THE OXFORD DICTIONARY, THESAURUS, AND WORDPOWER GUIDE

The Oxford Dictionary, Thesaurus, and Wordpower Guide

Dictionary Editor: Catherine Soanes

Thesaurus Editor: Maurice Waite

Project Editor: Sara Hawker

OXFORD
UNIVERSITY PRESS

OXFORD
UNIVERSITY PRESS

Great Clarendon Street, Oxford OX2 6DP

Oxford University Press is a department of the University of Oxford.
It furthers the University's objective of excellence in research, scholarship, and education by publishing worldwide in

Oxford New York

Athens Auckland Bangkok Bogotá Buenos Aires Cape Town Chennai Dar es Salaam Delhi Florence Hong Kong Istanbul Karachi Kolkata Kuala Lumpur Madrid Melbourne Mexico City Mumbai Nairobi Paris São Paulo Shanghai Singapore Taipei Tokyo Toronto Warsaw

with associated companies in Berlin Ibadan

Published in the United States
by Oxford University Press Inc., New York

First published 2001

British Library Cataloguing in Publication Data
Data available

Library of Congress Cataloging in Publication Data
Data available

ISBN 0–19–860373-8

10 9 8 7 6 5 4 3 2 1

Typeset in Monotype Nimrod and Arial
by Morton Word Processing Ltd
Printed in Italy by
La Tipografica Varese

Contents

Introduction

The *Oxford Dictionary, Thesaurus, and Wordpower Guide* is a handy three-in-one resource which has been compiled to provide a wide variety of information about the English language and a plentiful source of material with which to enrich and develop your vocabulary. The dictionary and thesaurus texts are combined in a way that enables convenient and easy reference to both: the top section of each page contains the dictionary text, while the lower section gives matching thesaurus entries for many of the words covered by the dictionary.

The dictionary text is derived from the *Oxford Compact English Dictionary*, part of the range of new generation dictionaries based on the *New Oxford Dictionary of English*. It presents up-to-date information on a broad range of vocabulary, concentrating on the standard core of English as an international language but also including a wide selection of terms used in technical and specialist contexts. Definitions focus on the central meanings of words and are written in clear, concise, and accessible language. Pronunciations are given using a simple system which will be easily understood by everyone able to write and speak English. The dictionary also provides over two hundred usage notes within the text, giving clear guidance on difficult or controversial points of grammar and usage.

The thesaurus text is derived from the *Oxford Paperback Thesaurus* and provides lists of synonyms for over 15,000 entries in the dictionary text. Within thesaurus entries, synonym lists are divided into numbered sections relating to particular meanings of the words in question. At the start of almost every synonym list is a 'core synonym': the term which is closest in meaning to the entry word in that particular sense. (At **obstinate**, for example, the core synonym is *stubborn*.) Subsequent synonyms are arranged according to their closeness in meaning to the entry word, while those whose usage is restricted in some way, such as regionalisms or informal terms, are placed at the end of each synonym list and clearly labelled. Antonyms (words with opposite meanings) are provided for most entry words and, where appropriate, 'related words' are also given. These are terms which are closely connected to an entry word, but are not synonyms: for example the entry for **back** has a section containing the related adjectives *dorsal* and *lumbar*.

The Wordpower Guide is made up of seven sections designed to help you explore the richness of the English language and to provide help and inspiration with creative writing, essays, or word games. The Vocabulary Builder section contains a wide range of words and phrases associated with various keywords: the entry for **eye**, for example, includes the names of the different parts of the human eye, the term for an eye specialist, and the names of various eye defects or diseases. The Right Word section gives guidance about the subtle differences between words sharing the same basic meaning, for example **artificial**, **synthetic**, and **man-made**. A Common Confusables section explains the difference between words which are similar in sound or spelling and which are consequently easy to confuse, for example **loath** and **loathe** or **chord** and **cord**. A section of Weird and Wonderful Words gives definitions and histories for some of the stranger and more colourful words in the language, for example **callithumpian** or **snollygoster**. There are also sections on Foreign Words and Phrases, Collective Names for Animals and Birds, and a Games and Puzzles Wordbuilder which gives lists of words which can be particularly useful for word-game players.

The Oxford Dictionary, Thesaurus, and Wordpower Guide is an ideal companion for anyone who wants comprehensive, up-to-date guidance on using the English language in more confident, informed, and effective way.

Guide to the use of the dictionary and thesaurus

1. Structure of dictionary entries

The dictionary section is designed to be as straightforward and self-explanatory as possible and the use of special symbols and conventions has been kept to a minimum. Those that are used are explained below.

Verb inflections

acquit ● verb (**acquitted**, **acquitting**) **1** formally declare that (someone) is not guilty of a criminal charge. **2** (**acquit oneself**) behave or perform in a specified way.
– DERIVATIVES **acquittal** noun.
– ORIGIN Latin *acquitare* 'pay a debt', from *quitare* 'set free'.

Word origin

Variant pronunciations

acumen /akyoomən, əkyōōmən/ ● **noun** the ability to make good judgements and take quick decisions.
– ORIGIN Latin, 'sharpness, point'.

Grammatical information (in round brackets)

Sense number

aesthetics (US also **esthetics**) ● **plural noun** (usu. treated as sing.) **1** a set of principles concerned with the nature of beauty, especially in art. **2** the branch of philosophy which deals with questions of beauty and artistic taste.

Part of speech

Information on plural use

aircraft ● **noun** (pl. same) an aeroplane, helicopter, or other machine capable of flight.

Label (showing regional distribution)

airplane ● **noun** N. Amer. an aeroplane.

aisle /īl/ ● **noun** **1** a passage between rows of seats. **2** a passage between sets of shelves in a supermarket or other shop. **3** Architecture a lateral division of a church parallel to, and divided by pillars from, a nave, choir, or transept.
– PHRASES **lead someone up the aisle** get married to someone.
– DERIVATIVES **aisled** adjective.
– ORIGIN Latin *ala* 'wing'.

Subject label

Phrases and idioms

Label (showing level of formality)

alight[1] ● **verb** **1** formal, chiefly Brit. descend from a vehicle. **2** **alight on** chance to notice.
– ORIGIN Old English.

Typical pattern (in bold)

Homonym number (indicates different word with the same spelling)

alight[2] **adverb & adjective** **1** on fire. **2** shining brightly.

alternate ● **verb** /awltərnayt/ **1** occur or do in turn repeatedly. **2** change repeatedly between two contrasting conditions.
● **adjective** /awlternət/ **1** every other. **2** (of two things) each following and succeeded by the other in a regular pattern. **3** chiefly N. Amer. another term for ALTERNATIVE.
– DERIVATIVES **alternately** adverb **alternation** noun.
– USAGE The use of **alternate** to mean **alternative** (as in *we will need to find alternate sources of fuel*) is common in North American English, though still regarded as incorrect by many in Britain.
– ORIGIN Latin *alternare* 'do by turns', from *alter* other.

Derivatives (in alphabetical order)

Usage note

Cross reference (in small capitals)

Pronunciation (for selected words) — Plural form

amigo /əmeegō/ ● **noun** (pl. **amigos**) informal, chiefly N. Amer. a friend.
– ORIGIN Spanish.

● Introduces new part of speech

Example of use (taken from real evidence) — Subject label

appeal ● **verb 1** make a serious or heartfelt request. **2** be attractive or interesting: *activities that appeal to all.* **3** Law apply to a higher court for a reversal of a lower court's decision. **4** Cricket (of the bowler or fielders) call on the umpire to declare a batsman out.
● **noun 1** an act of appealing. **2** the quality of being attractive or interesting.
– ORIGIN Latin *appellare* 'to address'.

Variant spelling — Label (showing currency)

aught /awt/ (also **ought**) ● **pronoun** archaic anything at all.
– ORIGIN Old English.

2. Structure of thesaurus entries

The organization of the thesaurus text is very straightforward and largely self-explanatory. The different parts of an entry are explained below.

Sense number

● Introduces new part of speech

Form of the entry word for which the following synonyms can be substituted

Example of use to help distinguish different senses

Core synonym (in small capitals), the synonym closest in meaning to the entry word

Label showing level of formality of following synonyms

bag ● **noun 1** *I dug around in my bag for my lipstick* HANDBAG, shoulder bag, clutch bag, evening bag, pochette; N. Amer. pocketbook, purse; historical reticule, scrip. **2** *she began to unpack her bags* SUITCASE, case, valise, portmanteau, holdall, grip, overnighter; backpack, rucksack, knapsack, haversack, kitbag, duffel bag; satchel; (**bags**) luggage, baggage.
● **verb 1** *locals bagged the most fish* CATCH, land, capture, trap, snare, ensnare; kill, shoot. **2** *he bagged seven medals* GET, secure, obtain, acquire, pick up; win, achieve, attain; commandeer, grab, appropriate, take; informal get one's hands on, land, net.

Label showing currency of following synonym

chest ● **noun 1** *a bullet wound in the chest* BREAST, upper body, torso, trunk; technical thorax. **2** *a large chest* BUST, bosom; archaic embonpoint. **3** *an oak chest* BOX, case, casket, crate, trunk, coffer, strongbox.
– RELATED TERMS pectoral, thoracic.
get something off one's chest (informal) CONFESS, disclose, divulge, reveal, make known, make public, make a clean breast of, bring into the open, tell all about, get a load off one's mind.

Phrase for which synonyms are offered

Words which are closely related to the entry word but which are not direct synonyms

sluggish ● **adjective 1** *Alex felt tired and sluggish* LETHARGIC, listless, lacking in energy, lifeless, inert, inactive, slow, torpid, languid, apathetic, weary, tired, fatigued, sleepy, drowsy, enervated; lazy, idle, indolent, slothful, sluggardly; Medicine asthenic; N. Amer. logy; informal dozy, dopey. **2** *the economy is sluggish* INACTIVE, quiet, slow, slack, flat, depressed, stagnant.
– OPPOSITES VIGOROUS.

Label showing subject field of following synonym

Label showing regional distribution of following synonym

Words which mean the opposite of the entry word

Label showing level of formality of this sense of the entry word

bucket ● **noun 1** *a bucket of water* PAIL, scuttle, can, tub. **2** (informal) *everyone wept buckets* FLOODS, gallons, oceans.
● **verb** (Brit. informal) **1** *it was bucketing down* RAIN HEAVILY, rain cats and dogs, rain hard, pour, pelt, lash, teem; Brit. tip. **2** *the car came bucketing out of a side road. See* SPEED *verb sense 1.*

Cross reference (in small capitals)

3. Labels

Unless otherwise stated, the words and senses in the dictionary and thesaurus sections are all part of standard English. Some words, however, are appropriate only to certain situations or are found only in certain contexts, and where this is the case a label (or combination of labels) is used.

Register labels

Register labels refer to the particular level of use in the language—indicating whether a term is formal or informal, historical or archaic, and so on:

formal: normally used only in writing, in contexts such as official documents.

informal: normally used only in spoken contexts or informal written contexts.

dated: no longer used by the majority of English speakers, but still encountered, especially among the older generation.

archaic: old-fashioned language, not in ordinary use today, though sometimes used to give a deliberately old-fashioned effect and also encountered in the literature of the past.

historical: still used today, but only in reference to some practice or artefact that is no longer part of the modern world, e.g. **baldric** or **doubloon**.

literary: found only or mainly in literature.

technical: normally used only in technical and specialist language, though not necessarily restricted to any specific subject field.

rare: not in normal use today or in previous times.

humorous: used with the intention of sounding funny or playful.

euphemistic: used in place of a more direct or vulgar term.

dialect: not used in the standard language, but still widely used in certain local regions of the English-speaking world.

offensive: likely to cause offence, especially racial offence, whether the speaker intends it or not.

derogatory: intended to convey a low opinion or cause offence.

vulgar slang: very informal language, especially that relating to sexual activity or other bodily functions, which is widely regarded as taboo and may cause offence.

Geographical labels

The main regional standards for the language of English are British, US and Canadian, Australian and New Zealand, South African, Indian, and West Indian. The vast majority of words and senses listed in the dictionary and thesaurus are common to all the major regional standard varieties of English, but where important local differences exist these are recorded.

The geographical label 'Brit.' implies that the use is found typically in standard British English but is not found in standard American English, though it may be found in other varieties such as Australian or South African English. The label 'US', on the other hand, implies that the use is typically US and is not standard in British English, though it may be found elsewhere.

Subject labels

Subject labels are used to indicate that a word or sense is associated with a particular subject field or specialist activity, such as Medicine, Aeronautics, or Baseball.

4. Pronunciations

The dictionary section uses a respelling system for pronunciation which is easy to use for anyone who can write and speak English. Stressed syllables are shown in bold. The dictionary's policy is to give pronunciations for words which may be less familiar or which can present problems even to native English speakers. The dictionary does not give pronunciations for ordinary everyday words assumed to be familiar to English speakers, such as *bake*, *baby*, *boastful*, and *budget*.

List of respelling symbols

Vowels	Examples	Consonants	Examples
a	*as in* **pat**	b, bb	*as in* **bay**, **rubber**
aa	*as in* **palm**	ch	*as in* **church**
aar	*as in* **farm**	d, dd	*as in* **dog**, **puddle**
air	*as in* **fair**, **mayor**	f, ff	*as in* **fit**, **coffee**
arr	*as in* **carry**	g, gg	*as in* **get**, **struggle**
aw	*as in* **law**, **caught**	h	*as in* **head**
awr	*as in* **warm**	j	*as in* **judge**, **carriage**
ay	*as in* **day**	k, kk	*as in* **kick**, **wicked**
e	*as in* **men**	ks	*as in* **mix**
ee	*as in* **feet**	kw	*as in* **quick**
eer	*as in* **hear**, **souvenir**	<u>kh</u>	*as in* **loch**
er	*as in* **fern**	l, ll	*as in* **like**, **silly**
err	*as in* **ferry**	'l	*as in* **bottle**, **candle**
ə	*as in* **along**	m, mm	*as in* **may**, **hammer**
ər	*as in* **parade**, **bitter**	'm	*as in* **chasm**, **idealism**
i	*as in* **pin**	n, nn	*as in* **nun**, **runner**
ī	*as in* **time**, **buy**	N	*as in* **en route**, **croissant**
īr	*as in* **fire**, **desire**		
irr	*as in* **lyrics**	'n	*as in* **wooden**, **button**
o	*as in* **rob**	ng	*as in* **sing**, **sink**
ō	*as in* **go**, **hotel**	ngg	*as in* **single**, **anger**
ö	*as in* **colonel**, **jeu**	p, pp	*as in* **pit**, **supper**
oo	*as in* **unite**, **speculate**	r, rr	*as in* **run**, **fir**, **spirit**
ŏŏ	*as in* **wood**, **sugar**	s	*as in* **sit**, **messy**
ōō	*as in* **food**, **music**	sh	*as in* **shut**, **passion**
oor	*as in* **tour**, **jury**	t, tt	*as in* **taste**, **butter**
or	*as in* **door**, **corner**	th	*as in* **thin**, **truth**
orr	*as in* **sorry**, **warrior**	<u>th</u>	*as in* **then**, **mother**
ör	*as in* **fleur de lys**, **voyeur**	v, vv	*as in* **vet**, **civil**
ow	*as in* **mouse**, **coward**	w	*as in* **way**
owr	*as in* **powerful**	y	*as in* **yet**, **tortilla**
oy	*as in* **boy**, **noisy**	z, zz	*as in* **zero**, **fuzzy**
u	*as in* **cut**, **blood**	<u>zh</u>	*as in* **measure**, **vision**
ur	*as in* **curl**, **journey**		
urr	*as in* **hurry**		

5. Abbreviations used in the dictionary and thesaurus

adj.	adjective
Austral.	Australian
Brit.	British
fem.	feminine
masc.	masculine
N. Amer.	North American
N. English	Northern English
NZ	New Zealand
part.	participle
pl.	plural
pronunc.	pronunciation
S. African	South African
sing.	singular
US	American
usu.	usually
W. Indian	West Indian

Note on trademarks and proprietary status

The dictionary and thesaurus sections include some words which have, or are asserted to have, proprietary status as trademarks or otherwise. Their inclusion does not imply that they have acquired for legal purposes a non-proprietary or general significance, nor any other judgement concerning their legal status. In cases where the editorial staff have some evidence that a word has proprietary status this is indicated in the entry for that word by the label trademark, but no judgement concerning the legal status of such words is made or implied thereby.

Aa

A[1] (also **a**) ● **noun** (pl. **As** or **A's**) **1** the first letter of the alphabet. **2** denoting the first, best, or most important in a set. **3** Music the sixth note of the diatonic scale of C major. **4** the human blood type (in the ABO system) containing the A antigen and lacking the B.
– PHRASES **from A to B** from one's starting point to one's destination. **from A to Z** over the entire range.

A[2] ● **abbreviation** **1** ampere(s). **2** (Å) ångstrom(s). **3** (in showing goals or points conceded) against. **4** answer.

a[1] (**an** before a vowel sound) ● **determiner** **1** used when mentioning someone or something for the first time; the indefinite article. **2** one single: *a hundred.* **3** someone like (the name specified). **4** per: *typing 60 words a minute.*
– ORIGIN Old English.

a[2] ● **abbreviation** **1** (in travel timetables) arrives. **2** (used before a date) before. [ORIGIN from Latin *ante.*] **3** Brit. (with reference to sporting fixtures) away.

a-[1] (often **an-** before a vowel) ● **prefix** not; without: *atheistic.*
– ORIGIN from Greek.

a-[2] ● **prefix** **1** to; towards: *aside.* **2** in the process of: *a-hunting.* **3** in a specified state: *aflutter.*
– ORIGIN Old English.

a-[3] ● **prefix** **1** of: *anew.* **2** utterly: *abash.*
– ORIGIN Old French *a-*, from Latin *ex* 'of, from'.

A1 ● **adjective** informal excellent.
– ORIGIN used at Lloyd's Register of Shipping to refer to ships in first-class condition as to hull (A) and stores (1).

A3 ● **noun** a standard European size of paper, 420 × 297 mm.

A4 ● **noun** a standard European size of paper, 297 × 210 mm.

A5 ● **noun** a standard European size of paper, 210 × 148 mm.

AA ● **abbreviation** **1** Alcoholics Anonymous. **2** anti-aircraft. **3** Automobile Association.

aardvark /aardvaark/ ● **noun** a badger-sized African burrowing mammal, with a tubular snout and a long tongue, feeding on ants and termites.
– ORIGIN South African Dutch, from *aarde* 'earth' + *vark* 'pig'.

Aaron's rod ● **noun** mullein.
– ORIGIN alluding to *Aaron* in the Bible, whose staff was said to have flowered.

AB[1] ● **noun** the human blood type (in the ABO system) containing both the A and B antigens.

AB[2] ● **abbreviation** **1** able seaman. **2** Alberta. **3** US Bachelor of Arts. [ORIGIN from Latin *Artium Baccalaureus.*]

ab- (also **abs-**) ● **prefix** away; from: *abdicate.*
– ORIGIN Latin.

aback ● **adverb** archaic towards or situated to the rear.
– PHRASES **take aback** shock or surprise (someone).
– ORIGIN Old English.

abacus /abbəkəss/ ● **noun** (pl. **abacuses**) a frame with rows of wires or grooves along which beads are slid, used for calculating.
– ORIGIN Greek *abax* 'slab, drawing board'.

abaft /əbaaft/ ● **adverb & preposition** Nautical in or behind the stern of a ship.
– ORIGIN from archaic *baft* 'in the rear'.

abalone /abbəlōni/ ● **noun** an edible mollusc with an ear-shaped shell lined with mother-of-pearl.
– ORIGIN from an American Indian language.

abandon ● **verb** **1** desert or leave permanently. **2** give up (an action or practice) completely. **3** (**abandon oneself to**) indulge in (a desire or impulse) without restraint. ● **noun** complete lack of inhibition or restraint.
– DERIVATIVES **abandonment** noun.
– ORIGIN Old French *abandoner.*

abandoned ● **adjective** unrestrained; uninhibited.

abase /əbayss/ ● **verb** (**abase oneself**) behave in a way that lessens others' respect for one.
– DERIVATIVES **abasement** noun.
– ORIGIN Old French *abaissier* 'to lower'.

abashed ● **adjective** embarrassed, disconcerted, or ashamed.
– ORIGIN from Old French *esbair* 'utterly astound'.

abate /əbayt/ ● **verb** **1** (of something bad) become less intense or widespread. **2** Law reduce or remove (a nuisance).
– DERIVATIVES **abatement** noun.
– ORIGIN Old French *abatre* 'to fell', from Latin *battere* 'to beat'.

abattoir /abbətwaar/ ● **noun** a slaughterhouse.
– ORIGIN French, from *abattre* 'to fell'.

abbacy /abbəsi/ ● **noun** (pl. **abbacies**) the office of an abbot or

Thesaurus

aback ● **adverb**
– PHRASES **take someone aback** SURPRISE, shock, stun, stagger, astound, astonish, startle, take by surprise; dumbfound, nonplus, stop someone in their tracks; shake (up), jolt, throw, unnerve, disconcert, unsettle, bewilder; *informal* flabbergast, knock sideways, floor; *Brit. informal* knock for six.

abandon ● **verb** **1** *the party abandoned policies which made it unelectable* RENOUNCE, relinquish, dispense with, disclaim, disown, disavow, discard, wash one's hands of; give up, drop, jettison, do away with, axe; *informal* ditch, scrap, scrub, junk; *formal* forswear. **2** *by that stage, she had abandoned painting* GIVE UP, stop, cease, drop, forgo, desist from, have done with, abstain from, discontinue, break off, refrain from, set aside; *informal* cut out, kick, pack in, quit; *Brit. informal* jack in; *formal* abjure. **3** *he abandoned his wife* DESERT, leave, leave high and dry, turn one's back on, cast aside, break (up) with; jilt, strand, leave stranded, leave in the lurch, throw over; *informal* walk out on, run out on, dump, ditch; *poetic/literary* forsake. **4** *the skipper gave the order to abandon ship* VACATE, leave, depart from, withdraw from, quit, evacuate. **5** *a vast expanse of territory was abandoned to the invaders* RELINQUISH, surrender, give up, cede, yield, leave. **6** *she abandoned herself to the sensuousness of the music* INDULGE IN, give way to, give oneself up to, yield to, lose oneself to/in.
– OPPOSITES keep, retain, continue.
● **noun** *reckless abandon* UNINHIBITEDNESS, recklessness, lack of restraint, lack of inhibition, wildness, impulsiveness, impetuosity, immoderation, wantonness.
– OPPOSITES self-control.

abandoned ● **adjective** **1** *an abandoned child* DESERTED, forsaken, cast aside/off; jilted, stranded, rejected; *informal* dumped, ditched. **2** *an abandoned tin mine* UNUSED, disused, neglected, idle; deserted, unoccupied, uninhabited, empty. **3** *a wild, abandoned dance* UNINHIBITED, reckless, unrestrained, wild, unbridled, impulsive, impetuous; immoderate, wanton.

abase ● **verb** HUMBLE, humiliate, belittle, demean, lower, degrade, debase, cheapen, discredit, bring low; (**abase oneself**) grovel, kowtow, bow and scrape, toady, fawn; *informal* crawl, suck up to someone, lick someone's boots.

abasement ● **noun** HUMILIATION, belittlement, lowering, degradation, debasement.

abashed ● **adjective** EMBARRASSED, ashamed, shamefaced, remorseful, mortified, conscience-stricken, humiliated, humbled, chagrined, crestfallen, sheepish, red-faced, blushing, put out of countenance, discountenanced, with one's tail between one's legs.

abate ● **verb** **1** *the storm had abated* SUBSIDE, die down/away/out, lessen, ease (off), let up, decrease, diminish, moderate, decline, fade, dwindle, recede, tail off, peter out, taper off, wane, ebb, weaken, come to an end; *archaic* remit. **2** *nothing abated his crusading zeal* DECREASE, lessen, diminish, reduce, moderate, ease, soothe, dampen, calm, tone down, allay, temper.
– OPPOSITES intensify, increase.

abatement ● **noun** **1** *the storm still rages with no sign of abatement* SUBSIDING, dying down/away/out, lessening, easing (off), let-up, decrease, moderation, decline, ebb. **2** *noise abatement* DE-

a

abbess.

abbatial /əbaysh'l/ ● adjective relating to an abbey, abbot, or abbess.

abbé /abbay/ ● noun (in France) an abbot or other cleric.

– ORIGIN French.

abbess /abbiss/ ● noun a woman who is the head of an abbey of nuns.

abbey ● noun (pl. **abbeys**) an establishment occupied by a community of monks or nuns.

– ORIGIN Old French *abbeie*, from Latin *abbas* 'abbot'.

abbot ● noun a man who is the head of an abbey of monks.

– ORIGIN Greek *abbas* 'father', from Aramaic.

abbreviate /əbreeviayt/ ● verb shorten (a word, phrase, or text).

– ORIGIN Latin *abbreviare*, from *brevis* 'short'.

abbreviation ● noun **1** a shortened form of a word or phrase. **2** the process or result of abbreviating.

ABC[1] ● noun **1** the alphabet. **2** an alphabetical guide. **3** the rudiments of a subject.

ABC[2] ● abbreviation Australian Broadcasting Corporation.

abdabs (also **habdabs**) ● plural noun (often in phrase **the screaming abdabs**) Brit. informal nervous anxiety or tension.

– ORIGIN of unknown origin.

abdicate /abdikayt/ ● verb **1** (of a monarch) renounce the throne. **2** fail to fulfil or undertake (a duty).

– DERIVATIVES **abdication** noun.

– ORIGIN Latin *abdicare* 'renounce'.

abdomen /abdəmən/ ● noun **1** the part of the body containing the digestive and reproductive organs; the belly. **2** Zoology the rear part of the body of an arthropod.

– DERIVATIVES **abdominal** /abdommin'l/ adjective **abdominally** adverb.

– ORIGIN Latin.

abduct ● verb take (someone) away by force or deception.

– DERIVATIVES **abductee** noun **abduction** noun **abductor** noun.

– ORIGIN Latin *abducere* 'lead away'.

abeam ● adverb at right angles to a ship's or an aircraft's length.

abed ● adverb archaic in bed.

Aberdeen Angus ● noun a breed of hornless black beef cattle originating in Scotland.

Aberdonian /abbərdōniən/ ● adjective relating to Aberdeen. ● noun a person from Aberdeen.

– ORIGIN from Latin *Aberdonia*.

aberrant /əberrənt/ ● adjective departing from an accepted standard or normal type.

– DERIVATIVES **aberrance** noun **aberrancy** noun **aberrantly** adverb.

aberration /abbəraysh'n/ ● noun **1** a departure from what is normal or acceptable. **2** a mental or moral lapse. **3** Optics the failure of rays to converge at one focus because of a defect in a lens or mirror.

– DERIVATIVES **aberrational** adjective.

– ORIGIN Latin, from *aberrare* 'to stray'.

abet /əbet/ ● verb (**abetted**, **abetting**) (usu. in phrase **aid and abet**) encourage or assist (someone) to do something wrong, in particular to commit a crime.

– DERIVATIVES **abetment** noun **abetter** (also **abettor**) noun.

– ORIGIN Old French *abeter*, from *beter* 'hound, urge on'.

abeyance /əbayənss/ ● noun (in phrase **in/into abeyance**) temporarily suspended or not used.

– ORIGIN from Old French *abeer* 'aspire after'.

ABH ● abbreviation actual bodily harm.

abhor /əbhor/ ● verb (**abhorred**, **abhorring**) detest; hate.

– ORIGIN Latin *abhorrere*, from *horrere* 'to shudder'.

abhorrent ● adjective inspiring disgust and loathing.

– DERIVATIVES **abhorrence** noun.

abide ● verb **1** (**abide by**) accept or observe (a rule or decision). **2** informal tolerate: *he could not abide conflict.* **3** (of a feeling or memory) endure. **4** archaic live; dwell.

– ORIGIN Old English, 'wait'; related to BIDE.

abiding ● adjective continuing through time; enduring.

– DERIVATIVES **abidingly** adverb.

ability ● noun (pl. **abilities**) **1** the power or capacity to do something. **2** skill or talent.

– ORIGIN Latin *habilitas*, from *habilis* 'able'.

ab initio /ab inishiō/ ● adverb & adjective from the beginning.

Thesaurus

CREASE, reduction, lowering.

abattoir ● noun SLAUGHTERHOUSE; *Brit.* butchery; *archaic* shambles.

abbey ● noun MONASTERY, CONVENT, priory, cloister, friary, nunnery; *historical* charterhouse; *rare* coenobium.

abbreviate ● verb SHORTEN, reduce, cut, contract, condense, compress, abridge, truncate, pare down, prune, shrink, telescope; summarize, abstract, precis, synopsize, digest, edit.

– OPPOSITES lengthen, expand.

abbreviated ● adjective SHORTENED, reduced, cut, condensed, abridged, concise, compact, succinct; summary, thumbnail, synoptic; *formal* compendious.

– OPPOSITES long.

abbreviation ● noun SHORTENED FORM, short form, contraction, acronym, initialism, symbol, diminutive; elision.

abdicate ● verb **1** *the king abdicated in 1936* RESIGN, retire, stand down, step down, bow out, renounce the throne; *archaic* demit. **2** *Ferdinand abdicated the throne* RESIGN FROM, relinquish, renounce, give up, surrender, vacate, cede; *Law* disclaim; *formal* abjure. **3** *the state abdicated all responsibility for their welfare* DISOWN, reject, renounce, give up, refuse, relinquish, repudiate, abandon, turn one's back on, wash one's hands of; *formal* abjure; *poetic/literary* forsake.

abdication ● noun **1** *Edward VIII's abdication* RESIGNATION, retirement; relinquishment, renunciation, surrender; *formal* abjuration; *archaic* demission. **2** *an abdication of responsibility* DISOWNING, renunciation, rejection, refusal, relinquishment, repudiation, abandonment.

abdomen ● noun STOMACH, belly, gut, middle, intestines; *informal* tummy, tum, insides, guts, maw, breadbasket, pot, paunch; *Austral. informal* bingy; *dated* corporation.

abdominal ● adjective GASTRIC, intestinal, stomach, stomachic, enteric, duodenal, visceral, coeliac, ventral.

abduct ● verb KIDNAP, carry off, seize, capture, run away/off with, make off with, spirit away, hold hostage, hold to ransom; *informal* snatch.

aberrant ● adjective DEVIANT, deviating, divergent, abnormal, atypical, anomalous, irregular, rogue; strange, odd, peculiar, uncommon, freakish; twisted, warped, perverted.

– OPPOSITES normal, typical.

aberration ● noun *a statistical aberration* ANOMALY, deviation, departure from the norm, divergence, abnormality, irregularity, variation, freak, rarity, oddity, peculiarity, curiosity; mistake.

abet ● verb ASSIST, aid, help, lend a hand, support, back, encourage; cooperate with, collaborate with, work with, collude with, be in collusion with, be hand in glove with, side with; second, endorse, sanction; promote, champion, further, expedite, connive at.

– OPPOSITES hinder.

abeyance ● noun SUSPENSION, a state of suspension, a state of uncertainty, remission; (**in abeyance**) pending, suspended, deferred, postponed, put off, put to one side, unresolved, up in the air; *informal* in cold storage, on ice, on the back burner, hanging fire.

abhor ● verb DETEST, hate, loathe, despise, execrate, regard with disgust, shrink from, recoil from, shudder at; *formal* abominate.

– OPPOSITES love, admire.

abhorrence ● noun HATRED, loathing, detestation, execration, revulsion, abomination, disgust, repugnance, horror, odium, aversion.

abhorrent ● adjective DETESTABLE, hateful, loathsome, despicable, abominable, execrable, repellent, repugnant, repulsive, revolting, disgusting, distasteful, horrible, horrid, horrifying, awful, heinous, reprehensible, obnoxious, odious, nauseating, offensive, contemptible.

– OPPOSITES admirable.

abide ● verb **1** *he expected everybody to abide by the rules* COMPLY WITH, obey, observe, follow, keep to, hold to, conform to, adhere to, stick to, stand by, act in accordance with, uphold, heed, accept, go along with, acknowledge, respect, defer to. **2** (*informal*) *I can't abide the smell of cigarettes* TOLERATE, bear, stand, put up with, endure, take, countenance; *informal* stomach; *Brit. informal* stick; *formal* brook; *archaic* suffer. **3** *at least one memory will abide* CONTINUE, remain, survive, last, persist, stay, live on.

– OPPOSITES flout, disobey.

abiding ● adjective ENDURING, lasting, persisting, long-lasting, lifelong, continuing, remaining, surviving, standing, durable, everlasting, perpetual, eternal, unending, constant, permanent, unchanging, steadfast, immutable.

– OPPOSITES short-lived, ephemeral.

– ORIGIN Latin.

abiotic /aybīottik/ ● **adjective** not involving or derived from living organisms.

abject /abjekt/ ● **adjective** **1** extremely unpleasant and degrading: *abject poverty.* **2** completely without pride or dignity: *an abject apology.*

– DERIVATIVES **abjection** noun **abjectly** adverb **abjectness** noun.

– ORIGIN Latin *abjectus* 'rejected', from *jacere* 'to throw'.

abjure /əbjoor/ ● **verb** formal swear to give up (a belief or claim).

– DERIVATIVES **abjuration** noun.

– ORIGIN Latin *abjurare*, from *jurare* 'swear'.

ablation /əblaysh'n/ ● **noun** **1** the loss of solid material by melting, evaporation, or erosion. **2** the surgical removal of body tissue.

– ORIGIN Latin, from *auferre* 'take away'.

ablative /ablətiv/ ● **adjective** **1** Grammar (of a case) indicating an agent, instrument, or source, expressed by 'by', 'with', or 'from' in English. **2** involving ablation.

ablaze ● **adjective** burning fiercely.

able ● **adjective** (**abler**, **ablest**) **1** having the power, skill, or means to do something. **2** skilful and competent.

– DERIVATIVES **ably** adverb.

– ORIGIN Latin *habilis* 'handy'.

-able ● **suffix** forming adjectives meaning: **1** able to be: *calculable.* **2** subject to; relevant to: *taxable.* **3** having the quality to: *suitable.*

– DERIVATIVES **-ability** suffix **-ably** suffix.

able-bodied ● **adjective** not physically unfit or disabled.

able seaman ● **noun** a rank of sailor in the Royal Navy above ordinary seaman and below leading seaman.

ablutions /əbloosh'nz/ ● **plural noun** formal or humorous the act of washing oneself.

– DERIVATIVES **ablutionary** adjective.

– ORIGIN Latin, from *abluere* 'wash away'.

ABM ● **abbreviation** anti-ballistic-missile.

abnegate /abnigayt/ ● **verb** formal renounce or reject (something desired or valuable).

– DERIVATIVES **abnegation** noun.

– ORIGIN Latin, from *negare* 'deny'.

abnormal ● **adjective** deviating from what is normal.

– DERIVATIVES **abnormality** noun **abnormally** adverb.

– ORIGIN Greek *anōmalos* 'uneven', related to ANOMALOUS.

Abo /abō/ ● **noun** (pl. **Abos**) Austral. informal, offensive an Aboriginal.

aboard ● **adverb & preposition** on or into (a ship, train, or other vehicle).

abode ● **noun** formal or literary **1** a house or home. **2** residence: *right of abode.*

– ORIGIN from ABIDE.

abolish ● **verb** formally put an end to (a practice or institution).

– ORIGIN Latin *abolere* 'destroy'.

abolition ● **noun** the abolishing of a system, practice, or institution.

abolitionist ● **noun** a person who favours the abolition of something, especially capital punishment or (formerly) slavery.

– DERIVATIVES **abolitionism** noun.

A-bomb ● **noun** short for ATOM BOMB.

abominable ● **adjective** **1** causing moral revulsion. **2** informal very bad; terrible.

– DERIVATIVES **abominably** adverb.

– ORIGIN Latin *abominabilis*, from *abominari* 'deprecate'.

Abominable Snowman ● **noun** the yeti.

abominate /əbomminayt/ ● **verb** formal detest.

abomination ● **noun** **1** an object of disgust or hatred. **2** a feeling of hatred.

Thesaurus

ability ● **noun** **1** *the ability to read and write* CAPACITY, capability, potential, potentiality, power, faculty, aptness, facility; wherewithal, means. **2** *the president's leadership ability* TALENT, skill, expertise, adeptness, aptitude, skilfulness, savoir faire, prowess, mastery, accomplishment; competence, proficiency; dexterity, adroitness, deftness, cleverness, flair, finesse, gift, knack, genius; qualification, resources; *informal* know-how.

abject ● **adjective** **1** *abject poverty* WRETCHED, miserable, hopeless, pathetic, pitiful, pitiable, piteous, sorry, woeful, lamentable, degrading, appalling, atrocious, awful. **2** *an abject sinner* CONTEMPTIBLE, base, low, vile, worthless, debased, degraded, despicable, ignominious, mean, unworthy, ignoble. **3** *an abject apology* OBSEQUIOUS, grovelling, fawning, toadyish, servile, cringing, sycophantic, submissive, craven.

abjure ● **verb** *(formal)* RENOUNCE, relinquish, reject, forgo, disavow, abandon, deny, repudiate, give up, wash one's hands of; eschew, abstain from, refrain from; *informal* kick, pack in; *Brit. informal* jack in; *Law* disaffirm; *poetic/literary* forsake; *formal* forswear, abnegate.

ablaze ● **adjective** **1** *several vehicles were ablaze* ON FIRE, alight, aflame, in flames, flaming, burning, blazing; *poetic/literary* afire. **2** *every window was ablaze with light* LIT UP, alight, gleaming, glowing, aglow, illuminated, bright, shining, radiant, shimmering, sparkling, flashing, dazzling, luminous, incandescent. **3** *his eyes were ablaze with fury* PASSIONATE, impassioned, aroused, excited, stimulated, eager, animated, intense, ardent, fervent, frenzied.

able ● **adjective** **1** *he will soon be able to resume his duties* CAPABLE OF, competent to, equal to, up to, fit to, prepared to, qualified to; allowed to, free to, in a position to. **2** *an able student* INTELLIGENT, clever, talented, skilful, skilled, accomplished, gifted; proficient, apt, good, adroit, adept; capable, competent, efficient, effective.

– OPPOSITES incompetent, incapable.

able-bodied ● **adjective** HEALTHY, FIT, in good health, robust, strong, sound, sturdy, vigorous, hardy, hale and hearty, athletic, muscular, strapping, burly, brawny, lusty; in good shape, in good trim, in fine fettle, fighting fit, as fit as a fiddle, as fit as a flea; *informal* husky; *dated* stalwart.

– OPPOSITES infirm, frail, disabled.

ablutions ● **plural noun** *(formal)* WASHING, cleansing, bathing, showering, scrubbing; wash, bath, shower, toilet, soak, dip, douche; *rare* lavage, lavation.

abnegation ● **noun** *(formal)* **1** *a serious abnegation of their responsibilities* RENUNCIATION, rejection, refusal, abandonment, abdication, surrender, relinquishment, repudiation, denial; *formal* abjuration. **2** *people capable of abnegation and unselfishness* SELF-DENIAL, self-sacrifice, abstinence, temperance, continence, asceticism, abstemiousness, austerity.

– OPPOSITES acceptance, self-indulgence.

abnormal ● **adjective** UNUSUAL, uncommon, atypical, untypical, non-typical, unrepresentative, rare, isolated, irregular, anomalous, deviant, divergent, aberrant, freak, freakish; STRANGE, odd, peculiar, curious, bizarre, weird, queer; eccentric, idiosyncratic, quirky; unexpected, unfamiliar, unconventional, surprising, unorthodox, singular, exceptional, extraordinary, out of the ordinary, out of the way; unnatural, perverse, perverted, twisted, warped, unhealthy, distorted; *Brit.* out of the common; *informal* funny, freaky, kinky.

– OPPOSITES normal, typical, common.

abnormality ● **noun** **1** *babies born with physical or mental abnormalities* MALFORMATION, deformity, irregularity, flaw, defect. **2** *the abnormality of such behaviour* UNUSUALNESS, uncommonness, atypicality, irregularity, anomalousness, deviation, divergence, aberrance, aberration, freakishness; strangeness, oddness, peculiarity, unexpectedness, singularity.

abode ● **noun** *(formal)* HOME, house, place of residence, accommodation, seat; quarters, lodgings, rooms; address; *informal* pad, digs; *formal* dwelling, dwelling place, residence, habitation.

abolish ● **verb** PUT AN END TO, get rid of, scrap, end, stop, terminate, axe, eradicate, eliminate, exterminate, destroy, annihilate, stamp out, obliterate, wipe out, extinguish, quash, expunge, extirpate; annul, cancel, invalidate, nullify, void, dissolve; rescind, repeal, revoke, overturn; discontinue, remove, excise, drop, jettison; *informal* do away with, ditch, junk, scrub, dump, chop, give something the chop, knock something on the head; *formal* abrogate.

– OPPOSITES retain, create.

abolition ● **noun** SCRAPPING, ending, termination, eradication, elimination, extermination, destruction, annihilation, obliteration, extirpation; annulment, cancellation, invalidation, nullification, dissolution; revocation, repeal, rescindment, discontinuation, removal; *formal* abrogation.

abominable ● **adjective** LOATHSOME, detestable, hateful, odious, obnoxious, despicable, contemptible, damnable, diabolical; disgusting, revolting, repellent, repulsive, offensive, repugnant, abhorrent, reprehensible, atrocious, horrifying, execrable, foul, vile, wretched, base, horrible, awful, dreadful, appalling, nauseating; horrid, nasty, disagreeable, unpleasant, distasteful; *informal* terrible, shocking, God-awful; *Brit. informal* beastly; *dated* cursed, accursed.

– OPPOSITES good, admirable.

abominate ● **verb** *(formal)* DETEST, loathe, hate, abhor, despise, exe-

a

aboriginal • adjective **1** inhabiting or existing in a land from the earliest times or from before the arrival of colonists; indigenous. **2** (**Aboriginal**) relating to the Australian Aboriginals. • noun **1** an aboriginal inhabitant. **2** (**Aboriginal**) a member of one of the indigenous peoples of Australia.

aborigine /abbərijini/ • noun **1** an aboriginal person, animal, or plant. **2** (**Aborigine**) an Australian aboriginal.
– ORIGIN from Latin *ab origine* 'from the beginning'.

abort • verb **1** carry out or undergo the abortion of (a fetus). **2** Biology (of an embryonic organ or organism) remain undeveloped; fail to mature. **3** bring to a premature end because of a problem or fault.
– ORIGIN Latin *aboriri* 'miscarry'.

abortifacient /əbortifaysh'nt/ Medicine • adjective (of a drug) causing abortion. • noun an abortifacient drug.

abortion • noun **1** the deliberate termination of a human pregnancy. **2** the natural expulsion of a fetus from the womb before it is able to survive independently. **3** informal, derogatory something imperfectly planned or made.
– DERIVATIVES **abortionist** noun (chiefly derogatory).

abortive • adjective failing to produce the intended result; unsuccessful.
– DERIVATIVES **abortively** adverb.

ABO system • noun a system of four basic types (A, AB, B, and O) into which human blood may be classified according to the presence or absence of particular antigens.

abound • verb **1** exist in large numbers or amounts. **2** (**abound in/with**) have in large numbers or amounts.
– ORIGIN Latin *abundare* 'overflow'.

about • preposition & adverb **1** on the subject of; concerning. **2** used to indicate movement within a particular area or location in a particular place. **3** approximately.
– PHRASES **be about to** be on the point of.
– ORIGIN Old English, related to BUT.

about-turn (also chiefly N. Amer. **about-face**) • noun Brit. **1** Military a turn made so as to face the opposite direction. **2** a complete change of opinion or policy.

above • preposition & adverb **1** at a higher level than. **2** in preference to. **3** (in printed text) mentioned earlier.
– PHRASES **above board** legitimate and honest. **above oneself** conceited. **not be above** be capable of doing (something unworthy).
– ORIGIN Old English.

abracadabra • exclamation a word said by conjurors when performing a magic trick.
– ORIGIN Latin, from a Greek base.

abrade /əbrayd/ • verb scrape or wear away.
– ORIGIN Latin *abradere*, from *radere* 'to scrape'.

abrasion /əbrayzh'n/ • noun **1** the action or process of abrading or being abraded. **2** an area of scraped skin.

abrasive /əbraysiv/ • adjective **1** capable of polishing or cleaning a hard surface by rubbing or grinding. **2** harsh or rough in

Thesaurus

crate, shudder at, recoil from, shrink from, be repelled by.
– OPPOSITES like, love.

abomination • noun **1** *in both wars, internment was an abomination* ATROCITY, disgrace, horror, obscenity, outrage, evil, crime, monstrosity, anathema, bane. **2** *he had a Calvinist abomination of indulgence* DETESTATION, loathing, hatred, aversion, antipathy, revulsion, repugnance, abhorrence, odium, execration, disgust, horror, hostility.
– OPPOSITES liking, love.

aboriginal • adjective *the area's aboriginal inhabitants* INDIGENOUS, native; original, earliest, first; ancient, primitive, primeval, primordial; rare autochthonous, autochthonic.
• noun *the social structure of the aboriginals* NATIVE, aborigine, original inhabitant; rare autochthon, indigene.

abort • verb **1** *I decided not to abort the pregnancy* TERMINATE, end. **2** *the organism can cause pregnant ewes to abort* MISCARRY, have a miscarriage. **3** *the crew aborted the take-off* HALT, stop, end, axe, call off, cut short, discontinue, terminate, arrest; informal pull the plug on. **4** *the mission aborted* COME TO A HALT, end, terminate, fail, miscarry, go wrong, fall through, collapse, founder, come to grief.

abortion • noun TERMINATION, miscarriage; rare feticide.

abortive • adjective UNSUCCESSFUL, failed, vain, thwarted, futile, useless, worthless, ineffective, ineffectual, to no effect, to no avail, inefficacious, fruitless, unproductive, unavailing, sterile, nugatory; archaic bootless.
– OPPOSITES successful, fruitful.

abound • verb **1** *cafes and bars abound in the narrow streets* BE PLENTIFUL, be abundant, be numerous, proliferate, superabound, be thick on the ground; informal grow on trees, be two/ten a penny. **2** *a stream which abounded with trout and eels* BE FULL OF, overflow with, teem with, be packed with, be crowded with, be thronged with; be alive with, be crawling with, be overrun by/with, swarm with, bristle with, be infested with, be thick with; informal be lousy with, be stuffed with, be jam-packed with, be chock-a-block with, be chock-full of.

abounding • adjective ABUNDANT, plentiful, superabundant, considerable, copious, ample, lavish, luxuriant, profuse, boundless, prolific, inexhaustible, generous; galore; poetic/literary plenteous.
– OPPOSITES meagre, scanty.

about • preposition **1** *a book about ancient Greece* REGARDING, concerning, with reference to, referring to, with regard to, with respect to, respecting, relating to, on, touching on, dealing with, relevant to, connected with, in connection with, on the subject of, in the matter of, apropos, re. **2** *two hundred people were milling about the room* AROUND, round, throughout, over, through, on every side of.
• adverb **1** *there were babies crawling about in the grass* AROUND, here and there, to and fro, back and forth, from place to place, hither and thither, in all directions. **2** *I knew he was about somewhere* NEAR, nearby, around, hereabouts, not far off/away, close by, in the vicinity, in the neighbourhood. **3** *the explosion caused about £15,000 worth of damage* APPROXIMATELY, roughly, around, round about, in the region of, circa, of the order of, something like; or so, or thereabouts, there or thereabouts, more or less, give or take a few, not far off; Brit. getting on for; informal as near as dammit; N. Amer. informal in the ballpark of. **4** *there's a lot of flu about* AROUND, in circulation, in existence, current, going on, prevailing, prevalent, happening, in the air, abroad.
– PHRASES **about to** (JUST) GOING TO, ready to, all set to, preparing to, intending to, soon to; on the point of, on the verge of, on the brink of, within an ace of.

about-turn (Brit.) • noun **1** *he saluted and did an about-turn* ABOUT-FACE, volte-face, turnaround, turnabout, U-turn; informal U-ey, one-eighty. **2** *the government was forced to make an about-turn* VOLTE-FACE, U-turn, reversal, retraction, backtracking, swing, swerve; change of heart, change of mind, sea change.

above • preposition **1** *a tiny window above the door* OVER, higher (up) than; on top of, atop, on, upon. **2** *those above the rank of Colonel* SUPERIOR TO, senior to, over, higher (up) than, more powerful than; in charge of, commanding. **3** *you must be above suspicion* BEYOND, not liable to, not open to, not vulnerable to, out of reach of; immune to, exempt from. **4** *the Chinese valued pearls above gold* MORE THAN, over, before, rather than, in preference to, instead of. **5** *an increase above the rate of inflation* GREATER THAN, more than, higher than, exceeding, in excess of, over, over and above, beyond, surpassing, upwards of.
– OPPOSITES below, under, beneath.
• adverb **1** *in the darkness above, something moved* OVERHEAD, on/at the top, high up, on high, up above, (up) in the sky, high above one's head, aloft. **2** *the two cases described above* EARLIER, previously, before, formerly.
• adjective *the above example* PRECEDING, previous, earlier, former, foregoing, prior, above-stated, aforementioned, aforesaid.
– PHRASES **above all** MOST IMPORTANTLY, before everything, beyond everything, first of all, most of all, chiefly, primarily, in the first place, first and foremost, mainly, principally, predominantly, especially, essentially, basically, in essence, at bottom; informal at the end of the day, when all is said and done. **above oneself** CONCEITED, proud, arrogant, self-important, cocky, haughty, disdainful, snobbish, snobby, supercilious; informal stuck-up, high and mighty, snooty, uppity, big-headed, swollen-headed, too big for one's boots.

above board • adjective *the proceedings were completely above board* LEGITIMATE, lawful, legal, licit, honest, fair, open, frank, straight, overt, candid, forthright, unconcealed, trustworthy, unequivocal; informal legit, kosher, pukka, by the book, fair and square, square, on the level, on the up and up, upfront.
– OPPOSITES dishonest, shady.

abrade • verb WEAR AWAY/DOWN, erode, scrape away, corrode, eat away at, gnaw away at.

abrasion • noun **1** *he had abrasions to his forehead* GRAZE, cut, scrape, scratch, gash, laceration, injury, contusion; sore, ulcer;

manner. ● noun a substance used for abrading.
– DERIVATIVES **abrasively** adverb **abrasiveness** noun.
abreaction ● noun Psychoanalysis the expression and consequent release of a previously repressed emotion, achieved through hypnosis or suggestion.
– ORIGIN German *Abreagierung*.
abreast ● adverb **1** side by side and facing the same way. **2** alongside. **3** (**abreast of**) up to date with.
abridge ● verb shorten (a text or film).
– DERIVATIVES **abridgement** (also **abridgment**) noun **abridger** noun.
– ORIGIN Old French *abregier*, from Latin *abbreviare* 'abbreviate'.
abroad ● adverb **1** in or to a foreign country or countries. **2** in different directions; over a wide area. **3** at large; in circulation. **4** archaic out of doors. ● noun foreign countries collectively.
abrogate /abrəgayt/ ● verb formal repeal or do away with (a law or agreement).
– DERIVATIVES **abrogation** noun **abrogator** noun.
– ORIGIN Latin *abrogare* 'repeal'.
abrupt ● adjective **1** sudden and unexpected. **2** brief to the point of rudeness; curt. **3** steep.
– DERIVATIVES **abruptly** adverb **abruptness** noun.
– ORIGIN Latin *abruptus* 'broken off, steep', from *rumpere* 'break'.
ABS ● abbreviation anti-lock braking system.
abscess ● noun a swollen area within body tissue, containing pus.
– ORIGIN Latin *abscessus*, from *abscedere* 'go away'.
abscissa /absissə/ ● noun (pl. **abscissae** /absissee/ or **abscissas**) Mathematics the distance from a point on a graph to the vertical or *y*-axis; the *x*-coordinate.
– ORIGIN from Latin *abscissa linea* 'cut-off line'.
abscission /əbsizh'n/ ● noun Botany the process by which parts of a plant, e.g. dead leaves, break off naturally.
– ORIGIN Latin, from *abscindere* 'cut off'.
abscond /əbskond/ ● verb leave hurriedly and secretly to escape from custody or avoid arrest.
– DERIVATIVES **absconder** noun.
– ORIGIN Latin *abscondere* 'hide'.
abseil /absayl, -zīl/ ● verb descend a near-vertical surface using a rope coiled round the body and fixed at a higher point.
– DERIVATIVES **abseiler** noun **abseiling** noun.
– ORIGIN German *abseilen*, from *ab* 'down' + *Seil* 'rope'.
absence ● noun **1** the state of being away from a place or person. **2** (**absence of**) the non-existence or lack of.
– PHRASES **absence makes the heart grow fonder** proverb you feel more affection for those you love when parted from them.
absent ● adjective /abs'nt/ **1** not present. **2** showing a lack of attention. ● verb /əbsent/ (**absent oneself**) stay or go away.
– DERIVATIVES **absently** adverb.
– ORIGIN from Latin *abesse* 'to be away'.
absentee ● noun a person who is absent.
absenteeism ● noun frequent absence from work or school without good reason.
absent-minded ● adjective inattentive or forgetful.
– DERIVATIVES **absent-mindedly** adverb **absent-mindedness** noun.
absinth /absinth/ ● noun **1** the shrub wormwood. **2** (usu. **absinthe**) a green aniseed-flavoured liqueur formerly made with wormwood.
– ORIGIN French, from Greek *apsinthion* 'wormwood'.
absolute ● adjective **1** not qualified or diminished in any way; total. **2** having unlimited power: *an absolute ruler*. **3** not relative or comparative: *absolute moral principles*. **4** Grammar (of a construction) syntactically independent of the rest of the sentence, as in *dinner being over, we left the table*; (of an adjective or transitive verb) used without an expressed noun or object (e.g. *the brave, guns kill*). **5** Law (of a decree) final. ● noun Philosophy a value or principle which is universally valid or able to be viewed without relation to other things.
– DERIVATIVES **absoluteness** noun.
– ORIGIN Latin *absolutus* 'freed, unrestricted', from *absolvere* 'set free'.
absolutely ● adverb **1** with no qualification, restriction, or limi-

Thesaurus

Medicine trauma. **2** *the metal is resistant to abrasion* EROSION, wearing away/down, corrosion.
abrasive ● adjective **1** *abrasive kitchen cleaners* CORROSIVE, corroding, erosive; caustic, harsh, coarse. **2** *her abrasive manner* CAUSTIC, cutting, biting, acerbic; rough, harsh, hard, tough, sharp, curt, brusque, stern, severe; wounding, nasty, cruel, callous, insensitive, unfeeling, unsympathetic, inconsiderate; *N. Amer.* acerb.
– OPPOSITES kind, gentle.
abreast ● adverb **1** *they walked three abreast* IN A ROW, side by side, alongside, level, beside each other, shoulder to shoulder. **2** *try to keep abreast of current affairs* UP TO DATE WITH, up with, in touch with, informed about, acquainted with, knowledgeable about, conversant with, familiar with, au courant with, au fait with.
abridge ● verb SHORTEN, cut, cut short/down, curtail, truncate, trim, crop, clip, pare down, prune; abbreviate, condense, contract, compress, reduce, decrease, shrink; summarize, sum up, abstract, precis, synopsize, give a digest of, put in a nutshell, edit; *rare* epitomize.
– OPPOSITES lengthen.
abridged ● adjective SHORTENED, cut, cut down, concise, condensed, abbreviated; summary, outline, thumbnail; bowdlerized, censored, expurgated; *informal* potted.
abridgement ● noun SUMMARY, abstract, synopsis, precis, outline, résumé, sketch, digest.
abroad ● adverb **1** *he regularly travels abroad* OVERSEAS, out of the country, to/in foreign parts, to/in a foreign country/land. **2** *rumours were abroad* IN CIRCULATION, circulating, widely current, everywhere, in the air, {here, there, and everywhere}; about, around; at large.
abrogate ● verb *(formal)* REPEAL, revoke, rescind, repudiate, overturn, annul, cancel, invalidate, nullify, void, negate, dissolve, countermand, declare null and void, discontinue; reverse, retract, remove, withdraw, abolish, put an end to, do away with, get rid of, end, stop, quash, scrap; *Law* disaffirm.
– OPPOSITES institute, introduce.
abrogation ● noun *(formal)* REPEAL, revocation, repudiation, rescindment, overturning, annulment, cancellation, invalidation, nullification, negation, dissolution, discontinuation; reversal, retraction, removal, withdrawal, abolition; *formal* rescission; *Law* disaffirmation.
abrupt ● adjective **1** *an abrupt halt | an abrupt change of subject* SUDDEN, unexpected, without warning, unanticipated, unforeseen, precipitate, surprising, startling; quick, swift, rapid, hurried, hasty, immediate, instantaneous. **2** *an abrupt manner* CURT, brusque, blunt, short, sharp, terse, brisk, crisp, gruff, rude, discourteous, uncivil, snappish, unceremonious, offhand, rough, harsh; bluff, no-nonsense, to the point; *informal* snappy. **3** *abrupt, epigrammatic paragraphs* DISJOINTED, jerky, uneven, disconnected, inelegant. **4** *an abrupt slope* STEEP, sheer, precipitous, bluff, sharp, sudden; perpendicular, vertical, dizzy, vertiginous.
– OPPOSITES gradual, gentle.
abscess ● noun ULCER, ulceration, cyst, boil, blister, sore, pustule, carbuncle, pimple, wen, whitlow, canker; inflammation, infection, eruption.
abscond ● verb RUN AWAY, escape, bolt, flee, make off, take flight, take off, decamp; make a break for it, take to one's heels, make a quick getaway, beat a hasty retreat, show a clean pair of heels, run for it, make a run for it; disappear, vanish, slip away, steal away, sneak away; *informal* do a moonlight flit, clear out, cut and run, skedaddle, skip, head for the hills, do a disappearing act, fly the coop, take French leave, scarper, vamoose; *Brit. informal* do a bunk, do a runner; *N. Amer. informal* take a powder.
absence ● noun **1** *his prolonged absence from the office* NON-ATTENDANCE, non-appearance, absenteeism; TRUANCY, playing truant; leave, holiday, vacation, sabbatical. **2** *the absence of any other suitable candidate* LACK, want, non-existence, unavailability, deficiency, dearth; need.
– OPPOSITES presence.
absent ● adjective **1** *she was absent from work* AWAY, off, out, non-attending, truant; off duty, on holiday, on leave; gone, missing, lacking, unavailable, non-existent; *informal* AWOL. **2** *an absent look* DISTRACTED, preoccupied, inattentive, vague, absorbed, abstracted, unheeding, oblivious, distrait, absent-minded, dreamy, far away, in a world of one's own, lost in thought, in a brown study; blank, empty, vacant; *informal* miles away.
– OPPOSITES present, attentive, alert.
● verb *Rose absented herself from the occasion* STAY AWAY, be absent, withdraw, retire, take one's leave, remove oneself.
absent-minded ● adjective FORGETFUL, distracted, preoccupied, inattentive, vague, abstracted, unheeding, oblivious, distrait, in a brown study, wool-gathering; lost in thought, pensive, thoughtful, brooding; *informal* scatterbrained, miles away, having a mind/

a

tation. **2** used for emphasis or to express agreement. **3** not viewed in relation to other things or factors.
absolute majority ● noun a majority over all rivals combined; more than half.
absolute pitch ● noun Music **1** perfect pitch. **2** pitch according to a fixed standard defined by the frequency of the sound vibration.
absolute temperature ● noun a temperature measured from absolute zero in kelvins.
absolute zero ● noun the lowest temperature theoretically possible (zero kelvins, -273.15°C).
absolution ● noun **1** formal release from guilt, obligation, or punishment. **2** formal declaration by a priest that a person's sins are forgiven.
– ORIGIN Latin, from *absolvere* 'set free, acquit'.
absolutism ● noun **1** the principle that those in government should have unlimited power. **2** belief in absolute principles in philosophy.
– DERIVATIVES **absolutist** noun & adjective.
absolve /əbzolv/ ● verb **1** declare (someone) free from guilt or responsibility. **2** give absolution for (a sin).
– ORIGIN Latin *absolvere* 'set free, acquit'.
absorb /əbzorb, -sorb/ ● verb **1** soak up (liquid or another substance). **2** take in (information). **3** assimilate or take over (something less powerful). **4** use up (time or resources). **5** reduce the effect or intensity of (sound or an impact). **6** (usu. as **absorbed** or **absorbing**) engross the attention of.
– DERIVATIVES **absorbable** adjective **absorber** noun.
– ORIGIN Latin *absorbere* 'suck in'.
absorbent ● adjective able to soak up liquid easily.
– DERIVATIVES **absorbency** noun.
absorption ● noun the process of absorbing or the action of being absorbed.
– DERIVATIVES **absorptive** adjective.
abstain ● verb **1** restrain oneself from doing or indulging in something. **2** formally choose not to vote.
– DERIVATIVES **abstainer** noun.
– ORIGIN Latin *abstinere* 'hold from'.
abstemious /əbsteemiəss/ ● adjective not self-indulgent, especially as regards eating and drinking.
– DERIVATIVES **abstemiously** adverb **abstemiousness** noun.
– ORIGIN Latin *abstemius*, from *ab-* 'from' + a word related to *temetum* 'alcoholic liquor'.
abstention /əbstensh'n/ ● noun **1** an instance of abstaining from a vote. **2** abstinence.
abstinence /abstinənss/ ● noun the practice of abstaining, especially from drinking alcohol.
– DERIVATIVES **abstinent** adjective.
– ORIGIN Latin *abstinentia*, from *abstinere*, 'hold from'.
abstract ● adjective /abstrakt/ **1** theoretical rather than physical or concrete. **2** (of art) achieving its effect through colour and shapes rather than attempting to represent recognizable reality. ● verb /əbstrakt/ **1** extract or remove. **2** consider theoretically or separately from something else. **3** make a written summary of. ● noun /abstrakt/ **1** a summary of a book or article. **2** an abstract work of art.
– DERIVATIVES **abstractly** adverb **abstractor** noun.
– ORIGIN from Latin *abstrahere* 'draw away'.
abstracted ● adjective not concentrating on what is happening; preoccupied.
– DERIVATIVES **abstractedly** adverb.
abstract expressionism ● noun a development of abstract art aiming at subjective emotional expression with particular emphasis on spontaneous creativity (e.g. action painting).
abstraction ● noun **1** the quality of being abstract. **2** something which exists only as an idea. **3** a preoccupied state. **4** abstracting or removing something.
abstruse /əbstroōss/ ● adjective difficult to understand; obscure.

Thesaurus

memory like a sieve.
absolute ● adjective **1** *absolute silence | an absolute disgrace* COMPLETE, total, utter, out-and-out, outright, entire, perfect, pure, decided; thorough, thoroughgoing, undivided, unqualified, unadulterated, unalloyed, unmodified, unreserved, downright, undiluted, consummate, unmitigated, sheer, arrant, rank, dyed-in-the wool. **2** *the absolute truth* DEFINITE, certain, positive, unconditional, categorical, unquestionable, incontrovertible, undoubted, unequivocal, decisive, conclusive, confirmed, infallible. **3** *absolute power* UNLIMITED, unrestricted, unrestrained, unbounded, boundless, infinite, ultimate, total, supreme, unconditional. **4** *an absolute monarch* AUTOCRATIC, despotic, dictatorial, tyrannical, tyrannous, authoritarian, arbitrary, autonomous, sovereign, autarchic, omnipotent. **5** *absolute moral standards* UNIVERSAL, fixed, independent, non-relative, non-variable, absolutist.
– OPPOSITES partial, qualified, limited, conditional.
absolutely ● adverb *you're absolutely right* COMPLETELY, totally, utterly, perfectly, entirely, wholly, fully, quite, thoroughly, unreservedly; definitely, certainly, positively, unconditionally, categorically, unquestionably, undoubtedly, without (a) doubt, without question, surely, unequivocally; exactly, precisely, decisively, conclusively, manifestly, in every way/respect, one hundred per cent, every inch, to the hilt; *informal* dead.
● exclamation (*informal*) *'Have I made myself clear?' 'Absolutely!'* YES, indeed, of course, definitely, certainly, quite, without (a) doubt, without question, unquestionably; by all means.
absolution ● noun FORGIVENESS, pardon, exoneration, remission, dispensation, indulgence, clemency, mercy; discharge, acquittal; freedom, deliverance, release; vindication; *informal* let-off; *formal* exculpation; *archaic* shrift.
absolve ● verb **1** *this fact does not absolve you from responsibility* EXONERATE, discharge, acquit, vindicate; release, relieve, liberate, free, deliver, clear, exempt, let off; *formal* exculpate. **2** *I absolve you from your sins* FORGIVE, pardon.
– OPPOSITES blame, condemn.
absorb ● verb **1** *a sponge-like material which absorbs water* SOAK UP, suck up, draw up/in, take up/in, blot up, mop up, sop up. **2** *she absorbed the information in silence* ASSIMILATE, digest, take in. **3** *the company was absorbed into the new concern* INCORPORATE, assimilate, integrate, take in, subsume, include, co-opt, swallow up. **4** *these roles absorb most of his time and energy* USE (UP), consume, take up, occupy. **5** *she was totally abosrbed in her book* ENGROSS, captivate, occupy, preoccupy, engage, rivet, grip, hold, interest, intrigue, immerse, involve, enthral, spellbind, fascinate.
absorbent ● adjective POROUS, spongy, sponge-like, permeable, pervious, absorptive; *technical* spongiform; *rare* sorbefacient.
absorbing ● adjective FASCINATING, interesting, captivating, gripping, engrossing, compelling, compulsive, enthralling, riveting, spellbinding, intriguing, thrilling, exciting; *informal* unputdownable.
– OPPOSITES boring, uninteresting.
absorption ● noun **1** *the absorption of water* SOAKING UP, sucking up; *technical* osmosis. **2** *the company's absorption into a larger concern* INCORPORATION, assimilation, integration, inclusion. **3** *her total absorption in the music* INVOLVEMENT, immersion, raptness, engrossment, occupation, preoccupation, engagement, captivation, fascination, enthralment.
abstain ● verb **1** *Benjamin abstained from wine* REFRAIN, desist, hold back, forbear; give up, renounce, avoid, shun, eschew, forgo, go without, do without; refuse, decline; *informal* cut out; *formal* abjure. **2** *most pregnant women abstain, or drink very little* BE TEETOTAL, take the pledge; *informal* be on the wagon. **3** *262 voted against, 38 abstained* NOT VOTE, decline to vote.
abstemious ● adjective SELF-DENYING, temperate, abstinent, moderate, self-disciplined, restrained, self-restrained, sober, austere, ascetic, puritanical, spartan, self-abnegating, hair-shirt.
– OPPOSITES self-indulgent.
abstinence ● noun SELF-DENIAL, self-restraint; teetotalism, temperance, sobriety, abstemiousness, abstention.
abstract ● adjective **1** *abstract concepts* THEORETICAL, conceptual, notional, intellectual, metaphysical, philosophical, academic; *rare* ideational. **2** *abstract art* NON-REPRESENTATIONAL, non-pictorial.
– OPPOSITES actual, concrete.
● verb **1** *staff abstract material for an online database* SUMMARIZE, precis, abridge, condense, compress, shorten, cut down, abbreviate, synopsize; *rare* epitomize. **2** *a scheme to abstract more water from the river* EXTRACT, pump, draw (off), withdraw, remove, take out/away; separate, isolate.
● noun *an abstract of her speech* SUMMARY, synopsis, precis, résumé, outline, abridgement, digest, summation; *N. Amer.* wrap-up; *archaic* argument.
abstracted ● adjective ABSENT-MINDED, distracted, preoccupied, in a world of one's own, with one's head in the clouds, daydreaming, dreamy, inattentive, thoughtful, pensive, lost in thought, deep in thought, immersed in thought, wool-gathering, in a brown study, musing, brooding, absent, distrait; *informal* miles away.

– DERIVATIVES **abstrusely** adverb **abstruseness** noun.
– ORIGIN Latin *abstrusus* 'concealed'.
absurd ● adjective completely unreasonable, illogical, or inappropriate.
– DERIVATIVES **absurdity** noun **absurdly** adverb.
– ORIGIN Latin *absurdus* 'out of tune', hence 'irrational'.
absurdism ● noun the belief that human beings exist in a purposeless, chaotic universe.
– DERIVATIVES **absurdist** adjective & noun.
ABTA ● abbreviation Association of British Travel Agents.
abundance /əbundənss/ ● noun **1** a very large quantity. **2** the state of having a very large quantity; plentifulness: *vines grew in abundance.* **3** the amount of something present in a particular area, volume, or sample.
– ORIGIN Latin *abundantia*, from *abundare* 'overflow'.
abundant ● adjective **1** existing or available in large quantities; plentiful. **2** (**abundant in**) having plenty of.
– DERIVATIVES **abundantly** adverb.
abuse ● verb /əbyōōz/ **1** use improperly or to excess. **2** treat with cruelty or violence, especially assault sexually. **3** speak to in an insulting and offensive way. ● noun /əbyōōss/ **1** the improper use of something. **2** cruel and violent treatment, especially sexual assault. **3** insulting and offensive language.
– DERIVATIVES **abuser** noun.
– ORIGIN Latin *abuti* 'misuse'.
abusive ● adjective **1** extremely offensive and insulting. **2** involving cruelty and violence.
– DERIVATIVES **abusively** adverb **abusiveness** noun.
abut /əbut/ ● verb (**abutted, abutting**) **1** be next to or share a boundary with. **2** touch or lean on.
– ORIGIN Old French *abouter*, from *bouter* 'strike, butt'.
abutilon /əbyōōtilon/ ● noun a herbaceous plant or shrub growing in warm climates, with showy yellow, red, or mauve flowers.
– ORIGIN Latin, from an Arabic word meaning 'Indian mallow'.
abutment ● noun a structure supporting the side of an arch, especially at the end of a bridge.
abysmal ● adjective **1** informal extremely bad. **2** literary very deep.
– DERIVATIVES **abysmally** adverb.
abyss /əbiss/ ● noun a very deep chasm.
– ORIGIN from Greek *abussos* 'bottomless'.
abyssal ● adjective **1** relating to the depths of the ocean. **2** Geology plutonic.
Abyssinian /abissiniən/ ● adjective historical relating to Abyssinia (the former name of Ethiopia). ● noun **1** historical a person from Abyssinia. **2** a breed of cat having long ears and short brown hair flecked with grey.
AC ● abbreviation **1** alternating current. **2** air conditioning. **3** Aircraftman. **4** appellation contrôlée. **5** athletic club.
Ac ● symbol the chemical element actinium.
a/c ● abbreviation **1** account. **2** (also **A/C**) air conditioning.
acacia /əkayshə/ ● noun a tree or shrub of warm climates with yellow or white flowers.
– ORIGIN Greek *akakia*.
academe /akkədeem/ ● noun (often in phrase **the groves of academe**) academia.
academia /akkədeemiə/ ● noun the academic environment or community.
academic ● adjective **1** relating to education and scholarship. **2** scholarly rather than technical or practical. **3** of only theoretical interest. ● noun a teacher or scholar in an institute of higher education.
– DERIVATIVES **academically** adverb.
academician /əkaddəmish'n/ ● noun **1** a member of an academy. **2** N. Amer. an academic.
academicism /akkədemmisiz'm/ ● noun adherence to formal or conventional rules and traditions in art or literature.
academy ● noun (pl. **academies**) **1** a place of study or training in a special field. **2** a society or institution of distinguished scholars, artists, or scientists that aims to promote and maintain standards in its field. **3** US & Scottish a secondary school.
– ORIGIN Greek *akadēmeia*, from *Akadēmos*, the name of the garden where Plato taught.
Academy award ● noun an award given by the Academy of Motion Picture Arts and Sciences for achievement in the film industry; an Oscar.

Thesaurus

– OPPOSITES attentive.
abstraction ● noun **1** *philosophical abstractions* CONCEPT, idea, notion, thought, theory, hypothesis. **2** *she sensed his momentary abstraction* ABSENT-MINDEDNESS, distraction, preoccupation, dreaminess, inattentiveness, inattention, wool-gathering; thoughtfulness, pensiveness. **3** *the abstraction of metal from ore* EXTRACTION, removal, separation.
abstruse ● adjective OBSCURE, arcane, esoteric, little known, recherché, rarefied, recondite, difficult, hard, puzzling, perplexing, cryptic, Delphic, complex, complicated, involved, over/above one's head, incomprehensible, unfathomable, impenetrable, mysterious.
absurd ● adjective PREPOSTEROUS, ridiculous, ludicrous, farcical, laughable, risible, idiotic, stupid, foolish, silly, inane, imbecilic, insane, hare-brained; unreasonable, irrational, illogical, nonsensical, pointless, senseless; *informal* crazy; *Brit. informal* barmy, daft.
– OPPOSITES reasonable, sensible.
absurdity ● noun PREPOSTEROUSNESS, ridiculousness, ludicrousness, risibility, idiocy, stupidity, foolishness, folly, silliness, inanity, insanity; unreasonableness, irrationality, illogicality, pointlessness, senselessness; *informal* craziness.
abundance ● noun PROFUSION, plentifulness, profuseness, copiousness, amplitude, lavishness, bountifulness; host, cornucopia, riot; plenty, quantities, scores, multitude; *informal* millions, sea, ocean(s), wealth, lot(s), heap(s), mass(es), stack(s), pile(s), load(s), bags, mountain(s), ton(s), slew, scads, oodles; *Brit. informal* shedload; *N. Amer. informal* gobs; *formal* plenitude.
– OPPOSITES lack, scarcity.
abundant ● adjective *an abundant supply of food* PLENTIFUL, copious, ample, profuse, rich, lavish, liberal, generous, bountiful, large, huge, great, bumper, overflowing, prolific, teeming; in plenty, in abundance; *informal* a gogo, galore; *poetic/literary* plenteous, bounteous.
– OPPOSITES scarce, sparse.
– PHRASES **be abundant** ABOUND, be plentiful, be numerous, proliferate, be thick on the ground; *informal* grow on trees, be two/ten a penny.
abuse ● verb **1** *the judge abused his power* MISUSE, misapply, misemploy; exploit, take advantage of. **2** *he was accused of abusing children* MISTREAT, maltreat, ill-treat, treat badly; molest, interfere with, indecently assault, sexually abuse, sexually assault; injure, hurt, harm, damage. **3** *the referee was abused by players from both teams* INSULT, be rude to, swear at, curse, call someone names, taunt, shout at, revile, inveigh against, vilify, slander, cast aspersions on; *Brit. informal* slag off.
● noun **1** *the abuse of power* MISUSE, misapplication, misemployment; exploitation. **2** *the abuse of children* MISTREATMENT, maltreatment, ill-treatment; molestation, interference, indecent assault, sexual abuse, sexual assault; injury, hurt, harm, damage. **3** *the scheme is open to administrative abuse* CORRUPTION, injustice, wrongdoing, wrong, misconduct, misdeed(s), offence(s), crime(s), sin(s). **4** *torrents of abuse* INSULTS, curses, jibes, expletives, swear words; swearing, cursing, name-calling; invective, vilification, vituperation, slander; *Brit. informal* verbal(s); *N. Amer. informal* trash talk; *archaic* contumely.
abusive ● adjective INSULTING, rude, vulgar, offensive, disparaging, belittling, derogatory, disrespectful, denigratory, uncomplimentary, pejorative, vituperative; defamatory, slanderous, libellous, scurrilous, blasphemous; *informal* bitchy; *archaic* contumelious.
abut ● verb ADJOIN, be adjacent to, border, neighbour, join, touch, meet, reach, be contiguous with.
abysmal ● adjective *(informal) some of the teaching was abysmal* VERY BAD, dreadful, awful, terrible, frightful, atrocious, disgraceful, deplorable, shameful, hopeless, lamentable, laughable; *informal* rotten, appalling, crummy, pathetic, pitiful, woeful, useless, lousy, dire, poxy, the pits; *Brit. informal* chronic, shocking.
abyss ● noun CHASM, gorge, ravine, canyon, fissure, rift, crevasse, hole, gulf, pit, cavity, void, bottomless pit.
academic ● adjective **1** *an academic institution* EDUCATIONAL, scholastic, instructional, pedagogical. **2** *his academic turn of mind* SCHOLARLY, studious, literary, well read, intellectual, clever, erudite, learned, educated, cultured, bookish, highbrow, pedantic, donnish, cerebral; *informal* brainy; *dated* lettered. **3** *the debate has been largely academic* THEORETICAL, conceptual, notional, philosophical, hypothetical, speculative, conjectural, suppositional, putative; impractical, unrealistic, ivory-tower.
● noun *a group of Russian academics* SCHOLAR, lecturer, don, teacher, tutor, professor, fellow, man/woman of letters, thinker, blue-

a

Acadian /əkaydiən/ ● adjective relating to the former French colony of Acadia (now Nova Scotia) in Canada. ● noun a person from Acadia.

acanthus /əkanthəss/ ● noun **1** a plant or shrub with bold flower spikes and spiny decorative leaves. **2** Architecture a representation of an acanthus leaf.
– ORIGIN Greek *akanthos*, from *akantha* 'thorn'.

a cappella /a kəpellə/ ● adjective & adverb (of music) sung without instrumental accompaniment.
– ORIGIN Italian, 'in chapel style'.

acaricide ● noun a substance poisonous to mites or ticks.
– ORIGIN from Greek *akari* 'mite, tick'.

ACAS /aykass/ ● abbreviation (in the UK) Advisory, Conciliation, and Arbitration Service.

accede /əkseed/ ● verb (usu. **accede to**) formal **1** assent or agree to a demand, request, or treaty. **2** take up an office or position.
– ORIGIN Latin *accedere* 'come to'.

accelerando /əksellərandō, əchel-/ ● adverb & adjective Music with a gradual increase of speed.
– ORIGIN Italian.

accelerant ● noun a substance used to help fire spread.

accelerate /əksellərayt/ ● verb **1** begin or cause to move more quickly. **2** increase in rate, amount, or extent.
– DERIVATIVES **acceleration** noun.
– ORIGIN Latin *accelerare* 'hasten', from *celer* 'swift'.

accelerator ● noun **1** a foot pedal which controls the speed of a vehicle's engine. **2** Physics an apparatus for accelerating charged particles to high velocities. **3** a substance that speeds up a chemical process.

accelerometer /əksellərommitər/ ● noun an instrument for measuring acceleration.

accent ● noun /aks'nt, -sent/ **1** a way of pronouncing a language, associated with a country, area, or social class. **2** an emphasis given to a syllable, word, or note. **3** a mark on a letter or word indicating how a sound is pronounced or stressed. **4** a particular emphasis: *the accent is on participation.* ● verb /aksent/ **1** (**accented**) spoken with a particular accent: *accented English.* **2** stress or emphasize.
– DERIVATIVES **accentual** adjective.
– ORIGIN Latin *accentus* 'tone, signal, or intensity'.

accentuate /əksentyooayt/ ● verb make more noticeable or prominent.
– DERIVATIVES **accentuation** noun.

accept ● verb **1** agree to receive or undertake (something offered or proposed). **2** regard favourably or with approval. **3** believe or receive as valid or correct. **4** take on (a responsibility or liability). **5** tolerate or submit to.
– DERIVATIVES **acceptance** noun **acceptor** noun.
– ORIGIN Latin *acceptare*, from *capere* 'take'.

acceptable ● adjective **1** able to be accepted. **2** adequate, though not outstanding or perfect.
– DERIVATIVES **acceptability** noun **acceptably** adverb.

access ● noun **1** the means or opportunity to approach or enter a place. **2** the right or opportunity to use something or see someone. **3** retrieval of information stored in a computer's memory. **4** an attack or outburst of an emotion: *an access of rage.* ● verb **1** gain access to; make accessible. **2** approach or enter (a place).
– ORIGIN Latin *accessus*, from *accedere* 'come to'.

accessible ● adjective **1** able to be accessed. **2** friendly and easy to talk to; approachable. **3** easily understood or appreciated.
– DERIVATIVES **accessibility** noun **accessibly** adverb.

accession ● noun **1** the attainment of a position of rank. **2** the formal acceptance of a treaty or joining of an association. **3** a

Thesaurus

stocking; *informal* egghead, bookworm; *formal* pedagogue.

academy ● noun EDUCATIONAL INSTITUTION, school, college, university, institute, seminary, conservatory, conservatoire.

accede ● verb (*formal*) **1** *he acceded to the government's demands* AGREE TO, consent to, accept, assent to, acquiesce in, comply with, go along with, concur with, surrender to, yield to, give in to, give way to, defer to. **2** *Elizabeth I acceded to the throne in 1558* SUCCEED TO, come to, assume, inherit, take. **3** *Albania acceded to the IMF in 1990* JOIN, become a member of, sign up to.

accelerate ● verb **1** *the car accelerated down the hill* SPEED UP, go faster, gain momentum, increase speed, pick up speed, gather speed, put on a spurt. **2** *inflation started to accelerate* INCREASE, rise, go up, leap up, surge, escalate, spiral. **3** *the university accelerated the planning process* HASTEN, expedite, precipitate, speed up, quicken, make faster, step up, advance, further, forward, promote, give a boost to, stimulate, spur on; *informal* crank up.
– OPPOSITES decelerate, delay.

acceleration ● noun **1** *the car's acceleration is sensational* INCREASE IN SPEED, increasing speed, gain in momentum. **2** *the acceleration of the industrial process* HASTENING, precipitation, speeding up, quickening, stepping up, advancement, furtherance, boost, stimulation, spur. **3** *an acceleration in the divorce rate* INCREASE, rise, leap, surge, escalation.

accent ● noun **1** *a Scottish accent* PRONUNCIATION, intonation, enunciation, articulation, inflection, tone, modulation, cadence, timbre, manner of speaking, delivery; brogue, burr, drawl, twang. **2** *the accent is on the first syllable* STRESS, emphasis, accentuation, force, prominence; beat; *technical* ictus. **3** *the accent is on comfort* EMPHASIS, stress, priority; importance, prominence. **4** *an acute accent* MARK, diacritic, diacritical mark.
● verb *fabrics which accent the background colours in the room* FOCUS ATTENTION ON, draw attention to, point up, underline, underscore, accentuate, highlight, spotlight, foreground, feature, play up, bring to the fore, heighten, stress, emphasize.

accentuate ● verb FOCUS ATTENTION ON, draw attention to, point up, underline, underscore, accent, highlight, spotlight, foreground, feature, play up, bring to the fore, heighten, stress, emphasize.

accept ● verb **1** *he accepted a pen as a present* RECEIVE, take, get, gain, obtain, acquire. **2** *he accepted the job immediately* TAKE ON, undertake, assume, take responsibility for. **3** *she accepted an invitation to lunch* SAY YES TO, reply in the affirmative, agree to. **4** *she was accepted as one of the family* WELCOME, receive, embrace, adopt. **5** *he accepted Ellen's explanation* BELIEVE, regard as true, give credence to, credit, trust; *informal* buy, swallow. **6** *we have agreed to accept his decision* GO ALONG WITH, agree to, consent to, acquiesce in, concur with, assent to, comply with, abide by, follow, adhere to, act in accordance with, defer to, yield to, surrender to, bow to, give in to, submit to, respect; *formal* accede to. **7** *she will just have to accept the consequences* TOLERATE, endure, put up with, bear, take, submit to, stomach, swallow; reconcile oneself to, resign oneself to, get used to, adjust to, learn to live with, make the best of; face up to.
– OPPOSITES refuse, reject.

acceptable ● adjective **1** *an acceptable standard of living* SATISFACTORY, adequate, reasonable, quite good, fair, decent, good enough, sufficient, sufficiently good, fine, not bad, all right, average, tolerable, passable, middling, moderate; *informal* OK, so-so, fair-to-middling. **2** *a most acceptable present* WELCOME, appreciated; pleasing, agreeable, delightful, desirable, satisfying, gratifying, to one's liking. **3** *the risk had seemed acceptable at the time* BEARABLE, tolerable, allowable, admissible, sustainable, justifiable, defensible.

acceptance ● noun **1** *the acceptance of an award* RECEIPT, receiving, taking, obtaining. **2** *the acceptance of responsibility* UNDERTAKING, assumption. **3** *acceptances to an invitation* YES, affirmative reply, confirmation. **4** *her acceptance as one of the family* WELCOME, favourable reception, adoption. **5** *his acceptance of Matilda's explanation* BELIEF, credence, trust, faith. **6** *their acceptance of the decision* COMPLIANCE, acquiescence, agreement, consent, concurrence, assent, adherence, deference, surrender, submission, respect. **7** *the acceptance of pain* TOLERATION, endurance, forbearance.

accepted ● adjective RECOGNIZED, acknowledged, established, traditional, orthodox; usual, customary, common, normal, general, prevailing, accustomed, familiar, wonted, popular, expected, routine, standard, stock.

access ● noun **1** *the building has a side access* ENTRANCE, entry, way in, means of entry; approach, means of approach. **2** *they were denied access to the stadium* ADMISSION, admittance, entry, entrée, ingress, right of entry. **3** *students have access to a photocopier* (THE) USE OF, permission to use. **4** *an access of rage* FIT, attack, outburst, outpouring, eruption, explosion, burst, outbreak, flare-up, blow-up, blaze, paroxysm, bout, rush; outflow, outflowing, welling up.
● verb *the program used to access the data* RETRIEVE, gain access to, obtain; read.

accessible ● adjective **1** *the village is only accessible on foot | an easily accessible reference tool* REACHABLE, attainable, approachable; obtainable, available; *informal* get-at-able. **2** *his accessible style of writing* UNDERSTANDABLE, comprehensible, easy to understand, intelligible. **3** *Professor Cooper is very accessible* APPROACHABLE,

a

new item added to a library or museum collection.
accessorize (also **accessorise**) ● verb add a fashion accessory to (a garment).
accessory (also **accessary**) ● noun (pl. **accessories**) **1** a thing which can be added to something else to make it more useful, versatile, or attractive. **2** a small article carried or worn to complement a garment. **3** Law a person who helps someone commit a crime without taking part in it. ● adjective chiefly technical subsidiary or supplementary.
– ORIGIN Latin *accessorius* 'additional thing'.
acciaccatura /əchakkətoorə/ ● noun (pl. **acciaccaturas** or **acciaccature** /əchakkətooray/) Music a grace note performed as quickly as possible before an essential note of a melody.
– ORIGIN Italian, from *acciaccare* 'to crush'.
accident ● noun **1** an unfortunate incident that happens unexpectedly and unintentionally. **2** an incident that happens by chance or without apparent cause. **3** chance.
– PHRASES **accidents will happen in the best regulated families** proverb however careful you try to be, it is inevitable that some unfortunate or unforeseen events will occur.
– ORIGIN from Latin *accidere* 'to fall or happen'.
accidental ● adjective **1** happening by accident. **2** incidental; subsidiary. ● noun Music a sign indicating a momentary departure from the key signature by raising or lowering a note.
– DERIVATIVES **accidentally** adverb.
accidie /aksidee/ ● noun depression, apathy, or listlessness.
– ORIGIN Greek *akēdia* 'listlessness'.
acclaim ● verb praise enthusiastically and publicly. ● noun enthusiastic public praise.
– ORIGIN Latin *acclamare*, from *clamare* 'to shout'.
acclamation ● noun loud and enthusiastic approval or praise.
– PHRASES **by acclamation** (of election, agreement, etc.) by shouting approval rather than by voting.
acclimate /aklimayt, əkli-/ ● verb chiefly N. Amer. acclimatize.
– DERIVATIVES **acclimation** noun.
acclimatize (also **acclimatise**) ● verb make or become accustomed to a new climate or new conditions.
– DERIVATIVES **acclimatization** noun.
– ORIGIN French *acclimater*, from *climat* 'climate'.
acclivity /əklivviti/ ● noun (pl. **acclivities**) an upward slope.
– ORIGIN Latin *acclivitas*, from *clivus* 'a slope'.
accolade /akkəlayd, akkəlayd/ ● noun something given as a special honour or in recognition of merit.
– ORIGIN originally meaning 'a touch on a person's shoulders with a sword when knighting them': from Provençal *acolada* 'embrace around the neck', from Latin *collum* 'neck'.
accommodate ● verb **1** provide lodging or sufficient space for. **2** adapt to or fit in with.
– ORIGIN Latin *accommodare*, from *commodus* 'fitting'.
accommodating ● adjective willing to help or fit in with someone's wishes.
– DERIVATIVES **accommodatingly** adverb.
accommodation ● noun **1** a room, building, or space where someone may live or stay. **2** (**accommodations**) N. Amer. lodgings. **3** a settlement or compromise. **4** adaptation to changing circumstances.

Thesaurus

friendly, agreeable, obliging, congenial, affable, cordial, welcoming, easy-going, pleasant.
accession ● noun **1** *the Queen's accession to the throne* SUCCESSION, assumption, inheritance. **2** *accession to the Treaty of Rome was effected in 1971* ASSENT, consent, agreement; acceptance, acquiescence, compliance, concurrence. **3** *recent accessions to the museum* ADDITION, acquisition, new item, gift, purchase.
accessorize ● verb COMPLEMENT, enhance, set off, show off; go with, accompany; decorate, adorn, ornament, trim.
accessory ● noun **1** *camera accessories such as tripods and flashguns* ATTACHMENT, extra, addition, add-on, adjunct, appendage, appurtenance, fitment, supplement. **2** *fashion accessories* ADORNMENT, embellishment, ornament, ornamentation, decoration; frills, trimmings. **3** *she was charged as an accessory to murder* ACCOMPLICE, partner in crime, associate, collaborator, fellow conspirator; henchman.
● adjective *an accessory gearbox* ADDITIONAL, extra, supplementary, supplemental, auxiliary, ancillary, secondary, subsidiary, reserve, add-on.
accident ● noun **1** *an accident at work* MISHAP, misadventure, unfortunate incident, mischance, misfortune, disaster, tragedy, catastrophe, calamity; technical casualty. **2** *an accident on the motorway* CRASH, collision, smash, bump, car crash, road traffic accident, RTA; derailment; N. Amer. wreck; informal smash-up, pile-up; Brit. informal prang, shunt. **3** *it is no accident that there is a similarity between them* CHANCE, mere chance, coincidence, twist of fate, freak, hazard; fluke, bit of luck, serendipity; fate, fortuity, fortune, providence, happenstance.
accidental ● adjective **1** *an accidental meeting* FORTUITOUS, chance, adventitious, fluky, coincidental, casual, serendipitous, random; unexpected, unforeseen, unanticipated, unlooked-for, unintentional, unintended, inadvertent, unplanned, unpremeditated, unthinking, unwitting. **2** *the location is accidental and contributes nothing to the poem* INCIDENTAL, unimportant, by the way, by the by, supplementary, subsidiary, subordinate, secondary, accessory, peripheral, tangential, extraneous, extrinsic, irrelevant, non-essential, inessential.
– OPPOSITES intentional, deliberate.
accidentally ● adverb BY ACCIDENT, by chance, by a mere chance, by a twist of fate, as luck would have it, fortuitously, by a fluke, by happenstance, coincidentally, adventitiously; unexpectedly, unintentionally, inadvertently, unwittingly.
acclaim ● verb *the booklet has been widely acclaimed by teachers* PRAISE, applaud, cheer, commend, approve, welcome, pay tribute to, speak highly of, eulogize, compliment, celebrate, sing the praises of, rave about, heap praise on, wax lyrical about, lionize, exalt, admire, hail, extol, honour, hymn; informal crack someone/something up; N. Amer. informal ballyhoo; formal laud.
– OPPOSITES criticize.
● noun *she has won acclaim for her commitment to democracy* PRAISE, applause, cheers, ovation, tribute, accolade, acclamation, salutes, plaudits, bouquets; approval, approbation, admiration, congratulations, commendation, welcome, homage; compliment, a pat on the back.
– OPPOSITES criticism.
acclaimed ● adjective CELEBRATED, admired, highly rated, lionized, honoured, esteemed, exalted, well thought of, well received, acknowledged; eminent, great, renowned, distinguished, prestigious, illustrious, pre-eminent.
acclamation ● noun PRAISE, applause, cheers, ovation, tribute, accolade, acclaim, salutes, plaudits, bouquets; approval, admiration, approbation, congratulations, commendation, homage; compliment, a pat on the back.
– OPPOSITES criticism.
acclimatization ● noun ADJUSTMENT, adaptation, accommodation, habituation, acculturation, familiarization, inurement; naturalization; N. Amer. acclimation.
acclimatize ● verb ADJUST, adapt, accustom, accommodate, habituate, acculturate; get used, become inured, reconcile oneself, resign oneself; familiarize oneself; find one's feet, get one's bearings, become seasoned, become naturalized; N. Amer. acclimate.
accolade ● noun **1** *he received the accolade of knighthood* HONOUR, privilege, award, gift, title; prize, laurels, bays, palm. **2** *the hotel won a top accolade from the inspectors* TRIBUTE, commendation, praise, testimonial, compliment, pat on the back; salutes, plaudits, congratulations, bouquets; informal rave.
accommodate ● verb **1** *refugees were accommodated in army camps* LODGE, house, put up, billet, quarter, board, take in, shelter, give someone a roof over their head; harbour. **2** *the cottages accommodate up to six people* HOLD, take, have room for. **3** *our staff will make every effort to accommodate you* HELP, assist, aid, oblige; meet the needs/wants of, cater for, fit in with, satisfy. **4** *she tried to accommodate herself to her new situation* ADJUST, adapt, accustom, habituate, acclimatize, acculturate, get accustomed, get used, come to terms with; N. Amer. acclimate. **5** *the bank would be glad to accommodate you with a loan* PROVIDE, supply, furnish, grant.
accommodating ● adjective OBLIGING, cooperative, helpful, eager to help, adaptable, amenable, considerate, unselfish, generous, willing, kindly, hospitable, neighbourly, kind, friendly, pleasant, agreeable; Brit. informal decent.
accommodation ● noun **1** *temporary accommodation* HOUSING, lodging(s), living quarters, quarters, rooms; place to stay, billet; shelter, a roof over one's head; informal digs, pad; formal abode, residence, place of residence, dwelling, dwelling place, habitation. **2** *lifeboat accommodation for 1,178 people* SPACE, room, seating; places. **3** *an accommodation between the two parties was reached* ARRANGEMENT, understanding, settlement, accord, deal, bargain,

a

accommodation address • noun Brit. an address used by a person unable or unwilling to give a permanent address.
accompaniment • noun **1** a musical part which accompanies an instrument, voice, or group. **2** something that supplements or complements something else.
accompanist • noun a person who provides a musical accompaniment.
accompany • verb (**accompanies, accompanied**) **1** go somewhere with (someone). **2** be present or occur at the same time as. **3** play musical support or backing for (an instrument, voice, or group).
– ORIGIN Old French *accompagner*, from *compaignon* 'companion'.
accomplice /əkumpliss/ • noun a person who helps another commit a crime.
– ORIGIN from Latin *complex* 'allied'.
accomplish • verb achieve or complete successfully.
– ORIGIN Old French *acomplir*, from Latin *complere* 'to complete'.
accomplished • adjective highly trained or skilled.
accomplishment • noun **1** something that has been achieved successfully. **2** the successful achievement of a task. **3** an activity that one can do well.
accord • verb **1** give or grant someone (power or recognition). **2** (**accord with**) be in agreement or consistent with. • noun **1** an official agreement or treaty. **2** agreement in opinion or feeling.
– PHRASES **of one's own accord** voluntarily or without outside intervention. **with one accord** in a united way.
– ORIGIN Old French *acorder* 'reconcile, be of one mind', from Latin *cor* 'heart'.
accordance • noun (in phrase **in accordance with**) in a manner conforming with.
according • adverb **1** (**according to**) as stated by or in. **2** (**according to**) corresponding or in proportion to. **3** (**according as**) depending on whether.
accordingly • adverb **1** appropriately. **2** consequently.
accordion /əkordiən/ • noun a musical instrument played by stretching and squeezing with the hands to work a bellows, the melody and chords being sounded by buttons or keys.
– DERIVATIVES **accordionist** noun.
– ORIGIN from Italian *accordare* 'to tune'.
accost • verb approach and address boldly or aggressively.
– ORIGIN originally in the sense 'go or lie alongside': from French *accoster*, from Latin *costa* 'rib, side'.
account • noun **1** a description of an event or experience. **2** a record of financial expenditure and receipts. **3** a service through a bank or similar organization by which funds are held on behalf of a client or goods or services are supplied on credit. **4** importance: *money was of no account to her.* • verb consider or regard in a specified way.
– PHRASES **account for 1** supply or make up (a specified amount). **2** give a satisfactory record or explanation of. **3** succeed in killing or defeating. **call** (or **bring**) **to account** require (someone) to explain a mistake or poor performance. **on someone's account** for a specified person's benefit. **on account of** because of. **on no account** under no circumstances. **on one's own account** with one's own money or assets. **take account of** consider along with other factors before reaching a decision. **there's no accounting for tastes** (or **taste**) proverb it's impossible to explain why different people like different things, especially those things which the speaker considers unappealing. **turn to** (**good**) **account** turn to one's advantage.
– ORIGIN Old French *acont*, from *conter* 'to count'.
accountable • adjective **1** required or expected to justify actions or decisions. **2** understandable.
– DERIVATIVES **accountability** noun **accountably** adverb.
accountancy • noun the profession or duties of an accountant.

Thesaurus

compromise. **4** *their accommodation to changing economic circumstances* ADJUSTMENT, adaptation, habituation, acclimatization, acculturation; inurement; *N. Amer.* acclimation.
accompaniment • noun **1** *a musical accompaniment* BACKING, support, background, soundtrack. **2** *the wine makes a superb accompaniment to cheese* COMPLEMENT, supplement, addition, adjunct, appendage, companion, accessory.
accompany • verb **1** *the driver accompanied her to the door* GO WITH, travel with, keep someone company, tag along with, partner, escort, chaperone, attend, show, see, usher, conduct. **2** *the illness is often accompanied by nausea* OCCUR WITH, co-occur with, coexist with, go with, go together with, go hand in hand with, appear with, attend by. **3** *he accompanied the choir on the piano* BACK, play with, play for, support.
accomplice • noun PARTNER IN CRIME, associate, accessory, confederate, collaborator, fellow conspirator; henchman; *informal* sidekick.
accomplish • verb FULFIL, achieve, succeed in, realize, attain, manage, bring about/off, carry out/through, execute, effect, perform, do, discharge, complete, finish, consummate, conclude; *formal* effectuate.
accomplished • adjective EXPERT, skilled, skilful, masterly, virtuoso, master, consummate, complete, proficient, talented, gifted, adept, adroit, deft, dexterous, able, good, competent, capable, efficient, experienced, seasoned, trained, practised, professional, polished, ready, apt; *informal* great, mean, nifty, crack, ace, wizard; *Brit. informal* a dab hand at; *N. Amer. informal* crackerjack.
accomplishment • noun **1** *the reduction of inflation was a remarkable accomplishment* ACHIEVEMENT, act, deed, exploit, performance, attainment, effort, feat, move, coup. **2** *typing was another of her accomplishments* TALENT, skill, gift, ability, attainment, achievement, forte, knack. **3** *a poet of considerable accomplishment* EXPERTISE, skill, skilfulness, talent, adeptness, adroitness, deftness, dexterity, ability, prowess, mastery, competence, capability, proficiency, aptitude, artistry, art; *informal* know-how.
accord • verb **1** *the national assembly accorded him more power* GIVE, grant, present, award, vouchsafe; confer on, bestow on, vest in, invest with. **2** *his views accorded with mine* CORRESPOND, agree, tally, match, concur, be consistent, harmonize, be in harmony, be compatible, be in tune, correlate; conform to; *informal* square.
– OPPOSITES withhold, disagree, differ.
• noun **1** *a peace accord* PACT, treaty, agreement, settlement, deal, entente, concordat, protocol, contract, convention. **2** *the two sides failed to reach accord* AGREEMENT, consensus, unanimity, harmony, unison, unity; *formal* concord.
– PHRASES **of one's own accord** VOLUNTARILY, of one's own free will, of one's own volition, by choice; willingly, freely, readily. **with one accord** UNANIMOUSLY, in complete agreement, with one mind, without exception, as one, of one voice, to a man.
accordance • noun *a ballot held in accordance with trade union rules* IN AGREEMENT WITH, in conformity with, in line with, true to, in the spirit of, observing, following, heeding.
according • adjective **1** *she had a narrow escape, according to the doctors* AS STATED BY, as claimed by, on the authority of, in the opinion of. **2** *cook the rice according to the instructions* AS SPECIFIED BY, as per, in accordance with, in compliance with, in agreement with. **3** *salary will be fixed according to experience* IN PROPORTION TO, proportional to, commensurate with, in relation to, relative to, in line with, corresponding to.
accordingly • adverb **1** *they appreciated the danger and acted accordingly* APPROPRIATELY, correspondingly, suitably. **2** *accordingly, he returned home to Yorkshire* THEREFORE, for that reason, consequently, so, as a result, as a consequence, in consequence, hence, thus, that being the case, ergo.
accost • verb SPEAK TO, call to, shout to, hail, address; approach, confront, detain, stop, waylay; *informal* buttonhole, collar; *Brit. informal* nobble.
account • noun **1** *his account of the incident* DESCRIPTION, report, version, story, narration, narrative, statement, explanation, exposition, delineation, portrayal, tale; chronicle, history, record, log; view, impression. **2** *a sensitive account of the Debussy Sonata* PERFORMANCE, interpretation, rendering, rendition, execution. **3** *the firm's quarterly accounts* FINANCIAL RECORD, ledger, balance sheet, financial statement; (**accounts**) books. **4** *I pay the account off in full each month* BILL, invoice, tally; debt, charges; *N. Amer.* check; *informal* tab. **5** *his background is of no account* IMPORTANCE, import, significance, consequence, substance, note; *formal* moment.
• verb *her visit could not be accounted a success* CONSIDER, regard as, reckon, hold to be, think, look on as, view as, see as, judge, adjudge, count, deem, rate.
– PHRASES **account for 1** *they must account for the delay* EXPLAIN, answer for, give reasons for, rationalize, justify. **2** *excise duties account for over half the price of Scotch* CONSTITUTE, make up, comprise, form, compose, represent. **on account of** BECAUSE OF, owing to, due to, as a consequence of, thanks to, by/in virtue of, in view of. **on no account** NEVER, under no circumstances, not for any reason.
accountability • noun RESPONSIBILITY, liability, answerability.

a

accountant ● noun a person who keeps or inspects financial accounts.
accounting ● noun the keeping of financial accounts.
accoutre /əkōōtər/ (US **accouter**) ● verb (**accoutred, accoutring**; US **accoutered, accoutering**) clothe or equip.
– ORIGIN French *accoutrer*, from *cousture* 'sewing'.
accoutrement /əkōōtrəmənt, -tərmənt/ (US **accouterment**) ● noun **1** an additional item of dress or equipment. **2** (**accoutrements**) a soldier's outfit other than weapons and garments.
accredit ● verb (**accredited, accrediting**) **1** (**accredit to**) attribute (something) to (someone). **2** give official authorization to. **3** send (a diplomat or journalist) to a particular place or post.
– DERIVATIVES **accreditation** noun.
– ORIGIN French *accréditer*, from *crédit* 'credit'.
accrete /əkreet/ ● verb grow or form by gradual accumulation.
– ORIGIN Latin *accrescere* 'grow'.
accretion /əkreesh'n/ ● noun **1** growth or increase by gradual accumulation. **2** a thing formed or added in this way.
accrue /əkrōō/ ● verb (**accrues, accrued, accruing**) **1** (of a benefit or sum of money) be received in regular or increasing amounts. **2** accumulate or receive (payments or benefits).
– DERIVATIVES **accrual** noun.
– ORIGIN Old French *acreistre* 'increase', from Latin *accrescere* 'grow'.
acculturate /əkulchərayt/ ● verb absorb and integrate into a different culture.
– DERIVATIVES **acculturation** noun.
accumulate /əkyōōmyoolayt/ ● verb **1** gather together a number or quantity of. **2** gather or build up.
– DERIVATIVES **accumulation** noun **accumulative** adjective.
– ORIGIN Latin *accumulare* 'heap up', from *cumulus* 'a heap'.
accumulator ● noun **1** a person or thing that accumulates. **2** Brit. a large rechargeable electric cell. **3** Brit. a bet placed on a series of events, the winnings and stake from each being placed on the next.
accurate /akyoorət/ ● adjective **1** correct in all details. **2** capable of or successful in reaching the intended target.
– DERIVATIVES **accuracy** noun **accurately** adverb.
– USAGE On the distinction between **accurate** and **precise**, see the note at PRECISE.
– ORIGIN from Latin *accurare* 'do with care', from *cura* 'care'.
accursed /əkursid, əkurst/ ● adjective **1** literary under a curse. **2** dated horrible; hateful.
accusation ● noun a charge or claim that someone has done something illegal or wrong.
accusative /əkyōōzətiv/ ● adjective Grammar (of a case) expressing the object of an action or the goal of motion.
– ORIGIN from Latin *casus accusativus* 'the case showing cause'.
accuse ● verb (often **accuse of**) **1** charge with an offence or crime. **2** claim that (someone) has done (something wrong).
– DERIVATIVES **accusatory** adjective **accuser** noun.
– ORIGIN Latin *accusare* 'call to account', from *causa* 'reason, motive, lawsuit'.
accustom ● verb **1** (**accustom to**) make used to. **2** (**be accustomed to**) be used to.
– ORIGIN Old French *acostumer*, from *costume* 'custom'.
accustomed ● adjective customary; usual.
AC/DC ● adjective **1** alternating current/direct current. **2** informal bisexual.
ace ● noun **1** a playing card with a single spot on it, the highest card in its suit in most games. **2** informal a person who is very good at a particular activity. **3** Tennis a service that an opponent is unable to return. **4** Golf a hole in one. ● adjective informal very good. ● verb informal (in tennis) serve an ace against.
– PHRASES **ace up one's sleeve** a plan or piece of information kept secret until required. **hold all the aces** have all the advantages. **within an ace of** very close to.
– ORIGIN Latin *as* 'unity, a unit'.
acellular ● adjective Biology **1** not divided into or containing cells. **2** consisting of one cell only.
-aceous ● suffix **1** Botany forming adjectives from family names: *ericaceous*. **2** chiefly Biology & Geology forming adjectives describing similarity: *olivaceous*.
– ORIGIN from Latin *-aceus*.
acephalous /ayseffələss, -kef-/ ● adjective without a head.
– ORIGIN Greek *akephalos*, from *kephalē* 'head'.
acer /aysər/ ● noun a maple or related tree, with five-lobed leaves.
– ORIGIN Latin.
acerbic /əserbik/ ● adjective **1** sharp and forthright. **2** archaic or

Thesaurus

accountable ● adjective **1** *the government was held accountable for the food shortage* RESPONSIBLE, liable, answerable; to blame. **2** *the game's popularity is barely accountable* EXPLICABLE, explainable; understandable, comprehensible.
accoutrements ● plural noun EQUIPMENT, paraphernalia, stuff, things, apparatus, tackle, kit, implements, material(s), rig, outfit, regalia, appurtenances, impedimenta, odds and ends, bits and pieces, bits and bobs, trappings, accessories.
accredit ● verb **1** *he was accredited with being one of the world's fastest sprinters* RECOGNIZE AS, credit with. **2** *the discovery of distillation is usually accredited to the Arabs* ASCRIBE, attribute. **3** *professional bodies accredit these research degrees* RECOGNIZE, authorize, approve, certify, license.
accredited ● adjective OFFICIAL, appointed, recognized, authorized, approved, certified, licensed.
accretion ● noun **1** *the accretion of sediments* ACCUMULATION, formation, collecting, cumulation, accrual; growth, increase. **2** *architectural accretions* ADDITION, extension, appendage, add-on, supplement.
accrue ● verb **1** *financial benefits will accrue from restructuring* RESULT, arise, follow, ensue; be caused by. **2** *interest is added to the account as it accrues* ACCUMULATE, collect, build up, mount up, grow, increase.
accumulate ● verb GATHER, collect, amass, stockpile, pile up, heap up, store (up), hoard, cumulate, lay in/up; increase, multiply, accrue; run up.
accumulation ● noun MASS, build-up, pile, heap, stack, collection, stock, store, stockpile, reserve, hoard; amassing, gathering, cumulation, accrual, accretion.
accuracy ● noun CORRECTNESS, precision, exactness; factuality, literalness, fidelity, faithfulness, truth, truthfulness, veracity, authenticity, realism, verisimilitude.
accurate ● adjective **1** *accurate information* | *an accurate representation of the situation* CORRECT, precise, exact, right, error-free, perfect; FACTUAL, fact-based, literal, faithful, true, truthful, true to life, authentic, realistic; informal on the mark, on the beam, on the nail; Brit. informal spot on, bang on; N. Amer. informal on the money, on the button; formal veracious. **2** *an accurate shot* WELL AIMED, on target, unerring, deadly, lethal, sure, true, on the mark.
accursed ● adjective **1** (dated) *that accursed woman* HATEFUL, detestable, loathsome, foul, abominable, damnable, odious, obnoxious, despicable, horrible, horrid, ghastly, awful, dreadful, terrible; annoying, irritating, infuriating, exasperating; informal damned, damn, blasted, pesky, pestilential, infernal; Brit. informal beastly. **2** (poetic/literary) *he and his line are accursed* CURSED, damned, doomed, condemned, ill-fated, ill-omened, jinxed.
– OPPOSITES pleasant, blessed.
accusation ● noun ALLEGATION, charge, claim, assertion, imputation; indictment, arraignment; suit, lawsuit; Law, Brit. plaint; N. Amer. impeachment.
accuse ● verb **1** *four people were accused of assault* CHARGE WITH, indict for, arraign for; summons, cite, prefer charges against; N. Amer. impeach for. **2** *the companies were accused of causing job losses* BLAME FOR, lay the blame on, hold responsible for, hold accountable for; condemn for, criticize for, denounce for; informal lay at the door of, point the finger at, stick on, pin on.
– OPPOSITES absolve, exonerate.
accustom ● verb ADAPT, adjust, acclimatize, habituate, accommodate, acculturate; reconcile oneself, become reconciled, get used to, come to terms with, learn to live with, become inured; N. Amer. acclimate.
accustomed ● adjective CUSTOMARY, usual, normal, habitual, regular, routine, ordinary, typical, traditional, established, common, general; poetic/literary wonted.
ace (informal) ● noun *a rowing ace* EXPERT, master, genius, virtuoso, maestro, adept, past master, doyen, champion, star; informal demon, hotshot, wizard, whizz; Brit. informal dab hand; N. Amer. informal maven, crackerjack.
– OPPOSITES amateur.
● adjective *an ace tennis player* EXCELLENT, first-rate, first-class, marvellous, wonderful, magnificent, outstanding, superlative, formidable, virtuoso, masterly, expert, champion, consummate, skilful, adept; informal great, terrific, tremendous, superb, fantastic, sensational, fabulous, fab, crack, hotshot, A1, mean, demon, awesome,

a

technical tasting sour or bitter.
– DERIVATIVES **acerbically** adverb **acerbity** noun.
– ORIGIN from Latin *acerbus* 'sour-tasting'.

acetaldehyde /assitaldihī/ ● **noun** Chemistry a colourless volatile liquid aldehyde.

acetaminophen /əseetəminnəfen/ ● **noun** North American term for PARACETAMOL.

acetate /assitayt/ ● **noun 1** Chemistry a salt or ester of acetic acid. **2** fibre or plastic made of cellulose acetate. **3** a transparency made of cellulose acetate film.

acetic acid /əseetik/ ● **noun** the acid that gives vinegar its characteristic taste.
– ORIGIN from Latin *acetum* 'vinegar'.

acetone /assitōn/ ● **noun** a colourless volatile liquid ketone used as a solvent and in chemical synthesis.
– ORIGIN from ACETIC ACID.

acetylene /əsettileen/ ● **noun** a gas which burns with a bright flame, used in welding.
– ORIGIN from ACETIC ACID.

Achaean /əkeeən/ ● **noun 1** a person from Achaea in ancient Greece. **2** literary a Greek. ● **adjective** relating to Achaea.

ache ● **noun** a continuous or prolonged dull pain. ● **verb 1** suffer from an ache. **2** (**ache for/to do**) feel intense desire for or to do.
– DERIVATIVES **aching** adjective.
– ORIGIN Old English.

achene /əkeen/ ● **noun** Botany a small, dry one-seeded fruit that does not open to release the seed.
– ORIGIN Latin *achaenium*, from *a-* 'not' + Greek *khainein* 'to gape'.

achieve ● **verb** bring about or accomplish by effort, skill, or courage.
– DERIVATIVES **achievable** adjective **achiever** noun.
– ORIGIN Old French *achever* 'come or bring to a head', from *a chief* 'to a head'.

achievement ● **noun 1** a thing that is achieved. **2** the process or fact of achieving.

Achilles heel /əkilleez/ ● **noun** a weakness or vulnerable point.
– ORIGIN from the mythological Greek hero *Achilles*, whose mother plunged him into the River Styx when he was a baby, thus making his body invulnerable except for the heel by which she held him.

Achilles tendon ● **noun** the tendon connecting calf muscles to the heel.

achondroplasia /əkondrōplayziə, aykon-/ ● **noun** Medicine a hereditary condition in which the growth of long bones is retarded, resulting in short limbs.
– ORIGIN from A-[1] + Greek *khondros* 'cartilage' + *plasis* 'moulding'.

achromatic /akrōmattik/ ● **adjective 1** transmitting light without separating it into colours. **2** without colour.

achy (also **achey**) ● **adjective** (**achier**, **achiest**) suffering from an ache or aches.

acid ● **noun 1** a substance with chemical properties including turning litmus red, neutralizing alkalis, and dissolving some metals. **2** informal the drug LSD. ● **adjective 1** having the properties of an acid; having a pH of less than 7. **2** sharp-tasting or sour. **3** (of a remark) bitter or cutting.
– DERIVATIVES **acidly** adverb **acidy** adjective.
– ORIGIN Latin *acidus*, from *acere* 'be sour'.

acid drop ● **noun** Brit. a boiled sweet with a sharp taste.

acid house ● **noun** a kind of fast, repetitive synthesized dance music.

acidify ● **verb** (**acidifies**, **acidified**) make or become acid.
– DERIVATIVES **acidification** noun.

acidity ● **noun 1** the level of acid in something. **2** bitterness or sharpness in a person's remarks or tone.

acid jazz ● **noun** a kind of dance music incorporating elements of jazz, funk, soul, and hip hop.

acid rain ● **noun** rainfall made acidic by sulphur and nitrogen oxides from the industrial burning of fossil fuels.

acid test ● **noun** a conclusive test of success or value.
– ORIGIN from the original use denoting a test for gold using nitric acid.

acidulate /əsidyoolayt/ ● **verb** make slightly acidic.

acidulous /əsidyooləss/ ● **adjective** sharp-tasting; sour.

-acious ● **suffix** (forming adjectives) inclined to; having as a capacity: *capacious*.
– ORIGIN from Latin *-ax*, *-ac-*.

-acity ● **suffix** forming nouns of quality or state corresponding to adjectives ending in *-acious*.
– ORIGIN from Latin *-acitas*.

ack-ack ● **noun** Military, informal anti-aircraft gunfire or guns.
– ORIGIN signallers' former name for the letters *AA*.

ackee /akkee/ (also **akee**) ● **noun** the fruit of a West African tree, eaten as a vegetable.
– ORIGIN from Kru (a West African language).

ackers ● **plural noun** Brit. informal money.
– ORIGIN probably from an Arabic word meaning 'small change, coins', and originally used by British troops in Egypt as a name for the piastre.

acknowledge ● **verb 1** accept or admit the existence or truth of. **2** confirm receipt of or gratitude for. **3** greet with words or gestures.
– ORIGIN from the obsolete verb *knowledge* (in the same sense).

acknowledgement (also **acknowledgment**) ● **noun 1** the action or fact of acknowledging. **2** an act or instance of acknowledging. **3** (**acknowledgements**) (in a book) a printed expression of the author's gratitude to others.

Thesaurus

magic, tip-top, top-notch; *Brit. informal* smashing, brilliant, brill.
– OPPOSITES mediocre.

acerbic ● **adjective** SHARP, sarcastic, sardonic, mordant, trenchant, cutting, razor-edged, biting, stinging, searing, scathing, caustic, astringent, abrasive; *N. Amer.* acerb; *Brit. informal* sarky; *N. Amer. informal* snarky.

ache ● **noun 1** *a stomach ache* PAIN, cramp, twinge, pang; gnawing, stabbing, stinging, smarting; soreness, tenderness, irritation, discomfort. **2** *the ache in her heart* SORROW, sadness, misery, grief, anguish, suffering, pain, agony, torture, hurt.
● **verb 1** *my legs were aching* HURT, be sore, be painful, be in pain, throb, pound, twinge; smart, burn, sting; *informal* give someone gyp; *Brit. informal* play up. **2** *her heart ached for poor Philippa* GRIEVE, sorrow, be in distress, be miserable, be in anguish, bleed. **3** *Marie ached for his affection* LONG, yearn, hunger, thirst, hanker, pine, itch; crave, desire.

achieve ● **verb** ATTAIN, reach, arrive at; realize, bring off/about, pull off, accomplish, carry out/through, fulfil, execute, perform, engineer, conclude, complete, finish, consummate; earn, win, gain, acquire, obtain, come by, get, secure, clinch, net; *informal* wrap up, wangle, swing; *formal* effectuate.

achievement ● **noun 1** *the achievement of a high rate of economic growth* ATTAINMENT, realization, accomplishment, fulfilment, implementation, execution, performance; conclusion, completion, close, consummation. **2** *they felt justifiably proud of their achievement* ACCOMPLISHMENT, attainment, feat, performance, undertaking, act, action, deed, effort, exploit; work, handiwork.

Achilles' heel ● **noun** WEAK SPOT, weak point, weakness, soft underbelly, shortcoming, failing, imperfection, flaw, defect, chink in one's armour.
– OPPOSITES strength.

aching ● **adjective 1** *his aching back* PAINFUL, achy, sore, stiff, hurt, tender, uncomfortable; hurting, in pain, throbbing, pounding, smarting, burning, stinging. **2** *her aching heart* SORROWFUL, sad, miserable, grieving, upset, distressed, anguished, grief-stricken, heavy.

acid ● **adjective 1** *a slightly acid flavour* ACIDIC, SOUR, tart, bitter, sharp, acrid, pungent, acerbic, vinegary, acetic, acetous. **2** *acid remarks* ACERBIC, sarcastic, sharp, sardonic, scathing, cutting, razor-edged, biting, stinging, caustic, trenchant, mordant, bitter, acrimonious, astringent, harsh, abrasive, wounding, hurtful, unkind, vitriolic, venomous, waspish, spiteful, malicious; *N. Amer.* acerb; *informal* bitchy, catty; *Brit. informal* sarky; *N. Amer. informal* snarky.
– OPPOSITES sweet, pleasant.

acknowledge ● **verb 1** *the government acknowledged the need to begin talks* ADMIT, accept, grant, allow, concede, confess, own, recognize. **2** *he did not acknowledge Colin, but hurried past* GREET, salute, address; nod to, wave to, raise one's hat to, say hello to. **3** *Douglas was glad to acknowledge her help* EXPRESS GRATITUDE FOR, show appreciation for, thank someone for. **4** *few people acknowledged my letters* ANSWER, reply to, respond to.
– OPPOSITES reject, deny, ignore.

acknowledged ● **adjective** RECOGNIZED, accepted, approved, ac-

a

acme /akmi/ • noun the highest point of achievement or excellence.
– ORIGIN Greek *akmē* 'highest point'.
acne • noun a skin condition marked by numerous red pimples on the face.
– ORIGIN Greek *aknas*, a misreading of *akmas*, a plural of *akmē* 'highest point, peak, or facial eruption'; compare with ACME.
acolyte /akkəlit/ • noun **1** an assistant or follower. **2** a person assisting a priest in a religious service.
– ORIGIN Latin *acolytus*, from Greek *akolouthos* 'follower'.
aconite /akkənit/ • noun **1** a poisonous plant bearing spikes of hooded pink or purple flowers. **2** (also **winter aconite**) a small plant bearing yellow flowers in early spring.
– ORIGIN Greek *akoniton*.
acorn • noun the fruit of the oak, a smooth oval nut in a cup-like base.
– ORIGIN Old English, related to ACRE, later associated with OAK and CORN[1].
acoustic /əkoōstik/ • adjective **1** relating to sound or hearing. **2** (of popular music or musical instruments) not having electrical amplification. • noun **1** the properties of a room or building that determine how sound is transmitted in it. **2** (**acoustics**) (treated as sing.) the branch of physics concerned with the properties of sound.
– DERIVATIVES **acoustical** adjective **acoustically** adverb **acoustician** noun.
– ORIGIN Greek *akoustikos*, from *akouein* 'hear'.
acquaint • verb **1** (**acquaint with**) make (someone) aware of or familiar with. **2** (**be acquainted with**) know personally. **3** (**be acquainted**) (of two or more people) know each other personally.
– ORIGIN Latin *accognitare*, from *cognoscere* 'come to know'.
acquaintance • noun **1** familiarity with or knowledge of someone or something. **2** a person one knows slightly.
acquiesce /akwiess/ • verb accept or consent to something without protest.
– ORIGIN Latin *acquiescere*, from *quiescere* 'to rest'.
acquiescent • adjective ready to accept or do something without protest.
– DERIVATIVES **acquiescence** noun.
acquire • verb **1** come to possess. **2** learn or develop (a skill, quality, etc.).
– DERIVATIVES **acquirement** noun **acquirer** noun.
– ORIGIN Latin *acquirere* 'get in addition', from *quaerere* 'seek'.
acquired taste • noun a thing that one learns to like over time.
acquisition /akwizish'n/ • noun **1** an object that has recently been acquired. **2** the act of acquiring.
acquisitive • adjective excessively interested in acquiring money or material things.
– DERIVATIVES **acquisitively** adverb **acquisitiveness** noun.
acquit • verb (**acquitted**, **acquitting**) **1** formally declare that (someone) is not guilty of a criminal charge. **2** (**acquit oneself**) behave or perform in a specified way.
– DERIVATIVES **acquittal** noun.
– ORIGIN Latin *acquitare* 'pay a debt', from *quitare* 'set free'.
acre /aykər/ • noun a unit of land area equal to 4,840 square yards (0.405 hectare).
– DERIVATIVES **acreage** noun.
– ORIGIN Old English, originally denoting the amount of land a pair of oxen could plough in a day.
acrid /akrid/ • adjective unpleasantly bitter or pungent.
– DERIVATIVES **acridity** noun **acridly** adverb.
– ORIGIN from Latin *acer* 'sharp, pungent'.
acrimonious /akrimōniəss/ • adjective angry and bitter.
– DERIVATIVES **acrimoniously** adverb.
acrimony /akriməni/ • noun bitterness or ill feeling.
– ORIGIN originally in the sense 'bitter taste or smell': from Latin *acrimonia*, from *acer* 'pungent, acrid'.
acrobat • noun an entertainer who performs acrobatics.
– ORIGIN Greek *akrobatēs*, from *akrobatos* 'walking on tiptoe'.
acrobatic • adjective involving or adept at spectacular gymnastic feats.
– DERIVATIVES **acrobatically** adverb.
acrobatics • plural noun (usu. treated as sing.) spectacular gymnastic feats.

Thesaurus

credited, confirmed, declared, confessed, avowed.
acknowledgement • noun **1** *acknowledgement of the need to take new initiatives* ACCEPTANCE, admission, concession, confession, recognition. **2** *a smile of acknowledgement* GREETING, welcome, salutation. **3** *she left without a word of acknowledgement* THANKS, gratitude, appreciation, recognition. **4** *I sent off the form, but there was no acknowledgement* ANSWER, reply, response.
acme • noun PEAK, pinnacle, zenith, height, high point, crown, crest, summit, top, apex, apogee; climax, culmination.
– OPPOSITES nadir.
acolyte • noun ASSISTANT, helper, attendant, minion, underling, lackey, henchman; follower, disciple, supporter, votary; *informal* sidekick, groupie, hanger-on.
acquaint • verb *he will need to acquaint himself with the regulations* FAMILIARIZE, make familiar, make aware of, inform of, advise of, apprise of, let know, get up to date; brief, prime; *informal* fill in on, gen up on, clue in on.
acquaintance • noun **1** *a business acquaintance* CONTACT, associate, colleague. **2** *my acquaintance with George* ASSOCIATION, relationship, contact. **3** *the pupils had little acquaintance with the language* FAMILIARITY WITH, knowledge of, experience of, awareness of, understanding of, comprehension of, grasp of.
acquainted • adjective **1** *she was well acquainted with Gothic literature* FAMILIAR, conversant, at home, up to date, abreast, au fait, au courant, well versed, knowledgeable, well informed; informed, apprised; *informal* genned up, clued in; *formal* cognizant. **2** *I am not personally acquainted with him* FRIENDLY, on friendly terms.
acquiesce • verb *he acquiesced in the cover-up* ACCEPT, consent to, agree to, allow, concede, assent to, concur with, give the nod to; comply with, cooperate with, give in to, bow to, yield to, submit to; *informal* go along with.
acquiescence • noun CONSENT, agreement, acceptance, concurrence, assent, leave; compliance, concession, cooperation; submission.
acquiescent • adjective COMPLIANT, cooperative, willing, obliging, agreeable, amenable, tractable, persuadable, pliant, unprotesting; submissive, self-effacing, unassertive, yielding, biddable, docile.
acquire • verb OBTAIN, come by, get, receive, gain, earn, win, come into, be given; buy, purchase, procure, possess oneself of, secure, pick up; *informal* get one's hands on, get hold of, land, bag, score.
– OPPOSITES lose.
acquirement • noun **1** *her many acquirements* ATTAINMENT, achievement, accomplishment, skill, talent. **2** *the acquirement of money* ACQUISITION, obtaining, gaining, earning, winning, procurement.
acquisition • noun **1** *a new acquisition* PURCHASE, buy, gain, accession, addition, investment, possession. **2** *the acquisition of funds* OBTAINING, acquirement, gaining, earning, winning, procurement, collection.
acquisitive • adjective GREEDY, covetous, avaricious, possessive, grasping, grabbing, predatory, avid, rapacious, mercenary, materialistic; *informal* money-grubbing.
acquisitiveness • noun GREED, greediness, covetousness, cupidity, possessiveness, avarice, avidity, rapaciousness, rapacity, materialism.
acquit • verb **1** *the jury acquitted her* CLEAR, exonerate, find innocent, absolve; discharge, release, free, set free; *informal* let off (the hook); *formal* exculpate. **2** *the boys acquitted themselves well* BEHAVE, conduct oneself, perform, act; *formal* comport oneself. **3** (archaic) *they acquitted themselves of their duty* CARRY OUT, perform, discharge, execute.
– OPPOSITES convict.
acquittal • noun **1** *the acquittal of the defendants* CLEARING, exoneration; discharge, release, freeing; *informal* let-off; *formal* exculpation. **2** (archaic) *the acquittal of these duties* DISCHARGE, carrying out, execution, performance.
– OPPOSITES conviction.
acrid • adjective PUNGENT, bitter, sharp, sour, tart, harsh, acid, acidic, vinegary, acetic, acetous; stinging, burning.
acrimonious • adjective BITTER, angry, rancorous, caustic, acerbic, scathing, sarcastic, acid, harsh, sharp, cutting; virulent, spiteful, vicious, vitriolic, hostile, venomous, nasty, bad-tempered, ill-natured, mean, malign, malicious, malignant, waspish; *informal* bitchy, catty.
acrimony • noun BITTERNESS, anger, rancour, resentment, ill feeling, ill will, bad blood, animosity, hostility, enmity, antagonism, waspishness, spleen, malice, spitefulness, venom.
– OPPOSITES goodwill.

a

acromegaly /akrōmeggəli/ ● noun abnormal growth of the hands, feet, and face caused by overproduction of growth hormone by the pituitary gland.
– DERIVATIVES **acromegalic** /akrōmigalik/ adjective.
– ORIGIN from Greek *akron* 'tip, extremity' + *megas* 'great'.

acronym /akrənim/ ● noun a word formed from the initial letters of other words (e.g. *laser, Aids*).
– ORIGIN from Greek *akron* 'end, tip' + *onoma* 'name'.

acrophobia /akrəfōbiə/ ● noun extreme or irrational fear of heights.
– DERIVATIVES **acrophobic** adjective.
– ORIGIN from Greek *akron* 'summit'.

acropolis /əkroppəliss/ ● noun a citadel or fortified part of an ancient Greek city, built on high ground.
– ORIGIN Greek, from *akron* 'summit' + *polis* 'city'.

across ● preposition & adverb from one side to the other of (something).
– PHRASES **across the board** applying to all.
– ORIGIN from Old French *a croix, en croix* 'in or on a cross'.

acrostic /əkrostik/ ● noun a poem or puzzle in which certain letters in each line form a word or words.
– ORIGIN Greek *akrostikhis*, from *akron* 'end' + *stikhos* 'row, line of verse'.

acrylic ● adjective of or relating to polymers of **acrylic acid**, an organic acid used in making synthetic resins. ● noun acrylic paint or textile fabric.
– ORIGIN from Latin *acer* 'pungent' + *oleum* 'oil'.

ACT ● abbreviation Australian Capital Territory.

act ● verb **1** take action; do something. **2** take effect or have a particular effect. **3** behave in a specified way. **4** (**act as**) fulfil the function of. **5** (**act for/on behalf of**) represent on a contractual or legal basis. **6** (**acting**) temporarily doing the duties of another. **7** perform a fictional role in a play or film. ● noun **1** a thing done. **2** a law passed formally by a parliament. **3** a simulation or pretence: *putting on an act*. **4** a main division of a play, ballet, or opera. **5** a set performance or performing group. **6** dated a record of the decisions or proceedings of a committee or academic body.
– PHRASES **act of contrition** (in the Roman Catholic Church) a penitential prayer. **act of God** an instance of uncontrollable natural forces in operation. **act of grace** a privilege or concession that cannot be claimed as a right. **act up** informal behave badly. **get in on the act** informal become involved in a particular activity to share its benefits.
– ORIGIN Latin *actus* 'event, thing done', from *agere* 'do, act'.

actinic /aktinnik/ ● adjective (of light) able to cause chemical reactions through having a significant short-wavelength or ultraviolet component.
– ORIGIN from Greek *aktis* 'ray'.

actinide /aktinīd/ ● noun Chemistry any of the series of fifteen radioactive metallic elements from actinium to lawrencium in the periodic table.

actinium /aktinniəm/ ● noun a rare radioactive metallic chemical element found in uranium ores.
– ORIGIN from Greek *aktis* 'ray'.

action ● noun **1** the process of doing something to achieve an aim. **2** a thing done. **3** the effect or influence of something such as a chemical. **4** a lawsuit. **5** armed conflict. **6** the way in which something works or moves. **7** informal exciting or notable activity. ● verb take action on or deal with.
– PHRASES **actions speak louder than words** proverb what someone actually does means more than what they say they will do. **in action** engaged in an activity; in operation. **out of action** not working.

actionable ● adjective Law giving sufficient reason to take legal action.

action painting ● noun a technique and style of painting in which paint is thrown or poured on to the canvas.

action replay ● noun Brit. a playback of part of a television broadcast, especially one in slow motion.

action stations ● plural noun chiefly Brit. the positions taken up by military personnel in preparation for action.

activate ● verb **1** make active or operative. **2** convert (a substance, molecule, etc.) into a reactive form.
– DERIVATIVES **activation** noun **activator** noun.

activated carbon (also **activated charcoal**) ● noun charcoal that has been treated to increase its ability to absorb gases and dissolved substances.

active ● adjective **1** moving or tending to move about vigorously or frequently. **2** (of a person's mind) alert and lively. **3** participating in a particular sphere or activity. **4** working; operative. **5** (of an electric circuit) capable of automatic change in response to input or feedback. **6** (of a volcano) erupting or having erupted in historical times. **7** having a chemical or biological effect on something. **8** Grammar (of verbs) in which the subject is the person or thing performing the action and which can take a direct object (e.g. *she loved him* as opposed to the passive form *he was loved*).
– DERIVATIVES **actively** adverb.
– ORIGIN Latin *activus*, from *agere* 'act, do'.

active matrix ● noun Electronics a display system in which each pixel is individually controlled.

Thesaurus

acrobat ● noun TUMBLER, gymnast, tightrope walker, wire walker, trapeze artist; *rare* funambulist.

acrobatics ● plural noun **1** *staggering feats of acrobatics* GYMNASTICS, tumbling; agility; *rare* funambulism. **2** *the acrobatics required to negotiate an international contract* MENTAL AGILITY, skill, quick thinking, alertness, inventiveness.

act ● verb **1** *the Government must act to remedy the situation* TAKE ACTION, take steps, take measures, move, react. **2** *he was acting on the orders of the party leader* FOLLOW, act in accordance with, obey, heed, comply with; fulfil, meet, discharge. **3** *an estate agent acting for a prospective buyer* REPRESENT, act on behalf of; stand in for, fill in for, deputize for, take the place of. **4** *Alison began to act oddly* BEHAVE, conduct oneself, react; *formal* comport oneself. **5** *the scents act as a powerful aphrodisiac* OPERATE, work, function, serve. **6** *the drug acted directly on the blood vessels* AFFECT, have an effect on, work on; have an impact on, impact on, influence. **7** *he acted in a highly successful film* PERFORM, play a part, take part, appear; *informal* tread the boards. **8** *we laughed, but most of us were just acting* PRETEND, play-act, put it on, fake it, feign it, dissemble, dissimulate.
● noun **1** *acts of kindness | a criminal act* DEED, action, feat, exploit, move, gesture, performance, undertaking, stunt, operation; achievement, accomplishment. **2** *the act raised the tax on tobacco* LAW, decree, statute, bill, act of Parliament, enactment, resolution, edict, dictum, ruling, measure; *N. Amer. formal* ordinance. **3** *the first act of the play* DIVISION, section, subsection, part, segment. **4** *a music hall act* PERFORMANCE, turn, routine, number, sketch, skit. **5** *it was all just an act* PRETENCE, show, front, facade, masquerade, charade, posture, pose, affectation, sham, fake; *informal* a put-on.
– PHRASES **act up** (*informal*) **1** *all children act up from time to time* MISBEHAVE, behave badly, get up to mischief; *Brit. informal* play up. **2** *the plane's engine was acting up* MALFUNCTION, go wrong, be defective, be faulty; *informal* be on the blink; *Brit. informal* play up.

acting ● noun *the theory and practice of acting* DRAMA, the theatre, the stage, the performing arts, thespianism, dramatics, dramaturgy, stagecraft, theatricals; *informal* treading the boards.
● adjective *the bank's acting governor* TEMPORARY, interim, caretaker, pro tem, provisional, stopgap; deputy, stand-in, fill-in; *N. Amer. informal* pinch-hitting.
– OPPOSITES permanent.

action ● noun **1** *there can be no excuse for their actions* DEED, act, move, undertaking, exploit, manoeuvre, endeavour, effort, exertion; behaviour, conduct, activity. **2** *the need for local community action* MEASURES, steps, activity, movement, work, operation. **3** *a man of action* ENERGY, vitality, vigour, forcefulness, drive, initiative, spirit, liveliness, vim, pep; activity; *informal* get-up-and-go. **4** *the action of hormones on the pancreas* EFFECT, influence, working; power. **5** *he missed all the action while he was away* EXCITEMENT, activity, happenings, events, incidents; *informal* goings-on. **6** *twenty-nine men died in the action* FIGHTING, hostilities, battle, conflict, combat, warfare; engagement, clash, encounter, skirmish. **7** *a civil action for damages* LAWSUIT, legal action, suit (at law), case, prosecution, litigation, proceedings.

activate ● verb OPERATE, switch on, turn on, start (up), set going, trigger (off), set in motion, actuate, energize; trip.

active ● adjective **1** *despite her illness she remained active* ENERGETIC, lively, sprightly, spry, mobile, vigorous, vital, dynamic, sporty; busy, occupied; *informal* on the go, full of beans. **2** *an active member of the union* HARD-WORKING, busy, industrious, diligent, tireless, contributing, effective, enterprising, involved, enthusiastic, keen, committed, devoted, zealous. **3** *the watermill was active until 1960* OPERATIVE, working, functioning, functional, operating,

a

active service ● noun direct participation in military operations as a member of the armed forces.

activism ● noun the use of vigorous campaigning to bring about political or social change.
– DERIVATIVES **activist** noun & adjective.

activity ● noun (pl. **activities**) **1** a condition in which things are happening or being done. **2** busy or vigorous action or movement. **3** an action taken in pursuit of an objective. **4** a recreational pursuit. **5** the degree to which something displays its characteristic property or behaviour.

actor ● noun **1** a person whose profession is acting. **2** a participant in an action or process.

actress ● noun a female actor.
– DERIVATIVES **actressy** adjective.

actual ● adjective **1** existing in fact. **2** existing now; current: *actual income.*
– ORIGIN Latin *actualis*, from *actus* 'event, thing done'.

actual bodily harm ● noun Law minor injury inflicted on a person by the deliberate action of another, considered less serious than grievous bodily harm.

actuality ● noun (pl. **actualities**) **1** actual existence or fact, as opposed to what was intended or expected. **2** (**actualities**) existing conditions or facts.

actualize (also **actualise**) ● verb make a reality of.
– DERIVATIVES **actualization** noun.

actually ● adverb **1** as the truth or facts of a situation. **2** as a matter of fact; even.

actuary /akchooəri/ ● noun (pl. **actuaries**) a person who compiles and analyses statistics in order to calculate insurance risks and premiums.
– DERIVATIVES **actuarial** adjective.
– ORIGIN Latin *actuarius* 'bookkeeper'.

actuate /akchooayt/ ● verb **1** cause to operate. **2** motivate to act in a particular way.
– DERIVATIVES **actuation** noun **actuator** noun.

acuity /əkyōōiti/ ● noun sharpness or keenness of thought, vision, or hearing.
– ORIGIN Latin *acuitas*, from *acus* 'needle'.

acumen /akyoomən, əkyōōmən/ ● noun the ability to make good judgements and take quick decisions.
– ORIGIN Latin, 'sharpness, point'.

acupressure /akyoopreshər/ ● noun a system of complementary medicine in which manual pressure is applied to the body at specific points along supposed lines of energy.

acupuncture /akyoopungkchər/ ● noun a system of complementary medicine in which fine needles are inserted in the skin at specific points along supposed lines of energy.
– DERIVATIVES **acupuncturist** noun.
– ORIGIN from Latin *acu* 'with a needle' + PUNCTURE.

acute ● adjective **1** (of something bad) critical; serious. **2** (of an illness) coming sharply to a crisis. Often contrasted with CHRONIC. **3** perceptive; shrewd. **4** (of a physical sense or faculty) highly developed. **5** (of an angle) less than 90°.
– DERIVATIVES **acutely** adverb **acuteness** noun.
– ORIGIN Latin *acutus* 'sharpened', from *acus* 'needle'.

acute accent ● noun a mark (´) placed over certain letters in some languages to indicate a feature such as altered sound quality (e.g. in *fiancée*).

-acy ● suffix forming nouns of state or quality: *celibacy.*
– ORIGIN from Latin *-atia* or from Greek *-ateia*.

AD ● abbreviation Anno Domini (used to indicate that a date comes the specified number of years after the traditional date of Christ's birth).
– USAGE AD is normally written in small capitals and should be placed **before** the numerals, as in AD *375.* However, when the date is spelled out, it is normal to write *the third century* AD.
– ORIGIN Latin, 'in the year of the Lord'.

ad ● noun informal an advertisement.

ad- (also **a-** before *sc, sp, st*; **ac-** before *c, k, q*; **af-** before *f*; **ag-** before *g*; **al-** before *l*; **an-** before *n*; **ap-** before *p*; **ar-** before *r*; **as-** before *s*; **at-** before *t*) ● prefix **1** denoting motion or direction to: *advance.* **2** denoting reduction or change into: *adulterate.* **3** denoting addition or increase: *adjunct.*
– ORIGIN from Latin *ad* 'to'.

adage /addij/ ● noun a proverb or short statement expressing a general truth.
– ORIGIN Latin *adagium* 'saying', from *aio* 'I say'.

adagio /ədaazhiō/ Music ● adverb & adjective in slow time. ● noun (pl. **adagios**) an adagio passage.
– ORIGIN Italian, from *ad agio* 'at ease'.

adamant ● adjective refusing to be persuaded or to change one's mind.
– DERIVATIVES **adamantly** adverb.
– ORIGIN Greek *adamas* 'untameable, invincible'.

adamantine /adəmantīn/ ● adjective literary unbreakable.

Adam's ale ● noun dated, humorous water.

Adam's apple ● noun a projection at the front of the neck formed by the thyroid cartilage of the larynx.
– ORIGIN so named from the notion that a piece of the forbidden fruit became lodged in Adam's throat.

adapt ● verb **1** make suitable for a new use or purpose. **2** become adjusted to new conditions.
– DERIVATIVES **adaptive** adjective.
– ORIGIN Latin *adaptare*, from *aptus* 'fit'.

Thesaurus

operational, in action, in operation; live; *informal* up and running.
– OPPOSITES listless, passive.

activity ● noun **1** *there was a lot of activity in the area* BUSTLE, hustle and bustle, busyness, action, liveliness, movement, life, stir, flurry; happenings, occurrences, proceedings, events, incidents; *informal* toing and froing, comings and goings. **2** *a wide range of activities* PURSUIT, occupation, interest, hobby, pastime, recreation, diversion; venture, undertaking, enterprise, project, scheme, business, entertainment; act, action, deed, exploit.

actor, actress ● noun PERFORMER, player, trouper, thespian; film star, matinee idol, star, starlet; *informal* ham; *Brit. informal* luvvy; *N. Amer. informal* hambone.
– RELATED TERMS histrionic.

actual ● adjective REAL, true, genuine, authentic, verified, attested, confirmed, definite, hard, plain, veritable; existing, existent, manifest, substantial, factual, de facto, bona fide; *informal* real live.
– OPPOSITES notional.

actuality ● noun *the journalistic debate about actuality and fiction* REALITY, fact, truth, real life.
– PHRASES **in actuality** IN (ACTUAL) FACT, actually, really, in reality, in point of fact, in truth, if truth be told, to tell the truth; *archaic* in sooth.

actually ● adverb *I looked upset but actually I was terribly excited* REALLY, in (actual) fact, in point of fact, as a matter of fact, in reality, in actuality, in truth, if truth be told, to tell the truth; *archaic* in sooth.

actuate ● verb **1** *the sprinkler system was actuated by the fire* ACTIVATE, operate, switch on, turn on, start (up), set going, trigger (off), trip, set in motion, energize. **2** *the defendant was actuated by malice* MOTIVATE, prompt, stimulate, move, drive, influence, incite, spur on, impel.

acumen ● noun ASTUTENESS, shrewdness, acuity, sharpness, sharp-wittedness, cleverness, smartness, brains; judgement, understanding, awareness, sense, common sense, canniness, discernment, wisdom, wit, sagacity, perspicacity, insight, perception, penetration; *informal* nous, savvy, know-how, horse sense; *N. Amer. informal* smarts; *formal* perspicuity.

acute ● adjective **1** *the acute food shortages* SEVERE, critical, drastic, dire, dreadful, terrible, awful, grave, bad, serious, desperate, parlous, dangerous. **2** *acute stomach pains* SHARP, severe, stabbing, excruciating, agonizing, racking, searing. **3** *his acute mind* ASTUTE, shrewd, sharp, sharp-witted, razor-sharp, rapier-like, quick, quick-witted, agile, nimble, clever, intelligent, brilliant, smart, canny, discerning, perceptive, perspicacious, penetrating, insightful, incisive, piercing, discriminating, sagacious, wise, judicious; *informal* on the ball, quick off the mark, quick on the uptake, streetwise, savvy; *N. Amer. informal* heads-up. **4** *an acute sense of smell* KEEN, sharp, good, penetrating, discerning, sensitive.
– OPPOSITES mild, dull.

acutely ● adverb EXTREMELY, exceedingly, very, markedly, severely, intensely, deeply, profoundly, keenly, painfully, desperately, tremendously, enormously, thoroughly, heartily; *informal* awfully, terribly.
– OPPOSITES slightly.

adage ● noun SAYING, maxim, axiom, proverb, aphorism, apophthegm, saw, dictum, precept, motto, truism, platitude, cliché, commonplace.

adamant ● adjective UNSHAKEABLE, immovable, inflexible, unwavering, unswerving, uncompromising, resolute, resolved, determined, firm, steadfast; stubborn, unrelenting, unyielding, un-

a

adaptable • adjective able to adjust to or be modified for new conditions or uses.
– DERIVATIVES **adaptability** noun **adaptably** adverb.
adaptation (also **adaption**) • noun **1** the action or process of adapting or being adapted. **2** a film or play adapted from a written work. **3** Biology a change by which an organism becomes better suited to its environment.
adaptogen /ədaptəjən/ • noun (in herbal medicine) a natural substance considered to help the body adapt to stress.
– DERIVATIVES **adaptogenic** adjective.
adaptor (also **adapter**) • noun **1** a device for connecting pieces of equipment. **2** Brit. a device for connecting more than one plug at a time or plugs of a non-standard type to an electrical socket.
ADC • abbreviation **1** aide-de-camp. **2** analogue to digital converter.
add • verb **1** join to or put with something else. **2** put together (two or more numbers or amounts) to calculate their total value. **3** (**add up**) increase in amount, number, or degree. **4** say as a further remark. **5** (**add up**) informal make sense.
– ORIGIN Latin *addere*, from *ad-* 'to' + *dare* 'put'.
addendum /ədendəm/ • noun (pl. **addenda** /ədendə/) an extra item added at the end of a book or text.
– ORIGIN Latin, 'that which is to be added'.
adder • noun a venomous snake with a dark zigzag pattern on its back.
– ORIGIN Old English *nædre* 'serpent, adder'; the initial *n* was lost by wrong division of *a naddre*.
addict • noun a person who is addicted to something.
addicted • adjective **1** physically dependent on a particular substance. **2** devoted to a particular interest or activity.
– ORIGIN from Latin *addicere* 'assign'.
addiction • noun the fact or condition of being addicted.
– DERIVATIVES **addictive** adjective.
addition • noun **1** the action or process of adding. **2** a person or thing added.
additional • adjective added, extra, or supplementary.
– DERIVATIVES **additionally** adverb.
additive • noun a substance added to improve or preserve something. • adjective relating to or produced by addition.
addle • verb **1** confuse. **2** (**addled**) (of an egg) rotten. • adjective unsound; muddled.
– ORIGIN from Old English, 'liquid filth'.
address • noun **1** the details of the place where someone lives or an organization is situated. **2** Computing a number identifying a location in a data storage system or computer memory. **3** a formal speech. • verb **1** write someone's name and address on (an envelope or parcel). **2** speak formally to. **3** think about and begin to deal with.
– DERIVATIVES **addressee** noun **addresser** noun.
– ORIGIN from Latin *ad-* 'towards' + *directus* 'direct'.
adduce /ədyo͞oss/ • verb cite as evidence.
– ORIGIN Latin *adducere*, from *ad-* 'towards' + *ducere* 'to lead'.
adenine /addineen/ • noun Biochemistry a compound which is one of the four constituent bases of DNA.
– ORIGIN from Greek *adēn* 'gland'.
adenoids /addinoydz/ • plural noun a mass of lymphoid tissue between the back of the nose and the throat, sometimes enlarged and hindering speech or breathing in the young.
– DERIVATIVES **adenoidal** adjective.
– ORIGIN from Greek *adēn* 'gland'.
adenoma /addinōmə/ • noun (pl. **adenomas** or **adenomata** /addinōmətə/) Medicine a benign tumour occurring in glandular tissue or formed from glandular structures.
– ORIGIN Latin, from Greek *adēn* 'gland'.
adenosine /ədennəseen/ • noun Biochemistry a compound (adenine combined with ribose) which occurs in living cells in the form of phosphates, whose breakdown provides energy for muscle action and other processes.

Thesaurus

bending, rigid, obdurate, inexorable, intransigent, dead set.
adapt • verb **1** *we've adapted the hotels to suit their needs* MODIFY, alter, change, adjust, convert, redesign, restyle, refashion, remodel, reshape, revamp, rework, rejig, redo, reconstruct, reorganize; customize, tailor; improve, amend, refine; *informal* tweak. **2** *he has adapted well to his new home* ADJUST, acclimatize oneself, accommodate oneself, habituate oneself, become habituated, get used, orient oneself, reconcile oneself, come to terms, get one's bearings, find one's feet, acculturate, assimilate, blend in, fit in; *N. Amer.* acclimate.
adaptable • adjective **1** *competent and adaptable staff* FLEXIBLE, versatile, cooperative, accommodating, amenable. **2** *an adaptable piece of furniture* VERSATILE, modifiable, convertible, alterable, adjustable, changeable; multi-purpose, all-purpose.
adaptation • noun **1** *the adaptation of old buildings* CONVERSION, alteration, modification, redesign, remodelling, revamping, reconstruction. **2** *the adaptation of an ethnic community to British society* ADJUSTMENT, acclimatization, accommodation, habituation, acculturation, assimilation, integration; *N. Amer.* acclimation.
add • verb **1** *the front porch was added in 1751* ATTACH, build on, join, append, affix, connect, annex; include, incorporate. **2** *they added all the figures up* TOTAL, count (up), compute, reckon up, tally; *Brit.* tot up. **3** *the subsidies added up to £1700* AMOUNT TO, come to, run to, make, total, equal, number. **4** *the recent riots add up to a deepening crisis* AMOUNT TO, constitute; signify, signal, mean, indicate, denote, point to, be evidence of, be symptomatic of; *informal* spell. **5** *her decision just added to his woe* INCREASE, magnify, amplify, augment, intensify, heighten, deepen; exacerbate, aggravate, compound, reinforce; add fuel to the fire, fan the flames, rub salt on the wound. **6** *she added that she had every confidence in Laura* GO ON TO SAY, state further, continue, carry on.
– OPPOSITES subtract.
– PHRASES **add up** *(informal) the situation just didn't add up* MAKE SENSE, stand to reason, hold up, hold water, ring true, be convincing.
addendum • noun APPENDIX, codicil, postscript, afterword, tailpiece, rider, coda, supplement; adjunct, appendage, addition, add-on, attachment.
addict • noun **1** *a heroin addict* ABUSER, user; *informal* junkie, druggy, -freak, -head, pill-popper; *N. Amer. informal* hophead. **2** *(informal) skiing addicts* ENTHUSIAST, fan, lover, devotee, aficionado; *informal* freak, nut, fiend, fanatic, maniac.
addicted • adjective **1** *he was addicted to tranquillizers* DEPENDENT ON; *informal* hooked on. **2** *she became addicted to the theatre* DEVOTED TO, obsessed with, fixated on, fanatical about, passionate about, a slave to; *informal* hooked on, mad on, crazy about.
addiction • noun **1** *his heroin addiction* DEPENDENCY, dependence, habit; *informal* monkey. **2** *a slavish addiction to fashion* DEVOTION TO, dedication to, obsession with, infatuation with, passion for, love of, mania for, enslavement to.
addictive • adjective HABIT-FORMING; compulsive; *Brit. informal* moreish.
addition • noun **1** *the soil is improved by the addition of compost* ADDING, incorporation, inclusion, introduction. **2** *an addition to the existing regulations* SUPPLEMENT, adjunct, addendum, appendage, add-on, extra; rider.
– PHRASES **in addition 1** *conditions were harsh and in addition some soldiers fell victim to snipers* ADDITIONALLY, as well, what's more, furthermore, moreover, also, into the bargain, to boot. **2** *eight presidential candidates in addition to the General* BESIDES, as well as, on top of, plus, over and above.
additional • adjective EXTRA, added, supplementary, supplemental, further, auxiliary, ancillary; more, other, another, new, fresh.
additionally • adverb ALSO, in addition, as well, too, besides, on top (of that), moreover, further, furthermore, what's more, over and above that, into the bargain, to boot; *archaic* withal.
additive • noun ADDED INGREDIENT, addition; preservative, colouring; *Brit. informal* E-number.
addled • adjective MUDDLED, confused, muzzy, fuddled, befuddled, dazed, disoriented, disorientated, fuzzy; *informal* woozy.
address • noun **1** *the address on the envelope* inscription, superscription; directions. **2** *our officers called at the address* HOUSE, flat, apartment, home; *formal* residence, dwelling, dwelling place, habitation, abode, domicile. **3** *his address to the European Parliament* SPEECH, lecture, talk, monologue, dissertation, discourse, oration, peroration; sermon, homily, lesson.
• verb **1** *I addressed the envelope by hand* inscribe, superscribe. **2** *the preacher addressed a crowded congregation* TALK TO, give a talk to, speak to, make a speech to, give a lecture to, lecture, hold forth to; PREACH TO, give a sermon to. **3** *the question of how to address one's parents-in-law* CALL, name, designate; speak to, write to; *formal* denominate. **4** *correspondence should be addressed to the Banking Ombudsman* DIRECT, send, communicate, convey, remit. **5** *the minister failed to address the issue of subsidies* ATTEND TO, apply oneself to, tackle, see to, deal with, confront, get to grips with, get down to, turn one's hand to, take in hand, undertake,

a

adept ● adjective /addept, ədept/ very skilled or proficient. ● noun /addept/ a person who is adept at something.
– DERIVATIVES **adeptly** adverb **adeptness** noun.
– ORIGIN from Latin *adipisci* 'obtain, attain'.
adequate ● adjective satisfactory or acceptable.
– DERIVATIVES **adequacy** noun **adequately** adverb.
– ORIGIN from Latin *adaequare* 'make equal to'.
à deux /aa dö/ ● adverb for or involving two people.
– ORIGIN French.
adhere /ədheer/ ● verb (**adhere to**) **1** stick fast to. **2** remain faithful to.
– DERIVATIVES **adherence** noun.
– ORIGIN Latin *adhaerere* 'stick to'.
adherent ● noun a person who supports a particular party, person, or set of ideas. ● adjective sticking fast to an object or surface.
adhesion /ədheezh'n/ ● noun **1** the action or process of adhering. **2** technical the sticking together of different substances. Compare with COHESION. **3** Medicine an abnormal union of surfaces due to inflammation or injury.
adhesive /ədheessiv/ ● adjective causing adherence; sticky. ● noun an adhesive substance.
– DERIVATIVES **adhesively** adverb **adhesiveness** noun.
ad hoc /ad hok/ ● adjective & adverb formed or done for a particular purpose only.
– ORIGIN Latin, 'to this'.
ad hominem /ad homminem/ ● adverb & adjective (of an argument) personal rather than objective.
– ORIGIN Latin, 'to the person'.
adiabatic /aydīəbattik/ ● adjective Physics **1** relating to a process or condition in which heat does not enter or leave the system concerned. **2** impassable to heat.
– DERIVATIVES **adiabatically** adverb.
– ORIGIN Greek *adiabatos* 'impassable'.
adieu /ədyoo/ ● exclamation chiefly literary goodbye.
– ORIGIN Old French, from *a* 'to' + *Dieu* 'God'.
ad infinitum /ad infinītəm/ ● adverb endlessly; forever.
– ORIGIN Latin, 'to infinity'.
adios /addioss/ ● exclamation Spanish term for GOODBYE.
– ORIGIN Spanish, from *a* 'to' + *Dios* 'God'.
adipose /addipōz/ ● adjective technical denoting body tissue used for the storage of fat.
– DERIVATIVES **adiposity** noun.
– ORIGIN Latin *adiposus*, from *adeps* 'fat'.
adit /addit/ ● noun an access or drainage passage leading horizontally into a mine.
– ORIGIN Latin *aditus* 'approach, entrance'.
adjacent /əjays'nt/ ● adjective next to or adjoining something else.
– DERIVATIVES **adjacency** noun.
– ORIGIN from Latin *adjacere* 'lie near to'.
adjective ● noun Grammar a word used to describe or modify a noun, such as *sweet*, *red*, or *technical*.
– DERIVATIVES **adjectival** adjective.
– ORIGIN Old French *adjectif*, from Latin *adicere* 'add'.
adjoin ● verb be next to and joined with.
– ORIGIN Old French *ajoindre*, from Latin *adjungere* 'join to'.
adjourn /əjurn/ ● verb **1** break off (a meeting) with the intention of resuming it later. **2** postpone (a resolution or sentence).
– DERIVATIVES **adjournment** noun.
– ORIGIN Old French *ajorner*, from *a jorn nome* 'to an appointed day'.
adjudge ● verb decide or award judicially.
– ORIGIN Latin *adjudicare*, from *ad-* 'to' + *judicare* 'to judge'.
adjudicate /əjoodikayt/ ● verb **1** make a formal judgement on a disputed matter. **2** judge a competition.
– DERIVATIVES **adjudication** noun **adjudicative** adjective **adjudicator** noun.
– ORIGIN Latin *adjudicare* 'adjudge'.
adjunct /ajungkt/ ● noun **1** an additional and supplementary part. **2** Grammar a word or phrase in a sentence other than the verb or predicate. ● adjective connected in an auxiliary way.
– DERIVATIVES **adjunctive** adjective.
– ORIGIN from Latin *adjungere* 'adjoin'.

Thesaurus

concentrate on, focus on, devote oneself to.
adduce ● verb CITE, quote, name, mention, instance, point out, refer to; put forward, present, offer, advance, propose, proffer.
adept ● adjective *an adept negotiator* EXPERT, proficient, accomplished, skilful, talented, masterly, consummate, virtuoso; adroit, dexterous, deft, artful; brilliant, splendid, marvellous, formidable, outstanding, first-rate, first-class, excellent, fine; informal great, top-notch, tip-top, A1, ace, mean, hotshot, crack, nifty, deadly; Brit. informal a dab hand at; N. Amer. informal crackerjack.
– OPPOSITES inept.
● noun *kung fu adepts* EXPERT, past master, master, genius, maestro, doyen; informal wizard, demon, ace, hotshot, whizz; N. Amer. informal maven, crackerjack.
– OPPOSITES amateur.
adequacy ● noun **1** *the adequacy of the existing services* SATISFACTORINESS, acceptability, acceptableness; sufficiency. **2** *he had deep misgivings about his own adequacy* CAPABILITY, competence, ability, aptitude, suitability; effectiveness, fitness; formal efficacy.
adequate ● adjective **1** *he lacked adequate financial resources* SUFFICIENT, enough, requisite. **2** *the company provides an adequate service* ACCEPTABLE, passable, reasonable, satisfactory, tolerable, fair, decent, quite good, pretty good, goodish, moderate, unexceptional, unremarkable, undistinguished, ordinary, average, not bad, all right, middling; informal OK, so-so, fair-to-middling, nothing to write home about. **3** *the workstations were small but seemed adequate to the task* EQUAL TO, up to, capable of, suitable for, able to do, fit for, sufficient for.
adhere ● verb **1** *a dollop of cream adhered to her nose* STICK (FAST), cohere, cling, bond, attach; be stuck, be fixed, be glued. **2** *they adhere scrupulously to Judaic law* ABIDE BY, stick to, hold to, comply with, act in accordance with, conform to, submit to; follow, obey, heed, observe, respect, uphold, fulfil.
– OPPOSITES flout, ignore.
adherent ● noun FOLLOWER, supporter, upholder, defender, advocate, disciple, votary, devotee, partisan, member, friend, stalwart, sectary; believer, worshipper.
– OPPOSITES opponent.
adhesion ● noun **1** *the adhesion of the gum strip to the paper fibres* STICKING, adherence. **2** *the front tyres were struggling for adhesion* TRACTION, grip, purchase.
adhesive ● noun *a spray adhesive* GLUE, fixative, gum, paste, cement; N. Amer. mucilage; N. Amer. informal stickum.
● adjective *adhesive mortar* STICKY, tacky, gluey, gummed; viscous, viscid; technical adherent.
adieu ● noun & exclamation (poetic/literary) GOODBYE, farewell, until we meet again; informal bye-bye, ta-ta, bye, cheerio, cheers, ciao, so long; informal, dated toodle-oo, toodle-pip.
ad infinitum ● adverb FOREVER, for ever and ever, evermore, always, for all time, until the end of time, in perpetuity, until hell freezes over; perpetually, eternally, endlessly, interminably, unceasingly, unendingly; Brit. for evermore; informal until the cows come home, until the twelfth of never, until doomsday, until kingdom come; archaic for aye.
adjacent ● adjective ADJOINING, neighbouring, next-door, abutting, contiguous, proximate; (**adjacent to**) close to, near, next to, by, by the side of, bordering on, beside, alongside, attached to, touching, cheek by jowl with.
adjoin ● verb BE NEXT TO, be adjacent to, border (on), abut, be contiguous with, communicate with, extend to; join, conjoin, connect with, touch, meet.
adjoining ● adjective CONNECTING, connected, interconnecting, adjacent, neighbouring, bordering, next-door; contiguous, proximate; attached, touching.
adjourn ● verb **1** *the hearing was adjourned* SUSPEND, break off, discontinue, interrupt, prorogue, stay, recess. **2** *sentencing was adjourned until June 9* POSTPONE, put off/back, defer, delay, hold over, shelve. **3** *they adjourned to the sitting room for liqueurs* WITHDRAW, retire, retreat, take oneself; formal repair, remove; poetic/literary betake oneself.
adjournment ● noun SUSPENSION, discontinuation, interruption, postponement, deferment, deferral, stay, prorogation; break, pause, recess.
adjudge ● verb JUDGE, deem, find, pronounce, proclaim, rule, hold, determine; consider, think, rate, reckon, perceive, regard as, view as, see as, believe to be.
adjudicate ● verb JUDGE, try, hear, examine, arbitrate; pronounce on, give a ruling on, pass judgement on, decide, determine, settle, resolve.
adjudication ● noun JUDGEMENT, decision, pronouncement, ruling, settlement, resolution, arbitration, finding, verdict, sentence; Law

a

adjure /əjoor/ ● verb formal solemnly urge to do something.
– ORIGIN Latin *adjurare*, from *ad-* 'to' + *jurare* 'swear'.
adjust ● verb **1** alter slightly so as to achieve a desired result. **2** become used to a new situation. **3** assess (loss or damages) when settling an insurance claim.
– DERIVATIVES **adjustability** noun **adjustable** adjective **adjuster** noun **adjustment** noun.
– ORIGIN Old French *ajoster* 'to approximate', from Latin *juxta* 'near'.
adjutant /ajoot'nt/ ● noun a military officer acting as an administrative assistant to a senior officer.
– ORIGIN from Latin *adjutare*, from *adjuvare* 'help towards'.
adjuvant /adjoov'nt/ ● adjective (of medical treatment) applied after initial treatment for cancer to prevent the formation of secondary tumours. ● noun a substance used to enhance the body's immune response to an infection or foreign body.
– ORIGIN from Latin *adjuvare* 'help towards'.
ad-lib ● verb (**ad-libbed**, **ad-libbing**) speak or perform in public without preparing in advance. ● adverb & adjective **1** spoken without advance preparation. **2** Music with free rhythm and expression. ● noun an ad-lib remark or speech.
– ORIGIN abbreviation of Latin *ad libitum* 'according to pleasure'.
ad litem /ad lītem/ ● adjective Law acting in a lawsuit on behalf of people who cannot represent themselves.
– ORIGIN Latin, 'for the lawsuit'.
administer ● verb **1** attend to the organization or implementation of. **2** dispense (a drug or remedy).
– DERIVATIVES **administrable** adjective.
– ORIGIN Latin *administrare*, from *ministrare* 'wait upon'.
administrate ● verb administer; carry out administration.
– DERIVATIVES **administrative** adjective **administrator** noun.
administration ● noun **1** the organization and running of a business or system. **2** the action of administering. **3** the government in power. **4** chiefly N. Amer. the term of office of a political leader or government.
admirable /admirəb'l/ ● adjective arousing or deserving respect and approval.
– DERIVATIVES **admirably** adverb.
admiral ● noun **1** the most senior commander of a fleet or navy. **2** (**Admiral**) a naval officer of the second most senior rank, above vice admiral and below Admiral of the Fleet.
– ORIGIN originally denoting an emir: from Old French *amiral* from an Arabic word meaning 'commander'.
Admiral of the Fleet ● noun the highest rank of admiral in the Royal Navy.
Admiralty ● noun (pl. **Admiralties**) (in the UK) the government department that formerly administered the Royal Navy, now used only in titles.
admire ● verb **1** regard with respect or warm approval. **2** look at with pleasure.
– DERIVATIVES **admiration** noun **admirer** noun **admiring** adjective.
– ORIGIN Latin *admirari* 'wonder at'.
admissible ● adjective **1** acceptable or valid. **2** having the right to be admitted to a place.
– DERIVATIVES **admissibility** noun.
admission ● noun **1** a confession. **2** the process or fact of being admitted to a place. **3** a person admitted to hospital for treatment.
admit ● verb (**admitted**, **admitting**) **1** confess to be true or to be the case. **2** allow to enter. **3** receive into a hospital for treatment. **4** accept as valid. **5** (**admit of**) allow the possibility of.
– ORIGIN Latin *admittere* 'let into'.
admittance ● noun the process or fact of entering or being allowed to enter.

Thesaurus

determination.
adjudicator ● noun JUDGE, arbitrator, arbiter; referee, umpire.
adjunct ● noun SUPPLEMENT, addition, extra, add-on, accessory, accompaniment, complement, appurtenance; attachment, appendage, addendum.
adjust ● verb **1** *Kate had adjusted to her new life* ADAPT, become accustomed, get used, accommodate, acclimatize, orient oneself, reconcile oneself, habituate oneself, assimilate; come to terms with, blend in with, fit in with, find one's feet in; N. Amer. acclimate. **2** *he adjusted the brakes* MODIFY, alter, regulate, tune, fine-tune, calibrate, balance; adapt, rearrange, change, rejig, rework, revamp, remodel, reshape, convert, tailor, improve, enhance, customize; repair, fix, correct, rectify, overhaul, put right; informal tweak.
adjustable ● adjective ALTERABLE, adaptable, modifiable, convertible, variable, multiway, versatile.
adjustment ● noun **1** *a period of adjustment* ADAPTATION, accommodation, acclimatization, habituation, acculturation, naturalization, assimilation; N. Amer. acclimation. **2** *the car will run on unleaded petrol with no adjustment* MODIFICATION, alteration, regulation, adaptation, rearrangement, change, reconstruction, customization, refinement; repair, correction, amendment, overhaul, improvement.
ad-lib ● verb *she ad-libbed half the speech* IMPROVISE, extemporize, speak impromptu, play it by ear, make it up as one goes along; informal busk it, wing it.
● adverb *she spoke ad lib* IMPROMPTU, extempore, without preparation, without rehearsal, extemporaneously; informal off the cuff, off the top of one's head.
● adjective *a live, ad-lib commentary* IMPROMPTU, extempore, extemporaneous, extemporary, improvised, unprepared, unrehearsed, unscripted; informal off-the-cuff, spur-of-the-moment.
administer ● verb **1** *the union is administered by a central executive* MANAGE, direct, control, operate, regulate, conduct, handle, run, organize, supervise, superintend, oversee, preside over, govern, rule, lead, head, steer; be in control of, be in charge of, be responsible for, be at the helm of; informal head up. **2** *the lifeboat crew administered first aid* DISPENSE, issue, give, provide, apply, allot, distribute, hand out, dole out, disburse. **3** *a gym shoe was used to administer punishment* INFLICT, mete out, deal out, deliver.
administration ● noun **1** *the day-to-day administration of the company* MANAGEMENT, direction, control, command, charge, conduct, operation, running, leadership, government, governing, superintendence, supervision, regulation, overseeing. **2** *the previous Labour administration* GOVERNMENT, cabinet, ministry, regime, executive, authority, directorate, council, leadership, management; parliament, congress, senate; rule, term of office, incumbency. **3** *the administration of anti-inflammatory drugs* PROVISION, issuing, issuance, application, dispensing, dispensation, distribution, disbursement.
administrative ● adjective MANAGERIAL, management, directorial, executive, organizational, supervisory, regulatory.
administrator ● noun MANAGER, director, executive, controller, head, chief, leader, governor, superintendent, supervisor; informal boss.
admirable ● adjective COMMENDABLE, praiseworthy, laudable, estimable, meritorious, creditable, exemplary, worthy, deserving, respectable, worthwhile, good, sterling, fine, masterly, great.
– OPPOSITES deplorable.
admiration ● noun *his patience commanded widespread admiration* RESPECT, approval, approbation, appreciation, (high) regard, esteem; commendation, acclaim, applause, praise, compliments, tributes, accolades, plaudits; formal laudation.
– OPPOSITES scorn.
admire ● verb **1** *I admire your courage* RESPECT, approve of, esteem, think highly of, rate highly, hold in high regard, applaud, praise, commend, acclaim. **2** *Simon had admired her for a long time* ADORE, love, worship, dote on, be enamoured of, be infatuated with; be taken with, be attracted to, find attractive; informal carry a torch for, have a thing about.
– OPPOSITES despise.
admirer ● noun **1** *a great admirer of Henry James* FAN, devotee, enthusiast, aficionado; supporter, adherent, follower, disciple. **2** *a handsome admirer of hers* SUITOR, wooer, sweetheart, lover, boyfriend, young man; poetic/literary swain; dated beau.
admissible ● adjective VALID, allowable, allowed, permissible, permitted, acceptable, satisfactory, justifiable, defensible, supportable, well founded, tenable, sound; legitimate, lawful, legal, licit; informal OK, legit, kosher, pukka.
admission ● noun **1** *membership entitles you to free admission* ADMITTANCE, entry, entrance, right of entry, access, right of access, ingress; entrée. **2** *admission is fifty pence* ENTRANCE FEE, entry charge, ticket. **3** *a written admission of liability* CONFESSION, acknowledgement, acceptance, concession, disclosure, divulgence.
admit ● verb **1** *he unlocked the door to admit her* LET IN, allow entry, permit entry, take in, usher in, show in, receive, welcome. **2** *he was admitted as a scholar to Winchester College* ACCEPT, take on, receive, enrol, enlist, register, sign up. **3** *Paul admitted that he was angry* CONFESS, acknowledge, own, concede, grant, accept, allow; reveal, disclose, divulge. **4** *he admitted three offences of*

a

admix ● verb chiefly technical mix with something else.
– DERIVATIVES **admixture** noun.
admonish ● verb **1** reprimand firmly. **2** earnestly urge or warn.
– DERIVATIVES **admonishment** noun **admonition** noun **admonitory** adjective.
– ORIGIN Latin *admonere* 'urge by warning'.
ad nauseam /ad nawziam/ ● adverb to a tiresomely excessive degree.
– ORIGIN Latin, 'to sickness'.
ado ● noun trouble; fuss.
– ORIGIN originally in the sense 'action, business': from northern dialect *at do* 'to do'.
adobe /ədōbi/ ● noun a kind of clay used to make sun-dried bricks.
– ORIGIN from Spanish *adobar* 'to plaster', from an Arabic word meaning 'bricks'.
adolescent ● adjective in the process of developing from a child into an adult. ● noun an adolescent boy or girl.
– DERIVATIVES **adolescence** noun.
– ORIGIN from Latin *adolescere* 'come to maturity'.
Adonis /ədōniss/ ● noun an extremely handsome young man.
– ORIGIN from the name of a beautiful youth in Greek mythology.
adopt ● verb **1** legally take (another's child) and bring it up as one's own. **2** choose to take up or follow (an option or course of action). **3** Brit. choose as a candidate for office. **4** assume (an attitude or position). **5** formally approve or accept.
– DERIVATIVES **adoptable** adjective **adoptee** noun **adopter** noun **adoption** noun.
– ORIGIN Latin *adoptare*, from *optare* 'choose'.
adoptive ● adjective **1** (of a child or parent) in that relationship by adoption. **2** denoting a place chosen as one's permanent place of residence.
adorable ● adjective inspiring great affection.
– DERIVATIVES **adorably** adverb.
adore ● verb love and respect deeply.
– DERIVATIVES **adoration** noun **adorer** noun **adoring** adjective.
– ORIGIN Latin *adorare* 'to worship', from *orare* 'speak, pray'.
adorn ● verb make more attractive or beautiful; decorate.
– DERIVATIVES **adornment** noun.
– ORIGIN Latin *adornare* 'deck out, decorate'.
adrenal /ədreen'l/ ● adjective relating to a pair of glands (the **adrenal glands**), situated above the kidneys and secreting adrenalin and other hormones.
adrenalin /ədrennəlin/ (also **adrenaline**) ● noun a hormone that increases rates of blood circulation, breathing, and carbohydrate metabolism, secreted by the adrenal glands (especially in conditions of stress).
adrenalized /ədrennəlīzd/ (also **adrenalised**) ● adjective excited, tense, or highly charged.
Adriatic /aydriattik/ ● adjective of the region of the **Adriatic Sea**, the arm of the Mediterranean between Italy and the Balkans.
adrift ● adjective & adverb **1** (of a boat) drifting without control. **2** Brit. informal no longer fixed in position.
adroit /ədroyt/ ● adjective clever or skilful in using the hands or mind.
– ORIGIN from French *à droit* 'according to right, properly'.
adsorb /ədzorb, -sorb/ ● verb (of a solid) hold (molecules of a gas, liquid, or dissolved substance) in a layer on its surface.
– DERIVATIVES **adsorbable** adjective **adsorption** noun **adsorptive** adjective.
adsorbent ● noun a substance which adsorbs another. ● adjec-

Thesaurus

reckless driving CONFESS (TO), plead guilty to, own up to, make a clean breast of.
– OPPOSITES exclude, deny.
admittance ● noun ENTRY, right of entry, admission, entrance, access, right of access, ingress; entrée.
– OPPOSITES exclusion.
admonish ● verb **1** *he was severely admonished by his father* REPRIMAND, rebuke, scold, reprove, reproach, upbraid, chastise, chide, berate, criticize, take to task, pull up, read the Riot Act to, haul over the coals; *informal* tell off, dress down, bawl out, rap over the knuckles, give someone hell; *Brit. informal* tick off, give someone a rocket, have a go at, carpet, tear someone off a strip; *N. Amer. informal* chew out; *formal* castigate; *rare* reprehend. **2** *she admonished him to drink less* ADVISE, recommend, counsel, urge, exhort, bid, enjoin; *formal* adjure.
admonition ● noun **1** *a breach of the rules which led to an admonition* REPRIMAND, rebuke, reproof, remonstrance, reproach, reproval, stricture, criticism, recrimination, scolding, censure; *informal* telling-off, dressing-down, talking-to, tongue-lashing, rap over the knuckles, slap on the wrist, flea in one's ear, earful; *Brit. informal* rocket, rollicking, wigging, ticking-off; *formal* castigation. **2** *an admonition to proceed carefully* EXHORTATION, warning, piece of advice, recommendation, counsel.
ado ● noun FUSS, trouble, bother, upset, agitation, commotion, stir, hubbub, confusion, excitement, hurly-burly, flurry; palaver, rigmarole, brouhaha; *N. Amer.* fuss and feathers; *informal* hassle, to-do, hoo-ha, ballyhoo, song and dance, performance, kerfuffle; *Brit. informal* carry-on.
adolescence ● noun TEENAGE YEARS, teens, youth; pubescence, puberty.
adolescent ● noun *an awkward adolescent* TEENAGER, youngster, young person, youth, boy, girl; juvenile, minor; *informal* teen, teeny-bopper.
● adjective **1** *an adolescent boy* TEENAGE, pubescent, young; juvenile; *informal* teen. **2** *adolescent silliness* IMMATURE, childish, juvenile, infantile, puerile, jejune.
– OPPOSITES adult, mature.
adopt ● verb **1** *the child was adopted by an American family* take as one's child, be adoptive parents to, take in, take care of. **2** *a republican constitution was adopted in 1971* ESPOUSE, take on/up, embrace, assume; appropriate, arrogate. **3** *the people adopted him as their patron saint* CHOOSE, select, pick, vote for, elect, settle on, decide on, opt for; name, nominate, appoint.
– OPPOSITES abandon.
adorable ● adjective LOVABLE, appealing, charming, cute, sweet, enchanting, bewitching, captivating, engaging, endearing, dear, darling, delightful, lovely, beautiful, attractive, gorgeous, winsome, winning, fetching; *Scottish & N. English* bonny.
– OPPOSITES hateful.
adoration ● noun **1** *the girl gazed at him with adoration* LOVE, devotion, care, fondness; admiration, high regard, awe, idolization, worship, hero-worship, adulation. **2** *our day of prayer and adoration* WORSHIP, glory, glorification, praise, thanksgiving, homage, exaltation, extolment, veneration, reverence; *archaic* magnification.
adore ● verb **1** *he adored his mother* LOVE DEARLY, love, be devoted to, dote on, hold dear, cherish, treasure, prize, think the world of; admire, hold in high regard, look up to, idolize, worship; *informal* put on a pedestal. **2** *the people had come to pray and adore God* WORSHIP, glorify, praise, revere, reverence, exalt, extol, venerate, pay homage to; *formal* laud; *archaic* magnify. **3** *(informal) I adore oysters* LIKE, love, be very fond of, be very keen on, be partial to, have a weakness for; delight in, revel in, relish, savour; *informal* be crazy about, be wild about, have a thing about, be hooked on, go a bundle on; *Brit. informal* be potty about.
– OPPOSITES hate.
adorn ● verb DECORATE, embellish, ornament, enhance; beautify, prettify, grace, bedeck, deck (out), dress (up), trim, swathe, wreathe, festoon, garland, array, emblazon; *poetic/literary* bedizen, caparison.
adornment ● noun DECORATION, embellishment, ornamentation, ornament, enhancement; beautification, prettification; frills, accessories, trimmings, finishing touches.
adrift ● adjective **1** *their empty boat was spotted adrift* DRIFTING, unmoored, unanchored. **2** *(Brit. informal) the pipe of my breathing apparatus came adrift* LOOSE, free; detached, unsecured, unfastened, untied, unknotted, undone. **3** *he was adrift in a strange country* LOST, off course; disorientated, disoriented, confused, (all) at sea; drifting, rootless, unsettled, directionless, aimless, purposeless, without purpose. **4** *(Brit. informal) his instincts were not entirely adrift.* See WRONG adjective sense 1.
adroit ● adjective SKILFUL, adept, dexterous, deft, nimble, able, capable, skilled, expert, masterly, masterful, master, practised, polished, slick, proficient, accomplished, gifted, talented; quick-witted, quick-thinking, clever, smart, sharp, cunning, wily, resourceful, astute, shrewd, canny; *informal* nifty, crack, mean, wizard, demon, ace, A1, on the ball, savvy; *N. Amer. informal* crackerjack.
– OPPOSITES inept, clumsy.
adroitness ● noun SKILL, skilfulness, prowess, expertise, adeptness, dexterity, deftness, nimbleness, ability, capability, mastery, proficiency, accomplishment, artistry, art, facility, aptitude, flair,

a

tive able to adsorb substances.

aduki /ədōōki/ ● noun variant of ADZUKI.

adulation /adyoolaysh'n/ ● noun excessive admiration.
– DERIVATIVES **adulate** verb **adulatory** adjective.
– ORIGIN Latin, from *adulari* 'fawn on'.

adult /addult, ədult/ ● noun **1** a person who is fully grown and developed. **2** Law a person who has reached the age of majority. ● adjective **1** fully grown and developed. **2** for or characteristic of adults.
– DERIVATIVES **adulthood** noun.
– ORIGIN Latin *adultus*, from *adolescere* 'come to maturity'.

adulterate /ədultərayt/ ● verb make poorer in quality by adding another substance.
– DERIVATIVES **adulterant** adjective **adulteration** noun.
– ORIGIN Latin *adulterare* 'to corrupt'.

adulterer ● noun (fem. **adulteress**) a person who has committed adultery.
– ORIGIN from Latin *adulterare* 'debauch, corrupt'.

adultery ● noun voluntary sexual intercourse between a married person and a person who is not their spouse.
– DERIVATIVES **adulterous** adjective.

adumbrate /addumbrayt/ ● verb formal **1** give a faint or general idea of. **2** foreshadow.
– DERIVATIVES **adumbration** noun.
– ORIGIN Latin *adumbrare* 'shade, overshadow'.

advance ● verb **1** move forwards. **2** make or cause to make progress. **3** put forward (a theory or suggestion). **4** hand over (payment) to (someone) as a loan or before it is due. ● noun **1** a forward movement. **2** a development or improvement. **3** an amount of money advanced. **4** an approach made with the aim of initiating a sexual or amorous relationship. ● adjective done, sent, or supplied beforehand.
– DERIVATIVES **advancer** noun.
– ORIGIN Old French *avancer*, from Latin *abante* 'in front'.

advanced ● adjective **1** far on in progress or life. **2** complex; not elementary. **3** very modern.

advanced level ● noun fuller form of A LEVEL.

advanced subsidiary level ● noun (in the UK except Scotland) a GCE examination at a level between GCSE and advanced level.

advancement ● noun **1** the process of promoting a cause or plan. **2** the promotion of a person in rank or status. **3** a development or improvement.

advantage ● noun **1** a condition or circumstance that puts one in a favourable position. **2** Tennis a score marking a point interim between deuce and winning the game. ● verb be of benefit to.
– PHRASES **take advantage of 1** make unfair use of for one's own benefit. **2** dated seduce. **3** make good use of the opportunities offered.
– DERIVATIVES **advantageous** /advəntayjəss/ adjective.
– ORIGIN Old French *avantage*, from Latin *abante* 'in front'.

advent /advent/ ● noun **1** the arrival of a notable person or thing. **2** (**Advent**) Christian Theology the coming or second coming of Christ. **3** (**Advent**) the first season of the Church year, leading up to Christmas.
– ORIGIN Latin *adventus* 'arrival'.

Advent calendar ● noun a calendar containing small numbered flaps, one of which is opened on each day of Advent to reveal a seasonal picture.

Adventist ● noun a member of a Christian sect emphasizing belief in the imminent second coming of Christ.
– DERIVATIVES **Adventism** noun.

adventitious /adventishəss/ ● adjective **1** happening according to chance. **2** Botany (of roots) growing directly from the stem or other upper part of a plant.
– DERIVATIVES **adventitiously** adverb.
– ORIGIN Latin *adventicius* 'coming to us from abroad'.

Thesaurus

finesse, talent; quick-wittedness, cleverness, sharpness, cunning, astuteness, shrewdness, resourcefulness, savoir faire; *informal* know-how, savvy.

adulation ● noun HERO-WORSHIP, worship, idolization, adoration, admiration, veneration, awe, devotion, glorification, praise, flattery, blandishments.

adulatory ● adjective FLATTERING, complimentary, highly favourable, enthusiastic, glowing, reverential, rhapsodic, eulogistic, laudatory; fulsome, honeyed.
– OPPOSITES disparaging.

adult ● adjective **1** *an adult woman* MATURE, grown-up, fully grown, full-grown, fully developed, of age. **2** *an adult movie* SEXUALLY EXPLICIT, pornographic, obscene, smutty, dirty, rude, erotic, sexy, suggestive, titillating; *informal* porn, porno, naughty, blue, X-rated, skin.

adulterate ● verb MAKE IMPURE, degrade, debase, spoil, taint, contaminate; doctor, tamper with, dilute, water down, weaken; bastardize, corrupt; *informal* cut, spike, dope.
– OPPOSITES purify.

adulterer ● noun PHILANDERER, deceiver, womanizer, ladies' man, Don Juan, Casanova, Lothario; *informal* cheat, two-timer, love rat; *formal* fornicator.

adulterous ● adjective UNFAITHFUL, faithless, disloyal, untrue, inconstant, false, false-hearted, deceiving, deceitful, treacherous; extramarital; *informal* cheating, two-timing.
– OPPOSITES faithful.

adultery ● noun INFIDELITY, unfaithfulness, falseness, disloyalty, cuckoldry, extramarital sex; affair, liaison, amour; *informal* carryings-on, hanky-panky, a bit on the side, playing around; *formal* fornication.
– OPPOSITES fidelity.

advance ● verb **1** *the battalion advanced rapidly* MOVE FORWARD, proceed, press on, push on, push forward, make progress, make headway, gain ground, approach, come closer, draw nearer, near; *archaic* draw nigh. **2** *the court may advance the date of the hearing* BRING FORWARD, put forward, move forward. **3** *the move advanced his career* PROMOTE, further, forward, help, aid, assist, boost, strengthen, improve, benefit, foster. **4** *our technology has advanced in the last few years* PROGRESS, make progress, make headway, develop, evolve, make strides, move forward (in leaps and bounds), move ahead; improve, thrive, flourish, prosper. **5** *the hypothesis I wish to advance in this article* PUT FORWARD, present, submit, suggest, propose, introduce, offer, adduce, moot. **6** *a relative advanced him some money* LEND, loan, put up, come up with; *Brit. informal* sub.
– OPPOSITES retreat, hinder, postpone, retract, borrow.
● noun **1** *the advance of the aggressors* PROGRESS, forward movement; approach. **2** *a significant medical advance* BREAKTHROUGH, development, step forward, step in the right direction, (quantum) leap; find, finding, discovery, invention. **3** *share prices showed significant advances* INCREASE, rise, upturn, upsurge, upswing, growth; *informal* hike. **4** *the writer is going to be given a huge advance* DOWN PAYMENT, retainer, prepayment, deposit, front money, money up front. **5** *unwelcome sexual advances* PASS, proposition.
● adjective **1** *an advance party of settlers* PRELIMINARY, sent (on) ahead, first, exploratory; pilot, test, trial. **2** *advance warning* EARLY, prior, beforehand.
– PHRASES **in advance** BEFOREHAND, before, ahead of time, earlier, previously; in readiness.

advanced ● adjective **1** *advanced manufacturing techniques* STATE-OF-THE-ART, new, modern, up to date, up to the minute, the newest, the latest; progressive, avant-garde, ahead of the times, pioneering, innovatory, sophisticated. **2** *advanced further-education courses* HIGHER-LEVEL, higher, tertiary.
– OPPOSITES primitive.

advancement ● noun **1** *the advancement of computer technology* DEVELOPMENT, progress, evolution, growth, improvement, advance, furtherance; headway. **2** *employees must be offered opportunities for advancement* PROMOTION, preferment, career development, upgrading, a step up the ladder, progress, improvement, betterment, growth.

advantage ● noun **1** *the advantages of belonging to a union* BENEFIT, value, good point, strong point, asset, plus, bonus, boon, blessing, virtue; attraction, beauty, usefulness, helpfulness, convenience, advantageousness, profit. **2** *they appeared to be gaining the advantage over their opponents* UPPER HAND, edge, lead, whip hand, trump card; superiority, dominance, ascendancy, supremacy, power, mastery. **3** *there is no advantage to be gained from delaying the process* BENEFIT, profit, gain, good; *informal* mileage, percentage.
– OPPOSITES disadvantage, drawback, detriment.

advantageous ● adjective **1** *an advantageous position* SUPERIOR, dominant, powerful; good, fortunate, lucky, favourable. **2** *the arrangement is advantageous to both sides* BENEFICIAL, of benefit, helpful, of assistance, useful, of use, of value, of service, profitable, fruitful; convenient, expedient, in everyone's interests.

a

adventure ● noun **1** an unusual, exciting, and daring experience. **2** excitement arising from or associated with danger or risk.
– DERIVATIVES **adventuresome** adjective.
– ORIGIN from Latin *adventurus* 'about to happen', from *advenire* 'arrive'.
adventurer ● noun (fem. **adventuress**) **1** a person willing to take risks or use dishonest methods for personal gain: *a political adventurer.* **2** a person who enjoys or seeks adventure.
adventurism ● noun willingness to take risks in business or politics.
– DERIVATIVES **adventurist** noun & adjective.
adventurous ● adjective open to or involving new or daring methods or experiences.
– DERIVATIVES **adventurously** adverb **adventurousness** noun.
adverb ● noun Grammar a word or phrase that modifies the meaning of an adjective, verb, or other adverb, or of a sentence (e.g *gently, very, fortunately*).
– ORIGIN Latin *adverbium*, from *ad-* 'to' + *verbum* 'word, verb'.
adverbial Grammar ● noun a word or phrase functioning as a major clause constituent and typically expressing place (*in the garden*), time (*in May*), or manner (*in a strange way*). ● adjective relating to or functioning as an adverb or adverbial.
adversarial /advəsairiəl/ ● adjective involving or characterized by conflict or opposition.
– DERIVATIVES **adversarially** adverb.
adversary /advərsəri/ ● noun (pl. **adversaries**) an opponent.
– ORIGIN Latin *adversarius* 'opposed, opponent'.
adverse /adverss/ ● adjective harmful; unfavourable.
– DERIVATIVES **adversely** adverb.
– USAGE A common error is to use **adverse** instead of **averse**, as in *I am not adverse to helping out*, rather than the correct form *I am not averse to helping out.*
– ORIGIN Latin *adversus* 'against, opposite', from *advertere* 'turn to'.
adversity ● noun (pl. **adversities**) difficulty; misfortune.
advert[1] /advert/ ● noun Brit. informal an advertisement.
advert[2] /ədvert/ ● verb (**advert to**) formal refer to.
– ORIGIN Latin *advertere* 'turn to'.
advertise ● verb **1** present or describe (a product, service, or event) in a public medium so as to promote sales. **2** seek to fill (a vacancy) by placing a notice in a newspaper or other medium. **3** make (a quality or fact) known.
– DERIVATIVES **advertiser** noun **advertising** noun.
– ORIGIN Old French *advertir*, from Latin *advertere* 'turn to'.
advertisement ● noun a notice or display advertising something.
advertorial /advertoriəl/ ● noun an advertisement in the style of an editorial or objective journalistic article.
advice ● noun **1** guidance or recommendations offered with regard to future action. **2** a formal notice of a sale or other transaction.
– ORIGIN Old French *avis*, from Latin *ad* 'to' + *videre* 'to see'.
advisable ● adjective to be recommended; sensible.
– DERIVATIVES **advisability** noun.
advise ● verb **1** recommend (a course of action). **2** inform about a fact or situation. **3** offer advice to.
– DERIVATIVES **adviser** (also **advisor**) noun.
– ORIGIN Old French *aviser*, from Latin *ad-* 'to' + *videre* 'to see'.
advised ● adjective behaving as someone would recommend; sensible.
– DERIVATIVES **advisedly** adverb.
advisory ● adjective having the power to make recommendations but not to enforce them.
advocaat /advəkaat/ ● noun a liqueur made with eggs, sugar, and brandy.
– ORIGIN Dutch, 'advocate' (being originally considered a lawyer's drink).
advocate ● noun /advəkət/ **1** a person who publicly supports or recommends a particular cause or policy. **2** a person who pleads a case on someone else's behalf. **3** Scottish term for BARRISTER. ● verb /advəkayt/ publicly recommend or support.
– DERIVATIVES **advocacy** noun.
– ORIGIN Latin *advocare* 'call (to one's aid)'.
adze /adz/ (US **adz**) ● noun a tool similar to an axe, with an arched blade at right angles to the handle.
– ORIGIN Old English.
adzuki /ədzōōki/ (also **aduki**) ● noun (pl. **adzukis**) a small dark-

Thesaurus

– OPPOSITES disadvantageous, detrimental.
advent ● noun ARRIVAL, appearance, emergence, materialization, occurrence, dawn, birth, rise, development; approach, coming.
adventitious ● adjective **1** *he felt that the conversation was not entirely adventitious* UNPLANNED, unpremeditated, accidental, chance, fortuitous, serendipitous, coincidental, casual, random. **2** *the adventitious population* FOREIGN, alien, non-native.
adventure ● noun **1** *her recent adventures in Italy* EXPLOIT, escapade, deed, feat, experience; stunt. **2** *they set off in search of adventure* EXCITEMENT, thrill, stimulation; risk, danger, hazard, peril, uncertainty, precariousness.
adventurer ● noun DAREDEVIL, hero, heroine; swashbuckler, knight errant.
adventurous ● adjective **1** *an adventurous traveller* DARING, daredevil, intrepid, venturesome, bold, fearless, brave, unafraid, unshrinking, dauntless; *informal* gutsy, spunky. **2** *adventurous activities* RISKY, dangerous, perilous, hazardous, precarious, uncertain; exciting, thrilling.
– OPPOSITES cautious.
adversary ● noun OPPONENT, rival, enemy, antagonist, combatant, challenger, contender, competitor, opposer; opposition, competition; *poetic/literary* foe.
– OPPOSITES ally, supporter.
adverse ● adjective **1** *adverse weather conditions* UNFAVOURABLE, disadvantageous, inauspicious, unpropitious, unfortunate, unlucky, untimely, untoward. **2** *the drug's adverse side effects* HARMFUL, dangerous, injurious, detrimental, hurtful, deleterious. **3** *an adverse response from the public* HOSTILE, UNFAVOURABLE, antagonistic, unfriendly, ill-disposed, negative.
– OPPOSITES favourable, auspicious, beneficial.
adversity ● noun MISFORTUNE, ill luck, bad luck, trouble, difficulty, hardship, distress, disaster, suffering, affliction, sorrow, misery, tribulation, woe, pain, trauma; mishap, misadventure, accident, upset, reverse, setback, crisis, catastrophe, tragedy, calamity, trial, cross, burden, blow, vicissitude; hard times, trials and tribulations.
advertise ● verb PUBLICIZE, make public, make known, announce, broadcast, proclaim, trumpet, call attention to, bill; promote, market, beat/bang the drum for, trail, huckster; *informal* push, plug, hype, boost; *N. Amer. informal* ballyhoo, flack.
advertisement ● noun NOTICE, announcement, bulletin; commercial, promotion, blurb, write-up; poster, leaflet, pamphlet, flyer, bill, handbill, handout, circular, brochure, sign, placard; *informal* ad, push, plug, puff, bumph; *Brit. informal* advert.
advice ● noun GUIDANCE, counselling, counsel, help, direction; information, recommendations, guidelines, suggestions, hints, tips, pointers, ideas, opinions, views.
advisability ● noun WISDOM, desirability, preferability, prudence, sense, appropriateness, aptness, fitness, suitability, judiciousness; expediency, advantageousness, advantage, benefit, profit, profitability.
advisable ● adjective WISE, desirable, preferable, well, best, sensible, prudent, proper, appropriate, apt, suitable, fitting, judicious, recommended, suggested; expedient, politic, advantageous, beneficial, profitable, in one's (best) interests.
advise ● verb **1** *her grandmother advised her to reconsider her decision* COUNSEL, give guidance, guide, offer suggestions, give hints/tips/pointers. **2** *he advised caution* ADVOCATE, recommend, suggest, urge, encourage, enjoin. **3** *you will be advised of the requirements* INFORM, notify, give notice, apprise, warn, forewarn; acquaint with, make familiar with, make known to, update about; *informal* fill in on.
adviser ● noun COUNSELLOR, mentor, guide, consultant, confidant, confidante; coach, teacher, tutor, guru.
advisory ● adjective CONSULTATIVE, consultatory, advising; recommendatory.
– OPPOSITES executive.
advocacy ● noun SUPPORT, backing, promotion, championing; recommendation, prescription; *N. Amer.* boosterism.
advocate ● noun *an advocate of children's rights* CHAMPION, upholder, supporter, backer, promoter, proponent, exponent, spokesman, spokeswoman, spokesperson, campaigner, fighter, crusader; propagandist, apostle, apologist; *N. Amer.* booster.
– OPPOSITES critic.
● verb *heart specialists advocate a diet low in cholesterol* RECOMMEND, prescribe, advise, urge; support, back, favour, uphold, sub-

a

red edible bean.
– ORIGIN Japanese.
Aegean /ijeeən/ ● adjective of the region of the **Aegean Sea**, the part of the Mediterranean between Greece and Turkey.
aegis /eejiss/ ● noun the protection, backing, or support of someone.
– ORIGIN Greek *aigis* 'shield of Zeus'.
-aemia (also **-haemia**, US **-emia** or **-hemia**) ● combining form in nouns denoting that a substance is present in the blood: *septicaemia.*
– ORIGIN Greek *-aimia*, from *haima* 'blood'.
aeolian /eeōliən/ (US **eolian**) ● adjective chiefly Geology relating to or arising from the action of the wind.
– ORIGIN from *Aeolus*, the Greek god of the winds.
aeolian harp ● noun a stringed instrument that produces musical sounds when a current of air passes through it.
aeon /eeon/ (US or technical also **eon**) ● noun **1** an indefinite and very long period of time. **2** a major division of geological time, subdivided into eras. **3** Astronomy & Geology a unit of time equal to a thousand million years.
– ORIGIN Greek *aiōn* 'age'.
aerate /airayt/ ● verb introduce air into.
– DERIVATIVES **aeration** noun **aerator** noun.
– ORIGIN from Latin *aer* 'air'.
aerated ● adjective **1** (of a liquid) made effervescent by being charged with carbon dioxide. **2** Brit. informal agitated, angry, or over-excited.
aerial ● noun a structure that transmits or receives radio or television signals. ● adjective **1** existing or taking place in the air. **2** involving the use of aircraft.
– ORIGIN from Greek *aēr* 'air'.
aerie ● noun US spelling of EYRIE.
aero- /airō-/ ● combining form **1** relating to air: *aerobic.* **2** relating to aircraft: *aerodrome.*
– ORIGIN from Greek *aēr* 'air'.
aerobatics ● plural noun (treated as sing. or pl.) feats of flying performed for display.
– DERIVATIVES **aerobatic** adjective.
aerobic /airōbik/ ● adjective **1** relating to physical exercise intended to improve the absorption and transportation of oxygen. **2** Biology using oxygen from the air.
– DERIVATIVES **aerobically** adverb.
– ORIGIN from AERO- + Greek *bios* 'life'.
aerobics ● plural noun (treated as sing. or pl.) aerobic exercises.
aerodrome ● noun Brit. a small airport or airfield.
aerodynamic ● adjective **1** relating to aerodynamics. **2** having a shape which reduces the drag from air moving past.
– DERIVATIVES **aerodynamically** adverb.
aerodynamics ● plural noun **1** (treated as sing.) the branch of science concerned with the interaction between the air and solid bodies moving through it. **2** (treated as pl.) aerodynamic properties.
– DERIVATIVES **aerodynamicist** noun.
aerofoil ● noun Brit. a structure designed to give the most favourable ratio of lift to drag in flight.
aerogramme (US **aerogram**) ● noun another term for AIR LETTER.
aeronautics ● plural noun (usu. treated as sing.) the study or practice of travel through the air.
– DERIVATIVES **aeronautic** adjective **aeronautical** adjective.
– ORIGIN Latin *aeronautica* 'matters relating to aeronautics', from Greek *aēr* 'air' + *nautēs* 'sailor'.
aeroplane ● noun chiefly Brit. a powered flying vehicle with fixed wings and a weight greater than that of the air it displaces.
– ORIGIN from French *aéro-* 'air' + Greek *-planos* 'wandering'.
aerosol ● noun **1** a substance enclosed under pressure and released as a fine spray. **2** Chemistry a suspension of submicroscopic particles dispersed in air or gas.
– DERIVATIVES **aerosolize** (also **aerosolise**) verb.
– ORIGIN from AERO- + SOL².
aerospace ● noun the branch of technology and industry concerned with aviation and space flight.
aesthete /eestheet/ (US also **esthete**) ● noun a person who is appreciative of art and beauty.
aesthetic /eessthettik/ (US also **esthetic**) ● adjective **1** concerned with beauty or the appreciation of beauty. **2** of pleasing appearance. ● noun a set of principles underlying the work of a particular artist or artistic movement.
– DERIVATIVES **aesthetically** adverb **aestheticism** noun **aestheticize** (also **aestheticise**) verb.
– ORIGIN Greek *aisthētikos*, from *aisthesthai* 'perceive'.
aesthetics (US also **esthetics**) ● plural noun (usu. treated as sing.) **1** a set of principles concerned with the nature of beauty, especially in art. **2** the branch of philosophy which deals with questions of beauty and artistic taste.
aether ● noun variant spelling of ETHER (in senses 3 and 4).
aetiology /eetiolləji/ (US **etiology**) ● noun **1** Medicine the cause of a disease or condition. **2** the investigation of cause or a reason.
– DERIVATIVES **aetiological** adjective.
– ORIGIN from Greek *aitia* 'a cause'.
afar ● adverb chiefly literary at or to a distance.
AFC ● abbreviation **1** Air Force Cross. **2** Association Football Club.
affable ● adjective good-natured and sociable.
– DERIVATIVES **affability** noun **affably** adverb.
– ORIGIN Latin *affabilis*, from *ad-* 'to' + *fari* 'speak'.
affair ● noun **1** an event of a specified kind or that has previously been referred to. **2** a matter that is a particular person's responsibility. **3** a love affair. **4** (**affairs**) matters of public interest and importance.
– ORIGIN from Old French *à faire* 'to do'.
affaire /affair/ (also **affaire de** or **du cœur** /affair də kör, dyoo/) ● noun a love affair.
– ORIGIN French, 'affair (of the heart)'.
affect¹ /əfekt/ ● verb **1** make a difference to; have an effect on. **2** touch the feelings of.
– DERIVATIVES **affecting** adjective.
– USAGE **Affect** and **effect** are frequently confused. **Affect** is primarily a verb meaning 'make a difference to', as in *the changes will affect everyone.* **Effect** is used both as a noun meaning 'a result' (e.g. *the substance has a pain-killing effect*) and as a verb meaning 'bring about (a result)', as in *she effected a cost-cutting exercise.*
– ORIGIN Latin *afficere* 'affect'.
affect² /əfekt/ ● verb **1** pretend to have or feel. **2** use, wear, or assume pretentiously or so as to impress.
– ORIGIN Latin *affectare* 'aim at', from *afficere* 'affect, influence'.
affect³ /affekt/ ● noun Psychology emotion or desire as influencing behaviour.
– DERIVATIVES **affectless** adjective.
– ORIGIN German *Affekt*, from Latin *affectus* 'disposition'.

Thesaurus

scribe to, champion, campaign on behalf of, speak for, argue for, lobby for, promote.
aegis ● noun *negotiations conducted under the aegis of the UN* PROTECTION, backing, support, patronage, sponsorship, charge, care, guidance, guardianship, trusteeship, agency, safeguarding, shelter, umbrella, aid, assistance; auspices.
aeon ● noun *the age of piracy was stamped out aeons ago* AGES, an age, an eternity, a long time, a lifetime; years; *informal* donkey's years; *Brit. informal* yonks.
aesthetic ● adjective ARTISTIC, tasteful, in good taste; graceful, elegant, exquisite, beautiful, attractive, pleasing, lovely.
affability ● noun FRIENDLINESS, amiability, geniality, congeniality, cordiality, warmth, pleasantness, likeability, good humour, good nature, kindliness, kindness, courtesy, courteousness, civility, approachability, amenability, sociability, gregariousness, neighbourliness.
affable ● adjective FRIENDLY, amiable, genial, congenial, cordial, warm, pleasant, nice, likeable, personable, charming, agreeable, sympathetic, good-humoured, good-natured, kindly, kind, courteous, civil, gracious, approachable, accessible, amenable, sociable, outgoing, gregarious, clubbable, neighbourly, welcoming, hospitable, obliging; *Scottish* couthy.
affair ● noun **1** *what you do in your spare time is your affair* BUSINESS, concern, matter, responsibility, province, preserve; problem, worry; *Brit. informal* lookout. **2** (**affairs**) *his financial affairs* TRANSACTIONS, concerns, matters, activities, dealings, undertakings, ventures, business. **3** *the board admitted responsibility for the affair* EVENT, incident, happening, occurrence, eventuality, episode; case, matter, business. **4** *his affair with Anthea was over* RELATIONSHIP, love affair, affaire (de cœur), romance, fling, flirtation, dalliance, liaison, involvement, intrigue, amour; *informal* hanky-panky; *Brit. informal* carry-on.
affect¹ ● verb **1** *this development may have affected the judge's decision* HAVE AN EFFECT ON, influence, act on, work on, have an im-

a

affectation /affektaysh'n/ ● noun behaviour, speech, or writing that is artificial and designed to impress.
affected ● adjective artificial and designed to impress.
– DERIVATIVES **affectedly** adverb.
affection ● noun a feeling of fondness or liking.
affectionate ● adjective readily showing affection.
– DERIVATIVES **affectionately** adverb.
affective ● adjective chiefly Psychology relating to moods, feelings, and attitudes.
afferent /affərənt/ ● adjective Physiology relating to the conduction of nerve impulses or blood inwards or towards something. The opposite of EFFERENT.
– ORIGIN from Latin *afferre* 'bring towards'.
affiance /əfīənss/ ● verb **(be affianced)** literary be engaged to marry.
– ORIGIN Old French *afiancer*, from Latin *affidare* 'declare on oath'.
affidavit /affidayvit/ ● noun Law a written statement confirmed by oath or affirmation, for use as evidence in court.
– ORIGIN Latin, 'he has stated on oath'.
affiliate ● verb /əfilliayt/ officially attach or connect to an organization. ● noun /əfilliət/ an affiliated person or organization.
– DERIVATIVES **affiliation** noun **affiliative** adjective.
– ORIGIN Latin *affiliare* 'adopt as a son'.
affinity ● noun (pl. **affinities**) **1** a natural liking or sympathy for someone or something. **2** a close relationship based on a common origin or structure. **3** relationship by marriage. **4** the tendency of a substance to combine with another.
– ORIGIN Latin *affinitas*, from *affinis* 'related'.
affirm ● verb **1** state emphatically or publicly. **2** Law make a formal declaration rather than taking an oath.
– DERIVATIVES **affirmation** noun.
– ORIGIN Latin *affirmare*, from *firmus* 'strong'.
affirmative ● adjective agreeing with or consenting to a statement or request. ● noun an affirmative statement or word. ● exclamation chiefly N. Amer. yes.
– DERIVATIVES **affirmatively** adverb.
affirmative action ● noun chiefly N. Amer. action favouring those who tend to suffer from discrimination.
affix ● verb /əfiks/ attach or fasten to something else. ● noun /affiks/ Grammar an addition to a word in order to modify its meaning or create a new word.
– DERIVATIVES **affixation** noun.
– ORIGIN Latin *affixare*, from *figere* 'to fix'.
afflict ● verb cause pain or suffering to.
– DERIVATIVES **affliction** noun.
– ORIGIN Latin *afflictare* 'knock about, harass', or *affligere* 'knock down, weaken'.
affluent ● adjective wealthy.
– DERIVATIVES **affluence** noun.
– ORIGIN from Latin *affluere* 'flow towards, flow freely'.
afford ● verb **1 (can/could afford)** have sufficient money, time, or means for. **2** provide (an opportunity or facility).
– DERIVATIVES **affordability** noun **affordable** adjective.
– ORIGIN Old English, 'promote, perform'; related to FORTH.
afforest /əforrist/ ● verb convert (land) into forest.
– DERIVATIVES **afforestation** noun.
affray ● noun Law, dated a breach of the peace by fighting in a public place.
– ORIGIN from Old French *afrayer* 'disturb, startle'.

Thesaurus

pact on; change, alter, modify, transform, form, shape, sway, bias. **2** *he was visibly affected by the experience* MOVE, touch, make an impression on, hit (hard), tug at someone's heartstrings; UPSET, trouble, distress, disturb, agitate, shake (up). **3** *the disease affected his lungs* ATTACK, infect; hit, strike.
affect² ● verb **1** *he deliberately affected a republican stance* ASSUME, take on, adopt, embrace, espouse. **2** *Paul affected an air of injured innocence* PRETEND, feign, fake, simulate, make a show of, make a pretence of, sham; *informal* put on; *N. Amer. informal* make like.
affectation ● noun **1** *George had always abhorred affectation* PRETENSION, pretentiousness, affectedness, artificiality, posturing, posing; airs (and graces); *informal* la-di-da; *Brit. informal* side. **2** *an affectation of calm* FACADE, front, show, appearance, pretence, simulation, posture, pose.
affected ● adjective PRETENTIOUS, artificial, contrived, unnatural, stagy, studied, mannered, ostentatious; insincere, unconvincing, feigned, false, fake, sham, simulated; *informal* la-di-da, phoney, pretend, put on.
– OPPOSITES natural, unpretentious, genuine.
affecting ● adjective TOUCHING, moving, emotive, emotional; stirring, soul-stirring, heart-warming; poignant, pathetic, pitiful, piteous, tear-jerking, heart-rending, heartbreaking, disturbing, distressing, upsetting, sad, haunting.
affection ● noun FONDNESS, love, liking, tenderness, warmth, devotion, endearment, care, caring, attachment, friendship; warm feelings.
affectionate ● adjective LOVING, fond, adoring, devoted, caring, doting, tender, warm, warm-hearted, soft-hearted, friendly; demonstrative, cuddly; *informal* touchy-feely, lovey-dovey.
– OPPOSITES cold.
affianced ● adjective *(poetic/literary)*. See ENGAGED sense 2.
affiliate ● verb *the society is not affiliated to any political party* ASSOCIATE WITH, unite with, combine with, join (up) with, join forces with, link up with, ally with, align with, federate with, amalgamate with, merge with; attach to, annex to, incorporate into, integrate into.
affiliated ● adjective ASSOCIATED, allied, related, federated, confederated, amalgamated, unified, connected, linked; in league, in partnership.
affiliation ● noun ASSOCIATION, connection, alliance, alignment, link, attachment, tie, relationship, fellowship, partnership, coalition, union; amalgamation, incorporation, integration, federation, confederation.
affinity ● noun **1** *her affinity with animals and birds* EMPATHY, rapport, sympathy, accord, harmony, relationship, bond, fellow feeling, like-mindedness, closeness, understanding; liking, fondness; *informal* chemistry. **2** *the semantic affinity between the two words* SIMILARITY, resemblance, likeness, kinship, relationship, association, link, analogy, similitude, correspondence.
– OPPOSITES aversion, dislike, dissimilarity.
affirm ● verb **1** *he affirmed that they would lend military assistance* DECLARE, state, assert, proclaim, pronounce, attest, swear, avow, guarantee, pledge, give an undertaking; *formal* aver; *rare* asseverate. **2** *the referendum affirmed the republic's right to secede* UPHOLD, support, confirm, ratify, endorse.
– OPPOSITES deny.
affirmation ● noun **1** *an affirmation of faith* DECLARATION, statement, assertion, proclamation, pronouncement, attestation; oath, avowal, guarantee, pledge; deposition; *formal* averment; *rare* asseveration. **2** *the poem ends with an affirmation of pastoral values* CONFIRMATION, ratification, endorsement.
– OPPOSITES denial.
affirmative ● adjective *an affirmative answer* POSITIVE, assenting, consenting, corroborative, favourable.
– OPPOSITES negative.
● noun *she took his grunt as an affirmative* AGREEMENT, acceptance, assent, acquiescence, concurrence; OK, yes.
– OPPOSITES disagreement.
affix ● verb **1** *he affixed a stamp to the envelope* STICK, glue, paste, gum; attach, fasten, fix; clip, tack, pin; tape. **2** *(formal) affix your signature to the document* APPEND, add, attach.
afflict ● verb TROUBLE, burden, distress, cause suffering to, beset, harass, worry, oppress; torment, plague, blight, bedevil, rack, smite, curse; *archaic* ail.
affliction ● noun **1** *a herb reputed to cure a variety of afflictions* DISORDER, disease, malady, complaint, ailment, illness, indisposition, handicap; scourge, plague, trouble. **2** *he bore his affliction with great dignity* SUFFERING, distress, pain, trouble, misery, wretchedness, hardship, misfortune, adversity, sorrow, torment, tribulation, woe.
affluence ● noun WEALTH, prosperity, fortune; riches, money, resources, assets, possessions, property, substance, means.
– OPPOSITES poverty.
affluent ● adjective WEALTHY, rich, prosperous, well off, moneyed, well-to-do; propertied, substantial, of means, of substance, plutocratic; *informal* well heeled, rolling in it, made of money, filthy rich, stinking rich, loaded, on easy street, worth a packet.
– OPPOSITES poor, impoverished.
afford ● verb **1** *I can't afford a new car* PAY FOR, bear the expense of, have the money for, spare the price of; run to, stretch to, manage. **2** *it took more time than he could afford* SPARE, allow (oneself). **3** *the rooftop terrace affords beautiful views* PROVIDE, supply, furnish, offer, give, make available, yield.
affray ● noun *(Law, dated)* FIGHT, brawl, confrontation, clash, skir-

a

affront • noun an action or remark that causes offence. • verb offend the modesty or values of.
– ORIGIN from Old French *afronter* 'to slap in the face, insult'.
Afghan /afgan/ • noun a person from Afghanistan. • adjective relating to Afghanistan.
– ORIGIN Pashto.
Afghan coat • noun Brit. a kind of sheepskin coat with the skin outside.
Afghan hound • noun a silky-haired breed of dog used for hunting.
afghani /afgaani/ • noun (pl. **afghanis**) the basic monetary unit of Afghanistan, equal to 100 puls.
– ORIGIN Pashto.
aficionado /əfissyənaadō/ • noun (pl. **aficionados**) a person who is very knowledgeable and enthusiastic about an activity or subject.
– ORIGIN Spanish, 'amateur'.
afield • adverb to or at a distance.
AFL • abbreviation Australian Football League.
aflame • adjective in flames.
afloat • adjective & adverb **1** floating in water. **2** on board a ship or boat. **3** out of debt or difficulty.
AFM • abbreviation Air Force Medal.
afoot • adverb & adjective **1** in preparation or progress. **2** chiefly N. Amer. on foot.
afore • preposition archaic or dialect before.
afore- • prefix before; previously: *aforementioned.*
aforementioned • adjective denoting a thing or person previously mentioned.
a fortiori /ay fortiorī/ • adverb for an even stronger reason.
– ORIGIN Latin, from *a fortiori argumento* 'from stronger argument'.
afoul • adverb N. Amer. into conflict or difficulty with.
afraid • adjective fearful or anxious.
– PHRASES **I'm afraid** expressing polite apology or regret.
– ORIGIN from Old French *afrayer* 'disturb, startle'.
A-frame • noun a timber frame shaped like a capital letter A.
afresh • adverb in a new or different way.
African • noun **1** a person from Africa, especially a black person. **2** a person of black African descent. • adjective relating to Africa or people of African descent.
– DERIVATIVES **Africanize** (also **Africanise**) verb.
African American chiefly US • noun an American of African origin. • adjective relating to African Americans.
Afrikaans /afrikaanss/ • noun a language of southern Africa derived from Dutch, an official language of South Africa.
– ORIGIN Dutch, 'African'.
Afrikaner /afrikaanər/ • noun an Afrikaans-speaking white person in South Africa.
– DERIVATIVES **Afrikanerdom** noun.
Afro • noun a hairstyle consisting of a mass of very tight curls all round the head, like the natural hair of some black people.
Afro- • combining form African: *Afro-American.*
Afro-American • adjective & noun chiefly N. Amer. another term for AFRICAN AMERICAN.
Afro-Caribbean • noun a person of African descent living in or coming from the Caribbean. • adjective relating to Afro-Caribbeans.
aft /aaft/ • adverb & adjective at, near, or towards the stern of a ship or tail of an aircraft.
– ORIGIN probably related to ABAFT.
after • preposition **1** in the time following (an event or another period of time). **2** behind. **3** in pursuit of. **4** next to and following in order or importance. **5** in allusion or reference to. • conjunction & adverb in the time following (an event). • adjective **1** archaic later. **2** nearer the stern of a ship.
– PHRASES **after all** in spite of any indications to the contrary. **after hours** after normal working or opening hours.
– ORIGIN Old English.
afterbirth • noun the placenta and fetal membranes discharged from the womb after a birth.
afterburner • noun an auxiliary burner in the exhaust of a jet engine.
aftercare • noun care of a person after a stay in hospital or on release from prison.
after-effect • noun an effect that follows after the primary action of something.
afterglow • noun light remaining in the sky after the sun has set.
after-image • noun an impression of a vivid image retained by the eye after the stimulus has ceased.
afterlife • noun **1** (in some religions) life after death. **2** later life.
aftermath • noun the consequences of an unpleasant or disastrous event.
– ORIGIN from AFTER + dialect *math* 'mowing'.
afternoon • noun the time from noon or lunchtime to evening.
afters • plural noun Brit. informal the dessert course of a meal.
aftershave • noun a scented lotion for applying to the skin after shaving.

Thesaurus

mish, scuffle, tussle; fracas, altercation, disturbance, breach of the peace; *informal* scrap, dust-up, punch-up, set-to, shindig, free-for-all.
affront • noun *an affront to public morality* INSULT, offence, indignity, slight, snub, put-down, provocation, injury; outrage, atrocity, scandal; *informal* slap in the face, kick in the teeth.
• verb *she was affronted by his familiarity* INSULT, offend, mortify, provoke, pique, wound, hurt; put out, irk, displease, bother, rankle, vex, gall; outrage, scandalize, disgust; *informal* put someone's back up, needle.
aficionado • noun CONNOISSEUR, expert, authority, specialist, pundit; enthusiast, devotee; *informal* buff, freak, nut, fiend, maniac, fanatic, addict.
aflame • adjective BURNING, ablaze, alight, on fire, in flames, blazing; *poetic/literary* afire.
afloat • adverb & adjective BUOYANT, floating, buoyed up, on/above the surface, (keeping one's head) above water.
afoot • adjective & adverb GOING ON, happening, around, about, abroad, stirring, circulating, in circulation, at large, in the air/wind; brewing, looming, in the offing, on the horizon.
aforesaid • adjective PREVIOUSLY MENTIONED, aforementioned, aforenamed; foregoing, preceding, earlier, previous; above.
afraid • adjective **1** *they ran away because they were afraid* FRIGHTENED, scared, terrified, fearful, petrified, scared witless, scared to death, terror-stricken, terror-struck, frightened/scared out of one's wits, shaking in one's shoes, shaking like a leaf; intimidated, alarmed, panicky; faint-hearted, cowardly; *informal* scared stiff, in a (blue) funk, in a cold sweat; *N. Amer. informal* spooked; *archaic* afeared, affrighted. **2** *don't be afraid to ask awkward questions* RELUCTANT, hesitant, unwilling, disinclined, loath, slow, chary, shy. **3** *I'm afraid that your daughter is ill* SORRY, sad, distressed, regretful, apologetic.
– RELATED TERMS -phobe.
– OPPOSITES brave, confident.
afresh • adverb ANEW, again, over/once again, once more, another time.
after • preposition **1** *he made a speech after the performance* FOLLOWING, subsequent to, at the close/end of, in the wake of; *formal* posterior to. **2** *Guy shut the door after them* BEHIND, following. **3** *after the way he treated my sister I never want to speak to him again* BECAUSE OF, as a result/consequence of, in view of, owing to, on account of. **4** *is he still going to marry her, after all that's happened?* DESPITE, in spite of, regardless of, notwithstanding. **5** *the policeman ran after him* IN PURSUIT OF, in someone's direction, following. **6** *I'm after information, and I'm willing to pay for it* IN SEARCH OF, in quest/pursuit of, trying to find, looking for. **7** *they asked after Dad* ABOUT, concerning, regarding, with regard/respect/reference to. **8** *the village was named after a Roman officer* IN HONOUR OF, as a tribute to; with the name of. **9** *animal studies after Bandinelli* IN THE STYLE OF, in the manner of, in imitation of; similar to, like, characteristic of.
– RELATED TERMS post-.
– OPPOSITES before, preceding.
• adverb **1** *the week after, we went to Madrid* LATER, afterwards, after this/that, subsequently. **2** *porters were following on after with their bags* BEHIND, in the rear, at the back, in someone's wake.
– OPPOSITES previously, before, ahead, in front.
– PHRASES **after all** MOST IMPORTANTLY, above all, beyond everything, ultimately; *informal* when all's said and done, at the end of the day, when push comes to shove.
after-effect • noun REPERCUSSION, aftermath, consequence; *Medicine* sequela.
afterlife • noun LIFE AFTER DEATH, the next world, the hereafter, the

a

aftershock • noun a smaller earthquake following the main shock of a large earthquake.
aftertaste • noun a strong or unpleasant taste lingering in the mouth after eating or drinking.
afterthought • noun something thought of or added later.
afterwards (US also **afterward**) • adverb at a later or future time.
afterword • noun a concluding section in a book, typically by a person other than the author.
afterworld • noun a world entered after death.
Ag • symbol the chemical element silver.
– ORIGIN from Latin *argentum*.
again /əgen, əgayn/ • adverb **1** once more. **2** returning to a previous position or condition. **3** in addition to what has already been mentioned.
– ORIGIN Old English.
against • preposition **1** in opposition to. **2** to the disadvantage of. **3** in resistance to. **4** in anticipation of and preparation for (a difficulty). **5** in relation to (money owed, due, or lent) so as to reduce, cancel, or secure it. **6** in or into contact with. **7** (in betting) in anticipation of the failure of.
– PHRASES **have something against** dislike or bear a grudge against.
agape[1] /əgayp/ • adjective (of a person's mouth) wide open.
agape[2] /aggəpay/ • noun Christian love as distinct from erotic love or simple affection.
– ORIGIN Greek, 'brotherly love'.
agar /aygaar/ (also **agar-agar** /aygaaraygaar/) • noun a jelly-like substance obtained from red seaweed and used in biological cultures and as a thickener in foods.
– ORIGIN Malay.
agaric /aggərik/ • noun a fungus with gills on the underside of the cap, e.g. a mushroom.
– ORIGIN Greek *agarikon* 'tree fungus'.
agate /aggət/ • noun an ornamental stone consisting of a hard variety of chalcedony.
– ORIGIN Greek *akhatēs*.
agave /əgayvi/ • noun an American plant with narrow spiny leaves and tall flower spikes.
– ORIGIN from Greek *Agauē*, the name of one of the daughters of Cadmus in Greek mythology.
age • noun **1** the length of time that a person or thing has existed. **2** a particular stage in someone's life. **3** the latter part of existence; old age. **4** a distinct period of history. **5** a division of geological time that is a subdivision of an epoch. • verb (**ageing** or **aging**) **1** grow or cause to appear old or older. **2** (with reference to an alcoholic drink, cheese, etc.) mature.
– PHRASES **act** (or **be**) **one's age** behave in a manner appropriate to someone of one's age. **come of age** reach adult status (in UK law at 18).
– DERIVATIVES **ageing** noun & adjective.
– ORIGIN Old French, from Latin *aevum* 'age, era'.
-age • suffix forming nouns: **1** denoting an action or its result: *leverage*. **2** denoting an aggregate or number of: *mileage*. **3** denoting a place or abode: *vicarage*. **4** fees payable for: *postage*.
– ORIGIN Latin *-aticum*.
aged • adjective **1** /ayjd/ of a specified age. **2** /ayjid/ old. **3** /ayjd/ having been subjected to ageing.
ageism • noun prejudice or discrimination on the grounds of age.
– DERIVATIVES **ageist** adjective & noun.
ageless • adjective not ageing or appearing to age.
– DERIVATIVES **agelessness** noun.
agency • noun **1** an organization providing a particular service. **2** a government office or department providing a specific service. **3** action or intervention to produce a particular result.
agenda • noun **1** a list of items of business to be discussed at a meeting. **2** a list of matters to be addressed.
– ORIGIN Latin, 'things to be done'.
agent • noun **1** a person who provides a particular service, typically liaising between two other parties. **2** a spy. **3** a person or thing that takes an active role or produces a specified effect.
– ORIGIN from Latin *agere* 'to do'.
agent noun • noun a noun denoting a person or thing that performs the action of a verb, usually ending in *-er* or *-or*, e.g. *worker, accelerator*.
agent provocateur /aazhon prəvokkətör/ • noun (pl. **agents provocateurs** pronunc. same) a person employed to induce suspected offenders to commit criminal acts and thus be convicted.
– ORIGIN French, 'provocative agent'.
age of consent • noun the age at which a person's consent to sexual intercourse is legally valid.
age-old • adjective having existed for a very long time.
agglomerate • verb /əglommərayt/ collect or form into a mass. • noun /əglommərət/ a mass or collection of things.
– DERIVATIVES **agglomeration** noun.
– ORIGIN Latin *agglomerare* 'add to'.
agglutinate /əglootinayt/ • verb firmly stick together to form a mass.
– DERIVATIVES **agglutination** noun.
– ORIGIN Latin *agglutinare* 'cause to adhere'.
aggrandize /əgrandīz/ (also **aggrandise**) • verb **1** increase the power, status, or wealth of. **2** artificially enhance the reputation of.
– DERIVATIVES **aggrandizement** noun.
– ORIGIN French *agrandir*, from Latin *grandis* 'large'.
aggravate • verb **1** make worse. **2** informal annoy or exasperate.

Thesaurus

afterworld; immortality.
aftermath • noun REPERCUSSIONS, after-effects, consequences, effects, results, fruits.
afterwards • adverb LATER, later on, subsequently, then, next, after this/that; at a later time/date, in due course.
again • adverb **1** *her spirits lifted again* ONCE MORE, another time, afresh, anew. **2** *this can add half as much again to the price* EXTRA, in addition, additionally, on top. **3** *again, evidence was not always consistent* ALSO, furthermore; moreover, besides.
– PHRASES **again and again** REPEATEDLY, over and over (again), time and (time) again, many times, many a time; often, frequently, continually, constantly.
against • preposition **1** *a number of delegates were against the motion* OPPOSED TO, in opposition to, hostile to, averse to, antagonistic towards, inimical to, unsympathetic to, resistant to, at odds with, in disagreement with, dead set against; informal anti, agin. **2** *he was swimming against the tide* IN OPPOSITION TO, counter to, contrary to, in the opposite direction to. **3** *his age is against him* DISADVANTAGEOUS TO, unfavourable to, damaging to, detrimental to, prejudicial to, deleterious to, harmful to, injurious to, a drawback for. **4** *she leaned against the wall* TOUCHING, in contact with, up against, on.
– RELATED TERMS anti-.
– OPPOSITES in favour of, pro.
age • noun **1** *he is 35 years of age* NUMBER OF YEARS, length of life; stage of life, generation, age group. **2** *her hearing had deteriorated with age* ELDERLINESS, old age, oldness, senescence, seniority, maturity; one's advancing/advanced/declining years; poetic/literary eld; archaic caducity. **3** *the Elizabethan age* ERA, epoch, period, time. **4** (informal) *you haven't been in touch with me for ages* A LONG TIME, days/months/years on end, an eternity; informal ages and ages, donkey's years, a month of Sundays; Brit. informal yonks.
• verb *Cabernet Sauvignon ages well | the experience has aged her* MATURE, mellow, ripen; grow/become/make old, (cause to) decline.
aged • adjective ELDERLY, old, mature, older, senior, ancient, senescent, advanced in years, in one's dotage, long in the tooth, as old as the hills, past one's prime, not as young as one used to be; informal getting on, over the hill, no spring chicken.
– OPPOSITES young.
agency • noun **1** *an advertising agency* BUSINESS, organization, company, firm, office, bureau. **2** *the infection is caused by the agency of insects* ACTION, activity, means, effect, influence, force, power, vehicle, medium. **3** *regional policy was introduced through the agency of the Board of Trade* INTERVENTION, intercession, involvement, good offices; auspices, aegis.
agenda • noun LIST OF ITEMS, schedule, programme, timetable, line-up, list, plan.
agent • noun **1** *the sale was arranged through an agent* REPRESENTATIVE, emissary, envoy, go-between, proxy, negotiator, broker, spokesperson, spokesman, spokeswoman; informal rep. **2** *a travel agent* AGENCY, business, organization, company, firm, bureau. **3** *a CIA agent* SPY, secret agent, undercover agent, operative, fifth columnist, mole, Mata Hari; N. Amer. informal spook, G-man; archaic intelligencer. **4** *the agents of destruction* PERFORMER, author, executor, perpetrator, producer, instrument, catalyst. **5** *a cleansing agent* MEDIUM, means, instrument, vehicle.

a

– DERIVATIVES **aggravating** adjective **aggravation** noun.
– USAGE **Aggravate** in the sense 'annoy or exasperate' is in widespread use in modern English and dates back to the 17th century, but the use is still regarded as incorrect by some traditionalists.
– ORIGIN Latin *aggravare* 'make heavy'.
aggravated • adjective Law (of an offence) made more serious by related circumstances.
aggregate • noun /agrigət/ **1** a whole formed by combining several different elements. **2** the total score of a player or team in a fixture comprising more than one game or round. • adjective /agrigət/ formed or calculated by the combination of many separate items. • verb /agrigayt/ combine into a whole.
– DERIVATIVES **aggregation** noun **aggregative** /agrigətiv/ adjective.
– ORIGIN from Latin *aggregare* 'herd together'.
aggression • noun hostile or violent behaviour or attitudes.
– ORIGIN Latin, from *aggredi* 'to attack'.
aggressive • adjective **1** characterized by or resulting from aggression. **2** unduly forceful.
– DERIVATIVES **aggressively** adverb **aggressiveness** noun.
aggressor • noun a person or country that attacks without being provoked.
aggrieved • adjective resentful because of unfair treatment.
– ORIGIN from Old French *agrever* 'make heavier', from Latin *aggravare* (see AGGRAVATE).
aggro • noun Brit. informal **1** aggressive behaviour. **2** difficulties.
– ORIGIN abbreviation of *aggravation*.
aghast /əgaast/ • adjective filled with horror or shock.
– ORIGIN from obsolete *gast* 'frighten'; spelling probably influenced by GHOST (compare with GHASTLY).
agile • adjective **1** able to move quickly and easily. **2** quick-witted or shrewd.
– DERIVATIVES **agilely** adverb **agility** noun.
– ORIGIN Latin *agilis*, from *agere* 'do'.
agitate • verb **1** make troubled or nervous. **2** campaign to arouse public concern about an issue. **3** stir or disturb (a liquid) briskly.
– DERIVATIVES **agitation** noun.
– ORIGIN Latin *agitare* 'agitate, drive'.
agitator • noun a person who urges others to protest or rebel.
agitprop /ajitprop/ • noun political propaganda, especially in the arts.
– ORIGIN Russian.
aglet /aglət/ • noun a metal or plastic tube fixed round each end of a shoelace.
– ORIGIN French *aiguillette* 'small needle'.
AGM • abbreviation annual general meeting.
agnostic /agnostik/ • noun a person who believes that nothing can be known concerning the existence of God. • adjective relating to agnostics.
– DERIVATIVES **agnosticism** noun.
ago • adverb before the present (used with a measurement of time).
– ORIGIN from the obsolete verb *ago* 'to pass'.
agog • adjective very eager to hear or see something.
– ORIGIN from Old French *en gogues*, from *en* 'in' + *gogue* 'fun'.
agonize (also **agonise**) • verb **1** worry greatly. **2** cause agony to.
– DERIVATIVES **agonizing** adjective.
agony • noun (pl. **agonies**) extreme suffering.
– ORIGIN Greek *agōnia*, from *agōn* 'contest'.
agony aunt (or **agony uncle**) • noun Brit. informal a person who answers letters in an agony column.
agony column • noun Brit. informal a column in a newspaper or magazine offering advice on readers' personal problems.
agora[1] /aggərə/ • noun (pl. **agorae** /aggəree/ or **agoras**) (in an-

Thesaurus

agglomeration • noun COLLECTION, mass, cluster, lump, clump, pile, heap; accumulation, build-up; miscellany, jumble, hotchpotch, mixed bag.
aggravate • verb **1** *the new law could aggravate the situation* WORSEN, make worse, exacerbate, inflame, compound; add fuel to the fire/flames, add insult to injury, rub salt in the wound. **2** *(informal) you don't have to aggravate people to get what you want* ANNOY, irritate, exasperate, put out, nettle, provoke, antagonize, get on someone's nerves, ruffle (someone's feathers), try someone's patience; *Brit.* rub up the wrong way; *informal* peeve, needle, bug, miff, hack off, get someone's goat, get under someone's skin, get up someone's nose; *Brit. informal* wind up, nark, get at, get across, get on someone's wick; *N. Amer. informal* tick off.
– OPPOSITES alleviate, improve.
aggravation • noun **1** *the recession led to the aggravation of unemployment problems* WORSENING, exacerbation, compounding. **2** *(informal) no amount of money is worth the aggravation* NUISANCE, annoyance, irritation, hassle, trouble, difficulty, inconvenience, bother; *informal* aggro.
aggregate • noun **1** *the specimen is an aggregate of rock and mineral fragments* COLLECTION, mass, agglomeration, assemblage; mixture, mix, combination, blend; compound, alloy, amalgam. **2** *he won with an aggregate of 325* TOTAL, sum total, sum, grand total. • adjective *an aggregate score* TOTAL, combined, gross, overall, composite.
aggression • noun **1** *an act of aggression* HOSTILITY, aggressiveness, belligerence, bellicosity, force, violence; pugnacity, pugnaciousness, militancy, warmongering. **2** *he played the game with unceasing aggression* CONFIDENCE, self-confidence, boldness, determination, forcefulness, vigour, energy, dynamism, zeal.
aggressive • adjective **1** *aggressive and disruptive behaviour* VIOLENT, confrontational, antagonistic, truculent, pugnacious, macho; quarrelsome, argumentative. **2** *aggressive foreign policy* WARMONGERING, warlike, warring, belligerent, bellicose, hawkish, militaristic; offensive, expansionist; *informal* gung-ho. **3** *an aggressive promotional drive* ASSERTIVE, pushy, forceful, vigorous, energetic, dynamic; bold, audacious; *informal* in-your-face, feisty.
– OPPOSITES peaceable, peaceful.
aggressor • noun ATTACKER, assaulter, assailant; invader.
aggrieved • adjective **1** *the manager looked aggrieved at the suggestion* RESENTFUL, affronted, indignant, disgruntled, discontented, upset, offended, piqued, riled, nettled, vexed, irked, irritated, annoyed, put out, chagrined; *informal* peeved, miffed, in a huff; *Brit. informal* cheesed off; *N. Amer. informal* sore, steamed. **2** *the aggrieved party* WRONGED, injured, harmed.
– OPPOSITES pleased.
aghast • adjective HORRIFIED, appalled, dismayed, thunderstruck, stunned, shocked, staggered; *informal* flabbergasted; *Brit. informal* gobsmacked.
agile • adjective **1** *she was as agile as a monkey* NIMBLE, lithe, supple, limber, acrobatic, fleet-footed, light-footed, light on one's feet; *informal* nippy, twinkle-toed; *poetic/literary* fleet, lightsome. **2** *an agile mind* ALERT, sharp, acute, shrewd, astute, perceptive, quick-witted.
– OPPOSITES clumsy, stiff.
agitate • verb **1** *any mention of Clare agitates my grandmother* UPSET, perturb, fluster, ruffle, disconcert, unnerve, disquiet, disturb, distress, unsettle; *informal* rattle, faze; *N. Amer. informal* discombobulate. **2** *she agitated for the appointment of more women* CAMPAIGN, strive, battle, fight, struggle, push, press. **3** *agitate the water to disperse the oil* STIR, whisk, beat.
agitated • adjective UPSET, perturbed, flustered, ruffled, disconcerted, unnerved, disquieted, disturbed, distressed, unsettled; nervous, jumpy, on edge, tense, keyed up; *informal* rattled, fazed, in a dither, in a flap, in a state, in a lather, jittery, in a tizz/tizzy; *Brit. informal* having kittens, in a (flat) spin; *N. Amer. informal* discombobulated.
– OPPOSITES calm, relaxed.
agitation • noun **1** *Freddie gritted his teeth in agitation* ANXIETY, perturbation, disquiet, distress, concern, alarm, worry; *rare* disconcertment. **2** *an upsurge in nationalist agitation* CAMPAIGNING, striving, battling, fighting, struggling. **3** *the vigorous agitation of the components* STIRRING, whisking, beating.
agitator • noun TROUBLEMAKER, rabble-rouser, agent provocateur, demagogue, incendiary; revolutionary, firebrand, rebel, insurgent, subversive; *informal* stirrer.
agnostic • noun SCEPTIC, doubter, doubting Thomas; unbeliever, disbeliever, non-believer; rationalist; *rare* nullifidian.
– OPPOSITES believer, theist.
ago • adverb IN THE PAST, before, earlier, back, since, previously; *formal* heretofore.
agog • adverb EAGER, excited, impatient, keen, anxious, avid, in suspense, on tenterhooks, on the edge of one's seat, on pins and needles, waiting with bated breath.
agonize • verb WORRY, fret, fuss, brood, upset oneself, rack one's brains, wrestle with oneself, be worried/anxious, feel uneasy, exercise oneself; *informal* stew; *archaic* pore on.
agonizing • adjective EXCRUCIATING, harrowing, racking, searing, extremely painful, acute, severe, torturous, tormenting, piercing;

cient Greece) a public open space used for assemblies and markets.
– ORIGIN Greek.
agora² /aggəraa/ ● noun (pl. **agorot** or **agoroth** /aggərōt/) a monetary unit of Israel, equal to one hundredth of a shekel.
– ORIGIN Hebrew, 'small coin'.
agoraphobia /aggərəfōbiə/ ● noun irrational fear of open or public places.
– DERIVATIVES **agoraphobic** adjective & noun.
– ORIGIN from Greek *agora* 'marketplace'
agrarian /əgrairiən/ ● adjective relating to agriculture.
– ORIGIN Latin *agrarius*, from *ager* 'field'.
agree ● verb (**agrees**, **agreed**, **agreeing**) **1** have the same opinion about something. **2** (**be agreed**) (of two or more parties) be in agreement. **3** (**agree to**) express willingness to comply with (a request, suggestion, etc.). **4** chiefly Brit. reach agreement about. **5** (**agree with**) be consistent with. **6** be good for: *she ate something which didn't agree with her.*
– ORIGIN Old French *agreer*, from Latin *gratus* 'pleasing'.
agreeable ● adjective **1** pleasant. **2** willing to agree to something. **3** acceptable.
– DERIVATIVES **agreeableness** noun **agreeably** adverb.
agreement ● noun **1** accordance in opinion or feeling. **2** a negotiated and typically legally binding arrangement. **3** consistency or conformity between two things.
agriculture ● noun the science or practice of farming, including the rearing of crops and animals.
– DERIVATIVES **agricultural** adjective **agriculturalist** noun **agriculturally** adverb **agriculturist** noun.
– ORIGIN Latin *agricultura*, from *ager* 'field' + *cultura* 'cultivation'.
agrimony /agriməni/ ● noun (pl. **agrimonies**) a plant of the rose family, with slender spikes of yellow flowers.
– ORIGIN Greek *argemōnē* 'poppy'.
agrochemical ● noun a chemical used in agriculture.
agronomy /əgronnəmi/ ● noun the science of soil management and crop production.
– DERIVATIVES **agronomic** adjective **agronomist** noun.
– ORIGIN French, from Greek *agros* 'field' + *-nomos* 'arranging'.
aground ● adjective & adverb (with reference to a ship) on or on to the bottom in shallow water.
ague /aygyoo/ ● noun archaic **1** malaria or some other illness involving fever and shivering. **2** a fever or shivering fit.
– ORIGIN from Latin *acuta febris* 'acute fever'.
ahead ● adverb **1** further forward in space or time. **2** in advance. **3** in the lead.
– PHRASES **ahead of 1** before. **2** earlier than planned or expected.
ahistorical ● adjective lacking historical perspective or context.
ahoy ● exclamation Nautical a call to attract attention.
AI ● abbreviation artificial intelligence.
AID ● abbreviation artificial insemination by donor.
aid ● noun **1** help or support. **2** material help given to a country in need. ● verb help.
– PHRASES **in aid of** chiefly Brit. in support of.
– ORIGIN Old French *aide*, from Latin *adjuvare*, from *juvare* 'help'.
aide /ayd/ ● noun an assistant to a political leader.
aide-de-camp /ayddəkon/ ● noun (pl. **aides-de-camp** pronunc. same) a military officer acting as a confidential assistant to a senior officer.
– ORIGIN French.
aide-memoire /aydmemwaar/ ● noun (pl. **aides-memoires** or **aides-memoire** pronunc. same) **1** a note, object, or device used to aid the memory. **2** a diplomatic memorandum.
– ORIGIN French.
Aids ● noun a disease, caused by the HIV virus and transmitted in body fluids, in which the sufferer loses immunity to infection and some forms of cancer.
– ORIGIN acronym from *acquired immune deficiency syndrome.*
aikido /īkeedō/ ● noun a Japanese form of self-defence and martial art that uses locks, holds, throws, and the opponent's own movements.
– ORIGIN Japanese, 'way of adapting the spirit'.
ail ● verb archaic trouble or afflict in mind or body.
– ORIGIN Old English.
aileron /aylərон/ ● noun a hinged surface in the trailing edge of an aircraft's wing, used to control the roll of the aircraft about its longitudinal axis.
– ORIGIN French, 'small wing'.
ailing ● adjective in poor health.

Thesaurus

informal hellish, killing; *formal* grievous.
agony ● noun PAIN, hurt, suffering, torture, torment, anguish, affliction, trauma; pangs, throes; *rare* excruciation.
agrarian ● adjective AGRICULTURAL, rural, rustic, pastoral, countryside, farming; *poetic/literary* georgic, sylvan, Arcadian, agrestic.
agree ● verb **1** *I agree with you* CONCUR, be of the same mind/opinion, see eye to eye, be in sympathy, be united, be as one man. **2** *they had agreed to a ceasefire* CONSENT, assent, acquiesce, accept, approve, say yes, give one's approval, give the nod; *formal* accede. **3** *the plan and the drawing do not agree with each other* MATCH (UP), accord, correspond, conform, coincide, fit, tally, be in harmony/agreement, be consistent/equivalent; *informal* square. **4** *they agreed on a price* SETTLE, decide, arrive at, negotiate, reach an agreement, come to terms, strike a bargain, make a deal, shake hands.
– OPPOSITES differ, contradict, reject.
agreeable ● adjective **1** *an agreeable atmosphere of rural tranquillity* PLEASANT, pleasing, enjoyable, pleasurable, nice, to one's liking, appealing, charming, delightful. **2** *an agreeable fellow* LIKEABLE, charming, amiable, affable, pleasant, nice, friendly, good-natured, sociable, genial, congenial. **3** *we should get together for a talk, if you're agreeable* WILLING, amenable, in accord/agreement.
– OPPOSITES unpleasant.
agreement ● noun **1** *all heads nodded in agreement* ACCORD, concurrence, consensus; assent, acceptance, consent, acquiescence, endorsement. **2** *an agreement on military cooperation* CONTRACT, compact, treaty, covenant, pact, accord, concordat, protocol. **3** *there is some agreement between my view and that of the author* CORRESPONDENCE, consistency, compatibility, accord; similarity, resemblance, likeness, similitude.
– OPPOSITES discord.
agricultural ● adjective **1** *an agricultural labourer* FARM, farming, agrarian; rural, rustic, pastoral, countryside; *poetic/literary* georgic, sylvan, Arcadian, agrestic. **2** *agricultural land* FARMED, farm, agrarian, cultivated, tilled.
– OPPOSITES urban.
agriculture ● noun FARMING, cultivation, tillage, tilling, husbandry, land/farm management; agribusiness, agronomy.
– RELATED TERMS agri-, agro-.
aground ● adverb & adjective GROUNDED, ashore, beached, stuck, shipwrecked, high and dry, on the rocks, on the ground/bottom.
ahead ● adverb **1** *he peered ahead, but could see nothing* FORWARD(S), towards the front, frontwards. **2** *he had ridden on ahead* IN FRONT, at the head, in the lead, at the fore, in the vanguard, in advance. **3** *she was preparing herself for what lay ahead* IN THE FUTURE, in time, in time to come, in the fullness of time, at a later date, after this, henceforth, later on, in due course, next. **4** *they are ahead by six points* LEADING, winning, in the lead, (out) in front, first, coming first.
– OPPOSITES behind, at the back, in the past.
– PHRASES **ahead of 1** *Blanche went ahead of the others* IN FRONT OF, before. **2** *we have a demanding trip ahead of us* IN STORE FOR, waiting for. **3** *two months ahead of schedule* IN ADVANCE OF, before, earlier than. **4** *in terms of these amenities, Britain is ahead of other European countries* MORE ADVANCED THAN, further on than, superior to, surpassing, exceeding, better than.
aid ● noun **1** *with the aid of his colleagues he prepared a manifesto* ASSISTANCE, support, help, backing, cooperation, succour; a helping hand. **2** *humanitarian aid* RELIEF, charity, financial assistance, donations, contributions, subsidies, handouts, subvention; debt remission; *historical* alms. **3** *a hospital aid* HELPER, assistant, girl/man Friday.
– OPPOSITES hindrance.
● verb **1** *he provided an army to aid the King of England* HELP, assist, abet, come to someone's aid, give assistance, lend a hand, be of service; avail, succour, sustain. **2** *essences can aid restful sleep* FACILITATE, promote, encourage, help, further, boost; speed up, hasten, accelerate, expedite.
– OPPOSITES hinder.
aide ● noun ASSISTANT, helper, adviser, right-hand man, man/girl Friday, adjutant, deputy, second (in command); subordinate, junior, underling, acolyte; *N. Amer.* cohort.
ail ● verb *(archaic)* TROUBLE, afflict, pain, distress, bother, worry, be the matter with.

a

ailment • noun a minor illness.
ailurophobia /īlyo͞orəfōbiə/ • noun extreme or irrational fear of cats.
– DERIVATIVES **ailurophobe** noun.
– ORIGIN from Greek *ailuros* 'cat'.
aim • verb **1** point (a weapon or camera) at a target. **2** direct at someone or something. **3** try to achieve something. • noun **1** a purpose or intention. **2** the aiming of a weapon or missile.
– PHRASES **take aim** point a weapon or camera at a target.
– DERIVATIVES **aimless** adjective.
– ORIGIN Old French *amer*, from Latin *aestimare* 'assess, estimate'.
ain't • contraction informal **1** am not; are not; is not. **2** has not; have not.
– USAGE In modern English the use of **ain't** is non-standard and should not be used in formal or written contexts, despite being widespread in many dialects and in informal speech.
air • noun **1** the invisible gaseous substance surrounding the earth, a mixture mainly of oxygen and nitrogen. **2** the open space above the surface of the earth. **3** (before another noun) indicating the use of aircraft: *air travel.* **4** the earth's atmosphere as a medium for transmitting radio waves. **5** one of the four elements (air, earth, fire, and water) in ancient and medieval philosophy and in astrology. **6** Music a tune or short melodious composition. **7** (**an air of**) an impression of. **8** (**airs**) an affected and condescending manner. • verb **1** express (an opinion or grievance) publicly. **2** broadcast (a programme) on radio or television. **3** expose to fresh or warm air.
– PHRASES **airs and graces** an affectation of superiority. **in the air** noticeable all around. **on** (or **off**) **the air** being (or not being) broadcast on radio or television. **take the air** go out of doors. **up in the air** unresolved. **walk** (or **tread**) **on air** feel elated.
– DERIVATIVES **airless** adjective.
– ORIGIN Greek *aēr*.
air bag • noun a safety device in a vehicle, that inflates rapidly when there is a sudden impact, so cushioning the occupant.
airbase • noun a base for military aircraft.
air bed • noun Brit. an inflatable mattress.
air bladder • noun an air-filled bladder or sac found in certain animals and plants.
airborne • adjective **1** carried or spread through the air. **2** (of an aircraft) flying.
air brake • noun **1** a brake worked by air pressure. **2** a movable flap or other device on an aircraft to reduce its speed.
airbrick • noun Brit. a brick perforated with small holes for ventilation.
airbrush • noun an artist's device for spraying paint by means of compressed air. • verb **1** paint with an airbrush. **2** alter or conceal (a photograph or a part of a photograph) using an airbrush.
airburst • noun an explosion in the air, especially of a nuclear bomb.
air chief marshal • noun a high rank of RAF officer, above air marshal and below Marshal of the RAF.
air commodore • noun a rank of RAF officer, above group captain and below air vice-marshal.
air conditioning • noun a system for controlling the humidity, ventilation, and temperature in a building or vehicle.
– DERIVATIVES **air-conditioned** adjective **air conditioner** noun.
air corridor • noun a route over a foreign country which aircraft must take.
aircraft • noun (pl. same) an aeroplane, helicopter, or other machine capable of flight.
aircraft carrier • noun a large warship from which aircraft can take off and land.
aircraftman (or **aircraftwoman**) • noun the lowest rank in the RAF, below leading aircraftman (or leading aircraftwoman).
aircrew • noun (pl. **aircrews**) (treated as sing. or pl.) the crew of an aircraft.
air cushion • noun **1** an inflatable cushion. **2** the layer of air supporting a hovercraft or similar vehicle.
airdrop • noun an act of dropping supplies, troops, or equipment by parachute.
Airedale • noun a large rough-coated black-and-tan breed of terrier.
– ORIGIN from *Airedale*, a district in Yorkshire.
airer • noun Brit. a frame or stand for airing or drying laundry.
airfield • noun an area of land set aside for the take-off, landing, and maintenance of aircraft.
air force • noun a branch of the armed forces concerned with fighting or defence in the air.
airframe • noun the body of an aircraft as distinct from its engine.
airfreight • noun the carriage of goods by aircraft.
air-freshener • noun a scented substance or device for masking unpleasant odours in a room.
air gun • noun **1** a gun which uses compressed air to fire pellets. **2** a tool using very hot air to strip paint.
airhead • noun informal a stupid person.
air hostess • noun Brit. a stewardess in a passenger aircraft.
airing • noun **1** an exposure to warm or fresh air. **2** a public expression of an opinion or discussion of a subject.
air kiss • noun a restrained embrace, in which the lips are pursed as if kissing but without making contact.
air letter • noun a sheet of light paper folded and sealed to form a letter for sending by airmail.
airlift • noun an act of transporting supplies by aircraft, typically in an emergency.
airline • noun **1** an organization providing a regular passenger air service. **2** (**air line**) a pipe or tube supplying air.
airliner • noun a large passenger aircraft.
airlock • noun **1** a stoppage of the flow in a pump or pipe, caused by an air bubble. **2** a compartment with controlled pres-

Thesaurus

ailing • adjective **1** *his ailing mother* ILL, unwell, sick, sickly, poorly, weak, indisposed, in poor/bad health, infirm, debilitated, delicate, valetudinarian, below par; *Brit.* off colour; *informal* laid up, under the weather. **2** *the country's ailing economy* FAILING, in poor condition, weak, poor, deficient.
– OPPOSITES healthy.
ailment • noun ILLNESS, disease, disorder, affliction, malady, complaint, infirmity; *informal* bug, virus; *Brit. informal* lurgy.
aim • verb **1** *he aimed the rifle* POINT, direct, train, sight, line up. **2** *she aimed at the target* TAKE AIM, fix on, zero in on, draw a bead on. **3** *undergraduates aiming for a first degree* WORK TOWARDS, be after, set one's sights on, try for, strive for, aspire to, endeavour to achieve; *formal* essay. **4** *this system is aimed at the home entertainment market* TARGET, intend, destine, direct, design, tailor, market, pitch. **5** *we aim to give you the best possible service* INTEND, mean, have in mind/view; plan, resolve, propose, design.
• noun *our aim is to develop gymnasts to the top level* OBJECTIVE, object, goal, end, target, design, desire, desired result, intention, intent, plan, purpose, object of the exercise; ambition, aspiration, wish, dream, hope, raison d'être.
aimless • adjective **1** *Flavia set out on an aimless walk* PURPOSELESS, objectless, goalless, without purpose, without goal. **2** *aimless men standing outside the bars* UNOCCUPIED, idle, at a loose end; purposeless, undirected.
– OPPOSITES purposeful.
air • noun **1** *hundreds of birds hovered in the air* SKY, atmosphere; heavens, ether. **2** *open the windows to get some air into the room* BREEZE, draught, wind; breath/blast of air, gust/puff of wind. **3** *an air of defiance* EXPRESSION, appearance, look, impression, aspect, aura, mien, countenance, manner, bearing, tone. **4** *women putting on airs* AFFECTATIONS, pretension, pretentiousness, affectedness, posing, posturing, airs and graces; *Brit. informal* side. **5** *a traditional Scottish air* TUNE, melody, song; *poetic/literary* lay.
– RELATED TERMS aerial, aero-.
• verb **1** *a chance to air your views* EXPRESS, voice, make public, ventilate, articulate, state, declare, give expression/voice to; have one's say. **2** *the windows were opened to air the room* VENTILATE, freshen, refresh, cool. **3** *the film was aired nationwide* BROADCAST, transmit, screen, show, televise, telecast.
airborne • adjective FLYING, in flight, in the air, on the wing.
airily • adverb LIGHTLY, breezily, flippantly, casually, nonchalantly, heedlessly, without consideration.
– OPPOSITES seriously.
airing • noun **1** *give the bedroom a good airing* VENTILATING, ventilation, freshening, refreshing, cooling. **2** *they went to the park for an airing* STROLL, walk, saunter, turn, amble, promenade; *dated* constitutional. **3** *the airing of different views* EXPRESSION, voicing, venting, ventilation, articulation, stating, declaration, communication. **4** *I hope the BBC gives the play another airing* BROADCAST, transmission, screening, showing, televising, telecast.

a

sure and parallel sets of doors, to permit movement between areas at different pressures.

airmail ● noun a system of transporting mail overseas by air.

airman (or **airwoman**) ● noun **1** a pilot or member of the crew of an aircraft in an air force. **2** a member of the RAF below commissioned rank.

air marshal ● noun a high rank of RAF officer, above air vice-marshal and below air chief marshal.

air mile ● noun **1** a nautical mile used as a measure of distance flown by aircraft. **2** (**Air Miles**) trademark points (equivalent to miles of free air travel) accumulated by buyers of airline tickets and other products.

air pistol (or **air rifle**) ● noun a gun which uses compressed air to fire pellets.

airplane ● noun N. Amer. an aeroplane.

air plant ● noun a tropical American epiphytic plant with long narrow leaves that absorb water and nutrients from the atmosphere.

airplay ● noun broadcasting time devoted to a particular record, performer, or musical genre.

air pocket ● noun **1** a cavity containing air. **2** a region of low pressure causing an aircraft to lose height suddenly.

airport ● noun a complex of runways and buildings for the take-off, landing, and maintenance of civil aircraft, with facilities for passengers.

air quality ● noun the degree to which the ambient air is pollution-free.

air raid ● noun an attack in which bombs are dropped from aircraft on to a ground target.

air-sea rescue ● noun a rescue from the sea using aircraft.

airship ● noun a power-driven aircraft kept buoyant by a body of gas (usually helium) which is lighter than air.

airspace ● noun the part of the air above and subject to the jurisdiction of a particular country.

airspeed ● noun the speed of an aircraft relative to the air through which it is moving.

airstream ● noun a current of air.

airstrip ● noun a strip of ground for the take-off and landing of aircraft.

airtight ● adjective **1** not allowing air to escape or pass through. **2** unassailable: *an airtight alibi.*

airtime ● noun time during which a broadcast is being transmitted.

air traffic control ● noun the ground-based personnel and equipment concerned with controlling and monitoring air traffic within a particular area.

air vice-marshal ● noun a high rank of RAF officer, above air commodore and below air marshal.

airwaves ● plural noun the radio frequencies used for broadcasting.

airway ● noun **1** the passage by which air reaches the lungs. **2** a tube for supplying air to the lungs in an emergency. **3** a recognized route followed by aircraft.

airworthy ● adjective (of an aircraft) safe to fly.
– DERIVATIVES **airworthiness** noun.

airy ● adjective (**airier**, **airiest**) **1** spacious and well ventilated. **2** light as air; delicate. **3** casual; dismissive.
– DERIVATIVES **airily** adverb **airiness** noun.

airy-fairy ● adjective informal, chiefly Brit. foolishly idealistic and vague.

aisle /īl/ ● noun **1** a passage between rows of seats. **2** a passage between sets of shelves in a supermarket or other shop. **3** Architecture a lateral division of a church parallel to, and divided by pillars from, a nave, choir, or transept.
– PHRASES **lead someone up the aisle** get married to someone.
– DERIVATIVES **aisled** adjective.
– ORIGIN Latin *ala* 'wing'.

aitch ● noun the letter H.
– PHRASES **drop one's aitches** fail to pronounce the letter *h* at the beginning of words.
– ORIGIN Old French *ache.*

aitchbone ● noun **1** the buttock or rump bone of cattle. **2** a cut of beef lying over this.
– ORIGIN from dialect *nache* 'rump', from Old French, from Latin *natis* 'buttock', + BONE; the initial *n* was lost by wrong division of *a nache bone.*

ajar ● adverb & adjective (of a door or window) slightly open.
– ORIGIN from Old English, 'a turn'.

AK ● abbreviation Alaska.

aka ● abbreviation also known as.

Akan /aakən/ ● noun (pl. same) **1** a member of a people inhabiting southern Ghana and adjacent parts of Ivory Coast. **2** the language of this people.
– ORIGIN Akan.

akee ● noun variant spelling of ACKEE.

akimbo ● adverb with hands on the hips and elbows turned outwards.
– ORIGIN probably from Old Norse.

akin ● adjective **1** of similar character. **2** related by blood.
– ORIGIN contracted form of *of kin.*

akvavit /akvəvit/ ● noun variant spelling of AQUAVIT.

AL ● abbreviation Alabama.

Al ● symbol the chemical element aluminium.

-al ● suffix **1** (forming adjectives) relating to; of the kind of: *tidal.* **2** forming nouns chiefly denoting verbal action: *arrival.*
– ORIGIN from Latin *-alis.*

alabaster /aləbaastər, -bastər/ ● noun a translucent form of gypsum, typically white, often carved into ornaments. ● adjective literary smooth and white: *pale, alabaster skin.*
– ORIGIN Greek *alabastos, alabastros.*

à la carte /aa laa **kaart**/ ● adjective & adverb (with reference to a menu or meal) offering or ordered as dishes that are separately priced, rather than part of a set meal.
– ORIGIN French, 'according to the card'.

alack (also **alack-a-day**) ● exclamation archaic an expression of regret or dismay.

alacrity ● noun brisk eagerness or enthusiasm.
– ORIGIN Latin *alacritas,* from *alacer* 'brisk'.

Aladdin's cave ● noun a place filled with a great number of interesting or precious items.
– ORIGIN from the story of *Aladdin* in the *Arabian Nights' Entertainments.*

à la mode /aa laa **mōd**/ ● adverb & adjective up to date; fashionable.
– ORIGIN French.

alanine /ələneen/ ● noun Biochemistry an amino acid which is a constituent of most proteins.
– ORIGIN from German *Alanin,* from ALDEHYDE.

alarm ● noun **1** anxious or frightened awareness of danger. **2** a warning of danger. **3** a warning sound or device. ● verb **1** frighten or disturb. **2** (**be alarmed**) be fitted or protected with an alarm.
– ORIGIN from Italian *all' arme!* 'to arms!'

alarm clock ● noun a clock that can be preset to sound an

Thesaurus

airless ● adjective STUFFY, close, stifling, suffocating, oppressive; unventilated, badly/poorly ventilated.
– OPPOSITES airy, ventilated.

airport ● noun *Brit.* aerodrome; *N. Amer.* airdrome; *informal* drome.

airtight ● adjective **1** *an airtight container* SEALED, hermetically sealed, closed/shut tight. **2** *an airtight alibi* INDISPUTABLE, unquestionable, incontrovertible, undeniable, incontestable, irrefutable, watertight, beyond dispute/question/doubt.

airy ● adjective **1** *the conservatory is light and airy* WELL VENTILATED, fresh; spacious, uncluttered; light, bright. **2** *an airy gesture* NONCHALANT, casual, breezy, flippant, insouciant, heedless. **3** *airy clouds* DELICATE, soft, fine, feathery, insubstantial.
– OPPOSITES stuffy.

airy-fairy ● adjective *(informal)* IMPRACTICAL, unrealistic, idealistic, fanciful.
– OPPOSITES practical.

aisle ● noun PASSAGE, passageway, gangway, walkway.

ajar ● adjective & adverb SLIGHTLY OPEN, half open, agape.
– OPPOSITES closed, wide open.

akin ● adjective SIMILAR, related, close, near, corresponding, comparable, equivalent; connected, alike, analogous.
– OPPOSITES unlike.

alacrity ● noun EAGERNESS, willingness, readiness; enthusiasm, ardour, fervour, keenness; promptness, haste, swiftness, dispatch, speed.

alarm ● noun **1** *the girl spun round in alarm* FEAR, anxiety, apprehension, trepidation, nervousness, unease, distress, agitation, consternation, disquiet, perturbation, fright, panic. **2** *a smoke alarm* SIREN, warning sound, danger/distress signal; warning device, alarm bell; *archaic* tocsin.

a

alarm at a particular time, used to wake someone from sleep.

alarmist ● noun a person who exaggerates a danger, so causing needless alarm. ● adjective creating needless alarm.
– DERIVATIVES **alarmism** noun.

alarum /əlaarəm/ ● noun archaic term for ALARM.
– PHRASES **alarums and excursions** humorous confused activity and uproar.

alas ● exclamation literary or humorous an expression of grief, pity, or concern.
– ORIGIN Old French *a las, a lasse*, from Latin *lassus* 'weary'.

alb ● noun a white robe reaching to the feet, worn by clergy and servers in some Christian Churches.
– ORIGIN from Latin *tunica alba* 'white garment'.

albacore /albəkor/ ● noun a tuna of warm seas which travels in large schools and is an important food fish.
– ORIGIN Arabic, probably from a word meaning 'premature, precocious'.

Albanian ● noun **1** a person from Albania. **2** the Indo-European language of Albania. ● adjective relating to Albania.

albatross ● noun (pl. **albatrosses**) **1** a very large seabird with long narrow wings, found chiefly in the southern oceans. **2** a burden or encumbrance (in allusion to Coleridge's *The Rime of the Ancient Mariner*).
– ORIGIN alteration (influenced by Latin *albus* 'white') of *alcatras* (a 16th-century word applied to various seabirds), from an Arabic word meaning 'the diver'.

albedo /albeedō/ ● noun (pl. **albedos**) chiefly Astronomy the proportion of the incident light that is reflected by a surface.
– ORIGIN Latin, 'whiteness'.

albeit /awlbeeit/ ● conjunction though.
– ORIGIN from *all be it*.

albino /albeenō/ ● noun (pl. **albinos**) a person or animal born with an absence of pigment in the skin and hair (which are white) and the eyes (which are usually pink).
– DERIVATIVES **albinism** /albiniz'm/ noun.
– ORIGIN from Latin *albus* 'white'.

Albion ● noun literary Britain or England.
– ORIGIN Latin, probably of Celtic origin and related to Latin *albus* 'white' (in allusion to the white cliffs of Dover).

album ● noun **1** a blank book for the insertion of photographs, stamps, or other items forming a collection. **2** a collection of recordings issued as a single item.
– ORIGIN Latin, 'blank tablet', from *albus* 'white'.

albumen /albyoomin/ ● noun egg white, or the protein contained in it.
– ORIGIN Latin, from *albus* 'white'.

albumin /albyoomin/ ● noun Biochemistry a water-soluble form of protein found especially in blood serum and egg white and coagulable by heat.
– DERIVATIVES **albuminous** /albyoominəss/ adjective.

alcazar /alkəzaar/ ● noun a Spanish palace or fortress of Moorish origin.
– ORIGIN Spanish, from an Arabic word meaning 'the castle'.

alchemy /alkəmi/ ● noun **1** the medieval forerunner of chemistry, concerned particularly with attempts to convert common metals into gold or to find a universal elixir. **2** a mysterious or paradoxical process.
– DERIVATIVES **alchemical** adjective **alchemist** noun **alchemize** (also **alchemise**) verb.
– ORIGIN from an Arabic word based on Greek *khēmia, khēmeia* 'art of transmuting metals'.

alcheringa /alchəringgə/ ● noun (in Australian Aboriginal mythology) a 'golden age' when the first ancestors were created.
– ORIGIN Aranda (an Aboriginal language), 'in the dreamtime'.

alcohol ● noun **1** a colourless volatile liquid compound which is the intoxicating ingredient in drinks such as wine, beer, and spirits. **2** drink containing this. **3** Chemistry any organic compound containing a hydroxyl group –OH: *propyl alcohol*.
– ORIGIN originally in the sense 'a fine powder, especially kohl, produced by sublimation': from an Arabic word meaning 'the kohl'.

alcoholic ● adjective relating to the consumption of alcohol. ● noun a person suffering from alcoholism.

alcoholism ● noun addiction to alcoholic liquor.

alcopop ● noun Brit. informal a ready-mixed carbonated drink containing alcohol.

alcove ● noun a recess, typically in the wall of a room.
– ORIGIN French, from an Arabic word meaning 'the vault'.

aldehyde /aldihīd/ ● noun Chemistry an organic compound containing the group –CHO, formed by the oxidation of alcohols.
– ORIGIN from Latin *alcohol dehydrogenatum* 'alcohol deprived of hydrogen'.

al dente /al dentay/ ● adjective & adverb (of food) cooked so as to be still firm when bitten.
– ORIGIN Italian, 'to the tooth'.

alder ● noun a tree of the birch family, which bears catkins and has toothed leaves.
– ORIGIN Old English.

alderman ● noun **1** chiefly historical a co-opted member of an English county or borough council, next in status to the Mayor. **2** (also **alderwoman**) N. Amer. & Austral. an elected member of a city council.
– DERIVATIVES **aldermanship** noun.
– ORIGIN Old English, 'chief, patriarch'.

aldosterone /aldostərōn/ ● noun Biochemistry a corticosteroid hormone which stimulates absorption of sodium by the kidneys and so regulates water and salt balance.
– ORIGIN blend of ALDEHYDE and STEROID.

ale ● noun **1** chiefly Brit. beer other than lager, stout, or porter. **2** N. Amer. beer brewed by top fermentation.
– ORIGIN Old English.

aleatory /ayliətəri/ (also **aleatoric**) ● adjective **1** depending on the throw of a dice or on chance. **2** relating to music or other forms of art involving elements of random choice during their composition or performance.
– ORIGIN from Latin *aleator* 'dice player'.

alembic /əlembik/ ● noun an apparatus formerly used for distilling, consisting of a gourd-shaped container and a cap with a long spout.
– ORIGIN from an Arabic word meaning 'the still', from Greek *ambix* 'cup'.

alert ● adjective **1** quick to notice and respond to danger or unusual circumstances. **2** quick-thinking; intelligent. ● noun **1** the state of being alert. **2** a warning of danger. ● verb warn of a danger or problem.
– DERIVATIVES **alertly** adverb **alertness** noun.
– ORIGIN from Italian *all' erta* 'to the watchtower'.

Thesaurus

– OPPOSITES calmness, composure.
● verb *the news had alarmed her* FRIGHTEN, scare, panic, unnerve, distress, agitate, upset, disconcert, shock, dismay, disturb; *informal* rattle, spook, scare the living daylights out of; *Brit. informal* put the wind up.

alarming ● adjective FRIGHTENING, unnerving, shocking; distressing, upsetting, disconcerting, perturbing, dismaying, disquieting, disturbing; *informal* scary.
– OPPOSITES reassuring.

alarmist ● noun SCAREMONGER, gloom-monger, doom-monger, doomster, doomsayer, Cassandra; *informal* doom and gloom merchant.
– OPPOSITES optimist.

alchemy ● noun CHEMISTRY; magic, sorcery, witchcraft.

alcohol ● noun LIQUOR, intoxicating liquor, strong/alcoholic drink, drink, spirits; *informal* booze, hooch, the hard stuff, firewater, rotgut, moonshine, grog, tipple, the demon drink, the bottle; *Brit. informal* gut-rot; *N. Amer. informal* juice; *technical* ethyl alcohol, ethanol.

alcoholic ● adjective *alcoholic drinks* INTOXICATING, inebriating, containing alcohol; strong, hard, stiff; *formal* spirituous.
● noun *his father's an alcoholic* DIPSOMANIAC, drunk, drunkard, heavy/hard/serious drinker, problem drinker, alcohol-abuser, person with a drink problem; tippler, sot, inebriate; *informal* boozer, lush, alky, dipso, soak, tosspot, wino, sponge, barfly; *Austral./NZ informal* hophead; *archaic* toper.

alcove ● noun RECESS, niche, nook, inglenook, bay.

alert ● adjective **1** *police have asked neighbours to keep alert* VIGILANT, watchful, attentive, observant, wideawake, circumspect; on the lookout, on one's guard/toes, on the qui vive; *informal* keeping one's eyes open/peeled. **2** *mentally alert* QUICK-WITTED, sharp, bright, quick, keen, perceptive, wideawake, on one's toes; *informal* on the ball, quick on the uptake, all there, with it.
– OPPOSITES inattentive.
● noun **1** *a state of alert* VIGILANCE, watchfulness, attentiveness, alertness, circumspection. **2** *a flood alert* WARNING, notification, notice; siren, alarm, signal, danger/distress signal.

A level ● noun (in the UK except Scotland) the higher of the two main levels of the GCE examination.
– ORIGIN abbreviation of ADVANCED LEVEL.

Alexander technique ● noun a system designed to promote well-being through the control of posture.
– ORIGIN named after the Australian-born actor and elocutionist Frederick Matthias *Alexander* (1869–1955).

alexandrine /aligzandrin/ Poetry ● adjective (of a line of verse) having six iambic feet. ● noun an alexandrine line.
– ORIGIN French, from the name of Alexander the Great, the subject of an Old French poem in this metre.

alfalfa /alfalfə/ ● noun a plant with clover-like leaves and bluish flowers, grown in warm climates for fodder.
– ORIGIN Spanish, from an Arabic word meaning 'a green fodder'.

alfresco /alfreskō/ ● adverb & adjective in the open air.
– ORIGIN Italian *al fresco*.

alga /algə/ ● noun (pl. **algae** /aljee, algee/) any of a large group of simple plants containing chlorophyll but lacking true stems, roots, and leaves, e.g. seaweed.
– DERIVATIVES **algal** adjective.
– ORIGIN Latin, 'seaweed'.

algebra /aljibrə/ ● noun the branch of mathematics in which letters and other symbols are used to represent numbers and quantities in formulae and equations.
– DERIVATIVES **algebraic** /aljibrayik/ adjective **algebraist** noun.
– ORIGIN Latin, from an Arabic word meaning 'the reunion of broken parts'.

Algerian ● noun a person from Algeria. ● adjective relating to Algeria.

-algia ● combining form denoting pain in a specified part of the body: *neuralgia*.
– DERIVATIVES **-algic** combining form in corresponding adjectives.
– ORIGIN from Greek *algos* 'pain'.

Algonquian /algongkwiən/ (also **Algonkian** /algongkiən/) ● noun **1** a large family of North American Indian languages, including Cree, Blackfoot, and Cheyenne. **2** a speaker of any of these languages. ● adjective relating to this family of languages or its speakers.

Algonquin /algongkwin/ (also **Algonkin**) /algongkin/ ● noun **1** a member of an American Indian people living in Canada along and westwards of the Ottawa River. **2** the Algonquian language of this people. ● adjective relating to this people.
– ORIGIN French, from a Micmac word meaning 'at the place of spearing fish and eels'.

algorithm /algərithəm/ ● noun a process or set of rules used in calculations or other problem-solving operations.
– DERIVATIVES **algorithmic** adjective.
– ORIGIN Latin *algorismus*, from an Arabic word meaning 'the man of Kwārizm', referring to a 9th-century mathematician.

alias /ayliəss/ ● adverb also known as. ● noun **1** a false identity. **2** Computing an identifying label used to access a file, command, or address.
– DERIVATIVES **aliasing** noun.
– ORIGIN Latin, 'at another time, otherwise'.

alibi /alibī/ ● noun (pl. **alibis**) a claim or piece of evidence that one was elsewhere when an alleged act took place. ● verb (**alibis**, **alibied**, **alibiing**) informal provide an alibi for.
– ORIGIN from Latin, 'elsewhere'.

Alice band ● noun a flexible band worn to hold back the hair.
– ORIGIN named after the heroine of *Alice's Adventures in Wonderland* by Lewis Carroll.

alien ● adjective **1** belonging to a foreign country. **2** unfamiliar and distasteful. **3** (of a plant or animal species) introduced from another country and later naturalized. **4** relating to beings from other worlds. ● noun **1** a foreigner. **2** an alien plant or animal species. **3** a being from another world.
– DERIVATIVES **alienness** noun.
– ORIGIN Latin *alienus*, from *alius* 'other'.

alienable ● adjective Law able to be transferred to new ownership.

alienate ● verb **1** cause to feel isolated. **2** lose the support or sympathy of.
– DERIVATIVES **alienation** noun.
– ORIGIN Latin *alienare* 'estrange', from *alius* 'other'.

alight[1] ● verb **1** formal, chiefly Brit. descend from a vehicle. **2** (**alight on**) chance to notice.
– ORIGIN Old English.

alight[2] ● adverb & adjective **1** on fire. **2** shining brightly.

align ● verb **1** place or arrange in a straight line or into correct relative positions. **2** (**align oneself with**) ally oneself to.
– DERIVATIVES **alignment** noun.
– ORIGIN French *aligner*, from *à ligne* 'into line'.

alike ● adjective similar. ● adverb in a similar way.
– ORIGIN Old English.

alimentary ● adjective providing nourishment or sustenance.
– ORIGIN from Latin *alimentum* 'nourishment'.

alimentary canal ● noun the passage along which food passes through the body.

alimony ● noun chiefly N. Amer. maintenance for a spouse after separation or divorce.
– ORIGIN originally in the sense 'nourishment, means of subsistence': from Latin *alimonia*, from *alere* 'nourish'.

A-line ● adjective (of a garment) slightly flared from a narrow waist or shoulders.

aliphatic /alifattik/ ● adjective Chemistry (of an organic compound) containing an open chain of carbon atoms in its molecule (as in the alkanes), not an aromatic ring.
– ORIGIN from Greek *aleiphar* 'fat'.

aliquot /alikwot/ ● noun **1** a portion of a larger whole, especially a sample taken for chemical analysis or other treatment. **2** (also **aliquot part** or **portion**) Mathematics a quantity which can be divided into another a whole number of times. ● verb divide

Thesaurus

● verb *police were alerted by a phone call* WARN, notify, apprise, forewarn, put on one's guard, put on the qui vive; *informal* tip off, clue in.

alias ● noun *he is known under several aliases* ASSUMED NAME, false name, pseudonym, sobriquet, incognito; pen/stage name, nom de plume/guerre.
● adverb *Cassius Clay, alias Muhammed Ali* ALSO KNOWN AS, aka, also called, otherwise known as.

alibi ● noun *we've both got a good alibi for last night* DEFENCE, justification, explanation, reason; *informal* story, line.
● verb *(informal) her brother agreed to alibi her* COVER FOR, give an alibi to, provide with an alibi.

alien ● adjective **1** *alien cultures* FOREIGN, overseas, non-native. **2** *an alien landscape* UNFAMILIAR, unknown, strange, peculiar; exotic, foreign. **3** *a vicious role alien to his nature* INCOMPATIBLE, opposed, conflicting, contrary, in conflict, at variance; *rare* oppugnant. **4** *alien beings* EXTRATERRESTRIAL, unearthly; Martian.
– OPPOSITES native, familiar, earthly.
● noun **1** *an illegal alien* FOREIGNER, non-native, immigrant, emigrant, émigré, incomer. **2** *the alien's spaceship crashed* EXTRATERRESTRIAL, ET; Martian; *informal* little green man.

alienate ● verb **1** *his homosexuality alienated him from his conservative father* ESTRANGE, divide, distance, put at a distance, isolate, cut off; set against, turn away, drive apart, disunite, set at variance/odds, drive a wedge between. **2** *(Law) they tried to prevent the land from being alienated* TRANSFER, pass on, hand over; *Law* convey, devolve.

alienation ● verb **1** *she shared my deep sense of alienation* ISOLATION, detachment, estrangement, distance, separation, division; cutting off, turning away. **2** *(Law) most leases contain restrictions against alienation* TRANSFER, passing on, handing over; *Law* conveyance, devolution.

alight[1] ● verb *(formal)* **1** *he alighted from the train* GET OFF, step off, disembark, pile out; detrain, deplane. **2** *a swallow alighted on a branch* LAND, come to rest, settle, perch; *archaic* light.
– OPPOSITES get on, board.

alight[2] ● adjective **1** *the bales of hay were alight* BURNING, ablaze, aflame, on fire, in flames, blazing; *poetic/literary* afire. **2** *her face was alight with laughter* LIT UP, gleaming, glowing, aglow, ablaze, bright, shining, radiant.

align ● verb **1** *the desks are aligned in straight rows* LINE UP, put in order, put in rows/columns, place, position, situate, set, range. **2** *he aligned himself with the workers* ALLY, affiliate, associate, join, side, unite, combine, join forces, form an alliance, team up, band together, throw in one's lot, make common cause.

alike ● adjective *all the doors looked alike* SIMILAR, (much) the same, indistinguishable, identical, uniform, interchangeable, cut from the same cloth, like (two) peas in a pod, (like) Tweedledum and Tweedledee; *informal* much of a muchness.
– OPPOSITES different.
● adverb *great minds think alike* SIMILARLY, (just) the same, in the same way/manner/fashion, identically.

a

into aliquots; take aliquots from.
– ORIGIN from Latin, 'some, so many'.
alive ● adjective **1** living; not dead. **2** continuing in existence or use. **3** alert and active. **4** having interest and meaning. **5** (**alive with**) swarming or teeming with.
– DERIVATIVES **aliveness** noun.
alkali /alkəli/ ● noun (pl. **alkalis** or US also **alkalies**) a compound, such as lime or caustic soda, with particular chemical properties including turning litmus blue and neutralizing or effervescing with acids.
– DERIVATIVES **alkalize** (also **alkalise**) verb.
– ORIGIN originally denoting a saline substance derived from the ashes of plants: from an Arabic word meaning 'fry, roast'.
alkaline ● adjective containing an alkali or having the properties of an alkali; having a pH greater than 7.
– DERIVATIVES **alkalinity** noun.
alkaloid /alkəloyd/ ● noun Chemistry any of a class of nitrogenous organic compounds of plant origin which have pronounced physiological actions on humans.
alkane /alkayn/ ● noun Chemistry any of the series of saturated hydrocarbons including methane, ethane, propane, and higher members.
– ORIGIN from ALKYL.
alkene /alkeen/ ● noun Chemistry any of the series of unsaturated hydrocarbons containing a double bond, including ethylene and propene.
– ORIGIN from ALKYL.
alkyl /alkīl/ ● noun Chemistry a hydrocarbon radical derived from an alkane by removal of a hydrogen atom.
– ORIGIN German *Alkohol* 'alcohol'.
alkyne /alkīn/ ● noun Chemistry any of the series of unsaturated hydrocarbons containing a triple bond, including acetylene.
– ORIGIN from ALKYL.
all ● predeterminer & determiner **1** the whole quantity or extent of: *all her money*. **2** any whatever: *he denied all knowledge*. **3** the greatest possible: *with all speed*. ● pronoun everything or everyone. ● adverb **1** completely. **2** indicating an equal score: *one-all*.
– PHRASES **all along** from the beginning. **all and sundry** everyone. **all but 1** very nearly. **2** all except. **all for** informal strongly in favour of. **all in** informal exhausted. **all in all** on the whole. **all out** using all one's strength or resources. **all over** informal **1** everywhere. **2** informal typical of the person mentioned. **all over the place** informal **1** everywhere. **2** in a state of disorder. **all round 1** in all respects. **2** for or by each person: *drinks all round*. **all told** in total. **at all** in any way. **in all** in total. **on all fours** on hands and knees. **one's all** one's whole strength or resources.
– ORIGIN Old English.
Allah /alə/ ● noun the name of God among Muslims (and Arab Christians).
– ORIGIN Arabic.
allay /əlay/ ● verb **1** diminish or end (fear or concern). **2** alleviate (pain or hunger).
– ORIGIN Old English, 'lay down or aside'.
all-clear ● noun a signal that danger or difficulty is over.
allegation ● noun a claim that someone has done something illegal or wrong, typically made without proof.
allege /əlej/ ● verb claim that someone has done something illegal or wrong, typically without proof.
– DERIVATIVES **alleged** adjective **allegedly** adverb.
– ORIGIN originally in the sense 'declare on oath': from Old French *esligier*, from Latin *lis* 'lawsuit'; confused in sense with Latin *allegare* 'allege'.
allegiance /əleejənss/ ● noun loyalty of a subordinate to a superior or of an individual to a group or cause.
– ORIGIN Old French *ligeance*; related to LIEGE.
allegorical ● adjective constituting or containing allegory.
– DERIVATIVES **allegoric** adjective **allegorically** adverb.
allegory /aligəri/ ● noun (pl. **allegories**) a story, poem, or picture which can be interpreted to reveal a hidden meaning.
– DERIVATIVES **allegorist** noun **allegorization** (also **allegorisation**) noun **allegorize** (also **allegorise**) verb.
– ORIGIN Greek *allēgoria*, from *allos* 'other' + *-agoria* 'speaking'.
allegretto /aligrettō/ ● adverb & adjective Music at a fairly brisk speed.
– ORIGIN Italian, from ALLEGRO.
allegro /əlegrō/ Music ● adverb & adjective at a brisk speed. ● noun (pl. **allegros**) an allegro movement, passage, or composition.
– ORIGIN Italian, 'lively'.
allele /aleel/ ● noun Genetics one of two or more alternative forms of a gene that arise by mutation and are found at the same place on a chromosome.
– DERIVATIVES **allelic** adjective.
– ORIGIN German *Allel*, abbreviation of ALLELOMORPH.
allelomorph /əleelōmorf/ ● noun an allele.
– DERIVATIVES **allelomorphic** adjective.
– ORIGIN from Greek *allēl-* 'one another' + *morphē* 'form'.
alleluia /aliloōyə/ ● exclamation & noun variant spelling of HALLELUJAH.
Allen key ● noun trademark a spanner designed to fit into and turn an Allen screw.
Allen screw ● noun trademark a screw with a hexagonal socket in the head.
– ORIGIN from the name of the *Allen* Manufacturing Company, Connecticut.
allergen /alərjən/ ● noun a substance that causes an allergic reaction.
allergenic ● adjective likely to cause an allergic reaction.
allergic ● adjective **1** caused by or relating to an allergy. **2** having an allergy.
allergy ● noun (pl. **allergies**) an adverse reaction by the body to a substance to which it has become hypersensitive.

Thesaurus

alimony ● noun FINANCIAL SUPPORT, maintenance, support; child support.
alive ● adjective **1** *he was last seen alive on Boxing Day* LIVING, live, breathing, animate, sentient; *informal* alive and kicking; *archaic* quick. **2** *the synagogue has kept the Jewish faith alive* ACTIVE, existing, in existence, existent, functioning, in operation; on the map. **3** *the thrills that kept him really alive* ANIMATED, lively, full of life, alert, active, energetic, vigorous, spry, sprightly, vital, vivacious, buoyant, exuberant, ebullient, zestful, spirited; *informal* full of beans, bright-eyed and bushy-tailed, chirpy, chipper, peppy, full of vim and vigour. **4** *teachers need to be alive to their pupils' backgrounds* ALERT, awake, aware, conscious, mindful, heedful, sensitive, familiar; *informal* wise; *formal* cognizant. **5** *the place was alive with mice* TEEMING, swarming, overrun, crawling, bristling, infested; crowded, packed; *informal* lousy.
– OPPOSITES dead, inanimate, inactive, lethargic.
all ● determiner **1** *all the children went | all creatures need sleep* EACH OF, each/every one of, every single one of; every (single), each and every. **2** *the sun shone all week* THE WHOLE OF THE, every bit of the, the complete, the entire. **3** *in all honesty | with all speed* COMPLETE, entire, total, full; greatest (possible), maximum.
– RELATED TERMS omni-, pan-, panto-.
– OPPOSITES no, none of.
● pronoun **1** *all are welcome* EVERYONE, everybody, each/every person. **2** *all of the cups were broken* EACH ONE, the sum, the total, the whole lot. **3** *they took all of it* EVERYTHING, every part, the whole/total amount, the (whole) lot, the entirety.
– OPPOSITES none, nobody, nothing.
● adverb *he was dressed all in black* COMPLETELY, fully, entirely, totally, wholly, absolutely, utterly; in every respect, in all respects, without reservation/exception.
– OPPOSITES partly.
allay ● verb REDUCE, diminish, decrease, lessen, assuage, alleviate, ease, relieve, soothe, soften, calm, take the edge off.
– OPPOSITES increase, intensify.
allegation ● noun CLAIM, assertion, charge, accusation, declaration, statement, contention, argument, affirmation, attestation; *formal* averment.
allege ● verb CLAIM, assert, charge, accuse, declare, state, contend, argue, affirm, attest, testify, swear; *formal* aver.
alleged ● adjective SUPPOSED, so-called, claimed, professed, purported, ostensible, putative, unproven.
allegedly ● adverb REPORTEDLY, supposedly, reputedly, purportedly, ostensibly, apparently, putatively, by all accounts, so the story goes.
allegiance ● noun LOYALTY, faithfulness, fidelity, obedience, adherence, homage, devotion; *historical* fealty; *formal* troth.
– OPPOSITES disloyalty, treachery.
allegorical ● adjective SYMBOLIC, metaphorical, figurative, representative, emblematic.
allegory ● noun PARABLE, analogy, metaphor, symbol, emblem.
allergic ● adjective **1** *she was allergic to nuts* HYPERSENSITIVE, sensi-

a

– DERIVATIVES **allergist** noun.
– ORIGIN from Greek *allos* 'other'.

alleviate /əleeviayt/ ● verb make (pain or difficulty) less severe.
– DERIVATIVES **alleviation** noun **alleviator** noun.
– ORIGIN Latin *alleviare* 'lighten'.

alley ● noun (pl. **alleys**) **1** a narrow passageway between or behind buildings. **2** a path in a park or garden. **3** a long, narrow area in which skittles and bowling are played.
– ORIGIN Old French *alee* 'walking or passage', from Latin *ambulare* 'to walk'.

alley cat ● noun a stray urban cat.

alleyway ● noun an alley between or behind buildings.

alliance ● noun **1** the state of being allied or associated. **2** a union or association between countries or organizations. **3** a relationship or connection.

allied ● adjective **1** joined by or relating to an alliance. **2** (**Allied**) relating to Britain and its allies in the First and Second World Wars. **3** (**allied to/with**) in combination or working together with.

alligator ● noun a large semiaquatic reptile similar to a crocodile but with a broader and shorter head.
– ORIGIN from Spanish *el lagarto* 'the lizard'.

alligator pear ● noun North American term for AVOCADO.

all-in ● adjective Brit. (especially of a price) inclusive of everything.

all-in wrestling ● noun chiefly Brit. wrestling with few or no restrictions.

alliteration ● noun the occurrence of the same letter or sound at the beginning of adjacent or closely connected words.
– DERIVATIVES **alliterate** verb **alliterative** adjective **alliteratively** adverb.
– ORIGIN Latin, from *littera* 'letter'.

allium /aliəm/ ● noun (pl. **alliums**) a bulbous plant of a genus that includes onions, leeks, garlic, and chives.
– ORIGIN Latin, 'garlic'.

allocate ● verb assign or distribute to.
– DERIVATIVES **allocable** adjective **allocation** noun **allocative** adjective **allocator** noun.
– ORIGIN Latin *allocare*.

allopathy /əloppəthi/ ● noun the treatment of disease by conventional means, i.e. with drugs having effects opposite to the symptoms. Often contrasted with HOMEOPATHY.
– DERIVATIVES **allopath** noun **allopathic** adjective **allopathist** noun.

allosaurus /aləsorəss/ ● noun a large bipedal carnivorous dinosaur of the late Jurassic period.
– ORIGIN from Greek *allos* 'other' + *sauros* 'lizard'.

allot ● verb (**allotted**, **allotting**) apportion or assign to.
– DERIVATIVES **allottee** noun.
– ORIGIN Old French *aloter*, from Latin *loter* 'divide into lots'.

allotment ● noun **1** Brit. a plot of land rented by an individual from a local authority, for growing vegetables or flowers. **2** the action of allotting. **3** an amount of something allotted.

allotrope /alətrōp/ ● noun Chemistry each of two or more different physical forms in which an element can exist (e.g. graphite, charcoal, and diamond as forms of carbon).
– DERIVATIVES **allotropic** adjective **allotropy** /əlotrəpi/ noun.
– ORIGIN from Greek *allotropos* 'of another form'.

allow ● verb **1** admit as legal or acceptable. **2** permit to do something. **3** (**allow for**) take into consideration when making plans or calculations. **4** provide or set aside for a particular purpose. **5** admit the truth of.
– DERIVATIVES **allowable** adjective **allowably** adverb **allowedly** adverb.
– ORIGIN Old French *alouer*, from Latin *allaudare* 'to praise', reinforced by Latin *allocare* 'allocate'.

allowance ● noun **1** the amount of something allowed. **2** a sum of money paid regularly to a person. **3** an amount of money that can be earned or received free of tax.
– PHRASES **make allowances for 1** take into consideration. **2** treat (someone) leniently because of their difficult circumstances.

Thesaurus

tive, sensitized. **2** (*informal*) *boys are allergic to washing* AVERSE, opposed, hostile, inimical, antagonistic, antipathetic, resistant, (dead) set against.

allergy ● noun **1** *an allergy to feathers* HYPERSENSITIVITY, sensitivity, allergic reaction. **2** (*informal*) *their allergy to free enterprise* AVERSION, antipathy, opposition, hostility, antagonism, dislike, distaste.

alleviate ● verb REDUCE, ease, relieve, take the edge off, deaden, dull, diminish, lessen, weaken, lighten, attenuate, allay, assuage, palliate, damp, soothe, help, soften, temper.
– OPPOSITES aggravate.

alley ● noun PASSAGE, passageway, alleyway, back alley, backstreet, lane, path, pathway, walk, allée.

alliance ● noun **1** *a defensive alliance* ASSOCIATION, union, league, confederation, federation, confederacy, coalition, consortium, affiliation, partnership. **2** *an alliance between medicine and morality* RELATIONSHIP, affinity, association, connection.

allied ● adjective **1** *a group of allied nations* FEDERATED, confederated, associated, in alliance, in league, in partnership; unified, united, amalgamated, integrated. **2** *agricultural and allied industries* ASSOCIATED, related, connected, interconnected, linked; similar, like, comparable, equivalent.
– OPPOSITES independent, unrelated.

all-important ● adjective VITAL, essential, indispensable, crucial, key, vitally important, of the utmost importance; critical, life-and-death, paramount, pre-eminent, high-priority; urgent, pressing, burning.
– OPPOSITES inessential.

allocate ● verb ALLOT, assign, distribute, apportion, share out, portion out, deal out, dole out, give out, dish out, parcel out, ration out, divide out/up; *informal* divvy up.

allocation ● noun **1** *the efficient allocation of resources* ALLOTMENT, assignment, distribution, apportionment, sharing out, handing out, dealing out, doling out, giving out, dishing out, parcelling out, rationing out, dividing out/up; *informal* divvying up. **2** *our annual allocation of funds* ALLOWANCE, allotment, quota, share, ration, grant, slice; *informal* cut; *Brit. informal* whack.

allot ● verb ALLOCATE, assign, apportion, distribute, issue, grant; earmark for, designate for, set aside for; hand out, deal out, dish out, dole out, give out; *informal* divvy up.

allotment ● noun **1** *the allotment of shares by a company* ALLOCATION, assignment, distribution, apportionment, issuing, sharing out, handing out, dealing out, doling out, giving out, dishing out, parcelling out, rationing out, dividing out/up; *informal* divvying up. **2** *each member received an allotment of new shares* QUOTA, share, ration, grant, allocation, allowance, slice; *informal* cut; *Brit. informal* whack.

all out ● adverb *I'm working all out to finish my novel* STRENUOUSLY, energetically, vigorously, hard, with all one's might (and main), eagerly, enthusiastically, industriously, diligently, assiduously, sedulously, indefatigably, with application/perseverance; *informal* like mad, like crazy; *Brit. informal* like billy-o.
– OPPOSITES lackadaisically.
● adjective *an all-out attack* STRENUOUS, energetic, vigorous, forceful, forcible; spirited, mettlesome, plucky, determined, resolute, aggressive, eager, keen, enthusiastic, zealous, ardent, fervent.
– OPPOSITES half-hearted.

allow ● verb **1** *the police allowed him to go home* PERMIT, let, authorize, give permission/authorization/leave, sanction, grant someone the right, license, enable, entitle; consent, assent, give one's consent/assent/blessing, give the nod, acquiesce, agree, approve; *informal* give the go-ahead, give the thumbs up, OK, give the OK, give the green light; *formal* accede. **2** *allow an hour or so for driving* SET ASIDE, allocate, allot, earmark, designate, assign. **3** *the house was demolished to allow for road widening* PROVIDE, get ready, cater, take into consideration, take into account, make provision, make preparations, prepare, plan, make plans. **4** *she allowed that all people had their funny little ways* ADMIT, acknowledge, recognize, agree, accept, concede, grant.
– OPPOSITES prevent, forbid.

allowable ● adjective *the maximum allowable number of users* PERMISSIBLE, permitted, allowed, admissible, acceptable, legal, lawful, legitimate, licit, authorized, sanctioned, approved, in order; *informal* OK, legit.
– OPPOSITES forbidden.

allowance ● noun **1** *your baggage allowance* PERMITTED AMOUNT/QUANTITY, allocation, allotment, quota, share, ration, grant, limit, portion, slice. **2** *her father gave her an allowance* PAYMENT, pocket money, sum of money, contribution, grant, subsidy, maintenance, financial support. **3** *a tax allowance* CONCESSION, reduction, decrease, discount.
– PHRASES **make allowance(s) for 1** *you must make allowances for delays* TAKE INTO CONSIDERATION, take into account, bear in mind,

alloy • noun /aloy/ **1** a metal made by combining two or more metallic elements, especially to give greater strength or resistance to corrosion. **2** an inferior metal mixed with a precious one. • verb /əloy/ **1** mix (metals) to make an alloy. **2** spoil by adding something inferior.
– ORIGIN Old French *aloier, aleier* 'combine', from Latin *alligare* 'bind'.
all right • adjective **1** satisfactory; acceptable. **2** permissible. • adverb fairly well. • exclamation expressing or asking for agreement or acceptance.
all-round (US **all-around**) • adjective **1** having a great many abilities or uses. **2** in many or all respects.
all-rounder • noun Brit. a person competent in a range of skills.
All Saints' Day • noun a Christian festival in honour of all the saints, held (in the Western Church) on 1 November.
All Souls' Day • noun a Catholic festival with prayers for the souls of the dead in purgatory, held on 2 November.
allspice • noun the dried aromatic fruit of a Caribbean tree, used as a culinary spice.
all-time • adjective hitherto unsurpassed: *the all-time record.*
allude • verb (**allude to**) **1** hint at. **2** mention in passing.
– ORIGIN Latin *alludere*, from *ludere* 'to play'.
allure • noun powerful attractiveness or charm. • verb strongly attract or charm.
– DERIVATIVES **allurement** noun.
– ORIGIN Old French *aleurier*, from Latin *luere* 'a lure'.
alluring • adjective attractive; tempting.
– DERIVATIVES **alluringly** adverb.
allusion • noun an indirect reference to something.
– DERIVATIVES **allusive** adjective **allusively** adverb **allusiveness** noun.
alluvium /əlo͝oviəm/ • noun a fertile deposit of clay, silt, and sand left by river flood water.
– DERIVATIVES **alluvial** adjective.
– ORIGIN Latin, from *luere* 'to wash'.
ally /alī/ • noun (pl. **allies**) **1** a person, organization, or country that cooperates with another. **2** (**the Allies**) the countries that fought with Britain in the First and Second World Wars. • verb /əlī/ (**allies, allied**) (**ally to/with**) **1** beneficially combine (a resource or commodity) with. **2** (**ally oneself with**) side with.
– ORIGIN from Old French *alier*, from Latin *alligare* 'bind together'.
-ally • suffix forming adverbs from adjectives ending in *-al* (such as *radically* from *radical*).
alma mater /almə maatər, maytər/ • noun the school, college, or university that one once attended.
– ORIGIN Latin, 'bountiful mother'.
almanac /awlmənak, ol-/ (also **almanack**) • noun **1** a calendar giving important dates and information, such as the phases of the moon. **2** an annual handbook containing information of general or specialist interest.
– ORIGIN Greek *almenikhiaka.*
almighty • adjective **1** omnipotent. **2** informal enormous. • noun (**the Almighty**) a name or title for God.
almond • noun the oval edible nut-like kernel of the almond tree.
– ORIGIN Old French *alemande*, from Greek *amugdalē.*
almond eyes • plural noun eyes that are narrow and oval with pointed ends.
almond paste • noun marzipan.
almoner /aamənər/ • noun historical an official distributor of alms.
– DERIVATIVES **almonry** noun.
almost • adverb very nearly.
– ORIGIN Old English.
alms /aamz/ • plural noun (in historical contexts) charitable donations of money or food to the poor.
– ORIGIN from Greek *eleēmosunē* 'compassion'.
almshouse • noun a house founded by charity, offering accommodation for the poor.
aloe /alō/ • noun **1** a succulent tropical plant with thick tapering leaves and bell-shaped flowers. **2** (**aloes** or **bitter aloes**) a strong laxative obtained from the bitter juice of various kinds of aloe. **3** (also **aloes wood**) the heartwood of a tropical Asian tree, yielding a fragrant resin.
– ORIGIN Greek *aloē.*
aloe vera • noun a jelly-like substance obtained from a kind of aloe, used as a soothing treatment for the skin.
– ORIGIN Latin, 'true aloe'.
aloft • adjective & adverb up in or into the air.
– ORIGIN Old Norse.
alone • adjective & adverb **1** on one's own; by oneself. **2** isolated and lonely. **3** only; exclusively.
– PHRASES **leave** (or **let**) **alone 1** abandon or desert. **2** stop interfering with.

Thesaurus

have regard to, provide for, plan for, make plans for, get ready for, cater for, allow for, make provision for, make preparations for, prepare for. **2** *she made allowances for his faults* EXCUSE, make excuses for, forgive, pardon, overlook.
alloy • noun MIXTURE, mix, amalgam, fusion, meld, blend, compound, combination, composite, union; *technical* admixture.
all-powerful • adjective OMNIPOTENT, almighty, supreme, pre-eminent; dictatorial, despotic, totalitarian, autocratic.
– OPPOSITES powerless.
all right • adjective **1** *the tea was all right* SATISFACTORY, acceptable, adequate, fairly good, passable, reasonable; *informal* so-so, OK. **2** *are you all right?* UNHURT, uninjured, unharmed, unscathed, in one piece, safe (and sound); well, fine, alive and well; *informal* OK. **3** *it's all right for you to go now* PERMISSIBLE, permitted, allowed, allowable, admissible, acceptable, legal, lawful, legitimate, licit, authorized, sanctioned, approved, in order; *informal* OK, legit.
– OPPOSITES unsatisfactory, hurt, forbidden.
• adverb **1** *the system works all right* SATISFACTORILY, adequately, fairly well, passably, acceptably, reasonably; *informal* OK. **2** *it's him all right* DEFINITELY, certainly, unquestionably, undoubtedly, indubitably, undeniably, assuredly, without (a) doubt, beyond (any) doubt, beyond the shadow of a doubt; *archaic* in sooth, verily.
• exclamation *all right, I'll go* VERY WELL (THEN), right (then), fine, good, yes, agreed, wilco; *informal* OK, okey-dokey, roger; *Brit. informal* righto.
allude • verb REFER, touch on, suggest, hint, imply, mention (in passing), make an allusion to; *formal* advert.
allure • noun *the allure of Paris* ATTRACTION, lure, draw, pull, appeal, allurement, enticement, temptation, charm, seduction, fascination.
• verb *will sponsors be allured by such opportunities?* ATTRACT, lure, entice, tempt, appeal to, captivate, draw, win over, charm, seduce, fascinate, whet the appetite of, make someone's mouth water.
– OPPOSITES repel.
alluring • adjective ENTICING, tempting, attractive, appealing, inviting, captivating, fetching, seductive; enchanting, charming, fascinating; *informal* come-hither.
allusion • noun REFERENCE, mention, suggestion, hint, comment, remark.
ally • noun *close political allies* ASSOCIATE, colleague, friend, confederate, partner, supporter.
– OPPOSITES enemy, opponent.
• verb **1** *he allied his racing experience with business acumen* COMBINE, marry, couple, merge, amalgamate, join, fuse. **2** *the Catholic powers allied with Philip II* UNITE, combine, join (up), join forces, band together, team up, collaborate, side, align oneself, form an alliance, throw in one's lot, make common cause.
– OPPOSITES split.
almanac • noun YEARBOOK, calendar, register, annual; manual, handbook.
almighty • adjective **1** *I swear by almighty God* ALL-POWERFUL, omnipotent, supreme, pre-eminent. **2** (*informal*) *an almighty explosion* VERY GREAT, huge, enormous, immense, colossal, massive, prodigious, stupendous, tremendous, monumental, mammoth, vast, gigantic, giant, mighty, Herculean, epic; very loud, deafening, earsplitting, ear-piercing, booming, thundering, thunderous; *informal* whopping, thumping, astronomical, mega, monster, humongous, jumbo; *Brit. informal* whacking, ginormous.
– OPPOSITES powerless, insignificant.
almost • adverb NEARLY, (just) about, more or less, practically, virtually, all but, as good as, close to, near, not quite, not far from/off, to all intents and purposes; approaching, bordering on, verging on; *informal* pretty nearly/much/well; *poetic/literary* well-nigh, nigh on.
– RELATED TERMS quasi-.
alms • plural noun (*historical*) GIFT(S), donation(s), handout(s), offering(s), charity, baksheesh, largesse; *rare* donative.
aloft • adjective & adverb **1** *he hoisted the Cup aloft* UPWARDS, up, high, into the air/sky, skyward, heavenward. **2** *the airships*

– DERIVATIVES **aloneness** noun.
– ORIGIN from ALL + ONE.
along • preposition & adverb **1** moving in a constant direction on (a more or less horizontal surface). **2** extending in a more or less horizontal line on. **3** in or into company with others.
– PHRASES **along with** in company with or at the same time as. **be** (or **come**) **along** arrive.
– ORIGIN Old English, related to LONG[1].
alongside (N. Amer. also **alongside of**) • preposition **1** close to the side of; next to. **2** at the same time as or in coexistence with.
aloof • adjective cool and distant.
– DERIVATIVES **aloofly** adverb **aloofness** noun.
– ORIGIN from LUFF; originally in nautical use meaning 'away and to windward!', i.e. with the ship kept away from a lee shore or other hazard.
alopecia /aləpeeshə/ • noun Medicine abnormal loss of hair.
– ORIGIN Greek *alōpekia*, 'fox mange'.
aloud • adverb not silently; audibly.
ALP • abbreviation Australian Labor Party.
alp • noun **1** a high mountain. **2** (the **Alps**) a high range of mountains in Switzerland and adjoining countries. **3** (in Switzerland) an area of green pasture on a mountainside.
– ORIGIN Greek *Alpeis*.
alpaca /alpakkə/ • noun (pl. same or **alpacas**) **1** a long-haired domesticated South American mammal related to the llama. **2** the wool of the alpaca.
– ORIGIN Spanish, from an American Indian word.
alpenhorn /alpənhorn/ (also **alphorn**) • noun a very long valveless wooden wind instrument played like a horn and used for signalling in the Alps.
– ORIGIN German, 'Alp horn'.
alpenstock /alpənstok/ • noun a long iron-tipped stick used by hillwalkers.
– ORIGIN German, 'Alp stick'.
alpha /alfə/ • noun **1** the first letter of the Greek alphabet (Α, α), transliterated as 'a'. **2** Brit. a first-class mark given for a piece of work.
– PHRASES **alpha and omega** the beginning and the end.
– ORIGIN Greek.
alphabet • noun an ordered set of letters or symbols used to represent the basic speech sounds of a language.
– DERIVATIVES **alphabetize** (also **alphabetise**) verb.
– ORIGIN from Greek *alpha* and *bēta*, the first two letters of the Greek alphabet.
alphabetical • adjective in the order of the letters of the alphabet.
– DERIVATIVES **alphabetic** adjective **alphabetically** adverb.
alphanumeric /alfənyoomerrik/ • adjective consisting of or using both letters and numerals.
alpha particle (also **alpha ray**) • noun Physics a helium nucleus, especially as emitted by some radioactive substances.
alpha testing • noun trials of a new product carried out before beta-testing.
alphorn /alphorn/ • noun another term for ALPENHORN.
alpine • adjective **1** relating to high mountains. **2** growing or found on high mountains. **3** (**Alpine**) relating to the Alps. • noun an alpine plant.
alpinist /alpinist/ • noun a climber of high mountains, especially in the Alps.
already • adverb **1** before the time in question. **2** as surprisingly soon or early as this.
alright • adjective, adverb, & exclamation variant spelling of ALL RIGHT.
– USAGE The spelling **alright** (rather than **all right**) is considered by many to be unacceptable in formal writing, even though other single-word forms such as **altogether** have long been accepted.
Alsatian • noun **1** Brit. a German shepherd dog. **2** a person from Alsace, a region of NE France. • adjective relating to Alsace.
also • adverb in addition.
– ORIGIN Old English.
also-ran • noun a loser in a race or contest.
altar • noun **1** a table or flat-topped block on which religious offerings are made. **2** the table in a Christian church at which the bread and wine are consecrated in communion services.
– PHRASES **lead to the altar** marry (a woman).
– ORIGIN Latin, from *altus* 'high'.
altar boy • noun a boy who acts as a priest's assistant during a service.
altarpiece • noun a painting or other work of art set above and behind an altar.
alter • verb change in character, appearance, direction, etc.
– DERIVATIVES **alterable** adjective **alteration** noun.
– ORIGIN Latin *alterare*, from *alter* 'other'.
altercation • noun a noisy argument or disagreement.
– ORIGIN Latin, from *altercari* 'to wrangle'.
alter ego /altər eegō, awltər eggō/ • noun **1** a person's secondary or alternative personality. **2** a close friend who is very like oneself.
– ORIGIN Latin, 'other self'.
alternate • verb /awltərnayt/ **1** occur or do in turn repeatedly. **2** change repeatedly between two contrasting conditions. • adjective /awlternət/ **1** every other. **2** (of two things) each following and succeeded by the other in a regular pattern. **3** chiefly N. Amer. another term for ALTERNATIVE.
– DERIVATIVES **alternately** adverb **alternation** noun.
– USAGE The use of **alternate** to mean **alternative** (as in *we will need to find alternate sources of fuel*) is common in North American English, though still regarded as incorrect by many in Britain.
– ORIGIN Latin *alternare* 'do by turns', from *alter* 'other'.

Thesaurus

stayed aloft for many hours IN THE AIR, in the sky, high up, up (above), on high, overhead.
– OPPOSITES down.
alone • adjective & adverb **1** *she was alone in the house* BY ONESELF, on one's own, all alone, solitary, single, singly, solo, solus; unescorted, partnerless, companionless; *Brit. informal* on one's tod, on one's lonesome, on one's Jack Jones; *Austral./NZ informal* on one's Pat Malone. **2** *he managed alone* UNAIDED, unassisted, without help/assistance, single-handedly, solo, on one's own. **3** *she felt terribly alone* LONELY, isolated, solitary, deserted, abandoned, forlorn, friendless. **4** *a house standing alone* APART, by itself/oneself, separate, detached, isolated. **5** *you alone can inspire me* ONLY, solely, just; and no one else, and nothing else, no one but, nothing but.
– OPPOSITES in company, with help, among others.
along • preposition **1** *she walked along the corridor* DOWN, from one end of —— to the other. **2** *trees grew along the river bank* BESIDE, by the side of, on the edge of, alongside. **3** *they'll stop along the way* ON, at a point on, in the course of.
• adverb **1** *Maurice moved along past the other exhibits* ONWARDS, on, ahead, forward(s). **2** *I invited a friend along* AS COMPANY, with one, to accompany one, as a partner.
– PHRASES **along with** TOGETHER WITH, accompanying, accompanied by; at the same time as; as well as, in addition to, plus, besides.
aloof • adjective DISTANT, detached, unfriendly, unsociable, remote, unapproachable, formal, stiff, austere, withdrawn, reserved, unforthcoming, uncommunicative; *informal* stand-offish.
– OPPOSITES familiar, friendly.
aloud • adverb AUDIBLY, out loud, for all to hear.
– OPPOSITES silently.
alphabet • noun ABC, letters, writing system, syllabary.
already • adverb **1** *Anna had suffered a great deal already* BY THIS/THAT TIME, by now/then, thus/so far, before now/then, until now/then, up to now/then. **2** *is it 3 o'clock already?* AS EARLY AS THIS/THAT, as soon as this/that, so soon.
also • adverb TOO, as well, besides, in addition, additionally, furthermore, further, moreover, into the bargain, on top (of that), what's more, to boot, equally; *informal* and all; *archaic* withal, forbye.
alter • verb **1** *Eliot was persuaded to alter the passage* CHANGE, make changes to, make different, make alterations to, adjust, make adjustments to, adapt, amend, modify, revise, revamp, rework, redo, refine, vary, transform; *informal* tweak; *technical* permute. **2** *the state of affairs has altered* CHANGE, become different, undergo a (sea) change, adjust, adapt, transform, evolve.
– OPPOSITES preserve, stay the same.
alteration • noun CHANGE, adjustment, adaptation, modification, variation, revision, amendment; rearrangement, reordering, restyling, rejigging, reworking, revamping; transformation, sea change; *humorous* transmogrification.
altercation • noun ARGUMENT, quarrel, squabble, fight, shouting match, disagreement, difference of opinion, falling-out, dispute, disputation, wrangle, war of words; *informal* tiff, run-in, slanging match, spat, scrap; *Brit. informal* row, barney, ding-dong, bust-up, bit of argy-bargy; *N. Amer. informal* rhubarb; *archaic* broil, miff.
alternate • verb **1** *rows of trees alternate with dense shrub* BE

a

alternate angles • plural noun two equal angles formed on opposite side of a line crossing two parallel lines.
alternating current • noun an electric current that reverses its direction many times a second. Compare with DIRECT CURRENT.
alternative • adjective **1** (of one or more things) available as another possibility. **2** (of two things) mutually exclusive. **3** departing from or challenging traditional practices. • noun one of two or more available possibilities.
– DERIVATIVES **alternatively** adverb.
– USAGE Some people maintain that you can only have a maximum of two alternatives (because the word **alternative** comes from Latin *alter* 'other of two'). References to more than two alternatives are, however, normal in modern standard English.
alternative energy • noun energy fuelled in ways that do not use up natural resources or harm the environment.
alternative medicine • noun therapy regarded as unorthodox by the medical profession, e.g. herbalism.
alternator • noun a dynamo that generates an alternating current.
although • conjunction **1** in spite of the fact that. **2** but.
altimeter /altimeetər/ • noun an instrument which indicates the altitude reached, especially in an aircraft.
altiplano /altiplaanō/ • noun (pl. **altiplanos**) the high tableland of central South America.
– ORIGIN Spanish.
altitude • noun the height of an object or point in relation to sea level or ground level.
– DERIVATIVES **altitudinal** adjective.
– ORIGIN Latin *altitudo*, from *altus* 'high'.
altitude sickness • noun illness resulting from shortage of oxygen at high altitude.
alto /altō/ • noun (pl. **altos**) **1** the highest adult male or lowest female singing voice. **2** (before another noun) referring to the second or third highest of a family of instruments: *an alto sax*.
– ORIGIN from Italian *alto canto* 'high song'.
altocumulus • noun (pl. **altocumuli**) rounded masses of cloud with a level base, at medium altitude.
altogether • adverb **1** completely. **2** in total. **3** on the whole.
– PHRASES **in the altogether** informal naked.
– USAGE Note that **altogether** and **all together** do not mean the same thing. **Altogether** means 'in total', as in *there are six bedrooms altogether*, whereas **all together** means 'all in one place' or 'all at once', as in *it was good to have a group of friends all together; they came in all together*.
altostratus • noun a continuous uniform layer of cloud at medium altitude.
altruism /altroo-iz'm/ • noun **1** unselfish concern for others. **2** Zoology behaviour of an animal that benefits another at its own expense.
– DERIVATIVES **altruist** noun **altruistic** adjective **altruistically** adverb.
– ORIGIN from Italian *altrui* 'somebody else', from Latin *alteri huic* 'to this other'.

alum /aləm/ • noun a crystalline compound consisting of a double sulphate of aluminium and potassium, used in dyeing and tanning.
– ORIGIN Latin *alumen*.
alumina /əlo͞omină/ • noun aluminium oxide, a constituent of many clays and found crystallized as corundum and sapphire.
– ORIGIN from Latin *alumen* 'alum', on the pattern of words such as *magnesia*.
aluminium /alyoominniəm/ (US **aluminum** /əlo͞ominəm/) • noun a strong, light, corrosion-resistant silvery-grey metallic element.
– DERIVATIVES **aluminous** adjective.
aluminize /əlo͞ominīz/ (also **aluminise**) • verb coat with aluminium.
aluminosilicate /əlo͞ominōsillikayt/ • noun a silicate mineral in which aluminium replaces some of the silicon.
alumnus /əlumnəss/ • noun (pl. **alumni** /əlumnī/; fem. **alumna** /əlumnə/, pl. **alumnae** /əlumnee/) a former pupil or student of a particular school, college, or university.
– ORIGIN Latin, 'pupil', from *alere* 'nourish'.
alveolus /alveeələss, alviōləss/ • noun (pl. **alveoli** /alveeəlī, alviōlī/) Anatomy **1** any of the many tiny air sacs in the lungs. **2** the bony socket for the root of a tooth.
– DERIVATIVES **alveolar** adjective.
– ORIGIN Latin, 'small cavity'.
always • adverb **1** on all occasions; at all times. **2** forever. **3** repeatedly. **4** failing all else.
alyssum /alisəm/ • noun (pl. **alyssums**) a herbaceous plant with small white or yellow flowers.
– ORIGIN Greek *alusson*, from *a-* 'without' + *lussa* 'rabies' (referring to its former use in herbalism).
Alzheimer's disease /alts-himərz/ • noun a form of progressive mental deterioration occurring in middle or old age.
– ORIGIN named after the German neurologist Alois *Alzheimer* (1864–1915).
AM • abbreviation amplitude modulation.
Am • symbol the chemical element americium.
am first person singular present of BE.
a.m. • abbreviation before noon.
– ORIGIN from Latin *ante meridiem*.
amah /aamə/ • noun a nursemaid or maid in the Far East or India.
– ORIGIN Portuguese *ama*.
amalgam /əmalgəm/ • noun **1** a mixture or blend. **2** Chemistry an alloy of mercury with another metal, especially one used for dental fillings.
– ORIGIN Greek *malagma* 'an emollient'.
amalgamate /əmalgəmayt/ • verb **1** combine or unite to form one organization or structure. **2** Chemistry alloy (a metal) with mercury.
– DERIVATIVES **amalgamation** noun.
amanuensis /əmanyooensiss/ • noun (pl. **amanuenses**

Thesaurus

INTERSPERSED, occur in turn/rotation, rotate, follow one another; take turns, take it in turns, work/act in sequence. **2** *we could alternate the groups so that no one felt they had been left out* GIVE TURNS TO, take in turn, rotate, take in rotation; swap, exchange, interchange.
• adjective **1** *she attended on alternate days* EVERY OTHER, every second. **2** *place the leeks and noodles in alternate layers* ALTERNATING, interchanging, following in sequence, sequential, occurring in turns. **3** (N. Amer.) *an alternate plan*. See ALTERNATIVE adjective sense 1.
alternative • adjective **1** *an alternative route* DIFFERENT, other, another, second, possible, substitute, replacement; standby, emergency, reserve, back-up, auxiliary, fallback; N. Amer. alternate. **2** *an alternative lifestyle* UNORTHODOX, unconventional, nonstandard, unusual, uncommon, out of the ordinary, radical, revolutionary, nonconformist, avant-garde; informal off the wall, oddball, offbeat, way-out.
• noun *we have no alternative* OPTION, choice, other possibility; substitute, replacement.
alternatively • adverb ON THE OTHER HAND, as an alternative, or; otherwise, instead, if not, then again; N. Amer. alternately.
although • conjunction IN SPITE OF THE FACT THAT, despite the fact that, notwithstanding (the fact) that, even though/if, for all that, while, whilst.
altitude • noun HEIGHT, elevation, distance above the sea/ground.
altogether • adverb **1** *he wasn't altogether happy* COMPLETELY, totally, entirely, absolutely, wholly, fully, thoroughly, utterly, perfectly, one hundred per cent, in all respects. **2** *we have five offices altogether* IN ALL, all told, in toto. **3** *altogether it was a great evening* ON THE WHOLE, overall, all in all, all things considered, on balance, on average, for the most part, in the main, in general, generally, by and large.
altruism • noun UNSELFISHNESS, selflessness, compassion, kindness, public-spiritedness; charity, benevolence, beneficence, philanthropy, humanitarianism; poetic/literary bounty, bounteousness.
– OPPOSITES selfishness.
always • adverb **1** *he's always late* EVERY TIME, each time, at all times, all the time, without fail, consistently, invariably, regularly, habitually, unfailingly. **2** *she's always complaining* CONTINUALLY, continuously, constantly, forever, perpetually, incessantly, ceaselessly, unceasingly, endlessly, the entire time; informal 24-7. **3** *the place will always be dear to me* FOREVER, for always, for good (and all), for evermore, for ever and ever, until the end of time, eternally, for eternity, until hell freezes over; informal for keeps, until the cows come home; archaic for aye. **4** *you can always take it back to the shop* AS A LAST RESORT, no matter what, in any event/case, come what may.
– OPPOSITES never, seldom, sometimes.
amalgamate • verb COMBINE, merge, unite, fuse, blend, meld; join (together), join forces, band (together), link (up), team up, go into

/əmanyooenseez/) a literary assistant, in particular one who takes dictation.
– ORIGIN Latin, from *servus a manu* 'slave at handwriting, secretary'.
amaranth /ammərangh/ ● noun love-lies-bleeding or a related plant.
– ORIGIN from Greek *amarantos* 'not fading'.
amaretti /ammərettі/ ● plural noun Italian almond-flavoured biscuits.
– ORIGIN Italian, from *amaro* 'bitter'.
amaretto /ammərettō/ ● noun a brown almond-flavoured liqueur produced in Italy.
amaryllis /ammərilliss/ ● noun a bulbous plant with large trumpet-shaped flowers.
– ORIGIN from Greek *Amarullis*, a name for a country girl in pastoral poetry.
amass ● verb accumulate over time.
– DERIVATIVES **amasser** noun.
– ORIGIN Latin *amassare*, related to MASS.
amateur ● noun **1** a person who takes part in a sport or other activity without being paid. **2** a person regarded as incompetent at a particular activity. ● adjective **1** non-professional. **2** inept.
– DERIVATIVES **amateurism** noun.
– ORIGIN French, 'lover'.
amateurish ● adjective incompetent; unskilful.
– DERIVATIVES **amateurishly** adverb **amateurishness** noun.
amatory /ammətəri/ ● adjective relating to or induced by sexual love or desire.
– ORIGIN Latin *amatorius*, from *amare* 'to love'.
amaze ● verb surprise greatly; astonish.
– DERIVATIVES **amazement** noun.
– ORIGIN Old English.
amazing ● adjective **1** causing great surprise or wonder; astonishing. **2** informal very good or impressive.
– DERIVATIVES **amazingly** adverb.
Amazon /amməz'n/ ● noun **1** a member of a legendary race of female warriors. **2** a very tall, strong woman.
– ORIGIN Greek *Amazōn*, explained by the Greeks as meaning 'breastless' (as if from *a-* 'without' + *mazos* 'breast'), with reference to the fable that the Amazons cut off the right breast so as to draw a bow more easily.
Amazonian /amməzōniən/ ● adjective **1** relating to the River Amazon. **2** (of a woman) very tall and strong.
ambassador ● noun **1** a diplomat sent by a state as its permanent representative in a foreign country. **2** a representative or promoter of an activity.
– DERIVATIVES **ambassadorial** adjective **ambassadress** noun.
– ORIGIN Italian *ambasciator*, from Latin *ambactus* 'servant'.
amber ● noun **1** hard translucent fossilized resin, typically yellowish in colour, used in jewellery. **2** a honey-yellow colour.
– ORIGIN Old French *ambre*, from an Arabic word originally meaning 'ambergris'.
ambergris /ambərgreess/ ● noun a wax-like substance secreted from the intestines of the sperm whale, found floating in tropical seas and used in perfume manufacture.
– ORIGIN from Old French *ambre gris* 'grey amber'.
ambidextrous /ambidekstrəss/ ● adjective able to use the right and left hands equally well.
– DERIVATIVES **ambidexterity** noun **ambidextrously** adverb **ambidextrousness** noun.
– ORIGIN from Latin *ambi-* 'on both sides' + *dexter* 'right-handed'.
ambience /ambiənss/ (also **ambiance**) ● noun **1** the character and atmosphere of a place. **2** character given to a sound recording by the space in which the sound occurs.
ambient /ambiənt/ ● adjective **1** relating to the immediate surroundings of something. **2** (of music) electronic and having no vocals or persistent beat, used to create atmosphere.
– ORIGIN Latin, from *ambire* 'go round'.
ambiguity /ambigyōōiti/ ● noun (pl. **ambiguities**) uncertain or inexact meaning.
ambiguous /ambigyōōəss/ ● adjective **1** (of language) having more than one meaning. **2** not clear or decided.
– DERIVATIVES **ambiguously** adverb.
– ORIGIN Latin *ambiguus* 'doubtful'.
ambit ● noun the scope, extent, or bounds of something.
– ORIGIN Latin *ambitus* 'circuit'.
ambition ● noun **1** a strong desire to do or achieve something. **2** desire for success, wealth, or fame.
– ORIGIN Latin, from *ambire* 'go around (canvassing for votes)'.
ambitious ● adjective **1** having or showing ambition. **2** intended to meet a high standard and therefore difficult to achieve.
– DERIVATIVES **ambitiously** adverb **ambitiousness** noun.
ambivalent /ambivvələnt/ ● adjective having mixed feelings or contradictory ideas about something or someone.
– DERIVATIVES **ambivalence** noun **ambivalently** adverb.
– ORIGIN from Latin *ambi-* 'on both sides' + *valere* 'be worth'.
amble ● verb walk at a leisurely pace. ● noun a leisurely walk.

Thesaurus

partnership; *poetic/literary* commingle.
– OPPOSITES separate.
amalgamation ● noun COMBINATION, union, blend, mixture, fusion, coalescence, synthesis, composite, amalgam.
amass ● verb GATHER, collect, assemble; accumulate, stockpile, store (up), cumulate, accrue, lay in/up, garner; *informal* stash (away).
– OPPOSITES dissipate.
amateur ● noun **1** *the crew were all amateurs* NON-PROFESSIONAL, non-specialist, layman, layperson; dilettante. **2** *what a bunch of amateurs* BUNGLER, incompetent, bumbler; *Brit. informal* bodger.
– OPPOSITES professional, expert.
● adjective **1** *an amateur sportsman* NON-PROFESSIONAL, lay, non-specialist; dilettante. **2** *their amateur efforts* INCOMPETENT, inept, unskilful, inexpert, amateurish, clumsy, maladroit, bumbling; *Brit. informal* bodged.
amateurish ● adjective. See AMATEUR adjective sense 2.
amatory ● adjective SEXUAL, erotic, amorous, romantic, sensual, passionate, sexy; *informal* randy, steamy, naughty.
amaze ● verb ASTONISH, astound, surprise, stun, stagger, nonplus, shock, startle, stupefy, stop someone in their tracks, leave open-mouthed, leave aghast, take someone's breath away, dumbfound; *informal* bowl over, flabbergast; *Brit. informal* knock for six; **(amazed)** thunderstruck, at a loss for words, speechless; *Brit. informal* gobsmacked.
amazement ● noun ASTONISHMENT, surprise, shock, stupefaction, incredulity, disbelief, speechlessness, awe, wonder, wonderment.
amazing ● adjective ASTONISHING, astounding, surprising, stunning, staggering, shocking, startling, stupefying, breathtaking; awesome, awe-inspiring, sensational, remarkable, spectacular, stupendous, phenomenal, extraordinary, incredible, unbelievable; *informal* mind-blowing, flabbergasting; *poetic/literary* wondrous.
ambassador ● noun **1** *the American ambassador* ENVOY, plenipotentiary, emissary, (papal) nuncio, representative, diplomat; *archaic* legate. **2** *a great ambassador for the sport* CAMPAIGNER, representative, promoter, champion, supporter, backer; *N. Amer.* booster.
ambience ● noun ATMOSPHERE, air, aura, climate, mood, feel, feeling, vibrations, character, quality, impression, flavour, look, tone; *informal* vibes.
ambiguity ● noun AMBIVALENCE, equivocation; obscurity, vagueness, abstruseness, doubtfulness, uncertainty; *formal* dubiety.
ambiguous ● adjective EQUIVOCAL, ambivalent, arguable, debatable; open to debate/argument, obscure, unclear, vague, abstruse, doubtful, dubious, uncertain.
– OPPOSITES clear.
ambit ● noun SCOPE, extent, range, breadth, width, reach, sweep; terms of reference, field of reference, jurisdiction, remit; area, sphere, field, realm, compass.
ambition ● noun **1** *young people with ambition* DRIVE, determination, enterprise, initiative, eagerness, motivation, enthusiasm, zeal, commitment, a sense of purpose; *informal* get-up-and-go. **2** *her ambition was to become a model* ASPIRATION, intention, goal, aim, objective, object, purpose, intent, plan, desire, wish, design, target, dream.
ambitious ● adjective **1** *an energetic and ambitious politician* ASPIRING, determined, forceful, pushy, enterprising, motivated, enthusiastic, energetic, zealous, committed, purposeful, power-hungry; *informal* go-ahead, go-getting. **2** *he was ambitious to make it to the top* EAGER, determined, intent on, enthusiastic, anxious, hungry, impatient, striving. **3** *an ambitious task* DIFFICULT, exacting, demanding, formidable, challenging, hard, arduous, onerous, tough; *archaic* toilsome.
– OPPOSITES laid-back.
ambivalent ● adjective EQUIVOCAL, uncertain, unsure, doubtful, indecisive, inconclusive, irresolute, in two minds, undecided, torn,

a

– ORIGIN Latin *ambulare* 'to walk'.
ambrosia • noun **1** Greek & Roman Mythology the food of the gods. **2** something very pleasing to taste or smell. **3** honey or pollen used as food by bees.
– DERIVATIVES **ambrosial** adjective.
– ORIGIN Greek, 'elixir of life'.
ambulance • noun a vehicle equipped for taking sick or injured people to and from hospital.
– ORIGIN French, from *hôpital ambulant* 'mobile field hospital', from Latin *ambulare* 'walk'.
ambulance-chaser • noun derogatory, chiefly N. Amer. a lawyer who specializes in bringing cases seeking damages for personal injury.
ambulant /ambyoolənt/ • adjective Medicine able to walk about; not confined to bed.
ambulatory /ambyoolətəri/ • adjective **1** relating to walking or able to walk. **2** movable; mobile. • noun (pl. **ambulatories**) an aisle or cloister in a church or monastery.
ambuscade /ambəskayd/ archaic • noun an ambush. • verb attack by ambushing.
– ORIGIN French *embuscade*, from a Latin word meaning 'to place in a wood'.
ambush • noun a surprise attack by people lying in wait in a concealed position. • verb attack in such a way.
– ORIGIN Old French *embusche*, from a Latin word meaning 'to place in a wood'; related to BUSH[1].
ameba • noun (pl. **amebae** or **amebas**) US spelling of AMOEBA.
ameliorate /əmeeliərayt/ • verb formal make (something) better.
– DERIVATIVES **amelioration** noun **ameliorative** adjective.
– ORIGIN from Latin *meliorare*.
amen /aamen, aymen/ • exclamation said at the end of a prayer or hymn, meaning 'so be it'.
– ORIGIN Greek, from a Hebrew word meaning 'truth, certainty'.
amenable /əmeenəb'l/ • adjective **1** willing to respond to persuasion or suggestions. **2** (**amenable to**) capable of being acted on.
– DERIVATIVES **amenability** noun **amenably** adverb.
– ORIGIN from Old French *amener* 'bring to', from Latin *minari* 'threaten'.
amend • verb make minor improvements to (a document, proposal, etc.).
– DERIVATIVES **amendable** adjective.
– USAGE On the difference between **amend** and **emend**, see the note at EMEND.
– ORIGIN Latin *emendare* 'to correct'.
amendment • noun **1** a minor improvement. **2** (**Amendment**) an article added to the US Constitution.
amends • plural noun (in phrase **make amends**) compensate or make up for a wrongdoing.
amenity /əmeeniti/ • noun (pl. **amenities**) a useful or desirable feature of a place.
– ORIGIN Latin *amoenitas*, from *amoenus* 'pleasant'.
amenorrhoea /əmennəreeə/ (US **amenorrhea**) • noun abnormal failure to menstruate.
Amerasian /ammərayzh'n, -sh'n/ • adjective having one American and one Asian parent. • noun an Amerasian person.
American • adjective relating to the United States or to the continents of America. • noun a person from the United States or any of the countries of North, South, or Central America.
– DERIVATIVES **Americanize** (also **Americanise**) verb.
Americana /əmerrikaanə/ • plural noun things associated with the United States.
American dream • noun the ideal of equality of opportunity associated with the US.
American football • noun a kind of football played in the US with an oval ball on a field marked out as a gridiron.
American Indian • noun a member of the indigenous peoples of America, especially North America.
– USAGE **American Indian** has been steadily replaced in the US by the term **Native American**, especially in official contexts. However, **American Indian** is still widespread in general use even in the US, and is generally acceptable to American Indians themselves.
Americanism • noun **1** a word or phrase used or originating in the US. **2** the qualities typical of America and Americans.
americium /ammərissiəm/ • noun a radioactive metallic chemical element made by high-energy atomic collisions.
– ORIGIN from *America*, where it was first made.
Amerindian /ammərindiən/ (also **Amerind** /ammərind/) • noun & adjective another term for AMERICAN INDIAN.
amethyst /ammәthist/ • noun a precious stone consisting of a violet or purple variety of quartz.
– ORIGIN Greek *amethustos* 'not drunken' (because the stone was believed to prevent intoxication).
Amharic /amharrik/ • noun the Semitic official language of Ethiopia.
– ORIGIN from *Amhara*, a region of central Ethiopia.
amiable • adjective friendly and pleasant in manner.
– DERIVATIVES **amiability** noun **amiably** adverb.
– ORIGIN Old French, from Latin *amicabilis* 'friendly, amicable'.
amicable /ammikəb'l/ • adjective friendly and without disagreement.
– DERIVATIVES **amicably** adverb.
– ORIGIN Latin *amicabilis*, from *amicus* 'friend'.
amice /ammiss/ • noun a white cloth worn on the neck and shoulders by a priest celebrating the Eucharist.
– ORIGIN Latin *amicia*.
amid • preposition surrounded by; in the middle of.
amide /aymid, ammid/ • noun Chemistry **1** an organic compound containing the group $-C(O)NH_2$. **2** a salt-like compound containing the anion NH_2^-.
– ORIGIN from AMMONIA.
amidships (US also **amidship**) • adverb & adjective in the middle of a ship.
amidst • preposition literary variant of AMID.
amigo /əmeegō/ • noun (pl. **amigos**) informal, chiefly N. Amer. a friend.
– ORIGIN Spanish.
amine /aymeen/ • noun Chemistry an organic compound derived from ammonia by replacement of one or more hydrogen atoms

Thesaurus

in a dilemma, on the horns of a dilemma, in a quandary, on the fence, hesitating, wavering, vacillating, equivocating, blowing hot and cold; *informal* iffy.
– OPPOSITES unequivocal, certain.
amble • verb STROLL, saunter, wander, ramble, promenade, walk, go for a walk, take a walk; *informal* mosey, tootle; *Brit. informal* pootle, mooch; *formal* perambulate.
ambush • noun *seven soldiers were killed in an ambush* SURPRISE ATTACK, trap; *archaic* ambuscade.
• verb *twenty youths ambushed their patrol car* ATTACK BY SURPRISE, surprise, pounce on, lay a trap for, set an ambush for, lie in wait for, waylay; *N. Amer.* bushwhack; *archaic* ambuscade.
ameliorate • verb IMPROVE, make better, better, make improvements to, enhance, help, benefit, boost, amend; relieve, ease, mitigate; *informal* tweak, patch up.
– OPPOSITES worsen.
amenable • adjective **1** *an amenable child* COMPLIANT, acquiescent, biddable, manageable, controllable, governable, persuadable, tractable, responsive, pliant, malleable, complaisant, easily handled; *rare* persuasible. **2** *many cancers are amenable to treatment* SUSCEPTIBLE, receptive, responsive; *archaic* susceptive.
– OPPOSITES uncooperative.
amend • verb REVISE, alter, change, modify, qualify, adapt, adjust; edit, copy-edit, rewrite, redraft, rephrase, reword, rework, revamp.
amends • plural noun *I wanted to make amends* COMPENSATION, recompense, reparation, restitution, redress, atonement, expiation.
– PHRASES **make amends** COMPENSATE, recompense, indemnify, make it up to; atone for, make up for, make good, expiate.
amenity • noun **1** *basic amenities* FACILITY, service, convenience, resource, appliance, aid, comfort, benefit, advantage. **2** *a loss of amenity* PLEASANTNESS, agreeableness, niceness.
America • noun. See UNITED STATES OF AMERICA.
amiable • adjective FRIENDLY, affable, amicable, cordial; warm, warm-hearted, good-natured, nice, pleasant, agreeable, likeable, genial, good-humoured, charming, easy to get on/along with, companionable, sociable, personable; *informal* chummy; *Brit. informal* matey; *N. Amer. informal* regular.
– OPPOSITES unfriendly, disagreeable.
amicable • adjective FRIENDLY, good-natured, cordial, easy, easy-going, neighbourly, harmonious, cooperative, civilized.
– OPPOSITES unfriendly.
amid • preposition **1** *the jeep was concealed amid pine trees* IN THE MIDDLE OF, surrounded by, among, amongst; *poetic/literary* amidst, in

by organic radicals.
amino acid ● noun any of a class of about twenty organic compounds which form the basic constituents of proteins and contain both acid and amine groups.
amir /əmeer/ ● noun variant spelling of EMIR.
Amish /aamish, ay-/ ● plural noun a strict US Protestant sect living mainly in Pennsylvania and Ohio.
– ORIGIN from the name of the Swiss preacher Jakob *Amman* (*c.*1645–*c.*1730).
amiss ● adjective not quite right; inappropriate. ● adverb wrongly or inappropriately.
– PHRASES **not go amiss** be welcome and useful. **take amiss** be offended by (something said).
– ORIGIN probably from Old Norse, 'so as to miss'.
amity /ammiti/ ● noun friendly relations.
– ORIGIN Old French *amitie*, from Latin *amicus* 'friend'.
ammeter /ammitər/ ● noun an instrument for measuring electric current in amperes.
ammo ● noun informal ammunition.
ammonia /əmōniə/ ● noun a colourless, intensely pungent gas, forming a strongly alkaline solution in water which is used as a cleaning fluid.
– DERIVATIVES **ammoniacal** /ammənīək'l/ adjective.
– ORIGIN from SAL AMMONIAC.
ammonite /ammənīt/ ● noun an extinct marine mollusc with a spiral shell, found as a fossil.
– ORIGIN from Latin *cornu Ammonis* 'horn of Ammon', from the fossil's resemblance to the ram's horn associated with the god Jupiter Ammon.
ammonium /əmōniəm/ ● noun Chemistry the ion NH_4^+, present in solutions of ammonia and in salts derived from ammonia.
ammunition ● noun **1** a supply or quantity of bullets and shells. **2** points used to support one's case in argument.
– ORIGIN from French *la munition* 'the fortification'.
amnesia /amneeziə/ ● noun loss of memory.
– DERIVATIVES **amnesiac** noun & adjective **amnesic** adjective & noun.
– ORIGIN Greek, 'forgetfulness'.
amnesty ● noun (pl. **amnesties**) **1** an official pardon for people convicted of political offences. **2** a period where no action is taken against people admitting to particular offences. ● verb (**amnesties**, **amnestied**) grant an amnesty to.
– ORIGIN Greek *amnēstia* 'forgetfulness'.
amniocentesis /amniōsenteessiss/ ● noun (pl. **amniocenteses** /amniōsenteeseez/) the sampling of amniotic fluid to check for abnormalities in the fetus.
– ORIGIN from AMNION + Greek *kentēsis* 'pricking'.
amnion /amniən/ ● noun (pl. **amnions** or **amnia**) the innermost membrane surrounding an embryo.
– DERIVATIVES **amniotic** adjective.
– ORIGIN Greek, 'caul'.
amniotic fluid ● noun the fluid surrounding a fetus within the amnion.
amoeba /əmeebə/ (US also **ameba**) ● noun (pl. **amoebas** or **amoebae** /əmeebee/) a microscopic single-celled animal which is able to change shape.
– DERIVATIVES **amoebic** adjective **amoeboid** adjective.
– ORIGIN from Greek *amoibē* 'change, alternation'.
amok /əmok/ (also **amuck**) ● adverb (in phrase **run amok**) behave uncontrollably and disruptively.
– ORIGIN Malay, 'rushing in a frenzy'.
among (chiefly Brit. also **amongst**) ● preposition **1** surrounded by; in the middle of. **2** included or occurring in. **3** shared by; between.
– ORIGIN Old English.
amontillado /əmontilaadō/ ● noun (pl. **amontillados**) a medium dry sherry.
– ORIGIN Spanish, from *Montilla*, a town in southern Spain.
amoral /aymorrəl/ ● adjective having no moral sense; unconcerned with right or wrong.
– DERIVATIVES **amoralist** noun **amorality** noun.
amorous ● adjective showing or feeling sexual desire.
– DERIVATIVES **amorously** adverb **amorousness** noun.
– ORIGIN Latin *amorosus*, from *amor* 'love'.
amorphous /əmorfəss/ ● adjective **1** without a definite shape or form. **2** technical not crystalline.
– ORIGIN from Greek *a-* 'without' + *morphē* 'form'.
amortize /əmortīz/ (also **amortise**) ● verb gradually write off (a cost) or reduce (a debt).
– DERIVATIVES **amortization** noun.
– ORIGIN Old French *amortir*, from Latin *mors* 'death'.
amount ● noun **1** the total number, size, value, or extent of something. **2** a quantity. ● verb (**amount to**) **1** come to be (a total) when added together. **2** be the equivalent of.
– ORIGIN from Old French *amont* 'upward', from Latin *ad montem*.
amour /əmoor/ ● noun a lover or love affair, especially a secret one.
– ORIGIN Old French, from Latin *amor* 'love'.
amour propre /amoor proprə/ ● noun self-respect.
– ORIGIN French.
amp[1] ● noun short for AMPERE.
amp[2] ● noun informal short for AMPLIFIER.
Ampakine /ampəkīn/ ● noun (trademark in the US) any of a class of synthetic compounds which facilitate transmission of nerve impulses in the brain and appear to improve memory and learning capacity.
– ORIGIN from *AMPA* (an acronym denoting certain receptors in the brain) + Greek *kinein* 'to move'.
amperage /ampərij/ ● noun the strength of an electric current in amperes.
ampere /ampair/ ● noun the SI base unit of electric current, equal to a flow of one coulomb per second.

Thesaurus

the midst of. **2** *the truce collapsed amid fears of a revolt* AT A TIME OF, in an atmosphere of, against a background of; as a result of.
amiss ● adjective *an inspection revealed nothing amiss* WRONG, awry, faulty, out of order, defective, unsatisfactory, incorrect; inappropriate, improper.
– OPPOSITES right, in order.
– PHRASES **not come/go amiss** BE WELCOME, be appropriate, be useful. **take something amiss** BE OFFENDED, take offence, be upset.
amity ● noun FRIENDSHIP, friendliness, harmony, harmoniousness, understanding, accord, cooperation, amicableness, goodwill, cordiality, warmth; formal concord.
– OPPOSITES animosity, enmity.
ammunition ● noun *police seized arms and ammunition* BULLETS, shells, projectiles, missiles, rounds, shot, slugs, cartridges, munitions; informal ammo.
amnesty ● noun *an amnesty for political prisoners* PARDON, pardoning, reprieve; release, discharge; informal let-off.
● verb *the guerrillas were amnestied* PARDON, grant an amnesty to, reprieve; release, discharge, liberate, free, spare; informal let off, let off the hook.
amok ● adverb
– PHRASES **run amok** GO BERSERK, get out of control, rampage, riot, run riot, go on the rampage, behave like a maniac, behave wildly/uncontrollably, become violent/destructive; informal raise hell.
among, amongst ● preposition **1** *you're among friends* SURROUNDED BY, in the company of, amongst, amid, in the middle of; poetic/literary amidst, in the midst of. **2** *a child was among the injured* INCLUDED IN, one/some of, in the group/number of. **3** *he distributed the proceeds among his creditors* BETWEEN, to each of.
– RELATED TERMS inter-.
– PHRASES **between ourselves/yourselves/themselves** JOINTLY, with one another, together, mutually, reciprocally.
amoral ● adjective *their amoral attitude to sex* UNPRINCIPLED, without standards/morals/scruples.
– OPPOSITES principled.
amorous ● adjective LUSTFUL, sexual, erotic, amatory, ardent, passionate, impassioned; in love, enamoured, lovesick; informal lovey-dovey, kissy, smoochy, goo-goo, hot; Brit. informal randy; archaic sportive.
– OPPOSITES unloving.
amorphous ● adjective SHAPELESS, formless, structureless, indeterminate.
– OPPOSITES shaped, definite.
amount ● noun QUANTITY, number, total, aggregate, sum, quota, group, size, mass, weight, volume, bulk, quantum.
– PHRASES **amount to 1** *the bill amounted to £50* ADD UP TO, come to, run to, be, make, total; Brit. tot up to. **2** *the delays amounted to maladministration* CONSTITUTE, comprise, be tantamount, come down, boil down; signify, signal, mean, indicate, suggest, denote, point to, be evidence, be symptomatic; poetic/literary betoken. **3** *her relationships had never amounted to anything significant* BECOME,

a

– ORIGIN named after the French physicist André-Marie *Ampère* (1775–1836).

ampersand /ampərsand/ ● noun the sign &, standing for *and* or the Latin *et.*

– ORIGIN alteration of *and per se and* '& by itself is *and*', chanted as an aid to learning the sign.

amphetamine /amfettəmeen, -min/ ● noun a synthetic drug used illegally as a stimulant.

– ORIGIN abbreviation of its chemical name.

amphibian ● noun **1** a cold-blooded animal with an aquatic larval stage and a terrestrial adult stage, e.g. a frog, toad, or newt. **2** an aircraft or vehicle that can operate on land and on water.

– ORIGIN Greek *amphibion*, from *amphi* 'both' + *bios* 'life'.

amphibious /amfibbiəss/ ● adjective **1** living in or suited for both land and water. **2** (of a military operation) involving forces landed from the sea.

– DERIVATIVES **amphibiously** adverb.

amphibole /amfibōl/ ● noun a mineral with fibrous or columnar crystals, found in many rocks.

– ORIGIN from Latin *amphibolus* 'ambiguous' (because of the varied structure of the minerals).

amphitheatre (US **amphitheater**) ● noun **1** a round building consisting of tiers of seats surrounding a central space for dramatic or sporting events. **2** a semicircular seating gallery in a theatre.

– ORIGIN Greek *amphitheatron*, from *amphi* 'on both sides' + *theatron* 'theatre'.

amphora /amfərə/ ● noun (pl. **amphorae** /amfəree/ or **amphoras**) a tall ancient Greek or Roman jar or jug with two handles and a narrow neck.

– ORIGIN Latin, from Greek *amphi-* 'on both sides' + *phoreus* 'bearer'.

ample ● adjective (**ampler**, **amplest**) **1** enough or more than enough; plentiful. **2** large and accommodating.

– DERIVATIVES **amply** adverb.

– ORIGIN Latin *amplus* 'large, abundant'.

amplifier ● noun **1** an electronic device for increasing the strength of electrical signals. **2** a device of this kind combined with a loudspeaker, used to amplify electric guitars and other musical instruments.

amplify ● verb (**amplifies**, **amplified**) **1** increase the volume or strength of (sound or electrical signals). **2** add detail to (a story or statement).

– DERIVATIVES **amplification** noun.

– ORIGIN Latin *amplificare*, from *amplus* 'large, abundant'.

amplitude ● noun **1** Physics the maximum extent of a vibration or oscillation from the point of equilibrium. **2** breadth, range, or magnitude.

amplitude modulation ● noun the modulation of a wave by varying its amplitude, used as a means of broadcasting an audio signal by radio.

ampoule /ampool/ (US also **ampul** or **ampule** /ampyool/) ● noun a small sealed glass capsule containing a measured quantity of liquid ready for injecting.

– ORIGIN Latin *ampulla* (see AMPULLA).

ampulla /ampoollə/ ● noun (pl. **ampullae** /ampoollee/) **1** a roughly spherical ancient Roman flask with two handles. **2** a flask for holding consecrated oil.

– ORIGIN Latin, related to AMPHORA.

amputate /ampyootayt/ ● verb cut off (a limb) in a surgical operation.

– DERIVATIVES **amputation** noun.

– ORIGIN Latin *amputare* 'lop off'.

amputee ● noun a person who has had a limb amputated.

amuck /əmuk/ ● adverb variant spelling of AMOK.

amulet /amyoolit/ ● noun an ornament or small piece of jewellery worn as protection against evil.

– ORIGIN Latin *amuletum.*

amuse ● verb **1** cause (someone) to laugh or smile. **2** entertain.

– DERIVATIVES **amused** adjective **amusing** adjective.

– ORIGIN Old French *amuser* 'entertain, deceive', from *muser* 'stare stupidly'.

amusement ● noun **1** the state of being amused. **2** the provision or enjoyment of entertainment. **3** Brit. a game machine or other device for providing entertainment.

amusement arcade ● noun Brit. an indoor area containing coin-operated game machines.

amyl /aymīl, ammil/ ● noun Chemistry the straight-chain pentyl radical $-C_5H_{11}$.

– ORIGIN from Latin *amylum* 'starch'.

amylase /ammilayz/ ● noun an enzyme found chiefly in saliva and pancreatic fluid, that converts starch into simple sugars.

amyl nitrite ● noun a synthetic liquid that is used in medicine to expand blood vessels and is sometimes inhaled for its stimulatory effects.

an ● determiner the form of 'a' (the indefinite article) used before words beginning with a vowel sound.

– USAGE There is some divergence of opinion over whether to use **a** or **an** before certain words beginning with **h-** when the first syllable is unstressed (eg. **historical** and **hotel**). The form depends on whether the initial **h** is sounded or not: **an** was formerly common because **h** was not usually pronounced for these words. In current English the norm is for the initial **h** to be pronounced, and therefore the indefinite article **a** is used; however, the older form, with the silent **h** and **an**, is still encountered.

an- ● prefix variant spelling of A-[1] before a vowel (as in *anaemia*).

-an ● suffix **1** forming adjectives and nouns, especially from names of places, systems, or zoological classes: *Cuban.* **2** Chemistry forming names of organic compounds, chiefly polysaccharides: *dextran.*

– ORIGIN from Latin *-anus, -ana, -anum.*

ana- (usu. **an-** before a vowel) ● prefix **1** up: *anabatic.* **2** back: *anamnesis.* **3** again: *anabiosis.*

– ORIGIN from Greek *ana* 'up'.

-ana ● suffix forming plural nouns denoting things associated with a person, place, or interest: *Victoriana.*

– ORIGIN from Latin, neuter plural of the adjectival ending *-anus.*

Anabaptism /annəbaptiz'm/ ● noun the doctrine that baptism should only be administered to believing adults.

– DERIVATIVES **Anabaptist** noun & adjective.

anabolic steroid ● noun a synthetic hormone used to promote muscle growth and illegally to enhance performance in sport.

anabolism /ənabbəliz'm/ ● noun Biochemistry the synthesis of complex molecules in living organisms from simpler ones together with the storage of energy. The opposite of CATABOLISM.

Thesaurus

grow/develop into, prove to be, turn out to be. **the full amount** THE GRAND TOTAL, the total, the aggregate; *informal* the whole caboodle/shebang, the full nine yards.

ample ● adjective **1** *there is ample time for discussion* ENOUGH, sufficient, adequate, plenty of, more than enough, enough and to spare. **2** *an ample supply of wine* PLENTIFUL, abundant, copious, profuse, rich, lavish, liberal, generous, bountiful, large, huge, great, bumper; *informal* a gogo, galore; *poetic/literary* plenteous. **3** *his ample tunic* SPACIOUS, capacious, roomy, sizeable; voluminous, loose-fitting, baggy, sloppy; *formal* commodious.

– OPPOSITES insufficient, meagre.

amplify ● verb **1** *many frogs amplify their voices* MAKE LOUDER, louden, turn up, magnify, intensify, increase, boost, step up, raise. **2** *these notes amplify our statement* EXPAND, enlarge on, elaborate on, add to, supplement, develop, flesh out, add detail to, go into detail about.

– OPPOSITES reduce, quieten.

amplitude ● noun MAGNITUDE, size, volume; extent, range, compass; breadth, width.

amputate ● verb CUT OFF, sever, remove (surgically), saw/chop off.

amulet ● noun LUCKY CHARM, charm, talisman, fetish, mascot, totem, idol, juju; *archaic* periapt.

amuse ● verb **1** *her annoyance simply amused him* ENTERTAIN, make laugh, delight, divert, cheer (up), please, charm, tickle; *informal* tickle pink, crack up; *Brit. informal* crease up. **2** *he amused himself by writing poetry* OCCUPY, engage, busy, employ, distract, absorb, engross, hold someone's attention; interest, entertain, divert.

– OPPOSITES bore.

amusement ● noun **1** *we looked with amusement at the cartoon* MIRTH, merriment, light-heartedness, hilarity, glee, delight, gaiety, joviality, fun; enjoyment, pleasure, high spirits, cheerfulness. **2** *I read the book for amusement* ENTERTAINMENT, pleasure, leisure, relaxation, fun, enjoyment, interest, diversion; *informal* R and R; *N. Amer. informal* rec; *archaic* disport. **3** *a wide range of amusements* ACTIVITY, entertainment, diversion; game, sport.

amusing ● adjective ENTERTAINING, funny, comical, humorous, light-hearted, jocular, witty, mirthful, hilarious, droll, diverting; *infor-*

– DERIVATIVES **anabolic** adjective.
– ORIGIN from Greek *anabolē* 'ascent'.
anachronism /ənakrəniz'm/ ● noun **1** a thing which seems to belong to a period other than the one in which it exists. **2** something placed in the wrong historical period.
– DERIVATIVES **anachronistic** adjective **anachronistically** adverb.
– ORIGIN from Greek *ana-* 'backwards' + *khronos* 'time'.
anaconda /annəkondə/ ● noun a very large snake of the boa family, native to tropical South America.
– ORIGIN Sinhalese, 'whip snake'.
anaemia /əneemiə/ (US **anemia**) ● noun a shortage of red cells or haemoglobin in the blood, resulting in pallor and weariness.
– ORIGIN from Greek *an-* 'without' + *haima* 'blood'.
anaemic (US **anemic**) ● adjective **1** suffering from anaemia. **2** lacking spirit or vitality.
anaerobic /annairōbik/ ● adjective Biology not using oxygen from the air.
– DERIVATIVES **anaerobically** adverb.
anaesthesia /annisstheeziə/ (US **anesthesia**) ● noun insensitivity to pain, especially as induced by an anaesthetic before a surgical operation.
– ORIGIN Greek *anaisthēsia*, from *an-* 'without' + *aisthēsis* 'sensation'.
anaesthesiology /anniss-theeziolləji/ (US **anesthesiology**) ● noun the branch of medicine concerned with anaesthetics.
– DERIVATIVES **anaesthesiologist** noun.
anaesthetic /anissthettik/ (US **anesthetic**) ● noun a drug or gas that causes insensitivity to pain. ● adjective inducing or relating to anaesthesia.
anaesthetist /əneessthətist/ (US **anesthetist**) ● noun a medical specialist who administers anaesthetics.
anaesthetize /əneessthətīz/ (also **anaesthetise**, US **anesthetize**) ● verb administer an anaesthetic to.
– DERIVATIVES **anaesthetization** noun.
anagram /annəgram/ ● noun a word or phrase formed by rearranging the letters of another.
– ORIGIN from Greek *ana-* 'back, anew' + *gramma* 'letter'.
anal /ayn'l/ ● adjective **1** relating to the anus. **2** anal-retentive.
– DERIVATIVES **anally** adverb.
analeptic /annəleptik/ ● adjective (of a drug) reinvigorating and reviving, especially through stimulating the central nervous system. ● noun an analeptic drug.
– ORIGIN Greek *analēptikos*.
analgesia /annəljeeziə/ ● noun Medicine relief of pain.
– ORIGIN Greek *analgēsia* 'painlessness', from *an-* 'not' + *algein* 'feel pain'.
analgesic /annəljeezik/ Medicine ● adjective relieving pain. ● noun a pain-relieving drug.
analogous /ənaləgəss/ ● adjective comparable in certain respects.
– DERIVATIVES **analogously** adverb.
– ORIGIN Greek *analogos* 'proportionate'.
analogue /annəlog/ (US also **analog**) ● noun an analogous person or thing. ● adjective (also **analog**) based on a continuously variable physical quantity (e.g. voltage) rather than digital information.
analogy /ənaləji/ ● noun (pl. **analogies**) **1** a comparison between one thing and another made to explain or clarify. **2** a correspondence or partial similarity.
– DERIVATIVES **analogical** adjective.
anal-retentive ● adjective Psychoanalysis excessively orderly and fussy (supposedly because of conflict over toilet-training in infancy).
analysand /ənalisand/ ● noun a person undergoing psychoanalysis.
analyse (US **analyze**) ● verb **1** examine in detail the elements or structure of. **2** psychoanalyse.
– DERIVATIVES **analysable** adjective **analyser** noun.
analysis /ənalisiss/ ● noun (pl. **analyses** /ənaliseez/) **1** a detailed examination of the elements or structure of something. **2** the separation of something into its constituent elements. **3** psychoanalysis.
– ORIGIN Greek *analusis*, from *analuein* 'unloose'.
analyst ● noun **1** a person who conducts analysis. **2** a psychoanalyst.
analytical (also **analytic**) ● adjective relating to or using analysis or logical reasoning.
– DERIVATIVES **analytically** adverb.
analyze ● verb US spelling of ANALYSE.
anamnesis /annəmneessiss/ ● noun (pl. **anamneses** /annəmneeseez/) recollection, especially of a supposed previous existence.
– ORIGIN Greek, 'remembrance'.
anamorphosis /annəmorfəsiss/ ● noun a distorted image which appears normal when viewed from a particular point or with a suitable mirror or lens.
– DERIVATIVES **anamorphic** adjective.
– ORIGIN Greek *anamorphōsis* 'transformation'.
anaphora /ənaffərə/ ● noun **1** Grammar the use of a word to refer back to a word used earlier, to avoid repetition (for example the verb *do* in *I like it and so do they*). **2** the repetition of a word or phrase at the beginning of successive clauses as a rhetorical device.
– DERIVATIVES **anaphoric** /annəforrik/ adjective.
– ORIGIN Greek, 'repetition'.
anaphylactic shock /annəfilaktik/ ● noun Medicine an extreme allergic reaction to something that the body has become hypersensitive to.
– ORIGIN from Greek *ana-* 'again' + *phulaxis* 'guarding'.
anarchic ● adjective with no controlling rules or principles.
– DERIVATIVES **anarchical** adjective **anarchically** adverb.
anarchism ● noun belief in the abolition of all government and the organization of society on a cooperative basis.
– DERIVATIVES **anarchist** noun & adjective **anarchistic** adjective.
anarchy ● noun **1** a state of disorder due to lack of government or control. **2** a society founded on the principles of anarchism.
– ORIGIN Greek *anarkhia*, from *an-* 'without' + *arkhos* 'chief, ruler'.
Anasazi /annəsaazi/ ● noun (pl. same or **Anasazis**) a member of an ancient American Indian people of the south-western US.
– ORIGIN Navajo, 'ancient one' or 'enemy ancestor'.
anastomosis /ənastəmōsiss/ ● noun (pl. **anastomoses** /ənastəmōseez/) technical a connection between channels, tubes, blood vessels, etc.
– ORIGIN Greek, from *anastomoun* 'provide with a mouth'.
anathema /ənathəmə/ ● noun **1** something that one vehemently dislikes: *racism was anathema to her*. **2** a Church decree excommunicating a person or denouncing a doctrine.
– ORIGIN Greek, 'thing dedicated', (later) 'thing devoted to evil'.
anathematize /ənathəmətīz/ (also **anathematise**) ● verb

Thesaurus

mal wacky, side-splitting, rib-tickling.
– OPPOSITES boring, solemn.
anaemic ● adjective **1** *his anaemic face* COLOURLESS, bloodless, pale, pallid, wan, ashen, grey, sallow, pasty-faced, whey-faced, peaky, sickly, etiolated. **2** *an anaemic description of her feelings* FEEBLE, weak, insipid, wishy-washy, vapid, bland; lame, tame, lacklustre, spiritless, lifeless, ineffective, ineffectual, etiolated; *informal* pathetic.
anaesthetic ● noun NARCOTIC, painkiller, painkilling drug, pain reliever, sedative, anodyne, analgesic; general, local.
analgesic ● adjective PAINKILLING, pain-relieving, anodyne, narcotic, palliative.
analogous ● adjective COMPARABLE, parallel, similar, like, corresponding, related, kindred, equivalent; *formal* cognate.
– OPPOSITES unrelated.
analogy ● noun SIMILARITY, parallel, correspondence, likeness, resemblance, correlation, relation, kinship, equivalence, similitude.
– OPPOSITES dissimilarity.
analyse ● verb EXAMINE, inspect, survey, study, scrutinize, look over; investigate, explore, probe, research, go over (with a fine-tooth comb), review, evaluate, break down, dissect, anatomize.
analysis ● noun EXAMINATION, investigation, inspection, survey, study, scrutiny; exploration, probe, research, review, evaluation, interpretation, anatomization, dissection.
analytical, analytic ● adjective SYSTEMATIC, logical, scientific, methodical, (well) organized, ordered, orderly, meticulous, rigorous.
– OPPOSITES unsystematic.
anarchic ● adjective LAWLESS, without law and order, in disorder/turmoil, unruly, chaotic, turbulent.
– OPPOSITES ordered.
anarchist ● noun NIHILIST, insurgent, agitator, subversive, terrorist, revolutionary, revolutionist, insurrectionist.
anarchy ● noun LAWLESSNESS, nihilism, mobocracy, revolution, in-

a

curse; condemn.

Anatolian /annətōliən/ ● **adjective** relating to Anatolia in western Asia Minor. ● **noun** a person from Anatolia.

anatomize (also **anatomise**) ● **verb** **1** dissect (a body). **2** examine and analyse in detail.

anatomy ● **noun** (pl. **anatomies**) **1** the scientific study of bodily structure. **2** the bodily structure of a person, animal, or plant. **3** a detailed examination or analysis.
– DERIVATIVES **anatomical** adjective **anatomically** adverb **anatomist** noun.
– ORIGIN from Greek *ana-* 'up' + *tomia* 'cutting'.

ANC ● **abbreviation** African National Congress.

-ance ● **suffix** forming nouns: **1** denoting a quality or state: *perseverance.* **2** denoting an action: *utterance.*
– ORIGIN French, from Latin *-antia, -entia.*

ancestor ● **noun** **1** a person, typically one more remote than a grandparent, from whom one is descended. **2** something from which a later species or version has evolved.
– DERIVATIVES **ancestral** adjective **ancestrally** adverb **ancestress** noun.
– ORIGIN Latin *antecessor,* from *antecedere* 'go before'.

ancestry ● **noun** (pl. **ancestries**) a person's ancestors or ethnic origins.

anchor ● **noun** a heavy object used to moor a ship to the sea bottom, typically having a metal shank with a pair of curved, barbed flukes. ● **verb** **1** moor with an anchor. **2** secure firmly in position.
– ORIGIN Greek *ankura.*

anchorage ● **noun** **1** a place where ships may anchor safely. **2** the state of anchoring or being anchored.

anchorite /angkərīt/ ● **noun** historical a religious recluse.
– ORIGIN Greek *anakhōrētēs,* from *anakhōrein* 'retire'.

anchorman (or **anchorwoman**) ● **noun** a person who presents a live television or radio programme involving other contributors.

anchovy /anchəvi, anchōvi/ ● **noun** (pl. **anchovies**) a small fish of the herring family, with a strong flavour.
– ORIGIN Spanish and Portuguese *anchova.*

ancien régime /ONSYAN rez͟heem/ ● **noun** (pl. **anciens régimes** pronunc. same) a political or social system that has been replaced by a more modern one.
– ORIGIN French, 'old rule'.

ancient ● **adjective** **1** belonging to or originating in the very distant past. **2** chiefly humorous very old. ● **noun** **1** archaic or humorous an old man. **2** (**the ancients**) the people of ancient times.
– DERIVATIVES **anciently** adverb.
– ORIGIN Old French *ancien,* from Latin *ante* 'before'.

ancient lights ● **plural noun** (usually treated as sing.) English Law the established right of access to light of a property, used to prevent the construction of buildings which would obstruct such access.

Ancient of Days ● **noun** God.

ancillary /ansillәri/ ● **adjective** **1** providing subsidiary support. **2** additional; supplementary.
– ORIGIN Latin *ancillaris,* from *ancilla* 'maidservant'.

-ancy ● **suffix** forming nouns denoting a quality or state: *expectancy.*
– ORIGIN from Latin *-antia.*

and ● **conjunction** **1** used to connect words, clauses, or sentences. **2** used to connect two identical words to emphasize progressive change or great duration: *getting better and better.* **3** (connecting two numbers) plus. **4** informal (after a verb) to: *try and do it.*
– USAGE As with other conjunctions such as **but** and **because**, it is widely held that it is incorrect to begin a sentence with **and**, the argument being that such a sentence expresses an incomplete thought. It has, however, long been used in this way in both written and spoken English (typically for rhetorical effect), and is quite acceptable.
– ORIGIN Old English.

-and ● **suffix** (forming nouns) denoting a person or thing to be treated in a specified way.
– ORIGIN from Latin gerundive ending *-andus.*

Andalusian /andəlo͞oziən/ ● **noun** a person from Andalusia in southern Spain. ● **adjective** relating to Andalusia.

andante /andantay/ Music ● **adverb & adjective** in a moderately slow tempo. ● **noun** an andante passage.
– ORIGIN Italian, 'going'.

Andean /andeeən, andiən/ ● **adjective** relating to the Andes, a mountain system running the length of the Pacific coast of South America.

andiron /andīrn/ ● **noun** a metal support, typically one of a pair, for wood burning in a fireplace.
– ORIGIN Old French *andier.*

Andorran /andorən/ ● **noun** a person from Andorra, a small autonomous principality in the southern Pyrenees. ● **adjective** relating to Andorra.

andouille /ONdo͞oi/ ● **noun** **1** (in France) a pork sausage made from chitterlings. **2** (in Cajun cooking) a spicy smoked-pork sausage.
– ORIGIN French.

androgen /andrəjən/ ● **noun** a male sex hormone, such as testosterone.
– ORIGIN from Greek *anēr* 'man' + -GEN.

androgyne /andrəjīn/ ● **noun** **1** an androgynous individual. **2** a hermaphrodite.

androgynous /androjinəss/ ● **adjective** partly male and partly female; of indeterminate sex.
– DERIVATIVES **androgyny** noun.
– ORIGIN from Greek *anēr* 'man' + *gunē* 'woman'.

android /androyd/ ● **noun** (in science fiction) a robot with a human appearance.

-ane ● **suffix** Chemistry forming names of saturated hydrocarbons.

anecdotage /annikdōtij/ ● **noun** **1** anecdotes collectively. **2** humorous old age in which anecdotes are told excessively.

anecdote /annikdōt/ ● **noun** **1** a short entertaining story about a real incident or person. **2** an account regarded as unreliable or as being hearsay.
– DERIVATIVES **anecdotal** adjective **anecdotalist** noun **anecdotally** adverb.
– ORIGIN from Greek *anekdota* 'things unpublished'.

Thesaurus

surrection, disorder, chaos, tumult, turmoil.
– OPPOSITES government, order.

anathema ● **noun** **1** *racial hatred was anathema to her* ABHORRENT, hateful, repugnant, repellent, offensive; ABOMINATION, outrage, bane, bugbear, bête noire. **2** *the Vatican Council issued an anathema* CURSE, ban, excommunication, proscription, debarment, denunciation.

anatomy ● **noun** **1** *a cat's anatomy* STRUCTURE, make-up, composition, constitution, form. **2** *an anatomy of society* ANALYSIS, examination, inspection, survey, study, investigation, review, evaluation.

ancestor ● **noun** **1** *he could trace his ancestors back to King James I* FOREBEAR, forefather, predecessor, antecedent, progenitor, primogenitor. **2** *the instrument is an ancestor of the lute* FORERUNNER, precursor, predecessor.
– OPPOSITES descendant, successor.

ancestral ● **adjective** INHERITED, hereditary, familial.

ancestry ● **noun** ANCESTORS, forebears, forefathers, progenitors, antecedents; family tree; lineage, genealogy, roots.

anchor ● **noun** **1** *the anchor of the new coalition* MAINSTAY, cornerstone, linchpin, bulwark, foundation. **2** *a CBS news anchor* PRESENTER, announcer, anchorman, anchorwoman, broadcaster. ● **verb** **1** *the ship was anchored in the bay* MOOR, berth, be at anchor; *archaic* harbour. **2** *the fish anchors itself to the coral* SECURE, fasten, attach, affix, fix.

anchorage ● **noun** MOORINGS, moorage, roads, roadstead, harbourage.

anchorite ● **noun** *(historical)* HERMIT, recluse, ascetic; *historical* stylite; *archaic* eremite.

ancient ● **adjective** **1** *ancient civilizations* OF LONG AGO, early, prehistoric, primeval, primordial, primitive; *poetic/literary* of yore; *archaic* foregone. **2** *an ancient custom* OLD, very old, age-old, archaic, antediluvian, time-worn, time-honoured. **3** *I feel positively ancient* ANTIQUATED, aged, elderly, decrepit, antediluvian, in one's dotage; old-fashioned, out of date, outmoded, démodé, passé; *informal* out of the ark; *Brit. informal* past its/one's sell-by date.
– RELATED TERMS archaeo-, palaeo-.
– OPPOSITES recent, contemporary.

ancillary ● **adjective** ADDITIONAL, auxiliary, supporting, helping, extra, supplementary, accessory; *Medicine* adjuvant; *rare* adminicular.
– RELATED TERMS para-.

and ● **conjunction** TOGETHER WITH, along with, with, as well as, in addition to, also, too; besides, furthermore; *informal* plus.

anechoic /annikōik/ ● adjective technical free from echo; tending to absorb or deaden sound.
anemia ● noun US spelling of ANAEMIA.
anemic ● adjective US spelling of ANAEMIC.
anemometer /annimommitər/ ● noun an instrument for measuring the speed of the wind or other flowing gas.
– ORIGIN from Greek *anemos* 'wind'.
anemone /ənemməni/ ● noun **1** a plant with brightly coloured flowers and deeply divided leaves. **2** a sea anemone.
– ORIGIN from Greek, 'windflower', apparently because the flowers open only when the wind blows.
aneroid /annəroyd/ ● adjective (of a barometer) measuring air pressure by the action of the air in deforming the elastic lid of a box containing a vacuum.
– ORIGIN from Greek *a-* 'without' + *nēros* 'water'.
anesthesia etc. ● noun US spelling of ANAESTHESIA etc.
aneurysm /anyooriz'm/ (also **aneurism**) ● noun Medicine an excessive localized swelling of the wall of an artery.
– DERIVATIVES **aneurysmal** adjective.
– ORIGIN Greek *aneurusma* 'dilatation'.
anew ● adverb chiefly literary **1** in a new or different way. **2** once more; again.
angel ● noun **1** a spiritual being believed to act as an attendant or messenger of God, conventionally represented as being of human form with wings. **2** a person of great beauty, kindness, or virtue. **3** informal a financial backer. **4** a former English coin bearing the figure of the archangel Michael killing a dragon.
– PHRASES **on the side of the angels** on the side of what is right.
– ORIGIN Greek *angelos* 'messenger'.
angel cake (N. Amer. also **angel food cake**) ● noun a very light, pale sponge cake typically baked in a ring shape and covered with soft icing.
angel dust ● noun informal the hallucinogenic drug phencyclidine hydrochloride.
Angeleno /anjəleenō/ (also **Los Angeleno**) ● noun (pl. **Angelenos**) a person from Los Angeles.
– ORIGIN American Spanish.
angelfish ● noun a fish with a deep, laterally compressed body and large dorsal and anal fins, often vividly coloured or patterned.
angel hair ● noun a type of pasta consisting of very fine long strands.
angelic ● adjective **1** relating to angels. **2** exceptionally beautiful, innocent, or kind.
– DERIVATIVES **angelically** adverb.
angelica /anjellikə/ ● noun a tall aromatic plant, the candied stalks of which are used in confectionery and cake decoration.
– ORIGIN from Latin *herba angelica* 'angelic herb', so named because it was believed to be effective against poisoning and disease.
angelus /anjələss/ ● noun **1** a Roman Catholic devotion commemorating the Incarnation of Jesus and including the Hail Mary. **2** a ringing of bells announcing this.
– ORIGIN from the Latin phrase *Angelus domini* 'the angel of the Lord', the opening words of the devotion.
anger ● noun a strong feeling of annoyance, displeasure, or hostility. ● verb provoke anger in.
– ORIGIN Old Norse, 'grief'.
angina /anjīnə/ (also **angina pectoris** /pektəriss/) ● noun a condition marked by severe pain in the chest, arising from an inadequate blood supply to the heart.
– ORIGIN Latin, 'quinsy', from Greek *ankhonē* 'strangling'; *pectoris* means 'of the chest' in Latin.
angiography /anjiogrəfi/ ● noun radiography of blood or lymph vessels, carried out after introduction of a radiopaque substance.
– DERIVATIVES **angiogram** noun **angiographic** adjective.
– ORIGIN from Greek *angeion* 'vessel'.
angioplasty /anjiōplasti/ ● noun (pl. **angioplasties**) a surgical operation to repair or unblock a blood vessel, especially a coronary artery.
angiosperm ● noun Botany a plant of a large group that have flowers and produce seeds enclosed within a carpel, including herbaceous plants, shrubs, grasses, and most trees. Compare with GYMNOSPERM.
Angle ● noun a member of an ancient Germanic people who came to England in the 5th century AD and founded kingdoms in Mercia, Northumbria, and East Anglia.
– ORIGIN Latin *Anglus* 'inhabitant of *Angul*' (in northern Germany); related to ANGLE² (because Angul's shape resembled a fishing hook) and ENGLISH.
angle¹ ● noun **1** the space (usually measured in degrees) between two intersecting lines or surfaces at or close to the point where they meet. **2** a corner, especially an external projection or internal recess. **3** a position from which something is viewed or along which it travels or acts. **4** a particular way of approaching an issue or problem. ● verb **1** direct, move, or incline at an angle. **2** present (information) to reflect a particular view or have a particular focus.
– DERIVATIVES **angled** adjective.
– ORIGIN Latin *angulus* 'corner'.
angle² ● verb **1** fish with a rod and line. **2** seek something desired by indirectly prompting someone to offer it: *she was angling for sympathy.*
– DERIVATIVES **angler** noun **angling** noun.
– ORIGIN Old English.
angle bracket ● noun **1** either of a pair of marks in the form < >, used to enclose words or figures so as to separate them from their context. **2** another term for BRACKET (in sense 3).
angle grinder ● noun a device with a rotating abrasive disc, used to grind, polish, or cut metal and other materials.
angle iron ● noun a constructional material consisting of pieces of iron or steel with an L-shaped cross section, able to be bolted together.
angle of incidence ● noun Physics the angle which an incident line or ray makes with a perpendicular to the surface at the point of incidence.
anglepoise ● noun trademark a type of desk lamp with a jointed arm and counterbalancing springs that hold it in any position to which it is adjusted.
anglerfish ● noun a marine fish that lures prey within reach of its mouth with a fleshy filament arising from its snout.
Anglican ● adjective relating to the Church of England or any Church in communion with it. ● noun a member of any of these Churches.

Thesaurus

anecdotal ● adjective **1** *anecdotal evidence* UNSCIENTIFIC, unreliable, based on hearsay. **2** *her book is anecdotal and chatty* NARRATIVE, full of stories.
anecdote ● noun STORY, tale, narrative; urban myth; *informal* yarn.
anew ● adverb AGAIN, afresh, once more/again, over again.
angel ● noun **1** *God sent an angel* MESSENGER OF GOD, divine/heavenly messenger, divine being. **2** *she's an absolute angel* PARAGON OF VIRTUE, saint; gem, treasure, darling, dear; *informal* star; *Brit. informal, dated* brick. **3** *(informal) a financial angel* BACKER, sponsor, benefactor, promoter, patron.
– OPPOSITES devil.
angelic ● adjective **1** *angelic beings* DIVINE, heavenly, celestial, holy, seraphic; *poetic/literary* empyrean. **2** *Sophie's angelic appearance* INNOCENT, pure, virtuous, good, saintly, wholesome.
– OPPOSITES demonic, infernal.
anger ● noun *his face was livid with anger* ANNOYANCE, vexation, exasperation, crossness, irritation, irritability, indignation, pique; rage, fury, wrath, outrage, irascibility, ill temper/humour; *informal* aggravation; *poetic/literary* ire, choler.
– RELATED TERMS irascible.
– OPPOSITES pleasure, good humour.
● verb *she was angered by his terse reply* ANNOY, irritate, exasperate, irk, vex, put out; enrage, incense, infuriate, make someone's hackles rise; *Brit.* rub up the wrong way; *informal* make someone's blood boil, get someone's back up, make someone see red, get someone's dander up, rattle someone's cage; aggravate, get someone, rile, hack off; *Brit. informal* wind up, nark; *N. Amer. informal* tee off, tick off, burn up, gravel; *informal, dated* give someone the pip.
– OPPOSITES pacify, placate.
angle¹ ● noun **1** *the wall is sloping at an angle of 33°* GRADIENT, slant, inclination. **2** *the angle of the roof* CORNER, intersection, point, apex. **3** *consider the problem from a different angle* PERSPECTIVE, point of view, viewpoint, standpoint, position, aspect, slant, direction.
● verb **1** *Anna angled her camera towards the tree* TILT, slant, direct, turn. **2** *angle your answer so that it is relevant* PRESENT, slant, orient, twist, bias.
angle² ● verb *he was angling for an invitation* TRY TO GET, seek to

a

– DERIVATIVES **Anglicanism** noun.
– ORIGIN Latin *Anglicanus*, from *Anglus* 'Angle'.
Anglicism ● noun **1** a word or phrase that is peculiar to British English. **2** the quality of being typically English or of favouring English things.
anglicize (also **anglicise**) ● verb make English in form or character.
– DERIVATIVES **anglicization** noun.
Anglo- ● combining form **1** English: *anglophone*. **2** English or British and ...: *Anglo-Latin*.
– ORIGIN from Latin *Anglus* 'English'.
Anglo-Catholicism ● noun a tradition within the Anglican Church which is close to Catholicism in its doctrine and worship and is broadly identified with High Church Anglicanism.
– DERIVATIVES **Anglo-Catholic** adjective & noun.
Anglocentric ● adjective centred on or considered in terms of England or Britain.
Anglo-Indian ● adjective **1** relating to or involving both Britain and India. **2** of mixed British and Indian parentage. **3** chiefly historical of British descent or birth but having lived long in India. ● noun an Anglo-Indian person.
Anglo-Irish ● adjective **1** relating to both Britain and Ireland (or specifically the Republic of Ireland). **2** of mixed English and Irish parentage. **3** of English descent but born or resident in Ireland.
Anglophile ● noun a person who is fond of or greatly admires England or Britain.
– DERIVATIVES **Anglophilia** noun.
anglophone ● adjective English-speaking.
Anglo-Saxon ● noun **1** a Germanic inhabitant of England between the 5th century and the Norman Conquest. **2** a person of English descent. **3** chiefly N. Amer. any white, English-speaking person. **4** the Old English language. **5** informal plain English, in particular vulgar slang.
Angolan /anggōlən/ ● noun a person from Angola, a country in SW Africa. ● adjective relating to Angola.
angora /anggorə/ ● noun **1** a cat, goat, or rabbit of a long-haired breed. **2** a fabric made from the hair of the angora goat or rabbit.
– ORIGIN from *Angora* (now Ankara) in Turkey.
angostura /anggəstyoorə/ ● noun **1** an aromatic bitter bark from South America, used as a flavouring. **2** (also **Angostura bitters** trademark) a kind of tonic.
– ORIGIN from *Angostura* (now Ciudad Bolívar) in Venezuela.
angry ● adjective (**angrier**, **angriest**) **1** feeling or showing anger. **2** (of a wound or sore) red and inflamed.
– DERIVATIVES **angrily** adverb.
angst /angst/ ● noun a profound feeling of generalized anxiety or dread.
– DERIVATIVES **angsty** adjective.
– ORIGIN German, 'fear'.
angstrom /angstrəm/ (also **ångström** /ongstrerm/) ● noun Physics a unit of length equal to one hundred-millionth of a centimetre, 10^{-10} metre.
– ORIGIN named after the Swedish physicist A. J. *Ångström* (1814–74).
anguish ● noun severe mental or physical pain or suffering.
– ORIGIN Latin *angustia* 'tightness', (in plural) 'straits, distress'.
anguished ● adjective experiencing or expressing anguish.
angular /anggyoolər/ ● adjective **1** having angles or sharp corners. **2** (of a person) lean and having a prominent bone structure. **3** placed or directed at an angle. **4** Physics measured with reference to angles, especially those associated with rotation.
– DERIVATIVES **angularity** noun **angularly** adverb.
anhydrous /anhīdrəss/ ● adjective Chemistry containing no water.
– ORIGIN from Greek *an-* 'without' + *hudōr* 'water'.
aniline /annileen, -lin/ ● noun an oily liquid found in coal tar, used in the manufacture of dyes, drugs, and plastics.
– ORIGIN from an Arabic word meaning 'indigo' (from which it was originally obtained).
anima /annimə/ ● noun Psychoanalysis **1** (in Jungian psychology) the feminine part of a man's personality. Compare with ANIMUS. **2** the part of the psyche which is directed inwards, in touch with the subconscious. Compare with PERSONA.
– ORIGIN Latin, 'mind, soul'.
animadvert /annimədvert/ ● verb (**animadvert on/upon/against**) formal criticize or censure.
– DERIVATIVES **animadversion** noun.
– ORIGIN Latin *animadvertere*, from *animus* 'mind' + *advertere* 'to turn'.
animal ● noun **1** a living organism which feeds on organic matter, has specialized sense organs and nervous system, and is able to move about and to respond rapidly to stimuli. **2** a mammal, as opposed to a bird, reptile, fish, or insect. **3** a very cruel, violent, or uncivilized person. **4** (before another noun) physical rather than spiritual or intellectual: *animal lust*. **5** a particular type of person or thing: *a political animal*.
– ORIGIN from Latin *animalis* 'having breath'.
animalcule /annimalkyōōl/ ● noun archaic a microscopic animal.
animalism ● noun behaviour characteristic of animals; animality.
– DERIVATIVES **animalistic** adjective.
animality ● noun human behaviour characteristic of animals, especially in being physical and instinctive.
animal liberation ● noun the freeing of animals from exploitation and cruel treatment by humans.
animal magnetism ● noun **1** a quality of powerful sexual attractiveness. **2** historical a supposed physical force to which the action of mesmerism was ascribed.
animate ● verb /annimayt/ **1** bring to life or activity. **2** give (a film or character) the appearance of movement using animation. ● adjective /annimət/ alive; having life.
– DERIVATIVES **animator** noun.
– ORIGIN Latin *animare*, from *anima* 'life, soul'.

Thesaurus

obtain, fish for, hope for, be after.
angler ● noun FISHERMAN, rod; *archaic* fisher.
angry ● adjective **1** *Vivienne got angry* IRATE, annoyed, cross, vexed, irritated, indignant, irked; furious, enraged, infuriated, in a temper, incensed, raging, incandescent, fuming, seething, beside oneself, outraged; *informal* (hopping) mad, wild, livid, apoplectic, as cross as two sticks, hot under the collar, up in arms, foaming at the mouth, steamed up, in a lather/paddy, fit to be tied; *Brit. informal* aerated, shirty; *N. Amer. informal* sore, bent out of shape, teed off, ticked off; *Austral./NZ informal* ropeable, snaky; *poetic/literary* wrathful; *archaic* wroth. **2** *an angry debate* HEATED, passionate, stormy, 'lively'; bad-tempered, ill-tempered, acrimonious, bitter. **3** *angry sores* INFLAMED, red, swollen, sore, painful.
– OPPOSITES pleased, good-humoured.
– PHRASES **get angry** LOSE ONE'S TEMPER, become enraged, go into a rage, go berserk, flare up; *informal* go mad/crazy/wild, go bananas, hit the roof, go through the roof, go up the wall, see red, go off the deep end, fly off the handle, blow one's top, blow a fuse/gasket, lose one's rag, flip (one's lid), have a fit, foam at the mouth, explode, go non-linear, go ballistic; *Brit. informal* go spare, do one's nut; *N. Amer. informal* flip one's wig, blow one's lid/stack, have a conniption fit.
angst ● noun ANXIETY, fear, apprehension, worry, foreboding, trepidation, malaise, disquiet, disquietude, unease, uneasiness.
anguish ● noun AGONY, pain, torment, torture, suffering, distress, angst, misery, sorrow, grief, heartache, desolation, despair; *poetic/literary* dolour.
– OPPOSITES happiness.
anguished ● adjective AGONIZED, tormented, tortured; grief-stricken, wretched, heartbroken, desolate, devastated; *informal* cut up; *poetic/literary* dolorous.
angular ● adjective **1** *an angular shape* SHARP-CORNERED, pointed, V-shaped, Y-shaped. **2** *an angular face* BONY, raw-boned, lean, rangy, spare, thin, gaunt.
– OPPOSITES rounded, curving.
animal ● noun **1** *endangered animals* CREATURE, beast, living thing; (**animals**) wildlife, fauna; *N. Amer. informal* critter. **2** *the man was an animal* BRUTE, beast, monster, devil, demon, fiend; *informal* swine, bastard, pig.
– RELATED TERMS ZOO-.
● adjective **1** *animal life* ZOOLOGICAL, animalistic; *rare* zoic. **2** *a grunt of animal passion* CARNAL, fleshly, bodily, physical; brutish, unrefined, uncultured, coarse.
animate ● verb *a sense of excitement animated the whole school* ENLIVEN, vitalize, breathe (new) life into, energize, invigorate, revive, vivify, liven up; inspire, inspirit, exhilarate, thrill, excite, fire, arouse, rouse; *N. Amer.* light a fire under; *informal* buck up, pep up, give someone a buzz.
– OPPOSITES depress.
● adjective *an animate being* LIVING, alive, live, breathing; *archaic*

a

animated ● adjective **1** lively. **2** (of a film) made using animation.
– DERIVATIVES **animatedly** adverb.
animation ● noun **1** the state of being full of life or vigour. **2** the technique of filming a sequence of drawings or positions of models to create an illusion of movement. **3** (also **computer animation**) the creation of moving images by means of a computer.
animatronics /annimətronniks/ ● plural noun (treated as sing.) the creation and operation of lifelike robots, especially for use in films.
– DERIVATIVES **animatronic** adjective.
anime /annimay, annimə/ ● noun Japanese animated films, typically having a science fiction theme.
– ORIGIN Japanese.
animism /annimiz'm/ ● noun the belief that plants and inanimate objects have souls.
– DERIVATIVES **animist** noun **animistic** adjective.
– ORIGIN from Latin *anima* 'life, soul'.
animosity /annimossiti/ ● noun (pl. **animosities**) strong hostility.
– ORIGIN Latin *animositas*, from *animus* 'spirit, mind'.
animus /annimәss/ ● noun **1** hostility or ill feeling. **2** Psychoanalysis (in Jungian psychology) the masculine part of a woman's personality. Compare with ANIMA.
– ORIGIN Latin, 'spirit, mind'.
anion /anniən/ ● noun Chemistry a negatively charged ion. The opposite of CATION.
– DERIVATIVES **anionic** adjective.
– ORIGIN from ANODE + ION.
anise /anniss/ ● noun a plant grown for its aromatic seeds (aniseed).
– ORIGIN Greek *anison* 'anise, dill'.
aniseed ● noun the seed of the plant anise, used as a flavouring.
ankh /angk/ ● noun an ancient Egyptian symbol of life in the shape of a cross with a loop instead of the top arm.
– ORIGIN Egyptian, 'life, soul'.
ankle ● noun **1** the joint connecting the foot with the leg. **2** the narrow part of the leg between this and the calf.
– ORIGIN Old English.
anklet ● noun a chain or band worn round the ankle.
ankylosaur /angkiləsor/ ● noun a heavily built plant-eating dinosaur of the Cretaceous period, armoured with bony plates.
– ORIGIN from Greek *ankulos* 'crooked' + *sauros* 'lizard'.
ankylosing spondylitis ● noun a form of spinal arthritis chiefly affecting young males.
ankylosis /angkilōsiss/ ● noun Medicine abnormal stiffening and immobility of a joint due to fusion of the bones.
– ORIGIN from Greek *ankuloun* 'make crooked'.
anna ● noun a former monetary unit of India and Pakistan, equal to one sixteenth of a rupee.
– ORIGIN Hindi.
annal /ann'l/ ● noun **1** (**annals**) a history of events year by year. **2** a record of the events of one year.
– DERIVATIVES **annalist** noun.
– ORIGIN from Latin *annales libri* 'yearly books'.
annatto /ənattō/ ● noun (pl. **annattos**) an orange-red dye obtained from a tropical fruit, used for colouring foods.
– ORIGIN Carib.
anneal /əneel/ ● verb heat (metal or glass) and allow it to cool slowly, so as to toughen it.
– ORIGIN Old English, 'set on fire'.
annelid /annəlid/ ● noun a worm with a segmented body, such as an earthworm or leech.
– ORIGIN from Latin *annelus* 'small ring'.
annex ● verb /aneks/ **1** seize (territory) and add it to one's own. **2** add as an extra or subordinate part. ● noun /anneks/ (chiefly Brit. also **annexe**) (pl. **annexes**) **1** a building joined to or associated with a main building. **2** an addition to a document.
– DERIVATIVES **annexation** noun.
– ORIGIN Latin *annectere* 'connect'.
annihilate /ənīilayt/ ● verb **1** destroy completely. **2** informal defeat completely.
– DERIVATIVES **annihilation** noun **annihilator** noun.
– ORIGIN Latin *annihilare* 'reduce to nothing'.
anniversary ● noun (pl. **anniversaries**) the date on which an event took place in a previous year.
– ORIGIN from Latin *anniversarius* 'returning yearly'.
Anno Domini /annō domminī/ ● adverb full form of AD.
annotate /annətayt/ ● verb add explanatory notes to.
– DERIVATIVES **annotation** noun **annotator** noun.
– ORIGIN Latin *annotare* 'to mark'.
announce ● verb **1** make a public declaration about. **2** be a sign of: *lilies announce the arrival of summer.*
– DERIVATIVES **announcer** noun.
– ORIGIN Latin *annuntiare*, from *nuntius* 'messenger'.
announcement ● noun **1** a public declaration. **2** the action of announcing.
annoy ● verb **1** make slightly angry. **2** pester or harass. **3** archaic harm or attack repeatedly.
– DERIVATIVES **annoyance** noun **annoyed** adjective **annoying** adjective.
– ORIGIN Old French *anoier*, from Latin *mihi in odio est* 'it is hateful to me'.

Thesaurus

quick.
– OPPOSITES inanimate.
animated ● adjective LIVELY, spirited, high-spirited, energetic, full of life, excited, enthusiastic, eager, alive, active, vigorous, vibrant, vital, vivacious, buoyant, exuberant, ebullient, effervescent, bouncy, bubbly, perky; *informal* bright-eyed and bushy-tailed, full of beans, bright and breezy, chirpy, chipper, peppy.
– OPPOSITES lethargic, lifeless.
animosity ● noun ANTIPATHY, hostility, friction, antagonism, enmity, animus, bitterness, rancour, resentment, dislike, ill feeling/will, bad blood, hatred, hate, loathing; malice, spite, spitefulness.
– OPPOSITES goodwill, friendship.
annals ● plural noun RECORDS, archives, chronicles, accounts, registers; *Law* muniments.
annex ● verb **1** *ten amendments were annexed to the constitution* ADD, append, attach, tack on, tag on. **2** *Charlemagne annexed northern Italy* TAKE OVER, take possession of, appropriate, seize, conquer, occupy.
● noun (also **annexe**) EXTENSION, addition; wing; *N. Amer.* ell.
annexation ● noun SEIZURE, occupation, invasion, conquest, takeover, appropriation.
annihilate ● verb DESTROY, wipe out, obliterate, wipe off the face of the earth; kill, slaughter, exterminate, eliminate, liquidate; *informal* take out, rub out, snuff out, waste.
– OPPOSITES create.
annotate ● verb COMMENT ON, add notes/footnotes to, gloss, interpret; *archaic* margin.
annotation ● noun NOTE, notation, comment, gloss, footnote; commentary, explanation, interpretation.
announce ● verb **1** *their financial results were announced* MAKE PUBLIC, make known, report, declare, state, give out, notify, publicize, broadcast, publish, advertise, circulate, proclaim, blazon abroad. **2** *Victor announced the guests* INTRODUCE, present, name. **3** *strains of music announced her arrival* SIGNAL, indicate, give notice of, herald, proclaim; *poetic/literary* betoken.
announcement ● noun **1** *an announcement by the Minister* STATEMENT, report, declaration, proclamation, pronouncement, rescript; bulletin, communiqué; *N. Amer.* advisory. **2** *the announcement of the decision* DECLARATION, notification, reporting, publishing, broadcasting, proclamation; *archaic* annunciation.
announcer ● noun PRESENTER, anchorman, anchorwoman, anchor; newsreader, newscaster, broadcaster.
annoy ● verb IRRITATE, vex, make angry/cross, anger, exasperate, irk, gall, pique, put out, antagonize, nettle, get on someone's nerves, ruffle someone's feathers, make someone's hackles rise; *Brit.* rub up the wrong way; *informal* aggravate, peeve, hassle, miff, rile, needle, get (to), bug, hack off, get up someone's nose, get someone's goat, get someone's back up, give someone the hump, drive mad/crazy, drive round the bend/twist, drive up the wall, get someone's dander up; *Brit. informal* wind up, nark, get on someone's wick; *N. Amer. informal* tee off, tick off, burn up, rankle, gravel; *informal, dated* give someone the pip.
– OPPOSITES please, gratify.
annoyance ● noun **1** *much to his annoyance, Louise didn't even notice* IRRITATION, exasperation, vexation, indignation, anger, displeasure, chagrin; *informal* aggravation. **2** *they found him an annoyance* NUISANCE, pest, bother, irritant, inconvenience, thorn in one's flesh; *informal* pain (in the neck), bind, bore, hassle; *N. Amer. informal* nudnik, burr in/under someone's saddle; *Austral./NZ informal* nark.

annual ● adjective **1** occurring once a year. **2** calculated over or covering a year. **3** (of a plant) living for a year or less. ● noun **1** a book or magazine of a series published once a year. **2** an annual plant.
– DERIVATIVES **annually** adverb.
– ORIGIN Latin *annualis*, from *annus* 'year'.
annuity ● noun (pl. **annuities**) a fixed yearly allowance, especially one provided by a form of investment.
– ORIGIN Latin *annuitas*, from *annuus* 'yearly'.
annul /ənul/ ● verb (**annulled**, **annulling**) declare (a law, marriage, or other legal contract) invalid.
– DERIVATIVES **annulment** noun.
– ORIGIN Latin *annullare*, from *nullum* 'nothing'.
annular /anyoolər/ ● adjective technical ring-shaped.
– ORIGIN Latin *annularis*, from *anulus* 'small ring'.
annulate /anyoolət/ ● adjective chiefly Zoology marked with or formed of rings.
annunciation ● noun **1** (**the Annunciation**) the announcement of the Incarnation by the angel Gabriel to Mary (Gospel of Luke, chapter 1). **2** a Church festival commemorating this, held on 25 March.
annus horribilis /annəs horeebiliss/ ● noun a year of disaster or misfortune.
– ORIGIN Latin, suggested by ANNUS MIRABILIS.
annus mirabilis /annəss miraabiliss/ ● noun a remarkable or auspicious year.
– ORIGIN Latin, 'wonderful year'.
anode /annōd/ ● noun a positively charged electrode. The opposite of CATHODE.
– ORIGIN Greek *anodos* 'way up'.
anodized /annədīzd/ (also **anodised**) ● adjective (of metal, especially aluminium) coated with a protective oxide layer by electrolysis.
anodyne /annədīn/ ● adjective unlikely to cause offence or disagreement; bland. ● noun a painkilling drug or medicine.
– ORIGIN Greek *anōdunos* 'painless'.
anoint ● verb **1** smear or rub with oil, especially as part of a religious ceremony. **2** ceremonially confer office on (a priest or monarch) by anointing them.
– ORIGIN Old French *enoindre*, from Latin *inungere*.
anomalous ● adjective differing from what is standard or normal.
– DERIVATIVES **anomalously** adverb **anomalousness** noun.
– ORIGIN from Greek *an-* 'not' + *homalos* 'even'.
anomaly /ənomməli/ ● noun (pl. **anomalies**) something that deviates from what is standard or normal.
anomie /annəmi/ (also **anomy**) ● noun lack of the usual social or moral standards.
– ORIGIN French, from Greek *anomos* 'lawless'.
anon ● adverb archaic or informal soon; shortly.
– ORIGIN Old English, 'in or into (one state or course)'.
anonymous ● adjective **1** not identified by name; of unknown identity. **2** lacking character; featureless.
– DERIVATIVES **anonymity** /annənimmiti/ noun **anonymously** adverb.
– ORIGIN Greek *anōnumos* 'nameless'.
anopheles /ənoffileez/ ● noun a mosquito of a genus which includes the species that transmits malaria.
– ORIGIN from Greek, 'useless'.
anorak ● noun **1** a waterproof jacket, usually with a hood. **2** Brit. informal a socially inept person with an obsessive interest in something.
– ORIGIN Greenland Eskimo.
anorexia /annəreksiə/ (also **anorexia nervosa**) ● noun an emotional disorder characterized by an obsessive desire to lose weight by refusing to eat.
– ORIGIN from Greek *an-* 'without' + *orexis* 'appetite'.
anorexic (also **anorectic**) ● adjective relating to or suffering from anorexia. ● noun **1** a person suffering from anorexia. **2** (**anorectic**) a medicine which produces a loss of appetite.
another ● determiner & pronoun **1** one more; a further. **2** different from one that already mentioned.
answer ● noun **1** something said or written in reaction to a question or statement. **2** the solution to a problem. ● verb **1** respond with an answer. **2** (**answer back**) respond impudently. **3** (**answer to/for**) be responsible to or for. **4** satisfy (a need). **5** defend oneself against (a charge or accusation).
– ORIGIN Old English, related to SWEAR.
answerable ● adjective (**answerable to/for**) responsible to or for.
answering machine ● noun a device which supplies a recorded answer to a telephone call and can record a message from the caller.
answerphone ● noun Brit. an answering machine.
ant ● noun a small insect, usually wingless, living in a complex social colony.
– PHRASES **have ants in one's pants** informal be fidgety.
– ORIGIN Old English.
-ant ● suffix **1** (forming adjectives) having a quality or state: *arrogant*. **2** (forming nouns) performing a function: *deodorant*.
– ORIGIN Latin.
antacid /antassid/ ● adjective preventing or correcting acidity in the stomach.
antagonism /antaggəniz'm/ ● noun open hostility or opposition.
antagonist ● noun an open opponent or enemy.
– DERIVATIVES **antagonistic** adjective.
– ORIGIN Greek *antagōnistēs*, from *antagōnizesthai* 'struggle

Thesaurus

annoyed ● adjective IRRITATED, cross, angry, vexed, exasperated, irked, piqued, displeased, put out, disgruntled, in a bad mood, in a temper, nettled; *informal* aggravated, peeved, miffed, miffy, riled, hacked off, hot under the collar; *Brit. informal* narked, shirty; *N. Amer. informal* teed off, ticked off, sore, bent out of shape; *Austral./NZ informal* snaky, crook; *archaic* wroth.
annoying ● adjective IRRITATING, infuriating, exasperating, maddening, trying, tiresome, troublesome, bothersome, irksome, vexing, vexatious, galling; *informal* aggravating, pesky.
annual ● adjective YEARLY, once-a-year; year-long, twelve-month.
annually ● adverb YEARLY, once a year, each year, per annum.
annul ● verb DECLARE INVALID, declare null and void, nullify, invalidate, void; repeal, reverse, rescind, revoke; *Law* vacate; *formal* abrogate; *archaic* recall.
– OPPOSITES restore, enact.
anodyne ● noun PAINKILLER, painkilling drug, pain reliever, analgesic, narcotic.
● adjective *the conversation was anodyne* BLAND, inoffensive, innocuous, neutral, unobjectionable.
anoint ● verb **1** *the head of the infant was anointed* SMEAR/RUB WITH OIL; *archaic* anele. **2** *he was anointed and crowned* CONSECRATE, bless, ordain; *formal* hallow.
anomalous ● adjective ABNORMAL, atypical, irregular, aberrant, exceptional, freak, freakish, odd, bizarre, peculiar, unusual, out of the ordinary.
– OPPOSITES normal, typical.
anomaly ● noun ODDITY, peculiarity, abnormality, irregularity, inconsistency, incongruity, aberration, quirk.
anon ● adverb *(informal)* SOON, shortly, in a little while, presently, before long, by and by; *dated* directly; *poetic/literary* ere long.
anonymous ● adjective **1** *an anonymous donor* UNNAMED, of unknown name, nameless, incognito, unidentified, unknown; *rare* innominate. **2** *an anonymous letter* UNSIGNED, unattributed. **3** *an anonymous housing estate* CHARACTERLESS, nondescript, impersonal, faceless.
– OPPOSITES known, identified.
another ● determiner **1** *have another drink* ONE MORE, a further, an additional; an extra, a spare. **2** *she left him for another man* A DIFFERENT, some other, an alternative.
– OPPOSITES the same.
answer ● noun **1** *her answer was unequivocal* REPLY, response, rejoinder, reaction; retort, riposte; *informal* comeback. **2** *the answer is 150* SOLUTION, key. **3** *a new filter is the answer* SOLUTION, remedy, way out.
– OPPOSITES question.
● verb **1** *Steve was about to answer* REPLY, respond, make a rejoinder, rejoin; retort, riposte. **2** *he has yet to answer the charges* REBUT, refute, defend oneself against. **3** *a man answering this description* MATCH, fit, correspond to, be similar to. **4** *we're trying to answer the needs of our audience* SATISFY, meet, fulfil, fill, measure up to. **5** *I answer to the Commissioner* REPORT, work for/under, be subordinate, be accountable, be answerable, be responsible.
– PHRASES **answer someone back** RESPOND CHEEKILY TO, be cheeky to, be impertinent to, talk back to, cheek; *N. Amer. informal* sass. **answer for 1** *he will answer for his crime* PAY FOR, be punished for, suffer for; make amends for, make reparation for, atone for. **2** *the*

against'.
antagonize (also **antagonise**) ● verb make hostile.
Antarctic ● adjective relating to the region surrounding the South Pole.
– ORIGIN Greek *antarktikos* 'opposite to the north'.
ante /anti/ ● noun a stake put up by a player in poker or brag before receiving cards. ● verb (**antes**, **anted**, **anteing**) (**ante up**) put up (an amount) as an ante.
– PHRASES **up** (or **raise**) **the ante** increase what is at stake or under discussion.
– ORIGIN from Latin, 'before'.
ante- /anti/ ● prefix before; preceding: *antecedent.*
anteater ● noun a mammal with a long snout, feeding on ants and termites.
antebellum /antibelləm/ ● adjective occurring or existing before a particular war.
– ORIGIN Latin, from *ante* 'before' and *bellum* 'war'.
antecedent /antiseed'nt/ ● noun **1** a thing that existed before or precedes another. **2** (**antecedents**) a person's ancestors and social background. **3** Grammar an earlier word, phrase, or clause to which a following pronoun refers back. ● adjective preceding in time or order.
– ORIGIN from Latin *antecedere* 'go before'.
antechamber ● noun an ante-room.
antedate ● verb **1** come before in time. **2** indicate that (a document or event) belongs to an earlier date.
antediluvian /antidilōōviən/ ● adjective **1** belonging to the time before the biblical Flood. **2** chiefly humorous ridiculously old-fashioned.
– ORIGIN from ANTE- + Latin *diluvium* 'deluge'.
antelope ● noun a swift-running deer-like animal with upward-pointing horns, native to Africa and Asia.
– ORIGIN Greek *antholops* (originally the name of a fierce mythical creature).
antenatal ● adjective before birth; during or relating to pregnancy.
antenna /antennə/ ● noun (pl. **antennae** /antennnee/) **1** each of a pair of long, thin sensory appendages on the heads of insects, crustaceans, etc. **2** (pl. also **antennas**) an aerial.
– ORIGIN Latin, alteration of *antemna* 'yard' (of a ship's mast).
antepenultimate ● adjective last but two in a series.
ante-post ● adjective Brit. (of a bet) placed before the runners are known, on a horse thought likely to be entered.
anterior ● adjective **1** technical at or nearer the front. The opposite of POSTERIOR. **2** (**anterior to**) formal before.
– ORIGIN Latin, comparative of *ante* 'before'.
ante-room ● noun a small room leading to a more important one.
anthelmintic /anthelmintik/ ● adjective Medicine used to destroy parasitic worms.
– ORIGIN from *anth-* 'against' + Greek *helmins* 'worm'.
anthem ● noun **1** an uplifting song associated with a group or cause, especially a patriotic one adopted by a country as an expression of national identity. **2** a musical setting of a religious text to be sung by a choir during a church service.
– DERIVATIVES **anthemic** adjective.
– ORIGIN Old English, from Latin *antiphona* 'antiphon'.
anther ● noun the part of a flower's stamen that contains the pollen.
– ORIGIN Greek *anthos* 'flower'.
anthill ● noun a mound-shaped nest built by ants or termites.
anthology ● noun (pl. **anthologies**) a collection of poems or other pieces of writing or music.
– DERIVATIVES **anthologist** noun **anthologize** (also **anthologise**) verb.
– ORIGIN from Greek *anthos* 'flower' + *-logia* 'collection'.
anthracite /anthrəsīt/ ● noun hard coal that burns with little flame and smoke.
– ORIGIN Greek *anthrakitēs*, from *anthrax* 'coal'.
anthrax /anthraks/ ● noun a serious bacterial disease of sheep and cattle, able to be transmitted to humans.
– ORIGIN Greek *anthrax* 'coal, carbuncle'.
anthropogenic /anthrəpəjennik/ ● adjective (chiefly of pollution) originating in human activity.
– DERIVATIVES **anthropogenically** adverb.
anthropoid ● adjective referring to the higher primates including monkeys, apes, and humans.
– ORIGIN from Greek *anthrōpos* 'human being'.
anthropology /anthrəpolləji/ ● noun the study of humankind, especially the study of societies and cultures and human origins.
– DERIVATIVES **anthropological** adjective **anthropologist** noun.
– ORIGIN from Greek *anthrōpos* 'human being'.
anthropomorphic /anthrəpəmorfik/ ● adjective **1** attributing human form or feelings to a god, animal, or object. **2** having human characteristics.
– DERIVATIVES **anthropomorphism** noun.
anthropophagi /anthrəpoffəgī/ ● plural noun (in legends or fables) cannibals.
– ORIGIN from Greek *anthrōpophagos* 'man-eating'.
anthropophagy /anthrəpoffəji/ ● noun cannibalism.
anti ● preposition opposed to; against.
anti- ● prefix **1** opposed to; against: *anti-aircraft.* **2** preventing or relieving: *antibacterial.* **3** the opposite of: *anticlimax.*
– ORIGIN Greek.
antibacterial ● adjective active against bacteria.
antibiotic ● noun a medicine that inhibits the growth of or destroys bacteria.
– ORIGIN from Greek *biōtikos* 'fit for life'.
antibody ● noun (pl. **antibodies**) a protein produced in the blood to counteract an antigen.
Antichrist ● noun an enemy of Christ believed by the early Church to appear before the end of the world.
anticipate ● verb **1** be aware of (a future event) and prepare for it. **2** regard as probable. **3** look forward to. **4** act or happen before.
– DERIVATIVES **anticipator** noun **anticipatory** adjective.
– ORIGIN Latin *anticipare*, from *ante-* 'before' + *capere* 'take'.

Thesaurus

government has a lot to answer for BE ACCOUNTABLE FOR, be responsible for, be liable for, take the blame for; *informal* take the rap for.
answerable ● adjective *the Attorney General is answerable only to Parliament* ACCOUNTABLE, responsible, liable; subject.
antagonism ● noun HOSTILITY, friction, enmity, antipathy, animus, opposition, dissension, rivalry; acrimony, bitterness, rancour, resentment, aversion, dislike, ill/bad feeling, ill will; *Brit. informal* needle.
– OPPOSITES rapport, friendship.
antagonist ● noun ADVERSARY, opponent, enemy, rival; (**antagonists**) opposition, competition.
– OPPOSITES ally.
antagonistic ● adjective **1** *he was antagonistic to the reforms* HOSTILE, against, (dead) set against, opposed, inimical, antipathetic, ill-disposed, resistant, in disagreement; *informal* anti. **2** *an antagonistic group of bystanders* HOSTILE, aggressive, belligerent, bellicose, pugnacious; *rare* oppugnant.
– OPPOSITES pro.
antagonize ● verb AROUSE HOSTILITY IN, alienate; anger, annoy, provoke, vex, irritate; *Brit.* rub up the wrong way; *informal* aggravate, rile, needle, rattle someone's cage, get someone's back up, get someone's dander up, make someone's hackles rise; *Brit. informal* nark, get on someone's wick.
– OPPOSITES pacify, placate.
antecedent ● noun **1** *her antecedents have been traced* ANCESTOR, forefather, forebear, progenitor, primogenitor; (**antecedents**) ancestry, family tree, lineage, genealogy, roots. **2** *the guitar's antecedent* PRECURSOR, forerunner, predecessor.
– OPPOSITES descendant.
● adjective *antecedent events* PREVIOUS, earlier, prior, preceding, precursory; *formal* anterior.
– OPPOSITES subsequent.
antedate ● verb PRECEDE, predate, come/go before.
antediluvian ● adjective **1** *antediluvian animals* PREHISTORIC, primeval, primordial, primal, ancient, early. **2** *his antediluvian attitudes* OUT OF DATE, outdated, outmoded, old-fashioned, antiquated, behind the times, passé.
ante-room ● noun ANTECHAMBER, vestibule, lobby, foyer; *Architecture* narthex.
anthem ● noun HYMN, song, chorale, psalm, paean.
anthology ● noun COLLECTION, selection, compendium, treasury, miscellany; *archaic* garland.
anticipate ● verb **1** *the police did not anticipate trouble* EXPECT, foresee, predict, be prepared for, bargain on, reckon on; *N. Amer. informal* figure on. **2** *Elaine anticipated her meeting with Will* LOOK FORWARD TO, await, lick one's lips over. **3** *warders can't always an-*

a

anticipation • noun the action of anticipating; expectation or prediction.
anticlimax • noun a disappointing end to an exciting series of events.
– DERIVATIVES **anticlimactic** adjective.
anticline /antiklīn/ • noun a ridge or fold of stratified rock in which the strata slope downwards from the crest. Compare with SYNCLINE.
– ORIGIN from ANTI- + Greek *klinein* 'lean'.
anticlockwise • adverb & adjective Brit. in the opposite direction to the way in which the hands of a clock move round.
anticoagulant • adjective preventing the blood from clotting.
anticonvulsant • adjective preventing or reducing the severity of epileptic fits or other convulsions. • noun an anticonvulsant drug.
antics • plural noun foolish, outrageous, or amusing behaviour.
– ORIGIN from Italian *antico* 'antique', also 'grotesque'.
anticyclone • noun an area of high atmospheric pressure around which air slowly circulates, usually resulting in calm, fine weather.
– DERIVATIVES **anticyclonic** adjective.
antidepressant • adjective used to alleviate depression. • noun an antidepressant drug.
antidote • noun **1** a medicine taken to counteract a poison. **2** something that counteracts an unpleasant feeling or situation: *laughter is a good antidote to stress.*
– ORIGIN Greek *antidoton*, from *anti-* 'against' + *didonai* 'give'.
anti-emetic • adjective preventing vomiting. • noun an anti-emetic drug.
antifreeze • noun a liquid added to water to prevent it from freezing, especially as used in the radiator of a motor vehicle.
antigen • noun a harmful substance which causes the body to produce antibodies.
– DERIVATIVES **antigenic** adjective.
Antiguan /anteegwən/ • noun a person from Antigua, or the country of Antigua and Barbuda, in the West Indies. • adjective relating to Antigua or Antigua and Barbuda.
anti-hero (or **anti-heroine**) • noun a central character in a story, film, or play who lacks conventional heroic qualities.
antihistamine • noun a drug that counteracts the effects of histamine, used in treating allergies.
anti-inflammatory • adjective (of a drug) used to reduce inflammation.
antilogarithm • noun the number of which a given number is the logarithm.
antimacassar /antimәkassәr/ • noun a piece of cloth put over the back of a chair to protect it from grease and dirt.
– ORIGIN from ANTI- + *Macassar*, a kind of hair oil formerly used by men, represented as consisting of ingredients from Makassar (the former name for the seaport of Ujung Pandang in Indonesia).
antimatter • noun matter consisting of the antiparticles of the particles making up normal matter.
antimony /antimәni/ • noun a brittle silvery-white metallic element.
– ORIGIN Latin *antimonium.*
antinomian /antinōmiәn/ • adjective believing that Christians are released by grace from obeying moral laws. • noun a person with such a belief.
– DERIVATIVES **antinomianism** noun.
– ORIGIN from Greek *anti-* 'against' + *nomos* 'law'.
antinomy /antinnәmi/ • noun (pl. **antinomies**) a paradox.
antioxidant • noun a substance that counteracts oxidation.
antiparticle • noun a subatomic particle with the same mass as a given particle but an opposite electric charge or magnetic effect.
antipasto /antipastō/ • noun (pl. **antipasti** /antipasti/) an Italian hors d'oeuvre.
– ORIGIN Italian, from *anti-* 'before' + *pasto* 'food'.
antipathy /antippәthi/ • noun (pl. **antipathies**) a strong feeling of dislike.
– DERIVATIVES **antipathetic** adjective.
– ORIGIN Greek *antipatheia*, from *anti-* 'against' + *pathos* 'feeling'.
anti-personnel • adjective (of weapons) designed to kill or injure people rather than to damage buildings or equipment.
antiperspirant • noun a substance applied to the skin to prevent or reduce perspiration.
antiphon /antif'n/ • noun a short chant sung before or after a psalm or canticle.
– ORIGIN from Greek *antiphōna* 'harmonies'.
antiphonal /antiffәn'l/ • adjective (of church music) sung, recited, or played alternately by two groups.
Antipodes /antippәdeez/ • plural noun **1** (**the Antipodes**) Australia and New Zealand (in relation to the northern hemisphere). **2** (**antipodes** or **antipode**) the direct opposite of something.
– DERIVATIVES **antipodal** adjective **Antipodean** adjective & noun.
– ORIGIN from Greek *antipodes* 'having the feet opposite'.
antipyretic • adjective used to prevent or reduce fever.
antiquarian /antikwairiәn/ • adjective relating to the collection or study of antiques, rare books, or antiquities. • noun (also **antiquary**) a person who studies or collects antiquarian items.
– DERIVATIVES **antiquarianism** noun.
antiquated • adjective old-fashioned or outdated.
antique • noun a decorative object or piece of furniture that is valuable because of its age. • adjective **1** valuable because of its age. **2** old-fashioned or outdated. **3** literary ancient.
– ORIGIN Latin *antiquus* 'former, ancient'.
antiquity • noun (pl. **antiquities**) **1** the distant past, especially before the Middle Ages. **2** an object from the distant past. **3** great age.
antirrhinum /antirīnәm/ • noun (pl. **antirrhinums**) a snapdragon.
– ORIGIN Greek *antirrhinon*, from *anti-* 'counterfeiting' + *rhis* 'nose' (from the flower's resemblance to an animal's snout).
antiscorbutic • adjective preventing or curing scurvy.
anti-Semitism • noun hostility to or prejudice against Jews.
– DERIVATIVES **anti-Semite** noun **anti-Semitic** adjective.
antiseptic • adjective **1** preventing the growth of micro-organisms that cause disease or infection. **2** so clean or pure as to lack character. • noun an antiseptic substance.
antiserum • noun (pl. **antisera**) a blood serum containing antibodies against specific antigens.
antisocial • adjective **1** contrary to accepted social customs and

Thesaurus

ticipate the actions of prisoners PRE-EMPT, forestall, second-guess; *informal* beat someone to the punch. **4** *her plays anticipated her film work* FORESHADOW, precede, antedate, come/go before.
anticipation • noun **1** *my anticipation is that we will see a rise in rates* EXPECTATION, prediction, forecast. **2** *her eyes sparkled with anticipation* EXPECTANCY, expectation, excitement, suspense.
– PHRASES **in anticipation of** IN THE EXPECTATION OF, in preparation for, ready for.
anticlimax • noun LET-DOWN, disappointment, comedown, non-event; disillusionment; *Brit.* damp squib; *informal* washout.
antics • plural noun CAPERS, pranks, larks, high jinks, skylarking; *Brit. informal* monkey tricks.
antidote • noun **1** *the antidote to this poison* ANTITOXIN, antiserum, antivenin. **2** *laughter is a good antidote to stress* REMEDY, cure, nostrum.
antipathetic • adjective HOSTILE, against, (dead) set against, opposed, antagonistic, ill-disposed, unsympathetic; *informal* anti, down on.
– OPPOSITES pro.
antipathy • noun HOSTILITY, antagonism, animosity, aversion, animus, enmity, dislike, distaste, hatred, hate, abhorrence, loathing.
– OPPOSITES liking, affinity.
antiquated • adjective OUTDATED, out of date, outmoded, outworn, behind the times, old-fashioned, anachronistic, old-fangled, passé, démodé; *informal* out of the ark, mouldy; *N. Amer. informal* horse and buggy, mossy, clunky.
– OPPOSITES modern, up to date.
antique • noun COLLECTOR'S ITEM, period piece, antiquity, object of virtu, objet d'art.
• adjective **1** *antique furniture* OLD, antiquarian, collectable. **2** *statues of antique gods* ANCIENT, of long ago; *poetic/literary* of yore. **3** *antique work practices.* See ANTIQUATED.
– OPPOSITES modern, state-of-the-art.
antiquity • noun **1** *the civilizations of antiquity* ANCIENT TIMES, the ancient past, classical times, the distant past. **2** *Islamic antiquities* ANTIQUE, period piece, collector's item. **3** *a church of great antiquity* AGE, oldness, ancientness.
antiseptic • adjective **1** *an antiseptic substance* DISINFECTANT, germicidal, bactericidal. **2** *antiseptic bandages* STERILE, aseptic, germ-free, uncontaminated, disinfected. **3** *their antiseptic surroundings*

a

causing annoyance. **2** avoiding the company of others.
– DERIVATIVES **antisocially** adverb.

antithesis /antithəsiss/ ● noun (pl. **antitheses** /antithəseez/) **1** a person or thing that is the direct opposite of another. **2** the putting together of contrasting ideas or words to produce a rhetorical effect.
– ORIGIN from Greek *antitithenai* 'set against'.

antithetical /antithettikk'l/ ● adjective **1** mutually opposed or incompatible. **2** (in rhetoric) using antithesis.

antitoxin ● noun an antibody that counteracts a toxin.

antitrust ● adjective chiefly US (of legislation) preventing or controlling monopolies.

antivenin /antivennin/ ● noun an antiserum containing antibodies against poisons in the venom of snakes.

antivivisection ● adjective opposed to the use of live animals for scientific research.
– DERIVATIVES **antivivisectionist** noun & adjective.

antler ● noun each of a pair of branched horns on the head of an adult deer.
– ORIGIN Old French *antoillier*.

antonym /antənim/ ● noun a word opposite in meaning to another.
– ORIGIN from Greek *anti-* 'against' + *onoma* 'a name'.

anus /aynəss/ ● noun the opening at the end of the digestive system through which solid waste matter leaves the body.
– ORIGIN Latin.

anvil ● noun a heavy iron block on which metal can be hammered and shaped.
– ORIGIN Old English.

anxiety ● noun (pl. **anxieties**) an anxious feeling or state.

anxious ● adjective **1** experiencing worry or unease. **2** very eager and concerned to do something.
– DERIVATIVES **anxiously** adverb **anxiousness** noun.
– ORIGIN Latin *anxius*, from *angere* 'to choke'.

any ● determiner & pronoun **1** one or some of a thing or number of things, no matter how much or how many. **2** whichever or whatever one chooses. ● adverb at all; in some degree.
– USAGE When used as a pronoun **any** can be used with either a singular or a plural verb, depending on the context: *we needed more sugar but there wasn't any left* (**singular verb**) or *are any of the new videos available?* (**plural verb**).
– ORIGIN Old English.

anybody ● pronoun anyone.

anyhow ● adverb **1** anyway. **2** in a careless or haphazard way.

anyone ● pronoun any person or people.

anything ● pronoun a thing of any kind, no matter what.
– PHRASES **anything but** not at all.

anyway ● adverb **1** used to emphasize something just said. **2** used in conversations to change the subject or to resume after interruption. **3** nevertheless.

anywhere ● adverb in or to any place. ● pronoun any place.

Anzac /anzak/ ● noun **1** a soldier in the Australian and New Zealand Army Corps (1914–18). **2** informal a person from Australia or New Zealand.

AOB ● abbreviation Brit. (at the end of an agenda for a meeting) any other business.

aïoli /īōli/ (also **aioli**) ● noun mayonnaise seasoned with garlic.
– ORIGIN French, from Provençal *ai* 'garlic' + *oli* 'oil'.

aorta /ayortə/ ● noun the main artery supplying blood from the heart to the rest of the body.
– DERIVATIVES **aortic** adjective.
– ORIGIN Greek *aortē*, from *aeirein* 'raise'.

apace ● adverb literary swiftly; quickly.
– ORIGIN from Old French *a pas* 'at (a considerable) pace'.

Apache /əpachi/ ● noun (pl. same or **Apaches**) a member of an American Indian people living chiefly in New Mexico and Arizona.
– ORIGIN probably from a word in an American Indian language meaning 'enemy'.

apart ● adverb **1** separated by a distance in time or space. **2** to or on one side. **3** into pieces.
– PHRASES **apart from 1** except for. **2** as well as.
– ORIGIN from Latin *a parte* 'at the side'.

apartheid /əpaartayt/ ● noun the official system of segregation or discrimination on racial grounds formerly in force in South Africa.
– ORIGIN Afrikaans, 'separateness'.

apartment ● noun **1** chiefly N. Amer. a set of rooms forming one residence; a flat. **2** (**apartments**) a private suite of rooms in a very large house.
– ORIGIN Italian *appartamento*, from *appartare* 'to separate'.

apathetic ● adjective not interested or enthusiastic.
– DERIVATIVES **apathetically** adverb.

apathy /appəthi/ ● noun lack of interest or enthusiasm.
– ORIGIN Greek *apatheia*, from *apathēs* 'without feeling'.

apatosaurus /əpattəsawrəss/ ● noun a huge herbivorous dinosaur of the late Jurassic period, with a long neck and tail. Also called BRONTOSAURUS.

Thesaurus

CHARACTERLESS, colourless, soulless; clinical, institutional.
– OPPOSITES contaminated.
● noun DISINFECTANT, germicide, bactericide.

antisocial ● adjective **1** *antisocial behaviour* OBJECTIONABLE, offensive, unacceptable, distasteful, disruptive; sociopathic. **2** *I'm feeling a bit antisocial* UNSOCIABLE, unfriendly, uncommunicative, reclusive, misanthropic.

antithesis ● noun (DIRECT) OPPOSITE, converse, reverse, inverse, obverse, the other side of the coin; informal the flip side.

antithetical ● adjective (DIRECTLY) OPPOSED, contrasting, contrary, contradictory, conflicting, incompatible, irreconcilable, inconsistent, poles apart, at variance/odds; rare oppugnant.
– OPPOSITES identical, like.

anxiety ● noun **1** *his anxiety grew* WORRY, concern, apprehension, apprehensiveness, uneasiness, unease, fearfulness, fear, disquiet, disquietude, perturbation, agitation, angst, nervousness, nerves, tension, tenseness; informal butterflies (in one's stomach), jitteriness, twitchiness, collywobbles, jim-jams. **2** *an anxiety to please* EAGERNESS, keenness, desire.
– OPPOSITES serenity.

anxious ● adjective **1** *I'm anxious about her* WORRIED, concerned, apprehensive, fearful, uneasy, perturbed, troubled, bothered, disturbed, distressed, fretful, agitated, nervous, edgy, unquiet, on edge, tense, overwrought, worked up, keyed up, jumpy, worried sick, with one's stomach in knots, with one's heart in one's mouth; informal uptight, on tenterhooks, with butterflies in one's stomach, like a cat on a hot tin roof, jittery, twitchy, in a stew/twitter, all of a dither/lather, in a tizz/tizzy, het up; Brit. informal strung up, windy, having kittens, in a (flat) spin, like a cat on hot bricks; N. Amer. informal antsy, spooky, squirrelly, in a twit; Austral./NZ informal toey; dated overstrung. **2** *she was anxious for news* EAGER, keen, desirous, impatient.
– OPPOSITES carefree, unconcerned.

any ● determiner **1** *is there any cake left?* SOME, a piece/part/bit of. **2** *it doesn't make any difference to me* THE SLIGHTEST BIT OF, a scrap/shred/jot/whit of, an iota of. **3** *any job will do* WHICHEVER, no matter which, never mind which; informal any old.
● pronoun *you don't know any of my friends* A SINGLE ONE, (even) one; anyone, anybody.
● adverb *is your father any better?* AT ALL, in the least, to any extent, in any degree.

anyhow ● adverb **1** *anyhow, it doesn't really matter* ANYWAY, in any case/event, at any rate; however, be that as it may; N. Amer. informal anyways. **2** *her clothes were strewn about anyhow* HAPHAZARDLY, carelessly, heedlessly, negligently, in a muddle; informal all over the place; Brit. informal all over the shop; N. Amer. informal all over the lot.

apace ● adverb (poetic/literary) QUICKLY, fast, swiftly, rapidly, speedily, briskly, without delay, post-haste, expeditiously.
– OPPOSITES slowly.

apart ● adverb **1** *the villages are two miles apart* AWAY/DISTANT FROM EACH OTHER. **2** *Isabel stood apart* TO ONE SIDE, aside, separately, alone, by oneself/itself. **3** *his parents are living apart* SEPARATELY, independently, on one's own. **4** *the car was blown apart* TO PIECES/BITS, up; poetic/literary asunder.
– PHRASES **apart from** EXCEPT FOR, but for, aside from, with the exception of, excepting, excluding, bar, barring, besides, other than; informal outside of; formal save.

apartment ● noun **1** *a rented apartment* FLAT, penthouse; Austral. home unit; N. Amer. informal crib. **2** *the royal apartments* SUITE (OF ROOMS), rooms, living quarters, accommodation.

apathetic ● adjective UNINTERESTED, indifferent, unconcerned, unmoved, uninvolved, unemotional, emotionless, dispassionate, lukewarm, unmotivated; informal couldn't-care-less; rare Laodicean.

apathy ● noun INDIFFERENCE, lack of interest/enthusiasm/concern, unconcern, uninterestedness, unresponsiveness, impassivity,

a

– ORIGIN from Greek *apatē* 'deceit' (because of a deceptive similarity between some of its bones and those of other dinosaurs) + *sauros* 'lizard'.

APC ● abbreviation armoured personnel carrier.

ape ● noun **1** a large tailless primate of a group including gorillas, chimpanzees, and gibbons. **2** informal an unintelligent or clumsy person. ● verb imitate in an absurd or unthinking way.

– ORIGIN Old English.

aperçu /appərsyoō/ ● noun (pl. **aperçus**) a comment which makes an illuminating or entertaining point.

– ORIGIN French, 'thing perceived'.

aperient /əpeeriənt/ ● adjective (of a drug) used to relieve constipation.

– ORIGIN from Latin *aperire* 'to open'.

aperitif /əperriteef/ ● noun an alcoholic drink taken before a meal to stimulate the appetite.

– ORIGIN French, from Latin *aperire* 'to open'.

aperture /appərtyoor/ ● noun **1** an opening, hole, or gap. **2** the variable opening by which light enters a camera.

– ORIGIN Latin *apertura*, from *aperire* 'to open'.

Apex /aypeks/ ● noun a system of reduced fares for air or rail journeys booked in advance.

– ORIGIN from *A*dvance *P*urchase *Ex*cursion.

apex /aypeks/ ● noun (pl. **apexes** or **apices** /aypiseez/) the top or highest part, especially one forming a point.

– ORIGIN Latin, 'peak, tip'.

aphasia /əfayziə/ ● noun inability to understand or produce speech, as a result of brain damage.

– DERIVATIVES **aphasic** adjective & noun.

– ORIGIN from Greek *aphatos* 'speechless'.

aphelion /apheeliən/ ● noun (pl. **aphelia** /apheeliə/) the point in a planet's orbit at which it is furthest from the sun. The opposite of PERIHELION.

– ORIGIN from Greek *aph' hēlion* 'from the sun'.

aphid /ayfid/ ● noun a greenfly or similar small insect feeding on the sap of plants.

– ORIGIN Greek *aphis*.

aphorism /afføriz'm/ ● noun a concise witty remark which contains a general truth.

– DERIVATIVES **aphoristic** adjective.

– ORIGIN Greek *aphorismos* 'definition'.

aphrodisiac /afrədizziak/ ● noun a food, drink, or drug that arouses sexual desire.

– ORIGIN Greek *aphrodisiakos*, from *Aphrodite*, the goddess of love.

apiary /aypiəri/ ● noun (pl. **apiaries**) a place where bees are kept.

– DERIVATIVES **apiarist** noun.

– ORIGIN Latin *apiarium*, from *apis* 'bee'.

apical /aypik'l, ap-/ ● adjective technical relating to or forming an apex.

– ORIGIN from Latin *apex* 'peak, tip'.

apices plural of APEX.

apiculture /aypikulchər/ ● noun technical bee-keeping.

– ORIGIN from Latin *apis* 'bee'.

apiece ● adverb to, for, or by each one.

aplenty ● adjective in abundance: *he has work aplenty*.

aplomb /əplom/ ● noun self-confidence or calm assurance.

– ORIGIN French, from *à plomb* 'according to a plumb line, perpendicularly'.

apnoea /apneeə/ (US **apnea**) ● noun a medical condition when a person temporarily stops breathing, especially during sleep.

– ORIGIN Greek *apnoia*, from *apnous* 'breathless'.

apocalypse /əpokkəlips/ ● noun **1** an event involving great and widespread destruction. **2** (**the Apocalypse**) the final destruction of the world, as described in the biblical book of Revelation.

– ORIGIN Greek *apokalupsis*, from *apokaluptein* 'uncover, reveal'.

apocalyptic ● adjective resembling the end of the world in being momentous or catastrophic.

– DERIVATIVES **apocalyptically** adverb.

Apocrypha /əpokrifə/ ● plural noun (treated as sing. or pl.) those books of the Old Testament not accepted as part of Hebrew scripture and excluded from the Protestant Bible at the Reformation.

– ORIGIN from Latin *apocrypha scripta* 'hidden writings'.

apocryphal ● adjective **1** widely circulated but unlikely to be true: *an apocryphal story*. **2** of or belonging to the Apocrypha.

apogee /appəjee/ ● noun **1** Astronomy the point in the orbit of the moon or a satellite at which it is furthest from the earth. The opposite of PERIGEE. **2** a culmination or climax.

– ORIGIN from Greek *apogaion diastēma*, 'distance away from earth'.

apolitical ● adjective not interested or involved in politics.

apologetic ● adjective regretfully acknowledging an offence.

– DERIVATIVES **apologetically** adverb.

apologetics ● plural noun (treated as sing. or pl.) reasoned arguments defending a theory or doctrine.

apologia /appəlōjiə/ ● noun a formal written defence of one's opinions or conduct.

– ORIGIN Latin, 'apology'.

apologist ● noun a person who offers an argument in defence of something controversial.

apologize (also **apologise**) ● verb express regret for something that one has done wrong.

apology ● noun (pl. **apologies**) **1** a regretful acknowledgement of an offence or failure. **2** (**an apology for**) informal a very poor example of. **3** a justification or defence.

– ORIGIN Greek *apologia* 'a speech in one's own defence'.

apophthegm /appəthem/ (US **apothegm**) ● noun a concise saying stating a general truth.

– ORIGIN Greek *apothegma*, from *apophthengesthai* 'speak out'.

apoplectic /appəplektik/ ● adjective **1** informal overcome with anger. **2** dated relating to apoplexy (stroke).

apoplexy /appəpleksi/ ● noun (pl. **apoplexies**) **1** dated unconsciousness or incapacity resulting from a cerebral haemorrhage or stroke. **2** informal extreme anger.

– ORIGIN Greek *apoplexia*, from *apoplēssein* 'disable by a stroke'.

apoptosis /appəptōsiss/ ● noun Biology the death of cells which occurs as a normal part of an organism's development.

– ORIGIN Greek *apoptōsis* 'falling off'.

aporia /əporiə/ ● noun an irresolvable internal contradiction in

Thesaurus

dispassion, dispassionateness, lethargy, languor, ennui, accidie.

– OPPOSITES enthusiasm, passion.

ape ● noun PRIMATE, simian; monkey; *technical* anthropoid.
● verb *he aped Barbara's accent* IMITATE, mimic, copy, do an impression of; *informal* take off, send up; *archaic* monkey.

aperture ● noun OPENING, hole, gap, slit, slot, vent, crevice, chink, crack, interstice; *technical* orifice, foramen.

apex ● noun **1** *the apex of a pyramid* TIP, peak, summit, pinnacle, top, vertex. **2** *the apex of his career* CLIMAX, culmination, apotheosis; peak, pinnacle, zenith, acme, apogee, high(est) point.

– RELATED TERMS apical.

– OPPOSITES bottom, nadir.

aphorism ● noun SAYING, maxim, axiom, adage, epigram, dictum, gnome, proverb, saw, tag, apophthegm.

aphrodisiac ● noun LOVE POTION, philtre.
● adjective EROTIC, sexy, sexually arousing.

apiece ● adverb EACH, respectively, per item; *informal* a throw.

aplenty ● adjective IN ABUNDANCE, in profusion, galore, in large quantities/numbers, by the dozen; *informal* a gogo, by the truckload.

aplomb ● noun POISE, self-assurance, self-confidence, calmness, composure, collectedness, level-headedness, sangfroid, equilibrium, equanimity; *informal* unflappability.

apocryphal ● adjective FICTITIOUS, made-up, untrue, fabricated, false, spurious; unverified, unauthenticated, unsubstantiated.

– OPPOSITES authentic.

apologetic ● adjective REGRETFUL, sorry, contrite, remorseful, penitent, repentant; conscience-stricken, shamefaced, ashamed.

– OPPOSITES unrepentant.

apologia ● noun DEFENCE, justification, vindication, explanation; argument, case.

apologist ● noun DEFENDER, supporter, upholder, advocate, proponent, exponent, propagandist, champion, campaigner.

– OPPOSITES critic.

apologize ● verb SAY SORRY, express regret, be apologetic, make an apology, ask forgiveness, ask for pardon, eat humble pie.

apology ● noun **1** *I owe you an apology* EXPRESSION OF REGRET, one's regrets; *Austral./NZ informal* beg-pardon; *poetic/literary* amende honorable. **2** *(informal) an apology for a flat* TRAVESTY, inadequate/poor example; *informal* excuse.

apoplectic ● adjective *(informal)* FURIOUS, enraged, infuriated, incensed, raging; incandescent, fuming, seething; *informal* (hopping)

a text, argument, or theory.
– ORIGIN Greek, from *aporos* 'impassable'.

apostasy /əpostəsi/ ● noun abandonment of a belief or principle.
– ORIGIN Greek *apostasis* 'desertion'.

apostate /appəstayt/ ● noun a person who renounces a belief or principle.

apostatize /əpostətīz/ (also **apostatise**) ● verb abandon a belief or principle.

a posteriori /ay posterriorī/ ● adjective & adverb involving reasoning based on known facts to deduce causes.
– ORIGIN Latin, 'from what comes after'.

apostle ● noun 1 (**Apostle**) each of the twelve chief disciples of Jesus Christ. 2 an enthusiastic and pioneering supporter of an idea or cause.
– ORIGIN Greek *apostolos* 'messenger'.

apostolate /əpostəlayt/ ● noun 1 the position or authority of a religious leader. 2 evangelistic activity.

apostolic /appəstollik/ ● adjective 1 relating to the Apostles. 2 relating to the Pope, regarded as the successor to St Peter.

apostrophe /əpostrəfi/ ● noun 1 a punctuation mark (') used to indicate either possession (e.g. *Harry's book*) or the omission of letters or numbers (e.g. *can't; Jan. '99*). 2 Rhetoric a passage that turns away from the subject to address an absent person or thing.
– ORIGIN Greek *apostrophos*, from *apostrephein* 'turn away'.

apostrophize (also **apostrophise**) ● verb 1 Rhetoric address an apostrophe to. 2 punctuate with an apostrophe.

apothecaries' measure (also **apothecaries' weight**) ● noun historical a system of units formerly used in pharmacy for liquid volume (or weight), based on the fluid ounce and the ounce troy.

apothecary /əpothəkəri/ ● noun (pl. **apothecaries**) archaic a person who prepared and sold medicines.
– ORIGIN Latin *apothecarius* from Greek *apothēkē* 'storehouse'.

apothegm ● noun US spelling of APOPHTHEGM.

apotheosis /əpothiōsiss/ ● noun (pl. **apotheoses** /əpothiōseez/) 1 the culmination or highest point: *the apotheosis of his career.* 2 elevation to divine status.
– DERIVATIVES **apotheosize** (also **apotheosise**) verb.
– ORIGIN Greek, from *apotheoun* 'make a god of'.

appal (US **appall**) ● verb (**appalled, appalling**) 1 greatly dismay or horrify. 2 (**appalling**) informal very bad or displeasing.
– DERIVATIVES **appallingly** adverb.
– ORIGIN Old French *apalir* 'grow pale'.

apparatchik /appəraatchik/ ● noun (pl. **apparatchiks** or **apparatchiki** /appəraatchikkee/) 1 chiefly historical a member of the administrative system of a communist party. 2 derogatory or humorous an official in a large political organization.
– ORIGIN Russian, from German *Apparat* 'apparatus'.

apparatus /appəraytəss/ ● noun (pl. **apparatuses**) 1 the equipment needed for a particular activity or purpose. 2 a complex structure within an organization: *the apparatus of government.*
– ORIGIN Latin, from *apparare* 'make ready for'.

apparel /əparrəl/ ● noun formal clothing. ● verb (**apparelled, apparelling**; US **appareled, appareling**) archaic clothe.
– ORIGIN Old French *apareillier*, from Latin *ad-* 'to' + *par* 'equal'.

apparent ● adjective 1 clearly seen or understood; obvious. 2 seeming real, but not necessarily so.
– DERIVATIVES **apparently** adverb.
– ORIGIN from Latin *apparere* 'appear'.

apparition ● noun a remarkable thing making a sudden appearance, especially a ghost.

appeal ● verb 1 make a serious or heartfelt request. 2 be attractive or interesting: *activities that appeal to all.* 3 Law apply to a higher court for a reversal of a lower court's decision. 4 Cricket (of the bowler or fielders) call on the umpire to declare a batsman out. ● noun 1 an act of appealing. 2 the quality of being attractive or interesting.
– ORIGIN Latin *appellare* 'to address'.

appealing ● adjective attractive or interesting.
– DERIVATIVES **appealingly** adverb.

appear ● verb 1 become visible or evident. 2 give a particular impression; seem. 3 present oneself publicly or formally, especially as a performer or in a law court. 4 be published.
– ORIGIN Latin *apparere*, from *parere* 'come into view'.

appearance ● noun 1 the way that someone or something looks or seems. 2 an act of appearing.
– PHRASES **keep up appearances** maintain an impression of wealth or well-being.

Thesaurus

mad, livid, as cross as two sticks, foaming at the mouth, fit to be tied; *poetic/literary* wrathful.

apostate ● noun DISSENTER, heretic, defector, turncoat; *archaic* recreant; *rare* tergiversator.
– OPPOSITES follower.

apostle ● noun 1 *the 12 apostles* DISCIPLE, follower. 2 *the apostles of the Slavs* MISSIONARY, evangelist, proselytizer. 3 *an apostle of capitalism* ADVOCATE, apologist, proponent, exponent, promoter, supporter, upholder, champion; *N. Amer.* booster.

apotheosis ● noun CULMINATION, climax, peak, pinnacle, zenith, acme, apogee, high(est) point.
– OPPOSITES nadir.

appal ● verb HORRIFY, shock, dismay, distress, outrage, scandalize; disgust, repel, revolt, sicken, nauseate, offend, make someone's blood run cold.

appalling ● adjective 1 *an appalling crime* SHOCKING, horrific, horrifying, horrible, terrible, awful, dreadful, ghastly, hideous, horrendous, frightful, atrocious, abominable, abhorrent, outrageous, gruesome, grisly, monstrous, heinous, egregious. 2 *(informal) your schoolwork is appalling* DREADFUL, awful, terrible, frightful, atrocious, disgraceful, deplorable, hopeless, lamentable; *informal* rotten, crummy, pathetic, pitiful, woeful, useless, lousy, abysmal, dire; *Brit. informal* chronic, shocking.

apparatus ● noun 1 *laboratory apparatus* EQUIPMENT, gear, rig, tackle, gadgetry; appliance, instrument, machine, mechanism, device, contraption. 2 *the apparatus of government* STRUCTURE, system, framework, organization, network.

apparel ● noun *(formal)* CLOTHES, clothing, garments, dress, attire, wear, garb; *informal* gear, togs, duds; *Brit. informal* clobber, kit; *N. Amer. informal* threads; *archaic* raiment, habit, habiliments.

apparent ● adjective 1 *their relief was all too apparent* EVIDENT, plain, obvious, clear, manifest, visible, discernible, perceptible; unmistakable, crystal clear, palpable, patent, blatant, as plain as a pikestaff, writ large; *informal* as plain as the nose on one's face, written all over one's face. 2 *his apparent lack of concern* SEEMING, ostensible, outward, superficial; supposed, alleged, professed.
– OPPOSITES unclear.

apparently ● adverb SEEMINGLY, evidently, it seems/appears (that), as far as one knows, by all accounts; ostensibly, outwardly, on the face of it, so the story goes, so I'm told; allegedly, reputedly.

apparition ● noun 1 *a monstrous apparition* GHOST, phantom, spectre, spirit, wraith; vision, hallucination; *informal* spook; *poetic/literary* phantasm, revenant, shade, visitant, wight; *rare* eidolon. 2 *the apparition of a strange man* APPEARANCE, manifestation, materialization, emergence; visitation.

appeal ● verb 1 *police are appealing for information* ASK URGENTLY/EARNESTLY, make an urgent/earnest request, call, make a plea, plead. 2 *Andrew appealed to me to help them* IMPLORE, beg, entreat, call on, plead with, exhort, ask, request, petition; *formal* adjure; *poetic/literary* beseech. 3 *the thought of travelling appealed to me* ATTRACT, be attractive to, interest, take someone's fancy, fascinate, tempt, entice, allure, lure, draw, whet someone's appetite; *informal* float someone's boat.
● noun 1 *an appeal for help* PLEA, urgent/earnest request, entreaty, cry, call, petition, supplication, cri de cœur; *rare* obsecration. 2 *the cultural appeal of the island* ATTRACTION, attractiveness, allure, charm; fascination, magnetism, drawing power, pull. 3 *the court allowed the appeal* RETRIAL, re-examination.

appealing ● adjective ATTRACTIVE, engaging, alluring, enchanting, captivating, bewitching, fascinating, tempting, enticing, seductive, irresistible, winning, winsome, charming, desirable; *Brit. informal* tasty; *dated* taking.
– OPPOSITES disagreeable, off-putting.

appear ● verb 1 *a cloud of dust appeared on the horizon* BECOME VISIBLE, come into view/sight, materialize, pop up. 2 *fundamental differences were beginning to appear* BE REVEALED, emerge, surface, manifest itself, become apparent/evident, come to light; arise, crop up. 3 *(informal) Bill still hadn't appeared* ARRIVE, turn up, put in an appearance, come, get here/there; *informal* show (up), pitch up, fetch up, roll in, blow in. 4 *they appeared to be completely devoted* SEEM, look, give the impression, come across as, strike someone as. 5 *the paperback edition didn't appear for two years* BECOME AVAILABLE, come on the market, go on sale, come out, be published, be produced. 6 *he appeared on Broadway* PERFORM, play,

a

appease ● verb placate (someone) by agreeing to their demands.
– DERIVATIVES **appeasement** noun **appeaser** noun.
– ORIGIN Old French *apaisier*, from *pais* 'peace'.
appellant /əpellənt/ ● noun Law a person who appeals against a court ruling.
appellate /əpellət/ ● adjective Law (of a court) dealing with appeals.
appellation /appəlaysh'n/ ● noun formal a name or title.
– ORIGIN Latin, from *appellare* 'to address'.
appellation contrôlée /appelassyon kəntrōlay/ (also **appellation d'origine** /dorrizheen/ **contrôlée**) ● noun a guarantee that a French wine was produced in the region stated and in the approved manner.
– ORIGIN French, 'controlled appellation'.
append ● verb add to the end of a document or piece of writing.
– ORIGIN Latin *appendere* 'hang on'.
appendage ● noun a thing attached to or projecting from something larger or more important.
appendectomy /appendektəmi/ (Brit. also **appendicectomy** /əpendisektəmi/) ● noun (pl. **appendectomies**) a surgical operation to remove the appendix.
appendicitis ● noun inflammation of the appendix.
appendix ● noun (pl. **appendices** or **appendixes**) **1** a small tube of tissue attached to the lower end of the large intestine. **2** a section of additional information at the end of a book.
– ORIGIN Latin, from *appendere* 'hang on'.
appertain /appərtayn/ ● verb **1** (**appertain to**) relate to. **2** be appropriate.
– ORIGIN Latin *appertinere*, from *pertinere* 'pertain'.
appetite ● noun **1** a natural desire to satisfy a bodily need, especially for food. **2** a liking or inclination: *my appetite for study had gone.*
– DERIVATIVES **appetitive** adjective.
– ORIGIN Latin *appetitus* 'desire for', from *appetere* 'seek after'.
appetizer (also **appetiser**) ● noun a small dish of food or a drink taken before a meal to stimulate the appetite.
appetizing (also **appetising**) ● adjective stimulating the appetite.
applaud ● verb **1** show approval by clapping. **2** express approval of: *the world applauded his courage.*
– ORIGIN Latin *applaudere*, from *plaudere* 'to clap'.
applause ● noun approval shown by clapping.
apple ● noun the rounded fruit of a tree of the rose family, with green or red skin and crisp flesh.
– PHRASES **the apple never falls far from the tree** proverb salient family characteristics are usually inherited. **the apple of one's eye** a person of whom one is extremely fond and proud. [ORIGIN originally denoting the pupil of the eye, extended as a symbol of something cherished.] **a rotten** (or **bad**) **apple** informal a corrupt person in a group, likely to have a detrimental influence on the others. **upset the apple cart** spoil a plan.
– DERIVATIVES **appley** adjective.
– ORIGIN Old English.
apple-pie order ● noun perfect order.
applet /applit/ ● noun Computing a small application running within a larger program.
appliance ● noun **1** a device designed to perform a specific task. **2** Brit. the application of something.
applicable ● adjective relevant or appropriate.
– DERIVATIVES **applicability** noun.
applicant ● noun a person who applies for something.
application ● noun **1** a formal request to an authority. **2** the action of applying. **3** practical use or relevance. **4** sustained effort. **5** a computer program designed to fulfil a particular purpose.

Thesaurus

act.
– OPPOSITES vanish.
appearance ● noun **1** *her dishevelled appearance* LOOK(S), air, aspect, mien. **2** *an appearance of respectability* IMPRESSION, air, (outward) show; semblance, facade, veneer, front, pretence. **3** *the sudden appearance of her daughter* ARRIVAL, advent, coming, emergence, materialization. **4** *the appearance of these symptoms* OCCURRENCE, manifestation, development.
appease ● verb **1** *an attempt to appease his critics* CONCILIATE, placate, pacify, propitiate, reconcile, win over; informal sweeten. **2** *I'd wasted a lot of money to appease my vanity* SATISFY, fulfil, gratify, indulge; assuage, relieve, take the edge off.
– OPPOSITES provoke, inflame.
appeasement ● noun **1** *a policy of appeasement* CONCILIATION, placation, pacification, propitiation, reconciliation; peacemaking, peace-mongering. **2** *appeasement for battered consciences* SATISFACTION, fulfilment, gratification, indulgence; assuagement, relief.
– OPPOSITES provocation.
appellation ● noun (formal) NAME, title, designation, tag, sobriquet, byname, nickname, cognomen; informal moniker, handle; formal denomination.
append ● verb ADD, attach, affix, tack on, tag on; formal subjoin.
appendage ● noun **1** *I am not just an appendage to the family* ADDITION, attachment, adjunct, addendum, appurtenance, accessory. **2** *a pair of feathery appendages* PROTUBERANCE, projection; technical process.
appendix ● noun SUPPLEMENT, addendum, postscript, codicil; coda, epilogue, afterword, tailpiece, back matter.
appertain ● verb
– PHRASES **appertain to** PERTAIN TO, be pertinent to, apply to, relate to, concern, be concerned with, have to do with, be relevant to, have reference to, have a bearing on, bear on; archaic regard.
appetite ● noun **1** *a walk sharpens the appetite* HUNGER, ravenousness, hungriness; taste, palate; rare edacity. **2** *my appetite for learning* CRAVING, longing, yearning, hankering, hunger, thirst, passion; enthusiasm, keenness, eagerness, desire; informal yen; archaic appetency.
appetizer ● noun STARTER, first course, hors d'oeuvre, amuse-gueule, antipasto.
appetizing ● adjective **1** *an appetizing lunch* MOUTH-WATERING, inviting, tempting; tasty, delicious, flavoursome, toothsome; informal scrumptious, scrummy, yummy, moreish. **2** *the least appetizing part of election campaigns* APPEALING, attractive, inviting, alluring.
– OPPOSITES bland, unappealing.
applaud ● verb **1** *the audience applauded* CLAP, give a standing ovation, put one's hands together; show one's appreciation; informal give someone a big hand. **2** *police have applauded the decision* PRAISE, commend, acclaim, salute, welcome, celebrate, express admiration for, express approval of, look on with favour, approve of, sing the praises of, pay tribute to, speak highly of, take one's hat off to, express respect for.
– OPPOSITES boo, criticize.
applause ● noun **1** *a massive round of applause* CLAPPING, handclapping, (standing) ovation; acclamation. **2** *the museum's design won general applause* PRAISE, acclaim, acclamation, admiration, commendation, adulation, favour, approbation, approval, respect; compliments, accolades, tributes.
appliance ● noun **1** *domestic appliances* DEVICE, machine, instrument, gadget, contraption, apparatus, utensil, implement, tool, mechanism, contrivance, labour-saving device; informal gizmo, mod con. **2** *the appliance of science* APPLICATION, use, exercise, employment, implementation, utilization, practice, applying, discharge, execution, prosecution, enactment; formal praxis.
applicable ● adjective *the laws applicable to the dispute* RELEVANT, appropriate, pertinent, appurtenant, apposite, germane, material, significant, related, connected; fitting, suitable, apt, befitting, to the point, useful, helpful; formal ad rem.
– OPPOSITES inappropriate, irrelevant.
applicant ● noun CANDIDATE, interviewee, competitor, contestant, contender, entrant; claimant, suppliant, supplicant, petitioner, postulant; prospective student/employee, job-seeker, job-hunter, auditioner.
application ● noun **1** *an application for an overdraft* REQUEST, appeal, petition, entreaty, plea, solicitation, supplication, requisition, suit, approach, claim, demand. **2** *the application of anti-inflation policies* IMPLEMENTATION, use, exercise, employment, utilization, practice, applying, discharge, execution, prosecution, enactment; formal praxis. **3** *the argument is clearest in its application to the theatre* RELEVANCE, relevancy, bearing, significance, pertinence, aptness, appositeness, germaneness, importance. **4** *the application of make-up* PUTTING ON, rubbing in, applying. **5** *an application to relieve muscle pain* OINTMENT, lotion, cream, rub, salve, emollient, preparation, liniment, embrocation, balm, unguent, poultice. **6** *the job takes a great deal of application* DILIGENCE, industriousness, industry, assiduity, commitment, dedication, devotion, conscientiousness, perseverance, persistence, tenacity, doggedness, sedulousness; concentration, attention, attentiveness, steadiness, patience, endurance; effort, hard work, labour, en-

a

applicator ● noun a device for inserting something or applying a substance to a surface.

applied ● adjective practical rather than theoretical: *applied chemistry.*

appliqué /əpleekay/ ● noun decorative needlework in which fabric shapes are sewn or fixed on to a fabric background.
– DERIVATIVES **appliquéd** adjective.
– ORIGIN French, 'applied'.

apply ● verb (**applies**, **applied**) **1** make a formal request for something to be done, such as asking to be considered for a job. **2** bring into operation or use. **3** be relevant. **4** put (a substance) on a surface. **5** (**apply oneself**) put all one's efforts into a task.
– ORIGIN Latin *applicare* 'fold, fasten to'.

appoint ● verb **1** assign a job or role to. **2** decide on (a time or place).
– DERIVATIVES **appointee** noun.
– ORIGIN Old French *apointer*, from *a point* 'to a point'.

appointed ● adjective **1** (of a time or place) pre-arranged. **2** equipped or furnished: *a luxuriously appointed lounge.*

appointment ● noun **1** an arrangement to meet. **2** a job or position. **3** the action of appointing or the process of being appointed. **4** (**appointments**) furniture or fittings.
– PHRASES **by appointment (to the Queen)** selling goods or services to the Queen.

apportion ● verb share out; assign.
– DERIVATIVES **apportionment** noun.
– ORIGIN Latin *apportionare*, from *portionare* 'divide into portions'.

apposite /appəzit/ ● adjective very appropriate; apt.
– ORIGIN from Latin *apponere* 'apply'.

apposition ● noun **1** chiefly technical the positioning of things next to each other. **2** Grammar a relationship in which a word or phrase is placed next to another in order to qualify or explain it (e.g. *my friend Sue*).
– DERIVATIVES **appositive** adjective & noun.

appraisal ● noun **1** the action or an instance of assessing. **2** a formal assessment of an employee's performance at work.

appraise ● verb **1** assess the quality or nature of. **2** give (an employee) an appraisal. **3** (of an official valuer) set a price on.
– DERIVATIVES **appraisee** noun **appraiser** noun.
– USAGE **Appraise** is frequently confused with **apprise**. **Appraise** means 'assess', while **apprise** means 'inform' and is often used in the structure *apprise someone of something*.
– ORIGIN alteration of APPRISE.

appreciable ● adjective large or important enough to be noticed.
– DERIVATIVES **appreciably** adverb.

appreciate /əpreeshiayt, -siayt/ ● verb **1** recognize the value or significance of. **2** understand (a situation) fully. **3** be grateful for. **4** rise in value or price.
– DERIVATIVES **appreciator** noun.
– ORIGIN Latin *appretiare* 'appraise', from *pretium* 'price'.

appreciation ● noun **1** recognition of the value or significance of something. **2** gratitude. **3** a favourable written assessment of a person or their work. **4** increase in monetary value.

appreciative ● adjective feeling or showing gratitude or pleasure.
– DERIVATIVES **appreciatively** adverb **appreciativeness** noun.

apprehend ● verb **1** intercept in the course of unlawful or wrongful action. **2** seize or arrest. **3** understand; perceive. **4** archaic anticipate with fear or unease.
– ORIGIN Latin *apprehendere*, from *prehendere* 'lay hold of'.

apprehension ● noun **1** uneasy or fearful anticipation. **2** understanding. **3** the action of arresting someone.

Thesaurus

deavour. **7** *a vector graphics application* PROGRAM, software, routine.

apply ● verb **1** *300 people applied for the job* PUT IN AN APPLICATION, put in, try, bid, appeal, petition, sue, register, audition; request, seek, solicit, claim, ask, try to obtain. **2** *the Act did not apply to Scotland* BE RELEVANT, have relevance, have a bearing, appertain, pertain, relate, concern, affect, involve, cover, deal with, touch; be pertinent, be appropriate, be significant. **3** *she applied some ointment* PUT ON, rub in, work in, spread, smear. **4** *a steady pressure should be applied* EXERT, administer, implement, use, exercise, employ, utilize, bring to bear.
– PHRASES **apply oneself** BE DILIGENT, be industrious, be assiduous, show commitment, show dedication; work hard, exert oneself, make an effort, try hard, do one's best, give one's all, buckle down, put one's shoulder to the wheel, keep one's nose to the grindstone; strive, endeavour, struggle, labour, toil; pay attention, commit oneself, devote oneself; persevere, persist; informal put one's back in it, knuckle down, get stuck in.

appoint ● verb **1** *he was appointed chairman* NOMINATE, name, designate, install as, commission, engage, co-opt; select, choose, elect, vote in; Military detail. **2** *the arbitrator shall appoint a date for the meeting* SPECIFY, determine, assign, designate, allot, set, fix, arrange, choose, decide on, establish, settle, ordain, prescribe, decree.
– OPPOSITES reject.

appointed ● adjective **1** *at the appointed time* SCHEDULED, arranged, pre-arranged, specified, decided, agreed, determined, assigned, designated, allotted, set, fixed, chosen, established, settled, preordained, ordained, prescribed, decreed. **2** *a well appointed room* FURNISHED, decorated, outfitted, fitted out, provided, supplied.

appointment ● noun **1** *a six o'clock appointment* MEETING, engagement, interview, arrangement, consultation, session; date, rendezvous, assignation; commitment, fixture; poetic/literary tryst. **2** *the appointment of directors* NOMINATION, naming, designation, installation, commissioning, engagement, co-option; selection, choosing, election, voting in; Military detailing. **3** *he held an appointment at the university* JOB, post, position, situation, employment, place, office; dated station.

apportion ● verb SHARE, divide, allocate, distribute, allot, assign, give out, hand out, mete out, deal out, dish out, dole out; ration, measure out; split; informal divvy up.

apposite ● adjective APPROPRIATE, suitable, fitting, apt, befitting; relevant, pertinent, appurtenant, to the point, applicable, germane, material, congruous, felicitous; formal ad rem.
– OPPOSITES inappropriate.

appraisal ● noun **1** *an objective appraisal of the book* ASSESSMENT, evaluation, estimation, judgement, rating, gauging, sizing up, summing-up, consideration. **2** *a free insurance appraisal* VALUATION, estimate, estimation, quotation, pricing; survey.

appraise ● verb **1** *they appraised their handiwork* ASSESS, evaluate, judge, rate, gauge, review, consider; informal size up. **2** *his goods were appraised at £1,800* VALUE, price, estimate, quote; survey.

appreciable ● adjective CONSIDERABLE, substantial, significant, sizeable, goodly, fair, reasonable, marked; perceptible, noticeable, visible; informal tidy.
– OPPOSITES negligible.

appreciate ● verb **1** *I'd appreciate your advice* BE GRATEFUL, be thankful, be obliged, be indebted, be in your debt, be appreciative. **2** *the college appreciated her greatly* VALUE, treasure, admire, respect, hold in high regard, think highly of, think much of. **3** *we appreciate the problems* RECOGNIZE, acknowledge, realize, know, be aware of, be conscious of, be sensitive to, understand, comprehend; informal be wise to. **4** *a home that will appreciate in value* INCREASE, gain, grow, rise, go up, escalate, soar, rocket.
– OPPOSITES disparage, depreciate, decrease.

appreciation ● noun **1** *he showed his appreciation* GRATITUDE, thanks, gratefulness, thankfulness, recognition, sense of obligation. **2** *her appreciation of literature* VALUING, treasuring, admiration, respect, regard, esteem, high opinion. **3** *an appreciation of the value of teamwork* ACKNOWLEDGEMENT, recognition, realization, knowledge, awareness, consciousness, understanding, comprehension. **4** *the appreciation of the franc against the pound* INCREASE, gain, growth, rise, inflation, escalation. **5** *an appreciation of the professor's work* REVIEW, critique, criticism, critical analysis, assessment, evaluation, judgement, rating; Brit. informal crit.
– OPPOSITES ingratitude, unawareness, depreciation, decrease.

appreciative ● adjective **1** *we are appreciative of all your efforts* GRATEFUL, thankful, obliged, indebted, in someone's debt. **2** *an appreciative audience* SUPPORTIVE, encouraging, sympathetic, responsive; enthusiastic, admiring, approving, complimentary.
– OPPOSITES ungrateful, disparaging.

apprehend ● verb **1** *the thieves were quickly apprehended* ARREST, catch, capture, seize; take prisoner, take into custody, detain, put in jail, put behind bars, imprison, incarcerate; informal collar, nab, nail, run in, pinch, bust, pick up, pull in, feel someone's collar; Brit. informal nick, do. **2** *they are slow to apprehend danger* APPRECIATE, recognize, discern, perceive, make out, take in, realize, grasp, understand, comprehend; informal get the picture; Brit. informal twig, suss (out).

a

apprehensive • adjective anticipating something with anxiety or fear.
– DERIVATIVES **apprehensively** adverb **apprehensiveness** noun.
apprentice • noun a person learning a skilled practical trade from an employer. • verb employ as an apprentice.
– DERIVATIVES **apprenticeship** noun.
– ORIGIN Old French *aprentis*, from Latin *apprehendere* 'apprehend'.
apprise • verb inform; tell.
– USAGE On the confusion of **apprise** and **appraise**, see APPRAISE.
– ORIGIN French, from *apprendre* 'learn, teach', from Latin *apprehendere* 'apprehend'.
approach • verb **1** come near to in distance, time, or standard. **2** go to (someone) with a proposal or request. **3** start to deal with in a certain way. • noun **1** a way of dealing with something. **2** an initial proposal or request. **3** the action of approaching. **4** a way leading to a place.
– ORIGIN Old French *aprochier*, from Latin *appropiare* 'draw near'.
approachable • adjective **1** friendly and easy to talk to. **2** able to be reached from a particular direction or by a particular means.
– DERIVATIVES **approachability** noun.
approbation • noun approval; praise.
– DERIVATIVES **approbative** adjective **approbatory** adjective.
– ORIGIN Latin, from *approbare* 'approve'.
appropriate • adjective /əprōpriət/ suitable; proper. • verb /əprōpriayt/ **1** take for one's own use without permission. **2** devote (money) to a special purpose.
– DERIVATIVES **appropriately** adverb **appropriateness** noun **appropriation** noun **appropriator** noun.
– ORIGIN from Latin *appropriare* 'make one's own', from *proprius* 'own, proper'.
approval • noun **1** the opinion that something is good. **2** official acknowledgement that something is satisfactory.
– PHRASES **on approval** (of goods) able to be returned if unsatisfactory.
approve • verb **1** (often **approve of**) believe that someone or something is good or acceptable. **2** officially acknowledge as satisfactory.
– ORIGIN Old French *aprover*, from Latin *approbare*.
approved school • noun Brit. historical a residential institution for young offenders.
approximate • adjective /əproksimət/ fairly accurate but not totally precise. • verb /əproksimayt/ **1** come close in quality or quantity. **2** estimate fairly accurately.
– DERIVATIVES **approximately** adverb **approximation** noun **approximative** adjective.
– ORIGIN Latin *approximatus*, from *proximus* 'very near'.
appurtenance /əpurtinənss/ • noun an accessory associated with a particular activity.
– ORIGIN Old French *apertenance*, from Latin *appertinere* 'belong to'.
APR • abbreviation annual (or annualized) percentage rate.

Thesaurus

apprehension • noun **1** *he was filled with apprehension* ANXIETY, worry, unease, nervousness, nerves, misgivings, disquiet, concern, tension, trepidation, perturbation, consternation, angst, dread, fear, foreboding; *informal* butterflies, the willies, the heebie-jeebies. **2** *her quick apprehension of their wishes* APPRECIATION, recognition, discernment, perception, realization, grasp, understanding, comprehension, awareness. **3** *the apprehension of a perpetrator* ARREST, capture, seizure; detention, imprisonment, incarceration; *informal* collar, nabbing, bust; *Brit. informal* nick.
– OPPOSITES confidence.
apprehensive • adjective ANXIOUS, worried, uneasy, nervous, concerned, agitated, tense, afraid, scared, frightened, fearful; *informal* on tenterhooks.
– OPPOSITES confident.
apprentice • noun TRAINEE, learner, probationer, novice, beginner, starter; pupil, student; *N. Amer.* tenderfoot; *informal* rookie; *N. Amer. informal* greenhorn.
– OPPOSITES veteran.
apprenticeship • noun TRAINEESHIP, training period, studentship, novitiate; *historical* indentureship.
apprise • verb INFORM, tell, notify, advise, brief, make aware, enlighten, update, keep posted; *informal* clue in, fill in, put wise, put in the picture.
approach • verb **1** *she approached the altar* MOVE TOWARDS, come/go towards, advance towards, go/come/draw/move nearer, go/come/draw/move closer, near; close in, gain on; reach, arrive at. **2** *the trade deficit is approaching £20 million* BORDER ON, verge on, approximate, touch, nudge, get on for, near, come near to, come close to. **3** *she approached him about leaving his job* SPEAK TO, talk to; make advances, make overtures, make a proposal, sound out, proposition. **4** *he approached the problem in the best way* TACKLE, set about, address oneself to, undertake, get down to, launch into, embark on, go about, get to grips with.
– OPPOSITES leave.
• noun **1** *the traditional British approach* METHOD, procedure, technique, modus operandi, MO, style, way, manner; strategy, tactic, system, means, line of action. **2** *he considered an approach to the High Court* PROPOSAL, proposition, submission, application, appeal, plea, request. **3** (*dated*) *his approaches were repulsed* ADVANCES, overtures, suggestions, attentions; suit. **4** *the dog barked at the approach of any intruder* ADVANCE, coming, nearing; arrival, appearance; advent. **5** *the approach to the castle* DRIVEWAY, drive, access road, road, avenue; way.
approachable • adjective **1** *students found the staff approachable* FRIENDLY, welcoming, pleasant, agreeable, congenial, affable, cordial; obliging, communicative, helpful. **2** *the south landing is approachable by boat* ACCESSIBLE, attainable, reachable; *informal* get-at-able.
– OPPOSITES aloof, inaccessible.
approbation • noun APPROVAL, acceptance, endorsement, appreciation, respect, admiration, commendation, praise, congratulations, acclaim, esteem, applause.
– OPPOSITES criticism.
appropriate • adjective *this isn't the appropriate time* SUITABLE, proper, fitting, apt, right; relevant, pertinent, apposite; convenient, opportune; seemly, befitting; *formal* ad rem; *archaic* meet.
– OPPOSITES unsuitable.
• verb **1** *the barons appropriated church lands* SEIZE, commandeer, expropriate, annex, arrogate, sequestrate, sequester, take over, hijack; steal, take; *informal* swipe, nab, bag; *Brit. informal* pinch, half-inch, nick. **2** *his images have been appropriated by advertisers* PLAGIARIZE, copy; poach, steal, 'borrow'; *informal* rip off. **3** *we are appropriating funds for these expenses* ALLOCATE, assign, allot, earmark, set aside, devote, apportion.
approval • noun **1** *their proposals went to the ministry for approval* ACCEPTANCE, agreement, consent, assent, permission, leave, the nod; rubber stamp, sanction, endorsement, ratification, authorization, validation; support, backing; *informal* the go-ahead, the green light, the OK, the thumbs up. **2** *Lily looked at him with approval* APPROBATION, appreciation, favour, liking, admiration, regard, esteem, respect, praise. **3** *we will send you the goods on approval* TRIAL, sale or return; *Brit. informal* appro.
– OPPOSITES refusal, dislike.
approve • verb **1** *his boss doesn't approve of his lifestyle* AGREE WITH, hold with, endorse, support, back, uphold, subscribe to, recommend, advocate, be in favour of, favour, think well of, like, appreciate, take kindly to; be pleased with, admire, applaud, praise. **2** *the government approved the proposals* ACCEPT, agree to, consent to, assent to, give one's blessing to, bless, rubber-stamp, give the nod; ratify, sanction, endorse, authorize, validate, pass; support, back; *informal* give the go-ahead, give the green light, give the OK, give the thumbs-up.
– OPPOSITES condemn, refuse.
approximate • adjective *all measurements are approximate* ESTIMATED, rough, imprecise, inexact, indefinite, broad, loose; *N. Amer. informal* ballpark.
– OPPOSITES precise.
• verb *this scenario probably approximates to the truth* BE/COME CLOSE TO, be/come near to, approach, border on, verge on; resemble, be similar to, be not unlike.
approximately • adverb ROUGHLY, about, around, circa, round about, more or less, in the neighbourhood of, in the region of, of the order of, something like, give or take (a few); near to, close to, nearly, almost, approaching; *Brit.* getting on for; *informal* pushing; *N. Amer. informal* in the ballpark of.
– OPPOSITES precisely.
approximation • noun **1** *the figure is only an approximation* ESTIMATE, estimation, guess, rough calculation; *informal* guesstimate; *N. Amer. informal* ballpark figure. **2** *an approximation to the truth* SEMBLANCE, resemblance, likeness, similarity, correspondence.

apraxia /əpraksiə/ ● noun Medicine inability to perform particular activities as a result of brain damage.
– ORIGIN Greek, 'inaction'.
après-ski ● noun social activities following a day's skiing.
– ORIGIN French, 'after skiing'.
apricot ● noun an orange-yellow fruit resembling a small peach.
– ORIGIN Portuguese *albricoque* or Spanish *albaricoque*, from an Arabic word based on Latin *praecox* 'early-ripe'.
April ● noun the fourth month of the year.
– ORIGIN Latin *Aprilis*.
April Fool's Day ● noun 1 April, traditionally an occasion for playing tricks.
a priori /ay prīorī/ ● adjective & adverb based on theoretical reasoning rather than actual observation.
– ORIGIN Latin, 'from what is before'.
apron ● noun **1** a protective garment covering the front of one's clothes and tied at the back. **2** an area on an airfield used for manoeuvring or parking aircraft. **3** (also **apron stage**) a strip of stage projecting in front of the curtain. **4** an endless conveyor made of overlapping plates.
– PHRASES **tied to someone's apron strings** under someone's influence and control to an excessive extent.
– ORIGIN Old French *naperon* 'small tablecloth', from Latin *mappa* 'napkin'; the *n* was lost by wrong division of *a napron*.
apropos /aprəpō/ ● preposition with reference to.
– ORIGIN French *à propos*.
apse /aps/ ● noun a large semicircular or polygonal recess with a domed roof, typically at a church's eastern end.
– DERIVATIVES **apsidal** /apsid'l/ adjective.
– ORIGIN Greek *apsis* 'arch, vault'.
apt ● adjective **1** appropriate; suitable. **2** (**apt to**) having a tendency to. **3** quick to learn.
– DERIVATIVES **aptly** adverb **aptness** noun.
– ORIGIN Latin *aptus* 'fitted'.
aptitude ● noun a natural ability or inclination.
– ORIGIN Old French, from Latin *aptus* 'fitted'.
aqua- /akwə/ ● combining form relating to water: *aqualung*.
– ORIGIN Latin *aqua* 'water'.
aqualung ● noun a portable breathing apparatus for divers.
aquamarine ● noun **1** a light bluish-green variety of beryl. **2** a light bluish-green colour.
– ORIGIN from Latin *aqua marina* 'seawater'.
aquanaut ● noun a diver.
– ORIGIN from Latin *aqua* 'water' + Greek *nautēs* 'sailor'.
aquaplane ● noun a board for riding on water, pulled by a speedboat. ● verb **1** ride on an aquaplane. **2** (of a vehicle) slide uncontrollably on a wet surface.
– ORIGIN from Latin *aqua* 'water' + PLANE[1].
aqua regia /akwə reejiə/ ● noun Chemistry a highly corrosive mixture of concentrated nitric and hydrochloric acids.
– ORIGIN Latin, 'royal water': so called because it is able to dissolve gold.
aquarelle /akwərel/ ● noun the technique of painting with thin, transparent watercolours.
– ORIGIN French, from Italian *acquarella* 'watercolour'.
aquarist /akwərist/ ● noun a person who keeps an aquarium.
aquarium ● noun (pl. **aquaria** or **aquariums**) a water-filled glass tank for keeping fish and other aquatic life.
– ORIGIN Latin, from *aquarius* 'of water'.
Aquarius /əkwairiəss/ ● noun **1** Astronomy a large constellation (the Water Bearer), said to represent a man pouring water from a jar. **2** Astrology the eleventh sign of the zodiac, which the sun enters about 21 January.
– DERIVATIVES **Aquarian** noun & adjective.
aquatic /əkwattik/ ● adjective **1** relating to water. **2** living in or near water. ● noun an aquatic plant or animal.
aquatint ● noun a print resembling a watercolour, made using a copper plate etched with nitric acid.
– ORIGIN French, from Italian *acqua tinta* 'coloured water'.
aquavit /akwəveet/ (also **akvavit** /akvəveet/) ● noun an alcoholic spirit made from potatoes.
– ORIGIN from Norwegian, Swedish, and Danish *akvavit*, 'water of life'.
aqua vitae /akwə veetī/ ● noun archaic strong alcoholic spirit, especially brandy.
– ORIGIN Latin, 'water of life'.
aqueduct /akwidukt/ ● noun a long channel or elevated bridge-like structure, used for channelling water over a distance.
– ORIGIN from Latin *aquae ductus* 'conduit'.
aqueous /aykwiəss/ ● adjective relating to or containing water.
– ORIGIN from Latin *aqua* 'water'.
aqueous humour ● noun the clear fluid in the eyeball in front of the lens.
aquifer /akwifər/ ● noun a body of rock that holds water or through which water flows.
aquilegia /akwileejə/ ● noun a plant bearing showy flowers with backward-pointing spurs.
– ORIGIN probably from Latin *aquilegus* 'water-collecting'.
aquiline /akwilīn/ ● adjective **1** like an eagle. **2** (of a nose) curved like an eagle's beak.
– ORIGIN Latin *aquilinus*, from *aquila* 'eagle'.
AR ● abbreviation US Arkansas.
Ar ● symbol the chemical element argon.
-ar ● suffix **1** (forming adjectives) of the kind specified: *molecular*. **2** forming nouns such as *scholar*.
– ORIGIN from Latin *-aris*.
Arab ● noun **1** a member of a Semitic people inhabiting much of the Middle East and North Africa. **2** a breed of horse originating in Arabia.
– DERIVATIVES **Arabize** (also **Arabise**) verb.
– ORIGIN Arabic.
arabesque /arrəbesk/ ● noun **1** Ballet a posture in which one leg is extended horizontally backwards and the arms are outstretched. **2** an ornamental design consisting of intertwined flowing lines. **3** Music a passage with a highly ornamented melody.
– ORIGIN French, from Italian *arabesco* 'in the Arabic style'.
Arabian ● noun **1** historical a person from Arabia. **2** an Arab horse. ● adjective relating to Arabia or its people.
Arabic ● noun the Semitic language of the Arabs, written from right to left in a cursive script. ● adjective relating to the Arabs or Arabic.
arabica /ərabbikə/ ● noun a type of coffee bean widely grown in tropical Asia and Africa.
– ORIGIN Latin, 'Arabic'.
Arabic numeral ● noun any of the numerals 0, 1, 2, 3, 4, 5, 6, 7, 8, and 9.
Arabism ● noun **1** Arab culture or identity. **2** an Arabic word or phrase.
– DERIVATIVES **Arabist** noun & adjective.
arable ● adjective **1** (of land) able to be ploughed and used for the cultivation of crops. **2** (of crops) cultivated on ploughed land.
– ORIGIN Latin *arabilis*, from *arare* 'to plough'.
arachnid /əraknid/ ● noun a member of a class of arthropods

Thesaurus

appurtenances ● plural noun ACCESSORIES, trappings, appendages, accoutrements, equipment, paraphernalia, impedimenta, bits and pieces, things; *informal* stuff.
a priori ● adjective *a priori reasoning* THEORETICAL, deduced, deductive, inferred, postulated, suppositional; scientific.
– OPPOSITES empirical.
● adverb *the results cannot be predicted a priori* THEORETICALLY, deductively, scientifically.
apron ● noun PINAFORE, overall; *informal* pinny.
apropos ● preposition *he was asked a question apropos his resignation* WITH REFERENCE TO, with regard to, with respect to, regarding, concerning, on the subject of, connected with, about, re.
● adjective *the word 'conglomerate' was decidedly apropos* APPROPRIATE, pertinent, relevant, apposite, apt, applicable, suitable, germane, material.
– OPPOSITES inappropriate.
– PHRASES **apropos of nothing** IRRELEVANTLY, arbitrarily, at random, for no reason, illogically.
apt ● adjective **1** *a very apt description of how I felt* SUITABLE, fitting, appropriate, befitting, relevant, applicable, apposite; *Brit. informal* spot on. **2** *they are apt to get a mite slipshod* INCLINED, given, likely, liable, disposed, predisposed, prone. **3** *an apt pupil* CLEVER, quick, bright, sharp, smart, intelligent, able, gifted, adept, astute.
– OPPOSITES inappropriate, unlikely, slow.
aptitude ● noun TALENT, gift, flair, bent, skill, knack, facility, ability, capability, potential, capacity, faculty, genius.
aquatic ● adjective MARINE, water, saltwater, freshwater, seawater, sea, oceanic, river; *technical* pelagic, thalassic.

a

including the spiders, scorpions, mites, and ticks.
– ORIGIN from Greek *arakhnē* 'spider'.

arachnophobia /əraknəfōbiə/ ● noun extreme fear of spiders.
– DERIVATIVES **arachnophobe** noun **arachnophobic** adjective.
– ORIGIN from Greek *arakhnē* 'spider'.

arak /ərak/ ● noun variant spelling of ARRACK.

Aramaic /arrəmayik/ ● noun a branch of the Semitic family of languages, used as a lingua franca in the Near East from the 6th century BC and still spoken in some communities. ● adjective relating to this language.
– ORIGIN Greek *Aramaios* 'of *Aram*' (the biblical name of Syria).

Aran ● adjective (of knitwear) featuring patterns of cable stitch and diamond designs, as made traditionally in the Aran Islands off the west coast of Ireland.

Arapaho /ərappəhō/ ● noun (pl. same or **Arapahos**) **1** a member of a North American Indian people living on the Great Plains. **2** the Algonquian language of this people.
– ORIGIN from an American Indian word meaning 'many tattoo marks'.

Arawak /arrəwak/ ● noun (pl. same or **Arawaks**) **1** a member of a group of native peoples of the Greater Antilles and northern and western South America. **2** any of the languages of these peoples.
– DERIVATIVES **Arawakan** adjective & noun.
– ORIGIN Carib.

arbiter ● noun **1** a person who settles a dispute. **2** a person who has influence over something.
– ORIGIN Latin, 'judge, supreme ruler'.

arbitrage /aarbitraazh, -trij/ ● noun Economics the simultaneous buying and selling of assets in different markets or in derivative forms, taking advantage of the differing prices.
– DERIVATIVES **arbitrageur** /aarbitraazhör/noun.
– ORIGIN French, from *arbitrer* 'give judgement'.

arbitrary /aarbitrəri, -tri/ ● adjective **1** based on random choice or personal whim. **2** (of power or authority) used without constraint; autocratic.
– DERIVATIVES **arbitrarily** adverb **arbitrariness** noun.
– ORIGIN Latin *arbitrarius*, from *arbiter* 'judge, supreme ruler'.

arbitrate ● verb act as an arbitrator to settle a dispute.
– ORIGIN Latin *arbitrari*, from *arbiter* 'judge, supreme ruler'.

arbitration ● noun the use of an arbitrator to settle a dispute.

arbitrator ● noun an independent person or body officially appointed to settle a dispute.

arbor[1] ● noun **1** an axle on which something revolves. **2** a device holding a tool in a lathe.
– ORIGIN French *arbre* 'tree, axis', influenced by Latin *arbor* 'tree'.

arbor[2] ● noun US spelling of ARBOUR.

arboreal /aarboriəl/ ● adjective **1** relating to trees. **2** living in trees.
– DERIVATIVES **arboreality** noun.
– ORIGIN from Latin *arbor* 'tree'.

arboretum /aarbəreetəm/ ● noun (pl. **arboretums** or **arboreta**) a garden devoted to the study and display of trees.
– ORIGIN Latin, from *arbor* 'tree'.

arboriculture /aarbərikulchər/ ● noun the cultivation of trees and shrubs.

arbour (US **arbor**) ● noun a shady recess in a garden, with a canopy of trees or climbing plants.
– ORIGIN Old French *erbier*, from Latin *herba* 'grass, herb'; influenced by Latin *arbor* 'tree'.

arc ● noun **1** a curve forming part of the circumference of a circle. **2** a curving trajectory. **3** a luminous electrical discharge between two points. ● verb (**arced**, **arcing**) **1** move with a curving trajectory. **2** (**arcing**) the forming of an electric arc.
– ORIGIN Latin *arcus* 'bow, curve'.

arcade ● noun **1** a covered passage with arches along one or both sides. **2** chiefly Brit. a covered walk with shops along one or both sides. **3** Architecture a series of arches supporting a wall.
– DERIVATIVES **arcading** noun.
– ORIGIN French, from Latin *arcus* 'bow, curve'.

Arcadian ● noun **1** a person from Arcadia, a mountainous region of southern Greece. **2** literary an idealized country dweller. ● adjective **1** relating to Arcadia in Greece. **2** rustic in an idealized way.

Arcady /aarkədi/ ● noun literary an ideal rustic paradise.
– ORIGIN Greek *Arkadia* 'Arcadia', a region of Greece.

arcane /aarkayn/ ● adjective understood by few; mysterious.
– DERIVATIVES **arcanely** adverb.
– ORIGIN Latin *arcanus*, from *arca* 'chest'.

arcanum /aarkaynəm/ ● noun (pl. **arcana**) a hidden thing; a mystery or profound secret.
– ORIGIN Latin, from *arca* 'chest'.

arch[1] ● noun **1** a curved structure spanning an opening or supporting the weight of a bridge, roof, or wall. **2** the inner side of the foot. ● verb form or cause to form an arch.
– DERIVATIVES **arched** adjective.
– ORIGIN Old French *arche*, from Latin *arcus* 'bow'.

arch[2] ● adjective self-consciously playful or teasing.
– DERIVATIVES **archly** adverb **archness** noun.
– ORIGIN from ARCH-, by association with the sense 'rogue' in combinations such as *arch-scoundrel*.

arch- ● combining form **1** chief; principal: *archbishop*. **2** pre-eminent of its kind: *an arch-enemy*.
– ORIGIN from Greek *arkhos* 'chief'.

archaea /aarkeeə/ ● plural noun Biology micro-organisms which are similar to bacteria in size and simplicity of structure but constitute an ancient group intermediate between the bacteria and eukaryotes.
– ORIGIN from Greek *arkhaios* 'ancient'.

Archaean /aarkeeən/ (US **Archean**) ● adjective Geology relating to the earlier part of the Precambrian aeon (before about 2,500 million years ago).
– ORIGIN from Greek *arkhaios* 'ancient'.

archaeology (US also **archeology**) ● noun the study of human history and prehistory through the excavation of sites and the analysis of physical remains.
– DERIVATIVES **archaeologic** adjective **archaeological** adjective **archaeologist** noun.
– ORIGIN from Greek *arkhaios* 'ancient'.

archaeopteryx /aarkiopteriks/ ● noun the oldest known fossil bird, of the late Jurassic period, which had feathers and wings like a bird, but teeth and a bony tail like a dinosaur.
– ORIGIN from Greek *arkhaios* 'ancient' + *pterux* 'wing'.

Thesaurus

aqueduct ● noun CONDUIT, race, channel, watercourse, sluice, sluiceway, spillway; bridge, viaduct.

aquiline ● adjective HOOKED, curved, bent, angular; beak-like.

arable ● adjective FARMABLE, cultivable, cultivatable; fertile, productive, fecund.

arbiter ● noun **1** *an arbiter between Moscow and Washington.* See ARBITRATOR. **2** *the great arbiter of fashion* AUTHORITY, judge, controller, director; master, expert, pundit.

arbitrary ● adjective **1** *an arbitrary decision* CAPRICIOUS, whimsical, random, chance, unpredictable; casual, wanton, unmotivated, motiveless, unreasoned, unsupported, irrational, illogical, groundless, unjustified. **2** *the arbitrary power of a prince* AUTOCRATIC, dictatorial, autarchic, undemocratic, despotic, tyrannical, authoritarian; absolute, uncontrolled, unlimited, unrestrained.
– OPPOSITES reasoned, democratic.

arbitrate ● verb ADJUDICATE, judge, referee, umpire; mediate, conciliate, intervene, intercede; settle, decide, resolve, pass judgement.

arbitration ● noun ADJUDICATION, judgement, arbitrament; mediation, mediatorship, conciliation, intervention, interposition.

arbitrator ● noun ADJUDICATOR, arbiter, judge, referee, umpire; mediator, conciliator, intervenor, intercessor, go-between.

arbour ● noun BOWER, alcove, grotto, recess, pergola, gazebo.

arc ● noun *the arc of a circle* CURVE, arch, crescent, semicircle, half-moon; curvature, convexity.
● verb *I sent the ball arcing out over the river* CURL, curve; arch.

arcade ● noun **1** *a classical arcade* GALLERY, colonnade, cloister, loggia, portico, peristyle, stoa. **2** *she went to a cafe in the arcade* SHOPPING CENTRE, shopping precinct; *N. Amer.* plaza, mall, shopping mall.

arcane ● adjective MYSTERIOUS, secret, covert, clandestine; enigmatic, esoteric, obscure, abstruse, recondite, recherché, impenetrable, opaque.

arch[1] ● noun **1** *a stone arch* ARCHWAY, vault, span, dome. **2** *the arch of his spine* CURVE, bow, bend, arc, curvature, convexity; hunch, crook.
● verb *she arched her eyebrows* CURVE, arc; raise.

arch[2] ● adjective *an arch grin* MISCHIEVOUS, teasing, saucy, knowing, playful, roguish, impish, cheeky, tongue-in-cheek.

arch- ● combining form *his arch-enemy* CHIEF, principal, foremost,

archaic /aarkayik/ ● adjective **1** belonging to former or ancient times. **2** old or in an old-fashioned style.
– DERIVATIVES **archaically** adverb.
– ORIGIN Greek *arkhaios* 'ancient'.
archaism ● noun **1** the use of archaic features in language or art. **2** an archaic word or style.
archangel /aarkaynjəl/ ● noun an angel of high rank.
– DERIVATIVES **archangelic** adjective.
archbishop ● noun the chief bishop responsible for a large district.
archdeacon ● noun a senior Christian cleric to whom a bishop delegates certain responsibilities.
archduchess ● noun **1** the wife or widow of an archduke. **2** historical a daughter of the Emperor of Austria.
archduke ● noun **1** a chief duke. **2** historical a son of the Emperor of Austria.
– DERIVATIVES **archducal** adjective **archduchy** noun.
Archean ● adjective US spelling of ARCHAEAN.
arch-enemy ● noun a chief enemy.
archeology ● noun US spelling of ARCHAEOLOGY.
archer ● noun a person who shoots with a bow and arrows.
– ORIGIN Old French *archier*, from Latin *arcus* 'bow'.
archerfish ● noun an Asian and Australasian freshwater fish that knocks insect prey off vegetation by shooting water from its mouth.
archery ● noun shooting with a bow and arrows.
archetype /aarkitīp/ ● noun **1** a very typical example. **2** an original model. **3** a recurrent motif in literature or art.
– DERIVATIVES **archetypal** adjective **archetypical** adjective.
– ORIGIN Greek *arkhetupon*, from *arkhe-* 'primitive' + *tupos* 'a model'.
archiepiscopal /aarki-ipiskəp'l/ ● adjective relating to an archbishop.
– DERIVATIVES **archiepiscopacy** noun (pl. **archiepiscopacies**) **archiepiscopate** noun.
Archimedean screw ● noun a device invented by the Greek mathematician Archimedes (*c.*287–212 BC) for raising water by means of a helix rotating within a tube.
Archimedes' principle ● noun Physics a law stating that a body immersed in a fluid is subject to an upward force equal to the weight of fluid the body displaces.
archipelago /aarkipelləgō/ ● noun (pl. **archipelagos** or **archipelagoes**) an extensive group of islands.
– ORIGIN from Greek *arkhi-* 'chief' + *pelagos* 'sea' (originally a name for the Aegean Sea, notable for its large number of islands).
architect ● noun **1** a person who designs buildings and supervises their construction. **2** a person responsible for the invention or realization of something. ● verb Computing design and make (a program or system).
– ORIGIN Greek *arkhitektōn* 'chief builder'.
architectonic /aarkitektonnik/ ● adjective **1** relating to architecture or architects. **2** having a clearly defined and artistically pleasing structure. ● noun (**architectonics**) (treated as sing.) **1** the scientific study of architecture. **2** musical, literary, or artistic structure.
– DERIVATIVES **architectonically** adverb.
architecture ● noun **1** the art or practice of designing and constructing buildings. **2** the style in which a building is designed and constructed. **3** the complex structure of something.
– DERIVATIVES **architectural** adjective.
architrave /aarkitrayv/ ● noun **1** (in classical architecture) a main beam resting across the tops of columns. **2** the frame around a doorway or window.
– ORIGIN French, from Latin *trabs* 'a beam'.
archive /aarkīv/ ● noun a collection of historical documents or records. ● verb **1** place in an archive. **2** Computing transfer (data) to a less frequently used storage medium.
– DERIVATIVES **archival** adjective.
– ORIGIN French *archives* (plural), from Greek *arkheia* 'public records'.
archivist /aarkivist/ ● noun a person who is in charge of archives.
archosaur /aarkəsor/ ● noun a reptile of a large group that includes the crocodilians together with the extinct dinosaurs and pterosaurs.
– ORIGIN from Greek *arkhos* 'chief' or *arkhōn* 'ruler' + *sauros* 'lizard'.
archway ● noun a curved structure forming a passage or entrance.
-archy /aarki/ ● combining form forming nouns denoting a type of rule or government, corresponding to nouns ending in *-arch*: *monarchy*.
arc lamp (also **arc light**) ● noun a light source using an electric arc.
Arctic ● adjective **1** relating to the regions around the North Pole. **2** living or growing in such regions. **3** (**arctic**) informal (of weather) very cold. ● noun (**the Arctic**) the regions around the North Pole.
– ORIGIN from Greek *arktos* 'bear, Ursa Major, pole star'.
arcuate /aarkyooət/ ● adjective technical curved.
– ORIGIN from Latin *arcuare* 'to curve'.
ardent ● adjective **1** very enthusiastic; passionate. **2** archaic or literary burning; glowing.
– DERIVATIVES **ardency** noun **ardently** adverb.
– ORIGIN Latin *ardens*, from *ardere* 'to burn'.
ardour (US **ardor**) ● noun great enthusiasm; passion.
– ORIGIN Latin *ardor*, from *ardere* 'to burn'.
arduous ● adjective difficult and tiring.
– DERIVATIVES **arduously** adverb **arduousness** noun.
– ORIGIN Latin *arduus* 'steep, difficult'.
are[1] second person singular present and first, second, third person plural present of BE.
are[2] /aar/ ● noun historical a metric unit of measurement, equal to

Thesaurus

leading, main, major, prime, premier, greatest; *informal* number-one.
– OPPOSITES minor.
archaic ● adjective OBSOLETE, out of date, old-fashioned, outmoded, behind the times, bygone, anachronistic, antiquated, superannuated, antediluvian, olde worlde, old-fangled; ancient, old, extinct, defunct; *informal* out of the arc; *poetic/literary* of yore.
– OPPOSITES modern.
arched ● adjective VAULTED, domed, curved, bowed; *poetic/literary* embowed.
archer ● noun BOWMAN.
– RELATED TERMS toxophily.
archetypal ● adjective QUINTESSENTIAL, classic, most typical, representative, model, exemplary, textbook, copybook; stock, stereotypical, prototypical.
– OPPOSITES atypical.
archetype ● noun QUINTESSENCE, essence, typification, representative, model, embodiment, prototype, stereotype; original, pattern, standard, paradigm.
architect ● noun **1** *the architect of Durham Cathedral* DESIGNER, planner, draughtsman. **2** *the architect of the National Health Service* ORIGINATOR, author, creator, founder, (founding) father; engineer, inventor, mastermind; *poetic/literary* begetter.
architecture ● noun **1** *modern architecture* BUILDING DESIGN, building style, planning, building, construction; *formal* architectonics. **2** *the architecture of a computer system* STRUCTURE, construction, organization, layout, design, build, anatomy, make-up; *informal* set-up.
archive ● noun **1** *she delved into the family archives* RECORDS, annals, chronicles, accounts; papers, documents, files; history; *Law* muniments. **2** *the National Sound Archive* RECORD OFFICE, registry, repository, museum, chancery.
● verb *the videos are archived for future use* FILE, log, catalogue, document, record, register; store, cache.
arctic ● adjective **1** *Arctic waters* POLAR, far northern; *poetic/literary* hyperborean; *technical* boreal. **2** *arctic weather conditions* (BITTERLY) COLD, wintry, freezing, frozen, icy, glacial, gelid, sub-zero, polar, Siberian.
– OPPOSITES Antarctic, tropical.
● noun FAR NORTH, North Pole, Arctic circle.
– OPPOSITES Antarctic.
ardent ● adjective PASSIONATE, fervent, zealous, wholehearted, vehement, intense, fierce; enthusiastic, keen, eager, avid, committed, dedicated.
– OPPOSITES apathetic.
ardour ● noun PASSION, fervour, zeal, vehemence, intensity, fire, emotion; enthusiasm, eagerness, gusto, keenness, dedication.
arduous ● adjective ONEROUS, taxing, difficult, hard, heavy, laborious, burdensome, strenuous, vigorous, back-breaking; demanding, tough, challenging, formidable; exhausting, tiring, punish-

a

100 square metres.
– ORIGIN Latin *area* 'piece of level ground'.
area ● noun **1** a part of an expanse or surface. **2** the extent or measurement of a surface. **3** a space allocated for a specific use. **4** a subject or range of activity. **5** a sunken enclosure giving access to a basement.
– DERIVATIVES **areal** adjective.
– ORIGIN Latin, 'piece of level ground'.
area code ● noun a dialling code.
arena ● noun **1** a level area surrounded by seating, in which public events and entertainments are held. **2** a sphere of activity.
– ORIGIN Latin *harena, arena* 'sand, sand-strewn place of combat'.
aren't ● contraction **1** are not. **2** am not (only used in questions).
areola /əreeələ/ ● noun (pl. **areolae** /əreeəlee/) Anatomy a small circular area, in particular the pigmented skin surrounding a nipple.
– DERIVATIVES **areolar** adjective **areolate** adjective.
– ORIGIN Latin 'small open space'.
arête /əret/ ● noun a sharp mountain ridge.
– ORIGIN French, from Latin *arista* 'ear of corn, spine'.
argent ● adjective & noun literary & Heraldry silver.
– ORIGIN Latin *argentum* 'silver'.
Argentine ● noun & adjective another term for ARGENTINIAN.
argentine /aarjəntīn/ ● adjective archaic of or resembling silver.
– ORIGIN from Latin *argentum* 'silver'.
Argentinian ● noun a person from Argentina. ● adjective relating to Argentina.
arginine /aarjineen/ ● noun Biochemistry an amino acid which is an essential nutrient in the diet.
– ORIGIN German *Arginin*, perhaps from Greek *arginoeis* 'bright-shining, white'.
argon /aargon/ ● noun an inert gaseous chemical element, present in small amounts in the air.
– ORIGIN Greek, from *argos* 'idle'.
argosy ● noun (pl. **argosies**) literary a large merchant ship, originally one from Ragusa (now Dubrovnik) or Venice.
– ORIGIN from Italian *Ragusea nave* 'vessel of *Ragusa*'.
argot /aargō/ ● noun the jargon or slang of a particular group.
– ORIGIN French.
arguable ● adjective **1** able to be argued or asserted. **2** open to disagreement.
– DERIVATIVES **arguably** adverb.
argue ● verb (**argues, argued, arguing**) **1** exchange diverging or opposite views heatedly. **2** give reasons or cite evidence in support of something.
– PHRASES **argue the toss** informal, chiefly Brit. dispute a decision already made.
– DERIVATIVES **arguer** noun.
– ORIGIN Latin *arguere* 'prove, accuse'.
argument ● noun **1** a heated exchange of diverging or opposite views. **2** a set of reasons given in support of something.
argumentation ● noun systematic reasoning in support of something.
argumentative ● adjective **1** given to arguing. **2** using or characterized by systematic reasoning.
– DERIVATIVES **argumentatively** adverb **argumentativeness** noun.
argy-bargy /aarjibaarji/ ● noun informal, chiefly Brit. noisy quarrelling.
– ORIGIN rhyming jingle based on ARGUE.
argyle /aargīl/ ● noun a pattern used in knitwear, consisting of coloured diamonds on a plain background.
– ORIGIN from *Argyll*, the Scottish clan on whose tartan the pattern is based.
aria /aariə/ ● noun Music a long accompanied song for a solo voice in an opera or oratorio.
– ORIGIN Italian, from Latin *aer* 'air'.
Arian (also **Arien**) /airiən/ ● noun a person born under the sign of Aries. ● adjective relating to a person born under the sign of Aries.
arid ● adjective **1** very dry; having little or no rain. **2** uninteresting; unsatisfying.
– DERIVATIVES **aridity** noun **aridly** adverb **aridness** noun.
– ORIGIN Latin *aridus*, from *arere* 'be dry or parched'.
Aries /aireez/ ● noun **1** Astronomy a small constellation (the Ram), said to represent the ram whose Golden Fleece was sought by Jason and the Argonauts. **2** Astrology the first sign of the zodiac, which the sun enters about 20 March.
– ORIGIN Latin.
aright ● adverb dialect correctly; properly.
– ORIGIN Old English.
aril /arril/ ● noun Botany an extra covering around a seed, e.g. the red fleshy cup of a yew berry.
– ORIGIN Latin *arillus*.
arise ● verb (past **arose**; past part. **arisen**) **1** originate or become apparent. **2** (**arise from/out of**) occur as a result of. **3** formal or literary get or stand up.
– ORIGIN Old English, related to RISE.
aristocracy ● noun (pl. **aristocracies**) a class comprising people of noble birth with hereditary titles.
– ORIGIN Greek *aristokratia*, from *aristos* 'best' + *-kratia* 'power'.
aristocrat ● noun a member of the aristocracy.

Thesaurus

ing, gruelling; *informal* killing; *Brit. informal* knackering; *archaic* toilsome.
– OPPOSITES easy.
area ● noun **1** *an inner-city area* DISTRICT, region, zone, sector, quarter; locality, locale, neighbourhood, parish, patch; tract, belt; *informal* neck of the woods; *Brit. informal* manor; *N. Amer. informal* turf. **2** *specific areas of scientific knowledge* FIELD, sphere, discipline, realm, domain, sector, province, territory, line. **3** *the dining area* SECTION, space; place, room. **4** *the area of a circle* EXPANSE, extent, size, scope, compass; dimensions, proportions.
arena ● noun **1** *an ice-hockey arena* STADIUM, amphitheatre, coliseum; ground, field, ring, rink, pitch, court; *N. Amer.* bowl, park; *historical* circus. **2** *the political arena* SCENE, sphere, realm, province, domain, sector, forum, territory, world.
argot ● noun JARGON, slang, idiom, cant, parlance, vernacular, patois; dialect, speech, language; *informal* lingo.
arguable ● adjective **1** *he had an arguable claim for asylum* TENABLE, defendable, defensible, supportable, sustainable, able to hold water; reasonable, viable, acceptable. **2** *it is arguable whether these routes are worthwhile* DEBATABLE, questionable, open to question, controversial, contentious, doubtful, uncertain, moot.
– OPPOSITES untenable, certain.
arguably ● adverb POSSIBLY, conceivably, feasibly, plausibly, probably, maybe, perhaps.
argue ● verb **1** *they argued that the government was to blame* CONTEND, assert, maintain, insist, hold, claim, reason, swear, allege; *Law* depose; *formal* aver, represent, opine. **2** *the children are always arguing* QUARREL, disagree, row, squabble, fall out, bicker, fight, wrangle, dispute, feud, have words, cross swords, lock horns, be at each other's throats; *informal* argufy, spat; *archaic* altercate. **3** *it is hard to argue the point* DISPUTE, debate, discuss, controvert.
argument ● noun **1** *he had an argument with Tony* QUARREL, disagreement, squabble, fight, dispute, wrangle, clash, altercation, feud, contretemps, disputation, falling-out; *informal* tiff, barney, slanging match; *Brit. informal* row. **2** *arguments for the existence of God* REASONING, justification, explanation, rationalization; case, defence, vindication; evidence, reasons, grounds. **3** *(archaic) the argument of the book* THEME, topic, subject matter; summary, synopsis, precis, gist, outline.
argumentative ● adjective QUARRELSOME, disputatious, captious, contrary, cantankerous, contentious; belligerent, bellicose, combative, antagonistic, truculent, pugnacious; *rare* oppugnant.
arid ● adjective **1** *an arid landscape* DRY, dried up, waterless, moistureless, parched, scorched, baked, thirsty, droughty, desert; BARREN, infertile. **2** *this town has an arid, empty feel* DREARY, dull, drab, dry, sterile, colourless, unstimulating, uninspiring, flat, boring, uninteresting, lifeless.
– OPPOSITES wet, fertile, vibrant.
aright ● adverb *(dialect)* CORRECTLY, rightly, right, all right; accurately, properly, precisely, perfectly; *informal* OK.
arise ● verb **1** *many problems arose* COME TO LIGHT, become apparent, appear, emerge, crop up, turn up, surface, spring up; occur; *poetic/literary* befall, come to pass. **2** *injuries arising from defective products* RESULT, proceed, follow, ensue, derive, stem, originate; be caused by. **3** *(formal) the beast arose* STAND UP, rise, get to one's feet, get up.
aristocracy ● noun NOBILITY, peerage, gentry, upper class, ruling class, elite, high society, establishment, haut monde; aristocrats, lords, ladies, peers (of the realm), nobles, noblemen, noblewomen; *informal* upper crust, top drawer, aristos; *Brit. informal* nobs, toffs.
– OPPOSITES working class.
aristocrat ● noun NOBLEMAN, noblewoman, lord, lady, peer (of the

a

aristocratic ● adjective belonging to or having the characteristics of the aristocracy.
– DERIVATIVES **aristocratically** adverb.
Aristotelian /arristəteeliən/ ● adjective relating to the theories of the Greek philosopher Aristotle (384–322 BC). ● noun a student or follower of Aristotle or his philosophy.
arithmetic ● noun /ərithmətik/ **1** the branch of mathematics concerned with the properties and manipulation of numbers. **2** the use of numbers in counting and calculation. ● adjective /arrithmettik/ relating to arithmetic.
– DERIVATIVES **arithmetical** adjective **arithmetically** adverb **arithmetician** noun.
– ORIGIN from Greek *arithmētikē tekhnē* 'art of counting', from *arithmos* 'number'.
arithmetic progression (also **arithmetic series**) ● noun a sequence of numbers in which each differs from the preceding one by a constant quantity (e.g. 1, 2, 3, 4, etc.; 9, 7, 5, 3, etc.).
-arium ● suffix forming nouns denoting a place: *planetarium.*
– ORIGIN from Latin.
ark ● noun **1** (in the Bible) the ship built by Noah to save his family and two of every kind of animal from the Flood. **2** (also **Holy Ark**) a chest or cupboard housing the Torah scrolls in a synagogue. **3** (**Ark of the Covenant**) the chest which contained the tablets of the laws of the ancient Israelites.
– PHRASES **out of the ark** informal very old or old-fashioned.
– ORIGIN Latin *arca* 'chest'.
arm[1] ● noun **1** each of the two upper limbs of the human body from the shoulder to the hand. **2** a side part of a chair supporting a sitter's arm. **3** a narrow body of water or land projecting from a larger body. **4** a branch or division of an organization.
– PHRASES **arm in arm** with arms linked. **cost an arm and a leg** informal be extremely expensive. **in arms** (of a baby) too young to walk. **keep at arm's length** avoid intimacy or close contact with. **with open arms** with great affection or enthusiasm.
– DERIVATIVES **armful** noun **armless** adjective.
– ORIGIN Old English.
arm[2] ● verb **1** supply with weapons. **2** provide with essential equipment for a task or situation. **3** activate the fuse of (a bomb) so that it is ready to explode.
– ORIGIN Latin *armare*, from *arma* 'armour, arms'.
armada /aarmaadə/ ● noun a fleet of warships.
– ORIGIN Spanish, from Latin *armare* 'to arm'.
armadillo ● noun (pl. **armadillos**) a nocturnal insect-eating mammal native to Central and South America, with large claws and a body covered in bony plates.
– ORIGIN Spanish, 'little armed man'.
Armageddon /aarməgedd'n/ ● noun **1** (in the New Testament) the last battle between good and evil before the Day of Judgement. **2** a catastrophic conflict.
– ORIGIN Greek, from a Hebrew phrase meaning 'hill of Megiddo' (Book of Revelation, chapter 16).
Armagnac /aarmənyak/ ● noun a type of brandy made in Aquitaine in SW France.
– ORIGIN from the former name of a district in Aquitaine.
armament /aarməmənt/ ● noun **1** (also **armaments**) military weapons and equipment. **2** the process of equipping military forces for war.
– ORIGIN Latin *armamentum*, from *armare* 'to arm'.
armature /aarməchər/ ● noun **1** the rotating coil of a dynamo or electric motor. **2** any moving part of an electrical machine in which a voltage is induced by a magnetic field. **3** a piece of iron acting as a keeper for a magnet. **4** Biology the protective covering of an animal or plant. **5** archaic armour.
– ORIGIN Latin *armatura* 'armour'.
armband ● noun **1** a band worn around the upper arm to hold up a shirtsleeve or as a form of identification. **2** an inflatable plastic band worn around the upper arm as a swimming aid.
armchair ● noun **1** a large, upholstered chair with side supports for the sitter's arms. **2** (before another noun) experiencing something through reading, television, etc. rather than at first hand: *an armchair traveller.*
armed ● adjective equipped with or involving a firearm.
armed forces ● plural noun a country's army, navy, and air force.
Armenian /aarmeeniən/ ● noun **1** a person from Armenia. **2** the Indo-European language of Armenia. ● adjective relating to Armenia.
armistice /aarmistiss/ ● noun a truce.
– ORIGIN French, from Latin *arma* 'armour, arms' + *-stitium* 'stoppage'.
armlet ● noun a bracelet worn round the upper arm.
armlock ● noun a method of restraining someone by holding their arm bent tightly behind their back.
armoire /arrmwaar/ ● noun a cupboard or wardrobe.
– ORIGIN French, from Latin *armarium* 'closet'.
armor ● noun US spelling of ARMOUR.
armorer ● noun US spelling of ARMOURER.
armory[1] ● noun heraldry.
– DERIVATIVES **armorial** adjective.
– ORIGIN Old French *armoierie*, from *armoier* 'to blazon', from Latin *arma* 'arms'.
armory[2] ● noun US spelling of ARMOURY.
armour (US **armor**) ● noun **1** the metal coverings formerly worn to protect the body in battle. **2** (also **armour plate**) the tough metal layer covering a military vehicle or ship. **3** military vehicles collectively. **4** the protective layer or shell of some animals and plants.
– DERIVATIVES **armoured** adjective.
– ORIGIN Old French *armure*, from Latin *armatura*, from *arma* 'armour, arms'.
armourer (US **armorer**) ● noun **1** a maker or supplier of weapons or armour. **2** an official in charge of the arms of a warship or regiment.
armour-plated ● adjective covered with armour plate.
armoury (US **armory**) ● noun (pl. **armouries**) **1** a store or supply of arms. **2** a set of resources available for a particular purpose.
armpit ● noun a hollow under the arm at the shoulder.
armrest ● noun an arm of a chair.
arms ● plural noun **1** guns and other weapons. **2** emblems originally displayed on the shields of knights to distinguish them in battle, surviving today as coats of arms.
– PHRASES **a call to arms** a call to make ready for fighting. **up in arms** protesting vigorously.
– ORIGIN Latin *arma*.
arms control ● noun international agreement to limit the production and accumulation of arms.
arms race ● noun a situation in which nations compete for superiority in the development and accumulation of weapons.
arm-wrestling ● noun a contest in which two people engage hands and try to force each other's arm down on to a surface.
army ● noun (pl. **armies**) **1** an organized military force equipped for fighting on land. **2** a large number of similar people or things.
– ORIGIN Old French *armee*, from Latin *armare* 'to arm'.

Thesaurus

realm), peeress, grandee; *informal* aristo; *Brit. informal* toff, nob.
– OPPOSITES commoner.
aristocratic ● adjective **1** *an aristocratic family* NOBLE, titled, upper-class, blue-blooded, high-born, well born, elite; *Brit.* upmarket; *informal* upper crust, top drawer; *Brit. informal* posh; *archaic* gentle. **2** *an aristocratic manner* REFINED, polished, courtly, dignified, decorous, gracious, fine, gentlemanly, ladylike; haughty, proud.
– OPPOSITES working-class, vulgar.
arm[1] ● noun **1** *the arm of her jacket* SLEEVE. **2** *an arm of the sea* INLET, creek, cove, fjord, bay, voe; estuary, firth, strait(s), sound, channel. **3** *the political arm of the group* BRANCH, section, department, division, wing, sector, detachment, offshoot, extension. **4** *the long arm of the law* REACH, power, authority, influence.
arm[2] ● verb **1** *he armed himself with a revolver* EQUIP, provide, supply, furnish, issue, fit out. **2** *arm yourself against criticism* PREPARE, forearm, make ready, brace, steel, fortify.
armada ● noun FLEET, flotilla, squadron; *poetic/literary* navy.
armaments ● plural noun ARMS, weapons, weaponry, firearms, guns, ordnance, artillery, munitions, materiel.
armistice ● noun TRUCE, ceasefire, peace, suspension of hostilities.
armour ● noun PROTECTIVE COVERING, armour plate; *historical* chain mail, coat of mail, panoply.
armoured ● adjective ARMOUR-PLATED, steel-plated, ironclad; bulletproof, bombproof; reinforced, toughened.
armoury ● noun ARSENAL, arms depot, arms cache, ordnance depot, magazine, ammunition dump.
arms ● plural noun **1** *the illegal export of arms* WEAPONS, weaponry, firearms, guns, ordnance, artillery, armaments, munitions, materiel. **2** *the family arms* CREST, emblem, coat of arms, heraldic de-

a

arnica /aarnikə/ ● noun a plant bearing yellow daisy-like flowers, used medicinally for the treatment of bruises.
– ORIGIN Latin.
aroha /aarohə/ ● noun NZ **1** love; affection. **2** sympathy.
– ORIGIN Maori.
aroma ● noun a pleasant and distinctive smell.
– ORIGIN Greek, 'spice'.
aromatherapy ● noun the use of aromatic plant extracts and essential oils for healing and cosmetic purposes.
– DERIVATIVES **aromatherapeutic** adjective **aromatherapist** noun.
aromatic ● adjective **1** having an aroma. **2** Chemistry (of an organic compound) containing a flat ring of atoms in its molecule (as in benzene). ● noun an aromatic plant, substance, or compound.
– DERIVATIVES **aromatically** adverb.
arose past of ARISE.
around ● adverb **1** located or situated on every side. **2** so as to face in the opposite direction. **3** in or to many places throughout a locality. **4** here and there. **5** available or present. **6** approximately. ● preposition **1** on every side of. **2** in or to many places throughout (a locality). **3** so as to encircle or embrace. **4** following an approximately circular route round.
arouse ● verb **1** bring about (a feeling or response) in someone. **2** excite sexually. **3** awaken from sleep.
– DERIVATIVES **arousal** noun.
– ORIGIN from ROUSE, on the pattern of *rise, arise*.
ARP ● abbreviation Brit. historical air-raid precautions.
arpeggio /aarpejiō/ ● noun (pl. **arpeggios**) Music the notes of a chord played in rapid succession.
– ORIGIN Italian, from *arpeggiare* 'play the harp'.
arrack /arrək/ (also **arak**) ● noun an alcoholic spirit made from the sap of the coco palm or from rice.
– ORIGIN from an Arabic word meaning 'sweat'.
arraign /ərayn/ ● verb call before a court to answer a criminal charge.
– DERIVATIVES **arraignment** noun.
– ORIGIN Old French *araisnier*, from Latin *ad-* 'to' + *ratio* 'reason, account'.
arrange ● verb **1** put tidily or in a particular order. **2** organize or plan. **3** Music adapt (a composition) for performance with instruments or voices other than those originally specified.
– DERIVATIVES **arrangeable** adjective **arranger** noun.
– ORIGIN Old French *arangier*, from *rang* 'rank'.
arrangement ● noun **1** the result of arranging things in an attractive or ordered way. **2** a plan for a future event. **3** Music an arranged composition.
arrant /arrənt/ ● adjective utter; complete.
– DERIVATIVES **arrantly** adverb.
– ORIGIN variant of ERRANT, originally in phrases such as *arrant thief*, meaning 'outlawed, roving thief'.
arras /arrənt/ ● noun a tapestry wall hanging.
– ORIGIN named after the French town of *Arras*, where tapestries were made.
array ● noun **1** an impressive display or range of a particular thing. **2** an ordered arrangement of troops. **3** literary elaborate or beautiful clothing. ● verb **1** display or arrange in a neat or impressive way. **2** (**be arrayed in**) be elaborately clothed in.
– ORIGIN Old French *arei*.
arrears ● plural noun money owed that should already have been paid.
– PHRASES **in arrears 1** behind with paying money that is owed. **2** (of wages or rent) paid at the end of each period of work or occupation.
– ORIGIN Old French *arere*, from Latin *retro* 'backwards'.
arrest ● verb **1** seize by legal authority and take into custody. **2** stop or check (progress or a process). **3** (**arresting**) attracting attention. ● noun **1** the action of arresting someone. **2** a sudden cessation of motion.
– DERIVATIVES **arrestingly** adverb.
– ORIGIN Old French *arester*, from Latin *restare* 'remain, stop'.
arrhythmia /ərrithmiə/ ● noun Medicine a condition in which

Thesaurus

vice, insignia, escutcheon, shield.
– RELATED TERMS heraldic.
army ● noun **1** *the invading army* ARMED FORCE, military force, land force, military, soldiery, infantry, militia; troops, soldiers; archaic host. **2** *an army of tourists* CROWD, swarm, multitude, horde, mob, gang, throng, mass, flock, herd, pack.
– RELATED TERMS military, martial.
aroma ● noun SMELL, odour, fragrance, scent, perfume, bouquet, nose; poetic/literary redolence.
aromatic ● adjective FRAGRANT, scented, perfumed, fragranced, odoriferous; poetic/literary redolent.
around ● adverb **1** *there were houses scattered around* ON EVERY SIDE, on all sides, throughout, all over (the place), everywhere; about, here and there. **2** *he turned around* IN THE OPPOSITE DIRECTION, to face the other way, backwards, to the rear. **3** *there was no one around* NEARBY, near, about, close by, close (at hand), at hand, in the vicinity, at close range.
● preposition **1** *the palazzo is built around a courtyard* ON ALL SIDES OF, about, encircling, surrounding. **2** *they drove around town* ABOUT, all over, in/to all parts of. **3** *around three miles* APPROXIMATELY, about, round about, circa, roughly, something like, more or less, in the region of, in the neighbourhood of, give or take (a few); nearly, close to, approaching; Brit. getting on for; N. Amer. informal in the ballpark of.
arouse ● verb **1** *they had aroused his suspicion* INDUCE, prompt, trigger, stir up, bring out, kindle, fire, spark off, provoke, engender, cause, foster; poetic/literary enkindle. **2** *his ability to arouse the masses* STIR UP, rouse, galvanize, excite, electrify, stimulate, inspire, inspirit, move, fire up, whip up, get going, inflame, agitate, goad, incite. **3** *his touch aroused her* EXCITE, stimulate (sexually), titillate; informal turn on, get going, give a thrill to, light someone's fire. **4** *she was aroused from her sleep* WAKE (UP), awaken, bring to/round, rouse; Brit. informal knock up; poetic/literary waken.
– OPPOSITES allay, pacify, turn off.
arraign ● verb **1** *he was arraigned for murder* INDICT, prosecute, put on trial, bring to trial, take to court, lay/file/prefer charges against, summons, cite; accuse of, charge with; N. Amer. impeach; informal do; archaic inculpate. **2** *they bitterly arraigned the government* CRITICIZE, censure, attack, condemn, chastise, lambaste, rebuke, admonish, remonstrate with, take to task, berate, reproach; informal knock, slam, blast, lay into; Brit. informal slate, slag off; formal castigate, excoriate.
– OPPOSITES acquit, praise.
arrange ● verb **1** *she arranged the flowers* ORDER, set out, lay out, array, position, dispose, present, display, exhibit; group, sort, organize, tidy. **2** *they hoped to arrange a meeting* ORGANIZE, fix (up), plan, schedule, pencil in, contrive, settle on, decide, determine, agree. **3** *he arranged the piece for a full orchestra* ADAPT, set, score, orchestrate, instrument.
arrangement ● noun **1** *the arrangement of the furniture* POSITIONING, disposition, order, presentation, display; grouping, organization, alignment. **2** *the arrangements for my trip* PREPARATION, plan, provision; planning, groundwork. **3** *we had an arrangement* AGREEMENT, deal, understanding, bargain, settlement, pact, modus vivendi. **4** *an arrangement of Beethoven's symphonies* ADAPTATION, orchestration, instrumentation.
arrant ● adjective *what arrant nonsense!* UTTER, complete, total, absolute, downright, outright, thorough, out-and-out, sheer, pure, unmitigated, unqualified; blatant, flagrant; Brit. informal right.
array ● noun **1** *a huge array of cars* RANGE, collection, selection, assortment, diversity, variety; arrangement, assemblage, line-up, formation; display, exhibition. **2** (poetic/literary) *she arrived in silken array* DRESS, attire, clothing, garb, garments; finery; formal apparel.
● verb **1** *a buffet was arrayed on the table* ARRANGE, assemble, group, order, range, place, position, set out, lay out, dispose; display. **2** *he was arrayed in grey flannel* DRESS, attire, clothe, garb, deck (out), outfit, get up, turn out; archaic apparel, habit.
arrears ● plural noun *rent arrears* MONEY OWING, outstanding payment(s), debt(s), liabilities, dues.
– PHRASES **in arrears** BEHIND, behindhand, late, overdue, in the red, in debt.
arrest ● verb **1** *police arrested him for murder* APPREHEND, take into custody, take prisoner, detain, put in jail; informal pick up, pull in, pinch, bust, nab, do, collar; Brit. informal nick. **2** *the spread of the disease can be arrested* STOP, halt, check, block, hinder, restrict, limit, inhibit, impede, curb; prevent, obstruct; poetic/literary stay. **3** *she tried to arrest his attention* ATTRACT, capture, catch, hold, engage; absorb, occupy, engross.
– OPPOSITES release, start.
● noun **1** *a warrant for your arrest* DETENTION, apprehension, seizure, capture. **2** *a cardiac arrest* STOPPAGE, halt, interruption.
arresting ● adjective *an arresting image* STRIKING, eye-catching, conspicuous, engaging, impressive, imposing, spectacular, dra-

the heart beats with an irregular or abnormal rhythm.
– DERIVATIVES **arrhythmic** adjective.
– ORIGIN Greek *arruthmia* 'lack of rhythm'.
arrival • noun **1** the action or process of arriving. **2** a newly arrived person or thing.
arrive • verb **1** reach a destination. **2** be brought or delivered. **3** (of a particular moment) come about. **4** (**arrive at**) reach (a conclusion or decision). **5** informal become successful and well known.
– ORIGIN originally in the sense 'reach the shore after a voyage': from Old French *ariver*, from Latin *ripa* 'shore'.
arriviste /arreeveest/ • noun often derogatory a person who has recently gained social or financial status or is ambitious to do so.
– ORIGIN French.
arrogant • adjective having an exaggerated sense of one's own importance or abilities.
– DERIVATIVES **arrogance** noun **arrogantly** adverb.
– ORIGIN Old French, from Latin *arrogare* 'claim for oneself'.
arrogate /arrəgayt/ • verb take or claim for oneself without justification.
– DERIVATIVES **arrogation** noun.
– ORIGIN Latin *arrogare* 'claim for oneself'.
arrondissement /aroNdeessmoN/ • noun **1** (in France) a subdivision of a local government department. **2** an administrative district of Paris.
– ORIGIN French, from *arrondir* 'make round'.
arrow • noun **1** a stick with a sharp pointed head, designed to be shot from a bow. **2** a symbol resembling this, used to show direction or position. • verb move swiftly and directly.
– DERIVATIVES **arrowed** adjective.
– ORIGIN Old Norse.
arrowroot • noun a plant that yields a fine-grained starch used in cookery and medicine.
– ORIGIN from an Arawak word meaning 'meal of meals', by association with ARROW and ROOT[1], the plant's tubers being used to absorb poison from arrow wounds.
arroyo /əroyō/ • noun (pl. **arroyos**) US a deep and usually dry gully cut by an intermittent river or stream.
– ORIGIN Spanish.
arse • noun Brit. vulgar slang a person's bottom.
– ORIGIN Old English.
arsenal • noun a store of weapons and ammunition.
– ORIGIN French, or obsolete Italian *arzanale*, from an Arabic phrase meaning 'house of industry'.
arsenic • noun a brittle steel-grey chemical element with many highly poisonous compounds.
– DERIVATIVES **arsenical** adjective **arsenide** noun.
– ORIGIN originally in the sense 'orpiment': from Greek *arsenikon*, from Arabic.
arson • noun the criminal act of deliberately setting fire to property.
– DERIVATIVES **arsonist** noun.
– ORIGIN Old French, from Latin *ardere* 'to burn'.
art[1] • noun **1** the expression of creative skill through a visual medium such as painting or sculpture. **2** the product of such a process; paintings, drawings, and sculpture collectively. **3** (**the arts**) the various branches of creative activity, such as painting, music, and drama. **4** (**arts**) subjects of study primarily concerned with human culture (as contrasted with scientific or technical subjects). **5** a skill: *the art of conversation*.
– ORIGIN Latin *ars*.
art[2] archaic or dialect second person singular present of BE.
art deco • noun a decorative style prominent in the 1920s and 1930s, characterized by precise geometric shapes.
– ORIGIN French *art décoratif* 'decorative art'.
artefact /aartifakt/ (US **artifact**) • noun a functional or decorative man-made object.
– ORIGIN from Latin *arte* 'using art' + *factum* 'something made'.
arteriole /aarteeriōl/ • noun Anatomy a small branch of an artery leading into capillaries.
– DERIVATIVES **arteriolar** adjective.
arteriosclerosis /aarteeriōskleerōsiss/ • noun Medicine thickening and hardening of the walls of the arteries.
artery • noun (pl. **arteries**) **1** any of the muscular-walled tubes through which blood flows from the heart around the body. **2** an important route in a transport system.
– DERIVATIVES **arterial** adjective.
– ORIGIN Greek *artēria*.
artesian /aarteezh'n/ • adjective (of a well) bored vertically into a layer of water-bearing rock that is lying at an angle, with the result that natural pressure forces the water upwards.
– ORIGIN from *Artois*, a region in France.
artful • adjective cunningly clever.
– DERIVATIVES **artfully** adverb **artfulness** noun.
art house • noun a cinema which shows artistic or experimental films.
arthritis /aarthrītis/ • noun painful inflammation and stiffness of the joints.
– DERIVATIVES **arthritic** adjective & noun.
– ORIGIN Greek, from *arthron* 'joint'.
arthropod /aarthrəpod/ • noun Zoology an invertebrate animal with a segmented body, external skeleton, and jointed limbs, such as an insect, spider, or crustacean.
– ORIGIN from Greek *arthron* 'joint' + *pous* 'foot'.
arthroscope • noun Medicine an instrument for inspecting or operating on the interior of a joint.
– DERIVATIVES **arthroscopic** adjective **arthroscopy** noun.
Arthurian /aarthyoorian/ • adjective relating to the reign of the legendary King Arthur of Britain.
artichoke • noun (also **globe artichoke**) the unopened flower head of a thistle-like plant, eaten as a vegetable.
– ORIGIN Italian *articiocco*, from Arabic.
article • noun **1** a particular object. **2** a piece of writing included in a newspaper or magazine. **3** a separate clause or

Thesaurus

matic, breathtaking, dazzling, stunning, awe-inspiring, remarkable, outstanding, distinctive.
– OPPOSITES inconspicuous.
arrival • noun **1** *they awaited Ruth's arrival* COMING, appearance, entrance, entry, approach. **2** *staff greeted the late arrivals* COMER, entrant, incomer; visitor, caller, guest. **3** *the arrival of democracy* EMERGENCE, appearance, advent, coming, dawn, onset, inauguration, origin, birth.
– OPPOSITES departure, end.
arrive • verb **1** *more police arrived* COME, turn up, get here/there, make it, appear, enter, present oneself, come along, materialize; informal show (up), roll in/up, blow in, show one's face. **2** *we arrived at his house* REACH, get to, come to, make, make it to, gain, end up at; informal wind up at. **3** *they arrived at an agreement* REACH, achieve, attain, gain, accomplish; work out, draw up, put together, strike, settle on; informal clinch. **4** *the wedding finally arrived* HAPPEN, occur, take place, come about; present itself, crop up; poetic/literary come to pass. **5** *quadraphony had arrived* EMERGE, appear, surface, dawn, be born, come into being, arise. **6** (informal) *their Rolls Royce proved that they had arrived* SUCCEED, be a success, do well, reach the top, make good, prosper, thrive; informal make it, make one's mark, do all right for oneself.
– OPPOSITES depart, leave.
arriviste • noun SOCIAL CLIMBER, status seeker, would-be, self-seeker; upstart, parvenu(e), vulgarian; (**arrivistes**) nouveau riche, new money; informal go-getter.
arrogant • adjective HAUGHTY, conceited, self-important, egotistic, full of oneself, superior; overbearing, pompous, bumptious, imperious, overweening; proud, immodest; informal high and mighty, too big for one's boots, big-headed; rare hubristic.
– OPPOSITES modest.
arrogate • verb ASSUME, take, claim, appropriate, seize, expropriate, wrest, usurp, commandeer.
arrow • noun **1** *a bow and arrow* SHAFT, bolt, dart; historical quarrel. **2** *the arrow pointed right* POINTER, indicator, marker, needle.
arsenal • noun **1** *Britain's nuclear arsenal* WEAPONS, weaponry, arms, armaments. **2** *mutineers broke into the arsenal* ARMOURY, arms depot, arms cache, ordnance depot, magazine, ammunition dump.
arson • noun INCENDIARISM, pyromania; Brit. fire-raising.
arsonist • noun INCENDIARY, pyromaniac; Brit. fire-raiser; informal firebug, pyro; N. Amer. informal torch.
art • noun **1** *he studied art* FINE ART, artwork, design. **2** *the art of writing* SKILL, craft, technique, knack, facility, ability. **3** *she uses art to achieve her aims* CUNNING, artfulness, slyness, craftiness, guile; deceit, duplicity, artifice, wiles.
artery • noun *the main arteries out of town* MAIN ROAD, trunk road, high road, highway.
artful • adjective SLY, crafty, cunning, wily, scheming, devious, Machiavellian, sneaky, tricky, conniving, designing, calculating;

a

paragraph of a legal document. **4** (**articles**) a period of professional training as a solicitor, architect, surveyor, or accountant. **5** Grammar the definite or indefinite article. ● **verb** employ under contract as a trainee.
– ORIGIN Latin *articulus* 'small joint or connecting part'.
articled clerk ● **noun** a law student employed as a trainee.
article of faith ● **noun** a firmly held belief.
articular ● **adjective** Anatomy of or relating to a joint.
articulate ● **adjective** /aartikyoolət/ **1** fluent and clear in speech. **2** technical having joints or jointed segments. ● **verb** /aartikyoolayt/ **1** pronounce (words) distinctly. **2** clearly express (an idea or feeling). **3** form a joint. **4** (**articulated**) having two or more sections connected by a flexible joint.
– DERIVATIVES **articulacy** noun **articulately** adverb **articulateness** noun **articulation** noun.
– ORIGIN from Latin *articulare* 'divide into joints, utter distinctly'.
artifact ● **noun** US spelling of ARTEFACT.
artifice /aartifiss/ ● **noun** the use of cunning plans or devices in order to trick or deceive.
– ORIGIN Latin *artificium*, from *ars* 'art' + *facere* 'make'.
artificer /aartiffissər/ ● **noun** **1** a person skilled in making or contriving things. **2** a skilled mechanic in the armed forces.
artificial ● **adjective** **1** made as a copy of something natural. **2** contrived or affected.
– DERIVATIVES **artificiality** noun **artificially** adverb.
– ORIGIN from Latin *artificium*, from *ars* 'art' + *facere* 'make'.
artificial insemination ● **noun** the veterinary or medical procedure of injecting semen into the vagina or uterus.
artificial intelligence ● **noun** the performance by computer systems of tasks normally requiring human intelligence.
artificial respiration ● **noun** the restoration or maintenance of someone's breathing by manual, mechanical, or mouth-to-mouth methods.
artillery ● **noun** **1** large-calibre guns used in warfare on land. **2** a branch of the armed forces trained to use artillery.
– ORIGIN Old French *artillerie*, from *atillier* 'equip, arm'.
artisan ● **noun** a skilled worker who makes things by hand.
– DERIVATIVES **artisanal** adjective.
– ORIGIN French, from Latin *artire* 'instruct in the arts'.
artist ● **noun** **1** a person who paints or draws as a profession or hobby. **2** a person who practises or performs any of the creative arts. **3** informal a habitual practitioner of a specified activity: *a con artist*.
– DERIVATIVES **artistry** noun.
– ORIGIN French *artiste*, from Latin *ars* 'art'.
artiste /aarteest/ ● **noun** a professional entertainer, especially a singer or dancer.
– ORIGIN French, 'artist'.
artistic ● **adjective** **1** having or revealing creative skill. **2** relating to or characteristic of art or artists: *an artistic temperament*. **3** aesthetically pleasing: *artistic designs*.
– DERIVATIVES **artistically** adverb.
artless ● **adjective** **1** without guile or pretension. **2** clumsy.
– DERIVATIVES **artlessly** adverb.
art nouveau /aar noovō/ ● **noun** a style of decorative art and architecture prominent in the late 19th and early 20th centuries, characterized by intricate linear designs and flowing curves.
– ORIGIN French, 'new art'.
artwork ● **noun** illustrations or other non-textual material prepared for inclusion in a publication.
arty (chiefly N. Amer. also **artsy**) ● **adjective** (**artier**, **artiest**) informal overtly artistic or interested in the arts.
– DERIVATIVES **artiness** noun.
arugula /əroogyoolə/ ● **noun** N. Amer. the salad vegetable rocket.
– ORIGIN Italian dialect *arucula*, from Italian *ruca* 'rocket'.
arum /airəm/ ● **noun** cuckoo pint (*Arum maculatum*) or a related plant.
– ORIGIN Greek *aron*.
arum lily ● **noun** a tall lily-like African plant of the arum family.
arvo ● **noun** (pl. **arvos**) Austral./NZ informal afternoon.
-ary ● **suffix** **1** forming adjectives such as *budgetary* or *capillary*. **2** forming nouns such as *dictionary*.
Aryan /airiən/ ● **noun** **1** a member of a people speaking an Indo-European language who spread into northern India in the 2nd millennium BC. **2** the language of this people. **3** (in Nazi ideology) a person of Caucasian race not of Jewish descent. ● **adjective** relating to the Aryan people.
– ORIGIN from Sanskrit, 'noble'.
As ● **symbol** the chemical element arsenic.
as ● **adverb** used in comparisons to refer to the extent or degree of something. ● **conjunction** **1** used to indicate simultaneous occurrence. **2** used to indicate by comparison the way that something happens. **3** because. **4** even though. ● **preposition** **1** used to refer to the function or character of someone or something: *it came as a shock*. **2** during the time of being.
– PHRASES **as for** with regard to. **as yet** until now or that time.
– ORIGIN Old English, 'similarly'.

Thesaurus

canny, shrewd; deceitful, duplicitous, disingenuous, underhand; *informal* foxy, shifty; *archaic* subtle.
– OPPOSITES ingenuous.
article ● **noun** **1** *small household articles* OBJECT, thing, item, artefact, commodity, product. **2** *an article in The Times* REPORT, account, story, write-up, feature, item, piece (of writing), column, review, commentary. **3** *the crucial article of the treaty* CLAUSE, section, subsection, point, item, paragraph, division, subdivision, part, portion.
articulate ● **adjective** *an articulate speaker* ELOQUENT, fluent, effective, persuasive, lucid, expressive, silver-tongued; intelligible, comprehensible, understandable.
– OPPOSITES unintelligible.
● **verb** *they were unable to articulate their emotions* EXPRESS, voice, vocalize, put in words, communicate, state; air, ventilate, vent, pour out; utter, say, speak, enunciate, pronounce; *informal* come out with.
articulated ● **adjective** HINGED, jointed, segmented; *technical* articulate.
artifice ● **noun** TRICKERY, deceit, deception, duplicity, guile, cunning, artfulness, wiliness, craftiness, slyness, chicanery; fraud, fraudulence.
artificial ● **adjective** **1** *artificial flowers* SYNTHETIC, fake, imitation, mock, ersatz, substitute, replica, reproduction; man-made, manufactured, fabricated; plastic; *informal* pretend. **2** *an artificial smile* INSINCERE, feigned, false, unnatural, contrived, put-on, exaggerated, forced, laboured, strained, hollow; *informal* pretend, phoney.
– OPPOSITES natural, genuine.
artillery ● **noun** ORDNANCE, (big) guns, cannon(s), cannonry.
artisan ● **noun** CRAFTSMAN, craftswoman, craftsperson; skilled worker, technician; smith, wright, journeyman; *archaic* artificer.
artist ● **noun** **1** *a Belfast mural artist* DESIGNER, creator, originator, producer; old master. **2** *the surgeon is an artist with the knife* EXPERT, master, maestro, past master, virtuoso, genius; *informal* pro, ace; *Brit. informal* dab hand.
– OPPOSITES novice.
artiste ● **noun** ENTERTAINER, performer, showman, artist; player, musician, singer, dancer, actor, actress; star.
artistic ● **adjective** **1** *he's very artistic* CREATIVE, imaginative, inventive, expressive; sensitive, perceptive, discerning. **2** *artistic dances* AESTHETIC, aesthetically pleasing, beautiful, attractive, fine; decorative, ornamental; tasteful, stylish, elegant, exquisite.
– OPPOSITES unimaginative, inelegant.
artistry ● **noun** CREATIVE SKILL, creativity, art, skill, talent, genius, brilliance, flair, proficiency, virtuosity, finesse, style; craftsmanship, workmanship.
artless ● **adjective** NATURAL, ingenuous, naive, simple, innocent, childlike, guileless; candid, open, sincere, unaffected.
– OPPOSITES scheming.
as ● **conjunction** **1** *she saw him as he disappeared* WHILE, just as, even as, just when, at the time that, at the moment that. **2** *we all felt as Frank did* IN THE (SAME) WAY THAT, the (same) way; *informal* like. **3** *do as you're told* WHAT, that which. **4** *they were free, as the case had not been proved* BECAUSE, since, seeing that/as, in view of the fact that, owing to the fact that; *informal* on account of; *poetic/literary* for. **5** *try as she did, she couldn't smile* THOUGH, although, even though, in spite of the fact that, despite the fact that, notwithstanding that, for all that, albeit, however. **6** *relatively short distances, as Paris to Lyons* SUCH AS, like, for instance, for example, e.g. **7** *I'm away a lot, as you know* WHICH, a fact which.
● **preposition** **1** *he was dressed as a policeman* LIKE, in the guise of, so as to appear to be. **2** *I'm speaking to you as your friend* IN THE ROLE OF, being, acting as.
– PHRASES **as for/as to** CONCERNING, with respect to, on the subject

asafoetida /assəfettidə/ (US **asafetida**) ● noun an unpleasant-smelling gum obtained from the roots of a plant of the parsley family, used in herbal medicine and Indian cooking.
– ORIGIN Latin, from *asa* (from a Persian word meaning 'mastic') + *foetida* 'stinking'.

asap ● abbreviation as soon as possible.

asbestos ● noun a highly heat-resistant fibrous silicate mineral, used in fire-resistant and insulating materials.
– ORIGIN from Greek, 'unquenchable'.

asbestosis /asbestōsiss/ ● noun a serious lung disease, often accompanied by cancer, resulting from breathing asbestos dust.

ascend ● verb **1** go up; climb or rise. **2** rise in status. **3** (of a voice or sound) rise in pitch.
– ORIGIN Latin *ascendere*.

ascendant ● adjective **1** holding a position of increasing status or influence. **2** Astrology (of a planet, zodiacal degree, or sign) on or close to the intersection of the ecliptic with the eastern horizon. ● noun Astrology the ascendant point.
– PHRASES **in the ascendant** rising in power or influence.
– DERIVATIVES **ascendancy** noun.

ascension ● noun **1** the action of ascending in status. **2** (**Ascension**) the ascent of Christ into heaven on the fortieth day after the Resurrection.
– DERIVATIVES **ascensional** adjective.

ascent ● noun **1** an instance of ascending. **2** a climb up a mountain. **3** an upward slope.

ascertain /assərtayn/ ● verb find out for certain.
– DERIVATIVES **ascertainable** adjective **ascertainment** noun.
– ORIGIN Old French *acertener*, from Latin *certus* 'settled, sure'.

ascetic /əsettik/ ● adjective strictly self-disciplined and avoiding any sensory pleasures or luxuries. ● noun an ascetic person.
– DERIVATIVES **ascetically** adverb **asceticism** noun.
– ORIGIN from Greek *askētēs* 'monk', from *askein* 'to exercise'.

ASCII /aski/ ● abbreviation Computing American Standard Code for Information Interchange.

ascites /əsīteez/ ● noun Medicine the accumulation of fluid in the peritoneal cavity, causing abdominal swelling.
– ORIGIN Greek *askitēs*, from *askos* 'wineskin'.

ascorbic acid /əskorbik/ ● noun vitamin C, a compound found in citrus fruits and green vegetables, essential in maintaining healthy connective tissue.
– ORIGIN from Latin *scorbutus* 'scurvy'.

ascribe ● verb (**ascribe to**) **1** attribute (a particular cause, person, or period) to. **2** regard (a quality) as belonging to.
– DERIVATIVES **ascribable** adjective **ascription** noun.
– ORIGIN Latin *ascribere*, from *scribere* 'write'.

asdic ● noun a form of sonar developed by the British in the Second World War to detect submarines.
– ORIGIN acronym from *Allied Submarine Detection Investigation Committee*.

aseptic /ayseptik/ ● adjective marked by the absence of bacteria, viruses, and other micro-organisms. Compare with ANTISEPTIC.

asexual ● adjective **1** Biology without sex or sexual organs. **2** (of reproduction) not involving the fusion of gametes. **3** without sexual feelings or associations.
– DERIVATIVES **asexuality** noun **asexually** adverb.

ash[1] ● noun **1** the powder remaining after something has been burned. **2** (**ashes**) the remains of a human body after cremation. **3** (**the Ashes**) a cricket trophy awarded for winning a test match series between England and Australia. [ORIGIN from a mock obituary (1882) referring to the symbolic remains of English cricket after an Australian victory.]
– PHRASES **ashes in one's mouth** something that is bitterly disappointing.
– DERIVATIVES **ashy** adjective.
– ORIGIN Old English.

ash[2] ● noun **1** a tree with compound leaves, winged fruits, and hard pale wood. **2** an Old English letter, ᚫ.
– ORIGIN Old English.

ashamed ● adjective feeling embarrassed or guilty.
– DERIVATIVES **ashamedly** adverb.
– ORIGIN Old English.

Ashanti /əshanti/ (also **Asante**) ● noun (pl. same) a member of a people of south central Ghana.
– ORIGIN the name in Akan (an African language).

ash blonde (also **ash blond**) ● adjective (of hair) very pale blonde.

ashcan ● noun US a dustbin.

ashen ● adjective very pale through shock, fear, or illness.

Ashkenazi /ashkənaazi/ ● noun (pl. **Ashkenazim** /ashkənaazim/) a Jew of central or eastern European descent. Compare with SEPHARDI.
– ORIGIN from *Ashkenaz*, a grandson of Noah.

ashlar /ashlər/ ● noun large square-cut stones used as the surface layer of a wall.
– ORIGIN Old French *aisselier*, from Latin *axilla* 'little plank'.

ashore ● adverb to or on the shore or land.

ashram /ashrəm/ ● noun an Indian religious retreat or community.
– ORIGIN Sanskrit, 'hermitage'.

ashtray ● noun a small receptacle for tobacco ash and cigarette ends.

Ash Wednesday ● noun the first day of Lent in the Western Christian Church.
– ORIGIN from the custom of marking the foreheads of penitents with ashes on that day.

Asian /ayshən, -zhn/ ● noun a person from Asia or a person of Asian descent. ● adjective relating to Asia.
– USAGE In Britain **Asian** is used to refer to people who come from (or whose parents came from) the Indian subcontinent, while in North America it is used to refer to people from the Far East.

Asiatic /ayshiattik, ayzi-/ ● adjective relating to Asia.

A-side ● noun the side of a pop single regarded as the main one.

aside ● adverb **1** to one side; out of the way. **2** in reserve. ● noun **1** an actor's remark addressed to the audience rather than the other characters. **2** an incidental remark.
– PHRASES **aside from** apart from. **set aside 1** temporarily remove (land) from agricultural production. **2** annul (a legal decision or process).

Thesaurus

of, in the matter of, as regards, with regard to, regarding, with reference to, re, in re, apropos, vis-à-vis. **as it were** SO TO SPEAK, in a manner of speaking, to some extent, so to say; *informal* sort of. **as yet** SO FAR, thus far, yet, still, up till now, up to now.

ascend ● verb CLIMB, go up/upwards, move up/upwards, rise (up); mount, scale, conquer; take to the air, take off.
– OPPOSITES descend.

ascendancy ● noun DOMINANCE, domination, supremacy, superiority, paramountcy, predominance, primacy, dominion, hegemony, authority, control, command, power, rule, sovereignty, lordship, leadership, influence.
– OPPOSITES subordination.

ascendant ● adjective RISING (IN POWER), on the rise, on the way up, up-and-coming, flourishing, prospering, burgeoning.
– OPPOSITES declining.

ascent ● noun **1** *the first ascent of the Matterhorn* CLIMB, scaling, conquest. **2** *a balloon ascent* RISE, climb, launch, take-off, lift-off, blast-off. **3** *the ascent grew steeper* (UPWARD) SLOPE, incline, rise, upward gradient, inclination, acclivity.
– OPPOSITES descent, drop.

ascertain ● verb FIND OUT, discover, get to know, work out, make out, fathom (out), learn, deduce, divine, discern, see, understand, comprehend; establish, determine, verify, confirm; *informal* figure out; *Brit. informal* suss (out).

ascetic ● adjective *an ascetic life* AUSTERE, self-denying, abstinent, abstemious, self-disciplined, self-abnegating; simple, puritanical, monastic; reclusive, eremitic, hermitic; celibate, chaste.
– OPPOSITES sybaritic.
● noun *a desert ascetic* ABSTAINER, puritan, recluse, hermit, solitary; fakir, Sufi, dervish, sadhu, muni; *historical* anchorite; *archaic* eremite.
– OPPOSITES sybarite.

ascribe ● verb ATTRIBUTE, assign, put down, accredit, credit, chalk up, impute; blame on, lay at the door of; connect with, associate with.

ash ● noun CINDERS, ashes, clinker.

ashamed ● adjective **1** *she felt ashamed that she had hit him* SORRY, shamefaced, abashed, sheepish, guilty, contrite, remorseful, repentant, penitent, regretful, rueful, apologetic; embarrassed, mortified. **2** *he was ashamed to admit it* RELUCTANT, loath, unwilling, disinclined, indisposed, afraid.
– OPPOSITES proud, pleased.

ashen ● adjective PALE, wan, pasty, grey, colourless, pallid, white, waxen, ghostly, bloodless.

a

asinine /assinin/ ● adjective extremely stupid or foolish.
– DERIVATIVES **asininity** noun.
– ORIGIN Latin *asininus*, from *asinus* 'ass'.

-asis (also **-iasis**) ● suffix forming the names of diseases: *psoriasis.*
– ORIGIN Greek.

ask ● verb **1** say something in order to get an answer or some information. **2** say that one wants someone to do, give, or allow something. **3** (**ask for**) request to speak to. **4** expect or demand (something) of someone. **5** invite (someone) to a social occasion. **6** (**ask out**) invite (someone) out on a date. **7** (**ask after**) enquire about the well-being of (someone).
– PHRASES **a big ask** Austral./NZ informal a difficult demand to fulfil. **for the asking** for little or no effort or cost.
– ORIGIN Old English.

askance /əskanss, əskaanss/ ● adverb with a suspicious or disapproving look.
– ORIGIN of unknown origin.

askari /əskaari/ ● noun (pl. same or **askaris**) (in East Africa) a soldier or police officer.
– ORIGIN Arabic, 'soldier'.

askew /əskyoō/ ● adverb & adjective not straight or level.

asking price ● noun the price at which something is offered for sale.

aslant ● adverb at a slant. ● preposition across at a slant.

asleep ● adjective & adverb **1** in or into a state of sleep. **2** not attentive or alert. **3** (of a limb) numb.

asp /asp/ ● noun **1** a small viper with an upturned snout. **2** the Egyptian cobra.
– ORIGIN Greek *aspis.*

asparagine /əsparrəjeen/ ● noun Biochemistry an amino acid which is a constituent of most proteins.
– ORIGIN from ASPARAGUS (which contains it).

asparagus /əsparrəgəss/ ● noun a vegetable consisting of the tender young shoots of a tall plant.
– ORIGIN Greek *asparagos.*

aspartame /əspaartaym/ ● noun a low-calorie artificial sweetener.
– ORIGIN from *aspartic acid,* a related chemical named after *asparagus.*

aspartic acid /əspaartik/ ● noun an acidic amino acid present in many proteins and in sugar cane.
– ORIGIN from Latin *asparagus.*

aspect ● noun **1** a particular part or feature of a matter. **2** appearance or quality. **3** the side of a building facing a particular direction.
– DERIVATIVES **aspectual** adjective.
– ORIGIN Latin *aspectus,* from *aspicere* 'look at'.

aspect ratio ● noun **1** the ratio of the width to the height of an image on a television screen. **2** Aeronautics the ratio of the span to the mean chord of an aerofoil.

aspen ● noun a poplar tree with small rounded long-stalked leaves.
– ORIGIN from dialect *asp* (in the same sense).

Asperger's syndrome /asperjərz/ ● noun Psychiatry a mild autistic disorder characterized by awkwardness in social interaction, pedantry in speech, and preoccupation with very narrow interests.
– ORIGIN named after the Austrian psychiatrist Hans *Asperger* (1906–80).

asperity /əsperriti/ ● noun (pl. **asperities**) **1** harshness of tone or manner. **2** a rough edge on a surface.
– ORIGIN Latin *asperitas,* from *asper* 'rough'.

aspersion /əspersh'n/ ● noun (often in phrase **cast aspersions on**) an attack on someone's character or reputation.
– ORIGIN originally denoting the sprinkling of water at baptism: Latin, from *aspergere* 'sprinkle'.

asphalt /asfalt/ ● noun a dark tar-like substance used in surfacing roads or waterproofing buildings.
– DERIVATIVES **asphaltic** adjective.
– ORIGIN Greek *asphalton.*

asphodel /asfədel/ ● noun a plant of the lily family with long, slender leaves and flowers borne on a spike.
– ORIGIN Greek *asphodelos*; related to DAFFODIL.

asphyxia /əsfiksiə/ ● noun a condition caused by the body being deprived of oxygen, leading to unconsciousness or death.
– DERIVATIVES **asphyxiant** adjective & noun.
– ORIGIN Greek *asphuxia,* from *a-* 'without' + *sphuxis* 'pulse'.

asphyxiate ● verb kill or be killed by asphyxia; suffocate.
– DERIVATIVES **asphyxiation** noun.

aspic ● noun a savoury jelly made with meat stock.
– ORIGIN French, 'asp', from the colours of the jelly as compared with those of the snake.

aspidistra /aspidistrə/ ● noun a plant of the lily family with broad tapering leaves.
– ORIGIN from Greek *aspis* 'shield' (because of the shape of the stigma).

aspirant /aspīrənt/ ● adjective aspiring towards a particular achievement or status. ● noun a person who has such aspirations.

aspirate ● verb /aspərayt/ **1** Phonetics pronounce with an exhalation of breath or with the sound of *h.* **2** Medicine draw (fluid) by suction from a vessel or cavity. **3** technical inhale. ● noun /aspərət/ Phonetics an aspirated consonant or sound of *h.*
– ORIGIN Latin *aspirare,* from *spirare* 'breathe'

aspiration ● noun **1** a hope or ambition. **2** the action of aspirating.
– DERIVATIVES **aspirational** adjective.

Thesaurus

ashore ● adverb ON TO (THE) LAND, on to the shore; shorewards, landwards; on the shore, on (dry) land.

aside ● adverb **1** *they stood aside* TO ONE SIDE, to the side, on one side; apart, away, separately. **2** *that aside, he seemed a nice man* APART, notwithstanding.
● noun *'Her parents died,' said Mrs Manton in an aside* WHISPERED REMARK, confidential remark, stage whisper; digression, incidental remark, obiter dictum, deviation.
– PHRASES **aside from** APART FROM, besides, in addition to, not counting, barring, other than, but (for), excluding, not including, except (for), excepting, leaving out, save (for).

asinine ● adjective FOOLISH, stupid, brainless, mindless, senseless, idiotic, imbecilic, ridiculous, ludicrous, absurd, nonsensical, fatuous, silly, inane, witless, empty-headed; *informal* half-witted, dumb, moronic; *Brit. informal* daft; *Scottish & N. English informal* glaikit.
– OPPOSITES intelligent, sensible.

ask ● verb **1** *he asked what time we opened* ENQUIRE, query, want to know; question, interrogate, quiz. **2** *they want to ask a few questions* PUT (FORWARD), pose, raise, submit. **3** *don't be afraid to ask for advice* REQUEST, demand; solicit, seek, crave, apply, petition, call, appeal, sue. **4** *let's ask them to dinner* INVITE, bid, summon, have someone over/round.
– OPPOSITES answer.

askance ● adverb *they look askance at anything foreign* SUSPICIOUSLY, sceptically, cynically, mistrustfully, distrustfully, doubtfully, dubiously; disapprovingly, contemptuously, scornfully, disdainfully.
– OPPOSITES approvingly.

askew ● adjective CROOKED, lopsided, tilted, angled, at an angle, skew, skewed, slanted, aslant, awry, squint, out of true, to/on one side, uneven, off centre, asymmetrical; *informal* cock-eyed, wonky; *Brit. informal* skew-whiff.
– OPPOSITES straight.

asleep ● adjective **1** *she was asleep in bed* SLEEPING, in a deep sleep, napping, catnapping, dozing, drowsing; *informal* snoozing, dead to the world; *Brit. informal* kipping; *humorous* in the land of Nod; *poetic/literary* slumbering. **2** *my leg's asleep* NUMB, with no feeling, numbed, benumbed, dead, insensible, insensate, unfeeling.
– OPPOSITES awake.

aspect ● noun **1** *the photos depict every aspect of life* FEATURE, facet, side, characteristic, particular, detail; angle, slant. **2** *his face had a sinister aspect* APPEARANCE, look, air, cast, mien, demeanour, expression; atmosphere, mood, quality, ambience, feeling. **3** *a summer house with a southern aspect* OUTLOOK, view, exposure; situation, position, location. **4** *the front aspect of the hotel* FACE, elevation, facade, side.

asperity ● noun HARSHNESS, sharpness, abrasiveness, severity, acerbity, astringency, tartness, sarcasm.

aspersions ● plural noun VILIFICATION, disparagement, denigration, defamation, condemnation, criticism, denunciation, slander, libel, calumny; slurs, smears, insults, slights; *informal* mudslinging, bad-mouthing; *Brit. informal* slagging off; *formal* castigation.
– PHRASES **cast aspersions on** VILIFY, disparage, denigrate, defame, run down, impugn, belittle, criticize, condemn, decry, denounce, pillory; malign, slander, libel, discredit; *informal* pull apart, throw mud at, knock, bad-mouth; *Brit. informal* rubbish, slate, slag off.

aspirator ● noun Medicine an instrument or apparatus for aspirating fluid from a vessel or cavity.

aspire ● verb (usu. **aspire to/to do**) have ambitions to be or do something.
– DERIVATIVES **aspiring** adjective.
– ORIGIN Latin *aspirare*, from *spirare* 'breathe'.

aspirin ● noun (pl. same or **aspirins**) a medicine used in tablet form to relieve pain and reduce fever and inflammation.
– ORIGIN from the chemical name, *acetylated salicylic acid*.

ass[1] ● noun **1** a donkey or similar horse-like animal with long ears and a braying call. **2** informal a foolish or stupid person.
– ORIGIN Latin *asinus*.

ass[2] ● noun North American form of ARSE.

assail ● verb **1** attack violently. **2** (of an unpleasant feeling) come upon (someone) strongly.
– ORIGIN Latin *assalire*, from *salire* 'to leap'.

assailant ● noun a person who attacks another.

assassin ● noun a person who assassinates someone.
– ORIGIN Arabic, 'hashish-eater', with reference to a fanatical Muslim sect who ruled part of northern Persia 1094–1256 and were reputed to use hashish before murder missions.

assassinate ● verb murder (a political or religious leader).
– DERIVATIVES **assassination** noun.

assault ● noun **1** a violent attack. **2** Law an act that threatens physical harm to a person. **3** a concentrated attempt to do something difficult. ● verb make an assault on.
– DERIVATIVES **assaultive** adjective.
– ORIGIN from Old French *assauter*, from Latin *saltare* 'to leap'.

assault and battery ● noun Law the action of threatening a person together with making physical contact with them.

assault course ● noun Brit. a course providing a series of physical challenges, used for training soldiers.

assay /assay, əsay/ ● noun the testing of a metal or ore to determine its ingredients and quality. ● verb **1** carry out an assay on. **2** archaic attempt.
– DERIVATIVES **assayer** noun.
– ORIGIN Old French *assai, essai* 'trial'.

assay office ● noun **1** a place where ores and metals are tested. **2** Brit. an institution which awards hallmarks to things made of precious metals.

assegai /assigī/ ● noun (pl. **assegais**) a slender iron-tipped spear used by southern African peoples.
– ORIGIN Arabic, 'the spear'.

assemblage ● noun **1** a collection or gathering. **2** something made of pieces fitted together.

assemble ● verb **1** come or bring together. **2** fit together the component parts of.
– DERIVATIVES **assembler** noun.
– ORIGIN Old French *asembler*, from Latin *ad-* 'to' + *simul* 'together'.

assembly ● noun (pl. **assemblies**) **1** a group of people gathered together. **2** a body with powers to make decisions and laws. **3** a regular gathering of teachers and pupils in a school. **4** the action of assembling component parts. **5** a unit consisting of assembled parts.

assembly line ● noun a series of machines by which identical items are assembled in successive stages.

assent /əsent/ ● noun the expression of approval or agreement. ● verb (usu. **assent to**) express assent.
– DERIVATIVES **assenter** (also **assentor**) noun.
– ORIGIN from Latin *assentire*, from *sentire* 'feel, think'.

assert ● verb **1** state (a fact or belief) confidently and forcefully. **2** cause others to recognize (something) by confident and forceful behaviour. **3** (**assert oneself**) be confident and forceful.
– ORIGIN Latin *asserere* 'claim, affirm'.

assertion ● noun **1** a confident and forceful statement. **2** the action of asserting.

assertive ● adjective confident and forceful.

Thesaurus

asphyxiate ● verb CHOKE (TO DEATH), suffocate, smother, stifle; throttle, strangle.

aspiration ● noun DESIRE, hope, dream, wish, longing, yearning; aim, ambition, expectation, goal, target.

aspire ● verb DESIRE, hope, dream, long, yearn, set one's heart on, wish, want, be desirous of; aim, seek, pursue, set one's sights on.

aspiring ● adjective WOULD-BE, aspirant, hopeful, budding; potential, prospective, future; ambitious, determined; *informal* wannabe.

ass ● noun **1** *he rode on an ass* DONKEY, jackass, jenny; *Scottish* cuddy; *Brit. informal* moke, neddy. **2** *(informal) don't be a silly ass* FOOL, idiot, dolt, simpleton, imbecile; *informal* ninny, nincompoop, dimwit, donkey, chump, halfwit, dum-dum, loon, jackass, cretin, jerk, nerd, fathead, blockhead, numbskull, dunce, dipstick, lamebrain, pea-brain, thickhead, woodenhead, pinhead, airhead, birdbrain; *Brit. informal* nitwit, twit, clot, plonker, berk, prat, pillock, wally, twerp, charlie; *Scottish informal* nyaff, balloon, gowk; *N. Amer. informal* schmuck, bozo, turkey, goofball, putz, wiener, weeny; *Austral./NZ informal* drongo, galah; *dated* tomfool, muttonhead.

assail ● verb **1** *the army moved in to assail the enemy* ATTACK, assault, pounce on, set upon/about, fall on, charge, rush, storm; *informal* lay into, tear into, pitch into. **2** *she was assailed by doubts* PLAGUE, torment, rack, beset, dog, trouble, disturb, worry, bedevil, nag, vex. **3** *critics assailed the policy* CRITICIZE, censure, attack, condemn, pillory, revile; *informal* knock, slam; *Brit. informal* slate, slag off; *formal* castigate.

assailant ● noun ATTACKER, mugger, assaulter; *rare* assailer.

assassin ● noun MURDERER, killer, gunman; executioner; *informal* hit man, hired gun; *poetic/literary* slayer; *dated* homicide.

assassinate ● verb MURDER, kill, slaughter; eliminate, execute; *N. Amer.* terminate; *informal* hit; *poetic/literary* slay.

assassination ● noun MURDER, killing, slaughter, homicide; political execution, elimination; *N. Amer.* termination; *informal* hit; *poetic/literary* slaying.

assault ● verb **1** *he assaulted a police officer* ATTACK, hit, strike, punch, beat up, thump; pummel, pound, batter; *informal* clout, wallop, belt, clobber, bop, biff, sock, deck, slug, plug, lay into, do over, rough up; *Austral. informal* quilt; *poetic/literary* smite. **2** *they left to assault the hill* ATTACK, assail, pounce on, set upon, strike, fall on, swoop on, rush, storm, besiege. **3** *he first assaulted then murdered her* RAPE, sexually assault, molest, interfere with.
● noun **1** *he was charged with assault* BATTERY, violence; sexual assault, rape; *Brit.* grievous bodily harm, GBH, actual bodily harm, ABH. **2** *an assault on the city* ATTACK, strike, onslaught, offensive, charge, push, thrust, invasion, bombardment, sortie, incursion, raid, blitz, campaign.

assay ● noun *new plate was brought for assay* EVALUATION, assessment, appraisal, analysis, examination, tests, inspection, scrutiny.
● verb *gold is assayed to determine its purity* EVALUATE, assess, appraise, analyse, examine, test, inspect, scrutinize, probe.

assemblage ● noun COLLECTION, accumulation, conglomeration, gathering, group, grouping, cluster, aggregation, mass, number; assortment, selection, array.

assemble ● verb **1** *a crowd had assembled* GATHER, collect, get together, congregate, convene, meet, muster, rally; *formal* foregather. **2** *he assembled the suspects* BRING/CALL TOGETHER, gather, collect, round up, marshal, muster, summon; *formal* convoke. **3** *how to assemble the kite* CONSTRUCT, build, fabricate, manufacture, erect, set up, put/piece together, connect, join.
– OPPOSITES disperse, dismantle.

assembly ● noun **1** *an assembly of dockers* GATHERING, meeting, congregation, convention, rally, convocation, assemblage, group, body, crowd, throng, company; *informal* get-together. **2** *the labour needed in car assembly* CONSTRUCTION, manufacture, building, fabrication, erection.

assent ● noun *they are likely to give their assent* AGREEMENT, acceptance, approval, approbation, consent, acquiescence, compliance, concurrence, the nod; sanction, endorsement, confirmation; permission, leave, blessing; *informal* the go-ahead, the green light, the OK, the thumbs up.
– OPPOSITES dissent, refusal.
● verb *he assented to the change* AGREE TO, accept, approve, consent to, acquiesce in, concur in, give one's blessing to, give the nod; sanction, endorse, confirm; *informal* give the go-ahead, give the green light, give the OK, OK, give the thumbs up; *formal* accede to.
– OPPOSITES refuse.

assert ● verb **1** *they asserted that all aboard were safe* DECLARE, maintain, contend, argue, state, claim, propound, proclaim, announce, pronounce, swear, insist, avow; *formal* aver, opine; *rare* asseverate. **2** *we find it difficult to assert our rights* INSIST ON, stand up for, uphold, defend, contend, establish, press/push for, stress.
– PHRASES **assert oneself** BEHAVE/SPEAK CONFIDENTLY, be assertive, put oneself forward, make one's presence felt; *informal* put one's foot down.

assertion ● noun **1** *I questioned his assertion* DECLARATION, contention, statement, claim, opinion, proclamation, announcement,

a

– DERIVATIVES **assertively** adverb **assertiveness** noun.

asses plural of ASS[1], ASS[2].

assess ● verb **1** evaluate or estimate. **2** set the value of a tax, fine, etc. for (a person or property).
– DERIVATIVES **assessable** adjective **assessment** noun **assessor** noun.
– ORIGIN Old French *assesser*, from Latin *assidere* 'sit by' (later 'levy tax)'.

asset ● noun **1** a useful or valuable thing or person. **2** (**assets**) property owned by a person or company.
– ORIGIN originally in the sense 'sufficient estate to allow discharge of a will': from Old French *asez* 'enough'.

asset-stripping ● noun the taking over of a company in financial difficulties and selling each of its assets at a profit.

asseveration /əsevvəraysh'n/ ● noun formal a solemn or emphatic declaration or statement.
– DERIVATIVES **asseverate** verb.
– ORIGIN Latin, from *asseverare*, from *severus* 'serious'.

assiduity /assidyōōiti/ ● noun (pl. **assiduities**) constant or close attention to what one is doing.

assiduous /əsidyooəss/ ● adjective showing great care and perseverance.
– DERIVATIVES **assiduously** adverb **assiduousness** noun.
– ORIGIN Latin *assiduus*, from *assidere* 'sit by'.

assign ● verb **1** allocate (a task or duty) to someone. **2** give (someone) a job or task. **3** regard (something) as belonging to or being caused by. **4** transfer (legal rights or liabilities).
– DERIVATIVES **assignable** adjective **assigner** (also **assignor**) noun.
– ORIGIN Latin *assignare*, from *signare* 'to sign'.

assignation ● noun **1** a secret arrangement to meet, especially by lovers. **2** the action of assigning.

assignee ● noun chiefly Law **1** a person to whom a right or liability is legally transferred. **2** a person appointed to act for another.

assignment ● noun **1** a task allocated to someone as part of a job or course of study. **2** the action of assigning.

assimilate ● verb **1** take in and understand (information or ideas). **2** absorb and integrate into a people or culture. **3** absorb and digest (food or nutrients). **4** regard as or make similar.
– DERIVATIVES **assimilable** adjective **assimilation** noun **assimilative** adjective **assimilator** noun.
– ORIGIN Latin *assimilare* 'absorb, incorporate', from *similis* 'like'.

assist ● verb help (someone). ● noun chiefly N. Amer. an act of helping someone.
– ORIGIN Latin *assistere* 'take one's stand by'.

assistance ● noun help or support.

assistant ● noun **1** a person who ranks below a senior person. **2** a person who helps in particular work.

assize /əsīz/ (also **assizes**) ● noun historical a court which sat at intervals in each county of England and Wales.
– ORIGIN Old French *assise*, from Latin *assidere* 'sit by'.

associate ● verb /əsōsiayt, -shiayt/ **1** connect in the mind. **2** frequently meet or have dealings. **3** (**be associated with** or **associate oneself with**) be involved with. ● noun /əsōsiət, -shiət/ **1** a work partner or colleague. **2** a person with subordinate membership of an organization. ● adjective /əsōsiət, -shiət/ **1** connected with an organization or business. **2** having membership but with lower status.
– ORIGIN Latin *associare* 'join', from *socius* 'sharing, allied'.

association ● noun **1** a group of people organized for a joint purpose. **2** a connection or link between people or organizations. **3** a mental connection between ideas.
– DERIVATIVES **associational** adjective.

Association Football ● noun more formal term for SOCCER.

Thesaurus

pronouncement, protestation, avowal; *formal* averment; *rare* asseveration. **2** *an assertion of the right to march* DEFENCE, upholding; insistence on.

assertive ● adjective CONFIDENT, self-confident, bold, decisive, assured, self-assured, self-possessed; authoritative, strong-willed, forceful, insistent, determined, commanding, pushy; *informal* feisty; *dated* pushful.
– OPPOSITES timid.

assess ● verb **1** *the committee's power is hard to assess* EVALUATE, judge, gauge, rate, estimate, appraise, get the measure of, determine, weigh up, analyse; *informal* size up. **2** *the damage was assessed at £5 billion* VALUE, calculate, work out, determine, fix, cost, price, estimate.

assessment ● noun **1** *a teacher's assessment of the pupil's abilities* EVALUATION, judgement, rating, estimation, appraisal, analysis, opinion. **2** *some assessments valued the estate at £2 million* VALUATION, calculation, costing, pricing, estimate.

asset ● noun **1** *he sees his age as an asset* BENEFIT, advantage, blessing, good point, strong point, strength, forte, virtue, recommendation, attraction, resource, boon, merit, bonus, plus, pro. **2** *the seizure of all their assets* PROPERTY, resources, estate, holdings, possessions, effects, goods, valuables, belongings, chattels.
– OPPOSITES liability.

assiduous ● adjective DILIGENT, careful, meticulous, thorough, sedulous, attentive, conscientious, punctilious, painstaking, rigorous, particular; persevering.

assign ● verb **1** *a young doctor was assigned the task* ALLOCATE, allot, give, set; charge with, entrust with. **2** *she was assigned to a new post* APPOINT, promote, delegate, commission, post, co-opt; select for, choose for, install in; *Military* detail. **3** *we assign large sums of money to travel budgets* EARMARK, designate, set aside, reserve, appropriate, allot, allocate, apportion. **4** *he assigned the opinion to the Prince* ASCRIBE, attribute, put down, accredit, credit, chalk up, impute; pin on, lay at the door of. **5** *he may assign the money to a third party* TRANSFER, make over, give, pass, hand over/down, convey, consign; *Law* attorn, devise.

assignation ● noun RENDEZVOUS, date, appointment, meeting; *poetic/literary* tryst.

assignment ● noun **1** *I'm going to finish this assignment tonight* TASK, piece of work, job, duty, chore, mission, errand, undertaking, exercise, business, endeavour, enterprise; project, homework. **2** *the assignment of tasks* ALLOCATION, allotment, issuance, designation; sharing out, apportionment, distribution, handing out, dispensation. **3** *the assignment of property* TRANSFER, making over, giving, hand down, consignment; *Law* conveyance, devise, attornment.

assimilate ● verb **1** *the amount of information he can assimilate* ABSORB, take in, acquire, pick up, grasp, comprehend, understand, learn, master; digest, ingest. **2** *many tribes were assimilated by Turkic peoples* SUBSUME, incorporate, integrate, absorb, engulf, acculturate; co-opt, adopt, embrace, admit.

assist ● verb **1** *I spend my time assisting the chef* HELP, aid, abet, lend a (helping) hand to, oblige, accommodate, serve; collaborate with, work with; support, back (up), second; *informal* pitch in with; *Brit. informal* muck in with. **2** *the exchange rates assisted the firm's expansion* FACILITATE, aid, ease, expedite, spur, promote, boost, benefit, foster, encourage, stimulate, precipitate, accelerate, advance, further, forward.
– OPPOSITES hinder, impede.

assistance ● noun HELP, aid, support, backing, reinforcement, succour, relief, intervention, cooperation, collaboration; a (helping) hand, a good turn; *informal* a break, a leg up.
– OPPOSITES hindrance.

assistant ● noun **1** *a photographer's assistant* SUBORDINATE, deputy, second (in command), number two, right-hand man/woman, aide, personal assistant, PA, attendant, mate, apprentice, junior, auxiliary; hired hand, hired help, helper, man/girl Friday; *informal* sidekick, gofer; *Brit. informal* dogsbody, skivvy. **2** *an assistant in the local shop* SALES ASSISTANT, salesperson, saleswoman/girl, salesman, server, checkout operator; seller, vendor; *N. Amer.* clerk; *informal* counter-jumper; *dated* shop boy/girl.

associate ● verb **1** *the colours that we associate with fire* LINK, connect, relate, identify, equate, bracket, set side by side. **2** *I was forced to associate with them* MIX, keep company, mingle, socialize, go around, rub shoulders, fraternize, consort, have dealings; *N. Amer.* rub elbows; *informal* hobnob, hang out/around/round, be thick with; *Brit. informal* hang about. **3** *the firm is associated with a local charity* AFFILIATE, align, connect, join, attach, team up, be in league, ally; merge, integrate, confederate.
● noun *his business associate* PARTNER, colleague, co-worker, workmate, comrade, ally, confederate; connection, contact, acquaintance; collaborator, partner; *informal* crony; *Brit. informal* oppo; *Austral./NZ informal* offsider.

associated ● adjective **1** *salaries and associated costs* RELATED, connected, linked, correlated, similar, corresponding; attendant, accompanying, incidental. **2** *their associated company* AFFILIATED, allied, integrated, amalgamated, federated, confederated, syndicated, connected, related.
– OPPOSITES unrelated.

association ● noun **1** *a trade association* ALLIANCE, consortium,

associative ● adjective **1** of or involving association. **2** Mathematics unchanged in result by varying the grouping of quantities, as long as their order remains the same, such that for example $(a \times b) \times c = a \times (b \times c)$.

assonance /assənənss/ ● noun resemblance of sound between words arising from the rhyming of vowels only (e.g. *sonnet, porridge*) or from use of identical consonants with different vowels (e.g. *cold, culled*).
– DERIVATIVES **assonant** adjective.
– ORIGIN from Latin *assonare* 'respond to'.

assorted ● adjective of various sorts put together.
– ORIGIN from Old French *assorter*, from *sorte* 'sort, kind'.

assortment ● noun a miscellaneous collection.

assuage /əswayj/ ● verb **1** make (an unpleasant feeling) less intense. **2** satisfy (an appetite or desire).
– DERIVATIVES **assuagement** noun.
– ORIGIN Old French *assouagier*, from Latin *suavis* 'sweet'.

assume ● verb **1** accept as true without proof. **2** take (responsibility or control). **3** begin to have (a quality, appearance, or extent). **4** pretend to have; adopt falsely.
– ORIGIN Latin *assumere*, from *sumere* 'take'.

assuming ● conjunction based on the assumption that.

assumption ● noun **1** a thing that is assumed to be true. **2** the action of assuming responsibility or control. **3** (**Assumption**) the reception of the Virgin Mary bodily into heaven, according to Roman Catholic doctrine.

assurance ● noun **1** a positive declaration intended to give confidence. **2** confidence or certainty in one's own abilities. **3** chiefly Brit. life insurance.
– USAGE In the context of life insurance, a technical distinction is made between **assurance** and **insurance**. **Assurance** is used of policies under whose terms a payment is guaranteed, either after a fixed term or on the death of the insured person; **insurance** is the general term, and is used in particular of policies under whose terms a payment would be made only in certain circumstances (e.g. accident or death within a limited period).

assure ● verb **1** tell (someone) something positively to dispel doubts. **2** make (something) certain to happen. **3** chiefly Brit. cover by assurance.
– DERIVATIVES **assurer** noun.
– ORIGIN Old French *assurer*, from Latin *securus* 'free from care'.

assured ● adjective **1** confident. **2** protected against change or ending.
– DERIVATIVES **assuredly** adverb.

Assyrian /əsirriən/ ● noun an inhabitant of Assyria, an ancient country in what is now Iraq. ● adjective relating to Assyria.

astatine /astəteen/ ● noun a very unstable radioactive chemical element belonging to the halogen group.
– ORIGIN from Greek *astatos* 'unstable'.

aster /astər/ ● noun a Michaelmas daisy or related plant, typically with purple or pink rayed flowers.
– ORIGIN Greek, 'star'.

asterisk ● noun a symbol (*) used in text as a pointer to an annotation or footnote. ● verb mark with an asterisk.
– ORIGIN Greek *asteriskos* 'small star'.

asterism /astəriz'm/ ● noun a group of three asterisks (⁂) drawing attention to following text.

astern ● adverb behind or towards the rear of a ship or aircraft.

asteroid /astəroyd/ ● noun a small rocky body orbiting the sun.
– ORIGIN from Greek *asteroeidēs* 'starlike'.

asthma /asmə/ ● noun a medical condition marked by difficulty in breathing.
– DERIVATIVES **asthmatic** adjective & noun.
– ORIGIN Greek, from *azein* 'breathe hard'.

astigmatism /əstigmətiz'm/ ● noun a defect of the eye or a lens, resulting in distorted images.
– DERIVATIVES **astigmatic** /astigmattik/ adjective.
– ORIGIN from Greek *stigma* 'point'.

astilbe /əstilbi/ ● noun a plant with plumes of tiny white, pink, or red flowers.
– ORIGIN Latin, from Greek *a-* 'not' + *stilbē* 'glittering'.

astir ● adjective **1** in a state of excited movement. **2** awake and out of bed.

astonish ● verb surprise or impress greatly.
– DERIVATIVES **astonished** adjective **astonishing** adjective **astonishment** noun.
– ORIGIN Old French *estoner* 'stun, stupefy', from Latin *tonare* 'to thunder'.

astound ● verb shock or greatly surprise.
– DERIVATIVES **astounded** adjective **astounding** adjective.
– ORIGIN related to ASTONISH.

astrakhan /astrəkan/ ● noun the dark curly fleece of young

Thesaurus

coalition, union, league, guild, syndicate, federation, confederation, confederacy, conglomerate, cooperative, partnership, affiliation. **2** *the association between man and environment* RELATIONSHIP, relation, interrelation, connection, interconnection, link, bond, union, tie, attachment, interdependence, affiliation.

assorted ● adjective VARIOUS, miscellaneous, mixed, varied, varying, diverse, eclectic, multifarious, sundry; poetic/literary divers.

assortment ● noun MIXTURE, variety, array, mixed bag, mix, miscellany, selection, medley, diversity, ragbag, pot-pourri, salmagundi, farrago, gallimaufry, omnium gatherum.

assuage ● verb **1** *a pain that could never be assuaged* RELIEVE, ease, alleviate, soothe, mitigate, allay, palliate, abate, suppress, subdue, tranquillize; moderate, lessen, diminish, reduce. **2** *her hunger was quickly assuaged* SATISFY, gratify, appease, fulfil, indulge, relieve, slake, sate, satiate, quench, check.
– OPPOSITES aggravate, intensify.

assume ● verb **1** *I assumed he wanted me to keep the book* PRESUME, suppose, take it (as given), take for granted, take as read, conjecture, surmise, conclude, deduce, infer, reckon, reason, think, fancy, believe, understand, gather; N. Amer. figure; archaic ween. **2** *he assumed a Southern accent* AFFECT, adopt, impersonate, put on, simulate, feign, fake. **3** *the disease may assume epidemic proportions* ACQUIRE, take on, come to have. **4** *they are to assume more responsibility* ACCEPT, shoulder, bear, undertake, take on/up, manage, handle, deal with. **5** *he assumed control of their finances* SEIZE, take (over), appropriate, commandeer, expropriate, hijack, wrest, usurp.

assumed ● adjective FALSE, fictitious, invented, made-up, fake, bogus, sham, spurious, make-believe, improvised, adopted; informal pretend, phoney; Brit. informal cod.
– OPPOSITES genuine.

assumption ● noun **1** *an informed assumption* SUPPOSITION, presumption, belief, expectation, conjecture, speculation, surmise, guess, premise, hypothesis; conclusion, deduction, inference, notion, impression. **2** *her assumption of ease* PRETENCE, simulation, affectation. **3** *the early assumption of community obligation* ACCEPTANCE, shouldering, tackling, undertaking. **4** *the assumption of power by revolutionaries* SEIZURE, arrogation, appropriation, expropriation, commandeering, confiscation, hijacking, wresting.

assurance ● noun **1** *her calm assurance* SELF-CONFIDENCE, confidence, self-assurance, self-possession, nerve, poise, aplomb, level-headedness; calmness, composure, sangfroid, equanimity; informal cool, unflappability. **2** *you have my assurance* WORD (OF HONOUR), promise, pledge, vow, avowal, oath, bond, undertaking, guarantee, commitment. **3** *there is no assurance of getting one's money back* GUARANTEE, certainty, certitude, surety, confidence, expectation. **4** *life assurance* INSURANCE, indemnity, indemnification, protection, security, cover.
– OPPOSITES self-doubt, uncertainty.

assure ● verb **1** *we must assure him of our loyal support* REASSURE, convince, satisfy, persuade, guarantee, promise, tell; affirm, pledge, swear, vow. **2** *he wants to assure a favourable vote* ENSURE, secure, guarantee, seal, clinch, confirm; informal sew up. **3** *they guarantee to assure your life* INSURE, provide insurance, cover, indemnify.

assured ● adjective **1** *an assured voice* CONFIDENT, self-confident, self-assured, self-possessed, poised, phlegmatic, level-headed; calm, composed, equanimous, imperturbable, unruffled; informal unflappable, together. **2** *an assured supply of weapons* GUARANTEED, certain, sure, secure, reliable, dependable, sound; infallible, unfailing; informal sure-fire.
– OPPOSITES doubtful, uncertain.

astonish ● verb AMAZE, astound, stagger, surprise, startle, stun, confound, dumbfound, stupefy, daze, nonplus, take aback, leave open-mouthed, leave aghast; informal flabbergast, bowl over; Brit. informal knock for six.

astonished ● adjective AMAZED, astounded, staggered, surprised, startled, stunned, thunderstruck, aghast, taken aback, dumbfounded, dumbstruck, stupefied, dazed, nonplussed, awestruck; informal flabbergasted; Brit. informal gobsmacked.

astonishing ● adjective AMAZING, astounding, staggering, surprising, breathtaking; remarkable, extraordinary, incredible, un-

a

karakul lambs from central Asia.
– ORIGIN named after the city of *Astrakhan* in Russia.
astral /astrəl/ • **adjective** relating to the stars.
– ORIGIN Latin *astralis*, from *astrum* 'star'.
astray • **adverb** away from the correct path or direction.
– ORIGIN from Old French *estraie*, from Latin *extra* 'out of bounds' + *vagari* 'wander'.
astride • **1 preposition & adverb** with a leg on each side of. **2 adverb** (of a person's legs) apart.
astringent /əstrinjənt/ • **adjective 1** causing the contraction of body tissues. **2** (of taste or smell) sharp or bitter. **3** harsh or severe. • **noun** an astringent lotion applied for medical or cosmetic purposes.
– DERIVATIVES **astringency** noun **astringently** adverb.
– ORIGIN from Latin *astringere* 'pull tight'.
astro- /astrō/ • **combining form** relating to the stars or to outer space: *astronaut*.
– ORIGIN from Greek *astron* 'star'.
astrodome • **noun 1** chiefly US an enclosed stadium with a domed roof. **2** a domed window in an aircraft for astronomical observations.
astrolabe /astrəlayb/ • **noun** an instrument formerly used for making astronomical measurements and in navigation for calculating latitude.
– ORIGIN Latin *astrolabium*, from Greek *astrolabos* 'star-taking'.
astrology • **noun** the study of the movements and relative positions of celestial bodies and their supposed influence on human affairs.
– DERIVATIVES **astrologer** noun **astrological** adjective **astrologically** adverb.
astronaut • **noun** a person trained to travel in a spacecraft.
– ORIGIN from Greek *astron* 'star' + *nautēs* 'sailor'.
astronautics • **plural noun** (treated as sing.) the science and technology of space travel and exploration.
astronomical • **adjective 1** relating to astronomy. **2** informal extremely large: *astronomical fees*.
– DERIVATIVES **astronomic** adjective **astronomically** adverb.
astronomical unit • **noun** a unit of measurement equal to the mean distance from the earth to the sun, 149.6 million kilometres.
astronomy • **noun** the science of celestial objects, space, and the physical universe.
– DERIVATIVES **astronomer** noun.
astrophysics • **plural noun** (treated as sing.) the branch of astronomy concerned with the physical nature of celestial bodies.
– DERIVATIVES **astrophysical** adjective **astrophysicist** noun.
AstroTurf • **noun** trademark an artificial grass surface, used for sports fields.
– ORIGIN from sense 1 of ASTRODOME.
astute • **adjective** good at making accurate judgements; shrewd.
– DERIVATIVES **astutely** adverb **astuteness** noun.
– ORIGIN Latin *astutus*, from *astus* 'craft'.
asunder • **adverb** archaic or literary apart.
– ORIGIN Old English.
asylum • **noun 1** shelter or protection. **2** protection granted by a state to a political refugee. **3** dated an institution for the mentally ill.
– ORIGIN Greek *asulon* 'refuge'.
asymmetrical • **adjective** lacking symmetry.
– DERIVATIVES **asymmetric** adjective **asymmetrically** adverb.
asymmetric bars • **plural noun** a pair of bars of different heights used in women's gymnastics.
asymmetry /aysimmitri/ • **noun** (pl. **asymmetries**) lack of symmetry.
asymptomatic • **adjective** Medicine producing or showing no symptoms.
asymptote /assimptōt/ • **noun** a straight line that continually approaches a given curve but does not meet it.
– DERIVATIVES **asymptotic** /assimptottik/ adjective **asymptotically** adverb.
– ORIGIN from Latin *asymptota linea* 'line not meeting'.
asynchronous • **adjective** not existing or occurring at the same time.
– DERIVATIVES **asynchronously** adverb.
At • **symbol** the chemical element astatine.
at[1] • **preposition 1** expressing location or arrival. **2** expressing the time when an event takes place. **3** denoting a value, rate, or point on a scale. **4** expressing a state or condition. **5** expressing the object or target of a look, shot, action, or plan. **6** expressing the means by which something is done.
– PHRASES **at that** in addition; furthermore. **where it's at** informal the focus of fashion.
– ORIGIN Old English.
at[2] • **noun** a monetary unit of Laos, equal to one hundredth of a kip.
– ORIGIN Thai.
atavistic /attəvistik/ • **adjective** returning to something ancient or ancestral.
– DERIVATIVES **atavism** noun **atavistically** adverb.
– ORIGIN from Latin *atavus* 'forefather'.
ataxia /ətaksiə/ • **noun** Medicine the loss of full control of bodily movements.
– DERIVATIVES **ataxic** adjective.
– ORIGIN Greek, 'disorder'.
ATC • **abbreviation 1** air traffic control or controller. **2** Air Training Corps.
ate past of EAT.
-ate[1] • **suffix** forming nouns denoting: **1** status, office, or function: *doctorate*. **2** a group: *electorate*. **3** Chemistry a salt or ester: *chlorate*. **4** a product of a chemical process: *condensate*.
– ORIGIN Old French *-at* or Latin *-atus*.
-ate[2] • **suffix 1** forming adjectives and nouns such as *associate*. **2** forming verbs such as *fascinate*.
– ORIGIN Latin *-atus*.
atelier /ətelliay/ • **noun** a workshop or studio.
– ORIGIN French, from Latin *astula* 'splinter of wood'.
atheism /aythi-iz'm/ • **noun** the belief that God does not exist.
– DERIVATIVES **atheist** noun **atheistic** adjective **atheistical** adjective.
– ORIGIN from Greek *a-* 'without' + *theos* 'god'.
atheling /athəling/ • **noun** a prince or lord in Anglo-Saxon Eng-

Thesaurus

believable, phenomenal; *informal* mind-boggling.
astonishment • **noun** AMAZEMENT, surprise, stupefaction, incredulity, disbelief, speechlessness, awe, wonder.
astound • **verb** AMAZE, astonish, stagger, surprise, startle, stun, confound, dumbfound, stupefy, daze, nonplus, take aback, leave open-mouthed, leave aghast; *informal* flabbergast, bowl over; *Brit. informal* knock for six.
astounding • **adjective** AMAZING, astonishing, staggering, surprising, breathtaking, remarkable, extraordinary, incredible, unbelievable, phenomenal; *informal* mind-boggling.
astray • **adverb 1** *the shots went astray* OFF TARGET, wide of the mark, awry, off course. **2** *the older boys lead him astray* INTO WRONGDOING, into sin, into iniquity, away from the straight and narrow.
astringent • **adjective 1** *the lotion has an astringent effect on pores* CONSTRICTING, constrictive, contracting; styptic. **2** *her astringent words* SEVERE, sharp, stern, harsh, acerbic, acidulous, caustic, mordant, trenchant; scathing, cutting, incisive, waspish; *N. Amer.* acerb.
astrology • **noun** HOROSCOPY; horoscopes; *rare* astromancy.
astronaut • **noun** SPACEMAN/WOMAN, cosmonaut, space traveller, space cadet; *N. Amer. informal* jock.
astronomical • **adjective 1** *astronomical alignments* PLANETARY, stellar; celestial. **2** *(informal) the sums he has paid are astronomical* HUGE, enormous, very large, prodigious, monumental, colossal, vast, gigantic, massive; substantial, considerable, sizeable, hefty; inordinate; *informal* astronomic, whopping, humongous; *Brit. informal* ginormous.
– OPPOSITES tiny.
astute • **adjective** SHREWD, sharp, acute, quick, clever, intelligent, bright, smart, canny, intuitive, perceptive, insightful, incisive, sagacious, wise; *informal* on the ball, quick on the uptake, savvy; *Brit. informal* suss; *N. Amer. informal* heads-up; *rare* argute.
– OPPOSITES stupid.
asunder • **adverb** *(poetic/literary) the fabric of society may be torn asunder* APART, up, in two; to pieces, to shreds.
asylum • **noun 1** *he appealed for political asylum* REFUGE, sanctuary, shelter, safety, protection, security, immunity; a safe haven. **2** *(dated) his father was confined to an asylum* PSYCHIATRIC HOSPITAL, mental hospital, mental institution, mental asylum; *informal* madhouse, loony bin, funny farm; *N. Amer. informal* bughouse; *dated* lunatic asylum; *archaic* bedlam.
asymmetrical • **adjective** LOPSIDED, unsymmetrical, uneven, unbalanced, crooked, awry, askew, skew, squint, misaligned; dispro-

a

land.
– ORIGIN Old English.
Athenian /əthe̅eniən/ • noun a person from Athens in Greece. • adjective relating to Athens.
atherosclerosis /athərōskleerōsiss/ • noun a disease of the arteries in which fatty material is deposited on their inner walls.
– DERIVATIVES **atherosclerotic** adjective.
– ORIGIN from Greek *athērē* 'groats' + *sklērōsis* 'hardening'.
athlete • noun **1** a person who is good at sports. **2** a person who competes in track and field events.
– ORIGIN Greek *athlētēs*, from *athlon* 'prize'.
athlete's foot • noun a form of ringworm infection affecting the skin between the toes.
athletic • adjective **1** fit and good at sport. **2** relating to athletics.
– DERIVATIVES **athletically** adverb **athleticism** noun.
athletics • plural noun (usu. treated as sing.) **1** chiefly Brit. the sport of competing in track and field events. **2** N. Amer. physical sports and games.
at-home • noun a social gathering in a person's home.
athwart /əthwawrt/ • preposition & adverb from side to side of something; across.
– ORIGIN from an archaic sense of THWART, meaning 'across'.
-ation • suffix (forming nouns) denoting an action or its result: *exploration.*
– ORIGIN French or Latin.
Atlantic • adjective of or adjoining the Atlantic Ocean.
– ORIGIN from the name of the god *Atlas* (see ATLAS); the term originally referred to Mount Atlas in Libya.
atlas • noun **1** a book of maps or charts. **2** Anatomy the topmost vertebra of the backbone.
– ORIGIN from the name of the Greek god *Atlas*, who held up the pillars of the universe: his picture appeared at the front of early atlases.
ATM • abbreviation automated teller machine.
atmosphere • noun **1** the envelope of gases surrounding the earth or another planet. **2** the quality of the air in a place. **3** a pervading tone or mood. **4** a unit of pressure equal to mean atmospheric pressure at sea level, 101,325 pascals (roughly 14.7 pounds per square inch).
– ORIGIN from Greek *atmos* 'vapour' + *sphaira* 'globe'.
atmospheric • adjective **1** relating to the atmosphere of the earth or another planet. **2** creating a distinctive mood, typically of romance, mystery, or nostalgia.
– DERIVATIVES **atmospherically** adverb.
atmospherics • plural noun electrical disturbances in the atmosphere, that interfere with telecommunications.
ATOL /attol/ • abbreviation (in the UK) Air Travel Organizer's Licence.
atoll /attol/ • noun a ring-shaped reef or chain of islands formed of coral.
– ORIGIN Maldivian.
atom • noun **1** the smallest particle of a chemical element, consisting of a positively charged nucleus surrounded by negatively charged electrons. **2** an extremely small amount: *she did not have an atom of strength left.*
– ORIGIN from Greek *atomos* 'indivisible'.
atom bomb • noun a bomb whose explosive power comes from the fission of heavy atomic nuclei.
atomic • adjective **1** relating to an atom or atoms. **2** of or forming a single indivisible unit or component in a larger system. **3** relating to nuclear energy.
– DERIVATIVES **atomically** adverb.
atomic bomb • noun an atom bomb.
atomic clock • noun an extremely accurate type of clock which is regulated by the vibrations of an atomic or molecular system such as caesium.
atomicity • noun **1** the number of atoms in the molecule of an element. **2** the state or fact of being composed of atoms.
atomic mass • noun the mass of an atom of a chemical element expressed in atomic mass units.
atomic mass unit • noun a unit of mass used to express atomic and molecular weights, equal to one twelfth of the mass of an atom of carbon-12.
atomic number • noun the number of protons in the nucleus of a chemical element's atom, which determines its place in the periodic table.
atomic theory • noun the theory that all matter is made up of tiny indivisible particles (atoms).
atomic weight • noun another term for RELATIVE ATOMIC MASS.
atomize (also **atomise**) • verb **1** convert (a substance) into very fine particles or droplets. **2** fragment.
– DERIVATIVES **atomization** noun **atomizer** noun.
atonal /aytōn'l/ • adjective Music not written in any key or mode.
– DERIVATIVES **atonality** noun.
atone • verb (**atone for**) make amends for.
– ORIGIN from *at one.*
atonement • noun **1** amends for a wrong or injury. **2** (**the Atonement**) Christian Theology the reconciliation of God and mankind through the death of Jesus Christ.
atop • preposition literary on the top of.
atopic /aytoppik/ • adjective relating to a form of allergy in which a hypersensitivity reaction such as eczema or asthma may occur in a part of the body not in contact with the allergen.
– DERIVATIVES **atopy** /attəpi/ noun.
– ORIGIN from Greek *atopia* 'unusualness'.
ATP • abbreviation Brit. automatic train protection.
atrabilious /atrəbilliəss/ • adjective literary melancholy or ill-tempered.
– ORIGIN from Latin *atra bilis* 'black bile'.
atrium /aytriəm/ • noun (pl. **atria** /aytriə/ or **atriums**) **1** a central hall rising through several storeys and having a glazed roof. **2** an open central court in an ancient Roman house. **3** Anatomy each of the two upper cavities of the heart.
– DERIVATIVES **atrial** adjective.
– ORIGIN Latin.
atrocious • adjective **1** horrifyingly wicked. **2** informal extremely bad or unpleasant.
– DERIVATIVES **atrociously** adverb.
– ORIGIN from Latin *atrox* 'cruel'.
atrocity • noun (pl. **atrocities**) an extremely wicked or cruel act.
atrophy /atrəfi/ • verb (**atrophies, atrophied**) **1** (of body tissue

Thesaurus

portionate, unequal, irregular; *informal* cock-eyed; *Brit. informal* skew-whiff, wonky.
atheism • noun NON-BELIEF, disbelief, unbelief, scepticism, doubt, agnosticism; nihilism.
atheist • noun NON-BELIEVER, disbeliever, unbeliever, sceptic, doubter, doubting Thomas, agnostic; nihilist; *rare* nullifidian.
– OPPOSITES believer.
athlete • noun SPORTSMAN, sportswoman, sportsperson; Olympian; runner; *N. Amer. informal* jock.
athletic • adjective **1** *his athletic physique* MUSCULAR, muscly, sturdy, strapping, well built, strong, powerful, robust, able-bodied, vigorous, hardy, lusty, hearty, brawny, burly, broad-shouldered, Herculean; FIT, in good shape, in trim; *informal* sporty, husky, hunky, beefy; *poetic/literary* thewy, stark. **2** *athletic events* SPORTING, sports; Olympic.
– OPPOSITES puny.
athletics • plural noun TRACK AND FIELD EVENTS, sporting events, sports, games, races; contests.
atmosphere • noun **1** *the gases present in the atmosphere* AIR, aerospace; sky; *poetic/literary* the heavens, the firmament, the blue, the azure, the ether. **2** *the hotel has a relaxed atmosphere* AMBIENCE, air, mood, feel, feeling, character, tone, tenor, aura, quality, undercurrent, flavour; *informal* vibe.
atom • noun **1** *they build tiny circuits atom by atom* PARTICLE, molecule, bit, piece, fragment, fraction. **2** *there wasn't an atom of truth in the allegations* GRAIN, iota, jot, whit, mite, scrap, shred, ounce, scintilla; *Irish* stim; *informal* smidgen.
atone • verb MAKE AMENDS, make reparation, make up for, compensate, pay, recompense, expiate, make good, offset; do penance.
atrocious • adjective **1** *atrocious cruelties* BRUTAL, barbaric, barbarous, savage, vicious; wicked, cruel, nasty, heinous, monstrous, vile, inhuman, black-hearted, fiendish, ghastly, horrible; abominable, outrageous, hateful, disgusting, despicable, contemptible, loathsome, odious, abhorrent, sickening, horrifying, unspeakable, execrable, egregious. **2** *(informal) the weather was atrocious* APPALLING, dreadful, terrible, very bad, unpleasant, miserable; *informal* abysmal, dire, rotten, lousy, God-awful; *Brit. informal* shocking, chronic.
– OPPOSITES admirable, superb.
atrocity • noun **1** *press reports detailed a number of atrocities*

a

or an organ) waste away. **2** gradually become less effective or vigorous. ● **noun** the condition or process of atrophying.
– DERIVATIVES **atrophic** /ətroffik/ adjective.
– ORIGIN from Greek *atrophia* 'lack of food'.

atropine /atrəpeen, -pin/ ● **noun** a poisonous compound found in deadly nightshade, used in medicine as a muscle relaxant.
– ORIGIN from *Atropos*, one of the Fates in Greek mythology.

attach ● **verb** **1** fasten; join. **2** include (a condition) as part of an agreement. **3** assign or attribute. **4** appoint (someone) for special or temporary duties. **5** Law, archaic seize (a person or property) by legal authority.
– DERIVATIVES **attachable** adjective.
– ORIGIN Old French *atachier* 'fasten, fix'.

attaché /ətashay/ ● **noun** a person on an ambassador's staff with specialized duties.
– ORIGIN French, 'attached'.

attaché case ● **noun** a small, flat briefcase for carrying documents.

attached ● **adjective** affectionate; fond: *Mark became increasingly attached to Tara.*

attachment ● **noun** **1** an extra part or extension attached to something. **2** the action of attaching. **3** affection or fondness. **4** Brit. temporary secondment to an organization. **5** a computer file appended to an email.

attack ● **verb** **1** take aggressive action against. **2** (of a disease, chemical, etc.) act harmfully on. **3** criticize or oppose fiercely and publicly. **4** begin to deal with (a problem or task) in a determined way. **5** (in sport) attempt to score goals or points. ● **noun** **1** an instance of attacking. **2** a sudden short bout of an illness. **3** the players in a team whose role is to attack.
– DERIVATIVES **attacker** noun.
– ORIGIN Italian *attaccare* 'join battle'.

attain ● **verb** **1** succeed in accomplishing. **2** reach (a specified age, size, or amount).
– DERIVATIVES **attainable** adjective.
– ORIGIN Latin *attingere*, from *tangere* 'to touch'.

attainder /ətayndər/ ● **noun** historical the forfeiting of land and civil rights as a consequence of a death sentence.
– ORIGIN from Old French *ateindre* 'accomplish, convict, bring to justice'.

attainment ● **noun** **1** the action of achieving. **2** an achievement.

attar /attaar/ ● **noun** a fragrant essential oil made from rose petals.
– ORIGIN Arabic, 'perfume, essence'.

attempt ● **verb** make an effort to achieve or complete (something). ● **noun** an act of attempting.
– ORIGIN Latin *attemptare*, from *temptare* 'to tempt'.

attend ● **verb** **1** be present at. **2** go regularly to (a school, church, etc). **3** (**attend to**) deal with or pay attention to. **4** occur at the same time as or as a result of. **5** escort and wait on (an important person).
– DERIVATIVES **attendee** noun **attender** noun.
– ORIGIN Latin *attendere*, from *tendere* 'stretch'.

attendance ● **noun** **1** the action of attending. **2** the number of people present at a particular occasion.

Thesaurus

ABOMINATION, cruelty, enormity, outrage, horror, monstrosity, obscenity, violation, crime, abuse. **2** *conflict and atrocity around the globe* BARBARITY, barbarism, brutality, savagery, inhumanity, cruelty, wickedness, evil, iniquity, horror.

atrophy ● **verb** **1** *muscles atrophy in microgravity* WASTE AWAY, become emaciated, wither, shrivel (up), shrink; decay, decline, deteriorate, degenerate, weaken. **2** *the campaign atrophied* DWINDLE, deteriorate, decline, wane, fade, peter out, crumble, disintegrate, collapse, slump, go downhill.
– OPPOSITES strengthen, flourish.
● **noun** *muscular atrophy* WASTING, emaciation, withering, shrivelling, shrinking; decay, decline, deterioration, degeneration, weakening, debilitation, enfeeblement.
– OPPOSITES strengthening.

attach ● **verb** **1** *a lead weight is attached to the cord* FASTEN, fix, affix, join, connect, link, secure, make fast, tie, bind, chain; stick, adhere, glue, fuse; append. **2** *he attached himself to the Liberal Party* AFFILIATE, associate, align, ally, unite, integrate, join; be in league with, form an alliance with. **3** *they attached importance to research* ASCRIBE, assign, attribute, accredit, impute. **4** *the medical officer attached to HQ* ASSIGN, appoint, allocate, second; Military detail.
– OPPOSITES detach, separate.

attached ● **adjective** **1** *I'm not interested in you—I'm attached* MARRIED, engaged, promised in marriage; going out, spoken for, involved; informal hitched, spliced, shackled, going steady; dated betrothed; formal wed, wedded; poetic/literary affianced; archaic espoused. **2** *she was very attached to her brother* FOND OF, devoted to; informal mad about, crazy about.
– OPPOSITES single.

attachment ● **noun** **1** *he has a strong attachment to his mother* BOND, closeness, devotion, loyalty; fondness for, love for, affection for, feeling for; relationship with. **2** *the shower had a massage attachment* ACCESSORY, fitting, fitment, extension, add-on, appendage. **3** *the attachment of safety restraints* FIXING, fastening, linking, coupling, connection. **4** *he was on attachment from another regiment* ASSIGNMENT, appointment, secondment, transfer; Military detail. **5** *his family's Conservative attachment* AFFILIATION, association, alliance, alignment, connection; links, ties, sympathies.

attack ● **verb** **1** *Chris had been brutally attacked* ASSAULT, assail, set upon, beat up; batter, pummel, punch; N. Amer. beat up on; informal do over, work over, rough up; Brit. informal duff up. **2** *the French had still not attacked* STRIKE, charge, pounce; bombard, shell, blitz, strafe, fire. **3** *the clergy attacked government policies* CRITICIZE, censure, condemn, pillory, savage, revile, vilify; informal knock, slam, bash, lay into; Brit. informal slate, slag off, rubbish; N. Amer. informal pummel. **4** *they have to attack the problem soon* ADDRESS, attend to, deal with, confront, apply oneself to, get to work on, undertake, embark on; informal get stuck into, get cracking on, get weaving on. **5** *the virus attacks the liver* AFFECT, have an effect on, strike; infect, damage, injure.
– OPPOSITES defend, praise, protect.
● **noun** **1** *an attack on their home* ASSAULT, onslaught, offensive, strike, blitz, raid, charge, rush, invasion, incursion. **2** *she wrote a hostile attack on him* CRITICISM, censure, rebuke, admonishment, reprimand, reproval; condemnation, denunciation, revilement, vilification; tirade, diatribe, polemic; informal roasting, caning; Brit. informal slating, rollicking, blast. **3** *an asthmatic attack* FIT, seizure, spasm, convulsion, paroxysm, outburst, bout.
– OPPOSITES defence, commendation.

attacker ● **noun** ASSAILANT, assaulter, aggressor; mugger, rapist, killer, murderer.

attain ● **verb** ACHIEVE, accomplish, reach, obtain, gain, procure, secure, get, hook, net, win, earn, acquire; realize, fulfil; informal clinch, bag, wrap up.

attainable ● **adjective** ACHIEVABLE, obtainable, accessible, within reach, securable, realizable; practicable, workable, realistic, reasonable, viable, feasible, possible; informal doable, get-at-able.

attainment ● **noun** **1** *the attainment of common goals* ACHIEVEMENT, accomplishment, realization, fulfilment, completion; formal effectuation, reification. **2** *educational attainment* ACHIEVEMENT, accomplishment, proficiency, competence; qualification; skill, aptitude, ability.

attempt ● **verb** *I attempted to answer the question* TRY, strive, aim, venture, endeavour, seek, undertake, make an effort; have a go at, try one's hand at; informal go all out, bend over backwards, bust a gut, have a crack at, have a shot at, have a stab at; formal essay; archaic assay.
● **noun** *an attempt to put the economy to rights* EFFORT, endeavour, try, venture, trial; informal crack, go, shot, stab; formal essay; archaic assay.

attend ● **verb** **1** *they attended a carol service* BE PRESENT AT, sit in on, take part in; appear at, present oneself at, turn up at, visit, go to; informal show up at, show one's face at. **2** *he had not attended to the regulations* PAY ATTENTION, pay heed, be attentive, listen; concentrate, take note, bear in mind, take into consideration, heed, observe, mark. **3** *the wounded were attended to nearby* CARE FOR, look after, minister to, see to; tend, treat, nurse, help, aid, assist, succour; informal doctor. **4** *he attended to the boy's education* DEAL WITH, see to, manage, organize, sort out, handle, take care of, take charge of, take in hand, tackle. **5** *the queen was attended by an usher* ESCORT, accompany, chaperone, squire, guide, lead, conduct, usher, shepherd; assist, help, serve, wait on. **6** *her giddiness was attended with a fever* BE ACCOMPANIED BY, occur with, coexist with, be associated with, connected with, be linked with; be produced by, originate from/in, stem from, result from, arise from.
– OPPOSITES miss, disregard, ignore, neglect.

attendance ● **noun** **1** *you requested the attendance of a doctor*

a

attendant • noun 1 a person employed to provide a service to the public. 2 an assistant to an important person. • adjective occurring at the same time or as a result of.

attention • noun 1 the mental faculty of considering or taking notice. 2 special care or consideration. 3 (**attentions**) attentive treatment or sexual advances. 4 an erect posture assumed by a soldier, with the feet together and the arms straight down the sides of the body.
– DERIVATIVES **attentional** adjective.

attention deficit disorder • noun a condition found in children, marked by concentration, hyperactivity, and learning difficulties.

attentive • adjective 1 paying close attention. 2 considerately attending to the comfort or wishes of others.
– DERIVATIVES **attentively** adverb **attentiveness** noun.

attenuate /ətenyooayt/ • verb 1 reduce the strength, effect, or value of. 2 make thin or thinner.
– DERIVATIVES **attenuation** noun.
– ORIGIN Latin *attenuare* 'make slender'.

attest /ətest/ • verb 1 provide or serve as clear evidence of. 2 declare that something exists or is the case.
– DERIVATIVES **attestation** noun.
– ORIGIN Latin *attestari*, from *testari* 'to witness'.

Attic /attik/ • adjective relating to Attica in Greece, or to ancient Athens.

attic • noun a space or room inside the roof of a building.
– ORIGIN originally a term in classical architecture: from Latin *Atticus* 'Attic'.

attire • noun clothes, especially fine or formal ones. • verb (**be attired**) be dressed in clothes of a specified kind.
– ORIGIN from Old French *atirer* 'equip', from *a tire* 'in order'.

attitude • noun 1 a settled way of thinking or feeling. 2 a posture of the body. 3 informal, chiefly N. Amer. self-confident or aggressively uncooperative behaviour.
– DERIVATIVES **attitudinal** adjective.
– ORIGIN Italian *attitudine* 'fitness, posture', from Latin *aptus* 'fit'.

attitudinize /attityoōdiniz/ (also **attitudinise**) • verb adopt or express a particular attitude for effect.

atto- • combining form denoting a factor of one million million millionth (10^{-18}).
– ORIGIN from Danish or Norwegian *atten* 'eighteen'.

attorney /əturni/ • noun (pl. **attorneys**) 1 a person appointed to act for another in legal matters. 2 chiefly US a lawyer.
– ORIGIN from Old French *atorner* 'assign'.

Attorney-General • noun (pl. **Attorneys General**) the principal legal officer of the Crown or a state.

attract • verb 1 draw in by offering something interesting or advantageous. 2 cause (a specified reaction). 3 (often **be attracted to**) cause to have a liking for or interest in. 4 draw (something) closer by exerting a force.
– DERIVATIVES **attractor** noun.
– ORIGIN Latin *attrahere* 'draw near'.

attractant • noun a substance which attracts. • adjective tending to attract.

attraction • noun 1 the action or power of attracting. 2 something that attracts interest. 3 Physics a force under the influence of which objects tend to move towards each other.

attractive • adjective 1 pleasing or appealing to the senses. 2 arousing interest. 3 relating to attraction between physical objects.
– DERIVATIVES **attractively** adverb **attractiveness** noun.

attribute • verb /ətribyoōt/ (**attribute to**) regard as belonging to or being caused by. • noun /atribyoōt/ 1 a characteristic or inherent quality or feature. 2 an object that represents a person, status, or office.
– DERIVATIVES **attributable** /ətribyootəb'l/ adjective **attribution** noun.
– ORIGIN Latin *attribuere* 'assign to'.

Thesaurus

PRESENCE, appearance; attention. 2 *their gig attendances grew* AUDIENCE, turnout, house, gate; crowd, congregation, gathering; Austral. informal muster.
– OPPOSITES absence.
– PHRASES **in attendance** PRESENT, here, there, near, nearby, at hand, available; assisting, supervising.

attendant • noun 1 *a sleeping car attendant* STEWARD, waiter, waitress, garçon, porter, servant; N. Amer. waitperson. 2 *a royal attendant* ESCORT, companion, retainer, aide, lady in waiting, equerry, chaperone; servant, manservant, valet, gentleman's gentleman, maidservant, maid; N. Amer. houseman; Brit. informal skivvy; Military, dated batman.
• adjective *new discoveries and the attendant excitement* ACCOMPANYING, associated, related, connected, concomitant; resultant, resulting, consequent.

attention • noun 1 *the issue needs further attention* CONSIDERATION, contemplation, deliberation, thought, study, observation, scrutiny, investigation, action. 2 *he tried to attract the attention of a policeman* AWARENESS, notice, observation, heed, regard, scrutiny, surveillance. 3 *adequate medical attention* CARE, treatment, ministration, succour, relief, aid, help, assistance. 4 *he was effusive in his attentions* OVERTURES, approaches, suit, wooing, courting; compliments, flattery.

attentive • adjective 1 *a bright and attentive scholar* PERCEPTIVE, observant, alert, acute, aware, heedful, vigilant; intent, focused, committed, studious, diligent, conscientious, earnest; informal not missing a trick, on the ball. 2 *the most attentive of husbands* CONSCIENTIOUS, considerate, thoughtful, kind, caring, solicitous, understanding, sympathetic, obliging, accommodating, gallant, chivalrous; dutiful, responsible.
– OPPOSITES inconsiderate.

attenuated • adjective 1 *attenuated fingers* THIN, slender, narrow, slim, skinny, spindly, bony; poetic/literary extenuated; rare attenuate. 2 *his muscle activity was much attenuated* WEAKENED, reduced, lessened, decreased, diminished, impaired.
– OPPOSITES plump, broad, strengthened.

attest • verb CERTIFY, corroborate, confirm, verify, substantiate, authenticate, evidence, demonstrate, show, prove; endorse, support, affirm, bear out, give credence to, vouch for; formal evince.
– OPPOSITES disprove.

attic • noun LOFT, roof space, cock loft; garret, mansard.

attire • noun *Thomas preferred formal attire* CLOTHING, clothes, garments, dress, wear, outfits, garb, costume; informal gear, togs, duds, get-up; Brit. informal clobber; N. Amer. informal threads; formal apparel; archaic raiment, habiliments.
• verb *she was attired in black crêpe* DRESS (UP), clothe, garb, robe, array, costume, swathe, deck (out), turn out, fit out, trick out/up, rig out; informal get up; archaic apparel, invest, habit.

attitude • noun 1 *you seem ambivalent in your attitude* VIEW, viewpoint, outlook, perspective, stance, standpoint, position, inclination, orientation, approach, reaction; opinion, ideas, convictions, feelings, thinking. 2 *an attitude of prayer* POSITION, posture, pose, stance.

attorney • noun LAWYER, legal practitioner, legal executive, legal representative, member of the bar, counsel; Brit. barrister, Queen's counsel, QC; Scottish advocate; N. Amer. counselor(-at-law); informal brief.

attract • verb 1 *positive ions are attracted to the negatively charged terminal* DRAW, pull, magnetize. 2 *he was attracted by her smile* ENTICE, allure, lure, tempt, charm, win over, woo, engage, enchant, entrance, captivate, beguile, bewitch, seduce; excite, titillate, arouse; informal turn on.
– OPPOSITES repel.

attraction • noun 1 *the stars are held together by gravitational attraction* PULL, draw; magnetism. 2 *she had lost whatever attraction she had ever had* APPEAL, attractiveness, desirability, seductiveness, seduction, allure, animal magnetism; charisma, charm, beauty, good looks; informal come-on. 3 *the fair offers sideshows and other attractions* ENTERTAINMENT, activity, diversion, interest.
– OPPOSITES repulsion.

attractive • adjective 1 *a more attractive career* APPEALING, inviting, tempting, irresistible; agreeable, pleasing, interesting. 2 *she has no idea how attractive she is* GOOD-LOOKING, beautiful, pretty, handsome, lovely, stunning, striking, arresting, gorgeous, prepossessing, fetching, captivating, bewitching, beguiling, engaging, charming, enchanting, appealing, delightful; sexy, seductive, alluring, tantalizing, irresistible, ravishing, desirable; Scottish & N. English bonny; informal fanciable, tasty, hot, easy on the eye, drop-dead gorgeous; Brit. informal fit; N. Amer. informal cute, foxy; Austral./NZ informal spunky; poetic/literary beauteous; archaic comely, fair.
– OPPOSITES uninviting, ugly.

attribute • verb *they attributed their success to him* ASCRIBE, assign, accredit, credit, impute; put down, chalk up, hold responsible, pin on; connect with, associate with.
• noun 1 *he has all the attributes of a top player* QUALITY, characteristic, trait, feature, element, aspect, property, sign, hallmark,

a

attributive /ətribyootiv/ • adjective Grammar (of an adjective) preceding the word that it modifies, as *old* in *the old dog*. Contrasted with PREDICATIVE.
– DERIVATIVES **attributively** adverb.
attrition /ətrish'n/ • noun **1** gradual wearing down through sustained attack or pressure. **2** wearing away by friction.
– DERIVATIVES **attritional** adjective.
– ORIGIN Latin, from *atterere* 'to rub'.
attune • verb adjust or accustom to a particular situation.
atypical • adjective not typical.
– DERIVATIVES **atypically** adverb.
Au • symbol the chemical element gold.
– ORIGIN from Latin *aurum*.
aubade /ōbaad/ • noun a poem or piece of music appropriate to the dawn.
– ORIGIN French, from Spanish *albada*, from *alba* 'dawn'.
auberge /ōbairzh/ • noun an inn in French-speaking countries.
– ORIGIN French, from Provençal *alberga* 'lodging'.
aubergine /ōbərzheen/ • noun chiefly Brit. a purple egg-shaped fruit eaten as a vegetable.
– ORIGIN French, from Arabic.
aubretia /awbreeshə/ (also **aubrietia**) • noun a trailing plant with dense masses of foliage and purple, pink, or white flowers.
– ORIGIN named after the French botanist Claude *Aubriet* (1668–1743).
auburn /awbərn/ • noun a reddish-brown colour.
– ORIGIN Old French *auborne*, from Latin *albus* 'white'; the original sense was 'yellowish white', but the word became associated with *brown* because it was formerly spelt *abrune* or *abroun*.
au courant /ō kooron/ • adjective up to date and well informed.
– ORIGIN French, 'in the (regular) course'.
auction /awksh'n/ • noun a public sale in which goods or property are sold to the highest bidder. • verb sell at an auction.
– ORIGIN Latin, 'increase, auction', from *augere* 'to increase'.
auctioneer • noun a person who conducts auctions.
audacious /awdayshəss/ • adjective **1** willing to take bold risks. **2** impudent.
– DERIVATIVES **audaciously** adverb **audaciousness** noun **audacity** noun.
– ORIGIN from Latin *audax* 'bold'.
audible • adjective able to be heard.
– DERIVATIVES **audibility** noun **audibly** adverb.
– ORIGIN Latin *audibilis*, from *audire* 'hear'.
audience • noun **1** the assembled spectators or listeners at an event. **2** a formal interview with a person in authority.
– ORIGIN Latin *audientia*, from *audire* 'hear'.
audio- • combining form relating to hearing or sound, especially when recorded, transmitted, or reproduced: *audio-visual*.
– ORIGIN from Latin *audire* 'hear'.
audio frequency • noun a frequency capable of being perceived by the human ear, generally between 20 and 20,000 hertz.
audiology /awdiolləji/ • noun the branch of science and medicine concerned with the sense of hearing.
– DERIVATIVES **audiological** adjective **audiologist** noun.
audio tape • noun magnetic tape on which sound can be recorded.
audio typist • noun a typist who transcribes from recorded dictation.
audio-visual • adjective using both sight and sound, typically in the form of slides or video and speech or music.
audit /awdit/ • noun an official inspection of an organization's accounts. • verb (**audited, auditing**) make an audit of.
– ORIGIN from Latin *audire* 'hear' (because an audit was originally presented orally).
audition • noun an interview for a performer in which they give a practical demonstration of their skill. • verb assess or be assessed by an audition.
auditor • noun **1** a person who conducts an audit. **2** a listener.
auditorium • noun (pl. **auditoriums** or **auditoria**) **1** the part of a theatre or hall in which the audience sits. **2** chiefly N. Amer. a large public hall.
– ORIGIN Latin.
auditory • adjective relating to the sense of hearing.
au fait /ō fay/ • adjective (**au fait with**) having a good or detailed knowledge of.
– ORIGIN French, 'to the point'.
auger /awgər/ • noun a tool resembling a large corkscrew, for boring holes.
– ORIGIN Old English *nafogār*; the *n* was lost by wrong division of *a nauger*.
aught /awt/ (also **ought**) • pronoun archaic anything at all.
– ORIGIN Old English.
augment /awgment/ • verb make greater by addition; increase.
– DERIVATIVES **augmentation** noun.
– ORIGIN Latin *augmentare*, from *augere* 'to increase'.
augmented • adjective Music (of an interval) one semitone greater than the corresponding major or perfect interval.
au gratin /ō graton/ • adjective (after a noun) sprinkled with breadcrumbs or grated cheese and browned.
– ORIGIN French, 'by grating'.

Thesaurus

mark, distinction. **2** *the hourglass is the attribute of Father Time* SYMBOL, mark, sign, hallmark, trademark.
attrition • noun **1** *a gradual attrition of the market economy* WEARING DOWN/AWAY, weakening, debilitation, enfeebling, sapping, attenuation. **2** *the attrition of the edges of the teeth* ABRASION, friction, erosion, corrosion, grinding, wearing (away); deterioration, damaging; rare detrition.
attune • verb ACCUSTOM, adjust, adapt, acclimatize, condition, accommodate, assimilate; N. Amer. acclimate.
atypical • adjective UNUSUAL, untypical, uncommon, unconventional, unorthodox, irregular, abnormal, aberrant, deviant, unrepresentative; strange, odd, peculiar, bizarre, weird, queer, freakish; exceptional, singular, rare, out of the way, out of the ordinary, extraordinary; Brit. out of the common; informal funny, freaky.
– OPPOSITES normal.
auburn • adjective REDDISH-BROWN, red-brown, Titian (red), tawny, russet, chestnut, copper, coppery, rufous.
au courant • adjective UP TO DATE, au fait, in touch, familiar, at home, acquainted, conversant; abreast, apprised, in the know, well informed, knowledgeable, well versed, enlightened; informal clued up, wise to, hip to.
audacious • adjective **1** *his audacious exploits* BOLD, daring, fearless, intrepid, brave, courageous, valiant, heroic, plucky; daredevil, devil-may-care, death-or-glory, reckless, madcap; venturesome, mettlesome; informal gutsy, spunky, ballsy; poetic/literary temerarious. **2** *an audacious remark* IMPUDENT, impertinent, insolent, presumptuous, cheeky, irreverent, discourteous, disrespectful, insubordinate, ill-mannered, unmannerly, rude, brazen, shameless, pert, defiant, cocky, bold (as brass); informal brass-necked, fresh, saucy; N. Amer. informal sassy, nervy; archaic malapert, contumelious.
– OPPOSITES timid, polite.
audacity • noun **1** *a traveller of extraordinary audacity* BOLDNESS, daring, fearlessness, intrepidity, bravery, courage, heroism, pluck, grit; recklessness; spirit, mettle; informal guts, gutsiness, spunk; Brit. informal bottle; N. Amer. informal moxie. **2** *he had the audacity to contradict me* IMPUDENCE, impertinence, insolence, presumption, cheek, bad manners, effrontery, nerve, gall, defiance, temerity; informal brass (neck), chutzpah; Brit. informal sauce; N. Amer. informal sass.
audible • adjective HEARABLE, perceptible, discernible, detectable, appreciable; clear, distinct, loud.
– OPPOSITES faint.
audience • noun **1** *the audience applauded* SPECTATORS, LISTENERS, viewers, onlookers, patrons; crowd, throng, congregation, turnout; house, gallery, stalls; Brit. informal punters. **2** *the radio station's teenage audience* MARKET, PUBLIC, following, fans; listenership, viewership. **3** *an audience with the Pope* MEETING, consultation, conference, hearing, reception, interview.
audit • noun *an audit of the party accounts* INSPECTION, examination, scrutiny, probe, investigation, assessment, appraisal, evaluation, review, analysis; informal going-over, once-over.
• verb *we audited their accounts* INSPECT, examine, survey, go through, scrutinize, probe, vet, investigate, assess, appraise, evaluate, review, analyse, study, check; informal give something a/the once-over, give something a going-over.
auditorium • noun THEATRE, hall, assembly room; chamber, room.
au fait • adjective FAMILIAR, acquainted, conversant, at home, up to date, au courant, in touch; abreast, apprised, in the know, well informed, knowledgeable, well versed, enlightened; informal clued up, wise to, hip to.
augment • verb INCREASE, add to, supplement, top up, build up, enlarge, expand, extend, raise, multiply, swell; magnify, amplify,

a

augur /awgər/ ● verb be a sign of (a likely outcome). ● noun (in ancient Rome) a religious official who interpreted the significance of natural signs.
– ORIGIN from Latin, 'diviner'.

augury /awgyəri/ ● noun (pl. **auguries**) **1** an omen. **2** the interpretation of omens.

August ● noun the eighth month of the year.
– ORIGIN named after *Augustus* Caesar, the first Roman emperor.

august /awgust/ ● adjective inspiring respect and admiration.
– ORIGIN Latin *augustus* 'consecrated, venerable'.

Augustan /awgustən/ ● adjective **1** relating to the reign of the Roman emperor Augustus (a notable period of Latin literature). **2** relating to a classical style of 17th- and 18th-century English literature. ● noun a writer of the Augustan age.

Augustinian /awgəstiniən/ ● adjective **1** relating to St Augustine (354-430). **2** relating to a religious order observing a rule derived from St Augustine's writings. ● noun a member of an Augustinian order.

auk /awk/ ● noun a short-winged black and white diving seabird.
– ORIGIN Old Norse.

auld /awld/ ● adjective Scottish form of OLD.
– PHRASES **auld lang syne** times long past. [ORIGIN literally 'old long since'.]

aumbry /awmbri/ ● noun (pl. **aumbries**) a small recess or cupboard in the wall of a church.
– ORIGIN Latin *armarium* 'closet'.

au naturel /ō natyoorel/ ● adjective & adverb in the most simple or natural way.
– ORIGIN French.

aunt ● noun the sister of one's father or mother or the wife of one's uncle.
– ORIGIN Old French *ante*, from Latin *amita*.

Aunt Sally ● noun (pl. **Aunt Sallies**) **1** a game in which players throw sticks or balls at a wooden dummy. **2** an easy target for criticism.

au pair /ō pair/ ● noun a foreign girl employed to help with housework and childcare in exchange for board and lodging.
– ORIGIN French, 'on equal terms'.

aura /awrə/ ● noun (pl. **aurae** /awree/ or **auras**) **1** the distinctive atmosphere or quality associated with someone or something. **2** a supposed invisible force surrounding a living creature.
– ORIGIN Greek, 'breeze, breath'.

aural /awrəl/ ● adjective relating to the ear or the sense of hearing.
– DERIVATIVES **aurally** adverb.
– ORIGIN from Latin *auris* 'ear'.

auralize /awrəlīz/ ● verb **1** imagine or hear in the mind. **2** make aurally perceptible.

aurar plural of EYRIR.

aureate /awriət/ ● adjective made of or having the colour of gold.
– ORIGIN Latin *aureatus*, from *aurum* 'gold'.

aureole /awriōl/ (also **aureola** /awreeələ/) ● noun **1** (in paintings) a radiant circle surrounding a person to represent holiness. **2** a circle of light around the sun or moon.
– ORIGIN from Latin *aureola corona* 'golden crown'.

au revoir /ō rəvwaar/ ● exclamation goodbye.
– ORIGIN French, 'to the seeing again'.

auricle /awrik'l/ ● noun **1** the external part of the ear. **2** an atrium of the heart.
– ORIGIN Latin *auricula* 'little ear'.

auricular /awrikyoolər/ ● adjective **1** relating to the ear or hearing. **2** relating to or shaped like an auricle.

aurochs /awroks/ ● noun (pl. same) a large extinct wild ox that was the ancestor of domestic cattle.
– ORIGIN German.

aurora /awrorə/ ● noun (pl. **auroras** or **aurorae** /awroree/) the northern lights (**aurora borealis** /borriayliss/) or southern lights (**aurora australis** /awstrayliss/), streamers of coloured light seen in the sky near the earth's magnetic poles.
– ORIGIN Latin, 'dawn, goddess of the dawn'.

auscultation /awskəltaysh'n/ ● noun listening to sounds from the heart, lungs, or other organs with a stethoscope.
– ORIGIN Latin, from *auscultare* 'listen to'.

auspice /awspiss/ ● noun archaic an omen.
– PHRASES **under the auspices of** with the support or protection of.
– ORIGIN Latin *auspicium*, from *auspex* 'observer of birds'.

auspicious /awspishəss/ ● adjective indicating a good chance of success; favourable.
– DERIVATIVES **auspiciously** adverb.

Aussie (also **Ozzie**) ● noun (pl. **Aussies**) & adjective informal Australia or Australian.

austere /osteer/ ● adjective (**austerer**, **austerest**) **1** severe or strict in appearance or manner. **2** lacking comforts, luxuries, or adornment.
– DERIVATIVES **austerely** adverb **austerity** noun.
– ORIGIN Greek *austēros* 'severe'.

austral /awstrəl/ ● adjective technical **1** of the southern hemisphere. **2** (**Austral**) of Australia or Australasia.
– ORIGIN Latin *australis*, from *Auster* 'the south, the south wind'.

Australasian /ostrəlayzh'n, -sh'n/ ● adjective relating to Australasia, a region consisting of Australia, New Zealand, and islands of the SW Pacific. ● noun a person from Australasia.

Australian ● noun a person from Australia. ● adjective relating to Australia.
– ORIGIN from Latin *Terra Australis* 'the southern land', the name of the supposed southern continent.

Australian Rules ● plural noun (treated as sing.) a form of football played on an oval field with an oval ball by teams of eighteen players.

Australopithecus /ostrəlōpithikəss/ ● noun a genus of fossil primates with both ape-like and human characteristics, found in Pliocene and Lower Pleistocene deposits in Africa.
– DERIVATIVES **australopithecine** /ostrəlōpithiseen/ noun & adjective.
– ORIGIN from Latin *australis* 'southern' + Greek *pithēkos* 'ape'.

Austrian ● noun a person from Austria. ● adjective relating to Austria.

Austrian blind ● noun a ruched blind extending part-way down a window.

autarchy /awtaarki/ ● noun (pl. **autarchies**) **1** another term for AUTOCRACY. **2** variant spelling of AUTARKY.

autarky (also **autarchy**) ● noun **1** economic independence or self-sufficiency. **2** an economically independent state or society.
– DERIVATIVES **autarkic** adjective.
– ORIGIN from Greek *autarkēs* 'self-sufficiency'.

auteur /ōtör/ ● noun a film director regarded as the author of their films.
– ORIGIN French, 'author'.

authentic ● adjective of undisputed origin; genuine.
– DERIVATIVES **authentically** adverb **authenticity** noun.
– ORIGIN Greek *authentikos* 'principal, genuine'.

Thesaurus

escalate; improve, boost; *informal* up, jack up, hike up, bump up.
– OPPOSITES decrease.

augur ● verb *these successes augur well for the future* BODE, portend, herald, be a sign, warn, forewarn, foreshadow, be an omen, presage, indicate, signify, signal, promise, threaten, spell, denote; predict, prophesy; *poetic/literary* betoken, foretoken, forebode.

august ● adjective DISTINGUISHED, respected, eminent, venerable, hallowed, illustrious, prestigious, renowned, celebrated, honoured, acclaimed, esteemed, exalted; great, important, lofty, noble; imposing, impressive, awe-inspiring, stately, grand, dignified.

aura ● noun ATMOSPHERE, ambience, air, quality, character, mood, feeling, feel, flavour, tone, tenor; emanation, vibration; *informal* vibe.

auspices ● plural noun PATRONAGE, aegis, umbrella, protection, keeping, care; support, backing, guardianship, trusteeship, guidance, supervision.

auspicious ● adjective FAVOURABLE, propitious, promising, rosy, good, encouraging; opportune, timely, lucky, fortunate, providential, felicitous, advantageous.

austere ● adjective **1** *an outwardly austere man* SEVERE, stern, strict, harsh, steely, flinty, dour, grim, cold, frosty, unemotional, unfriendly; formal, stiff, reserved, aloof, forbidding; grave, solemn, serious, unsmiling, unsympathetic, unforgiving; hard, unyielding, unbending, inflexible, illiberal; *informal* hard-boiled. **2** *an austere life* ASCETIC, self-denying, self-disciplined, non-indulgent, frugal, spartan, puritanical, abstemious, abstinent, self-sacrificing, strict, temperate, sober, simple, restrained; celibate, chaste. **3** *the buildings were austere* PLAIN, simple, basic, functional, modest, unadorned, unembellished, unfussy, restrained; stark, bleak, bare, clinical, spartan, ascetic; *informal* no frills.

a

authenticate ● verb prove or show to be authentic.
– DERIVATIVES **authentication** noun **authenticator** noun.
author ● noun **1** a writer of a book or article. **2** a person who originates a plan or idea. ● verb be the author of.
– DERIVATIVES **authoress** noun **authorial** /awthoriəl/ adjective **authorship** noun.
– ORIGIN Latin *auctor*, from *augere* 'increase, originate'.
authoritarian /awthorritairiən/ ● adjective favouring or enforcing strict obedience to authority. ● noun an authoritarian person.
– DERIVATIVES **authoritarianism** noun.
authoritative /awthorritətiv/ ● adjective **1** reliable because true or accurate. **2** commanding and self-confident. **3** supported by authority; official.
– DERIVATIVES **authoritatively** adverb **authoritativeness** noun.
authority ● noun (pl. **authorities**) **1** the power or right to give orders and enforce obedience. **2** a person or organization having official power. **3** recognized knowledge or expertise. **4** an authoritative person or book.
– ORIGIN Old French *autorite*, from Latin *auctor* 'originator'.
authorize (also **authorise**) ● verb give official permission for or approval to.
– DERIVATIVES **authorization** noun.
Authorized Version ● noun an English translation of the Bible made in 1611, at the order of James I.
autism /awtiz'm/ ● noun a mental condition characterized by great difficulty in communicating with others and in using language and abstract concepts.
– DERIVATIVES **autistic** adjective & noun.
– ORIGIN from Greek *autos* 'self'.
auto ● adjective & noun short for AUTOMATIC.
auto-[1] (usu. **aut-** before a vowel) ● combining form **1** self: *autocrat.* **2** one's own: *autograph.* **3** automatic; spontaneous: *autoxidation.*
– ORIGIN from Greek *autos* 'self'.
auto-[2] ● combining form relating to cars: *autocross.*
– ORIGIN from AUTOMOBILE.
Autobahn /awtōbaan/ ● noun a motorway in a German-speaking country.
– ORIGIN German, from *Auto* 'motor car' + *Bahn* 'path, road'.
autobiography ● noun (pl. **autobiographies**) an account of a person's life written by that person.
– DERIVATIVES **autobiographer** noun **autobiographic** adjective **autobiographical** adjective.
autochthon /awtokthən/ ● noun (pl. **autochthons** or **autochthones** /awtokthəneez/) an original or indigenous inhabitant of a place.
– ORIGIN Greek, from *autos* 'self' + *khthōn* 'earth'.
autochthonous /awtokthənəss/ ● adjective indigenous.
autoclave /awtəklayv/ ● noun a strong heated container used for processes using high pressures and temperatures, e.g. steam sterilization.
– ORIGIN from Greek *auto-* 'self' + Latin *clavus* 'nail' or *clavis* 'key' (because it is self-fastening).
autocracy /awtokrəsi/ ● noun (pl. **autocracies**) **1** a system of government by one person with absolute power. **2** a state governed in this way.
– ORIGIN from Greek *autos* 'self' + *kratos* 'power'.
autocrat ● noun **1** a ruler who has absolute power. **2** a domineering person.
– DERIVATIVES **autocratic** adjective **autocratically** adverb.
autocue ● noun trademark a device used as a television prompt in which a script is projected on to a screen visible only to the speaker or performer.
auto-da-fé /awtōdaafay/ ● noun (pl. **autos-da-fé** /awtōzdaafay/) the burning of a heretic by the Spanish Inquisition.
– ORIGIN Portuguese, 'act of the faith'.
autodidact /awtōdidakt/ ● noun a self-taught person.
– DERIVATIVES **autodidactic** adjective.
auto-erotic ● adjective relating to sexual excitement generated by stimulating one's own body.
– DERIVATIVES **auto-eroticism** noun.
autogenic /awtəjennik/ ● adjective technical self-generated.
autogenous /awtojinəss/ ● adjective **1** arising from within or from a thing itself. **2** (of welding) done either without a filler or with a filler of the same metal as the pieces being welded.
autogiro (also **autogyro**) ● noun (pl. **autogiros**) a form of aircraft with unpowered rotors and a propeller.

Thesaurus

– OPPOSITES genial, immoderate, ornate.
Australia ● noun *informal* Oz, Aussie, down under.
authentic ● adjective **1** *an authentic document* GENUINE, real, bona fide, true, veritable, simon-pure; legitimate, lawful, legal, valid; *informal* the real McCoy, the real thing, pukka, kosher; *Austral./NZ informal* dinkum. **2** *an authentic depiction of the situation* RELIABLE, dependable, trustworthy, authoritative, honest, faithful; accurate, factual, true, truthful; *formal* veridical, veracious.
– OPPOSITES fake, unreliable.
authenticate ● verb **1** *the evidence will authenticate his claim* VERIFY, validate, prove, substantiate, corroborate, confirm, support, back up, attest to, give credence to. **2** *a mandate authenticated by the popular vote* VALIDATE, ratify, confirm, seal, sanction, endorse.
authenticity ● noun **1** *the authenticity of the painting* GENUINENESS, bona fides; legitimacy, legality, validity. **2** *the authenticity of this account* RELIABILITY, dependability, trustworthiness, credibility; accuracy, truth, veracity, fidelity.
author ● noun **1** *modern Canadian authors* WRITER, wordsmith; novelist, playwright, poet, essayist, biographer; columnist, reporter; *informal* penman, penwoman, scribe, scribbler. **2** *the author of the peace plan* ORIGINATOR, creator, instigator, founder, father, architect, designer, deviser, producer; cause, agent.
– RELATED TERMS auctorial.
authoritarian ● adjective *his authoritarian manner* AUTOCRATIC, dictatorial, despotic, tyrannical, draconian, oppressive, repressive, illiberal, undemocratic; disciplinarian, domineering, overbearing, high-handed, peremptory, imperious, strict, rigid, inflexible; *informal* bossy.
– OPPOSITES democratic, liberal.
● noun *the army is dominated by authoritarians* AUTOCRAT, despot, dictator, tyrant; disciplinarian, martinet.
authoritative ● adjective **1** *authoritative information* RELIABLE, dependable, trustworthy, sound, authentic, valid, attested, verifiable; accurate. **2** *the authoritative edition* DEFINITIVE, most reliable, best; authorized, accredited, recognized, accepted, approved. **3** *his authoritative manner* ASSURED, confident, assertive; commanding, masterful, lordly; domineering, imperious, overbearing, authoritarian; *informal* bossy.
– OPPOSITES unreliable, timid.
authority ● noun **1** *a rebellion against those in authority* POWER, jurisdiction, command, control, charge, dominance, rule, sovereignty, supremacy; influence; *informal* clout. **2** *the authority to arrest drug traffickers* AUTHORIZATION, right, power, mandate, prerogative, licence. **3** *the money was spent without parliamentary authority* AUTHORIZATION, permission, consent, leave, sanction, licence, dispensation, assent, acquiescence, agreement, approval, endorsement, clearance; *informal* the go-ahead, the thumbs up, the OK, the green light. **4** *the authorities* OFFICIALS, officialdom; government, administration, establishment; police; *informal* the powers that be. **5** *an authority on the stock market* EXPERT, specialist, aficionado, pundit, doyen(ne), guru, sage; *informal* boffin. **6** *he cites the nuns' testimony as an authority* SOURCE, reference, citation, quotation, passage. **7** *on good authority* EVIDENCE, testimony, witness, attestation, word, avowal; *Law* deposition.
authorization ● noun PERMISSION, consent, leave, sanction, licence, dispensation, clearance, the nod; assent, agreement, approval, endorsement; authority, right, power, mandate; *informal* the go-ahead, the thumbs up, the OK, the green light.
– OPPOSITES refusal.
authorize ● verb **1** *they authorized further action* SANCTION, permit, allow, approve, consent to, assent to; ratify, endorse, validate; *informal* give the green light, give the go-ahead, OK, give the thumbs up. **2** *the troops were authorized to fire* EMPOWER, mandate, commission; entitle.
– OPPOSITES forbid.
authorized ● adjective APPROVED, recognized, sanctioned; accredited, licensed, certified; official, lawful, legal, legitimate.
– OPPOSITES unofficial.
autobiography ● noun MEMOIRS, life story, personal history.
autocracy ● noun ABSOLUTISM, totalitarianism, dictatorship, despotism, tyranny, monocracy, autarchy.
– OPPOSITES democracy.
autocrat ● noun ABSOLUTE RULER, dictator, despot, tyrant, monocrat.
autocratic ● adjective DESPOTIC, tyrannical, dictatorial, totalitar-

a

– ORIGIN Spanish, from *auto-* 'self' + *giro* 'gyration'.
autograph • noun **1** a celebrity's signature written for an admirer. **2** a manuscript or musical score in an author's or composer's own handwriting. • verb write one's signature on.
– DERIVATIVES **autographic** adjective.
– ORIGIN from Greek *autographos* 'written with one's own hand'.
autoharp • noun a kind of zither on which chords may be played by damping selected strings.
autoimmune • adjective (of disease) caused by antibodies or lymphocytes produced against substances naturally present in the body.
autolysis /awtollisiss/ • noun Biology the destruction of cells or tissues by their own enzymes.
– DERIVATIVES **autolytic** adjective.
automate • verb convert (a process or facility) to operation by automatic equipment.
– DERIVATIVES **automation** noun.
automated teller machine • noun a machine that provides cash and other banking services on insertion of a special card.
automatic • adjective **1** operating with little or no direct human control. **2** (of a firearm) self-loading and able to fire continuously. **3** done or occurring without conscious thought. **4** (of a penalty) imposed inevitably as a result of a fixed rule. • noun an automatic machine or device.
– DERIVATIVES **automatically** adverb **automaticity** noun.
– ORIGIN Greek *automatos* 'acting by itself'.
automatic pilot • noun a device for keeping an aircraft on a set course.
– PHRASES **on automatic pilot** doing something out of habit without concentration or conscious thought.
automatic writing • noun writing said to be produced by a spiritual, occult, or subconscious means.
automatism /awtommətiz'm/ • noun Psychiatry action which does not involve conscious thought or intention.
automaton /awtommət'n/ • noun (pl. **automata** /awtommətə/ or **automatons**) **1** a moving mechanical device resembling a human being. **2** a machine which operates according to coded instructions.
– ORIGIN Greek, from *automatos* 'acting of itself'.
automobile • noun chiefly N. Amer. a motor car.
automotive /awtəmōtiv/ • adjective relating to motor vehicles.
autonomic /awtənommik/ • adjective relating to the part of the nervous system that controls involuntary bodily functions such as circulation and digestion.
autonomous • adjective self-governing or independent.
– DERIVATIVES **autonomously** adverb.
autonomy /awtonnəməss/ • noun **1** self-government. **2** freedom of action.
– ORIGIN Greek *autonomia*, from *autonomos* 'having its own laws'.
autopilot • noun short for AUTOMATIC PILOT.
autopsy /awtopsi/ • noun (pl. **autopsies**) an examination of a dead body to discover the cause of death or the extent of disease.
– ORIGIN Greek *autopsia*, from *autoptēs* 'eyewitness'.
autoroute • noun a French motorway.
– ORIGIN French.
autostrada /awtōstraadə/ • noun (pl. **autostradas** or **autostrade** /awtōstraade/) an Italian motorway.
– ORIGIN Italian, from *auto* 'automobile' + *strada* 'road'.
auto-suggestion • noun the hypnotic or subconscious adoption of an idea which one has originated oneself.
autumn • noun chiefly Brit. the season after summer and before winter.
– DERIVATIVES **autumnal** adjective.
– ORIGIN Latin *autumnus*.
auxiliary /awgzilyəri/ • adjective providing supplementary or additional help and support. • noun (pl. **auxiliaries**) an auxiliary person or thing.
– ORIGIN Latin *auxiliarius*, from *auxilium* 'help'.
auxiliary verb • noun Grammar a verb used in forming the tenses, moods, and voices of other verbs (e.g. *be*, *do*, and *have*).
avail • verb **1** (**avail oneself of**) use or take advantage of. **2** help or benefit. • noun use or benefit: *his protests were to little avail.*
– ORIGIN Latin *valere* 'be strong, be of value'.
available • adjective **1** able to be used or obtained. **2** not otherwise occupied.
– DERIVATIVES **availability** noun.
avalanche /avvəlaansh/ • noun **1** a mass of snow and ice falling rapidly down a mountainside. **2** an overwhelming deluge.
– ORIGIN French.
avant-garde /avvoNgaard/ • adjective (in the arts) new and experimental. • noun (**the avant-garde**) avant-garde ideas or artists.
– DERIVATIVES **avant-gardism** noun **avant-gardist** noun.
– ORIGIN French, 'vanguard'.
avarice • noun extreme greed for wealth or material gain.
– DERIVATIVES **avaricious** adjective.
– ORIGIN from Latin *avarus* 'greedy'.
avast /əvaast/ • exclamation Nautical stop; cease.
– ORIGIN Dutch *hou'vast* 'hold fast!'
avatar /avvətaar/ • noun chiefly Hinduism a deity appearing in bodily form on earth.
– ORIGIN Sanskrit, 'descent'.
Ave Maria /aavay məreeə/ • noun a prayer to the Virgin Mary used in Catholic worship.
– ORIGIN the opening words in Latin, 'hail, Mary!'
avenge • verb inflict harm in return for (a wrong).
– DERIVATIVES **avenger** noun.
– ORIGIN Old French *avengier*, from Latin *vindicare* 'vindicate'.
avenue • noun **1** a broad road or path. **2** a means of approach.
– ORIGIN from French *avenir* 'arrive, approach'.
aver /əver/ • verb (**averred**, **averring**) formal assert to be the

Thesaurus

ian, autarchic; undemocratic, one-party, monocratic; domineering, draconian, overbearing, high-handed, peremptory, imperious; harsh, rigid, inflexible, illiberal, oppressive.
autograph • noun *fans pestered him for his autograph* SIGNATURE; *N. Amer. informal* John Hancock.
• verb *Jack autographed copies of his book* SIGN.
automatic • adjective **1** *automatic garage doors* MECHANIZED, mechanical, automated, computerized, electronic, robotic; self-activating. **2** *an automatic reaction* INSTINCTIVE, involuntary, unconscious, reflex, knee-jerk, instinctual, subconscious; spontaneous, impulsive, unthinking; mechanical; *informal* gut. **3** *he is the automatic choice for the team* INEVITABLE, unavoidable, inescapable, mandatory, compulsory; certain, definite, undoubted, assured.
– OPPOSITES manual, deliberate.
autonomous • adjective SELF-GOVERNING, self-ruling, self-determining, independent, sovereign, free.
autonomy • noun SELF-GOVERNMENT, self-rule, home rule, self-determination, independence, sovereignty, freedom.
autopsy • noun POST-MORTEM, PM, necropsy.
auxiliary • adjective **1** *an auxiliary power source* ADDITIONAL, supplementary, supplemental, extra, reserve, back-up, emergency, fallback, other. **2** *auxiliary nursing staff* ANCILLARY, assistant, support.
• noun *a nursing auxiliary* ASSISTANT, helper, ancillary.
avail • verb **1** *guests can avail themselves of the facilities* USE, take advantage of, utilize, employ. **2** *his arguments cannot avail him* HELP, aid, assist, benefit, profit, be of service.
– PHRASES **to no avail** IN VAIN, without success, unsuccessfully, fruitlessly, for nothing.
available • adjective **1** *refreshments will be available* OBTAINABLE, accessible, to/at hand, at one's disposal, handy, convenient; on sale, procurable; untaken, unengaged, unused; *informal* up for grabs, on tap, gettable. **2** *I'll see if he's available* FREE, unoccupied; present, in attendance; contactable.
– OPPOSITES busy, engaged.
avalanche • noun **1** SNOWSLIDE, icefall; rockslide, landslide, landslip; *Brit.* snow-slip. **2** *an avalanche of press comment* BARRAGE, volley, flood, deluge, torrent, tide, shower, wave.
avant-garde • adjective *an avant-garde composer* INNOVATIVE, innovatory, original, experimental, left-field, inventive, ahead of the times, new, modern, advanced, forward-looking, state-of-the-art, trendsetting, pioneering, progressive, ground-breaking, trailblazing, revolutionary; unfamiliar, unorthodox, unconventional; *informal* offbeat, way-out.
– OPPOSITES conservative.
avarice • noun GREED, acquisitiveness, cupidity, covetousness, rapacity, materialism, mercenariness, Mammonism; *informal* money-grubbing.
– OPPOSITES generosity.
avenge • verb REQUITE, punish, repay, pay back, take revenge for, get even for.
avenue • noun **1** *tree-lined avenues* ROAD, street, drive, parade,

a

case.
– ORIGIN Old French *averer*, from Latin *verus* 'true'.
average • noun **1** the result obtained by adding several amounts together and then dividing the total by the number of amounts. **2** a usual amount or level. • adjective **1** constituting an average. **2** usual or ordinary. **3** mediocre. • verb **1** amount to or achieve as an average. **2** calculate the average of.
– DERIVATIVES **averagely** adverb **averageness** noun.
– ORIGIN French *avarie* 'damage to ship or cargo', from Arabic; the modern sense arose from the equitable sharing of liability for losses at sea between the owners of the vessel and of the cargo.
averse • adjective (**averse to**) strongly disliking or opposed to.
– USAGE On the confusion of **averse** and **adverse**, see ADVERSE.
– ORIGIN from Latin *avertere* (see AVERT).
aversion • noun a strong dislike or disinclination.
– DERIVATIVES **aversive** adjective.
avert • verb **1** turn away (one's eyes). **2** prevent or ward off (an undesirable occurrence).
– ORIGIN Latin *avertere*, from *vertere* 'to turn'.
avian /ayviən/ • adjective relating to birds.
– ORIGIN from Latin *avis* 'bird'.
aviary /ayviəri/ • noun (pl. **aviaries**) a large enclosure for keeping birds in.
aviation • noun the activity of operating and flying aircraft.
– ORIGIN French, from Latin *avis* 'bird'.
aviator • noun dated a pilot.
aviculture /ayvikulchər/ • noun the breeding of birds.
– DERIVATIVES **avicultural** adjective **aviculturist** noun.
avid • adjective keenly interested or enthusiastic.
– DERIVATIVES **avidity** noun **avidly** adverb.
– ORIGIN Latin *avidus*, from *avere* 'crave'.
avionics • plural noun (usu. treated as sing.) electronics used in aviation.
avo /aavō/ • noun (pl. **avos**) a monetary unit of Macao, equal to one hundredth of a pataca.
– ORIGIN Portuguese.
avocado • noun (pl. **avocados**) a pear-shaped fruit with a rough skin, pale green flesh, and a large stone.
– ORIGIN Spanish, from Nahuatl.
avocation /avvəkaysh'n/ • noun a hobby or minor occupation.
– ORIGIN Latin, from *avocare* 'call away'.
avocet /avvəset/ • noun a long-legged wading bird with an upturned bill.
– ORIGIN French.
avoid • verb **1** keep away or refrain from. **2** prevent from doing or happening.
– DERIVATIVES **avoidable** adjective **avoidably** adverb **avoidance** noun.
– ORIGIN Old French *evuider* 'clear out, get rid of'.
avoirdupois /avvərdəpoyz/ • noun a system of weights based on a pound of 16 ounces or 7,000 grains. Compare with TROY.
– ORIGIN from Old French *aveir de peis* 'goods of weight'.
avow • verb assert or confess openly.
– DERIVATIVES **avowal** noun **avowed** adjective.
– ORIGIN Old French *avouer* 'acknowledge', from Latin *advocare* 'summon in defence'.
avuncular /əvungkyoolər/ • adjective like an uncle in being friendly towards a younger person.
– ORIGIN from Latin *avunculus* 'maternal uncle'.
AWACS /aywaks/ • abbreviation airborne warning and control system.
await • verb wait for.
awake • verb (past **awoke**; past part. **awoken**) **1** stop sleeping. **2** make or become active again. • adjective not asleep.
awaken • verb **1** awake. **2** rouse (a feeling).
– DERIVATIVES **awakening** noun & adjective.
award • verb give officially as a prize or reward. • noun **1** something awarded. **2** the action of awarding.
– ORIGIN Old French *esguarder* 'consider, ordain'.
aware • adjective having knowledge or perception of a situation or fact.
– DERIVATIVES **awareness** noun.
– ORIGIN Old English.
awash • adjective covered or flooded with water.

Thesaurus

boulevard, broadway, thoroughfare. **2** *possible avenues of research* LINE, path; method, approach.
aver • verb *(formal)* DECLARE, maintain, claim, assert, state, swear, avow, vow; *rare* asseverate.
average • noun *the price is above the national average* MEAN, median, mode; norm, standard, rule, par.
• adjective **1** *the average temperature in May* MEAN, median, modal. **2** *a woman of average height* ORDINARY, standard, normal, typical, regular. **3** *a very average director* MEDIOCRE, second-rate, undistinguished, ordinary, middle-of-the-road, unexceptional, unexciting, unremarkable, unmemorable, indifferent, pedestrian, lacklustre, forgettable, amateurish; *informal* OK, so-so, fair-to-middling, no great shakes, not up to much; *Brit. informal* not much cop; *N. Amer. informal* bush-league; *NZ informal* half-pie.
– OPPOSITES outstanding, exceptional.
– PHRASES **on average** NORMALLY, usually, ordinarily, generally, in general, for the most part, as a rule, typically; overall, by and large, on the whole.
averse • adjective OPPOSED, against, antipathetic, hostile, ill-disposed, resistant; disinclined, reluctant, loath; *informal* anti.
– OPPOSITES keen.
aversion • noun DISLIKE, antipathy, distaste, abhorrence, hatred, loathing, detestation, hostility; reluctance, disinclination; *archaic* disrelish.
– OPPOSITES liking.
avert • verb **1** *she averted her head* TURN ASIDE, turn away. **2** *an attempt to avert political chaos* PREVENT, avoid, stave off, ward off, forestall, preclude.
aviator • noun *(dated)* PILOT, airman/woman, flyer; *dated* aeronaut.
avid • adjective KEEN, eager, enthusiastic, ardent, passionate, zealous; devoted, dedicated, wholehearted, earnest; *Brit. informal* as keen as mustard.
– OPPOSITES apathetic.
avoid • verb **1** *I avoid situations that stress me* KEEP AWAY FROM, steer clear of, give a wide berth to, fight shy of. **2** *he is trying to avoid responsibility* EVADE, dodge, sidestep, escape, run away from; *informal* duck, wriggle out of, get out of, cop out of; *Austral./NZ informal* duck-shove. **3** *she moved to avoid a blow* DODGE, duck, get out of the way of. **4** *you've been avoiding me all evening* SHUN, stay away from, evade, keep one's distance, elude, hide from; ignore. **5** *he should avoid drinking alcohol* REFRAIN FROM, abstain from, desist from, eschew.
– OPPOSITES confront, face up to, seek out.
avoidable • adjective PREVENTABLE, stoppable, avertable, escapable.
– OPPOSITES inescapable.
avow • verb ASSERT, declare, state, maintain, swear, vow, insist; *formal* aver; *rare* asseverate.
avowed • adjective SELF-CONFESSED, self-declared, acknowledged, admitted; open, overt.
await • verb **1** *Peter was awaiting news* WAIT FOR, expect, anticipate. **2** *many dangers await them* BE IN STORE FOR, lie ahead of, lie in wait for, be waiting for.
awake • verb **1** *she awoke the following morning* WAKE (UP), awaken, stir, come to, come round; *poetic/literary* waken. **2** *the alarm awoke him at 7.30* WAKE (UP), awaken, rouse, arouse; *Brit. informal* knock up. **3** *they finally awoke to the extent of the problem* REALIZE, become aware of, become conscious of; *informal* get wise to.
• adjective **1** *she was still awake* WAKEFUL, sleepless, restless, restive; *archaic* watchful; *rare* insomnolent. **2** *too few are awake to the dangers* AWARE OF, conscious of, mindful of, alert to; *formal* cognizant of; *archaic* ware of.
– OPPOSITES asleep, oblivious.
awaken • verb **1** *I awakened early* | *the jolt awakened her*. See AWAKE senses 1, 2. **2** *he had awakened strong emotions in her* AROUSE, rouse, bring out, engender, evoke, trigger, stir up, stimulate, kindle; revive; *poetic/literary* enkindle.
award • verb *the society awarded him a silver medal* GIVE, grant, accord, assign; confer on, bestow on, present to, endow with, decorate with.
• noun **1** *an award for high-quality service* PRIZE, trophy, medal, decoration; reward; *informal* gong. **2** *a libel award* PAYMENT, settlement, compensation. **3** *the Arts Council gave him an award of £1,500* GRANT, scholarship, endowment; *Brit.* bursary. **4** *the award of an honorary doctorate* CONFERRAL, conferment, bestowal, presentation.
aware • adjective **1** *she is aware of the dangers* CONSCIOUS OF, mindful of, informed about, acquainted with, familiar with, alive to, alert to; *informal* wise to, in the know about, hip to; *formal* cognizant of; *archaic* ware of. **2** *we need to be more environmentally aware* KNOWLEDGEABLE, enlightened, well informed, au fait; *informal* clued

away ● adverb **1** to or at a distance. **2** into an appropriate place for storage. **3** towards or into non-existence. **4** constantly, persistently, or continuously. ● adjective (of a sports fixture) played at the opponents' ground.
– ORIGIN Old English.
awe ● noun a feeling of great respect mixed with fear. ● verb inspire with awe.
– ORIGIN Old English.
aweigh ● adjective Nautical (of an anchor) raised just clear of the seabed.
awesome ● adjective **1** inspiring awe. **2** informal excellent.
awful ● adjective **1** very bad or unpleasant. **2** used for emphasis: *an awful lot.* **3** archaic inspiring awe.
– DERIVATIVES **awfulness** noun.
awfully ● adverb **1** informal very or very much: *I'm awfully sorry.* **2** very badly or unpleasantly.
awhile ● adverb for a short time.
awkward ● adjective **1** hard to do or deal with. **2** causing or feeling embarrassment. **3** inconvenient. **4** clumsy.
– DERIVATIVES **awkwardly** adverb **awkwardness** noun.
– ORIGIN from obsolete *awk* 'clumsy', from Old Norse.
awl ● noun a small pointed tool used for piercing holes.
– ORIGIN Old English.
awn /awn/ ● noun Botany a stiff bristle growing from the ear or flower of barley, rye, and grasses.
– ORIGIN Old Norse.
awning ● noun a sheet of canvas stretched on a frame and used to shelter a shop window or doorway.
– ORIGIN of unknown origin.
awoke past of AWAKE.
awoken past participle of AWAKE.
AWOL /aywol/ ● adjective Military absent but without intent to desert.
– ORIGIN acronym from *absent without (official) leave.*
awry ● adverb & adjective away from the expected course or position.
– ORIGIN from WRY.
axe (US also **ax**) ● noun **1** a heavy-bladed tool used for chopping wood. **2** (**the axe**) severe cost-cutting action. ● verb cancel or dismiss suddenly and ruthlessly.
– PHRASES **have an axe to grind** have a private reason for doing something.
– ORIGIN Old English.
axel /aks'l/ ● noun a jump in skating with one (or more) and a half turns in the air.
– ORIGIN named after the Norwegian skater *Axel* R. Paulsen (1885–1938).
axes plural of AXIS.
axial /aksiəl/ ● adjective forming, relating to, or around an axis.
– DERIVATIVES **axially** adverb.
axil /aksil/ ● noun Botany the upper angle where a leaf joins a stem.
– ORIGIN Latin *axilla.*
axiom /aksiəm/ ● noun a proposition regarded as self-evidently true.
– DERIVATIVES **axiomatic** adjective.
– ORIGIN Greek *axiōma* 'what is thought fitting'.
axis ● noun (pl. **axes** /akseez/) **1** an imaginary line through a body, about which it rotates. **2** an imaginary line about which a regular figure is symmetrically arranged. **3** Mathematics a fixed reference line for the measurement of coordinates. **4** (**the Axis**) the alliance between Germany and Italy in the Second World War.
– ORIGIN Latin, 'axle, pivot'.
axle /aks'l/ ● noun a rod or spindle passing through the centre of a wheel or group of wheels.
– ORIGIN Old Norse.
axolotl /aksəlott'l/ ● noun a Mexican salamander which retains

Thesaurus

up, genned up; *Brit. informal* switched-on.
– OPPOSITES ignorant.
awareness ● noun CONSCIOUSNESS, recognition, realization; understanding, grasp, appreciation, knowledge, insight; familiarity; *formal* cognizance.
awash ● adjective **1** *the road was awash* FLOODED, under water, submerged, submersed. **2** *the city was awash with journalists* INUNDATED, flooded, swamped, teeming, overflowing, overrun; *informal* knee-deep in.
away ● adverb **1** *she began to walk away* OFF, from here, from there. **2** *stay away from the trouble* AT A DISTANCE FROM, apart from. **3** *Bernice pushed him away* ASIDE, off, to one side. **4** *we'll be away for two weeks* ELSEWHERE, abroad; gone, absent; on holiday, on vacation.
awe ● noun WONDER, wonderment; admiration, reverence, respect; dread, fear.
awe-inspiring ● adjective. See AWESOME.
awesome ● adjective BREATHTAKING, awe-inspiring, magnificent, amazing, stunning, staggering, imposing, stirring, impressive; formidable, fearsome; *informal* mind-boggling, mind-blowing; *poetic/literary* wondrous; *archaic* awful.
– OPPOSITES unimpressive.
awestruck ● adjective AWED, wonderstruck, amazed, lost for words, open-mouthed; reverential; terrified, afraid, fearful.
awful ● adjective **1** *the place smelled awful* DISGUSTING, nasty, terrible, dreadful, ghastly, horrible, vile, foul, revolting, repulsive, repugnant, odious, sickening, nauseating; *informal* yucky, sick-making, gross; *Brit. informal* beastly; *poetic/literary* noisome. **2** *an awful book* DREADFUL, terrible, frightful, atrocious, execrable; inadequate, inferior, substandard, lamentable; *informal* crummy, pathetic, rotten, woeful, lousy, appalling, abysmal, dire, poxy; *Brit. informal* duff, rubbish. **3** *an awful accident* SERIOUS, grave, bad, terrible, dreadful. **4** *you look awful—go and lie down* ILL, unwell, sick, peaky, queasy, nauseous; *Brit.* off colour, poorly; *informal* rough, lousy, rotten, terrible, dreadful; *Brit. informal* grotty, ropy; *Scottish informal* wabbit, peely-wally; *Austral./NZ informal* crook; *dated* queer, seedy. **5** *I felt awful for getting so angry* REMORSEFUL, guilty, ashamed, contrite, sorry, regretful, repentant, self-reproachful. **6** *(archaic) the awful sights of nature* AWE-INSPIRING, awesome, impressive; dread, fearful.
– OPPOSITES wonderful.
awfully ● adverb **1** *(informal) an awfully nice man* VERY, extremely, really, exceedingly, immensely, thoroughly, dreadfully, exceptionally, remarkably, extraordinarily; *N. English* right; *informal* terrifically, terribly, devilishly, seriously, majorly; *Brit. informal* jolly, ever so, dead, well; *N. Amer. informal* real, mighty, awful; *informal, dated* frightfully; *archaic* exceeding. **2** *(informal) thanks awfully* VERY MUCH, a lot; *informal* a million. **3** *we played awfully* VERY BADLY, terribly, dreadfully, atrociously, appallingly, execrably; *informal* abysmally, pitifully, diabolically.
awhile ● adverb FOR A MOMENT, for a (little) while, for a short time; *informal* for a bit.
awkward ● adjective **1** *the box was awkward to carry* DIFFICULT, tricky; cumbersome, lumbersome, unwieldy; *Brit. informal* fiddly. **2** *an awkward time* INCONVENIENT, inappropriate, inopportune, unseasonable, difficult. **3** *he put her in a very awkward position* EMBARRASSING, uncomfortable, unpleasant, delicate, tricky, problematic(al), troublesome, thorny; humiliating, compromising; *informal* sticky, dicey, hairy; *Brit. informal* dodgy. **4** *she felt awkward alone with him* UNCOMFORTABLE, uneasy, tense, nervous, edgy, unquiet; self-conscious, embarrassed. **5** *his awkward movements* CLUMSY, ungainly, uncoordinated, graceless, inelegant, gauche, gawky, wooden, stiff; unskilful, maladroit, inept, blundering; *informal* clodhopping, ham-fisted, ham-handed, cack-handed; *Brit. informal* all (fingers and) thumbs. **6** *(Brit.) you're being damned awkward* UNREASONABLE, uncooperative, unhelpful, disobliging, difficult, obstructive; contrary, perverse; stubborn, obstinate; *Brit. informal* bloody-minded, bolshie; *N. Amer. informal* balky; *formal* refractory.
– OPPOSITES easy, convenient, at ease, graceful, amenable.
awning ● noun CANOPY, shade, sunshade, shelter, cover; *Brit.* blind, sunblind.
awry ● adjective **1** *something was awry* AMISS, wrong; *informal* up. **2** *his wig looked awry* ASKEW, crooked, lopsided, tilted, skewed, skew, squint, to one side, off-centre, uneven; *informal* cock-eyed; *Brit. informal* skew-whiff, wonky.
– OPPOSITES straight.
axe ● noun HATCHET, cleaver, tomahawk, adze, poleaxe; *Brit.* chopper; *historical* battleaxe.
● verb **1** *the show was axed* CANCEL, withdraw, drop, scrap, discontinue, terminate, end; *informal* ditch, dump, pull the plug on. **2** *500 staff were axed* DISMISS, make redundant, lay off, let go, discharge, get rid of; *informal* sack, fire, give someone the sack, give someone the bullet, give someone their marching orders; *Brit. informal* give someone their cards.
axiom ● noun ACCEPTED TRUTH, general truth, dictum, truism; maxim, adage, aphorism, apophthegm, gnome.

a

its aquatic newt-like larval form throughout life.
– ORIGIN Nahuatl, 'water servant'.
axon ● noun the long thread-like part of a nerve cell.
– DERIVATIVES **axonal** adjective.
– ORIGIN Greek, 'axis'.
ayah /īə/ ● noun a nanny employed by Europeans in the former British Empire, especially India.
– ORIGIN Portuguese *aia* 'nurse'.
ayatollah /īətollə/ ● noun a Shiite religious leader in Iran.
– ORIGIN from Arabic, 'token of God'.
aye[1] /ī/ (also **ay**) ● exclamation archaic or dialect yes. ● noun a vote for a proposal.
– ORIGIN probably from *I*, first person personal pronoun, expressing assent.
aye[2] /ay, ī/ ● adverb archaic or Scottish always; still.
– ORIGIN Old Norse.
AZ ● abbreviation Arizona.
azalea /əzayliə/ ● noun a deciduous flowering shrub with brightly coloured flowers.
– ORIGIN from Greek *azaleos* 'dry' (because the shrubs flourish in dry soil).
Azerbaijani /azzərbījaani/ ● noun (pl. **Azerbaijanis**) a person from Azerbaijan. ● adjective relating to Azerbaijan or Azerbaijanis.
azimuth /azziməth/ ● noun Astronomy the horizontal direction of a celestial object, measured from the north or south point of the horizon.
– DERIVATIVES **azimuthal** adjective.
– ORIGIN Arabic, 'the way, direction'.
azo dye /ayzō/ ● noun Chemistry a synthetic dye whose molecule contains two adjacent nitrogen atoms between carbon atoms.
– ORIGIN from obsolete *azote* 'nitrogen', from French, from Greek *a-* 'without' + *zōē* 'life'.
Aztec /aztek/ ● noun a member of the American Indian people dominant in Mexico before the Spanish conquest.
– ORIGIN Nahuatl, 'person of Aztlan', their legendary place of origin.
azure /azyər/ ● adjective bright blue in colour like a cloudless sky. ● noun a bright blue colour.
– ORIGIN Old French *azur*, from Persian, 'lapis lazuli'.

Thesaurus

axis ● noun **1** *the earth revolves on its axis* CENTRE LINE, vertical, horizontal. **2** *the Anglo-American axis* ALLIANCE, coalition, bloc, union, confederation, confederacy, league.
axle ● noun SHAFT, spindle, rod, arbor, mandrel, pivot.
azure ● adjective SKY-BLUE, bright blue, blue; *poetic/literary* cerulean; *rare* cyanic.

Bb

B[1] (also **b**) ● noun (pl. **Bs** or **B's**) **1** the second letter of the alphabet. **2** denoting the second item in a set. **3** Music the seventh note of the diatonic scale of C major. **4** the human blood type containing the B antigen and lacking the A.

B[2] ● abbreviation **1** (in chess) bishop. **2** black (used in describing grades of pencil lead). ● symbol the chemical element boron.

b ● abbreviation **1** (**b.**) born. **2** Cricket bowled by. **3** Cricket bye(s).

BA ● abbreviation **1** Bachelor of Arts. **2** British Airways.

Ba ● symbol the chemical element barium.

baa ● verb (**baas**, **baaed**, **baaing**) (of a sheep or lamb) bleat. ● noun the cry of a sheep or lamb.
– ORIGIN imitative.

baba /baabaa/ (also **rum baba**) ● noun a rich sponge cake, soaked in rum-flavoured syrup.
– ORIGIN Polish, 'married peasant woman'.

babble ● verb **1** talk rapidly in a foolish, excited, or incomprehensible way. **2** (of a stream) make a continuous murmur as the water flows over stones. ● noun the sound of babbling.
– DERIVATIVES **babbler** noun.
– ORIGIN Low German *babbelen*, or an independent English formation, based on the repeated syllable *ba*, typical of a child's early speech.

babe ● noun **1** literary a baby. **2** informal a sexually attractive young woman.

babel /bayb'l/ ● noun a confused noise made by a number of voices.
– ORIGIN from the biblical Tower of *Babel*, where God confused the languages of the builders.

baboon ● noun a large ground-dwelling monkey with a long snout.
– ORIGIN originally denoting a grotesque figure used in architecture: from Old French *babuin* or Latin *babewynus*.

babushka /bəbōōshkə/ ● noun (in Russia) an old woman or grandmother.
– ORIGIN Russian, 'grandmother'.

baby ● noun (pl. **babies**) **1** a child or animal that is newly or recently born. **2** a timid or childish person. **3** informal a person with whom one is having a romantic relationship. **4** (**one's baby**) one's particular responsibility, achievement, or concern. ● adjective comparatively small or immature of its kind. ● verb (**babies**, **babied**) be overprotective towards.
– PHRASES **be left holding the baby** informal be left with an unwelcome responsibility. **throw the baby out with the bathwater** discard something valuable along with things that are undesirable.
– DERIVATIVES **babyhood** noun **babyish** adjective.
– ORIGIN probably imitative of an infant's first attempts at speech.

baby blue ● noun a pale shade of blue.

baby boom ● noun informal a temporary marked increase in the birth rate, especially the one following the Second World War.
– DERIVATIVES **baby boomer** noun.

baby bust ● noun N. Amer. informal a temporary marked decrease in the birth rate.
– DERIVATIVES **baby buster** noun.

baby doll ● noun a girl or woman with pretty, childlike looks. ● adjective referring to a style of women's clothing resembling that traditionally worn by a young child.

Babylonian /babilōniən/ ● noun a person from Babylon or Babylonia, an ancient city and kingdom in Mesopotamia. ● adjective relating to Babylon or Babylonia.

babysit ● verb (**babysitting**; past and past part. **babysat**) look after a child or children while the parents are out.
– DERIVATIVES **babysitter** noun.

baby walker ● noun a device for helping a baby learn to walk, consisting of a harness set into a frame on wheels.

baccalaureate /bakkəlawriət/ ● noun **1** an examination qualifying candidates for higher education. **2** a university bachelor's degree.
– ORIGIN Latin *baccalaureatus*, from *baccalaureus* 'bachelor'.

baccarat /bakkəraa/ ● noun a gambling card game in which players bet against a banker.
– ORIGIN French *baccara*.

bacchanal /bakkən'l/ chiefly literary ● noun **1** a wild and drunken party or celebration. **2** a follower of Bacchus, the Greek or Roman god of wine.
– ORIGIN Latin *bacchanalis*, from the name of the god *Bacchus*.

Bacchanalia /bakkənayliə/ ● plural noun (also treated as sing.) **1** the ancient Roman festival of the god Bacchus. **2** (**bacchanalia**) drunken revelry.
– DERIVATIVES **bacchanalian** adjective.

bacchant /bakkənt/ ● noun (pl. **bacchants**; fem. **bacchante** /bəkanti/, pl. **bacchantes** /bəkanteez/) a priest or follower of Bacchus.

baccy ● noun Brit. informal tobacco.

bachata /bachaatə/ ● noun a style of romantic music originating in the Dominican Republic.
– ORIGIN Caribbean Spanish, 'party, good time'.

bachelor ● noun **1** a man who has never been married. **2** a person who holds a first degree from a university.
– DERIVATIVES **bachelorhood** noun.
– ORIGIN Old French *bacheler* 'a young man aspiring to knighthood'.

bachelorette ● noun N. Amer. a young unmarried woman.

bacillus /bəsilləss/ ● noun (pl. **bacilli** /bəsillī/) a rod-shaped bacterium.
– DERIVATIVES **bacillary** adjective.
– ORIGIN Latin, 'little stick'.

back ● noun **1** the rear surface of the human body from the shoulders to the hips. **2** the corresponding upper surface of an animal's body. **3** the side or part of something away from the viewer. **4** the side or part of an object that is not normally seen or used. **5** a player in a team game who plays in a defensive position behind the forwards. ● adverb **1** in the opposite direction from that in which one is facing or travelling. **2** so as to return to an earlier or normal position. **3** into the past. **4** in re-

Thesaurus

babble ● verb **1** *Betty babbled away* PRATTLE, rattle on, gabble, chatter, jabber, twitter, go on, run on, prate, ramble, burble, blather, blether; *informal* gab, yak, yabber, yatter, yammer, blabber, jaw, gas, shoot one's mouth off; *Brit. informal* witter, rabbit, chunter, natter, waffle; *N. Amer. informal* run off at the mouth. **2** *a brook babbled gently* BURBLE, murmur, gurgle, purl, tinkle; *poetic/literary* plash.
● noun *his inarticulate babble* PRATTLE, gabble, chatter, jabber, prating, rambling, blather, blether; *informal* gab, yak, yabbering, yatter; *Brit. informal* wittering, waffle, natter, chuntering.

babe ● noun *(poetic/literary)*. See BABY noun.

babel ● noun CLAMOUR, din, racket, confused noise, tumult, uproar, hubbub; babble, babbling, shouting, yelling, screaming; *informal* hullabaloo; *Brit. informal* row.

baby ● noun *a newborn baby* INFANT, newborn, child, tot, little one; *Scottish & N. English* bairn; *informal* sprog, tiny; *poetic/literary* babe, babe in arms; *technical* neonate.
– RELATED TERMS infantile.
● adjective *baby carrots* MINIATURE, mini, little, small, small-scale, scaled-down, toy, pocket, midget, dwarf; *Scottish* wee; *N. Amer.* vest-pocket; *informal* teeny, teeny-weeny, teensy, teensy-weensy, itsy-bitsy, itty-bitty, tiddly, bite-sized; *Brit. informal* titchy; *N. Amer. informal* little-bitty.
– OPPOSITES large.
● verb *her aunt babied her* PAMPER, mollycoddle, spoil, cosset, coddle, indulge, overindulge, pet, nanny, pander to.

b

turn. ● verb **1** give support to. **2** walk or drive backwards. **3** bet money on (a person or animal) winning a race or contest. **4** (**back on/on to**) (of a building or other structure) have its back facing or adjacent to. **5** cover the back of. **6** provide musical accompaniment to (a singer or musician). **7** (of the wind) change direction anticlockwise around the points of the compass. ● adjective **1** of or at the back. **2** in a remote or subsidiary position. **3** relating to the past.
– PHRASES **back and forth** to and fro. **the back of beyond** a very remote place. **back down** concede defeat. **back off** draw back from confrontation. **back out** withdraw from a commitment. **back to front** Brit. with the back at the front and the front at the back. **back up** Computing make a spare copy of (data or a disk). **behind someone's back** without a person's knowledge. **get** (or **put**) **someone's back up** annoy someone. **put one's back into** approach (a task) with vigour. **turn one's back on** ignore; reject. **with one's back to** (or **up against**) **the wall** in a desperate situation.
– DERIVATIVES **backer** noun **backless** adjective.
– ORIGIN Old English.

backbeat ● noun Music a strong accent on one of the normally unaccented beats of the bar.

back bench ● noun (in the UK) any of the benches in the House of Commons occupied by members of parliament who do not hold office.
– DERIVATIVES **back-bencher** noun.

backbiting ● noun malicious talk about an absent person.

backblocks ● plural noun Austral./NZ land in the remote and sparsely inhabited interior.

back boiler ● noun Brit. a boiler supplying hot water, built in behind a fireplace or integral to a gas fire.

backbone ● noun **1** the spine. **2** the chief support of a system or organization. **3** strength of character.

back-breaking ● adjective (of manual labour) physically demanding.

back-burner ● verb US postpone action on.
– PHRASES **on the back burner** having low priority.

backchat ● noun Brit. informal rude or impudent remarks.

backcloth ● noun Brit. a backdrop.

backcomb ● verb chiefly Brit. comb (the hair) towards the scalp to make it look thicker.

backdate ● verb Brit. **1** make retrospectively valid. **2** put an earlier date to (a document or agreement) than the actual one.

back door ● adjective underhand; clandestine.
– PHRASES **by** (or **through**) **the back door** in a clandestine or underhand way.

backdrop ● noun **1** a painted cloth hung at the back of a theatre stage as part of the scenery. **2** the setting or background for a scene or event.

backfire ● verb **1** (of a vehicle or its engine) undergo a mistimed explosion in the cylinder or exhaust. **2** (of a plan or action) go wrong, having the opposite effect to what was intended.

back-formation ● noun a word that is formed from what appears to be its derivative (e.g. *edit* from *editor*).

backgammon ● noun a board game in which two players move their pieces around triangular points according to the throw of dice.
– ORIGIN from BACK + an Old English word meaning 'game'.

background ● noun **1** part of a scene or description that forms a setting for the main figures or events. **2** information or circumstances that influence or explain something. **3** a person's education, experience, and social circumstances. **4** a persistent low level of radioactivity, radiation, noise, etc. present in a particular environment. **5** tasks or processes running on a computer that do not need input from the user.

backhand ● noun (in racket sports) a stroke played with the back of the hand facing in the direction of the stroke. ● verb strike with a backhanded blow or stroke.

backhanded ● adjective **1** made with the back of the hand facing in the direction of movement. **2** indirect or ambiguous: *a backhanded compliment.*

Thesaurus

babyish ● adjective CHILDISH, immature, infantile, juvenile, puerile, adolescent.
– OPPOSITES mature.

back ● noun **1** *she's broken her back* SPINE, backbone, spinal column, vertebral column. **2** *the back of the house* REAR, rear side, other side; *Nautical* stern. **3** *the back of the queue* END, tail end, rear end, tail; *N. Amer.* tag end. **4** *the back of a postcard* REVERSE, other side, underside; verso; *informal* flip side.
– RELATED TERMS dorsal, lumbar.
– OPPOSITES front, head, face.
● adverb **1** *he pushed his chair back* BACKWARDS, behind one, to one's rear, rearwards; away, off. **2** *a few months back* AGO, earlier, previously, before, in the past.
– OPPOSITES forward.
● verb **1** *the record companies backed the scheme with a few hundred pounds* SPONSOR, finance, put up the money for, fund, subsidize, underwrite, be a patron of, act as guarantor of; *informal* foot the bill for, pick up the tab for; *N. Amer. informal* bankroll, stake. **2** *most people backed the idea* SUPPORT, endorse, sanction, approve of, give one's blessing to, smile on, favour, advocate, promote, uphold, champion; vote for, ally oneself with, stand behind, side with, be on the side of, defend, take up the cudgels for; second; *informal* throw one's weight behind. **3** *he backed the horse at 33–1* BET ON, gamble on, stake money on. **4** *he backed away* REVERSE, draw back, step back, move/drive backwards, back off, pull back, retreat, withdraw, give ground, backtrack, retrace one's steps.
– OPPOSITES oppose, advance.
● adjective **1** *the back seats* REAR, rearmost, hind, hindmost, hinder, posterior. **2** *a back copy* PAST, old, previous, earlier, former, out of date.
– OPPOSITES front, current, future.
– PHRASES **back down** GIVE IN, concede defeat, surrender, yield, submit, climb down, concede, reconsider; backtrack, back-pedal. **back out of** RENEGE ON, go back on, withdraw from, pull out of, retreat from, fail to honour, abandon, default on, repudiate, backpedal on. **back something up** SUBSTANTIATE, corroborate, confirm, support, bear out, endorse, bolster, reinforce, lend weight to. **back someone up** SUPPORT, stand by, give one's support to, side with, be on someone's side, take someone's side, take someone's part; vouch for. **behind someone's back** SECRETLY, without someone's knowledge, on the sly, slyly, sneakily, covertly, surreptitiously, furtively.

backbiting ● noun MALICIOUS TALK, spiteful talk, slander, libel, defamation, abuse, character assassination, disparagement, denigration; slurs, aspersions; *informal* bitching, bitchiness, cattiness, mud-slinging, bad-mouthing; *Brit. informal* slagging off, rubbishing.

backbone ● noun **1** *an injured backbone* SPINE, spinal column, vertebral column, vertebrae; back; *Anatomy* dorsum, rachis. **2** *infantry are the backbone of most armies* MAINSTAY, cornerstone, foundation, chief support, buttress, pillar. **3** *he has enough backbone to see us through* STRENGTH OF CHARACTER, strength of will, firmness of purpose, firmness, resolution, resolve, grit, determination, fortitude, mettle, spirit; *informal* guts, spunk; *Brit. informal* bottle.
– RELATED TERMS spinal.

back-breaking ● adjective GRUELLING, arduous, strenuous, onerous, punishing, crushing, demanding, exacting, taxing, exhausting, draining; *informal* killing; *Brit. informal* knackering; *archaic* toilsome.
– OPPOSITES easy.

backchat ● noun (*Brit. informal*) IMPUDENCE, impertinence, cheek, cheekiness, effrontery, insolence, rudeness, rude retorts; answering back, talking back; *informal* mouth, lip; *N. Amer. informal* sass, smart mouth, back talk; *rare* contumely.

backer ● noun **1** *£3 million was provided by the project's backers* SPONSOR, investor, underwriter, financier, patron, benefactor, benefactress; *informal* angel. **2** *the backers of the proposition* SUPPORTER, defender, advocate, promoter, proponent; seconder; *N. Amer.* booster.

backfire ● verb *Bernard's plan backfired on him* REBOUND, boomerang, come back; fail, miscarry, go wrong; *informal* blow up in someone's face; *archaic* redound on.

background ● noun **1** *a background of palm trees* BACKDROP, backcloth, surrounding(s), setting, scene. **2** *students from many different backgrounds* SOCIAL CIRCUMSTANCES, family circumstances; environment, class, culture, tradition; upbringing. **3** *her nursing background* EXPERIENCE, record, history, past, training, education, grounding, knowledge. **4** *the political background* CIRCUMSTANCES, context, conditions, situation, environment, milieu, scene, scenario.
– OPPOSITES foreground.
– PHRASES **in the background** *maybe there was a sugar daddy in*

backhander • noun **1** a backhand stroke or blow. **2** Brit. informal a bribe.
backhoe (Brit. also **backhoe loader**) • noun a mechanical digger with a bucket attached to a hinged boom.
backing • noun **1** support. **2** a layer of material that forms or strengthens the back of something. **3** (especially in popular music) accompaniment to the main singer.
backing track • noun a recorded musical accompaniment.
backlash • noun **1** a strong and adverse reaction by a large number of people. **2** recoil or degree of play arising between parts of a mechanism.
backlist • noun a publisher's list of books published before the current season and still in print.
backlog • noun an accumulation of matters needing to be dealt with.
backlot • noun an outdoor area in a film studio where large exterior sets are made and some outside scenes are filmed.
backpack • noun a rucksack. • verb travel or hike carrying one's belongings in a rucksack.
– DERIVATIVES **backpacker** noun.
back passage • noun Brit. euphemistic a person's rectum.
back-pedal • verb **1** move the pedals of a bicycle backwards in order to brake. **2** hastily reverse one's previous action or opinion.
back room • noun a place where secret planning work is done. • adjective relating to secret work or planning.
backscratching • noun informal mutual exchange of favours or help.
back-seat driver • noun informal a passenger in a car who gives the driver unwanted advice.
backside • noun informal a person's bottom.
backslapping • noun the offering of hearty congratulations or praise.
backslash • noun a backward-sloping diagonal line (\).
backslide • verb (past **backslid**; past part. **backslid** or **backslidden**) relapse into bad ways.
– DERIVATIVES **backslider** noun **backsliding** noun.
backspace • noun a key on a typewriter or computer keyboard used to move the carriage or cursor backwards. • verb move a typewriter carriage or computer cursor backwards.
backspin • noun a backward spin given to a moving ball, causing it to stop more quickly or rebound at a steeper angle.
back-stabbing • noun criticizing someone while pretending to be friendly. • adjective behaving in such a way.
backstage • adverb in or to the area behind the stage in a theatre. • adjective relating to this area in a theatre.
backstairs • plural noun **1** stairs at the back or side of a building. **2** (before another noun) underhand; clandestine: *backstairs deals.*
backstitch • noun a method of sewing with overlapping stitches. • verb sew using backstitch.
backstreet • noun **1** a minor street. **2** (before another noun) secret, especially because illegal: *backstreet abortions.*
backstroke • noun a swimming stroke performed on the back with the arms lifted out of the water in a backward circular motion.
back-to-back • adjective **1** chiefly Brit. (of houses) built in a terrace backing on to another terrace, with a wall or a narrow alley between. **2** following consecutively.
back-to-nature • adjective relating to reversion to a simpler way of life.
backtrack • verb **1** retrace one's steps. **2** reverse one's previous position or opinion.
back-up • noun **1** support. **2** a person or thing held in reserve. **3** Computing the procedure for making a spare copy of data.
backward • adjective **1** directed behind or to the rear. **2** having made less progress than is normal or expected. • adverb variant of BACKWARDS.
– PHRASES **not backward in** not lacking the confidence to do.
– DERIVATIVES **backwardly** adverb **backwardness** noun.
backwards (also **backward**) • adverb **1** in the direction of one's back. **2** back towards the starting point. **3** in reverse of the usual direction or order.
– PHRASES **bend over backwards** informal make every effort to be fair or helpful. **know backwards** be entirely familiar with.
backwash • noun receding waves flowing outwards behind a ship.
backwater • noun **1** a part of a river not reached by the current, where the water is stagnant. **2** a place or state in which no development is taking place.
backwoods • plural noun chiefly N. Amer. **1** remote uncleared forest land. **2** a remote or sparsely inhabited region.
backwoodsman • noun chiefly N. Amer. an inhabitant of backwoods.
backyard • noun **1** Brit. a yard at the back of a house or other building. **2** N. Amer. a back garden. **3** informal the area close to where one lives.
bacon • noun salted or smoked meat from the back or sides of a pig.
– PHRASES **bring home the bacon** informal achieve material success.
– ORIGIN Old French.
bacteria plural of BACTERIUM.
bactericide /bakteerisīd/ • noun a substance which kills bacteria.
– DERIVATIVES **bactericidal** adjective.
bacteriological • adjective **1** relating to bacteriology or bacteria. **2** relating to germ warfare.
bacteriology • noun the study of bacteria.
– DERIVATIVES **bacteriologist** noun.
bacterium • noun (pl. **bacteria**) a member of a large group of microscopic single-celled organisms which have cell walls but lack an organized nucleus, and include many kinds which can cause disease.
– DERIVATIVES **bacterial** adjective.
– USAGE **Bacteria**, the plural form of **bacterium**, should always be

Thesaurus

the background BEHIND THE SCENES, out of the public eye, out of the spotlight, out of the limelight, backstage; inconspicuous, unobtrusive, unnoticed.
backhanded • adjective INDIRECT, ambiguous, oblique, equivocal; double-edged, two-edged; tongue-in-cheek.
– OPPOSITES direct.
backing • noun **1** *he has the backing of his colleagues* SUPPORT, help, assistance, aid; approval, endorsement, sanction, blessing. **2** *financial backing* SPONSORSHIP, funding, patronage; money, investment, funds, finance; grant, contribution, subsidy. **3** *musical backing* ACCOMPANIMENT; harmony, obbligato.
backlash • noun ADVERSE REACTION, counterblast, comeback; retaliation, reprisal.
backlog • noun ACCUMULATION, logjam, pile-up.
back-pedal • verb *the government has back-pedalled on its plans* CHANGE ONE'S MIND, go into reverse, backtrack, back down, climb down, do an about-face, do a U-turn, renege, go back on, back out of, fail to honour, withdraw, take back, default on; *Brit.* do an about-turn.
backslide • verb *many things can cause slimmers to backslide* RELAPSE, lapse, regress, retrogress, weaken, lose one's resolve, give in to temptation, go astray, leave the straight and narrow.
– OPPOSITES persevere.
backslider • noun RECIDIVIST, regressor; apostate, fallen angel.
back-up • noun HELP, support, assistance, aid; reinforcements, reserves, additional resources.
backward • adjective **1** *a backward look* REARWARD, to/towards the rear, to/towards the back, behind one, reverse. **2** *the decision was a backward step* RETROGRADE, retrogressive, regressive, for the worse, in the wrong direction, downhill, negative. **3** *an economically backward country* UNDERDEVELOPED, undeveloped; primitive, benighted. **4** *he was not backward in displaying his talents* HESITANT, reticent, reluctant; shy, diffident, bashful, timid; unwilling, afraid, loath, averse.
– OPPOSITES forward, progressive, advanced, confident.
• adverb *the car rolled slowly backward.* See BACKWARDS.
backwards • adverb **1** *Penny glanced backwards* TOWARDS THE REAR, rearwards, backward, behind one. **2** *count backwards from twenty to ten* IN REVERSE, in reverse order.
– OPPOSITES forwards.
backwash • noun **1** *a ship's backwash* WAKE, wash, slipstream, backflow. **2** *the backwash of the Cuban missile crisis* REPERCUSSIONS, reverberations, after-effects, aftermath, fallout.
backwoods • plural noun THE BACK OF BEYOND, remote areas, the wilds, the hinterlands, a backwater; *N. Amer.* the backcountry, the backland; *informal* the middle of nowhere, the sticks; *N. Amer. informal* the boondocks, the boonies; *Austral./NZ informal* beyond the black stump.

used with the plural form of the verb: *the bacteria causing salmonella are killed by thorough cooking*, **not** *the bacteria causing salmonella is killed by thorough cooking*.
– ORIGIN Latin, from Greek *baktērion* 'little rod' (because the first ones to be discovered were rod-shaped).

b

Bactrian camel • noun the two-humped camel, native to central Asia.
– ORIGIN named after *Bactria*, an ancient empire in central Asia.
bad • adjective (**worse**, **worst**) **1** of poor quality or a low standard. **2** unwelcome; unpleasant. **3** severe; serious. **4** offending moral standards or accepted conventions. **5** (**bad for**) harmful to. **6** injured, ill, or diseased. **7** (of food) decayed. **8** guilty; ashamed. **9** (**badder**, **baddest**) informal, chiefly N. Amer. good; excellent.
– PHRASES **to the bad** to ruin or downfall. **too bad** informal regrettable but unable to be changed.
– DERIVATIVES **badness** noun.
– ORIGIN perhaps from an Old English word meaning 'hermaphrodite, womanish man'.
bad blood • noun ill feeling.
bad debt • noun a debt that cannot be recovered.
baddy (also **baddie**) • noun (pl. **baddies**) informal a villain in a book, film, etc.
bade /bayd, bad/ past of BID².
bad faith • noun intent to deceive.
bad form • noun an offence against social conventions.
badge • noun a small flat object worn to show a person's name, rank, job, or membership of an organization.
– ORIGIN of unknown origin.
badger • noun a heavily built nocturnal mammal, typically having a grey and black coat and a white-striped head. • verb repeatedly and annoyingly ask (someone) to do something.
– ORIGIN perhaps from BADGE, with reference to the animal's distinctive head markings.
bad hair day • noun informal, chiefly US a day on which everything goes wrong.
badinage /baddinaazh/ • noun witty conversation.
– ORIGIN French, from *badiner* 'to joke'.
badlands • plural noun heavily eroded land on which little can grow or be grown.
badly • adverb (**worse**, **worst**) **1** in an unsatisfactory, unacceptable, or incompetent way. **2** severely; seriously. **3** very much.
– PHRASES **badly off** poor.
badminton • noun a game with rackets in which a shuttlecock is hit back and forth across a net.
– ORIGIN named after *Badminton* in SW England, where the game was first played.
bad-mouth • verb informal criticize maliciously.
bad-tempered • adjective easily angered.
baffle • verb totally bewilder. • noun a device used to restrain or regulate the flow of sound, light, gas, or a fluid.
– DERIVATIVES **bafflement** noun **baffling** adjective.
– ORIGIN perhaps related to French *bafouer* 'ridicule'.
bag • noun **1** a flexible container with an opening at the top. **2** (**bags**) loose folds of skin under a person's eyes. **3** (**bags of**) informal, chiefly Brit. plenty of. **4** informal an unpleasant or unattractive woman. **5** (**one's bag**) informal one's particular interest or taste. • verb (**bagged**, **bagging**) **1** put in a bag. **2** succeed in killing or catching (an animal). **3** succeed in obtaining. **4** (of clothes) form loose bulges. **5** Austral. informal criticize.
– PHRASES **bags** (or **bags I**) Brit. informal a child's expression used to make a claim to something. **in the bag** informal as good as secured.
– DERIVATIVES **bagful** noun **bagger** noun **baggy** adjective (**baggier**, **baggiest**).
– ORIGIN perhaps from Old Norse.
bagasse /bəgass/ • noun the dry pulpy residue left after the extraction of juice from sugar cane.

Thesaurus

bacteria • plural noun MICRO-ORGANISMS, microbes, germs, bacilli, pathogens; *informal* bugs.
bad • adjective **1** *bad workmanship* SUBSTANDARD, poor, inferior, second-rate, second-class, unsatisfactory, inadequate, unacceptable, not up to scratch, not up to par, deficient, imperfect, defective, faulty, shoddy, amateurish, careless, negligent, miserable, sorry; incompetent, inept, inexpert, ineffectual; *informal* crummy, rotten, pathetic, useless, woeful, bum, lousy, ropy, not up to snuff; *Brit. informal* duff, rubbish. **2** *the alcohol had a really bad effect on me* HARMFUL, damaging, detrimental, injurious, hurtful, inimical, destructive, ruinous, deleterious; unhealthy, unwholesome. **3** *the bad guys* WICKED, sinful, immoral, evil, morally wrong, corrupt, base, black-hearted, reprobate, amoral; criminal, villainous, nefarious, iniquitous, dishonest, dishonourable, unscrupulous, unprincipled; *informal* crooked, bent, dirty; *dated* dastardly. **4** *you bad girl!* NAUGHTY, badly behaved, disobedient, wayward, wilful, self-willed, defiant, unruly, insubordinate, undisciplined. **5** *bad news* UNPLEASANT, disagreeable, unwelcome; unfortunate, unlucky, unfavourable; terrible, dreadful, awful, grim, distressing. **6** *a bad time to arrive* INAUSPICIOUS, unfavourable, inopportune, unpropitious, unfortunate, disadvantageous, adverse, inappropriate, unsuitable, untoward. **7** *a bad accident* SEVERE, serious, grave, critical, acute; *formal* grievous. **8** *the meat's bad* ROTTEN, off, decayed, decomposed, decomposing, putrid, putrefied, mouldy, mouldering; sour, rancid, rank, unfit for human consumption; addled. **9** *if you still feel bad, stay in bed.* See ILL adjective sense 1. **10** *a bad knee* INJURED, wounded, diseased; *Brit. informal* gammy, knackered; *Austral./NZ informal* crook. **11** *I felt bad about leaving them* GUILTY, conscience-stricken, remorseful, guilt-ridden, ashamed, contrite, sorry, full of regret, regretful, shamefaced. **12** *a bad cheque* INVALID, worthless; counterfeit, fake, false, bogus, fraudulent; *informal* phoney, dud. **13** *bad language* OFFENSIVE, vulgar, crude, foul, obscene, rude, coarse, smutty, dirty, filthy, indecent, indecorous; blasphemous, profane.
– OPPOSITES good, beneficial, virtuous, well behaved, minor, slight, fresh, unrepentant.
– PHRASES **not bad** ALL RIGHT, adequate, good enough, reasonable, fair, decent, average, tolerable, acceptable, passable, middling, moderate, fine; *informal* OK, so-so, fair-to-middling.
badge • noun **1** *a name badge* pin, brooch; *N. Amer.* button. **2** *a badge of success* SIGN, symbol, indication, signal, mark; hallmark, trademark.
badger • verb PESTER, harass, bother, plague, torment, hound, nag, chivvy, harry, keep on at, go on at; *informal* hassle, bug.
badinage • noun BANTER, repartee, witty conversation, raillery, wordplay, cut and thrust; witticisms, bons mots, ripostes, sallies, quips; *N. Amer. informal* josh.
badly • adverb **1** *the job had been badly done* POORLY, incompetently, ineptly, inexpertly, inefficiently, imperfectly, deficiently, defectively, unsatisfactorily, inadequately, incorrectly, faultily, shoddily, amateurishly, carelessly, negligently; *informal* crummily, pitifully, woefully. **2** *try not to think badly of me* UNFAVOURABLY, ill, critically, disapprovingly. **3** *stop behaving badly* NAUGHTILY, disobediently, wilfully, reprehensibly, mischievously. **4** *he had been badly treated* CRUELLY, wickedly, unkindly, harshly, shamefully; unfairly, unjustly, wrongly, improperly. **5** *it turned out badly* UNSUCCESSFULLY, unfavourably, adversely, unfortunately, unhappily, unluckily. **6** *some of the victims are badly hurt* SEVERELY, seriously, gravely, acutely, critically; *formal* grievously. **7** *she badly needs help* DESPERATELY, sorely, intensely, seriously, very much, greatly, exceedingly.
– OPPOSITES well, slightly.
bad-tempered • adjective IRRITABLE, irascible, tetchy, testy, grumpy, grouchy, crotchety, in a (bad) mood, cantankerous, curmudgeonly, ill-tempered, ill-humoured, peevish, having got out of bed on the wrong side, cross, as cross as two sticks, fractious, pettish, crabby; *informal* snappish, on a short fuse; *Brit. informal* shirty, stroppy, ratty; *N. Amer. informal* cranky, ornery; *Austral./NZ informal* snaky; *informal, dated* miffy.
– OPPOSITES good-humoured, affable.
baffle • verb PERPLEX, puzzle, bewilder, mystify, bemuse, confuse, confound, nonplus; *informal* flummox, faze, stump, beat, fox, make someone scratch their head, be all Greek to, floor; *N. Amer. informal* discombobulate, buffalo.
– OPPOSITES enlighten.
baffling • adjective PUZZLING, BEWILDERING, perplexing, mystifying, bemusing, confusing, unclear; inexplicable, incomprehensible, impenetrable, cryptic, opaque.
– OPPOSITES clear, comprehensible.
bag • noun **1** *I dug around in my bag for my lipstick* HANDBAG, shoulder bag, clutch bag, evening bag, pochette; *N. Amer.* pocketbook, purse; *historical* reticule, scrip. **2** *she began to unpack her bags* SUITCASE, case, valise, portmanteau, holdall, grip, overnighter; backpack, rucksack, knapsack, haversack, kitbag, duffel bag; satchel; (**bags**) luggage, baggage.
• verb **1** *locals bagged the most fish* CATCH, land, capture, trap,

– ORIGIN French, from Spanish *bagazo* 'pulp'.
bagatelle /baggətel/ ● **noun 1** a game in which small balls are hit into numbered holes on a board. **2** something unimportant.
– ORIGIN Italian *bagatella*.
bagel /bayg'l/ ● **noun** a dense, ring-shaped bread roll that is simmered before baking.
– ORIGIN Yiddish.
baggage ● **noun 1** personal belongings packed in suitcases for travelling. **2** experiences or long-held opinions perceived as encumbrances: *emotional baggage*. **3** dated a cheeky or disagreeable girl or woman.
– ORIGIN Old French *bagage*, from *baguer* 'tie up', or from *bagues* 'bundles'.
bag lady ● **noun** informal a homeless woman who carries her possessions in shopping bags.
bagman ● **noun 1** Brit. informal, dated a travelling salesman. **2** US & Austral. informal an agent who collects or distributes the proceeds of illicit activities.
bagpipe ● **noun** a musical instrument with reed pipes that are sounded by wind squeezed from a bag.
– DERIVATIVES **bagpiper** noun.
baguette /baget/ ● **noun** a long, narrow French loaf.
– ORIGIN French, from Latin *baculum* 'staff'.
bah ● **exclamation** an expression of contempt.
Baha'i /baahī/ (also **Bahai**) ● **noun** (pl. **Baha'is**) **1** a monotheistic religion founded in Persia in the 19th century, emphasizing the essential oneness of humankind and of all religions and seeking world peace. **2** an adherent of the Baha'i faith.
– ORIGIN Persian, from Arabic, 'splendour'.
Bahamian /bəhaymiən/ ● **noun** a person from the Bahamas. ● **adjective** relating to the Bahamas.
Bahraini /baarayni/ ● **noun** a person from Bahrain. ● **adjective** relating to Bahrain.
baht /baat/ ● **noun** (pl. same) the basic monetary unit of Thailand, equal to 100 satangs.
– ORIGIN Thai.
Bahutu plural of HUTU.
bail[1] ● **noun 1** the temporary release of an accused person awaiting trial, sometimes on condition that a sum of money is lodged to guarantee their appearance in court. **2** money paid by or for such a person as security. ● **verb** release or secure the release of (an accused person) on payment of bail.
– PHRASES **go** (or **stand**) **bail** act as surety for an accused person. **jump bail** informal fail to appear for trial after being released on bail.
– ORIGIN Old French, 'custody, jurisdiction', from Latin *bajulare* 'bear a burden'.
bail[2] ● **noun 1** Cricket either of the two crosspieces bridging the stumps. **2** a bar on a typewriter or computer printer which holds the paper steady. **3** a bar separating horses in an open stable. **4** Austral./NZ a framework for securing the head of a cow during milking. ● **verb** Austral./NZ **1** secure (a cow) during milking. **2** confront with intent to rob. **3** detain in conversation.
– ORIGIN Old French *baile* 'palisade, enclosure'.
bail[3] (Brit. also **bale**) ● **verb 1** scoop water out of (a ship or boat). **2** (**bail out**) make an emergency parachute descent from an aircraft. **3** (**bail out**) rescue from a difficulty.
– ORIGIN from French *baille* 'bucket', from Latin *bajulus* 'carrier'.
bailey ● **noun** (pl. **baileys**) the outer wall of a castle.
– ORIGIN probably from Old French *baile* 'palisade, enclosure'.
Bailey bridge ● **noun** a prefabricated lattice steel bridge designed for rapid assembly, especially in military operations.
– ORIGIN named after the English engineer Sir Donald *Bailey* (1901–85).
bailiff ● **noun 1** chiefly Brit. a sheriff's officer who serves writs, seizes property to clear rent arrears, and carries out arrests. **2** Brit. the agent of a landlord.
– ORIGIN Old French *baillif*, from Latin *bajulus* 'carrier, manager'.
bailiwick /bayliwik/ ● **noun** Law the district or jurisdiction of a bailiff.
– ORIGIN from BAILIFF + Old English *wick* 'dwelling place'.
Baily's beads ● **plural noun** Astronomy a string of bright points seen at the edge of the darkened moon at the beginning or end of totality in an eclipse of the sun, caused by the uneven lunar surface.
– ORIGIN named after the English astronomer Francis *Baily* (1774–1844).
bain-marie /banmərее/ ● **noun** (pl. **bains-marie** or **bain-maries** pronunc. same) a pan of hot water in which a cooking container is placed for slow cooking.
– ORIGIN French, 'bath of Maria', said to be the name of an alchemist.
bairn ● **noun** chiefly Scottish & N. English a child.
– ORIGIN Old English.
bait ● **noun 1** food put on a hook or in a trap to entice fish or other animals. **2** variant spelling of BATE. ● **verb 1** taunt or tease. **2** set dogs on (a trapped or restrained animal). **3** put bait on or in.
– PHRASES **rise to the bait** react to a provocation exactly as intended.
– ORIGIN Old Norse, 'pasture, food'.
baiza /bīzaa/ ● **noun** (pl. same or **baizas**) a monetary unit of Oman, equal to one thousandth of a rial.
baize ● **noun** a felt-like material that is typically green, used for covering billiard and card tables.
– ORIGIN French *baies*, from *bai* 'chestnut-coloured'.
bake ● **verb 1** cook (food) by dry heat in an oven. **2** heat, especially so as to dry or harden. **3** informal be or become extremely hot in prolonged hot weather. ● **noun** a dish consisting of a number of ingredients mixed together and baked.
– ORIGIN Old English.
baked Alaska ● **noun** a dessert consisting of sponge cake and ice cream in a meringue covering, cooked briefly in a hot oven.
baked beans ● **plural noun** baked haricot beans, typically cooked in tomato sauce and tinned.
Bakelite ● **noun** trademark an early brittle form of plastic.
– ORIGIN named after Leo H. *Baekeland* (1863–1944), the Belgian-born American chemist who invented it.
baker ● **noun** a person whose trade is making bread and cakes.
– PHRASES **baker's dozen** a group of thirteen. [ORIGIN from the former bakers' custom of adding an extra loaf to a dozen sold to a retailer.]
– DERIVATIVES **bakery** noun.
Bakewell tart ● **noun** Brit. a baked open tart consisting of a pastry case lined with jam and filled with almond sponge cake.
– ORIGIN named after the town of *Bakewell* in Derbyshire.
baking powder ● **noun** a mixture of sodium bicarbonate and cream of tartar, used as a raising agent in baking.
baking soda ● **noun** sodium bicarbonate.
baklava /bakləvə/ ● **noun** a Middle Eastern dessert made of filo pastry filled with chopped nuts and soaked in honey.
– ORIGIN Turkish.
baksheesh /baksheesh/ ● **noun** (in some eastern countries and the Indian subcontinent) a small sum of money given as alms, a tip, or a bribe.
– ORIGIN Persian.
balaclava ● **noun** a close-fitting woollen hat covering the head and encircling the neck.
– ORIGIN named after the village of *Balaclava* in the Crimea: the hat was worn originally by soldiers in the Crimean War.
balafon /baləfon/ ● **noun** a large xylophone with hollow gourds

Thesaurus

snare, ensnare; kill, shoot. **2** *he bagged seven medals* GET, secure, obtain, acquire, pick up; win, achieve, attain; commandeer, grab, appropriate, take; *informal* get one's hands on, land, net.
baggage ● **noun** LUGGAGE, suitcases, cases, bags.
baggy ● **adjective** LOOSE-FITTING, loose, roomy, generously cut, full, ample, voluminous, billowing; oversized, shapeless, ill-fitting, tent-like, sack-like.
– OPPOSITES tight.
bail ● **noun** *he was released on bail* SURETY, security, assurance, indemnity, indemnification; bond, guarantee, pledge; *archaic* gage.
– PHRASES **bail out** *the pilot bailed out* EJECT, parachute to safety. **bail someone/something out** *the government bailed out loss-making industries* RESCUE, save, relieve; finance, help (out), assist, aid; *informal* save someone's bacon/neck/skin.
bait ● **noun 1** *the fish let go of the bait* LURE, decoy, fly, troll, jig, plug. **2** *was she the bait to lure him into a trap?* ENTICEMENT, lure, decoy, snare, trap, siren, carrot, attraction, draw, magnet, incentive, temptation, inducement; *informal* come-on.
● **verb** *he was baited at school* TAUNT, tease, goad, pick on, torment, persecute, plague, harry, harass, hound; *informal* needle; *Brit. informal* wind up, nark.
bake ● **verb 1** *bake the fish for 15–20 minutes* COOK, oven-bake,

b

as resonators, used in West African music.
– ORIGIN from a West African language meaning 'xylophone' and 'to play'.

balalaika /baləlīkə/ ● noun a Russian musical instrument like a guitar with a triangular body and three strings.
– ORIGIN Russian.

balance ● noun **1** an even distribution of weight ensuring stability. **2** mental or emotional stability. **3** a condition in which different elements are equal or in the correct proportions. **4** an apparatus for weighing, especially one with a beam and central pivot. **5** a preponderance: *the balance of opinion was that work was important.* **6** a figure representing the difference between credits and debits in an account. ● verb **1** be or put in a steady position. **2** compare the value of (one thing) with another. **3** establish equal or appropriate proportions of elements in.
– PHRASES **balance of payments** the difference in total value between payments into and out of a country over a period. **balance of power 1** a situation in which states of the world have roughly equal power. **2** the power held by a small group when larger groups are of equal strength. **balance of trade** the difference in value between a country's imports and exports. **be** (or **hang**) **in the balance** be in an uncertain or critical state. **on balance** when all factors are taken into consideration.
– DERIVATIVES **balancer** noun.
– ORIGIN Old French, from Latin *libra bilanx* 'balance having two scale-pans'.

balance sheet ● noun a written statement of the assets, liabilities, and capital of a business.

balboa /balbōə/ ● noun the basic monetary unit of Panama, equal to 100 centésimos.
– ORIGIN named after the Spanish explorer Vasco Núñez de *Balboa* (1475–1519).

balcony ● noun (pl. **balconies**) **1** an enclosed platform on the outside of a building, with access from an upper-floor window or door. **2** the highest tier of seats in a theatre or cinema.
– DERIVATIVES **balconied** adjective.
– ORIGIN Italian *balcone*.

bald ● adjective **1** having a scalp with very little or no hair. **2** (of an animal) not covered by the usual fur, hair, or feathers. **3** (of a tyre) having the tread worn away. **4** without any extra detail or explanation; plain or blunt.
– DERIVATIVES **balding** adjective **baldish** adjective **baldly** adverb **baldness** noun.
– ORIGIN probably from an obsolete base meaning 'white patch'.

baldachin /bawldəkin/ (also **baldaquin** /bawldəkin/) ● noun a ceremonial canopy over an altar, throne, or doorway.
– ORIGIN originally denoting a rich brocade from Baghdad: from Italian *Baldacco* 'Baghdad'.

bald eagle ● noun a white-headed North American eagle, the national bird of the US.

balderdash ● noun senseless talk or writing.
– ORIGIN originally denoting a frothy liquid or an unappetizing mixture of drinks: of unknown origin.

baldric /bawldrik/ ● noun historical a belt for a sword, worn over one shoulder and reaching down to the opposite hip.
– ORIGIN Old French *baudre*.

bale[1] ● noun a large wrapped or bound bundle of paper, hay, or cotton. ● verb make up into bales.
– DERIVATIVES **baler** noun.
– ORIGIN probably from Dutch.

bale[2] ● noun & verb Brit. variant spelling of BAIL[3].

baleen ● noun whalebone.
– ORIGIN Latin *balaena* 'whale'.

baleen whale ● noun any of the kinds of whale that have plates of whalebone in the mouth for straining plankton from the water.

baleful ● adjective **1** menacing. **2** having a harmful effect.
– DERIVATIVES **balefully** adverb.
– ORIGIN from an Old English word meaning 'evil'.

Balinese /baalineez/ ● noun (pl. same) a person from Bali. ● adjective relating to Bali.

balk ● verb & noun chiefly US variant spelling of BAULK.

Balkan /bawlkən/ ● adjective relating to the countries occupying the part of south-east Europe bounded by the Adriatic, Ionian, Aegean, and the Black Seas. ● noun (**the Balkans**) the Balkan countries.
– ORIGIN Turkish.

Balkanize (also **Balkanise**) ● verb divide (a region or body) into smaller mutually hostile states or groups.
– DERIVATIVES **Balkanization** noun.

balky /bawlki/ ● adjective (**balkier**, **balkiest**) chiefly N. Amer. awkward; uncooperative.

ball[1] ● noun **1** a solid or hollow sphere, especially one that is kicked, thrown, or hit in a game. **2** a single throw or kick of the ball in a game. **3** N. Amer. a game played with a ball, especially baseball. ● verb squeeze or form into a ball.
– PHRASES **the ball is in your court** it is up to you to make the next move. **the ball of the foot** the rounded part of the foot at the base of the big toe. **keep one's eye on** (or **take one's eye off**) **the ball** keep (or fail to keep) one's attention focused on the matter in hand. **on the ball** alert to new ideas, methods, and trends. **play ball** informal cooperate. **start** (or **get** or **set**) **the ball rolling** make a start.
– ORIGIN Old Norse.

ball[2] ● noun a formal social gathering for dancing.
– PHRASES **have a ball** informal enjoy oneself greatly.
– ORIGIN French *bal* 'a dance', from Latin *ballare* 'to dance'.

ballad ● noun **1** a poem or song telling a popular story. **2** a slow

Thesaurus

roast, dry-roast, pot-roast. **2** *the earth was baked by the sun* SCORCH, burn, sear, parch, dry (up), desiccate; *N. Amer.* broil.

balance ● noun **1** *I tripped and lost my balance* STABILITY, equilibrium, steadiness, footing. **2** *political balance in broadcasting* FAIRNESS, justice, impartiality, egalitarianism, equal opportunity; parity, equity, equilibrium, equipoise, evenness, symmetry, correspondence, uniformity, equality, equivalence, comparability. **3** *this stylistic development provides a balance to the rest of the work* COUNTERBALANCE, counterweight, stabilizer, compensation. **4** *the food was weighed on a balance* SCALE(S), weighing machine, weighbridge. **5** *the balance of the rent* REMAINDER, outstanding amount, rest, residue, remaining part/number/quantity, difference.
– OPPOSITES instability, imbalance.
● verb **1** *she balanced the book on her head* STEADY, stabilize, poise, level. **2** *he balanced his radical remarks with more familiar declarations* COUNTERBALANCE, balance out, offset, even out/up, counteract, compensate for, make up for. **3** *their income and expenditure do not balance* CORRESPOND, agree, tally, match up, concur, coincide, be in agreement, be consistent, equate, be equal. **4** *you need to balance cost against benefit* WEIGH, weigh up, compare, evaluate, consider, assess, appraise, judge.
– PHRASES **in the balance** UNCERTAIN, undetermined, unsettled, unresolved, unsure, pending, in limbo, up in the air, at a turning point, critical, at a critical stage, at a crisis. **on balance** OVERALL, all in all, all things considered, by and large, taking everything into consideration/account, on average.

balanced ● adjective **1** *a balanced view* FAIR, equitable, just, unbiased, unprejudiced, objective, impartial, dispassionate. **2** *a balanced diet* MIXED, varied; healthy, sensible. **3** *a balanced individual* LEVEL-HEADED, well balanced, well adjusted, mature, stable, sensible, practical, realistic, with both feet on the ground, pragmatic, reasonable, rational, sane, even-tempered, commonsensical, full of common sense; *informal* together.
– OPPOSITES partial, unhealthy, neurotic.

balcony ● noun **1** *the balcony of the villa* veranda, loggia, terrace, patio. **2** *the applause from the balcony* GALLERY, upper circle; *informal* the gods.

bald ● adjective **1** *a bald head* HAIRLESS, smooth, shaven, depilated; bald-headed. **2** *a few bald bushes* LEAFLESS, bare, uncovered. **3** *a bald statement* PLAIN, simple, unadorned, unvarnished, unembellished, undisguised, unveiled, stark, severe, austere, brutal, harsh; blunt, direct, forthright, plain-spoken, straight, straightforward, candid, honest, truthful, realistic, true to life, frank, outspoken; *informal* upfront.
– OPPOSITES hairy.

balderdash ● noun. See NONSENSE sense 1.

baldness ● noun HAIR LOSS, hairlessness; *Medicine* alopecia.

bale[1] ● noun *a bale of cotton* BUNDLE, truss, bunch, pack, package, parcel.

bale[2] ● verb
– PHRASES **bale out.** See BAIL.

baleful ● adjective MENACING, threatening, unfriendly, hostile, antagonistic, evil, evil-intentioned, vindictive, malevolent, malicious, malignant, malign, sinister; harmful, injurious, dangerous, noxious, pernicious, deadly, venomous, poisonous; *poetic/literary*

sentimental or romantic song.
– DERIVATIVES **balladeer** noun **balladry** noun.
– ORIGIN Provençal *balada* 'dance, song to dance to', from Latin *ballare* 'to dance'.
ballade /balaad/ • noun **1** a poem with sets of three verses, each ending with the same line, and a short verse in conclusion. **2** a short, lyrical piece of music, especially one for piano.
– ORIGIN earlier spelling of BALLAD.
ball-and-socket joint • noun a joint in which a rounded end lies in a socket, allowing movement in all directions.
ballast • noun **1** a heavy substance carried by a ship or hot air balloon to keep it stable. **2** gravel or coarse stone used to form the base of a railway track or road. **3** a passive component used in an electric circuit to moderate changes in current.
– ORIGIN probably Low German or Scandinavian.
ball bearing • noun **1** a bearing in which the parts are separated by a ring of small metal balls which reduce friction. **2** a ball used in such a bearing.
ballboy (or **ballgirl**) • noun a boy (or girl) who retrieves balls that go out of play during a tennis match or baseball game.
ballcock • noun a valve which automatically tops up a cistern when liquid is drawn from it.
ballerina • noun a female ballet dancer.
– ORIGIN from Italian *ballerino* 'dancing master', from Latin *ballare* 'to dance'.
ballet • noun **1** an artistic dance form performed to music, using formalized steps and gestures. **2** a creative work of this form or the music written for it.
– DERIVATIVES **balletic** adjective.
– ORIGIN Italian *balletto* 'a little dance'.
balletomane /balitōmayn/ • noun a ballet enthusiast.
ball game • noun **1** a game played with a ball. **2** informal a situation that is completely different from a previous one.
ballistic /bəlistik/ • adjective **1** relating to projectiles or their flight. **2** moving under the force of gravity only.
– PHRASES **go ballistic** informal fly into a rage.
– ORIGIN from Greek *ballein* 'to throw'.
ballistic missile • noun a missile which is initially powered and guided but falls under gravity on to its target.
ballistics • plural noun (treated as sing.) the science of projectiles and firearms.
ballocks • plural noun variant spelling of BOLLOCKS.
balloon • noun **1** a small rubber bag which is inflated and used as a toy or a decoration. **2** a large bag filled with hot air or gas to make it rise in the air, with a basket for passengers hanging from it. **3** a rounded outline in which the words or thoughts of characters in a comic strip or cartoon are written. • verb **1** swell out in a spherical shape. **2** increase rapidly.
– PHRASES **when the balloon goes up** informal when the action or trouble starts.
– DERIVATIVES **ballooning** noun **balloonist** noun.
– ORIGIN French *ballon* or Italian *ballone* 'large ball'.
balloon angioplasty • noun Medicine surgical widening of a blood vessel by means of a catheter incorporating a small inflatable balloon.
ballot • noun **1** a procedure by which people vote secretly on an issue. **2** (**the ballot**) the total number of votes cast in such a process. **3** a lottery held to decide the allocation of tickets or other things among a number of applicants. • verb (**balloted**, **balloting**) **1** obtain a secret vote from (members). **2** cast one's vote on an issue. **3** allocate by drawing lots.
– ORIGIN originally denoting a ball placed in a container to register a vote: from Italian *ballotta* 'little ball'.
ballpark chiefly N. Amer. • noun **1** a baseball ground. **2** informal a particular area or range. • adjective informal approximate: *a ballpark figure.*
ballpoint pen • noun a pen with a tiny ball as its writing point.
ballroom • noun a large room for formal dancing.
ballroom dancing • noun formal social dancing in couples.
balls vulgar slang • plural noun **1** testicles. **2** courage; nerve. **3** (treated as sing.) Brit. nonsense. • verb (**balls up**) bungle.
balls-up • noun Brit. vulgar slang a bungled task or action.
ballsy • adjective (**ballsier**, **ballsiest**) informal bold and confident.
bally /bali/ • adjective & adverb Brit. old-fashioned euphemism for BLOODY[2].
ballyhoo • noun informal extravagant publicity or fuss.
– ORIGIN of unknown origin.
balm • noun **1** a fragrant ointment used to heal or soothe the skin. **2** something that soothes or heals.
– ORIGIN Old French *basme*, from Latin *balsamum* 'balsam'.
balmy • adjective (**balmier**, **balmiest**) (of the weather) pleasantly warm.
baloney /bəlōni/ (also **boloney**) • noun informal nonsense.
– ORIGIN perhaps from BOLOGNA.
balsa (also **balsa wood**) /bolsə/ • noun very lightweight timber obtained from a tropical American tree, used chiefly for making models and rafts.
– ORIGIN Spanish, 'raft'.
balsam /bolsəm/ • noun **1** an aromatic resin obtained from certain trees and shrubs, used in perfumes and medicines. **2** a herbaceous plant grown for its pink or purple flowers.
– DERIVATIVES **balsamic** adjective.
– ORIGIN Greek *balsamon.*
balsamic vinegar • noun dark, sweet Italian vinegar that has been matured in wooden barrels.
balti /bolti/ • noun (pl. **baltis**) a type of Pakistani cuisine in which the food is cooked in a small two-handled pan.
– ORIGIN Urdu, 'pail'.
Baltic • adjective **1** relating to the Baltic sea or those states on its eastern shores. **2** relating to the Baltic languages. • noun an Indo-European branch of languages consisting of Lithuanian, Latvian, and Old Prussian.
– ORIGIN from Latin *Balthae* 'dwellers near the Baltic Sea'.
baluster /baləstər/ • noun a short pillar forming part of a series supporting a rail.
– ORIGIN from Italian *balaustra* 'wild pomegranate flower' (because of the resemblance to part of the flower).
balustrade /baləstrayd/ • noun a railing supported by balusters.
– DERIVATIVES **balustraded** adjective.
bambino /bambeenō/ • noun (pl. **bambini** /bambeeni/) a baby or young child.
– ORIGIN Italian, 'little silly'.
bamboo • noun a giant tropical grass with hollow woody stems.
– ORIGIN Malay.
bamboo shoot • noun a young shoot of bamboo, eaten as a vegetable.
bamboozle /bambo͞oz'l/ • verb informal **1** cheat or deceive. **2** confuse.
– ORIGIN of unknown origin.
ban[1] • verb (**banned**, **banning**) officially prohibit. • noun an official prohibition.
– ORIGIN Old English, 'summon by a public proclamation'.

Thesaurus

malefic, maleficent.
– OPPOSITES benevolent, friendly.
balk • verb. See BAULK.
ball[1] • noun **1** *a ball of dough* SPHERE, globe, orb, globule, spherule, spheroid, ovoid. **2** *a musket ball* BULLET, pellet, slug, projectile.
ball[2] • noun *a fancy-dress ball* DANCE, dinner dance, masked ball, masquerade; *N. Amer.* hoedown, prom; *informal* hop, disco, bop.
ballad • noun SONG, folk song, shanty, ditty, canzone; poem, tale, saga.
balloon • noun hot-air balloon, barrage balloon; airship, dirigible, Zeppelin; envelope, gasbag; *informal* blimp.
• verb **1** *her long skirt ballooned in the wind* SWELL (OUT), puff out/up, bulge (out), bag, belly (out), fill (out), billow (out). **2** *the company's debt has ballooned* INCREASE RAPIDLY, soar, rocket, shoot up, escalate, mount, surge, spiral; *informal* go through the roof, sky-rocket.
– OPPOSITES plummet.
ballot • noun VOTE, poll, election, referendum, plebiscite, show of hands.
ballyhoo • noun *(informal)* PUBLICITY, advertising, promotion, marketing, propaganda, push, puffery, build-up, boosting; fuss, excitement; *informal* hype, spiel, hoo-ha, hullabaloo, song and dance, splash.
balm • noun **1** *a skin balm* OINTMENT, lotion, cream, salve, liniment, embrocation, rub, gel, emollient, unguent, balsam, moisturizer; *dated* pomade; *technical* demulcent, humectant; *archaic* unction. **2** *balm for troubled spirits* RELIEF, comfort, ease, succour, consolation, cheer, solace; *poetic/literary* easement.
balmy • adjective MILD, gentle, temperate, summery, calm, tranquil, clement, fine, pleasant, benign, soothing, soft.

b

ban² /baan/ ● noun (pl. **bani** /baani/) a monetary unit of Romania, equal to one hundredth of a leu.
– ORIGIN Romanian.
banal /bənaal/ ● adjective tediously unoriginal or ordinary.
– DERIVATIVES **banality** noun (pl. **banalities**) **banally** adverb.
– ORIGIN originally meaning 'compulsory', hence 'common': from French *ban* 'proclamation, summons'.
banana ● noun a long curved fruit with yellow skin and soft flesh, which grows on a tropical or subtropical tree-like plant.
– PHRASES **go** (or **be**) **bananas** informal become (or be) mad or angry.
– ORIGIN from an African language.
banana republic ● noun derogatory a small politically unstable country whose economy is dependent on a single export controlled by foreign concerns.
banana split ● noun a sweet dish made with bananas cut down the middle and filled with ice cream, sauce, and nuts.
band¹ ● noun **1** a flat, thin strip or loop of material used as a fastener, for reinforcement, or as decoration. **2** a stripe or strip of a different colour or composition from its surroundings: *a band of cloud.* **3** a range of values or a specified category within a series: *the lower-rate tax band.* **4** a range of frequencies or wavelengths in a spectrum: *the UHF band.* **5** a belt or strap transmitting motion between two wheels or pulleys. ● verb **1** fit a band on or round. **2** mark with a stripe or stripes. **3** allocate to a range or category.
– DERIVATIVES **banding** noun.
– ORIGIN Old English, related to BIND.
band² ● noun **1** a small group of musicians and vocalists who play pop, jazz, or rock music. **2** a group of musicians who play brass, wind, or percussion instruments. **3** a group of people with a common purpose or sharing a common feature. ● verb form a group for a common purpose.
– ORIGIN Old French *bande*; related to BANNER.
bandage ● noun a strip of material used to bind up a wound or to protect an injury. ● verb bind with a bandage.
– ORIGIN French, from *bande* 'band'.
bandanna /bandannə/ ● noun a large coloured handkerchief or neckerchief.
– ORIGIN Hindi.
bandbox ● noun a circular cardboard box for carrying hats.
bandeau /bandō/ ● noun (pl. **bandeaux** /bandōz/) **1** a narrow band worn round the head to hold the hair in position. **2** a woman's strapless top consisting of a band of fabric fitting around the bust.
– ORIGIN Old French *bandel* 'small band'.
banderilla /bandərilyə/ ● noun a decorated dart thrust into a bull's neck or shoulders during a bullfight.
– ORIGIN Spanish, 'small banner'.
banderillero /bandərilyairō/ ● noun (pl. **banderillos**) a bullfighter who uses banderillas.
– ORIGIN Spanish.
bandicoot /bandikōōt/ ● noun a mainly insectivorous marsupial native to Australia and New Guinea.
– ORIGIN from an Indian language, meaning 'pig-rat'.
bandicoot rat ● noun an Asian rat that is a destructive pest.
bandit ● noun (pl. **bandits** or **banditti** /bandeeti/) a member of a gang of armed robbers.
– DERIVATIVES **banditry** noun.
– ORIGIN from Italian *bandito* 'banned'.
bandog ● noun a fighting dog bred for its strength and ferocity.
– ORIGIN from BAND¹, because the dog was originally kept on a chain or 'band'.
bandolier /bandəleer/ (also **bandoleer**) ● noun a shoulder belt with loops or pockets for cartridges.
– ORIGIN French *bandoulière*.
bandsaw ● noun a saw consisting of an endless moving steel belt with a serrated edge.
bandstand ● noun a covered outdoor platform for a band to play on.
bandwagon ● noun an activity or cause that has suddenly become fashionable or popular: *the company is jumping on the Green bandwagon.*
– ORIGIN from the former use of a wagon to carry a band in a parade.
bandwidth ● noun **1** a range of frequencies, especially one used in telecommunications. **2** the transmission capacity of a computer network or other telecommunication system.
bandy¹ ● adjective (**bandier**, **bandiest**) (of a person's legs) curved outwards so that the knees are wide apart.
– ORIGIN perhaps from obsolete *bandy* 'curved hockey stick'.
bandy² ● verb (**bandies**, **bandied**) (usu. **bandy about/around**) pass on or mention (an idea, term, or rumour) in a casual or uninformed way.
– PHRASES **bandy words** exchange angry remarks.
– ORIGIN perhaps from French *bander* 'take sides at tennis'; related to BAND².
bane ● noun a cause of great distress or annoyance.
– ORIGIN Old English, 'thing causing death, poison'.
bang ● noun **1** a sudden loud sharp noise. **2** a sudden painful blow. **3** (**bangs**) chiefly N. Amer. a fringe of hair cut straight across the forehead. ● verb **1** strike or put down forcefully and

Thesaurus

– OPPOSITES harsh, wintry.
bamboozle ● verb *(informal)*. See TRICK verb.
ban ● verb **1** *smoking was banned* PROHIBIT, forbid, veto, proscribe, disallow, outlaw, make illegal, embargo, bar, debar, block, stop, suppress, interdict; *Law* enjoin, restrain. **2** *Gary was banned from the playground* EXCLUDE, banish, expel, eject, evict, drive out, force out, oust, remove, get rid of; *informal* boot out, kick out; *Brit. informal* turf out.
– OPPOSITES permit, admit.
● noun **1** *a ban on smoking* PROHIBITION, veto, proscription, embargo, bar, suppression, stoppage, interdict, interdiction, moratorium, injunction. **2** *a ban from international football* EXCLUSION, banishment, expulsion, ejection, eviction, removal.
– OPPOSITES permission, admission.
banal ● adjective TRITE, hackneyed, clichéd, platitudinous, vapid, commonplace, ordinary, common, stock, conventional, stereotyped, overused, overdone, overworked, stale, worn out, time-worn, tired, threadbare, hoary, hack, unimaginative, unoriginal, uninteresting, dull; *informal* old hat, corny, played out; *N. Amer. informal* cornball, dime-store.
– OPPOSITES original.
banality ● noun **1** *the banality of most TV sitcoms* TRITENESS, platitudinousness, vapidity, staleness, unimaginativeness, lack of originality, prosaicness, dullness; *informal* corniness. **2** *they exchanged banalities* PLATITUDE, cliché, truism, commonplace, old chestnut, bromide.
– OPPOSITES originality, epigram, witticism.
band¹ ● noun **1** *a band round her waist* BELT, sash, girdle, strap, tape, ring, hoop, loop, circlet, circle, cord, tie, string, thong, ribbon, fillet, strip; *poetic/literary* cincture. **2** *the green band round his pullover* STRIPE, strip, streak, line, bar, belt, swathe; *technical* stria, striation.
band² ● noun **1** *a band of robbers* GROUP, gang, mob, pack, troop, troupe, company, party, crew, body, working party, posse; team, side, line-up; association, society, club, circle, fellowship, partnership, guild, lodge, order, fraternity, confraternity, sodality, brotherhood, sisterhood, sorority, union, alliance, affiliation, institution, league, federation, clique, set, coterie; *informal* bunch. **2** *the band played on* (MUSICAL) GROUP, pop group, ensemble, orchestra; *informal* combo.
● verb *local people banded together* JOIN (UP), team up, join forces, pool resources, club together, get together; amalgamate, unite, form an alliance, form an association, affiliate, federate.
– OPPOSITES split up.
bandage ● noun *she had a bandage on her foot* DRESSING, covering, gauze, compress, plaster, tourniquet; *trademark* Elastoplast, Band-Aid.
● verb *she bandaged my knee* BIND, bind up, dress, cover, wrap, swaddle, strap (up).
bandit ● noun *they were robbed by bandits* ROBBER, thief, raider, mugger; freebooter, outlaw, hijacker, looter, marauder, gangster; *dated* desperado; *poetic/literary* brigand; *historical* rustler, highwayman, footpad, reaver; *Scottish historical* mosstrooper.
bandy¹ ● adjective *bandy legs* BOWED, curved, bent; bow-legged, bandy-legged.
– OPPOSITES straight.
bandy² ● verb **1** *lots of figures were bandied about* SPREAD (ABOUT/AROUND), put about, toss about, discuss, rumour, mention, repeat; *poetic/literary* bruit about/abroad. **2** *I'm not going to bandy words with you* EXCHANGE, swap, trade.
bane ● noun SCOURGE, plague, curse, blight, pest, nuisance, headache, nightmare, trial, hardship, cross to bear, burden, thorn in

noisily. **2** make or cause to make a bang. **3** vulgar slang (of a man) have sexual intercourse with. ● **adverb** informal, chiefly Brit. exactly: *bang on time.*
– PHRASES **bang away at** informal do persistently or doggedly. **bang goes ——** informal a plan or hope is suddenly destroyed. **bang on** Brit. informal exactly right. **bang on about** informal talk at tedious length about. **bang up** Brit. informal imprison. **with a bang** suddenly or spectacularly.
– ORIGIN imitative, perhaps Scandinavian.
banger ● **noun** chiefly Brit. **1** informal a sausage. **2** informal an old car. **3** a loud explosive firework.
Bangladeshi /banggləddeshi/ ● **noun** (pl. same or **Bangladeshis**) a person from Bangladesh. ● **adjective** relating to Bangladesh.
bangle ● **noun** a rigid ornamental band worn around the arm.
– ORIGIN Hindi.
bang-up ● **adjective** N. Amer. informal excellent.
bani plural of BAN².
banish ● **verb** **1** make (someone) leave a place, especially as an official punishment. **2** get rid of; drive away.
– DERIVATIVES **banishment** noun.
– ORIGIN Old French *banir.*
banister (also **bannister**) ● **noun** **1** (also **banisters**) the uprights and handrail at the side of a staircase. **2** a single upright at the side of a staircase.
– ORIGIN from BALUSTER.
banjax /banjaks/ ● **verb** informal ruin or incapacitate.
– ORIGIN Anglo-Irish.
banjo ● **noun** (pl. **banjos** or **banjoes**) a stringed musical instrument with a circular body and a long neck.
– DERIVATIVES **banjoist** noun.
– ORIGIN from a black American alteration of *bandore,* denoting a kind of lute.
bank¹ ● **noun** **1** the land alongside or sloping down to a river or lake. **2** a long, raised mound or mass: *mud banks.* **3** a set of similar things grouped together in rows. ● **verb** **1** heap or form into a mass or mound. **2** (of an aircraft or vehicle) tilt sideways in making a turn. **3** build (a road, railway, or sports track) higher at the outer edge of a bend.
– ORIGIN Old Norse, related to BENCH.
bank² ● **noun** **1** an organization offering financial services, especially the safekeeping of customers' money until required and making loans at interest. **2** a stock or supply available for use: *a blood bank.* **3** a site or container where something may be left for recycling: *a paper bank.* **4** (**the bank**) the store of money or tokens held by the banker in some gambling or board games. ● **verb** **1** deposit in a bank. **2** have an account at a bank. **3** (**bank on**) rely on.
– PHRASES **break the bank** informal cost more than one can afford.
– ORIGIN originally denoting a money dealer's table: from Latin *banca* 'bench'.
bankable ● **adjective** certain to bring profit and success.
bank card ● **noun** a cheque card.
banker¹ ● **noun** **1** a person who manages or owns a bank. **2** the person who keeps the bank in some gambling or board games.
banker² ● **noun** Austral./NZ informal a river flooded to the top of its banks.
bank holiday ● **noun** Brit. a public holiday, when banks are officially closed.
banking¹ ● **noun** the business conducted or services offered by a bank.
banking² ● **noun** an embankment or artificial bank.
banknote ● **noun** a piece of paper money issued by a central bank.
bank rate ● **noun** another term for BASE RATE or DISCOUNT RATE.
bankroll ● **noun** N. Amer. **1** a roll of banknotes. **2** available funds. ● **verb** informal support financially.
bankrupt ● **adjective** **1** declared in law unable to pay one's debts. **2** completely lacking in a particular good quality or value: *morally bankrupt.* ● **noun** a person legally declared as bankrupt. ● **verb** reduce to a bankrupt state.
– DERIVATIVES **bankruptcy** noun (pl. **bankruptcies**).
– ORIGIN from Italian *banca rotta* 'broken bench'.
banksia /bangksiə/ ● **noun** an evergreen Australian shrub with flowers resembling bottlebrushes.
– ORIGIN named after the English botanist Sir Joseph *Banks* (1743–1820).
banner ● **noun** a long strip of cloth bearing a slogan or design, hung up or carried on poles. ● **adjective** N. Amer. excellent; outstanding: *a banner year.*
– ORIGIN Old French *baniere.*
bannister ● **noun** variant spelling of BANISTER.

Thesaurus

one's flesh/side, bitter pill, affliction, trouble, misery, woe, tribulation, misfortune; *informal* pain.
bang ● **noun** **1** *the door slammed with a bang* THUD, thump, bump, crack, crash, smack, boom, clang, peal, clap, knock, tap, clunk, clonk; stamp, stomp, clump, clomp; report, explosion, detonation; *informal* wham, whump, whomp. **2** *a nasty bang on the head* BLOW, knock, thump, bump, hit, smack, crack; *informal* bash, whack, thwack.
● **verb** **1** *he banged the table* HIT, strike, beat, thump, hammer, knock, rap, pound, thud, punch, bump, smack, crack, slap, slam, welt, cuff, pummel, buffet; *informal* bash, whack, thwack, clobber, clout, clip, wallop, belt, tan, biff, bop, sock, lam, whomp; *Brit. informal* slosh; *N. Amer. informal* boff, bust, slug, whale. **2** *fireworks banged in the air* GO BANG, go off with a bang, thud, thump, boom, peal, clap, pound, crack, crash, explode, detonate, burst, blow up.
● **adverb** *(informal)* **1** *bang in the middle of town | bang on time* PRECISELY, exactly, right, directly, immediately, squarely, dead; promptly, prompt, dead on, on the stroke of ——, on the dot of ——; sharp, on the dot; *informal* smack, slap, slap bang, plumb; *N. Amer. informal* on the button, on the nose, smack dab, spang. **2** *bang up to date* COMPLETELY, absolutely, totally, entirely, wholly, fully, thoroughly, in all respects, utterly, perfectly, quite, altogether, one hundred per cent.
bangle ● **noun** BRACELET, wristlet, anklet, armlet.
banish ● **verb** **1** *he was banished for his crime* EXILE, expel, deport, eject, expatriate, extradite, repatriate, transport; cast out, oust, evict, throw out, exclude, shut out, ban. **2** *he tried to banish his fear* DISPEL, dismiss, disperse, scatter, dissipate, drive away, chase away, shut out, quell, allay.
– OPPOSITES admit, engender.
banister ● **noun** HANDRAIL, railing, rail; baluster; balustrade.
bank¹ ● **noun** **1** *the banks of Lake Michigan* EDGE, side, embankment, levee, border, verge, boundary, margin, rim, fringe; *poetic/literary* marge, bourn, skirt. **2** *a grassy bank* SLOPE, rise, incline, gradient, ramp; mound, ridge, hillock, hummock, knoll; bar, reef, shoal, shelf; accumulation, pile, heap, mass, drift. **3** *a bank of switches* ARRAY, row, line, tier, group, series.
– RELATED TERMS riparian, riverain.
● **verb** **1** *they banked up the earth* PILE (UP), heap (up), stack (up); accumulate, amass, assemble, put together. **2** *the aircraft banked* TILT, LEAN, tip, slant, incline, angle, slope, list, camber, pitch, dip, cant.
bank² ● **noun** **1** *money in the bank* FINANCIAL INSTITUTION, merchant bank, savings bank, finance company, finance house; *Brit.* building society; *N. Amer.* savings and loan (association), thrift. **2** *a blood bank* STORE, reserve, accumulation, stock, stockpile, supply, pool, fund, cache, hoard, deposit; storehouse, reservoir, repository, depository.
● **verb** **1** *I banked the money* DEPOSIT, pay in. **2** *they bank with Barclays* HAVE AN ACCOUNT AT, deposit one's money with, use, be a customer of.
– PHRASES **bank on** RELY ON, depend on, count on, place reliance on, bargain on, plan on, reckon on, calculate on; anticipate, expect; be confident of, be sure of, pin one's hopes/faith on; *N. Amer. informal* figure on.
banknote ● **noun** NOTE; *N. Amer.* bill; *US informal* greenback; *US & historical* Treasury note; (**banknotes**) paper money.
bankrupt ● **adjective** **1** *the company was declared bankrupt* INSOLVENT, failed, ruined, in debt, owing money, in the red, in arrears; *Brit.* in administration, in receivership; *informal* bust, belly up, gone to the wall, broke, flat broke; *informal, dated* smashed; *Brit. informal* skint, stony broke, in Queer Street; *Brit. informal, dated* in Carey Street. **2** *this government is bankrupt of ideas* BEREFT, devoid, empty, destitute; completely lacking, without, in need of, wanting; *informal* minus, sans.
– OPPOSITES solvent, teeming with.
● **verb** *the strike nearly bankrupted the union* RUIN, impoverish, reduce to penury/destitution, bring to ruin, bring someone to their knees, wipe out, break, pauperize; *rare* beggar.
bankruptcy ● **noun** *many companies were facing bankruptcy* INSOLVENCY, liquidation, failure, (financial) ruin; *Brit.* administration, receivership.

b

bannock /bannək/ • noun Scots & N. English a round, flat loaf.
– ORIGIN Old English.
banns • plural noun a public announcement of an intended marriage read out in a parish church.
– ORIGIN plural of BAN[1].
banoffi pie /bənoffee/ (also **banoffee pie**) • noun a flan filled with bananas, toffee, and cream.
– ORIGIN from BANANA + TOFFEE.
banquet /bangkwit/ • noun an elaborate and formal meal for many people. • verb (**banqueted**, **banqueting**) entertain with a banquet.
– ORIGIN French, 'little bench'.
banquette /bangket/ • noun an upholstered bench along a wall.
– ORIGIN French, from Italian *banchetta* 'little bench'.
banshee /banshee/ • noun (in Irish legend) a female spirit whose wailing warns of a death in a house.
– ORIGIN from Old Irish *ben síde* 'woman of the fairies'.
bantam • noun a chicken of a small breed.
– ORIGIN apparently named after the province of *Bantam* in Java.
bantamweight • noun a weight in boxing and other sports between flyweight and featherweight.
banter • noun the good-humoured exchange of teasing remarks. • verb engage in banter.
– ORIGIN of unknown origin.
Bantu /bantoo/ • noun (pl. same or **Bantus**) **1** a member of a large group of peoples of central and southern Africa. **2** the group of languages spoken by these peoples.
– USAGE **Bantu** is a strongly offensive word in South African English, especially when used of individual people, but is still used outside South Africa to refer to the group of languages and their speakers collectively.
– ORIGIN Bantu, 'people'.
banyan /banyən/ (also **banian**) • noun an Indian fig tree, whose branches produce aerial roots which later become new trunks.
– ORIGIN originally applied by Europeans to a tree under which traders had built a pagoda: from Gujarati, 'trader'.
banzai /baanzī/ • exclamation a cry used by the Japanese when going into battle or in greeting their emperor. • adjective informal fierce and reckless.
– ORIGIN Japanese, 'ten thousand years (of life to you)'.
baobab /bayōbab/ • noun a short African tree with a very thick trunk and large edible fruit.
– ORIGIN probably from an African language.
bap • noun Brit. a soft, round, flattish bread roll.
– ORIGIN of unknown origin.
baptism • noun the Christian rite of sprinkling a person with water or immersing them in it, symbolizing purification and admission to the Christian Church.
– PHRASES **baptism of fire** a difficult new experience.
– DERIVATIVES **baptismal** adjective.
– ORIGIN from Greek *baptizein* 'immerse, baptize'.
Baptist • noun a member of a Protestant Christian denomination believing that baptism should be by total immersion and of adult believers only.
baptistery (also **baptistry**) • noun (pl. **baptisteries**) a building or part of a church used for baptism.
baptize (also **baptise**) • verb **1** administer baptism to. **2** give a name or nickname to.
– ORIGIN Greek *baptizein* 'immerse, baptize'.
bar[1] • noun **1** a long rigid piece of wood, metal, etc. **2** a counter, room, or place where alcoholic drinks or refreshments are served. **3** a small shop or counter serving refreshments or providing a service: *a snack bar*. **4** a barrier or obstacle. **5** any of the short units into which a piece of music is divided, shown on a score by vertical lines. **6** (**the bar**) a partition in a court room, now usually imaginary, at which an accused person stands. **7** (**the Bar**) the profession of barrister. **8** (**the Bar**) barristers or (N. Amer.) lawyers collectively. **9** Brit. a metal strip added to a medal as an additional distinction. • verb (**barred**, **barring**) **1** fasten with a bar or bars. **2** prohibit from doing something or going somewhere. • preposition chiefly Brit. except for.
– PHRASES **be called** (or **go**) **to the Bar** Brit. be admitted as a barrister. **behind bars** in prison.
– DERIVATIVES **barred** adjective.
– ORIGIN Old French *barre*.
bar[2] • noun a unit of pressure equivalent to a hundred thousand newtons per square metre.
– ORIGIN Greek *baros* 'weight'.
barathea /barrətheeə/ • noun a fine woollen cloth.
– ORIGIN of unknown origin.
barb • noun **1** a sharp projection near the end of an arrow, fish hook, etc., which is angled away from the main point so as to make extraction difficult. **2** a deliberately hurtful remark.
– DERIVATIVES **barbless** adjective.
– ORIGIN originally denoting a piece of linen worn by nuns over or under the chin: from Latin *barba* 'beard'.
Barbadian /baarbaydiən/ • noun a person from Barbados. • adjective relating to Barbados.
barbarian • noun **1** (in ancient times) a member of a people not belonging to the Greek, Roman, or Christian civilizations. **2** an uncivilized or cruel person. • adjective uncivilized or cruel.
– ORIGIN from Greek *barbaros* 'foreign'.
barbaric • adjective **1** savagely cruel. **2** primitive; unsophisticated.
– DERIVATIVES **barbarically** adverb.
barbarism • noun **1** extreme cruelty. **2** an uncivilized or primitive state. **3** a word or expression which is badly formed according to traditional rules, e.g. the word *television*, which is formed from two different languages.
– DERIVATIVES **barbarity** noun.
barbarous • adjective **1** exceedingly cruel. **2** primitive; uncivil-

Thesaurus

– OPPOSITES solvency.
banner • noun **1** *students waved banners* PLACARD, sign, poster, notice. **2** *banners fluttered above the troops* FLAG, standard, ensign, colour(s), pennant, banderole, guidon; *Brit.* pendant; *Nautical* burgee.
banquet • noun FEAST, dinner; *informal* spread, blowout; *Brit. informal* nosh-up, slap-up meal; *Brit. informal, dated* tuck-in.
– OPPOSITES snack.
banter • noun *a brief exchange of banter* REPARTEE, witty conversation, raillery, wordplay, cut and thrust, badinage; *N. Amer. informal* josh.
• verb *sightseers were bantering with the guards* JOKE, jest, quip; *informal* josh, wisecrack.
baptism • noun **1** *the baptism ceremony* CHRISTENING, naming; *rare* lustration. **2** *his baptism as a politician* INITIATION, debut, introduction, inauguration, launch, rite of passage.
baptize • verb **1** *he was baptized as a baby* CHRISTEN; *rare* lustrate. **2** *they were baptized into the church* ADMIT, initiate, enrol, recruit, convert. **3** *he was baptized Enoch* NAME, give the name, call, dub; *formal* denominate.
bar • noun **1** *an iron bar* ROD, pole, stick, batten, shaft, rail, paling, spar, strut, crosspiece, beam. **2** *a bar of chocolate* BLOCK, slab, cake, tablet, brick, loaf, wedge, ingot. **3** *your drinks are on the bar* COUNTER, table, buffet, stand. **4** *she had a drink in a bar* HOSTELRY, tavern, inn, taproom; *Brit.* pub, public house; *informal* watering hole; *Brit. informal* local, boozer; *dated* alehouse; *N. Amer. historical* saloon. **5** *a bar to promotion* OBSTACLE, impediment, hindrance, obstruction, block, hurdle, barrier, stumbling block. **6** *members of the Bar* BARRISTERS, advocates, counsel. **7** *the bar across the river mouth* SANDBANK, shoal, shallow, reef.
– OPPOSITES aid.
• verb **1** *they have barred the door* BOLT, lock, fasten, secure, block, barricade, obstruct. **2** *I was barred from entering* PROHIBIT, debar, preclude, forbid, ban, interdict, inhibit; exclude, keep out; obstruct, hinder, block; *Law* enjoin.
– OPPOSITES open, admit.
• preposition *everyone bar me*. See EXCEPT preposition.
barb • noun **1** *the hook has a nasty barb* SPIKE, prong, spur, thorn, needle, prickle, spine, quill. **2** *the barbs from his critics* INSULT, sneer, jibe, cutting remark, shaft, slight, brickbat, slur, jeer, taunt; (**barbs**) abuse, disparagement, scoffing, scorn, sarcasm, goading; *informal* dig, put-down.
barbarian • noun *the city was besieged by barbarians* SAVAGE, heathen, brute, beast, wild man/woman; ruffian, thug, lout, vandal, hoodlum, hooligan; *informal* roughneck; *Brit. informal* yobbo, yob, lager lout.
• adjective *the barbarian hordes* SAVAGE, uncivilized, barbaric, primitive, heathen, wild, brutish, Neanderthal.
– OPPOSITES civilized.
barbaric • adjective **1** *barbaric crimes* BRUTAL, barbarous, brutish, bestial, savage, vicious, wicked, cruel, ruthless, merciless, villainous, murderous, heinous, monstrous, vile, inhuman, infernal, dark, fiendish, diabolical. **2** *barbaric cultures* SAVAGE, barbarian,

ized.
– DERIVATIVES **barbarously** adverb.
barbecue • noun **1** an outdoor meal or party at which food is grilled on a rack over a charcoal fire. **2** a grill used at a barbecue. • verb (**barbecues**, **barbecued**, **barbecuing**) cook (food) on a barbecue.
– ORIGIN originally in the sense 'wooden framework for sleeping on, or for drying meat or fish on': from Spanish *barbacoa*, perhaps from Arawak, 'wooden frame on posts'.
barbecue sauce • noun a highly seasoned sauce containing vinegar, spices, and usually chillies.
barbed • adjective **1** having a barb or barbs. **2** (of a remark) deliberately hurtful.
barbed wire • noun wire with clusters of short, sharp spikes at intervals along it.
barbel /baarb'l/ • noun **1** a fleshy filament growing from the mouth or snout of certain fish. **2** a large freshwater fish with barbels hanging from the mouth.
– ORIGIN Latin *barbellus* 'small barbel', from *barba* 'beard'.
barbell /baarbel/ • noun a long metal bar to which discs of varying weights are attached at each end, used for weightlifting.
barber • noun a person who cuts men's hair and shaves or trims beards as an occupation. • verb cut or trim (a man's hair).
– ORIGIN Old French *barbe* 'beard'.
barberry • noun another term for BERBERIS.
– ORIGIN Old French *berberis*.
barbershop • noun a style of unaccompanied close harmony singing, typically for four male voices.
barber's pole • noun a red-and-white striped pole mounted outside a barber's shop as a business sign.
barbican /baarbikən/ • noun a double tower above a gate or drawbridge of a castle or fortified city.
– ORIGIN Old French *barbacane*.
bar billiards • plural noun (treated as sing.) Brit. a form of billiards in which balls are struck into holes guarded by pegs.
barbiturate /baarbityoorət/ • noun any of a class of sedative drugs related to a synthetic compound (**barbituric acid**) derived from uric acid.
– ORIGIN from *barbituric acid*, from German *Barbitursäure*, from the name *Barbara* + *Ursäure* 'uric acid'
Barbour /baarbər/ (also **Barbour jacket**) • noun trademark a type of green waxed outdoor jacket.
– ORIGIN named after John *Barbour* & Sons Ltd., English clothing manufacturers.
bar chart (also **bar graph**) • noun a diagram in which different quantities are represented by rectangles of varying height.
bar code • noun a code in the form of a set of stripes of varying widths that can be read by a computer, printed on a product and identifying it for stock control.
bard[1] • noun **1** archaic or literary a poet, traditionally one reciting epics. **2** (**the Bard**) Shakespeare. **3** (**Bard**) the winner of a prize for Welsh verse at an Eisteddfod.
– DERIVATIVES **bardic** adjective.
– ORIGIN Celtic.
bard[2] • verb cover (meat or game) with rashers of fat bacon before roasting.
– ORIGIN from French *barde*, formerly also meaning 'armour for the breast of a warhorse'.
Bardolino /baardəleenō/ • noun a red wine from the Veneto region of Italy.
– ORIGIN Italian.
bare • adjective **1** not clothed or covered. **2** without the appropriate or usual covering or contents: *a big, bare room.* **3** without elaboration; basic: *the bare facts.* **4** only just sufficient: *a bare majority.* • verb uncover and reveal.
– PHRASES **with one's bare hands** without using tools or weapons.
– DERIVATIVES **barely** adverb **bareness** noun.
– ORIGIN Old English.
bareback • adverb & adjective on an unsaddled horse.
bareboat • adjective (of a boat or ship) hired without a crew.
barefaced • adjective shameless and undisguised: *a barefaced lie.*
barf • verb informal, chiefly N. Amer. vomit.
– ORIGIN of unknown origin.
bargain • noun **1** an agreement made between people as to what each will do for the other. **2** a thing bought or offered for sale for a low price. • verb **1** negotiate the terms of an agreement. **2** (**bargain for/on**) expect.
– PHRASES **drive a hard bargain** press forcefully for a deal in one's favour. **into the bargain** in addition.
– DERIVATIVES **bargainer** noun.
– ORIGIN Old French *bargaine*.
barge • noun **1** a long flat-bottomed boat for carrying freight on canals and rivers. **2** a large ornamental boat used for pleasure or on ceremonial occasions. • verb **1** move forcefully or roughly. **2** (**barge in**) intrude or interrupt rudely or awkwardly.
– ORIGIN Old French, perhaps from Greek *baris* 'Egyptian boat'.
bargeboard • noun an ornamental board fixed to the gable end of a roof to hide the ends of the roof timbers.

Thesaurus

primitive, heathen, wild, brutish, Neanderthal.
– OPPOSITES civilized.
barbarity • noun **1** *the barbarity of slavery* BRUTALITY, brutalism, cruelty, bestiality, barbarism, barbarousness, savagery, viciousness, wickedness, villainy, baseness, inhumanity. **2** *the barbarities of the last war* ATROCITY, act of brutality, act of savagery, crime, outrage, enormity.
– OPPOSITES benevolence.
barbarous • adjective. See BARBARIC sense 1.
barbecue • noun *she held a barbecue* MEAL COOKED OUTDOORS, —— roast; *N. Amer.* cookout; *informal* barbie, BBQ.
• verb *they barbecued some steaks* COOK OUTDOORS, grill, spit-roast; *N. Amer.* broil, charbroil.
barbed • adjective HURTFUL, wounding, cutting, stinging, mean, spiteful, nasty, cruel, vicious, unkind, snide, scathing, pointed, bitter, acid, caustic, sharp, vitriolic, venomous, poisonous, hostile, malicious, malevolent, vindictive; *informal* bitchy, catty.
– OPPOSITES kindly.
bard • noun *(poetic/literary)*. See POET.
bare • adjective **1** *he was bare to the waist* NAKED, unclothed, undressed, uncovered, stripped, having nothing on, nude, in the nude, stark naked; *informal* without a stitch on, in one's birthday suit, in the raw, in the altogether, in the buff, in the nuddy; *Brit. informal* starkers; *Scottish informal* in the scud, scuddy; *N. Amer. informal* buck naked. **2** *a bare room* EMPTY, unfurnished, cleared; stark, austere, spartan, unadorned, unembellished, unornamented, plain. **3** *a cupboard bare of food* EMPTY, devoid, bereft; without, lacking, wanting, free from. **4** *a bare landscape* BARREN, bleak, exposed, desolate, stark, arid, desert, lunar; treeless, deforested. **5** *the bare facts* BASIC, essential, fundamental, plain, straightforward, simple, pure, stark, bald, cold, hard, brutal, harsh. **6** *a bare minimum* MERE, no more than, simple; slim, slight, slender, paltry, minimum.
– OPPOSITES clothed, furnished, embellished, lush.
• verb *he bared his arm* UNCOVER, strip, lay bare, undress, unclothe, denude, expose.
– OPPOSITES cover.
barefaced • adjective FLAGRANT, blatant, glaring, obvious, undisguised, unconcealed; shameless, unabashed, unashamed, impudent, audacious, unblushing, brazen, brass-necked.
barely • adverb HARDLY, scarcely, just, only just, narrowly, by the skin of one's teeth, by a hair's breadth; almost not; *informal* by a whisker.
– OPPOSITES easily.
bargain • noun **1** *I'll make a bargain with you* AGREEMENT, arrangement, understanding, deal; contract, pact, compact; pledge, promise. **2** *these boots are a bargain at £40* GOOD BUY, cheap buy; (good) value for money, surprisingly cheap; *informal* snip, steal, giveaway.
– OPPOSITES rip-off.
• verb *they bargained over the contract* HAGGLE, negotiate, discuss terms, hold talks, deal, barter, dicker; *formal* treat.
– PHRASES **bargain for/on** EXPECT, anticipate, be prepared for, allow for, plan for, reckon with, take into account/consideration, contemplate, imagine, envisage, foresee, predict; count on, rely on, depend on, bank on, plan on, reckon on; *N. Amer. informal* figure on. **into the bargain** ALSO, as well, in addition, additionally, besides, on top (of that), over and above that, to boot, for good measure; *N. Amer.* in the bargain.
barge • noun lighter, canal boat; *Brit.* narrowboat, wherry; *N. Amer.* scow.
• verb *he barged us out of the way* PUSH, shove, force, elbow, shoul-

b

– ORIGIN from *barge-* (used in terms relating to the gable of a building), perhaps from Latin *bargus* 'gallows'.
bargee /baarjee/ • noun chiefly Brit. a person in charge of or working on a barge.
bargepole • noun a long pole used to propel a barge and fend off obstacles.
– PHRASES **would not touch with a bargepole** informal would refuse to have anything to do with.
bar graph • noun a bar chart.
barite • noun variant spelling of BARYTE.
baritone • noun **1** an adult male singing voice between tenor and bass. **2** (before another noun) denoting an instrument that is second lowest in pitch in its family: *a baritone sax.*
– ORIGIN Greek *barutonos*, from *barus* 'heavy' + *tonos* 'tone'.
barium /bairiəm/ • noun a soft, reactive metallic chemical element.
– ORIGIN from BARYTE.
barium meal • noun a preparation containing barium sulphate, opaque to X-rays, which is swallowed so that the stomach or intestines can be studied radiologically.
bark[1] • noun the sharp explosive cry of a dog, fox, or seal. • verb **1** give a bark. **2** utter (a command or question) abruptly or aggressively.
– PHRASES **one's bark is worse than one's bite** one is not as ferocious as one seems. **be barking up the wrong tree** informal be pursuing a mistaken line of thought or course of action.
– ORIGIN Old English.
bark[2] • noun the tough protective outer sheath of the trunk and branches of a tree or woody shrub. • verb **1** strip the bark from. **2** scrape the skin off (one's shin) by accidentally hitting it.
– ORIGIN Old Norse.
bark[3] • noun archaic or literary a ship or boat.
– ORIGIN variant of BARQUE.
barker • noun informal a tout at an auction or sideshow who calls out to passers-by to attract custom.
barking • adjective Brit. informal completely mad.
barley • noun a hardy cereal with coarse bristles extending from the ears, used chiefly in brewing and animal feed.
– ORIGIN Old English.
barley sugar • noun an amber-coloured sweet made of boiled sugar.
barley water • noun a drink made from water and a boiled barley mixture.
barley wine • noun a strong English ale.
barm • noun the froth on fermenting malt liquor.
– ORIGIN Old English.
barmaid • noun a woman who serves drinks in a bar or public house.
barman • noun chiefly Brit. a man who serves drinks in a bar or public house.
bar mitzvah /baa mitsvə/ • noun the religious initiation ceremony of a Jewish boy who has reached the age of 13.
– ORIGIN Hebrew, 'son of the commandment'.
barmy • adjective (**barmier**, **barmiest**) informal, chiefly Brit. extremely foolish; mad.
– DERIVATIVES **barmily** adverb **barminess** noun.
– ORIGIN originally in the sense 'frothy': from BARM.
barn • noun a large farm building used for storage or for housing livestock.
– ORIGIN Old English, 'barley house'.
barnacle /baarnək'l/ • noun a marine crustacean which attaches itself permanently to underwater surfaces.
– DERIVATIVES **barnacled** adjective.
– ORIGIN Latin *bernaca*.
barnacle goose • noun a goose with a white face and black neck, breeding in arctic tundra.
– ORIGIN from the former belief that the bird hatched from barnacles.
barn dance • noun **1** an informal social gathering for country dancing. **2** a dance for a number of couples moving round a circle, typically involving changes of partner.
barnet /baarnit/ • noun Brit. informal a person's hair.
– ORIGIN from rhyming slang *barnet fair* (a horse fair held at *Barnet*, Herts).
barney • noun (pl. **barneys**) Brit. informal a noisy quarrel.
– ORIGIN of unknown origin.
barn owl • noun a pale-coloured owl with a heart-shaped face, typically nesting in farm buildings.
barnstorm • verb chiefly N. Amer. **1** tour rural districts giving theatrical performances, formerly often in barns. **2** make a rapid tour as part of a political campaign.
barnstorming • adjective flamboyantly vigorous and effective.
barnyard • noun N. Amer. a farmyard.
barograph • noun a barometer that records its readings on a moving chart.
Barolo /bərōlō/ • noun a full-bodied red wine from Barolo, in the Piedmont region of Italy.
barometer • noun **1** an instrument measuring atmospheric pressure, used especially in forecasting the weather. **2** an indicator of change: *furniture is a barometer of changing tastes.*
– DERIVATIVES **barometric** adjective.
– ORIGIN from Greek *baros* 'weight'.
baron • noun **1** a member of the lowest order of the British nobility. **2** historical a person who held lands or property from the sovereign or an overlord. **3** a powerful person in business or industry: *a press baron.*
– DERIVATIVES **baronial** /bərōniəl/ adjective.
– ORIGIN Latin *baro* 'man, warrior'.
baronage • noun (treated as sing. or pl.) barons or nobles collectively.
baroness • noun **1** the wife or widow of a baron. **2** a woman holding the rank of baron.
baronet • noun a member of the lowest hereditary titled British order.
– DERIVATIVES **baronetcy** noun.
baron of beef • noun Brit. a joint of beef consisting of two sirloins joined at the backbone.
barony • noun (pl. **baronies**) the rank and estates of a baron.
baroque /bərok/ • noun a highly ornate and complex style of European architecture, art, and music of the 17th and 18th centuries. • adjective **1** in or relating to this style or period. **2** highly ornate and extravagant in style.
– ORIGIN French, from Portuguese *barroco* 'irregularly shaped pearl'.
barouche /bəroosh/ • noun historical a four-wheeled horse-drawn carriage with a collapsible hood over the rear half.
– ORIGIN Italian *baroccio* 'two-wheeled carriage'.
barque /baark/ • noun **1** a sailing ship in which the foremast and mainmast are square-rigged and the mizzenmast is rigged fore and aft. **2** literary a boat.
– ORIGIN Latin *barca* 'ship's boat'.
barrack[1] • verb provide (soldiers) with accommodation.
barrack[2] • verb **1** Brit. & Austral./NZ jeer loudly at (a performer or speaker). **2** (**barrack for**) Austral./NZ support and encourage.
– ORIGIN probably from Northern Irish dialect.
barrack-room lawyer • noun Brit. a person who speaks with apparent authority on subjects in which they are not qualified.
barracks • plural noun (often treated as sing.) a large building or

Thesaurus

der, jostle, bulldoze, muscle.
– PHRASES **barge in** BURST IN, break in, butt in, cut in, interrupt, intrude, encroach; gatecrash; *informal* horn in.
bark[1] • noun *the bark of a dog* WOOF, yap, yelp, bay.
• verb **1** *the dog barked* WOOF, yap, yelp, bay. **2** *'Okay, outside!' he barked* SAY BRUSQUELY, say abruptly, say angrily, snap; shout, bawl, cry, yell, roar, bellow, thunder; *informal* holler.
– OPPOSITES whisper.
bark[2] • noun *the bark of a tree* RIND, skin, peel, covering; integument; cork; *technical* cortex.
– RELATED TERMS corticate.
• verb *he barked his shin* SCRAPE, graze, scratch, abrade, scuff, rasp, skin.
barmy • adjective *(Brit. informal).* See FOOLISH.
barn • noun OUTBUILDING, shed, outhouse, shelter; stable, stall; *Brit.* byre; *archaic* grange, garner.
baron • noun **1** *he was created a baron* LORD, noble, nobleman, aristocrat, peer. **2** *a press baron* MAGNATE, tycoon, mogul, captain of industry, nabob, mandarin.
baroque • adjective **1** *the baroque exuberance of his printed silk shirts* ORNATE, fancy, over-elaborate, extravagant, rococo, fussy, busy, ostentatious, showy. **2** *baroque prose* FLOWERY, florid, flamboyant, high-flown, high-sounding, magniloquent, grandiloquent, orotund, overblown, convoluted, pleonastic; *informal* highfalutin, purple; *rare* fustian.
– OPPOSITES plain.

group of buildings for housing soldiers.
– ORIGIN Italian *baracca* or Spanish *barraca* 'soldier's tent'.
barracouta /barrəkōōtə/ • noun (pl. same or **barracoutas**) **1** a long, slender fish of southern oceans, used as food. **2** NZ a long loaf of bread.
– ORIGIN alteration of BARRACUDA.
barracuda /barrəkōōdə/ • noun (pl. same or **barracudas**) a large, slender predatory fish of tropical seas.
– ORIGIN of unknown origin.
barrage /barraazh/ • noun **1** a concentrated artillery bombardment over a wide area. **2** an overwhelming succession of questions or complaints. **3** Brit. an artificial barrier across a river to control the water level. • verb bombard with questions or complaints.
– ORIGIN French, from *barrer* 'to bar'.
barrage balloon • noun a large anchored balloon, typically with netting suspended from it, used as an obstacle to low-flying enemy aircraft.
barramundi /barrəmundi/ • noun (pl. same or **barramundis**) a large, chiefly freshwater fish of Australia and SE Asia.
– ORIGIN probably from an Aboriginal language.
barre /baar/ • noun a horizontal bar at waist level used by ballet dancers as a support during exercises.
– ORIGIN French.
barrel • noun **1** a large cylindrical container bulging out in the middle and with flat ends. **2** a measure of capacity for oil and beer (36 imperial gallons for beer and 35 for oil). **3** a cylindrical tube forming part of an object such as a gun or a pen. • verb (**barrelled**, **barrelling**; US **barreled**, **barreling**) **1** informal, chiefly N. Amer. drive or move very fast. **2** put into a barrel or barrels.
– PHRASES **over a barrel** informal in a severely disadvantageous position.
– ORIGIN Latin *barriclus* 'small cask'.
barrel organ • noun a small pipe organ that plays a preset tune when a handle is turned.
barrel vault • noun Architecture a vault forming a half cylinder.
barren • adjective **1** (of land) too poor to produce vegetation. **2** (of a female animal) unable to bear young. **3** bleak and lifeless. **4** (**barren of**) without.
– DERIVATIVES **barrenness** noun.
– ORIGIN Old French *barhaine*.
barrette /baret/ • noun a hairslide.
– ORIGIN French, 'small bar'.
barricade /barrikayd/ • noun an improvised barrier erected to block a road or entrance. • verb block or defend with a barricade.
– ORIGIN French, from Spanish *barrica* 'cask'; related to BARREL (barrels being used to build the first barricades in Paris).
barrier • noun **1** an obstacle that prevents movement or access. **2** an obstacle to communication or progress: *a language barrier*.
– ORIGIN Old French *barriere*.
barrier cream • noun Brit. a cream used to protect the skin from damage or infection.
barrier method • noun contraception using a device or preparation which prevents sperm from reaching an ovum.
barrier reef • noun a coral reef close to the shore but separated from it by a channel of deep water.
barring • preposition except for; if not for.
barrio /barriō/ • noun (pl. **barrios**) **1** (in a Spanish-speaking country) a district of a town. **2** (in the US) the Spanish-speaking quarter of a town or city.
– ORIGIN Spanish.
barrister • noun chiefly Brit. a lawyer entitled to practise as an advocate, particularly in the higher courts. Compare with SOLICITOR.
– ORIGIN from BAR[1].
barrow[1] • noun Brit. a two-wheeled handcart used by street traders.
– ORIGIN Old English, 'stretcher, bier'.
barrow[2] • noun Archaeology an ancient burial mound.
– ORIGIN Old English.
Barsac /baarsak/ • noun a sweet white wine from the district of Barsac in SW France.
Bart • abbreviation Baronet.
bartender • noun a person serving drinks at a bar.
barter • verb exchange (goods or services) for other goods or services. • noun trading by bartering.
– ORIGIN probably from Old French *barater* 'deceive'.
baryon /barrion/ • noun Physics a subatomic particle with a mass equal to or greater than that of a proton, such as a nucleon.
– ORIGIN from Greek *barus* 'heavy'.
baryte /barīt/ (also **barytes** /bərīteez/, **barite**) • noun a colourless or white mineral consisting of barium sulphate.
– ORIGIN from Greek *barus* 'heavy'.
basal /bays'l/ • adjective forming or belonging to a base.
basal metabolic rate • noun the rate at which the body uses energy while at rest to maintain vital functions such as breathing and keeping warm.
basalt /bassawlt/ • noun a dark fine-grained volcanic rock that sometimes displays a columnar structure.
– DERIVATIVES **basaltic** /bəsawltik/ adjective.
– ORIGIN Latin *basaltes*, from Greek *basanos* 'touchstone'.
bascule bridge /baskyōōl/ • noun a type of bridge with a section which can be raised and lowered using counterweights.
– ORIGIN French *bascule* 'see-saw', from *battre* 'to bump' + *cul* 'buttocks'.
base[1] • noun **1** the lowest part or edge of something, especially the part on which it rests. **2** a foundation, support, or starting point: *the town's economic base collapsed.* **3** the main place where a person works or stays. **4** a centre of operations: *a military base.* **5** a main element or ingredient to which others are added. **6** Chemistry a substance capable of reacting with an acid to form a salt and water. **7** the root or stem of a word. **8** Mathematics a number used as the basis of a numeration scale. **9** Baseball each of the four stations that must be reached in turn to score a run. • verb **1** use something as the foundation for. **2** situate at a centre of operations.
– PHRASES **get to first base** informal, chiefly N. Amer. achieve the first step towards one's objective. **touch base** informal, chiefly N. Amer. briefly make or renew contact.
– DERIVATIVES **based** adjective.
– ORIGIN Greek *basis* 'base, pedestal'.
base[2] • adjective **1** without moral principles; ignoble. **2** archaic of low social class. **3** (of coins) not made of precious metal.

Thesaurus

barrack • verb *(Brit. & Austral./NZ)* JEER, heckle, shout at/down; interrupt, boo, hiss.
– OPPOSITES applaud.
barracks • plural noun GARRISON, camp, encampment, depot, billet, quarters, fort, cantonment.
barrage • noun **1** *an artillery barrage* BOMBARDMENT, cannonade; gunfire, shelling; salvo, volley, fusillade; *historical* broadside. **2** *a barrage of criticism* DELUGE, stream, storm, torrent, onslaught, flood, spate, tide, avalanche, hail, blaze; abundance, mass, profusion. **3** *a barrage across the river* DAM, barrier, weir, dyke, embankment, wall.
barrel • noun CASK, keg, butt, vat, tun, drum, hogshead, kilderkin, pin, pipe; *historical* firkin.
– RELATED TERMS cooper, stave, hoop.
barren • adjective **1** *barren land* UNPRODUCTIVE, infertile, unfruitful, sterile, arid, desert. **2** *a barren woman* INFERTILE, sterile, childless; *technical* infecund. **3** *a barren exchange of courtesies* POINTLESS, futile, worthless, profitless, valueless, unrewarding, purposeless, useless, vain, aimless, hollow, empty, vacuous, vapid.
– OPPOSITES fertile.
barricade • noun *a barricade across the street* BARRIER, roadblock, blockade; obstacle, obstruction.
• verb *they barricaded the building* SEAL (UP), close up, block off, shut off/up; defend, protect, fortify, occupy.
barrier • noun **1** *the barrier across the entrance* FENCE, railing, barricade, hurdle, bar, blockade, roadblock. **2** *a barrier to international trade* OBSTACLE, obstruction, hurdle, stumbling block, bar, block, impediment, hindrance, curb.
barring • preposition EXCEPT FOR, with the exception of, excepting, if there is/are no, bar, discounting, short of, apart from, but for, other than, aside from, excluding, omitting, leaving out, save for, saving; *informal* outside of.
barrister • noun COUNSEL, Queen's Counsel, QC, lawyer; *Scottish* advocate; *N. Amer.* attorney, counselor(-at-law); *informal* brief; (**barristers**) the Bar.
barter • verb **1** *they bartered grain for salt* TRADE, swap, exchange, sell. **2** *you can barter for souvenirs* HAGGLE, bargain, negotiate, discuss terms, deal, dicker; *formal* treat.

b

– DERIVATIVES **baseness** noun.
– ORIGIN Latin *bassus* 'short'.
baseball ● noun a game played with a bat and ball between two teams on a diamond-shaped circuit of four bases, around all of which a batsman must run to score.
baseball cap ● noun a cotton cap with a large peak.
base jump ● noun a parachute jump from a fixed point, e.g. a high building or promontory.
– ORIGIN from *b*uilding, *a*ntenna-tower, *s*pan, *e*arth (denoting the types of structure used).
baseless ● adjective not based on fact; untrue.
baseline ● noun **1** a minimum or starting point used for comparisons. **2** (in tennis, volleyball, etc.) the line marking each end of a court.
basement ● noun a room or floor partly or entirely below ground level.
– ORIGIN probably from archaic Dutch, 'foundation'.
base metal ● noun a common non-precious metal such as copper, tin, or zinc.
base rate ● noun the interest rate set by the Bank of England for lending to other banks, used as the basis for interest rates generally.
bases plural of BASE[1] and BASIS.
bash informal ● verb **1** strike hard and violently. **2** (**bash out**) produce rapidly and carelessly. ● noun **1** a heavy blow. **2** a party or social event. **3** Brit. an attempt: *she'll have a bash at anything.*
– ORIGIN perhaps a blend of BANG and SMASH.
bashful ● adjective shy and easily embarrassed.
– DERIVATIVES **bashfully** adverb **bashfulness** noun.
– ORIGIN from obsolete *bash* 'make or become abashed'.
BASIC ● noun a simple high-level computer programming language.
– ORIGIN from *Beginners' All-purpose Symbolic Instruction Code.*
basic ● adjective **1** forming an essential foundation; fundamental. **2** consisting of the minimum required or offered: *a basic wage.* **3** Chemistry containing or having the properties of a base; alkaline. ● noun (**basics**) essential facts or principles.
basically ● adverb **1** fundamentally. **2** in fact; essentially: *they basically did the same thing every day.*
basil ● noun an aromatic plant of the mint family, used in cookery.
– ORIGIN from Greek *basilikos* 'royal'.
basilar /bassilər/ ● adjective Anatomy & Zoology referring to or situated at the base of something, especially of the skull.
– ORIGIN Latin *basilaris.*
basilica /bəzillikə/ ● noun **1** a large oblong building with double colonnades and an apse, used in ancient Rome as a law court or for public assemblies. **2** a Christian church of a similar plan.
– ORIGIN Latin, 'royal palace', from Greek *basilikos* 'royal'.
basilisk /bazzilisk/ ● noun **1** a mythical reptile with a lethal gaze or breath. **2** a long, slender Central American lizard, the male of which has a crest running from the head to the tail.
– ORIGIN Greek *basiliskos* 'little king, serpent'.
basin ● noun **1** a large bowl or open container for preparing food or holding liquid. **2** a broadly circular valley or natural depression. **3** an area drained by a river and its tributaries. **4** an enclosed area of water for mooring boats.
– ORIGIN Latin *bacinus*, from *bacca* 'water container'.
basis ● noun (pl. **bases** /bayseez/) **1** the foundation of a theory or process. **2** the principles according to which an activity is carried on.
– ORIGIN Greek, 'step, pedestal'; related to BASE[1].
bask ● verb **1** lie exposed to warmth and sunlight for pleasure. **2** (**bask in**) revel in (something pleasing).
– ORIGIN perhaps related to an Old Norse word meaning 'bathe'.
basket ● noun **1** a container for holding or carrying things, made from interwoven strips of cane or wire. **2** Basketball a net fixed on a hoop, used as the goal. **3** a group, category, or range: *a basket of currencies.*
– ORIGIN Old French.
basketball ● noun a team game in which goals are scored by throwing a ball through a netted hoop fixed at each end of the court.
basket case ● noun informal a useless person or thing.
– ORIGIN originally US slang, denoting a soldier who had lost all four limbs.
basketry ● noun **1** the craft of basket-making. **2** baskets collectively.
basking shark ● noun a large shark which feeds on plankton and typically swims slowly close to the surface.
basmati rice /bazmaati/ ● noun a kind of long-grain Indian

Thesaurus

● noun *an economy based on barter* TRADING, trade, exchange, business, commerce, buying and selling, dealing.
base[1] ● noun **1** *the base of the tower* FOUNDATION, bottom, foot, support, stand, pedestal, plinth. **2** *the system uses existing technology as its base* BASIS, foundation, bedrock, starting point, source, origin, root(s), core, key component, heart, backbone. **3** *the troops returned to their base* HEADQUARTERS, camp, site, station, settlement, post, centre, starting point.
– OPPOSITES top.
● verb **1** *he based his idea on a movie* FOUND, build, construct, form, ground, root; use as a basis; (**be based on**) derive from, spring from, stem from, originate in, have its origin in. **2** *the company was based in London* LOCATE, situate, position, install, station, site, establish, garrison.
base[2] ● adjective *base motives* SORDID, ignoble, low, low-minded, mean, immoral, improper, unseemly, unscrupulous, unprincipled, dishonest, dishonourable, shameful, bad, wrong, evil, wicked, iniquitous, sinful.
– OPPOSITES noble.
baseless ● adjective *baseless accusations* GROUNDLESS, unfounded, ill-founded, without foundation; unsubstantiated, unproven, unsupported, uncorroborated, unconfirmed, unverified, unattested; unjustified, unwarranted; speculative, conjectural; unsound, unreliable, spurious, specious, untrue, fabricated, trumped up.
– OPPOSITES valid.
basement ● noun CELLAR, vault, crypt, undercroft; *Brit.* lower ground floor; *Scottish* dunny.
bash (*informal*) ● verb **1** *she bashed him with her stick* STRIKE, hit, beat, thump, slap, smack, clip, bang, knock, batter, pound, pummel; *informal* wallop, clout, belt, whack, thwack, clobber, bop, biff, sock; *archaic* smite. **2** *they bashed into one another* CRASH, run, bang, smash, slam, cannon, knock, bump; collide with, hit, meet head-on.
● noun **1** *a bash on the head* BLOW, rap, hit, knock, bang, slap, crack, thump, tap, clip; *informal* wallop, clout, belt, whack, thwack, bop, biff, sock; *archaic* smite. **2** *Harry's birthday bash.* See PARTY noun sense 1. **3** (*Brit.*) *I'll have a bash at it.* See ATTEMPT.
bashful ● adjective SHY, reserved, diffident, inhibited, retiring, reticent, reluctant, shrinking; hesitant, timid, apprehensive, nervous, wary.
– OPPOSITES bold, confident.
basic ● adjective **1** *basic human rights* FUNDAMENTAL, essential, primary, principal, cardinal, elementary, elemental, quintessential, intrinsic, central, pivotal, critical, key, focal; vital, necessary, indispensable. **2** *basic cooking facilities* PLAIN, simple, unsophisticated, straightforward, adequate; unadorned, undecorated, unornamented, without frills; spartan, stark, severe, austere, limited, meagre, rudimentary, patchy, sketchy, minimal; unfussy, homely, homespun; rough (and ready), crude, makeshift; *informal* bog-standard.
– OPPOSITES secondary, unimportant, elaborate.
basically ● adverb FUNDAMENTALLY, essentially, in essence; firstly, first of all, first and foremost, primarily; at heart, at bottom, au fond; principally, chiefly, above all, most of all, mostly, mainly, on the whole, by and large, substantially; intrinsically, inherently; *informal* at the end of the day, when all is said and done.
basics ● plural noun FUNDAMENTALS, essentials, rudiments, (first) principles, preliminaries, groundwork; essence, basis, core; *informal* nitty-gritty, brass tacks, nuts and bolts, ABC.
basin ● noun **1** *she poured water into the basin* BOWL, dish, pan. **2** *a basin among low hills* VALLEY, hollow, dip, depression.
basis ● noun **1** *the basis of his method* FOUNDATION, support, base; reasoning, rationale, defence; reason, grounds, justification, motivation. **2** *the basis of discussion* STARTING POINT, base, point of departure, beginning, premise, fundamental point/principle, principal constituent, main ingredient, cornerstone, core, heart, thrust, essence, kernel, nub. **3** *on a part-time basis* FOOTING, condition, status, position; arrangement, system, method.
bask ● verb **1** *I basked in the sun* LAZE, lie, lounge, relax, sprawl, loll; sunbathe, sun oneself. **2** *she's basking in all the glory* REVEL, delight, luxuriate, wallow, take pleasure, rejoice, glory, indulge oneself; enjoy, relish, savour, lap up.

rice with a delicate fragrance.
– ORIGIN Hindi, 'fragrant'.
Basque /bask, baask/ ● **noun 1** a member of a people living in the western Pyrenees in France and Spain. **2** the language of this people.
– ORIGIN Latin *Vasco* 'inhabitant of Vasconia' (the Latin name also of Gascony in SW France).
basque /bask/ ● **noun** a woman's close-fitting bodice, typically having a short continuation below waist level.
– ORIGIN from BASQUE, referring to traditional Basque dress.
bas-relief /basrileef/ ● **noun** Art low relief.
– ORIGIN Italian *basso-rilievo*.
bass¹ /bayss/ ● **noun 1** the lowest adult male singing voice. **2** (before another noun) denoting the member of a family of instruments that is the lowest in pitch: *a bass clarinet.* **3** informal a bass guitar or double bass. **4** the low-frequency output of transmitted or reproduced sound.
– DERIVATIVES **bassist** noun.
– ORIGIN alteration of BASE².
bass² /bass/ ● **noun** (pl. same or **basses**) a fish with a spiny dorsal fin, related to or resembling the perch.
– ORIGIN alteration of dialect *barse*.
bass clef ● **noun** Music a clef placing F below middle C on the second-highest line of the stave.
basset (also **basset hound**) ● **noun** a breed of sturdy hunting dog with a long body, short legs, and long, drooping ears.
– ORIGIN French, from *bas* 'low'.
bassinet /bassinet/ ● **noun** a child's wicker cradle.
– ORIGIN French, 'little basin'.
basso /bassō/ ● **noun** (pl. **bassos** or **bassi** /bassi/) a bass voice or vocal part.
– ORIGIN Italian, 'low'.
bassoon ● **noun** a large bass woodwind instrument of the oboe family.
– DERIVATIVES **bassoonist** noun.
– ORIGIN Italian *bassone*, from *basso* 'low'.
basso profundo /prəfundō/ ● **noun** (pl. **bassos profundos** or **bassi profundi** /prəfundi/) a bass singer with an exceptionally low range.
bast /bast/ ● **noun** fibre obtained from plants and used for matting and cord.
– ORIGIN Old English.
bastard /baastərd/ ● **noun 1** archaic or derogatory an illegitimate person. **2** informal an unpleasant or despicable person. **3** informal a person of a specified kind: *the poor bastard.* ● **adjective 1** archaic or derogatory illegitimate. **2** no longer in its pure or original form.
– ORIGIN Latin *bastardus*.
bastardize (also **bastardise**) ● **verb 1** debase by adding new elements. **2** archaic declare (someone) illegitimate.
– DERIVATIVES **bastardization** noun.
bastardy ● **noun** archaic illegitimacy.
baste¹ ● **verb** pour fat or juices over (meat) during cooking.
– DERIVATIVES **baster** noun
– ORIGIN of unknown origin.
baste² ● **verb** tack with long, loose stitches in preparation for sewing.
– ORIGIN Old French *bastir* 'sew lightly'.
bastinado /bastinaydō/ ● **noun** chiefly historical a form of punishment or torture that involves caning the soles of someone's feet.
– ORIGIN Spanish *bastonada*, from *bastón* 'stick, cudgel'.
bastion /bastiən/ ● **noun 1** a projecting part of a fortification allowing an increased angle of fire. **2** something protecting or preserving particular principles or activities: *the town was a bastion of Conservatism.*
– ORIGIN Italian *bastione*, from *bastire* 'build'.
bat¹ ● **noun** an implement with a handle and a solid surface, used in sports for hitting the ball. ● **verb** (**batted, batting**) **1** (in sport) take the role of hitting rather than throwing the ball. **2** hit with the flat of one's hand. **3** (**bat around/about**) informal, chiefly N. Amer. casually discuss (an idea).
– PHRASES **off one's own bat** Brit. informal of one's own accord.
– ORIGIN Old English, 'club, stick, staff'.
bat² ● **noun 1** a flying nocturnal mammal with membranous wings that extend between the fingers and limbs. **2** (**old bat**) informal an unattractive and unpleasant woman.
– PHRASES **have bats in the belfry** informal be eccentric or mad.
– ORIGIN Scandinavian; sense 2 is from *bat*, an old slang term for 'prostitute', or from BATTLEAXE.
bat³ ● **verb** (**batted, batting**) flutter (one's eyelashes).
– PHRASES **not bat an eyelid** informal show no surprise or concern.
– ORIGIN variant of obsolete *bate* 'to flutter'.
batch ● **noun 1** a quantity of goods produced or dispatched at one time. **2** a quantity of loaves or rolls baked together. **3** Computing a group of records processed as a single unit. ● **verb** arrange in batches.
– ORIGIN Old English, related to BAKE.
batch file ● **noun** a computer file containing a list of instructions to be carried out in turn.
bate (also **bait**) ● **noun** Brit. informal, dated an angry mood.
– ORIGIN from BAIT.
bated ● **adjective** (in phrase **with bated breath**) in great suspense.
– ORIGIN from obsolete *bate* 'restrain', from ABATE.
bath ● **noun 1** a large tub that is filled with water for immersing and washing one's body. **2** an act of washing in a bath. **3** (also **baths**) a building containing a public swimming pool or washing facilities. **4** a container holding a liquid in which an object is immersed in chemical processing. ● **verb** wash in a bath.
– PHRASES **take a bath** informal suffer a heavy financial loss.
– ORIGIN Old English.
Bath bun ● **noun** Brit. a round currant bun topped with icing or sugar.
– ORIGIN named after the city of *Bath* in SW England.
bath chair ● **noun** dated an invalid's wheelchair.
– ORIGIN named after *Bath* in SW England, frequented for its supposedly curative hot springs.
bathe /bayth/ ● **verb 1** wash by immersing one's body in water. **2** chiefly Brit. take a swim. **3** soak or wipe gently with liquid to clean or soothe. **4** suffuse or envelop: *my desk is bathed in sunlight.* ● **noun** a swim.
– DERIVATIVES **bather** noun.
– ORIGIN Old English.
bathing machine ● **noun** historical a wheeled hut drawn to the edge of the sea, for changing in and bathing from.
bathing suit (Brit. also **bathing costume**) ● **noun** a swimming costume.
batholith /bathəlith/ ● **noun** Geology a very large igneous intrusion extending to an unknown depth in the earth's crust.
– ORIGIN from Greek *bathos* 'depth' + *lithos* 'stone'.
bathos /baythoss/ ● **noun** (in literature) an unintentional change in mood from the important and serious to the trivial

Thesaurus

basket ● **noun** WICKERWORK BOX, hamper, creel, pannier, punnet, trug.
bass ● **adjective** *his bass tones* LOW, deep, low-pitched, resonant, sonorous, rumbling, booming, resounding; baritone.
– OPPOSITES high.
bastard ● **noun 1** *(archaic) he had fathered a bastard* ILLEGITIMATE CHILD, child born out of wedlock; *dated* love child, by-blow; *archaic* natural child/son/daughter. **2** *(informal) he's a real bastard.* See SCOUNDREL.
● **adjective 1** *(archaic) a bastard child* ILLEGITIMATE, born out of wedlock; *archaic* natural. **2** *a bastard Darwinism* ADULTERATED, alloyed, impure, inferior; hybrid, mongrel, patchwork.
bastardize ● **verb** ADULTERATE, corrupt, contaminate, weaken, dilute, taint, pollute, debase, distort.
bastion ● **noun 1** *the town wall and bastions* PROJECTION, outwork, breastwork, barbican; *Architecture* bartizan. **2** *a bastion of respectability* STRONGHOLD, bulwark, defender, support, supporter, guard, protection, protector, defence, prop, mainstay.
batch ● **noun** GROUP, quantity, lot, bunch, mass, cluster, raft, set, collection, bundle, pack; consignment, shipment.
bath ● **noun 1** *he lay soaking in the bath* BATHTUB, tub, hot tub, whirlpool, sauna, steam bath, Turkish bath; *trademark* jacuzzi. **2** *she had a quick bath* WASH, soak, dip; shower.
– RELATED TERMS balneal, balneary.
● **verb** *I bathed quickly | bath your baby gently* BATHE, have/take a bath, wash; shower.
bathe ● **verb 1** *she bathed and dressed.* See BATH verb. **2** *(Brit.) I bathed in the local swimming pool* SWIM, go swimming, take a dip. **3** *they bathed his wounds* CLEAN, wash, rinse, wet, soak, immerse. **4** *the room was bathed in light* SUFFUSE, permeate, pervade, envelop, flood, cover, wash, fill.
● **noun** *we had a bathe* SWIM, dip, paddle.

or ridiculous.
– DERIVATIVES **bathetic** /bəthettik/ adjective.
– ORIGIN Greek, 'depth'.

b

bathrobe ● noun a dressing gown made of towelling.
bathroom ● noun **1** a room containing a bath and usually also a washbasin and toilet. **2** N. Amer. a room containing a toilet.
bath salts ● plural noun crystals that are dissolved in bathwater to soften or perfume it.
bathysphere ● noun a manned spherical chamber for deep-sea observation.
– ORIGIN from Greek *bathus* 'deep'.
batik /bəteek/ ● noun a method (originating in Java) of producing coloured designs on cloth by waxing the parts not to be dyed.
– ORIGIN from Javanese, 'painted'.
batiste /bateest/ ● noun a fine linen or cotton fabric.
– ORIGIN French; probably related to *battre* 'to beat'.
batman ● noun dated (in the British armed forces) an officer's personal valet or attendant.
– ORIGIN from Old French *bat* 'packsaddle'; the word originally refered to an orderly in charge of the *bat horse* which carried the officer's baggage.
bat mitzvah /bat mitsvə/ ● noun a religious initiation ceremony for a Jewish girl at the age of twelve years and a day.
– ORIGIN Hebrew, 'daughter of commandment'.
baton ● noun **1** a thin stick used to conduct an orchestra or choir. **2** a short stick passed from runner to runner in a relay race. **3** a stick carried and twirled by a drum major. **4** a police officer's truncheon. **5** a staff of office or authority.
– PHRASES **pass** (or **take up**) **the baton** hand over (or take up) a duty or responsibility.
– ORIGIN French, from Latin *bastum* 'stick'.
baton round ● noun Brit. a large rubber or plastic bullet used in riot control.
batrachian /bətraykiən/ ● noun a frog or toad.
– ORIGIN from Greek *batrakhos* 'frog'.
bats ● adjective informal mad.
– ORIGIN from *have bats in the belfry* (see BAT²).
batsman ● noun a player who bats in cricket.
battalion /bətaliən/ ● noun a large body of troops, forming part of a brigade.
– ORIGIN French *bataillon*, from Italian *battaglia* 'battle'.
batten¹ ● noun a long, flat wooden or metal strip for strengthening or securing something. ● verb strengthen or fasten with battens.
– PHRASES **batten down the hatches 1** secure a ship's tarpaulins. **2** prepare for a difficulty or crisis.
– ORIGIN Old French *batant*, from *batre* 'to beat'.
batten² ● verb (**batten on**) thrive or prosper at the expense of.
– ORIGIN Old Norse, 'get better'.
Battenberg ● noun chiefly Brit. an oblong marzipan-covered sponge cake in two colours.
– ORIGIN named after the town of *Battenberg* in Germany.
batter¹ ● verb strike repeatedly with hard blows.
– DERIVATIVES **batterer** noun.
– ORIGIN Old French *batre* 'to beat'.
batter² ● noun a mixture of flour, egg, and milk or water, used for making pancakes or coating food before frying.
– ORIGIN from Old French *batre* 'to beat'.
batter³ ● noun a player who bats in baseball.
battered ● adjective (of food) coated in batter and fried.
battering ram ● noun a heavy object swung or rammed against a door to break it down.
– ORIGIN the object was originally in the form of a heavy beam with a carved ram's head at the end.
battery ● noun (pl. **batteries**) **1** a device containing one or more electrical cells, for use as a source of power. **2** an extensive series or range: *a battery of tests.* **3** chiefly Brit. a series of small cages for the intensive rearing of poultry. **4** Law the infliction of unlawful personal violence on another person. **5** a fortified emplacement for heavy guns. **6** an artillery subunit of guns, men, and vehicles.
– ORIGIN originally in the sense 'metal articles made by hammering', later 'a collection of artillery': from Old French *baterie*, from Latin *battuere* 'to beat'.
battle ● noun **1** a sustained fight between organized armed forces. **2** a lengthy and difficult struggle or contest: *a battle of wits.* ● verb fight or struggle tenaciously.
– DERIVATIVES **battler** noun.
– ORIGIN Old French *bataille*, from Latin *battuere* 'to beat'.
battleaxe ● noun **1** a large axe used in ancient warfare. **2** informal a formidably aggressive older woman.
battlecruiser ● noun an early 20th-century warship that was faster and more lightly armoured than a battleship.
battledore /batt'ldor/ ● noun **1** (also **battledore and shuttlecock**) a game played with a shuttlecock and rackets, a forerunner of badminton. **2** the small racket used in this.
– ORIGIN perhaps from Provençal *batedor* 'beater'.
battledress ● noun combat dress worn by soldiers.
battlefield (also **battleground**) ● noun the piece of ground on which a battle is fought.
battlement ● noun a parapet with gaps at intervals for firing from, forming part of a fortification.
– DERIVATIVES **battlemented** adjective.
– ORIGIN from Old French *bataillier* 'fortify with movable defence turrets'.
battle royal ● noun (pl. **battles royal**) a fiercely contested fight or dispute.
battleship ● noun a heavily armoured warship with large-calibre guns.
batty ● adjective (**battier**, **battiest**) informal mad.
– DERIVATIVES **battiness** noun.
– ORIGIN from BAT².
batwing ● adjective (of a sleeve) having a deep armhole and a tight cuff.
bauble /bawb'l/ ● noun a small, showy trinket or decoration.
– ORIGIN Old French *baubel* 'child's toy'.
baud /baud/ ● noun (pl. same or **bauds**) Computing a unit of trans-

Thesaurus

bathing costume *(Brit.)* ● noun SWIMSUIT, bathing suit; swimming trunks, bikini; swimwear; *Brit.* swimming costume; *informal* cossie; *Austral./NZ informal* bathers.
bathos ● noun ANTICLIMAX, let-down, disappointment, disillusionment; absurdity; *informal* comedown.
baton ● noun **1** *the conductor's baton* STICK, rod, staff, wand. **2** *police batons* TRUNCHEON, club, cudgel, bludgeon, stick, mace, shillelagh; *N. Amer.* nightstick, blackjack; *Brit. informal* cosh.
battalion ● noun **1** *an infantry battalion* regiment, brigade, force, division, squadron, squad, company, section, detachment, contingent, legion, corps, cohort. **2** *a battalion of supporters.* See CROWD noun sense 1.
batten ● noun *a timber batten* BAR, bolt, rail, shaft; board, strip.
● verb *Stephen was battening down the shutters* FASTEN, fix, secure, clamp, lash, make fast, nail, seal.
batter ● verb PUMMEL, pound, hit repeatedly, rain blows on, buffet, belabour, thrash, beat up; *informal* knock about/around, beat the living daylights out of, give someone a good hiding, lay into, lace into, do over, rough up.
battered ● adjective DAMAGED, shabby, run down, worn out, falling to pieces, falling apart, dilapidated, rickety, ramshackle, crumbling, the worse for wear, on its last legs.
battery ● noun **1** *a flat battery* CELL, accumulator. **2** *a gun battery* EMPLACEMENT, artillery unit; cannonry, ordnance. **3** *a battery of equipment* ARRAY, set, bank, group, row, line, line-up, collection. **4** *a battery of tests* SERIES, sequence, cycle, string, succession. **5** *assault and battery* VIOLENCE, assault, mugging; *Brit.* grievous bodily harm, GBH, actual bodily harm, ABH.
battle ● noun **1** *he was killed in the battle* FIGHT, armed conflict, clash, struggle, skirmish, engagement, fray, duel; war, campaign, crusade; fighting, warfare, combat, action, hostilities; *informal* scrap, dogfight, shoot-out. **2** *a legal battle* CONFLICT, clash, contest, competition, struggle; disagreement, argument, altercation, dispute, controversy.
● verb **1** *he has been battling against illness* FIGHT, combat, contend with; resist, withstand, stand up to, confront; war, feud; struggle, strive, work. **2** *Mark battled his way to the bar* FORCE, push, elbow, shoulder, fight; struggle, labour.
battleaxe ● noun **1** *a severe blow from a battleaxe* POLEAXE, axe, pike, halberd, tomahawk. **2** *(informal) she's a real battleaxe.* See HARRIDAN.
battle cry ● noun **1** *the army's battle cry* WAR CRY, war whoop, rallying call/cry. **2** *the battle cry of the feminist movement* SLOGAN, motto, watchword, catchphrase.
battlefield ● noun BATTLEGROUND, field of battle, field of operations, combat zone, theatre (of war), front.

mission speed for electronic signals, corresponding to one information unit or event per second.
– ORIGIN named after the French engineer Jean M. E. *Baudot* (1845–1903).

baulk /bawlk, bawk/ (chiefly US also **balk**) ● verb **1** (**baulk at**) hesitate to accept (an idea). **2** thwart or hinder (a plan or person). **3** (of a horse) refuse to go on. ● noun a roughly squared timber beam.
– ORIGIN originally in the sense 'unploughed ridge', later 'obstacle': from Old Norse, 'partition'.

baulky ● adjective British spelling of BALKY.

bauxite /bawksit/ ● noun a clayey rock that is the chief ore of aluminium.
– ORIGIN from *Les Baux*, a village in SE France, where it was first found.

Bavarian /bəvairiən/ ● noun a person from Bavaria, a region in southern Germany. ● adjective relating to Bavaria.

bavarois /bavvəwaa/ (also **bavaroise** /bavvəwaaz/) ● noun a dessert containing gelatin and whipped cream.
– ORIGIN French, 'Bavarian'.

bawd /bawd/ ● noun archaic a woman in charge of a brothel.
– ORIGIN Old French *baudestroyt* 'procuress', from *baude* 'shameless'.

bawdy ● adjective (**bawdier**, **bawdiest**) humorously indecent.
– DERIVATIVES **bawdiness** noun.

bawdy house ● noun archaic a brothel.

bawl ● verb **1** shout out noisily. **2** (**bawl out**) informal reprimand angrily. **3** weep noisily. ● noun a loud shout.
– ORIGIN imitative.

bay[1] ● noun a broad curved inlet of the sea.
– ORIGIN Old French *baie*, from Old Spanish *bahia*.

bay[2] (also **bay laurel** or **sweet bay**) ● noun an evergreen Mediterranean shrub, with aromatic leaves that are used in cookery.
– ORIGIN Old French *baie*, from Latin *baca* 'berry'.

bay[3] ● noun **1** a window area that projects outwards from a wall. **2** a section of wall in a church between two buttresses or columns. **3** an area specially allocated or marked off: *a loading bay*. **4** a compartment with a particular function in an aircraft, motor vehicle, or ship: *a bomb bay*.
– ORIGIN Old French *baie*, from Latin *batare* 'to gape'.

bay[4] ● adjective (of a horse) reddish-brown with black points. ● noun a bay horse.
– ORIGIN Old French *bai*, from Latin *badius*.

bay[5] ● verb (of a dog) bark or howl loudly. ● noun the sound of baying.
– PHRASES **at bay** trapped or cornered. **bay for blood** demand retribution. **hold** (or **keep**) **at bay** prevent from approaching or having an effect.
– ORIGIN Old French *abaiier* 'to bark'.

bayberry ● noun (pl. **bayberries**) a North American shrub with aromatic leathery leaves and waxy berries.

bayonet ● noun **1** a long blade fixed to the muzzle of a rifle for hand-to-hand fighting. **2** (before another noun) denoting a type of fitting for a light bulb which is pushed into a socket and then twisted into place. ● verb (**bayoneted**, **bayoneting**) stab with a bayonet.
– ORIGIN originally denoting a short dagger: from French *baïonnette*, from *Bayonne*, a town in SW France where the daggers were first made.

bayou /bīoo/ ● noun (pl. **bayous**) (in the southern US) a marshy outlet of a lake or river.
– ORIGIN Louisiana French, from an American Indian word.

bay rum ● noun a perfume for the hair, distilled originally from rum and bayberry leaves.

bay window ● noun a window built to project outwards from a wall.

bazaar /bəzaar/ ● noun **1** a market in a Middle-Eastern country. **2** a fund-raising sale of goods.
– ORIGIN Persian, 'market'.

bazooka ● noun **1** a short-range rocket launcher used against tanks. **2** a kazoo shaped like a trumpet.
– ORIGIN apparently from US slang *bazoo* in the sense 'kazoo'.

B. & B. ● abbreviation bed and breakfast.

BBC ● abbreviation British Broadcasting Corporation.

bbl. ● abbreviation barrels (especially of oil).

BBQ ● abbreviation informal a barbecue.

BC ● abbreviation **1** before Christ (used to indicate that a date is before the Christian era). **2** British Columbia.
– USAGE BC is normally written in small capitals and placed **after** the numerals, as in *72* BC.

bcc ● abbreviation blind carbon copy.

BCE ● abbreviation before the Common Era (indicating dates before the Christian era, used especially by non-Christians).

BCG ● abbreviation Bacillus Calmette-Guérin, an anti-tuberculosis vaccine.

BD ● abbreviation Bachelor of Divinity.

BE ● abbreviation **1** Bachelor of Education. **2** Bachelor of Engineering.

Be ● symbol the chemical element beryllium.

be ● verb (sing. present **am**; **are**; **is**; pl. present **are**; 1st and 3rd sing. past **was**; 2nd sing. past and pl. past **were**; present subjunctive **be**; past subjunctive **were**; present part. **being**; past part. **been**) **1** (usu. **there is/are**) exist; be present. **2** occur; take place. **3** have the specified state, nature, or role. **4** come; go; visit. ● auxiliary verb **1** used with a present participle to form continuous tenses. **2** used with a past participle to form the passive voice. **3** used to indicate something that is due to, may, or should happen.
– PHRASES **the be-all and end-all** informal the most important aspect of something. **not be oneself** not feel in one's usual physical or mental state. **-to-be** of the future: *his bride-to-be*.
– ORIGIN Old English: an irregular verb whose full conjugation derives from several originally distinct verbs.

be- ● prefix forming verbs: **1** all over; all round: *bespatter*. **2** thoroughly; excessively: *bewilder*. **3** expressing transitive action: *bemoan*. **4** affect with or cause to be: *befog*. **5** (forming adjectives ending in *-ed*) having; covered with: *bejewelled*.
– ORIGIN Old English, related to BY.

Thesaurus

battlement ● noun CASTELLATION, crenellation, parapet, rampart, wall.

batty ● adjective (*informal*). See MAD sense 1.

bauble ● noun TRINKET, knick-knack, ornament, frippery, gewgaw, gimcrack, bibelot; *N. Amer.* kickshaw; *N. Amer. informal* tchotchke, tsatske; *archaic* gaud.

baulk ● verb **1** *I baulk at paying that much* BE UNWILLING TO, draw the line at, jib at, be reluctant to, hesitate over; eschew, resist, scruple to, refuse to, take exception to; draw back from, flinch from, shrink from, recoil from, demur from, not like to, hate to. **2** *they were baulked by traffic* IMPEDE, obstruct, thwart, hinder, prevent, check, stop, curb, halt, bar, block, forestall, frustrate.
– OPPOSITES accept, assist.

bawdy ● adjective RIBALD, indecent, risqué, racy, rude, spicy, sexy, suggestive, titillating, naughty, improper, indelicate, indecorous, off colour, earthy, broad, locker-room, Rabelaisian; pornographic, obscene, vulgar, crude, coarse, gross, lewd, dirty, filthy, smutty, unseemly, salacious, prurient, lascivious, licentious, X-rated, near the bone, near the knuckle; *informal* blue, raunchy, nudge-nudge; *euphemistic* adult.
– OPPOSITES clean, innocent.

bawl ● verb **1** *'Come on!' he bawled* SHOUT, yell, roar, bellow, screech, scream, shriek, howl, whoop, bark, trumpet, thunder; *informal* yammer, holler. **2** *the children continued to bawl* CRY, sob, weep, shed tears, wail, whine, howl, squall, ululate; *Scottish informal* greet.
– OPPOSITES whisper.
● noun *a terrifying bawl* SHOUT, yell, roar, bellow, screech, scream, howl, whoop; *informal* holler.
– OPPOSITES whisper.
– PHRASES **bawl someone out** (*informal*). See REPRIMAND verb.

bay[1] ● noun *ships were anchored in the bay* COVE, inlet, indentation, gulf, bight, basin, fjord, arm; natural harbour, anchorage.

bay[2] ● noun *there was a bay let into the wall* ALCOVE, recess, niche, nook, opening, hollow, cavity, inglenook.

bay[3] ● verb **1** *the hounds bayed* HOWL, bark, yelp, yap, cry, bellow, roar. **2** *the crowd bayed for an encore* CLAMOUR, shout, call, press, yell, scream, shriek, roar; demand, insist on.
– PHRASES **at bay** AT A DISTANCE, away, off, at arm's length.

bayonet ● noun *a man armed with a bayonet* sword, knife, blade, spear, lance, pike, javelin.
● verb *stragglers were bayoneted* STAB, spear, knife, gore, spike, stick, impale, run through, transfix, gash, slash.

bazaar ● noun **1** *a Turkish bazaar* MARKET, market place, souk, mart, exchange. **2** *the church bazaar* FÊTE, fair, jumble sale, bring-and-buy sale, car boot sale, carnival; fund-raiser, charity

b

beach ● noun a pebbly or sandy shore at the edge of the sea or a lake. ● verb bring or come on to a beach from the water.
– ORIGIN perhaps related to an Old English word meaning 'brook'.

beachcomber ● noun **1** a person who searches beaches for articles of value. **2** a long wave rolling in from the sea.

beachhead ● noun a fortified position on a beach taken by landing forces.

beacon ● noun **1** a fire lit on the top of a hill as a signal. **2** a light serving as a signal for ships or aircraft. **3** a radio transmitter signalling the position of a ship or aircraft.
– ORIGIN Old English, 'sign, portent, ensign'.

bead ● noun **1** a small piece of glass, stone, etc., threaded in a string with others to make a necklace or rosary. **2** a drop of a liquid on a surface. **3** a small knob forming the foresight of a gun. **4** the reinforced inner edge of a tyre. ● verb **1** decorate or cover with beads. **2** form into a string like beads.
– PHRASES **draw a bead on** chiefly N. Amer. take aim at with a gun.
– DERIVATIVES **beaded** adjective.
– ORIGIN Old English, 'prayer' (each bead on a rosary representing a prayer).

beadle ● noun Brit. **1** a ceremonial officer of a church, college, etc. **2** historical a parish officer dealing with petty offenders.
– ORIGIN Old English, 'a person who makes a proclamation'.

beady ● adjective (of a person's eyes) small, round, and observing things clearly.
– DERIVATIVES **beadily** adverb.

beagle ● noun a small, short-legged breed of hound, originally for hunting hares.
– ORIGIN perhaps from Old French *beegueule* 'open-mouthed'.

beagling ● noun hunting with beagles.

beak ● noun **1** a bird's horny projecting jaws; a bill. **2** a projection at the prow of an ancient warship, used in attacking enemy ships. **3** Brit. informal a magistrate or schoolmaster.
– DERIVATIVES **beaked** adjective **beaky** adjective.
– ORIGIN Latin *beccus*.

beaker ● noun Brit. **1** a tall plastic cup. **2** a cylindrical glass container used in laboratories.
– ORIGIN Old Norse.

beam ● noun **1** a long piece of timber or metal used as a support in building. **2** a narrow horizontal length of timber for balancing on in gymnastics. **3** a ray or shaft of light or particles. **4** a radiant smile. **5** a ship's breadth at its widest point. **6** the side of a ship: *there was land in sight on the port beam.* ● verb **1** transmit (a radio signal). **2** shine brightly. **3** smile radiantly.
– PHRASES **a beam in one's eye** a fault that is greater in oneself than in the person one is criticizing. [ORIGIN with biblical allusion to the Gospel of Matthew, chapter 7.] **off beam** informal on the wrong track. **on her** (or **its**) **beam ends** (of a ship) on its side.
– ORIGIN Old English, 'tree, beam'.

bean ● noun **1** an edible seed growing in long pods on certain plants. **2** the hard seed of a coffee or cocoa plant. **3** informal a very small amount or nothing at all: *there is not a bean of truth in the report.* **4** informal, dated a person's head. ● verb informal, chiefly N. Amer. hit on the head.
– PHRASES **full of beans** informal lively; in high spirits. **old bean** Brit. informal, dated a friendly form of address.
– ORIGIN Old English.

beanbag ● noun **1** a small bag filled with dried beans and used in children's games. **2** a large cushion filled with polystyrene beads, used as a seat.

bean counter ● noun informal an excessively careful accountant or bureaucrat.

bean curd ● noun another term for TOFU.

beanery ● noun (pl. **beaneries**) N. Amer. informal a cheap restaurant.

beanfeast ● noun Brit. informal a party with plentiful food and drink.
– ORIGIN originally referring to an annual dinner given to employees, which always featured beans and bacon.

beanie ● noun (pl. **beanies**) a small close-fitting hat worn on the back of the head.
– ORIGIN perhaps from BEAN (in the sense 'head').

beano ● noun (pl. **beanos**) Brit. informal a party.
– ORIGIN abbreviation of BEANFEAST.

beanpole ● noun informal a tall, thin person.

bean sprouts ● plural noun the edible sprouting seeds of certain beans.

bear[1] ● verb (past **bore**; past part. **borne**) **1** carry. **2** have as a quality or visible mark. **3** support (a weight). **4** (**bear oneself**) behave in a specified manner: *she bore herself with dignity.* **5** manage to tolerate; endure: *I can't bear it.* **6** (**cannot bear**) strongly dislike. **7** give birth to (a child). **8** (of a tree or plant) produce (fruit or flowers). **9** turn and proceed in a specified direction: *bear left.*
– PHRASES **bear down on** approach in a purposeful or intimidating manner. **bear fruit** yield positive results. **bear someone a grudge** nurture a feeling of resentment against someone. **bear in mind** remember and take into account. **bear on** be relevant to. **bear out** support or confirm. **bear up** remain cheerful in difficult circumstances. **bear with** be patient or tolerant with. **bear witness** (or **testimony**) **to** testify to. **be borne in upon** come to be realized by. **bring to bear 1** prepare and use to effect. **2** aim (a weapon).
– ORIGIN Old English.

bear[2] ● noun **1** a large, heavy mammal with thick fur and a very short tail. **2** Stock Exchange a person who sells shares hoping to buy them back later at a lower price. Often contrasted with BULL[1]. [ORIGIN said to be from a proverb warning against 'selling the bear's skin before one has caught the bear'.] **3** a rough or bad-mannered person.
– PHRASES **like a bear with a sore head** Brit. informal very irritable.
– ORIGIN Old English.

Thesaurus

event; *N. Amer.* tag sale.

be ● verb **1** *there was once a king* EXIST, have being, have existence; live, be alive, have life, breathe, draw breath, be extant. **2** *is there a cafe here?* BE PRESENT, be around, be available, be near, be nearby, be at hand. **3** *the trial is tomorrow at one-thirty* OCCUR, happen, take place, come about, arise, crop up, transpire, fall, materialize, ensue; *poetic/literary* come to pass, befall, betide. **4** *the bed is over there* BE SITUATED, be located, be found, be present, be set, be positioned, be placed, be installed. **5** *it has been like this for hours* REMAIN, stay, last, continue, survive, endure, persist, prevail; wait, linger, hold on, hang on. **6** *I'm at college* ATTEND, go to, be present at, take part in; frequent, haunt, patronize.

beach ● noun *a sandy beach* SEASIDE, seashore, shore, coast, coastline, coastal region, littoral, seaboard, foreshore, water's edge; sands, lido; *dated* plage; *poetic/literary* strand.
● verb *they beached the boat* LAND, ground, strand, run aground, run ashore.

beachcomber ● noun SCAVENGER, forager, collector.

beached ● adjective STRANDED, grounded, aground, ashore, marooned, high and dry, stuck.

beacon ● noun WARNING LIGHT/FIRE, signal (light/fire), danger signal, bonfire; lighthouse, light-tower.

bead ● noun **1** *a string of beads* BALL, pellet, pill, globule, sphere, spheroid, oval, ovoid, orb, round; (**beads**) necklace; rosary, chaplet. **2** *beads of sweat* DROPLET, drop, blob, dot, dewdrop, teardrop.
– PHRASES **draw/get a bead on** *(N. Amer.)* AIM AT, fix on, focus on, zero in on, sight.

beak ● noun **1** *a bird's beak* BILL, nib, mandible; *Scottish & N. English* neb. **2** *(informal) he blew his beak loudly.* See NOSE noun sense 1.

beaker ● noun CUP, tumbler, glass, mug.

beam ● noun **1** *an oak beam* JOIST, lintel, rafter, purlin; spar, girder, baulk, timber, plank; support, strut; scantling, transom, stringer. **2** *a beam of light* RAY, shaft, stream, streak, pencil, finger; flash, gleam, glow, glimmer, glint, flare. **3** *the beam on her face* GRIN, smile, happy expression, bright look.
– OPPOSITES frown.
● verb **1** *the signal is beamed out* BROADCAST, transmit, relay, send/put out, disseminate; direct, aim. **2** *the sun beamed down* SHINE, radiate, give off light, glare, gleam. **3** *he beamed broadly* GRIN, grin from ear to ear, grin like a Cheshire cat, smile, smirk; *informal* be all smiles.
– OPPOSITES frown.
– PHRASES **off beam** *(informal)* MISTAKEN, incorrect, inaccurate, wrong, erroneous, off target, out, on the wrong track, wide of the mark, awry. **on the beam** *(informal)* CORRECT, right, accurate, true, on the right track, on the right lines; *informal* on the money, on the mark; *Brit. informal* spot on.

bear ● verb **1** *she was bearing a box of cookies* CARRY, bring, transport, move, convey, take, fetch, deliver; *informal* tote. **2** *the bag bore my name* DISPLAY, exhibit, be marked with, show, carry, have.

bearable ● adjective able to be endured.
– DERIVATIVES **bearably** adverb.
bear-baiting ● noun historical a form of entertainment which involved setting dogs to attack a captive bear.
beard ● noun **1** a growth of hair on the chin and lower cheeks of a man's face. **2** a tuft of hairs or bristles on certain animals or plants. ● verb boldly confront or challenge (someone formidable).
– DERIVATIVES **bearded** adjective **beardless** adjective.
– ORIGIN Old English.
bearded dragon ● noun an Australian lizard with a large throat pouch bearing sharp spines.
bearer ● noun **1** a person or thing that carries something. **2** a person who presents a cheque or other order to pay money.
bear garden (also **bear pit**) ● noun a scene of uproar and confusion.
– ORIGIN originally meaning 'place used for bear-baiting'.
beargrass ● noun a North American plant with long, coarse, grass-like leaves, especially a wild yucca.
bear hug ● noun a rough, tight embrace.
bearing ● noun **1** a person's way of standing, moving, or behaving. **2** relation; relevance: *the case has no bearing on the issues.* **3** (**bearings**) a device that allows two parts to rotate or move in contact with each other. **4** direction or position relative to a fixed point. **5** (**one's bearings**) awareness of one's position relative to one's surroundings. **6** Heraldry a device or charge.
bearish ● adjective **1** resembling or likened to a bear. **2** Stock Exchange characterized by falling share prices.
bear market ● noun Stock Exchange a market in which share prices are falling.
Béarnaise sauce /bayaarnayz/ ● noun a rich sauce thickened with egg yolks and flavoured with tarragon.
– ORIGIN named after *Béarn*, a region of SW France.
bear's breech ● noun a plant with large deep-cut leaves and tall spikes of purple and white flowers.
bearskin ● noun a tall cap of black fur worn ceremonially by certain troops.
beast ● noun **1** an animal, especially a large or dangerous mammal. **2** a very cruel or wicked person.
– ORIGIN Latin *bestia*.
beastie ● noun (pl. **beasties**) Scottish or humorous a small animal or insect.
beastly Brit. informal ● adjective very unpleasant. ● adverb dated to an extreme and unpleasant degree.
– DERIVATIVES **beastliness** noun.
beast of burden ● noun an animal used for carrying loads.
beast of prey ● noun an animal that kills and eats other animals.
beat ● verb (past **beat**; past part. **beaten**) **1** strike (someone) repeatedly and violently. **2** strike repeatedly to flatten or make a noise. **3** defeat, surpass, or overcome. **4** informal baffle. **5** (of the heart) pulsate. **6** (of a bird) move (the wings) up and down. **7** stir (cooking ingredients) vigorously. **8** move across (land) to raise game birds for shooting. ● noun **1** a main accent in music or poetry. **2** a pulsation of the heart. **3** a movement of a bird's wings. **4** a brief pause or moment of hesitation. **5** an area allocated to a police officer and patrolled on foot. ● adjective informal completely exhausted.
– PHRASES **beat about the bush** discuss a matter without coming to the point. **beat the bounds** historical mark parish boundaries by walking round them and striking certain points with rods. **beat down** force (someone) to reduce the price of something. **beat it** informal leave. **beat off** succeed in resisting (an attacker). **beat up** attack (someone) and hit them repeatedly. **beat a retreat** withdraw. **off the beaten track** isolated.
– DERIVATIVES **beatable** adjective **beater** noun.
– ORIGIN Old English.
beatbox ● noun informal **1** a drum machine. **2** a radio or radio

Thesaurus

3 *will it bear his weight?* SUPPORT, carry, hold up, prop up. **4** *they can't bear the cost alone* SUSTAIN, carry, support, shoulder, absorb, take on. **5** *she bore no grudge* HARBOUR, foster, entertain, cherish, nurse, nurture, brood over. **6** *such a solution does not bear close scrutiny* WITHSTAND, stand up to, stand, put up with, take, cope with, handle, sustain, accept. **7** *I can't bear having him around* ENDURE, tolerate, put up with, stand, abide, submit to, experience, undergo, go through, countenance, brave, weather, stomach, support; Scottish thole; informal hack, swallow; Brit. informal stick, wear, be doing with; formal brook; archaic suffer. **8** *she bore a son* GIVE BIRTH TO, bring forth, deliver, be delivered of, have, produce, spawn; N. Amer. birth; informal drop; poetic/literary beget. **9** *a shrub that bears yellow berries* PRODUCE, yield, give forth, give, grow, provide, supply. **10** *bear left at the junction* VEER, curve, swerve, fork, diverge, deviate, turn, bend.
– PHRASES **bear oneself** CONDUCT ONESELF, carry oneself, acquit oneself, act, behave, perform; formal comport oneself. **bear down on** ADVANCE ON, close in on, move in on, converge on. **bear fruit** YIELD RESULTS, get results, succeed, meet with success, be successful, be effective, be profitable, work, go as planned; informal pay off, come off, pan out, do the trick, do the business. **bear something in mind** TAKE INTO ACCOUNT, take into consideration, remember, consider, be mindful, mind, mark, heed, not forget. **bear on** BE RELEVANT TO, appertain to, pertain to, relate to, have a bearing on, have relevance to, apply to, be pertinent to. **bear something out** CONFIRM, corroborate, substantiate, endorse, vindicate, give credence to, support, ratify, warrant, uphold, justify, prove, authenticate, verify. **bear up** REMAIN CHEERFUL, grin and bear it; cope, manage, get by; informal hack it. **bear with** BE PATIENT WITH, show forbearance towards, make allowances for, tolerate, put up with, endure. **bear witness/testimony to** TESTIFY TO, be evidence of, be proof of, attest to, evidence, prove, vouch for; demonstrate, show, establish, indicate, reveal, bespeak.
bearable ● adjective TOLERABLE, endurable, supportable, sustainable.
beard ● noun *a black beard* FACIAL HAIR, whiskers, stubble, designer stubble, five o'clock shadow, bristles; goatee, imperial, Vandyke. ● verb *I bearded him when he was on his own* CONFRONT, face, challenge, brave, come face to face with, meet head on; defy, oppose, stand up against, square up to, dare, throw down the gauntlet to, beard the lion in his den.
bearded ● adjective UNSHAVEN, whiskered, whiskery, bewhiskered; stubbly, bristly.
– OPPOSITES clean shaven.
bearer ● noun **1** *a lantern-bearer* CARRIER, porter. **2** *the bearer of bad news* MESSENGER, agent, conveyor, carrier, emissary. **3** *the bearer of the documents* HOLDER, possessor, owner.
bearing ● noun **1** *a man of military bearing* POSTURE, stance, carriage, gait; Brit. deportment; formal comportment. **2** *a rather regal bearing* DEMEANOUR, manner, air, aspect, attitude, behaviour, mien, style. **3** *this has no bearing on the matter* RELEVANCE, pertinence, connection, appositeness, germaneness, importance, significance, application. **4** *a bearing of 015°* DIRECTION, orientation, course, trajectory, heading, tack, path, line, run. **5** *he tormented her beyond bearing* ENDURANCE, tolerance, toleration. **6** *I lost my bearings* ORIENTATION, sense of direction; whereabouts, location, position.
beast ● noun **1** *the beasts of the forest* ANIMAL, creature, brute; N. Amer. informal critter. **2** *he is a cruel beast* MONSTER, brute, savage, barbarian, animal, swine, pig, ogre, fiend, sadist, demon, devil.
– RELATED TERMS bestial.
beastly (Brit. informal) ● adjective **1** *politics is a beastly profession* AWFUL, horrible, rotten, nasty, foul, objectionable, unpleasant, disagreeable, offensive, vile, hateful, detestable; informal terrible, God-awful. **2** *why are you being so beastly to her?* UNKIND, malicious, mean, nasty, unpleasant, unfriendly, spiteful, cruel, vicious, base, foul, malevolent, despicable, contemptible; informal horrible, horrid, rotten.
– OPPOSITES pleasant, kind.
beat ● verb **1** *they were beaten with truncheons* HIT, strike, batter, thump, bang, hammer, punch, knock, thrash, pound, pummel, slap, rain blows on; assault, attack, abuse; cudgel, club, birch; informal wallop, belt, bash, whack, thwack, clout, clobber, slug, tan, biff, bop, sock, deck, plug, beat the living daylights out of, give someone a good hiding. **2** *the waves beat all along the shore* BREAK ON/AGAINST, dash against; lash, strike, lap, wash; splash, ripple, roll; poetic/literary plash, lave. **3** *the metal is beaten into a die* HAMMER, forge, form, shape, mould, work, stamp, fashion, model. **4** *her heart was still beating* PULSATE, pulse, palpitate, vibrate, throb; pump, pound, thump, thud, hammer, drum; pitter-patter, go pit-a-pat. **5** *the eagle beat its wings* FLAP, flutter, thresh, thrash, wave, vibrate, oscillate. **6** *beat the cream into the mixture* WHISK, mix, blend, whip. **7** *she beat a path through the grass* TREAD, tramp, trample, wear, flatten, press down. **8** *the team they need to beat* DEFEAT, conquer, win against, get the better of, vanquish, trounce, rout, overpower, overcome, subdue; informal lick, thrash,

b

cassette player for playing loud music.

beat generation • noun a movement of young people in the 1950s and early 1960s who rejected conventional society.

beatific /beeətiffik/ • adjective **1** feeling or expressing blissful happiness. **2** Christian Theology bestowing holy bliss.
– DERIVATIVES **beatifically** adverb.

beatify /beeattifī/ • verb (**beatifies**, **beatified**) (in the Roman Catholic Church) announce that (a dead person) is in a state of bliss, the first step towards making them a saint.
– DERIVATIVES **beatification** noun.
– ORIGIN Latin *beatificare*, from *beatus* 'blessed'.

beatitude /biattityōōd/ • noun **1** supreme blessedness. **2** (**the Beatitudes**) the blessings listed by Jesus in the Sermon on the Mount (Gospel of Matthew, chapter 5).

beatnik • noun a young member of a subculture associated with the beat generation.

beat-up • adjective informal worn out by overuse.

beau /bō/ • noun (pl. **beaux** or **beaus** /bōz, bō/) dated **1** a boyfriend or male admirer. **2** a dandy.
– ORIGIN from French, 'handsome'.

Beaufort scale /bōfərt/ • noun a scale of wind speed ranging from force 0 to force 12.
– ORIGIN named after the English admiral Sir Francis *Beaufort* (1774–1857).

Beaujolais /bōzhəlay/ • noun a light red wine produced in the Beaujolais district of SE France.

Beaujolais Nouveau /nōōvō/ • noun a Beaujolais wine sold in the first year of a vintage.
– ORIGIN from French *nouveau* 'new'.

beau monde /bō mond/ • noun fashionable society.
– ORIGIN French, 'fine world'.

Beaune /bōn/ • noun a red burgundy wine from the region around Beaune in eastern France.

beauteous • adjective literary beautiful.

beautician • noun a person whose job is to give beauty treatments.

beautiful • adjective **1** very pleasing to the senses or mind aesthetically. **2** of a very high standard; excellent.
– DERIVATIVES **beautifully** adverb.

beautify • verb (**beautifies**, **beautified**) make beautiful.
– DERIVATIVES **beautification** noun.

beauty • noun (pl. **beauties**) **1** a combination of qualities that delights the aesthetic senses. **2** (before another noun) intended to make someone more attractive: *beauty treatment.* **3** a beautiful woman. **4** an excellent example. **5** an attractive feature or advantage.
– PHRASES **beauty is in the eye of the beholder** proverb something which one person finds beautiful or admirable may not appeal to another. **beauty is only skin-deep** proverb a pleasing appearance is not a guide to character.
– ORIGIN Old French *beaute*, from Latin *bellus* 'beautiful, fine'.

beauty contest • noun a contest in which the winner is the woman judged the most beautiful.

beauty queen • noun the winner of a beauty contest.

beauty salon (also **beauty parlour**) • noun an establishment in which hairdressing and cosmetic treatments are carried out.

beauty sleep • noun humorous sleep that helps one remain young and attractive.

beauty spot • noun **1** a place with beautiful scenery. **2** a small artificial mole worn by a woman on the face.

beaux plural of BEAU.

beaver • noun (pl. same or **beavers**) **1** a large semiaquatic rodent noted for gnawing through trees in order to make dams. **2** a hat made of felted beaver fur. **3** a very hard-working person. • verb (often **beaver away**) informal work hard.
– ORIGIN Old English.

bebop /beebop/ • noun a type of jazz originating in the 1940s and characterized by complex harmony and rhythms.
– ORIGIN imitative.

becalm • verb (**be becalmed**) (of a sailing ship) be unable to move through lack of wind.

became past participle of BECOME.

because • conjunction for the reason that; since.
– PHRASES **because of** by reason of.
– USAGE On starting a sentence with **because**, see the note at AND.
– ORIGIN from the phrase *by cause.*

béchamel /beshəmel/ • noun a rich white sauce made with milk infused with herbs and other flavourings.
– ORIGIN named after the Marquis Louis de *Béchamel* (died 1703).

beck[1] • noun N. English a stream.
– ORIGIN Old Norse.

beck[2] • noun (in phrase **at someone's beck and call**) always having to be ready to obey someone's orders.
– ORIGIN abbreviated form of BECKON.

beckon • verb **1** make a gesture to encourage or instruct someone to approach or follow. **2** seem appealing or inviting: *the wide open spaces of Australia beckoned.*
– ORIGIN Old English, related to BEACON.

Thesaurus

whip, wipe the floor with, clobber. **9** *he beat the record* SURPASS, exceed, better, improve on, go one better than, eclipse, transcend, top, trump, cap.
• noun **1** *the song has a good beat* RHYTHM, pulse, metre, time, measure, cadence; stress, accent. **2** *the beat of hooves* POUNDING, banging, thumping, thudding, booming, hammering, battering, crashing. **3** *the beat of her heart* PULSE, pulsating, vibration, throb, palpitation, reverberation; pounding, thump, thud, hammering, drumming; pit-a-pat. **4** *a policeman on his beat* CIRCUIT, round, route, way, path.
• adjective *(informal) phew, I'm beat!* See EXHAUSTED sense 1.
– PHRASES **beat a (hasty) retreat.** See RETREAT verb sense 1. **beat it** *(informal).* See RUN verb sense 2. **beat someone/something off** REPEL, fight off, fend off, stave off, repulse, drive away/back, force back, beat back, push back, put to flight. **beat someone up** ASSAULT, attack, mug, thrash; *informal* knock about/around, do over, work over, rough up, fill in, lay into, lace into, sail into, beat the living daylights out of, let someone have it; *Brit. informal* duff someone up; *N. Amer. informal* beat up on.

beatific • adjective **1** *a beatific smile* RAPTUROUS, joyful, ecstatic, seraphic, blissful, serene, happy, beaming. **2** *a beatific vision* BLESSED, exalted, sublime, heavenly, holy, divine, celestial, paradisical, glorious.

beatify • verb CANONIZE, bless, sanctify, hallow, consecrate, make holy.

beatitude • noun BLESSEDNESS, benediction, grace; bliss, ecstasy, exaltation, supreme happiness, divine joy/rapture; saintliness, sainthood.

beau • noun *(dated)* **1** *Sally and her beau* BOYFRIEND, sweetheart, lover, darling, partner, significant other, escort, young man, admirer, suitor. **2** *an eighteenth-century beau* DANDY, fop, man about town; *informal, dated* swell; *archaic* coxcomb, popinjay.

beautiful • adjective ATTRACTIVE, pretty, handsome, good-looking, alluring, prepossessing; lovely, charming, delightful, appealing, engaging, winsome; ravishing, gorgeous, stunning, arresting, glamorous, bewitching, beguiling; graceful, elegant, exquisite, aesthetic, artistic, decorative, magnificent; *Scottish & N. English* bonny; *informal* tasty, divine, knockout, drop-dead gorgeous, fanciable; *Brit. informal* smashing; *N. Amer. informal* cute, foxy; *Austral./NZ informal* beaut, spunky; *formal* beauteous; *archaic* comely, fair.
– OPPOSITES ugly.

beautify • verb ADORN, embellish, enhance, decorate, ornament, garnish, gild, smarten, prettify, enrich, glamorize, spruce up, deck (out), trick out, grace; *informal* get up, do up, do out, tart up.
– OPPOSITES spoil, uglify.

beauty • noun **1** *a woman of great beauty* ATTRACTIVENESS, prettiness, good looks, comeliness, allure; loveliness, charm, appeal, heavenliness; winsomeness, grace, elegance, exquisiteness; splendour, magnificence, grandeur, impressiveness, decorativeness; gorgeousness, glamour; *Scottish & N. English* bonniness; *poetic/literary* beauteousness, pulchritude. **2** *she is a beauty* BEAUTIFUL WOMAN, belle, vision, Venus, goddess, beauty queen, English rose, picture; *informal* looker, good looker, lovely, stunner, knockout, bombshell, dish, cracker, peach, eyeful, bit of all right; *Brit. informal* smasher. **3** *the beauty of this plan* ADVANTAGE, attraction, strength, benefit, boon, blessing, good thing, strong point, virtue, merit, selling point; *informal* plus.
– OPPOSITES ugliness, drawback.

beaver • verb
– PHRASES **beaver away** *(informal).* See SLOG verb sense 1.

becalmed • adjective MOTIONLESS, still, at a standstill, at a halt, unmoving, stuck.

because • conjunction SINCE, as, in view of the fact that, owing to the fact that, seeing that/as; *informal* on account of; *poetic/literary* for.
– OPPOSITES despite.
– PHRASES **because of** ON ACCOUNT OF, as a result of, as a conse-

become ● verb (past **became**; past part. **become**) **1** begin to be. **2** turn into. **3** (**become of**) happen to. **4** (of clothing) look good when worn by (someone). **5** be appropriate to.
– ORIGIN Old English, from BE- + COME.

becoming ● adjective **1** (of clothing) looking good on someone. **2** decorous; proper.
– DERIVATIVES **becomingly** adverb.

becquerel /bekkərel/ ● noun Physics the SI unit of radioactivity, corresponding to one disintegration per second.
– ORIGIN named after the French physicist A-H. *Becquerel* (1852–1908).

BEd ● abbreviation Bachelor of Education.

bed ● noun **1** a piece of furniture incorporating a mattress or other surface for sleeping or resting on. **2** informal a bed as a place for sexual activity. **3** an area of ground where flowers and plants are grown. **4** a flat base or foundation. **5** a layer of rock. **6** the bottom of the sea or a lake or river. ● verb (**bedded**, **bedding**) **1** provide with or settle in sleeping accommodation. **2** informal have sexual intercourse with. **3** (often **bed in/down**) fix or be fixed firmly. **4** (**bed out**) transfer (a plant) from a pot to the ground.
– PHRASES **a bed of roses** usu. with negative a comfortable or easy situation or activity. **get out of bed on the wrong side** start the day in a bad mood, which continues all day long. **put to bed** informal make (a newspaper) ready for press.
– DERIVATIVES **bedded** adjective.
– ORIGIN Old English.

bed and board ● noun lodging and food.

bed and breakfast ● noun **1** sleeping accommodation and breakfast in a guest house or hotel. **2** a guest house.

bedazzle ● verb greatly impress with brilliance or skill.

bedbug ● noun a wingless bug which sucks the blood of sleeping humans.

bedchamber ● noun archaic a bedroom.

bedclothes ● plural noun coverings for a bed, such as sheets and blankets.

beddable /beddəb'l/ ● adjective informal sexually attractive or available.

bedding ● noun **1** bedclothes. **2** straw or similar material for animals to sleep on. **3** a base or bottom layer.

bedding plant ● noun an annual plant produced for planting in a bed in the spring.

bedeck ● verb decorate lavishly.

bedevil ● verb (**bedevilled**, **bedevilling**; US **bedeviled**, **bedeviling**) cause continual trouble to.

bedfellow ● noun **1** a person sharing a bed with another. **2** a person or thing closely associated with another.

bedhead ● noun Brit. an upright board or panel fixed at the head of a bed.

bedizen /bidīz'n/ ● verb literary dress up or decorate gaudily.
– ORIGIN from obsolete *dizen* 'deck out'.

bedjacket ● noun a soft loose jacket worn when sitting up in bed.

bedlam /bedləm/ ● noun **1** a scene of uproar and confusion. **2** archaic an asylum.
– ORIGIN early form of *Bethlehem*, referring to the hospital of St Mary of Bethlehem in London, used as an asylum for the insane.

bedlinen ● noun sheets, pillowcases, and duvet covers.

Bedouin /beddoo-in/ (also **Beduin**) ● noun (pl. same) a nomadic Arab of the desert.
– ORIGIN Old French, from an Arabic word meaning 'dwellers in the desert'.

bedpan ● noun a receptacle used as a toilet by a bedridden patient.

bedpost ● noun any of the four upright supports of a bedstead.

bedraggled ● adjective dishevelled.

bedridden ● adjective confined to bed by sickness or old age.

bedrock ● noun **1** solid rock underlying loose deposits such as soil. **2** the fundamental principles on which something is based.

bedroom ● noun a room for sleeping in.

bedside manner ● noun the manner in which a doctor attends a patient.

bedsit (also **bedsitter** or **bed-sitting room**) ● noun Brit. informal a rented room consisting of a combined bedroom and living room, with cooking facilities.

bedsocks ● plural noun chiefly Brit. thick socks worn in bed.

bedsore ● noun a sore that develops as a result of lying in bed in one position for a prolonged period.

bedspread ● noun a decorative cloth used to cover a bed.

bedstead ● noun the framework of a bed.

bedstraw ● noun a plant with small flowers and slender leaves, formerly used for stuffing mattresses.

Bedu /beddōō/ ● noun another term for BEDOUIN.
– ORIGIN Arabic.

bed-wetting ● noun involuntary urination during the night.

bee ● noun **1** a stinging winged insect which collects nectar and pollen from flowers and produces wax and honey. **2** a meeting for communal work or amusement: *a sewing bee*.
– PHRASES **the bee's knees** informal an outstandingly good person or thing. **have a bee in one's bonnet** informal be obsessed with something.
– ORIGIN Old English.

beech ● noun a large tree with smooth grey bark and hard, pale wood.
– ORIGIN Old English.

beechmast ● noun the angular brown nuts of the beech tree,

Thesaurus

quence of, owing to, due to; thanks to, by/in virtue of; *formal* by reason of.

beckon ● verb **1** *the guard beckoned to Benny* GESTURE, signal, wave, gesticulate, motion. **2** *the moorland and miles of coastal path beckon many walkers* ENTICE, invite, tempt, coax, lure, charm, attract, draw, call.

become ● verb **1** *she became rich* GROW, get, turn, come to be, get to be; *poetic/literary* wax. **2** *he became a tyrant* TURN INTO, change into, be transformed into, be converted into. **3** *he became Foreign Secretary* BE APPOINTED (AS), be assigned as, be nominated, be elected (as), be made. **4** *the dress becomes her* SUIT, flatter, look good on; set off, show to advantage; *informal* do something for. **5** *it ill becomes him to preach the gospel* BEFIT, suit; *formal* behove.
– PHRASES **become of** HAPPEN TO, be the fate of, be the lot of, overtake; *poetic/literary* befall, betide.

becoming ● adjective FLATTERING, fetching; attractive, lovely, pretty, handsome; stylish, elegant, chic, fashionable, tasteful; *archaic* comely.

bed ● noun **1** *she got into bed* couch, cot, cradle, berth, billet; *informal* the sack, the hay; *Brit. informal* one's pit; *Scottish informal* one's kip. **2** *a flower bed* PATCH, plot, border, strip. **3** *granite blocks set on a bed of cobblestones* BASE, foundation, support, prop, substructure, substratum. **4** *a river bed* BOTTOM, floor, ground.
● verb **1** *the tiles are bedded in mortar* EMBED, set, fix, insert, inlay, implant, bury, base, plant, settle. **2** *time to bed out the seedlings* PLANT (OUT), transplant.
– PHRASES **bed down.** See GO TO BED. **go to bed** RETIRE, call it a day; go to sleep, have/take a nap, have a doze, get some sleep; *informal* hit the sack, hit the hay, turn in, snatch forty winks, get some shut-eye; *Brit. informal* have a kip, get some kip, hit the pit; *N. Amer. informal* catch some Zs.

bedaub ● verb (*poetic/literary*) SMEAR, daub, bespatter, spatter, splatter, cover, coat; *poetic/literary* besmirch, begrime.

bedclothes ● plural noun BEDDING, sheets and blankets; bed linen; bedcovers, covers.

bedding ● noun. See BEDCLOTHES.

bedeck ● verb *a church bedecked with flowers* DECORATE, adorn, ornament, embellish, furnish, garnish, trim, deck, grace, enrich, dress up, trick out; swathe, wreathe, festoon; *informal* get up, do out; *poetic/literary* furbelow.

bedevil ● verb AFFLICT, torment, beset, assail, beleaguer, plague, blight, rack, oppress, harry, curse, dog; harass, distress, trouble, worry, torture.

bedlam ● noun UPROAR, pandemonium, commotion, mayhem, confusion, disorder, chaos, anarchy, lawlessness; furore, upheaval, hubbub, hurly-burly, turmoil, riot, ruckus, rumpus, tumult; *informal* hullabaloo, ructions, snafu.
– OPPOSITES calm.

bedraggled ● adjective DISHEVELLED, disordered, untidy, unkempt, tousled, disarranged, in a mess; *N. Amer. informal* mussed.
– OPPOSITES neat, clean, dry.

bedridden ● adjective CONFINED TO BED, immobilized; *informal* laid up, flat on one's back.

bedrock ● noun *this fact is the bedrock of our authority* CORE, basis, base, foundation, roots, heart, backbone, principle, essence, nitty-gritty; *informal* nuts and bolts.

b

pairs of which are enclosed in a prickly case.

bee-eater ● noun a brightly coloured insect-eating bird with a curved bill and long tail.

beef ● noun **1** the flesh of a cow, bull, or ox, used as food. **2** (pl. **beeves** /beevz/ or US also **beefs**) a cow, bull, or ox fattened for its meat. **3** informal flesh with well-developed muscle. **4** informal strength or power. **5** (pl. **beefs**) informal a complaint or grievance. ● verb informal **1** (**beef up**) make stronger or more substantial. **2** complain.
– ORIGIN Old French *boef*, from Latin *bos* 'ox'.

beefburger ● noun a fried or grilled cake of minced beef eaten in a bun.

beefcake ● noun informal men with well-developed muscles.

beefeater ● noun a Yeoman Warder or Yeoman of the Guard in the Tower of London.
– ORIGIN originally a derogatory term for a well-fed servant.

beefsteak ● noun a thick slice of steak, especially rump steak.

beef tea ● noun Brit. a hot drink made with a beef extract.

beef tomato (chiefly N. Amer. also **beefsteak tomato**) ● noun a large, firm variety of tomato.

beef Wellington ● noun a dish consisting of beef coated in pâté and wrapped in puff pastry.

beefy ● adjective **1** informal muscular or robust. **2** tasting like beef.
– DERIVATIVES **beefily** adverb **beefiness** noun.

beehive ● noun **1** a structure in which bees are kept. **2** a woman's domed and lacquered hairstyle popular in the 1960s.

bee-keeping ● noun the occupation of owning and breeding bees for their honey.
– DERIVATIVES **bee-keeper** noun.

beeline ● noun (in phrase **make a beeline for**) hurry directly to.
– ORIGIN with reference to the straight line supposedly taken instinctively by a bee when returning to the hive.

Beelzebub /bielzibub/ ● noun the Devil.
– ORIGIN Hebrew, 'lord of flies', the name of a Philistine god.

been past participle of BE.

beep ● noun a short, high-pitched sound emitted by electronic equipment or a vehicle horn. ● verb produce a beep.
– DERIVATIVES **beeper** noun.
– ORIGIN imitative.

beer ● noun an alcoholic drink made from yeast-fermented malt flavoured with hops.
– PHRASES **beer and skittles** Brit. amusement or enjoyment.
– ORIGIN from Latin *biber* 'a drink', from *bibere* 'to drink'.

beer belly (or **beer gut**) ● noun informal a man's protruding stomach, caused by excessive consumption of beer.

beer cellar ● noun **1** an underground room for storing beer. **2** a basement bar where beer is served.

beer garden ● noun a garden attached to a public house, where beer is served.

beer mat ● noun a small cardboard mat for resting glasses on in a public house.

beery ● adjective informal **1** drinking a lot of beer. **2** smelling or tasting of beer.

beestings ● plural noun (treated as sing.) the first milk produced by a cow or goat after giving birth.
– ORIGIN Old English.

bee-stung ● adjective informal (of a woman's lips) full and red.

beeswax ● noun **1** wax secreted by bees to make honeycombs, used for wood polishes and candles. **2** N. Amer. informal a person's concern: *that's none of your beeswax.*

beeswing /beezwing/ ● noun a filmy crust on old port.

beet ● noun a plant with a fleshy root, cultivated as food and for processing into sugar.
– ORIGIN Latin *beta*.

beetle[1] ● noun an insect with the forewings modified into hard wing cases that cover the hindwings and abdomen. ● verb informal hurry along with short, quick steps.
– ORIGIN Old English, 'biter'.

beetle[2] ● noun **1** a very heavy mallet. **2** a machine used for making cloth more lustrous by pressing it with rollers.
– ORIGIN Old English, related to BEAT.

beetle[3] ● verb project or overhang.
– ORIGIN from BEETLE-BROWED: apparently used as a nonce-word by Shakespeare and later adopted by other writers.

beetle-browed ● adjective having prominent or bushy eyebrows.
– ORIGIN origin uncertain.

beetle-crusher ● noun Brit. humorous a large boot or shoe.

beetroot ● noun chiefly Brit. the edible dark-red root of a variety of beet.

beeves plural of BEEF (in sense 2 of the noun).

beezer ● adjective Brit. informal excellent.
– ORIGIN of unknown origin.

BEF ● abbreviation British Expeditionary Force.

befall ● verb (past **befell**; past part. **befallen**) literary (especially of something bad) happen to.

befit ● verb (**befitted**, **befitting**) be appropriate for.
– DERIVATIVES **befitting** adjective.

before ● preposition, conjunction, & adverb **1** during the period of time preceding. **2** in front of. **3** in preference to; rather than.
– ORIGIN Old English, from BY + FORE.

beforehand ● adverb in advance.

befriend ● verb become a friend to.

befuddle ● verb muddle or confuse.
– DERIVATIVES **befuddled** adjective **befuddlement** noun.

beg ● verb (**begged**, **begging**) **1** ask earnestly or humbly for something. **2** ask for food or money as charity. **3** (of a dog) sit up with the front paws raised in the hope of a reward.
– PHRASES **beg off** withdraw from a promise or undertaking. **beg**

Thesaurus

bedspread ● noun BEDCOVER, coverlet, quilt, throwover, blanket; *Brit.* eiderdown; *N. Amer.* throw, spread, comforter; *dated* counterpane.

beef *(informal)* ● noun **1** *there's plenty of beef on him* MUSCLE, brawn, bulk; strength, power. **2** *his beef was about the cost* COMPLAINT, criticism, objection, cavil, quibble, grievance, grumble, grouse; *informal* gripe, grouch, moan, whinge.
● verb *security was being beefed up* TOUGHEN UP, strengthen, build up, reinforce, consolidate, invigorate, improve.

beefy ● adjective *(informal)* MUSCULAR, brawny, hefty, burly, hulking, strapping, well built, solid, strong, powerful, heavy, robust, sturdy; *informal* hunky, husky.
– OPPOSITES puny.

beer ● noun ALE, brew; *Brit. informal* wallop, pint, jar; *Austral./NZ informal* hop, sherbet.

beetle ● noun
– RELATED TERMS coleopteran, coleopterous.
● verb *(informal) he beetled past* SCURRY, scamper, scuttle, bustle, hurry, hasten, rush, dash; *informal* scoot, zip.

beetling ● adjective PROJECTING, protruding, prominent, overhanging, sticking out, jutting out.

befall ● verb *(poetic/literary)* **1** *the same fate befell him* HAPPEN TO, overtake, come upon, be visited on. **2** *tell us what befell* HAPPEN, occur, take place, come about, transpire, materialize; ensue, follow, result; *N. Amer. informal* go down; *poetic/literary* come to pass, betide; *formal* eventuate.

befitting ● preposition IN KEEPING WITH, as befits, appropriate to, fit for, suitable for, suited to, proper to, right for, compatible with, consistent with, in character with; *archaic* meet for.

befogged ● adjective CONFUSED, muddled, fuddled, befuddled, groggy, dizzy, muzzy; *informal* dopey, woozy, not with it.
– OPPOSITES lucid.

before ● preposition **1** *he dressed up before going out* PRIOR TO, previous to, earlier than, preparatory to, in preparation for, preliminary to, in anticipation of, in expectation of; in advance of, ahead of, leading up to, on the eve of; *rare* anterior to. **2** *he appeared before the judge* IN FRONT OF, in the presence of, in the sight of. **3** *death before dishonour* IN PREFERENCE TO, rather than, sooner than.
– RELATED TERMS pre-.
– OPPOSITES after.
● adverb **1** *she has ridden before* PREVIOUSLY, before now/then, until now/then, up to now/then; earlier, formerly, hitherto, in the past, in days gone by; *formal* heretofore. **2** *a small party went on before* AHEAD, in front, in advance.
– OPPOSITES behind.

beforehand ● adverb IN ADVANCE, in readiness, ahead of time; before, before now/then, earlier (on), previously, already, sooner.
– OPPOSITES afterwards.

befriend ● verb MAKE FRIENDS WITH, make a friend of; look after, help, protect, stand by.

befuddled ● adjective CONFUSED, muddled, addled, bewildered, disorientated, all at sea, fazed, perplexed, dazed, dizzy, stupefied, groggy, muzzy, foggy, fuzzy, dopey, woozy; *informal* mixed up; *N.*

the question 1 (of a fact or action) invite a question or point that has not been dealt with. **2** assume the truth of a proposition without arguing it. **go begging** be available because unwanted by others.
– ORIGIN probably Old English.
began past of BEGIN.
begat archaic past of BEGET.
beget /biget/ ● verb (**begetting**; past **begot**; past part. **begotten**) archaic or literary **1** produce (a child). **2** cause.
– DERIVATIVES **begetter** noun.
– ORIGIN Old English, 'get, obtain by effort'.
beggar ● noun **1** a person who lives by begging for food or money. **2** informal a person of a specified type: *lucky beggar!* ● verb reduce to poverty.
– PHRASES **beggar belief** (or **description**) be too extraordinary to be believed or described. **beggars can't be choosers** proverb people with no other options must be content with what is offered.
beggarly ● adjective **1** meagre and ungenerous. **2** poverty-stricken.
beggary ● noun a state of extreme poverty.
begin ● verb (**beginning**; past **began**; past part. **begun**) **1** perform or undergo the first part of (an action or activity). **2** come into being. **3** have as its starting point. **4** (**begin on/upon**) set to work on. **5** informal have any chance of doing: *circuitry that Karen could not begin to comprehend.*
– DERIVATIVES **beginner** noun **beginning** noun.
– ORIGIN Old English.
begone ● exclamation archaic go away at once!
begonia /bigōniə/ ● noun a plant having flowers with brightly coloured sepals but no petals.
– ORIGIN named after the French botanist Michel *Bégon* (1638–1710).
begorra /bigorrə/ ● exclamation an exclamation of surprise traditionally attributed to the Irish.
– ORIGIN alteration of *by God*.
begot past of BEGET.
begotten past participle of BEGET.
begrudge ● verb **1** feel envious that (someone) possesses or enjoys (something). **2** give reluctantly or resentfully.
beguile ● verb **1** charm, enchant, or trick. **2** archaic or literary help (time) pass pleasantly.
– DERIVATIVES **beguiling** adjective.
beguine /baygeen/ ● noun a popular dance of Caribbean origin, similar to the foxtrot.
– ORIGIN from French *béguin* 'infatuation'.
begum /baygəm/ ● noun Indian **1** a Muslim woman of high rank. **2** (**Begum**) the title of a married Muslim woman.
– ORIGIN Turkish, 'princess'.
begun past participle of BEGIN.
behalf ● noun (in phrase **on** (US also **in**) **behalf of** or **on someone's behalf**) **1** in the interests of a person, group, or principle. **2** as a representative of.
– ORIGIN from a mixture of the earlier phrases *on his halve* and *bihalve him*, both meaning 'on his side'.
behave ● verb **1** act in a specified way. **2** (also **behave oneself**) act in a polite or proper way.
– ORIGIN from BE- + HAVE in the sense 'bear (oneself) in a particular way'.
behaved ● adjective acting in a specified way: *a well-behaved child.*
behaviour (US **behavior**) ● noun the way in which someone or

Thesaurus

Amer. informal discombobulated.
– OPPOSITES clear.
beg ● verb **1** *he begged on the streets* ASK FOR MONEY, seek charity/alms; *informal* sponge, cadge, scrounge, bum; *Brit. informal* scab; *N. Amer. informal* mooch; *Austral./NZ informal* bludge. **2** *we begged for mercy* ASK FOR, request, plead for, appeal for, call for, sue for, solicit, seek, press for. **3** *he begged her not to go* IMPLORE, entreat, plead with, appeal to, supplicate, pray to, importune; ask, request, call on, petition; *poetic/literary* beseech.
beget ● verb *(poetic/literary)* **1** *he begat a son* FATHER, sire, have, bring into the world, give life to, bring into being, spawn; *archaic* engender. **2** *violence begets violence* CAUSE, give rise to, lead to, result in, bring about, create, produce, generate, engender, spawn, occasion, bring on, precipitate, prompt, provoke, kindle, trigger, spark off, touch off, stir up, whip up, induce, inspire, promote; *poetic/literary* enkindle.
beggar ● noun **1** *he never turned any beggar from his kitchen door* TRAMP, beggarman, beggarwoman, vagrant, vagabond, mendicant; *N. Amer.* hobo; *informal* scrounger, sponger, cadger, freeloader; *Brit. informal* dosser; *N. Amer. informal* bum, moocher, mooch, schnorrer; *Austral./NZ informal* bagman, bludger; *rare* clochard. **2** *(informal) the lucky beggar!* See PERSON.
● verb *the fare beggared her for a week* IMPOVERISH, make poor, reduce to penury, bankrupt, make destitute, pauperize, ruin, wipe out, break, cripple; bring someone to their knees.
beggarly ● adjective **1** *a beggarly sum* MEAGRE, paltry, pitiful, miserable, miserly, ungenerous, scant, scanty, skimpy, puny, inadequate, insufficient, insubstantial; *informal* measly, stingy, pathetic, piddling, piffling, mingy; *formal* exiguous. **2** *in beggarly circumstances* WRETCHED, miserable, sordid, squalid, shabby, mean; poor, poverty-stricken, impoverished, distressed, needy, destitute.
– OPPOSITES considerable, affluent.
beggary ● noun POVERTY, penury, destitution, ruin, ruination, indigence, impecuniousness, impoverishment, need, privation, pauperism, mendicity, want, hardship, reduced circumstances, straitened circumstances, debt, financial ruin; *rare* pauperdom.
begin ● verb **1** *we began work* START, commence, set about, go about, embark on, launch into, get down to, take up; initiate, set in motion, institute, inaugurate, get ahead with; *informal* get cracking on, get going on. **2** *he began by saying hello* OPEN, lead off, get under way, get going, get off the ground, start (off), go ahead, commence; *informal* start the ball rolling, kick off, get the show on the road, fire away, take the plunge. **3** *when did the illness begin?* APPEAR, arise, become apparent, make an appearance, spring up, crop up, turn up, come into existence, come into being, originate, start, commence, develop; *poetic/literary* come to pass.
– RELATED TERMS incipient, inceptive, inchoate, embryonic.
– OPPOSITES finish, end, disappear.
beginner ● noun NOVICE, starter, (raw) recruit, newcomer, tyro, fledgling, neophyte, initiate, fresher, freshman, cub, probationer; postulant, novitiate; *N. Amer.* tenderfoot; *informal* rookie, new kid (on the block), newie, newbie; *N. Amer. informal* greenhorn, probie, punk.
– OPPOSITES expert, veteran.
beginning ● noun **1** *the beginning of socialism* DAWN, birth, inception, conception, origination, genesis, emergence, rise, start, commencement, starting point, launch, onset, outset; day one; *informal* kick-off. **2** *the beginning of the article* OPENING, start, commencement, first part, introduction, preamble, opening statement. **3** *the therapy has its beginnings in China* ORIGIN, source, roots, starting point, birthplace, fons et origo, cradle, spring, early stages, fountainhead; genesis, creation; *poetic/literary* fount, well spring.
– OPPOSITES end, conclusion.
begrime ● verb *(poetic/literary)* DIRTY, soil, sully, stain, mark, muddy; smear, daub, spatter, bespatter, splatter; *poetic/literary* besmirch.
begrudge ● verb **1** *she begrudged Brian his affluence* ENVY, grudge; resent, be jealous of, be envious of. **2** *don't begrudge the cost* RESENT, feel aggrieved about, feel bitter about, be annoyed about, be resentful of, grudge, mind, object to, take exception to, regret; give unwillingly/reluctantly.
beguile ● verb **1** *she was beguiled by its beauty* CHARM, attract, enchant, entrance, win over, woo, captivate, bewitch, spellbind, dazzle, hypnotize, mesmerize, seduce. **2** *(poetic/literary) the programme has been beguiling children for years* ENTERTAIN, amuse, delight, please, occupy, absorb, engage, distract, divert, fascinate, enthral, engross.
– OPPOSITES repel, bore.
beguiling ● adjective CHARMING, enchanting, entrancing, charismatic, captivating, bewitching, spellbinding, hypnotizing, mesmerizing, magnetic, alluring, enticing, tempting, inviting, seductive, irresistible; *informal* come-hither.
– OPPOSITES unappealing.
behalf ● noun
– PHRASES **on behalf of, on someone's behalf 1** *I am writing on behalf of my client* AS A REPRESENTATIVE OF, as a spokesperson for, for, in the name of, in place of, on the authority of, at the behest of. **2** *a campaign on behalf of cycling* IN THE INTERESTS OF, in support of, for, for the benefit of, for the good of, for the sake of.
behave ● verb **1** *she behaved badly* CONDUCT ONESELF, act, acquit oneself, bear oneself; *formal* comport oneself; *archaic* deport oneself. **2** *the children behaved themselves* ACT CORRECTLY, act properly, conduct oneself well, be well behaved, be good; be polite, show good

b

something behaves.
– DERIVATIVES **behavioural** adjective.
behaviourism (US **behaviorism**) ● noun Psychology the theory that behaviour can be explained in terms of conditioning, and that psychological disorders are best treated by altering behaviour patterns.
– DERIVATIVES **behaviourist** noun & adjective.
behead ● verb execute (someone) by cutting off their head.
beheld past and past participle of BEHOLD.
behemoth /bi**hee**moth/ ● noun a huge or monstrous creature.
– ORIGIN Hebrew, 'monstrous beast'.
behest /bi**hest**/ ● noun (usu. in phrase **at the behest of**) literary a person's order or command.
– ORIGIN Old English, 'a vow'.
behind ● preposition & adverb **1** at or to the back or far side of. **2** further back than other members of a moving group. **3** in support of. **4** responsible for (an event or plan). **5** less advanced than. **6** late in accomplishing or paying something. **7** remaining after the departure or death of. ● noun informal a person's bottom.
– ORIGIN Old English.
behindhand ● adjective late or slow in doing something.
behold ● verb (past and past part. **beheld**) archaic or literary see or observe.
– DERIVATIVES **beholder** noun.
– ORIGIN Old English.
beholden ● adjective (usu. **beholden to**) owing a debt; indebted.
behove /bi**hōv**/ (US **behoove** /bi**hoōv**/) ● verb (**it behoves someone to do**) formal it is a duty, responsibility, or appropriate response for someone to do.
– ORIGIN Old English.
beige ● noun a pale sandy fawn colour.
– ORIGIN French.
being ● noun **1** existence. **2** the nature or essence of a person. **3** a living creature: *alien beings.*
bejabers /bi**jay**bərz/ (also **bejabbers** /bi**jab**bərz/) ● exclamation Irish expressing surprise.
– ORIGIN alteration of *by Jesus.*
bejewelled (US **bejeweled**) ● adjective adorned with jewels.
belabour (US **belabor**) ● verb **1** attack physically or verbally. **2** argue or discuss in excessive detail.
belated ● adjective coming late or too late.
– DERIVATIVES **belatedly** adverb **belatedness** noun.
belay /**bee**lay, bi**lay**/ ● verb **1** fix (a rope) round a rock, pin, or other object to secure it. **2** nautical slang stop! ● noun **1** an act of belaying. **2** something used for belaying.
bel canto /bel **kan**tō/ ● noun a style of operatic singing using a full, rich, broad tone.
– ORIGIN Italian, 'fine song'.
belch ● verb **1** noisily emit wind from the stomach through the mouth. **2** forcefully emit (smoke or flames). ● noun an act of belching.
– ORIGIN Old English, probably imitative.
beldam /**bel**dəm/ (also **beldame**) ● noun archaic an old woman.
– ORIGIN from Old French *bel* 'beautiful' + DAM[2].
beleaguered ● adjective **1** under siege. **2** in difficulties; harassed.
– ORIGIN from Dutch *belegeren* 'camp round'.
belemnite /**bel**ləmnīt/ ● noun an extinct marine cephalopod mollusc with a bullet-shaped internal shell, found as a fossil.
– ORIGIN from Greek *belemnon* 'dart'.
belfry ● noun (pl. **belfries**) the place in a bell tower or steeple in which bells are housed.
– ORIGIN Old French *belfrei.*
Belgian ● noun a person from Belgium. ● adjective relating to Belgium.
Belial /**bee**liəl/ ● noun the Devil.
– ORIGIN Hebrew, 'worthlessness'.
belie ● verb (**belying**) **1** fail to give a true idea of. **2** show to be untrue or unjustified.
– ORIGIN Old English, 'deceive by lying'.
belief ● noun **1** a feeling that something exists or is true, espe-

Thesaurus

manners, mind one's manners, mind one's Ps and Qs.
– OPPOSITES misbehave.
behaviour ● noun **1** *his behaviour last night was inexcusable* CONDUCT, deportment, bearing, etiquette; actions, doings; manners, ways; *formal* comportment. **2** *the behaviour of these organisms* FUNCTIONING, action, performance, operation, working, reaction, response.
behead ● verb DECAPITATE, cut someone's head off, guillotine.
behest ● noun *(poetic/literary)* INSTRUCTION, requirement, demand, insistence, bidding, request, wish, desire, will; command, order, decree, ruling, directive; *informal* say-so.
behind ● preposition **1** *he hid behind a tree* AT THE BACK/REAR OF, beyond, on the far/other side of; *N. Amer.* in back of. **2** *a guard ran behind him* AFTER, following, at the back/rear of, hard on the heels of, in the wake of. **3** *you are behind the rest of the class* LESS ADVANCED THAN, slower than, weaker than, inferior to. **4** *he was behind the bombings* RESPONSIBLE FOR, at the bottom of, the cause of, the source of, the organizer of; to blame for, culpable of, guilty of. **5** *they have the nation behind them* SUPPORTING, backing, for, on the side of, in agreement with; financing, *informal* rooting for.
– OPPOSITES in front of, ahead of.
● adverb **1** *a man followed behind* AFTER, afterwards, at the back/end, in the rear. **2** *I looked behind* OVER ONE'S SHOULDER, to/towards the back, to/towards the rear, backwards. **3** *we're behind, so don't stop* (RUNNING) LATE, behind schedule, behindhand, not on time, behind time. **4** *he was behind with his subscription* IN ARREARS, overdue; late, unpunctual, behindhand.
– OPPOSITES in front, ahead.
● noun *(informal) he sat on his behind.* See BOTTOM noun sense 6.
– PHRASES **put something behind one** CONSIGN TO THE PAST, put down to experience, regard as water under the bridge, forget about, ignore.
behindhand ● adverb BEHIND, behind schedule/time; late, belated, unpunctual, slow.
– OPPOSITES ahead.
behold ● verb *(poetic/literary) no eyes beheld them* SEE, observe, view, look at, watch, survey, gaze at/upon, regard, contemplate, inspect, eye; catch sight of, glimpse, spot, spy, notice; *informal* clap eyes on, have/take a gander at, get a load of; *Brit. informal* have/take a dekko at, have/take a butcher's at, have/take a shufti at, clock; *N. Amer. informal* eyeball; *poetic/literary* espy, descry.
● exclamation *(archaic) behold, here I am!* LOOK, see; *archaic* lo.
beholden ● adjective INDEBTED, in someone's debt, obligated, under an obligation; grateful, owing a debt of gratitude.
behove ● verb *(formal)* **1** *it behoves me to go* BE INCUMBENT ON, be obligatory for, be required of, be expected of, be appropriate for. **2** *it ill behoves them to comment* BEFIT, become, suit.
beige ● adjective FAWN, pale brown, buff, sand, sandy, oatmeal, biscuit, coffee, coffee-coloured, café au lait, camel, ecru.
being ● noun **1** *she is warmed by his very being* EXISTENCE, living, life, reality, actuality, essential nature, lifeblood, vital force; *Philosophy* esse. **2** *God is alive in the being of man* SOUL, spirit, nature, essence, inner being, inner self, psyche; heart, bosom, breast; *Philosophy* quiddity, pneuma. **3** *an enlightened being* CREATURE, life form, living entity, living thing, (living) soul, individual, person, human (being).
belabour ● verb **1** *he belaboured the driver about the head* BEAT, hit, strike, smack, batter, pummel, pound, buffet, rain blows on, thrash; *N. Amer.* beat up on; *informal* wallop, whack, clout, clobber, bop, biff, sock, plug; *N. Amer. informal* whale; *archaic* smite. **2** *he was belaboured in the press* CRITICIZE, attack, berate, censure, condemn, denounce, denigrate, revile, pillory, flay, lambaste, savage, tear/pull to pieces, run down; *informal* knock, slam, pan, bash, take apart, crucify, hammer, lay into, roast; *Brit. informal* slate, rubbish, slag off; *N. Amer. informal* pummel, cut up; *formal* castigate, excoriate. **3** *don't belabour the point* OVER-ELABORATE, labour, dwell on, harp on about, hammer away at; overdo, overplay, over-dramatize, make too much of, place too much emphasis on; *informal* flog to death, drag out, make a big thing of, blow out of all proportion; *N. Amer. informal* do over.
– OPPOSITES praise, understate.
belated ● adjective LATE, overdue, behindhand, behind time, behind schedule, delayed, tardy, unpunctual.
– OPPOSITES early.
belch ● verb **1** *onions make me belch* bring up wind; *informal* BURP; *Scottish & N. English informal* rift. **2** *the furnace belched flames* EMIT, give off, give out, pour out, discharge, disgorge, spew out, spit out, vomit, cough up; *poetic/literary* disembogue.
● noun *he gave a loud belch informal* BURP; *Scottish & N. English informal* rift; *formal* eructation.
beleaguered ● adjective **1** *the beleaguered garrison* BESIEGED, under siege, blockaded, surrounded, encircled, hemmed in, under

cially one without proof. **2** a firmly held opinion. **3** (**belief in**) trust or confidence in. **4** religious faith.
– PHRASES **beyond belief** astonishing; incredible.
– ORIGIN Old English.

believe ● verb **1** accept that (something) is true or (someone) is telling the truth. **2** (**believe in**) have faith in the truth or existence of. **3** have religious faith. **4** think or suppose.
– DERIVATIVES **believable** adjective **believer** noun.

Belisha beacon /bəleeshə/ ● noun (in the UK) an orange ball containing a flashing light, mounted on a post at each end of a zebra crossing.
– ORIGIN named after Leslie Hore-*Belisha* (1893–1957), British Minister of Transport when the beacons were introduced.

belittle ● verb dismiss as unimportant.

Belizean /beleeziən/ (also **Belizian**) ● noun a person from Belize, a country on the Caribbean coast of Central America. ● adjective relating to Belize.

bell ● noun **1** a deep inverted metal cup that sounds a clear musical note when struck. **2** a device that buzzes or rings to give a signal. **3** (**bells**) a musical instrument consisting of a set of metal tubes, played by being struck. **4** Nautical the time as indicated every half-hour of a watch by the striking of the ship's bell one to eight times: *at five bells in the forenoon of June 11.* **5** a bell-shaped object or part. ● verb **1** summon or indicate with a bell. **2** flare outwards in the shape of a bell.
– PHRASES **bell the cat** take the danger of a shared enterprise upon oneself. [ORIGIN an allusion to a fable in which the mice suggest hanging a bell around the cat's neck to have warning of its approach.] **bells and whistles** attractive additional features or trimmings. **give someone a bell** Brit. informal telephone someone. **ring a bell** informal sound vaguely familiar.
– ORIGIN Old English.

belladonna /belladonnə/ ● noun **1** deadly nightshade. **2** a drug made from deadly nightshade.
– ORIGIN from Italian *bella donna* 'fair lady', perhaps from the cosmetic use of its juice to dilate the pupils.

bell-bottoms ● plural noun trousers with a marked flare below the knee.

bellboy (also **bellhop**) ● noun chiefly N. Amer. a porter in a hotel or club.

bell curve ● noun Statistics a graph of a normal distribution, with a large rounded peak which tapers away at each end.

belle /bel/ ● noun a beautiful girl or woman.
– ORIGIN French, from Latin *bellus* 'beautiful'.

belle époque /bel epok/ ● noun the period of settled and comfortable life before the First World War.
– ORIGIN French, 'fine period'.

belles-lettres /bel letrə/ ● plural noun literary works written and read for their elegant style.
– ORIGIN French, 'fine letters'.

bellflower ● noun a plant with blue, purple, or white bell-shaped flowers.

bellicose /bellikōs/ ● adjective aggressive and ready to fight.
– DERIVATIVES **bellicosity** /bellikossiti/ noun.
– ORIGIN Latin *bellicosus*, from *bellum* 'war'.

belligerence /bəlijərənss/ (also **belligerency**) ● noun aggressive or warlike behaviour.

belligerent ● adjective **1** hostile and aggressive. **2** engaged in a war or conflict. ● noun a nation or person engaged in war or conflict.
– DERIVATIVES **belligerently** adverb.
– ORIGIN from Latin *belligerare* 'wage war'.

Bellini /bəleeni/ ● noun (pl. **Bellinis**) a cocktail consisting of peach juice mixed with champagne.
– ORIGIN named after the Venetian painter Giovanni *Bellini* (*c.*1430–1516); the cocktail was said to have been invented in Venice.

bell jar ● noun a bell-shaped glass cover for use in a laboratory.

bell metal ● noun an alloy of copper and tin for making bells.

bellow ● verb **1** emit a loud, deep roar of pain or anger. **2** shout or sing very loudly. ● noun a loud, deep shout or sound.
– ORIGIN perhaps from Old English.

bellows ● plural noun **1** a device consisting of a bag with two handles, used for blowing air into a fire. **2** an object or device with sides that allow it to expand and contract.
– ORIGIN probably from the plural of the Old English word for 'belly'.

bell-ringing ● noun the activity or pastime of ringing church bells or handbells.

Bell's palsy ● noun paralysis of the facial nerve causing muscular weakness in one side of the face.
– ORIGIN named after the Scottish anatomist Sir Charles *Bell* (1774–1842).

bellwether ● noun **1** the leading sheep of a flock, often with a bell on its neck. **2** a leader or indicator.

belly ● noun (pl. **bellies**) **1** the front part of the human body below the ribs, containing the stomach and bowels. **2** a person's stomach. **3** the rounded underside of a ship or aircraft. **4** the top surface of a violin or similar instrument, over which the strings are placed. ● verb (**bellies, bellied**) swell or bulge.

Thesaurus

attack. **2** *a beleaguered government* HARD-PRESSED, troubled, in difficulties, under pressure, under stress, with one's back to the wall, in a tight corner, in a tight spot; *informal* up against it.

belie ● verb **1** *his eyes belied his words* CONTRADICT, be at odds with, call into question, give the lie to, show/prove to be false, disprove, debunk, discredit, controvert, negative; *formal* confute. **2** *his image belies his talent* CONCEAL, cover, disguise; misrepresent, falsify, give a false idea/account of.
– OPPOSITES testify to, reveal.

belief ● noun **1** *it's my belief that age is irrelevant* OPINION, view, conviction, judgement, thinking, way of thinking, idea, impression, theory, conclusion, notion. **2** *belief in God* FAITH, trust, reliance, confidence, credence. **3** *traditional beliefs* IDEOLOGY, principle, ethic, tenet, canon; doctrine, teaching, dogma, article of faith, creed, credo.
– OPPOSITES disbelief, doubt.

believable ● adjective CREDIBLE, plausible, tenable, able to hold water, conceivable, likely, probable, possible, feasible, reasonable, with a ring of truth.

believe ● verb **1** *I don't believe you* BE CONVINCED BY, trust, have confidence in, consider honest, consider truthful. **2** *do you believe that story?* REGARD AS TRUE, accept, be convinced by, give credence to, credit, trust, put confidence in; *informal* swallow, buy, go for. **3** *I believe he worked for you* THINK, be of the opinion that, have an idea that, imagine, suspect, suppose, assume, presume, take it, conjecture, surmise, conclude, deduce, understand, be given to understand, gather, fancy, guess, dare say; *informal* reckon, figure; *archaic* ween.
– OPPOSITES doubt.
– PHRASES **believe in 1** *she believed in God* BE CONVINCED/SURE/PERSUADED OF THE EXISTENCE OF, believe in the existence of. **2** *I believe in lots of exercise* HAVE FAITH IN, pin one's faith on, trust in, have every confidence in, cling to, set (great) store by, value, be convinced by, be persuaded by; subscribe to, approve of; *informal* swear by, rate.

believer ● noun DEVOTEE, adherent, disciple, follower, supporter, upholder, worshipper.
– OPPOSITES infidel, sceptic.

belittle ● verb DISPARAGE, denigrate, run down, deprecate, depreciate, downgrade, play down, trivialize, minimize, make light of, treat lightly; *informal* do down, pooh-pooh; *formal* derogate; *rare* misprize.
– OPPOSITES praise, magnify.

belle ● noun BEAUTY, vision, picture, pin-up, beauty queen, English rose, goddess, Venus; *informal* looker, good looker, lovely, stunner, knockout, bombshell, dish, cracker, bobby-dazzler, peach, honey, eyeful, sight for sore eyes, bit of all right; *Brit. informal* smasher.

bellicose ● adjective BELLIGERENT, aggressive, hostile, antagonistic, pugnacious, truculent, confrontational, contentious, militant, combative; *informal* spoiling for a fight; *Brit. informal* stroppy, bolshie; *N. Amer. informal* scrappy; *rare* oppugnant.
– OPPOSITES peaceable.

belligerent ● adjective **1** *a belligerent stare* HOSTILE, aggressive, threatening, antagonistic, pugnacious, bellicose, truculent, confrontational, contentious, militant, combative; *informal* spoiling for a fight; *Brit. informal* stroppy, bolshie; *N. Amer. informal* scrappy; *rare* oppugnant. **2** *the belligerent states* WARRING, at war, combatant, fighting, battling.
– OPPOSITES peaceable, neutral.

bellow ● verb *she bellowed in his ear* ROAR, shout, bawl, thunder, trumpet, boom, bark, yell, shriek, howl, scream; raise one's voice; *informal* holler.
– OPPOSITES whisper.
● noun *a bellow of pain* ROAR, shout, bawl, bark, yell, yelp, shriek,

– PHRASES **go belly up** informal go bankrupt.
– DERIVATIVES **bellied** adjective.
– ORIGIN Old English, 'bag'.
bellyache informal ● noun a stomach pain. ● verb complain noisily or persistently.
belly button ● noun informal a person's navel.
bellyflop ● noun informal a dive into water, landing flat on one's front.
bellyful ● noun a sufficient amount to eat.
– PHRASES **have a bellyful of** informal have more than enough of.
belly laugh ● noun a loud unrestrained laugh.
belong ● verb **1** be rightly put into a particular position or class. **2** fit or be acceptable in a particular place or environment. **3** (**belong to**) be a member of. **4** (**belong to**) be the property or possession of.
belongings ● plural noun a person's movable possessions.
Belorussian /bellōrush'n/ (also **Byelorussian**) ● noun a person from Belarus in eastern Europe. ● adjective relating to Belarus.
beloved ● adjective dearly loved. ● noun a much loved person.
below ● preposition & adverb **1** at a lower level than. **2** (in printed text) mentioned further down.
– PHRASES **below stairs** Brit. dated in the basement of a house (occupied by servants).
Bel Paese /bel paa-ayzay/ ● noun trademark a rich, mild, creamy white cheese from Italy.
– ORIGIN Italian, 'fair country'.
belt ● noun **1** a strip of leather or other material worn round the waist to support or hold in clothes or to carry weapons. **2** a continuous band in machinery that transfers motion from one wheel to another. **3** a strip or encircling area: *the asteroid belt.* **4** informal a heavy blow. ● verb **1** fasten or secure with a belt. **2** informal beat or hit very hard. **3** (**belt out**) informal sing or play (something) loudly and forcefully. **4** informal rush or dash. **5** (**belt up**) informal be quiet.
– PHRASES **below the belt** unfair; disregarding the rules. [ORIGIN from the notion of an illegal blow in boxing.] **belt and braces** Brit. providing double security, by using more than one means to the same end. **tighten one's belt** cut one's spending. **under one's belt** safely or satisfactorily achieved or acquired.
– DERIVATIVES **belted** adjective.
– ORIGIN Latin *balteus* 'girdle'.
Beltane /beltayn/ ● noun an ancient Celtic festival celebrated on May Day.
– ORIGIN Scottish Gaelic.
belter ● noun informal **1** an outstanding example of something. **2** a loud, forceful singer or song.
beltway ● noun US a ring road.
beluga /bəlōōgə/ ● noun (pl. same or **belugas**) **1** a small white toothed whale of Arctic waters. **2** a very large sturgeon from which caviar is obtained.
– ORIGIN from Russian, 'white'.
belvedere /belvideer/ ● noun a summer house or open-sided gallery positioned to command a fine view.
– ORIGIN from Italian, 'fair sight'.
belying present participle of BELIE.
BEM ● abbreviation British Empire Medal.
bemoan ● verb lament or express sorrow for.
bemuse ● verb confuse or bewilder.
– DERIVATIVES **bemused** adjective **bemusement** noun.
ben ● noun Scottish a high mountain.
– ORIGIN Scottish Gaelic and Irish.
bench ● noun **1** a long seat for more than one person. **2** a long, sturdy work table in a workshop or laboratory. **3** (**the bench**) the office of judge or magistrate. **4** (**the bench**) a seat at the side of a sports field for coaches and players not taking part in a game.
– ORIGIN Old English, related to BANK[1].
bencher ● noun Law (in the UK) a senior member of any of the Inns of Court.
benchmark ● noun **1** a standard or point of reference. **2** a surveyor's mark cut in a wall and used as a reference point in measuring altitudes.

Thesaurus

howl, scream; *informal* holler.
– OPPOSITES whisper.
belly ● noun *he scratched his belly* STOMACH, abdomen, paunch, middle, midriff, girth; *informal* tummy, tum, gut, guts, insides, pot, pot belly, beer belly, beer gut, bread basket; *Scottish informal* kyte; *N. Amer. informal* bay window; *dated, humorous* corporation.
● verb *her skirt bellied out* BILLOW (OUT), bulge (out), balloon (out), bag (out), fill (out); distend.
– OPPOSITES sag, flap.
belong ● verb **1** *the house belongs to his mother* BE OWNED BY, be the property of, be the possession of, be held by, be in the hands of. **2** *I belong to a trade union* BE A MEMBER OF, be in, be affiliated to, be allied to, be associated with, be linked to, be an adherent of. **3** *the garden belongs to the basement flat* BE PART OF, be attached to, be an adjunct of, go with. **4** *these creatures belong with bony fish* BE CLASSED, be classified, be categorized, be included, have a place, be located, be situated, be found, lie. **5** *she doesn't belong here* FIT IN, be suited to, have a rightful place, have a home; *informal* go, click.
belonging ● noun AFFILIATION, ACCEPTANCE, association, attachment, integration, closeness; rapport, fellow feeling, fellowship.
– OPPOSITES alienation.
belongings ● plural noun POSSESSIONS, effects, worldly goods, chattels, property; *informal* gear, tackle, kit, things, stuff, bits and pieces, bits and bobs; *Brit. informal* clobber, gubbins.
beloved ● adjective *her beloved brother | Tuscany is beloved by artists* DARLING, dear, dearest, precious, adored, much loved, cherished, treasured, prized, highly regarded, admired, esteemed, worshipped, revered, venerated, idolized.
● noun *he watched his beloved* SWEETHEART, love, darling, dearest, lover, girlfriend, boyfriend, young lady, young man, lady friend, man friend; *informal* steady, baby, angel, honey, pet; *poetic/literary* swain; *dated* beau; *archaic* paramour, doxy.
below ● preposition **1** *the water rushed below them* BENEATH, under, underneath, further down than, lower than. **2** *the sum is below average* LESS THAN, lower than, under, not as much as, smaller than. **3** *a captain is below a major* LOWER THAN, under, inferior to, subordinate to, subservient to.
– RELATED TERMS hypo-, sub-.
– OPPOSITES above, over, more than.
● adverb **1** *I could see what was happening below* FURTHER DOWN, lower down, in a lower position, underneath, beneath. **2** *the statements below* UNDERNEATH, following, further on, at a later point.
belt ● noun **1** *the belt of her coat* GIRDLE, sash, strap, cummerbund, band; *poetic/literary* cincture; *historical* baldric. **2** *farmers in the cotton belt* REGION, area, district, zone, sector, territory; tract, strip, stretch. **3** *(informal) a belt across the face* BLOW, punch, smack, crack, slap, bang, thump, knock, box; *informal* clout, bash, clip, biff, whack, thwack, wallop, sock, swipe; *Brit. informal* slosh; *N. Amer. informal* boff, bust, slug, whale; *archaic* smite.
● verb **1** *she belted the children in* FASTEN, tie, bind; *poetic/literary* gird. **2** *(informal) a guy belted him in the face* HIT, strike, smack, slap, bang, beat, punch, thump, welt; *informal* clout, bash, biff, whack, thwack, wallop, sock, slog, clobber, bop, lam, larrup; *N. Amer. informal* boff, bust, slug, whale; *archaic* smite. **3** *(informal) he belted down the hill.* See SPEED verb sense 1.
– PHRASES **below the belt** UNFAIR, unjust, unacceptable, inequitable; unethical, unprincipled, immoral, unscrupulous, unsporting, sneaky, dishonourable, dishonest, underhand; *informal* low-down, dirty; *Brit. informal* out of order, off, a bit thick, not cricket. **belt up** *(informal)* BE QUIET, quieten down, be silent, fall silent, hush, stop talking, hold your tongue; *informal* shut up, shut your face/mouth/trap, button your lip, pipe down, cut the cackle, put a sock in it; *Brit. informal* shut your gob, wrap up; *N. Amer. informal* save it.
bemoan ● verb LAMENT, bewail, mourn, grieve over, sorrow over, cry over; deplore, complain about; *archaic* plain over.
– OPPOSITES rejoice at, applaud.
bemused ● adjective BEWILDERED, confused, puzzled, perplexed, baffled, mystified, nonplussed, muddled, dumbfounded, at sea, at a loss, taken aback, disoriented, disconcerted; *informal* flummoxed, bamboozled, clueless, fazed; *N. Amer. informal* discombobulated.
bemusement ● noun BEWILDERMENT, confusion, puzzlement, perplexity, bafflement, befuddlement, stupefaction, mystification, disorientation; *informal* bamboozlement; *N. Amer. informal* discombobulation.
bench ● noun **1** *he sat on a bench* PEW, form, stall, settle. **2** *a laboratory bench* WORKBENCH, work table, worktop, work surface, counter. **3** *the bench heard the evidence* JUDGES, magistrates, judiciary; court.
benchmark ● noun STANDARD, point of reference, gauge, criterion, specification, canon, convention, guide, guideline, guiding prin-

b

bench press ● noun an exercise in which one lies on a bench with feet on the floor and raises a weight with both arms.

bench test (also **bench run**) ● noun a test carried out on a product before it is released.

bend[1] ● verb (past and past part. **bent**) **1** give or have a curved or angled shape, form, or course. **2** lean or curve the body downwards; stoop. **3** force or be forced to give in. **4** interpret or modify (a rule) to suit oneself. **5** direct (one's attention or energies) to a task. ● noun **1** a curved or angled part or course. **2** a kind of knot used to join two ropes together, or one rope to another object. **3** (**the bends**) (treated as sing.) decompression sickness.
– PHRASES **bend someone's ear** informal talk to someone at length or in an unwelcome way. **round the bend** informal mad.
– DERIVATIVES **bendable** adjective **bendy** adjective.
– ORIGIN Old English, 'put in bonds, tension a bow'; related to BAND[1].

bend[2] ● noun Heraldry a broad diagonal stripe from top left to bottom right of a shield.
– ORIGIN Old French *bende* 'flat strip'.

bender ● noun informal **1** a drinking bout. **2** Brit. a shelter made by covering a framework of bent branches with canvas. **3** derogatory a male homosexual.

bend sinister ● noun Heraldry a broad diagonal stripe from top right to bottom left of a shield (a supposed sign of bastardy).

beneath ● preposition & adverb extending or directly underneath. ● preposition of lower status or worth than.
– ORIGIN Old English.

Benedictine ● noun **1** /bennidiktin/ a monk or nun of a Christian religious order following the rule of St Benedict. **2** /bennidikteen/ trademark a liqueur based on brandy, originally made by Benedictine monks in France. ● adjective /bennidiktin/ of St Benedict or the Benedictines.

benediction ● noun **1** the utterance of a blessing. **2** the state of being blessed.
– ORIGIN Latin, from *benedicere* 'bless'.

benefaction /bennifaksh'n/ ● noun formal a donation or gift.
– ORIGIN Latin, from *bene facere* 'do good (to)'.

benefactor ● noun a person who gives money or other help.
– DERIVATIVES **benefactress** noun.

benefice /bennifiss/ ● noun a Church office whereby a member of the clergy receives accommodation and income in return for pastoral duties.
– ORIGIN Latin *beneficium* 'favour, support', from *bene facere* 'do good'.

beneficent /bineffis'nt/ ● adjective doing or resulting in good.
– DERIVATIVES **beneficence** noun **beneficently** adverb.

beneficial ● adjective favourable or advantageous.
– DERIVATIVES **beneficially** adverb.

beneficiary ● noun (pl. **beneficiaries**) a person who benefits from something, especially a trust or will.

benefit ● noun **1** advantage or profit. **2** a payment made by the state or an insurance scheme to someone entitled to receive it, e.g. an unemployed person. **3** a public performance to raise money for a charity. ● verb (**benefited** or **benefitted**, **benefiting** or **benefitting**) **1** receive an advantage; profit. **2** bring advantage to.
– PHRASES **benefit of clergy 1** historical exemption of the English clergy and nuns from the jurisdiction of the ordinary civil courts. **2** ecclesiastical sanction or approval. **the benefit of the doubt** a concession that a person must be regarded as correct or innocent if the opposite has not been proven.
– ORIGIN Latin *benefactum* 'good deed', from *bene facere* 'do good'.

benevolent ● adjective **1** well meaning and kindly. **2** (of an organization) charitable rather than profit-making.
– DERIVATIVES **benevolence** noun **benevolently** adverb.
– ORIGIN Old French *benivolent*, from Latin *bene* 'well' + *velle* 'to wish'.

Bengali /benggawli/ ● noun (pl. **Bengalis**) **1** a person from Bengal in the north-east of the Indian subcontinent. **2** the Indic language of Bangladesh and West Bengal. ● adjective relating to Bengal.
– ORIGIN Hindi.

benighted ● adjective **1** ignorant or unenlightened. **2** archaic unable to travel further because darkness has fallen.

benign ● adjective **1** genial and kindly. **2** favourable; not harm-

Thesaurus

ciple, norm, touchstone, yardstick, barometer, indicator, measure, model, exemplar, pattern.

bend ● verb **1** *the frames can be bent to fit your face* CURVE, crook, flex, angle, hook, bow, arch, buckle, warp, contort, distort, deform. **2** *the highway bent to the left* TURN, curve, incline, swing, veer, deviate, diverge, fork, change course, curl, loop. **3** *he bent down to tie his shoe* STOOP, bow, crouch, hunch, lean down/over. **4** *they want to bend me to their will* MOULD, shape, manipulate, direct, force, press, influence, incline, sway. **5** *he bent his mind to the question* DIRECT, turn, train, steer, set.
– OPPOSITES straighten.
● noun *he came to a bend in the road* CURVE, turn, corner, kink, angle, arc, crescent, twist, crook, deviation, deflection, loop; dogleg, oxbow, zigzag; Brit. hairpin bend, hairpin turn, hairpin; rare incurvation.
– OPPOSITES straight.
– PHRASES **bend over backwards** (*informal*) TRY ONE'S HARDEST, do one's best, do one's utmost, do all one can, give one's all, make every effort; informal do one's damnedest, go all out, pull out all the stops, bust a gut, move heaven and earth.

beneath ● preposition **1** *we sat beneath the trees* UNDER, underneath, below, at the foot of, at the bottom of; lower than. **2** *the rank beneath theirs* INFERIOR TO, below, not so important as, lower in status than, subordinate to, subservient to. **3** *such an attitude was beneath her* UNWORTHY OF, unbecoming to, degrading to, below.
– OPPOSITES above.
● adverb *sand with rock beneath* UNDERNEATH, below, further down, lower down.
– OPPOSITES above.

benediction ● noun **1** *the priest said a benediction* BLESSING, prayer, invocation; grace. **2** *filled with heavenly benediction* BLESSEDNESS, beatitude, bliss, grace.

benefactor, benefactress ● noun PATRON, supporter, backer, sponsor; donor, contributor, subscriber; informal angel.

beneficent ● adjective BENEVOLENT, charitable, altruistic, humanitarian, neighbourly, public-spirited, philanthropic; GENEROUS, magnanimous, munificent, unselfish, unstinting, open-handed, liberal, lavish, bountiful; poetic/literary bounteous.
– OPPOSITES unkind, mean.

beneficial ● adjective ADVANTAGEOUS, favourable, helpful, useful, of use, of benefit, of assistance, valuable, of value, profitable, rewarding, gainful.
– OPPOSITES disadvantageous.

beneficiary ● noun HEIR, heiress, inheritor, legatee; recipient; Law devisee, cestui que trust; Scottish Law heritor.

benefit ● noun **1** *for the benefit of others* GOOD, sake, welfare, well-being, advantage, comfort, ease, convenience; help, aid, assistance, service. **2** *the benefits of working for a large firm* ADVANTAGE, reward, merit, boon, blessing, virtue; bonus; value; informal perk; formal perquisite. **3** *state benefit* SOCIAL SECURITY PAYMENTS, public assistance allowance, welfare; charity, donations, gifts, financial assistance; informal the dole; Scottish informal the buroo, the broo.
– OPPOSITES detriment, disadvantage.
● verb **1** *the deal benefited them both* BE ADVANTAGEOUS TO, be beneficial to, be of advantage to, be to the advantage of, profit, do good to, be of service to, serve, be useful to, be of use to, be helpful to, be of help to, help, aid, assist, be of assistance to; better, improve, strengthen, boost, advance, further. **2** *they may benefit from drugs* PROFIT, gain, reap benefits, reap reward, make money; make the most of, exploit, turn to one's advantage, put to good use, do well out of; informal cash in, make a killing.
– OPPOSITES damage, suffer.

benevolence ● noun KINDNESS, kind-heartedness, big-heartedness, goodness, goodwill, charity, altruism, humanitarianism, compassion, philanthropism; generosity, magnanimity, munificence, unselfishness, open-handedness, beneficence; poetic/literary bounty, bounteousness.
– OPPOSITES spite, miserliness.

benevolent ● adjective **1** *a benevolent patriarch* KIND, kindly, kind-hearted, big-hearted, good-natured, good, benign, compassionate, caring, altruistic, humanitarian, philanthropic; generous, magnanimous, munificent, unselfish, open-handed, beneficent; poetic/literary bounteous. **2** *a benevolent institution* CHARITABLE, non-profit-making, non-profit, not-for-profit; formal eleemosynary.
– OPPOSITES unkind, tight-fisted.

benighted ● adjective IGNORANT, unenlightened, uneducated, uninformed, backward, simple; primitive, uncivilized, unsophisti-

b

ful. **3** (of a tumour) not malignant.
– DERIVATIVES **benignity** noun **benignly** adverb.
– ORIGIN Latin *benignus*, probably from *bene* 'well' + *-genus* '-born'.
benignant /bənignənt/ ● adjective less common term for BENIGN.
– DERIVATIVES **benignancy** noun.
Beninese /bennineez/ ● noun a person from Benin, a country in West Africa. ● adjective relating to Benin.
benison /benniz'n/ ● noun literary a blessing.
– ORIGIN Old French *beneiçun*, from Latin *benedictio* 'benediction'.
bent[1] past and past participle of BEND[1]. ● adjective **1** having an angle or sharp curve. **2** informal, chiefly Brit. dishonest; corrupt. **3** Brit. informal, derogatory homosexual. **4** (**bent on**) determined to do or have. ● noun a natural talent or inclination.
bent[2] ● noun a stiff grass used for lawns and in hay grasses.
– ORIGIN Old English.
benthos ● noun Biology the flora and fauna found on the bottom of a sea or lake.
– DERIVATIVES **benthic** adjective.
– ORIGIN Greek, 'depth of the sea'.
bentonite ● noun a kind of absorbent clay formed by breakdown of volcanic ash, used especially as a filler.
– ORIGIN named after Fort *Benton* in Montana, US, where it was first found.
benumb ● verb deprive of feeling.
Benzedrine /benzidreen/ ● noun trademark for AMPHETAMINE.
benzene /benzeen/ ● noun Chemistry a volatile liquid hydrocarbon present in coal tar and petroleum.
– ORIGIN from BENZOIC ACID.
benzine /benzeen/ (also **benzin** /-zin/) ● noun a mixture of liquid hydrocarbons obtained from petroleum.
benzodiazepine /benzōdiayzipeen/ ● noun Medicine any of a class of organic compounds used as tranquillizers, such as Librium and Valium.
benzoic acid ● noun Chemistry a white crystalline compound present in some plant resins and used as a food preservative.
– DERIVATIVES **benzoate** noun.
– ORIGIN from *benzoin* (denoting a gum resin), from French *benjoin*, from an Arabic word meaning 'incense of Java'.
bequeath /bikweeth/ ● verb **1** leave (property) to someone by a will. **2** hand down or pass on.
– ORIGIN Old English, related to QUOTH.
bequest ● noun **1** the action of bequeathing. **2** something that is bequeathed.
berate ● verb scold or criticize angrily.
Berber /berbər/ ● noun a member of the indigenous people of North Africa.
– ORIGIN Arabic, from Greek *barbaros* 'foreigner'.
berberis /berbəriss/ ● noun a spiny shrub with yellow flowers and red berries.
– ORIGIN Latin *barbaris*.
bereave ● verb (**be bereaved**) be deprived of a close relation or friend through their death.
– DERIVATIVES **bereavement** noun.
– ORIGIN Old English.
bereft ● adjective **1** (**bereft of**) deprived of; without. **2** lonely and abandoned.
– ORIGIN archaic past participle of BEREAVE.
beret /berray/ ● noun a flattish round cap of felt or cloth.
– ORIGIN French, 'Basque cap', from Latin *birrus* 'hooded cape'.
bergamot /bergəmot/ ● noun **1** an oily substance extracted from a variety of Seville orange, used as flavouring in Earl Grey tea. **2** an aromatic herb of the mint family.
– ORIGIN named after *Bergamo* in northern Italy.
beriberi /berriberri/ ● noun a disease causing inflammation of the nerves and heart failure, due to a deficiency of vitamin B_1.
– ORIGIN Sinhalese, from a word meaning 'weakness'.
berk /berk/ ● noun Brit. informal a stupid person.
– ORIGIN abbreviation of *Berkeley* or *Berkshire Hunt*, rhyming slang for 'cunt'.
berkelium /berkeeliəm/ ● noun a radioactive metallic chemical element made by high-energy atomic collisions.
– ORIGIN named after the University of *Berkeley* in California (where it was first made).
berm /berm/ ● noun a raised bank or flat strip of land bordering a river, canal, or road.
– ORIGIN French *berme*.
Bermudan /bərmyōōdən/ (also **Bermudian**) ● noun a person from Bermuda. ● adjective relating to Bermuda.
Bermuda shorts (also **Bermudas**) ● plural noun casual knee-length shorts.
berry ● noun (pl. **berries**) **1** a small roundish juicy fruit without a stone. **2** Botany a fruit that has its seeds enclosed in a fleshy pulp, e.g. a banana or tomato.
– ORIGIN Old English.
berserk /bərzerk/ ● adjective out of control; wild and frenzied. ● noun (also **berserker**) an ancient Norse warrior who fought with frenzy.
– ORIGIN Old Norse, probably from *bjorn* 'bear' + *serkr* 'coat', or possibly from *berr* 'bare' (i.e. without armour).
berth ● noun **1** a ship's place at a wharf or dock. **2** a fixed bunk on a ship or train. ● verb **1** moor in a berth. **2** provide a berth for (a passenger).
– PHRASES **give a wide berth** stay well away from.

Thesaurus

cated, philistine, barbarian, barbaric, barbarous; *poetic/literary* nescient; *archaic* rude.
– OPPOSITES enlightened.
benign ● adjective **1** *a benign grandfatherly role* KINDLY, kind, warm-hearted, good-natured, friendly, warm, affectionate, agreeable, amiable, genial, congenial, cordial, approachable, tender-hearted, gentle, sympathetic, compassionate, caring, well disposed, benevolent. **2** *a benign climate* TEMPERATE, mild, gentle, balmy, soft, pleasant; healthy, wholesome, salubrious, health-giving. **3** *a benign tumour* HARMLESS, non-malignant, non-cancerous, innocent, benignant.
– OPPOSITES unfriendly, hostile, unhealthy, unfavourable, malignant.
bent ● adjective **1** *the bucket had a bent handle* TWISTED, CROOKED, warped, contorted, deformed, misshapen, out of shape, irregular; bowed, arched, curved, angled, hooked, kinked; *N. Amer. informal* pretzeled. **2** *(Brit. informal) a bent policeman.* See CORRUPT adjective sense 1. **3** *(Brit. informal).* See HOMOSEXUAL adjective.
– OPPOSITES straight, law-abiding, heterosexual.
● noun *an artistic bent* INCLINATION, leaning, tendency; talent, gift, flair, aptitude, facility, skill, capability, capacity; predisposition, disposition, instinct, orientation, predilection, proclivity, propensity.
– PHRASES **bent on** INTENT ON, determined on, set on, insistent on, resolved on, hell-bent on; committed to, single-minded about, obsessed with, fanatical about, fixated on.
benumbed ● adjective NUMB, unfeeling, insensible, stupefied, groggy, foggy, fuzzy, muzzy, dazed, dizzy; befuddled, fuddled, disoriented, confused, bewildered, all at sea; *informal* dopey, woozy, mixed up; *N. Amer. informal* discombobulated.
– OPPOSITES perceptive.
bequeath ● verb LEAVE (IN ONE'S WILL), will, make over, pass on, hand on/down, entrust, grant, transfer; donate, give; endow on, bestow on, confer on; *Law* demise, devise, convey.
bequest ● noun LEGACY, inheritance, endowment, settlement; estate, heritage; bestowal, bequeathal; *Law* devise; *Law, dated* hereditament.
berate ● verb SCOLD, rebuke, reprimand, reproach, reprove, admonish, chide, criticize, upbraid, take to task, pull up, read someone the Riot Act, haul over the coals; *informal* tell off, give someone a talking-to, give someone a telling-off, give someone a dressing-down, give someone a roasting, rap over the knuckles, send someone away with a flea in their ear, bawl out, come down on, tear into, put on the mat, slap down, blast; *Brit. informal* tick off, have a go at, carpet, give someone a rocket, give someone a rollicking, tear someone off a strip; *Brit. informal, dated* give someone a wigging; *N. Amer. informal* chew out, ream out, take to the woodshed; *Austral. informal* monster; *formal* castigate; *dated* call down, rate; *rare* reprehend, objurgate.
– OPPOSITES praise.
bereaved ● adjective orphaned, widowed.
bereavement ● noun DEATH IN THE FAMILY, loss, passing (away), demise; *formal* decease.
bereft ● adjective DEPRIVED, robbed, stripped, devoid, bankrupt; wanting, in need of, lacking, without; *informal* minus, sans, clean out of.
berry ● noun FRUIT, currant.
berserk ● adjective MAD, crazy, insane, out of one's mind, hysterical, frenzied, crazed, demented, maniacal, manic, frantic, raving, wild, out of control, amok, on the rampage; *informal* off one's head,

– ORIGIN probably from a nautical use of BEAR[1] + -TH[2].

beryl /berril/ ● noun a transparent pale green, blue, or yellow mineral used as a gemstone.
– ORIGIN Greek *bērullos*.

beryllium /bərilliəm/ ● noun a hard, grey, lightweight metallic chemical element of which the mineral beryl is a compound.

beseech ● verb (past and past part. **besought** or **beseeched**) chiefly literary ask (someone) fervently for something.
– ORIGIN Old English, related to SEEK.

beset ● verb (**besetting**; past and past part. **beset**) trouble or harass persistently.
– ORIGIN Old English.

beside ● preposition **1** at the side of; next to. **2** compared with. **3** in addition to; apart from.
– PHRASES **beside oneself** distraught.

besides ● preposition in addition to; apart from. ● adverb in addition; as well.

besiege ● verb **1** surround (a place) with armed forces in order to capture it or force it to surrender. **2** harass or oppress with requests or complaints.
– DERIVATIVES **besieger** noun.
– ORIGIN Old French *asegier*.

besmirch /bismurch/ ● verb **1** damage (someone's reputation). **2** literary make dirty; soil.

besom /beez'm/ ● noun **1** a broom made of twigs tied round a stick. **2** derogatory, chiefly Scottish & N. English a woman or girl.
– ORIGIN Old English.

besotted /bisottid/ ● adjective strongly infatuated.
– ORIGIN from obsolete *besot* 'make foolishly affectionate', from SOT.

besought past and past participle of BESEECH.

bespatter ● verb spatter with liquid.

bespeak ● verb (past **bespoke**; past part. **bespoken**) **1** be evidence of. **2** order or reserve in advance.

bespectacled ● adjective wearing glasses.

bespoke ● adjective Brit. (of goods) made to order.

best ● adjective **1** of the most excellent or desirable type or quality. **2** most suitable, appropriate, or sensible. ● adverb **1** to the highest degree; most. **2** to the highest standard. **3** most suitably, appropriately, or sensibly. ● noun **1** (**the best**) that which is the most excellent or desirable. **2** (**one's best**) the highest standard one can reach. **3** (in sport) a record performance. ● verb informal outwit or defeat.
– PHRASES **at best** taking the most optimistic view. **be for the best** be desirable in the end, although not at first seeming so. **best end** Brit. the rib end of a neck of lamb or other meat. **the best-laid plans of mice and men gang aft agley** proverb even the most careful planning doesn't necessarily ensure success. [ORIGIN see GANG[2].] **the best of three** (or **five** etc.) victory achieved by winning the majority of a specified odd number of games. **the best part of** most of. **get the best of** overcome. **give someone best** Brit. admit that someone is superior. **had best** find it most sensible to. **make the best of** derive what limited advantage one can from. **six of the best** Brit. a caning as a punishment, traditionally with six strokes of the cane.
– ORIGIN Old English.

best boy ● noun the assistant to the chief electrician of a film crew.

bestial /bestiəl/ ● adjective **1** of or like a beast. **2** savagely cruel and wicked.

b

Thesaurus

off the deep end, ape, bananas, bonkers, nuts, hyper; *Brit. informal* spare, crackers, barmy; *N. Amer. informal* postal.

berth ● noun **1** *a 4-berth cabin* BUNK, bed, cot, couch, hammock. **2** *the vessel left its berth* MOORING, dock.
● verb **1** *the ship berthed in London Docks* DOCK, moor, land, tie up, make fast. **2** *the boats each berth six* ACCOMMODATE, sleep.
– PHRASES **give someone/something a wide berth** AVOID, shun, keep away from, stay away from, steer clear of, keep at arm's length, have nothing to do with; dodge, sidestep, circumvent, skirt round.

beseech ● verb (*poetic/literary*) IMPLORE, beg, entreat, plead with, appeal to, call on, supplicate, importune, pray to, ask, request, petition.

beset ● verb **1** *he is beset by fears* PLAGUE, bedevil, assail, beleaguer, afflict, torment, rack, oppress, trouble, worry, harass, dog. **2** *they were beset by enemy forces* SURROUND, besiege, hem in, shut in, fence in, box in, encircle, ring round.

beside ● preposition **1** *Kate walked beside him* ALONGSIDE, by/at the side of, next to, parallel to, abreast of, at someone's elbow; adjacent to, next door to, cheek by jowl with; bordering, abutting, neighbouring. **2** *beside Paula, she felt clumsy* COMPARED WITH/TO, in comparison with/to, by comparison with, next to, against, contrasted with, in contrast to/with.
– RELATED TERMS para-.
– PHRASES **beside oneself** DISTRAUGHT, overcome, out of one's mind, frantic, desperate, distracted, at one's wits' end, frenzied, wound up, worked up; hysterical, unhinged, mad, crazed, berserk, demented. **beside the point.** See POINT[1].

besides ● preposition *who did you ask besides Mary?* IN ADDITION TO, as well as, over and above, above and beyond, on top of; apart from, other than, aside from, but for, save for, not counting, excluding, not including, except, with the exception of, excepting, leaving aside; *N. Amer. informal* outside of; *archaic* forbye.
● adverb **1** *there's a lot more besides* IN ADDITION, as well, too, also, into the bargain, on top of that, to boot; *archaic* therewithal. **2** *besides, he's a man* FURTHERMORE, moreover, further; anyway, anyhow, in any case, be that as it may; *informal* what's more; *N. Amer. informal* anyways.

besiege ● verb **1** *the English army besieged Leith* LAY SIEGE TO, beleaguer, blockade, surround; *archaic* invest. **2** *fans besieged his hotel* SURROUND, mob, crowd round, swarm round, throng round, ring round, encircle. **3** *guilt besieged him* OPPRESS, torment, torture, rack, plague, afflict, haunt, harrow, beset, beleaguer, trouble, bedevil, prey on. **4** *he was besieged with requests* OVERWHELM, inundate, deluge, flood, swamp, snow under; bombard.

besmirch ● verb SULLY, tarnish, blacken, drag through the mud/mire, stain, taint, smear, disgrace, dishonour, bring discredit to, damage, ruin.
– OPPOSITES honour, enhance.

besotted ● adjective INFATUATED, smitten, in love, head over heels in love, obsessed; doting on, greatly enamoured of; *informal* bowled over by, swept off one's feet by, struck on, crazy about, mad about, wild about, gone on, carrying a torch for; *Brit. informal* potty about.

bespatter ● verb SPLATTER, spatter, splash, speck, fleck, spot; dirty, soil; *Scottish & Irish* slabber; *informal* splotch, splodge, splosh.

bespeak ● verb **1** *a tree-lined road which bespoke money* INDICATE, be evidence of, be a sign of, denote, point to, testify to, evidence, reflect, demonstrate, show, manifest, display, signify; reveal, betray; *informal* spell; *poetic/literary* betoken. **2** *he had bespoken a room* ORDER, reserve, book; *informal* bag.
– OPPOSITES belie.

best ● adjective **1** *the best hotel in Paris* FINEST, greatest, top, foremost, leading, pre-eminent, premier, prime, first, chief, principal, supreme, of the highest quality, superlative, par excellence, unrivalled, second to none, without equal, nonpareil, unsurpassed, peerless, matchless, unparalleled, unbeaten, unbeatable, optimum, optimal, ultimate, incomparable, ideal, perfect; highest, record-breaking; *informal* star, number-one, a cut above the rest, top-drawer; *formal* unexampled. **2** *do whatever you think best* MOST ADVANTAGEOUS, most useful, most suitable, most fitting, most appropriate; most prudent, most sensible, most advisable.
– OPPOSITES worst.
● adverb **1** *the best-dressed man* TO THE HIGHEST STANDARD, in the best way. **2** *the food he liked best* MOST, to the highest/greatest degree. **3** *this is best done at home* MOST ADVANTAGEOUSLY, most usefully, most suitably, most fittingly, most appropriately; most sensibly, most prudently, most wisely; better.
– OPPOSITES worst, least.
● noun **1** *only the best will do* FINEST, choicest, top, cream, choice, prime, elite, crème de la crème, flower, jewel in the crown, nonpareil; *informal* tops, pick of the bunch. **2** *she dressed in her best* BEST CLOTHES, finery, Sunday best; *informal* best bib and tucker, glad rags. **3** *give her my best* BEST WISHES, regards, kind/kindest regards, greetings, compliments, felicitations, respects; love.
● verb (*informal*) *she was not to be bested* DEFEAT, beat, get the better of, outdo, outwit, outsmart, worst, be more than a match for, prevail over, vanquish, trounce, triumph over; surpass, outclass, outshine, put someone in the shade, overshadow, eclipse; *informal* lick, get one over on.
– PHRASES **at one's best** ON TOP FORM, at one's peak, in one's prime, in the pink, in the best of health. **do one's best** DO ONE'S UTMOST, try one's hardest, make every effort, do all one can, give one's all; *informal* bend over backwards, do one's damnedest, go all out, pull

b

– DERIVATIVES **bestially** adverb.
– ORIGIN Latin *bestialis*, from *bestia* 'beast'.
bestiality • noun **1** savagely cruel and wicked behaviour. **2** sexual intercourse between a person and an animal.
bestiary /bestiəri/ • noun (pl. **bestiaries**) a treatise on animals, especially a moralizing medieval work.
bestir • verb (**bestirred**, **bestirring**) (**bestir oneself**) exert or rouse oneself.
best man • noun a male friend or relative chosen by a bridegroom to assist him at his wedding.
bestow • verb give or grant (an honour, right, or gift).
– DERIVATIVES **bestowal** noun.
– ORIGIN from Old English *stōw* 'place'.
bestrew • verb (past part. **bestrewed** or **bestrewn**) literary scatter or lie scattered over (a surface).
bestride • verb (past **bestrode**; past part. **bestridden**) stand astride over; span or straddle.
best-seller • noun a book or other product that sells in very large numbers.
bet • verb (**betting**; past and past part. **bet** or **betted**) **1** risk money or property against another's on the basis of the outcome of an unpredictable event such as a race or game. **2** informal feel sure. • noun **1** an act of betting. **2** a sum of money staked. **3** informal a candidate or option with a specified likelihood of success: *Allen looked a good bet for victory.* **4** (**one's bet**) informal one's opinion.
– PHRASES **you bet** informal you may be sure; certainly.
– DERIVATIVES **bettor** (also **better**) noun.
– ORIGIN perhaps a shortening of obsolete *abet* 'abetment'.
beta /beetə/ • noun **1** the second letter of the Greek alphabet (Β, β), transliterated as 'b'. **2** Brit. a second-class mark given for a piece of work.
– ORIGIN Greek.
beta blocker • noun a drug which prevents increased cardiac action, used to treat angina and reduce high blood pressure.
beta decay • noun radioactive decay in which an electron is emitted.
betake • verb (past **betook**; past part. **betaken**) (**betake oneself to**) literary go to.
beta particle (or **ray**) • noun Physics a fast-moving electron emitted by some radioactive substances.
beta rhythm • noun Physiology the normal electrical activity of the brain when conscious and alert.
beta testing • noun independent trials of a new product carried out in the final stages of development (after alpha testing).
betatron /beetətron/ • noun Physics an apparatus for accelerating electrons in a circular path by magnetic induction.
betel /beet'l/ • noun the leaf of an evergreen Asian plant related to pepper, which in the East is chewed as a mild stimulant.
– ORIGIN Portuguese, from a Dravidian language.
betel nut • noun the astringent seed of an areca palm, chewed with betel leaves.
bête noire /bet nwaar/ • noun (pl. **bêtes noires** pronunc. same) (**one's bête noire**) a person or thing that one particularly dislikes.
– ORIGIN French, 'black beast'.
bethink • verb (past and past part. **bethought**) (**bethink oneself**) formal come to think.
betide • verb literary happen; befall.
betimes • adverb literary in good time; early.
bêtise /beteez/ • noun a foolish remark or action.
– ORIGIN French, from *bête* 'foolish'.
betoken • verb literary be a warning or sign of.
betony /bettəni/ • noun (pl. **betonies**) a plant of the mint family bearing spikes of showy purple flowers.
– ORIGIN Latin *betonica*.
betook past of BETAKE.
betray • verb **1** act treacherously towards (a person, country, etc.) by revealing information to or otherwise aiding an enemy. **2** be disloyal to. **3** unintentionally reveal; be evidence of.
– DERIVATIVES **betrayal** noun **betrayer** noun.
– ORIGIN from Old French *trair*, from Latin *tradere* 'hand over'.
betrothed dated • adjective formally engaged to be married. • noun (**one's betrothed**) the person to whom one is engaged.
– DERIVATIVES **betrothal** noun.
better • adjective **1** more desirable, satisfactory, or effective. **2** partly or fully recovered from illness or injury. • adverb **1** more satisfactorily or effectively. **2** to a greater degree; more. • noun **1** that which is better; the better one. **2** (**one's betters**) chiefly dated or humorous one's superiors in social class or ability. • verb **1** improve on or surpass. **2** (**better oneself**) achieve a higher social position or status.
– PHRASES **better the devil you know than the devil you don't**

Thesaurus

out all the stops, bust a gut, break one's neck, move heaven and earth. **had best** OUGHT TO, should.
bestial • adjective **1** *Stanley's bestial behaviour* SAVAGE, brutish, brutal, barbarous, barbaric, cruel, vicious, violent, inhuman, subhuman; depraved, degenerate, perverted, immoral, warped. **2** *man's bestial ancestors* ANIMAL, beast-like, animalistic; *rare* zoic.
– OPPOSITES civilized, humane.
bestir • verb
– PHRASES **bestir oneself** EXERT ONESELF, make an effort, rouse oneself, get going, get moving, get on with it; *informal* shake a leg, look lively, get cracking, get weaving, get one's finger out, get off one's backside; *Brit. informal, dated* stir one's stumps.
bestow • verb CONFER ON, grant, accord, afford, endow someone with, vest in, present, award, give, donate, entrust with, vouchsafe.
bestride • verb **1** *the oilfield bestrides the border* EXTEND ACROSS, lie on both sides of, straddle, span, bridge. **2** *he bestrode his horse* STRADDLE, sit/stand astride. **3** *Italy bestrode Europe in opera* DOMINATE, tower over/above.
best-seller • noun great success, brand leader; *informal* blockbuster, chart-topper, chartbuster, hit, smash (hit).
– OPPOSITES failure, flop.
best-selling • adjective VERY SUCCESSFUL, very popular; *informal* number-one, chart-topping, hit, smash.
bet • verb **1** *he bet £10 on the favourite* WAGER, gamble, stake, risk, venture, hazard, chance; put/lay money, speculate; *informal* punt; *Brit. informal* have a flutter, chance one's arm. **2** *(informal) I bet it was your idea* BE CERTAIN, be sure, be convinced, be confident; expect, predict, forecast, guess; *Brit. informal* put one's shirt on.
• noun **1** *a £20 bet* WAGER, gamble, stake, ante; *Brit. informal* flutter, punt. **2** *(informal) my bet is that they'll lose* PREDICTION, forecast, guess; opinion, belief, feeling, view, theory. **3** *(informal) your best bet is to go early* OPTION, choice, alternative, course of action, plan.
bête noire • noun BUGBEAR, pet hate, bogey; a thorn in one's flesh/side, the bane of one's life; *N. Amer.* bugaboo.
– OPPOSITES favourite.
betide • verb *(poetic/literary)* HAPPEN, occur, take place, come about, transpire, arise, chance; result, ensue, follow, develop, supervene; *N. Amer. informal* go down; *formal* eventuate; *poetic/literary* come to pass, befall; *archaic* hap, bechance.
betoken • verb *(poetic/literary)* **1** *a small gift betokening regret* INDICATE, be a sign of, be evidence of, evidence, manifest, mean, signify, denote, represent, show, demonstrate, bespeak; *informal* spell. **2** *the blue sky betokened a day of good weather* FORETELL, signal, give notice of, herald, proclaim, prophesy, foreshadow, presage, be a harbinger of, portend, augur, be an omen of, be a sign of, be a warning of, warn of, bode; *poetic/literary* foretoken, forebode.
betray • verb **1** *he betrayed his own brother* BREAK ONE'S PROMISE TO, be disloyal to, be unfaithful to, break faith with, play someone false; inform on/against, give away, denounce, sell out, stab in the back; *informal* split on, rat on, peach on, stitch up, do the dirty on, sell down the river, squeal on; *Brit. informal* grass on, shop, sneak on; *N. Amer. informal* rat out, drop a/the dime on, finger; *Austral./NZ informal* dob on, point the bone at. **2** *he betrayed a secret* REVEAL, disclose, divulge, tell, give away, leak; unmask, expose, bring out into the open; let slip, let out, let drop, blurt out; *informal* blab, spill.
– OPPOSITES be loyal to, hide.
betrayal • noun DISLOYALTY, treachery, bad faith, faithlessness, falseness, Punic faith; duplicity, deception, double-dealing; breach of faith, breach of trust, stab in the back; double-cross, sell-out; *poetic/literary* perfidy.
– OPPOSITES loyalty.
betrayer • noun TRAITOR, back-stabber, Judas, double-crosser; renegade, quisling, double agent, collaborator, informer, mole, stool pigeon; turncoat, defector; *informal* snake in the grass, rat, scab; *Brit. informal* grass, supergrass, nark; *N. Amer. informal* fink, stoolie.
betrothal • noun *(dated)* ENGAGEMENT, marriage contract; *archaic* espousal.
betrothed • adjective *(dated)* ENGAGED (TO BE MARRIED), promised/pledged in marriage, attached; *informal* spoken for; *poetic/literary*

know proverb it's wiser to deal with an undesirable but familiar person or situation than to risk a change that might lead to a situation with worse difficulties or a person whose faults you have yet to discover. **better off** in a more advantageous position, especially in financial terms. **the better part of** almost all of; most of. **better safe than sorry** proverb it's wiser to be cautious and careful than to be hasty or rash and so do something you may later regret. **for better or worse** whether the outcome is good or bad. **get the better of** defeat or overcome. **had better** would find it wiser to.
– USAGE In the phrase **had better do something** the word **had** acts like an auxiliary verb and in informal spoken contexts it is often dropped, as in *you better not come tonight*. In writing, the **had** may be contracted to **'d** but it should not be dropped altogether.
– ORIGIN Old English.

better half ● noun informal a person's spouse or partner.

betterment ● noun improvement.

bettong /bettong/ ● noun a short-nosed Australian rat-kangaroo.
– ORIGIN Dharuk (an Aboriginal language).

between ● preposition & adverb **1** at, into, or across the space separating (two objects, places, or points). **2** in the period separating (two points in time). ● preposition **1** indicating a connection or relationship involving (two or more parties). **2** by combining the resources or actions of (two or more parties).
– PHRASES **between ourselves** (or **you and me**) in confidence.
– USAGE A preposition such as **between** takes the object case and is correctly followed by object pronouns such as **me** rather than subject pronouns such as **I**. It is therefore correct to say **between you and me** rather than **between you and I**.
– ORIGIN Old English, related to TWO.

betwixt ● preposition & adverb archaic between.
– PHRASES **betwixt and between** informal neither one thing nor the other.
– ORIGIN Old English, related to TWO.

bevel ● noun **1** (in carpentry) a surface or edge which slopes away from a horizontal or vertical surface. **2** (also **bevel square**) a tool for marking angles in carpentry and stonework. ● verb (**bevelled**, **bevelling**; US **beveled**, **beveling**) cut a bevel on.
– ORIGIN Old French, from *baif* 'open-mouthed', from *baer* 'gape'.

beverage ● noun a drink other than water.
– ORIGIN Old French *bevrage*, from Latin *bibere* 'to drink'.

bevvy ● noun (pl. **bevvies**) Brit. informal an alcoholic drink.
– DERIVATIVES **bevvied** adjective.
– ORIGIN abbreviation of BEVERAGE.

bevy /bevvi/ ● noun (pl. **bevies**) a large group of people or things.
– ORIGIN of unknown origin.

bewail ● verb greatly regret or lament.
– DERIVATIVES **bewailer** noun.

beware ● verb be cautious and alert to risks or dangers.
– ORIGIN from the phrase *be ware* 'be aware'.

bewilder ● verb perplex or confuse.
– DERIVATIVES **bewildering** adjective **bewilderment** noun.
– ORIGIN from obsolete *wilder* 'lead or go astray'.

bewitch ● verb **1** cast a spell over. **2** enchant and delight.
– DERIVATIVES **bewitcher** noun **bewitching** adjective **bewitchment** noun.
– ORIGIN from WITCH.

bey /bay/ ● noun (pl. **beys**) historical the governor of a district or province in the Ottoman Empire.
– ORIGIN Turkish *beg* 'prince, governor'.

beyond ● preposition & adverb **1** at or to the further side of. **2** more extensive or extreme than. **3** happening or continuing after. **4** having reached or progressed further than (a specified level or amount). **5** to or in a degree where a specified action is impossible. **6** apart from; except. ● noun (**the beyond**) the unknown, especially in references to life after death.
– ORIGIN Old English.

bezel /bezz'l/ ● noun a groove holding a gemstone or the glass cover of a watch in position.
– ORIGIN Old French.

bezique /bizeek/ ● noun a trick-taking card game for two, played with a double pack of 64 cards.
– ORIGIN French *bésigue*, perhaps from a Persian word meaning 'juggler'.

Bh ● symbol the chemical element bohrium.

bhaji /baaji/ (also **bhajia**) /baajə/ ● noun (pl. **bhajis**, **bhajia**) (in Indian cooking) a small flat cake or ball of vegetables, fried in batter.
– ORIGIN Hindi, 'fried vegetables'.

bhang /bang/ (also **bang**) ● noun (in India) the leaves and flower-tops of cannabis, used as a narcotic.
– ORIGIN Hindi.

bhangra /baanggrə/ ● noun a type of popular music combining Punjabi folk traditions with Western pop music.
– ORIGIN Punjabi.

bhindi /bindi/ ● noun Indian term for OKRA.
– ORIGIN Hindi.

b.h.p. ● abbreviation brake horsepower.

Bhutanese /bōōtəneez/ ● noun a person from Bhutan, a small kingdom in the Himalayas. ● adjective relating to Bhutan.

Thesaurus

affianced; *archaic* plighted, espoused.
– OPPOSITES unattached.

better ● adjective **1** *better facilities* SUPERIOR, finer, of higher quality; preferable; *informal* a cut above, streets ahead, head and shoulders above, ahead of the pack/field. **2** *there couldn't be a better time* MORE ADVANTAGEOUS, more suitable, more fitting, more appropriate, more useful, more valuable, more desirable. **3** *are you better?* HEALTHIER, fitter, stronger; well, cured, healed, recovered; recovering, on the road to recovery, making progress, improving; *informal* on the mend.
– OPPOSITES worse, inferior.
● adverb **1** *I played much better today* TO A HIGHER STANDARD, in a superior/finer way. **2** *this may suit you better* MORE, to a greater degree/extent. **3** *the money could be better spent* MORE WISELY, more sensibly, more suitably, more fittingly, more advantageously.
● verb **1** *he bettered the record* SURPASS, improve on, beat, exceed, top, cap, trump, eclipse. **2** *refugees who want to better their lot* IMPROVE, ameliorate, raise, advance, further, lift, upgrade, enhance.
– OPPOSITES worsen.

betterment ● noun IMPROVEMENT, amelioration, advancement, furtherance, upgrading, enhancement.

between ● preposition **1** *Philip stood between his parents* IN THE SPACE SEPARATING, in the middle of, with one on either side; *archaic* betwixt. **2** *the bond between her and her mother* CONNECTING, linking, joining; uniting, allying.
– RELATED TERMS inter-.

bevel ● noun SLOPE, slant, angle, cant, chamfer.

beverage ● noun DRINK, liquid refreshment; *humorous* libation; *archaic* potation.

bevy ● noun GROUP, crowd, herd, flock, horde, army, galaxy, assemblage, gathering, band, body, pack; knot, cluster; *informal* bunch, gaggle, posse.

bewail ● verb LAMENT, bemoan, mourn, grieve over, sorrow over, cry over; deplore, complain about; *archaic* plain over.
– OPPOSITES rejoice at, applaud.

beware ● verb BE ON YOUR GUARD, watch out, look out, mind out, be alert, be on the lookout, keep your eyes open/peeled, keep an eye out, keep a sharp lookout, be on the qui vive; take care, be careful, be cautious, have a care, watch your step; *Brit. school slang, dated* cave; *Golf* fore; *Hunting* ware.

bewilder ● verb BAFFLE, mystify, bemuse, perplex, puzzle, confuse, confound, nonplus; *informal* flummox, faze, stump, beat, fox, make someone scratch their head, be all Greek to, floor; *N. Amer. informal* discombobulate, buffalo.
– OPPOSITES enlighten.

bewildered ● adjective BAFFLED, mystified, bemused, perplexed, puzzled, confused, nonplussed, at sea, at a loss, disorientated, taken aback; *informal* flummoxed, bamboozled; *N. Amer. informal* discombobulated.

bewitch ● verb **1** *that evil woman bewitched him* CAST/PUT A SPELL ON, enchant; possess, witch, curse; *N. Amer.* hex, hoodoo; *Austral.* point the bone at. **2** *she was bewitched by her surroundings* CAPTIVATE, enchant, entrance, enrapture, charm, beguile, delight, fascinate, enthral.
– OPPOSITES repel.

beyond ● preposition **1** *beyond the trees* ON THE FAR SIDE OF, on the other side of, further away than, behind, past, after. **2** *beyond six o'clock* LATER THAN, past, after. **3** *inflation beyond 10 per cent* GREATER THAN, more than, exceeding, in excess of, above, over and above, above and beyond, upwards of. **4** *little beyond food was*

Bi ● symbol the chemical element bismuth.
bi- (also **bin-** before a vowel) ● combining form **1** two; having two: *biathlon.* **2** occurring twice in every one or once in every two: *bicentennial.* **3** lasting for two: *biennial.*
– ORIGIN Latin, 'doubly, having two'.
biannual ● adjective occurring twice a year. Compare with BIENNIAL.
– DERIVATIVES **biannually** adverb.
bias ● noun **1** inclination or prejudice in favour of a particular person, thing, or viewpoint. **2** a slanting direction across the grain of a fabric. **3** the tendency of a ball in the game of bowls to swerve because of the way it is weighted. **4** Electronics a steady voltage, applied to an electronic device, that can be adjusted to change the way the device operates. ● verb (**biased**, **biasing** or **biassed**, **biassing**) influence unfairly; prejudice.
– ORIGIN originally in the sense 'oblique' or 'oblique line': from French *biais.*
bias binding ● noun a narrow strip of fabric cut on the bias, used to bind edges.
biathlon ● noun a sporting event in which the competitors combine cross-country skiing and rifle shooting.
– DERIVATIVES **biathlete** noun.
– ORIGIN from Greek *athlon* 'contest'.
bib ● noun **1** a piece of cloth or plastic fastened under a child's chin to keep its clothes clean while it is eating. **2** the upper front part of an apron or pair of dungarees. **3** a common inshore fish of the cod family.
– PHRASES **one's best bib and tucker** informal one's smartest clothes.
– ORIGIN probably from Latin *bibere* 'to drink'.
bibelot /beebəlō/ ● noun a small ornament or trinket.
– ORIGIN French, a fanciful formation from *bel* 'beautiful'.
Bible ● noun **1** the Christian scriptures, consisting of the Old and New Testaments. **2** the Jewish scriptures. **3** (**bible**) informal a book regarded as authoritative.
– ORIGIN Greek *biblion* 'book'.
Bible Belt ● noun those areas of the southern and middle western US and western Canada where many Protestants believe in a literal interpretation of the Bible.
biblical ● adjective relating to or contained in the Bible.
– DERIVATIVES **biblically** adverb.
bibliography /bibliogrəfi/ ● noun (pl. **bibliographies**) **1** a list of books or documents on a particular subject or by a particular author. **2** the study of books in terms of their classification, printing, and publication. **3** a list of the books referred to in a scholarly work.
– DERIVATIVES **bibliographer** noun **bibliographic** adjective.
– ORIGIN from Greek *biblion* 'book'.
bibliomania ● noun passionate enthusiasm for collecting and possessing books.
– DERIVATIVES **bibliomaniac** noun & adjective.
bibliophile /bibliōfīl/ ● noun a person who collects or has a great love of books.
– DERIVATIVES **bibliophilic** adjective **bibliophily** noun.
bibulous /bibyooləss/ ● adjective formal very fond of drinking alcohol.
– DERIVATIVES **bibulously** adverb **bibulousness** noun.
– ORIGIN Latin *bibulus* 'freely drinking', from *bibere* 'to drink'.
bicameral /bīkammərəl/ ● adjective (of a legislative body) having two chambers.
– DERIVATIVES **bicameralism** noun.
– ORIGIN from Latin *camera* 'chamber'.
bicarbonate ● noun **1** Chemistry a salt containing the anion HCO_3^-. **2** (also **bicarbonate of soda**) sodium bicarbonate.
bicentenary ● noun (pl. **bicentenaries**) the two-hundredth anniversary of a significant event.
– DERIVATIVES **bicentennial** noun & adjective.
biceps /bīseps/ ● noun (pl. same) **1** a large muscle in the upper arm which flexes the arm and forearm and turns the hand to face palm uppermost. **2** (also **leg biceps**) a muscle in the back of the thigh which helps to flex the leg.
– ORIGIN Latin, 'two-headed' (because the muscle has two points of attachment).
bichon frise /beeshən freez/ ● noun a breed of toy dog with a fine, curly, white coat.
– ORIGIN from French *barbichon* 'little water spaniel' + *frisé* 'curly-haired'.
bicker ● verb argue about trivial matters.
– ORIGIN of unknown origin.
bicuspid ● adjective having two cusps or points. ● noun a tooth with two cusps, especially a human premolar tooth.
– ORIGIN from Latin *cuspis* 'sharp point'.
bicycle ● noun a vehicle consisting of two wheels held in a frame one behind the other, propelled by pedals and steered with handlebars attached to the front wheel. ● verb ride a bicycle.
– DERIVATIVES **bicyclist** noun.
– ORIGIN from Greek *kuklos* 'wheel'.
bid[1] ● verb (**bidding**; past and past part. **bid**) **1** offer (a certain price) for something, especially at an auction. **2** (**bid for**) (of a contractor) tender for (work). **3** (**bid for**) make an effort to obtain or achieve. ● noun **1** an offer to buy something. **2** an offer to do work or supply goods at a stated price. **3** an effort to obtain or achieve something.
– DERIVATIVES **bidder** noun **bidding** noun.
– ORIGIN Old English.
bid[2] ● verb (**bidding**; past **bid** or **bade**; past part. **bid**) **1** utter (a greeting or farewell) to. **2** archaic or literary command (someone) to do something.
– ORIGIN Old English, 'ask'.
biddable ● adjective meekly ready to accept and follow instructions.
bidden archaic or literary past participle of BID[2].
biddy ● noun (pl. **biddies**) informal a woman, especially an old one.
– ORIGIN originally denoting a chicken: of unknown origin.
bide ● verb archaic or dialect remain or stay in a place.
– PHRASES **bide one's time** wait quietly for a good opportunity to do something.
– ORIGIN Old English.
bidet /beeday/ ● noun a low oval basin used for washing one's genital and anal area.
– ORIGIN French, 'pony'.

Thesaurus

provided APART FROM, except, other than, besides; *informal* outside of; *formal* save.
● adverb *a house with a garden beyond* FURTHER AWAY/OFF.
bias ● noun **1** *he accused the media of bias* PREJUDICE, partiality, partisanship, favouritism, unfairness, one-sidedness; bigotry, intolerance, discrimination, a jaundiced eye; leaning, tendency, inclination, predilection. **2** *a dress cut on the bias* DIAGONAL, cross, slant, angle.
– OPPOSITES impartiality.
● verb *this may have biased the result* PREJUDICE, influence, colour, sway, weight, predispose; distort, skew, slant.
biased ● adjective PREJUDICED, partial, partisan, blinkered, one-sided; bigoted, intolerant, discriminatory; jaundiced, distorted, warped, twisted, skewed.
– OPPOSITES impartial.
Bible ● noun **1** *he read the Bible* THE (HOLY) SCRIPTURES, Holy Writ, the Good Book, the Book of Books. **2** *(informal) the taxi driver's bible* HANDBOOK, manual, ABC, companion, guide, vade mecum.
bibliophile ● noun BOOK LOVER, avid reader; *informal* book worm; *rare* bibliomaniac.
bicker ● verb SQUABBLE, argue, quarrel, wrangle, fight, disagree, dispute, spar, have words, be at each other's throats, lock horns; *informal* scrap, argufy, spat; *archaic* altercate.
– OPPOSITES agree.
bicycle ● noun CYCLE, two-wheeler, pedal cycle; *informal* bike, pushbike.
bid[1] ● verb **1** *United bid £1 million for the striker* OFFER, make an offer of, put in a bid of, put up, tender, proffer, propose. **2** *she is bidding for a place in the England team* TRY TO OBTAIN, try to get, make a pitch for, make a bid for.
● noun **1** *a bid of £3,000* OFFER, tender, proposal. **2** *a bid to cut crime* ATTEMPT, effort, endeavour, try; *informal* crack, go, shot, stab; *formal* essay.
bid[2] ● verb **1** *she bid him farewell* WISH; utter. **2** *(poetic/literary) I did as he bade me* ORDER, command, tell, instruct, direct, enjoin, charge. **3** *(poetic/literary) he bade his companions enter* INVITE TO, ask to, request to.
biddable ● adjective OBEDIENT, acquiescent, compliant, tractable, amenable, complaisant, cooperative, dutiful, submissive; *rare* persuasible.
– OPPOSITES disobedient, uncooperative.
bidding ● noun COMMAND, order, instruction, decree, injunction,

Biedermeier /beedərmīər/ ● adjective denoting a 19th-century German style of furniture and decoration characterized by restraint and utilitarianism.
– ORIGIN from the name of a fictitious German schoolmaster created by L. Eichrodt (1854).

biennial ● adjective **1** taking place every other year. Compare with BIANNUAL. **2** (of a plant) taking two years to grow from seed to fruition and die. ● noun **1** a biennial plant. **2** an event celebrated or taking place every two years.
– DERIVATIVES **biennially** adverb.
– ORIGIN from Latin *annus* 'year'.

bier /beer/ ● noun a movable platform on which a coffin or corpse is placed before burial.
– ORIGIN Old English, related to BEAR¹.

biff informal ● verb strike roughly with the fist. ● noun a sharp blow with the fist.
– ORIGIN probably imitative.

bifid /bīfid/ ● adjective Botany & Zoology (of a part of a plant or animal) divided by a deep cleft or notch into two parts.
– ORIGIN Latin *bifidus* 'doubly split'.

bifocal ● adjective denoting a lens having two parts each with a different focal length, one for distant and one for near vision. ● noun (**bifocals**) a pair of glasses with bifocal lenses.

bifurcate ● verb /bīfəkayt/ divide into two branches or forks. ● adjective /bīfurkət/ forked; branched.
– DERIVATIVES **bifurcation** noun.
– ORIGIN Latin *bifurcare*, from *furca* 'a fork'.

big ● adjective (**bigger**, **biggest**) **1** of considerable size, physical power, or extent. **2** of considerable importance or seriousness. **3** informal exciting great interest or popularity. **4** informal, often ironic generous: *'That's big of you!'*
– PHRASES **the big screen** informal the cinema. **big with child** archaic advanced in pregnancy. **in a big way** informal to a great extent or high degree. **talk big** informal talk confidently or boastfully. **think big** informal be ambitious. **too big for one's boots** informal conceited.
– DERIVATIVES **biggish** adjective **bigness** noun.
– ORIGIN of unknown origin.

bigamy ● noun the offence of marrying someone while already married to another person.
– DERIVATIVES **bigamist** noun **bigamous** adjective.
– ORIGIN Old French *bigamie*, from BI- + Greek *-gamos* 'married'.

big band ● noun a large group of musicians playing jazz or swing music.

big bang ● noun the rapid expansion of matter from a state of extremely high density and temperature which, according to current cosmological theories, marked the origin of the universe.

Big Brother ● noun a person or organization exercising total control over people's lives.
– ORIGIN from the name of the fictitious head of state in George Orwell's *Nineteen Eighty-four* (1949).

big crunch ● noun a contraction of the universe to a state of extremely high density and temperature (a hypothetical opposite of the BIG BANG).

big dipper ● noun **1** Brit. a roller coaster. **2** (**the Big Dipper**) North American term for PLOUGH (in sense 2).

big end ● noun (in a piston engine) the larger end of the connecting rod, encircling the crankpin.

Bigfoot ● noun (pl. **Bigfeet**) a large, hairy ape-like creature, supposedly found in NW America.

big game ● noun large animals hunted for sport.

big-head ● noun informal a conceited person.

bight /bīt/ ● noun **1** a curve or recess in a coastline or other geographical feature. **2** a loop of rope.
– ORIGIN Old English.

big mouth ● noun informal an indiscreet or boastful person.
– DERIVATIVES **big-mouthed** adjective.

bigot /biggət/ ● noun a person who is prejudiced in their views and intolerant of the opinions of others.
– DERIVATIVES **bigoted** adjective **bigotry** noun.
– ORIGIN French.

big top ● noun the main tent in a circus.

big wheel ● noun a Ferris wheel.

bigwig ● noun informal an important person.

bijou /beezhoo/ ● adjective small and elegant. ● noun (pl. **bijoux** pronunc. same) archaic a jewel or trinket.
– ORIGIN French, from Breton *bizou* 'finger-ring', from *biz* 'finger'.

bike informal ● noun a bicycle or motorcycle. ● verb ride a bicycle or motorcycle.
– DERIVATIVES **biker** noun.

bikini ● noun (pl. **bikinis**) a women's two-piece swimsuit.
– ORIGIN named after *Bikini* atoll in the western Pacific, where an atom bomb was exploded in 1946 (because of the supposed 'explosive' effect created by the garment).

bilateral ● adjective **1** having two sides. **2** involving two parties.
– DERIVATIVES **bilaterally** adverb.

bilberry ● noun (pl. **bilberries**) the small blue edible berry of a hardy dwarf shrub found on heathland and high ground.
– ORIGIN probably Scandinavian.

Bildungsroman /bildoongzrōmaan/ ● noun a novel dealing with someone's formative years or spiritual education.
– ORIGIN German, from *Bildung* 'education' + *Roman* 'a novel'.

bile ● noun **1** a bitter fluid which aids digestion, secreted by the liver and stored in the gall bladder. **2** anger; irritability.
– ORIGIN Latin *bilis*.

bile duct ● noun the tube which conveys bile from the liver and the gall bladder to the duodenum.

Thesaurus

demand, mandate, direction, summons, call; wish, desire; request; *poetic/literary* behest; *archaic* hest.

big ● adjective **1** *a big building* LARGE, sizeable, substantial, great, huge, immense, enormous, extensive, colossal, massive, mammoth, vast, tremendous, gigantic, giant, monumental, mighty, gargantuan, elephantine, titanic, mountainous, Brobdingnagian; towering, tall, high, lofty; outsize, oversized; goodly; capacious, voluminous, spacious; king-size(d), man-size, family-size(d), economy-size(d); *informal* jumbo, whopping, thumping, bumper, mega, humongous, monster, astronomical, almighty, dirty great, socking great; *Brit. informal* whacking, ginormous; *formal* commodious. **2** *a big man* WELL BUILT, sturdy, brawny, burly, broad-shouldered, muscular, muscly, rugged, lusty, Herculean, bulky, hulking, strapping, thickset, stocky, solid, hefty; tall, huge, gigantic; fat, stout, portly, plump, fleshy, paunchy, corpulent, obese; *informal* hunky, beefy, husky; *poetic/literary* thewy, stark. **3** *my big brother* GROWN-UP, adult, mature, grown; elder, older. **4** *a big decision* IMPORTANT, significant, major, momentous, weighty, consequential, far-reaching, key, vital, critical, crucial. **5** *(informal) a big man in the government* POWERFUL, important, prominent, influential, high-powered, leading; *N. Amer.* major-league. **6** *(informal) he has big plans* AMBITIOUS, far-reaching, grandiose, on a grand scale. **7** *she's got a big heart* GENEROUS, kind, kindly, caring, compassionate, loving. **8** *(informal) African bands are big in Britain* POPULAR, successful, in demand, sought-after, all the rage; *informal* hot, in, cool, trendy, now, hip; *Brit. informal, dated* all the go.
– OPPOSITES small, minor, unimportant, modest, mean.
– PHRASES **too big for one's boots** *(informal)* CONCEITED, full of oneself, cocky, arrogant, cocksure, above oneself, self-important; vain, self-satisfied, pleased with oneself, smug, complacent; *informal* big-headed, swollen-headed; *poetic/literary* vainglorious.

big-headed ● adjective *(informal)* CONCEITED, full of oneself, cocky, arrogant, cocksure, above oneself, self-important; vain, self-satisfied, pleased with oneself, smug, complacent; *informal* swollen-headed, too big for one's boots; *poetic/literary* vainglorious.
– OPPOSITES modest.

big-hearted ● adjective GENEROUS, magnanimous, munificent, open-handed, bountiful, unstinting, unselfish, altruistic, charitable, philanthropic, benevolent; kind, kindly, kind-hearted; *poetic/literary* bounteous.
– OPPOSITES mean.

bigot ● noun DOGMATIST, partisan, sectarian; racist, sexist, chauvinist, jingoist.

bigoted ● adjective PREJUDICED, biased, partial, one-sided, sectarian, discriminatory; opinionated, dogmatic, intolerant, narrow-minded, blinkered, illiberal; racist, sexist, chauvinistic, jingoistic; jaundiced, warped, twisted, distorted.
– OPPOSITES open-minded.

bigotry ● noun PREJUDICE, bias, partiality, partisanship, sectarianism, discrimination; dogmatism, intolerance, narrow-mindedness; racism, sexism, chauvinism, jingoism.
– OPPOSITES open-mindedness.

bigwig ● noun *(informal)* VIP, important person, notable, dignitary, grandee; celebrity; *informal* somebody, heavyweight, big shot, big noise, big gun, big cheese, big fish; *Brit. informal* brass hat; *N. Amer. informal* big wheel.

b

bilge ● noun **1** the area on the outer surface of a ship's hull where the bottom curves to meet the vertical sides. **2** (**bilges**) the lowest internal portion of the hull. **3** (also **bilge water**) dirty water that collects inside the bilges. **4** informal nonsense; rubbish.
– ORIGIN probably a variant of BULGE.

bilharzia /bilhaartsiə/ ● noun a chronic disease caused by infestation with blood flukes, endemic in parts of Africa and South America.
– ORIGIN named after the German physician T. *Bilharz* (1825–62), who discovered the parasite.

bilingual ● adjective **1** speaking two languages fluently. **2** expressed in or using two languages.
– DERIVATIVES **bilingualism** noun.

bilious ● adjective **1** relating to bile. **2** affected by nausea or vomiting. **3** spiteful; bad-tempered.
– DERIVATIVES **biliously** adverb **biliousness** noun.

bilk ● verb informal **1** cheat or defraud. **2** obtain (money) fraudulently.
– DERIVATIVES **bilker** noun.
– ORIGIN originally used in cribbage meaning 'spoil one's opponent's score': perhaps a variant of BAULK.

Bill ● noun (**the Bill** or **the Old Bill**) Brit. informal the police.
– ORIGIN familiar form of the given name *William*.

bill[1] ● noun **1** a printed or written statement of the money owed for goods or services. **2** a draft of a proposed law presented to parliament for discussion. **3** a programme of entertainment at a theatre or cinema. **4** N. Amer. a banknote. **5** a poster or handbill. ● verb **1** list (a person or event) in a programme. **2** (**bill as**) describe or proclaim as. **3** send a bill to. **4** charge (a sum of money).
– PHRASES **bill of lading** a detailed list of a ship's cargo given by the master of the ship to the person consigning the goods. **a clean bill of health** a declaration or confirmation of good health or condition. **fit the bill** be suitable for a particular purpose.
– DERIVATIVES **billable** adjective **billing** noun.
– ORIGIN Old French *bille*, probably from Latin *bulla* 'seal, sealed document'.

bill[2] ● noun **1** the beak of a bird. **2** a narrow promontory: *Portland Bill.* ● verb (of birds, especially doves) stroke bill with bill during courtship.
– PHRASES **bill and coo** informal behave or talk in a loving and sentimental way.
– ORIGIN Old English.

billabong ● noun Austral. a branch of a river forming a backwater or stagnant pool.
– ORIGIN from an Aboriginal language.

billboard ● noun a hoarding.

billet[1] ● noun a civilian house where soldiers are lodged temporarily. ● verb (**billeted, billeting**) lodge (soldiers) in a civilian house.
– ORIGIN originally denoting a short written document, later a written order requiring a householder to lodge the bearer: from Old French *billette* 'little bill'; related to BILL[1].

billet[2] ● noun **1** a thick piece of wood. **2** a small bar of metal for further processing.
– ORIGIN Old French *billette* and *billot* 'little tree trunk', from Latin *billa, billus* 'branch, trunk'.

billet-doux /billidoo/ ● noun (pl. **billets-doux** /billidooz/) dated or humorous a love letter.
– ORIGIN French, 'sweet note'.

billfold ● noun N. Amer. a wallet.

billhook ● noun a tool having a sickle-shaped blade with a sharp inner edge, used for pruning or lopping branches.

billiards ● plural noun (treated as sing.) a game for two people, played on a billiard table with three balls.
– ORIGIN French *billard* 'billiard cue, billiards', from Old French *bille* 'tree trunk'.

billiard table ● noun a cloth-covered rectangular table used in billiards, snooker, and some forms of pool, with six pockets at the corners and sides into which balls are struck with cues.

billion ● cardinal number (pl. **billions** or (with numeral or quantifying word) same) **1** the number equivalent to the product of a thousand and a million; 1,000,000,000 or 10^9. **2** dated, chiefly Brit. a million million (1,000,000,000,000 or 10^{12}). **3** (**billions**) informal a very large number or amount.
– DERIVATIVES **billionth** ordinal number.
– ORIGIN French, from *million*, by substitution of the prefix *bi-* 'two' for the initial letters.

billionaire ● noun a person possessing assets worth at least a billion pounds or dollars.

bill of exchange ● noun a written order requiring a person to make a specified payment to the signatory or to a named payee.

bill of rights ● noun a statement of rights, in particular the English constitutional settlement of 1689 and the first ten amendments to the Constitution of the US, ratified in 1791.

billow ● noun **1** a large undulating mass of cloud, smoke, or steam. **2** archaic a large sea wave. ● verb **1** (of fabric) fill with air and swell outwards. **2** (of smoke, cloud, or steam) move or flow outward with an undulating motion.
– DERIVATIVES **billowy** adjective.
– ORIGIN Old Norse.

billposter (also **billsticker**) ● noun a person who pastes up advertisements or other notices on hoardings.

billy (also **billycan**) ● noun (pl. **billies**) a tin or enamel cooking pot with a lid and folding handle, used in camping.
– ORIGIN perhaps from an Aboriginal word meaning 'water'.

billy goat ● noun a male goat.
– ORIGIN from *Billy*, familiar form of the given name *William*.

bimbo ● noun (pl. **bimbos**) informal, derogatory an attractive but unintelligent or frivolous young woman.
– DERIVATIVES **bimbette** noun.
– ORIGIN originally in the sense 'fellow': from Italian, 'little child'.

bimonthly ● adjective & adverb appearing or taking place twice a month or every two months.

bin ● noun **1** a container for rubbish. **2** a large container for storing a specified substance. **3** a partitioned stand or case for storing bottles of wine. ● verb (**binned, binning**) throw (something) away by putting it in a bin.
– ORIGIN Old English.

binary /bīnəri/ ● adjective **1** composed of or involving two things. **2** using or denoting a system of numbers with two as its base, employing the digits 0 and 1. ● noun (pl. **binaries**) **1** the binary system of notation. **2** Astronomy a system of two stars revolving round their common centre.

Thesaurus

– OPPOSITES nonentity.

bijou ● adjective SMALL, little, compact, snug, cosy.

bilge ● noun *(informal).* See NONSENSE sense 1.

bilious ● adjective **1** *I felt bilious* NAUSEOUS, sick, queasy, nauseated, green about the gills; *N. Amer. informal* barfy. **2** *his bilious disposition* BAD-TEMPERED, irritable, irascible, tetchy, testy, crotchety, ill-tempered, ill-natured, ill-humoured, peevish, fractious, pettish, crabby, waspish, prickly, crusty, shrewish, quick-tempered; *N. Amer. informal* cranky, ornery. **3** *a bilious green and pink colour scheme* LURID, garish, loud, violent; sickly, nauseating.
– OPPOSITES well, good-humoured, muted.

bilk ● verb *(informal).* See SWINDLE verb.

bill[1] ● noun **1** *a bill for £600* INVOICE, account, statement, list of charges; *N. Amer.* check; *informal, humorous* the damage; *N. Amer. informal* tab; *archaic* reckoning, score. **2** *a parliamentary bill* DRAFT LAW, proposed piece of legislation, proposal, measure. **3** *she was top of the bill* PROGRAMME (OF ENTERTAINMENT), line-up; *N. Amer.* playbill. **4** *(N. Amer.) a $10 bill* BANKNOTE, note; *US informal* greenback; *US & historical* Treasury note. **5** *he had been posting bills* POSTER, advertisement, public notice, announcement; flyer, leaflet, handbill; *Brit.* flyposter; *N. Amer.* dodger; *informal* ad; *Brit. informal* advert.
● verb **1** *please bill me for the work* INVOICE, charge, debit, send a statement to. **2** *the concert went ahead as billed* ADVERTISE, announce; schedule, programme, timetable; *N. Amer.* slate. **3** *he was billed as the new Sean Connery* DESCRIBE, call, style, label, dub; promote, publicize, talk up; *informal* hype.

bill[2] ● noun *a bird's bill* BEAK; *Scottish & N. English* neb; *technical* mandibles.

billet ● noun *the troops' billets* QUARTERS, rooms; accommodation, lodging, housing; barracks, cantonment.
● verb *two soldiers were billeted here* ACCOMMODATE, quarter, put up, lodge, house; station, garrison.

billow ● noun **1** *billows of smoke* CLOUD, mass. **2** *(archaic) the billows that break upon the shore* WAVE, roller, boomer, breaker.
● verb **1** *her dress billowed around her* PUFF UP/OUT, balloon (out), swell, fill (out), belly out. **2** *smoke billowed from the chimney* SWIRL, spiral, roll, undulate, eddy; pour, flow.

billowing ● adjective ROLLING, swirling, undulating, surging, heav-

– ORIGIN Latin *binarius*, from *bini* 'two together'.

bind ● verb (past and past part. **bound**) **1** tie or fasten tightly together. **2** restrain (someone) by tying their hands and feet. **3** wrap or encircle tightly. **4** hold in a united or cohesive group or mass. **5** impose a legal or contractual obligation on. **6** (**be bound by**) be hampered or constrained by. **7** (**bind someone over**) (of a court of law) require someone to fulfil an obligation, typically by paying a sum of money as surety. **8** secure (a contract), typically with a sum of money. **9** fix together and enclose (the pages of a book) in a cover. **10** trim (the edge of a piece of material) with a fabric strip. ● noun **1** informal an annoyance. **2** a statutory constraint. **3** Music another term for TIE.
– ORIGIN Old English.

binder ● noun **1** a cover for holding magazines or loose sheets of paper together. **2** a reaping machine that binds grain into sheaves. **3** a bookbinder.

bindery ● noun (pl. **binderies**) a workshop or factory in which books are bound.

bindi /bindee/ ● noun (pl. **bindis**) a decorative mark worn in the middle of the forehead by Indian women.
– ORIGIN Hindi.

binding ● noun **1** a strong covering holding the pages of a book together. **2** fabric cut or woven in a strip, used for binding the edges of a piece of material. **3** (also **ski binding**) Skiing a device fixed to a ski to grip a ski boot. ● adjective (of an agreement) involving a contractual obligation.

bindweed ● noun a twining plant with trumpet-shaped flowers, several kinds of which are invasive weeds.

bine /bīn/ ● noun a long, flexible stem of a climbing plant.
– ORIGIN originally a dialect form of BIND.

bin-end ● noun Brit. one of the last bottles from a bin of wine.

binge informal ● noun a short period of excessive indulgence. ● verb (**bingeing** or US also **binging**) indulge in an activity, especially eating, to excess.
– DERIVATIVES **binger** noun.
– ORIGIN of unknown origin.

bingo ● noun a game in which players mark off randomly called numbers on printed cards, the winner being the first to mark off all their numbers. ● exclamation **1** a call by someone who wins a game of bingo. **2** expressing satisfaction at a sudden positive event or outcome.
– ORIGIN of unknown origin.

binnacle ● noun a built-in housing for a ship's compass.
– ORIGIN from Spanish *bitácula, bitácora* or Portuguese *bitacola*, from Latin *habitaculum* 'dwelling place'.

binocular /binokyoolər/ ● adjective adapted for or using both eyes.
– ORIGIN from Latin *bini* 'two together' + *oculus* 'eye'.

binoculars ● plural noun an optical instrument with a separate lens for each eye, used for viewing distant objects.

binocular vision ● noun vision using two eyes with overlapping fields of view, allowing good perception of depth.

binomial /bīnōmiəl/ ● noun **1** Mathematics an algebraic expression of the sum or the difference of two terms. **2** Biology the two-part Latin name of a species (the genus followed by the species name). ● adjective consisting of two terms.
– ORIGIN from Latin *bi-* 'having two' + Greek *nomos* 'part, portion'.

bint ● noun Brit. informal, derogatory a girl or woman.
– ORIGIN Arabic, 'daughter, girl'.

bio- ● combining form **1** of or relating to life: *biosynthesis.* **2** biological; relating to biology: *biohazard.* **3** of living beings: *biogenesis.*
– ORIGIN from Greek *bios* 'human life', the sense being extended in modern scientific usage to mean 'organic life'.

biochemistry ● noun the branch of science concerned with the chemical processes which occur within living organisms.
– DERIVATIVES **biochemical** adjective **biochemist** noun.

biochip ● noun a device acting like a silicon chip, with components made from biological molecules or structures.

biocide ● noun **1** a substance that is poisonous to living organisms, such as a pesticide. **2** the destruction of life.
– DERIVATIVES **biocidal** adjective.

biodegradable ● adjective capable of being decomposed by bacteria or other living organisms.
– DERIVATIVES **biodegradability** noun **biodegradation** noun **biodegrade** verb.

bio-diesel ● noun a biofuel intended as a substitute for diesel.

biodiversity ● noun the variety of plant and animal life in the world or in a particular habitat.

bioengineering ● noun **1** another term for GENETIC ENGINEERING. **2** the use of artificial tissues or organs in the body. **3** the use in engineering or industry of organisms or biological processes.
– DERIVATIVES **bioengineer** noun & verb.

biofeedback ● noun the use of electronic monitoring of a normally automatic bodily function in order to train someone to acquire voluntary control of that function.

bioflavonoid ● noun any of a group of compounds occurring mainly in fruit, sometimes regarded as vitamins.

biofuel ● noun fuel derived directly from living matter.

biogas ● noun gaseous fuel, especially methane, produced by the fermentation of organic matter.

biogeography ● noun the branch of biology concerned with the geographical distribution of plants and animals.
– DERIVATIVES **biogeographer** noun **biogeographic** adjective **biogeographical** adjective.

biography ● noun (pl. **biographies**) an account of a person's life written by someone else.
– DERIVATIVES **biographer** noun **biographic** adjective **biographical** adjective.

biohazard ● noun a risk to human health or the environment arising from biological research.

bioinformatics /bīōinfəmattiks/ ● plural noun (treated as sing.) the science of collecting and analysing complex biological data such as genetic codes.

biological ● adjective **1** relating to biology or living organisms. **2** (of a parent or child) related by blood; natural. **3** relating to the use of micro-organisms or toxins of biological origin as weapons of war. **4** (of a detergent) containing enzymes to assist cleaning.
– DERIVATIVES **biologically** adverb.

biological clock ● noun an innate mechanism that controls the cyclical physiological activities of an organism.

biological control ● noun the control of a pest by the introduction of a natural enemy or predator.

biology ● noun **1** the scientific study of living organisms. **2** the plants and animals of a particular area. **3** the features of a particular organism or class of organisms.
– DERIVATIVES **biologist** noun.

bioluminescence ● noun the biochemical emission of light by living organisms such as glow-worms and deep-sea fishes.
– DERIVATIVES **bioluminescent** adjective.

biomass ● noun **1** the total quantity or weight of organisms in a given area or volume. **2** organic matter used as a fuel, especially in the generation of electricity.

biome ● noun a large naturally occurring community of flora and fauna occupying a major habitat, such as forest or tundra.

biomorph ● noun **1** a decorative form or object resembling a

Thesaurus

ing, billowy, swelling, rippling.

bin ● noun CONTAINER, receptacle, holder; drum, canister, caddy, can, tin.

bind ● verb **1** *they bound her hands and feet* TIE (UP), fasten (together), hold together, secure, make fast, attach; rope, strap, lash, truss, tether. **2** *Shelley bound up the wound with a clean dressing* BANDAGE, dress, cover, wrap; strap up, tape up. **3** *the experience had bound them together* UNITE, join, bond, knit together, draw together, yoke together. **4** *we have not bound ourselves to join* COMMIT ONESELF, undertake, pledge, vow, promise, swear, give one's word. **5** *the edges are bound in a contrasting colour* TRIM, hem, edge, border, fringe; finish. **6** *they are bound by the agreement* CONSTRAIN, restrict, restrain, trammel, tie hand and foot, tie down, shackle; hamper, hinder, inhibit.
– OPPOSITES untie, separate.
● noun (*informal*) **1** *starting so early is a bind* NUISANCE, annoyance, inconvenience, bore, bother, source of irritation, irritant, trial; *informal* pain, pain in the neck/backside, headache, hassle, drag; *N. Amer. informal* pain in the butt. **2** *he is in a political bind* PREDICAMENT, difficult/awkward situation, quandary, dilemma, plight, cleft stick; *informal* spot, tight spot, hole.

binding ● adjective IRREVOCABLE, unalterable, inescapable, unbreakable, contractual; compulsory, obligatory, mandatory, imperative, incumbent.

binge ● noun (*informal*) DRINKING BOUT, debauch; *informal* bender, session, booze-up, blind; *Scottish informal* skite; *N. Amer. informal* jag, toot;

living organism. **2** a graphical representation of an organism generated on a computer.
– DERIVATIVES **biomorphic** adjective.

b

bionic ● adjective **1** relating to the use of electrically-operated artificial body parts. **2** informal having ordinary human powers increased by or as if by the aid of such devices.
– DERIVATIVES **bionically** adverb **bionics** plural noun.

biophysics ● plural noun (treated as sing.) the science of the application of the laws of physics to biological phenomena.
– DERIVATIVES **biophysical** adjective **biophysicist** noun.

biopic ● noun informal a biographical film.

biopiracy ● noun bioprospecting, regarded as a form of exploitation of developing countries.

bioprospecting ● noun the search for plant and animal species from which medicinal drugs and other commercially valuable compounds can be obtained.
– DERIVATIVES **bioprospector** noun.

biopsy ● noun (pl. **biopsies**) an examination of tissue taken from the body, to discover the presence, cause, or extent of a disease.
– ORIGIN from Greek *bios* 'life' + *opsis* 'sight'.

biorhythm ● noun a recurring cycle in the physiology or functioning of an organism, such as the daily cycle of sleeping and waking.
– DERIVATIVES **biorhythmic** adjective.

biosphere ● noun the regions of the surface and atmosphere of the earth occupied by living organisms.
– DERIVATIVES **biospheric** adjective.

biosynthesis ● noun the production of complex molecules within living organisms or cells.
– DERIVATIVES **biosynthetic** adjective.

biota ● noun the animal and plant life of a particular region, habitat, or geological period.
– ORIGIN Greek *biotē* 'life'.

biotechnology ● noun the exploitation of biological processes for industrial and other purposes, especially the genetic manipulation of micro-organisms for the production of antibiotics, hormones, etc.
– DERIVATIVES **biotechnological** adjective **biotechnologist** noun.

biotic ● adjective relating to living things and the effect they have on each other.
– ORIGIN Greek *biōtikos*, from *bios* 'life'.

biotin /bīətin/ ● noun a vitamin of the B complex, found in egg yolk, liver, and yeast, involved in the synthesis of fatty acids and glucose.
– ORIGIN from Greek *bios* 'life'.

biotype ● noun a group of organisms having an identical genetic constitution.

bipartisan ● adjective involving the agreement or cooperation of two political parties.
– DERIVATIVES **bipartisanship** noun.

bipartite ● adjective **1** involving two separate parties. **2** technical consisting of two parts.

biped /bīped/ ● noun an animal that walks on two feet.
– DERIVATIVES **bipedal** /bīpeed'l/ adjective.
– ORIGIN from Latin *bi-* 'having two' + *pes* 'foot'.

biplane ● noun an early type of aircraft with two pairs of wings, one above the other.

bipolar ● adjective having or relating to two poles or extremities.
– DERIVATIVES **bipolarity** noun.

birch ● noun **1** a slender hardy tree having a peeling, typically silver-grey or white, bark and yielding a hard fine-grained wood. **2** (**the birch**) chiefly historical a punishment in which a person is flogged with a bundle of birch twigs. ● verb chiefly historical punish with the birch.
– ORIGIN Old English.

bird ● noun **1** a warm-blooded egg-laying vertebrate animal which has feathers, wings, and a beak, and typically is able to fly. **2** informal a person of a specified kind or character: *she's a sharp old bird.* **3** Brit. informal a young woman or girlfriend.
– PHRASES **the bird has flown** the person one is looking for has escaped or left. **a bird in the hand is worth two in the bush** proverb it's better to be content with what you have than to risk losing everything by seeking to get more. **birds of a feather flock together** proverb people of the same sort or with the same tastes and interests will be found together. **do (one's) bird** Brit. informal serve a prison sentence. [ORIGIN *bird* from rhyming slang *birdlime* 'time'.]
– ORIGIN Old English, 'chick, fledgling'.

birdbrain ● noun informal a stupid person.

bird dog ● noun N. Amer. **1** a gun dog trained to retrieve birds. **2** informal a talent scout in the field of sport.

birder ● noun informal a birdwatcher.

birdie ● noun (pl. **birdies**) **1** informal a little bird. **2** Golf a score of one stroke under par at a hole. ● verb (**birdying**) Golf play (a hole) with a score of one stroke under par.
– ORIGIN the golf term is from US slang *bird*, meaning any first-rate thing.

birding ● noun informal birdwatching.

birdlime ● noun a sticky substance spread on to twigs to trap small birds.

bird of paradise ● noun (pl. **birds of paradise**) a tropical bird, the male of which is noted for the brilliance of its plumage and its spectacular courtship display.

bird of passage ● noun (pl. **birds of passage**) **1** dated a migratory bird. **2** a person who passes through a place without staying for long.

bird of prey ● noun (pl. **birds of prey**) a bird that feeds on animal flesh, typically having a hooked bill and sharp talons (e.g. an eagle, hawk, or owl).

bird's-eye view ● noun a general view from above.

birdshot ● noun the smallest size of shot for sporting rifles or other guns.

bird's nest soup ● noun (in Chinese cookery) a soup made from the dried gelatinous coating of the nests of swifts and other birds.

birdsong ● noun the musical vocalizations of birds.

bird table ● noun Brit. a small raised platform in a garden on which food for birds is placed.

birdwatching ● noun a hobby involving the observation of birds in their natural environment.

biretta /birettə/ ● noun a square cap with three flat projections on top, worn by Roman Catholic clergymen.
– ORIGIN Italian *berretta* or Spanish *birreta*, from Latin *birrus* 'hooded cape'.

biriani /birriaani/ (also **biriyani** or **biryani**) ● noun an Indian dish made with highly seasoned rice and meat, fish, or vegetables.
– ORIGIN Urdu, from Persian, 'fried, grilled'.

biro ● noun (pl. **biros**) Brit. trademark a kind of ballpoint pen.
– ORIGIN named after László József *Biró* (1899–1985), Hungarian inventor of the ballpoint.

birr /bur/ ● noun the basic monetary unit of Ethiopia, equal to 100 cents.
– ORIGIN Amharic.

birth ● noun **1** the emergence of a baby or other young from the body of its mother; the start of life as a physically separate being. **2** the beginning of something. **3** origin or ancestry: *he is of noble birth.*
– DERIVATIVES **birthing** noun.
– PHRASES **give birth** bear a child or young.
– ORIGIN Old Norse, related to BEAR[1].

birth certificate ● noun an official document recording a person's place and date of birth and identifying them by name and by the name of their parents.

birth control ● noun the prevention of unwanted pregnancies, especially through the use of contraception.

birthday ● noun the annual anniversary of the day on which a person was born.

birthing pool ● noun a large circular tub in which a woman is able to give birth to her baby while lying in water.

birthmark ● noun a coloured mark on the body which is there from birth.

Thesaurus

dated souse; *poetic/literary* bacchanal, bacchanalia; *archaic* wassail.

biography ● noun LIFE STORY, life, memoir; *informal* bio, biog.

bird ● noun fowl; chick, fledgling, nestling; (**birds**) avifauna; *informal* feathered friend, birdie.
– RELATED TERMS avian.

birth ● noun **1** *the birth of a child* CHILDBIRTH, delivery, nativity, birthing; *formal* parturition; *dated* confinement; *archaic* accouchement, childbed. **2** *the birth of science* BEGINNING(S), emergence, genesis, dawn, dawning, rise, start. **3** *he is of noble birth* ANCESTRY, lineage, blood, descent, parentage, family, extraction, origin, genealogy, heritage, stock, kinship.
– RELATED TERMS natal.

birth mother ● noun a woman who has given birth to a child, as opposed to an adoptive mother.
birthplace ● noun the place where a person was born.
birth rate ● noun the number of live births per thousand of population per year.
birthright ● noun **1** a particular right or privilege that a person has from birth, especially as an eldest son. **2** a natural or moral right, possessed by everyone.
birth sign ● noun Astrology the zodiacal sign through which the sun is passing when a person is born.
birthstone ● noun a gemstone popularly associated with the month or astrological sign of a person's birth.
biryani ● noun variant spelling of BIRIANI.
bis /bis/ ● adverb Music to be repeated.
– ORIGIN Latin, 'twice'.
biscuit ● noun **1** Brit. a small, flat, crisp unleavened cake. **2** N. Amer. a small, soft round cake like a scone. **3** porcelain or other pottery which has been fired but not glazed.
– PHRASES **take the biscuit** (or chiefly N. Amer. **cake**) informal be the most remarkable or foolish of its kind.
– DERIVATIVES **biscuity** adjective.
– ORIGIN Old French *bescuit*, from Latin *bis* 'twice' + *coquere* 'to cook' (because biscuits were originally cooked in a twofold process: first baked and then dried out in a slow oven).
bisect ● verb divide into two parts.
– DERIVATIVES **bisection** noun **bisector** noun.
– ORIGIN from Latin *secare* 'to cut'.
bisexual ● adjective **1** sexually attracted to both men and women. **2** Biology having characteristics of both sexes. ● noun a person who is sexually attracted to both men and women.
– DERIVATIVES **bisexuality** noun.
bishop ● noun **1** a senior member of the Christian clergy, usually in charge of a diocese and empowered to confer holy orders. **2** a chess piece, typically having a top shaped like a mitre, that can move in any direction along a diagonal.
– ORIGIN Greek *episkopos* 'overseer'.
bishopric ● noun **1** the office or rank of a bishop. **2** a diocese.
bismuth /bizmәth/ ● noun a brittle reddish-tinged grey metallic chemical element resembling lead.
– ORIGIN from *bisemutum*, Latinization of German *Wismut*.
bison ● noun (pl. same) a humpbacked shaggy-haired wild ox.
– ORIGIN Latin.
bisque[1] /bisk/ ● noun a rich soup made from lobster or other shellfish.
– ORIGIN French.
bisque[2] ● noun another term for BISCUIT (in sense 3).
bistable /bīstayb'l/ ● adjective (chiefly of an electronic circuit) having two stable states.
bistro /beestro/ ● noun (pl. **bistros**) a small, inexpensive restaurant.
– ORIGIN French.
bisulphate (US **bisulfate**) ● noun Chemistry a salt containing the anion HSO_4^-.
bit[1] ● noun **1** a small piece or quantity. **2** (**a bit**) a short time or distance. **3** (also **bit of fluff** or **stuff**) informal a girl or young woman.
– PHRASES **a bit** somewhat. **bit by bit** gradually. **bit on the side** informal **1** a person with whom one is unfaithful to one's partner. **2** money earned outside one's normal job. **do one's bit** informal make a useful contribution. **to bits 1** into pieces. **2** informal very much; to a great degree.
– ORIGIN Old English, 'bite, mouthful'.
bit[2] past of BITE.
bit[3] ● noun **1** a metal mouthpiece attached to a bridle, used to control a horse. **2** a tool or piece for boring or drilling. **3** the part of a key that engages with the lock lever.
– PHRASES **get the bit between one's teeth** begin to tackle something in a determined way.
– ORIGIN Old English, 'biting, a bite'.
bit[4] ● noun Computing a unit of information expressed as either a 0 or 1 in binary notation.
– ORIGIN blend of BINARY and DIGIT.
bitch ● noun **1** a female dog, wolf, fox, or otter. **2** informal a woman whom one considers to be malicious or unpleasant. **3** black English a woman (used in a non-derogatory sense). **4** (**a bitch**) informal a difficult or unpleasant thing or situation. ● verb informal make spiteful comments.
– ORIGIN Old English.
bitchy ● adjective (**bitchier**, **bitchiest**) informal malicious; spiteful.
– DERIVATIVES **bitchily** adverb **bitchiness** noun.
bite ● verb (past **bit**; past part. **bitten**) **1** use the teeth to cut into something. **2** (of a snake, insect, or spider) wound with a sting, pincers, or fangs. **3** (of a fish) take the bait or lure on the end of a fishing line into the mouth. **4** (of a tool, tyre, boot, etc.) grip or take hold on a surface. **5** (of a policy or situation) take effect, with unpleasant consequences. **6** (**bite back**) refrain with difficulty from saying. **7** informal annoy or worry: *what's biting you today?* ● noun **1** an act or instance of biting. **2** a piece cut off by biting. **3** Dentistry the bringing together of the teeth when the jaws are closed. **4** informal a quick snack. **5** a sharpness or pungency in flavour. **6** a feeling of cold in the air.
– PHRASES **bite the bullet** decide to do something difficult or unpleasant that one has been hesitating over. [ORIGIN from the old custom of giving wounded soldiers a bullet to bite on when undergoing surgery without anaesthetic.] **bite the dust** informal die or be killed. **bite the hand that feeds one** deliberately hurt or offend a benefactor. **bite off more than one can chew** take on a commitment one cannot fulfil. **bite one's tongue** make a desperate effort to avoid saying something. **once bitten, twice shy** an unpleasant experience causes one to be cautious when in a similar situation again.
– DERIVATIVES **biter** noun.
– ORIGIN Old English.
biting ● adjective **1** (of a wind or the air) painfully cold. **2** (of wit

Thesaurus

– OPPOSITES death, demise, end.
– PHRASES **give birth to** HAVE, bear, produce, be delivered of, bring into the world; *N. Amer.* birth; *informal* drop; *archaic* bring forth.
birthmark ● noun NAEVUS, mole, blemish.
birthright ● noun PATRIMONY, inheritance, heritage; right, due, prerogative, privilege; primogeniture.
biscuit ● noun *(Brit.)* CRACKER, wafer; *N. Amer.* cookie; *informal* bicky.
bisect ● verb CUT IN HALF, halve, divide/cut/split in two, split down the middle; cross, intersect.
bisexual ● adjective **1** *a bisexual actor* AMBISEXUAL; *informal* AC/DC, bi, swinging both ways, ambidextrous; *N. Amer. informal* switch-hitting. **2** *bisexual crustaceans* HERMAPHRODITE, hermaphroditic, intersex; androgynous, epicene; *technical* monoclinous, gynandrous, gynandromorphic.
bishop ● noun diocesan, metropolitan, suffragan; *formal* prelate.
– RELATED TERMS episcopal.
bishopric ● noun DIOCESE, see.
bit ● noun **1** *a bit of bread* PIECE, portion, segment, section, part; chunk, lump, hunk, slice; fragment, scrap, shred, crumb, grain, speck; SPOT, drop, pinch, dash, soupçon, modicum; morsel, mouthful, bite, sample; iota, jot, tittle, whit, atom, particle, trace, touch, suggestion, hint, tinge; snippet, snatch; *informal* smidgen, tad. **2** *wait a bit* MOMENT, minute, second, (little) while; *informal* sec, jiffy; *Brit. informal* mo, tick.
– PHRASES **a bit** RATHER, fairly, slightly, somewhat, quite, moderately; *informal* pretty, sort of, kind of. **bit by bit** GRADUALLY, little by little, in stages, step by step, piecemeal, slowly. **in a bit** SOON, in a (little) while, in a second, in a minute, in a moment, shortly; *informal* anon, in a jiffy, in two shakes; *Brit. informal* in a tick, in two ticks, in a mo; *N. Amer. informal* in a snap; *dated* directly; *poetic/literary* ere long.
bitch ● noun *(informal)* **1** *she's such a bitch* SHREW, vixen, she-devil, hellcat; *informal* cow, cat; *archaic* grimalkin. **2** *a bitch of a job* NIGHTMARE; *informal* bastard, bummer, —— from hell, swine, pig, stinker. ● verb **1** *big men bitched about the price of oil* COMPLAIN, whine, grumble, grouse; *informal* whinge, moan, grouch, gripe. **2** *he's always bitching about colleagues* BE SPITEFUL ABOUT, criticize, run down, speak ill of, slander, malign; *informal* knock, pull to pieces, take apart, bad-mouth, do a hatchet job on; *N. Amer. informal* trash; *Brit. informal* slag off.
– PHRASES **bitch something up** *(informal)* MAKE A MESS OF, mess up, spoil, ruin, wreck; bungle; *informal* botch, muck up, make a hash of, screw up, louse up, muff; *Brit. informal* make a pig's ear of, cock up; *N. Amer. informal* flub, goof up.
bitchy ● adjective *(informal)*. See SPITEFUL.
bite ● verb **1** *the dog bit his arm* SINK ONE'S TEETH INTO, chew, munch, crunch, champ, tear at. **2** *the acid bites into the copper* CORRODE, eat into, eat away at, burn (into), etch, dissolve. **3** *my boots failed to bite* GRIP, hold, get a purchase. **4** *the measures begin to bite* TAKE EFFECT, have an effect, be effective, work, act, have results. **5** *a*

b

or criticism) harsh or cruel.
– DERIVATIVES **bitingly** adverb.
bitmap ● noun a representation in which each item corresponds to one or more bits of information, especially the information used to control the display of a computer screen.
bit part ● noun a small acting role in a play or a film.
bitstream ● noun Electronics a stream of data in binary form.
bitten past participle of BITE.
bitter ● adjective **1** having a sharp, pungent taste or smell; not sweet. **2** causing pain or unhappiness. **3** feeling anger, hurt, and resentment. **4** (of a conflict) harsh and acrimonious. **5** (of wind or weather) intensely cold. ● noun **1** Brit. beer that is strongly flavoured with hops and has a bitter taste. **2** (**bitters**) (treated as sing.) liquor that is flavoured with bitter plant extracts and used as an ingredient in cocktails.
– PHRASES **to the bitter end** to the very end, in spite of harsh difficulties.
– DERIVATIVES **bitterly** adverb **bitterness** noun.
– ORIGIN Old English.
bitter lemon ● noun Brit. a carbonated semi-sweet soft drink flavoured with lemons.
bittern ● noun a marshbird of the heron family, noted for the male's deep booming call.
– ORIGIN Old French *butor*, from Latin *butio* 'bittern' + *taurus* 'bull' (because of its call).
bitter orange ● noun another term for SEVILLE ORANGE.
bittersweet ● adjective **1** sweet with a bitter aftertaste. **2** arousing pleasure tinged with sadness or pain. ● noun **1** another term for WOODY NIGHTSHADE. **2** a vine-like American climbing plant bearing clusters of bright orange pods.
bitty ● adjective (**bittier**, **bittiest**) informal **1** chiefly Brit. made up of small parts that seem unrelated. **2** N. Amer. (with another adjective) tiny: *a little-bitty girl*.
– DERIVATIVES **bittily** adverb **bittiness** noun.
bitumen /bityoomən/ ● noun a black viscous mixture of hydrocarbons obtained naturally or as a residue from petroleum distillation, used for road surfacing and roofing.
– DERIVATIVES **bituminous** adjective.
– ORIGIN Latin.
bituminous coal ● noun black coal with a relatively high volatile content, burning with a characteristically bright smoky flame.
bivalve ● noun an aquatic mollusc which has a compressed body enclosed within two hinged shells, such as an oyster, mussel, or scallop. ● adjective **1** (also **bivalved**) having a hinged double shell. **2** Botany having two valves.
bivouac /bivvoo-ak/ ● noun a temporary camp without tents or cover. ● verb (**bivouacked**, **bivouacking**) stay in such a camp.
– ORIGIN French, probably from Swiss German *Bîwacht* 'additional guard at night'.
bivvy informal ● noun (pl. **bivvies**) a small tent or temporary shelter. ● verb (**bivvies**, **bivvied**) use such a tent or shelter.
– ORIGIN abbreviation of BIVOUAC.
biweekly ● adjective & adverb appearing or taking place every two weeks or twice a week. ● noun (pl. **biweeklies**) a periodical that appears biweekly.
biyearly ● adjective & adverb appearing or taking place every two years or twice a year.
biz ● noun informal business.
bizarre /bizaar/ ● adjective strange; unusual.
– DERIVATIVES **bizarrely** adverb **bizarreness** noun.
– ORIGIN French, from Italian *bizzarro* 'angry'.
Bk ● symbol the chemical element berkelium.
blab informal ● verb (**blabbed**, **blabbing**) reveal secrets by indiscreet talk. ● noun a person who blabs.
– ORIGIN imitative.
blabber informal ● verb talk indiscreetly or excessively. ● noun **1** a person who blabbers. **2** indiscreet or excessive talk.
blabbermouth ● noun informal a person who talks indiscreetly or excessively.
black ● adjective **1** of the very darkest colour owing to the absence of or complete absorption of light. **2** deeply stained with dirt. **3** (of coffee or tea) served without milk. **4** relating to a human group having dark-coloured skin, especially of African or Australian Aboriginal ancestry. **5** characterized by tragedy, disaster, or despair. **6** (of humour) presenting tragic or harrowing situations in comic terms. **7** full of anger or hatred. ● noun **1** black colour or pigment. **2** a member of a dark-skinned people, especially one of African or Australian Aboriginal ancestry. **3** Brit. informal blackcurrant cordial. ● verb **1** make black, especially by the application of black polish, make-up, etc. **2** Brit. dated refuse to handle (goods) or have dealings with (a person or business) as a way of taking industrial action.
– PHRASES **black someone's eye** hit someone in the eye so as to cause bruising. **black out 1** make (a room or building) dark by extinguishing lights and covering windows. **2** obscure completely. **3** undergo a sudden loss of consciousness; faint. **in the black** not owing any money. **in someone's black books** informal in disfavour with someone. **look on the black side** informal view a situation from a pessimistic angle.
– DERIVATIVES **blackish** adjective **blackly** adverb **blackness** noun.
– USAGE To refer to African peoples and their descendants, **black** is the word most generally accepted in Britain today, in preference to **coloured** or **Negro**. In the US **African American** and **Afro-American** are often used.
– ORIGIN Old English.

Thesaurus

hundred or so retailers should bite ACCEPT, agree, respond; be lured, be enticed, be tempted; take the bait.
● noun **1** *he took a bite at his sandwich* CHEW, munch, nibble, gnaw, nip, snap. **2** *he ate it in two bites* MOUTHFUL, piece, bit, morsel. **3** *do you fancy a bite?* SNACK, light meal, mouthful, soupçon; refreshments; *informal* a little something. **4** *the appetizer had a fiery bite* PIQUANCY, pungency, spiciness, strong flavour, tang, zest, sharpness, tartness; *informal* kick, punch, zing.
biting ● adjective **1** *biting comments* VICIOUS, harsh, cruel, savage, cutting, sharp, bitter, scathing, caustic, acid, acrimonious, acerbic, stinging; vitriolic, hostile, spiteful, venomous, mean, nasty; *informal* bitchy, catty. **2** *the biting wind* FREEZING, icy, arctic, glacial; bitter, piercing, penetrating, raw, wintry.
– OPPOSITES mild.
bitter ● adjective **1** *bitter coffee* SHARP, acid, acidic, acrid, tart, sour, biting, unsweetened, vinegary; *N. Amer.* acerb; *technical* acerbic. **2** *a bitter woman* RESENTFUL, embittered, aggrieved, grudge-bearing, begrudging, rancorous, spiteful, jaundiced, ill-disposed, sullen, sour, churlish, morose, petulant, peevish, with a chip on one's shoulder. **3** *a bitter blow* PAINFUL, unpleasant, disagreeable, nasty, cruel, awful, distressing, upsetting, harrowing, heartbreaking, heart-rending, agonizing, traumatic, tragic, chilling; *formal* grievous. **4** *a bitter wind* FREEZING, icy, arctic, glacial; biting, piercing, penetrating, raw, wintry. **5** *a bitter row* ACRIMONIOUS, virulent, angry, rancorous, spiteful, vicious, vitriolic, savage, ferocious, hate-filled, venomous, poisonous, acrid, nasty, ill-natured.
– OPPOSITES sweet, magnanimous, content, welcome, warm, amicable.
bitterness ● noun **1** *the bitterness of the medicine* SHARPNESS, acidity, acridity, tartness, sourness, harshness, vinegariness; *technical* acerbity. **2** *his bitterness grew* RESENTMENT, rancour, indignation, grudge, spite, sullenness, sourness, churlishness, moroseness, petulance, pique, peevishness. **3** *the bitterness of war* TRAUMA, pain, agony, grief; unpleasantness, disagreeableness, nastiness; heartache, heartbreak, distress, desolation, despair, tragedy. **4** *there was no bitterness between them* ACRIMONY, hostility, antipathy, antagonism, enmity, animus, friction, rancour, vitriol, hatred, loathing, venom, poison, nastiness, ill feeling, ill will, bad blood.
– OPPOSITES sweetness, magnanimity, contentment, warmth, goodwill.
bitty ● adjective (*informal*) DISJOINTED, incoherent, fragmented, fragmentary, scrappy, piecemeal; inconsistent, unsystematic, jumbled; uneven, erratic, patchy.
– OPPOSITES coherent.
bizarre ● adjective STRANGE, peculiar, odd, funny, curious, outlandish, outré, eccentric, unconventional, unorthodox, queer, extraordinary; *informal* weird, wacky, oddball, way out, freaky, off the wall, offbeat; *Brit. informal* rum; *N. Amer. informal* wacko.
– OPPOSITES normal.
blab ● verb (*informal*) **1** *she blabbed to the press* TALK, give the game away; *informal* let the cat out of the bag, spill the beans; *Brit. informal* blow the gaff, cough. **2** *I do not blab secrets* BLURT OUT, let slip, let out, tell, reveal, betray, disclose, give away, divulge, leak; *informal* let on, spill.
blabber ● verb (*informal*). See BABBLE verb.
blabbermouth ● noun (*informal*) TALKER, chatterer, prattler; *N. Amer.* blatherskite; *informal* chatterbox, windbag, gasbag, bigmouth; *Brit.*

blackamoor /blakkəmor/ ● noun archaic a black African or a very dark-skinned person.
– ORIGIN from BLACK + MOOR.
black and tan ● noun **1** a breed of terrier with a black back and tan markings on the face, flanks, and legs. **2** (**Black and Tans**) an armed force recruited by the British government to fight Sinn Fein in Ireland in 1921. [ORIGIN so named because of the colours of their uniform.]
black and white ● adjective (of a situation or debate) involving clearly defined opposing principles or issues.
black art (also **black arts**) ● noun black magic.
blackball ● verb reject or vote against (a candidate applying to become a member of a private club).
– ORIGIN from the practice of registering an adverse vote by placing a black ball in a ballot box.
black bean ● noun a cultivated variety of soy bean.
black belt ● noun a black belt worn by an expert in judo, karate, and other martial arts.
blackberry ● noun (pl. **blackberries**) the edible soft fruit of a prickly climbing shrub, consisting of a cluster of purple-black drupels. ● verb (**blackberries**, **blackberried**) (usu. **blackberrying**) gather blackberries.
blackbird ● noun **1** a thrush of which the male has all-black plumage and a yellow bill. **2** an American songbird with largely black plumage.
blackboard ● noun a large board with a dark surface for writing on with chalk.
black box ● noun a flight recorder in an aircraft.
blackcap ● noun a warbler of which the male has a black cap.
blackcurrant ● noun the small round edible black berry of a shrub.
black economy ● noun the part of a country's economic activity which is not recorded or taxed by its government.
blacken ● verb **1** become or make black or dark. **2** damage or destroy (someone's reputation).
black eye ● noun an area of bruised skin around the eye resulting from a blow.
black-figure ● noun a type of ancient Greek pottery in which figures are painted in black, details being added by incising through to the red clay background..
blackfly ● noun **1** a black or dark green aphid which is a common pest of crops. **2** a small black bloodsucking fly.
Blackfoot ● noun (pl. same or **Blackfeet**) a member of a confederacy of North American Indian peoples of the north-western plains consisting of three closely related tribes: the Blackfoot proper or Siksika, the Bloods, and the Peigan.
blackguard /blaggaard/ ● noun dated a man who behaves in a dishonourable or contemptible way.
– DERIVATIVES **blackguardly** adjective.
– ORIGIN originally denoting a body of servants, especially the menials in charge of kitchen utensils; the exact significance of 'black' is uncertain.
blackhead ● noun a plug of oily matter in a hair follicle.
black hole ● noun Astronomy a region of space having a gravitational field so intense that no matter or radiation can escape.
black ice ● noun a transparent coating of ice on a road surface.
blacking ● noun black paste or polish.
blackjack ● noun **1** chiefly N. Amer. a gambling card game in which players try to acquire cards with a face value totalling exactly 21. **2** N. Amer. a flexible lead-filled truncheon.
blackleg ● noun Brit. derogatory a person who continues working when fellow workers are on strike.
blacklist ● noun a list of people or groups regarded as unacceptable or untrustworthy. ● verb put on a blacklist.
black magic ● noun magic involving the supposed summoning of evil spirits.
blackmail ● noun **1** the demanding of money from someone in return for not revealing discreditable information. **2** the use of threats or manipulation in an attempt to influence someone's actions. ● verb subject to blackmail.
– DERIVATIVES **blackmailer** noun.
– ORIGIN from obsolete *mail* 'tribute, rent', from Old Norse, 'speech, agreement'.
Black Maria ● noun informal a police vehicle for transporting prisoners.
– ORIGIN said to be named after a black woman, *Maria* Lee, who kept a boarding house in Boston and helped police in escorting drunk and disorderly customers to jail.
black mark ● noun informal a note of a person's misdemeanour or discreditable action.
black market ● noun an illegal trade in officially controlled or scarce commodities.
– DERIVATIVES **black marketeer** noun.
black mass ● noun a travesty of the Roman Catholic Mass in worship of the Devil.
blackout ● noun **1** a period when all lights must be turned out to prevent them being seen by the enemy during an air raid. **2** a sudden failure or dimming of electric lights. **3** a temporary loss of consciousness. **4** an official suppression of information: *a total news blackout.*
black pudding ● noun Brit. a black sausage containing pork, dried pig's blood, and suet.
Black Rod (in full **Gentleman Usher of the Black Rod**) ● noun (in the UK) the chief usher of the Lord Chamberlain's department of the royal household, who is also usher to the House of Lords.
black sheep ● noun informal a member of a family or other group who is regarded as a disgrace to it.

Thesaurus

informal natterer.
black ● adjective **1** *a black horse* DARK, pitch-black, jet-black, coal-black, inky; *Heraldry* sable; *rare* nigrescent. **2** *a black night* UNLIT, dark, starless, moonless; *poetic/literary* tenebrous, Stygian. **3** *the blackest day of the war* TRAGIC, disastrous, calamitous, catastrophic, cataclysmic, fateful, wretched, woeful, awful, terrible; *formal* grievous. **4** *Mary was in a black mood* MISERABLE, unhappy, sad, wretched, broken-hearted, heartbroken, grief-stricken, grieving, sorrowful, sorrowing, anguished, desolate, despairing, disconsolate, downcast, dejected, cheerless, melancholy, morose, gloomy, glum, mournful, doleful, funereal, dismal, forlorn, woeful, abject; *informal* blue; *poetic/literary* dolorous. **5** *black humour* CYNICAL, macabre, weird, unhealthy, ghoulish, morbid, perverted, gruesome; *informal* sick. **6** *a black look.* See ANGRY sense 1. **7** *(archaic) a black deed.* See WICKED sense 1.
– RELATED TERMS melan-.
– OPPOSITES white, clear, bright, joyful, cheerful, pleasant, friendly.
● verb **1** *the steps of the houses were neatly blacked* BLACKEN, darken; dirty, make sooty, make smoky, stain, grime, soil. **2** *she blacked his eye* BRUISE, contuse; hit, punch, injure. **3** *(Brit. dated) trade union members blacked the work* BOYCOTT, embargo, blacklist, proscribe.
– PHRASES **black out** FAINT, lose consciousness, pass out, swoon; *informal* flake out, go out. **black something out** DARKEN, shade, turn off the lights in; keep the light out of. **in the black** IN CREDIT, in funds, debt-free, out of debt, solvent, financially sound, able to pay one's debts, creditworthy; *rare* unindebted. **black and white 1** *a black-and-white picture* MONOCHROME, greyscale. **2** *I wish to see the proposals in black and white* IN PRINT, printed, written down, set down, on paper, recorded, on record, documented. **3** *in black-and-white terms* CATEGORICAL, unequivocal, absolute, uncompromising, unconditional, unqualified, unambiguous, clear, clear-cut.
blackball ● verb REJECT, debar, bar, ban, vote against, blacklist, exclude, shut out.
– OPPOSITES admit.
blacken ● verb **1** *they blackened their faces* BLACK, darken; dirty, make sooty, make smoky, stain, grime, soil. **2** *the sky blackened* GROW/BECOME BLACK, darken, dim, grow dim, cloud over. **3** *someone has blackened my name* SULLY, tarnish, besmirch, drag through the mud/mire, stain, taint, smear, disgrace, dishonour, bring discredit to, damage, ruin; slander, defame.
– OPPOSITES whiten, clean, lighten, brighten, clear.
blackguard ● noun *(dated).* See VILLAIN.
blacklist ● verb BOYCOTT, ostracize, avoid, embargo, steer clear of, ignore; refuse to employ; *Brit. dated* black.
black magic ● noun SORCERY, witchcraft, wizardry, necromancy, the black arts, devilry; malediction, voodoo, witching, witchery.
blackmail ● noun *he was accused of blackmail* EXTORTION, demanding money with menaces; *informal* hush money; *formal* exaction.
● verb **1** *he was blackmailing the murderer* EXTORT MONEY FROM, threaten, hold to ransom; *informal* demand hush money from. **2** *she blackmailed me to work for her* COERCE, pressurize, pressure, force; *informal* lean on, put the screws on, twist someone's arm.
blackout ● noun **1** *a power blackout* POWER CUT, power failure, failure of the electricity supply; brown-out. **2** *a news blackout* SUPPRESSION, silence, censorship, reporting restrictions. **3** *he had a*

b

blackshirt • noun a member of a Fascist organization.
– ORIGIN so named because of the black uniforms worn by the Italian Fascists before and during the Second World War.
blacksmith • noun **1** a person who makes and repairs things in iron by hand. **2** a person who shoes horses; a farrier.
black spot • noun **1** Brit. a place marked by a particular problem or difficulty: *an accident black spot.* **2** a plant disease producing black blotches on the leaves.
black stump • noun Austral. informal a notional place regarded as the last outpost of civilization.
black swan • noun a mainly black swan with white flight feathers, native to Australia.
blackthorn • noun a thorny shrub which bears white flowers, followed by blue-black fruits (sloes).
black tie • noun men's formal evening wear.
blackwater fever • noun a severe form of malaria in which blood cells are rapidly destroyed, resulting in dark urine.
black widow • noun a highly venomous American spider having a black body with red markings.
bladder • noun **1** a sac in the abdomen which receives urine from the kidneys and stores it for excretion. **2** an inflated or hollow flexible bag or chamber.
– ORIGIN Old English.
bladderwort • noun an aquatic plant with small air-filled bladders which keep the plant afloat and trap tiny animals.
bladderwrack • noun a brown seaweed with strap-like fronds containing air bladders.
blade • noun **1** the flat cutting edge of a knife or other tool or weapon. **2** the broad flat part of an oar, leaf, or other object. **3** a long narrow leaf of grass. **4** a shoulder bone in a joint of meat, or the joint itself. **5** informal, dated a dashing young man.
– ORIGIN Old English.
blag Brit. informal • noun **1** a violent robbery. **2** an act of using clever talk or lying to obtain something. • verb (**blagged**, **blagging**) **1** steal in a violent robbery. **2** obtain by clever talk or lying.
– DERIVATIVES **blagger** noun.
– ORIGIN perhaps from French *blaguer* 'tell lies'.
blame • verb hold responsible and criticize for a fault or wrong. • noun **1** responsibility for a fault or wrong. **2** criticism for a fault or wrong.
– PHRASES **be to blame** be responsible for a fault or wrong.
– DERIVATIVES **blameable** (US also **blamable**) adjective **blameworthy** adjective.
– ORIGIN Old French *blasmer*, from Greek *blasphēmein* 'blaspheme'.
blameless • adjective innocent of wrongdoing.
– DERIVATIVES **blamelessly** adverb **blamelessness** noun.
blanch • verb **1** make or become white or pale. **2** prepare (vegetables) by immersing briefly in boiling water. **3** peel (almonds) by scalding them.
– ORIGIN Old French *blanchir*, from *blanc* 'white'.
blancmange /blәmonj/ • noun a sweet jelly-like dessert made with cornflour and milk.
– ORIGIN from Old French *blanc mangier*, from *blanc* 'white' + *mangier* 'eat'.
blanco • noun Brit. a white substance used for whitening belts and other items of military equipment.
– ORIGIN from French *blanc* 'white'.
bland • adjective **1** lacking strong features or characteristics and therefore uninteresting. **2** (of food or drink) lacking flavour or seasoning.
– DERIVATIVES **blandly** adverb **blandness** noun.
– ORIGIN Latin *blandus* 'soft, smooth'.
blandishments • plural noun flattery intended to persuade or cajole.
blank • adjective **1** not marked or decorated; bare or plain. **2** not comprehending or reacting. **3** complete; absolute: *a blank refusal.* • noun **1** a space left to be filled in a document. **2** a cartridge containing gunpowder but no bullet. **3** an empty space or period of time. **4** an object with no mark or design on it. • verb **1** (often **blank out**) cross out or obscure. **2** Brit. informal deliberately ignore (someone).
– PHRASES **draw a blank** fail to obtain a favourable response.
– DERIVATIVES **blankly** adverb **blankness** noun.
– ORIGIN Old French *blanc* 'white'.
blank cheque • noun **1** a cheque with the amount left for the payee to fill in. **2** an unlimited freedom of action.
blanket • noun **1** a large piece of woollen material used as a covering for warmth. **2** a thick mass or layer of a specified material: *a blanket of cloud.* • adjective covering all cases or instances; total: *a blanket ban.* • verb (**blanketed**, **blanketing**) cover completely with a thick layer.
– PHRASES **born on the wrong side of the blanket** dated illegitimate.
– DERIVATIVES **blanketing** noun.
– ORIGIN originally denoting undyed woollen cloth: from Old French *blanc* 'white'.
blanket bath • noun Brit. an all-over wash given to a person confined to bed.
blanket stitch • noun a buttonhole stitch used on the edges of material too thick to be hemmed.
blanket weed • noun a common green freshwater alga forming mats of long filaments.
blank verse • noun verse without rhyme.
blanquette /bloNket/ • noun a dish consisting of white meat in

Thesaurus

blackout FAINTING FIT, faint, loss of consciousness, passing out, swoon, collapse; *Medicine* syncope.
blame • verb **1** *he always blames other people* HOLD RESPONSIBLE, hold accountable, condemn, accuse, find/consider guilty, assign fault/liability/guilt to; *archaic* inculpate. **2** *they blame youth crime on unemployment* ASCRIBE TO, attribute to, impute to, lay at the door of, put down to; *informal* pin.
– OPPOSITES absolve.
• noun *he was cleared of all blame* RESPONSIBILITY, guilt, accountability, liability, culpability, fault.
blameless • adjective INNOCENT, guiltless, above reproach, irreproachable, unimpeachable, in the clear, exemplary, perfect, virtuous, pure, impeccable; *informal* squeaky clean.
– OPPOSITES blameworthy.
blameworthy • adjective CULPABLE, reprehensible, indefensible, inexcusable, guilty, criminal, delinquent, wrong, evil, wicked; to blame, at fault, reproachable, responsible, answerable, erring, errant, in the wrong.
– OPPOSITES blameless.
blanch • verb **1** *the moon blanches her hair* TURN PALE, whiten, lighten, wash out, fade, blench, etiolate. **2** *his face blanched* PALE, turn pale, turn white, whiten, lose its colour, lighten, fade, blench. **3** *blanch the spinach leaves* SCALD, boil briefly.
– OPPOSITES colour, darken.
bland • adjective **1** *bland food* TASTELESS, flavourless, insipid, weak, watery, spiceless, wishy-washy. **2** *a bland film* UNINTERESTING, dull, boring, tedious, monotonous, dry, drab, dreary, wearisome; unexciting, unimaginative, uninspiring, uninspired, lacklustre, vapid, flat, stale, trite, vacuous, wishy-washy. **3** *a bland expression* UNEMOTIONAL, emotionless, dispassionate, passionless; unexpressive, cool, impassive; expressionless, blank, wooden, stony, deadpan, hollow, undemonstrative, imperturbable.
– OPPOSITES tangy, interesting, emotional.
blandishments • plural noun FLATTERY, cajolery, coaxing, wheedling, persuasion, honeyed words, smooth talk, blarney; *informal* sweet talk, soft soap, buttering up.
blank • adjective **1** *a blank sheet of paper* EMPTY, unmarked, unused, clear, free, bare, clean, plain. **2** *a blank face* EXPRESSIONLESS, deadpan, wooden, stony, impassive, unresponsive, poker-faced, vacuous, empty, glazed, fixed, lifeless, inscrutable. **3** *'What?' said Maxim, looking blank* BAFFLED, mystified, puzzled, perplexed, stumped, at a loss, stuck, bewildered, nonplussed, bemused, lost, uncomprehending, (all) at sea, confused; *informal* flummoxed, bamboozled. **4** *a blank refusal* OUTRIGHT, absolute, categorical, unqualified, complete, flat, straight, positive, certain, explicit, unequivocal, clear, clear-cut.
– OPPOSITES full, expressive, qualified.
• noun SPACE, gap, lacuna.
blanket • noun *a blanket of cloud* COVERING, layer, coating, carpet, overlay, cloak, mantle, veil, pall, shroud.
• adjective *blanket coverage* complete, total, comprehensive, overall, general, mass, umbrella, inclusive, all-inclusive, all-round, wholesale, outright, across the board, sweeping, indiscriminate, thorough; universal, global, worldwide, international, nationwide, countrywide, coast-to-coast.
– OPPOSITES partial, piecemeal.
• verb **1** *snow blanketed the mountains* COVER, coat, carpet, overlay; cloak, shroud, swathe, envelop; *poetic/literary* mantle. **2** *double*

a white sauce.
– ORIGIN French, from *blanc* 'white'.
blare ● verb sound loudly and harshly. ● noun a loud, harsh sound.
– ORIGIN Dutch or Low German *blaren*.
blarney ● noun talk intended to be charming or flattering.
– ORIGIN named after *Blarney* Castle in Ireland, where there is a stone said to give persuasive speech to anyone who kisses it.
blasé /blaazay/ ● adjective unimpressed with something because of over-familiarity.
– ORIGIN French, from *blaser* 'cloy'.
blaspheme /blasfeem/ ● verb speak irreverently about God or sacred things.
– DERIVATIVES **blasphemer** noun.
– ORIGIN Greek *blasphēmein*, from *blasphēmos* 'evil-speaking'.
blasphemous ● adjective sacrilegious against God or sacred things; profane.
– DERIVATIVES **blasphemously** adverb.
blasphemy /blasfəmi/ ● noun (pl. **blasphemies**) irreverent talk about God or sacred things.
blast ● noun **1** an explosion, or the destructive wave of highly compressed air spreading outwards from it. **2** a strong gust of wind or air. **3** a single loud note of a horn or whistle. **4** informal a severe reprimand. **5** N. Amer. informal an enjoyable experience. ● verb **1** blow up with explosives. **2** (**blast off**) (of a rocket or spacecraft) take off. **3** produce loud music or noise. **4** informal criticize fiercely. **5** kick or strike (a ball) hard. **6** literary (of wind) wither (a plant). ● exclamation Brit. informal expressing annoyance.
– PHRASES **(at) full blast** at maximum power or intensity.
– DERIVATIVES **blaster** noun.
– ORIGIN Old English.
blasted ● adjective informal used to express annoyance.
blast furnace ● noun a smelting furnace into which a blast of hot compressed air can be introduced.
blatant ● adjective open and unashamed; flagrant.
– DERIVATIVES **blatancy** noun **blatantly** adverb.
– ORIGIN first used by the poet Edmund Spenser in *blatant beast* to describe a thousand-tongued monster, then in the sense 'clamorous': perhaps from Scots *blatand* 'bleating'.
blather (also **blither**) ● verb talk at length without making much sense. ● noun rambling talk with no real substance.
– ORIGIN from Old Norse, 'nonsense'.
blaze ● noun **1** a very large or fiercely burning fire. **2** a very bright light or display of colour. **3** a conspicuous outburst: *a blaze of publicity.* **4** a white stripe down the face of a horse or other animal. **5** (**blazes**) informal a euphemism for 'hell': *go to blazes!* **6** a cut made on a tree to mark a route. ● verb **1** burn or shine fiercely or brightly. **2** shoot repeatedly or indiscriminately. **3** present (news) in a prominent or sensational manner.
– PHRASES **blaze a trail 1** mark out a path or route. **2** be the first to do something; pioneer.
– DERIVATIVES **blazing** adjective.
– ORIGIN Old English; sense 3 of the verb is from Low German or Dutch *blāzen* 'to blow'.
blazer ● noun **1** a jacket worn by schoolchildren or sports players as part of a uniform. **2** a man's smart jacket not forming part of a suit.
blazon /blayz'n/ ● verb **1** display or depict prominently or vividly. **2** Heraldry describe or depict (a coat of arms). ● noun **1** a correct description of armorial bearings. **2** archaic a coat of arms.
– ORIGIN from Old French *blason* 'shield'.
bleach ● verb **1** make white or lighter by a chemical process or by exposure to sunlight. **2** clean or sterilize with bleach. ● noun a chemical used to bleach things and also to sterilize drains, sinks, etc.
– ORIGIN Old English, related to BLEAK.
bleacher ● noun **1** a person or thing that bleaches. **2** N. Amer. a cheap bench seat in an uncovered part of a sports ground.
bleaching powder ● noun a powder containing calcium hypochlorite, used to bleach materials.
bleak ● adjective **1** bare and exposed to the elements. **2** charmless and inhospitable. **3** (of a situation) not hopeful or encouraging.
– DERIVATIVES **bleakly** adverb **bleakness** noun.
– ORIGIN Old English or Old Norse, 'white, shining'.

Thesaurus

glazing blankets the noise a bit MUFFLE, deaden, soften, mute, silence, quieten, smother, dampen.
– OPPOSITES amplify.
blare ● verb *sirens blared* BLAST, sound loudly, trumpet, clamour, boom, roar, thunder, bellow, resound.
– OPPOSITES murmur.
● noun *the blare of the siren* BLAST, trumpeting, clamour, boom, roar, thunder, bellow.
– OPPOSITES murmur.
blarney ● noun BLANDISHMENTS, honeyed words, smooth talk, flattery, cajolery, coaxing, wheedling, persuasion; charm offensive; *informal* sweet talk, soft soap, smarm, buttering up.
blasé ● adjective INDIFFERENT, unconcerned, uncaring, casual, nonchalant, offhand, uninterested, apathetic, unimpressed, unmoved, unresponsive, phlegmatic; *informal* laid-back; *rare* pococurante.
– OPPOSITES concerned, responsive.
blaspheme ● verb SWEAR, curse, take the Lord's name in vain; *informal* cuss; *archaic* execrate.
blasphemous ● adjective SACRILEGIOUS, profane, irreligious, irreverent, impious, ungodly, godless.
– OPPOSITES reverent.
blasphemy ● noun PROFANITY, sacrilege, irreligion, irreverence, taking the Lord's name in vain, swearing, curse, cursing, impiety, desecration; *archaic* execration.
– OPPOSITES reverence.
blast ● noun **1** *the blast from the bomb* SHOCK WAVE, pressure wave. **2** *Friday's blast killed two people* EXPLOSION, detonation, discharge, burst. **3** *a sudden blast of cold air* GUST, rush, gale, squall, wind, draught, waft, puff, flurry. **4** *the shrill blast of the trumpets* BLARE, wail, roar, screech, shriek, hoot, honk, beep. **5** *(informal) I braced myself for the inevitable blast.* See REPRIMAND noun.
● verb **1** *bombers were blasting enemy airfields* BLOW UP, bomb, blow (to pieces), dynamite, explode. **2** *guns were blasting away* FIRE, shoot, blaze, let fly, discharge. **3** *he blasted his horn* HONK, beep, toot, sound. **4** *radios blasting out pop music* BLARE, boom, roar, thunder, bellow, pump, shriek, screech. **5** *Fowler was blasted with an air gun* SHOOT, gun down, mow down, cut down, put a bullet in; *informal* pot, plug. **6** *(informal) he blasted the pupils for being late.* See REPRIMAND.
– PHRASES **blast off** BE LAUNCHED, take off, lift off, leave the ground, become airborne, take to the air.
blasted ● adjective *(informal).* See DAMNED sense 2.
blast-off ● noun LAUNCH, lift-off, take-off, ascent, firing.
– OPPOSITES touchdown.
blatant ● adjective FLAGRANT, glaring, obvious, undisguised, unconcealed, open; shameless, barefaced, unabashed, unashamed, unblushing, brazen, brass-necked.
– OPPOSITES inconspicuous, shamefaced.
blather ● verb *he just blathered on* PRATTLE, babble, chatter, twitter, prate, go on, run on, rattle on, yap, jibber-jabber, maunder, ramble, burble, drivel; *informal* yak, yatter; *Brit. informal* witter, rabbit, chunter, waffle.
● noun *mindless blather* PRATTLE, chatter, twitter, babble, prating, gabble, jabber, rambling; *informal* yatter, twaddle; *Brit. informal* wittering, chuntering.
blaze ● noun **1** *firemen fought the blaze* FIRE, flames, conflagration, inferno, holocaust. **2** *a blaze of light* GLARE, gleam, flash, burst, flare, streak, radiance, brilliance, beam. **3** *a blaze of anger* OUTBURST, burst, eruption, flare-up, explosion, outbreak; blast, attack, fit, spasm, paroxysm, access, rush, storm.
● verb **1** *the fire blazed merrily* BURN, be alight, be on fire, be in flames, flame. **2** *headlights blazed* SHINE, flash, flare, glare, gleam, glint, dazzle, glitter, glisten. **3** *soldiers blazed away* FIRE, shoot, blast, let fly.
blazon ● verb **1** *their name is blazoned across the sails* DISPLAY, exhibit, present, spread, emblazon, plaster. **2** *the newspapers blazoned the news abroad* PUBLICIZE, make known, make public, announce, report, communicate, spread, circulate, give out, publish, broadcast, trumpet, proclaim, promulgate.
bleach ● verb **1** *the blinds had been bleached by the sun* TURN WHITE, whiten, turn pale, blanch, lighten, fade, decolour, decolorize, peroxide. **2** *they saw bones bleaching in the sun* TURN WHITE, whiten, turn pale, pale, blanch, lose its colour, lighten, fade.
– OPPOSITES darken.
bleak ● adjective **1** *a bleak landscape* BARE, exposed, desolate, stark, desert, lunar, open, empty, windswept; treeless, without vegetation, denuded. **2** *the future is bleak* UNPROMISING, unfavourable, unpropitious, inauspicious; discouraging, disheartening, depressing,

b

bleary • adjective (**blearier**, **bleariest**) (of the eyes) dull and unfocused from sleep or tiredness.
– DERIVATIVES **blearily** adverb.
– ORIGIN probably related to High German *blerre* 'blurred vision' and Low German *blarroged* 'bleary-eyed'.

bleat • verb **1** (of a sheep or goat) make a weak, wavering cry. **2** speak or complain in a weak or foolish way. • noun a bleating sound.
– ORIGIN Old English.

bleb • noun a small blister or bubble.
– ORIGIN variant of BLOB.

bleed • verb (past and past part. **bled**) **1** lose blood from the body as a result of injury or illness. **2** draw blood from (someone) as a former method of medical treatment. **3** informal drain of money or resources. **4** (of dye or colour) seep into an adjacent colour or area. **5** allow (fluid or gas) to escape from a closed system through a valve. • noun an instance of bleeding.
– ORIGIN Old English.

bleeder • noun Brit. informal a person regarded with contempt, disrespect, or pity: *lucky little bleeder!*

bleeding • adjective Brit. informal used for emphasis, or to express annoyance.

bleeding edge • noun the very forefront of technological development.
– ORIGIN after LEADING EDGE, CUTTING EDGE.

bleeding heart • noun **1** informal, derogatory a person considered to be excessively soft-hearted or liberal. **2** a plant with red heart-shaped flowers.

bleep • noun a short high-pitched sound made by an electronic device as a signal or to attract attention. • verb **1** make a bleep. **2** (in broadcasting) censor (a word or phrase) by substituting a bleep. **3** summon with a bleeper.
– ORIGIN imitative.

bleeper • noun Brit. a small portable electronic device which bleeps when someone wants to contact the wearer.

blemish • noun **1** a small flaw which spoils the appearance of something. **2** a moral defect. • verb spoil the appearance of.
– ORIGIN from Old French *blesmir* 'make pale, injure'.

blench • verb make a sudden flinching movement out of fear or pain.
– ORIGIN Old English, 'deceive'.

blend • verb **1** mix and combine with something else. **2** form a harmonious combination or part of a whole. • noun a mixture of different things or people.
– ORIGIN probably Scandinavian.

blender • noun an electric device used for liquidizing or chopping food.

blenny • noun (pl. **blennies**) a small coastal fish with scaleless skin and spiny fins.
– ORIGIN from Greek *blennos* 'mucus' (because of its mucous coating).

bless • verb **1** call on God to protect or treat favourably. **2** consecrate by a religious rite. **3** praise (God). **4** (**be blessed with**) be endowed with or granted (something greatly desired).
– PHRASES **bless you!** said to a person who has just sneezed.
– ORIGIN Old English, related to BLOOD (perhaps originally in the sense 'mark or consecrate with blood').

blessed /blessid, blest/ • adjective **1** made holy. **2** granted God's favour and protection. **3** bringing welcome pleasure or relief: *blessed sleep.* **4** informal used in mild expressions of exasperation.
– DERIVATIVES **blessedly** adverb **blessedness** noun.

blessing • noun **1** God's favour and protection. **2** a prayer asking for blessing. **3** a beneficial thing for which one is grateful. **4** a person's sanction or support.
– PHRASES **a blessing in disguise** an apparent misfortune that eventually has good results.

blew past of BLOW[1].

blewit /bloōit/ (also **blewits**) • noun an edible mushroom with a pale buff or lilac cap.
– ORIGIN probably from BLUE[1].

blight • noun **1** a plant disease, especially one caused by fungi. **2** a thing that spoils or damages something. **3** ugly or neglected urban landscape. • verb **1** infect (plants) with blight. **2** spoil or destroy.
– ORIGIN originally denoting inflammation of the skin: of unknown origin.

blighter • noun Brit. informal a person regarded with contempt, irritation, or pity.

Thesaurus

dim, gloomy, black, dark, grim, hopeless.
– OPPOSITES lush, promising.

bleary • adjective BLURRED, blurry, unfocused; fogged, clouded, dull, misty, watery, rheumy; *archaic* blear.
– OPPOSITES clear.

bleat • verb **1** *the sheep were bleating* BAA; *N. Amer. informal* blat. **2** *don't bleat to me about fairness* COMPLAIN, grouse, carp, fuss, snivel; *Scottish & Irish* girn; *informal* gripe, beef, whinge, bellyache, moan, go on; *N. English informal* mither; *N. Amer. informal* kvetch.

bleed • verb **1** *his arm was bleeding* LOSE BLOOD, haemorrhage. **2** *the doctor bled him* DRAW BLOOD FROM; *Medicine* exsanguinate; *archaic* phlebotomize. **3** *one colour bled into another* FLOW, run, seep, filter, percolate, leach. **4** *sap was bleeding from the trunk* FLOW, run, ooze, seep, exude, weep. **5** *(informal) the country was bled dry by poachers* DRAIN, sap, deplete, milk, exhaust. **6** *my heart bleeds for them* GRIEVE, ache, sorrow, mourn, lament, feel, suffer; sympathize with, pity.

blemish • noun **1** *not a blemish marred her skin* IMPERFECTION, flaw, defect, fault, deformity, discoloration, disfigurement; bruise, scar, pit, pock, scratch, cut, gash; mark, streak, spot, smear, speck, blotch, smudge, smut; birthmark; *Medicine* stigma. **2** *government is not without blemish* DEFECT, fault, failing, flaw, imperfection, foible, vice; shortcoming, weakness, deficiency, limitation; taint, stain, dishonour, disgrace.
– OPPOSITES virtue.
• verb **1** *nothing blemished the coast* MAR, spoil, impair, disfigure, blight, deface, mark, scar; ruin. **2** *his reign has been blemished by controversy* SULLY, tarnish, besmirch, blacken, blot, taint; spoil, mar, ruin, disgrace, damage, undermine, degrade, dishonour; *formal* vitiate.
– OPPOSITES enhance.

blench • verb FLINCH, start, shy (away), recoil, shrink, pull back, cringe, wince, quail, cower.

blend • verb **1** *blend the ingredients until smooth* MIX, mingle, combine, merge, fuse, meld, coalesce, integrate, intermix; stir, whisk, fold in; *technical* admix; *poetic/literary* commingle. **2** *the new buildings blend with the older ones* HARMONIZE, go (well), fit (in), be in tune, be compatible, match, complement, coordinate.
• noun *a blend of bananas, raisins, and ginger* MIXTURE, mix, combination, amalgamation, amalgam, union, marriage, fusion, meld, synthesis; *technical* admixture.

bless • verb **1** *the chaplain blessed the couple* ASK/INVOKE GOD'S FAVOUR FOR, give a benediction for. **2** *the Cardinal blessed the memorial plaque* CONSECRATE, sanctify, dedicate (to God), make holy, make sacred; *formal* hallow. **3** *bless the name of the Lord* PRAISE, worship, glorify, honour, exalt, pay homage to, venerate, reverence, hallow; *archaic* magnify. **4** *the gods blessed us with magical voices* ENDOW, bestow, furnish, accord, give, favour, grace; confer on; *poetic/literary* endue. **5** *I bless the day you came here* GIVE THANKS FOR, be grateful for, thank; appreciate. **6** *the government refused to bless the undertaking* SANCTION, consent to, endorse, agree to, approve, back, support; *informal* give the thumbs up to, give the green light to, OK.
– OPPOSITES curse, trouble, rue, oppose.

blessed • adjective **1** *a blessed place* HOLY, sacred, hallowed, consecrated, sanctified; ordained, canonized, beatified. **2** *blessed are the meek* FAVOURED, fortunate, lucky, privileged, enviable. **3** *the fresh air made a blessed change* WELCOME, pleasant, agreeable, refreshing, favourable, gratifying, heartening, much needed.
– OPPOSITES cursed, wretched, unwelcome.

blessing • noun **1** *may God give us his blessing* PROTECTION, favour. **2** *a special blessing from the priest* BENEDICTION, invocation, prayer, intercession; grace. **3** *she gave the plan her blessing* SANCTION, endorsement, approval, approbation, favour, consent, assent, agreement; backing, support; *informal* the thumbs up. **4** *it was a blessing they didn't have far to go* BOON, godsend, advantage, benefit, help, bonus, plus; stroke of luck, windfall; *poetic/literary* benison.
– OPPOSITES condemnation, affliction.

blight • noun **1** *potato blight* DISEASE, canker, infestation, fungus, mildew, mould. **2** *the blight of aircraft noise* AFFLICTION, scourge, bane, curse, plague, menace, misfortune, woe, trouble, ordeal, trial, nuisance, pest.
– OPPOSITES blessing.
• verb **1** *a tree blighted by leaf curl* INFECT, mildew; kill, destroy. **2** *scandal blighted the careers of several politicians* RUIN, wreck,

Blighty ● noun Brit. informal Britain or England, as used by soldiers serving abroad.
– ORIGIN first used by soldiers in the Indian army: from Urdu, 'foreign, European'.
blimey ● exclamation Brit. informal expressing surprise, excitement, or alarm.
– ORIGIN altered form of *God blind* (or *blame*) *me!*
blimp ● noun informal **1** (also **Colonel Blimp**) Brit. a pompous, reactionary person. **2** a small airship or barrage balloon. **3** N. Amer. an obese person.
– DERIVATIVES **blimpish** adjective.
– ORIGIN sense 1 derives from a character invented by the cartoonist David Low.
blind ● adjective **1** lacking the power of sight; unable to see. **2** done without being able to see or without necessary information. **3** lacking perception, judgement, or reason. **4** concealed, closed, or blocked off. **5** (of flying) using instruments only. **6** informal the slightest: *it didn't do a blind bit of good.* ● verb **1** make blind. **2** deprive of understanding or judgement. **3** (**blind with**) confuse or overawe (someone) with (something they do not understand). ● noun **1** a screen for a window. **2** something designed to conceal one's real intentions. ● adverb without being able to see clearly.
– PHRASES **bake blind** bake (a flan case) without a filling. **blind drunk** informal extremely drunk. **turn a blind eye** pretend not to notice. [ORIGIN said to be in allusion to Nelson, who lifted a telescope to his blind eye at the Battle of Copenhagen (1801), thus not seeing the signal to 'discontinue the action'.] **when the blind lead the blind, both shall fall into a ditch** proverb those people without knowledge or experience should not try to guide others in a similar position.
– DERIVATIVES **blindly** adverb **blindness** noun.
– ORIGIN Old English.
blind alley ● noun **1** a cul-de-sac. **2** a course of action leading nowhere.
blind date ● noun a social engagement with a person one has not previously met, designed to have a romantic aim.
blinder ● noun Brit. informal an excellent performance in a game or race.
blindfold ● noun a piece of cloth tied around the head to cover someone's eyes. ● verb deprive of sight with a blindfold. ● adverb with a blindfold covering the eyes.
– ORIGIN from obsolete *blindfell* 'strike blind, blindfold', from Old English.
blinding ● adjective **1** (of light) very bright. **2** suddenly and overwhelmingly obvious. **3** informal (of an action) remarkably skilful and exciting.
– DERIVATIVES **blindingly** adverb.
blind man's buff (US also **blind man's bluff**) ● noun a game in which a blindfold player tries to catch others while being pushed about by them.
– ORIGIN from *buff* 'a blow', from Old French.
blind side ● noun a direction in which a person has a poor view.
blind spot ● noun **1** Anatomy the point of entry of the optic nerve on the retina, insensitive to light. **2** an area where a person's view is obstructed. **3** an area in which a person lacks understanding or impartiality. **4** a point within the normal range of a transmitter where there is unusually weak reception.
blindworm ● noun another term for SLOW-WORM.
blini /bleeni/ (also **blinis**) ● plural noun (sing. **blin**) pancakes made from buckwheat flour.
– ORIGIN Russian.
blink ● verb **1** shut and open the eyes quickly. **2** (**blink at**) react to (something) with surprise or disapproval. **3** (of a light) shine unsteadily or intermittently. ● noun an act of blinking.
– PHRASES **on the blink** informal (of a machine) not working properly; out of order.
– ORIGIN Scots variant of BLENCH.
blinker ● noun chiefly Brit. **1** (**blinkers**) a pair of small screens attached to a horse's bridle to prevent the horse seeing sideways. **2** (**blinkers**) a thing that prevents someone from understanding a situation fully. **3** a vehicle indicator light that flashes on and off. ● verb **1** put blinkers on (a horse). **2** cause to have a narrow outlook.
blinking ● adjective Brit. informal used to express annoyance.
blintze /blints/ ● noun a thin rolled pancake filled with cheese or fruit and then fried or baked.
– ORIGIN Russian *blinets* 'little pancake'.
blip ● noun **1** a very short high-pitched sound made by an electronic device. **2** an unexpected, minor, and usually temporary deviation from a general trend. **3** a small flashing point of light on a radar screen. ● verb (**blipped**, **blipping**) (of an electronic device) make a blip.
– ORIGIN imitative.
blipvert ● noun a television advert of a few seconds' duration.
bliss ● noun **1** perfect happiness; great joy. **2** a state of spiritual blessedness. ● verb (**bliss out** or **be blissed out**) informal be in a state of perfect happiness, oblivious to everything else.
– ORIGIN Old English, related to BLITHE.
blissful ● adjective extremely happy; full of joy.
– DERIVATIVES **blissfully** adverb.
blister ● noun **1** a small bubble on the skin filled with serum and typically caused by friction or burning. **2** a similar swelling, filled with air or fluid, on a surface. ● verb be or cause to be affected with blisters.
– ORIGIN perhaps from Old French *blestre* 'swelling, pimple'.
blistering ● adjective **1** (of heat) intense. **2** (of criticism) very vehement. **3** (in sport) extremely fast, forceful, or impressive.
– DERIVATIVES **blisteringly** adverb.

Thesaurus

spoil, mar, frustrate, disrupt, undo, end, scotch, destroy, shatter, devastate, demolish; *informal* mess up, foul up, put paid to, put the kibosh on, stymie; *Brit. informal* scupper; *archaic* bring to naught.
blind ● adjective **1** *he has been blind since birth* SIGHTLESS, unsighted, visually impaired, visionless, unseeing; partially sighted, purblind; *informal* as blind as a bat. **2** *she was ignorant, but not blind* IMPERCEPTIVE, unperceptive, insensitive, slow, obtuse, uncomprehending; stupid, unintelligent; *informal* dense, dim, thick, dumb, dopey; *Brit. informal* dozy; *Scottish & N. English informal* glaikit. **3** *you should be blind to failure* UNMINDFUL OF, mindless of, careless of, heedless of, oblivious to, insensible to, unconcerned about, indifferent to. **4** *blind acceptance of conventional opinion* UNCRITICAL, unreasoned, unthinking, unconsidered, mindless, undiscerning, indiscriminate. **5** *a blind rage* IMPETUOUS, impulsive, uncontrolled, uncontrollable, unrestrained, immoderate, intemperate, wild, irrational, unbridled. **6** *a blind alley* WITHOUT EXIT, blocked, closed, barred, impassable; dead end.
– OPPOSITES sighted, perceptive, mindful, discerning.
● verb **1** *he was blinded in a car crash* MAKE BLIND, deprive of sight, render sightless; put someone's eyes out. **2** *scaffolding blinded the windows* OBSCURE, cover, blot out, mask, shroud, block, eclipse, obstruct. **3** *he was blinded by his faith* DEPRIVE OF JUDGEMENT, deprive of perception, deprive of reason, deprive of sense. **4** *they try to blind you with science* OVERAWE, intimidate, daunt, deter, discourage, cow, abash, subdue, dismay; disquiet, discomfit, unsettle, disconcert; confuse, bewilder, confound, perplex, overwhelm; *informal* faze, psych out.
● noun **1** *a window blind* SCREEN, shade, sunshade, curtain, awning, canopy; louvre, jalousie, shutter. **2** *some crook had sent the card as a blind* DECEPTION, camouflage, smokescreen, front, facade, cover, pretext, masquerade, feint; trick, ploy, ruse, machination.
blindly ● adverb **1** *he stared blindly ahead* SIGHTLESSLY, unseeingly. **2** *he ran blindly upstairs* IMPETUOUSLY, impulsively, recklessly, heedlessly, uncontrolledly. **3** *they blindly followed US policy* UNCRITICALLY, unthinkingly, mindlessly, indiscriminately.
blink ● verb **1** *his eyes did not blink* flutter, flicker, wink, bat; *technical* nictitate, nictate. **2** *several red lights began to blink* FLASH, flicker, wink. **3** *no one even blinks at the 'waitresses' in drag* BE SURPRISED, look twice; *informal* boggle.
blinkered ● adjective NARROW-MINDED, inward-looking, parochial, provincial, insular, small-minded, close-minded, short-sighted; hidebound, inflexible, entrenched, prejudiced, bigoted; *Brit.* parish-pump.
– OPPOSITES broad-minded.
bliss ● noun **1** *she gave a sigh of bliss* JOY, happiness, pleasure, delight, ecstasy, elation, rapture, euphoria. **2** *religions promise perfect bliss after death* BLESSEDNESS, benediction, beatitude, glory, heavenly joy, divine happiness; heaven, paradise.
– OPPOSITES misery, hell.
blissful ● adjective ECSTATIC, euphoric, joyful, elated, rapturous, on cloud nine, in seventh heaven; delighted, thrilled, overjoyed, joyous; *informal* over the moon, on top of the world; *Austral. informal* wrapped.
blister ● noun **1** *a blister on each heel* bleb; *Medicine* bulla, pustule,

b

blithe /blīth/ ● adjective **1** cheerfully or thoughtlessly indifferent. **2** literary happy or joyous.
– DERIVATIVES **blithely** adverb **blitheness** noun.
– ORIGIN Old English, related to BLISS.
blither ● verb & noun variant spelling of BLATHER.
blithering ● adjective informal complete; utter: *a blithering idiot.*
BLitt ● abbreviation Bachelor of Letters.
– ORIGIN from Latin *Baccalaureus Litterarum.*
blitz ● noun **1** an intensive or sudden military attack. **2** (**the Blitz**) the German air raids on Britain in 1940–1. **3** informal a sudden and concerted effort. ● verb **1** attack or seriously damage in a blitz. **2** succeed in overwhelming or defeating utterly.
– ORIGIN abbreviation of BLITZKRIEG.
blitzkrieg /blitskreeg/ ● noun an intense military campaign intended to bring about a swift victory.
– ORIGIN German, 'lightning war'.
blizzard ● noun a severe snowstorm with high winds.
– ORIGIN of unknown origin.
bloat ● verb cause to swell with fluid or gas.
– DERIVATIVES **bloated** adjective.
– ORIGIN perhaps from an Old Norse word meaning 'soft, flabby'.
bloater ● noun a herring cured by salting and light smoking.
blob ● noun **1** a drop of a thick liquid or viscous substance. **2** an indeterminate roundish mass or shape.
– DERIVATIVES **blobby** adjective.
bloc ● noun a group of countries or political parties who have formed an alliance.
– ORIGIN French, 'block'.
block ● noun **1** a large solid piece of material with flat surfaces on each side. **2** chiefly Brit. a large single building subdivided into separate flats or offices. **3** a group of buildings bounded by four streets. **4** a large quantity of things regarded as a unit. **5** an obstacle to progress. **6** a solid area of colour on a surface. **7** (also **cylinder block** or **engine block**) a large metal moulding containing the cylinders of an internal-combustion engine. **8** a pulley or system of pulleys mounted in a case. ● verb **1** prevent movement or flow in. **2** impede or prevent (an action or movement). **3** (**block out/in**) mark out (an outline) or shade in roughly.
– PHRASES **knock someone's block off** informal hit someone about the head. **put one's head** (or **neck**) **on the block** informal put one's standing or reputation at risk.
– DERIVATIVES **blocker** noun **blocky** adjective.
– ORIGIN Dutch.
blockade ● noun an act of sealing off a place to prevent goods or people from entering or leaving. ● verb set up a blockade of.
– PHRASES **run a blockade** (of a ship) manage to enter or leave a blockaded port.
blockage ● noun an obstruction which makes movement or flow difficult or impossible.
block and tackle ● noun a lifting mechanism consisting of ropes, a pulley block, and a hook.
blockbuster ● noun informal a film or book that is a great commercial success.
– DERIVATIVES **blockbusting** adjective.
block capitals ● plural noun plain capital letters.
blockhead ● noun informal a very stupid person.
blockhouse ● noun **1** a reinforced concrete shelter used as an observation point. **2** US a house made of squared logs.
blockish ● adjective **1** bulky or crude in form. **2** unintelligent; stupid.
block release ● noun Brit. a system of allowing employees the whole of a stated period off work for education.
block vote ● noun Brit. a vote proportional in power to the number of people a delegate represents.
bloke ● noun Brit. informal a man.
– ORIGIN Shelta.
blokeish (also **blokish** or **blokey**) ● adjective Brit. informal stereotypically male in behaviour and interests.
blonde ● adjective (also **blond**) **1** (of hair) fair or pale yellow. **2** having fair hair and a light complexion. ● noun **1** a woman with blonde hair. **2** the colour of blonde hair.
– ORIGIN French, from Latin *blundus, blondus* 'yellow'.
Blood /blud/ ● noun (pl. same or **Bloods**) a member of a North American Indian people belonging to the Blackfoot Confederacy.
blood ● noun **1** the red liquid that circulates in the arteries and veins, carrying oxygen and carbon dioxide. **2** family background: *she must have Irish blood.* **3** violence involving bloodshed. **4** fiery or passionate temperament. **5** dated a fashionable and dashing young man. ● verb **1** initiate in a particular activity. **2** smear the face of (a novice hunter) with the blood of the kill.
– PHRASES **blood and thunder** informal unrestrained and violent action or behaviour. **blood is thicker than water** proverb family relationships are the most important ones. **blood, sweat, and tears** extremely hard work. **first blood 1** the first shedding of blood in a fight. **2** the first point or advantage gained in a contest. **give blood** allow blood to be removed medically from one's body for use in transfusions. **have blood on one's hands** be responsible for someone's death. **in one's blood** ingrained in or fundamental to one's character. **make someone's blood boil** informal infuriate someone. **make someone's blood run cold** horrify someone. **new** (or **fresh**) **blood** new members admitted to a group. **of the blood** (**royal**) literary royal. **young blood** a younger member or members of a group as an invigor-

Thesaurus

vesicle, vesication. **2** *check for blisters in the roofing felt* BUBBLE, swelling, bulge, protuberance.
blistering ● adjective **1** *blistering heat* INTENSE, extreme, ferocious, fierce; SCORCHING, searing, blazing, baking, burning, fiery; *informal* boiling, roasting, sweltering. **2** *a blistering attack on the government* SAVAGE, vicious, fierce, bitter, harsh, scathing, devastating, caustic, searing, vitriolic. **3** *a blistering pace* VERY FAST, breakneck; *informal* blinding.
– OPPOSITES mild, leisurely.
blithe ● adjective **1** *a blithe disregard for the rules* CASUAL, indifferent, unconcerned, unworried, untroubled, uncaring, careless, heedless, thoughtless; nonchalant, blasé. **2** *(poetic/literary) his blithe, smiling face* HAPPY, cheerful, jolly, merry, joyful, joyous, blissful, ecstatic, euphoric, elated; *poetic/literary* blithesome; *dated* gay.
– OPPOSITES thoughtful, sad.
blitz ● noun *the blitz on London* BOMBARDMENT, bombing, onslaught, barrage; attack, assault, raid, strike, blitzkrieg.
● verb *the town was blitzed in the war* BOMBARD, attack, bomb, shell, torpedo, strafe; destroy, devastate, ravage.
blizzard ● noun SNOWSTORM, white-out.
bloated ● adjective SWOLLEN, distended, tumefied, bulging, inflated, enlarged, expanded, dilated.
blob ● noun **1** *a blob of cold gravy* DROP, droplet, globule, bead, bubble; *informal* glob. **2** *a blob of ink* SPOT, dab, blotch, blot, dot, smudge; *informal* splotch, splodge.
● verb *masking fluid is blobbed on freely* DAUB, dab, spot, slop.
bloc ● noun ALLIANCE, coalition, federation, confederation, league, union, partnership, axis, body, association, group.
block ● noun **1** *a block of cheese* CHUNK, hunk, lump, wedge, cube, brick, slab, piece; *Brit. informal* wodge. **2** *an apartment block* BUILDING, complex, structure, development. **3** *a block of shares* BATCH, group, set, quantity. **4** *a sketching block* PAD, notepad, sketchpad, jotter, tablet. **5** *a block to Third World development* OBSTACLE, bar, barrier, impediment, hindrance, check, hurdle, stumbling block, handicap, deterrent. **6** *a block in the pipe* BLOCKAGE, obstruction, stoppage, congestion, occlusion, clot.
– OPPOSITES aid.
● verb **1** *weeds can block drainage ditches* CLOG (UP), stop up, choke, plug, obstruct, gum up, dam up, congest, jam, close; *informal* bung up; *Brit. informal* gunge up; *technical* occlude. **2** *picket lines blocked access to the factory* HINDER, hamper, obstruct, impede, inhibit, restrict, limit; halt, stop, bar, check, prevent. **3** *he blocked a shot on the goal line* PARRY, stop, deflect, fend off, hold off, repel, repulse.
– OPPOSITES facilitate.
– PHRASES **block something off** CLOSE UP, shut off, seal off, barricade, bar, obstruct. **block something out 1** *trees blocked out the light* CONCEAL, keep out, blot out, exclude, obliterate, blank out, stop. **2** *block out an area in charcoal* ROUGH OUT, sketch out, outline, delineate, draft.
blockade ● noun **1** *a naval blockade of the island* SIEGE; *rare* besiegement. **2** *they erected blockades in the streets* BARRICADE, barrier, roadblock; obstacle, obstruction.
● verb *rebels blockaded the capital* BARRICADE, block off, shut off, seal; BESIEGE, surround.
blockage ● noun OBSTRUCTION, stoppage, block, occlusion, congestion.
bloke ● noun *(Brit. informal).* See FELLOW sense 1.
blonde, masc. **blond** ● adjective FAIR, light, yellow, flaxen, tow-

ating force.

– ORIGIN Old English.

bloodbath ● noun an event in which many people are killed violently.

blood brother ● noun a man who has sworn to treat another man as a brother.

blood count ● noun a determination of the number of corpuscles in a specific volume of blood.

blood-curdling ● adjective horrifying; very frightening.

blood doping (also **blood boosting**) ● noun the injection of oxygenated blood into an athlete before an event in an (illegal) attempt to enhance performance.

blood feud ● noun a lengthy conflict between families involving a cycle of retaliatory killings.

blood group ● noun any of various types of human blood classified according to their compatibility in transfusion, especially by means of the ABO system.

bloodhound ● noun a large hound with a very keen sense of smell, used in tracking.

bloodless ● adjective **1** (of a conflict) without violence or killing. **2** (of the skin) drained of colour. **3** lacking in vitality; feeble. **4** cold or ruthless.

– DERIVATIVES **bloodlessly** adverb **bloodlessness** noun.

bloodletting ● noun **1** historical the surgical removal of some of a patient's blood for therapeutic purposes. **2** violence during a war or conflict.

bloodline ● noun a pedigree or set of ancestors.

blood money ● noun **1** money paid in compensation to the family of someone who has been killed. **2** money paid to a hired killer.

blood orange ● noun an orange of a variety with red flesh.

blood poisoning ● noun a diseased state due to the presence of micro-organisms or their toxins in the blood.

blood pressure ● noun the pressure of the blood in the circulatory system, which is closely related to the force and rate of the heartbeat.

blood pudding (also **blood sausage**) ● noun black pudding.

blood relation (also **blood relative**) ● noun a person who is related to another by birth rather than by marriage.

bloodshed ● noun the killing or wounding of people.

bloodshot ● adjective (of the eyes) inflamed or tinged with blood.

blood sport ● noun a sport involving the hunting, wounding, or killing of animals.

bloodstock ● noun thoroughbred horses considered collectively.

bloodstream ● noun the blood circulating through the body of a person or animal.

bloodsucker ● noun **1** an animal or insect that sucks blood. **2** informal a person who extorts money or otherwise lives off other people.

– DERIVATIVES **bloodsucking** adjective.

blood sugar ● noun the concentration of glucose in the blood.

bloodthirsty ● adjective (**bloodthirstier**, **bloodthirstiest**) eager to kill and maim.

blood vessel ● noun a tubular structure carrying blood through the tissues and organs; a vein, artery, or capillary.

bloody[1] ● adjective (**bloodier**, **bloodiest**) **1** covered with or composed of blood. **2** involving much violence or cruelty. ● verb (**bloodies**, **bloodied**) cover or stain with blood.

– DERIVATIVES **bloodily** adverb **bloodiness** noun.

bloody[2] ● adjective informal, chiefly Brit. **1** used to express anger or shock, or for emphasis. **2** dated unpleasant: *don't be too bloody to Nigel.*

– ORIGIN perhaps connected with the 'bloods' or aristocratic rowdies of the 17th and 18th centuries; to be *bloody drunk* (= as drunk as a blood) meant 'very drunk indeed'.

Bloody Mary ● noun (pl. **Bloody Marys**) a drink consisting of vodka and tomato juice.

bloody-minded ● adjective Brit. informal deliberately uncooperative.

bloom ● verb **1** produce flowers; be in flower. **2** be or become very healthy. ● noun **1** a flower, especially one cultivated for its beauty. **2** the state or period of blooming. **3** a youthful or healthy glow in a person's complexion. **4** a delicate powdery surface deposit on fruits.

– ORIGIN Old Norse.

bloomer[1] ● noun Brit. a large loaf with diagonal slashes on a rounded top.

– ORIGIN of unknown origin.

bloomer[2] ● noun Brit. informal a stupid mistake.

– ORIGIN equivalent to *blooming error*.

bloomers ● plural noun **1** women's loose-fitting knee-length knickers. **2** historical women's loose-fitting trousers, gathered at the knee or ankle.

– ORIGIN named after Mrs Amelia J. *Bloomer* (1818–94), an American social reformer who advocated a similar garment.

blooming ● adjective Brit. informal used to express annoyance or for emphasis.

bloop informal, chiefly N. Amer. ● verb (of an electronic device) emit a short low-pitched noise. ● noun a short low-pitched noise emitted by an electronic device.

– ORIGIN imitative.

blooper ● noun informal, chiefly N. Amer. an embarrassing error.

blossom ● noun **1** a flower or a mass of flowers on a tree or bush. **2** the state or period of flowering. ● verb **1** (of a tree or bush) produce blossom. **2** develop in a promising or healthy way.

– ORIGIN Old English, related to BLOOM.

blot ● noun **1** a dark mark or stain, especially one made by ink. **2** a thing that mars something that is otherwise good. ● verb (**blotted**, **blotting**) **1** dry with an absorbent material. **2** mark, stain, or mar. **3** (**blot out**) obscure (a view). **4** (**blot out**) obliterate or ignore (a painful memory or thought).

– PHRASES **blot one's copybook** Brit. tarnish one's good reputation.

Thesaurus

coloured, golden, platinum, ash blonde, strawberry blonde; bleached, peroxide.

– OPPOSITES dark.

blood ● noun **1** *he had lost too much blood* gore, vital fluid; *poetic/literary* lifeblood, ichor. **2** *a woman of noble blood* ANCESTRY, lineage, bloodline, descent, parentage, family, birth, extraction, origin, genealogy, heritage, stock, kinship.

– RELATED TERMS haemal, haemic, haematic, sanguineous.

blood-curdling ● adjective TERRIFYING, frightening, spine-chilling, chilling, hair-raising, horrifying, alarming; eerie, sinister, horrible; *Scottish* eldritch; *informal* scary.

bloodless ● adjective **1** *a bloodless revolution* NON-VIOLENT, peaceful, peaceable, pacifist. **2** *his face was bloodless* ANAEMIC, pale, wan, pallid, ashen, colourless, chalky, waxen, white, grey, pasty, drained, drawn, deathly. **3** *a bloodless Hollywood mogul* HEARTLESS, unfeeling, cruel, ruthless, merciless, pitiless, uncharitable; cold, hard, stony-hearted, cold-blooded, callous. **4** *a bloodless chorus* FEEBLE, spiritless, lifeless, listless, half-hearted, unenthusiastic, lukewarm.

– OPPOSITES bloody, ruddy, charitable, powerful.

bloodshed ● noun SLAUGHTER, massacre, killing, wounding; carnage, butchery, bloodletting, bloodbath; violence, fighting, warfare, battle; *poetic/literary* slaying.

bloodthirsty ● adjective MURDEROUS, homicidal, violent, vicious, barbarous, barbaric, savage, brutal, cut-throat; fierce, ferocious, inhuman.

bloody ● adjective **1** *his bloody nose* BLEEDING. **2** *bloody medical waste* BLOODSTAINED, blood-soaked, gory; *archaic* sanguinary. **3** *a bloody civil war* VICIOUS, ferocious, savage, fierce, brutal, murderous, gory; *archaic* sanguinary. **4** *(Brit. informal) a bloody nuisance!* See DAMNED.

bloody-minded ● adjective *(Brit. informal)* UNCOOPERATIVE, awkward, disobliging, recalcitrant, unaccommodating, inflexible, uncompromising, contrary, perverse, obstinate, stubborn; difficult; *informal* pig-headed; *Brit. informal* bolshie, stroppy.

– OPPOSITES compliant.

bloom ● noun **1** *orchid blooms* FLOWER, blossom, floweret, floret. **2** *a girl in the bloom of youth* PRIME, perfection, acme, peak, height, heyday; salad days. **3** *the bloom of her skin* RADIANCE, lustre, sheen, glow, freshness; BLUSH, rosiness, pinkness, colour. ● verb **1** *the geraniums bloomed* FLOWER, blossom, open; mature. **2** *the children bloomed in the Devonshire air* FLOURISH, thrive, prosper, progress, burgeon; *informal* be in the pink.

– OPPOSITES wither, decline.

blossom ● noun *pink blossoms* FLOWER, bloom, floweret, floret. ● verb **1** *the snowdrops have blossomed* BLOOM, flower, open, unfold; mature. **2** *the whole region had blossomed* DEVELOP, grow, mature, progress, evolve; flourish, thrive, prosper, bloom, burgeon.

b

– ORIGIN probably Scandinavian.

blotch ● noun a large irregular patch or unsightly mark. ● verb cover or mark with blotches.
– DERIVATIVES **blotchy** adjective.
– ORIGIN alteration of obsolete *plotch*.

blotter ● noun blotting paper inserted into a frame.

blotting paper ● noun absorbent paper used for soaking up excess ink when writing.

blotto ● adjective informal extremely drunk.

blouse ● noun **1** a woman's upper garment resembling a shirt. **2** a loose smock or tunic. **3** a type of jacket worn as part of military uniform. ● verb make (a garment) hang in loose folds.
– PHRASES **big girl's blouse** Brit. informal a weak, cowardly, or over-sensitive man.
– ORIGIN French.

blouson /blo͞ozon/ ● noun a short loose-fitting jacket.
– ORIGIN French.

blow[1] ● verb (past **blew**; past part. **blown**) **1** (of wind) move creating an air current. **2** propel or be propelled by the wind. **3** expel air through pursed lips. **4** force air through the mouth into (an instrument) to make a sound. **5** sound (the horn of a vehicle). **6** (of an explosion) displace violently. **7** burst or burn out through pressure or overheating. **8** force air through a tube into (molten glass) to create an artefact. **9** informal spend (money) recklessly. **10** informal completely bungle (an opportunity). **11** informal expose (a stratagem): *his cover was blown.* ● noun **1** a strong wind. **2** an act of blowing.
– PHRASES **blow a fuse** (or **gasket**) informal lose one's temper. **blow away** informal kill by shooting. **blow hot and cold** vacillate. **blow someone's mind** informal impress or affect someone very strongly. **blow one's nose** clear one's nose of mucus by blowing through it. **blow off** informal **1** lose one's temper and shout. **2** break wind noisily. **blow over** (of trouble) fade away without serious consequences. **blow one's top** informal lose one's temper. **blow up 1** explode. **2** lose one's temper. **3** (of a wind or storm) begin to develop. **4** (of a scandal or dispute) emerge or become public. **5** inflate.
– ORIGIN Old English.

blow[2] ● noun **1** a powerful stroke with a hand or weapon. **2** a sudden shock or disappointment.
– PHRASES **come to blows** start fighting after a disagreement.
– ORIGIN of unknown origin.

blow-by-blow ● adjective (of a description of an event) giving all the details in the order in which they occurred.

blow-dry ● verb arrange (the hair) while drying it with a hand-held dryer.

blower ● noun **1** a device for creating a current of air to dry or heat something. **2** informal, chiefly Brit. a telephone.

blowfish ● noun a fish that is able to inflate its body when alarmed.

blowfly ● noun a bluebottle or similar large fly which lays its eggs on meat and carcasses.

blowhard ● noun N. Amer. informal a person who blusters and boasts in an unpleasant way.

blowhole ● noun **1** the nostril of a whale or dolphin on the top of its head. **2** a hole in ice for breathing or fishing through. **3** a vent for air or smoke in a tunnel.

blow job ● noun vulgar slang an act of fellatio.

blowlamp ● noun British term for BLOWTORCH.

blown past participle of BLOW[1].

blowout ● noun **1** an occasion when a vehicle tyre bursts or an electric fuse melts. **2** informal a large, lavish meal.

blowpipe ● noun **1** a weapon consisting of a long tube through which an arrow or dart is blown. **2** a long tube by means of which molten glass is blown.

blowsy /blowzi/ (also **blowzy**) ● adjective (of a woman) coarse, untidy, and red-faced.
– ORIGIN from obsolete *blowze* 'beggar's female companion'.

blowtorch ● noun a portable device producing a hot flame, typically used to burn off paint.

blowy ● adjective (**blowier**, **blowiest**) windy or windswept.

BLT ● noun a sandwich filled with bacon, lettuce, and tomato.

blub ● verb (**blubbed**, **blubbing**) informal sob noisily.
– ORIGIN abbreviation of BLUBBER[2].

blubber[1] ● noun the fat of sea mammals, especially whales and seals.
– DERIVATIVES **blubbery** adjective.
– ORIGIN originally denoting the foaming of the sea: perhaps sym-

Thesaurus

– OPPOSITES fade, decline.
– PHRASES **in blossom** IN FLOWER, flowering, blossoming, blooming, in (full) bloom, open, out.

blot ● noun **1** *an ink blot* SPOT, dot, mark, blotch, smudge, patch, dab; *informal* splotch; *Brit. informal* splodge. **2** *the only blot on a clean campaign* BLEMISH, taint, stain, blight, flaw, fault; disgrace, dishonour. **3** *a blot on the landscape* EYESORE, monstrosity, carbuncle, mess; *informal* sight.
● verb **1** *blot the excess water* SOAK UP, absorb, sponge up, mop up; dry up/out; dab, pat. **2** *the writing was messy and blotted* SMUDGE, smear, blotch, mark. **3** *he had blotted our name forever* TARNISH, taint, stain, blacken, sully, mar; dishonour, disgrace, besmirch.
– OPPOSITES honour.
– PHRASES **blot something out 1** *Mary blotted out her picture* ERASE, obliterate, delete, efface, rub out, blank out, expunge; cross out, strike out. **2** *clouds were starting to blot out the stars* CONCEAL, hide, obscure, exclude, obliterate; shadow, eclipse. **3** *he urged her to blot out the memory* ERASE, efface, eradicate, expunge, wipe out.

blotch ● noun **1** *pink flowers with dark blotches* PATCH, smudge, dot, spot, blot, dab, daub; *informal* splotch; *Brit. informal* splodge. **2** *his face was covered in blotches* PATCH, mark, freckle, birthmark, discoloration, eruption, naevus.
● verb *her face was blotched and swollen* SPOT, mark, smudge, streak, blemish.

blotchy ● adjective MOTTLED, dappled, blotched, patchy, spotty, spotted, smudged, marked; *informal* splotchy; *Brit. informal* splodgy.

blow[1] ● verb **1** *the icy wind blew around us* GUST, puff, flurry, blast, roar, bluster, rush, storm. **2** *his ship was blown on to the rocks* SWEEP, carry, toss, drive, push, force. **3** *leaves blew across the road* DRIFT, flutter, waft, float, glide, whirl, move. **4** *he blew a smoke ring* EXHALE, puff; emit, expel, discharge, issue. **5** *Uncle Albert was puffing and blowing* WHEEZE, puff, pant, gasp. **6** *he blew a trumpet* SOUND, blast, toot, pipe, trumpet; play. **7** *a rear tyre had blown* BURST, explode, blow out, split, rupture, puncture. **8** *the bulb had blown* FUSE, short-circuit, burn out, break, go. **9** *(informal) he blew his money on gambling* SQUANDER, waste, misspend, throw away, fritter away, go through, lose, lavish, dissipate, use up; spend recklessly; *informal* splurge; *Brit. informal, dated* blue. **10** *(informal) don't blow this opportunity* SPOIL, ruin, bungle, mess up, fudge, muff; WASTE, lose, squander; *informal* botch, screw up, foul up; *Brit. informal* cock up, bodge. **11** *(informal) his cover was blown* EXPOSE, reveal, uncover, disclose, divulge, unveil, betray, leak.
● noun **1** *a severe blow* GALE, storm, tempest, hurricane; wind, breeze, gust, draught, flurry. **2** *a blow on the guard's whistle* TOOT, blast, blare; whistle.
– PHRASES **blow out 1** *the matches will not blow out in a strong wind* BE EXTINGUISHED, go out, be put out, stop burning. **2** *the front tyre blew out.* See BLOW[1] verb sense 7. **3** *the windows blew out* SHATTER, rupture, crack, smash, splinter, disintegrate; burst, explode, fly apart; *informal* bust. **blow something out** EXTINGUISH, put out, snuff, douse, quench, smother. **blow over** ABATE, subside, drop off, lessen, ease (off), let up, diminish, fade, dwindle, slacken, recede, tail off, peter out, pass, die down, fizzle out. **blow up 1** *a lorry-load of shells blew up* EXPLODE, detonate, go off, ignite, erupt. **2** *he blows up at whoever's in his way* LOSE ONE'S TEMPER, get angry, rant and rave, go berserk, flare up, erupt; *informal* go mad, go crazy, go wild, go ape, hit the roof, fly off the handle. **3** *a crisis blew up* BREAK OUT, erupt, flare up, boil over; emerge, arise. **blow something up 1** *they blew the plane up* BOMB, blast, destroy; explode, detonate. **2** *blow up the balloons* INFLATE, pump up, fill up, puff up, swell, expand, aerate. **3** *things get blown up out of all proportion* EXAGGERATE, overstate, overstress, overestimate, magnify, amplify; aggrandize, embellish, elaborate. **4** *I blew the picture up on a photocopier* ENLARGE, magnify, expand, increase.

blow[2] ● noun **1** *a blow on the head* KNOCK, BANG, hit, punch, thump, smack, crack, rap; *informal* whack, thwack, bash, clout, sock, wallop. **2** *losing his wife must have been a blow* SHOCK, surprise, bombshell, thunderbolt, jolt; calamity, catastrophe, disaster, upset, setback.

blowout ● noun **1** *the steering is automatic in the event of blowouts* PUNCTURE, flat tyre, burst tyre; *informal* flat. **2** *(informal) this meal is our last real blowout* FEAST, banquet, celebration, party; *informal* shindig, do, binge; *Brit. informal* beanfeast, bunfight, nosh-up.

blowsy ● adjective UNTIDY, sloppy, scruffy, messy, dishevelled, unkempt, frowzy, slovenly; coarse; RED-FACED, ruddy, florid, raddled.
– OPPOSITES tidy, respectable.

bolic.

blubber[2] • verb informal sob noisily and uncontrollably.
– ORIGIN probably imitative.

bludge Austral./NZ informal • verb **1** live off the efforts of others. **2** cadge or scrounge. • noun an easy job or assignment.

bludgeon • noun a thick stick with a heavy end, used as a weapon. • verb **1** beat with a bludgeon. **2** bully into doing something.
– ORIGIN of unknown origin.

bludger • noun Austral./NZ informal a scrounger or idler.
– ORIGIN originally British slang denoting a pimp who robbed his prostitute's clients: abbreviation of *bludgeoner*.

blue[1] • adjective (**bluer**, **bluest**) **1** of a colour intermediate between green and violet, as of the sky on a sunny day. **2** informal melancholy or depressed. **3** informal (of a film, joke, or story) with sexual or pornographic content. **4** (of a cat, fox, or rabbit) having fur of a smoky grey colour. **5** Brit. informal politically conservative. • noun **1** blue colour, pigment, or material. **2** Brit. a person who has represented Cambridge University or Oxford University in a particular sport. **3** Austral./NZ informal a nickname for a redheaded person. **4** Austral./NZ informal an argument or fight.
– PHRASES **once in a blue moon** informal very rarely. [ORIGIN because a 'blue moon' is a phenomenon that never occurs.] **out of the blue** informal unexpectedly. **talk a blue streak** N. Amer. informal speak continuously and at great length.
– DERIVATIVES **blueness** noun.
– ORIGIN Old French *bleu*.

blue[2] • verb (**blues**, **blued**, **bluing** or **blueing**) Brit. informal, dated squander or spend recklessly.
– ORIGIN perhaps from BLOW[1].

blue baby • noun a baby with cyanosis.

bluebell • noun a woodland plant which produces clusters of blue bell-shaped flowers.

blueberry • noun (pl. **blueberries**) the small blue-back berry of a North American dwarf shrub.

bluebird • noun an American songbird, the male of which has a blue head, back, and wings.

blue-blooded • adjective of noble birth.

blue book • noun (in the UK) a report bound in a blue cover and issued by Parliament or the Privy Council.

bluebottle • noun a common blowfly with a metallic-blue body.

blue cheese • noun cheese containing veins of blue mould, such as Stilton.

blue-chip • adjective denoting companies or their shares considered to be a reliable investment.
– ORIGIN from the *blue chip* used in gambling games, which usually has a high value.

blue-collar • adjective chiefly N. Amer. relating to manual work or workers.

blue-eyed boy • noun Brit. informal, chiefly derogatory a person highly regarded and treated with special favour.

bluegrass • noun **1** (also **Kentucky bluegrass**) a meadow grass introduced into North America and grown for fodder. **2** a kind of country music characterized by virtuosic playing of banjos and guitars.

blue-green algae • plural noun cyanobacteria.

blue heeler • noun Austral./NZ a cattle dog with a dark speckled body.

blueish • adjective variant spelling of BLUISH.

Blue Peter • noun a blue flag with a white square in the centre, raised by a ship about to leave port.

blueprint • noun **1** a design plan or other technical drawing. **2** something which acts as a plan, model, or template.
– ORIGIN from the original process in which prints were composed of white lines on a blue ground or of blue lines on a white ground.

blue riband • noun (also **blue ribbon**) a ribbon of blue silk given to the winner of a competition or as a mark of great distinction. • adjective (**blue-ribbon**) N. Amer. of the highest quality; first-class.

blues • plural noun **1** (treated as sing. or pl.) melancholic music of black American folk origin. **2** (**the blues**) informal feelings of melancholy or depression.
– DERIVATIVES **bluesy** adjective.
– ORIGIN from *blue devils* 'depression or delirium tremens'.

blue-sky • adjective informal not yet practicable or profitable.

bluestocking • noun often derogatory an intellectual or literary woman.
– ORIGIN in reference to literary parties held in London around 1750 by three society ladies, where some of the men favoured less formal dress (blue worsted stockings as opposed to the more formal black silk ones).

blue tit • noun a common titmouse with a blue cap and yellow underparts.

blue whale • noun a bluish-grey rorqual which is the largest living animal.

bluey • adjective almost or partly blue. • noun (pl. **blueys**) Austral./NZ informal, archaic **1** a bundle of possessions carried by a bushman. [ORIGIN so named because the covering was generally a blue blanket.] **2** a nickname for a red-headed person.

bluff[1] • noun an attempt to deceive someone into believing that one can or will do something. • verb try to deceive someone as to one's abilities or intentions.
– PHRASES **call someone's bluff** challenge someone to carry out a stated intention, in the expectation of being able to expose it as a pretence.
– DERIVATIVES **bluffer** noun.
– ORIGIN from Dutch *bluffen* 'brag'.

bluff[2] • adjective good-naturedly frank and direct.
– DERIVATIVES **bluffly** adverb **bluffness** noun.
– ORIGIN originally in the sense 'surly, abrupt': figurative use of BLUFF[3].

bluff[3] • noun a steep cliff, bank, or promontory. • adjective (of a cliff or a ship's bows) having a vertical or steep broad front.
– ORIGIN of unknown origin.

bluish (also **blueish**) • adjective having a blue tinge.

blunder • noun a stupid or careless mistake. • verb **1** make a blunder. **2** move clumsily or as if unable to see.
– ORIGIN probably Scandinavian.

blunderbuss • noun **1** historical a short large-bored gun. **2** an un-

Thesaurus

blowy • adjective WINDY, windswept, blustery, gusty, breezy; stormy, squally.
– OPPOSITES still.

blubber[1] • noun *whale blubber* FAT, fatty tissue.

blubber[2] • verb (informal) *she started to blubber* CRY, sob, weep, howl, snivel; informal blub, boohoo.

bludgeon • noun *hooligans wielding bludgeons* CUDGEL, club, stick, truncheon, baton; N. Amer. nightstick, blackjack; Brit. informal cosh.
• verb **1** *he was bludgeoned to death* BATTER, cudgel, club, beat, thrash; informal clobber. **2** *I let him bludgeon me into marriage* COERCE, force, compel, pressurize, pressure, bully, browbeat, hector, dragoon, steamroller; informal strong-arm, railroad.

blue • adjective **1** *bright blue eyes* sky-blue, azure, cobalt, sapphire, navy, Oxford blue, Cambridge blue, ultramarine, aquamarine, cyan; poetic/literary cerulean. **2** (informal) *Mum was feeling a bit blue* DEPRESSED, down, sad, unhappy, melancholy, miserable, gloomy, dejected, downhearted, downcast, despondent, low, glum; informal down in the dumps, down in the mouth, fed up. **3** (informal) *a blue movie* PORNOGRAPHIC, racy, risqué, naughty, spicy; indecent, dirty, lewd, smutty, filthy, obscene, sordid; erotic, arousing, sexy, titillating, explicit; informal porn, porno, X-rated, raunchy; euphemistic adult.
– OPPOSITES happy, clean.

blueprint • noun **1** *blueprints of the aircraft* PLAN, design, diagram, drawing, sketch, map, layout, representation. **2** *a blueprint for similar measures in other countries* MODEL, plan, template, framework, pattern, example, guide, prototype, pilot.

blues • plural noun (informal) *a fit of blues* DEPRESSION, sadness, unhappiness, melancholy, misery, sorrow, gloom, dejection, despondency, despair; the doldrums.

bluff[1] • noun *this offer was denounced as a bluff* DECEPTION, subterfuge, pretence, sham, fake, deceit, feint, hoax, fraud, charade; trick, ruse, scheme, machination; informal put-on.
• verb **1** *they are bluffing to hide their guilt* PRETEND, sham, fake, feign, lie, hoax, pose, posture, masquerade, dissemble. **2** *I managed to bluff the board into believing me* DECEIVE, delude, mislead, trick, fool, hoodwink, dupe, hoax, beguile, gull; informal con, kid, have on.

bluff[2] • adjective *a bluff man* PLAIN-SPOKEN, straightforward, blunt, direct, no-nonsense, frank, open, candid, forthright, unequivocal; hearty, genial, good-natured; informal upfront.

bluff[3] • noun *an impregnable high bluff* CLIFF, promontory, headland, crag, bank, peak, escarpment, scarp.

blunder • noun *he shook his head at his blunder* MISTAKE, error,

b

subtle and imprecise action or method.
– ORIGIN Dutch *donderbus* 'thunder gun'.

blunt • adjective **1** lacking a sharp edge or point. **2** having a flat or rounded end. **3** uncompromisingly forthright in manner. • verb **1** make or become blunt. **2** weaken or reduce the force of.
– DERIVATIVES **bluntly** adverb **bluntness** noun.
– ORIGIN perhaps Scandinavian.

blur • verb (**blurred**, **blurring**) make or become unclear or less distinct. • noun something that cannot be seen, heard, or recalled clearly.
– DERIVATIVES **blurry** adjective (**blurrier**, **blurriest**).
– ORIGIN perhaps related to BLEARY.

blurb • noun a short promotional description of a book, film, or other product.
– ORIGIN coined by the American humorist Gelett Burgess (died 1951).

blurt • verb say suddenly and without careful consideration.
– ORIGIN probably imitative.

blush • verb become red in the face through shyness or embarrassment. • noun **1** an instance of blushing. **2** literary a pink or pale red tinge.
– PHRASES **at first blush** at the first glimpse or impression.
– DERIVATIVES **blushing** adjective.
– ORIGIN Old English.

blusher • noun a cosmetic used to give a warm reddish tinge to the cheeks.

bluster • verb **1** talk in a loud or aggressive way with little effect. **2** (of wind or rain) blow or beat fiercely and noisily. • noun blustering talk.
– DERIVATIVES **blusterer** noun **blustery** adjective.
– ORIGIN imitative.

BM • abbreviation **1** Bachelor of Medicine. **2** British Museum.

BMA • abbreviation British Medical Association.

B-movie • noun a low-budget film used as a supporting feature in a cinema programme.

BMX • abbreviation bicycle motocross (referring to bicycles designed for cross-country racing).

boa • noun **1** a large snake which kills its prey by constriction. **2** a long, thin stole of feathers or fur worn around a woman's neck.
– ORIGIN Latin.

boab /bōab/ • noun Austral. another term for BAOBAB.

boar • noun (pl. same or **boars**) **1** (also **wild boar**) a tusked wild pig. **2** an uncastrated domestic male pig.
– ORIGIN Old English.

board • noun **1** a long, thin, flat piece of wood used in building. **2** a thin, flat, rectangular piece of stiff material used for various purposes. **3** the decision-making body of an organization. **4** the provision of regular meals in return for payment. • verb **1** get on or into (a ship, aircraft, or other vehicle). **2** receive meals and accommodation in return for payment. **3** (of a pupil) live in school during term time. **4** (**board up/over**) cover or seal with pieces of wood.
– PHRASES **go by the board** (of a plan or principle) be abandoned or rejected. [ORIGIN from nautical use meaning 'fall overboard', the 'board' meaning the side of a ship.] **on board** on or in a ship, aircraft, or other vehicle. **take on board** informal fully consider or assimilate (a new idea or situation). **tread the boards** informal appear on stage as an actor.
– ORIGIN Old English.

boarder • noun **1** a person who boards, in particular a pupil who lives in school during term time. **2** a person who forces their way on to a ship in an attack.

board game • noun a game that involves the movement of counters or other objects around a board.

boarding house • noun a private house providing food and lodging for paying guests.

boarding school • noun a school in which the pupils live during term time.

boardroom • noun a room in which a board of directors meets regularly.

boardsailing • noun another term for WINDSURFING.
– DERIVATIVES **boardsailor** noun.

boardwalk • noun **1** a wooden walkway across sand or marshy ground. **2** N. Amer. a promenade along a beach or waterfront.

boast • verb **1** talk about oneself with excessive pride. **2** possess (a feature that is a source of pride). • noun an act of boasting.
– DERIVATIVES **boaster** noun.
– ORIGIN of unknown origin.

boastful • adjective showing excessive pride and self-satisfaction in oneself.
– DERIVATIVES **boastfully** adverb **boastfulness** noun.

boat • noun **1** a vessel for travelling on water. **2** a boat-shaped

Thesaurus

gaffe, slip, oversight, faux pas; *informal* botch, slip-up, boo-boo; *Brit. informal* clanger, boob; *N. Amer. informal* blooper.
• verb **1** *the government admitted it had blundered* MAKE A MISTAKE, err, miscalculate, bungle, trip up, be wrong; *informal* slip up, screw up, blow it, goof; *Brit. informal* boob. **2** *she blundered down the steps* STUMBLE, lurch, stagger, flounder, struggle, fumble, grope.

blunt • adjective **1** *a blunt knife* UNSHARPENED, dull, worn, edgeless. **2** *the leaf is broad with a blunt tip* ROUNDED, flat, obtuse, stubby. **3** *a blunt message* STRAIGHTFORWARD, frank, plain-spoken, candid, direct, bluff, forthright, unequivocal; BRUSQUE, abrupt, curt, terse, bald, brutal, harsh; stark, undisguised, unvarnished; *informal* upfront.
– OPPOSITES sharp, pointed, subtle.
• verb **1** *ebony blunts tools very rapidly* DULL, make less sharp. **2** *age hasn't blunted my passion for life* DULL, deaden, dampen, numb, weaken, sap, cool, temper, allay, abate; diminish, reduce, decrease, lessen, deplete.
– OPPOSITES sharpen, intensify.

blur • verb **1** *she felt tears blur her vision* CLOUD, fog, obscure, dim, make hazy, unfocus, soften; *poetic/literary* bedim; *archaic* blear. **2** *films blur the difference between villains and victims* OBSCURE, make vague, confuse, muddle, muddy, obfuscate, cloud, weaken. **3** *memories of the picnic had blurred* BECOME DIM, dull, numb, deaden, mute; lessen, decrease, diminish.
– OPPOSITES sharpen, focus.
• noun *a blur on the horizon* INDISTINCT SHAPE; haze, cloud, mist.

blurred • adjective INDISTINCT, blurry, fuzzy, hazy, misty, foggy, shadowy, faint; unclear, vague, indefinite, unfocused, obscure, nebulous.

blurt • verb
– PHRASES **blurt something out** BURST OUT WITH, exclaim, call out; DIVULGE, disclose, reveal, betray, let slip, give away; *informal* blab, gush, let on, spill the beans, let the cat out of the bag; *dated* ejaculate.

blush • verb *Joan blushed at the compliment* REDDEN, turn/go pink, turn/go red, flush, colour, burn up; feel shy, feel embarrassed.
• noun *the darkness hid her fiery blush* FLUSH, rosiness, pinkness, bloom, high colour.

bluster • verb **1** *he started blustering about the general election* RANT, thunder, bellow, sound off; be overbearing; *informal* throw one's weight about/around. **2** *storms bluster in from the sea* BLAST, gust, storm, roar, rush.
• noun *his bluster turned to cooperation* RANTING, thundering, hectoring, bullying; bombast, bumptiousness, braggadocio.

blustery • adjective STORMY, gusty, blowy, windy, squally, wild, tempestuous, turbulent; howling, roaring.
– OPPOSITES calm.

board • noun **1** *a wooden board* PLANK, beam, panel, slat, batten, timber, lath. **2** *the board of directors* COMMITTEE, council, panel, directorate, commission, group. **3** *your room and board will be free* FOOD, meals, provisions, refreshments, diet, table, bread; keep, maintenance; *informal* grub, nosh, eats, chow; *Brit. informal* scoff.
• verb **1** *he boarded the aircraft* GET ON, go aboard, enter, mount, ascend; embark, emplane, entrain; catch; *informal* hop on. **2** *a number of students boarded with them* LODGE, live, reside, be housed; *N. Amer.* room; *informal* put up, have digs. **3** *they run a facility for boarding dogs* ACCOMMODATE, lodge, take in, put up, house; keep, feed, cater for.
– PHRASES **board something up/over** COVER UP/OVER, close up, shut up, seal.

boast • verb **1** *his mother had been boasting about him* BRAG, crow, blow one's trumpet, swagger, swank, gloat, show off; exaggerate, overstate; *informal* talk big, lay it on thick; *Austral./NZ informal* skite. **2** *the hotel boasts a wide selection of facilities* POSSESS, have, own, enjoy, pride oneself/itself on.
• noun **1** *the government's main boast seemed undone* BRAG, self-praise; exaggeration, overstatement, fanfaronade; *informal* swank; *Austral./NZ informal* skite. **2** *the hall is the boast of the county* PRIDE, joy, wonder, delight, treasure, gem.

serving dish for sauce or gravy. • verb travel in a boat for pleasure.
– PHRASES **be in the same boat** informal be in the same difficult circumstances as others. **miss the boat** see MISS[1]. **push the boat out** Brit. informal be extravagant. **rock the boat** informal disturb an existing situation.
– DERIVATIVES **boating** noun **boatload** noun.
– ORIGIN Old English.
boatel • noun **1** a waterside hotel with facilities for mooring boats. **2** a moored ship used as a hotel.
– ORIGIN blend of BOAT and HOTEL.
boater • noun **1** a flat-topped straw hat with a brim. [ORIGIN originally worn while boating.] **2** a person who travels in a boat.
boathook • noun a long pole with a hook and a spike at one end, used for moving boats.
boatman • noun a person who provides transport by boat.
boat people • plural noun refugees who have left a country by sea.
boatswain /bōs'n/ (also **bo'sun** or **bosun**) • noun a ship's officer in charge of equipment and the crew.
– ORIGIN from BOAT + SWAIN.
boat train • noun a train scheduled to connect with the arrival or departure of a boat.
Bob • noun (in phrase **Bob's your uncle**) Brit. informal an expression signifying the simplicity of completing a task.
bob[1] • verb (**bobbed**, **bobbing**) **1** make or cause to make a quick, short movement up and down. **2** curtsy briefly. • noun a quick, short movement up and down.
– PHRASES **bob for apples** try to catch floating apples with one's mouth, as a game.
– ORIGIN of unknown origin.
bob[2] • noun **1** a short hairstyle hanging evenly all round. **2** a weight on a pendulum, plumb line, or kite-tail. **3** a bobsleigh. • verb (**bobbed**, **bobbing**) cut (hair) in a bob.
– ORIGIN originally denoting a bunch or cluster: of unknown origin.
bob[3] • noun (pl. same) Brit. informal a shilling.
– ORIGIN of unknown origin.
bobbin • noun a cylinder, cone, or reel holding thread.
– ORIGIN French *bobine*.
bobble[1] • noun a small ball made of strands of wool.
– DERIVATIVES **bobbly** adjective.
– ORIGIN from BOB[2].
bobble[2] informal • verb move with an irregular bouncing motion. • noun an irregular bouncing motion.
– ORIGIN from BOB[1].
bobby • noun (pl. **bobbies**) Brit. informal, dated a police officer.
– ORIGIN after Sir *Robert* Peel (1788–1850), the British Prime Minister who established the Metropolitan Police.
bobcat • noun a small North American lynx with a barred and spotted coat and a short tail.
– ORIGIN from BOB[2], with reference to its short tail.
bobsleigh (N. Amer. **bobsled**) • noun a mechanically steered and braked sledge used for racing down an ice-covered run.
– DERIVATIVES **bobsleighing** noun.
bobsy-die /bobzidī/ • noun dialect & NZ a great deal of fuss or trouble.
– ORIGIN contraction of *Bob's-a-dying*.
bobtail • noun a docked tail of a horse or dog.
Boche /bosh/ • noun (**the Boche**) informal, dated Germans, especially German soldiers, collectively.
– ORIGIN French soldiers' slang, literally 'rascal', applied to Germans in World War I.
bod • noun informal **1** a body. **2** chiefly Brit. a person.
bodacious /bōdayshəss/ • adjective N. Amer. informal excellent, admirable, or attractive.
– ORIGIN perhaps a variant of south-western dialect *boldacious*, a blend of BOLD and AUDACIOUS.
bode • verb (**bode well/ill**) be a portent of a good or bad outcome.
– ORIGIN Old English, 'proclaim, foretell'; related to BID[1].
bodega /bədaygə/ • noun (in Spanish-speaking countries) a cellar or shop selling wine, or both wine and groceries.
– ORIGIN Spanish, from Greek *apothēkē* 'storehouse'; related to BOUTIQUE.
bodge • verb Brit. informal make or repair badly or clumsily.
– DERIVATIVES **bodger** noun.
– ORIGIN alteration of BOTCH.
bodgie • noun (pl. **bodgies**) Austral./NZ informal a flawed or worthless thing.
– ORIGIN probably from **bodger** (see BODGE).
bodhrán /bowraan/ • noun a shallow one-sided Irish drum.
– ORIGIN Irish.
bodh tree • noun variant of BO TREE.
bodice • noun **1** the upper front part of a woman's dress. **2** a woman's sleeveless undergarment, often laced at the front.
– ORIGIN originally *bodies*, plural of BODY.
bodice-ripper • noun informal, humorous a sexually explicit historical novel or film.
bodiless • adjective **1** lacking a body. **2** incorporeal; insubstantial.
bodily • adjective **1** relating to the body. **2** material or physical. • adverb by taking hold of a person's body with force.
bodkin • noun **1** a thick, blunt needle with a large eye, used for drawing tape or cord through a hem. **2** historical a long pin used to fasten women's hair.
– ORIGIN perhaps of Celtic origin and related to Irish *bod*, Welsh *bidog*, Scottish Gaelic *biodag* 'dagger'.
body • noun (pl. **bodies**) **1** the physical structure, including the bones, flesh, and organs, of a person or an animal. **2** the torso. **3** a corpse. **4** the main or central part of something. **5** a mass or collection. **6** an organized group of people with a common function: *a regulatory body*. **7** technical a piece of matter; a material object: *the path taken by the falling body*. **8** a full flavour in wine. **9** fullness of a person's hair. **10** a bodysuit. • verb (**bodies**, **bodied**) (**body forth**) give material form to.
– PHRASES **keep body and soul together** stay alive in difficult circumstances. **over my dead body** informal used to express strong opposition.
– DERIVATIVES **bodied** adjective.
– ORIGIN Old English.
body bag • noun a bag used for carrying a corpse from the scene of an accident or crime.
body blow • noun **1** a heavy punch to the body. **2** a severe setback.
bodyboard • noun a short, light surfboard ridden in a prone position.
bodybuilder • noun a person who strengthens and enlarges their muscles through exercise such as weightlifting.
body clock • noun a person's biological clock.

Thesaurus

boastful • adjective BRAGGING, swaggering, bumptious, puffed up, full of oneself; cocky, conceited, arrogant, egotistical; *informal* swanky, big-headed, swollen-headed; *N. Amer. informal* blowhard; *poetic/literary* vainglorious.
– OPPOSITES modest.
boat • noun *a rowing boat* VESSEL, craft, watercraft, ship; *poetic/literary* keel, barque.
• verb *he insisted on boating into the lake* SAIL, yacht, cruise.
bob • verb **1** *their yacht bobbed about* MOVE UP AND DOWN, bounce, toss, skip, dance, jounce; wobble, jiggle, joggle, jolt, jerk. **2** *the bookie's head bobbed* NOD, incline, dip; wag, waggle. **3** *the maid bobbed and left the room* CURTSY, bow.
• noun **1** *a bob of his head* NOD, inclination, dip; wag, waggle. **2** *the maid scurried away with a bob* CURTSY, bow, obeisance.
bode • verb AUGUR, portend, herald, be a sign of, warn of, foreshadow, be an omen of, presage, indicate, signify, promise, threaten, spell; prophesy, predict; *poetic/literary* betoken, forebode.
bodily • adjective *bodily sensations* PHYSICAL, corporeal, corporal, somatic, fleshly; concrete, real, actual, tangible.
– OPPOSITES spiritual, mental.
• adverb *he hauled her bodily from the van* FORCEFULLY, forcibly, violently; wholly, completely, entirely.
body • noun **1** *the human body* FIGURE, frame, form, physique, anatomy, skeleton; soma; *informal* bod. **2** *he was hit by shrapnel in the head and body* TORSO, trunk. **3** *his body was washed up on the shore* CORPSE, carcass, skeleton, remains; *informal* stiff; *Medicine* cadaver. **4** *the body of the article* MAIN PART, central part, core, heart, hub. **5** *the body of the ship* BODYWORK, hull; fuselage. **6** *a body of water* EXPANSE, mass, area, stretch, tract, sweep, extent. **7** *a growing body of evidence* QUANTITY, amount, volume, collection, mass, corpus. **8** *the representative body of the employers* ASSOCIATION, organization, group, party, company, society, circle, syndicate, guild, corporation, contingent. **9** *a heavenly body* OBJECT, entity. **10** *add body to your hair* FULLNESS, thickness, substance, bounce,

b

body double • noun a stand-in for a film actor during stunt or nude scenes.
bodyguard • noun a person employed to protect a rich or famous person.
body language • noun the conscious and unconscious bodily movements by which feelings are communicated.
body politic • noun the people of a nation or society considered as an organized group of citizens.
body-popping • noun a kind of dancing characterized by jerky robotic movements of the joints.
body shop • noun a garage where repairs to the bodywork of vehicles are carried out.
bodysnatcher • noun historical a person who illicitly disinterred corpses for dissection.
body stocking • noun a woman's one-piece undergarment covering the torso and legs.
bodysuit • noun a woman's close-fitting stretch garment for the upper body.
bodysurf • verb surf without using a board.
body warmer • noun a sleeveless padded jacket.
bodywork • noun the metal outer shell of a vehicle.
Boer /bōər, boor/ • noun a member of the Dutch and Huguenot population which settled in southern Africa in the late 17th century. • adjective relating to the Boers.
– ORIGIN Dutch, 'farmer'.
boeuf bourguignon /berf boorginyon/ • noun a dish consisting of beef stewed in red wine.
– ORIGIN French, 'Burgundy beef'.
boff N. Amer. informal • verb **1** hit or strike. **2** have sexual intercourse with. • noun **1** a blow or punch. **2** an act of sexual intercourse.
– ORIGIN imitative.
boffin • noun informal, chiefly Brit. a scientist.
– DERIVATIVES **boffiny** adjective.
– ORIGIN of unknown origin.
boffo N. Amer. informal • adjective **1** (of a play or film) very successful. **2** (of a laugh) deep and unrestrained. • noun (pl. **boffos**) a success.
– ORIGIN from BOFF in the former sense 'roaring success'.
bog • noun **1** an area of soft, wet, muddy ground. **2** Brit. informal a toilet. • verb (**bogged**, **bogging**) **1** (**bog down**) cause to become stuck; hinder the progress of. **2** (**bog in**) Austral./NZ informal start a task enthusiastically.
– DERIVATIVES **bogginess** noun **boggy** adjective.
– ORIGIN Irish or Scottish Gaelic *bogach*, from *bog* 'soft'.
bogey[1] Golf • noun (pl. **bogeys**) a score of one stroke over par at a hole. • verb (**bogeys**, **bogeyed**) play (a hole) in one stroke over par.
– ORIGIN perhaps from *Bogey*, denoting the Devil (see BOGEY[2]), regarded as an imaginary player.
bogey[2] (also **bogy**) • noun (pl. **bogeys**) **1** an evil or mischievous spirit. **2** a cause of fear or alarm: *the bogey of recession.* **3** Brit. informal a piece of nasal mucus.
– ORIGIN originally as *Bogey*, a name applied to the Devil.
bogeyman (also **bogyman**) • noun an evil spirit.
boggle • verb informal **1** be astonished or baffled. **2** (**boggle at**) hesitate to do.
– ORIGIN probably related to BOGEY[2].
bogie /bōgi/ • noun (pl. **bogies**) chiefly Brit. **1** an undercarriage with four or six wheels pivoted beneath the end of a railway vehicle. **2** chiefly N. English a low truck on four small wheels.
– ORIGIN of unknown origin.
bog-standard • adjective informal, derogatory ordinary; basic.
bogus • adjective not genuine or true.
– DERIVATIVES **bogusly** adverb **bogusness** noun.
– ORIGIN originally US, denoting a machine for making counterfeit money: of unknown origin.
bogy • noun (pl. **bogies**) variant spelling of BOGEY[2].
Bohemian /bōheemiən/ • noun **1** a person from Bohemia, a region of the Czech Republic. **2** a socially unconventional person, especially an artist or writer. • adjective **1** relating to Bohemia. **2** socially unconventional.
– DERIVATIVES **Bohemianism** noun.
– ORIGIN sense 2 is from French *bohémien* 'gypsy' (because gypsies were thought to come from Bohemia).
bohrium /boriəm/ • noun a very unstable chemical element made by high-energy atomic collisions.
– ORIGIN named after the Danish physicist Niels *Bohr* (1885–1962).
boil[1] • verb **1** (with reference to a liquid) reach or cause to reach the temperature at which it bubbles and turns to vapour. **2** (with reference to food) cook or be cooked by immersing in boiling water. **3** seethe like boiling liquid. **4** (**boil down to**) amount to. • noun **1** the act or process of boiling; boiling point. **2** a state of vigorous activity or excitement: *the team have gone off the boil this season.*
– ORIGIN Old French *boillir*, from Latin *bullire* 'to bubble'.
boil[2] • noun an inflamed pus-filled swelling on the skin.
– ORIGIN Old English.
boiled sweet • noun Brit. a hard sweet made of boiled sugar.
boiler • noun **1** a fuel-burning apparatus for heating water, especially a device providing a domestic hot-water supply or serving a central heating system. **2** Brit. informal a chicken suitable for cooking only by boiling.
boilerplate • noun **1** rolled steel plates for making boilers. **2** chiefly N. Amer. stereotyped or clichéd writing. **3** standardized pieces of text for use as clauses in contracts or as part of a computer program.
boiler suit • noun Brit. a one-piece suit worn as overalls for heavy manual work.
boiling • adjective **1** at or near boiling point. **2** informal extremely hot.
boiling point • noun the temperature at which a liquid boils.
boisterous • adjective **1** noisy, energetic, and cheerful. **2** literary (of weather or water) wild or stormy.

Thesaurus

lift, shape.
– PHRASES **body and soul** COMPLETELY, entirely, totally, utterly, fully, thoroughly, wholeheartedly, unconditionally, to the hilt.
bodyguard • noun MINDER, guard, protector, guardian, defender; *informal* heavy.
boffin • noun *(Brit. informal)* EXPERT, specialist, authority, genius, mastermind; SCIENTIST, technician, inventor; *informal* egghead, Einstein.
bog • noun MARSH, swamp, mire, quagmire, morass, slough, fen, wetland; *Brit.* carr; *Scottish & N. English* moss.
– PHRASES **bog someone/something down** MIRE, stick, entangle, ensnare, embroil; hamper, hinder, impede, delay, stall, detain; swamp, overwhelm.
bogey • noun **1** *water bogies frighten children from pools* EVIL SPIRIT, bogle, spectre, phantom, hobgoblin, demon; *informal* spook. **2** *the guild is the bogey of bankers* BUGBEAR, pet hate, bane, anathema, abomination, nightmare, horror, dread, curse; *N. Amer.* bugaboo.
boggle • verb *(informal)* **1** *this data makes the mind boggle* MARVEL, wonder, be astonished, be overwhelmed, be staggered; gape, goggle; *informal* gawk. **2** *you never boggle at plain speaking* DEMUR, baulk; shrink from, shy away from, be shy about; hesitate, waver, falter; *informal* be cagey about.
boggy • adjective MARSHY, swampy, miry, fenny, muddy, waterlogged, wet, soggy, sodden, squelchy; spongy, heavy, sloughy.
bogus • adjective FAKE, spurious, false, fraudulent, sham, deceptive; COUNTERFEIT, forged, feigned; make-believe, dummy, pseudo; *informal* phoney, pretend.
– OPPOSITES genuine.
bohemian • noun *he is an artist and a real bohemian* NONCONFORMIST, avant-gardist, free spirit, dropout; hippy, beatnik.
– OPPOSITES conservative.
• adjective *a bohemian student life* UNCONVENTIONAL, nonconformist, unorthodox, avant-garde, irregular, alternative; artistic; *informal* arty-farty, way-out, offbeat.
– OPPOSITES conventional.
boil[1] • verb **1** *boil the potatoes* BRING TO THE BOIL, simmer; cook. **2** *the soup is boiling* SIMMER, bubble, stew. **3** *a huge cliff with the sea boiling below* CHURN, seethe, froth, foam; *poetic/literary* roil. **4** *she boiled at his lack of consideration* FUME, seethe, rage, smoulder, bristle, be angry, be furious; get worked up; *informal* see red, get steamed up.
• noun *bring the stock to the boil* BOILING POINT, 100 degrees centigrade.
– PHRASES **boil something down** CONDENSE, reduce, concentrate, thicken. **boil down to** COME DOWN TO, amount to, add up to, be in essence.
boil[2] • noun *a boil on her neck* SWELLING, SPOT, pimple, blister, pustule, eruption, carbuncle, wen, abscess, ulcer; *technical* furuncle.
boiling • adjective **1** *boiling water* AT BOILING POINT, at 100 degrees centigrade; very hot, piping hot; bubbling. **2** *(informal) it was a boil-*

b

– DERIVATIVES **boisterously** adverb **boisterousness** noun.
– ORIGIN from earlier *boistuous* 'rustic, coarse, boisterous', of unknown origin.

bolas /bōləss/ ● **noun** (treated as sing. or pl.) (especially in South America) a missile consisting of a number of balls connected by strong cord, thrown to entangle the limbs of cattle or other animals.
– ORIGIN Spanish and Portuguese, plural of *bola* 'ball'.

bold ● **adjective** **1** confident and courageous. **2** dated audacious; impudent. **3** (of a colour or design) strong or vivid. **4** (of type) having thick strokes. ● **noun** a bold typeface.
– PHRASES **be so bold as to** dare to. **as bold as brass** confident to the point of impudence.
– DERIVATIVES **boldly** adverb **boldness** noun.
– ORIGIN Old English.

bole ● **noun** a tree trunk.
– ORIGIN Old Norse.

bolero /bəlairō/ ● **noun** (pl. **boleros**) **1** a Spanish dance in simple triple time. **2** /bollərō/ a woman's short open jacket.
– ORIGIN Spanish.

boletus /bəleetəss/ (also **bolete**) ● **noun** (pl. **boletuses**) a toadstool with pores rather than gills on the underside of the cap, and a thick stem.
– ORIGIN Greek *bōlitēs*.

bolide /bōlid/ ● **noun** a large meteor which explodes in the atmosphere.
– ORIGIN French, from Greek *bolis* 'missile'.

bolivar /bolivaar/ ● **noun** the basic monetary unit of Venezuela, equal to 100 centimos.
– ORIGIN named after the Venezuelan Simon *Bolívar* (1783–1830), who liberated Venezuela from the Spanish.

Bolivian ● **noun** a person from Bolivia. ● **adjective** relating to Bolivia.

boliviano ● **noun** (pl. **bolivianos**) the basic monetary unit of Bolivia, equal to 100 centavos or cents.
– ORIGIN Spanish, 'Bolivian'.

boll /bōl/ ● **noun** the rounded seed capsule of plants such as cotton or flax.
– ORIGIN Dutch *bolle* 'rounded object'.

bollard ● **noun** **1** Brit. a short post used to prevent traffic from entering an area. **2** a short post on a ship or quayside for securing a rope.
– ORIGIN perhaps from Old Norse, 'bole'.

bollocking (also **ballocking**) ● **noun** Brit. vulgar slang a severe reprimand.
– DERIVATIVES **bollock** verb.

bollocks (also **ballocks**) ● **plural noun** Brit. vulgar slang **1** the testicles. **2** (treated as sing.) nonsense; rubbish.
– ORIGIN related to BALL[1].

bollworm ● **noun** a moth caterpillar which is a pest of cotton and other crops.

Bollywood ● **noun** informal the Indian popular film industry, based in Bombay.
– ORIGIN blend of *Bombay* and *Hollywood*.

bologna /bəlōnyə/ ● **noun** a smoked sausage made chiefly of bacon, veal, and pork suet.
– ORIGIN named after the city of *Bologna* in northern Italy.

bolometer /bəlommitər/ ● **noun** Physics an electrical instrument for measuring radiant energy.
– DERIVATIVES **bolometric** adjective.
– ORIGIN from Greek *bolē* 'ray of light'.

boloney ● **noun** variant spelling of BALONEY.

bolo tie /bōlō/ ● **noun** N. Amer. a tie consisting of a cord around the neck with a large ornamental fastening at the throat.
– ORIGIN alteration of *bola tie*, from its resemblance to the BOLAS.

Bolshevik /bolshivik/ ● **noun** historical **1** a member of the majority faction of the Russian Social Democratic Party, which seized power in the Revolution of 1917. **2** a person with politically subversive or radical views. ● **adjective** relating to or characteristic of Bolsheviks or Bolshevism.
– DERIVATIVES **Bolshevism** noun **Bolshevist** noun.
– ORIGIN Russian, from *bol'she* 'greater' (with reference to the greater faction).

bolshie (also **bolshy**) Brit. informal ● **adjective** deliberately combative or uncooperative.
– DERIVATIVES **bolshiness** noun.
– ORIGIN from BOLSHEVIK.

bolster ● **noun** **1** a long, firm pillow. **2** a part in a tool, vehicle, or structure providing support or reducing friction. ● **verb** support or strengthen.
– DERIVATIVES **bolsterer** noun.
– ORIGIN Old English.

bolt[1] ● **noun** **1** a long metal pin with a head that screws into a nut, used to fasten things together. **2** a bar that slides into a socket to fasten a door or window. **3** the sliding piece of the breech mechanism of a rifle. **4** a short, heavy arrow shot from a crossbow. **5** a flash of lightning across the sky. ● **verb** fasten with a bolt.
– PHRASES **a bolt from** (or **out of**) **the blue** a sudden and unexpected event. **bolt upright** with the back very straight. **have shot one's bolt** informal have done everything possible but still not succeeded.
– ORIGIN Old English.

bolt[2] ● **verb** **1** run away suddenly. **2** (of a plant) grow quickly upwards and stop flowering as seeds develop. **3** eat (food) quickly.
– PHRASES **make a bolt for** try to escape by running suddenly towards.
– DERIVATIVES **bolter** noun.
– ORIGIN from BOLT[1], expressing the sense 'fly like an arrow'.

bolt[3] ● **noun** a roll of fabric, originally as a measure.
– ORIGIN transferred use of BOLT[1].

bolt hole ● **noun** chiefly Brit. an escape route or hiding place.

bolus /bōləss/ ● **noun** (pl. **boluses**) **1** a small rounded mass of something, especially of food being swallowed. **2** a large pill used in veterinary medicine. **3** Medicine a single dose of a drug given all at once.
– ORIGIN Greek *bōlos* 'clod'.

bomb ● **noun** **1** a container of explosive or incendiary material, designed to explode on impact or when detonated by a timer or remote-control. **2** (**the bomb**) nuclear weapons collectively. **3** (**a bomb**) Brit. informal a large sum of money. ● **verb** **1** attack with a bomb or bombs. **2** Brit. informal move or travel very quick-

Thesaurus

ing day VERY HOT, scorching, blistering, sweltering, sultry, torrid; *informal* roasting, baking.
– OPPOSITES freezing.

boisterous ● **adjective** **1** *a boisterous game of handball* LIVELY, animated, exuberant, spirited; rowdy, unruly, wild, uproarious, unrestrained, undisciplined, uninhibited, uncontrolled, rough, disorderly, riotous; noisy, loud, clamorous; *Brit. informal* rumbustious. **2** *a boisterous wind* BLUSTERY, gusty, windy, stormy, wild, squally, tempestuous; howling, roaring; *informal* blowy.
– OPPOSITES restrained, calm.

bold ● **adjective** **1** *bold adventurers* DARING, intrepid, brave, courageous, valiant, valorous, fearless, dauntless, audacious, daredevil; adventurous, heroic, plucky, spirited, confident, assured; *informal* gutsy, spunky, feisty. **2** *a bold pattern* STRIKING, vivid, bright, strong, eye-catching, prominent; gaudy, lurid, garish. **3** *departure times are in bold type* HEAVY, thick, pronounced.
– OPPOSITES timid, pale.

bolshie ● **adjective** *(Brit. informal)* UNCOOPERATIVE, awkward, disobliging, unhelpful, recalcitrant, contrary, perverse, obstinate, stubborn, difficult, unreasonable, exasperating, trying; *Brit. informal* bloody-minded, stroppy.
– OPPOSITES compliant.

bolster ● **noun** *the bed was strewn with bolsters* PILLOW, cushion, pad.
● **verb** *a break would bolster her morale* STRENGTHEN, reinforce, boost, fortify, renew; support, buoy up, shore up, maintain, aid, help; augment, increase.
– OPPOSITES undermine.

bolt ● **noun** **1** *the bolt on the shed door* BAR, LOCK, catch, latch, fastener. **2** *nuts and bolts* RIVET, pin, peg, screw. **3** *a bolt whirred over my head* ARROW, quarrel, dart, shaft; *poetic/literary* reed. **4** *a bolt of lightning* FLASH, shaft, streak, burst, flare. **5** *Mark made a bolt for the door* DASH, dart, run, sprint, leap, bound. **6** *a bolt of cloth* ROLL, reel, spool; quantity, amount.
● **verb** **1** *he bolted the door* LOCK, bar, latch, fasten, secure. **2** *the lid was bolted down* RIVET, pin, peg, screw; fasten, fix. **3** *Anna bolted from the room* DASH, dart, run, sprint, hurtle, rush, fly, shoot, bound; flee; *informal* tear, scoot, leg it. **4** *he bolted down his breakfast* GOBBLE, gulp, wolf, guzzle, devour; *informal* demolish, polish off, shovel down; *Brit. informal* shift, gollop, scoff; *N. Amer. informal* scarf, snarf.
– OPPOSITES open.

b

ly. **3** informal fail badly.
– PHRASES **go down a bomb** Brit. informal be very well received. **go like a bomb** Brit. informal **1** be very successful. **2** move very fast.
– ORIGIN French *bombe*, probably from Greek *bombos* 'booming, humming', of imitative origin.

bombard /bombaard/ ● verb **1** attack continuously with bombs or other missiles. **2** subject to a continuous flow of questions or information. **3** Physics direct a stream of high-speed particles at (a substance). ● noun /**bom**baard/ an early form of cannon, which fired a stone ball.
– DERIVATIVES **bombardment** noun.
– ORIGIN from Old French *bombarde* 'a cannon' or French *bombarder*, probably from Greek *bombos* 'booming'.

bombardier /bombərdeer/ ● noun **1** a rank of non-commissioned officer in certain artillery regiments, equivalent to corporal. **2** a member of a bomber crew in the US air force responsible for sighting and releasing bombs.
– ORIGIN French.

bombardier beetle ● noun a beetle that discharges an irritant vapour from its anus with an audible pop when alarmed.

bombast /**bom**bast/ ● noun grandiose but empty language.
– ORIGIN originally denoting cotton wool used as padding: from Old French *bombace*, from Latin *bombyx* 'silkworm'.

bombastic /bombastik/ ● adjective grandiose but with little meaning.
– DERIVATIVES **bombastically** adverb.

Bombay duck ● noun dried bummalo fish eaten as an accompaniment with curries.
– ORIGIN alteration of BUMMALO by association with the city of *Bombay* in India, from which bummalo were exported.

Bombay mix ● noun an Indian spiced snack consisting of lentils, peanuts, and deep-fried strands of gram flour.

bombazine /**bom**bəzeen/ ● noun a twilled dress fabric of worsted and silk or cotton.
– ORIGIN French *bombasin*, from Latin *bombycinus* 'silken', from Greek *bombux* 'silkworm'.

bombe /bomb/ ● noun a frozen dome-shaped dessert.
– ORIGIN French, 'bomb'.

bombed ● adjective **1** subjected to bombing. **2** informal intoxicated by drink or drugs.

bomber ● noun **1** an aircraft that drops bombs. **2** a person who plants bombs, especially as a terrorist. **3** informal a large cannabis cigarette.

bomber jacket ● noun a short jacket gathered at the waist and cuffs by elasticated bands and having a zip front.

bombinate /**bom**binayt/ ● verb literary buzz; hum.
– ORIGIN Latin *bombinare* 'buzz', from *bombus* 'booming'.

bombora /bomborə/ ● noun Austral. a wave which forms over a submerged offshore reef or rock, producing a dangerous stretch of broken water.
– ORIGIN from an Aboriginal word.

bombshell ● noun **1** something that comes as a great surprise and shock. **2** informal a very attractive woman.

bona fide /bōnə fīdi/ ● adjective genuine; real. ● adverb chiefly Law without intention to deceive.
– ORIGIN Latin, 'with good faith'.

bona fides /bōnə fīdeez/ ● noun **1** honesty and sincerity of intention. **2** (treated as pl.) informal a person's credentials.
– ORIGIN Latin, 'good faith'.

bonanza ● noun a source of wealth, profit, or good fortune.
– ORIGIN Spanish, 'fair weather, prosperity', from Latin *bonus* 'good'.

bon appétit /bon appetee/ ● exclamation used to wish someone an enjoyable meal.
– ORIGIN French, 'good appetite'.

bonbon ● noun a sweet.
– ORIGIN French, from *bon* 'good'.

bonce ● noun Brit. informal a person's head.
– ORIGIN originally denoting a large marble: of unknown origin.

bond ● noun **1** a thing used to tie or fasten things together. **2** (**bonds**) physical restraints used to hold someone prisoner. **3** a force or feeling that unites people. **4** a binding agreement. **5** a certificate issued by a government or a public company promising to repay borrowed money at a fixed rate of interest at a specified time. **6** (also **chemical bond**) a strong force of attraction holding atoms together in a molecule. **7** Building any of the various patterns in which bricks are laid to ensure strength in the resulting structure. ● verb **1** join or be joined securely to something else. **2** establish a relationship based on shared feelings or experiences. **3** lay (bricks) in a strong overlapping pattern. **4** place (dutiable goods) in bond.
– PHRASES **in bond** (of dutiable goods) stored by customs until duty is paid by the importer.
– ORIGIN variant of BAND[1].

bondage ● noun **1** the state of being a slave or feudal serf. **2** sexual practice that involves the tying up or restraining of one partner.
– ORIGIN from obsolete *bond* 'serf'; influenced by BOND.

bonded ● adjective **1** joined securely together, especially by an adhesive, heat process, or pressure. **2** bound by a legal agreement.

bonded warehouse ● noun a customs-controlled warehouse for the retention of dutiable goods held in bond.

bond paper ● noun high-quality writing paper.

bondsman ● noun **1** a person who stands surety for a bond. **2** archaic a slave or feudal serf.

bone ● noun **1** any of the pieces of hard, whitish tissue making up the skeleton in vertebrates. **2** the hard material of which bones consist. **3** a thing resembling a bone, such as a strip of stiffening for an undergarment. ● verb **1** remove the bones from (meat or fish) before cooking. **2** (**bone up on**) informal study (a subject) intensively.
– PHRASES **bone of contention** a source of continuing disagreement. **close to the bone 1** (of a remark) accurate to the point of causing discomfort. **2** (of a joke or story) near the limit of decency. **have a bone to pick with** informal have reason to disagree or be annoyed with. **in one's bones** felt or believed deeply or instinctively. **make no bones about** be straightforward in stating or dealing with. **off** (or **on**) **the bone** (of meat or fish) having had the bones removed (or left in). **what's bred in the bone will come out in the flesh** (or **blood**) proverb a person's behaviour or characteristics are determined by their heredity. **work one's fingers to the bone** work very hard.
– DERIVATIVES **boneless** adjective.
– ORIGIN Old English.

bone china ● noun white porcelain containing the mineral resi-

Thesaurus

– PHRASES **a bolt from/out of the blue** SHOCK, surprise, bombshell, thunderbolt, revelation; *informal* turn-up for the books. **bolt upright** STRAIGHT, rigidly, stiffly.

bomb ● noun **1** *they saw bombs bursting on the runway* EXPLOSIVE, incendiary (device); missile, projectile; *dated* blockbuster, bombshell. **2** *the world has lived with the bomb* NUCLEAR WEAPONS, nuclear bombs, atom bombs, A-bombs. **3** *(Brit. informal) a new superstore will cost a bomb.* See FORTUNE sense 5.
● verb **1** *their headquarters were bombed* BOMBARD, blast, shell, blitz, strafe, pound; attack, assault; blow up, destroy, demolish, flatten, devastate. **2** *(Brit. informal) she bombed across Texas.* See SPEED verb sense 1. **3** *(informal) the film bombed at the box office.* See FAIL sense 1.

bombard ● verb **1** *gun batteries bombarded the islands* SHELL, pound, blitz, strafe, bomb; assail, attack, assault, batter, blast, pelt. **2** *we were bombarded with information* INUNDATE, swamp, flood, deluge, snow under; besiege, overwhelm.

bombast ● noun BLUSTER, pomposity, empty talk, humbug, turgidity, verbosity, verbiage; pretentiousness, ostentation, grandiloquence; *informal* hot air; *rare* fustian.

bombastic ● adjective POMPOUS, blustering, turgid, verbose, orotund, high-flown, high-sounding, overwrought, pretentious, ostentatious, grandiloquent; *informal* highfalutin; *rare* fustian.

bona fide ● adjective AUTHENTIC, genuine, real, true, actual; legal, legitimate, lawful, valid, proper; *informal* legit, pukka, the real McCoy.
– OPPOSITES bogus.

bonanza ● noun WINDFALL, godsend, boon, blessing, bonus, stroke of luck; *informal* jackpot.

bond ● noun **1** *the women forged a close bond* FRIENDSHIP, relationship, fellowship, partnership, association, affiliation, alliance, attachment. **2** *the prisoner struggled with his bonds* CHAINS, fetters, shackles, manacles, irons, restraints. **3** *I've broken my bond* PROMISE, pledge, vow, oath, word (of honour), guarantee, assurance; agreement, contract, pact, bargain, deal.
● verb *the extensions are bonded to your hair* JOIN, fasten, fix, affix, attach, secure, bind, stick, fuse.

bondage ● noun SLAVERY, enslavement, servitude, subjugation,

due of burnt bones.
bone dry • adjective extremely dry.
bonehead • noun informal a stupid person.
bone idle • adjective extremely idle.
– ORIGIN expressing *idle through to the bone.*
bonemeal • noun ground bones used as a fertilizer.
boner • noun **1** informal a stupid mistake. **2** vulgar slang, chiefly N. Amer. an erection of the penis.
boneshaker • noun Brit. informal **1** an old vehicle with poor suspension. **2** an early type of bicycle without rubber tyres.
boneyard • noun informal a cemetery.
bonfire • noun an open-air fire lit to burn rubbish or as a celebration.
– ORIGIN originally denoting a fire on which bones were burnt, or for burning heretics.
Bonfire Night • noun (in the UK) 5 November, on which fireworks are let off, bonfires lit, and effigies of Guy Fawkes burnt, in memory of the Gunpowder Plot of 1605.
bongo • noun (pl. **bongos** or **bongoes**) each of a pair of small drums, held between the knees and played with the fingers.
– ORIGIN Latin American Spanish *bongó.*
bonhomie /bonnəmee/ • noun good-natured friendliness.
– DERIVATIVES **bonhomous** adjective.
– ORIGIN French, from *bonhomme* 'good fellow'.
bonito /bəneetō/ • noun (pl. **bonitos**) a small tuna with dark stripes, important as a food and game fish.
– ORIGIN Spanish.
bonk informal • verb **1** hit so as to cause a reverberating sound. **2** Brit. have sexual intercourse. • noun **1** a reverberating sound. **2** Brit. an act of sexual intercourse.
– ORIGIN imitative.
bonkers • adjective informal mad; crazy.
– ORIGIN of unknown origin.
bon mot /BON mō/ • noun (pl. **bons mots** pronunc. same or /BON mōz/) a clever or witty remark.
– ORIGIN French, 'good word'.
bonne femme /bon fam/ • adjective (of fish, stews, and soups) cooked in a simple way: *sole bonne femme.*
– ORIGIN from French *à la bonne femme* 'in the manner of a good housewife'.
bonnet • noun **1** a woman's or child's hat tied under the chin and with a brim framing the face. **2** a soft brimless hat like a beret, worn by men and boys in Scotland. **3** Brit. the hinged metal canopy covering the engine of a motor vehicle.
– DERIVATIVES **bonneted** adjective.
– ORIGIN Old French *bonet*, from Latin *abonnis* 'headgear'.
bonny (also **bonnie**) • adjective (**bonnier**, **bonniest**) chiefly Scottish & N. English **1** physically attractive; healthy-looking. **2** sizeable; considerable.
– DERIVATIVES **bonnily** adverb **bonniness** noun.
– ORIGIN perhaps related to Old French *bon* 'good'.
bonsai /bonsī/ • noun the art of growing ornamental, artificially dwarfed varieties of trees or shrubs.
– ORIGIN Japanese, 'tray planting'.
bonus • noun **1** a sum of money added seasonally to a person's wages for good performance. **2** Brit. an extra dividend or issue paid to shareholders. **3** an unexpected and welcome event.
– ORIGIN Latin, 'good'.
bon vivant /BON veevON/ • noun (pl. **bon vivants** or **bons vivants** pronunc. same) a person indulging in a sociable and luxurious lifestyle.
– ORIGIN French, 'person living well'.
bon viveur /BON veevör/ • noun (pl. **bon viveurs** or **bons viveurs** pronunc. same) another term for BON VIVANT.
– ORIGIN pseudo-French, from French *bon* 'good' and *viveur* 'a living person'.
bon voyage /bon vwaayaazh/ • exclamation have a good journey.
– ORIGIN French, 'good journey'.
bony • adjective (**bonier**, **boniest**) **1** of, like, or containing bones. **2** so thin that the bones can be seen.
– DERIVATIVES **boniness** noun.
bony fish • noun a fish with a skeleton of bone, as opposed to a cartilaginous fish.
bonzer • adjective Austral./NZ informal excellent.
– ORIGIN perhaps an alteration of BONANZA.
boo • exclamation **1** said suddenly to surprise someone. **2** said to show disapproval or contempt. • verb (**boos**, **booed**) say 'boo' to show disapproval or contempt.
– PHRASES **wouldn't say boo to a goose** is very shy or reticent.
– ORIGIN imitative of the lowing of oxen.
booay /bōōī/ (also **booai**) • noun (**the booay**) NZ remote rural districts.
– PHRASES **up the booay** informal completely wrong or astray.
– ORIGIN perhaps from the place name *Puhoi* in North Auckland, New Zealand.
boob[1] informal • noun **1** Brit. an embarrassing mistake. **2** N. Amer. a stupid person. • verb Brit. make an embarrassing mistake.
– ORIGIN from BOOBY[1].
boob[2] • noun informal a woman's breast.
– ORIGIN from BOOBY[2].
boo-boo • noun informal a mistake.
– ORIGIN reduplication of BOOB[1].
boob tube • noun **1** Brit. informal a woman's tight-fitting strapless top. **2** N. Amer. informal television; a television set.
booby[1] • noun (pl. **boobies**) **1** informal a stupid person. **2** a large tropical seabird of the gannet family.
– ORIGIN probably from Spanish *bobo*, from Latin *balbus* 'stammering'.
booby[2] • noun (pl. **boobies**) informal a woman's breast.
– ORIGIN from dialect *bubby*; perhaps related to German dialect *Bübbi* 'teat'.
booby prize • noun a prize given to the person who comes last in a contest.
booby trap • noun an object containing a concealed explosive device designed to detonate when someone touches it.
boodle • noun informal money, especially that gained or spent dishonestly.
– ORIGIN originally denoting a pack or crowd: from Dutch *boedel*, *boel* 'possessions, disorderly mass'.
boogie • noun (also **boogie-woogie**) (pl. **boogies**) **1** a style of blues played on the piano with a strong, fast beat. **2** informal a dance to pop or rock music. • verb (**boogieing**) informal dance to pop or rock music.
– ORIGIN originally US in the sense 'party': of unknown origin.
boogie board • noun a short, light surfboard ridden in a prone position.
book • noun **1** a written or printed work consisting of pages glued or sewn together along one side and bound in covers. **2** a main division of a literary work or of the Bible. **3** a bound set of blank sheets for writing in: *an exercise book.* **4** (**books**) a set of records or accounts. **5** a set of tickets, stamps, matches, etc., bound together. **6** a bookmaker's record of bets accepted and money paid out. • verb **1** reserve (accommodation, a ticket, etc.). **2** (**book in**) register one's arrival at a hotel. **3** engage (a performer or guest) for an event. **4** (**be booked up**) have all places or dates reserved. **5** make an official note of the details of (someone who has broken a law or rule).

Thesaurus

subjection, oppression, domination, exploitation, persecution; *historical* serfdom, vassalage; *archaic* enthralment.
– OPPOSITES liberty.
bonhomie • noun GENIALITY, affability, conviviality, cordiality, amiability, sociability, friendliness, warmth, joviality.
– OPPOSITES coldness.
bon mot • noun WITTICISM, quip, pun, pleasantry, jest, joke; *informal* wisecrack, one-liner.
bonny • adjective *(Scottish & N. English)* BEAUTIFUL, attractive, pretty, gorgeous, fetching, prepossessing; lovely, nice, sweet, cute, appealing, endearing, adorable, lovable, charming, winsome; *informal* divine; *Austral./NZ informal* beaut; *poetic/literary* beauteous; *archaic* fair, comely.
– OPPOSITES unattractive.
bonus • noun **1** *the extra work's a real bonus* BENEFIT, advantage, boon, blessing, godsend, stroke of luck, asset, plus, pro, attraction; *informal* perk; *formal* perquisite. **2** *she's on a good salary and she gets a bonus* GRATUITY, handout, gift, present, reward, prize; incentive, inducement; *informal* perk, sweetener; *formal* perquisite.
– OPPOSITES disadvantage.
bon viveur, bon vivant • noun HEDONIST, pleasure-seeker, sensualist, sybarite, voluptuary; epicure, gourmet, gastronome.
– OPPOSITES puritan.
bony • adjective GAUNT, ANGULAR, skinny, thin, lean, spare, spindly, skin-and-bones, skeletal, emaciated, underweight; *informal* like a bag of bones.

b

– PHRASES **bring someone to book** officially call someone to account for their behaviour. **by the book** strictly according to the rules. **in someone's bad** (or **good**) **books** in disfavour (or favour) with someone. **in my book** in my opinion. **on the books** contained in a list of members, employees, or clients. **take a leaf out of someone's book** imitate someone in a particular way. **throw the book at** informal charge or punish (someone) as severely as possible. **you can't judge a book by its cover** proverb outward appearances are not a reliable indication of the true character of someone or something.
– DERIVATIVES **bookable** adjective **booker** noun **booking** noun.
– ORIGIN Old English, 'to grant by charter'.
bookbinder • noun a person skilled in the craft of binding books.
bookcase • noun an open cabinet containing shelves on which to keep books.
book club • noun an organization which sells its subscribers selected books by mail order at reduced prices.
bookend • noun a support placed at the end of a row of books to keep them upright.
bookie • noun (pl. **bookies**) informal a bookmaker.
bookish • adjective **1** devoted to reading and studying. **2** (of language) literary in style.
– DERIVATIVES **bookishly** adverb **bookishness** noun.
bookkeeping • noun the activity of keeping records of financial affairs.
booklet • noun a small, thin book with paper covers.
bookmaker • noun a person whose job is to take bets, calculate odds, and pay out winnings.
bookmark • noun **1** a strip of leather or card used to mark a place in a book. **2** Computing a record of the address of a file, Internet page, etc. enabling quick access by a user.
bookplate • noun a decorative label pasted in the front of a book, bearing the name of its owner.
book token • noun Brit. a voucher which can be exchanged for books costing up to a specified amount.
book value • noun the value of a security or asset as entered in a firm's books. Often contrasted with MARKET VALUE.
bookworm • noun informal a person who enjoys and spends much time reading.
Boolean /bo͞oliən/ • adjective denoting a system of notation used to represent logical propositions by means of the binary digits 0 (false) and 1 (true), especially in computing and electronics.
– ORIGIN named after the English mathematician George *Boole* (1815–64).
boom[1] • noun a loud, deep, resonant sound. • verb make this sound.
– DERIVATIVES **booming** adjective **boomy** adjective.
– ORIGIN imitative; perhaps from Dutch *bommen* 'to hum, buzz'.
boom[2] • noun a period of great prosperity or rapid economic growth. • verb experience a boom.
– DERIVATIVES **boomy** adjective.
– ORIGIN probably from BOOM[1].
boom[3] • noun **1** a pivoted spar to which the foot of a vessel's sail is attached. **2** a movable arm carrying a microphone or film camera. **3** a floating beam used to contain oil spills or to form a barrier across the mouth of a harbour.
– ORIGIN Dutch, 'beam, tree, pole', related to BEAM.
boomerang • noun a curved flat piece of wood that can be thrown so as to return to the thrower, used by Australian Aboriginals as a hunting weapon.
– ORIGIN from an Aboriginal language.
boon • noun **1** a thing that is helpful or beneficial. **2** archaic a favour or request.
– ORIGIN Old Norse.
boon companion • noun a close friend.
– ORIGIN originally in the sense 'good fellow', referring to a drinking companion: *boon* from Old French *bon*, from Latin *bonus* 'good'.
boondocks • plural noun (**the boondocks**) N. Amer. informal rough or isolated country.
– ORIGIN from a Tagalog word meaning 'mountain'.
boondoggle N. Amer. informal • noun an unnecessary, wasteful, or fraudulent project. • verb waste money or time on such projects.
– ORIGIN of unknown origin.
boonies • plural noun short for BOONDOCKS.
boor /boor/ • noun a rough and bad-mannered person.
– DERIVATIVES **boorish** adjective **boorishly** adverb **boorishness** noun.
– ORIGIN Low German *būr* or Dutch *boer* 'farmer'.
boost • verb help or encourage to increase or improve. • noun a source of help or encouragement.
– ORIGIN of unknown origin.
booster • noun **1** Medicine a dose of a vaccine increasing or renewing the effect of an earlier one. **2** the part of a rocket or spacecraft used to give initial acceleration. **3** a source of help or encouragement. **4** a device for increasing electrical voltage or signal strength.

Thesaurus

– OPPOSITES plump.
booby • noun *(informal)*. See IDIOT.
book • noun **1** *he published his first book in 1610* VOLUME, tome, publication, title; novel, storybook, treatise, manual; paperback, hardback, softback. **2** *he scribbled in his book* NOTEPAD, notebook, pad, memo pad, exercise book; ledger, logbook, journal, diary; *Brit.* jotter, pocketbook; *N. Amer.* scratch pad. **3** *the council had to balance its books* ACCOUNTS, records; account book, record book, ledger, balance sheet.
• verb **1** *she booked a table at the restaurant* RESERVE, make a reservation, pre-arrange, order; *informal* bag; *formal* bespeak. **2** *we booked a number of events in the Festival* ARRANGE, programme, schedule, timetable, line up, lay on; *N. Amer.* slate.
– PHRASES **by the book** ACCORDING TO THE RULES, within the law, lawfully, legally, legitimately; honestly, fairly; *informal* on the level, fair and square. **book in** REGISTER, check in, enrol.
booking • noun RESERVATION, pre-arrangement; appointment, date.
bookish • adjective STUDIOUS, scholarly, academic, intellectual, highbrow, erudite, learned, educated, knowledgeable; cerebral, serious, earnest, thoughtful.
booklet • noun PAMPHLET, brochure, leaflet, handbill, flyer, tract; *N. Amer.* folder, mailer.
boom • noun **1** *the boom of the waves on the rocks* REVERBERATION, resonance, thunder, echoing, crashing, drumming, pounding, roar, rumble. **2** *an unprecedented boom in sales* UPTURN, upsurge, upswing, increase, advance, growth, boost, escalation, improvement.
– OPPOSITES slump.
• verb **1** *thunder boomed overhead* REVERBERATE, resound, resonate; rumble, thunder, blare, echo; crash, roll, clap, explode, bang. **2** *a voice boomed at her* BELLOW, roar, thunder, shout, bawl; *informal* holler. **3** *the market continued to boom* FLOURISH, burgeon, thrive, prosper, progress, improve, pick up, expand, mushroom, snowball.
– OPPOSITES whisper, slump.
boomerang • verb BACKFIRE, recoil, reverse, rebound, come back, ricochet; be self-defeating; *informal* blow up in one's face.
booming • adjective **1** *a booming voice* RESONANT, sonorous, ringing, resounding, reverberating, carrying, thunderous; strident, stentorian, strong, powerful. **2** *booming business* FLOURISHING, burgeoning, thriving, prospering, prosperous, successful, strong, buoyant; profitable, fruitful, lucrative; expanding.
boon[1] • noun *their help was such a boon* BLESSING, godsend, bonus, plus, benefit, advantage, help, aid, asset; stroke of luck; *informal* perk; *formal* perquisite.
– OPPOSITES curse.
boon[2] • adjective *a boon companion* CLOSE, intimate, bosom, inseparable, faithful; favourite, best.
boor • noun LOUT, oaf, ruffian, thug, yahoo, barbarian, Neanderthal, brute, beast; *informal* clod, roughneck, peasant, pig; *Brit. informal* yobbo, yob, oik.
boorish • adjective COARSE, uncouth, rude, ill-bred, ill-mannered, uncivilized, unrefined, common, rough, thuggish, loutish; vulgar, unsavoury, gross, brutish, Neanderthal; *informal* cloddish, plebby; *Brit. informal* yobbish; *Austral. informal* ocker.
– OPPOSITES refined.
boost • noun **1** *a boost to one's morale* UPLIFT, lift, spur, encouragement, help, inspiration, stimulus, fillip. **2** *a boost in sales* INCREASE, expansion, upturn, upsurge, upswing, rise, escalation, improvement, advance, growth, boom; *informal* hike.
– OPPOSITES decrease.
• verb **1** *he phones her to boost her morale* IMPROVE, raise, uplift, increase, enhance, encourage, heighten, help, promote, foster, stimulate, invigorate, revitalize; *informal* buck up. **2** *they used advertising to boost sales* INCREASE, raise, escalate, improve, strengthen, inflate, push up, promote, advance, foster, stimulate; facili-

boot[1] ● noun **1** a sturdy item of footwear covering the foot and ankle, and sometimes the lower leg. **2** informal a hard kick. **3** Brit. a space at the back of a car for carrying luggage. ● verb **1** kick hard. **2** (**boot out**) informal force to leave. **3** start (a computer) and put it into a state of readiness for operation. [ORIGIN from BOOTSTRAP.]
– PHRASES **the boot is on the other foot** the situation is now reversed. **give** (or **get**) **the boot** informal dismiss (or be dismissed) from a job. **old boot** informal an ugly or disliked old woman. **put the boot in** Brit. informal kick or attack someone when they are already on the ground. **with one's heart in one's boots** very depressed or anxious.
– DERIVATIVES **bootable** adjective **booted** adjective.
– ORIGIN Old Norse, or Old French *bote.*

boot[2] ● noun (in phrase **to boot**) as well.
– ORIGIN Old English, 'advantage, remedy'.

bootblack ● noun a person who makes their living by polishing boots and shoes.

bootboy ● noun informal a rowdy youth with close-cropped hair and heavy boots.

boot camp ● noun chiefly N. Amer. **1** a military training camp with very harsh discipline. **2** a prison for young offenders, run on military lines.

bootee (also **bootie**) ● noun **1** a baby's soft shoe. **2** a woman's short boot.

booth ● noun **1** a small temporary structure used for selling goods or staging shows at a market or fair. **2** an enclosed compartment allowing privacy when telephoning, voting, etc.
– ORIGIN from Old Norse, 'dwell'.

bootlace ● noun a cord or leather strip for lacing boots.

bootleg ● adjective (of alcoholic drink or a recording) made or distributed illegally. ● noun an illegal musical recording.
– DERIVATIVES **bootlegger** noun **bootlegging** noun.
– ORIGIN from a practice among smugglers of hiding bottles in their boots.

bootless ● adjective archaic (of an action) ineffectual; useless.
– ORIGIN Old English, 'not able to be compensated for by payment'.

bootlicker ● noun informal an obsequious person.

bootstrap ● noun **1** a loop at the back of a boot, used to pull it on. **2** Computing the action of loading a program into a computer by means of a few initial instructions which enable the introduction of the rest of the program from an input device.
– PHRASES **pull oneself up by one's bootstraps** improve one's position by one's own efforts.

booty ● noun valuable stolen goods.
– ORIGIN Low German *būte, buite* 'exchange, distribution'.

booze informal ● noun alcoholic drink. ● verb drink large quantities of alcohol.
– DERIVATIVES **boozy** adjective (**boozier**, **booziest**).
– ORIGIN from Dutch *būsen* 'drink to excess'.

boozer ● noun informal **1** a person who drinks large quantities of alcohol. **2** Brit. a pub.

booze-up ● noun informal a heavy drinking session.

bop[1] informal ● noun chiefly Brit. **1** a dance to pop music. **2** a social occasion with dancing. ● verb (**bopped**, **bopping**) dance to pop music.
– DERIVATIVES **bopper** noun.
– ORIGIN shortening of BEBOP.

bop[2] informal ● verb (**bopped**, **bopping**) hit or punch quickly. ● noun a quick blow or punch.
– ORIGIN imitative.

bora /borə/ ● noun a cold, dry NE wind blowing in the upper Adriatic.
– ORIGIN Italian, from Latin *boreas* (see BOREAL).

boracic /bərassik/ ● adjective **1** consisting of, containing, or denoting boric acid. **2** Brit. informal having no money. [ORIGIN from *boracic lint*, rhyming slang for 'skint'.]

borage /borrij/ ● noun a herbaceous plant with bright blue flowers and hairy leaves.
– ORIGIN Latin *borrago*, perhaps from an Arabic word meaning 'father of roughness' (referring to the leaves).

borax /boraks/ ● noun a white mineral consisting of hydrated sodium borate, found in some alkaline salt deposits and used in making glass and as a metallurgical flux.
– ORIGIN Latin, from Aramaic.

Bordeaux /bordō/ ● noun (pl. same or /bordōz/) a wine from Bordeaux, a district of SW France.

bordello /bordellō/ ● noun (pl. **bordellos**) chiefly N. Amer. a brothel.
– ORIGIN Italian, probably from Old French *bordel*, from *borde* 'small farm or cottage'.

border ● noun **1** a boundary between two countries or other areas. **2** a decorative band around the edge of something. **3** a strip of ground along the edge of a lawn for planting flowers or shrubs. ● verb **1** form a border around or along. **2** (of a country or area) be adjacent to (another). **3** (**border on**) come close to (an extreme condition).
– ORIGIN Old French *bordeure.*

borderer ● noun a person living near the border between two countries.

borderline ● noun a line marking a boundary. ● adjective only just acceptable in quality or as belonging to a category: *references may be requested in borderline cases.*

Thesaurus

tate, help, assist, aid; *informal* hike, bump up.
– OPPOSITES decrease.

boot[1] ● noun **1** *muddy boots* GUMBOOT, wellington, wader, walking boot, riding boot, moon boot, thigh boot, ankle boot, pixie boot, desert boot; *informal* welly; *trademark* Doc Martens; *historical* top boot. **2** *(informal) a boot in the stomach* KICK, blow, knock.
● verb **1** *his shot was booted away by the goalkeeper* KICK, punt, bunt, tap; propel, drive, knock. **2** *boot up your computer* START UP, fire up.
– PHRASES **boot someone out** *(informal).* See DISMISS sense 1. **give someone the boot** *(informal).* See DISMISS sense 1.

boot[2] ● noun
– PHRASES **to boot** AS WELL, also, too, besides, into the bargain, in addition, additionally, on top, what's more, moreover, furthermore; *informal* and all.

booth ● noun **1** *booths for different traders* STALL, stand, kiosk. **2** *a phone booth* CUBICLE, kiosk, box, enclosure, cabin.

bootleg ● adjective ILLEGAL, illicit, unlawful, unauthorized, unlicensed, pirated; contraband, smuggled, black-market.

bootless ● adjective *(archaic).* See FRUITLESS.

bootlicker ● noun *(informal)* SYCOPHANT, toady, fawner, flatterer, creep, crawler, lickspittle, truckler, groveller, kowtower; *informal* yes-man; *archaic* toad-eater.

booty ● noun LOOT, plunder, pillage, haul, spoils, stolen goods, ill-gotten gains, pickings; *informal* swag.

booze *(informal)* ● noun *fill him up with food and booze* ALCOHOL, alcoholic drink, (intoxicating) liquor, drink, spirits, intoxicants; *informal* grog, firewater, rotgut, the hard stuff, the bottle, Dutch courage, hooch, moonshine; *Brit. informal* bevvies; *N. Amer. informal* juice, the sauce.
● verb *I was boozing with my mates* DRINK (ALCOHOL), tipple, imbibe, indulge; *informal* hit the bottle, knock a few back, swill; *Brit. informal* bevvy; *N. Amer. informal* bend one's elbow.

boozer ● noun **1** *(informal) he's a notorious boozer* DRINKER, drunk, drunkard, alcoholic, dipsomaniac, tippler, imbiber, sot, inebriate; *informal* lush, alky, dipso, soak, tosspot, wino, sponge, barfly; *Austral./NZ informal* hophead; *archaic* toper. **2** *(Brit. informal) I'm off down the boozer* BAR, wine bar, inn, roadhouse; *Brit.* pub, public house; *N. Amer.* tavern; *informal* watering hole; *Brit. informal* local; *dated* alehouse; *N. Amer. historical* saloon; *archaic* hostelry.

bop ● noun *(Brit. informal)* **1** *I fancy a bop* DANCE; *informal* boogie, jive. **2** *a college bop* DISCOTHEQUE; *informal* disco, hop.
● verb *(informal) they were bopping to disco music* DANCE, jig; *informal* boogie, jive, groove, disco, rock, stomp, hoof it; *N. Amer. informal* get down, cut a/the rug.

bordello ● noun *(N. Amer.)* BROTHEL, whorehouse; *Law* disorderly house; *Brit. informal* knocking shop; *N. Amer. informal* cathouse; *euphemistic* massage parlour; *archaic* bawdy house, house of ill fame, house of ill repute.

border ● noun **1** *the border of a medieval manuscript* EDGE, MARGIN, perimeter, circumference, periphery; rim, fringe, verge; sides. **2** *the Soviet border* FRONTIER, boundary, borderline, perimeter; marches, bounds.
● verb **1** *the fields were bordered by hedges* SURROUND, enclose, encircle, circle, edge, fringe, bound, flank. **2** *the straps are bordered with gold braid* EDGE, fringe, hem; trim, pipe, finish. **3** *the forest bordered on Broadmoor* ADJOIN, abut, be next to, be adjacent to, be contiguous with, touch, join, meet, reach.
– PHRASES **border on** VERGE ON, approach, come close to, be comparable to, approximate to, be tantamount to, be similar to, be not

b

bore[1] ● verb **1** make (a hole) in something with a drill or other tool. **2** hollow out (a gun barrel or other tube). ● noun **1** the hollow part inside a gun barrel or other tube. **2** the diameter of this: *a small-bore rifle.*
– DERIVATIVES **borer** noun.
– ORIGIN Old English.

bore[2] ● noun a dull and uninteresting person or activity. ● verb cause to feel weary and uninterested by being dull and tedious.
– DERIVATIVES **boring** adjective.
– ORIGIN of unknown origin.

bore[3] ● noun a steep-fronted wave caused by the meeting of two tides or by a tide rushing up a narrow estuary.
– ORIGIN perhaps from an Old Norse word meaning 'wave'.

bore[4] past of BEAR[1].

boreal /boriəl/ ● adjective of the North or northern regions.
– ORIGIN from Latin *Boreas*, denoting the god of the north wind, from Greek.

bored ● adjective feeling weary and impatient because one is unoccupied or has no interest in one's current activity.
– USAGE The constructions **bored by** or **bored with** should be used rather than **bored of**. Although **bored of** mirrors the accepted construction **tired of** and is often used informally, it is not considered acceptable in standard English.

boredom ● noun the state of feeling bored.

boreen /boreen/ ● noun Irish a narrow country road.
– ORIGIN Irish.

borehole ● noun a deep, narrow hole in the ground made to locate water or oil.

boric /borik/ ● adjective Chemistry of boron.

boric acid ● noun Chemistry a weakly acid crystalline compound derived from borax, used as a mild antiseptic.

borlotti bean /borlotti/ ● noun a type of kidney bean with a pink speckled skin that turns brown when cooked.
– ORIGIN Italian *borlotti*, plural of *borlotto* 'kidney bean'.

born ● adjective **1** existing as a result of birth. **2** (**born of**) existing as a result of (a situation or feeling). **3** having a natural ability to do a particular job or task: *a born engineer.* **4** (**-born**) having a specific nationality: *a German-born philosopher.*
– PHRASES **born and bred** by birth and upbringing. **in all one's born days** throughout one's life (used for emphasis). **not know one is born** not realize how easy one's life is. **I** (or **she**, etc.) **wasn't born yesterday** I am (or she, etc. is) not foolish or gullible.
– ORIGIN Old English, past participle of BEAR[1].

born-again ● adjective **1** relating to or denoting a person who has converted to a personal faith in Christ. **2** showing the great enthusiasm of a person newly converted to a cause: *born-again environmentalists.*

borne past participle of BEAR[1].

-borne ● adjective carried by the thing specified: *water-borne bacteria.*

Bornean /borniən/ ● noun a person from Borneo. ● adjective relating to Borneo.

boron /boron/ ● noun a non-metallic chemical element which can be prepared as a brown powder or (if pure) a black crystalline semiconductor.
– DERIVATIVES **boride** noun.
– ORIGIN from BORAX.

boronia /bərōniə/ ● noun a sweet-scented Australian shrub, cultivated for its perfume and flowers.
– ORIGIN named after the Italian botanist Francesco *Borone* (1769–94).

borough /burrə/ ● noun **1** Brit. a town (as distinct from a city) with a corporation and privileges granted by a royal charter. **2** an administrative division of London. **3** a municipal corporation in certain US states. **4** each of five divisions of New York City.
– ORIGIN Old English, 'fortress, citadel'.

borrow ● verb **1** take and use (something belonging to someone else) with the intention of returning it. **2** take and use (money) from a person or bank under agreement to pay it back later.
– PHRASES **be (living) on borrowed time** be surviving against expectations.
– DERIVATIVES **borrower** noun.
– ORIGIN Old English.

borscht /borsht/ (also **borsch** /borsh/) ● noun a Russian or Polish soup made with beetroot.
– ORIGIN Russian *borshch.*

borstal /borst'l/ ● noun Brit. historical a custodial institution for young offenders.
– ORIGIN named after the village of *Borstal* in southern England, where the first of these was established.

borzoi /borzoy/ ● noun (pl. **borzois**) a breed of large Russian wolfhound with a narrow head and silky coat.
– ORIGIN from Russian *borzyĭ* 'swift'.

bosh ● noun informal nonsense.
– ORIGIN from Turkish *boş* 'empty, worthless'.

bosky /boski/ ● adjective literary covered by trees or bushes.
– ORIGIN from obsolete *bosk*, variant of BUSH[1].

Bosnian /bozniən/ ● noun a person from Bosnia. ● adjective relating to Bosnia.

bosom ● noun **1** a woman's breast or chest. **2** the breast as the seat of emotions. **3** a person's loving care or protection: *the bosom of his family.* ● adjective (of a friend) very close.
– DERIVATIVES **bosomy** adjective.
– ORIGIN Old English.

boson /bōzon/ ● noun Physics a subatomic particle, such as a photon, which has a spin of zero or a whole number.
– ORIGIN named after the Indian physicist S. N. *Bose* (1894–1974).

boss[1] informal ● noun a person who is in charge of an employee or organization. ● verb give orders in a domineering manner. ● adjective N. Amer. excellent.
– ORIGIN Dutch *baas* 'master'.

boss[2] ● noun **1** a projecting knob or stud on the centre of a shield, propeller, or similar object. **2** Architecture an ornamental carving at the point where the ribs in a ceiling cross.

Thesaurus

unlike, resemble.

borderline ● noun *the borderline between old and antique* DIVIDING LINE, divide, division, demarcation line, line, cut-off point; threshold, margin, border, boundary.
● adjective *borderline cases* MARGINAL, uncertain, indefinite, unsettled, undecided, doubtful, indeterminate, unclassifiable, equivocal; questionable, debatable, controversial, contentious, problematic; *informal* iffy.

bore[1] ● verb *bore a hole in the ceiling* DRILL, pierce, perforate, puncture, punch, cut; tunnel, burrow, mine, dig, gouge, sink.
● noun **1** *a well bore* BOREHOLE, hole, well, shaft, pit. **2** *the canon has a bore of 890 millimetres* CALIBRE, diameter, gauge.

bore[2] ● verb *the television news bored Philip* STULTIFY, pall on, stupefy, weary, tire, fatigue, send to sleep, leave cold; bore to death, bore to tears; *informal* turn off.
– OPPOSITES interest.
● noun *you can be such a bore* TEDIOUS PERSON/THING, tiresome person/thing, bother, nuisance, pest, annoyance, trial, vexation, thorn in one's flesh/side; *informal* drag, pain (in the neck), headache, hassle; *N. Amer. informal* nudnik.

boredom ● noun WEARINESS, ennui, apathy, unconcern, accidie; frustration, dissatisfaction, restlessness, restiveness; tedium, dullness, monotony, repetitiveness, flatness, dreariness; *informal* deadliness.

boring ● adjective TEDIOUS, dull, monotonous, repetitive, unrelieved, unvaried, unimaginative, uneventful; characterless, featureless, colourless, lifeless, insipid, uninteresting, unexciting, uninspiring, unstimulating, jejune, flat, bland, dry, stale, tired, banal, lacklustre, stodgy, dreary, humdrum, mundane; mind-numbing, soul-destroying, wearisome, tiring, tiresome, irksome, trying, frustrating; *informal* deadly, not up to much; *Brit. informal* samey; *N. Amer. informal* dullsville.

borrow ● verb **1** *we borrowed a lot of money* LOAN, take as a loan; lease, hire; *informal* cadge, scrounge, bum; *Brit. informal* scab; *N. Amer. informal* mooch; *Austral./NZ informal* bludge. **2** *(informal) they 'borrowed' all of his tools* TAKE, help oneself to, appropriate, commandeer, abscond with, carry off; steal, purloin; *informal* filch, rob, swipe, nab, rip off, lift, 'liberate', snaffle; *Brit. informal* nick, pinch, half-inch, whip, knock off; *N. Amer. informal* heist, glom. **3** *adventurous chefs borrow foreign techniques* ADOPT, take on, acquire, embrace.
– OPPOSITES lend.

bosom ● noun **1** *the gown was set low over her bosom* BUST, chest; breasts, mammary glands, mammae; *informal* boobs, knockers, bubbies; *Brit. informal* bristols, charlies; *N. Amer. informal* bazooms; *archaic* embonpoint. **2** *(poetic/literary) the family took Gill into its bosom* PROTECTION, shelter, safety, refuge; heart, core; *poetic/literary* midst. **3** *love was kindled within his bosom* HEART, breast, soul, core, spirit.

– ORIGIN Old French *boce*.
bossa nova /bossə nōvə/ ● noun a dance like the samba, originating in Brazil.
– ORIGIN Portuguese, 'new tendency'.
boss-eyed ● adjective Brit. informal cross-eyed; squinting.
– ORIGIN related to dialect *boss* 'miss, bungle', of unknown origin.
bossy ● adjective (**bossier**, **bossiest**) informal fond of giving orders; domineering.
– DERIVATIVES **bossily** adverb **bossiness** noun.
bossyboots ● noun Brit. informal a bossy person.
bosun /bōs'n/ (also **bo'sun**) ● noun variant spelling of BOATSWAIN.
bot ● noun Computing an autonomous program on a network which can interact with systems or users, especially in the manner of a player in some computer games.
– ORIGIN shortening of ROBOT.
botanical ● adjective relating to botany. ● noun a substance obtained from a plant and used as an additive.
– DERIVATIVES **botanically** adverb.
botanical garden (also **botanic garden**) ● noun a place where plants are grown for scientific study and display to the public.
botany /bottəni/ ● noun the scientific study of plants.
– DERIVATIVES **botanic** adjective **botanist** noun.
– ORIGIN from Greek *botanē* 'plant'.
botch informal ● verb perform (an action or task) badly or carelessly. ● noun (also **botch-up**) a badly performed action or task.
– DERIVATIVES **botcher** noun.
– ORIGIN of unknown origin.
both ● predeterminer, determiner, & pronoun two people or things, regarded and identified together. ● adverb applying equally to each of two alternatives.
– PHRASES **have it both ways** benefit from two incompatible ways of thinking or behaving.
– USAGE When **both** is used in constructions with **and**, the structures following the two words should be symmetrical: *both at home and at work* is better than *both at home and work*.
– ORIGIN Old Norse.
bother ● verb **1** take the trouble to do. **2** worry, disturb, or upset. **3** (**bother with/about**) feel concern about or interest in. ● noun **1** trouble and fuss. **2** (**a bother**) a cause of trouble or fuss. ● exclamation chiefly Brit. used to express mild irritation.
– ORIGIN originally in the dialect senses 'noise, chatter' or 'confuse with noise': from Anglo-Irish.
bothersome ● adjective annoying; troublesome.
bothy /bothi/ (also **bothie**) ● noun (pl. **bothies**) (in Scotland) a small hut or cottage for farm labourers or as a mountain refuge.
– ORIGIN related to Gaelic *both*, *bothan*, and perhaps to BOOTH.
bo tree /bō/ (also **bodh tree**) ● noun a fig tree native to India and SE Asia, regarded as sacred by Buddhists because it was under such a tree that Buddha's enlightenment took place.
– ORIGIN representing a Sinhalese word meaning 'tree of knowledge'.
botrytis /bətrītiss/ ● noun a greyish powdery mould of plants, deliberately cultivated on the grapes used for certain wines.
– ORIGIN from Greek *botrus* 'cluster of grapes'.
Botswanan /botswaanən/ ● noun a person from Botswana, a country of southern Africa. ● adjective relating to Botswana.
bottle ● noun **1** a container with a narrow neck, used for storing liquids. **2** Brit. informal one's courage or confidence. ● verb **1** place in bottles for storage. **2** (**bottle up**) repress or conceal (one's feelings). **3** (**bottle out**) Brit. informal lose one's nerve and decide not to do something. **4** informal hit with a glass bottle.
– PHRASES **hit the bottle** informal start to drink alcohol heavily.
– ORIGIN Old French *boteille*, from Latin *butticula* 'small cask'; related to BUTT[4].
bottle bank ● noun Brit. a place where used glass bottles may be deposited for recycling.
bottlebrush ● noun **1** a cylindrical brush for cleaning inside bottles. **2** an Australian shrub or small tree with spikes of flowers resembling bottlebrushes.
bottle-feed ● verb (**bottle-feeds**, **bottle-feeding**, **bottle-fed**) feed (a baby) with milk from a bottle.
bottle green ● adjective dark green.
bottleneck ● noun **1** the neck or mouth of a bottle. **2** a narrow section of road or a junction where traffic flow is restricted.
bottom ● noun **1** the lowest point or part of something. **2** the furthest point or part of something. **3** the lowest position in a competition or ranking. **4** chiefly Brit. a person's buttocks. **5** (also **bottoms**) the lower half of a two-piece garment. ● adjective **1** in the lowest position. **2** in the furthest position away in a downhill direction. ● verb **1** (of a ship) touch the bottom of the sea. **2** (**bottom out**) (of a situation) reach the lowest point before stabilizing or improving. **3** Austral./NZ excavate to the level of a mineral-bearing stratum.
– PHRASES **at bottom** fundamentally. **be at the bottom of** be the fundamental cause or origin of. **the bottom falls** (or **drops**) **out of something** something suddenly fails or collapses. **bottoms up!** informal said as a toast before drinking. **get to the bottom of** find an explanation for (a mystery).
– DERIVATIVES **bottomless** adjective **bottommost** adjective.
– ORIGIN Old English.
bottom drawer ● noun Brit. dated household linen and other

Thesaurus

● adjective *bosom friends* CLOSE, boon, intimate, inseparable, faithful, constant, devoted; good, best, firm, favourite.
boss *(informal)* ● noun *the boss of a large company* HEAD, chief, principal, director, president, chief executive, chair, manager(ess); supervisor, foreman, overseer, controller; employer, owner, proprietor, patron; *informal* number one, kingpin, top dog, bigwig; *Brit. informal* gaffer, governor; *N. Amer. informal* head honcho, padrone, sachem, big kahuna.
● verb *you have no right to boss me about* ORDER ABOUT/AROUND, dictate to, lord it over, bully, push around/about, domineer, dominate, pressurize, browbeat; call the shots, lay down the law; *informal* bulldoze, walk all over, railroad.
bossy ● adjective *(informal)* DOMINEERING, pushy, overbearing, imperious, officious, high-handed, authoritarian, dictatorial, controlling; *informal* high and mighty.
– OPPOSITES submissive.
botch *(informal)* ● verb *examiners botched the marking* BUNGLE, mismanage, mishandle, make a mess of; *informal* mess up, make a hash of, muff, fluff, foul up, screw up; *Brit. informal* bodge, cock up; *N. Amer. informal* flub.
● noun *I've made a botch of things* MESS, blunder, failure, wreck, fiasco, debacle; *informal* hash; *Brit. informal* bodge, cock-up, pig's ear.
– OPPOSITES success.
bother ● verb **1** *no one bothered her* DISTURB, trouble, inconvenience, pester, badger, harass, molest, plague, nag, hound, harry, annoy, upset, irritate; *informal* hassle, bug, get up someone's nose, get in someone's hair; *N. English informal* mither; *N. Amer. informal* ride. **2** *the incident was too small to bother about* MIND, care, concern oneself, trouble oneself, worry oneself; *informal* give a damn, give a hoot. **3** *there was something bothering him* WORRY, trouble, concern, perturb, disturb, disquiet, disconcert, unnerve; fret, upset, distress, agitate, gnaw at, weigh down; *informal* rattle.
● noun **1** *I don't want to put you to any bother* TROUBLE, effort, exertion, inconvenience, fuss, pains; *informal* hassle. **2** *the food was such a bother to cook* NUISANCE, pest, palaver, rigmarole, job, trial, bind, bore, drag, inconvenience, trouble, problem; *informal* hassle, headache, pain (in the neck). **3** *a spot of bother in the public bar* DISORDER, fighting, trouble, ado, disturbance, agitation, commotion, uproar; *NZ* bobsy-die; *informal* hoo-ha, aggro, argy-bargy, kerfuffle.
bothersome ● adjective ANNOYING, irritating, vexatious, maddening, exasperating; tedious, wearisome, tiresome; troublesome, trying, taxing, awkward; *informal* aggravating, pesky, pestilential.
bottle ● noun **1** *a bottle of whisky* carafe, flask, decanter, pitcher, flagon, carboy, demijohn. **2** *(informal) a world blurred by the bottle.* See ALCOHOL. **3** *(Brit. informal) no one had the bottle to stand up to McGregor* COURAGE, bravery, valour, nerve, confidence, daring, audacity, pluck, spirit, grit, mettle, spine, backbone; *informal* guts, spunk, gumption; *N. Amer. informal* moxie.
– PHRASES **bottle something up** SUPPRESS, repress, restrain, withhold, hold in, rein in, inhibit, smother, stifle, contain, conceal, hide; *informal* keep a lid on.
bottleneck ● noun TRAFFIC JAM, jam, congestion, hold-up, gridlock, tailback; constriction, narrowing, restriction, obstruction, blockage; *informal* snarl-up.
bottom ● noun **1** *the bottom of the stairs* FOOT, lowest part, lowest point, base; foundation, substructure, underpinning. **2** *the bottom of the car* UNDERSIDE, underneath, undersurface, undercarriage, underbelly. **3** *the bottom of Lake Ontario* FLOOR, bed, depths. **4** *the bottom of his garden* FARTHEST POINT, far end, extremity. **5** *the bottom of his class* LOWEST LEVEL, lowest position. **6** *(Brit.) I've got a tattoo on my bottom* REAR (END), rump, backside, seat; buttocks,

b

items stored by a woman in preparation for her marriage.

bottom feeder • noun **1** any marine creature that lives on the seabed and feeds by scavenging. **2** N. Amer. informal a member of a group of very low social status who survives by whatever means possible.

bottom line • noun informal **1** the final total of an account or balance sheet. **2** the underlying and most important factor.

botty • noun (pl. **botties**) Brit. informal a person's bottom.

botulism /botyooliz'm/ • noun a dangerous form of food poisoning caused by a bacterium growing on improperly sterilized foods.
– ORIGIN German *Botulismus*, originally 'sausage poisoning', from Latin *botulus* 'sausage'.

bouclé /booklay/ • noun yarn with a looped or curled ply.
– ORIGIN French, 'buckled, curled'.

boudin /boodaN/ • noun (pl. same) a French type of black pudding.
– ORIGIN French.

boudoir /boodwaar/ • noun a woman's bedroom or small private room.
– ORIGIN French, 'sulking-place', from *bouder* 'pout, sulk'.

bouffant /boofoN/ • adjective (of hair) styled so as to stand out from the head in a rounded shape. • noun a bouffant hairstyle.
– ORIGIN French, 'swelling'.

bougainvillea /boogənvilliə/ (also **bougainvillaea**) • noun an ornamental climbing plant widely cultivated in the tropics, with brightly coloured papery bracts surrounding the flowers.
– ORIGIN named after the French explorer L. A. de *Bougainville* (1729–1811).

bough • noun a main branch of a tree.
– ORIGIN Old English 'bough or shoulder'; related to BOW³.

bought past and past participle of BUY.

bouillabaisse /booyəbess/ • noun a rich fish stew or soup, as made originally in Provence.
– ORIGIN French.

bouillon /booyoN/ • noun thin soup or stock made by stewing meat, fish, or vegetables.
– ORIGIN French, from *bouillir* 'to boil'.

boulder • noun a large rock.
– DERIVATIVES **bouldery** adjective.
– ORIGIN Scandinavian.

boulder clay • noun clay containing many large stones, formed by deposition from melting glaciers.

boule /bool/ (also **boules** pronunc. same) • noun a French game similar to bowls, played with metal balls.
– ORIGIN French, 'bowl'.

boulevard /booləvaard/ • noun a wide street, typically one lined with trees.
– ORIGIN French, 'rampart' (later 'a promenade on the site of a rampart'), from German *Bollwerk* 'bulwark'.

boulevardier /booləvaardeer/ • noun a wealthy, fashionable socialite.
– ORIGIN French, 'person who frequents boulevards'.

boulle /bool/ (also **buhl**) • noun brass, tortoiseshell, or other material used for inlaying furniture.
– ORIGIN French *boule*, from the name of the French cabinetmaker André *Boulle* (1642–1732).

bounce • verb **1** spring quickly up or away from a surface after hitting it. **2** move or jump up and down repeatedly. **3** (of light or sound) reflect back from a surface. **4** (**bounce back**) recover well after a setback or problem. **5** informal (of a cheque) be returned by a bank when there are insufficient funds in an account to meet it. **6** Brit. informal pressurize (someone) into doing something. **7** informal, chiefly N. Amer. dismiss from a job. • noun **1** a rebound of a ball or other object. **2** an act of bouncing up and down. **3** exuberant self-confidence. **4** health and body in a person's hair.
– PHRASES **bounce an idea off someone** informal discuss an idea with another person in order to test or improve it.
– ORIGIN perhaps imitative, or from Low German *bunsen* 'beat' or Dutch *bons* 'a thump'.

bouncer • noun a person employed by a nightclub to prevent troublemakers entering or to eject them from the premises.

bouncing • adjective (of a baby) vigorous and healthy.

bouncy • adjective (**bouncier**, **bounciest**) **1** able to bounce or making something bounce well. **2** confident and lively.
– DERIVATIVES **bouncily** adverb **bounciness** noun.

bouncy castle • noun a large inflatable structure on which children can jump and play.

bound¹ • verb walk or run with leaping strides. • noun a leaping movement towards or over something.
– ORIGIN French *bondir* 'resound', later 'rebound', from Latin *bombus* 'humming'.

bound² • noun **1** a boundary. **2** a limitation or restriction. • verb **1** form the boundary of. **2** restrict.
– PHRASES **out of bounds 1** (in sport) beyond the field of play. **2** beyond the acceptable or permitted limits.
– ORIGIN Old French *bodne*, from Latin *bodina*.

bound³ • adjective going towards somewhere: *a train bound for Edinburgh.*
– ORIGIN from Old Norse, 'get ready'.

bound⁴ past and past participle of BIND. • adjective **1** (**-bound**) restricted or confined to or by a place or situation: *his job kept him city-bound.* **2** destined or certain to be, do, or have. **3** obliged to do.
– PHRASES **I'll be bound** I am sure.

boundary • noun (pl. **boundaries**) **1** a line marking the limits of an area. **2** Cricket a hit crossing the limits of the field, scoring four or six runs.
– ORIGIN from BOUND².

Thesaurus

cheeks; *informal* behind, BTM, sit-upon, derrière; *Brit. informal* bum, botty, jacksie; *N. Amer. informal* butt, fanny, tush, tail, buns, booty, heinie; *humorous* fundament, posterior, stern; *Anatomy* nates. **7** *police got to the bottom of the mystery* ORIGIN, cause, root, source, basis, foundation; heart, kernel; reality, essence.
– OPPOSITES top, surface.
• adjective *she sat on the bottom step* LOWEST, last, bottommost; *technical* basal.
– OPPOSITES top.
– PHRASES **from top to bottom** THOROUGHLY, fully, extensively, completely, comprehensively, rigorously, exhaustively, scrupulously, meticulously.

bottomless • adjective **1** *the bottomless pits of hell* FATHOMLESS, unfathomable, endless, infinite, immeasurable. **2** *George's appetite was bottomless* UNLIMITED, limitless, boundless, infinite, inexhaustible, endless, never-ending, everlasting; vast, huge, enormous.
– OPPOSITES limited.

bough • noun BRANCH, limb, arm, offshoot.

boulder • noun ROCK, stone; *Austral./NZ* gibber.

boulevard • noun AVENUE, street, road, drive, lane, parade, broadway, thoroughfare.

bounce • verb **1** *the ball bounced* REBOUND, spring back, ricochet, jounce; *N. Amer.* carom. **2** *William bounced down the stairs* BOUND, leap, jump, spring, bob, hop, skip, trip, prance.
• noun **1** *he reached the door in a single bounce* BOUND, leap, jump, spring, hop, skip. **2** *the pitch's uneven bounce* SPRINGINESS, resilience, elasticity, give. **3** *she had lost her bounce* VITALITY, vigour, energy, vivacity, liveliness, animation, sparkle, verve, spirit, enthusiasm, dynamism; cheerfulness, happiness, buoyancy, optimism; *informal* get-up-and-go, pep, zing.
– PHRASES **bounce back** RECOVER, revive, rally, pick up, be on the mend; perk up, cheer up, brighten up, liven up; *informal* buck up.

bouncing • adjective VIGOROUS, thriving, flourishing, blooming; HEALTHY, strong, robust, fit, in fine fettle; *informal* in the pink.

bouncy • adjective **1** *a bouncy bridge* SPRINGY, flexible, resilient, elastic, stretchy, rubbery. **2** *a rather bouncy ride* BUMPY, jolting, jerky, jumpy, jarring, rough. **3** *she was always bouncy* LIVELY, energetic, perky, frisky, jaunty, dynamic, vital, vigorous, vibrant, animated, spirited, buoyant, bubbly, sparkling, vivacious; enthusiastic, upbeat; *informal* peppy, zingy, chirpy.

bound¹ • adjective **1** *he raised his bound ankles* TIED, chained, fettered, shackled, secured. **2** *she seemed bound to win* CERTAIN, sure, very likely, destined. **3** *you're bound by the Official Secrets Act to keep quiet* OBLIGATED, obliged, compelled, required, constrained. **4** *religion and morality are bound up with one another* CONNECTED, linked, tied, united, allied.

bound² • verb *hares bound in the fields* LEAP, jump, spring, bounce, hop; skip, bob, dance, prance, gambol, gallop.
• noun *he crossed the room with a single bound* LEAP, jump, spring, bounce, hop.

bound³ • verb **1** *corporate freedom is bounded by law* LIMIT, restrict, confine, circumscribe, demarcate, delimit. **2** *the heath is bounded by a hedge* ENCLOSE, surround, encircle, circle, border; close in/off, hem in. **3** *the garden was bounded by Swan Lane* BORDER, adjoin,

bounden /bowndən/ archaic past participle of BIND.
– PHRASES **a bounden duty** an obligatory responsibility.
bounder ● noun Brit. informal, dated a dishonourable man.
boundless ● adjective unlimited.
– DERIVATIVES **boundlessly** adverb **boundlessness** noun.
bounteous ● adjective archaic bountiful.
– DERIVATIVES **bounteously** adverb **bounteousness** noun.
– ORIGIN from Old French *bontif* 'benevolent', from *bonte* 'bounty, goodness'.
bountiful ● adjective **1** abundant. **2** giving generously.
– PHRASES **Lady Bountiful** a woman who engages in ostentatious acts of charity. [ORIGIN from the name of a character in Farquhar's *The Beaux' Stratagem* (1707).]
– DERIVATIVES **bountifully** adverb.
bounty ● noun (pl. **bounties**) **1** a reward paid for killing or capturing someone. **2** historical a sum paid by the state to encourage trade. **3** chiefly historical a sum paid by the state to army or navy recruits on enlistment. **4** literary something given or occurring in generous amounts. **5** literary generosity: *people along the Nile depend on its bounty.*
– ORIGIN Old French *bonte* 'goodness', from Latin *bonus* 'good'.
bounty hunter ● noun a person who pursues a criminal for a reward.
bouquet /bookay, bō-/ ● noun **1** a bunch of flowers. **2** the characteristic scent of a wine or perfume.
– ORIGIN French, (earlier 'clump of trees'), from Old French *bos*, variant of *bois* 'wood'.
bouquet garni /bookay gaarni, bō-/ ● noun (pl. **bouquets garnis**) a bunch of herbs used for flavouring a stew or soup.
– ORIGIN French, 'garnished bouquet'.
bourbon /burb'n/ ● noun a kind of American whisky distilled from maize and rye.
– ORIGIN named after *Bourbon* County, Kentucky, where it was first made.
bourgeois /boorzhwaa/ (also **bourgeoise**) /boorzhwaaz/ ● adjective **1** characteristic of the middle class, especially in being materialistic or conventional. **2** (in Marxist contexts) capitalist. ● noun (pl. same) a bourgeois person.
– ORIGIN French, from Latin *burgus* 'castle, fortified town'; related to BOROUGH and BURGESS.
bourgeoisie /boorzhwaazee/ ● noun (treated as sing. or pl.) **1** the middle class. **2** (in Marxist contexts) the capitalist class.
– ORIGIN French.
bourn[1] /born/ ● noun dialect a small stream.
– ORIGIN Southern English variant of BURN[2].
bourn[2] /born/ (also **bourne**) ● noun literary **1** a boundary. **2** a goal or destination.
– ORIGIN French *borne*, from Old French *bodne* 'boundary'.
bourrée /bŏoray/ ● noun **1** a lively French dance like a gavotte. **2** Ballet a series of very fast little steps performed on the tips of the toes with the feet close together.
– ORIGIN French, 'faggot of twigs' (the dance being performed around a twig fire).
bourse /boorss/ ● noun a stock market in a non-English-speaking country, especially France.
– ORIGIN French, 'purse', from Greek *bursa* 'leather'.
bout /bowt/ ● noun **1** a short period of illness or intense activity. **2** a wrestling or boxing match.
– ORIGIN from dialect *bought* 'bend, loop'.
boutique /bōoteek/ ● noun a small shop selling fashionable clothes.
– ORIGIN French, 'small shop', from Greek *apothēkē* 'storehouse'.
bouzouki /boozōoki/ ● noun (pl. **bouzoukis**) a long-necked Greek form of mandolin.
– ORIGIN modern Greek *mpouzouki*, perhaps related to Turkish *bozuk* 'spoilt' (with reference to roughly made instruments).
bovine /bōvīn/ ● adjective **1** relating to or resembling cattle. **2** sluggish or stupid. ● noun an animal of the cattle group, which also includes buffaloes and bisons.
– DERIVATIVES **bovinely** adverb.
– ORIGIN Latin *bovinus*, from *bos* 'ox'.
bovine spongiform encephalopathy ● noun see BSE.
bovver ● noun Brit. informal hooliganism or trouble-making.
– ORIGIN cockney pronunciation of BOTHER.
bow[1] /bō/ ● noun **1** a knot tied with two loops and two loose ends. **2** a weapon for shooting arrows, made of curved wood joined at both ends by a taut string. **3** a rod with horsehair stretched along its length, used for playing some stringed instruments. ● verb play (a stringed instrument) using a bow.
– PHRASES **have another string to one's bow** Brit. have a further resource available.
– ORIGIN Old English, 'bend, bow, arch'; related to BOW[2].
bow[2] /bow/ ● verb **1** bend the head or upper body as a sign of respect, greeting, or shame. **2** bend with age or under a heavy weight. **3** submit to pressure or demands. **4** (**bow out**) withdraw or retire from an activity. ● noun an act of bowing.
– PHRASES **bow and scrape** behave in an obsequious way. **take a bow** acknowledge applause by bowing.
– ORIGIN Old English, 'bend, stoop'; related to BOW[1].
bow[3] /bow/ (also **bows**) ● noun the front end of a ship.
– PHRASES **a shot across the bows** a warning statement or gesture.
– ORIGIN Low German *boog* or Dutch *boeg* 'shoulder or ship's bow'; related to BOUGH.

Thesaurus

abut; be next to, be adjacent to.
boundary ● noun **1** *the boundary between Israel and Jordan* BORDER, frontier, borderline, partition. **2** *the boundary between art and advertising* DIVIDING LINE, divide, division, borderline, cut-off point. **3** *the boundary of his estate* BOUNDS, confines, limits, margins, edges, fringes; border, periphery, perimeter. **4** *the boundaries of accepted behaviour* LIMITS, parameters, bounds, confines; ambit, compass.
boundless ● adjective LIMITLESS, unlimited, unbounded, untold, immeasurable, abundant; inexhaustible, endless, infinite, interminable, unfailing, ceaseless, everlasting.
– OPPOSITES limited.
bounds ● plural noun **1** *we keep rents within reasonable bounds* LIMITS, confines, proportions. **2** *land within the forest bounds* BORDERS, boundaries, confines, limits, margins, edges; periphery, perimeter.
– PHRASES **out of bounds** OFF LIMITS, restricted; forbidden, banned, proscribed, illegal, illicit, unlawful, unacceptable, taboo; *informal* no go.
bountiful ● adjective **1** *their bountiful patron* GENEROUS, magnanimous, munificent, open-handed, unselfish, unstinting, lavish; benevolent, beneficent, charitable. **2** *a bountiful supply of fresh food* ABUNDANT, plentiful, ample, bumper, superabundant, inexhaustible, prolific, profuse, copious; lavish, generous, handsome, rich; *informal* whopping; *poetic/literary* plenteous.
– OPPOSITES mean, meagre.
bounty ● noun **1** *a bounty for each man killed* REWARD, prize, award, commission, premium, dividend, bonus, gratuity, tip, donation, handout; incentive, inducement; money; *informal* perk, sweetener; *formal* perquisite. **2** (*poetic/literary*) *I thank the Lord for all his bounty* GENEROSITY, magnanimity, munificence, bountifulness, largesse, lavishness; benevolence, beneficence, charity, goodwill; blessings, favours.
bouquet ● noun **1** *her bridal bouquet* BUNCH OF FLOWERS, posy, nosegay, tussie-mussie, spray, corsage. **2** *bouquets go to Ann for a well-planned event* COMPLIMENT, commendation, tribute, accolade; praise, congratulations, applause. **3** *the Chardonnay has a fine bouquet* AROMA, nose, smell, fragrance, perfume, scent, odour.
bourgeois ● adjective **1** *a bourgeois family* MIDDLE-CLASS, propertied; CONVENTIONAL, conservative, conformist; provincial, suburban, small-town. **2** *bourgeois decadence* CAPITALISTIC, materialistic, money-oriented, commercial.
– OPPOSITES proletarian, communist.
● noun *a proud bourgeois* MEMBER OF THE MIDDLE CLASS, property owner.
bout ● noun **1** *a short bout of exercise* SPELL, period, time, stretch, stint, session; burst, flurry, spurt. **2** *a coughing bout* ATTACK, fit, spasm, paroxysm, convulsion, eruption, outburst. **3** *he is fighting only his fifth bout* CONTEST, match, round, heat, competition, event, meeting, fixture; fight, prizefight.
bovine ● adjective **1** *large, bovine eyes* COW-LIKE, calf-like, taurine. **2** *an expression of bovine amazement* STUPID, slow, ignorant, unintelligent, imperceptive, half-baked, vacuous, mindless, witless, doltish; *informal* dumb, dense, dim, dim-witted, dopey, birdbrained, pea-brained; *Brit. informal* dozy, daft; *Scottish & N. English informal* glaikit.
● noun COW, heifer, bull, bullock, calf, ox; *N. Amer. informal* boss, bossy; *Farming* beef.
bow[1] ● verb **1** *the officers bowed* INCLINE THE BODY, incline the head, nod, salaam, curtsy, bob. **2** *the mast quivered and bowed* BEND,

b

bowdlerize /bowdlərīz/ (also **bowdlerise**) ● verb remove indecent or offensive material from (a text).
– ORIGIN from the name of Dr Thomas *Bowdler* (1754–1825), an American who published an expurgated edition of Shakespeare.
bowel /bowəl/ ● noun **1** the intestine. **2** (**bowels**) the deepest inner parts of something.
– ORIGIN Latin *botellus* 'little sausage'.
bowel movement ● noun an act of defecation.
bower /bowr/ ● noun **1** a pleasant shady place under trees. **2** literary a lady's private room. **3** literary a summer house or country cottage.
– ORIGIN Old English.
bowerbird ● noun an Australasian bird noted for the male's habit of constructing an elaborate bower adorned with feathers, shells, etc. to attract the female.
bow-fronted ● adjective having a convexly curved front.
bowie knife /bō-i/ ● noun a long knife with a blade double-edged at the point.
– ORIGIN named after the American frontiersman Jim *Bowie* (1799–1836).
bowl[1] ● noun **1** a round, deep dish or basin. **2** a rounded, concave part of an object. **3** a natural basin. **4** chiefly N. Amer. a stadium for sporting or musical events.
– ORIGIN Old English, related to BOLL.
bowl[2] ● verb **1** roll (a round object) along the ground. **2** Cricket (of a bowler) throw (the ball) towards the wicket, or dismiss (a batsman) by hitting the wicket with a bowled ball. **3** move rapidly and smoothly. **4** (**bowl over**) knock down. **5** (**bowl over**) informal completely overwhelm or astonish. ● noun **1** a wooden or hard rubber ball used in the game of bowls. **2** a large ball used in tenpin bowling or skittles.
– ORIGIN Old French *boule*, from Latin *bulla* 'bubble'.
bow-legged ● adjective having legs that curve outwards at the knee.
bowler[1] ● noun **1** Cricket a member of the fielding side who bowls. **2** a player at bowls, tenpin bowling, or skittles.
bowler[2] ● noun a man's hard felt hat with a round dome-shaped crown.
– ORIGIN named after the 19th-century English hatter William *Bowler*.
bowline /bōlin/ ● noun **1** a rope attaching the weather side of a square sail to a ship's bow. **2** a simple knot for forming a non-slipping loop at the end of a rope.
bowling ● noun the game of bowls, tenpin bowling, or skittles.
bowling alley ● noun a long narrow track along which balls are rolled in skittles or tenpin bowling.
bowling green ● noun an area of closely mown grass on which the game of bowls is played.
bowls /bōlz/ ● plural noun (treated as sing.) a game played with heavy wooden bowls, the object of which is to propel one's bowl as close as possible to a small white ball (the jack).
bowser /bowzər/ ● noun trademark **1** a tanker used for fuelling aircraft or supplying water. **2** Austral./NZ a petrol pump.
– ORIGIN from the name of a company of oil storage engineers.
bowsprit /bōsprit/ ● noun a spar running out from a ship's bow, to which the forestays are fastened.
Bow Street Runners /bō/ ● plural noun (in the early 19th century) the London police.
– ORIGIN named after *Bow Street* in London, site of the chief metropolitan magistrates' court.
bow tie ● noun a necktie in the form of a bow.
bow window ● noun a curved bay window.
bowyer /bōyər/ ● noun a person who makes or sells archers' bows.
box[1] ● noun **1** a container with a flat base and sides and a lid. **2** an area enclosed within straight lines on a page or computer screen. **3** an enclosed area reserved for a group of people in a theatre or sports ground, or for witnesses or the jury in a law court. **4** a facility at a newspaper office for receiving replies to an advertisement, or at a post office for keeping letters until collected. **5** Brit. a shield for protecting a man's genitals in sport. **6** Brit. a small country house used when shooting or fishing. **7** (**the box**) informal, chiefly Brit. television. **8** (**the box**) Soccer, informal the penalty area. ● verb **1** put in a box. **2** (**box in**) restrict or confine.
– ORIGIN Old English, probably related to BOX[3].
box[2] ● verb fight an opponent with the fists in padded gloves as a sport. ● noun a slap on the side of a person's head.
– PHRASES **box clever** Brit. informal act so as to outwit someone. **box someone's ears** slap someone on the side of the head.
– DERIVATIVES **boxing** noun.
– ORIGIN of unknown origin.
box[3] ● noun a slow-growing evergreen shrub with small glossy leaves and hard wood.
– ORIGIN Greek *puxos*.
box[4] ● verb (in phrase **box the compass**) recite the compass points in correct order.
– ORIGIN perhaps from Spanish *bojar* 'sail round', from Low German *bōgen* 'bend'.
boxcar ● noun N. Amer. an enclosed railway freight wagon.
boxer ● noun **1** a person who boxes as a sport. **2** a medium-sized breed of dog with a smooth brown coat and pug-like face.
boxer shorts ● plural noun men's underpants resembling shorts.
box girder ● noun a hollow girder with a square cross section.
Boxing Day ● noun chiefly Brit. a public holiday on the first day

Thesaurus

buckle, stoop, curve, flex, deform. **3** *the government bowed to foreign pressure* YIELD, submit, give in, surrender, succumb, capitulate, defer, conform; comply with, accept, heed, observe. **4** *a footman bowed her in* USHER, conduct, show, lead, guide, direct, steer, shepherd.
● noun *a perfunctory bow* OBEISANCE, salaam, bob, curtsy, nod; *archaic* reverence.
– PHRASES **bow out** WITHDRAW, resign, retire, step down, pull out, back out; give up, quit, leave; *informal* pack in, chuck (in); *Brit. informal* jack in.
bow[2] ● noun *the bow of the tanker* PROW, front, stem, nose, head, cutwater; *Brit. humorous* sharp end.
bow[3] ● noun **1** *she tied a bow in her hair* LOOP, knot; ribbon. **2** *he bent the rod into a bow* ARC, curve, bend; crescent, half-moon. **3** *an archer's bow* longbow, crossbow; *Archery* recurve.
bowdlerize ● verb EXPURGATE, censor, blue-pencil, cut, edit; sanitize, water down, emasculate.
bowel ● noun **1** *a disorder of the bowels* INTESTINE(S), small intestine, large intestine, colon; *informal* guts, insides. **2** *the bowels of the ship* INTERIOR, inside, core, belly; depths, recesses; *informal* innards.
bower ● noun **1** *a rose-scented bower* ARBOUR, pergola, grotto, alcove, sanctuary. **2** *(poetic/literary) the lady's bower* BEDROOM; *historical* boudoir; *archaic* bedchamber, chamber.
bowl[1] ● verb **1** *he bowled a hundred or so balls* PITCH, throw, propel, hurl, toss, lob, loft, fling, launch, deliver; spin, roll; *informal* chuck, sling, bung, heave, buzz; *dated* shy. **2** *the car bowled along the roads* TRUNDLE, drive, motor, travel; hurtle, speed, shoot, sweep; *informal* belt, tear, scoot; *Brit. informal* bomb; *N. Amer. informal* clip.
– PHRASES **bowl someone over 1** *the explosion bowled us over* KNOCK DOWN/OVER, fell, floor, prostrate. **2** *(informal) I have been bowled over by your generosity* OVERWHELM, astound, astonish, overawe, dumbfound, stagger, stun, daze, shake, take aback, leave aghast; *informal* knock sideways, flabbergast, blow away; *Brit. informal* knock for six.
bowl[2] ● noun **1** *she cracked two eggs into a bowl* DISH, basin, pot, crock, crucible, mortar; container, vessel, receptacle; *historical* jorum, porringer. **2** *the town lay in a shallow bowl* VALLEY, hollow, dip, depression, trough, crater. **3** *(N. Amer.) the Hollywood Bowl* STADIUM, arena, amphitheatre, colosseum; ground; *informal* park. **4** *the bowl of a tobacco pipe* HOLLOW, depression.
box[1] ● noun **1** *a box of cigars* CARTON, pack, packet; case, crate, chest, coffer, casket; container, receptacle. **2** *a telephone box* BOOTH, cubicle, kiosk, cabin, hut; compartment, carrel, alcove, bay, recess.
● verb *Muriel boxed up his clothes* PACKAGE, pack, parcel, wrap, bundle, bale, crate.
– PHRASES **box something/someone in** HEM IN, fence in, close in, shut in; trap, confine, imprison, intern; surround, enclose, encircle, circle.
box[2] ● verb **1** *he began boxing professionally* FIGHT, prizefight, spar; battle, brawl; *informal* scrap. **2** *he boxed my ears* CUFF, smack, strike, hit, thump, slap, swat, punch, jab, wallop; *Scottish & N. English* skelp; *informal* belt, bop, biff, sock, clout, clobber, whack, plug, slug; *Brit. informal* slosh, dot; *N. Amer. informal* boff, bust.
● noun *a box on the ear* CUFF, hit, thump, slap, smack, swat, punch, jab, hook; *Scottish & N. English* skelp; *informal* belt, bop, biff,

after Christmas Day.
– ORIGIN from the former custom of giving tradespeople a Christmas box on this day.

box junction • noun Brit. a road area at a junction marked with a yellow grid, which a vehicle should enter only if its exit is clear.

box number • noun a number identifying an advertisement in a newspaper, used as an address for replies.

box office • noun a place at a theatre, cinema, etc. where tickets are sold.

box pleat • noun a pleat consisting of two parallel creases forming a raised band.

boxroom • noun Brit. a very small room.

boxy • adjective (**boxier**, **boxiest**) **1** squarish in shape. **2** (of a room or space) cramped.

boy • noun **1** a male child or youth. **2** (**boys**) informal men who mix socially or belong to a particular group. • exclamation informal used to express strong feelings.
– DERIVATIVES **boyhood** noun **boyish** adjective.
– ORIGIN of unknown origin.

boyar /bōyaar/ • noun a member of the old aristocracy in Russia, next in rank to a prince.
– ORIGIN Russian *boyarin* 'grandee'.

boycott • verb refuse to have commercial or social dealings with (a person, organization, or country) as a punishment or protest. • noun an act of boycotting.
– ORIGIN from Captain Charles C. *Boycott*, an Irish land agent so treated in 1880 in an attempt to get rents reduced.

boyfriend • noun a person's regular male companion in a romantic or sexual relationship.

Boyle's law • noun Chemistry a law stating that the pressure of a given mass of an ideal gas is inversely proportional to its volume at a constant temperature.
– ORIGIN named after the English scientist Robert *Boyle* (1627–91).

boyo • noun (pl. **boyos**) Welsh & Irish informal a boy or man.

Boy Scout • noun old-fashioned term for SCOUT (in sense 3).

boysenberry /boyz'nbəri/ • noun (pl. **boysenberries**) a large red edible blackberry-like fruit.
– ORIGIN named after the American horticulturalist Robert *Boysen* (died 1950).

bozo /bōzō/ • noun (pl. **bozos**) informal, chiefly N. Amer. a stupid or insignificant person.
– ORIGIN of unknown origin.

BP • abbreviation **1** before the present (era). **2** blood pressure. **3** British Petroleum.

Bq • abbreviation becquerel.

Br • symbol the chemical element bromine.

bra • noun a woman's undergarment worn to support the breasts.
– DERIVATIVES **braless** adjective.
– ORIGIN abbreviation of BRASSIERE.

brace • noun **1** (**braces**) Brit. a pair of straps passing over the shoulders and fastening to the top of trousers to hold them up. **2** a strengthening or supporting piece or part. **3** a wire device fitted in the mouth to straighten the teeth. **4** (also **brace and bit**) a drilling tool with a crank handle and a socket to hold a bit. **5** a rope attached to the yard of a ship for trimming the sail. **6** (pl. same) a pair of things, especially birds or mammals killed in hunting. **7** either of two connecting marks { and }, used in printing and music. • verb **1** make stronger or firmer with a brace. **2** press (one's body) firmly against something to stay balanced. **3** (**brace oneself**) prepare for something difficult or unpleasant.
– ORIGIN from Old French *bracier* 'embrace', from *brace* 'two arms', from Latin *bracchium* 'arm'.

bracelet • noun an ornamental band or chain worn on the wrist or arm.
– ORIGIN Old French, from *bras* 'arm'.

brachiopod /brakiəpod/ • noun Zoology a marine invertebrate resembling a bivalve mollusc, with tentacles used for filter-feeding.
– ORIGIN from Greek *brakhiōn* 'arm' + *pous* 'foot'.

brachiosaurus /brakiəsawrəss/ • noun a huge herbivorous dinosaur with forelegs much longer than the hind legs.
– ORIGIN from Greek *brakhiōn* 'arm' + *sauros* 'lizard'.

bracing • adjective fresh and invigorating.
– DERIVATIVES **bracingly** adverb.

bracken • noun a tall fern with coarse lobed fronds.
– ORIGIN Scandinavian.

bracket • noun **1** each of a pair of marks ( ) [ ] { } < > used to enclose words or figures. **2** a category of similar people or things: *a high income bracket.* **3** a right-angled support projecting from a wall. • verb (**bracketed**, **bracketing**) **1** enclose (words or figures) in brackets. **2** place in the same category or group. **3** hold or attach by means of a bracket.
– ORIGIN Spanish *bragueta* 'codpiece, bracket', from Latin *bracae* 'breeches'.

brackish • adjective (of water) slightly salty, as in river estuaries.
– ORIGIN from obsolete *brack* 'salty', from Low German, Dutch *brac.*

bract • noun Botany a modified leaf with a flower or flower cluster in its axil.
– ORIGIN Latin *bractea* 'thin metal plate'.

brad • noun a nail with a rectangular cross section and a small asymmetrical head.
– ORIGIN Old Norse.

bradawl /braddawl/ • noun a tool for boring holes, resembling a screwdriver.

brae /bray/ • noun Scottish a steep bank or hillside.
– ORIGIN Old Norse, 'eyelash'.

brag • verb (**bragged**, **bragging**) say something boastfully. • noun **1** a simplified form of poker. **2** an act of bragging.
– DERIVATIVES **bragger** noun.
– ORIGIN of unknown origin (French *braguer* is recorded only later).

braggadocio /braggədōchiō/ • noun boastful or arrogant behaviour.

Thesaurus

sock, clout, whack, plug, slug.

boxer • noun FIGHTER, pugilist, ringster, prizefighter, kick-boxer; *informal* bruiser, scrapper.

boxing • noun PUGILISM, fighting, sparring, fisticuffs; kick-boxing, prizefighting; the (prize) ring.

boy • noun LAD, schoolboy, male child, youth, young man, stripling; *Scottish & N. English* laddie; *derogatory* brat. See also CHILD.

boycott • verb *they boycotted the elections* SPURN, snub, shun, avoid, abstain from, wash one's hands of, turn one's back on, reject, veto.
– OPPOSITES support.
• noun *a boycott on the use of tropical timbers* BAN, veto, embargo, prohibition, sanction, restriction; avoidance, rejection, refusal.

boyfriend • noun LOVER, sweetheart, beloved, darling, dearest, young man, man friend, man, escort, suitor; PARTNER, significant other; *informal* fella, flame, fancy man, toy boy, sugar daddy; *N. Amer. informal* squeeze; *poetic/literary* swain; *dated* beau; *archaic* paramour.

boyish • adjective YOUTHFUL, young, childlike, adolescent, teenage; immature, juvenile, infantile, childish, babyish, puerile.

brace • noun **1** *the saw is best used with a brace* VICE, clamp, press. **2** *power drills run faster than a brace* DRILL, boring tool, rotary tool. **3** *the aquarium is supported by wooden braces* PROP, beam, joist, batten, rod, post, strut, stay, support, stanchion, bracket. **4** *a brace on his right leg* SUPPORT, caliper. **5** *a brace of partridges* PAIR, couple, duo, twosome; two. **6** *(Printing) the term within braces* BRACKET, parenthesis.
• verb **1** *the plane's wing is braced by a system of rods* SUPPORT, shore up, prop up, hold up, buttress, underpin; strengthen, reinforce. **2** *he braced his hand on the railing* STEADY, secure, stabilize, fix, poise; tense, tighten. **3** *brace yourself for disappointment* PREPARE, get ready, gear up, nerve, steel, galvanize, gird, strengthen, fortify; *informal* psych oneself up.

bracelet • noun BANGLE, band, circlet, armlet, wristlet; manilla, rakhi, kara.

bracing • adjective INVIGORATING, refreshing, stimulating, energizing, exhilarating, reviving, restorative, rejuvenating, revitalizing, rousing, fortifying, strengthening; FRESH, brisk, keen.

bracket • noun **1** *each speaker is fixed on a separate bracket* SUPPORT, prop, stay, batten, joist; rest, mounting, rack, frame. **2** *put the words in brackets* PARENTHESIS; *Printing* brace. **3** *a higher tax bracket* GROUP, category, grade, classification, set, division, order.
• verb *women were bracketed with minors* GROUP, CLASSIFY, class, categorize, grade, list, sort, place, assign; couple, pair, twin; liken, compare.

brackish • adjective SLIGHTLY SALTY, saline, salt.

b

– ORIGIN from *Braggadocchio*, a boastful character in Spenser's *Faerie Queene*.

braggart /braggərt/ ● noun a person who brags.
– ORIGIN French *bragard*, from *braguer* 'to brag'.

Brahman /braamən/ ● noun (pl. **Brahmans**) **1** (also **Brahmin**) a member of the highest Hindu caste, that of the priesthood. **2** (also **Brahma**) the ultimate reality underlying all phenomena in the Hindu scriptures.
– ORIGIN Sanskrit.

Brahmin /braamin/ ● noun **1** variant spelling of BRAHMAN (in sense 1). **2** US a socially or culturally superior person.
– DERIVATIVES **Brahminical** adjective.

braid ● noun **1** threads woven into a decorative band. **2** a length of hair made up of interlaced strands. ● verb **1** form a braid with (hair). **2** edge or trim with braid.
– ORIGIN Old English, 'make a sudden movement', also 'interweave'.

Braille /brayl/ ● noun a written language for the blind, in which characters are represented by patterns of raised dots.
– ORIGIN named after the blind French educationist Louis *Braille* (1809–52).

brain ● noun **1** an organ of soft nervous tissue contained in the skull, functioning as the coordinating centre of sensation and intellectual and nervous activity. **2** intellectual capacity. **3** (**the brains**) informal the main organizer or planner within a group. ● verb informal hit hard on the head with an object.
– PHRASES **have on the brain** informal be obsessed with.
– DERIVATIVES **brained** adjective.
– ORIGIN Old English.

brainbox ● noun Brit. informal a very clever person.

brainchild ● noun informal an idea or invention originated by a specified person.

brain-dead ● adjective **1** having suffered brain death. **2** informal extremely stupid.

brain death ● noun irreversible brain damage causing the end of independent breathing.

brain drain ● noun informal the emigration of highly skilled or qualified people from a country.

brainiac ● noun N. Amer. informal a very intelligent person.
– ORIGIN from the name of a super-intelligent alien character of the Superman comic strip.

brainless ● adjective stupid; very foolish.
– DERIVATIVES **brainlessly** adverb **brainlessness** noun.

brainpan ● noun informal, chiefly N. Amer. a person's skull.

brainstem ● noun the central trunk of the brain, consisting of the medulla oblongata, pons, and midbrain.

brainstorm ● noun **1** informal a moment in which one is suddenly unable to think clearly. **2** a spontaneous group discussion to produce ideas. ● verb have a spontaneous discussion to produce ideas.

brains trust ● noun a group of experts who give impromptu answers to questions.

brain-teaser ● noun informal a problem or puzzle.

brainwash ● verb subject (someone) to a prolonged process to transform their attitudes and beliefs totally.

brainwave ● noun **1** an electrical impulse in the brain. **2** informal a sudden clever idea.

brainy ● adjective (**brainier**, **brainiest**) informal intelligent.
– DERIVATIVES **brainily** adverb **braininess** noun.

braise ● verb fry (food) lightly and then stew slowly in a closed container.
– ORIGIN French *braiser*, from *braise* 'live coals' (in which the container was placed).

brake[1] ● noun a device for slowing or stopping a moving vehicle. ● verb slow or stop a vehicle with a brake.
– ORIGIN of unknown origin.

brake[2] ● noun historical an open horse-drawn carriage with four wheels.
– ORIGIN variant of synonymous *break*, also denoting a two-wheeled carriage for breaking in young horses; of unknown origin.

brake[3] ● noun **1** a toothed instrument for crushing flax and hemp. **2** (also **brake harrow**) a heavy machine formerly used for breaking up large lumps of earth.
– ORIGIN perhaps related to BREAK.

brake[4] ● noun archaic or literary a thicket.
– ORIGIN Old English.

brake drum ● noun a broad, short cylinder attached to a wheel, against which the brake shoes press to cause braking.

brake horsepower ● noun an imperial unit equal to one horsepower, used in expressing the power available at the shaft of an engine.

brake shoe ● noun a long curved block which presses on to a brake drum.

bramble ● noun **1** a prickly scrambling shrub of the rose family, especially a blackberry. **2** chiefly Brit. the fruit of the blackberry.
– ORIGIN Old English, related to BROOM.

brambling ● noun a finch with a white rump, related to the chaffinch.
– ORIGIN perhaps from obsolete German *Brämling* in the same sense; related to BRAMBLE.

Bramley (also **Bramley's seedling**) ● noun (pl. **Bramleys**) a variety of large English cooking apple with green skin.
– ORIGIN named after the 19th-century English butcher Matthew *Bramley*, in whose garden it first grew.

bran ● noun pieces of grain husk separated from flour after milling.
– ORIGIN Old French.

branch ● noun **1** a part of a tree which grows out from the trunk or a bough. **2** a river, road, or railway extending out from a main one. **3** a division of a large organization, group, etc. ● verb **1** divide into or send out one or more branches. **2** (**branch out**) extend one's activities or interests in a new direction.
– ORIGIN Old French *branche*, from Latin *branca* 'paw'.

Thesaurus

brag ● verb BOAST, crow, swagger, swank, bluster, gloat, show off; blow one's own trumpet, sing one's own praises; *informal* talk big, lay it on thick; *Austral./NZ informal* skite.

braggart ● noun *he was a prodigious braggart and a liar* BOASTER, bragger, swaggerer, poser, poseur, egotist; *informal* big-head, loudmouth, show-off, swank; *N. Amer. informal* showboat, blowhard; *Austral./NZ informal* skite; *Brit. informal, dated* swankpot.

braid ● noun **1** *straps bordered with gold braid* CORD, bullion, thread, tape, binding, rickrack, ribbon; cordon, torsade; *Military slang* scrambled egg. **2** *her hair was in braids* PLAIT, pigtail, twist; cornrows, dreadlocks.
● verb **1** *she began to braid her hair* PLAIT, entwine, intertwine, interweave, weave, twist, twine. **2** *the sleeves are braided in scarlet* TRIM, edge, border, pipe, hem, fringe.

brain ● noun **1** *the disease attacks cells in the brain* CEREBRUM, cerebral matter, encephalon. **2** *success requires brains as well as brawn* INTELLIGENCE, intellect, brainpower, cleverness, wit(s), reasoning, wisdom, acumen, discernment, judgement, understanding, sense; *informal* nous, grey matter, savvy; *N. Amer. informal* smarts. **3** *(informal) Janice is the brains of the family* CLEVER PERSON, intellectual, intellect, thinker, mind, scholar; genius, Einstein; *informal* egghead, bright spark; *Brit. informal* brainbox, clever clogs; *N. Amer. informal* brainiac, rocket scientist.
– RELATED TERMS cerebral, encephalic.
– OPPOSITES dunce.

brainless ● adjective STUPID, FOOLISH, witless, unintelligent, ignorant, idiotic, simple-minded, empty-headed, half-baked; *informal* dumb, half-witted, brain-dead, moronic, cretinous, thick, dopey, dozy, birdbrained, pea-brained, dippy, wooden-headed; *Brit. informal* divvy; *Scottish & N. English informal* glaikit; *N. Amer. informal* dumb-ass, chowderheaded.
– OPPOSITES clever.

brain-teaser ● noun *(informal)* PUZZLE, problem, riddle, conundrum, poser.

brainwash ● verb INDOCTRINATE, condition, re-educate, persuade, influence.

brainy ● adjective *(informal)* CLEVER, intelligent, bright, brilliant, gifted; intellectual, erudite, academic, scholarly, studious, bookish; *informal* smart; *Brit. informal* swotty.
– OPPOSITES stupid.

brake ● noun *a brake on research* CURB, check, restraint, restriction, constraint, control, limitation.
● verb *she braked at the traffic lights* SLOW (DOWN), decelerate, reduce speed.
– OPPOSITES accelerate.

branch ● noun **1** *the branches of a tree* BOUGH, limb, arm, offshoot. **2** *a branch of the river* TRIBUTARY, feeder, side stream. **3** *the judicial branch of government* DIVISION, subdivision, section, subsec-

brand ● noun **1** a type of product manufactured by a company under a particular name. **2** a brand name. **3** an identifying mark burned on livestock with a heated iron. **4** a piece of burning or smouldering wood. ● verb **1** mark with a branding iron. **2** mark out as having a particular shameful quality: *she was branded a liar*. **3** give a brand name to.
– ORIGIN from Old English, 'burning'.

brandish ● verb wave or flourish (something) as a threat or in anger or excitement.
– ORIGIN Old French *brandir*, related to BRAND.

brandling ● noun a red earthworm with rings of a brighter colour, used in compost and as bait by anglers.

brand name ● noun a name given by the maker to a product or range of products.

brand new ● adjective completely new.
– ORIGIN with the idea 'straight from the fire'.

brandy ● noun (pl. **brandies**) a strong alcoholic spirit distilled from wine or fermented fruit juice.
– ORIGIN from earlier *brandwine*, from Dutch *branden* 'burn, distil' + *wijn* 'wine'.

brandy butter ● noun Brit. a stiff sauce of brandy, butter, and sugar.

brandy snap ● noun a crisp rolled gingerbread wafer.

bran tub ● noun Brit. a lucky dip in which items are buried in bran.

brash ● adjective self-assertive in a rude, noisy, or overbearing way.
– DERIVATIVES **brashly** adverb **brashness** noun.
– ORIGIN perhaps a form of RASH[1].

brass ● noun **1** a yellow alloy of copper and zinc. **2** (also **horse brass**) a flat brass ornament for the harness of a draught horse. **3** Brit. a memorial consisting of a flat piece of inscribed brass in the wall or floor of a church. **4** brass wind instruments forming a band or section of an orchestra. **5** (also **top brass**) informal people in authority. **6** Brit. informal money.
– PHRASES **brassed off** Brit. informal disgruntled. **cold enough to freeze the balls off a brass monkey** informal extremely cold. [ORIGIN from a type of brass rack or 'monkey' in which cannonballs were stored and which contracted in very cold weather, ejecting the balls.] **get down to brass tacks** informal start to consider the basic facts.
– ORIGIN Old English.

brass band ● noun a group of musicians playing brass instruments.

brasserie /brassəri/ ● noun (pl. **brasseries**) an inexpensive French or French-style restaurant.
– ORIGIN French, 'brewery'.

brass hat ● noun Brit. informal a high-ranking officer in the armed forces.

brassica /brassikə/ ● noun a plant of a family that includes cabbage, swede, rape, and mustard.
– ORIGIN Latin, 'cabbage'.

brassiere /brazziər/ ● noun full form of BRA.
– ORIGIN French, 'bodice, child's vest'.

brass rubbing ● noun reproduction of the design on an engraved brass by rubbing heelball or chalk over paper laid on it.

brassy ● adjective (**brassier**, **brassiest**) **1** resembling brass in colour. **2** harsh or blaring like a brass instrument. **3** tastelessly showy or loud.

brat ● noun informal a badly behaved child.
– DERIVATIVES **brattish** adjective.
– ORIGIN perhaps an abbreviation of Scots *bratchet*, from Old French *brachet* 'hound, bitch'.

brat pack ● noun informal a rowdy and ostentatious group of young celebrities.

bratwurst /bratvurst/ ● noun a type of fine German pork sausage.
– ORIGIN German, from *Brat* 'a spit' + *Wurst* 'sausage'.

bravado ● noun boldness intended to impress or intimidate.
– ORIGIN Spanish *bravada*, from *bravo* 'brave'.

brave ● adjective having or showing courage. ● noun dated an American Indian warrior. ● verb endure or face (unpleasant conditions) with courage.
– DERIVATIVES **bravely** adverb **bravery** noun.
– ORIGIN Italian or Spanish *bravo* 'bold, untamed', from Latin *barbarus* 'barbarous'.

bravo[1] /braavō/ ● exclamation shouted to express approval for a performer.
– ORIGIN from Italian, 'bold, brave'.

bravo[2] /braavō/ ● noun (pl. **bravos** or **bravoes**) a thug or hired assassin.
– ORIGIN Italian, 'bold (one)'.

bravura /brəvyoorə/ ● noun **1** great skill and brilliance. **2** the display of great daring.
– ORIGIN Italian, from *bravo* 'bold'.

braw /braw/ ● adjective Scottish fine; splendid.
– ORIGIN variant of BRAVE.

brawl ● noun a rough or noisy fight or quarrel. ● verb take part in a brawl.
– DERIVATIVES **brawler** noun.
– ORIGIN perhaps imitative and related to BRAY.

brawn ● noun **1** physical strength as opposed to intelligence. **2** Brit. cooked meat from a pig's or calf's head, pressed with jelly.
– DERIVATIVES **brawny** adjective.
– ORIGIN Old French *braon* 'fleshy part of the leg'.

Thesaurus

tion, department, sector, part, side, wing. **4** *the corporation's New York branch* OFFICE, bureau, agency; subsidiary, offshoot, satellite. ● verb **1** *the place where the road branches* FORK, bifurcate, divide, subdivide, split. **2** *narrow paths branched off the road* DIVERGE FROM, deviate from, split off from; fan out from, radiate from.
– PHRASES **branch out** EXPAND, open up, extend; diversify, broaden one's horizons.

brand ● noun **1** *a new brand of margarine* MAKE, line, label, marque; type, kind, sort, variety; trade name, trademark, proprietary name. **2** *her particular brand of humour* TYPE, kind, sort, variety, class, category, genre, style, ilk; *N. Amer.* stripe. **3** *the brand on a sheep* IDENTIFICATION, marker, earmark. **4** *the brand of dipsomania* STIGMA, shame, disgrace; taint, blot, mark.
● verb **1** *the letter M was branded on each animal* MARK, stamp, burn, sear. **2** *the scene was branded on her brain* ENGRAVE, stamp, etch, imprint. **3** *the media branded us as communists* STIGMATIZE, mark out; denounce, discredit, vilify; label.

brandish ● verb FLOURISH, wave, shake, wield; swing, swish; display, flaunt.

brash ● adjective **1** *a brash man* SELF-ASSERTIVE, pushy, cocksure, cocky, self-confident, arrogant, bold, audacious, brazen; forward, impudent, insolent, rude. **2** *brash colours* GARISH, gaudy, loud, flamboyant, showy, tasteless; *informal* flashy, tacky.
– OPPOSITES meek, muted.

brassy ● adjective **1** BRAZEN, forward, bold, self-assertive, pushy, cocksure, cocky, brash; shameless, immodest; loud, vulgar, showy, ostentatious; *informal* flashy. **2** *brassy music* LOUD, blaring, noisy, deafening, strident; raucous, harsh, dissonant, discordant, cacophonous; tinny.
– OPPOSITES demure, soft.

brat ● noun *(informal)* RASCAL, wretch, imp; minx, chit; *informal* monster, horror, whippersnapper.

bravado ● noun BOLDNESS, swaggering, bluster; machismo; boasting, bragging, bombast, braggadocio; *informal* showing off.

brave ● adjective **1** *they put up a brave fight* COURAGEOUS, plucky, valiant, valorous, intrepid, heroic, lionhearted, bold, fearless, daring, audacious; unflinching, unshrinking, unafraid, dauntless, doughty, mettlesome, stout-hearted, spirited; *informal* game, gutsy, spunky. **2** *(poetic/literary) his medals made a brave show* SPLENDID, magnificent, impressive, fine, handsome.
– OPPOSITES cowardly.
● noun *(dated) an Indian brave* WARRIOR, soldier, fighter.
● verb *fans braved freezing temperatures to see them play* ENDURE, put up with, bear, withstand, weather, suffer, go through; face, confront, defy.

bravery ● noun COURAGE, pluck, valour, intrepidity, nerve, daring, fearlessness, audacity, boldness, dauntlessness, stout-heartedness, heroism; backbone, grit, spine, spirit, mettle; *informal* guts, spunk; *Brit. informal* bottle; *N. Amer. informal* moxie.

bravo ● exclamation WELL DONE, congratulations; encore.

bravura ● noun *a display of bravura* SKILL, brilliance, virtuosity, expertise, artistry, talent, ability, flair.
● adjective *a bravura performance* VIRTUOSO, masterly, outstanding, excellent, superb, brilliant, first-class; *informal* mean, ace, A1.

brawl ● noun *a drunken brawl* FIGHT, skirmish, scuffle, tussle, fray, melee, free-for-all, scrum; fisticuffs; *informal* scrap, dust-up, set-to; *Brit. informal* punch-up, ruck; *Scottish informal* rammy; *N. Amer. informal* rough house, brannigan; *Law, dated* affray.

b

Braxton Hicks contractions /brakstən **hiks**/ ● plural noun Medicine intermittent weak contractions of the uterus occurring during pregnancy.
– ORIGIN named after the English gynaecologist John *Braxton Hicks* (1823–97).
bray ● noun the loud, harsh cry of a donkey. ● verb make such a sound.
– ORIGIN from Old French *braire* 'to cry'.
braze ● verb solder with an alloy of copper and zinc. ● noun a brazed joint.
– ORIGIN French *braser* 'solder'.
brazen ● adjective **1** bold and shameless. **2** literary made of brass. ● verb (**brazen it out**) endure a difficult situation with apparent confidence and lack of shame.
– DERIVATIVES **brazenly** adverb.
– ORIGIN Old English, 'made of brass'.
brazier[1] /brayziər/ ● noun **1** a portable heater holding lighted coals. **2** N. Amer. a barbecue.
– ORIGIN French *brasier*, from *braise* 'hot coals'.
brazier[2] /brayziər/ ● noun a worker in brass.
Brazilian ● noun a person from Brazil. ● adjective relating to Brazil.
brazil nut ● noun the large three-sided nut of a South American forest tree.
breach ● verb **1** make a gap or hole in; break through. **2** break (a rule or agreement). ● noun **1** a gap made in a wall or barrier. **2** an act of breaking a rule or agreement. **3** a break in relations.
– PHRASES **breach of the peace** chiefly Brit. the criminal offence of behaving in a violent or noisy way that causes a public disturbance. **breach of promise** the breaking of a sworn assurance. **step into the breach** replace someone who is suddenly unable to do a job.
– ORIGIN Old French *breche*, related to BREAK.
bread ● noun **1** food made of flour, water, and yeast mixed together and baked. **2** informal money.
– PHRASES **bread and butter** a person's livelihood or main source of income. **bread and circuses** entertainment or political policies intended to keep the masses happy and docile. **break bread** celebrate the Eucharist. **cast one's bread upon the waters** do good without expecting gratitude or reward. [ORIGIN with biblical allusion to the Book of Ecclesiastes, chapter 11.] **know which side one's bread is buttered** informal know where one's advantage lies.
– ORIGIN Old English.
breadcrumb ● noun a small fragment of bread.
breaded ● adjective (of food) coated with breadcrumbs and fried.
breadfruit ● noun a large round starchy fruit of a tropical tree, used as a vegetable and to make a substitute for flour.
breadline ● noun **1** (usu. in phrase **on the breadline**) Brit. the poorest condition in which it is acceptable to live. **2** N. Amer. a queue of people waiting to receive free food.
bread sauce ● noun sauce made with milk and breadcrumbs, eaten with roast turkey.
breadth ● noun **1** the distance or measurement from side to side of something. **2** wide range: *breadth of experience*. **3** dated a piece of cloth of standard or full width.
– ORIGIN obsolete *brede*, related to BROAD.
breadwinner ● noun a person who supports their family with the money they earn.
break ● verb (past **broke**; past part. **broken**) **1** separate into pieces as a result of a blow, shock, or strain. **2** make or become inoperative; stop working. **3** interrupt (a continuity, sequence, or course). **4** fail to observe (a law, regulation, or agreement). **5** crush the strength or spirit of. **6** surpass (a record). **7** succeed in deciphering (a code). **8** make a sudden rush or dash. **9** lessen the impact of (a fall). **10** suddenly make or become public. **11** (of a person's voice) falter and change tone. **12** (of a boy's voice) change in tone and register at puberty. **13** (of the weather) change suddenly, especially after a fine spell. **14** (of a storm) begin violently. **15** (of dawn or a day) begin as the sun rises. **16** use (a banknote) to pay for something and receive change. **17** make the first stroke at the beginning of a game of billiards, pool, or snooker. ● noun **1** an interruption, pause, or gap. **2** a short rest or pause in work. **3** an instance of breaking, or the point where something is broken. **4** a sudden rush or dash. **5** informal an opportunity or chance. **6** (also **break of serve** or **service break**) Tennis the winning of a game against an opponent's serve. **7** Snooker & Billiards a consecutive series of successful shots. **8** a short solo in jazz or popular music.
– PHRASES **break away** escape from control or influence. **break one's back** (or **neck**) put great effort into achieving something. **break the back of** accomplish the main or hardest part of. **break cover** (of game being hunted) emerge into the open. **break down 1** suddenly cease to function or continue. **2** lose control of one's emotions when in distress. **break in 1** force entry to a building. **2** interject. **3** accustom (a horse) to being ridden. **4** make (new shoes) comfortable by wearing them. **breaking and entering** (in North American, and formerly also British, law) the crime of entering a building by force to commit burglary. **break into** burst forth into (laughter, song, or faster movement). **break a leg!** theatrical slang good luck! **break of day** dawn. **break off** abruptly end or discontinue. **break out 1** (of something undesirable) start suddenly. **2** escape. **3** informal open and start using (something). **break out in** be suddenly affected by an unpleasant sensation or condition. **break someone's serve** win a game in a tennis match against an opponent's service. **break up 1** (of a gathering or relationship) end or part. **2** Brit. end the school term. **break wind** release gas from the anus. **break with 1** quarrel with. **2** go against (a custom or tradition). **give someone a break** informal stop putting pressure on someone.
– DERIVATIVES **breakable** adjective.
– ORIGIN Old English.

Thesaurus

● verb *he ended up brawling with photographers* FIGHT, skirmish, scuffle, tussle, exchange blows, grapple, wrestle; *informal* scrap; *N. Amer. informal* rough-house.
brawn ● noun PHYSICAL STRENGTH, muscle(s), burliness, huskiness, toughness, power, might; *informal* beef, beefiness.
brawny ● adjective STRONG, muscular, muscly, well built, powerful, mighty, Herculean, strapping, burly, sturdy, husky, rugged; bulky, hefty, meaty, solid; *informal* beefy, hunky, hulking.
– OPPOSITES puny, weak.
bray ● verb **1** *a donkey brayed* NEIGH, whinny, hee-haw. **2** *Billy brayed with laughter* ROAR, bellow, trumpet.
brazen ● adjective **1** *brazen defiance* BOLD, shameless, as bold as brass, unashamed, unabashed, unembarrassed; defiant, impudent, impertinent, cheeky; barefaced, blatant, flagrant; *Brit. informal* saucy. **2** *(poetic/literary) brazen objects* BRASS.
– OPPOSITES timid.
– PHRASES **brazen it out** PUT ON A BOLD FRONT, stand one's ground, be defiant, be unrepentant, be unabashed.
breach ● noun **1** *a clear breach of the regulations* CONTRAVENTION, violation, infringement, infraction, transgression, neglect; *Law* delict. **2** *a breach between government and Church* RIFT, schism, division, gulf, chasm; disunion, estrangement, discord, dissension, disagreement; split, break, rupture, scission; *Brit. informal* bust-up. **3** *a breach in the sea wall* BREAK, rupture, split, crack, fracture; opening, gap, hole, fissure.
● verb **1** *the river breached its bank* BREAK (THROUGH), burst, rupture; *informal* bust. **2** *the changes breached union rules* BREAK, contravene, violate, infringe; defy, disobey, flout, fly in the face of; *Law* infract.
bread ● noun **1** *(informal) his job puts bread on the table.* See FOOD sense 1. **2** *(informal) I hate doing this, but I need the bread.* See MONEY sense 1.
breadth ● noun **1** *a breadth of 100 metres* WIDTH, broadness, wideness, thickness; span; diameter. **2** *the breadth of his knowledge* RANGE, extent, scope, depth, reach, compass, scale, degree.
break ● verb **1** *the mirror broke* SHATTER, smash, crack, snap, fracture, fragment, splinter, fall to bits, fall to pieces; split, burst; *informal* bust. **2** *she had broken her leg* FRACTURE, crack. **3** *the bite had barely broken the skin* PIERCE, puncture, penetrate, perforate; cut. **4** *the coffee machine has broken* STOP WORKING, break down, give out, go wrong, malfunction; crash; *informal* go kaput, conk out, be on the blink, give up the ghost; *Brit. informal* pack up. **5** *traders who break the law* CONTRAVENE, violate, infringe, breach; defy, flout, disobey, fly in the face of. **6** *his concentration was broken* INTERRUPT, disturb, interfere with. **7** *they broke for coffee* STOP, pause, have a rest; *N. Amer.* recess; *informal* knock off, take five. **8** *a pile of carpets broke his fall* CUSHION, soften the impact of, take the edge off. **9** *the film broke box-office records* EXCEED, surpass, beat, better, cap, top, outdo, outstrip, eclipse; *informal* leave standing. **10** *habits are very difficult to break* GIVE UP, relinquish, drop; *informal* kick,

breakage ● noun **1** the action of breaking something or the fact of being broken. **2** a thing that has been broken.

breakaway ● noun **1** a withdrawal from something established or long-standing. **2** a sudden rush away from a main group.

break-dancing ● noun an energetic and acrobatic style of street dancing, developed by US blacks.

breakdown ● noun **1** a failure or collapse. **2** an explanatory analysis, especially of statistics.

breaker ● noun **1** a heavy sea wave that breaks on the shore. **2** a person that breaks up old machinery.

breakfast ● noun a meal eaten in the morning, the first of the day. ● verb eat this meal.
– PHRASES **have for breakfast** informal deal with or defeat with contemptuous ease.
– ORIGIN from BREAK + FAST².

break-in ● noun an illegal forced entry in order to steal something.

breakneck ● adjective dangerously fast.

breakthrough ● noun a sudden important development or success.

breakthrough bleeding ● noun bleeding from the uterus occurring abnormally between menstrual periods.

breakwater ● noun a barrier built out into the sea to protect a coast or harbour from the force of waves.

bream ● noun (pl. same) a deep-bodied greenish-bronze freshwater fish.
– ORIGIN Old French *bresme*.

breast ● noun **1** either of the two soft, protruding organs on a woman's chest which secrete milk after pregnancy. **2** a person's or animal's chest region. ● verb **1** face and move forwards against or through. **2** reach the top of (a hill).
– DERIVATIVES **breasted** adjective.
– ORIGIN Old English.

breastbone ● noun a thin flat bone running down the centre of the chest and connecting the ribs; the sternum.

breastfeed ● verb (**breastfeeds**, **breastfeeding**, **breastfed**) feed (a baby) with milk from the breast.

breastplate ● noun a piece of armour covering the chest.

breaststroke ● noun a style of swimming in which the arms are pushed forwards and then swept back while the legs are alternately tucked in and kicked out.

breastwork ● noun a low temporary defence or parapet.

breath ● noun **1** air taken into or expelled from the lungs. **2** an instance of breathing in or out. **3** a slight movement of air. **4** a sign, hint, or suggestion: *he avoided the slightest breath of scandal.*
– PHRASES **breath of fresh air** a refreshing change. **catch one's breath 1** cease breathing momentarily in surprise or fear. **2** rest after exercise to restore normal breathing. **draw breath** breathe in. **hold one's breath** cease breathing temporarily. **out of breath** gasping for air. **take breath** pause to recover normal breathing. **take someone's breath away** astonish or inspire someone. **under one's breath** in a very quiet voice.
– ORIGIN Old English, 'smell, scent'.

Thesaurus

shake, pack in, quit. **11** *the strategies used to break the union* DESTROY, crush, quash, defeat, vanquish, overcome, overpower, overwhelm, suppress, cripple; weaken, subdue, cow, undermine. **12** *her self-control finally broke* GIVE WAY, crack, cave in, yield, go to pieces. **13** *four thousand pounds wouldn't break him* BANKRUPT, ruin, pauperize. **14** *he tried to break the news gently* REVEAL, disclose, divulge, impart, tell; announce, release. **15** *he broke the encryption code* DECIPHER, decode, decrypt, unravel, work out; informal figure out. **16** *the day broke fair and cloudless* DAWN, begin, start, emerge, appear. **17** *a political scandal broke* ERUPT, break out. **18** *the weather broke* CHANGE, alter, shift. **19** *waves broke against the rocks* CRASH, dash, beat, pound, lash. **20** *her voice broke as she relived the experience* FALTER, quaver, quiver, tremble, shake.
– OPPOSITES repair, keep, resume.
● noun **1** *the magazine has been published without a break since 1950* INTERRUPTION, interval, gap, hiatus; discontinuation, suspension, disruption, cut-off; stop, stoppage, cessation. **2** *a break in the weather* CHANGE, alteration, variation. **3** *let's have a break* REST, respite, recess; stop, pause; interval, intermission; informal time out, breather, down time. **4** *a weekend break* HOLIDAY; N. Amer. vacation; Brit. informal vac. **5** *a break in diplomatic relations* RIFT, schism, split, break-up, severance, rupture; Brit. informal bust-up. **6** *a break in the wall* GAP, opening, space, hole, breach, chink, crack, fissure; tear, split. **7** (informal) *the actress got her first break in 1951* OPPORTUNITY, chance, opening.
– PHRASES **break away 1** *she attempted to break away from his grip* ESCAPE, get away, run away, flee, make off; break free, break loose, get out of someone's clutches; informal leg it, cut and run. **2** *a group broke away from the main party* LEAVE, secede from, split off from, separate from, part company with, defect from; form a splinter group. **break down 1** *his van broke down.* See BREAK verb sense 4. **2** *pay negotiations broke down* FAIL, collapse, founder, fall through, disintegrate; informal fizzle out. **3** *Vicky broke down, sobbing loudly* BURST INTO TEARS; lose control, be overcome, go to pieces, crumble, disintegrate; informal crack up, lose it. **break something down 1** *the police broke the door down* KNOCK DOWN, kick down, smash in, pull down, tear down, demolish. **2** *break big tasks down into smaller parts* DIVIDE, separate. **3** *graphs show how the information can be broken down* ANALYSE, categorize, classify, sort out, itemize, organize; dissect. **break in 1** *thieves broke in and took her cheque book* COMMIT BURGLARY, break and enter; force one's way in, burst in. **2** *'I don't want to interfere,' Mrs Hendry broke in* INTERRUPT, butt in, cut in, interject, interpose, intervene, chime in; Brit. informal chip in. **break someone in** TRAIN, initiate; informal show someone the ropes. **break into 1** *thieves broke into a house in Perth Street* BURGLE, rob; force one's way into, burst into. **2** *Phil broke into the discussion* INTERRUPT, butt into, cut in on, intervene in. **3** *he broke into a song* BURST INTO, launch into. **break off** SNAP OFF, come off, become detached, become separated. **break something off 1** *I broke off a branch from the tree* SNAP OFF, pull off, sever, detach. **2** *they threatened to break off diplomatic relations* END, terminate, stop, cease, call a halt to, finish, dissolve; SUSPEND, discontinue; informal pull the plug on. **break out 1** *he broke out of the detention centre* ESCAPE FROM, abscond from, flee from; get free. **2** *fighting broke out* FLARE UP, start suddenly, erupt, burst out. **break up 1** *the meeting broke up* END, finish, stop, terminate; adjourn; N. Amer. recess. **2** *the crowd began to break up* DISPERSE, scatter, disband, part company. **3** *Danny and I broke up last year* SPLIT UP, separate, part (company); divorce. **4** (informal) *the whole cast broke up* BURST OUT LAUGHING, dissolve into laughter; informal fall about, crack up, crease up; theatrical slang corpse. **break something up 1** *police tried to break up the crowd* DISPERSE, scatter, disband. **2** *I'm not going to let you break up my marriage* WRECK, ruin, destroy.

breakable ● adjective FRAGILE, delicate, flimsy, insubstantial; destructible; formal frangible.

breakaway ● adjective *a breakaway group* SEPARATIST, secessionist, schismatic, splinter; rebel, renegade.

breakdown ● noun **1** *the breakdown of the negotiations* FAILURE, collapse, disintegration, foundering. **2** *on the death of her father she suffered a breakdown* NERVOUS BREAKDOWN; informal crack-up. **3** *the breakdown of the computer system* MALFUNCTION, failure, crash. **4** *a breakdown of the figures* ANALYSIS, classification, examination, investigation, dissection.

breaker ● noun WAVE, roller, comber, white horse; informal boomer; N. Amer. informal kahuna.

break-in ● noun BURGLARY, robbery, theft, raid; informal smash-and-grab.

breakneck ● adjective *the breakneck pace of change* EXTREMELY FAST, rapid, speedy, high-speed, lightning, whirlwind.
– PHRASES **at breakneck speed** DANGEROUSLY FAST, at full tilt, flat out, ventre à terre; informal hell for leather, like the wind, like a bat out of hell, like greased lightning; Brit. informal like the clappers.

breakthrough ● noun ADVANCE, development, step forward, success, improvement; discovery, innovation, revolution.
– OPPOSITES setback.

break-up ● noun **1** *the break-up of negotiations* END, dissolution; breakdown, failure, collapse, disintegration. **2** *their break-up was very amicable* SEPARATION, split, parting, divorce; estrangement, rift; Brit. informal bust-up. **3** *the break-up of the Soviet Union* DIVISION, partition.

breakwater ● noun SEA WALL, jetty, mole, groyne, pier.

breast ● noun **1** *the curve of her breasts* mammary gland, mamma; (**breasts**) BOSOM(S), bust, chest; informal boobs, knockers, bubbies; Brit. informal bristols, charlies; N. Amer. informal bazooms. **2** *feelings of frustration were rising up in his breast* HEART, bosom, soul, core.

breath ● noun **1** *I took a deep breath* INHALATION, inspiration, gulp of air; exhalation, expiration; Medicine respiration. **2** *I had barely enough breath to reply* wind; informal puff. **3** *a breath of wind* PUFF,

b

breathable ● adjective **1** (of air) fit to breathe. **2** (of clothing) admitting air to the skin and allowing sweat to evaporate.

breathalyser (US trademark **Breathalyzer**) ● noun a device used by police for measuring the amount of alcohol in a driver's breath.
– DERIVATIVES **breathalyse** (US **breathalyze**) verb.
– ORIGIN blend of BREATH and ANALYSE.

breatharian /breethairiən/ ● noun a person who believes that it is possible, through meditation, to reach a level of consciousness where one can exist on air alone.

breathe ● verb **1** take air into the lungs and then expel it as a regular physical process. **2** say with quiet intensity. **3** admit or emit air or moisture. **4** give an impression of.
– PHRASES **breathe down someone's neck 1** follow closely behind someone. **2** constantly check up on someone. **breathe one's last** die.

breather ● noun informal a brief pause for rest.

breathing space ● noun an opportunity to pause, relax, or decide what to do next.

breathless ● adjective **1** gasping for breath. **2** feeling or causing great excitement, fear, etc.
– DERIVATIVES **breathlessly** adverb **breathlessness** noun.

breathtaking ● adjective astonishing or awe-inspiring.
– DERIVATIVES **breathtakingly** adverb.

breath test ● noun a test in which a driver is made to blow into a breathalyser.

breathy ● adjective (of a voice) having an audible sound of breathing.
– DERIVATIVES **breathily** adverb.

breccia /brechə/ ● noun Geology rock consisting of angular fragments cemented by finer calcareous material.
– ORIGIN Italian, 'gravel'.

bred past and past participle of BREED.

breech ● noun the back part of a rifle or gun barrel.
– ORIGIN Old English, 'garment covering the loins and thighs', later 'the buttocks'.

breech birth ● noun a birth in which the baby's buttocks or feet are delivered first.

breeches ● plural noun short trousers fastened just below the knee, now worn for riding or as part of ceremonial dress.

breeches buoy ● noun a lifebuoy on a rope with a canvas support by means of which a person may be held and transported.

breed ● verb (past and past part. **bred**) **1** (of animals) mate and then produce offspring. **2** keep (animals) for the purpose of producing young. **3** bring up (someone) to behave in a particular way. **4** produce or lead to. ● noun **1** a distinctive type within a species of animals or plants, especially one deliberately developed. **2** a sort or kind.
– ORIGIN Old English, related to BROOD.

breeder ● noun **1** a person or animal that breeds. **2** a nuclear reactor which creates another fissile material (plutonium-239) as a by-product of energy production by fission of uranium-238.

breeding ● noun upper-class good manners regarded as being passed on by heredity.

breeze ● noun **1** a gentle wind. **2** informal something easy to do. ● verb informal come or go in a casual or light-hearted manner.
– ORIGIN originally in the sense 'north-east wind': probably from Old Spanish and Portuguese *briza*.

breeze block ● noun Brit. a lightweight building brick made from cinders mixed with sand and cement.
– ORIGIN *breeze* from French *braise* 'live coals'.

breezy ● adjective (**breezier**, **breeziest**) **1** pleasantly windy. **2** relaxed, informal, and cheerily brisk.
– DERIVATIVES **breezily** adverb **breeziness** noun.

Bren gun ● noun a lightweight quick-firing machine gun used by the Allies in the Second World War.
– ORIGIN blend of *Brno* in the Czech Republic (where it was originally made) and *Enfield* (where it was later made).

brethren archaic plural of BROTHER. ● plural noun fellow Christians or members of a male religious order.

Breton /brett'n/ ● noun **1** a person from Brittany. **2** the language of Brittany, derived from Cornish.
– ORIGIN Old French, 'Briton'.

breve ● noun **1** Music a note twice as long as a semibreve, represented as a semibreve with two short bars either side, or as a square. **2** a written or printed mark (˘) indicating a short or unstressed vowel.
– ORIGIN variant of BRIEF: the musical term was originally used in a series where a *long* was of greater time value than a *breve*.

brevet /brevvit/ ● noun a former type of military commission by which an officer was promoted to a higher rank without the corresponding pay.
– ORIGIN originally denoting an official letter: from Old French *brievet* 'little letter'.

breviary /breeviəri/ ● noun (pl. **breviaries**) a book containing the service for each day, recited by those in orders in the Roman Catholic Church.
– ORIGIN Latin *breviarium* 'summary, abridgement'.

brevity /brevviti/ ● noun **1** concise and exact use of words. **2** shortness of time.
– PHRASES **brevity is the soul of wit** proverb the essence of a witty statement lies in its concise wording and delivery. [ORIGIN from Shakespeare's *Hamlet* (II. ii. 90).]
– ORIGIN Latin *brevitas*, from *brevis* 'brief'.

brew ● verb **1** make (beer) by soaking, boiling, and fermentation. **2** make (tea or coffee) by mixing it with hot water. **3** (of

Thesaurus

waft, faint breeze. **4** *a breath of scandal* HINT, suggestion, trace, touch, whisper, suspicion, whiff, undertone. **5** *(archaic) there was no breath left in him* LIFE (FORCE).
– RELATED TERMS respiratory.
– PHRASES **take someone's breath away** ASTONISH, astound, amaze, stun, startle, stagger, shock, take aback, dumbfound, jolt, shake up; awe, overawe, thrill; *informal* knock sideways, flabbergast, blow away, bowl over; *Brit. informal* knock for six.

breathe ● verb **1** *she breathed deeply* inhale and exhale, respire, draw breath; puff, pant, blow, gasp, wheeze; *Medicine* inspire, expire; *poetic/literary* suspire. **2** *at least I'm still breathing* BE ALIVE, be living, live. **3** *he would breathe new life into his firm* INSTIL, infuse, inject, impart. **4** *'Together at last,' she breathed* WHISPER, murmur, purr, sigh, say. **5** *the room breathed an air of hygiene* SUGGEST, indicate, have all the hallmarks of.

breather ● noun *(informal)* BREAK, REST, respite, breathing space, pause, interval, recess.

breathless ● adjective **1** *Will arrived flushed and breathless* OUT OF BREATH, panting, puffing, gasping, wheezing; winded, puffed out, short of breath; *informal* out of puff. **2** *the crowd were breathless with anticipation* AGOG, open-mouthed, waiting with bated breath, on the edge of one's seat, on tenterhooks, in suspense; excited, impatient.

breathtaking ● adjective SPECTACULAR, magnificent, wonderful, awe-inspiring, awesome, astounding, astonishing, amazing, stunning, incredible; thrilling, exciting; *informal* sensational, out of this world; *poetic/literary* wondrous.

breed ● verb **1** *elephants breed readily in captivity* REPRODUCE, produce offspring, procreate, multiply; mate. **2** *she was born and bred in the village* BRING UP, rear, raise, nurture. **3** *the political system bred discontent* CAUSE, bring about, give rise to, lead to, produce, generate, foster, result in; stir up; *poetic/literary* beget.
● noun **1** *a breed of cow* VARIETY, stock, strain; type, kind, sort. **2** *a new breed of journalist* TYPE, kind, sort, variety, class, genre, generation; *N. Amer.* stripe.

breeding ● noun **1** *individual birds pair for breeding* REPRODUCTION, procreation; mating. **2** *the breeding of rats* REARING, raising, nurturing. **3** *her aristocratic breeding* UPBRINGING, rearing; parentage, family, pedigree, blood, birth. **4** *people of rank and breeding* (GOOD) MANNERS, gentility, refinement, cultivation, polish, urbanity; *informal* class.

breeding ground ● noun *the school is a breeding ground for communists* NURSERY, cradle, nest, den; hotbed.

breeze ● noun **1** *a breeze ruffled the leaves* GENTLE WIND, puff of air, gust; *Meteorology* light air(s); *poetic/literary* zephyr. **2** *(informal) travelling through London was a breeze* EASY TASK, five-finger exercise, walkover; child's play, nothing; *informal* doddle, piece of cake, cinch, kids' stuff, cakewalk; *N. Amer. informal* duck soup, snap; *Austral./NZ informal* bludge; *dated* snip.
● verb *(informal) Roger breezed into her office* SAUNTER, stroll, sail, cruise.

breezy ● adjective **1** *a bright, breezy day* WINDY, fresh, brisk, airy; blowy, blustery, gusty. **2** *his breezy manner* JAUNTY, CHEERFUL, cheery, brisk, carefree, easy, casual, relaxed, informal, light-hearted, lively, buoyant, sunny; *informal* upbeat, bright-eyed and bushy-tailed; *dated* gay.

brevity ● noun **1** *the report is notable for its brevity* CONCISENESS, concision, succinctness, economy of language, pithiness, incisive-

an unwelcome situation) begin to develop. ● noun something brewed.
– DERIVATIVES **brewer** noun.
– ORIGIN Old English.

brewery ● noun (pl. **breweries**) a place where beer is made commercially.

briar[1] (also **brier**) ● noun a prickly scrambling shrub, especially a wild rose.
– ORIGIN Old English.

briar[2] (also **briar pipe**, **brier**) ● noun a tobacco pipe made from the woody nodules of a white-flowered shrub of the heather family.
– ORIGIN French *bruyère* 'heath, heather', from Latin *brucus*.

bribe ● verb dishonestly persuade (someone) to act in one's favour by paying them or giving other inducement. ● noun an inducement offered in an attempt to bribe.
– DERIVATIVES **bribery** noun.
– ORIGIN originally in the sense 'rob, extort', later 'money extorted or demanded': from Old French *briber, brimber* 'beg'.

bric-a-brac ● noun miscellaneous objects and ornaments of little value.
– ORIGIN French, from obsolete *à bric et à brac* 'at random'.

brick ● noun **1** a small rectangular block of fired or sun-dried clay, used in building. **2** Brit. a child's toy building block. **3** Brit. informal, dated a generous, helpful, and reliable person. ● verb block or enclose with a wall of bricks.
– PHRASES **bricks and mortar** buildings, especially housing. **like a ton of bricks** informal with crushing weight, force, or authority. **you can't make bricks without straw** proverb nothing can be made or accomplished without adequate material or information.
– ORIGIN Low German, Dutch *bricke, brike*.

brickbat ● noun **1** a piece of brick used as a missile. **2** a critical remark or reaction.

brickfield ● noun an area of ground where bricks are made.

brickie ● noun (pl. **brickies**) Brit. informal a bricklayer.

bricklayer ● noun a person whose job is to build structures with bricks.

brick red ● noun a deep brownish red.

bricolage /brikkəlaazh/ ● noun (pl. same or **bricolages**) **1** (in art or literature) construction or creation from a diverse range of available things. **2** something created in this way.
– ORIGIN French.

bridal ● adjective of or concerning a bride or a newly married couple.
– ORIGIN from Old English, 'wedding feast'.

bride ● noun a woman on her wedding day or just before and after the event.
– ORIGIN Old English.

bridegroom ● noun a man on his wedding day or just before and after the event.
– ORIGIN Old English, 'bride man'.

bridesmaid ● noun a girl or woman who accompanies a bride on her wedding day.

bridewell ● noun archaic a prison or reform school for petty offenders.
– ORIGIN named after *St Bride's Well* in London, near which such a building stood.

bridge[1] ● noun **1** a structure carrying a road, path, or railway across a river, road, etc. **2** the platform on a ship from which the captain and officers direct operations. **3** the upper bony part of a person's nose. **4** a partial denture supported by natural teeth on either side. **5** the part on a stringed instrument over which the strings are stretched. **6** (also **bridge passage**) Music a transitional section or middle eight in a composition. ● verb be or make a bridge over or between.
– ORIGIN Old English.

bridge[2] ● noun a card game related to whist, played by two partnerships of two players.
– ORIGIN of unknown origin.

bridgehead ● noun a strong position secured by an army inside enemy territory.

bridge roll ● noun Brit. a small, soft bread roll with a long, thin shape.

bridging loan ● noun chiefly Brit. a sum of money lent by a bank to cover an interval between two transactions, typically the buying of one house and the selling of another.

bridie ● noun (pl. **bridies**) Scottish a meat pasty.
– ORIGIN perhaps from obsolete *bride's pie*.

bridle ● noun the headgear used to control a horse, consisting of buckled straps to which a bit and reins are attached. ● verb **1** put a bridle on. **2** bring under control. **3** show resentment or anger.
– ORIGIN Old English.

bridleway (also **bridle path**) ● noun Brit. a path or track along which horse riders have right of way.

Brie /bree/ ● noun a kind of soft, mild, creamy cheese with a firm, white skin.
– ORIGIN named after *Brie* in northern France.

brief ● adjective **1** lasting a short time. **2** concise; using few words. **3** (of clothing) not covering much of the body. ● noun **1** chiefly Brit. a summary of the facts in a case given to a barrister to argue in court. **2** informal a solicitor or barrister. **3** chiefly Brit. a set of instructions about a task. **4** a letter from the Pope on a matter of discipline. ● verb instruct or inform thoroughly in preparation for a task.
– PHRASES **hold a brief for** Brit. be retained as counsel for. **hold no brief for** not support.
– DERIVATIVES **briefly** adverb.
– ORIGIN Old French, from Latin *brevis* 'short'.

briefcase ● noun a flat rectangular case for carrying books and documents.

Thesaurus

ness, shortness, compactness. **2** *the brevity of human life* SHORTNESS, briefness, transience, ephemerality, impermanence.
– OPPOSITES verbosity.

brew ● verb **1** *this beer is brewed in Frankfurt* FERMENT, make. **2** *I'll brew some tea* PREPARE, infuse, make, stew; *Brit. informal* mash. **3** *there's trouble brewing* DEVELOP, loom, impend, be imminent, be on the horizon, be in the offing, be just around the corner.
● noun **1** *home brew* BEER, ale. **2** *a hot reviving brew* DRINK, beverage; tea, coffee. **3** *a dangerous brew of political turmoil and violent conflict* MIXTURE, mix, blend, combination, amalgam.

bribe ● verb *he used his wealth to bribe officials* BUY OFF, pay off, suborn; *informal* grease someone's palm, keep someone sweet, fix, square; *Brit. informal* nobble.
● noun *he accepted bribes* INDUCEMENT, incentive, douceur; *informal* backhander, pay-off, kickback, sweetener, carrot; *Brit. informal* bung; *N. Amer. informal* schmear.

bribery ● noun SUBORNATION; *N. Amer.* payola; *informal* palm-greasing, graft, hush money.

bric-a-brac ● noun ORNAMENTS, knick-knacks, trinkets, bibelots, gewgaws, gimcracks; bits and pieces, bits and bobs, odds and ends, things, stuff; *informal* junk.

brick ● noun **1** *bricks and mortar* breeze block, adobe, clinker; header, stretcher, bondstone; *Brit.* airbrick. **2** *a brick of ice cream* BLOCK, cube, bar, cake.

bridal ● adjective *the bridal party* WEDDING, nuptial, marriage, matrimonial, marital, conjugal.

bride ● noun WIFE, marriage partner; newly-wed.

bridge ● noun **1** *a bridge over the river* VIADUCT, flyover, overpass, aqueduct. **2** *a bridge between rival groups* LINK, connection, bond, tie.
● verb **1** *a walkway bridged the motorway* SPAN, cross (over), extend across, traverse, arch over. **2** *an attempt to bridge the gap between cultures* JOIN, link, connect, unite; straddle; overcome, reconcile.

bridle ● noun *a horse's bridle* HARNESS, headgear.
● verb **1** *she bridled at his tone* BRISTLE, take offence, take umbrage, be affronted, be offended, get angry. **2** *he bridled his indignation* CURB, restrain, hold back, control, check, rein in/back; suppress, stifle; *informal* keep a/the lid on.

brief ● adjective **1** *a brief account* CONCISE, succinct, short, pithy, incisive, abridged, condensed, compressed, abbreviated, compact, thumbnail, potted; *formal* compendious. **2** *a brief visit* SHORT, flying, fleeting, hasty, hurried, quick, cursory, perfunctory; temporary, short-lived, momentary, transient; *informal* quickie. **3** *a pair of brief shorts* SKIMPY, scanty, short; revealing. **4** *the boss was rather brief with him* BRUSQUE, abrupt, curt, short, blunt, sharp.
– OPPOSITES lengthy.
● noun **1** *a barrister's brief* SUMMARY, case, argument, contention; dossier. **2** (informal) *his brief's eloquence saved him.* See LAWYER. **3** *a brief of our requirements* OUTLINE, summary, synopsis, precis, sketch, digest.
● verb *employees were briefed about the decision* INFORM, tell, up-

b

briefing ● noun a meeting for giving information or instructions.

briefs ● plural noun short, close-fitting underpants or knickers.

brier[1] ● noun variant spelling of BRIAR[1].

brier[2] ● noun variant spelling of BRIAR[2].

brig[1] ● noun **1** a two-masted square-rigged ship. **2** informal a prison on a warship.
– ORIGIN abbreviation of BRIGANTINE.

brig[2] ● noun Scottish & N. English a bridge.
– ORIGIN Old Norse.

brigade ● noun **1** a subdivision of an army, typically consisting of a small number of battalions and forming part of a division. **2** informal, often derogatory a particular group of people: *the anti-smoking brigade.*
– ORIGIN French, from Italian *brigata* 'company', from *brigare* 'contend'.

brigadier ● noun a rank of officer in the British army, above colonel and below major general.

brigadier general ● noun a rank of officer in the US army, air force, and marine corps, above colonel and below major general.

brigalow /briggəlō/ ● noun an Australian acacia tree.
– ORIGIN from an Aboriginal word.

brigand /briggənd/ ● noun literary a member of a gang of bandits, especially in forested and mountainous areas.
– DERIVATIVES **brigandage** noun.
– ORIGIN Italian *brigante* '(person) contending', related to BRIGADE.

brigantine /briggənteen/ ● noun a two-masted sailing ship with a square-rigged foremast and a mainmast rigged fore and aft.
– ORIGIN Italian *brigantino*, from *brigante* 'brigand'.

bright ● adjective **1** giving out much light, or filled with light. **2** (of colour) vivid and bold. **3** intelligent and quick-witted. **4** (of sound) clear and high-pitched. **5** cheerfully lively. **6** (of prospects) good.
– PHRASES **bright-eyed and bushy-tailed** informal alert and lively.
– DERIVATIVES **brightly** adverb **brightness** noun.
– ORIGIN Old English.

brighten ● verb **1** make or become brighter. **2** make or become happier and more cheerful.

Bright's disease ● noun a disease involving chronic inflammation of the kidneys.
– ORIGIN named after the English physician Richard *Bright* (1789–1858).

bright spark ● noun ironic a clever or witty person.

brill ● noun a flatfish similar to the turbot.
– ORIGIN of unknown origin.

brilliant ● adjective **1** (of light or colour) very bright or vivid. **2** exceptionally clever or talented. **3** Brit. informal excellent; marvellous.
– DERIVATIVES **brilliance** (also **brilliancy**) noun **brilliantly** adverb.
– ORIGIN French *brillant*, from *briller* 'shine', probably from Latin *beryllus* 'beryl'.

brilliantine ● noun dated scented oil used on men's hair to make it look glossy.

brim ● noun **1** the projecting edge around the bottom of a hat. **2** the lip of a cup, bowl, etc. ● verb (**brimmed**, **brimming**) fill or be full to the point of overflowing.
– DERIVATIVES **brimful** adjective **brimmed** adjective.
– ORIGIN originally denoting the edge of a body of water: perhaps related to German *Bräme* 'trimming'.

brimstone /brimstōn/ ● noun **1** archaic sulphur. **2** a large bright yellow or greenish-white butterfly.
– ORIGIN Old English, probably from *bryne* 'burning' + *stān* 'stone'.

brindle (also **brindled**) ● adjective (of a domestic animal) brownish or tawny with streaks of other colour.
– ORIGIN probably Scandinavian.

brine ● noun water saturated or strongly impregnated with salt, e.g. seawater.
– ORIGIN Old English.

bring ● verb (past and past part. **brought**) **1** carry or accompany to a place. **2** cause to be in a particular position, state, or condition. **3** cause (someone) to receive (specified income or profit). **4** (**bring oneself to do**) force oneself to do (something unpleasant). **5** initiate (legal action).
– PHRASES **bring about 1** cause (something) to happen. **2** cause (a ship) to head in a different direction. **bring forward 1** move (something scheduled) to an earlier time. **2** propose (an idea) for consideration. **bring the house down** make an audience laugh or applaud very enthusiastically. **bring off** achieve (something) successfully. **bring on 1** encourage or help (someone) to develop or improve. **2** cause (something unpleasant) to occur. **bring out 1** produce and launch (a new product or publication). **2** emphasize (a feature). **3** encourage (someone) to feel

Thesaurus

date, notify, advise, apprise; prepare, prime, instruct; *informal* fill in, clue in, put in the picture.

briefing ● noun **1** *a press briefing* CONFERENCE, meeting, interview; *N. Amer.* backgrounder. **2** *this briefing explains the systems* INFORMATION, rundown, guidance; instructions, directions, guidelines.

briefly ● adverb **1** *Henry paused briefly* MOMENTARILY, temporarily, for a moment, fleetingly. **2** *briefly, the plot is as follows* IN SHORT, in brief, to cut a long story short, in a word, in sum, in a nutshell, in essence.

briefs ● plural noun UNDERPANTS, pants, knickers, Y-fronts, G-string, thong; *N. Amer.* shorts, undershorts; *informal* panties, undies, frillies; *Brit. informal* kecks, smalls.

brigade ● noun **1** *a brigade of soldiers* UNIT, contingent, battalion, regiment, division, squadron, company, platoon, section, corps, troop. **2** *the volunteer ambulance brigade* SQUAD, team, group, band, party, crew, force, outfit.

brigand ● noun *(poetic/literary)*. See BANDIT.

bright ● adjective **1** *the bright surface of the metal* SHINING, brilliant, dazzling, beaming, glaring; sparkling, flashing, glittering, scintillating, gleaming, glowing, luminous, radiant; shiny, lustrous, glossy. **2** *a bright morning* SUNNY, sunshiny, cloudless, clear, fair, fine. **3** *bright colours* VIVID, brilliant, intense, strong, bold, glowing, rich; fluorescent, gaudy, lurid, garish. **4** *bright flowers* COLOURFUL, brightly-coloured, vivid, vibrant; *dated* gay. **5** *a bright guitar sound* CLEAR, vibrant, pellucid; high-pitched. **6** *a bright young graduate* CLEVER, intelligent, quick-witted, smart, canny, astute, intuitive, perceptive; ingenious, resourceful; gifted, brilliant; *informal* brainy. **7** *a bright smile* HAPPY, cheerful, cheery, jolly, merry, sunny, beaming; lively, exuberant, buoyant, bubbly, bouncy, perky, chirpy; *dated* gay. **8** *a bright future* PROMISING, rosy, optimistic, hopeful, favourable, propitious, auspicious, encouraging, good, golden.
– OPPOSITES dull, dark, stupid.
● adverb *(poetic/literary) the moon shone bright* BRIGHTLY, brilliantly, intensely.

brighten ● verb **1** *sunshine brightened the room* ILLUMINATE, light up, lighten, make bright, make brighter, cast/shed light on. **2** *you can brighten up the shadiest of corners* ENHANCE, embellish, enrich, dress up, prettify, beautify; *informal* jazz up. **3** *Sarah brightened up as she thought of Emily's words* CHEER UP, perk up, rally; be enlivened, feel heartened, be uplifted, be encouraged, take heart; *informal* buck up, pep up.

brilliance ● noun **1** *a philosopher of great brilliance* GENIUS, talent, ability, prowess, skill, expertise, aptitude, flair, finesse, panache; greatness, distinction; intelligence, wisdom, sagacity, intellect. **2** *the brilliance and beauty of Paris* SPLENDOUR, magnificence, grandeur, resplendence. **3** *the brilliance of the sunshine* BRIGHTNESS, vividness, intensity; sparkle, glitter, glittering, glow, blaze, beam, luminosity, radiance.

brilliant ● adjective **1** *a brilliant student* GIFTED, talented, able, adept, skilful; bright, intelligent, clever, smart, astute, intellectual; elite, superior, first-class, first-rate, excellent; *informal* brainy. **2** *his brilliant career* SUPERB, glorious, illustrious, impressive, remarkable, exceptional. **3** *(Brit. informal) we had a brilliant time* EXCELLENT, marvellous, superb, very good, first-rate, first-class, wonderful, splendid; *informal* great, terrific, tremendous, fantastic, sensational, fabulous, fab, ace, cool, awesome, magic, wicked; *Brit. informal* smashing, brill; *Austral./NZ informal* bonzer. **4** *a shaft of brilliant light* BRIGHT, shining, blazing, dazzling, vivid, intense, gleaming, glaring, luminous, radiant; *poetic/literary* irradiant, coruscating. **5** *brilliant green* VIVID, intense, bright, bold, dazzling.
– OPPOSITES stupid, bad, dark.

brim ● noun **1** *the brim of his hat* peak, visor, shield, shade. **2** *the cup was filled to its brim* RIM, lip, brink, edge.
● verb **1** *the pan was brimming with water* BE FULL (UP), be filled to the top; overflow, run over. **2** *her eyes were brimming with tears* FILL, fill up; overflow.

brimful ● adjective FULL (UP), brimming, filled/full to the brim, filled to capacity, overfull, running over; *informal* chock-full.
– OPPOSITES empty.

more confident. **bring round 1** restore (someone) to consciousness. **2** persuade (someone) to adopt one's own point of view. **bring to 1** restore (someone) to consciousness. **2** cause (a boat) to stop, especially by turning into the wind. **bring to bear** exert (influence or pressure). **bring to pass** chiefly literary cause (something) to happen. **bring up 1** look after (a child) until it is an adult. **2** raise (a matter) for discussion. **3** (of a ship) come to a stop.
– DERIVATIVES **bringer** noun.
– ORIGIN Old English.

bring and buy sale ● noun Brit. a charity sale at which people donate things to sell.

brink ● noun **1** the extreme edge of land before a steep slope or a body of water. **2** the threshold of a state or situation, typically a bad one.
– ORIGIN Scandinavian.

brinkmanship /bringkmənship/ (US also **brinksmanship**) ● noun the pursuit of a dangerous policy to the limits of safety before stopping.

briny /brīni/ ● adjective of salty water or the sea; salty. ● noun (**the briny**) Brit. informal the sea.

brio /breeō/ ● noun vigour or vivacity.
– ORIGIN Italian.

brioche /breeosh/ ● noun a small, round, sweet French roll.
– ORIGIN French, from *brier* 'split up into small pieces'.

briquette /briket/ (also **briquet**) ● noun a block of compressed coal dust or peat used as fuel.
– ORIGIN French, 'small brick'.

brisk ● adjective **1** active and energetic. **2** slightly brusque.
– DERIVATIVES **briskly** adverb **briskness** noun.
– ORIGIN probably from French *brusque* 'lively, fierce'.

brisket ● noun meat from the breast of a cow.
– ORIGIN perhaps from Old Norse, 'cartilage, gristle'.

brisling /brizling/ ● noun (pl. same or **brislings**) a sprat, especially one seasoned, smoked, and canned.
– ORIGIN Norwegian and Danish.

bristle ● noun **1** a short, stiff hair on an animal's skin or a man's face. **2** a stiff animal or artificial hair, used to make a brush. ● verb **1** (of hair or fur) stand upright away from the skin. **2** react angrily or defensively. **3** (**bristle with**) be covered with or abundant in.
– DERIVATIVES **bristly** adjective.
– ORIGIN Old English.

Bristol fashion ● adjective Brit. informal, dated in good order.
– ORIGIN originally in nautical use, referring to the prosperity brought to the English city and port of Bristol from its shipping.

bristols ● plural noun Brit. informal a woman's breasts.
– ORIGIN from rhyming slang *Bristol Cities* 'titties'.

Brit ● noun informal a British person.

Britannia /britanyə/ ● noun the personification of Britain, usually depicted as a helmeted woman with shield and trident.
– ORIGIN the Latin name for Britain.

Britannic /britannik/ ● adjective dated of Britain or the British Empire.

British ● adjective relating to Great Britain or the United Kingdom.
– DERIVATIVES **Britishness** noun.
– ORIGIN Old English, from Latin *Britto* or Celtic.

Britisher ● noun informal (especially in North America) a British person.

British thermal unit ● noun a unit of heat equal to the amount of heat needed to raise 1 lb of water at maximum density through one degree Fahrenheit.

Briton ● noun **1** a British person. **2** a native of southern Britain before and during Roman times.
– ORIGIN Old French *Breton*, from Latin *Britto* or Celtic.

brittle ● adjective **1** hard but liable to break or shatter easily. **2** hard or superficial in a way that masks nervousness or instability. ● noun a brittle sweet made from nuts and set melted sugar.
– DERIVATIVES **brittleness** noun.
– ORIGIN related to an Old English word meaning 'break up'.

brittle bone disease ● noun a disease in which the bones be-

b

Thesaurus

brindle, brindled ● adjective TAWNY, brownish, brown; DAPPLED, streaked, mottled, speckled, flecked.

bring ● verb **1** *he brought over a tray* CARRY, fetch, bear, take; convey, transport; move, haul, shift. **2** *Philip brought his bride to his mansion* ESCORT, conduct, guide, lead, usher, show, shepherd. **3** *the wind changed and brought rain* CAUSE, produce, create, generate, precipitate, lead to, give rise to, result in; stir up, whip up, promote; *poetic/literary* beget. **4** *the police contemplated bringing charges* PUT FORWARD, prefer, lay, submit, present, initiate, institute. **5** *this job brings him a regular salary* EARN, make, fetch, bring in, yield, net, gross, return, produce; command, attract.
– PHRASES **bring something about 1** *the affair that brought about her death* CAUSE, produce, give rise to, result in, lead to, occasion, bring to pass; provoke, generate, engender, precipitate; *formal* effectuate. **2** *he brought the ship about* TURN (ROUND/AROUND), reverse, change the direction of. **bring something back 1** *the smell brought back memories* REMIND ONE OF, put one in mind of, bring/call to mind, conjure up, evoke, summon up; take one back. **2** *bring back capital punishment* REINTRODUCE, reinstate, re-establish, revive, resurrect. **bring someone down 1** *he was brought down by a clumsy challenge* TRIP, knock over/down; foul. **2** *I couldn't bear to bring her down* DEPRESS, sadden, upset, get down, dispirit, dishearten, discourage. **bring something down 1** *we will bring down the price* DECREASE, reduce, lower, cut, drop; *informal* slash. **2** *the unrest brought down the government* UNSEAT, overturn, topple, overthrow, depose, oust. **bring something forward** PROPOSE, suggest, advance, raise, table, present, move, submit, lodge. **bring someone in** INVOLVE, include, count in. **bring something in 1** *he brought in a private member's bill* INTRODUCE, launch, inaugurate, initiate, institute. **2** *the event brings in one million pounds each year.* See BRING sense 5. **bring something off** ACHIEVE, accomplish, attain, bring about, pull off, manage, realize, complete, finish; execute, perform, discharge; *formal* effectuate. **bring something on.** See BRING SOMETHING ABOUT sense 1. **bring something out 1** *they were bringing out a new magazine* LAUNCH, establish, begin, start, found, set up, instigate, inaugurate, market; publish, print, issue, produce. **2** *the shawl brings out the colour of your eyes* ACCENTUATE, highlight, emphasize, accent, set off. **bring someone round 1** *she administered artificial respiration and brought him round* WAKE UP, return to consciousness, rouse, bring to. **2** *we would have brought him round, given time* PERSUADE, convince, talk round, win over, sway, influence. **bring oneself to** *she could not bring herself to complain* FORCE ONESELF TO, make oneself, bear to, stand to. **bring someone up** REAR, raise, care for, look after, nurture, provide for. **bring something up** MENTION, allude to, touch on, raise, broach, introduce; voice, air, suggest, propose, submit, put forward, table.

brink ● noun **1** *the brink of the abyss* EDGE, verge, margin, rim, lip; border, boundary, perimeter, periphery, limit(s). **2** *two countries on the brink of war* VERGE, threshold, point, edge.

brio ● noun VIGOUR, vivacity, gusto, verve, zest, enthusiasm, vitality, dynamism, animation, spirit, energy; *informal* pep, vim, get-up-and-go.

brisk ● adjective **1** *a brisk pace* QUICK, rapid, fast, swift, speedy, hurried; energetic, lively, vigorous; *informal* nippy. **2** *the bar was doing a brisk trade* BUSY, bustling, lively, hectic; good. **3** *his tone became brisk* NO-NONSENSE, decisive, businesslike; brusque, abrupt, short, sharp, curt, blunt, terse, gruff; *informal* snappy. **4** *a brisk breeze* BRACING, fresh, crisp, invigorating, refreshing, stimulating, energizing; biting, keen, chilly, cold; *informal* nippy.
– OPPOSITES slow, quiet.

bristle ● noun **1** *the bristles on his chin* HAIR, whisker; (**bristles**) stubble, five o'clock shadow; *Zoology* seta. **2** *a hedgehog's bristles* SPINE, prickle, quill, barb.
● verb **1** *the hair on the back of his neck bristled* RISE, stand up, stand on end; *poetic/literary* horripilate. **2** *she bristled at his tone* BRIDLE, take offence, take umbrage, be affronted, be offended; get angry, be irritated. **3** *the roof bristled with antennae* ABOUND, overflow, be packed, be crowded, be jammed, be full, be covered; *informal* be thick, be jam-packed, be chock-full.

bristly ● adjective **1** *bristly little bushes* PRICKLY, spiky, thorny, scratchy, brambly. **2** *the bristly skin of his cheek* STUBBLY, hairy, fuzzy, unshaven, whiskered, whiskery; scratchy, rough, coarse, prickly; *Zoology* hispid.
– OPPOSITES smooth.

Britain ● noun THE UNITED KINGDOM, the UK, Great Britain, the British Isles; *Brit. informal* Blighty; *poetic/literary* Albion.

brittle ● adjective **1** *glass is a brittle material* BREAKABLE, fragile, delicate; splintery; *formal* frangible. **2** *a brittle laugh* HARSH, hard, sharp, grating. **3** *a brittle young woman* EDGY, nervy, anxious, un-

b

come brittle, especially osteoporosis.
broach ● verb **1** raise (a sensitive subject) for discussion. **2** pierce or open (a cask or container) to draw out liquid.
– ORIGIN Old French *brochier*, from Latin *brocchus* 'projecting'.
broad ● adjective **1** having a distance larger than usual from side to side; wide. **2** of a specified distance wide. **3** large in area or scope. **4** without detail; general: *a broad outline*. **5** (of a hint) clear and unambiguous. **6** (of a regional accent) very noticeable and strong. **7** somewhat coarse and indecent. ● noun N. Amer. informal a woman.
– PHRASES **broad daylight** full daylight; day.
– DERIVATIVES **broadly** adverb **broadness** noun.
– ORIGIN Old English.
broad bean ● noun a large flat green bean which is usually eaten without the pod.
broad-brush ● adjective lacking in detail and finesse.
broadcast ● verb (past **broadcast**; past part. **broadcast** or **broadcasted**) **1** transmit by radio or television. **2** tell to many people. **3** scatter (seeds) rather than placing in drills or rows. ● noun a radio or television programme or transmission.
– DERIVATIVES **broadcaster** noun.
Broad Church ● noun a tradition or group within the Anglican Church favouring a liberal interpretation of doctrine.
broadcloth ● noun a fine cloth of wool or cotton.
broaden ● verb make or become broader.
broad gauge ● noun a railway gauge which is wider than the standard gauge of 4 ft 8½ in (1.435 m).
broadleaved (also **broadleaf**) ● adjective (of trees or herbaceous plants) having relatively wide flat leaves, as opposed to conifers or grasses.
broadloom ● noun carpet woven in wide widths.
broad-minded ● adjective tolerant or liberal.
broadsheet ● noun **1** a large piece of paper printed with information on one side only. **2** a newspaper with a large format.
broadside ● noun **1** historical a firing of all the guns from one side of a warship. **2** the side of a ship above the water between the bow and quarter. **3** a strongly worded critical attack.
– PHRASES **broadside on** sideways on.
broadsword ● noun a sword with a wide blade, used for cutting rather than thrusting.
Brobdingnagian /brobdingnaggiən/ ● adjective gigantic.
– ORIGIN from *Brobdingnag*, a land in *Gulliver's Travels* where everything is of huge size.
brocade ● noun a rich fabric woven with a raised pattern, usually with gold or silver thread.
– DERIVATIVES **brocaded** adjective.
– ORIGIN Spanish and Portuguese *brocado*, from Italian *brocco* 'twisted thread'.
broccoli /brokkəli/ ● noun a vegetable with heads of small green or purplish flower buds.
– ORIGIN Italian, plural of *broccolo* 'cabbage sprout, head'.
brochette /broshet/ ● noun a dish of meat or fish chunks barbecued, grilled, or roasted on a skewer.
– ORIGIN French, 'little skewer'.
brochure /brōshər/ ● noun a magazine containing pictures and information about a product or service.
– ORIGIN French, 'something stitched', related to BROACH and BROOCH.
broderie anglaise /brōdəri ONGglayz/ ● noun open embroidery on fine white cotton or linen.
– ORIGIN French, 'English embroidery'.
brogue ● noun **1** a strong outdoor shoe with ornamental perforated patterns in the leather. **2** a marked accent, especially Irish or Scottish, when speaking English.
– ORIGIN originally denoting a rough shoe: from Scottish Gaelic and Irish *bróg*; sense 2 perhaps arose as an allusion to the rough footwear of Irish peasants.
broil ● verb chiefly N. Amer. **1** cook (meat or fish) by exposure to direct heat. **2** become very hot.
– ORIGIN Old French *bruler* 'to burn'.
broiler ● noun **1** a young chicken suitable for roasting, grilling, or barbecuing. **2** N. Amer. a gridiron or grill for broiling meat or fish.
broke past (and archaic past participle) of BREAK. ● adjective informal having completely run out of money.
– PHRASES **go for broke** informal risk everything in an all-out effort.
broken past participle of BREAK. ● adjective (of a language) spoken falteringly and with many mistakes, as by a foreigner.
– DERIVATIVES **brokenly** adverb **brokenness** noun.
broken-down ● adjective **1** worn out and dilapidated. **2** not working.

Thesaurus

stable, highly strung, tense, excitable, jumpy, skittish, neurotic; *informal* uptight.
– OPPOSITES flexible, resilient, soft, relaxed.
broach ● verb **1** *I broached the matter with my parents* BRING UP, raise, introduce, talk about, mention, touch on, air. **2** *he broached a barrel of beer* PIERCE, puncture, tap; OPEN, uncork; *informal* crack open.
broad ● adjective **1** *a broad flight of steps* WIDE. **2** *the leaves are two inches broad* WIDE, across, in breadth, in width. **3** *a broad expanse of prairie* EXTENSIVE, vast, immense, great, spacious, expansive, sizeable, sweeping, rolling. **4** *a broad range of opportunities* COMPREHENSIVE, inclusive, extensive, wide, all-embracing, eclectic, unlimited. **5** *this report gives a broad outline* GENERAL, non-specific, unspecific, rough, approximate, basic; loose, vague. **6** *a broad hint* OBVIOUS, unsubtle, explicit, direct, plain, clear, straightforward, bald, patent, transparent, undisguised, overt. **7** *his broad humour has been toned down* INDECENT, coarse, indelicate, ribald, risqué, racy, rude, suggestive, naughty, off colour, earthy, smutty, dirty, filthy, vulgar; *informal* blue, near the knuckle. **8** *a broad Somerset accent* PRONOUNCED, noticeable, strong, thick. **9** *he was attacked in broad daylight* FULL, complete, total; clear, bright.
– OPPOSITES narrow, limited, detailed, subtle.
broadcast ● verb **1** *the show will be broadcast worldwide* TRANSMIT, relay, air, beam, show, televise, telecast, screen. **2** *the result was broadcast far and wide* REPORT, announce, publicize, proclaim; spread, circulate, air, blazon, trumpet. **3** *don't broadcast too much seed* SCATTER, sow, disperse, sprinkle, spread, distribute. ● noun *radio and television broadcasts* PROGRAMME, show, production, transmission, telecast, screening; *informal* prog.
broaden ● verb **1** *her smile broadened* WIDEN, expand, stretch (out), draw out, spread; deepen. **2** *the government tried to broaden its political base* EXPAND, enlarge, extend, widen, swell; increase, augment, add to, amplify; develop, enrich, improve, build on.
broadly ● adverb **1** *the pattern is broadly similar for men and women* IN GENERAL, on the whole, as a rule, in the main, mainly, predominantly; loosely, roughly, approximately. **2** *he was smiling broadly now* WIDELY, openly.
broad-minded ● adjective LIBERAL, tolerant, open-minded, free-thinking, indulgent, progressive, permissive, unshockable; unprejudiced, unbiased, unbigoted.
– OPPOSITES intolerant.
broadside ● noun **1** *(historical) the gunners fired broadsides* SALVO, volley, cannonade, barrage, blast, fusillade. **2** *a broadside against the economic reforms* CRITICISM, censure, polemic, diatribe, tirade; attack, onslaught; *poetic/literary* philippic.
brochure ● noun BOOKLET, prospectus, catalogue; pamphlet, leaflet, handbill, handout; *N. Amer.* folder.
broil ● verb *(N. Amer.)* GRILL, toast, barbecue, bake; cook.
broke ● adjective *(informal)*. See PENNILESS.
broken ● adjective **1** *a broken bottle* SMASHED, shattered, fragmented, splintered, crushed, snapped; in bits, in pieces; destroyed, disintegrated; cracked, split; *informal* in smithereens. **2** *a broken arm* FRACTURED, damaged, injured. **3** *his video's broken* DAMAGED, faulty, defective, not working, malfunctioning, in disrepair, inoperative, out of order, broken-down, down; *informal* on the blink, kaput, bust, busted, conked out, acting up, done for; *Brit. informal* knackered. **4** *broken skin* CUT, ruptured, punctured, perforated. **5** *a broken marriage* FAILED, ended. **6** *broken promises* FLOUTED, violated, infringed, contravened, disregarded, ignored. **7** *he was left a broken man* DEFEATED, beaten, subdued; DEMORALIZED, dispirited, discouraged, crushed, humbled; dishonoured, ruined. **8** *a night of broken sleep* INTERRUPTED, disturbed, fitful, disrupted, discontinuous, intermittent, unsettled, troubled. **9** *he pressed on over the broken ground* UNEVEN, rough, irregular, bumpy; rutted, pitted. **10** *she spoke in broken English* HALTING, hesitating, disjointed, faltering, imperfect.
– OPPOSITES working, uninterrupted, smooth, perfect.
broken-down ● adjective **1** *a broken-down hotel* DILAPIDATED, run down, ramshackle, tumbledown, in disrepair, battered, crumbling, deteriorated, gone to rack and ruin. **2** *a broken-down car* DEFECTIVE, broken, faulty; not working, malfunctioning, inoperative, non-functioning; *informal* kaput, conked out, clapped out, done

broken-hearted • adjective overwhelmed by grief or disappointment.
– DERIVATIVES **broken-heartedness** noun.

broken home • noun a family in which the parents are divorced or separated.

broker • noun a person who buys and sells goods or assets for others. • verb arrange or negotiate (a deal or plan).
– DERIVATIVES **brokerage** noun.
– ORIGIN Old French *brocour*.

broker-dealer • noun (in the UK) a person combining the former functions of a broker and jobber on the Stock Exchange.

broking • noun Brit. the business or service of buying and selling goods or assets for others.

brolga /brolgə/ • noun a large grey Australian crane with an elaborate courtship display.
– ORIGIN from an Aboriginal word.

brolly • noun (pl. **brollies**) Brit. informal an umbrella.

bromeliad /brəmeeliad/ • noun a tropical plant of an American family (Bromeliaceae), typically with short stems with rosettes of stiff, spiny leaves.
– ORIGIN named after the Swedish botanist Olaf *Bromel* (1639–1705).

bromide • noun **1** Chemistry a compound of bromine with another element or group. **2** dated a sedative preparation containing potassium bromide. **3** a trite and unoriginal idea or remark, especially one intended to placate: *I was too hard-headed to accept their official bromides.*

bromine /brōmeen/ • noun a dark red liquid chemical element of the halogen group, with a choking irritating smell.
– ORIGIN from Greek *brōmos* 'a stink'.

bronchi plural of BRONCHUS.

bronchial /brongkiəl/ • adjective relating to the bronchi or bronchioles.

bronchiole /brongkiōl/ • noun Anatomy any of the minute branches into which a bronchus divides.
– ORIGIN Latin *bronchiolus*.

bronchitis • noun inflammation of the mucous membrane in the bronchial tubes.
– DERIVATIVES **bronchitic** adjective & noun.

bronchopneumonia /brongkōnyōōmōniə/ • noun inflammation of the lungs, arising in the bronchi or bronchioles.

bronchoscope • noun a fibre-optic cable that is passed into the windpipe in order to view the bronchi.
– DERIVATIVES **bronchoscopy** noun.

bronchus • noun (pl. **bronchi** /brongkī/) any of the major air passages of the lungs which diverge from the windpipe.
– ORIGIN Greek *bronkhos* 'windpipe'.

bronco • noun (pl. **broncos**) a wild or half-tamed horse of the western US.
– ORIGIN from Spanish, 'rough, rude'.

brontosaurus /brontəsawrəss/ • noun former term for APATOSAURUS.
– ORIGIN from Greek *brontē* 'thunder' + *sauros* 'lizard'.

bronze • noun **1** a yellowish-brown alloy of copper and tin. **2** a yellowish-brown colour. **3** a work of sculpture or other object made of bronze. • verb **1** give a bronze surface to. **2** make suntanned.
– DERIVATIVES **bronzy** adjective.
– ORIGIN Italian *bronzo*, probably from a Persian word meaning 'brass'.

Bronze Age • noun a historical period that followed the Stone Age and preceded the Iron Age, when weapons and tools were made of bronze.

bronze medal • noun a medal made of or coloured bronze, customarily awarded for third place in a race or competition.

brooch • noun an ornament fastened to clothing with a hinged pin and catch.
– ORIGIN Old French *broche* 'spit for roasting', from Latin *brocchus* 'projecting'.

brood • noun **1** a family of young animals produced at one hatching or birth. **2** informal all the children in a family. • verb **1** think deeply about an unpleasant subject. **2** (**brooding**) appearing darkly menacing. **3** (of a bird) sit on (eggs) to hatch them. • adjective (of an animal) kept to be used for breeding.
– ORIGIN Old English, related to BREED.

brooder • noun a heated house for chicks or piglets.

broody • adjective (**broodier**, **broodiest**) **1** (of a hen) inclined to incubate eggs. **2** informal (of a woman) having a strong desire to have a baby. **3** thoughtful and unhappy.
– DERIVATIVES **broodily** adverb **broodiness** noun.

brook[1] • noun a small stream.
– DERIVATIVES **brooklet** noun.
– ORIGIN Old English.

brook[2] • verb formal tolerate or allow (opposition): *she would brook no criticism.*
– ORIGIN Old English 'use, possess' (later 'digest, stomach').

broom • noun **1** a long-handled brush used for sweeping. **2** a shrub with many yellow flowers and small or few leaves.
– PHRASES **a new broom sweeps clean** proverb people newly appointed to positions of responsibility tend to make far-reaching changes.
– ORIGIN Old English, related to BRAMBLE.

broomball • noun N. Amer. a game similar to ice hockey in which players use rubber brooms or broom handles to manoeuvre a ball.

broomrape • noun a leafless parasitic plant with tubular flowers, which attaches itself to the roots of its host plant.
– ORIGIN from BROOM + Latin *rapum* 'tuber'.

broomstick • noun the handle of a broom, on which witches are said to fly.

Bros • plural noun brothers (in names of companies).

brose /brōz/ • noun chiefly Scottish a kind of porridge made with oatmeal or dried peas.
– ORIGIN Old French, related to BROTH.

broth • noun **1** soup consisting of meat or vegetable chunks cooked in stock. **2** a liquid nutrient medium for the culture of bacteria.
– ORIGIN Old English, related to BREW.

brothel • noun a house where men visit prostitutes.
– ORIGIN originally in the sense 'worthless man, prostitute': related to an Old English word meaning 'degenerate, deteriorate'.

brother • noun **1** a man or boy in relation to other children of his parents. **2** a male associate or fellow member of an organization. **3** (pl. also **brethren**) a (male) fellow Christian. **4** a member of a religious order of men: *a Benedictine brother.* **5** N. Amer. informal a black man. • exclamation used to express annoyance or surprise.
– DERIVATIVES **brotherly** adjective.
– ORIGIN Old English.

brotherhood • noun **1** the relationship between brothers. **2** a

Thesaurus

for; *Brit. informal* knackered.
– OPPOSITES smart.

broken-hearted • adjective HEARTBROKEN, grief-stricken, desolate, devastated, inconsolable, miserable, depressed, melancholy, wretched, sorrowful, sad, forlorn, heavy-hearted, woeful, doleful, downcast, woebegone, down; *informal* down in the mouth; *poetic/literary* heartsick.
– OPPOSITES overjoyed.

broker • noun *a top City broker* DEALER, broker-dealer, agent; middleman, intermediary, mediator; factor, liaison; stockbroker, arbitrageur.
• verb *an agreement was brokered by the secretariat* ARRANGE, organize, orchestrate, work out, settle, clinch, bring about; negotiate, mediate.

bronze • noun *Scotland won the bronze* BRONZE MEDAL, third prize.

bronzed • adjective TANNED, suntanned, tan, bronze, brown, reddish-brown.

brooch • noun BREASTPIN, pin, clip, badge.

brood • noun **1** *the bird flew to feed its brood* OFFSPRING, young, progeny; family, hatch, clutch; *formal* progeniture. **2** *(informal) Gill was the youngest of the brood* FAMILY, household; children, offspring, youngsters, progeny; *informal* kids.
• verb **1** *once the eggs are laid the male broods them* INCUBATE, hatch. **2** *he slumped in his armchair, brooding* WORRY, fret, agonize, mope, sulk; think, ponder, contemplate, meditate, muse, ruminate.

brook[1] • noun *a babbling brook* STREAM, streamlet, rill, brooklet, runnel, runlet, gill; *N. English* beck; *Scottish & N. English* burn; *S. English* bourn; *N. Amer. & Austral./NZ* creek.

brook[2] • verb *(formal) we brook no violence* TOLERATE, allow, stand, bear, abide, put up with, endure; accept, permit, countenance; *informal* stomach, stand for, hack; *Brit. informal* stick; *archaic* suffer.

brothel • noun WHOREHOUSE; *N. Amer.* bordello; *Brit. informal* knocking shop; *N. Amer. informal* cathouse, creepjoint; *euphemistic* massage par-

b

feeling of kinship and closeness. **3** an association or community of people.

brother-in-law ● noun (pl. **brothers-in-law**) **1** the brother of one's wife or husband. **2** the husband of one's sister or sister-in-law.

brougham /broōəm, broōm/ ● noun historical **1** a horse-drawn carriage with a roof, four wheels, and an open driver's seat in front. **2** a motor car with an open driver's seat.

– ORIGIN named after Lord *Brougham* (1778–1868), who designed the carriage.

brought past and past participle of BRING.

brouhaha /broōhaahaa/ ● noun a noisy and overexcited reaction.

– ORIGIN French.

brow ● noun **1** a person's forehead. **2** an eyebrow. **3** the summit of a hill or pass.

– DERIVATIVES **browed** adjective.

– ORIGIN Old English.

browbeat ● verb (past **browbeat**; past part. **browbeaten**) intimidate with words or looks.

brown ● adjective **1** of a colour produced by mixing red, yellow, and blue, as of dark wood or rich soil. **2** dark-skinned or suntanned. ● noun brown colour, pigment, or material. ● verb **1** make or become brown by cooking. **2** (**be browned off**) informal be irritated or depressed.

– DERIVATIVES **brownish** adjective **browny** adjective.

– ORIGIN Old English.

brown ale ● noun Brit. dark, mild beer sold in bottles.

brown bear ● noun a large bear with a coat colour ranging from cream to black.

brown belt ● noun a belt of a brown colour marking a level of proficiency below that of a black belt in judo, karate, or other martial arts.

brown coal ● noun lignite.

brown dwarf ● noun Astronomy a celestial object intermediate in size between a giant planet and a small star.

brownfield ● adjective (of an urban site) having had previous development on it. Compare with GREENFIELD.

brown goods ● plural noun television sets, audio equipment, and similar household appliances. Compare with WHITE GOODS.

Brownian motion ● noun Physics the erratic movement of microscopic particles in a fluid, as a result of collisions with the surrounding molecules.

– ORIGIN named after the Scottish botanist Robert *Brown* (1773–1858).

Brownie ● noun (pl. **Brownies**) **1** (Brit. also **Brownie Guide**) a member of the junior branch of the Guides Association. **2** (**brownie**) a small square of rich chocolate cake. **3** (**brownie**) a benevolent elf supposedly doing housework secretly.

– PHRASES **brownie point** informal, humorous a notional award given for an attempt to please.

browning ● noun Brit. darkened flour for colouring gravy.

brown-nose N. Amer. informal ● noun (also **brown-noser**) a person who acts in a grossly obsequious way. ● verb curry favour with (someone) by acting in such a way.

brownout ● noun chiefly N. Amer. a partial blackout.

brown owl ● noun another term for TAWNY OWL.

brown rice ● noun unpolished rice with only the husk of the grain removed.

brown sauce ● noun a commercially prepared relish containing vinegar and spices.

Brownshirt ● noun a member of a Nazi militia founded by Hitler in 1921 and suppressed in 1934, with brown uniforms.

brownstone ● noun N. Amer. **1** a kind of reddish-brown sandstone used for building. **2** a building faced with such sandstone.

brown sugar ● noun unrefined or partially refined sugar.

brown trout ● noun (pl. same) the common trout of European lakes and rivers, typically with dark spotted skin.

browse ● verb **1** survey goods or text in a leisurely way. **2** Computing read or survey (data files) via a network. **3** (of an animal) feed on leaves, twigs, etc. ● noun an act of browsing.

– DERIVATIVES **browsable** adjective.

– ORIGIN from Old French *brost* 'young shoot'.

browser ● noun **1** a person or animal that browses. **2** Computing a program with a graphical user interface for displaying HTML files, used to navigate the World Wide Web.

brucellosis /broōssəlōsiss/ ● noun a bacterial disease chiefly affecting cattle and causing undulant fever in humans.

– ORIGIN from *Brucella*, the name of the bacterium responsible.

bruise ● noun **1** an injury appearing as an area of discoloured skin on the body, caused by a blow rupturing underlying blood vessels. **2** a similar area of damage on a fruit, vegetable, or plant. ● verb **1** inflict a bruise on. **2** be susceptible to bruising.

– ORIGIN Old English.

bruiser ● noun informal, derogatory a tough, aggressive person.

bruit /broōt/ ● verb spread (a report or rumour) widely.

– ORIGIN Old French *bruire* 'to roar'.

brumby /brumbi/ ● noun (pl. **brumbies**) (in Australia) a wild or unbroken horse.

– ORIGIN of unknown origin.

brume ● noun literary mist or fog.

– DERIVATIVES **brumous** adjective.

– ORIGIN French, from Latin *bruma* 'winter'.

Brummie (also **Brummy**) Brit. informal ● noun (pl. **Brummies**) a person from Birmingham. ● adjective **1** Brit. relating to Birmingham. **2** (**brummy**) Austral./NZ counterfeit, showy, or cheaply made.

brunch ● noun a late morning meal eaten instead of breakfast and lunch.

Bruneian /broōniən/ ● noun a person from the sultanate of Brunei. ● adjective relating to Brunei.

brunette (US also **brunet**) ● noun a woman or girl with dark brown hair.

– ORIGIN from French *brun* 'brown'.

brunt ● noun the chief impact of something bad.

– ORIGIN of unknown origin.

bruschetta /broōskettə/ ● noun toasted Italian bread drenched

Thesaurus

lour; *Law* disorderly house; *archaic* bawdy house, house of ill fame, house of ill repute.

brother ● noun **1** *she had a younger brother informal* bro. **2** *they were brothers in crime* COLLEAGUE, associate, partner, comrade, fellow, friend; *informal* pal, chum; *Brit. informal* mate. **3** *a brother of the Order* MONK, cleric, friar, religious, monastic.

– RELATED TERMS fraternal.

brotherhood ● noun **1** *the ideals of justice and brotherhood* COMRADESHIP, fellowship, brotherliness, fraternalism, kinship; camaraderie, friendship. **2** *a masonic brotherhood* SOCIETY, fraternity, association, alliance, union, league, guild, order, body, community, club, lodge, circle.

brotherly ● adjective **1** *their brotherly rivalry* FRATERNAL, sibling. **2** *brotherly love* FRIENDLY, comradely; affectionate, amicable, kind, devoted, loyal.

brow ● noun **1** *the doctor wiped his brow* FOREHEAD, temple; *Zoology* frons. **2** *heavy black brows* EYEBROW. **3** *the brow of the hill* SUMMIT, peak, top, crest, crown, head, pinnacle, apex.

browbeat ● verb BULLY, hector, intimidate, force, coerce, compel, dragoon, bludgeon, pressure, pressurize, tyrannize, terrorize, menace; harass, harry, hound; *informal* bulldoze, railroad.

brown ● adjective **1** *brown eyes* hazel, chocolate-coloured, coffee-coloured, cocoa-coloured, nut-brown; brunette; sepia, mahogany, umber, burnt sienna; beige, buff, tan, fawn, camel, café au lait, caramel, chestnut. **2** *his skin was brown* TANNED, suntanned, browned, bronze, bronzed; dark, swarthy, dusky. **3** *brown bread* WHOLEMEAL.

● verb *the grill browns food evenly* GRILL, toast, singe, sear, crisp (up); barbecue, bake, cook.

browned off ● adjective (*informal*) FED UP, irritated, annoyed, irked, put out, peeved, disgruntled; disheartened, depressed; *informal* hacked off; *Brit. informal* brassed off, cheesed off, narked.

browse ● verb **1** *I browsed among the little shops* LOOK AROUND/ROUND, window-shop, peruse. **2** *she browsed through the newspaper* SCAN, skim, glance, look, peruse; thumb, leaf, flick; dip into. **3** *three cows were browsing in the meadow* GRAZE, feed, crop; ruminate.

● noun *this brochure is well worth a browse* SCAN, read, skim, glance, look.

bruise ● noun *a bruise across her forehead* CONTUSION, lesion, mark, injury; swelling, lump, bump, welt; *Medicine* ecchymosis.

● verb **1** *her face was badly bruised* CONTUSE, injure, mark, discolour. **2** *every one of the apples is bruised* MARK, discolour, blemish; damage, spoil. **3** *Eric's ego was bruised* UPSET, offend, insult, affront, hurt, wound, injure, crush.

brunette ● adjective BROWN-HAIRED, dark, dark-haired.

in olive oil.
– ORIGIN Italian.
brush[1] ● noun **1** an implement with a handle and a block of bristles, hair, or wire, used especially for cleaning, smoothing, or painting. **2** an act of brushing. **3** a slight and fleeting touch. **4** a brief encounter with something bad or unwelcome. **5** the bushy tail of a fox. **6** a piece of carbon or metal serving as an electrical contact with a moving part in a motor or alternator. ● verb **1** clean, smooth, or apply with a brush. **2** touch or push lightly. **3** (**brush off**) dismiss abruptly or contemptuously. **4** (**brush up on** or **brush up**) work to regain (a previously learned skill).
– ORIGIN Old French *broisse*.
brush[2] ● noun chiefly N. Amer. & Austral./NZ undergrowth, small trees, and shrubs.
– ORIGIN Old French *broce*.
brushed ● adjective **1** (of fabric) having a soft raised nap. **2** (of metal) finished with a non-reflective surface.
brushtail ● noun a tree-dwelling Australian marsupial with a pointed muzzle and a furred tail with a naked tip.
brushwood ● noun undergrowth, twigs, and small branches.
brusque /brŏosk/ ● adjective abrupt or offhand.
– DERIVATIVES **brusquely** adverb **brusqueness** noun.
– ORIGIN French, 'lively, fierce', from Italian *brusco* 'sour'.
Brussels sprout (also **Brussel sprout**) ● noun a vegetable consisting of the small compact bud of a variety of cabbage.
brut /brŏot/ ● adjective (of sparkling wine) very dry.
– ORIGIN French, 'raw, rough'.
brutal ● adjective **1** savagely violent. **2** without any attempt to disguise unpleasantness.
– DERIVATIVES **brutality** noun **brutally** adverb.
brutalism ● noun cruelty and savageness.
brutalize (also **brutalise**) ● verb **1** make brutal by frequent exposure to violence. **2** treat brutally.
– DERIVATIVES **brutalization** noun.
brute ● noun **1** a violent or savage person or animal. **2** informal a cruel or insensitive person. ● adjective **1** unreasoning and animal-like. **2** merely physical. **3** harsh or inescapable.
– DERIVATIVES **brutish** adjective.
– ORIGIN Latin *brutus* 'dull, stupid'.
bryony /brīəni/ ● noun (pl. **bryonies**) a climbing hedgerow plant with red berries.
– ORIGIN Greek *bruōnia*.
bryophyte /brīəfīt/ ● noun Botany a member of the division of plants (Bryophyta) which comprises the mosses and liverworts.
– ORIGIN from Greek *bruon* 'moss' + *phuton* 'plant'.
bryozoan ● noun Zoology a minute sedentary colonial aquatic animal found encrusting rocks or seaweed or forming stalked fronds.
– ORIGIN from Greek *bruon* 'moss' + *zōia* 'animals'.
BS ● abbreviation **1** Bachelor of Surgery. **2** British Standard(s).
BSc ● abbreviation Bachelor of Science.
BSE ● abbreviation bovine spongiform encephalopathy, a fatal disease of cattle which affects the central nervous system and is believed to be related to Creutzfeldt–Jakob disease in humans.
BSI ● abbreviation British Standards Institution.
B-side ● noun the side of a pop single regarded as the less important one.
BST ● abbreviation **1** bovine somatotrophin, especially as an additive in cattle feed. **2** British Summer Time.
BT ● abbreviation British Telecom.
B2B ● abbreviation business-to-business, referring to trade conducted via the Internet between businesses.
Btu (also **BTU**) ● abbreviation British thermal unit(s).
btw ● abbreviation by the way.
bubble ● noun **1** a thin sphere of liquid enclosing air or another gas. **2** an air- or gas-filled spherical cavity in a liquid or a solidified liquid such as glass. **3** a transparent domed cover. ● verb **1** (of a liquid) be agitated by rising bubbles of air or gas. **2** (**bubble with**) be filled with (an irrepressible positive feeling). **3** (**bubble up**) (of a feeling) intensify to the point of being expressed.
– ORIGIN partly imitative, partly an alteration of BURBLE.
bubble and squeak ● noun Brit. a dish of cooked cabbage fried with cooked potatoes.
bubble bath ● noun fragrant liquid added to bathwater to make it foam.
bubblegum ● noun **1** chewing gum that can be blown into bubbles. **2** (before another noun) chiefly N. Amer. simplistic or adolescent in style: *bubblegum pop music*.
bubble wrap ● noun (trademark in the US) protective plastic packaging in sheets containing numerous small air cushions.
bubbly ● adjective (**bubblier**, **bubbliest**) **1** containing bubbles. **2** cheerful and high-spirited. ● noun informal champagne.
bubo /byŏobō/ ● noun (pl. **buboes**) a swollen inflamed lymph node in the armpit or groin.
– DERIVATIVES **bubonic** adjective.
– ORIGIN Greek *boubōn* 'groin or swelling in the groin'.
bubonic plague ● noun a form of plague transmitted by rat fleas and characterized by the formation of buboes.
buccal /bukk'l/ ● adjective technical relating to the cheek or mouth.
– ORIGIN from Latin *bucca* 'cheek'.

b

Thesaurus

brunt ● noun (FULL) FORCE, impact, shock, burden, pressure, weight; effect, repercussions, consequences.
brush[1] ● noun **1** *a dustpan and brush* BROOM, sweeper, besom, whisk. **2** *he gave the seat a brush with his hand* CLEAN, sweep, wipe, dust. **3** *a fox's brush* TAIL. **4** *the brush of his lips against her cheek* TOUCH, stroke, skim, graze, nudge, contact; kiss. **5** *a brush with the law* ENCOUNTER, clash, confrontation, conflict, altercation, incident; *informal* run-in, to-do; *Brit. informal* spot of bother.
● verb **1** *he spent his day brushing the floors* SWEEP, clean, buff, scrub. **2** *she brushed her hair* GROOM, comb, neaten, tidy, smooth, arrange, fix, do; curry. **3** *she felt his lips brush her cheek* TOUCH, stroke, caress, skim, sweep, graze, contact; kiss. **4** *she brushed a wisp of hair away* PUSH, move, sweep, clear.
– PHRASES **brush something aside** DISREGARD, ignore, dismiss, shrug off, wave aside; overlook, pay no attention to, take no notice of, neglect, forget about, turn a blind eye to; reject, spurn; laugh off, make light of, trivialize; *informal* pooh-pooh. **brush someone off** REBUFF, dismiss, spurn, reject; slight, scorn, disdain; ignore, disregard, snub, cut, turn one's back on, give someone the cold shoulder, freeze out; jilt, cast aside, discard, throw over, drop, leave; *informal* knock back. **brush up (on)** REVISE, read up, go over, relearn, cram, study; improve, sharpen (up), polish up; hone, refine, perfect; *informal* bone up; *Brit. informal* swot up, gen up.
brush[2] ● noun *an area covered in dense brush* UNDERGROWTH, underwood, scrub, brushwood, shrubs, bushes; *N. Amer.* underbrush, chaparral.
brush-off ● noun (*informal*) REJECTION, refusal, rebuff, repulse; snub, slight, cut; *informal* knock-back; *N. Amer. informal* kiss-off.
brusque ● adjective CURT, abrupt, blunt, short, sharp, terse, brisk, peremptory, gruff, bluff; offhand, discourteous, impolite, rude; *informal* snappy.
– OPPOSITES polite.
brutal ● adjective **1** *a brutal attack* SAVAGE, cruel, vicious, ferocious, barbaric, barbarous, wicked, murderous, bloodthirsty, cold-blooded, callous, heartless, merciless, sadistic; heinous, monstrous, abominable, atrocious. **2** *brutal honesty* UNSPARING, unstinting, unembellished, unvarnished, bald, naked, stark, blunt, direct, straightforward, frank, outspoken, forthright, plain-spoken; complete, total.
– OPPOSITES gentle.
brutalize ● verb **1** *the men were brutalized by life in the trenches* DESENSITIZE, dehumanize, harden, toughen, inure. **2** *they were brutalized by the police* ATTACK, assault, beat, batter; abuse.
– OPPOSITES humanize.
brute ● noun **1** *a callous brute* SAVAGE, beast, monster, animal, barbarian, fiend, ogre; sadist; thug, lout, ruffian; *informal* swine, pig. **2** *the alsatian was a vicious-looking brute* ANIMAL, beast, creature; *N. Amer. informal* critter.
● adjective *brute strength* PHYSICAL, bodily; crude, violent.
bubble ● noun *the bubbles in his mineral water* globule, bead, blister; air pocket; (**bubbles**) sparkle, fizz, effervescence, froth, head.
● verb **1** *this wine bubbled nicely on the tongue* SPARKLE, fizz, effervesce, foam, froth. **2** *the milk was bubbling above the flame* BOIL, simmer, seethe, gurgle. **3** *she was bubbling over with enthusiasm* OVERFLOW, brim over, be filled, gush.
bubbly ● adjective **1** *a glass of bubbly wine* SPARKLING, bubbling, fizzy, effervescent, gassy, aerated, carbonated; spumante, pétillant, mousseux; frothy, foamy. **2** *she was bubbly and full of life* VIVACIOUS, animated, ebullient, lively, high-spirited, zestful; sparkling, bouncy, buoyant, carefree; merry, happy, cheerful, perky, sunny, bright; *informal* upbeat, chirpy.

b

buccaneer /bukkəneer/ ● **noun 1** historical a pirate, originally one preying on ships in the Caribbean. **2** a recklessly adventurous and unscrupulous person.
– DERIVATIVES **buccaneering** adjective.
– ORIGIN originally denoting European hunters in the Caribbean: from French *boucanier*, from *boucan* 'a frame on which to cook or cure meat'.

buck[1] ● **noun 1** the male of some animals, especially deer and antelopes. **2** S. African an antelope (of either sex). **3** a vertical jump performed by a horse. **4** archaic a fashionable young man. ● **verb 1** (of a horse) perform a buck. **2** oppose or resist. **3** (**buck up**) informal make or become more cheerful.
– PHRASES **buck up one's ideas** become more serious and hard-working.
– ORIGIN Old English.

buck[2] ● **noun** N. Amer. & Austral./NZ informal a dollar.
– PHRASES **a fast buck** easily and quickly earned money.
– ORIGIN of unknown origin.

buck[3] ● **noun** an object placed in front of a poker player whose turn it is to deal.
– PHRASES **the buck stops here** informal the responsibility for something cannot be avoided. **pass the buck** informal shift responsibility to someone else.
– ORIGIN of unknown origin.

buckaroo ● **noun** N. Amer. dated a cowboy.
– ORIGIN alteration of VAQUERO.

buckboard ● **noun** N. Amer. an open horse-drawn carriage with four wheels and seating that is attached to a plank between the front and rear axles.
– ORIGIN from *buck* 'body of a cart' + BOARD.

bucket ● **noun 1** a cylindrical open container with a handle used to carry liquids. **2** (**buckets**) informal large quantities of liquid. **3** a scoop on a waterwheel, dredger, digger, etc. ● **verb** (**bucketed, bucketing**) (**bucket down**) Brit. informal rain heavily.
– DERIVATIVES **bucketful** noun.
– ORIGIN Old French *buquet* 'tub, pail'.

bucket seat ● **noun** a vehicle seat with a rounded back to fit one person.

bucket shop ● **noun** informal, derogatory **1** an unauthorized office speculating with the funds of unwitting investors. **2** Brit. a travel agency providing cheap air tickets.

buckeye ● **noun 1** an American tree or shrub related to the horse chestnut. **2** the shiny brown nut of the buckeye.

buck fever ● **noun** N. Amer. nervousness felt by novice hunters on first sighting game.

buckhorn ● **noun** horn of a deer used for knife handles and rifle sights.

buckjump Austral./NZ ● **verb** (of a horse) jump vertically with its head lowered, back arched, and legs drawn together. ● **noun** an act of buckjumping.
– DERIVATIVES **buckjumper** noun.

buckle ● **noun** a flat frame with a hinged pin, used for fastening a belt or strap. ● **verb 1** fasten with a buckle. **2** bend and give way under pressure. **3** (**buckle down**) tackle a task with determination.
– ORIGIN Latin *buccula* 'cheek strap of a helmet', from *bucca* 'cheek'; sense 2 is from French *boucler* 'to bulge'.

buckler ● **noun** historical a small round shield held by a handle or worn on the forearm.
– ORIGIN from Old French *escu bocler*, 'shield with a boss'.

Buckley's ● **noun** (in phrase **have Buckley's chance**) Austral./NZ informal have little or no chance.
– ORIGIN perhaps from William *Buckley* (died 1856), who, despite dire predictions as to his chances of survival, lived with the Aboriginals for many years.

buckram ● **noun** coarse linen or other cloth stiffened with paste, used as interfacing and in bookbinding.
– ORIGIN Old French *boquerant*.

Bucks ● **abbreviation** Buckinghamshire.

Buck's Fizz ● **noun** Brit. champagne or sparkling white wine mixed with orange juice as a cocktail.
– ORIGIN named after *Buck's Club* in London.

buckshee ● **adjective** informal, chiefly Brit. free of charge.
– ORIGIN alteration of BAKSHEESH.

buckshot ● **noun** coarse lead shot used in shotgun shells.

buckskin ● **noun 1** the skin of a male deer. **2** (**buckskins**) clothes or shoes made from buckskin. **3** thick smooth cotton or woollen fabric.

buckthorn ● **noun** a thorny shrub or small tree which bears black berries.

buck-tooth ● **noun** an upper tooth that projects over the lower lip.
– DERIVATIVES **buck-toothed** adjective.

buckwheat ● **noun** a plant producing starchy seeds used for fodder or milled into flour.
– ORIGIN Dutch *boecweite* 'beech wheat', its grains being shaped like beechmast.

bucolic /byookollik/ ● **adjective** relating to rural or pastoral life.
– ORIGIN Greek *boukolikos*, from *boukolos* 'herdsman'.

bud ● **noun 1** a knob-like growth on a plant which develops into a leaf, flower, or shoot. **2** Biology an outgrowth from an organism that separates to form a new individual asexually. ● **verb** (**budded, budding**) form a bud or buds.
– ORIGIN of unknown origin.

Buddhism /bŏŏddiz'm/ ● **noun** a religion or philosophy, founded by Siddartha Gautama (Buddha; *c.*563–*c.*460 BC), which teaches that elimination of the self is the route to enlightenment.
– DERIVATIVES **Buddhist** noun & adjective **Buddhistic** adjective.

budding ● **adjective** beginning and showing signs of promise: *their budding relationship.*

buddleia /budliə/ ● **noun** a shrub with clusters of fragrant lilac, white, or yellow flowers.
– ORIGIN named after the English botanist Adam *Buddle* (died 1715).

buddy ● **noun** (pl. **buddies**) informal, chiefly N. Amer. **1** a close friend. **2** a working companion with whom close cooperation is required.
– ORIGIN perhaps an alteration of BROTHER.

budge ● **verb 1** make or cause to make the slightest movement. **2** change or cause to change an opinion.
– ORIGIN French *bouger* 'to stir', from Latin *bullire* 'to boil'.

budgerigar ● **noun** a small Australian parakeet which is green with a yellow head in the wild.
– ORIGIN of Aboriginal origin.

budget ● **noun 1** an estimate of income and expenditure for a

Thesaurus

– OPPOSITES still, listless.
● **noun** *(informal) a bottle of bubbly* CHAMPAGNE, sparkling wine; mousseux, spumante, cava; *informal* champers, fizz.

buccaneer ● **noun** *(archaic)* PIRATE, marauder, raider, freebooter, plunderer, cut-throat, privateer.

buck ● **verb** *it takes guts to buck the system* RESIST, oppose, defy, fight, kick against.
– PHRASES **buck up** *(informal)* CHEER UP, perk up, take heart, pick up, bounce back. **buck someone up** *(informal)* CHEER UP, buoy up, ginger up, perk up, hearten, uplift, encourage, enliven, give someone a lift; *informal* pep up.

bucket ● **noun 1** *a bucket of water* PAIL, scuttle, can, tub. **2** *(informal) everyone wept buckets* FLOODS, gallons, oceans.
● **verb** *(Brit. informal)* **1** *it was bucketing down* RAIN HEAVILY, rain cats and dogs, rain hard, pour, pelt, lash, teem; *Brit.* tip. **2** *the car came bucketing out of a side road.* See SPEED verb sense 1.

buckle ● **noun** *a belt buckle* CLASP, clip, catch, hasp, fastener.
● **verb 1** *he buckled the belt round his waist* FASTEN, do up, hook, strap, secure, clasp, clip. **2** *the front axle buckled* WARP, bend, twist, curve, distort, contort, deform; bulge, arc, arch; crumple, collapse, give way.
– PHRASES **buckle down** GET (DOWN) TO WORK, set to work, get down to business; work hard, apply oneself, make an effort, be industrious, be diligent, focus; *informal* pull one's finger out; *Brit. informal* get stuck in.

bucolic ● **adjective** RUSTIC, rural, pastoral, country, countryside; *poetic/literary* Arcadian, sylvan, georgic.

bud ● **noun** *fresh buds* SPROUT, shoot; *Botany* plumule.
● **verb** *trees began to bud* SPROUT, shoot, germinate, swell; *dated* vegetate.

budding ● **adjective** PROMISING, up-and-coming, rising, in the making, aspiring, future, prospective, potential, fledgling, developing; *informal* would-be, wannabe.

budge ● **verb 1** *the horses wouldn't budge* MOVE, shift, stir, go. **2** *I couldn't budge the door* DISLODGE, shift, move, reposition. **3** *they refuse to budge on the issue* GIVE WAY, give in, yield, change one's mind, acquiesce, compromise, do a U-turn. **4** *our customers won't be budged on price alone* INFLUENCE, sway, convince, persuade, in-

set period of time. **2** the amount of money needed or available for a purpose. **3** (**Budget**) a regular estimate of national revenue and expenditure put forward by a finance minister. ● verb (**budgeted**, **budgeting**) allow or provide for in a budget. ● adjective inexpensive.
– DERIVATIVES **budgetary** adjective.
– ORIGIN originally denoting a pouch or wallet: from Old French *bougette* 'little leather bag', from Latin *bulga* 'leather bag, knapsack'; in the 18th century the Chancellor of the Exchequer, in presenting his annual statement, was said 'to open the budget'.

budgie ● noun (pl. **budgies**) informal term for BUDGERIGAR.

buff[1] ● noun **1** a yellowish-beige colour. **2** a dull yellow leather with a velvety surface. ● verb **1** polish. **2** give (leather) a velvety finish.
– PHRASES **in the buff** informal naked.
– ORIGIN originally denoting a buffalo: probably from French *buffle*, from Latin *bufalus* 'buffalo'.

buff[2] ● noun informal a person who is interested in and very knowledgeable about a particular subject.
– ORIGIN from BUFF[1], originally applied to enthusiastic fire-watchers, because of the buff uniforms worn by New York firemen.

buffalo ● noun (pl. same or **buffaloes**) **1** a heavily built wild ox with backward-curving horns. **2** the North American bison.
– ORIGIN Latin *bufalus*, from Greek *boubalos* 'antelope, wild ox'.

buffer[1] ● noun **1** (**buffers**) Brit. projecting shock-absorbing pistons at the end of a railway track or on a railway vehicle. **2** a person or thing that reduces a shock or forms a barrier between adversaries. **3** (also **buffer solution**) Chemistry a solution which resists changes in pH when acid or alkali is added to it. **4** Computing a temporary memory area or queue used when creating or editing text, or when transferring data.
– ORIGIN probably from the obsolete verb *buff* 'deaden the force of something'.

buffer[2] ● noun Brit. informal an unworldly or incompetent elderly man.
– ORIGIN probably from obsolete *buff* (see BUFFER[1]), or from dialect *buff* 'stutter, splutter'.

buffet[1] /bŏofay, buffay/ ● noun **1** a meal consisting of several dishes from which guests serve themselves. **2** a room or counter selling light meals or snacks. **3** /**buff**it/ a sideboard or cupboard for crockery.
– ORIGIN Old French *bufet* 'stool'.

buffet[2] /buffit/ ● verb (**buffeted**, **buffeting**) (especially of wind or waves) strike repeatedly and violently. ● noun dated a blow.
– ORIGIN Old French *buffeter*, from *bufe* 'a blow'.

buffoon ● noun a ridiculous but amusing person.
– DERIVATIVES **buffoonery** noun **buffoonish** adjective.

– ORIGIN French *bouffon*, from Latin *buffo* 'clown'.

bug ● noun **1** an insect of an order including aphids and many other insects. **2** informal any small insect. **3** informal a harmful micro-organism or an illness caused by a micro-organism. **4** informal an enthusiasm for something: *the sailing bug*. **5** a microphone used for secret recording. **6** an error in a computer program or system. ● verb (**bugged**, **bugging**) **1** conceal a microphone in (a room or telephone). **2** informal annoy; bother.
– ORIGIN of unknown origin.

bugaboo ● noun chiefly N. Amer. an object of fear.
– ORIGIN probably of Celtic origin.

bugbear ● noun a cause of anxiety or irritation.
– ORIGIN probably from the obsolete *bug* 'evil spirit' + BEAR[2].

bug-eyed ● adjective with bulging eyes.

bugger vulgar slang, chiefly Brit. ● noun **1** derogatory a person who commits buggery. **2** a person regarded with contempt or pity. **3** an annoying or awkward thing. ● verb **1** practise buggery with. **2** cause serious harm or trouble to. **3** (**bugger off**) go away. ● exclamation used to express annoyance.
– PHRASES **bugger about/around** act stupidly or carelessly. **bugger all** nothing.
– ORIGIN Old French *bougre* 'heretic', from Latin *Bulgarus* 'Bulgarian' (particularly one belonging to the Orthodox Church and regarded as a heretic by the Roman Catholic Church).

buggery ● noun anal intercourse.

buggy ● noun (pl. **buggies**) **1** a small motor vehicle with an open top. **2** historical a light horse-drawn vehicle for one or two people.
– ORIGIN of unknown origin.

bugle[1] ● noun a brass instrument like a small trumpet, traditionally used for military signals. ● verb sound a bugle.
– DERIVATIVES **bugler** noun.
– ORIGIN Latin *buculus* 'little ox', from *bos* 'ox': the horn of an ox was used to give signals.

bugle[2] ● noun a creeping plant with blue flowers on upright stems.
– ORIGIN Latin *bugula*.

bugloss /byōōgloss/ ● noun a bristly plant with bright blue flowers.
– ORIGIN Greek *buglōssos* 'ox-tongued'.

buhl /bōōl/ ● noun variant spelling of BOULLE.

build ● verb (past and past part. **built**) **1** construct by putting parts or materials together. **2** (often **build up**) increase in size or intensity over time. **3** (**build on**) use as a basis for further progress or development. **4** (**build in/into**) incorporate (something) as a permanent part of. ● noun **1** the proportions of a person's or animal's body. **2** the style or form of construction of something.
– DERIVATIVES **builder** noun.
– ORIGIN Old English, related to BOWER.

Thesaurus

duce, entice, tempt, lure, cajole, bring round.
– PHRASES **budge up/over** *(informal)* MOVE UP/OVER, shift up/over, make room, make space.

budget ● noun **1** *your budget for the week* FINANCIAL PLAN, forecast; accounts, statement. **2** *the defence budget* ALLOWANCE, allocation, quota; grant, award, funds, resources, capital.
● verb **1** *we have to budget £7,000 for the work* ALLOCATE, allot, allow, earmark, designate, set aside. **2** *budget your finances* SCHEDULE, plan, cost, estimate; ration.
● adjective *a budget hotel* CHEAP, inexpensive, economy, low-cost, low-price, cut-price, discount, bargain.
– OPPOSITES expensive.

buff[1] ● adjective *a plain buff envelope* BEIGE, yellowish, yellowish-brown, light brown, fawn, sandy, wheaten, biscuit, camel.
● verb *he buffed the glass* POLISH, burnish, shine, clean, rub.
– PHRASES **in the buff** *(informal)*. See NAKED sense 1.

buff[2] ● noun *(informal) a film buff* ENTHUSIAST, fan, devotee, lover, admirer; expert, aficionado, authority, pundit; *informal* freak, nut, fanatic, addict.

buffer ● noun *a buffer against market fluctuations* CUSHION, bulwark, shield, barrier, guard, safeguard.
● verb *a massage helped to buffer the strain* CUSHION, absorb, soften, lessen, diminish, moderate, allay.
– OPPOSITES intensify.

buffet[1] ● noun **1** *a sumptuous buffet* COLD TABLE, self-service meal, smorgasbord. **2** *a station buffet* CAFE, cafeteria, snack bar, canteen, restaurant. **3** *the plates are kept in the buffet* SIDEBOARD, cabinet, cupboard.

buffet[2] ● verb **1** *rough seas buffeted the coast* BATTER, pound, lash, strike, hit. **2** *he has been buffeted by bad publicity* AFFLICT, trouble, harm, burden, bother, beset, harass, torment, blight, bedevil.
● noun **1** *(dated) I rained buffets on the door* BLOW, punch, thump, box, knock, rap; *informal* whack, wallop, clout. **2** *all the buffets of this world* SHOCK, upset, setback, crisis, blow; misfortune, trouble, problem, hardship, adversity; affliction, sorrow, tribulation, tragedy, vicissitude.

buffoon ● noun *he regarded the chaplain as a buffoon* FOOL, idiot, dunce, ignoramus, simpleton, jackass; *informal* chump, blockhead, nincompoop, numbskull, dope, twit, nitwit, halfwit, clot, birdbrain, twerp.

bug ● noun **1** *bugs were crawling everywhere* INSECT, mite; *informal* creepy-crawly, beastie. **2** *(informal) a stomach bug* ILLNESS, ailment, disorder, infection, disease, sickness, complaint, upset, condition; bacterium, germ, virus; *Brit. informal* lurgy. **3** *(informal) he caught the journalism bug* OBSESSION, enthusiasm, craze, fad, mania, passion, fixation. **4** *the bug planted on his phone* LISTENING DEVICE, hidden microphone, wire, wiretap, tap. **5** *the program developed a bug* FAULT, error, defect, flaw; virus; *informal* glitch, gremlin.
● verb **1** *her conversations were bugged* RECORD, eavesdrop on, spy on, overhear; wiretap, tap, monitor. **2** *(informal) she really bugs me.* See ANNOY.

bugbear ● noun PET HATE, bête noire, bogey; bane, irritation, vexation, anathema, thorn in one's flesh/side; nightmare, horror; *informal* peeve, pain (in the neck), hang-up; *N. Amer.* bugaboo.

build ● verb **1** *a supermarket had been built* CONSTRUCT, erect, put up, assemble. **2** *they were building a snowman* MAKE, construct,

b

building ● noun **1** a structure with a roof and walls. **2** the process or trade of building houses and other structures.

building society ● noun Brit. a financial organization which pays interest on members' investments and lends capital for mortgages.

build-up ● noun **1** a gradual accumulation. **2** a period of excitement and preparation before an event.

built past and past participle of BUILD. ● adjective of a specified physical build: *a slightly built woman.*

built-in ● adjective **1** forming an integral part of a structure. **2** inherent; innate.

built-up ● adjective (of an area) densely covered by buildings.

bulb ● noun **1** a rounded underground storage organ present in some plants, consisting of a short stem surrounded by fleshy leaf bases. **2** a light bulb. **3** an expanded or rounded part at the end of something.
– ORIGIN Greek *bolbos* 'onion, bulbous root'.

bulbil ● noun Botany a small bulb-like structure which may fall to form a new plant.
– ORIGIN Latin *bulbillus* 'small bulb'.

bulbous ● adjective **1** round or bulging in shape. **2** (of a plant) growing from a bulb.

Bulgarian ● noun **1** a person from Bulgaria. **2** the Slavic language spoken in Bulgaria. ● adjective relating to Bulgaria.

bulgar wheat ● noun a cereal food made from whole wheat partially boiled then dried.
– ORIGIN Turkish *bulgur* 'bruised grain'.

bulge ● noun **1** a rounded swelling distorting a flat surface. **2** Military a piece of land projecting outwards from an otherwise regular line. **3** informal a temporary increase. ● verb **1** swell or protrude to an unnatural extent. **2** be full of and distended with.
– DERIVATIVES **bulging** adjective **bulgy** adjective.
– ORIGIN originally denoting a wallet or bag: from Old French *boulge*, from Latin *bulga* 'leather bag'.

bulimia /byoolimmiə/ (also **bulimia nervosa**) ● noun an emotional disorder characterized by bouts of overeating, typically alternating with fasting or self-induced vomiting.
– DERIVATIVES **bulimic** adjective & noun.
– ORIGIN Greek *boulimia* 'ravenous hunger', from *bous* 'ox' + *limos* 'hunger'.

bulk ● noun **1** the mass or size of something large. **2** the greater part. **3** a large mass or shape. **4** (before another noun) large in quantity: *bulk orders.* **5** roughage in food. ● verb **1** be of great size or importance. **2** treat (a product) so that its quantity appears greater than it is.
– PHRASES **in bulk** (of goods) in large quantities.
– ORIGIN probably from an Old Norse word meaning 'cargo'.

bulkhead ● noun a barrier between separate compartments inside a ship, aircraft, etc.
– ORIGIN from Old Norse, 'partition' + HEAD.

bulky ● adjective (**bulkier**, **bulkiest**) large and unwieldy.

bull[1] ● noun **1** an uncastrated male bovine animal. **2** a large male animal, e.g. a whale or elephant. **3** Brit. a bullseye. **4** Stock Exchange a person who buys shares hoping to sell them at a higher price later. Often contrasted with BEAR[2].
– PHRASES **like a bull in a china shop** behaving clumsily in a delicate situation. **take the bull by the horns** deal decisively with a difficult situation.
– ORIGIN Old Norse.

bull[2] ● noun a papal edict.
– ORIGIN Latin *bulla* 'bubble, rounded object', later 'seal or sealed document'.

bull[3] ● noun informal nonsense.
– ORIGIN of unknown origin.

bull bar ● noun a grille fitted to the front of a motor vehicle to protect against impact damage.

bulldog ● noun a breed of dog with a protruding lower jaw, a flat wrinkled face, and a broad chest.

bulldog clip ● noun Brit. trademark a sprung metal device with two flat plates, used to hold papers together.

bulldoze ● verb **1** clear or destroy with a bulldozer. **2** informal use force to deal with or coerce.
– ORIGIN from BULL[1] + *-doze*, an alteration of the noun DOSE.

bulldozer ● noun a tractor with a broad curved blade at the front for clearing ground.

bullet ● noun **1** a projectile fired from a small firearm. **2** (**the bullet**) informal dismissal from employment. **3** Printing a solid circle printed before each in a list of items.
– ORIGIN French *boulet* 'small ball', from Latin *bulla* 'bubble'.

bulletin ● noun **1** a short official statement or summary of news. **2** a regular newsletter or report.
– ORIGIN Italian *bullettino* 'little passport', from *bulla* 'seal, bull'.

bulletin board ● noun **1** N. Amer. a noticeboard. **2** Computing an

Thesaurus

form, create, fashion, model, shape. **3** *they are building a business strategy* ESTABLISH, found, set up, institute, inaugurate, initiate.
● noun *a man of slim build* PHYSIQUE, frame, body, figure, form, shape, stature, proportions; *informal* vital statistics.
– PHRASES **build something in/into** INCORPORATE IN/INTO, include in, absorb into, subsume into, assimilate into. **build on** EXPAND ON, enlarge on, develop, elaborate, flesh out, embellish, amplify; refine, improve, perfect. **build up** INCREASE, grow, mount up, intensify, escalate; strengthen. **build something up 1** *he built up a huge business* ESTABLISH, set up, found, institute, start, create; develop, expand, enlarge. **2** *he built up his stamina* BOOST, strengthen, increase, improve, augment, raise, enhance, swell; *informal* beef up. **3** *I have built up a collection of prints* ACCUMULATE, amass, collect, gather; stockpile, hoard.

builder ● noun **1** *a canal builder* DESIGNER, planner, architect, deviser, creator, maker, constructor. **2** *the builders must finish the job in time* CONSTRUCTION WORKER, bricklayer, labourer; *Brit.* ganger; *Brit. dated* navvy.

building ● noun **1** *a brick building* STRUCTURE, construction, edifice, erection, pile; property, premises, establishment. **2** *the building of power stations* CONSTRUCTION, erection, fabrication, assembly.
– RELATED TERMS tectonic.

build-up ● noun **1** *the build-up of military strength* INCREASE, growth, expansion, escalation, development, proliferation. **2** *the build-up of carbon dioxide* ACCUMULATION, accretion. **3** *the build-up for the World Cup* PUBLICITY, promotion, advertising, marketing; *informal* hype, ballyhoo.

built-in ● adjective **1** *a built-in cupboard* FITTED, integral, integrated, incorporated. **2** *built-in advantages* INHERENT, intrinsic, inbuilt; essential, implicit, basic, fundamental, deep-rooted.

bulb ● noun TUBER, corm, rhizome.

bulbous ● adjective BULGING, protuberant, round, fat, rotund; swollen, tumid, distended, bloated.

bulge ● noun **1** *a bulge in his pocket* SWELLING, bump, lump, protuberance, prominence. **2** *(informal) a bulge in the population* SURGE, upsurge, rise, increase, escalation.
● verb *his eyes were bulging* SWELL, stick out, puff out, balloon (out), fill out, belly, distend; project, protrude, stand out.

bulk ● noun **1** *the sheer bulk of the bags* SIZE, volume, dimensions, proportions, mass, scale, magnitude, immensity, vastness. **2** *the bulk of entrants were British* MAJORITY, generality, main part, major part, lion's share, preponderance; most, almost all.
– OPPOSITES minority.
● verb *some meals are bulked out with fat* EXPAND, pad out, fill out, eke out; augment, increase.
– PHRASES **bulk large** BE IMPORTANT, loom large, dominate; be significant, be influential, be of consequence, carry weight; count, matter, signify.

bulky ● adjective **1** *bulky items of refuse* LARGE, big, huge, sizeable, substantial, massive; king-size, outsize, oversized, considerable; CUMBERSOME, unmanageable, unwieldy, heavy, weighty; *informal* jumbo, whopping, hulking; *Brit. informal* ginormous. **2** *a bulky man* HEAVILY BUILT, stocky, thickset, sturdy, well built, burly, strapping, solid, heavy, hefty, meaty; stout, fat, plump, chubby, portly, rotund, round, chunky; overweight, obese, fleshy, corpulent; *informal* tubby, pudgy, roly-poly, beefy, porky, blubbery; *Brit. informal* podgy.
– OPPOSITES small, slight.

bulldoze ● verb **1** *they plan to bulldoze the park* DEMOLISH, knock down, tear down, pull down, flatten, level, raze, clear. **2** *(informal) he bulldozed his way through* FORCE, push, shove, barge, elbow, shoulder, jostle; plunge, crash, sweep, bundle. **3** *(informal) she tends to bulldoze everyone* BULLY, hector, browbeat, intimidate, steamroller, dragoon, bludgeon, domineer, pressurize, tyrannize, strong-arm; *informal* railroad, lean on, boss.

bullet ● noun ball, shot; *informal* slug; (**bullets**) lead.

bulletin ● noun **1** *a news bulletin* REPORT, dispatch, story, press release, newscast, flash; statement, announcement, message, communication, communiqué. **2** *the society's monthly bulletin* NEWS-

information storage system designed to permit any authorized user to access and add to it from a remote terminal.
bullfighting • noun the sport of baiting and killing a bull as a public spectacle.
– DERIVATIVES **bullfight** noun **bullfighter** noun.
bullfinch • noun a finch with mainly grey and black plumage, of which the male has a pink breast.
bullfrog • noun a very large frog with a deep croak.
bullheaded • adjective determined and obstinate.
bullhorn • noun chiefly N. Amer. a megaphone.
bullion • noun gold or silver in bulk before coining.
– ORIGIN Old French *bouillon*, based on Latin *bullire* 'to boil'.
bullish • adjective **1** aggressively confident and self-assertive. **2** Stock Exchange characterized or influenced by rising share prices.
– DERIVATIVES **bullishly** adverb **bullishness** noun.
bull market • noun Stock Exchange a market in which share prices are rising.
bullock • noun a castrated male bovine animal raised for beef.
– ORIGIN Old English.
bullring • noun an arena where bullfights are held.
bullrush • noun variant spelling of BULRUSH.
bullseye • noun **1** the centre of the target in sports such as archery and darts. **2** a hard peppermint-flavoured sweet.
bullshit vulgar slang • noun nonsense. • verb (**bullshitted**, **bullshitting**) talk nonsense in an attempt to deceive.
– DERIVATIVES **bullshitter** noun.
bull terrier • noun a dog that is a cross-breed of bulldog and terrier.
bully[1] • noun (pl. **bullies**) a person who deliberately intimidates or persecutes those who are weaker. • verb (**bullies**, **bullied**) intimidate.
– ORIGIN probably from Dutch *boele* 'lover'.
bully[2] • adjective informal, chiefly N. Amer. excellent.
– PHRASES **bully for you!** (or **him** etc.) often ironic an expression of admiration or approval.
– ORIGIN from BULLY[1].
bully[3] • noun (pl. **bullies**) (also **bully off**) the start of play in field hockey. • verb (**bullies**, **bullied**) start play in this way.
– ORIGIN of unknown origin.
bully[4] (also **bully beef**) • noun informal corned beef.
– ORIGIN from French *bouilli* 'boiled'.
bulrush (also **bullrush**) • noun a reed mace or similar waterside plant.
– ORIGIN probably from BULL[1] in the sense 'large, coarse'.
bulwark /bŏŏlwərk/ • noun **1** a defensive wall. **2** an extension of a ship's sides above deck level.
– ORIGIN from Low German and Dutch *bolwerk*.
bum[1] • noun Brit. informal a person's bottom.
– ORIGIN of unknown origin.
bum[2] informal • noun N. Amer. **1** a vagrant. **2** a lazy or worthless person. **3** a devotee of a particular activity: *a surf bum*. • verb (**bummed**, **bumming**) **1** get by asking or begging. **2** (**bum around**) chiefly N. Amer. pass one's time idly. • adjective bad; wrong.
– PHRASES **give the bum's rush** chiefly N. Amer. forcibly eject (someone).
– ORIGIN probably from BUMMER.
bumbag • noun Brit. informal a small pouch for valuables on a belt, worn round the hips.
bumble • verb **1** act or speak in an awkward or confused manner. **2** (of an insect) buzz or hum.
– DERIVATIVES **bumbler** noun.
– ORIGIN from BOOM[1].
bumblebee • noun a large hairy bee with a loud hum.
bumf (also **bumph**) • noun informal, chiefly Brit. **1** useless or tedious printed information. **2** dated toilet paper.
– ORIGIN abbreviation of slang *bum-fodder*, in the same sense.
bummalo /bumməlō/ • noun (pl. same) a small elongated South Asian fish, dried as food.
– ORIGIN perhaps from an Indian language.
bummer • noun informal **1** an annoying or disappointing thing. **2** N. Amer. a vagrant or loafer.
– ORIGIN perhaps from German *Bummler*, from *bummeln* 'stroll, loaf about'.
bump • noun **1** a light blow or a jolting collision. **2** a protuberance on a level surface. • verb **1** knock or run into with a jolt. **2** move with much jolting. **3** (**bump into**) meet by chance. **4** (**bump off**) informal murder. **5** (**bump up**) informal make larger or apparently larger.
– DERIVATIVES **bumpy** adjective (**bumpier**, **bumpiest**).
– ORIGIN perhaps Scandinavian.
bumper • noun **1** a protective horizontal bar across the front or back of a motor vehicle. **2** (also **bumper race**) Horse Racing a flat race for horses intended for future steeplechases. **3** archaic a large glass of an alcoholic drink. • adjective exceptionally large or successful.
bumper car • noun a dodgem.
bumph • noun variant spelling of BUMF.
bumpkin • noun an unsophisticated person from the country-side.
– ORIGIN perhaps from Dutch *boomken* 'little tree' or earlier *bommekijn* 'little barrel', denoting a dumpy person.
bumptious • adjective irritatingly self-assertive or conceited.
– DERIVATIVES **bumptiously** adverb **bumptiousness** noun.
– ORIGIN from BUMP, on the pattern of *fractious*.

b

Thesaurus

LETTER, news-sheet, proceedings; newspaper, magazine, digest, gazette, review.
bullish • adjective CONFIDENT, positive, assertive, self-assertive, assured, self-assured, bold, determined; optimistic, buoyant, sanguine; *informal* feisty, upbeat.
bully • noun *the village bully* PERSECUTOR, oppressor, tyrant, tormentor, intimidator; tough guy, bully boy, thug.
• verb **1** *the others bully him* PERSECUTE, oppress, tyrannize, browbeat, intimidate, dominate; *informal* push around/about. **2** *she was bullied into helping* COERCE, pressure, pressurize, press, push, lean on; force, strong-arm, compel; badger, goad, prod, browbeat, bludgeon, intimidate, dragoon, strong-arm; *informal* bulldoze, railroad.
bulwark • noun **1** *ancient bulwarks* WALL, rampart, fortification, parapet, stockade, palisade, barricade, embankment, earthwork. **2** *a bulwark of liberty* PROTECTOR, defender, protection, guard, defence, supporter, buttress; mainstay, bastion, stronghold.
bum[1] • noun *(Brit. informal)*. See BOTTOM noun sense 6.
bum[2] *(informal)* • noun *(N. Amer.)* **1** *the bums sleeping on the sidewalk*. See TRAMP noun sense 1. **2** *you lazy bum* IDLER, loafer, good-for-nothing, ne'er-do-well, layabout, lounger, shirker; *informal* waster, loser, scrounger.
• verb **1** *he bummed around Florida* LOAF, lounge, idle, moon, amble, wander, drift, meander, dawdle; *informal* mooch; *N. Amer. informal* lollygag. **2** *they bummed money off him* BEG, borrow; *informal* scrounge, cadge, sponge; *Brit. informal* scab; *N. Amer. informal* mooch; *Austral./NZ informal* bludge.
• adjective *a bum deal* BAD, poor, second-rate, third-rate, second-class, unsatisfactory, inadequate, unacceptable; dreadful, awful, terrible, deplorable, lamentable; *informal* crummy, rotten, pathetic, lousy, pitiful, dire, poxy; *Brit. informal* duff, rubbish.
– OPPOSITES excellent.
bumble • verb **1** *they bumbled around the house* BLUNDER, lurch, stumble, stagger, lumber, flounder, totter. **2** *the speakers bumbled* MUTTER, mumble, stumble, babble, burble, drivel, gibber.
bumbling • adjective BLUNDERING, bungling, inept, clumsy, maladroit, awkward, muddled; oafish, clodhopping, lumbering; crude; *informal* botched, ham-fisted, cack-handed.
– OPPOSITES efficient.
bump • noun **1** *I landed with a bump* JOLT, crash, smash, smack, crack, bang, thud, thump; *informal* whack, thwack, bash, wallop. **2** *I was woken by a bump* BANG, crack, boom, clang, knock, thud, thump, clunk, crash, smash; stomp, clump, clomp; *informal* whump. **3** *a bump in the road* HUMP, lump, ridge, bulge, knob, protuberance. **4** *a bump on his head* SWELLING, lump, bulge, injury, contusion; outgrowth, growth, carbuncle, protuberance; *Anatomy* bulla.
• verb **1** *cars bumped into each other* HIT, crash, smash, slam, bang, knock, run, plough; ram, collide with, strike; *N. Amer.* impact. **2** *a cart bumping along the road* BOUNCE, jolt, jerk, rattle, shake.
– PHRASES **bump into** MEET (BY CHANCE), encounter, run into/across, come across, chance on, happen on. **bump someone off** *(informal)*. See KILL verb sense 1.
bumper • adjective ABUNDANT, rich, bountiful, good, fine; large, big, huge, plentiful, profuse, copious; *informal* whopping; *poetic/literary* plenteous, bounteous.
– OPPOSITES meagre.
bumpkin • noun YOKEL, peasant, provincial, rustic, country cousin, countryman/woman; *N. Amer. informal* hayseed, hillbilly,

b

bun ● noun **1** a small cake or bread roll. **2** a hairstyle in which the hair is drawn into a tight coil at the back of the head. **3** (**buns**) N. Amer. informal a person's buttocks.
– PHRASES **have a bun in the oven** informal be pregnant.
– ORIGIN of unknown origin.

bunch ● noun **1** a number of things growing or fastened together. **2** informal a group of people. **3** informal, chiefly N. Amer. a lot. ● verb collect or form into a bunch.
– PHRASES **bunch of fives** Brit. informal a punch.
– DERIVATIVES **bunchy** adjective.
– ORIGIN of unknown origin.

bund ● noun (in India and Pakistan) an embankment or causeway.
– ORIGIN Persian.

bundle ● noun **1** a collection of things or quantity of material tied or wrapped up together. **2** a set of nerve, muscle, or other fibres running in parallel. **3** informal a large amount of money. ● verb **1** tie or roll up in or as if in a bundle. **2** (**be bundled up**) be dressed in many warm clothes. **3** informal push or carry forcibly.
– PHRASES **a bundle of fun** (or **laughs**) informal, often ironic something extremely amusing or pleasant. **go a bundle on** Brit. informal be very keen on.
– ORIGIN perhaps from Old English, 'a binding'.

bunfight ● noun Brit. informal, humorous a grand or official tea party or other function.

bung[1] ● noun a stopper for a hole in a container. ● verb **1** close with a bung. **2** (**bung up**) block up.
– ORIGIN Dutch *bonghe*.

bung[2] Brit. informal ● verb put or throw somewhere casually. ● noun a bribe.
– ORIGIN symbolic.

bung[3] ● adjective Austral./NZ informal ruined or useless.
– PHRASES **go bung** fail completely.
– ORIGIN from an extinct Aboriginal language.

bungalow ● noun a house with only one main storey.
– ORIGIN Hindi, 'belonging to Bengal'.

bungee /bunji/ ● noun (also **bungee cord** or **rope**) a long nylon-cased rubber band used for securing luggage and in the sport of bungee jumping.
– ORIGIN of unknown origin.

bungee jumping ● noun the sport of leaping from a high place, secured by a bungee around the ankles.
– DERIVATIVES **bungee jump** noun **bungee jumper** noun.

bungle ● verb **1** perform (a task) clumsily or incompetently. **2** (**bungling**) prone to making mistakes. ● noun a mistake or failure.
– DERIVATIVES **bungler** noun.
– ORIGIN of unknown origin.

bunion ● noun a painful swelling on the big toe.
– ORIGIN Old French *buignon*, from *buigne* 'bump on the head'.

bunk[1] ● noun a narrow shelf-like bed. ● verb chiefly N. Amer. sleep in a bunk or improvised bed in shared quarters.
– ORIGIN of unknown origin; perhaps related to BUNKER.

bunk[2] ● verb Brit. informal abscond from school or work.
– PHRASES **do a bunk** make a hurried departure.
– ORIGIN of unknown origin.

bunk[3] ● noun informal, dated nonsense.
– ORIGIN abbreviation of BUNKUM.

bunk bed ● noun a piece of furniture consisting of two beds, one above the other.

bunker ● noun **1** a large container for storing fuel. **2** an underground shelter for use in wartime. **3** a hollow filled with sand, used as an obstacle on a golf course. ● verb refuel (a ship).
– ORIGIN originally Scots, denoting a seat or bench.

bunkhouse ● noun a building with sleeping accommodation for workers.

bunkum (also **buncombe**) ● noun informal, dated nonsense.
– ORIGIN named after *Buncombe* County in North Carolina, mentioned in a speech made by its congressman solely to please his constituents (*c.*1820).

bunny ● noun (pl. **bunnies**) informal **1** a child's term for a rabbit. **2** (also **bunny girl**) a club hostess or waitress wearing a skimpy costume with ears and a tail.
– ORIGIN dialect *bun* 'squirrel, rabbit'.

bunny-hop ● verb jump forward in a crouched position. ● noun an act of bunny-hopping.

Bunsen burner ● noun a small adjustable gas burner used in laboratories.
– ORIGIN named after the German chemist Robert *Bunsen* (1811–99).

bunting[1] ● noun a seed-eating songbird of a large group typically with brown streaked plumage and a boldly marked head.
– ORIGIN of unknown origin.

bunting[2] ● noun flags and streamers used as festive decorations.
– ORIGIN of unknown origin.

bunyip /bunyip/ ● noun Austral. **1** a mythical monster said to inhabit inland waterways. **2** an impostor or pretender.
– ORIGIN from an Aboriginal word.

buoy /boy/ ● noun an anchored float serving as a navigation mark or for mooring. ● verb **1** keep afloat. **2** (often **be buoyed up**) cause to become or remain cheerful and confident. **3** cause (a price) to rise to or remain high.
– ORIGIN probably from Dutch *boye*, *boeie*; the verb is from Spanish *boyar* 'to float'.

buoyant ● adjective **1** able to keep afloat. **2** cheerful and optimistic. **3** (of an economy or market) engaged in much activity.
– DERIVATIVES **buoyancy** noun **buoyantly** adverb.

Thesaurus

hick; *Austral. informal* bushy; *Irish informal* culchie.

bumptious ● adjective SELF-IMPORTANT, conceited, arrogant, self-assertive, pushy, swollen-headed, pompous, overbearing, cocky, swaggering; proud, haughty, overweening, egotistical; *informal* snooty, uppity.
– OPPOSITES modest.

bumpy ● adjective **1** *a bumpy road* UNEVEN, rough, rutted, pitted, potholed, holey; lumpy, rocky. **2** *a bumpy ride* BOUNCY, rough, uncomfortable, jolting, lurching, jerky, jarring, bone-shaking. **3** *a bumpy start* INCONSISTENT, variable, irregular, fluctuating, intermittent, erratic, patchy; rocky, unsettled, unstable, turbulent, chaotic, full of ups and downs.
– OPPOSITES smooth.

bunch ● noun **1** *a bunch of flowers* BOUQUET, posy, nosegay, tussie-mussie, spray, corsage; wreath, garland. **2** *a bunch of keys* CLUSTER, clump, knot; group. **3** *(informal) a great bunch of people* GROUP, set, circle, company, collection, bevy, band; *informal* gang, crowd, load. **4** *(N. Amer. informal) a whole bunch of things.* See LOT pronoun.
● verb **1** *he bunched the reins in his hand* BUNDLE, clump, cluster, group, gather; pack. **2** *his trousers bunched around his ankles* GATHER, ruffle, pucker, fold, pleat. **3** *the runners bunched up behind him* CLUSTER, huddle, gather, congregate, collect, amass, group, crowd.

bundle ● noun *a bundle of clothes* BUNCH, roll, clump, wad, parcel, sheaf, bale, bolt; pile, stack, heap, mass; *informal* load, wodge.
● verb **1** *she bundled up her things* TIE, pack, parcel, wrap, roll, fold, bind, truss, bale. **2** *she was bundled in furs* WRAP, envelop, clothe, cover, muffle, swathe, swaddle, shroud, drape, enfold. **3** *(informal) he was bundled into a van* HUSTLE, manhandle, frogmarch, hurry, rush; shove, push, thrust.

bung ● noun STOPPER, plug, cork, spigot, spile, seal; *N. Amer.* stopple.

bungle ● verb MISHANDLE, mismanage, mess up, spoil, ruin; *informal* botch, muff, fluff, make a hash of, foul up, screw up; *Brit. informal* make a pig's ear of, cock up; *N. Amer. informal* flub, goof up.

bungler ● noun BLUNDERER, incompetent, amateur, bumbler, clown; *informal* botcher, butterfingers; *Brit. informal* bodger; *N. Amer. informal* jackleg.

bungling ● adjective INCOMPETENT, blundering, amateurish, inept, unskilful, clumsy, awkward, bumbling; *informal* ham-fisted, cack-handed.

bunk[1] ● noun BERTH, cot, bed.

bunk[2] *(Brit. informal)* ● verb *he bunked off school* (PLAY) TRUANT FROM, skip, avoid, shirk; *Brit. informal* skive off; *N. Amer. informal* play hookey from, goof off, cut; *Austral./NZ informal* wag.
– PHRASES **do a bunk.** See ABSCOND.

bunk[3] ● noun *(informal).* See NONSENSE sense 1.

bunkum ● noun *(informal, dated).* See NONSENSE sense 1.

buoy ● noun *a mooring buoy* FLOAT, marker, beacon.
● verb *the party was buoyed by an election victory* CHEER (UP), hearten, rally, invigorate, uplift, lift, encourage, stimulate, inspirit; *informal* pep up, perk up, buck up.
– OPPOSITES depress.

buoyancy ● noun **1** *the drum's buoyancy* ABILITY TO FLOAT, lightness, floatability. **2** *her natural buoyancy* CHEERFULNESS, happiness, light-heartedness, joy, bounce, sunniness, breeziness, jollity; liveliness, ebullience, high spirits, vivacity, vitality, verve, sparkle,

BUPA /bōōpə/ ● abbreviation British United Provident Association, a private health insurance organization.
bur ● noun see BURR.
burble ● verb **1** make a continuous murmuring noise. **2** speak unintelligibly and at length. ● noun **1** continuous murmuring noise. **2** rambling speech.
– ORIGIN imitative.
burbot /burbət/ ● noun an elongated bottom-dwelling fish that is the only freshwater member of the cod family.
– ORIGIN Old French *borbete*, probably from *borbe* 'mud, slime'.
burden ● noun **1** a heavy load. **2** a cause of hardship, worry, or grief. **3** the main responsibility for a task. **4** the main theme of a speech, book, or argument. **5** a ship's carrying capacity. ● verb **1** load heavily. **2** cause worry, hardship, or grief.
– PHRASES **burden of proof** the obligation to prove an assertion.
– ORIGIN Old English.
burdensome ● adjective onerous or troublesome.
burdock ● noun a herbaceous plant of the daisy family, with large leaves and prickly flowers.
– ORIGIN from BUR + DOCK³.
bureau /byoorō/ ● noun (pl. **bureaux** or **bureaus**) **1** Brit. a writing desk with drawers and an angled top opening downwards to form a writing surface. **2** N. Amer. a chest of drawers. **3** an office for transacting particular business: *a news bureau*. **4** a government department.
– ORIGIN French, originally in the sense 'baize' (used to cover writing desks), from Old French *burel*, probably from *bure* 'dark brown'.
bureaucracy /byoorokrəsi/ ● noun (pl. **bureaucracies**) **1** a system of government in which most decisions are taken by state officials rather than by elected representatives. **2** excessively complicated administrative procedure.
– DERIVATIVES **bureaucratization** (also **bureaucratisation**) noun **bureaucratize** (also **bureaucratise**) verb.
bureaucrat ● noun an official perceived as being overly concerned with procedural correctness.
– DERIVATIVES **bureaucratic** adjective.
bureau de change /byoorō də shonzh/ ● noun (pl. **bureaux de change** pronunc. same) a place where one can exchange foreign money.
– ORIGIN French, 'office of exchange'.
burette /byooret/ (US also **buret**) ● noun a graduated glass tube with a tap at one end, for delivering known volumes of a liquid.
– ORIGIN French, from *buire* 'jug'.
burgeon /burjən/ ● verb grow or increase rapidly.
– ORIGIN Old French *bourgeonner* 'put out buds', from Latin *burra* 'wool'.
burger ● noun a hamburger.
burgess ● noun **1** Brit. archaic a citizen of a town or borough. **2** Brit. historical a Member of Parliament for a borough, corporate town, or university. **3** (in the US and historically in the UK) a magistrate or member of the governing body of a town.
– ORIGIN Old French *burgeis*, from Latin *burgus* 'castle, fortified town'.
burgh /burrə/ ● noun archaic or Scottish a borough or chartered town.
– ORIGIN Scots form of BOROUGH.
burgher /burgər/ ● noun archaic a citizen of a town or city.
burglar ● noun a person who commits burglary.
– ORIGIN from Old French *burgier* 'pillage'.
burglarize (also **burglarise**) ● verb North American term for BURGLE.
burglary ● noun (pl. **burglaries**) illegal entry into a building with intent to commit a crime such as theft.
burgle ● verb commit burglary in (a building).
burgundy ● noun (pl. **burgundiies**) **1** a red wine from Burgundy, a region of east central France. **2** a deep red colour.
burial ● noun **1** the burying of a dead body. **2** Archaeology a grave or the remains found in it.
– ORIGIN Old English.
burin /byoorin/ ● noun **1** a steel tool used for engraving. **2** Archaeology a flint tool with a chisel point.
– ORIGIN French.
Burkinan /burkeenən/ ● noun a person from Burkina Faso, a country in western Africa. ● adjective relating to Burkina Faso or Burkinans.
burl ● noun **1** a lump in wool or cloth. **2** N. Amer. a rounded knotty growth on a tree.
– ORIGIN Old French *bourle* 'tuft of wool', from Latin *burra* 'wool'.
burlap /burlap/ ● noun coarse canvas woven from jute or hemp, used for sacking.
– ORIGIN of unknown origin.
burlesque ● noun **1** a comically exaggerated imitation, especially in a literary or dramatic work. **2** N. Amer. a variety show, typically including striptease. ● verb (**burlesques**, **burlesqued**, **burlesquing**) parody.
– ORIGIN French, from Italian *burla* 'mockery'.
burly ● adjective (**burlier**, **burliest**) (of a person) large and strong.
– DERIVATIVES **burliness** noun.
– ORIGIN probably from an Old English word meaning 'stately, fit for the bower'.
Burman ● noun (pl. **Burmans**) & adjective another term for

Thesaurus

zest; optimism; *informal* pep. **3** *the buoyancy of the market* VIGOUR, strength, resilience, growth, improvement, expansion.
buoyant ● adjective **1** *a buoyant substance* ABLE TO FLOAT, floating, floatable. **2** *a buoyant mood* CHEERFUL, cheery, happy, light-hearted, carefree, bright, merry, joyful, bubbly, bouncy, sunny, jolly; lively, jaunty, high-spirited, perky; optimistic, confident, positive; *informal* peppy, upbeat. **3** *sales were buoyant* BOOMING, strong, vigorous, thriving; improving, expanding, mushrooming, snowballing.
burble ● verb **1** *the exhaust was burbling* GURGLE, bubble, murmur, purr, whirr, drone, hum, rumble. **2** *he burbled on* PRATTLE, blather, blether, babble, gabble, prate, drivel, rattle, ramble, maunder, go on, run on; *informal* jabber, blabber, yatter, gab; *Brit. informal* rabbit, witter, waffle, chunter; *N. Amer. informal* run off at the mouth.
burden ● noun **1** *they shouldered their burdens* LOAD, cargo, weight; pack, bundle. **2** *a financial burden* RESPONSIBILITY, onus, charge, duty, obligation, liability; trouble, care, problem, worry, difficulty, strain, encumbrance. **3** *the burden of his message* GIST, substance, drift, thrust, meaning, significance, essence, import, message.
● verb **1** *he was burdened with a heavy pack* LOAD, charge, weigh down, encumber, hamper; overload, overburden. **2** *avoid burdening them with guilt* OPPRESS, trouble, worry, harass, upset, distress; haunt, afflict, strain, stress, tax, overwhelm.
burdensome ● adjective ONEROUS, oppressive, troublesome, weighty, worrisome, stressful; vexatious, irksome, trying, difficult; arduous, strenuous, hard, laborious, exhausting, tiring, taxing, demanding, punishing, gruelling.
bureau ● noun **1** *an oak bureau* DESK, writing table, secretaire, escritoire; *Brit.* davenport. **2** *a marriage bureau* AGENCY, service, office, business, company, firm. **3** *the intelligence bureau* DEPARTMENT, division, branch, section.
bureaucracy ● noun **1** *the ranks of the bureaucracy* CIVIL SERVICE, government, administration; establishment, system, powers that be; ministries, authorities. **2** *unnecessary bureaucracy* RED TAPE, rules and regulations, protocol, officialdom, paperwork.
bureaucrat ● noun OFFICIAL, administrator, civil servant, minister, functionary, mandarin; *Brit.* jack-in-office; *derogatory* apparatchik.
bureaucratic ● adjective **1** *bureaucratic structure* ADMINISTRATIVE, official, governmental, ministerial, state, civic. **2** *current practice is far too bureaucratic* RULE-BOUND, rigid, inflexible, complicated.
burgeon ● verb FLOURISH, thrive, prosper, improve; expand, escalate, swell, grow, boom, mushroom, snowball, rocket.
burglar ● noun HOUSEBREAKER, robber, cat burglar, thief, raider, looter, safe-breaker/-cracker; intruder; *N. Amer. informal* yegg; *informal, dated* cracksman.
burglary ● noun **1** *a sentence for burglary* HOUSEBREAKING, breaking and entering, theft, stealing, robbery, larceny, thievery, looting. **2** *a series of burglaries* BREAK-IN, theft, robbery, raid; *informal* smash and grab; *N. Amer. informal* heist.
burgle ● verb ROB, loot, steal from, plunder, rifle, pillage; break into; *informal* do.
burial ● noun BURYING, interment, committal, inhumation, entombment; funeral, obsequies; *formal* exequies; *archaic* sepulture.
– RELATED TERMS funerary, sepulchral.
– OPPOSITES exhumation.
burial ground ● noun CEMETERY, graveyard, churchyard, necropolis, garden of remembrance; *Scottish* kirkyard; *N. Amer.* memorial

b

BURMESE.

Burmese ● noun (pl. same) **1** a member of the largest ethnic group of Burma (now Myanmar) in SE Asia. **2** a person from Burma. **3** (also **Burmese cat**) a cat of a short-coated breed originating in Asia. ● adjective relating to Burma or the Burmese.

burn[1] ● verb (past and past part. **burned** or chiefly Brit. **burnt**) **1** (of a fire) flame or glow while consuming a fuel. **2** be or cause to be harmed or destroyed by fire. **3** use (a fuel) as a source of heat or energy. **4** (of the skin) become red and painful through exposure to the sun. **5** (**be burning with**) be entirely possessed by (a desire or emotion). **6** (**burn out**) become exhausted through overwork. **7** informal drive very fast. **8** produce (a CD) by copying from an original or master copy. ● noun an injury caused by burning.

– PHRASES **burn one's boats** (or **bridges**) do something which makes turning back impossible. **burn the candle at both ends** go to bed late and get up early. **burn a hole in one's pocket** (of money) tempt one to spend it. **burn the midnight oil** work late into the night. **burn rubber** informal drive very quickly.

– ORIGIN Old English.

burn[2] ● noun Scottish & N. English a small stream.

– ORIGIN Old English.

burned ● adjective variant spelling of BURNT.

burner ● noun **1** a part of a cooker, lamp, etc. that emits a flame. **2** an apparatus for burning something.

burning ● adjective **1** very deeply felt. **2** of urgent interest and importance.

– DERIVATIVES **burningly** adverb.

burnish ● verb polish by rubbing. ● noun the shine on a polished surface.

– DERIVATIVES **burnisher** noun.

– ORIGIN Old French *brunir* 'make brown', from *brun* 'brown'.

burnous /burnōōss/ (US also **burnoose**) ● noun a long hooded cloak worn by Arabs.

– ORIGIN Arabic, from Greek *birros* 'cloak'.

burnout ● noun **1** the reduction of a fuel or substance to nothing through use or combustion. **2** overheating of an electrical device or component. **3** physical or mental collapse.

burnt (also **burned**) past and past participle of BURN[1].

burp informal ● verb **1** belch. **2** make (a baby) belch after feeding. ● noun a belch.

– ORIGIN imitative.

burr ● noun **1** a whirring sound. **2** a rough pronunciation of the letter *r*, as in some regional accents. **3** (also **bur**) a prickly seed case or flower head that clings to clothing and animal fur. **4** (also **bur**) a rough edge left on a metal object by the action of a tool. **5** (also **bur**) a small drill used in woodworking, dentistry, or surgery. ● verb **1** make a whirring sound. **2** form a rough edge on (metal).

– ORIGIN probably Scandinavian.

burrito /bəreetō/ ● noun (pl. **burritos**) a Mexican dish consisting of a tortilla rolled round a filling of minced beef or beans.

– ORIGIN Latin American Spanish, from Spanish *burro*, 'donkey'.

burro /bōōrō/ ● noun (pl. **burros**) chiefly US a small donkey used as a pack animal.

– ORIGIN Spanish.

burrow ● noun a hole or tunnel dug by a small animal as a dwelling. ● verb **1** make a burrow. **2** hide underneath or delve into something.

– DERIVATIVES **burrower** noun.

– ORIGIN variant of BOROUGH.

bursa /bursə/ ● noun (pl. **bursae** /bursee/ or **bursas**) Anatomy a fluid-filled sac or cavity, especially at a joint.

– ORIGIN Latin, 'bag, purse'.

bursar ● noun **1** chiefly Brit. a person who manages the financial affairs of a college or school. **2** Scottish a student holding a bursary.

– ORIGIN Latin *bursarius*, from *bursa* 'bag, purse'.

bursary ● noun (pl. **bursaries**) chiefly Brit. a grant, especially one awarded to a student.

bursitis /bursītiss/ ● noun Medicine inflammation of a bursa, typically in a shoulder joint.

burst ● verb (past and past part. **burst**) **1** break suddenly and violently apart. **2** be very full. **3** move or be opened suddenly and forcibly. **4** (**be bursting with**) feel (an irrepressible emotion or impulse). **5** suddenly do something as an expression of a strong feeling: *she burst out crying*. ● noun **1** an instance or the result of bursting. **2** a sudden brief outbreak of something violent or noisy. **3** a period of continuous effort.

– PHRASES **burst someone's bubble** shatter someone's illusions.

– ORIGIN Old English.

burton ● noun (in phrase **go for a burton**) Brit. informal be ruined, destroyed, or killed.

– ORIGIN originally RAF slang: perhaps referring to *Burton* ale, from Burton-upon-Trent.

Burundian /bōōrōōndiən/ ● noun a person from Burundi, a country in central Africa. ● adjective relating to Burundi.

bury ● verb (**buries**, **buried**) **1** put or hide underground. **2** place (a dead body) in the earth or a tomb. **3** cause to disappear or become unnoticeable. **4** (**bury oneself**) involve oneself deeply in something.

– PHRASES **bury one's head in the sand** ignore unpleasant realities.

– ORIGIN Old English.

bus ● noun (pl. **buses**; US also **busses**) **1** a large motor vehicle carrying customers along a fixed route. **2** Computing a distinct set of conductors within a computer system, to which pieces of equipment may be connected in parallel. ● verb (**buses** or **bus-**

Thesaurus

park; *informal* boneyard; *archaic* God's acre; *historical* potter's field.

burlesque ● noun PARODY, caricature, satire, lampoon, skit; *informal* send-up, take-off, spoof.

burly ● adjective STRAPPING, well built, sturdy, brawny, strong, muscular, muscly, thickset, big, hefty, bulky, stocky, Herculean; *informal* hunky, beefy, husky, hulking.

– OPPOSITES puny.

burn ● verb **1** *the coal was burning* BE ON FIRE, be alight, be ablaze, blaze, go up (in smoke), be in flames, be aflame; smoulder, glow. **2** *he burned the letters* SET FIRE TO, set on fire, set alight, set light to, light, ignite, touch off; incinerate; *informal* torch. **3** *I burned my dress with the iron* SCORCH, singe, sear, char, blacken, brand; scald. **4** *her face burned* BE HOT, be warm, be feverish, be on fire; blush, redden, go red, flush, colour. **5** *she was burning with curiosity* BE CONSUMED, be eaten up, be obsessed, be tormented, be beside oneself. **6** *Meredith burned to know the secret* YEARN, long, ache, desire, want, wish, hanker, crave, hunger, thirst; *informal* have a yen, yen, itch, be dying. **7** *the energy they burn up* CONSUME, use up, expend, get/go through, eat up; dissipate.

burning ● adjective **1** *burning coals* BLAZING, flaming, fiery, ignited, glowing, red-hot, smouldering; raging, roaring. **2** *burning desert sands* EXTREMELY HOT, red-hot, fiery, blistering, scorching, searing, sweltering, torrid; *informal* baking, boiling (hot), roasting, sizzling. **3** *a burning desire* INTENSE, passionate, deep-seated, profound, wholehearted, strong, ardent, fervent, urgent, fierce, eager, frantic, consuming, uncontrollable. **4** *burning issues* IMPORTANT, crucial, significant, vital, essential, pivotal; urgent, pressing, compelling, critical.

burnish ● verb POLISH (UP), shine, buff (up), rub (up).

burp (*informal*) ● verb BELCH, bring up wind; *Scottish & N. English informal* rift.
● noun BELCH; wind; *Scottish & N. English informal* rift; *formal* eructation.

burrow ● noun *a rabbits' burrow* WARREN, tunnel, hole, dugout; lair, set, den, earth.
● verb *the mouse burrows a hole* TUNNEL, dig (out), excavate, grub, mine, bore, channel; hollow out, gouge out.

burst ● verb **1** *one balloon burst* SPLIT (OPEN), rupture, break, tear. **2** *a shell burst* EXPLODE, blow up, detonate, go off. **3** *smoke burst through the hole* BREAK, erupt, surge, gush, rush, stream, flow, pour, spill; spout, spurt, jet, spew. **4** *he burst into the room* PLUNGE, charge, barge, plough, hurtle, career, rush, dash, tear. **5** *she burst into tears* BREAK OUT IN, erupt in, have a fit of.
● noun **1** *a burst in the tyre* RUPTURE, puncture, breach, split, blowout. **2** *mortar bursts* EXPLOSION, detonation, blast, eruption, bang. **3** *a burst of gunfire* VOLLEY, salvo, fusillade, barrage, discharge; hail, rain. **4** *a burst of activity* OUTBREAK, eruption, flare-up, blaze, attack, fit, rush, gale, storm, surge, upsurge, spurt; *informal* splurt.

– PHRASES **burst out 1** *'I don't care!' she burst out* EXCLAIM, blurt, cry, shout, yell; *dated* ejaculate. **2** *he burst out crying* SUDDENLY START.

bury ● verb **1** *the dead were buried* INTER, lay to rest, entomb; *informal* put six feet under, plant; *poetic/literary* inhume. **2** *she buried her face in her hands* HIDE, conceal, cover, enfold, engulf, tuck, cup, sink. **3** *the bullet buried itself in the wood* EMBED, sink, implant, submerge; drive into. **4** *he buried himself in his work* ABSORB, en-

ses, **bused** or **bussed**, **busing** or **bussing**) **1** transport or travel in a bus. **2** N. Amer. clear (dirty crockery) in a restaurant or cafeteria.
– ORIGIN shortening of OMNIBUS.
busby ● noun (pl. **busbies**) a tall fur hat with a cloth flap hanging down on the right-hand side, worn by certain regiments of hussars and artillerymen.
– ORIGIN originally denoting a bushy wig: of unknown origin.
bush[1] ● noun **1** a shrub or clump of shrubs with stems of moderate length. **2** (**the bush**) (in Australia and Africa) wild or uncultivated country. **3** vulgar slang a woman's pubic hair. ● verb spread out into a thick clump.
– ORIGIN Old French *bois* 'wood'.
bush[2] ● noun Brit. **1** a metal lining for a round hole, especially one in which an axle revolves. **2** a sleeve that protects an electric cable where it passes through a panel.
– ORIGIN Dutch *busse*.
bushbaby ● noun (pl. **bushbabies**) a small nocturnal African primate with very large eyes.
bushed ● adjective informal **1** exhausted. **2** Austral./NZ lost in the bush. **3** Canadian & Austral./NZ mad.
bushel ● noun **1** Brit. a measure of capacity equal to 8 gallons (equivalent to 36.4 litres). **2** US a measure of capacity equal to 64 US pints (equivalent to 35.2 litres).
– ORIGIN Old French *boissel*.
bushido /boosheedō/ ● noun the code of honour and morals of the Japanese samurai.
– ORIGIN from Japanese words meaning 'samurai' + 'way'.
bushing ● noun another term for BUSH[2].
Bushman ● noun **1** a member of any of several aboriginal peoples of southern Africa. **2** old-fashioned term for SAN (the languages of these people). **3** (**bushman**) a person who lives or travels in the Australian bush.
bushranger ● noun **1** US a person living far from civilisation. **2** Austral./NZ historical an outlaw living in the bush.
bush telegraph ● noun a rapid informal network by which information or gossip is spread.
bushwhack ● verb **1** N. Amer. & Austral./NZ live or travel in the bush. **2** N. Amer. & Austral./NZ work clearing scrub and felling trees. **3** N. Amer. ambush.
– DERIVATIVES **bushwhacker** noun.
bushwhacked ● adjective exhausted.
bushy[1] ● adjective (**bushier**, **bushiest**) **1** growing thickly: *a bushy beard*. **2** covered with bush or bushes.
– DERIVATIVES **bushily** adverb **bushiness** noun.
bushy[2] ● noun (pl. **bushies**) Austral./NZ informal a person who lives in the bush.
business ● noun **1** a person's regular occupation or trade. **2** work to be done or matters to be attended to. **3** a person's concern. **4** commercial activity. **5** a commercial organization. **6** informal a difficult or problematic matter. **7** (**the business**) informal an excellent person or thing. **8** actions other than dialogue in a play.
– PHRASES **in business** informal operating or able to begin operation. **in the business of** engaged in or prepared to engage in. **like nobody's business** informal extraordinarily. **mind one's own business** avoid meddling in other people's affairs.
– ORIGIN Old English, 'anxiety' (from BUSY + -NESS); the sense 'a duty', from which other senses developed, dates from Middle English.
business end ● noun informal the functional part of a tool or device.
businesslike ● adjective efficient and practical.
businessman (or **businesswoman**) ● noun a person who works in commerce, especially at executive level.
busk ● verb **1** play music in the street for voluntary donations. **2** (**busk it**) informal improvise.
– DERIVATIVES **busker** noun.
– ORIGIN from obsolete French *busquer* 'seek'.
buskin ● noun historical a calf-high or knee-high boot, as worn by ancient Athenian tragic actors.
– ORIGIN probably from Old French *bouzequin*.
busman ● noun a bus driver.
– PHRASES **a busman's holiday** leisure time spent doing the same thing that one does at work.
bust[1] ● noun **1** a woman's breasts. **2** a sculpture of a person's head, shoulders, and chest.
– ORIGIN French *buste*, from Latin *bustum* 'tomb, sepulchral monument'.
bust[2] informal ● verb (past and past part. **busted** or **bust**) **1** break, split, or burst. **2** chiefly N. Amer. strike violently. **3** chiefly N. Amer. raid, search, or arrest. **4** chiefly US demote (a soldier). ● noun **1** a period of economic difficulty or depression. **2** a police raid. ● adjective **1** damaged; broken. **2** bankrupt.
– ORIGIN variant of BURST.
bustard /bustərd/ ● noun a large swift-running bird of open country.
– ORIGIN perhaps a blend of Old French *bistarde* and *oustarde*, from Latin *avis tarda* 'slow bird'.
buster ● noun informal, chiefly N. Amer. a form of address to a man or boy.
bustier /bustiay/ ● noun a close-fitting strapless top for women.
– ORIGIN French.
bustle[1] ● verb **1** move energetically or noisily. **2** (of a place) be full of activity. ● noun excited activity and movement.
– DERIVATIVES **bustling** adjective.
– ORIGIN perhaps from obsolete *busk* 'prepare'.
bustle[2] ● noun historical a pad or frame worn under a skirt to puff it out behind.
– ORIGIN of unknown origin.
bust-up ● noun informal a serious quarrel or fight.
busty ● adjective (**bustier**, **bustiest**) informal having large breasts.

Thesaurus

gross, immerse, occupy, engage, busy, involve.
– OPPOSITES exhume.
bush ● noun **1** *a rose bush* SHRUB; (**bushes**) undergrowth, shrubbery. **2** *the bush* WILDS, wilderness; backwoods, hinterland(s); *N. Amer.* backcountry, backland(s); *Austral./NZ* outback, backblocks, booay; *N. Amer. informal* boondocks, tall timbers; *Austral./NZ informal* Woop Woop, beyond the black stump.
bushy ● adjective THICK, shaggy, fuzzy, bristly, fluffy, woolly; luxuriant; *informal* jungly.
busily ● adverb ACTIVELY, energetically, vigorously, enthusiastically; industriously, purposefully, diligently.
business ● noun **1** *she has to smile in her business* WORK, line of work, occupation, profession, career, employment, job, position; vocation, calling; field, sphere, trade, craft; *informal* racket, game; *archaic* employ. **2** *who do you do business with?* TRADE, trading, commerce, dealing, traffic, merchandising; dealings, transactions, negotiations. **3** *her own business* FIRM, company, concern, enterprise, venture, organization, operation, undertaking; office, agency, franchise, practice; *informal* outfit, set-up. **4** *none of your business* CONCERN, affair, responsibility, duty, function, obligation; problem, worry; *informal* bailiwick; *Brit. informal* pigeon, lookout. **5** *(informal) an odd business* AFFAIR, matter, thing, case, circumstance, situation, event, incident, happening, occurrence; episode.
– RELATED TERMS corporate.
businesslike ● adjective PROFESSIONAL, efficient, slick, competent, methodical, disciplined, systematic, orderly, organized, structured, practical, pragmatic.
businessman, businesswoman ● noun ENTREPRENEUR, business person, industrialist, manufacturer, tycoon, magnate, employer; dealer, trader, broker, merchant, buyer, seller, marketeer, merchandiser, vendor, tradesman, retailer, supplier.
bust[1] ● noun **1** *her large bust* CHEST, bosom; breasts, mammary glands, mammae; *informal* boobs, knockers, bubbies; *Brit. informal* bristols, charlies; *N. Amer. informal* bazooms. **2** *a bust of Caesar* SCULPTURE, carving, effigy, statue; head and shoulders.
bust[2] *(informal)* ● verb **1** *the lock has bust* BREAK, crack, snap, smash, fracture, shatter, disintegrate; split, burst. **2** *he promised to bust the mafia* OVERTHROW, destroy, topple, bring down, ruin, break, overturn, overcome, defeat, get rid of, oust, dislodge. **3** *they were busted for drugs.* See ARREST verb sense 1. **4** *(N. Amer.) my apartment got busted.* See RAID verb sense 3.
– PHRASES **go bust** FAIL, collapse, fold, go under, founder; go bankrupt, go into receivership, go into liquidation, be wound up; *informal* crash, go broke, go to the wall, go belly up, flop.
bustle ● verb **1** *people bustled about* RUSH, dash, hurry, scurry, scuttle, scamper, scramble; run, tear, charge; *informal* scoot, beetle, buzz, zoom. **2** *she bustled us into the kitchen* HUSTLE, bundle, sweep, push, whisk.
● noun *the bustle of the market* ACTIVITY, action, liveliness, hustle and bustle, excitement; tumult, hubbub, whirl; *informal* toing and froing, comings and goings.
bustling ● adjective BUSY, crowded, swarming, teeming, thronged;

b

busy • adjective (**busier**, **busiest**) **1** having a great deal to do. **2** currently occupied with an activity. **3** excessively detailed or decorated. • verb (**busies**, **busied**) (**busy oneself**) keep occupied.
– DERIVATIVES **busily** adverb **busyness** noun.
– ORIGIN Old English.
busybody • noun a meddling or prying person.
busy Lizzie • noun Brit. a plant with abundant red, pink, or white flowers.
but • conjunction **1** nevertheless. **2** on the contrary. **3** with negative or in questions other than; otherwise than. **4** with negative archaic without it being the case that. • preposition except; apart from. • adverb **1** only. **2** Austral./NZ, N. English, & Scottish informal though, however: *he was a nice bloke but.* • noun an objection.
– PHRASES **but for 1** except for. **2** if it were not for. **but then** on the other hand.
– USAGE On starting a sentence with **but**, see the note at AND.
– ORIGIN Old English, 'outside, without, except'.
butane /byōōtayn/ • noun a flammable hydrocarbon gas present in petroleum and natural gas and used as a fuel.
– ORIGIN ultimately from Latin *butyrum* 'butter'.
butch • adjective informal aggressively or ostentatiously masculine.
– ORIGIN perhaps an abbreviation of BUTCHER.
butcher • noun **1** a person who cuts up and sells meat as a trade. **2** a person who slaughters animals for food. **3** a person who kills brutally or indiscriminately. • verb **1** slaughter or cut up (an animal) for food. **2** kill (someone) brutally. **3** ruin deliberately or through incompetence.
– PHRASES **have** (or **take**) **a butcher's** Brit. informal have a look. [ORIGIN *butcher's* from *butcher's hook*, rhyming slang for a 'look'.]
– DERIVATIVES **butchery** noun.
– ORIGIN Old French *bochier*, from *boc* 'he-goat'.
butcher bird • noun a shrike, so called from its habit of impaling prey on thorns.
butler • noun the chief manservant of a house.
– ORIGIN Old French *bouteillier* 'cup-bearer', from *bouteille* 'bottle'.
butt[1] • verb **1** hit with the head or horns. **2** (**butt in**) interrupt or intrude on a conversation or activity. **3** (**butt out**) N. Amer. informal stop interfering. • noun a rough push with the head.
– ORIGIN Old French *boter*.
butt[2] • noun **1** an object of criticism or ridicule. **2** a target or range in archery or shooting. **3** a position taken up by a person shooting grouse.
– ORIGIN Old French *but*.
butt[3] • noun **1** the thicker end of a tool or a weapon. **2** the square end of a plank or plate meeting the end or side of another. **3** the stub of a cigar or a cigarette. **4** N. Amer. informal a person's bottom. • verb **1** meet end to end. **2** join (pieces of timber) with the ends or sides flat against each other.
– ORIGIN from Dutch *bot* 'stumpy', related to BUTTOCK.
butt[4] • noun a cask used for wine, ale, or water.
– ORIGIN Latin *buttis*.
butte /byōōt/ • noun N. Amer. & technical an isolated hill with steep sides and a flat top.
– ORIGIN French, 'mound'.
butter • noun a pale yellow fatty substance made by churning cream and used as a spread or in cooking. • verb **1** spread with butter. **2** (**butter up**) informal flatter (someone).
– PHRASES **look as if butter wouldn't melt in one's mouth** informal appear innocent while being the opposite.
– ORIGIN Latin *butyrum*, from Greek *bouturon*.
butter bean • noun a lima bean of a variety with large flat white seeds.
buttercream • noun a mixture of butter and icing sugar used as a filling or topping for a cake.
buttercup • noun a plant with bright yellow cup-shaped flowers, common as a garden weed.
butterfat • noun the natural fat contained in milk and dairy products.
butterfingers • noun informal a clumsy person, especially one who fails to hold a catch.
butterfly • noun **1** an insect with two pairs of large, typically colourful wings held erect when at rest, feeding on nectar and active by day. **2** a showy or frivolous person. **3** (**butterflies**) informal a fluttering and nauseous sensation felt in the stomach when one is nervous. **4** a stroke in swimming in which both arms are raised out of the water and lifted forwards together.
– ORIGIN Old English: perhaps from the cream or yellow colour of common species, or from a former belief that the insects stole butter.
butterfly bush • noun a buddleia with large spikes of

Thesaurus

buzzing, hectic, lively.
– OPPOSITES deserted.
busy • adjective **1** *they are busy raising money* OCCUPIED (IN), engaged in, involved in, employed in, working at, hard at work (on); rushed off one's feet, hard-pressed; on the job, absorbed, engrossed, immersed, preoccupied; *informal* (as) busy as a bee, on the go, hard at it; *Brit. informal* on the hop. **2** *she is busy at the moment* UNAVAILABLE, engaged, occupied; working, in a meeting, on duty; *informal* tied up. **3** *a busy day* HECTIC, active, lively, full, eventful; energetic, tiring. **4** *the town was busy* CROWDED, bustling, hectic, swarming, teeming, full, thronged. **5** *a busy design* ORNATE, overelaborate, overblown, overwrought, overdone, fussy, cluttered, overworked.
– OPPOSITES idle, free, quiet.
• verb *he busied himself with paperwork* OCCUPY, involve, engage, concern, absorb, engross, immerse, preoccupy; distract, divert.
busybody • noun MEDDLER, interferer, mischief-maker, troublemaker; gossip, scandalmonger; eavesdropper, gawker; *informal* nosy parker, snoop, snooper, rubberneck; *Brit. informal* gawper; *informal, dated* Paul Pry.
but • conjunction **1** *he stumbled but didn't fall* YET, nevertheless, nonetheless, even so, however, still, notwithstanding, despite that, in spite of that, for all that, all the same, just the same; though, although. **2** *I am clean but you aren't* WHEREAS, conversely, but then, then again, on the other hand, by/in contrast, on the contrary. **3** *one cannot but sympathize* (DO) OTHER THAN, (do) otherwise than; except.
• preposition *everyone but him* EXCEPT (FOR), apart from, other than, besides, aside from, with the exception of, bar, excepting, excluding, leaving out, save (for), saving.
• adverb *he is but a shadow of his former self* ONLY, just, simply, merely, no more than, nothing but; a mere; *N. English* nobbut.
– PHRASES **but for** EXCEPT FOR, if it were not for, were it not for, barring, notwithstanding.
butch • adjective *(informal)* MASCULINE, manly; mannish, manlike, unfeminine, unladylike; *informal* macho.
– OPPOSITES effeminate.
butcher • noun **1** *a butcher's shop* MEAT SELLER, meat trader; slaughterer; *Scottish* flesher. **2** *a Nazi butcher* MURDERER, slaughterer, killer, assassin; *N. Amer.* terminator; *poetic/literary* slayer; *dated* cut-throat, homicide.
• verb **1** *the goat was butchered* SLAUGHTER, cut up, carve up, joint. **2** *they butchered 150 people* MASSACRE, murder, slaughter, kill, destroy, exterminate, assassinate; *N. Amer.* terminate; *informal* dispose of; *poetic/literary* slay. **3** *the studio butchered the film* SPOIL, ruin, mutilate, mangle, mess up, wreck; *informal* make a hash of, screw up.
butchery • noun **1** *the butchery trade* MEAT SELLING. **2** *(Brit.) the cattle went to the butchery* ABATTOIR, slaughterhouse. **3** *(Brit.) a butchery* BUTCHER'S (SHOP), meat market, meat counter. **4** *the butchery in the war* SLAUGHTER, massacre, mass murder; *poetic/literary* slaying.
butt[1] • verb *she butted him* RAM, headbutt, bunt; bump, buffet, push, shove; *N. English* tup.
– PHRASES **butt in** INTERRUPT, break in, cut in, chime in, interject, intervene, interfere; *informal* poke one's nose in, put one's oar in; *Brit. informal* chip in.
butt[2] • noun *the butt of a joke* TARGET, victim, object, subject; laughing stock.
butt[3] • noun **1** *the butt of a gun* STOCK, end, handle, hilt, haft, helve. **2** *a cigarette butt* STUB, end, tail end, stump, remnant; *informal* fag end, dog end. **3** *(N. Amer. informal) sitting on his butt.* See BOTTOM noun sense 6.
• verb *the shop butts up against the house* ADJOIN, abut, be next to, be adjacent to, border (on), neighbour, be connected to; join, touch.
butt[4] • noun *a brandy butt* BARREL, cask, keg, vat, tun; tub, bin, drum, canister.
butter • verb
– PHRASES **butter someone up** *(informal)* FLATTER, court, wheedle, persuade, blarney, coax, get round, prevail on; be obsequious towards, be sycophantic towards, toady to, fawn on, make up to,

purplish-lilac or white flowers.

butterfly effect • noun (in chaos theory) the phenomenon whereby a tiny localized change in a complex system can have large effects elsewhere.
– ORIGIN from the notion that a butterfly fluttering in Rio de Janeiro could change the weather in Chicago.

butterfly nut • noun another term for WING NUT.

butter icing • noun another term for BUTTERCREAM.

buttermilk • noun the slightly sour liquid left after butter has been churned.

butter muslin • noun Brit. loosely woven cotton cloth, formerly used for wrapping butter.

butterscotch • noun a brittle yellow-brown sweet made with butter and brown sugar.

buttery[1] • adjective containing, tasting like, or covered with butter.

buttery[2] • noun (pl. **butteries**) Brit. a room in a college where food is kept and sold to students.
– ORIGIN Old French *boterie* 'butt-store'.

buttie • noun (pl. **butties**) variant spelling of BUTTY.

buttock • noun either of the two round fleshy parts of the human body that form the bottom.
– ORIGIN Old English, probably related to BUTT[3].

button • noun **1** a small disc or knob sewn on to a garment to fasten it by being pushed through a buttonhole. **2** a knob on a piece of electrical or electronic equipment which is pressed to operate it. **3** chiefly N. Amer. a decorative badge pinned to clothing. **4** Fencing a knob fitted to the point of a foil to make it harmless. • verb **1** fasten or be fastened with buttons. **2** (**button up**) informal complete satisfactorily.
– PHRASES **button one's lip** informal stop or refrain from talking. **buttoned-up** informal formal and inhibited in manner. **on the button** informal, chiefly N. Amer. precisely.
– DERIVATIVES **buttoned** adjective.
– ORIGIN Old French *bouton*.

button-down • adjective (of a shirt collar) having points which are buttoned to the garment.

buttonhole • noun **1** a slit made in a garment to receive a button for fastening. **2** Brit. a flower or spray worn in a lapel buttonhole. • verb informal accost and detain (someone) in conversation.

button mushroom • noun a young unopened mushroom.

button-through • adjective Brit. (of clothing) fastened with buttons from top to bottom.

buttress /butriss/ • noun **1** a projecting support built against a wall. **2** a projecting portion of a hill or mountain. • verb **1** support with buttresses. **2** support or strengthen.
– ORIGIN from Old French *ars bouterez* 'thrusting arch'.

butty (also **buttie**) • noun (pl. **butties**) informal, chiefly N. English a sandwich.
– ORIGIN from BUTTER.

butyl /byoōtil/ • noun Chemistry the radical $-C_4H_9$, derived from butane.

buxom /buksəm/ • adjective (of a woman) attractively plump and large-breasted.
– ORIGIN originally in the sense 'compliant', later 'lively and good-tempered': from Old English, 'to bend'.

buy • verb (**buys**, **buying**; past and past part. **bought**) **1** obtain in exchange for payment. **2** get (something) by sacrifice or great effort. **3** informal accept the truth of. • noun informal a purchase.
– PHRASES **buy out 1** pay (someone) to give up an interest or share in something. **2** (**buy oneself out**) obtain one's release from the armed services by payment. **buy time** delay an event temporarily so as to have longer to improve one's own position. **have bought it** informal be killed.
– ORIGIN Old English.

buyer • noun **1** a person who buys. **2** a person employed to select and purchase stock for a retail or manufacturing business.

buyer's market • noun an economic situation in which goods or shares are plentiful and buyers can keep prices down.

buyout • noun the purchase of a controlling share in a company, especially by its own managers.

buzz • noun **1** a low, continuous humming or murmuring sound. **2** the sound of a buzzer or telephone. **3** an atmosphere of excitement and activity. **4** informal a thrill. **5** informal a rumour. • verb **1** make a humming sound. **2** signal with a buzzer. **3** move quickly. **4** (**buzz off**) informal go away. **5** have an air of excitement or purposeful activity. **6** informal (of an aircraft) fly very close to (something) at high speed.
– ORIGIN imitative.

buzzard /buzzərd/ • noun **1** a large bird of prey typically seen soaring in wide circles. **2** N. Amer. a vulture.
– ORIGIN Old French *busard*, from Latin *buteo* 'falcon'.

buzz cut • noun a very short haircut in which the hair is clipped close to the head with a razor.

buzzer • noun an electrical device that makes a buzzing noise to attract attention.

buzz saw • noun North American term for CIRCULAR SAW.

buzzword • noun informal a technical word or phrase that has become fashionable.

buzzy • adjective informal (of a place or atmosphere) lively and exciting.

BVM • abbreviation Blessed Virgin Mary.

bwana /bwaanə/ • noun (in East Africa) a form of address for a boss or master.
– ORIGIN Swahili.

by • preposition **1** through the agency or means of. **2** indicating a quantity or amount, or the size of a margin. **3** expressing multiplication, especially in dimensions. **4** indicating the end of a time period. **5** near to; beside. **6** past and beyond. **7** during. **8** according to. • adverb so as to go past. • noun (pl. **byes**) variant spelling of BYE[1].
– PHRASES **by and by** before long. **by the by** (or **bye**) incidentally. **by and large** on the whole. [ORIGIN originally in nautical use, describing the handling of a ship both to the wind and off it.] **by oneself 1** alone. **2** unaided.
– ORIGIN Old English.

by- (also **bye-**) • prefix subordinate; incidental; secondary: *by-election*.

by-blow • noun Brit. dated a man's illegitimate child.

Thesaurus

play up to, ingratiate oneself with, rub up the right way, curry favour with; *informal* suck up to, be all over, keep someone sweet, sweet-talk, soft-soap.

butterfly • noun LEPIDOPTERAN.

buttocks • plural noun CHEEKS; rear (end), rump, backside, seat; *Brit.* bottom; *informal* behind, BTM, sit-upon, derrière; *Brit. informal* bum, botty, jacksie; *N. Amer. informal* butt, fanny, tush, tail, buns, booty, heinie; *humorous* fundament, posterior, stern; *Anatomy* nates.

button • noun **1** *shirt buttons* FASTENER, stud, toggle; hook, catch, clasp. **2** *press the button* SWITCH, knob, control; lever, handle.

buttonhole • verb *(informal)*. See ACCOST.

buttress • noun **1** *stone buttresses* PROP, support, abutment, shore, pier, reinforcement, stanchion. **2** *a buttress against social collapse* SAFEGUARD, defence, protection, guard; support, prop; bulwark.
• verb *authority was buttressed by religion* STRENGTHEN, reinforce, fortify, support, bolster, shore up, underpin, cement, uphold, defend, back up.

buxom • adjective LARGE-BREASTED, big-breasted, big-bosomed, bosomy; shapely, ample, plump, rounded, full-figured, voluptuous, curvaceous, Rubenesque; *informal* busty, chesty, well endowed, curvy.

buy • verb **1** *they bought a new house* PURCHASE, acquire, obtain, get, pick up, snap up; take, procure, pay for; invest in; *informal* get hold of, score. **2** *he could not be bought* BRIBE, buy off, suborn, corrupt; *informal* grease someone's palm, give a backhander to, get at, fix, square; *Brit. informal* nobble.
– OPPOSITES sell.
• noun *(informal) a good buy* PURCHASE, investment, acquisition, gain; deal, bargain.

buyer • noun PURCHASER, customer, consumer, shopper, investor; (**buyers**) clientele, patronage, market; *Law* vendee.

buzz • noun **1** *the buzz of the bees* HUM, humming, buzzing, murmur, drone; *Brit. informal* zizz. **2** *an insistent buzz from her control panel* WARNING SOUND, purr, ring, note, tone, beep, bleep, warble, alarm. **3** *(informal) give me a buzz.* See CALL noun sense 3. **4** *(informal) the buzz is that he's gone.* See RUMOUR. **5** *(informal) I get a real buzz out of flying* THRILL, stimulation, glow, tingle; *informal* kick; *N. Amer. informal* charge.
• verb **1** *bees buzzed* HUM, drone, bumble, murmur; *Brit. informal* zizz. **2** *the intercom buzzed* PURR, warble, sound, ring, beep, bleep. **3** *he buzzed around* BUSTLE, scurry, scuttle, hurry, rush, race, dash, tear, chase; *informal* scoot, beetle, whizz, zoom, zip. **4** *the club is buzzing with excitement* HUM, throb, vibrate, pulse, bustle.

by • preposition **1** *I broke it by forcing the lid* THROUGH, as a result of,

b

bye[1] ● noun **1** the transfer of a competitor directly to the next round of a competition because they have no opponent assigned to them. **2** Cricket a run scored from a ball that passes the batsman without being hit.
– PHRASES **by the bye** variant spelling of **by the by** (see BY).
– ORIGIN originally denoting an incidental matter; from BY.
bye[2] ● exclamation informal goodbye.
bye-bye ● exclamation informal goodbye.
– ORIGIN child's reduplication.
by-election ● noun Brit. an election held in a single constituency to fill a vacancy arising during a government's term of office.
Byelorussian /byellōrush'n/ ● adjective & noun variant spelling of BELORUSSIAN.
by-form ● noun a secondary form of a word.
bygone ● adjective belonging to an earlier time.
– PHRASES **let bygones be bygones** forget past differences and be reconciled.
by-law (also **bye-law**) ● noun **1** Brit. a regulation made by a local authority or corporation. **2** a rule made by a company or society to control the actions of its members.
– ORIGIN probably from obsolete *byrlaw* 'local law or custom', from an Old Norse word meaning 'town'.
byline ● noun **1** a line in a newspaper naming the writer of an article. **2** (also **byeline**) (in soccer) the part of the goal line to either side of the goal.
byname ● noun a nickname.
bypass ● noun **1** a road passing round a town for through traffic. **2** a secondary channel or connection to allow a flow when the main one is closed or blocked. **3** a surgical operation to make an alternative passage to aid the circulation of blood.
● verb go past or round.
byplay ● noun subsidiary action in a play or film.
by-product ● noun **1** an incidental or secondary product made in the manufacture of something else. **2** an unintended but inevitable secondary result.
byre /bīr/ ● noun Brit. a cowshed.
– ORIGIN Old English.
byroad ● noun a minor road.
Byronic /bīronnik/ ● adjective **1** characteristic of Lord Byron (1788–1824) or his poetry. **2** (of a man) alluringly dark, mysterious, and moody.
bystander ● noun a person who is present at an event or incident but does not take part.
byte /bīt/ ● noun Computing a group of binary digits (usually eight) operated on as a unit.
– ORIGIN based on BIT[4] and BITE.
byway ● noun a minor road or path.
byword ● noun **1** a notable example or embodiment of something. **2** a proverb or saying.
Byzantine /bizantīn, bī-, bizzən-, -teen/ ● adjective **1** relating to Byzantium (later called Constantinople, now Istanbul), the Byzantine Empire, or the Eastern Orthodox Church. **2** excessively complicated and detailed. **3** very devious or underhand. ● noun a citizen of Byzantium or the Byzantine Empire.

Thesaurus

because of, by dint of, by way of, via, by means of; with the help of, with the aid of, by virtue of. **2** *be there by midday* NO LATER THAN, in good time for, at, before. **3** *a house by the lake* NEXT TO, beside, alongside, by/at the side of, adjacent to, side by side with; near, close to, neighbouring, adjoining, bordering, overlooking; connected to, contiguous with, attached to. **4** *go by the building* PAST, in front of, beyond. **5** *all right by me* ACCORDING TO, with, as far as —— is concerned.
● adverb *people hurried by* PAST, on, along.
– PHRASES **by and by** EVENTUALLY, ultimately, finally, in the end, one day, some day, sooner or later, in time, in a while, in the long run, in the fullness of time, in time to come, at length, in the future, in due course. **by oneself** ALONE, on one's own, singly, separately, solitarily, unaccompanied, companionless, unattended, unescorted, solo; unaided, unassisted, without help, by one's own efforts, under one's own steam, independently, single-handed(ly), off one's own bat, on one's own initiative; informal by one's lonesome; Brit. informal on one's tod, on one's Jack Jones.
bygone ● adjective PAST, former, olden, earlier, previous, one-time, long-ago, of old, ancient, antiquated; departed, dead, extinct, defunct, out of date, outmoded; poetic/literary of yore.
– OPPOSITES present, recent.
bypass ● noun RING ROAD, detour, diversion, alternative route; Brit. relief road.
● verb **1** *bypass the farm* GO ROUND, go past, make a detour round; avoid. **2** *an attempt to bypass the problem* AVOID, evade, dodge, escape, elude, circumvent, get round, skirt, sidestep, steer clear of; informal duck. **3** *they bypassed the regulations* IGNORE, pass over, omit, neglect, go over the head of; informal short-circuit.
by-product ● noun SIDE EFFECT, consequence, entailment, corollary; ramification, repercussion, spin-off, fallout; fruits; Brit. knock-on effect.
bystander ● noun ONLOOKER, looker-on, passer-by, nonparticipant, observer, spectator, eyewitness, witness, watcher; informal gawper, rubberneck.
byword ● noun **1** *his name became a byword for luxury* PERFECT EXAMPLE, classic case, model, exemplar, embodiment, incarnation, personification, epitome, typification. **2** *reality was his byword* SLOGAN, motto, maxim, mantra, catchword, watchword, formula; middle name.

Cc

C[1] (also **c**) ● noun (pl. **Cs** or **C's**) **1** the third letter of the alphabet. **2** denoting the third item in a set. **3** Music the first note of the diatonic scale of C major. **4** the Roman numeral for 100. [ORIGIN abbreviation of Latin *centum* 'hundred'.]

C[2] ● abbreviation **1** (**C.**) Cape (chiefly on maps). **2** Celsius or centigrade. **3** (in names of sports clubs) City. **4** (©) copyright. **5** (in Britain) Conservative. **6** Physics coulomb(s). ● symbol the chemical element carbon.

c ● abbreviation **1** Cricket caught by. **2** cent(s). **3** (preceding a date or amount) circa. **4** (**c.**) century or centuries. ● symbol Physics the speed of light in a vacuum.

CA ● abbreviation California.

Ca ● symbol the chemical element calcium.

ca. ● abbreviation (preceding a date or amount) circa.

CAA ● abbreviation (in the UK) Civil Aviation Authority.

CAB ● abbreviation Citizens' Advice Bureau.

cab ● noun **1** (also **taxi cab**) a taxi. **2** the driver's compartment in a truck, bus, or train. **3** historical a horse-drawn vehicle for public hire.
– ORIGIN abbreviation of CABRIOLET.

cabal /kəbal/ ● noun a secret political clique or faction.
– ORIGIN Latin *cabala* 'Kabbalah' (its original sense in English).

Cabala ● noun variant spelling of KABBALAH.

cabaret /kabbəray/ ● noun **1** entertainment held in a nightclub or restaurant while the audience sit at tables. **2** a nightclub or restaurant where such entertainment is performed.
– ORIGIN Old French, 'wooden structure, inn'.

cabbage ● noun **1** a vegetable with thick green or purple leaves surrounding a spherical heart or head of young leaves. **2** Brit. informal, derogatory a person with a very dull or limited life. **3** Brit. informal, offensive a person who is severely handicapped or brain-damaged.
– ORIGIN Old French *caboche* 'head'.

cabbage white ● noun a white butterfly whose caterpillars are pests of cabbages and related plants.

Cabbala ● noun variant spelling of KABBALAH.

cabbalistic /kabbəlistik/ ● adjective relating to or associated with mystical interpretations or esoteric doctrine.
– ORIGIN variant of **Kabbalistic** (see KABBALAH).

cabby (also **cabbie**) ● noun (pl. **cabbies**) informal a taxi driver.

caber /kaybər/ ● noun a roughly trimmed tree trunk used in the Scottish Highland sport of tossing the caber.
– ORIGIN Scottish Gaelic *cabar* 'pole'.

Cabernet Franc /kabbərnay froN/ ● noun a variety of black wine grape grown chiefly in parts of the Loire Valley and NE Italy.
– ORIGIN French.

Cabernet Sauvignon /kabbərnay sōvinyoN/ ● noun a variety of black wine grape originally from the Bordeaux area of France.
– ORIGIN French.

cabin ● noun **1** a private room or compartment on a ship. **2** the passenger compartment in an aircraft. **3** a small wooden shelter or house.
– ORIGIN Old French *cabane*, from Latin *capanna*.

cabin boy ● noun chiefly historical a boy employed to wait on a ship's officers or passengers.

cabin class ● noun the intermediate class of accommodation on a passenger ship.

cabin cruiser ● noun a motor boat with living accommodation.

cabinet ● noun **1** a cupboard with drawers or shelves for storing or displaying articles. **2** a wooden box or piece of furniture housing a radio, television, or speaker. **3** (also **Cabinet**) a committee of senior ministers responsible for controlling government policy.
– DERIVATIVES **cabinetry** noun.
– ORIGIN from CABIN; sense 3 derives from the obsolete sense 'small private room'.

cabinetmaker ● noun a skilled joiner who makes furniture or similar high-quality woodwork.

cabin fever ● noun informal, chiefly N. Amer. depression and irritability resulting from long confinement indoors during the winter.

cable ● noun **1** a thick rope of wire or hemp. **2** an insulated wire or wires for transmitting electricity or telecommunication signals. **3** historical a cablegram. **4** the chain of a ship's anchor. **5** Nautical a length of 200 yards (182.9 m) or (in the US) 240 yards (219.4 m). ● verb dated send a cablegram to.
– ORIGIN Old French *chable*, from Latin *capulum* 'halter'.

cable car ● noun a small carriage suspended on a continuous moving cable and travelling up and down a mountainside.

cablegram ● noun historical a telegraph message sent by cable.

cable stitch ● noun a combination of knitted stitches resembling twisted rope.

cable television ● noun a system in which television programmes are transmitted to the sets of subscribers by cable.

cabochon /kabbəshon/ ● noun a gem that is polished but not given facets.
– ORIGIN French, 'small head'.

caboodle ● noun (in phrase **the whole caboodle** or **the whole kit and caboodle**) informal the whole number or quantity of people or things in question.
– ORIGIN originally US: perhaps from the phrase *kit and boodle*, in the same sense.

caboose ● noun **1** N. Amer. a wagon with accommodation for the crew on a freight train. **2** archaic a kitchen on a ship's deck.
– ORIGIN Dutch *kabuis*.

cabriole leg ● noun a kind of curved leg characteristic of Chippendale and Queen Anne furniture.
– ORIGIN from French *cabriole* 'light leap', so named from the resemblance to the front leg of a leaping animal.

cabriolet /kabriōlay/ ● noun **1** a car with a roof that folds down. **2** a light two-wheeled carriage with a hood, drawn by one horse.
– ORIGIN French, from *cabriole* 'light leap'; so named because of the carriage's motion.

cacao /kəkayō/ ● noun the bean-like seeds of a tropical American tree, from which cocoa, cocoa butter, and chocolate are made.
– ORIGIN Nahuatl.

cache /kash/ ● noun **1** a hidden store of things. **2** Computing an auxiliary memory from which high-speed retrieval is possible.

Thesaurus

cab ● noun **1** *she hailed a cab* TAXI, taxi cab; *Brit* minicab, hackney carriage; *N. Amer.* hack; *historical* fiacre. **2** *a truck driver's cab* (DRIVER'S) COMPARTMENT, cabin.

cabal ● noun CLIQUE, faction, coterie, cell, sect, camarilla; pressure group; *Brit.* ginger group.

cabaret ● noun **1** *the evening's cabaret* ENTERTAINMENT, (floor) show, performance. **2** *the cabarets of Montreal* NIGHTCLUB, club, boîte; *N. Amer.* cafe; *informal* nightspot, niterie, clip joint; *N. Amer. informal* honky-tonk.

cabin ● noun **1** *a first-class cabin* BERTH, stateroom, deckhouse; *historical* roundhouse. **2** *a cabin by the lake* HUT, log cabin, shanty, shack; chalet; *Scottish* bothy; *N. Amer.* cabana; *Austral.* mia-mia; *archaic* cot; *N. Amer. archaic* shebang. **3** *the driver's cabin* CAB, compartment.

cabinet ● noun **1** *a walnut cabinet* CUPBOARD, bureau, chest of drawers. **2** *the new cabinet* SENIOR MINISTERS, ministry, council, executive.

cable ● noun **1** *a thick cable moored the ship* ROPE, cord, line, guy; *Nautical* hawser, stay, bridle, topping lift; *N. Amer.* choker. **2** *electric cables* WIRE, lead; power line; *Brit.* flex. **3** *(historical) he immediately sent them a cable* TELEGRAM, telemessage, radiogram; *informal* wire;

C

● **verb** store in a cache.
– ORIGIN French, from *cacher* 'to hide'.
cache-sexe /kashseks/ ● **noun** (pl. pronounced same) a covering for a person's genitals, worn by erotic dancers or tribal peoples.
– ORIGIN French, from *cacher* 'to hide' and *sexe* 'genitals'.
cachet /kashay/ ● **noun** **1** prestige. **2** a distinguishing mark or seal. **3** a flat capsule enclosing a dose of unpleasant-tasting medicine.
– ORIGIN French, from *cacher* in the sense 'to press'.
cachexia /kəkeksiə/ ● **noun** Medicine weakness and wasting of the body due to severe chronic illness.
– DERIVATIVES **cachectic** adjective.
– ORIGIN Greek *kakhexia*, from *kakos* 'bad' + *hexis* 'habit'.
cacique /kəseek/ ● **noun** **1** (in Latin America or the Spanish-speaking Caribbean) a native chief. **2** (in Spain or Latin America) a local political boss.
– ORIGIN from Taino (an extinct Caribbean language).
cack ● **noun** Brit. informal excrement.
– ORIGIN Old English, from Latin *cacare* 'defecate'.
cack-handed ● **adjective** Brit. informal **1** inept; clumsy. **2** derogatory left-handed.
cackle ● **noun** a raucous clucking cry, as made by a hen or goose. ● **verb** **1** give a cackle. **2** talk inconsequentially and at length.
– PHRASES **cut the cackle** informal stop talking aimlessly and come to the point.
– ORIGIN probably from Low German *kākelen*.
cacophony /kəkoffəni/ ● **noun** (pl. **cacophonies**) a harsh discordant mixture of sounds.
– DERIVATIVES **cacophonous** adjective.
– ORIGIN Greek *kakophōnia*, from *kakophōnos* 'ill-sounding'.
cactus ● **noun** (pl. **cacti** /kaktī/ or **cactuses**) a succulent plant with a thick fleshy stem bearing spines but no leaves.
– ORIGIN Greek *kaktos* 'cardoon'.
cad ● **noun** dated or humorous a man who behaves dishonourably, especially towards a woman.
– DERIVATIVES **caddish** adjective.
– ORIGIN originally denoting a passenger picked up by the driver of a horse-drawn coach for personal profit: abbreviation of CADDIE or CADET.
cadaver /kədaavər/ ● **noun** Medicine or literary a corpse.
– ORIGIN Latin, from *cadere* 'to fall'.
cadaverous ● **adjective** resembling a corpse in being very pale, thin, or bony.
caddie (also **caddy**) ● **noun** (pl. **caddies**) a person who carries a golfer's clubs and provides other assistance during a match. ● **verb** (**caddying**) work as a caddie.
– ORIGIN originally Scots, denoting a gentleman who joined the army without a commission, later coming to mean 'odd-job man': from French *cadet* (see CADET).
caddis /kaddis/ (also **caddis fly**) ● **noun** a small moth-like insect having aquatic larvae that build protective cases of sticks, stones, etc.
– ORIGIN of unknown origin.
caddy ● **noun** (pl. **caddies**) a small storage container, especially for tea.
– ORIGIN from earlier *catty*, denoting a unit of weight of 1⅓ lb (0.61 kg), from Malay.
cadence /kayd'nss/ ● **noun** **1** a modulation or inflection of the voice. **2** Music a sequence of notes or chords comprising the close of a musical phrase. **3** rhythm.
– DERIVATIVES **cadenced** adjective.
– ORIGIN Italian *cadenza*, from Latin *cadere* 'to fall'.
cadenza /kədenzə/ ● **noun** Music a virtuoso solo passage in a concerto or other work, typically near the end.
– ORIGIN Italian (see CADENCE).
cadet ● **noun** **1** a young trainee in the armed services or police. **2** formal or archaic a younger son or daughter.
– DERIVATIVES **cadetship** noun.
– ORIGIN French, ultimately from Latin *caput* 'head'.
cadge ● **verb** informal ask for or obtain (something to which one is not entitled).
– DERIVATIVES **cadger** noun.
– ORIGIN from *cadger*, a northern English and Scottish word meaning 'itinerant dealer'.
cadmium /kadmiəm/ ● **noun** a silvery-white metallic chemical element resembling zinc.
– ORIGIN from Latin *cadmia* 'calamine', so named because it is found with calamine in zinc ore.
cadmium yellow ● **noun** a bright yellow pigment containing cadmium sulphide.
cadre /kaadər/ ● **noun** **1** a small group of people trained for a particular purpose or profession. **2** /also kaydər/ a group of activists in a revolutionary organization.
– ORIGIN French, from Latin *quadrus* 'square'.
caduceus /kədyōōssiəss/ ● **noun** (pl. **caducei** /kədyōōssi-ī/) an ancient Greek or Roman herald's wand, typically one with two serpents twined round it, carried by the messenger god Hermes or Mercury.
– ORIGIN Latin, from Greek *kērux* 'herald'.
caecilian /sisilliən/ ● **noun** a burrowing worm-like amphibian with poorly developed eyes and no limbs.
– ORIGIN from Latin *caecilia* 'slow-worm'.
caecum /seekəm/ (US **cecum**) ● **noun** (pl. **caeca**) a pouch connected to the junction of the small and large intestines.
– DERIVATIVES **caecal** adjective.
– ORIGIN from Latin *intestinum caecum* 'blind gut'.
Caerns. ● **abbreviation** Caernarfonshire.
Caerphilly /kairfilli, kər-/ ● **noun** a kind of mild white cheese, originally made in Caerphilly in Wales.
Caesar /seezər/ ● **noun** a title of Roman emperors, especially those from Augustus to Hadrian.
– ORIGIN family name of the Roman statesman Gaius Julius *Caesar*.
Caesarean /sizairiən/ (also **Caesarian**) ● **adjective** relating to Julius Caesar or the Caesars. ● **noun** a Caesarean section.
Caesarean section ● **noun** a surgical operation for delivering a child by cutting through the wall of the mother's abdomen.
– ORIGIN from the story that Julius Caesar was delivered by this method.
caesium /seeziəm/ (US **cesium**) ● **noun** a soft, silvery, extremely reactive metallic chemical element.
– ORIGIN from Latin *caesius* 'greyish-blue' (because it has characteristic lines in the blue part of the spectrum).
caesura /sizyoorə/ ● **noun** **1** (in Greek and Latin verse) a break between words within a metrical foot. **2** (in modern verse) a pause near the middle of a line.
– ORIGIN Latin, from *caedere* 'cut'.
cafard /kafaar/ ● **noun** melancholia.
– ORIGIN French.
cafe /kaffay/ ● **noun** **1** a small restaurant selling light meals and drinks. **2** N. Amer. a bar or nightclub.
– ORIGIN French, 'coffee or coffee house'.

Thesaurus

historical cablegram.
● **verb** *(dated) the secretariat cabled a reply* RADIO, send, transmit; *informal* wire.
cache ● **noun** **1** *a cache of arms* HOARD, store, stockpile, stock, supply, reserve; arsenal; *informal* stash. **2** *a niche used as a cache* HIDING PLACE, secret place; *informal* hidey-hole; *informal, dated* stash.
cachet ● **noun** PRESTIGE, prestigiousness, status, standing, kudos, snob value, stature, pre-eminence, eminence; street credibility.
cackle ● **verb** **1** *the geese cackled at him* SQUAWK, cluck. **2** *Noel cackled with glee* LAUGH LOUDLY, guffaw, crow, chortle, chuckle.
cacophonous ● **adjective** LOUD, noisy, ear-splitting, raucous, discordant, dissonant, inharmonious, unmelodious, unmusical, tuneless; *archaic* absonant.
– OPPOSITES harmonious.
cacophony ● **noun** DIN, racket, noise, discord, dissonance, discordance.
cad ● **noun** *(dated).* See SCOUNDREL.
cadaver ● **noun** *(Medicine)* CORPSE, (dead) body, remains, carcass; *informal* stiff; *archaic* corse.
cadaverous ● **adjective** (DEATHLY) PALE, pallid, ashen, grey, whey-faced, etiolated, corpse-like; as thin as a rake, bony, skeletal, emaciated, skin-and-bones, haggard, gaunt, drawn, pinched, hollow-cheeked, hollow-eyed; *informal* like a bag of bones, anorexic; *archaic* starveling.
– OPPOSITES rosy, plump.
cadence ● **noun** RHYTHM, tempo, metre, beat, pulse; intonation, modulation, lilt.
cadge ● **verb** *(informal)* SCROUNGE, borrow; *informal* bum, touch someone for, sponge; *Brit. informal* scab; *N. Amer. informal* mooch; *Austral./NZ informal* bludge.

cafe curtain ● noun a curtain covering the lower half of a window.
cafe society ● noun people who spend a lot of time in fashionable restaurants and nightclubs.
cafeteria ● noun a self-service restaurant.
– ORIGIN Latin American Spanish, 'coffee shop'.
cafetière /kaffətyair/ ● noun a coffee pot containing a plunger with which the grounds are pushed to the bottom before the coffee is poured.
– ORIGIN French.
caffeine /kaffeen/ ● noun a compound which is found in tea and coffee plants and is a stimulant of the central nervous system.
– DERIVATIVES **caffeinated** adjective.
– ORIGIN French *caféine*, from *café* 'coffee'.
caftan ● noun variant spelling of KAFTAN.
cage ● noun **1** a structure of bars or wires in which birds or other animals are confined. **2** any similar structure, in particular the compartment in a lift. ● verb confine in or as if in a cage.
– ORIGIN Old French, from Latin *cavea*.
cagey (also **cagy**) ● adjective informal uncommunicative owing to caution or suspicion.
– DERIVATIVES **cagily** adverb **caginess** (also **cageyness**) noun.
– ORIGIN of unknown origin.
cagoule /kəgool/ (also **kagoul**) ● noun a lightweight, hooded, thigh-length waterproof jacket.
– ORIGIN French, 'cowl'.
cahoots /kəhoots/ ● plural noun (in phrase **in cahoots**) informal colluding or conspiring together secretly.
– ORIGIN of unknown origin.
caiman /kaymən/ (also **cayman**) ● noun a tropical American reptile similar to an alligator.
– ORIGIN Carib.
Cain ● noun (in phrase **raise Cain**) informal create trouble or a commotion.
– ORIGIN from *Cain*, eldest son of Adam and Eve and murderer of his brother Abel (Genesis 4).
caique /kīeek/ ● noun **1** a light rowing boat used on the Bosporus. **2** a small eastern Mediterranean sailing ship.
– ORIGIN Turkish *kayık*.
cairn ● noun **1** a mound of rough stones built as a memorial or landmark. **2** (also **cairn terrier**) a small breed of terrier with a shaggy coat.
– ORIGIN Scottish Gaelic *carn*.
caisson /kays'n, kəsoon/ ● noun **1** a large watertight chamber in which underwater construction work may be carried out. **2** a vessel or structure used as a gate across the entrance of a dry dock or basin.
– ORIGIN French, 'large chest'.
caitiff /kaytif/ ● noun archaic a contemptible or cowardly person.
– ORIGIN Old French *caitif* 'captive', from Latin *captivus*.
cajole /kəjōl/ ● verb persuade (someone) to do something by sustained coaxing or flattery.
– DERIVATIVES **cajolery** noun.
– ORIGIN French *cajoler*.
Cajun /kayjən/ ● noun a member of a French-speaking community in the bayou areas of southern Louisiana, descended from French Canadians. ● adjective relating to the Cajuns.
– ORIGIN alteration of *Acadian* 'relating to Acadia', a former French colony in Canada (now Nova Scotia).
cake ● noun **1** an item of soft sweet food made from baking a mixture of flour, fat, eggs, and sugar. **2** a flat, round item of savoury food that is baked or fried. **3** the amount of money available for sharing: *a fair slice of the education cake.* ● verb (of a thick or sticky substance) cover and become encrusted on.
– PHRASES **a piece of cake** informal something easily achieved. **sell like hot cakes** informal be sold quickly and in large quantities. **take the cake** see **take the biscuit** at BISCUIT. **you can't have your cake and eat it (too)** proverb you can't enjoy both of two desirable but mutually exclusive alternatives.
– ORIGIN Scandinavian.
cakehole ● noun Brit. informal a person's mouth.
cakewalk ● noun **1** informal a very easy task. **2** a strutting dance popular at the end of the 19th century, developed from an American black contest in graceful walking which had a cake as a prize.
Cal ● abbreviation large calorie(s).
cal ● abbreviation small calorie(s).
calabash /kaləbash/ ● noun a water container, tobacco pipe, or other object made from the dried shell of a gourd.
– ORIGIN Spanish *calabaza*, perhaps from a Persian word meaning 'melon'.
calaboose /kaləbooss/ ● noun US informal a prison.
– ORIGIN Spanish *calabozo* 'dungeon'.
calabrese /kaləbreez/ ● noun a bright green variety of broccoli.
– ORIGIN Italian, meaning 'from Calabria', a region of SW Italy.
calamari /kaləmaari/ (also **calamares** /kaləmaarayz/) ● plural noun squid served as food.
– ORIGIN Italian, from Greek *kalamos* 'pen' (with reference to the squid's long tapering internal shell and its ink).
calamine /kaləmīn/ ● noun a pink powder consisting of zinc carbonate and ferric oxide, used to make a soothing lotion or ointment.
– ORIGIN Latin *calamina*, from Greek *kadmeia gē* 'Cadmean earth', from the name of *Cadmus*, the legendary founder of Thebes.
calamity ● noun (pl. **calamities**) an event causing great and sudden damage or distress.
– DERIVATIVES **calamitous** adjective **calamitously** adverb.
– ORIGIN Latin *calamitas*.
calando /kəlandō/ ● adverb Music gradually decreasing in speed and volume.
– ORIGIN Italian, 'slackening'.
calash ● noun another term for CALECHE.
calcareous /kalkairiəss/ ● adjective containing calcium carbonate; chalky.
– ORIGIN Latin *calcarius*, from *calx* 'lime'.
calceolaria /kalsiəlairiə/ ● noun a South American plant with brightly coloured slipper- or pouch-shaped flowers.
– ORIGIN Latin *calceolus* 'little shoe'.
calces plural of CALX.
calciferol /kalsifferol/ ● noun Biochemistry vitamin D_2, essential for the deposition of calcium in bones.
calciferous /kalsifferəss/ ● adjective containing or producing calcium salts, especially calcium carbonate.
calcify /kalsifī/ ● verb (**calcifies**, **calcified**) harden by deposition of or conversion into calcium carbonate or other calcium salts.
– DERIVATIVES **calcification** noun.
calcine /kalsīn, -sin/ ● verb reduce, oxidize, or dry (a substance) by roasting or strong heat.
– DERIVATIVES **calcination** noun.

Thesaurus

cadre ● noun CORPS, body, team, group.
cafe ● noun SNACK BAR, cafeteria, buffet; coffee bar/shop, tea room/shop; bistro, brasserie; *N. Amer.* diner; *informal* eatery, noshery; *Brit. informal* caff.
cafeteria ● noun SELF-SERVICE RESTAURANT, canteen, cafe, buffet.
cage ● noun *animals in cages* ENCLOSURE, pen, pound; coop, hutch; birdcage, aviary; *N. Amer.* corral.
● verb *many animals are caged* CONFINE, shut in/up, pen, coop up, immure, impound; *N. Amer.* corral.
cagey ● adjective *(informal)* SECRETIVE, guarded, non-committal, tight-lipped, reticent, evasive; *informal* playing one's cards close to one's chest.
– OPPOSITES open.
cahoots ● plural noun
– PHRASES **in cahoots** *(informal)* IN LEAGUE, colluding, in collusion, conspiring, collaborating, hand in glove.
cajole ● verb PERSUADE, wheedle, coax, talk into, prevail on, blarney; *informal* sweet-talk, soft-soap, twist someone's arm; *archaic* blandish.
cajolery ● noun PERSUASION, wheedling, coaxing, inveiglement, cajolement; blandishments, blarney; *informal* sweet talk, soft soap, arm-twisting; *formal* suasion.
cake ● noun **1** *cream cakes* BUN, pastry, gateau. **2** *a cake of soap* BAR, tablet, block, slab, lump.
● verb **1** *boots caked with mud* COAT, encrust, plaster, cover. **2** *the blood was beginning to cake* CLOT, congeal, coagulate, solidify, set, inspissate.
calamitous ● adjective DISASTROUS, catastrophic, cataclysmic, devastating, dire, tragic; *poetic/literary* direful.
calamity ● noun DISASTER, catastrophe, tragedy, cataclysm, adver-

C

– ORIGIN Latin *calcinare*, from *calx* 'lime'.
calcite /kalsīt/ ● noun a white or colourless mineral consisting of calcium carbonate.
– ORIGIN German *Calcit*.
calcium ● noun a soft grey reactive metallic chemical element.
– ORIGIN from Latin *calx* 'lime'.
calcium carbonate ● noun a white insoluble compound occurring naturally as chalk, limestone, marble, and calcite, and forming mollusc shells.
calculate ● verb **1** determine mathematically. **2** (**calculate on**) include as an essential element in one's plans. **3** intend (an action) to have a particular effect.
– DERIVATIVES **calculable** adjective.
– ORIGIN Latin *calculare* 'count', from *calculus* 'small pebble' (as used on an abacus).
calculated ● adjective done with awareness of the likely consequences.
– DERIVATIVES **calculatedly** adverb.
calculating ● adjective selfishly scheming.
– DERIVATIVES **calculatingly** adverb.
calculation ● noun **1** a mathematical determination of quantity or extent. **2** an assessment of the risks or effects of a course of action.
calculator ● noun something used for making mathematical calculations, in particular a small electronic device with a keyboard and a visual display.
calculus /kalkjooləss/ ● noun (pl. **calculi** /kalkyoolī/ or **calculuses**) **1** the branch of mathematics concerned with finding derivatives and integrals of functions by methods based on the summation of infinitesimal differences. **2** Medicine a stone formed by deposition of minerals in the kidney, gall bladder, or other organ.
– ORIGIN Latin, 'small pebble' (as used on an abacus).
caldera /kaaldairə/ ● noun a large volcanic crater, especially one formed by the collapse of the volcano's mouth.
– ORIGIN Spanish, from Latin *caldaria* 'boiling pot'.
caldron ● noun chiefly US variant spelling of CAULDRON.
caleche /kəlesh/ (also **calash**) ● noun historical **1** a light low-wheeled carriage with a removable folding hood. **2** a woman's hooped silk hood.
– ORIGIN French, from Polish from *kolo* 'wheel'.
Caledonian /kalidōniən/ ● adjective relating to Scotland or the Scottish Highlands.
– ORIGIN from *Caledonia*, the Latin name for northern Britain.
calendar /kalindər/ ● noun **1** a chart or series of pages showing the days, weeks, and months of a particular year. **2** a system by which the beginning, length, and subdivisions of the year are fixed. **3** a list or schedule of special days, events, or activities.
– DERIVATIVES **calendrical** /kalendrik'l/ adjective.
– ORIGIN Latin *kalendarium* 'account book', from *kalendae* (see CALENDS).
calender /kalindər/ ● noun a machine in which cloth or paper is pressed by rollers to glaze or smooth it.
– ORIGIN French *calendre*.
calends /kalendz/ (also **kalends**) ● plural noun the first day of the month in the ancient Roman calendar.
– ORIGIN Latin *kalendae*, *calendae* 'first day of the month' (when the order of days was proclaimed).
calendula /kəlendyoolə/ ● noun a plant of a family that includes the common or pot marigold.
– ORIGIN Latin, from *calendae* (see CALENDS); perhaps because it flowers for most of the year.
calf[1] ● noun (pl. **calves**) **1** a young bovine animal, especially a domestic cow or bull in its first year. **2** the young of some other large mammals, such as elephants. **3** a floating piece of ice detached from an iceberg.
– ORIGIN Old English.
calf[2] ● noun (pl. **calves**) the fleshy part at the back of a person's leg below the knee.
– ORIGIN Old Norse.
calf love ● noun another term for PUPPY LOVE.
calibrate /kalibrayt/ ● verb **1** mark (a gauge or instrument) with a standard scale of readings. **2** compare the readings of (an instrument) with those of a standard. **3** adjust (experimental results) to take external factors into account or to allow comparison with other data.
– DERIVATIVES **calibration** noun **calibrator** noun.
– ORIGIN from CALIBRE.
calibre /kalibər/ (US **caliber**) ● noun **1** quality of character or level of ability. **2** the internal diameter of a gun barrel, or the diameter of a bullet or shell.
– ORIGIN originally in the sense 'social standing': from French, perhaps from an Arabic word meaning 'mould'.
calico /kalikō/ ● noun (pl. **calicoes** or US also **calicos**) **1** Brit. a type of plain white or unbleached cotton cloth. **2** N. Amer. printed cotton fabric.
– ORIGIN alteration of *Calicut*, a seaport in SW India where the fabric originated.
Californian ● noun a person from California. ● adjective relating to California.
californium /kaliforniəm/ ● noun a radioactive metallic chemical element made by high-energy atomic collisions.
– ORIGIN named after *California* University (where it was first made).
caliper /kalipər/ (also **calliper**) ● noun **1** (also **calipers**) a measuring instrument with two hinged legs and in-turned or out-turned points. **2** a motor-vehicle or bicycle brake consisting of two or more hinged components. **3** a metal support for a person's leg.
– ORIGIN probably an alteration of CALIBRE.
caliph /kaylif/ ● noun historical the chief Muslim civil and religious ruler, regarded as the successor of Muhammad.
– DERIVATIVES **caliphate** noun.
– ORIGIN Arabic, 'deputy of God'.
calisthenics ● plural noun US spelling of CALLISTHENICS.
calix ● noun variant spelling of CALYX.
calk ● noun & verb US spelling of CAULK.
call ● verb **1** cry out to (someone) in order to summon them or attract their attention. **2** telephone. **3** (of a bird or animal) make its characteristic cry. **4** pay a brief visit. **5** give a specified name or description to. **6** fix a date or time for (a meeting, election, or strike). **7** predict the result of (a vote or contest). **8** bring (a witness) into court to give evidence. **9** inspire or urge to do something. ● noun **1** a cry made as a summons or to attract attention. **2** a telephone communication. **3** the characteristic cry of a bird or animal. **4** a brief visit. **5** (**call for**) demand or need for: *there is little call for antique furniture.* **6** a vocation. **7** a shout by an official in a game indicating that the ball has gone out of play or that a rule has been breached.
– PHRASES **call for** require; demand. **call in** require payment of (a loan). **call off** cancel (an event or agreement). **call on/upon** turn to as a source of help. **call of nature** euphemistic a need to urinate or defecate. **call the shots** (or **tune**) take the initiative in deciding how something should be done. **call up 1** summon (someone) to serve in the army or to play in a team. **2** bring (something stored) into use. **on call 1** available to provide a professional service if necessary. **2** (of money lent) repayable on demand.
– DERIVATIVES **caller** noun.
– ORIGIN Old Norse.

Thesaurus

sity, tribulation, affliction, misfortune, misadventure.
– OPPOSITES godsend.
calculate ● verb **1** *the interest is calculated on a daily basis* COMPUTE, work out, reckon, figure; add up/together, count up, tally, total; *Brit.* tot up. **2** *his words were calculated to wound her* INTEND, mean, design. **3** *we had calculated on a quiet Sunday* EXPECT, anticipate, reckon, bargain; *N. Amer. informal* figure on.
calculated ● adjective DELIBERATE, premeditated, planned, preplanned, preconceived, intentional, intended; *Law, dated* prepense.
– OPPOSITES unintentional.
calculating ● adjective CUNNING, crafty, wily, shrewd, scheming, devious, designing, Machiavellian; *informal* foxy; *archaic* subtle.
– OPPOSITES ingenuous.
calculation ● noun **1** *the calculation of the overall cost* COMPUTATION, reckoning, adding up, counting up, working out, figuring; *Brit.* totting up. **2** *political calculations* ASSESSMENT, judgement; forecast, projection, prediction.
calendar ● noun **1** ALMANAC. **2** *my social calendar* SCHEDULE, programme, diary.
calibre ● noun **1** *a man of his calibre* QUALITY, merit, distinction, stature, excellence, pre-eminence; ability, expertise, talent, capability, capacity, proficiency. **2** *rugby of this calibre* STANDARD,

call centre ● noun an office in which large numbers of telephone calls, especially from customers, are handled for an organization.

call girl ● noun a female prostitute who accepts appointments by telephone.

calligraphy ● noun decorative handwriting or handwritten lettering.
– DERIVATIVES **calligrapher** noun **calligraphic** adjective.
– ORIGIN Greek *kalligraphia*, from *kalligraphos* 'person who writes beautifully'.

calling ● noun **1** a profession or occupation. **2** a vocation.

calling card ● noun chiefly N. Amer. a visiting card or business card.

calliope /kəlīəpi/ ● noun chiefly historical an American keyboard instrument resembling an organ but with the notes produced by steam whistles.
– ORIGIN from *Calliope*, the Greek Muse of epic poetry (literally 'beautiful-voiced').

calliper ● noun variant spelling of CALIPER.

callipygian /kalipijiən/ (also **callipygean**) ● adjective literary having well-shaped buttocks.
– ORIGIN from Greek *kallos* 'beauty' + *pūgē* 'buttocks'.

callisthenics /kalissthenniks/ (US **calisthenics**) ● plural noun gymnastic exercises to achieve bodily fitness and grace of movement.
– ORIGIN from Greek *kallos* 'beauty' + *sthenos* 'strength'.

callosity /kəlossiti/ ● noun (pl. **callosities**) technical a callus.

callous ● adjective insensitive and cruel. ● noun variant spelling of CALLUS.
– DERIVATIVES **callously** adverb **callousness** noun.
– ORIGIN Latin *callosus* 'hard-skinned'.

callow ● adjective (of a young person) inexperienced and immature.
– DERIVATIVES **callowly** adverb **callowness** noun.
– ORIGIN Old English, 'bald', probably from Latin *calvus* 'bald', later 'unfledged'.

call sign (also **call signal**) ● noun a message or tune broadcast on radio to identify the broadcaster or transmitter.

callus /kaləss/ (also **callous**) ● noun **1** a thickened and hardened part of the skin or soft tissue. **2** Botany a hard formation of tissue formed over a wound.
– DERIVATIVES **callused** adjective.
– ORIGIN Latin, 'hardened skin'.

calm ● adjective **1** not showing or feeling nervousness, anger, or other emotions. **2** peaceful and undisturbed. ● noun **1** a calm state or period. **2** (**calms**) an area of the sea without wind. ● verb (often **calm down**) make or become tranquil and quiet.
– DERIVATIVES **calmly** adverb **calmness** noun.
– ORIGIN from Greek *kauma* 'heat of the day'.

calmative ● adjective (of a drug) having a sedative effect.

calomel /kaləmel/ ● noun mercurous chloride, a white powder formerly used as a purgative.
– ORIGIN from Greek *kalos* 'beautiful' + *melas* 'black' (perhaps because it was originally obtained from a black mixture of mercury and mercuric chloride).

Calor gas /kalər/ ● noun Brit. trademark liquefied butane stored under pressure in portable containers, used as a substitute for mains gas.
– ORIGIN from Latin *calor* 'heat'.

caloric /kəlorrik, kalərik/ ● adjective chiefly N. Amer. or technical relating to heat; calorific.

calorie ● noun (pl. **calories**) **1** (also **large calorie**) a unit of energy, often used in specifying the energy value of foods, equal to the energy needed to raise the temperature of 1 kilogram of water through 1°C (4.1868 kilojoules). **2** (also **small calorie**) a unit of energy equal to one-thousandth of a large calorie.
– ORIGIN from Latin *calor* 'heat'.

calorific ● adjective chiefly Brit. **1** relating to the amount of energy contained in food or fuel. **2** high in calories.

calorimeter /kalərimmitər/ ● noun an apparatus for measuring the amount of heat involved in a chemical reaction or other process.
– DERIVATIVES **calorimetric** adjective **calorimetry** noun.

caltrop /kaltrəp/ (also **caltrap**) ● noun **1** a spiked metal ball thrown on the ground to impede wheeled vehicles or (formerly) cavalry horses. **2** a creeping plant with hard spines.
– ORIGIN from Latin *calx* 'heel' or *calcare* 'to tread' + a word related to TRAP[1].

Thesaurus

level, quality. **3** *the calibre of a gun* BORE, diameter, gauge.

call ● verb **1** *'Wait for me!' she called* CRY (OUT), shout, yell, bellow, roar, bawl, scream, vociferate; informal holler. **2** *Mum called me in the morning* WAKE (UP), awaken, rouse; Brit. informal knock up; poetic/literary waken. **3** *I'll call you tomorrow* PHONE, telephone, get someone on the phone, give someone a call; Brit. ring (up), give someone a ring; informal call up, give someone a buzz; Brit. informal give someone a bell/tinkle, get someone on the blower; N. Amer. informal get someone on the horn. **4** *Rose called a taxi* SUMMON, send for, order. **5** *he called at Ashgrove Cottage* PAY A (BRIEF) VISIT TO, visit, pay a call on, call/drop/look in on, drop/stop by, pop into. **6** *the prime minister called a meeting* CONVENE, summon, assemble; formal convoke. **7** *they called their daughter Hannah* NAME, christen, baptize; designate, style, term, dub; formal denominate. **8** *I would call him a friend* DESCRIBE AS, regard as, look on as, consider to be. ● noun **1** *I heard calls from the auditorium* CRY, shout, yell, roar, scream, exclamation, vociferation; informal holler. **2** *the call of the water rail* CRY, song, sound. **3** *I'll give you a call tomorrow* PHONE CALL, telephone call; Brit. ring; informal buzz; Brit. informal bell, tinkle. **4** *he paid a call on Harold* VISIT, social call. **5** *a call for party unity* APPEAL, request, plea, entreaty. **6** *the last call for passengers on flight BA701* SUMMONS, request. **7** *there's no call for that kind of language* NEED, necessity, reason, justification, excuse. **8** *there's no call for expensive wine here* DEMAND, desire, market. **9** *the call of the Cairngorms* ATTRACTION, appeal, lure, allure, spell, pull, draw.
– PHRASES **call for 1** *desperate times call for desperate measures* REQUIRE, need, necessitate; justify, warrant. **2** *I'll call for you around seven* PICK UP, collect, fetch. **call something off** CANCEL, abandon, scrap, drop, axe; informal scrub, nix; N. Amer. informal redline. **call on 1** *I might call on her later* VISIT, pay a call on, go and see, look/drop in on; N. Amer. visit with; informal look up, pop in on. **2** *he called on the government to hold a plebiscite* APPEAL TO, ask, request, petition, urge. **3** *we are able to call on qualified staff* HAVE RECOURSE TO, avail oneself of, draw on, make use of. **call the shots** BE IN CHARGE, be in control, be at the helm/wheel, be in the driving seat, pull the strings; informal run the show, be the boss. **call to mind 1** *this calls to mind Cézanne's works* EVOKE, bring to mind, call up, conjure up. **2** *I cannot call to mind where I have seen you* REMEMBER, recall, recollect. **call someone up 1** (informal) *Roland called me up*. See CALL verb sense 3. **2** *they called up the reservists* ENLIST, recruit, conscript; US draft. **3** *he was called up for the England team* SELECT, pick, choose; Brit. cap. **on call** ON DUTY, on standby, available.

call girl ● noun PROSTITUTE, whore, sex worker, fille de joie; informal tart, pro, working girl; N. Amer. informal hooker, hustler; euphemistic escort, masseuse; dated woman of the streets; archaic strumpet, harlot, trollop.

calling ● noun PROFESSION, occupation, vocation, career, work, employment, job, business, trade, craft, line (of work); archaic employ.

callous ● adjective HEARTLESS, unfeeling, uncaring, cold, cold-hearted, hard, as hard as nails, hard-hearted, stony-hearted, insensitive, lacking compassion, hardbitten, unsympathetic.
– OPPOSITES kind, compassionate.

callow ● adjective IMMATURE, inexperienced, juvenile, adolescent, naive, green, raw, untried, unworldly, unsophisticated; informal wet behind the ears.
– OPPOSITES mature.

calm ● adjective **1** *she seemed very calm* SERENE, tranquil, relaxed, unruffled, unperturbed, unflustered, untroubled; equable, even-tempered; placid, unexcitable, unemotional, phlegmatic; composed, {cool, calm, and collected}, cool-headed, self-possessed; informal unflappable, unfazed. **2** *the night was calm* WINDLESS, still, tranquil, quiet. **3** *the calm waters of the lake* TRANQUIL, still, smooth, glassy, like a millpond; poetic/literary stilly.
– OPPOSITES excited, nervous, stormy.
● noun **1** *calm prevailed* TRANQUILLITY, stillness, calmness, quiet, quietness, quietude, peace, peacefulness. **2** *his usual calm deserted him* COMPOSURE, coolness, calmness, self-possession, sangfroid; serenity, tranquillity, equanimity, equability, placidness, placidity; informal cool, unflappability.
● verb **1** *I tried to calm him down* SOOTHE, pacify, placate, mollify, appease, conciliate; Brit. quieten (down); Austral. square off; poetic/literary dulcify. **2** *she forced herself to calm down* COMPOSE ONESELF, recover/regain one's composure, control oneself, pull oneself together, simmer down, cool down/off, take it easy; Brit. quieten down; informal get a grip, keep one's shirt on, wind down; N. Amer.

C

calumet /kalyoomet/ ● noun a North American Indian peace pipe.
– ORIGIN French, from Latin *calamellus* 'little reed'.
calumniate /kəlumniayt/ ● verb formal make false and defamatory statements about.
– DERIVATIVES **calumniator** noun.
calumny /kaləmni/ ● noun (pl. **calumnies**) the making of false and defamatory statements about someone. ● verb (**calumnies, calumnied**) formal calumniate.
– DERIVATIVES **calumnious** /kəlumniəss/ adjective.
– ORIGIN Latin *calumnia*.
Calvados /kalvədoss/ ● noun apple brandy, traditionally made in the Calvados region of Normandy.
calve ● verb **1** give birth to a calf. **2** (of a mass of ice) split off from an iceberg or glacier.
– ORIGIN Old English.
calves plural of CALF[1], CALF[2].
Calvinism ● noun the Protestant theological system of John Calvin (1509–64) and his successors, centring on the doctrine of predestination.
– DERIVATIVES **Calvinist** noun **Calvinistic** adjective.
calx /kalks/ ● noun (pl. **calces** /kalseez/) Chemistry, archaic a powdery metallic oxide formed when an ore or mineral has been heated.
– ORIGIN Latin, 'lime'.
calypso /kəlipsō/ ● noun (pl. **calypsos**) a kind of West Indian music or song in syncopated African rhythm, typically with words improvised on a topical theme.
– ORIGIN of unknown origin.
calyx /kayliks/ (also **calix**) ● noun (pl. **calyces** /kayliseez/ or **calyxes**) **1** Botany the sepals of a flower, forming a protective layer around a flower in bud. **2** Zoology a cup-like cavity or structure.
– ORIGIN Greek *kalux* 'case of a bud, husk'.
calzone /kaltsōnay/ ● noun (pl. **calzoni** or **calzones**) a type of pizza that is folded in half before cooking to contain a filling.
– ORIGIN Italian dialect, probably a special use of *calzone* 'trouser leg'.
cam ● noun **1** a projection on a rotating part in machinery, designed to make sliding contact with another part while rotating and impart motion to it. **2** a camshaft.
– ORIGIN Dutch *kam* 'comb'
camaraderie /kamməraadəri/ ● noun mutual trust and friendship.
– ORIGIN French, from *camarade* 'comrade'.
camber /kambər/ ● noun **1** a slightly convex or arched shape of a road, aircraft wing, or other horizontal surface. **2** Brit. a tilt built into a road at a bend or curve. **3** the slight sideways inclination of the front wheels of a motor vehicle.
– DERIVATIVES **cambered** adjective.
– ORIGIN from Old French *chambre* 'arched', from Latin *camurus* 'curved inwards'.
cambium /kambiəm/ ● noun (pl. **cambia** or **cambiums**) Botany a layer of cells in a plant stem between the xylem and phloem, from which new tissue grows by cellular division.
– ORIGIN Latin, 'change, exchange'.
Cambodian /kambōdiən/ ● noun **1** a person from Cambodia. **2** the Khmer language. ● adjective relating to Cambodia.
Cambrian /kambriən/ ● adjective **1** Welsh. **2** Geology relating to the first period in the Palaeozoic era (between the Precambrian aeon and the Ordovician period, about 570 to 510 million years ago).
– ORIGIN from Latin *Cambria*, from Welsh *Cymru* 'Wales'.
cambric /kambrik/ ● noun a lightweight, closely woven white linen or cotton fabric.
– ORIGIN named after the town of *Cambrai* in northern France; compare with CHAMBRAY.
Cambs. ● abbreviation Cambridgeshire.
camcorder ● noun a portable combined video camera and video recorder.
came past tense of COME.
camel ● noun a large, long-necked mammal of arid country, with long slender legs, broad cushioned feet, and either one or two humps on the back.
– ORIGIN Greek *kamēlos*, from Semitic.
camel hair ● noun **1** a fabric made from the hair of a camel. **2** fine, soft hair from a squirrel's tail, used in artists' brushes.
camellia /kəmeeliə/ ● noun an evergreen shrub with showy flowers and shiny leaves.
– ORIGIN named after the Moravian botanist Joseph *Kamel* (1661–1706) (Latinized as *Camellus*).
camelopard /kamməlәpaard, kəmel-/ ● noun archaic a giraffe.
– ORIGIN from Greek *kamēlos* 'camel' + *pardalis* 'leopard'.
Camelot /kammәlot/ ● noun **1** the place where King Arthur held his legendary court. **2** a place associated with glittering romance and optimism.
Camembert /kamməmbair/ ● noun a kind of rich, soft, creamy cheese originally made near Camembert in Normandy.
cameo /kammiō/ ● noun (pl. **cameos**) **1** a piece of jewellery consisting of a portrait in profile carved in relief on a background of a different colour. **2** a short piece of writing which neatly encapsulates something. **3** a small distinctive part played by a distinguished actor.
– ORIGIN Latin *cammaeus*.
camera ● noun a device for recording visual images in the form of photographs, cinema film, or video signals.
– PHRASES **in camera** chiefly Law in private, in particular in the private chambers of a judge. [ORIGIN Latin, 'in the chamber'.]
– ORIGIN Latin, 'vault, arched chamber'.
camera obscura /kammərə obskyoorə/ ● noun a darkened box or building with a lens or aperture for projecting the image of an external object on to a screen inside.
– ORIGIN Latin, 'dark chamber'.
camera-ready ● adjective in the right form to be reproduced photographically on to a printing plate.
Cameroonian /kammərōōniən/ ● noun a person from Cameroon, a country on the west coast of Africa. ● adjective relating to Cameroon.
camiknickers ● plural noun Brit. a woman's one-piece undergarment which combines a camisole and a pair of French knickers.
camisole /kammisōl/ ● noun a woman's loose-fitting undergarment for the upper body.
– ORIGIN French, from Latin *camisia* 'shirt or nightgown'.
camomile ● noun variant spelling of CHAMOMILE.
camouflage /kamməflaazh/ ● noun **1** the disguising of military personnel and equipment by painting or covering them to make them blend in with their surroundings. **2** clothing or materials used for such a purpose. **3** the natural colouring or form of an animal which enables it to blend in with its surroundings. ● verb hide or disguise by means of camouflage.
– ORIGIN French, from *camoufler* 'to disguise'.
camp[1] ● noun **1** a place where tents are temporarily set up. **2** a complex of huts and other buildings for soldiers, holidaymakers, or detainees. **3** the supporters of a particular party or doctrine regarded collectively. **4** a fortified prehistoric site, especially an Iron Age hill fort. ● verb lodge in a tent or caravan while on holiday.
– PHRASES **break camp** take down a tent or the tents of an encampment ready to leave.
– ORIGIN Latin *campus* 'level ground'.
camp[2] informal ● adjective **1** (of a man) ostentatiously and extravagantly effeminate. **2** deliberately exaggerated and theatrical in style. ● noun camp behaviour or style. ● verb (usu. **camp it up**) behave in a camp way.
– DERIVATIVES **campy** adjective.
– ORIGIN of unknown origin.
campaign ● noun **1** a series of military operations intended to

Thesaurus

informal chill out, hang/stay loose, decompress.
– OPPOSITES excite, upset.
calumny ● noun SLANDER, defamation (of character), character assassination, calumniation, libel; vilification, traducement, obloquy, verbal abuse, revilement, scurrility; *informal* mud-slinging; *archaic* contumely.
camaraderie ● noun FRIENDSHIP, comradeship, fellowship, companionship; mutual support, team spirit, esprit de corps.
camouflage ● noun **1** *pieces of turf served for camouflage* DISGUISE, concealment. **2** *her indifference was merely camouflage* FACADE, (false) front, smokescreen, cover-up, mask, blind, screen, masquerade, dissimulation, pretence.
● verb *the caravan was camouflaged with branches* DISGUISE, hide, conceal, keep hidden, mask, screen, cover (up).
camp[1] ● noun **1** *an army camp* BIVOUAC, encampment; campsite, camping ground. **2** *the liberal and conservative camps* FACTION,

achieve an objective in a particular area. **2** an organized course of action to achieve a goal. ● **verb** work in an organized way towards a goal.
– DERIVATIVES **campaigner** noun.
– ORIGIN French *campagne* 'open country', from Latin *campus* 'level ground'; the modern sense arose from an army's practice of moving from a fortress or town to open country at the onset of summer.

campanile /kampəneelay/ ● **noun** a bell tower, especially a free-standing one.
– ORIGIN Italian, from *campana* 'bell'.

campanology ● **noun** the art or practice of bell-ringing.
– DERIVATIVES **campanological** adjective **campanologist** noun.
– ORIGIN from Latin *campana* 'bell'.

campanula /kampanyoolə/ ● **noun** another term for BELLFLOWER.
– ORIGIN from Latin *campana* 'bell'.

camp bed ● **noun** Brit. a folding portable bed.

camper ● **noun** **1** a person who spends a holiday in a tent or holiday camp. **2** (also **camper van**) a large motor vehicle with living accommodation.

campesino /kampəseenō/ ● **noun** (pl. **campesinos** /kampəseenōz/) (in Spanish-speaking countries) a peasant farmer.
– ORIGIN Spanish.

campfire ● **noun** an open-air fire in a camp.

camp follower ● **noun** **1** a civilian working in or attached to a military camp. **2** a person who associates with a group without being a full member of it.

camphor /kamfər/ ● **noun** a white volatile crystalline substance with an aromatic smell and bitter taste, occurring in certain essential oils.
– ORIGIN Latin *camphora*, from Sanskrit.

campion ● **noun** a plant of the pink family, typically having pink or white flowers with notched petals.
– ORIGIN perhaps related to CHAMPION, the name originally being applied to a plant of this kind said to have been used for victors' garlands in ancient times.

campo /kampō/ ● **noun** (pl. **campos**) **1** (**the campo**) (in South America, especially Brazil) a grass plain with occasional stunted trees. **2** a square in an Italian or Spanish town.
– ORIGIN Spanish, Portuguese, and Italian, 'field'.

campsite ● **noun** a place used for camping, especially one equipped for holidaymakers.

campus ● **noun** (pl. **campuses**) **1** the grounds and buildings of a university or college. **2** N. Amer. the grounds of a college, school, hospital, or other institution.
– ORIGIN Latin, 'level ground'.

campylobacter /kampilōbaktər/ ● **noun** a genus of bacterium responsible for some food poisoning in humans and spontaneous abortion in animals.
– ORIGIN from Greek *kampulos* 'bent' + BACTERIUM.

camshaft /kamshaaft/ ● **noun** a shaft with one or more cams attached to it, especially one operating the valves in an internal-combustion engine.

can[1] ● **modal verb** (3rd sing. present **can**; past **could**) **1** be able to. **2** used to express doubt or surprise: *he can't have finished.* **3** used to indicate that something is typically the case: *he could be very moody.* **4** be permitted to.
– USAGE On whether it is better to use **can** or **may** when requesting permission, see the note at MAY.
– ORIGIN Old English, 'know'.

can[2] ● **noun** **1** a cylindrical metal container, in particular one in which food or drink is hermetically sealed for long-term storage. **2** (**the can**) N. Amer. informal prison. **3** (**the can**) N. Amer. informal the toilet. ● **verb** (**canned**, **canning**) preserve in a can.
– PHRASES **a can of worms** a complex matter that once acknowledged will prove difficult to manage. **in the can** informal on tape or film and ready to be broadcast or released.
– DERIVATIVES **canner** noun.
– ORIGIN Old English.

Canada goose ● **noun** a common brownish-grey North American goose, introduced in Britain and elsewhere.

Canadian ● **noun** a person from Canada. ● **adjective** relating to Canada.
– DERIVATIVES **Canadianism** noun.

canaille /kanī/ ● **noun** derogatory the common people; the masses.
– ORIGIN French, from Italian *canaglia* 'pack of dogs', from *cane* 'dog'.

canal ● **noun** **1** an artificial waterway allowing the passage of boats inland or conveying water for irrigation. **2** a tubular duct in a plant or animal conveying food, liquid, or air.
– ORIGIN Latin *canalis* 'pipe, groove, channel', from *canna* 'cane'.

canalize /kannəlīz/ (also **canalise**) ● **verb** **1** convert (a river) into a navigable canal. **2** convey through a duct or channel. **3** give a direction or purpose to.
– DERIVATIVES **canalization** noun.

canapé /kannəpay/ ● **noun** **1** a small piece of bread or pastry with a savoury topping, often served with drinks. **2** a sofa, especially a decorative French antique.
– ORIGIN French, 'sofa, couch'; the first sense is a figurative extension of this (a 'couch' on which to place toppings); related to CANOPY.

canard /kənaard, kannaard/ ● **noun** an unfounded rumour or story.
– ORIGIN French, 'duck', also 'hoax', from Old French *caner* 'to quack'.

canary ● **noun** (pl. **canaries**) **1** a bright yellow finch with a melodious song, popular as a cage bird. **2** (also **canary yellow**) a bright yellow colour.
– ORIGIN from the *Canary* Islands, to which one species of the bird is native; the name of the islands is from Latin *canaria insula* 'island of dogs'.

canasta /kənastə/ ● **noun** a card game resembling rummy, using two packs and usually played by two pairs of partners.
– ORIGIN Spanish, 'basket'.

cancan ● **noun** a lively, high-kicking stage dance originating in 19th-century Parisian music halls.
– ORIGIN French, child's word for *canard* 'duck', from Old French *caner* 'to quack'.

cancel ● **verb** (**cancelled**, **cancelling**; US also **canceled**, **canceling**) **1** decide that (a planned event) will not take place. **2** annul or revoke. **3** (**cancel out**) neutralize or negate the effect of. **4** mark (a stamp, ticket, etc.) to show that it has been used and is no longer valid.
– DERIVATIVES **cancellation** noun **canceller** noun.
– ORIGIN Latin *cancellare*, from *cancelli* 'crossbars'.

Cancer ● **noun** **1** Astronomy a constellation (the Crab), said to represent a crab crushed under the foot of Hercules. **2** Astrology the fourth sign of the zodiac, which the sun enters at the northern summer solstice (about 21 June).
– DERIVATIVES **Cancerian** /kanseeriən/ noun & adjective.
– ORIGIN Latin, 'crab'.

cancer ● **noun** **1** a disease caused by an uncontrolled division of abnormal cells in a part of the body. **2** a malignant growth or tumour resulting from such a division of cells. **3** something evil or destructive that is hard to contain or eradicate.
– DERIVATIVES **cancerous** adjective.

Thesaurus

wing, group, lobby, caucus, bloc, coterie, sect, cabal.
● **verb** *they camped in a field* PITCH TENTS, set up camp, encamp, bivouac.

camp[2] (informal) ● **adjective** **1** *a highly camp actor* EFFEMINATE, effete, mincing; *informal* campy, limp-wristed; *Brit. informal* poncey. **2** *camp humour* EXAGGERATED, theatrical, affected; *informal* over the top, OTT, camped up.
– OPPOSITES macho.
– PHRASES **camp it up** POSTURE, behave theatrically/affectedly, overact; *informal* ham it up.

campaign ● **noun** **1** *Napoleon's Russian campaign* MILITARY OPERATION(S), manoeuvre(s); crusade, war, battle, offensive, attack. **2** *the campaign to reduce vehicle emissions* CRUSADE, drive, push, struggle; operation, strategy, battle plan.
● **verb** **1** *they are campaigning for political reform* CRUSADE, fight, battle, push, press, strive, struggle, lobby. **2** *she campaigned as a political outsider* RUN/STAND FOR OFFICE, canvass, electioneer; *N. Amer.* stump.

campaigner ● **noun** CRUSADER, fighter, activist; champion, advocate, promoter.

can ● **noun** TIN, canister; jerrycan, oilcan.

canal ● **noun** **1** *barges chugged up the canal* INLAND WATERWAY, watercourse. **2** *the ear canal* DUCT, tube, passage.

cancel ● **verb** **1** *the match was cancelled* CALL OFF, abandon, scrap, drop, axe; *informal* scrub, nix; *N. Amer. informal* redline. **2** *his visa has been cancelled* ANNUL, invalidate, nullify, declare null and void, void; revoke, rescind, retract, countermand, withdraw; *Law* vacate, discharge. **3** *rising unemployment cancelled out earlier eco-*

– ORIGIN Latin, 'crab or creeping ulcer', said to have been applied to tumours because the swollen veins around them resembled the limbs of a crab.

candela /kandellə/ ● noun Physics the SI unit of luminous intensity.
– ORIGIN Latin, 'candle'.

candelabrum /kandilaabrəm/ ● noun (pl. **candelabra** /kandilaabrə/) a large branched candlestick or holder for several candles or lamps.
– USAGE Based on the Latin forms, the correct singular is **candelabrum** and the correct plural is **candelabra**, but these forms are often not observed in practice: the singular form is assumed to be **candelabra** and hence its plural is interpreted as **candelabras**.
– ORIGIN Latin, from *candela* 'candle'.

candid ● adjective truthful and straightforward; frank.
– DERIVATIVES **candidly** adverb **candidness** noun.
– ORIGIN originally in the sense 'white': from Latin *candidus* 'white'.

candida /kandidə/ ● noun a yeast-like parasitic fungus that sometimes causes thrush.
– ORIGIN from Latin *candidus* 'white'.

candidate /kandidət/ ● noun **1** a person who applies for a job or is nominated for election. **2** a person taking an examination. **3** a person or thing regarded as suitable for a particular fate, treatment, or position: *she was the perfect candidate for a biography.*
– DERIVATIVES **candidacy** noun **candidature** noun (Brit.).
– ORIGIN from Latin *candidatus* 'white-robed', also denoting a candidate for office (who traditionally wore a white toga), from *candidus* 'white'.

candle ● noun a stick or block of wax or tallow with a central wick which is lit to produce light as it burns.
– PHRASES **be unable to hold a candle to** informal be not nearly as good as. **not worth the candle** not justifying the cost or trouble involved.
– ORIGIN Latin *candela*, from *candere* 'be white or glisten'.

Candlemas /kand'lməss, -mass/ ● noun a Christian festival held on 2 February to commemorate the purification of the Virgin Mary (after childbirth, according to Jewish law) and the presentation of Christ in the Temple.

candlepower ● noun the illuminating power of a light source.
– ORIGIN from the former use of *candle* for a unit of luminous intensity, superseded by the *candela*.

candlestick ● noun a support or holder for a candle.

candlewick ● noun a thick, soft cotton fabric with a raised, tufted pattern.

candour (US **candor**) ● noun the quality of being open and honest.
– ORIGIN Latin *candor* 'whiteness, purity'.

candy ● noun (pl. **candies**) (also **sugar candy**) **1** N. Amer. sweets. **2** chiefly Brit. sugar crystallized by repeated boiling and slow evaporation. ● verb (**candies**, **candied**) preserve (fruit) by coating and impregnating it with a sugar syrup.
– ORIGIN from French *sucre candi* 'crystallized sugar', from Arabic.

candyfloss ● noun Brit. **1** a mass of pink or white fluffy spun sugar wrapped round a stick. **2** something worthless or insubstantial.

candy-striped ● adjective patterned with alternating stripes of white and another colour, typically pink.

candytuft ● noun a plant with small heads of white, pink, or purple flowers, grown as a garden or rockery plant.
– ORIGIN from *Candy*, obsolete form of *Candia*, former name of Crete.

cane ● noun **1** the hollow jointed stem of tall reeds, grasses, etc., especially bamboo. **2** the slender, pliant stem of plants such as rattan. **3** a woody stem of a raspberry or related plant. **4** a length of cane or a slender stick used as a support for plants, a walking stick, or an instrument of punishment. ● verb beat with a cane as a punishment.
– DERIVATIVES **caner** noun.
– ORIGIN Greek *kanna, kannē.*

caned ● adjective **1** (of furniture) made or repaired with cane. **2** Brit. informal intoxicated with drink or drugs.

canine /kaynīn/ ● adjective relating to or resembling a dog. ● noun **1** a dog or other animal of the dog family. **2** (also **canine tooth**) a pointed tooth between the incisors and premolars, often greatly enlarged in carnivores.
– ORIGIN Latin *caninus*, from *canis* 'dog'.

canister ● noun a round or cylindrical container.
– ORIGIN Greek *kanastron* 'wicker basket', from *kanna* 'cane'.

canker ● noun **1** a destructive fungal disease of trees that results in damage to the bark. **2** an open lesion in plant tissue caused by infection or injury. **3** fungal rot in parsnips, tomatoes, or other vegetables. **4** an ulcerous condition in animals, especially an inflammation of the ear caused by a mite infestation. ● verb **1** become infected with canker. **2** (**cankered**) infected with a pervasive and corrupting bitterness.
– DERIVATIVES **cankerous** adjective.
– ORIGIN originally denoting a tumour: from Old French *chancre*, from Latin *cancer* 'crab, creeping ulcer'.

canna ● noun a lily-like tropical American plant with bright flowers and ornamental strap-like leaves.
– ORIGIN Latin *canna*; related to CANE.

cannabis ● noun a psychotropic drug in the form of a resinous extract or dried preparation, obtained from the hemp plant.
– ORIGIN Latin (used as the botanical name for hemp); from Greek *kannabis*.

canned ● adjective **1** preserved in a sealed can. **2** informal, chiefly derogatory (of music, applause, etc.) pre-recorded.

cannellini bean /kannəleeni/ ● noun a kidney-shaped bean of a medium-sized creamy-white variety.
– ORIGIN Italian *cannellini*, 'small tubes'.

cannelloni /kannəlōni/ ● plural noun rolls of pasta stuffed with a meat or vegetable mixture, usually cooked in a cheese sauce.
– ORIGIN Italian, 'large tubes'.

cannery ● noun (pl. **canneries**) a factory where food is canned.

cannibal ● noun a person who eats the flesh of other human beings.
– DERIVATIVES **cannibalism** noun **cannibalistic** adjective.
– ORIGIN Spanish *Canibales*, a variant of *Caribes*, a West Indian people reputed to eat humans; related to CARIB.

cannibalize (also **cannibalise**) ● verb **1** use (a machine) as a source of spare parts for another, similar machine. **2** (of an animal) eat (an animal of its own kind).
– DERIVATIVES **cannibalization** noun.

cannon ● noun (pl. usu. same) **1** a large, heavy piece of artillery formerly used in warfare. **2** an automatic heavy gun that fires shells from an aircraft or tank. ● verb chiefly Brit. (**cannon into/off**) collide with forcefully or at an angle.
– ORIGIN Italian *cannone* 'large tube', from Latin *canna* 'cane'.

Thesaurus

nomic gains NEUTRALIZE, counterbalance, counteract, balance (out), countervail; negate, nullify, wipe out, negative.

cancer ● noun **1** *most skin cancers are curable* MALIGNANT GROWTH, cancerous growth, tumour, malignancy; *technical* carcinoma, sarcoma, melanoma, lymphoma, myeloma. **2** *racism is a cancer* EVIL, blight, scourge, poison, canker, plague; *archaic* pestilence.
– RELATED TERMS carcinomatous, carcin-.

candid ● adjective **1** *his responses were remarkably candid* FRANK, outspoken, forthright, blunt, open, honest, truthful, sincere, direct, plain-spoken, bluff; *informal* upfront, on the level; *N. Amer. informal* on the up and up; *archaic* round, free-spoken. **2** *candid shots* UNPOSED, informal, uncontrived, impromptu, natural.
– OPPOSITES guarded.

candidate ● noun **1** *candidates should be computer-literate* (JOB) APPLICANT, job-seeker, interviewee; contender, nominee, possible; *Brit. informal* runner. **2** *A-level candidates* EXAMINEE, entrant.

candour ● noun FRANKNESS, openness, honesty, candidness, truthfulness, sincerity, forthrightness, directness, plain-spokenness, bluffness, bluntness, outspokenness; *informal* telling it like it is.

candy ● noun (*N. Amer.*) See CONFECTIONERY.

cane ● noun **1** *a silver-topped cane* (WALKING) STICK, staff; alpenstock; crook; *Austral./NZ* waddy. **2** *tie the shoot to a cane* STICK, stake, upright, pole. **3** *he was been beaten with a cane* STICK, rod, birch; *N. Amer. informal* paddle; *historical* ferule.
● verb *Matthew was caned for bullying* BEAT, strike, hit, flog, thrash, lash, birch, flagellate; *informal* give someone a hiding, larrup; *N. Amer. informal* whale.

canker ● noun **1** *this plant is susceptible to canker* FUNGAL DISEASE, plant rot; blight. **2** *ear cankers* ULCER, ulceration, infection, sore, abscess. **3** *racism remains a canker.* See CANCER sense 2.

cannabis ● noun MARIJUANA, hashish, bhang, hemp, kif, ganja, sinsemilla, skunkweed; *informal* hash, grass, skunk, pot, blow,

cannonade /kannənayd/ ● noun a period of continuous heavy gunfire. ● verb discharge heavy guns continuously.
cannonball ● noun a round metal or stone projectile fired from a cannon.
cannon bone ● noun a long tube-shaped bone between a horse's fetlock and the knee or hock.
cannon fodder ● noun soldiers regarded merely as material to be expended in war.
cannot ● contraction can not.
cannula /kanyoolə/ ● noun (pl. **cannulae** /kanyoolee/ or **cannulas**) Surgery a thin tube inserted into the body to administer medication, drain off fluid, or introduce a surgical instrument.
– ORIGIN Latin, 'small reed'.
canny ● adjective (**cannier**, **canniest**) **1** shrewd, especially in financial or business matters. **2** N. English & Scottish pleasant; nice.
– DERIVATIVES **cannily** adverb **canniness** noun.
– ORIGIN from CAN[1], in the obsolete sense 'know'.
canoe ● noun a narrow keelless boat with pointed ends, propelled with a paddle. ● verb (**canoes**, **canoed**, **canoeing**) travel in or paddle a canoe.
– DERIVATIVES **canoeist** noun.
– ORIGIN Spanish *canoa*, from Carib.
canon[1] ● noun **1** a general rule or principle by which something is judged. **2** a Church decree or law. **3** a collection of authentic sacred books. **4** the authentic works of a particular author or artist. **5** a list of literary works considered to be permanently established as being of the highest quality. **6** Music a passage or piece of music in which a theme is taken up by two or more parts that overlap.
– ORIGIN Greek *kanōn* 'rule'.
canon[2] ● noun **1** a member of a cathedral chapter. **2** (also **canon regular** or **regular canon**) (fem. **canoness**) a member of certain orders of Roman Catholic clergy that live communally like monks or nuns.
– ORIGIN from Latin *canonicus*, from Greek *kanon* 'rule'.
canonic /kənonnik/ ● adjective **1** Music in the form of a canon. **2** another term for CANONICAL.
– DERIVATIVES **canonicity** noun.
canonical ● adjective **1** according to canon law. **2** accepted as being authentic, accurate, and authoritative. **3** of or relating to a cathedral chapter or a member of it. ● noun (**canonicals**) the prescribed official dress of the clergy.
– DERIVATIVES **canonically** adverb.
canonize (also **canonise**) ● verb **1** (in the Roman Catholic Church) officially declare (a dead person) to be a saint. **2** sanction by Church authority.
– DERIVATIVES **canonization** noun.
– ORIGIN Latin *canonizare* 'admit as authoritative'.
canon law ● noun ecclesiastical law, especially that laid down by papal pronouncements.
canonry ● noun (pl. **canonries**) the office or benefice of a canon.
canoodle ● verb informal kiss and cuddle amorously.
– ORIGIN of unknown origin.
canopy ● noun (pl. **canopies**) **1** a cloth covering hung or held up over a throne or bed. **2** a roof-like projection or shelter. **3** the expanding, umbrella-like part of a parachute. **4** the uppermost branches of the trees in a forest, forming a roof-like cover of foliage. ● verb (**canopies**, **canopied**) cover or provide with a canopy.
– ORIGIN Latin *conopeum* 'mosquito net over a bed', from Greek *kōnōps* 'mosquito'.
cant[1] /kant/ ● noun **1** hypocritical and sanctimonious talk. **2** derogatory language peculiar to a specified group. **3** (before another noun) denoting a phrase or catchword temporarily current: *a cant word.* ● verb dated talk hypocritically and sanctimoniously.
– ORIGIN originally in the sense 'singing', later 'whining speech' (as of a beggar): probably from Latin *cantare* 'to sing'.
cant[2] /kant/ ● verb be or cause to be in a slanting or oblique position; tilt. ● noun **1** a slope or tilt. **2** a wedge-shaped block of wood remaining after the better-quality pieces have been cut off.
– ORIGIN Low German *kant*, *kante*, Dutch *cant*, 'point, side, edge'.
can't ● contraction cannot.
Cantab. /kantab/ ● abbreviation of Cambridge University.
– ORIGIN from Latin *Cantabrigia* 'Cambridge'.
cantabile /kantaabilay/ ● adverb & adjective Music in a smooth singing style.
– ORIGIN Italian, 'singable'.
cantaloupe /kantəloop/ ● noun a small round variety of melon with orange flesh and ribbed skin.
– ORIGIN French *cantaloup*, from *Cantaluppi* near Rome.
cantankerous ● adjective bad-tempered, argumentative, and uncooperative.
– DERIVATIVES **cantankerously** adverb **cantankerousness** noun.
– ORIGIN perhaps a blend of Anglo-Irish *cant* 'auction' and *rancorous*.
cantata /kantaatə/ ● noun a medium-length narrative or descriptive piece of music with vocal solos and normally a chorus and orchestra.
– ORIGIN from Italian *cantata aria* 'sung air'.
canteen ● noun **1** a restaurant in a workplace or educational establishment. **2** Brit. a specially designed case containing a set of cutlery. **3** a small water bottle, as used by soldiers or campers.
– ORIGIN originally denoting a shop selling provisions or alcohol in a barracks: from Italian *cantina* 'cellar'.
canter ● noun a pace of a horse between a trot and a gallop, with not less than one foot on the ground at any time. ● verb move at a canter.
– PHRASES **in** (or **at**) **a canter** Brit. without much effort; easily.
– ORIGIN short for *Canterbury pace*, from the supposed easy pace of medieval pilgrims to Canterbury.
Canterbury bell ● noun a tall cultivated bellflower with large pale blue flowers.

C

Thesaurus

draw, the weed, reefer; *Brit. informal* wacky baccy; *N. Amer. informal* locoweed.
cannibal ● noun MANEATER, people-eater.
cannon ● noun MOUNTED GUN, field gun, piece of artillery; mortar, howitzer; *historical* carronade, bombard, culverin, falconet, serpentine; *Brit. historical* pom-pom.
● verb *the couple behind cannoned into us* COLLIDE WITH, hit, run/crash/smash/plough into.
cannonade ● noun BOMBARDMENT, shelling, gunfire, artillery fire, barrage, pounding.
canny ● adjective SHREWD, astute, sharp, sharp-witted, discerning, penetrating, discriminating, perceptive, perspicacious, wise, sagacious; cunning, crafty, wily; *N. Amer.* as sharp as a tack; *informal* smart, savvy; *Brit. informal* suss, sussed; *N. Amer. informal* heads-up; *dated* long-headed; *rare* argute.
canoe ● noun KAYAK, dugout, outrigger, bidarka, pirogue, waka.
canon[1] ● noun **1** *the canons of fair play and equal opportunity* PRINCIPLE, rule, law, tenet, precept; standard, convention, criterion, measure. **2** *a set of ecclesiastical canons* LAW, decree, edict, statute, dictate, decretal. **3** *the Shakespeare canon* (LIST OF) WORKS, writings, oeuvre.
canon[2] ● noun *a canon assists the bishop* PREBENDARY, clergyman, ecclesiastic.
canonical ● adjective **1** *the canonical method* RECOGNIZED, authoritative, authorized, accepted, sanctioned, approved, established, orthodox. **2** *canonical rites* ACCORDING TO ECCLESIASTICAL LAW, official, sanctioned.
– OPPOSITES unorthodox.
canonize ● verb **1** *the saint was canonized* BEATIFY, declare to be a saint. **2** *we canonize freedom of speech* GLORIFY, acclaim, regard as sacred; enshrine.
canopy ● noun AWNING, shade, sunshade; baldachin, tester, chuppah, velarium.
cant[1] ● noun **1** *religious cant* HYPOCRISY, sanctimoniousness, sanctimony, humbug, pietism. **2** *(derogatory) thieves' cant* SLANG, jargon, idiom, argot, patois, speech, terminology, language; *informal* lingo, -speak, -ese.
cant[2] ● verb *the deck canted some twenty degrees* TILT, lean, slant, slope, incline; tip, list, bank, heel.
● noun *the cant of the walls* SLOPE, slant, tilt, angle, inclination.
cantankerous ● adjective BAD-TEMPERED, irascible, irritable, grumpy, grouchy, crotchety, tetchy, testy, crusty, curmudgeonly, ill-tempered, ill-humoured, peevish, cross, fractious, pettish, crabbed, crabby, prickly, touchy; *informal* snappish, snappy, chippy; *Brit. informal* shirty, stroppy, narky, ratty; *N. Amer. informal* cranky, ornery; *Austral./NZ informal* snaky; *informal, dated* miffy.
– OPPOSITES affable.
canteen ● noun **1** *the staff canteen* RESTAURANT, cafeteria, refec-

C

– ORIGIN named after the bells on Canterbury pilgrims' horses.
canticle /kantik'l/ ● noun a hymn or chant forming a regular part of a church service.
– ORIGIN Latin *canticulum* 'little song'.
cantilever /kantileevər/ ● noun **1** a long projecting beam or girder fixed at only one end, used chiefly in bridge construction. **2** a bracket or beam projecting from a wall to support a balcony, cornice, etc. ● verb support by a cantilever or cantilevers.
– ORIGIN of unknown origin.
canto /kantō/ ● noun (pl. **cantos**) one of the sections into which some long poems are divided.
– ORIGIN Italian, 'song', from Latin *cantus*.
canton /kanton/ ● noun **1** a political or administrative subdivision of a country. **2** a state of the Swiss Confederation.
– DERIVATIVES **cantonal** /kantən'l/ adjective.
– ORIGIN Old French, 'corner'.
Cantonese /kantəneez/ ● noun (pl. same) **1** a person from Canton (another name for Guangzhou), a city in China. **2** a form of Chinese spoken mainly in SE China and Hong Kong. ● adjective relating to Canton or Cantonese.
cantonment /kantoonmənt/ ● noun a military station in British India.
– ORIGIN French *cantonnement*, from *cantonner* 'to quarter'.
cantor /kantor/ ● noun **1** (in Jewish worship) an official who sings liturgical music and leads prayer in a synagogue. **2** (in formal Christian worship) a person who sings solo verses to which the choir or congregation respond.
– ORIGIN Latin, 'singer'.
Canuck /kənuk/ ● noun informal a Canadian, especially a French Canadian.
– ORIGIN apparently from *Canada*.
canvas ● noun (pl. **canvases** or **canvasses**) **1** a strong, coarse unbleached cloth used to make sails, tents, etc. **2** a piece of canvas prepared for use as the surface for an oil painting. **3** (**the canvas**) the floor of a boxing or wrestling ring, having a canvas covering. **4** either of a racing boat's tapering ends, originally covered with canvas. ● verb (**canvassed**, **canvassing**; US **canvased**, **canvasing**) cover with canvas.
– PHRASES **under canvas 1** in a tent or tents. **2** with sails spread.
– ORIGIN Old French *canevas*, from Latin *cannabis* 'hemp'.
canvass ● verb **1** visit (someone) in order to seek their vote in an election. **2** question (someone) to find out their opinion. **3** Brit. propose (an idea or plan) for discussion. ● noun an act of canvassing.
– DERIVATIVES **canvasser** noun.
– ORIGIN originally in the sense 'toss in a canvas sheet' (as a sport or punishment).
canyon ● noun a deep gorge, especially one with a river flowing through it.
– ORIGIN Spanish *cañón* 'tube', from Latin *canna* 'cane'.
canyoning ● noun the sport of jumping into a fast-flowing mountain stream and being carried downstream.
CAP ● abbreviation Common Agricultural Policy.
cap ● noun **1** a soft, flat hat without a brim and usually with a peak. **2** a soft, close-fitting head covering worn for a particular purpose. **3** a protective lid or cover for a bottle, pen, etc. **4** Dentistry an artificial protective covering for a tooth. **5** an upper limit imposed on spending or borrowing. **6** chiefly Brit. a cap awarded to members of a sports team. **7** (also **Dutch cap**) Brit. informal a contraceptive diaphragm. **8** the broad upper part of a mushroom or toadstool. **9** short for PERCUSSION CAP. ● verb (**capped**, **capping**) **1** put or form a cap, lid, or cover on. **2** provide a fitting climax or conclusion to. **3** place a limit on (prices, expenditure, etc.). **4** (**be capped**) chiefly Brit. be chosen as a member of a sports team. **6** Scottish & NZ confer a university degree on.
– PHRASES **cap in hand** humbly asking for a favour. **set one's cap at** dated (of a woman) try to attract (a man). **to cap it all** as the final unfortunate incident in a long series.
– DERIVATIVES **capful** noun **capper** noun.
– ORIGIN Latin *cappa*, perhaps from *caput* 'head'.
capability ● noun (pl. **capabilities**) the power or ability to do something.
capable ● adjective **1** (**capable of**) having the ability or quality necessary to do. **2** able to achieve efficiently whatever one has to do.
– DERIVATIVES **capably** adverb.
– ORIGIN French, from Latin *capere* 'take or hold'.
capacious ● adjective having a lot of space inside; roomy.
– DERIVATIVES **capaciously** adverb **capaciousness** noun.
– ORIGIN from Latin *capax* 'capable'.
capacitance /kəpassitənss/ ● noun Physics the ability of a circuit or object to store electric charge, equivalent to the ratio of the change in electric charge to the corresponding change in electric potential.
capacitate ● verb **1** make capable. **2** make legally competent.
– DERIVATIVES **capacitation** noun.
capacitor ● noun a device used to store electric charge, consisting of one or more pairs of conductors separated by an insulator.
capacity ● noun (pl. **capacities**) **1** the maximum amount that something can contain or produce. **2** (before another noun) fully occupying the available space: *a capacity crowd.* **3** the total cylinder volume that is swept by the pistons in an internal-combustion engine. **4** the ability or power to do something. **5** a specified role or position: *I was engaged in a voluntary capacity.*
– ORIGIN Latin *capacitas*, from *capere* 'take or hold'.
caparison /kəparris'n/ ● noun an ornamental covering spread over a horse's saddle or harness. ● verb (**be caparisoned**) be decked out in rich decorative coverings.
– ORIGIN Spanish *caparazón* 'saddlecloth', from *capa* 'hood'.
cape[1] ● noun **1** a cloak, specially a short one. **2** a part of a longer coat or cloak that falls loosely over the shoulders from the neckband.
– DERIVATIVES **caped** adjective.
– ORIGIN French, from Latin *cappa* 'covering for the head'.
cape[2] ● noun a headland or promontory.
– ORIGIN Old French *cap*, from Latin *caput* 'head'.
Cape gooseberry ● noun the soft edible yellow berry of a tropical South American plant, enclosed in a lantern-shaped husk.
capelin /kaplin/ (also **caplin**) ● noun a small food fish of the

Thesaurus

tory, mess hall; *Brit. Military* NAAFI; *N. Amer.* lunchroom. **2** *a canteen of water* CONTAINER, flask, bottle.
canvass ● verb **1** *he's canvassing for the Green Party* CAMPAIGN, electioneer; *N. Amer.* stump; *Brit. informal* doorstep. **2** *they promised to canvass all members* POLL, question, ask, survey, interview. **3** *they're canvassing support* SEEK, try to obtain. **4** *(Brit.) early retirement was canvassed as a solution* PROPOSE, suggest, discuss, debate, consider.
canyon ● noun RAVINE, gorge, gully, defile, couloir; chasm, abyss, gulf; *N. Amer.* gulch, coulee.
cap ● noun **1** *a white plastic cap* LID, top, stopper, cork, bung, spile; *N. Amer.* stopple. **2** *cap and gown* MORTAR BOARD, academic cap; *Brit.* square; *dated* trencher. **3** *the cap on spending* (UPPER) LIMIT, ceiling; curb, check.
● verb **1** *mountains capped with snow* TOP, crown, cover, coat. **2** *his innings capped a great day* ROUND OFF, crown, be a fitting climax to. **3** *they tried to cap each other's stories* BEAT, better, improve on, surpass, outdo, outshine, top, upstage. **4** *(Brit.) he was capped for England* CHOOSE, select, pick, give someone the nod. **5** *budgets will be capped* SET A LIMIT ON, limit, restrict; curb, control, peg.
capability ● noun ABILITY, capacity, power, potential; competence, proficiency, accomplishment, adeptness, aptitude, faculty, experience, skill, skilfulness, talent, flair; *informal* know-how.
capable ● adjective *a very capable young woman* COMPETENT, able, efficient, effective, proficient, accomplished, adept, handy, experienced, skilful, skilled, talented, gifted; *informal* useful; *rare* habile.
– OPPOSITES incompetent.
– PHRASES **be capable of 1** *I'm quite capable of looking after myself* HAVE THE ABILITY TO, be equal to (the task of), be up to; *informal* have what it takes to. **2** *the strange events are capable of rational explanation* BE OPEN/SUSCEPTIBLE TO, admit of, allow of.
capacious ● adjective ROOMY, spacious, ample, big, large, sizeable, generous; *formal* commodious.
– OPPOSITES cramped, small.
capacity ● noun **1** *the capacity of the freezer* VOLUME, size, magnitude, dimensions, measurements, proportions. **2** *his capacity to inspire trust.* See CAPABILITY. **3** *in his capacity as Commander-in-Chief* POSITION, post, job, office; role, function.
cape[1] ● noun *a woollen cape* CLOAK, mantle, cope, wrap, stole, tip-

smelt family, found in North Atlantic coastal waters.
– ORIGIN French, from Latin *cappa* 'cap or cape'.
capellini /kappəleeni/ ● plural noun pasta in the form of very thin strands.
– ORIGIN Italian, 'small hairs'.
caper[1] ● verb skip or dance about in a lively or playful way. ● noun **1** a playful skipping movement. **2** informal an illicit or ridiculous activity or escapade.
– PHRASES **cut a caper** make a playful, skipping movement.
– DERIVATIVES **caperer** noun.
– ORIGIN from Latin *capreolus* 'little goat'.
caper[2] ● noun a flower bud of a southern European shrub, pickled for use in cooking.
– ORIGIN Greek *kapparis*.
capercaillie /kappəkayli/ (Scottish also **capercailzie** /-kaylzi/) ● noun (pl. **capercaillies**) a large turkey-like grouse of mature pine forests in northern Europe.
– ORIGIN from Scottish Gaelic *capull coille*, 'horse of the wood'.
capillarity ● noun the tendency of a liquid in a narrow tube or pore to rise or fall as a result of surface tension.
capillary /kəpilləri/ ● noun **1** Anatomy any of the fine branching blood vessels that form a network between the arterioles and venules. **2** (also **capillary tube**) a tube with an internal diameter of hair-like thinness. ● adjective relating to capillaries or capillarity.
– ORIGIN Latin *capillaris*, from *capillus* 'hair'.
capillary action ● noun another term for CAPILLARITY.
capital[1] ● noun **1** the most important city or town of a country or region, usually its seat of government and administrative centre. **2** wealth owned by a person or organization or invested, lent, or borrowed. **3** the excess of a company's assets over its liabilities. **4** a capital letter. ● adjective **1** (of an offence or charge) liable to the death penalty. **2** (of a letter of the alphabet) large in size and of the form used to begin sentences and names. **3** informal, dated excellent.
– PHRASES **make capital out of** use to advantage.
– ORIGIN Latin *capitalis*, from *caput* 'head'.
capital[2] ● noun Architecture the top part of a pillar or column.
– ORIGIN Latin *capitellum* 'little head'.
capital gain ● noun a profit from the sale of property or an investment.
capital goods ● plural noun goods that are used in producing other goods, rather than being bought by consumers.
capitalism ● noun an economic and political system in which a country's trade and industry are controlled by private owners for profit, rather than by the state.
– DERIVATIVES **capitalist** noun & adjective **capitalistic** adjective.
capitalize (also **capitalise**) ● verb **1** (**capitalize on**) take the chance to gain advantage from. **2** provide with financial capital. **3** convert into financial capital. **4** write or print (a word or letter) in capital letters or with an initial capital.
– DERIVATIVES **capitalization** noun.
capital punishment ● noun the legally authorized killing of someone as punishment for a crime.
capital sum ● noun a lump sum of money payable to an insured person or paid as an initial fee or investment.
capitation ● noun the payment of a fee or grant to a doctor, school, etc., the amount being determined by the number of patients, pupils, etc.
– ORIGIN Latin, from *caput* 'head'.
capitol /kappit'l/ ● noun **1** (in the US) a building housing a legislative assembly. **2** (**the Capitol**) the seat of the US Congress in Washington DC. **3** (**the Capitol**) the temple of Jupiter on the Capitoline Hill in ancient Rome.
– ORIGIN Old French *capitolie*, from Latin *caput* 'head'.
capitulate /kəpityoolayt/ ● verb give in to an opponent or an unwelcome demand.
– DERIVATIVES **capitulation** noun **capitulator** noun.
– ORIGIN originally in the sense 'parley': from Latin *capitulare* 'draw up under headings', from *caput* 'head'.
caplet ● noun trademark a coated oral medicinal tablet.
– ORIGIN blend of CAPSULE and TABLET.
caplin ● noun variant spelling of CAPELIN.
capo[1] /kappō/ (also **capo tasto**) ● noun (pl. **capos**) a clamp fastened across all the strings of a fretted musical instrument to raise their tuning.
– ORIGIN from Italian *capo tasto*, 'head stop'.
capo[2] /kappō/ ● noun (pl. **capos**) chiefly N. Amer. the head or branch head of a crime syndicate, especially the Mafia.
– ORIGIN Italian, from Latin *caput* 'head'.
capoeira /kappooayrə/ ● noun a system of physical discipline and movement featuring elements from dance and the martial arts, originating among Brazilian slaves.
– ORIGIN Portuguese.
capon /kayp'n/ ● noun a castrated domestic cock fattened for eating.
– ORIGIN Old French, from Latin *capo*.
cappuccino /kappoocheenō/ ● noun (pl. **cappuccinos**) coffee made with milk that has been frothed up with pressurized steam.
– ORIGIN Italian, 'Capuchin' (because the colour of the coffee resembles that of a Capuchin's habit).
caprice /kəpreess/ ● noun a sudden and unaccountable change of mood or behaviour.
– ORIGIN French, from Italian *capriccio* 'head with the hair standing on end', later 'sudden start'.
capricious /kəprishəss/ ● adjective given to sudden and unaccountable changes of mood or behaviour.
– DERIVATIVES **capriciously** adverb **capriciousness** noun.
Capricorn /kaprikorn/ ● noun Astrology the tenth sign of the zodiac (the Goat), which the sun enters at the northern winter solstice (about 21 December).
– DERIVATIVES **Capricornian** noun & adjective.
– ORIGIN Latin *capricornus*, from *caper* 'goat' + *cornu* 'horn'.
caprine /kaprīn/ ● adjective relating to or resembling a goat or goats.
– ORIGIN Latin *caprinus*, from *caper* 'goat'.
capri pants /kəpree/ (also **capris**) ● plural noun close-fitting tapered trousers for women.
– ORIGIN from *Capri*, an island off the west coast of Italy.
capsicum /kapsikəm/ ● noun (pl. **capsicums**) the fruit of a tropical American plant, of which sweet peppers and chilli peppers are varieties.
– ORIGIN Latin, perhaps from *capsa* 'container, case'.
capsize ● verb (of a boat) be overturned in the water.
– ORIGIN perhaps from Spanish *capuzar* 'sink (a ship) by the

Thesaurus

pet, poncho; *historical* pelisse, pelerine, mantlet.
cape[2] ● noun *the ship rounded the cape* HEADLAND, promontory, point, head, foreland; horn, hook, bill, ness, mull.
caper ● verb *children were capering about* SKIP, dance, romp, frisk, gambol, cavort, prance, frolic, leap, hop, jump; *rare* curvet, rollick. ● noun **1** *she did a little caper* DANCE, skip, hop, leap, jump, curvet, gambado. **2** *(informal) I'm too old for this kind of caper* ESCAPADE, stunt, prank, trick, mischief, antics, high jinks, skylarking; *informal* lark, shenanigans.
capital ● noun **1** *Warsaw is the capital of Poland* FIRST CITY, seat of government, metropolis. **2** *he had enough capital to pull off the deal* MONEY, finance(s), funds, the wherewithal, the means, assets, wealth, resources, investment capital; *informal* dough, bread, loot; *Brit. informal* dosh, brass, lolly, spondulicks; *US informal* greenbacks; *N. Amer. informal* bucks; *Austral./NZ informal* Oscar. **3** *he wrote the name in capitals* CAPITAL LETTER, upper-case letter, block capital; *informal* cap. ● adjective **1** *capital letters* UPPER-CASE, block. **2** *(informal, dated) he's a really capital fellow.* See SPLENDID sense 2.
capitalism ● noun PRIVATE ENTERPRISE, free enterprise, the free market.
– OPPOSITES communism.
capitalist ● noun FINANCIER, investor, industrialist; magnate, tycoon.
capitalize ● verb *the capacity to capitalize new ventures* FINANCE, fund, underwrite, provide capital for, back; *N. Amer. informal* bankroll, stake.
– PHRASES **capitalize on** *an attempt to capitalize on the government's embarrassment* TAKE ADVANTAGE OF, profit from, make the most of, exploit; *informal* cash in on.
capitulate ● verb SURRENDER, give in, yield, concede defeat, give up the struggle, submit; lay down one's arms, raise/show the white flag, throw in the towel/sponge.
– OPPOSITES resist, hold out.
caprice ● noun **1** *his wife's caprices* WHIM, whimsy, vagary, fancy, fad, quirk, eccentricity, foible. **2** *the staff tired of his caprice* FICKLENESS, changeableness, volatility, capriciousness, unpredictability.
capricious ● adjective FICKLE, inconstant, changeable, variable,

C

head'.
cap sleeve ● noun a short sleeve which tapers to nothing under the arm.
capstan /**kap**stən/ ● noun a broad revolving cylinder with a vertical axis, used for winding a rope or cable.
– ORIGIN Provençal *cabestan*, from Latin *capere* 'seize'.
capstone ● noun a stone placed on top of a wall, tomb, or other structure.
capsule ● noun **1** a small soluble case of gelatin containing a dose of medicine, swallowed whole. **2** a small case or container. **3** a space capsule. **4** Botany a dry fruit that releases its seeds by bursting open when ripe.
– DERIVATIVES **capsular** adjective **capsulate** adjective.
– ORIGIN Latin *capsula* 'small case or container'.
captain ● noun **1** the person in command of a ship. **2** the pilot in command of a civil aircraft. **3** a rank of naval officer above commander and below commodore. **4** a rank of officer in the army and in the US and Canadian air forces, above lieutenant and below major. **5** (in the US) a police officer in charge of a precinct. **6** the leader of a team, especially in sports. ● verb serve as the captain of.
– DERIVATIVES **captaincy** noun.
– ORIGIN Old French *capitain* 'chief', from Latin *caput* 'head'.
caption ● noun **1** a title or brief explanation appended to an illustration or cartoon. **2** a piece of text appearing on screen as part of a film or television broadcast. ● verb provide with a caption.
– ORIGIN originally in the sense 'capture': from Latin, from *capere* 'take, seize'.
captious /**kap**shəss/ ● adjective tending to find fault or raise petty objections.
– DERIVATIVES **captiously** adverb **captiousness** noun.
– ORIGIN Old French *captieux*, from Latin *capere* 'take, seize'; related to CAPTION.
captivate ● verb attract and hold the interest and attention of; charm.
– DERIVATIVES **captivating** adjective **captivation** noun.
– ORIGIN from Latin *captivare* 'take captive'.
captive ● noun a person who has been taken prisoner or held in confinement. ● adjective **1** imprisoned or confined. **2** having no freedom to choose an alternative. **3** (of a facility or service) controlled by and reserved for a particular organization.
– DERIVATIVES **captivity** noun.
– ORIGIN Latin *captivus*, from *capere* 'seize, take'.
captor ● noun a person who imprisons or confines another.
capture ● verb **1** take into one's possession or control by force. **2** record or express accurately in words or pictures. **3** cause (data) to be stored in a computer. ● noun **1** the action of capturing or of being captured. **2** a person or thing that has been captured.
– DERIVATIVES **capturer** noun.
– ORIGIN Latin *captura*, from *capere* 'seize, take'.
Capuchin /**kap**pŏŏchin/ ● noun **1** a friar belonging to a strict branch of the Franciscan order. **2** a cloak and hood formerly worn by women. **3** (**capuchin**) a South American monkey with a cowl-like cap of hair on the head.
– ORIGIN from Italian *cappuccino* 'small hood', from Latin *cappa* 'covering for the head'.
capybara /kappi**baa**rə/ ● noun (pl. same or **capybaras**) a large South American rodent resembling a long-legged guinea pig.
– ORIGIN Spanish *capibara* or Portuguese *capivara*, from an American Indian word meaning 'grass-eater'.
car ● noun **1** a powered road vehicle designed to carry a small number of people. **2** a railway carriage or (N. Amer.) wagon.
– ORIGIN originally meaning 'wheeled vehicle': from Latin *carrus*.
carabiner ● noun variant spelling of KARABINER.
carabiniere /karrəbi**nyair**i/ ● noun (pl. **carabinieri** pronunc. same) a member of the Italian paramilitary police.
– ORIGIN Italian, 'soldier armed with a carbine'.
caracul ● noun variant spelling of KARAKUL.
carafe /kə**raf**/ ● noun an open-topped glass flask typically used for serving wine in a restaurant.
– ORIGIN French, from Italian *caraffa*, probably from an Arabic word meaning 'draw water'.
carambola /karrəm**bō**lə/ ● noun a golden-yellow fruit with a star-shaped cross section; starfruit.
– ORIGIN Portuguese, probably from an Indian language.
caramel ● noun **1** sugar or syrup heated until it turns brown, used as a flavouring or colouring for food or drink. **2** a soft toffee made with sugar and butter that have been melted and further heated.
– DERIVATIVES **caramelize** (also **caramelise**) verb.
– ORIGIN French, from Spanish *caramelo*.
carapace /**karr**əpayss/ ● noun the hard upper shell of a tortoise or crustacean.
– ORIGIN French, from Spanish *carapacho*.
carat /**karr**ət/ ● noun **1** a unit of weight for precious stones and pearls, equivalent to 200 milligrams. **2** (US also **karat**) a measure of the purity of gold, pure gold being 24 carats.
– ORIGIN French, from Greek *keration* 'fruit of the carob' (also denoting a unit of weight).
caravan ● noun **1** Brit. a vehicle equipped for living in, usually designed to be towed. **2** N. Amer. a covered truck. **3** historical a group of people travelling together across a desert in Asia or North Africa.
– DERIVATIVES **caravanner** noun **caravanning** noun.
– ORIGIN French *caravane*, from Persian.
caravanserai /karrə**van**sərī, -ri/ (US also **caravansary**) ● noun (pl. **caravanserais** or **caravansaries**) **1** historical an inn with a central courtyard for travellers in the desert regions of Asia or North Africa. **2** a group of people travelling together; a caravan.

Thesaurus

mercurial, volatile, unpredictable, temperamental; whimsical, fanciful, flighty, quirky, faddish.
– OPPOSITES consistent.
capsize ● verb OVERTURN, turn over, turn upside down, upend, flip/tip/keel over, turn turtle; *Nautical* pitchpole; *archaic* overset.
– OPPOSITES right.
capsule ● noun **1** *he swallowed a capsule* PILL, tablet, lozenge, pastille, drop; *informal* tab. **2** *the bottle's capsule* COVER, seal, cap, top. **3** *a space capsule* MODULE, craft, probe.
captain ● noun **1** *the ship's captain* COMMANDER, master; *informal* skipper. **2** *the team's captain* LEADER, head; *informal* boss, skipper. **3** *a captain of industry* MAGNATE, tycoon, industrialist; chief, head, leader, principal; *informal* boss, number one, bigwig, big shot/gun, honcho, top dog; *N. Amer. informal* kahuna, top banana.
● verb *a vessel captained by a cut-throat* COMMAND, run, be in charge of, control, manage, govern; *informal* skipper.
caption ● noun TITLE, heading, wording, head, legend, rubric, slogan.
captious ● adjective CRITICAL, fault-finding, quibbling, cavilling; hypercritical, pedantic, hair-splitting; *informal* nit-picking, pernickety.
– OPPOSITES forgiving.
captivate ● verb ENTHRAL, charm, enchant, bewitch, fascinate, beguile, entrance, enrapture, delight, attract, allure.
– OPPOSITES repel, bore.
captive ● noun *the captives were released* PRISONER, convict, detainee, inmate; prisoner of war, POW, internee; *informal* jailbird, con; *Brit. informal* (old) lag; *N. Amer. informal* yardbird.
● adjective *captive wild animals* CONFINED, caged, incarcerated, locked up; jailed, imprisoned, in prison, interned, detained, in captivity, under lock and key, behind bars.
captivity ● noun IMPRISONMENT, confinement, internment, incarceration, detention; *archaic* duress, durance.
– OPPOSITES freedom.
captor ● noun JAILER, guard, incarcerator, keeper.
capture ● verb **1** *the spy was captured in Moscow* CATCH, apprehend, seize, arrest; take prisoner/captive, imprison, detain, put/throw in jail, put behind bars, put under lock and key, incarcerate; *informal* nab, collar, lift, pick up, pull in; *Brit. informal* nick. **2** *guerrillas captured a strategic district* OCCUPY, invade, conquer, seize, take (possession of). **3** *the music captured the atmosphere of a summer morning* EXPRESS, reproduce, represent, encapsulate. **4** *the tales of pirates captured the children's imaginations* ENGAGE, attract, catch, seize, hold.
– OPPOSITES free.
● noun *he tried to evade capture* ARREST, apprehension, seizure, being taken prisoner/captive, imprisonment.
car ● noun **1** *he drove up in his car* MOTOR (CAR), automobile; *informal* wheels; *N. Amer. informal* auto. **2** *the dining car* CARRIAGE, coach; *Brit.* saloon.
carafe ● noun FLASK, jug, pitcher, decanter, flagon.
caravan ● noun **1** (*Brit.*) *a fishing holiday in a caravan* MOBILE HOME,

– ORIGIN Persian, 'caravan palace'.

caravel /karrəvel/ (also **carvel**) ● noun historical a small, fast Spanish or Portuguese ship of the 15th–17th centuries.

– ORIGIN Portuguese *caravela*, from Greek *karabos* 'horned beetle' or 'light ship'.

caraway /karrəway/ ● noun the seeds of a plant of the parsley family, used for flavouring.

– ORIGIN Latin *carui*, probably ultimately from Greek *karon* 'cumin'.

carbide ● noun Chemistry a compound of carbon with a metal or other element.

carbine ● noun **1** a light automatic rifle. **2** historical a short rifle or musket used by cavalry.

– ORIGIN French *carabine*, from *carabin* 'mounted musketeer'.

carbohydrate ● noun any of a large group of compounds (including sugars, starch, and cellulose) which contain carbon, hydrogen, and oxygen, occur in foods and living tissues, and can be broken down to release energy in the body.

carbolic acid (also **carbolic**) ● noun phenol, especially when used as a disinfectant.

carbon ● noun a non-metallic chemical element which has two main forms (diamond and graphite), occurs in impure form in charcoal, soot, and coal, and is present in all organic compounds.

– DERIVATIVES **carbonaceous** adjective.

– ORIGIN Latin *carbo* 'coal, charcoal'.

carbonara /kaarbənaarə/ ● adjective denoting a pasta sauce made with bacon or ham, egg, and cream.

– ORIGIN from Italian, 'charcoal kiln'.

carbonate /kaarbənayt/ ● noun a salt of the anion CO_3^{2-}, typically formed by reaction of carbon dioxide with bases. ● verb (usu. as adj. **carbonated**) dissolve carbon dioxide in.

– DERIVATIVES **carbonation** noun.

carbon black ● noun a fine carbon powder used as a pigment.

carbon copy ● noun **1** a copy made with carbon paper. **2** a person or thing identical to another.

carbon dating ● noun the determination of the age of an organic object from the relative proportions of the isotopes carbon-12 and carbon-14 that it contains.

carbon dioxide ● noun a colourless, odourless gas produced by burning carbon and organic compounds and by respiration, and absorbed by plants in photosynthesis.

carbon fibre ● noun a material consisting of thin, strong crystalline filaments of carbon.

carbonic /kaarbonnik/ ● adjective relating to carbon or carbon dioxide.

carbonic acid ● noun a very weak acid formed when carbon dioxide dissolves in water.

Carboniferous /kaarbəniffərəss/ ● adjective Geology relating to the fifth period of the Palaeozoic era (between the Devonian and Permian periods, about 363 to 290 million years ago), a time when extensive coal-bearing strata were formed.

carbonize (also **carbonise**) ● verb convert into carbon, by heating or burning.

– DERIVATIVES **carbonization** noun.

carbon monoxide ● noun a colourless, odourless toxic flammable gas formed by incomplete combustion of carbon.

carbon paper ● noun thin paper coated with carbon, used for making a second impression as a document is being written or typed.

carbon steel ● noun steel in which the main alloying element is carbon, and whose properties depend on the percentage of carbon present.

carbon tax ● noun a tax on petrol and other fossil fuels.

carbonyl /kaarbənīl, -nil/ ● noun (before another noun) Chemistry referring to the radical formed of a carbon atom and an oxygen atom, present in aldehydes, ketones, and many other organic compounds: *carbonyl group.*

car boot sale ● noun Brit. an outdoor sale at which people sell things from the boots of their cars.

carborundum /kaarbərundəm/ ● noun a very hard black solid consisting of silicon carbide, used as an abrasive.

– ORIGIN blend of CARBON and CORUNDUM.

carboxyl /kaarboksil, -sil/ ● noun (before another noun) Chemistry referring to the radical formed from a carbonyl and a hydroxyl radical, present in organic acids: *carboxyl group.*

carboxylic acid /kaarboksillik/ ● noun Chemistry an acid containing a carboxyl group, such as formic and acetic acids.

carboy ● noun a large globular glass bottle with a narrow neck, used for holding acids or other corrosive liquids.

– ORIGIN from a Persian word meaning 'large glass flagon'.

carbuncle /kaarbungk'l/ ● noun **1** a severe abscess or multiple boil in the skin. **2** a bright red gem, in particular a polished garnet.

– DERIVATIVES **carbuncular** adjective.

– ORIGIN Latin *carbunculus* 'small coal', from *carbo* 'coal, charcoal'.

carburettor /kaarbərettər/ (also **carburetter**, US **carburetor**) ● noun a device in an internal-combustion engine for mixing air with a fine spray of liquid fuel.

– DERIVATIVES **carburetted** (US **carbureted**) adjective.

– ORIGIN from archaic *carburet* 'combine or charge with carbon'.

carcass (Brit. also **carcase**) ● noun **1** the dead body of an animal, especially one prepared for cutting up as meat. **2** the remains of a cooked bird after all the edible parts have been removed. **3** the structural framework of a building, ship, or piece of furniture.

– ORIGIN Old French *carcois* and in later use from French *carcasse*.

carcinogen /kaarsinnəjən/ ● noun a substance capable of causing cancer.

– DERIVATIVES **carcinogenic** adjective.

– ORIGIN from CARCINOMA.

carcinogenic /kaarsinnəjennik/ ● adjective having the potential to cause cancer.

– DERIVATIVES **carcinogenesis** noun **carcinogenicity** noun.

carcinoma /kaarsinōmə/ ● noun (pl. **carcinomas** or **carcinomata** /kaarsinōmətə/) a cancer arising in the tissues of the skin or of the lining of the internal organs.

– DERIVATIVES **carcinomatous** adjective.

– ORIGIN from Greek *karkinos* 'crab'.

card[1] ● noun **1** thick, stiff paper or thin cardboard. **2** a piece of card for writing on, especially a postcard or greetings card. **3** a business card or visiting card. **4** a small rectangular piece of plastic containing machine-readable personal data, e.g. a credit card or cash card. **5** a playing card. **6** (**cards**) a game played with playing cards. **7** (**cards**) Brit. informal documents relating to an employee, especially for tax and national insurance, held by the employer. **8** informal, dated or N. Amer. an odd or amusing person. ● verb write on a card, especially for indexing.

– PHRASES **a card up one's sleeve** Brit. a plan or asset that is kept secret until it is needed. **give someone their cards** (or **get one's cards**) Brit. informal dismiss someone (or be dismissed) from employment. **hold all the cards** be in a very strong position. **on the cards** informal possible or likely. **play the —— card** exploit a specified issue or idea, especially for political advantage: *he plays the race card.* **play one's cards right** make the best use of one's assets and opportunities. **put** (or **lay**) **one's cards on the table** be completely open and honest in declaring one's intentions.

– ORIGIN Old French *carte*, from Greek *khartēs* 'papyrus leaf'.

card[2] ● verb comb and clean (raw wool or similar material) with a sharp-toothed instrument to disentangle the fibres before spinning. ● noun a toothed implement or machine for this purpose.

– DERIVATIVES **carder** noun.

– ORIGIN Provençal *carda*, from *cardar* 'tease, comb', from Latin *carduus* 'thistle'.

C

Thesaurus

camper, caravanette; *N. Amer.* trailer; *Brit. trademark* Dormobile. **2** *a gypsy caravan* WAGON, covered cart. **3** *a refugee caravan* CONVOY, procession, column, train.

carbuncle ● noun BOIL, sore, abscess, pustule, wen, whitlow; *technical* furuncle.

carcass ● noun **1** *a lamb carcass* CORPSE, (dead) body, remains; *Medicine* cadaver; *informal* stiff; *archaic* corse. **2** *(informal) shift your carcass* BODY, self; backside; *N. Amer. informal* butt.

card ● noun **1** *a piece of stiff card* CARDBOARD, pasteboard, board. **2** *I'll send her a card* GREETINGS CARD, postcard. **3** *she produced her card* IDENTIFICATION, ID, credentials; business card. **4** *she paid with her card* CREDIT CARD, debit card, cash card, swipe card; *informal* plastic. **5** *the cards were dealt* PLAYING CARD; (**cards**) pack of cards. **6** *(informal, dated) he said she was a card* ECCENTRIC, character; JOKER, wit, wag, jester, clown; *informal* laugh, scream, hoot, riot; *informal, dated* caution.

C

cardamom /kaardəməm/ (also **cardamum**) • noun the aromatic seeds of a plant of the ginger family, used as a spice.
– ORIGIN from Greek *kardamon* 'cress' + *amōmon*, a kind of spice plant.
cardboard • noun **1** pasteboard or stiff paper. **2** (before another noun) (of a fictional character) lacking depth and realism.
cardboard city • noun chiefly Brit. an urban area where homeless people congregate under makeshift shelters.
card-carrying • adjective registered as a member of a political party or trade union.
cardiac /kaardiak/ • adjective of or relating to the heart.
– ORIGIN from Greek *kardia* 'heart'.
cardigan • noun a knitted jumper fastening with buttons down the front.
– ORIGIN named after the 7th Earl of *Cardigan* (1797–1868), whose troops fighting in the Crimean War first wore such garments.
cardinal • noun **1** a leading dignitary of the Roman Catholic Church, nominated by and having the power to elect the Pope. **2** a deep scarlet colour like that of a cardinal's cassock. **3** an American songbird of which the male is partly or mostly red and which typically has a crest. • adjective of the greatest importance; fundamental.
– DERIVATIVES **cardinalate** noun **cardinally** adverb **cardinalship** noun.
– ORIGIN Latin *cardinalis*, from *cardo* 'hinge'; sense 1 has arisen from the function of such priests as 'pivots' of church life.
cardinal humour • noun see HUMOUR.
cardinal number • noun a number denoting quantity (one, two, three, etc.), as opposed to an ordinal number (first, second, third, etc.).
cardinal point • noun each of the four main points of the compass (north, south, east, and west).
cardinal virtue • noun each of the chief moral attributes of scholastic philosophy: justice, prudence, temperance, and fortitude.
card index • noun a catalogue in which each item is entered on a separate card.
cardiogram • noun a record of muscle activity within the heart made by a cardiograph.
cardiograph • noun an instrument for recording heart muscle activity.
– DERIVATIVES **cardiographer** noun **cardiography** noun.
– ORIGIN from Greek *kardia* 'heart'.
cardiology • noun the branch of medicine concerned with diseases and abnormalities of the heart.
– DERIVATIVES **cardiological** adjective **cardiologist** noun.
– ORIGIN from Greek *kardia* 'heart'.
cardiopulmonary • adjective Medicine of or relating to the heart and the lungs.
cardiovascular • adjective Medicine of or relating to the heart and blood vessels.
cardoon • noun a tall thistle-like plant related to the globe artichoke, with edible leaves and roots.
– ORIGIN French *cardon*, from Latin *carduus* 'thistle, artichoke'.
card sharp (also **card sharper**) • noun a person who cheats at cards.
card vote • noun Brit. another term for BLOCK VOTE.
cardy (also **cardie**) • noun (pl. **cardies**) Brit. informal a cardigan.
care • noun **1** the provision of what is necessary for the welfare and protection of someone or something. **2** Brit. protective custody or guardianship provided for children by a local authority. **3** serious attention or consideration applied to avoid damage, risk, or error: *handle with care.* **4** a feeling of or occasion for anxiety. • verb **1** feel concern or interest. **2** feel affection or liking. **3** (**care for/to do**) like to have or be willing to do. **4** (**care for**) look after and provide for the needs of.
– PHRASES **care of** at the address of. **take care 1** be cautious. **2** make sure (to do). **take care of 1** keep safe and provided for. **2** deal with.
– DERIVATIVES **caring** noun & adjective.
– ORIGIN Old English.
careen /kəreen/ • verb **1** turn (a ship) on its side for cleaning or repair. **2** (of a ship) tilt; lean over. **3** move in an uncontrolled way; career.
– ORIGIN from Latin *carina* 'a keel'.
career • noun **1** an occupation undertaken for a significant period of a person's life, usually with opportunities for progress. **2** (before another noun) working with long-term commitment in a particular profession: *a career diplomat.* **3** (before another noun) (of a woman) choosing to pursue a profession rather than devoting her time to childcare or housekeeping. • verb move swiftly and in an uncontrolled way in a specified direction.
– ORIGIN originally denoting a road or racecourse: from French *carrière*, from Latin *carrus* 'wheeled vehicle'.
careerist • noun a person who is intent on gaining advancement in their profession.
– DERIVATIVES **careerism** noun.
carefree • adjective free from anxiety or responsibility.
– DERIVATIVES **carefreeness** noun.
careful • adjective **1** taking care to avoid mishap or harm; cautious. **2** (**careful with**) prudent in the use of. **3** done with or showing thought and attention.
– DERIVATIVES **carefully** adverb **carefulness** noun.
careless • adjective **1** not giving sufficient attention or thought to avoiding harm or mistakes. **2** (**careless of/about**) not concerned or worried about. **3** showing no interest or effort; casual.
– DERIVATIVES **carelessly** adverb **carelessness** noun.

Thesaurus

– PHRASES **give someone their cards** (Brit. informal) DISMISS, get rid of, lay off, make redundant, let someone go, discharge; informal sack, fire, kick/boot out, give someone their marching orders, give someone the (old) heave-ho, give someone the elbow/push. **on the cards** (informal) LIKELY, possible, probable, expected, in the wind, in the offing.
cardinal • adjective FUNDAMENTAL, basic, main, chief, primary, prime, principal, paramount, pre-eminent, highest, key, essential.
– OPPOSITES unimportant.
care • noun **1** *the care of the child* SAFE KEEPING, supervision, custody, charge, protection, control, responsibility; guardianship, wardship. **2** *handle with care* CAUTION, carefulness, heedfulness, heed, attention, attentiveness. **3** *she chose her words with care* DISCRETION, judiciousness, forethought, thought, regard, heed, mindfulness; accuracy, precision. **4** *the cares of the day* WORRY, anxiety, trouble, concern, stress, pressure, strain; sorrow, woe, hardship. **5** *constant care for others* CONCERN, consideration, thought, regard, solicitude.
– OPPOSITES neglect, carelessness.
• verb *the teachers didn't care about our work* BE CONCERNED, worry (oneself), trouble/concern oneself, bother, mind, be interested; informal give a damn/hoot/rap.
– PHRASES **care for 1** *he cares for his children* LOVE, be fond of, be devoted to, treasure, adore, dote on, think the world of, worship, idolize. **2** *would you care for a cup of coffee?* LIKE, want, desire, fancy, feel like. **3** *the hospice cares for the terminally ill* LOOK AFTER, take care of, tend, attend to, minister to, nurse; be responsible for, keep safe, keep an eye on.
career • noun **1** *a business career* PROFESSION, occupation, vocation, calling, employment, line (of work), walk of life, métier. **2** *a chequered career* EXISTENCE, life, course, passage, path.
• adjective *a career politician* PROFESSIONAL, permanent, full-time.
• verb *they careered down the hill* RUSH, hurtle, streak, shoot, race, bolt, dash, speed, run, whizz, zoom, flash, blast, charge, hare, fly, pelt, go like the wind; informal belt, scoot, tear, zap, zip, whip, go like a bat out of hell; Brit. informal bomb, bucket; N. Amer. informal hightail, clip.
carefree • adjective UNWORRIED, untroubled, blithe, airy, nonchalant, insouciant, happy-go-lucky, free and easy, easy-going, relaxed; informal laid back.
– OPPOSITES careworn.
careful • adjective **1** *be careful when you go up the stairs* CAUTIOUS, heedful, alert, attentive, watchful, vigilant, wary, on guard, circumspect. **2** *Roland was careful of his reputation* MINDFUL, heedful, protective. **3** *careful with money* PRUDENT, thrifty, economical, sparing, frugal, scrimping, abstemious; informal stingy. **4** *careful consideration of the facts* ATTENTIVE, conscientious, painstaking, meticulous, diligent, assiduous, sedulous, scrupulous, punctilious, methodical; informal pernickety; archaic nice.
– OPPOSITES careless, extravagant.
careless • adjective **1** *careless motorists* INATTENTIVE, incautious, negligent, remiss; heedless, irresponsible, impetuous, reckless. **2** *careless work* SHODDY, slapdash, slipshod, scrappy, slovenly, negligent, lax, slack, disorganized, hasty, hurried; informal sloppy, slap-happy. **3** *a careless remark* THOUGHTLESS, insensitive, indiscreet, unguarded, incautious, inadvertent. **4** *she was very careless*

carer ● noun Brit. a family member or paid helper who regularly looks after a sick, elderly, or disabled person.

caress ● verb touch or stroke gently or lovingly. ● noun a gentle or loving touch.
– DERIVATIVES **caressing** adjective **caressingly** adverb.
– ORIGIN French *caresser*, from Latin *carus* 'dear'.

caret /karrət/ ● noun a mark (‸, ⁁) placed below a line of text to indicate a proposed insertion.
– ORIGIN Latin, 'is lacking'.

caretaker ● noun **1** a person employed to look after a public building. **2** (before another noun) holding power temporarily: *a caretaker government.*

careworn ● adjective tired and unhappy because of prolonged worry.

cargo ● noun (pl. **cargoes** or **cargos**) goods carried commercially on a ship, aircraft, or truck.
– ORIGIN Spanish, from Latin *carricare* 'to load', from *carrus* 'wheeled vehicle'.

cargo pants ● plural noun loose-fitting casual cotton trousers with large patch pockets halfway down each leg.

Carib /karrib/ ● noun **1** a member of an indigenous South American people living mainly in coastal regions of French Guiana, Suriname, Guyana, and Venezuela. **2** the language of the Carib.
– ORIGIN Spanish *caribe*, from Haitian Creole.

Caribbean /karribeeən, kəribbiən/ ● adjective relating to the region consisting of the Caribbean Sea, its islands (including the West Indies), and the surrounding coasts.
– USAGE There are two acceptable pronunciations of **Caribbean**: the British pronunciation puts the stress on the **-be-**, while in the US and the Caribbean itself the stress is on the **-rib-**.

caribou /karriboo/ ● noun (pl. same) N. Amer. a reindeer.
– ORIGIN Canadian French, from an American Indian word meaning 'snow-shoveller'.

caricature /karrikətyoor/ ● noun a depiction of a person in which distinguishing characteristics are exaggerated for comic or grotesque effect. ● verb make a caricature of.
– DERIVATIVES **caricatural** adjective **caricaturist** noun.
– ORIGIN Italian *caricatura*, from Latin *carricare* 'to load'.

caries /kaireez/ ● noun decay and crumbling of a tooth or bone.
– DERIVATIVES **carious** adjective.
– ORIGIN Latin.

carillon /kərilyən/ ● noun a set of bells sounded from a keyboard or by an automatic mechanism.
– ORIGIN French, from Old French *quarregnon* 'peal of four bells', from Latin *quattuor* 'four'.

carjacking ● noun chiefly N. Amer. the action of stealing a car after violently ejecting its driver.

Carmelite /kaarməlīt/ ● noun a friar or nun of an order founded at Mount Carmel in NW Israel during the Crusades (*c.*1154). ● adjective relating to the Carmelites.

carminative /kaarminətiv/ Medicine ● adjective relieving flatulence. ● noun a carminative drug.
– ORIGIN from Latin *carminare* 'heal by incantation', from *carmen* 'song, verse, incantation'.

carmine /kaarmīn/ ● noun a vivid crimson pigment made from cochineal.
– ORIGIN French *carmin*, from an Arabic word meaning 'kermes'; related to CRIMSON.

carnage /kaarnij/ ● noun the killing of a large number of people.
– ORIGIN French, from Latin *caro* 'flesh'.

carnal ● adjective relating to physical, especially sexual, needs and activities.
– DERIVATIVES **carnality** noun **carnally** adverb.
– ORIGIN Latin *carnalis*, from *caro* 'flesh'.

carnal knowledge ● noun dated, chiefly Law sexual intercourse.

carnation ● noun a double-flowered cultivated variety of clove pink, with grey-green leaves and showy pink, white, or red flowers.
– ORIGIN perhaps based on a misreading of an Arabic word meaning 'clove or clove pink', influenced by French *carnation* 'flesh colour or rosy pink', from Latin *caro* 'flesh'.

carnelian /kaarneeliən/ (also **cornelian**) ● noun a dull red or pink semi-precious variety of chalcedony.
– ORIGIN Old French *corneline*, the prefix *car-* being suggested by Latin *caro* 'flesh'.

carnival ● noun **1** an annual period of public revelry involving processions, music, and dancing. **2** N. Amer. a travelling funfair or circus.
– DERIVATIVES **carnivalesque** adjective.
– ORIGIN Italian *carnevale*, from Latin *carnelevamen* 'Shrovetide', from *caro* 'flesh' + *levare* 'put away'.

carnivore /kaarnivor/ ● noun a carnivorous animal.

carnivorous /kaarnivvərəss/ ● adjective (of an animal) feeding on flesh.
– DERIVATIVES **carnivorously** adverb **carnivorousness** noun.
– ORIGIN Latin *carnivorus*, from *caro* 'flesh'.

carnosaur ● noun a large bipedal carnivorous dinosaur of a group including tyrannosaurus, allosaurus, and megalosaurus.

carob /karrəb/ ● noun the edible brownish-purple pod of an Arabian tree, from which a powder is extracted for use as a substitute for chocolate.
– ORIGIN Old French *carobe*, from Arabic.

carol ● noun a religious song or popular hymn associated with Christmas. ● verb (**carolled**, **carolling**; US **caroled**, **caroling**) **1** (**go carolling**) sing carols in the streets. **2** sing or say happily.
– DERIVATIVES **caroller** (US **caroler**) noun.
– ORIGIN Old French *carole*.

Carolingian /karrəlinjiən/ (also **Carlovingian**) ● adjective **1** relating to the Frankish dynasty founded by Charlemagne's father (Pepin III), which ruled in western Europe from 750 to 987. **2** denoting a script developed in France during the time of Charlemagne, on which modern lower-case letters are largely based. ● noun a member of the Carolingian dynasty.
– ORIGIN alteration of earlier *Carlovingian*, by association with Latin *Carolus* 'Charles'.

carotene /karrəteen/ ● noun an orange or red plant pigment found notably in carrots, important in the formation of vitamin A.
– DERIVATIVES **carotenoid** /kərottinoyd/ noun.
– ORIGIN from Latin *carota* 'carrot'.

carotid /kərottid/ ● adjective Anatomy relating to the two main arteries carrying blood to the head and neck.
– ORIGIN from Greek *karōtides*, plural of *karōtis* 'drowsiness, stupor' (because compression of these arteries was thought to cause stupor).

Thesaurus

of investments NEGLIGENT, heedless, improvident, unconcerned, indifferent, oblivious. **5** *careless masculine grace* UNSTUDIED, artless, casual, effortless, nonchalant, insouciant, languid.
– OPPOSITES careful, meticulous.

caress ● verb STROKE, touch, fondle, brush, skim, nuzzle.

caretaker ● noun JANITOR, attendant, porter, custodian, concierge; *N. Amer.* superintendent.
● adjective *the caretaker manager* TEMPORARY, short-term, provisional, substitute, acting, interim, pro tem, stand-in, fill-in, stopgap; *N. Amer. informal* pinch-hitting.
– OPPOSITES permanent.

careworn ● adjective WORRIED, anxious, harassed, strained, stressed; drained, drawn, gaunt, haggard; *informal* hassled.
– OPPOSITES carefree.

cargo ● noun FREIGHT, load, haul, consignment, delivery, shipment; goods, merchandise; *archaic* lading.

caricature ● noun *a caricature of the Prime Minister* CARTOON, parody, satire, lampoon, burlesque; *informal* send-up, take-off.
● verb *she has turned to caricaturing her fellow actors* PARODY, satirize, lampoon, make fun of, burlesque; *informal* send up, take off.

caring ● adjective KIND, kind-hearted, warm-hearted, tender; concerned, attentive, thoughtful, solicitous, considerate; affectionate, loving, doting, fond; sympathetic, understanding, compassionate, feeling.
– OPPOSITES cruel.

carnage ● noun SLAUGHTER, massacre, mass murder, butchery, bloodbath, bloodletting; holocaust, pogrom, ethnic cleansing.

carnal ● adjective SEXUAL, sensual, erotic, lustful, lascivious, libidinous, lecherous, licentious; physical, bodily, corporeal, fleshly.
– OPPOSITES spiritual.

carnival ● noun **1** *the town's carnival* FESTIVAL, fiesta, fête, gala, jamboree, celebration. **2** *(N. Amer.) he worked at a carnival* FUNFAIR, circus, fair, amusement show.

carnivorous ● adjective MEAT-EATING, predatory, of prey.
– OPPOSITES herbivorous.

carol ● noun *children sang carols* CHRISTMAS SONG, hymn, canticle.

C

carouse /kərowz/ ● verb drink alcohol and enjoy oneself with others in a noisy, lively way. ● noun a noisy, lively drinking party.
– DERIVATIVES **carousal** noun **carouser** noun.
– ORIGIN originally meaning 'right out, completely' in the phrase *drink carouse*, from German *gar aus trinken*.

carousel /karrəsel/ ● noun **1** a merry-go-round at a fair. **2** a rotating machine or device, in particular a conveyor system for baggage collection at an airport.
– ORIGIN originally in the sense 'an equestrian tournament among knights': from Italian *carosello*, perhaps from *carro* 'chariot'.

carp[1] ● noun (pl. same) a deep-bodied freshwater fish, often kept in ponds and sometimes farmed for food.
– ORIGIN Latin *carpa*.

carp[2] ● verb complain or find fault continually.
– DERIVATIVES **carper** noun.
– ORIGIN originally in the sense 'talk, chatter': from Old Norse, 'brag', later influenced by Latin *carpere* 'slander, pluck at'.

carpaccio /kaarpachiō/ ● noun an Italian hors d'oeuvre consisting of thin slices of raw beef or fish served with a sauce.
– ORIGIN named after the Italian painter Vittore *Carpaccio* (*c.*1455–1525), from his use of red pigments.

carpal Anatomy & Zoology ● adjective relating to the carpus. ● noun a bone of the carpus.

carpal tunnel syndrome ● noun a painful condition of the hand and fingers caused by compression of a major nerve where it passes over the carpal bones.

carpe diem /kaarpay deeem/ ● exclamation make the most of the present time.
– ORIGIN Latin, 'seize the day!'.

carpel ● noun Botany the female reproductive organ of a flower, consisting of an ovary, a stigma, and usually a style.
– DERIVATIVES **carpellary** adjective.
– ORIGIN Greek *karpos* 'fruit'.

carpenter ● noun a person who makes wooden objects and structures. ● verb make by shaping wood.
– DERIVATIVES **carpentry** noun.
– ORIGIN Old French *carpentier*, from Latin *carpentarius artifex* 'carriage-maker'; related to CAR.

carpenter trousers ● plural noun loose-fitting trousers with many pockets of various sizes and loops for tools at the top or sides of the legs.

carpet ● noun **1** a floor covering made from thick woven fabric. **2** a large rug. **3** a thick or soft expanse or layer: *a carpet of bluebells*. ● verb (**carpeted**, **carpeting**) **1** cover with a carpet. **2** Brit. informal reprimand severely.
– PHRASES **on the carpet** informal being severely reprimanded by someone in authority. **sweep under the carpet** conceal or ignore (a problem) in the hope that it will be forgotten.
– DERIVATIVES **carpeting** noun.
– ORIGIN originally denoting a thick cover for a table or bed: from obsolete Italian *carpita* 'woollen counterpane', from Latin *carpere* 'pluck, pull to pieces'; the phrase 'on the carpet' and the related verb sense are in reference to the covering over the council table before which one would be summoned.

carpet bag ● noun a travelling bag of a kind originally made of carpet-like fabric.

carpetbagger ● noun derogatory, chiefly N. Amer. **1** a politician who seeks election in an area where they have no local connections. **2** an unscrupulous opportunist.

carpet-bomb ● verb bomb (an area) intensively.

carpet slipper ● noun a soft slipper with an upper of wool or thick cloth.

carport ● noun an open-sided shelter for a car, projecting from the side of a house.

carpus /kaarpəss/ ● noun (pl. **carpi** /kaarpī/) the group of small bones in the wrist.
– ORIGIN Greek *karpos* 'wrist'.

carrack /karrək/ ● noun a large European merchant ship of a kind operating from the 14th to the 17th century.
– ORIGIN Old Fench *caraque*.

carrageen /karrəgeen/ (also **carrageen moss**) ● noun an edible red shoreline seaweed with flattened branching fronds.
– ORIGIN Irish.

carrel /karrəl/ ● noun **1** a small cubicle with a desk for a reader in a library. **2** historical a small enclosure or study in a cloister.
– ORIGIN apparently related to CAROL in the obsolete sense 'a ring or enclosure'.

carriage ● noun **1** a four-wheeled passenger vehicle pulled by two or more horses. **2** Brit. any of the separate passenger vehicles of a train. **3** Brit. the conveying of goods from one place to another. **4** a person's bearing or deportment. **5** a moving part of a machine that carries other parts into the required position. **6** a wheeled support for moving a heavy object such as a gun.
– ORIGIN Old French *cariage*, from *carier* 'carry'.

carriage clock ● noun Brit. a portable clock in a rectangular case with a handle on top.

carriageway ● noun Brit. **1** each of the two sides of a dual carriageway or motorway. **2** the part of a road intended for vehicles.

carrier ● noun **1** a person or thing that carries or holds something. **2** a person or company that transports goods or people for payment. **3** a person or animal that transmits a disease to others without suffering from it themselves.

carrier bag ● noun Brit. a plastic or paper bag with handles, for carrying shopping.

carrier pigeon ● noun a homing pigeon trained to carry messages.

carrion ● noun the decaying flesh of dead animals.
– ORIGIN Old French *caroine*, *charoigne*, from Latin *caro* 'flesh'.

carrion crow ● noun a common black crow.

carrot ● noun **1** the tapering orange root of a plant of the parsley family, eaten as a vegetable. **2** something enticing offered as a means of persuasion: *training that relies more on the carrot than on the stick*.
– ORIGIN Greek *karōton*.

carroty ● adjective (of a person's hair) orange-red.

carry ● verb (**carries**, **carried**) **1** move or transport from one place to another. **2** have on one's person wherever one goes. **3** support the weight of. **4** assume or accept (responsibility or blame). **5** have as a feature or consequence: *the bike carries a ten-year guarantee*. **6** conduct or transmit. **7** take or develop (an idea or activity) to a particular point. **8** approve (a proposed measure) by a majority of votes: *the motion was carried by one vote*. **9** persuade to support one's policy. **10** publish or broadcast. **11** (of a sound or voice) travel a specific distance: *his voice carried clearly across the room*. **12** (**carry oneself**) stand and move in a specified way. **13** be pregnant with. ● noun (pl. **carries**) an act of carrying.
– PHRASES **be/get carried away** lose self-control. **carry all before one** overcome all opposition. **carry the can** Brit. informal take responsibility for a mistake or misdeed. **carry the day** be victorious or successful. **carry forward** transfer (figures) to a new page or account. **carry off 1** take away by force. **2** (of a disease) kill. **3** succeed in doing. **carry on 1** continue. **2** engage in (an activity). **3** informal, chiefly Brit. be engaged in a love affair.

Thesaurus

● verb *Boris carolled happily* SING, trill, warble, chirp; *archaic* wassail.

carouse ● verb DRINK AND MAKE MERRY, go on a drinking bout, go on a spree; revel, celebrate, roister; *informal* booze, go boozing, binge, go on a binge, go on a bender, paint the town red, party, rave, make whoopee, whoop it up; *Brit. informal* go on the bevvy; *archaic* wassail.

carp ● verb COMPLAIN, cavil, grumble, grouse, whine, bleat, nag; *informal* gripe, grouch, beef, bellyache, moan, bitch, whinge; *Brit. informal* be on at someone; *N. English informal* mither; *N. Amer. informal* kvetch.
– OPPOSITES praise.

carpenter ● noun WOODWORKER, joiner, cabinet-maker; *Brit. informal* chippy.

carpet ● noun **1** *a Turkish carpet* RUG, mat, matting, floor covering. **2** *a carpet of wild flowers* COVERING, blanket, layer, cover, cloak, mantle.
● verb **1** *the gravel was carpeted in moss* COVER, coat, overlay, overspread, blanket. **2** *(Brit. informal) an officer was carpeted for leaking information*. See REPRIMAND verb.

carriage ● noun **1** *a railway carriage* COACH, car; *Brit.* saloon. **2** *a horse and carriage* WAGON, hackney, hansom, gig, landau, trap. **3** *the carriage of bikes on trains* TRANSPORT, transportation, conveyance, carrying, movement, shipment. **4** *an erect carriage* POSTURE, bearing, stance, gait; attitude, manner, demeanour; *Brit.* deportment.

carry out perform (a task). **carry over 1** keep to use or deal with in a new context. **2** postpone. **carry through** bring to completion. **carry weight** be influential.
– ORIGIN Old French *carier*, from Latin *carrus* 'wheeled vehicle'.
carryall ● noun N. Amer. a large bag or case.
carrycot ● noun Brit. a small portable baby's cot.
carry-on noun Brit. informal ● 1 a fuss. **2** (also **carryings-on**) questionable or improper behaviour.
cart ● noun **1** an open horse-drawn vehicle with two or four wheels, used for carrying loads or passengers. **2** a shallow open container on wheels, pulled or pushed by hand. ● verb **1** convey in a cart or similar vehicle. **2** informal carry (a heavy or cumbersome object) somewhere with difficulty. **3** convey or remove unceremoniously: *the demonstrators were carted off by the police.*
– PHRASES **put the cart before the horse** reverse the proper order or procedure.
– DERIVATIVES **carter** noun.
– ORIGIN Old Norse.
carte blanche /kaart **blaansh**/ ● noun complete freedom to act as one wishes.
– ORIGIN French, 'blank paper'.
cartel /kaartel/ ● noun an association of manufacturers or suppliers formed to maintain high prices and restrict competition.
– ORIGIN used originally to refer to the coalition of the Conservative and National Liberal parties in Germany (1887): from German *Kartell*, from Italian *cartello* 'little card'.
Cartesian /kaarteeziən/ ● adjective relating to the French philosopher René Descartes (1596–1650) and his ideas. ● noun a follower of Descartes.
– DERIVATIVES **Cartesianism** noun.
– ORIGIN from *Cartesius*, Latinized form of *Descartes*.
Cartesian coordinates ● plural noun a coordinate system using two (or three) mutually perpendicular axes.
Carthaginian /kaarthəjinniən/ ● noun a person from the ancient city of Carthage on the coast of North Africa. ● adjective relating to Carthage or its people.
carthorse ● noun Brit. a large, strong horse suitable for heavy work.
Carthusian /kaarthyoōziən/ ● noun a monk or nun of an austere contemplative order founded by St Bruno in 1084. ● adjective relating to this order.
– ORIGIN from *Carthusia*, the Latin name for *Chartreuse* in France, where the order was founded.
cartilage /kaartilij/ ● noun firm, flexible connective tissue which covers the ends of joints and forms structures such as the larynx and the external ear.
– DERIVATIVES **cartilaginous** /kaartilajinəss/ adjective.
– ORIGIN Latin *cartilago*.
cartilaginous fish ● noun a fish with a skeleton of cartilage rather than bone, e.g. a shark or ray.
cartography /kaartogrəfi/ ● noun the science or practice of drawing maps.
– DERIVATIVES **cartographer** noun **cartographic** adjective.
– ORIGIN from French *carte* 'card, map'.
carton ● noun a light cardboard box or container.
– ORIGIN French, from Italian *cartone* 'cartoon'.
cartoon ● noun **1** a drawing executed in an exaggerated style for humorous or satirical effect. **2** (also **cartoon strip**) a narrative sequence of humorous drawings with captions in a comic, newspaper, or magazine. **3** a film made from a sequence of drawings, using animation techniques to give the appearance of movement. **4** a full-size drawing made as a preliminary design for a painting or other work of art. ● verb represent in a cartoon.
– DERIVATIVES **cartoonish** adjective **cartoonist** noun **cartoony** adjective.
– ORIGIN Italian *cartone*, from Latin *carta*, *charta* 'card, map'.
cartouche /kaartoōsh/ ● noun **1** a carved decoration or drawing representing a scroll with rolled-up ends, often bearing an inscription. **2** an oval or oblong enclosing Egyptian hieroglyphs, typically representing the name and title of a monarch.
– ORIGIN French, from Latin *carta*, *charta* 'card, map'.
cartridge ● noun **1** a container holding a spool of film, a quantity of ink, or other item or substance, designed for insertion into a mechanism. **2** a casing containing a charge and a bullet or shot for small arms or an explosive charge for blasting.
– ORIGIN variant of CARTOUCHE.
cartridge paper ● noun thick, rough-textured drawing paper originally used for making cartridge casings.
cartwheel ● noun a circular sideways handspring with the arms and legs extended. ● verb perform cartwheels.
cartwright ● noun chiefly historical a person whose job is making carts.
carve ● verb **1** cut into or shape (a hard material) to produce an object or design. **2** produce (a design or object) by carving. **3** cut (cooked meat) into slices for eating. **4** (**carve out**) develop (a career, reputation, etc.) through painstaking effort. **5** (**carve up**) divide up ruthlessly. **6** (**carve up**) aggressively overtake (another driver).
– ORIGIN Old English.
carvel /kaarv'l/ ● noun variant spelling of CARAVEL.

C

Thesaurus

carrier ● noun BEARER, conveyor, transporter; porter, courier, haulier.
carry ● verb **1** *she carried the box into the kitchen* CONVEY, transfer, move, take, bring, bear, lug, fetch; *informal* cart, hump. **2** *a coach operator carrying 12 million passengers a year* TRANSPORT, convey, move, handle. **3** *satellites carry the signal over the Atlantic* TRANSMIT, conduct, relay, communicate, convey, dispatch, beam. **4** *the dinghy can carry the weight of the baggage* SUPPORT, sustain, stand; prop up, shore up, bolster. **5** *managers carry most responsibility* UNDERTAKE, accept, assume, bear, shoulder, take on (oneself). **6** *she was carrying his baby* BE PREGNANT WITH, bear, expect; *technical* be gravid with. **7** *she carried herself with assurance* CONDUCT, bear, hold; act, behave, acquit; *formal* comport; *archaic* deport. **8** *a resolution was carried* APPROVE, vote for, accept, endorse, ratify; agree to, assent to, rubber-stamp; *informal* OK, give the thumbs up to. **9** *I carried the whole audience* WIN OVER, sway, convince, persuade, influence; motivate, stimulate. **10** *today's paper carried an article on housing policy* PUBLISH, print, communicate, distribute; broadcast, transmit. **11** *we carry a wide range* SELL, stock, keep (in stock), offer, have (for sale), retail, supply. **12** *most toxins carry warnings* DISPLAY, bear, exhibit, show, be marked with. **13** *it carries a penalty of two years' imprisonment* ENTAIL, involve, result in, occasion, have as a consequence. **14** *his voice carried across the quay* BE AUDIBLE, travel, reach.
– PHRASES **be/get carried away** LOSE SELF-CONTROL, get overexcited, go too far; *informal* flip, lose it. **carry someone off** KILL (OFF), cause the death of, take/end the life of, finish off; *informal* do in. **carry something off 1** *she carried off four awards* WIN, secure, gain, achieve, collect; *informal* land, net, bag, scoop. **2** *he has carried it off* SUCCEED, triumph, be victorious, be successful, do well, make good; *informal* crack it. **carry on 1** *they carried on arguing* CONTINUE, keep (on), go on; persist in, persevere in; *informal* stick with/at. **2** *(informal) the English way of carrying on* BEHAVE, act, conduct oneself, acquit oneself; *formal* comport oneself; *archaic* deport oneself. **3** *(informal) she was carrying on with other men* HAVE AN AFFAIR, commit adultery, have a fling; *informal* play around, mess about/around; *Brit. informal* play away; *N. Amer. informal* fool around. **4** *(informal) I was always carrying on* MISBEHAVE, behave badly, get up to mischief, cause trouble, get up to no good, be naughty; clown about/around, fool about/around, mess about/around; *informal* act up; *Brit. informal* muck about/around, play up. **carry something on** ENGAGE IN, conduct, undertake, be involved in, carry out, perform. **carry something out 1** *they carried out a Caesarean* CONDUCT, perform, implement, execute. **2** *I carried out my promise to her* FULFIL, carry through, honour, redeem, make good; keep, observe, abide by, comply with, adhere to, stick to, keep faith with.
carry-on ● noun *(Brit. informal)* FUSS, commotion, trouble, bother, excitement, palaver; *informal* hoo-ha, ballyhoo, song and dance, performance, kerfuffle.
cart ● noun **1** *a horse-drawn cart* WAGON, carriage, dray; *archaic* wain. **2** *a man with a cart took their luggage* HANDCART, pushcart, trolley, barrow.
● verb *(informal) he had the wreckage carted away* TRANSPORT, convey, haul, move, shift, take; carry, lug, heft; *informal* hump.
carton ● noun BOX, package, cardboard box, container, pack, packet.
cartoon ● noun **1** *a cartoon of the Prime Minister* CARICATURE, parody, lampoon, satire; *informal* take-off, send-up. **2** *he was reading cartoons* COMIC STRIP, comic, graphic novel. **3** *they watched cartoons on television* ANIMATED FILM, animation. **4** *detailed cartoons for a full-size portrait* SKETCH, rough, outline, preliminary drawing,

carvel-built ● adjective (of a boat) having external planks which do not overlap. Compare with CLINKER-BUILT.
carver ● noun **1** a person or tool that carves. **2** Brit. the principal chair, with arms, in a set of dining chairs, intended for the person carving meat.
carvery ● noun (pl. **carveries**) chiefly Brit. a buffet or restaurant where cooked joints are carved as required.
carving ● noun an object or design carved from wood or stone as a work of art.
car wash ● noun a structure through which a vehicle is driven while being washed automatically.
caryatid /karriattid/ ● noun (pl. **caryatides** /karriattideez/ or **caryatids**) Architecture a supporting pillar in the form of a draped female figure.
– ORIGIN from Greek *karuatides* 'priestesses of Artemis at Caryae', from *Karuai* (Caryae) in Laconia.
Casanova /kassənōvə/ ● noun a man notorious for seducing women.
– ORIGIN from the name of the Italian adventurer Giovanni Jacopo *Casanova* (1725–98).
casbah ● noun variant spelling of KASBAH.
cascade ● noun **1** a small waterfall, especially one in a series. **2** a mass of something that falls, hangs, or occurs in large quantities. **3** a succession of devices or stages in a process, each of which triggers or initiates the next. ● verb **1** pour downwards rapidly and in large quantities. **2** arrange in a series or sequence.
– ORIGIN Italian *cascata*, from *cascare* 'to fall'; related to CASE¹.
cascara /kaskaarə/ (also **cascara sagrada** /səgraadə/) ● noun a laxative made from the dried bark of a North American buckthorn.
– ORIGIN Spanish, '(sacred) bark'.
case¹ ● noun **1** an instance of a particular situation or set of circumstances. **2** an instance of a disease, injury, or problem. **3** an incident under official investigation by the police. **4** a legal action that is to be or has been decided in a court of law. **5** a set of facts or arguments supporting one side of a debate or lawsuit. **6** a person or their situation as a subject of medical or welfare attention. **7** Grammar an inflected form of a noun, adjective, or pronoun expressing the semantic relation of the word to other words in the sentence: *the possessive case.*
– PHRASES **be the case** be so. **in case** so as to provide for the possibility of something happening or being true. **on** (or **off**) **someone's case** informal continually (or no longer) criticizing or harassing someone.
– ORIGIN Latin *casus* 'fall, occurrence, chance'.
case² ● noun **1** a container or protective covering. **2** Brit. a suitcase. **3** a box containing twelve bottles of wine or other drink, sold as a unit. **4** each of the two forms, capital or minuscule, in which a letter of the alphabet may be written or printed. ● verb **1** enclose within a case. **2** informal reconnoitre (a place) before carrying out a robbery.
– ORIGIN Old French *casse*, from Latin *capsa* 'box, receptacle'; sense 4 derives from a container for holding type in printing; two cases were set on a stand, the higher one for capitals (upper case) and the lower for minuscule (lower case).
casebook ● noun Brit. a written record of cases, kept by a doctor, investigator, lawyer, etc.
case-harden ● verb **1** harden the surface of (a material). **2** (**case-hardened**) made callous or tough by experience.
case history ● noun a record of a person's background or medical history kept by a doctor or social worker.
casein /kayseen/ ● noun the main protein present in milk and (in coagulated form) in cheese.
– ORIGIN from Latin *caseus* 'cheese'.
case law ● noun the law as established by the outcome of former cases rather than by legislation.
caseload ● noun the number of cases being dealt with by a doctor, lawyer, or social worker at one time.
casement ● noun a window set on a vertical hinge so that it opens like a door.
– ORIGIN Anglo-Latin *cassimentum*, from Latin *capsa* 'box, receptacle'.
case-sensitive ● adjective Computing differentiating between capital and lower-case letters.
case study ● noun **1** a detailed study of the development of a particular person, group, or situation over a period of time. **2** a particular instance used to illustrate a thesis or principle.
casework ● noun social work directly concerned with individuals and their personal circumstances.
cash ● noun **1** money in coins or notes. **2** money as an available resource: *he was always short of cash.* ● verb **1** give or obtain notes or coins for (a cheque or money order). **2** (**cash in**) convert (an insurance policy, savings account, etc.) into money. **3** (**cash in on**) informal take advantage of (a situation). **4** (**cash up**) Brit. count and check takings at the end of a day's trading.
– PHRASES **cash down** with immediate and full payment at the time of purchase. **cash in one's chips** informal die. **cash in hand** payment in cash rather than by cheque or other means.
– DERIVATIVES **cashable** adjective **cashless** adjective.
– ORIGIN originally denoting a box for money: from Old French *casse*, from Latin *capsa* 'box, receptacle'.
cash and carry ● noun a system of wholesale trading whereby goods are paid for in full and taken away by the purchaser.
cashback ● noun **1** a cash refund offered as an incentive to buyers. **2** a facility whereby a customer may withdraw cash when making a debit card purchase.
cash book ● noun a book in which receipts and payments of money are recorded.
cash card ● noun Brit. a plastic card issued by a bank or building society which enables the holder to withdraw money from a cash dispenser.
cash cow ● noun informal a business or investment that provides a steady income or profit.
cash crop ● noun a crop produced for its commercial value rather than for use by the grower.
cash desk ● noun Brit. a counter or compartment in a shop or restaurant where payments are made.

Thesaurus

underdrawing; *Computing* wireframe.
cartridge ● noun **1** *a toner cartridge* CASSETTE, magazine, canister, container. **2** *a rifle cartridge* BULLET, round, shell, charge, shot.
carve ● verb **1** *he carved horn handles* SCULPT, sculpture; cut, hew, whittle; form, shape, fashion. **2** *I carved my initials on the tree* ENGRAVE, etch, incise, score. **3** *he carved the roast chicken* SLICE, cut up, chop.
– PHRASES **carve something up** DIVIDE, partition, apportion, subdivide, split up, break up; share out, dole out; *informal* divvy up.
carving ● noun SCULPTURE, model, statue, statuette, figure, figurine.
– RELATED TERMS glyptic.
cascade ● noun WATERFALL, cataract, falls, rapids, white water.
● verb *rain cascaded from the roof* POUR, gush, surge, spill, stream, flow, issue, spurt, jet.
case¹ ● noun **1** *a classic case of overreaction* INSTANCE, occurrence, manifestation, demonstration, exposition, exhibition; example, illustration, specimen, sample, exemplification. **2** *if that is the case I will have to find somebody else* SITUATION, position, state of affairs, the lie of the land; circumstances, conditions, facts, how things stand; *Brit.* state of play; *informal* score. **3** *the officers on the case* INVESTIGATION, enquiry, examination, exploration, probe, search, inquest. **4** *urgent cases* PATIENT, sick person, invalid, sufferer, victim. **5** *he lost his case* LAWSUIT, (legal) action, legal dispute, suit, trial, legal/judicial proceedings, litigation. **6** *a strong case* ARGUMENT, contention, reasoning, logic, defence, justification, vindication, exposition, thesis.
case² ● noun **1** *a cigarette case* CONTAINER, box, canister, receptacle, holder; *dated* etui. **2** *a seed case* CASING, cover, covering, sheath, sheathing, envelope, sleeve, jacket, integument. **3** *(Brit.) she threw some clothes into a case* SUITCASE, (travelling) bag, valise, portmanteau; (**cases**) luggage, baggage. **4** *a case of wine* CRATE, box, pack. **5** *a glass display case* CABINET, cupboard.
● verb **1** *the rifle is cased in wood* COVER, surround, encase, sheathe, envelop. **2** *(informal) a thief casing the joint* RECONNOITRE, inspect, examine, survey, explore; *informal* recce, make a recce of, check out.
cash ● noun **1** *a wallet stuffed with cash* MONEY, currency, hard cash; (bank) notes, coins, change; *N. Amer.* bills; *informal* dough, bread, loot, readies, moolah; *Brit. informal* dosh, brass, lolly, spondulicks; *US informal* greenbacks; *N. Amer. informal* bucks, dinero; *Austral./NZ informal* Oscar; *Brit. dated* l.s.d. **2** *a lack of cash* FINANCE, money, resources, funds, assets, the means, the wherewithal.
– OPPOSITES cheque, credit.
● verb *the bank cashed her cheque* EXCHANGE, change, convert into cash/money; honour, pay, accept; *Brit.* encash.

cash dispenser ● noun Brit. another term for AUTOMATED TELLER MACHINE.

cashew /kashoo/ ● noun (also **cashew nut**) the edible kidney-shaped nut of a tropical American tree.
– ORIGIN Tupi.

cash flow ● noun the total amount of money passing into and out of a business, especially as affecting liquidity.

cashier[1] ● noun a person handling payments and receipts in a shop, bank, or business.
– ORIGIN French *caissier*, from *caisse* 'cash'.

cashier[2] ● verb dismiss from the armed forces because of a serious misdemeanour.
– ORIGIN French *casser* 'revoke, dismiss', from Latin *quassare* 'quash'.

cashmere ● noun fine soft wool, originally that obtained from a breed of Himalayan goat.
– ORIGIN an early spelling of *Kashmir*, a region on the northern border of India and NE Pakistan.

cashpoint ● noun Brit. another term for AUTOMATED TELLER MACHINE.

cash register ● noun a machine used in shops for totalling and recording the amount of each sale and storing the money received.

casing ● noun **1** a cover or shell that protects or encloses something. **2** the frame round a door or window.

casino ● noun (pl. **casinos**) a public building or room for gambling.
– ORIGIN Italian, 'little house'.

cask ● noun a large barrel for the storage of liquid, especially alcoholic drinks.
– ORIGIN French *casque* or Spanish *casco* 'helmet'.

cask beer ● noun draught beer left to mature naturally in the cask from which it is served.

cask-conditioned ● adjective (of beer) undergoing a secondary fermentation in the cask and not further processed before serving.

casket ● noun **1** a small ornamental box or chest for holding valuable objects. **2** chiefly N. Amer. a coffin.
– ORIGIN perhaps a variant of Old French *cassette* 'little box'.

Cassandra /kəsandrə/ ● noun a prophet of disaster.
– ORIGIN from *Cassandra* in Greek mythology, whose prophecies, though true, were doomed by Apollo to be disbelieved.

cassata /kəsaatə/ ● noun a Neapolitan ice cream dessert containing candied or dried fruit and nuts.
– ORIGIN Italian.

cassava /kəsaavə/ ● noun the starchy tuberous root of a tropical American tree, used as food.
– ORIGIN from Taino (an extinct Caribbean language).

casserole ● noun **1** a large dish with a lid, used for cooking food slowly in an oven. **2** a kind of stew cooked slowly in an oven. ● verb cook slowly in a casserole.
– ORIGIN French, from Greek *kuathion* 'little cup'.

cassette ● noun a sealed plastic case containing audio tape, videotape, film, etc., for insertion into a recorder, camera, etc.
– ORIGIN French, 'little box'.

cassia /kassiə/ ● noun **1** a tree or plant of warm climates, producing senna and other products. **2** the aromatic bark of an East Asian tree, yielding an inferior kind of cinnamon.
– ORIGIN Latin, from Hebrew, 'bark resembling cinnamon'.

cassis /kaseess/ (also **crème de cassis**) ● noun a syrupy blackcurrant liqueur.
– ORIGIN French, 'blackcurrant'.

cassock ● noun a long garment worn by some Christian clergy and members of church choirs.
– ORIGIN Italian *casacca* 'riding coat'.

cassoulet /kassoolay/ ● noun a stew made with meat and beans.
– ORIGIN French, 'small stew pan'.

cassowary /kassəwairi/ ● noun (pl. **cassowaries**) a very large flightless bird related to the emu, native mainly to New Guinea.
– ORIGIN Malay.

cast ● verb (past and past part. **cast**) **1** throw forcefully or so as to spread over an area. **2** cause (light or shadow) to appear on a surface. **3** direct (one's eyes or thoughts) towards something. **4** express: *journalists cast doubt on this account.* **5** register (a vote). **6** assign a part to (an actor) or allocate parts in (a play or film). **7** discard or shed. **8** throw the hooked and baited end of (a fishing line) out into the water. **9** shape (metal or other material) by pouring it into a mould while molten. **10** produce by casting: *a figure cast in bronze.* **11** arrange and present in a specified form or style. **12** cause (a magic spell) to take effect. **13** Hunting (of a dog) search around for a scent. ● noun **1** the actors taking part in a play or film. **2** an object made by casting metal or other material. **3** (also **plaster cast**) a bandage stiffened with plaster of Paris, moulded to support and protect a broken limb. **4** an act of casting. **5** form, appearance, or character: *minds of a philosophical cast.* **6** a slight squint.
– PHRASES **be cast away** be stranded after a shipwreck. **be cast down** feel depressed. **cast about** (or **around** or **round**) search far and wide. **cast off 1** Knitting take the stitches off the needle by looping each over the next. **2** set a boat or ship free from its moorings. **cast on** Knitting make the first row of loops on the needle.
– ORIGIN Old Norse.

castanets ● plural noun a pair of small concave pieces of wood, ivory, or plastic, clicked together by the fingers as an accompaniment to Spanish dancing.
– ORIGIN Spanish *castañeta* 'little chestnut'.

castaway ● noun a person who has been shipwrecked and stranded in an isolated place.

caste ● noun **1** each of the hereditary classes of Hindu society, distinguished by relative degrees of ritual purity or pollution and of social status. **2** any exclusive social class.
– ORIGIN Spanish and Portuguese *casta* 'lineage, breed', from Latin *castus* 'chaste'.

castellated /kastəlaytid/ ● adjective having battlements.
– DERIVATIVES **castellation** noun.
– ORIGIN Latin *castellatus*, from *castellum* 'little fort'.

caster ● noun **1** a person or machine that casts. **2** variant spelling of CASTOR.

caster sugar (also **castor sugar**) ● noun Brit. finely granulated white sugar.
– ORIGIN because suitable for sprinkling from a castor.

castigate /kastigayt/ ● verb formal reprimand severely.

C

Thesaurus

– PHRASES **cash in on** *(informal)* TAKE ADVANTAGE OF, exploit, milk; make money from, profit from; *informal* make a killing out of.

cashier[1] ● noun *the cashier took the cheque* CLERK, bank clerk, teller, banker, treasurer, bursar, purser.

cashier[2] ● verb *(Military) he was found guilty and cashiered* DISMISS, discharge, expel, throw/cast out, get rid of; *informal* sack, fire, kick/boot out, give someone their marching orders, give someone the bullet, give someone the elbow/push.

casing ● noun COVER, case, shell, envelope, sheath, sheathing, sleeve, jacket, housing.

casino ● noun GAMBLING HOUSE, gambling club, gambling den; *dated* gaming house.

cask ● noun BARREL, keg, butt, tun, vat, drum, hogshead; *historical* puncheon, firkin.

casket ● noun **1** *a small casket* BOX, chest, case, container, receptacle. **2** *(N. Amer.) the casket of a dead soldier* COFFIN; *informal* box; *humorous* wooden overcoat.

cast ● verb **1** *he cast the stone into the stream* THROW, toss, fling, pitch, hurl, lob; *informal* chuck, sling, bung; *dated* shy. **2** *fishermen cast their nets* SPREAD, throw, open out. **3** *she cast a fearful glance over her shoulder* DIRECT, shoot, throw, send. **4** *each citizen cast a vote* REGISTER, record, enter, file, vote. **5** *the fire cast a soft light* EMIT, give off, send out, radiate. **6** *the figures cast dancing shadows* FORM, create, produce; project, throw. **7** *the stags' antlers are cast each year* SHED, lose, discard, slough off. **8** *a figure cast by hand* MOULD, fashion, form, shape, model; sculpt, sculpture, forge. **9** *they were cast as extras* CHOOSE, select, pick, name, nominate.
● noun **1** *a cast of the writer's hand* MOULD, die, matrix, shape, casting, model. **2** *a cast of the dice* THROW, toss, fling, pitch, hurl, lob; *informal* chuck, sling, bung; *dated* shy. **3** *an enquiring cast of mind* TYPE, sort, kind, character, variety, class, style, stamp, nature. **4** *a cast in one eye* SQUINT, strabismus. **5** *the cast of 'The Barber of Seville'* ACTORS, performers, players, company; dramatis personae, characters.
– PHRASES **cast something aside** DISCARD, reject, throw away/out, get rid of, dispose of, abandon. **cast someone away** SHIPWRECK, wreck; strand, leave stranded, maroon. **cast down** DEPRESSED, downcast, unhappy, sad, miserable, gloomy, down, low; dejected, dispirited, discouraged, disheartened, downhearted, demoralized, disconsolate, crestfallen, despondent; *informal* blue.

– DERIVATIVES **castigation** noun **castigator** noun.
– ORIGIN Latin *castigare* 'reprove', from *castus* 'pure, chaste'.
Castilian /kastiliən/ ● noun **1** a person from the Spanish region of Castile. **2** the language of Castile, being the standard spoken and literary Spanish. ● adjective relating to Castile or Castilian.
casting ● noun an object made by casting molten metal or other material.
casting vote ● noun an extra vote used by a chairperson to decide an issue when votes on each side are equal.
– ORIGIN from an obsolete sense of *cast* 'turn the scale'.
cast iron ● noun **1** a hard alloy of iron and carbon which can be readily cast in a mould. **2** (before another noun) firm and unchangeable: *a cast-iron guarantee.*
castle ● noun **1** a large fortified building or group of buildings, typically of the medieval period. **2** Chess, informal old-fashioned term for ROOK².
– PHRASES **castles in the air** (or **in Spain**) unattainable schemes existing only in the imagination.
– ORIGIN Latin *castellum* 'little fort'.
cast-off ● adjective abandoned or discarded. ● noun a cast-off garment.
castor /kaastər/ (also **caster**) ● noun **1** each of a set of small swivelling wheels fixed to the legs or base of a piece of furniture. **2** a small container with holes in the top, used for sprinkling salt, sugar, etc.
– ORIGIN variant of CASTER.
castor oil ● noun a pale yellow purgative oil obtained from the seeds of an African shrub.
– ORIGIN Greek *kastōr* 'beaver': perhaps so named because in medicinal use it succeeded an oily substance secreted by beavers.
castor sugar ● noun variant spelling of CASTER SUGAR.
castrate ● verb **1** remove the testicles of. **2** deprive of power or vigour.
– DERIVATIVES **castration** noun **castrator** noun.
– ORIGIN Latin *castrare.*
castrato /kastraatō/ ● noun (pl. **castrati** /kastraatee/) historical a male singer castrated in boyhood so as to retain a soprano or alto voice.
– ORIGIN Italian.
casual ● adjective **1** relaxed and unconcerned. **2** showing insufficient care or forethought: *a casual remark.* **3** not regular or firmly established; occasional or temporary: *casual jobs.* **4** happening by chance; accidental. **5** informal. ● noun **1** a temporary or occasional worker. **2** (**casuals**) clothes or shoes suitable for informal everyday wear.
– DERIVATIVES **casually** adverb **casualness** noun.
– ORIGIN Latin *casualis,* from *casus* 'fall'.
casualization (also **casualisation**) ● noun the replacement of a permanently employed workforce by casual workers.
casualty ● noun (pl. **casualties**) **1** a person killed or injured in a war or accident. **2** a person or thing badly affected by an event or situation: *the firm was one of the casualties of the recession.*
– ORIGIN originally in the sense 'a chance occurrence': from Latin *casualitas,* from *casualis* (see CASUAL).
casualty department (also **casualty**) ● noun the department of a hospital providing immediate treatment for emergency cases.
casuarina /kassyooəreenə/ ● noun a tree with slender, jointed, drooping twigs bearing tiny scale-like leaves, native to Australia and SE Asia.
– ORIGIN Latin *casuarius* 'cassowary' (from the resemblance of the branches to the bird's feathers).
casuistry /kazhoo-istri/ ● noun the use of clever but false reasoning, especially in relation to moral issues.
– DERIVATIVES **casuist** noun **casuistic** adjective **casuistical** adjective.
– ORIGIN from Spanish *casuista,* from Latin *casus* 'fall, chance, occurrence'.
casus belli /kaysəss belli/ ● noun (pl. same) an act or situation provoking or justifying war.
– ORIGIN from Latin *casus* 'case' and *belli* 'of war'.
CAT ● abbreviation Medicine computerized axial tomography.
cat ● noun **1** a small domesticated carnivorous mammal with soft fur, a short snout, and retractile claws. **2** a wild animal resembling this, in particular a lion, tiger, or other member of the cat family. **3** informal a malicious or spiteful woman.
– PHRASES **all cats are grey in the dark** proverb distinguishing qualities are obscured in some circumstances, and if they can't be perceived they don't matter. **a cat may look at a king** proverb even a person of low status or importance has rights. **let the cat out of the bag** informal reveal a secret by mistake. **like a cat on a hot tin roof** (Brit. also **on hot bricks**) informal very agitated or anxious. **put** (or **set**) **the cat among the pigeons** Brit. say or do something likely to cause trouble. **when** (or **while**) **the cat's away, the mice will play** proverb it is natural for people to do as they like in the absence of someone in authority.
– DERIVATIVES **catlike** adjective.
– ORIGIN Old English.
cata- (also **cat-**) ● prefix **1** down; downwards: *catabolism.* **2** wrongly; badly: *catachresis.* **3** completely: *cataclysm.* **4** against; alongside: *catechize.*
– ORIGIN from Greek *kata* 'down'.
catabolism /kətabbəliz'm/ ● noun the breakdown of complex molecules in living organisms to form simpler ones, together with the release of energy. The opposite of ANABOLISM.
– DERIVATIVES **catabolic** adjective.
– ORIGIN from Greek *katabolē* 'throwing down'.
catachresis /kattəkreessiss/ ● noun (pl. **catachreses** /kattəkreeseez/) the incorrect use of a word.
– ORIGIN Greek, from *katakhrēsthai* 'misuse'.
cataclysm /kattəkliz'm/ ● noun a violent upheaval or disaster.
– DERIVATIVES **cataclysmic** adjective **cataclysmically** adverb.
– ORIGIN originally denoting the biblical Flood: from Greek *kataklusmos* 'deluge'.
catacomb /kattəkōōm, -kōm/ ● noun an underground cemetery consisting of a gallery with recesses for tombs.
– ORIGIN Latin *catacumbas,* the name of the subterranean cemetery of St Sebastian near Rome.
catafalque /kattəfalk/ ● noun a decorated wooden framework

Thesaurus

caste ● noun (SOCIAL) CLASS, social order, rank, level, stratum, echelon, status; *dated* estate, station.
castigate ● verb *(formal)* REPRIMAND, rebuke, admonish, chastise, chide, upbraid, reprove, reproach, scold, berate, take to task, lambaste, give someone a piece of one's mind, haul over the coals, censure; *informal* tell off, give someone an earful, give someone a roasting, rap someone on the knuckles, slap someone's wrist, dress down, bawl out, give someone hell, blow up at, pitch into, lay into, blast; *Brit. informal* tick off, have a go at, carpet, tear someone off a strip, give someone what for, give someone a rocket; *N. Amer. informal* chew out, ream out; *Austral. informal* monster; *dated* give someone a rating; *rare* reprehend, objurgate.
– OPPOSITES praise, commend.
castle ● noun FORTRESS, fort, stronghold, fortification, keep, citadel.
castrate ● verb NEUTER, geld, cut, desex, sterilize, fix; *N. Amer. & Austral.* alter; *Brit. informal* doctor; *archaic* emasculate.
casual ● adjective **1** *a casual attitude to life* INDIFFERENT, apathetic, uncaring, unconcerned; lackadaisical, blasé, nonchalant, insouciant, offhand, flippant; easy-going, free and easy, blithe, carefree, devil-may-care; *informal* laid-back. **2** *a casual remark* OFFHAND, spontaneous, unpremeditated, unthinking, unconsidered, impromptu, throwaway, unguarded; *informal* off-the-cuff. **3** *a casual glance* CURSORY, perfunctory, superficial, passing, fleeting; hasty, brief, quick. **4** *a casual acquaintance* SLIGHT, superficial. **5** *casual work* TEMPORARY, part-time, freelance, impermanent, irregular, occasional. **6** *casual sex* PROMISCUOUS, recreational, extramarital, free. **7** *a casual meeting changed his life* CHANCE, accidental, unplanned, unintended, unexpected, unforeseen, unanticipated, fortuitous, serendipitous, adventitious. **8** *a casual shirt* INFORMAL, comfortable, leisure, sportif, everyday; *informal* sporty. **9** *the inn's casual atmosphere* RELAXED, friendly, informal, unceremonious, easy-going, free and easy; *informal* laid-back.
– OPPOSITES careful, planned, formal.
● noun *we employ ten casuals* TEMPORARY WORKER, part-timer, freelance, freelancer; *informal* temp.
casualty ● noun VICTIM, fatality, loss, MIA; (**casualties**) dead and injured, missing (in action).
casuistry ● noun SOPHISTRY, specious reasoning, speciousness.
cat ● noun FELINE, tomcat, tom, kitten, mouser; *informal* pussy (cat), puss; *Brit. informal* moggie, mog; *archaic* grimalkin.
cataclysm ● noun DISASTER, catastrophe, calamity, tragedy, devastation, holocaust, ruin, ruination, upheaval, convulsion.
cataclysmic ● adjective DISASTROUS, catastrophic, calamitous, tra-

to support a coffin.
– ORIGIN Italian *catafalco*.
Catalan /kattəlan/ ● noun **1** a person from Catalonia in NE Spain. **2** the language of Catalonia. ● adjective relating to Catalonia.
– ORIGIN Spanish, related to Catalan *català* 'Catalan'.
catalepsy /kattəlepsi/ ● noun a medical condition in which a person suffers a trance or seizure with a loss of sensation and consciousness accompanied by rigidity of the body.
– DERIVATIVES **cataleptic** adjective & noun.
– ORIGIN Greek *katalēpsis*, from *katalambanein* 'seize upon'.
catalogue (US also **catalog**) ● noun **1** a complete list of items arranged in alphabetical or other systematic order. **2** a publication containing details of items for sale. **3** a series of bad things: *a catalogue of failures.* ● verb (**catalogues**, **catalogued**, **cataloguing**; US also **catalogs**, **cataloged**, **cataloging**) list in a catalogue.
– DERIVATIVES **cataloguer** noun.
– ORIGIN Greek *katalogos*, from *katalegein* 'pick out or enrol'.
Catalonian /kattəlōniən/ ● adjective & noun another term for CATALAN.
catalpa /kətalpə/ ● noun a tree with heart-shaped leaves and trumpet-shaped flowers, native to North America and east Asia.
– ORIGIN from an American Indian language.
catalyse /kattəlīz/ (US **catalyze**) ● verb cause or accelerate (a reaction) by acting as a catalyst.
– DERIVATIVES **catalyser** noun.
catalysis /kətalississ/ ● noun the acceleration of a chemical reaction by a catalyst.
– DERIVATIVES **catalytic** /kattəlittik/ adjective.
– ORIGIN Greek *katalusis* 'dissolution'.
catalyst ● noun **1** a substance that increases the rate of a chemical reaction without itself undergoing any permanent chemical change. **2** a person or thing that precipitates an event.
catalytic converter ● noun a device in the exhaust system of a motor vehicle, containing a catalyst for converting pollutant gases into less harmful ones.
catamaran /kattəməran/ ● noun a yacht or other boat with twin hulls in parallel.
– ORIGIN Tamil, 'tied wood'.
catamite /kattəmīt/ ● noun archaic a boy kept for homosexual practices.
– ORIGIN Latin *catamitus*, from Greek *Ganumēdēs* 'Ganymede' (Zeus's cup-bearer in Greek mythology).
cataplexy /kattəpleksi/ ● noun a medical condition in which strong emotion or laughter causes a person to suffer sudden physical collapse though remaining conscious.
– ORIGIN Greek *kataplēxis* 'stupefaction', from *kata-* 'down' + *plēssein* 'strike'.
catapult ● noun **1** chiefly Brit. a forked stick with an elastic band fastened to the two prongs, used for shooting small stones. **2** historical a military machine for hurling large stones or other missiles. **3** a mechanical device for launching a glider or aircraft. ● verb **1** hurl or launch with or as if with a catapult. **2** move suddenly or at great speed.
– ORIGIN Latin *catapulta*, from Greek *kata-* 'down' + *pallein* 'hurl'.
cataract /kattərakt/ ● noun **1** a large waterfall. **2** a medical condition in which the lens of the eye becomes progressively opaque, resulting in blurred vision.
– ORIGIN Latin *cataracta* 'waterfall, floodgate', also 'portcullis' (sense 2 probably being a figurative use of this), from Greek *kataraktēs* 'down-rushing'.
catarrh /kətaar/ ● noun excessive discharge of mucus in the nose or throat.
– DERIVATIVES **catarrhal** adjective.
– ORIGIN Latin *catarrhus*, from Greek *katarrhein* 'flow down'.
catastrophe /kətastrəfi/ ● noun an event causing great damage or suffering.
– DERIVATIVES **catastrophic** adjective.
– ORIGIN Greek *katastrophē* 'overturning, sudden turn'.
catatonia /kattətōniə/ ● noun **1** abnormality of movement and behaviour arising from a disturbed mental state. **2** informal a state of immobility and stupor.
– DERIVATIVES **catatonic** adjective.
– ORIGIN from Greek *tonos* 'tone or tension'.
catboat ● noun a single-masted sailing boat with only one sail.
– ORIGIN perhaps from obsolete *cat* (a former type of merchant ship used in NE England).
cat burglar ● noun a thief who enters a building by climbing to an upper storey.
catcall ● noun a shrill whistle or shout of mockery or disapproval. ● verb make a catcall.
catch ● verb (past and past part. **caught**) **1** intercept and hold (something thrown, propelled, or dropped). **2** seize or take hold of. **3** capture after a chase or in a trap, net, etc. **4** be in time to board (a train, bus, etc.) or to see (a person, programme, etc.). **5** entangle or become entangled: *she caught her foot in the bedspread.* **6** (**be caught in**) unexpectedly find oneself in (an unwelcome situation). **7** surprise (someone) in an awkward or incriminating situation. **8** engage (a person's interest or imagination). **9** perceive, hear, or understand: *he said something Jess couldn't catch.* **10** strike (someone or a part of one's body). **11** become infected with (an illness). **12** ignite and start burning. **13** Cricket dismiss (a batsman) by catching the ball before it touches the ground. ● noun **1** an act of catching. **2** a device for securing a door, window, etc. **3** a hidden problem or disadvantage. **4** an unevenness in a person's voice caused by emotion. **5** informal a person considered desirable as a partner or spouse. **6** an amount of fish caught.
– PHRASES **catch one's breath 1** draw one's breath in sharply to express an emotion. **2** recover one's breath after exertion. **catch someone's eye 1** be noticed by someone. **2** attract someone's attention by making eye contact. **catch the light** shine in the light. **catch on** informal **1** (of a practice or fashion) become popular. **2** understand what is meant. **catch out** Brit. **1** discover that (someone) has done something wrong. **2** take unawares: *you might get caught out by the weather.* **catch the sun 1** be in a sunny position. **2** Brit. become tanned or sunburnt. **catch up 1** succeed in reaching a person ahead. **2** do tasks which one should have done earlier. **3** (**be/get caught up in**) become involved in.
– DERIVATIVES **catchable** adjective **catcher** noun.
– ORIGIN Old French *chacier*, from Latin *captare* 'try to catch'.
catch-22 ● noun a difficult situation from which there is no escape because it involves mutually conflicting or dependent conditions.
– ORIGIN title of a novel by Joseph Heller (1961).
catch-all ● noun a term or category intended to cover all possi-

Thesaurus

gic, devastating, ruinous, terrible, violent, awful.
catacombs ● plural noun UNDERGROUND CEMETERY, crypt, vault, tomb, ossuary.
catalogue ● noun **1** *a library catalogue* DIRECTORY, register, index, list, listing, record, archive, inventory. **2** *a mail-order catalogue* BROCHURE, magalogue, mailer; *N. Amer. informal* wish book.
● verb *the collection is fully catalogued* CLASSIFY, categorize, systematize, index, list, archive, make an inventory of, inventory, record, itemize.
catapult ● noun *a boy fired the catapult* SLING, slingshot; *Austral./NZ* shanghai; *historical* ballista, trebuchet.
● verb *Sam was catapulted into the sea* PROPEL, launch, hurl, fling, send flying, fire, blast, shoot.
cataract ● noun WATERFALL, cascade, falls, rapids, white water.
catastrophe ● noun DISASTER, calamity, cataclysm, holocaust, ruin, ruination, tragedy; adversity, blight, trouble, trial, tribulation.
catastrophic ● adjective DISASTROUS, calamitous, cataclysmic, ruinous, tragic, fatal, dire, awful, terrible, dreadful; *poetic/literary* direful.
catcall ● noun WHISTLE, boo, hiss, jeer, raspberry, hoot, taunt; (**catcalls**) scoffing, abuse, taunting, derision.
catch ● verb **1** *he caught the ball* SEIZE, grab, snatch, seize/grab/take hold of, grasp, grip, clutch, clench; receive, get, intercept. **2** *we've caught the thief* CAPTURE, seize; apprehend, arrest, take prisoner/captive, take into custody; trap, snare, ensnare; net, hook, land; *informal* nab, collar, run in, bust; *Brit. informal* nick. **3** *her heel caught in a hole* BECOME TRAPPED, become entangled, snag. **4** *she caught the 7.45 bus* BE IN TIME FOR, make, get; board, get on, step aboard. **5** *they were caught siphoning petrol* DISCOVER, find, come upon/across, stumble on, chance on; surprise, catch red-handed, catch in the act. **6** *it caught his imagination* ENGAGE, capture, attract, draw, grab, grip, seize; hold, absorb, engross. **7** *she caught a trace of aftershave* PERCEIVE, notice, observe,

C

bilities.

catch crop ● noun Brit. a crop grown in the space or interval between two main crops.

catching ● adjective informal (of a disease) infectious.

catchline ● noun Brit. **1** a short, eye-catching headline or title. **2** an advertising slogan.

catchment (also **catchment area**) ● noun **1** the area from which a hospital's patients or a school's pupils are drawn. **2** the area from which rainfall flows into a river, lake, or reservoir.

catchpenny ● adjective having a cheap superficial attractiveness designed to encourage quick sales.

catchphrase ● noun a well-known sentence or phrase.

catchword ● noun **1** a popular word or phrase encapsulating a particular concept. **2** a word printed or placed so as to attract attention.

catchy ● adjective (**catchier**, **catchiest**) (of a tune or phrase) instantly appealing and memorable.
– DERIVATIVES **catchiness** noun.

catechesis /kattikeesiss/ ● noun religious instruction given in preparation for Christian baptism or confirmation.
– ORIGIN via Latin from Greek *katēkhēsis* 'oral instruction'.

catechetical /kattikettikk'l/ ● adjective **1** relating to catechesis. **2** denoting religious teaching by means of questions and answers.

catechism /kattikiz'm/ ● noun a summary of the principles of Christian religion in the form of questions and answers, used for teaching.

catechist ● noun a Christian teacher, especially one using a catechism.

catechize (also **catechise**) ● verb instruct by question and answer, especially by using a catechism.
– ORIGIN Greek *katēkhizein*, from *katēkhein* 'instruct orally'.

catechumen /kattikyoōmen/ ● noun a Christian preparing for baptism or confirmation.
– ORIGIN from Greek *katēkhoumenos* 'being instructed', from *katēkhein* 'instruct orally'.

categorical (also **categoric**) ● adjective unambiguously explicit and direct.
– DERIVATIVES **categorically** adverb.

categorize (also **categorise**) ● verb place in a particular category; classify.
– DERIVATIVES **categorization** noun.

category ● noun (pl. **categories**) a class or division of people or things having shared characteristics.
– ORIGIN Greek *katēgoria* 'statement, accusation'.

catenary /kəteenəri/ ● noun (pl. **catenaries**) a curve formed by a wire, chain, etc. hanging freely from two points on the same horizontal level. ● adjective involving or denoting a catenary.
– ORIGIN from Latin *catena* 'chain'.

cater ● verb chiefly Brit. **1** (**cater for**) provide food and drink at (a social event). **2** (**cater for/to**) provide with what is needed or required. **3** (**cater for**) take into account. **4** (**cater to**) satisfy (a need or demand).
– DERIVATIVES **caterer** noun.
– ORIGIN Old French *acater* 'buy', from Latin *captare* 'seize'.

cater-cornered /kaytərkornərd/ (also **kitty-corner**) ● adjective & adverb N. Amer. situated diagonally opposite.
– ORIGIN from dialect *cater* 'diagonally', from *cater* denoting the four on dice, from French *quatre* 'four'.

caterpillar ● noun **1** the larva of a butterfly or moth. **2** (also **caterpillar track** or **tread**) trademark an articulated steel band passing round the wheels of a vehicle for travel on rough ground.
– ORIGIN perhaps from a variant of Old French *chatepelose* 'hairy cat', influenced by obsolete *piller* 'ravager'.

caterwaul /kattərwawl/ ● verb make a shrill howling or wailing noise. ● noun a shrill howling or wailing noise.

catfish ● noun a freshwater or marine fish with whisker-like barbels round the mouth.

cat flap ● noun a small hinged flap in an outer door through which a cat may pass.

catgut ● noun material used for the strings of musical instruments and for surgical sutures, made of the dried intestines of sheep or horses (but not cats).
– ORIGIN the association with CAT remains unexplained.

catharsis /kəthaarsiss/ ● noun the release of pent-up emotions, for example through drama.
– DERIVATIVES **cathartic** adjective & noun.
– ORIGIN Greek *katharsis*, from *kathairein* 'cleanse'.

cathedral ● noun the principal church of a diocese.
– ORIGIN from Greek *kathedra* 'seat' (the full term was originally *cathedral church*, being a church containing the bishop's throne).

Catherine wheel ● noun Brit. a firework in the form of a spinning coil.
– ORIGIN named after St *Catherine*, who was martyred on a spiked wheel.

catheter /kathitər/ ● noun a flexible tube inserted into a body cavity, particularly the bladder, for removing fluid.
– ORIGIN Greek *kathetēr*, from *kathienai* 'send or let down'.

cathode /kathōd/ ● noun a negatively charged electrode. The opposite of ANODE.
– ORIGIN Greek *kathodos* 'way down'.

Thesaurus

discern, detect, note, make out; *Brit. informal* clock. **8** *I couldn't catch what she was saying* HEAR, perceive, discern, make out; understand, comprehend, grasp, apprehend; *informal* get, get the drift of, figure out; *Brit. informal* twig, suss (out). **9** *it caught the flavour of the sixties* EVOKE, conjure up, call to mind, recall, encapsulate, capture. **10** *the blow caught her on the side of her face* HIT, strike, slap, smack, bang. **11** *he caught malaria* BECOME INFECTED WITH, contract, get, be taken ill with, develop, come down with, be struck down with; *Brit.* go down with; *informal* take ill with; *N. Amer. informal* take sick with. **12** *the kindling wouldn't catch* IGNITE, start burning, catch fire, kindle. **13** *the generator caught immediately* START (RUNNING), fire, begin working.
– OPPOSITES drop, release, miss.
● noun **1** *he inspected the catch* HAUL, net, bag, yield. **2** *(informal) Giles is a good catch* ELIGIBLE MAN/WOMAN, marriage prospect. **3** *he slipped the catch* LATCH, lock, fastener, clasp, hasp. **4** *he is always looking for the catch* SNAG, disadvantage, drawback, stumbling block, hitch, fly in the ointment, pitfall, complication, problem, hiccup, difficulty; trap, trick, snare; *informal* con. **5** *a catch in her voice* TREMOR, unevenness, shake, quiver, wobble.
– PHRASES **catch it** *(informal)* BE REPRIMANDED, be scolded, be rebuked, be taken to task, be chastised, get into trouble, be hauled over the coals; *informal* be told off, be for the high jump, be in hot water, get a dressing-down, get an earful, get a roasting, get a rap over the knuckles, get a slap on the wrist; *Brit. informal* be for it; *formal* be castigated. **catch on** *(informal)* **1** *radio soon caught on* BECOME POPULAR/FASHIONABLE, take off, boom, flourish, thrive. **2** *I caught on fast* UNDERSTAND, comprehend, learn, see the light; *informal* cotton on, latch on, get the picture/message, get wise. **catch (someone) up** DRAW LEVEL (WITH), reach; gain on.

catching ● adjective *(informal)* INFECTIOUS, contagious, communicable, transmittable, transmissible; *dated* infective.

catchphrase ● noun SAYING, quotation, quote, slogan, catchword; *N. Amer. informal* tag line.

catchword ● noun MOTTO, watchword, slogan, byword, catchphrase; *informal* buzzword.

catchy ● adjective MEMORABLE, unforgettable; appealing, popular; singable, melodious, tuneful.

catechize ● verb INTERROGATE, question, cross-examine, cross-question, quiz, sound out, give the third degree to; *informal* grill, pump.

categorical ● adjective UNQUALIFIED, unconditional, unequivocal, absolute, explicit, unambiguous, definite, direct, downright, outright, emphatic, positive, point-blank, conclusive, without reservations, out-and-out; *formal* apodictic.
– OPPOSITES qualified, equivocal.

categorize ● verb CLASSIFY, class, group, grade, rate, designate; order, arrange, sort, rank; file, catalogue, list, index.

category ● noun CLASS, classification, group, grouping, bracket, heading, set; type, sort, kind, variety, species, breed, brand, make, model; grade, order, rank.

cater ● verb
– PHRASES **cater for 1** *we cater for vegetarians* PROVIDE FOOD FOR, feed, serve, cook for; *dated* victual. **2** *a resort catering for older holidaymakers* SERVE, provide for, meet the needs/wants of, accommodate. **3** *he seemed to cater for all tastes* TAKE INTO ACCOUNT/CONSIDERATION, allow for, consider, bear in mind, make provision for, have regard for. **cater to** SATISFY, indulge, pander to, gratify, accommodate, minister to, give in to, fulfil.

caterwaul ● verb HOWL, wail, bawl, cry, yell, scream, screech,

cathode ray ● noun a beam of electrons emitted from the cathode of a high-vacuum tube.
cathode ray tube ● noun a high-vacuum tube in which cathode rays produce a luminous image on a fluorescent screen, used in televisions and visual display units.
catholic ● adjective 1 including a wide variety of things: *catholic tastes.* 2 (**Catholic**) Roman Catholic. 3 (**Catholic**) of or including all Christians. ● noun (**Catholic**) a Roman Catholic.
– DERIVATIVES **Catholicism** noun **catholicity** noun **Catholicize** (also **Catholicise**) verb.
– ORIGIN Greek *katholikos* 'universal'.
cation /kattīən/ ● noun Chemistry a positively charged ion. The opposite of ANION.
– DERIVATIVES **cationic** /kattīonnik/ adjective.
– ORIGIN from CATHODE + ION.
catkin ● noun a spike of small soft flowers hanging from trees such as willow and hazel.
– ORIGIN from obsolete Dutch *katteken* 'kitten'.
catlick ● noun a perfunctory wash.
catmint ● noun a plant with a pungent smell attractive to cats.
catnap ● noun a short sleep during the day. ● verb (**catnapped, catnapping**) have a catnap.
catnip ● noun another term for CATMINT.
– ORIGIN from CAT + Latin *nepeta* 'catmint'.
cat-o'-nine-tails ● noun historical a rope whip with nine knotted cords, used for flogging.
cat's cradle ● noun a child's game in which patterns are constructed in a loop of string held between the fingers of each hand.
cat's eye ● noun 1 a semi-precious stone. 2 (**catseye**) Brit. trademark each of a series of reflective studs marking the lanes or edges or a road.
cat's paw ● noun a person used by another to carry out an unpleasant task.
catsuit ● noun chiefly Brit. a woman's close-fitting one-piece garment with trouser legs.
catsup /katsəp/ ● noun US another term for KETCHUP.
cat's whisker ● noun a fine adjustable wire in a crystal radio receiver.
– PHRASES **the cat's whiskers** (also **the cat's pyjamas**) informal an excellent person or thing.
cattery ● noun (pl. **catteries**) a boarding or breeding establishment for cats.
cattish ● adjective another term for CATTY.
cattle ● plural noun large ruminant animals with horns and cloven hoofs, domesticated for meat or milk or as beasts of burden; cows and oxen.
– ORIGIN Old French *chatel* 'chattel'.
cattle cake ● noun Brit. concentrated food for cattle in a compressed flat form.
cattle grid (N. Amer. **cattle guard**) ● noun a metal grid covering a ditch, allowing vehicles and pedestrians to cross but not animals.
catty ● adjective (**cattier, cattiest**) informal spiteful.
– DERIVATIVES **cattily** adverb.
CATV ● abbreviation community antenna television (cable television).
catwalk ● noun 1 a narrow walkway or open bridge, especially in an industrial installation. 2 a narrow platform along which models walk to display clothes.
Caucasian /korkayziən, -ayzh'n/ ● adjective 1 relating to a broad division of humankind covering peoples from Europe, western Asia, and parts of India and North Africa. 2 white-skinned; of European origin. 3 relating to the region of the Caucasus in SE Europe. ● noun a Caucasian person.
caucus /kawkəss/ ● noun (pl. **caucuses**) 1 a meeting of the members of a legislative body of a political party, to select candidates or decide policy. 2 a group of people with shared concerns within a larger organization.
– ORIGIN perhaps from an Algonquian word meaning 'adviser'.
caudal /kawd'l/ ● adjective 1 of or like a tail. 2 at or near the posterior part of the body.
– DERIVATIVES **caudally** adverb.
– ORIGIN from Latin *cauda* 'tail'.
caught past and past participle of CATCH.
caul /kawl/ ● noun the amniotic membrane enclosing a fetus, part of which is occasionally found on a baby's head at birth.
– ORIGIN perhaps from Old French *cale* 'head covering'.
cauldron (also **caldron**) ● noun a large metal pot, used for cooking over an open fire.
– ORIGIN Old French *caudron*, from Latin *caldarium* 'hot bath', *caldaria* 'cooking pot'.
cauliflower ● noun a variety of cabbage with a large flower head of small creamy-white flower buds, eaten as a vegetable.
– ORIGIN from obsolete French *chou fleuri* 'flowered cabbage'.
cauliflower ear ● noun a person's ear that has become thickened or deformed as a result of repeated blows.
caulk /kawk/ (US also **calk**) ● noun a waterproof filler and sealant, used in building work and repairs. ● verb 1 seal with caulk. 2 make (a boat or its seams) watertight.
– ORIGIN from Latin *calcare* 'to tread'.
causal ● adjective relating to or acting as a cause.
– DERIVATIVES **causally** adverb.
– ORIGIN Latin *causalis*, from *causa* 'cause'.
causality ● noun 1 the relationship between cause and effect. 2 the principle that everything has a cause.
causation ● noun 1 the action of causing. 2 the relationship between cause and effect.
causative ● adjective 1 acting as a cause. 2 Grammar expressing causation.
cause ● noun 1 a person or thing that produces an effect. 2 reasonable grounds for a belief or action: *cause for concern.* 3 a principle or movement which one is prepared to support or advocate. 4 a lawsuit. ● verb be the cause of; make happen.
– PHRASES **cause and effect** the principle of causation. **make common cause** unite in order to achieve a shared aim.
– DERIVATIVES **causeless** adjective.
– ORIGIN Latin *causa*.
cause célèbre /kawz selebrə/ ● noun (pl. **causes célèbres** pronunc. same) a controversial issue arousing great public interest.
– ORIGIN French, 'famous case'.
causeway ● noun a raised road or track across low or wet ground.
– ORIGIN from Old French *causee*, from Latin *calx* 'lime, limestone' (used for paving roads).
caustic /kawstik/ ● adjective 1 able to burn or corrode organic tissue by chemical action. 2 scathingly sarcastic. ● noun a caustic substance.
– DERIVATIVES **caustically** adverb.
– ORIGIN Greek *kaustikos*, from *kaustos* 'combustible'.
caustic soda ● noun sodium hydroxide.

C

Thesaurus

yowl, ululate.
catharsis ● noun PURGING, purgation, purification, cleansing, (emotional) release, relief; *Psychoanalysis* abreaction.
catholic ● adjective DIVERSE, diversified, wide, broad, broad-based, eclectic, liberal; comprehensive, all-encompassing, all-embracing, all-inclusive.
– OPPOSITES narrow.
cattle ● plural noun cows, bovines, oxen, bulls; stock, livestock.
– RELATED TERMS bovine.
catty ● adjective *(informal) a catty remark*. See SPITEFUL.
caucus ● noun 1 *caucuses will be held in eleven states* MEETING, assembly, gathering, congress, conference, convention, rally, convocation. 2 *the right-wing caucus* FACTION, camp, bloc, group, set, band, ring, cabal, coterie, pressure group; *Brit.* ginger group.
cause ● noun 1 *the cause of the fire* SOURCE, root, origin, beginning(s), starting point; mainspring, base, basis, foundation, fountainhead; originator, author, creator, producer, agent; *formal* radix. 2 *there is no cause for alarm* REASON, grounds, justification, call, need, necessity, occasion, excuse, pretext. 3 *the cause of human rights | a good cause* PRINCIPLE, ideal, belief, conviction; object, end, aim, objective, purpose; charity. 4 *he went to plead his cause* CASE, suit, lawsuit, action, dispute.
– RELATED TERMS -genic, -facient.
– OPPOSITES effect, result.
● verb *flooding and snow caused chaos in the region* BRING ABOUT, give rise to, lead to, result in, create, produce, generate, engender, spawn, bring on, precipitate, prompt, provoke, trigger, spark off, make happen, induce, inspire, promote, foster; *poetic/literary* beget, enkindle.
– OPPOSITES result from.
caustic ● adjective 1 *a caustic cleaner* CORROSIVE, corroding, mordant, acid. 2 *a caustic comment* SARCASTIC, cutting, biting, mor-

cauterize /kawtərīz/ (also **cauterise**) ● verb burn the skin or flesh of (a wound) to stop bleeding or prevent infection.
– DERIVATIVES **cauterization** noun.
– ORIGIN Greek *kautēriazein*, from *kautērion* 'branding iron'.
cautery /kawtəri/ ● noun (pl. **cauteries**) **1** an instrument or caustic substance used for cauterizing. **2** the action of cauterizing.

C

caution ● noun **1** care taken to avoid danger or mistakes. **2** warning: *advisers sounded a note of caution.* **3** Law, chiefly Brit. a formal warning given to someone who has committed a minor offence but has not been charged. ● verb **1** warn or advise. **2** chiefly Brit. issue a legal caution to. **3** chiefly Brit. (of a police officer) advise (someone) of their legal rights when arresting them.
– PHRASES **throw caution to the wind** act in a reckless manner.
– ORIGIN Latin, from *cavere* 'take heed'.
cautionary ● adjective serving as a warning.
cautious ● adjective careful to avoid potential problems or dangers.
– DERIVATIVES **cautiously** adverb **cautiousness** noun.
cava /kaavə/ ● noun a Spanish sparkling wine made in the same way as champagne.
– ORIGIN Spanish.
cavalcade /kavvəlkayd/ ● noun a procession of vehicles, riders, or people on foot.
– ORIGIN Italian *cavalcata*, from *cavalcare* 'to ride'.
cavalier ● noun **1** (**Cavalier**) historical a supporter of King Charles I in the English Civil War. **2** archaic or literary a courtly gentleman. ● adjective showing a lack of proper concern.
– DERIVATIVES **cavalierly** adverb.
– ORIGIN Italian *cavaliere*, from Latin *caballus* 'horse'.
cavalry ● noun (pl. **cavalries**) (usu. treated as pl.) soldiers who fight on horses or in armoured vehicles.
– DERIVATIVES **cavalryman** noun.
– ORIGIN Italian *cavalleria*, from *cavallo* 'horse'.
cavalry twill ● noun strong woollen twill of a khaki or light brown colour.
cave ● noun a large natural underground chamber. ● verb (**cave in**) **1** subside or collapse. **2** submit under pressure.
– DERIVATIVES **caver** noun.
– ORIGIN from Latin *cavus* 'hollow'.
caveat /kavviat/ ● noun a warning or proviso of specific conditions.
– ORIGIN Latin, 'let a person beware'.
caveat emptor /kavviat emptor/ ● noun the principle that the buyer is responsible for checking the quality and suitability of goods before purchase.
– ORIGIN Latin, 'let the buyer beware'.
caveman (or **cavewoman**) ● noun a prehistoric person who lived in caves.
cavern ● noun **1** a large cave, or chamber in a cave. **2** a vast, dark space.
– DERIVATIVES **cavernous** adjective.
– ORIGIN Latin *caverna*, from *cavus* 'hollow'.
caviar /kavviaar/ (also **caviare**) ● noun the pickled roe of sturgeon or other large fish, eaten as a delicacy.
– ORIGIN French.
cavil /kavv'l/ ● verb (**cavilled, cavilling**; US **caviled, caviling**) make petty objections. ● noun a petty objection.
– ORIGIN Latin *cavillari*, from *cavilla* 'mockery'.
caving ● noun exploring caves as a sport.
cavitation ● noun the formation of bubbles in a liquid.
cavity ● noun (pl. **cavities**) **1** a hollow space within a solid object. **2** a decayed part of a tooth.
– ORIGIN Latin *cavitas*, from *cavus* 'hollow'.
cavity wall ● noun a wall formed from two thicknesses of bricks with a space between them.
cavort ● verb jump or dance around excitedly.
– ORIGIN perhaps an alteration of CURVET.
cavy /kayvi/ ● noun (pl. **cavies**) a guinea pig or related South American rodent.
– ORIGIN Latin *cavia*, from Carib.
caw ● noun the harsh cry of a rook, crow, or similar bird. ● verb utter a caw.
– ORIGIN imitative.
cayenne /kayen/ (also **cayenne pepper**) ● noun a pungent, hot-tasting red powder prepared from dried chillies.
– ORIGIN Tupi, later associated with *Cayenne* in French Guiana.
cayman ● noun variant spelling of CAIMAN.
Cayuga /kayōōgə, kī-/ ● noun (pl. same or **Cayugas**) a member of an American Indian people formerly inhabiting part of New York State.
– ORIGIN from a place name.
Cayuse /kīyōōss/ ● noun (pl. same or **Cayuses**) a member of an American Indian people of Washington State and Oregon.
– ORIGIN the name in Chinook Jargon.
CB ● abbreviation **1** Citizens' Band. **2** (in the UK) Companion of the Order of the Bath.
CBE ● abbreviation (in the UK) Commander of the Order of the British Empire.
CBI ● abbreviation Confederation of British Industry.
CC ● abbreviation **1** Brit. City Council. **2** Brit. County Council. **3** Cricket Club.
cc (also **c.c.**) ● abbreviation **1** carbon copy (an indication that a duplicate has been or should be sent to another person). **2** cubic centimetre(s).
CCTV ● abbreviation closed-circuit television.
CD ● abbreviation compact disc.
Cd ● symbol the chemical element cadmium.
cd ● abbreviation candela.

Thesaurus

dant, sharp, bitter, scathing, derisive, sardonic, ironic, scornful, trenchant, acerbic, vitriolic, acidulous; *Brit. informal* sarky; *formal* mordacious.
– OPPOSITES kind.
cauterize ● verb BURN, sear, singe, scorch; disinfect, sterilize.
caution ● noun **1** *proceed with caution* CARE, carefulness, heedfulness, heed, attention, attentiveness, alertness, watchfulness, vigilance, circumspection, discretion, prudence. **2** *a first offender may receive a caution* WARNING, admonishment, injunction; reprimand, rebuke, reproof, scolding; *informal* telling-off, dressing-down, talking-to; *Brit. informal* ticking-off, carpeting. **3** *(informal, dated) her uncle's a caution.* See CLOWN noun sense 2.
● verb **1** *advisers cautioned against tax increases* ADVISE, warn, counsel, urge. **2** *he was cautioned by the police* WARN, admonish; reprimand, rebuke, reprove, scold; *informal* tell off, give someone a dressing-down, give someone a talking-to; *Brit. informal* give someone a ticking-off, carpet.
cautious ● adjective CAREFUL, heedful, attentive, alert, watchful, vigilant, circumspect, prudent.
– OPPOSITES reckless.
cavalcade ● noun PROCESSION, parade, motorcade, cortège; *Brit.* march past.
cavalier ● noun **1** *(historical) Cavaliers dying for King Charles* ROYALIST, king's man. **2** *(archaic) the lady and her cavalier* ESCORT, gentleman; *dated* beau. **3** *(archaic) foot soldiers and cavaliers* HORSEMAN, equestrian; cavalryman, trooper, knight.
– OPPOSITES Roundhead.
● adjective *a cavalier disregard for danger* OFFHAND, indifferent, casual, dismissive, insouciant, unconcerned; supercilious, patronizing, condescending, disdainful, scornful, contemptuous; *informal* couldn't-care-less.
cavalry ● plural noun MOUNTED TROOPS, cavalrymen, troopers, horse; *historical* dragoons, lancers, hussars.
cave ● noun CAVERN, grotto, pothole, underground chamber.
– RELATED TERMS speleology, speleologist; *N. Amer.* spelunking.
– PHRASES **cave in 1** *the roof caved in* COLLAPSE, fall in/down, give (way), crumble, subside. **2** *the manager caved in to their demands* YIELD, surrender, capitulate, give in, back down, make concessions, throw in the towel/sponge.
caveat ● noun WARNING, caution, admonition; proviso, condition, stipulation, provision, clause, rider, qualification.
caveman, cavewoman ● noun CAVE-DWELLER, troglodyte, primitive man/woman, prehistoric man/woman.
cavern ● noun LARGE CAVE, grotto, underground chamber/gallery.
cavernous ● adjective VAST, huge, large, immense, spacious, roomy, airy, capacious, voluminous, extensive, deep; hollow, gaping, yawning; *formal* commodious.
– OPPOSITES small.
cavil ● verb COMPLAIN, carp, grumble, grouse, whine, bleat, quibble, niggle; *informal* gripe, grouch, beef, bellyache, moan, bitch, whinge, kick up a fuss; *Brit. informal* chunter, create; *N. English informal* mither; *N. Amer. informal* kvetch.
cavity ● noun SPACE, chamber, hollow, hole, pocket, pouch; orifice, aperture; socket, gap, crater, pit.

CD-I • abbreviation compact disc (interactive).
CD-ROM • noun a compact disc used in a computer as a read-only device for displaying data.
– ORIGIN from *compact disc read-only memory*.
CDV • abbreviation compact disc video.
CE • abbreviation **1** Church of England. **2** Common Era.
Ce • symbol the chemical element cerium.
ceanothus /seeənōthəss/ • noun a North American shrub with dense clusters of small blue flowers.
– ORIGIN Greek *keanōthos*, a kind of thistle.
cease • verb come or bring to an end; stop.
– PHRASES **without cease** without stopping.
– ORIGIN Latin *cessare*, from *cedere* 'to yield'.
ceasefire • noun a temporary suspension of fighting.
ceaseless • adjective constant and unending.
– DERIVATIVES **ceaselessly** adverb.
cecum • noun (pl. **ceca**) US spelling of CAECUM.
cedar • noun a tall coniferous tree with hard, fragrant wood.
– ORIGIN Greek *kedros*.
cede /seed/ • verb give up (power or territory).
– ORIGIN Latin *cedere* 'to yield'.
cedi /seedi/ • noun (pl. same or **cedis**) the basic monetary unit of Ghana, equal to 100 pesewas.
– ORIGIN Ghanaian, perhaps an alteration of SHILLING.
cedilla /sidillə/ • noun a mark (¸) written under the letter *c*, especially in French, to show that it is pronounced like an *s* (e.g. *façade*).
– ORIGIN Spanish *zedilla* 'little 'z''.
ceilidh /kayli/ • noun a social event with Scottish or Irish folk music and singing, traditional dancing, and storytelling.
– ORIGIN Old Irish *céilide* 'visit, visiting'.
ceiling • noun **1** the upper inside surface of a room. **2** an upper limit set on prices, wages, or expenditure. **3** the maximum altitude an aircraft can reach.
– ORIGIN from obsolete *ceil* 'line or plaster the roof of (a building)', perhaps from Latin *celare* 'conceal'.
celandine /selləndīn/ • noun **1** (also **lesser celandine**) a common yellow-flowered plant of the buttercup family. **2** (**greater celandine**) a yellow-flowered plant of the poppy family, with toxic sap.
– ORIGIN from Greek *khelidōn* 'swallow' (the flowering of the plant being associated with the arrival of swallows).
celebrant /sellibrənt/ • noun **1** a person who performs a rite, especially a priest at the Eucharist. **2** a person who celebrates something.
celebrate • verb **1** mark (a significant occasion) with an enjoyable activity. **2** engage in festivities to mark a significant occasion. **3** honour or praise publicly. **4** perform (a religious ceremony), in particular officiate at (the Eucharist).
– DERIVATIVES **celebration** noun **celebrator** noun **celebratory** adjective.
– ORIGIN Latin *celebrare*, from *celeber* 'frequented or honoured'.
celebrity • noun (pl. **celebrities**) **1** a famous person. **2** the state of being famous.
celeriac /silerriak/ • noun a variety of celery which forms a large swollen edible root.
– ORIGIN from CELERY.
celerity /silerriti/ • noun archaic or literary swiftness of movement.
– ORIGIN Latin *celeritas*, from *celer* 'swift'.
celery • noun a garden plant with crisp juicy stalks, used in salads or as a vegetable.
– ORIGIN French *céleri*, from Greek *selinon* 'parsley'.
celesta /silestə/ (also **celeste** /silest/) • noun a small keyboard instrument in which felted hammers strike a row of steel plates suspended over wooden resonators.
– ORIGIN from French *céleste* 'heavenly' (with reference to the instrument's ethereal sound).
celestial • adjective **1** positioned in or relating to the sky or outer space. **2** belonging or relating to heaven.
– DERIVATIVES **celestially** adverb.
– ORIGIN Latin *caelestis*, from *caelum* 'heaven'.
celestial equator • noun the projection into space of the earth's equator.
celestial pole • noun Astronomy the point on the celestial sphere directly above either of the earth's geographic poles, around which the stars appear to rotate.
celestial sphere • noun an imaginary sphere of which the observer is the centre and on which all celestial objects are considered to lie.
celiac • noun US spelling of COELIAC.
celibate /sellibət/ • adjective **1** abstaining from marriage and sexual relations for religious reasons. **2** having or involving no sexual relations. • noun a person who is celibate.
– DERIVATIVES **celibacy** noun.
– ORIGIN from Latin *caelibatus* 'unmarried state'.
cell • noun **1** a small room for a prisoner, monk, or nun. **2** Biology the smallest structural and functional unit of an organism, consisting of cytoplasm and a nucleus enclosed in a membrane. **3** a small compartment in a larger structure such as a honeycomb. **4** a small group forming a nucleus of political activity. **5** a device or unit in which electricity is generated using chemical energy or light, or in which electrolysis takes place.
– ORIGIN Latin *cella* 'storeroom or chamber'.
cellar • noun **1** a storage space or room below ground level in a house. **2** a stock of wine.
– ORIGIN Latin *cellarium* 'storehouse', from *cella* 'storeroom or

Thesaurus

cavort • verb SKIP, dance, romp, jig, caper, frisk, gambol, prance, frolic, lark; bounce, trip, leap, jump, bound, spring, hop; *rare* rollick.
cease • verb **1** *hostilities had ceased* COME TO AN END, come to a halt, end, halt, stop, conclude, terminate, finish, draw to a close, be over. **2** *they ceased all military activity* BRING TO AN END, bring to a halt, end, halt, stop, conclude, terminate, finish, wind up, discontinue, suspend, break off; *informal* leave off.
– OPPOSITES start, continue.
– PHRASES **without cease** CONTINUOUSLY, incessantly, unendingly, unremittingly, without a pause/break, on and on.
ceaseless • adjective CONTINUAL, constant, continuous; incessant, unceasing, unending, endless, never-ending, interminable, nonstop, uninterrupted, unremitting, relentless, unrelenting, unrelieved, sustained, persistent, eternal, perpetual.
– OPPOSITES intermittent.
cede • verb SURRENDER, concede, relinquish, yield, part with, give up; hand over, deliver up, give over, make over, transfer; abandon, forgo, sacrifice; *poetic/literary* forsake.
ceiling • noun UPPER LIMIT, maximum, limitation.
celebrate • verb **1** *they were celebrating their wedding anniversary* COMMEMORATE, observe, mark, keep, honour, remember, memorialize. **2** *let's celebrate!* ENJOY ONESELF, make merry, have fun, have a good/wild time, have a party, revel, roister, carouse; *N. Amer.* step out; *informal* party, go out on the town, paint the town red, whoop it up, make whoopee, live it up, have a ball. **3** *the priest celebrated mass* PERFORM, observe, officiate at. **4** *he was celebrated for his achievements* PRAISE, extol, glorify, eulogize, reverence, honour, pay tribute to; *formal* laud; *archaic* emblazon.
celebrated • adjective ACCLAIMED, admired, highly rated, lionized, revered, honoured, esteemed, exalted, vaunted, well thought of; eminent, great, distinguished, prestigious, illustrious, pre-eminent, estimable, notable, of note, of repute; *formal* lauded.
– OPPOSITES unsung.
celebration • noun **1** *the celebration of his 50th birthday* COMMEMORATION, observance, marking, keeping. **2** *a cause for celebration* JOLLIFICATION, merrymaking, enjoying oneself, carousing, revelry, revels, festivities; *informal* partying. **3** *a birthday celebration* PARTY, function, gathering, festivities, festival, fête, carnival, jamboree; *informal* do, bash, rave; *Brit. informal* rave-up, knees-up, beanfeast, bunfight, beano. **4** *the celebration of the Eucharist* OBSERVANCE, performance, officiation, solemnization.
celebrity • noun **1** *his celebrity grew* FAME, prominence, renown, eminence, pre-eminence, stardom, popularity, distinction, note, notability, prestige, stature, repute, reputation. **2** *a sporting celebrity* FAMOUS PERSON, VIP, very important person, personality, (big) name, famous/household name, star, superstar; *informal* celeb, somebody, someone, megastar.
– OPPOSITES obscurity.
celestial • adjective **1** *a celestial body* (IN) SPACE, heavenly, astronomical, extraterrestrial, stellar, planetary. **2** *celestial beings* HEAVENLY, holy, saintly, divine, godly, godlike, ethereal; immortal, angelic, seraphic, cherubic.
– OPPOSITES earthly, hellish.
celibate • adjective UNMARRIED, single, unwed, spouseless; chaste, virginal, virgin, maidenly, maiden, intact, abstinent, self-denying.
– OPPOSITES married.
cell • noun **1** *a prison cell* ROOM, cubicle, chamber; dungeon, oubli-

C

chamber'.

cello /chellō/ ● noun (pl. **cellos**) a bass instrument of the violin family, held upright on the floor between the legs of the seated player.
– DERIVATIVES **cellist** noun.
– ORIGIN shortening of VIOLONCELLO.

cellophane /selləfayn/ ● noun trademark a thin transparent wrapping material made from viscose.
– ORIGIN from CELLULOSE + *-phane* (from Latin *diaphanus* 'diaphanous').

cellphone ● noun a mobile phone.

cellular /selyoolər/ ● adjective **1** relating to or consisting of living cells. **2** relating to a mobile telephone system that uses a number of short-range radio stations to cover the area it serves. **3** (of fabric) woven with an open mesh to trap air for extra insulation. **4** consisting of small compartments or rooms.
– ORIGIN Latin *cellularis*, from *cellula* 'little chamber'.

cellulite /selyoolīt/ ● noun persistent subcutaneous fat causing dimpling of the skin.
– ORIGIN French, from *cellule* 'small cell'.

cellulitis ● noun Medicine inflammation of connective tissue immediately under the skin.

celluloid ● noun **1** a transparent flammable plastic made from camphor and nitrocellulose, formerly used for cinematographic film. **2** the cinema as a genre.

cellulose /selyoolōz, -lōss/ ● noun **1** an insoluble substance derived from glucose, forming the main constituent of plant cell walls and of vegetable fibres such as cotton. **2** paint or lacquer consisting principally of cellulose acetate or nitrate in solution.
– DERIVATIVES **cellulosic** adjective.
– ORIGIN French, from *cellule* 'small cell'.

cellulose acetate ● noun a non-flammable polymer produced from cellulose, used as the basis of artificial fibres and plastic.

Celsius /selsiəss/ ● adjective of or denoting a scale of temperature on which water freezes at 0° and boils at 100°.
– USAGE **Celsius** rather than **centigrade** is the standard accepted term when giving temperatures.
– ORIGIN named after the Swedish astronomer Anders *Celsius* (1701–44).

Celt /kelt, selt/ ● noun **1** a member of a group of peoples inhabiting much of Europe and Asia Minor in pre-Roman times. **2** a native of a modern nation or region in which a Celtic language is (or was) spoken.
– ORIGIN from Greek *Keltoi* 'Celts'.

Celtic /keltik, sel-/ ● noun a group of languages including Irish, Scottish Gaelic, Welsh, Breton, Manx, and Cornish. ● adjective relating to Celtic or to the Celts.

cement ● noun **1** a powdery substance made by calcining lime and clay, used in making mortar and concrete. **2** a soft glue that hardens on setting. ● verb **1** fix with cement. **2** establish or strengthen: *the occasion cemented our friendship.*
– DERIVATIVES **cementation** noun.
– ORIGIN Latin *caementum* 'quarry stone', from *caedere* 'hew'.

cemetery ● noun (pl. **cemeteries**) a large burial ground.
– ORIGIN Greek *koimētērion* 'dormitory'.

cenobite ● noun variant spelling of COENOBITE.

cenotaph /sennətaaf/ ● noun a monument to someone buried elsewhere, especially a war memorial.
– ORIGIN from Greek *kenos* 'empty' + *taphos* 'tomb'.

Cenozoic /seenəzōik/ (also **Cainozoic**) ● adjective Geology of or relating to the era following the Mesozoic era (from about 65 million years ago to the present).
– ORIGIN from Greek *kainos* 'new' + *zōion* 'animal'.

censer ● noun a container in which incense is burnt.
– ORIGIN Old French *censier*, from *encens* 'incense'.

censor ● noun an official who examines material that is to be published and suppresses parts considered offensive or a threat to security. ● verb suppress or remove unacceptable parts of (a book, film, etc.).
– DERIVATIVES **censorship** noun.
– ORIGIN Latin (denoting a magistrate in ancient Rome who held censuses and supervised public morals), from *censere* 'assess'.

censorious /sensoriəss/ ● adjective severely critical.
– DERIVATIVES **censoriously** adverb **censoriousness** noun.

censure /senshər/ ● verb express strong disapproval of. ● noun strong disapproval or criticism.
– DERIVATIVES **censurable** adjective.
– ORIGIN from Latin *censura* 'judgement, assessment', from *censere* 'assess'.

census ● noun (pl. **censuses**) an official count or survey of a population.
– ORIGIN Latin, from *censere* 'assess'.

cent ● noun a monetary unit equal to one hundredth of a dollar or other decimal currency unit.
– ORIGIN from Latin *centum* 'hundred'.

centas /sentass/ ● noun (pl. same) a monetary unit of Lithuania, equal to one hundredth of a litas.
– ORIGIN Lithuanian.

centaur /sentawr/ ● noun Greek Mythology a creature with the head, arms, and torso of a man and the body and legs of a horse.
– ORIGIN Greek *kentauros*, the Greek name for a people of Thessaly who were expert horsemen.

centavo /sentaavō/ ● noun (pl. **centavos**) a monetary unit of Portugal, Mexico, Brazil, and certain other countries, equal to one hundredth of the basic unit.
– ORIGIN Spanish and Portuguese, from Latin *centum* 'a hundred'.

centenarian ● noun a person a hundred or more years old. ● adjective a hundred or more years old.

centenary /senteenəri, -tennəri/ ● noun (pl. **centenaries**) chiefly Brit. the hundredth anniversary of an event.
– ORIGIN from Latin *centenarius* 'containing a hundred', from *centum* 'a hundred'.

centennial ● adjective relating to a hundredth anniversary. ● noun a hundredth anniversary.
– ORIGIN from Latin *centum* 'a hundred'.

center etc. ● noun US spelling of CENTRE etc.

centesimo /chentessimō/ ● noun (pl. **centesimos**) a monetary unit of Italy, worth one hundredth of a lira.
– ORIGIN Italian.

centésimo /sentessimō/ ● noun (pl. **centésimos**) a monetary unit of Uruguay and Panama, equal to one hundredth of the basic unit.
– ORIGIN Spanish.

centi- ● combining form **1** one hundredth: *centilitre.* **2** hundred: *centipede.*
– ORIGIN from Latin *centum* 'hundred'.

centigrade ● adjective of or denoting the Celsius scale of temperature, with a hundred degrees between the freezing and boiling points of water.
– USAGE On using **centigrade** or **Celsius**, see the note at CELSIUS.
– ORIGIN from Latin *centum* 'a hundred' + *gradus* 'step'.

centigram (also **centigramme**) ● noun a metric unit of mass equal to one hundredth of a gram.

centilitre (US **centiliter**) ● noun a metric unit of capacity equal to one hundredth of a litre.

centime /sonteem/ ● noun a monetary unit of France, Belgium, Switzerland, and certain other countries, equal to one hun-

Thesaurus

ette, lock-up. **2** *each cell of the honeycomb* COMPARTMENT, cavity, hole, hollow, section. **3** *terrorist cells* UNIT, faction, arm, section, coterie, group.

cellar ● noun BASEMENT, vault, underground room, lower ground floor; crypt, undercroft.
– OPPOSITES attic.

cement ● noun *polystyrene cement* ADHESIVE, glue, fixative, gum, paste; superglue, epoxy resin; *N. Amer.* mucilage; *N. Amer. informal* stickum.
● verb *he cemented the sample to a microscope slide* STICK, bond; fasten, fix, affix, attach, secure, bind, glue, gum, paste.

cemetery ● noun GRAVEYARD, churchyard, burial ground, necropolis; *informal* boneyard; *historical* potter's field; *archaic* God's acre.

censor ● noun *the film censors* EXPURGATOR, bowdlerizer; examiner, inspector, editor.
● verb *letters home were censored* CUT, delete parts of, make cuts in, blue-pencil; edit, expurgate, bowdlerize, sanitize; *informal* clean up.

censorious ● adjective HYPERCRITICAL, overcritical, disapproving, condemnatory, denunciatory, deprecatory, disparaging, reproachful, reproving, censuring, captious; *formal* castigatory.

censure ● verb *he was censured for his conduct.* See REPRIMAND verb.
● noun *a note of censure* CONDEMNATION, criticism, attack, abuse; reprimand, rebuke, admonishment, reproof, reproval, upbraiding, disapproval, reproach, reprehension, obloquy; *formal* excoriation,

dredth of a franc or other decimal currency unit.
– ORIGIN from Latin *centesimus* 'hundredth'.
centimetre (US **centimeter**) ● **noun** a metric unit of length equal to one hundredth of a metre.
centimo /sentimō/ ● **noun** (pl. **centimos**) a monetary unit of Spain and a number of Latin American countries, equal to one hundredth of the basic unit.
– ORIGIN Spanish.
centipede ● **noun** an arthropod with an elongated body composed of many segments, most of which bear a pair of legs.
– ORIGIN from Latin *centum* 'a hundred' + *pes* 'foot'.
central ● **adjective 1** in or near the centre. **2** very important; essential.
– DERIVATIVES **centrality** noun **centrally** adverb.
central bank ● **noun** a national bank that provides services for its country's government and commercial banking system, and issues currency.
central heating ● **noun** a system for warming a building by heating water or air in one place and circulating it through pipes and radiators or vents.
centralize (also **centralise**) ● **verb** concentrate (control or power) under a single authority.
– DERIVATIVES **centralism** noun **centralist** noun & adjective **centralization** noun.
central nervous system ● **noun** the complex of nerve tissues that controls the activities of the body.
central processing unit (also **central processor**) ● **noun** the part of a computer in which operations are controlled and executed.
central reservation ● **noun** Brit. the strip of land between the carriageways of a motorway or other major road.
centre (US **center**) ● **noun 1** a point in the middle of something that is equally distant from all of its sides, ends, or surfaces. **2** a place where a specified activity is concentrated. **3** a point from which something spreads or to which something is directed: *the city was a centre of discontent.* **4** a political group whose opinions avoid extremes. **5** the middle player in some team games. ● **verb 1** place in the centre. **2** (**centre on/around**) have as a major concern or theme.
– ORIGIN Latin *centrum*, from Greek *kentron* 'sharp point, stationary point of a pair of compasses'.
centre back ● **noun** Soccer a defender who plays in the middle of the field.
centreboard (US **centerboard**) ● **noun** a pivoted board lowered through the keel of a sailing boat to reduce sideways movement.
centrefold (US **centerfold**) ● **noun** the two middle pages of a magazine.
centre forward ● **noun** Soccer & Hockey an attacker who plays in the middle of the field.
centre half ● **noun** Soccer another term for CENTRE BACK.
centre of gravity ● **noun** the point from which the weight of a body appears to act.
centre of mass ● **noun** a point representing the mean position of all the matter in a body (in uniform gravity, the same as the centre of gravity).
centrepiece (US **centerpiece**) ● **noun** the most important item in a display.
centre stage ● **noun 1** the centre of a stage. **2** the most prominent position. ● **adverb** in or towards this position.
-centric ● **combining form 1** having a specified centre: *geocentric.* **2** originating from a specified viewpoint: *Eurocentric.*
– DERIVATIVES **-centricity** combining form in corresponding nouns.
– ORIGIN from Greek *kentrikos*.
centrifugal /sentrifyo͞og'l, sentrifyoog'l/ ● **adjective** Physics moving away from a centre.
– DERIVATIVES **centrifugally** adverb.
– ORIGIN from Latin *centrum* 'centre' + *-fugus* 'fleeing'.
centrifugal force ● **noun** Physics a force, arising from the body's inertia, which appears to act on a body moving in a circular path and is directed away from the centre around which the body is moving.
centrifuge /sentrifyo͞oj/ ● **noun** a machine with a rapidly rotating container, used chiefly to separate liquids from solids. ● **verb** subject to the action of a centrifuge.
– DERIVATIVES **centrifugation** /sentrifyoogaysh'n/ noun.
centripetal /sentrippit'l/ ● **adjective** Physics moving towards a centre.
– DERIVATIVES **centripetally** adverb.
– ORIGIN from Latin *centrum* 'centre' + *-petus* 'seeking'.
centripetal force ● **noun** Physics a force which acts on a body moving in a circular path and is directed towards the centre around which the body is moving.
centrist ● **noun** a person having moderate political views or policies.
– DERIVATIVES **centrism** noun.
centurion ● **noun** the commander of a century in the ancient Roman army.
– ORIGIN Latin, from *centuria* 'century'.
century ● **noun** (pl. **centuries**) **1** a period of one hundred years. **2** a batsman's score of a hundred runs in cricket. **3** a company of a hundred men in the ancient Roman army.
– USAGE Strictly speaking, centuries run from 01 to 100, meaning that the new century begins on the first day of the year 01 (e.g. 1 January 2001). In practice and in popular perception, however, the new century is held to begin when the significant digits in the date change, e.g. on 1 January 2000, when 1999 becomes 2000.
– ORIGIN Latin *centuria*, from *centum* 'hundred'.
CEO ● **abbreviation** chief executive officer.
cep /sep/ ● **noun** an edible mushroom with a smooth brown cap.
– ORIGIN French *cèpe*, from Latin *cippus* 'stake'.
cephalic /sifalik, ke-/ ● **adjective** relating to the head.
– ORIGIN from Greek *kephalē* 'head'.
cephalopod /seffəlәpod/ ● **noun** Zoology a mollusc of a class including octopuses and squids.
– ORIGIN from Greek *kephalē* 'head' + *pous* 'foot'.
ceramic ● **adjective 1** made of clay that is permanently hardened by heat. **2** relating to ceramic articles. ● **noun** (**ceramics**) **1** ceramic articles. **2** (usu. treated as sing.) the art of making ceramics.
– DERIVATIVES **ceramicist** noun.
– ORIGIN Greek *keramikos*, from *keramos* 'pottery'.
ceratopsian /serrətopsiən, kerr-/ ● **noun** a gregarious plant-eating dinosaur of a group including triceratops, with a bony frill around the neck.
– ORIGIN from Greek *keras* 'horn' + *ops* 'face'.
cereal ● **noun 1** a grain used for food, for example wheat, maize, or rye. **2** a grass producing such grain. **3** a breakfast food made from a cereal grain or grains.
– ORIGIN Latin, from *Ceres*, the Roman goddess of agriculture.
cerebellum /serribelləm/ ● **noun** (pl. **cerebellums** or **cerebella**) Anatomy the part of the brain at the back of the skull, which coordinates muscular activity.
– DERIVATIVES **cerebellar** adjective.
– ORIGIN Latin, 'little brain'.
cerebral /serribrəl/ ● **adjective 1** relating to the cerebrum of the brain. **2** intellectual rather than emotional or physical.
– DERIVATIVES **cerebrally** adverb.
cerebral palsy ● **noun** a condition marked by impaired muscle coordination and spastic paralysis, caused by damage to the brain before or at birth.
cerebration /serribraysh'n/ ● **noun** the working of the brain; thinking.

C

Thesaurus

castigation; *rare* objurgation.
– OPPOSITES approval.
central ● **adjective 1** *occupying a central position* MIDDLE, centre, halfway, midway, mid, median, medial, mean; *Anatomy* mesial. **2** *central London* INNER, innermost, middle, mid. **3** *their central campaign issue* MAIN, chief, principal, primary, leading, foremost, first, most important, predominant, dominant, key, crucial, vital, essential, basic, fundamental, core, prime, premier, paramount, major, overriding; *informal* number-one.
– OPPOSITES side, outer, subordinate.
centralize ● **verb** CONCENTRATE, consolidate, amalgamate, condense, unify, streamline, focus, rationalize.
– OPPOSITES devolve.
centre ● **noun** *the centre of the town* MIDDLE, nucleus, heart, core, hub; middle point, midpoint, halfway point, mean, median.
– OPPOSITES edge.
● **verb** *the story centres on a doctor* FOCUS, concentrate, pivot, revolve, be based.
centrepiece ● **noun** HIGHLIGHT, main feature, high point/spot, best part, climax; focus of attention, focal point, centre of

cerebrospinal /serribrōspīn'l/ ● adjective Anatomy relating to the brain and spine.
cerebrospinal fluid ● noun Anatomy the clear watery fluid which fills the space between membranes in the brain and the spinal chord.
cerebrum /serribrəm/ ● noun (pl. **cerebra** /serribrə/) Anatomy the principal part of the brain, located in the front area of the skull.
– ORIGIN Latin, 'brain'.
cerecloth /seerkloth/ ● noun historical waxed cloth, used especially for wrapping a corpse.
– ORIGIN from Latin *cera* 'wax'.
ceremonial ● adjective **1** relating to or used for ceremonies. **2** (of a post or role) involving only nominal authority or power. ● noun another term for CEREMONY.
– DERIVATIVES **ceremonially** adverb.
ceremonious ● adjective relating or appropriate to grand and formal occasions.
– DERIVATIVES **ceremoniously** adverb **ceremoniousness** noun.
ceremony ● noun (pl. **ceremonies**) **1** a formal occasion, typically celebrating a particular event or anniversary. **2** the ritual procedures observed at such occasions.
– PHRASES **stand on ceremony** observe formalities. **without ceremony** without formality or politeness.
– ORIGIN Latin *caerimonia* 'religious worship'.
cerise /səreess/ ● noun a light, clear red colour.
– ORIGIN French, 'cherry'.
cerium /serriəm/ ● noun a silvery-white metallic chemical element, the most abundant of the lanthanide series.
– ORIGIN named after the asteroid *Ceres*, discovered in 1801, shortly before cerium was identified.
cert ● noun Brit. informal **1** an event regarded as inevitable. **2** a competitor, candidate, etc. regarded as certain to win.
cert. ● abbreviation **1** certificate. **2** certified.
certain ● adjective **1** able to be relied on to happen or be the case. **2** completely convinced of something. **3** specific but not explicitly named or stated. ● pronoun (**certain of**) some but not all.
– ORIGIN Latin *certus* 'settled, sure'.
certainly ● adverb **1** definitely; undoubtedly. **2** yes; by all means.
certainty ● noun (pl. **certainties**) **1** the quality or state of being certain. **2** a fact that is true or an event that is definitely going to take place.
certifiable ● adjective able or needing to be certified.
certificate ● noun /sərtiffikət/ **1** an official document recording a particular fact, event, or level of achievement. **2** an official classification awarded to a cinema film, indicating its suitability for a particular age group. ● verb /sərtiffikayt/ provide with a certificate.
– DERIVATIVES **certification** noun.
certify ● verb (**certifies**, **certified**) **1** formally confirm. **2** officially recognize as meeting certain standards. **3** officially declare insane.
– ORIGIN Latin *certificare*, from *certus* 'certain'.
certiorari /sertiōraari/ ● noun Law a writ by which a higher court reviews a case tried in a lower court.
– ORIGIN Latin, 'to be informed', a phrase originally occurring at the start of the writ.
certitude ● noun a feeling of absolute certainty.
– ORIGIN Latin *certitudo*, from *certus* 'certain'.
cerulean /sirōōliən/ ● adjective deep blue in colour like a clear sky.
– ORIGIN Latin *caeruleus*, from *caelum* 'sky'.
cervical /servik'l, servīk'l/ ● adjective Anatomy **1** relating to the cervix. **2** relating to the neck.
– ORIGIN Latin *cervicalis*, from *cervix* 'neck'.
cervical smear ● noun Brit. a specimen of cellular material from the cervix spread on a microscope slide for examination for cancerous cells or precancerous changes.
cervix /serviks/ ● noun (pl. **cervices** /serviseez/) **1** the narrow neck-like passage forming the lower end of the womb. **2** technical the neck.
– ORIGIN Latin.
Cesarean (also **Cesarian**) ● adjective & noun US spelling of CAESAREAN.
cesium ● noun US spelling of CAESIUM.
cessation ● noun the fact or process of ceasing.
– ORIGIN Latin, from *cessare* 'cease'.
cession ● noun the formal giving up of rights, property, or territory by a state.
– ORIGIN Latin, from *cedere* 'cede'.
cesspit ● noun a pit for the disposal of liquid waste and sewage.
– ORIGIN from *cess* in CESSPOOL.
cesspool ● noun an underground container for the temporary storage of liquid waste and sewage.
– ORIGIN probably from archaic *suspiral* 'vent, water pipe, settling tank', from Old French *souspirail* 'air hole'.
c'est la vie /say laa vee/ ● exclamation that's life.
– ORIGIN French.

Thesaurus

attention/interest, magnet, cynosure.
ceramics ● plural noun POTTERY, pots, china.
ceremonial ● adjective *a ceremonial occasion* FORMAL, official, state, public; ritual, ritualistic, prescribed, stately, courtly, solemn.
– OPPOSITES informal.
● noun *diplomatic ceremonial* RITUAL, ceremony, rite, formality, pomp, protocol; formal praxis.
ceremonious ● adjective DIGNIFIED, majestic, imposing, impressive, solemn, stately, formal, courtly; regal, imperial, elegant, grand, glorious, splendid, magnificent, resplendent, portentous; informal starchy.
ceremony ● noun **1** *a wedding ceremony* RITE, ritual, ceremonial, observance; service, sacrament, liturgy, worship, celebration. **2** *the new Queen was proclaimed with due ceremony* POMP, protocol, formalities, niceties, decorum, etiquette, punctilio, politesse.
certain ● adjective **1** *I'm certain he's guilty* SURE, confident, positive, convinced, in no doubt, satisfied, assured, persuaded. **2** *it is certain that more changes are in the offing* UNQUESTIONABLE, sure, definite, beyond question, not in doubt, indubitable, undeniable, irrefutable, indisputable; obvious, evident, recognized, confirmed, accepted, acknowledged, undisputed, undoubted, unquestioned, as sure as eggs is eggs. **3** *they are certain to win* SURE, very likely, bound, destined. **4** *certain defeat* INEVITABLE, assured, destined, predestined; unavoidable, inescapable, inexorable, ineluctable. **5** *there is no certain cure* RELIABLE, dependable, trustworthy, foolproof, tried and tested, effective, guaranteed, sure, unfailing, infallible; informal sure-fire; dated sovereign. **6** *a certain sum of money* DETERMINED, definite, fixed, established, precise. **7** *a certain lady* PARTICULAR, specific, individual, special. **8** *to a certain extent that is true* MODERATE, modest, medium, middling; limited, small.
– OPPOSITES doubtful, possible, unlikely.
certainly ● adverb **1** *this is certainly a late work* UNQUESTIONABLY, surely, assuredly, definitely, beyond/without question, without doubt, indubitably, undeniably, irrefutably, indisputably; obviously, patently, evidently, plainly, clearly, unmistakably, undisputedly, undoubtedly, as sure as eggs is eggs. **2** *our revenues are certainly lower* ADMITTEDLY, without question, definitely, undoubtedly, without a doubt.
– OPPOSITES possibly.
● exclamation *'Shall we eat now?' 'Certainly.'* YES, definitely, absolutely, sure, by all means, indeed, of course, naturally; affirmative; Brit. dated rather.
certainty ● noun **1** *she knew with certainty that he was telling the truth* CONFIDENCE, sureness, positiveness, conviction, certitude, assurance. **2** *he accepted defeat as a certainty* INEVITABILITY, foregone conclusion; informal sure thing; Brit. informal cert, dead cert.
– OPPOSITES doubt, possibility.
certificate ● noun GUARANTEE, certification, document, authorization, authentication, credentials, accreditation, licence, diploma.
certify ● verb **1** *the aircraft was certified as airworthy* VERIFY, guarantee, attest, validate, confirm, substantiate, endorse, vouch for, testify to; provide evidence, give proof, prove, demonstrate. **2** *a certified hospital* ACCREDIT, recognize, license, authorize, approve, warrant.
certitude ● noun CERTAINTY, confidence, sureness, positiveness, conviction, assurance.
– OPPOSITES doubt.
cessation ● noun END, ending, termination, stopping, halting, ceasing, finish, finishing, stoppage, conclusion, winding up, discontinuation, abandonment, suspension, breaking off, cutting short.
– OPPOSITES start, resumption.
cession ● noun SURRENDER, surrendering, ceding, concession, re-

cetacean /sitaysh'n/ Zoology ● **noun** a marine mammal of an order including whales and dolphins. ● **adjective** relating to cetaceans.
– ORIGIN from Greek *kētos* 'whale'.
ceteris paribus /kaytəriss parriboŏss/ ● **adverb** other things being equal.
– ORIGIN Latin.
CF ● **abbreviation** cystic fibrosis.
Cf ● **symbol** the chemical element californium.
cf. ● **abbreviation** compare with.
– ORIGIN from Latin *confer* 'compare'.
CFC ● **abbreviation** chlorofluorocarbon, any of a class of synthetic compounds of carbon, hydrogen, chlorine, and fluorine, used as refrigerants and aerosol propellants and harmful to the ozone layer.
CFE ● **abbreviation** (in the UK) College of Further Education.
CFS ● **abbreviation** chronic fatigue syndrome.
cg ● **abbreviation** centigram(s).
CGT ● **abbreviation** capital gains tax.
CH ● **abbreviation** (in the UK) Companion of Honour.
ch. ● **abbreviation** chapter.
Chablis /shabli/ ● **noun** a dry white burgundy wine from Chablis in eastern France.
cha-cha ● **noun** a ballroom dance with small steps and swaying hip movements, performed to a Latin American rhythm.
– ORIGIN Latin American Spanish.
chaconne /shəkon/ ● **noun** Music **1** a composition in a series of varying sections in slow triple time. **2** a stately dance performed to such music.
– ORIGIN Spanish *chacona*.
chacun à son goût /shakön a son goō/ ● **exclamation** each to their own taste.
– ORIGIN French.
Chadian /chaddiən/ ● **noun** a person from Chad in central Africa. ● **adjective** relating to Chad or Chadians.
chador /chuddər/ (also **chuddar**) ● **noun** a piece of dark-coloured cloth that is wrapped around the head and upper body leaving only the face exposed, worn by Muslim women.
– ORIGIN Persian, 'sheet or veil'.
chafe ● **verb 1** make or become sore by rubbing. **2** (of an object) rub abrasively against another. **3** rub (a part of the body) to restore warmth or sensation. **4** become impatient because of a restriction or inconvenience. ● **noun** wear or damage caused by rubbing.
– ORIGIN Old French *chaufer* 'make hot', from Latin *calere* 'be hot'.
chafer ● **noun** a large flying beetle of a group including the cockchafer and June bug.
– ORIGIN Old English.
chaff[1] /chaaf/ ● **noun 1** the husks of grain or other seed separated by winnowing or threshing. **2** chopped hay and straw used as fodder.
– PHRASES **separate** (or **sort**) **the wheat from the chaff** distinguish valuable people or things from worthless ones.
– ORIGIN Old English.
chaff[2] /chaaf, chaff/ ● **noun** light-hearted joking. ● **verb** tease.
– ORIGIN perhaps from CHAFE.
chaffinch ● **noun** a common finch, the male of which has a bluish head, pink underparts, and dark wings with a white flash.
– ORIGIN Old English.
chafing dish ● **noun 1** a cooking pot with an outer pan of hot water, used for keeping food warm. **2** a metal pan with a heating device below it, used for cooking at table.
– ORIGIN from the original (now obsolete) sense of CHAFE 'become warm, warm up'.
chagrin /shagrin/ ● **noun** annoyance or shame at having failed. ● **verb** (**be chagrined**) feel annoyed or ashamed.
– ORIGIN French, 'rough skin, shagreen'.
chain ● **noun 1** a connected series of metal links used for fastening or pulling, or as jewellery. **2** a connected series, set, or sequence. **3** a part of a molecule consisting of a number of atoms bonded together in a series. **4** a measure of length equal to 66 ft. ● **verb** fasten or confine with a chain.
– ORIGIN Old French *chaine*, from Latin *catena*.
chain gang ● **noun** a group of convicts chained together while working outside the prison.
chain letter ● **noun** one of a sequence of letters, each recipient in the sequence being requested to send copies to a number of other people.
chain mail ● **noun** historical armour made of small metal rings linked together.
chain reaction ● **noun 1** a chemical reaction in which the products themselves spread the reaction. **2** a series of events, each caused by the previous one.
chainsaw ● **noun** a power-driven saw with teeth set on a moving chain.
chain-smoke ● **verb** smoke cigarettes in continuous succession.
chain stitch ● **noun** an ornamental embroidery or crochet stitch resembling a chain.
chain store ● **noun** one of a series of shops owned by one firm and selling the same goods.
chair ● **noun 1** a separate seat for one person, with a back and four legs. **2** the person in charge of a meeting or an organization. **3** a professorship. **4** (**the chair**) US short for ELECTRIC CHAIR. ● **verb 1** act as chairperson of. **2** carry aloft in a chair or sitting position to celebrate a victory.
– ORIGIN Old French *chaiere*, from Greek *kathedra*.
chairlift ● **noun** a series of chairs hung from a moving cable, used for carrying passengers up and down a mountain.
chairman (or **chairwoman**) ● **noun** a person in charge of a meeting or organization.
chairperson ● **noun** a chairman or chairwoman.
chaise /shayz/ ● **noun** chiefly historical a horse-drawn carriage for one or two people, especially one with an open top and two wheels.
– ORIGIN French.
chaise longue /shayz longg/ (US also **chaise lounge**) ● **noun** (pl. **chaises longues** pronunc. same) **1** a sofa with a backrest at only one end. **2** N. Amer. a sunbed or other chair with a lengthened seat.
– ORIGIN French, 'long chair'.
chakra /chukrə/ ● **noun** (in Indian thought) each of the centres of spiritual power in the human body, usually considered to be seven in number.
– ORIGIN Sanskrit, 'wheel or circle'.

C

Thesaurus

linquishment, yielding, giving up; handing over, transfer; abandonment, sacrifice; *poetic/literary* forsaking.
chafe ● **verb 1** *the collar chafed his neck* ABRADE, graze, rub against, gall, scrape, scratch; *Medicine* excoriate. **2** *I chafed her feet* RUB, warm (up). **3** *material chafed by the rock* WEAR AWAY/DOWN, erode, abrade, scour, scrape away. **4** *the bank chafed at the restrictions* BE ANGRY, be annoyed, be irritated, fume, be exasperated, be frustrated.
chaff[1] ● **noun 1** *separating the chaff from the grain* HUSKS, hulls, pods, shells, bran; *N. Amer.* shucks. **2** *the proposals were so much chaff* RUBBISH, dross; *N. Amer.* garbage, trash; *Austral./NZ* mullock; *informal* junk.
chaff[2] ● **noun** *good-natured chaff* BANTER, repartee, teasing, ragging, joking, jesting, raillery, badinage, wisecracks, witticism(s); *informal* kidding, ribbing; *formal* persiflage.
● **verb** *the pleasures of chaffing your mates* TEASE, make fun of, poke fun at, rag; *informal* take the mickey out of, rib, josh, kid, have on, pull someone's leg; *Brit. informal* wind up; *N. Amer. informal* goof on, rag on, razz; *Austral./NZ informal* poke mullock at, poke borak at; *informal, dated* twit; *archaic* make sport of.
chagrin ● **noun** ANNOYANCE, irritation, vexation, exasperation, displeasure, dissatisfaction, discontent; anger, rage, fury, wrath, indignation, resentment; embarrassment, mortification, humiliation, shame.
– OPPOSITES delight.
chain ● **noun 1** *he was held in chains* FETTERS, shackles, irons, leg-irons, manacles, handcuffs; *informal* cuffs, bracelets; *Brit. archaic, informal* darbies; *historical* bilboes; *archaic* gyves. **2** *a chain of events* SERIES, succession, string, sequence, train, course. **3** *a chain of shops* GROUP, multiple shop/store, multiple.
● **verb** *she chained her bicycle to the railings* SECURE, fasten, tie, tether, hitch; restrain, shackle, fetter, manacle, handcuff.
chair ● **noun 1** *he sat down on a chair* SEAT. **2** *the chair of the committee.* See CHAIRMAN. **3** *a university chair* PROFESSORSHIP. **4** *(N. Amer.) he was sent to the chair* ELECTRIC CHAIR, electrocution, execution.
● **verb** *she chairs the economic committee* PRESIDE OVER, take the chair of; lead, direct, run, manage, control, be in charge of, be in control of.

C

chalcedony /kalseddəni/ ● **noun** (pl. **chalcedonies**) quartz occurring in a microcrystalline form such as onyx and agate.
– ORIGIN Greek *khalkēdōn*.

chalet /shalay/ ● **noun 1** a wooden house with overhanging eaves, typically found in the Swiss Alps. **2** a small wooden cabin used by holidaymakers.
– ORIGIN Old French *chasel* 'farmstead'.

chalice ● **noun 1** historical a goblet. **2** the wine cup used in the Christian Eucharist.
– ORIGIN Latin *calix* 'cup'.

chalk ● **noun 1** a white soft limestone (calcium carbonate) formed from the skeletal remains of sea creatures. **2** a similar substance (calcium sulphate), made into sticks and used for drawing or writing. ● **verb 1** draw or write with chalk. **2** Brit. charge (drinks bought in a pub or bar) to a person's account. **3** (**chalk up**) achieve (something) noteworthy. **4** (**chalk up**) ascribe (something) to a particular cause.
– PHRASES **as different as chalk and cheese** Brit. fundamentally different. **by a long chalk** Brit. by far.
– DERIVATIVES **chalky** adjective (**chalkier**, **chalkiest**).
– ORIGIN Latin *calx* 'lime'.

chalkboard ● **noun** North American term for BLACKBOARD.

challenge ● **noun 1** a call to someone to participate in a contest. **2** a call to prove something. **3** a demanding task or situation. **4** an attempt to win a sporting contest. ● **verb 1** dispute the truth or validity of. **2** invite (someone) to engage in a contest. **3** Law object to (a jury member). **4** compete with. **5** (of a sentry) call on (someone) to prove their identity.
– DERIVATIVES **challenger** noun **challenging** adjective.
– ORIGIN Old French *chalenge*, from Latin *calumnia* 'calumny'.

challenged ● **adjective 1** euphemistic suffering from impairment or disability in a specified respect: *physically challenged.* **2** humorous lacking or deficient in a specified respect: *vertically challenged.*

challis /shalliss, shalli/ ● **noun** a lightweight soft clothing fabric made from silk and worsted.
– ORIGIN origin uncertain.

chalybeate /kəlibbiət/ ● **adjective** denoting natural mineral springs containing iron salts.
– ORIGIN Latin *chalybeatus*, from Greek *khalups* 'steel'.

chamaeleon ● **noun** variant spelling of CHAMELEON.

chamber ● **noun 1** a large room used for formal or public events. **2** one of the houses of a parliament. **3** (**chambers**) Law, Brit. rooms used by a barrister or barristers. **4** literary or archaic a private room, especially a bedroom. **5** an enclosed space or cavity. **6** (before another noun) Music of or for a small group of instruments: *a chamber orchestra.* **7** the part of a gun bore that contains the charge.
– DERIVATIVES **chambered** adjective.
– ORIGIN Old French *chambre*, from Latin *camera* 'vault, arched chamber', from Greek *kamara* 'object with an arched cover'.

chamberlain /chaymbərlin/ ● **noun** historical **1** an officer who managed the household of a monarch or noble. **2** Brit. an officer who received revenue on behalf of a corporation or public body.
– ORIGIN Old French.

chambermaid ● **noun** a woman who cleans rooms in a hotel.

chamber music ● **noun** instrumental music played by a small ensemble, such as a string quartet.

Chamber of Commerce ● **noun** a local association to promote the interests of the business community.

chamber pot ● **noun** a bowl kept in a bedroom and used as a toilet.

chambray /shambray/ ● **noun** a linen-finished cloth with a white weft and a coloured warp.
– ORIGIN from *Cambrai* (see CAMBRIC).

chameleon /kəmeeliən/ (also **chamaeleon**) ● **noun** a small slow-moving lizard with a long extensible tongue, protruding eyes, and the ability to change colour.
– DERIVATIVES **chameleonic** adjective.
– ORIGIN Greek *khamaileōn*, from *khamai* 'on the ground' + *leōn* 'lion'.

chamfer /chamfər/ Carpentry ● **verb** cut away (a right-angled edge or corner) to make a symmetrical sloping edge. ● **noun** a chamfered edge or corner.
– ORIGIN French *chamfrain*, from *chant* 'point, side, edge' + *fraint* 'broken'.

chamois ● **noun** (pl. same) **1** /shamwaa/ (pl. pronounced same or /shamwaaz/) an agile goat-antelope found in mountainous areas of southern Europe. **2** /shammi/ (pl. pronounced /shammiz/) (also **chamois leather**) soft pliable leather made from the skin of sheep, goats, or deer.
– ORIGIN French.

chamomile /kamməmīl/ (also **camomile**) ● **noun** an aromatic plant with white and yellow flowers.
– ORIGIN Latin *chamomilla*, from Greek *khamaimēlon* 'earth-apple' (because of the apple-like smell of its flowers).

champ[1] ● **verb 1** munch enthusiastically or noisily. **2** fret impatiently.
– PHRASES **champ at the bit** be very impatient.
– ORIGIN probably imitative.

champ[2] ● **noun** informal a champion.

champagne /shampayn/ ● **noun** a white sparkling wine from Champagne, a region in NE France.

champers ● **noun** informal, chiefly Brit. champagne.

champion ● **noun 1** a person who has won a sporting contest or other competition. **2** a defender of a cause or person. ● **verb** support the cause of. ● **adjective** Brit. informal or dialect excellent.
– ORIGIN Latin *campion* 'fighter', from *campus* 'level ground'.

championship ● **noun 1** a sporting contest for the position of champion. **2** the vigorous defence of a person or cause.

chance ● **noun 1** a possibility of something happening. **2** (**chances**) the probability of something happening. **3** an opportunity. **4** the occurrence of events in the absence of any obvious design. ● **verb 1** do something by accident. **2** informal risk.
– PHRASES **by any chance** possibly. **chance one's arm** Brit. informal risk doing something. **on the (off) chance** just in case. **stand a chance** have a prospect of success. **take a chance** (or **chances**) expose oneself to the risk of danger or failure.
– ORIGIN Old French *cheance*, from *cheoir* 'fall, befall'.

Thesaurus

chairman, chairwoman ● **noun** CHAIR, chairperson, president, leader, convener; spokesperson, spokesman, spokeswoman.

chalk ● **verb**
– PHRASES **chalk something up 1** *he has chalked up another success* ACHIEVE, attain, accomplish, gain, earn, win, succeed in making, make, get, obtain, notch up, rack up. **2** *I forgot completely—chalk it up to age* ATTRIBUTE, assign, ascribe, put down; blame on, pin on, lay at the door of.

chalky ● **adjective 1** *chalky skin* PALE, bloodless, pallid, colourless, wan, ashen, white, pasty. **2** *chalky bits at the bottom of the glass* POWDERY, gritty, granular; *archaic* pulverulent.

challenge ● **noun 1** *he accepted the challenge* DARE, provocation; summons. **2** *a challenge to his leadership* TEST, questioning, dispute, stand, opposition, confrontation. **3** *it was proving quite a challenge* PROBLEM, difficult task, test, trial.
● **verb 1** *we challenged their statistics* QUESTION, disagree with, dispute, take issue with, protest against, call into question, object to. **2** *he challenged one of my men to a duel* DARE, summon, throw down the gauntlet to. **3** *changes that would challenge them* TEST, tax, strain, make demands on; stretch, stimulate, inspire, excite.

challenging ● **adjective** DEMANDING, testing, taxing, exacting; stretching, exciting, stimulating, inspiring; difficult, tough, hard, formidable, onerous, arduous, strenuous, gruelling; *formal* exigent.
– OPPOSITES easy, uninspiring.

chamber ● **noun 1** *a debating chamber* ROOM, hall, assembly room, auditorium. **2** *(archaic) we slept safely in our chamber* BEDROOM, room; *poetic/literary* bower; *historical* boudoir; *archaic* bedchamber. **3** *the left chamber of the heart* COMPARTMENT, cavity; *Anatomy* auricle, ventricle.

champagne ● **noun** SPARKLING WINE; mousseux, spumante, cava; *informal* champers, bubbly, fizz.

champion ● **noun 1** *the world champion* WINNER, title-holder, defending champion, gold medallist; prizewinner, victor (ludorum); *informal* champ, number one. **2** *a champion of change* ADVOCATE, proponent, promoter, supporter, defender, upholder, backer, exponent; campaigner, lobbyist, crusader, apologist; *N. Amer.* booster. **3** *(historical) the king's champion* KNIGHT, man-at-arms, warrior.
● **verb** *championing the rights of tribal peoples* ADVOCATE, promote, defend, uphold, support, back, stand up for, take someone's part; campaign for, lobby for, fight for, crusade for, stick up for.
– OPPOSITES oppose.

chance ● **noun 1** *there was a chance he might be released* POSSIBILITY, prospect, probability, likelihood, likeliness, expectation, anticipation; risk, threat, danger. **2** *I gave her a chance to answer*

chancel /chaans'l/ ● noun the part of a church near the altar, reserved for the clergy and choir.
– ORIGIN from Latin *cancelli* 'crossbars'.
chancellery /chaansələri/ ● noun (pl. **chancelleries**) the position, office, or department of a chancellor.
chancellor ● noun **1** a senior state or legal official of various kinds. **2** (**Chancellor**) the head of the government in some European countries.
– DERIVATIVES **chancellorship** noun.
– ORIGIN Latin *cancellarius* 'porter, secretary' (originally a court official stationed at the grating separating public from judges), from *cancelli* 'crossbars'.
Chancellor of the Exchequer ● noun the finance minister of the United Kingdom.
chancer ● noun informal a person who fully exploits any opportunity.
chancery ● noun (pl. **chanceries**) (**Chancery** or **Chancery Division**) Law (in the UK) the Lord Chancellor's court, a division of the High Court of Justice.
– ORIGIN contraction of CHANCELLERY.
chancre /shangkər/ ● noun Medicine a painless ulcer, particularly one developing on the genitals in venereal disease.
– ORIGIN Latin *cancer* 'creeping ulcer'.
chancroid /shangkroyd/ ● noun a venereal infection causing ulceration of the lymph nodes in the groin.
chancy ● adjective (**chancier**, **chanciest**) informal uncertain; risky.
– DERIVATIVES **chancily** adverb.
chandelier ● noun a large hanging light with branches for several light bulbs or candles.
– ORIGIN French, from *chandelle* 'candle'.
chandler /chaandlər/ ● noun **1** (also **ship chandler**) a dealer in supplies and equipment for ships. **2** historical a dealer in household items such as oil and groceries.
– DERIVATIVES **chandlery** noun.
– ORIGIN originally denoting a candlemaker or candle seller: from Old French *chandelier*, from *chandelle* (see CHANDELIER).
change ● verb **1** make or become different. **2** exchange for another. **3** move from one to (another). **4** (**change over**) move from one system or situation to another. **5** exchange (a sum of money) for the same sum in a different currency or denomination. ● noun **1** the action of changing. **2** an instance of becoming different. **3** money returned to someone as the balance of the sum paid or money given in exchange for the same sum in larger units. **4** coins as opposed to banknotes. **5** a clean garment or garments as replacement clothing. **6** an order in which a peal of bells can be rung.
– PHRASES **change hands 1** (of a business or building) pass to a different owner. **2** (of money) pass to another person in the course of a business transaction. **a change is as good as a rest** proverb a change of work or occupation can be as refreshing as a period of relaxation. **change one's tune** express a very different attitude. **for a change** contrary to how things usually happen. **get no change out of** Brit. informal fail to get information or a desired reaction from. **ring the changes** vary the ways of doing something. [ORIGIN with allusion to the different orders in which a peal of bells may be rung.]
– DERIVATIVES **changeless** adjective **changer** noun.
– ORIGIN Old French *changer*, from Latin *cambire* 'barter'.
changeable ● adjective **1** liable to unpredictable variation. **2** able to be changed.
– DERIVATIVES **changeability** noun.
changeling ● noun a child believed to have been secretly substituted by fairies for the parents' real child.
changeover ● noun a change from one system or situation to another.
channel ● noun **1** a length of water wider than a strait, joining two larger areas of water, especially two seas. **2** (**the Channel**) the English Channel. **3** Biology a tubular passage or duct for liquid. **4** an electric circuit which acts as a path for a signal. **5** a band of frequencies used in radio and television transmission. **6** a medium for communication or the passage of information. **7** a navigable passage in a stretch of water otherwise unsafe for vessels. ● verb (**channelled**, **channelling**; US **channeled**, **channeling**) **1** direct towards a particular end. **2** cause to pass along or through a specified route or medium.
– ORIGIN Latin *canalis* 'pipe, groove, channel', from *canna* 'cane, reed'.
channel-hop ● verb (**channel-hopped**, **channel-hopping**) informal change frequently from one television channel to another.
chant ● noun **1** a repeated rhythmic phrase, typically one shouted or sung in unison by a group. **2** a monotonous or repetitive song. **3** a tune to which the words of psalms or other works with irregular rhythm are fitted by singing several syllables or words to the same note. ● verb say, shout, or sing in a chant.
– ORIGIN Old French *chanter*, from Latin *canere* 'sing'.
chanter ● noun the pipe of a bagpipe with finger holes, on which the melody is played.
chanterelle /chantərel/ ● noun an edible woodland mushroom with a yellow funnel-shaped cap.

C

Thesaurus

OPPORTUNITY, opening, occasion, turn, time, window (of opportunity); *N. Amer. & Austral./NZ* show; *informal* shot, look-in. **3** *Nigel took an awful chance* RISK, gamble, venture, speculation, long shot, leap in the dark. **4** *pure chance* ACCIDENT, coincidence, serendipity, fate, destiny, fortuity, providence, happenstance; good fortune, (good) luck, fluke.
● adjective *a chance discovery* ACCIDENTAL, fortuitous, adventitious, fluky, coincidental, serendipitous; unintentional, unintended, inadvertent, unplanned.
– OPPOSITES intentional.
● verb **1** *I chanced to meet him* HAPPEN. **2** *(informal) she chanced another look* RISK, hazard, venture, try; *formal* essay.
– PHRASES **by chance** FORTUITOUSLY, by accident, accidentally, coincidentally, serendipitously; unintentionally, inadvertently. **chance on/upon** COME ACROSS/UPON, run across/into, happen on, light on, stumble on, find by chance, meet (by chance); *informal* bump into; *archaic* run against.
chancy ● adjective *(informal)* RISKY, unpredictable, uncertain, precarious; unsafe, insecure, tricky, high-risk, hazardous, perilous, parlous; *informal* dicey, hairy; *Brit. informal* dodgy.
– OPPOSITES predictable.
change ● verb **1** *this could change the face of Britain | things have changed* ALTER, make/become different, adjust, adapt, amend, modify, revise, refine; reshape, refashion, redesign, restyle, revamp, rework, remodel, reorganize, reorder; vary, transform, transfigure, transmute, metamorphose, evolve; *informal* tweak; *technical* permute. **2** *he's changed his job* EXCHANGE, substitute, swap, switch, replace, alternate, interchange.
– OPPOSITES preserve, keep.
● noun **1** *a change of plan* ALTERATION, modification, variation, revision, amendment, adjustment, adaptation; remodelling, reshaping, rearrangement, reordering, restyling, reworking; metamorphosis, transformation, evolution, mutation; *humorous* transmogrification. **2** *a change of government* EXCHANGE, substitution, swap, switch, replacement, alternation, interchange. **3** *I've no change* COINS, loose/small change, (hard) cash, silver, coppers, specie.
– PHRASES **have a change of heart.** See HEART.
changeable ● adjective **1** *the weather will be changeable | changeable moods* VARIABLE, inconstant, varying, changing, fluctuating, irregular; erratic, inconsistent, unstable, unsettled, turbulent, changeful, protean; fickle, capricious, temperamental, volatile, mercurial, unpredictable, blowing hot and cold; *informal* up and down; *poetic/literary* fluctuant. **2** *the colours are changeable* ALTERABLE, adjustable, modifiable, variable, mutable, exchangeable, interchangeable, replaceable.
– OPPOSITES constant.
changeless ● adjective UNCHANGING, unvarying, timeless, static, fixed, permanent, constant, unchanged, consistent, uniform; stable, steady, unchangeable, unalterable, invariable, immutable.
– OPPOSITES variable.
channel ● noun **1** *the English Channel* STRAIT(S), sound, narrows, (sea) passage. **2** *the water ran down a channel* DUCT, gutter, conduit, trough, culvert, sluice, spillway, race, drain. **3** *a channel for their extraordinary energy* USE, medium, vehicle, way of harnessing; release (mechanism), safety valve, vent. **4** *a channel of communication* MEANS, medium, instrument, mechanism, agency, vehicle, route, avenue.
● verb **1** *she channelled out a groove* HOLLOW OUT, gouge (out), cut (out). **2** *many countries channel their aid through charities* CONVEY, transmit, conduct, direct, guide, relay, pass on, transfer.
chant ● noun **1** *the protesters' chants* SHOUT, cry, (rallying) call, slogan. **2** *the melodious chant of the monks* INCANTATION, intonation, singing, song, recitative; *rare* cantillation.

C

– ORIGIN Latin *cantharellus*, from Greek *kantharos*, denoting a kind of drinking container.

chanteuse /shaantöz/ ● noun a female singer of popular songs.
– ORIGIN French, from *chanter* 'sing'.

chantry ● noun (pl. **chantries**) a chapel or other part of a church endowed for the celebration of masses for the donor's soul.
– ORIGIN Old French *chanterie*, from *chanter* 'sing'.

chanty /shanti/ ● noun (pl. **chanties**) variant spelling of SHANTY².

Chanukkah ● noun variant spelling of HANUKKAH.

chaos ● noun **1** complete disorder and confusion. **2** the formless matter supposed to have existed before the creation of the universe.
– DERIVATIVES **chaotic** adjective **chaotically** adverb.
– ORIGIN Greek *khaos* 'vast chasm, void'.

chaos theory ● noun the branch of science concerned with the behaviour of complex systems in which tiny changes can have major effects, and which therefore seem unpredictable.

chap¹ ● verb (**chapped**, **chapping**) **1** (of the skin) crack and become sore through exposure to cold weather. **2** (of cold weather) cause (skin) to crack in this way.
– ORIGIN of unknown origin.

chap² ● noun informal, chiefly Brit. a man or a boy.
– ORIGIN abbreviation of CHAPMAN.

chaparral /shappəral/ ● noun N. Amer. vegetation consisting chiefly of tangled shrubs and thorny bushes.
– ORIGIN Spanish, from *chaparra* 'dwarf evergreen oak'.

chapatti /chəpaati/ ● noun (pl. **chapattis**) (in Indian cookery) a thin pancake of unleavened wholemeal bread cooked on a griddle.
– ORIGIN from Hindi, 'roll out'.

chapbook ● noun historical a small pamphlet containing tales, ballads, or tracts, sold by pedlars.
– ORIGIN from CHAPMAN.

chapel ● noun **1** a small building for Christian worship, typically one attached to an institution or private house. **2** a part of a large church with its own altar and dedication. **3** Brit. a place of worship for Nonconformist congregations. **4** Brit. the members or branch of a print or newspaper trade union at a particular place of work.
– ORIGIN Old French *chapele*, from Latin *cappella*, 'little cape' (the first chapel being a sanctuary in which St Martin's cloak was preserved).

chaperone /shappərōn/ (also **chaperon** /shappəron/) ● noun dated an older woman responsible for the behaviour of an unmarried girl at social occasions. ● verb accompany and look after.
– DERIVATIVES **chaperonage** /shappərənij/ noun.
– ORIGIN originally denoting a hood, regarded as giving protection: from French, from *chape* 'cap, hood'.

chaplain ● noun a member of the clergy attached to a private chapel, institution, etc.
– DERIVATIVES **chaplaincy** noun.
– ORIGIN Latin *cappellanus*, originally denoting a custodian of the cloak of St Martin, from *cappella* (see CHAPEL).

chaplet ● noun **1** a circlet for a person's head. **2** a string of 55 beads for counting prayers.
– ORIGIN Old French *chapelet* 'little hat', from Latin *cappa* 'cap'.

chapman ● noun archaic a pedlar.
– ORIGIN Old English, related to CHEAP.

chaps ● plural noun N. Amer. leather overtrousers without a seat, worn by a cowboy to protect the legs.
– ORIGIN short for *chaparajos*, from Mexican Spanish *chaparreras*, from *chaparra* (with reference to protection from the thorny vegetation of the *chaparral*).

chaptalization /chaptəlīzaysh'n/ (also **chaptalisation**) ● noun (in winemaking) the correction or improvement of must by the addition of calcium carbonate or sugar.
– DERIVATIVES **chaptalize** (also **chaptalise**) verb.
– ORIGIN from Jean A. *Chaptal* (1756–1832), the French chemist who invented the process.

chapter ● noun **1** a main division of a book. **2** a particular period in history or in a person's life. **3** the governing body of a cathedral or other religious community. **4** chiefly N. Amer. a local branch of a society.
– PHRASES **chapter and verse** an exact reference or authority. **a chapter of accidents** a series of unfortunate events.
– ORIGIN Old French *chapitre*, from Latin *capitulum* 'little head'.

char¹ ● verb (**charred**, **charring**) partially burn so as to blacken the surface.
– ORIGIN apparently from CHARCOAL.

char² Brit. informal ● noun a charwoman. ● verb (**charred**, **charring**) work as a charwoman.

char³ (also **cha** /chaa/ or **chai** /chī/) ● noun Brit. informal tea.
– ORIGIN Chinese.

char⁴ ● noun variant spelling of CHARR.

charabanc /sharrəbang/ ● noun Brit. an early form of bus.
– ORIGIN French *char-à-bancs* 'carriage with benches'.

character ● noun **1** the qualities distinctive to an individual. **2** the distinctive nature of something. **3** a person in a novel, play, or film. **4** a part played by an actor. **5** a printed or written letter or symbol. **6** strength and originality in a person's nature. **7** a person's good reputation. **8** informal an eccentric or amusing person.
– DERIVATIVES **characterful** adjective **characterless** adjective.
– ORIGIN Old French *caractere*, from Greek *kharaktēr* 'a stamping tool'.

character actor ● noun an actor who specializes in playing unusual people rather than leading roles.

characteristic ● adjective typical of a particular person, place, or thing. ● noun a feature or quality typical of a person, place, or thing.
– DERIVATIVES **characteristically** adverb.

characterize (also **characterise**) ● verb **1** describe the distinctive character of. **2** (of a feature or quality) be characteristic of.

Thesaurus

● verb **1** *protesters were chanting slogans* SHOUT, chorus, repeat. **2** *the choir chanted Psalm 118* SING, intone, incant; *rare* cantillate.

chaos ● noun DISORDER, disarray, disorganization, confusion, mayhem, bedlam, pandemonium, havoc, turmoil, tumult, commotion, disruption, upheaval, uproar; a muddle, a mess, a shambles, a mare's nest; anarchy, lawlessness; *informal* hullabaloo, all hell broken loose.
– OPPOSITES order.

chaotic ● adjective DISORDERLY, disordered, in disorder, in chaos, in disarray, disorganized, topsy-turvy, in pandemonium, in turmoil, in uproar; in a muddle, in a mess, messy, in a shambles; anarchic, lawless.

chap¹ ● verb *my skin chapped in the wind* BECOME RAW, become sore, become inflamed, chafe, crack.

chap² ● noun *(Brit. informal) he's a nice chap* MAN, boy, character; *informal* fellow, guy, geezer; *Brit. informal* bloke, lad, bod; *N. Amer. informal* dude, hombre; *Brit. informal, dated* cove.

chaperone ● noun *Aunt Millie went as chaperone* COMPANION, duenna, escort, protectress, protector, minder.
● verb *she was chaperoned by her mother* ACCOMPANY, escort, attend, watch over, keep an eye on, protect, mind.

chapter ● noun **1** *the first chapter of the book* SECTION, division, part, portion. **2** *a new chapter in our history* PERIOD, phase, page, stage, epoch, era. **3** *(N. Amer.) a local chapter of the American Cancer Society* BRANCH, division, subdivision, section, department, lodge, wing, arm. **4** *the cathedral chapter* GOVERNING BODY, council, assembly, convocation, synod, consistory.

char ● verb SCORCH, burn, singe, sear, blacken; *informal* toast.

character ● noun **1** *a forceful character | the character of a town* PERSONALITY, nature, disposition, temperament, temper, mentality, make-up; features, qualities, properties, traits; spirit, essence, identity, ethos, complexion, tone, feel, feeling. **2** *a woman of character* INTEGRITY, honour, moral strength/fibre, rectitude, uprightness; fortitude, strength, backbone, resolve, grit, will power; *informal* guts, gutsiness; *Brit. informal* bottle. **3** *a stain on his character* REPUTATION, (good) name, standing, stature, position, status. **4** *(informal) a bit of a character* ECCENTRIC, oddity, madcap, crank, individualist, nonconformist, rare bird; *informal* oddball; *Brit. informal* odd bod; *informal, dated* card, caution. **5** *a boorish character* PERSON, man, woman, soul, creature, individual, customer; *informal* cookie; *Brit. informal* bod, guy; *informal, dated* body, dog. **6** *the characters develop throughout the play* PERSONA, role, part; (**characters**) dramatis personae. **7** *thirty characters* LETTER, figure, symbol, sign, mark.

characteristic ● noun *interesting characteristics* ATTRIBUTE, feature, (essential) quality, property, trait, aspect, element, facet; mannerism, habit, custom, idiosyncrasy, peculiarity, quirk, oddity, foible.
● adjective *his characteristic eloquence* TYPICAL, usual, normal, pre-

– DERIVATIVES **characterization** noun.
charade /shəraad/ ● noun **1** an absurd pretence. **2** (**charades**) (treated as sing.) a game of guessing a word or phrase from written or acted clues.
– ORIGIN Provençal *charrado* 'conversation'.
charbroil ● verb N. Amer. grill (food, especially meat) on a rack over charcoal.
charcoal ● noun **1** a porous black form of carbon obtained when wood is heated in the absence of air. **2** a dark grey colour.
– ORIGIN probably related to COAL in the early sense 'charcoal'.
charcuterie /shaarkōōtəri/ ● noun (pl. **charcuteries**) **1** cold cooked meats collectively. **2** a shop selling such meats.
– ORIGIN French, from obsolete *char* 'flesh' + *cuite* 'cooked'.
chard /chaard/ ● noun (also **Swiss chard**) a beet of a variety with edible broad white leaf stalks and green blades.
– ORIGIN French *carde*.
Chardonnay /shaardənay/ ● noun **1** a variety of white wine grape used for making champagne and other wines. **2** a wine made from this grape.
– ORIGIN French.
charentais /sharrəntay/ ● noun a small variety of melon with a green rind and orange flesh.
– ORIGIN French, 'from the Charentes region'.
charge ● verb **1** demand (an amount) as a price for a service rendered or goods supplied. **2** accuse (someone) of something, especially an offence under law. **3** rush forward in attack. **4** entrust with a task. **5** store electrical energy in (a battery). **6** technical or formal load or fill (a container, gun, etc.) to the full or proper extent. **7** fill with a quality or emotion. ● noun **1** a price asked. **2** a formal accusation made against a prisoner brought to trial. **3** a financial liability or commitment. **4** responsibility for care or control. **5** a person or thing entrusted to someone's care. **6** a headlong rush forward, typically in attack. **7** the property of matter that is responsible for electrical phenomena, existing in a positive or negative form. **8** the quantity of this carried by a body. **9** energy stored chemically in a battery for conversion into electricity. **10** a quantity of explosive to be detonated in order to fire a gun or similar weapon.
– PHRASES **press charges** accuse someone formally of a crime so that they can be brought to trial.
– DERIVATIVES **chargeable** adjective **charged** adjective.
– ORIGIN Old French *charger*, from Latin *carricare* 'to load'.
charge account ● noun an account to which goods and services may be charged on credit.
charge card ● noun a credit card for use with an account which must be paid in full when a statement is issued.
chargé d'affaires /shaarzhay dafair/ (also **chargé**) ● noun (pl. **chargés** pronunc. same) **1** an ambassador's deputy. **2** a state's diplomatic representative in a minor country.
– ORIGIN French, 'a person in charge of affairs'.
chargehand ● noun Brit. a worker with supervisory duties ranking below a foreman.
charge nurse ● noun Brit. a nurse in charge of a ward in a hospital.
charger[1] ● noun **1** a device for charging a battery. **2** a horse ridden by a knight or cavalryman.
charger[2] ● noun archaic a large flat dish.
– ORIGIN Old French *chargeour*, from Latin *carricare* 'to load'.
chargrill ● verb grill (food, typically meat or fish) quickly at a very high heat.
chariot ● noun a two-wheeled vehicle drawn by horses, used in ancient warfare and racing.
– DERIVATIVES **charioteer** noun.
– ORIGIN Old French, from *char* 'cart' from Latin *carrus* 'wheeled vehicle'.
charisma /kərizmə/ ● noun **1** compelling attractiveness or charm. **2** (pl. **charismata** /kərizmətə/) Christian Theology a divinely conferred talent.
– ORIGIN Greek *kharisma*, from *kharis* 'favour, grace'.
charismatic ● adjective **1** having charisma. **2** relating to a movement within certain Christian Churches that emphasizes the inspirational power of the Holy Spirit. ● noun an adherent of the charismatic movement.
– DERIVATIVES **charismatically** adverb.
charitable ● adjective **1** relating to the assistance of those in need. **2** tolerant in judging others.
– DERIVATIVES **charitably** adverb.
charity ● noun (pl. **charities**) **1** an organization set up to help those in need. **2** the voluntary giving of money or other help to those in need. **3** help or money given in this way. **4** tolerance in judging others.
– PHRASES **charity begins at home** proverb a person's first responsibility is for the needs of their own family and friends.
– ORIGIN Latin *caritas*, from *carus* 'dear'.
charlatan /shaarlət'n/ ● noun a person falsely claiming to have a certain expertise.
– DERIVATIVES **charlatanism** noun **charlatanry** noun.
– ORIGIN Italian *ciarlatano*, from *ciarlare* 'to babble'.
Charles's law ● noun Chemistry a law stating that the volume of

C

Thesaurus

dictable, habitual; distinctive, particular, special, especial, peculiar, idiosyncratic, singular, unique.
characterize ● verb **1** *the period was characterized by scientific advancement* DISTINGUISH, make distinctive, mark, typify, set apart. **2** *the women are characterized as prophets of doom* PORTRAY, depict, present, represent, describe; categorize, class, style, brand.
charade ● noun FARCE, pantomime, travesty, mockery, parody, act, masquerade.
charge ● verb **1** *he didn't charge much* ASK (IN PAYMENT), levy, demand, exact; bill, invoice. **2** *the subscription will be charged to your account* BILL, debit from, take from. **3** *two men were charged with affray* ACCUSE, indict, arraign; prosecute, try, put on trial; N. Amer. impeach; archaic inculpate. **4** *they charged him with reforming the system* ENTRUST, burden, encumber, saddle, tax. **5** *the cavalry charged the tanks* ATTACK, storm, assault, assail, fall on, swoop on, descend on; informal lay into, tear into. **6** *riot police charged into the crowd* RUSH, storm, stampede, push, plough, launch oneself, go headlong; informal steam; N. Amer. informal barrel. **7** *charge your glasses!* | *the guns were charged* FILL (UP), top up; load (up), arm, prepare to fire. **8** *his work was charged with energy* SUFFUSE, pervade, permeate, saturate, infuse, imbue, fill. **9** *I charge you to stop* ORDER, command, direct, instruct, exhort, enjoin; formal adjure; poetic/literary bid.
● noun **1** *all customers pay a charge* FEE, payment, price, tariff, amount, sum, fare, levy. **2** *he pleaded guilty to the charge* ACCUSATION, allegation, indictment, arraignment; N. Amer. impeachment; archaic inculpation. **3** *an infantry charge* ATTACK, assault, offensive, onslaught, drive, push, thrust. **4** *the child was in her charge* CARE, protection, safe keeping, control; custody, guardianship, wardship; hands; archaic ward. **5** *his charge was to save the business* DUTY, responsibility, task, job, assignment, mission, function; Brit. informal pigeon. **6** *the safety of my charge* WARD, protégé, dependant. **7** *the judge gave a careful charge to the jury* INSTRUCTION, direction, directive, order, command, dictate, exhortation. **8** (N. Amer. informal) *I get a real charge out of working hard* THRILL, tingle, glow; excitement, stimulation, enjoyment, pleasure; informal kick, buzz.
– PHRASES **in charge of** RESPONSIBLE FOR, in control of, at the helm/wheel of; MANAGING, running, administering, directing, supervising, overseeing, controlling; informal running the show.
charisma ● noun CHARM, presence, (force of) personality, strength of character; (animal) magnetism, attractiveness, appeal, allure.
charismatic ● adjective CHARMING, fascinating, strong in character; magnetic, captivating, beguiling, attractive, appealing, alluring.
charitable ● adjective **1** *charitable activities* PHILANTHROPIC, humanitarian, altruistic, benevolent, public-spirited; non-profit-making; formal eleemosynary. **2** *charitable people* BIG-HEARTED, generous, open-handed, free-handed, liberal, munificent, bountiful, beneficent; poetic/literary bounteous. **3** *he was charitable in his judgements* MAGNANIMOUS, generous, liberal, tolerant, easy-going, broad-minded, considerate, sympathetic, lenient, indulgent, forgiving.
charity ● noun **1** *an AIDS charity* NON-PROFIT-MAKING ORGANIZATION, voluntary organization, charitable institution; fund, trust, foundation. **2** *we don't need charity* FINANCIAL ASSISTANCE, aid, welfare, (financial) relief; handouts, gifts, presents, largesse; historical alms. **3** *his actions are motivated by charity* PHILANTHROPY, humanitarianism, humanity, altruism, public-spiritedness, social conscience, benevolence, beneficence, munificence. **4** *show a bit of charity* GOODWILL, compassion, consideration, concern, kindness, kind-heartedness, tenderness, tender-heartedness, sympathy, indulgence, tolerance, leniency, caritas; poetic/literary bounteousness.
charlatan ● noun QUACK, mountebank, sham, fraud, fake, impostor, hoodwinker, hoaxer, cheat, deceiver, double-dealer,

an ideal gas at constant pressure is directly proportional to the absolute temperature.
– ORIGIN named after the French physicist Jacques A. C. *Charles* (1746–1823).

charleston ● noun a lively dance of the 1920s which involved turning the knees inwards and kicking out the lower legs.
– ORIGIN named after the city of *Charleston* in South Carolina, US.

C

charlie ● noun (pl. **charlies**) informal **1** Brit. a fool. **2** cocaine.
– ORIGIN from the male given name *Charles*.

charlotte ● noun a pudding made of stewed fruit with a casing or covering of bread, sponge cake, biscuits, or breadcrumbs.
– ORIGIN French, from the female given name *Charlotte*.

charm ● noun **1** the power or quality of delighting or fascinating others. **2** a small ornament worn on a necklace or bracelet. **3** an object, act, or saying believed to have magic power. ● verb **1** delight greatly. **2** use one's charm in order to influence someone.
– DERIVATIVES **charmer** noun **charmless** adjective.
– ORIGIN Old French *charme*, from Latin *carmen* 'song, verse, incantation'.

charmed ● adjective (of a person's life) unusually lucky as though protected by magic. ● exclamation dated expressing polite pleasure at an introduction.

charming ● adjective **1** delightful; attractive. **2** very polite, friendly, and likeable. ● exclamation used as an ironic expression of displeasure.
– DERIVATIVES **charmingly** adverb.

charm offensive ● noun a campaign of flattery designed to achieve the support of others.

charnel house ● noun historical a building or vault in which corpses or bones were piled.
– ORIGIN from Latin *carnalis* 'relating to flesh'.

Charolais /sharrəlay/ ● noun (pl. same) an animal of a breed of large white beef cattle.
– ORIGIN named after the *Monts du Charollais*, hills in eastern France where the breed originated.

charpoy /chaarpoy/ ● noun Indian a light bedstead.
– ORIGIN Persian.

charr /chaar/ (also **char**) ● noun (pl. same) a trout-like northern freshwater or marine fish.
– ORIGIN perhaps Celtic.

chart ● noun **1** a sheet of information in the form of a table, graph, or diagram. **2** a geographical map, especially one used for navigation by sea or air. **3** (**the charts**) a weekly listing of the current best-selling pop records. ● verb **1** make a map of. **2** plot or record on a chart.
– ORIGIN Latin *charta*, from Greek *khartēs* 'papyrus leaf'.

charter ● noun **1** a written grant by a sovereign or legislature, by which a body such as a university is created or its rights defined. **2** a written constitution or description of an organization's functions. **3** (in the UK) a written statement of the rights of a specified group of people. **4** the hiring of an aircraft, ship, or motor vehicle. ● verb **1** grant a charter to (a city, university, etc.). **2** hire (an aircraft, ship, or motor vehicle).
– DERIVATIVES **charterer** noun.
– ORIGIN Latin *chartula*, from *charta* 'paper'.

chartered ● adjective Brit. (of an accountant, engineer, etc.) qualified as a member of a professional body that has a royal charter.

charter flight ● noun a flight by an aircraft chartered for a specific journey, not part of an airline's regular schedule.

Chartism ● noun a UK parliamentary reform movement of 1837–48, the principles of which were set out in a manifesto called *The People's Charter*.
– DERIVATIVES **Chartist** noun & adjective.

chartreuse /shaartröz/ ● noun a pale green or yellow liqueur made from brandy.
– ORIGIN named after *La Grande Chartreuse*, the Carthusian monastery near Grenoble where the liqueur was first made.

charwoman ● noun Brit. dated a woman employed as a cleaner in a house or office.
– ORIGIN from obsolete *char* or *chare* 'a chore'.

chary /chairi/ ● adjective (**charier**, **chariest**) cautiously reluctant: *leaders are chary of reform.*
– ORIGIN Old English, 'sorrowful, anxious'.

chase[1] ● verb **1** pursue in order to catch. **2** rush or cause to go in a specified direction. **3** try to obtain (something owed or required). ● noun **1** an act of chasing. **2** (**the chase**) hunting as a sport.
– PHRASES **give chase** go in pursuit.
– ORIGIN Old French *chacier*, from Latin *captare* 'continue to take'.

chase[2] ● verb engrave (metal, or a design on metal).
– ORIGIN apparently from earlier *enchase*, from Old French *enchasser* 'enclose'.

chaser ● noun **1** a person or thing that chases. **2** a horse for steeplechasing. **3** informal a strong alcoholic drink taken after a weaker one.

Chasid /khassid/ ● noun variant spelling of HASID.

Chasidism /khassidiz'm/ ● noun variant spelling of HASIDISM.

chasm ● noun **1** a deep fissure. **2** a profound difference between people, viewpoints, feelings, etc.
– ORIGIN Greek *khasma* 'gaping hollow'.

Thesaurus

(confidence) trickster, swindler, fraudster; *informal* phoney, shark, con man/artist, flimflammer; *Brit. informal* twister; *N. Amer. informal* bunco artist, gold brick, chiseller; *Austral. informal* magsman, illywhacker; *dated* confidence man/woman.

charm ● noun **1** *people were captivated by her charm* ATTRACTIVENESS, beauty, glamour, loveliness; appeal, allure, desirability, seductiveness, sexual/animal magnetism, charisma; *informal* pulling power. **2** *these traditions retain a lot of charm* APPEAL, drawing power, attraction, allure, fascination. **3** *magical charms* SPELL, incantation, conjuration, rune, magic formula/word; *N. Amer.* mojo, hex. **4** *a lucky charm* TALISMAN, fetish, amulet, mascot, totem, juju; *archaic* periapt.
● verb **1** *he charmed them with his singing* DELIGHT, please, win (over), attract, captivate, allure, lure, dazzle, fascinate, enchant, enthral, enrapture, seduce, spellbind. **2** *he charmed his mother into agreeing* COAX, cajole, wheedle; *informal* sweet-talk, soft-soap; *archaic* blandish.

charming ● adjective DELIGHTFUL, pleasing, pleasant, agreeable, likeable, endearing, lovely, lovable, adorable, appealing, attractive, good-looking, prepossessing; alluring, delectable, ravishing, winning, winsome, fetching, captivating, enchanting, entrancing, fascinating, seductive; *informal* heavenly, divine, gorgeous, easy on the eye; *Brit. informal* smashing; *poetic/literary* beauteous; *archaic* fair, comely.
– OPPOSITES repulsive.

chart ● noun **1** *check your ideal weight on the chart* GRAPH, table, diagram, histogram; bar chart, pie chart, flow chart; *Computing* graphic. **2** *the pop charts* TOP TWENTY, list, listing; *dated* hit parade.
● verb **1** *the changes were charted accurately* TABULATE, plot, graph, record, register, represent; make a chart/diagram of. **2** *the book charted his progress* FOLLOW, trace, outline, describe, detail, record, document, chronicle, log.

charter ● noun **1** *a Royal charter* AUTHORITY, authorization, sanction, dispensation, consent, permission; permit, licence, warrant, franchise. **2** *the UN Charter* CONSTITUTION, code, canon; fundamental principles, rules, laws. **3** *the charter of a yacht* HIRE, hiring, lease, leasing, rent, rental, renting; booking, reservation.
● verb *they chartered a bus* HIRE, lease, rent; book, reserve.

chary ● adjective WARY, cautious, circumspect, heedful, careful, on one's guard; distrustful, mistrustful, sceptical, suspicious, dubious, hesitant, reluctant, leery, nervous, apprehensive, uneasy; *informal* cagey, iffy.

chase[1] ● verb **1** *the dogs chased the fox* PURSUE, run after, give chase to, follow; hunt, track, trail; *informal* tail. **2** *chasing young girls* WOO, pursue, run after, make advances to, flirt with, pay court to; *informal* chat up, come on to; *dated* court, romance, set one's cap at, make love to. **3** *she chased away the donkeys* DRIVE, send, scare; *informal* send packing. **4** *she chased away all thoughts of him* DISPEL, banish, dismiss, drive away, shut out, put out of one's mind. **5** *photographers chased on to the runway* RUSH, dash, race, speed, streak, shoot, charge, scramble, scurry, hurry, fly, pelt; *informal* scoot, belt, tear, zip, whip; *N. Amer. informal* boogie, hightail, clip; *archaic* hie.
● noun *they gave up the chase* PURSUIT, hunt, trail.
– PHRASES **chase someone/something up** PESTER, harass, harry, nag; seek out, find, go after; *informal* hassle.

chase[2] ● verb *the figures are chased on the dish* ENGRAVE, etch, carve, inscribe, cut, chisel.

chasm ● noun **1** *a deep chasm* GORGE, abyss, canyon, ravine, gully, gulf, defile, couloir, crevasse, fissure, crevice; *N. Amer.* gulch, cou-

chassé /shassay/ • noun a gliding step in dancing in which one foot displaces the other.
– ORIGIN French, 'chased'.
Chassid /khassid/ • noun variant spelling of HASID.
chassis /shassi/ • noun (pl. same /shassiz/) **1** the base frame of a motor vehicle or other wheeled conveyance. **2** the outer structural framework of a piece of audio, radio, or computer equipment.
– ORIGIN French, 'frame'.
chaste • adjective **1** abstaining from extramarital, or from all, sexual intercourse. **2** without unnecessary ornamentation.
– ORIGIN Latin *castus* 'morally pure'.
chasten • verb (of a reproof or misfortune) have a restraining or demoralizing effect on.
– ORIGIN Old French *chastier*, from Latin *castigare* 'castigate'.
chastise • verb reprimand severely.
– DERIVATIVES **chastisement** noun **chastiser** noun.
chastity • noun the practice of refraining from sexual intercourse.
chastity belt • noun historical a garment or device designed to prevent the woman wearing it from having sexual intercourse.
chasuble /chazyoob'l/ • noun a sleeveless outer vestment worn by a priest when celebrating Mass.
– ORIGIN Latin *casubla*, from *casula* 'hooded cloak or little cottage'.
chat • verb (**chatted**, **chatting**) **1** talk in an informal way. **2** (**chat up**) informal engage in flirtatious conversation. • noun an informal conversation.
– ORIGIN shortening of CHATTER.
chateau /shattō/ • noun (pl. **chateaux** pronunc. same or /shattōz/) a large French country house or castle.
– ORIGIN French.
chatelaine /shattəlayn/ • noun dated a woman in charge of a large house.
– ORIGIN French, from *châtelain* 'castellan'.
chatline • noun a telephone service which allows conversation among a number of separate callers.
chat room • noun an area on the Internet or other computer network where users can communicate.
chat show • noun Brit. a television or radio programme in which celebrities are invited to talk informally.
chattel /chatt'l/ • noun a personal possession.
– ORIGIN Old French *chatel*, from Latin *caput* 'head'.
chatter • verb **1** talk at length about trivial matters. **2** (of a person's teeth) click repeatedly together from cold or fear. • noun **1** incessant trivial talk. **2** a series of short quick high-pitched sounds.
– PHRASES **the chattering classes** derogatory educated people considered as a social group given to liberal opinions.
– DERIVATIVES **chatterer** noun.
– ORIGIN imitative.
chatterbox • noun informal a person who chatters.
chatty • adjective (**chattier**, **chattiest**) **1** fond of chatting. **2** (of a conversation, letter, etc.) informal and lively.
– DERIVATIVES **chattily** adverb **chattiness** noun.
chauffeur • noun a person employed to drive a car. • verb drive (a car or a passenger in a car) as a chauffeur.
– ORIGIN French, 'stoker' (by association with steam engines).
chauvinism /shōviniz'm/ • noun **1** exaggerated or aggressive patriotism. **2** excessive or prejudiced support for one's own cause, group, or sex.
– ORIGIN named after Nicolas *Chauvin*, a Napoleonic veteran noted for his extreme patriotism.
chauvinist • noun a person displaying excessive or prejudiced support for their own country, cause, group, or sex. • adjective relating to such excessive or prejudiced support.
– DERIVATIVES **chauvinistic** adjective.
cheap • adjective **1** low in price. **2** charging low prices. **3** inexpensive because of poor quality. **4** of little worth because achieved in a discreditable way. **5** N. Amer. informal miserly. • adverb at or for a low price.
– DERIVATIVES **cheapish** adjective **cheaply** adverb **cheapness** noun.
– ORIGIN Old English 'bargaining, trade', from Latin *caupo* 'small trader, innkeeper'.

Thesaurus

lee. **2** *the chasm between their views* BREACH, gulf, rift; difference, separation, division, dissension, schism, scission.
chassis • noun FRAMEWORK, frame, structure, substructure, shell, casing, bodywork, body.
chaste • adjective **1** *chaste girlhood* VIRGINAL, virgin, intact, maidenly, unmarried, unwed; celibate, abstinent, self-restrained, self-denying, continent; innocent, virtuous, pure (as the driven snow), sinless, undefiled, unsullied; *Christianity* immaculate; *poetic/literary* vestal. **2** *a chaste kiss on the cheek* NON-SEXUAL, platonic, innocent. **3** *the dark, chaste interior* PLAIN, simple, bare, unadorned, undecorated, unornamented, unembellished, functional, no-frills, austere.
– OPPOSITES promiscuous, passionate.
chasten • verb **1** *both men were chastened* SUBDUE, humble, cow, squash, deflate, flatten, take down a peg or two, put someone in their place; *informal* cut down to size, settle someone's hash. **2** *(archaic) the Heaven that chastens us.* See CHASTISE sense 1.
chastise • verb **1** *the staff were chastised for arriving late* SCOLD, upbraid, berate, reprimand, reprove, rebuke, admonish, chide, censure, lambaste, lecture, give someone a piece of one's mind, take to task, haul over the coals; *informal* tell off, dress down, bawl out, blow up at, give someone an earful, give someone a roasting, come down on someone like a ton of bricks, have someone's guts for garters, slap someone's wrist, rap over the knuckles, give someone hell; *Brit. informal* carpet, tick off, have a go at, tear someone off a strip, give someone what for, give someone a rocket; *N. Amer. informal* chew out, ream out; *Austral. informal* monster; *dated* give someone a rating; *formal* castigate; *archaic* chasten; *rare* reprehend, objurgate. **2** *(dated) her mistress chastised her with a whip.* See BEAT verb sense 1.
– OPPOSITES praise.
chastity • noun CELIBACY, chasteness, virginity, abstinence, self-restraint, self-denial, continence; singleness, maidenhood; innocence, purity, virtue, morality; *Christianity* immaculateness.
chat • noun *I popped in for a chat* TALK, conversation, gossip, chatter, heart-to-heart, tête-à-tête, blather; *informal* jaw, gas, confab; *Brit. informal* natter, chinwag, rabbit; *N. Amer. informal* rap, bull session; *formal* confabulation, colloquy.
• verb *they chatted with their guests* TALK, gossip, chatter, speak, converse, engage in conversation, tittle-tattle, prattle, jabber, babble; *informal* gas, jaw, chew the rag/fat, yap, yak, yabber, yatter, yammer; *Brit. informal* natter, rabbit, chunter, have a chinwag; *N. Amer. informal* shoot the breeze/bull, visit; *Austral./NZ informal* mag; *formal* confabulate; *archaic* clack.
– PHRASES **chat someone up** *(informal)* FLIRT WITH, make advances to; *informal* come on to; *dated* make love to, set one's cap at, romance.
chatter • noun *she tired him with her chatter* CHAT, talk, gossip, chit-chat, patter, jabbering, jabber, prattling, prattle, babbling, babble, tittle-tattle, blathering, blather; *informal* yabbering, yammering, yattering, yapping, jawing, chewing the rag/fat; *Brit. informal* nattering, chuntering, rabbiting on; *formal* confabulation, colloquy; *archaic* clack.
• verb *they chattered excitedly.* See CHAT verb.
chatterbox • noun *(informal)* TALKER, chatterer, prattler; *N. Amer.* blatherskite; *informal* windbag, gasbag, blabbermouth; *Brit. informal* natterer.
chatty • adjective **1** *he was a chatty person* TALKATIVE, communicative, expansive, unreserved, gossipy, gossiping, garrulous, loquacious, voluble, verbose; *informal* mouthy, gabby, gassy; *Brit. informal* able to talk the hind legs off a donkey. **2** *a chatty letter* CONVERSATIONAL, gossipy, informal, casual, familiar, friendly; *informal* newsy.
– OPPOSITES taciturn.
chauvinist • adjective *chauvinist sentiments* JINGOISTIC, chauvinistic, excessively patriotic, excessively nationalistic, flag-waving, xenophobic, racist, racialist, ethnocentric; sexist, male chauvinist, anti-feminist, misogynist, woman-hating.
• noun *he's a chauvinist* SEXIST, anti-feminist, misogynist, woman-hater; *informal* male chauvinist pig, MCP.
cheap • adjective **1** *cheap tickets* INEXPENSIVE, low-priced, low-cost, economical, competitive, affordable, reasonable, reasonably priced, budget, economy, bargain, cut-price, reduced, discounted, discount, rock-bottom, giveaway, bargain-basement; *informal* dirt cheap. **2** *plain without looking cheap* POOR-QUALITY, second-rate, third-rate, substandard, low-grade, inferior, vulgar, shoddy, trashy, tawdry, meretricious, cheap and nasty, cheapjack, gimcrack, Brummagem, pinchbeck; *informal* rubbishy, cheapo, junky, tacky, kitsch; *Brit. informal* naff, duff, ropy, grotty; *N. Amer. informal* two-bit, dime-store. **3** *the cheap exploitation of suffering* DESPICABLE, contemptible, immoral, unscrupulous, unprincipled, unsavoury, distasteful, vulgar, ignoble, shameful; *archaic* scurvy. **4** *he*

cheapen ● verb **1** lower the price of. **2** degrade the worth of.
cheapjack ● adjective chiefly N. Amer. of inferior quality.
cheapskate ● noun informal a miserly person.
– ORIGIN from *skate* 'a disreputable or contemptible person'.
cheat ● verb **1** act dishonestly or unfairly in order to gain an advantage. **2** deprive of something by deceitful or unfair means. **3** avoid (something undesirable) by luck or skill: *she cheated death in a spectacular crash.* ● noun **1** a person who cheats. **2** an act of cheating.
– ORIGIN shortening of ESCHEAT.
Chechen /chechen/ ● noun (pl. same or **Chechens**) a person from Chechnya, an autonomous republic in SW Russia.
– ORIGIN Russian.
check[1] ● verb **1** examine the accuracy, quality, or condition of. **2** stop or slow the progress of. **3** Chess move a piece or pawn to a square where it directly attacks (the opposing king). ● noun **1** an examination to check accuracy, quality, or condition. **2** an act of checking progress. **3** a means of control or restraint. **4** Chess an act of checking the opposing king. **5** N. Amer. the bill in a restaurant. **6** (also **check mark**) North American term for TICK[1] (in sense 1).
– PHRASES **check in 1** register at a hotel or airport. **2** have (one's baggage) weighed and put into the hold of an aircraft. **check out 1** settle one's hotel bill before leaving. **2** informal establish the truth of or inform oneself about. **check up on** investigate. **in check 1** under control. **2** Chess (of a king) directly attacked by an opponent's piece or pawn.
– DERIVATIVES **checkable** adjective.
– ORIGIN Old French *eschequier* 'play chess, put in check', ultimately from a Persian word meaning 'king'.
check[2] ● noun a pattern of small squares. ● adjective (also **checked**) having such a pattern.
– ORIGIN probably from CHEQUER.
check[3] ● noun US spelling of CHEQUE.
checker[1] ● noun **1** a person or thing that checks. **2** US a cashier in a supermarket.
checker[2] ● noun & verb US spelling of CHEQUER.
checkerboard ● noun US spelling of CHEQUERBOARD.
checking account (Canadian **chequing account**) ● noun N. Amer. a current account at a bank.
checklist ● noun a list of items required or things to be done or considered.
checkmate ● noun **1** Chess a position of check from which a king cannot escape. **2** a final defeat or deadlock. ● verb **1** Chess put into checkmate. **2** defeat or frustrate totally.
– ORIGIN from Persian, 'the king is dead'.
checkout ● noun a point at which goods are paid for in a supermarket or similar store.
checkpoint ● noun a barrier where security checks are carried out on travellers.
check-up ● noun a thorough medical or dental examination to detect any problems.
Cheddar ● noun a kind of firm smooth cheese originally made in Cheddar in SW England.
cheek ● noun **1** either side of the face below the eye. **2** either of the buttocks. **3** impertinence; audacity. ● verb speak impertinently to.
– PHRASES **cheek by jowl** close together. **turn the other cheek** refrain from retaliating after an attack or insult. [ORIGIN with biblical allusion to the Gospel of Matthew, chapter 5.]
– ORIGIN Old English.
cheekbone ● noun the bone below the eye.
cheeky ● adjective (**cheekier**, **cheekiest**) impudent or irreverent.
– DERIVATIVES **cheekily** adverb **cheekiness** noun.
cheep ● noun **1** a shrill squeaky cry made by a young bird. **2** informal the slightest sound: *there hasn't been a cheep from anybody.* ● verb make a cheep.
– ORIGIN imitative.
cheer ● verb **1** shout for joy or in praise or encouragement. **2** praise or encourage with shouts. **3** (**cheer up**) make or become less miserable. **4** give comfort or support to. ● noun **1** a shout of joy, encouragement, or praise. **2** (also **good cheer**) cheerfulness; optimism. **3** food and drink provided for a festive occasion.
– ORIGIN originally in the sense 'face', later 'expression, mood': from Old French *chiere* 'face', from Greek *kara* 'head'.
cheerful ● adjective **1** noticeably happy and optimistic. **2** bright

Thesaurus

made me feel cheap ASHAMED, humiliated, mortified, debased, degraded. **5** *(N. Amer. informal) he made the other guests look cheap.* See MEAN[2] sense 1.
– OPPOSITES expensive.
cheapen ● verb **1** *cheapening the cost of exports* REDUCE, lower (in price), cut, mark down, discount; informal slash. **2** *Hetty never cheapened herself* DEMEAN, debase, degrade, lower, humble, devalue, abase, discredit, disgrace, dishonour, shame, humiliate, mortify, prostitute.
cheat ● verb **1** *customers were cheated* SWINDLE, defraud, deceive, trick, dupe, hoodwink, double-cross, gull; informal diddle, rip off, con, fleece, shaft, sting, bilk, rook, gyp, finagle, flimflam, put one over on, pull a fast one on; N. Amer. informal sucker, gold-brick, stiff; Austral. informal pull a swifty on; formal mulct; poetic/literary cozen; archaic chicane. **2** *she cheated Ryan out of his fortune* DEPRIVE OF, deny, prevent from gaining; informal do out of. **3** *the boy cheated death* AVOID, escape, evade, elude; foil, frustrate, thwart. **4** *cheating husbands* COMMIT ADULTERY, be unfaithful, stray; informal two-time, play about/around; Brit. informal play away.
● noun **1** *a liar and a cheat* SWINDLER, cheater, fraudster, (confidence) trickster, deceiver, hoaxer, hoodwinker, double-dealer, double-crosser, sham, fraud, fake, charlatan, quack, mountebank; informal con man/artist, shark, sharper, phoney, flimflammer; Brit. informal twister; N. Amer. informal grifter, bunco artist, gold brick, chiseller; Austral. informal magsman, illywhacker; dated confidence man, confidence woman. **2** *a sure cheat for generating cash* SWINDLE, fraud, deception, deceit, hoax, sham, trick, ruse; informal con.
check ● verb **1** *troops checked all vehicles | I checked her background* EXAMINE, inspect, look at/over, scrutinize, survey; study, investigate, research, probe, look into, enquire into; informal check out, give something a/the once-over. **2** *he checked that the gun was cocked* MAKE SURE, confirm, verify. **3** *two defeats checked their progress* HALT, stop, arrest, cut short; bar, obstruct, hamper, impede, inhibit, frustrate, foil, thwart, curb, block, stall, hold up, retard, delay, slow down; poetic/literary stay. **4** *her tears could not be checked* SUPPRESS, repress, restrain, control, curb, rein in, stifle, hold back, choke back; informal keep a lid on.
● noun **1** *a check of the records* EXAMINATION, inspection, scrutiny, scrutinization, perusal, study, investigation, probe, analysis; test, trial, monitoring; check-up; informal once-over, look-see. **2** *a check on the abuse of authority* CONTROL, restraint, constraint, curb, limitation. **3** *(N. Amer.) the waitress arrived with the check* BILL, account, invoice, statement; N. Amer. informal tab; archaic reckoning.
– PHRASES **check in** REPORT (ONE'S ARRIVAL), book in, register. **check out** LEAVE, vacate, depart; pay the bill, settle up. **check something out** *(informal)* **1** *the police checked out the leads* INVESTIGATE, look into, enquire into, probe, research, examine, go over; assess, weigh up, analyse, evaluate; follow up; informal give something a/the once-over; N. Amer. informal scope out. **2** *she checked herself out in the mirror* LOOK AT, survey, regard, inspect, contemplate; informal have a gander/squint at; Brit. informal have a dekko/butcher's at, clock; N. Amer. informal eyeball. **keep something in check** CURB, restrain, hold back, keep a tight rein on, rein in/back; control, govern, master, suppress, stifle; informal keep a lid on.
check-up ● noun EXAMINATION, inspection, evaluation, analysis, survey, probe, test, appraisal; check, health check; informal once-over, going-over.
cheek ● noun *that's enough of your cheek!* IMPUDENCE, impertinence, insolence, cheekiness, presumption, effrontery, gall, pertness, impoliteness, disrespect, bad manners, overfamiliarity, cockiness; answering back, talking back; informal brass (neck), lip, mouth, chutzpah; Brit. informal sauce, backchat; N. Amer. informal sass, sassiness, nerviness, back talk; archaic assumption.
● verb *they were cheeking the dinner lady* ANSWER BACK, talk back, be cheeky, be impertinent; Brit. informal backchat; N. Amer. informal sass, be sassy.
cheeky ● adjective IMPUDENT, impertinent, insolent, presumptuous, forward, pert, bold (as brass), brazen, cocky, overfamiliar, discourteous, disrespectful, impolite, bad-mannered; informal brass-necked, lippy, mouthy, fresh, saucy; N. Amer. informal sassy, nervy; archaic assumptive.
– OPPOSITES respectful, polite.
cheep ● verb CHIRP, chirrup, twitter, tweet, peep, chitter, chirr, trill, warble, sing.
cheer ● noun **1** *the cheers of the crowd* HURRAH, hurray, whoop,

and pleasant: *a cheerful room.*
– DERIVATIVES **cheerfully** adverb **cheerfulness** noun.
cheerio ● exclamation Brit. informal goodbye.
cheerleader ● noun (in North America) a girl belonging to a group that performs organized chanting and dancing in support of a team at sporting events.
cheerless ● adjective gloomy; depressing.
– DERIVATIVES **cheerlessly** adverb **cheerlessness** noun.
cheers ● exclamation informal **1** expressing good wishes before drinking. **2** chiefly Brit. said to express gratitude or on parting.
cheery ● adjective (**cheerier**, **cheeriest**) happy and optimistic.
– DERIVATIVES **cheerily** adverb **cheeriness** noun.
cheese[1] ● noun a food made from the pressed curds of milk, having a texture either firm and elastic or soft and semi-liquid.
– PHRASES **hard cheese** Brit. informal, dated used to express sympathy over a petty matter.
– ORIGIN Latin *caseus.*
cheese[2] ● verb (usu. **be cheesed off**) Brit. informal exasperate, frustrate, or bore.
– ORIGIN of unknown origin.
cheeseboard ● noun **1** a board on which cheese is served and cut. **2** a selection of cheeses served as a course of a meal.
cheeseburger ● noun a beefburger with a slice of cheese on it, served in a bread roll.
cheesecake ● noun **1** a rich sweet tart made with cream and soft cheese on a biscuit base. **2** informal images portraying women according to a stereotyped ideal of sexual attractiveness.
cheesecloth ● noun thin, loosely woven cotton cloth.
cheese-paring ● noun excessive care with money; parsimony.
cheese plant ● noun see SWISS CHEESE PLANT.
cheesy ● adjective (**cheesier**, **cheesiest**) **1** like cheese in taste, smell, or consistency. **2** informal cheap or blatantly artificial.
– DERIVATIVES **cheesiness** noun.
cheetah /cheetə/ ● noun a large swift-running spotted cat found in Africa and parts of Asia.
– ORIGIN Hindi.
chef ● noun a professional cook, especially the chief cook in a restaurant or hotel.
– ORIGIN French, 'head'.
chef-d'œuvre /shay dövrə/ ● noun (pl. **chefs-d'œuvre** pronunc. same) a masterpiece.
– ORIGIN French, 'chief work'.
chela /keelə/ ● noun (pl. **chelae** /keeli/) a pincer-like claw, especially of a crab or other crustacean.
– ORIGIN Greek *khēlē* 'claw'.
Chelsea boot ● noun an elastic-sided boot with a pointed toe.
– ORIGIN named after *Chelsea*, a district of London.
Chelsea bun ● noun Brit. a flat, spiral-shaped currant bun sprinkled with sugar.
Chelsea pensioner ● noun an inmate of the Chelsea Royal Hospital for old or disabled soldiers.
chemical ● adjective relating to chemistry or chemicals. ● noun a distinct compound or substance, especially one which has been artificially prepared or purified.
– DERIVATIVES **chemically** adverb.
– ORIGIN French *chimique*, from Latin *alchimia* 'alchemy'.
chemical engineering ● noun the branch of engineering concerned with the design and operation of industrial chemical plants.
chemin de fer /shəmaɴ də fair/ ● noun a card game which is a variety of baccarat.
– ORIGIN French, 'railway'.
chemise /shəmeez/ ● noun **1** a dress hanging straight from the shoulders, popular in the 1920s. **2** a woman's loose-fitting undergarment or nightdress.
– ORIGIN Old French, from Latin *camisia* 'shirt or nightgown'.
chemist ● noun **1** Brit. a person who is authorized to dispense medicinal drugs. **2** Brit. a shop where medicinal drugs are dispensed and toiletries and other medical goods are sold. **3** a person engaged in chemical research or experiments.
– ORIGIN Latin *alchimista* 'alchemist'.
chemistry ● noun (pl. **chemistries**) **1** the branch of science concerned with the properties and interactions of the substances of which matter is composed. **2** the chemical properties of a substance or body. **3** attraction or interaction between two people.
chemotherapy /keemətherrəpi/ ● noun the treatment of disease, especially cancer, by the use of chemical substances.
chenille /shəneel/ ● noun fabric made from a tufted velvety yarn, typically used for furnishings or clothing.
– ORIGIN French, 'hairy caterpillar', from Latin *canicula* 'small dog'.
cheongsam /chiongsam/ ● noun a straight, close-fitting silk dress with a high neck, worn by Chinese and Indonesian women.
– ORIGIN Chinese.
cheque (US **check**) ● noun a written order to a bank to pay a stated sum from an account to a specified person.
– ORIGIN variant of CHECK[1], in the sense 'device for checking the amount of an item'.
cheque card ● noun Brit. a card issued by a bank to guarantee the honouring of cheques up to a stated amount.
chequer (US **checker**) ● noun **1** (**chequers**) a pattern of alternately coloured squares. **2** (**checkers**) (treated as sing.) N. Amer. the game of draughts. ● verb **1** (**be chequered**) be divided into or marked with chequers. **2** (**chequered**) marked by periods of fluctuating fortune.
– ORIGIN from EXCHEQUER, originally in the sense 'chessboard'.
chequerboard (US **checkerboard**) ● noun a board for playing checkers and similar games, having a regular chequered pattern in black and white.

Thesaurus

bravo, shout; hosanna, alleluia; (**cheers**) acclaim, acclamation, clamour, applause, ovation. **2** *a time of cheer* HAPPINESS, joy, joyousness, cheerfulness, cheeriness, gladness, merriment, gaiety, jubilation, jollity, jolliness, high spirits, joviality, jocularity, conviviality, light-heartedness; merrymaking, pleasure, rejoicing, revelry. **3** *Christmas cheer* FARE, food, foodstuffs, eatables, provender; drink, beverages; *informal* eats, nibbles, nosh, grub, chow; *Brit. informal* scoff; *dated* victuals; *formal* comestibles; *poetic/literary* viands.
– OPPOSITES boo, sadness.
● verb **1** *they cheered their team* ACCLAIM, hail, salute, shout for, hurrah, hurray, applaud, clap, put one's hands together for; bring the house down; *informal* holler for, give someone a big hand; *N. Amer. informal* ballyhoo. **2** *the bad weather did little to cheer me* RAISE SOMEONE'S SPIRITS, make happier, brighten, buoy up, enliven, exhilarate, hearten, gladden, uplift, perk up, encourage, inspirit; *informal* buck up.
– OPPOSITES boo, depress.
– PHRASES **cheer someone on** ENCOURAGE, urge on, spur on, drive on, motivate, inspire, fire (up), inspirit; *N. Amer.* light a fire under. **cheer up** PERK UP, brighten (up), become more cheerful, liven up, rally, revive, bounce back, take heart; *informal* buck up. **cheer someone up.** See CHEER verb sense 2.
cheerful ● adjective **1** *he arrived looking cheerful* HAPPY, jolly, merry, bright, glad, sunny, joyful, joyous, light-hearted, in good/high spirits, full of the joys of spring, sparkling, bubbly, exuberant, ebullient, cock-a-hoop, elated, gleeful, breezy, airy, cheery, jaunty, animated, radiant, smiling; jovial, genial, good-humoured; carefree, unworried, untroubled, without a care in the world; *informal* upbeat, chipper, chirpy, peppy, bright-eyed and bushy-tailed, full of beans; *dated* gay; *formal* jocund; *poetic/literary* gladsome, blithe, blithesome. **2** *a cheerful room* PLEASANT, attractive, agreeable, cheering, bright, sunny, happy, friendly, welcoming.
– OPPOSITES sad.
cheerio ● exclamation *(Brit. informal)* GOODBYE, farewell, adieu, au revoir, ciao, adios, auf Wiedersehen, sayonara; *Austral./NZ* hooray; *informal* bye, bye-bye, so long, see you (later), later(s); *Brit. informal* cheers, ta-ta, ta-ra; *informal, dated* pip pip, toodle-oo.
cheerless ● adjective GLOOMY, dreary, dull, dismal, bleak, drab, sombre, dark, dim, dingy, funereal; austere, stark, bare, comfortless, unwelcoming, uninviting; miserable, wretched, joyless, depressing, disheartening, dispiriting.
cheers ● exclamation **1** *(informal) he raised his glass and said 'Cheers!'* HERE'S TO YOU, good health, your health, skol, prosit, salut; *informal* bottoms up, down the hatch; *Brit. informal* here's mud in your eye; *Brit. informal, dated* cheerio, chin-chin. **2** *(Brit. informal) cheers, see you later!* See CHEERIO. **3** *(Brit. informal) cheers, mate* (MANY) THANKS, thanks a lot, thank you (kindly), much obliged; *informal* thanks a million; *Brit. informal* ta.
cheery ● adjective. See CHEERFUL sense 1.
chef ● noun COOK, cordon bleu cook, food preparer; chef de cuisine, chef de partie, commis chef; pastry cook, saucier; *N. Amer. informal*

C

chequered flag ● noun Motor Racing a flag with a black-and-white chequered pattern, displayed to drivers at the end of a race.
cherish ● verb **1** protect and care for lovingly. **2** have (a hope or ambition) over a long period.
– ORIGIN Old French *cherir*, from *cher* 'dear'.
Cherokee /cherrəkee/ ● noun (pl. same or **Cherokees**) a member of an American Indian people formerly inhabiting much of the southern US.
– ORIGIN the Cherokees' name for themselves.
cheroot /shəroot/ ● noun a cigar with both ends open.
– ORIGIN French *cheroute*, from a Tamil word meaning 'roll of tobacco'.
cherry ● noun (pl. **cherries**) **1** the small, round bright or dark red stone fruit of a tree of the rose family. **2** a bright deep red colour. **3** (**one's cherry**) informal one's virginity.
– PHRASES **a bite at the cherry** an attempt or opportunity. **a bowl of cherries** a very pleasant situation: *life is no bowl of cherries.* **the cherry on the cake** a desirable thing providing the finishing touch to something already good.
– ORIGIN Old French *cherise*, from Greek *kerasos*.
cherry brandy ● noun a sweet liqueur made with brandy in which cherries have been steeped.
cherry-pick ● verb selectively choose (the best things or people) from those available.
cherry tomato ● noun a miniature tomato with a strong flavour.
chert /chert/ ● noun a hard, dark, very fine-grained rock composed of silica, of which flint is a nodular form.
– ORIGIN of unknown origin.
cherub ● noun **1** (pl. **cherubim** or **cherubs**) a winged angelic being represented as a chubby child with wings. **2** (pl. **cherubs**) a beautiful or innocent-looking child.
– DERIVATIVES **cherubic** adjective **cherubically** adverb.
– ORIGIN Hebrew.
chervil /chervil/ ● noun a plant with delicate fern-like leaves which are used as a culinary herb.
– ORIGIN Greek *khairephullon*.
Ches. ● abbreviation Cheshire.
Cheshire /cheshər/ ● noun a kind of firm crumbly cheese, originally made in Cheshire.
Cheshire cat ● noun a cat depicted with a broad fixed grin, as in Lewis Carroll's *Alice's Adventures in Wonderland* (1865).
– ORIGIN of unknown origin, but it is said that *Cheshire* cheeses used to be marked with the face of a smiling cat.
chess ● noun a board game for two players, the object of which is to put the opponent's king under a direct attack, leading to checkmate.
– ORIGIN from Old French *esches* plural of *eschec* 'a check', from a Persian word meaning 'king'.
chessboard ● noun a square board divided into sixty-four alternating dark and light squares, used for playing chess or draughts.
chest ● noun **1** the front surface of a person's body between the neck and the stomach. **2** the circumference of a person's upper body. **3** a large strong box for storage or transport. **4** Brit. the treasury or financial resources of an institution.
– PHRASES **get something off one's chest** informal say something that one has wanted to say for a long time. **keep** (or **play**) **one's cards close to one's chest** informal be extremely secretive about one's intentions.
– DERIVATIVES **chested** adjective.
– ORIGIN Greek *kistē* 'box'.
chesterfield ● noun **1** a sofa having padded arms and back of the same height and curved outwards at the top. **2** a man's plain straight overcoat, typically with a velvet collar.
– ORIGIN named after a 19th-century Earl of *Chesterfield*.
chestnut ● noun **1** a glossy hard brown nut which develops within a bristly case and can be roasted and eaten. **2** (also **sweet chestnut** or **Spanish chestnut**) the large tree that produces these nuts. **3** a deep reddish-brown colour. **4** a horse of a reddish-brown or yellowish-brown colour. **5** (usu. **old chestnut**) a joke, story, or subject that has become uninteresting through constant repetition.
– ORIGIN from Greek *kastanea* + NUT.
chest of drawers ● noun a piece of furniture consisting of an upright frame into which drawers are fitted.
chesty ● adjective informal **1** Brit. having a lot of catarrh in the lungs. **2** (of a woman) having large or prominent breasts.
– DERIVATIVES **chestiness** noun.
chetrum /chetroom/ ● noun (pl. same or **chetrums**) a monetary unit of Bhutan, equal to one hundredth of a ngultrum.
– ORIGIN from Dzongkha, the official language of Bhutan.
cheval glass /shəval/ (also **cheval mirror**) ● noun a tall mirror fitted at its middle to an upright frame so that it can be tilted.
– ORIGIN French *cheval* 'horse, frame'.
chevalier /shevvəleer/ ● noun **1** historical a knight. **2** a member of certain orders of knighthood or of modern French orders such as the Legion of Honour.
– ORIGIN Old French, from Latin *caballus* 'horse'.
Cheviot /chevviət, cheev-/ ● noun a large sheep of a breed with short thick wool.
– ORIGIN from the *Cheviot* Hills in northern England and Scotland.
chèvre /shevrə/ ● noun French cheese made with goat's milk.
– ORIGIN French, 'goat'.
chevron ● noun **1** a V-shaped line or stripe, especially one on the sleeve of a uniform indicating rank or length of service. **2** Heraldry a broad inverted V-shape.
– ORIGIN Old French, from Latin *caper* 'goat'.
chevrotain /shevrətayn/ ● noun a small deer-like mammal with small tusks, found in tropical rainforests.
– ORIGIN French, 'little goat'.
chew ● verb **1** bite and work (food) in the mouth to make it easier to swallow. **2** (**chew over**) discuss or consider at length. **3** (**chew out**) N. Amer. informal reprimand severely. ● noun **1** an instance of chewing. **2** a thing, especially a sweet, for chewing.
– PHRASES **chew the fat** (or **rag**) informal chat in a leisurely way.
– DERIVATIVES **chewable** adjective **chewer** noun.
– ORIGIN Old English.
chewing gum ● noun flavoured gum for chewing.
chewy ● adjective suitable for chewing, or requiring much chewing.
– DERIVATIVES **chewiness** noun.
Cheyenne /shīan/ ● noun (pl. same or **Cheyennes**) a member of an American Indian people formerly living between the Missouri and Arkansas Rivers.

Thesaurus

short-order cook.
chef-d'œuvre ● noun MASTERPIECE, masterwork, finest work, magnum opus, pièce de résistance, tour de force.
chequered ● adjective **1** *a chequered tablecloth* CHECKED, multicoloured, many-coloured. **2** *a chequered history* VARIED, mixed, full of ups and downs, vicissitudinous; unstable, irregular, erratic, inconstant; *informal* up and down.
cherish ● verb **1** *a woman he could cherish* ADORE, hold dear, love, dote on, be devoted to, revere, esteem, admire; think the world of, set great store by, hold in high esteem; care for, look after, protect, preserve, keep safe. **2** *I cherish her letters* TREASURE, prize, value highly, hold dear. **3** *they cherished dreams of glory* HARBOUR, entertain, possess, hold (on to), cling to, keep in one's mind, foster, nurture.
cherub ● noun **1** *she was borne up to heaven by cherubs* ANGEL, seraph. **2** *a cherub of 18 months* BABY, infant, toddler; pretty child, loveable child, innocent child, little angel; *informal* (tiny) tot, tiny; *poetic/literary* babe (in arms).
cherubic ● adjective ANGELIC, sweet, cute, adorable, appealing, loveable; innocent, seraphic, saintly.
chest ● noun **1** *a bullet wound in the chest* BREAST, upper body, torso, trunk; *technical* thorax. **2** *a large chest* BUST, bosom; *archaic* embonpoint. **3** *an oak chest* BOX, case, casket, crate, trunk, coffer, strongbox.
– RELATED TERMS pectoral, thoracic.
– PHRASES **get something off one's chest** *(informal)* CONFESS, disclose, divulge, reveal, make known, make public, make a clean breast of, bring into the open, tell all about, get a load off one's mind.
chew ● verb *Carolyn chewed a mouthful of toast* MASTICATE, munch, champ, crunch, nibble, gnaw, eat, consume; *formal* manducate.
– PHRASES **chew something over** MEDITATE ON, ruminate on, think about/over/through, mull over, consider, weigh up, ponder on, deliberate on, reflect on, muse on, dwell on, give thought to, turn over in one's mind; brood over, puzzle over, wrestle with, rack one's brains about; *N. Amer.* think on; *informal* kick around/about,

– ORIGIN from a Dakota word meaning 'speak incoherently'.
chez /shay/ ● **preposition** chiefly humorous at the home of.
– ORIGIN French.
chi[1] /kī/ ● **noun** the twenty-second letter of the Greek alphabet (Χ, χ), transliterated as 'kh' or 'ch'.
– ORIGIN Greek.
chi[2] /kee/ (also **qi** or **ki**) ● **noun** the circulating life force whose existence and properties are the basis of much Chinese philosophy and medicine.
– ORIGIN Chinese, 'air, breath'.
Chianti /kianti/ ● **noun** (pl. **Chiantis**) a dry red Italian wine produced in Tuscany.
– ORIGIN named after the *Chianti* Mountains, Italy.
chiaroscuro /ki-aarəskoorō/ ● **noun** the treatment of light and shade in drawing and painting.
– ORIGIN Italian, from *chiaro* 'clear, bright' + *oscuro* 'dark, obscure'.
chiasma /kīazmə/ (also **optic chiasma**) ● **noun** (pl. **chiasmata** /kīazmətə/) Anatomy the X-shaped structure below the brain where the optic nerves from the left and right eyes cross over each other.
– ORIGIN Greek, 'crosspiece, cross-shaped mark'.
chiasmus /kīazməss/ ● **noun** the inversion in a second phrase or clause of the order of words in the first.
– ORIGIN Greek *khiasmos* 'crosswise arrangement'.
chic /sheek/ ● **adjective** (**chicer**, **chicest**) elegantly and stylishly fashionable. ● **noun** stylishness and elegance.
– DERIVATIVES **chicly** adverb.
– ORIGIN French.
chicane /shikayn/ ● **noun 1** a sharp double bend created to form an obstacle on a motor-racing track. **2** archaic chicanery.
– ORIGIN from French *chicaner* 'quibble'.
chicanery ● **noun** the use of trickery to achieve one's purpose.
Chicano /chikaanō/ ● **noun** (pl. **Chicanos**; fem. **Chicana**, pl. **Chicanas**) chiefly US a North American of Mexican origin or descent.
– ORIGIN from Spanish *mejicano* 'Mexican'.
chichi /sheeshee/ ● **adjective** over-elaborate and affected; fussy.
– ORIGIN French.
chick ● **noun 1** a young bird, especially one newly hatched. **2** informal a young woman.
– ORIGIN abbreviation of CHICKEN.
chickadee ● **noun** North American term for TIT[1].
– ORIGIN imitative of its call.
chicken ● **noun 1** a domestic fowl kept for its eggs or meat, especially a young one. **2** a coward. **3** informal a game in which the first person to lose their nerve and withdraw from a dangerous situation is the loser. ● **adjective** informal cowardly. ● **verb** (**chicken out**) informal be too scared to do something.
– PHRASES **chicken-and-egg** (of a situation) in which each of two things appears to be necessary to the other. [ORIGIN from the question 'What came first, the chicken or the egg?'] **like a headless chicken** informal frenziedly.
– ORIGIN Old English.
chicken feed ● **noun** informal a paltry sum of money.
chickenpox ● **noun** an infectious disease causing a mild fever and a rash of itchy inflamed pimples; varicella.
– ORIGIN probably so named because of its mildness, as compared to smallpox.
chicken wire ● **noun** light wire netting with a hexagonal mesh.
chickpea ● **noun** a round yellowish seed which is a pulse of major importance as food.
– ORIGIN from Latin *cicer* 'chickpea'.
chickweed ● **noun** a small white-flowered plant, often growing as a garden weed.
chicle /chikk'l/ ● **noun** the milky latex of the sapodilla tree, used to make chewing gum.
– ORIGIN Nahuatl.
chicory /chikkəri/ ● **noun** (pl. **chicories**) **1** a blue-flowered plant with edible leaves and a root which is used as an additive to or substitute for coffee. **2** North American term for ENDIVE.
– ORIGIN Greek *kikhorion.*
chide /chīd/ ● **verb** (past **chided** or **chid** /chid/; past part. **chided** or archaic **chidden** /chidd'n/) scold or rebuke.
– ORIGIN Old English.
chief ● **noun 1** a leader or ruler of a people. **2** the head of an organization. ● **adjective 1** having the highest rank or authority. **2** most important: *the chief reason.*
– DERIVATIVES **chiefdom** noun.
– ORIGIN Old French, from Latin *caput* 'head'.
chief constable ● **noun** Brit. the head of the police force of a county or other region.
chiefly ● **adverb** mainly; mostly.
chief of staff ● **noun** the senior staff officer of a service or command.
chieftain ● **noun** the leader of a people or clan.
– DERIVATIVES **chieftaincy** noun (pl. **chieftaincies**) **chieftainship** noun.
– ORIGIN Old French *chevetaine*, from Latin *capitaneus* 'chief'.
chiffchaff ● **noun** a common warbler with drab plumage and a repetitive call.
– ORIGIN imitative of its call.
chiffon ● **noun** a light, transparent fabric of silk or nylon.
– ORIGIN French, from *chiffe* 'rag'.
chiffonier /shiffəneer/ ● **noun 1** Brit. a low cupboard used as a sideboard or having a bookshelf on top. **2** N. Amer. a tall chest of drawers.
– ORIGIN French, 'ragpicker', also 'chest of drawers for oddments'.
chigger /chiggər/ (also **jigger**) ● **noun** a tropical flea, the female of which lays eggs beneath the host's skin, causing painful sores.
– ORIGIN variant of CHIGOE.
chignon /sheenyON/ ● **noun** a knot or coil of hair arranged on the back of a woman's head.
– ORIGIN French, 'nape of the neck'.
chigoe /chiggō/ ● **noun** another term for CHIGGER
– ORIGIN French *chique*, from a West African language.
chihuahua /chiwaawə/ ● **noun** a very small breed of dog with smooth hair and large eyes.
– ORIGIN named after *Chihuahua* in northern Mexico.

Thesaurus

bat around/about; *formal* cogitate about; *archaic* pore on. **chew the fat/rag** *(informal)*. See CHAT verb.
chic ● **adjective** STYLISH, smart, elegant, sophisticated, dressy, dapper, dashing, trim; fashionable, high-fashion, in vogue, up to date, up to the minute, contemporary, à la mode; *informal* trendy, with it, snappy, snazzy, natty, swish; *N. Amer. informal* fly, spiffy, kicky, tony.
– OPPOSITES unfashionable.
chicanery ● **noun** TRICKERY, deception, deceit, deceitfulness, duplicity, dishonesty, deviousness, unscrupulousness, sharp practice, underhandedness, subterfuge, fraud, fraudulence, skulduggery, swindling, cheating, duping, hoodwinking; *informal* crookedness, monkey business, hanky-panky, shenanigans; *Brit. informal* jiggery-pokery; *N. Amer. informal* monkeyshines; *archaic* management, knavery.
chide ● **verb** SCOLD, chastise, upbraid, berate, reprimand, reprove, rebuke, admonish, censure, lambaste, lecture, give someone a piece of one's mind, take to task, haul over the coals; *informal* tell off, dress down, bawl out, blow up at, give someone an earful, give someone a roasting, come down on someone like a ton of bricks, have someone's guts for garters, slap someone's wrist, rap over the knuckles, give someone hell; *Brit. informal* carpet, tick off, have a go at, tear someone off a strip, give someone what for, give someone a rocket; *N. Amer. informal* chew out, ream out; *Austral. informal* monster; *formal* castigate; *dated* give someone a rating; *archaic* chasten; *rare* reprehend, objurgate.
– OPPOSITES praise.
chief ● **noun 1** *a Highland chief* LEADER, chieftain, head, headman, ruler, overlord, master, commander, seigneur, liege (lord), potentate. **2** *the chief of the central bank* HEAD, principal, chief executive, president, chair, chairman, chairwoman, chairperson, governor, director, manager, manageress; employer, proprietor; *N. Amer.* chief executive officer, CEO; *informal* skipper, numero uno, (head) honcho, boss; *Brit. informal* gaffer, guv'nor; *N. Amer. informal* padrone, sachem.
● **adjective 1** *the chief rabbi* HEAD, leading, principal, premier, highest, foremost, supreme, arch. **2** *their chief aim* MAIN, principal, most important, primary, prime, first, cardinal, central, key, crucial, essential, predominant, pre-eminent, paramount, overriding; *informal* number-one.
– RELATED TERMS arch-.
– OPPOSITES subordinate, minor.
chiefly ● **adverb** MAINLY, in the main, primarily, principally, predominantly, mostly, for the most part; usually, habitually, typic-

C

chilblain ● noun a painful, itching swelling on a hand or foot caused by poor circulation in the skin when exposed to cold.
– ORIGIN from CHILL + archaic *blain*, from an Old English word meaning 'inflamed swelling or sore'.

child ● noun (pl. **children**) **1** a young human being below the age of full physical development. **2** a son or daughter of any age. **3** derogatory an immature or irresponsible person. **4** (**children**) archaic the descendants of a family or people.
– PHRASES **child's play** a task which is easily accomplished. **with child** archaic pregnant.
– DERIVATIVES **childless** adjective.
– ORIGIN Old English.

childbed ● noun archaic childbirth.

child benefit ● noun (in the UK) regular payment by the state to the parents of a child up to a certain age.

childbirth ● noun the action of giving birth to a child.

childhood ● noun the state or period of being a child.

childish ● adjective **1** of, like, or appropriate to a child. **2** silly and immature.
– DERIVATIVES **childishly** adverb **childishness** noun.

childlike ● adjective (of an adult) having the good qualities, such as innocence, associated with a child.

childminder ● noun Brit. a person who looks after children in their own house for payment.

children plural of CHILD.

Chilean /chilliən/ ● noun a person from Chile. ● adjective relating to Chile.

chili ● noun (pl. **chilies**) US spelling of CHILLI.

chiliastic /killiastik/ ● adjective another term for MILLENARIAN.
– ORIGIN from Greek *khilias* 'a thousand years'.

chill ● noun **1** an unpleasant feeling of coldness. **2** a feverish cold. ● verb **1** make cold. **2** horrify or frighten. **3** (usu. **chill out**) informal, chiefly N. Amer. calm down and relax. ● adjective chilly.
– DERIVATIVES **chilling** adjective **chillness** noun.
– ORIGIN Old English.

chiller ● noun **1** a cold cabinet or refrigerator for keeping stored food a few degrees above freezing point. **2** short for **spine-chiller**.

chill factor ● noun the perceived lowering of the air temperature caused by the wind.

chilli (also **chilli pepper**, **chile**, US **chili**) ● noun (pl. **chillies**, **chiles**, or US **chilies**) **1** a small hot-tasting pod of a variety of capsicum, used in sauces, relishes, and spice powders. **2** chilli powder or chilli con carne.
– ORIGIN Nahuatl.

chilli con carne /chilli kon kaarni/ ● noun a stew of minced beef and beans flavoured with chilli.
– ORIGIN Spanish *chile con carne* 'chilli pepper with meat'.

chilli powder ● noun a hot-tasting mixture of ground dried red chillies and other spices.

chillum /chilləm/ ● noun (pl. **chillums**) **1** a hookah. **2** a pipe used for smoking cannabis.
– ORIGIN Hindi.

chilly ● adjective (**chillier**, **chilliest**) **1** unpleasantly cold. **2** unfriendly.
– DERIVATIVES **chilliness** noun.

chimaera ● noun variant spelling of CHIMERA.

chime ● noun **1** a melodious ringing sound. **2** a bell or a metal bar or tube used in a set to produce chimes when struck. ● verb **1** (of a bell or clock) make a melodious ringing sound. **2** (**chime in with**) be in agreement with. **3** (**chime in**) interject a remark.
– ORIGIN probably from CYMBAL (interpreted as *chime bell*).

chimera /kīmeerə/ (also **chimaera**) ● noun **1** Greek Mythology a fire-breathing female monster with a lion's head, a goat's body, and a serpent's tail. **2** something hoped for but illusory or impossible to achieve. **3** Biology an organism containing a mixture of genetically different tissues.
– ORIGIN Greek *khimaira* 'she-goat or chimera'.

chimerical /kīmerrik'l/ ● adjective **1** like a mythical chimera. **2** illusory or impossible to achieve.
– DERIVATIVES **chimerically** adverb.

chimney ● noun (pl. **chimneys**) **1** a vertical pipe which conducts smoke and gases up from a fire or furnace. **2** a glass tube protecting the flame of a lamp. **3** a very steep narrow cleft by which a rock face may be climbed.
– ORIGIN Old French *cheminee*, from Greek *kaminos* 'oven'.

chimney breast ● noun a part of an interior wall that projects to surround a chimney.

chimney piece ● noun Brit. a mantelpiece.

chimney pot ● noun an earthenware or metal pipe at the top of a chimney.

chimney stack ● noun the part of a chimney that projects above a roof.

chimp ● noun informal term for CHIMPANZEE.

chimpanzee ● noun an anthropoid ape native to west and central Africa.
– ORIGIN Kikongo (a language of the Congo and surrounding areas).

chin ● noun the protruding part of the face below the mouth. ● verb informal hit or punch on the chin.

Thesaurus

ally, commonly, generally, on the whole, largely, by and large, as a rule, almost always.

child ● noun YOUNGSTER, little one, boy, girl; baby, newborn, infant, toddler; schoolboy, schoolgirl, minor, junior; son, daughter, descendant; (**children**) offspring, progeny; *Scottish & N. English* bairn, laddie, lassie, lass; *informal* kid, kiddie, kiddiewink, nipper, tiny, (tiny) tot, shaver, young 'un, lad; *Brit. informal* sprog; *N. Amer. informal* rug rat; *Austral./NZ informal* ankle-biter; *derogatory* brat, guttersnipe; *poetic/literary* babe (in arms).
– RELATED TERMS paedo-.

childbirth ● noun LABOUR, delivery, giving birth, birthing; *formal* parturition; *dated* confinement; *poetic/literary* travail; *archaic* lying-in, accouchement, childbed.
– RELATED TERMS obstetric, puerperal.

childhood ● noun YOUTH, early years/life, infancy, babyhood, boyhood, girlhood, pre-teens, pre-pubescence, minority; the springtime of life, one's salad days; *formal* nonage, juvenescence.
– OPPOSITES adulthood.

childish ● adjective **1** *childish behaviour* IMMATURE, babyish, infantile, juvenile, puerile; silly, inane, jejune, foolish, irresponsible. **2** *a round childish face* CHILDLIKE, youthful, young, young-looking, girlish, boyish.
– OPPOSITES mature, adult.

childlike ● adjective **1** *grandmother looked almost childlike* YOUTHFUL, young, young-looking, girlish, boyish. **2** *geniuses tend to be rather childlike* INNOCENT, artless, guileless, unworldly, unsophisticated, naive, ingenuous, trusting, unsuspicious, unwary, credulous, gullible; unaffected, without airs, uninhibited, natural, spontaneous; *informal* wet behind the ears.

chill ● noun **1** *a chill in the air* COLDNESS, chilliness, coolness, iciness, rawness, bitterness, nip. **2** *he had a chill* COLD, dose of flu/influenza; *archaic* grippe. **3** *the chill in their relations* UNFRIENDLINESS, lack of warmth/understanding, chilliness, coldness, coolness.
– OPPOSITES warmth.
● verb **1** *the dessert is best chilled* MAKE COLD, make colder, cool (down/off); refrigerate, ice. **2** *his quiet tone chilled Ruth* SCARE, frighten, petrify, terrify, alarm; make someone's blood run cold, chill to the bone/marrow, make someone's flesh crawl; *informal* scare the pants off; *Brit. informal* put the wind up; *archaic* affright.
– OPPOSITES warm.
● adjective *a chill wind* COLD, chilly, cool, fresh; wintry, frosty, icy, ice-cold, icy-cold, glacial, polar, arctic, raw, bitter, bitterly cold, biting, freezing, frigid, gelid; *informal* nippy; *Brit. informal* parky.
– PHRASES **chill out** *(N. Amer. informal) a place to chill out.* See RELAX sense 1.

chilly ● adjective **1** *the weather had turned chilly* COLD, cool, crisp, fresh, wintry, frosty, icy, ice-cold, icy-cold, chill, glacial, polar, arctic, raw, bitter, bitterly cold, freezing, frigid, gelid; *informal* nippy; *Brit. informal* parky. **2** *I woke up feeling chilly* COLD, frozen (stiff), frozen to the marrow/core/bone, freezing (cold), bitterly cold, shivery, chilled. **3** *a chilly reception* UNFRIENDLY, unwelcoming, cold, cool, frosty, gelid; *informal* stand-offish, offish.
– OPPOSITES warm.

chime ● verb **1** *the bells began to chime* RING, peal, toll, sound; ding, dong, clang, boom; *poetic/literary* knell. **2** *the clock chimed eight o'clock* STRIKE, sound.
● noun *the chimes of the bells* PEAL, pealing, ringing, carillon, toll, tolling; ding-dong, clanging, tintinnabulation; *poetic/literary* knell.
– PHRASES **chime in 1** *'Yes, you do that,' Doreen chimed in* INTERJECT, interpose, interrupt, butt in, cut in, join in; *Brit. informal* chip in. **2** *his remarks chimed in with the ideas of Adam Smith* ACCORD, correspond, be consistent, be compatible, agree, be in agreement, fit in, be in tune, be consonant; *informal* square.

– PHRASES **keep one's chin up** informal remain cheerful in difficult circumstances. **take it on the chin** informal accept misfortune stoically.
– DERIVATIVES **chinned** adjective.
– ORIGIN Old English.
china • noun **1** a fine white or translucent ceramic material. **2** household objects made from china. **3** Brit. informal a friend. [ORIGIN from rhyming slang *china plate* 'mate'.]
– ORIGIN from Persian, 'relating to China'.
china blue • noun a pale greyish blue.
china clay • noun another term for KAOLIN.
chinagraph pencil • noun Brit. a waxy pencil used to write on china, glass, or other hard surfaces.
Chinaman • noun chiefly archaic or derogatory a native of China.
China syndrome • noun a hypothetical sequence of events following the meltdown of a nuclear reactor, in which the core melts deep into the earth.
– ORIGIN so named because China is on the opposite side of the earth from a reactor in the US.
China tea • noun tea made from a small-leaved type of tea plant grown in China, often smoked or with flower petals added.
Chinatown • noun a district of a non-Chinese town in which the population is predominantly of Chinese origin.
chinchilla /chinchillə/ • noun **1** a small South American rodent with soft grey fur and a long bushy tail. **2** a breed of cat or rabbit with silver-grey or grey fur.
– ORIGIN Aymara or Quechua (South American Indian languages).
chin-chin • exclamation Brit. informal, dated a toast made before drinking.
– ORIGIN representing a pronunciation of a Chinese phrase.
Chindit /chindit/ • noun a member of the Allied forces behind the Japanese lines in Burma (now Myanmar) in 1943–5.
– ORIGIN from the Burmese name for a mythical creature.
chine[1] /chīn/ • noun **1** the backbone of an animal, or a joint of meat containing part of it. **2** a mountain ridge.
– ORIGIN Old French *eschine*, from Latin *spina* 'spine'.
chine[2] /chīn/ • noun (in the Isle of Wight or Dorset) a deep narrow ravine.
– ORIGIN Old English, 'cleft, chink'.
chine[3] /chīn/ • noun the angle where the planks or plates at the bottom of a boat or ship meet the side.
– ORIGIN Old English.
Chinese • noun (pl. same) **1** the language of China. **2** a person from China. • adjective relating to China.
Chinese box • noun each of a nest of boxes.
Chinese burn • noun informal a burning sensation inflicted on a person by placing both hands on their arm and then twisting it.
Chinese cabbage • noun another term for CHINESE LEAVES.
Chinese chequers (US **Chinese checkers**) • plural noun (treated as sing.) a board game in which players attempt to move marbles or counters from one corner to the opposite one on a star-shaped board.
Chinese lantern • noun **1** a collapsible paper lantern. **2** a plant with white flowers and globular orange fruits enclosed in a papery orange-red calyx.
Chinese leaves (also **Chinese cabbage**) • plural noun an oriental variety of cabbage which does not form a firm heart.
Chinese puzzle • noun an intricate puzzle consisting of many interlocking pieces.
Chinese wall • noun an insurmountable barrier, especially to the passage of information.
Chinese whispers • plural noun (treated as sing.) a game in which a message is distorted by being passed around in a whisper.
Chink (also **Chinky**) • noun informal, offensive a Chinese person.
chink[1] • noun **1** a narrow opening or crack. **2** a beam of light admitted by a chink.
– ORIGIN related to CHINE[3].
chink[2] • verb make a light, high-pitched ringing sound, as of glasses or coins striking together. • noun a high-pitched ringing sound.
– ORIGIN imitative.
chinless • adjective **1** lacking a well-defined chin. **2** informal lacking strength of character.
chino /cheenō/ • noun **1** a cotton twill fabric. **2** (**chinos**) casual trousers made from such fabric.
– ORIGIN Latin American Spanish, 'toasted' (referring to the typical colour).
chinoiserie /shinwaazəri/ • noun **1** the use of Chinese motifs and techniques in Western art, furniture, and architecture. **2** objects or decorations in this style.
– ORIGIN French, from *chinois* 'Chinese'.
Chinook /chinoōk/ • noun (pl. same or **Chinooks**) a member of an American Indian people originally living in Oregon.
– ORIGIN Salish.
chinook /chinoōk/ • noun **1** a warm, dry wind which blows down the east side of the Rocky Mountains at the end of winter. **2** a large North Pacific salmon which is an important commercial food fish.
Chinook Jargon • noun an extinct pidgin composed of elements from Chinook, English, French, and other languages, formerly used in the Pacific North-West of North America.
chintz • noun printed multicoloured cotton fabric with a glazed finish, used for curtains and upholstery.
– ORIGIN Hindi, 'spattering, stain'.
chintzy • adjective (**chintzier**, **chintziest**) **1** decorated with or resembling chintz. **2** colourful but fussy and tasteless.
chinwag • noun Brit. informal a chat.
chip • noun **1** a small, thin piece removed in the course of cutting or breaking a hard material. **2** a blemish left by the removal of such a piece. **3** chiefly Brit. a long rectangular piece of deep-fried potato. **4** (also **potato chip**) chiefly N. Amer. a potato crisp. **5** a microchip. **6** a counter used in certain gambling games to represent money. **7** (in football or golf) a short lofted kick or shot. • verb (**chipped**, **chipping**) **1** cut or break (a chip) from a hard material. **2** break at the edge or on the surface. **3** (**chip away**) gradually and relentlessly make something smaller or weaker. **4** (in football or golf) strike (the ball) to produce a short lofted shot or pass. **5** (**chipped**) Brit. (of potatoes) cut into chips.
– PHRASES **chip in 1** contribute one's share of a joint activity. **2** Brit. informal make an interjection. **a chip off the old block** informal someone who resembles their parent in character. **a chip on one's shoulder** informal a deeply ingrained grievance. **have had one's chips** Brit. informal be dead or out of contention. **when the chips are down** informal when a very serious situation arises.
– ORIGIN from an Old English word meaning 'cut off'.
chipboard • noun material made from compressed wood chips and resin.
chipmunk • noun a burrowing ground squirrel with light and dark stripes running down the body.
– ORIGIN Ojibwa (an American Indian language).
chipolata • noun Brit. a small thin sausage.
– ORIGIN Italian *cipollata* 'dish of onions'.
Chippendale /chippəndayl/ • adjective (of furniture) neoclassical with elements of French rococo and chinoiserie, as designed by or after the style of the English furniture-maker Thomas Chippendale (1718–79).
chipper • adjective informal cheerful and lively.
– ORIGIN perhaps from northern English dialect *kipper* 'lively'.
chipping • noun Brit. a small fragment of stone, wood, or similar material.
chippy informal • noun (also **chippie**) (pl. **chippies**) **1** Brit. a fish-and-chip shop. **2** Brit. a carpenter. **3** N. Amer. a prostitute. • adjec-

C

Thesaurus

chimera • noun ILLUSION, fantasy, delusion, dream, fancy.
chimney • noun STACK, smokestack; flue, funnel, vent.
china • noun **1** *a china cup* PORCELAIN. **2** *a table laid with the best china* DISHES, plates, cups and saucers, crockery, tableware, dinner service, tea service.
chink[1] • noun *a chink in the curtains* OPENING, gap, space, hole, aperture, crack, fissure, crevice, cranny, cleft, split, slit, slot.
chink[2] • verb *the glasses chinked* JINGLE, jangle, clink, tinkle.
chip • noun **1** *wood chips* FRAGMENT, sliver, splinter, spell, shaving, paring, flake. **2** *a chip in the glass* NICK, crack, scratch; flaw, fault. **3** *fish and chips* chipped potatoes, potato chips; *Brit.* French fried potatoes; *N. Amer.* French fries. **4** *gambling chips* COUNTER, token, jetton; *N. Amer.* check.
• verb **1** *the teacup was chipped* NICK, crack, scratch; damage. **2** *the plaster had chipped* BREAK (OFF), crack, crumble. **3** *chip the flint to the required shape* WHITTLE, hew, chisel.
– PHRASES **chip in 1** *'He's right,' Gloria chipped in* INTERRUPT, interject, interpose, cut in, chime in, butt in. **2** *parents and staff*

tive touchy and irritable.

chiral /kīrəl/ ● adjective Chemistry (of a molecule) not able to be superimposed on its mirror image.
– DERIVATIVES **chirality** noun.
– ORIGIN from Greek *kheir* 'hand'.

chirography /kīrogrəfi/ ● noun handwriting, especially as distinct from typography.
– DERIVATIVES **chirographic** adjective.

chiromancy /kīrəmansi/ ● noun the prediction of a person's future from the lines on the palms of their hands; palmistry.
– ORIGIN from Greek *kheir* 'hand'.

chiropody /kiroppədi/ ● noun the treatment of the feet and their ailments.
– DERIVATIVES **chiropodist** noun.
– ORIGIN from Greek *kheir* 'hand' + *pous* 'foot'.

chiropractic /kīrəpraktik/ ● noun a system of complementary medicine based on the manipulative treatment of misalignments of the joints, especially those of the spinal column.
– DERIVATIVES **chiropractor** noun.
– ORIGIN from Greek *kheir* 'hand' + *praktikos* 'practical'.

chirp ● verb **1** (of a small bird or a grasshopper) utter a short, sharp, high-pitched sound. **2** say something in a lively and cheerful way. ● noun a chirping sound.
– ORIGIN imitative.

chirpy ● adjective (**chirpier**, **chirpiest**) informal cheerful and lively.
– DERIVATIVES **chirpily** adverb **chirpiness** noun.

chirr /chur/ (also **churr**) ● verb (of a bird or insect) make a prolonged low trilling sound. ● noun a low trilling sound.
– ORIGIN imitative.

chirrup ● verb (**chirruped**, **chirruping**) (of a small bird) make repeated short high-pitched sounds. ● noun a chirruping sound.
– DERIVATIVES **chirrupy** adjective.
– ORIGIN alteration of CHIRP.

chisel ● noun a long-bladed hand tool with a bevelled cutting edge, used to cut or shape wood, stone, or metal. ● verb (**chiselled**, **chiselling**; US **chiseled**, **chiseling**) **1** cut or shape with a chisel. **2** (**chiselled**) (of a man's facial features) strongly defined. **3** informal, chiefly N. Amer. cheat or swindle.
– DERIVATIVES **chiseller** noun.
– ORIGIN Old French, from Latin *caedere* 'to cut'.

chit[1] ● noun derogatory an impudent or arrogant young woman.
– ORIGIN originally meaning 'whelp, cub, or kitten': perhaps related to dialect *chit* 'sprout'.

chit[2] ● noun a short official note recording a sum owed.
– ORIGIN Hindi, 'note, pass'.

chital /cheet'l/ ● noun a deer with curved antlers and a white-spotted fawn coat, native to India and Sri Lanka.
– ORIGIN Sanskrit, 'spotted'.

chit-chat informal ● noun inconsequential conversation. ● verb talk about trivial matters.

chitin /kītin/ ● noun Biochemistry a fibrous substance which forms the exoskeleton of arthropods and the cell walls of fungi.
– DERIVATIVES **chitinous** adjective.
– ORIGIN Greek *khitōn* (see CHITON).

chiton /kīton/ ● noun **1** a long woollen tunic worn in ancient Greece. **2** a marine mollusc that has an oval flattened body with a shell of overlapping plates.
– ORIGIN Greek *khitōn* 'tunic'.

chitter ● verb **1** make a twittering or chattering sound. **2** Scottish & dialect shiver with cold.
– ORIGIN imitative.

chitterlings /chittərlingz/ ● plural noun the smaller intestines of a pig, cooked for food.
– ORIGIN perhaps related to synonymous German *Kutteln*.

chivalrous ● adjective **1** (of a man) courteous and gallant, especially towards women. **2** relating to the historical notion of chivalry.
– DERIVATIVES **chivalrously** adverb.

chivalry ● noun **1** the medieval knightly system with its religious, moral, and social code. **2** the combination of qualities expected of an ideal knight, especially courage, honour, courtesy, justice, and a readiness to help the weak. **3** courteous behaviour, especially that of a man towards women.
– DERIVATIVES **chivalric** adjective.
– ORIGIN Old French *chevalerie*, from Latin *caballarius* 'horseman'.

chives ● plural noun a small plant with long tubular leaves used as a culinary herb.
– ORIGIN Old French, from Latin *cepa* 'onion'.

chivvy (also **chivy**) ● verb (**chivvies**, **chivvied**) tell (someone) repeatedly to do something.
– ORIGIN originally meaning 'a hunting cry': probably from the ballad *Chevy Chase*, celebrating a skirmish on the Scottish border.

chlamydia /kləmiddiə/ ● noun (pl. same or **chlamydiae** /kləmiddi-ee/) a very small parasitic bacterium.
– ORIGIN Greek *khlamus* 'cloak'.

chloral /klorəl/ ● noun Chemistry a viscous liquid used as a sedative in the form of a crystalline derivative (**chloral hydrate**).
– ORIGIN French, blend of *chlore* 'chlorine' and *alcool* 'alcohol'.

chlorate ● noun Chemistry a salt containing the anion ClO_3^-.

chloride /klorīd/ ● noun a compound of chlorine with another element or group.

chlorinate /klorinayt/ ● verb impregnate or treat with chlorine.
– DERIVATIVES **chlorination** noun.

chlorine /kloreen/ ● noun a poisonous, irritant, pale green gaseous chemical element.
– ORIGIN from Greek *khlōros* 'green'.

chlorofluorocarbon /klorōfloorōkaarb'n/ ● noun see CFC.

chloroform ● noun a sweet-smelling liquid used as a solvent and formerly as a general anaesthetic. ● verb make unconscious with this substance.
– ORIGIN from CHLORINE + FORMIC ACID.

chlorophyll /klorrəfil/ ● noun a green pigment which is responsible for the absorption of light by plants to provide energy for photosynthesis.
– ORIGIN from Greek *khlōros* 'green' + *phullon* 'leaf'.

chloroplast /klorrəplast/ ● noun a structure in green plant cells which contains chlorophyll and in which photosynthesis takes place.
– ORIGIN from Greek *khlōros* 'green' + *plastos* 'formed'.

chlorosis /klərōsiss/ ● noun **1** loss of the normal green coloration of the leaves of plants. **2** anaemia caused by iron deficiency, causing a pale, faintly greenish complexion.
– DERIVATIVES **chlorotic** adjective.

chocaholic ● noun variant spelling of CHOCOHOLIC.

choc ice ● noun Brit. a small bar of ice cream with a thin coating of chocolate.

chock ● noun **1** a wedge or block placed against a wheel to prevent it from moving. **2** a ring with a gap at the top, through which a rope or line is run.
– ORIGIN Old French *çoche* 'block, log'.

chock-a-block ● adjective informal crammed full.
– ORIGIN originally in nautical use, with reference to blocks in tackle running close together.

chock-full ● adjective informal filled to overflowing.
– ORIGIN of unknown origin; later associated with CHOCK.

chocoholic (also **chocaholic**) ● noun informal a person who is very fond of chocolate.

chocolate ● noun **1** a food made from roasted and ground cacao seeds, typically sweetened and eaten as confectionery. **2** a sweet covered with chocolate. **3** a drink made by mixing

Thesaurus

chipped in to raise the cash CONTRIBUTE, club together, make a contribution/donation, pay; *informal* fork out, shell out, cough up; *Brit. informal* stump up; *N. Amer. informal* kick in.

chirp ● verb TWEET, twitter, chirrup, cheep, peep, chitter, chirr; sing, warble, trill.

chirpy ● adjective *(informal) a chirpy mood.* See CHEERFUL sense 2.

chit-chat ● noun *(informal)* SMALL TALK, chat, chatting, chatter, prattle; *Brit. informal* nattering, chuntering.

chivalrous ● adjective **1** *his chivalrous treatment of women* GALLANT, gentlemanly, honourable, respectful, considerate; courteous, polite, gracious, well mannered, mannerly; *archaic* gentle. **2** *chivalrous pursuits* KNIGHTLY, noble, chivalric; brave, courageous, bold, valiant, valorous, heroic, daring, intrepid.
– OPPOSITES rude, cowardly.

chivalry ● noun **1** *acts of chivalry* GALLANTRY, gentlemanliness, considerateness; courtesy, courteousness, politeness, graciousness, mannerliness, good manners. **2** *the values of chivalry* KNIGHT ERRANTRY, courtly manners, knightliness, courtliness, nobility; bravery, courage, boldness, valour, heroism, daring, intrepidity.
– OPPOSITES rudeness.

milk or water with chocolate. **4** a deep brown colour.
– DERIVATIVES **chocolatey** (also **chocolaty**) adjective.
– ORIGIN Nahuatl.
chocolate-box ● **adjective** (of a view or picture) pretty in a trite, conventional way.
chocolatier /chokkəlattiər/ ● **noun** (pl. pronounced same) a maker or seller of chocolate.
– ORIGIN French.
Choctaw /choktaw/ ● **noun** (pl. same or **Choctaws**) a member of an American Indian people now living mainly in Mississippi.
– ORIGIN Choctaw.
choice ● **noun 1** an act of choosing. **2** the right or ability to choose. **3** a range from which to choose. **4** something chosen. ● **adjective 1** of very good quality. **2** (of language) rude and abusive.
– ORIGIN from Old French *chois*, from *choisir* 'choose'.
choir ● **noun 1** an organized group of singers, especially one that takes part in church services. **2** the part of a large church between the altar and the nave, used by the choir and clergy.
– ORIGIN Old French *quer*, from Latin *chorus* (see CHORUS).
choirboy (or **choirgirl**) ● **noun** a boy (or girl) who sings in a church or cathedral choir.
choisya /choyziə/ ● **noun** an evergreen shrub with sweet-scented white flowers.
– ORIGIN named after the Swiss botanist Jacques D. *Choisy* (1799–1859).
choke[1] ● **verb 1** prevent (someone) from breathing by constricting or obstructing the throat or depriving of air. **2** have trouble breathing. **3** (often **be choked with**) fill (a space) so as to hinder movement. **4** make speechless with strong emotion. ● **noun 1** a valve in the carburettor of a petrol engine used to reduce the amount of air in the fuel mixture. **2** an inductance coil used to smooth the variations of an alternating current or to alter its phase.
– ORIGIN Old English, related to CHEEK.
choke[2] ● **noun** the inedible mass of silky fibres at the centre of a globe artichoke.
– ORIGIN probably a confusion of the ending of *artichoke* with CHOKE[1].
choke-damp ● **noun** choking or suffocating gas found in mines and other underground spaces.
choker ● **noun 1** a close-fitting necklace or ornamental neckband. **2** a clerical or other high collar.
chokey ● **noun** Brit. informal, dated prison.
– ORIGIN Hindi, 'customs or toll house, police station'.
choko /chōkō/ ● **noun** (pl. **chokos**) Austral./NZ the fruit of the chayote, eaten as a vegetable.
– ORIGIN Spanish *chocho*.
choky ● **adjective 1** having or causing difficulty in breathing. **2** breathless with emotion.
cholecalciferol /kollikalsiffərol/ ● **noun** Biochemistry a form of vitamin D (vitamin D_3), produced naturally in the skin by the action of sunlight.
choler /kollər/ ● **noun 1** (in medieval science and medicine) one of the four bodily humours, identified with bile, believed to be associated with a peevish or irascible temperament. **2** archaic or literary anger or irascibility.
– ORIGIN Latin *cholera* from Greek *kholē* 'bile'.
cholera /kollərə/ ● **noun** an infectious disease of the small intestine, typically contracted from infected water and causing severe vomiting and diarrhoea.
– ORIGIN Latin, 'diarrhoea, bile'.
choleric /kollərik/ ● **adjective** bad-tempered or irritable.
cholesterol /kəlestərol/ ● **noun** a compound of the steroid type which occurs normally in most body tissues and is believed to promote atherosclerosis if present in high concentrations in the blood (e.g. as a result of a diet high in animal fat).
– ORIGIN from Greek *kholē* 'bile' + *stereos* 'stiff'.
chomp ● **verb** munch or chew noisily or vigorously.
– ORIGIN imitative.
chook /cho͝ok/ ● **noun** informal, chiefly Austral./NZ a chicken or fowl.
– ORIGIN probably from English dialect *chuck* 'chicken', of imitative origin.
choose ● **verb** (past **chose**; past part. **chosen**) **1** pick out as being the best of two or more alternatives. **2** decide on a course of action.
– DERIVATIVES **chooser** noun.
– ORIGIN Old English.
choosy ● **adjective** (**choosier**, **choosiest**) informal excessively fastidious in making a choice.
– DERIVATIVES **choosiness** noun.
chop[1] ● **verb** (**chopped**, **chopping**) **1** cut with repeated sharp, heavy blows of an axe or knife. **2** strike with a short, heavy blow. **3** ruthlessly abolish or reduce in size. ● **noun 1** a downward cutting blow or movement. **2** (**the chop**) Brit. informal dismissal, cancellation, or killing. **3** a thick slice of meat, especially pork or lamb, adjacent to and usually including a rib.
– PHRASES **chop logic** argue in a tiresomely pedantic way. [ORIGIN from a dialect use of *chop* meaning 'bandy words'.]
– ORIGIN variant of CHAP[1].
chop[2] ● **verb** (**chopped**, **chopping**) (in phrase **chop and change**) Brit. informal repeatedly change one's opinions or behaviour.
– ORIGIN originally in the sense 'barter, exchange', related to CHAPMAN.
chop-chop ● **adverb & exclamation** quickly.
– ORIGIN pidgin English, from Chinese dialect; related to CHOPSTICK.
chopper ● **noun 1** Brit. a short axe with a large blade. **2** (**choppers**) informal teeth. **3** informal a helicopter. **4** informal a type of motorcycle with high handlebars. **5** vulgar slang a man's penis.
choppy ● **adjective** (of the sea) having many small waves.
– DERIVATIVES **choppiness** noun.

Thesaurus

chivvy ● **verb** NAG, badger, hound, harass, harry, pester, keep on at, go on at; *informal* hassle, bug, breathe down someone's neck; *N. Amer. informal* ride.
choice ● **noun 1** *their choice of candidate | freedom of choice* SELECTION, election, choosing, picking; decision, say, vote. **2** *you have no other choice* OPTION, alternative, possible course of action. **3** *an extensive choice of wines* RANGE, variety, selection, assortment. **4** *the perfect choice* APPOINTEE, nominee, candidate, selection.
● **adjective 1** *choice plums* SUPERIOR, first-class, first-rate, prime, premier, grade A, best, finest, excellent, select, quality, high-quality, top, top-quality, high-grade, prize, fine, special; hand-picked, carefully chosen; *informal* tip-top, A1, top-notch. **2** *a few choice words* RUDE, abusive, insulting, offensive.
– OPPOSITES inferior.
choir ● **noun** SINGERS, chorus, chorale.
– RELATED TERMS choral.
choke ● **verb 1** *Christopher started to choke* GAG, retch, cough, fight for breath. **2** *thick dust choked her* SUFFOCATE, asphyxiate, smother, stifle. **3** *she had been choked to death* STRANGLE, throttle; asphyxiate, suffocate; *informal* strangulate. **4** *the guttering was choked with leaves* CLOG (UP), bung up, stop up, block, obstruct, plug; *technical* occlude.
– PHRASES **choke something back** SUPPRESS, hold back, fight back, bite back, swallow, check, restrain, control, repress, smother, stifle; *informal* keep a/the lid on.
choleric ● **adjective** BAD-TEMPERED, irascible, irritable, grumpy, grouchy, crotchety, tetchy, testy, crusty, cantankerous, curmudgeonly, ill-tempered, peevish, cross, fractious, crabbed, crabby, waspish, prickly, peppery, touchy, short-tempered; *informal* snappish, snappy, chippy, short-fused; *Brit. informal* shirty, stroppy, narky, ratty; *N. Amer. informal* cranky, ornery, soreheaded; *Austral./NZ informal* snaky.
– OPPOSITES good-natured, affable.
choose ● **verb 1** *we chose a quiet country hotel* SELECT, pick (out), opt for, plump for, settle on, decide on, fix on; appoint, name, nominate, vote for. **2** *I'll stay as long as I choose* WISH, want, desire, feel/be inclined, please, like, see fit.
choosy ● **adjective** (*informal*) FUSSY, finicky, fastidious, over-particular, difficult/hard to please, exacting, demanding; *informal* picky, pernickety; *N. Amer. informal* persnickety; *archaic* nice.
chop ● **verb 1** *chop the potatoes into pieces* CUT UP, cut into pieces, chop up, cube, dice; *N. Amer.* hash. **2** *chopping wood* CHOP UP, cut up, cut into pieces, hew, split. **3** *four fingers were chopped off* SEVER, cut off, hack off, slice off, lop off, saw off, shear off. **4** *they chopped down large areas of rainforest* CUT DOWN, fell, hack down. **5** (*informal*) *their training courses were chopped* REDUCE DRASTICALLY, cut; abolish, axe, scrap; *informal* slash.
– PHRASES **the chop** (*Brit. informal*) NOTICE; *informal* the sack, the boot, the elbow, the push, one's marching orders; *Brit. informal* one's cards.

C

chops • plural noun informal **1** a person's or animal's mouth, jaws, or cheeks. **2** the technical skill of a jazz or rock musician.
– ORIGIN of unknown origin.
chopstick • noun each of a pair of small, thin, tapered sticks held in one hand and used as eating utensils by the Chinese and Japanese.
– ORIGIN pidgin English, from a Chinese dialect word meaning 'nimble ones'.
chop suey /chop sōōi/ • noun a Chinese-style dish of meat with bean sprouts, bamboo shoots, and onions.
– ORIGIN Chinese, 'mixed bits'.
choral • adjective of, for, or sung by a choir or chorus.
– DERIVATIVES **chorally** adverb.
chorale • noun **1** a simple, stately hymn tune, or a composition consisting of a harmonized version of one. **2** chiefly US a choir or choral society.
– ORIGIN from Latin *cantus choralis*.
chord[1] • noun a group of three or more notes sounded together in harmony.
– DERIVATIVES **chordal** adjective.
– ORIGIN from ACCORD; the spelling was influenced by CHORD[2].
chord[2] • noun **1** a straight line joining the ends of an arc. **2** the width of an aircraft's wing from leading to trailing edge. **3** Engineering each of the two principal members of a truss. **4** Anatomy variant spelling of CORD.
– PHRASES **strike** (or **touch**) **a chord** affect or stir someone's emotions.
– ORIGIN a later spelling (influenced by Latin *chorda* 'rope') of CORD.
chordate /kordayt/ • noun Zoology an animal of a large group (the phylum Chordata) which includes all the vertebrates together with the sea squirts and lancelets (which possess a notochord).
– ORIGIN from Latin *chorda* 'rope', on the pattern of words such as *vertebrate*.
chore • noun a routine or tedious task, especially a household one.
– ORIGIN variant of obsolete *char* or *chare* (see CHARWOMAN).
chorea /koreeə/ • noun a neurological disorder characterized by jerky involuntary movements.
– ORIGIN Greek *khoreia* 'dancing in unison'.
choreograph /korriəgraaf/ • verb compose the sequence of steps and moves for (a dance performance).
– DERIVATIVES **choreographer** noun.
choreography /korriografi/ • noun **1** the sequence of steps and movements in dance. **2** the practice of designing such sequences.
– DERIVATIVES **choreographic** adjective **choreographically** adverb.
– ORIGIN from Greek *khoreia* 'dancing in unison', from *khoros* 'chorus'.
chorine /koreen/ • noun a chorus girl.
chorion /koriən/ • noun the outermost membrane surrounding an embryo.
– ORIGIN Greek *khorion*.
chorister • noun **1** a member of a choir, especially a choirboy or choirgirl. **2** US a person who leads the singing of a church choir or congregation.
– ORIGIN Old French *cueriste*, from *quer* (see CHOIR).
chorizo /chəreezō/ • noun (pl. **chorizos**) a spicy Spanish pork sausage.
– ORIGIN Spanish.
chortle • verb laugh in a breathy, gleeful way. • noun a breathy, gleeful laugh.
– ORIGIN coined by Lewis Carroll in *Through the Looking Glass*; probably a blend of CHUCKLE and SNORT.
chorus • noun (pl. **choruses**) **1** a part of a song which is repeated after each verse. **2** something said at the same time by many people. **3** a large group of singers, especially one performing with an orchestra. **4** a piece of choral music, especially one forming part of an opera or oratorio. **5** (in ancient Greek tragedy) a group of performers who comment on the main action. • verb (**chorused**, **chorusing**) (of a group of people) say the same thing at the same time.
– ORIGIN Latin, from Greek *khoros*.
chorus girl • noun a young woman who sings or dances in the chorus of a musical.
chose past of CHOOSE.
chosen past participle of CHOOSE.
choucroute /shōōkrōōt/ • noun sauerkraut.
– ORIGIN French, from German dialect *Surkrut*.
chough /chuf/ • noun a black bird of the crow family with a red or yellow downcurved bill.
– ORIGIN probably from the sound of the bird's call.
choux pastry /shōō/ • noun very light pastry made with egg, used for eclairs and profiteroles.
– ORIGIN French, from *chou* 'cabbage, rosette'.
chow /chow/ • noun **1** informal, chiefly N. Amer. food. **2** (also **chow chow**) a Chinese breed of dog with a tail curled over its back, a bluish-black tongue, and a thick coat. • verb (**chow down**) N. Amer. informal eat.
– ORIGIN shortened from *chow chow*, a pidgin English word originally meaning 'mixed pickle'.
chowder • noun a rich soup containing fish, clams, or corn with potatoes and onions.
– ORIGIN perhaps from French *chaudière* 'stew pot', related to CAULDRON.
chow mein /chow mayn/ • noun a Chinese-style dish of fried noodles with shredded meat or seafood and vegetables.
– ORIGIN Chinese, 'stir-fried noodles'.
chrism /krizz'm/ • noun a consecrated oil used for anointing in the Catholic, Orthodox, and Anglican Churches.
– ORIGIN Greek *khrisma* 'anointing'.
Christ • noun the title given to Jesus. • exclamation used to express irritation, dismay, or surprise.
– DERIVATIVES **Christlike** adjective **Christly** adjective.
– ORIGIN Greek *Khristos* 'anointed one', translating a Hebrew word meaning 'Messiah'.
Christadelphian /kristədelfiən/ • noun a member of a Christian sect claiming to return to the beliefs and practices of the earliest disciples and expecting a second coming of Christ. • adjective relating to this sect.
– ORIGIN from Greek *Khristos* 'Christ' + *adelphos* 'brother'.
christen • verb **1** name (a baby) at baptism as a sign of admission to a Christian Church. **2** informal use for the first time.
– DERIVATIVES **christening** noun.
– ORIGIN Old English 'make Christian', from Latin *Christus* 'Christ'.
Christendom • noun dated the worldwide body of Christians.
Christian • adjective relating to or professing Christianity or its teachings. • noun a person who has received Christian baptism or is a believer in Christianity.
– DERIVATIVES **Christianize** (also **Christianise**) verb.
– ORIGIN Latin *Christianus*, from *Christus* 'Christ'.
Christian era • noun the era beginning with the traditional date of Christ's birth.
Christianity • noun the religion based on the person and teachings of Jesus Christ.
Christian name • noun a forename, especially one given at baptism.
Christian Science • noun the beliefs and practices of the Church of Christ Scientist, a Christian sect.
– DERIVATIVES **Christian Scientist** noun.
Christingle /kristingg'l/ • noun a lighted candle symbolizing Christ, held by children especially at Advent services.
– ORIGIN probably from German dialect *Christkindl* 'Christ-child, Christmas gift'.
Christmas • noun (pl. **Christmases**) **1** (also **Christmas Day**) the annual Christian festival celebrating Christ's birth, held on 25 December. **2** the period immediately before and after this.
– ORIGIN Old English, 'Mass of Christ'.

Thesaurus

chopper • noun *(Brit.)* AXE, cleaver, hatchet.
choppy • adjective ROUGH, turbulent, heavy, heaving, stormy, tempestuous, squally.
– OPPOSITES calm.
chore • noun TASK, job, duty, errand; (domestic) work.
chortle • verb CHUCKLE, laugh, giggle, titter, tee-hee, snigger.
chorus • noun **1** *the chorus sang powerfully* CHOIR, ensemble, choral group, choristers, (group of) singers. **2** *they sang the chorus* REFRAIN.
– PHRASES **in chorus** IN UNISON, together, simultaneously, as one; in concert, in harmony.
Christ • noun JESUS (CHRIST), the Messiah, the Son of God, the Lamb of God, the Prince of Peace, the Nazarene, the Galilean.
christen • verb **1** *she was christened Sara* BAPTIZE, name, give the

Christmas box ● noun Brit. a present given at Christmas to tradespeople and employees.

Christmas cake ● noun Brit. a rich fruit cake covered with marzipan and icing, eaten at Christmas.

Christmas pudding ● noun Brit. a rich pudding eaten at Christmas, made with flour, suet, and dried fruit.

Christmas rose ● noun a small white-flowered winter-blooming hellebore.

Christmas tree ● noun an evergreen tree decorated with lights and ornaments at Christmas.

chromate /krōmayt/ ● noun Chemistry a salt in which the anion contains both chromium and oxygen.

chromatic ● adjective **1** Music relating to or using notes not belonging to the diatonic scale of the key of a passage. **2** (of a scale) ascending or descending by semitones. **3** relating to or produced by colour.
– ORIGIN Greek *khrōmatikos*, from *khrōma* 'colour, chromatic scale'.

chromatid /krōmətid/ ● noun Biology each of the two thread-like strands into which a chromosome divides during cell division.

chromatin /krōmətin/ ● noun Biology the material of which non-bacterial chromosomes are composed, consisting of DNA or RNA and proteins.

chromatography ● noun Chemistry a technique for the separation of a mixture by passing it through a medium in which the components move at different rates.
– DERIVATIVES **chromatogram** noun **chromatograph** noun **chromatographic** adjective.
– ORIGIN from Greek *khrōma* 'colour' (early separations being displayed as coloured bands or spots).

chrome ● noun **1** chromium plate as a finish. **2** (before another noun) denoting compounds or alloys of chromium: *chrome steel.*
– DERIVATIVES **chromed** adjective.
– ORIGIN Greek *khrōma* 'colour' (some chromium compounds having brilliant colours).

chrome yellow ● noun a bright yellow pigment made from lead chromate.

chromite ● noun the main ore of chromium, a brownish-black oxide of chromium and iron.

chromium ● noun a hard white metallic chemical element used in stainless steel and other alloys.

chromosome ● noun Biology a thread-like structure found in the nuclei of most living cells, carrying genetic information in the form of genes.
– DERIVATIVES **chromosomal** adjective.
– ORIGIN from Greek *khrōma* 'colour' + *sōma* 'body'.

chromosphere ● noun Astronomy a reddish gaseous layer immediately above the photosphere of the sun or another star.
– DERIVATIVES **chromospheric** adjective.

chronic ● adjective **1** (of an illness or problem) persisting for a long time. **2** having a persistent illness or bad habit. **3** Brit. informal very bad.
– DERIVATIVES **chronically** adverb **chronicity** noun.
– ORIGIN Greek *khronikos* 'of time', from *khronos* 'time'.

chronic fatigue syndrome ● noun a medical condition of unknown cause, with fever, aching, and prolonged tiredness and depression.

chronicle ● noun a written account of historical events in the order of their occurrence. ● verb record (a series of events) in a detailed way.
– DERIVATIVES **chronicler** noun.
– ORIGIN Greek *khronika* 'annals', from *khronikos* 'of time'.

chronograph ● noun an instrument for recording time with great accuracy.

chronological ● adjective **1** relating to the establishment of dates and time sequences. **2** (of a record of events) starting with the earliest and following the order in which they occurred.
– DERIVATIVES **chronologically** adverb.

chronology /krənolləji/ ● noun (pl. **chronologies**) **1** the study of records to establish the dates of past events. **2** the arrangement of events or dates in the order of their occurrence.
– DERIVATIVES **chronologist** noun.
– ORIGIN from Greek *khronos* 'time'.

chronometer /krənommitər/ ● noun an instrument for measuring time accurately in spite of motion or varying conditions.

chronometry ● noun the science of accurate time measurement.
– DERIVATIVES **chronometric** adjective.

chrysalis /krissəliss/ ● noun (pl. **chrysalises**) **1** an insect pupa, especially of a butterfly or moth. **2** the hard outer case enclosing this.
– ORIGIN Greek *khrusallis*, from *khrusos* 'gold' (because of the metallic sheen of some pupae).

chrysanthemum /krizanthiməm/ ● noun (pl. **chrysanthemums**) a garden plant with brightly coloured flowers.
– ORIGIN from Greek *khrusos* 'gold' + *anthemon* 'flower'.

chthonic /kthonnik/ (also **chthonian** /kthōniən/) ● adjective relating to or inhabiting the underworld.
– ORIGIN from Greek *khthōn* 'earth'.

chub ● noun a thick-bodied river fish with a grey-green back and white underparts.
– ORIGIN of unknown origin.

Chubb ● noun trademark a lock with a device for fixing the bolt to prevent it from being picked.
– ORIGIN named after the London locksmith Charles *Chubb* (1773–1845).

chubby ● adjective (**chubbier**, **chubbiest**) plump and rounded.
– DERIVATIVES **chubbily** adverb **chubbiness** noun.
– ORIGIN from CHUB.

chuck[1] ● verb informal **1** throw (something) carelessly or casually. **2** give up. **3** (**chuck up**) vomit.
– PHRASES **chuck it down** rain heavily.
– DERIVATIVES **chucker** noun.
– ORIGIN from CHUCK[2].

chuck[2] ● verb touch playfully under the chin. ● noun a playful touch under the chin.
– ORIGIN probably from Old French *chuquer* 'to knock, bump'.

chuck[3] ● noun **1** a device for holding a workpiece in a lathe or a tool in a drill. **2** a cut of beef extending from the neck to the ribs.
– ORIGIN a variant of CHOCK.

chuck[4] ● noun N. English used as a familiar form of address.
– ORIGIN alteration of CHICK.

chuckle ● verb laugh quietly or inwardly. ● noun a quiet laugh.
– ORIGIN from obsolete *chuck* 'to cluck'.

chucklehead ● noun informal a stupid person.
– ORIGIN from obsolete *chuckle* 'big and clumsy'.

chuddies /chudeez/ (also **chuddis** /chudiss/) ● plural noun Indian underpants.
– ORIGIN perhaps an alteration of CHADOR.

chuff ● verb (of a steam engine) move with a regular puffing

Thesaurus

name of, call. **2** *a group who were christened 'The Magic Circle'* CALL, name, dub, style, term, designate, label, nickname, give the name of; *formal* denominate.

Christmas ● noun NOEL; *informal* Xmas; *Brit. informal* Chrimbo, Chrissie; *archaic* Yule, Yuletide.

chronic ● adjective **1** *a chronic illness* PERSISTENT, long-standing, long-term; incurable. **2** *chronic economic problems* CONSTANT, continuing, ceaseless, unabating, unending, persistent, long-lasting; severe, serious, acute, grave, dire. **3** *a chronic liar* INVETERATE, hardened, dyed-in-the-wool, incorrigible; compulsive; *informal* pathological. **4** *(Brit. informal) the film was chronic.* See SUBSTANDARD.
– OPPOSITES acute, temporary.

chronicle ● noun *a chronicle of the region's past* RECORD, written account, history, annals, archive(s); log, diary, journal.
● verb *the events that followed have been chronicled* RECORD, put on record, write down, set down, document, register, report.

chronicler ● noun ANNALIST, historian, archivist, diarist, recorder, reporter.

chronological ● adjective SEQUENTIAL, consecutive, in sequence, in order (of time).

chubby ● adjective PLUMP, tubby, fat, rotund, portly, dumpy, chunky, well upholstered, well covered, well rounded; *informal* roly-poly, pudgy, blubbery; *Brit. informal* podgy; *N. Amer. informal* zaftig, corn-fed; *archaic* pursy.
– OPPOSITES skinny.

chuck ● verb *(informal)* **1** *he chucked the letter onto the table* THROW, toss, fling, hurl, pitch, cast, lob; *informal* sling, bung, buzz; *Austral. informal* hoy; *NZ informal* bish. **2** *I chucked the rubbish* THROW AWAY/OUT, discard, dispose of, get rid of, dump, bin, scrap, jettison; *informal* ditch, junk; *N. Amer. informal* trash. **3** *I've chucked my job* GIVE UP, leave, resign from; *informal* quit, pack in; *Brit. informal* jack in. **4** *Mary chucked him for another guy* LEAVE, throw over, finish

sound.
– ORIGIN imitative.
chuffed • adjective Brit. informal delighted.
– ORIGIN from dialect *chuff* 'plump or pleased'.
chug • verb (**chugged**, **chugging**) move with or give out a series of muffled explosive sounds, as of an engine running slowly. • noun a sound of this type.
– ORIGIN imitative.
chukka • noun each of a number of periods (typically six) into which play in a game of polo is divided.
– ORIGIN Sanskrit, 'circle or wheel'.
chum informal • noun a close friend. • verb (**chummed**, **chumming**) (**chum up**) form a friendship with someone.
– DERIVATIVES **chummy** adjective.
– ORIGIN originally Oxford University slang for a room-mate: probably short for *chamber-fellow*; compare with CRONY.
chump • noun **1** informal, dated a foolish person. **2** Brit. the thick end of something, especially a loin of lamb or mutton.
– ORIGIN originally in the sense 'thick lump of wood': probably a blend of CHUNK[1] and LUMP[1] or STUMP.
chunder informal, chiefly Austral./NZ • verb vomit. • noun vomit.
– ORIGIN probably from rhyming slang *Chunder Loo* 'spew', from the name of a cartoon character.
chunk[1] • noun **1** a thick, solid piece. **2** a large amount.
– ORIGIN apparently an alteration of CHUCK[3].
chunk[2] • verb make a muffled, metallic sound.
– ORIGIN imitative.
chunky • adjective (**chunkier**, **chunkiest**) **1** (of a person) short and sturdy. **2** containing chunks.
– DERIVATIVES **chunkily** adverb **chunkiness** noun.
chunter • verb Brit. informal **1** chatter or grumble monotonously. **2** move slowly and noisily.
– ORIGIN probably imitative.
church • noun **1** a building used for public Christian worship. **2** (**Church**) a particular Christian organization with its own distinctive doctrines. **3** institutionalized religion as a political or social force.
– ORIGIN from Greek *kuriakon dōma* 'Lord's house', from *kurios* 'master or lord'.
churchman (or **churchwoman**) • noun a member of the Christian clergy or of a Church.
Church of England • noun the English branch of the Western Christian Church, which rejects the Pope's authority and has the monarch as its head.
Church of Scotland • noun the national (Presbyterian) Christian Church in Scotland.
churchwarden • noun either of two elected lay representatives in an Anglican parish.
churchy • adjective **1** excessively pious. **2** resembling or appropriate to a church.
churchyard • noun an enclosed area surrounding a church, especially as used for burials.
churinga /churinggə/ • noun (pl. same or **churingas**) (among Australian Aboriginals) a sacred amulet or other object.
– ORIGIN from an Aboriginal word meaning 'object from the dreaming'.
churl • noun **1** an impolite and mean-spirited person. **2** archaic a peasant.
– ORIGIN Old English.
churlish • adjective rude, mean-spirited, and surly.
– DERIVATIVES **churlishly** adverb **churlishness** noun.
churn • noun **1** a machine for making butter by agitating milk or cream. **2** Brit. a large metal milk can. • verb **1** agitate (milk or cream) in a churn to produce butter. **2** (with reference to liquid) move about vigorously. **3** (**churn out**) produce mechanically and in large quantities. **4** (as adj. **churned up**) upset or nervous.
– ORIGIN Old English.
chute[1] (also **shoot**) • noun **1** a sloping channel for conveying things to a lower level. **2** a water slide into a swimming pool.
– ORIGIN French, 'fall' (of water or rocks).
chute[2] • noun informal a parachute.
chutney • noun (pl. **chutneys**) a spicy condiment made of fruits or vegetables with vinegar, spices, and sugar.
– ORIGIN Hindi.
chutzpah /khootspə/ • noun informal shameless audacity.
– ORIGIN Yiddish.
chyle /kīl/ • noun Physiology a milky fluid which drains from the small intestine into the lymphatic system during digestion.
– DERIVATIVES **chylous** adjective.
– ORIGIN Greek *khūlos* 'juice'.
chyme /kīm/ • noun Physiology the fluid which passes from the stomach to the small intestine, consisting of gastric juices and partly digested food.
– ORIGIN Greek *khūmos* 'juice'.
Ci • abbreviation curie.
CIA • abbreviation Central Intelligence Agency.
ciabatta /chəbaatə/ • noun a flattish Italian bread made with olive oil.
– ORIGIN Italian, 'slipper' (from its shape).
ciao /chow/ • exclamation informal used as a greeting at meeting or parting.
– ORIGIN Italian, from dialect *schiavo* 'I am your slave'.
cicada /sikaadə/ • noun a large bug with long transparent wings, which makes a shrill droning noise after dark.
– ORIGIN Latin.
cicatrix /sikkətriks/ (also **cicatrice** /sikkətriss/) • noun (pl. **cicatrices** /sikkətrīseez/) **1** a scar. **2** Botany a mark on a stem left after a leaf or other part has become detached.
– DERIVATIVES **cicatricial** /sikkətrish'l/ adjective.
– ORIGIN Latin.
cicatrize /sikkətrīz/ (also **cicatrise**) • verb heal by scar formation.
cicely /sissəli/ (also **sweet cicely**) • noun (pl. **cicelies**) an aromatic white-flowered plant with fern-like leaves.
– ORIGIN Greek *seselis*.
cicerone /chichərōni, sissə-/ • noun (pl. **ciceroni** pronunc. same) a guide who gives information to sightseers.
– ORIGIN Italian, from the name of the Roman writer *Cicero* (106–43 BC), apparently alluding to the guides' learning.
cichlid /siklid/ • noun Zoology a perch-like freshwater fish.
– ORIGIN Greek *kikhlē*.
CID • abbreviation (in the UK) Criminal Investigation Department.
-cide • combining form **1** denoting a person or substance that kills: *insecticide*. **2** denoting an act of killing: *suicide*.
– ORIGIN from Latin *-cida*, *-cidium*, from *caedere* 'to kill'.
cider • noun Brit. an alcoholic drink made from fermented apple juice.

Thesaurus

with, break off with, jilt; *informal* dump, ditch, give someone the elbow; *Brit. informal* give someone the push, give someone the big E.
chuckle • verb CHORTLE, giggle, titter, tee-hee, snicker, snigger.
chum • noun *(informal)* FRIEND, companion, intimate; playmate, classmate, schoolmate, workmate; *informal* pal, spar, crony; *Brit. informal* mate, oppo, china, mucker; *N. Amer. informal* buddy, amigo, compadre, homeboy.
– OPPOSITES enemy, stranger.
chummy • adjective *(informal)* FRIENDLY, on good terms, close, familiar, intimate; *informal* thick, matey, pally, buddy-buddy, palsy-walsy.
chunk • noun LUMP, hunk, wedge, block, slab, square, nugget, brick, cube, bar, cake; *informal* wodge; *N. Amer. informal* gob.
chunky • adjective **1** *a chunky young man* STOCKY, sturdy, thickset, heavily built, well built, burly, bulky, brawny, solid, heavy; *Austral./NZ* nuggety; *Brit. informal* fubsy. **2** *a chunky sweater* THICK, bulky, heavy-knit.
– OPPOSITES slight, light.
church • noun **1** *a village church* PLACE OF WORSHIP, house of God; cathedral, minster, abbey, chapel, basilica; *Scottish & N. English* kirk. **2** *the Methodist Church* DENOMINATION, sect, creed; faith.
– RELATED TERMS ecclesiastical.
churchyard • noun GRAVEYARD, cemetery, necropolis, burial ground, garden of remembrance; *Scottish* kirkyard; *N. Amer.* memorial park; *archaic* God's acre.
churlish • adjective RUDE, ill-mannered, ill-bred, discourteous, impolite, unmannerly, uncivil, ungentlemanly, unchivalrous; inconsiderate, uncharitable, mean-spirited, ungracious, surly, sullen; *informal* ignorant.
– OPPOSITES polite.
churn • verb **1** *village girls churned the milk* STIR, agitate, beat, whip, whisk. **2** *the sea churned* HEAVE, boil, swirl, toss, seethe; *poetic/literary* roil. **3** *the propellers churned up the water* DISTURB, stir up, agitate; *poetic/literary* roil.
– PHRASES **churn something out** PRODUCE, make, turn out; *informal* crank out, bang out.

– ORIGIN Old French *sidre*, from a Hebrew word meaning 'strong drink'.
ci-devant /seedəvON/ ● adjective former.
– ORIGIN French, 'heretofore'.
cigar ● noun a cylinder of tobacco rolled in tobacco leaves for smoking.
– ORIGIN French *cigare*, probably from a Mayan word meaning 'smoking'.
cigarette (US also **cigaret**) ● noun a cylinder of finely cut tobacco rolled in paper for smoking.
– ORIGIN French, 'little cigar'.
cigarette card ● noun Brit. a collectable card with a picture on it, formerly included in packets of cigarettes.
cigarette paper ● noun a thin paper for rolling around tobacco to make a cigarette.
cigarillo /siggərillō/ ● noun (pl. **cigarillos**) a small cigar.
– ORIGIN Spanish, 'little cigar'.
ciliary /silliəri/ ● adjective **1** Biology relating to or involving cilia. **2** Anatomy relating to the eyelashes or eyelids.
cilium /silliəm/ ● noun (pl. **cilia** /silliə/) **1** Biology a microscopic hair-like vibrating structure, occurring on the surface of certain cells. **2** Anatomy an eyelash.
– ORIGIN Latin.
cill ● noun chiefly Building variant spelling of SILL.
cimbalom /simbələm/ ● noun a large Hungarian dulcimer.
– ORIGIN Hungarian, from Latin *cymbalum* 'cymbal'.
C.-in-C. ● abbreviation Commander-in-Chief.
cinch ● noun informal **1** an extremely easy task. **2** a certainty.
– ORIGIN from Spanish *cincha* 'girth'.
cinchona /singkōnə/ ● noun a medicinal drug obtained from the bark of a South American tree, containing quinine and related compounds.
– ORIGIN named after the Countess of *Chinchón* (died 1641), who brought the drug to Spain.
cinder ● noun a piece of burnt coal or wood that has stopped giving off flames but still has combustible matter in it.
– DERIVATIVES **cindery** adjective.
– ORIGIN Old English.
cine ● adjective cinematographic.
cineaste /sinniast/ ● noun an enthusiast of the cinema.
– ORIGIN French.
cinema ● noun chiefly Brit. **1** a theatre where films are shown. **2** the production of films as an art or industry.
– ORIGIN Greek *kinēma* 'movement', from *kinein* 'to move'.
cinematic ● adjective relating to or characteristic of the cinema.
– DERIVATIVES **cinematically** adverb.
cinematograph ● noun historical, chiefly Brit. an apparatus for showing films.
cinematography ● noun the art of photography and camerawork in film-making.
– DERIVATIVES **cinematographer** noun **cinematographic** adjective.
cinéma-vérité /sinimə verritay/ ● noun a style of film-making characterized by realistic films avoiding artistic effect.
– ORIGIN French, 'cinema truth'.
cinephile ● noun an enthusiast of the cinema.
cineraria /sinnərairiə/ ● noun a winter-flowering plant of the daisy family.
– ORIGIN from Latin *cinerarius* 'of ashes' (because of the ash-coloured down on the leaves).
cinerary urn /sinnərəri/ ● noun an urn for holding a person's ashes after cremation.
– ORIGIN from Latin *cinerarius* 'of ashes'.
cingulum /singyooləm/ ● noun (pl. **cingula** /singyoolə/) Anatomy **1** a curved bundle of nerve fibres in the brain. **2** a ridge of enamel on the crown of a tooth.
– DERIVATIVES **cingulate** adjective.
– ORIGIN Latin, 'belt'.
cinnabar /sinnəbaar/ ● noun **1** a bright red mineral consisting of mercury sulphide. **2** (also **cinnabar moth**) a day-flying moth with black and red wings.
– ORIGIN Greek *kinnabari*.
cinnamon ● noun **1** an aromatic spice made from the dried and rolled bark of an Asian tree. **2** a yellowish-brown colour resembling cinnamon.
– ORIGIN Greek *kinnamōmon*.
cinquecento /chingkwichentō/ ● noun the 16th century as a period of Italian art and literature.
– ORIGIN Italian, 'five hundred'.
cinquefoil /singkfoyl/ ● noun **1** a plant with compound leaves of five leaflets and five-petalled yellow flowers. **2** Art an ornamental design of five lobes arranged in a circle.
– ORIGIN from Latin *quinque* 'five' + *folium* 'leaf'.
cipher (also **cypher**) ● noun **1** a code. **2** a key to a code. **3** an unimportant person or thing. **4** dated a zero. ● verb encode (a message).
– ORIGIN Old French *cifre*, from Arabic.
circa /surkə/ ● preposition approximately.
– ORIGIN Latin.
circadian /surkaydiən/ ● adjective (of biological processes) recurring on a twenty-four-hour cycle.
– ORIGIN from Latin *circa* 'about' + *dies* 'day'.
circle ● noun **1** a round plane figure whose boundary consists of points equidistant from the centre. **2** a group of people or things forming a circle. **3** a curved upper tier of seats in a theatre. **4** a group of people with a shared profession, interests, or acquaintances. ● verb **1** move or be situated all the way around. **2** draw a line around.
– PHRASES **come** (or **turn**) **full circle** return to a previous position or situation. **go** (or **run**) **round in circles** informal do something for a long time without achieving anything.
– ORIGIN Latin *circulus* 'small ring', from *circus* 'ring'.
circlet ● noun an ornamental circular band worn on the head.
circlip ● noun Brit. a metal ring sprung into a slot to hold something in place.
– ORIGIN blend of CIRCLE or CIRCULAR and CLIP[1].
circuit ● noun **1** a roughly circular line, route, or movement. **2** Brit. a track used for motor racing. **3** a system of conductors and components forming a complete path for an electric current. **4** an established series of sporting events or entertainments. **5** a series of physical exercises performed in one training session. **6** a regular journey by a judge around a district to hear court cases. ● verb move all the way around.
– ORIGIN Latin *circuitus*, from *circumire* 'go round'.
circuit-breaker ● noun an automatic safety device for stopping the flow of current in an electric circuit.
circuitous /surkyōōitəss/ ● adjective (of a route) longer than the most direct way.
– DERIVATIVES **circuitously** adverb **circuitousness** noun.

C

Thesaurus

chute ● noun **1** *a refuse chute* CHANNEL, slide, shaft, funnel, conduit. **2** *water chutes* (WATER) SLIDE, flume.
cigarette ● noun filter tip, king-size; *informal* ciggy, cig, smoke, cancer stick, coffin nail; *Brit. informal* fag, snout, roll-up.
cinch ● noun *(informal)* **1** *it's a cinch* EASY TASK, child's play, five-finger exercise, gift, walkover; *informal* doddle, piece of cake, picnic, breeze, kids' stuff, cakewalk, pushover; *Brit. informal* doss; *N. Amer. informal* duck soup, snap; *Austral./NZ informal* bludge, snack; *dated* snip. **2** *he was a cinch to take a prize* CERTAINTY, sure thing; *Brit. informal* (dead) cert.
– OPPOSITES challenge.
cinders ● plural noun ASHES, ash, embers.
cinema ● noun **1** *the local cinema* multiplex, cinematheque; *N. Amer.* movie theatre/house; *dated* picture palace/theatre; *historical* nickelodeon. **2** *I hardly ever go to the cinema* THE PICTURES, the movies; *informal* the flicks. **3** *British cinema* FILMS, movies, pictures, motion pictures.
cipher ● noun **1** *information in cipher* CODE, secret writing; cryptograph. **2** *working as a cipher* NOBODY, nonentity, unimportant person. **3** *(dated) a row of ciphers* ZERO, nought, nil, 0.
circa ● preposition APPROXIMATELY, (round) about, around, in the region of, roughly, something like, of the order of, or so, or thereabouts, more or less; *informal* as near as dammit; *N. Amer. informal* in the ballpark of.
– OPPOSITES exactly.
circle ● noun **1** *a circle of gold stars* RING, band, hoop, circlet; halo, disc; *technical* annulus. **2** *her circle of friends* GROUP, set, company, coterie, clique; crowd, band; *informal* gang, bunch, crew. **3** *illustrious circles* SPHERE, world, milieu; society.
● verb **1** *seagulls circled above* WHEEL, move round, revolve, rotate, whirl, spiral. **2** *satellites circling the earth* GO ROUND, travel round, circumnavigate; orbit, revolve round. **3** *the abbey was circled by a wall* SURROUND, encircle, ring, enclose, encompass; *poetic/literary* gird.
circuit ● noun **1** *two circuits of the village green* LAP, turn, round, circle. **2** *(Brit.) a racing circuit* TRACK, racetrack, running track,

circuitry ● noun (pl. **circuitries**) electric circuits collectively.

circular ● adjective **1** having the form of a circle. **2** Logic (of an argument) false because already containing an assumption of what is to be proved. **3** (of a letter or advertisement) for distribution to a large number of people. ● noun a circular letter or advertisement.
– DERIVATIVES **circularity** noun **circularly** adverb.

circularize (also **circularise**) ● verb distribute a large number of letters, leaflets, etc. to.

circular saw ● noun a power saw with a rapidly rotating toothed disc.

circulate ● verb **1** move continuously through a closed system or area. **2** pass from place to place or person to person. **3** move around a social function and talk to many people.
– DERIVATIVES **circulator** noun.

circulating library ● noun historical a small library with books lent for a fee.

circulation ● noun **1** movement to and fro or around something. **2** the continuous motion of blood round the body. **3** the public availability of something. **4** the number of copies sold of a newspaper or magazine.
– DERIVATIVES **circulatory** adjective.

circum- ● prefix about; around: *circumambulate.*
– ORIGIN from Latin *circum* 'round'.

circumambient /surkəmambiənt/ ● adjective chiefly literary surrounding.

circumambulate /surkəmambyoolayt/ ● verb formal walk all the way round.
– DERIVATIVES **circumambulation** noun.

circumcircle ● noun Geometry a circle touching all the vertices of a triangle or polygon.

circumcise ● verb **1** cut off the foreskin of (a young boy or man) as a Jewish or Islamic rite. **2** cut off the clitoris, and sometimes the labia, of (a girl or young woman).
– DERIVATIVES **circumcision** noun.
– ORIGIN Latin *circumcidere* 'cut around'.

circumference ● noun **1** the enclosing boundary of a circle. **2** the distance around something.
– DERIVATIVES **circumferential** adjective.
– ORIGIN Latin *circumferentia*, from *circum* 'around' + *ferre* 'carry'.

circumflex ● noun a mark (ˆ) placed over a vowel in some languages to indicate contraction, length, or another quality.
– ORIGIN Latin *circumflexus*, from *circum* 'around' + *flectere* 'to bend'.

circumlocution /surkəmləkyo͞osh'n/ ● noun the use of many words where fewer would do.
– DERIVATIVES **circumlocutory** adjective.
– ORIGIN Latin, from *circum* 'around' + *loqui* 'speak'.

circumnavigate ● verb sail all the way around.
– DERIVATIVES **circumnavigation** noun.

circumpolar ● adjective **1** situated or occurring around one of the earth's poles. **2** Astronomy (of a star) above the horizon at all times in a given latitude.

circumscribe ● verb **1** restrict; limit. **2** Geometry draw (a figure) round another, touching it at points but not cutting it.
– DERIVATIVES **circumscription** noun.
– ORIGIN Latin *circumscribere*, from *circum* 'around' + *scribere* 'write'.

circumspect ● adjective cautious or prudent.
– DERIVATIVES **circumspection** noun **circumspectly** adverb.
– ORIGIN Latin *circumspectus*, from *circumspicere* 'look around'.

circumstance ● noun **1** a fact or condition connected with an event or action. **2** unforeseen events outside one's control: *a victim of circumstance.* **3** (**circumstances**) one's state of financial or material welfare.
– PHRASES **under** (or **in**) **the circumstances** given the difficult nature of the situation. **under** (or **in**) **no circumstances** never.
– ORIGIN Latin *circumstantia*, from *circumstare* 'encircle, encompass'.

circumstantial ● adjective **1** (of evidence) consisting of facts that strongly suggest something, but do not provide conclusive proof. **2** containing full details.
– DERIVATIVES **circumstantiality** noun **circumstantially** adverb.

circumvent /surkəmvent/ ● verb find a way around (an obstacle).
– DERIVATIVES **circumvention** noun.
– ORIGIN Latin *circumvenire* 'skirt around'.

circus ● noun (pl. **circuses**) **1** a travelling company of acrobats, trained animals, and clowns. **2** (in ancient Rome) a rounded sporting arena lined with seats. **3** informal a scene of frantic activity: *a media circus.*
– ORIGIN Latin, 'ring or circus'.

cirque /surk/ ● noun Geology a steep-sided hollow at the head of a valley or on a mountainside.
– ORIGIN French, from Latin *circus.*

cirrhosis /sirōsiss/ ● noun a chronic liver disease marked by degeneration of cells and thickening of tissue.
– DERIVATIVES **cirrhotic** adjective.
– ORIGIN from Greek *kirrhos* 'tawny' (the colour of the liver in many cases).

cirrocumulus /sirrōkyo͞omyooləss/ ● noun cloud forming a broken layer of small fleecy clouds at high altitude.

cirrostratus /sirrōstraatəss/ ● noun cloud forming a thin, uniform semi-translucent layer at high altitude.

cirrus /sirrəss/ ● noun (pl. **cirri** /sirrī/) **1** cloud forming wispy streaks at high altitude. **2** Zoology & Botany a slender tendril or hair-like filament.
– ORIGIN Latin, 'a curl'.

CIS ● abbreviation Commonwealth of Independent States.

cisalpine /sisalpīn/ ● adjective on the southern side of the Alps.
– ORIGIN Latin *cisalpinus.*

cisco /siskō/ ● noun (pl. **ciscoes**) a northern freshwater whitefish, important as a food fish.
– ORIGIN of unknown origin.

cissy ● noun & adjective variant spelling of SISSY.

Cistercian /sistersh'n/ ● noun a monk or nun of an order that is a stricter branch of the Benedictines. ● adjective relating to this order.
– ORIGIN from *Cistercium*, the Latin name of *Citeaux* in France, where the order was founded.

cistern ● noun **1** a water storage tank, especially as part of a flushing toilet. **2** an underground reservoir for rainwater.
– ORIGIN Latin *cisterna*, from *cista* 'box'.

Thesaurus

course. **3** *the judge's circuit* TOUR (OF DUTY), rounds.

circuitous ● adjective **1** *a circuitous route* ROUNDABOUT, indirect, winding, meandering, serpentine. **2** *a circuitous discussion* INDIRECT, oblique, roundabout, circumlocutory, periphrastic.
– OPPOSITES direct.

circular ● adjective *a circular window* ROUND, disc-shaped, ring-shaped, annular.
● noun *a free circular* LEAFLET, pamphlet, handbill, flyer; *N. Amer.* mailer, folder, dodger.

circulate ● verb **1** *the news was widely circulated* SPREAD (ABOUT/AROUND), communicate, disseminate, make known, make public, broadcast, publicize, advertise; distribute, give out, pass around. **2** *fresh air circulates freely* FLOW, course, move round. **3** *they circulated among their guests* SOCIALIZE, mingle.

circumference ● noun **1** *the circumference of the pit* PERIMETER, border, boundary; edge, rim, verge, margin, fringe; *poetic/literary* marge, bourn. **2** *the circumference of his arm* GIRTH, width.

circumlocution ● noun PERIPHRASIS, tautology, repetitiveness, repetitiousness, discursiveness, long-windedness, verbosity, wordiness, prolixity, verbiage, redundancy, pleonasm.

circumscribe ● verb RESTRICT, limit, keep within bounds, curb, confine, restrain; regulate, control.

circumspect ● adjective CAUTIOUS, wary, careful, chary, guarded, on one's guard; watchful, alert, attentive, heedful, vigilant, leery; *informal* cagey, playing one's cards close to one's chest.
– OPPOSITES unguarded.

circumstances ● plural noun **1** *favourable economic circumstances* SITUATION, conditions, state of affairs, position; (turn of) events, incidents, occurrences, happenings; factors, context, background, environment; *informal* circs. **2** *Jane explained the circumstances to him* THE FACTS, the details, the particulars, how things stand, the lie of the land; *Brit.* the state of play; *N. Amer.* the lay of the land; *informal* what's what, the score. **3** *reduced circumstances* FINANCIAL POSITION, lot, lifestyle; resources, means, finances, income; *dated* station in life.

circumstantial ● adjective **1** *circumstantial evidence* INDIRECT, inferred, deduced, conjectural; inconclusive, unprovable. **2** *the picture was so circumstantial that it began to be convincing* DETAILED, particularized, comprehensive, thorough, exhaustive; explicit, specific.

cistus ● noun a shrub with large white or red flowers.
– ORIGIN Greek *kistos*.

citadel ● noun a fortress protecting or dominating a city.
– ORIGIN French *citadelle* or Italian *cittadella*, from Latin *civitas* 'city'.

citation ● noun **1** a quotation from or reference to a book or author. **2** a mention of a praiseworthy act in an official report. **3** a note accompanying an award, giving reasons for it.

cite ● verb **1** quote (a book or author) as evidence for an argument. **2** praise for a courageous act in an official dispatch. **3** Law summon to appear in court.
– ORIGIN Latin *citare*, from *cire* 'to call'.

citified ● adjective chiefly derogatory characteristic of or adjusted to a city.

citizen ● noun **1** a legally recognized subject or national of a state or commonwealth. **2** an inhabitant of a town or city.
– DERIVATIVES **citizenry** noun **citizenship** noun.
– ORIGIN Old French *citezein*, from Latin *civitas* 'city'.

Citizens' Band ● noun a range of radio frequencies which are allocated for local communication by private individuals.

citric ● adjective derived from or related to citrus fruit.
– ORIGIN from Latin *citrus* 'citron tree'.

citric acid ● noun a sharp-tasting acid present in the juice of lemons and other sour fruits.
– DERIVATIVES **citrate** noun.

citrine /sitrin/ ● noun a glassy yellow variety of quartz.
– ORIGIN from Old French *citrin* 'lemon-coloured', from Latin *citrus* 'citron tree'.

citron ● noun the large, lemon-like fruit of a shrubby Asian tree.
– ORIGIN Latin *citrus* 'citron tree', on the pattern of *limon* 'lemon'.

citronella ● noun a fragrant natural oil obtained from a South Asian grass, used as an insect repellent and in perfume.

citrus ● noun (pl. **citruses**) **1** a tree of a genus that includes citron, lemon, lime, orange, and grapefruit. **2** (also **citrus fruit**) a fruit from such a tree.
– DERIVATIVES **citrusy** adjective.
– ORIGIN Latin, 'citron tree'.

cittern /sittərn/ ● noun a lute-like stringed instrument with a flattened back, used in 16th- and 17th-century Europe.
– ORIGIN Greek *kithara*, denoting a kind of harp.

city ● noun (pl. **cities**) **1** a large town, in particular (Brit.) a town created a city by charter and containing a cathedral. **2** (**the City**) the part of London governed by the Lord Mayor and the Corporation. **3** the financial and commercial institutions in this part of London.
– ORIGIN Old French *cite*, from Latin *civitas*, from *civis* 'citizen'.

city father ● noun a person concerned with the administration of a city.

city hall ● noun (treated as sing.) N. Amer. municipal offices or officers collectively.

cityscape ● noun a city landscape.

city slicker ● noun a person with the sophisticated tastes or values associated with city dwellers.

city state ● noun a city and surrounding territory that forms an independent state.

City Technology College ● noun (in the UK) a type of secondary school set up to teach technology and science in inner-city areas.

civet ● noun **1** a slender nocturnal cat native to Africa and Asia. **2** a strong musky perfume obtained from the scent glands of the civet.
– ORIGIN Arabic.

civic ● adjective relating to a city or town.
– DERIVATIVES **civically** adverb.
– ORIGIN Latin *civicus*, from *civis* 'citizen'.

civic centre ● noun **1** the area of a town where municipal offices are situated. **2** a building containing municipal offices.

civics ● plural noun (treated as sing.) the study of the rights and duties of citizenship.

civil ● adjective **1** relating to ordinary citizens, as distinct from military or ecclesiastical matters. **2** Law non-criminal: *a civil court*. **3** courteous and polite.
– DERIVATIVES **civilly** adverb.
– ORIGIN Latin *civilis*, from *civis* 'citizen'.

civil defence ● noun the organization and training of civilians for their protection during wartime.

civil disobedience ● noun the refusal to comply with certain laws or to pay taxes, as a political protest.

civil engineer ● noun an engineer who designs roads, bridges, dams, etc.

civilian ● noun a person not in the armed services or the police force. ● adjective relating to a civilian.
– ORIGIN Old French *civilien*, in the phrase *droit civilien* 'civil law'.

civility ● noun (pl. **civilities**) **1** politeness and courtesy. **2** (**civilities**) polite remarks used in formal conversation.

civilization (also **civilisation**) ● noun **1** an advanced stage or system of human social development. **2** the process of achieving this. **3** a civilized nation or region.

civilize (also **civilise**) ● verb **1** bring to an advanced stage of social development. **2** (**civilized**) polite and good-mannered.
– DERIVATIVES **civilizer** noun.

civil law ● noun **1** law concerned with ordinary citizens, rather than criminal, military, or religious affairs. **2** the system of law predominant on the European continent, influenced by that of ancient Rome.

civil liberty ● noun **1** freedom of action and speech subject to laws established for the good of the community. **2** (**civil liberties**) one's rights to this.
– DERIVATIVES **civil libertarian** noun.

Civil List ● noun (in the UK) an annual allowance voted by Parliament for the royal family's household expenses.

civil marriage ● noun a marriage without religious ceremony.

civil rights ● plural noun the rights of citizens to political and social freedom and equality.

civil servant ● noun a member of the civil service.

Thesaurus

circumvent ● verb AVOID, get round/past, evade, bypass, sidestep, dodge; *N. Amer.* end-run; *informal* duck.

cistern ● noun TANK, reservoir, container, butt.

citadel ● noun FORTRESS, fort, stronghold, fortification, castle, burg; *archaic* hold.

citation ● noun **1** *a citation from an eighteenth-century text* QUOTATION, quote, extract, excerpt, passage, line; reference, allusion; *N. Amer.* cite. **2** *a citation for gallantry* COMMENDATION, (honourable) mention. **3** *(Law) a traffic citation* SUMMONS, subpoena, writ, court order.

cite ● verb **1** *cite the passage in full* QUOTE, reproduce. **2** *he cited the case of Leigh v. Gladstone* REFER TO, make reference to, mention, allude to, adduce, instance; specify, name. **3** *he has been cited many times* COMMEND, pay tribute to, praise. **4** *(Law) the writ cited four of the signatories* SUMMON, summons, serve with a writ, subpoena.

citizen ● noun **1** *a British citizen* SUBJECT, national, passport holder, native. **2** *the citizens of Edinburgh* INHABITANT, resident, native, townsman, townswoman; *formal* denizen; *archaic* burgher; *Brit. archaic* burgess.

city ● noun TOWN, municipality, metropolis, megalopolis; conurbation, urban area, metropolitan area; *Scottish* burgh; *informal* big smoke; *N. Amer. informal* burg.
– RELATED TERMS urban, civic.

civic ● adjective MUNICIPAL, city, town, urban, metropolitan; public, civil, community.

civil ● adjective **1** *a civil marriage* SECULAR, non-religious, lay; *formal* laic. **2** *civil aviation* NON-MILITARY, civilian. **3** *a civil war* INTERNAL, domestic, interior, national. **4** *he behaved in a civil manner* POLITE, courteous, well mannered, well bred, gentlemanly, chivalrous, gallant, ladylike; cordial, genial, pleasant, affable.
– OPPOSITES religious, military, international, rude.

civilian ● noun NON-MILITARY PERSON, non-combatant person, ordinary/private citizen; *informal* civvy.

civility ● noun **1** *he treated me with civility* COURTESY, courteousness, politeness, good manners, graciousness, consideration, respect, politesse, comity. **2** *she didn't waste time on civilities* POLITE REMARK, politeness, courtesy; formality.
– OPPOSITES rudeness.

civilization ● noun **1** *a higher stage of civilization* HUMAN DEVELOPMENT, advancement, progress, enlightenment, culture, refinement, sophistication. **2** *ancient civilizations* CULTURE, society, nation, people.

civilize ● verb ENLIGHTEN, edify, improve, educate, instruct, refine, cultivate, polish, socialize, humanize.

civilized ● adjective POLITE, courteous, well mannered, civil, gentlemanly, ladylike, mannerly; cultured, cultivated, refined, polished, sophisticated; enlightened, educated, advanced, developed.

C

civil service ● noun the branches of state administration, excluding military and judicial branches and elected politicians.
civil war ● noun a war between citizens of the same country.
civvy ● noun (pl. **civvies**) informal **1** a civilian. **2** (**civvies**) civilian clothes.
– PHRASES **Civvy Street** Brit. informal civilian life.
CJD ● abbreviation Creutzfeldt–Jakob disease.
Cl ● symbol the chemical element chlorine.
cl ● abbreviation centilitre.
clack ● verb make a sharp sound as of a hard object striking another. ● noun a clacking sound.
– ORIGIN imitative.
clad archaic or poetic past participle of CLOTHE. ● adjective **1** clothed. **2** provided with cladding. ● verb (**cladding**; past and past part. **cladded** or **clad**) cover with cladding.
cladding ● noun a covering or coating on a structure or material.
clade /klayd/ ● noun Biology a group of organisms comprising all the evolutionary descendants of a common ancestor.
– ORIGIN Greek *klados* 'branch'.
cladistics /klədistiks/ ● plural noun (treated as sing.) Biology a method of classification of animals and plants based on clades.
– DERIVATIVES **cladistic** adjective.
claim ● verb **1** state as being the case, without being able to give proof. **2** demand as one's due. **3** call for (someone's attention). **4** request (money) under the terms of an insurance policy. **5** cause the loss of (someone's life). ● noun **1** a statement that something is the case. **2** a demand for something considered one's due. **3** a request for compensation under the terms of an insurance policy.
– DERIVATIVES **claimable** adjective **claimant** noun.
– ORIGIN Latin *clamare* 'call out'.
clairvoyance /klairvoyənss/ ● noun the supposed faculty of perceiving events in the future or beyond normal sensory contact.
– ORIGIN from French *clair* 'clear' + *voir* 'to see'.
clairvoyant ● noun a person claiming to have clairvoyance. ● adjective having clairvoyance.
clam ● noun a large marine bivalve mollusc with shells of equal size. ● verb (**clammed**, **clamming**) (**clam up**) informal stop talking abruptly.
– ORIGIN Old English, 'a bond or bondage'; related to CLAMP.
clamber ● verb climb or move in an awkward and laborious way. ● noun an act of clambering.
– ORIGIN probably from *clamb*, obsolete past tense of CLIMB.
clamdiggers ● plural noun close-fitting calf-length trousers for women.
clammy ● adjective (**clammier**, **clammiest**) **1** unpleasantly damp and sticky. **2** (of air) cold and damp.
– DERIVATIVES **clammily** adverb **clamminess** noun.
– ORIGIN from dialect *clam* 'to be sticky'; related to CLAY.
clamour (US **clamor**) ● noun **1** a loud and confused noise. **2** a vehement protest or demand. ● verb (of a group) make a clamour.
– DERIVATIVES **clamorous** adjective.
– ORIGIN Latin *clamor*, from *clamare* 'cry out'.
clamp ● noun a brace, band, or clasp for strengthening or holding things together. ● verb **1** fasten in place or together with a clamp. **2** (**clamp down**) suppress or prevent something. **3** fit a wheel clamp to (an illegally parked car).
– DERIVATIVES **clamper** noun.
– ORIGIN probably Dutch and related to CLAM.
clampdown ● noun informal a concerted attempt to suppress something.
clan ● noun **1** a group of close-knit and interrelated families, especially in the Scottish Highlands. **2** a group with a strong common interest.
– ORIGIN Scottish Gaelic, 'offspring, family', from Latin *planta* 'sprout'.
clandestine /klandestin/ ● adjective surreptitious or secretive.
– DERIVATIVES **clandestinely** adverb **clandestinity** noun.
– ORIGIN Latin *clandestinus*, from *clam* 'secretly'.
clang ● noun a loud metallic sound. ● verb make a clang.
– ORIGIN imitative, influenced by Latin *clangere* 'resound'.
clanger ● noun informal, chiefly Brit. a mistake.
clangour /klanggər/ (US **clangor**) ● noun a continuous clanging sound.
– DERIVATIVES **clangorous** adjective.
– ORIGIN Latin *clangor*, from *clangere* 'resound'.
clank ● noun a loud, sharp sound as of pieces of metal being struck together. ● verb make a clank.
– DERIVATIVES **clanking** adjective.
– ORIGIN imitative.
clannish ● adjective tending to exclude others outside the group.
– DERIVATIVES **clannishly** adverb **clannishness** noun.
clansman ● noun a male member of a clan.

Thesaurus

– OPPOSITES rude, unsophisticated.
civil servant ● noun PUBLIC SERVANT, government official; bureaucrat, mandarin, official, administrator, functionary.
clad ● adjective DRESSED, clothed, attired, got up, garbed, rigged out, costumed; wearing, sporting; *archaic* apparelled.
claim ● verb **1** *Davies claimed that she was lying* ASSERT, declare, profess, maintain, state, hold, affirm, avow; argue, contend, allege; *formal* aver; *archaic* avouch. **2** *no one claimed the items* LAY CLAIM TO, assert ownership of, formally request. **3** *you can claim compensation* REQUEST, ask for, apply for; demand, exact. **4** *the fire claimed four lives* TAKE, cause/result in the loss of.
● noun **1** *her claims that she was raped* ASSERTION, declaration, profession, affirmation, avowal, protestation; contention, allegation. **2** *a claim for damages* REQUEST, application; demand, petition. **3** *we have first claim on their assets* ENTITLEMENT TO, title to, right to.
claimant ● noun APPLICANT, candidate, supplicant; petitioner, plaintiff, litigant, appellant.
clairvoyance ● noun SECOND SIGHT, psychic powers, ESP, extrasensory perception, sixth sense; telepathy.
clairvoyant ● noun PSYCHIC, fortune teller, crystal-gazer; medium, spiritualist; telepathist, telepath, mind-reader.
● adjective *I'm not clairvoyant* PSYCHIC, having second sight, having a sixth sense; telepathic.
clamber ● verb SCRAMBLE, climb, scrabble, claw one's way.
clammy ● adjective **1** *his clammy hands* MOIST, damp, sweaty, sticky; slimy, slippery. **2** *the clammy atmosphere* DAMP, dank, wet; humid, close, muggy, heavy.
– OPPOSITES dry.
clamorous ● adjective NOISY, loud, vocal, vociferous, raucous, rowdy; importunate, demanding, insistent, vehement.
– OPPOSITES quiet.
clamour ● noun **1** *her voice rose above the clamour* DIN, racket, rumpus, loud noise, uproar, tumult, shouting, yelling, screaming, baying, roaring; commotion, brouhaha, hue and cry, hubbub; *informal* hullabaloo; *Brit. informal* row. **2** *the clamour for her resignation* DEMAND(S), call(s), urging. **3** *the clamour of protectionists* PROTESTS, complaints, outcry.
● verb **1** *clamouring crowds* YELL, shout loudly, bay, scream, roar. **2** *scientists are clamouring for a ban* DEMAND, call, press, push, lobby.
clamp ● noun **1** *a clamp was holding the wood* BRACE, vice, press, clasp; *Music* capo (tasto); *Climbing* jumar. **2** *clamps had been fitted to the car* IMMOBILIZER, wheel clamp; *N. Amer.* boot.
● verb **1** *the sander is clamped on to the workbench* FASTEN, secure, fix, attach; screw, bolt. **2** *a pipe was clamped between his teeth* CLENCH, grip, hold, press, clasp. **3** *his car was clamped* IMMOBILIZE, wheel-clamp; *N. Amer.* boot.
– PHRASES **clamp down on** SUPPRESS, prevent, stop, put a stop/end to, stamp out; crack down on, limit, restrict, control, keep in check.
clampdown ● noun *(informal)* SUPPRESSION, prevention, stamping out; crackdown, restriction, restraint, curb, check.
clan ● noun **1** *the Macleod clan* GROUP OF FAMILIES, sept; family, house, dynasty, tribe; *Anthropology* sib, kinship group. **2** *a clan of art collectors* GROUP, set, circle, clique, coterie; crowd, band; *informal* gang, bunch.
clandestine ● adjective SECRET, covert, furtive, surreptitious, stealthy, cloak-and-dagger, hole-and-corner, closet, backstairs, hugger-mugger; *informal* hush-hush.
clang ● noun *the clang of the church bells* REVERBERATION, ringing, ring, ding-dong, bong, peal, chime, toll.
● verb *the huge bells clanged* REVERBERATE, resound, ring, bong, peal, chime, toll.
clanger ● noun *(Brit. informal)*. See BLUNDER noun.
clank ● noun *the clank of rusty chains* JANGLING, clanging, rattling, clinking, jingling; clang, jangle, rattle, clangour, clink, jingle.
● verb *I could hear the chain clanking* JANGLE, rattle, clink, clang,

clap[1] ● verb (**clapped**, **clapping**) **1** strike the palms of (one's hands) together repeatedly, especially to applaud. **2** slap encouragingly on the back. **3** place (a hand) briefly over one's face as a gesture of dismay. **4** (of a bird) flap (its wings) audibly. ● noun **1** an act of clapping. **2** an explosive sound, especially of thunder.
– PHRASES **clap in jail** (or **irons**) put in prison (or in chains).
– ORIGIN Old English, 'throb, beat'.
clap[2] ● noun informal a venereal disease, especially gonorrhoea.
– ORIGIN Old French *clapoir*.
clapboard /klapbord, klabbərd/ ● noun chiefly N. Amer. one of a series of long planks of wood with edges horizontally overlapping, covering the outer walls of buildings.
– ORIGIN Low German *klappholt* 'barrel stave'.
clapped-out ● adjective informal, chiefly Brit. worn out from age or heavy use.
clapper ● noun the tongue or striker of a bell.
– PHRASES **like the clappers** Brit. informal very fast or hard.
clapperboard ● noun hinged boards that are struck together at the beginning of filming to synchronize the picture and sound machinery.
claptrap ● noun nonsense.
– ORIGIN originally denoting something designed to elicit applause.
claque /klak, klaak/ ● noun **1** a group of people hired to applaud or heckle a performer. **2** a group of sycophantic followers.
– ORIGIN French, from *claquer* 'to clap'.
claret /klarrət/ ● noun **1** a red wine, especially from Bordeaux. **2** a deep purplish red colour.
– ORIGIN from Latin *claratum vinum* 'clarified wine', from *clarus* 'clear'.
clarify ● verb (**clarifies**, **clarified**) **1** make more comprehensible. **2** melt (butter) to separate out the impurities.
– DERIVATIVES **clarification** noun **clarifier** noun.
– ORIGIN Old French *clarifier*, from Latin *clarus* 'clear'.
clarinet ● noun a woodwind instrument with a single-reed mouthpiece, a cylindrical tube, and holes stopped by keys.
– DERIVATIVES **clarinettist** (US **clarinetist**) noun.
– ORIGIN from French *clarine*, denoting a kind of bell.
clarion /klarriən/ ● noun chiefly historical a shrill war trumpet. ● adjective loud and clear.
– PHRASES **clarion call** a strongly expressed demand for action.
– ORIGIN Latin, from *clarus* 'clear'.
clarity ● noun **1** the state or quality of being clear and easily perceived or understood. **2** transparency or purity.
– ORIGIN Latin *claritas*, from *clarus* 'clear'.
clarsach /klaarsəkh/ ● noun a small harp with wire strings, used in the folk and early music of Scotland and Ireland.
– ORIGIN Scottish Gaelic, perhaps from *clar* 'table, board'.
clash ● verb **1** (of opposing groups) come into violent conflict. **2** disagree or be at odds. **3** (of colours) appear discordant when placed together. **4** (of dates or events) occur inconveniently at the same time. **5** strike together, producing a loud discordant sound. ● noun an act or sound of clashing.
– ORIGIN imitative.
clasp ● verb **1** grasp tightly with one's hand. **2** place (one's arms) around something so as to hold it tightly. **3** press (one's hands) together with the fingers interlaced. **4** fasten with a clasp. ● noun **1** a device with interlocking parts used for fastening. **2** a bar on a medal ribbon. **3** an act of clasping.
– PHRASES **clasp hands** shake hands warmly.
– ORIGIN of unknown origin.
clasp knife ● noun a knife with a blade that folds into the handle.
class ● noun **1** a set or category of things having a common characteristic and differentiated from others by kind or quality. **2** a system that divides members of a society into sets based on social or economic status. **3** a set in a society ordered by social or economic status. **4** a group of students or pupils who are taught together. **5** a lesson. **6** Biology a principal taxonomic category that ranks above order and below phylum or division. **7** informal impressive stylishness. **8** Brit. a division of candidates according to merit in a university examination. ● verb assign to a particular category. ● adjective informal showing stylish excellence: *a class player*.
– ORIGIN Latin *classis* 'a division of the Roman people, a grade, or a class of pupils'.
class action ● noun Law, chiefly N. Amer. a law suit filed or defended by an individual acting on behalf of a group.
classic ● adjective **1** judged over a period of time to be of the highest quality. **2** typical. ● noun **1** a work of art of established value. **2** (**Classics**) the study of ancient Greek and Latin literature, philosophy, and history. **3** (**the classics**) the works of ancient Greek and Latin writers.
– ORIGIN Latin *classicus* 'belonging to a class or division', later 'of the highest class'.
classical ● adjective **1** relating to ancient Greek or Latin literature, art, or culture. **2** (of a form of art or a language) representing an exemplary standard within a long-established form.

Thesaurus

jingle.
clannish ● adjective CLIQUEY, cliquish, insular, exclusive; unfriendly, unwelcoming.
clap ● verb **1** *the audience clapped* APPLAUD, clap one's hands, give someone a round of applause, put one's hands together; *informal* give someone a (big) hand; *N. Amer. informal* give it up. **2** *he clapped Owen on the back* SLAP, strike, hit, smack, thump; pat; *informal* whack, thwack. **3** *the dove clapped its wings* FLAP, beat, flutter.
● noun **1** *everybody gave him a clap* ROUND OF APPLAUSE, handclap; *informal* hand. **2** *a clap on the shoulder* SLAP, blow, smack, thump; pat; *informal* whack, thwack. **3** *a clap of thunder* CRACK, crash, bang, boom; thunderclap.
claptrap ● noun *sentimental claptrap*. See NONSENSE sense 1.
clarify ● verb **1** *their report clarified the situation* MAKE CLEAR, shed/throw light on, elucidate, illuminate; EXPLAIN, explicate, define, spell out, clear up. **2** *clarified butter* PURIFY, refine; filter, fine.
– OPPOSITES confuse.
clarity ● noun **1** *the clarity of his account* LUCIDITY, lucidness, clearness, coherence; *formal* perspicuity. **2** *the clarity of the image* SHARPNESS, clearness, crispness, definition. **3** *the crystal clarity of the water* LIMPIDITY, limpidness, clearness, transparency, translucence, pellucidity.
– OPPOSITES vagueness, blurriness, opacity.
clash ● noun **1** *clashes between armed gangs* CONFRONTATION, skirmish, fight, battle, engagement, encounter, conflict. **2** *an angry clash* ARGUMENT, altercation, confrontation, shouting match; contretemps, quarrel, disagreement, dispute; *informal* run-in, slanging match. **3** *a clash of tweeds and a striped shirt* MISMATCH, discordance, discord, lack of harmony. **4** *a clash of dates* COINCIDENCE, concurrence; conflict. **5** *the clash of cymbals* STRIKING, bang, clang, crash.
● verb **1** *protesters clashed with police* FIGHT, skirmish, contend, come to blows, come into conflict; do battle. **2** *the prime minister clashed with union leaders* DISAGREE, differ, wrangle, dispute, cross swords, lock horns, be at loggerheads. **3** *her red coat clashed with her hair* BE INCOMPATIBLE, not match, not go, be discordant. **4** *the dates clash* CONFLICT, coincide, occur simultaneously. **5** *she clashed the cymbals together* BANG, strike, clang, crash.
clasp ● verb **1** *Ruth clasped his hand* GRASP, grip, clutch, hold tightly; take hold of, seize, grab. **2** *he clasped Joanne in his arms* EMBRACE, hug, enfold, fold, envelop; hold, squeeze.
● noun **1** *a gold clasp* FASTENER, fastening, catch, clip, pin; buckle, hasp. **2** *his tight clasp* EMBRACE, hug, cuddle; grip, grasp.
class ● noun **1** *a hotel of the first class* CATEGORY, grade, rating, classification, group, grouping. **2** *a new class of heart drug* KIND, sort, type, variety, genre, brand; species, genus, breed, strain; *N. Amer.* stripe. **3** *the middle class* SOCIAL DIVISION, social stratum, rank, level, echelon, group, grouping; social status; *archaic* estate, condition. **4** *there are 30 pupils in the class* FORM, study group, set, stream. **5** *a Maths class* LESSON, period; seminar, tutorial, workshop. **6** *(informal) a woman of class* STYLE, stylishness, elegance, chic, sophistication, taste, refinement, quality, excellence.
● verb *the 12-seater is classed as a commercial vehicle* CLASSIFY, categorize, group, grade; order, sort, codify; bracket, designate, label, pigeonhole.
● adjective *(informal) a class player*. See EXCELLENT.
classic ● adjective **1** *the classic work on the subject* DEFINITIVE, authoritative; outstanding, first-rate, first-class, best, finest, excellent, superior, masterly. **2** *a classic example of Norman design* TYPICAL, archetypal, quintessential, vintage; model, representative, perfect, prime, textbook. **3** *a classic style* SIMPLE, elegant, understated; traditional, timeless, ageless.
– OPPOSITES atypical.

3 (of music) of long-established form or style or (more specifically) written in the European tradition between approximately 1750 and 1830. **4** relating to the first significant period of an area of study: *classical Marxism*.
– DERIVATIVES **classically** adverb.

classicism ● noun the following of ancient Greek or Roman principles and style in art and literature, generally associated with harmony and restraint.

classicist ● noun **1** a person who studies Classics. **2** a follower of classicism.

classicizing (also **classicising**) ● adjective imitating a classical style.

classification ● noun **1** the action or process of classifying. **2** a category into which something is put.
– DERIVATIVES **classificatory** adjective.

classified ● adjective **1** (of newspaper or magazine advertisements) organized in categories. **2** (of information or documents) designated as officially secret. ● noun (**classifieds**) classified advertisements.

classify ● verb (**classifies**, **classified**) **1** arrange (a group) in classes according to shared characteristics. **2** assign to a particular class or category. **3** designate (documents or information) as officially secret.
– DERIVATIVES **classifiable** adjective **classifier** noun **classifying** adjective.

classless ● adjective **1** (of a society) not divided into social classes. **2** not showing characteristics of a particular social class.
– DERIVATIVES **classlessness** noun.

classroom ● noun a room in which a class of pupils or students is taught.

class struggle ● noun (in Marxist ideology) the conflict of interests between the workers and the ruling class in a capitalist society.

classy ● adjective (**classier**, **classiest**) informal stylish and sophisticated.
– DERIVATIVES **classily** adverb **classiness** noun.

clatter ● noun a loud rattling sound as of hard objects striking each other. ● verb **1** make a clatter. **2** fall or move with a clatter.
– ORIGIN Old English, of imitative origin.

clause ● noun **1** a unit of grammatical organization next below the sentence in rank, and in traditional grammar said to consist of a subject and predicate. **2** a particular and separate article, stipulation, or proviso in a treaty, bill, or contract.
– DERIVATIVES **clausal** adjective.
– ORIGIN Old French, from Latin *claudere* 'shut, close'.

claustrophobia /klawstrəfōbiə/ ● noun extreme or irrational fear of confined places.
– DERIVATIVES **claustrophobe** noun **claustrophobic** adjective.
– ORIGIN from Latin *claustrum* 'lock, bolt'.

clavichord /klavvikord/ ● noun a small, rectangular keyboard instrument with a soft tone.
– ORIGIN from Latin *clavis* 'key' + *chorda* 'string'.

clavicle ● noun Anatomy technical term for COLLARBONE.
– DERIVATIVES **clavicular** adjective.
– ORIGIN Latin *clavicula* 'small key' (because of its shape).

claw ● noun **1** a curved, pointed horny nail on each digit of the foot in birds, lizards, and some mammals. **2** the pincer of a crab, scorpion, or other arthropod. ● verb **1** scratch or tear at with the claws or fingernails. **2** (**claw away**) try desperately to move (something) with the hands. **3** (**claw one's way**) haul oneself forward with one's hands. **4** (**claw back**) regain or recover (money, power, etc.) laboriously or harshly.
– PHRASES **get one's claws into** informal have a controlling influence over.
– DERIVATIVES **clawed** adjective.
– ORIGIN Old English.

claw hammer ● noun a hammer with one side of the head split and curved, used for extracting nails.

clay ● noun **1** a sticky impermeable earth that can be moulded when wet and baked to make bricks and pottery. **2** literary the substance of the human body.
– DERIVATIVES **clayey** adjective.
– ORIGIN Old English, related to CLEAVE² and CLIMB.

claymore ● noun historical a type of broadsword used in Scotland.
– ORIGIN Scottish Gaelic *claidheamh* 'great sword'.

clay pigeon ● noun a saucer-shaped piece of baked clay or other material thrown up in the air as a target for shooting.

clay pipe ● noun a tobacco pipe made of hardened clay.

clean ● adjective **1** free from dirt, pollutants, or harmful substances. **2** morally pure: *clean living*. **3** not obscene. **4** attentive to personal hygiene. **5** showing or having no record of offences or crimes: *a clean driving licence*. **6** played or done according to the rules: *a good clean fight*. **7** free from irregularities; smooth: *a clean fracture*. **8** (of an action) smoothly and skilfully done. ● adverb **1** so as to be free from dirt. **2** informal completely. ● verb **1** make clean. **2** (**clean out**) informal use up or take (all someone's money or resources). **3** (**clean out**) steal the entire contents of (a place). **4** (**clean up**) informal make a substantial gain or profit. ● noun chiefly Brit. an act of cleaning.
– PHRASES **a clean sheet** (or **slate**) an absence of existing restraints or commitments. **come clean** informal fully confess something. **keep one's hands clean** remain uninvolved in an immoral or illegal act. **make a clean breast of it** fully confess something. **make a clean sweep 1** remove all unwanted people or things ready to start afresh. **2** win all of a group of related sporting contests.
– DERIVATIVES **cleanable** adjective **cleanness** noun.
– ORIGIN Old English.

Thesaurus

● noun *a classic of the genre* DEFINITIVE EXAMPLE, model, epitome, paradigm, exemplar; great work, masterpiece.

classical ● adjective **1** *classical mythology* ancient Greek, Hellenic, Attic; Latin, ancient Roman. **2** *classical music* TRADITIONAL, long-established; serious, highbrow, heavyweight. **3** *a classical style* SIMPLE, pure, restrained, plain, austere; well proportioned, harmonious, balanced, symmetrical, elegant.
– OPPOSITES modern.

classification ● noun **1** *the classification of diseases* CATEGORIZATION, categorizing, classifying, grouping, grading, ranking, organization, sorting, codification, systematization. **2** *a series of classifications* CATEGORY, class, group, grouping, grade, grading, ranking, bracket.

classify ● verb *we can classify the students into two groups* CATEGORIZE, group, grade, rank, rate, order, organize, range, sort, type, codify, bracket, systematize, systemize; catalogue, list, file, index; *archaic* assort.

classy ● adjective *(informal) a classy hotel* STYLISH, high-class, superior, exclusive, chic, elegant, smart, sophisticated; *Brit.* upmarket; *N. Amer.* high-toned; *informal* posh, ritzy, plush, swanky; *Brit. informal* swish.

clatter ● verb *the cups clattered on the tray* RATTLE, clank, clink, clunk, clang.

clause ● noun *a new clause in the treaty* SECTION, paragraph, article, subsection; stipulation, condition, proviso, rider.

claw ● noun **1** *a bird's claw* TALON, nail; *technical* unguis. **2** *a crab's claw* PINCER, nipper; *technical* chela.
● verb *her fingers clawed his shoulders* SCRATCH, lacerate, tear, rip, scrape, graze, dig into.

clay ● noun **1** *the soil is mainly clay* EARTH, soil, loam. **2** *potter's clay* argil, china clay, kaolin, adobe, ball clay, pug; fireclay.

clean ● adjective **1** *keep the wound clean* WASHED, scrubbed, cleansed, cleaned; spotless, unsoiled, unstained, unsullied, unblemished, immaculate, pristine, dirt-free, as clean as a whistle; hygienic, sanitary, disinfected, sterilized, sterile, aseptic, decontaminated; laundered; *informal* squeaky clean. **2** *a clean sheet of paper* BLANK, empty, clear, plain; unused, new, pristine, fresh, unmarked. **3** *clean air* PURE, clear, fresh, crisp, refreshing; unpolluted, uncontaminated. **4** *a clean life* VIRTUOUS, good, upright, upstanding; honourable, respectable, reputable, decent, righteous, moral, exemplary; innocent, pure, chaste; *informal* squeaky clean. **5** *the firm is clean* INNOCENT, guiltless, blameless, guilt-free, crime-free, above suspicion; *informal* squeaky clean. **6** *a good clean fight* FAIR, honest, sporting, sportsmanlike, honourable, according to the rules; *informal* on the level. **7** *(informal) they are trying to stay clean* SOBER, teetotal, dry, non-drinking; DRUG-FREE, off drugs; *informal* on the wagon. **8** *a clean cut* NEAT, smooth, crisp, straight, precise. **9** *a clean break* COMPLETE, thorough, total, absolute, conclusive, decisive, final, irrevocable. **10** *clean lines* SIMPLE, elegant, graceful, streamlined, smooth.
– OPPOSITES dirty, polluted.
● adverb *(informal) I clean forgot* COMPLETELY, entirely, totally, fully, quite, utterly, absolutely.
● verb **1** *Dad cleaned the windows* WASH, cleanse, wipe, sponge,

clean and jerk ● noun a weightlifting exercise in which a weight is raised above the head following an initial lift to shoulder level.

clean-cut ● adjective **1** sharply outlined. **2** (of a person) clean and neat.

cleaner ● noun a person or thing that cleans.
– PHRASES **take to the cleaners** informal **1** defraud of a large portion of money or resources. **2** inflict a crushing defeat on.

cleanly ● adverb /kleenli/ in a clean manner. ● adjective /klenli/ (**cleanlier**, **cleanliest**) archaic habitually clean.
– DERIVATIVES **cleanliness** noun.

cleanse ● verb **1** make thoroughly clean. **2** rid of something unpleasant or unwanted. ● noun an act of cleansing.
– DERIVATIVES **cleanser** noun **cleansing** adjective.
– ORIGIN Old English.

clean-shaven ● adjective (of a man) without a beard or moustache.

clear ● adjective **1** easy to perceive or understand. **2** leaving or feeling no doubt. **3** transparent; unclouded. **4** free of obstructions or unwanted objects. **5** (of a period of time) free of commitments. **6** free from disease, contamination, or guilt. **7** (**clear of**) not touching; away from. **8** complete: *seven clear days' notice.* **9** (of a sum of money) net. ● adverb **1** so as to be out of the way of or uncluttered by. **2** with clarity. ● verb **1** make or become clear. **2** get past or over (something) safely or without touching it. **3** show or declare to be innocent. **4** give official approval or authorization to or for. **5** cause people to leave (a building or place). **6** (of a cheque) pass through a clearing house so that the money enters the payee's account. **7** earn or gain (an amount of money) as a net profit. **8** discharge (a debt).
– PHRASES **clear the air 1** make the air less sultry. **2** defuse a tense situation by frank discussion. **clear the decks** prepare for something by dealing beforehand with anything that might hinder progress. **clear off** informal go away. **clear out** informal **1** empty. **2** leave quickly. **clear up 1** tidy (something) by removing unwanted items. **2** solve or explain. **3** (of an illness or other medical condition) become cured. **4** (of the weather) become brighter; stop raining. **in the clear** no longer in danger or under suspicion.
– DERIVATIVES **clearness** noun.
– ORIGIN Old French *cler*, from Latin *clarus*.

clearance ● noun **1** the action or an act of clearing or the process of being cleared. **2** official authorization for something to take place. **3** clear space allowed for a thing to move past or under another.

clear-cut ● adjective sharply defined; easy to perceive or understand.

clearing ● noun an open space in a forest.

clearing bank ● noun Brit. a bank which is a member of a clearing house.

clearing house ● noun **1** a bankers' establishment where cheques and bills from member banks are exchanged. **2** an agency which collects and distributes information.

clearly ● adverb **1** with clarity. **2** obviously; without doubt.

clear-sighted ● adjective thinking clearly; perspicacious.

clearway ● noun Brit. a main road other than a motorway on which vehicles are not permitted to stop.

cleat ● noun **1** a T-shaped or similar projection to which a rope may be attached. **2** a projecting wedge on a spar, tool, etc., to prevent slippage.
– DERIVATIVES **cleated** adjective.
– ORIGIN Germanic, related to CLOT and CLOUT.

cleavage ● noun **1** a sharp division; a split. **2** the cleft between a woman's breasts. **3** Biology cell division, especially of a fertilized egg cell. **4** the splitting of rocks or crystals in a preferred plane or direction.

cleave[1] ● verb (past **clove** or **cleft** or **cleaved**; past part. **cloven** or **cleft** or **cleaved**) **1** split or sever along a natural grain or line. **2** divide; split.
– ORIGIN Old English.

C

Thesaurus

scrub, mop, rinse, scour, swab, hose down, sluice (down), disinfect; shampoo; poetic/literary lave. **2** *I got my clothes cleaned* LAUNDER, dry-clean. **3** *she cleaned the fish* GUT, draw, dress; formal eviscerate.
– OPPOSITES dirty.
– PHRASES **clean someone out** (informal) BANKRUPT, ruin, make insolvent, make penniless, wipe out. **come clean** (informal) TELL THE TRUTH, tell all, make a clean breast of it; confess, own up, admit guilt, admit to one's crimes/sins; informal fess up.

cleanse ● verb **1** *the wound was cleansed* CLEAN (UP), wash, bathe, rinse, disinfect. **2** *cleansing the environment of traces of lead* RID, clear, free, purify, purge. **3** *only God can cleanse us from sin* PURIFY, purge, absolve, free; deliver.

clear ● adjective **1** *clear instructions* UNDERSTANDABLE, comprehensible, intelligible, plain, uncomplicated, explicit, lucid, coherent, simple, straightforward, unambiguous, clear-cut, crystal clear; formal perspicuous. **2** *a clear case of harassment* OBVIOUS, evident, plain, crystal clear; sure, definite, unmistakable, manifest, indisputable, patent, incontrovertible, irrefutable, beyond doubt, beyond question; palpable, visible, discernible, conspicuous, overt, blatant, glaring; as plain as a pikestaff, as plain as day; informal as plain as the nose on one's face. **3** *clear water* TRANSPARENT, limpid, pellucid, translucent, crystal clear; unclouded. **4** *a clear blue sky* BRIGHT, cloudless, unclouded, without a cloud in the sky. **5** *her clear complexion* UNBLEMISHED, spot-free. **6** *Rosa's clear voice* DISTINCT, bell-like, as clear as a bell. **7** *the road was clear | a clear view* UNOBSTRUCTED, unblocked, passable, open; unrestricted, unhindered. **8** *the algae were clear of toxins* FREE, devoid, without, unaffected by; rid, relieved. **9** *a clear conscience* UNTROUBLED, undisturbed, unperturbed, unconcerned, having no qualms; peaceful, at peace, tranquil, serene, calm, easy. **10** *two clear days' notice* WHOLE, full, entire, complete.
– OPPOSITES vague, opaque, cloudy, obstructed.
● adverb **1** *stand clear of the doors* AWAY FROM, apart from, at a (safe) distance from, out of contact with. **2** *Tommy's voice came loud and clear* DISTINCTLY, clearly, as clear as a bell, plainly, audibly. **3** *he has time to get clear away* COMPLETELY, entirely, fully, wholly, totally, utterly; informal clean.
● verb **1** *the sky cleared briefly* BRIGHTEN (UP), lighten, clear up, become bright/brighter/lighter, become fine/sunny. **2** *the drizzle had cleared* DISAPPEAR, go away, end; peter out, fade, wear off, decrease, lessen, diminish. **3** *together they cleared the table* EMPTY, unload, unburden, strip. **4** *clearing drains* UNBLOCK, unstop. **5** *staff cleared the building* EVACUATE, empty; leave. **6** *Karen cleared the dirty plates* REMOVE, take away, carry away, tidy away/up. **7** *I'm clearing my debts* PAY (OFF), repay, settle, discharge. **8** *I cleared the bar at my first attempt* GO OVER, pass over, sail over; jump (over), vault (over), leap (over), hurdle. **9** *he was cleared by an appeal court* ACQUIT, declare innocent, find not guilty; absolve, exonerate; informal let off (the hook); formal exculpate. **10** *I was cleared to work on the atomic project* AUTHORIZE, give permission, permit, allow, pass, accept, endorse, license, sanction, give approval/consent to; informal OK, give the OK, give the thumbs up, give the green light, give the go-ahead. **11** *I cleared £50,000 profit* NET, make/realize a profit of, take home, pocket; gain, earn, make, get, bring in, pull in.
– PHRASES **clear off** (informal) GO AWAY, get out, leave; be off with you, shoo, on your way; informal beat it, push off, shove off, scram, scoot, buzz off, clear out; Brit. informal hop it, sling your hook; Austral./NZ informal rack off; N. Amer. informal bug off, take a hike; poetic/literary begone. **clear out** (informal). See LEAVE[1] sense 1. **clear something out 1** *we cleared out the junk room* EMPTY (OUT); tidy (up), clear up. **2** *clear out the rubbish* GET RID OF, throw out/away, discard, dispose of, dump, bin, scrap, jettison; informal chuck (out/away), ditch, get shut of; Brit. informal get shot of; N. Amer. informal trash. **clear up.** See CLEAR verb sense 1. **clear something up 1** *clear up the garden* TIDY (UP), put in order, straighten up, clean up, spruce up. **2** *we've cleared up the problem* SOLVE, resolve, straighten out, find an/the answer to; get to the bottom of, explain; informal crack, figure out, suss out.

clearance ● noun **1** *slum clearance* REMOVAL, clearing, demolition. **2** *you must have Home Office clearance* AUTHORIZATION, permission, consent, approval, blessing, leave, sanction, licence, dispensation, assent, agreement, endorsement; informal the green light, the go-ahead, the thumbs up, the OK, the say-so. **3** *the clearance of a debt* REPAYMENT, payment, paying (off), settling, discharge. **4** *there is plenty of clearance* SPACE, room (to spare), margin, leeway.

clear-cut ● adjective DEFINITE, distinct, clear, well defined, precise, specific, explicit, unambiguous, unequivocal, black and white, cut and dried.
– OPPOSITES vague.

clearing ● noun GLADE, dell, gap, opening.

clearly ● adverb **1** *write clearly* INTELLIGIBLY, plainly, distinctly, comprehensibly, with clarity; legibly, audibly; formal perspicuously. **2** *clearly, substantial changes are needed* OBVIOUSLY, evidently,

C

cleave[2] ● verb (**cleave to**) literary **1** stick fast to. **2** become strongly involved with or emotionally attached to.
– ORIGIN Old English, related to CLAY and CLIMB.

cleaver ● noun a tool with a heavy broad blade, used for chopping meat.

clef ● noun Music any of several symbols placed on a stave, indicating the pitch of the notes written on the stave.
– ORIGIN French, from Latin *clavis* 'key'.

cleft past participle of CLEAVE[1]. ● adjective split, divided, or partially divided into two. ● noun **1** a fissure or split in rock or the ground. **2** an indentation in a person's forehead or chin, or a hollow between two parts of the body.
– PHRASES **be** (or **be caught**) **in a cleft stick** chiefly Brit. be in a situation in which any action one takes will have adverse consequences.

cleft lip ● noun a congenital split in the upper lip on one or both sides of the centre, often associated with a cleft palate.

cleft palate ● noun a congenital split in the roof of the mouth.

clematis /klemmətiss, kləmaytiss/ ● noun an ornamental climbing plant bearing white, pink, or purple flowers and feathery seeds.
– ORIGIN Greek *klēmatis*, from *klēma* 'vine branch'.

clement ● adjective **1** (of weather) mild. **2** merciful.
– DERIVATIVES **clemency** noun.
– ORIGIN Latin *clemens*.

clementine /klemməntīn, -teen/ ● noun a deep orange-red variety of tangerine grown around the Mediterranean and in South Africa.
– ORIGIN French, from the male given name *Clément*.

clench ● verb **1** (with reference to one's fist or teeth) close or press together tightly, in response to stress or anger. **2** (with reference to a set of muscles) contract sharply. **3** grasp tightly. ● noun the action of clenching or the state of being clenched.
– ORIGIN Old English, 'fix securely'; related to CLING.

clerestory /kleerstori/ (US also **clearstory**) ● noun (pl. **clerestories**) the upper part of the nave, choir, and transepts of a large church, incorporating a series of windows which admit light to the central parts of the building.
– ORIGIN from CLEAR + STOREY.

clergy /klerji/ ● noun (pl. **clergies**) (usu. treated as pl.) the body of people ordained for religious duties in the Christian Church.
– ORIGIN Latin *clericus* 'cleric, clergyman'.

clergyman (or **clergywoman**) ● noun a priest or minister of a Christian church.

cleric ● noun a priest or religious leader.
– ORIGIN Latin *clericus*, from Greek *klēros* 'lot, heritage' (with reference to Acts of the Apostles, chapter 1).

clerical ● adjective **1** relating to the routine work of an office clerk. **2** of or relating to the clergy.
– DERIVATIVES **clericalism** noun **clericalist** noun **clerically** adverb.

clerical collar ● noun a stiff upright white collar which fastens at the back, worn by the clergy in some churches.

clerical error ● noun a mistake made in copying or writing out a document.

clerihew /klerrihyoo/ ● noun a short comic verse consisting of two rhyming couplets with lines of unequal length, typically referring to a famous person.
– ORIGIN named after Edmund *Clerihew* Bentley (1875–1956), the English writer who invented it.

clerk ● noun **1** a person employed in an office or bank to keep records or accounts and to undertake other routine administrative duties. **2** an official in charge of the records of a local council or court. **3** a senior official in Parliament. **4** a lay officer of a cathedral, church, or chapel. **5** (also **desk clerk**) N. Amer. a receptionist in a hotel. **6** (also **sales clerk**) N. Amer. an assistant in a shop. ● verb N. Amer. work as a clerk.
– DERIVATIVES **clerkish** adjective **clerkly** adjective **clerkship** noun.
– ORIGIN Latin *clericus* 'cleric, clergyman'; reinforced by Old French *clerc*, from the same source.

clever ● adjective (**cleverer**, **cleverest**) **1** quick to understand, learn, and devise or apply ideas. **2** skilled at doing something.
– DERIVATIVES **cleverly** adverb **cleverness** noun.
– ORIGIN originally in the sense 'quick to catch hold': perhaps of Dutch or German origin, and related to CLEAVE[2].

clew ● noun **1** the lower or after corner of a sail. **2** (**clews**) Nautical the cords by which a hammock is suspended. ● verb (**clew a sail up/down**) draw a sail up or let it down by the clews when preparing for furling or when unfurling.
– ORIGIN originally denoting a ball of thread: related to CLUE.

cliché /kleeshay/ (also **cliche**) ● noun **1** a hackneyed or overused phrase or opinion. **2** a very predictable or unoriginal thing or person.
– DERIVATIVES **clichéd** (also **cliché'd**) adjective.
– ORIGIN French, from *clicher* 'to stereotype'.

click ● noun **1** a short, sharp sound as of two hard objects coming smartly into contact. **2** Computing an act of pressing one of the buttons on a mouse. ● verb **1** make or cause to make a click. **2** move or become secured with a click. **3** Computing press (a mouse button). **4** informal become suddenly clear and understandable. **5** informal become friendly and compatible.
– DERIVATIVES **clickable** adjective **clicker** noun **clicky** adjective.
– ORIGIN imitative.

Thesaurus

patently, unquestionably, undoubtedly, without doubt, indubitably, plainly, undeniably, incontrovertibly, irrefutably, doubtless, it goes without saying, needless to say.

cleave[1] ● verb **1** *cleaving wood for the fire* SPLIT (OPEN), cut (up), hew, hack, chop up; *poetic/literary* sunder; *archaic* rive. **2** *cleaving a path through the traffic* PLOUGH, drive, bulldoze, carve.

cleave[2] ● verb
– PHRASES **cleave to** *(poetic/literary)* **1** *her tongue clove to the roof of her mouth* STICK (FAST) TO, adhere to, be attached to. **2** *cleaving too closely to Moscow's line* ADHERE TO, hold to, abide by, be loyal/faithful to.

cleaver ● noun CHOPPER, hatchet, axe, knife; butcher's knife, kitchen knife.

cleft ● noun **1** *a deep cleft in the rocks* SPLIT, slit, crack, fissure, crevice, rift, break, fracture, rent, breach. **2** *the cleft in his chin* DIMPLE.
● adjective *a cleft tail* SPLIT, divided, cloven.

clemency ● noun MERCY, mercifulness, leniency, lenience, mildness, indulgence, quarter; compassion, humanity, pity, sympathy.
– OPPOSITES ruthlessness.

clench ● verb **1** *he stood there clenching his hands* SQUEEZE TOGETHER, clamp together, close/shut tightly; make into a fist. **2** *he clenched the back of chair* GRIP, grasp, grab, clutch, clasp, hold tightly, seize, press, squeeze.
● noun *the clench of his fists* CONTRACTION, tightening, tensing, constricting.

clergy ● noun CLERGYMEN, clergywomen, churchmen, churchwomen, clerics, priests, ecclesiastics, men/women of God; ministry, priesthood, holy orders, the church, the cloth.
– RELATED TERMS clerical.
– OPPOSITES laity.

clergyman, clergywoman ● noun PRIEST, churchman, churchwoman, man/woman of the cloth, man/woman of God; cleric, minister, preacher, chaplain, father, ecclesiastic, bishop, pastor, vicar, rector, parson, curate, deacon, deaconess; *Scottish* kirkman; *N. Amer.* dominie; *informal* reverend, padre, Holy Joe, sky pilot; *Austral. informal* josser.

clerical ● adjective **1** *clerical jobs* OFFICE, desk, back-room; administrative, secretarial; white-collar. **2** *a clerical minister* ECCLESIASTICAL, church, priestly, religious, spiritual, sacerdotal; holy, divine.
– OPPOSITES secular.

clerk ● noun OFFICE WORKER, clerical worker, administrator; bookkeeper; cashier, teller; *informal* pen-pusher; *historical* scrivener.

clever ● adjective **1** *a clever young woman* INTELLIGENT, bright, smart, astute, quick-witted, shrewd; talented, gifted, brilliant, capable, able, competent, apt; educated, learned, knowledgeable, wise; *informal* brainy, savvy. **2** *a clever scheme* INGENIOUS, canny, cunning, crafty, artful, slick, neat. **3** *she was clever with her hands* SKILFUL, dexterous, adroit, adept, deft, nimble, handy; skilled, talented, gifted. **4** *a clever remark* WITTY, amusing, droll, humorous, funny.
– OPPOSITES stupid.

cliché ● noun PLATITUDE, hackneyed phrase, commonplace, banality, truism, stock phrase, trite phrase; *informal* old chestnut; *dated* bromide.

click ● noun CLACK, snick, snap, pop, tick; clink.
● verb **1** *cameras clicked* CLACK, snap, snick, tick, pop; clink. **2** *(informal) that night it clicked* BECOME CLEAR, fall into place, come home, make sense, dawn, register, get through, sink in. **3** *(informal) we just clicked* TAKE TO EACH OTHER, get along, be compatible, be like-minded, feel a rapport, see eye to eye; *informal* hit it off, get on like

client • noun a person using the services of a professional person or organization.
– ORIGIN originally denoting a person under the protection and patronage of another: from Latin *cliens*, from *cluere* 'hear or obey'.

clientele /kleeontel/ • noun clients or customers collectively.
– ORIGIN French.

cliff • noun a steep rock face, especially at the edge of the sea.
– DERIVATIVES **cliffy** adjective.
– ORIGIN Old English.

cliffhanger • noun a story or event that is full of suspense because its ending or outcome is uncertain.

climacteric /klīmaktərik, klīmakterrik/ • noun **1** Medicine the period of life when fertility is in decline; (in women) the menopause. **2** a critical period or event. • adjective **1** having extreme and far-reaching implications or results; critical. **2** Medicine characteristic of or undergoing a climacteric.
– ORIGIN from Greek *klimaktēr* 'critical period', from *klimax* 'ladder, climax'.

climactic /klīmaktik/ • adjective forming an exciting climax.
– DERIVATIVES **climactically** adverb.

climate • noun **1** the general weather conditions prevailing in an area over a long period. **2** a prevailing trend or public attitude.
– DERIVATIVES **climatology** noun **climatological** adjective.
– ORIGIN originally denoting a zone of the earth between two lines of latitude: from Greek *klima* 'slope, zone'.

climatic /klīmattik/ • adjective relating to climate.
– DERIVATIVES **climatically** adverb.

climax • noun **1** the most intense, exciting, or important point of something. **2** an orgasm. • verb reach or bring to a climax.
– ORIGIN Greek *klimax* 'ladder, climax'.

climb • verb **1** go or come up to a higher position. **2** go up or scale (a hill, rock face, etc.) **3** (of a plant) grow up (a supporting structure) by clinging to or twining round it. **4** move with effort into or out of a confined space. **5** increase in scale, value, or power. **6** (**climb down**) withdraw from a position taken up in argument or negotiation. • noun **1** an act of climbing. **2** a recognized route up a mountain or cliff.
– PHRASES **be climbing the walls** informal feel frustrated, helpless, and trapped.
– DERIVATIVES **climbable** adjective.
– ORIGIN Old English, related to CLAY and CLEAVE².

climber • noun **1** a person who climbs rocks or mountains as a sport. **2** a climbing plant.

climbing frame • noun Brit. a structure of joined bars for children to climb on.

clime • noun chiefly literary a region considered with reference to its climate: *sunnier climes.*
– ORIGIN Greek *klima* 'slope, zone'.

clinch • verb **1** conclusively settle (a contract or contest). **2** (of two people) grapple at close quarters. **3** come together in an embrace. **4** secure (a nail or rivet) by driving the point sideways when it has penetrated. • noun **1** a struggle or scuffle at close quarters. **2** an embrace.
– ORIGIN from CLENCH.

clincher • noun informal a fact, argument, or event that settles a matter conclusively.

cline /klīn/ • noun a continuum with an infinite number of gradations from one end to the other.
– ORIGIN from Greek *klinein* 'to slope'.

cling • verb (past and past part. **clung**) (**cling to/on to**) **1** hold on tightly to. **2** adhere or stick to. **3** remain persistently faithful to. **4** be emotionally dependent on.
– ORIGIN Old English, related to CLENCH.

cling film • noun Brit. a thin clinging transparent plastic film used as a wrapping or covering for food.

clingy • adjective (**clingier, clingiest**) liable to cling; clinging.
– DERIVATIVES **clinginess** noun.

clinic • noun **1** a place where specialized medical treatment or advice is given. **2** a gathering at a hospital bedside for the teaching of medicine or surgery. **3** chiefly N. Amer. a conference or short course on a particular subject.
– ORIGIN from Greek *klinikē tekhnē* 'bedside art', from *klinē* 'bed'.

clinical • adjective **1** relating to the observation and treatment of patients (rather than theoretical studies). **2** efficient and coldly detached. **3** (of a place) bare, functional, and clean.
– DERIVATIVES **clinically** adverb.

clinical psychology • noun the branch of psychology concerned with the assessment and treatment of mental illness.

clinician • noun a doctor having direct contact with and responsibility for treating patients, rather than one involved with theoretical studies.

clink[1] • noun a sharp ringing sound, such as that made when metal or glass are struck. • verb make or cause to make a clink.
– ORIGIN from Dutch *klinken.*

clink[2] • noun informal prison.
– ORIGIN of unknown origin.

Thesaurus

a house on fire, be on the same wavelength. **4** (*informal*) *this issue hasn't clicked with the voters* GO DOWN WELL, prove popular, be a hit, succeed.

client • noun CUSTOMER, buyer, purchaser, shopper, consumer, user; patient; patron, regular; (**clients**) clientele, patronage, public, market; *Brit. informal* punter; *Law* vendee.

clientele • noun CLIENTS. See CLIENT.

cliff • noun PRECIPICE, rock face, crag, bluff, ridge, escarpment, scar, scarp, overhang.

climactic • adjective FINAL, ending, closing, concluding, ultimate; exciting, thrilling, gripping, riveting, dramatic, hair-raising; crucial, decisive, critical.

climate • noun **1** *a mild climate* WEATHER CONDITIONS, weather; atmospheric conditions. **2** *they come from colder climates* REGION, area, zone, country, place; *poetic/literary* clime. **3** *the political climate* ATMOSPHERE, mood, feeling, ambience, tenor; tendency, ethos, attitude; milieu; *informal* vibe(s).

climax • noun **1** *the climax of his career* PEAK, pinnacle, height, high(est) point, top; acme, zenith; culmination, crowning point, crown, crest; highlight, high spot, high water mark. **2** ORGASM; ejaculation.
– OPPOSITES nadir.
• verb **1** *the event will climax with a concert* CULMINATE, peak, reach a pinnacle, come to a crescendo, come to a head. **2** ORGASM; ejaculate; *informal* come, feel the earth move; *poetic/literary* die.

climb • verb **1** *we climbed the hill* ASCEND, mount, scale, scramble up, clamber up, shin up; go up, walk up; conquer, gain. **2** *the plane climbed* RISE, ascend, go up, gain altitude. **3** *the road climbs steeply* SLOPE UPWARDS, rise, go uphill, incline upwards. **4** *the shares climbed to 550 pence* INCREASE, rise, go up; shoot up, soar, rocket. **5** *he climbed through the ranks* ADVANCE, rise, move up, progress, work one's way. **6** *he climbed out of his car* CLAMBER, scramble; step.
– OPPOSITES descend, drop, fall.
• noun *a steep climb* ASCENT, clamber.
– OPPOSITES descent.
– PHRASES **climb down 1** *Sandy climbed down the ladder* DESCEND, go/come down, move down, shin down. **2** *the Government had to climb down* BACK DOWN, admit defeat, surrender, capitulate, yield, give in, give way, submit; retreat, backtrack; eat one's words, eat humble pie; do a U-turn; *Brit.* do an about-turn; *N. Amer. informal* eat crow.

clinch • verb **1** *he clinched the deal* SECURE, settle, conclude, close, pull off, bring off, complete, confirm, seal, finalize; *informal* sew up, wrap up. **2** *these findings clinched the matter* SETTLE, decide, determine; resolve; *informal* sort out. **3** *they clinched the title* WIN, secure; be victorious, come first, triumph, prevail. **4** *they clinch every nail* SECURE, fasten, fix, pinion. **5** *the boxers clinched* GRAPPLE, wrestle, struggle, scuffle.
– OPPOSITES lose.
• noun *a passionate clinch* EMBRACE, hug, cuddle, squeeze, hold, clasp.

cling • verb *rice grains tend to cling together* STICK, adhere, hold, cohere, bond, bind.
– PHRASES **cling (on) to 1** *she clung to him* HOLD ON, clutch, grip, grasp, clasp, attach oneself to, hang on; embrace, hug. **2** *they clung to their beliefs* ADHERE TO, hold to, stick to, stand by, abide by, cherish, remain true to, have faith in; *informal* swear by, stick with.

clinic • noun MEDICAL CENTRE, health centre, outpatients' department, surgery, doctor's.

clinical • adjective **1** *he seemed so clinical* DETACHED, impersonal, dispassionate, objective, uninvolved, distant, remote, aloof, removed, cold, indifferent, neutral, unsympathetic, unfeeling, unemotional. **2** *the room was clinical* PLAIN, simple, unadorned, unembellished, stark, austere, spartan, bleak, bare; clean; function-

C

clinker ● noun **1** the stony residue from burnt coal or from a furnace. **2** a brick with a vitrified surface.
– ORIGIN from Dutch *klinken* 'to clink'.

clinker-built ● adjective (of a boat) having external planks which overlap downwards and are secured with clinched nails. Compare with CARVEL-BUILT.
– ORIGIN from CLINCH.

clip[1] ● noun **1** a flexible or spring-loaded device for holding an object or objects together or in place. **2** a piece of jewellery that can be fastened on to a garment with a clip. **3** a metal holder containing cartridges for an automatic firearm. ● verb (**clipped**, **clipping**) fasten or be fastened with a clip or clips.
– ORIGIN Old English.

clip[2] ● verb (**clipped**, **clipping**) **1** cut, trim, or cut out with shears or scissors. **2** trim the hair or wool of (an animal). **3** strike smartly or with a glancing blow. ● noun **1** an act of clipping. **2** a short sequence taken from a film or broadcast. **3** informal a smart or glancing blow. **4** informal a rapid or specified speed: *they went by at a fast clip.*
– ORIGIN Old Norse.

clip art ● noun pre-drawn pictures and symbols provided with word-processing software and drawing packages.

clipboard ● noun a small board with a spring clip at the top, used for holding papers and providing support for writing.

clip joint ● noun informal a nightclub or bar that charges exorbitant prices.

clipped ● adjective (of speech) having short, sharp vowel sounds and clear pronunciation.

clipper ● noun **1** (**clippers**) an instrument for clipping. **2** a fast sailing ship, especially one of 19th-century design with concave bows and raked masts.

clipping ● noun **1** a small piece trimmed from something: *grass clippings.* **2** an article cut from a newspaper or magazine.

clique /kleek/ ● noun a small group of people who spend time together and do not readily allow others to join them.
– DERIVATIVES **cliquey** adjective **cliquish** adjective.
– ORIGIN French, from Old French *cliquer* 'make a noise'.

clitoridectomy /klittəridektəmi/ ● noun (pl. **clitoridectomies**) excision of the clitoris; female circumcision.

clitoris /klittəriss/ ● noun a small sensitive and erectile part of the female genitals at the front end of the vulva.
– DERIVATIVES **clitoral** adjective.
– ORIGIN Greek *kleitoris.*

cloaca /klōaykə/ ● noun (pl. **cloacae** /klōaysee/) (in some animals) a common cavity at the end of the digestive tract for the release of both excretory and genital products.
– DERIVATIVES **cloacal** adjective.
– ORIGIN Latin, 'sewer'.

cloak ● noun **1** an overgarment that hangs loosely from the shoulders over the arms to the knees or ankles. **2** something that hides or covers: *a cloak of secrecy.* **3** (**cloaks**) Brit. a cloakroom. ● verb dress or hide in a cloak.
– ORIGIN Old French *cloke,* from *cloche* 'bell, cloak', from Latin *clocca* 'bell'; related to CLOCK.

cloak-and-dagger ● adjective involving intrigue and secrecy.

cloakroom ● noun **1** a room in a public building where outdoor clothes and bags may be left. **2** Brit. a room that contains a toilet or toilets.

clobber[1] ● noun Brit. informal clothing and personal belongings.
– ORIGIN of unknown origin.

clobber[2] ● verb informal **1** hit hard. **2** defeat heavily.
– ORIGIN of unknown origin.

cloche /klosh/ ● noun **1** a small translucent cover for protecting or forcing outdoor plants. **2** (also **cloche hat**) a woman's close-fitting, bell-shaped hat.
– ORIGIN French, 'bell'.

clock ● noun **1** an instrument that measures and indicates the time by means of a dial or a digital display. **2** informal a measuring device resembling a clock, such as a speedometer. ● verb informal **1** attain or register (a specified time, distance, or speed). **2** (**clock in/out** or Brit. **on/off**) register one's arrival at or departure from work by means of an automatic recording clock. **3** Brit. see or watch. **4** chiefly Brit. hit on the head. **5** illegally wind back the milometer of (a car).
– PHRASES **round** (or **around**) **the clock** all day and all night. **turn** (or **put**) **back the clock** return to the past or to a previous way of doing things.
– DERIVATIVES **clocker** noun.
– ORIGIN Latin *clocca* 'bell'; related to CLOAK.

clock-watching ● noun working no longer than one's allotted hours.

clockwise ● adverb & adjective in a curve corresponding in direction to the movement of the hands of a clock.

clockwork ● noun a mechanism with a spring and toothed gearwheels, used to drive a mechanical clock, toy, or other device.
– PHRASES **like clockwork** very smoothly and easily.

clod ● noun **1** a lump of earth. **2** informal a stupid person.
– ORIGIN variant of CLOT.

cloddish ● adjective foolish, awkward, or clumsy.

clodhopper ● noun informal **1** a large, heavy shoe. **2** a foolish, awkward, or clumsy person.

clog ● noun **1** a shoe with a thick wooden sole. **2** an encumbrance. ● verb (**clogged**, **clogging**) (often **clog up**) block or become blocked.
– ORIGIN originally in the sense 'block of wood to impede an animal's movement': origin unknown.

cloisonné /klwaazonay/ ● noun enamel work in which different colours are separated by strips of flattened wire placed edgeways on a metal backing.
– ORIGIN French, 'partitioned'.

cloister /kloystər/ ● noun **1** a covered, and typically colonnaded, passage round an open court in a convent, monastery, college, or cathedral. **2** (**the cloister**) the secluded life of a monk or nun. ● verb seclude or shut up in a convent or monastery.
– DERIVATIVES **cloistral** adjective.
– ORIGIN Old French *cloistre,* from Latin *claustrum* 'lock, enclosed place', from *claudere* 'to close'.

cloistered ● adjective **1** having or enclosed by a cloister. **2** shel-

Thesaurus

al, basic, institutional, impersonal, characterless.
– OPPOSITES emotional, luxurious.

clip[1] ● noun **1** *a briefcase clip* FASTENER, clasp, hasp, catch, hook, buckle, lock. **2** *a diamanté clip* BROOCH, pin, badge. **3** *his clip was empty* MAGAZINE, cartridge, cylinder.
● verb *he clipped the pages together* FASTEN, attach, fix, join; pin, staple, tack.

clip[2] ● verb **1** *I clipped the hedge* TRIM, prune, cut, snip, shorten, crop, shear, pare; lop; neaten, shape. **2** *clip the coupon below* REMOVE, cut out, snip out, tear out, detach. **3** *his lorry clipped a van* HIT, strike, touch, graze, glance off, run into. **4** *Mum clipped his ear* HIT, cuff, strike, smack, slap, box; *informal* clout, whack, wallop, clobber, biff, sock.
● noun **1** *I gave the dog a clip* TRIM, cut, crop, haircut; shear. **2** *a film clip* EXTRACT, excerpt, snippet, cutting, fragment; trailer. **3** *(informal) a clip round the ear* SMACK, cuff, slap, box; *informal* clout, whack, wallop, biff, sock. **4** *(informal) the truck went at a good clip* SPEED, rate, pace, velocity; *informal* lick.
– PHRASES **clip someone's wings** RESTRICT SOMEONE'S FREEDOM, impose limits on, keep under control, stand in the way of; obstruct, impede, frustrate, thwart, fetter, hamstring.

clipping ● noun CUTTING, snippet, extract, excerpt.

clique ● noun COTERIE, set, circle, ring, in-crowd, group; club, society, fraternity, sorority; cabal, caucus; *informal* gang.

cloak ● noun **1** *the cloak over his shoulders* CAPE, robe, mantle, shawl, wrap, stole, tippet; poncho, serape, djellaba; cope; *historical* pelisse. **2** *a cloak of secrecy* COVER, veil, mantle, shroud, screen, mask, shield, blanket.
● verb *a peak cloaked in mist* CONCEAL, hide, cover, veil, shroud, mask, obscure, cloud; envelop, swathe, surround.

clobber[1] ● noun *(Brit. informal).* See CLOTHES.

clobber[2] ● verb *(informal).* See HIT verb sense 1.

clock ● noun **1** *a grandfather clock* TIMEPIECE, timekeeper, timer; chronometer, chronograph. **2** *(informal) the car had 50,000 miles on the clock* MILOMETER, counter; taximeter.
● verb *(informal)* **1** *the UK clocked up record exports* REGISTER, record, log, notch up; achieve, attain, accomplish, make; *informal* chalk up, bag. **2** *(Brit.) Liz was first to clock the change.* See NOTICE verb.

clod ● noun **1** *clods of earth* LUMP, clump, chunk, hunk, wedge. **2** *(informal) an insensitive clod.* See IDIOT.

clog ● noun *a wooden clog* sabot.
● verb *the pipes were clogged* BLOCK, obstruct, congest, jam, choke, bung up, plug, stop up, fill up; *Brit. informal* gunge up.

cloister ● noun **1** *the convent cloisters* WALKWAY, covered walk, ar-

tered from the outside world.

clomp • verb walk with a heavy tread. • noun the sound of a heavy tread.
– ORIGIN imitative.

clompy • adjective variant spelling of CLUMPY (in sense 1).

clone • noun **1** Biology an organism produced asexually from one ancestor to which it is genetically identical. **2** a person or thing regarded as identical with another; a copy or double. • verb **1** propagate as a clone. **2** make an identical copy of.
– DERIVATIVES **clonal** adjective.
– ORIGIN Greek *klōn* 'twig'.

clonk • noun a sound made by an abrupt and heavy impact. • verb **1** move with or make a clonk. **2** informal hit.
– DERIVATIVES **clonky** adjective.
– ORIGIN imitative.

clop • noun a sound made by a horse's hooves on a hard surface. • verb (**clopped**, **clopping**) move with such a sound.

close[1] /klōss/ • adjective **1** only a short distance away or apart in space or time. **2** (of a connection or resemblance) strong. **3** denoting someone who is part of a person's immediate family. **4** (of a relationship or the people conducting it) very affectionate or intimate. **5** (of observation or examination) done in a careful and thorough way. **6** (of information) carefully guarded. **7** not willing to give away money or information. **8** uncomfortably humid or airless. • adverb so as to be very near; with very little space between. • noun **1** Brit. a residential street without through access. **2** Brit. the precinct surrounding a cathedral.
– PHRASES **close-fisted** unwilling to spend money; mean. **close-knit** (of a group of people) united or bound together by strong relationships and common interests. **close-mouthed** reticent; discreet. **at** (or **from**) **close quarters** (or **range**) close to or from a position close to someone or something. **close-run** (of a contest or objective) won or lost by a very small margin. **close shave** (also **close call**) informal a narrow escape from danger or disaster.
– DERIVATIVES **closely** adverb **closeness** noun.
– ORIGIN Old French *clos*, from Latin *claudere* 'close, enclose, shut'.

close[2] /klōz/ • verb **1** move so as to cover an opening. **2** (also **close up**) bring two parts of (something) together. **3** (**close on/in on/up on**) gradually get nearer to or surround. **4** (**close in**) (of bad weather or darkness) gradually surround one. **5** (**close in**) (of days or nights) feature nightfall at an increasingly early hour with the approach of the winter solstice. **6** (**close around/over**) encircle and hold. **7** bring or come to an end. **8** finish speaking or writing. **9** (often **close down/up**) (with reference to a business or other organization) cease or cause to cease to trade or operate. **10** bring (a transaction or arrangement) to a conclusion. • noun **1** the end of an event or of a period of time or activity. **2** a shut position.
– DERIVATIVES **closable** adjective **closer** noun.
– ORIGIN Old French *clore*, from Latin *claudere*.

closed • adjective **1** not open or allowing access. **2** not communicating with or influenced by others.
– PHRASES **behind closed doors** taking place secretly. **a closed book** a subject or person about which one knows nothing.

closed-circuit television • noun a television system in which the video signals are transmitted from one or more cameras by cable to a restricted set of monitors.

closed shop • noun a place of work where all employees must belong to an agreed trade union.

close harmony • noun Music harmony in which the notes of the chord are close together, typically in vocal music.

close season (also chiefly N. Amer. **closed season**) • noun **1** a period between specified dates when fishing or the killing of particular game is officially forbidden. **2** Brit. a part of the year when a particular sport is not played.

closet • noun **1** chiefly N. Amer. a tall cupboard or wardrobe. **2** a small room. **3** archaic a toilet. **4** (**the closet**) (especially with reference to homosexuality) a state of secrecy or concealment. **5** (before another noun) secret; covert: *a closet socialist.* • verb (**closeted**, **closeting**) **1** shut away in private conference or study. **2** (**closeted**) keeping the fact of being homosexual secret.
– ORIGIN Old French, from *clos* 'close'.

close-up • noun a photograph or film sequence taken at close range and showing the subject on a large scale.

clostridium /klostriddiəm/ • noun (pl. **clostridia** /klostriddiə/) Biology an anaerobic bacterium which causes disease, e.g. tetanus and botulism.
– DERIVATIVES **clostridial** adjective.
– ORIGIN from Greek *klōstēr* 'spindle'.

closure • noun **1** an act or process of closing. **2** a device that closes or seals. **3** (in a legislative assembly) a procedure for ending a debate and taking a vote.
– ORIGIN Latin *clausura*, from *claudere* 'to close'.

clot • noun **1** a thick mass of coagulated liquid, especially blood, or of material stuck together. **2** Brit. informal a foolish or clumsy person. • verb (**clotted**, **clotting**) form or cause to form into clots.
– ORIGIN Old English.

cloth • noun (pl. **cloths**) **1** woven, knitted, or felted fabric made

Thesaurus

cade, loggia, gallery. **2** *I was educated in the cloister* ABBEY, monastery, friary, convent, priory, nunnery.
• verb *they were cloistered at home* CONFINE, isolate, shut away, sequester, seclude, closet.

cloistered • adjective SECLUDED, sequestered, sheltered, protected, insulated; shut off, isolated, confined; solitary, monastic, hermitic, reclusive.

close[1] • adjective **1** *the town is close to Leeds* NEAR, adjacent; in the vicinity of, in the neighbourhood of, within reach of; neighbouring, adjoining, abutting, alongside, on the doorstep, a stone's throw away; nearby, at hand, at close quarters; informal within spitting distance; archaic nigh. **2** *flying in close formation* DENSE, compact, tight, close-packed, packed, solid; crowded, cramped, congested. **3** *I was close to tears* NEAR, on the verge of, on the brink of, on the point of. **4** *a very close match* EVENLY MATCHED, even, neck and neck, with nothing to choose between them; informal fifty-fifty, even-steven(s). **5** *close relatives* IMMEDIATE, direct, near. **6** *close friends* INTIMATE, dear, bosom; close-knit, inseparable, attached, devoted, faithful; special, good, best, fast, firm; informal (as) thick as thieves. **7** *a close resemblance* STRONG, marked, distinct, pronounced. **8** *a close examination* CAREFUL, detailed, thorough, minute, searching, painstaking, meticulous, rigorous, scrupulous, conscientious; attentive, focused. **9** *keep a close eye on them* VIGILANT, watchful, keen, alert. **10** *a close translation* STRICT, faithful, exact, precise, literal; word for word, verbatim. **11** *he's close about his deals* RETICENT, secretive, uncommunicative, unforthcoming, tight-lipped, guarded, evasive. **12** *Sylvie was close with money* MEAN, miserly, niggardly, parsimonious, penny-pinching; informal tight-fisted, stingy, tight. **13** *the weather was close* HUMID, muggy, stuffy, airless, heavy, sticky, sultry, oppressive, stifling.
– OPPOSITES far, distant, one-sided, slight, loose, generous, fresh.
• noun (Brit.) *a small close of houses* CUL-DE-SAC, street, road; courtyard, quadrangle, enclosure.

close[2] • verb **1** *she closed the door* SHUT, pull to, push to, slam; fasten, secure. **2** *close the hole* BLOCK (UP/OFF), stop up, plug, seal (up/off), shut up/off, cork, stopper, bung (up); clog (up), choke, obstruct. **3** *the enemy were closing fast* CATCH UP, creep up, near, approach, gain on someone. **4** *the gap is closing* NARROW, reduce, shrink, lessen, get smaller, diminish, contract. **5** *his arms closed around her* MEET, join, connect; form a circle. **6** *he closed the meeting* END, conclude, finish, terminate, wind up, break off, halt, discontinue, dissolve; adjourn, suspend. **7** *the factory is to close* SHUT DOWN, close down, cease production, cease trading, be wound up, go out of business, go bankrupt, go into receivership, go into liquidation; informal fold, go to the wall, go bust. **8** *he closed a deal* CLINCH, settle, secure, seal, confirm, establish; transact, pull off; complete, conclude, fix, agree, finalize; informal wrap up.
– OPPOSITES open, widen, begin.
• noun *the close of the talks* END, finish, conclusion, termination, cessation, completion, resolution; climax, denouement.
– OPPOSITES beginning.
– PHRASES **close down.** See CLOSE[2] verb sense 7.

closet • noun *a clothes closet* CUPBOARD, wardrobe, cabinet, locker.
• adjective *a closet gay* SECRET, covert, private; surreptitious, clandestine, underground, furtive.
• verb *David was closeted in his den* SHUT AWAY, sequester, seclude, cloister, confine, isolate.

closure • noun CLOSING DOWN, shutdown, winding up; termination, discontinuation, cessation, finish, conclusion; failure; informal folding.

clot • noun **1** *blood clots* LUMP, clump, mass; thrombus, thrombosis, embolus; informal glob; Brit. informal gob. **2** (Brit. informal) *a clumsy clot.*

from a soft fibre such as wool or cotton. **2** a piece of cloth for a particular purpose. **3** (**the cloth**) the clergy; the clerical profession.
– ORIGIN Old English.
cloth cap ● noun Brit. **1** a man's flat woollen cap with a peak. **2** (before another noun) relating to the working class.
clothe ● verb (past and past part. **clothed** or archaic or literary **clad**) **1** provide with clothes. **2** (**be clothed in**) be dressed in.
– ORIGIN from the same Old English word as CLOTH.
clothes ● plural noun items worn to cover the body.
– ORIGIN Old English.
clothes horse ● noun a frame on which washed clothes are hung to dry.
clothes line ● noun a rope or wire on which washed clothes are hung to dry.
clothes moth ● noun a small brown moth whose larvae can be destructive to textile fibres.
clothes peg (also N. Amer. **clothespin**) ● noun Brit. a clip or forked device for securing clothes to a clothes line.
clothier /klōthiər/ ● noun a person who makes or sells clothes or cloth.
clothing ● noun clothes collectively.
clotted cream ● noun chiefly Brit. thick cream obtained by heating milk slowly and then allowing it to cool while the cream content rises to the top in coagulated lumps.
clotting factor ● noun any of a number of substances in the blood which are involved in the clotting process, such as factor VIII.
cloud ● noun **1** a visible mass of condensed watery vapour floating in the atmosphere, typically high above the general level of the ground. **2** an indistinct or billowing mass of smoke, dust, etc. **3** a large number of insects or birds moving together. **4** a state or cause of gloom or anxiety. ● verb **1** (usu. **cloud over**) (of the sky) become full of clouds. **2** make or become less clear or transparent. **3** (of someone's face or eyes) show sadness, anxiety, or anger. **4** make unclear or uncertain.
– PHRASES **have one's head in the clouds** be full of idealistic dreams. **on cloud nine** (or **seven**) extremely happy. [ORIGIN with reference to a ten-part classification of clouds in which 'nine' was next to the highest.] **under a cloud** under suspicion or discredited.
– DERIVATIVES **cloudiness** noun **cloudless** adjective **cloudlet** noun **cloudy** adjective (**cloudier**, **cloudiest**).
– ORIGIN Old English, 'mass of rock or earth'; probably related to CLOT.
cloudburst ● noun a sudden violent rainstorm.
cloud cuckoo land ● noun a state of unrealistic or absurdly over-optimistic fantasy.
– ORIGIN translation of Greek *Nephelokokkugia*, the name of a city built by the birds in Aristophanes' comedy *Birds*, from *nephelē* 'cloud' + *kokkux* 'cuckoo'.
clout ● noun **1** informal a heavy blow. **2** informal influence or power. **3** archaic a piece of cloth or clothing. ● verb informal hit hard.
– PHRASES **ne'er cast a clout till May be out** proverb do not discard your winter clothes until the end of May.
– ORIGIN Old English, 'a patch or metal plate'; related to CLEAT and CLOT.
clove[1] ● noun **1** the dried flower bud of a tropical tree, used as a pungent aromatic spice. **2** (**oil of cloves**) an aromatic oil extracted from these buds and used for the relief of dental pain. **3** (also **clove pink** or **clove gillyflower**) a clove-scented pink which is the original type from which the carnation and other double pinks have been bred.
– ORIGIN from Old French *clou de girofle*, 'nail of gillyflower' (from its shape), GILLYFLOWER being originally the name of the spice and later applied to the similarly scented pink.
clove[2] ● noun any of the small bulbs making up a compound bulb of garlic, shallot, etc.
– ORIGIN Old English, related to CLEAVE[1].
clove[3] past of CLEAVE[1].
clove hitch ● noun a knot by which a rope is secured by passing it twice round a spar or another rope that it crosses at right angles in such a way that both ends pass under the loop of rope at the front.
– ORIGIN *clove*, past tense of CLEAVE[1] (because the rope appears as separate parallel lines at the back of the knot).
cloven past participle of CLEAVE[1].
cloven hoof (also **cloven foot**) ● noun the divided hoof or foot of ruminants such as cattle, sheep, goats, antelopes, and deer.
clover ● noun a herbaceous plant with globular white or deep pink flower heads and three-lobed leaves.
– PHRASES **in clover** in ease and luxury.
– ORIGIN Old English.
clown ● noun **1** a comic entertainer, especially one in a circus, wearing a traditional costume and exaggerated make-up. **2** a playful, extrovert person. ● verb act comically or playfully.
– DERIVATIVES **clownish** adjective.
– ORIGIN perhaps of Low German origin.
cloy ● verb disgust or sicken with an excess of sweetness, richness, or sentiment.
– DERIVATIVES **cloying** adjective **cloyingly** adverb.
– ORIGIN shortening of obsolete *accloy* 'block up', from Old French *encloyer* 'drive a nail into', from Latin *clavus* 'a nail'.
club[1] ● noun **1** an association dedicated to a particular interest

Thesaurus

See FOOL noun sense 1.
● verb *the blood is likely to clot* COAGULATE, set, congeal, curdle, thicken, solidify.
cloth ● noun **1** *a maker of cloth* FABRIC, material, textile(s); *Brit.* soft goods. **2** *a cloth to wipe the table* RAG, wipe, duster, sponge; flannel, towel; *Austral.* washer; *UK trademark* J-cloth. **3** *a gentleman of the cloth* THE CLERGY, the church, the priesthood, the ministry; clergymen, clerics, priests.
clothe ● verb **1** *they were clothed in silk* DRESS, attire, robe, garb, array, costume, swathe, deck (out), turn out, fit out, rig (out); *informal* get up; *archaic* apparel, habit, invest. **2** *a valley clothed in conifers* COVER, blanket, carpet; envelop, swathe.
clothes ● plural noun CLOTHING, garments, attire, garb, dress, wear, costume; *informal* gear, togs, duds, get-up; *Brit. informal* clobber; *N. Amer. informal* threads; *formal* apparel; *archaic* raiment, habiliments, vestments.
– RELATED TERMS sartorial.
clothing ● noun. See CLOTHES.
cloud ● noun **1** *dark clouds* storm cloud, cloudbank; mackerel sky. **2** *a cloud of exhaust smoke* MASS, billow; pall, mantle, blanket. **3** *a cloud of rooks* FLOCK, swarm, mass, multitude, host, throng, crowd.
● verb **1** *the sky clouded* BECOME CLOUDY, cloud over, become overcast, lour, blacken, darken. **2** *the sand is churned up, clouding the water* MAKE CLOUDY, make murky, dirty, darken, blacken. **3** *anger clouded my judgement* CONFUSE, muddle, obscure, fog, muddy, mar.
– PHRASES **on cloud nine** ECSTATIC, rapturous, joyful, elated, blissful, euphoric, in seventh heaven, walking on air, transported, in raptures, delighted, thrilled, overjoyed, very happy; *informal* over the moon, on top of the world; *Austral. informal* wrapped.
cloudy ● adjective **1** *a cloudy sky* OVERCAST, clouded; dark, grey, black, leaden, murky; sombre, dismal, heavy, gloomy; sunless, starless; hazy, misty, foggy. **2** *cloudy water* MURKY, muddy, milky, dirty, opaque, turbid. **3** *his eyes grew cloudy* TEARFUL, teary, weepy, lachrymose; moist, watery; misty, blurred. **4** *avoid cloudy phrases* VAGUE, imprecise, foggy, hazy, confused, muddled, nebulous, obscure.
– OPPOSITES clear.
clout (*informal*) ● noun **1** *a clout on the ear* SMACK, slap, thump, punch, blow, hit, cuff, box, clip; *informal* whack, wallop. **2** *his clout in the business world* INFLUENCE, power, weight, sway, leverage, control, say; dominance, authority; *informal* teeth, muscle.
● verb *he clouted me* HIT, strike, punch, smack, slap, cuff, thump, buffet; *informal* wallop, belt, whack, clobber, sock, bop, biff.
cloven ● adjective SPLIT, divided, cleft.
clown ● noun **1** *a circus clown* COMIC ENTERTAINER, comedian; *historical* jester, fool, zany; *archaic* merry andrew. **2** *the class clown* JOKER, comedian, comic, humorist, wag, wit, prankster, jester, buffoon; *informal* laugh, kidder, wisecracker; *Austral./NZ informal* hard case. **3** *bureaucratic clowns* FOOL, idiot, dolt, ass, simpleton, ignoramus; bungler, blunderer; *informal* moron, jackass, chump, numbskull, nincompoop, halfwit, bonehead, fathead, birdbrain; *Brit. informal* prat, berk, twit, nitwit, twerp.
● verb *Harvey clowned around* FOOL AROUND/ABOUT, play the fool, play about/around, monkey about/around; joke, jest; *informal* mess about/around, lark (about/around), horse about/around; *Brit. informal* muck about/around; *dated* play the giddy goat.
cloy ● verb SICKEN, disgust; become sickening, become nauseating, pall; be excessive.
cloying ● adjective SICKLY, syrupy, saccharine, oversweet; sicken-

or activity. **2** an organization offering members social amenities, meals, and temporary residence. **3** a nightclub with dance music. ● verb (**clubbed**, **clubbing**) **1** (**club together**) combine with others to do something, especially to collect a sum of money. **2** informal go out to nightclubs.
– DERIVATIVES **clubber** noun.
– ORIGIN formed obscurely from CLUB².
club² ● noun **1** a heavy stick with a thick end, used as a weapon. **2** (also **golf club**) a club used to hit the ball in golf, with a heavy wooden or metal head on a slender shaft. **3** (**clubs**) one of the four suits in a conventional pack of playing cards, denoted by a black trefoil. ● verb (**clubbed**, **clubbing**) beat with a club or similar implement.
– ORIGIN Old Norse; related to CLUMP.
clubbable ● adjective sociable and popular.
– DERIVATIVES **clubbability** noun.
club class ● noun Brit. the intermediate class of seating on an aircraft, designed especially for business travellers.
club foot ● noun a deformed foot which is twisted so that the sole cannot be placed flat on the ground.
clubhouse ● noun a building having a bar and other facilities for the members of a club.
clubmoss ● noun a low-growing flowerless plant belonging to a group of plants resembling large mosses.
clubroot ● noun a disease of cabbages, turnips, etc. in which the root becomes swollen and distorted.
club sandwich ● noun a sandwich consisting typically of chicken and bacon, tomato, and lettuce, layered between three slices of bread.
cluck ● noun the characteristic short, guttural sound made by a hen. ● verb **1** make a cluck. **2** (**cluck over/around**) express fussy concern about.
– DERIVATIVES **clucky** adjective.
– ORIGIN imitative.
clue ● noun a fact or piece of evidence that helps to clarify a mystery or solve a problem. ● verb (**clues**, **clued**, **clueing**) (**clue in**) informal inform.
– PHRASES **not have a clue** informal be bewildered, incompetent, or ignorant.
– ORIGIN originally denoting a ball of thread, hence one used to guide a person out of a labyrinth: variant of CLEW.
clued-up (also chiefly N. Amer. **clued-in**) ● adjective informal well informed about a particular subject.
clueless ● adjective informal having no knowledge, understanding, or ability.
– DERIVATIVES **cluelessly** adverb **cluelessness** noun.
clump ● noun **1** a small group of trees or plants growing closely together. **2** a compacted mass or lump of something. **3** another term for CLOMP. ● verb **1** form into a clump or mass. **2** another term for CLOMP.
– ORIGIN originally denoting a heap or lump; related to CLUB².
clumpy ● adjective **1** (also **clompy**) (of shoes or boots) heavy and inelegant. **2** forming or tending to form clumps.
clumsy ● adjective (**clumsier**, **clumsiest**) **1** awkward in movement or performance. **2** difficult to use; unwieldy. **3** tactless.
– DERIVATIVES **clumsily** adverb **clumsiness** noun.
– ORIGIN from obsolete *clumse* 'make or be numb', probably of Scandinavian origin.
clung past and past participle of CLING.
Cluniac /kloōniak/ ● noun a monk of a reformed Benedictine monastic order founded at Cluny in eastern France in 910.
clunk ● noun a dull, heavy sound such as that made by thick pieces of metal striking together. ● verb move with or make a clunk.
– ORIGIN imitative.
cluster ● noun a group of similar things positioned or occurring closely together. ● verb form a cluster.
– ORIGIN Old English, probably related to CLOT.
cluster bomb ● noun a bomb which releases a number of projectiles on impact.
clutch¹ ● verb grasp tightly. ● noun **1** a tight grasp. **2** (**clutches**) power; control. **3** a mechanism for connecting and disconnecting the engine and the transmission system in a vehicle.
– ORIGIN originally in the sense 'bend, crook': variant of obsolete *clitch* 'close the hand', from Old English.
clutch² ● noun **1** a group of eggs fertilized at the same time and laid in a single session. **2** a brood of chicks. **3** a small group of people or things.
– ORIGIN Old Norse.
clutch bag ● noun a slim, flat handbag without handles or a strap.
clutter ● noun **1** things lying about untidily. **2** an untidy state. ● verb cover or fill with clutter.
– ORIGIN variant of dialect *clotter* 'to clot', influenced by CLUSTER and CLATTER.
Cm ● symbol the chemical element curium.
cm ● abbreviation centimetre or centimetres.
CMG ● abbreviation (in the UK) Companion of St Michael and St George (or Companion of the Order of St Michael and St George).
CMV ● abbreviation cytomegalovirus.
CNAA ● abbreviation Council for National Academic Awards.
CND ● abbreviation Campaign for Nuclear Disarmament.
CO ● abbreviation **1** Colorado. **2** Commanding Officer.
Co ● symbol the chemical element cobalt.
Co. ● abbreviation **1** company. **2** county.

Thesaurus

ing, nauseating; mawkish, sentimental; *Brit.* twee; *informal* over the top, OTT, mushy, slushy, sloppy, gooey, cheesy, corny; *N. Amer. informal* cornball, sappy.
club¹ ● noun **1** *a canoeing club* SOCIETY, association, organization, institution, group, circle, band, body, ring, crew; alliance, league, union. **2** *the city has great clubs* NIGHTCLUB, disco, discotheque, bar; *informal* niterie. **3** *the top club in the league* TEAM, squad, side, lineup.
– PHRASES **club together** POOL RESOURCES, join forces, team up, band together, get together, pull together, collaborate, ally; *informal* have a whip-round.
club² ● noun *a wooden club* CUDGEL, truncheon, bludgeon, baton, stick, mace, bat; *N. Amer.* blackjack, nightstick; *Brit. informal* cosh.
● verb *he was clubbed with an iron bar* CUDGEL, bludgeon, bash, beat, hit, strike, batter, belabour; *informal* clout, clobber; *Brit. informal* cosh.
clue ● noun **1** *police are searching for clues* HINT, indication, sign, signal, pointer, trace, indicator; lead, tip, tip-off; evidence, information. **2** *a crossword clue* QUESTION, problem, puzzle, riddle, poser, conundrum.
– PHRASES **clue someone in/up** *(informal)* INFORM, notify, make aware, prime; keep up to date, keep posted; *informal* tip off, give the gen, give the low-down, fill in on, gen up on, put in the picture, put wise, keep up to speed. **not have a clue** *(informal)* HAVE NO IDEA, be ignorant, not have an inkling; be baffled, be mystified, be at a loss; *informal* be clueless, not have the faintest.
clump ● noun **1** *a clump of trees* CLUSTER, thicket, group, bunch, assemblage. **2** *a clump of earth* LUMP, clod, mass, gobbet, wad; *informal* glob; *Brit. informal* gob.
● verb **1** *galaxies clump together* CLUSTER, group, collect, gather, assemble, congregate, mass. **2** *they were clumping around upstairs* STAMP, stomp, clomp, tramp, lumber; thump, thud, bang; *informal* galumph.
clumsy ● adjective **1** *she was terribly clumsy* AWKWARD, uncoordinated, ungainly, graceless, inelegant; inept, maladroit, unskilful, unhandy, accident-prone, like a bull in a china shop, all fingers and thumbs; *informal* cack-handed, ham-fisted, butterfingered, having two left feet; *N. Amer. informal* klutzy. **2** *a clumsy contraption* UNWIELDY, cumbersome, bulky, awkward. **3** *a clumsy remark* GAUCHE, awkward, graceless; unsubtle, uncouth, boorish, crass; tactless, insensitive, thoughtless, undiplomatic, indelicate, ill-judged.
– OPPOSITES graceful, elegant, tactful.
cluster ● noun **1** *clusters of berries* BUNCH, clump, mass, knot, group, clutch, bundle, truss. **2** *a cluster of spectators* CROWD, group, knot, huddle, bunch, throng, flock, pack, band; *informal* gang, gaggle.
● verb *they clustered around the television* CONGREGATE, gather, collect, group, assemble; huddle, crowd, flock.
clutch¹ ● verb *she clutched his arm* GRIP, grasp, clasp, cling to, hang on to, clench, hold.
– PHRASES **clutch at** REACH FOR, snatch at, make a grab for, catch at, claw at.
clutch² ● noun **1** *a clutch of eggs* GROUP, batch. **2** *a clutch of awards* GROUP, collection; raft, armful; *informal* load, bunch.
clutches ● plural noun POWER, control, domination, command, rule, tyranny; hands, hold, grip, grasp, claws, jaws; custody.
clutter ● noun **1** *a clutter of toys* MESS, jumble, litter, heap, tangle, muddle, hotchpotch. **2** *a desk full of clutter* DISORDER, chaos, dis-

C

c/o • abbreviation care of.
co- • prefix **1** (forming nouns) joint; mutual; common: *co-driver*. **2** (forming adjectives) jointly; mutually: *coequal*. **3** (forming verbs) together with another or others: *co-produce*.
– ORIGIN Latin, originally a form of COM-.
coach[1] • noun **1** chiefly Brit. a comfortably equipped single-decker bus used for longer journeys. **2** a railway carriage. **3** a closed horse-drawn carriage. • verb travel or convey by coach.
– ORIGIN French *coche*, from Hungarian *kocsi szekér* 'wagon from *Kocs*', a town in Hungary.
coach[2] • noun **1** an instructor or trainer in sport. **2** a tutor who gives private or specialized teaching. • verb train or teach as a coach.
– ORIGIN a figurative extension of COACH[1].
coach-built • adjective Brit. (of a vehicle) having specially or individually built bodywork.
– DERIVATIVES **coachbuilder** noun.
coaching inn • noun historical an inn along a route followed by horse-drawn coaches, at which horses could be changed.
coachwork • noun the bodywork of a road or railway vehicle.
coagulant /kōagyoolənt/ • noun a substance that causes coagulation.
coagulate /kōagyoolayt/ • verb (of a fluid, especially blood) change to a solid or semi-solid state.
– DERIVATIVES **coagulable** adjective **coagulation** noun **coagulator** noun.
– ORIGIN Latin *coagulare* 'curdle'.
coal • noun **1** a combustible black rock consisting mainly of carbonized plant matter and used as fuel. **2** Brit. a piece of coal.
– PHRASES **coals to Newcastle** something supplied to a place where it is already plentiful. **haul over the coals** reprimand severely.
– DERIVATIVES **coaly** adjective.
– ORIGIN Old English.
coalesce /kōəless/ • verb come or bring together to form one mass or whole.
– DERIVATIVES **coalescence** noun **coalescent** adjective.
– ORIGIN Latin *coalescere*, from *alescere* 'grow up'.
coalface • noun an exposed surface of coal in a mine.
– PHRASES **at the coalface** engaged in work in a particular field at an active rather than theoretical level.
coalfield • noun an extensive area containing a number of underground coal strata.
coal gas • noun a mixture of gases obtained by distilling coal, formerly used for lighting and heating.
coalition /kōəlish'n/ • noun a temporary alliance, especially of political parties forming a government.
– DERIVATIVES **coalitionist** noun.
– ORIGIN Latin, from *coalescere* 'coalesce'.
coal tar • noun a thick black liquid distilled from coal, containing organic chemicals including benzene, naphthalene, phenols, and aniline.
coal tit (also **cole tit**) • noun a small titmouse with a grey back, black cap and throat, and white cheeks.
coaming /kōming/ (also **coamings**) • noun a raised border round the cockpit or hatch of a boat to keep out water.
– ORIGIN of unknown origin.
coarse • adjective **1** rough or harsh in texture. **2** consisting of large grains or particles. **3** rude or vulgar in behaviour or speech. **4** of inferior quality.
– DERIVATIVES **coarsely** adverb **coarseness** noun.
– ORIGIN originally in the sense 'ordinary or inferior': perhaps related to COURSE.
coarse fish • noun (pl. same) Brit. any freshwater fish other than salmon and trout.
coarsen • verb make or become coarse.
coast • noun **1** land adjoining or near the sea. **2** the easy movement of a vehicle without the use of power. • verb **1** move easily without using power. **2** act or make progress without making much effort: *United coasted to victory*. **3** sail along the coast.
– PHRASES **the coast is clear** there is no danger of being observed or caught.
– DERIVATIVES **coastal** adjective.
– ORIGIN originally in the sense 'side of the body': from Latin *costa* 'rib, flank, side'.
coaster • noun **1** a ship carrying cargo along the coast from port to port. **2** a small mat for a glass.
coastguard • noun an organization or person that keeps watch over coastal waters to assist people or ships in danger and to prevent smuggling.
coastline • noun a length of coast: *a rugged coastline*.
coat • noun **1** a full-length outer garment with sleeves. **2** an animal's covering of fur or hair. **3** an enclosing or covering layer or structure. **4** a single application of paint or similar material. • verb provide with or form a layer or covering.
– ORIGIN Old French *cote*.
coat dress • noun a woman's tailored dress that resembles a coat.
coati /kōaati/ • noun (pl. **coatis**) a raccoon-like animal found in Central and South America, with a long flexible snout and a ringed tail.
– ORIGIN Spanish and Portuguese, from a Tupi word incorporating elements meaning 'belt' and 'nose'.
coating • noun a thin layer or covering.
coat of arms • noun the distinctive heraldic bearings or shield of a person, family, corporation, or country.
coat of mail • noun historical a jacket composed of metal rings or plates, serving as armour.
coat-tail • noun each of the flaps formed by the back of a tailcoat.
– PHRASES **on someone's coat-tails** undeservedly benefiting from another's success.
coax /kōks/ • verb **1** persuade gradually or by flattery to do something. **2** manipulate carefully into a particular situation or position.
– ORIGIN originally in the sense 'pet, fondle': from obsolete *cokes* 'simpleton'.
coaxial /kōaksiəl/ • adjective **1** having a common axis. **2** (of a cable or line) transmitting by means of two concentric conductors separated by an insulator.

Thesaurus

array, untidiness, mess, confusion; litter, rubbish.
• verb *the garden was cluttered with tools* LITTER, mess up, disarrange; be strewn, be scattered; poetic/literary bestrew.
coach[1] • noun **1** *a journey by coach* BUS, minibus; dated omnibus, charabanc. **2** *a railway coach* CARRIAGE, wagon, compartment, van, Pullman; N. Amer. car. **3** *a coach and horses* HORSE-DRAWN CARRIAGE, trap, hackney, hansom, gig, landau, brougham.
coach[2] • noun *a football coach* INSTRUCTOR, trainer; teacher, tutor, mentor, guru.
• verb *he coached Richard in maths* INSTRUCT, teach, tutor, school, educate; drill, cram; train.
coagulate • verb CONGEAL, clot, thicken, gel; solidify, harden, set, dry.
coalesce • verb MERGE, unite, join together, combine, fuse, mingle, blend; amalgamate, consolidate, integrate, homogenize, converge.
coalition • noun ALLIANCE, union, partnership, bloc, caucus; federation, league, association, confederation, consortium, syndicate, combine; amalgamation, merger.
coarse • adjective **1** *coarse blankets* ROUGH, scratchy, prickly, wiry. **2** *his coarse features* LARGE, rough, rough-hewn, heavy; ugly. **3** *a coarse boy* OAFISH, loutish, boorish, uncouth, rude, impolite, ill-mannered, uncivil; vulgar, common, rough, uncultured, crass. **4** *a coarse innuendo* VULGAR, crude, rude, off colour, dirty, filthy, smutty, indelicate, improper, unseemly, crass, tasteless, lewd, prurient; informal blue, farmyard.
– OPPOSITES soft, delicate, refined.
coarsen • verb **1** *hands coarsened by work* ROUGHEN, toughen, harden. **2** *I had been coarsened by the army* DESENSITIZE, dehumanize; dull, deaden.
– OPPOSITES soften, refine.
coast • noun *the west coast* SEABOARD, coastal region, coastline, seashore, shore, foreshore, shoreline, seaside, waterfront, littoral; poetic/literary strand.
• verb *the car coasted down a hill* FREEWHEEL, cruise, taxi, drift, glide, sail.
coat • noun **1** *a winter coat* OVERCOAT, jacket. **2** *a dog's coat* FUR, hair, wool, fleece; hide, pelt, skin. **3** *a coat of paint* LAYER, covering, coating, skin, film, wash; plating, glaze, varnish, veneer, patina; deposit.
• verb *the tube was coated with wax* COVER, paint, glaze, varnish, wash; surface, veneer, laminate, plate, face; daub, smear, cake, plaster.
coating • noun. See COAT noun sense 3.

– DERIVATIVES **coaxially** adverb.

cob ● noun **1** Brit. a loaf of bread. **2** a corncob. **3** (also **cobnut**) a hazelnut or filbert. **4** a powerfully built, short-legged horse. **5** a male swan. **6** a roundish lump of coal.
– ORIGIN originally denoting a strong man or leader: of unknown origin.

cobalt /kōbawlt/ ● noun a hard silvery-white metallic chemical element with magnetic properties, used in alloys.
– ORIGIN German *Kobalt* 'imp, demon' (from the belief that cobalt was harmful to the ores with which it occurred).

cobalt blue ● noun a deep blue pigment containing cobalt and aluminium oxides.

cobber ● noun Austral./NZ informal a companion or friend.
– ORIGIN perhaps related to English dialect *cob* 'take a liking to'.

cobble[1] ● noun (also **cobblestone**) a small round stone used to cover road surfaces.
– DERIVATIVES **cobbled** adjective.
– ORIGIN from COB.

cobble[2] ● verb **1** (**cobble together**) roughly assemble from available parts or elements. **2** dated repair (shoes).
– ORIGIN back-formation from COBBLER.

cobbler ● noun **1** a person whose job is mending shoes. **2** chiefly N. Amer. a fruit pie with a rich, cake-like crust. **3** (**cobblers**) Brit. informal nonsense. [ORIGIN originally in the sense 'testicles': from rhyming slang *cobbler's awls* 'balls'.]
– PHRASES **let the cobbler stick to his last** proverb people should only concern themselves with things they know something about. [ORIGIN translating Latin *ne sutor ultra crepidam*.]
– ORIGIN of unknown origin.

cobra /kōbrə/ ● noun a highly venomous snake that spreads the skin of its neck into a hood when disturbed, native to Africa and Asia.
– ORIGIN from Portuguese *cobra de capello* 'snake with hood'.

cobweb ● noun a spider's web, especially an old or dusty one.
– DERIVATIVES **cobwebbed** adjective **cobwebby** adjective.
– ORIGIN originally *coppeweb*: from obsolete *coppe* 'spider', from Old English.

coca /kōkə/ ● noun a tropical American shrub grown for its leaves, which are the source of cocaine.
– ORIGIN Spanish, from an American Indian word.

cocaine /kōkayn/ ● noun an addictive drug derived from coca or prepared synthetically, used as an illegal stimulant and sometimes medicinally as a local anaesthetic.
– ORIGIN from COCA.

coccus /kokkəss/ ● noun (pl. **cocci** /kokkī/) Biology any spherical or roughly spherical bacterium.
– DERIVATIVES **coccal** adjective **coccoid** adjective.
– ORIGIN originally denoting a scale insect: from Greek *kokkos* 'berry'.

coccyx /koksiks/ ● noun (pl. **coccyges** /koksijeez/ or **coccyxes**) a small triangular bone at the base of the spinal column in humans and some apes, formed of fused vestigial vertebrae.
– DERIVATIVES **coccygeal** /koksijiəl/ adjective.
– ORIGIN Greek *kokkux* 'cuckoo' (because the shape of the human bone resembles the cuckoo's bill).

cochineal /kochineel/ ● noun a scarlet dye used for colouring food, made from the crushed dried bodies of a female scale insect.
– ORIGIN French *cochenille* or Spanish *cochinilla*, from Latin *coccinus* 'scarlet'.

cochlea /kokliə/ ● noun (pl. **cochleae** /kokli-ee/) the spiral cavity of the inner ear, containing an organ which produces nerve impulses in response to sound vibrations.
– DERIVATIVES **cochlear** adjective.
– ORIGIN Latin, 'snail shell or screw', from Greek *kokhlias*.

cock ● noun **1** a male bird, especially of a domestic fowl. **2** vulgar slang a man's penis. **3** Brit. informal nonsense. **4** a firing lever in a gun which can be raised to be released by the trigger. **5** a stopcock. ● verb **1** tilt or bend (something) in a particular direction. **2** raise the cock of (a gun) to make it ready for firing. **3** (**cock up**) Brit. informal spoil or ruin.
– PHRASES **cock one's ear** (of a dog) raise its ears to an erect position.
– ORIGIN Latin *coccus*; reinforced by Old French *coq*.

cockabully /kokkəbŏŏlli/ ● noun (pl. **cockabullies**) NZ a small blunt-nosed freshwater fish.
– ORIGIN Maori.

cockade /kokayd/ ● noun a rosette or knot of ribbons worn in a hat as a badge of office or as part of a livery.
– DERIVATIVES **cockaded** adjective.
– ORIGIN French *cocarde*, from obsolete *coquard* 'saucy'.

cock-a-doodle-doo ● exclamation used to represent the sound made by a cock when it crows.

cock-a-hoop ● adjective extremely pleased.
– ORIGIN from the phrase *set cock a hoop*, apparently denoting the action of turning on a tap and allowing liquor to flow.

cock-a-leekie ● noun a soup traditionally made in Scotland with chicken and leeks.

cock and bull story ● noun informal a ridiculous and implausible story.

cockatiel /kokkəteel/ ● noun a small crested Australian parrot with a mainly grey body and a yellow and orange face.
– ORIGIN Dutch *kaketielje*, probably from a Malay word meaning 'cockatoo'.

cockatoo /kokkətōō/ ● noun a parrot with an erectile crest.
– ORIGIN Dutch *kaketoe*, from Malay.

cockatrice /kokkətriss/ ● noun **1** another term for BASILISK (in sense 1). **2** Heraldry a mythical animal depicted as a two-legged dragon with a cock's head.
– ORIGIN Old French *cocatris*, from Latin *calcatrix* 'tracker'.

cockchafer /kokchayfər/ ● noun a large brown flying beetle which is a destructive plant pest.
– ORIGIN from COCK (expressing size) + CHAFER.

cockcrow ● noun literary dawn.

cocked hat ● noun a brimless triangular hat pointed at the front, back, and top.
– PHRASES **knock into a cocked hat** completely defeat or outdo.

cockerel ● noun a young domestic cock.

cocker spaniel ● noun a small breed of spaniel with a silky coat.
– ORIGIN from COCK, because the dog was bred to flush game birds such as woodcock.

cock-eyed ● adjective informal **1** crooked or askew; not level. **2** absurd; impractical. **3** having a squint.

cockfighting ● noun the sport (illegal in the UK and some other countries) of setting two cocks to fight each other.
– DERIVATIVES **cockfight** noun.

cockle[1] ● noun **1** an edible burrowing bivalve mollusc with a strong ribbed shell. **2** (also **cockleshell**) literary a small shallow boat.
– PHRASES **warm the cockles of one's heart** give one a comforting feeling of contentment.
– DERIVATIVES **cockling** noun.
– ORIGIN Old French *coquille* 'shell', from Greek *konkhē* 'conch'.

cockle[2] ● verb (of paper) wrinkle or pucker.
– ORIGIN French *coquiller* 'blister (bread in cooking)', from *coquille* (see COCKLE[1]).

cockney /kokni/ ● noun (pl. **cockneys**) **1** a native of the East End of London, traditionally one born within the sound of Bow Bells. **2** the dialect or accent prevailing in this area.
– ORIGIN originally denoting a pampered child, later a town-dweller regarded as affected or puny: origin uncertain.

cockpit ● noun **1** a compartment for the pilot and crew in an aircraft or spacecraft. **2** the driver's compartment in a racing car. **3** a place where cockfights are held.
– ORIGIN from COCK + PIT[1]; sense 1 derives from an 18th-century use denoting an area in the aft lower deck of a ship where the

Thesaurus

coax ● verb PERSUADE, wheedle, cajole, get round; beguile, seduce, inveigle, manoeuvre; *informal* sweet-talk, soft-soap, butter up, twist someone's arm.

cobble ● verb
– PHRASES **cobble something together** PREPARE ROUGHLY/HASTILY, make roughly/hastily, throw together; improvise, contrive, rig (up), whip up; *informal* rustle up; *Brit. informal* knock up.

cock ● noun ROOSTER, cockerel, capon.
● verb **1** *he cocked his head* TILT, tip, angle, incline, dip. **2** *she cocked her little finger* BEND, flex, crook, curve. **3** *the dog cocked its leg* LIFT, raise, hold up.

cock-eyed ● adjective (*informal*) **1** *that picture is cock-eyed* CROOKED, awry, askew, lopsided, tilted, off-centre, skewed, skew, squint, misaligned; *Brit. informal* skew-whiff, wonky. **2** *a cock-eyed scheme* ABSURD, preposterous, ridiculous, ludicrous, farcical, laughable, risible, idiotic, stupid, foolish, silly, inane, imbecilic, hare-

wounded were taken, later coming to mean 'the 'pit' or well from which a yacht was steered'.

cockroach ● noun a beetle-like scavenging insect with long antennae and legs, some kinds of which are household pests.
– ORIGIN Spanish *cucaracha*.

cockscomb ● noun the crest or comb of a domestic cock.

cocksure ● adjective presumptuously or arrogantly confident.
– DERIVATIVES **cocksureness** noun.
– ORIGIN from archaic *cock* (a euphemism for *God*) + SURE; later associated with COCK.

C

cocktail ● noun **1** an alcoholic drink consisting of a spirit mixed with other ingredients, such as fruit juice. **2** (before another noun) relating to or associated with cocktail drinking or formal social occasions: *a cocktail dress.* **3** a dish consisting of a mixture of small pieces of food. **4** a mixture of diverse substances or factors, especially when dangerous or unpleasant.
– ORIGIN originally denoting a horse with a docked tail, later a racehorse which was not a thoroughbred through having a cock-tailed horse in its pedigree: from COCK + TAIL[1].

cock-up ● noun Brit. informal something done badly or inefficiently.

cocky[1] ● adjective (**cockier**, **cockiest**) conceited in a bold or cheeky way.
– DERIVATIVES **cockily** adverb **cockiness** noun.
– ORIGIN originally in the sense 'lecherous': from COCK.

cocky[2] ● noun (pl. **cockies**) Austral./NZ informal a cockatoo.

cocoa ● noun **1** a powder made from roasted and ground cacao seeds. **2** a hot drink made from cocoa powder mixed with milk or water.
– ORIGIN alteration of CACAO.

cocoa bean ● noun a cacao seed.

cocoa butter ● noun a fatty substance obtained from cocoa beans, used in making confectionery and cosmetics.

coco de mer /kōkō də **mair**/ ● noun a tall palm tree native to the Seychelles, having an immense nut in a hard woody shell.
– ORIGIN French, 'coco from the sea' (because the tree was first known from nuts found floating in the sea).

coconut ● noun **1** the large brown seed of a tropical palm, consisting of a hard woody husk surrounded by fibre, lined with edible white flesh and containing a clear liquid (**coconut milk**). **2** the edible white flesh of a coconut.
– ORIGIN from Spanish and Portuguese *coco* 'grinning face' (because of the appearance of the base of the coconut).

coconut ice ● noun Brit. a sweet made from sugar and desiccated coconut.

coconut shy ● noun Brit. a fairground sideshow where balls are thrown at coconuts in an attempt to knock them off stands.

cocoon /kəkoon/ ● noun **1** a silky case spun by the larvae of many insects for protection during the pupal stage. **2** a covering that prevents the corrosion of metal equipment. **3** something that envelops in a protective or comforting way. ● verb **1** wrap in a cocoon. **2** N. Amer. retreat from the stressful conditions of public life.
– DERIVATIVES **cocooner** noun.
– ORIGIN French *cocon*, from Provençal *coucoun* 'eggshell, cocoon'.

cocotte /kəkot/ ● noun (usu. in phrase **en cocotte**) a small casserole in which individual portions of food can be cooked and served.
– ORIGIN French, from *cocasse*, from Latin *cucuma* 'cooking pot'.

COD ● abbreviation cash on delivery.

cod[1] (also **codfish**) ● noun (pl. same) a large marine fish with a small barbel on the chin, important as a food fish.
– ORIGIN perhaps the same word as Old English *codd* 'bag', because of the fish's appearance.

cod[2] ● adjective Brit. informal not authentic; fake.
– ORIGIN perhaps from slang *cod* 'a fool'.

cod[3] ● noun Brit. informal, dated nonsense.
– ORIGIN abbreviation of CODSWALLOP.

coda /kōdə/ ● noun **1** Music the concluding passage of a piece or movement, typically forming an addition to the basic structure. **2** a concluding event, remark, or section.
– ORIGIN Italian, from Latin *cauda* 'tail'.

coddle ● verb **1** treat in an indulgent or overprotective way. **2** cook (an egg) in water below boiling point.
– DERIVATIVES **coddler** noun.
– ORIGIN origin uncertain; sense 1 is probably a variant of obsolete *caudle* 'administer invalids' gruel'.

code ● noun **1** a system of words, figures, or symbols used to represent others, especially for the purposes of secrecy. **2** (also **dialling code**) a sequence of numbers dialled to connect a telephone line with another exchange. **3** Computing program instructions. **4** a systematic collection of laws or statutes: *the penal code.* **5** a set of conventions governing behaviour. ● verb **1** convert into a code. **2** (usu. **coded**) express in an indirect or euphemistic way.
– DERIVATIVES **coder** noun.
– ORIGIN originally denoting a collection of statutes in ancient Rome: from Latin *codex* 'block of wood'.

codeine /kōdeen/ ● noun a sleep-inducing and painkilling drug derived from morphine.
– ORIGIN from Greek *kōdeia* 'poppy head'.

codependency ● noun excessive emotional or psychological reliance on a partner, typically one with an illness or addiction who requires support.
– DERIVATIVES **codependence** noun **codependent** adjective & noun.

codex /kōdeks/ ● noun (pl. **codices** /kōdiseez/ or **codexes**) **1** an ancient manuscript text in book form. **2** an official list of medicines, chemicals, etc.
– ORIGIN originally denoting a collection of statutes: from Latin, 'block of wood', later denoting a block for writing on, hence a book.

codger ● noun informal, derogatory an elderly man.
– ORIGIN perhaps a variant of *cadger* (see CADGE).

codicil /kōdisil, kod-/ ● noun an addition or supplement that explains, modifies, or revokes a will or part of one.
– ORIGIN Latin *codicillus* 'little book', from *codex* 'block of wood'.

codify /kōdifī/ ● verb (**codifies**, **codified**) organize (procedures or rules) into a system or code.
– DERIVATIVES **codification** noun **codifier** noun.

codling[1] ● noun an immature cod.

codling[2] ● noun any of several varieties of cooking apple having a long tapering shape.
– ORIGIN perhaps from the surname *Codlin*, from Old French *quer de lion* 'lion-heart'.

codling moth ● noun a small greyish moth whose larvae feed on apples.

cod liver oil ● noun oil pressed from the fresh liver of cod, which is rich in vitamins D and A.

codpiece ● noun a pouch to cover the genitals on a pair of man's breeches, worn in the 15th and 16th centuries.
– ORIGIN from earlier *cod* 'scrotum', from Old English, 'bag'.

codswallop ● noun Brit. informal nonsense.
– ORIGIN origin uncertain, but perhaps named after Hiram *Codd*, who invented a bottle for fizzy drinks (1875).

co-ed informal ● noun N. Amer. dated a female student at a co-educational institution. ● adjective co-educational.

co-education ● noun the education of pupils of both sexes together.
– DERIVATIVES **co-educational** adjective.

coefficient /kō-ifish'nt/ ● noun **1** Mathematics a quantity placed before and multiplying the variable in an algebraic expression (e.g. *4* in $4x^2$). **2** Physics a multiplier or factor that measures

Thesaurus

brained, half-baked; impractical, unfeasible; irrational, illogical, nonsensical; *informal* crazy; *Brit. informal* barmy, daft.

cocksure ● adjective ARROGANT, conceited, overweening, overconfident, cocky, proud, vain, self-important, swollen-headed, egotistical, presumptuous; smug, patronizing, pompous; *informal* high and mighty.
– OPPOSITES modest.

cocky ● adjective ARROGANT, conceited, overweening, overconfident, cocksure, self-important, swollen-headed, egotistical, presumptuous, boastful, self-assertive; bold, forward, insolent, cheeky.
– OPPOSITES modest.

cocoon ● verb **1** *he cocooned her in a towel* WRAP, swathe, swaddle, muffle, cloak, enfold, envelop, cover, fold. **2** *he was cocooned in the upper classes* PROTECT, shield, shelter, screen, cushion, insulate, isolate, cloister.

coddle ● verb PAMPER, cosset, mollycoddle; spoil, indulge, overindulge, pander to; wrap in cotton wool; baby, mother, wait on hand and foot.
– OPPOSITES neglect.

code ● noun **1** *a secret code* CIPHER, key; hieroglyphics; cryptogram. **2** *a strict social code* MORALITY, convention, etiquette, protocol. **3** *the penal code* LAW(S), rules, regulations; constitution, system.

some property.

coelacanth /seeləkanth/ ● noun a large bony marine fish with a three-lobed tail fin, known only from fossils until one was found alive in 1938.
– ORIGIN from Greek *koilos* 'hollow' + *akantha* 'spine' (because its fins have hollow spines).

coelenterate /seelentərayt/ ● noun Zoology a member of a large group of aquatic invertebrate animals (phylum Cnidaria), including jellyfish, corals, and sea anemones, which typically have a tube- or cup-shaped body with a single opening ringed with tentacles.
– ORIGIN from Greek *koilos* 'hollow' + *enteron* 'intestine'.

coeliac /seeliak/ (US **celiac**) ● adjective Anatomy & Medicine of or relating to the abdomen.
– ORIGIN Greek *koiliakos*, from *koilia* 'belly'.

coeliac disease ● noun a chronic failure to digest food caused by hypersensitivity of the small intestine to gluten.

coelurosaur /silyoorəsawr/ ● noun a small slender carnivorous dinosaur with long forelimbs.
– ORIGIN from Greek *koilos* 'hollow' + *oura* 'tail' + *sauros* 'lizard'.

coenobite /seenəbīt/ (also **cenobite**) ● noun a member of a monastic community.
– DERIVATIVES **coenobitic** /seenəbittik/ adjective.
– ORIGIN Old French *cenobite*, from Greek *koinobion* 'convent'.

coenzyme ● noun Biochemistry a non-protein compound that is essential for the functioning of an enzyme.

coequal ● adjective having the same rank or importance. ● noun a person or thing equal with another.
– DERIVATIVES **coequality** noun.

coerce /kōerss/ ● verb persuade (an unwilling person) to do something by using force or threats.
– DERIVATIVES **coercion** noun **coercive** adjective.
– ORIGIN Latin *coercere* 'restrain'.

coeval /kōeev'l/ ● adjective having the same age or date of origin; contemporary. ● noun a person of roughly the same age as oneself; a contemporary.
– ORIGIN Latin *coaevus*, from *co-* 'in common' + *aevum* 'age'.

coexist ● verb **1** exist at the same time or in the same place. **2** exist in harmony.
– DERIVATIVES **coexistence** noun **coexistent** adjective.

coextensive ● adjective extending over the same area, extent, or time.

C. of E. ● abbreviation Church of England.

coffee ● noun **1** a hot drink made from the roasted and ground bean-like seeds of a tropical shrub. **2** the roasted and ground seeds used to make this drink.
– ORIGIN Arabic.

coffee table ● noun a small, low table.

coffee-table book ● noun a large, lavishly illustrated book.

coffer ● noun **1** a small chest for holding valuables. **2** (**coffers**) the funds or financial reserves of an institution. **3** a decorative sunken panel in a ceiling.
– ORIGIN Old French *coffre* 'chest', from Greek *kophinos* 'basket'.

cofferdam ● noun a watertight enclosure pumped dry to permit construction work below the waterline, as when building bridges or repairing a ship.

coffered ceiling ● noun a ceiling decorated with a coffer or coffers.

coffin ● noun a long, narrow box in which a dead body is buried or cremated. ● verb (**coffined**, **coffining**) place in a coffin.
– ORIGIN Old French *cofin* 'little basket', from Greek *kophinus* 'basket'.

cog ● noun **1** a wheel or bar with a series of projections on its edge, which transfers motion by engaging with projections on another wheel or bar. **2** any one of these projections.
– DERIVATIVES **cogged** adjective.
– ORIGIN probably Scandinavian.

cogent /kōjənt/ ● adjective (of an argument or case) clear, logical, and convincing.
– DERIVATIVES **cogency** noun **cogently** adverb.
– ORIGIN from Latin *cogere* 'compel'.

cogitate /kojitayt/ ● verb formal meditate or reflect.
– DERIVATIVES **cogitation** noun **cogitative** adjective **cogitator** noun.
– ORIGIN Latin *cogitare* 'to consider'.

cognac /konyak/ ● noun a high-quality brandy distilled in Cognac in western France.

cognate /kognayt/ ● adjective **1** (of a word) having the same etymological derivation as another (e.g. English *father*, German *Vater*, and Latin *pater*). **2** formal related; connected. ● noun a cognate word.
– ORIGIN Latin *cognatus* 'born together'.

cognition /kognish'n/ ● noun the mental acquisition of knowledge through thought, experience, and the senses.
– DERIVATIVES **cognitional** adjective.
– ORIGIN Latin, from *cognoscere* 'get to know'.

cognitive /kognitiv/ ● adjective of or relating to cognition.
– DERIVATIVES **cognitively** adverb.

cognitive therapy ● noun a type of psychotherapy in which negative patterns of thought about the self and the world are challenged.

cognizance /kogniz'nss/ (also **cognisance**) ● noun formal knowledge or awareness.
– PHRASES **take cognizance of** formal take account of.
– DERIVATIVES **cognizant** adjective **cognize** (also **cognise**) verb.
– ORIGIN Old French *conoisance*, from Latin *cognoscere* 'get to know'.

cognomen /kognōmən/ ● noun an extra personal name given to an ancient Roman citizen, functioning rather like a nickname and often passed down from father to son.
– ORIGIN Latin, from *co-* 'together with' + *gnomen* 'name'.

cognoscenti /konyəshenti/ ● plural noun people who are well informed about a particular subject.
– ORIGIN Italian, 'people who know', from Latin *cognoscere* 'get to know'.

cohabit ● verb (**cohabited**, **cohabiting**) **1** live together and have a sexual relationship without being married. **2** coexist.
– DERIVATIVES **cohabitant** noun **cohabitation** noun **cohabitee** noun.
– ORIGIN Latin *cohabitare* 'live together'.

cohere /kōheer/ ● verb **1** hold firmly together; form a whole. **2** (of an argument or theory) be logically consistent.
– ORIGIN Latin *cohaerere* 'stick together'.

coherent ● adjective **1** (of an argument or theory) logical and consistent. **2** able to speak clearly and logically. **3** holding together to form a whole.
– DERIVATIVES **coherence** noun **coherently** adverb.

cohesion /kōheezh'n/ ● noun the action or fact of holding to-

Thesaurus

codify ● verb SYSTEMATIZE, systemize, organize, arrange, order, structure; tabulate, catalogue, list, sort, index, classify, categorize, file, log.

coerce ● verb PRESSURE, pressurize, press, push, constrain; force, compel, oblige, browbeat, bludgeon, bully, threaten, intimidate, dragoon, twist someone's arm; *informal* railroad, lean on.

coercion ● noun FORCE, compulsion, constraint, duress, oppression, enforcement, harassment, intimidation, threats, arm-twisting, pressure.

coffee ● noun *N. Amer. informal* joe, java.

coffer ● noun **1** *every church had a coffer* STRONGBOX, money box, cash box, money chest, treasure chest, safe; casket, box. **2** *the Imperial coffers* FUND(S), reserves, resources, money, finances, wealth, cash, capital, purse; treasury, exchequer.

coffin ● noun sarcophagus; *N. Amer.* casket; *informal* box; *humorous* wooden overcoat.

cogent ● adjective CONVINCING, compelling, strong, forceful, powerful, potent, weighty, effective; valid, sound, plausible, telling; impressive, persuasive, eloquent, credible, influential; conclusive, authoritative; logical, reasoned, rational, reasonable, lucid, coherent, clear.

cogitate ● verb *(formal)* THINK (ABOUT), contemplate, consider, mull over, meditate, muse, ponder, reflect, deliberate, ruminate; dwell on, brood on, chew over, weigh up; *informal* put on one's thinking cap.

cognate ● adjective *(formal)* ASSOCIATED, related, connected, allied, linked; similar, like, alike, akin, kindred, comparable, parallel, corresponding, analogous.

cognition ● noun PERCEPTION, discernment, apprehension, learning, understanding, comprehension, insight; reasoning, thinking, thought.

cognizance ● noun *(formal)*. See AWARENESS.

cognizant ● adjective *(formal)*. See AWARE sense 1.

cohabit ● verb LIVE TOGETHER, live with; *informal* shack up (with); *informal, dated* live in sin.

cohere ● verb **1** *the stories cohere into a convincing whole* STICK TOGETHER, hold together, be united, bind, fuse. **2** *this view does not cohere with others* BE CONSISTENT, hang together.

gether or forming a united whole.

cohesive ● adjective characterized by or causing cohesion.
– DERIVATIVES **cohesively** adverb **cohesiveness** noun.

cohort /kōhort/ ● noun **1** an ancient Roman military unit, comprising six centuries and equal to one tenth of a legion. **2** a number of people banded together or treated as a group. **3** derogatory, chiefly N. Amer. a supporter or companion.
– ORIGIN Latin *cohors* 'yard, retinue'.

C

coif /koyf/ ● noun a close-fitting cap worn by nuns under a veil. ● verb /kwaaf, kwof/ (**coiffed**, **coiffing**; US also **coifed**, **coifing**) style or arrange (someone's hair).
– ORIGIN Old French *coife* 'headdress', from Latin *cofia* 'helmet'.

coiffeur /kwaaför/ ● noun (fem. **coiffeuse** /kwaföz/) a hairdresser.
– ORIGIN French, from *coiffer* 'arrange the hair'.

coiffure /kwaafyoor/ ● noun a person's hairstyle.
– DERIVATIVES **coiffured** adjective.

coign /koyn/ ● noun a projecting corner or angle of a wall.
– PHRASES **coign of vantage** a favourable position for observation or action.
– ORIGIN variant of COIN.

coil ● noun **1** a length of something wound in a joined sequence of concentric loops. **2** an intrauterine contraceptive device in the form of a coil. **3** an electrical device consisting of a coiled wire, for converting the level of a voltage, producing a magnetic field, or adding inductance to a circuit. ● verb arrange or form into a coil.
– ORIGIN Old French *coillir*, from Latin *colligere* 'gather together'.

coin ● noun a flat disc or piece of metal with an official stamp, used as money. ● verb **1** make (coins) by stamping metal. **2** Brit. informal earn (large amounts of money) quickly and easily. **3** invent (a new word or phrase).
– DERIVATIVES **coiner** noun.
– ORIGIN Old French, 'wedge, corner, die', from Latin *cuneus* 'wedge'.

coinage ● noun **1** coins collectively. **2** the action or process of producing coins. **3** a system or type of coins in use. **4** the invention of a new word or phrase. **5** a newly invented word or phrase.

coincide /kō-insīd/ ● verb **1** occur at the same time or place. **2** correspond in nature; tally. **3** be in agreement.
– ORIGIN Latin *coincidere* 'occur together.'.

coincidence ● noun **1** a remarkable concurrence of events or circumstances without apparent causal connection. **2** correspondence in nature or in time of occurrence.
– DERIVATIVES **coincident** adjective **coincidental** adjective **coincidentally** adverb.

Cointreau /kwuntrō/ ● noun trademark a colourless orange-flavoured liqueur.
– ORIGIN named after the *Cointreau* family, liqueur producers based in Angers, France.

coir /koyər/ ● noun fibre from the outer husk of the coconut, used in potting compost and for making ropes and matting.
– ORIGIN from a Dravidian word.

coitus /kōitəss/ ● noun technical sexual intercourse.
– DERIVATIVES **coital** adjective.
– ORIGIN Latin, from *coire* 'go together'.

coitus interruptus /intəruptəss/ ● noun sexual intercourse in which the penis is withdrawn before ejaculation.

cojones /kəhōnayz/ ● plural noun informal, chiefly N. Amer. **1** a man's testicles. **2** courage; guts.
– ORIGIN Spanish.

coke[1] ● noun **1** a solid fuel made by heating coal in the absence of air so that the volatile components are driven off. **2** carbon residue left after the incomplete combustion or distillation of petrol or other fuels. ● verb (usu. **coking**) convert (coal) into coke.
– ORIGIN originally in the sense 'charcoal': of unknown origin.

coke[2] ● noun informal term for COCAINE.

Col. ● abbreviation Colonel.

col ● noun the lowest point of a ridge or saddle between two peaks.
– ORIGIN French, 'neck'.

cola ● noun **1** a brown carbonated drink flavoured with an extract of cola nuts, or with a similar flavouring. **2** (also **kola**) a small tropical evergreen tree whose seed (the **cola nut**) contains caffeine.
– ORIGIN Temne (an African language).

colander /kulləndər/ ● noun a perforated bowl used to strain off liquid from food.
– ORIGIN from Latin *colare* 'to strain'.

colcannon /kolkannən/ ● noun an Irish and Scottish dish of cabbage and potatoes boiled and mashed together.
– ORIGIN from COLE + perhaps CANNON (it is said that cannonballs were used to pound vegetables such as spinach).

colchicum /kolchikəm/ ● noun (pl. **colchicums**) **1** a plant of a genus that includes meadow saffron or autumn crocus. **2** the dried corm or seed of meadow saffron, used medicinally.
– ORIGIN from Greek *kolkhikon* 'of Colchis' (an ancient region east of the Black Sea), with allusion to Medea in classical mythology, a woman from Colchis who was a skilled poisoner.

cold ● adjective **1** of or at a low or relatively low temperature. **2** not feeling or showing emotion or affection. **3** not affected by emotion; objective: *cold statistics.* **4** (of a colour) containing pale blue or grey and giving no impression of warmth. **5** (of a scent or trail) no longer fresh and easy to follow. **6** (in children's games) far from finding or guessing what is sought. **7** without preparation or rehearsal; unawares. **8** informal unconscious. ● noun **1** cold weather or surroundings. **2** a common infection in which the mucous membrane of the nose and throat becomes inflamed, causing running at the nose and sneezing.
– PHRASES **cold comfort** poor or inadequate consolation. **get cold feet** lose one's nerve. **the cold shoulder** intentional unfriendliness or rejection. **in cold blood** without feeling or mercy.
– DERIVATIVES **coldly** adverb **coldness** noun.
– ORIGIN Old English.

cold-blooded ● adjective **1** (of animals, e.g. reptiles and fish)

Thesaurus

coherent ● adjective LOGICAL, reasoned, reasonable, rational, sound, cogent, consistent; clear, lucid, articulate; intelligible, comprehensible.
– OPPOSITES muddled.

cohesion ● noun UNITY, togetherness, solidarity, bond, coherence; connection, linkage.

cohort ● noun **1** *a Roman army cohort* UNIT, force, corps, division, brigade, battalion, regiment, squadron, company, troop, contingent, legion. **2** *the 1940–4 birth cohort of women* GROUP, grouping, category, class, set, division, batch, list; age group, generation.

coil ● noun *coils of rope* LOOP, twist, turn, curl, convolution; spiral, helix, corkscrew.
● verb *he coiled her hair around his finger* WIND, loop, twist, curl, curve, bend, twine, entwine; spiral, corkscrew.

coin ● noun **1** *a gold coin* PIECE. **2** *large amounts of coin* COINAGE, coins, specie; (loose) change, small change, silver, copper(s), gold.
– RELATED TERMS numismatic.
● verb **1** *guineas were coined* MINT, stamp, strike, cast, punch, die, mould, forge, make. **2** *he coined the term* INVENT, create, make up, conceive, originate, think up, dream up.

coincide ● verb **1** *the events coincided* OCCUR SIMULTANEOUSLY, happen together, be concurrent, concur, coexist. **2** *their interests do not always coincide* TALLY, correspond, agree, accord, concur, match, fit, be consistent, equate, harmonize, be compatible, dovetail, correlate; *informal* square.
– OPPOSITES differ.

coincidence ● noun **1** *too close to be mere coincidence* ACCIDENT, chance, serendipity, fortuity, providence, happenstance, fate; a fluke. **2** *the coincidence of inflation and unemployment* CO-OCCURRENCE, coexistence, conjunction, simultaneity, contemporaneity, concomitance. **3** *a coincidence of interests* CORRESPONDENCE, agreement, accord, concurrence, consistency, conformity, harmony, compatibility.

coincident ● adjective **1** *algae blooms coincident with dolphin deaths* CONCURRENT, coinciding, simultaneous, contemporaneous, concomitant, coexistent. **2** *their aims are coincident* IN AGREEMENT, in harmony, in accord, consistent, compatible, congruent, in step, in tune; the same.

coincidental ● adjective **1** *a coincidental resemblance* ACCIDENTAL, chance, fluky, random; fortuitous, adventitious, serendipitous; unexpected, unforeseen, unintentional, inadvertent, unplanned. **2** *the coincidental disappearance of the two men* SIMULTANEOUS, concurrent, coincident, contemporaneous, concomitant.

coitus ● noun *(technical).* See SEX noun sense 1.

cold ● adjective **1** *a cold day* CHILLY, chill, cool, freezing, icy, snowy, wintry, frosty, frigid, gelid; bitter, biting, raw; *informal* nippy,

having a body whose temperature varies with that of the environment. **2** without emotion; callous.
– DERIVATIVES **cold-bloodedly** adverb **cold-bloodedness** noun.
cold-call ● verb make an unsolicited visit or telephone call to (someone) in an attempt to sell goods or services.
cold chisel ● noun a toughened chisel used for cutting metal.
cold cream ● noun a cream for cleansing and softening the skin.
cold cuts ● plural noun slices of cold cooked meats.
cold frame ● noun a frame with a glass top in which small plants are grown and protected.
cold fusion ● noun nuclear fusion supposedly occurring at or close to room temperature.
cold-hearted ● adjective lacking affection or warmth; unfeeling.
– DERIVATIVES **cold-heartedly** adverb **cold-heartedness** noun.
cold sore ● noun an inflamed blister in or near the mouth, caused by infection with the herpes simplex virus.
cold sweat ● noun a state of sweating induced by nervousness or illness.
cold turkey ● noun informal **1** abrupt withdrawal from a drug to which one is addicted. **2** symptoms such as sweating and nausea caused by this.
cold war ● noun a state of hostility between the Soviet bloc countries and the Western powers after the Second World War.
cole ● noun chiefly archaic cabbage, kale, or a similar plant.
– ORIGIN Latin *caulis* 'stem, cabbage'; compare with KALE.
coleopteran /kolliοptərən/ ● noun an insect of the order Coleoptera, comprising the beetles.
– DERIVATIVES **coleopterous** adjective.
– ORIGIN from Greek *koleos* 'sheath' + *pteron* 'wing'.
coleslaw ● noun a salad dish of shredded raw cabbage and carrots mixed with mayonnaise.
– ORIGIN Dutch *koolsla*, from *kool* 'cabbage' + *sla* 'salad'.
coleus /kōliəss/ ● noun a tropical plant with brightly coloured variegated leaves.
– ORIGIN Greek *koleos* 'sheath' (because the stamens are joined together, resembling a sheath).
coley /kōli/ ● noun (pl. same or **coleys**) another term for SAITHE.
– ORIGIN perhaps from *coalfish*, an alternative name for the fish.
colic ● noun severe pain in the abdomen caused by wind or obstruction in the intestines.
– DERIVATIVES **colicky** adjective.
– ORIGIN Latin *colicus*, from *colon* 'colon'.
coliform /kolliform/ ● adjective belonging to a group of rod-shaped bacteria typified by *E. coli*.
– ORIGIN from Latin *coli* 'of the colon'.
coliseum /kolliseeəm/ (also **colosseum**) ● noun (in names) a large theatre, cinema, or stadium.
– ORIGIN from the *Colosseum*, the vast amphitheatre of ancient Rome, from Latin *colosseus* 'gigantic'.
colitis /kəlitiss/ ● noun inflammation of the lining of the colon.
collaborate /kəlabbərayt/ ● verb **1** work jointly on an activity or project. **2** cooperate traitorously with an enemy.
– DERIVATIVES **collaboration** noun **collaborationist** noun & adjective **collaborative** adjective **collaborator** noun.
– ORIGIN Latin *collaborare* 'work together'.
collage /kollaazh/ ● noun **1** a form of art in which various materials are arranged and stuck to a backing. **2** a combination or collection of various things.
– ORIGIN French, 'gluing'.
collagen /kolləjən/ ● noun the main structural protein found in animal connective tissue, yielding gelatin when boiled.
– ORIGIN French *collagène*, from Greek *kolla* 'glue'.
collapsar /kəlapsaar/ ● noun Astronomy an old star that has collapsed under its own gravity to form a white dwarf, neutron star, or black hole.
– ORIGIN from COLLAPSE, on the pattern of words such as *pulsar*.
collapse ● verb **1** suddenly fall down or give way. **2** (of a person) fall down as a result of physical breakdown. **3** fail suddenly and completely. ● noun **1** an instance of a structure collapsing. **2** a sudden failure or breakdown.
– ORIGIN Latin *collabi*, from *labi* 'to slip'.
collapsible ● adjective able to be folded down.
collar ● noun **1** a band of material around the neck of a shirt or other garment, either upright or turned over. **2** a band put around the neck of a domestic animal. **3** a connecting band or pipe in a piece of machinery. **4** Brit. a piece of meat rolled up and tied. ● verb informal seize or apprehend (someone).
– DERIVATIVES **collared** adjective **collarless** adjective.
– ORIGIN Latin *collare* 'band for the neck', from *collum* 'neck'.
collarbone ● noun either of the pair of bones joining the breastbone to the shoulder blades; the clavicle.
collate /kəlayt/ ● verb **1** collect and combine (texts or information). **2** compare and analyse (two or more sources of information). **3** Printing examine (a book) to make sure the sheets are in the correct order.
– DERIVATIVES **collator** noun.
– ORIGIN originally in the sense 'confer (a benefice) upon': from Latin *collatus* 'brought together', from *conferre* (see CONFER).
collateral /kəlattərəl/ ● noun **1** something pledged as security for repayment of a loan. **2** a person descended from the same ancestor as another but through a different line. ● adjective **1** additional but subordinate; secondary. **2** descended from the same stock but by a different line. **3** situated side by side; parallel.
– DERIVATIVES **collaterally** adverb.
– ORIGIN Latin *collateralis*, from *latus* 'side'.
collateral damage ● noun inadvertent casualties and destruction in civilian areas caused by military operations.
collation /kəlaysh'n/ ● noun **1** the action of collating. **2** a light informal meal.
colleague ● noun a person with whom one works.
– ORIGIN Latin *collega* 'partner in office'.
collect[1] /kəlekt/ ● verb **1** bring or gather together. **2** systemat-

Thesaurus

brass monkeys, arctic; *Brit. informal* parky. **2** *I'm very cold* CHILLY, chilled, cool, freezing, frozen, shivery, numb, benumbed; hypothermic. **3** *a cold reception* UNFRIENDLY, inhospitable, unwelcoming, forbidding, cool, frigid, frosty, glacial, lukewarm, indifferent, unfeeling, unemotional, formal, stiff.
– OPPOSITES hot, warm.
cold-blooded ● adjective CRUEL, callous, sadistic, inhuman, inhumane, pitiless, merciless, ruthless, unforgiving, unfeeling, uncaring, heartless; savage, brutal, barbaric, barbarous; cold, cold-hearted, unemotional.
cold-hearted ● adjective UNFEELING, unloving, uncaring, unsympathetic, unemotional, unfriendly, uncharitable, unkind, insensitive; hard-hearted, stony-hearted, heartless, hard, cold.
collaborate ● verb **1** *they collaborated on the project* COOPERATE, join forces, team up, band together, work together, participate, combine, ally; pool resources, club together. **2** *they collaborated with the enemy* FRATERNIZE, conspire, collude, cooperate, consort, sympathize.
collaborator ● noun **1** *his collaborator on the book* CO-WORKER, partner, associate, colleague, confederate; assistant. **2** *a wartime collaborator* QUISLING, fraternizer, collaborationist, colluder, (enemy) sympathizer; traitor, fifth columnist.
collapse ● verb **1** *the roof collapsed* CAVE IN, fall in, subside, fall down, give (way), crumple, sag, slump. **2** *he collapsed last night* FAINT, pass out, black out, lose consciousness, keel over, swoon; *informal* flake out, conk out. **3** *she collapsed in tears* BREAK DOWN, go to pieces, lose control, be overcome, crumble; *informal* crack up. **4** *peace talks collapsed* BREAK DOWN, fail, fall through, fold, founder, miscarry, come to grief, be unsuccessful; end; *informal* flop, fizzle out.
● noun **1** *the collapse of the roof* CAVE-IN, subsidence. **2** *her collapse on stage* FAINTING FIT, faint, blackout, loss of consciousness, swoon; *Medicine* syncope. **3** *the collapse of the talks* BREAKDOWN, failure, disintegration; end. **4** *he suffered a collapse* (NERVOUS) BREAKDOWN, personal crisis, psychological trauma; *informal* crack-up.
collar ● noun **1** *a shirt collar* NECKBAND, choker; *historical* ruff, gorget, bertha. **2** *a collar round the pipe* RING, band, collet, sleeve, flange.
● verb *(informal)* **1** *he collared a thief* APPREHEND, arrest, catch, capture, seize; take prisoner, take into custody, detain; *informal* nab, pinch, bust, pick up, pull in, feel someone's collar; *Brit. informal* nick. **2** *she collared me in the street* ACCOST, waylay, hail, approach, detain, stop, halt, catch, confront, importune; *informal* buttonhole; *Brit. informal* nobble.
collate ● verb **1** *the system is used to collate information* COLLECT, gather, accumulate, assemble; combine, aggregate, put together; arrange, organize. **2** *we must collate these two sources* COMPARE, contrast, set side by side, juxtapose, weigh against.
collateral ● noun SECURITY, surety, guarantee, guaranty, insurance, indemnity, indemnification; backing.
colleague ● noun CO-WORKER, fellow worker, workmate, team-

C

ically acquire (items of a particular kind) as a hobby. **3** call for and take away; fetch. **4** call for and receive as a right or due. **5** (**collect oneself**) regain control of oneself. **6** Austral./NZ informal collide with. ● **adverb & adjective** N. Amer. (of a telephone call) to be paid for by the person receiving it.
– ORIGIN Latin *colligere* 'gather together'.
collect[2] /kollekt/ ● **noun** (in church use) a short prayer, especially one assigned to a particular day or season.
– ORIGIN Latin *collecta* 'a gathering', from *colligere* 'gather together'.
collectable (also **collectible**) ● **adjective** **1** worth collecting; of interest to a collector. **2** able to be collected. ● **noun** an item valued and sought by collectors.
– DERIVATIVES **collectability** noun.
collected ● **adjective** **1** calm and unperturbed. **2** (of works) brought together in one volume or edition.
collection ● **noun** **1** the action of collecting. **2** a regular removal of mail for dispatch or of refuse for disposal. **3** an instance of collecting donations. **4** a group of things collected or accumulated.
collective ● **adjective** **1** done by or belonging to all the members of a group. **2** taken as a whole; aggregate. ● **noun** an enterprise owned or operated cooperatively.
– DERIVATIVES **collectively** adverb **collectivity** noun.
collective bargaining ● **noun** negotiation of wages and other conditions of employment by an organized body of employees.
collective farm ● **noun** a jointly operated amalgamation of several smallholdings, especially one owned by the state.
collective noun ● **noun** a noun that denotes a group of individuals (e.g. *assembly, family*).
collectivism ● **noun** **1** the giving of priority to a group over each individual in it. **2** the ownership of land and the means of production by the people or the state.
– DERIVATIVES **collectivist** adjective & noun **collectivize** (also **collectivise**) verb.
collector ● **noun** **1** a person who collects things of a specified type. **2** an official who is responsible for collecting money owed.
colleen /kolleen/ ● **noun** Irish a girl or young woman.
– ORIGIN Irish *cailín* 'country girl'.
college ● **noun** **1** an educational establishment providing higher education or specialized training. **2** (in Britain) any of the independent institutions into which some universities are separated. **3** an organized group of professional people.
– ORIGIN Latin *collegium* 'partnership', from *collega* 'partner'.
College of Arms ● **noun** (in the UK) a corporation which officially records and grants armorial bearings.
collegial /kəleejət/ ● **adjective** **1** another term for COLLEGIATE (in sense 1). **2** involving shared responsibility.
collegian /kəleejən/ ● **noun** a member of a college.
collegiate /kəleejət/ ● **adjective** **1** relating to a college or college students. **2** (of a university) composed of different colleges.
collegiate church ● **noun** a church endowed for a chapter of canons but without a bishop's see.
collide ● **verb** **1** hit by accident when moving. **2** come into conflict or opposition.
– ORIGIN Latin *collidere*, from *laedere* 'to strike'.
collie ● **noun** (pl. **collies**) a breed of sheepdog with a long, pointed nose and thick long hair.
– ORIGIN perhaps from COAL (the breed originally being black).
collier /kolliər/ ● **noun** chiefly Brit. **1** a coal miner. **2** a ship carrying coal.
colliery ● **noun** (pl. **collieries**) a coal mine.
collimate /kollimayt/ ● **verb** **1** make (rays of light or particles) accurately parallel. **2** align (an optical system) accurately.
– DERIVATIVES **collimation** noun **collimator** noun.
– ORIGIN Latin *collimare*, a mistaken reading of *collineare* 'align or aim'.
collinear /kəlinniər/ ● **adjective** Geometry (of points) lying in the same straight line.
– DERIVATIVES **collinearity** noun.
collision ● **noun** an instance of colliding.
– DERIVATIVES **collisional** adjective.
collocate ● **verb** /kolləkayt/ (of a word) form a collocation with another. ● **noun** /kolləkət/ a word that forms a collocation with another.
collocation ● **noun** **1** the habitual occurrence of a word with another word or words with a frequency greater than chance. **2** a word or group of words that habitually occur together (e.g. *heavy drinker*).
– ORIGIN Latin, from *collocare* 'place together'.
colloid /kolloyd/ ● **noun** **1** a homogeneous substance consisting of submicroscopic particles of one substance dispersed in another, as in an emulsion or gel. **2** a gelatinous substance.
– DERIVATIVES **colloidal** adjective.
– ORIGIN from Greek *kolla* 'glue'.
collop /kolləp/ ● **noun** dialect & N. Amer. a slice of meat.
– ORIGIN Scandinavian.
colloquial /kəlōkwiəl/ ● **adjective** (of language) used in ordinary or familiar conversation; not formal or literary.
– DERIVATIVES **colloquially** adverb.
– ORIGIN from Latin *colloquium* 'conversation'.
colloquialism ● **noun** a colloquial word or phrase.
colloquium /kəlōkwiəm/ ● **noun** (pl. **colloquiums** or **colloquia** /kəlōkwiə/) an academic conference or seminar.
– ORIGIN Latin.
colloquy /kolləkwi/ ● **noun** (pl. **colloquies**) **1** formal a conference or conversation. **2** a gathering for discussion of theological questions.
– ORIGIN Latin *colloquium* 'conversation'.
collude /kəlo͞od/ ● **verb** come to a secret understanding; conspire.
– ORIGIN Latin *colludere* 'have a secret agreement', from *ludere* 'to play'.

Thesaurus

mate, associate, partner, collaborator, ally, confederate; Brit. informal oppo.
collect ● **verb** **1** *he collected the rubbish* GATHER, accumulate, assemble; amass, stockpile, pile up, heap up, store (up), hoard, save; mass, accrue. **2** *a crowd soon collected* GATHER, assemble, meet, muster, congregate, convene, converge, flock together. **3** *I must collect the children* FETCH, go/come to get, call for, meet. **4** *they collect money for charity* RAISE, appeal for, ask for, solicit; obtain, acquire, gather. **5** *he paused to collect himself* RECOVER, regain one's composure, pull oneself together, steady oneself; informal get a grip (on oneself). **6** *she collected her thoughts* MUSTER, summon (up), gather, get together, marshal.
– OPPOSITES disperse, distribute.
collected ● **adjective** CALM, cool, self-possessed, self-controlled, composed, poised; serene, tranquil, relaxed, unruffled, unperturbed, untroubled; placid, quiet, sedate, phlegmatic; informal unfazed, together, laid-back.
– OPPOSITES excited, hysterical.
collection ● **noun** **1** *a collection of stolen items* HOARD, pile, heap, stack, stock, store, stockpile; accumulation, reserve, supply, bank, pool, fund, mine, reservoir. **2** *a collection of shoppers* GROUP, crowd, body, assemblage, gathering, throng; knot, cluster; multitude, bevy, party, band, horde, pack, flock, swarm, mob; informal gang, load, gaggle. **3** *a collection of Victorian dolls* SET, series; array, assortment. **4** *a collection of short stories* ANTHOLOGY, selection, compendium, treasury, compilation, miscellany, pot-pourri. **5** *a collection for the poor* DONATIONS, contributions, gifts, subscription(s); informal whip-round; historical alms. **6** *a church collection* OFFERING, offertory, tithe.
collective ● **adjective** COMMON, shared, joint, combined, mutual, communal, pooled; united, allied, cooperative, collaborative.
– OPPOSITES individual.
college ● **noun** **1** *a college of technology* SCHOOL, academy, university, polytechnic, institute, seminary, conservatoire, conservatory. **2** *the College of Heralds* ASSOCIATION, society, club, institute, body, fellowship, guild, lodge, order, fraternity, league, union, alliance.
collide ● **verb** **1** *the trains collided with each other* CRASH, impact; hit, strike, run into, bump into, meet head-on, cannon into, plough into; N. Amer. informal barrel into. **2** *politics and metaphysics collide* CONFLICT, clash; differ, diverge, disagree, be at odds, be incompatible.
collision ● **noun** **1** *a collision on the ring road* CRASH, accident, impact, smash, bump, hit; Brit. RTA (road traffic accident); N. Amer. wreck; informal pile-up; Brit. informal prang, shunt. **2** *a collision between two ideas* CONFLICT, clash; disagreement, incompatibility, contradiction.
colloquial ● **adjective** INFORMAL, conversational, everyday, nonliterary; unofficial, idiomatic, slangy, vernacular, popular, demotic.

collusion • noun secret cooperation in order to cheat or deceive.
– DERIVATIVES **collusive** adjective.

collywobbles • plural noun informal, chiefly humorous **1** stomach pain or queasiness. **2** intense anxiety.
– ORIGIN formed from COLIC and WOBBLE.

colobus /kolləbəss/ • noun (pl. same) a slender leaf-eating African monkey with silky fur.
– ORIGIN from Greek *kolobos* 'curtailed' (with reference to its shortened thumbs).

cologne /kəlōn/ • noun eau de cologne or similarly scented toilet water.

Colombian /kəlombiən/ • noun a person from Colombia. • adjective relating to Colombia.

colon[1] /kōlən/ • noun a punctuation mark (:) used to precede a list of items, a quotation, or an expansion or explanation.
– ORIGIN Greek *kōlon* 'limb, clause'.

colon[2] /kōlon/ • noun the main part of the large intestine, which passes from the caecum to the rectum.
– ORIGIN Greek *kolon* 'food, meat'.

colón /kolon/ • noun (pl. **colones**) the basic monetary unit of Costa Rica and El Salvador, equal to 100 centimos in Costa Rica and 100 centavos in El Salvador.
– ORIGIN from Cristóbal *Colón*, the Spanish name of Christopher Columbus.

colonel /kön'l/ • noun a rank of officer in the army and in the US air force, above a lieutenant colonel and below a brigadier or brigadier general.
– DERIVATIVES **colonelcy** noun (pl. **colonelcies**).
– ORIGIN from Italian *colonnello* 'column of soldiers'.

colonial • adjective **1** relating to or characteristic of a colony or of colonialism. **2** in a style characteristic of the period of the British colonies in America before independence. **3** (of animals or plants) living in colonies. • noun a person who lives in a colony.
– DERIVATIVES **colonially** adverb.

colonialism • noun the practice of acquiring control over another country, occupying it with settlers, and exploiting it economically.
– DERIVATIVES **colonialist** noun & adjective.

colonic /kəlonnik/ • adjective Anatomy relating to or affecting the colon.

colonic irrigation • noun a therapeutic treatment in which water is inserted via the anus to flush out the colon.

colonist • noun an inhabitant of a colony.

colonize (also **colonise**) • verb **1** establish a colony in (a place). **2** take over (a place) for one's own use.
– DERIVATIVES **colonization** noun **colonizer** noun.

colonnade /kollənayd/ • noun a row of evenly spaced columns supporting a roof or other structure.
– DERIVATIVES **colonnaded** adjective.
– ORIGIN French, from Latin *columna* 'column'.

colonoscopy /kōlənoskəpi/ • noun (pl. **colonoscopies**) examination of the colon with a fibre-optic instrument inserted through the anus.

colony • noun (pl. **colonies**) **1** a country or area under the control of another country and occupied by settlers from that country. **2** a group of people of one nationality or race living in a foreign place. **3** a place where a group of people with the same occupation or interest live together: *a nudist colony*. **4** a community of animals or plants of one kind living close together.
– ORIGIN Latin *colonia* 'settlement, farm', from *colere* 'cultivate'.

colophon /kolləfən/ • noun a publisher's emblem or imprint.
– ORIGIN Greek *kolophōn* 'summit or finishing touch'.

color • noun & verb US spelling of COLOUR.

Colorado beetle • noun a yellow- and black-striped American beetle whose larvae are highly destructive to potato plants.
– ORIGIN named after the US state of *Colorado*.

coloration (also **colouration**) • noun **1** arrangement or scheme of colour; colouring. **2** character or tone, especially of music.

coloratura /kollərətyoorə/ • noun **1** elaborate ornamentation of a vocal melody. **2** a soprano skilled in such singing.
– ORIGIN Italian, 'colouring'.

colossal • adjective extremely large.
– DERIVATIVES **colossally** adverb.
– ORIGIN from Latin *colossus* (see COLOSSUS).

colosseum • noun variant spelling of COLISEUM.

colossus /kəlossəss/ • noun (pl. **colossi** /kəlossi/ or **colossuses**) a person or thing of enormous size, in particular a statue that is much bigger than life size.
– ORIGIN Latin, from Greek *kolossos*.

colostomy /kəlostəmi/ • noun (pl. **colostomies**) a surgical operation in which the colon is shortened and the cut end diverted to an opening in the abdominal wall.
– ORIGIN from COLON[2] + Greek *stoma* 'mouth'.

colostrum /kəlostrəm/ • noun the first secretion from the mammary glands after giving birth.
– ORIGIN Latin.

colour (US **color**) • noun **1** the property possessed by an object of producing different sensations on the eye as a result of the way it reflects or emits light. **2** one, or any mixture, of the constituents into which light can be separated in a spectrum or rainbow. **3** the use of all colours, not only black and white, in photography or television. **4** pigmentation of the skin as an indication of someone's race. **5** redness of the complexion. **6** interest, excitement, and vitality. **7** (**colours**) chiefly Brit. an item or items of a particular colour worn for identification, especially in sport. **8** (**colours**) the flag of a regiment or ship. • verb **1** give a colour to. **2** show embarrassment by becoming red; blush. **3** influence, especially in a negative way: *the experiences had coloured her whole existence.*
– PHRASES **show one's true colours** reveal one's real character or intentions, especially when these are disreputable.
– ORIGIN Latin *color*.

colourant (US **colorant**) • noun a dye or pigment used to colour something.

colouration • noun variant spelling of COLORATION.

colour-blind • adjective unable to distinguish certain colours.
– DERIVATIVES **colour blindness** noun.

coloured (US **colored**) • adjective **1** having a colour or colours. **2** dated or offensive wholly or partly of non-white descent. **3** S. African of mixed ethnic origin. • noun **1** dated or offensive a person who is wholly or partly of non-white descent. **2** S. African an Afrikaans- or English-speaking person of mixed descent. **3** (**coloureds**) clothes, sheets, etc. that are any colour but white.
– USAGE In reference to skin colour **coloured** was the accepted term until the 1960s, when it was superseded by **black**; it is now widely regarded as offensive except in historical contexts. In South Africa, on the other hand, the term is used to refer to

Thesaurus

– OPPOSITES formal.

collude • verb CONSPIRE, connive, collaborate, plot, scheme; *informal* be in cahoots.

colonist • noun SETTLER, colonizer, colonial, pioneer; immigrant, incomer, newcomer; *N. Amer. historical* homesteader.
– OPPOSITES native.

colonize • verb SETTLE (IN), people, populate; occupy, take over, seize, capture, subjugate.

colonnade • noun ROW OF COLUMNS; portico, stoa, peristyle; arcade, covered walk.

colony • noun **1** *a French colony* TERRITORY, dependency, protectorate, satellite, settlement, outpost, province. **2** *the British colony in New York* POPULATION, community. **3** *an artists' colony* COMMUNITY, commune; quarter, district, ghetto.

colossal • adjective HUGE, massive, enormous, gigantic, very big, giant, mammoth, vast, immense, monumental, prodigious, mountainous, titanic, towering, king-size(d); *informal* monster, whopping, humongous, jumbo; *Brit. informal* ginormous.
– OPPOSITES tiny.

colour • noun **1** *the lights changed colour* HUE, shade, tint, tone, coloration. **2** *oil colour* PAINT, pigment, colourant, dye, stain, tint, wash. **3** *the colour in her cheeks* REDNESS, pinkness, rosiness, ruddiness, blush, flush, bloom. **4** *people of every colour* SKIN COLOURING, skin tone, colouring; race, ethnic group. **5** *anecdotes add colour to the text* VIVIDNESS, life, liveliness, vitality, excitement, interest, richness, zest, spice, piquancy, impact, force; *informal* oomph, pizzazz, punch, kick; *poetic/literary* salt. **6** *the colours of the Oxford City club* STRIP, kit, uniform, costume, livery, regalia. **7** *the regimental colours.* See FLAG[1] noun.
– RELATED TERMS chromatic.
• verb **1** *the wood was coloured blue* TINT, dye, stain, paint, pigment, wash. **2** *she coloured up* BLUSH, redden, go pink, go red, flush. **3** *the experience coloured her outlook* INFLUENCE, affect, taint, warp, skew, distort, bias, prejudice. **4** *they colour evidence to*

C

people of mixed-race parentage rather than as a synonym for **black**, and in this context is not considered offensive or derogatory.
colour-fast ● adjective dyed in colours that will not fade or be washed out.
colourful (US **colorful**) ● adjective **1** having many or varied colours. **2** lively and exciting; vivid.
– DERIVATIVES **colourfully** adverb **colourfulness** noun.
colouring (US **coloring**) ● noun **1** the process or art of applying colour. **2** visual appearance with regard to colour. **3** the natural hues of a person's skin, hair, and eyes. **4** a substance used to colour something, especially food.
colourist (US **colorist**) ● noun an artist or designer who uses colour in a special or skilful way.
colourless (US **colorless**) ● adjective **1** without colour. **2** lacking character or interest; dull.
colour scheme ● noun an arrangement or combination of colours.
colour sergeant ● noun a rank of non-commissioned officer in the Royal Marines, above sergeant and below warrant officer (responsible for carrying one of the regiment's colours in a guard of honour).
colour supplement ● noun Brit. a magazine printed in colour and issued with a newspaper.
colourway (US **colorway**) ● noun any of a range of combinations of colours in which something is available.
colposcopy /kolposkəpi/ ● noun surgical examination of the vagina and the cervix of the womb.
– ORIGIN from Greek *kolpos* 'womb'.
colt /kōlt/ ● noun **1** a young uncastrated male horse, in particular one less than four years old. **2** a member of a junior sports team.
– ORIGIN Old English.
colter ● noun US spelling of COULTER.
coltish ● adjective energetic but awkward in one's movements or behaviour.
coltsfoot ● noun a plant with yellow flowers and large heart-shaped leaves.
colubrine /kolyoobrīn/ ● adjective of or resembling a snake.
– ORIGIN Latin *colubrinus*, from *coluber* 'snake'.
columbine /kolləmbīn/ ● noun a plant with long-spurred, typically purplish-blue flowers.
– ORIGIN from Latin *columba* 'dove' (from the supposed resemblance of the flower to a cluster of five doves).
column ● noun **1** an upright pillar supporting an arch or other structure or standing alone as a monument. **2** a line of people or vehicles moving in the same direction. **3** a vertical division of a page or text. **4** a regular section of a newspaper or magazine on a particular subject or by a particular person. **5** an upright shaft used for controlling a machine.
– DERIVATIVES **columnar** adjective **columned** adjective.
– ORIGIN Latin *columna* 'pillar'.
columnist /kolləm(n)ist/ ● noun a journalist who writes a column in a newspaper or magazine.
com- (also **co-**, **col-**, **con-**, or **cor-**) ● prefix with; together; jointly; altogether: *combine*.
– ORIGIN from Latin *cum* 'with'.
coma /kōmə/ ● noun a state of prolonged deep unconsciousness.
– ORIGIN Greek *kōma* 'deep sleep'.
Comanche /kəmanchi/ ● noun (pl. same or **Comanches**) a member of an American Indian people of the south-western US.
– ORIGIN the Comanches' name for themselves.
comatose /kōmətōz/ ● adjective **1** of or in a state of coma. **2** informal extremely tired or lethargic.
comb ● noun **1** an article with a row of narrow teeth, used for untangling or arranging the hair. **2** a device for separating and dressing textile fibres. **3** the red fleshy crest on the head of a domestic fowl, especially a cock. **4** a honeycomb. ● verb **1** untangle or arrange (the hair) by drawing a comb through it. **2** prepare (wool, flax, or cotton) for manufacture with a comb. **3** search carefully and systematically.
– ORIGIN Old English.
combat ● noun fighting, especially between armed forces. ● verb (**combated** or **combatted**, **combating** or **combatting**) take action to reduce or prevent (something bad or undesirable).
– ORIGIN from Latin *combattere* 'fight with'.
combatant /kombətənt/ ● noun a person or nation engaged in fighting during a war. ● adjective engaged in fighting during a war.
combative /kombətiv/ ● adjective ready or eager to fight or argue.
– DERIVATIVES **combatively** adverb **combativeness** noun.
combat trousers ● plural noun loose trousers with large patch pockets halfway down each leg, typically made of hard-wearing cotton.
combe /koōm/ (also **coomb** or **coombe**) ● noun Brit. a short valley or hollow on a hillside or coastline.
– ORIGIN Old English, related to CWM.
comber /kōmər/ ● noun **1** a long curling sea wave. **2** a person or machine that combs cotton or wool.
combination ● noun **1** the action of combining two or more different things. **2** something in which the component elements are individually distinct. **3** a sequence of numbers or letters used to open a combination lock. **4** (**combinations**) dated a single undergarment covering the body and legs.
– DERIVATIVES **combinational** adjective.
combination lock ● noun a lock that is opened by rotating a set of marked dials to show a specific sequence of letters or

Thesaurus

make a story saleable EXAGGERATE, overstate, embroider, embellish, dramatize, enhance, varnish; falsify, misreport, manipulate.
colourful ● adjective **1** *a colourful picture* BRIGHTLY COLOURED, vivid, vibrant, brilliant, radiant, rich; gaudy, glaring, garish; multicoloured, multicolour, rainbow, varicoloured, harlequin, polychromatic, psychedelic; *informal* jazzy. **2** *a colourful account* VIVID, graphic, lively, animated, dramatic, fascinating, interesting, stimulating, scintillating, evocative.
colourless ● adjective **1** *a colourless liquid* UNCOLOURED, white, bleached; *poetic/literary* achromatic. **2** *her colourless face* PALE, pallid, wan, anaemic, bloodless, ashen, white, waxen, pasty, peaky, sickly, drained, drawn, ghostly, deathly. **3** *a colourless personality* UNINTERESTING, dull, boring, tedious, dry, dreary; unexciting, bland, weak, insipid, vapid, vacuous, feeble, wishy-washy, lame, lifeless, spiritless, anaemic, bloodless; nondescript, characterless.
– OPPOSITES colourful, rosy.
column ● noun **1** *arches supported by massive columns* PILLAR, post, support, upright, baluster, pier, pile, pilaster, stanchion; obelisk, monolith. **2** *a column in the paper* ARTICLE, piece, item, story, report, account, write-up, feature, review, notice, editorial, leader. **3** *we walked in a column* LINE, file, queue, procession, rank, row, chain, train, cavalcade, convoy; *informal* crocodile.
columnist ● noun WRITER, contributor, journalist, correspondent, newspaperman, newspaperwoman, newsman, newswoman; wordsmith, penman; critic, reviewer, commentator; *informal* scribbler, pen-pusher, hack(ette), journo.
coma ● noun STATE OF UNCONSCIOUSNESS; *Medicine* persistent vegetative state, PVS.
comatose ● adjective **1** *he was comatose after the accident* UNCONSCIOUS, in a coma, insensible, insensate. **2** *(informal) she lay comatose in the sun* INERT, inactive, lethargic, sluggish, torpid, languid; somnolent, sleeping, dormant.
comb ● verb **1** *she combed her hair* GROOM, brush, untangle, smooth, straighten, neaten, tidy, arrange; curry. **2** *the wool was combed* SEPARATE, dress, card, tease, hackle, heckle. **3** *police combed the area* SEARCH, scour, explore, sweep, probe, hunt through, forage through, poke about/around in, go over, go over with a fine-tooth comb; leave no stone unturned.
combat ● noun *he was killed in combat* BATTLE, fighting, action, hostilities, conflict, war, warfare.
● verb *they tried to combat the disease* FIGHT, battle, tackle, attack, counter, resist, withstand; impede, block, thwart, inhibit; stop, halt, prevent, check, curb.
combatant ● noun **1** *a combatant in the war* FIGHTER, soldier, serviceman/woman, warrior, trooper. **2** *combatants in the computer market* CONTENDER, adversary, opponent, competitor, challenger, rival.
● adjective *combatant armies* WARRING, at war, opposing, belligerent, fighting, battling.
combative ● adjective PUGNACIOUS, aggressive, antagonistic, quarrelsome, argumentative, contentious, hostile, truculent, belligerent, bellicose, militant; *informal* spoiling for a fight.
– OPPOSITES conciliatory.
combination ● noun **1** *a combination of ancient and modern* AMALGAMATION, amalgam, merge, blend, mixture, mix, fusion, marriage, coalition, integration, incorporation, synthesis, composite.

numbers.

combine ● verb /kəmbīn/ **1** join or mix together. **2** do or engage in simultaneously. **3** Chemistry unite to form a compound. ● noun /kombīn/ a group of people or companies acting together for a commercial purpose.
– DERIVATIVES **combiner** noun.
– ORIGIN Latin *combinare* 'join two by two', from *bini* 'two together'.

combine harvester ● noun an agricultural machine that reaps, threshes, and cleans a cereal crop in one operation.

combining form ● noun a form of a word normally used in combination with another element to form a word (e.g. *bio-* 'life' in *biology*).

comb jelly ● noun a marine animal with a jellyfish-like body bearing rows of fused cilia for propulsion.

combo ● noun (pl. **combos**) informal **1** a small jazz, rock, or pop band. **2** chiefly N. Amer. a combination.

combust /kəmbust/ ● verb consume or be consumed by fire.
– DERIVATIVES **combustible** adjective & noun.
– ORIGIN Latin *comburere* 'burn up'.

combustion ● noun **1** the process of burning. **2** Chemistry rapid chemical combination with oxygen, involving the production of heat and light.

come ● verb (past **came**; past part. **come**) **1** move, travel, or reach towards or into a place thought of as near or familiar to the speaker. **2** arrive. **3** happen; take place. **4** occupy or achieve a specified position in space, order, or priority: *she came second.* **5** pass into a specified state or reach a certain condition or state of mind: *his shirt came undone.* **6** be sold or available in a specified form. **7** (also **come, come**) said to correct, reassure, or urge on someone. **8** (**coming**) likely to be important or successful in the future: *a coming man.* **9** informal have an orgasm. ● preposition informal when a specified time is reached or event happens. ● noun informal semen ejaculated at an orgasm.
– PHRASES **come about 1** happen; take place. **2** (of a ship) change direction. **come across 1** (also chiefly Brit. **come over**) give a specified impression. **2** meet or find by chance. **3** informal hand over what is wanted. **come back** chiefly N. Amer. reply or respond, especially vigorously. **come by** manage to acquire or obtain. **come down on 1** criticize or punish harshly. **2** reach a decision in favour of one side or another. **come down to** be dependent on (a factor). **come forward** volunteer for a task or to give evidence. **come from** originate in. **come in** prove to be: *it came in handy.* **come in for** receive (a negative reaction). **come into** inherit (money or property). **come of 1** result from. **2** be descended from. **come off 1** succeed; be accomplished. **2** fare in a specified way. **come off it** informal said when vigorously expressing disbelief. **come on 1** (of a state or condition) start to arrive or happen. **2** (also **come upon**) meet or find by chance. **3** said to encourage or correct someone or hurry them up. **come on to** informal make sexual advances towards. **come out 1** (of a fact) become known. **2** declare oneself as being for or against something. **3** acquit oneself or fare in a specified way. **4** (of a photograph) be produced satisfactorily or in a specified way. **5** (of the result of a calculation or measurement) emerge at a specified figure. **6** informal openly declare that one is homosexual. **7** Brit. dated (of a young upper-class woman) make one's debut in society. **come out with** say in a sudden, rude, or incautious way. **come over 1** (of a feeling) begin to affect. **2** Brit. informal suddenly start to feel a specified way. **come round** chiefly Brit. (chiefly US also **come around**) **1** recover consciousness. **2** be converted to another person's opinion. **3** (of a date or regular occurrence) be imminent again. **come to 1** recover consciousness. **2** (of an expense) amount to. **3** (of a ship) come to a stop. **come to pass** chiefly literary happen. **come up 1** (of a situation or problem) occur or present itself. **2** (of a time or event) approach or draw near. **come up with** produce (something), especially when pressured or challenged. **come upon 1** attack by surprise. **2** see come on (sense 2). **come what may** no matter what happens. **have it coming** (**to one**) informal be due for retribution.
– ORIGIN Old English.

C

Thesaurus

2 *he acted in combination with his brother* COOPERATION, collaboration, association, union, partnership, league.

combine ● verb **1** *he combines comedy with tragedy* AMALGAMATE, integrate, incorporate, merge, mix, fuse, blend; bind, join, marry, unify. **2** *teachers combined to tackle the problem* COOPERATE, collaborate, join forces, get together, club together, unite, team up, throw in one's lot; *informal* gang up.

combustible ● adjective INFLAMMABLE, flammable, incendiary, ignitable.

combustion ● noun BURNING; kindling, ignition.

come ● verb **1** *come and listen* MOVE NEARER, move closer, approach, advance, draw close/closer, draw near/nearer; proceed; *archaic* draw nigh. **2** *they came last night* ARRIVE, get here/there, make it, appear, come on the scene; approach, enter, turn up, come along, materialize; *informal* show (up), roll in/up, blow in, show one's face. **3** *they came to a stream* REACH, arrive at, get to, make it to, make, gain; come across, run across, happen on, chance on, come upon, stumble on; end up at; *informal* wind up at. **4** *the dress comes to her ankles* EXTEND, stretch, reach, come as far as. **5** *she comes from Belgium* BE FROM, be a native of, hail from, originate in; live in, reside in. **6** *attacks came without warning* HAPPEN, occur, take place, come about, transpire, fall, present itself, crop up, materialize, arise, arrive, appear; ensue, follow; *poetic/literary* come to pass, befall. **7** *the car does not come in red* BE AVAILABLE, be for sale; be made, be produced. **8** *(informal)* CLIMAX, orgasm.
– OPPOSITES go, leave.
– PHRASES **come about** HAPPEN, occur, take place, transpire, fall; crop up, materialize, arise, arrive, appear, surface; ensue, follow; *poetic/literary* come to pass, befall. **come across 1** *they came across his friends* MEET/FIND BY CHANCE, meet, run into, run across, come upon, chance on, stumble on, happen on; discover, encounter, find, locate; *informal* bump into. **2** *the emotion comes across* BE COMMUNICATED, be perceived, get across, be clear, be understood, register, sink in, strike home. **3** *she came across as cool* SEEM, appear, look, sound, look to be; *Brit.* come over; *N. Amer.* come off. **4** *(informal) she had come across with more information* HAND OVER, give, deliver, produce, part with; *informal* come up with, cough up; *N. Amer. informal* ante up. **come along 1** *the puppies are coming along nicely* PROGRESS, develop, shape up; come on, turn out; improve, get better, pick up, rally, recover. **2** *Come along!* HURRY (UP), be quick, get a move on, come along, look lively, speed up, move faster; *informal* get moving, get cracking, step on it, move it, buck up, shake a leg, make it snappy; *Brit. informal* get your skates on; *N. Amer. informal* get a wiggle on; *dated* make haste. **come apart** BREAK UP, fall to bits, fall to pieces, disintegrate, come unstuck, separate, split, tear. **come back** RETURN, get back, arrive home, come home; come again. **come between** ALIENATE, estrange, separate, divide, split up, break up, disunite, set at odds. **come by** OBTAIN, acquire, gain, get, find, pick up, procure, secure; buy, purchase; *informal* get one's hands on, get hold of, bag, score, swing. **come down** DECIDE, conclude, settle; choose, opt. **come down on.** See REPRIMAND verb. **come down to** AMOUNT TO, add up to, constitute, boil down to, be equivalent to. **come down with** FALL ILL WITH, fall sick with, be taken ill with, show symptoms of, become infected with, get, catch, develop, contract, fall victim to; *Brit.* go down with. **come forward** VOLUNTEER, offer one's services, make oneself available. **come in** ENTER, gain admission, cross the threshold. **come into** INHERIT, be left, be willed, be bequeathed. **come in for** RECEIVE, experience, sustain, undergo, go through, encounter, face, be subjected to, bear, suffer. **come off 1** *this soufflé rarely comes off* SUCCEED, work, turn out well, work out, go as planned, produce the desired result, get results. **2** *she always came off worse* END UP, finish up. **come on** PROGRESS, develop, shape up, take shape, come along, turn out; improve. **come out 1** *it came out that he'd been to Rome* BECOME KNOWN, become apparent, come to light, emerge, transpire; get out, be discovered, be uncovered, be revealed, leak out, be disclosed. **2** *my book is coming out* BE PUBLISHED, be issued, be released, be brought out, be printed, go on sale. **3** *the flowers have come out* BLOOM, flower, open. **4** *it will come out all right* END, finish, conclude, work out, turn out; *informal* pan out. **5** *the MP came out voluntarily* declare that one is homosexual, come out of the closet. **6** *(Brit. dated) she came out in 1929* ENTER SOCIETY, make one's debut in society. **come out with** UTTER, say, let out, blurt out, burst out with. **come round 1** *he has just come round from anaesthetic* REGAIN CONSCIOUSNESS, come to, come to one's senses, recover, revive, awake, wake up. **2** *I came round to her view* BE CONVERTED, be won over (by), agree (with), change one's mind, be persuaded (by); give way, yield, relent. **3** *Friday the 13th comes round every few months* OCCUR, take place, happen, come up, crop up, arise; recur, reoccur, return, reappear. **4** *come round for a drink* VISIT, call (in/round), look in, stop by, drop by/in/round/over, come over; *informal* pop in/round/over. **come**

C

comeback • noun **1** a return to prominence or fashionability. **2** informal a quick reply to a critical remark. **3** informal opportunity to seek redress.
comedian • noun (fem. **comedienne**) **1** an entertainer whose act is intended to arouse laughter. **2** a comic actor.
comedown • noun informal **1** a loss of status or importance. **2** a feeling of disappointment or depression. **3** a lessening of the sensations generated by a narcotic drug as its effects wear off.
comedy • noun (pl. **comedies**) **1** entertainment consisting of jokes and sketches intended to make an audience laugh. **2** a film, play, or programme intended to arouse laughter. **3** a humorous or satirical play in which the characters ultimately triumph over adversity.
– DERIVATIVES **comedic** /kəmeedik/ adjective.
– ORIGIN Greek *kōmōidia*, from *kōmos* 'revel' + *aoidos* 'singer'.
comedy of manners • noun a play, novel, or film that satirizes behaviour in a particular social group.
come-hither • adjective informal flirtatious or coquettish.
comely /kumli/ • adjective (**comelier**, **comeliest**) archaic or humorous pleasant to look at; attractive.
– DERIVATIVES **comeliness** noun.
– ORIGIN probably shortened from *becomely* 'fitting, becoming'.
come-on • noun informal a gesture or remark intended to attract someone sexually.
comestible /kəmestib'l/ formal or humorous • noun an item of food. • adjective edible.
– ORIGIN Latin *comestibilis*, from *comedere* 'eat up'.
comet /kommit/ • noun a celestial object moving around the solar system, consisting of a nucleus of ice and dust and, when near the sun, a diffuse tail.
– DERIVATIVES **cometary** adjective.
– ORIGIN Greek *komētēs* 'long-haired star'.
comeuppance • noun informal a punishment or fate that someone deserves.
comfit /kumfit/ • noun a sweet consisting of a nut or other centre coated in sugar.
– ORIGIN Old French *confit*, from Latin *conficere* 'put together'.
comfort • noun **1** a state of physical ease and freedom from pain or constraint. **2** (**comforts**) things that contribute to comfort. **3** consolation for grief or anxiety. • verb cause to feel less unhappy; console.
– DERIVATIVES **comforting** adjective.
– ORIGIN Old French *confort*, from Latin *confortare* 'strengthen'.
comfortable • adjective **1** providing or enjoying physical comfort. **2** free from financial worry. **3** (of a victory) with a wide margin.
– DERIVATIVES **comfortably** adverb.
comforter • noun **1** a person or thing that provides consolation. **2** Brit. a baby's dummy. **3** N. Amer. a warm quilt.
comfort station • noun N. Amer. euphemistic a public toilet.
comfrey /kumfri/ • noun (pl. **comfreys**) a plant with large hairy leaves and clusters of purplish or white bell-shaped flowers.
– ORIGIN Old French *cumfirie*, from Latin *confervere* 'heal' (referring to the plant's medicinal use).
comfy • adjective (**comfier**, **comfiest**) informal comfortable.
– DERIVATIVES **comfily** adverb **comfiness** noun.
comic • adjective **1** causing or meant to cause laughter. **2** relating to or in the style of comedy. • noun **1** a comedian. **2** a children's periodical containing comic strips.
– ORIGIN Greek *kōmikos*, from *kōmos* 'revel'.
comical • adjective causing laughter, especially through being ludicrous.
– DERIVATIVES **comically** adverb.
comic opera • noun an opera that portrays humorous situations and characters, with much spoken dialogue.
comic relief • noun humorous content in a dramatic or literary work which offsets more serious parts.
comic strip • noun a sequence of drawings in boxes that tell an amusing story.

Thesaurus

through SURVIVE, get through, ride out, weather, live through, pull through; withstand, stand up to, endure, surmount, overcome; *informal* stick out. **come to 1** *the bill came to £17.50* AMOUNT TO, add up to, run to, total, equal; *Brit.* tot up to. **2** *I came to in the hospital* REGAIN CONSCIOUSNESS, come round, come to one's senses, recover, revive, awake, wake up. **come up** ARISE, occur, happen, come about, transpire, emerge, surface, crop up, turn up, pop up. **come up to 1** *she came up to his shoulder* REACH, come to, be as tall as, extend to. **2** *he never came up to her expectations* MEASURE UP TO, match up to, live up to, fulfil, satisfy, meet, equal, compare with; be good enough; *informal* hold a candle to. **come up with** PRODUCE, devise, think up; propose, put forward, submit, suggest, recommend, advocate, introduce, moot.
comeback • noun **1** *he made a determined comeback* RESURGENCE, recovery, return, rally, upturn; *Brit.* fightback. **2** *(informal) one of my best comebacks* RETORT, riposte, return, rejoinder; answer, reply, response.
comedian • noun **1** *a famous comedian* COMIC, comedienne, funny man/woman, humorist, gagster, stand-up; *N. Amer.* tummler. **2** *Dad was such a comedian* JOKER, jester, wit, wag, comic, wisecracker, jokester; prankster, clown, fool, buffoon; *informal* laugh, hoot, case; *informal, dated* card, caution.
comedienne • noun. See COMEDIAN sense 1.
comedown • noun *(informal)* **1** *a bit of a comedown for a sergeant* LOSS OF STATUS, loss of face, humiliation, belittlement, demotion, degradation, disgrace. **2** *it's such a comedown after Christmas* ANTICLIMAX, let-down, disappointment, disillusionment, deflation, decline.
comedy • noun **1** *he excels in comedy* LIGHT ENTERTAINMENT, comic play, comic film, farce, situation comedy, satire, pantomime, comic opera; burlesque, slapstick; *informal* sitcom. **2** *the comedy in their work* HUMOUR, fun, funny side, comical aspect, absurdity, drollness, farce.
– OPPOSITES tragedy, gravity.
comely • adjective *(archaic)*. See ATTRACTIVE sense 2.
come-on • noun *(informal)* INDUCEMENT, incentive, attraction, lure, pull, draw, enticement, bait, carrot, temptation; fascination, charm, appeal, allure.
comeuppance • noun *(informal)* JUST DESERTS, just punishment, due, retribution, requital.
comfort • noun **1** *travel in comfort* EASE, relaxation, repose, serenity, tranquillity, contentment, cosiness; luxury, opulence, prosperity; bed of roses. **2** *words of comfort* CONSOLATION, solace, condolence, sympathy, commiseration; support, reassurance, cheer.
• verb *a friend tried to comfort her* CONSOLE, solace, condole with, commiserate with, sympathize with; support, succour, ease, reassure, soothe, calm; cheer, hearten, uplift; *informal* buck up.
– OPPOSITES distress, depress.
comfortable • adjective **1** *a comfortable lifestyle* PLEASANT, free from hardship; affluent, well-to-do, luxurious, opulent. **2** *a comfortable room* COSY, snug, warm, pleasant, agreeable; restful, homelike, homely; *informal* comfy. **3** *comfortable clothes* LOOSE, loose-fitting, casual; *informal* comfy. **4** *a comfortable pace* LEISURELY, unhurried, relaxed, easy, gentle, sedate, undemanding, slow; *informal* laid-back. **5** *they feel comfortable with each other* AT EASE, relaxed, secure, safe, unworried, contented, happy.
– OPPOSITES hard, spartan, tense.
comforting • adjective CONSOLING, sympathetic, compassionate, solicitous, tender, warm, caring, loving; supportive, reassuring, soothing, calming; cheering, heartening, encouraging.
comfortless • adjective **1** *a comfortless house* GLOOMY, dreary, dismal, bleak, grim, sombre; joyless, cheerless, depressing, disheartening, dispiriting, unwelcoming, uninviting; austere, spartan, institutional. **2** *he left her comfortless* MISERABLE, heartbroken, grief-stricken, unhappy, sad, distressed, desolate, devastated, inconsolable, disconsolate, downcast, downhearted, dejected, cheerless, depressed, melancholy, gloomy, glum; *informal* blue, down in the mouth, down in the dumps.
– OPPOSITES cosy, happy.
comic • adjective *a comic play* HUMOROUS, funny, droll, amusing, hilarious, uproarious; comical, farcical, silly, slapstick, zany; witty, jocular; *informal* priceless, side-splitting, rib-tickling; *informal, dated* killing.
– OPPOSITES serious.
• noun **1** *a music hall comic* COMEDIAN, comedienne, funny man/woman, comedy actor/actress, humorist, wit; joker, clown; *informal* kidder, wisecracker. **2** *Tony read his comic* CARTOON PAPER, comic paper, comic book, graphic novel; *informal* funny.
comical • adjective **1** *he could be quite comical* FUNNY, comic, humorous, droll, witty, jocular, hilarious, amusing, diverting, entertaining; *informal* jokey, wacky, waggish, side-splitting, rib-tickling, priceless, a scream, a laugh; *informal, dated* killing, a card, a caution. **2** *they look comical in those suits* SILLY, absurd, ridiculous, laughable, risible, ludicrous, preposterous, foolish; *informal* wacky,

comity /kommiti/ ● noun (pl. **comities**) **1** an association of nations for their mutual benefit. **2** (also **comity of nations**) the mutual recognition by nations of the laws and customs of others. **3** formal polite and considerate behaviour towards others.
– ORIGIN Latin *comitas*, from *comis* 'courteous'.

comma ● noun **1** a punctuation mark (,) indicating a pause between parts of a sentence or separating items in a list. **2** a butterfly with orange and brown wings and a white comma-shaped mark on the underside of the hindwing.
– ORIGIN Greek *komma* 'piece cut off, short clause'.

command ● verb **1** give an authoritative order. **2** be in charge of (a military unit). **3** dominate (a strategic position) from a superior height. **4** be in a position to receive or secure: *emeralds command a high price.* ● noun **1** an authoritative order. **2** authority, especially over armed forces: *the officer in command.* **3** a group of officers exercising control over a particular group or operation. **4** the ability to use or control something: *his command of English.* **5** an instruction causing a computer to perform one of its basic functions.
– ORIGIN Latin *commandare*, from *mandare* 'commit, command'.

commandant /kommәndant/ ● noun an officer in charge of a force or institution.

command economy ● noun another term for PLANNED ECONOMY.

commandeer /kommәndeer/ ● verb **1** officially take possession of for military purposes. **2** seize for one's own purposes.
– ORIGIN Afrikaans *kommandeer*, from Dutch *commanderen* 'command'.

commander ● noun **1** a person in authority, especially in a military context. **2** a rank of naval officer next below captain. **3** an officer in charge of a Metropolitan Police district in London. **4** a member of a higher class in some orders of knighthood.

commander-in-chief ● noun (pl. **commanders-in-chief**) an officer in charge of all of the armed forces of a country.

commanding ● adjective **1** indicating or expressing authority; imposing. **2** possessing or giving superior strength: *a commanding lead.*
– DERIVATIVES **commandingly** adverb.

commandment ● noun a divine rule, especially one of the Ten Commandments.

commando ● noun (pl. **commandos**) **1** a soldier specially trained for carrying out raids. **2** a unit of such troops.
– ORIGIN Portuguese, from *commandar* 'to command'.

commando knife ● noun a long, slender knife suitable for hand-to-hand combat.

Command Paper ● noun (in the UK) a document laid before Parliament by order of the Crown, though in practice by the government.

command performance ● noun a presentation of a play, concert, or film at the request of royalty.

comme ci, comme ça /kom see komsaa/ ● adverb neither very good nor very bad.
– ORIGIN French, 'like this, like that'.

commedia dell'arte /komaydiә dellaartay/ ● noun an Italian kind of improvised comedy popular in the 16th–18th centuries, based on stock characters.
– ORIGIN Italian, 'comedy of art'.

comme il faut /kom eel fō/ ● adjective correct in behaviour or etiquette.
– ORIGIN French, 'as is necessary'.

commemorate ● verb honour the memory of as a mark of respect.
– DERIVATIVES **commemoration** noun **commemorative** adjective.
– ORIGIN Latin *commemorare* 'bring to remembrance'.

commence ● verb begin.
– ORIGIN Old French *commencier*, from Latin *initiare* 'begin'.

commencement ● noun **1** the beginning of something. **2** N. Amer. a ceremony in which degrees or diplomas are conferred.

commend ● verb **1** praise formally or officially. **2** present as suitable or good; recommend. **3** (**commend to**) formal or archaic entrust to.
– DERIVATIVES **commendation** noun **commendatory** adjective.
– ORIGIN Latin *commendare*, from *mandare* 'commit, entrust'.

commendable ● adjective deserving praise.
– DERIVATIVES **commendably** adverb.

commensal /kәmens'l/ ● adjective Biology relating to an association between two organisms in which one benefits and the other derives neither benefit nor harm.
– ORIGIN Latin *commensalis*, from *com-* 'sharing' + *mensa* 'a table'.

commensurable /kәmenshәrәb'l, -syoorәb'l/ ● adjective **1** measurable by the same standard. **2** (**commensurable to**) proportionate to. **3** Mathematics (of numbers) in a ratio equal to a ratio of integers.
– ORIGIN Latin *commensurabilis*, from *mensurare* 'to measure'.

commensurate /kәmenshәrәt, -syoorәt/ ● adjective corresponding in size or degree; in proportion.
– DERIVATIVES **commensurately** adverb.

C

Thesaurus

crazy.
– OPPOSITES sensible.

coming ● adjective *the coming election* FORTHCOMING, imminent, impending, approaching; future, expected, anticipated; close, at hand, in store, in the offing, in the pipeline, on the horizon, on the way; *informal* on the cards.
● noun *the coming of spring* APPROACH, advance, advent, arrival, appearance, emergence, onset.

command ● verb **1** *he commanded his men to retreat* ORDER, tell, direct, instruct, call on, require; *poetic/literary* bid. **2** *Jones commanded a tank squadron* BE IN CHARGE OF, be in command of, be the leader of; head, lead, control, direct, manage, supervise, oversee; *informal* head up. **3** *they command great respect* RECEIVE, get, gain, secure.
● noun **1** *officers shouted commands* ORDER, instruction, directive, direction, commandment, injunction, demand, stipulation, requirement, exhortation, bidding, request. **2** *he had 160 men under his command* AUTHORITY, control, charge, power, direction, dominion, guidance; leadership, rule, government, management, supervision, jurisdiction. **3** *a brilliant command of English* KNOWLEDGE, mastery, grasp, comprehension, understanding.

commandeer ● verb SEIZE, take, requisition, appropriate, expropriate, sequestrate, sequester, confiscate, annex, take over, claim, pre-empt; hijack, arrogate, help oneself to; *informal* walk off with; *Law* distrain; *Scottish Law* poind.

commander ● noun LEADER, head, chief, overseer, controller; commander-in-chief, C in C, commanding officer, CO, officer; *informal* boss, boss man, skipper, numero uno, number one, top dog, kingpin, head honcho; *Brit. informal* gaffer, guv'nor.

commanding ● adjective **1** *a commanding position* DOMINANT, dominating, controlling, superior, powerful, prominent, advantageous, favourable. **2** *a commanding voice* AUTHORITATIVE, masterful, assertive, firm, emphatic, insistent, imperative; peremptory, imperious, dictatorial; *informal* bossy.

commemorate ● verb CELEBRATE, pay tribute to, pay homage to, honour, salute, toast; remember, recognize, acknowledge, observe, mark.

commemorative ● adjective MEMORIAL, remembrance; celebratory.

commence ● verb BEGIN, start; get the ball rolling, get going, get under way, get off the ground, set about, embark on, launch into, lead off; open, initiate, inaugurate; *informal* kick off, get the show on the road.
– OPPOSITES conclude.

commencement ● noun BEGINNING, start, opening, outset, onset, launch, initiation, inception, origin; *informal* kick-off.

commend ● verb **1** *we should commend him* PRAISE, compliment, congratulate, applaud, salute, honour; sing the praises of, pay tribute to, take one's hat off to, pat on the back; *formal* laud. **2** *I commend her to you without reservation* RECOMMEND, suggest, propose; endorse, advocate, vouch for, speak for, support, back. **3** *(formal) I commend them to your care* ENTRUST, trust, deliver, commit, hand over, give, turn over, consign, assign.
– OPPOSITES criticize.

commendable ● adjective ADMIRABLE, praiseworthy, creditable, laudable, estimable, meritorious, exemplary, noteworthy, honourable, respectable, fine, excellent.
– OPPOSITES reprehensible.

commendation ● noun **1** *letters of commendation* PRAISE, congratulation, appreciation; acclaim, credit, recognition, respect, esteem, admiration, homage, tribute. **2** *a commendation for bravery* AWARD, accolade, prize, honour, (honourable) mention, citation.

commensurate ● adjective **1** *they had privileges but commensurate duties* EQUIVALENT, equal, corresponding, correspondent, comparable, proportionate, proportional. **2** *a salary commensurate with your qualifications* APPROPRIATE TO, in keeping with, in line

C

comment ● noun **1** a remark expressing an opinion or reaction. **2** discussion, especially of a critical nature, of an issue or event. ● verb express an opinion or reaction.
– ORIGIN Latin *commentum* 'contrivance, interpretation', from *comminisci* 'devise'.
commentary ● noun (pl. **commentaries**) **1** the expression of opinions or offering of explanations about an event or situation. **2** a broadcast spoken account of a sports match or other event as it happens. **3** a set of explanatory or critical notes on a text.
commentate ● verb provide a commentary on a sports match or other event.
commentator ● noun **1** a person who comments on events or texts, especially in the media. **2** a person who provides a commentary on a sports match or other event.
commerce ● noun **1** the activity of buying and selling, especially on a large scale. **2** dated social dealings between people.
– ORIGIN Latin *commercium* 'trade, trading', from *merx* 'merchandise'.
commercial ● adjective **1** concerned with or engaged in commerce. **2** making or intended to make a profit. **3** (of television or radio) funded by the revenue from broadcast advertisements. ● noun a television or radio advertisement.
– DERIVATIVES **commerciality** noun **commercially** adverb.
commercialism ● noun emphasis on the maximizing of profit.
commercialize (also **commercialise**) ● verb manage or exploit in a way designed to make a profit.
– DERIVATIVES **commercialization** noun.
commercial traveller ● noun Brit. dated a travelling sales representative.
Commie ● noun (pl. **Commies**) informal, derogatory a communist.
commingle /kəmingg'l/ ● verb literary mix; blend.
comminuted /komminyo͞otid/ ● adjective **1** technical reduced to minute particles or fragments. **2** Medicine (of a fracture) producing multiple bone splinters.
– DERIVATIVES **comminution** noun.
– ORIGIN from Latin *comminuere* 'break into pieces'.
commis chef /kommi/ ● noun a junior chef.
– ORIGIN French, 'deputy chef'.
commiserate /kəmizzərayt/ ● verb express sympathy or pity; sympathize.
– DERIVATIVES **commiseration** noun.
– ORIGIN Latin *commiserari*, from *miserari* 'to lament'.
commissar /kommisaar/ ● noun a Communist official, especially in Soviet Russia or China, responsible for political education.
– ORIGIN Russian *komissar*, from Latin *commissarius* 'person in charge'.
commissariat /kommisairiət/ ● noun chiefly Military a department for the supply of food and equipment.
commissary /kommissəri/ ● noun (pl. **commissaries**) **1** a deputy or delegate. **2** N. Amer. a restaurant or food store in a military base or other institution.
commission ● noun **1** an instruction, command, or duty. **2** an order for something to be produced specially. **3** a group of people given official authority to do something. **4** a sum paid to an agent in a commercial transaction. **5** a warrant conferring the rank of military officer. **6** the action of committing a crime or offence. **7** archaic the authority to perform a task. ● verb **1** order or authorize the production of. **2** bring into working order. **3** appoint to the rank of military officer.
– PHRASES **in** (or **out of**) **commission** in (or not in) use or working order.
– ORIGIN Latin, from *committere* 'join, entrust'.
commissionaire /kəmishənair/ ● noun chiefly Brit. a uniformed door attendant at a hotel, theatre, or other building.
– ORIGIN French.
commissioner ● noun **1** a person appointed by, or as a member of, a commission. **2** a representative of the supreme authority in an area. **3** the head of the Metropolitan Police in London.
commissioner for oaths ● noun Brit. a solicitor authorized to administer an oath to a person making an affidavit.
commissure /kommisyoor/ ● noun Anatomy a seam or join, especially between the hemispheres of the brain or the two sides of the spinal cord.
– ORIGIN Latin *commissura* 'junction'.
commit ● verb (**committed**, **committing**) **1** carry out or perform (a crime, immoral act, or mistake). **2** pledge or dedicate to a course, policy, or use. **3** (**commit oneself to**) resolve to remain in a long-term emotional relationship with (someone). **4** transfer for safekeeping or permanent preservation. **5** send to prison or psychiatric hospital, or for trial in a higher court.
– ORIGIN Latin *committere* 'join, entrust', from *mittere* 'put or send'.
commitment ● noun **1** dedication to a cause or policy. **2** a pledge or undertaking. **3** an engagement or obligation that restricts freedom of action.
committal ● noun **1** the sending of someone to prison or psy-

Thesaurus

with, consistent with, corresponding to, according to, relative to; dependent on, based on.
comment ● noun **1** *their comments on her appearance* REMARK, observation, statement, utterance; pronouncement, judgement, reflection, opinion, view; criticism. **2** *a great deal of comment* DISCUSSION, debate; interest. **3** *a comment in the margin* NOTE, annotation, footnote, gloss, commentary, explanation.
● verb **1** *they commented on the food* REMARK ON, speak about, talk about, discuss, mention. **2** *'It will soon be night,' he commented* REMARK, observe, reflect, say, state, declare, announce; interpose, interject.
commentary ● noun **1** *the test match commentary* NARRATION, description, account, report, review. **2** *textual commentary* EXPLANATION, elucidation, interpretation, exegesis, analysis; assessment, appraisal, criticism; notes, comments.
commentator ● noun **1** *a television commentator* NARRATOR, announcer, presenter, anchorman, anchorwoman, anchor; reporter, journalist, newscaster, sportscaster; *informal* talking head. **2** *a political commentator* CRITIC, analyst, pundit, monitor, observer; writer, speaker.
commerce ● noun **1** *eastern commerce* TRADE, trading, buying and selling, business, dealing, traffic; (financial) transactions, dealings. **2** *(dated) human commerce* RELATIONS, dealings, socializing, communication, association, contact, intercourse.
commercial ● adjective **1** *a vessel built for commercial purposes* TRADE, trading, business, private enterprise, mercantile, sales. **2** *we turn good ideas into commercial products* LUCRATIVE, money-making, money-spinning, profitable, remunerative, fruitful, gainful; viable, successful. **3** *public opinion was commercial* PROFIT-ORIENTATED, money-orientated, materialistic, mercenary.
● noun *a TV commercial* ADVERTISEMENT, promotion, display; *informal* ad, plug; *Brit. informal* advert.
commercialized ● adjective PROFIT-ORIENTATED, money-orientated, commercial, materialistic, mercenary.
commiserate ● verb (**commiserate with**) OFFER SYMPATHY TO, be sympathetic to, offer condolences to, condole with, sympathize with, empathize with, feel pity for, feel sorry for, feel for; comfort, console.
commiseration ● noun CONDOLENCE(S), sympathy, pity, comfort, solace, consolation; compassion, understanding.
commission ● noun **1** *the dealer's commission* PERCENTAGE, brokerage, share, portion, dividend, premium, fee, consideration, bonus; *informal* cut, take, rake-off, slice; *Brit. informal* whack, divvy. **2** *the commission of building a palace* TASK, employment, job, project, mission, assignment, undertaking; duty, charge, responsibility. **3** *items made under royal commission* WARRANT, licence, sanction, authority. **4** *an independent commission* COMMITTEE, board, council, panel, directorate, delegation. **5** *the commission of an offence* PERPETRATION, committing, committal, execution.
● verb **1** *he was commissioned to paint a portrait* ENGAGE, contract, charge, employ, hire, recruit, retain, appoint, enlist, co-opt, book, sign up. **2** *they commissioned a sculpture* ORDER; authorize; *formal* bespeak.
– PHRASES **in commission** IN SERVICE, in use; working, functional, operative, up and running, in operation, in working order. **out of commission** NOT IN SERVICE, not in use, unserviceable; not working, inoperative, out of order; down.
commit ● verb **1** *he committed a murder* CARRY OUT, do, perpetrate, engage in, enact, execute, effect, accomplish; be responsible for; *informal* pull off. **2** *she was committed to their care* ENTRUST, consign, assign, deliver, give, hand over, relinquish; *formal* commend. **3** *they committed themselves to the project* PLEDGE, devote, apply, give, dedicate. **4** *the judge committed him to prison* CONSIGN, send, deliver, confine. **5** *her husband had her committed* HOSPITALIZE, confine, institutionalize, put away; certify.
commitment ● noun **1** *the pressure of his commitments* RESPONSI-

chiatric hospital, or for trial. **2** the burial of a corpse.

committed ● adjective **1** dedicated to a cause, activity, job, etc. **2** in a long-term emotional relationship.

committee /kəmitti/ ● noun **1** (treated as sing. or pl.) a group of people appointed for a specific function by a larger group. **2** /kommitee/ Law, Brit. a person to whom another person or another person's property is entrusted.
– PHRASES **Committee of the whole House** the whole House of Commons when sitting as a committee.

committee stage ● noun the third of five stages of a bill's progress through Parliament, when it may be debated and amended.

commode ● noun **1** a piece of furniture containing a concealed chamber pot. **2** a chest of drawers of a decorative type popular in the 18th century.
– ORIGIN French, 'convenient, suitable'.

commodify /kəmoddifī/ ● verb (**commodifies, commodified**) turn into or treat as a mere commodity.
– DERIVATIVES **commodification** noun.

commodious /kəmōdiəss/ ● adjective formal roomy and comfortable.
– ORIGIN Latin *commodus* 'convenient'.

commodity /kəmodditi/ ● noun (pl. **commodities**) **1** a raw material or agricultural product that can be bought and sold. **2** something useful or valuable.
– ORIGIN Latin *commoditas*, from *commodus* 'convenient'.

commodore /kommədor/ ● noun **1** a naval rank above captain and below rear admiral. **2** the president of a yacht club. **3** the senior captain of a shipping line.
– ORIGIN probably from Dutch *komandeur* 'commander'.

common ● adjective (**commoner, commonest**) **1** occurring, found, or done often; not rare. **2** without special qualities, rank, or position; ordinary. **3** of the most familiar type. **4** showing a lack of taste and refinement supposedly typical of the lower classes; vulgar. **5** shared by two or more people or things. **6** belonging to or affecting the whole of a community: *common land.* **7** Grammar (of a noun in Latin, Dutch, and certain other languages) belonging to a gender conventionally regarded as masculine or feminine. ● noun **1** a piece of open land for public use. **2** a form of Christian service used for each of a group of occasions.
– PHRASES **common or garden** Brit. informal of the usual or ordinary type. **in common** in joint use or possession; shared. **in common with** in the same way as.
– DERIVATIVES **commonness** noun.
– ORIGIN Latin *communis*.

commonality ● noun (pl. **commonalities**) **1** the sharing of features or attributes. **2** (**the commonality**) another term for COMMONALTY.

commonalty /kommənəlti/ ● noun (treated as pl.) (**the commonalty**) chiefly historical people without special rank or position.

common denominator ● noun **1** Mathematics a common multiple of the denominators of several fractions. **2** a feature shared by all members of a group.

commoner ● noun one of the ordinary or common people, as opposed to the aristocracy or to royalty.

Common Era ● noun another term for CHRISTIAN ERA.

common ground ● noun views shared by each of two or more parties.

common law ● noun law derived from custom and judicial precedent rather than statutes.

common-law husband (or **wife**) ● noun **1** a partner in a marriage recognized in some jurisdictions (excluding the UK) as valid by common law, though not brought about by a civil or ecclesiastical ceremony. **2** a partner in a relationship in which a man and woman cohabit for long enough to suggest stability.

commonly ● adverb very often; frequently.

common market ● noun **1** a group of countries imposing few or no duties on trade with one another and a common tariff on trade with other countries. **2** (**the Common Market**) the European Economic Community or European Union.

common noun ● noun a noun referring to a class of objects or a concept as opposed to a particular individual.

commonplace ● adjective not unusual or original; ordinary or trite. ● noun **1** a usual or ordinary thing. **2** a trite saying or topic; a platitude.

common room ● noun chiefly Brit. a room in an educational institution for use of students or staff outside teaching hours.

commons ● plural noun **1** (**the Commons**) the House of Commons. **2** (**the Commons**) historical the common people regarded as a part of a political system. **3** archaic provisions shared in common; rations.

common sense ● noun good sense and sound judgement in practical matters.

commonsensical ● adjective possessing or marked by common sense.

common time ● noun Music a rhythmic pattern in which there are two or four beats in a bar.

commonweal /kommənweel/ ● noun (**the commonweal**) archaic the welfare of the public.

commonwealth ● noun **1** an independent state or community, especially a democratic republic. **2** (**the Commonwealth** or in full **the Commonwealth of Nations**) an association consisting of the UK together with states that were previously part of the British Empire, and dependencies. **3** an aggregate or grouping of states or other bodies. **4** (**the Commonwealth**) the republican period of government in Britain between the execution of Charles I in 1649 and the Restoration of Charles II in 1660. **5** (**the commonwealth**) archaic the general good.

commotion ● noun a state of confused and noisy disturbance.
– ORIGIN Latin, from *com-* 'altogether' + *motio* 'motion'.

communal /komyoon'l, kəmyōōn'l/ ● adjective **1** shared or done

Thesaurus

BILITY, obligation, duty, tie, liability; task; engagement, arrangement. **2** *her commitment to her students* DEDICATION, devotion, allegiance, loyalty, faithfulness, fidelity. **3** *he made a commitment* VOW, promise, pledge, oath; contract, pact, deal; decision, resolution.

committed ● adjective DEVOUT, devoted, dedicated, loyal, faithful, staunch, firm, steadfast, unwavering, wholehearted, keen, passionate, ardent, fervent, sworn, pledged; dutiful, diligent; *informal* card-carrying, true blue, deep-dyed.
– OPPOSITES apathetic.

commodious ● adjective *(formal)* ROOMY, capacious, spacious, ample, generous, sizeable, large, big, extensive.
– OPPOSITES cramped.

commodity ● noun ITEM, material, product, article, object; import, export.

common ● adjective **1** *the common folk* ORDINARY, normal, average, unexceptional; simple. **2** *a very common art form* USUAL, ordinary, familiar, regular, frequent, recurrent, everyday; standard, typical, conventional, stock, commonplace, run-of-the-mill. **3** *a common belief* WIDESPREAD, general, universal, popular, mainstream, prevalent, prevailing, rife, established, conventional, traditional, orthodox, accepted. **4** *the common good* COLLECTIVE, communal, community, public, popular, general; shared, combined. **5** *they are far too common* UNCOUTH, vulgar, coarse, rough, boorish, unladylike, ungentlemanly, ill-bred, uncivilized, unsophisticated, unrefined; lowly, low-born, low-class, inferior, proletarian, plebeian; *informal* plebby; *Brit. informal* common as muck.
– OPPOSITES unusual, rare, individual, refined.
● noun *(Brit. informal) use your common!* See COMMON SENSE.

commonly ● adverb OFTEN, frequently, regularly, repeatedly, time and (time) again, all the time, routinely, habitually, customarily; *N. Amer.* oftentimes; *informal* lots.

commonplace ● adjective **1** *a commonplace writing style* ORDINARY, run-of-the-mill, unremarkable, unexceptional, average, mediocre, pedestrian, prosaic, lacklustre, dull, bland, uninteresting, mundane; hackneyed, trite, banal, clichéd, predictable, stale, tired, unoriginal; *informal* (plain) vanilla, bog-standard, a dime a dozen; *Brit. informal* common or garden; *N. Amer. informal* ornery, bush-league. **2** *a commonplace occurrence* COMMON, normal, usual, ordinary, familiar, routine, standard, everyday, daily, regular, frequent, habitual, typical.
– OPPOSITES original, unusual.
● noun **1** *early death was a commonplace* EVERYDAY EVENT, routine. **2** *a great store of commonplaces* PLATITUDE, cliché, truism, hackneyed phrase, trite phrase, old chestnut, banality; *dated* bromide.

common sense ● noun SENSIBLENESS, (good) sense, (native) wit, judgement, level-headedness, prudence, discernment, canniness, astuteness, shrewdness, wisdom, insight, perception, perspicacity; practicality, capability, resourcefulness, enterprise; *informal* horse sense, gumption, nous, savvy; *Brit. informal* common; *N. Amer. informal* smarts.
– OPPOSITES folly.

by all members of a community. **2** (of conflict) between different communities, especially those having different religions or ethnic origins.
– DERIVATIVES **communality** noun **communally** adverb.
– ORIGIN Latin *communalis*, from *communis* 'common'.
communard /komyoonaard/ • noun **1** a member of a commune. **2** (**Communard**) historical a supporter of the Paris Commune.
commune[1] /komyo͞on/ • noun **1** a group of people living together and sharing possessions and responsibilities. **2** the smallest French territorial division for administrative purposes. **3** (**the Commune**) the government elected in Paris in 1871, advocating communal organization of society.
– ORIGIN Latin *communia*, from *communis* 'common'.
commune[2] /kəmyo͞on/ • verb (**commune with**) share one's intimate thoughts or feelings with.
– ORIGIN Old French *comuner* 'to share'.
communicable • adjective (especially of a disease) able to be communicated to others.
communicant • noun a person who receives Holy Communion.
communicate • verb **1** share or exchange information or ideas. **2** pass on, transmit, or convey (an emotion, disease, heat, etc.). **3** (**communicating**) (of two rooms) having a common connecting door. **4** receive Holy Communion.
– DERIVATIVES **communicator** noun.
– ORIGIN Latin *communicare* 'to share', from *communis* 'common'.
communication • noun **1** the action of communicating. **2** a letter or message. **3** (**communications**) means of sending or receiving information, such as telephone lines or computers. **4** (**communications**) means of travelling or of transporting goods, such as roads or railways.
– DERIVATIVES **communicational** adjective.
communication cord • noun Brit. a cord or chain which a train passenger may pull in an emergency, causing the train to brake.
communicative • adjective willing or eager to talk or impart information.
– DERIVATIVES **communicatively** adverb.
communion • noun **1** the sharing of intimate thoughts and feelings. **2** (also **Holy Communion**) the service of Christian worship at which bread and wine are consecrated and shared; the Eucharist. **3** an allied group of Christian Churches or communities: *the Anglican communion.*
communiqué /kəmyo͞onikay/ • noun an official announcement or statement, especially one made to the media.
– ORIGIN French, 'communicated'.
communism • noun **1** a political and social system whereby all property is owned by the community and each person contributes and receives according to their ability and needs. **2** a system of this kind derived from Marxism, practised in China and formerly in the Soviet Union.
– DERIVATIVES **communist** noun & adjective **communistic** adjective.
– ORIGIN French *communisme*, from *commun* 'common'.
communitarianism /kəmyo͞onitairiəniz'm/ • noun **1** a system of social organization based on small self-governing communities. **2** an ideology which emphasizes the responsibility of the individual to the community and the importance of the family unit.
– DERIVATIVES **communitarian** adjective & noun.
community • noun (pl. **communities**) **1** a group of people living together in one place. **2** (**the community**) the people of an area or country considered collectively; society. **3** a group of people with a common religion, race, or profession: *the scientific community.* **4** the holding of certain attitudes and interests in common. **5** a group of interdependent plants or animals growing or living together or occupying a specified habitat.
– ORIGIN Old French *comunete*, from Latin *communis* 'common'.
community care • noun long-term care for mentally ill, elderly, and disabled people within the community rather than in hospitals or institutions.
community centre • noun a place providing educational or recreational activities for a neighbourhood.
community service • noun socially useful work that an offender is required to do instead of going to prison.
community singing • noun singing by a large crowd.
commutate /komyootayt/ • verb regulate or reverse the direction of (an alternating electric current), especially to make it a direct current.
commutation • noun **1** the commuting of a judicial sentence. **2** the commutating of an electric current.
commutative /kəmyo͞otətiv/ • adjective Mathematics unchanged in result by interchanging the order of quantities, such that for example $a \times b = b \times a$.
commutator /komyo͞otaytər/ • noun an attachment connected with the armature of a motor or dynamo, through which electrical contact is made and which ensures the current flows as direct current.
commute • verb **1** travel some distance between one's home

Thesaurus

commotion • noun DISTURBANCE, uproar, tumult, rumpus, ruckus, brouhaha, furore, hue and cry, fuss, stir, storm; turmoil, disorder, confusion, chaos, mayhem, havoc, pandemonium; unrest, fracas, riot, breach of the peace; *Irish, N. Amer., & Austral.* donnybrook; *informal* ruction(s), ballyhoo, kerfuffle, hoo-ha, to-do, hullabaloo; *Brit. informal* carry-on, row, aggro, argy-bargy; *Law, dated* affray.
communal • adjective **1** *the kitchen was communal* SHARED, joint, common. **2** *they farm on a communal basis* COLLECTIVE, cooperative, community, communalist, combined.
– OPPOSITES private, individual.
commune • noun *she lives in a commune* COLLECTIVE, cooperative, communal settlement, kibbutz.
• verb **1** *we pray to commune with God* COMMUNICATE, speak, talk, converse, interface. **2** *she likes to commune with nature* EMPATHIZE, identify, have a rapport, feel at one; relate to, feel close to.
communicable • adjective CONTAGIOUS, INFECTIOUS, transmittable, transmissible, transferable, spreadable; *informal* catching; *dated* infective.
communicate • verb **1** *he communicated the news to his boss* CONVEY, tell, impart, relay, transmit, pass on, announce, report, recount, relate, present; divulge, disclose, mention; spread, disseminate, promulgate, broadcast. **2** *they communicate daily* LIAISE, be in touch, be in contact, have dealings, interface, commune, meet; talk, speak, converse; *informal* have a confab, powwow. **3** *learn how to communicate better* GET ONE'S MESSAGE ACROSS, explain oneself, be understood, get through to someone. **4** *the disease is communicated easily* TRANSMIT, transfer, spread, carry, pass on. **5** *each bedroom communicates with a bathroom* CONNECT WITH, join up with, open on to, lead into.
communication • noun **1** *the communication of news* TRANSMISSION, conveyance, divulgence, divulgation, disclosure; dissemination, promulgation, broadcasting. **2** *there was no communication between them* CONTACT, dealings, relations, connection, association, socializing, intercourse; correspondence, dialogue, talk, conversation, discussion; *dated* commerce. **3** *an official communication* MESSAGE, statement, announcement, report, dispatch, communiqué, letter, bulletin, correspondence. **4** *road and rail communications* LINKS, connections; services, routes.
communicative • adjective FORTHCOMING, expansive, expressive, unreserved, uninhibited, vocal, outgoing, frank, open, candid; talkative, chatty, loquacious; *informal* gabby.
communion • noun **1** *a sense of communion with others* AFFINITY, fellowship, kinship, friendship, fellow feeling, togetherness, closeness, harmony, understanding, rapport, connection, communication, empathy, accord, unity. **2** *Christ's presence at Communion* EUCHARIST, Holy Communion, Lord's Supper, Mass.
communiqué • noun OFFICIAL COMMUNICATION, press release, bulletin, message, missive, dispatch, statement, report, announcement, declaration, proclamation; *N. Amer.* advisory; *informal* memo.
communism • noun COLLECTIVISM, state ownership, (radical) socialism; Sovietism, Bolshevism, Marxism, Leninism, Trotskyism, Maoism.
communist • noun & adjective COLLECTIVIST, leftist, (radical) socialist; Soviet, Bolshevik, Bolshevist, Marxist, Leninist, Trotskyist, Trotskyite, Maoist; *informal, derogatory* Commie, Bolshie, red, lefty.
community • noun **1** *work done for the community* POPULATION, populace, people, citizenry, (general) public, collective; residents, inhabitants, citizens. **2** *a rural community* DISTRICT, region, zone, area, locality, locale, neighbourhood; *informal* neck of the woods, turf; *Brit. informal* manor; *N. Amer. informal* hood, nabe. **3** *gays are not one homogenous community* GROUP, body, set, circle, clique, faction; *informal* gang, bunch. **4** *a monastic community* BROTHERHOOD, sisterhood, fraternity, sorority, sodality; colony, order. **5** *commu-*

and place of work on a regular basis. **2** reduce (a judicial sentence, especially a sentence of death) to a less severe one. **3** change (one kind of payment or obligation) for (another).
– DERIVATIVES **commutable** adjective **commuter** noun.
– ORIGIN Latin *commutare*, from *mutare* 'to change'; sense 1 derives from *commutation ticket*, the US term for a season ticket (because the daily fare is commuted to a single payment).
compact[1] ● adjective /kəmpakt/ **1** closely and neatly packed together; dense. **2** having all the necessary components or features neatly fitted into a small space. ● verb /kəmpakt/ exert force on to make more dense; compress. ● noun /kompakt/ a small flat case containing face powder, a mirror, and a powder puff.
– DERIVATIVES **compaction** noun **compactly** adverb **compactness** noun **compactor** noun.
– ORIGIN from Latin *compingere* 'fasten together'.
compact[2] /kompakt/ ● noun a formal agreement or contract between two or more parties.
– ORIGIN Latin *compactum*, from *compacisci* 'make a covenant with'.
compact disc ● noun a small plastic disc on which music or other digital information is stored in the form of a pattern of metal-coated pits from which it can be read using laser light reflected off the disc.
compadre /kompaadray/ ● noun (pl. **compadres**) informal, chiefly N. Amer. a friend or companion.
– ORIGIN Spanish, 'godfather'.
companion ● noun **1** a person with whom one spends time or travels. **2** each of a pair of things intended to complement or match each other. **3** (**Companion**) a member of the lowest grade of certain orders of knighthood.
– DERIVATIVES **companionship** noun.
– ORIGIN Old French *compaignon* 'one who breaks bread with another', from Latin *panis* 'bread'.
companionable ● adjective friendly and sociable.
– DERIVATIVES **companionably** adverb.
companionate /kəmpanyənət/ ● adjective formal (of a marriage or relationship) between partners or spouses as equal companions.
companionway ● noun a set of steps leading from a ship's deck down to a cabin or lower deck.
– ORIGIN from obsolete Dutch *kompanje* 'quarterdeck'.
company ● noun (pl. **companies**) **1** a commercial business. **2** companionship, especially of a specified kind: *she is excellent company*. **3** a guest or guests: *we're expecting company*. **4** a number of people gathered together. **5** a body of soldiers, especially the smallest subdivision of an infantry battalion. **6** a group of actors, singers, or dancers who perform together.
– PHRASES **in company with** together with. **keep someone company** spend time with someone to prevent them feeling lonely or bored. **keep company with** associate with habitually.
– ORIGIN Old French *compainie*; related to *compaignon* (see COMPANION).
comparable /kompərəb'l/ ● adjective **1** able to be likened to another; similar. **2** of equivalent quality.
– DERIVATIVES **comparability** noun **comparably** adverb.
comparative /kəmparrətiv/ ● adjective **1** measured or judged by comparison; relative. **2** involving comparison between two or more subjects or branches of science. **3** (of an adjective or adverb) expressing a higher degree of a quality, but not the highest possible (e.g. *braver*; *more fiercely*). Contrasted with POSITIVE, SUPERLATIVE.
comparatively ● adverb to a moderate degree as compared to something else; relatively.
comparator /kəmparrətər/ ● noun **1** a device for comparing something measurable with a reference or standard. **2** something used as a standard for comparison.
compare ● verb **1** (often **compare to/with**) estimate, measure, or note the similarity or dissimilarity between. **2** (**compare to**) point out or describe the resemblances of (something) with. **3** (usu. **compare with**) be similar to or have a specified relationship with another thing or person.
– PHRASES **beyond** (or **without**) **compare** surpassing all others of the same kind. **compare notes** exchange ideas or information about a subject.
– ORIGIN Latin *comparare*, from *compar* 'like, equal'.
comparison ● noun **1** the action or an instance of comparing. **2** the quality of being similar or equivalent.
compartment ● noun **1** a separate section of a structure or container. **2** a division of a railway carriage marked by partitions.
– DERIVATIVES **compartmental** adjective **compartmentally** adverb.

C

Thesaurus

nity of interests SIMILARITY, likeness, comparability, correspondence, agreement, closeness, affinity. **6** *the community of goods* JOINT OWNERSHIP, common ownership, shared possession.
commute ● verb **1** *they commute on a train* TRAVEL TO AND FROM WORK, travel to and fro, travel back and forth. **2** *his sentence was commuted* REDUCE, lessen, lighten, shorten, cut, attenuate, moderate. **3** *knight service was commuted for a payment* EXCHANGE, change, substitute, swap, trade, switch.
– OPPOSITES increase.
commuter ● noun (DAILY) TRAVELLER, traveller, passenger; *informal* straphanger.
compact[1] ● adjective **1** *a compact rug* DENSE, close-packed, tightly packed; thick, tight, firm. **2** *a compact camera* SMALL, little, petite, miniature, mini, small-scale; *Scottish* wee; *informal* teeny, teeny-weeny; *Brit. informal* dinky; *N. Amer.* little-bitty. **3** *her tale is compact* CONCISE, succinct, condensed, brief, pithy; short and sweet; *informal* snappy; *formal* compendious.
– OPPOSITES loose, large, rambling.
● verb *the snow has been compacted* COMPRESS, condense, pack down, press down, tamp (down), flatten.
compact[2] ● noun *the warring states signed a compact* TREATY, pact, accord, agreement, contract, bargain, deal, settlement, covenant, concordat; pledge, promise, bond.
companion ● noun **1** *Harry and his companion* ASSOCIATE, partner, escort, compatriot, confederate; friend, intimate, confidant(e), comrade; *informal* pal, chum, crony, sidekick; *Brit. informal* mate, oppo, china, mucker; *N. Amer. informal* buddy, amigo, compadre; *Austral./NZ informal* offsider. **2** *a lady's companion* ATTENDANT, aide, helper, assistant, valet, equerry, lady in waiting; chaperone; carer, minder. **3** *the tape is a companion to the book* COMPLEMENT, counterpart, twin, match; accompaniment, supplement, addition, adjunct, accessory. **4** *The Gardener's Companion* HANDBOOK, manual, guide, reference book, ABC, primer, vade mecum; *informal* bible.
companionable ● adjective FRIENDLY, affable, cordial, genial, congenial, amiable, easy-going, good-natured, comradely; sociable, convivial, outgoing, gregarious; *informal* chummy, pally; *Brit. informal* matey; *N. Amer. informal* buddy-buddy, clubby.
companionship ● noun FRIENDSHIP, fellowship, closeness, togetherness, amity, intimacy, rapport, camaraderie, brotherhood, sisterhood; company, society, social contact.
company ● noun **1** *an oil company* FIRM, business, corporation, establishment, agency, office, bureau, institution, organization, concern, enterprise; conglomerate, consortium, syndicate, multinational; *informal* outfit. **2** *I enjoy his company* COMPANIONSHIP, friendship, fellowship, amity, camaraderie; society, association. **3** *I'm expecting company* GUESTS, visitors, callers, people; someone. **4** *a company of poets* GROUP, crowd, party, band, assembly, cluster, flock, herd, troupe, throng, congregation; *informal* bunch, gang. **5** *a company of infantry* UNIT, section, detachment, troop, corps, squad, squadron, platoon, battalion, division.
– RELATED TERMS corporate.
comparable ● adjective **1** *comparable incomes* SIMILAR, close, near, approximate, akin, equivalent, commensurate, proportional, proportionate; like, matching. **2** *nobody is comparable with him* EQUAL TO, as good as, in the same league as, able to hold a candle to, on a par with, on a level with; a match for.
comparative ● adjective RELATIVE; in/by comparison.
compare ● verb **1** *we compared the data sets* CONTRAST, juxtapose, collate, differentiate, weigh up. **2** *he was compared to Wagner* LIKEN, equate, analogize; class with, bracket with, set side by side with. **3** *the porcelain compares with Dresden's fine china* BE AS GOOD AS, be comparable to, bear comparison with, be the equal of, match up to, be on a par with, be in the same league as, come close to, hold a candle to, be not unlike; match, resemble, emulate, rival, approach.
– PHRASES **beyond compare** WITHOUT EQUAL, second to none, in a class of one's own; peerless, matchless, unmatched, incomparable, inimitable, supreme, outstanding, consummate, unique, singular, perfect.
comparison ● noun **1** *a comparison of the results* JUXTAPOSITION, collation, differentiation. **2** *there's no comparison between them* RE-

C

– ORIGIN French *compartiment*, from Latin *compartiri* 'divide'.

compartmentalize (also **compartmentalise**) ● verb divide into categories or sections.

– DERIVATIVES **compartmentalization** noun.

compass ● noun **1** an instrument containing a magnetized pointer which shows the direction of magnetic north and bearings from it. **2** (also **compasses**) an instrument for drawing circles and arcs and measuring distances between points, consisting of two arms linked by a movable joint. **3** range or scope. ● verb archaic **1** circle or surround. **2** manage to accomplish.

– ORIGIN Old French *compas*, from Latin *com-* 'together' + *passus* 'a step or pace'.

compassion ● noun sympathetic pity and concern for the sufferings or misfortunes of others.

– ORIGIN Latin, from *compati* 'suffer with'.

compassionate ● adjective feeling or showing compassion.

– DERIVATIVES **compassionately** adverb.

compassionate leave ● noun leave from work granted in recognition of personal circumstances, especially the death of a close relative.

compatible ● adjective **1** able to exist or be used together without problems or conflict. **2** (of two people) able to have a harmonious relationship; well suited. **3** (usu. **compatible with**) consistent or in keeping.

– DERIVATIVES **compatibility** noun **compatibly** adverb.

– ORIGIN Latin *compatibilis*, from *compati* 'suffer with'.

compatriot /kəmpatriət, -payt-/ ● noun a person from the same country; a fellow citizen.

– ORIGIN French, from Latin *patriota* 'fellow countryman'.

compeer /kəmpeer/ ● noun **1** formal a person of equal rank, status, or ability. **2** archaic a companion or associate.

– ORIGIN Old French *comper*, from Latin *par* 'equal'; compare with PEER².

compel ● verb (**compelled**, **compelling**) **1** force or oblige to do something. **2** bring about by force or pressure.

– ORIGIN Latin *compellere*, from *pellere* 'drive'.

compelling ● adjective powerfully evoking attention or admiration.

– DERIVATIVES **compellingly** adverb.

compendious ● adjective formal presenting the essential facts in a comprehensive but concise way.

– DERIVATIVES **compendiously** adverb.

– ORIGIN Latin *compendiosus* 'advantageous, brief'.

compendium /kəpendiəm/ ● noun (pl. **compendiums** or **compendia** /kəpendiə/) **1** a collection of concise but detailed information about a particular subject. **2** a collection of similar items.

– ORIGIN Latin, 'profit, saving' (literally 'what is weighed together'), from *compendere* 'weigh together'.

compensate ● verb **1** give (someone) something to reduce or balance the bad effect of loss, suffering, or injury. **2** (**compensate for**) make up for (something undesirable) by exerting an opposite force or effect.

– DERIVATIVES **compensator** noun **compensatory** adjective.

– ORIGIN Latin *compensare* 'weigh against'.

compensation ● noun **1** something given to compensate for loss, suffering, or injury. **2** something that compensates for an undesirable state of affairs. **3** the action or process of compensating. **4** chiefly N. Amer. salary or wages.

compère /kompair/ Brit. ● noun a person who introduces the acts in a variety show. ● verb act as a compère for.

– ORIGIN French, 'godfather'.

compete ● verb strive to gain or win something by defeating or establishing superiority over others.

– ORIGIN Latin *competere*, from *petere* 'aim at, seek'.

competence (also **competency**) ● noun **1** the quality or extent of being competent. **2** dated an income large enough to live on.

competent ● adjective **1** having the necessary skill or knowledge to do something successfully. **2** satisfactory or adequate, though not outstanding: *she spoke quite competent French.* **3** having legal authority to deal with a particular matter.

– DERIVATIVES **competently** adverb.

– ORIGIN from Latin *competere* in the sense 'be fit or proper'.

competition ● noun **1** the activity of competing against others. **2** an event or contest in which people compete. **3** the person or people with whom one is competing.

Thesaurus

SEMBLANCE, likeness, similarity, correspondence, correlation, parallel, parity, comparability.

compartment ● noun **1** *a secret compartment* SECTION, part, bay, recess, chamber, cavity; pocket. **2** *they put science and religion in separate compartments* DOMAIN, field, sphere, department; category, pigeonhole, bracket, group, set.

compartmentalize ● verb CATEGORIZE, pigeonhole, bracket, group, classify, characterize, stereotype, label, brand; sort, rank, rate.

compass ● noun SCOPE, range, extent, reach, span, breadth, ambit, limits, parameters, bounds.

compassion ● noun PITY, sympathy, empathy, fellow feeling, care, concern, solicitude, sensitivity, warmth, love, tenderness, mercy, leniency, tolerance, kindness, humanity, charity.

– OPPOSITES indifference, cruelty.

compassionate ● adjective SYMPATHETIC, empathetic, understanding, caring, solicitous, sensitive, warm, loving; merciful, lenient, tolerant, considerate, kind, humane, charitable, big-hearted.

compatibility ● noun LIKE-MINDEDNESS, similarity, affinity, closeness, fellow feeling, harmony, rapport, empathy, sympathy.

compatible ● adjective **1** *they were never compatible* (WELL) SUITED, well matched, like-minded, in tune, in harmony; reconcilable. **2** *her bruising is compatible with a fall* CONSISTENT, congruous, congruent; in keeping.

compatriot ● noun FELLOW COUNTRYMAN/WOMAN, countryman, countrywoman, fellow citizen.

compel ● verb **1** *he compelled them to leave their land* FORCE, pressurize, pressure, press, push, urge; dragoon, browbeat, bully, intimidate; oblige, require, make; *informal* lean on, put the screws on. **2** *they can compel compliance* EXACT, extort, demand, insist on, force, necessitate.

compelling ● adjective **1** *a compelling performance* ENTHRALLING, captivating, gripping, riveting, spellbinding, mesmerizing, absorbing, irresistible. **2** *a compelling argument* CONVINCING, persuasive, cogent, irresistible, powerful, strong, weighty, plausible, credible, sound, valid, telling, conclusive, irrefutable, unanswerable.

– OPPOSITES boring, weak.

compendious ● adjective *(formal)* SUCCINCT, pithy, short and to the point, concise, compact, condensed, compressed, abridged, summarized, synoptic; *informal* snappy.

– OPPOSITES expanded.

compendium ● noun COLLECTION, compilation, anthology, treasury, digest; summary, synopsis, precis, outline.

compensate ● verb **1** *you must compensate for what you did* MAKE AMENDS, make up, make reparation, recompense, atone, requite, pay; expiate, make good, rectify. **2** *we agreed to compensate him for his loss* RECOMPENSE, repay, pay back, reimburse, remunerate, recoup, requite, indemnify. **3** *his flair compensated for his faults* BALANCE (OUT), counterbalance, counteract, offset, make up for, cancel out, neutralize, negative.

compensation ● noun RECOMPENSE, repayment, reimbursement, remuneration, requital, indemnification, indemnity, redress; damages; *N. Amer. informal* comp.

compère ● noun HOST, presenter, anchor, anchorman/woman, master of ceremonies, MC, announcer; *N. Amer. informal* emcee.

compete ● verb **1** *they competed in a tennis tournament* TAKE PART, participate, play, be a competitor, be involved; enter, go in for. **2** *they had to compete with other firms* CONTEND, vie, battle, wrangle, jockey, go head to head; strive against, pit oneself against; challenge, take on. **3** *no one can compete with him* RIVAL, challenge, keep up with, keep pace with, compare with, match, be in the same league as, come near to, come close to, touch; *informal* hold a candle to.

competence ● noun **1** *my technical competence* CAPABILITY, ability, competency, proficiency, accomplishment, expertise, adeptness, skill, prowess, mastery, talent; *informal* savvy, know-how. **2** *the competence of the system* ADEQUACY, appropriateness, suitability, fitness; effectiveness; *formal* efficacy. **3** *matters within the competence of the courts* AUTHORITY, power, control, jurisdiction, ambit, scope, remit.

competent ● adjective **1** *a competent carpenter* CAPABLE, able, proficient, adept, adroit, accomplished, complete, skilful, skilled, gifted, talented, expert; good, excellent; *informal* great, mean, wicked, nifty, ace. **2** *she spoke competent French* ADEQUATE, acceptable, satisfactory, reasonable, fair, decent, not bad, all right, average, tolerable, passable, moderate, middling; *informal* OK, okay, so-so. **3** *the court was not competent to hear the case* FIT, suitable,

competitive ● adjective **1** relating to or characterized by competition. **2** strongly desiring to be more successful than others. **3** as good as or better than others of a comparable nature.
– DERIVATIVES **competitively** adverb **competitiveness** noun.

competitor ● noun **1** a person who takes part in a sporting contest. **2** an organization engaged in commercial or economic competition with others.

compilation ● noun **1** the action or process of compiling. **2** a thing, especially a book or record, compiled from different sources.

compile ● verb **1** produce (a book, report, etc.) by assembling material from other sources. **2** gather (material) to produce a book, report, etc.
– ORIGIN Latin *compilare* 'plunder or plagiarize'.

compiler ● noun **1** a person who compiles information. **2** a computer program that translates instructions from a high-level language into a machine-code or lower-level form which can be executed by the computer.

complacent /kəmplaysənt/ ● adjective smug and uncritically satisfied with oneself or one's achievements.
– DERIVATIVES **complacency** (also **complacence**) noun **complacently** adverb.
– ORIGIN from Latin *complacere* 'to please'.

complain ● verb **1** express dissatisfaction or annoyance. **2** (**complain of**) state that one is suffering from (a symptom of illness).
– DERIVATIVES **complainer** noun.
– ORIGIN Old French *complaindre*, from Latin *complangere* 'bewail'.

complainant ● noun Law a plaintiff in certain lawsuits.

complaint ● noun **1** an act of complaining. **2** a reason for dissatisfaction. **3** the expression of dissatisfaction: *a letter of complaint.* **4** an illness or medical condition, especially a relatively minor one.

complaisant /kəmplayz'nt/ ● adjective willing to please others or to accept their behaviour without protest.
– DERIVATIVES **complaisance** noun.
– ORIGIN French, from Latin *complacere* 'to please'.

complected /kəmplektid/ ● adjective N. Amer. having a specified complexion.

complement ● noun /kompliмənt/ **1** a thing that contributes extra features to something else so as to enhance or improve it. **2** the number or quantity that makes something complete. **3** a word or words used with a verb to complete the meaning of the predicate (e.g. *happy* in the sentence *we are happy*). **4** Geometry the amount by which a given angle is less than 90°. ● verb /kompliment/ serve as a complement to.
– USAGE **Complement** and **compliment** are frequently confused. As a verb, **complement** means 'add to in a way that enhances or improves', while **compliment** means 'politely congratulate or praise'.
– ORIGIN Latin *complementum*, from *complere* 'fill up'.

complementarity ● noun (pl. **complementarities**) a situation in which two or more different things enhance each other or form a balanced whole.

complementary ● adjective **1** combining so as to form a complete whole or to enhance each other. **2** relating to complementary medicine.

complementary angle ● noun either of two angles whose sum is 90°.

complementary colour ● noun a colour that combined with a given colour makes white or black.

complementary medicine ● noun medical therapy that falls beyond the scope of scientific medicine but may be used alongside it, e.g. acupuncture and osteopathy.

complete ● adjective **1** having all the necessary or appropriate parts; entire. **2** having run its full course; finished. **3** to the greatest extent or degree; total. **4** skilled at every aspect of an activity: *the complete footballer.* **5** (**complete with**) having as an additional part or feature. ● verb **1** finish making or doing. **2** provide with the items necessary to make (something) complete. **3** write the required information on (a form). **4** Brit. conclude the sale of a property.
– DERIVATIVES **completeness** noun.
– ORIGIN from Latin *complere* 'fill up, finish, fulfil'.

completely ● adverb totally; utterly.

completion ● noun **1** the action of completing or the state of being completed. **2** Brit. the final stage in the sale of a property, at which point it legally changes ownership.

completist ● noun an obsessive fan who wants to own every-

Thesaurus

suited, appropriate; qualified, empowered, authorized.
– OPPOSITES inadequate, unfit.

competition ● noun **1** *Stephanie won the competition* CONTEST, tournament, match, game, heat, fixture, event; trials, stakes. **2** *I'm not interested in competition* RIVALRY, competitiveness, vying; conflict, feuding, fighting; *informal* keeping up with the Joneses. **3** *we must stay ahead of the competition* OPPOSITION, other side, field; enemy; challengers, opponents, rivals, adversaries; *poetic/literary* foe.

competitive ● adjective **1** *a competitive player* AMBITIOUS, zealous, keen, pushy, combative, aggressive; *informal* go-ahead. **2** *a highly competitive industry* RUTHLESS, aggressive, fierce; *informal* dog-eat-dog, cut-throat. **3** *competitive prices* REASONABLE, moderate, keen; low, inexpensive, cheap, budget, bargain, reduced, discount; rock-bottom, bargain-basement.
– OPPOSITES apathetic, exorbitant.

competitor ● noun **1** *the competitors in the race* CONTESTANT, contender, challenger, participant, entrant; runner, player. **2** *our European competitors* RIVAL, challenger, opponent, adversary; competition, opposition.
– OPPOSITES ally.

compilation ● noun COLLECTION, selection, anthology, treasury, compendium, album, corpus, collectanea; pot-pourri.

compile ● verb ASSEMBLE, put together, make up, collate, compose, organize, arrange; gather, collect.

complacency ● noun SMUGNESS, self-satisfaction, self-regard, self-congratulation; gloating, triumph, pride; satisfaction, contentment.

complacent ● adjective SMUG, self-satisfied, self-congratulatory, self-regarding; gloating, triumphant, proud; pleased, satisfied, content, contented; *informal* like the cat that got the cream, I'm-all-right-Jack; *N. Amer. informal* wisenheimer.

complain ● verb PROTEST, grumble, whine, bleat, carp, cavil, grouse, make a fuss; object to, speak out against, oppose, criticize, find fault with; *informal* whinge, kick up a fuss, bellyache, moan, beef, bitch, sound off; *Brit. informal* gripe, chunter, create; *N. Amer. informal* kvetch.

complaint ● noun **1** *they lodged a complaint* PROTEST, objection, grievance, grouse, cavil, quibble, grumble; charge, accusation, criticism; *informal* beef, gripe, whinge; *Law, Brit.* plaint. **2** *little cause for complaint* PROTESTATION, objection, exception, grievance, grumbling; criticism, fault-finding, condemnation, disapproval, dissatisfaction; *informal* whingeing, grousing, bellyaching, nit-picking. **3** *a kidney complaint* DISORDER, disease, infection, affliction, illness, ailment, sickness; condition, problem, upset, trouble; *informal* bug, virus.

complaisant ● adjective WILLING, acquiescent, agreeable, amenable, cooperative, accommodating, obliging; biddable, compliant, docile, obedient.

complement ● noun **1** *the perfect complement to the food* ACCOMPANIMENT, companion, addition, supplement, accessory, trimming. **2** *a full complement of lifeboats* AMOUNT, total, contingent, capacity, allowance, quota.
● verb *this sauce complements the dessert* ACCOMPANY, go with, round off, set off, suit, harmonize with; enhance, complete.

complementary ● adjective HARMONIOUS, compatible, corresponding, matching, twin, complemental; supportive, reciprocal, interdependent.
– OPPOSITES incompatible.

complete ● adjective **1** *the complete interview* ENTIRE, whole, full, total; uncut, unabridged. **2** *their research was complete* FINISHED, ended, concluded, completed, finalized; accomplished, achieved, discharged, settled, done; *informal* wrapped up, sewn up, polished off. **3** *a complete fool* ABSOLUTE, out-and-out, utter, total, real, downright, thoroughgoing, veritable, prize, perfect, unqualified, unmitigated, sheer, arrant; *N. Amer.* full-bore; *Brit. informal* right.
– OPPOSITES partial, unfinished.
● verb **1** *he had to complete his training* FINISH, end, conclude, finalize, wind up; *informal* wrap up, sew up, polish off. **2** *the outfit was completed with a veil* FINISH OFF, round off, top off, crown, cap, complement. **3** *complete the application form* FILL IN/OUT, answer.

completely ● adverb TOTALLY, entirely, wholly, thoroughly, fully, utterly, absolutely, perfectly, unreservedly, unconditionally, quite, altogether, downright; in every way, in every respect, one

thing produced by a particular person or group.

complex ● adjective **1** consisting of many different and connected parts. **2** not easy to understand; complicated. ● noun **1** a group of similar buildings or facilities on the same site. **2** an interlinked system; a network. **3** a related group of repressed feelings or ideas which lead to abnormal mental states or behaviour. **4** informal an obsession or preoccupation.

– DERIVATIVES **complexity** noun **complexly** adverb.

– ORIGIN Latin *complexus*, from *complectere* 'embrace, comprise', later associated with *complexus* 'plaited'.

complexion ● noun **1** the natural tone and texture of the skin of a person's face. **2** the general aspect or character of something.

– DERIVATIVES **-complexioned** adjective.

– ORIGIN Latin, 'combination', from *complectere* 'embrace, comprise'.

complex number ● noun Mathematics a number containing both a real and an imaginary part.

compliance /kəmplīənss/ ● noun **1** the action or fact of complying. **2** excessive acquiescence.

compliant ● adjective **1** tending to be excessively obedient or acquiescent. **2** complying with rules or standards.

– DERIVATIVES **compliantly** adverb.

complicate ● verb **1** make more intricate or confusing. **2** Medicine introduce complications in (an existing condition).

– ORIGIN Latin *complicare* 'fold together'.

complicated ● adjective **1** consisting of many interconnecting elements; intricate. **2** involving many confusing aspects.

complication ● noun **1** a circumstance that complicates something; a difficulty. **2** an involved or confused state. **3** Medicine a secondary disease or condition aggravating an already existing one.

complicit /kəmplissit/ ● adjective involved with others in an unlawful activity.

complicity ● noun involvement with others in an unlawful activity.

– ORIGIN from Old French *complice* 'an associate', from Latin *complicare* 'fold together'.

compliment ● noun /kompliment/ **1** an expression of praise or admiration, either in words or by an action. **2** (**compliments**) formal greetings. ● verb /kompliment/ politely congratulate or praise.

– PHRASES **return the compliment** retaliate or respond in kind. **with the compliments of someone** given without charge.

– USAGE On the confusion of **compliment** and **complement**, see the note at COMPLEMENT.

– ORIGIN Italian *complimento* 'fulfilment of the requirements of courtesy', from Latin *complementum* 'completion, fulfilment'.

complimentary ● adjective **1** expressing a compliment; praising or approving. **2** given free of charge.

compline /komplin/ ● noun (in the Roman Catholic and High Anglican Church) an evening service traditionally said before retiring for the night.

– ORIGIN from Old French *complie* 'completed', from Latin *complere* 'fill up'.

comply /kəmplī/ ● verb (**complies, complied**) (often **comply with**) **1** act in accordance with a wish or command. **2** meet specified standards.

– ORIGIN Latin *complere* 'fulfil, fill up'.

component /kəmpōnənt/ ● noun a part or element of a larger whole. ● adjective being part of a larger whole.

– ORIGIN from Latin *componere* 'put together'.

comport /kəmport/ ● verb (**comport oneself**) formal conduct oneself; behave.

– ORIGIN Latin *comportare*, from *portare* 'carry, bear'.

comportment ● noun formal behaviour or bearing.

compose ● verb **1** create (a work of art, especially music or poetry). **2** constitute or make up (a whole). **3** arrange in an orderly or artistic way. **4** (often **composed**) calm or settle (one's features or thoughts). **5** prepare (a text) for printing by setting up the characters to be printed.

– ORIGIN Old French *composer*, from Latin *componere* 'put together'.

composer ● noun a person who writes music.

Thesaurus

hundred per cent, every inch, to the hilt; *informal* dead, deadly.

completion ● noun REALIZATION, accomplishment, achievement, fulfilment, consummation, finalization, resolution; finish, end, conclusion, close, cessation.

complex ● adjective **1** *a complex situation* COMPLICATED, involved, intricate, convoluted, elaborate, impenetrable, Gordian; difficult, knotty, tricky, thorny; *Brit. informal* fiddly. **2** *a complex structure* COMPOUND, composite, multiplex.

– OPPOSITES simple.

● noun **1** *a complex of roads* NETWORK, system, nexus, web, tissue; combination, aggregation. **2** *(informal) he had a complex about losing his hair* OBSESSION, fixation, preoccupation; neurosis; *informal* hang-up, thing, bee in one's bonnet.

complexion ● noun **1** *a pale complexion* SKIN, skin colour, skin tone; pigmentation. **2** *this puts an entirely new complexion on things* PERSPECTIVE, angle, slant, interpretation; appearance, light, look. **3** *governments of all complexions* TYPE, kind, sort; nature, character, stamp, ilk, kidney.

complexity ● noun COMPLICATION, problem, difficulty; twist, turn, intricacy, complicatedness.

compliance ● noun **1** *compliance with international law* OBEDIENCE TO, observance of, adherence to, conformity to, respect for. **2** *he mistook her silence for compliance* ACQUIESCENCE, agreement, assent, consent, acceptance; complaisance, pliability, docility, meekness, submission.

– OPPOSITES violation, defiance.

compliant ● adjective ACQUIESCENT, amenable, biddable, tractable, complaisant, accommodating, cooperative; obedient, docile, malleable, pliable, submissive, tame, yielding, controllable, unresisting, persuadable, persuasible.

– OPPOSITES recalcitrant.

complicate ● verb MAKE (MORE) DIFFICULT, make complicated, mix up, confuse, muddle; *informal* mess up, screw up, snarl up.

– OPPOSITES simplify.

complicated ● adjective COMPLEX, intricate, involved, convoluted, tangled, impenetrable, knotty, tricky, thorny, labyrinthine, tortuous; confusing, bewildering, perplexing; *Brit. informal* fiddly.

– OPPOSITES straightforward.

complication ● noun **1** *a complication concerning ownership* DIFFICULTY, problem, obstacle, hurdle, stumbling block; drawback, snag, catch, hitch; *informal* fly in the ointment, prob, headache, facer; *Brit. informal* spanner in the works. **2** *the complication of life in modern society* COMPLEXITY, complicatedness, intricacy, convolutedness.

complicity ● noun COLLUSION, involvement, collaboration, connivance; conspiracy; *informal* being in cahoots.

compliment ● noun **1** *an unexpected compliment* FLATTERING REMARK, tribute, accolade, commendation, bouquet, pat on the back; (**compliments**) praise, acclaim, admiration, flattery, blandishments, honeyed words. **2** *my compliments on your cooking* CONGRATULATIONS, commendations, praise. **3** *Margaret sends her compliments* GREETINGS, regards, respects, good wishes, best wishes, salutations, felicitations.

– OPPOSITES insult.

● verb *they complimented his performance* PRAISE, pay tribute to, speak highly/well of, flatter, wax lyrical about, make much of, commend, acclaim, applaud, salute, honour; congratulate, pat on the back.

– OPPOSITES criticize.

complimentary ● adjective **1** *complimentary remarks* FLATTERING, appreciative, congratulatory, admiring, approving, commendatory, favourable, glowing, adulatory; *informal* rave. **2** *complimentary tickets* FREE (OF CHARGE), gratis, for nothing, on the house; courtesy.

– OPPOSITES derogatory.

comply ● verb *Myra complied with his wishes* ABIDE BY, observe, obey, adhere to, conform to, follow, respect; agree to, assent to, go along with, yield to, submit to, defer to; satisfy, fulfil.

– OPPOSITES ignore, disobey.

component ● noun *the components of electronic devices* PART, piece, bit, element, constituent, ingredient; unit, module, section.

● adjective *the molecule's component elements* CONSTITUENT, integral; basic, essential.

comport ● verb

– PHRASES **comport oneself** *(formal)* BEHAVE, conduct oneself, act, acquit oneself; *archaic* deport oneself.

compose ● verb **1** *a poem composed by Shelley* WRITE, formulate, devise, make up, think up, produce, invent, concoct; pen, author, draft; *poetic/literary* rhyme. **2** *compose a still life* ORGANIZE, arrange, set out. **3** *the congress is composed of ten senators* MAKE UP, consti-

composite /kompəzit/ ● adjective **1** made up of various parts or elements. **2** (**Composite**) relating to a classical order of architecture consisting of elements of the Ionic and Corinthian orders. **3** /**kom**pəzīt/ (of a plant) having flower heads consisting of numerous florets, such as a daisy or chrysanthemum. ● noun **1** a thing made up of several parts or elements. **2** /**kom**pəzit/ a motion for debate composed of two or more related resolutions.
– ORIGIN from Latin *componere* 'put together'.
composition ● noun **1** the constitution of something made up from different elements: *the molecular composition of cells.* **2** a work of music, literature, or art. **3** a thing composed of various elements. **4** the action of composing. **5** the artistic arrangement of the parts of a picture.
– DERIVATIVES **compositional** adjective.
compositor /kəmpozzitər/ ● noun a person who arranges type for printing or who keys text into a composing machine.
compos mentis /komposs **men**tiss/ ● adjective having full control of one's mind.
– ORIGIN Latin.
compost ● noun **1** decayed organic material used as a fertilizer for growing plants. **2** a mixture of compost with loam soil used as a growing medium. ● verb make into or treat with compost.
– ORIGIN Latin *composita* 'something put together', from *componere* 'compose'.
composure ● noun the state of being calm and self-controlled.
compote /**kom**pōt, -pot/ ● noun fruit preserved or cooked in syrup.
– ORIGIN French, related to COMPOST.
compound[1] ● noun /**kom**pownd/ **1** a thing composed of two or more separate elements. **2** a substance formed from two or more elements chemically united in fixed proportions. **3** a word made up of two or more existing words. ● adjective /**kom**pownd/ **1** made up or consisting of several parts or elements. **2** (of interest) payable on both capital and the accumulated interest. Compare with SIMPLE. **3** (of a leaf, flower, or eye) consisting of two or more simple parts or individuals in combination. ● verb /kəm**pownd**/ **1** make up (a composite whole). **2** make (something bad) worse. **3** mix (ingredients or constituents). **4** Law forbear from prosecuting (a felony) in exchange for money or other consideration.
– DERIVATIVES **compounder** noun.
– ORIGIN from Latin *componere* 'put together'.
compound[2] /**kom**pownd/ ● noun **1** a large open area enclosed by a fence, e.g. around a factory or within a prison. **2** another term for POUND[3].
– ORIGIN Malay, 'enclosure, hamlet'.
compound fracture ● noun an injury in which a broken bone pierces the skin.
compound time ● noun Music musical rhythm or metre in which each beat in a bar is subdivided into three smaller units, so having the value of a dotted note.
comprehend /kompri**hend**/ ● verb **1** grasp mentally; understand. **2** formal include or encompass.
– ORIGIN Latin *comprehendere*, from *prehendere* 'to grasp'.
comprehensible ● adjective able to be understood; intelligible.
– DERIVATIVES **comprehensibility** noun.
comprehension ● noun **1** the action of understanding. **2** the ability to understand; range of understanding: *mysteries beyond human comprehension.*
comprehensive ● adjective **1** including or dealing with all or nearly all aspects of something. **2** Brit. (of a system of secondary education) in which children of all abilities are educated in one school. **3** (of motor-vehicle insurance) providing cover for most risks. **4** (of a victory or defeat) by a large margin. ● noun Brit. a comprehensive school.
– DERIVATIVES **comprehensively** adverb **comprehensiveness** noun.
compress ● verb /kəm**press**/ **1** flatten by pressure; force into less space. **2** squeeze or press (two things) together. ● noun /**kom**press/ a pad of absorbent material pressed on to part of the body to relieve inflammation or stop bleeding.
– DERIVATIVES **compressibility** noun **compressible** adjective **compressive** adjective.
– ORIGIN Old French *compresser*, from Latin *comprimere* 'press together'.
compressed air ● noun air that is at more than atmospheric pressure.
compression ● noun **1** the action of compressing or being compressed. **2** the reduction in volume (causing an increase in pressure) of the fuel mixture in an internal-combustion engine before ignition.
– DERIVATIVES **compressional** adjective.
compressor ● noun **1** an instrument or device for compressing something. **2** a machine used to supply air or other gas at increased pressure.

Thesaurus

tute, form, comprise.
– PHRASES **compose oneself** CALM DOWN, control oneself, regain one's composure, pull oneself together, collect oneself, steady oneself, keep one's head; *informal* get a grip, keep one's cool; *N. Amer. informal* decompress.
composed ● adjective CALM, collected, cool (as a cucumber), self-controlled, self-possessed; serene, tranquil, relaxed, at ease, unruffled, unperturbed, untroubled; equable, even-tempered, imperturbable; *informal* unflappable, together, laid-back.
– OPPOSITES excited.
composer ● noun melodist, symphonist, songwriter, songster, writer; *informal* tunesmith, songsmith.
composite ● adjective *a composite structure* COMPOUND, complex; combined, blended, mixed.
● noun *a composite of plastic and metal* AMALGAMATION, amalgam, combination, compound, fusion, synthesis, mixture, blend; alloy.
composition ● noun **1** *the composition of the council* MAKE-UP, constitution, configuration, structure, formation, form, framework, fabric, anatomy, organization; *informal* set-up. **2** *a literary composition* WORK (OF ART), creation, opus, oeuvre, piece, arrangement. **3** *the composition of a poem* WRITING, creation, formulation, invention, concoction, compilation. **4** *a school composition* ESSAY, paper, study, piece of writing; *N. Amer.* theme. **5** *the composition of the painting* ARRANGEMENT, disposition, layout; proportions, balance, symmetry. **6** *an adhesive composition* MIXTURE, compound, amalgam, blend, mix.
compost ● noun FERTILIZER, mulch, manure, bonemeal, fishmeal, guano; humus, peat; plant food, top-dressing.
composure ● noun SELF-CONTROL, self-possession, calm, equanimity, equilibrium, serenity, tranquillity; aplomb, poise, presence of mind, sangfroid; imperturbability, placidness, impassivity; *informal* cool.
compound ● noun *a compound of two elements* AMALGAM, amalgamation, combination, composite, blend, mixture, mix, fusion, synthesis; alloy.
● adjective *a compound substance* COMPOSITE, complex; blended, fused, combined.
– OPPOSITES simple.
● verb **1** *a smell compounded of dust and mould* BE COMPOSED OF, be made up of, be formed from. **2** *soap compounded with disinfectant* MIX, combine, blend, amalgamate, fuse, synthesize. **3** *his illness compounds their problems* AGGRAVATE, exacerbate, worsen, add to, augment, intensify, heighten, increase, magnify; complicate.
– OPPOSITES alleviate.
comprehend ● verb **1** *Katie couldn't comprehend his message* UNDERSTAND, grasp, take in, see, apprehend, follow, make sense of, fathom, get to the bottom of; unravel, decipher, interpret; *informal* work out, figure out, make head or tail of, get one's head around, take on board, get the drift of, catch on to, get; *Brit. informal* twig, suss (out). **2** *(formal) a divine order comprehending all men* COMPRISE, include, encompass, embrace, involve, contain.
– OPPOSITES exclude.
comprehensible ● adjective INTELLIGIBLE, understandable, accessible; lucid, coherent, clear, plain, explicit, unambiguous, straightforward, fathomable.
– OPPOSITES opaque.
comprehension ● noun UNDERSTANDING, grasp, conception, apprehension, cognition, ken, knowledge, awareness, perception; interpretation.
– OPPOSITES ignorance.
comprehensive ● adjective INCLUSIVE, all-inclusive, complete; thorough, full, extensive, all-embracing, exhaustive, detailed, in-depth, encyclopedic, universal, catholic; far-reaching, radical, sweeping, across the board, wholesale; broad, wide-ranging; *informal* wall-to-wall.
– OPPOSITES limited.
compress ● verb **1** *the skirt can be compressed into a bag* SQUEEZE, press, squash, crush, cram, jam, stuff; tamp, pack, compact; constrict; *informal* scrunch. **2** *Polly compressed her lips* PURSE, press together, pucker. **3** *the text was compressed* ABRIDGE, condense,

C

comprise ● verb **1** be made up of; consist of. **2** (also **be comprised of**) make up; constitute.
– USAGE Traditionally, **comprise** means 'consist of' and should not be used to mean 'constitute or make up (a whole)'. However, a passive use of **comprise** is becoming part of standard English: this use (as *in the country is comprised of twenty states*) is more or less synonymous with the traditional active sense (as in *the country comprises twenty states*).
– ORIGIN from French, 'comprised', from *comprendre* 'comprehend'.
compromise ● noun **1** an agreement reached by each side making concessions. **2** an intermediate state between conflicting opinions, reached by mutual concession. ● verb **1** settle a dispute by mutual concession. **2** expediently accept standards that are lower than is desirable. **3** bring into disrepute or danger by indiscreet or reckless behaviour.
– DERIVATIVES **compromiser** noun.
– ORIGIN Old French *compromis*, from Latin *compromittere*, from *promittere* 'promise'.
compromising ● adjective revealing an embarrassing or incriminating secret.
comptroller /kəntrōlər/ ● noun a controller (used in the title of some financial officers).
– ORIGIN variant of CONTROLLER.
compulsion ● noun **1** the action or state of compelling or being compelled. **2** an irresistible urge to behave in a certain way.
compulsive ● adjective **1** resulting from or acting on an irresistible urge. **2** irresistibly interesting or exciting.
– DERIVATIVES **compulsively** adverb **compulsiveness** noun.
compulsory ● adjective required by law or a rule; obligatory.
– DERIVATIVES **compulsorily** adverb.
compulsory purchase ● noun Brit. the officially enforced purchase of privately owned land or property for public use.
compunction ● noun a feeling of guilt or moral scruple that prevents or follows wrongdoing: *he felt no compunction in letting her worry.*
– DERIVATIVES **compunctious** adjective.
– ORIGIN Latin, from *compungere* 'prick sharply'.
computation ● noun **1** mathematical calculation. **2** the use of computers, especially as a subject of research or study.
– DERIVATIVES **computational** adjective.
compute ● verb reckon or calculate (a figure or amount).
– DERIVATIVES **computable** adjective.
– ORIGIN Latin *computare*, from *putare* 'settle (an account)'.
computer ● noun an electronic device capable of storing and processing information in accordance with a predetermined set of instructions.
computerate ● adjective informal computer-literate.
computerize (also **computerise**) ● verb convert to a system or form which is controlled, stored, or processed by computer.
– DERIVATIVES **computerization** noun.
computer-literate ● adjective having sufficient knowledge and skill to be able to use computers.
computing ● noun the use or operation of computers.
comrade ● noun **1** (among men) a companion who shares one's activities or is a fellow member of an organization. **2** (also **comrade-in-arms**) a fellow soldier. **3** a fellow socialist or communist.
– DERIVATIVES **comradely** adjective **comradeship** noun.
– ORIGIN Spanish *camarada* 'room-mate'.
con[1] informal ● verb (**conned**, **conning**) deceive (someone) into doing or believing something by lying. ● noun a deception of this kind.
– ORIGIN abbreviation of CONFIDENCE, as in *confidence trick*.
con[2] ● noun (usu. in phrase **pros and cons**) a disadvantage of or argument against something.
– ORIGIN from Latin *contra* 'against'.
con[3] ● noun informal a convict.
con[4] (US also **conn**) ● verb (**conned**, **conning**) direct the steering of (a ship).
– ORIGIN apparently from obsolete *cond* 'conduct, guide', from Old French *conduire*.
con- ● prefix variant spelling of COM- assimilated before *c, d, f, g, j, n, q, s, t, v*, and sometimes before vowels (as in *concord, confide*, etc.).
concatenate /kənkattinayt/ ● verb formal or technical link together in a chain or series.
– DERIVATIVES **concatenation** noun.
– ORIGIN Latin *concatenare* 'link together'.
concave /konkayv/ ● adjective having an outline or surface that curves inwards like the interior of a sphere. Compare with CONVEX.
– DERIVATIVES **concavity** noun.
– ORIGIN Latin *concavus*, from *cavus* 'hollow'.
conceal ● verb prevent from being seen or known.
– DERIVATIVES **concealer** noun **concealment** noun.
– ORIGIN Latin *concelare*, from *celare* 'hide'.
concede ● verb **1** finally admit or agree that something is true. **2** surrender (a possession, advantage, or right). **3** admit defeat in (a match or contest). **4** fail to prevent an opponent scoring (a goal or point).
– ORIGIN Latin *concedere*, from *cedere* 'yield'.
conceit ● noun **1** excessive pride in oneself. **2** an elaborate metaphor or artistic effect. **3** a fanciful notion.

Thesaurus

shorten, cut, abbreviate, truncate; summarize, precis.
– OPPOSITES expand.
comprise ● verb **1** *the country comprises twenty states* CONSIST OF, be made up of, be composed of, contain, encompass, incorporate; include; *formal* comprehend. **2** *this breed comprises half the herd* MAKE UP, constitute, form, compose; account for.
compromise ● noun **1** *they reached a compromise* AGREEMENT, understanding, settlement, terms, deal, trade-off, bargain; middle ground, happy medium, balance. **2** *a happy marriage needs compromise* GIVE AND TAKE, concession, cooperation.
– OPPOSITES intransigence.
● verb **1** *we compromised* MEET EACH OTHER HALFWAY, come to an understanding, make a deal, make concessions, find a happy medium, strike a balance; give and take. **2** *his actions could compromise his reputation* UNDERMINE, weaken, damage, harm; jeopardize, prejudice; discredit, dishonour, shame, embarrass.
compulsion ● noun **1** *he is under no compulsion to go* OBLIGATION, constraint, coercion, duress, pressure, intimidation. **2** *a compulsion to tell the truth* URGE, impulse, need, desire, drive; obsession, fixation, addiction; temptation.
compulsive ● adjective **1** *a compulsive desire* IRRESISTIBLE, uncontrollable, compelling, overwhelming, urgent; obsessive. **2** *compulsive eating* OBSESSIVE, obsessional, addictive, uncontrollable. **3** *a compulsive liar* INVETERATE, chronic, incorrigible, incurable, hardened, hopeless, persistent; obsessive, addicted, habitual; *informal* pathological, hooked. **4** *it's compulsive viewing* FASCINATING, compelling, gripping, riveting, engrossing, enthralling, captivating.
compulsory ● adjective OBLIGATORY, mandatory, required, requisite, necessary, essential; imperative, unavoidable, enforced, demanded, prescribed.
– OPPOSITES optional.
compunction ● noun SCRUPLES, misgivings, qualms, worries, unease, uneasiness, doubts, reluctance, reservations; guilt, regret, contrition, self-reproach.
compute ● verb CALCULATE, work out, reckon, determine, evaluate, quantify; add up, count up, tally, total, totalize; *Brit.* tot up.
comrade ● noun COMPANION, friend; colleague, associate, partner, co-worker, workmate; *informal* pal, crony; *Brit. informal* mate, chum, oppo; *N. Amer. informal* buddy.
con *(informal)* ● verb & noun. See SWINDLE.
concatenation ● noun SERIES, sequence, succession, chain.
concave ● adjective INCURVED, curved inwards, hollow, depressed, sunken; indented, recessed.
– OPPOSITES convex.
conceal ● verb **1** *clouds concealed the sun* HIDE, screen, cover, obscure, block out, blot out, mask, shroud, secrete. **2** *he concealed his true feelings* HIDE, cover up, disguise, mask, veil; keep secret, keep dark, draw a veil over; suppress, repress, bottle up; *informal* keep a/the lid on, keep under one's hat.
– OPPOSITES reveal, confess.
concealed ● adjective HIDDEN, not visible, out of sight, invisible, covered, disguised, camouflaged, obscured; private, secret.
concealment ● noun **1** *the concealment of his weapon* HIDING, secretion. **2** *the concealment of the bushes* COVER, shelter, protection, screen; privacy, seclusion; secrecy. **3** *the deliberate concealment of facts* SUPPRESSION, hiding, cover-up, hushing up; whitewash.
concede ● verb **1** *I had to concede that I'd overreacted* ADMIT, acknowledge, accept, allow, grant, recognize, own, confess; agree. **2** *he conceded the Auvergne to the king* SURRENDER, yield, give up, relinquish, cede, hand over.

– ORIGIN from CONCEIVE.
conceited ● adjective excessively proud of oneself.
conceivable ● adjective capable of being imagined or understood.
– DERIVATIVES **conceivably** adverb.
conceive ● verb **1** become pregnant with (a child). **2** devise in the mind; imagine.
– ORIGIN Latin *concipere*, from *capere* 'take'.
concentrate ● verb **1** (often **concentrate on**) focus all one's attention or mental effort on an object or activity. **2** gather together in numbers or a mass at one point. **3** focus on: *concentrate your energy on breathing.* **4** increase the strength of (a solution). ● noun a concentrated substance or solution.
– DERIVATIVES **concentrator** noun.
– ORIGIN from Latin *con-* 'together' + *centrum* 'centre' or from French *concentrer* 'to concentrate'.
concentration ● noun **1** the action or power of concentrating. **2** a close gathering of people or things. **3** the relative amount of a particular substance contained within a solution or mixture.
concentration camp ● noun a camp for detaining political prisoners, especially in Nazi Germany.
concentric ● adjective (of circles or arcs) sharing the same centre.
– DERIVATIVES **concentrically** adverb **concentricity** noun.
– ORIGIN Latin *concentricus*, from *con-* 'together' + *centrum* 'centre'.
concept ● noun **1** an abstract idea. **2** an idea to help sell or publicize a commodity.
– ORIGIN Latin *conceptum* 'something conceived'.
conception ● noun **1** the action of conceiving a child or of one being conceived. **2** the devising of a plan or idea. **3** a concept. **4** ability to imagine or understand.
conceptual ● adjective relating to mental concepts.
– DERIVATIVES **conceptually** adverb.
conceptualize (also **conceptualise**) ● verb form a concept of.
– DERIVATIVES **conceptualization** noun.
concern ● verb **1** relate to; be about. **2** be relevant to; affect or involve. **3** make anxious or worried. ● noun **1** worry; anxiety. **2** a matter of interest or importance. **3** a business.
– PHRASES **have no concern with** have nothing to do with. **to whom it may concern** used to address a reader whose identity is unknown.
– ORIGIN Latin *concernere*, from *cernere* 'sift, discern'.
concerned ● adjective worried or anxious.
concerning ● preposition about.
concert ● noun /konsert/ **1** a musical performance given in public, typically of several compositions. **2** formal agreement; harmony. ● verb /kənsert/ formal arrange by mutual agreement or coordination.
– PHRASES **in concert 1** acting jointly. **2** giving a live public performance.
– ORIGIN Italian *concerto*, from *concertare* 'harmonize'.
concerted ● adjective **1** jointly arranged or carried out: *a concerted campaign.* **2** using exertion: *a concerted effort.*
concertina /konserteenə/ ● noun a small musical instrument played by stretching and squeezing a central bellows between the hands to blow air over reeds, each note being sounded by a button. ● verb (**concertinas**, **concertinaed** or **concertina'd**, **concertinaing**) compress in folds like those of a concertina.
concerto /kənchertō/ ● noun (pl. **concertos** or **concerti**) a musical composition for an orchestra and one or more solo instruments.

C

Thesaurus

– PHRASES **concede defeat** CAPITULATE, give in, surrender, yield, give up, submit, raise the white flag; back down, climb down, throw in the towel.
conceit ● noun **1** *his extraordinary conceit* VANITY, narcissism, conceitedness, self-admiration, self-regard, egotism; pride, arrogance, hubris, self-importance; self-satisfaction, smugness; *informal* bigheadedness, swollen-headedness; *poetic/literary* vainglory. **2** *the conceits of Shakespeare's verse* IMAGE, imagery, metaphor, simile, trope. **3** *the conceit of time travel* IDEA, notion, fancy.
– OPPOSITES humility.
conceited ● adjective VAIN, narcissistic, self-centred, egotistic, egotistical, egocentric; proud, arrogant, boastful, full of oneself, self-important, immodest, swaggering; self-satisfied, smug; supercilious, haughty, snobbish; *informal* big-headed, too big for one's boots, stuck-up, high and mighty, uppity, snotty; *Brit. informal* toffee-nosed; *N. Amer. informal* chesty; *poetic/literary* vainglorious.
conceivable ● adjective IMAGINABLE, possible; plausible, tenable, credible, believable, thinkable, feasible; understandable, comprehensible.
conceive ● verb **1** *she was unable to conceive* BECOME PREGNANT, become impregnated. **2** *the project was conceived in 1977* THINK UP, think of, dream up, devise, formulate, design, originate, create, develop; hatch; *informal* cook up. **3** *I could hardly conceive what it must be like* IMAGINE, envisage, visualize, picture, think, envision; grasp, appreciate, apprehend.
concentrate ● verb **1** *the government concentrated its efforts* FOCUS, direct, centre, centralize. **2** *she concentrated on the film* FOCUS ON, pay attention to, keep one's mind on, devote oneself to; be absorbed in, be engrossed in, be immersed in; *informal* get stuck into. **3** *troops concentrated on the horizon* COLLECT, gather, congregate, converge, mass, cluster, rally. **4** *the liquid is filtered and concentrated* CONDENSE, boil down, reduce, thicken.
– OPPOSITES disperse, dilute.
● noun *a fruit concentrate* EXTRACT, decoction, distillation.
concentrated ● adjective **1** *a concentrated effort* STRENUOUS, concerted, intensive, intense; *informal* all-out. **2** *a concentrated solution* CONDENSED, reduced, evaporated, thickened; strong, undiluted.
– OPPOSITES half-hearted, diluted.
concentration ● noun **1** *a task requiring concentration* CLOSE ATTENTION, attentiveness, application, single-mindedness, absorption. **2** *the concentration of effort* FOCUSING, centralization. **3** *concentrations of barnacle geese* GATHERING, cluster, mass, flock, congregation, assemblage.
– OPPOSITES inattention.
concept ● noun IDEA, notion, conception, abstraction; theory, hypothesis; belief, conviction, opinion; image, impression, picture.
conception ● noun **1** *the fertility treatment resulted in conception* INCEPTION OF PREGNANCY, conceiving, fertilization, impregnation, insemination. **2** *the product's conception* INCEPTION, genesis, origination, creation, invention; beginning, origin. **3** *his original conception* PLAN, scheme, project, proposal; intention, aim, idea. **4** *my conception of democracy* IDEA, concept, notion, understanding, abstraction; theory, hypothesis; perception, image, impression. **5** *they had no conception of our problems* UNDERSTANDING, comprehension, appreciation, knowledge, grasp; idea, inkling; *informal* clue.
concern ● verb **1** *the report concerns the war* BE ABOUT, deal with, cover; discuss, go into, examine, study, review, analyse; relate to, pertain to. **2** *that doesn't concern you* AFFECT, involve, be relevant to, apply to, have a bearing on, impact on; be important to, interest. **3** *I won't concern myself with your affairs* INVOLVE ONESELF IN, take an interest in, busy oneself with, devote one's time to, bother oneself with. **4** *one thing still concerns me* WORRY, disturb, trouble, bother, perturb, unsettle, make anxious.
● noun **1** *a voice full of concern* ANXIETY, worry, disquiet, apprehensiveness, unease, consternation. **2** *his concern for others* SOLICITUDE, solicitousness, consideration, care, sympathy, regard. **3** *housing is the concern of the council* RESPONSIBILITY, business, affair, charge, duty, job; province, preserve; problem, worry; *informal* pigeon, bag, bailiwick *Brit. informal* lookout. **4** *issues that are of concern to women* INTEREST, importance, relevance, significance. **5** *Aboriginal concerns* AFFAIR, issue, matter, question, consideration. **6** *a publishing concern* COMPANY, business, firm, organization, operation, corporation, establishment, house, office, agency; *informal* outfit, set-up.
– OPPOSITES indifference.
concerned ● adjective **1** *her mother looked concerned* WORRIED, anxious, perturbed, troubled, distressed, upset, uneasy, apprehensive, agitated. **2** *he is concerned about your welfare* SOLICITOUS, caring; attentive to, considerate of. **3** *all concerned parties* INTERESTED, involved, affected; connected, related, implicated.
concerning ● preposition ABOUT, regarding, relating to, with reference to, referring to, with regard to, as regards, with respect to, respecting, dealing with, on the subject of, in connection with, re, apropos of.
concert ● noun MUSICAL PERFORMANCE, show, production, presentation; recital; *informal* gig.
– PHRASES **in concert** TOGETHER, jointly, in combination, in collaboration, in cooperation, in league, side by side; in unison.
concerted ● adjective **1** *make a concerted effort* STRENUOUS, vigorous, intensive, intense, concentrated; *informal* all-out. **2** *concerted action was taken* JOINT, united, collaborative, collective, combined,

C

– ORIGIN Italian.
concert performance ● noun Brit. a performance of a piece of music written for an opera or ballet without the accompanying dramatic action.
concert pitch ● noun **1** a standard for the tuning of musical instruments, in which the note A above middle C has a frequency of 440 hertz. **2** a state of readiness and keenness.
concession ● noun **1** a thing conceded. **2** a reduction in price for a certain category of person. **3** the right to use land or other property for a specified purpose, granted by a government or other controlling body. **4** a commercial operation set up within the premises of a larger concern.
– DERIVATIVES **concessionary** adjective **concessive** adjective.
– ORIGIN Latin, from *concedere* 'concede'.
concessionaire /kənseshənair/ (also **concessionnaire**) ● noun the holder of a concession or grant, especially for the use of land or trading rights.
conch /kongk, konch/ ● noun (pl. **conchs** /kongks/ or **conches** /**kon**chiz/) a tropical marine mollusc with a spiral shell.
– ORIGIN Greek *konkhē* 'mussel, cockle, or shell-like cavity'.
conchology /kong**koll**əji/ ● noun the scientific study or collection of mollusc shells.
– DERIVATIVES **conchologist** noun.
concierge /**kon**siairzh/ ● noun **1** (especially in France) a resident caretaker of a block of flats or small hotel. **2** a hotel employee who assists guests by booking tours, making theatre and restaurant reservations, etc.
– ORIGIN French.
conciliate /kən**sil**liayt/ ● verb **1** make calm and content; placate. **2** mediate in a dispute.
– DERIVATIVES **conciliation** noun **conciliator** noun **conciliatory** adjective.
– ORIGIN Latin *conciliare* 'combine, gain', from *concilium* 'assembly'.
concise ● adjective giving a lot of information clearly and in few words.
– DERIVATIVES **concisely** adverb **conciseness** noun **concision** noun.
– ORIGIN Latin *concisus* 'cut up, cut down'.
conclave /**kon**klayv/ ● noun **1** a private meeting. **2** (in the Roman Catholic Church) the assembly of cardinals for the election of a pope.
– ORIGIN Latin, 'lockable room', from *clavis* 'key'.
conclude ● verb **1** bring or come to an end. **2** arrive at a judgement or opinion by reasoning. **3** formally settle or arrange (a treaty or agreement).
– ORIGIN Latin *concludere*, from *claudere* 'to shut'.
conclusion ● noun **1** an end or finish. **2** the summing-up of an argument or text. **3** a judgement or decision reached by reasoning. **4** the settling of a treaty or agreement.
conclusive ● adjective decisive or convincing.
– DERIVATIVES **conclusively** adverb **conclusiveness** noun.
concoct /kən**kokt**/ ● verb **1** make (a dish or meal) by combining ingredients. **2** invent or devise (a story or plan).
– DERIVATIVES **concocter** noun **concoction** noun.
– ORIGIN Latin *concoquere* 'cook together'.
concomitant /kən**kom**mitənt/ formal ● adjective naturally accompanying or associated. ● noun a concomitant phenomenon.
– DERIVATIVES **concomitance** noun **concomitantly** adverb.
– ORIGIN from Latin *concomitari* 'accompany', from *comes* 'companion'.
concord ● noun formal **1** agreement; harmony. **2** a treaty.
– ORIGIN Latin *concordia*, from *concors* 'of one mind'.
concordance /kən**kord**'ns/ ● noun **1** an alphabetical list of the important words in a text, usually with citations of the passages concerned. **2** formal agreement.
– ORIGIN from Latin *concordare* 'agree on'.
concordant ● adjective in agreement; consistent.
concordat /kən**kor**dat/ ● noun an agreement or treaty, especially one between the Vatican and a secular state.
concourse ● noun **1** a large open area inside or in front of a public building. **2** formal a crowd of people.
– ORIGIN Latin *concursus*, from *concurrere* 'assemble in crowds'.
concrete ● adjective **1** existing in a material or physical form; not abstract. **2** specific; definite: *concrete proof*. ● noun a building material made from gravel, sand, cement, and water, hardening when dry into a stone-like mass. ● verb cover or fix solidly with concrete.
– DERIVATIVES **concretely** adverb **concreteness** noun.
– ORIGIN Latin *concretus* 'grown together'.
concrete jungle ● noun an urban area with a high density of

Thesaurus

cooperative.
– OPPOSITES half-hearted, individual.
concession ● noun **1** *the government made several concessions* COMPROMISE, allowance, exception, sop. **2** *a concession of failure* ADMISSION, acknowledgement, acceptance, recognition, confession. **3** *the concession of territory* SURRENDER, relinquishment, sacrifice, handover. **4** *tax concessions* REDUCTION, cut, discount, deduction, decrease; rebate; *informal* break. **5** *a logging concession* RIGHT, privilege; licence, permit, franchise, warrant, authorization.
– OPPOSITES denial, acquisition.
conciliate ● verb **1** *he tried to conciliate the peasantry* APPEASE, placate, pacify, mollify, assuage, soothe, humour, reconcile, win over, make peace with. **2** *he conciliated in the dispute* MEDIATE, act as peacemaker, arbitrate; pour oil on troubled waters.
– OPPOSITES provoke.
conciliator ● noun PEACEMAKER, mediator, go-between, middleman, intermediary, intercessor; dove.
– OPPOSITES troublemaker.
conciliatory ● adjective PROPITIATORY, placatory, appeasing, pacifying, pacific, mollifying, peacemaking.
concise ● adjective SUCCINCT, pithy, incisive, brief, short and to the point, short and sweet; abridged, condensed, compressed, abbreviated, compact, potted; *informal* snappy.
– OPPOSITES lengthy, wordy.
conclave ● noun (PRIVATE) MEETING, gathering, assembly, conference, council, summit; *informal* parley, powwow, get-together.
conclude ● verb **1** *the meeting concluded at ten* FINISH, end, draw to a close, be over, stop, cease. **2** *he concluded the press conference* BRING TO AN END, close, wind up, terminate, dissolve; round off; *informal* wrap up. **3** *an attempt to conclude a ceasefire* NEGOTIATE, broker, agree, come to terms on, settle, clinch, finalize, tie up; bring about, arrange, effect, engineer; *informal* sew up. **4** *I concluded that he was rather unpleasant* DEDUCE, infer, gather, judge, decide, conjecture, surmise; *N. Amer.* figure; *informal* reckon.
– OPPOSITES commence.
conclusion ● noun **1** *the conclusion of his speech* END, ending, finish, close, termination, wind-up, cessation; culmination, denouement, coda. **2** *the conclusion of a trade agreement* NEGOTIATION, brokering, settlement, completion, arrangement, resolution. **3** *his conclusions have been verified* DEDUCTION, inference, interpretation, reasoning; opinion, judgement, verdict; assumption, presumption, supposition.
– OPPOSITES beginning.
– PHRASES **in conclusion** FINALLY, in closing, to conclude, last but not least; to sum up, in short.
conclusive ● adjective **1** *conclusive proof* INCONTROVERTIBLE, undeniable, indisputable, irrefutable, unquestionable, unassailable, convincing, certain, decisive, definitive, definite, positive, categorical, unequivocal; airtight, watertight. **2** *a conclusive win* EMPHATIC, resounding, convincing.
– OPPOSITES unconvincing.
concoct ● verb **1** *she began to concoct her dinner* PREPARE, make, assemble; *informal* fix, rustle up; *Brit. informal* knock up. **2** *this story she has concocted* MAKE UP, dream up, fabricate, invent, trump up; formulate, hatch, brew; *informal* cook up.
concoction ● noun **1** *a concoction containing gin and vodka* MIXTURE, brew, preparation, potion. **2** *a strange concoction of styles* BLEND, mixture, mix, combination, hybrid. **3** *her story is an improbable concoction* FABRICATION, invention, falsification; *informal* fairy story, fairy tale.
concomitant ● adjective *(formal)* ATTENDANT, accompanying, associated, related, connected; resultant, consequent.
– OPPOSITES unrelated.
concord ● noun *(formal)* **1** *council meetings rarely ended in concord* AGREEMENT, harmony, accord, consensus, concurrence, unity. **2** *a concord was to be drawn up* TREATY, agreement, accord, pact, compact, settlement.
– OPPOSITES discord.
concourse ● noun **1** *the station concourse* ENTRANCE, foyer, lobby, hall. **2** *(formal) a vast concourse of onlookers* CROWD, group, gathering, assembly, body, company, throng, flock, mass.
concrete ● adjective **1** *concrete objects* SOLID, material, real, physical, tangible, palpable, substantial, visible, existing. **2** *concrete proof* DEFINITE, firm, positive, conclusive, definitive; real, genuine,

large, unattractive, modern buildings.

concretion ● noun a hard solid mass formed by accumulation of matter.

concubine /kongkyoobīn/ ● noun **1** chiefly historical (in polygamous societies) a woman who lives with a man but has lower status than his wife or wives. **2** archaic a mistress.
– ORIGIN Latin *concubina*, from *con-* 'with' + *cubare* 'to lie'.

concupiscence /kənkyoōpis'ns/ ● noun formal lust.
– DERIVATIVES **concupiscent** adjective.
– ORIGIN Latin *concupiscentia*, from *concupiscere* 'begin to desire'.

concur /kənkur/ ● verb (**concurred**, **concurring**) **1** (often **concur with**) agree. **2** happen at the same time.
– ORIGIN Latin *concurrere* 'run together, assemble in crowds'.

concurrent ● adjective **1** existing or happening at the same time. **2** Mathematics (of three or more lines) meeting at or tending towards one point.
– DERIVATIVES **concurrence** noun **concurrently** adverb.

concussion ● noun **1** temporary unconsciousness or confusion caused by a blow on the head. **2** a violent shock as from a heavy blow.
– DERIVATIVES **concuss** verb **concussive** adjective.
– ORIGIN Latin, from *concutere* 'dash together, shake'.

condemn ● verb **1** express complete disapproval of. **2** (usu. **condemn to**) sentence to a punishment, especially death. **3** force (someone) to endure something unpleasant. **4** officially declare to be unfit for use. **5** prove the guilt of.
– DERIVATIVES **condemnation** noun **condemnatory** adjective.
– ORIGIN Latin *condemnare*, from *damnare* 'inflict loss on'.

condensation ● noun **1** water from humid air collecting as droplets on a cold surface. **2** the conversion of a vapour or gas to a liquid. **3** a concise version of something.

condense ● verb **1** make denser or more concentrated. **2** change from a gas or vapour to a liquid. **3** express (a piece of writing or speech) in fewer words.
– ORIGIN Latin *condensare*, from *condensus* 'very thick'.

condensed milk ● noun milk that has been thickened by evaporation and sweetened.

condenser ● noun **1** an apparatus for condensing vapour. **2** a lens or system of lenses for collecting and directing light. **3** another term for CAPACITOR.

condescend ● verb **1** show that one feels superior. **2** do something despite regarding it as below one's dignity: *he condescended to see me at my hotel.*
– DERIVATIVES **condescension** noun.
– ORIGIN Latin *condescendere*, from *descendere* 'descend'.

condescending ● adjective feeling or showing a patronizing attitude.
– DERIVATIVES **condescendingly** adverb.

condign /kəndīn/ ● adjective formal (of punishment) fitting and deserved.
– ORIGIN Latin *condignus*, from *dignus* 'worthy'.

condiment ● noun a seasoning or relish for food, such as salt or mustard.
– ORIGIN Latin *condimentum*, from *condire* 'to pickle'.

condition ● noun **1** the state of something or someone, with regard to appearance, fitness, or working order. **2** (**conditions**) circumstances affecting the functioning or existence of something. **3** a state of affairs that must exist before something else is possible: *for a country to borrow money, three conditions must be met.* **4** an illness or medical problem. ● verb **1** have a significant influence on; determine. **2** bring into a good or desirable state or condition. **3** train or accustom to behave in a certain way: *the child is conditioned to dislike food.* **4** set prior requirements on (something) before it can occur.
– PHRASES **in** (or **out of**) **condition** in a fit (or unfit) physical state. **on condition that** with the stipulation that.
– ORIGIN Latin *condicion* 'agreement', from *condicere* 'agree upon'.

conditional ● adjective **1** subject to one or more conditions being met. **2** (of a clause, phrase, conjunction, or verb form) expressing a condition. ● noun the conditional mood of a verb, for example *should* in *if I should die*.
– DERIVATIVES **conditionality** noun **conditionally** adverb.

conditioner ● noun a thing used to improve the condition of something, especially a liquid applied to the hair.

condo ● noun (pl. **condos**) N. Amer. informal short for CONDOMINIUM (in sense 2).

condole /kəndōl/ ● verb (**condole with**) express sympathy for.
– ORIGIN Latin *condolere* 'grieve or suffer with'.

condolence ● noun an expression of sympathy, especially on the occasion of a death.

C

Thesaurus

bona fide.
– OPPOSITES abstract, imaginary.

concubine ● noun *(archaic)* MISTRESS, kept woman; lover; *informal* fancy woman, bit on the side; *archaic* paramour.

concupiscence ● noun *(formal).* See LUST noun sense 1.

concur ● verb **1** *we concur with this view* AGREE, be in agreement, go along, fall in, be in sympathy; see eye to eye, be of the same mind, be of the same opinion. **2** *the two events concurred* COINCIDE, be simultaneous, be concurrent, coexist.
– OPPOSITES disagree.

concurrent ● adjective **1** *nine concurrent life sentences* SIMULTANEOUS, coincident, contemporaneous, parallel. **2** *concurrent lines* CONVERGENT, converging, meeting, intersecting.

concussion ● noun **1** *he suffered concussion* temporary unconsciousness; brain injury. **2** *the concussion of the blast* FORCE, impact, shock, jolt.

condemn ● verb **1** *he condemned the suspended players* CENSURE, criticize, denounce, revile, blame, chastise, berate, reprimand, rebuke, reprove, take to task, find fault with; *informal* slam, blast, lay into; *Brit. informal* slate, slag off, have a go at; *formal* castigate. **2** *he was condemned to death* SENTENCE; convict, find guilty. **3** *the house has been condemned* DECLARE UNFIT, declare unsafe. **4** *her mistake had condemned her* INCRIMINATE, implicate; *archaic* inculpate. **5** *his illness condemned him to a lonely life* DOOM, destine, damn; consign, assign.
– OPPOSITES praise.

condemnation ● noun CENSURE, criticism, flak, strictures, denunciation, vilification; reproof, disapproval; *informal* a bad press; *formal* castigation.

condemnatory ● adjective CENSORIOUS, critical, damning; reproving, reproachful, deprecatory, disapproving, unfavourable; *formal* castigatory.

condensation ● noun **1** *windows misty with condensation* MOISTURE, water droplets, steam. **2** *the condensation of the vapour* PRECIPITATION, liquefaction, deliquescence. **3** *a condensation of recent literature* ABRIDGEMENT, summary, synopsis, precis, digest. **4** *the condensation of the report* SHORTENING, abridgement, abbreviation, summarization.

condense ● verb **1** *the water vapour condenses* PRECIPITATE, liquefy, become liquid, deliquesce. **2** *he condensed the play* ABRIDGE, shorten, cut, abbreviate, compact; summarize, synopsize, precis; truncate, curtail.
– OPPOSITES vaporize, expand.

condensed ● adjective **1** *a condensed text* ABRIDGED, shortened, cut, compressed, abbreviated, reduced, truncated, concise; outline, thumbnail; *informal* potted. **2** *condensed soup* CONCENTRATED, evaporated, reduced; undiluted.
– OPPOSITES diluted.

condescend ● verb **1** *don't condescend to your reader* PATRONIZE, talk down to, look down one's nose at, look down on, put down. **2** *he condescended to see us* DEIGN, stoop, descend, lower oneself, demean oneself; vouchsafe, see fit, consent.

condescending ● adjective PATRONIZING, supercilious, superior, snobbish, snobby, disdainful, lofty, haughty; *informal* snooty, stuck-up; *Brit. informal* toffee-nosed.

condition ● noun **1** *check the condition of your wiring* STATE, shape, order; *Brit. informal* nick. **2** *they lived in appalling conditions* CIRCUMSTANCES, surroundings, environment, situation, set-up, setting, habitat; *informal* circs. **3** *she was in tip-top condition* FITNESS, health, form, shape, trim, fettle. **4** *a liver condition* DISORDER, problem, complaint, illness, disease, ailment, sickness, affliction, infection, upset; *informal* bug, virus; *Brit. informal* lurgy. **5** *a condition of employment* STIPULATION, constraint, prerequisite, precondition, requirement, rule, term, specification, provision, proviso.
● verb **1** *their choices are conditioned by the economy* CONSTRAIN, control, govern, determine, decide; affect, touch, impact on; form, shape, guide, sway, bias. **2** *our minds are conditioned by habit* TRAIN, teach, educate, guide; accustom, adapt, habituate, mould, inure. **3** *condition the boards with water* TREAT, prepare, prime, temper, process, acclimatize, acclimate, season. **4** *a product to condition your skin* IMPROVE, nourish, tone (up), moisturize.

conditional ● adjective **1** *their approval is conditional on success* SUBJECT TO, dependent on, contingent on, based on, determined by, controlled by, tied to. **2** *a conditional offer* CONTINGENT, dependent,

C

condom ● noun a thin rubber sheath worn on the penis during sexual intercourse as a contraceptive or to protect against infection.
– ORIGIN of unknown origin.
condominium /kondəminniəm/ ● noun (pl. **condominiums**) **1** the joint control of a state's affairs by other states. **2** N. Amer. a building or complex containing a number of individually owned flats or houses. **3** N. Amer. a flat or house in a condominium.
– ORIGIN Latin, from *con-* 'together with' + *dominium* 'sovereignty, dominion'
condone /kəndōn/ ● verb accept or forgive (an offence or wrongdoing).
– DERIVATIVES **condonation** /kondənaysh'n/ noun.
– ORIGIN Latin *condonare* 'refrain from punishing'.
condor ● noun a very large South American vulture with a bare head and mainly black plumage.
– ORIGIN Spanish, from Quechua.
conduce ● verb (**conduce to**) formal help to bring about.
– ORIGIN Latin *conducere* 'bring together'.
conducive ● adjective (**conducive to**) contributing or helping towards.
conduct ● noun /kondukt/ **1** the manner in which a person behaves. **2** management or direction: *the conduct of foreign affairs.* ● verb /kəndukt/ **1** organize and carry out. **2** direct the performance of (a piece of music or an orchestra or choir). **3** guide to or around a place. **4** (**conduct oneself**) behave in a specified way. **5** transmit (heat, electricity, etc.) by conduction.
– ORIGIN from Latin *conducere* 'bring together'.
conductance ● noun the degree to which a material conducts electricity.
conduction ● noun the transmission of heat or electricity directly through a substance, without motion of the material.
– DERIVATIVES **conductive** adjective.
conductivity ● noun the degree to which a specified material conducts electricity or heat.
conductor ● noun **1** a person who conducts an orchestra or choir. **2** a material or device that conducts heat or electricity. **3** a person who collects fares on a bus. **4** N. Amer. a guard on a train.
– DERIVATIVES **conductorship** noun **conductress** noun.
conduit /kondit, -dyoo-it/ ● noun **1** a channel for conveying water or other fluid. **2** a tube or trough protecting electric wiring.
– ORIGIN Old French, from Latin *conductus*, from *conducere* 'bring together'.
cone ● noun **1** an object which tapers from a circular or roughly circular base to a point. **2** (also **traffic cone**) a plastic cone used to separate off sections of a road. **3** the cone-shaped dry fruit of a conifer. **4** one of two types of light-sensitive cell in the retina of the eye, responsible for sharpness of vision and colour perception. Compare with ROD.
– ORIGIN Greek *kōnos*.
coney /kōni/ (also **cony**) ● noun (pl. **coneys**) Brit. a rabbit.
– ORIGIN Old French *conin*, from Latin *cuniculus*.
confab ● noun informal an informal conversation or discussion.
confabulate /kənfabyoolayt/ ● verb formal converse.
– DERIVATIVES **confabulation** noun.
– ORIGIN Latin *confabulari* 'chat together'.
confect /kənfekt/ ● verb make (something elaborate or dainty).
– ORIGIN Latin *conficere* 'put together'.
confection ● noun **1** an elaborate sweet dish or delicacy. **2** an elaborately constructed thing: *a confection of marble and gilt.*
confectioner ● noun a person who makes or sells confectionery.
confectionery ● noun (pl. **confectioneries**) sweets and chocolates collectively.
confederacy ● noun (pl. **confederacies**) **1** a league or alliance, especially of confederate states. **2** (**the Confederacy**) the Confederate states of the US.
confederate ● adjective /kənfeddərət/ **1** joined by an agreement or treaty. **2** (**Confederate**) denoting the southern states which separated from the US in 1860–1. ● noun /kənfeddərət/ an accomplice or fellow worker. ● verb /kənfeddərayt/ (usu. **confederated**) bring into an alliance.
– ORIGIN Latin *confoederatus*, from *foedus* 'league'.
confederation ● noun **1** an alliance of a number of parties or groups. **2** a union of states with some political power vested in a central authority. **3** the action of confederating or the state of being confederated.
confer /kənfer/ ● verb (**conferred**, **conferring**) **1** grant (a title, degree, benefit, or right). **2** have discussions.
– DERIVATIVES **conferment** noun **conferral** noun.
– ORIGIN Latin *conferre* 'bring together'.
conferee ● noun **1** a person who attends a conference. **2** a person on whom something is conferred.
conference ● noun **1** a formal meeting for discussion or debate. **2** an association in commerce for regulation or exchange of information. **3** a league of sports teams or clubs.
confess ● verb **1** admit to a crime or wrongdoing. **2** acknowledge reluctantly. **3** declare one's sins formally to a priest. **4** (of a priest) hear the confession of.
– ORIGIN Old French *confesser*, from Latin *confiteri* 'acknowledge'.
confessedly ● adverb by one's own admission.

Thesaurus

qualified, with reservations, limited, provisional, provisory.
condolences ● plural noun SYMPATHY, commiseration(s), compassion, pity, support, comfort, consolation, understanding.
condom ● noun CONTRACEPTIVE, sheath; *N. Amer.* prophylactic; *Brit. trademark* Durex, Femidom; *Brit. informal* johnny; *N. Amer. informal* rubber, safe; *Brit. informal, dated* French letter; *dated* protective.
condone ● verb DISREGARD, accept, allow, let pass, turn a blind eye to, overlook, forget; forgive, pardon, excuse, let go.
– OPPOSITES condemn.
conducive ● adjective FAVOURABLE, beneficial, advantageous, opportune, propitious, encouraging, promising, convenient, good, helpful, instrumental, productive, useful.
– OPPOSITES unfavourable.
conduct ● noun **1** *they complained about her conduct* BEHAVIOUR, performance, demeanour; actions, activities, deeds, doings, exploits; habits, manners; *formal* comportment. **2** *the conduct of the elections* MANAGEMENT, running, direction, control, supervision, regulation, administration, organization, coordination, orchestration, handling.
● verb **1** *the election was conducted lawfully* MANAGE, direct, run, administer, organize, coordinate, orchestrate, handle, control, oversee, supervise, regulate, carry out/on. **2** *he was conducted through the corridors* ESCORT, guide, lead, usher, show; shepherd, see, bring, take, help. **3** *aluminium conducts heat* TRANSMIT, convey, carry, transfer, impart, channel, relay; disseminate, diffuse, radiate.
– PHRASES **conduct oneself** BEHAVE, act, acquit oneself, bear oneself; *formal* comport oneself; *archaic* deport oneself.
conduit ● noun CHANNEL, duct, pipe, tube, gutter, trench, culvert, cut, sluice, spillway, flume, chute.
confectionery ● noun SWEETS, chocolates, bonbons; *N. Amer.* candy; *informal* sweeties; *archaic* sweetmeats.
confederacy ● noun FEDERATION, confederation, alliance, league, association, coalition, consortium, syndicate, group, circle; bloc, axis.
confederate ● adjective *confederate councils* FEDERAL, confederated, federated, allied, associated, united.
– OPPOSITES split.
● noun *he met his confederate in the street* ASSOCIATE, partner, accomplice, helper, assistant, ally, collaborator, colleague; *Brit. informal* oppo; *Austral./NZ informal* offsider.
confederation ● noun ALLIANCE, league, confederacy, federation, association, coalition, consortium, conglomerate, cooperative, syndicate, group, circle; society, union.
confer ● verb **1** *she conferred a knighthood on him* BESTOW ON, present to, grant to, award to, decorate with, honour with, give to, endow with, extend to, vouchsafe to. **2** *she went to confer with her colleagues* CONSULT, talk, speak, converse, have a chat, have a tête-à-tête, parley; *informal* have a confab, powwow.
conference ● noun **1** *an international conference* CONGRESS, meeting, convention, seminar, colloquium, symposium, forum, summit. **2** *he gathered them for a conference* DISCUSSION, consultation, debate, talk, conversation, dialogue, chat, tête-à-tête, parley; *informal* confab; *formal* confabulation.
confess ● verb **1** *he confessed that he had done it* ADMIT, acknowledge, reveal, disclose, divulge, avow, declare, profess; own up, tell all. **2** *they could not make him confess* OWN UP, plead guilty, accept the blame; tell the truth, tell all, make a clean breast of it; *informal* come clean, spill the beans, let the cat out of the bag, get something off one's chest, let on; *Brit. informal* cough. **3** *I confess I*

confession ● noun **1** an act of confessing, especially a formal statement admitting to a crime. **2** a formal admission of one's sins privately to a priest. **3** (also **confession of faith**) a statement setting out essential religious doctrine.

confessional ● noun **1** an enclosed stall in a church, in which a priest sits to hear confessions. **2** a confession. ● adjective **1** (of speech or writing) in which a person admits to private thoughts or incidents in their past. **2** relating to religious confession.

confessor ● noun **1** a priest who hears confessions. **2** a person who makes a confession.

confetti ● noun small pieces of coloured paper traditionally thrown over a bride and groom after a marriage ceremony.
– ORIGIN Italian, 'sweets' (from the Italian custom of throwing sweets during carnivals).

confidant /**kon**fidant/ ● noun (fem. **confidante** pronunc. same) a person in whom one confides.

confide /kən**fīd**/ ● verb **1** (often **confide in**) tell someone about a secret or private matter in confidence. **2** (**confide to**) dated entrust (something) to the care of.
– ORIGIN Latin *confidere* 'have full trust'.

confidence ● noun **1** the belief that one can have faith in or rely on someone or something. **2** self-assurance arising from an appreciation of one's abilities. **3** the telling of private matters or secrets with mutual trust. **4** a secret or private matter told to someone under a condition of trust.
– PHRASES **in someone's confidence** in a position of trust with someone. **take into one's confidence** tell one's secrets to.

confidence trick (N. Amer. also **confidence game**) ● noun an act of cheating someone by gaining their trust.

confident ● adjective **1** feeling confidence in oneself. **2** feeling certainty about something.
– DERIVATIVES **confidently** adverb.

confidential ● adjective **1** intended to be kept secret. **2** entrusted with private information: *a confidential secretary.*
– DERIVATIVES **confidentiality** noun **confidentially** adverb.

configuration /kənfigyoo**ray**sh'n/ ● noun an arrangement of parts or elements in a particular form or figure.
– DERIVATIVES **configurational** adjective.

configure ● verb **1** arrange in a particular configuration. **2** arrange or order (a computer system) so as to fit it for a designated task.
– DERIVATIVES **configurable** adjective.
– ORIGIN Latin *configurare* 'shape after a pattern'; related to FIGURE.

confine ● verb /kən**fīn**/ **1** (**confine to**) restrict (someone or something) within certain limits of (space, scope, or time). **2** (**be confined to**) be unable to leave (one's bed, home, etc.) due to illness or disability. **3** (**be confined**) dated (of a woman) remain in bed for a period before, during, and after giving birth. ● noun /**kon**fīn/ (**confines**) limits or boundaries.
– DERIVATIVES **confinement** noun.
– ORIGIN from Latin *confinis* 'bordering', from *finis* 'end, limit'.

confined ● adjective (of a space) enclosed; cramped.

confirm ● verb **1** establish the truth or correctness of. **2** state with assurance that something is true. **3** make definite or formally valid. **4** (**confirm in**) reinforce (someone) in (an opinion or feeling). **5** (usu. **be confirmed**) administer the religious rite of confirmation to.
– DERIVATIVES **confirmatory** adjective.
– ORIGIN Latin *confirmare*, from *firmus* 'firm'.

confirmation ● noun **1** the action of confirming or the state of being confirmed. **2** the rite at which a baptized person affirms their belief and is admitted as a full member of the Christian Church. **3** the Jewish ceremony of bar mitzvah.

confirmed ● adjective firmly established in a habit, belief, or way of life: *a confirmed bachelor.*

confiscate /**kon**fiskayt/ ● verb **1** take or seize (property) with authority. **2** appropriate to the public treasury as a penalty.
– DERIVATIVES **confiscation** noun **confiscatory** adjective.
– ORIGIN Latin *confiscare* 'put away in a chest, consign to the public treasury', from *fiscus* 'chest, treasury'.

confit /**kon**fi/ ● noun duck or other meat cooked very slowly in its own fat.
– ORIGIN French, 'conserved'.

conflagration /konflə**gray**sh'n/ ● noun an extensive and destructive fire.
– ORIGIN Latin, from *flagrare* 'to blaze'.

C

Thesaurus

don't know ACKNOWLEDGE, admit, concede, grant, allow, own, declare, affirm.
– OPPOSITES deny.

confession ● noun ADMISSION, acknowledgement, profession; revelation, disclosure, divulgence, avowal; guilty plea.

confidant, fem. **confidante** ● noun CLOSE FRIEND, bosom friend, best friend; intimate, familiar; *informal* chum, pal, crony; *Brit. informal* mate, oppo, mucker; *N. Amer. informal* buddy.

confide ● verb **1** *he confided his fears to his mother* REVEAL, disclose, divulge, lay bare, betray, impart, declare, intimate, uncover, expose, vouchsafe, tell; confess, admit, give away; *informal* blab, spill. **2** *I need him to confide in* OPEN ONE'S HEART TO, unburden oneself to, confess to, tell all to.

confidence ● noun **1** *I have little confidence in these figures* TRUST, belief, faith, credence, conviction. **2** *she's brimming with confidence* SELF-ASSURANCE, self-confidence, self-possession, assertiveness; poise, aplomb, phlegm; courage, boldness, mettle, nerve. **3** *the girls exchanged confidences* SECRET, confidentiality, intimacy.
– OPPOSITES scepticism, doubt.

confident ● adjective **1** *we are confident that business will improve* OPTIMISTIC, hopeful, sanguine; sure, certain, positive, convinced, in no doubt, satisfied, assured, persuaded. **2** *a confident girl* SELF-ASSURED, assured, self-confident, positive, assertive, self-possessed, self-reliant, poised; cool-headed, phlegmatic, level-headed, unperturbed, imperturbable, unruffled, at ease; *informal* together.

confidential ● adjective **1** *a confidential chat* PRIVATE, personal, intimate, quiet; secret, sensitive, classified, restricted, unofficial, unrevealed, undisclosed, unpublished; *informal* hush-hush, mum; *formal* sub rosa; *archaic* privy. **2** *a confidential friend* TRUSTED, trustworthy, trusty, faithful, reliable, dependable; close, bosom, intimate.

confidentially ● adverb PRIVATELY, in private, in confidence, between ourselves/themselves, off the record, quietly, secretly, in secret, behind closed doors; *formal* sub rosa.

configuration ● noun ARRANGEMENT, layout, geography, design, organization, order, grouping, positioning, disposition, alignment; shape, form, appearance, formation, structure, format.

confine ● verb **1** *they were confined in the house* ENCLOSE, incarcerate, imprison, intern, impound, hold captive, trap; shut in/up, keep, lock in/up, coop (up); fence in, hedge in, wall in/up. **2** *he confined his remarks to the weather* RESTRICT, limit.

confined ● adjective CRAMPED, constricted, restricted, limited, small, narrow, compact, tight, poky, uncomfortable, inadequate.
– OPPOSITES roomy.

confinement ● noun **1** *solitary confinement* IMPRISONMENT, internment, incarceration, custody, captivity, detention, restraint; house arrest. **2** *the confinement of an animal* CAGING, enclosure; quarantine. **3** (dated) *she went to hospital for her confinement* LABOUR, delivery, birthing; birth, childbirth; *formal* parturition; *archaic* lying-in, childbed.

confines ● plural noun LIMITS, margins, extremities, edges, borders, boundaries, fringes, marches; periphery, perimeter.

confirm ● verb **1** *records confirm the latest evidence* CORROBORATE, verify, prove, validate, authenticate, substantiate, justify, vindicate; support, uphold, back up. **2** *he confirmed that help was on the way* AFFIRM, reaffirm, assert, assure someone, repeat; promise, guarantee. **3** *his appointment was confirmed by the President* RATIFY, validate, sanction, endorse, formalize, authorize, warrant, accredit, approve, accept.
– OPPOSITES contradict, deny.

confirmation ● noun **1** *independent confirmation of the deaths* CORROBORATION, verification, proof, testimony, endorsement, authentication, substantiation, evidence. **2** *confirmation of your appointment* RATIFICATION, approval, authorization, validation, sanction, endorsement, formalization, accreditation, acceptance.

confirmed ● adjective ESTABLISHED, long-standing, committed, dyed-in-the-wool, through and through; staunch, loyal, faithful, devoted, dedicated, steadfast; habitual, compulsive, persistent; unapologetic, unashamed, inveterate, chronic, incurable; *informal* deep-dyed, card-carrying.

confiscate ● verb IMPOUND, seize, commandeer, requisition, appropriate, expropriate, sequester, sequestrate, take (away); *Law* distrain; *Scottish Law* poind.
– OPPOSITES return.

confiscation ● noun SEIZURE, requisition, appropriation, expropriation, sequestration, commandeering; *Law* distraint, distrain-

C

conflate ● verb combine into one.
– DERIVATIVES **conflation** noun.
– ORIGIN Latin *conflare* 'kindle, fuse'.
conflict ● noun /konflikt/ **1** a serious disagreement or argument. **2** a prolonged armed struggle. **3** an incompatibility between opinions, principles, etc.: *a conflict of interests.* ● verb /kənflikt/ be incompatible or at variance with.
– DERIVATIVES **conflictual** adjective.
– ORIGIN Latin *conflictus* 'a contest'.
confluence /konflooənss/ ● noun **1** the junction of two rivers. **2** an act or process of merging.
– DERIVATIVES **confluent** adjective.
– ORIGIN from Latin *confluere* 'flow together'.
conform ● verb **1** comply with rules, standards, or conventions. **2** be similar in form or type.
– ORIGIN Latin *conformare*, from *formare* 'to form'.
conformable ● adjective (usu. **conformable to**) **1** disposed or accustomed to conform. **2** similar in nature; consistent.
conformance ● noun another term for CONFORMITY.
conformation ● noun the shape or structure of something.
– DERIVATIVES **conformational** adjective.
conformist ● noun a person who conforms to accepted behaviour or established practices. ● adjective conventional.
– DERIVATIVES **conformism** noun.
conformity ● noun **1** compliance with conventions, rules, or laws. **2** similarity in form or type.
confound ● verb **1** surprise or bewilder. **2** prove wrong. **3** defeat (a plan, aim, or hope).
– ORIGIN Latin *confundere* 'pour together, mix up'.
confounded ● adjective informal, dated used to express annoyance.
– DERIVATIVES **confoundedly** adverb.
confraternity ● noun (pl. **confraternities**) a brotherhood, especially with a religious or charitable purpose.
– ORIGIN Latin *confraternitas*, from *confrater* 'confrère'.
confrère /konfrair/ ● noun a fellow member of a profession.
– ORIGIN French, from Latin *confrater*, from *frater* 'brother'.
confront ● verb **1** meet face to face in hostility or defiance. **2** (of a problem) present itself to. **3** face up to and deal with (a problem). **4** compel to face or consider something.
– DERIVATIVES **confrontation** noun **confrontational** adjective.
– ORIGIN Latin *confrontare*, from *frons* 'face'.
Confucian /kənfyoosh'n/ ● adjective relating to the Chinese philosopher Confucius (551–479 BC) or his philosophy. ● noun a follower of Confucius or his philosophy.
– DERIVATIVES **Confucianism** noun **Confucianist** noun & adjective.
confuse ● verb **1** make bewildered or perplexed. **2** make less easy to understand. **3** mistake (one for another).
– DERIVATIVES **confusable** adjective.
– ORIGIN from Latin *confusus*, from *confundere* 'mix up'.
confused ● adjective **1** bewildered. **2** lacking order and so difficult to understand or distinguish.
– DERIVATIVES **confusedly** adverb.
confusion ● noun **1** the state of being confused; uncertainty or bewilderment. **2** a situation or state of panic or disorder. **3** the mistaking of one person or thing for another.
confute ● verb formal prove to be wrong.
– DERIVATIVES **confutation** noun.
– ORIGIN Latin *confutare* 'restrain, answer conclusively'.
conga /konggə/ ● noun **1** a Latin American dance of African origin, performed by people in single file and consisting of three steps forward followed by a kick. **2** (also **conga drum**) a tall, narrow drum beaten with the hands.

Thesaurus

ment; *Scottish Law* poind.
conflagration ● noun FIRE, blaze, flames, inferno, firestorm.
conflict ● noun **1** *industrial conflicts* DISPUTE, quarrel, squabble, disagreement, dissension, clash; discord, friction, strife, antagonism, hostility, disputation, contention; feud, schism. **2** *the Vietnam conflict* WAR, campaign, battle, fighting, (armed) confrontation, engagement, encounter, struggle, hostilities; warfare, combat. **3** *a conflict between his business and domestic life* CLASH, incompatibility, incongruity, friction; mismatch, variance, difference, divergence, contradiction, inconsistency.
– OPPOSITES agreement, peace, harmony.
● verb *their interests sometimes conflict* CLASH, be incompatible, vary, be at odds, be in conflict, differ, diverge, disagree, contrast, collide.
conflicting ● adjective CONTRADICTORY, incompatible, inconsistent, irreconcilable, incongruous, contrary, opposite, opposing, antithetical, clashing, discordant, divergent; at odds.
confluence ● noun CONVERGENCE, meeting, junction, conflux, watersmeet.
conform ● verb **1** *visitors have to conform to our rules* COMPLY WITH, abide by, obey, observe, follow, keep to, stick to, adhere to, uphold, heed, accept, go along with, fall in with, respect, defer to; satisfy, meet, fulfil. **2** *they refuse to conform* FOLLOW CONVENTION, be conventional, fit in, adapt, adjust, follow the crowd; comply, acquiesce, toe the line, follow the rules; submit, yield; *informal* play it by the book, play by the rules. **3** *goods must conform to their description* MATCH, fit, suit, answer, agree with, be like, correspond to, be consistent with, measure up to, tally with, square with.
– OPPOSITES flout, rebel.
conformist ● noun CONVENTIONALIST, traditionalist, conservative, stickler, formalist, diehard, reactionary; *informal* stick-in-the-mud, stuffed shirt.
– OPPOSITES eccentric, rebel.
confound ● verb **1** *the figures confounded analysts* AMAZE, astonish, dumbfound, stagger, surprise, startle, stun, nonplus; throw, shake, discompose, bewilder, baffle, mystify, bemuse, perplex, puzzle, confuse; take aback, shake up, catch off balance; *informal* flabbergast, blow someone's mind, blow away, flummox, faze, stump, beat, fox; *N. Amer. informal* discombobulate. **2** *he has always confounded expectations* CONTRADICT, counter, invalidate, negate, go against, drive a coach and horses through; quash, explode, demolish, shoot down, destroy, disprove; *informal* shoot full of holes.
confront ● verb **1** *Jones confronted the burglar* CHALLENGE, square up to, face (up to), come face to face with, meet, accost, waylay; stand up to, brave, beard, tackle; *informal* collar; *Brit. informal* nobble. **2** *the problems that confront us* TROUBLE, bother, burden, distress, worry, oppress, annoy, strain, stress, tax, torment, plague, blight, curse; face, beset. **3** *they must confront their problems* TACKLE, address, face, get to grips with, grapple with, take on, attend to, see to, deal with, take care of, handle, manage; *informal* get stuck into. **4** *she confronted him with the evidence* PRESENT, face.
– OPPOSITES avoid.
confrontation ● noun CONFLICT, clash, fight, battle, encounter, head-to-head, face-off, engagement, skirmish; hostilities, fighting; *informal* set-to, run-in, dust-up, showdown.
confuse ● verb **1** *don't confuse students with too much detail* BEWILDER, baffle, mystify, bemuse, perplex, puzzle, confound, nonplus; *informal* flummox, faze, stump, fox; *N. Amer. informal* discombobulate. **2** *the authors have confused the issue* COMPLICATE, muddle, jumble, garble, blur, obscure, cloud. **3** *some confuse strokes with heart attacks* MIX UP, muddle up, confound; mistake for.
– OPPOSITES enlighten, simplify.
confused ● adjective **1** *they are confused about what is going on* BEWILDERED, bemused, puzzled, perplexed, baffled, mystified, nonplussed, muddled, dumbfounded, at sea, at a loss, taken aback, disoriented, disconcerted; *informal* flummoxed, bamboozled, clueless, fazed; *N. Amer. informal* discombobulated. **2** *her confused elderly mother* DEMENTED, bewildered, muddled, addled, befuddled, disoriented, disorientated; unbalanced, unhinged; senile. **3** *a confused recollection* VAGUE, unclear, indistinct, imprecise, blurred, hazy, woolly, shadowy, dim; imperfect, sketchy. **4** *a confused mass of bones* DISORDERLY, disordered, disorganized, disarranged, out of order, untidy, muddled, jumbled, mixed up, chaotic, topsy-turvy; *informal* higgledy-piggledy; *Brit. informal* shambolic.
– OPPOSITES lucid, clear, precise, neat.
confusing ● adjective BEWILDERING, baffling, unclear, perplexing, puzzling, mystifying, disconcerting; ambiguous, misleading, inconsistent, contradictory; unaccountable, inexplicable, impenetrable, unfathomable; complex, complicated.
confusion ● noun **1** *there is confusion about the new system* UNCERTAINTY, incertitude, unsureness, doubt, ignorance; *formal* dubiety. **2** *she stared in confusion* BEWILDERMENT, bafflement, perplexity, puzzlement, mystification, befuddlement; shock, daze, wonder, wonderment, astonishment; *informal* bamboozlement; *N. Amer. informal* discombobulation. **3** *her life was in utter confusion* DISORDER, disarray, disorganization, untidiness, chaos, mayhem; turmoil, tumult, disruption, upheaval, uproar, hurly-burly, muddle, mess; *informal* shambles. **4** *a confusion of boxes* JUMBLE, muddle, mess, heap, tangle; *informal* shambles.
– OPPOSITES certainty, order.
confute ● verb (*formal*) DISPROVE, contradict, controvert, refute, deny, rebut, belie, negate, invalidate, explode, discredit, debunk,

– ORIGIN Spanish, from *congo* 'Congolese'.

congeal /kənjeel/ ● verb become semi-solid, especially on cooling.
– DERIVATIVES **congelation** /konjəlaysh'n/ noun.
– ORIGIN Latin *congelare*, from *gelare* 'freeze'.

congener /kənjeenər/ ● noun a person or thing of the same kind as another.
– DERIVATIVES **congeneric** /konjinerrik/ adjective.
– ORIGIN Latin, from *con-* 'together with' + *genus* 'race, stock'.

congenial /kənjeeniəl/ ● adjective **1** pleasant because of qualities or interests similar to one's own: *congenial company.* **2** suited to one's taste or inclination.
– DERIVATIVES **congeniality** noun **congenially** adverb.

congenital /kənjennit'l/ ● adjective **1** (of a disease or abnormality) present from birth. **2** having a particular trait from or as if from birth: *a congenital liar.*
– DERIVATIVES **congenitally** adverb.
– ORIGIN from Latin *congenitus* 'born together'.

conger /konggə/ (also **conger eel**) ● noun a large predatory eel of shallow coastal waters.
– ORIGIN Greek *gongros.*

congeries /konjeereez/ ● noun (pl. same) a disorderly collection.
– ORIGIN Latin, 'heap, pile'.

congested ● adjective **1** so crowded as to hinder or prevent freedom of movement. **2** abnormally full of blood. **3** blocked with mucus.
– DERIVATIVES **congestion** noun.
– ORIGIN from Latin *congerere* 'heap up'.

congestive ● adjective Medicine involving or produced by congestion of a part of the body.

conglomerate ● noun /kənglommərət/ **1** something consisting of a number of different and distinct things. **2** a large corporation formed by the merging of separate firms. **3** Geology a coarse-grained sedimentary rock composed of rounded fragments cemented together. ● adjective /kənglommərət/ relating to a conglomerate. ● verb /kənglommərayt/ gather into or form a conglomerate.
– DERIVATIVES **conglomeration** noun.
– ORIGIN from Latin *conglomerare* 'roll or heap together'.

Congolese /konggəleez/ ● noun (pl. same) **1** a person from the Congo or the Democratic Republic of Congo (formerly Zaire). **2** any of the languages spoken in the Congo region. ● adjective relating to the Congo or the Democratic Republic of Congo.

congratulate ● verb **1** express good wishes or praise at the happiness, success, or good fortune of. **2** (**congratulate oneself**) think oneself fortunate or clever.
– DERIVATIVES **congratulatory** adjective.
– ORIGIN Latin *congratulari*, from *gratus* 'pleasing'.

congratulation ● noun **1** (**congratulations**) praise or good wishes on a special occasion. **2** the action of congratulating.

congregant /konggrigənt/ ● noun a member of a congregation.

congregate ● verb gather into a crowd or mass.
– ORIGIN Latin *congregare* 'collect (into a flock)', from *grex* 'a flock'.

congregation ● noun **1** a group of people assembled for religious worship. **2** a gathering or collection of people or things. **3** the action of congregating.

congregational ● adjective **1** relating to a congregation. **2** (**Congregational**) of or adhering to Congregationalism.

Congregationalism ● noun a system of organization among Christian churches whereby individual churches are largely self-governing.
– DERIVATIVES **Congregationalist** noun & adjective.

congress ● noun **1** a formal meeting or series of meetings between delegates. **2** (**Congress**) a national legislative body, especially that of the US. **3** the action of coming together.
– DERIVATIVES **congressional** adjective.
– ORIGIN Latin *congressus*, from *congredi* 'meet'.

congressman (or **congresswoman**) ● noun a male (or female) member of the US Congress.

congruent /konggrooənt/ ● adjective **1** in agreement or harmony. **2** Geometry (of figures) identical in form.
– DERIVATIVES **congruence** noun.
– ORIGIN from Latin *congruere* 'agree, meet together'.

congruous /konggrooəss/ ● adjective in agreement or harmony.
– DERIVATIVES **congruity** /konggrōōiti/ noun.

conic /konnik/ ● adjective of a cone.

conical ● adjective shaped like a cone.

conic section ● noun the figure of a circle, ellipse, parabola, or hyperbola formed by the intersection of a plane and a circular cone.

conifer /konnifər, kōn-/ ● noun a tree bearing cones and evergreen needle-like or scale-like leaves, e.g. a pine or cypress.
– DERIVATIVES **coniferous** adjective.
– ORIGIN Latin, 'cone-bearing'.

Thesaurus

quash, drive a coach and horses through; *informal* shoot full of holes; *formal* gainsay.
– OPPOSITES prove.

congeal ● verb COAGULATE, clot, thicken, gel, inspissate, cake, set, curdle.

congenial ● adjective **1** *very congenial people* LIKE-MINDED, compatible, kindred, well suited; companionable, sociable, sympathetic, comradely, convivial, hospitable, genial, personable, agreeable, friendly, pleasant, likeable, amiable, nice. **2** *a congenial environment* PLEASANT, pleasing, agreeable, enjoyable, pleasurable, nice, appealing, satisfying, gratifying, delightful, relaxing, welcoming, hospitable; suitable, well suited, favourable.
– OPPOSITES unpleasant.

congenital ● adjective **1** *congenital defects* INBORN, inherited, hereditary, innate, inbred, constitutional, inbuilt, natural, inherent. **2** *a congenital liar* INVETERATE, compulsive, persistent, chronic, regular, habitual, obsessive, confirmed; incurable, incorrigible, irredeemable, hopeless; unashamed, shameless; *informal* pathological.
– OPPOSITES acquired.

congested ● adjective CROWDED, overcrowded, full, overflowing, packed, jammed, thronged, teeming, swarming; obstructed, blocked, clogged, choked; *informal* snarled up, gridlocked, jam-packed; *Brit. informal* like Piccadilly Circus.
– OPPOSITES clear.

congestion ● noun CROWDING, overcrowding; obstruction, blockage; traffic jam, bottleneck; *informal* snarl-up, gridlock.

conglomerate ● noun **1** *the conglomerate was broken up* CORPORATION, combine, group, consortium, partnership; firm, company, business, multinational. **2** *a conglomerate of disparate peoples* MIXTURE, mix, combination, amalgamation, union, marriage, fusion, composite, synthesis; miscellany, hotchpotch.
● adjective *a conglomerate mass* AGGREGATE, agglomerate, amassed, combined.
● verb *the debris conglomerated into planets* COALESCE, unite, join, combine, merge, fuse, consolidate, amalgamate, integrate, mingle, intermingle.

congratulate ● verb **1** *she congratulated him on his marriage* SEND ONE'S BEST WISHES, wish someone good luck, wish someone joy; drink someone's health, toast. **2** *they are to be congratulated* PRAISE, commend, applaud, salute, honour; pay tribute to, regard highly, pat on the back, take one's hat off to.
– OPPOSITES criticize.
– PHRASES **congratulate oneself** TAKE PRIDE, feel proud, flatter oneself, preen oneself, pat oneself on the back; feel satisfaction, take pleasure, glory, bask, delight.

congratulations ● plural noun **1** *her congratulations on their wedding* GOOD WISHES, best wishes, compliments, felicitations. **2** *you all deserve congratulations* PRAISE, commendation, applause, salutes, honour, acclaim, cheers, bouquets; approval, admiration, compliments, kudos, adulation; a pat on the back.
– OPPOSITES blame.

congregate ● verb ASSEMBLE, gather, collect, come together, convene, rally, rendezvous, muster, meet, cluster, group.
– OPPOSITES disperse.

congregation ● noun **1** *the chapel congregation* PARISHIONERS, parish, churchgoers, flock, faithful, followers, believers, fellowship, communicants, laity, brethren; throng, company, assemblage, audience. **2** *congregations of birds* GATHERING, assembly, flock, swarm, bevy, pack, group, body, crowd, mass, multitude, horde, host, mob, throng.

congress ● noun **1** *a congress of mathematicians* CONFERENCE, convention, seminar, colloquium, symposium, forum, meeting, assembly, gathering, rally, summit. **2** *elections for the new Congress* LEGISLATURE, legislative assembly, parliament, convocation, diet, council, senate, chamber, house.

congruence ● noun COMPATIBILITY, consistency, conformity, match, balance, consonance, congruity; agreement, accord, con-

C

conjecture /kənjekchər/ ● noun an opinion or conclusion based on incomplete information; a guess. ● verb form a conjecture; guess.
– DERIVATIVES **conjectural** adjective.
– ORIGIN Latin *conjectura*, from *conicere* 'put together in thought'.
conjoin ● verb formal join; combine.
conjoint ● adjective combined or united.
conjugal /konjoog'l/ ● adjective relating to marriage or the relationship between husband and wife.
– ORIGIN Latin *conjugalis*, from *conjux* 'spouse'.
conjugal rights ● plural noun the rights, especially to sexual relations, regarded as exercisable in law by each partner in a marriage.
conjugate ● verb /**kon**joogayt/ **1** give the different forms of (a verb). **2** (of bacteria or unicellular organisms) become temporarily united in order to exchange genetic material. ● adjective /**kon**joogət/ **1** technical joined or related as a pair. **2** Biology (of gametes) fused. ● noun /**kon**joogət/ a conjugate thing.
– DERIVATIVES **conjugation** noun.
– ORIGIN Latin *conjugare* 'yoke together'.
conjunct ● adjective /kən**jungkt**/ joined together, combined, or associated. ● noun /**kon**jungkt/ **1** each of two or more joined or associated things. **2** Grammar an adverbial joining two sentences or clauses (e.g. *however*).
– ORIGIN Latin *conjunctus*, from *conjungere* 'conjoin'.
conjunction ● noun **1** a word used to connect clauses or sentences or to coordinate words in the same clause (e.g. *and*, *if*). **2** an instance of two or more events occurring at the same point in time or space. **3** Astronomy & Astrology an alignment of two planets so that they appear to be in the same place in the sky.
– PHRASES **in conjunction** together.
conjunctiva /konjungk**tī**və, kən**jungk**tivə/ ● noun the mucous membrane that covers the front of the eye and lines the inside of the eyelids.
– DERIVATIVES **conjunctival** adjective.
– ORIGIN from Latin *membrana conjunctiva* 'conjunctive membrane'.
conjunctive ● adjective relating to or forming a conjunction. ● noun a word or expression acting as a conjunction.
conjunctivitis /kənjungkti**vī**tiss/ ● noun inflammation of the conjunctiva.
conjuncture ● noun **1** a combination of events. **2** a state of affairs.
conjure /**kun**jər/ ● verb (usu. **conjure up**) **1** cause to appear as if by magic. **2** call to the mind. **3** call upon (a spirit) to appear by magic. **4** /kən**joor**/ archaic implore to do something.
– PHRASES **a name to conjure with** a name of great importance within a particular field.
– ORIGIN Latin *conjurare* 'band together by an oath, conspire'.
conjuring ● noun the performance of seemingly magical tricks, often involving sleight of hand.
conjuror (also **conjurer**) ● noun a performer of conjuring tricks.
conk[1] ● verb (**conk out**) informal **1** (of a machine) break down. **2** faint or go to sleep. **3** die.
– ORIGIN of unknown origin.
conk[2] ● noun Brit. informal a person's nose.
– ORIGIN perhaps an alteration of CONCH.
conker ● noun Brit. **1** the hard shiny dark brown nut of a horse chestnut tree. **2** (**conkers**) (treated as sing.) a children's game in which each has a conker on a string and tries to break another's with it.
– ORIGIN dialect, 'snail shell' (with which the game was originally played).
con man ● noun informal a man who cheats others using confidence tricks.
conn ● verb US spelling of CON[4].
connect ● verb **1** bring together so as to establish a link. **2** join together so as to provide access and communication. **3** (**be connected**) be related in some respect. **4** put into contact by telephone. **5** (of a train, bus, etc.) arrive at its destination just before another departs so that passengers can transfer.
– DERIVATIVES **connectable** adjective **connector** noun.
– ORIGIN Latin *connectere*, from *nectere* 'bind'.
connecting rod ● noun the rod connecting the piston and the crankpin in an engine or pump.
connection (Brit. also **connexion**) ● noun **1** a link or relationship. **2** the action of connecting. **3** (**connections**) influential people with whom one has contact or to whom one is related. **4** an opportunity for catching a connecting train, bus, etc.
– PHRASES **in connection with** concerning. **in this** (or **that**) **connection** with reference to this (or that).
connective ● adjective connecting. ● noun something that connects.
connective tissue ● noun bodily tissue that connects, supports, binds, or separates other tissues or organs, typically consisting of relatively few cells embedded in fibrous material or fat.
connectivity ● noun **1** the state or extent of being connected. **2** Computing capacity for the interconnection of platforms, systems, and applications.
connexion ● noun variant spelling of CONNECTION.
conning tower /**kon**ning/ ● noun the superstructure of a submarine, containing the periscope.
connive /kə**nīv**/ ● verb **1** (**connive at/in**) secretly allow (a wrongdoing). **2** (often **connive with**) conspire.
– DERIVATIVES **connivance** noun.
– ORIGIN Latin *connivere* 'shut the eyes (to)'.
connoisseur /konnə**sör**/ ● noun an expert judge in matters of taste.
– DERIVATIVES **connoisseurship** noun.
– ORIGIN French, from *connaître* 'know'.
connotation /konnə**tay**sh'n/ ● noun an idea or feeling invoked

Thesaurus

sensus, harmony, unity; *formal* concord.
– OPPOSITES conflict.
conical ● adjective CONE-SHAPED, tapered, tapering, pointed, funnel-shaped; *informal* pointy; *Zoology* conoid.
conjectural ● adjective SPECULATIVE, suppositional, suppositious, theoretical, hypothetical, putative, notional; postulated, inferred, presumed, assumed, presupposed, tentative.
conjecture ● noun *the information is merely conjecture* SPECULATION, guesswork, surmise, fancy, presumption, assumption, theory, postulation, supposition; inference, extrapolation; estimate; *informal* guesstimate, a shot in the dark.
– OPPOSITES fact.
● verb *I conjectured that the game was over* GUESS, speculate, surmise, infer, fancy, imagine, believe, think, suspect, presume, assume, hypothesize, suppose.
– OPPOSITES know.
conjugal ● adjective MARITAL, matrimonial, nuptial, marriage, bridal; *Law* spousal; *poetic/literary* connubial.
conjunction ● noun CO-OCCURRENCE, concurrence, coincidence, coexistence, simultaneity, contemporaneity, concomitance, synchronicity, synchrony.
conjure ● verb **1** *he conjured a cigarette out of the air* PRODUCE, make something appear, materialize, magic, summon. **2** *the picture that his words conjured up* BRING TO MIND, call to mind, evoke, summon up, recall, recreate; echo, allude to, suggest, awaken.
conjuring ● noun MAGIC, illusion, sleight of hand, legerdemain; *formal* prestidigitation.
conjuror ● noun MAGICIAN, illusionist; *formal* prestidigitator.
connect ● verb **1** *electrodes were connected to the device* ATTACH, join, fasten, fix, affix, couple, link, secure, hitch; stick, adhere, fuse, pin, screw, bolt, clamp, clip, hook (up); add, append. **2** *customs connected with Easter* ASSOCIATE, link, couple; identify, equate, bracket, relate to.
connection ● noun **1** *the connection between commerce and art* LINK, relationship, relation, interconnection, interdependence, association; bond, tie, tie-in, correspondence, parallel, analogy. **2** *a poor connection in the plug* ATTACHMENT, joint, fastening, coupling. **3** *he has the right connections* CONTACT, friend, acquaintance, ally, colleague, associate; relation, relative, kin.
– PHRASES **in connection with** REGARDING, concerning, with reference to, with regard to, with respect to, respecting, relating to, in relation to, on, connected with, on the subject of, in the matter of, apropos, re, in re.
connivance ● noun COLLUSION, complicity, collaboration, involvement, assistance; tacit consent, conspiracy, intrigue.
connive ● verb **1** *wardens connived at offences* DELIBERATELY IGNORE, overlook, disregard, pass over, take no notice of, make allowances for, turn a blind eye to, wink at, excuse, condone, let go; look the other way, let something ride. **2** *the government connived with security forces* CONSPIRE, collude, collaborate, intrigue, be hand in glove, plot, scheme; *informal* be in cahoots.
conniving ● adjective SCHEMING, cunning, crafty, calculating, devi-

by a word in addition to its primary or literal meaning.
connote /kənōt/ ● verb **1** (of a word) imply or suggest in addition to its primary or literal meaning. **2** imply as a consequence or condition.
– DERIVATIVES **connotative** /konnətaytiv/ adjective.
– USAGE **Connote** does not mean the same as **denote**: whereas **denote** refers to the literal, primary meaning of something, **connote** refers to other characteristics suggested or implied by that thing. Thus, one might say that a word like **mother** *denotes* 'a woman who is a parent' but *connotes* qualities such as protection and affection.
– ORIGIN Latin *connotare* 'mark in addition'.
connubial /kənyoobiəl/ ● adjective literary conjugal.
– ORIGIN Latin *connubialis*, from *connubium* 'marriage'.
conquer ● verb **1** overcome and take control of by military force. **2** successfully overcome (a problem) or climb (a mountain).
– DERIVATIVES **conquerable** adjective **conqueror** noun.
– ORIGIN Latin *conquirere* 'gain, win'.
conquest ● noun **1** the action of conquering. **2** a conquered territory. **3** a person whose affection or favour has been won.
conquistador /konkwistədor, -kis-/ ● noun (pl. **conquistadores** /konkwistədorayz, -kistə-/ or **conquistadors**) a Spanish conqueror of Mexico or Peru in the 16th century.
– ORIGIN Spanish.
consanguineous /konsanggwinniəss/ ● adjective descended from the same ancestor.
– DERIVATIVES **consanguinity** noun.
– ORIGIN Latin *consanguineus* 'of the same blood'.
conscience ● noun a person's moral sense of right and wrong, chiefly as it affects their own behaviour.
– PHRASES **in (all) conscience** in fairness.
– DERIVATIVES **conscienceless** adjective.
– ORIGIN Latin *conscientia* 'knowledge within oneself', from *scire* 'to know'.
conscientious /konshienshəss/ ● adjective **1** diligent and thorough in carrying out one's work or duty. **2** relating to a person's conscience.
– DERIVATIVES **conscientiously** adverb **conscientiousness** noun.
conscientious objector ● noun a person who refuses to serve in the armed forces for reasons of conscience.
conscious ● adjective **1** aware of and responding to one's surroundings. **2** (usu. **conscious of**) aware. **3** deliberate: *a conscious effort.*
– DERIVATIVES **consciously** adverb.
– ORIGIN Latin *conscius* 'knowing with others or in oneself'.
consciousness ● noun **1** the state of being conscious. **2** one's awareness or perception of something.
conscript ● verb /kənskript/ call up for compulsory military service. ● noun /konskript/ a conscripted person.
– DERIVATIVES **conscription** noun.
– ORIGIN from Latin *conscriptus*, from *conscribere* 'enrol'.
consecrate /konsikrayt/ ● verb **1** make or declare sacred. **2** ordain to a sacred office, typically that of bishop. **3** (in Christian belief) make (bread or wine) into the body and blood of Christ.
– DERIVATIVES **consecration** noun.
– ORIGIN Latin *consecrare* 'dedicate, devote as sacred'.
consecutive /kənsekyootiv/ ● adjective **1** following in unbroken or logical sequence. **2** Grammar expressing consequence or result.
– DERIVATIVES **consecutively** adverb.
– ORIGIN Latin *consecutivus*, from *consequi* 'follow closely'.
consensual /kənsensyooəl, -shooəl/ ● adjective relating to or involving consent or consensus.
consensus /kənsensəss/ ● noun general agreement.
– ORIGIN Latin, 'agreement'.
consent ● noun permission or agreement. ● verb **1** give permission. **2** agree to do.
– ORIGIN from Latin *consentire* 'agree'.
consenting adult ● noun an adult who willingly agrees to engage in a sexual act.
consequence ● noun **1** a result or effect. **2** importance or relevance: *the past is of no consequence.* **3** dated social distinction.

C

Thesaurus

ous, wily, sly, tricky, artful, guileful; manipulative, Machiavellian, disingenuous, deceitful, underhand, treacherous; *informal* foxy.
connoisseur ● noun EXPERT, authority, specialist, pundit, savant; arbiter of taste, aesthete; gourmet, epicure, gastronome; *informal* buff; *N. Amer. informal* maven.
connotation ● noun OVERTONE, undertone, undercurrent, implication, hidden meaning, nuance, hint, echo, vibrations, association, intimation, suggestion, suspicion, insinuation.
connote ● verb IMPLY, suggest, indicate, signify, hint at, give the impression of, smack of, be associated with, allude to.
conquer ● verb **1** *the Franks conquered the Visigoths* DEFEAT, beat, vanquish, trounce, triumph over, be victorious over, get the better of, worst; overcome, overwhelm, overpower, overthrow, subdue, subjugate, best, quell, quash, crush, rout; *informal* lick, hammer, clobber, thrash, paste, demolish, annihilate, wipe the floor with, walk all over, make mincemeat of, massacre, slaughter; *Brit. informal* stuff; *N. Amer. informal* cream, shellac, skunk. **2** *Peru was conquered by Spain* SEIZE, take (over), appropriate, subjugate, capture, occupy, invade, annex, overrun. **3** *the first men to conquer Mount Everest* CLIMB, ascend, mount, scale, top, crest. **4** *the way to conquer fear* OVERCOME, get the better of, control, master, get a grip on, deal with, cope with, surmount, rise above, get over; quell, quash, beat, triumph over; *informal* lick.
– OPPOSITES lose.
conqueror ● noun VANQUISHER, conquistador; victor, winner, champion, conquering hero.
conquest ● noun **1** *the conquest of the Aztecs* DEFEAT, vanquishment, annihilation, overthrow, subjugation, rout, mastery, crushing; victory over, triumph over. **2** *their conquest of the valley* SEIZURE, takeover, capture, occupation, invasion, acquisition, appropriation, subjugation, subjection. **3** *the conquest of Everest* ASCENT. **4** *she's his latest conquest* CATCH, acquisition, prize, slave; admirer, fan, worshipper; lover, boyfriend, girlfriend; *informal* fancy man, fancy woman.
– OPPOSITES victory, surrender.
conscience ● noun SENSE OF RIGHT AND WRONG, moral sense, inner voice; morals, standards, values, principles, ethics, beliefs; compunction, scruples, qualms.
conscience-stricken ● adjective GUILT-RIDDEN, remorseful, ashamed, shamefaced, apologetic, sorry; chastened, contrite, guilty, regretful, rueful, repentant, penitent, self-reproachful, abashed, sheepish, compunctious.
– OPPOSITES unrepentant.
conscientious ● adjective DILIGENT, industrious, punctilious, painstaking, sedulous, assiduous, dedicated, careful, meticulous, thorough, attentive, hard-working, studious, rigorous, particular; religious, strict.
– OPPOSITES casual.
conscious ● adjective **1** *the patient was conscious* AWARE, awake, alert, responsive, sentient, compos mentis. **2** *he became conscious of people talking* AWARE OF, alert to, mindful of, sensible of; *formal* cognizant of; *archaic* ware of. **3** *a conscious effort* DELIBERATE, intentional, intended, purposeful, purposive, knowing, considered, calculated, wilful, premeditated, planned, volitional; *Law, dated* prepense.
– OPPOSITES unaware.
conscript ● verb *they were conscripted into the army* CALL UP, enlist, recruit; *US* draft; *historical* press, impress.
● noun *an army conscript* compulsorily enlisted soldier, recruit; *US* draftee.
– OPPOSITES volunteer.
consecrate ● verb SANCTIFY, bless, make holy, make sacred; dedicate to God, devote, reserve, set apart; anoint, ordain; *formal* hallow.
consecutive ● adjective SUCCESSIVE, succeeding, following, in succession, running, in a row, one after the other, back-to-back, continuous, straight, uninterrupted; *informal* on the trot.
consensus ● noun **1** *there was consensus among delegates* AGREEMENT, harmony, concurrence, accord, unity, unanimity, solidarity; *formal* concord. **2** *the consensus was that they should act* GENERAL OPINION, majority opinion, common view.
– OPPOSITES disagreement.
consent ● noun *the consent of all members* AGREEMENT, assent, acceptance, approval, approbation; permission, authorization, sanction, leave; backing, endorsement, support; *informal* go-ahead, thumbs up, green light, OK.
– OPPOSITES dissent.
● verb *she consented to surgery* AGREE, assent, yield, give in, submit; allow, give permission for, sanction, accept, approve, go

C

– ORIGIN Latin *consequentia*, from *consequi* 'follow closely'.
consequent ● adjective following as a consequence.
– DERIVATIVES **consequential** adjective **consequently** adverb.
conservancy /kənservənsi/ ● noun (pl. **conservancies**) **1** an organization concerned with the preservation of natural resources. **2** a commission controlling a port, river, or catchment area. **3** conservation.
conservation ● noun **1** preservation or restoration of the natural environment and wildlife. **2** preservation and repair of archaeological, historical, and cultural sites and artefacts. **3** careful use of a resource: *energy conservation*. **4** Physics the principle by which the total value of a quantity (e.g. mass or energy) remains constant in a closed system.
– DERIVATIVES **conservationist** noun.
conservative ● adjective **1** averse to change and holding traditional values. **2** (in a political context) favouring free enterprise, private ownership, and socially conservative ideas. **3** (**Conservative**) relating to a Conservative Party. **4** (of an estimate) purposely low for the sake of caution. ● noun **1** a conservative person. **2** (**Conservative**) a supporter or member of a Conservative Party.
– DERIVATIVES **conservatism** noun **conservatively** adverb.
conservatoire /kənservətwaar/ ● noun a college for the study of classical music or other arts.
– ORIGIN French.
conservator /kənservətər, **kon**sərvaytər/ ● noun a person involved in conservation.
conservatory ● noun (pl. **conservatories**) **1** Brit. a room with a glass roof and walls, attached to a house and used as a sun lounge or a greenhouse. **2** chiefly N. Amer. a conservatoire.
conserve /kənserv/ ● verb **1** protect from harm, destruction, or wasteful overuse. **2** Physics maintain (a quantity) at a constant overall total. ● noun /also **kon**serv/ fruit jam.
– ORIGIN Latin *conservare* 'to preserve'.
consider ● verb **1** think carefully about. **2** believe or think. **3** take into account when making a judgement. **4** look attentively at.
– ORIGIN Latin *considerare* 'examine', perhaps from *sidus* 'star'.
considerable ● adjective **1** notably large. **2** significant or notable.
– DERIVATIVES **considerably** adverb.
considerate ● adjective careful not to harm or inconvenience others.
– DERIVATIVES **considerately** adverb.
consideration ● noun **1** careful thought. **2** a fact taken into account when making a decision. **3** thoughtfulness towards others. **4** a payment or reward.
– PHRASES **in consideration of** in return for.
considering ● preposition & conjunction taking into consideration. ● adverb informal taking everything into account.
consign /kənsīn/ ● verb **1** deliver to someone's possession or care. **2** send (goods) by a public carrier. **3** (**consign to**) put (someone or something) in (a place) so as to be rid of them.
– DERIVATIVES **consignee** noun **consignor** noun.
– ORIGIN Latin *consignare* 'mark with a seal'.
consignment ● noun a batch of goods consigned.

Thesaurus

along with.
– OPPOSITES forbid.
consequence ● noun **1** *a consequence of inflation* RESULT, upshot, outcome, out-turn, effect, repercussion, ramification, corollary, concomitant, aftermath; fruit(s), product, by-product, end result; *informal* pay-off; *Medicine* sequela. **2** *the past is of no consequence* IMPORTANCE, import, significance, account, substance, note, mark, prominence, value, concern, interest; *formal* moment.
– OPPOSITES cause.
consequent ● adjective RESULTING, resultant, ensuing, consequential; following, subsequent, successive; attendant, accompanying, concomitant; collateral, associated, related.
consequential ● adjective **1** *a fire and the consequential smoke damage* RESULTING, resultant, ensuing, consequent; following, subsequent; attendant, accompanying, concomitant; collateral, associated, related. **2** *one of his more consequential initiatives* IMPORTANT, significant, major, momentous, weighty, material, appreciable, memorable, far-reaching, serious.
– OPPOSITES insignificant.
consequently ● adverb AS A RESULT, as a consequence, so, thus, therefore, ergo, accordingly, hence, for this/that reason, because of this/that, on this/that account; inevitably, necessarily.
conservation ● noun PRESERVATION, protection, safeguarding, safe keeping; care, guardianship, husbandry, supervision; upkeep, maintenance, repair, restoration; ecology, environmentalism.
conservative ● adjective **1** *the conservative wing of the party* RIGHT-WING, reactionary, traditionalist; *Brit.* Tory, blimpish; *US* Republican; *informal* true blue. **2** *the conservative trade-union movement* TRADITIONALIST, traditional, conventional, orthodox, old-fashioned, dyed-in-the-wool, hidebound, unadventurous, set in one's ways; moderate, middle-of-the-road; *informal* stick in the mud. **3** *a conservative suit* CONVENTIONAL, sober, modest, plain, unobtrusive, restrained, subtle, low-key, demure; *informal* square, straight. **4** *a conservative estimate* LOW, cautious, understated, moderate, reasonable.
– OPPOSITES socialist, radical, ostentatious.
● noun *liberals and conservatives have found common ground* RIGHT-WINGER, reactionary, rightist, diehard; *Brit.* Tory, blimp; *US* Republican.
conservatory ● noun **1** *a frost-free conservatory* SUMMER HOUSE, belvedere; glasshouse, greenhouse, hothouse. **2** *a teaching job at the conservatory* CONSERVATOIRE, music school, drama school.
conserve ● verb *fossil fuel should be conserved* PRESERVE, protect, save, safeguard, keep, look after; sustain, prolong, perpetuate; store, reserve, husband.
– OPPOSITES squander.
● noun *cherry conserve* JAM, preserve, jelly, marmalade, confiture.
consider ● verb **1** *Isabel considered her choices* THINK ABOUT, contemplate, reflect on, examine, review; mull over, ponder, deliberate on, chew over, meditate on, ruminate on; assess, evaluate, weigh up, appraise; *informal* size up. **2** *I consider him irresponsible* DEEM, think, believe, judge, adjudge, rate, count, find; regard as, hold to be, reckon to be, view as, see as. **3** *he considered the ceiling* LOOK AT, contemplate, observe, regard, survey, view, scrutinize, scan, examine, inspect; *informal* check out; *N. Amer. informal* eyeball. **4** *the inquiry will consider those issues* TAKE INTO CONSIDERATION, take account of, make allowances for, bear in mind, be mindful of, remember, mind, mark, respect, heed, note, make provision for.
– OPPOSITES ignore.
considerable ● adjective **1** *a considerable amount of money* SIZEABLE, substantial, appreciable, significant; goodly, fair, hefty, handsome, decent, worthwhile; ample, plentiful, abundant, great, large, generous; *informal* tidy, not to be sneezed at. **2** *considerable success* MUCH, great, a lot of, lots of, a great deal of, plenty of, a fair amount of. **3** *a considerable cricketer* DISTINGUISHED, noteworthy, important, significant, prominent, eminent, influential, illustrious; renowned, celebrated, acclaimed.
– OPPOSITES paltry, minor.
considerably ● adverb GREATLY, (very) much, a great deal, a lot, lots; significantly, substantially, appreciably, markedly, noticeably; *informal* plenty, seriously.
considerate ● adjective ATTENTIVE, thoughtful, solicitous, mindful, heedful; obliging, accommodating, helpful, cooperative, patient; kind, unselfish, compassionate, sympathetic, caring, charitable, altruistic, generous; polite, sensitive, tactful.
consideration ● noun **1** *your case needs careful consideration* THOUGHT, deliberation, reflection, contemplation, rumination, meditation; examination, inspection, scrutiny, analysis, discussion; attention, regard; *formal* cogitation. **2** *his health is the prime consideration* FACTOR, issue, matter, concern, detail, aspect, feature. **3** *firms should show more consideration* ATTENTIVENESS, concern, care, thoughtfulness, solicitude; kindness, understanding, respect, sensitivity, tact, discretion; compassion, charity, benevolence. **4** *I might do it, for a consideration* PAYMENT, fee, premium, remuneration, compensation; commission, percentage, dividend; *informal* cut, slice, piece of the action; *formal* emolument.
– PHRASES **take something into consideration** CONSIDER, give thought to, take into account, allow for, provide for, plan for, make provision for, accommodate, bargain for, reckon with; foresee, anticipate.
considering ● preposition *considering his size he was speedy* BEARING IN MIND, taking into consideration, taking into account, keeping in mind, in view of, in the light of.
● adverb *(informal) he'd been lucky, considering* ALL THINGS CONSIDERED, all in all, on the whole, at the end of the day, when all's said and done.
consign ● verb **1** *he was consigned to prison* SEND, deliver, hand

consist • verb **1** (**consist of**) be composed of. **2** (**consist in**) have as an essential feature.
– ORIGIN Latin *consistere* 'stand firm or still, exist'.
consistency (also **consistence**) • noun (pl. **consistencies**) **1** the state of being consistent. **2** the degree of thickness or viscosity of a substance.
consistent • adjective **1** conforming to a regular pattern; unchanging. **2** (usu. **consistent with**) in agreement.
– DERIVATIVES **consistently** adverb.
consistory /kənsistəri/ • noun (pl. **consistories**) **1** (in the Roman Catholic Church) the council of cardinals, with or without the Pope. **2** (also **consistory court**) (in the Church of England) a court presided over by a bishop, for the administration of ecclesiastical law in a diocese.
– ORIGIN Latin *consistorium*, from *consistere* 'stand firm, exist'.
consolation /konsəlaysh'n/ • noun **1** comfort received after a loss or disappointment. **2** a source of such comfort.
– DERIVATIVES **consolatory** /kənsollətri/ adjective.
consolation prize • noun a prize given to a competitor who just fails to win.
console[1] /kənsōl/ • verb comfort in a time of grief of disappointment.
– ORIGIN Latin *consolari*, from *solari* 'soothe'.
console[2] /konsōl/ • noun **1** a panel or unit accommodating a set of controls. **2** (also **games console**) a small machine for playing computerized video games. **3** the cabinet containing the keyboards, stops, etc. of an organ. **4** an ornamental bracket or corbel.
– ORIGIN French.
consolidate /kənsollidayt/ • verb **1** make stronger or more solid. **2** combine into a single unit.
– DERIVATIVES **consolidation** noun **consolidator** noun.
– ORIGIN Latin *consolidare*, from *solidus* 'solid'.
consommé /kənsommay/ • noun a clear soup made with concentrated stock.
– ORIGIN French, 'consummated, completed'.
consonance /konsənənss/ • noun **1** agreement or compatibility. **2** the recurrence of similar-sounding consonants, especially in prosody.
consonant /konsənənt/ • noun **1** a speech sound in which the breath is at least partly obstructed and which forms a syllable when combined with a vowel. **2** a letter representing such a sound. • adjective (**consonant with**) in agreement or harmony with.
– DERIVATIVES **consonantal** adjective.
– ORIGIN Latin *consonare* 'sound together', from *sonus* 'sound'.
consort[1] • noun /konsort/ **1** a wife, husband, or companion, especially the spouse of a monarch. **2** a ship sailing in company with another. • verb /kənsort/ (**consort with**) habitually associate with.
– ORIGIN Latin *consors* 'sharing, partner'.
consort[2] /konsort/ • noun a small group of musicians performing together, typically playing Renaissance music.
– ORIGIN earlier form of CONCERT.
consortium /kənsortiəm/ • noun (pl. **consortia** /kənsortiə/ or **consortiums**) an association, typically of several companies.
– ORIGIN Latin, 'partnership'.
conspectus /kənspektəss/ • noun a summary or overview of a subject.
– ORIGIN Latin, 'a view or survey'.
conspicuous /kənspikyooəss/ • adjective **1** clearly visible. **2** attracting notice; notable: *conspicuous bravery*.
– DERIVATIVES **conspicuously** adverb.
– ORIGIN Latin *conspicuus*, from *conspicere* 'look at attentively'.
conspiracist • noun a supporter of a conspiracy theory.
conspiracy • noun (pl. **conspiracies**) **1** a secret plan by a group to do something unlawful or harmful. **2** the action of conspiring.
conspiracy theory • noun a belief that some covert but influential organization is responsible for an unexplained event.
conspire • verb **1** jointly make secret plans to commit a wrongful act. **2** (of circumstances) seem to be acting together in bringing about an unfortunate result.
– DERIVATIVES **conspirator** noun **conspiratorial** adjective **conspiratorially** adverb.
– ORIGIN Latin *conspirare* 'agree, plot', from *spirare* 'breathe'.
constable • noun Brit. a police officer.
– ORIGIN originally denoting the governor of a royal castle: from Old French *conestable*, from Latin *comes stabuli* 'count, or head officer, of the stable'.
constabulary /kənstabyooləri/ • noun (pl. **constabularies**) chiefly Brit. a police force.
constant • adjective **1** occurring continuously. **2** remaining the

Thesaurus

over, turn over, sentence; confine in, imprison in, incarcerate in, lock up in; *informal* put away, put behind bars; *Brit. informal* bang up. **2** *the picture was consigned for sale* ASSIGN, allocate, place, put, remit, hand down. **3** *the package was consigned by a local company* SEND (OFF), dispatch, transmit, convey, post, mail, ship. **4** *I consigned her picture to the bin* DEPOSIT, commit, banish, relegate.
consignment • noun DELIVERY, shipment, load, boatload, truckload, cargo; batch; goods.
consist • verb **1** *the exhibition consists of 180 drawings* BE COMPOSED, be made up, be formed; comprise, contain, include, incorporate. **2** *style consists in the choices that writers make* BE INHERENT, lie, reside, be present, be contained; be expressed by.
consistency • noun **1** *the trend shows a degree of consistency* UNIFORMITY, constancy, regularity, evenness, steadiness, stability, equilibrium; dependability, reliability. **2** *cream of pouring consistency* THICKNESS, density, viscosity, heaviness, texture; firmness, solidity.
consistent • adjective **1** *consistent opinion-poll evidence* CONSTANT, regular, uniform, steady, stable, even, unchanging, undeviating, unfluctuating; dependable, reliable, predictable. **2** *her injuries were consistent with a knife attack* COMPATIBLE, congruous, consonant, in tune, in line, reconcilable; corresponding to, conforming to.
– OPPOSITES irregular, incompatible.
consolation • noun COMFORT, solace, sympathy, compassion, pity, commiseration; relief, help, (moral) support, encouragement, reassurance.
console[1] • verb *she tried to console him* COMFORT, solace, condole with, sympathize with, commiserate with, show compassion for; help, support, cheer (up), hearten, encourage, reassure, soothe.
– OPPOSITES upset.
console[2] • noun *a digital console* CONTROL PANEL, instrument panel, dashboard, keyboard, keypad; *informal* dash.
consolidate • verb **1** *we consolidated our position in the market* STRENGTHEN, secure, stabilize, reinforce, fortify; enhance, improve. **2** *consolidate the results into an action plan* COMBINE, unite, merge, integrate, amalgamate, fuse, synthesize, bring together, unify.
consonance • noun AGREEMENT, accord, harmony, unison; compatibility, congruity, congruence; *formal* concord.
consonant • adjective
– PHRASES **consonant with** IN AGREEMENT WITH, consistent with, in accordance with, in harmony with, compatible with, congruous with, in tune with.
consort • noun *the queen and her consort* PARTNER, companion, mate; spouse, husband, wife.
• verb *he consorted with other women* ASSOCIATE, keep company, mix, go around, spend time, socialize, fraternize, have dealings; *informal* run around, hang around/round, hang out, be thick; *Brit. informal* hang about.
conspicuous • adjective EASILY SEEN, clear, visible, noticeable, discernible, perceptible, detectable; obvious, manifest, evident, apparent, marked, pronounced, prominent, patent, crystal clear; striking, eye-catching, overt, blatant, writ large; distinct, recognizable, unmistakable, inescapable; *informal* as plain as the nose on one's face, standing out like a sore thumb, standing out a mile.
conspiracy • noun **1** *a conspiracy to manipulate the race results* PLOT, scheme, plan, machination, ploy, trick, ruse, subterfuge; *informal* racket. **2** *conspiracy to murder* PLOTTING, collusion, intrigue, connivance, machination, collaboration; treason.
conspirator • noun PLOTTER, schemer, intriguer, colluder, collaborator, conniver, machinator.
conspire • verb **1** *they admitted conspiring to steal cars* PLOT, scheme, plan, intrigue, machinate, collude, connive, collaborate, work hand in glove; *informal* be in cahoots. **2** *circumstances conspired against them* ACT TOGETHER, work together, combine, unite, join forces; *informal* gang up.
constancy • noun **1** *constancy between lovers* FIDELITY, faithfulness, loyalty, commitment, dedication, devotion; dependability, reliability, trustworthiness. **2** *the constancy of Henry's views* STEADFASTNESS, resolution, resolve, firmness, fixedness; determin-

same. **3** faithful and dependable. ● **noun 1** an unchanging situation. **2** Mathematics & Physics a number or quantity that does not change its value.
– DERIVATIVES **constancy** noun **constantly** adverb.
– ORIGIN Old French, from Latin *constare* 'stand firm'.
constellation ● **noun** a group of stars forming a recognized pattern and typically named after a mythological or other figure.
– ORIGIN Latin, from *stella* 'star'.
consternation ● **noun** anxiety or dismay.
– ORIGIN Latin, from *consternare* 'terrify, prostrate'.
constipate ● **verb** (usu. **be constipated**) affect with constipation.
– ORIGIN Latin *constipare* 'crowd or press together'.
constipation ● **noun** a difficulty in emptying the bowels, associated with hardened faeces.
constituency /kənstityooənsi/ ● **noun** (pl. **constituencies**) **1** a body of voters in a specified area who elect a representative to a legislative body. **2** chiefly Brit. the area represented in this way.
constituent ● **adjective 1** being a part of a whole. **2** having the power to appoint or elect. **3** able to make or change a political constitution. ● **noun 1** a member of a constituency. **2** a component part.
– ORIGIN Latin, from *constituere* 'establish, appoint'.
constitute /konstityoot/ ● **verb 1** be (a part) of a whole. **2** be or be equivalent to. **3** (usu. **be constituted**) establish by law.
– ORIGIN Latin *constituere* 'establish, appoint', from *statuere* 'set up'.
constitution ● **noun 1** a body of fundamental principles or established precedents according to which a state or organization is governed. **2** composition or formation. **3** a person's physical or mental state.
constitutional ● **adjective 1** relating to or in accordance with a constitution. **2** relating to a person's physical or mental state. ● **noun** dated a walk taken regularly to maintain good health.
– DERIVATIVES **constitutionality** noun **constitutionally** adverb.
constitutive ● **adjective 1** having the power to establish something. **2** forming a constituent of something.
– DERIVATIVES **constitutively** adverb.
constrain ● **verb 1** compel or force towards a course of action. **2** (**constrained**) appearing forced. **3** severely restrict the scope, extent, or activity of.
– DERIVATIVES **constrainedly** adverb.
– ORIGIN Old French *constraindre*, from Latin *constringere* 'bind tightly together'.
constraint ● **noun 1** a limitation or restriction. **2** stiffness of manner and inhibition.
constrict ● **verb 1** make or become narrower, especially by encircling pressure; tighten. **2** deprive of freedom of movement.
– DERIVATIVES **constriction** noun **constrictive** adjective.
– ORIGIN from Latin *constringere* 'bind tightly together'.
constrictor ● **noun 1** a snake that kills by constricting and asphyxiating its prey, such as a boa or python. **2** a muscle whose contraction narrows a vessel or passage.
construct ● **verb** /kənstrukt/ **1** build or erect. **2** form (a theory) from various conceptual elements. ● **noun** /konstrukt/ **1** an idea or theory containing various conceptual elements. **2** a thing constructed.
– DERIVATIVES **constructor** noun.
– ORIGIN from Latin *construere* 'heap together, build'.
construction ● **noun 1** the action or process of constructing. **2** a building or other structure. **3** the industry of erecting buildings. **4** an interpretation or explanation.
– DERIVATIVES **constructional** adjective.
constructive ● **adjective 1** serving a useful purpose. **2** Law derived by inference; not stated explicitly.

Thesaurus

ation, perseverance, tenacity, doggedness, staunchness, staying power, obstinacy. **3** *a constancy of human motive* CONSISTENCY, permanence, persistence, durability, endurance; uniformity, immutability, regularity, stability, steadiness.
constant ● **adjective 1** *the constant background noise* CONTINUAL, continuous, persistent, sustained, round-the-clock; ceaseless, unceasing, perpetual, incessant, never-ending, eternal, endless, unabating, non-stop, unrelieved; interminable, unremitting, relentless. **2** *keep a constant speed* CONSISTENT, regular, steady, uniform, even, invariable, unvarying, unchanging, undeviating, unfluctuating. **3** *a constant friend* FAITHFUL, loyal, devoted, true, fast, firm, unswerving; steadfast, staunch, dependable, trustworthy, trusty, reliable, dedicated, committed. **4** *constant vigilance* STEADFAST, steady, resolute, determined, tenacious, dogged, unwavering, unflagging.
– OPPOSITES fitful, variable, fickle.
● **noun** *dread of cancer has been a constant* UNCHANGING FACTOR, given.
constantly ● **adverb** ALWAYS, all the time, continually, continuously, persistently; round-the-clock, night and day, {morning, noon, and night}; endlessly, non-stop, incessantly, unceasingly, perpetually, eternally, forever; interminably, unremittingly, relentlessly; Scottish aye; informal 24-7.
– OPPOSITES occasionally.
consternation ● **noun** DISMAY, perturbation, distress, disquiet, discomposure; surprise, amazement, astonishment; alarm, panic, fear, fright, shock.
– OPPOSITES satisfaction.
constituent ● **adjective** *constituent parts* COMPONENT, integral; elemental, basic, essential, inherent.
● **noun 1** *MPs must listen to their constituents* VOTER, elector, member of a constituency. **2** *the constituents of tobacco* COMPONENT, ingredient, element; part, piece, bit, unit; section, portion.
constitute ● **verb 1** *farmers constituted 10 per cent of the population* AMOUNT TO, add up to, account for, form, make up, compose, comprise. **2** *this constitutes a breach of copyright* BE EQUIVALENT TO, be, embody, be tantamount to, be regarded as. **3** *the courts were constituted in 1875* INAUGURATE, establish, initiate, found, create, set up, start, form, organize, develop; commission, charter, invest, appoint, install, empower.
constitution ● **noun 1** *the constitution guarantees our rights* CHARTER, social code, law; bill of rights; rules, regulations, fundamental principles. **2** *the chemical constitution of the dye* COMPOSITION, make-up, structure, construction, arrangement, configuration, formation, anatomy; informal set-up. **3** *she has the constitution of an ox* HEALTH, physique, physical condition, shape, fettle.
constitutional ● **adjective 1** *constitutional powers* LEGAL, lawful, legitimate, authorized, permitted; sanctioned, ratified, warranted, constituted, statutory, chartered, vested, official; by law. **2** *a constitutional weakness* INHERENT, intrinsic, innate, fundamental, essential, organic; congenital, inborn, inbred.
● **noun** *(dated) she went out for a constitutional.* See WALK noun sense 1.
constrain ● **verb 1** *he felt constrained to explain* COMPEL, force, drive, impel, oblige, coerce, prevail on, require; press, push, pressure, pressurize. **2** *prices were constrained by state controls* RESTRICT, limit, curb, check, restrain, contain, rein in, hold back, keep down.
constrained ● **adjective** *his constrained manner* UNNATURAL, awkward, self-conscious, forced, stilted, strained; restrained, reserved, reticent, guarded.
– OPPOSITES relaxed.
constraint ● **noun 1** *financial constraints* RESTRICTION, limitation, curb, check, restraint, control, damper, rein; hindrance, impediment, obstruction, handicap. **2** *they were able to talk without constraint* INHIBITION, uneasiness, embarrassment; restraint, reticence, guardedness, formality; self-consciousness, forcedness, awkwardness, stiltedness.
constrict ● **verb 1** *fat constricts the blood vessels* NARROW, make narrower, tighten, compress, contract, squeeze, strangle, strangulate; archaic straiten. **2** *fear of crime constricts many people's lives* RESTRICT, impede, limit, inhibit, obstruct, interfere with, hinder, hamper.
– OPPOSITES expand, dilate.
constriction ● **noun** TIGHTNESS, pressure, compression, contraction; obstruction, blockage, impediment; Medicine stricture, stenosis.
construct ● **verb 1** *a new motorway was being constructed* BUILD, erect, put up, set up, raise, establish, assemble, manufacture, fabricate, create, make. **2** *he constructed a faultless argument* FORMULATE, form, put together, create, devise, design, compose, work out; fashion, mould, shape, frame.
– OPPOSITES demolish.
construction ● **noun 1** *the construction of a new airport* BUILDING, erection, putting up, setting up, establishment; assembly, manufacture, fabrication, creation. **2** *the station was a spectacular construction* STRUCTURE, building, edifice, pile. **3** *you could put an hon-*

– DERIVATIVES **constructively** adverb **constructiveness** noun.
constructive dismissal ● noun the changing of an employee's job with the aim of forcing resignation.
construe ● verb (**construes**, **construed**, **construing**) (often **be construed**) interpret in a particular way.
– DERIVATIVES **construable** adjective **construal** noun.
– ORIGIN Latin *construere* 'heap together, build'.
consubstantiation /konsəbstanshiaysh'n/ ● noun Christian Theology the doctrine that the substance of the bread and wine coexists with the body and blood of Christ in the Eucharist. Compare with TRANSUBSTANTIATION.
consul /kons'l/ ● noun **1** a state official living in a foreign city and protecting the state's citizens and interests there. **2** (in ancient Rome) one of two elected chief magistrates who ruled the republic jointly for a year.
– DERIVATIVES **consular** /**kon**syoolər/ adjective **consulship** noun.
– ORIGIN Latin, related to *consulere* 'take counsel'.
consulate ● noun **1** the place where a consul works. **2** (in ancient Rome) the period of office of a consul or the system of government by consuls.
consult ● verb **1** seek information or advice from. **2** seek permission or approval from. **3** (**consulting**) engaged in the business of giving advice to others in the same field.
– DERIVATIVES **consultation** noun **consultative** adjective **consultee** noun.
– ORIGIN Latin *consultare*, from *consulere* 'take counsel'.
consultancy ● noun (pl. **consultancies**) a professional practice giving expert advice in a particular field.
consultant ● noun **1** a person who provides expert advice professionally. **2** Brit. a hospital doctor of senior rank.
consumable ● adjective intended to be used up and then replaced. ● noun a consumable commodity.
consume ● verb **1** eat or drink. **2** use up. **3** (especially of a fire) completely destroy. **4** (of a feeling) absorb all of the attention and energy of.
– DERIVATIVES **consuming** adjective.
– ORIGIN Latin *consumere*, from *sumere* 'take up'.
consumer ● noun a person who buys a product or service for personal use.
consumerism ● noun **1** the protection or promotion of the interests of consumers. **2** the preoccupation of society with the acquisition of goods.
– DERIVATIVES **consumerist** adjective & noun.
consummate ● verb /**kon**syoomayt/ **1** make (a marriage or relationship) complete by having sexual intercourse. **2** complete (a transaction). ● adjective /**kon**syoomət, **kon**səmət/ showing great skill and flair.
– DERIVATIVES **consummately** adverb **consummation** noun **consummator** noun.
– ORIGIN Latin *consummare* 'bring to completion'.
consumption ● noun **1** the action or process of consuming. **2** an amount consumed. **3** dated a wasting disease, especially tuberculosis.
– DERIVATIVES **consumptive** adjective & noun (dated).
contact ● noun /**kon**takt/ **1** the state or condition of physical touching. **2** (before another noun) caused by or operating through physical touch: *contact dermatitis.* **3** the state or condition of communicating or meeting. **4** a meeting or communication set up with someone. **5** a person who may be asked for information or assistance. **6** a person who has associated with a patient with a contagious disease. **7** a connection for the passage of an electric current from one thing to another. ● verb /**kon**takt, kən**takt**/ get in touch or communication with.
– DERIVATIVES **contactable** adjective.
– ORIGIN Latin *contactus*, from *contingere* 'touch, border on'.
contact lens ● noun a thin plastic lens placed directly on the surface of the eye to correct visual defects.
contact print ● noun a photographic print made by placing a negative directly on to sensitized paper, glass, or film and illuminating it.
contact sport ● noun a sport in which the participants necessarily come into bodily contact with one another.
contagion /kən**tay**jən/ ● noun the communication of disease from one person to another by close contact.
– ORIGIN Latin, from *con-* 'together with' + *tangere* 'to touch'.
contagious ● adjective **1** (of a disease) spread by direct or indirect contact between people or organisms. **2** having a contagious disease. **3** (of an emotion, attitude, etc.) likely to spread to and affect others.
– DERIVATIVES **contagiously** adverb **contagiousness** noun.
contain ● verb **1** have or hold within. **2** control or restrain. **3** prevent (a problem) from becoming worse.
– DERIVATIVES **containable** adjective.
– ORIGIN Latin *continere*, from *tenere* 'to hold'.

Thesaurus

est construction on their conduct INTERPRETATION, reading, meaning, explanation, explication, construal; *informal* take.
constructive ● adjective USEFUL, helpful, productive, positive, encouraging; practical, valuable, profitable, worthwhile.
construe ● verb INTERPRET, understand, read, see, take, take to mean, regard.
consul ● noun AMBASSADOR, diplomat, chargé d'affaires, attaché, envoy, emissary, plenipotentiary; *archaic* legate.
consult ● verb **1** *you need to consult a solicitor* SEEK ADVICE FROM, ask, take counsel from, call on/upon, speak to, turn to, have recourse to; *informal* pick someone's brains. **2** *the government must consult with interested parties* CONFER, have discussions, talk things over, exchange views, communicate, parley, deliberate; *informal* put their heads together. **3** *she consulted her diary* REFER TO, turn to, look at.
consultant ● noun **1** *an engineering consultant* ADVISER, expert, specialist, authority, pundit. **2** *a consultant at Guy's hospital* SENIOR DOCTOR, specialist.
consultation ● noun **1** *the need for further consultation with industry* DISCUSSION, dialogue, discourse, debate, negotiation, deliberation. **2** *a 30-minute consultation* MEETING, talk, discussion, interview, audience, hearing; appointment, session; *formal* confabulation, colloquy.
consume ● verb **1** *vast amounts of food and drink were consumed* EAT, devour, ingest, swallow, gobble up, wolf down, guzzle, feast on, snack on; DRINK, gulp down, imbibe, sup; *informal* tuck into, put away, polish off, dispose of, pig oneself on, down, neck, sink, swill; *Brit. informal* scoff, gollop, shift; *N. Amer. informal* scarf (down/up), snarf (down/up). **2** *natural resources are being consumed at an alarming rate* USE (UP), utilize, expend; deplete, exhaust; waste, squander, drain, dissipate, fritter away. **3** *the fire consumed fifty houses* DESTROY, demolish, lay waste, wipe out, annihilate, devastate, gut, ruin, wreck. **4** *Carolyn was consumed with guilt* EAT UP, devour, obsess, grip, overwhelm; absorb, preoccupy.
consumer ● noun PURCHASER, buyer, customer, shopper; user, end-user; client; (**the consumer** or consumers) the public, the market.
consuming ● adjective ABSORBING, compelling, compulsive, besetting, obsessive, overwhelming; intense, ardent, strong, powerful, burning, raging, fervid, profound, deep-seated.
consummate ● verb *the deal was finally consummated* COMPLETE, conclude, finish, accomplish, achieve; execute, carry out, perform; *informal* sew up, wrap up; *formal* effectuate.
● adjective *his consummate skill | a consummate politician* SUPREME, superb, superlative, superior, accomplished, expert, proficient, skilful, skilled, masterly, master, first-class, talented, gifted, polished, practised, perfect, ultimate; complete, total, utter, absolute, pure.
consumption ● noun **1** *food unfit for human consumption* EATING, drinking, ingestion. **2** *the consumption of fossil fuels* USE, using up, utilization, expending, depletion; waste, squandering, dissipation.
contact ● noun **1** *a disease transmitted through direct contact with rats* TOUCH, touching; proximity, exposure. **2** *foreign diplomats were asked to avoid all contact with him* COMMUNICATION, correspondence, touch; association, connection, intercourse, relations, dealings; *archaic* traffic. **3** *he had many contacts in Germany* CONNECTION, acquaintance, associate, friend.
● verb *anyone with information should contact the police* GET IN TOUCH WITH, communicate with, make contact with, approach, notify; telephone, phone, call, ring up, speak to, talk to, write to; *informal* get hold of.
contagion ● noun *(dated)* DISEASE, infection, illness, plague, blight; *informal* bug, virus; *archaic* pestilence.
contagious ● adjective INFECTIOUS, communicable, transmittable, transmissible, spreadable; *informal* catching; *dated* infective.
contain ● verb **1** *the archive contains much unpublished material* INCLUDE, comprise, take in, incorporate, involve, encompass, embrace; consist of, be made up of, be composed of. **2** *the boat contained four people* HOLD, carry, accommodate, seat. **3** *he must con-*

C

container ● noun **1** a box, cylinder, or similar object for holding something. **2** a large standard-sized metal box for the transport of goods by road, rail, sea, or air.

containerize (also **containerise**) ● verb pack into or transport by container.
– DERIVATIVES **containerization** noun.

containment ● noun the action of keeping something harmful under control.

contaminate ● verb make impure by exposure to or addition of a poisonous or polluting substance.
– DERIVATIVES **contaminant** noun **contamination** noun **contaminator** noun.
– ORIGIN Latin *contaminare* 'make impure', from *contamen* 'contact, pollution'.

contemn /kəntem/ ● verb archaic treat or regard with contempt.
– DERIVATIVES **contemner** /kəntemm(n)ər/ noun.
– ORIGIN Latin *contemnere*, from *temnere* 'despise'.

contemplate /kontəmplayt/ ● verb **1** look at thoughtfully. **2** think about. **3** think profoundly and at length. **4** have as a probable intention.
– DERIVATIVES **contemplator** noun.
– ORIGIN Latin *contemplari* 'survey, observe, contemplate', from *templum* 'place for observation'.

contemplation ● noun **1** the action of contemplating. **2** religious meditation.

contemplative /kəntemplətiv/ ● adjective expressing or involving contemplation. ● noun a person whose life is devoted to prayer, especially in a monastery or convent.
– DERIVATIVES **contemplatively** adverb.

contemporaneous /kəntempərayniəss/ ● adjective existing at or occurring in the same period of time.
– DERIVATIVES **contemporaneity** noun **contemporaneously** adverb **contemporaneousness** noun.
– ORIGIN Latin, from *tempus* 'time'.

contemporary /kəntempərəri/ ● adjective **1** living, occurring, or originating at the same time. **2** belonging to or occurring in the present. **3** modern in style or design. ● noun (pl. **contemporaries**) **1** a person or thing existing at the same time as another. **2** a person of roughly the same age as another.
– ORIGIN Latin *contemporarius*, from *tempus* 'time'.

contempt ● noun **1** the feeling that a person or a thing is worthless or beneath consideration. **2** (also **contempt of court**) the offence of being disobedient to or disrespectful of a court of law.
– PHRASES **beneath contempt** utterly worthless or despicable. **hold in contempt** despise.
– ORIGIN Latin *contemptus*, from *temnere* 'despise'.

contemptible ● adjective deserving contempt.
– DERIVATIVES **contemptibly** adverb.

contemptuous ● adjective showing contempt.
– DERIVATIVES **contemptuously** adverb **contemptuousness** noun.

contend ● verb **1** (**contend with/against**) struggle to deal with (a difficulty). **2** (**contend for**) engage in a struggle or campaign to achieve. **3** assert as a position in an argument.
– DERIVATIVES **contender** noun.
– ORIGIN Latin *contendere*, from *tendere* 'stretch, strive'.

content[1] /kəntent/ ● adjective in a state of peaceful happiness or satisfaction. ● verb **1** satisfy; please. **2** (**content oneself with**) accept (something) as adequate despite wanting something more or better. ● noun **1** a state of happiness or satisfaction. **2** a member of the British House of Lords who votes for a motion.
– PHRASES **to one's heart's content** to the full extent of one's desires.
– DERIVATIVES **contentment** noun.
– ORIGIN Latin *contentus* 'satisfied', from *tenere* 'to hold'.

content[2] /kontent/ ● noun **1** (**contents**) the things that are contained in something. **2** the amount of a particular constituent occurring in a substance: *soya milk has a low fat content.* **3** (**contents** or **table of contents**) a list of chapters or sections at the front of a book or periodical. **4** the material dealt with in a speech or text as distinct from its form or style.
– ORIGIN Latin *contentum* 'thing contained'.

contented ● adjective **1** happy and at ease. **2** willing to accept something; satisfied.
– DERIVATIVES **contentedly** adverb **contentedness** noun.

contention ● noun **1** heated disagreement. **2** an assertion.
– PHRASES **in contention** having a good chance of success in a contest.
– ORIGIN Latin, from *contendere* 'contend'.

contentious ● adjective **1** causing or likely to cause disagree-

Thesaurus

tain his anger RESTRAIN, curb, rein in, suppress, repress, stifle, subdue, quell, swallow, bottle up, hold in, keep in check; control, master.

container ● noun RECEPTACLE, vessel, holder, repository.

contaminate ● verb POLLUTE, adulterate; defile, debase, corrupt, taint, infect, foul, spoil, soil, stain, sully; poison.
– OPPOSITES purify.

contemplate ● verb **1** *she contemplated her image in the mirror* LOOK AT, view, regard, examine, inspect, observe, survey, study, scrutinize, scan, stare at, gaze at, eye. **2** *he contemplated his fate* THINK ABOUT, ponder, reflect on, consider, mull over, muse on, dwell on, deliberate over, meditate on, ruminate on, chew over, brood on/about, turn over in one's mind; formal cogitate. **3** *he was contemplating action for damages* CONSIDER, think about, have in mind, intend, plant, propose; envisage, foresee.

contemplation ● noun **1** *the contemplation of beautiful objects* VIEWING, examination, inspection, observation, survey, study, scrutiny. **2** *the monks sat in quiet contemplation* THOUGHT, reflection, meditation, consideration, rumination, deliberation, reverie, introspection, brown study; formal cogitation, cerebration.

contemplative ● adjective THOUGHTFUL, pensive, reflective, meditative, musing, ruminative, introspective, brooding, deep/lost in thought, in a brown study.

contemporary ● adjective **1** *contemporary sources* OF THE TIME, of the day, contemporaneous, concurrent, coeval, coexisting, coexistent. **2** *contemporary society* MODERN, present-day, present, current, present-time. **3** *a very contemporary design* MODERN, up to date, up to the minute, fashionable; modish, latest, recent; informal trendy, with it.
– OPPOSITES old-fashioned, out of date.
● noun *Chaucer's contemporaries* PEER, fellow; formal compeer.

contempt ● noun **1** *she regarded him with contempt* SCORN, disdain, disrespect, scornfulness, contemptuousness, derision; disgust, loathing, hatred, abhorrence; archaic despite. **2** *he is guilty of contempt of court* DISRESPECT, disregard, slighting.
– OPPOSITES respect.

contemptible ● adjective DESPICABLE, detestable, hateful, reprehensible, deplorable, unspeakable, disgraceful, shameful, ignominious, abject, low, mean, cowardly, unworthy, discreditable, petty, worthless, shabby, cheap, beyond contempt, beyond the pale, sordid; archaic scurvy.
– OPPOSITES admirable.

contemptuous ● adjective SCORNFUL, disdainful, disrespectful, insulting, insolent, derisive, mocking, sneering, scoffing, withering, scathing, snide; condescending, supercilious, haughty, proud, superior, arrogant, dismissive, aloof; informal high and mighty, snotty, sniffy; archaic contumelious.
– OPPOSITES respectful.

contend ● verb **1** *the pilot had to contend with torrential rain* COPE WITH, face, grapple with, deal with, take on, pit oneself against. **2** *three main groups were contending for power* COMPETE, vie, contest, fight, battle, tussle, go head to head; strive, struggle. **3** *he contends that the judge was wrong* ASSERT, maintain, hold, claim, argue, insist, state, declare, profess, affirm; allege; formal aver.

content[1] ● adjective *she seemed content with life* CONTENTED, satisfied, pleased, gratified, fulfilled, happy, cheerful, glad; unworried, untroubled, at ease, at peace, tranquil, serene.
– OPPOSITES discontented, dissatisfied.
● verb *her reply seemed to content him* SATISFY, please; soothe, pacify, placate, appease, mollify.
● noun *a time of content.* See CONTENTMENT.

content[2] ● noun **1** *foods with a high fibre content* AMOUNT, proportion, quantity. **2** (**contents**) *the contents of a vegetarian sausage* CONSTITUENTS, ingredients, components, elements. **3** (**contents**) *the book's list of contents* CHAPTERS, sections, divisions. **4** *the content of the essay* SUBJECT MATTER, subject, theme, argument, thesis, message, thrust, substance, matter, material, text, ideas.

contented ● adjective *a contented man.* See CONTENT[1] adjective.

contention ● noun **1** *a point of contention* DISAGREEMENT, dispute, disputation, argument, discord, conflict, friction, strife, dissension, disharmony. **2** *the Marxist contention that capitalism equals exploitation* ARGUMENT, claim, plea, submission, allegation, assertion, declaration; opinion, stand, position, view, belief, thesis, case.

ment or controversy. **2** given to provoking argument. **3** Law relating to or involving differences between contending parties.
– DERIVATIVES **contentiously** adverb **contentiousness** noun.

conterminous /konterminəss/ ● adjective **1** sharing a common boundary. **2** having the same area, context, or meaning.
– DERIVATIVES **conterminously** adverb.
– ORIGIN Latin *conterminus*, from *terminus* 'boundary'.

contest ● noun /**kon**test/ **1** an event in which people compete for supremacy. **2** a dispute or conflict. ● verb /kən**test**/ **1** compete to attain (a position of power). **2** take part in (a competition or election). **3** challenge or dispute.
– PHRASES **no contest** a decision to declare a boxing match invalid on the grounds that one or both of the boxers are not making serious efforts.
– DERIVATIVES **contestable** adjective **contester** noun.
– ORIGIN originally in the sense 'swear to, attest': from Latin *contestari* 'call upon to witness, initiate an action (by calling witnesses)'.

contestant ● noun a person who takes part in a contest.

context ● noun **1** the circumstances that form the setting for an event, statement, or idea. **2** the parts that immediately precede and follow a word or passage and clarify its meaning.
– DERIVATIVES **contextual** adjective **contextualize** (also **contextualise**) verb **contextually** adverb.
– ORIGIN originally denoting the construction of a text: from Latin *contextus*, from *texere* 'to weave'.

contiguous /kəntigyooəss/ ● adjective **1** sharing a common border. **2** next or together in sequence.
– DERIVATIVES **contiguity** noun **contiguously** adverb.
– ORIGIN Latin *contiguus* 'touching'.

continent[1] ● noun **1** any of the world's main continuous expanses of land (Europe, Asia, Africa, North and South America, Australia, Antarctica). **2** (also **the Continent**) the mainland of Europe as distinct from the British Isles.
– ORIGIN from Latin *terra continens* 'continuous land'.

continent[2] ● adjective **1** able to control movements of the bowels and bladder. **2** exercising self-restraint, especially sexually.
– DERIVATIVES **continence** noun **continently** adverb.
– ORIGIN from Latin *continere*, from *tenere* 'to hold'.

continental ● adjective **1** forming or belonging to a continent. **2** (also **Continental**) coming from or characteristic of mainland Europe. ● noun (also **Continental**) a person from mainland Europe.

continental breakfast ● noun a light breakfast of coffee and bread rolls with butter and jam.

continental climate ● noun a relatively dry climate with very hot summers and very cold winters, characteristic of the central parts of Asia and North America.

continental drift ● noun the gradual movement of the continents across the earth's surface through geological time.

continental quilt ● noun Brit. a duvet.

continental shelf ● noun an area of seabed around a large land mass where the sea is relatively shallow.

contingency /kəntinjənsi/ ● noun (pl. **contingencies**) **1** a future event or circumstance which is possible but cannot be predicted with certainty. **2** a provision for such an event or circumstance. **3** the absence of certainty in events.

contingent /kən**tin**jənt/ ● adjective **1** subject to chance. **2** (**contingent on/upon**) dependent on. **3** (of losses, liabilities, etc.) that can be anticipated to arise if a particular event occurs. ● noun **1** a group of people with a common feature, forming part of a larger group. **2** a body of troops or police sent to join a larger force.
– DERIVATIVES **contingently** adverb.
– ORIGIN from Latin *contingere* 'befall'.

continual ● adjective **1** constantly or frequently occurring. **2** having no interruptions.
– DERIVATIVES **continually** adverb.

continuance ● noun formal **1** the state of continuing. **2** the time for which a situation or action lasts.

continuation ● noun **1** the action of continuing or the state of being continued. **2** a part that is attached to and is an extension of something else.

continue ● verb (**continues**, **continued**, **continuing**) **1** persist in an activity or process. **2** remain in existence, operation, or a specified state. **3** carry on with. **4** carry on travelling in the same direction. **5** recommence or resume.
– DERIVATIVES **continuator** noun.
– ORIGIN Latin *continuare*, from *continuus* 'uninterrupted'.

continuity /kontinyooiti/ ● noun (pl. **continuities**) **1** the unbroken and consistent existence or operation of something. **2** a connection or line of development with no sharp breaks. **3** the maintenance of continuous action and self-consistent detail in the scenes of a film or broadcast. **4** the linking of broadcast items by a spoken commentary.

Thesaurus

– OPPOSITES agreement.
– PHRASES **in contention** IN COMPETITION, competing, contesting, contending, vying; striving, struggling.

contentious ● adjective **1** *a contentious issue* CONTROVERSIAL, disputable, debatable, disputed, open to debate, moot, vexed. **2** *a contentious debate* HEATED, vehement, fierce, violent, intense, impassioned. **3** *contentious people.* See QUARRELSOME.

contentment ● noun CONTENTEDNESS, content, satisfaction, gratification, fulfilment, happiness, pleasure, cheerfulness; ease, comfort, well-being, peace, equanimity, serenity, tranquillity.

contest ● noun **1** *a boxing contest* COMPETITION, match, tournament, game, meet, event, trial, bout, heat, fixture, tie, race. **2** *the contest for the party leadership* FIGHT, battle, tussle, struggle, competition, race.
● verb **1** *he intended to contest the seat* COMPETE FOR, contend for, vie for, fight for, try to win, go for, throw one's hat in the ring. **2** *we contested the decision* OPPOSE, object to, challenge, take a stand against, take issue with, question, call into question. **3** *the issues have been hotly contested* DEBATE, argue about, dispute, quarrel over.

contestant ● noun COMPETITOR, participant, player, contender, candidate, aspirant, entrant; rival, opponent, adversary, antagonist.

context ● noun **1** *the wider historical context* CIRCUMSTANCES, conditions, factors, state of affairs, situation, background, scene, setting. **2** *a quote taken out of context* FRAME OF REFERENCE, contextual relationship; text, subject, theme, topic.

contiguous ● adjective ADJACENT, neighbouring, adjoining, bordering, next-door; abutting, connecting, touching, in contact, proximate.

continent ● adjective SELF-RESTRAINED, self-disciplined, abstemious, abstinent, self-denying, ascetic; chaste, celibate, monkish, monastic, virginal.

contingency ● noun EVENTUALITY, (chance) event, incident, happening, occurrence, juncture, possibility, fortuity, accident, chance, emergency.

contingent ● adjective **1** *the merger is contingent on government approval* DEPENDENT ON, conditional on, subject to, determined by, hinging on, resting on. **2** *contingent events* CHANCE, accidental, fortuitous, possible, unforeseeable, unpredictable, random, haphazard.
● noun **1** *a contingent of Japanese businessmen* GROUP, party, body, band, company, cohort, deputation, delegation; informal bunch, gang. **2** *a contingent of marines* DETACHMENT, unit, group.

continual ● adjective **1** *a service disrupted by continual breakdowns* FREQUENT, repeated, constant, recurrent, recurring, regular. **2** *she was in continual pain* CONSTANT, continuous, unending, never-ending, unremitting, unabating, relentless, unrelenting, unrelieved, chronic, uninterrupted, unbroken, round-the-clock.
– OPPOSITES occasional, temporary.

continuance ● noun. See CONTINUATION.

continuation ● noun CARRYING ON, continuance, extension, prolongation, protraction, perpetuation.
– OPPOSITES end.

continue ● verb **1** *he was unable to continue with his job* CARRY ON, proceed, pursue, go on, keep on, persist, press on, persevere, keep at; informal stick at, soldier on. **2** *discussions continued throughout the year* GO ON, carry on, last, extend, be prolonged, run on, drag on. **3** *we are keen to continue this relationship* MAINTAIN, keep up, sustain, keep going, keep alive, preserve. **4** *his willingness to continue in office* REMAIN, stay, carry on, keep going. **5** *we continued our conversation after supper* RESUME, pick up, take up, carry on with, return to, recommence.
– OPPOSITES stop, break off.

continuing ● adjective ONGOING, continuous, sustained, persistent, steady, relentless, uninterrupted, unabating, unremitting, unrelieved, unceasing.
– OPPOSITES sporadic.

C

continuo /kəntinyoo-ō/ (also **basso continuo**) ● noun (pl. **continuos**) (in baroque music) an accompanying part which includes a bass line and harmonies, typically played on a keyboard instrument.
– ORIGIN from Italian *basso continuo* 'continuous bass'.

continuous ● adjective **1** without interruption. **2** forming a series with no exceptions or reversals.
– DERIVATIVES **continuously** adverb **continuousness** noun.

continuous assessment ● noun Brit. the evaluation of a pupil's progress throughout a course of study, as distinct from by examination.

continuum ● noun (pl. **continua**) a continuous sequence in which adjacent elements are not perceptibly different from each other, but the extremes are quite distinct.
– ORIGIN Latin, from *continuus* 'uninterrupted'.

contort ● verb twist or bend out of its normal shape.
– DERIVATIVES **contortion** noun.
– ORIGIN Latin *contorquere* 'twist round, brandish'.

contortionist ● noun an entertainer who twists and bends their body into strange and unnatural positions.

contour ● noun **1** an outline, especially one representing or bounding the shape or form of something. **2** (also **contour line**) a line on a map joining points of equal height above or below sea level. ● verb **1** mould into a specific shape. **2** (**contoured**) (of a map or diagram) marked with contours. **3** (of a road or railway) follow the outline of (a topographical feature).
– ORIGIN French, from Italian *contornare* 'draw in outline'.

contra- ● prefix **1** against; opposite: *contraception*. **2** (of musical instruments or organ stops) pitched an octave below: *contrabass*.
– ORIGIN Latin *contra* 'against'.

contraband /kontrəband/ ● noun **1** goods that have been imported or exported illegally. **2** trade in smuggled goods. ● adjective **1** imported or exported illegally. **2** relating to traffic in illegal goods.
– DERIVATIVES **contrabandist** noun.
– ORIGIN Italian *contrabando*, from *contra-* 'against' + *bando* 'proclamation, ban'.

contraception ● noun the use of contraceptives.

contraceptive ● adjective **1** preventing conception. **2** relating to contraception. ● noun a device or drug used to prevent conception.

contract ● noun /kontrakt/ **1** a written or spoken agreement intended to be enforceable by law. **2** informal an arrangement for someone to be killed by a hired assassin. ● verb /kəntrakt/ **1** decrease in size, number, or range. **2** (of a muscle) become shorter and tighter in order to move part of the body. **3** shorten (a word or phrase) by omitting or merging letters or words. **4** enter into a formal and legally binding agreement. **5** (**contract in/out**) Brit. choose to be or not to be involved in. **6** (**contract out**) arrange for (work) to be done by another organization. **7** catch or develop (a disease). **8** become liable to pay (a debt).
– DERIVATIVES **contractive** adjective **contractual** adjective **contractually** adverb.
– ORIGIN from Latin *contractus*, from *contrahere* 'draw together, tighten'.

contractable ● adjective (of a disease) able to be caught.

contract bridge ● noun the standard form of the card game bridge, in which only tricks bid and won count towards the game.

contractible ● adjective able to be shrunk or capable of contracting.

contractile /kəntraktīl/ ● adjective Biology & Physiology capable of or producing contraction.
– DERIVATIVES **contractility** noun.

contraction ● noun **1** the process of contracting. **2** a shortening of the muscles of the womb occurring at intervals during childbirth. **3** a word or group of words resulting from contracting an original form.

contractor ● noun a person who undertakes a contract to provide materials or labour for a job.

contradict ● verb **1** deny the truth of (a statement) by asserting the opposite. **2** challenge (someone) by making a statement opposing one made by them.
– DERIVATIVES **contradictor** noun.
– ORIGIN Latin *contradicere* 'speak against'.

contradiction ● noun **1** a combination of statements, ideas, or features which are opposed to one another. **2** the statement of a position opposite to one already made.
– PHRASES **contradiction in terms** a statement or group of words associating incompatible objects or ideas.

contradictory ● adjective **1** mutually opposed or inconsistent. **2** containing inconsistent elements.
– DERIVATIVES **contradictorily** adverb **contradictoriness** noun.

contradistinction ● noun distinction made by contrasting the different qualities of two things.

contraflow ● noun Brit. a temporary arrangement by which the lanes of a dual carriageway or motorway normally carrying traffic in one direction become two-directional.

contraindicate ● verb Medicine (of a condition or circumstance) suggest or indicate that (a particular technique or drug) should not be used.
– DERIVATIVES **contraindication** noun.

contralto /kəntraltō/ ● noun (pl. **contraltos**) the lowest female singing voice.
– ORIGIN Italian.

contraption ● noun a machine or device that appears strange

Thesaurus

continuity ● noun CONTINUOUSNESS, uninterruptedness, flow, progression.

continuous ● adjective CONTINUAL, uninterrupted, unbroken, constant, ceaseless, incessant, steady, sustained, solid, continuing, ongoing, unceasing, without a break, non-stop, round-the-clock, persistent, unremitting, relentless, unrelenting, unabating, unrelieved, without respite, endless, unending, never-ending, perpetual, everlasting, eternal, interminable; consecutive, running; N. Amer. without surcease.
– OPPOSITES intermittent.

contort ● verb TWIST, bend out of shape, distort, misshape, warp, buckle, deform.

contour ● noun OUTLINE, shape, form; lines, curves, figure; silhouette, profile.

contraband ● noun *contraband was suspected* SMUGGLING, illegal traffic, black marketeering, bootlegging; the black market.
● adjective *contraband goods* SMUGGLED, black-market, bootleg, under the counter, illegal, illicit, unlawful; prohibited, banned, proscribed, forbidden; informal hot.

contract ● noun *a legally binding contract* AGREEMENT, commitment, arrangement, settlement, understanding, compact, covenant, bond; deal, bargain; Law indenture.
● verb **1** *the market for such goods began to contract* SHRINK, get smaller, decrease, diminish, reduce, dwindle, decline. **2** *her stomach muscles contracted* TIGHTEN, tense, flex, constrict, draw in, narrow. **3** *she contracted her brow* WRINKLE, knit, crease, purse, pucker. **4** *his name was soon contracted to 'Jack'* SHORTEN, abbreviate, cut, reduce; elide. **5** *the company contracted to rebuild the stadium* UNDERTAKE, pledge, promise, covenant, commit oneself, engage, agree, enter an agreement, make a deal. **6** *she contracted German measles* DEVELOP, catch, get, pick up, come down with, be struck down by, be stricken with, succumb to; Brit. go down with. **7** *he contracted a debt of £3,300* INCUR, run up.
– OPPOSITES expand, relax, lengthen.
– PHRASES **contract something out** SUBCONTRACT, outsource, farm out.

contraction ● noun **1** *the contraction of the industry* SHRINKING, shrinkage, decline, decrease, diminution, dwindling. **2** *the contraction of muscles* TIGHTENING, tensing, flexing. **3** *my contractions started at midnight* LABOUR PAINS, labour; cramps; poetic/literary travail. **4** *'goodbye' is a contraction of 'God be with you'* ABBREVIATION, short form, shortened form, elision, diminutive.

contradict ● verb **1** *he contradicted the government's account of the affair* DENY, refute, rebut, dispute, challenge, counter, controvert; formal gainsay. **2** *nobody dared to contradict him* ARGUE AGAINST, go against, challenge, oppose; formal gainsay. **3** *this research contradicts previous computer models* CONFLICT WITH, be at odds with, be at variance with, be inconsistent with, run counter to, disagree with.
– OPPOSITES confirm, agree with.

contradiction ● noun **1** *the contradiction between his faith and his lifestyle* CONFLICT, clash, disagreement, opposition, inconsistency, mismatch, variance. **2** *a contradiction of his statement* DENIAL, refutation, rebuttal, countering, counterstatement.
– OPPOSITES confirmation, agreement.

contradictory ● adjective OPPOSED, in opposition, opposite, anti-

or unnecessarily complicated.
– ORIGIN perhaps from CONTRIVE, by association with TRAP[1].
contrapuntal /kontrəpunt'l/ ● *adjective* Music of or in counterpoint.
– DERIVATIVES **contrapuntally** adverb **contrapuntist** noun.
– ORIGIN from Italian *contrapunto* 'counterpoint'.
contrariety /kontrərīəti/ ● *noun* opposition or inconsistency between two things.
contrariwise /kəntrairiwīz/ ● *adverb* **1** in the opposite way. **2** on the other hand.
contrary /kontrəri/ ● *adjective* **1** opposite in nature, direction, or meaning. **2** (of two or more statements, beliefs, etc.) opposed to one another. **3** /kəntrairi/ perversely inclined to do the opposite of what is expected or desired. ● *noun* (**the contrary**) the opposite.
– PHRASES **to the contrary** with the opposite meaning or implication.
– DERIVATIVES **contrarily** adverb **contrariness** noun.
– ORIGIN Latin *contrarius*, from *contra* 'against'.
contrast ● *noun* /kontraast/ **1** the state of being noticeably different from something else when put or considered together. **2** a thing or person noticeably different from another. **3** the degree of difference between tones in a television picture, photograph, etc. **4** enhancement of appearance provided by juxtaposing different colours or textures. ● *verb* /kəntraast/ **1** differ noticeably. **2** compare so as to emphasize differences.
– DERIVATIVES **contrastive** adjective.
– ORIGIN Latin *contrastare*, from *stare* 'stand'.
contravene /kontrəveen/ ● *verb* **1** commit an act that is not in accordance with (a law, treaty, etc.). **2** conflict with (a right, principle, etc.).
– DERIVATIVES **contravener** noun **contravention** noun.
– ORIGIN Latin *contravenire*, from *venire* 'come'.
contretemps /kontrətoN/ ● *noun* (pl. same or /kontrətoNz/) a minor dispute or disagreement.
– ORIGIN originally meaning 'motion out of time' and denoting a thrust in fencing made at an inopportune moment: from French.
contribute /kəntribyoot, kontribyoot/ ● *verb* **1** give in order to help achieve or provide something. **2** (**contribute to**) help to cause or bring about.
– DERIVATIVES **contribution** noun **contributive** /kəntribyootiv/ adjective **contributor** noun.
– USAGE The first pronunciation, which puts the stress on **-tri-**, is held to be the only correct one, despite the fact that the alternative, with the stress on **con-**, is older.
– ORIGIN Latin *contribuere* 'bring together, add'.
contributory ● *adjective* **1** playing a part in bringing something about. **2** (of a pension or insurance scheme) operated by means of a fund into which people pay.
con trick ● *noun* informal a confidence trick.
contrite /kəntrīt, kontrīt/ ● *adjective* feeling or expressing remorse.
– DERIVATIVES **contritely** adverb **contriteness** noun **contrition** noun.
– ORIGIN Latin *contritus*, from *conterere* 'grind down, wear away'.
contrivance ● *noun* **1** the action of contriving. **2** an ingenious device or scheme.
contrive /kəntrīv/ ● *verb* **1** devise or plan using skill and artifice. **2** manage to do something foolish.
– DERIVATIVES **contrivable** adjective **contriver** noun.
– ORIGIN Old French *controver* 'imagine, invent', from Latin *contropare* 'compare'.
contrived ● *adjective* deliberately created rather than arising spontaneously.
control ● *noun* **1** the power to influence people's behaviour or the course of events. **2** the restriction of an activity or phenomenon. **3** a means of limiting or regulating something: *exchange controls*. **4** a device by which a machine is regulated. **5** the place where something is verified or from which an activity is directed: *passport control*. **6** a person or thing used as a standard of comparison for checking the results of a survey or experiment. ● *verb* (**controlled**, **controlling**) **1** have control or command of. **2** limit or regulate.
– PHRASES **in control** able to direct a situation, person, or activity. **out of control** no longer manageable. **under control** (of a danger or emergency) being dealt with or contained successfully.
– DERIVATIVES **controllability** noun **controllable** adjective **control-**

C

Thesaurus

thetical, contrary, contrasting, conflicting, at variance, at odds, opposing, clashing, divergent, discrepant, different; inconsistent, incompatible, irreconcilable.
contraption ● *noun* DEVICE, gadget, apparatus, machine, appliance, mechanism, invention, contrivance; *informal* gizmo, widget; *Brit. informal* gubbins; *Austral. informal* bitzer.
contrary ● *adjective* **1** *contrary views* OPPOSITE, opposing, opposed, contradictory, clashing, conflicting, antithetical, incompatible, irreconcilable. **2** *she was sulky and contrary* PERVERSE, awkward, difficult, uncooperative, unhelpful, obstructive, disobliging, recalcitrant, wilful, self-willed, stubborn, obstinate, mulish, pigheaded, intractable; *informal* cussed; *Brit. informal* bloody-minded, bolshie, stroppy; *N. Amer. informal* balky; *formal* refractory; *archaic* froward.
– OPPOSITES compatible, accommodating.
● *noun* *in fact, the contrary is true* OPPOSITE, reverse, converse, antithesis.
– PHRASES **contrary to** IN CONFLICT WITH, against, at variance with, at odds with, in opposition to, counter to, incompatible with.
contrast ● *noun* **1** *the contrast between rural and urban trends* DIFFERENCE, dissimilarity, disparity, distinction, contradistinction, divergence, variance, variation, differentiation; contradiction, incongruity, opposition, polarity; *formal* dissimilitude. **2** *Jane was a complete contrast to Sarah* OPPOSITE, antithesis; foil, complement.
– OPPOSITES similarity.
● *verb* **1** *a view which contrasts with his earlier opinion* DIFFER FROM, be at variance with, be contrary to, conflict with, go against, be at odds with, be in opposition to, disagree with, clash with. **2** *people contrasted her with her sister* COMPARE, set side by side, juxtapose; measure against; distinguish from, differentiate from.
– OPPOSITES resemble, liken.
contravene ● *verb* **1** *he contravened the Official Secrets Act* BREAK, breach, violate, infringe; defy, disobey, flout. **2** *the prosecution contravened the rights of the individual* CONFLICT WITH, be in conflict with, be at odds with, be at variance with, run counter to.
– OPPOSITES comply with.
contravention ● *noun* BREACH, violation, infringement, neglect, dereliction.
contretemps ● *noun* ARGUMENT, quarrel, squabble, disagreement, difference of opinion, dispute; *informal* tiff, set-to, run-in, spat; *Brit. informal* row, barney; *Scottish informal* rammy.
contribute ● *verb* **1** *the government contributed a million pounds* GIVE, donate, put up, subscribe, hand out, grant, bestow, present, provide, supply, furnish; *informal* chip in, pitch in, fork out, shell out, cough up; *Brit. informal* stump up; *N. Amer. informal* kick in, ante up, pony up. **2** *an article contributed by Dr Clouson* SUPPLY, provide, submit. **3** *numerous factors contribute to job satisfaction* PLAY A PART IN, be instrumental in, be a factor in, have a hand in, be conducive to, make for, lead to, cause; *formal* conduce to.
contribution ● *noun* **1** *voluntary financial contributions* DONATION, gift, offering, present, handout, grant, subsidy, allowance, endowment, subscription; *formal* benefaction; *historical* alms. **2** *contributions from local authors* ARTICLE, piece, story, item, chapter, paper, essay.
contributor ● *noun* **1** *the magazine's regular contributors* WRITER, columnist, correspondent. **2** *campaign contributors* DONOR, benefactor, subscriber, supporter, backer, subsidizer, patron, sponsor.
contrite ● *adjective* REMORSEFUL, repentant, penitent, regretful, sorry, apologetic, rueful, sheepish, hangdog, ashamed, chastened, shamefaced, conscience-stricken, guilt-ridden, in sackcloth and ashes.
contrition ● *noun* REMORSE, remorsefulness, repentance, penitence, sorrow, sorrowfulness, regret, ruefulness, pangs of conscience; shame, guilt, compunction; *archaic* rue.
contrivance ● *noun* **1** *a mechanical contrivance* DEVICE, gadget, machine, appliance, contraption, apparatus, mechanism, implement, tool, invention; *informal* gizmo, widget; *Austral. informal* bitzer. **2** *her matchmaking contrivances* SCHEME, stratagem, tactic, manoeuvre, move, plan, ploy, gambit, wile, trick, ruse, plot, machination.
contrive ● *verb* BRING ABOUT, engineer, manufacture, orchestrate, stage-manage, create, devise, concoct, construct, plan, fabricate, plot, hatch; *informal* wangle, set up.
contrived ● *adjective* FORCED, strained, studied, artificial, affected,

C

lably adverb **controller** noun.
– ORIGIN originally in the sense 'verify accounts': from Old French *contreroller* 'keep a copy of a roll of accounts', from Latin *contrarotulus* 'copy of a roll'.
controlling interest • noun the holding by one person or group of a majority of the stock of a business.
control tower • noun a tall building from which the movements of air traffic are monitored and controlled.
controversial • adjective causing or likely to cause controversy.
– DERIVATIVES **controversialist** noun **controversially** adverb.
controversy /kontrəversi, kəntrovvərsi/ • noun (pl. **controversies**) debate or disagreement about a matter which arouses strongly contrasting opinions.
– USAGE The second pronunciation, putting the stress on **-trov-**, is widely held to be incorrect in standard English.
– ORIGIN Latin *controversia*, from *controversus* 'turned against, disputed'.
controvert • verb deny the truth of.
– DERIVATIVES **controvertible** adjective.
– ORIGIN from Latin *controversus* 'turned against, disputed'.
contumacious /kontyoomayshəss/ • adjective archaic or Law stubbornly or wilfully disobedient to authority.
– DERIVATIVES **contumaciously** adverb **contumacy** noun.
– ORIGIN from Latin *contumax*, perhaps from *tumere* 'to swell'.
contumely /kontyōōmli/ • noun (pl. **contumelies**) archaic insolent or insulting language or treatment.
– DERIVATIVES **contumelious** /kontyoomeeliəss/ adjective.
– ORIGIN Latin *contumelia*, perhaps from *tumere* 'to swell'.
contusion /kəntyōōzh'n/ • noun a bruise.
– DERIVATIVES **contuse** verb.
– ORIGIN Latin, from *contundere* 'to bruise, crush'.
conundrum /kənundrəm/ • noun (pl. **conundrums**) **1** a confusing and difficult problem or question. **2** a riddle.
– ORIGIN originally in the sense 'a crank or pedant': of unknown origin.
conurbation /konnurbaysh'n/ • noun an extended urban area, typically consisting of several towns merging with the suburbs of a central city.
– ORIGIN from Latin *urbs* 'city'.
convalesce /konvəless/ • verb gradually recover one's health after an illness or medical treatment.
– ORIGIN Latin *convalescere*, from *valescere* 'grow strong'.
convalescent • adjective recovering from an illness or medical treatment. • noun a convalescent person.
– DERIVATIVES **convalescence** noun.
convection • noun transference of mass or heat within a fluid caused by the tendency of warmer and less dense material to rise.
– DERIVATIVES **convect** verb **convectional** adjective **convective** adjective.
– ORIGIN Latin, from *convehere*, from *vehere* 'carry'.
convector • noun a heating appliance that circulates warm air by convection.
convene /kənveen/ • verb **1** call people together for (a meeting). **2** assemble for a common purpose.
– DERIVATIVES **convenable** adjective.
– ORIGIN Latin *convenire* 'assemble, agree, fit', from *venire* 'come'.
convener (also **convenor**) • noun **1** a person who convenes meetings of a committee. **2** Brit. a senior trade union official at a workplace.
convenience • noun **1** freedom from effort or difficulty. **2** a useful or helpful device or situation. **3** Brit. a public toilet.
– PHRASES **at one's convenience** when or where it suits one. **at one's earliest convenience** as soon as one can without difficulty.
– ORIGIN Latin *convenientia*, from *convenire* 'assemble, agree, fit'.
convenience food • noun a food that has been pre-prepared commercially and so requires little preparation by the consumer.
convenient • adjective **1** fitting in well with a person's needs, activities, and plans. **2** involving little trouble or effort.
– DERIVATIVES **conveniently** adverb.
convenor • noun variant spelling of CONVENER.
convent • noun **1** a Christian community of nuns living under monastic vows. **2** (also **convent school**) a school attached to and run by a convent.
– ORIGIN Old French, from Latin *conventus* 'assembly, company'.
conventicle /kənventik'l/ • noun historical a secret or unlawful religious meeting, especially of nonconformists.
– ORIGIN Latin *conventiculum* 'place of assembly', from *convenire* 'assemble, agree, fit'.
convention • noun **1** a way in which something is usually done. **2** socially acceptable behaviour. **3** an agreement between countries. **4** a large meeting or conference. **5** N. Amer. an assembly of the delegates of a political party to select candidates for office. **6** a body set up by agreement to deal with a particular issue.
– ORIGIN Latin, 'meeting, covenant'.
conventional • adjective **1** based on or in accordance with con-

Thesaurus

put-on, pretended, false, feigned, manufactured, unnatural; laboured, overdone, elaborate.
– OPPOSITES natural.
control • noun **1** *China retained control over the region* JURISDICTION, sway, power, authority, command, dominance, government, mastery, leadership, rule, sovereignty, supremacy, ascendancy; charge, management, direction, supervision, superintendence. **2** *strict import controls* RESTRAINT, constraint, limitation, restriction, check, curb, brake, rein; regulation. **3** *her control deserted her* SELF-CONTROL, self-restraint, self-possession, composure, calmness; *informal* cool. **4** *easy-to-use controls* SWITCH, knob, button, dial, handle, lever. **5** *mission control* HEADQUARTERS, HQ, base, centre of operations, command post.
• verb **1** *one family had controlled the company since its formation* BE IN CHARGE OF, run, manage, direct, administer, head, preside over, supervise, superintend, steer; command, rule, govern, lead, dominate, hold sway over, be at the helm; *informal* head up, be in the driving seat, run the show. **2** *she struggled to control her temper* RESTRAIN, keep in check, curb, check, contain, hold back, bridle, rein in, suppress, repress, master. **3** *public spending was controlled* LIMIT, restrict, curb, cap, constrain; *informal* put the brakes on.
controversial • adjective CONTENTIOUS, disputed, at issue, moot, disputable, debatable, arguable, vexed, tendentious.
controversy • noun DISAGREEMENT, dispute, argument, debate, dissension, contention, disputation, altercation, wrangle, wrangling, quarrel, quarrelling, war of words, storm; cause célèbre; *Brit. informal* row.
contusion • noun BRUISE, discoloration, black-and-blue mark, injury; *Medicine* ecchymosis.
conundrum • noun **1** *the conundrums facing policy-makers in the 1980s* PROBLEM, difficult question, vexed question, difficulty, quandary, dilemma; *informal* poser, facer. **2** *Roderick enjoyed conundrums and crosswords* RIDDLE, puzzle, wordgame; *informal* brainteaser.
convalesce • verb RECUPERATE, get better, recover, get well, get back on one's feet.
convalescence • noun RECUPERATION, recovery, return to health, rehabilitation, improvement.
convalescent • adjective RECUPERATING, recovering, getting better, on the road to recovery, improving; *informal* on the mend.
convene • verb **1** *he convened a secret meeting* SUMMON, call, call together, order; *formal* convoke. **2** *the committee convened for its final session* ASSEMBLE, gather, meet, come together, congregate; *formal* foregather.
convenience • noun **1** *the convenience of the arrangement* EXPEDIENCE, advantageousness, advantage, opportuneness, propitiousness, timeliness; suitability, appropriateness. **2** *for convenience, the handset is wall-mounted* EASE OF USE, usability, usefulness, utility, serviceability, practicality. **3** *the kitchen has all the modern conveniences* APPLIANCE, (labour-saving) device, gadget; amenity, facility; *informal* gizmo, mod con.
convenient • adjective **1** *a convenient time* SUITABLE, appropriate, fitting, fit, suited, opportune, timely, well timed, favourable, advantageous, seasonable, expedient. **2** *a hotel that's convenient for the beach* NEAR (TO), close to, within easy reach of, well situated for, handy for, not far from, just round the corner from; *informal* a stone's throw from, within spitting distance of.
convent • noun NUNNERY, priory, abbey, religious community.
convention • noun **1** *social conventions* CUSTOM, usage, practice, tradition, way, habit, norm; rule, code, canon, punctilio; propriety, etiquette, protocol; *formal* praxis; (**conventions**) mores. **2** *a convention signed by 74 countries* AGREEMENT, accord, protocol, compact, pact, treaty, concordat, entente; contract, bargain, deal.

vention. **2** following social conventions; not individual or adventurous. **3** (of weapons or power) non-nuclear.

– DERIVATIVES **conventionalist** noun **conventionality** noun **conventionalize** (also **conventionalise**) verb **conventionally** adverb.

converge /kənverj/ ● verb **1** come together from different directions so as eventually to meet. **2** (**converge on/upon**) come from different directions and meet at.

– DERIVATIVES **convergent** adjective.

– ORIGIN Latin *convergere*, from *vergere* 'incline'.

conversant ● adjective (**conversant with**) familiar with or knowledgeable about.

conversation ● noun an informal spoken exchange of news and ideas between two or more people.

– DERIVATIVES **conversational** adjective.

conversationalist ● noun a person who is good at or fond of engaging in conversation.

converse[1] ● verb /kənverss/ hold a conversation.

– DERIVATIVES **converser** noun.

– ORIGIN originally in the sense 'live among, be familiar with': from Latin *conversari* 'keep company with'.

converse[2] /konverss/ ● noun a situation, object, or statement that is the opposite of another. ● adjective opposite.

– DERIVATIVES **conversely** adverb.

– ORIGIN Latin *conversus* 'turned about'.

conversion ● noun **1** the action of converting or the state of being converted. **2** Brit. a building that has been converted to a new purpose. **3** Rugby a successful kick at goal after a try, scoring two points.

convert ● verb /kənvert/ **1** change in form, character, or function. **2** change (money, stocks, or units in which a quantity is expressed) into others of a different kind. **3** adapt (a building) to make it suitable for a new purpose. **4** change one's religious faith or other beliefs. **5** Rugby score extra points after (a try) by a successful kick at goal. ● noun /konvert/ a person who has changed their religious faith or other beliefs.

– DERIVATIVES **converter** (also **convertor**) noun.

– ORIGIN Latin *convertere* 'turn about'.

convertible ● adjective **1** able to be converted. **2** (of a car) having a folding or detachable roof. ● noun a convertible car.

– DERIVATIVES **convertibility** noun.

convex /konveks/ ● adjective having an outline or surface that curves outwards like the exterior of a sphere. Compare with CONCAVE.

– DERIVATIVES **convexity** noun **convexly** adverb.

– ORIGIN Latin *convexus* 'vaulted, arched'.

convey /kənvay/ ● verb **1** transport or carry to a place. **2** communicate (an idea, impression, or feeling). **3** Law transfer the title to (property).

– DERIVATIVES **conveyable** adjective **conveyor** (also **conveyer**) noun.

– ORIGIN Latin *conviare* 'escort', from *via* 'way'.

conveyance ● noun **1** the action or process of conveying. **2** formal a means of transport; a vehicle. **3** the legal process of transferring property from one owner to another.

– DERIVATIVES **conveyancer** noun **conveyancing** noun.

conveyor belt ● noun a continuous moving band used for transporting objects from one place to another.

convict ● verb /kənvikt/ declare to be guilty of a criminal offence by the verdict of a jury or the decision of a judge in a court of law. ● noun /konvikt/ a person convicted of a criminal offence and serving a sentence of imprisonment.

– ORIGIN from Latin *convictus* 'demonstrated, convicted', from *convincere* (see CONVINCE).

conviction ● noun **1** an instance of being convicted of a criminal offence. **2** the action or process of convicting. **3** a firmly held belief or opinion. **4** the quality of showing that one is convinced of what one believes or says.

convince ● verb **1** cause to believe firmly in the truth of something. **2** persuade to do something.

– DERIVATIVES **convincer** noun **convincible** adjective.

– ORIGIN Latin *convincere* 'overcome, demonstrate', from *vincere* 'conquer'.

convincing ● adjective **1** able to convince. **2** (of a victory or a winner) leaving no margin of doubt.

Thesaurus

3 *the party's biennial convention* CONFERENCE, meeting, congress, assembly, gathering, summit, convocation, synod, conclave.

conventional ● adjective **1** *the conventional wisdom of the day* ORTHODOX, traditional, established, accepted, received, mainstream, prevailing, prevalent, accustomed, customary. **2** *a conventional railway* NORMAL, standard, regular, ordinary, usual, traditional, typical, common. **3** *a very conventional woman* CONSERVATIVE, traditional, traditionalist, conformist, bourgeois, old-fashioned, of the old school, small-town, suburban; *informal* straight, square, stick-in-the-mud, fuddy-duddy. **4** *a conventional piece of work* UNORIGINAL, formulaic, predictable, stock, unadventurous, unremarkable.

– OPPOSITES unorthodox, original.

converge ● verb **1** *Oxford Circus, a station where three lines converge* MEET, intersect, cross, connect, link up, coincide, join, unite, merge. **2** *90,000 fans converged on Wembley* CLOSE IN ON, bear down on, approach, move towards.

– OPPOSITES diverge, leave.

conversant ● adjective FAMILIAR, acquainted, au fait, au courant, at home, well versed, well informed, knowledgeable, informed, abreast, up to date; *informal* up to speed, clued up, genned up; *formal* cognizant.

conversation ● noun DISCUSSION, talk, chat, gossip, tête-à-tête, heart-to-heart, head-to-head, exchange, dialogue; *informal* confab, jaw, chit-chat; *Brit. informal* chinwag, natter; *N. Amer. informal* gabfest, schmooze; *Austral./NZ informal* yarn; *formal* confabulation, colloquy.

conversational ● adjective **1** *conversational English* INFORMAL, chatty, relaxed, friendly; colloquial, idiomatic. **2** *a conversational man* TALKATIVE, chatty, communicative, forthcoming, expansive, loquacious, garrulous.

converse[1] ● verb *they conversed in low voices* TALK, speak, chat, have a conversation, discourse, communicate; *informal* chew the fat/rag, jaw; *Brit. informal* natter; *N. Amer. informal* visit, shoot the breeze/bull; *Austral./NZ informal* mag; *formal* confabulate.

converse[2] ● noun *the converse is also true* OPPOSITE, reverse, obverse, contrary, antithesis, other side of the coin; *informal* flip side.

conversion ● noun **1** *the conversion of waste into energy* CHANGE, changing, transformation, metamorphosis, transfiguration, transmutation, sea change; *humorous* transmogrification. **2** *the conversion of the building* ADAPTATION, alteration, modification, reconstruction, rebuilding, redevelopment, redesign, renovation, rehabilitation. **3** *his religious conversion* REBIRTH, regeneration, reformation.

convert ● verb **1** *plants convert the sun's energy into chemical energy* CHANGE, turn, transform, metamorphose, transfigure, transmute; *humorous* transmogrify; *technical* permute. **2** *the factory was converted into flats* ADAPT, turn, change, alter, modify, rebuild, reconstruct, redevelop, refashion, redesign, restyle, revamp, renovate, rehabilitate; *N. Amer.* bring up to code; *informal* do up; *N. Amer. informal* rehab. **3** *they sought to convert sinners* PROSELYTIZE, evangelize, bring to God, redeem, save, reform, re-educate, cause to see the light.

● noun *Christian converts* PROSELYTE, neophyte, new believer; *Christianity* catechumen.

convey ● verb **1** *taxis conveyed guests to the station* TRANSPORT, carry, bring, take, fetch, bear, move, ferry, shuttle, shift, transfer. **2** *he conveyed the information to me* COMMUNICATE, pass on, make known, impart, relay, transmit, send, hand on, relate, tell, reveal, disclose. **3** *it's impossible to convey how I felt* EXPRESS, communicate, get across/over, put across/over, indicate, say. **4** *he conveys an air of competence* PROJECT, exude, emit, emanate.

conveyance ● noun **1** *the conveyance of agricultural produce* TRANSPORTATION, transport, carriage, carrying, transfer, movement, delivery; haulage, portage, cartage, shipment, freightage. **2** (*formal*) *three-wheeled conveyances* VEHICLE, means/method of transport; car, bus, coach, van, lorry, truck, bicycle, motorbike, motorcycle.

convict ● verb *he was convicted of indecent assault* FIND GUILTY, sentence; *Brit. informal* be done for.

– OPPOSITES acquit.

● noun *two escaped convicts* PRISONER, inmate; trusty; criminal, offender, lawbreaker, felon; *informal* jailbird, con, (old) lag, crook; *N. Amer. informal* yardbird.

conviction ● noun **1** *his conviction for murder* DECLARATION OF GUILT, sentence, judgement. **2** *his political convictions* BELIEF, opinion, view, thought, persuasion, idea, position, stance, article of faith. **3** *she spoke with conviction* CERTAINTY, certitude, assurance, confidence, sureness, no shadow of a doubt.

– OPPOSITES acquittal, uncertainty.

convince ● verb **1** *he convinced me that I was wrong* MAKE CERTAIN, persuade, satisfy, prove to; assure, put/set someone's mind at

– DERIVATIVES **convincingly** adverb.
convivial /kənvivviəl/ ● adjective **1** (of an atmosphere or event) friendly and lively. **2** (of a person) cheerfully sociable.
– DERIVATIVES **conviviality** noun **convivially** adverb.
– ORIGIN originally in the sense 'fit for a feast': from Latin *convivium* 'a feast'.
convocation /konvəkaysh'n/ ● noun a large formal assembly of people.
– DERIVATIVES **convocational** adjective.
– ORIGIN Latin, from *convocare* 'call together'.
convoke /kənvōk/ ● verb formal call together (an assembly or meeting).
– ORIGIN Latin *convocare*, from *vocare* 'to call'.
convoluted /konvəlōōtid/ ● adjective **1** (of an argument, statement, etc.) extremely complex. **2** intricately folded, twisted, or coiled.
– DERIVATIVES **convolutedly** adverb.
convolution ● noun **1** a coil or twist. **2** the state of being or process of becoming coiled or twisted. **3** a complex argument, statement, etc.
– DERIVATIVES **convolutional** adjective.
– ORIGIN Latin, from *convolvere* 'roll together'.
convolvulus /kənvolvyooləss/ ● noun (pl. **convolvuluses**) a twining plant with trumpet-shaped flowers, some kinds of which are invasive weeds; bindweed.
– ORIGIN Latin, 'bindweed', from *convolvere* 'roll together'.
convoy /konvoy/ ● noun a group of ships or vehicles travelling together under armed protection. ● verb (of a warship or armed troops) accompany (a group of ships or vehicles) for protection.
– PHRASES **in convoy** travelling as a group.
– ORIGIN originally in the senses 'convey' and 'act as escort': from French *convoyer*, from Latin *conviare* 'convey'.
convulsant ● adjective producing convulsions. ● noun a convulsant drug.
convulse /kənvulss/ ● verb **1** suffer convulsions. **2** (**be convulsed**) be caused by an emotion, laughter, or physical stimulus to make sudden, violent, uncontrollable movements.
– DERIVATIVES **convulsive** adjective **convulsively** adverb.
– ORIGIN Latin *convellere* 'pull violently, wrench'.
convulsion ● noun **1** a sudden, violent, irregular movement of the body caused by involuntary contraction of muscles. **2** (**convulsions**) uncontrollable laughter. **3** a violent social or natural upheaval.
cony ● noun (pl. **conies**) variant spelling of CONEY.
coo ● verb (**coos, cooed**) **1** (of a pigeon or dove) make a soft murmuring sound. **2** (of a person) speak in a soft gentle voice. ● noun a cooing sound.
– ORIGIN imitative.
cooee informal ● exclamation used to attract attention.
– PHRASES **within cooee** Austral./NZ within reach.
– ORIGIN imitative of a signal used by Australian Aboriginals and copied by settlers.
cook ● verb **1** prepare (food or a meal) by mixing, combining, and heating the elements or ingredients. **2** (with reference to food) heat or be heated so as to reach an edible state. **3** informal alter dishonestly. **4** (**cook up**) informal concoct (a story, excuse, or plan). ● noun a person who cooks.
– PHRASES **cook someone's goose** informal spoil someone's plans. **too many cooks spoil the broth** proverb if too many people are involved in a task or activity, it will not be done well.
– ORIGIN from Latin *coquus* 'a cook'.
cooker ● noun Brit. **1** an appliance for cooking food, typically consisting of an oven, hob, and grill. **2** informal an apple or other fruit more suitable for cooking than for eating raw.
cookery ● noun (pl. **cookeries**) **1** the practice or skill of preparing and cooking food. **2** N. Amer. a kitchen.
cookhouse ● noun a building used for cooking, especially on a ranch, military camp, etc.
cookie ● noun (pl. **cookies**) **1** N. Amer. a sweet biscuit. **2** informal a person of a specified kind: *she's a tough cookie.*
– PHRASES **the way the cookie crumbles** informal, chiefly N. Amer. the way things turn out, especially when undesirable.
– ORIGIN Dutch *koekje* 'little cake'.
cookie cutter ● noun N. Amer. **1** a device with sharp edges for cutting biscuit dough into a particular shape. **2** (before another noun) denoting something mass-produced or lacking any distinguishing characteristics: *cookie-cutter songwriting.*
cookout ● noun N. Amer. a party or gathering where a meal is cooked and eaten outdoors.
Cook's tour ● noun informal a rapid tour of many places.
– ORIGIN named after the English travel agent Thomas *Cook* (1808–92).
cool ● adjective **1** of or at a fairly low temperature. **2** keeping one from becoming too hot. **3** unfriendly or unenthusiastic. **4** free from anxiety or excitement: *he kept a cool head.* **5** (of jazz) restrained and relaxed. **6** informal fashionably attractive or impressive. **7** informal excellent. **8** (**a cool ——**) informal used to emphasize a specified large amount of money: *a cool £50 million.* ● noun (**the cool**) a fairly low temperature, or a place or time characterized by this: *the cool of the day.* ● verb make or become cool.
– PHRASES **keep** (or **lose**) **one's cool** informal maintain (or fail to maintain) a calm and controlled attitude.
– DERIVATIVES **coolish** adjective **coolly** adverb **coolness** noun.
– ORIGIN Old English, related to COLD.
coolant ● noun a fluid used to cool an engine, nuclear reactor,

Thesaurus

rest. **2** *I convinced her to marry me* PERSUADE, induce, prevail on, get, talk into, win over, cajole, inveigle.
convincing ● adjective **1** *a convincing argument* COGENT, persuasive, plausible, powerful, potent, strong, forceful, compelling, irresistible, telling, conclusive. **2** *a convincing 5–0 win* RESOUNDING, emphatic, decisive, conclusive.
convivial ● adjective FRIENDLY, genial, affable, amiable, congenial, agreeable, good-humoured, cordial, warm, sociable, outgoing, gregarious, clubbable, companionable, hail-fellow-well-met, cheerful, jolly, jovial, lively; enjoyable, festive; *Scottish* couthy.
conviviality ● noun FRIENDLINESS, geniality, affability, amiability, bonhomie, congeniality, cordiality, warmth, good nature, sociability, gregariousness, cheerfulness, good cheer, joviality, jollity, gaiety, liveliness.
convocation ● noun ASSEMBLY, gathering, meeting, conference, convention, congress, council, symposium, colloquium, conclave, synod.
convoke ● verb *(formal)* CONVENE, summon, call together, call.
convoluted ● adjective COMPLICATED, complex, involved, elaborate, serpentine, labyrinthine, tortuous, tangled, Byzantine; confused, confusing, bewildering, baffling.
– OPPOSITES straightforward.
convolution ● noun **1** *crosses adorned with elaborate convolutions* TWIST, turn, coil, spiral, twirl, curl, helix, whorl, loop, curlicue; *Architecture* volute. **2** *the convolutions of the plot* COMPLEXITY, intricacy, complication, twist, turn, entanglement.
convoy ● noun *a convoy of vehicles* GROUP, fleet, cavalcade, motorcade, cortège, caravan, line, train.
● verb *the ship was convoyed by army gunboats* ESCORT, accompany, attend, flank; protect, defend, guard.
convulse ● verb SHAKE UNCONTROLLABLY, go into spasms, shudder, jerk, thrash about.
convulsion ● noun **1** *she had convulsions* FIT, seizure, paroxysm, spasm, attack; throes; *Medicine* ictus. **2** (**convulsions**) *the audience collapsed in convulsions* FITS OF LAUGHTER, paroxysms of laughter, uncontrollable laughter; *informal* hysterics. **3** *the political convulsions of the period* UPHEAVAL, eruption, cataclysm, turmoil, turbulence, tumult, disruption, agitation, disturbance, unrest, disorder.
convulsive ● adjective SPASMODIC, jerky, paroxysmal, violent, uncontrollable.
cook ● verb **1** *Iris had cooked dinner* PREPARE, make, put together; *informal* fix, rustle up; *Brit. informal* knock up. **2** *(informal) he'd been cooking the books* FALSIFY, alter, doctor, tamper with, interfere with, massage, manipulate; *Brit. informal* fiddle. **3** *(informal) what's cooking?* See HAPPEN sense 1.
– PHRASES **cook something up** *(informal)* CONCOCT, devise, contrive, fabricate, trump up, hatch, plot, plan, invent, make up, think up, dream up.
cooking ● noun CUISINE, cookery, baking; food.
– RELATED TERMS culinary.
cool ● adjective **1** *a cool breeze* CHILLY, chill, cold, bracing, brisk, crisp, fresh, refreshing, invigorating; draughty; *informal* nippy; *Brit. informal* parky. **2** *a cool response* UNENTHUSIASTIC, lukewarm, tepid, indifferent, uninterested, apathetic, half-hearted; unfriendly, distant, remote, aloof, cold, chilly, frosty, unwelcoming, unresponsive, offhand, uncommunicative, undemonstrative; *informal* standoffish. **3** *his ability to keep cool in a crisis* CALM, {cool, calm, and collected}, composed, as cool as a cucumber, collected, cool-

or other device.

cooler ● noun **1** a device or container for keeping things cool. **2** N. Amer. a refrigerator. **3** a long drink, especially a mixture of wine, fruit juice, and soda water. **4** (**the cooler**) informal prison or a prison cell.

coolibah /ko͞olibaa/ ● noun a North Australian gum tree which typically grows near watercourses and has very strong, hard wood.
– ORIGIN from an Aboriginal language.

coolie /ko͞oli/ ● noun (pl. **coolies**) **1** dated an unskilled native labourer in India, China, and some other Asian countries. **2** offensive a person from the Indian subcontinent or of Indian descent.
– ORIGIN from a Hindi word meaning 'day-labourer'.

coolie hat ● noun a broad conical hat as worn by labourers in some Asian countries.

cooling-off period ● noun **1** an interval during which the parties in a dispute can try to settle their differences before taking further action. **2** an interval after a sale contract is agreed during which the purchaser can decide to cancel without loss.

cooling tower ● noun a tall, open-topped, cylindrical concrete tower, used for cooling water or condensing steam from an industrial process.

coolth /ko͞olth/ ● noun **1** pleasantly low temperature. **2** informal articles, activities, or people perceived as fashionable.

coombe (also **coomb**) ● noun variant spelling of COMBE.

coon ● noun **1** N. Amer. short for RACCOON. **2** informal, offensive a black person. [ORIGIN slang use of sense 1, from an earlier sense '(sly) fellow'.]

coop /ko͞op/ ● noun a cage or pen for poultry. ● verb (usu. **be cooped up**) confine in a small space.
– ORIGIN Latin *cupa* 'cask, tub'.

co-op /kō op/ ● noun informal a cooperative organization.

cooper ● noun a person who makes or repairs casks and barrels.
– DERIVATIVES **cooperage** noun **coopery** noun.
– ORIGIN from Latin *cupa* 'cask, tub'.

cooperate /kōopərayt/ (also **co-operate**) ● verb **1** work jointly towards the same end. **2** comply with a request.
– DERIVATIVES **cooperant** noun **cooperation** noun **cooperator** noun.
– ORIGIN Latin *cooperari* 'work together'.

cooperative (also **co-operative**) ● adjective **1** involving cooperation. **2** willing to be of assistance. **3** (of a farm, business, etc.) owned and run jointly by its members, with profits or benefits shared among them. ● noun a cooperative organization.
– DERIVATIVES **cooperatively** adverb **cooperativeness** noun.

co-opt ● verb **1** appoint to membership of a committee or other body by invitation of the existing members. **2** divert to a role different from the usual or original one. **3** adopt (an idea or policy) for one's own use.
– DERIVATIVES **co-optation** noun **co-option** noun **co-optive** adjective.
– ORIGIN Latin *cooptare*, from *optare* 'choose'.

coordinate (also **co-ordinate**) ● verb /kōordinayt/ **1** bring the different elements of (a complex activity or organization) into a harmonious or efficient relationship. **2** (**coordinate with**) negotiate with (others) in order to work together effectively. **3** match or harmonize attractively. ● adjective /kōordinət/ equal in rank or importance. ● noun /kōordinət/ **1** Mathematics each of a group of numbers used to indicate the position of a point, line, or plane. **2** (**coordinates**) matching items of clothing.
– DERIVATIVES **coordinative** adjective **coordinator** noun.
– ORIGIN from Latin *ordinare* 'put in order', from *ordo* 'order'.

coordination (also **co-ordination**) ● noun **1** the action or process of coordinating. **2** the ability to move different parts of the body smoothly and at the same time.

coot ● noun **1** (pl. same) an aquatic bird of the rail family with black plumage and a white bill that extends back on to the forehead as a horny shield. **2** (usu. **old coot**) informal a stupid or eccentric person.
– ORIGIN probably Dutch or Low German.

cop informal ● noun a police officer. ● verb (**copped**, **copping**) **1** catch or arrest (an offender). **2** incur (something unwelcome). **3** (**cop off**) have a sexual encounter. **4** (**cop out**) avoid doing something that one ought to do.
– PHRASES **cop hold of** Brit. take hold of. **cop it** Brit. **1** get into trouble. **2** be killed. **not much cop** Brit. not very good.
– ORIGIN perhaps from Old French *caper* 'seize', from Latin *capere*.

copal /kōp'l/ ● noun resin from any of a number of tropical trees, used to make varnish.
– ORIGIN Spanish, from a Nahuatl word meaning 'incense'.

cope[1] ● verb deal effectively with something difficult.
– DERIVATIVES **coper** noun.
– ORIGIN originally in the sense 'meet in battle, come to blows': from Old French *coper*, from Greek *kolaphos* 'a blow with the fist'.

cope[2] ● noun a long, loose cloak worn by a priest or bishop on ceremonial occasions. ● verb (in building) cover (a joint or structure) with a coping.
– ORIGIN Latin *cappa* 'covering for the head', from *caput* 'head'.

copeck ● noun variant spelling of KOPEK.

Copernican system /kəpernikən/ (also **Copernican theory**) ● noun the theory proposed by the Polish astronomer Nicolaus Copernicus (1473–1543) that the sun is the centre of the solar system, with the planets (including the earth) orbiting round it. Compare with PTOLEMAIC SYSTEM.

copier ● noun a machine that makes exact copies of something.

co-pilot ● noun a second pilot in an aircraft.

coping ● noun the top, typically rounded or sloping, course of a

C

Thesaurus

headed, level-headed, self-possessed, controlled, self-controlled, poised, serene, tranquil, unruffled, unperturbed, unmoved, untroubled, imperturbable, placid, phlegmatic; *informal* unflappable, together, laid-back. **4** *a cool lack of morality* BOLD, audacious, nerveless; brazen, shameless, unabashed. **5** *(informal) she thinks she's so cool* FASHIONABLE, stylish, chic, up to the minute, sophisticated; *informal* trendy, funky, with it, hip, big, happening, groovy; *N. Amer. informal* kicky, tony, fly. **6** *(informal) a cool song.* See EXCELLENT.
– OPPOSITES warm, enthusiastic, agitated.
● noun **1** *the cool of the evening* CHILL, chilliness, coldness, coolness. **2** *Ken lost his cool* SELF-CONTROL, control, composure, self-possession, calmness, equilibrium, calm; aplomb, poise, sangfroid, presence of mind.
– OPPOSITES warmth.
● verb **1** *cool the sauce in the fridge* CHILL, refrigerate. **2** *her reluctance did nothing to cool his interest* LESSEN, moderate, diminish, reduce, dampen. **3** *Simpson's ardour had cooled* SUBSIDE, lessen, diminish, decrease, abate, moderate, die down, fade, dwindle, wane. **4** *after a while, she cooled off* CALM DOWN, recover/regain one's composure, compose oneself, control oneself, pull oneself together, simmer down.
– OPPOSITES heat, inflame, intensify.

coop ● noun *a hen coop* PEN, run, cage, hutch, enclosure.
● verb *he hates being cooped up at home* CONFINE, shut in/up, cage (in), pen up/in, keep, detain, trap, incarcerate, immure.

cooperate ● verb **1** *police and social services cooperated in the operation* COLLABORATE, work together, work side by side, pull together, band together, join forces, team up, unite, combine, pool resources, make common cause, liaise. **2** *he was happy to cooperate* BE OF ASSISTANCE, assist, help, lend a hand, be of service, do one's bit; *informal* play ball.

cooperation ● noun **1** *cooperation between management and workers* COLLABORATION, joint action, combined effort, teamwork, partnership, coordination, liaison, association, synergy, give and take, compromise. **2** *thank you for your cooperation* ASSISTANCE, helpfulness, help, helping hand, aid.

cooperative ● adjective **1** *a cooperative effort* COLLABORATIVE, collective, combined, common, joint, shared, mutual, united, concerted, coordinated. **2** *pleasant and cooperative staff* HELPFUL, eager to help, glad to be of assistance, obliging, accommodating, willing, amenable, adaptable.

coordinate ● verb **1** *exhibitions coordinated by a team of international scholars* ORGANIZE, arrange, order, systematize, harmonize, correlate, synchronize, bring together, fit together, dovetail. **2** *care workers coordinate at a local level* COOPERATE, liaise, collaborate, work together, negotiate, communicate, be in contact. **3** *floral designs coordinate with the decor* MATCH, complement, set off; harmonize, blend, fit in, go.

cop *(informal)* ● noun *a traffic cop.* See POLICE OFFICER.
● verb *he tried to cop out of his responsibilities.* See AVOID sense 2.

cope ● verb **1** *she couldn't cope on her own* MANAGE, survive, subsist, look after oneself, fend for oneself, shift for oneself, carry on, get by/through, bear up, hold one's own, keep one's end up, keep one's head above water; *informal* make it, hack it. **2** *his inability to cope with the situation* DEAL WITH, handle, manage, address, face

brick or stone wall.
– ORIGIN from COPE², originally meaning 'dress in a cope', hence 'to cover'.

copious • adjective abundant; plentiful.
– DERIVATIVES **copiously** adverb **copiousness** noun.
– ORIGIN from Latin *copia* 'plenty'.

C

copolymer /kōpollimər/ • noun Chemistry a polymer made by reaction of two different monomers, with units of more than one kind.

copper¹ • noun **1** a red-brown metallic chemical element which is used for electrical wiring and as a component of brass and bronze. **2** (**coppers**) Brit. coins of low value made of copper or bronze. **3** Brit. dated a large copper or iron container for boiling laundry. **4** a reddish-brown colour. • verb cover or coat with copper.
– DERIVATIVES **coppery** adjective.
– ORIGIN from Latin *cyprium aes* 'Cyprus metal' (so named because Cyprus was the chief source).

copper² • noun Brit. informal a police officer.
– ORIGIN from COP.

copper beech • noun a variety of beech tree with purplish-brown leaves.

copper-bottomed • adjective Brit. thoroughly reliable.
– ORIGIN with reference to copper sheathing applied to the bottom of a ship.

copperplate • noun **1** a polished copper plate with a design engraved or etched into it. **2** an elaborate looped style of handwriting. [ORIGIN the copybooks for this were originally printed from copperplates.]

copper sulphate • noun a blue crystalline solid used in electroplating and as a fungicide.

coppice • noun an area of woodland in which the trees or shrubs are periodically cut back to ground level to stimulate growth and provide wood. • verb cut back (a tree or shrub) in this way.
– ORIGIN Old French *copeiz*, from Greek *kolaphus* 'a blow with the fist'.

copra /koprə/ • noun dried coconut kernels, from which oil is obtained.
– ORIGIN Portuguese and Spanish, from an Indian word meaning 'coconut'.

coprolite /koprəlīt/ • noun Palaeontology a piece of fossilized dung.

coprophilia /koprəfilliə/ • noun abnormal interest and pleasure in faeces and defecation.
– ORIGIN from Greek *kopros* 'dung'.

copse • noun a small group of trees.
– ORIGIN shortened form of COPPICE.

Copt /kopt/ • noun **1** a native Egyptian in the Hellenistic and Roman periods. **2** a member of the Coptic Church, the native Christian Church in Egypt.
– ORIGIN Latin *Coptus*, from Greek *Aiguptios* 'Egyptian'.

Coptic • noun the language of the Copts, which survives only in the Coptic Church. • adjective relating to the Copts or their language.

copula /kopyoolə/ • noun Grammar a connecting word, in particular a form of the verb *be* connecting a subject and complement.
– DERIVATIVES **copular** adjective.
– ORIGIN Latin, 'connection, linking of words'.

copulate /kopyoolayt/ • verb have sexual intercourse.
– DERIVATIVES **copulation** noun **copulatory** adjective.
– ORIGIN Latin *copulare* 'fasten together'.

copy • noun (pl. **copies**) **1** a thing made to be similar or identical to another. **2** a single specimen of a particular book, record, etc. **3** matter to be printed. **4** material for a newspaper or magazine article. • verb (**copies**, **copied**) **1** make a copy of. **2** imitate the behaviour or style of.
– ORIGIN Latin *copia* 'abundance', later 'transcript'.

copybook • noun **1** a book containing models of handwriting for learners to imitate. **2** (before another noun) exactly in accordance with established standards: *a copybook landing*.

copycat • noun informal **1** a person who copies another. **2** (before another noun) denoting an action, especially a crime, carried out in imitation of another: *copycat attacks*.

copy-edit • verb edit (text) by checking its consistency and accuracy.
– DERIVATIVES **copy editor** noun.

copyist • noun **1** a person who makes copies. **2** a person who imitates the styles of others, especially in art.

copyright • noun the exclusive legal right, given to the originator or their assignee for a fixed number of years, to publish, perform, film, or record literary, artistic, or musical material, and to authorize others to do the same.

copy typist • noun a person whose job is to type transcripts of written drafts.

copywriter • noun a person who writes the text of advertisements or publicity material.

coq au vin /kok ō VAN/ • noun a casserole of chicken pieces cooked in red wine.
– ORIGIN French, 'cock in wine'.

coquette /kəket/ • noun a woman who flirts.
– DERIVATIVES **coquetry** noun **coquettish** adjective **coquettishly** adverb **coquettishness** noun.
– ORIGIN French, 'wanton female', from *coq* 'cock'.

coracle /korrək'l/ • noun a small, round boat made of wickerwork covered with a watertight material, propelled with a paddle.
– ORIGIN Welsh *corwgl*, related to Scottish Gaelic and Irish *curach* 'small boat'.

coral • noun **1** a hard stony substance secreted by certain marine animals as an external skeleton, typically forming large reefs. **2** precious red coral, used in jewellery. **3** the pinkish-red colour of red coral.
– ORIGIN Greek *korallion, kouralion*.

coralline /korrəlīn/ • adjective **1** derived or formed from coral. **2** pinkish-red. **3** resembling coral.

cor anglais /kor onglay/ • noun (pl. **cors anglais** pronunc. same) an alto woodwind instrument of the oboe family, having a bulbous bell and sounding a fifth lower than the oboe.
– ORIGIN French, 'English horn'.

corbel /korb'l/ • noun a projection jutting out from a wall to support a structure above it.
– DERIVATIVES **corbelled** (US **corbeled**) adjective **corbelling** (US **corbeling**) noun.
– ORIGIN Old French, 'little crow', from Latin *corvus* 'raven' (perhaps because the shape of a corbel is similar to that of a crow's beak).

cord • noun **1** long thin string or rope made from several twisted strands. **2** a length of cord. **3** an anatomical structure resembling a cord (e.g. the spinal cord). **4** an electric flex. **5** corduroy. **6** (**cords**) corduroy trousers. **7** a measure of cut wood (usually 128 cu. ft, 3.62 cubic metres). • verb (usu. **corded**) attach a cord to.
– DERIVATIVES **cording** noun.
– ORIGIN Greek *khordē* 'gut, string of a musical instrument'.

cordate /kordayt/ • adjective Botany & Zoology heart-shaped.
– ORIGIN originally in the sense 'wise', from Latin *cordatus* 'wise', later 'heart-shaped', from *cor* 'heart'.

Thesaurus

(up to), confront, tackle, get to grips with, get through, weather, come to terms with.

copious • adjective ABUNDANT, superabundant, plentiful, ample, profuse, full, extensive, generous, bumper, lavish, fulsome, liberal, overflowing, in abundance, many, numerous; *informal* a gogo, galore; *poetic/literary* plenteous.
– OPPOSITES sparse.

copse • noun THICKET, grove, wood, coppice, stand, clump, brake; *Brit.* spinney; *N. Amer. & Austral./NZ* brush; *archaic* hurst, holt, boscage.

copulate • verb. See HAVE SEX at SEX.

copulation • noun. See SEX sense 1.

copy • noun **1** *a copy of the report* DUPLICATE, facsimile, photocopy, carbon (copy), mimeograph, mimeo; transcript; reprint; *trademark* Xerox, photostat. **2** *a copy of a sketch by Leonardo da Vinci* REPLICA, reproduction, replication, print, imitation, likeness; counterfeit, forgery, fake; *informal* knock-off.
• verb **1** *each form had to be copied* DUPLICATE, photocopy, xerox, photostat, mimeograph, run off, reproduce. **2** *portraits copied from original paintings by Reynolds* REPRODUCE, replicate; forge, fake, counterfeit. **3** *their sound was copied by a lot of jazz players* IMITATE, reproduce, emulate, follow, echo, mirror, parrot, mimic, ape; plagiarize, steal; *informal* rip off.

coquettish • adjective FLIRTATIOUS, flirty, provocative, seductive, inviting, kittenish, coy, arch, teasing, playful; *informal* come-hither, vampish.

cord • noun STRING, thread, thong, lace, ribbon, strap, tape, tie,

cordial ● adjective **1** warm and friendly. **2** heartfelt and sincere. ● noun **1** Brit. a sweet fruit-flavoured drink, sold as a concentrate. **2** chiefly N. Amer. another term for LIQUEUR. **3** a pleasant-tasting medicine.
– DERIVATIVES **cordiality** noun **cordially** adverb.
– ORIGIN Latin *cordialis*, from *cor* 'heart'.

cordite ● noun a smokeless explosive made from nitrocellulose, nitroglycerine, and petroleum jelly.
– ORIGIN from CORD, because of its appearance.

cordless ● adjective (of an electrical appliance or telephone) working without connection to a mains supply or central unit.

cordoba /kordəbə/ ● noun the basic monetary unit of Nicaragua, equal to 100 centavos.
– ORIGIN named after F. Fernández de *Córdoba*, a 16th-century Spanish governor of Nicaragua.

cordon /kord'n/ ● noun **1** a line or circle of police, soldiers, or guards forming a barrier. **2** a fruit tree trained to grow as a single stem. ● verb (**cordon off**) prevent access to or from by means of a cordon.
– ORIGIN Italian *cordone* and French *cordon*; related to CORD.

cordon bleu /kordon blö/ ● adjective Cookery of the highest class. ● noun (pl. **cordons bleus** pronounc. same) a cook of the highest class.
– ORIGIN French, 'blue ribbon' (once signifying the highest order of chivalry in the reign of the Bourbon kings).

cordon sanitaire /kordon sannitair/ ● noun (pl. **cordons sanitaires** pronunc. same) **1** a line or circle of guards positioned around an area infected by disease, preventing anyone from leaving. **2** a measure designed to prevent communication or the spread of undesirable influences.
– ORIGIN French, 'sanitary line'.

corduroy /kordəroy/ ● noun a thick cotton fabric with velvety ribs.
– ORIGIN probably from CORD + *duroy*, denoting a former kind of lightweight worsted.

cordwainer /kordwaynər/ ● noun Brit. archaic a shoemaker.
– ORIGIN Old French *cordewan*, from Spanish *cordobán* 'from Cordoba', with reference to a soft leather originally produced there.

cordwood ● noun wood cut into cords or uniform lengths.

core ● noun **1** the tough central part of various fruits, containing the seeds. **2** the central or most important part of something. **3** the dense metallic or rocky central region of a planet. **4** the central part of a nuclear reactor, which contains the fissile material. ● verb remove the core from (a fruit).
– PHRASES **to the core** to the depths of one's being.
– DERIVATIVES **corer** noun.
– ORIGIN of unknown origin.

coreopsis /korriopsiss/ ● noun a plant of the daisy family, typically with yellow flowers.
– ORIGIN Latin, from Greek *koris* 'bug' + *opsis* 'appearance' (because of the shape of the seed).

co-respondent (also **corespondent**) ● noun a person cited in a divorce case as having committed adultery with the respondent.

core time ● noun Brit. the central part of the working day in a flexitime system, when an employee must be present.

corgi (also **Welsh corgi**) ● noun (pl. **corgis**) a breed of dog with short legs and a foxlike head.
– ORIGIN Welsh, from *cor* 'dwarf' + *ci* 'dog'.

coriander /korriandər/ ● noun an aromatic Mediterranean plant of the parsley family, the leaves and seeds of which are used in cookery.
– ORIGIN Old French *coriandre*, from Greek *koriannon*.

Corinthian /kərinthiən/ ● adjective **1** relating to Corinth, a city in southern Greece and a city state in ancient Greece. **2** denoting the most ornate of the classical orders of architecture, characterized by flared capitals with rows of acanthus leaves. ● noun a person from Corinth.

Coriolis force /korriōliss/ ● noun a force (perpendicular to the direction of motion and to the axis of rotation) which acts on a mass moving in a rotating system and tends to deflect moving objects on the earth (e.g. rotating weather systems) to the right in the northern hemisphere and to the left in the southern.
– ORIGIN named after the French engineer Gaspard *Coriolis* (1792–1843).

cork ● noun **1** the buoyant, light brown substance obtained from the bark of the cork oak. **2** a bottle stopper made of cork. **3** a piece of cork used as a float for a fishing line or net. ● verb **1** close or seal (a bottle) with a cork. **2** (**corked**) (of wine) spoilt by tannin from the cork.
– ORIGIN Dutch and Low German *kork*, from Spanish *alcorque* 'cork-soled sandal', ultimately from Latin *quercus* 'oak, cork oak'.

corkage ● noun a charge made by a restaurant or hotel for serving wine that has been brought in by a customer.

corker ● noun informal an excellent person or thing.
– DERIVATIVES **corking** adjective.

cork oak ● noun an evergreen Mediterranean oak, the bark of which is the source of cork.

corkscrew ● noun a device for pulling corks from bottles, consisting of a spiral metal rod that is inserted into the cork, and a handle. ● verb move or twist in a spiral.

corm ● noun a rounded underground storage organ present in plants such as crocuses and cyclamens, consisting of a swollen stem base covered with scale leaves.
– DERIVATIVES **cormlet** noun.
– ORIGIN Greek *kormos* 'trunk stripped of its boughs'.

cormorant /kormərənt/ ● noun a large diving seabird with a long neck, long hooked bill, and mainly black plumage.
– ORIGIN Old French *cormaran*, from Latin *corvus marinus* 'sea-raven'.

corn[1] ● noun **1** chiefly Brit. the chief cereal crop of a district, especially (in England) wheat or (in Scotland) oats. **2** N. Amer. & Austral./NZ maize. **3** informal something banal or sentimental. ● verb (**corned**) preserved with salt or brine.
– PHRASES **corn on the cob** maize when cooked and eaten straight from the cob.
– ORIGIN Old English.

corn[2] ● noun a small, painful area of thickened skin on the toes or foot, caused by pressure.
– ORIGIN Latin *cornu* 'horn'.

corncob ● noun the central woody part of an ear of maize, to which the grains are attached.

corncrake ● noun a secretive crake inhabiting coarse grasslands, with a distinctive double rasping call.

corn dolly ● noun Brit. a symbolic or decorative model of a human figure, made of plaited straw.

cornea /korniə/ ● noun the transparent layer forming the front of the eye.
– DERIVATIVES **corneal** adjective.
– ORIGIN from Latin *cornea tela* 'horny tissue'.

corned beef ● noun **1** Brit. beef preserved in brine, chopped and pressed and sold in tins. **2** N. Amer. beef brisket cured in brine and boiled, typically served cold.

cornelian /korneeliən/ ● noun variant spelling of CARNELIAN.

corner ● noun **1** a place or angle where two or more sides or edges meet. **2** a place where two streets meet. **3** a secluded or remote region or area. **4** a difficult or awkward position. **5** a position in which one dominates the supply of a particular commodity. **6** (also **corner kick**) Soccer a free kick taken by the attacking side from a corner of the field. **7** Boxing & Wrestling each of the diagonally opposite ends of the ring, where a contestant rests between rounds. ● verb **1** force into a place or situation

C

Thesaurus

line, rope, cable, wire, ligature; twine, yarn, elastic, braid, braiding.

cordial ● adjective *a cordial welcome* FRIENDLY, warm, genial, affable, amiable, pleasant, fond, affectionate, warm-hearted, good-natured, gracious, hospitable, welcoming, hearty.
● noun *fruit cordial* SQUASH, crush, concentrate.

cordon ● noun *a cordon of 500 police* BARRIER, line, row, chain, ring, circle; picket line.
● verb *troops cordoned off the area* CLOSE OFF, shut off, seal off, fence off, separate off, isolate, enclose, surround.

core ● noun **1** *the earth's core* CENTRE, interior, middle, nucleus; recesses, bowels, depths; *informal* innards; *poetic/literary* midst. **2** *the core of the argument* HEART, heart of the matter, nucleus, nub, kernel, marrow, meat, essence, quintessence, crux, gist, pith, substance, basis, fundamentals; *informal* nitty-gritty, brass tacks, nuts and bolts.
● adjective *this is the core issue* CENTRAL, key, basic, fundamental, principal, primary, main, chief, crucial, vital, essential; *informal* number-one.
– OPPOSITES peripheral.

C

from which it is hard to escape. **2** control (a market) by dominating the supply of a particular commodity. **3** go round a bend in a road.
– PHRASES **fight one's corner** defend one's position or interests.
– ORIGIN Latin *cornu* 'horn, tip, corner'.
corner shop ● noun Brit. a small shop selling groceries and general goods in a mainly residential area.
cornerstone ● noun **1** a stone that forms the base of a corner of a building, joining two walls. **2** a vital part or basis: *sugar was the cornerstone of the economy.*
cornet /kornit/ ● noun **1** a brass instrument resembling a trumpet but shorter and wider. **2** Brit. a cone-shaped wafer for holding ice cream.
– DERIVATIVES **cornetist** /kornettist/ (also **cornettist**) noun.
– ORIGIN Old French, 'little horn', from Latin *cornu* 'horn'.
cornflakes ● plural noun a breakfast cereal consisting of toasted flakes made from maize flour.
cornflour ● noun Brit. finely ground maize flour, used for thickening sauces.
cornflower ● noun a slender plant of the daisy family with deep blue flowers.
cornice /korniss/ ● noun **1** an ornamental moulding round the wall of a room just below the ceiling. **2** a horizontal moulded projection crowning a building or structure.
– DERIVATIVES **corniced** adjective **cornicing** noun.
– ORIGIN Italian, perhaps from Latin *cornix* 'crow' (compare with CORBEL).
corniche /korneesh/ ● noun a road cut into the edge of a cliff, especially one running along a coast.
– ORIGIN French, 'cornice'.
Cornish ● adjective relating to Cornwall. ● noun the ancient Celtic language of Cornwall.
Cornish pasty ● noun Brit. a pasty containing seasoned meat and vegetables, especially potato.
cornucopia /kornyookōpiə/ ● noun **1** a symbol of plenty consisting of a goat's horn overflowing with flowers, fruit, and corn. **2** an abundant supply of good things.
– DERIVATIVES **cornucopian** adjective.
– ORIGIN from Latin *cornu copiae* 'horn of plenty' (a mythical horn able to provide whatever is desired).
corny ● adjective (**cornier, corniest**) informal trite or mawkishly sentimental.
– DERIVATIVES **cornily** adverb **corniness** noun.
– ORIGIN originally in the sense 'rustic, appealing to country folk'.
corolla /kərollə/ ● noun the petals of a flower, typically forming a whorl within the sepals.
– ORIGIN Latin, 'little crown'.
corollary /kərolləri/ ● noun (pl. **corollaries**) **1** a logical proposition that follows from one already proved. **2** a direct consequence or result. ● adjective associated; supplementary.
– ORIGIN Latin *corollarium* 'money paid for a garland or chaplet; gratuity' (later 'a deduction'), from *corolla* 'little crown'.
corona /kərōnə/ ● noun (pl. **coronae** /kərōnee/) **1** the rarefied gaseous envelope of the sun or a star. **2** (also **corona discharge**) Physics the glow around a conductor at high potential. **3** a small circle of light seen round the sun or moon. **4** Anatomy a crown or crown-like structure. **5** Botany the trumpet-shaped central part of a daffodil or narcissus flower. **6** a long, straight-sided cigar.
– ORIGIN Latin, 'wreath, crown'; sense 6 comes from a proprietary name of a Havana cigar.
coronal /kərōn'l, korrən'l/ ● adjective relating to the crown or corona of something.
coronary ● adjective relating to or denoting the arteries which surround and supply the heart. ● noun (pl. **coronaries**) (also **coronary thrombosis**) a blockage of the flow of blood to the heart, caused by a clot in a coronary artery.
– ORIGIN Latin *coronarius* 'resembling or forming a crown'.
coronation ● noun the ceremony of crowning a sovereign or a sovereign's consort.
– ORIGIN Latin, from *coronare* 'to crown'.
coroner /korrənər/ ● noun an official who holds inquests into violent, sudden, or suspicious deaths, and (in Britain) inquiries into cases of treasure trove.
– ORIGIN originally denoting an official responsible for safeguarding the private property of the Crown: from Old French *coruner*, from *corune* 'crown'.
coronet /korrənit/ ● noun **1** a small or simple crown. **2** a decorative band encircling the head.
– ORIGIN Old French *coronete*, 'little crown'.
corpora plural of CORPUS.
corporal[1] ● noun a rank of non-commissioned officer in the army, above lance corporal or private first class and below sergeant.
– ORIGIN Italian *caporale*, probably from Latin *corpus* 'body (of troops)'.
corporal[2] ● adjective relating to the human body.
– ORIGIN Latin *corporalis*, from *corpus* 'body'.
corporal punishment ● noun physical punishment, such as caning or flogging.
corporate ● adjective **1** relating to a business corporation. **2** of or shared by all members of a group: *corporate responsibility.*
– DERIVATIVES **corporately** adverb.
– ORIGIN from Latin *corporare* 'form into a body', from *corpus* 'body'.
corporation ● noun **1** a large company or group of companies authorized to act as a single entity and recognized as such in law. **2** Brit. a group of people elected to govern a city, town, or borough.
corporation tax ● noun tax levied on companies' profits.
corporatism ● noun the control of a state or organization by large interest groups.
– DERIVATIVES **corporatist** adjective & noun.
corporeal /korporiəl/ ● adjective relating to a person's body; physical rather than spiritual.
– DERIVATIVES **corporeality** /korporialiti/ noun.
– ORIGIN Latin *corporealis*, from *corpus* 'body'.
corps /kor/ ● noun (pl. **corps** /korz/) **1** a main subdivision of an army in the field, consisting of two or more divisions. **2** a branch of an army assigned to a particular kind of work. **3** a body of people engaged in a particular activity: *the press corps.*
– ORIGIN French, from Latin *corpus* 'body'.
corps de ballet /kor də balay/ ● noun (treated as sing. or pl.) **1** the

Thesaurus

cork ● noun STOPPER, stop, plug, bung, peg, spigot, spile; *N. Amer.* stopple.
corn ● noun GRAIN, cereal (crop); wheat, barley, oats, rye.
corner ● noun **1** *the cart lurched round the corner* BEND, curve, crook, dog-leg; turn, turning, junction, fork, intersection; *Brit.* hairpin bend. **2** *a charming corner of Italy* DISTRICT, region, area, section, quarter, part; *informal* neck of the woods. **3** *he found himself in a tight corner* PREDICAMENT, plight, tight spot, mess, muddle, difficulty, problem, dilemma, quandary; *informal* pickle, jam, stew, fix, hole, hot water, bind.
● verb **1** *he was eventually cornered by police dogs* DRIVE INTO A CORNER, run to earth, bring to bay, cut off, block off, trap, hem in, pen in, surround, enclose; capture, catch. **2** *crime syndicates have cornered the stolen car market* GAIN CONTROL OF, take over, control, dominate, monopolize; capture; *informal* sew up.
cornerstone ● noun FOUNDATION, basis, keystone, mainspring, mainstay, linchpin, bedrock, base, backbone, key, centrepiece, core, heart, centre, crux.
corny ● adjective *(informal)* BANAL, trite, hackneyed, commonplace, clichéd, predictable, stereotyped, platitudinous, tired, stale, overworked, overused, well worn; mawkish, sentimental, cloying, syrupy, sugary, saccharine; *Brit.* twee; *informal* cheesy, schmaltzy, mushy, slushy, sloppy, cutesy, toe-curling; *Brit. informal* soppy; *N. Amer. informal* cornball, hokey.
corollary ● noun CONSEQUENCE, (end) result, upshot, effect, repercussion, product, by-product; *Brit.* knock-on effect.
coronet ● noun. See CROWN noun sense 1.
corporal ● adjective BODILY, fleshly, corporeal, somatic, carnal, physical, material.
– OPPOSITES spiritual.
corporation ● noun **1** *the chairman of the corporation* COMPANY, firm, business, concern, operation, house, organization, agency, trust, partnership; conglomerate, group, chain, multinational; *informal* outfit, set-up. **2** *(Brit.) the corporation refused two planning applications* COUNCIL, town council, municipal authority.
corporeal ● adjective BODILY, fleshly, carnal, corporal, human, mortal, earthly, physical, material, tangible, concrete, real, actual.
corps ● noun **1** *an army corps* UNIT, division, detachment, section, company, contingent, squad, squadron, regiment, battalion, bri-

members of a ballet company who dance together as a group. **2** the lowest rank of dancers in a ballet company.

corpse ● noun a dead body, especially of a human. ● verb theatrical slang spoil a piece of acting by forgetting one's lines or laughing uncontrollably.
– ORIGIN Latin *corpus*.

corpulent /korpyoolənt/ ● adjective (of a person) fat.
– DERIVATIVES **corpulence** noun.
– ORIGIN Latin *corpulentus*, from *corpus* 'body'.

corpus /korpəss/ ● noun (pl. **corpora** /korpərə/ or **corpuses**) **1** a collection of written texts. **2** a collection of written or spoken material in machine-readable form.
– ORIGIN Latin, 'body'.

Corpus Christi /korpəss **kris**ti/ ● noun a feast commemorating the institution of the Eucharist, observed on the Thursday after Trinity Sunday.
– ORIGIN Latin, 'body of Christ'.

corpuscle /**kor**pus'l/ ● noun a minute body or cell in an organism, especially a red or white blood cell.
– DERIVATIVES **corpuscular** adjective.
– ORIGIN Latin *corpusculum* 'small body'.

corpus delicti /korpəss di**lik**tī/ ● noun Law the facts and circumstances constituting a breach of a law.
– ORIGIN Latin, 'body of offence'.

corpus luteum /korpəss **lōō**tiəm/ ● noun (pl. **corpora lutea** /**lōō**tiə/) Anatomy a hormone-secreting structure that develops in an ovary after an ovum has been discharged but degenerates after a few days unless pregnancy has begun.
– ORIGIN Latin, 'yellow body'.

corral /kəraal/ ● noun N. Amer. a pen for livestock on a farm or ranch. ● verb (**corralled**, **corralling**) **1** N. Amer. put or keep (livestock) in a corral. **2** gather (a group) together.
– ORIGIN Spanish and Old Portuguese.

correct ● adjective **1** free from error; true; right. **2** conforming to accepted social standards. **3** conforming to a particular political or ideological orthodoxy: *environmentally correct*. ● verb **1** put right. **2** mark the errors in (a text). **3** tell (someone) that they are in error. **4** adjust so as to function accurately or accord with a standard.
– DERIVATIVES **correctable** adjective **correctly** adverb **correctness** noun **corrector** noun.
– ORIGIN from Latin *corrigere* 'make straight, amend'.

correction ● noun **1** the action or process of correcting. **2** a change that rectifies an error or inaccuracy.
– DERIVATIVES **correctional** adjective (chiefly N. Amer.).

correctitude ● noun correctness, especially conscious correctness in one's behaviour.

corrective ● adjective designed to correct something undesirable. ● noun a corrective measure.

correlate /**kor**rəlayt/ ● verb have or bring into a relationship in which one thing affects or depends on another. ● noun each of two or more related or complementary things.

correlation ● noun **1** a mutual relationship. **2** the process of correlating two or more things. **3** Statistics interdependence of variable quantities.

correlative /kə**rel**lətiv/ ● adjective **1** having a correlation. **2** (of words such as *neither* and *nor*) corresponding to each other and regularly used together. ● noun a correlative word or concept.
– ORIGIN Latin *correlativus*, from *relativus* 'having reference or relation'.

correspond ● verb **1** match or agree almost exactly. **2** be comparable or equivalent in character or form. **3** communicate by exchanging letters.
– ORIGIN Latin *correspondere*, from *respondere* 'answer'.

correspondence ● noun **1** the action or fact of corresponding. **2** letters sent or received.

correspondence course ● noun a course of study in which student and tutors communicate by post.

correspondent ● noun **1** a person who writes letters, especially on a regular basis. **2** a journalist reporting on a particular subject or from a particular country. ● adjective corresponding.

corrida /koreedə/ ● noun a bullfight.
– ORIGIN from Spanish *corrida de toros* 'running of bulls'.

corridor ● noun **1** a passage in a building or train, with doors leading into rooms or compartments. **2** a belt of land linking two other areas or following a road or river.
– PHRASES **the corridors of power** the senior levels of government or administration.
– ORIGIN Italian *corridore*, alteration of *corridoio* 'running-place'.

corrie /**kor**ri/ ● noun (pl. **corries**) a cirque, especially one in the mountains of Scotland.
– ORIGIN Scottish Gaelic and Irish *coire* 'cauldron, hollow'.

corrigendum /korri**jen**dəm/ ● noun (pl. **corrigenda** /korri**jen**də/) a thing to be corrected, especially an error in a

C

Thesaurus

gade, platoon. **2** *a corps of trained engineers* GROUP, body, band, cohort, party, gang, pack; team, crew.

corpse ● noun DEAD BODY, body, carcass, skeleton, remains; *informal* stiff; *Medicine* cadaver; *archaic* corse.
– RELATED TERMS necro-.

corpulent ● adjective FAT, obese, overweight, plump, portly, stout, chubby, paunchy, beer-bellied, heavy, bulky, chunky, well upholstered, well padded, well covered, meaty, fleshy, rotund, broad in the beam; *informal* tubby, pudgy, beefy, porky, roly-poly, blubbery; *Brit. informal* podgy, fubsy; *N. Amer. informal* corn-fed, zaftig; *rare* abdominous.
– OPPOSITES thin.

correct ● adjective **1** *the correct answer* RIGHT, accurate, true, exact, precise, unerring, faithful, strict, faultless, flawless, error-free, perfect, word-perfect; *informal* on the mark, on the beam, on the nail; *Brit. informal* spot on, bang on; *N. Amer. informal* on the money, on the button. **2** *correct behaviour* PROPER, seemly, decorous, decent, respectable, right, suitable, fit, fitting, befitting, appropriate, apt; approved, accepted, conventional, customary, traditional, orthodox, comme il faut.
– OPPOSITES wrong, improper.
● verb **1** *proofread your work and correct any mistakes* RECTIFY, put right, set right, right, amend, emend, remedy, repair. **2** *an attempt to correct the trade imbalance* COUNTERACT, offset, counterbalance, compensate for, make up for, neutralize. **3** *the brakes need correcting* ADJUST, regulate, fix, set, standardize, normalize, calibrate, fine-tune.

correction ● noun RECTIFICATION, rectifying, righting, amendment, emendation, repair, remedy; *archaic* reparation.

corrective ● adjective REMEDIAL, therapeutic, restorative, curative, reparatory, reparative, rehabilitative.

correctly ● adverb **1** *the questions were answered correctly* ACCURATELY, right, unerringly, precisely, faultlessly, flawlessly, perfectly, without error; *dated* aright. **2** *she behaved correctly at all times* PROPERLY, decorously, with decorum, decently, suitably, fittingly, appropriately, well.
– OPPOSITES incorrectly, inappropriately.

correlate ● verb **1** *socio-economic status often correlates with educational achievement* CORRESPOND, match, parallel, agree, tally, tie in, be consistent, be compatible, be consonant, coordinate, dovetail, relate, conform; *informal* square; *N. Amer. informal* jibe. **2** *consumption of such foods was correlated with a decreased risk for certain cancers* CONNECT, establish a relationship/connection between, associate, relate.
– OPPOSITES contrast.

correlation ● noun CONNECTION, association, link, tie-in, tie-up, relation, relationship, interrelationship, interdependence, interconnection, interaction; correspondence, parallel.

correspond ● verb **1** *their policies do not correspond with their statements* CORRELATE, agree, be in agreement, be consistent, be compatible, be consonant, accord, be in tune, concur, coincide, tally, tie in, dovetail, fit in; match, parallel; *informal* square; *N. Amer. informal* jibe. **2** *a rank corresponding to the British rank of sergeant* BE EQUIVALENT, be analogous, be comparable, equate. **3** *Debbie and I corresponded for years* EXCHANGE LETTERS, write, communicate, keep in touch/contact.

correspondence ● noun **1** *there is some correspondence between the two variables* CORRELATION, agreement, consistency, compatibility, consonance, conformity, similarity, resemblance, parallel, comparability, accord, concurrence, coincidence. **2** *his private correspondence* LETTERS, messages, missives, mail, post.

correspondent ● noun *the paper's foreign correspondent* REPORTER, journalist, columnist, writer, contributor, newspaperman, newspaperwoman, commentator; *Brit.* pressman; *informal* stringer, news hound, journo.
● adjective *a correspondent improvement in quality* CORRESPONDING, parallel, matching, equivalent, comparable, similar, analogous, commensurate.

corresponding ● adjective COMMENSURATE, parallel, correspondent, matching, correlated, relative, proportional, proportionate,

C

book.
– ORIGIN Latin.
corroborate /kərobbərayt/ • verb confirm or give support to (a statement or theory).
– DERIVATIVES **corroboration** noun **corroborative** adjective.
– ORIGIN Latin *corroborare* 'strengthen'.
corroboree /kərobbəri/ • noun an Australian Aboriginal dance ceremony in the form of a sacred ritual or informal gathering.
– ORIGIN from an Aboriginal word denoting a style of dancing.
corrode /kərōd/ • verb **1** (with reference to metal or other hard material) wear or be worn away slowly by chemical action. **2** gradually weaken or destroy.
– DERIVATIVES **corrosion** noun.
– ORIGIN Latin *corrodere*, from *rodere* 'gnaw'.
corrosive • adjective tending to cause corrosion. • noun a corrosive substance.
– DERIVATIVES **corrosively** adverb **corrosiveness** noun.
corrugate /korroogayt/ • verb contract into wrinkles or folds.
– ORIGIN Latin *corrugare* 'to wrinkle'.
corrugated • adjective shaped into alternate ridges and grooves.
– DERIVATIVES **corrugation** noun.
corrupt • adjective **1** willing to act dishonestly in return for money or personal gain. **2** evil or morally depraved. **3** (of a text or computer data) made unreliable by errors or alterations. **4** archaic rotten or putrid. • verb **1** make corrupt. **2** archaic infect; contaminate.
– DERIVATIVES **corrupter** noun **corruptible** adjective **corruption** noun **corruptive** adjective **corruptly** adverb.
– ORIGIN from Latin *corrumpere* 'mar, bribe, destroy'.
corsage /korsaazh/ • noun **1** a spray of flowers worn pinned to a woman's clothes. **2** the bodice of a woman's dress.
– ORIGIN French, from Old French *cors* 'body'.
corsair /korsair/ • noun **1** archaic a pirate. **2** historical a privateer, especially one operating along the southern shore of the Mediterranean.
– ORIGIN French *corsaire*, from Latin *cursus* 'a raid, plunder'.
corselette /korsəlet/ (also **corselet**) • noun a woman's undergarment combining corset and brassiere.
corset • noun **1** a woman's tightly fitting undergarment extending from below the chest to the hips, worn to shape the figure. **2** a similar garment worn to support a weak or injured back.
– DERIVATIVES **corseted** adjective **corsetry** noun.
– ORIGIN originally meaning 'a close-fitting outer bodice': from Old French, 'little body'.
Corsican • noun **1** a person from Corsica. **2** the language of Corsica. • adjective relating to Corsica.
cortège /kortezh/ • noun a solemn procession, especially for a funeral.
– ORIGIN Italian *corteggio* 'entourage or retinue'.
cortex /korteks/ • noun (pl. **cortices** /kortiseez/) Anatomy the outer layer of an organ or structure, especially the outer, folded layer of the brain (**cerebral cortex**).
– DERIVATIVES **cortical** adjective.
– ORIGIN Latin, 'bark'.
corticosteroid • noun Biochemistry any of a group of steroid hormones produced by the cortex of the adrenal glands.
cortisone /kortizōn/ • noun a steroid hormone produced by the adrenal cortex and used as an anti-inflammatory and anti-allergy agent.
– ORIGIN from elements of its chemical name.
corundum /kərundəm/ • noun extremely hard crystallized alumina, used as an abrasive.
– ORIGIN Tamil.
coruscate /korrəskayt/ • verb literary (of light) flash or sparkle.
– DERIVATIVES **coruscant** adjective **coruscation** noun.
– ORIGIN Latin *coruscare* 'glitter'.
corvette /korvet/ • noun a small warship designed for convoy escort duty.
– ORIGIN French, from Dutch *korf*, denoting a kind of ship.
corvine /korvīn/ • adjective of or like a raven or crow, especially in colour.
– ORIGIN from Latin *corvus* 'raven'.
corybantic /korribantik/ • adjective literary wild; frenzied.
– ORIGIN from Greek *Korubantes*, denoting the priests of the Phrygian goddess Cybele, who performed wild dances.
corymb /korrimb/ • noun Botany a flower cluster whose lower stalks are proportionally longer so that the flowers form a fairly flat head.
– ORIGIN Greek *korumbos* 'cluster'.
coryza /kərīzə/ • noun catarrhal inflammation of the mucous membrane in the nose, as caused by a cold.
– ORIGIN Greek *koruza* 'nasal mucus'.
cos[1] /koss/ • noun a variety of lettuce with crisp narrow leaves that form a tall head.
– ORIGIN named after the Greek island of *Cos*, where it originated.
cos[2] /koss, koz/ • abbreviation cosine.
cosec /kōsek/ • abbreviation cosecant.
cosecant /kōseekənt/ • noun Mathematics (in a right-angled triangle) the ratio of the hypotenuse to the side opposite an acute angle (the reciprocal of sine).
cosh Brit. • noun a thick heavy stick or bar used as a weapon. • verb hit on the head with a cosh.
– ORIGIN of unknown origin.
co-signatory • noun a person or state signing a treaty or other document jointly with others.
cosine /kōsīn/ • noun Mathematics (in a right-angled triangle) the ratio of the side adjacent to a particular acute angle to the hypotenuse.
cosmetic • adjective **1** relating to treatment intended to improve a person's appearance. **2** improving only the appearance of something. • noun (**cosmetics**) cosmetic preparations, especially for the face.
– DERIVATIVES **cosmetically** adverb.

Thesaurus

comparable, equivalent, analogous.
corridor • noun PASSAGE, passageway, aisle, gangway, hall, hallway, gallery, arcade.
corroborate • verb CONFIRM, verify, endorse, ratify, authenticate, validate, certify; support, back up, uphold, bear out, bear witness to, attest to, testify to, vouch for, give credence to, substantiate, sustain.
– OPPOSITES contradict.
corrode • verb **1** *the iron had corroded* RUST, become rusty, tarnish; wear away, disintegrate, crumble, perish, spoil; oxidize. **2** *acid rain corrodes buildings* WEAR AWAY, eat away (at), gnaw away (at), erode, abrade, consume, destroy.
corrosive • adjective CAUSTIC, corroding, erosive, abrasive, burning, stinging; destructive, damaging, harmful, harsh.
corrugated • adjective RIDGED, fluted, grooved, furrowed, crinkled, crinkly, puckered, creased, wrinkled, wrinkly, crumpled; technical striate, striated.
corrupt • adjective **1** *a corrupt official* | *corrupt practices* DISHONEST, unscrupulous, dishonourable, unprincipled, unethical, amoral, untrustworthy, underhand, double-dealing, fraudulent, venal, bribable, buyable; criminal, illegal, unlawful, nefarious; informal crooked, shady, dirty, mucky, sleazy; Brit. informal bent, dodgy. **2** *the earth was corrupt in God's sight* IMMORAL, depraved, degenerate, reprobate, vice-ridden, perverted, debauched, dissolute, dissipated, bad, wicked, evil, base, sinful, ungodly, unholy, irreligious, profane, impious, impure; informal warped. **3** *a corrupt text* IMPURE, bastardized, debased, adulterated.
– OPPOSITES honest, ethical, pure.
• verb **1** *the fear of firms corrupting politicians in the search for contracts* BRIBE, suborn, buy (off), pay off; informal grease someone's palm, give someone a backhander/sweetener, get at, square; Brit. informal nobble. **2** *a book that might corrupt its readers* DEPRAVE, pervert, debauch, degrade, warp, lead astray, defile, pollute, sully; archaic demoralize. **3** *the apostolic writings had been corrupted* ALTER, tamper with, interfere with, bastardize, debase, adulterate.
corruption • noun **1** *political corruption* DISHONESTY, unscrupulousness, double-dealing, fraud, fraudulence, misconduct, crime, criminality, wrongdoing; bribery, subornation, venality, extortion, profiteering, jobbery; N. Amer. payola; informal crookedness, sleaze; formal malversation. **2** *his fall into corruption* IMMORALITY, depravity, vice, degeneracy, perversion, pervertedness, debauchery, dissoluteness, decadence, wickedness, evil, sin, sinfulness, ungodliness; formal turpitude. **3** *these figures have been subject to corruption* ALTERATION, bastardization, debasement, adulteration.
– OPPOSITES honesty, morality, purity.
corsair • noun (archaic). See PIRATE noun sense 1.
corset • noun GIRDLE, panty girdle, foundation (garment), corselette; Brit. roll-on; informal, dated waspie; historical stays.
cortège • noun **1** *the funeral cortège* PROCESSION, parade, cavalcade, motorcade, convoy, caravan, train, column, file, line. **2** *the*

– ORIGIN Greek *kosmētikos*, from *kosmos* 'order or adornment'.
cosmic • adjective relating to the universe or cosmos, especially as distinct from the earth.
– DERIVATIVES **cosmical** adjective **cosmically** adverb.
cosmic dust • noun small particles of matter distributed throughout space.
cosmic radiation • noun radiation consisting of cosmic rays.
cosmic rays • plural noun highly energetic atomic nuclei or other particles travelling through space at a speed approaching that of light.
cosmogony /kozmoggəni/ • noun (pl. **cosmogonies**) the branch of science concerned with the origin of the universe, especially the solar system.
– DERIVATIVES **cosmogonic** /kozməgonnik/ adjective **cosmogonist** noun.
– ORIGIN from Greek *kosmos* 'order or world' + *-gonia* '-begetting'.
cosmography • noun (pl. **-ies**) **1** the branch of science which deals with the general features of the universe, including the earth. **2** a description or representation of the universe or the earth.
– DERIVATIVES **cosmographer** noun **cosmographic** adjective.
cosmology • noun (pl. **cosmologies**) **1** the science of the origin and development of the universe. **2** an account or theory of the origin of the universe.
– DERIVATIVES **cosmological** adjective **cosmologist** noun.
cosmonaut • noun a Russian astronaut.
– ORIGIN Russian *kosmonavt*, on the pattern of *astronaut*.
cosmopolitan /kozməpollit'n/ • adjective **1** consisting of people from many different countries and cultures: *a cosmopolitan metropolis.* **2** familiar with and at ease in many different countries and cultures. • noun a cosmopolitan person.
– DERIVATIVES **cosmopolitanism** noun.
– ORIGIN from Greek *kosmos* 'world' + *politēs* 'citizen'.
cosmos • noun the universe seen as a well-ordered whole.
– ORIGIN Greek *kosmos* 'order or world'.
Cossack /kossak/ • noun a member of a people of southern Russia, Ukraine, and Siberia, noted for their horsemanship and military skill.
– ORIGIN Turkic, 'vagabond, nomad'.
cosset • verb (**cosseted**, **cosseting**) care for and protect in an overindulgent way.
– ORIGIN orginally denoting a lamb brought up by hand, later a spoiled child: probably from Old English, 'cottar'.
cost • verb (past and past part. **cost**) **1** require the payment of (a specified sum) in order to be bought or obtained. **2** involve the loss of: *his heroism cost him his life.* **3** (past and past part. **costed**) estimate the cost of. • noun **1** an amount given or required as payment. **2** the effort or loss necessary to achieve something. **3** (**costs**) legal expenses.
– PHRASES **at all costs** (or **at any cost**) regardless of the price or the effort needed. **at cost** at cost price. **to someone's cost** with loss or disadvantage to someone.
– ORIGIN Old French *couster*, from Latin *constare* 'stand firm, stand at a price'.
co-star • noun a performer appearing with another or others of equal importance. • verb **1** appear in a production as a co-star. **2** (of a production) include as a co-star.
Costa Rican /kostə reekən/ • noun a person from Costa Rica, a republic in Central America. • adjective relating to Costa Rica.
cost-effective (also **cost-efficient**) • adjective effective or productive in relation to its cost.
costermonger /kostərmunggər/ • noun Brit. dated a person who sells fruit and vegetables from a handcart in the street.
– ORIGIN from *Costard* (a type of apple) + -MONGER.
costing • noun the estimated cost of producing or undertaking something.
costive /kostiv/ • adjective constipated.
– DERIVATIVES **costiveness** noun.
– ORIGIN Old French, from Latin *constipare* 'press together'.
costly • adjective (**costier**, **costiest**) **1** expensive. **2** causing suffering, loss, or disadvantage: *a costly mistake.*
– DERIVATIVES **costliness** noun.
cost price • noun the price at which goods are bought by a retailer.
costume • noun **1** a set of clothes in a style typical of a particular country or historical period. **2** a set of clothes worn by an actor or performer for a role. **3** Brit. dated a woman's matching jacket and skirt. • verb dress in a costume.
– ORIGIN Italian, 'custom, fashion, habit', from Latin *consuetudo* 'custom'.
costume drama • noun a television or cinema production set in a historical period.
costume jewellery • noun jewellery made with inexpensive materials or imitation gems.
costumier /kostyōōmiər/ (US also **costumer** /kostyōōmər/) • noun a maker or supplier of theatrical or fancy-dress costumes.
– ORIGIN French.
cosy (US **cozy**) • adjective (**cosier**, **cosiest**) **1** comfortable, warm, and secure. **2** not seeking or offering challenge or difficulty: *the cosy belief that man is master.* • noun (pl. **cosies**) a cover to keep a teapot or a boiled egg hot. • verb (**cosies**, **cosied**) informal **1** make (someone) feel cosy. **2** (**cosy up to**) ingratiate oneself with.
– DERIVATIVES **cosily** adverb **cosiness** noun.
– ORIGIN originally Scots: of unknown origin.
cot¹ • noun Brit. a small bed with high barred sides for a baby or very young child.
– ORIGIN Hindi, 'bedstead, hammock'.
cot² • noun **1** a small shelter for livestock. **2** archaic a small, simple cottage.
– ORIGIN Old English, related to COTE.
cot³ • abbreviation Mathematics cotangent.
cotangent /kōtanjənt/ • noun Mathematics (in a right-angled triangle) the ratio of the side (other than the hypotenuse) adjacent to a particular acute angle to the side opposite the angle (the

C

Thesaurus

prince's cortège ENTOURAGE, retinue, train, suite; attendants, companions, followers, retainers.
cosmetic • adjective *most of the changes were merely cosmetic* SUPERFICIAL, surface, skin-deep, outward, exterior, external.
– OPPOSITES fundamental.
• noun (**cosmetics**) *a new range of cosmetics* MAKE-UP, beauty products, maquillage, face paint; *informal* warpaint, paint, slap.
cosmic • adjective **1** *cosmic bodies* EXTRATERRESTRIAL, in space, from space. **2** *an epic of cosmic dimensions* VAST, huge, immense, enormous, massive, colossal, prodigious, immeasurable, incalculable, unfathomable, fathomless, measureless, infinite, limitless, boundless.
cosmonaut • noun ASTRONAUT, spaceman/woman, space traveller, space cadet; *N. Amer. informal* jock.
cosmopolitan • adjective **1** *the student body has a cosmopolitan character* MULTICULTURAL, multiracial, international, worldwide, global. **2** *a cosmopolitan audience* WORLDLY, worldly-wise, well travelled, experienced, unprovincial, cultivated, cultured, sophisticated, suave, urbane, glamorous, fashionable; *informal* jet-setting, cool.
cosset • verb PAMPER, indulge, overindulge, mollycoddle, coddle, baby, pet, mother, nanny, nursemaid, pander to, feather-bed, spoil; wrap in cotton wool, wait on someone hand and foot.
cost • noun **1** *the cost of the equipment* PRICE, asking price, market price, selling price, fee, tariff, fare, toll, levy, charge, rental; value, valuation, quotation, rate, worth; *informal, humorous* damage. **2** *the human cost of the conflict* SACRIFICE, loss, expense, penalty, toll, price. **3** (**costs**) *we need to make £10,000 to cover our costs* EXPENSES, outgoings, disbursements, overheads, running costs, operating costs, fixed costs; expenditure, spending, outlay.
• verb **1** *the chair costs £186* BE PRICED AT, sell for, be valued at, fetch, come to, amount to; *informal* set someone back, go for; *Brit. informal* knock someone back. **2** *the proposal has not yet been costed* PUT A PRICE ON, price, value, put a value on, put a figure on.
costly • adjective **1** *costly machinery* EXPENSIVE, dear, high-cost, highly priced, overpriced; *Brit.* over the odds; *informal* steep, pricey. **2** *a costly mistake* CATASTROPHIC, disastrous, calamitous, ruinous; damaging, harmful, injurious, deleterious, woeful, awful, terrible, dreadful; *formal* grievous.
– OPPOSITES cheap.
costume • noun **1** *Elizabethan costumes* (SET OF) CLOTHES, garments, robes, outfit, ensemble; dress, clothing, attire, garb, uniform, livery; *informal* get-up, gear, togs; *Brit. informal* clobber, kit; *N. Amer. informal* threads; *formal* apparel; *archaic* habit, habiliments, raiment. **2** *(Brit.) if you'd like a dip, we can lend you a costume.* See SWIMSUIT.
cosy • adjective **1** *a cosy country cottage* SNUG, comfortable, warm, homelike, homey, homely, welcoming; safe, sheltered, secure; *N.*

C

reciprocal of tangent).
cot death ● noun Brit. the unexplained death of a baby in its sleep.
cote ● noun a shelter for mammals or birds, especially pigeons.
– ORIGIN Old English, related to COT².
coterie /kōtəri/ ● noun (pl. **coteries**) a small exclusive group of people with shared interests or tastes.
– ORIGIN French, from Low German *kote* 'cote'.
coterminous /kōterminəss/ ● adjective having the same boundaries or extent.
– ORIGIN alteration of CONTERMINOUS.
cotillion /kətilyən/ ● noun **1** an 18th-century French dance related to the quadrille. **2** US a formal ball, especially one at which debutantes are presented.
– ORIGIN French *cotillon*, 'petticoat dance'.
cotoneaster /kətōniastər/ ● noun a small-leaved shrub with bright red berries, often grown as a hedging plant.
– ORIGIN from Latin *cotoneum* 'quince'.
cottage ● noun a small house, typically one in the country.
– DERIVATIVES **cottagey** adjective.
– ORIGIN Latin *cotagium*, from COT² or COTE.
cottage cheese ● noun soft, lumpy white cheese made from the curds of skimmed milk.
cottage hospital ● noun Brit. a small local hospital.
cottage industry ● noun a business or manufacturing activity carried on in people's homes.
cottage loaf ● noun Brit. a loaf made from two round pieces of dough, the smaller on top of the larger.
cottage pie ● noun Brit. a dish of minced meat topped with browned mashed potato.
cottager ● noun a person living in a cottage.
cottar /kottər/ (also **cotter**) ● noun historical (in Scotland and Ireland) a farm labourer or tenant occupying a cottage in return for labour.
– ORIGIN Old English.
cotter pin ● noun **1** a metal pin used to fasten two parts of a mechanism together. **2** a split pin that is opened out after being passed through a hole.
– ORIGIN of unknown origin.
cotton ● noun a soft white fibrous substance which surrounds the seeds of a tropical and subtropical plant, used to make cloth or thread for sewing. ● verb informal (**cotton on**) begin to understand.
– DERIVATIVES **cottony** adjective.
– ORIGIN Arabic.
cotton bud ● noun Brit. a small wad of cotton wool on a short thin stick, used for cosmetic purposes or cleaning the ears.
cotton wool ● noun **1** Brit. fluffy wadding of a kind originally made from raw cotton, used especially for applying or removing cosmetics or bathing wounds. **2** US raw cotton.
cotyledon /kottileed'n/ ● noun an embryonic leaf, the first leaf to grow from a germinating seed.
– ORIGIN Greek *kotulēdōn* 'cup-shaped cavity'.
couch¹ /kowch/ ● noun **1** a long upholstered piece of furniture for several people to sit on. **2** a long seat with a headrest at one end on which a psychoanalyst's subject or doctor's patient lies while undergoing treatment. ● verb **1** (usu. **be couched in**) express in language of a specified style. **2** literary lie down.
– ORIGIN Old French *couche*, from Latin *collocare* 'place together'.
couch² /kowch, kōōch/ (also **couch grass**) ● noun a coarse grass with long creeping roots.
– ORIGIN variant of QUITCH.
couchette /kōōshet/ ● noun **1** a railway carriage with seats convertible into sleeping berths. **2** a berth in such a carriage.
– ORIGIN French, 'small couch'.
couch potato ● noun informal a person who spends a great deal of time watching television.
cougar /kōōgər/ ● noun North American term for PUMA.
– ORIGIN French *couguar*, from Guarani.
cough ● verb **1** expel air from the lungs with a sudden sharp sound. **2** (of an engine) make a sudden harsh noise. **3** (**cough up**) informal give (something, especially money) reluctantly. **4** Brit. informal reveal information; confess. ● noun **1** an act or sound of coughing. **2** a condition of the respiratory organs causing coughing.
– DERIVATIVES **cougher** noun.
– ORIGIN of imitative origin.
cough mixture ● noun Brit. liquid medicine taken to relieve a cough.
could ● modal verb past of CAN¹.
couldn't ● contraction could not.
coulis /kōōli/ ● noun (pl. same) a thin fruit or vegetable purée, used as a sauce.
– ORIGIN French, from *couler* 'to flow'.
coulomb /kōōlom/ ● noun Physics the unit of electric charge in the SI system, equal to the quantity of electricity conveyed in one second by a current of one ampere.
– ORIGIN named after the French military engineer Charles-Augustin de *Coulomb* (1736–1806).
coulter /kōltər/ (US **colter**) ● noun a vertical cutting blade fixed in front of a ploughshare.
– ORIGIN Latin *culter* 'knife or ploughshare'.
council ● noun **1** a formally constituted advisory, deliberative, or administrative body. **2** a body elected to manage the affairs of a city, county, or district. **3** (before another noun) Brit. denoting housing provided by a local council.
– ORIGIN Latin *concilium* 'convocation, assembly'; compare with COUNSEL.
councillor (US also **councilor**) ● noun a member of a council.
council of war ● noun **1** a gathering of military officers in wartime. **2** a meeting held to plan a response to an emergency.
council tax ● noun a tax levied on households by local authorities in the UK, based on the estimated value of a property.
counsel ● noun **1** advice, especially that given formally. **2** (pl. same) a barrister or other legal adviser conducting a case. **3** archaic consultation, especially to seek advice. ● verb (**counselled**, **counselling**; US **counseled**, **counseling**) **1** give advice to. **2** give professional help and advice to (someone) to resolve personal or psychological problems. **3** recommend (a course of action).
– PHRASES **keep one's own counsel** not disclose one's plans or opinions.
– ORIGIN Latin *consilium* 'consultation, advice'.
counsellor (US **counselor**) ● noun **1** a person trained to give guidance on personal or psychological problems. **2** a senior officer in the diplomatic service. **3** (also **counselor-at-law**) US & Irish a barrister.
count¹ ● verb **1** determine the total number of. **2** recite numbers in ascending order. **3** take into account; include. **4** regard or be regarded as possessing a quality or fulfilling a role: *people she had counted as her friends.* **5** be significant; matter: *it's the thought that counts.* **6** (**count on**/**upon**) rely on. **7** (**count in** or

Thesaurus

Amer. down-home, homestyle; *informal* comfy, snug as a bug (in a rug). **2** *a cosy chat* INTIMATE, relaxed, informal, friendly.
coterie ● noun CLIQUE, set, circle, inner circle, crowd, in-crowd, band, community; *informal* gang.
cottage ● noun SMALL HOUSE, lodge, chalet, cabin; shack, shanty; *(in Russia)* dacha; *Scottish* bothy, but and ben; *Austral. informal* weekender; *poetic/literary* bower; *archaic* cot.
couch ● noun *she seated herself on the couch* SETTEE, sofa, divan, chaise longue, chesterfield, love seat, settle, ottoman; *Brit.* put-you-up; *N. Amer.* daybed, davenport, studio couch.
● verb *his reply was couched in deferential terms* EXPRESS, phrase, word, frame, put, formulate, style, convey, say, state, utter.
cough ● verb *he coughed loudly* HACK, hawk, bark, clear one's throat, hem.
● noun *a loud cough* HACK, bark; *informal* frog in one's throat.
– RELATED TERMS tussive.
– PHRASES **cough something up** PAY (UP), come up with, hand over, dish out, part with; *informal* fork out, shell out, lay out; *Brit. informal* stump up; *N. Amer. informal* ante up, pony up.
council ● noun **1** *the town council* LOCAL AUTHORITY, local government, municipal authority, administration, executive, chamber, assembly; *Brit.* corporation. **2** *the Schools Council* ADVISORY BODY, board, committee, commission, assembly, panel; synod, convocation. **3** *that evening, she held a family council* meeting, gathering, conference, conclave, assembly.
counsel ● noun **1** *his wise counsel* ADVICE, guidance, counselling, direction, information; recommendations, suggestions, guidelines, hints, tips, pointers, warnings. **2** *the counsel for the defence* BARRISTER, lawyer; *Scottish* advocate; *N. Amer.* attorney, counselor (-at-law); *informal* brief.
● verb *he counselled the team to withdraw from the deal* ADVISE, recommend, direct, advocate, encourage, urge, warn, caution; guide,

out) include (or not include) in a planned activity. **8** (**count down**) recite numbers backwards to zero to indicate remaining time, especially before the launch of a rocket. **9** (**count out**) complete a count of ten seconds over (a fallen boxer) to indicate defeat. ● noun **1** an act of counting. **2** the total determined by counting. **3** a point for discussion or consideration. **4** Law a separate charge in an indictment.
– PHRASES **count the days** (or **hours**) be impatient for time to pass. **keep** (or **lose**) **count** take note of (or forget) the number or amount when counting. **don't count your chickens before they're hatched** proverb don't be too confident in anticipating success before it is certain. **out for the count** Boxing defeated by being knocked to the ground and unable to rise within ten seconds.
– DERIVATIVES **countable** adjective.
– ORIGIN Old French *counter*, from Latin *computare* 'calculate'.

count[2] ● noun a foreign nobleman whose rank corresponds to that of an earl.
– ORIGIN Old French *conte*, from Latin *comes* 'companion, attendant'.

countdown ● noun **1** an act of counting down to zero, especially before the launch of a rocket. **2** the final moments before a significant event.

countenance /kowntənənss/ ● noun **1** a person's face or facial expression. **2** formal support or approval. ● verb admit as acceptable or possible.
– PHRASES **keep one's countenance** maintain one's composure. **out of countenance** disconcerted or unpleasantly surprised.
– ORIGIN Old French *contenance* 'bearing, behaviour', from *contenir* 'contain'.

counter[1] ● noun **1** a long flat-topped fitment over which goods are sold or served or across which business is conducted with customers. **2** a small disc used in board games for keeping the score or as a place marker. **3** a token representing a coin. **4** a factor used to give one party an advantage in negotiations. **5** a person or thing that counts something.
– PHRASES **over the counter** by ordinary retail purchase, with no need for a prescription or licence. **under the counter** (or **table**) (with reference to goods bought or sold) surreptitiously and illegally.
– ORIGIN Old French *conteor*, from Latin *computare* 'calculate'.

counter[2] ● verb **1** speak or act in opposition or response to. **2** Boxing give a return blow while parrying. ● adverb (**counter to**) in the opposite direction to or in conflict with. ● adjective responding to something of the same kind, especially in opposition: *argument and counter argument.* ● noun an act or speech which counters something else.
– ORIGIN from Latin *contra* 'against'.

counter- ● prefix **1** denoting opposition, retaliation, or rivalry: *counter-attack.* **2** denoting movement or effect in the opposite direction: *counterpoise.* **3** denoting correspondence, duplication, or substitution: *counterpart.*
– ORIGIN from Latin *contra* 'against'.

counteract ● verb act against (something) so as to reduce its force or neutralize it.
– DERIVATIVES **counteraction** noun **counteractive** adjective.

counter-attack ● noun an attack made in response to one by an enemy or opponent. ● verb attack in response.

counter-attraction ● noun a rival attraction.

counterbalance ● noun /kowntərbalənss/ **1** a weight that balances another. **2** a factor having the opposite effect to that of another, so neutralizing it. ● verb /kowntər**bal**ənss/ have an opposing and balancing effect on.

counterblast ● noun a strongly worded reply to someone else's views.

counterclockwise ● adverb & adjective North American term for ANTICLOCKWISE.

counterculture ● noun a way of life and set of attitudes at variance with the prevailing social norm.

counter-espionage ● noun activities designed to prevent or thwart spying by an enemy.

counterfeit /kowntərfit/ ● adjective made in exact imitation of something valuable with the intention to deceive or defraud. ● noun a forgery. ● verb **1** imitate fraudulently. **2** pretend to feel or possess (an emotion or quality).
– DERIVATIVES **counterfeiter** noun.
– ORIGIN Old French *contrefait* 'made in opposition'.

counterfoil ● noun chiefly Brit. the part of a cheque, ticket, etc. that is kept as a record by the person issuing it.

countermand /kowntər**maand**/ ● verb **1** revoke (an order). **2** declare (voting) invalid.
– ORIGIN Latin *contramandare*, from *mandare* 'to order'.

countermeasure ● noun an action taken to counteract a danger or threat.

counterpane ● noun dated a bedspread.
– ORIGIN Old French *contrepointe*, from Latin *culcitra puncta* 'quilted mattress'.

counterpart ● noun a person or thing that corresponds to or

Thesaurus

give guidance.

counsellor ● noun ADVISER, consultant, guide, mentor; expert, specialist.

count ● verb **1** *she counted the money again* ADD UP, add together, reckon up, figure up, total, tally, calculate, compute; *Brit.* tot up; *formal* enumerate; *dated* cast up. **2** *a company with 250 employees, not counting overseas staff* INCLUDE, take into account, take account of, take into consideration, allow for. **3** *I count it a privilege to be asked* CONSIDER, think, feel, regard, look on as, view as, hold to be, judge, deem, account. **4** *it's your mother's feelings that count* MATTER, be of consequence, be of account, be significant, signify, be important, carry weight; *informal* cut any ice.
● noun **1** *at the last count, the committee had 579 members* CALCULATION, computation, reckoning, tally; *formal* enumeration. **2** *her white blood cell count* AMOUNT, number, total.
– PHRASES **count on/upon 1** *you can count on me* RELY ON, depend on, bank on, trust (in), be sure of, have (every) confidence in, believe in, put one's faith in, take for granted, take as read. **2** *they hadn't counted on Rangers' indomitable spirit* EXPECT, reckon on, anticipate, envisage, allow for, be prepared for, bargain for/on; *N. Amer. informal* figure on. **out for the count**. See UNCONSCIOUS adjective sense 1.

countenance ● noun *his strikingly handsome countenance* FACE, features, physiognomy, profile; (facial) expression, look, appearance, aspect, mien; *informal* mug; *Brit. informal* mush, phizog, phiz, clock, boat race; *N. Amer. informal* puss; *poetic/literary* visage, lineaments.
● verb *he would not countenance the use of force* TOLERATE, permit, allow, agree to, consent to, give one's blessing to, go along with, hold with, put up with, endure, stomach, swallow; *Scottish* thole; *informal* stand for; *formal* brook.

counter[1] ● noun *a pile of counters* TOKEN, chip, disc, jetton, plaque; piece, man, marker; *N. Amer.* check.

counter[2] ● verb **1** *workers countered accusations of dishonesty with claims of oppression* RESPOND TO, parry, hit back at, answer, retort to. **2** *the second argument is more difficult to counter* OPPOSE, dispute, argue against/with, contradict, controvert, negate, counteract; challenge, contest; *formal* gainsay, confute.
– OPPOSITES support.
● adjective *a counter bid* OPPOSING, opposed, opposite.
– PHRASES **counter to** AGAINST, in opposition to, contrary to, at variance with, in defiance of, in contravention of, in conflict with, at odds with, against.

counteract ● verb **1** *new measures to counteract drug trafficking* PREVENT, thwart, frustrate, foil, impede, curb, hinder, hamper, check, put a stop/end to, defeat. **2** *a drug to counteract the possible effect on her heart* OFFSET, counterbalance, balance (out), cancel out, even out, counterpoise, countervail, compensate for, make up for, remedy; neutralize, nullify, negate, invalidate.
– OPPOSITES encourage, exacerbate.

counterbalance ● verb COMPENSATE FOR, make up for, offset, balance (out), even out, counterpoise, counteract, equalize, neutralize; nullify, negate, undo.

counterfeit ● adjective *counterfeit cassettes* FAKE, faked, bogus, forged, imitation, spurious, substitute, ersatz; *informal* phoney.
– OPPOSITES genuine.
● noun *the notes were counterfeits* FAKE, forgery, copy, reproduction, imitation; fraud, sham; *informal* phoney, knock-off.
– OPPOSITES original.
● verb **1** *his signature was hard to counterfeit* FAKE, forge, copy, reproduce, imitate. **2** *he grew tired of counterfeiting interest* FEIGN, simulate, pretend, fake, sham.

countermand ● verb REVOKE, rescind, reverse, undo, repeal, retract, withdraw, quash, overturn, overrule, cancel, annul, invalidate, nullify, negate; *Law* disaffirm, discharge, vacate; *formal* abrogate; *archaic* recall.

C

has the same function as another.

counterpoint • noun **1** the technique of writing or playing a melody or melodies in conjunction with another, according to fixed rules. **2** a melody played in conjunction with another. **3** an idea or theme contrasting with the main element. • verb **1** add counterpoint to (a melody). **2** emphasize by contrast.
– ORIGIN Old French *contrepoint*, from Latin *contrapunctum*, '(song) marked over against (the original melody)'.

counterpoise • noun a counterbalance. • verb counterbalance.

counterproductive • adjective having the opposite of the desired effect.

Counter-Reformation • noun the reform of the Church of Rome in the 16th and 17th centuries which was stimulated by the Protestant Reformation.

counter-revolution • noun a revolution opposing a former one or reversing its results.
– DERIVATIVES **counter-revolutionary** adjective & noun.

countersign • verb sign (a document already signed by another person).

countersink • verb (past and past part. **countersunk**) **1** enlarge and bevel the rim of (a drilled hole) so that a screw or bolt can be inserted flush with the surface. **2** drive (a screw or bolt) into such a hole.

countertenor • noun the highest male adult singing voice.

countervail /kowntərvayl/ • verb (usu. **countervailing**) offset the effect of (something) by countering it with something of equal force.
– ORIGIN from Latin *contra valere* 'be of worth against'.

counterweight • noun a counterbalancing weight.

countess • noun **1** the wife or widow of a count or earl. **2** a woman holding the rank of count or earl.

counting • preposition taking account of; including.

countless • adjective too many to be counted; very many.

count noun • noun a noun that can form a plural and, in the singular, can be used with the indefinite article, e.g. *books*, *a book*. Contrasted with MASS NOUN.

countrified (also **countryfied**) • adjective characteristic of the country, especially in being unsophisticated.

country • noun (pl. **countries**) **1** a nation with its own government, occupying a particular territory. **2** districts outside large urban areas. **3** an area with regard to its physical features: *hill country*.
– PHRASES **across country** not keeping to roads. **go to the country** Brit. test public opinion by dissolving Parliament and holding a general election. **line of country** Brit. a subject in which a person is skilled or knowledgeable.
– ORIGIN Old French *cuntree*, from Latin *contrata terra* 'land lying opposite'.

country and western • noun country music.

country club • noun a club with sporting and social facilities, set in a rural area.

country cousin • noun an unsophisticated and provincial person.

country dance • noun a traditional type of English dance, in particular one performed by couples facing each other in long lines.

countryman (or **countrywoman**) • noun **1** a person living or born in the country. **2** a person from the same country as someone else.

country music • noun a form of popular music originating in the rural southern US, characteristically featuring ballads and dance tunes accompanied by a guitar.

countryside • noun the land and scenery of a rural area.

county • noun (pl. **counties**) **1** a territorial division of some countries, forming the chief unit of local administration. **2** US a political and administrative division of a state. **3** (before another noun) Brit. of or denoting the upper-class landed families of a particular county: *loud county voices*.
– ORIGIN originally denoting a periodical meeting held to transact the business of a shire: from Old French *conte*, from Latin *comitatus* 'domain of a count'.

county council • noun (in the UK) the elected governing body of an administrative county.
– DERIVATIVES **county councillor** noun.

county court • noun **1** (in England and Wales) a judicial court for civil cases. **2** US a court for civil and criminal cases.

county town (N. Amer. **county seat**) • noun the town that is the administrative capital of a county.

coup /ko͞o/ • noun (pl. **coups** /ko͞oz/) **1** a coup d'état. **2** an unexpected and notably successful act.
– ORIGIN French, from Latin *colpus* 'a blow'.

coup de grâce /ko͞o də graass/ • noun (pl. **coups de grâce** pronunc. same) a final blow or shot given to kill a wounded person or animal.
– ORIGIN French, 'stroke of grace'.

coup d'état /ko͞o daytaa/ • noun (pl. **coups d'état** pronunc. same) a sudden violent seizure of power from a government.
– ORIGIN French, 'blow of state'.

coupe /ko͞op/ • noun a shallow glass or glass dish, typically with a stem, in which desserts or champagne are served.
– ORIGIN French, 'goblet'.

coupé /ko͞opay/ (also **coupe** /ko͞op/) • noun a car with a fixed roof, two doors, and a sloping rear.
– ORIGIN originally denoting an enclosed carriage for two passengers and a driver: from French *carrosse coupé* 'cut carriage'.

couple • noun **1** two individuals of the same sort considered together. **2** (treated as sing. or pl.) two people who are married or otherwise closely associated romantically or sexually. **3** informal an indefinite small number. **4** Mechanics a pair of equal and parallel forces acting in opposite directions and tending to cause rotation. • verb **1** (often **be coupled to/with**) connect or combine. **2** have sexual intercourse.

Thesaurus

– OPPOSITES uphold.

counterpane • noun *(dated)*. See BEDSPREAD.

counterpart • noun EQUIVALENT, opposite number, peer, equal, coequal, parallel, complement, analogue, match, twin, mate, fellow, brother, sister; *formal* compeer.

countless • adjective INNUMERABLE, numerous, untold, legion, without number, numberless, unnumbered, multitudinous, incalculable, limitless; *informal* umpteen, no end of, a slew of, loads of, stacks of, heaps of, masses of, oodles of, zillions of; *N. Amer. informal* gazillions of; *poetic/literary* myriad.
– OPPOSITES few.

countrified • adjective RURAL, rustic, pastoral, bucolic, country; idyllic, unspoilt; *poetic/literary* Arcadian, sylvan, georgic.
– OPPOSITES urban.

country • noun **1** *foreign countries* NATION, (sovereign) state, kingdom, realm, territory, province, principality, palatinate, duchy. **2** *he risked his life for his country* HOMELAND, native land, fatherland, motherland, the land of one's fathers. **3** *the whole country took to the streets* PEOPLE, public, population, populace, citizenry, nation, body politic; electors, voters, taxpayers, grass roots; *Brit. informal* Joe Public. **4** *thickly forested country* TERRAIN, land, territory, parts; landscape, scenery, setting, surroundings, environment. **5** *she hated living in the country* COUNTRYSIDE, green belt, great outdoors; provinces, rural areas, backwoods, back of beyond, hinterland; *Austral./NZ* outback, bush, back country, backblocks, booay; *informal* sticks, middle of nowhere; *N. Amer. informal* boondocks, boonies, tall timbers; *Austral. informal* beyond the black stump.
• adjective *country pursuits* RURAL, countryside, outdoor, rustic, pastoral, bucolic; *poetic/literary* sylvan, Arcadian, georgic.
– OPPOSITES urban.

countryman, countrywoman • noun **1** *the traditions of his countrymen* COMPATRIOT, fellow citizen. **2** *the countryman takes a great interest in the weather* COUNTRY DWELLER, country cousin, son/daughter of the soil, farmer; rustic, yokel, bumpkin, peasant, provincial; *Irish informal* culchie; *N. Amer. informal* hayseed, hick, hillbilly, rube; *Austral. informal* bushy; *archaic* swain, hind, kern, carl, cottier.

countryside • noun **1** *beautiful unspoilt countryside* LANDSCAPE, scenery, surroundings, setting, environment; country, terrain, land. **2** *I was brought up in the countryside*. See COUNTRY noun sense 5.

county • noun *the northern counties* SHIRE, province, territory, administrative unit, region, district, area.
• adjective *(Brit.) a county lady* UPPER-CLASS, aristocratic, landed, landowning; *informal* upper-crust, top-drawer, {huntin', shootin', and fishin'}, tweedy.

coup • noun **1** *a violent military coup* SEIZURE OF POWER, coup d'état, putsch, overthrow, takeover, deposition; (palace) revolution, rebellion, revolt, insurrection, mutiny, insurgence, uprising. **2** *a major publishing coup* SUCCESS, triumph, feat, accomplishment, achievement, scoop, master stroke, stroke of genius.

– DERIVATIVES **coupledom** noun **coupler** noun.
– ORIGIN Latin *copula* 'connection'; related to COPULATE.
couplet ● noun a pair of successive lines of verse, typically rhyming and of the same length.
coupling ● noun a device for connecting railway vehicles or parts of machinery together.
coupon ● noun **1** a voucher entitling the holder to a discount on a product or a quantity of something rationed. **2** a detachable form used to send for a purchase or information or to enter a competition.
– ORIGIN French, 'piece cut off'.
courage ● noun **1** the ability to do something that frightens one. **2** strength in the face of pain or grief.
– PHRASES **have the courage of one's convictions** act on one's beliefs despite danger or disapproval. **take one's courage in both hands** nerve oneself to do something that frightens one.
– ORIGIN Old French *corage*, from Latin *cor* 'heart'.
courageous ● adjective having courage; brave.
– DERIVATIVES **courageously** adverb **courageousness** noun.
courgette /koorzhet/ ● noun Brit. a variety of marrow harvested and eaten at an early stage of growth.
– ORIGIN French, 'little gourd'.
courier /koorriər/ ● noun **1** a messenger who transports goods or documents. **2** a person employed to guide and assist a group of tourists. ● verb send or transport by courier.
– ORIGIN Old French *coreor* or French *courrier*, from Latin *currere* 'to run'.
course ● noun **1** a direction followed or intended: *the aircraft changed course.* **2** the way in which something progresses or develops: *the course of history.* **3** a procedure adopted to deal with a situation. **4** a dish forming one of the successive parts of a meal. **5** a series of lectures or lessons in a particular subject. **6** a series of repeated treatments or doses of medication. **7** an area of land or water prepared for racing, golf, or another sport. **8** Architecture a continuous horizontal layer of brick or stone. ● verb **1** (of liquid) flow. **2** (often **coursing**) pursue (game, especially hares) with greyhounds using sight rather than scent.
– PHRASES **in (the) course of 1** in the process of. **2** during. **of course 1** as expected. **2** used to give agreement or permission.
– ORIGIN Old French *cours*, from Latin *currere* 'to run'.
coursebook ● noun Brit. a textbook designed for use on a particular course of study.
courser[1] ● noun literary a swift horse.
– ORIGIN Old French *corsier*, from Latin *cursus* 'course'.
courser[2] ● noun a person who goes coursing with greyhounds.
coursework ● noun work done during a course of study, typically counting towards a final mark.
court ● noun **1** (also **court of law**) a body of people before whom judicial cases are heard. **2** the place where such a body meets. **3** a quadrangular area marked out for ball games such as tennis. **4** a quadrangle surrounded by a building or group of buildings. **5** the establishment, retinue, and courtiers of a sovereign. ● verb **1** dated be involved with romantically, especially with a view to marriage. **2** attempt to win the support or favour of. **3** go to great lengths to win (favourable attention). **4** risk incurring (misfortune) because of the way one behaves. **5** (of a male bird or other animal) try to attract (a mate).
– PHRASES **hold court** be the centre of attention. **out of court** before a legal hearing can take place. **pay court to** pay flattering attention to.
– ORIGIN Old French *cort*, from Latin *cohors* 'yard or retinue'.
court card ● noun Brit. a playing card that is a king, queen, or jack of a suit.
– ORIGIN alteration of *coat card*, from the decorative dress of the figures depicted.
court circular ● noun Brit. a daily report of the activities and public engagements of royal family members.
courteous /kurtiəss/ ● adjective polite, respectful, and considerate.
– DERIVATIVES **courteously** adverb **courteousness** noun.
– ORIGIN Old French *corteis* 'having manners fit for a royal court'.
courtesan /kortizan/ ● noun archaic a prostitute, especially one with wealthy or upper-class clients.
– ORIGIN French *courtisane*, from obsolete Italian *cortigiana* 'female courtier'.
courtesy /kurtisi/ ● noun (pl. **courtesies**) **1** courteous behaviour. **2** a polite speech or action, especially one required by convention.
– PHRASES **(by) courtesy of** given or allowed by.

Thesaurus

coup de grâce ● noun DEATH BLOW, finishing blow, kiss of death; *informal* KO, kayo.
coup d'état ● noun. See COUP sense 1.
couple ● noun **1** *a couple of girls* PAIR, duo, twosome, two, brace, span, yoke; *archaic* twain. **2** *a honeymoon couple* HUSBAND AND WIFE, twosome, partners, lovers; *informal* item.
● verb **1** *a sense of hope is coupled with a sense of loss* COMBINE, accompany, mix, incorporate, link, associate, connect, ally; add to, join to; *formal* conjoin. **2** *a cable is coupled to one of the wheels* CONNECT, attach, join, fasten, fix, link, secure, tie, bind, strap, rope, tether, truss, lash, hitch, yoke, chain, hook (up).
– OPPOSITES detach.
coupon ● noun **1** *money-off coupons* VOUCHER, token, ticket, slip; *N. Amer. informal* ducat, comp, rain check. **2** *fill in the coupon below* FORM, tear-off slip.
courage ● noun BRAVERY, courageousness, pluck, pluckiness, valour, fearlessness, intrepidity, nerve, daring, audacity, boldness, grit, hardihood, heroism, gallantry; *informal* guts, spunk; *Brit. informal* bottle; *N. Amer. informal* moxie, cojones, sand.
– OPPOSITES cowardice.
courageous ● adjective BRAVE, plucky, fearless, valiant, valorous, intrepid, heroic, lionhearted, bold, daring, daredevil, audacious, undaunted, unflinching, unshrinking, unafraid, dauntless, indomitable, doughty, mettlesome, venturesome, stout-hearted, gallant, death-or-glory; *N. Amer.* rock-ribbed; *informal* game, gutsy, spunky, ballsy, have-a-go.
– OPPOSITES cowardly.
courier ● noun **1** *the documents were sent by courier* MESSENGER, dispatch rider, runner. **2** *a courier for a package holiday company* REPRESENTATIVE, (tour) guide; dragoman; *N. Amer.* tour director; *informal* rep.
course ● noun **1** *the island was not far off our course* ROUTE, way, track, direction, tack, path, line, trail, trajectory, bearing, heading, orbit. **2** *the course of history* PROGRESSION, development, progress, advance, evolution, flow, movement, sequence, order, succession, rise, march, passage, passing. **3** *what is the best course to adopt?* PROCEDURE, plan (of action), course/line of action, MO, modus operandi, practice, approach, technique, way, means, policy, strategy, programme; *formal* praxis. **4** *a waterlogged course* RACECOURSE, racetrack, track, ground. **5** *a French course* PROGRAMME OF STUDY, course of study, curriculum, syllabus; classes, lectures, studies. **6** *a course of antibiotics* PROGRAMME, series, sequence, system, schedule, regimen.
● verb *tears coursed down her cheeks* FLOW, pour, stream, run, rush, gush, cascade, flood, roll.
– PHRASES **in due course** AT THE APPROPRIATE TIME, when the time is ripe, in time, in the fullness of time, in the course of time, at a later date, by and by, sooner or later, in the end, eventually. **of course** NATURALLY, as might be expected, as you/one would expect, needless to say, certainly, to be sure, as a matter of course, obviously, it goes without saying; *informal* natch.
court ● noun **1** *the court found him guilty* COURT OF LAW, law court, bench, bar, judicature, tribunal, chancery, assizes. **2** *walking in the castle court* COURTYARD, quadrangle, square, close, enclosure, plaza, piazza, cloister; *informal* quad. **3** *the King's's court* ROYAL HOUSEHOLD, retinue, entourage, train, suite, courtiers, attendants. **4** *she made her way to the queen's court* ROYAL RESIDENCE, palace, castle, chateau.
● verb **1** *a newspaper editor who was courted by senior politicians* CURRY FAVOUR WITH, cultivate, try to win over, make up to, ingratiate oneself with; *informal* suck up to, butter up; *N. Amer. informal* shine up to; *archaic* blandish. **2** *he was busily courting public attention* SEEK, pursue, go after, strive for, solicit. **3** *he's often courted controversy* RISK, invite, attract, bring on oneself. **4** *(dated) he's courting her sister* WOO, go out with, pursue, run after, chase, pay court to; *informal* date, see, go steady with; *Austral. informal* track (square) with; *dated* set one's cap at, romance, seek the hand of, make love to.
courteous ● adjective POLITE, well mannered, civil, respectful, well behaved, well bred, well spoken, mannerly; gentlemanly, chivalrous, gallant; gracious, obliging, considerate, pleasant, cordial, urbane, polished, refined, courtly, civilized; *archaic* fair-spoken.
– OPPOSITES rude.
courtesan ● noun *(archaic)*. See PROSTITUTE noun.

C

courtesy light ● noun a small light in a car that is automatically switched on when a door is opened.
courtesy title ● noun a title given to someone, especially the son or daughter of a peer, that has no legal validity.
courthouse ● noun **1** a building in which a judicial court is held. **2** US a building containing the administrative offices of a county.
courtier /kortiər/ ● noun a sovereign's companion or adviser.
courtly ● adjective (**courtlier**, **courtliest**) very dignified and polite.
– DERIVATIVES **courtliness** noun.
court martial ● noun (pl. **courts martial** or **court martials**) a judicial court for trying members of the armed services accused of breaking military law. ● verb (**court-martial**) (**court-martialled**, **court-martialling**; US **court-martialed**, **court-martialing**) try by court martial.
court order ● noun a direction issued by a court or a judge requiring a person to do or not do something.
courtroom ● noun the room or building in which a court of law meets.
courtship ● noun **1** a period of courting. **2** the courting behaviour of male birds and other animals. **3** the action of courting.
court shoe ● noun Brit. a woman's plain, lightweight shoe that has a low-cut upper and no fastening.
courtyard ● noun an open area enclosed by walls or buildings, especially in a castle or large house.
couscous /kooskoos/ ● noun a North African dish of steamed or soaked semolina, usually served with spicy meat or vegetables.
– ORIGIN Arabic.
cousin ● noun **1** (also **first cousin**) a child of one's uncle or aunt. **2** a person of a kindred people or nation.
– PHRASES **first cousin once removed 1** a child of one's first cousin. **2** one's parent's first cousin. **second cousin** a child of one's parent's first cousin. **third cousin** a child of one's parent's second cousin.
– DERIVATIVES **cousinly** adjective **cousinship** noun.
– ORIGIN Old French *cosin*, from Latin *consobrinus* 'mother's sister's child'.
couture /kootyoor/ ● noun **1** the design and manufacture of fashionable clothes to a client's specific requirements. **2** clothes of this type.
– ORIGIN French, 'sewing, dressmaking'.
couturier /kootyooriay/ ● noun (fem. **couturière** /kootyooriair/) a person who designs and sells couture clothes.
covalent /kōvaylənt/ ● adjective (of a chemical bond) formed by the sharing of electrons between atoms. Often contrasted with IONIC.
– DERIVATIVES **covalency** noun **covalently** adverb.
cove[1] ● noun **1** a small sheltered bay. **2** Architecture a concave arch or arched moulding at the junction of a wall with a ceiling. ● verb (**coved**) Architecture having a cove.
– DERIVATIVES **coving** noun.
– ORIGIN Old English, 'chamber, cave'.
cove[2] ● noun informal, dated a man.
– ORIGIN perhaps from a Romany word meaning 'thing or person'.
coven /kuvv'n/ ● noun a group of witches who meet regularly.
– ORIGIN variant of archaic *covin* 'band of people', from Latin *convenire* 'come together'.
covenant /kuvvənənt/ ● noun **1** a solemn agreement. **2** a contract by which one undertakes to make regular payments to a charity. **3** an agreement held to be the basis of a relationship of commitment with God. ● verb agree or pay by covenant.
– DERIVATIVES **covenantal** adjective.
– ORIGIN Old French, 'agreeing', from Latin *convenire* 'come together'.
cover ● verb **1** put something over or in front of (someone or something) so as to protect or conceal. **2** spread or extend over. **3** deal with. **4** travel (a specified distance). **5** (of money) be enough to pay for. **6** (of insurance) protect against a liability, loss, or accident. **7** (**cover up**) try to hide or deny the fact of (a wrongful action). **8** (**cover for**) temporarily take over the job of. **9** aim a gun at. **10** protect (an exposed person) by shooting at the enemy. **11** (in team games) take up a position ready to defend against (an opponent). **12** record or perform a cover version of (a song). **13** (of a male animal, especially a stallion) copulate with (a female animal). ● noun **1** something that covers or protects. **2** a thick protective outer part or page of a book or magazine. **3** shelter: *they ran for cover.* **4** military support for someone in danger. **5** a means of concealing an illegal or secret activity. **6** Brit. protection by insurance. **7** a place setting at a table in a restaurant. **8** (also **cover version**) a recording or performance of a song previously recorded by a different artist.
– PHRASES **break cover** suddenly leave shelter when being pursued. **cover one's back** informal take steps to avoid attack or criticism. **under cover of 1** concealed by. **2** while pretending to do something. **under separate cover** in a separate envelope.
– DERIVATIVES **covering** noun.
– ORIGIN Old French *covrir*, from Latin *cooperire*, from *operire* 'to cover'.
coverage ● noun the extent to which something is covered.

Thesaurus

courtesy ● noun POLITENESS, courteousness, good manners, civility, respect, respectfulness; chivalry, gallantry; graciousness, consideration, thought, thoughtfulness, cordiality, urbanity, courtliness.
courtier ● noun ATTENDANT, lord, lady, lady-in-waiting, steward, equerry, page, squire; *historical* liegeman.
courtly ● adjective REFINED, polished, cultivated, civilized, elegant, urbane, suave, debonair; polite, civil, courteous, gracious, well mannered, well bred, chivalrous, gallant, gentlemanly, ladylike, aristocratic, dignified, decorous, formal, ceremonious, stately.
– OPPOSITES uncouth.
courtship ● noun **1** *a whirlwind courtship* ROMANCE, (love) affair; engagement. **2** *his courtship of Emma* WOOING, courting, suit, pursuit; *archaic* addresses.
courtyard ● noun QUADRANGLE, cloister, square, plaza, piazza, close, enclosure, yard; *informal* quad.
cove[1] ● noun *a small sandy cove* BAY, inlet, fjord, anchorage; *Scottish* (sea) loch; *Irish* lough.
cove[2] ● noun (*informal, dated*) *he's a funny cove.* See FELLOW sense 1.
covenant ● noun *a breach of the covenant* CONTRACT, agreement, undertaking, commitment, guarantee, warrant, pledge, promise, bond, indenture; pact, deal, settlement, arrangement, understanding.
● verb *the landlord covenants to repair the property* UNDERTAKE, contract, guarantee, pledge, promise, agree, engage, warrant, commit oneself, bind oneself.
cover ● verb **1** *she covered face with a towel* PROTECT, shield, shelter; hide, conceal, veil. **2** *his car was covered in mud* CAKE, coat, encrust, plaster, smother, daub, bedaub. **3** *snow covered the fields* BLANKET, overlay, overspread, carpet, coat; *poetic/literary* mantle. **4** *a course covering all aspects of the business* DEAL WITH, consider, take in, include, involve, comprise, incorporate, embrace. **5** *the trial was covered by a range of newspapers* REPORT ON, write about, describe, commentate on, publish/broadcast details of. **6** *he turned on the radio to cover their conversation* MASK, disguise, hide, camouflage, muffle, stifle, smother. **7** *I'm covering for Jill* STAND IN FOR, fill in for, deputize for, take over from, relieve, take the place of, sit in for, understudy, hold the fort; *informal* sub for; *N. Amer. informal* pinch-hit for. **8** *can you make enough to cover your costs?* PAY (FOR), be enough for, fund, finance; pay back, make up for, offset. **9** *your home is covered against damage and loss* INSURE, protect, secure, underwrite, assure, indemnify. **10** *we covered ten miles each day* TRAVEL, journey, go, do, traverse.
– OPPOSITES expose.
● noun **1** *a protective cover* COVERING, sleeve, wrapping, wrapper, envelope, sheath, housing, jacket, casing, cowling; awning, canopy, tarpaulin. **2** *a manhole cover* LID, top, cap. **3** *a book cover* BINDING, jacket, dust jacket, dust cover, wrapper. **4** (**covers**) *she pulled the covers over her head* BEDCLOTHES, bedding, sheets, blankets. **5** *a thick cover of snow* COATING, coat, covering, layer, carpet, blanket, overlay, dusting, film, sheet, veneer, crust, skin, cloak, mantle, veil, pall, shroud. **6** *panicking onlookers ran for cover* SHELTER, protection, refuge, sanctuary, haven, hiding place. **7** *there is considerable game cover around the lake* UNDERGROWTH, vegetation, greenery, woodland, trees, bushes, brush, scrub, plants; covert, thicket, copse, coppice. **8** *the company was a cover for an international swindle* FRONT, facade, smokescreen, screen, blind, camouflage, disguise, mask, cloak. **9** (*Brit.*) *your policy provides cover against damage by subsidence* INSURANCE, protection, security, assurance, indemnification, indemnity, compensation.
– PHRASES **cover something up** CONCEAL, hide, keep secret/dark, hush up, draw a veil over, suppress, sweep under the carpet,

cover charge ● noun a service charge per person added to the bill in a restaurant.
covering letter (N. Amer. **cover letter**) ● noun a letter explaining the contents of an accompanying enclosure.
coverlet ● noun a bedspread.
– ORIGIN from Old French *covrir* 'to cover' + *lit* 'bed'.
cover note ● noun Brit. a temporary certificate showing that a person has a current insurance policy.
covert ● adjective /kuvvərt, kōvərt/ not openly acknowledged or displayed. ● noun /kuvvərt/ **1** a thicket in which game can hide. **2** a feather covering the base of a bird's main flight or tail feather.
– DERIVATIVES **covertly** adverb.
– ORIGIN Old French, 'covered'.
cover-up ● noun an attempt to conceal a mistake or crime.
covet /kuvvit/ ● verb (**coveted**, **coveting**) yearn to possess (something belonging to someone else).
– DERIVATIVES **covetable** adjective.
– ORIGIN Old French *cuveitier*, from Latin *cupiditas* 'cupidity'.
covetous ● adjective longing to possess something.
– DERIVATIVES **covetously** adverb **covetousness** noun.
covey /kuvvi/ ● noun (pl. **coveys**) a small flock of birds, especially partridge.
– ORIGIN from Old French *cover*, from Latin *cubare* 'lie down'.
cow[1] ● noun **1** a fully grown female animal of a domesticated breed of ox. **2** the female of certain other large animals, such as the elephant or whale. **3** informal, derogatory a woman. **4** Austral./NZ an unpleasant person or thing.
– PHRASES **till the cows come home** informal for an indefinitely long time.
– ORIGIN Old English.
cow[2] ● verb (usu. **be cowed**) intimidate into submitting to one's wishes.
– ORIGIN probably from an Old Norse word meaning 'oppress'.
coward ● noun a person contemptibly lacking in courage.
– DERIVATIVES **cowardice** noun **cowardliness** noun **cowardly** adjective.
– ORIGIN Old French *couard*, from Latin *cauda* 'tail', perhaps with reference to an animal with its tail between its legs.
cowbell ● noun a bell hung round a cow's neck.
cowboy ● noun **1** a man on horseback who herds cattle, especially in the western US. **2** informal an unscrupulous or unqualified tradesman.
cowcatcher ● noun a metal frame at the front of a locomotive for pushing aside obstacles on the line.
cower ● verb crouch down or shrink back in fear.
– ORIGIN Low German *kūren* 'lie in wait'.
cowherd ● noun a person who tends grazing cattle.
cowl ● noun **1** a large loose hood forming part of a monk's habit. **2** a hood-shaped covering for a chimney or ventilation shaft. **3** another term for COWLING.
– DERIVATIVES **cowled** adjective.
– ORIGIN Latin *cucullus* 'hood of a cloak'.
cowlick ● noun a lock of hair hanging over the forehead.
cowling ● noun a removable cover for a vehicle or aircraft engine.
cow parsley ● noun a hedgerow plant of the parsley family with large, lacy heads of tiny white flowers.
cowpat ● noun a flat, round piece of cow dung.
cowpoke ● noun N. Amer. informal a cowboy.
cowpox ● noun a disease of cows' udders spread by a virus, which can be contracted by humans and resembles mild smallpox.
cowpuncher ● noun N. Amer. informal a cowboy.
cowrie /kowri/ (also **cowry**) ● noun (pl. **cowries**) a marine gastropod mollusc with a smooth, glossy, domed shell with a long, narrow opening.
– ORIGIN Hindi.
cowslip ● noun a wild primula with clusters of drooping fragrant yellow flowers in spring.
– ORIGIN Old English, 'cow slime'.
Cox (in full **Cox's orange pippin**) ● noun an eating apple of a variety with a red-tinged green skin.
– ORIGIN named after the English fruit grower R. *Cox* (*c.*1776–1845).
cox ● noun a coxswain. ● verb act as a coxswain for.
– DERIVATIVES **coxless** adjective.
coxcomb /koksкōm/ ● noun **1** archaic a vain and conceited man; a dandy. **2** variant spelling of COCKSCOMB.
coxswain /koks'n/ ● noun **1** the steersman of a boat. **2** the senior petty officer in a small ship or submarine in the Royal Navy.
– ORIGIN from obsolete *cock* 'small boat' + SWAIN.
coy ● adjective (**coyer**, **coyest**) **1** pretending shyness or modesty. **2** reluctant to give details about something sensitive: *he's coy about his age.*
– DERIVATIVES **coyly** adverb **coyness** noun.
– ORIGIN Old French *coi*, from Latin *quietus* 'quiet'.
coyote /koyōti, koyōt/ ● noun (pl. same or **coyotes**) a wolf-like wild dog native to North America.
– ORIGIN Nahuatl.
coypu /koypoo/ ● noun (pl. **coypus**) a large semiaquatic beaver-like South American rodent, farmed for its fur.
– ORIGIN from a Chilean language.
cozen /kuzz'n/ ● verb literary trick or deceive.
– ORIGIN perhaps from obsolete Italian *cozzonare* 'to cheat'.
cozy ● adjective US spelling of COSY.
CPR ● abbreviation cardiopulmonary resuscitation.
CPS ● abbreviation (in the UK) Crown Prosecution Service.
cps (also **c.p.s.**) ● abbreviation **1** Computing characters per second. **2** cycles per second.
CPU ● abbreviation Computing central processing unit.

Thesaurus

gloss over; *informal* whitewash, keep a/the lid on.
coverage ● noun REPORTAGE, reporting, description, treatment, handling, presentation, investigation, commentary; reports, articles, pieces, stories.
covering ● noun **1** *a canvas covering* AWNING, canopy, tarpaulin, cowling, casing, housing; wrapping, wrapper, cover, envelope, sheath, sleeve, jacket, lid, top, cap. **2** *a covering of snow* LAYER, coating, coat, carpet, blanket, overlay, topping, dusting, film, sheet, veneer, crust, skin, cloak, mantle, veil.
● adjective *a covering letter* ACCOMPANYING, explanatory, introductory, prefatory.
coverlet ● noun BEDSPREAD, bedcover, cover, throw, duvet, quilt; *Brit.* eiderdown; *N. Amer.* spread, comforter; *dated* counterpane.
covert ● adjective SECRET, furtive, clandestine, surreptitious, stealthy, cloak-and-dagger, hole-and-corner, backstairs, under-the-table, hugger-mugger, concealed, hidden, private, undercover, underground; *informal* hush-hush.
– OPPOSITES overt.
cover-up ● noun WHITEWASH, concealment, false front, facade, camouflage, disguise, mask.
– OPPOSITES exposé.
covet ● verb DESIRE, yearn for, crave, have one's heart set on, want, wish for, long for, hanker after/for, hunger after/for, ache for, thirst for.
covetous ● adjective GRASPING, greedy, acquisitive, desirous, possessive, envious, green with envy, green-eyed.
covey ● noun GROUP, gang, troop, troupe, party, company, band, bevy, flock, army, herd; knot, cluster; *informal* bunch, gaggle, posse, crew.
cow ● verb INTIMIDATE, daunt, browbeat, bully, tyrannize, scare, terrorize, frighten, dishearten, unnerve, subdue; *informal* psych out, bulldoze.
coward ● noun WEAKLING, milksop, namby-pamby, mouse; *informal* chicken, scaredy-cat, yellow-belly, sissy, baby; *Brit. informal* big girl's blouse; *N. Amer. informal* pussy; *Austral./NZ informal* dingo, sook; *archaic* poltroon, caitiff.
– OPPOSITES hero.
cowardly ● adjective FAINT-HEARTED, lily-livered, spineless, chicken-hearted, craven, timid, timorous, fearful, pusillanimous; *informal* yellow, chicken, weak-kneed, gutless, yellow-bellied, wimpish, wimpy; *Brit. informal* wet; *archaic* recreant.
– OPPOSITES brave.
cowboy ● noun **1** *cowboys on horseback* CATTLEMAN, cowhand, cowman, cowherd, herder, herdsman, drover, stockman, rancher, gaucho, vaquero; *N. Amer. informal* cowpuncher, cowpoke, broncobuster; *N. Amer. dated* buckaroo. **2** *(informal) the builders were complete cowboys* ROGUE, rascal, scoundrel, cheat, swindler, fraudster, fly-by-night.
cower ● verb CRINGE, shrink, crouch, recoil, flinch, pull back, draw back, tremble, shake, quake, blench, quail, grovel.
coy ● adjective ARCH, simpering, coquettish, flirtatious, kittenish, skittish; demure, shy, modest, bashful, reticent, diffident, self-

C

Cr ● symbol the chemical element chromium.

crab ● noun **1** a marine crustacean, some kinds of which are edible, with a broad shell and five pairs of legs, the first of which are modified as pincers. **2** (**crabs**) informal an infestation of crab lice. ● verb **1** move sideways or obliquely. **2** fish for crabs.
– PHRASES **catch a crab** Rowing make a faulty stroke in which the oar is jammed under the water or misses the water completely.
– DERIVATIVES **crabber** noun **crablike** adjective & adverb.
– ORIGIN Old English.

crab apple ● noun a small, sour kind of apple.
– ORIGIN perhaps an alteration of Scots and northern English *scrab*.

crabbed ● adjective **1** (of writing) hard to read or understand. **2** bad-tempered; crabby.
– ORIGIN from CRAB, because of the crab's sideways gait and habit of snapping.

crabby ● adjective (**crabbier**, **crabbiest**) bad-tempered; morose.
– DERIVATIVES **crabbily** adverb **crabbiness** noun.

crabgrass ● noun N. Amer. a creeping grass that can become a serious weed.

crab louse ● noun a louse that infests human body hair.

crabwise ● adverb & adjective (of movement) sideways, especially in an awkward way.

crack ● noun **1** a narrow opening between two parts of something which has split or been broken. **2** a sudden sharp or explosive noise. **3** a sharp blow. **4** informal a joke or jibe. **5** informal an attempt to do something. **6** Irish enjoyable entertainment; a good time. **7** (also **crack cocaine**) a potent hard crystalline form of cocaine broken into small pieces. ● verb **1** break with little or no separation of the parts. **2** give way under pressure or strain. **3** make a sudden sharp or explosive sound. **4** hit hard. **5** (of a person's voice) suddenly change in pitch, especially through strain. **6** informal solve, interpret, or decipher. **7** informal break into (a safe). ● adjective very good or skilful.
– PHRASES **crack down on** informal take severe measures against. **crack of dawn** daybreak. **crack of doom** a thunder peal announcing the Day of Judgement. **crack of the whip** Brit. informal a chance to try or participate in something. **crack on** informal proceed or progress quickly. **crack up** informal **1** suffer an emotional breakdown under pressure. **2** burst into laughter. **3** (**be cracked up to be**) informal be asserted to be: *acting isn't as glamorous as it's cracked up to be.* **get cracking** informal act quickly and energetically.
– ORIGIN Old English.

crackbrained ● adjective informal extremely foolish.

crackdown ● noun a series of severe measures against undesirable or illegal behaviour.

cracked ● adjective **1** having cracks. **2** informal crazy.

cracked wheat ● noun grains of wheat that have been crushed into small pieces.

cracker ● noun **1** a paper cylinder which, when pulled apart, makes a sharp noise and releases a small toy or other novelty. **2** a firework that explodes with a crack. **3** a thin dry biscuit of a kind eaten with cheese. **4** Brit. informal a fine example of something.

cracker-barrel ● adjective N. Amer. simple and unsophisticated.
– ORIGIN with reference to the barrels of soda crackers formerly found in country stores, where customers would air their opinions.

crackerjack ● noun informal, chiefly N. Amer. an exceptionally good person or thing.
– ORIGIN fanciful formation from CRACK or CRACKER.

crackers ● adjective informal, chiefly Brit. insane; crazy.

cracking ● adjective Brit. informal **1** excellent. **2** fast and exciting: *a cracking pace.*

crackle ● verb make a rapid succession of slight cracking noises. ● noun **1** a crackling sound. **2** a pattern of minute surface cracks.
– DERIVATIVES **crackly** adjective.

crackling ● noun the crisp fatty skin of roast pork.

cracknel /kraknəl/ ● noun **1** a light, crisp, savoury biscuit. **2** a brittle sweet made from set melted sugar.

crackpot informal ● noun an eccentric or foolish person. ● adjective eccentric; impractical.

cracksman ● noun informal, dated a thief who breaks into safes.

-cracy ● combining form denoting a particular form of government or rule: *democracy.*
– ORIGIN from Greek *-kratia* 'power, rule'.

cradle ● noun **1** a baby's bed or cot, especially one mounted on rockers. **2** a place or period in which something originates or flourishes: *the cradle of civilization.* **3** a supporting framework resembling a cradle, in particular for a boat under repair or for workers on the side of high building. ● verb **1** hold gently and protectively. **2** place in a cradle.
– ORIGIN Old English.

cradle-snatcher ● noun humorous a person who has a sexual relationship with a much younger person.

craft ● noun **1** an activity involving skill in making things by hand. **2** skill in carrying out one's work. **3** (**crafts**) things made by hand. **4** cunning. **5** (pl. same) a boat, ship, or aircraft. ● verb make (something) skilfully.
– DERIVATIVES **crafter** noun.
– ORIGIN Old English; sense 5 perhaps comes from the idea of vessels requiring skill to handle.

Thesaurus

effacing, shrinking, timid.
– OPPOSITES brazen.

cozen ● verb *(poetic/literary).* See TRICK verb.

crabbed ● adjective **1** *her crabbed handwriting* CRAMPED, ill-formed, bad, illegible, unreadable, indecipherable; shaky, spidery. **2** *a crabbed old man.* See CRABBY.

crabby ● adjective IRRITABLE, cantankerous, irascible, bad-tempered, grumpy, grouchy, crotchety, tetchy, testy, crusty, curmudgeonly, ill-tempered, ill-humoured, peevish, cross, fractious, pettish, crabbed, prickly, waspish; *informal* snappish, snappy, chippy; *Brit. informal* shirty, stroppy, narky, ratty; *N. Amer. informal* cranky, ornery; *Austral./NZ informal* snaky.
– OPPOSITES affable.

crack ● noun **1** *a crack in the glass* SPLIT, break, chip, fracture, rupture; crazing. **2** *a crack between two rocks* SPACE, gap, crevice, fissure, cleft, breach, rift, cranny, chink, interstice. **3** *the crack of a rifle* BANG, report, explosion, detonation, pop; clap, crash. **4** *a crack on the head* BLOW, bang, hit, knock, rap, punch, thump, bump, smack, slap; *informal* bash, whack, thwack, clout, wallop, clip, biff, bop. **5** *(informal) we'll have a crack at it* ATTEMPT, try; *informal* go, shot, stab, whack; *formal* essay. **6** *(informal) cheap cracks about her clothes* JOKE, witticism, quip; jibe, barb, taunt, sneer, insult; *informal* gag, wisecrack, funny, dig.
● verb **1** *the glass cracked in the heat* BREAK, split, fracture, rupture, snap. **2** *she cracked him across the forehead* HIT, strike, smack, slap, beat, thump, knock, rap, punch; *informal* bash, whack, thwack, clobber, clout, clip, wallop, belt, biff, bop, sock; *Brit. informal* slosh; *N. Amer. informal* boff, bust, slug. **3** *the witnesses cracked* BREAK DOWN, give way, cave in, go to pieces, crumble, lose control, yield, succumb. **4** *(informal) the naval code proved harder to crack* DECIPHER, interpret, decode, break, solve, resolve, work out, find the key to; *informal* figure out, suss out.
● adjective *a crack shot* EXPERT, skilled, skilful, formidable, virtuoso, masterly, consummate, excellent, first-rate, first-class, marvellous, wonderful, magnificent, outstanding, superlative; deadly; *informal* great, superb, fantastic, ace, hotshot, mean, demon; *Brit. informal* brilliant; *N. Amer. informal* crackerjack.
– OPPOSITES incompetent.
– PHRASES **crack down on** SUPPRESS, prevent, stop, put a stop to, put an end to, stamp out, eliminate, eradicate; clamp down on, get tough on, come down hard on, limit, restrain, restrict, check, keep in check, control, keep under control. **crack up** *(informal)* BREAK DOWN, have a breakdown, lose control, go to pieces, go out of one's mind, go mad; *informal* lose it, fall/come apart at the seams, go crazy, freak out.

cracked ● adjective **1** *a cracked cup* CHIPPED, broken, crazed, fractured, splintered, split; damaged, defective, flawed, imperfect. **2** *(informal) you're cracked!* See MAD sense 1.

crackle ● verb SIZZLE, fizz, hiss, crack, snap, sputter, crepitate; *technical* decrepitate.

cradle ● noun **1** *the baby's cradle* CRIB, bassinet, Moses basket, cot, carrycot. **2** *the cradle of democracy* BIRTHPLACE, fount, fountainhead, source, spring, fountain, origin, place of origin, seat; *poetic/literary* wellspring.
● verb *she cradled his head in her arms* HOLD, support, pillow, cushion, shelter, protect; rest, prop (up).

craft ● noun **1** *a player with plenty of craft* SKILL, skilfulness, ability, capability, competence, art, talent, flair, artistry, dexterity, craftsmanship, expertise, proficiency, adroitness, adeptness, deftness, virtuosity. **2** *the historian's craft* ACTIVITY, occupation, profes-

craftsman (or **craftswoman**) • noun a worker skilled in a particular craft.
– DERIVATIVES **craftsmanship** noun.
craftwork • noun **1** the making of things by hand. **2** items or work produced in such a way.
– DERIVATIVES **craftworker** noun.
crafty • adjective (**craftier**, **craftiest**) cunning or deceitful.
– DERIVATIVES **craftily** adverb **craftiness** noun.
– ORIGIN Old English.
crag • noun a steep or rugged cliff or rock face.
– ORIGIN Celtic.
craggy • adjective (**craggier**, **craggiest**) **1** having many crags. **2** (of a man's face) attractively rugged and rough-textured.
– DERIVATIVES **craggily** adverb **cragginess** noun.
crake • noun a bird of the rail family with a short bill, such as the corncrake.
– ORIGIN Old Norse, based on the bird's call.
cram • verb (**crammed**, **cramming**) **1** force (too many people or things) into a room or container. **2** fill (something) to the point of overflowing. **3** study intensively just before an examination.
– ORIGIN Old English.
crammer • noun Brit. a college that gives intensive preparation for examinations.
cramp • noun **1** painful involuntary contraction of a muscle or muscles. **2** a tool for clamping two objects together. **3** (also **cramp-iron**) a metal bar with bent ends for holding masonry together. • verb **1** restrict or inhibit the development of. **2** fasten with a cramp or cramps. **3** suffer from cramp.
– PHRASES **cramp someone's style** informal prevent a person from acting freely or naturally.
– ORIGIN Low German and Dutch.
cramped • adjective **1** uncomfortably small or crowded. **2** (of handwriting) small and difficult to read.
crampon /krampon/ • noun a spiked device fixed to a boot for climbing on ice or rock.
– ORIGIN Old French.
cranberry • noun (pl. **cranberries**) a small sour-tasting red berry used in cooking.
– ORIGIN German *Kranbeere* 'crane-berry'.
crane[1] • noun **1** a tall machine used for moving heavy objects by suspending them from a projecting arm. **2** a moving platform supporting a camera. • verb **1** stretch out (one's neck) to see something. **2** move by means of a crane.
– ORIGIN from CRANE[2].
crane[2] • noun a tall, long-legged, long-necked wading bird with white or grey plumage.
– ORIGIN Old English.
crane fly • noun a slender two-winged fly with very long legs; a daddy-long-legs.
cranesbill • noun a plant with lobed leaves and purple or violet flowers.
– ORIGIN so named because of the long spur on the fruit, thought to resemble a crane's beak.
cranial /krayniəl/ • adjective relating to the skull or cranium.
cranium /krayniəm/ • noun (pl. **craniums** or **crania** /krayniə/) the skull, especially the part enclosing the brain.
– ORIGIN Latin, from Greek *kranion*.
crank[1] • noun a part of an axle or shaft bent out at right angles, for converting reciprocal to circular motion and vice versa. • verb **1** turn a crankshaft or handle. **2** (**crank up**) informal increase the intensity of. **3** (**crank out**) informal, derogatory produce regularly and routinely.
– ORIGIN Old English, related to CRINGE.
crank[2] • noun **1** an eccentric or obsessive person. **2** N. Amer. a bad-tempered person.
– ORIGIN from CRANKY.
crankcase • noun a case or covering enclosing a crankshaft.
crankpin • noun a pin by which a connecting rod is attached to a crank.
crankshaft • noun a shaft driven by a crank.
cranky • adjective (**crankier**, **crankiest**) informal **1** eccentric, odd. **2** chiefly N. Amer. bad-tempered; irritable. **3** (of a machine) working erratically.
– DERIVATIVES **crankily** adverb **crankiness** noun.
– ORIGIN originally in the sense 'sickly, in poor health': perhaps from Dutch or German *krank* 'sick'.
cranny • noun (pl. **crannies**) a small, narrow space or opening.
– ORIGIN Latin *crena* 'notch'.
crap vulgar slang • noun **1** excrement; faeces. **2** nonsense; rubbish. • verb (**crapped**, **crapping**) defecate. • adjective extremely poor in quality.
– DERIVATIVES **crappy** adjective.
– ORIGIN originally meaning 'chaff', later 'residue from rendering fat' and 'dregs of beer': related to Dutch *krappe*.
crape • noun **1** variant spelling of CRÊPE. **2** black silk, formerly used for mourning clothes.
– ORIGIN French *crêpe* (see CRÊPE).
crap game • noun N. Amer. a game of craps.
craps • plural noun (treated as sing.) a North American gambling game played with two dice.
– ORIGIN perhaps from CRAB or *crab's eyes*, denoting a throw of two ones.
crapshoot • noun N. Amer. a game of craps.
crapulent /krapyoolənt/ • adjective literary relating to the drinking of alcohol or to drunkenness.
– DERIVATIVES **crapulence** noun **crapulous** adjective.
– ORIGIN Latin *crapulentus*, from *crapula* 'drunkenness'.
crash • verb **1** (of a vehicle) collide violently with an obstacle or

Thesaurus

sion, work, line of work, pursuit. **3** *she used craft and diplomacy* CUNNING, craftiness, guile, wiliness, artfulness, deviousness, slyness, trickery, duplicity, dishonesty, deceit, deceitfulness, deception, intrigue, subterfuge; wiles, ploys, ruses, schemes, stratagems, tricks. **4** *a sailing craft* VESSEL, ship, boat; *poetic/literary* barque.
craftsman, craftswoman • noun ARTISAN, artist, skilled worker; expert, master; *archaic* artificer, mechanic.
craftsmanship • noun WORKMANSHIP, artistry, craft, art, handiwork, work; skill, skilfulness, expertise, technique.
crafty • adjective CUNNING, wily, guileful, artful, devious, sly, tricky, scheming, calculating, designing, sharp, shrewd, astute, canny; duplicitous, dishonest, deceitful; *informal* foxy; *archaic* subtle.
– OPPOSITES honest.
crag • noun CLIFF, bluff, ridge, precipice, height, peak, tor, escarpment, scarp.
craggy • adjective **1** *the craggy cliffs* STEEP, precipitous, sheer, perpendicular; rocky, rugged, ragged. **2** *his craggy face* RUGGED, rough-hewn, strong, manly; weather-beaten, weathered.
cram • verb **1** *wardrobes crammed with clothes* FILL, stuff, pack, jam, fill to overflowing, fill to the brim, overload; crowd, throng, overcrowd. **2** *they all crammed into the car* CROWD, pack, pile, squash, wedge oneself, force one's way. **3** *he crammed his clothes into a suitcase* THRUST, push, shove, force, ram, jam, stuff, pack, pile, squash, compress, squeeze, wedge. **4** *most of the students are cramming for exams* REVISE, study intensively; *informal* swot, mug up, bone up.
cramp • noun *stomach cramps* MUSCLE/MUSCULAR SPASM, pain, shooting pain, pang, stitch; *Medicine* clonus, hyperkinesis.
• verb *tighter rules will cramp economic growth* HINDER, impede, inhibit, hamper, constrain, hamstring, interfere with, restrict, limit, shackle; slow down, check, arrest, curb, retard.
cramped • adjective **1** *cramped accommodation* POKY, uncomfortable, confined, restricted, constricted, small, tiny, narrow; crowded, packed, congested; *archaic* strait. **2** *cramped handwriting* SMALL, crabbed, illegible, unreadable, indecipherable.
– OPPOSITES spacious.
crane • noun DERRICK, winch, hoist, davit, windlass; block and tackle.
cranium • noun SKULL, head; *N. Amer. informal* brainpan.
crank[1] • verb *you crank the engine by hand* START, turn (over), get going.
– PHRASES **crank something up** *(informal)* INCREASE, intensify, amplify, heighten, escalate, add to, augment, build up, expand, extend, raise; speed up, accelerate; *informal* up, jack up, hike up, step up, bump up, pump up.
crank[2] • noun *they're nothing but a bunch of cranks* ECCENTRIC, oddity, madman/madwoman, lunatic; *informal* oddball, freak, weirdo, crackpot, loony, nut, nutcase, head case, maniac; *Brit. informal* nutter; *N. Amer. informal* screwball, kook.
cranky • adjective **1** *(informal) a cranky diet* ECCENTRIC, bizarre, weird, peculiar, odd, strange, unconventional, left-field, unorthodox, outlandish; silly, stupid, mad, crazy, idiotic; *informal* wacky, crackpot, nutty; *Brit. informal* daft, potty; *N. Amer. informal* wacko. **2** *(N. Amer. informal) the children were tired and cranky.* See IRRITABLE.
cranny • noun CHINK, crack, crevice, slit, split, fissure, rift, cleft,

another vehicle. **2** (of an aircraft) fall from the sky and violently hit the land or sea. **3** move with force, speed, and sudden loud noise. **4** make a sudden loud, deep noise. **5** (of shares) fall suddenly in value. **6** Computing fail suddenly. **7** (also **crash out**) informal fall deeply asleep. **8** informal gatecrash (a party). ● **noun** **1** an instance of crashing. **2** a sudden loud, deep noise. ● **adjective** rapid and concentrated: *a crash course in Italian.*
– ORIGIN imitative, perhaps partly suggested by CRAZE and DASH.

C

crash-dive ● **verb** (of an aircraft or submarine) dive rapidly or uncontrollably.
crash helmet ● **noun** a helmet worn by a motorcyclist to protect the head.
crashing ● **adjective** informal complete; total: *a crashing bore.*
– DERIVATIVES **crashingly** adverb.
crash-land ● **verb** land roughly in an emergency.
crash pad ● **noun** informal a place to sleep in an emergency.
crash-test ● **verb** deliberately crash (a new vehicle) in order to evaluate and improve its ability to withstand impact.
crashworthiness ● **noun** the degree to which a vehicle will protect its occupants from the effects of an accident.
crass ● **adjective** grossly insensitive and unintelligent.
– DERIVATIVES **crassly** adverb **crassness** noun.
– ORIGIN originally in the sense 'dense or coarse': from Latin *crassus* 'solid, thick'.
-crat ● **combining form** denoting a member or supporter of a particular form of government or rule: *democrat.*
– ORIGIN from Greek *-kratia* 'power, rule'.
crate ● **noun** **1** a slatted wooden case for transporting goods. **2** a square container divided into small individual units for holding bottles. **3** informal an old and dilapidated vehicle. ● **verb** pack in a crate for transportation.
– ORIGIN perhaps related to Dutch *krat* 'tailboard of a wagon'.
crater ● **noun** a large bowl-shaped cavity, especially one caused by an explosion or impact or forming the mouth of a volcano. ● **verb** form a crater or craters in.
– ORIGIN Greek *kratēr* 'mixing-bowl'.
-cratic ● **combining form** relating to a particular kind of government or rule: *democratic.*
cravat ● **noun** a strip of fabric worn by men round the neck and tucked inside an open-necked shirt.
– ORIGIN French *cravate*, from *Cravate* 'Croat', because of the scarves worn by Croatian mercenaries in 17th-century France.
crave ● **verb** **1** feel a powerful desire for. **2** dated ask for: *I must crave your indulgence.*
– ORIGIN Old English.
craven ● **adjective** contemptibly lacking in courage; cowardly.
– DERIVATIVES **cravenly** adverb.
– ORIGIN from obsolete *cravant* 'defeated', perhaps from Old French *cravanter* 'crush, overwhelm'.
craving ● **noun** a powerful desire for something.
craw ● **noun** dated the crop of a bird or insect.
– PHRASES **stick in one's craw** see STICK[2].
– ORIGIN related to Dutch *crāghe* or Low German *krage* 'neck, throat'.
crawfish ● **noun** chiefly N. Amer. a crayfish.
– ORIGIN variant of CRAYFISH.
crawl ● **verb** **1** move forward on the hands and knees or by dragging the body close to the ground. **2** (of an insect or small animal) move slowly along a surface. **3** move unusually slowly. **4** (**be crawling with**) be unpleasantly covered or crowded with. **5** feel an unpleasant sensation resembling something moving over the skin. **6** informal behave obsequiously or ingratiatingly. ● **noun** **1** an act of crawling. **2** an unusually slow rate of movement. **3** a swimming stroke involving alternate overarm movements and rapid kicks of the legs.
– DERIVATIVES **crawler** noun.
– ORIGIN possibly related to Swedish *kravla* and Danish *kravle.*
crayfish ● **noun** (pl. **same**) a freshwater or marine crustacean resembling a small lobster.
– ORIGIN Old French *crevice*, related to German *Krebs* 'crab'.
crayon ● **noun** a stick of coloured chalk or wax, used for drawing. ● **verb** draw with a crayon or crayons.
– ORIGIN French, from *craie* 'chalk'.
craze ● **noun** a widespread but short-lived enthusiasm for something. ● **verb** (**be crazed**) (of a surface) be covered with a network of fine cracks.
– ORIGIN originally in the sense 'break, shatter, produce cracks': perhaps Scandinavian.
crazed ● **adjective** wildly insane; demented.
crazy ● **adjective** (**crazier**, **craziest**) **1** informal insane or unbalanced, especially in a wild or aggressive way. **2** informal extremely enthusiastic about something. **3** informal absurdly unlikely: *a crazy idea.* **4** archaic full of cracks or flaws. ● **noun** (pl. **crazies**) informal, chiefly N. Amer. an insane person.
– PHRASES **like crazy** to a great degree.
– DERIVATIVES **crazily** adverb **craziness** noun.

Thesaurus

opening, gap, aperture, cavity, hole, hollow, niche, corner, nook, interstice.
crash ● **verb** **1** *the car crashed into a tree* SMASH INTO, collide with, be in collision with, hit, strike, ram, cannon into, plough into, meet head-on, run into; *N. Amer.* impact. **2** *he crashed his car* SMASH, wreck; *Brit.* write off; *Brit. informal* prang; *N. Amer. informal* total. **3** *waves crashed against the shore* DASH, batter, pound, lash, slam, be hurled. **4** *thunder crashed overhead* BOOM, crack, roll, clap, explode, bang, blast, blare, resound, reverberate, rumble, thunder, echo. **5** *(informal) his clothing company crashed* COLLAPSE, fold, fail, go under, go bankrupt, become insolvent, cease trading, go into receivership, go into liquidation, be wound up; *informal* go broke, go bust, go to the wall, go belly up.
● **noun** **1** *a crash on the motorway* ACCIDENT, collision, smash, road traffic accident, RTA; derailment; *N. Amer.* wreck; *informal* pile-up; *Brit. informal* prang, shunt. **2** *a loud crash* BANG, smash, smack, crack, bump, thud, clatter, clunk, clonk, clang; report, detonation, explosion; noise, racket, clangour, din. **3** *the crash of her company* COLLAPSE, failure, bankruptcy, insolvency, liquidation.
● **adjective** *a crash course* INTENSIVE, concentrated, rapid, short; accelerated-learning, total-immersion.
crass ● **adjective** STUPID, insensitive, mindless, thoughtless, witless, oafish, boorish, asinine, coarse, gross, graceless, tasteless, tactless, clumsy, heavy-handed, blundering; *informal* ignorant, pig-ignorant.
– OPPOSITES intelligent.
crate ● **noun** CASE, packing case, chest, tea chest, box; container, receptacle.
crater ● **noun** HOLLOW, bowl, basin, hole, cavity, depression; *Geology* caldera, maar, solfatara.
crave ● **verb** LONG FOR, yearn for, desire, want, wish for, hunger for, thirst for, sigh for, pine for, hanker after, covet, lust after, ache for, set one's heart on, dream of, be bent on; *informal* have a yen for, itch for, be dying for; *archaic* desiderate.
craven ● **adjective** COWARDLY, lily-livered, faint-hearted, chicken-hearted, spineless, timid, timorous, fearful, pusillanimous, weak, feeble; *informal* yellow, chicken, weak-kneed, gutless, yellow-bellied, wimpish; contemptible, abject, ignominious; *Brit. informal* wet; *archaic* recreant.
– OPPOSITES brave.
craving ● **noun** LONGING, yearning, desire, want, wish, hankering, hunger, thirst, appetite, greed, lust, ache, need, urge; *informal* yen, itch.
crawl ● **verb** **1** *they crawled under the table* CREEP, worm one's way, go on all fours, go on hands and knees, wriggle, slither, squirm, scrabble. **2** *(informal) I'm not going to go crawling to him* GROVEL TO, ingratiate oneself with, be obsequious to, kowtow to, pander to, toady to, truckle to, bow and scrape to, dance attendance on, curry favour with, make up to, fawn on/over; *informal* suck up to, lick someone's boots, butter up. **3** *the place was crawling with soldiers* BE FULL OF, overflow with, teem with, be packed with, be crowded with, be alive with, be overrun with, swarm with, be bristling with, be infested with, be thick with; *informal* be lousy with, be stuffed with, be jam-packed with, be chock-a-block with, be chock-full of.
craze ● **noun** FAD, fashion, trend, vogue, enthusiasm, mania, passion, rage, obsession, compulsion, fixation, fetish, fancy, taste, fascination, preoccupation; *informal* thing.
crazed ● **adjective** MAD, insane, out of one's mind, deranged, demented, certifiable, lunatic, psychopathic; wild, raving, berserk, manic, maniac, frenzied; *informal* crazy, mental, off one's head, out of one's head, raving mad. See also CRAZY sense 1.
– OPPOSITES sane.
crazy ● **adjective** *(informal)* **1** *a crazy old man* MAD, insane, out of one's mind, deranged, demented, not in one's right mind, crazed, lunatic, non compos mentis, unhinged, mad as a hatter, mad as a March hare; *informal* mental, off one's head, nutty (as a fruitcake), off one's rocker, not right in the head, round the bend, raving

crazy paving ● noun Brit. paving made of irregular pieces of flat stone.

creak ● verb **1** make a harsh high-pitched sound when being moved or when pressure is applied. **2** show weakness or frailty under strain. ● noun a creaking sound.
– ORIGIN imitative.

creaky ● adjective (**creakier**, **creakiest**) **1** making a creaking sound. **2** decrepit or dilapidated.

cream ● noun **1** the thick white or pale yellow fatty liquid which rises to the top when milk is left to stand. **2** a dessert or other food containing cream or having a creamy consistency. **3** a thick liquid or semi-solid cosmetic or medical preparation. **4** the very best of a group: *the cream of American society.* **5** a very pale yellow or off-white colour. ● verb **1** work (butter) to form a smooth soft paste. **2** mash (a cooked vegetable) and mix with milk or cream. **3** (**cream off**) take away (the best part of a group).
– ORIGIN Old French *cresme*, from Latin *chrisma* 'oil for anointing'.

cream cheese ● noun soft, rich cheese made from unskimmed milk and cream.

cream cracker ● noun Brit. a dry unsweetened biscuit eaten with cheese.

creamer ● noun **1** a cream or milk substitute for adding to coffee or tea. **2** N. Amer. a jug for cream. **3** historical a flat dish for skimming the cream off milk.

creamery ● noun (pl. **creameries**) a factory that produces butter and cheese.

cream puff ● noun **1** a cake made of puff pastry filled with cream. **2** informal a weak or ineffectual person.

cream sherry ● noun a full-bodied mellow sweet sherry.

cream soda ● noun a carbonated vanilla-flavoured soft drink.

cream tea ● noun Brit. an afternoon meal consisting of tea to drink with scones, jam, and cream.

creamy ● adjective (**creamier**, **creamiest**) resembling or containing a lot of cream.
– DERIVATIVES **creamily** adverb **creaminess** noun.

crease ● noun **1** a line or ridge produced on paper, cloth, etc. by folding, pressing, or crushing. **2** Cricket any of a number of lines marked on the pitch at specified places. ● verb **1** make a crease in. **2** become creased. **3** (**crease up**) Brit. informal burst out laughing.
– ORIGIN probably a variant of CREST.

create ● verb **1** bring into existence. **2** make (someone) a member of the nobility. **3** Brit. informal make a fuss; complain.
– ORIGIN Latin *creare* 'produce'.

creatine /kreeəteen/ ● noun Biochemistry a compound formed in protein metabolism and involved in the supply of energy for muscular contraction.
– ORIGIN from Greek *kreas* 'meat'.

creation ● noun **1** the action or process of creating. **2** a thing which has been made or invented, especially something showing artistic talent. **3** (**the Creation**) the creating of the universe regarded as an act of God. **4** (**Creation**) literary the universe.

creationism ● noun the belief that the universe and living creatures were created by God in accordance with the account given in the Old Testament.
– DERIVATIVES **creationist** noun & adjective.

creative ● adjective involving the use of the imagination or original ideas in order to create something.
– DERIVATIVES **creatively** adverb **creativeness** noun **creativity** noun.

creative accountancy (also **creative accounting**) ● noun informal the exploitation of loopholes in financial regulation to gain advantage or to present figures in a misleadingly favourable light.

creator ● noun **1** a person or thing that creates. **2** (**the Creator**) God.

creature ● noun **1** a living being, in particular an animal as distinct from a person. **2** a person under the complete control of another.
– ORIGIN originally in the sense 'something created': from Latin *creatura*, from *creare* 'produce'.

creature comforts ● plural noun material comforts such as good food and accommodation.

crèche /kresh/ ● noun Brit. a nursery where babies and young children are cared for during the working day.
– ORIGIN French, related to CRIB.

cred ● noun informal short for CREDIBILITY (in sense 2).

credal /kreed'l/ (also **creedal**) ● adjective relating to a creed.

credence /kreed'nss/ ● noun **1** belief in or acceptance of something as true. **2** the likelihood of something being true; plausibility.
– ORIGIN Latin *credentia*, from *credere* 'believe'.

credential /kridensh'l/ ● noun **1** a qualification, achievement, etc., that gives an indication of a person's suitability for some-

C

Thesaurus

mad, bats, batty, bonkers, cuckoo, loopy, loony, bananas, loco, with a screw loose, touched, gaga, doolally, not all there, out to lunch, away with the fairies; *Brit. informal* barmy, crackers, barking, potty, round the twist, off one's trolley, not the full shilling; *N. Amer. informal* nutso, out of one's tree, meshuga, wacko, gonzo; *Austral./NZ informal* bushed. **2** *a crazy idea* STUPID, foolish, idiotic, silly, absurd, ridiculous, ludicrous, preposterous, farcical, laughable, risible, nonsensical, imbecilic, hare-brained, half-baked, impracticable, unworkable, ill-conceived, senseless; *informal* cockeyed; *Brit. informal* barmy, daft. **3** *he's crazy about her* PASSIONATE ABOUT, very keen on, enamoured of, infatuated with, smitten with, devoted to; very enthusiastic about, fanatical about; *informal* wild/mad/nuts about, gone on; *Brit. informal* potty about.
– OPPOSITES sane, sensible, apathetic.

creak ● verb SQUEAK, grate, rasp; groan, complain.

cream ● noun **1** *skin creams* LOTION, ointment, moisturizer, emollient, unguent, cosmetic; salve, rub, embrocation, balm, liniment. **2** *the cream of the world's photographers* BEST, finest, pick, flower, crème de la crème, elite.
– OPPOSITES dregs.
● adjective *a cream dress* OFF-WHITE, whitish, cream-coloured, creamy, ivory, yellowish-white.

creamy ● adjective **1** *a creamy paste* SMOOTH, thick, velvety, whipped; rich, buttery. **2** *creamy flowers* OFF-WHITE, whitish, cream-coloured, cream, ivory, yellowish-white.
– OPPOSITES lumpy.

crease ● noun **1** *trousers with knife-edge creases* FOLD, line, ridge; pleat, tuck; furrow, groove, corrugation. **2** *the creases at the corners of her eyes* WRINKLE, line, crinkle, pucker; (**creases**) crow's feet.
● verb *her skirt was creased and stained* CRUMPLE, wrinkle, crinkle, line, scrunch up, rumple, ruck up.

create ● verb **1** *she has created a work of stunning originality* PRODUCE, generate, bring into being, make, fabricate, fashion, build, construct; design, devise, originate, frame, develop, shape, form, forge. **2** *regular socializing creates a good team spirit* BRING ABOUT, give rise to, lead to, result in, cause, breed, generate, engender, produce, make for, promote, foster, sow the seeds of, contribute to. **3** *the governments planned to create a free-trade zone* ESTABLISH, found, initiate, institute, constitute, inaugurate, launch, set up, form, organize, develop. **4** *she was created a life peer in 1990* APPOINT, make; invest as, install as.
– OPPOSITES destroy.

creation ● noun **1** *the creation of a coalition government* ESTABLISHMENT, formation, foundation, initiation, institution, inauguration, constitution; production, generation, fabrication, fashioning, building, construction, origination, development. **2** *the whole of creation* THE WORLD, the universe, the cosmos; the living world, the natural world, nature, life, living things. **3** *Dickens's literary creations* WORK, work of art, production, opus, oeuvre; achievement.
– OPPOSITES destruction.

creative ● adjective INVENTIVE, imaginative, innovative, innovatory, experimental, original; artistic, expressive, inspired, visionary; enterprising, resourceful.

creativity ● noun INVENTIVENESS, imagination, imaginativeness, innovation, innovativeness, originality, individuality; artistry, inspiration, vision; enterprise, initiative, resourcefulness.

creator ● noun **1** *the creator of the series* AUTHOR, writer, designer, deviser, maker, producer; originator, inventor, architect, mastermind, prime mover; *poetic/literary* begetter. **2** *the Sabbath is kept to honour the Creator.* See GOD sense 1.

creature ● noun **1** *the earth and its creatures* ANIMAL, beast, brute; living thing, living being; *N. Amer. informal* critter. **2** *you're such a lazy creature!* PERSON, individual, human being, character, soul, wretch, customer; *informal* devil, beggar, sort, type; *Brit. informal* bod; *archaic* wight. **3** *she was often denounced as a creature of the liberals* LACKEY, minion, hireling, servant, puppet, tool, cat's paw, pawn; *informal* stooge, yes-man; *Brit. informal* poodle.

thing. **2** a document or certificate proving a person's identity or qualifications. **3** a letter of introduction given by a government to an ambassador before a new posting.

credibility • noun **1** the quality of being credible. **2** (also **street credibility**) acceptability among fashionable young urban people.

credible • adjective able to be believed; convincing.
– DERIVATIVES **credibly** adverb.
– ORIGIN Latin *credibilis*, from *credere* 'believe'.

C

credit • noun **1** the facility of being able to obtain goods or services before payment, based on the trust that payment will be made in the future. **2** an entry in an account recording a sum received. **3** public acknowledgement or praise given for an achievement or quality. **4** a source of pride: *the fans are a credit to the club*. **5** a written acknowledgement of a contributor's role displayed at the beginning or end of a film or programme. **6** a unit of study counting towards a degree or diploma. **7** Brit. a grade above a pass in an examination. • verb (**credited**, **crediting**) **1** (often **credit to**) publicly acknowledge that someone participated in the production of (something). **2** (**credit with**) ascribe an achievement or good quality to. **3** add (an amount of money) to an account. **4** believe (something surprising or unlikely).
– PHRASES **be in credit** (of an account) have money in it. **do someone credit** make someone worthy of praise or respect.
– ORIGIN Latin *creditum*, from *credere* 'believe, trust'.

creditable • adjective deserving public acknowledgement and praise, although not necessarily outstanding or successful.
– DERIVATIVES **creditability** noun **creditably** adverb.

credit card • noun a plastic card allowing the holder to make purchases on credit.

creditor • noun a person or company to whom money is owing.

credit union • noun a non-profit-making cooperative whose members can borrow money at low interest rates.

creditworthy • adjective considered suitable to receive commercial credit.
– DERIVATIVES **creditworthiness** noun.

credo /kreedō, kraydō/ • noun (pl. **credos**) **1** a statement of a person's beliefs or aims. **2** (**Credo**) a creed of the Christian Church in Latin.
– ORIGIN Latin, 'I believe'.

credulous /kredyooləss/ • adjective excessively ready to believe things; gullible.
– DERIVATIVES **credulity** /kridyooliti/ noun **credulously** adverb.
– ORIGIN Latin *credulus*, from *credere* 'believe'.

Cree /kree/ • noun (pl. same or **Crees**) a member of an American Indian people of central Canada.
– ORIGIN Algonquian.

creed • noun **1** a system of religious belief; a faith. **2** a statement of beliefs or principles; a credo.
– ORIGIN from Latin *credo* 'I believe'.

creedal • adjective variant spelling of CREDAL.

Creek /kreek/ • noun (pl. same) a member of a confederacy of American Indian peoples of the south-eastern US.
– ORIGIN from CREEK, because they lived beside the waterways of the flatlands of Georgia and Alabama.

creek • noun **1** a small waterway such as an inlet in a shoreline or channel in a marsh. **2** N. Amer. & Austral./NZ a stream or minor tributary of a river.
– PHRASES **up the creek** informal **1** in severe difficulty or trouble. **2** Brit. stupid or misguided.
– ORIGIN Old French *crique* or Old Norse *kriki* 'nook'.

creel • noun **1** a large basket for carrying fish. **2** a rack holding bobbins or spools when spinning.
– ORIGIN originally Scots and northern English: of unknown origin.

creep • verb (past and past part. **crept**) **1** move slowly and carefully, especially to avoid being noticed. **2** move or progress very slowly and steadily. **3** (of a plant) grow along the ground or other surface by extending stems or branches. **4** (**creep to**) informal behave obsequiously towards. • noun **1** informal a contemptible person, especially one who behaves obsequiously. **2** very slow, steady movement or progress.
– PHRASES **give someone the creeps** informal make someone feel revulsion or fear. **make one's flesh creep** cause one to have an unpleasant sensation like that of something crawling over the skin.
– ORIGIN Old English.

creeper • noun **1** any plant that grows along the ground or another surface by extending stems or branches. **2** (**creepers**) informal soft-soled suede shoes.

creepy • adjective (**creepier**, **creepiest**) informal causing an unpleasant feeling of fear or unease.
– DERIVATIVES **creepily** adverb **creepiness** noun.

creepy-crawly • noun (pl. **creepy-crawlies**) informal a spider, worm, or other small creature.

cremate • verb dispose of (a dead person's body) by burning it to ashes.
– DERIVATIVES **cremation** noun.
– ORIGIN Latin *cremare* 'burn'.

crematorium /kremmətoriəm/ • noun (pl. **crematoria** or **crematoriums**) a building where the dead are cremated.

crème anglaise /krem ONglayz/ • noun a rich egg custard.
– ORIGIN French, 'English cream'.

Thesaurus

credence • noun **1** *the government placed little credence in the scheme* BELIEF, faith, trust, confidence, reliance. **2** *later reports lent credence to this view* CREDIBILITY, plausibility; *archaic* credit.

credentials • plural noun DOCUMENTS, documentation, papers, identity papers, bona fides, ID, ID card, identity card, passport, proof of identity; certificates, diplomas, certification.

credibility • noun **1** *the whole tale lacks credibility* PLAUSIBILITY, believability, tenability, probability, feasibility, likelihood, credence; authority, cogency; *archaic* credit. **2** *the party lacked moral credibility* TRUSTWORTHINESS, reliability, dependability, integrity.

credible • adjective BELIEVABLE, plausible, tenable, able to hold water, conceivable, likely, probable, possible, feasible, reasonable, with a ring of truth, persuasive.

credit • noun **1** *he never got much credit for the show's success* PRAISE, commendation, acclaim, acknowledgement, recognition, kudos, glory, esteem, respect, admiration, tributes, thanks, gratitude, appreciation; *informal* bouquets, brownie points. **2** *the speech did his credit no good in the House of Commons* REPUTATION, repute, image, (good) name, character, prestige, standing, status, estimation, credibility. **3** *(archaic) his theory has been given very little credit* CREDENCE, belief, faith, trust, reliance, confidence.
• verb **1** *the wise will seldom credit all they hear* BELIEVE, accept, give credence to, trust, have faith in; *informal* buy, swallow, fall for, take something as gospel. **2** *the scheme's success can be credited to the team's frugality* ASCRIBE, attribute, assign, accredit, chalk up, put down.
– PHRASES **on credit** ON HIRE PURCHASE, on (the) HP, by instalments, on account; *informal* on tick, on the slate; *Brit. informal* on the never-never.

creditable • adjective COMMENDABLE, praiseworthy, laudable, admirable, honourable, estimable, meritorious, worthy, deserving, respectable.
– OPPOSITES deplorable.

credulous • adjective GULLIBLE, naive, over-trusting, over-trustful, easily taken in, impressionable, unsuspecting, unsuspicious, unwary, unquestioning; innocent, ingenuous, inexperienced, unsophisticated, unworldly, wide-eyed; *informal* born yesterday, wet behind the ears.
– OPPOSITES suspicious.

creed • noun **1** *people of many creeds and cultures* FAITH, religion, religious belief, religious persuasion, Church, denomination, sect. **2** *his political creed* SYSTEM OF BELIEF, (set of) beliefs, principles, articles of faith, ideology, credo, doctrine, teaching, dogma, tenets, canons.

creek • noun INLET, arm of the sea, bay, estuary, bight, fjord, sound; *Scottish* firth, frith; *(in Orkney & Shetland)* voe.

creep • verb **1** *Tim crept out of the house* TIPTOE, steal, sneak, slip, slink, sidle, pad, edge, inch; skulk, prowl. **2** *(informal) they're always creeping to the boss* GROVEL TO, ingratiate oneself with, curry favour with, toady to, truckle to, kowtow to, bow and scrape to, pander to, fawn on/over, make up to; *informal* crawl to, suck up to, lick someone's boots, butter up.

creeper • noun CLIMBING PLANT, trailing plant; vine, climber, rambler.

creeps • plural noun
– PHRASES **give someone the creeps** *(informal)* REPEL, repulse, revolt, disgust, sicken, nauseate, make someone's flesh creep, make someone's skin crawl; scare, frighten, terrify, horrify; *N. Amer. informal* gross out.

creepy • adjective *(informal)* FRIGHTENING, eerie, disturbing, sinister,

crème brûlée /krem broōlay/ ● noun (pl. **crèmes brûlées** pronunc. same or **crème brûlées** /krem broōlayz/) a dessert of custard topped with caramelized sugar.
– ORIGIN French, 'burnt cream'.
crème caramel /krem karrəmel/ ● noun (pl. **crèmes caramel** pronunc. same or **crème caramels**) a custard dessert made with whipped cream and eggs and topped with caramel.
– ORIGIN French.
crème de cassis /krem də kaseess/ ● noun see CASSIS[1].
crème de la crème /krem də laa **krem**/ ● noun the best person or thing of a particular kind.
– ORIGIN French, 'cream of the cream'.
crème de menthe /krem də **month**/ ● noun a green peppermint-flavoured liqueur.
– ORIGIN French, 'cream of mint'.
crème fraiche /krem **fresh**/ ● noun a type of thick cream with buttermilk, sour cream, or yogurt.
– ORIGIN French, 'fresh cream'.
crenellated /krennəlaytid/ (also **crenelated**) ● adjective (of a building) having battlements.
– ORIGIN from Latin *crena* 'notch'.
crenellations ● plural noun battlements.
Creole /kreeōl/ ● noun **1** a person of mixed European and black descent. **2** a descendant of European settlers in the Caribbean or Central or South America. **3** a white descendant of French settlers in Louisiana. **4** a mother tongue formed from the contact of a European language with another language, especially an African language.
– ORIGIN French, from Spanish *criollo*, probably from Portuguese *crioulo* 'black person born in Brazil'.
creosote ● noun **1** a dark brown oil distilled from coal tar, used as a wood preservative. **2** a liquid distilled from wood tar and used as an antiseptic. ● verb treat with creosote.
– ORIGIN from Greek *kreas* 'flesh' + *sōtēr* 'preserver'.
crêpe /krayp/ (also **crape**) ● noun **1** a light, thin fabric with a wrinkled surface. **2** hard-wearing wrinkled rubber used for the soles of shoes. **3** /also krep/ a thin pancake.
– DERIVATIVES **crêpey** (also **crêpy**) adjective.
– ORIGIN French, from Old French *crespe* 'curled, frizzed'.
crêpe de Chine /krayp də **sheen**/ ● noun a fine crêpe of silk or similar fabric.
– ORIGIN French, 'crêpe of China'.
crêpe paper ● noun thin, crinkled paper used for making decorations.
crêpe Suzette ● noun (pl. **crêpes Suzette** pronunc. same) a thin dessert pancake flamed and served in alcohol.
crepitate /kreppitayt/ ● verb rare make a crackling sound.
– DERIVATIVES **crepitation** noun.
– ORIGIN Latin *crepitare*, from *crepare* 'to rattle'.
crept past and past participle of CREEP.
crepuscular /kripuskyoolər/ ● adjective resembling or relating to twilight.
– ORIGIN from Latin *crepusculum* 'twilight'.
crescendo /krishendō/ ● noun **1** (pl. **crescendos** or **crescendi** /krishendi/) a gradual increase in loudness in a piece of music. **2** the loudest or climactic point. ● adverb & adjective Music with a gradual increase in loudness. ● verb (**crescendoes, crescendoed**) increase in loudness or intensity.
– ORIGIN Italian, from *crescere* 'to increase'.
crescent /krezz'nt/ ● noun **1** the curved sickle shape of the waxing or waning moon. **2** a thing of this shape, in particular a street or terrace of houses forming an arc.
– ORIGIN from Latin *crescere* 'grow'.
cress ● noun **1** a plant with small white flowers and pungent leaves. **2** young sprouts of garden cress eaten in salads.
– ORIGIN Old English.
crest ● noun **1** a comb or tuft of feathers, fur, or skin on the head of a bird or other animal. **2** a plume of feathers on a helmet. **3** the top of a ridge, wave, etc. **4** a distinctive heraldic device representing a family or corporate body. ● verb **1** reach the top of. **2** (**be crested with**) have (something) attached at the top.
– PHRASES **on the crest of a wave** at a very successful point.
– DERIVATIVES **crested** adjective.
– ORIGIN Old French *creste*, from Latin *crista* 'tuft, plume'.
crestfallen ● adjective sad and disappointed.
– ORIGIN originally referring to an animal with a fallen or drooping crest.
Cretaceous /kritayshəss/ ● adjective relating to the last period of the Mesozoic era (between the Jurassic and Tertiary periods, about 146 to 65 million years ago), at the end of which dinosaurs and many other organisms died out.
– ORIGIN from Latin *creta* 'chalk'.
Cretan /kreet'n/ ● noun a person from the Greek island of Crete. ● adjective relating to Crete.
cretin /krettin/ ● noun **1** a stupid person. **2** Medicine, dated a person who is deformed and mentally handicapped because of congenital thyroid deficiency.
– DERIVATIVES **cretinism** noun.
– ORIGIN from Swiss French *crestin* 'Christian', apparently used to convey a reminder that handicapped people are human.
cretinous ● adjective very stupid.
cretonne /kreton/ ● noun a heavy cotton fabric, typically with a floral pattern, used for upholstery.
– ORIGIN French.
Creutzfeldt–Jakob disease /kroytsfeldyakkob/ ● noun a fatal degenerative disease affecting nerve cells in the brain.
– PHRASES **new variant Creutzfeldt–Jakob disease** a form of the disease possibly linked to BSE.
– ORIGIN named after the German neurologists H. G. *Creutzfeldt* and A. *Jakob*, who first described the disease in the early 1920s.
crevasse /krivass/ ● noun a deep open crack in a glacier or ice field.
– ORIGIN Old French *crevace* (see CREVICE).
crevice /krevviss/ ● noun a narrow opening or fissure in a rock or wall.
– ORIGIN Old French *crevace*, from *crever* 'to burst'.
crew[1] ● noun (treated as sing. or pl.) **1** a group of people who work on and operate a ship, boat, aircraft, or train. **2** such a group other than the officers. **3** informal, often derogatory a group of people. ● verb **1** provide with a crew. **2** act as a member of a crew.
– ORIGIN Old French *creue* 'augmentation, increase', from Latin *crescere* 'grow'.
crew[2] past of CROW[2].
crew cut ● noun a very short haircut for men and boys.
– ORIGIN apparently first adopted by boat crews of Harvard and Yale universities.
crewel /kroōəl/ ● noun a thin, loosely twisted, worsted yarn used for tapestry and embroidery.
– ORIGIN of unknown origin.
crew neck ● noun a close-fitting round neckline.
crib ● noun **1** chiefly N. Amer. a child's bed with barred or latticed sides; a cot. **2** a barred rack for animal fodder; a manger. **3** informal a translation of a text for use by students, especially in a surreptitious way. **4** informal, chiefly N. Amer. an apartment or house. **5** short for CRIBBAGE. **6** Austral./NZ a snack. ● verb (**cribbed, cribbing**) **1** informal copy (something) illicitly or without acknowledgement. **2** archaic steal.
– DERIVATIVES **cribber** noun.
– ORIGIN Old English.

Thesaurus

weird, hair-raising, menacing, threatening; *Scottish* eldritch; *informal* spooky, scary.
crescent ● noun HALF-MOON, sickle-shape, demilune, lunula, lunette; arc, curve, bow.
crest ● noun **1** *the bird's crest* COMB, plume, tuft of feathers. **2** *the crest of the hill* SUMMIT, peak, top, tip, pinnacle, brow, crown, apex. **3** *the Duke of Wellington's crest* INSIGNIA, regalia, badge, emblem, heraldic device, coat of arms, arms; *Heraldry* bearing, charge.
crestfallen ● adjective DOWNHEARTED, downcast, despondent, disappointed, disconsolate, disheartened, discouraged, dispirited, dejected, depressed, desolate, in the doldrums, sad, glum, gloomy, dismayed, doleful, miserable, unhappy, woebegone, forlorn; *informal* blue, down in the mouth, down in the dumps.
– OPPOSITES cheerful.
crevasse ● noun CHASM, abyss, fissure, cleft, crack, split, breach, rift, hole, cavity.
crevice ● noun CRACK, fissure, cleft, chink, interstice, cranny, nook, slit, split, rift, fracture, breach; opening, gap, hole.
crew ● noun **1** *the ship's crew* SAILORS, mariners, hands, ship's company, ship's complement. **2** *a crew of cameramen and sound engineers* TEAM, group, company, unit, corps, party, gang. **3** *(informal) a crew of inebriated locals* CROWD, group, band, gang, mob, pack, troop, swarm, herd, posse; *informal* bunch, gaggle.
crib ● noun **1** *the baby's crib* COT, cradle, bassinet, Moses basket,

C

cribbage ● noun a card game for two players, the objective of which is to play cards whose value reaches exactly 15 or 31.
– ORIGIN related to CRIB.

crick ● noun a painful stiff feeling in the neck or back. ● verb twist or strain (one's neck or back), causing painful stiffness.
– ORIGIN of unknown origin.

cricket[1] ● noun an open-air game played on a large grass field with bat and ball between teams of eleven players, the batsmen attempting to score runs by hitting the ball and running between the wickets.
– PHRASES **not cricket** Brit. informal not fair or honourable.
– DERIVATIVES **cricketer** noun **cricketing** adjective.
– ORIGIN of unknown origin.

cricket[2] ● noun an insect related to the grasshoppers but with shorter legs, of which the male produces a characteristic musical chirping sound.
– ORIGIN Old French *criquet*, from *criquer* 'to crackle'.

cri de cœur /kree də kör/ ● noun (pl. **cris de cœur** pronunc. same) a passionate appeal or complaint.
– ORIGIN French, 'cry from the heart'.

cried past and past participle of CRY.

crier ● noun an officer who makes public announcements in a court of justice.

crikey ● exclamation Brit. informal an expression of surprise.
– ORIGIN euphemism for CHRIST.

crime ● noun **1** an offence against an individual or the state which is punishable by law. **2** such actions collectively. **3** informal something shameful or deplorable.
– ORIGIN Latin *crimen* 'judgement, offence'.

crime passionnel /kreem pasyonel/ ● noun (pl. **crimes passionnels** pronunc. same) a crime committed in a fit of sexual jealousy.
– ORIGIN French, 'crime of passion'.

criminal ● noun a person who has committed a crime. ● adjective **1** relating to or constituting a crime. **2** informal deplorable and shocking.
– DERIVATIVES **criminality** noun **criminally** adverb.

criminalize (also **criminalise**) ● verb make (an activity) illegal.
– DERIVATIVES **criminalization** noun.

criminology /krimminolləji/ ● noun the scientific study of crime and criminals.
– DERIVATIVES **criminological** adjective **criminologist** noun.

crimp ● verb **1** compress into small folds or ridges. **2** make waves in (hair) with a hot iron. ● noun a curl, wave, or folded or compressed edge.
– ORIGIN Old English.

crimper ● noun informal a hairdresser.

crimplene /krimpleen/ ● noun trademark a synthetic crease-resistant fibre and fabric.
– ORIGIN probably from CRIMP + TERYLENE.

crimson /krimz'n/ ● noun a rich deep red colour inclining to purple. ● verb become flushed, especially through embarrassment.
– ORIGIN Arabic, related to KERMES.

cringe /krinj/ ● verb (**cringing**) **1** bend one's head and body in fear or in a servile manner. **2** have a sudden feeling of embarrassment or disgust. ● noun an act of cringing.
– ORIGIN from an Old English word meaning 'bend, yield, fall in battle'; related to CRANK[1], CRINKLE.

cringeworthy ● adjective informal causing feelings of embarrassment.

crinkle ● verb form small creases or wrinkles. ● noun a small crease or wrinkle.
– DERIVATIVES **crinkly** adjective.
– ORIGIN related to CRINGE.

crinoline /krinnəlin/ ● noun a stiffened or hooped petticoat formerly worn to make a long skirt stand out.
– ORIGIN French, from Latin *crinis* 'hair' + *linum* 'thread'.

cripes /krīps/ ● exclamation informal, dated an expression of surprise.
– ORIGIN euphemism for CHRIST.

cripple ● noun archaic or offensive a person who is unable to walk or move properly through disability or injury. ● verb **1** make (someone) unable to move or walk properly. **2** cause severe and disabling damage to (something).
– USAGE The word **cripple** as a noun has acquired offensive connotations and should be avoided. Broader terms such as 'disabled person' are preferable.
– ORIGIN Old English, related to CREEP.

crisis ● noun (pl. **crises**) **1** a time of intense difficulty or danger. **2** the turning point of a disease, when it becomes clear whether the patient will recover or not.
– ORIGIN Greek *krisis* 'decision', from *krinein* 'decide'.

crisp ● adjective **1** firm, dry, and brittle. **2** (of the weather) cool, fresh, and invigorating. **3** briskly decisive and matter-of-fact. ● noun (also **potato crisp**) Brit. a wafer-thin slice of potato fried until crisp and eaten as a snack. ● verb **1** give (food) a crisp surface by cooking in an oven or under a grill. **2** archaic curl into short, stiff, wavy folds or crinkles.
– DERIVATIVES **crisper** noun **crisply** adverb **crispness** noun **crispy** adjective (**crispier**, **crispiest**).
– ORIGIN Latin *crispus* 'curled'.

crispbread ● noun a thin crisp biscuit made from crushed rye or wheat.

criss-cross ● adjective containing a number of intersecting straight lines or paths. ● noun a criss-cross pattern. ● verb

Thesaurus

carrycot. **2** *the oxen's cribs* MANGER, stall, feeding trough, fodder rack.
● verb (*informal*) *she cribbed the plot from a Shakespeare play* COPY, plagiarize, poach, appropriate, steal, 'borrow'; *informal* rip off, lift; *Brit. informal* nick, pinch.

crick ● verb STRAIN, twist, rick, sprain, pull, wrench; injure, hurt, damage.

crime ● noun **1** *kidnapping is a very serious crime* OFFENCE, unlawful act, illegal act, felony, misdemeanour, misdeed, wrong; *Law* tort. **2** *the increase in crime* LAWBREAKING, delinquency, wrongdoing, criminality, misconduct, illegality, villainy; *informal* crookedness; *Law* malfeasance. **3** *a crime against humanity* SIN, evil, immoral act, wrong, atrocity, abomination, disgrace, outrage.

criminal ● noun *a convicted criminal* LAWBREAKER, offender, villain, delinquent, felon, convict, malefactor, wrongdoer, culprit, miscreant; thief, burglar, robber, armed robber, gunman, gangster, terrorist; *informal* crook, con, jailbird, (old) lag; *N. Amer. informal* hood, yardbird; *Austral./NZ informal* crim; *Law* malfeasant.
● adjective **1** *criminal conduct* UNLAWFUL, illegal, illicit, lawless, felonious, delinquent, fraudulent, actionable, culpable; villainous, nefarious, corrupt, wrong, bad, evil, wicked, iniquitous; *informal* crooked; *Brit. informal* bent; *Law* malfeasant. **2** (*informal*) *a criminal waste of taxpayer's money* DEPLORABLE, shameful, reprehensible, disgraceful, inexcusable, unforgivable, unpardonable, outrageous, monstrous, shocking, scandalous, wicked.
– OPPOSITES lawful.

crimp ● verb PLEAT, flute, corrugate, ruffle, fold, crease, crinkle, pucker, gather; pinch, compress, press together, squeeze together.

crimped ● adjective *crimped blonde hair* CURLY, wavy, curled, frizzy, ringlety.

cringe ● verb **1** *she cringed as he bellowed in her ear* COWER, shrink, recoil, shy away, flinch, blench, draw back; shake, tremble, quiver, quail, quake. **2** *it makes me cringe when I think of it* WINCE, shudder, squirm, feel embarrassed/mortified.

crinkle ● verb WRINKLE, crease, pucker, furrow, corrugate, line; rumple, scrunch up, ruck up.

crinkly ● adjective WRINKLED, wrinkly, crinkled, creased, crumpled, rumpled, crimped, corrugated, fluted, puckered, furrowed; wavy.

cripple ● verb **1** *the accident crippled her* DISABLE, paralyse, immobilize, lame, incapacitate, handicap. **2** *the company had been crippled by the recession* DEVASTATE, ruin, destroy, wipe out; paralyse, hamstring, bring to a standstill, put out of action, put out of business, bankrupt, break, bring someone to their knees.

crippled ● adjective DISABLED, paralysed, incapacitated, physically handicapped, lame, immobilized, bedridden, confined to a wheelchair; *euphemistic* physically challenged; *archaic* halt.

crisis ● noun **1** *the situation had reached a crisis* CRITICAL POINT, turning point, crossroads, climacteric, head, moment of truth, zero hour, point of no return, Rubicon, doomsday; *informal* crunch. **2** *the current economic crisis* EMERGENCY, disaster, catastrophe, calamity; predicament, plight, mess, trouble, dire straits, difficulty, extremity.

crisp ● adjective **1** *crisp bacon* CRUNCHY, crispy, brittle, crumbly, friable, breakable; firm, dry. **2** *a crisp autumn day* INVIGORATING, bracing, brisk, fresh, refreshing, exhilarating, tonic, energizing; cool, chill, chilly, cold; *informal* nippy; *Brit. informal* parky. **3** *her answer was crisp* BRISK, decisive, businesslike, no-nonsense, incisive, to the point, matter of fact, brusque; terse, succinct, concise, brief,

1 form a criss-cross pattern on (a place). **2** move or travel around (a place) by going back and forth repeatedly.
– ORIGIN originally denoting a figure of a cross preceding the alphabet in a hornbook: from *Christ-cross*.

criterion /krīteeriən/ ● noun (pl. **criteria** /krīteeriə/) a principle or standard by which something may be judged or decided.
– DERIVATIVES **criterial** adjective.
– USAGE The singular form is **criterion** and the plural form is **criteria**. Do not use **criteria** as if it were a singular, as in *a further criteria needs to be considered*.
– ORIGIN Greek *kritērion* 'means of judging', from *kritēs* 'a judge'.

critic ● noun **1** a person who expresses an unfavourable opinion of something. **2** a person who reviews literary or artistic works.
– ORIGIN Greek *kritikos*, from *kritēs* 'a judge'.

critical ● adjective **1** expressing adverse or disapproving comments or judgements. **2** expressing or involving an analysis of the merits and faults of a literary or artistic work. **3** having a decisive importance in the success or failure of something; crucial. **4** extremely ill and at risk of death. **5** Mathematics & Physics relating to a point of transition from one state to another. **6** (of a nuclear reactor or fuel) maintaining a self-sustaining chain reaction.
– DERIVATIVES **critically** adverb.

critical mass ● noun **1** Physics the minimum amount of fissile material needed to maintain a nuclear chain reaction. **2** the minimum amount of resources required to start or maintain a venture.

critical path ● noun the sequence of stages determining the minimum time needed for a complex operation.

criticism ● noun **1** expression of disapproval; finding fault. **2** the critical assessment of literary or artistic works.

criticize (also **criticise**) ● verb **1** indicate the faults of in a disapproving way. **2** form and express a critical assessment of (a literary or artistic work).

critique /kriteek/ ● noun a detailed analysis and assessment. ● verb (**critiques**, **critiqued**, **critiquing**) evaluate in a detailed and analytical way.
– ORIGIN French.

critter ● noun informal or dialect, chiefly N. Amer. a living creature.

croak ● noun a characteristic deep hoarse sound made by a frog or a crow. ● verb **1** utter a croak. **2** informal die.
– DERIVATIVES **croaker** noun **croakily** adverb **croaky** adjective (**croakier**, **croakiest**).
– ORIGIN imitative.

Croatian /krōaysh'n/ ● noun (also **Croat** /krōat/) **1** a person from Croatia. **2** the language of the Croats, almost identical to Serbian but written in the Roman alphabet. ● adjective relating to Croatia or Croatian.

crochet /krōshay/ ● noun a handicraft in which yarn is made up into a patterned fabric by means of a hooked needle. ● verb (**crocheted** /krōshayd/, **crocheting** /krōshaying/) make (a garment or piece of fabric) in this way.
– ORIGIN French, 'little hook'.

croci plural of CROCUS.

crock[1] informal ● noun **1** an old person considered to be feeble and useless. **2** Brit. an old worn-out vehicle. ● verb **1** Brit. cause an injury to. **2** (**crocked**) N. Amer. drunk.
– ORIGIN originally denoting an old ewe or horse: probably related to CRACK.

crock[2] ● noun **1** an earthenware pot or jar. **2** an item of crockery. **3** N. Amer. informal something considered to be complete nonsense.
– ORIGIN Old English.

crockery ● noun plates, dishes, cups, and similar items made of earthenware or china.
– ORIGIN from obsolete *crocker* 'potter'.

crocodile ● noun **1** a large predatory semiaquatic reptile with long jaws, long tail, short legs, and a horny textured skin. **2** leather made from crocodile skin. **3** Brit. informal a line of schoolchildren walking in pairs.
– ORIGIN Old French *cocodrille*, from Greek *krokodilos* 'worm of the stones'.

crocodile clip ● noun chiefly Brit. a sprung metal clip with long, serrated jaws, used to connect an electric cable to a battery.

crocodile tears ● plural noun insincere tears or expressions of sorrow.
– ORIGIN said to be so named from a belief that crocodiles wept while devouring or luring their prey.

crocus /krōkəss/ ● noun (pl. **crocuses** or **croci** /krōkī/) a small spring-flowering plant with bright yellow, purple, or white flowers.
– ORIGIN Greek *krokos*.

Croesus /kreesəss/ ● noun a person of great wealth.
– ORIGIN from the name of a famously wealthy king of Lydia *c.*560–546 BC.

croft Brit. ● noun **1** a small rented farm in Scotland or northern England. **2** a small enclosed field attached to a house. ● verb farm (land) as a croft or crofts.
– DERIVATIVES **crofter** noun.
– ORIGIN Old English.

Crohn's disease /krōnz/ ● noun a chronic disease of the intestines, especially the colon and ileum.
– ORIGIN named after the American pathologist Burrill B. *Crohn* (1884–1983).

croissant /krwusson/ ● noun a crescent-shaped French roll made of sweet flaky pastry.
– ORIGIN French, 'crescent'.

Cro-Magnon /krōmagnən, krōmənyon/ ● noun the earliest form of modern human in Europe, appearing *c.*35,000 years ago.
– ORIGIN the name of a hill in the Dordogne, France.

cromlech /kromlek/ ● noun **1** (in Wales) a megalithic tomb; a dolmen. **2** (in Brittany) a circle of standing stones.
– ORIGIN Welsh, 'arched flat stone'.

crone ● noun an ugly old woman.
– ORIGIN Old French *caroigne* 'carrion'.

crony /krōni/ ● noun (pl. **cronies**) informal, often derogatory a close friend or companion.
– ORIGIN originally Cambridge university slang: from Greek *khronios* 'long-lasting' (here used to mean 'contemporary'); compare with CHUM.

cronyism (also **croneyism**) ● noun derogatory the improper ap-

C

Thesaurus

short, short and sweet, laconic; *informal* snappy. **4** *crisp white bed-linen* SMOOTH, uncreased, ironed; starched.
– OPPOSITES soft, sultry, rambling.

criterion ● noun STANDARD, specification, measure, gauge, test, scale, benchmark, yardstick, touchstone, barometer; principle, rule, law, canon.

critic ● noun **1** *a literary critic* REVIEWER, commentator, evaluator, analyst, judge, pundit. **2** *critics of the government* DETRACTOR, attacker, fault-finder.

critical ● adjective **1** *a highly critical report* CENSORIOUS, condemnatory, condemning, denunciatory, disparaging, disapproving, scathing, fault-finding, judgemental, negative, unfavourable; *informal* nit-picking, picky. **2** *a critical essay* EVALUATIVE, analytical, interpretative, expository, explanatory. **3** *the situation is critical* GRAVE, serious, dangerous, risky, perilous, hazardous, precarious, touch-and-go, in the balance, uncertain, parlous, desperate, dire, acute, life-and-death. **4** *the choice of materials is critical for product safety* CRUCIAL, vital, essential, of the essence, all-important, paramount, fundamental, key, pivotal, decisive, deciding, climacteric.
– OPPOSITES complimentary, unimportant.

criticism ● noun **1** *she was stung by his criticism* CENSURE, condemnation, denunciation, disapproval, disparagement, opprobrium, fault-finding, attack, broadside, flak, brickbats, stricture, recrimination; *informal* a bad press, panning; *Brit. informal* stick, slating; *formal* excoriation. **2** *literary criticism* EVALUATION, assessment, appraisal, analysis, judgement; commentary, interpretation, explanation, explication, elucidation.

criticize ● verb FIND FAULT WITH, censure, denounce, condemn, attack, lambaste, pillory, rail against, inveigh against, arraign, cast aspersions on, pour scorn on, disparage, denigrate, give a bad press to, run down; *informal* knock, pan, slam, hammer, lay into, pull to pieces, pick holes in; *Brit. informal* slag off, slate, rubbish; *N. Amer. informal* pummel, trash; *Austral./NZ informal* bag, monster; *formal* excoriate.
– OPPOSITES praise.

critique ● noun ANALYSIS, evaluation, assessment, appraisal, appreciation, criticism, review, study, commentary, exposition, exegesis.

crock ● noun **1** *a crock of honey* POT, jar; jug, pitcher, ewer; container, receptacle, vessel. **2** (**crocks**) *a pile of dirty crocks.* See CROCKERY. **3** *(informal) he's a bit of an old crock* INVALID, valetudinar-

pointment of friends and associates to positions of authority.

crook • noun **1** a shepherd's hooked staff. **2** a bishop's crozier. **3** a bend, especially at the elbow in a person's arm. **4** informal a criminal or dishonest person. • verb bend (something, especially a finger). • adjective Austral./NZ informal **1** bad, unsound, or unwell. **2** dishonest; illegal.
– ORIGIN Old Norse, 'hook'.

C

crookbacked • adjective archaic hunchbacked.

crooked /krŏŏkkid/ • adjective **1** bent or twisted out of shape or position. **2** informal dishonest or illegal. **3** Austral./NZ informal annoyed; exasperated.
– DERIVATIVES **crookedly** adverb **crookedness** noun.

croon • verb hum, sing, or speak in a soft, low voice. • noun a soft, low voice or tone.
– DERIVATIVES **crooner** noun.
– ORIGIN Low German and Dutch *krōnen* 'groan, lament'.

crop • noun **1** a plant, especially a cereal, fruit, or vegetable, cultivated for food or other use. **2** an amount of a crop harvested at one time. **3** an amount of people or things appearing at one time: *the current crop of politicians.* **4** a very short hairstyle. **5** a riding crop or hunting crop. **6** a pouch in a bird's gullet where food is stored or prepared for digestion. • verb (**cropped**, **cropping**) **1** cut very short or trim off the edges of. **2** (of an animal) bite off and eat the tops of (plants). **3** (**crop up**) appear or occur unexpectedly. **4** harvest (a crop) from an area. **5** sow or plant (land) with plants that will produce a crop.
– ORIGIN Old English.

crop circle • noun an area of standing crops which has been flattened in the form of a circle or other pattern by unexplained means.

crop dusting • noun the spraying of powdered insecticide or fertilizer on crops from the air.

cropper • noun **1** a plant which yields a specified crop. **2** a machine or person that cuts or trims something. **3** chiefly US a person who raises a crop, especially as a sharecropper.
– PHRASES **come a cropper** informal **1** fall heavily. **2** suffer a defeat or disaster.

crop top (also **cropped top**) • noun a woman's casual garment for the upper body, cut short so that it reveals the stomach.

croque-monsieur /krok məsyör/ • noun a fried or grilled cheese and ham sandwich.
– ORIGIN French, 'bite a man'.

croquet /krōkay/ • noun **1** a game played on a lawn, in which wooden balls are driven through a series of hoops with a mallet. **2** an act of croqueting a ball. • verb (**croqueted** /krōkayd/, **croqueting** /krōkaying/) knock away (an opponent's ball) by holding one's own ball against it and striking this with a mallet.
– ORIGIN perhaps a dialect form of French *crochet* 'hook'.

croquette /krəket/ • noun a small ball or roll of vegetables, minced meat, or fish, fried in breadcrumbs.
– ORIGIN French, from *croquer* 'to crunch'.

crosier /krōziər/ • noun variant spelling of CROZIER.

cross • noun **1** a mark, object, or figure formed by two short intersecting lines or pieces (+ or ×). **2** an upright post with a transverse bar, as used in antiquity for crucifixion. **3** a cross-shaped decoration awarded for bravery or indicating rank in some orders of knighthood. **4** a thing that is unavoidable and has to be endured: *she's just a cross we have to bear.* **5** an animal or plant resulting from cross-breeding; a hybrid. **6** (**a cross between**) a mixture or compromise of (two things). **7** (in soccer) a pass of the ball across the field towards the centre close to one's opponents' goal. • verb **1** go or extend across or to the other side of (a path, obstacle, or area). **2** pass in an opposite or different direction; intersect. **3** place crosswise: *Michele crossed her legs.* **4** draw a line or lines across; mark with a cross. **5** Brit. mark or annotate (a cheque) with a pair of parallel lines to indicate that it must be paid into a named bank account. **6** Soccer pass (the ball) across the field towards the centre when attacking. **7** cause (an animal of one species, breed, or variety) to interbreed with one of another. **8** oppose or stand in the way of. • adjective annoyed.
– PHRASES **at cross purposes** misunderstanding or having different aims from one another. **cross one's fingers** put one finger across another as a sign of hoping for good luck. **cross the floor** Brit. join the opposing side in Parliament. **cross my heart (and hope to die)** used to emphasize the truthfulness and sincerity of what one is saying. **cross off** delete (an item) from a list. **cross oneself** make the sign of the cross in front of one's chest as a sign of Christian reverence or to invoke divine protection. **cross out/through** delete (a word or phrase) by drawing a line through it. **cross over** (of an artist) begin to appeal to a wider audience. **cross someone's palm with silver** often humorous pay someone for a service, especially fortune-telling. **cross swords** have an argument or dispute. **crossed line** a telephone connection that has been wrongly made with the result that another call can be heard. **get one's wires** (or **lines**) **crossed** have a misunderstanding.
– DERIVATIVES **crosser** noun **crossly** adverb **crossness** noun.
– ORIGIN Old Irish *cros*, from Latin *crux*.

Thesaurus

ian; geriatric, dotard; *informal* crumbly, wrinkly.

crockery • noun DISHES, crocks, china, tableware; plates, bowls, cups, saucers.

crony • noun *(informal)* FRIEND, companion, bosom friend, intimate, confidant(e), familiar, associate, comrade; *informal* pal, chum, sidekick; *Brit. informal* mate; *N. Amer. informal* buddy, amigo, compadre; *archaic* compeer.

crook • noun **1** *(informal) a small-time crook* CRIMINAL, lawbreaker, offender, villain, delinquent, felon, convict, malefactor, culprit, wrongdoer; rogue, scoundrel, cheat, swindler, racketeer, confidence trickster; thief, robber, burglar; *informal* (old) lag, shark, con man, con, jailbird; *N. Amer. informal* hood, yardbird; *Austral./NZ informal* crim; *Law* malfeasant. **2** *the crook of a tree branch* BEND, fork, curve, angle.
• verb *he crooked his finger and called the waiter* COCK, flex, bend, curve, curl.

crooked • adjective **1** *narrow, crooked streets* WINDING, twisting, zigzag, meandering, tortuous, serpentine. **2** *a crooked spine* BENT, twisted, misshapen, deformed, malformed, contorted, out of shape, wry, warped, bowed, distorted; *Scottish* thrawn. **3** *the picture over the bed looked crooked* LOPSIDED, askew, awry, off-centre, uneven, out of true, out of line, asymmetrical, tilted, at an angle, aslant, slanting, squint; *Scottish* agley; *informal* cock-eyed; *Brit. informal* skew-whiff, wonky. **4** *(informal) a crooked cop | crooked deals* DISHONEST, unscrupulous, unprincipled, untrustworthy, corrupt, corruptible, buyable, venal; criminal, illegal, unlawful, nefarious, fraudulent; *Brit. informal* bent, dodgy.
– OPPOSITES straight, honest.

croon • verb SING SOFTLY, hum, warble, trill.

crop • noun **1** *some farmers lost their entire crop* HARVEST, year's growth, yield; fruits, produce. **2** *a bumper crop of mail* BATCH, lot, assortment, selection, collection, supply, intake. **3** *the bird's crop* CRAW; gullet, throat. **4** *a rider's crop* WHIP, switch, cane, stick.
• verb **1** *she's had her hair cropped* CUT SHORT, cut, clip, shear, shave, lop off, chop off, hack off; dock. **2** *a flock of sheep were cropping the turf* GRAZE ON, browse on, feed on, nibble, eat. **3** *the hay was cropped several times this summer* HARVEST, reap, mow; gather (in), collect, pick, bring home.
– PHRASES **crop up** HAPPEN, occur, arise, turn up, spring up, pop up, emerge, materialize, surface, appear, come to light, present itself; *poetic/literary* come to pass, befall; *archaic* hap.

cross • noun **1** *a bronze cross* CRUCIFIX, rood. **2** *we all have our crosses to bear* BURDEN, trouble, worry, trial, tribulation, affliction, curse, bane, misfortune, adversity, hardship, vicissitude; millstone, albatross, thorn in one's flesh/side; misery, woe, pain, sorrow, suffering; *informal* hassle, headache. **3** *a cross between a yak and a cow* HYBRID, hybridization, cross-breed, half-breed, mongrel; mixture, amalgam, blend, combination.
• verb **1** *they crossed the hills on foot* TRAVEL ACROSS, traverse, range over; negotiate, navigate, cover. **2** *a lake crossed by a fine stone bridge* SPAN, bridge; extend/stretch across, pass over. **3** *the point where the two roads cross* INTERSECT, meet, join, connect, criss-cross. **4** *no one dared cross him* OPPOSE, resist, defy, obstruct, impede, hinder, hamper; contradict, argue with, quarrel with, stand up to, take a stand against, take issue with; *formal* gainsay. **5** *the breed was crossed with the similarly coloured Friesian* HYBRIDIZE, cross-breed, interbreed, cross-fertilize, cross-pollinate.
• adjective *Jane was getting cross* ANGRY, annoyed, irate, irritated, in a bad mood, vexed, irked, piqued, out of humour, put out, displeased; irritable, short-tempered, bad-tempered, snappish, crotchety, grouchy, grumpy, fractious, testy, tetchy, crabby; *informal* mad, hot under the collar, peeved, riled, snappy, on the warpath, up in arms, steamed up, in a paddy; *Brit. informal* aerated, shirty, stroppy, ratty; *N. Amer. informal* sore, bent out of shape, teed off,

crossbar ● noun a horizontal bar, in particular one between the two upright posts of a football goal or between the handlebars and saddle on a bicycle.
cross bench ● noun a seat in the House of Lords occupied by a member who is independent of any political party.
crossbill ● noun a thickset finch with a crossed bill adapted for extracting seeds from the cones of conifers.
crossbow ● noun a medieval bow fixed across a wooden support, having a groove for the bolt and a mechanism for drawing and releasing the string.
cross-breed ● noun an animal or plant produced by mating or hybridizing two different species, breeds, or varieties. ● verb breed in this way.
cross-check ● verb verify (figures or information) by using an alternative source or method. ● noun an instance of cross-checking figures or information.
cross-country ● adjective **1** across fields or countryside, as opposed to on roads or tracks. **2** across a region or country, in particular not keeping to main or direct routes. ● noun the sport of cross-country running, riding, skiing, or motoring.
cross-current ● noun **1** a current in a river or sea which flows across another. **2** a process or tendency which is in conflict with another.
cross-cut ● verb **1** cut (wood or stone) across its main grain or axis. **2** alternate (one sequence) with another when editing a film.
cross-cut saw ● noun a saw with a handle at each end, used by two people for cutting across the grain of timber.
cross-dressing ● noun the wearing of clothing typical of the opposite sex.
crosse /kross/ ● noun the stick used in women's field lacrosse.
– ORIGIN Old French *croce* 'bishop's crook'.
cross-examine ● verb question (a witness called by the other party) in a court of law to check or extend testimony already given.
– DERIVATIVES **cross-examination** noun.
cross-eyed ● adjective having one or both eyes turned inwards towards the nose, either temporarily or as a permanent condition.
cross-fertilize ● verb **1** fertilize (a plant) using pollen from another plant of the same species. **2** stimulate the development of (something) with an exchange of ideas or information.
– DERIVATIVES **cross-fertilization** noun.
crossfire ● noun gunfire from two or more directions passing through the same area.
cross-grained ● adjective **1** (of timber) having a grain that runs across the regular grain. **2** stubbornly contrary or bad-tempered.
cross hairs ● plural noun a pair of fine wires crossing at right angles at the focus of an optical instrument or gunsight.
cross-hatch ● verb shade (an area) with many intersecting parallel lines.
crossing ● noun **1** a place where things, especially roads or railway lines, cross. **2** a place at which one may safely cross a street or railway line. **3** the intersection of a church nave and the transepts.
cross-legged ● adjective & adverb (of a seated person) with the legs crossed at the ankles and the knees bent outwards.
crossover ● noun **1** a point or place of crossing. **2** the production of work or achieving of success in a new field or style, especially in popular music.
cross ownership ● noun the ownership by one corporation of different companies with related interests or commercial aims.
crosspatch ● noun informal a bad-tempered person.
– ORIGIN from obsolete *patch* 'fool, clown', perhaps from Italian *pazzo* 'madman'.
crosspiece ● noun a beam or bar fixed or placed across something else.
cross-ply ● adjective Brit. (of a tyre) having fabric layers with their threads running diagonally across each other.
cross-pollinate ● verb pollinate (a flower or plant) with pollen from another flower or plant.
cross-question ● verb question in great detail.
cross reference ● noun a reference to another text given in order to elaborate on a point.
crossroads ● noun **1** an intersection of two or more roads. **2** (**crossroad**) N. Amer. a road that crosses a main road or joins two main roads.
cross section ● noun **1** a surface or shape exposed by making a straight cut through something at right angles to the axis. **2** a typical or representative sample of a larger group.
cross stitch ● noun a stitch formed of two stitches crossing each other.
crosstalk ● noun **1** unwanted transfer of signals between communication channels. **2** witty conversation.
cross tie ● noun US a railway sleeper.
crosstrees ● plural noun a pair of horizontal struts attached to a sailing ship's mast to spread the rigging.
crosswalk ● noun N. Amer. & Austral. a pedestrian crossing.
crosswind ● noun a wind blowing across one's direction of travel.
crosswise (also **crossways**) ● adverb **1** in the form of a cross. **2** diagonally; transversely.
crossword ● noun a puzzle consisting of a grid of squares and blanks into which words crossing vertically and horizontally are written according to clues.
crostini /krosteeni/ ● plural noun small pieces of toasted or fried bread served with a topping as a starter or canapé.
– ORIGIN Italian, 'little crusts'.
crotch ● noun **1** the part of the human body between the legs where they join the torso. **2** a fork in a tree, road, or river.
– ORIGIN perhaps related to Old French *croche* 'shepherd's crook'; partly also a variant of CRUTCH.
crotchet /krochit/ ● noun **1** Music, chiefly Brit. a musical note having the time value of a quarter of a semibreve, represented by a large solid dot with a plain stem. **2** a perverse or unfounded belief or notion.
– ORIGIN Old French *crochet* 'little hook'.
crotchety ● adjective irritable.
crouch ● verb adopt a position where the knees are bent and the upper body is brought forward and down. ● noun a crouching stance or posture.
– ORIGIN perhaps from Old French *crochir* 'be bent', from *croche* 'shepherd's crook'.
croup[1] /kroop/ ● noun inflammation of the larynx and trachea in children, causing breathing difficulties.
– ORIGIN from dialect *croup* 'to croak'.
croup[2] /kroop/ ● noun the rump or hindquarters of a horse.
– ORIGIN Old French, related to CROP.
croupier /kroopiay/ ● noun the person in charge of a gaming table, gathering in and paying out money or tokens.
– ORIGIN originally denoting a person standing behind a gambler to give advice: from Old French *cropier* 'pillion rider'.
crouton /krooton/ ● noun a small piece of fried or toasted bread

Thesaurus

ticked off; *Austral./NZ informal* ropeable, snaky, crook.
– OPPOSITES pleased.
– PHRASES **cross something out** DELETE, strike out, ink out, score out, edit out, blue-pencil, cancel, obliterate; *Printing* dele.
cross-examine ● verb INTERROGATE, question, cross-question, quiz, catechize, give someone the third degree; *informal* grill, pump, put someone through the wringer/mangle.
cross-grained ● adjective BAD-TEMPERED, cantankerous, irascible, grumpy, grouchy; awkward, perverse, contrary, uncooperative, unhelpful, obstructive, disobliging, recalcitrant, stubborn, obstinate, mulish, pig-headed, intractable; *informal* cussed; *Brit. informal* bloody-minded, bolshie, stroppy; *N. Amer. informal* balky; *formal* refractory.
– OPPOSITES good-humoured.
crossing ● noun **1** *a busy road crossing* JUNCTION, crossroads, intersection, interchange; level crossing. **2** *a short ferry crossing* JOURNEY, passage, voyage.
crosswise, crossways ● adverb DIAGONALLY, obliquely, transversely, aslant, cornerwise, at an angle, on the bias; *N. Amer.* cater-cornered, kitty-corner.
crotch ● noun GROIN, crutch; lap.
crotchet ● noun WHIM, whimsy, fancy, notion, vagary, caprice; foible, quirk, eccentricity; *archaic* megrim.
crotchety ● adjective BAD-TEMPERED, irascible, irritable, grumpy, grouchy, cantankerous, short-tempered, tetchy, testy, curmudgeonly, ill-tempered, ill-humoured, peevish, cross, fractious, pettish, waspish, crabbed, crabby, crusty, prickly, touchy; *informal* snappish, snappy, chippy; *Brit. informal* shirty, stroppy, narky, ratty; *N. Amer. informal* cranky, ornery; *Austral./NZ informal* snaky.
– OPPOSITES good-humoured.

served with soup or used as a garnish.
– ORIGIN French, from *croûte* 'crust'.
Crow ● noun (pl. same or **Crows**) a member of an American Indian people of eastern Montana.
crow[1] ● noun **1** a large perching bird with mostly glossy black plumage, a heavy bill, and a raucous voice. **2** informal an old or ugly woman.
– PHRASES **as the crow flies** in a straight line across country.
– ORIGIN Old English, related to CROW[2].
crow[2] ● verb (past **crowed** or **crew**) **1** (of a cock) utter its characteristic loud cry. **2** express pride or triumph in a tone of gloating satisfaction. ● noun the cry of a cock.
– ORIGIN Old English, related to CROW[1]; imitative.
crowbar ● noun an iron bar with a flattened end, used as a lever.
crowd ● noun **1** a large number of people gathered together. **2** a large audience, especially at a sporting event. **3** a group of people with a common interest. ● verb **1** (of a number of people) fill (a space) almost completely. **2** move or come together as a crowd. **3** move or stand too close to. **4** (**crowd out**) exclude by taking the place of.
– ORIGIN from Old English, 'press, hasten'.
crowded ● adjective (of a place) filled almost completely by a large number of people.
crowd-puller ● noun informal an event or person that attracts a large audience.
crowfoot ● noun an aquatic plant with lobed or divided leaves and white or yellow flowers.
crown ● noun **1** a circular ornamental headdress worn by a monarch as a symbol of authority. **2** (**the Crown**) the monarchy or reigning monarch. **3** a wreath of leaves or flowers worn as an emblem of victory, especially in ancient Greece or Rome. **4** an award or distinction gained by a victory or achievement. **5** the top or highest part, in particular of a person's head or a hat. **6** the part of a tooth projecting from the gum. **7** an artificial replacement or covering for the upper part of a tooth. **8** a British coin with a face value of five shillings or 25 pence, now minted only for commemorative purposes. ● verb **1** ceremonially place a crown on the head of (someone) to invest them as a monarch. **2** rest on or form the top of. **3** be the triumphant culmination of (an effort or endeavour). **4** fit a crown to (a tooth). **5** informal hit on the head.
– ORIGIN Latin *corona* 'wreath, chaplet'.
Crown Colony ● noun a British colony controlled by the Crown.
Crown Court ● noun (in England and Wales) a court which deals with serious cases referred from the magistrates' courts.
Crown Derby ● noun a kind of soft-paste porcelain made at Derby in England, often marked with a crown above the letter 'D'.
crowned head ● noun a king or queen.
crown green ● noun Brit. a kind of bowling green which rises slightly towards the middle.
Crown jewels ● plural noun the crown and other jewellery worn or carried by the sovereign on state occasions.
Crown prince ● noun (in some countries) a male heir to a throne.
Crown princess ● noun **1** the wife of a Crown prince. **2** (in some countries) a female heir to a throne.
crown wheel ● noun a gearwheel or cogwheel with teeth that project from the face of the wheel at right angles.
crow's foot ● noun a branching wrinkle at the outer corner of a person's eye.
crow's-nest ● noun a platform at the masthead of a vessel for a lookout to watch from.
crozier /krōziər/ (also **crosier**) ● noun a hooked staff carried by a bishop.
– ORIGIN Old French *croisier* 'cross-bearer'.
CRT ● abbreviation cathode ray tube.
cru /kroo/ ● noun (pl. **crus** pronunc. same) (in France) a vineyard or group of vineyards, especially one of recognized superior quality.
– ORIGIN French, 'growth'.
cruces plural of CRUX.
crucial /kroosh'l/ ● adjective **1** decisive or critical. **2** informal very important. **3** informal excellent.
– DERIVATIVES **crucially** adverb.
– ORIGIN originally in the sense 'cross-shaped': from Latin *crux* 'cross'.
cruciate ligament ● noun either of a pair of ligaments in the knee which cross each other and connect the femur to the tibia.
– ORIGIN from Latin *cruciatus* 'cross-shaped'.
crucible /kroossib'l/ ● noun **1** a container in which metals or other substances may be melted or subjected to very high temperatures. **2** a situation of severe trial, or in which different elements interact to produce something new.
– ORIGIN Latin *crucibulum* 'night lamp, crucible', from *crux* 'cross'.
cruciferous /kroosifferəss/ ● adjective Botany of the cabbage family (Cruciferae), with four equal petals arranged in a cross.
– ORIGIN from Latin *crux* 'cross' + *-fer* 'bearing'.
crucifix /kroosifiks/ ● noun a representation of a cross with a figure of Christ on it.
– ORIGIN from Latin *cruci fixus* 'fixed to a cross'.
crucifixion ● noun **1** the execution of a person by crucifying them. **2** (**the Crucifixion**) the killing of Jesus Christ in such a way.
cruciform /kroosiform/ ● adjective having the shape of a cross.
crucify /kroosifī/ ● verb (**crucifies**, **crucified**) **1** put (someone) to death by nailing or binding them to a cross. **2** cause anguish to. **3** informal criticize severely.
– ORIGIN from Latin *crux* 'cross' + *figere* 'fix'.
crud ● noun informal **1** an unpleasantly dirty or messy substance.

Thesaurus

crouch ● verb SQUAT, bend (down), hunker down, hunch over, stoop, kneel (down); duck, cower.
crow ● verb **1** *a cock crowed* CRY, squawk, screech, caw. **2** *try to avoid crowing about your success* BOAST, brag, trumpet, swagger, swank, gloat, show off, preen oneself, sing one's own praises; *informal* talk big, blow one's own trumpet, lay it on thick; *Austral./NZ informal* skite.
crowd ● noun **1** *a crowd of people* THRONG, horde, mass, multitude, host, army, herd, flock, drove, swarm, sea, troupe, pack, press, crush, mob, rabble; collection, company, gathering, assembly, assemblage, congregation; *informal* gaggle, bunch, gang, posse; *archaic* rout. **2** *she wanted to stand out from the crowd* MAJORITY, multitude, common people, populace, general public, masses, rank and file; *Brit. informal* Joe Public. **3** *he's been hanging round with Hurley's crowd* SET, group, circle, clique, coterie; camp; *informal* gang, crew, lot. **4** *the final attracted a capacity crowd* AUDIENCE, spectators, listeners, viewers; house, turnout, attendance, gate; congregation; *Brit. informal* punters.
● verb **1** *reporters crowded round her* CLUSTER, flock, swarm, mill, throng, huddle, gather, assemble, congregate, converge. **2** *the guests all crowded into the dining room* SURGE, push one's way, jostle, elbow one's way; squeeze, pile, cram. **3** *the quayside was crowded with holidaymakers* THRONG, pack, jam, cram, fill. **4** *stop crowding me* PRESSURIZE, pressure; harass, hound, pester, harry, badger, nag; *informal* hassle, lean on.
crowded ● adjective PACKED, full, filled to capacity, full to bursting, congested, overcrowded, overflowing, teeming, swarming, thronged, populous, overpopulated; busy; *informal* jam-packed, stuffed, chock-a-block, chock-full, bursting at the seams, full to the gunwales, wall-to-wall; *Austral./NZ informal* chocker.
– OPPOSITES deserted.
crown ● noun **1** *a jewelled crown* CORONET, diadem, circlet; *poetic/literary* coronal; *historical* taj. **2** *the world heavyweight crown* TITLE, award, accolade, distinction; trophy, cup, medal, plate, shield, belt, prize; laurels, bays, palm. **3** *his family were loyal servants of the Crown* MONARCH, sovereign, king, queen, emperor, empress; monarchy, royalty; *informal* royals. **4** *the crown of the hill* TOP, crest, summit, peak, pinnacle, tip, head, brow, apex.
● verb **1** *David II was crowned in 1331* ENTHRONE, install; invest, induct. **2** *a teaching post at Harvard crowned his career* ROUND OFF, cap, be the climax of, be the culmination of, top off, consummate, perfect, complete, put the finishing touch(es) to. **3** *a steeple crowned by a gilded weathercock* TOP, cap, tip, head, surmount. **4** *(informal) someone crowned him with a poker.* See HIT verb sense 1.
crucial ● adjective **1** *negotiations were at a crucial stage* PIVOTAL, critical, key, climacteric, decisive, deciding; life-and-death. **2** *confidentiality is crucial in this case* ALL-IMPORTANT, of the utmost importance, of the essence, critical, pre-eminent, paramount, essential, vital.
– OPPOSITES unimportant.

2 nonsense; rubbish.
– DERIVATIVES **cruddy** adjective.
– ORIGIN variant of CURD.

crude • adjective **1** in a natural or raw state; not yet processed or refined. **2** (of an estimate or guess) likely to be only approximately accurate. **3** rudimentary or makeshift. **4** offensively coarse or rude. • noun natural mineral oil.
– DERIVATIVES **crudely** adverb **crudeness** noun **crudity** noun.
– ORIGIN Latin *crudus* 'raw, rough'.

crudités /kroōditay/ • plural noun mixed raw vegetables served with a sauce into which they may be dipped.
– ORIGIN plural of French *crudité* 'rawness, crudity'.

cruel • adjective (**crueller**, **cruellest** or **crueler**, **cruelest**) **1** disregarding or taking pleasure in the pain or suffering of others. **2** causing pain or suffering.
– DERIVATIVES **cruelly** adverb.
– ORIGIN Latin *crudelis*, related to *crudus* 'raw, rough'.

cruelty • noun (pl. **cruelties**) cruel behaviour or attitudes.

cruet /kroōit/ • noun **1** a small container for salt, pepper, oil, or vinegar for use at a dining table. **2** Brit. a stand holding such containers. **3** a small container for the wine or water to be used in the celebration of the Eucharist.
– ORIGIN Old French, 'small pot'; related to CROCK².

cruise • verb **1** move slowly around without a precise destination, especially for pleasure. **2** travel smoothly at a moderate or economical speed. **3** achieve an objective with ease. **4** informal wander about in search of a sexual partner. • noun **1** an instance of cruising. **2** a voyage on a ship taken as a holiday and usually calling in at several places.
– ORIGIN probably from Dutch *kruisen* 'to cross'.

cruise control • noun a device in a motor vehicle which maintains a selected constant speed without requiring use of the accelerator pedal.

cruise missile • noun a low-flying missile which is guided to its target by an on-board computer.

cruiser • noun **1** a fast warship larger than a destroyer and less heavily armed than a battleship. **2** a yacht or motor boat with passenger accommodation. **3** N. Amer. a police patrol car.

cruiserweight • noun chiefly Brit. another term for LIGHT HEAVYWEIGHT.

crumb • noun **1** a small fragment of bread, cake, or biscuit. **2** the soft inner part of a loaf of bread. **3** informal, chiefly N. Amer. an objectionable or contemptible person. • verb cover (food) with breadcrumbs.
– ORIGIN Old English.

crumble • verb **1** break or fall apart into small fragments. **2** gradually disintegrate or fail. • noun Brit. a pudding made with fruit and a topping of flour and fat rubbed to the texture of breadcrumbs.
– ORIGIN Old English.

crumbly • adjective (**crumblier**, **crumbliest**) easily crumbling.
– DERIVATIVES **crumbliness** noun.

crumbs • exclamation Brit. informal an expression of dismay or surprise.
– ORIGIN euphemism for CHRIST.

crumhorn • noun variant spelling of KRUMMHORN.

crummy (also **crumby**) • adjective (**crummier**, **crummiest**) informal bad, unpleasant, or of poor quality.

crumpet • noun **1** a thick, flat cake with a soft, porous texture, eaten toasted and buttered. **2** Brit. informal women regarded as objects of sexual desire.
– ORIGIN of unknown origin.

crumple • verb **1** crush so as to become creased and wrinkled. **2** suddenly lose force, effectiveness, or composure. • noun a crushed fold, crease, or wrinkle.
– ORIGIN from obsolete *crump* 'make or become curved'.

crumple zone • noun a part of a motor vehicle designed to crumple easily in a crash and absorb the main force of an impact.

crunch • verb **1** crush (something hard or brittle) with the teeth, making a marked grinding sound. **2** make or move with such a sound. • noun **1** a crunching sound. **2** (**the crunch**) informal the crucial point of a situation. **3** a sit-up.
– ORIGIN variant of obsolete *cranch*: probably imitative.

crunchy • adjective (**crunchier**, **crunchiest**) making a crunching noise when bitten or crushed.
– DERIVATIVES **crunchily** adverb **crunchiness** noun.

crupper /kruppər/ • noun a strap buckled to the back of a saddle and looped under the horse's tail to prevent the saddle or harness from slipping forward.
– ORIGIN Old French *cropiere*; related to CROUP².

crural /kroorəl/ • adjective Anatomy & Zoology relating to the leg or the thigh.
– ORIGIN Latin *cruralis*, from *crus* 'leg'.

crusade • noun **1** any of a series of medieval military expeditions made by Europeans to recover the Holy Land from the Muslims. **2** an energetic organized campaign with a political, social, or religious aim: *a crusade against crime*. • verb **1** lead or take part in a crusade. **2** (**crusading**) energetically campaigning for a particular aim.
– DERIVATIVES **crusader** noun.
– ORIGIN French *croisade*, from *croisée* 'the state of being marked with the cross'.

cruse /kroōz/ • noun archaic an earthenware pot or jar.
– ORIGIN Old English.

crush • verb **1** deform, squash, or pulverize by compressing forcefully. **2** crease or crumple (cloth or paper). **3** violently subdue (opposition or a rebellion). **4** cause (someone) to feel overwhelming disappointment or embarrassment. • noun **1** a crowd of people pressed closely together. **2** informal an intense infatu-

C

Thesaurus

crucify • verb **1** *two thieves were crucified with Jesus* NAIL TO A CROSS; execute, put to death, kill. **2** *she had been crucified by his departure* DEVASTATE, crush, shatter, cut to the quick, wound, pain, harrow, torture, torment, agonize. **3** (*informal*) *the fans would crucify us if we lost.* See CRITICIZE.

crude • adjective **1** *crude oil* UNREFINED, unpurified, unprocessed, untreated; unmilled, unpolished; coarse, raw, natural. **2** *a crude barricade* PRIMITIVE, simple, basic, homespun, rudimentary, rough, rough and ready, rough-hewn, make-do, makeshift, improvised, unfinished; *dated* rude. **3** *crude jokes* VULGAR, rude, naughty, suggestive, bawdy, off colour, indecent, obscene, offensive, lewd, salacious, licentious, ribald, coarse, uncouth, indelicate, tasteless, crass, smutty, dirty, filthy, scatological; *informal* blue.
– OPPOSITES refined, sophisticated.

cruel • adjective **1** *a cruel man* BRUTAL, savage, inhuman, barbaric, barbarous, brutish, bloodthirsty, murderous, vicious, sadistic, wicked, evil, fiendish, diabolical, monstrous, abominable; callous, ruthless, merciless, pitiless, remorseless, uncaring, heartless, stony-hearted, hard-hearted, cold-blooded, cold-hearted, unfeeling, unkind, inhumane; *dated* dastardly; *poetic/literary* fell. **2** *her death was a cruel blow* HARSH, severe, bitter, harrowing, heartbreaking, heart-rending, painful, agonizing, traumatic; *formal* grievous.
– OPPOSITES compassionate.

cruelty • noun BRUTALITY, savagery, inhumanity, barbarity, barbarousness, brutishness, bloodthirstiness, viciousness, sadism, wickedness; callousness, ruthlessness, lack of compassion.

cruise • noun *a cruise down the Nile* BOAT TRIP, sea trip; voyage, journey.
• verb **1** *she cruised across the Atlantic* SAIL, voyage, journey. **2** *a taxi cruised past* DRIVE SLOWLY, drift; *informal* mosey, tootle; *Brit. informal* pootle.

crumb • noun FRAGMENT, bit, morsel, particle, speck, scrap, shred, sliver, atom, grain, trace, tinge, mite, iota, jot, whit, ounce, scintilla, soupçon; *informal* smidgen, tad.

crumble • verb DISINTEGRATE, fall apart, fall to pieces, fall down, break up, collapse, fragment; decay, fall into decay, deteriorate, degenerate, go to rack and ruin, decompose, rot, moulder, perish.

crumbly • adjective BRITTLE, breakable, friable, powdery, granular; short; crisp, crispy.

crumple • verb **1** *she crumpled the note in her fist* CRUSH, scrunch up, screw up, squash, squeeze; *Brit.* scrumple. **2** *his trousers were dirty and crumpled* CREASE, wrinkle, crinkle, rumple, ruck up. **3** *her resistance crumpled* COLLAPSE, give way, cave in, go to pieces, break down, crumble, be overcome.

crunch • verb *she crunched the biscuit with relish* MUNCH, chomp, champ, scrunch, bite into.
• noun (*informal*) *when the crunch comes, she'll be forced to choose* MOMENT OF TRUTH, critical point, crux, crisis, decision time, zero hour, point of no return; showdown.

crusade • noun **1** *the medieval crusades* HOLY WAR; *Islam* jihad. **2** *a crusade against crime* CAMPAIGN, drive, push, movement, effort, struggle; battle, war, offensive.
• verb *she likes crusading for the cause of the underdog* CAMPAIGN, fight, do battle, battle, take up arms, take up the cudgels, work,

C

ation. **3** a drink made from the juice of pressed fruit.
– DERIVATIVES **crushable** adjective **crusher** noun.
– ORIGIN Old French *cruissir* 'gnash teeth or crack'.
crush bar ● noun Brit. a bar in a theatre that sells drinks in the interval.
crush barrier ● noun Brit. a barrier for restraining a crowd.
crushed velvet ● noun velvet which has its nap pointing in different directions in irregular patches.
crush zone ● noun another term for CRUMPLE ZONE.
crust ● noun **1** the tough outer part of a loaf of bread. **2** a hard, dry scrap of bread. **3** informal a living or livelihood: *earning a crust.* **4** a hardened layer, coating, or deposit on something soft. **5** a layer of pastry covering a pie. **6** the outermost layer of rock of which a planet consists, especially the part of the earth above the mantle. **7** a deposit formed in wine or port aged in the bottle. ● verb form into or cover with a crust.
– ORIGIN Latin *crusta* 'rind, shell, crust'.
crustacean /krustaysh'n/ ● noun an aquatic arthropod of a large group including crabs, lobsters, shrimps, woodlice, and barnacles.
– ORIGIN Latin, from *crusta* 'rind, shell, crust'.
crusty ● adjective (**crustier, crustiest**) **1** having or consisting of a crust. **2** (of an old person) conservative and easily irritated. ● noun (pl. **crusties**) informal a young person of a subculture characterized by a shabby appearance and a nomadic lifestyle.
– DERIVATIVES **crustiness** noun.
crutch ● noun **1** a long stick with a crosspiece at the top, used as a support by a lame person. **2** something used for support or reassurance. **3** the crotch of the body or a garment.
– ORIGIN Old English.
crux /kruks/ ● noun (pl. **cruxes** or **cruces** /kroōseez/) (**the crux**) **1** the decisive or most important point at issue. **2** a particular point of difficulty.
– ORIGIN Latin, 'cross'.
cry ● verb (**cries, cried**) **1** shed tears. **2** shout or scream loudly. **3** (of a bird or other animal) make a loud characteristic call. **4** (**cry out for**) demand as a self-evident requirement or solution. **5** (**cry off**) informal go back on a promise or fail to keep to an arrangement. ● noun (pl. **cries**) **1** a spell of shedding tears. **2** a loud shout or scream. **3** a distinctive call of a bird or other animal.
– PHRASES **cry for the moon** ask for what is unattainable or impossible. **for crying out loud** informal used to express irritation or impatience.
– ORIGIN Old French *crier*, from Latin *quiritare* 'raise a public outcry', literally 'call on the *Quirites* (Roman citizens) for help'.
crybaby ● noun (pl. **crybabies**) a person who sheds tears frequently or readily.
cryer ● noun archaic spelling of CRIER.
crying ● adjective very great: *it would be a crying shame.*
cryogenics /krīəjenniks/ ● plural noun (treated as sing.) **1** the branch of physics concerned with the production and effects of very low temperatures. **2** another term for CRYONICS.
– DERIVATIVES **cryogenic** adjective.
– ORIGIN from Greek *kruos* 'frost'.
cryonics /krīonniks/ ● plural noun (treated as sing.) the deep-freezing of the bodies of people who have died of an incurable disease, in the hope of a future cure.
– DERIVATIVES **cryonic** adjective.
– ORIGIN contraction of CRYOGENICS.
cryosurgery ● noun surgery using the local application of intense cold to destroy unwanted tissue.
crypt ● noun an underground room or vault beneath a church, used as a chapel or burial place.
– ORIGIN Greek *kruptē* 'a vault', from *kruptos* 'hidden'.
cryptic ● adjective **1** mysterious or obscure in meaning. **2** (of a crossword) having difficult clues which indicate the solutions indirectly. **3** Zoology serving to camouflage an animal in its natural environment.
– DERIVATIVES **cryptically** adverb.
– ORIGIN Greek *kruptikos*, from *kruptos* 'hidden'.
cryptobiosis /kriptəbīōsis/ ● noun Biology a state in which an organism's metabolic activity is reduced to an undetectable level without disappearing altogether.
– DERIVATIVES **cryptobiotic** adjective.
cryptogam /kriptəgam/ ● noun Botany, dated a plant with no true flowers or seeds, such as a fern, moss, liverwort, lichen, or alga.
– DERIVATIVES **cryptogamic** adjective.
– ORIGIN from Greek *kruptos* 'hidden' + *gamos* 'marriage' (because the means of reproduction was not apparent).
cryptogram /kriptəgram/ ● noun a text written in code.
cryptography ● noun the art of writing or solving codes.
– DERIVATIVES **cryptographer** noun **cryptographic** adjective.
cryptology ● noun the study of codes, or the art of writing and solving them.
– DERIVATIVES **cryptological** adjective **cryptologist** noun.
cryptosporidium /kriptōsporiddiəm/ ● noun a single-celled parasite found in the intestinal tract of many animals, where it sometimes causes disease.
– ORIGIN from Greek *kruptos* 'hidden' + Latin *sporidium* 'small spore'.
cryptozoology ● noun the search for animals whose existence is disputed or unsubstantiated, such as the Loch Ness monster.
crystal ● noun **1** a clear transparent mineral, especially quartz. **2** a piece of a solid substance having a natural geometrically

Thesaurus

strive, struggle, agitate, lobby, champion, promote.
crusader ● noun CAMPAIGNER, fighter, champion, advocate; reformer.
crush ● verb **1** *essential oils are released when the herbs are crushed* SQUASH, squeeze, press, compress; pulp, mash, macerate, mangle; flatten, trample on, tread on; *informal* squidge, splat; *N. Amer. informal* smush. **2** *your dress will get crushed* CREASE, crumple, rumple, wrinkle, crinkle, scrunch up, ruck up; *Brit.* scrumple up. **3** *crush the biscuits with a rolling pin* PULVERIZE, pound, grind, break up, smash, crumble; mill; *technical* triturate, comminute; *archaic* bray, levigate. **4** *he crushed her in his arms* HUG, squeeze, hold tight, embrace, enfold. **5** *the new regime crushed all popular uprisings* SUPPRESS, put down, quell, quash, stamp out, put an end to, overcome, overpower, defeat, triumph over, break, repress, subdue, extinguish. **6** *Alan was crushed by her words* MORTIFY, humiliate, abash, chagrin, deflate, demoralize, flatten, squash; devastate, shatter, put someone in their place; *informal* shoot down in flames, cut down to size, knock the stuffing out of.
● noun **1** *the crush of people* CROWD, throng, horde, swarm, sea, mass, pack, press, mob; *archaic* rout. **2** *(informal) a teenage crush* INFATUATION, obsession, love, passion; *informal* pash, puppy love, calf love. **3** *lemon crush* SQUASH, fruit juice, cordial, drink.
crust ● noun **1** *a crust of ice* COVERING, layer, coating, cover, coat, sheet, thickness, film, skin, topping; incrustation, scab. **2** *(informal) I'm just trying to earn an honest crust* LIVING, livelihood, income, daily bread, means of subsistence; *informal* bread and butter.
crusty ● adjective **1** *crusty French bread* CRISP, crispy, well baked; crumbly, brittle, friable. **2** *a crusty old man* IRRITABLE, cantankerous, irascible, bad-tempered, ill-tempered, grumpy, grouchy, crotchety, short-tempered, tetchy, testy, crabby, curmudgeonly, peevish, cross, fractious, pettish, crabbed, prickly, waspish, peppery, cross-grained; *informal* snappish, snappy, chippy; *Brit. informal* stroppy, narky, ratty; *N. Amer. informal* cranky, ornery; *Austral./NZ informal* snaky.
– OPPOSITES soft, good-natured.
crux ● noun NUB, heart, essence, central point, main point, core, centre, nucleus, kernel; *informal* the bottom line.
cry ● verb **1** *Mandy started to cry* WEEP, shed tears, sob, wail, cry one's eyes out, bawl, howl, snivel, whimper, squall, mewl, bleat; lament, grieve, mourn, keen; *Scottish* greet; *informal* boohoo, blub, blubber, turn on the waterworks; *Brit. informal* grizzle; *poetic/literary* pule. **2** *'Wait!' he cried* CALL, shout, exclaim, sing out, yell, shriek, scream, screech, bawl, bellow, roar, vociferate, squeal, yelp; *informal* holler; *dated* ejaculate.
– OPPOSITES laugh, whisper.
● noun **1** *Leonora had a good cry* SOB, weep, crying fit. **2** *a cry of despair* CALL, shout, exclamation, yell, shriek, scream, screech, bawl, bellow, roar, howl, yowl, squeal, yelp, interjection; *informal* holler; *dated* ejaculation. **3** *fund-raisers have issued a cry for help* APPEAL, plea, entreaty, cry from the heart, cri de cœur.
– PHRASES **cry someone/something down** *(dated)* DISPARAGE, run down, belittle, make light of, denigrate, decry, deprecate, depreciate, play down, trivialize, minimize; *archaic* hold cheap. **cry off** *(informal)* BACK OUT, pull out, cancel, withdraw, beg off, excuse oneself, change one's mind; *informal* get cold feet, cop out.
crypt ● noun TOMB, vault, mausoleum, burial chamber, sepulchre, catacomb, ossuary, undercroft.
cryptic ● adjective ENIGMATIC, mysterious, confusing, mystifying,

regular form with symmetrically arranged plane faces. **3** highly transparent glass with a high refractive index. **4** the glass over a watch face. **5** (before another noun) clear and transparent: *the crystal waters of the lake.*
– ORIGIN Greek *krustallos* 'ice, crystal'.
crystal ball ● noun a solid globe of glass or rock crystal, used for crystal-gazing.
crystal-gazing ● noun looking intently into a crystal ball with the aim of seeing images relating to future or distant events.
crystalline /kristəlīn/ ● adjective **1** having the structure and form of a crystal. **2** literary very clear.
crystalline lens ● noun the lens of the eye.
crystallize (also **crystallise**) ● verb **1** form crystals. **2** (**crystallized**) (of fruit) coated and impregnated with sugar. **3** make or become definite and clear.
– DERIVATIVES **crystallization** noun.
crystallography /kristəlogrəfi/ ● noun the branch of science concerned with the structure and properties of crystals.
– DERIVATIVES **crystallographer** noun **crystallographic** adjective.
crystal set ● noun a simple early form of radio receiver with a crystal touching a metal wire as the rectifier, lacking an amplifier or loudspeaker and necessitating headphones or an earphone.
crystal system ● noun each of seven categories of crystals (cubic, tetragonal, orthorhombic, trigonal, hexagonal, monoclinic, and triclinic) classified according to the possible relations of the crystal axes.
Cs ● symbol the chemical element caesium.
c/s ● abbreviation cycles per second.
CSA ● abbreviation Child Support Agency.
CSE ● abbreviation historical (in England and Wales) an examination for secondary-school pupils not taking O levels, replaced in 1988 by the GCSE.
– ORIGIN abbreviation for *Certificate of Secondary Education.*
CS gas ● noun a powerful form of tear gas used in the control of riots.
– ORIGIN from the initials of the American chemists Ben B. *Corson* and Roger W. *Stoughton.*
CST ● abbreviation Central Standard Time.
CT ● abbreviation **1** computerized (or computed) tomography. **2** Connecticut.
ct ● abbreviation **1** carat. **2** cent.
CTC ● abbreviation City Technology College.
CTS ● abbreviation carpal tunnel syndrome.
Cu ● symbol the chemical element copper.
– ORIGIN Latin *cuprum.*
cu. ● abbreviation cubic.
cub ● noun **1** the young of a fox, bear, lion, or other carnivorous mammal. **2** (also **Cub Scout**) a member of the junior branch of the Scout Association, for boys aged about 8 to 11. **3** archaic a young man. ● verb (**cubbed**, **cubbing**) **1** give birth to cubs. **2** hunt fox cubs.
– ORIGIN of unknown origin.
Cuban /kyoobən/ ● noun a person from Cuba. ● adjective relating to Cuba.
Cuban heel ● noun a moderately high straight-sided heel on a shoe or boot.
cubby ● noun (pl. **cubbies**) chiefly N. Amer. a cubbyhole.
cubbyhole ● noun a small enclosed space or room.
– ORIGIN originally meaning 'straw basket': related to dialect *cub* 'stall, pen, hutch'.
cube ● noun **1** a symmetrical three-dimensional shape contained by six equal squares. **2** Mathematics the product of a number multiplied by its square, represented by a superscript figure 3. ● verb **1** Mathematics multiply (a number) by its square; find the cube of. **2** cut (food) into small cubes.
– ORIGIN Greek *kubos.*
cube root ● noun the number which produces a given number when cubed.
cubic /kyoobik/ ● adjective **1** having the shape of a cube. **2** (of a unit of measurement) equal to the volume of a cube whose side is one of the linear unit specified: *a cubic metre.* **3** involving the cube (and no higher power) of a quantity or variable.
– DERIVATIVES **cubical** adjective.
cubicle ● noun a small partitioned-off area of a room.
– ORIGIN originally meaning 'bedroom': from Latin *cubiculum,* from *cubare* 'lie down'.
cubism ● noun an early 20th-century style of painting making use of simple geometric shapes and interlocking planes.
– DERIVATIVES **cubist** noun & adjective.
cubit /kyoobit/ ● noun an ancient measure of length, approximately equal to the length of a forearm.
– ORIGIN Latin *cubitum* 'elbow, forearm, cubit'.
cuboid /kyooboyd/ ● adjective more or less cubic in shape. ● noun a solid which has six rectangular faces at right angles to each other.
– DERIVATIVES **cuboidal** adjective.
cub reporter ● noun informal a young or inexperienced newspaper reporter.
cuckold /kukkōld/ ● noun the husband of an adulteress, regarded as an object of derision. ● verb make (a married man) a cuckold.
– DERIVATIVES **cuckoldry** noun.
– ORIGIN Old French *cucuault,* from *cucu* 'cuckoo' (from the cuckoo's habit of laying its egg in another bird's nest).
cuckoo ● noun a grey or brown bird known for the two-note call of the male and for the habit of laying its eggs in the nests of small songbirds. ● adjective informal crazy.
– ORIGIN Old French *cucu,* imitative of its call.
cuckoo clock ● noun a clock with a mechanical cuckoo that pops out on the hour making a sound like a cuckoo's call.
cuckoo pint ● noun a plant, the common wild arum, having a purple or green spadix followed by bright red berries.
– ORIGIN from earlier *cuckoo-pintle,* from PINTLE in the obsolete sense 'penis' (because of the shape of the spadix).
cuckoo spit ● noun whitish froth found in compact masses on leaves and plant stems, exuded by the larvae of froghoppers.
cucumber ● noun the long, green-skinned fruit of a climbing plant, which has watery flesh and is eaten raw in salads.
– ORIGIN Latin *cucumis.*
cud ● noun partly digested food returned from the first stomach of cattle or other ruminants to the mouth for further chewing.
– PHRASES **chew the cud** think or talk reflectively.
– ORIGIN Old English.
cuddle ● verb **1** hold close in one's arms as a way of showing love or affection. **2** (often **cuddle up to**) lie or sit close; nestle. ● noun a prolonged and affectionate hug.
– ORIGIN of unknown origin.
cuddly ● adjective (**cuddlier**, **cuddliest**) pleasantly soft or plump.
cudgel /kujəl/ ● noun a short thick stick used as a weapon. ● verb (**cudgelled**, **cudgelling**; US **cudgeled**, **cudgeling**) beat with a cudgel.
– PHRASES **cudgel one's brain** think hard about a problem. **take up cudgels** start to defend or support someone or something strongly.
– ORIGIN Old English.
cue[1] ● noun **1** a signal to an actor to enter or to begin their speech or performance. **2** a signal or prompt for action. **3** a facility for playing through an audio or video recording very rap-

Thesaurus

perplexing, puzzling, obscure, abstruse, arcane, oracular, Delphic, ambiguous, elliptical, oblique; informal as clear as mud.
– OPPOSITES clear.
cub ● noun **1** *a lioness and her cubs* (**cubs**) YOUNG, offspring, pups; archaic whelps. **2** *a cub reporter* TRAINEE, apprentice, probationer, novice, tyro, learner, beginner; N. Amer. tenderfoot; informal rookie, newbie; N. Amer. informal greenhorn, probie.
– OPPOSITES veteran.
cubbyhole ● noun SMALL ROOM, booth, cubicle; den, snug; N. Amer. cubby.
cube ● noun **1** *a shape that was neither a cube nor a sphere* HEXAHEDRON, cuboid, parallelepiped. **2** *a cube of soap* BLOCK, lump, chunk, brick.
cuddle ● verb **1** *she picked up the baby and cuddled her* HUG, embrace, clasp, hold tight, hold/fold in one's arms. **2** *the pair were kissing and cuddling* EMBRACE, hug, caress, pet, fondle; informal canoodle, smooch; informal, dated spoon, bill and coo. **3** *I cuddled up to him* SNUGGLE, nestle, curl, nuzzle, burrow against.
cuddly ● adjective HUGGABLE, cuddlesome; plump, curvaceous, rounded, buxom, soft, warm; attractive, endearing, lovable; N. Amer. informal zaftig.
cudgel ● noun *a thick wooden cudgel* CLUB, bludgeon, stick, truncheon, baton, blackthorn, shillelagh, mace; Brit. life preserver; N. Amer. blackjack, billy, nightstick; Brit. informal cosh.

idly until a desired starting point is reached. ● **verb** (**cues**, **cued**, **cueing** or **cuing**) **1** give a cue to or for. **2** set a piece of audio or video equipment in readiness to play (a particular part of a recording).
– PHRASES **on cue** at the correct moment.
– ORIGIN of unknown origin.

cue² ● **noun** a long tapering wooden rod for striking the ball in snooker, billiards, etc. ● **verb** (**cues**, **cued**, **cueing** or **cuing**) use a cue to strike the ball.
– ORIGIN originally meaning 'long plait or pigtail': variant of QUEUE.

C

cue ball ● **noun** the ball that is to be struck with the cue in snooker, billiards, etc.

cue card ● **noun** a card held beside a camera for a television broadcaster to read from while appearing to look into the camera.

cuff¹ ● **noun 1** the end part of a sleeve, where the material of the sleeve is turned back or a separate band is sewn on. **2** chiefly N. Amer. a trouser turn-up. **3** (**cuffs**) informal handcuffs. ● **verb** informal secure with handcuffs.
– PHRASES **off the cuff** informal without preparation. [ORIGIN as if from notes jotted on one's shirt cuffs.]
– DERIVATIVES **cuffed** adjective.
– ORIGIN of unknown origin.

cuff² ● **verb** strike with an open hand, especially on the head. ● **noun** a blow given with an open hand.
– ORIGIN of unknown origin.

cufflink ● **noun** a device for fastening together the sides of a shirt cuff.

cui bono? /kwee bonnō/ ● **exclamation** who stands to gain (i.e. from a crime, and so might have been responsible for it)?
– ORIGIN Latin, 'to whom (is it) a benefit?'

cuirass /kwirass/ ● **noun** historical a piece of armour consisting of breastplate and backplate fastened together.
– ORIGIN Old French, from Latin *corium* 'leather'.

cuirassier /kwirrəseer/ ● **noun** historical a cavalry soldier wearing a cuirass.
– ORIGIN French.

cuisine /kwizeen/ ● **noun** a style or method of cooking, especially as characteristic of a particular country or region.
– ORIGIN French, 'kitchen'.

cul-de-sac /kuldəsak/ ● **noun** (pl. **culs-de-sac** pronunc. same) a street or passage closed at one end.
– ORIGIN originally a term in anatomy: from French, 'bottom of a sack'.

-cule ● **suffix** forming nouns such as *molecule*, *reticule*, which were originally diminutives.
– ORIGIN from French *-cule* or Latin *-culus*, *-cula*, *-culum*.

culinary ● **adjective** of or for cooking.
– DERIVATIVES **culinarily** adverb.
– ORIGIN from Latin *culina* 'kitchen'.

cull ● **verb 1** reduce the numbers of (animals) by selective slaughter. **2** select or obtain from a large quantity or a variety of sources. ● **noun** a selective slaughter of animals.
– ORIGIN Old French *coillier*, from Latin *colligere* 'gather together'.

culminate /kulminayt/ ● **verb 1** (usu. **culminate in/with**) reach or be a climax or point of highest development. **2** archaic or Astrology (of a celestial body) reach or be at the meridian.
– DERIVATIVES **culmination** noun.
– ORIGIN Latin *culminare*, from *culmen* 'summit'.

culottes /kyoolot(s)/ ● **plural noun** women's knee-length trousers, cut with very full legs to resemble a skirt.
– ORIGIN French, 'knee breeches', from *cul* 'rump'.

culpable /kulpəb'l/ ● **adjective** deserving blame.
– DERIVATIVES **culpability** noun **culpably** adverb.
– ORIGIN Latin *culpabilis*, from *culpa* 'fault, blame'.

culprit ● **noun** a person who is responsible for a crime or offence.
– ORIGIN originally in the judicial formula *Culprit, how will you be tried?*, perhaps from a misinterpretation of the written abbreviation *cul. prist* for Old French *Culpable: prest d'averrer notre bille* '(You are) guilty: (We are) ready to prove our indictment'.

cult ● **noun 1** a system of religious worship directed towards a particular figure or object. **2** a small religious group regarded as strange or as imposing excessive control over members. **3** something popular or fashionable among a particular section of society.
– DERIVATIVES **cultish** adjective **cultist** noun.
– ORIGIN Latin *cultus* 'worship'.

cultivar /kultivaar/ ● **noun** a plant variety that has been produced in cultivation by selective breeding.
– ORIGIN blend of CULTIVATE and VARIETY.

cultivate ● **verb 1** prepare and use (land) for crops or gardening. **2** raise or grow (plants or crops). **3** grow or maintain (living cells or tissue) in an artificial medium containing nutrients. **4** try to acquire or develop (a quality or skill). **5** try to win the friendship or favour of. **6** (**cultivated**) refined and well educated.
– DERIVATIVES **cultivable** adjective **cultivatable** adjective **cultivation** noun.
– ORIGIN Latin *cultivare*, from *cultiva terra* 'arable land'.

cultivator ● **noun 1** a person or thing that cultivates something. **2** a mechanical implement for breaking up the ground.

cultural ● **adjective 1** relating to the culture of a society. **2** relating to the arts and to intellectual achievements.
– DERIVATIVES **culturally** adverb.

culture ● **noun 1** the arts and other manifestations of human intellectual achievement regarded collectively. **2** a refined understanding or appreciation of this. **3** the customs, institutions, and achievements of a particular nation, people, or group. **4** the cultivation of plants, breeding of animals, or production of cells or tissues. **5** a preparation of cells grown in an artificial

Thesaurus

● **verb** *she was cudgelled to death* BLUDGEON, club, beat, batter, bash; *Brit. informal* cosh.

cue ● **noun** SIGNAL, sign, indication, prompt, reminder; nod, word, gesture.

cuff ● **verb** *Cullam cuffed him on the head* HIT, strike, slap, smack, thump, beat, punch; *informal* clout, wallop, belt, whack, thwack, bash, clobber, bop, biff, sock; *Brit. informal* slosh; *N. Amer. informal* boff, slug; *archaic* smite.
– PHRASES **off the cuff** (*informal*) **1** *an off-the-cuff remark* IMPROMPTU, extempore, ad lib; unrehearsed, unscripted, unprepared, improvised, spontaneous, unplanned. **2** *I spoke off the cuff* WITHOUT PREPARATION, without rehearsal, impromptu, ad lib; *informal* off the top of one's head.

cuisine ● **noun** COOKING, cookery; haute cuisine, cordon bleu, nouvelle cuisine.

cul-de-sac ● **noun** NO THROUGH ROAD, blind alley, dead end.

cull ● **verb 1** *anecdotes culled from Greek history* SELECT, choose, pick, take, obtain, glean. **2** *he sees culling deer as a necessity* SLAUGHTER, kill, destroy.

culminate ● **verb** *the festival culminated in a dramatic fire-walking ceremony* COME TO A CLIMAX, come to a head, peak, climax, reach a pinnacle; build up to, lead up to; end with, finish with, conclude with.

culmination ● **noun** CLIMAX, pinnacle, peak, high point, highest point, height, high water mark, top, summit, crest, zenith, crowning moment, apotheosis, apex, apogee; consummation, completion, finish, conclusion.
– OPPOSITES nadir.

culpable ● **adjective** TO BLAME, guilty, at fault, in the wrong, answerable, accountable, responsible, blameworthy, censurable.
– OPPOSITES innocent.

culprit ● **noun** GUILTY PARTY, offender, wrongdoer, miscreant; criminal, malefactor, lawbreaker, felon, delinquent; *informal* baddy, crook.

cult ● **noun 1** *a religious cult* SECT, denomination, group, movement, church, persuasion, body, faction. **2** *the cult of youth in Hollywood* OBSESSION WITH, fixation on, mania for, passion for, idolization of, devotion to, worship of, veneration of.

cultivate ● **verb 1** *the peasants cultivated the land* TILL, plough, dig, hoe, farm, work, fertilize, mulch. **2** *they were encouraged to cultivate basic food crops* GROW, raise, rear, plant, sow. **3** *Tessa tried to cultivate her* WIN SOMEONE'S FRIENDSHIP, woo, court, pay court to, keep sweet, curry favour with, ingratiate oneself with; *informal* get in someone's good books, butter up, suck up to; *N. Amer. informal* shine up to. **4** *he wants to cultivate his mind* IMPROVE, better, refine, elevate; educate, train, develop, enrich.

cultivated ● **adjective** CULTURED, educated, well read, civilized, enlightened, discerning, discriminating, refined, polished; sophisticated, urbane, cosmopolitan.

cultural ● **adjective 1** *cultural differences* ETHNIC, racial, folk; soci-

medium containing nutrients. ● verb maintain (tissue cells, bacteria, etc.) in conditions suitable for growth.
– ORIGIN Latin *cultura* 'growing, cultivation', from *colere* 'cultivate'.
cultured ● adjective **1** refined and well educated. **2** (of a pearl) formed round a foreign body inserted into an oyster.
culture shock ● noun disorientation experienced when suddenly subjected to an unfamiliar culture or way of life.
culture vulture ● noun informal a person who is very interested in the arts.
culvert /**kul**vərt/ ● noun a tunnel carrying a stream or open drain under a road or railway.
– ORIGIN of unknown origin.
cum /kum/ ● preposition combined with; also used as: *a study-cum-bedroom.*
– ORIGIN Latin.
cumber /**kum**bər/ ● verb dated hamper, hinder, or obstruct.
– ORIGIN from ENCUMBER.
Cumberland sauce ● noun a piquant sauce made from redcurrant jelly, served with game and cold meats.
Cumberland sausage ● noun Brit. a type of sausage traditionally made in a continuous strip and cooked as a spiral.
cumbersome ● adjective **1** difficult to carry or use through size; unwieldy. **2** slow or complicated and therefore inefficient.
– DERIVATIVES **cumbersomely** adverb **cumbersomeness** noun.
cumbia /**ko͝om**biə/ ● noun a kind of dance music of Colombian origin, similar to salsa.
– ORIGIN Colombian Spanish.
cumbrous /**kum**brəss/ ● adjective literary cumbersome.
cum grano salis /kum graanō **saal**is/ ● adverb with a pinch of salt.
– ORIGIN Latin.
cumin /**kum**min/ (also **cummin**) ● noun the aromatic seeds of a plant of the parsley family, used as a spice, especially in curry powder.
– ORIGIN Greek *kuminon*, probably of Semitic origin.
cummerbund /**kum**mərbund/ ● noun a sash worn around the waist, especially as part of a man's formal evening suit.
– ORIGIN Urdu and Persian.
cumquat ● noun variant spelling of KUMQUAT.
cumulate ● verb /**kyo͞o**myoolayt/ accumulate or be accumulated.
– DERIVATIVES **cumulation** noun.
– ORIGIN Latin *cumulare*, from *cumulus* 'a heap'.
cumulative ● adjective increasing or increased by successive additions.
– DERIVATIVES **cumulatively** adverb.
cumulonimbus /kyo͞omyoolō**nim**bəss/ ● noun (pl. **cumulonimbi** /kyo͞omyoolō**nim**bī/) cloud forming a towering mass with a flat base at fairly low altitude, as in thunderstorms.
cumulus /**kyo͞o**myooləss/ ● noun (pl. **cumuli** /**kyo͞o**myooli/) cloud forming rounded masses heaped on each other above a flat base at fairly low altitude.
– ORIGIN Latin, 'heap'.
cuneiform /**kyo͞o**niform/ ● adjective **1** relating to the wedge-shaped characters used in the ancient writing systems of Mesopotamia, Persia, and Ugarit. **2** chiefly Biology wedge-shaped. ● noun cuneiform writing.
– ORIGIN from Latin *cuneus* 'wedge'.
cunnilingus /kunni**ling**gəss/ ● noun stimulation of the female genitals using the tongue or lips.
– ORIGIN from Latin *cunnus* 'vulva' + *lingere* 'lick'.
cunning ● adjective **1** skilled in achieving one's ends by deceit or evasion. **2** ingenious. **3** N. Amer. attractive; charming. ● noun **1** craftiness. **2** ingenuity.
– DERIVATIVES **cunningly** adverb.
– ORIGIN originally in the sense 'erudite or skilful': perhaps from an Old Norse word meaning 'knowledge', related to CAN[1].
cunt ● noun vulgar slang **1** a woman's genitals. **2** an unpleasant or stupid person.
– ORIGIN Germanic.
cup ● noun **1** a small bowl-shaped container for drinking from. **2** a cup-shaped trophy, usually with a stem and two handles, awarded as a prize in a sports contest. **3** a sports contest in which the winner is awarded a cup. **4** chiefly N. Amer. a measure of capacity used in cookery, equal to half a US pint (0.237 litre). **5** either of the two parts of a bra shaped to contain or support one breast. **6** a long mixed drink made from wine or cider and fruit juice. ● verb (**cupped**, **cupping**) **1** form (one's hand or hands) into the curved shape of a cup. **2** place one's curved hand or hands around.
– PHRASES **in one's cups** informal drunk. **not one's cup of tea** informal not what one likes or is interested in.
– ORIGIN Latin *cuppa*, probably from *cupa* 'tub'.
cupboard ● noun a piece of furniture or small recess with a door and usually shelves, used for storage.
– ORIGIN originally denoting a table or sideboard on which cups, plates, etc. were displayed.
cupboard love ● noun affection that is feigned so as to obtain something.
cupcake ● noun a small iced cake baked in a cup-shaped foil or paper container.
Cupid ● noun **1** Roman Mythology the god of love, represented as a naked winged boy with a bow and arrows. **2** (also **cupid**) a representation of a naked winged child carrying a bow.
cupidity /kyo͞o**pid**diti/ ● noun greed for money or possessions.
– ORIGIN Latin *cupiditas*, from *cupidus* 'desirous'.
Cupid's bow ● noun a pronounced double curve at the top edge of a person's upper lip, resembling the shape of the bow carried by Cupid.
cupola /**kyo͞o**pələ/ ● noun **1** a rounded dome forming or adorning a roof or ceiling. **2** a gun turret. **3** a cylindrical furnace for refining metals.
– ORIGIN Latin *cupula* 'small cask'.
cuppa ● noun Brit. informal a cup of tea.
cuprammonium /kyooprə**mō**niəm/ ● noun (before a noun) Chemistry of or referring to a complex ion containing copper bonded to ammonia, solutions of which are able to dissolve cellulose.
cupreous /**kyo͞o**priəss/ ● adjective of or like copper.
– ORIGIN Latin *cupreus*, from *cuprum* 'copper'.
cupro /**kyo͞o**prō/ ● noun a type of rayon made by dissolving cotton cellulose with cuprammonium salts and spinning the resulting solution into filaments.
– ORIGIN an invented word, probably from CUPRAMMONIUM.

Thesaurus

etal, lifestyle. **2** *cultural achievements* AESTHETIC, artistic, intellectual; educational, edifying, civilizing.
culture ● noun **1** *20th century popular culture* THE ARTS, the humanities, intellectual achievement; literature, music, painting, philosophy. **2** *a man of culture* INTELLECTUAL/ARTISTIC AWARENESS, education, cultivation, enlightenment, discernment, discrimination, good taste, taste, refinement, polish, sophistication. **3** *Afro-Caribbean culture* CIVILIZATION, society, way of life, lifestyle; customs, traditions, heritage, habits, ways, mores, values. **4** *the culture of crops* CULTIVATION, farming; agriculture, husbandry, agronomy.
cultured ● adjective CULTIVATED, intellectually/artistically aware, artistic, enlightened, civilized, educated, well educated, well read, well informed, learned, knowledgeable, discerning, discriminating, refined, polished, sophisticated; informal arty.
– OPPOSITES ignorant.
culvert ● noun CHANNEL, conduit, watercourse, trough; drain, gutter.
cumbersome ● adjective **1** *a cumbersome diving suit* UNWIELDY, unmanageable, awkward, clumsy, inconvenient, incommodious; bulky, large, heavy, hefty, weighty, burdensome; informal hulking, clunky. **2** *cumbersome procedures* COMPLICATED, complex, involved, inefficient, unwieldy, slow.
– OPPOSITES manageable, straightforward.
cumulative ● adjective INCREASING, accumulative, growing, mounting; collective, aggregate, amassed; Brit. knock-on.
cunning ● adjective *a cunning scheme* CRAFTY, wily, artful, guileful, devious, sly, scheming, designing, calculating, Machiavellian; shrewd, astute, clever, canny; deceitful, deceptive, duplicitous; informal foxy; archaic subtle.
– OPPOSITES honest.
● noun *his political cunning* GUILE, craftiness, deviousness, slyness, trickery, duplicity; shrewdness, astuteness.
cup ● noun **1** *a cup and saucer* teacup, coffee cup, demitasse; mug, beaker; historical chalice. **2** *the winner was presented with a silver cup* TROPHY, award, prize.
cupboard ● noun CABINET, sideboard, dresser, armoire, credenza, buffet; Brit. chiffonier; informal glory hole.
Cupid ● noun EROS, the god of love; amoretto.
cupidity ● noun GREED, avarice, avariciousness, acquisitiveness,

C

cupro-nickel • noun an alloy of copper and nickel, especially in the proportions 3:1 as used in 'silver' coins.
cup-tied • adjective Brit. (of a soccer player) ineligible to play for one's club in a cup competition as a result of having played for another club in an earlier round.
cur /kur/ • noun **1** an aggressive dog, especially a mongrel. **2** informal a despicable man.
– ORIGIN perhaps from Old Norse *kurr* 'grumbling'.
curaçao /kyoorəsō/ • noun (pl. **curaçaos**) a liqueur flavoured with the peel of bitter oranges.
– ORIGIN named after *Curaçao*, the Caribbean island where the oranges are grown.
curacy • noun (pl. **curacies**) the office of a curate.
curare /kyooraari/ • noun a paralysing poison obtained from South American plants and traditionally used by Indian peoples as an arrow poison.
– ORIGIN Carib.
curate[1] /kyoorət/ • noun a member of the clergy engaged as assistant to a parish priest.
– PHRASES **curate's egg** Brit. something that is partly good and partly bad. [ORIGIN from a cartoon in *Punch* (1895) depicting a meek curate who, given a stale egg when dining with the bishop, assures his host that 'parts of it are excellent'.]
– ORIGIN Latin *curatus*, from *cura* 'care'.
curate[2] /kyoorayt/ • verb select, organize, and look after the items in (a collection or exhibition).
– DERIVATIVES **curation** noun.
– ORIGIN back-formation from CURATOR.
curative • adjective able to cure disease. • noun a curative medicine or agent.
curator • noun a keeper of a museum or other collection.
– DERIVATIVES **curatorial** adjective.
– ORIGIN Latin, from *curare* 'take care of'.
curb • noun **1** a check or restraint. **2** a type of bit with a strap or chain attached which passes under a horse's lower jaw, used as a check. **3** US variant spelling of KERB. • verb keep in check.
– ORIGIN Old French *courber* 'bend, bow', from Latin *curvare* 'bend'.
curd • noun **1** (also **curds**) a soft, white substance formed when milk coagulates, used as the basis for cheese. **2** the edible head of a cauliflower or similar plant.
– ORIGIN of unknown origin.
curd cheese • noun a mild, soft, smooth cheese made from skimmed milk curd.
curdle • verb separate or cause to separate into curds or lumps.
– PHRASES **make one's blood curdle** fill one with horror.
cure • verb **1** relieve (someone) of the symptoms of a disease or condition. **2** end (a disease, condition, or problem) by treatment or appropriate action. **3** preserve (meat, fish, etc.) by salting, drying, or smoking. • noun **1** something that cures a disease, condition, or problem. **2** restoration to health. **3** the process of curing meat, fish, etc. **4** a Christian minister's area of responsibility.
– DERIVATIVES **curable** adjective **curer** noun.
– ORIGIN originally in the senses 'care, concern, responsibility', later 'medical care': from Latin *cura* 'care'.
curé /kyooray/ • noun a parish priest in a French-speaking country.
– ORIGIN French.
cure-all • noun a remedy that will supposedly cure any ailment or problem.
curettage /kyoorettij, kyooritaazh/ • noun Surgery the use of a curette, especially on the lining of the uterus.
– ORIGIN French, from CURETTE.
curette /kyooret/ • noun a small surgical instrument used to remove material by a scraping action. • verb clean or scrape with a curette.
– ORIGIN French, from *curer* 'cleanse'.
curfew /kurfyoo/ • noun **1** a regulation requiring people to remain indoors between specified hours, typically at night. **2** the time at which such a restriction begins.
– ORIGIN originally denoting a regulation requiring fires to be extinguished at a fixed hour in the evening: from Old French *cuevrefeu*, from *cuvrir* 'to cover' + *feu* 'fire'.
Curia /kyooriə/ • noun the papal court at the Vatican, by which the Roman Catholic Church is governed.
– DERIVATIVES **Curial** adjective.
– ORIGIN Latin, denoting a division of an ancient Roman tribe, (by extension) the senate of cities other than Rome, and later a feudal or Roman Catholic court of justice.
curie /kyoori/ • noun (pl. **curies**) a unit of radioactivity, corresponding to 3.7×10^{10} disintegrations per second.
– ORIGIN named after the French physicists Pierre and Marie *Curie* (1867–1934 and 1859–1906).
curio /kyooriō/ • noun (pl. **curios**) a rare, unusual, or intriguing object.
– ORIGIN abbreviation of CURIOSITY.
curiosity • noun (pl. **curiosities**) **1** a strong desire to know or learn something. **2** a unusual or interesting object or fact.
– PHRASES **curiosity killed the cat** proverb being inquisitive about other people's affairs may get you into trouble.
curious • adjective **1** eager to know or learn something. **2** strange; unusual.
– DERIVATIVES **curiously** adverb.
– ORIGIN Latin *curiosus* 'careful', from *cura* 'care'.
curium /kyooriəm/ • noun a radioactive metallic chemical element made by high-energy atomic collisions.
– ORIGIN named after Marie and Pierre *Curie*.
curl • verb **1** form or cause to form a curved or spiral shape. **2** move in a spiral or curved course. **3** (**curl up**) informal writhe with embarrassment, shame, or amusement. **4** play at the game of curling. • noun **1** something in the shape of a spiral or coil, especially a lock of hair. **2** a curling movement.
– PHRASES **make someone's hair curl** informal shock or horrify someone.
– DERIVATIVES **curly** adjective (**curlier**, **curliest**).
– ORIGIN from obsolete *crulle* 'curly', from Dutch *krul*.
curler • noun **1** a roller or clasp around which a lock of hair is

Thesaurus

covetousness, rapacity, materialism, mercenariness, Mammonism; *informal* money-grubbing, an itching palm.
– OPPOSITES generosity.
cur • noun **1** *a mangy cur* MONGREL, tyke; *N. Amer.* yellow dog; *NZ* kuri; *informal* mutt; *Austral. informal* mong, bitzer. **2** *(informal) Neil was beginning to feel like a cur.* See SCOUNDREL.
curable • adjective REMEDIABLE, treatable, medicable, operable.
curative • adjective HEALING, therapeutic, medicinal, remedial, corrective, restorative, tonic, health-giving; *archaic* sanative.
curator • noun CUSTODIAN, keeper, conservator, guardian, caretaker, steward.
curb • noun *a curb on public spending* RESTRAINT, restriction, check, brake, rein, control, limitation, limit, constraint; *informal* crackdown; *poetic/literary* trammel.
• verb *he tried to curb his temper* RESTRAIN, hold back/in, keep back, repress, suppress, fight back, bite back, keep in check, check, control, rein in, contain, bridle, subdue; *informal* keep a/the lid on.
curdle • verb CLOT, coagulate, congeal, solidify, thicken; turn, sour, ferment.
cure • verb **1** *he was cured of the disease* HEAL, restore to health, make well/better; *archaic* cleanse. **2** *economic equality cannot cure all social ills* RECTIFY, remedy, put/set right, right, fix, mend, repair, heal, make better; solve, sort out, be the answer/solution to; eliminate, end, put an end to. **3** *some farmers cured their own bacon* PRESERVE, smoke, salt, dry, pickle.
• noun **1** *a cure for cancer* REMEDY, medicine, medication, medicament, antidote, antiserum; treatment, therapy; *archaic* physic. **2** *interest rate cuts are not the cure for the problem* SOLUTION, answer, antidote, nostrum, panacea, cure-all; *informal* quick fix, magic bullet.
cure-all • noun PANACEA, cure for all ills, sovereign remedy, heal-all, nostrum; *informal* magic bullet.
curio • noun TRINKET, knick-knack, bibelot, ornament, bauble; objet d'art, collector's item, object of virtu, rarity, curiosity; *N. Amer.* kickshaw.
curiosity • noun **1** *his evasiveness roused my curiosity* INTEREST, spirit of inquiry, inquisitiveness. **2** *the shop is a treasure trove of curiosities* ODDITY, curio, conversation piece, object of virtu, collector's item.
curious • adjective **1** *she was curious to know what had happened* INTRIGUED, interested, eager/dying to know, agog; inquisitive. **2** *her curious behaviour* STRANGE, odd, peculiar, funny, unusual, bizarre, weird, eccentric, queer, unexpected, unfamiliar, extraordinary, abnormal, out of the ordinary, anomalous, surprising, incongruous, unconventional, unorthodox; *informal* offbeat; *Brit.* out of the

wrapped to curl it. **2** a player in the game of curling.
curlew /kurlyoo/ ● noun (pl. same or **curlews**) a large wading bird with a long downcurved bill and brown streaked plumage.
– ORIGIN Old French *courlieu*, derived from the sound of the bird's call.
curlicue /kurlikyoo/ ● noun a decorative curl or twist in calligraphy or in the design of an object.
– ORIGIN from **curly** + CUE² (in the sense 'pigtail'), or *-cue* representing the letter *q*.
curling ● noun a game played on ice, in which large circular flat stones are slid across the surface towards a mark.
curling tongs (also **curling iron**) ● plural noun a device incorporating a heated rod around which hair can be wound so as to curl it.
curmudgeon /kərmujən/ ● noun a bad-tempered or surly person.
– DERIVATIVES **curmudgeonly** adjective.
– ORIGIN of unknown origin.
currach /kurrə/ (also **curragh**) ● noun Irish and Scottish term for CORACLE.
– ORIGIN Irish and Scottish Gaelic *curach* 'small boat'.
currant ● noun **1** a dried fruit made from a small seedless variety of grape. **2** a shrub producing small edible black, red, or white berries.
– ORIGIN from Old French *raisins de Corauntz* 'grapes of Corinth' (the original source).
currawong /kurrəwong/ ● noun an Australian songbird with mainly black or grey plumage and a resonant call.
– ORIGIN from an Aboriginal word.
currency ● noun (pl. **currencies**) **1** a system of money in general use in a particular country. **2** the quality or period of being current.
current ● adjective **1** happening or being used or done now. **2** in common or general use. ● noun **1** a body of water or air moving in a definite direction through a surrounding body of water or air. **2** a flow of electrically charged particles.
– ORIGIN from Latin *currere* 'run'.
current account ● noun Brit. an account with a bank or building society from which money may be withdrawn without notice.
current assets ● plural noun cash and other assets that are expected to be converted to cash within a year. Compare with FIXED ASSETS.
currently ● adverb at the present time.
curricle /kurrik'l/ ● noun historical a light, open, two-wheeled carriage pulled by two horses side by side.
– ORIGIN Latin *curriculum* 'course, racing chariot'.
curriculum /kərikyooləm/ ● noun (pl. **curricula** or **curriculums**) the subjects comprising a course of study in a school or college.
– DERIVATIVES **curricular** adjective.
– ORIGIN Latin, 'course, racing chariot'.
curriculum vitae /kərikyooləm veeti/ ● noun (pl. **curricula vitae**) a brief account of a person's education, qualifications, and previous occupations, sent with a job application.
– ORIGIN Latin, 'course of life'.
currier /kurriər/ ● noun a person who curries leather.
curry¹ ● noun (pl. **curries**) a dish of meat, vegetables, etc., cooked in an Indian-style sauce of strong spices. ● verb (**curries, curried**) prepare or flavour with such a sauce.
– ORIGIN Tamil.
curry² ● verb (**curries, curried**) **1** chiefly N. Amer. groom (a horse) with a curry-comb. **2** historical treat (tanned leather) to improve its properties.
– PHRASES **curry favour** ingratiate oneself through obsequious behaviour. [ORIGIN from the name (*Favel*) of a horse in a medieval French romance who became a symbol of cunning and duplicity; hence 'to rub down Favel' meant to use cunning.]
– ORIGIN Old French *correier*.
curry-comb ● noun a hand-held device with serrated ridges, used for grooming horses.
curry powder ● noun a mixture of finely ground spices, such as turmeric and coriander, used for making curry.
curse ● noun **1** an appeal to a supernatural power to inflict harm on someone or something. **2** a cause of harm or misery. **3** an offensive word or phrase used to express anger or annoyance. ● verb **1** use a curse against. **2** (**be cursed with**) be afflicted with. **3** utter offensive words; swear.
– ORIGIN Old English.
cursed /kursid, kurst/ ● adjective informal, dated used to express annoyance or irritation.
cursive /kursiv/ ● adjective written with the characters joined. ● noun writing with such a style.
– DERIVATIVES **cursively** adverb.
– ORIGIN Latin *cursivus*, from *currere* 'run'.
cursor ● noun **1** a movable indicator on a computer screen identifying the point that will be affected by input from the user. **2** the transparent slide engraved with a hairline used to locate points on a slide rule.
– ORIGIN Latin, 'runner' (the first sense in English).
cursory /kursəri/ ● adjective hasty and therefore not thorough.
– DERIVATIVES **cursorily** adverb **cursoriness** noun.
curst ● adjective archaic spelling of CURSED.
curt ● adjective noticeably or rudely brief.
– DERIVATIVES **curtly** adverb **curtness** noun.
– ORIGIN Latin *curtus* 'cut short, abridged'.
curtail /kurtayl/ ● verb reduce in extent or quantity.
– DERIVATIVES **curtailment** noun.
– ORIGIN from obsolete *curtal* 'horse with a docked tail', from Latin *curtus*, influenced by TAIL¹.

Thesaurus

common; Scottish unco; Brit. informal rum.
– OPPOSITES uninterested, ordinary.
curl ● verb **1** *smoke curled up from his cigarette* SPIRAL, coil, wreathe, twirl, swirl; wind, curve, bend, twist (and turn), loop, meander, snake, corkscrew, zigzag. **2** *Ruth curled her arms around his neck* WIND, twine, entwine, wrap. **3** *she washed and curled my hair* CRIMP, perm, tong. **4** *they curled up together on the sofa* NESTLE, snuggle, cuddle; N. Amer. snug down.
● noun **1** *the tangled curls of her hair* RINGLET, corkscrew, kink; kiss-curl. **2** *a curl of smoke* SPIRAL, coil, twirl, swirl, twist, corkscrew, curlicue, helix.
curly ● adjective WAVY, curling, curled, ringlety, crimped, permed, frizzy, kinky, corkscrew.
– OPPOSITES straight.
currency ● noun **1** *foreign currency* MONEY, legal tender, cash, banknotes, notes, coins, coinage, specie; N. Amer. bills. **2** *a term which has gained new currency* PREVALENCE, circulation, exposure; acceptance, popularity.
current ● adjective **1** *current events* CONTEMPORARY, present-day, modern, present, contemporaneous; topical, in the news, live, burning. **2** *the idea is still current* PREVALENT, prevailing, common, accepted, in circulation, circulating, on everyone's lips, popular, widespread. **3** *a current driving licence* VALID, usable, up to date. **4** *the current prime minister* INCUMBENT, present, in office, in power; reigning.
– OPPOSITES past, out of date, former.
● noun **1** *a current of air* FLOW, stream, backdraught, slipstream; airstream, thermal, updraught, draught; undercurrent, undertow, tide. **2** *the current of human life* COURSE, progress, progression, flow, tide, movement. **3** *the current of opinion* TREND, drift, direction, tendency.
curriculum ● noun SYLLABUS, course/programme of study, subjects, modules.
curse ● noun **1** *she put a curse on him* MALEDICTION, the evil eye; N. Amer. hex; Irish cess; informal jinx; formal imprecation; poetic/literary anathema. **2** *the curse of racism* EVIL, blight, scourge, plague, cancer, canker, poison. **3** *the curse of unemployment* AFFLICTION, burden, cross to bear, bane. **4** *muffled curses* SWEAR WORD, expletive, oath, profanity, four-letter word, dirty word, obscenity, blasphemy; informal cuss, cuss word; formal imprecation.
● verb **1** *it seemed as if the family had been cursed* PUT A CURSE ON, put the evil eye on, hoodoo, anathematize, damn; N. Amer. hex; informal jinx; archaic imprecate. **2** *she was cursed with feelings of inadequacy* AFFLICT, trouble, plague, bedevil. **3** *drivers cursed and sounded their horns* SWEAR, blaspheme, take the Lord's name in vain; informal cuss, turn the air blue, eff and blind; archaic execrate.
cursed ● adjective **1** *a cursed city* UNDER A CURSE, damned, doomed, ill-fated, ill-starred; informal jinxed; poetic/literary accursed, star-crossed. **2** (informal, dated) *those cursed children*. See ANNOYING.
cursory ● adjective PERFUNCTORY, desultory, casual, superficial, token; hasty, quick, hurried, rapid, brief, passing, fleeting.
– OPPOSITES thorough.
curt ● adjective TERSE, brusque, abrupt, clipped, blunt, short, monosyllabic, summary; snappish, sharp, tart; gruff, offhand, uncere-

C

curtain ● noun **1** a piece of material suspended at the top to form a screen, hung at a window in pairs or between the stage and auditorium of a theatre. **2** (**the curtain**) the rise or fall of a stage curtain between acts or scenes. **3** (**curtains**) informal a disastrous outcome. ● verb **1** provide with a curtain or curtains. **2** conceal with a curtain.
– ORIGIN Latin *cortina*, translation of Greek *aulaia*, from *aulē* 'court'.
curtain call ● noun the appearance of one or more performers on stage after a performance to acknowledge the audience's applause.
curtain-raiser ● noun an entertainment or other event happening just before a longer or more important one.
– ORIGIN originally used in the theatre to mean a short opening piece performed before a play.
curtain wall ● noun **1** a fortified wall around a medieval castle, typically one linking towers together. **2** a wall which encloses the space within a building but does not support the roof.
curtilage /kurtilij/ ● noun an area of land attached to a house and forming one enclosure with it.
– ORIGIN Old French, from *courtil* 'small court'.
curtsy (also **curtsey**) ● noun (pl. **curtsies** or **curtseys**) a woman's or girl's formal greeting, made by bending the knees with one foot in front of the other. ● verb (**curtsies**, **curtsied** or **curtseys**, **curtseyed**) perform a curtsy.
– ORIGIN variant of COURTESY.
curvaceous /kurvayshəss/ ● adjective (especially of a woman or a woman's figure) having an attractively curved shape.
curvature /kurvəchər/ ● noun the fact of being curved or the degree to which something is curved.
curve ● noun **1** a line or outline which gradually deviates from being straight for some or all of its length. **2** a line on a graph showing how one quantity varies with respect to another. ● verb form or cause to form a curve.
– ORIGIN from Latin *curvus* 'bent'.
curvet /kurvet/ ● noun a graceful or energetic leap. ● verb (**curvetted**, **curvetting** or **curveted**, **curveting**) (especially of a horse) leap gracefully or energetically.
– ORIGIN Italian *corvetta* 'little curve'.
curvilinear /kurvilinniər/ ● adjective contained by or consisting of a curved line or lines.
curvy ● adjective (**curvier**, **curviest**) **1** having many curves. **2** informal curvaceous.
– DERIVATIVES **curviness** noun.
cusec /kyoōsek/ ● noun a unit of water flow equal to one cubic foot per second.
cushion ● noun **1** a bag of cloth stuffed with a mass of soft material, used as a comfortable support for sitting or leaning on. **2** a source of support or protection against impact. **3** the elastic lining of the sides of a billiard table, from which the ball rebounds. ● verb **1** soften the effect of an impact on. **2** lessen the adverse effects of.
– ORIGIN Old French *cuissin*, from a Latin word meaning 'cushion for the hip', from *coxa* 'hip, thigh'.
cushy ● adjective (**cushier**, **cushiest**) informal **1** (of a task or situation) easy and undemanding. **2** N. Amer. (of furniture) comfortable.
– DERIVATIVES **cushiness** noun.
– ORIGIN from Urdu, 'pleasure'.
cusp /kusp/ ● noun **1** a pointed end where two curves meet. **2** each of the pointed ends of a crescent, especially of the moon. **3** a cone-shaped prominence on the surface of a tooth. **4** Astrology the initial point of an astrological sign or house. **5** a point of transition between two different states: *those on the cusp of adulthood.*
– DERIVATIVES **cuspate** adjective **cusped** adjective.
– ORIGIN Latin *cuspis* 'point or apex'.
cuspidor /kuspidor/ ● noun N. Amer. a spittoon.
– ORIGIN Portuguese, 'spitter'.
cuss informal ● noun **1** an annoying or stubborn person or animal. **2** a source of harm of misery. ● verb use offensive language; swear or curse.
cussed /kussid/ ● adjective informal awkward; annoying.
– DERIVATIVES **cussedly** adverb **cussedness** noun.
custard ● noun a dessert or sweet sauce made with milk and eggs and thickened with cornflour, or milk and a proprietary powder.
– ORIGIN originally *crustarde* or *custarde*, denoting an open pie containing meat or fruit in a sauce thickened with eggs: from Old French *crouste* 'crust'.
custard apple ● noun a large fleshy tropical fruit with a sweet yellow pulp.
custard pie ● noun an open pie containing cold set custard, or a similar container of foam, as thrown in slapstick comedy.
custodian /kustōdiən/ ● noun a person who has responsibility for or looks after something.
custody /kustədi/ ● noun **1** protective care or guardianship. **2** Law parental responsibility, especially as allocated to one of two divorcing parents. **3** imprisonment.
– DERIVATIVES **custodial** /kustōdiəl/ adjective.
– ORIGIN Latin *custodia*, from *custos* 'guardian'.
custom ● noun **1** a traditional way of behaving or doing something that is specific to a particular society, place, or time. **2** chiefly Brit. regular dealings with a shop or business by customers. **3** Law established usage having the force of law or right.
– ORIGIN Old French *coustume*, from Latin *consuescere* 'accustom'.
customary ● adjective in accordance with custom; usual.
– DERIVATIVES **customarily** adverb.

Thesaurus

monious, ungracious, rude, impolite, discourteous, uncivil; informal snappy.
– OPPOSITES expansive.
curtail ● verb **1** *economic policies designed to curtail spending* REDUCE, cut, cut down, decrease, lessen, pare down, trim, retrench; restrict, limit, curb, rein in/back; informal slash. **2** *his visit was curtailed* SHORTEN, cut short, truncate.
– OPPOSITES increase, lengthen.
curtain ● noun *he drew the curtains* WINDOW HANGING, screen, blind; N. Amer. drape.
● verb *the bed was curtained off from the rest of the room* CONCEAL, hide, screen, shield; separate, isolate.
curtsy ● verb *she curtsied to the king* BEND ONE'S KNEE, drop/bob a curtsy, genuflect.
● noun *she made a curtsy* BOB, genuflection, obeisance.
curvaceous ● adjective SHAPELY, voluptuous, sexy, full-figured, buxom, full-bosomed, bosomy, Junoesque; cuddly; informal curvy, well endowed, pneumatic, busty; archaic comely.
– OPPOSITES skinny.
curve ● noun *the serpentine curves of the river* BEND, turn, loop, curl, twist, hook; arc, arch, bow, half-moon, undulation, curvature.
– RELATED TERMS sinuous.
● verb *the road curved back on itself* BEND, turn, loop, wind, meander, undulate, snake, spiral, twist, coil, curl; arc, arch.
curved ● adjective BENT, arched, bowed, crescent, curving, wavy, sinuous, serpentine, meandering, undulating, curvilinear, curvy.
– OPPOSITES straight.
cushion ● noun *a cushion against inflation* PROTECTION, buffer, shield, defence, bulwark.
● verb **1** *she cushioned her head on her arms* SUPPORT, cradle, prop (up), rest. **2** *to cushion the blow, wages and pensions were increased* SOFTEN, lessen, diminish, decrease, mitigate, temper, allay, alleviate, take the edge off, dull, deaden. **3** *residents are cushioned from the outside world* PROTECT, shield, shelter, cocoon.
cushy ● adjective (informal) *a cushy job* EASY, undemanding; comfortable, secure; Brit. informal jammy.
– OPPOSITES difficult.
custodian ● noun CURATOR, keeper, conservator, guardian, overseer, superintendent; caretaker, steward, protector.
custody ● noun *the parent who has custody of the child* CARE, guardianship, charge, keeping, safe keeping, wardship, responsibility, protection, tutelage; custodianship, trusteeship; archaic ward.
– PHRASES **in custody** IN PRISON, in jail, imprisoned, incarcerated, locked up, under lock and key, interned, detained; on remand; informal behind bars, doing time, inside; Brit. informal banged up.
custom ● noun **1** *his unfamiliarity with the local customs* TRADITION, practice, usage, observance, way, convention, formality, ceremony, ritual; shibboleth, sacred cow, unwritten rule; mores; formal praxis. **2** *it is our custom to visit the Lake District in October* HABIT, practice, routine, way, wont; policy, rule. **3** (Brit.) *if you keep me waiting I will take my custom elsewhere* BUSINESS, patronage, trade.
customarily ● adverb USUALLY, traditionally, normally, as a rule, generally, ordinarily, commonly; habitually, routinely.

custom-built (also **custom-made**) ● adjective made to a particular customer's order.
customer ● noun **1** a person who buys goods or services from a shop or business. **2** a person or thing of a specified kind that one has to deal with: *he's a tough customer.*
custom house (also **customs house**) ● noun chiefly historical the office at a port or frontier where customs duty is collected.
customize (also **customise**) ● verb modify (something) to suit a particular individual or task.
customs ● plural noun **1** the duties levied by a government on imported goods. **2** the official department that administers and collects such duties.
– ORIGIN originally meaning a customary due paid to a ruler, later duty levied on goods on their way to market.
customs union ● noun a group of states that have agreed to charge the same import duties as each other and usually to allow free trade between themselves.
cut ● verb (**cutting**; past and past part. **cut**) **1** make an opening, incision, or wound in (something) with a sharp implement. **2** shorten or divide into pieces with a sharp implement. **3** make, form, or remove with a sharp implement. **4** make or design (a garment) in a particular way: *an impeccably cut suit.* **5** reduce the amount or quantity of. **6** end or interrupt the provision of (a supply). **7** (of a line) cross or intersect (another line). **8** stop filming or recording. **9** move to another shot in a film. **10** make (a sound recording). **11** divide a pack of playing cards by lifting a portion from the top. **12** strike or kick (a ball) quickly and abruptly. **13** chiefly N. Amer. absent oneself deliberately from: *Rod was cutting class.* **14** chiefly N. Amer. dilute or adulterate (alcohol or a drug) by mixing it with another substance. ● noun **1** an act of cutting. **2** a result of cutting: *a cut on his jaw.* **3** a reduction in amount or size. **4** the way or style in which a garment or the hair is cut. **5** a piece of meat cut from a carcass. **6** informal a share of profits. **7** a version of a film after editing: *the director's cut.*
– PHRASES **be cut out for** (or **to be**) informal have exactly the right qualities for a particular role. **cut your coat according to your cloth** proverb undertake only what you have the money or ability to do and no more. **a cut above** informal noticeably superior to. **cut and dried** (of a situation) completely settled. [ORIGIN originally used to distinguish the herbs of herbalists' shops from growing herbs.] **cut and run** informal make a speedy departure from a difficult situation rather than deal with it. [ORIGIN originally a nautical phrase, meaning 'cut the anchor cable because of an emergency and make sail immediately'.] **cut and thrust** a difficult or competitive atmosphere or environment. [ORIGIN originally a fencing phrase.] **cut both ways 1** (of a point or statement) serve both sides of an argument. **2** (of an action or process) have both good and bad effects. **cut corners** do something in a perfunctory way to save time or money. **cut a dash** be stylish or impressive. **cut dead** completely ignore (someone). **be cut from the same cloth** be of the same nature. **cut in 1** interrupt. **2** pull in too closely in front of another vehicle. **3** (of a motor or other device) begin operating automatically. **4** informal include (someone) in a deal and give them a share of the profits. **cut it** informal, chiefly N. Amer. come up to expectations. [ORIGIN shortened form of the idiom *cut the mustard.*] **cut it out** informal stop it. **cut the mustard** informal reach the required standard. **cut no ice** informal have no influence or effect. **cut off 1** block the usual means of access to (a place). **2** deprive of a supply of power, water, etc. **3** break a telephone connection with (someone). **4** disinherit. **cut out 1** exclude (someone). **2** (of an engine) suddenly stop operating. **cut a** (or **the**) **rug** informal, chiefly N. Amer. dance. **cut one's teeth** acquire initial experience of an activity. **cut a tooth** (of a baby) have a tooth appear through the gum. **cut up** informal (of a driver) overtake (someone) and pull in too closely. **cut up rough** Brit. informal behave in an aggressive or awkward way.
– ORIGIN probably Germanic.
cut and paste ● verb (on a word processor or computer) move (an item) from one part of a text to another.
cutaneous /kyoōtayniəss/ ● adjective relating to or affecting the skin.
– ORIGIN from Latin *cutis* 'skin'.
cutaway ● adjective **1** (of a coat or jacket) having the front cut away below the waist. **2** (of a diagram of an object) having some external parts left out to reveal the interior.
cutback ● noun a reduction, especially in expenditure.
cute ● adjective **1** endearingly pretty. **2** N. Amer. informal sexually attractive. **3** informal, chiefly N. Amer. clever; shrewd.
– DERIVATIVES **cutely** adverb **cuteness** noun.
– ORIGIN shortening of ACUTE.
cutesy ● adjective informal cute to a sentimental or mawkish extent.

C

Thesaurus

– OPPOSITES occasionally.
customary ● adjective **1** *customary social practices* USUAL, traditional, normal, conventional, familiar, accepted, routine, established, time-honoured, regular, prevailing. **2** *her customary good sense* USUAL, accustomed, habitual, wonted.
– OPPOSITES unusual.
customer ● noun CONSUMER, buyer, purchaser, patron, client; shopper; *Brit. informal* punter.
customs ● plural noun. See TAX noun sense 1.
cut ● verb **1** *the knife slipped and cut his finger* GASH, slash, lacerate, sever, slit, pierce, penetrate, wound, injure; scratch, graze, nick, snick, incise, score; lance. **2** *cut the pepper into small pieces* CHOP, cut up, slice, dice, cube, mince; carve; *N. Amer.* hash. **3** *cut back the new growth to about half its length* TRIM, snip, clip, crop, barber, shear, shave; pare; prune, pollard, poll, lop, dock; mow. **4** *I went to cut some flowers* PICK, pluck, gather; *poetic/literary* cull. **5** *lettering had been cut into the stonework* CARVE, engrave, incise, etch, score; chisel, whittle. **6** *the government cut public expenditure* REDUCE, cut back/down on, decrease, lessen, retrench, trim, slim down; rationalize, downsize, slenderize; mark down, discount, lower; *informal* slash. **7** *the text has been substantially cut* SHORTEN, abridge, condense, abbreviate, truncate; edit; bowdlerize, expurgate. **8** *you need to cut at least ten lines per page* DELETE, remove, take out, excise, blue-pencil. **9** *oil supplies to the area had been cut* DISCONTINUE, break off, suspend, interrupt; stop, end, put an end to. **10** *the point where the line cuts the vertical axis* CROSS, intersect, bisect; meet, join. **11** *(dated) the banker's wife cut her at church* SNUB, ignore, shun, give someone the cold shoulder, cold-shoulder, cut dead, look right through, rebuff, turn one's back on; *informal* freeze out.
● noun **1** *a cut on his jaw* GASH, slash, laceration, incision, wound, injury; scratch, graze, nick, snick. **2** *a cut of beef* JOINT, piece, section. **3** *(informal) the directors are demanding their cut* SHARE, portion, bit, quota, percentage; *informal* slice of the cake, rake-off, piece of the action; *Brit. informal* whack. **4** *his hair was in need of a cut* HAIRCUT, trim, clip, crop. **5** *a smart cut of the whip* BLOW, slash, stroke. **6** *he followed this with the unkindest cut of all* INSULT, slight, affront, slap in the face, jibe, barb, cutting remark; *informal* put-down, dig. **7** *a cut in interest rates* REDUCTION, cutback, decrease, lessening; *N. Amer.* rollback. **8** *the elegant cut of his jacket* STYLE, design; tailoring, lines, fit.
– PHRASES **cut back** *companies cut back on foreign investment* REDUCE, cut, cut down on, decrease, lessen, retrench, economize on, trim, prune, slim down, scale down; rationalize, downsize, pull/draw in one's horns, tighten one's belt; *informal* slash. **cut someone/something down 1** *24 hectares of trees were cut down* FELL, chop down, hack down, saw down, hew. **2** *he was cut down in his prime* KILL, slaughter, shoot down, mow down, gun down; *informal* take out, blow away; *poetic/literary* slay. **cut and dried** DEFINITE, decided, settled, explicit, specific, precise, unambiguous, clear-cut, unequivocal, black and white, hard and fast. **cut in** INTERRUPT, butt in, break in, interject, interpose, chime in; *Brit. informal* chip in. **cut someone/something off 1** *they cut off his finger* SEVER, chop off, hack off; amputate. **2** *oil and gas supplies were cut off* DISCONTINUE, break off, disconnect, suspend; stop, end, bring to an end. **3** *a community cut off from the mainland by the flood waters* ISOLATE, separate, keep apart; seclude, closet, cloister, sequester. **cut out** STOP WORKING, stop, fail, give out, break down; *informal* die, give up the ghost, conk out; *Brit. informal* pack up. **cut someone/something out 1** *cut out all the diseased wood* REMOVE, take out, excise, extract; snip out, clip out. **2** *it's best to cut out alcohol altogether* GIVE UP, refrain from, abstain from, go without; *informal* quit, leave off, pack in, lay off, knock off. **3** *his mother cut him out of her will* EXCLUDE, leave out, omit, eliminate. **cut something short** BREAK OFF, shorten, truncate, curtail, terminate, end, stop, abort, bring to an untimely end. **cut someone short** INTERRUPT, cut off, butt in on, break in on.
cutback ● noun REDUCTION, cut, decrease; economy, saving; *N. Amer.* rollback.
– OPPOSITES increase.

C

cut glass ● noun glass ornamented by having patterns cut into it.
cuticle /kyōōtik'l/ ● noun **1** dead skin at the base of a fingernail or toenail. **2** the epidermis of the body. **3** a protective layer covering the epidermis of a plant or invertebrate.
– DERIVATIVES **cuticular** adjective.
– ORIGIN from Latin *cuticula* 'little skin'.
cutis /kyōōtiss/ ● noun Anatomy the true skin or dermis.
– ORIGIN Latin, 'skin'.
cutlass /kutləss/ ● noun a short sword with a slightly curved blade, formerly used by sailors.
– ORIGIN Latin *cultellus* 'little knife'.
cutler ● noun a person who makes or sells cutlery.
– ORIGIN Old French *coutelier*, from Latin *cultellus* 'little knife, ploughshare'.
cutlery ● noun knives, forks, and spoons used for eating or serving food.
cutlet ● noun **1** a portion of meat, especially a chop from just behind the neck. **2** a flat croquette of minced meat, nuts, or pulses.
– ORIGIN French *côtelette*, from *coste* 'rib'.
cut-off ● noun **1** a point or level marking a designated limit. **2** a device for interrupting a power or fuel supply. **3** (**cut-offs**) shorts made by cutting off the legs of a pair of jeans. **4** chiefly N. Amer. a short cut.
cut-out ● noun **1** a shape cut out of board or another material. **2** a hole cut for decoration or to allow the insertion of something. **3** a device that automatically breaks an electric circuit for safety.
cut-price (chiefly N. Amer. also **cut-rate**) ● adjective for sale at a reduced price; cheap.
cutpurse ● noun archaic a pickpocket.
– ORIGIN with reference to stealing by cutting purses suspended from a waistband.
cutter ● noun **1** a person or thing that cuts. **2** a light, fast patrol boat or sailing boat. **3** a ship's boat used for carrying light stores or passengers. **4** Cricket & Baseball a ball that deviates sharply on pitching.
cut-throat ● noun dated a murderer or other violent criminal. ● adjective ruthless and intense.
cut-throat razor ● noun Brit. a razor with a long blade which folds like a penknife.
cutting ● noun **1** a piece cut off from something, in particular an article cut from a newspaper or a piece cut from a plant for propagation. **2** an open passage excavated through higher ground for a railway, road, or canal. ● adjective **1** capable of cutting. **2** (of a remark) hurtful.
– DERIVATIVES **cuttingly** adverb.
cutting edge ● noun **1** the latest or most advanced stage; the forefront. **2** (as adjective) (**cutting-edge**) innovative; pioneering.
cuttlebone ● noun the flattened internal skeleton of the cuttlefish.
cuttlefish ● noun a swimming marine mollusc that resembles a broad-bodied squid, having eight arms and two long tentacles that are used for grabbing prey.
– ORIGIN related to Old English *codd* 'bag', with reference to its ink bag.
cut-up ● noun a film or sound recording made by cutting and editing material from pre-existing recordings.
cut up ● adjective informal very distressed.
cutwater ● noun **1** the forward edge of a ship's prow. **2** a wedge-shaped projection on the pier of a bridge.
cutworm ● noun a moth caterpillar that lives in the soil and eats through the stems of young plants at ground level.
cuvée /kyōōvay/ ● noun a type, blend, or batch of wine, especially champagne.
– ORIGIN French, 'vatful'.
CV ● abbreviation curriculum vitae.
CVO ● abbreviation (in the UK) Commander of the Royal Victorian Order.
CVS ● abbreviation chorionic villus sampling, a test made in early pregnancy to detect fetal abnormalities.
cwm /koōm/ ● noun a cirque, especially in the Welsh mountains.
– ORIGIN Welsh; related to COMBE.
cwt. ● abbreviation hundredweight.
– ORIGIN from Latin *centum* 'a hundred'.
-cy ● suffix **1** denoting state or condition: *bankruptcy*. **2** denoting rank or status: *baronetcy*.
– ORIGIN from Latin *-cia*, *-tia* and Greek *-keia*, *-teia*.
cyan /sīən/ ● noun a greenish-blue colour which is one of the primary colours, complementary to red.
– ORIGIN Greek *kuaneos* 'dark blue'.
cyanide /sīənīd/ ● noun a salt or ester of hydrocyanic acid, most kinds of which are extremely poisonous.
cyanobacteria /sīənōbakteeriə/ ● plural noun micro-organisms of a group comprising the blue-green algae, related to bacteria but capable of photosynthesis.
cyanocobalamin /sīənōkəbaləmin/ ● noun vitamin B_{12}, a cobalt-containing vitamin derived from liver, fish, and eggs, a deficiency of which can cause pernicious anaemia.
– ORIGIN from Greek *kuanos* 'dark blue' + a blend of COBALT and VITAMIN.
cyanogen /sīannəjən/ ● noun a highly poisonous gas made by oxidizing hydrogen cyanide.
– ORIGIN from Greek *kuanos* 'dark blue mineral', so named because it is a constituent of Prussian blue.
cyanosis /sīənōsis/ ● noun a bluish discoloration of the skin due to poor circulation or inadequate oxygenation of the blood.
– DERIVATIVES **cyanotic** adjective.
– ORIGIN Greek *kuanōsis* 'blueness'.
cyber- /sībər/ ● combining form relating to information technology, the Internet, and virtual reality: *cyberspace*.
– ORIGIN from CYBERNETICS.
cybernetics ● plural noun (treated as sing.) the science of communications and automatic control systems in both machines and living things.
– DERIVATIVES **cybernetic** adjective.
– ORIGIN from Greek *kubernētēs* 'steersman'.
cyberphobia ● noun extreme or irrational fear of computers or technology.
cyberpunk ● noun a genre of science fiction set in a lawless subculture of an oppressive society dominated by computer technology.
cyberspace ● noun the notional environment in which communication over computer networks occurs.
cybersquatting ● noun the practice of registering names, especially well-known company or brand names, as Internet domains, in the hope of reselling them at a profit.
cyborg /sīborg/ ● noun a fictional or hypothetical person whose physical abilities are extended beyond human limitations by mechanical elements built into the body.
– ORIGIN blend of CYBER- and ORGANISM.
cycad /sīkad/ ● noun a tall, cone-bearing, palm-like plant of warm regions.
– ORIGIN from supposed Greek *kukas*, an error for *koikas* 'Egyptian palms'.
cyclamate /sikləmayt, sīk-/ ● noun a salt of a synthetic organic acid, formerly used as an artificial sweetener.
– ORIGIN contraction of *cyclohexylsulphamate*.
cyclamen /sikləmən/ ● noun (pl. same or **cyclamens**) a plant having pink, red, or white flowers with backward-curving petals.
– ORIGIN Greek *kuklaminos*, perhaps from *kuklos* 'circle', with reference to its bulbous roots.

Thesaurus

cute ● adjective ENDEARING, adorable, lovable, sweet, lovely, appealing, engaging, delightful, dear, darling, winning, winsome, attractive, pretty; *informal* cutesy, twee *Brit. informal* dinky.
cut-price ● adjective CHEAP, marked down, reduced, on (special) offer, discount; *N. Amer.* cut-rate.
– OPPOSITES expensive.
cut-throat ● noun *(dated) a band of robbers and cut-throats* MURDERER, killer, assassin; *informal* hit-man; *dated* homicide.
● adjective *cut-throat competition between rival firms* RUTHLESS, merciless, fierce, intense, aggressive, dog-eat-dog.
cutting ● noun **1** *a newspaper cutting* CLIPPING, clip, snippet; article, piece, column, paragraph. **2** *plant cuttings* SCION, slip; graft. **3** *fabric cuttings* PIECE, bit, fragment; trimming.
● adjective **1** *a cutting remark* HURTFUL, wounding, barbed, pointed, scathing, acerbic, mordant, caustic, acid, sarcastic, sardonic, snide, spiteful, malicious, mean, nasty, cruel, unkind; *informal* bitchy, catty; *Brit. informal* sarky; *N. Amer. informal* snarky. **2** *cutting winter winds* ICY, icy-cold, freezing, arctic, Siberian, glacial, bitter, chilling, chilly, chill; biting, piercing, penetrating, raw, keen, sharp.

cycle ● noun **1** a series of events that are regularly repeated in the same order. **2** a complete sequence of changes associated with a recurring phenomenon such as an alternating current, wave, etc. **3** a series of musical or literary works composed around a particular theme. **4** a bicycle. ● verb **1** ride a bicycle. **2** move in or follow a cycle of events.
– ORIGIN Greek *kuklos* 'circle'.
cyclic /sīklik/ ● adjective **1** occurring in cycles. **2** Chemistry having a molecular structure containing one or more closed rings of atoms.
– DERIVATIVES **cyclical** adjective **cyclically** adverb.
cyclist ● noun a person who rides a bicycle.
cycloid /sīkloyd/ ● noun Mathematics a curve traced by a point on a circle being rolled along a straight line.
– DERIVATIVES **cycloidal** adjective.
cyclometer /sīklommitər/ ● noun **1** an instrument for measuring circular arcs. **2** an instrument attached to a bicycle for measuring distance.
cyclone /sīklōn/ ● noun **1** a system of winds rotating inwards to an area of low barometric pressure; a depression. **2** a tropical storm.
– DERIVATIVES **cyclonic** adjective.
– ORIGIN probably from Greek *kuklōma* 'wheel, coil of a snake'.
cyclopean /sīkləpeeən, sīklōpiən/ (also **cyclopian**) ● adjective **1** of or resembling a Cyclops. **2** (of ancient masonry) made with massive irregular blocks.
cyclopedia /sīkləpeediə/ (also **cyclopaedia**) ● noun archaic (except in book titles) an encyclopedia.
Cyclops /sīklops/ ● noun **1** (pl. **Cyclops**, **Cyclopses**, or **Cyclopes** /sīklōpeez/) Greek Mythology a member of a race of savage one-eyed giants. **2** (**cyclops**) a minute freshwater crustacean which has a cylindrical body with a single central eye.
– ORIGIN from Greek *Kuklōps*, 'round-eyed'.
cyclorama /sīkləraamə/ ● noun **1** a panoramic scene set on the inside of a cylindrical surface, to be viewed by a central spectator. **2** a cloth stretched tight in an arc around the back of a stage set, used to represent the sky.
cyclosporin /sīklōsporin/ (also **cyclosporine**) ● noun a drug used to prevent the rejection of grafts and transplants.
– ORIGIN from Latin *spora* 'spore' (because it is produced from a fungus).
cyclotron /sīklətron/ ● noun an apparatus in which charged atomic and subatomic particles are accelerated by an alternating electric field while following an outward spiral or circular path in a magnetic field.
cyder ● noun archaic spelling of CIDER.
cygnet /signit/ ● noun a young swan.
– ORIGIN Old French, from Greek *kuknos* 'swan'.
cylinder /sillindər/ ● noun **1** a three-dimensional shape with straight parallel sides and a circular or oval cross section. **2** a piston chamber in a steam or internal-combustion engine. **3** a cylindrical container for liquefied gas under pressure. **4** a rotating metal roller in a printing press.
– DERIVATIVES **cylindrical** /silindrik'l/ adjective **cylindrically** adverb.
– ORIGIN Greek *kulindros* 'roller'.
cylinder head ● noun the end cover of a cylinder in an internal-combustion engine, against which the piston compresses the cylinder's contents.
cymbal /simb'l/ ● noun a musical instrument consisting of a slightly concave round brass plate which is either struck against another one or struck with a stick.
– ORIGIN Greek *kumbalon*, from *kumbē* 'cup'.
cyme ● noun Botany a flower cluster with a central stem bearing a single terminal flower that develops first, the other flowers in the cluster developing on lateral stems. Compare with RACEME.
– ORIGIN French, 'summit, unopened flower head', from Latin *cyma*.
Cymric /kimrik/ ● adjective (of language or culture) Welsh. ● noun the Welsh language.
– ORIGIN from Welsh *Cymru* 'Wales'.
cynic /sinnik/ ● noun **1** a person who has little faith in the integrity or sincerity of others. **2** a sceptic. **3** (**Cynic**) (in ancient Greece) a member of a school of philosophers founded by Antisthenes, characterized by an ostentatious contempt for wealth and pleasure.
– DERIVATIVES **cynicism** noun.
– ORIGIN Greek *kunikos*; probably originally from *Kunosarges*, the name of a gymnasium where the philosopher Antisthenes taught, but popularly taken to mean 'doglike, churlish', *kuōn* 'dog' becoming a nickname for a Cynic.
cynical ● adjective **1** tending not to believe in the integrity or sincerity of others. **2** sceptical. **3** contemptuous; mocking. **4** concerned only with one's own interests.
– DERIVATIVES **cynically** adverb.
cynosure /sīnəzyoor, sin-/ ● noun a person or thing that is the centre of attention or admiration.
– ORIGIN originally denoting the constellation Ursa Minor, or the pole star which it contains: from Greek *kunosoura* 'dog's tail' (also 'Ursa Minor').
cypher ● noun variant spelling of CIPHER.
cypress ● noun an evergreen coniferous tree with flattened shoots bearing small scale-like leaves, whose dark foliage is sometimes associated with mourning.
– ORIGIN Greek *kuparissos*.
Cypriot ● noun **1** a person from Cyprus. **2** the dialect of Greek used in Cyprus. ● adjective relating to Cyprus.
– ORIGIN Greek *Kupriōtes*, from *Kupros* 'Cyprus'.
Cyrillic /sirillik/ ● adjective denoting the alphabet used for Russian, Ukrainian, Bulgarian, Serbian, and some other Slavic languages, ultimately derived from Greek uncials. ● noun the Cyrillic alphabet.
– ORIGIN named after the 9th-century Greek missionary St *Cyril*, its reputed inventor.
cyst /sist/ ● noun **1** a thin-walled sac or cavity of abnormal character in the body, containing fluid. **2** a tough protective capsule enclosing the larva of a parasitic worm or the resting stage of an organism.
– ORIGIN Greek *kustis* 'bladder'.
cystectomy ● noun (pl. **cystectomies**) **1** a surgical operation to remove the urinary bladder. **2** a surgical operation to remove an abnormal cyst.
cysteine /sisti-een/ ● noun Biochemistry a sulphur-containing amino acid which occurs in keratins and other proteins. Compare with CYSTINE.
cystic ● adjective **1** chiefly Medicine relating to or characterized by cysts. **2** Zoology (of a parasite or other organism) enclosed in a cyst. **3** relating to the urinary bladder or the gall bladder.
cystic fibrosis ● noun a hereditary disorder which affects the exocrine glands, resulting in the production of abnormally thick mucus and leading to the blockage of the pancreatic ducts, intestines, and bronchi.
cystine /sisteen/ ● noun Biochemistry an oxidized form of the amino acid cysteine.
– ORIGIN from Greek *kustis* 'bladder' (because it was first isolated from urinary calculi).
cystitis /sistītis/ ● noun inflammation of the urinary bladder, typically caused by infection and accompanied by frequent painful urination.
cytogenetics /sītōjənettiks/ ● plural noun (treated as sing.) the study of inheritance in relation to the structure and function of chromosomes.

Thesaurus

– OPPOSITES friendly, warm.
cut up ● adjective *(informal)* See UPSET adjective sense 1.
cycle ● noun **1** *the cycle of birth, death, and rebirth* ROUND, rotation; pattern, rhythm. **2** *the painting is one of a cycle of seven* SERIES, sequence, succession, run; set. **3** *cycles may be hired from the station.* See BICYCLE.
cyclical ● adjective RECURRENT, recurring, regular, repeated; periodic, seasonal, circular.
cyclone ● noun HURRICANE, typhoon, tropical storm, storm, tornado, windstorm, whirlwind, tempest; *Austral.* willy-willy; *N. Amer. informal* twister.
cynic ● noun SCEPTIC, doubter, doubting Thomas; pessimist, prophet of doom, doomsayer, Cassandra; *informal* doom (and gloom) merchant.
cynical ● adjective SCEPTICAL, doubtful, distrustful, suspicious, disbelieving; pessimistic, negative, world-weary, disillusioned, disenchanted, jaundiced, sardonic.
– OPPOSITES idealistic.
cynicism ● noun SCEPTICISM, doubt, distrust, mistrust, suspicion, disbelief; pessimism, negativity, world-weariness, disenchantment.
cyst ● noun GROWTH, lump; abscess, wen, boil, carbuncle.

– DERIVATIVES **cytogenetic** adjective **cytogeneticist** noun.
– ORIGIN from Greek *kutos* 'vessel'.

cytology /sītolləji/ ● noun the branch of biology concerned with the structure and function of plant and animal cells.
– DERIVATIVES **cytological** adjective **cytologically** adverb **cytologist** noun.

C

cytomegalovirus /sītōmeggəlōvīrəss/ ● noun Medicine a kind of herpesvirus which usually produces very mild symptoms in an infected person but may cause severe neurological damage in people with weakened immune systems and in the newborn.

cytoplasm /sītōplaz'm/ ● noun Biology the material or protoplasm within a living cell, excluding the nucleus.
– DERIVATIVES **cytoplasmic** adjective.

cytosine /sītəseen/ ● noun Biochemistry a compound which is one of the four constituent bases of DNA.

cytotoxic ● adjective toxic to living cells.
– DERIVATIVES **cytotoxicity** noun.

czar etc. ● noun variant spelling of TSAR etc.

Czech /chek/ ● noun **1** a person from the Czech Republic or (formerly) Czechoslovakia. **2** the Slavic language spoken in the Czech Republic, closely related to Slovak. ● adjective relating to the Czech Republic.
– ORIGIN Polish spelling of the Czech.

Czechoslovak /chekkəslōvak/ (also **Czechoslovakian**) ● noun a person from the former country of Czechoslovakia, now divided between the Czech Republic and Slovakia. ● adjective relating to the former country of Czechoslovakia.

Dd

D[1] (also **d**) ● noun (pl. **Ds** or **D's**) **1** the fourth letter of the alphabet. **2** denoting the fourth item in a set. **3** Music the second note of the diatonic scale of C major. **4** the Roman numeral for 500. [ORIGIN understood as half of CIↃ, an earlier form of M (= 1,000).]

D[2] ● abbreviation **1** (in the US) Democrat or Democratic. **2** depth (in the sense of the dimension of an object from front to back). **3** (with a numeral) dimension(s) or dimensional. **4** (in tables of sports results) drawn.

d ● abbreviation **1** (in genealogies) daughter. **2** deci-. **3** (in travel timetables) departs. **4** (**d.**) died (used to indicate a date of death). **5** Brit. penny or pence (of pre-decimal currency). [ORIGIN from Latin *denarius* 'penny'.]

'd ● contraction **1** had. **2** would.

DA ● abbreviation US district attorney.

D/A ● abbreviation Electronics digital to analogue.

dab[1] ● verb (**dabbed**, **dabbing**) **1** press lightly with absorbent material. **2** apply with light quick strokes. ● noun **1** a small amount lightly applied. **2** (**dabs**) Brit. informal fingerprints.
– ORIGIN symbolic of a light striking movement

dab[2] ● noun a small North Atlantic flatfish.
– ORIGIN of unknown origin.

dabble ● verb **1** move (one's hands or feet) around gently in water. **2** take part in an activity in a casual way.
– DERIVATIVES **dabbler** noun.
– ORIGIN from obsolete Dutch *dabbelen* or from DAB[1].

dabchick ● noun the little grebe.
– ORIGIN the first element is perhaps related to DIP and DEEP.

dab hand ● noun Brit. informal a person who is very skilled in a particular activity.
– ORIGIN of unknown origin.

da capo /daa kaapō/ ● adverb & adjective Music repeat or repeated from the beginning.
– ORIGIN Italian, 'from the head'.

dace /dayss/ ● noun (pl. same) a small freshwater fish related to the carp.
– ORIGIN Old French *dars* (see DART).

dacha /dachə/ (also **datcha**) ● noun (in Russia) a house or cottage in the country, used as a holiday home.
– ORIGIN Russian, originally meaning 'grant of land'.

dachshund /daks-hoond/ ● noun a breed of dog with a long body and very short legs.
– ORIGIN German, 'badger dog' (the breed was originally used to dig badgers out of their setts).

dacoit /dəkoyt/ ● noun a member of a band of armed robbers in India or Burma (Myanmar).
– ORIGIN Hindi, 'robbery by a gang'.

dacoity ● noun (pl. **dacoities**) a violent robbery committed by dacoits in India or Burma (Myanmar).

dactyl /daktil/ ● noun Poetry a metrical foot consisting of one stressed syllable followed by two unstressed syllables.
– DERIVATIVES **dactylic** adjective.
– ORIGIN Greek *daktulos* 'finger' (the three bones of the finger corresponding to the three syllables).

dad ● noun informal one's father.
– ORIGIN perhaps imitative of a child's first syllables *da, da*.

Dada /daadaa/ ● noun an early 20th-century movement in the arts which mocked conventions and emphasized the illogical and absurd.
– DERIVATIVES **Dadaism** noun **Dadaist** noun & adjective.
– ORIGIN French, 'hobby horse', the title of a review which appeared in Zurich in 1916.

daddy ● noun (pl. **daddies**) informal one's father.

daddy-long-legs ● noun Brit. informal a crane fly.

dado /daydō/ ● noun (pl. **dados**) **1** the lower part of the wall of a room, when decorated differently from the upper part. **2** Architecture the cube of a pedestal between the base and the cornice.
– ORIGIN Italian, 'dice or cube'.

dado rail ● noun a waist-high moulding round the wall of a room, separating the dado from the upper part of the wall.

daemon[1] /deemən/ (also **daimon**) ● noun **1** (in ancient Greek belief) a divinity or supernatural being of a nature between gods and humans. **2** archaic spelling of DEMON[1].
– DERIVATIVES **daemonic** adjective.
– ORIGIN Greek *daimon*.

daemon[2] /deemən/ ● noun variant spelling of DEMON[2].

daffodil ● noun a plant bearing bright yellow flowers with a long trumpet-shaped centre.
– ORIGIN originally as *affodill*: from Latin *asphodilus* 'asphodel'.

daffy ● adjective (**daffier, daffiest**) informal silly; mildly eccentric.
– DERIVATIVES **daffiness** noun.
– ORIGIN from northern English dialect *daff* 'simpleton'; perhaps related to DAFT.

daft ● adjective informal, chiefly Brit. silly; foolish.
– ORIGIN Old English, 'mild, meek'.

dag[1] ● noun Austral./NZ a lock of wool matted with dung hanging from the hindquarters of a sheep.
– ORIGIN possibly related to TAG[1].

dag[2] ● noun Austral./NZ informal a socially conservative person.
– ORIGIN originally denoting an eccentric person: from an English dialect word meaning 'a challenge'.

dagger ● noun **1** a short pointed knife, used as a weapon. **2** Printing an obelus.
– PHRASES **at daggers drawn** in bitter conflict. **look daggers at** glare angrily at.
– ORIGIN perhaps from obsolete *dag* 'pierce', influenced by Old French *dague* 'long dagger'.

daggy ● adjective (**daggier, daggiest**) Austral./NZ informal **1** (especially of clothes) scruffy. **2** not stylish; unfashionable.

dago /daygō/ ● noun (pl. **dagos** or **dagoes**) informal, offensive a Spanish, Portuguese, or Italian-speaking person.
– ORIGIN from the Spanish forename *Diego* 'James'.

daguerreotype /dəgerrətīp/ (also **daguerrotype**) ● noun a photograph taken by an early process using an iodine-sensitized silver-coated copper plate and mercury vapour.
– ORIGIN French, named after L.-J.-M. *Daguerre* (1789–1851), its French inventor.

dahlia /dayliə/ ● noun a garden plant with brightly coloured

Thesaurus

dab ● verb *she dabbed disinfectant on the cut* PAT, press, touch, blot, mop, swab; daub, apply, wipe, stroke.
● noun **1** *a dab of glue* DROP, spot, smear, splash, speck, taste, trace, touch, hint, bit; *informal* smidgen, tad, lick. **2** *apply concealer with light dabs* PAT, touch, blot, wipe.

dabble ● verb **1** *they dabbled their feet in rock pools* SPLASH, dip, paddle, trail; immerse. **2** *he dabbled in politics* TOY WITH, dip into, flirt with, tinker with, trifle with, play with, dally with.

dabbler ● noun AMATEUR, dilettante, layman, layperson; tinkerer, trifler.
– OPPOSITES professional.

daemon ● noun NUMEN, genius (loci), attendant spirit, tutelary spirit.

daft ● adjective *(Brit. informal)* **1** *a daft idea* ABSURD, preposterous, ridiculous, ludicrous, farcical, laughable; idiotic, stupid, foolish, silly, inane, fatuous, hare-brained, half-baked; *informal* crazy, cockeyed; *Brit. informal* barmy. **2** *are you daft?* SIMPLE-MINDED, stupid, idiotic, slow, witless, feeble-minded, empty-headed, vacuous, vapid; unhinged, insane, mad; *informal* thick, dim, dopey, dumb, dim-witted, half-witted, birdbrained, pea-brained, slow on the uptake, soft in the head, brain-dead, not all there, touched, crazy, mental, nuts, batty, bonkers; *Brit. informal* potty, not the full shilling, barmy, crackers; *N. Amer. informal* dumb-ass. **3** *she's daft about him* INFATUATED WITH, enamoured of, smitten with, besotted by, very fond of;

single or double flowers and tuberous roots.
– ORIGIN named after the Swedish botanist Andreas *Dahl* (1751–89).
Dáil /doyl/ (in full **Dáil Éireann** /doyl airən/) ● noun the lower House of Parliament in the Republic of Ireland.
– ORIGIN Irish, 'assembly' (in full 'assembly of Ireland').
daily ● adjective done, happening, or produced every day or every weekday. ● adverb every day. ● noun (pl. **dailies**) informal **1** a newspaper published every day except Sunday. **2** (also **daily help**) Brit. dated a domestic cleaner.

d

daimon /dīmōn/ ● noun variant spelling of DAEMON.
dainty ● adjective (**daintier**, **daintiest**) **1** delicately small and pretty. **2** fastidious and fussy when eating. ● noun (pl. **dainties**) a small appetizing item of food.
– DERIVATIVES **daintily** adverb **daintiness** noun.
– ORIGIN from Old French *daintie* 'choice morsel, pleasure', from Latin *dignitas* 'worthiness, beauty'.
daiquiri /dakkəri/ ● noun (pl. **daiquiris**) a cocktail containing rum and lime juice.
– ORIGIN from *Daiquiri*, a rum-producing district in Cuba.
dairy ● noun (pl. **dairies**) a building for the processing and distribution of milk and milk products. ● adjective **1** made from milk. **2** involved in milk production.
– DERIVATIVES **dairying** noun.
– ORIGIN Old English, 'female servant' (later 'dairymaid'); related to DOUGH.
dairymaid ● noun archaic a woman employed in a dairy.
dairyman ● noun a man who is employed in a dairy or who sells dairy products.
dais /dayiss/ ● noun a low platform for a lectern or throne.
– ORIGIN Old French *deis*, from Latin *discus* 'disc or plate' (later 'table'), from Greek *diskos* 'discus'.
daisy ● noun (pl. **daisies**) a small grassland plant having flowers with a yellow centre and white rays.
– PHRASES **pushing up (the) daisies** informal dead and buried.
– ORIGIN Old English, 'day's eye' (because the flower opens in the morning and closes at night).
daisy chain ● noun a string of daisies threaded together by their stems.
daisy wheel ● noun a spoked disc carrying printing characters, used in word processors and typewriters.
Dakota /dəkōtə/ ● noun (pl. same or **Dakotas**) a member of a North American Indian people.
– ORIGIN Dakota, 'allies'.
daks ● plural noun Austral. informal trousers.
– ORIGIN a proprietary name.
Dalai Lama /dalī laamə/ ● noun the spiritual head of Tibetan Buddhism and, until the establishment of Chinese communist rule, the spiritual and temporal ruler of Tibet.
– ORIGIN Tibetan, 'ocean monk', because he is regarded as 'the ocean of compassion'.
dalasi /daalaasee/ ● noun (pl. same or **dalasis**) the basic monetary unit of Gambia, equal to 100 butut.
– ORIGIN a local word.
dale ● noun a valley, especially in northern England.
– ORIGIN Old English, related to DELL.
dally ● verb (**dallies**, **dallied**) **1** act or move slowly. **2** (**dally with**) have a casual sexual liaison with. **3** (**dally with**) show a casual interest in.
– DERIVATIVES **dalliance** noun.
– ORIGIN Old French *dalier* 'to chat'.
Dalmatian ● noun **1** a breed of large dog with short white hair and dark spots. **2** a person from Dalmatia, a region in Croatia.
– ORIGIN the dog is believed to have originally come from Dalmatia.
dal segno /dal senyō/ ● adverb & adjective Music repeat or repeated from the point marked by a sign.
– ORIGIN Italian, 'from the sign'.
dam[1] ● noun a barrier constructed across a river to hold back water, in order to form a reservoir or prevent flooding. ● verb (**dammed**, **damming**) build a dam across.
– ORIGIN Low German or Dutch.
dam[2] ● noun the female parent of an animal, especially a mammal.
– ORIGIN from DAME.
damage ● noun **1** physical harm reducing the value, operation, or usefulness of something. **2** (**damages**) financial compensation for a loss or injury. ● verb cause damage to.
– PHRASES **what's the damage?** informal, humorous what does it cost?
– ORIGIN Old French, from Latin *damnum* 'loss or hurt'; related to DAMN.
damaging ● adjective harmful or undesirable.
Damascene /damməseen/ ● adjective **1** relating to the city of Damascus, the capital of Syria. **2** (of a change of belief or opinion) dramatic and sudden. [ORIGIN with reference to the account in the Bible of the conversion of St Paul on the road to Damascus.]
damascened ● adjective **1** (of iron or steel) given a wavy pattern by hammer-welding and repeated heating and forging. **2** (of metal) inlaid with gold or silver.
– ORIGIN from the city of *Damascus*, once famous for this metalwork.
damask /damməsk/ ● noun a rich heavy fabric with a pattern woven into it. ● adjective literary pink or light red.
– ORIGIN from *Damascus*, where the fabric was first produced.
damask rose ● noun a sweet-scented rose having pink or light red velvety petals.
dame ● noun **1** (**Dame**) (in the UK) the title of a woman awarded a knighthood, equivalent to *Sir*. **2** N. Amer. informal a woman. **3** (also **pantomime dame**) Brit. a comic female character in pantomime, played by a man.
– ORIGIN Old French, from Latin *domina* 'mistress'.
damn /dam/ ● verb **1** (**be damned**) (in Christian belief) be condemned by God to eternal punishment in hell. **2** harshly condemn. **3** curse. ● exclamation informal expressing anger or frustration. ● adjective informal used to emphasize anger or frustration.
– PHRASES **as near as damn it** as close to being accurate as makes no difference. **damn all** Brit. informal nothing. **damn with faint praise** praise so unenthusiastically as to suggest condem-

Thesaurus

informal crazy, mad, nuts; *Brit. informal* potty; *informal, dated* sweet on.
– OPPOSITES sensible.
daily ● adjective *a daily event* EVERYDAY, day-to-day, quotidian, diurnal, circadian.
● adverb *the museum is open daily* EVERY DAY, once a day, day after day, diurnally.
dainty ● adjective **1** *a dainty china cup* DELICATE, fine, neat, elegant, exquisite; *Brit. informal* dinky. **2** *a dainty morsel* TASTY, delicious, choice, palatable, luscious, mouth-watering, delectable, toothsome; appetizing, inviting, tempting; *informal* scrumptious, yummy, scrummy, finger-licking, moreish. **3** *a dainty eater* FASTIDIOUS, fussy, finicky, finical, faddish; particular, discriminating; *informal* choosy, pernickety, picky; *Brit. informal* faddy.
– OPPOSITES unwieldy, unpalatable, undiscriminating.
● noun *home-made dainties* DELICACY, titbit, fancy, luxury, treat; nibble, savoury, appetizer, confection, bonbon; *informal* goody; *archaic* sweetmeat.
dais ● noun PLATFORM, stage, podium, rostrum, stand, apron; soapbox, stump.
dale ● noun VALLEY, vale; hollow, basin, gully, gorge, ravine; *Brit.* dene, combe; *N. English* clough; *Scottish* glen, strath; *poetic/literary* dell.
dally ● verb **1** *don't dally on the way to work* DAWDLE, delay, loiter, linger, waste time; lag, trail, straggle, fall behind; amble, meander, drift; *informal* dilly-dally; *archaic* tarry. **2** *he likes dallying with film stars* TRIFLE, toy, amuse oneself, flirt, play fast and loose, philander, carry on; *informal* play around.
– OPPOSITES hurry.
dam ● noun *the dam burst* BARRAGE, barrier, wall, embankment, barricade, obstruction.
● verb *the river was dammed* BLOCK (UP), obstruct, bung up, close; *technical* occlude.
damage ● noun **1** *did the thieves do any damage?* HARM, destruction, vandalism; injury, impairment, desecration, vitiation, detriment; ruin, havoc, devastation. **2** *(informal, humorous) what's the damage?* COST, price, expense, charge, total. **3** *she won £4,300 damages* COMPENSATION, recompense, restitution, redress, reparation(s); indemnification, indemnity; *N. Amer. informal* comp.
● verb *the parcel had been damaged* HARM, deface, mutilate, mangle, impair, injure, disfigure, vandalize; tamper with, sabotage; ruin, destroy, wreck; *N. Amer. informal* trash; *formal* vitiate.
– OPPOSITES repair.
damaging ● adjective HARMFUL, detrimental, injurious, hurtful, inimical, dangerous, destructive, ruinous, deleterious; bad, malign, adverse, undesirable, prejudicial, unfavourable; unhealthy, un-

nation. **not be worth a damn** informal have no value.
– ORIGIN Latin *dampnare* 'inflict loss on', from *damnum* 'loss, damage'.
damnable ● adjective very bad or unpleasant.
– DERIVATIVES **damnably** adverb.
damnation /damnaysh'n/ ● noun condemnation to eternal punishment in hell. ● exclamation expressing anger or frustration.
damned /damd/ ● adjective informal **1** used to emphasize anger or frustration. **2** (**damnedest**) used to emphasize the surprising nature of something.
– PHRASES **do** (or **try**) **one's damnedest** do (or try) one's utmost.
damning ● adjective strongly suggestive of guilt.
damp ● adjective slightly wet. ● noun moisture in the air, on a surface, or in a solid. ● verb **1** make damp. **2** (**damp down**) control or restrain (a feeling or situation). **3** (**damp down**) make (a fire) burn less strongly by reducing its air supply. **4** reduce or stop the vibration of (the strings of a musical instrument).
– DERIVATIVES **dampish** adjective **damply** adverb **dampness** noun.
– ORIGIN originally in the sense 'noxious inhalation': from Germanic.
damp course (also **damp-proof course**) ● noun a layer of waterproof material in a wall near the ground, to prevent rising damp.
dampen ● verb **1** make damp. **2** make less strong or intense.
– DERIVATIVES **dampener** noun.
damper ● noun **1** a pad silencing a piano string. **2** a device for reducing vibration or oscillation. **3** a movable metal plate in a flue or chimney, used to regulate the draught.
– PHRASES **put a damper on** informal have a subduing effect on.
damp squib ● noun Brit. something that turns out to be much less impressive than expected.
damsel /damz'l/ ● noun archaic or literary a young unmarried woman.
– ORIGIN Old French *dameisele*, from Latin *domina* 'mistress'.
damselfly ● noun a slender insect related to the dragonflies.
damson /damz'n/ ● noun a small purple-black plum-like fruit.
– ORIGIN from Latin *damascenum prunum* 'plum of Damascus'.
dan ● noun **1** any of ten degrees of advanced proficiency in judo or karate. **2** a person who has achieved a dan.
– ORIGIN Japanese.
dance ● verb **1** move rhythmically to music, typically following a set sequence of steps. **2** move in a quick and lively way. ● noun **1** a series of steps and movements that match the rhythm of a piece of music. **2** a social gathering at which people dance. **3** (also **dance music**) music for dancing to, especially in a nightclub.
– PHRASES **dance attendance on** try hard to please. **dance to someone's tune** comply with someone's demands. **lead some one a merry dance** Brit. cause someone a great deal of trouble.
– DERIVATIVES **dancer** noun **dancing** noun.
– ORIGIN Old French *dancer*.
D and C ● abbreviation dilatation and curettage.
dandelion ● noun a weed with large bright yellow flowers followed by rounded heads of seeds with downy tufts.
– ORIGIN French *dent-de-lion* 'lion's tooth' (because of the jagged shape of the leaves).
dandelion clock ● noun the downy spherical seed head of a dandelion.
dander ● noun (in phrase **get/have one's dander up**) informal lose one's temper.
– ORIGIN of unknown origin.
dandified ● adjective **1** (of a man) excessively concerned about his appearance. **2** self-consciously elaborate.
dandle ● verb gently bounce (a young child) on one's knees or in one's arms.
– ORIGIN of unknown origin.
dandruff ● noun flakes of dead skin on a person's scalp and in the hair.
– ORIGIN origin uncertain.
dandy ● noun (pl. **dandies**) a man unduly concerned with a stylish and fashionable appearance. ● adjective (**dandier, dandiest**) informal, chiefly N. Amer. excellent.
– DERIVATIVES **dandyish** adjective.
– ORIGIN a familiar form of the given name *Andrew*.
Dane ● noun a person from Denmark.
– ORIGIN Old English.
danger ● noun **1** the possibility of suffering harm. **2** a cause of harm. **3** the possibility of something unpleasant.
– ORIGIN originally in the sense 'jurisdiction or power', specifically 'power to harm': from Old French *dangier*, from Latin *dominus* 'lord'.
danger list ● noun Brit. a list of those who are dangerously ill in a hospital.
danger money ● noun extra payment for working under dan-

d

Thesaurus

wholesome.
– OPPOSITES beneficial.
damn ● verb **1** *they were all were damning him* CURSE, put the evil eye on, hoodoo; anathematize; *N. Amer.* hex; *informal* jinx; *archaic* imprecate. **2** *we are not going to damn the new product* CONDEMN, censure, criticize, attack, denounce, revile; find fault with, give something a bad press, deprecate, disparage; *informal* slam, lay into, blast; *Brit. informal* slate, slag off, have a go at.
– OPPOSITES bless, praise.
● noun *(informal) I don't care a damn* JOT, whit, iota, rap, scrap, bit; *informal* hoot, two hoots.
damnable ● adjective **1** *a damnable nuisance* UNPLEASANT, disagreeable, objectionable, horrible, horrid, awful, nasty, dreadful, terrible; annoying, irritating, maddening, exasperating; hateful, detestable, loathsome, abominable; *Brit. informal* beastly. **2** *suicide was thought damnable* SINFUL, wicked, evil, iniquitous, heinous, base, execrable.
damnation ● noun CONDEMNATION TO HELL, eternal punishment, perdition, doom, hellfire; curse, anathema; *N. Amer.* hex; *formal* imprecation; *archaic* execration.
damned ● adjective **1** *damned souls* CURSED, doomed, lost, condemned to hell; anathematized; *poetic/literary* accursed. **2** *(informal) this damned car won't start* BLASTED, damn, damnable, flaming, confounded, rotten, wretched; *Brit. informal* blessed, flipping, blinking, blooming, bloody, bleeding, ruddy; *dated* accursed.
damning ● adjective INCRIMINATING, condemnatory, damnatory; damaging, derogatory; conclusive, strong.
damp ● adjective *her hair was damp* MOIST, moistened, wettish, dampened, dampish; humid, steamy, muggy, clammy, sweaty, sticky, dank, moisture-laden, wet, wetted, rainy, drizzly, showery, misty, foggy, vaporous, dewy.
– OPPOSITES dry.
● noun *the damp in the air* MOISTURE, dampness, humidity, wetness, wet, water, condensation, steam, vapour; clamminess, dankness; rain, dew, drizzle, precipitation, spray; perspiration, sweat.
– OPPOSITES dryness.
● verb **1** *sweat damped his hair.* See DAMPEN sense 1. **2** *nothing damped my enthusiasm.* See DAMPEN sense 2.
– OPPOSITES dry.
dampen ● verb **1** *the rain dampened her face* MOISTEN, damp, wet, dew, water; *poetic/literary* bedew. **2** *nothing could dampen her enthusiasm* LESSEN, decrease, diminish, reduce, moderate, damp, put a damper on, throw cold water on, cool, discourage; suppress, extinguish, quench, stifle, curb, limit, check, restrain, inhibit, deter.
– OPPOSITES dry, heighten.
damper ● noun CURB, check, restraint, restriction, limit, limitation, constraint, rein, brake, control, impediment; chill, pall, gloom.
dampness ● noun. See DAMP noun.
damsel ● noun *(poetic/literary)*. See GIRL sense 2.
dance ● verb **1** *he danced with her* sway, trip, twirl, whirl, pirouette, gyrate; *informal* bop, disco, shake a leg, hoof it, cut a rug, trip the light fantastic; *N. Amer. informal* get down. **2** *little girls danced round me* CAPER, cavort, frisk, frolic, skip, prance, gambol, jig; leap, jump, hop, bounce. **3** *flames danced in the fireplace* FLICKER, leap, dart, play, flit, quiver; twinkle, shimmer.
● noun *the school dance* BALL, discotheque; masquerade; *N. Amer.* prom, hoedown; *informal* disco, hop, bop.
dancer ● noun danseur, danseuse; *informal* bopper, hoofer.
dandle ● verb BOUNCE, jiggle, dance, rock.
dandy ● noun *he became something of a dandy* FOP, man about town, bright young thing, glamour boy, rake; *informal* sharp dresser, snappy dresser, trendy, dude, pretty boy; *informal, dated* swell; *dated* beau; *archaic* buck, coxcomb, popinjay.
● adjective *(N. Amer. informal) our trip was dandy.* See EXCELLENT.
danger ● noun **1** *an element of danger* PERIL, hazard, risk, jeopardy; perilousness, riskiness, precariousness, uncertainty, instability, insecurity. **2** *he is a danger to society* MENACE, hazard, threat, risk. **3** *a serious danger of fire* POSSIBILITY, chance, risk,

gerous conditions.

dangerous ● adjective **1** likely to cause harm. **2** likely to cause problems.
– DERIVATIVES **dangerously** adverb **dangerousness** noun.

dangle ● verb **1** hang so as to swing freely. **2** offer (an incentive) to someone.
– DERIVATIVES **dangler** noun **dangly** adjective.
– ORIGIN symbolic of something loose and hanging.

Danish /daynish/ ● adjective relating to Denmark or the Danes. ● noun the language of Denmark.

d

Danish blue ● noun a strong-flavoured blue-veined white cheese.

Danish pastry ● noun a cake of sweetened yeast pastry topped with icing, fruit, or nuts.

dank ● adjective damp and cold.
– DERIVATIVES **dankly** adverb **dankness** noun.
– ORIGIN probably Scandinavian.

daphne /dafni/ ● noun a small evergreen shrub with sweet-scented flowers.
– ORIGIN originally denoting the laurel or bay tree; from *Daphne*, a nymph in Greek mythology who was turned into a laurel bush.

daphnia /dafniə/ ● noun (pl. same) a minute semi-transparent freshwater crustacean.
– ORIGIN named after *Daphne* (see DAPHNE).

dapper ● adjective (of a man) neat in dress and appearance.
– ORIGIN probably from a Low German or Dutch word meaning 'strong, stout'.

dapple ● verb mark with spots or small patches. ● noun a patch of colour or light.
– ORIGIN perhaps related to an Old Norse word meaning 'spot'.

dapple grey ● adjective (of a horse) grey or white with darker ring-like markings.

Darby and Joan ● noun Brit. a devoted old married couple.
– ORIGIN from a poem (1735) in the *Gentleman's Magazine*.

dare ● verb (3rd sing. present usu. **dare** before an expressed or implied infinitive without 'to') **1** have the courage to do. **2** defy or challenge to do. ● noun a challenge, especially to prove courage.
– PHRASES **how dare you** used to express indignation. **I dare say** (or **daresay**) it is probable.
– ORIGIN Old English.

daredevil ● noun a person who enjoys doing dangerous things.

daring ● adjective audaciously or adventurously bold. ● noun adventurous courage.
– DERIVATIVES **daringly** adverb.

Darjeeling /daarjeeling/ ● noun a high-quality tea grown in northern India.
– ORIGIN from *Darjeeling*, a hill station in West Bengal.

dark ● adjective **1** with little or no light. **2** of a deep or sombre colour. **3** (of skin, hair, or eyes) brown or black. **4** secret or mysterious. **5** (**darkest**) humorous most remote or uncivilized. **6** depressing or cheerless. **7** evil. ● noun **1** (**the dark**) the absence of light. **2** nightfall. **3** a dark colour or shade.
– PHRASES **the darkest hour is just before the dawn** proverb when things seem to be at their worst they are about to start improving. **in the dark** in a state of ignorance. **a shot** (or **stab**) **in the dark** a wild guess.
– DERIVATIVES **darkish** adjective **darkly** adverb **darkness** noun.
– ORIGIN Old English.

Dark Ages ● plural noun **1** the period in Europe between the fall of the Roman Empire and the Middle Ages, *c.*500–1100, regarded as unenlightened. **2** any period regarded as unenlightened.

dark chocolate ● noun plain chocolate.

darken ● verb **1** make or become darker. **2** cast a shadow over; spoil. **3** become unhappy or angry.
– PHRASES **never darken someone's door** keep away from someone's home.

dark horse ● noun a person who is secretive about themselves.

darkie (also **darky**) ● noun (pl. **darkies**) informal, offensive a black person.

darkling ● adjective literary **1** characterized by darkness. **2** growing darker.

Thesaurus

probability, likelihood, fear, prospect.
– OPPOSITES safety.

dangerous ● adjective **1** *a dangerous animal* MENACING, threatening, treacherous; savage, wild, vicious, murderous, desperate; *rare* minacious. **2** *dangerous wiring* HAZARDOUS, perilous, risky, high-risk, unsafe, unpredictable, precarious, insecure, touch-and-go, chancy, treacherous; *informal* dicey, hairy; *Brit. informal* dodgy.
– OPPOSITES harmless, safe.

dangle ● verb **1** *a chain dangled from his belt* HANG (DOWN), droop, swing, sway, wave, trail, stream. **2** *he dangled the keys* WAVE, swing, jiggle, brandish, flourish. **3** *he dangled money in front of the locals* OFFER, hold out; entice someone with, tempt someone with.

dangling ● adjective HANGING, drooping, droopy, suspended, pendulous, pendent, trailing, flowing, tumbling.

dank ● adjective DAMP, musty, chilly, clammy, moist, wet, unaired, humid.
– OPPOSITES dry.

dapper ● adjective SMART, spruce, trim, debonair, neat, well dressed, well groomed, well turned out, elegant, chic, dashing; *informal* snazzy, snappy, natty, sharp; *N. Amer. informal* spiffy, fly.
– OPPOSITES scruffy.

dapple ● verb DOT, spot, fleck, streak, speck, speckle, mottle, marble.

dappled ● adjective SPECKLED, blotched, blotchy, spotted, spotty, dotted, mottled, marbled, flecked, freckled; piebald, pied, brindle, pinto, tabby; patchy, variegated; *informal* splotchy, splodgy.

dare ● verb **1** *nobody dared to say a word* BE BRAVE ENOUGH, have the courage; venture, have the nerve, have the temerity, be so bold as, have the audacity; risk, hazard, take the liberty of; *N. Amer.* take a flyer; *informal* stick one's neck out, go out on a limb. **2** *she dared him to go* CHALLENGE, defy, invite, bid, provoke, goad; throw down the gauntlet.
● noun *she accepted the dare* CHALLENGE, provocation, goad; gauntlet, invitation.

daredevil ● noun *a young daredevil crashed his car* MADCAP, hothead, adventurer, exhibitionist, swashbuckler; stuntman; *Brit.* tearaway; *informal* show-off.
● adjective *a daredevil skydiver* DARING, bold, audacious, intrepid, fearless, madcap, death-or-glory, dauntless; heedless, reckless, rash, impulsive, impetuous, foolhardy, incautious, imprudent; *Brit.* tearaway, harum-scarum.
– OPPOSITES cowardly, cautious.

daring ● adjective *a daring attack* BOLD, audacious, intrepid, venturesome, fearless, brave, unafraid, undaunted, dauntless, valiant, valorous, heroic, dashing; madcap, rash, reckless, heedless; *informal* gutsy, spunky.
● noun *his sheer daring* BOLDNESS, audacity, temerity, fearlessness, intrepidity, bravery, courage, valour, heroism, pluck, spirit, mettle; recklessness, rashness, foolhardiness; *informal* nerve, guts, spunk, grit; *Brit. informal* bottle; *N. Amer. informal* moxie, sand.

dark ● adjective **1** *a dark night* BLACK, pitch-black, jet-black, inky; unlit, unilluminated; starless, moonless; dingy, gloomy, dusky, shadowy, shady; *poetic/literary* Stygian. **2** *a dark secret* MYSTERIOUS, secret, hidden, concealed, veiled, covert, clandestine; enigmatic, arcane, esoteric, obscure, abstruse, impenetrable, incomprehensible, cryptic. **3** *dark hair* BRUNETTE, dark brown, chestnut, sable, jet-black, ebony. **4** *dark skin* SWARTHY, dusky, olive, black, ebony; tanned, bronzed. **5** *dark days* TRAGIC, disastrous, calamitous, catastrophic, cataclysmic; dire, awful, terrible, dreadful, horrible, horrendous, atrocious, nightmarish, harrowing; wretched, woeful. **6** *dark thoughts* GLOOMY, dismal, pessimistic, negative, downbeat, bleak, grim, fatalistic, black, sombre; despairing, despondent, hopeless, cheerless, melancholy, glum, grave, morose, mournful, doleful. **7** *a dark look* MOODY, brooding, sullen, dour, scowling, glowering, angry, forbidding, threatening, ominous. **8** *dark deeds* EVIL, wicked, sinful, immoral, bad, iniquitous, ungodly, unholy, base; vile, unspeakable, foul, monstrous, shocking, atrocious, abominable, hateful, despicable, odious, horrible, heinous, execrable, diabolical, fiendish, murderous, barbarous, black; sordid, degenerate, depraved; dishonourable, dishonest, unscrupulous; *informal* low-down, dirty, crooked, shady.
– OPPOSITES bright, blonde, pale, happy, good.
● noun **1** *he's afraid of the dark* DARKNESS, blackness, gloom, murkiness, shadow, shade; dusk, twilight, gloaming. **2** *she went out after dark* NIGHT, night-time, darkness; nightfall, evening, twilight, sunset.
– OPPOSITES light, day.
– PHRASES **in the dark** UNAWARE, ignorant, oblivious, uninformed, unenlightened, unacquainted, unconversant.

darken ● verb **1** *the sky darkened* GROW DARK, blacken, dim, cloud over, lour; shade, fog. **2** *his mood darkened* BLACKEN, become

dark matter ● noun Astronomy non-luminous material believed to exist in space.
darkroom ● noun a room for developing photographs, from which normal light is excluded.
darky ● noun variant spelling of DARKIE.
darling ● noun **1** used as an affectionate form of address. **2** an endearing person. **3** a person popular with a particular group. ● adjective **1** beloved. **2** pretty; charming.
– ORIGIN Old English, from DEAR.
darn[1] ● verb mend (knitted material) by interweaving yarn across it.
– DERIVATIVES **darning** noun.
– ORIGIN perhaps from an Old English word meaning 'to hide'.
darn[2] ● verb, adjective, & exclamation informal euphemism for DAMN.
darned ● adjective informal euphemism for DAMNED.
darning needle ● noun a long sewing needle with a large eye, used in darning.
dart ● noun **1** a small pointed missile thrown or fired as a weapon. **2** a small pointed missile with a flight, used in the game of darts. **3** (**darts**) (usu. treated as sing.) an indoor game in which darts are thrown at a dartboard. **4** a sudden rapid movement. **5** a tapered tuck in a garment. ● verb move suddenly or rapidly.
– ORIGIN Old French, from a Germanic word meaning 'spear, lance'.
dartboard ● noun a circular board used as a target in the game of darts.
Darwinism ● noun the theory of the evolution of species by natural selection, advanced by the English natural historian Charles Darwin (1809–82).
– DERIVATIVES **Darwinian** noun & adjective **Darwinist** noun & adjective.
dash ● verb **1** run or travel in a great hurry. **2** strike or throw with great force. **3** destroy or frustrate (hopes). **4** (**dash off**) write (something) hurriedly. ● exclamation Brit. informal used to express mild annoyance. ● noun **1** an act of dashing. **2** chiefly N. Amer. a sprint. **3** a small amount added: *a dash of soda*. **4** impressive style; flair. **5** a horizontal stroke in writing, marking a pause or omission. **6** the longer of the signals used in Morse code.
– ORIGIN probably symbolic of forceful movement.
dashboard ● noun the panel of instruments and controls facing the driver of a vehicle.
– ORIGIN originally denoting a board in front of a carriage, to keep out mud.
dashiki /daashiki/ ● noun (pl. **dashikis**) a loose, brightly coloured shirt, originally from West Africa.
– ORIGIN Yoruba or Hausa (a West African language).
dashing ● adjective excitingly attractive and stylish.
– DERIVATIVES **dashingly** adverb.
dastardly ● adjective dated or humorous wicked and cruel.
– ORIGIN from archaic *dastard* 'despicable person', probably from *dazed* and influenced by *dotard* and *bastard*.
DAT ● abbreviation digital audiotape.
data /daytə/ ● noun **1** facts and statistics used for reference or analysis. **2** the quantities, characters, or symbols on which operations are performed by a computer.
– USAGE Traditionally and in technical use **data** is treated as a plural, as in Latin it is the plural of **datum.** In modern nonscientific use, however, it is often treated as a singular, and sentences such as *data was collected over a number of years* are now acceptable.
– ORIGIN Latin, plural of DATUM.
databank ● noun a large store of data in a computer.
database ● noun a structured set of data held in a computer.
datable (also **dateable**) ● adjective able to be dated to a particular time.
data capture ● noun Computing the action of gathering data from an automatic device, control system, or sensor.
data protection ● noun Brit. legal control over access to data stored in computers.
datcha /dachə/ ● noun variant spelling of DACHA.
date[1] ● noun **1** the day of the month or year as specified by a number. **2** a day or year when a given event occurred or will occur. **3** informal a social or romantic appointment. **4** a musical or theatrical performance, especially as part of a tour. ● verb **1** establish or ascertain the date of. **2** mark with a date. **3** (**date back to**) start or originate at (a particular time in the past). **4** (**dated**) old-fashioned. **5** informal, chiefly N. Amer. go on a date or regular dates with.
– PHRASES **to date** until now.
– ORIGIN Latin *data*, from *dare* 'give'; from the Latin formula used in dating letters, *data epistola* 'letter given or delivered'.
date[2] ● noun **1** a sweet, dark brown, oval fruit with a hard stone, usually eaten dried. **2** (also **date palm**) a tall palm tree which bears this fruit, native to western Asia and North Africa.
– ORIGIN Greek *daktulos* 'finger' (because of the finger-like shape of the tree's leaves).

d

Thesaurus

angry, become annoyed; sadden, become gloomy, become unhappy, become depressed, become dejected, become dispirited, become troubled.
darkness ● noun **1** *lights shone in the darkness* DARK, blackness, gloom, dimness, murkiness, shadow, shade; dusk, twilight, gloaming. **2** *darkness fell* NIGHT, night-time, dark. **3** *the forces of darkness* EVIL, wickedness, sin, iniquity, immorality; devilry, the Devil.
darling ● noun **1** *good night, darling* DEAR, dearest, love, lover, sweetheart, sweet, beloved; *informal* honey, angel, pet, sweetie, sugar, babe, baby, poppet, treasure. **2** *the darling of the media* FAVOURITE, pet, idol, hero, heroine; *informal* blue-eyed boy/girl.
● adjective **1** *his darling wife* DEAR, dearest, precious, adored, loved, beloved, cherished, treasured, esteemed, worshipped. **2** *a darling little hat* ADORABLE, appealing, charming, cute, sweet, enchanting, bewitching, endearing, dear, delightful, lovely, beautiful, attractive, gorgeous, fetching; *Scottish & N. English* bonny.
darn ● verb *he was darning his socks* MEND, repair, reinforce; sew up, stitch, patch.
● noun *a sweater with darns in the elbows* PATCH, repair, reinforcement, stitch.
dart ● noun **1** *a poisoned dart* SMALL ARROW, flechette, bolt; missile, projectile. **2** *she made a dart for the door* DASH, rush, run, bolt, break, start, charge, sprint, bound, leap, dive; scurry, scamper, scramble.
● verb **1** *Karl darted across the road* DASH, rush, tear, run, bolt, fly, shoot, charge, race, sprint, bound, leap, dive, gallop, scurry, scamper, scramble; *informal* scoot. **2** *he darted a glance at her* DIRECT, cast, throw, shoot, send, flash.
dash ● verb **1** *he dashed home* RUSH, race, run, sprint, bolt, dart, gallop, career, charge, shoot, hurtle, hare, fly, speed, zoom, scurry, scuttle, scamper; *informal* tear, belt, pelt, scoot, zip, whip, hotfoot it, leg it; *Brit. informal* bomb, go like the clappers; *N. Amer. informal* barrel. **2** *he dashed the glass to the ground* HURL, smash, crash, slam, throw, toss, fling, pitch, cast, project, propel, send; *informal* chuck, heave, sling, bung; *N. Amer. informal* peg; *dated* shy. **3** *rain dashed against the walls* BE HURLED, crash, smash; batter, strike, beat, pound, lash. **4** *her hopes were dashed* SHATTER, destroy, wreck, ruin, crush, devastate, demolish, blight, overturn, scotch, spoil, frustrate, thwart, check; *informal* banjax, do for, blow a hole in, put paid to; *Brit. informal* scupper.
– OPPOSITES dawdle, raise.
● noun **1** *a dash for the door* RUSH, race, run, sprint, bolt, dart, leap, charge, bound, break; scramble. **2** *a dash of salt* PINCH, touch, sprinkle, taste, spot, drop, dab, speck, smattering, sprinkling, splash, bit, modicum, little; *informal* smidgen, tad, lick. **3** *he led off with such dash* VERVE, style, flamboyance, gusto, zest, confidence, self-assurance, elan, flair, vigour, vivacity, sparkle, brio, panache, éclat, vitality, dynamism; *informal* pizzazz, pep, oomph.
dashing ● adjective **1** *a dashing pilot* DEBONAIR, devil-may-care, raffish, sporty, spirited, lively, dazzling, energetic, animated, exuberant, flamboyant, dynamic, bold, intrepid, daring, adventurous, plucky, swashbuckling; romantic, attractive, gallant. **2** *he looked exceptionally dashing* STYLISH, smart, elegant, chic, dapper, spruce, trim, debonair; fashionable, modish, voguish; *informal* trendy, with it, hip, sharp, snazzy, classy, natty, swish; *N. Amer. informal* fly, spiffy.
dastardly ● adjective (*dated*) WICKED, evil, heinous, villainous, diabolical, fiendish, barbarous, cruel, black, dark, rotten, vile, monstrous, abominable, despicable, degenerate, sordid; bad, base, mean, low, dishonourable, dishonest, unscrupulous, unprincipled; *informal* low-down, dirty, shady, rascally, scoundrelly, crooked; *Brit. informal* beastly.
– OPPOSITES noble.
data ● noun FACTS, figures, statistics, details, particulars, specifics;

dateable ● adjective variant spelling of DATABLE.
date stamp ● noun **1** a stamped mark indicating a date. **2** an adjustable stamp used to make such a mark. ● verb (**date-stamp**) mark with a date stamp.
dating agency ● noun a service which arranges introductions for people seeking romantic partners or friends.
dative /daytiv/ Grammar ● adjective (in Latin, Greek, German, etc.) denoting a case of nouns and pronouns indicating an indirect object or recipient. ● noun a dative noun, pronoun, etc.
– ORIGIN from Latin *casus dativus* 'case of giving', from *dare* 'give'.

d

datum /daytəm/ ● noun (pl. **data**) **1** a piece of information. **2** an assumption or premise from which inferences may be drawn. **3** a fixed starting point of a scale or operation.
– ORIGIN Latin, 'something given'.
datura /dətyoorə/ ● noun a shrubby North American plant with trumpet-shaped flowers, containing toxic or narcotic substances used as hallucinogens by some American Indian peoples.
– ORIGIN Hindi.
daub /dawb/ ● verb **1** coat or smear carelessly or liberally with a thick substance. **2** spread (a thick substance) on a surface in such a way. ● noun **1** plaster, clay, or a similar substance, especially when mixed with straw and applied to laths or wattles to form a wall. **2** a patch or smear of a thick substance. **3** a painting executed without much skill.
– DERIVATIVES **dauber** noun.
– ORIGIN Old French *dauber*, from Latin *dealbare* 'whiten, whitewash', from *albus* 'white'.
daube /dōb/ ● noun a stew of meat, typically beef, braised in wine.
– ORIGIN French.
daughter ● noun **1** a girl or woman in relation to her parents. **2** a female descendant.
– DERIVATIVES **daughterly** adjective.
– ORIGIN Old English.
daughter-in-law ● noun (pl. **daughters-in-law**) the wife of one's son.
daunt /dawnt/ ● verb (usu. **be daunted**) cause to feel intimidated or apprehensive.
– DERIVATIVES **daunting** adjective.
– ORIGIN Old French *danter*, from Latin *domare* 'to tame'.
dauntless ● adjective fearless and determined.
– DERIVATIVES **dauntlessly** adverb **dauntlessness** noun.
dauphin /dōfaɴ/ ● noun historical the eldest son of the King of France.
– ORIGIN French, from the family name of the lords of the province of Dauphiné, ultimately a nickname meaning 'dolphin'.
daven /daavən/ ● verb (**davened**, **davening**) (in Judaism) pray.
– ORIGIN Yiddish.
davenport /davv'nport/ ● noun **1** Brit. an ornamental writing desk with drawers and a sloping surface for writing. **2** N. Amer. a large upholstered sofa.
– ORIGIN sense 1 is named after a Captain *Davenport*, for whom a desk of this type was made in the 18th century; sense 2 is probably a manufacturer's name.
davit /davvit, dayvit/ ● noun a small crane on a ship, especially one of a pair for lowering a lifeboat.
– ORIGIN Old French *daviot*, from *david*, denoting a kind of carpenter's tool.
Davy Jones's locker ● noun informal the bottom of the sea, regarded as the grave of those who drown.
– ORIGIN from 18th-century nautical slang *Davy Jones*, denoting the evil spirit of the sea.
Davy lamp ● noun historical a miner's portable safety lamp with the flame enclosed by wire gauze to reduce the risk of a gas explosion.
– ORIGIN named after the English chemist Sir Humphry *Davy* (1778–1829), who invented it.
dawdle ● verb move slowly; take one's time.
– DERIVATIVES **dawdler** noun.
– ORIGIN related to dialect *daddle*, *doddle* 'dally'.
dawn ● noun **1** the first appearance of light in the sky in the morning. **2** the beginning of something. ● verb **1** (of a day) begin. **2** come into existence. **3** (**dawn on**) become evident to.
– ORIGIN from Old English, 'to dawn'; related to DAY.
dawn chorus ● noun the early-morning singing of birds.
day ● noun **1** a period of twenty-four hours as a unit of time, reckoned from midnight to midnight and corresponding to a rotation of the earth on its axis. **2** the time between sunrise and sunset. **3** (usu. **days**) a particular period of the past. **4** (**the day**) the present time or the time in question. **5** (**one's day**) the youthful or successful period of one's life. **6** (before another noun) working or done during the day: *my day job*.
– PHRASES **any day** informal **1** at any time. **2** under any circumstances. **call it a day** decide to stop doing something. **day by day** gradually and steadily. **day in, day out** continuously or repeatedly over a long period. **one day** (or **some day** or **one of these days**) at some time in the future. **one of those days** a day when things go badly. **that will be the day** informal that is very unlikely. **these days** at present.
– ORIGIN Old English.

Thesaurus

information, intelligence, material, input; *informal* info, gen.
date ● noun **1** *the only date he has to remember* DAY (OF THE MONTH), occasion, time; year; anniversary. **2** *a later date is suggested for this bridge* AGE, time, period, era, epoch, century, decade, year. **3** *a lunch date* APPOINTMENT, meeting, engagement, rendezvous, assignation; commitment. **4** *(informal) a date for tonight* PARTNER, escort, girlfriend, boyfriend; *informal* steady, bird, fella.
● verb **1** *the sculpture can be dated accurately* ASSIGN A DATE TO, ascertain the date of, put a date on. **2** *the building dates from the 16th century* WAS MADE IN, was built in, originates in, comes from, belongs to, goes back to. **3** *the best films don't date* BECOME OLD-FASHIONED, become outmoded, become dated, show its age. **4** *(informal) he's dating Jill* GO OUT WITH, take out, go around with, be involved with, see, woo; *informal* go steady with; *dated* court.
– PHRASES **to date** SO FAR, thus far, yet, as yet, up to now, till now, until now, up to the present (time), hitherto.
dated ● adjective OLD-FASHIONED, outdated, outmoded, passé, behind the times, archaic, obsolete, antiquated; unfashionable, unstylish; crusty, olde worlde, prehistoric, antediluvian; *informal* old hat, out, out of the ark.
– OPPOSITES modern.
daub ● verb *he daubed a rock with paint* SMEAR, bedaub, plaster, splash, spatter, splatter, cake, cover, smother, coat.
● noun *daubs of paint* SMEAR, smudge, splash, blot, spot, patch, blotch; *informal* splodge, splotch.
daughter ● noun FEMALE CHILD, girl.
daunt ● verb DISCOURAGE, deter, demoralize, put off, dishearten, dispirit; intimidate, abash, take aback, throw, cow, overawe, awe, frighten, scare, unman, dismay, disconcert, discompose, perturb, unsettle, unnerve; throw off balance; *informal* rattle, faze, shake up.
– OPPOSITES hearten.
dauntless ● adjective FEARLESS, determined, resolute, indomitable, intrepid, doughty, plucky, spirited, mettlesome; undaunted, undismayed, unflinching, unshrinking, bold, audacious, valiant, brave, courageous, daring; *informal* gutsy, spunky, feisty.
dawdle ● verb **1** *they dawdled over breakfast* LINGER, dally, take one's time, be slow, waste time, idle; delay, procrastinate, stall; *informal* dilly-dally; *archaic* tarry. **2** *Ruth dawdled home* AMBLE, stroll, trail, walk slowly, move at a snail's pace; *informal* mosey, tootle; *Brit. informal* pootle, mooch.
– OPPOSITES hurry.
dawn ● noun **1** *we got up at dawn* DAYBREAK, sunrise, first light, daylight, cockcrow; first thing in the morning; *N. Amer.* sunup. **2** *the dawn of civilization* BEGINNING, start, birth, inception, origination, genesis, emergence, advent, appearance, arrival, dawning, rise, origin, onset; unfolding, development, infancy; *informal* kick-off.
– OPPOSITES dusk, end.
● verb **1** *Thursday dawned crisp and sunny* BEGIN, break, arrive, emerge. **2** *a bright new future has dawned* BEGIN, start, commence, be born, appear, arrive, emerge; arise, rise, break, unfold, develop. **3** *the reality dawned on him* OCCUR TO, come to, strike, hit, enter someone's mind, register with, enter someone's consciousness, cross someone's mind, suggest itself.
– OPPOSITES end.
day ● noun **1** *I stayed for a day* TWENTY-FOUR-HOUR PERIOD, twenty-four hours. **2** *enjoy the beach during the day* DAYTIME, daylight; waking hours. **3** *the leading architect of the day* PERIOD, time, age, era, generation. **4** *in his day he had great influence* HEYDAY, prime, time; peak, height, zenith, ascendancy; youth, springtime, salad days.
– RELATED TERMS diurnal.

Dayak /dīak/ (also **Dyak**) ● noun (pl. same or **Dayaks**) **1** a member of a group of indigenous peoples inhabiting parts of Borneo. **2** the group of languages spoken by these peoples.
– ORIGIN Malay, 'up-country'.
daybed ● noun **1** a couch for daytime rest. **2** N. Amer. a couch that can be made into a bed.
day boy (or **day girl**) ● noun Brit. a boy (or girl) who lives at home and attends a school that also takes boarders.
daybreak ● noun dawn.
day centre (also **day-care centre**) ● noun a place providing daytime care and recreation facilities for those who cannot be fully independent.
daydream ● noun a series of pleasant thoughts that distract one's attention from the present. ● verb indulge in a daydream.
– DERIVATIVES **daydreamer** noun.
daylight ● noun **1** the natural light of the day. **2** dawn. **3** visible distance between one person or thing and another. **4** (**the** (**living**) **daylights**) life: *he beat the living daylights out of them.*
– PHRASES **see daylight** begin to understand something.
daylight robbery ● noun Brit. informal blatant and unfair overcharging.
day lily ● noun a lily which bears large yellow, red, or orange flowers, each lasting only one day.
day off ● noun (pl. **days off**) a day's holiday from work or school.
day out ● noun (pl. **days out**) Brit. a trip or excursion for a day.
daypack ● noun chiefly N. Amer. a small rucksack.
day release ● noun Brit. a system in which employees are granted days off work to go on educational courses.
day return ● noun Brit. a ticket at a reduced rate for a return journey on public transport within one day.
day room ● noun a communal room in an institution, used during the day.
day school ● noun **1** a non-residential school. **2** a short educational course.
day surgery ● noun minor surgery that does not require an overnight stay in hospital.
daytime ● noun **1** the time between sunrise and sunset. **2** the period of time corresponding to normal working hours.
day-to-day ● adjective **1** happening regularly every day. **2** of a routine nature; ordinary.
day trip ● noun a journey or excursion completed in one day.
– DERIVATIVES **day tripper** noun.
daze ● verb cause to feel stunned or bewildered. ● noun a state of stunned confusion or bewilderment.
– DERIVATIVES **dazedly** adverb.
– ORIGIN from Old Norse, 'weary'.
dazzle ● verb **1** (of a bright light) blind temporarily. **2** overwhelm with an impressive quality. ● noun blinding brightness.
– DERIVATIVES **dazzlement** noun **dazzler** noun. **dazzling** adjective.
– ORIGIN from DAZE.
Db ● symbol the chemical element dubnium.
dB ● abbreviation decibel(s).
DBE ● abbreviation (in the UK) Dame Commander of the Order of the British Empire.
DBS ● abbreviation **1** direct broadcasting by satellite. **2** direct-broadcast satellite.
DC ● abbreviation **1** direct current. **2** District of Columbia.
DCB ● abbreviation (in the UK) Dame Commander of the Order of the Bath.
DCC ● abbreviation digital compact cassette.
DCM ● abbreviation (in the UK) Distinguished Conduct Medal.
DCMG ● abbreviation (in the UK) Dame Commander of the Order of St Michael and St George.
DCVO ● abbreviation (in the UK) Dame Commander of the Royal Victorian Order.
DD ● abbreviation Doctor of Divinity.
D-Day ● noun **1** the day (6 June 1944) in the Second World War on which Allied forces invaded northern France. **2** the day on which something important is to begin.
– ORIGIN from *D* for *day* + DAY.
DDI ● abbreviation dideoxyinosine.
DDR ● abbreviation historical German Democratic Republic.
– ORIGIN abbreviation of German *Deutsche Demokratische Republik.*
DDT ● abbreviation dichlorodiphenyltrichloroethane, a synthetic organic compound used as an insecticide but now banned in many countries.
DE ● abbreviation **1** Delaware. **2** (in the UK) Department of Employment.
de- ● prefix forming or added to verbs or their derivatives: **1** down; away: *deduct.* **2** completely: *denude.* **3** denoting removal or reversal: *de-ice.*
– ORIGIN from Latin *de* 'off, from' or *dis-* (expressing reversal).
deacon /deek'n/ ● noun **1** (in Catholic, Anglican, and Orthodox Churches) an ordained minister of an order ranking below that of priest. **2** (in some Protestant Churches) a lay officer assisting a minister.
– ORIGIN Greek *diakonos* 'servant'.
deaconess ● noun a woman with duties similar to those of a deacon.
deactivate ● verb make (equipment or a virus) inactive by dis-

d

Thesaurus

– OPPOSITES night, decline.
– PHRASES **day after day** REPEATEDLY, again and again, over and over (again), time and (time) again, frequently, often, time after time; {day in, day out}, night and day, all the time; persistently, recurrently, constantly, continuously, continually, relentlessly, regularly, habitually, unfailingly, always; *N. Amer.* oftentimes; *informal* 24-7; *poetic/literary* oft, oft-times. **day by day 1** *day by day they were forced to retreat* GRADUALLY, slowly, progressively; bit by bit, inch by inch, little by little, inchmeal. **2** *they follow the news day by day* DAILY, every day, day after day; diurnally. **day in, day out.** See DAY AFTER DAY.
daybreak ● noun DAWN, crack of dawn, sunrise, first light, first thing in the morning, cockcrow; daylight; *N. Amer.* sunup.
– OPPOSITES nightfall.
daydream ● noun **1** *she was lost in a daydream* REVERIE, trance, fantasy, vision, fancy, brown study; inattentiveness, woolgathering, preoccupation, absorption, self-absorption, absentmindedness, abstraction. **2** *a big house was one of her daydreams* DREAM, pipe dream, fantasy, castle in the air, castle in Spain, fond hope; wishful thinking; *informal* pie in the sky.
● verb *stop daydreaming!* DREAM, muse, stare into space; fantasize, be in cloud cuckoo land, build castles in the air, build castles in Spain.
daydreamer ● noun DREAMER, fantasist, fantasizer, romantic, wishful thinker, idealist; visionary, theorizer, utopian, Walter Mitty.
daylight ● noun **1** *do the test in daylight* NATURAL LIGHT, sunlight. **2** *she only went there in daylight* DAYTIME, day; broad daylight. **3** *police moved in at daylight* DAWN, daybreak, break of day, crack of dawn, sunrise, first light, first thing in the morning, early morning, cockcrow; *N. Amer.* sunup.
– OPPOSITES darkness, night-time, nightfall.
– PHRASES **see daylight 1** *Sam finally saw daylight* UNDERSTAND, comprehend, realize, see the light; *informal* cotton on, catch on, latch on, get the picture, get the message, get it; *Brit. informal* twig. **2** *his project never saw daylight* BE COMPLETED, be accomplished, see (the) light of day.
day-to-day ● adjective REGULAR, everyday, daily, routine, habitual, frequent, normal, standard, usual, typical.
daze ● verb **1** *he was dazed by his fall* STUN, stupefy; knock unconscious, knock out; *informal* knock the stuffing out of. **2** *she was dazed by the revelations* ASTOUND, amaze, astonish, startle, dumbfound, stupefy, overwhelm, stagger, shock, confound, bewilder, take aback, nonplus, shake up; *informal* flabbergast, knock sideways, bowl over, blow away; *Brit. informal* knock for six.
● noun *she is in a daze* STUPOR, trance, haze; spin, whirl, muddle, jumble.
dazzle ● verb **1** *she was dazzled by the headlights* BLIND TEMPORARILY, deprive of sight. **2** *I was dazzled by the exhibition* OVERWHELM, overcome, impress, move, stir, affect, touch, awe, overawe, leave speechless, take someone's breath away; spellbind, hypnotize; *informal* bowl over, blow away, knock out.
● noun **1** *dazzle can be a problem to sensitive eyes* GLARE, brightness, brilliance, shimmer, radiance, shine. **2** *the dazzle of the limelight* SPARKLE, glitter, brilliance, glory, splendour, magnificence, glamour; attraction, lure, allure, draw, appeal; *informal* razzle-dazzle, razzmatazz.
dazzling ● adjective **1** *the sunlight was dazzling* BRIGHT, blinding, glaring, brilliant. **2** *a dazzling performance* IMPRESSIVE, remarkable, extraordinary, outstanding, exceptional; incredible, amazing, astonishing, phenomenal, breathtaking, thrilling; excellent, wonderful, magnificent, marvellous, superb, first-rate, superla-

connecting or destroying it.
– DERIVATIVES **deactivation** noun **deactivator** noun.

dead ● adjective **1** no longer alive. **2** (of a part of the body) numb. **3** displaying no emotion. **4** no longer relevant or important. **5** lacking activity or excitement. **6** devoid of living things. **7** (of equipment) not functioning. **8** complete; absolute: *dead silence.* ● adverb **1** absolutely. **2** exactly. **3** straight; directly. **4** Brit. informal very.
– PHRASES **dead and buried** over; finished. **the dead of night** the quietest, darkest part of the night. **the dead of winter** the coldest part of winter. **dead on one's feet** informal extremely tired. **dead to the world** informal fast asleep. **from the dead** from being dead; from death.
– DERIVATIVES **deadness** noun.
– ORIGIN Old English, related to DIE[1].

deadbeat ● adjective (**dead beat**) informal completely exhausted. ● noun informal **1** an idle or feckless person. **2** N. Amer. a person who tries to evade paying debts.

deadbolt ● noun a bolt engaged by turning a knob or key, rather than by spring action.

dead centre ● noun **1** the position of a crank when it is in line with the connecting rod and not exerting torque. **2** exactly in the centre.

dead duck ● noun informal an unsuccessful or useless person or thing.
– ORIGIN from the old saying 'never waste powder on a dead duck'.

deaden ● verb **1** reduce the strength or intensity of (a noise or sensation). **2** make insensitive. **3** deprive of force or vitality.
– DERIVATIVES **deadener** noun.

dead end ● noun an end of a road or passage from which no exit is possible.

dead hand ● noun an undesirable persisting influence.

deadhead chiefly Brit. ● noun a faded flower head. ● verb remove dead flower heads from (a plant).

dead heat ● noun a race in which two or more competitors are exactly level.

dead letter ● noun **1** a law or treaty which has not been repealed but is defunct in practice. **2** a letter that has not been delivered or claimed.

deadline ● noun the latest time or date by which something should be completed.

deadlock ● noun **1** a situation in which no progress can be made. **2** Brit. a lock operated by a key, as distinct from a spring lock. ● verb cause to reach a deadlock.

dead loss ● noun an unproductive or useless person or thing.

deadly ● adjective (**deadlier, deadliest**) **1** causing or able to cause death. **2** (of a voice, glance, etc.) filled with hate. **3** extremely accurate or effective. **4** informal extremely boring. ● adverb **1** in a way that resembles or suggests death. **2** extremely: *she was deadly serious.*
– DERIVATIVES **deadliness** noun.

deadly nightshade ● noun a poisonous bushy plant with drooping purple flowers and black cherry-like fruit.

deadly sin ● noun (in Christian tradition) a sin regarded as leading to damnation.

dead-nettle ● noun a plant of the mint family, with leaves that resemble those of a nettle but without stinging hairs.

deadpan ● adjective impassive or expressionless.

dead reckoning ● noun the calculation of one's position, especially at sea, by estimating the direction and distance travelled.

dead ringer ● noun a person or thing closely resembling another.

dead set ● noun **1** firm in one's determination. **2** see SET[2] (sense 10).

deadweight ● noun **1** the weight of an inert person or thing. **2** the total weight of cargo, stores, etc. which a ship can carry.

dead wood ● noun useless or unproductive people or things.

deaf ● adjective **1** without the faculty of hearing or having impaired hearing. **2** (**deaf to**) unwilling to listen or respond to.
– PHRASES **fall on deaf ears** be ignored. **turn a deaf ear** refuse to listen or respond.
– DERIVATIVES **deafness** noun.
– ORIGIN Old English.

deaf aid ● noun Brit. a hearing aid.

deaf-blind ● adjective having severely impaired hearing and vision.

deafen ● verb **1** cause to become deaf. **2** (**deafening**) extremely loud.
– DERIVATIVES **deafeningly** adverb.

Thesaurus

tive, matchless; *informal* mind-blowing, out of this world, fabulous, fab, super, sensational, ace, A1, cool, awesome; *Brit. informal* smashing, brill.

dead ● adjective **1** *my parents are dead* PASSED ON/AWAY, expired, departed, gone, no more; late, lost, lamented; perished, fallen, slain, slaughtered, killed, murdered; lifeless, extinct; *informal* (as) dead as a doornail, six feet under, pushing up daisies; *formal* deceased; *euphemistic* with God, asleep. **2** *patches of dead ground* BARREN, lifeless, bare, desolate, sterile. **3** *a dead language* OBSOLETE, extinct, defunct, disused, abandoned, discarded, superseded, vanished, forgotten; archaic, antiquated, ancient; *poetic/literary* of yore. **4** *the phone was dead* NOT WORKING, out of order, inoperative, inactive, in disrepair, broken, malfunctioning, defective; *informal* kaput, conked out, on the blink, bust; *Brit. informal* knackered. **5** *a dead leg* NUMB, numbed, deadened, desensitized, unfeeling; paralysed, crippled, incapacitated, immobilized, frozen. **6** *she has dead eyes* EMOTIONLESS, unemotional, unfeeling, impassive, unresponsive, indifferent, dispassionate, inexpressive, wooden, stony, cold; deadpan, flat; blank, vacant. **7** *his affection for her was dead* EXTINGUISHED, quashed, stifled; finished, over, gone, no more; ancient history. **8** *a dead town* UNEVENTFUL, uninteresting, unexciting, uninspiring, dull, boring, flat, quiet, sleepy, slow, lacklustre, lifeless; *informal* one-horse, dead-and-alive; *N. Amer. informal* dullsville. **9** *dead silence* COMPLETE, absolute, total, utter, out-and-out, thorough, unmitigated. **10** *a dead shot* UNERRING, unfailing, impeccable, sure, true, accurate, precise; deadly, lethal; *Brit. informal* spot on, bang on.
– OPPOSITES alive, fertile, modern, lively, poor.
● adverb **1** *he was dead serious* COMPLETELY, absolutely, totally, utterly, deadly, perfectly, entirely, quite, thoroughly; definitely, certainly, positively, categorically, unquestionably, undoubtedly, surely; in every way, one hundred per cent. **2** *flares were seen dead ahead* DIRECTLY, exactly, precisely, immediately, right, straight, due, squarely; *informal* bang, slap bang. **3** *(Brit. informal) it's dead easy.* See VERY.

deadbeat ● noun *(informal)* LAYABOUT, loafer, idler, good-for-nothing; *informal* waster; *Brit. informal* skiver; *N. Amer. informal* bum; *poetic/literary* wastrel.

deaden ● verb **1** *surgeons tried to deaden the pain* NUMB, dull, blunt, suppress; alleviate, mitigate, diminish, reduce, lessen, ease, soothe, relieve, assuage. **2** *the wood panelling deadened any noise* MUFFLE, mute, smother, stifle, dull, damp (down); silence, quieten, soften; cushion, buffer, absorb. **3** *laughing might deaden us to the moral issue* DESENSITIZE, numb, anaesthetize; harden (one's heart), toughen.
– OPPOSITES intensify, amplify, sensitize.

deadline ● noun TIME LIMIT, limit, finishing date, target date, cut-off point.

deadlock ● noun **1** *the strike reached a deadlock* STALEMATE, impasse, checkmate, stand-off; standstill, halt, (full) stop, dead end. **2** *(Brit.) the deadlock is opened with a key* BOLT, lock, latch, catch; *Scottish* sneck, snib.

deadly ● adjective **1** *these drugs can be deadly* FATAL, lethal, mortal, death-dealing, life-threatening; dangerous, injurious, harmful, detrimental, deleterious, unhealthy; noxious, toxic, poisonous; *poetic/literary* deathly. **2** *deadly enemies* MORTAL, irreconcilable, implacable, unappeasable, unforgiving, remorseless, merciless, pitiless; bitter, hostile, antagonistic. **3** *deadly seriousness* INTENSE, great, marked, extreme. **4** *he was deadly pale* DEATHLY, ghostly, ashen, white, pallid, wan, pale; ghastly. **5** *his aim is deadly* UNERRING, unfailing, impeccable, perfect, flawless, faultless; sure, true, precise, accurate, exact; *Brit. informal* spot on, bang on. **6** *(informal) life here can be deadly.* See BORING.
– OPPOSITES harmless, mild, inaccurate, exciting.
● adverb *deadly calm* COMPLETELY, absolutely, totally, utterly, perfectly, entirely, wholly, quite, dead, thoroughly; in every way, one hundred per cent, to the hilt.

deadpan ● adjective BLANK, expressionless, unexpressive, impassive, inscrutable, poker-faced, straight-faced; stony, wooden, vacant, fixed, lifeless.
– OPPOSITES expressive.

deaf ● adjective **1** *she is deaf and blind* HARD OF HEARING, having impaired hearing; *informal* deaf as a post. **2** *she was deaf to their pleading* UNMOVED BY, untouched by, unaffected by, indifferent to, unresponsive to, unconcerned by; unaware of, oblivious to, im-

deaf mute • noun a person who is deaf and unable to speak.
– USAGE In modern use **deaf mute** has acquired offensive connotations. It is advisable to avoid it in favour of other terms such as **profoundly deaf**.

deal[1] • verb (past and past part. **dealt**) **1** distribute (cards) to players for a game or round. **2** (**deal out**) distribute or apportion. **3** take part in commercial trading of a commodity. **4** informal buy and sell illegal drugs. **5** (**deal with**) have commercial relations with. **6** (**deal with**) take measures to put right. **7** (**deal with**) cope with. **8** (**deal with**) have as a subject. **9** inflict (a blow) on. • noun **1** an agreement between two or more parties for their mutual benefit. **2** the process of dealing cards in a card game. **3** a particular form of treatment given or received: *working mothers get a bad deal.*
– PHRASES **a big deal** informal **1** an important thing. **2** (**big deal**) used ironically to express contempt for something regarded as unimpressive. **a deal of** a large amount of. **a good** (or **great**) **deal 1** a large amount. **2** to a considerable extent: *a good deal better.* **a square deal** a fair bargain or treatment.
– ORIGIN Old English, related to DOLE.

deal[2] • noun fir or pine wood (as a building material).
– ORIGIN Low German and Dutch *dele* 'plank'.

dealer • noun **1** a person who buys and sells goods. **2** a person who buys and sells shares or other financial assets as a principal (rather than as a broker or agent). **3** a player who deals cards in a card game.
– DERIVATIVES **dealership** noun.

dealt past participle of DEAL[1].

dean • noun **1** the head of a cathedral chapter. **2** the head of a university faculty or department or of a medical school. **3** a college officer with a disciplinary and advisory role.
– DERIVATIVES **deanery** noun.
– ORIGIN Old French *deien*, from Latin *decanus* 'chief of a group of ten'.

dear • adjective **1** regarded with deep affection. **2** used in the polite introduction to a letter. **3** expensive. • noun **1** an endearing person. **2** used as an affectionate form of address. • adverb at a high cost. • exclamation used in expressions of surprise or dismay.
– DERIVATIVES **dearness** noun.
– ORIGIN Old English.

dearest • adjective **1** most loved or cherished. **2** most expensive. • noun used as an affectionate form of address.

Dear John letter (also **Dear John**) • noun informal a letter from a woman to a man, ending a personal relationship.

dearly • adverb **1** very much. **2** at great cost.

dearth /derth/ • noun a scarcity or lack.
– ORIGIN originally in the sense 'dearness and shortage of food': from DEAR + -TH[2].

death • noun **1** the action or fact of dying. **2** an instance of a person or an animal dying. **3** the state of being dead. **4** the end of something.
– PHRASES **at death's door** so ill that one may die. **catch one's death (of cold)** informal catch a severe cold. **die a death** fail utterly or come to an end. **do to death** repeat to the point of tedium. **like death warmed up** informal extremely tired or ill. **put to death** execute. **to death 1** until dead. **2** used for emphasis: *sick to death of him.*
– DERIVATIVES **deathless** adjective.
– ORIGIN Old English, related to DIE[1].

deathbed • noun the bed where someone is dying or has died.

death camp • noun a prison camp in which many people die or are put to death.

death cap • noun a deadly poisonous toadstool with a pale olive-green cap and white gills.

death certificate • noun an official statement, signed by a doctor, detailing a person's death.

death duty • noun former name for INHERITANCE TAX.

death knell • noun **1** the tolling of a bell to mark a death. **2** an event that signals the end of something.

deathly • adjective (**deathlier**, **deathliest**) resembling or suggestive of death.

d

Thesaurus

pervious to.

deafen • verb MAKE DEAF, deprive of hearing, impair someone's hearing.

deafening • adjective VERY LOUD, very noisy, ear-splitting, ear-shattering, overwhelming, almighty, mighty, tremendous; booming, thunderous, roaring, resounding, resonant, reverberating.
– OPPOSITES quiet.

deal • noun *completion of the deal* AGREEMENT, understanding, pact, bargain, covenant, contract, treaty; arrangement, compromise, settlement; terms; transaction, sale, account; *Law* indenture.
• verb **1** *how to deal with difficult children* COPE WITH, handle, manage, treat, take care of, take charge of, take in hand, sort out, tackle, take on; control; act towards, behave towards. **2** *the article deals with advances in chemistry* CONCERN, be about, have to do with, discuss, consider, cover, pertain to; tackle, study, explore, investigate, examine, review, analyse. **3** *the company deals in high-tech goods* TRADE IN, buy and sell; sell, purvey, supply, stock, market, merchandise; traffic, smuggle; *informal* push; *Brit. informal* flog. **4** *the cards were dealt* DISTRIBUTE, give out, share out, divide out, hand out, pass out, pass round, dole out, dispense, allocate; *informal* divvy up. **5** *the court dealt a blow to government reforms* DELIVER, administer, dispense, inflict, give, impose; aim.
– PHRASES **a great deal/a good deal** A LOT, a large amount, a fair amount, much, plenty; *informal* lots, loads, heaps, bags, masses, tons; *Brit. informal* a shedload.

dealer • noun **1** *an antique dealer* TRADER, tradesman, tradesperson, merchant, salesman/woman, seller, vendor, purveyor, pedlar, hawker; buyer, merchandiser, distributor, supplier, shopkeeper, retailer, wholesaler; *Brit.* stockist. **2** *a dealer in a bank* STOCKBROKER, broker-dealer, broker, agent.

dealing • noun **1** *dishonest dealing* BUSINESS METHODS, business practices, business, commerce, trading, transactions; behaviour, conduct, actions. **2** *the UK's dealings with China* RELATIONS, relationship, association, connections, contact, intercourse; negotiations, bargaining, transactions; trade, trading, business, commerce, traffic; *informal* truck, doings.

dean • noun **1** *student must have the consent of the dean* FACULTY HEAD, department head, college head, provost, university official; chief, director, principal, president, governor. **2** *the dean of St Patrick's Cathedral* CHAPTER HEAD, supervisor.

dear • adjective **1** *a dear friend* BELOVED, loved, adored, cherished, precious; esteemed, respected, worshipped; close, intimate, bosom, boon, best. **2** *her pictures were too dear to part with* PRECIOUS, treasured, valued, prized, cherished, special. **3** *such a dear man* ENDEARING, adorable, lovable, appealing, engaging, charming, captivating, winsome, lovely, nice, pleasant, delightful, sweet, darling. **4** *rather dear meals* EXPENSIVE, costly, high-priced, overpriced, exorbitant, extortionate; *Brit.* over the odds; *informal* pricey, steep, stiff.
– OPPOSITES hated, disagreeable, cheap.
• noun **1** *don't worry, my dear* DARLING, dearest, love, beloved, sweetheart, sweet, precious, treasure; *informal* sweetie, sugar, honey, baby, pet, sunshine, poppet. **2** *he's such a dear* LOVABLE PERSON; darling, sweetheart, pet, angel, gem, treasure; *informal* star.
• adverb *they buy cheaply and sell dear* AT A HIGH PRICE, at an exorbitant price, at high cost.

dearly • adverb **1** *I love my son dearly* VERY MUCH, a great deal, greatly, deeply, profoundly, extremely; fondly, devotedly, tenderly. **2** *our freedom has been bought dearly* AT GREAT COST, at a high price, with much suffering, with much sacrifice.

dearth • noun LACK, scarcity, shortage, shortfall, want, deficiency, insufficiency, inadequacy, paucity, sparseness, scantiness, rareness; absence.
– OPPOSITES surfeit.

death • noun **1** *her father's death* DEMISE, dying, end, passing, loss of life; eternal rest, quietus; murder, assassination, execution, slaughter, massacre; *informal* curtains; *formal* decease; *archaic* expiry. **2** *the death of their dream* END, finish, termination, extinction, extinguishing, collapse, destruction, eradication, obliteration. **3** *Death gestured towards a grave* THE GRIM REAPER, the Dark Angel, the Angel of Death.
– OPPOSITES life, birth.
– PHRASES **put someone to death** EXECUTE, hang, behead, guillotine, decapitate, electrocute, shoot, gas, crucify, stone; kill, murder, assassinate, eliminate, terminate, exterminate, destroy; *informal* bump off, polish off, do away with, do in, knock off, top, string up, take out, croak, stiff, blow away; *N. Amer. informal* ice, rub out, waste, whack, smoke; *poetic/literary* slay.

deathless • adjective IMMORTAL, undying, imperishable, indestructible; enduring, everlasting, eternal; timeless, ageless.
– OPPOSITES mortal, ephemeral.

deathly • adjective **1** *a deathly pallor* DEATHLIKE, deadly, ghostly,

death mask ● noun a plaster cast of a person's face, made just after their death.
death penalty ● noun punishment by execution.
death rate ● noun the number of deaths per one thousand people per year.
death rattle ● noun a gurgling sound in a dying person's throat.
death row ● noun a prison block for those sentenced to death.
death toll ● noun the number of deaths resulting from a particular cause.
death trap ● noun a dangerous building, vehicle, etc.
death-watch beetle ● noun a beetle whose larvae bore into dead wood and structural timbers.
– ORIGIN so-called because it makes a sound like a watch ticking, formerly believed to portend death.
death wish ● noun an unconscious desire for one's own death.
deb ● noun informal a debutante.
debacle /daybaak'l/ ● noun an utter failure or disaster.
– ORIGIN French, from *débâcler* 'unleash'.
debag /deebag/ ● verb (**debagged**, **debagging**) Brit. informal remove the trousers of (someone) as a joke or punishment.
debar ● verb (**debarred**, **debarring**) exclude or prohibit officially from doing something.
– DERIVATIVES **debarment** noun.
– ORIGIN Old French *desbarrer* 'unbar'.
debark ● verb leave a ship or aircraft.
– ORIGIN French *débarquer*.
debase /dibayss/ ● verb lower the quality, value, or character of.
– DERIVATIVES **debasement** noun.
debatable ● adjective open to discussion or argument.
debate ● noun **1** a formal discussion in a public meeting or legislature, in which opposing arguments are presented. **2** an argument. ● verb **1** discuss or argue about. **2** consider; ponder.
– PHRASES **under debate** being discussed.
– DERIVATIVES **debater** noun.
– ORIGIN Old French, from Latin *battere* 'to fight'.
debauch /dibawch/ ● verb corrupt morally. ● noun a bout of excessive indulgence in sensual pleasures.
– ORIGIN Old French *desbaucher* 'turn away from one's duty'.
debauchee /dibbawchee/ ● noun a person given to debauchery.
debauchery ● noun excessive indulgence in sensual pleasures.
debenture /dibenchər/ ● noun Brit. a bond of a company acknowledging a debt and yielding a fixed rate of interest.
– ORIGIN Latin *debentur* 'are owing' (used as the first word of a certificate recording a debt), from *debere* 'owe'.
debilitate /dibillitayt/ ● verb severely weaken.
– DERIVATIVES **debilitation** noun.
– ORIGIN Latin *debilitare*, from *debilis* 'weak'.
debility ● noun (pl. **debilities**) physical weakness.
debit ● noun **1** an entry in an account recording a sum owed. **2** a payment made or owed. ● verb (**debited**, **debiting**) (of a bank) remove (money) from a customer's account.
– ORIGIN French, from Latin *debitum* 'something owed'.
debit card ● noun a card allowing the holder to debit a bank account electronically when making a purchase.
debonair ● adjective (of a man) confident, stylish, and charming.
– ORIGIN from Old French *de bon aire* 'of good disposition'.
debouch /dibowch, -boosh/ ● verb emerge from a confined space into a wide, open area.
– DERIVATIVES **debouchment** noun.
– ORIGIN French, from *bouche* 'mouth'.
debrief ● verb question in detail about a completed mission.
– DERIVATIVES **debriefing** noun.
debris /debree, daybree/ ● noun **1** scattered items or pieces of rubbish. **2** loose broken pieces of rock.
– ORIGIN French, from *débriser* 'break down'.
debt ● noun **1** a sum of money owed. **2** the state of owing money. **3** a feeling of gratitude for a favour or service.
– ORIGIN Latin *debitum* 'something owed', from *debere* 'owe'.
debt of honour ● noun a debt dependent on a moral but not a

Thesaurus

ghastly; ashen, chalky, white, pale, pallid, bloodless, wan, anaemic, pasty. **2** (poetic/literary) *the eagle's deathly grasp* DEADLY, fatal, lethal, mortal, death-dealing; terrible, baleful, dangerous, perilous.
debacle ● noun FIASCO, failure, catastrophe, disaster, mess, ruin; downfall, collapse, defeat; informal foul-up, screw-up, hash, botch, washout; Brit. informal cock-up, pig's ear, bodge; N. Amer. informal snafu.
debar ● verb **1** *women were debarred from the club* EXCLUDE, ban, bar, disqualify, declare ineligible, preclude, shut out, lock out, keep out, reject, blackball; N. Amer. disfellowship. **2** *the unions were debarred from striking* PREVENT, prohibit, proscribe, disallow, ban, interdict, block, stop; forbid to; Law enjoin, estop.
– OPPOSITES admit, allow.
debase ● verb **1** *the moral code has been debased* DEGRADE, devalue, demean, cheapen, prostitute, discredit, drag down, tarnish, blacken, blemish; disgrace, dishonour, shame; damage, harm, undermine. **2** *the added copper debases the silver* REDUCE IN VALUE, reduce in quality, depreciate; contaminate, adulterate, pollute, taint, sully, corrupt; dilute, alloy.
– OPPOSITES enhance.
debased ● adjective **1** *their debased amusements* IMMORAL, debauched, dissolute, perverted, degenerate, wicked, sinful, vile, base, iniquitous, corrupt; lewd, lascivious, lecherous, prurient, indecent. **2** *the myth lives on in a debased form* CORRUPT, corrupted, bastardized, adulterated, diluted, tainted, sullied.
– OPPOSITES honourable, original.
debatable ● adjective ARGUABLE, disputable, questionable, open to question, controversial, contentious; doubtful, dubious, uncertain, unsure, unclear; borderline, inconclusive, moot, unsettled, unresolved, unconfirmed, undetermined, undecided, up in the air; informal iffy.
debate ● noun *a debate on the reforms* DISCUSSION, discourse, parley, dialogue; argument, dispute, wrangle, war of words; argumentation, disputation, dissension, disagreement, contention, conflict; negotiations, talks; informal confab, powwow.
● verb **1** *MPs will debate our future* DISCUSS, talk over/through, talk about, thrash out, argue, dispute; informal kick around/about, bat around/about. **2** *he debated whether to call her* CONSIDER, think over/about, chew over, mull over, weigh up, ponder, deliberate, contemplate, muse, meditate; formal cogitate.
debauch ● verb **1** *public morals have been debauched* CORRUPT, debase, deprave, warp, pervert, lead astray, ruin. **2** (dated) *he debauched six schoolgirls* SEDUCE, deflower, defile, violate; poetic/literary ravish.
debauched ● adjective DISSOLUTE, dissipated, degenerate, corrupt, depraved, sinful, unprincipled, immoral; lascivious, lecherous, lewd, lustful, libidinous, licentious, promiscuous, loose, wanton, abandoned; decadent, profligate, intemperate, sybaritic.
debauchery ● noun DISSIPATION, degeneracy, corruption, vice, depravity; immodesty, indecency, perversion, iniquity, wickedness, sinfulness, impropriety, immorality; lasciviousness, salaciousness, lechery, lewdness, lust, promiscuity, wantonness, profligacy; decadence, intemperance, sybaritism; formal turpitude.
debilitate ● verb WEAKEN, enfeeble, enervate, devitalize, sap, drain, exhaust, weary, fatigue, prostrate; undermine, impair, indispose, incapacitate, cripple, disable, paralyse, immobilize, lay low; informal knock out, do in.
– OPPOSITES invigorate.
debility ● noun FRAILTY, weakness, enfeeblement, enervation, devitalization, lassitude, exhaustion, weariness, fatigue, prostration; incapacity, indisposition, infirmity, illness, sickness, sickliness; informal weediness; Medicine asthenia.
debonair ● adjective SUAVE, urbane, sophisticated, cultured, self-possessed, self-assured, confident, charming, gracious, courteous, gallant, chivalrous, gentlemanly, refined, polished, well bred, genteel, dignified, courtly; well groomed, elegant, stylish, smart, dashing; informal smooth, swish, sharp, cool.
– OPPOSITES unsophisticated.
debrief ● verb QUESTION, quiz, interview, examine, cross-examine, interrogate, probe, sound out; informal grill, pump.
debris ● noun DETRITUS, refuse, rubbish, waste, litter, scrap, dross, chaff, flotsam and jetsam; lumber, rubble, wreckage; remains, scraps, dregs; N. Amer. trash, garbage; Austral./NZ mullock; informal dreck, junk.
debt ● noun **1** *he couldn't pay his debts* BILL, account, dues, arrears, charges; financial obligation, outstanding payment, money owing; N. Amer. check; informal tab. **2** *his debt to the author* INDEBTEDNESS, obligation; gratitude, appreciation, thanks.
– PHRASES **in debt** OWING MONEY, in arrears, behind with payments, overdrawn; insolvent, bankrupt, ruined; Brit. in liquidation; informal in the red, in Queer Street, on the rocks. **in someone's debt** IN-

legal obligation.
debtor ● noun a person who owes money.
debug ● verb (**debugged**, **debugging**) remove errors from (computer hardware or software).
– DERIVATIVES **debugger** noun.
debunk ● verb **1** discredit (a widely held opinion). **2** reduce the inflated reputation of.
– DERIVATIVES **debunker** noun.
deburr /deebur/ (also **debur**) ● verb (**deburred**, **deburring**) smooth the rough edges of.
debut /daybyoo/ ● noun **1** a person's first appearance in a capacity or role. **2** (before another noun) denoting the first recording or publication of a singer or writer. ● verb make a debut.
– ORIGIN French, from *débuter* 'lead off'.
debutant /debyootant/ ● noun a person making a debut.
debutante /debyootaant/ ● noun a young upper-class woman making her first appearance in society.
Dec. ● abbreviation December.
deca- /dekkə/ (also **dec-** before a vowel) ● combining form ten; having ten: *decahedron.*
– ORIGIN Greek *deka* 'ten'.
decade /dekkayd/ ● noun a period of ten years.
– USAGE Pronunciation with the stress on **-cade** is disapproved of by some traditionalists.
– ORIGIN Old French, from Greek *deka* 'ten'.
decadent ● adjective **1** characterized by moral or cultural decline. **2** luxuriously self-indulgent.
– DERIVATIVES **decadence** noun **decadently** adverb.
– ORIGIN French, from Latin *decadentia*; related to DECAY.
decaffeinated /deekaffinaytid/ ● adjective (of tea or coffee) having had most or all of its caffeine removed.
decagon /dekkəgən/ ● noun a plane figure with ten straight sides and angles.
decahedron /dekkəheedrən/ ● noun (pl. **decahedra** or **decahedrons**) a solid figure with ten plane faces.
decal /deekal/ ● noun a design on prepared paper for transferring on to glass, porcelain, etc.
– ORIGIN abbreviation of *decalcomania*, from French *décalquer* 'transfer a tracing' + *-manie* '-mania'.
decalcified ● adjective (of rock or bone) containing a reduced quantity of calcium salts.
– DERIVATIVES **decalcification** noun.
decalitre (US **decaliter**, **dekaliter**) ● noun a metric unit of capacity, equal to 10 litres.
Decalogue /dekkəlog/ ● noun the Ten Commandments.
– ORIGIN from Greek *dekalogos biblos* 'book of the Ten Commandments'.
decametre (US **decameter**, **dekameter**) ● noun a metric unit of length, equal to 10 metres.
decamp ● verb depart suddenly or secretly.
decanal /dikayn'l, dekkən'l/ ● adjective relating to a dean or deanery.
– ORIGIN Latin *decanalis*, from *decanus* (see DEAN).
decant /dikant/ ● verb **1** pour from one container into another to separate liquid from sediment. **2** informal transfer (passengers) to another place.
– ORIGIN Latin *decanthare*, from *canthus* 'edge, rim'.
decanter ● noun a stoppered glass container into which wine or spirit is decanted.
decapitate /dikappitayt/ ● verb cut off the head of.
– DERIVATIVES **decapitation** noun.
– ORIGIN Latin *decapitare*, from *caput* 'head'.
decapod /dekkəpod/ ● noun a crustacean with five pairs of walking legs, such as a shrimp.
– ORIGIN from Greek *deka* 'ten' + *pous* 'foot'.
decarbonize (also **decarbonise**) ● verb remove carbon deposits from (an engine).
decathlon /dikathlən/ ● noun an athletic event in which each competitor takes part in the same ten events.
– DERIVATIVES **decathlete** noun.
– ORIGIN from Greek *deka* 'ten' + *athlon* 'contest'.
decay ● verb **1** rot through the action of bacteria and fungi. **2** decline in quality or vigour. **3** Physics (of a radioactive substance, particle, etc.) undergo change to a different form by emitting radiation. ● noun **1** the state or process of decaying. **2** rotten matter or tissue.
– ORIGIN Old French *decair*, from Latin *decidere* 'fall down or off'.
decease ● noun formal or Law death. ● verb archaic die.
– ORIGIN Latin *decessus* 'death', from *decedere* 'to die'.
deceased formal or Law ● noun (**the deceased**) the recently dead person in question. ● adjective recently dead.
deceit ● noun **1** the action or practice of deceiving. **2** a deceitful act or statement.
deceitful ● adjective acting to deceive others.

d

Thesaurus

DEBTED TO, beholden to, obliged to, duty-bound to, honour-bound to, obligated to; grateful, thankful, appreciative.
debtor ● noun BORROWER, mortgagor; bankrupt, insolvent, defaulter, non-payer.
– OPPOSITES creditor.
debunk ● verb EXPLODE, deflate, quash, drive a coach and horses through, discredit, disprove, contradict, controvert, invalidate, negate; challenge, call into question; *informal* shoot full of holes, blow sky-high; *formal* confute.
– OPPOSITES confirm.
debut ● noun FIRST APPEARANCE, first performance, launch, coming out, entrance, premiere, introduction, inception, inauguration; *informal* kick-off.
decadence ● noun **1** *the decadence of modern society* DISSIPATION, degeneracy, debauchery, corruption, depravity, vice, sin, moral decay, immorality; immoderateness, intemperance, licentiousness, self-indulgence, hedonism. **2** *the decadence of nations* DECLINE, fall, decay, degeneration, deterioration, degradation, retrogression.
– OPPOSITES morality, rise.
decadent ● adjective **1** *decadent city life* DISSOLUTE, dissipated, degenerate, corrupt, depraved, sinful, unprincipled, immoral; licentious, abandoned, profligate, intemperate; sybaritic, hedonistic, pleasure-seeking, self-indulgent. **2** *the decadent empire* DECLINING, decaying, ebbing, degenerating, deteriorating.
decamp ● verb **1** *he decamped with the profits* ABSCOND, make off, run off/away, flee, bolt, take flight, disappear, vanish, steal away, sneak away, escape, make a run for it, leave, depart; *informal* split, scram, vamoose, cut and run, do a disappearing act, head for the hills, go AWOL; *Brit. informal* do a bunk, do a runner, scarper; *N. Amer. informal* take a powder, go on the lam. **2** (archaic) *the armies decamped* STRIKE ONE'S TENTS, break camp, move on.
decant ● verb POUR OUT/OFF, draw off, siphon off, drain, tap; transfer.
decapitate ● verb BEHEAD, guillotine; *archaic* decollate.
decay ● verb **1** *the corpses had decayed* DECOMPOSE, rot, putrefy, go bad, go off, spoil, fester, perish, deteriorate; degrade, break down, moulder, mortify, shrivel, wither. **2** *the cities continue to decay* DETERIORATE, degenerate, decline, go downhill, slump, slide, go to rack and ruin, go to seed; disintegrate, fall to pieces, fall into disrepair; fail, collapse; *informal* go to pot, go to the dogs, go down the toilet; *Austral./NZ informal* go to the pack.
● noun **1** *signs of decay* DECOMPOSITION, putrefaction, festering; rot, mould, mildew, fungus. **2** *tooth decay* ROT, corrosion, decomposition; caries, cavities, holes. **3** *the decay of American values* DETERIORATION, degeneration, debasement, degradation, decline, weakening, atrophy; crumbling, disintegration, collapse.
decayed ● adjective DECOMPOSED, decomposing, rotten, putrescent, putrid, bad, off, spoiled, perished; mouldy, festering, fetid, rancid, rank; maggoty, wormy, flyblown.
decaying ● adjective **1** *decaying fish* DECOMPOSING, decomposed, rotting, rotten, putrescent, putrid, bad, off, perished; mouldy, festering, fetid, rancid, rank; maggoty, wormy, flyblown. **2** *a decaying city* DECLINING, degenerating, dying, crumbling; run down, tumbledown, ramshackle, shabby, decrepit; in decline, in ruins; *informal* on the way out.
decease ● noun (formal) *her decease was imminent* DEATH, dying, demise, end, passing, loss of life, quietus; *informal* curtains, croaking, snuffing; *archaic* expiry.
● verb (archaic) *he deceased at his palace.* See DIE sense 1.
deceased ● adjective (formal) DEAD, expired, departed, gone, no more, passed on/away; late, lost, lamented; perished, fallen, slain, slaughtered, killed, murdered; lifeless, extinct; *informal* (as) dead as a doornail, six feet under, pushing up daisies; *euphemistic* with God, asleep.
deceit ● noun **1** *her endless deceit* DECEPTION, deceitfulness, duplicity, double-dealing, fraud, cheating, trickery, chicanery, deviousness, slyness, wiliness, guile, bluff, lying, pretence, treachery; *informal* crookedness, monkey business, jiggery-pokery; *N. Amer. informal* monkeyshines. **2** *their life is a deceit* SHAM, fraud, pretence,

d

– DERIVATIVES **deceitfully** adverb **deceitfulness** noun.
deceive ● verb **1** deliberately mislead into believing something false. **2** (of a thing) give a mistaken impression.
– DERIVATIVES **deceiver** noun.
– ORIGIN Old French *deceivre*, from Latin *decipere* 'ensnare, cheat'.
decelerate /deesellərayt/ ● verb begin to move more slowly.
– DERIVATIVES **deceleration** noun.
December ● noun the twelfth month of the year.
– ORIGIN Latin, from *decem* 'ten' (being originally the tenth month of the Roman year).
decency ● noun (pl. **decencies**) **1** decent behaviour. **2** (**decencies**) standards of propriety.
decennial /disenniəl/ ● adjective lasting for or recurring every ten years.
– ORIGIN from Latin *decem* 'ten' + *annus* 'year'.
decent ● adjective **1** conforming with generally accepted standards of morality or respectability. **2** of an acceptable standard. **3** Brit. informal kind or generous.
– DERIVATIVES **decently** adverb.
– ORIGIN from Latin *decere* 'to be fit'.
decentralize (also **decentralise**) ● verb transfer (authority) from central to local government.
– DERIVATIVES **decentralist** noun & adjective **decentralization** noun.
deception ● noun **1** the action of deceiving. **2** a thing that deceives.
deceptive ● adjective giving an impression different from the true one.
deceptively ● adverb **1** to a lesser extent than appears the case. **2** to a greater extent than appears the case.
– USAGE Beware of confusion when using **deceptively**, as it can mean both one thing and also its complete opposite. A *deceptively smooth surface* is one which appears smooth but in fact is not smooth at all, while a *deceptively spacious room* is one that does not look spacious but is in fact more spacious than it appears.
deci- ● combining form one tenth: *decilitre.*
– ORIGIN from Latin *decimus* 'tenth'.
decibel /dessibel/ ● noun a unit of measurement expressing the intensity of a sound or the power of an electrical signal.
– ORIGIN from DECI- + *bel*, a unit (= 10 decibels) named after Alexander Graham *Bell* (1847–1922), inventor of the telephone.
decide ● verb **1** resolve in the mind as a result of consideration. **2** settle (an issue or contest). **3** give a judgement concerning a legal case.
– DERIVATIVES **decidable** adjective **deciding** adjective.
– ORIGIN Latin *decidere* 'determine', from *caedere* 'cut'.
decided ● adjective definite; clear.
– DERIVATIVES **decidedly** adverb.
decider ● noun a contest that settles the winner of a series of contests.
deciduous /disidyooəss/ ● adjective **1** (of a tree or shrub) shedding its leaves annually. Contrasted with EVERGREEN. **2** (of teeth or horns) shed after a time.
– ORIGIN Latin *deciduus*, from *decidere* 'fall down or off'.
decilitre (US **deciliter**) ● noun a metric unit of capacity, equal to one tenth of a litre.
decimal ● adjective relating to a system of numbers based on the number ten. ● noun a fraction whose denominator is a power of ten, expressed by numbers placed to the right of a decimal point.
– DERIVATIVES **decimalize** (also **decimalise**) verb **decimally** adverb.
– ORIGIN from Latin *decimus* 'tenth'.
decimal place ● noun the position of a digit to the right of a decimal point.
decimal point ● noun a full point placed after the figure representing units in a decimal fraction.
decimate /dessimayt/ ● verb **1** kill or destroy a large proportion of. **2** drastically reduce the strength of.
– DERIVATIVES **decimation** noun.
– USAGE The earliest sense of **decimate** was 'kill one in every ten of', a reference to the ancient Roman practice of killing one in every ten of a group of soldiers as a collective punishment.

Thesaurus

hoax, fake, blind, artifice; trick, stratagem, device, ruse, scheme, dodge, machination, deception, subterfuge; cheat, swindle; *informal* con, set-up, scam, flimflam; *N. Amer. informal* bunco.
– OPPOSITES honesty.
deceitful ● adjective **1** *a deceitful woman* DISHONEST, untruthful, mendacious, insincere, false, disingenuous, untrustworthy, unscrupulous, unprincipled, two-faced, duplicitous, double-dealing, underhand, crafty, cunning, sly, scheming, calculating, treacherous, Machiavellian; *informal* sneaky, tricky, foxy, crooked; *Brit. informal* bent. **2** *a deceitful allegation* FRAUDULENT, counterfeit, fabricated, invented, concocted, made up, trumped up, untrue, false, bogus, fake, spurious, fallacious, deceptive, misleading; *euphemistic* economical with the truth.
deceive ● verb **1** *she was deceived by a con man* SWINDLE, defraud, cheat, trick, hoodwink, hoax, dupe, take in, mislead, delude, fool, outwit, lead on, inveigle, beguile, double-cross, gull; *informal* con, bamboozle, do, gyp, diddle, swizzle, rip off, shaft, pull a fast one on, take for a ride, pull the wool over someone's eyes, sell a pup to; *N. Amer. informal* sucker, snooker, stiff. **2** *he deceived her with another woman* BE UNFAITHFUL TO, cheat on, betray, play someone false; *informal* two-time.
decelerate ● verb SLOW DOWN/UP, ease up, slack up, reduce speed, brake.
decency ● noun **1** *standards of taste and decency* PROPRIETY, decorum, good taste, respectability, dignity, correctness, good form, etiquette; morality, virtue, modesty, delicacy. **2** *he didn't have the decency to tell me* COURTESY, politeness, good manners, civility, respect; consideration, thoughtfulness, tact, diplomacy.
decent ● adjective **1** *a decent Christian burial* PROPER, correct, appropriate, apt, fitting, suitable; respectable, dignified, decorous, seemly; nice, tasteful; conventional, accepted, standard, traditional, orthodox; comme il faut; *informal* pukka. **2** (*Brit. informal*) *a very decent chap* HONOURABLE, honest, trustworthy, dependable; respectable, upright, clean-living, virtuous, good; obliging, helpful, accommodating, unselfish, generous, kind, thoughtful, considerate; neighbourly, hospitable, pleasant, agreeable, amiable. **3** *a job with decent pay* SATISFACTORY, reasonable, fair, acceptable, adequate, sufficient, ample; not bad, all right, tolerable, passable, suitable; *informal* OK, okay, up to snuff.
– OPPOSITES unpleasant, unsatisfactory.
deception ● noun **1** *they obtained money by deception* DECEIT, deceitfulness, duplicity, double-dealing, fraud, cheating, trickery, chicanery, deviousness, slyness, wiliness, guile, bluff, lying, pretence, treachery; *informal* crookedness, monkey business, jiggery-pokery; *N. Amer. informal* monkeyshines. **2** *it was all a deception* TRICK, deceit, sham, fraud, pretence, hoax, fake, blind, artifice; stratagem, device, ruse, scheme, dodge, machination, subterfuge; cheat, swindle; *informal* con, set-up, scam, flimflam; *N. Amer. informal* bunco.
deceptive ● adjective **1** *distances are very deceptive* MISLEADING, illusory, illusionary, specious; ambiguous; distorted; *poetic/literary* illusive. **2** *deceptive practices* DECEITFUL, duplicitous, fraudulent, counterfeit, underhand, cunning, crafty, sly, guileful, scheming, treacherous, Machiavellian; disingenuous, untrustworthy, unscrupulous, unprincipled, dishonest, insincere, false; *informal* crooked, sharp, shady, sneaky, tricky, foxy; *Brit. informal* bent.
decide ● verb **1** *she decided to become a writer* RESOLVE, determine, make up one's mind, make a decision; elect, choose, opt, plan, aim, have the intention, have in mind, set one's sights on. **2** *research to decide a variety of questions* SETTLE, resolve, determine, work out, answer; *informal* sort out, figure out. **3** *the court is to decide the case* ADJUDICATE, arbitrate, adjudge, judge; hear, try, examine; sit in judgement on, pronounce on, give a verdict on, rule on.
decided ● adjective **1** *they have a decided advantage* DISTINCT, clear, marked, pronounced, obvious, striking, noticeable, unmistakable, patent, manifest; definite, certain, positive, emphatic, undeniable, indisputable, unquestionable; assured, guaranteed. **2** *he was very decided* DETERMINED, resolute, firm, strong-minded, strong-willed, emphatic, dead set, unwavering, unyielding, unbending, inflexible, unshakeable, unrelenting, obstinate, stubborn; *N. Amer.* rock-ribbed. **3** *our future is decided* SETTLED, established, resolved, determined, agreed, designated, chosen, ordained, prescribed; set, fixed; *informal* sewn up, wrapped up.
decidedly ● adverb DISTINCTLY, clearly, markedly, obviously, noticeably, unmistakably, patently, manifestly; definitely, certainly, positively, absolutely, downright, undeniably, unquestionably; extremely, exceedingly, exceptionally, particularly, especially, very; *N. English* right; *informal* terrifically, devilishly, ultra, mega, majorly; *Brit. informal* jolly, ever so, dead, well; *N. Amer. informal* real, mighty, awful; *archaic* exceeding.

This has been more or less totally superseded by the sense 'kill or destroy a large proportion of', although some traditionalists argue that this later sense is incorrect.
– ORIGIN Latin *decimare* 'take as a tenth'.
decimetre (US **decimeter**) ● noun a metric unit of length, equal to one tenth of a metre.
decipher /disīfər/ ● verb **1** convert from code into normal language. **2** succeed in understanding (something hard to interpret).
– DERIVATIVES **decipherable** adjective **decipherment** noun.
decision ● noun **1** a conclusion or resolution reached after consideration. **2** the action or process of deciding. **3** the quality of being decisive.
decisive ● adjective **1** settling an issue quickly. **2** able to make decisions quickly.
– DERIVATIVES **decisively** adverb **decisiveness** noun.
deck ● noun **1** a floor of a ship, especially the upper level. **2** a floor or platform, as in a bus or car park. **3** chiefly N. Amer. a pack of cards. **4** a component in sound-reproduction equipment, incorporating a player or recorder for discs or tapes. ● verb **1** decorate brightly or festively. **2** informal knock to the ground with a punch.
– PHRASES **hit the deck** informal fall to the ground.
– DERIVATIVES **decked** adjective.
– ORIGIN Dutch *dec* 'covering, roof'.
deckchair ● noun a folding chair with a wooden frame and a canvas seat.
deckhand ● noun a member of a ship's crew performing cleaning or manual work.
decking ● noun material used in making a deck.
deckle /dekk'l/ ● noun a continuous belt on either side in a papermaking machine, used for controlling the size of paper produced.
– ORIGIN German, 'small covering'.
deckle edge ● noun the rough uncut edge of a sheet of paper.
declaim ● verb speak or recite in an emphatic or dramatic way.
– DERIVATIVES **declamatory** adjective.
– ORIGIN Latin *declamare*, from *clamare* 'to shout'.
declamation ● noun the action or art of declaiming.
declaration ● noun **1** a formal statement or announcement. **2** an act of declaring.
declarative /diklarrətiv/ ● adjective **1** of the nature of a declaration. **2** (of a sentence or phrase) taking the form of a simple statement.
declare ● verb **1** announce solemnly or officially. **2** (**declare oneself**) reveal one's intentions or identity. **3** (**declared**) having admitted that one is the specified thing: *a declared atheist*. **4** acknowledge possession of (income or goods on which tax or duty should be paid). **5** Cricket close an innings voluntarily with wickets remaining.
– DERIVATIVES **declaratory** adjective **declaredly** adverb **declarer** noun.
– ORIGIN Latin *declarare*, from *clarare* 'make clear'.
déclassé /dayklassay/ (also **déclassée**) ● adjective having fallen in social status.
– ORIGIN French.
declassify ● verb (**declassifies**, **declassified**) officially declare (information or documents) to be no longer secret.
– DERIVATIVES **declassification** noun.
declension /diklensh'n/ ● noun **1** the variation of the form of a noun, pronoun, or adjective that identifies its grammatical case, number, and gender. **2** the class to which a noun or adjective is assigned according to this variation.
– ORIGIN from Old French *decliner* 'to decline'.
declination /deklinaysh'n/ ● noun **1** Astronomy the angular distance of a point north or south of the celestial equator. **2** the angular deviation of a compass needle from true north.
decline ● verb **1** become smaller, weaker, or less in quality or quantity. **2** politely refuse. **3** (especially of the sun) move downwards. **4** Grammar form (a noun, pronoun, or adjective) according to case, number, and gender. ● noun a gradual and continuous loss of strength, numbers, or value.
– ORIGIN Latin *declinare* 'bend down, turn aside', from *clinare* 'to bend'.
declivity /diklivviti/ ● noun (pl. **declivities**) a downward slope.
– ORIGIN Latin *declivitas*, from *clivus* 'a slope'.
declutch ● verb disengage the clutch of a motor vehicle.
decoction ● noun a liquor containing the concentrated essence of a substance, produced as a result of heating or boiling.
– ORIGIN Latin, from *decoquere* 'boil down'.
decode ● verb **1** convert (a coded message) into intelligible language. **2** convert (audio or video signals), in particular from

Thesaurus

deciding ● adjective DETERMINING, decisive, conclusive, key, pivotal, crucial, critical, significant, major, chief, principal, prime.
decipher ● verb **1** *he deciphered the code* DECODE, decrypt, break, work out, solve, interpret, translate; make sense of, get to the bottom of, unravel; *informal* crack, figure out; *Brit. informal* twig, suss (out). **2** *the writing was hard to decipher* MAKE OUT, discern, perceive, read, follow, fathom, make sense of, interpret, understand, comprehend, grasp.
– OPPOSITES encode.
decision ● noun **1** *they came to a decision* RESOLUTION, conclusion, settlement, commitment, resolve, determination; choice, option, selection. **2** *the judge's decision* VERDICT, finding, ruling, recommendation, judgement, pronouncement, adjudication, arbitrament; order, rule; findings, results; *Law* determination; *N. Amer.* resolve. **3** *his order had a ring of decision* DECISIVENESS, determination, resolution, resolve, firmness; strong-mindedness, purpose, purposefulness.
decisive ● adjective **1** *a decisive man* RESOLUTE, firm, strong-minded, strong-willed, determined; purposeful, forceful, dead set, unwavering, unyielding, unbending, inflexible, unshakeable, obstinate, stubborn; *N. Amer.* rock-ribbed. **2** *the decisive factor* DECIDING, conclusive, determining; key, pivotal, critical, crucial, significant, influential, major, chief, principal, prime.
deck ● verb **1** *the street was decked with bunting* DECORATE, bedeck, adorn, ornament, trim, trick out, garnish, cover, hang, festoon, garland, swathe, wreathe; embellish, beautify, prettify, enhance, grace, set off; *informal* get up, do up, do out, tart up; *poetic/literary* bejewel, bedizen, caparison, furbelow. **2** *Ingrid was decked out in blue* DRESS (UP), clothe, attire, garb, robe, drape, turn out, fit out, rig out, outfit, costume; *informal* doll up, get up, do up.
declaim ● verb **1** *a preacher declaiming from the pulpit* MAKE A SPEECH, give an address, give a lecture, deliver a sermon; speak, hold forth, orate, preach, lecture, sermonize, moralize; *informal* sound off, spout, speechify, preachify. **2** *they loved to hear him declaim poetry* RECITE, read aloud, read out loud, read out; deliver; *informal* spout. **3** *he declaimed against the evils of society* SPEAK OUT, rail, inveigh, fulminate, rage, thunder; rant, expostulate; condemn, criticize, attack, decry, disparage.
declamation ● noun SPEECH, address, lecture, sermon, homily, discourse, oration, recitation, disquisition, monologue.
declaration ● noun **1** *they issued a declaration* ANNOUNCEMENT, statement, communication, pronouncement, proclamation, communiqué, edict; *N. Amer.* advisory. **2** *the declaration of war* PROCLAMATION, notification, announcement, revelation, disclosure, broadcasting. **3** *a declaration of faith* ASSERTION, profession, affirmation, acknowledgement, revelation, disclosure, manifestation, confirmation, testimony, validation, certification, attestation; pledge, avowal, vow, oath, protestation.
declare ● verb **1** *she declared her political principles* PROCLAIM, announce, state, reveal, air, voice, articulate, express, vent, set forth, publicize, broadcast; *informal* come out with, shout from the rooftops. **2** *he declared that they were guilty* ASSERT, maintain, state, affirm, contend, argue, insist, hold, profess, claim, avow, swear; *formal* aver. **3** *his speech declared him a gentleman* SHOW TO BE, reveal as, confirm as, prove to be, attest to someone's being.
decline ● verb **1** *she declined all invitations* TURN DOWN, reject, brush aside, refuse, rebuff, spurn, repulse, dismiss; forgo, deny oneself, pass up; abstain from, say no; *informal* give the thumbs down to, give something a miss, give someone the brush-off; *Brit. informal* knock back. **2** *the number of traders has declined* DECREASE, reduce, lessen, diminish, dwindle, contract, shrink, fall off, tail off; drop, fall, go down, slump, plummet; *informal* nosedive, take a header, crash. **3** *standards steadily declined* DETERIORATE, degenerate, decay, crumble, collapse, slump, slip, slide, go downhill, worsen; weaken, wane, ebb; *informal* go to pot, go to the dogs, go down the toilet; *Austral./NZ informal* go to the pack.
– OPPOSITES accept, increase, rise.
● noun **1** *a decline in profits* REDUCTION, decrease, downturn, downswing, devaluation, depreciation, diminution, ebb, drop, slump, plunge; *informal* nosedive, crash. **2** *forest decline* DETERIORATION, degeneration, degradation, shrinkage; death, decay.
– PHRASES **in decline** DECLINING, decaying, crumbling, collapsing,

analogue to digital.
– DERIVATIVES **decodable** adjective **decoder** noun.
decoke /deekōk/ ● verb Brit. informal remove carbon or carbonaceous material from.
décolletage /daykoltaazh/ ● noun a low neckline on a woman's dress or top.
– ORIGIN French, from *décolleter* 'expose the neck'.
décolleté /daykoltay/ ● adjective having a low neckline. ● noun a décolletage.
– ORIGIN French.

d

decolonize (also **decolonise**) ● verb withdraw from (a colony), leaving it independent.
– DERIVATIVES **decolonization** noun.
decommission ● verb **1** take (a ship) out of service. **2** dismantle and make safe (a nuclear reactor or weapon).
decompose ● verb **1** (of organic matter) decay. **2** break down into component elements.
– DERIVATIVES **decomposable** adjective **decomposition** noun.
decompress /deekəmpress/ ● verb **1** expand (compressed computer data) to its normal size. **2** subject (a diver) to decompression.
– DERIVATIVES **decompressor** noun.
decompression ● noun **1** reduction in air pressure. **2** the process of decompressing.
decompression chamber ● noun a small room in which the air pressure can be varied, used to allow deep-sea divers to adjust to normal air pressure.
decompression sickness ● noun a serious condition that results when too rapid decompression causes nitrogen bubbles to form in the tissues of the body.
decongestant /deekənjestənt/ ● adjective (of a medicine) used to relieve nasal congestion. ● noun a decongestant medicine.
deconsecrate ● verb transfer (a building) from sacred to secular use.
– DERIVATIVES **deconsecration** noun.
deconstruct /deekənstrukt/ ● verb **1** analyse by deconstruction. **2** dismantle and expose the workings of.
– DERIVATIVES **deconstructive** adjective.
deconstruction ● noun a method of critical analysis of language and text which emphasizes the relational quality of meaning and the assumptions implicit in forms of expression.
– DERIVATIVES **deconstructionism** noun **deconstructionist** adjective & noun.
decontaminate ● verb remove dangerous substances from.
– DERIVATIVES **decontamination** noun.
decontextualize (also **decontextualise**) ● verb consider (something) in isolation from its context.
– DERIVATIVES **decontextualization** noun.
decontrol ● verb (**decontrolled**, **decontrolling**) release (a commodity, market, etc.) from controls or restrictions.
decor /daykor/ ● noun the furnishing and decoration of a room.
– ORIGIN French, from Latin *decorare* 'embellish'.
decorate ● verb **1** make more attractive by adding ornamentation. **2** apply paint or wallpaper to. **3** confer an award or medal on. **4** (**Decorated**) denoting a stage of English Gothic church architecture of the 14th century with elaborate tracery.
– ORIGIN Latin *decorare* 'embellish', from *decus* 'honour or embellishment'.
decoration ● noun **1** the process or art of decorating. **2** a decorative object or pattern. **3** the way in which something is decorated. **4** a medal or award conferred as an honour.
decorative /dekkərətiv/ ● adjective **1** serving to make something look more attractive; ornamental. **2** relating to decoration.
– DERIVATIVES **decoratively** adverb **decorativeness** noun.
decorator ● noun a person who decorates, in particular (Brit.) a person whose job is to paint interior walls or hang wallpaper.
decorous /dekkərəss/ ● adjective in keeping with good taste and propriety; polite and restrained.
– DERIVATIVES **decorously** adverb **decorousness** noun.
– ORIGIN Latin *decorus* 'seemly'.
decorum /dikorəm/ ● noun **1** behaviour in keeping with good taste and propriety. **2** prescribed behaviour; etiquette.
– ORIGIN Latin, 'seemly thing'.
découpage /daykoopaazh/ ● noun the decoration of a surface with paper cut-outs.
– ORIGIN French, from *découper* 'cut out'.
decouple ● verb separate or disengage one thing from another.
decoy ● noun /deekoy/ **1** a bird or mammal, or an imitation of one, used by hunters to lure game. **2** a person or thing used to mislead or lure someone into a trap. **3** a pond from which narrow netted channels lead, into which wild duck may be enticed for capture. ● verb /dikoy/ lure by means of a decoy.
– ORIGIN from Dutch *de kooi* 'the decoy', from Latin *cavea* 'cage'.
decrease ● verb /dikreess/ make or become smaller or fewer in size, amount, intensity, or degree. ● noun /deekreess/ **1** an instance of decreasing. **2** the process of decreasing.
– ORIGIN Latin *decrescere*, from *crescere* 'grow'.
decree ● noun **1** an official order that has the force of law. **2** a judgement or decision of certain law courts. ● verb (**decrees**, **decreed**, **decreeing**) order by decree.
– ORIGIN Latin *decretum* 'something decided', from *decernere* 'decide'.
decree absolute ● noun (pl. **decrees absolute**) English Law a

Thesaurus

failing; disappearing, dying, moribund; *informal* on its last legs, on the way out.
decode ● verb DECIPHER, decrypt, work out, solve, interpret, translate; make sense of, get to the bottom of, unravel, find the key to; *informal* crack, figure out; *Brit. informal* twig, suss (out).
decompose ● verb **1** *the chemical prevents corpses decomposing* DECAY, rot, putrefy, go bad, go off, spoil, fester, perish, deteriorate; degrade, break down, moulder, mortify, shrivel, wither. **2** *some minerals decompose rapidly* BREAK UP, fragment, disintegrate, crumble, dissolve; break down, decay. **3** *decompose words into simpler elements* SEPARATE, divide, break down, dissect, resolve, reduce.
decomposition ● noun **1** *an advanced state of decomposition* DECAY, putrefaction, putrescence, putridity. **2** *the decomposition of granite* DISINTEGRATION, dissolution; breaking down, decay. **3** *the decomposition of a sentence* SEPARATION, division, breakdown; dissection, dissolution, resolution, analysis, reduction.
decontaminate ● verb SANITIZE, sterilize, disinfect, clean, cleanse, purify; fumigate.
decor ● noun DECORATION, furnishing, ornamentation; colour scheme.
decorate ● verb **1** *the door was decorated with a wreath* ORNAMENT, adorn, trim, embellish, garnish, furnish, enhance, grace, prettify; festoon, garland, bedeck. **2** *he started to decorate his home* PAINT, WALLPAPER, paper; refurbish, furbish, renovate, redecorate; *informal* do up, spruce up, do over, fix up, give something a facelift. **3** *he was decorated for courage* GIVE A MEDAL TO, honour, cite, reward.
decoration ● noun **1** *a ceiling with rich decoration* ORNAMENTATION, adornment, trimming, embellishment, garnishing, gilding; beautification, prettification; enhancements, enrichments, frills, accessories, trimmings, finery, frippery. **2** *internal decoration.* See DECOR. **3** *a Christmas tree decoration* ORNAMENT, bauble, trinket, knick-knack, spangle; trimming, tinsel. **4** *a decoration won on the battlefield* MEDAL, award, star, ribbon; laurel, trophy, prize; *Military slang* fruit salad; *Brit. informal* gong.
decorative ● adjective ORNAMENTAL, embellishing, garnishing; fancy, ornate, attractive, pretty, showy.
– OPPOSITES functional.
decorous ● adjective PROPER, seemly, decent, becoming, befitting, tasteful; correct, appropriate, suitable, fitting; tactful, polite, well mannered, genteel, respectable; formal, restrained, modest, demure, gentlemanly, ladylike.
– OPPOSITES unseemly.
decorum ● noun **1** *he had acted with decorum* PROPRIETY, seemliness, decency, good taste, correctness; politeness, courtesy, good manners; dignity, respectability, modesty, demureness. **2** *a breach of decorum* ETIQUETTE, protocol, good form, custom, convention; formalities, niceties, punctilios, politeness.
– OPPOSITES impropriety.
decoy ● noun *a decoy to distract their attention* LURE, bait, red herring; enticement, inducement, temptation, attraction, carrot; snare, trap.
● verb *he was decoyed to the mainland* LURE, entice, tempt; entrap, snare, trap.
decrease ● verb **1** *pollution levels decreased* LESSEN, reduce, drop, diminish, decline, dwindle, fall off; die down, abate, subside, tail off, ebb, wane; plummet, plunge. **2** *decrease the amount of fat in your body* REDUCE, lessen, lower, cut, curtail; slim down, tone down, deplete, minimize; *informal* slash.
– OPPOSITES increase.

final order by a court of law which officially ends a marriage.

decree nisi ● noun (pl. **decrees nisi**) English Law an order by a court of law that states the date on which a marriage will end, unless a good reason to prevent a divorce is produced.
– ORIGIN Latin *nisi* 'unless'.

decrement /dekrimənt/ ● noun **1** a reduction or diminution. **2** Physics the ratio of the amplitudes in successive cycles of a damped oscillation.
– ORIGIN Latin *decrementum* 'diminution', from *decrescere* 'to decrease'.

decrepit /dikreppit/ ● adjective **1** worn out or ruined because of age or neglect. **2** elderly and infirm.
– DERIVATIVES **decrepitude** noun.
– ORIGIN Latin *decrepitus*, from *crepare* 'rattle, creak'.

decretal /dikreet'l/ ● noun a papal decree concerning a point of canon law. ● adjective of the nature of a decree.
– ORIGIN Latin *decretale*, from *decernere* 'to decide'.

decriminalize (also **decriminalise**) ● verb cease to treat (something) as illegal.
– DERIVATIVES **decriminalization** noun.

decry /dikrī/ ● verb (**decries, decried**) publicly denounce.
– DERIVATIVES **decrier** noun.
– ORIGIN originally in the sense 'decrease the value of coins by royal proclamation': from French *décrier* 'cry down'.

decrypt /deekript/ ● verb make (a coded or unclear message) intelligible.
– DERIVATIVES **decryption** noun.

decurved ● adjective Biology (especially of a bird's bill) curved downwards.

dedicate ● verb **1** devote to a particular subject, task, or purpose. **2** address (a book) to a person as a sign of respect or affection. **3** ceremonially assign (a church or other building) to a deity or saint.
– DERIVATIVES **dedicatee** noun **dedicator** noun **dedicatory** adjective.
– ORIGIN Latin *dedicare* 'devote or consecrate'.

dedicated ● adjective **1** devoted to a task or purpose. **2** exclusively assigned or allocated to a particular purpose.
– DERIVATIVES **dedicatedly** adverb.

dedication ● noun **1** the quality of being devoted to a purpose or task. **2** the action of dedicating. **3** the words with which something is dedicated.

deduce ● verb arrive at (a fact or a conclusion) by reasoning.
– DERIVATIVES **deducible** adjective.
– ORIGIN Latin *deducere* 'to take or lead away'.

deduct ● verb subtract or take away from a total.
– ORIGIN Latin *deducere* 'to take or lead away'.

deductible ● adjective able to be deducted, especially from taxable income.
– DERIVATIVES **deductibility** noun.

deduction ● noun **1** the action of deducting. **2** an amount that is or may be deducted. **3** the inference of particular instances by reference to a general law or principle. Often contrasted with INDUCTION.
– DERIVATIVES **deductive** adjective **deductively** adverb.

deed ● noun **1** an action that is performed intentionally or consciously. **2** (usu. **deeds**) a legal document, especially one relating to property ownership or legal rights. ● verb N. Amer. convey or transfer by legal deed.
– ORIGIN Old English.

deed of covenant ● noun Brit. an agreement to pay a regular amount of money, particularly when this enables the recipient to reclaim any tax paid by the donor on the amount.

deed poll ● noun English Law a legal deed made and executed by one party only, especially to formalize a change of a person's name.
– ORIGIN so named because the parchment was 'polled' or cut even, not indented as in the case of a deed made by two parties.

deejay ● noun informal a disc jockey.

deem ● verb formal regard or consider in a specified way.
– ORIGIN Old English, related to DOOM.

deemster ● noun a judge (of whom there are two) in the Isle of Man.

deep ● adjective **1** extending far down or in from the top or surface. **2** extending a specified distance from the top, surface, or outer edge. **3** (of sound) low in pitch and full in tone; not shrill. **4** (of colour) dark and intense. **5** very intense, profound, or extreme: *a deep sleep.* **6** difficult to understand. **7** (in ball games) far down or across the field. ● noun **1** (**the deep**) literary the sea. **2** (usu. **deeps**) a deep part of something, especially the sea. ● adverb far down or in; deeply.
– PHRASES **go off the deep end** informal give way immediately to an emotional or irrational outburst. **in deep water** informal in trouble or difficulty. **jump** (or **be thrown**) **in at the deep end** informal face a difficult problem or undertaking with little experience.
– DERIVATIVES **deepness** noun.
– ORIGIN Old English, related to DIP.

deep-dyed ● adjective informal thoroughgoing; complete.

d

Thesaurus

● noun *a decrease in crime* REDUCTION, drop, decline, downturn, cut, cutback, diminution, ebb, wane.
– OPPOSITES increase.

decree ● noun **1** *a presidential decree* ORDER, edict, command, commandment, mandate, proclamation, dictum, fiat; law, statute, act; formal ordinance. **2** *a court decree* JUDGEMENT, verdict, adjudication, ruling, resolution, decision.
● verb *he decreed that a stadium should be built* ORDER, command, rule, dictate, pronounce, proclaim, ordain; direct, decide, determine.

decrepit ● adjective **1** *a decrepit old man* FEEBLE, infirm, weak, weakly, frail; disabled, incapacitated, crippled, doddering, tottering; old, elderly, aged, ancient, senile; informal past it, over the hill, no spring chicken. **2** *a decrepit house* DILAPIDATED, rickety, run down, tumbledown, ramshackle, derelict, ruined, in (a state of) disrepair, gone to rack and ruin; battered, decayed, crumbling, deteriorating.
– OPPOSITES strong, sound.

decry ● verb DENOUNCE, condemn, criticize, censure, attack, rail against, run down, pillory, lambaste, vilify, revile; disparage, deprecate, cast aspersions on; informal slam, blast, knock; Brit. informal slate.
– OPPOSITES praise.

dedicate ● verb **1** *she dedicated her life to the sick* DEVOTE, commit, pledge, give, surrender, sacrifice; set aside, allocate, consign. **2** *a book dedicated to a noblewoman* INSCRIBE, address; assign. **3** *the chapel was dedicated to the Virgin Mary* DEVOTE, assign; bless, consecrate, sanctify; formal hallow.

dedicated ● adjective **1** *a dedicated socialist* COMMITTED, devoted, staunch, firm, steadfast, resolute, unwavering, loyal, faithful, true, dyed-in-the-wool; wholehearted, single-minded, enthusiastic, keen, earnest, zealous, ardent, passionate, fervent; informal card-carrying, deep-dyed. **2** *data is accessed by a dedicated machine* EXCLUSIVE, custom built, customized.
– OPPOSITES indifferent.

dedication ● noun **1** *sport requires dedication* COMMITMENT, application, diligence, industry, resolve, enthusiasm, zeal, conscientiousness, perseverance, persistence, tenacity, drive, staying power; hard work, effort. **2** *her dedication to the job* DEVOTION, commitment, loyalty, adherence, allegiance. **3** *the book has a dedication to his wife* INSCRIPTION, address, message. **4** *the dedication of the church* BLESSING, consecration, sanctification, benediction.
– OPPOSITES apathy.

deduce ● verb CONCLUDE, reason, work out, infer; glean, divine, intuit, understand, assume, presume, conjecture, surmise, reckon; informal figure out; Brit. informal suss out.

deduct ● verb SUBTRACT, take away, take off, debit, dock, discount; abstract, remove; informal knock off.
– OPPOSITES add.

deduction ● noun **1** *the deduction of tax* SUBTRACTION, removal, debit, abstraction. **2** *gross pay, before deductions* STOPPAGE, subtraction. **3** *she was right in her deduction* CONCLUSION, inference, supposition, hypothesis, assumption, presumption; suspicion, conviction, belief, reasoning.

deed ● noun **1** *knightly deeds* ACT, action; feat, exploit, achievement, accomplishment, endeavour, undertaking, enterprise. **2** *unity must be established in deed and word* FACT, reality, actuality. **3** *mortgage deeds* LEGAL DOCUMENT, contract, indenture, instrument.

deem ● verb CONSIDER, regard as, judge, adjudge, hold to be, view as, see as, take for, class as, count, find, esteem, suppose, reckon; think, believe, feel.

deep ● adjective **1** *a deep ravine* CAVERNOUS, yawning, gaping, huge, extensive; bottomless, fathomless, unfathomable; archaic profound. **2** *two inches deep* IN DEPTH, downwards, inwards, in vertical ex-

deepen ● verb make or become deep or deeper.
deep freeze ● noun (also **deep freezer**) a freezer. ● verb (**deep-freeze**) store in or freeze using a deep freeze.
deep-fry ● verb fry (food) in an amount of fat or oil sufficient to cover it completely.
deeply ● adverb **1** far down or in. **2** intensely.
deep-seated (also **deep-rooted**) ● adjective firmly established.
deep space ● noun outer space.
deer ● noun (pl. same) a hoofed grazing or browsing animal, the male of which usually has branched bony antlers that are shed annually.
– ORIGIN Old English, originally also denoting any quadruped.
deerhound ● noun a large rough-haired breed of dog resembling the greyhound.
deerstalker ● noun a soft cloth cap, originally worn for hunting, with peaks in front and behind and ear flaps which can be tied together over the top.
de-escalate ● verb reduce the intensity of (a conflict or crisis).
– DERIVATIVES **de-escalation** noun.
def ● adjective black slang excellent.
– ORIGIN an alteration of DEATH, or shortened from DEFINITIVE or DEFINITE.
deface ● verb spoil the surface or appearance of.
– DERIVATIVES **defacement** noun.
de facto /day faktō/ ● adverb in fact, whether by right or not. Often contrasted with DE JURE. ● adjective existing in fact: *a de facto one-party system.*
– ORIGIN Latin, 'of fact'.
defalcate /deefalkayt/ ● verb formal embezzle (funds).
– DERIVATIVES **defalcation** noun.
– ORIGIN originally in the sense 'deduct, subtract': from Latin *defalcare* 'to lop'.
defame ● verb damage the good reputation of.
– DERIVATIVES **defamation** noun **defamatory** adjective.
– ORIGIN Latin *diffamare* 'spread evil report', from *fama* 'report'.
default ● noun **1** failure to fulfil an obligation, especially to repay a loan or appear in a law court. **2** a pre-selected option adopted by a computer program or other mechanism when no alternative is specified. ● verb **1** fail to fulfil an obligation, especially to repay a loan or to appear in court. **2** (**default to**) revert automatically to (a pre-selected option).
– PHRASES **by default** because of a lack of opposition or positive action. **in default of** in the absence of.
– ORIGIN from Old French *defaillir* 'to fail', from Latin *fallere* 'disappoint, deceive'.
defaulter ● noun **1** a person who defaults. **2** chiefly Brit. a member of the armed forces guilty of a military offence.
defeasible /difeezib'l/ ● adjective Law & Philosophy open to revision, valid objection, forfeiture, or annulment.
defeat ● verb **1** win a victory over. **2** prevent from achieving an aim or prevent (an aim) from being achieved. **3** reject or block (a proposal or motion). ● noun an instance of defeating or the state of being defeated.
– ORIGIN Old French *desfaire*, from Latin *disfacere* 'undo'.
defeatist ● noun a person who gives in to failure too readily. ● adjective showing ready acceptance of failure.
– DERIVATIVES **defeatism** noun.
defecate /deffikayt/ ● verb discharge faeces from the body.
– DERIVATIVES **defecation** noun **defecatory** adjective.
– ORIGIN Latin *defaecare*, from *faex* 'dregs'.
defect[1] /deefekt/ ● noun a shortcoming, imperfection, or lack.
– ORIGIN Latin *defectus*, from *deficere* 'desert or fail'.
defect[2] /difekt/ ● verb abandon one's country or cause in favour of an opposing one.
– DERIVATIVES **defection** noun **defector** noun.
– ORIGIN Latin *deficere* (see DEFECT[1]).

Thesaurus

tent. **3** *deep affection* INTENSE, heartfelt, wholehearted, deep-seated, deep-rooted; sincere, genuine, earnest, enthusiastic, great. **4** *a deep sleep* SOUND, heavy, intense. **5** *a deep thinker* PROFOUND, serious, philosophical, complex, weighty; abstruse, esoteric, recondite, mysterious, obscure; intelligent, intellectual, learned, wise, scholarly; discerning, penetrating, perceptive, insightful. **6** *he was deep in concentration* RAPT, absorbed, engrossed, preoccupied, immersed, lost, gripped, intent, engaged. **7** *a deep mystery* OBSCURE, mysterious, secret, unfathomable, opaque, abstruse, recondite, esoteric, enigmatic, arcane; puzzling, baffling, mystifying, inexplicable. **8** *his deep voice* LOW-PITCHED, low, bass, rich, powerful, resonant, booming, sonorous. **9** *a deep red* DARK, intense, rich, strong, bold, warm.
– OPPOSITES shallow, superficial, high, light.
● noun **1** (poetic/literary) *creatures of the deep* THE SEA, the ocean; informal the drink; Brit. informal the briny; poetic/literary the profound. **2** *the deep of night* THE MIDDLE, the midst; the depths, the dead, the thick.
● adverb **1** *I dug deep* FAR DOWN, way down, to a great depth. **2** *he brought them deep into woodland* FAR, a long way, a great distance.
deepen ● verb **1** *his love for her had deepened* GROW, increase, intensify, strengthen, heighten, amplify, augment; informal step up; Brit. informal hot up. **2** *they deepened the hole* DIG OUT, dig deeper, excavate.
deeply ● adverb PROFOUNDLY, greatly, enormously, extremely, very much; strongly, powerfully, intensely, keenly, acutely; thoroughly, completely, entirely; informal well, seriously, majorly.
deep-rooted ● adjective DEEP-SEATED, deep, profound, fundamental, basic; established, ingrained, entrenched, unshakeable, inveterate, inbuilt; secure; persistent, abiding, lingering.
– OPPOSITES superficial.
deep-seated ● adjective. See DEEP-ROOTED.
deface ● verb VANDALIZE, disfigure, mar, spoil, ruin, sully, damage, blight, impair; N. Amer. informal trash.
de facto ● adverb *the republic is de facto two states* IN PRACTICE, in effect, in fact, in reality, really, actually.
– OPPOSITES de jure.
● adjective *de facto control* ACTUAL, real, effective.
– OPPOSITES de jure.
defamation ● noun LIBEL, slander, calumny, character assassination, vilification; scandalmongering, malicious gossip, aspersions, muckraking, abuse; disparagement, denigration; smear, slur; informal mud-slinging.
defamatory ● adjective LIBELLOUS, slanderous, calumnious, calumniatory, scandalmongering, malicious, vicious, backbiting, muckraking; abusive, disparaging, denigratory, insulting; informal mudslinging, bitchy, catty.
defame ● verb LIBEL, slander, malign, cast aspersions on, smear, traduce, give someone a bad name, run down, speak ill of, vilify, besmirch, stigmatize, disparage, denigrate, discredit, decry; informal do a hatchet job on, drag through the mud; N. Amer. slur; informal bad-mouth; Brit. informal slag off; formal calumniate.
– OPPOSITES compliment.
default ● noun **1** *the incidence of defaults on loans* NON-PAYMENT, failure to pay, non-remittance. **2** *I became a teacher by default* INACTION, omission, lapse, neglect, negligence, disregard; absence, non-appearance.
● verb **1** *the customer defaulted* FAIL TO PAY, not pay, renege, back out; go back on one's word; informal welsh, bilk. **2** *the program will default to its own style* REVERT, select automatically.
defaulter ● noun **1** *a mortgage defaulter* NON-PAYER, debt-dodger; tax-dodger; N. Amer. delinquent. **2** (Brit. Military) *the defaulters' room* OFFENDER, wrongdoer, felon, delinquent.
defeat ● verb **1** *the army which defeated the Scots* BEAT, conquer, win against, triumph over, get the better of, vanquish; rout, trounce, overcome, overpower, crush, subdue; informal lick, thrash, whip, wipe the floor with, make mincemeat of, clobber, slaughter, demolish, cane; Brit. informal stuff; N. Amer. informal cream, skunk. **2** *these complex plans defeat their purpose* THWART, frustrate, foil, ruin, scotch, debar, snooker, derail; obstruct, impede, hinder, hamper; informal put the kibosh on, put paid to, stymie; Brit. informal scupper, nobble. **3** *the motion was defeated* REJECT, overthrow, throw out, dismiss, outvote, turn down; informal give the thumbs down. **4** *how to make it work defeats me* BAFFLE, perplex, bewilder, mystify, bemuse, confuse, confound, throw; informal beat, flummox, faze, stump, fox.
● noun **1** *a crippling defeat* LOSS, conquest, vanquishment; rout, trouncing; downfall; informal thrashing, hiding, drubbing, licking, pasting, massacre, slaughter. **2** *the defeat of his plans* FAILURE, downfall, collapse, ruin; rejection, frustration, abortion, miscarriage; undoing, reverse.
– OPPOSITES victory, success.
defeatist ● adjective *a defeatist attitude* PESSIMISTIC, fatalistic, negative, cynical, despondent, despairing, hopeless, bleak, gloomy.
– OPPOSITES optimistic.
● noun PESSIMIST, fatalist, cynic, prophet of doom; misery, killjoy, worrier; informal quitter, doomster, wet blanket.
– OPPOSITES optimist.

defective ● adjective **1** imperfect or faulty. **2** lacking or deficient.
– DERIVATIVES **defectively** adverb **defectiveness** noun.
defence (US **defense**) ● noun **1** the action of defending from or resisting attack. **2** military measures or resources for protecting a country. **3** (**defences**) fortifications against attack. **4** attempted justification or vindication. **5** the case presented by or on behalf of the party being accused or sued in a lawsuit. **6** (**the defence**) the counsel for the defendant in a lawsuit. **7** (in sport) the action of defending one's goal or wicket, or the players in a team who perform this role.
defenceless (US **defenseless**) ● adjective without defence or protection; completely vulnerable.
– DERIVATIVES **defencelessness** noun.
defend ● verb **1** resist an attack on; protect from harm or danger. **2** conduct the case for (the party being accused or sued) in a lawsuit. **3** attempt to justify. **4** compete to retain (a title or seat) in a contest or election. **5** (in sport) protect one's goal or wicket rather than attempt to score against one's opponents.
– DERIVATIVES **defendable** adjective **defender** noun.
– ORIGIN Latin *defendere* 'ward off, defend'.
defendant ● noun a person sued or accused in a court of law. Compare with PLAINTIFF.
defenestration /deefenistraysh'n/ ● noun formal or humorous the action of throwing someone out of a window.
– DERIVATIVES **defenestrate** verb.
– ORIGIN Latin, from *fenestra* 'window'.
defensible ● adjective **1** justifiable by argument. **2** able to be defended or protected.
– DERIVATIVES **defensibility** noun **defensibly** adverb.
defensive ● adjective **1** used or intended to defend or protect. **2** very anxious to challenge or avoid criticism.
– PHRASES **on the defensive** expecting or resisting criticism or attack.
– DERIVATIVES **defensively** adverb **defensiveness** noun.
defer[1] /difer/ ● verb (**deferred**, **deferring**) put off to a later time; postpone.
– DERIVATIVES **deferment** noun **deferral** noun.
– ORIGIN Latin *differre*, from *ferre* 'bring, carry'.
defer[2] /difer/ ● verb (**deferred**, **deferring**) (**defer to**) submit humbly to.
– ORIGIN Latin *deferre* 'carry away, refer'.
deference ● noun humble submission and respect.
deferential ● adjective showing deference; respectful.
– DERIVATIVES **deferentially** adverb.
defiance ● noun open resistance; bold disobedience.
– ORIGIN Old French, from *defier* 'defy'.
defiant ● adjective showing defiance.
– DERIVATIVES **defiantly** adverb.
defibrillation /deefibrilaysh'n/ ● noun Medicine the stopping of fibrillation of the heart by administering a controlled electric shock.
– DERIVATIVES **defibrillate** verb **defibrillator** noun.
deficiency ● noun (pl. **deficiencies**) **1** a lack or shortage. **2** a failing or shortcoming.
deficiency disease ● noun a disease caused by the lack of some essential element in the diet.
deficient /difish'nt/ ● adjective **1** not having enough of a

d

Thesaurus

defecate ● verb EXCRETE (FAECES), have a bowel movement, evacuate one's bowels, void excrement, relieve oneself, go to the lavatory; *informal* do number two, do a pooh.
defect[1] ● noun *he spotted a defect in my work* FAULT, flaw, imperfection, deficiency, weakness, weak spot, inadequacy, shortcoming, limitation, failing; kink, deformity, blemish; mistake, error; *informal* glitch, gremlin; *Computing* bug, virus.
defect[2] ● verb *his chief intelligence officer defected* DESERT, change sides, turn traitor, rebel, renege; abscond, quit, escape; break faith; secede from, revolt against; *informal* rat on; *Military* go AWOL; *poetic/literary* forsake; *rare* tergiversate.
defection ● noun DESERTION, absconding, decamping, flight; apostasy, secession; treason, betrayal, disloyalty; *poetic/literary* perfidy; *rare* tergiversation.
defective ● adjective **1** *a defective seat belt* FAULTY, flawed, imperfect, shoddy, inoperative, malfunctioning, out of order, unsound; in disrepair, broken; *informal* on the blink; *Brit. informal* knackered, duff. **2** *these methods are defective* LACKING, wanting, deficient, inadequate, insufficient. **3** *(dated) a mentally defective child* IMPAIRED, slow, simple, backward, retarded; *dated* deficient, subnormal, educationally subnormal, ESN.
– OPPOSITES perfect.
defector ● noun DESERTER, turncoat, traitor, renegade, Judas, quisling; *informal* rat; *rare* tergiversator.
defence ● noun **1** *the defence of the fortress* PROTECTION, guarding, security, fortification; resistance, deterrent. **2** *the enemy's defences* BARRICADE, fortification; fortress, keep, rampart, bulwark, bastion. **3** *he spoke in defence of his boss* VINDICATION, justification, support, advocacy, endorsement; apology, explanation, exoneration. **4** *more spending on defence* ARMAMENTS, weapons, weaponry, arms; the military, the armed forces. **5** *the prisoner's defence* VINDICATION, explanation, mitigation, justification, rationalization, excuse, alibi, reason; plea, pleading; testimony, declaration, case.
defenceless ● adjective **1** *defenceless animals* VULNERABLE, helpless, powerless, impotent, weak, susceptible. **2** *the country is wholly defenceless* UNDEFENDED, unprotected, unguarded, unshielded, unarmed; vulnerable, assailable, exposed, insecure, pregnable.
– OPPOSITES resilient.
defend ● verb **1** *a fort built to defend Ireland* PROTECT, guard, safeguard, secure, shield; fortify, garrison, barricade; uphold, support, watch over. **2** *he defended his policy* JUSTIFY, vindicate, argue for, support, make a case for, plead for; excuse, explain. **3** *the manager defended his players* SUPPORT, back, stand by, stick up for, stand up for, argue for, champion, endorse; *informal* throw one's weight behind.
– OPPOSITES attack, criticize.
defendant ● noun ACCUSED, prisoner (at the bar); appellant, litigant, respondent; suspect.
– OPPOSITES plaintiff.
defender ● noun **1** *defenders of the environment* PROTECTOR, guard, guardian, preserver; custodian, watchdog, keeper, overseer, superintendent, caretaker. **2** *a defender of colonialism* SUPPORTER, upholder, backer, champion, advocate, apologist, proponent, exponent, promoter; adherent, believer. **3** *he passed two defenders and scored* FULLBACK, back, sweeper; (**defenders**) back four.
defensible ● adjective **1** *a defensible attitude* JUSTIFIABLE, arguable, tenable, defendable, supportable; plausible, sound, sensible, reasonable, rational, logical; acceptable, valid, legitimate; excusable, pardonable, understandable. **2** *a defensible territory* SECURE, safe, fortified; invulnerable, impregnable, impenetrable, unassailable.
– OPPOSITES untenable, vulnerable.
defensive ● adjective **1** *troops in defensive positions* DEFENDING, protective; wary, watchful. **2** *a defensive response* SELF-JUSTIFYING, oversensitive, thin-skinned, prickly, paranoid, neurotic; *informal* uptight, twitchy.
defer[1] ● verb *the committee will defer their decision* POSTPONE, put off, delay, hold over/off, put back; shelve, suspend, stay, mothball; *N. Amer.* put over, table, take a rain check on; *informal* put on ice, put on the back burner, put in cold storage.
defer[2] ● verb *they deferred to Joseph's judgement* YIELD, submit, give way, give in, surrender, capitulate, acquiesce; respect, honour.
deference ● noun RESPECT, respectfulness, dutifulness; submissiveness, submission, obedience, surrender, accession, capitulation, acquiescence, complaisance, obeisance.
– OPPOSITES disrespect.
deferential ● adjective RESPECTFUL, humble, obsequious; dutiful, obedient, submissive, subservient, yielding, acquiescent, complaisant, compliant, tractable, biddable, docile.
deferment ● noun POSTPONEMENT, deferral, suspension, delay, adjournment, interruption, pause; respite, stay, moratorium, reprieve, grace.
defiance ● noun RESISTANCE, opposition, non-compliance, disobedience, insubordination, dissent, recalcitrance, subversion, rebellion; contempt, disregard, scorn, insolence, truculence.
– OPPOSITES obedience.
defiant ● adjective INTRANSIGENT, resistant, obstinate, uncooperative, non-compliant, recalcitrant; obstreperous, truculent, dissenting, disobedient, insubordinate, subversive, rebellious, mutinous; *informal* feisty; *Brit. informal* stroppy, bolshie.
– OPPOSITES cooperative.
deficiency ● noun **1** *a vitamin deficiency* INSUFFICIENCY, lack, shortage, want, dearth, inadequacy, deficit, shortfall; scarcity, paucity, absence, undersupply, deprivation, shortness. **2** *the team's big deficiency* DEFECT, fault, flaw, imperfection, weakness, weak point,

specified quality or ingredient. **2** insufficient or inadequate.
– ORIGIN Latin, from *deficere* 'fail'.
deficit /deffisit/ ● noun **1** the amount by which something, especially a sum of money, falls short. **2** an excess of expenditure or liabilities over income or assets.
– ORIGIN Latin, 'it is lacking'.
defilade /deffilayd/ ● noun Military protection against enemy observation or gunfire.
– ORIGIN from French *défiler* 'protect from the enemy'.
defile[1] /difīl/ ● verb **1** make dirty; spoil or pollute. **2** desecrate.
– DERIVATIVES **defilement** noun **defiler** noun.
– ORIGIN alteration of obsolete *defoul*, from Old French *defouler* 'trample down'.
defile[2] /difīl/ ● noun a steep-sided narrow gorge or passage (originally one requiring troops to march in single file).
– ORIGIN French, from *file* 'column, file'.
define ● verb **1** state or describe the exact nature or scope of. **2** give the meaning of (a word or phrase). **3** mark out the limits or outline of.
– DERIVATIVES **definable** adjective **definer** noun.
– ORIGIN Latin *definire*, from *finire* 'finish'.
definite ● adjective **1** clearly stated or decided; not vague or doubtful. **2** (of a person) certain or sure about something. **3** known to be true or real. **4** having exact and discernible physical limits.
– DERIVATIVES **definiteness** noun.
definite article ● noun Grammar a determiner (*the* in English) that introduces a noun and implies that the thing mentioned has already been mentioned, is common knowledge, or is about to be defined.
definitely ● adverb without doubt; certainly .
definition ● noun **1** a statement of the exact meaning of a word or the nature or scope of something. **2** the action or process of defining. **3** the degree of distinctness in outline of an object or image.
– PHRASES **by definition** by its very nature; intrinsically.
– DERIVATIVES **definitional** adjective.
definitive ● adjective **1** (of a conclusion or agreement) decisive and with authority. **2** (of a book or other text) the most authoritative of its kind. **3** (of a postage stamp) for general use, not special or commemorative.
– DERIVATIVES **definitively** adverb.
deflate ● verb **1** let air or gas out of (a tyre, balloon, etc.). **2** cause to feel suddenly dispirited. **3** reduce price levels in (an economy).
– DERIVATIVES **deflator** noun.
deflation ● noun **1** the action or process of deflating or being deflated. **2** reduction of the general level of prices in an economy.
– DERIVATIVES **deflationary** adjective.
deflect ● verb turn aside from from a straight course or intended purpose.
– DERIVATIVES **deflective** adjective **deflector** noun.
– ORIGIN Latin *deflectere*, from *flectere* 'to bend'.
deflection (also **deflexion**) ● noun the action or process of deflecting or being deflected.
defloration /deefloraysh'n/ ● noun dated or literary the taking of a woman's virginity.
deflower ● verb dated or literary deprive (a woman) of her virginity.
defoliant ● noun a chemical used to remove the leaves from trees and plants.
defoliate /deefōliayt/ ● verb remove leaves or foliage from (trees or plants).
– DERIVATIVES **defoliation** noun.
– ORIGIN Latin *defoliare*, from *folium* 'leaf'.
deforest ● verb clear of forest or trees.
– DERIVATIVES **deforestation** noun.
deform ● verb distort the shape or form of; make misshapen.
– DERIVATIVES **deformable** adjective **deformation** noun.
deformed ● adjective misshapen; distorted.
deformity ● noun (pl. **deformities**) **1** a deformed part, especially of the body. **2** the state of being deformed.
defraud ● verb illegally obtain money from (someone) by deception.
– DERIVATIVES **defrauder** noun.
– ORIGIN Latin *defraudare*, from *fraudare* 'to cheat'.
defray ● verb provide money to pay (a cost).
– DERIVATIVES **defrayal** noun.
– ORIGIN French *défrayer*, from obsolete *frai* 'cost, expenses'.

Thesaurus

inadequacy, shortcoming, limitation, failing.
– OPPOSITES surplus, strength.
deficient ● adjective **1** *a diet deficient in vitamin A* LACKING, wanting, inadequate, insufficient, limited, poor, scant; short of/on, low on. **2** *deficient leadership* DEFECTIVE, faulty, flawed, inadequate, imperfect, shoddy, weak, inferior, unsound, substandard, second-rate, poor; Brit. informal duff.
deficit ● noun SHORTFALL, deficiency, shortage, undersupply; debt, arrears; negative amount, loss.
– OPPOSITES surplus.
defile ● verb **1** *her capacity for love had been defiled* SPOIL, sully, mar, impair, debase, degrade; poison, taint, tarnish; destroy, ruin. **2** *the sacred bones were defiled* DESECRATE, profane, violate; contaminate, pollute, debase, degrade, dishonour. **3** (archaic) *she was defiled by a married man* RAPE, violate; poetic/literary ravish; dated deflower.
definable ● adjective DETERMINABLE, ascertainable, known, definite, clear-cut, precise, exact, specific.
define ● verb **1** *the dictionary defines it succinctly* EXPLAIN, expound, interpret, elucidate, describe, clarify; give the meaning of, put into words. **2** *he defined the limits of the middle class* DETERMINE, establish, fix, specify, designate, decide, stipulate, set out; demarcate, delineate. **3** *the farm buildings defined against the fields* OUTLINE, delineate, silhouette.
definite ● adjective **1** *a definite answer* EXPLICIT, specific, express, precise, exact, clear-cut, direct, plain, outright; fixed, established, confirmed, concrete. **2** *definite evidence* CERTAIN, sure, positive, conclusive, decisive, firm, concrete, unambiguous, unequivocal, clear, unmistakable, proven; guaranteed, assured, cut and dried. **3** *she had a definite dislike for Robert* UNMISTAKABLE, unequivocal, unambiguous, certain, undisputed, decided, marked, distinct. **4** *a definite geographical area* FIXED, marked, demarcated, delimited, stipulated, particular.
– OPPOSITES vague, ambiguous, indeterminate.
definitely ● adverb CERTAINLY, surely, for sure, unquestionably, without doubt, without question, undoubtedly, indubitably, positively, absolutely; undeniably, unmistakably, plainly, clearly, obviously, patently, palpably, transparently, unequivocally, as sure as eggs is eggs.
definition ● noun **1** *the definition of 'intelligence'* MEANING, denotation, sense; interpretation, explanation, elucidation, description, clarification, illustration. **2** *the definition of the picture* CLARITY, visibility, sharpness, crispness, acuteness; resolution, focus, contrast.
definitive ● adjective **1** *a definitive decision* CONCLUSIVE, final, ultimate; unconditional, unqualified, absolute, categorical, positive, definite. **2** *the definitive guide* AUTHORITATIVE, exhaustive, best, finest, consummate; classic, standard, recognized, accepted, official.
deflate ● verb **1** *he deflated the tyres* LET DOWN, flatten, void; puncture. **2** *the balloon deflated* GO DOWN, collapse, shrink, contract. **3** *the news had deflated him* SUBDUE, humble, cow, chasten; dispirit, dismay, discourage, dishearten; squash, crush, bring down, take the wind out of someone's sails; informal knock the stuffing out of. **4** *the budget deflated the economy* REDUCE, slow down, diminish; devalue, depreciate, depress.
– OPPOSITES inflate.
deflect ● verb **1** *she wanted to deflect attention from herself* TURN ASIDE/AWAY, divert, avert, sidetrack; distract, draw away; block, parry, fend off, stave off. **2** *the ball deflected off the wall* BOUNCE, glance, ricochet; diverge, deviate, veer, swerve, slew.
deform ● verb DISFIGURE, bend out of shape, contort, buckle, warp; damage, impair.
deformed ● adjective MISSHAPEN, distorted, malformed, contorted, out of shape; twisted, crooked, warped, buckled, gnarled; crippled, humpbacked, hunchbacked, disfigured, grotesque; injured, damaged, mutilated, mangled.
deformity ● noun MALFORMATION, misshapenness, distortion, crookedness; imperfection, abnormality, irregularity; disfigurement; defect, flaw, blemish.
defraud ● verb SWINDLE, cheat, rob; deceive, dupe, hoodwink, double-cross, trick; informal con, do, sting, diddle, rip off, shaft, bilk, rook, gyp, pull a fast one on, put one over on, sell a pup to; N. Amer. informal sucker, snooker, stiff; Austral. informal pull a swifty

defrock • verb deprive (a person in holy orders) of ecclesiastical status.
defrost • verb **1** free of accumulated ice. **2** thaw (frozen food).
deft • adjective quick and neatly skilful.
– DERIVATIVES **deftly** adverb **deftness** noun.
– ORIGIN variant of DAFT, in the obsolete sense 'meek'.
defunct /difungkt/ • adjective no longer existing or functioning.
– ORIGIN Latin *defunctus* 'dead', from *defungi* 'carry out, finish'.
defuse • verb **1** remove the fuse from (an explosive device) in order to prevent it from exploding. **2** reduce the danger or tension in (a difficult situation).
– USAGE The verbs **defuse** and **diffuse** have different meanings but are often confused. **Defuse** means 'reduce the danger or tension in', while **diffuse** means 'spread over a wide area'.
defy • verb (**defies, defied**) **1** openly resist or refuse to obey. **2** challenge to do or prove something.
– DERIVATIVES **defier** noun.
– ORIGIN Old French *desfier*, from Latin *fidus* 'faithful'.
dégagé /daygaazhay/ • adjective unconcerned or unconstrained.
– ORIGIN French, 'set free'.
degauss /deegowss/ • verb Physics remove unwanted magnetism from.
– ORIGIN named after the German physicist Karl Friedrich *Gauss* (1777–1855).
degenerate • adjective /dijennərət/ having lost normal and desirable qualities; showing evidence of moral or physical decline. • noun /dijennərət/ a morally degenerate person. • verb /dijennərayt/ deteriorate physically or morally.
– DERIVATIVES **degeneracy** noun **degenerately** adverb **degeneration** noun.
– ORIGIN Latin *degeneratus* 'no longer of its kind', from *genus* 'race, kind'.
degenerative • adjective (of a disease) characterized by progressive deterioration.
deglaze • verb dilute meat sediments in (a pan) to make a gravy or sauce.
degradation /degrədaysh'n/ • noun **1** the condition or process of degrading or being degraded. **2** Geology the wearing down of rock by disintegration.
degrade • verb **1** cause (someone) to suffer a loss of dignity or self-respect. **2** lower the character or quality of. **3** archaic reduce to a lower rank. **4** cause to break down or deteriorate chemically. **5** Physics reduce (energy) to a less readily convertible form.
– DERIVATIVES **degradable** adjective **degradative** adjective.
degrading • adjective causing a loss of self-respect; humiliating.
degree • noun **1** the amount, level, or extent to which something happens or is present. **2** a unit of measurement of angles, equivalent to one ninetieth of a right angle. **3** a unit in a scale of temperature, intensity, hardness, etc. **4** an academic rank conferred by a college or university after examination or completion of a course. **5** each of a set of grades (usually three) used to classify burns according to their severity. **6** chiefly N. Amer. a legal grade of crime, especially murder. **7** a step in direct genealogical descent. **8** archaic social or official rank.
– PHRASES **by degrees** gradually. **to a degree 1** to some extent. **2** dated to a considerable extent.
– ORIGIN Old French, from Latin *gradus* 'grade'.
de haut en bas /də ōt ON baa/ • adverb & adjective in a condescending or superior manner.
– ORIGIN French, 'from above to below'.
dehisce /dihiss/ • verb technical gape or burst open.
– DERIVATIVES **dehiscence** noun **dehiscent** adjective.
– ORIGIN Latin *dehiscere*, from *hiscere* 'begin to gape'.
dehumanize (also **dehumanise**) • verb deprive of positive human qualities.
– DERIVATIVES **dehumanization** noun.
dehumidify • verb (**dehumidifies, dehumidified**) remove moisture from (the air or a gas).
– DERIVATIVES **dehumidification** noun **dehumidifier** noun.
dehydrate /deehīdrayt, -hīdrayt/ • verb **1** cause (someone) to lose a large amount of water from their body. **2** remove water from (food) in order to preserve it.
– DERIVATIVES **dehydration** noun.
– ORIGIN from Greek *hudros* 'water'.
de-ice • verb remove ice from.
– DERIVATIVES **de-icer** noun.
deicide /deeisīd, day-/ • noun the killing of a god.
deify /deeifī, day-/ • verb (**deifies, deified**) make into or worship as a god.
– DERIVATIVES **deification** noun.
– ORIGIN Latin *deificare*, from *deus* 'god'.
deign /dayn/ • verb (**deign to do**) do something that one considers to be beneath one's dignity.
– ORIGIN Latin *dignare* 'deem worthy', from *dignus* 'worthy'.

d

Thesaurus

on.
defray • verb PAY (FOR), cover, meet, square, settle, clear, discharge; foot the bill for; N. Amer. informal pick up the tab for.
deft • adjective SKILFUL, adept, adroit, dexterous, agile, nimble, handy; able, capable, skilled, proficient, accomplished, expert, polished, slick, professional, masterly; clever, shrewd, astute, canny, sharp; informal nifty, nippy.
– OPPOSITES clumsy.
defunct • adjective DISUSED, unused, inoperative, non-functioning, unusable, obsolete; no longer existing, discontinued; extinct.
– OPPOSITES working, extant.
defuse • verb **1** *he tried to defuse the grenade* DEACTIVATE, disarm, disable, make safe. **2** *an attempt to defuse the tension* REDUCE, lessen, diminish, lighten, relieve, ease, alleviate, moderate, mitigate.
– OPPOSITES activate, intensify.
defy • verb **1** *he defied European law* DISOBEY, go against, flout, fly in the face of, disregard, ignore; break, violate, contravene, breach, infringe; informal cock a snook at. **2** *his actions defy belief* ELUDE, escape, defeat; frustrate, thwart, baffle. **3** *he glowered, defying her to mock him* CHALLENGE, dare.
– OPPOSITES obey.
degeneracy • noun CORRUPTION, decadence, moral decay, dissipation, dissolution, profligacy, vice, immorality, sin, sinfulness, ungodliness; debauchery; formal turpitude.
degenerate • adjective **1** *a degenerate form of classicism* DEBASED, degraded, corrupt, impure; formal vitiated. **2** *her degenerate brother* CORRUPT, decadent, dissolute, dissipated, debauched, reprobate, profligate, vice-ridden; sinful, ungodly, immoral, unprincipled, amoral, dishonourable, disreputable, unsavoury, sordid, low, ignoble.
– OPPOSITES pure, moral.
• noun *a group of degenerates* REPROBATE, debauchee, profligate, libertine, roué, loose-liver.
• verb **1** *their quality of life had degenerated* DETERIORATE, decline, slip, slide, worsen, lapse, slump, go downhill, regress, retrogress; go to rack and ruin; informal go to pot, go to the dogs, hit the skids, go down the toilet. **2** *the muscles started to degenerate* WASTE (AWAY), atrophy, weaken.
– OPPOSITES improve.
degradation • noun **1** *poverty brings with it degradation* HUMILIATION, shame, loss of self-respect, abasement, indignity, ignominy. **2** *the degradation of women* DEMEANING, debasement, discrediting. **3** *the degradation of the tissues* DETERIORATION, degeneration, atrophy, decay; breakdown.
degrade • verb **1** *prisons should not degrade prisoners* DEMEAN, debase, cheapen, devalue; shame, humiliate, humble, mortify, abase, dishonour; dehumanize, brutalize. **2** *the polymer will not degrade* BREAK DOWN, deteriorate, degenerate, decay.
– OPPOSITES dignify.
degraded • adjective **1** *I feel so degraded* HUMILIATED, demeaned, cheapened, cheap, ashamed. **2** *his degraded sensibilities* DEGENERATE, corrupt, depraved, dissolute, dissipated, debauched, immoral, base, sordid.
– OPPOSITES proud, moral.
degrading • adjective HUMILIATING, demeaning, shameful, mortifying, ignominious, undignified, inglorious, wretched; informal infra dig.
degree • noun LEVEL, standard, grade, mark; amount, extent, measure; magnitude, intensity, strength; proportion, ratio.
– PHRASES **by degrees** GRADUALLY, little by little, bit by bit, inch by inch, step by step, slowly; piecemeal. **to a degree** TO SOME EXTENT, to a certain extent, up to a point.
dehydrate • verb **1** *alcohol dehydrates the skin* DRY (OUT), desiccate, dehumidify, effloresce. **2** *frogs can dehydrate quickly* DRY UP/OUT, lose water.
– OPPOSITES hydrate.
deify • verb **1** *she was deified by the early Romans* WORSHIP, revere, venerate, reverence, hold sacred; immortalize. **2** *he was deified by the press* IDOLIZE, lionize, hero-worship, extol; idealize, glorify, aggrandize; informal put on a pedestal.

d

deindustrialization (also **deindustrialisation**) ● noun decline in industrial activity in a region or economy.
– DERIVATIVES **deindustrialized** adjective.
deinonychus /dīnonnikəss/ ● noun a fast-running predatory dinosaur of the mid Cretaceous period.
– ORIGIN from Greek *deinos* 'terrible' + *onux* 'claw'.
deism /deeiz'm, day-/ ● noun belief in the existence of a supreme being, specifically of a creator who does not intervene in the universe. Compare with THEISM.
– DERIVATIVES **deist** noun **deistic** adjective
deity /deeiti, day-/ ● noun (pl. **deities**) **1** a god or goddess. **2** divine status, quality, or nature.
– ORIGIN Latin *deitas*, from *deus* 'god'.
déjà vu /dayzhaa voo/ ● noun a feeling of having already experienced the present situation.
– ORIGIN French, 'already seen'.
dejected ● adjective sad and dispirited.
– DERIVATIVES **dejectedly** adverb.
dejection ● noun sadness or low sprits.
– ORIGIN Latin, from *deicere* 'throw down'.
de jure /day jooray/ ● adverb rightfully; by right. Often contrasted with DE FACTO. ● adjective rightful.
– ORIGIN Latin, 'of law'.
dekko /dekkō/ ● noun Brit. informal a quick look or glance.
– ORIGIN Hindi, 'look!'
Delaware /delləwair/ ● noun (pl. same or **Delawares**) a member of an American Indian people formerly inhabiting the Delaware River valley of New Jersey and eastern Pennsylvania.
delay ● verb **1** make late or slow. **2** loiter or hesitate. **3** postpone or defer. ● noun an instance of delaying or being delayed.
– ORIGIN Old French *delayer*.
dele /deeli/ ● noun a proofreader's sign (₰) indicating matter to be deleted. ● verb (**deled**, **deleing**) delete or mark for deletion.
– ORIGIN Latin, 'blot out! efface!'.
delectable ● adjective lovely, delightful, or delicious.
– DERIVATIVES **delectably** adverb.
delectation /deelektaysh'n/ ● noun chiefly humorous pleasure and delight.
– ORIGIN Latin, from *delectare* 'to charm'.
delegacy /delligəsi/ ● noun (pl. **delegacies**) a body of delegates; a committee or delegation.
delegate ● noun /delligət/ **1** a person sent to represent others, in particular at a conference. **2** a member of a committee. ● verb /delligayt/ **1** entrust (a task or responsibility) to another person. **2** authorize (someone) to act as a representative.
– DERIVATIVES **delegator** noun.
– ORIGIN from Latin *delegare* 'send away, assign'.
delegation ● noun **1** a body of delegates; a deputation. **2** the process of delegating or being delegated.
delete ● verb remove or erase (text).
– DERIVATIVES **deletion** noun.
– ORIGIN Latin *delere* 'to blot out'.
deleterious /delliteeriəss/ ● adjective causing harm or damage.
– DERIVATIVES **deleteriously** adverb.
– ORIGIN Greek *dēlētērios* 'noxious'.
delft /delft/ ● noun glazed earthenware, typically decorated in blue on a white background.
– ORIGIN named after the town of *Delft* in the Netherlands, where it originated.
deli ● noun (pl. **delis**) informal short for DELICATESSEN.
deliberate ● adjective /dilibbərət/ **1** done consciously and intentionally. **2** careful and unhurried. ● verb /dilibbərayt/ engage in long and careful consideration.
– DERIVATIVES **deliberately** adverb **deliberateness** noun.
– ORIGIN Latin *deliberare* 'consider carefully', from *librare* 'weigh'.
deliberation ● noun **1** long and careful consideration. **2** slow and careful movement or thought.
deliberative ● adjective relating to or involving consideration or discussion.

Thesaurus

– OPPOSITES demonize.
deign ● verb CONDESCEND, stoop, lower oneself, demean oneself, humble oneself; consent, vouchsafe; *informal* come down from one's high horse.
deity ● noun GOD, goddess, divine being, supreme being, divinity, immortal; creator, demiurge; godhead.
dejected ● adjective DOWNCAST, downhearted, despondent, disconsolate, dispirited, crestfallen, disheartened; depressed, crushed, desolate, heartbroken, in the doldrums, sad, unhappy, doleful, melancholy, miserable, woebegone, forlorn, fed up, wretched, glum, gloomy; *informal* blue, down in the mouth, down in the dumps; *Brit. informal* brassed off, cheesed off.
– OPPOSITES cheerful.
de jure ● adverb & adjective BY RIGHT, rightfully, legally, according to the law; rightful, legal.
– OPPOSITES de facto.
delay ● verb **1** *we were delayed by the traffic* DETAIN, hold up, make late, slow up/down, bog down; hinder, hamper, impede, obstruct. **2** *they delayed no longer* LINGER, dally, drag one's feet, be slow, hold back, dawdle, waste time; procrastinate, stall, hang fire, mark time, temporize, hesitate, dither, shilly-shally; *informal* dilly-dally; *archaic* tarry. **3** *he may delay the cut in interest rates* POSTPONE, put off, defer, hold over, shelve, suspend, stay; reschedule; *N. Amer.* put over, table; *informal* put on ice, put on the back burner, put in cold storage.
– OPPOSITES hurry, advance.
● noun **1** *drivers will face lengthy delays* HOLD-UP, wait, detainment; hindrance, impediment, obstruction, setback. **2** *the delay of his trial* POSTPONEMENT, deferral, deferment, stay, respite; adjournment. **3** *I set off without delay* PROCRASTINATION, stalling, hesitation, dithering, dallying, dawdling.
delectable ● adjective **1** *a delectable meal* DELICIOUS, mouthwatering, appetizing, flavoursome, flavourful, toothsome, palatable; succulent, luscious, tasty; *informal* scrumptious, delish, scrummy, yummy; *Brit. informal* moreish; *N. Amer. informal* finger-licking, nummy. **2** *the delectable Ms Davis* DELIGHTFUL, lovely, captivating, charming, enchanting, appealing, beguiling; beautiful, attractive, ravishing, gorgeous, stunning, alluring, sexy, seductive, desirable, luscious; *informal* divine, heavenly, dreamy; *Brit. informal* tasty.
– OPPOSITES unpalatable, unattractive.
delectation ● noun *(humorous)* ENJOYMENT, gratification, delight, pleasure, satisfaction, relish; entertainment, amusement, titillation.
delegate ● noun *trade union delegates* REPRESENTATIVE, envoy, emissary, commissioner, agent, deputy, commissary; spokesperson, spokesman/woman; ambassador, plenipotentiary.
● verb **1** *she must delegate routine tasks* ASSIGN, entrust, pass on, hand on/over, turn over, devolve, depute, transfer. **2** *they were delegated to negotiate with the States* AUTHORIZE, commission, depute, appoint, nominate, mandate, empower, charge, choose, designate, elect.
delegation ● noun **1** *the delegation from South Africa* DEPUTATION, delegacy, legation, (diplomatic) mission, commission; delegates, representatives, envoys, emissaries, deputies. **2** *the delegation of tasks to others* ASSIGNMENT, entrusting, giving, devolution, deputation, transference.
delete ● verb REMOVE, cut out, take out, edit out, expunge, excise, eradicate, cancel; cross out, strike out, blue-pencil, ink out, scratch out, obliterate, white out; rub out, erase, efface, wipe out, blot out; *Printing* dele.
– OPPOSITES add.
deleterious ● adjective HARMFUL, damaging, detrimental, injurious; bad, adverse, disadvantageous, unfavourable, unfortunate, undesirable.
– OPPOSITES beneficial.
deliberate ● adjective **1** *a deliberate attempt to provoke him* INTENTIONAL, calculated, conscious, intended, planned, studied, knowing, wilful, wanton, purposeful, purposive, premeditated, preplanned; voluntary, volitional; *Law, dated* prepense. **2** *small, deliberate steps* CAREFUL, cautious; measured, regular, even, steady. **3** *a deliberate worker* METHODICAL, systematic, careful, painstaking, meticulous, thorough.
– OPPOSITES accidental, hasty, careless.
● verb *she deliberated on his words* THINK ABOUT/OVER, ponder, consider, contemplate, reflect on, muse on, meditate on, ruminate on, mull over, give thought to, weigh up; brood over, dwell on; *N. Amer.* think on.
deliberately ● adverb **1** *he deliberately hurt me* INTENTIONALLY, on purpose, purposely, by design, knowingly, wittingly, consciously, purposefully; wilfully, wantonly; *Law* with malice aforethought. **2** *he walked deliberately down the aisle* CAREFULLY, cautiously, slowly, steadily, evenly.
deliberation ● noun **1** *after much deliberation, I accepted*

delicacy ● noun (pl. **delicacies**) **1** delicate texture or structure. **2** susceptibility to illness or adverse conditions. **3** discretion and tact. **4** a choice or expensive food.

delicate ● adjective **1** very fine in texture or structure. **2** easily broken or damaged; fragile. **3** susceptible to illness or adverse conditions. **4** requiring sensitive or careful handling. **5** skilful; deft. **6** (of food or drink) subtly and pleasantly flavoured.
– PHRASES **in a delicate condition** archaic, euphemistic pregnant.
– DERIVATIVES **delicately** adverb.
– ORIGIN originally in the sense 'delightful, charming': from Latin *delicatus*.

delicatessen /dellikətess'n/ ● noun a shop selling cooked meats, cheeses, and unusual or foreign prepared foods.
– ORIGIN German or Dutch, from French *délicatesse* 'delicacy'.

delicious ● adjective **1** highly pleasant to the taste. **2** delightful: *a delicious irony*.
– DERIVATIVES **deliciously** adverb **deliciousness** noun.
– ORIGIN Latin *deliciosus*, from *deliciae* 'delight, pleasure'.

delight ● verb **1** please greatly. **2** (**delight in**) take great pleasure in. ● noun **1** great pleasure. **2** a cause or source of great pleasure.
– ORIGIN Latin *delectare* 'to charm'.

delighted ● adjective feeling or showing great pleasure.
– DERIVATIVES **delightedly** adverb.

delightful ● adjective causing delight; very pleasing.
– DERIVATIVES **delightfully** adverb.

delimit /dilimmit/ ● verb (**delimited**, **delimiting**) determine the limits or boundaries of.
– DERIVATIVES **delimitation** noun **delimiter** noun.

delineate /dilinniayt/ ● verb describe or indicate precisely.
– DERIVATIVES **delineation** /dilinniaysh'n/ noun.
– ORIGIN Latin *delineare* 'to outline'.

delinquency ● noun (pl. **delinquencies**) **1** minor crime, especially that committed by young people. **2** formal neglect of one's duty. **3** chiefly US a failure to pay an outstanding debt.

delinquent /dilingkwənt/ ● adjective **1** (especially of young people) tending to commit crime. **2** formal failing in one's duty. **3** chiefly N. Amer. in arrears. ● noun a delinquent person.
– DERIVATIVES **delinquently** adverb.
– ORIGIN from Latin *delinquere* 'to offend'.

deliquesce /dellikwess/ ● verb **1** (of organic matter) become liquid, typically during decomposition. **2** Chemistry (of a solid) become liquid by absorbing moisture from the air.
– DERIVATIVES **deliquescence** noun **deliquescent** adjective.
– ORIGIN Latin *deliquescere* 'dissolve'.

delirious ● adjective **1** suffering from delirium. **2** extremely excited or happy.
– DERIVATIVES **deliriously** adverb.

delirium /dilirriəm/ ● noun an acutely disturbed state of mind characterized by restlessness, illusions, and incoherent thought and speech.
– ORIGIN Latin, from *delirare* 'deviate, be deranged' (literally 'deviate from the furrow').

delirium tremens /treemenz/ ● noun a condition typical of withdrawal in chronic alcoholics, involving tremors and hallucinations.
– ORIGIN Latin, 'trembling delirium'.

deliver ● verb **1** bring and hand over (a letter or goods) to the appropriate recipient. **2** provide (something promised or expected). **3** save or set free. **4** state or present in a formal manner. **5** assist in the birth of. **6** (also **be delivered of**) give birth to. **7** launch or aim (a blow or attack).
– PHRASES **deliver the goods** informal provide what is promised or expected.
– DERIVATIVES **deliverable** adjective **deliverer** noun.
– ORIGIN Old French *delivrer*, from Latin *liberare* 'set free'.

d

Thesaurus

THOUGHT, consideration, reflection, contemplation, meditation, rumination; *formal* cogitation. **2** *he replaced the glass with deliberation* CARE, carefulness, caution, steadiness.

delicacy ● noun **1** *the fabric's sheer delicacy* FINENESS, exquisiteness, delicateness, daintiness, airiness; flimsiness, gauziness, floatiness, silkiness. **2** *the children's delicacy* SICKLINESS, ill health, frailty, fragility, weakness, debility; infirmity, valetudinarianism. **3** *the delicacy of the situation* DIFFICULTY, trickiness; sensitivity, ticklishness, awkwardness. **4** *treat this matter with delicacy* CARE, sensitivity, tact, discretion, diplomacy, subtlety, sensibility. **5** *an Australian delicacy* CHOICE FOOD, gourmet food, dainty, treat, luxury, bonne bouche; speciality.

delicate ● adjective **1** *delicate embroidery* FINE, exquisite, intricate, dainty; flimsy, gauzy, filmy, floaty, diaphanous, wispy, insubstantial. **2** *a delicate shade of blue* SUBTLE, soft, muted; pastel, pale, light. **3** *delicate china cups* FRAGILE, breakable, frail; *formal* frangible. **4** *his wife is delicate* SICKLY, unhealthy, frail, feeble, weak, debilitated; unwell, infirm; *formal* valetudinarian. **5** *a delicate issue* DIFFICULT, tricky, sensitive, ticklish, awkward, problematical, touchy, prickly; embarrassing; *informal* sticky, dicey. **6** *the matter required delicate handling* CAREFUL, sensitive, tactful, diplomatic, discreet, kid-glove, softly-softly. **7** *his delicate palate* DISCRIMINATING, discerning; FASTIDIOUS, fussy, finicky, dainty; *informal* picky, choosy, pernickety. **8** *a delicate mechanism* SENSITIVE, precision, precise.
– OPPOSITES coarse, lurid, strong, robust, clumsy.

delicious ● adjective **1** *a delicious meal* DELECTABLE, mouthwatering, appetizing, tasty, flavoursome, flavourful, toothsome, palatable; succulent, luscious; *informal* scrumptious, delish, scrummy, yummy; *Brit. informal* moreish; *N. Amer. informal* finger-licking, nummy. **2** *a delicious languor stole over her* DELIGHTFUL, exquisite, lovely, pleasurable, pleasant; *informal* heavenly, divine.
– OPPOSITES unpalatable, unpleasant.

delight ● verb **1** *her manners delighted him* PLEASE GREATLY, charm, enchant, captivate, entrance, thrill; gladden, gratify, appeal to; entertain, amuse, divert; *informal* send, tickle pink, bowl over. **2** *Fabia delighted in his touch* TAKE PLEASURE, revel, luxuriate, wallow, glory; adore, love, relish, savour, lap up; *informal* get a kick out of, get a buzz out of, get a thrill out of, dig; *N. Amer. informal* get a charge out of.
– OPPOSITES dismay, disgust, dislike.
● noun *she squealed with delight* PLEASURE, happiness, joy, glee, gladness; excitement, amusement; bliss, rapture, elation, euphoria.
– OPPOSITES displeasure.

delighted ● adjective PLEASED, glad, happy, thrilled, overjoyed, ecstatic, elated; on cloud nine, walking on air, in seventh heaven, jumping for joy; enchanted, charmed; amused, diverted; gleeful, cock-a-hoop; *informal* over the moon, tickled pink, as pleased as Punch, on top of the world, as happy as Larry, blissed out; *Brit. informal* chuffed; *N. English informal* made up; *Austral. informal* wrapped.

delightful ● adjective **1** *a delightful evening* PLEASANT, lovely, pleasurable, enjoyable; amusing, entertaining, diverting; gratifying, satisfying; marvellous, wonderful, splendid, sublime, thrilling; *informal* great, super, fabulous, fab, terrific, heavenly, divine, grand; *Brit. informal* brilliant, brill, smashing; *N. Amer. informal* peachy, ducky; *Austral./NZ informal* beaut, bonzer. **2** *the delightful Sally* CHARMING, enchanting, captivating, bewitching, appealing; sweet, endearing, cute, lovely, adorable, delectable, delicious, gorgeous, ravishing, beautiful, pretty; *Scottish & N. English* bonny; *informal* dreamy, divine.

delimit ● verb DETERMINE, establish, set, fix, demarcate, define, delineate.

delineate ● verb **1** *the aims of the study as delineated by the boss* DESCRIBE, set forth/out, present, outline, depict, represent; map out, define, specify, identify. **2** *a section delineated in red marker pen* OUTLINE, trace, block in, mark (out/off), delimit.

delinquency ● noun **1** *teenage delinquency* CRIME, wrongdoing, lawbreaking, lawlessness, misconduct, misbehaviour; misdemeanours, offences, misdeeds. **2** *(formal) grave delinquency on the host's part* NEGLIGENCE, dereliction of duty, irresponsibility.

delinquent ● adjective **1** *delinquent teenagers* LAWLESS, lawbreaking, criminal; errant, badly behaved, troublesome, difficult, unruly, disobedient, uncontrollable. **2** *(formal) delinquent parents face tough penalties* NEGLIGENT, neglectful, remiss, irresponsible, lax, slack; *N. Amer.* derelict.
– OPPOSITES dutiful.
● noun *teenage delinquents* OFFENDER, wrongdoer, malefactor, lawbreaker, culprit, criminal; hooligan, vandal, ruffian, hoodlum; young offender; *informal* tearaway.

delirious ● adjective **1** *she was delirious but had lucid intervals* INCOHERENT, raving, babbling, irrational; feverish, frenzied; deranged, demented, unhinged, mad, insane, out of one's mind. **2** *the delirious crowd* ECSTATIC, euphoric, elated, thrilled, overjoyed, beside oneself, walking on air, on cloud nine, in seventh heaven, carried away, transported, rapturous; hysterical, wild, frenzied; *informal* blissed out, over the moon, on a high.

delirium ● noun **1** *she had fits of delirium* DERANGEMENT, dementia, madness, insanity; incoherence, irrationality, hysteria, feverishness, hallucination. **2** *the delirium of desire* ECSTASY, rapture,

deliverance ● noun **1** the process of being rescued or set free. **2** a formal or authoritative utterance.

delivery ● noun (pl. **deliveries**) **1** the action of delivering something, especially letters or goods. **2** the process of giving birth. **3** an act of throwing or bowling a ball, especially a cricket ball. **4** the manner or style of giving a speech.

dell ● noun literary a small valley.
– ORIGIN Old English, related to DALE.

Delphic /delfik/ ● adjective **1** relating to the ancient Greek oracle at Delphi. **2** deliberately obscure or ambiguous: *Delphic utterances.*

delphinium /delfinniəm/ ● noun (pl. **delphiniums**) a garden plant bearing tall spikes of blue flowers.
– ORIGIN Greek *delphinion* 'larkspur', from *delphin* 'dolphin' (because of the shape of the spur, thought to resemble a dolphin's back).

delta[1] ● noun **1** the fourth letter of the Greek alphabet (Δ, δ), transliterated as 'd'. **2** Brit. a fourth-class mark given for a piece of work.
– ORIGIN Greek, from Phoenician.

delta[2] ● noun a triangular area of sediment deposited at the mouth of a river where it diverges into several outlets.
– ORIGIN from the shape of the Greek letter *delta.*

delta wing ● noun a single triangular swept-back wing on some aircraft.

deltoid /deltoyd/ ● adjective technical triangular. ● noun (also **deltoid muscle**) a thick triangular muscle covering the shoulder joint and used for raising the arm away from the body.
– ORIGIN Greek *deltoeidēs.*

delude /dilo͞od/ ● verb persuade (someone) to believe something incorrect; mislead.
– ORIGIN Latin *deludere* 'to mock', from *ludere* 'to play'.

deluded ● adjective having a mistaken belief; misguided.

deluge /delyo͞oj/ ● noun **1** a severe flood or very heavy fall of rain. **2** a great quantity of something arriving at the same time: *a deluge of complaints.* ● verb **1** inundate; overwhelm. **2** flood.
– ORIGIN Old French, from Latin *diluvium,* from *diluere* 'wash away'.

delusion ● noun a belief or impression that is not in accordance with a generally accepted reality.
– DERIVATIVES **delusional** adjective **delusive** adjective **delusory** adjective.

de luxe /di luks/ ● adjective luxurious or sumptuous; of a superior kind.
– ORIGIN French, 'of luxury'.

delve ● verb **1** reach inside a receptacle and search for something. **2** research intensively into something. **3** literary dig or excavate.
– ORIGIN Old English.

demagnetize (also **demagnetise**) ● verb remove magnetic properties from.
– DERIVATIVES **demagnetization** noun.

demagogue /demməgog/ ● noun **1** a political leader who appeals to popular desires and prejudices. **2** (in ancient Greece and Rome) an orator who supported the cause of the common people.
– DERIVATIVES **demagogic** /demməgoggik/ adjective **demagoguery** /demməgoggəri/ noun **demagogy** noun.
– ORIGIN Greek *dēmagōgos,* from *dēmos* 'the people' + *agōgos* 'leading'.

demand ● noun **1** an insistent and peremptory request, made as of right. **2** (**demands**) pressing requirements. **3** the desire of purchasers or consumers for a particular commodity or service. ● verb **1** ask authoritatively or brusquely. **2** insist on having. **3** require; need.
– PHRASES **in demand** sought after. **on demand** as soon as or whenever required.
– ORIGIN Latin *demandare* 'hand over, entrust'.

demanding ● adjective requiring much skill or effort.
– DERIVATIVES **demandingly** adverb.

demarcate /deemaarkayt/ ● verb set the boundaries or limits of.

demarcation ● noun **1** the action of fixing boundaries or

Thesaurus

transports, wild emotion, passion, wildness, excitement, frenzy, feverishness, fever; euphoria, elation.
– OPPOSITES lucidity.

deliver ● verb **1** *the parcel was delivered to his house* BRING, take, convey, carry, transport; send, dispatch, remit. **2** *the money was delivered up to the official* HAND OVER, turn over, make over, sign over; surrender, give up, yield, cede; consign, commit, entrust, trust. **3** *he was delivered from his enemies* SAVE, rescue, free, liberate, release, extricate, emancipate, redeem. **4** *the court delivered its verdict* UTTER, give, make, read, broadcast; pronounce, announce, declare, proclaim, hand down, return, set forth. **5** *she delivered a blow to his head* ADMINISTER, deal, inflict, give; informal land. **6** *he delivered the first ball* BOWL, pitch, hurl, throw, cast, lob. **7** *the trip delivered everything she wanted* PROVIDE, supply, furnish. **8** *we must deliver on our commitments* FULFIL, live up to, carry out, carry through, make good; informal deliver the goods, come across. **9** *she returned home to deliver her child* GIVE BIRTH TO, bear, be delivered of, have, bring into the world; N. Amer. birth; informal drop.

deliverance ● noun **1** *their deliverance from prison* LIBERATION, release, delivery, discharge, rescue, emancipation; salvation. **2** *the tone he adopted for such deliverances* UTTERANCE, statement, announcement, pronouncement, declaration, proclamation; lecture, speech.

delivery ● noun **1** *the delivery of the goods* CONVEYANCE, carriage, transportation, transport, distribution; dispatch, remittance; freightage, haulage, shipment. **2** *we get several deliveries a day* CONSIGNMENT, load, shipment. **3** *the deliveries take place in hospital* BIRTH, childbirth; formal parturition. **4** *her delivery was stilted* SPEECH, pronunciation, enunciation, articulation, elocution; utterance, recitation, recital, execution.

delude ● verb MISLEAD, deceive, fool, take in, trick, dupe, hoodwink, gull, lead on; informal con, pull the wool over someone's eyes, lead up the garden path, take for a ride; N. Amer. informal sucker, snooker; Austral. informal pull a swifty on.

deluge ● noun **1** *homes were swept away by the deluge* FLOOD, torrent; Brit. spate. **2** *the deluge turned the pitch into a swamp* DOWNPOUR, torrential rain; thunderstorm, rainstorm, cloudburst. **3** *a deluge of complaints* BARRAGE, volley; flood, torrent, avalanche, stream, spate, rush, outpouring.
● verb **1** *homes were deluged by the rains* FLOOD, inundate, submerge, swamp, drown. **2** *we have been deluged with calls* INUNDATE, overwhelm, overrun, flood, swamp, snow under, engulf, bombard.

delusion ● noun **1** *a common male delusion* MISAPPREHENSION, misconception, misunderstanding, mistake, error, misinterpretation, misconstruction, misbelief; fallacy, illusion, fantasy. **2** *a web of delusion* DECEPTION, trickery.

de luxe ● adjective LUXURIOUS, luxury, sumptuous, palatial, opulent, lavish; grand, high-class, quality, exclusive, choice, fancy; expensive, costly; Brit. upmarket; informal plush, posh, classy, ritzy, swanky, pricey; Brit. informal swish; N. Amer. informal swank.
– OPPOSITES basic, cheap.

delve ● verb **1** *she delved in her pocket* RUMMAGE, search, hunt, scrabble about/around, root about/around, ferret, fish about/around in, dig; go through, rifle through; Brit. informal rootle around in. **2** *we must delve deeper into the matter* INVESTIGATE, enquire, probe, explore, research, look into, go into.

demagogue ● noun RABBLE-ROUSER, political agitator, soapbox orator, firebrand; informal tub-thumper.

demand ● noun **1** *I gave in to her demands* REQUEST, call, command, order, dictate, ultimatum, stipulation. **2** *the demands of a young family* REQUIREMENT, need, desire, wish, want; claim, imposition. **3** *the big demand for such toys* MARKET, call, appetite, desire; run on, rush on.
● verb **1** *workers demanded wage increases* CALL FOR, ask for, request, push for, hold out for; insist on, claim. **2** *Harvey demanded that I tell him the truth* ORDER, command, enjoin, urge; poetic/literary bid. **3** *'Where is she?' he demanded* ASK, inquire, question, interrogate; challenge. **4** *an activity demanding detailed knowledge* REQUIRE, need, necessitate, call for, involve, entail. **5** *they demanded complete anonymity* INSIST ON, stipulate, make a condition of; expect, look for.
– PHRASES **in demand** SOUGHT-AFTER, desired, coveted, wanted, requested; marketable, desirable, popular, all the rage, at a premium, like gold dust; informal big, trendy, hot.

demanding ● adjective **1** *a demanding task* DIFFICULT, challenging, taxing, exacting, tough, hard, onerous, burdensome, formidable; arduous, uphill, rigorous, gruelling, back-breaking, punishing. **2** *a demanding child* NAGGING, clamorous, importunate, insistent; trying, tiresome, hard to please.

limits. **2** a dividing line.
– ORIGIN Spanish *demarcación*, originally used with reference to the line dividing the New World between the Spanish and Portuguese, laid down by the Pope in 1493.
dematerialize (also **dematerialise**) ● verb **1** become no longer physically present. **2** become spiritual rather than physical.
– DERIVATIVES **dematerialization** noun.
demean[1] /dimeen/ ● verb **1** cause to suffer a loss of dignity or respect. **2** (**demean oneself**) do something that is beneath one's dignity.
– DERIVATIVES **demeaning** adjective.
– ORIGIN from DE- + MEAN², on the pattern of *debase*.
demean[2] /dimeen/ ● verb (**demean oneself**) archaic conduct oneself.
– ORIGIN Old French *demener* 'to lead'.
demeanour (US **demeanor**) ● noun outward behaviour or bearing.
– ORIGIN from DEMEAN².
demented ● adjective **1** suffering from dementia. **2** informal wild and irrational.
– DERIVATIVES **dementedly** adverb.
– ORIGIN from earlier *dement* 'drive mad', from Latin *demens* 'insane'.
dementia /dimenshə/ ● noun a mental disorder marked by memory failures, personality changes, and impaired reasoning.
– ORIGIN Latin.
dementia praecox /preekoks/ ● noun archaic schizophrenia.
– ORIGIN Latin, 'early insanity'.
demerara sugar /demmərairə/ ● noun light brown cane sugar coming originally from the region of Demerara in Guyana.
demerge ● verb Brit. separate (a company) from another with which it was merged.
– DERIVATIVES **demerger** noun.
demerit ● noun **1** something deserving blame or criticism; a fault. **2** N. Amer. a mark awarded against someone for a fault or offence.
demersal /dimers'l/ ● adjective living close to the seabed.
– ORIGIN from Latin *demergere* 'submerge, sink'.
demesne /dimayn, dimeen/ ● noun **1** historical land attached to a manor. **2** archaic a domain.
– ORIGIN from Old French *demeine* 'belonging to a lord', from Latin *dominus* 'lord, master'.
demi- ● prefix **1** half: *demisemiquaver*. **2** partially; in an inferior degree: *demigod*.
– ORIGIN from Latin *dimidius* 'half'.
demigod (or **demigoddess**) ● noun a partly divine being.
demijohn ● noun a bulbous narrow-necked bottle holding from 3 to 10 gallons of liquid.
– ORIGIN probably an alteration of French *dame-jeanne* 'Lady Jane'.
demilitarize (also **demilitarise**) ● verb remove all military forces from (an area).
– DERIVATIVES **demilitarization** noun.
demi-mondaine /demmimondayn/ ● noun a woman belonging to the demi-monde.
– ORIGIN French.
demi-monde /demmimond/ ● noun a group considered to be on the fringes of respectable society.
– ORIGIN French, 'half-world'.
demineralize (also **demineralise**) ● verb remove salts or minerals from.
– DERIVATIVES **demineralization** noun.
demi-pension /demmipONSYON/ ● noun hotel accommodation with bed, breakfast, and one main meal per day.
– ORIGIN French, 'half board'.
demise /dimīz/ ● noun **1** a person's death. **2** the end or failure of something.
– ORIGIN Old French, from Latin *dimittere* 'send away'.
demi-sec /demmisek/ ● adjective (of wine) medium dry.
– ORIGIN French, 'half-dry'.
demisemiquaver /demmisemmikwayvər/ ● noun Music, chiefly Brit. a note having the time value of half a semiquaver.
demist /deemist/ ● verb Brit. clear condensation from.
– DERIVATIVES **demister** noun.
demiurge /demmiurj, deemi-/ ● noun **1** the creator of the world in the works of the Greek philosopher Plato. **2** a heavenly being that controls the material world in the works of Gnostic philosophers.
– DERIVATIVES **demiurgic** /demmiurjik, deemi-/ adjective.
– ORIGIN Greek *dēmiourgos* 'craftsman'.
demo informal ● noun (pl. **demos**) **1** short for DEMONSTRATION. **2** a demonstration recording or piece of software. ● verb (**demos, demoed**) give a demonstration of.
demob /deemob/ Brit. informal ● verb (**demobbed, demobbing**) demobilize. ● noun demobilization.
demobilize /deemōbiliz/ (also **demobilise**) ● verb take (troops) out of active service.
– DERIVATIVES **demobilization** noun.
democracy /dimokrəsi/ ● noun (pl. **democracies**) **1** a form of government in which the people have a voice in the exercise of power, typically through elected representatives. **2** a state governed in such a way. **3** control of a group by the majority of its members.
– ORIGIN Greek *dēmokratia*, from *dēmos* 'the people' + *-kratia* 'power, rule'.
democrat ● noun **1** a supporter of democracy. **2** (**Democrat**) (in the US) a member of the Democratic Party.
democratic ● adjective **1** relating to or supporting democracy. **2** egalitarian. **3** (**Democratic**) (in the US) relating to the Democratic Party.
– DERIVATIVES **democratically** adverb.
democratize (also **democratise**) ● verb introduce a democratic system or democratic principles to.
– DERIVATIVES **democratization** noun.
démodé /daymōday/ ● adjective out of fashion.
– ORIGIN French.
demodulate ● verb Electronics reverse the modulation of.
– DERIVATIVES **demodulation** noun **demodulator** noun.
demography /dimogrəfi/ ● noun the study of the structure of human populations using statistics of births, deaths, wealth, disease, etc.
– DERIVATIVES **demographer** noun **demographic** /demməgraffik/ adjective **demographically** adverb.
demoiselle /demwaazel/ ● noun archaic or literary a young woman.
– ORIGIN French, related to DAMSEL.
demolish /dimollish/ ● verb **1** pull or knock down (a building). **2** comprehensively refute. **3** informal overwhelmingly defeat. **4** informal eat up (food) quickly.

d

Thesaurus

– OPPOSITES easy.
demarcate ● verb SEPARATE, divide, mark (out/off), delimit, delineate; bound.
demarcation ● noun **1** *clear demarcation of function* SEPARATION, distinction, differentiation, division, delimitation, definition. **2** *territorial demarcations* BOUNDARY, border, borderline, frontier; dividing line, divide.
demean ● verb DISCREDIT, lower, degrade, debase, devalue; cheapen, abase, humble, humiliate, disgrace, dishonour.
– OPPOSITES dignify.
demeaning ● adjective DEGRADING, humiliating, shameful, mortifying, abject, ignominious, undignified, inglorious; *informal* infra dig.
demeanour ● noun MANNER, air, attitude, appearance, look; bearing, carriage; behaviour, conduct; *formal* comportment.
demented ● adjective MAD, insane, deranged, out of one's mind, crazed, lunatic, unbalanced, unhinged, disturbed, non compos mentis; *informal* crazy, mental, off one's head, off one's rocker, nutty, round the bend, raving mad, batty, cuckoo, loopy, loony, bananas, screwy, touched, gaga, not all there, out to lunch; *Brit. informal* barmy, bonkers, crackers, barking, round the twist, off one's trolley, not the full shilling; *N. Amer. informal* buggy, nutso, squirrelly, wacko.
– OPPOSITES sane.
dementia ● noun MENTAL ILLNESS, madness, insanity, derangement, lunacy; Alzheimer's (disease).
demise ● noun **1** *her tragic demise* DEATH, dying, passing, loss of life, end, quietus; *formal* decease; *archaic* expiry. **2** *the demise of the Ottoman empire* END, break-up, disintegration, fall, downfall, collapse.
– OPPOSITES birth.
demobilize ● verb DISBAND, decommission, discharge; *Brit. informal* demob.
democracy ● noun REPRESENTATIVE GOVERNMENT, elective government, constitutional government; self-government, autonomy; republic, commonwealth.
– OPPOSITES dictatorship.

– ORIGIN Latin *demoliri*, from *moliri* 'construct'.
demolition /demməlish'n/ • noun the action or process of demolishing or being demolished.
demon¹ • noun **1** an evil spirit or devil. **2** an evil or destructive person or thing. **3** (before another noun) forceful or skilful: *a demon cook*. **4** another term for DAEMON¹.
– ORIGIN Greek *daimōn* 'deity, spirit'.
demon² (also **daemon**) • noun Computing a background process that handles requests for services such as print spooling, and is dormant when not required.
– ORIGIN perhaps from *disk and execution monitor* or *device monitor*, or a transferred use of DEMON¹.
demonetize /deemunnitīz/ (also **demonetise**) • verb deprive (a coin or precious metal) of its status as money.
– DERIVATIVES **demonetization** noun.
– ORIGIN French *démonétiser*, from Latin *moneta* 'money'.
demoniac /dimōniak/ • adjective demonic. • noun a person supposedly possessed by an evil spirit.
– DERIVATIVES **demoniacal** adjective.
demonic /dimonnik/ • adjective of, resembling, or characteristic of demons or evil spirits.
– DERIVATIVES **demonically** adverb.
demonize (also **demonise**) • verb portray as wicked and threatening.
– DERIVATIVES **demonization** noun.
demonolatry /deemənollətri/ • noun the worship of demons.
demonology • noun the study of demons or demonic belief.
demonstrable /demmənstrəb'l, dimon-/ • adjective clearly apparent or capable of being logically proved.
– DERIVATIVES **demonstrably** adverb.
demonstrate • verb **1** clearly show that (something) exists or is true. **2** give a practical exhibition and explanation of. **3** express or reveal (a feeling or quality) by one's actions. **4** take part in a public demonstration.
– DERIVATIVES **demonstrator** noun.
– ORIGIN Latin *demonstrare* 'point out'.
demonstration • noun **1** the action or an instance of demonstrating. **2** a public meeting or march expressing protest or other opinion on an issue.
demonstrative /dimonstrətiv/ • adjective **1** tending to show one's feelings openly. **2** serving to demonstrate something. **3** Grammar (of a determiner or pronoun) indicating the person or thing referred to (e.g. *this, that, those*). • noun Grammar a demonstrative determiner or pronoun.
– DERIVATIVES **demonstratively** adverb **demonstrativeness** noun.
demoralize (also **demoralise**) • verb cause to lose confidence or hope.
– DERIVATIVES **demoralization** noun **demoralized** adjective **demoralizing** adjective.
– ORIGIN French *démoraliser* 'corrupt, deprave'.
demote • verb reduce to a lower rank or less senior position.
– DERIVATIVES **demotion** noun.
– ORIGIN from DE- + a shortened form of PROMOTE.
demotic /dimottik/ • adjective **1** (of language) used by ordinary people; colloquial. **2** relating to demotic Greek. • noun **1** the form of modern Greek used in everyday speech and writing. **2** demotic language.
– ORIGIN Greek *dēmotikos*, from *dēmos* 'the people'.
demotivate • verb make less eager to work or make an effort.
– DERIVATIVES **demotivation** noun.
demountable • adjective able to be dismantled or removed and readily reassembled or repositioned.
demur /dimur/ • verb (**demurred**, **demurring**) raise doubts or objections; show reluctance. • noun the action of demurring: *they accepted without demur*.
– DERIVATIVES **demurral** noun.
– ORIGIN Old French *demourer*, from Latin *morari* 'delay'.
demure /dimyoor/ • adjective (**demurer**, **demurest**) (of a woman) reserved, modest, and shy.
– DERIVATIVES **demurely** adverb **demureness** noun.
– ORIGIN perhaps from Old French *demourer* 'remain, stay', influenced by *mur* 'grave'.

Thesaurus

democratic • adjective ELECTED, representative, parliamentary, popular; egalitarian, classless; self-governing, autonomous, republican.
demolish • verb **1** *they demolished a block of flats* KNOCK DOWN, pull down, tear down, bring down, destroy, flatten, raze (to the ground), level, bulldoze, topple; blow up; dismantle, disassemble. **2** *he demolished her credibility* DESTROY, ruin, wreck; refute, disprove, discredit, overturn, explode, drive a coach and horses through; *informal* shoot full of holes, do for. **3** *(informal) our team were demolished*. See TROUNCE. **4** *(informal) she demolished a sausage roll*. See DEVOUR sense 1.
– OPPOSITES construct, strengthen.
demolition • noun **1** *the demolition of the building* DESTRUCTION, levelling, bulldozing, clearance; obliteration. **2** *the demolition of his theory* DESTRUCTION, refutation. **3** *(informal) New Zealand's demolition of England*. See DEFEAT noun sense 1.
demon • noun **1** *the demons from hell* DEVIL, fiend, evil spirit, cacodemon; incubus, succubus; hellhound. **2** *the man was a demon* MONSTER, ogre, fiend, devil, brute, savage, beast, barbarian, animal. **3** *Surrey's fast-bowling demon* GENIUS, expert, master, virtuoso, maestro, past master, marvel; star; *informal* hotshot, whizz, buff, pro, ace. **4** *the demon of creativity*. See DAEMON.
– OPPOSITES angel, saint.
demonic, demoniac, demoniacal • adjective **1** *demonic powers* DEVILISH, fiendish, diabolical, satanic, Mephistophelean, hellish, infernal; evil, wicked. **2** *the demonic intensity of his playing* FRENZIED, wild, feverish, frenetic, frantic, furious, manic, like one possessed.
demonstrable • adjective VERIFIABLE, provable, attestable; verified, proven, confirmed; obvious, clear, clear-cut, evident, apparent, manifest, patent, distinct, noticeable; unmistakable, undeniable.
demonstrate • verb **1** *his findings demonstrate that boys commit more crimes* SHOW, indicate, determine, establish, prove, confirm, verify, corroborate, substantiate. **2** *she was asked to demonstrate quilting* GIVE A DEMONSTRATION OF, show how something is done; display, show, illustrate, exemplify. **3** *his work demonstrated an analytical ability* REVEAL, bespeak, indicate, signify, signal, denote, show, display, exhibit; bear witness to, testify to; imply, intimate, give away. **4** *they demonstrated against the Government* PROTEST, rally, march; stage a sit-in, picket, strike, walk out; mutiny, rebel.
demonstration • noun **1** *there is no demonstration of God's existence* PROOF, substantiation, confirmation, affirmation, corroboration, verification, validation; evidence, indication, witness, testament. **2** *a demonstration of woodcarving* EXHIBITION, presentation, display, exposition, teach-in; *informal* demo, expo, taster. **3** *his paintings are a demonstration of his talent* MANIFESTATION, indication, sign, mark, token, embodiment; expression. **4** *an anti-racism demonstration* PROTEST, march, rally, lobby, sit-in; stoppage, strike, walkout, picket (line); *informal* demo.
demonstrative • adjective **1** *a very demonstrative family* EXPRESSIVE, open, forthcoming, communicative, unreserved, emotional, effusive, gushing; affectionate, cuddly, loving, warm, friendly, approachable; *informal* touchy-feely, lovey-dovey. **2** *the successes are demonstrative of their skill* INDICATIVE, indicatory, suggestive, illustrative. **3** *demonstrative evidence of his theorem* CONVINCING, definite, positive, telling, conclusive, certain, decisive; incontrovertible, irrefutable, undeniable, indisputable, unassailable.
– OPPOSITES reserved, inconclusive.
demoralize • verb DISHEARTEN, dispirit, deject, cast down, depress, dismay, daunt, discourage, unman, unnerve, crush, shake, throw, cow, subdue; break someone's spirit; *informal* knock the stuffing out of, knock sideways; *Brit. informal* knock for six.
– OPPOSITES hearten.
demoralized • adjective DISPIRITED, disheartened, downhearted, dejected, downcast, low, depressed, despairing; disconsolate, crestfallen, disappointed, dismayed, daunted, discouraged; crushed, humbled, subdued.
demote • verb DOWNGRADE, relegate, declass, reduce in rank; depose, unseat, displace, oust; *Military* cashier, disrate.
– OPPOSITES promote.
demotic • adjective POPULAR, vernacular, colloquial, idiomatic, vulgar, common; informal, everyday, slangy.
– OPPOSITES formal.
demur • verb *Steed demurred when the suggestion was made* OBJECT, take exception, take issue, protest, cavil, dissent; voice reservations, be unwilling, be reluctant, baulk, think twice; drag one's heels, refuse; *informal* boggle, kick up a fuss.
• noun *they accepted without demur* OBJECTION, protest, protestation, complaint, dispute, dissent, opposition, resistance; reservation, hesitation, reluctance, disinclination; doubts, qualms, mis-

demurrer /dimurrər/ ● **noun** Law a pleading that an opponent's point is irrelevant.
demutualize (also **demutualise**) ● **verb** change (a mutual organization such as a building society) to one of a different kind.
demystify ● **verb** (**demystifies, demystified**) make (a subject) less difficult to understand.
– DERIVATIVES **demystification** noun.
demythologize (also **demythologise**) ● **verb** reinterpret (a subject) so that it is free of mythical elements.
den ● **noun** **1** a wild animal's lair or home. **2** informal a person's private room. **3** a place where people meet secretly or illicitly: *an opium den.*
– ORIGIN Old English.
denar /deenər/ ● **noun** the basic monetary unit of Macedonia.
– ORIGIN Latin *denarius*; compare with DINAR.
denarius /dinairiəss/ ● **noun** (pl. **denarii** /dinairi-ī/) an ancient Roman silver coin.
– ORIGIN Latin, 'containing ten', from *deni* 'in tens'.
denary /deenəri/ ● **adjective** relating to or based on the number ten.
denationalize (also **denationalise**) ● **verb** transfer from public to private ownership.
– DERIVATIVES **denationalization** noun.
denature /deenaychər/ ● **verb** **1** take away or alter the natural qualities of. **2** make (alcohol) unfit for drinking by adding poisonous or foul-tasting substances.
– DERIVATIVES **denaturation** noun.
dendrimer /dendrimər/ ● **noun** Chemistry a synthetic polymer with a treelike branching structure.
dendrite /dendrīt/ ● **noun** a short extension of a nerve cell that conducts impulses to the cell body.
– DERIVATIVES **dendritic** /dendrittik/ adjective.
– ORIGIN from Greek *dendritēs* 'tree-like'.
dendrochronology /dendrōkrənolləji/ ● **noun** a technique of dating based on the investigation of annual growth rings in tree trunks.
– DERIVATIVES **dendrochronological** adjective **dendrochronologist** noun.
– ORIGIN from Greek *dendron* 'tree'.
dene /deen/ ● **noun** Brit. a deep, narrow, wooded valley.
– ORIGIN Old English, related to DEN.
dengue /denggi/ (also **dengue fever**) ● **noun** a tropical disease transmitted by mosquitoes, causing sudden fever and acute pains in the joints.
– ORIGIN Swahili.
deniable ● **adjective** able to be denied.
– DERIVATIVES **deniability** noun.
denial ● **noun** **1** the action of denying. **2** Psychology refusal to acknowledge an unacceptable truth or emotion.
denier /denyər/ ● **noun** a unit by which the fineness of yarn is measured, equal to the weight in grams of 9,000 metres of the yarn.
– ORIGIN originally denoting a French small coin: from Latin *denarius.*
denigrate /dennigrayt/ ● **verb** criticize unfairly; disparage.
– DERIVATIVES **denigration** noun **denigrator** noun.
– ORIGIN originally in the sense 'blacken, make dark': from Latin *denigrare*, from *niger* 'black'.
denim ● **noun** **1** a hard-wearing cotton twill fabric, typically blue. **2** (**denims**) jeans or other clothes made of such fabric.
– ORIGIN from French *serge de Nîmes*, denoting serge from the manufacturing town of *Nîmes.*
denizen /denniz'n/ ● **noun** **1** formal or humorous an inhabitant or occupant. **2** Brit. historical a foreigner allowed certain rights in their adopted country.
– ORIGIN from Old French *deinz* 'within'.
denominate /dinomminayt/ ● **verb** **1** formal call; name. **2** (**be denominated**) (of sums of money) be expressed in a specified monetary unit.
– ORIGIN Latin *denominare*, from *nominare* 'to name'.
denomination ● **noun** **1** a recognized branch of a church or religion. **2** the face value of a banknote, coin, postage stamp, etc. **3** formal a name or designation.
denominational ● **adjective** relating to a particular religious denomination.
– DERIVATIVES **denominationalism** noun.
denominator ● **noun** Mathematics the number below the line in a vulgar fraction; a divisor.
de nos jours /də nō zhoor/ ● **adjective** contemporary.
– ORIGIN French, 'of our days'.
denote /dinōt/ ● **verb** **1** be a sign of; indicate. **2** be a name or symbol for.
– DERIVATIVES **denotation** noun **denotational** adjective **denotative** /dinōtətiv/ adjective.
– USAGE On the difference between **denote** and **connote**, see the note at CONNOTE.
– ORIGIN Latin *denotare*, from *notare* 'observe, note'.
denouement /daynoomon/ ● **noun** the final part of a play, film, or narrative, in which matters are explained or resolved.
– ORIGIN French, from *dénouer* 'unknot'.
denounce ● **verb** publicly declare to be wrong or evil.
– DERIVATIVES **denouncement** noun **denouncer** noun.
– ORIGIN Latin *denuntiare* 'give official information', from *nuntius* 'messenger'.
de novo /day nōvō/ ● **adverb & adjective** starting from the beginning; anew.
– ORIGIN Latin, 'from new'.
dense ● **adjective** **1** closely compacted in substance. **2** crowded closely together. **3** informal stupid.
– DERIVATIVES **densely** adverb **denseness** noun.
– ORIGIN Latin *densus.*
density ● **noun** (pl. **densities**) **1** the degree of compactness of a

d

Thesaurus

givings, second thoughts; a murmur, a word.
demure ● **adjective** MODEST, unassuming, meek, mild, reserved, retiring, quiet, shy, bashful, diffident, reticent, timid, shrinking, coy; decorous, decent, seemly, ladylike, respectable, proper, virtuous, pure, innocent, chaste; sober, sedate, staid, prim, goody-goody, strait-laced; *informal* butter-wouldn't-melt.
– OPPOSITES brazen.
den ● **noun** **1** *the mink left its den* LAIR, sett, earth, drey, burrow, hole, dugout, covert, shelter, hiding place, hideout. **2** *a notorious drinking den* HAUNT, site, hotbed, nest, pit, hole; *informal* joint, dive. **3** *the poet scribbled in his den* STUDY, studio, library; sanctum, retreat, sanctuary, hideaway, snug, cubbyhole; *informal* hidey-hole.
denial ● **noun** **1** *the reports met with a denial* CONTRADICTION, refutation, rebuttal, repudiation, disclaimer; negation, dissent; *Law* disaffirmation. **2** *the denial of insurance to certain people* REFUSAL, withholding; rejection, rebuff, repulse, veto, turndown; *informal* knock-back; *N. Amer. formal* declination. **3** *the denial of worldly values* RENUNCIATION, eschewal, repudiation, disavowal, rejection, abandonment, surrender, relinquishment.
denigrate ● **verb** DISPARAGE, belittle, deprecate, decry, cast aspersions on, criticize, attack; speak ill of, give someone a bad name, defame, slander, libel; run down, abuse, insult, revile, malign, vilify; *N. Amer.* slur; *informal* bad-mouth, pull to pieces; *Brit. informal* rubbish, slate, slag off; *formal* calumniate.
– OPPOSITES extol.
denizen ● **noun** *(formal)* INHABITANT, resident, townsman/woman, native, local; occupier, occupant, dweller; *archaic* burgher.
denominate ● **verb** *(formal)* CALL, name, term, designate, style, dub, label, entitle.
denomination ● **noun** **1** *a Christian denomination* RELIGIOUS GROUP, sect, cult, movement, body, branch, persuasion, order, school; Church. **2** *banknotes in a number of denominations* VALUE, unit, size. **3** *(formal) the invention's denomination still stands today* NAME, title, term, designation, epithet, label, tag; *informal* handle, moniker; *formal* appellation.
denote ● **verb** **1** *the headdresses denoted warriors* DESIGNATE, indicate, be a mark of, signify, signal, symbolize, represent, mean; typify, characterize, distinguish, mark, identify. **2** *his manner denoted an inner strength* SUGGEST, point to, smack of, indicate, show, reveal, intimate, imply, convey, betray, bespeak; *informal* spell.
denouement ● **noun** **1** *the film's denouement* FINALE, final scene, epilogue, coda, end, ending, finish, close; culmination, climax, conclusion, resolution, solution. **2** *the debate had an unexpected denouement* OUTCOME, upshot, consequence, result, end; *informal* pay-off.
– OPPOSITES beginning, origin.
denounce ● **verb** **1** *the pope denounced abortion* CONDEMN, criticize, attack, censure, decry, revile, vilify, discredit, damn, reject; proscribe; malign, rail against, run down; *N. Amer.* slur; *informal* knock, slam, hit out at, lay into; *Brit. informal* slate, slag off; *formal* castigate. **2** *he was denounced as a traitor* EXPOSE, betray, inform

substance; mass per unit volume. **2** the quantity of people or things in a given area or space.

dent ● noun a slight hollow in a surface made by a blow or pressure. ● verb **1** mark with a dent. **2** have an adverse effect on.
– ORIGIN variant of DINT.

dental ● adjective **1** relating to the teeth or to dentistry. **2** Phonetics (of a consonant) pronounced with the tip of the tongue against the upper front teeth (as *th*) or the alveolar ridge (as *n*, *d*, *t*).
– DERIVATIVES **dentally** adverb.
– ORIGIN Latin *dentalis*, from *dens* 'tooth'.

d

dental surgeon ● noun a dentist.

dental technician ● noun a person who makes and repairs artificial teeth.

dentate /dentayt/ ● adjective Botany & Zoology having a tooth-like or serrated edge.

dentifrice /dentifriss/ ● noun a paste or powder for cleaning the teeth.
– ORIGIN from Latin *dens* 'tooth' + *fricare* 'to rub'.

dentil /dentil/ ● noun Architecture one of a series of small tooth-like rectangular blocks used as a decoration under the moulding of a cornice.
– ORIGIN Italian *dentello* 'little tooth'.

dentine /denteen/ (US **dentin** /dentin/) ● noun hard dense bony tissue forming the bulk of a tooth.

dentist ● noun a person who is qualified to treat the diseases and conditions that affect the teeth and gums.
– DERIVATIVES **dentistry** noun.

dentition /dentish'n/ ● noun the arrangement or condition of the teeth in a particular species or individual.

denture /denchər/ ● noun a removable plate or frame holding one or more artificial teeth.

denude ● verb (often **be denuded of**) strip of covering or possessions; make bare.
– DERIVATIVES **denudation** noun.
– ORIGIN Latin *denudare*, from *nudare* 'to bare'.

denunciation /dinunsiaysh'n/ ● noun the action of denouncing.
– DERIVATIVES **denunciatory** adjective.

deny /dinī/ ● verb (**denies, denied**) **1** refuse to admit the truth or existence of. **2** refuse to give (something requested or desired) to. **3** (**deny oneself**) go without.
– ORIGIN Old French *deneier*, from Latin *denegare*, from *negare* 'say no'.

deodorant /diōdərənt/ ● noun a substance which removes or conceals unpleasant bodily odours.
– ORIGIN from Latin *odor* 'smell'.

deodorize (also **deodorise**) ● verb remove or conceal an unpleasant smell in.
– DERIVATIVES **deodorizer** noun.

deoxygenate /deeoksijənayt/ ● verb remove oxygen from.
– DERIVATIVES **deoxygenation** noun.

deoxyribonucleic acid /deeoksiribōnyooklayik/ ● noun see DNA.

depart ● verb **1** leave, especially to start a journey. **2** (**depart from**) deviate from (a course of action).
– ORIGIN Old French *departir*, from Latin *dispertire* 'to divide'.

departed ● adjective deceased.

department ● noun **1** a division of a large organization or building, dealing with a specific area of activity. **2** an administrative district in France and other countries. **3** (**one's department**) informal an area of special expertise or responsibility. **4** informal a specified aspect or quality: *he was a bit lacking in the height department.*
– DERIVATIVES **departmental** adjective **departmentalize** (also **departmentalise**) verb **departmentally** adverb.

department store ● noun a large shop stocking many types of goods in different departments.

departure ● noun the action or an instance of departing.

depend ● verb (**depend on**) **1** be controlled or determined by. **2** rely on.
– PHRASES **depending on** according to.
– ORIGIN Latin *dependere* 'hang down'.

dependable ● adjective trustworthy and reliable.
– DERIVATIVES **dependability** noun **dependably** adverb.

dependant (also **dependent**) ● noun a person who relies on another, especially a family member, for financial support.
– USAGE Until recently, the correct spelling of the noun was **dependant**, but the variant **dependent** is now acceptable. However, the adjective is always spelled **dependent**.

dependency ● noun (pl. **dependencies**) **1** a country or province controlled by another. **2** the state of being dependent.

Thesaurus

on; incriminate, implicate, cite, name, accuse; *archaic* inculpate.
– OPPOSITES praise.

dense ● adjective **1** *a dense forest* THICK, close-packed, tightly packed, closely set, crowded, compact, solid, tight; overgrown, jungly, impenetrable, impassable. **2** *dense smoke* THICK, heavy, opaque, soupy, murky, smoggy; concentrated, condensed. **3** *(informal) they were dense enough to believe me* STUPID, unintelligent, ignorant, brainless, mindless, foolish, slow, witless, simple-minded, empty-headed, vacuous, vapid, idiotic, imbecilic; *informal* thick, dim, moronic, dumb, dopey, dozy, wooden-headed, lamebrained, birdbrained, pea-brained; *Brit. informal* daft.
– OPPOSITES sparse, thin, clever.

density ● noun SOLIDITY, solidness, denseness, thickness, substance, mass; compactness, tightness, hardness.

dent ● noun **1** *I made a dent in his car* INDENTATION, dint, dimple, dip, depression, hollow, crater, pit, trough. **2** *a nasty dent in their finances* REDUCTION, depletion, deduction, cut.
– OPPOSITES increase.
● verb **1** *Jamie dented his bike* DINT, indent, mark. **2** *the experience dented her confidence* DIMINISH, reduce, lessen, shrink, weaken, erode, undermine, sap, shake, damage, impair.

dentist ● noun DENTAL SURGEON, orthodontist, periodontist, paedodontist.

denude ● verb STRIP, clear, deprive, bereave, rob; lay bare, uncover, expose; deforest, defoliate; *dated* divest.
– OPPOSITES cover.

deny ● verb **1** *the report was denied by witnesses* CONTRADICT, repudiate, challenge, contest, oppose; disprove, debunk, explode, discredit, refute, rebut, invalidate, negate, nullify, quash; *informal* shoot full of holes; *formal* gainsay; *Law* disaffirm. **2** *he denied the request* REFUSE, turn down, reject, rebuff, repulse, decline, veto, dismiss; *informal* knock back, give the thumbs down to, give the red light to. **3** *she had to deny her parents* RENOUNCE, eschew, repudiate, disavow, disown, wash one's hands of, reject, discard, cast aside, abandon, give up; *formal* forswear; *poetic/literary* forsake.
– OPPOSITES confirm, accept.

deodorant ● noun *an underarm deodorant* ANTIPERSPIRANT, body spray, perfume, scent.

deodorize ● verb FRESHEN, sweeten, purify, disinfect, sanitize, sterilize; fumigate, aerate, air, ventilate.

depart ● verb **1** *James departed after lunch* LEAVE, go (away), withdraw, absent oneself, abstract oneself, quit, exit, decamp, retreat, retire; make off, run off/away; set off/out, get under way, be on one's way; *informal* make tracks, up sticks, clear off/out, take off, split; *Brit. informal* sling one's hook. **2** *the budget departed from the norm* DEVIATE, diverge, digress, drift, stray, veer; differ, vary; contrast with.
– OPPOSITES arrive.

departed ● adjective DEAD, expired, gone, no more, passed on/away; perished, fallen; *informal* six feet under, pushing up daisies; *formal* deceased; *euphemistic* with God, asleep.

department ● noun **1** *the public health department* DIVISION, section, sector, unit, branch, arm, wing; office, bureau, agency, ministry. **2** *rural departments* DISTRICT, canton, province, territory, state, county, shire, parish; region, area. **3** *the food is Kay's department* DOMAIN, territory, province, area, line; responsibility, duty, function, business, affair, charge, task, concern; *informal* pigeon, baby, bag, bailiwick.

departure ● noun **1** *he tried to delay her departure* LEAVING, going, leave-taking, withdrawal, exit, egress, retreat. **2** *a departure from normality* DEVIATION, divergence, digression, shift; variation, change. **3** *an exciting departure for film-makers* CHANGE, innovation, novelty, rarity.

depend ● verb **1** *her career depends on a good reference* BE CONTINGENT ON, be conditional on, be dependent on, hinge on, hang on, rest on, rely on; be decided by. **2** *my family depends on me* RELY ON, lean on; count on, bank on, trust (in), have faith in, believe in; pin one's hopes on.

dependable ● adjective RELIABLE, trustworthy, trusty, faithful, loyal, unfailing, sure, steadfast, stable; honourable, sensible, responsible.

dependant ● noun CHILD, minor; ward, charge, protégé; relative;

dependent • adjective **1** (**dependent on**) contingent on or determined by. **2** relying on someone or something for financial or other support. **3** (**dependent on**) unable to do without. **4** Grammar subordinate to another clause, phrase, or word. • noun variant spelling of DEPENDANT.
– DERIVATIVES **dependence** noun **dependently** adverb.
depersonalize (also **depersonalise**) • verb deprive of human characteristics or individuality.
– DERIVATIVES **depersonalization** noun.
depict /dipikt/ • verb **1** represent by a drawing, painting, or other art form. **2** portray in words.
– DERIVATIVES **depiction** noun.
– ORIGIN Latin *depingere*, from *pingere* 'to paint'.
depilate /deppilayt/ • verb remove the hair from.
– DERIVATIVES **depilation** noun **depilator** noun.
– ORIGIN Latin *depilare*, from *pilus* 'hair'.
depilatory /dipillətri/ • adjective used to remove unwanted hair. • noun (pl. **depilatories**) a depilatory cream or lotion.
deplete /dipleet/ • verb **1** reduce the number or quantity of. **2** use up (energy, stocks, etc.); exhaust.
– DERIVATIVES **depletion** noun.
– ORIGIN Latin *deplere* 'empty out'.
depleted uranium • noun uranium from which most of the fissile isotope uranium-235 has been removed.
deplorable /diplorəb'l/ • adjective deserving strong condemnation; shockingly bad.
– DERIVATIVES **deplorably** adverb.
deplore • verb feel or express strong disapproval of.
– ORIGIN Latin *deplorare*, from *plorare* 'bewail'.
deploy /diploy/ • verb **1** bring or move into position for military action. **2** bring into effective action.
– DERIVATIVES **deployment** noun.
– ORIGIN French *déployer*, from Latin *displicare* 'unfold or explain'.
depoliticize (also **depoliticise**) • verb remove from political activity or influence.
– DERIVATIVES **depoliticization** noun.
deponent /dipōnənt/ • noun Law a person who makes a deposition or affidavit under oath.
– ORIGIN from Latin *deponere* 'put down'.
depopulate • verb substantially reduce the population of.
– DERIVATIVES **depopulation** noun.
deport • verb **1** expel (a foreigner or immigrant) from a country. **2** (**deport oneself**) archaic behave in a specified manner.
– DERIVATIVES **deportation** noun **deportee** noun.
– ORIGIN Latin *deportare*, from *portare* 'carry'.
deportment • noun **1** chiefly Brit. the way a person stands and walks. **2** N. Amer. a person's behaviour or manners.
depose • verb **1** remove from office suddenly and forcefully. **2** Law testify to or give (evidence) on oath, especially in writing.
– ORIGIN Old French *deposer*, from Latin *deponere* 'put down'.
deposit • noun **1** a sum of money placed in a bank or other account. **2** a sum payable as a first instalment or as a pledge. **3** a returnable sum paid to cover possible loss or damage. **4** a layer or body of accumulated matter. **5** the action or an act of depositing. • verb (**deposited**, **depositing**) **1** put down in a specific place. **2** store or entrust with someone for safekeeping. **3** pay as a deposit. **4** (of a natural agency) lay down (matter) as a layer or covering.
– PHRASES **lose one's deposit** (of a candidate in a UK parliamentary election) receive less than a certain proportion of the votes (thereby forfeiting a statutory financial deposit).
– DERIVATIVES **depositor** noun.
– ORIGIN Latin *depositum*, from *deponere* 'put down'.
deposit account • noun chiefly Brit. a bank account that pays interest and may not usually be drawn on without notice.
depositary (also **depository**) • noun (pl. **depositaries**) a person to whom something is entrusted.
deposition /deepəzish'n, dep-/ • noun **1** the action of deposing someone from office. **2** Law the process of giving sworn evidence. **3** Law a sworn statement to be used as evidence. **4** the action of depositing.

d

Thesaurus

(**dependants**) offspring, progeny.
dependence • noun. See DEPENDENCY senses 1, 2, 3.
dependency • noun **1** *her dependency on her husband* DEPENDENCE, reliance; need for. **2** *the association of retirement with dependency* HELPLESSNESS, dependence, weakness, defencelessness, vulnerability. **3** *drug dependency* ADDICTION, dependence, reliance; craving, compulsion, fixation, obsession; abuse. **4** *a British dependency* COLONY, protectorate, province, outpost, satellite state; holding, possession. **5** *a dependency of the firm* SUBSIDIARY, adjunct, offshoot, auxiliary, attachment, satellite, derivative.
– OPPOSITES independence.
dependent • adjective **1** *your placement is dependent on her decision* CONDITIONAL, contingent, based; subject to, determined by, influenced by. **2** *the army is dependent on volunteers* RELIANT ON, relying on, counting on; sustained by. **3** *she is dependent on drugs* ADDICTED TO, reliant on; *informal* hooked on. **4** *he is ill and dependent* RELIANT, needy; helpless, weak, infirm, invalid, incapable; debilitated, disabled. **5** *a UK dependent territory* SUBSIDIARY, subject; satellite, ancillary; puppet.
depict • verb **1** *the painting depicts the Last Supper* PORTRAY, represent, picture, illustrate, delineate, reproduce, render; draw, paint. **2** *the process depicted by Darwin's theory* DESCRIBE, detail, relate; present, set forth, set out, outline, delineate; represent, portray, characterize.
depiction • noun **1** *a depiction of Aphrodite* PICTURE, painting, portrait, drawing, sketch, study, illustration; image, likeness. **2** *the film's depiction of women* PORTRAYAL, representation, presentation, characterization.
deplete • verb EXHAUST, use up, consume, expend, drain, empty, milk; reduce, decrease, diminish; slim down, cut back.
– OPPOSITES augment.
depletion • noun EXHAUSTION, use, consumption, expenditure; reduction, decrease, diminution; impoverishment.
deplorable • adjective **1** *your conduct is deplorable* DISGRACEFUL, shameful, dishonourable, unworthy, inexcusable, unpardonable, unforgivable; reprehensible, despicable, abominable, contemptible, execrable, heinous, beyond the pale. **2** *the garden is in a deplorable state* LAMENTABLE, regrettable, unfortunate, wretched, atrocious, awful, terrible, dreadful, diabolical; sorry, poor, inadequate; *informal* appalling, dire, abysmal, woeful, lousy; *formal* grievous.
– OPPOSITES admirable.
deplore • verb **1** *we deplore violence* ABHOR, find unacceptable, frown on, disapprove of, take a dim view of, take exception to; detest, despise; condemn, denounce. **2** *he deplored their lack of flair* REGRET, lament, mourn, rue, bemoan, bewail, complain about, grieve over, sigh over.
– OPPOSITES applaud.
deploy • verb **1** *forces were deployed at strategic points* POSITION, station, post, place, install, locate, situate, site, establish; base; distribute, dispose. **2** *she deployed all her skills* USE, utilize, employ, take advantage of, exploit; bring into service, call on, turn to, resort to.
deport • verb **1** *they were fined and deported* EXPEL, banish, exile, transport, expatriate, extradite, repatriate; evict, oust, throw out; *informal* kick out, boot out, send packing; *Brit. informal* turf out. **2** *(archaic) he deported himself with dignity.* See BEHAVE sense 1.
– OPPOSITES admit.
deportment • noun **1** *(Brit.) poise is concerned with good deportment* POSTURE, carriage, bearing, stance, gait; *formal* comportment. **2** *(N. Amer.) unprofessional deportment* BEHAVIOUR, conduct, performance; manners, practices, actions.
depose • verb **1** *the president was deposed* OVERTHROW, unseat, dethrone, topple, remove, supplant, displace; dismiss, oust, drum out, throw out, expel, eject; *informal* chuck out, boot out, get rid of, show someone the door; *Brit. informal* turf out. **2** *(Law) a witness deposed that he had seen me* SWEAR, testify, attest, assert, declare, claim; *rare* asseverate.
deposit • noun **1** *a thick deposit of ash* ACCUMULATION, sediment; layer, covering, coating, blanket. **2** *a copper deposit* SEAM, vein, lode, layer, stratum, bed. **3** *they paid a deposit* DOWN PAYMENT, advance payment, prepayment, instalment, retainer, stake.
• verb **1** *she deposited her books on the table* PUT (DOWN), place, set (down), unload, rest; drop; *informal* dump, park, plonk; *N. Amer. informal* plunk. **2** *the silt deposited by flood water* LEAVE (BEHIND), precipitate, dump; wash up, cast up. **3** *the gold was deposited at the bank* LODGE, bank, house, store, stow, put away; *informal* stash, squirrel away.
deposition • noun **1** *the King's deposition* OVERTHROW, downfall, removal, dethronement, displacement, dismissal, expulsion, ejection; *N. Amer.* ouster. **2** *(Law) depositions from witnesses* STATEMENT, affidavit, attestation, affirmation, assertion; allegation, declar-

depository ● noun (pl. **depositories**) **1** a place where things are stored. **2** variant spelling of DEPOSITARY.
depot /deppō/ ● noun **1** a place for the storage of large quantities of goods. **2** a place where buses, trains, or other vehicles are housed and maintained. **3** N. Amer. /deepō/ a railway or bus station. **4** the headquarters of a regiment.
– ORIGIN French, from Latin *depositum* 'deposit'.
deprave /diprayv/ ● verb lead away from what is natural or right; corrupt.
– DERIVATIVES **depravity** /dipravviti/ noun.
– ORIGIN Latin *depravare*, from *pravus* 'crooked, perverse'.
depraved ● adjective morally corrupt.
deprecate /deprikayt/ ● verb **1** express disapproval of. **2** another term for DEPRECIATE (in sense 2).
– DERIVATIVES **deprecation** noun **deprecatory** adjective.
– ORIGIN originally in the sense 'pray to ward off evil': from Latin *deprecari*, from *precari* 'pray'.
depreciate /dipreeshiayt/ ● verb **1** reduce in value over a period of time. **2** disparage or belittle.
– DERIVATIVES **depreciation** noun **depreciatory** /dipreeshiətəri/ adjective.
– ORIGIN Latin *depreciare* 'lower in price, undervalue'.
depredation /depridaysh'n/ ● noun (usu. **depredations**) an act of attacking or plundering.
– ORIGIN Latin, from *depraedari* 'to plunder'.
depress ● verb **1** cause to feel utterly dispirited or dejected. **2** reduce the level of activity in (a system). **3** push or pull down.
– ORIGIN Latin *depressare*, from *deprimere* 'press down'.
depressant ● adjective reducing functional or nervous activity. ● noun a depressant drug or other agent.
depressed ● adjective **1** severely despondent and dejected. **2** suffering the damaging effects of economic recession: *depressed rural areas.*
depression ● noun **1** severe despondency and dejection, especially when long-lasting and accompanied by physical symptoms. **2** a long and severe recession in an economy or market. **3** the action of depressing. **4** a sunken place or hollow. **5** Meteorology a cyclonic weather system.
depressive ● adjective tending to causing depression. ● noun a person who tends to suffer from depression.
depressurize (also **depressurise**) ● verb release the pressure inside (a compartment or container).
– DERIVATIVES **depressurization** noun.
deprivation /deprivaysh'n/ ● noun **1** hardship resulting from the lack of basic material benefits. **2** the action of depriving or the state of being deprived.
deprive ● verb prevent from possessing, using, or enjoying something: *the city was deprived of its water supply.*
– ORIGIN Latin *deprivare*, from *privare* 'bereave, deprive'.
deprived ● adjective suffering a detrimental lack of basic material and cultural benefits.
Dept ● abbreviation Department.
depth ● noun **1** the distance from the top down, from the surface inwards, or from front to back. **2** complexity and profundity of thought: *the book has unexpected depth.* **3** comprehensiveness of study or detail. **4** creditable intensity of emotion. **5** (**the depths**) the deepest, lowest, or inmost part: *the depths of Devon.*
– PHRASES **out of one's depth 1** in water too deep to stand in.

Thesaurus

ation; testimony, evidence; *rare* asseveration. **3** *the deposition of calcium* DEPOSITING, accumulation, build-up, precipitation.
depository ● noun REPOSITORY, cache, store, storeroom, storehouse, warehouse; vault, strongroom, safe, treasury; container, receptacle; *informal* lock-up.
depot ● noun **1** *the bus depot* TERMINAL, terminus, station, garage; headquarters, base. **2** *an arms depot* STOREHOUSE, warehouse, store, repository, depository, cache; arsenal, magazine, armoury, ammunition dump.
deprave ● verb CORRUPT, lead astray, warp, subvert, pervert, debauch, debase, degrade, defile, sully, pollute.
depraved ● adjective CORRUPT, perverted, deviant, degenerate, debased, immoral, unprincipled; debauched, dissolute, licentious, lecherous, prurient, indecent, sordid; wicked, sinful, vile, iniquitous, nefarious; *informal* warped, twisted, pervy, sick.
depravity ● noun CORRUPTION, vice, perversion, deviance, degeneracy, immorality, debauchery, dissipation, profligacy, licentiousness, lechery, prurience, obscenity, indecency; wickedness, sin, iniquity; *informal* perviness; *formal* turpitude.
deprecate ● verb **1** *the school deprecates this behaviour* DEPLORE, abhor, disapprove of, frown on, take a dim view of, take exception to, detest, despise; criticize, censure. **2** *he deprecates the value of television* BELITTLE, disparage, denigrate, run down, discredit, decry, play down, trivialize, underrate, undervalue, underestimate, depreciate; scoff at, sneer at, scorn, disdain; *informal* pooh-pooh.
– OPPOSITES praise, overrate.
deprecatory ● adjective **1** *very deprecatory remarks* DISAPPROVING, censorious, critical, scathing, damning, condemnatory, denunciatory, disparaging, denigratory, derogatory, negative, unflattering; disdainful, derisive, snide. **2** *a deprecatory smile* APOLOGETIC, rueful, regretful, sorry, remorseful, contrite, penitent, repentant; shamefaced, sheepish.
depreciate ● verb **1** *these cars will depreciate* DECREASE IN VALUE, lose value, fall in price. **2** *the decision to depreciate property* DEVALUE, cheapen, reduce, lower in price, mark down, cut, discount; *informal* slash. **3** *they depreciate the importance of art* BELITTLE, disparage, denigrate, decry, deprecate, underrate, undervalue, underestimate, diminish, trivialize; disdain, sneer at, scoff at, scorn; *informal* knock, bad-mouth, sell short, pooh-pooh, do down; *Brit. informal* rubbish.
depredation ● noun PLUNDERING, plunder, looting, pillaging, robbery; devastation, destruction, damage, rape; ravages, raids.
depress ● verb **1** *the news depressed him* SADDEN, dispirit, cast down, get down, dishearten, demoralize, crush, shake, desolate, weigh down, oppress; upset, distress, grieve, haunt, harrow; *informal* give someone the blues, make someone fed up. **2** *new economic policies depressed sales* SLOW DOWN, reduce, lower, weaken, impair; limit, check, inhibit, restrict. **3** *imports will depress farm prices* REDUCE, lower, cut, cheapen, keep down, discount, deflate, depreciate, devalue, diminish, axe; *informal* slash. **4** *depress each key in turn* PRESS, push, hold down; thumb, tap; operate, activate.
– OPPOSITES encourage, raise.
depressant ● noun SEDATIVE, tranquillizer, calmative, sleeping pill, soporific, opiate, hypnotic; *informal* downer, trank, sleeper, dope; *Medicine* neuroleptic.
– OPPOSITES stimulant.
depressed ● adjective **1** *he felt lonely and depressed* SAD, unhappy, miserable, gloomy, glum, melancholy, dejected, disconsolate, downhearted, downcast, down, despondent, dispirited, low, heavy-hearted, morose, dismal, desolate; tearful, upset; *informal* blue, down in the dumps, down in the mouth, fed up. **2** *a depressed economy* WEAK, enervated, devitalized, impaired; inactive, flat, slow, slack, sluggish, stagnant. **3** *depressed prices* REDUCED, low, cut, cheap, marked down, discounted, discount; *informal* slashed. **4** *a depressed town* POVERTY-STRICKEN, poor, disadvantaged, deprived, needy, distressed; run down; *informal* slummy. **5** *a depressed fracture* SUNKEN, hollow, concave, indented, recessed.
– OPPOSITES cheerful, strong, inflated, prosperous, raised.
depressing ● adjective **1** *depressing thoughts* UPSETTING, distressing, painful, heartbreaking; dismal, bleak, black, sombre, gloomy, grave, unhappy, melancholy, sad; wretched, doleful; *informal* morbid, blue. **2** *a depressing room* GLOOMY, bleak, dreary, grim, drab, sombre, dark, dingy, funereal, cheerless, joyless, comfortless, uninviting.
depression ● noun **1** *she ate to ease her depression* UNHAPPINESS, sadness, melancholy, melancholia, misery, sorrow, woe, gloom, despondency, low spirits, heavy heart, despair, desolation, hopelessness; upset, tearfulness; *informal* the dumps, the doldrums, the blues, one's black dog, a (blue) funk; *Psychiatry* dysthymia. **2** *an economic depression* RECESSION, slump, decline, downturn, standstill; stagnation; *Economics* stagflation. **3** *a depression in the ground* HOLLOW, indentation, dent, dint, cavity, concavity, dip, pit, hole, sinkhole, trough, crater; basin, bowl.
deprivation ● noun **1** *unemployment and deprivation* POVERTY, impoverishment, penury, privation, hardship, destitution; need, want, distress, indigence, beggary, ruin; straitened circumstances; *rare* pauperdom. **2** *deprivation of political rights* DISPOSSESSION, withholding, withdrawal, removal, divestment, expropriation, seizure, confiscation; denial, forfeiture, loss; absence, lack.
– OPPOSITES wealth.
deprive ● verb DISPOSSESS, strip, divest, relieve, bereave, deny, rob; cheat out of; *informal* do out of.
deprived ● adjective DISADVANTAGED, underprivileged, poverty-

2 in a situation beyond one's capabilities.
– ORIGIN from DEEP + -TH².
depth charge • noun an explosive charge designed to explode under water, used for attacking submarines.
depthless • adjective 1 unfathomably deep. 2 shallow and superficial.
deputation • noun a group of people who undertake a mission on behalf of a larger group.
depute • verb /dipyo͞ot/ 1 appoint (someone) to perform a task for which one is responsible. 2 delegate (authority or a task). • noun /depyo͞ot/ Scottish a deputy.
– ORIGIN Latin *deputare* 'consider to be, assign'.
deputize /depyootīz/ • verb temporarily act on behalf of someone else.
deputy • noun (pl. **deputies**) 1 a person appointed to undertake the duties of a superior in the superior's absence. 2 a parliamentary representative in certain countries.
deracinate /deerassinayt/ • verb 1 literary tear up by the roots. 2 (**deracinated**) displaced from one's environment.
– DERIVATIVES **deracination** noun.
– ORIGIN French *déraciner* 'uproot'.
derail • verb 1 cause (a train) to leave the tracks. 2 obstruct (a process) by diverting it from its intended course.
– DERIVATIVES **derailment** noun.
derailleur /diraylər/ • noun a bicycle gear which works by lifting the chain from one sprocket wheel to another.
– ORIGIN French, from *dérailler* 'derail'.
derange • verb 1 make insane. 2 throw into disorder.
– DERIVATIVES **derangement** noun.
– ORIGIN French *déranger*, from Old French *desrengier*, 'move from orderly rows'.
Derby /daarbi/ • noun (pl. **Derbies**) 1 an annual flat race at Epsom in Surrey for three-year-old horses, founded in 1780 by the 12th Earl of Derby. 2 (in names) a similar race or other important sporting contest. 3 (**derby**; also **local derby**) a sports match between two rival teams from the same area. 4 (**derby**) /derbi/ N. Amer. a bowler hat.
deregulate • verb remove regulations or restrictions from.
– DERIVATIVES **deregulation** noun **deregulatory** adjective.
derelict • adjective 1 in a very poor condition as a result of disuse and neglect. 2 chiefly N. Amer. shamefully negligent. • noun 1 a destitute person. 2 a ship or other piece of property abandoned by its owner.
– ORIGIN from Latin *derelinquere* 'to abandon'.
dereliction • noun 1 the state of having been abandoned and become dilapidated. 2 (usu. **dereliction of duty**) shameful failure to fulfil one's obligations.

d

derestrict • verb remove restrictions from.
– DERIVATIVES **derestriction** noun.
deride /dirīd/ • verb express contempt for; ridicule.
– ORIGIN Latin *deridere* 'scoff at'.
de rigueur /də rigör/ • adjective required by etiquette or current fashion: *large bath suites are de rigueur*.
– ORIGIN French, 'in strictness'.
derision /dirizh'n/ • noun contemptuous ridicule or mockery.
– ORIGIN Latin, from *deridere* 'scoff at'.
derisive /dirīsiv/ • adjective expressing contempt or ridicule.
– DERIVATIVES **derisively** adverb.
derisory /dirīsəri/ • adjective 1 ridiculously small or inadequate. 2 another term for DERISIVE.
derivation • noun 1 the deriving of something from a source or origin. 2 the formation of a word from another word or from a root in the same or another language.
– DERIVATIVES **derivational** adjective.
derivative /dirivvətiv/ • adjective 1 chiefly derogatory imitative of the work of another artist, writer, etc. 2 (of a financial product) having a value deriving from an underlying variable asset. • noun 1 something which is derived from another source. 2 a derivative future, option, or other financial product. 3 Mathematics an expression representing the rate of change of a function with respect to an independent variable.
– DERIVATIVES **derivatively** adverb.

Thesaurus

stricken, impoverished, poor, destitute, needy, unable to make ends meet; *Brit.* on the bread line.
depth • noun 1 *the depth of the caves* DEEPNESS, distance downwards, distance inwards; drop, vertical extent; *archaic* profundity. 2 *the depth of his knowledge* EXTENT, range, scope, breadth, width; magnitude, scale, degree. 3 *her lack of depth* PROFUNDITY, deepness, wisdom, understanding, intelligence, sagacity, discernment, penetration, insight, astuteness, acumen, shrewdness; *formal* perspicuity. 4 *a work of great depth* COMPLEXITY, intricacy; profundity, gravity, weight. 5 *depth of colour* INTENSITY, richness, deepness, vividness, strength, brilliance. 6 *the depths of the sea* DEEPEST PART, bottom, floor, bed; abyss.
– OPPOSITES shallowness, triviality, surface.
– PHRASES **in depth** THOROUGHLY, extensively, comprehensively, rigorously, exhaustively, completely, fully; meticulously, scrupulously, painstakingly.
deputation • noun DELEGATION, delegacy, legation, commission, committee, (diplomatic) mission; contingent, group, party.
depute • verb 1 *he was deputed to handle negotiations* APPOINT, designate, nominate, assign, commission, charge, choose, select, elect; empower, authorize. 2 *the judge deputed smaller cases to others* DELEGATE, transfer, hand over, pass on, consign, assign, entrust, give.
deputize • verb STAND IN, sit in, fill in, cover, substitute, replace, take someone's place, understudy, be a locum, relieve, take over; hold the fort, step into the breach; act for, act on behalf of; *informal* sub.
deputy • noun *he handed over to his deputy* SECOND (IN COMMAND), number two, subordinate, junior, assistant, personal assistant, PA, aide, helper, right-hand man/woman, underling, man/girl Friday; substitute, stand-in, fill-in, relief, understudy, locum tenens; representative, proxy, agent, spokesperson; *Scottish* depute; *informal* sidekick, locum, temp.
• adjective *her deputy editor* ASSISTANT, substitute, stand-in, acting, reserve, fill-in, caretaker, temporary, provisional, stopgap, surrogate; pro tempore, ad interim; *informal* second-string.
deranged • adjective INSANE, mad, disturbed, unbalanced, unhinged, unstable, irrational; crazed, demented, berserk, frenzied, lunatic, certifiable; non compos mentis; *informal* touched, crazy, mental; *Brit. informal* barmy, barking (mad), round the twist.
– OPPOSITES rational.
derelict • adjective 1 *a derelict building* DILAPIDATED, ramshackle, run down, tumbledown, in ruins, falling apart; rickety, creaky, deteriorating, crumbling; neglected, untended, gone to rack and ruin. 2 *a derelict airfield* DISUSED, abandoned, deserted, discarded, rejected, neglected, untended. 3 *(N. Amer.) he was derelict in his duty* NEGLIGENT, neglectful, remiss, lax, careless, sloppy, slipshod, slack, irresponsible, delinquent.
• noun *the derelicts who survive on the streets* TRAMP, vagrant, vagabond, down and out, homeless person, drifter; beggar, mendicant; outcast; *informal* dosser, bag lady; *N. Amer. informal* hobo, bum.
dereliction • noun 1 *buildings were reclaimed from dereliction* DILAPIDATION, disrepair, deterioration, ruin, rack and ruin; abandonment, neglect, disuse. 2 *dereliction of duty* NEGLIGENCE, neglect, delinquency, failure; carelessness, laxity, sloppiness, slackness, irresponsibility; oversight, omission.
deride • verb RIDICULE, mock, scoff at, jibe at, make fun of, poke fun at, laugh at, hold up to ridicule, pillory; disdain, disparage, denigrate, dismiss, slight; sneer at, scorn, insult; *informal* knock, pooh-pooh, take the mickey out of.
– OPPOSITES praise.
de rigueur • adjective 1 *straight hair was de rigueur* FASHIONABLE, in fashion, in vogue, modish, up to date, up to the minute, all the rage; *informal* trendy, with it. 2 *an address is de rigueur for business cards* CUSTOMARY, standard, conventional, normal, orthodox, usual, comme il faut; compulsory; *informal* done.
derision • noun MOCKERY, ridicule, jeers, sneers, taunts; disdain, disparagement, denigration, disrespect, insults; scorn, contempt; lampooning, satire.
derisive • adjective MOCKING, jeering, scoffing, teasing, derisory, snide, sneering; disdainful, scornful, contemptuous, taunting, insulting; scathing, sarcastic; *informal* snidey; *Brit. informal* sarky.
derisory • adjective 1 *a derisory sum* INADEQUATE, insufficient, tiny, small; trifling, paltry, pitiful, miserly, miserable; negligible, token, nominal; ridiculous, laughable, ludicrous, preposterous, insulting; *informal* measly, stingy, lousy, pathetic, piddling, piffling, mingy, poxy. 2 *derisory calls from the crowd*. See DERISIVE.
derivation • noun 1 *the derivation of theories from empirical observation* DERIVING, induction, deduction, inference; extraction, eliciting. 2 *the derivation of a word* ORIGIN, etymology, root, etymon, provenance, source; origination, beginning, foundation, basis, cause; development, evolution.

d

derive /dirīv/ ● verb (**derive from**) **1** obtain (something) from (a source). **2** base (something) on a modification of. **3** have as a root or origin; originate from.
– DERIVATIVES **derivable** adjective.
– ORIGIN originally meaning 'draw a fluid through or into a channel': from Latin *derivare*, from *rivus* 'a stream'.

dermatitis /dermətītiss/ ● noun inflammation of the skin as a result of irritation by or allergic reaction to an external agent.
– ORIGIN from Greek *derma* 'skin'.

dermatology ● noun the branch of medicine concerned with skin disorders.
– DERIVATIVES **dermatological** adjective **dermatologically** adverb **dermatologist** noun.

dermatosis /dermətōsiss/ ● noun (pl. **dermatoses** /dermətōseez/) a disease of the skin, especially one that does not cause inflammation.

dermis /dermiss/ ● noun Anatomy the thick layer of the skin below the epidermis, consisting of living tissue.
– DERIVATIVES **dermal** adjective.
– ORIGIN Latin, suggested by *epidermis*.

dernier cri /dairniay kree/ ● noun the very latest fashion.
– ORIGIN French, 'last cry'.

derogate /derrəgayt/ ● verb formal **1** (**derogate from**) detract from. **2** (**derogate from**) deviate from. **3** disparage.
– DERIVATIVES **derogation** noun.
– ORIGIN Latin *derogare* 'abrogate'.

derogatory /diroggətri/ ● adjective showing a critical or disrespectful attitude.
– DERIVATIVES **derogatorily** adverb.

derrick /derrik/ ● noun **1** a kind of crane with a movable pivoted arm. **2** the framework over an oil well, holding the drilling machinery.
– ORIGIN originally denoting a hangman, also the gallows: from *Derrick*, the surname of a 17th-century London hangman.

derrière /derriair/ ● noun euphemistic or humorous a person's buttocks.
– ORIGIN French, 'behind'.

derring-do /derringdoo/ ● noun dated or humorous action displaying heroic courage.
– ORIGIN from a 16th-century misprint and misinterpretation of the Middle English phrase *dorryng do* 'daring to do'.

derris /derriss/ ● noun an insecticide made from the powdered roots of a tropical plant.
– ORIGIN Greek, 'leather covering' (referring to the plant's pods).

derv (also **DERV**) ● noun Brit. diesel oil for motor vehicles.
– ORIGIN acronym from *diesel-engined road-vehicle*.

dervish /dervish/ ● noun a member of a Muslim fraternity vowed to poverty and known for their wild rituals.
– ORIGIN Persian, 'religious beggar', also 'poor'.

desalinate /deesalinayt/ ● verb remove salt from (seawater).
– DERIVATIVES **desalination** noun **desalinator** noun.

descant ● noun /deskant/ an independent treble melody sung or played above a basic melody. ● verb /diskant/ talk tediously or at length.
– ORIGIN Latin *discantus* 'part song, refrain'.

descant recorder ● noun the most common size of recorder, with a range of two octaves above the C above middle C.

descend ● verb **1** move down or downwards. **2** slope or lead downwards. **3** (**descend to**) lower oneself to commit (a shameful act). **4** (**descend on**) make a sudden attack on or unwelcome visit to. **5** (**be descended from**) be a blood relative of (an ancestor). **6** (usu. **descend to**) pass by inheritance.
– DERIVATIVES **descendent** adjective **descender** noun.
– ORIGIN Latin *descendere* 'climb down'.

descendant ● noun a person, animal, etc. that is descended from a particular ancestor.

descent ● noun **1** an act or the action of descending. **2** a downward slope. **3** a person's origin or nationality. **4** (**descent on**) a sudden violent attack on.

describe ● verb **1** give a detailed account in words of. **2** mark out or draw (a geometrical figure).
– DERIVATIVES **describable** adjective **describer** noun.
– ORIGIN Latin *describere* 'write down'.

description ● noun **1** a spoken or written account. **2** the process of describing. **3** a sort, kind, or class: *people of any description.*

descriptive ● adjective **1** serving or seeking to describe. **2** describing or classifying without expressing judgement.
– DERIVATIVES **descriptively** adverb.

descry /diskrī/ ● verb (**descries, descried**) literary catch sight of.

Thesaurus

derivative ● adjective *her poetry was derivative* IMITATIVE, unoriginal, uninventive, unimaginative, uninspired; copied, plagiarized, plagiaristic, second-hand; trite, hackneyed, clichéd, stale, stock, banal; *informal* copycat, cribbed, old hat.
– OPPOSITES original.
● noun **1** *a derivative of opium* BY-PRODUCT, subsidiary product; spin-off. **2** *a derivative of a verb* DERIVED WORD.

derive ● verb **1** *he derives consolation from his poetry* OBTAIN, get, take, gain, acquire, procure, extract, attain, glean. **2** *'coffee' derives from the Turkish 'kahveh'* ORIGINATE IN, stem from, descend from, spring from, be taken from. **3** *his fortune derives from property* ORIGINATE IN, be rooted in; stem from, come from, spring from, proceed from, issue from.

derogate ● verb (*formal*) **1** *his contribution was derogated by critics* DISPARAGE, denigrate, belittle, deprecate, deflate; decry, discredit, cast aspersions on, run down, criticize; defame, vilify, abuse, insult, attack, pour scorn on; *informal* pull apart, drag through the mud, knock, slam, bash, bad-mouth; *Brit. informal* rubbish, slate, slag off. **2** *the act would derogate from the king's majesty* DETRACT FROM, devalue, diminish, reduce, lessen, depreciate; demean, cheapen. **3** *rules which derogate from an Act of Parliament* DEVIATE, diverge, depart, digress, stray; differ, vary; conflict with, be incompatible with.
– OPPOSITES praise, increase.

derogatory ● adjective DISPARAGING, denigratory, deprecatory, disrespectful, demeaning; critical, pejorative, negative, unfavourable, uncomplimentary, unflattering, insulting; offensive, personal, abusive, rude, nasty, mean, hurtful; defamatory, slanderous, libellous; *informal* bitchy, catty.
– OPPOSITES complimentary.

descend ● verb **1** *the plane started descending* GO DOWN, come down; drop, fall, sink, dive, plummet, plunge, nosedive. **2** *she descended the stairs* CLIMB DOWN, go down, come down; shin down. **3** *the road descends to a village* SLOPE, dip, slant, go down, fall away. **4** *she saw Leo descend from the bus* ALIGHT, disembark, get down, get off, dismount. **5** *they would not to descend to such mean tricks* STOOP, lower oneself, demean oneself, debase oneself; resort, be reduced, go as far as. **6** *the army descended into chaos* DEGENERATE, deteriorate, decline, sink, slide, fall. **7** *they descended on the pub* COME IN FORCE, arrive in hordes; attack, assail, assault, storm, invade, swoop on, charge. **8** *he is descended from a Flemish family* BE A DESCENDANT OF, originate from, issue from, spring from, derive from. **9** *his estates descended to his son* BE HANDED DOWN, be passed down; be inherited by.
– OPPOSITES ascend, climb, board.

descendant ● noun SUCCESSOR, scion; heir; (**descendants**) offspring, progeny, family, lineage; *Law* issue; *archaic* seed, fruit of one's loins.
– OPPOSITES ancestor.

descent ● noun **1** *the plane began its descent* DIVE, drop; fall, pitch. **2** *their descent of the mountain* DOWNWARD CLIMB. **3** *a steep descent* SLOPE, incline, dip, drop, gradient, declivity, slant; hill. **4** *his descent into alcoholism* DECLINE, slide, fall, degeneration, deterioration, regression. **5** *she is of Italian descent* ANCESTRY, parentage, ancestors, family, antecedents; extraction, origin, derivation, birth; lineage, line, genealogy, heredity, stock, pedigree, blood, bloodline; roots, origins. **6** *the descent of property* INHERITANCE, succession. **7** *the sudden descent of the cavalry* ATTACK, assault, raid, onslaught, charge, thrust, push, drive, incursion, foray.

describe ● verb **1** *he described his experiences* REPORT, recount, relate, tell of, set out, chronicle; detail, catalogue, give a rundown of; explain, illustrate, discuss, comment on. **2** *she described him as a pathetic figure* DESIGNATE, pronounce, call, label, style, dub; characterize, class; portray, depict, brand, paint. **3** *the pen described a circle* DELINEATE, mark out, outline, trace, draw.

description ● noun **1** *a description of my travels* ACCOUNT, report, rendition, explanation, illustration; chronicle, narration, narrative, story, commentary; portrayal, portrait; details. **2** *the description of coal as 'bottled sunshine'* DESIGNATION, labelling, naming, dubbing, pronouncement; characterization, classification, branding; portrayal, depiction. **3** *vehicles of every description* SORT, variety, kind, type, category, order, breed, class, designation, specification, genre, genus, brand, make, character, ilk; *N. Amer.* stripe.

– ORIGIN perhaps confused with obsolete *descry* 'describe', related to DESCRIBE.
desecrate /dessikrayt/ ● verb treat (something sacred) with violent disrespect.
– DERIVATIVES **desecration** noun **desecrator** noun.
– ORIGIN from DE- + a shortened form of CONSECRATE.
desegregate ● verb end a policy of racial segregation in.
– DERIVATIVES **desegregation** noun.
deselect ● verb Brit. reject the candidature of (an existing MP).
– DERIVATIVES **deselection** noun.
desensitize (also **desensitise**) ● verb **1** make less sensitive. **2** make indifferent to cruelty or suffering.
– DERIVATIVES **desensitization** noun.
desert[1] /dizert/ ● verb **1** leave without help or support; abandon. **2** leave (a place), causing it to appear empty. **3** illegally run away from military service.
– DERIVATIVES **desertion** noun.
– ORIGIN Latin *desertare*, from *desertus* 'left waste' (related to DESERT[2]).
desert[2] /dezzərt/ ● noun **1** a waterless, desolate area of land with little or no vegetation, typically covered with sand. **2** a situation or area considered dull and uninteresting: *a cultural desert.* ● adjective like a desert; uninhabited and desolate.
– ORIGIN Latin *desertum* 'something left waste', from *deserere* 'leave, forsake'.
deserter ● noun a member of the armed forces who deserts.
desertification /dizertifikaysh'n/ ● noun the process by which fertile land becomes desert.
deserts /dizerts/ ● plural noun (usu. in phrase **get** or **receive one's just deserts**) what a person deserves with regard to reward or punishment.
– ORIGIN Old French *desert*, from *deservir* 'serve well, deserve'.
deserve ● verb do something or show qualities worthy of (a reward or punishment as appropriate).
– DERIVATIVES **deservedly** adverb.
– ORIGIN Latin *deservire* 'serve well or zealously'.
deserving ● adjective worthy of favourable treatment or assistance.
desex ● verb **1** deprive of sexual qualities. **2** castrate or spay.
déshabillé /dezzabeeay/ (also **dishabille**) /dissabeel/ ● noun the state of being only partly or scantily clothed.
– ORIGIN French, 'undressed'.
desiccate /dessikayt/ ● verb (usu. **desiccated**) remove the moisture from.
– DERIVATIVES **desiccation** noun.
– ORIGIN Latin *desiccare* 'make thoroughly dry'.
desideratum /diziddəraatəm/ ● noun (pl. **desiderata** /diziddəraatə/) something that is needed or wanted.
– ORIGIN Latin, 'something desired'.
design ● noun **1** a plan or drawing produced to show the look and function or workings of something before it is built or made. **2** the art or action of producing such a plan or drawing. **3** underlying purpose or planning: *the appearance of design in the universe.* **4** a decorative pattern. ● verb **1** conceive and produce a design for. **2** plan or intend for a purpose.
– PHRASES **by design** intentionally. **have designs on** aim to obtain, especially in an underhand way.
– ORIGIN from Latin *designare* 'mark out, designate'.
designate ● verb /dezzignayt/ **1** officially give a specified status or name to; describe as. **2** appoint to a specified position. ● adjective /dezzignət/ (after a noun) appointed to an office or position but not yet installed: *the Director designate.*
– DERIVATIVES **designator** noun.
– ORIGIN Latin *designare* (see DESIGN).
designation ● noun **1** the action of designating. **2** an official title or description.
designedly ● adverb intentionally.
designer ● noun **1** a person who designs things. **2** (before another noun) made by a famous fashion designer: *designer jeans.*
designer drug ● noun a synthetic analogue of an illegal drug, devised to circumvent drug laws.
designing ● adjective acting in a calculating, deceitful way.

d

Thesaurus

descriptive ● adjective ILLUSTRATIVE, expressive, graphic, detailed, lively, vivid, striking; explanatory, elucidatory, explicative.
descry ● verb *(poetic/literary).* See NOTICE verb.
desecrate ● verb VIOLATE, profane, defile, debase, degrade, dishonour; vandalize, damage, destroy, deface.
desert[1] ● verb **1** *his wife deserted him* ABANDON, leave, turn one's back on; throw over, jilt, break up with; leave high and dry, leave in the lurch, leave behind, strand, maroon; *informal* walk out on, run out on, drop, dump, ditch; *poetic/literary* forsake. **2** *his allies were deserting the cause* RENOUNCE, repudiate, relinquish, wash one's hands of, abandon, turn one's back on, betray, disavow; *formal* abjure; *poetic/literary* forsake. **3** *soldiers deserted in droves* ABSCOND, defect, run away, make off, decamp, flee, turn tail, take French leave, depart, quit; *Military* go AWOL.
desert[2] ● noun *an African desert* WASTELAND, wastes, wilderness, wilds, barren land; dust bowl.
● adjective **1** *desert conditions* ARID, dry, moistureless, parched, scorched, hot; barren, bare, stark, infertile, unfruitful, dehydrated, sterile. **2** *a desert island* UNINHABITED, empty, lonely, desolate, bleak; wild, uncultivated.
– OPPOSITES fertile.
deserted ● adjective **1** *a deserted wife* ABANDONED, thrown over, jilted, cast aside; neglected, stranded, marooned; forlorn, bereft; *informal* dumped, ditched, dropped; *poetic/literary* forsaken. **2** *a deserted village* EMPTY, uninhabited, unoccupied, unpeopled, abandoned, evacuated, vacant; untenanted, tenantless, neglected; desolate, lonely, godforsaken.
– OPPOSITES populous.
deserter ● noun ABSCONDER, runaway, fugitive, truant, escapee; renegade, defector, turncoat, traitor.
desertion ● noun **1** *his wife's desertion of him* ABANDONMENT, leaving, jilting. **2** *the desertion of the president's colleagues* DEFECTION; betrayal, renunciation, repudiation, apostasy; *formal* abjuration. **3** *soldiers were executed for desertion* ABSCONDING, running away, truancy, going absent without leave, taking French leave, escape; defection, treason; *Military* going AWOL.
deserve ● verb MERIT, earn, warrant, rate, justify, be worthy of, be entitled to, have a right to, be qualified for.
deserved ● adjective WELL EARNED, merited, warranted, justified, justifiable; rightful, due, right, just, fair, fitting, appropriate, suitable, proper, apt; *archaic* meet.
deserving ● adjective **1** *the deserving poor* WORTHY, meritorious, commendable, praiseworthy, admirable, estimable, creditable; respectable, decent, honourable, righteous. **2** *a lapse deserving of punishment* MERITING, warranting, justifying, suitable for, worthy of.
desiccated ● adjective DRIED, dry, dehydrated, powdered.
– OPPOSITES moist.
desideratum ● noun REQUIREMENT, prerequisite, need, indispensable thing, sine qua non, essential, requisite, necessary.
design ● noun **1** *a design for the offices* PLAN, blueprint, drawing, sketch, outline, map, plot, diagram, draft, representation, scheme, model. **2** *tableware with a gold design* PATTERN, motif, device; style, composition, make-up, layout, construction, shape, form. **3** *his design of reaching the top* INTENTION, aim, purpose, plan, intent, objective, object, goal, end, target; hope, desire, wish, dream, aspiration, ambition.
● verb **1** *the church was designed by Hicks* PLAN, outline, map out, draft, draw. **2** *they designed a new engine* INVENT, originate, create, think up, come up with, devise, formulate, conceive; make, produce, develop, fashion; *informal* dream up. **3** *this paper is designed to provoke discussion* INTEND, aim; devise, contrive, purpose, plan; tailor, fashion, adapt, gear; mean, destine.
– PHRASES **by design** DELIBERATELY, intentionally, on purpose, purposefully; knowingly, wittingly, consciously, calculatedly.
designate ● verb **1** *some firms designate a press officer* APPOINT, nominate, depute, delegate; select, choose, pick, elect, name, identify, assign. **2** *the rivers are designated 'Sites of Special Scientific Interest'* CLASSIFY, class, label, tag; name, call, entitle, term, dub; *formal* denominate.
designation ● noun **1** *the designation of a leader* APPOINTMENT, nomination, naming, selection, election. **2** *the designation of nature reserves* CLASSIFICATION, specification, definition, earmarking, pinpointing. **3** *the designation 'Generalissimo'* TITLE, name, epithet, tag; nickname, byname, sobriquet; *informal* moniker, handle; *formal* denomination, appellation.
designer ● noun **1** *a designer of farmhouses* CREATOR, planner, deviser, inventor, originator; maker; architect, builder. **2** *young designers made the dress* COUTURIER, tailor, costumier, dressmaker.
designing ● adjective SCHEMING, calculating, conniving; cunning, crafty, artful, wily, devious, guileful, manipulative; treacherous, sly, underhand, deceitful, double-dealing; *informal* crooked, foxy.

d

desirable ● adjective **1** wished for as being attractive, useful, or necessary. **2** (of a person) arousing sexual desire. ● noun a desirable person or thing.
– DERIVATIVES **desirability** noun **desirableness** noun **desirably** adverb.
desire ● noun **1** a strong feeling of wanting to have something or wishing for something to happen. **2** strong sexual feeling or appetite. ● verb **1** strongly wish for or want. **2** want sexually. **3** archaic request or entreat.
– DERIVATIVES **desirous** adjective.
– ORIGIN Latin *desiderare*.
desist /dizist/ ● verb cease; abstain.
– ORIGIN Latin *desistere*, from *sistere* 'to stop'.
desk ● noun **1** a piece of furniture with a flat or sloping surface and often with drawers, for writing, reading, or other work. **2** a counter in a hotel, bank, airport, etc. **3** a specified section of a news organization: *the sports desk*. **4** a position in an orchestra at which two players share a music stand.
– ORIGIN from Latin *discus* 'plate' (later 'desk'), from Greek *diskos* 'discus'.
deskill ● verb reduce the level of skill required to carry out (a job).
desk job ● noun a clerical or administrative job.
desktop ● noun **1** the working surface of a desk. **2** a microcomputer suitable for use at an ordinary desk. **3** the working area of a computer screen regarded as representing a notional desktop.
desktop publishing ● noun the production of high-quality printed matter by means of a printer linked to a desktop computer.
desolate ● adjective /dessələt/ **1** giving an impression of bleak and dismal emptiness. **2** utterly wretched and unhappy. ● verb /dessəlayt/ make desolate.
– DERIVATIVES **desolation** noun.
– ORIGIN from Latin *desolare* 'abandon', from *solus* 'alone'.
despair ● noun the complete loss or absence of hope. ● verb lose or be without hope.
– PHRASES **be the despair of** be the cause of despair in (someone else).
– ORIGIN from Latin *desperare*, from *sperare* 'to hope'.
despatch ● verb & noun variant spelling of DISPATCH.
desperado /despəraadō/ ● noun (pl. **desperadoes** or **desperados**) dated a desperate or reckless criminal.
– ORIGIN pseudo-Spanish alteration of the obsolete noun *desperate* 'person in despair or in a desperate situation'.
desperate ● adjective **1** feeling, showing, or involving despair. **2** extremely bad or serious: *a desperate shortage*. **3** having a great need or desire for something: *desperate for a cigarette*. **4** violent or dangerous.
– PHRASES **desperate diseases must have desperate remedies** proverb extreme measures are justified as a response to a difficult or dangerous situation.
– DERIVATIVES **desperately** adverb.
– ORIGIN Latin *desperatus* 'deprived of hope', from *desperare* (see DESPAIR).
desperation ● noun a state of despair, especially as resulting in reckless behaviour.
despicable /dispikəb'l, despik-/ ● adjective deserving hatred

Thesaurus

desirability ● noun **1** *the desirability of the property* APPEAL, attractiveness, allure; agreeableness, worth, excellence. **2** *the desirability of a different economy* ADVISABILITY, advantage, expedience, benefit, merit, value, profit, profitability. **3** *her obvious desirability* ATTRACTIVENESS, sexual attraction, beauty, good looks; charm, seductiveness; *informal* sexiness.
desirable ● adjective **1** *a desirable location* ATTRACTIVE, sought-after, in demand, popular, desired, covetable, enviable; appealing, agreeable, pleasant; valuable, good, excellent; *informal* to die for. **2** *it is desirable that they should meet* ADVANTAGEOUS, advisable, wise, sensible, recommendable; helpful, useful, beneficial, worthwhile, profitable, preferable. **3** *a very desirable woman* (SEXUALLY) ATTRACTIVE, beautiful, pretty, appealing; seductive, alluring, enchanting, beguiling, captivating, bewitching, irresistible; *informal* sexy, beddable.
– OPPOSITES unattractive, unwise, ugly.
desire ● noun **1** *a desire to see the world* WISH, want, aspiration, fancy, inclination, impulse; yearning, longing, craving, hankering, hunger; eagerness, enthusiasm, determination; *informal* yen, itch. **2** *his eyes glittered with desire* LUST, sexual attraction, passion, sensuality, sexuality; lasciviousness, lechery, salaciousness, libidinousness; *informal* the hots, raunchiness, horniness; *Brit. informal* randiness.
● verb **1** *they desired peace* WANT, wish for, long for, yearn for, crave, hanker after, be desperate for, be bent on, covet, aspire to; fancy; *informal* have a yen for, yen for. **2** *she desired him* BE ATTRACTED TO, lust after, burn for, be infatuated by; *informal* fancy, have the hots for, have a crush on, be mad about.
desired ● adjective **1** *cut the cloth to the desired length* REQUIRED, necessary, proper, right, correct; appropriate, suitable; preferred, chosen, selected. **2** *the desired results* WISHED FOR, wanted, coveted; sought-after, longed for, yearned for.
desirous ● adjective EAGER, desiring, anxious, keen, craving, yearning, longing, hungry; ambitious, aspiring; covetous, envious; *informal* dying, itching.
desist ● verb ABSTAIN, refrain, forbear, hold back, keep; stop, cease, discontinue, suspend, give up, break off, drop, dispense with, eschew; *informal* lay off, give over, quit, pack in.
– OPPOSITES continue.
desk ● noun WRITING TABLE, bureau, escritoire, secretaire; *Brit.* davenport.
desolate ● adjective **1** *desolate moorlands* BLEAK, stark, bare, dismal, grim; wild, inhospitable; deserted, uninhabited, godforsaken, abandoned, unpeopled, untenanted, empty; unfrequented, unvisited, isolated, remote. **2** *she is desolate* MISERABLE, despondent, depressed, disconsolate, devastated, despairing, inconsolable, broken-hearted, grief-stricken, crushed, bereft; sad, unhappy, downcast, down, dejected, forlorn, upset, distressed; *informal* blue, cut up.
– OPPOSITES populous, joyful.
● verb **1** *droughts desolated the plains* DEVASTATE, ravage, ruin, lay waste to; level, raze, demolish, wipe out, obliterate. **2** *she was desolated by the loss of her husband* DISHEARTEN, depress, sadden, cast down, make miserable, weigh down, crush, upset, distress; *informal* shatter.
desolation ● noun **1** *the desolation of the Gobi desert* BLEAKNESS, starkness, barrenness, sterility; wildness; isolation, loneliness, remoteness. **2** *a feeling of utter desolation* MISERY, sadness, unhappiness, despondency, sorrow, depression, grief, woe; broken-heartedness, wretchedness, dejection, devastation, despair, anguish, distress.
despair ● noun HOPELESSNESS, disheartenment, discouragement, desperation, distress, anguish, unhappiness; despondency, depression, disconsolateness, melancholy, misery, wretchedness; defeatism, pessimism.
– OPPOSITES hope, joy.
● verb LOSE HOPE, abandon hope, give up, lose heart, be discouraged, be despondent, be demoralized, resign oneself; be pessimistic, look on the black side.
– PHRASES **be the despair of** BE THE BANE OF, be the scourge of, be a burden on, be a trial to, be a thorn in the flesh/side of.
despairing ● adjective HOPELESS, in despair, dejected, depressed, despondent, disconsolate, gloomy, miserable, wretched, desolate, inconsolable; disheartened, discouraged, demoralized, devastated; defeatist, pessimistic.
despatch ● verb & noun. See DISPATCH.
desperado ● noun (*dated*) BANDIT, criminal, outlaw, lawbreaker, villain, renegade; robber, cut-throat, gangster, pirate.
desperate ● adjective **1** *a desperate look* DESPAIRING, hopeless; anguished, distressed, wretched, desolate, forlorn, distraught, fraught; out of one's mind, at one's wits' end, beside oneself, at the end of one's tether. **2** *a desperate attempt to escape* LAST-DITCH, last-gasp, eleventh-hour, do-or-die, final; frantic, frenzied, wild; futile, hopeless, doomed. **3** *a desperate shortage of teachers* GRAVE, serious, critical, acute, risky, precarious; dire, awful, terrible, dreadful; urgent, pressing, crucial, vital, drastic, extreme; *informal* chronic. **4** *they were desperate for food* IN GREAT NEED OF, urgently requiring, in want of; eager, longing, yearning, hungry, crying out; *informal* dying. **5** *a desperate act* VIOLENT, dangerous, lawless; reckless, rash, hasty, impetuous, foolhardy, incautious, hazardous, risky; death-or-glory, do-or-die.
desperately ● adverb **1** *he screamed desperately for help* IN DESPERATION, in despair, despairingly, in anguish, in distress; wretchedly, hopelessly, desolately, forlornly. **2** *they are desperately ill* SERIOUSLY, critically, gravely, severely, acutely, dangerously, perilously; very, extremely, dreadfully; hopelessly, irretrievably; *infor-*

and contempt.
– DERIVATIVES **despicably** adverb.
– ORIGIN Latin *despicabilis*, from *despicari* 'look down on'.
despise /dispīz/ ● verb feel contempt or repugnance for.
– DERIVATIVES **despiser** noun.
– ORIGIN Latin *despicere* 'look down'.
despite /dispīt/ ● preposition in spite of.
– ORIGIN originally in the sense 'contempt, scorn': from Latin *despectus* 'looking down on', from *despicere* (see DESPISE).
despoil /dispoyl/ ● verb literary steal valuable possessions from.
– DERIVATIVES **despoiler** noun **despoliation** /dispōliaysh'n/ noun.
– ORIGIN Latin *despoliare* 'rob, plunder'.
despondent ● adjective in low spirits from loss of hope or courage.
– DERIVATIVES **despondency** noun **despondently** adverb.
– ORIGIN from Latin *despondere* 'give up, abandon'.
despot /despot/ ● noun a ruler with absolute power, especially one who exercises it in a cruel or oppressive way.
– DERIVATIVES **despotic** adjective **despotism** noun.
– ORIGIN Greek *despotēs* 'master, absolute ruler'.
des res /dez rez/ ● noun Brit. informal a desirable residence.
dessert /dizert/ ● noun the sweet course eaten at the end of a meal.
– ORIGIN French, from *desservir* 'clear the table'.
dessertspoon ● noun a spoon used for dessert, smaller than a tablespoon and larger than a teaspoon.
dessert wine ● noun a sweet wine drunk with or following dessert.
destabilize (also **destabilise**) ● verb upset the stability of.
– DERIVATIVES **destabilization** noun.
destination ● noun the place to which someone or something is going or being sent.
destine /destin/ ● verb (**be destined**) **1** be intended or chosen for a particular purpose or end: *he was destined to be an engineer.* **2** bound for a particular destination.
– ORIGIN originally in the sense 'predetermine, decree': from Latin *destinare* 'make firm, establish'.
destiny ● noun (pl. **destinies**) **1** the events that will happen to a person, regarded as predetermined by fate. **2** the hidden power believed to control this; fate.
– ORIGIN Latin *destinata*, from *destinare* 'make firm, establish'.
destitute /destityōōt/ ● adjective **1** extremely poor and lacking the means to provide for oneself. **2** (**destitute of**) not having.
– DERIVATIVES **destitution** noun.
– ORIGIN originally in the sense 'deserted, abandoned': from Latin *destituere* 'forsake'.
destrier /destrier/ ● noun literary a medieval knight's warhorse.
– ORIGIN Old French, from Latin *dextera* 'the right hand' (because the squire led the knight's horse with his right hand).
destroy ● verb **1** put out of existence by severe damage or attack. **2** completely ruin or spoil. **3** kill (an animal) by humane means.
– ORIGIN Latin *destruere*, from *struere* 'build'.
destroyer ● noun **1** a person or thing that destroys. **2** a small fast warship equipped for a defensive role against submarines and aircraft.
destruct ● verb cause the destruction of.
– DERIVATIVES **destructor** noun.
destructible ● adjective able to be destroyed.
destruction ● noun **1** the action of destroying or the state of being destroyed. **2** a cause of someone's ruin.
– ORIGIN Latin, from *destruere* 'destroy'.

d

Thesaurus

mal terribly. **3** *he desperately wanted to talk* URGENTLY, pressingly; intensely, eagerly.
desperation ● noun HOPELESSNESS, despair, distress; anguish, agony, torment, misery, wretchedness; disheartenment, discouragement.
despicable ● adjective CONTEMPTIBLE, loathsome, hateful, detestable, reprehensible, abhorrent, abominable, awful, heinous; odious, vile, low, mean, abject, shameful, ignominious, shabby, ignoble, disreputable, discreditable, unworthy; *informal* dirty, rotten, low-down; *Brit. informal* beastly; *archaic* scurvy.
– OPPOSITES admirable.
despise ● verb DETEST, hate, loathe, abhor, execrate, deplore, dislike; scorn, disdain, look down on, deride, sneer at, revile; spurn, shun; *formal* abominate.
– OPPOSITES adore.
despite ● preposition IN SPITE OF, notwithstanding, regardless of, in the face of, for all, even with.
despoil ● verb **1** *a village despoiled by invaders* PLUNDER, pillage, rob, ravage, raid, ransack, rape, loot, sack; devastate, lay waste, ruin. **2** *the robbers despoiled him of all he had* ROB, strip, deprive, dispossess, denude, divest, relieve, clean out.
despondency ● noun HOPELESSNESS, despair, disheartenment, discouragement, low spirits, wretchedness; melancholy, gloom, misery, desolation, disappointment, dejection, sadness, unhappiness; *informal* the blues, heartache.
despondent ● adjective DISHEARTENED, discouraged, dispirited, downhearted, downcast, crestfallen, down, low, disconsolate, despairing, wretched; melancholy, gloomy, morose, dismal, woebegone, miserable, depressed, dejected, sad; *informal* blue, down in the mouth, down in the dumps.
– OPPOSITES hopeful, cheerful.
despot ● noun TYRANT, oppressor, dictator, absolute ruler, totalitarian, autocrat.
despotic ● adjective AUTOCRATIC, dictatorial, totalitarian, absolutist, undemocratic, unaccountable; one-party, autarchic, monocratic; tyrannical, tyrannous, oppressive, repressive, draconian, illiberal.
– OPPOSITES democratic.
despotism ● noun TYRANNY, dictatorship, totalitarianism, absolute rule, absolutism; oppression, repression; autocracy, monocracy, autarchy.
dessert ● noun PUDDING, sweet, second course, last course; *Brit. informal* afters, pud.
destabilize ● verb UNDERMINE, weaken, damage, subvert, sabotage, unsettle, upset, disrupt.
– OPPOSITES strengthen.
destination ● noun JOURNEY'S END, end of the line; terminus, stop, stopping place, port of call; goal, target, end.
destined ● adjective **1** *he is destined to lead a troubled life* FATED, ordained, predestined, meant; certain, sure, bound, assured, likely; doomed. **2** *computers destined for Pakistan* HEADING, bound, en route, scheduled; intended, meant, designed, designated, allotted, reserved.
destiny ● noun **1** *master of his own destiny* FUTURE, fate, fortune, doom; lot; *archaic* portion. **2** *she was sent by destiny* FATE, providence; predestination; divine decree, God's will, kismet, the stars; luck, fortune, chance; karma.
destitute ● adjective **1** *she was left destitute* PENNILESS, poor, impoverished, poverty-stricken, impecunious, without a penny to one's name; needy, in straitened circumstances, distressed, badly off; *Brit.* on the breadline; *informal* hard up, (flat) broke, strapped (for cash), without a brass farthing, without two pennies to rub together, without a bean; *Brit. informal* stony broke, skint; *N. Amer. informal* stone broke, without a red cent. **2** *we were destitute of clothing* DEVOID, bereft, deprived, in need; lacking, without, deficient in, wanting.
– OPPOSITES rich.
destitution ● noun POVERTY, impoverishment, penury, pennilessness, privation, pauperism; hardship, need, want, straitened circumstances, dire straits, deprivation, (financial) distress.
destroy ● verb **1** *their offices were destroyed by bombing* DEMOLISH, knock down, level, raze (to the ground), fell; wreck, ruin, shatter; blast, blow up, dynamite, explode, bomb. **2** *traffic would destroy the conservation area* SPOIL, ruin, wreck, disfigure, blight, mar, impair, deface, scar, injure, harm, devastate, damage, wreak havoc on. **3** *illness destroyed his career chances* WRECK, ruin, spoil, disrupt, undo, upset, put an end to, put a stop to, terminate, frustrate, blight, crush, quash, dash, scotch; devastate, demolish, sabotage; *informal* mess up, muck up, foul up, put paid to, put the kibosh on, do for, queer, blow a hole in; *Brit. informal* scupper, throw a spanner in the works of; *archaic* bring to naught. **4** *the horse had to be destroyed* KILL, put down, put to sleep, slaughter, terminate, exterminate. **5** *we had to destroy the enemy* ANNIHILATE, wipe out, obliterate, wipe off the face of the earth, eliminate, eradicate, liquidate, finish off, erase; kill, slaughter, massacre, exterminate; *informal* take out, rub out, snuff out; *N. Amer. informal* waste.
– OPPOSITES build, preserve, raise, spare.
destruction ● noun **1** *the destruction by allied bombers* DEMOLITION, wrecking, ruination, blasting, bombing; wreckage, ruins. **2** *the destruction of the countryside* SPOLIATION, devastation, ruination, blighting, disfigurement, impairment, scarring, harm,

destructive • adjective **1** causing destruction. **2** negative and unhelpful: *destructive criticism.*
– DERIVATIVES **destructively** adverb **destructiveness** noun.

desuetude /disyōōityōōd/ • noun formal a state of disuse.
– ORIGIN Latin *desuetudo*, from *desuescere* 'make unaccustomed'.

desultory /dezzəltri/ • adjective **1** lacking purpose or enthusiasm. **2** going from one thing to another erratically and intermittently: *a desultory conversation.*
– DERIVATIVES **desultorily** adverb.
– ORIGIN Latin *desultorius* 'superficial' (literally 'relating to a vaulter'), from *desilire* 'leap down'.

d

detach • verb **1** disengage (something) and remove it. **2** (**detach oneself from**) leave or distance oneself from (a group or situation). **3** (**be detached**) Military be sent on a separate mission.
– DERIVATIVES **detachability** noun **detachable** adjective.
– ORIGIN originally in the sense 'discharge a gun': from French *détacher*, from *attacher* 'attach'.

detached • adjective **1** separate or disconnected. **2** (of a house) not joined to another on either side. **3** aloof and objective.
– DERIVATIVES **detachedly** adverb.

detachment • noun **1** the state of being objective or aloof. **2** a group of troops, ships, etc. sent away on a separate mission. **3** the action or process of detaching.

detail • noun **1** a small individual item or fact. **2** small items or facts collectively: *attention to detail.* **3** a small part of a picture reproduced separately for close study. **4** a small detachment of troops or police officers given a special duty. • verb **1** describe item by item. **2** assign to undertake a particular task.
– PHRASES **in detail** as regards every aspect; fully.
– ORIGIN French *détail*, from *tailler* 'to cut'.

detailed • adjective having many details.

detailing • noun small decorative features on a building, garment, or work of art.

detain • verb **1** keep from proceeding; delay. **2** keep in official custody.
– DERIVATIVES **detainer** noun **detainment** noun.
– ORIGIN Latin *detinere* 'keep back'.

detainee /deetaynee/ • noun a person detained in custody, especially for political reasons.

detect • verb **1** discover the presence or existence of. **2** discover or investigate (a crime or its perpetrators). **3** notice (something intangible or barely perceptible).
– DERIVATIVES **detectable** adjective **detectably** adverb **detection** noun.
– ORIGIN Latin *detegere* 'uncover' from *tegere* 'to cover'.

detective • noun a person, especially a police officer, whose occupation is to investigate crimes.

detector • noun a device designed to detect the presence of something and to emit a signal in response.

détente /daytoNt/ • noun the easing of hostility or strained relations between countries.
– ORIGIN French, 'loosening, relaxation'.

detention • noun **1** the action of detaining or the state of being detained. **2** the punishment of being kept in school after hours.

detention centre • noun an institution where people, especially refugees and people awaiting trial, are detained.

deter /diter/ • verb (**deterred, deterring**) **1** discourage from doing something through fear of the consequences. **2** prevent the occurrence of.
– ORIGIN Latin *deterrere*, from *terrere* 'frighten'.

detergent • noun a soluble cleansing agent which combines

Thesaurus

desolation. **3** *the destruction of cattle* SLAUGHTER, killing, putting down, extermination, termination. **4** *the destruction of the enemies' forces* ANNIHILATION, obliteration, elimination, eradication, liquidation; killing, slaughter, massacre, extermination.

destructive • adjective **1** *the most destructive war* DEVASTATING, ruinous, disastrous, catastrophic, calamitous, cataclysmic; harmful, damaging, detrimental, deleterious, injurious, crippling; violent, savage, fierce, brutal, deadly, lethal. **2** *destructive criticism* NEGATIVE, hostile, vicious, unfriendly; unhelpful, obstructive, discouraging.

desultory • adjective CASUAL, cursory, superficial, token, perfunctory, half-hearted, lukewarm; random, aimless, erratic, unmethodical, unsystematic, chaotic, inconsistent, irregular, intermittent, sporadic, fitful.
– OPPOSITES keen.

detach • verb **1** *he detached the lamp from its bracket* UNFASTEN, disconnect, disengage, separate, uncouple, remove, loose, unhitch, unhook, free, disunite; pull off, cut off, break off. **2** *he detached himself from the crowd* FREE, separate, segregate; move away, split off; leave, abandon. **3** *he has detached himself from his family* DISSOCIATE, divorce, alienate, separate, segregate, isolate, cut off; break away, disaffiliate, defect; leave, quit, withdraw from, break with.
– OPPOSITES attach, join.

detached • adjective **1** *a detached collar* UNFASTENED, disconnected, separated, separate, loosened; untied, unhitched, undone, unhooked, unbuttoned; free, severed, cut off. **2** *a detached observer* DISPASSIONATE, disinterested, objective, uninvolved, outside, neutral, unbiased, unprejudiced, impartial, non-partisan; indifferent, aloof, remote, distant, impersonal. **3** *a detached house* STANDING ALONE, separate.

detachment • noun **1** *she looked on everything with detachment* OBJECTIVITY, dispassion, disinterest, open-mindedness, neutrality, impartiality; indifference, aloofness. **2** *a detachment of soldiers* UNIT, detail, squad, troop, contingent, outfit, task force, patrol, crew; platoon, company, corps, regiment, brigade, battalion. **3** *the detachment of the wallpaper* LOOSENING, disconnection, disengagement, separation; removal.

detail • noun **1** *the picture is correct in every detail* PARTICULAR, respect, feature, characteristic, attribute, specific, aspect, facet, part, unit, component, constituent; fact, piece of information, point, element, circumstance, consideration. **2** *that's just a detail* UNIMPORTANT POINT, trivial fact, triviality, technicality, nicety, subtlety, trifle, fine point, incidental, inessential, nothing. **3** *records with a considerable degree of detail* PRECISION, exactness, accuracy, thoroughness, carefulness, scrupulousness, particularity. **4** *a guard detail* UNIT, detachment, squad, troop, contingent, outfit, task force, patrol. **5** *I got the toilet detail* DUTY, task, job, chore, charge, responsibility, assignment, function, mission, engagement, occupation, undertaking, errand.
• verb **1** *the report details our objections* DESCRIBE, explain, expound, relate, catalogue, list, spell out, itemize, particularize, identify, specify; state, declare, present, set out, frame; cite, quote, instance, mention, name. **2** *troops were detailed to prevent the escape* ASSIGN, allocate, appoint, delegate, commission, charge; send, post; nominate, vote, elect, co-opt.
– PHRASES **in detail** THOROUGHLY, in depth, exhaustively, minutely, closely, meticulously, rigorously, scrupulously, painstakingly, carefully; completely, comprehensively, fully, extensively.

detailed • adjective COMPREHENSIVE, full, complete, thorough, exhaustive, all-inclusive; elaborate, minute, intricate; explicit, specific, precise, exact, accurate, meticulous, painstaking; itemized, blow-by-blow.
– OPPOSITES general.

detain • verb **1** *they were detained for questioning* HOLD, take into custody, take (in), confine, imprison, lock up, put in jail, intern; arrest, apprehend, seize; informal pick up, run in, haul in, nab, collar; Brit. informal nick. **2** *don't let me detain you* DELAY, hold up, make late, keep, slow up/down; hinder, hamper, impede, obstruct.
– OPPOSITES release.

detect • verb **1** *no one detected the smell of diesel* NOTICE, perceive, discern, be aware of, note, make out, spot, recognize, distinguish, remark, identify, diagnose; catch, sense, see, smell, scent, taste; Brit. informal clock. **2** *they are responsible for detecting fraud* DISCOVER, uncover, find out, turn up, unearth, dig up, root out, expose, reveal. **3** *help the police to detect crime* SOLVE, clear up, get to the bottom of, find the person behind; informal crack. **4** *the hackers were detected* CATCH, hunt down, track down, find, expose, reveal, unmask, smoke out; apprehend, arrest; informal nail.

detection • noun **1** *the detection of methane* DISCERNMENT, perception, awareness, recognition, identification, diagnosis; sensing, sight, smelling, tasting. **2** *the detection of insider dealing* DISCOVERY, uncovering, unearthing, exposure, revelation. **3** *the detection rate for burglary* SOLVING, clear-up. **4** *he managed to escape detection* CAPTURE, identification, exposure; apprehension, arrest.

detective • noun INVESTIGATOR, private investigator, private detective, operative; Brit. enquiry agent; informal private eye, PI, sleuth, snoop; N. Amer. informal shamus, gumshoe; informal, dated dick.

detention • noun CUSTODY, imprisonment, confinement, incarceration, internment, detainment, captivity; arrest, house arrest; quarantine.

deter • verb **1** *the high cost deterred many* DISCOURAGE, dissuade,

with impurities and dirt to make them more soluble. ● **adjective** relating to detergents or their action.
– ORIGIN from Latin *detergere* 'wipe away'.
deteriorate /diteeriərayt/ ● **verb** become progressively worse.
– DERIVATIVES **deterioration** noun.
– ORIGIN Latin *deteriorare*, from *deterior* 'worse'.
determinant /diterminənt/ ● **noun 1** a factor which determines the nature or outcome of something. **2** Biology a gene determining the character and development of particular cells in an organism. **3** Mathematics a quantity obtained by adding products of the elements of a square matrix according to a given rule. ● **adjective** serving to determine or decide.
determinate /diterminət/ ● **adjective** of fixed and definite limits or nature.
– DERIVATIVES **determinacy** noun.
determination ● **noun 1** firmness of purpose; resolutenesss. **2** the action or process of determining.
determine ● **verb 1** be the decisive factor in: *it is biological age that determines our looks.* **2** firmly decide. **3** ascertain or establish by research or calculation.
– DERIVATIVES **determinable** adjective.
– ORIGIN Latin *determinare* 'limit, fix'.
determined ● **adjective** having firmness of purpose; resolute.
– DERIVATIVES **determinedly** adverb.
determiner ● **noun 1** a person or thing that determines. **2** Grammar a modifying word that determines the kind of reference a noun or noun group has, for example *a, the, every*.
determinism ● **noun** Philosophy the doctrine that all events and actions are determined by external forces acting on the will.
– DERIVATIVES **determinist** noun & adjective **deterministic** adjective.
deterrent /diterrənt/ ● **noun** a thing that deters or is intended to deter. ● **adjective** able or intended to deter.
– DERIVATIVES **deterrence** noun.
detest ● **verb** dislike intensely.
– ORIGIN Latin *detestari* 'denounce, abhor', from *testari* 'witness'.
detestable ● **adjective** deserving intense dislike.
detestation /deetestaysh'n/ ● **noun** intense dislike.
dethrone ● **verb 1** remove (a monarch) from power. **2** remove from a position of authority or dominance.
– DERIVATIVES **dethronement** noun.
detonate /dettənayt/ ● **verb** explode or cause to explode.
– DERIVATIVES **detonation** noun.
– ORIGIN Latin *detonare*, from *tonare* 'to thunder'.
detonator ● **noun** a device or charge used to detonate an explosive.
detour /deetoor/ ● **noun** a divergence from a direct or intended route. ● **verb** take a detour.
– ORIGIN French, 'change of direction'.
detox informal ● **noun** /**dee**toks/ detoxification. ● **verb** /deetoks/ detoxify.
detoxicate /deetoksikayt/ ● **verb** another term for DETOXIFY.
– DERIVATIVES **detoxication** noun.
detoxify ● **verb** (**detoxifies, detoxified**) **1** remove toxic substances from. **2** abstain or help to abstain from drink or drugs until the bloodstream is free of toxins.
– DERIVATIVES **detoxification** noun **detoxifier** noun.
detract ● **verb** (**detract from**) cause (something) to seem less valuable or impressive.
– DERIVATIVES **detraction** noun.
– ORIGIN Latin *detrahere* 'draw away'.
detractor ● **noun** a person who disparages someone or something.
detrain ● **verb** leave or cause to leave a train.
detriment /detrimənt/ ● **noun** harm or damage: *she fasted to the detriment of her health.*
– DERIVATIVES **detrimental** adjective **detrimentally** adjective.
– ORIGIN Latin *detrimentum*, from *deterere* 'wear away'.
detritus /ditrītəss/ ● **noun** debris or waste material.

d

Thesaurus

put off, scare off; dishearten, demoralize, daunt, intimidate. **2** *the presence of a caretaker deters crime* PREVENT, stop, avert, fend off, stave off, ward off, block, halt, check; hinder, impede, hamper, obstruct, foil, forestall, counteract, inhibit, curb.
– OPPOSITES encourage.
detergent ● **noun** *washing detergent* CLEANER, cleanser; washing powder, washing-up liquid; soap.
● **adjective** *detergent action* CLEANING, cleansing; surface-active.
deteriorate ● **verb 1** *his health deteriorated* WORSEN, decline, degenerate; fail, slump, slip, go downhill, go backwards, wane, ebb; informal go to pot. **2** *these materials deteriorate if stored wrongly* DECAY, degrade, degenerate, break down, decompose, rot, go off, spoil, perish; break up, disintegrate, crumble, fall apart.
– OPPOSITES improve.
deterioration ● **noun 1** *a deterioration in law and order* DECLINE, collapse, failure, drop, downturn, slump, slip, retrogression. **2** *deterioration of the roof structure* DECAY, degradation, degeneration, breakdown, decomposition, rot; atrophy, weakening; break-up, disintegration, dilapidation.
determinate ● **adjective** FIXED, settled, specified, established, defined, explicit, known, determined, definitive, conclusive, express, precise, categorical, positive, definite.
determination ● **noun 1** *it took great determination to win* RESOLUTION, resolve, will power, strength of character, single-mindedness, purposefulness, intentness; staunchness, perseverance, persistence, tenacity, staying power; strong-mindedness, backbone; stubbornness, doggedness, obstinacy; spirit, courage, pluck, grit, stout-heartedness; informal guts, spunk; formal pertinacity. **2** *the determination of the rent* SETTING, specification, settlement, designation, arrangement, establishment, prescription. **3** *the determination of the speed of light* CALCULATION, discovery, ascertainment, establishment, deduction, divination, diagnosis, discernment, verification, confirmation.
determine ● **verb 1** *chromosomes determine the sex of the embryo* CONTROL, decide, regulate, direct, dictate, govern; affect, influence, mould. **2** *he determined to sell up* RESOLVE, decide, make up one's mind, choose, elect, opt; formal purpose. **3** *the rent shall be determined by an accountant* SPECIFY, set, fix, decide on, settle, assign, designate, arrange, choose, establish, ordain, prescribe, decree. **4** *determine the composition of the fibres* ASCERTAIN, find out, discover, learn, establish, calculate, work out, make out, deduce, diagnose, discern; check, verify, confirm; informal figure out.
determined ● **adjective 1** *he was determined to have his way* INTENT ON, bent on, set on, insistent on, resolved to, firm about, committed to; single-minded about, obsessive about. **2** *a very determined man* RESOLUTE, purposeful, purposive, adamant, single-minded, unswerving, unwavering, undaunted, intent, insistent; steadfast, staunch, stalwart; persevering, persistent, indefatigable, tenacious; strong-minded, strong-willed, unshakeable, steely, foursquare, dedicated, committed; stubborn, dogged, obstinate, inflexible, intransigent, unyielding, immovable; N. Amer. rock-ribbed; formal pertinacious.
determining ● **adjective** DECIDING, decisive, conclusive, final, definitive, key, pivotal, crucial, critical, major, chief, prime.
deterrent ● **noun** DISINCENTIVE, discouragement, damper, curb, check, restraint; obstacle, hindrance, impediment, obstruction, block, barrier, inhibition.
– OPPOSITES incentive.
detest ● **verb** ABHOR, hate, loathe, despise, shrink from, be unable to bear, find intolerable, dislike, disdain, have an aversion to; formal abominate.
– OPPOSITES love.
detestable ● **adjective** ABHORRENT, hateful, loathsome, despicable, abominable, execrable, repellent, repugnant, repulsive, revolting, disgusting, distasteful, horrible, horrid, awful; heinous, reprehensible, obnoxious, odious, offensive, contemptible.
dethrone ● **verb** DEPOSE, unseat, uncrown, oust, topple, overthrow, bring down, dislodge, displace, supplant, usurp, eject, drum out.
– OPPOSITES crown.
detonate ● **verb 1** *the charge detonated under the engine* EXPLODE, go off, blow up, shatter, erupt; ignite; bang, blast, boom. **2** *they detonated the bomb* SET OFF, explode, discharge, let off, touch off, trigger; ignite, kindle.
detonation ● **noun** EXPLOSION, discharge, blowing up, ignition; blast, bang, report.
detour ● **noun** DIVERSION, roundabout route, indirect route, scenic route; bypass, ring road; digression, deviation; Brit. relief road.
detract ● **verb 1** *my reservations should not detract from the book's excellence* BELITTLE, take away from, diminish, reduce, lessen, minimize, play down, trivialize, decry, depreciate, devalue, deprecate. **2** *the patterns will detract attention from each other* DIVERT, distract, draw away, deflect, avert, shift one's attention.
detractor ● **noun** CRITIC, disparager, denigrator, deprecator, belittler, attacker, fault-finder, backbiter; slanderer, libeller; informal knocker.

d

– DERIVATIVES **detrital** adjective.
– ORIGIN Latin, from *deterere* 'wear away'.

de trop /də trō/ ● adjective not wanted; unwelcome.
– ORIGIN French, 'excessive'.

detumescence /deetyoomess'nss/ ● noun subsiding from a state of swelling or sexual arousal.
– DERIVATIVES **detumescent** adjective.
– ORIGIN Latin *detumescere*, from *tumescere* 'to swell'.

detune ● verb **1** cause (a musical instrument) to become out of tune. **2** reduce the performance of (a motor vehicle or engine) by adjustment.

deuce[1] /dyo͞oss/ ● noun **1** chiefly N. Amer. the number two on dice or playing cards. **2** Tennis the score of 40 all in a game, at which two consecutive points are needed to win the game.
– ORIGIN Old French *deus*, from Latin *duos* 'two'.

deuce[2] /dyo͞oss/ ● noun **(the deuce)** informal used as a euphemism for 'devil' in exclamations or for emphasis.
– ORIGIN Low German *duus*, probably of the same origin as DEUCE[1] (two aces at dice being the worst throw).

deus ex machina /dayəss eks **mak**kinə/ ● noun an unexpected event saving a seemingly hopeless situation, especially in a narrative.
– ORIGIN Latin, from Greek *theos ek mēkhanēs* 'god from the machinery' (referring to the actors representing gods suspended above the stage in ancient Greek theatre, who intervened in the play's outcome).

deuterium /dyooteeriəm/ ● noun Chemistry a stable isotope of hydrogen with a mass approximately twice that of the usual isotope.
– ORIGIN Latin, from Greek *deuteros* 'second'.

Deutschmark /**doych**maark/ (also **Deutsche Mark** /doychə **maark**/) ● noun the basic monetary unit of Germany, equal to 100 pfennig.
– ORIGIN from German *deutsche Mark* 'German mark'.

devalue ● verb **(devalues, devalued, devaluing) 1** reduce the worth of. **2** reduce the official value of (a currency) in relation to other currencies.
– DERIVATIVES **devaluation** noun.

devastate /devvəstayt/ ● verb **1** destroy or ruin. **2** overwhelm with severe shock or grief.
– DERIVATIVES **devastation** noun **devastator** noun.
– ORIGIN Latin *devastare*, from *vastare* 'lay waste'.

devastating ● adjective **1** highly destructive. **2** extremely distressing or shocking. **3** informal very impressive or attractive.
– DERIVATIVES **devastatingly** adverb.

develop ● verb **(developed, developing) 1** become or make larger or more advanced. **2** start to exist, experience, or possess. **3** convert (land) to a new purpose, especially by constructing buildings. **4** treat (a photographic film) with chemicals to make a visible image.
– DERIVATIVES **developable** adjective **developer** noun.
– ORIGIN originally in the sense 'unfold': from French *développer*, from Latin *dis-* 'un-' + a second element found also in ENVELOP.

developing country ● noun a poor agricultural country that is seeking to become more advanced economically and socially.

development ● noun **1** the action of developing or the state of being developed. **2** a new product or idea. **3** a new stage in a changing situation. **4** an area of land with new buildings on it.
– DERIVATIVES **developmental** adjective **developmentally** adverb.

deviant ● adjective diverging from normal standards, especially in social or sexual behaviour. ● noun a deviant person.
– DERIVATIVES **deviance** noun **deviancy** noun.

deviate ● verb /deeviayt/ diverge from an established course or from normal standards.
– ORIGIN Latin *deviare* 'turn out of the way', from *via* 'way'.

deviation ● noun **1** the action or an act of deviating. **2** Statistics the amount by which a single measurement differs from a fixed value.

device ● noun **1** a thing made for a particular purpose, especially a mechanical or electronic contrivance. **2** a plan, scheme, or trick. **3** a drawing or design.
– PHRASES **leave someone to their own devices** leave someone to do as they wish.
– ORIGIN originally in sense 'desire or intention': from Old French *devis*, from Latin *dividere* 'to divide'.

devil ● noun **1 (the Devil)** (in Christian and Jewish belief) the supreme spirit of evil. **2** an evil spirit; a demon. **3** a very wicked or cruel person. **4** a mischievously clever or self-willed

Thesaurus

detriment ● noun HARM, damage, injury, hurt, impairment, loss, disadvantage, disservice, mischief.
– OPPOSITES benefit.

detrimental ● adjective HARMFUL, damaging, injurious, hurtful, inimical, deleterious, destructive, ruinous, disastrous, bad, malign, adverse, undesirable, unfavourable, unfortunate; unhealthy, unwholesome.
– OPPOSITES benign.

detritus ● noun DEBRIS, waste, refuse, rubbish, litter, scrap, flotsam and jetsam, lumber, rubble; remains, remnants, fragments, scraps, dregs, leavings, sweepings, dross, scum; *N. Amer.* trash, garbage; *Austral./NZ* mullock; *informal* dreck.

devalue ● verb BELITTLE, depreciate, disparage, denigrate, decry, deprecate, treat lightly, discredit, underrate, undervalue, underestimate, deflate, diminish, trivialize, run down; *informal* knock, sell short, put down, pooh-pooh, do down, pick holes in; *Brit. informal* rubbish.

devastate ● verb **1** *the city was devastated by an earthquake* DESTROY, ruin, wreck, lay waste, ravage, demolish, raze (to the ground), level, flatten. **2** *he was devastated by the news* SHATTER, shock, stun, daze, dumbfound, traumatize, crush, overwhelm, overcome, distress; *informal* knock sideways; *Brit. informal* knock for six.

devastating ● adjective **1** *a devastating cyclone* DESTRUCTIVE, ruinous, disastrous, catastrophic, calamitous, cataclysmic; harmful, damaging, injurious, detrimental; crippling, violent, savage, fierce, dangerous, fatal, deadly, lethal. **2** *devastating news* SHATTERING, shocking, traumatic, overwhelming, crushing, distressing, terrible. **3** *(informal) he presented devastating arguments* INCISIVE, highly effective, penetrating, cutting; withering, blistering, searing, scathing, fierce, savage, stinging, biting, caustic, harsh, unsparing.

devastation ● noun **1** *the hurricane left a trail of devastation* DESTRUCTION, ruin, desolation, havoc, wreckage; ruins, ravages. **2** *the devastation of Prussia* DESTRUCTION, wrecking, ruination, despoliation; demolition, annihilation. **3** *the devastation you have caused the family* SHOCK, trauma, distress, stress, strain, pain, anguish, suffering, upset, agony, misery, heartache.

develop ● verb **1** *the industry developed rapidly* GROW, expand, spread; advance, progress, evolve, mature; prosper, thrive, flourish, blossom. **2** *a plan was developed* INITIATE, instigate, set in motion; originate, invent, form, establish, generate. **3** *children should develop their talents* EXPAND, augment, broaden, supplement, reinforce; enhance, refine, improve, polish, perfect. **4** *a row developed* START, begin, emerge, erupt, break out, burst out, arise, break, unfold, happen. **5** *he developed the disease last week* FALL ILL WITH, be stricken with, succumb to; contract, catch, get, pick up, come down with, become infected with.

development ● noun **1** *the development of the firm* EVOLUTION, growth, maturation, expansion, enlargement, spread, progress; success. **2** *the development of an idea* FORMING, establishment, initiation, instigation, origination, invention, generation. **3** *keep abreast of developments* EVENT, occurrence, happening, circumstance, incident, situation, issue. **4** *a housing development* ESTATE, complex, site.

deviant ● adjective *deviant behaviour* ABERRANT, abnormal, atypical, anomalous, irregular, non-standard; nonconformist, perverse, uncommon, unusual; freakish, strange, odd, peculiar, bizarre, eccentric, idiosyncratic, unorthodox, exceptional; warped, perverted; *informal* kinky, quirky.
– OPPOSITES normal.
● noun *we were seen as deviants* NONCONFORMIST, eccentric, maverick, individualist; outsider, misfit; *informal* oddball, weirdo, freak; *N. Amer. informal* screwball, kook.

deviate ● verb DIVERGE, digress, drift, stray, slew, veer, swerve; get sidetracked, branch off; differ, vary, run counter to, contrast with.

deviation ● noun DIVERGENCE, digression, departure; difference, variation, variance; aberration, abnormality, irregularity, anomaly, inconsistency, discrepancy.

device ● noun **1** *a device for measuring pressure* IMPLEMENT, gadget, utensil, tool, appliance, apparatus, instrument, machine, mechanism, contrivance, contraption; *informal* gizmo, widget. **2** *an ingenious legal device* PLOY, tactic, move, stratagem, scheme, plot, trick, ruse, manoeuvre, machination, contrivance, expedient, dodge, wile; *Brit. informal* wheeze. **3** *their shields bear his device* EMBLEM,

person. **5** informal a person with specified characteristics: *the poor devil.* **6** (**the devil**) fighting spirit; wildness. **7** (**the devil**) a thing that is very difficult to deal with. **8** (**the devil**) expressing surprise or annoyance.
– PHRASES **be a devil!** informal said to encourage a hesitant person. **between the devil and the deep blue sea** caught in a dilemma. **the devil can quote scripture for his purpose** proverb people may conceal unworthy motives by reciting words that sound morally authoritative. **the devil finds work for idle hands to do** proverb if someone doesn't have enough work to occupy them, they are liable to cause or get into trouble. **the devil looks after his own** proverb success or good fortune often seem to come to those who least deserve it. **devil-may-care** cheerful and reckless. **the devil's in the detail** the details of a matter are its most problematic aspect. **the devil to pay** serious trouble to be dealt with. **give the devil his due** proverb if someone or something bad has any redeeming features these should be acknowledged. **like the devil** with great speed or energy. **speak** (or **talk**) **of the devil** said when a person appears just after being mentioned.
– ORIGIN Greek *diabolos* 'accuser, slanderer'.
devilish ● adjective **1** like a devil in evil and cruelty. **2** mischievous. **3** very difficult to deal with. ● adverb informal, dated very; extremely: *a devilish clever chap.*
– DERIVATIVES **devilishly** adverb **devilishness** noun.
devilled ● adjective cooked with hot seasoning.
devilment ● noun reckless mischief; wild spirits.
devilry ● noun **1** wicked activity. **2** reckless mischief.
devil's advocate ● noun a person who expresses a contentious opinion in order to provoke debate.
devil's food cake ● noun chiefly N. Amer. a rich chocolate cake.
devious /deeviəss/ ● adjective **1** skilful in using underhand tactics. **2** (of a route or journey) deviating from the most direct course; circuitous.
– DERIVATIVES **deviously** adverb **deviousness** noun.
– ORIGIN Latin *devius* 'out of the way', from *via* 'way'
devise /dīvīz/ ● verb **1** plan or invent (a complex procedure or mechanism). **2** Law leave (real property) to someone in a will.
– DERIVATIVES **deviser** noun.
– ORIGIN Old French *deviser*, from Latin *dividere* 'force apart, remove'.
devitalize (also **devitalise**) ● verb deprive of strength and vigour.
– DERIVATIVES **devitalization** noun.
devoid /divoyd/ ● adjective (**devoid of**) entirely lacking in.
– ORIGIN from Old French *devoidier* 'cast out'.
devolution /deevəloōsh'n/ ● noun the devolving of power by central government to local or regional administration.
– DERIVATIVES **devolutionary** adjective **devolutionist** noun.
devolve /divolv/ ● verb **1** transfer (power) to a lower level, especially from central government to local or regional administration. **2** (**devolve on/to**) (of duties or responsibility) pass to (a deputy or successor). **3** (**devolve on/to**) Law (of property) pass from one owner to (another), especially by inheritance.
– ORIGIN Latin *devolvere* 'roll down'.
Devonian /divōniən/ ● adjective Geology relating to the fourth period of the Palaeozoic era (about 409 to 363 million years ago), a time when the first amphibians appeared.
devoré /dəvoray/ ● noun a velvet fabric with a pattern formed by burning the pile away with acid.
– ORIGIN French, 'devoured'.
devote ● verb (**devote to**) give (time or resources) to.
– ORIGIN originally in the sense 'dedicate formally, consecrate': from Latin *devovere* 'consecrate'.
devoted ● adjective very loving or loyal.
– DERIVATIVES **devotedly** adverb.
devotee /devvətee/ ● noun **1** a person who is very enthusiastic about someone or something. **2** a follower of a particular religion or god.
devotion ● noun **1** great love or loyalty. **2** religious worship. **3** (**devotions**) prayers or religious observances.
– DERIVATIVES **devotional** adjective.

d

Thesaurus

symbol, logo, badge, crest, insignia, coat of arms, escutcheon, seal, mark, design, motif; monogram, hallmark, trademark.
devil ● noun **1** *God and the Devil* SATAN, Beelzebub, Lucifer, the Lord of the Flies, the Prince of Darkness; *informal* Old Nick. **2** *they drove out the devils from their bodies* EVIL SPIRIT, demon, cacodemon, fiend, bogie; *informal* spook. **3** *look what the cruel devil has done* BRUTE, beast, monster, fiend; villain, sadist, barbarian, ogre. **4** *he's a naughty little devil* RASCAL, rogue, imp, fiend, monkey, wretch; *informal* monster, horror, scamp, tyke; *Brit. informal* perisher; *N. Amer. informal* varmint. **5** *(informal) the poor devils looked ill* WRETCH, unfortunate, creature, soul, person, fellow; *informal* beggar.
devilish ● adjective **1** *a devilish grin* DIABOLICAL, fiendish, demonic, satanic, demoniac, demoniacal; hellish, infernal. **2** *a devilish torture* WICKED, evil, iniquitous, vile, foul, abominable, unspeakable, loathsome, monstrous, atrocious, heinous, hideous, odious, horrible, appalling, dreadful, awful, terrible, ghastly, abhorrent, despicable, depraved, dark, black, immoral; vicious, cruel, savage, barbaric. **3** *a devilish job* DIFFICULT, tricky, ticklish, troublesome, thorny, awkward, problematic.
devil-may-care ● adjective RECKLESS, rash, incautious, heedless, impetuous, impulsive, daredevil, hot-headed, wild, foolhardy, audacious, death-or-glory; nonchalant, casual, breezy, flippant, insouciant, happy-go-lucky, easy-going, unworried, untroubled, unconcerned, harum-scarum; *Brit.* tearaway.
devilment ● noun. See DEVILRY sense 2.
devilry, deviltry ● noun **1** *some devilry was afoot* WICKEDNESS, evil, sin, iniquity, vileness, badness, wrongdoing, dishonesty, unscrupulousness, villainy, delinquency, devilishness, fiendishness; *informal* crookedness, shadiness. **2** *she had a perverse sense of devilry* MISCHIEF, mischievousness, naughtiness, badness, perversity, impishness; misbehaviour, troublemaking, misconduct; pranks, tricks, roguery, devilment; *informal* monkey business, shenanigans. **3** *they dabbled in devilry* BLACK MAGIC, sorcery, witchcraft, wizardry, necromancy, enchantment, spell-working, incantation; the supernatural, occultism, the occult, the black arts, divination, voodoo, witchery; *N. Amer.* mojo, orenda.
devious ● adjective **1** *the devious ways in which they bent the rules* UNDERHAND, deceitful, dishonest, dishonourable, unethical, unprincipled, immoral, unscrupulous, fraudulent, dubious, unfair, treacherous, duplicitous; crafty, cunning, calculating, artful, conniving, scheming, sly, wily; sneaky, furtive, secret, clandestine, surreptitious, covert; *N. Amer.* snide, snidey; *informal* crooked, shady, dirty, low-down; *Brit. informal* dodgy. **2** *a devious route around the coast* CIRCUITOUS, roundabout, indirect, meandering, tortuous.
devise ● verb CONCEIVE, think up, dream up, work out, formulate, concoct; design, invent, coin, originate; compose, construct, fabricate, create, produce, develop; discover, hit on; hatch, contrive; *informal* cook up.
devitalize ● verb WEAKEN, enfeeble, debilitate, enervate, sap, drain, tax, exhaust, weary, tire (out), fatigue, wear out, prostrate; indispose, incapacitate, lay low; *informal* knock out, do in, shatter, whack, bush, frazzle, poop; *Brit. informal* knacker.
– OPPOSITES strengthen.
devoid ● adjective FREE, empty, vacant, bereft, denuded, deprived, destitute, bankrupt; (**devoid of**) lacking, without, wanting; *informal* minus.
devolution ● noun DECENTRALIZATION, delegation; redistribution, transfer; surrender, relinquishment.
devolve ● verb DELEGATE, depute, pass (down/on), hand down/over/on, transfer, transmit, assign, consign, convey, entrust, turn over, give, cede, surrender, relinquish, deliver; bestow, grant.
devote ● verb ALLOCATE, assign, allot, commit, give (over), apportion, consign, pledge; dedicate, consecrate; set aside, earmark, reserve, designate.
devoted ● adjective LOYAL, faithful, true (blue), staunch, steadfast, constant, committed, dedicated, devout; fond, loving, affectionate, caring, admiring.
devotee ● noun **1** *a devotee of rock music* ENTHUSIAST, fan, lover, aficionado, admirer; *informal* buff, freak, nut, fiend, fanatic, addict, maniac. **2** *devotees thronged the temple* FOLLOWER, adherent, supporter, advocate, disciple, votary, member, stalwart, fanatic, zealot; believer, worshipper.
devotion ● noun **1** *her devotion to her husband* LOYALTY, faithfulness, fidelity, constancy, commitment, adherence, allegiance, dedication; fondness, love, admiration, affection, care. **2** *a life of devotion* DEVOUTNESS, piety, religiousness, spirituality, godliness, holiness, sanctity. **3** *morning devotions* (RELIGIOUS) WORSHIP, religious observance; prayers, vespers, matins; prayer meeting, church service.
devotional ● adjective RELIGIOUS, sacred, spiritual, divine, church,

devour /divowr/ ● verb **1** eat greedily. **2** (of fire or a similar force) consume destructively. **3** read quickly and eagerly. **4** (**be devoured**) be totally absorbed by an emotion.
– DERIVATIVES **devourer** noun.
– ORIGIN Latin *devorare*, from *vorare* 'to swallow'.
devout /divowt/ ● adjective **1** deeply religious. **2** earnestly sincere: *my devout hope*.
– DERIVATIVES **devoutly** adverb **devoutness** noun.
– ORIGIN Latin *devotus* 'devoted', from *devovere* 'consecrate'.
dew ● noun **1** tiny drops of water that form when atmospheric vapour condenses on cool surfaces at night. **2** beaded or glistening liquid.
– ORIGIN Old English.
dewberry ● noun (pl. **dewberries**) the edible blue-black fruit of a trailing bramble, with a dewy white bloom.
Dewey decimal classification ● noun a decimal system of library classification which uses a three-figure code from 000 to 999 to represent the major branches of knowledge.
– ORIGIN named after the American librarian Melvil *Dewey* (1851–1931).
dewlap ● noun a fold of loose skin hanging from the neck or throat of an animal or bird, especially that present in many cattle.
dew point ● noun the atmospheric temperature below which dew can form.
dewy ● adjective (**dewier, dewiest**) **1** wet with dew. **2** (of a person's skin) appearing soft and lustrous.
dewy-eyed ● adjective naively sentimental.
Dexedrine /deksədreen/ ● noun trademark a form of amphetamine.
dexter /dekstər/ ● adjective Heraldry on or towards the bearer's right-hand side and the observer's left of a coat of arms. The opposite of SINISTER.
– ORIGIN Latin, 'on the right'.
dexterity /deksterriti/ ● noun skill in performing tasks, especially with the hands.
– ORIGIN Latin *dexteritas*, from *dexter* 'on the right'.
dexterous /dekstrəss/ (also **dextrous**) ● adjective showing dexterity; adroit.
– DERIVATIVES **dexterously** adverb.
dextral /dekstrəl/ technical ● adjective **1** of or on the right side or the right hand. **2** right-handed. ● noun a right-handed person.
dextrose ● noun a naturally occurring form of glucose.
– ORIGIN from Latin *dexter* 'on the right', because solutions of dextrose rotate the plane of polarized light to the right.
dextrous ● adjective variant spelling of DEXTEROUS.
DFC ● abbreviation (in the UK) Distinguished Flying Cross.
DFE ● abbreviation Department for Education.
DFM ● abbreviation (in the UK) Distinguished Flying Medal.
DG ● abbreviation director general.
dhal /daal/ (also **dal**) ● noun (in Indian cookery) split pulses.
– ORIGIN Hindi.
dhansak /dansak/ ● noun an Indian dish of meat or vegetables cooked with lentils and coriander.
– ORIGIN Gujarati.
dharma /daarmə/ ● noun (in Indian religion) the eternal law of the cosmos.
– ORIGIN Sanskrit, 'decree or custom'.
dhobi /dōbi/ ● noun (pl. **dhobis**) (in the Indian subcontinent) a person whose occupation is washing clothes.
– ORIGIN Hindi.
dhoti /dōti/ ● noun (pl. **dhotis**) a loincloth worn by male Hindus.
– ORIGIN Hindi.
dhow /dow/ ● noun a lateen-rigged ship with one or two masts, used chiefly in the Arabian region.
– ORIGIN Arabic.
dhurrie /durri/ ● noun (pl. **dhurries**) a heavy cotton rug of Indian origin.
– ORIGIN Hindi.
di- /dī, di/ ● combining form twice; two-; double: *dioxide*.
– ORIGIN from Greek *dis* 'twice'.
dia- (also **di-** before a vowel) ● prefix **1** through; across: *diameter*. **2** apart: *diaeresis*.
– ORIGIN Greek *dia* 'through'.
diabetes /dīəbeeteez/ ● noun a disorder of the metabolism causing the production of large amounts of urine.
– ORIGIN Greek, 'siphon'.
diabetes mellitus /milītəss/ ● noun the commonest form of diabetes, caused by a deficiency of the pancreatic hormone insulin, which results in a failure to metabolize sugars and starch.
– ORIGIN *mellitus* is Latin for 'sweet'.
diabetic ● adjective having or relating to diabetes. ● noun a person with diabetes.
diabolical ● adjective **1** (also **diabolic**) of or like the Devil, especially in being evil or cruel. **2** informal very bad: *a diabolical voice*.
– DERIVATIVES **diabolically** adverb.
– ORIGIN from Greek *diabolos* 'accuser, slanderer' (see DEVIL).
diabolism /dīabbəliz'm/ ● noun worship of the Devil.
– DERIVATIVES **diabolist** noun.
diachronic /dīəkronnik/ ● adjective concerned with the way in which something, especially language, has developed through time. Often contrasted with SYNCHRONIC.
– DERIVATIVES **diachronically** adverb **diachrony** /dīakrəni/ noun.
– ORIGIN from Greek *khronos* 'time'.
diaconal /dīakkən'l/ ● adjective relating to a deacon or deacons.
– ORIGIN from Latin *diaconus* 'deacon'.
diaconate /dīakkənayt, -nət/ ● noun **1** the office of deacon. **2** a body of deacons.
diacritic /dīəkrittik/ ● noun a sign, such as an accent, written above or below a letter to indicate a difference in pronunciation from the same letter when unmarked.
– DERIVATIVES **diacritical** adjective.
– ORIGIN Greek *diakritikos*, from *diakrinein* 'distinguish'.
diadem /dīədem/ ● noun a jewelled crown or headband worn as a symbol of sovereignty.
– ORIGIN Greek *diadēma*, from *diadein* 'bind round'.

Thesaurus

ecclesiastical.
– OPPOSITES secular.
devour ● verb **1** *he devoured his meal* EAT HUNGRILY, eat greedily, gobble (up/down), guzzle, gulp (down), bolt (down), cram down, gorge oneself on, wolf (down), feast on, consume, eat up; *informal* pack away, demolish, dispose of, make short work of, polish off, shovel down, stuff oneself with, pig oneself on, put away, get outside of; *Brit. informal* scoff. **2** *flames devoured the house* CONSUME, engulf, envelop; destroy, demolish, lay waste, devastate; gut, ravage, ruin, wreck. **3** *he was devoured by remorse* AFFLICT, plague, bedevil, trouble, harrow, rack; consume, swallow up, overcome, overwhelm.
devout ● adjective **1** *a devout Christian* PIOUS, religious, devoted, dedicated, reverent, God-fearing; holy, godly, saintly, faithful, dutiful, righteous, churchgoing, orthodox. **2** *a devout soccer fan* DEDICATED, devoted, committed, loyal, faithful, staunch, genuine, firm, steadfast, unwavering, sincere, wholehearted, keen, enthusiastic, zealous, passionate, ardent, fervent, active, sworn, pledged; *informal* card-carrying, true blue, deep-dyed.
dexterity ● noun **1** *painting china demanded dexterity* DEFTNESS, adeptness, adroitness, agility, nimbleness, handiness, ability, talent, skill, proficiency, expertise, experience, efficiency, mastery, delicacy, knack, artistry, finesse. **2** *his political dexterity* SHREWDNESS, astuteness, sharp-wittedness, acumen, acuity, intelligence; ingenuity, inventiveness, cleverness, smartness; canniness, sense, discernment, insight, understanding, penetration, perception, perspicacity, discrimination; cunning, artfulness, craftiness; *informal* nous, horse sense, savvy.
dexterous ● adjective **1** *a dexterous flick of the wrist* DEFT, adept, adroit, agile, nimble, neat, handy, able, capable, skilful, skilled, proficient, expert, practised, polished; efficient, effortless, slick, professional, masterly; *informal* nifty, mean, ace. **2** *his dexterous accounting abilities* SHREWD, ingenious, inventive, clever, intelligent, brilliant, smart, sharp, acute, astute, canny, intuitive, discerning, perceptive, insightful, incisive, judicious; cunning, artful, crafty, wily; *informal* on the ball, quick off the mark, quick on the uptake, brainy, savvy; *Brit. informal* suss.
– OPPOSITES clumsy, stupid.
diabolical, diabolic ● adjective **1** *his diabolical skill* DEVILISH, fiendish, satanic, demonic, demoniacal, hellish, infernal, evil, wicked, ungodly, unholy. **2** *(informal) a diabolical performance* VERY BAD, dreadful, awful, terrible, disgraceful, shameful, lamentable, deplorable, appalling, atrocious; inferior, substandard, unsatisfactory, inadequate, second-rate, third-rate, shoddy, inept; *informal* crummy, dire, dismal, God-awful, abysmal, rotten, pathetic, pitiful, lousy; *Brit. informal* duff, rubbish, ropy. **3** *(informal) a diabolical*

diaeresis /dīeerəsiss/ (US **dieresis**) ● noun (pl. **diaereses** /dīeerəseez/) a mark (¨) placed over a vowel to indicate that it is sounded separately, as in *Brontë*.
– ORIGIN Greek *diairesis* 'separation'.
diagnose /dīəgnōz/ ● verb **1** make a diagnosis of. **2** identify the medical condition of (someone).
– DERIVATIVES **diagnosable** adjective.
diagnosis ● noun (pl. **diagnoses**) the identification of the nature of an illness or other problem by examination of the symptoms.
– ORIGIN Greek, from *diagignōskein* 'distinguish, discern'.
diagnostic /dīəgnostik/ ● adjective **1** concerned with diagnosis. **2** (of a symptom) distinctive, and so indicating the nature of an illness: *infections which are diagnostic of Aids.* ● noun **1** a distinctive symptom or characteristic. **2** (**diagnostics**) (treated as sing. or pl.) the practice or techniques of diagnosis.
– DERIVATIVES **diagnostically** adverb **diagnostician** noun.
diagonal /dīaggən'l/ ● adjective **1** denoting a straight line joining opposite corners of a rectangle, square, or other figure. **2** (of a line) straight and at an angle; slanting. ● noun a diagonal line.
– DERIVATIVES **diagonally** adverb.
– ORIGIN Greek *diagōnios* 'from angle to angle'.
diagram ● noun a drawing giving a schematic representation of the appearance or structure of something. ● verb (**diagrammed, diagramming**; US **diagramed, diagraming**) represent by means of a diagram.
– DERIVATIVES **diagrammatic** adjective **diagrammatically** adverb.
– ORIGIN Greek *diagramma*, from *diagraphein* 'mark out by lines'.
dial ● noun **1** a disc marked to show the time on a clock or to indicate a reading or measurement by means of a pointer. **2** a disc with numbered holes on a telephone, turned to make a call. **3** a disc turned to select a setting on a radio, cooker, etc. **4** Brit. informal a person's face. ● verb (**dialled, dialling**; US **dialed, dialing**) call (a telephone number) by turning a dial or using a keypad.
– DERIVATIVES **dialler** (also **dialer**) noun.
– ORIGIN Latin *diale* 'clock dial', from *dies* 'day'.
dialect /dīəlekt/ ● noun a form of a language which is peculiar to a specific region or social group.
– DERIVATIVES **dialectal** adjective.
– ORIGIN originally in the sense 'dialectic': from Greek *dialektos* 'discourse, way of speaking'.
dialectic /dīəlektik/ Philosophy ● noun (also **dialectics**) (usu. treated as sing.) **1** the investigation of the truth of opinions, especially by logical discussion. **2** enquiry into metaphysical contradictions and their solutions. **3** the existence or action of opposing social forces, concepts, etc. ● adjective of or relating to dialectic or dialectics.
– ORIGIN from Greek *dialektikē tekhnē* 'art of debate', from *dialegesthai* 'converse with'.
dialectical ● adjective **1** relating to the logical discussion of opinions. **2** concerned with or acting through opposing forces.
– DERIVATIVES **dialectically** adverb.
dialectical materialism ● noun the Marxist theory that political and historical events result from the conflict of social forces (as caused by material needs).
dialectician /dīəlektish'n/ ● noun a person skilled in philosophical debate.
dialectology /dīəlektolləji/ ● noun the branch of linguistics concerned with the study of dialects.
– DERIVATIVES **dialectological** adjective **dialectologist** noun.
dialling code ● noun Brit. a sequence of numbers dialled to connect a telephone to an exchange in another area or country.
dialling tone (N. Amer. **dial tone**) ● noun a sound produced by a telephone that indicates that a caller may start to dial.
dialog box (Brit. also **dialogue box**) ● noun a small area on a computer screen in which the user is prompted to provide information or select commands.
dialogic /dīəlojik/ ● adjective relating to or in the form of dialogue.
– DERIVATIVES **dialogical** adjective.
dialogue (US also **dialog**) ● noun **1** conversation between two or more people as a feature of a book, play, or film. **2** discussion directed towards exploration of a subject or resolution of a problem. ● verb chiefly N. Amer. take part in dialogue.
– ORIGIN Greek *dialogos*, from *dialegesthai* 'converse with'.
dialyse /dīəlīz/ (US **dialyze**) ● verb purify (a mixture) or treat (a patient) by means of dialysis.
dialysis /dīalisiss/ ● noun (pl. **dialyses** /dīaliseez/) **1** Chemistry the separation of particles in a liquid on the basis of differences in their ability to pass through a membrane. **2** the clinical purification of blood by this technique, as a substitute for the normal function of the kidney.
– ORIGIN Greek *dialusis*, from *dialuein* 'split, separate'.
diamanté /dīəmontay/ ● adjective decorated with artificial jewels. ● noun fabric or costume jewellery decorated with artificial jewels.
– ORIGIN French, 'set with diamonds'.
diameter /dīammitər/ ● noun a straight line passing from side to side through the centre of a circle or sphere.
– ORIGIN from Greek *diametros grammē* 'line measuring across'.
diametrical /dīəmetrik'l/ ● adjective **1** (of opposites) complete; absolute. **2** of or along a diameter.
– DERIVATIVES **diametric** adjective **diametrically** adverb.
diamond ● noun **1** a precious stone consisting of a clear and colourless crystalline form of pure carbon, the hardest naturally occurring substance. **2** a figure with four straight sides of equal length forming two opposite acute angles and two opposite obtuse angles; a rhombus. **3** (**diamonds**) one of the four suits in a conventional pack of playing cards, denoted by a red diamond shape.
– DERIVATIVES **diamondiferous** /dīəməndiffərəss/ adjective.
– ORIGIN Old French *diamant*, from Latin *adamans* 'invincible'; related to ADAMANT.
diamond jubilee ● noun the sixtieth anniversary of a notable event.
diamond wedding ● noun the sixtieth anniversary of a wedding.
diamorphine /dīəmorfeen/ ● noun technical heroin.
– ORIGIN short for *diacetylmorphine* in the same sense.
dianthus /dīanthəss/ ● noun (pl. **dianthuses**) a flowering plant of a group that includes the pinks and carnations.
– ORIGIN from Greek *Dios* 'of Zeus' + *anthos* 'flower'.
diapason /dīəpayzən/ ● noun **1** an organ stop sounding a main register of flue pipes. **2** a grand swelling burst of harmony.
– ORIGIN from Greek *dia pasōn khordōn* 'through all notes'.
diaper /dīəpər/ ● noun **1** N. Amer. a baby's nappy. **2** a fabric woven in a pattern of small diamonds. **3** a repeating geometric-

d

Thesaurus

liberty EXTREME, excessive, undue, inordinate, immoderate, unconscionable, outrageous; intolerable, unacceptable, unreasonable, unjustifiable, unwarrantable, inexcusable, unpardonable.
diadem ● noun CROWN, coronet, tiara, circlet, chaplet; *poetic/literary* coronal; *historical* taj.
diagnose ● verb IDENTIFY, determine, distinguish, recognize, detect, pinpoint.
diagnosis ● noun **1** *the diagnosis of coeliac disease* IDENTIFICATION, detection, recognition, determination, discovery, pinpointing. **2** *the results confirmed his diagnosis* OPINION, judgement, verdict, conclusion.
diagonal ● adjective CROSSWISE, crossways, slanting, slanted, aslant, squint, oblique, angled, at an angle, cornerways, cornerwise; *N. Amer.* cater-cornered, kitty-cornered.
diagram ● noun DRAWING, line drawing, sketch, representation, draft, illustration, picture, plan, outline, delineation, figure; *Computing* graphic.
diagrammatic ● adjective GRAPHIC, graphical, representational, representative, schematic, simplified.
dial ● verb PHONE, telephone, call, ring, make/place a call (to); *informal* buzz; *Brit. informal* get on the blower; *N. Amer. informal* get someone on the horn.
dialect ● noun REGIONAL LANGUAGE, local language, local speech, vernacular, patois, idiom; regionalisms, localisms; *informal* lingo.
dialectic ● noun DISCUSSION, debate, dialogue, logical argument, reasoning, argumentation, polemics; *formal* ratiocination.
dialogue ● noun **1** *a book consisting of a series of dialogues* CONVERSATION, talk, discussion, interchange, discourse; chat, tête-à-tête; *informal* confab; *formal* colloquy, confabulation; *archaic* converse. **2** *they called for a serious political dialogue* DISCUSSION, exchange, debate, exchange of views, talk, head-to-head, consultation, conference, parley; talks, negotiations; *informal* powwow; *N. Amer. informal* skull session.
diameter ● noun BREADTH, width, thickness; calibre, bore, gauge.

d

al pattern. ● verb **1** N. Amer. put a nappy on (a baby). **2** decorate with a repeating geometrical pattern.
– ORIGIN from Greek *diaspros*, from *dia* 'across' + *aspros* 'white'.
diaphanous /dīaffənəss/ ● adjective light, delicate, and translucent.
– ORIGIN Greek *diaphanēs*, from *dia* 'through' + *phainein* 'to show'.
diaphragm /dīəfram/ ● noun **1** a dome-shaped muscular partition separating the thorax from the abdomen in mammals. **2** a taut flexible membrane in mechanical or acoustic systems. **3** a thin contraceptive cap fitting over the cervix. **4** a device for varying the effective aperture of the lens in a camera or other optical system.
– DERIVATIVES **diaphragmatic** adjective.
– ORIGIN Latin *diaphragma*, from Greek *dia* 'through, apart' + *phragma* 'a fence'.
diarist ● noun a person who writes a diary.
diarrhoea /dīəreeə/ (US **diarrhea**) ● noun a condition in which faeces are discharged from the bowels frequently and in a liquid form.
– DERIVATIVES **diarrhoeal** adjective **diarrhoeic** adjective.
– ORIGIN Greek *diarrhoia*, from *diarrhein* 'flow through'.
diary ● noun (pl. **diaries**) **1** a book in which one keeps a daily record of events and experiences. **2** a book marked with each day's date, in which to note appointments.
– ORIGIN Latin *diarium*, from *dies* 'day'.
diaspora /dīaspərə/ ● noun **1** (**the diaspora**) the dispersion of the Jews beyond Israel, chiefly in the 8th to 6th centuries BC. **2** the dispersion of any people from their traditional homeland.
– ORIGIN Greek, from *diaspeirein* 'disperse'.
diastole /dīastəli/ ● noun the phase of the heartbeat when the heart muscle relaxes and the chambers fill with blood. Often contrasted with SYSTOLE.
– DERIVATIVES **diastolic** adjective.
– ORIGIN Greek, 'separation, expansion'.
diathermy /dīəthermi/ ● noun a medical and surgical technique in which high-frequency electric currents are passed through a part of the body, producing heat and increased circulation of the blood.
– ORIGIN from Greek *thermon* 'heat'.
diatom /dīətəm/ ● noun Biology a single-celled alga which has a cell wall of silica.
– DERIVATIVES **diatomaceous** adjective.
– ORIGIN from Greek *diatomos* 'cut in two'.
diatomic /dīətommik/ ● adjective Chemistry consisting of two atoms.
diatonic /dīətonnik/ ● adjective Music involving only the notes of the major or minor scale, without chromatic alteration.
– ORIGIN Greek *diatonikos* 'at intervals of a tone'.
diatribe /dīətrīb/ ● noun a harsh and forceful verbal attack.
– ORIGIN Greek, 'spending of time, discourse'.
diazepam /diazzipam/ ● noun a tranquillizing drug used to relieve anxiety. Also called VALIUM (trademark).
dibber ● noun Brit. another term for DIBBLE.
dibble ● noun a pointed hand tool for making holes in the ground for seeds or young plants.
– ORIGIN origin uncertain.
dibs ● plural noun informal (often in phrase **have first dibs**) N. Amer. the right to share or choose something.
– ORIGIN originally denoting pebbles used in a children's game, from earlier *dib-stones*.
dice ● noun (pl. same; sing. also **die**) a small cube with faces bearing from one to six spots, used in games of chance. See also DIE². ● verb cut (food) into small cubes.
– PHRASES **dice with death** take serious risks. **no dice** informal, chiefly N. Amer. used to indicate an unsuccessful attempt or request.
– USAGE Historically, **dice** is the plural of **die**, but in modern standard English **dice** is used as both the singular and the plural.
– ORIGIN Old French *des*, plural of *de*, from Latin *datum* 'something given or played'.
dicey ● adjective (**dicier**, **diciest**) informal difficult or potentially dangerous.
dichotomize (also **dichotomise**) ● verb regard or represent as divided or opposed.
dichotomy /dīkottəmi/ ● noun (pl. **dichotomies**) a separation or contrast between two things.
– DERIVATIVES **dichotomous** adjective.
– ORIGIN Greek *dikhotomia* 'a cutting in two'.
dick¹ ● noun vulgar slang **1** a penis. **2** Brit. a stupid or contemptible person.
– ORIGIN familiar form of the given name *Richard*.
dick² ● noun informal, dated, chiefly N. Amer. a detective.
– ORIGIN perhaps a shortening of DETECTIVE, or from obsolete slang *dick* 'look', from Romany.
dickens /dikkinz/ ● noun informal used to express annoyance or surprise when asking questions: *what the dickens is going on?*
– ORIGIN a euphemism for 'devil'.
Dickensian /dikenziən/ ● adjective reminiscent of the novels of Charles Dickens (1812–1870), especially in terms of the urban poverty that they portray.
dicker ● verb **1** engage in petty argument or bargaining. **2** toy or fiddle with something.
– ORIGIN perhaps from obsolete *dicker* 'set of ten hides', used as a unit of trade, from Latin *decem* 'ten'.
dickhead ● noun vulgar slang a stupid, irritating, or ridiculous man.
dicky ● adjective (**dickier**, **dickiest**) Brit. informal not strong, healthy, or functioning reliably.
– ORIGIN perhaps from the given name *Dick*, in the old saying *as queer as Dick's hatband*.
dicotyledon /dīkotileed'n/ ● noun a plant with an embryo bearing two cotyledons (seed leaves).
dicta plural of DICTUM.
Dictaphone /diktəfōn/ ● noun trademark a small cassette recorder used to record speech.
dictate ● verb /diktayt/ **1** state or order authoritatively. **2** say or read aloud (words to be typed or written down). **3** control or determine. ● noun /diktayt/ an order or principle that must be obeyed.
– DERIVATIVES **dictation** noun.
– ORIGIN Latin *dictare*.
dictator ● noun a ruler with total power over a country.
– DERIVATIVES **dictatorial** adjective.
dictatorship ● noun **1** government by a dictator. **2** a country

Thesaurus

diametrical, diametric ● adjective DIRECT, absolute, complete, exact, extreme, polar, antipodal.
diaphanous ● adjective SHEER, fine, delicate, light, thin, insubstantial, floaty, flimsy, filmy, silken, chiffony, gossamer, gossamer-thin, gauzy; translucent, transparent, see-through.
– OPPOSITES thick, opaque.
diarrhoea ● noun loose motions; *informal* the runs, the trots, gippy tummy, holiday tummy, Delhi belly, Montezuma's revenge; *Brit. informal* the squits; *N. Amer. informal* turista; *archaic* the flux.
– OPPOSITES constipation.
diary ● noun **1** *he put the date in his diary* APPOINTMENT BOOK, engagement book, personal organizer; *trademark* Filofax. **2** *her World War II diaries* JOURNAL, memoir, chronicle, log, logbook, history, annal, record; *N. Amer.* daybook.
diatribe ● noun TIRADE, harangue, onslaught, attack, polemic, denunciation, broadside, fulmination, condemnation, censure, criticism; *informal* blast; *poetic/literary* philippic.
dicey ● adjective *(informal)* RISKY, uncertain, unpredictable, touch-and-go, precarious, unsafe, dangerous, fraught with danger, hazardous, perilous, high-risk, difficult; *informal* chancy, hairy, iffy; *Brit. informal* dodgy; *N. Amer. informal* gnarly.
– OPPOSITES safe.
dichotomy ● noun CONTRAST, difference, polarity, conflict; gulf, chasm, division, separation, split; *rare* contrariety.
dicky ● adjective *(Brit. informal)* WEAK, unhealthy, ailing, poorly, sickly, frail; unsound, unreliable, unsteady.
– OPPOSITES robust.
dictate ● verb **1** *the tsar's attempts to dictate policy* PRESCRIBE, lay down, impose, set down, order, command, decree, ordain, direct, determine, decide, control, govern. **2** *you are in no position to dictate to me* GIVE ORDERS TO, order about/around, lord it over; lay down the law; *informal* boss about/around, push around/about, throw one's weight about/around. **3** *choice is often dictated by availability* DETERMINE, control, govern, decide, influence, affect.
● noun *the dictates of his superior* ORDER, command, commandment, decree, edict, ruling, dictum, diktat, directive, direction, instruction, pronouncement, mandate, requirement, stipulation, injunction, demand; *formal* ordinance; *poetic/literary* behest.

governed by a dictator.
diction ● noun **1** the choice and use of words in speech or writing. **2** the style of enunciation in speaking or singing.
– ORIGIN Latin, from *dicere* 'to say'.
dictionary ● noun (pl. **dictionaries**) a book that lists the words of a language and gives their meaning, or their equivalent in a different language.
– ORIGIN from Latin *dictionarium manuale* or *dictionarius liber* 'manual or book of words'.
dictum /diktəm/ ● noun (pl. **dicta** /diktə/ or **dictums**) **1** a formal pronouncement from an authoritative source. **2** a short statement that expresses a general principle.
– ORIGIN Latin, 'something said'.
did past of DO[1].
didactic /dīdaktik/ ● adjective intended to teach or give moral instruction.
– DERIVATIVES **didactically** adverb **didacticism** noun.
– ORIGIN Greek *didaktikos*, from *didaskein* 'teach'.
diddle ● verb informal cheat or swindle.
– ORIGIN probably from Jeremy *Diddler*, a character in the farce *Raising the Wind* (1803) who constantly borrowed small sums of money.
diddly-squat /didliskwot/ ● pronoun N. Amer. informal anything at all.
– ORIGIN probably from US slang *doodle* 'excrement' + *squat* in the sense 'defecate'.
didgeridoo /dijəridoo/ ● noun an Australian Aboriginal wind instrument in the form of a long wooden tube, blown to produce a deep resonant sound.
– ORIGIN from an Aboriginal language.
didicoi /diddikoy/ (also **diddicoy**) ● noun (pl. **didicois**) dialect a gypsy or itinerant tinker.
– ORIGIN perhaps from a Romany phrase meaning 'look here'.
didn't ● contraction did not.
didst archaic second person singular past of DO[1].
die[1] ● verb (**dying**) **1** stop living. **2** (**die out**) become extinct. **3** (often **die away/down**) become less loud or strong. **4** (**be dying for/to do**) informal be very eager for.
– PHRASES **die hard** disappear or change very slowly. **never say die** do not give up hope. **to die for** informal extremely good or desirable.
– ORIGIN Old Norse, related to DEAD.
die[2] ● noun **1** singular form of DICE. **2** (pl. **dies**) a device for cutting or moulding metal or for stamping a design onto coins or medals.
– PHRASES **the die is cast** an event has happened that cannot be changed. (**as**) **straight as a die 1** completely straight. **2** entirely open and honest.
– USAGE In modern English the singular **die** (rather than **dice**) for sense 1 is now uncommon. **Dice** is widely used for both the singular and the plural.
– ORIGIN Old French *de*, from Latin *datum* 'something given or played'.
dieback ● noun a condition in which a tree or shrub begins to die from the tip of its leaves or roots backwards.
die-cast ● adjective (of a metal object) formed by pouring molten metal into a mould.
diehard ● noun a person who supports something uncompromisingly.
dielectric /dī-ilektrik/ Physics ● adjective non-conducting of electricity; insulating. ● noun an insulator.
dieresis ● noun US spelling of DIAERESIS.
diesel /deez'l/ ● noun **1** an internal-combustion engine in which the heat of compressed air is used to ignite the fuel. **2** a form of petroleum used to fuel diesel engines.
– ORIGIN named after the German engineer Rudolf *Diesel* (1858–1913).
diet[1] ● noun **1** the kinds of food that a person, animal, or community habitually eats. **2** a restricted regime of eating, followed in order to lose weight or for medical reasons. **3** (before another noun) (of food or drink) with reduced fat or sugar content.
● verb (**dieted**, **dieting**) restrict oneself to a special diet to lose weight.
– DERIVATIVES **dietary** adjective **dieter** noun.
– ORIGIN Greek *diaita* 'a way of life'.
diet[2] ● noun **1** a legislative assembly in certain countries. **2** historical a regular meeting of the states of a confederation.
– ORIGIN Latin *dieta* 'day's work', also 'meeting of councillors'.
dietetics ● plural noun (treated as sing.) the branch of knowledge concerned with the diet and its effects on health.
– DERIVATIVES **dietetic** adjective.
dietitian /dīətish'n/ (also **dietician**) ● noun an expert on diet and nutrition.
differ ● verb **1** be unlike or dissimilar. **2** disagree.
– PHRASES **agree to differ** amicably stop arguing because agreement will not be reached. **beg to differ** politely disagree.
– ORIGIN Latin *differre*, from *ferre* 'bring, carry'.
difference ● noun **1** a way in which people or things are dissimilar. **2** the state or condition of being dissimilar. **3** a disagreement, quarrel, or dispute. **4** the remainder left after subtraction of one value from another.
different ● adjective **1** not the same as another or each other.

Thesaurus

dictator ● noun AUTOCRAT, absolute ruler, despot, tyrant, oppressor, autarch.
dictatorial ● adjective **1** *a dictatorial regime* AUTOCRATIC, undemocratic, totalitarian, authoritarian, autarchic, despotic, tyrannical, tyrannous, absolute, unrestricted, unlimited, unaccountable, arbitrary. **2** *his dictatorial manner* DOMINEERING, autocratic, authoritarian, oppressive, imperious, officious, overweening, overbearing, peremptory, dogmatic, high and mighty; severe, strict; *informal* bossy, high-handed.
– OPPOSITES democratic, meek.
dictatorship ● noun ABSOLUTE RULE, undemocratic rule, despotism, tyranny, autocracy, autarchy, authoritarianism, totalitarianism, Fascism; oppression, repression.
– OPPOSITES democracy.
diction ● noun **1** *his careful diction* ENUNCIATION, articulation, elocution, locution, pronunciation, speech, intonation, inflection; delivery. **2** *the need for contemporary diction in poetry* PHRASEOLOGY, phrasing, turn of phrase, wording, language, usage, vocabulary, terminology, expressions, idioms.
dictionary ● noun LEXICON, wordbook, word list, glossary.
– RELATED TERMS lexicographic.
dictum ● noun **1** *he received the head's dictum with evident reluctance* PRONOUNCEMENT, proclamation, direction, injunction, dictate, command, commandment, order, decree, edict, mandate, diktat. **2** *the old dictum 'might is right'* SAYING, maxim, axiom, proverb, adage, aphorism, saw, precept, epigram, motto, truism, commonplace; expression, phrase, tag.
didactic ● adjective INSTRUCTIVE, instructional, educational, educative, informative, informational, edifying, improving, preceptive, pedagogic, moralistic.
die ● verb **1** *her father died last year* PASS AWAY, pass on, lose one's life, expire, breathe one's last, meet one's end, meet one's death, lay down one's life, perish, go the way of all flesh, go to one's last resting place, go to meet one's maker, cross the great divide; *informal* give up the ghost, kick the bucket, croak, buy it, turn up one's toes, cash in one's chips, shuffle off this mortal coil; *Brit. informal* snuff it, peg out, pop one's clogs; *N. Amer. informal* bite the big one, buy the farm; *archaic* decease, depart this life. **2** *the wind had died down* ABATE, subside, drop, lessen, ease (off), let up, moderate, fade, dwindle, peter out, wane, ebb, relent, weaken; melt away, dissolve, vanish, disappear; *archaic* remit. **3** *(informal) the engine died* FAIL, cut out, give out, stop, break down, stop working; *informal* conk out, go kaput, give up the ghost; *Brit. informal* pack up. **4** *(informal) she's dying to meet you* LONG, yearn, burn, ache; *informal* itch.
– OPPOSITES live, intensify.
diehard ● adjective HARD-LINE, reactionary, ultra-conservative, conservative, traditionalist, dyed-in-the-wool, deep-dyed, intransigent, inflexible, uncompromising, rigid, entrenched, set in one's ways; staunch, steadfast; *informal* blimpish.
diet[1] ● noun *health problems related to your diet* SELECTION OF FOOD, food, foodstuffs; *informal* grub, nosh.
● verb *she dieted for most of her life* BE ON A DIET, eat sparingly; slim, lose weight, watch one's weight; *N. Amer.* reduce; *informal* weight-watch; *N. Amer. informal* slenderize.
diet[2] ● noun *the diet's lower house* LEGISLATIVE ASSEMBLY, legislature, parliament, congress, senate, council, assembly.
differ ● verb **1** *the second set of data differed from the first* CONTRAST WITH, be different/dissimilar to, be unlike, vary from, diverge from, deviate from, conflict with, run counter to, be incompatible with, be at odds with, go against, contradict. **2** *the two sides differed over this issue* DISAGREE, conflict, be at variance/odds, be in

2 distinct; separate. **3** informal novel and unusual.
– DERIVATIVES **differently** adverb **differentness** noun.
– USAGE There is little difference in sense between **different from**, **different to**, and **different than**. **Different from** is generally regarded as the correct use in British English, while **different than** is largely restricted to North America.
differentia /diffərenshiə/ • noun (pl. **differentiae** /diffərenshiee/) a distinguishing mark or characteristic.
– ORIGIN Latin.
differentiable /diffərenshiəb'l/ • adjective able to be differentiated.
– DERIVATIVES **differentiability** noun.
differential /diffərensh'l/ • adjective chiefly technical constituting or depending on a difference; differing or varying according to circumstances or relevant factors. • noun **1** Brit. a difference in wages between industries or between categories of employees in the same industry. **2** Mathematics an infinitesimal difference between successive values of a variable. **3** a gear allowing a vehicle's driven wheels to revolve at different speeds in cornering. **4** chiefly technical a difference.
– DERIVATIVES **differentially** adverb.
differential calculus • noun Mathematics the part of calculus concerned with the derivatives of functions.
differential equation • noun an equation involving derivatives of a function or functions.
differentiate /diffərenshiayt/ • verb **1** recognize or identify as different; distinguish. **2** cause to appear different or distinct. **3** Mathematics transform (a function) into its derivative.
– DERIVATIVES **differentiation** noun **differentiator** noun.
difficult • adjective **1** needing much effort or skill to accomplish, deal with, or understand. **2** not easy to please or satisfy; awkward.
difficulty • noun (pl. **difficulties**) **1** the state or condition of being difficult. **2** a difficult or dangerous situation or circumstance.
– ORIGIN Latin *difficultas*, from *facultas* 'ability, opportunity'.
diffident • adjective lacking in self-confidence.
– DERIVATIVES **diffidence** noun **diffidently** adverb.
– ORIGIN Latin, from *diffidere* 'fail to trust'.
diffraction • noun Physics the process by which a beam of light or other system of waves is spread out as a result of passing through a narrow aperture or across an edge.
– DERIVATIVES **diffract** verb **diffractive** adjective.
– ORIGIN Latin, from *diffringere* 'break into pieces'.
diffuse • verb /difyo͞oz/ **1** spread over a wide area. **2** Physics (of a gas or liquid) travel or spread by diffusion. • adjective /difyo͞oss/ **1** spread out over a large area; not concentrated. **2** lacking clarity or conciseness.
– DERIVATIVES **diffusely** /difyo͞osli/ adverb **diffuser** (also **diffusor**) noun.
– USAGE Do not confuse with **defuse**.
– ORIGIN Latin *diffundere* 'pour out'.
diffusion • noun **1** the action or process of becoming spread over a wide area. **2** Physics the intermingling of substances by the natural movement of their particles.
– DERIVATIVES **diffusive** adjective.
dig • verb (**digging**; past and past part. **dug**) **1** break up and turn over or move earth. **2** make (a hole) by digging. **3** (often **dig up**) extract from the ground by digging. **4** poke or jab sharply. **5** (**dig into/through**) search or rummage in. **6** (**dig out/up**) discover (facts). **7** (**dig in**) begin eating heartily. **8** informal, dated like; appreciate. • noun **1** an act of digging. **2** an archaeological excavation. **3** a sharp push or poke. **4** informal a mocking or critical remark. **5** (**digs**) informal, chiefly Brit. lodgings.
– PHRASES **dig in one's heels** stubbornly refuse to compromise.
– ORIGIN perhaps from an Old English word meaning 'ditch'.

Thesaurus

dispute, not see eye to eye.
– OPPOSITES resemble, agree.
difference • noun **1** *the difference between the two sets of data* DISSIMILARITY, contrast, distinction, differentiation, variance, variation, divergence, disparity, deviation, polarity, gulf, gap, imbalance, contradiction, contradistinction; formal dissimilitude. **2** *we've had our differences in the past* DISAGREEMENT, difference of opinion, dispute, argument, quarrel, wrangle, contretemps, altercation; informal tiff, set-to, run-in, spat; Brit. informal row. **3** *I am willing to pay the difference* BALANCE, remainder, rest, remaining amount, residue.
– OPPOSITES similarity.
different • adjective **1** *people with different lifestyles* DISSIMILAR, unalike, unlike, contrasting, contrastive, divergent, differing, varying, disparate; poles apart, incompatible, mismatched, conflicting, clashing; informal like chalk and cheese. **2** *suddenly everything in her life was different* CHANGED, altered, transformed, new, unfamiliar, unknown, strange. **3** *two different occasions* DISTINCT, separate, individual, discrete, independent. **4** (informal) *he wanted to try something different* UNUSUAL, out of the ordinary, unfamiliar, unusual, novel, new, fresh, original, unconventional, exotic, uncommon.
– OPPOSITES similar, related, ordinary.
differential • adjective (technical) **1** *the differential achievements of boys and girls* DIFFERENT, dissimilar, contrasting, unalike, divergent, disparate, contrastive. **2** *the differential features between benign and malignant tumours* DISTINCTIVE, distinguishing.
– OPPOSITES similar.
differentiate • verb **1** *he unable to differentiate between fantasy and reality* DISTINGUISH, discriminate, make/draw a distinction, tell the difference, tell apart. **2** *this differentiates their business from all other booksellers* MAKE DIFFERENT, distinguish, set apart, single out, separate, mark off.
differentiation • noun DISTINCTION, distinctness, difference; separation, demarcation, delimitation.
difficult • adjective **1** *a very difficult job* HARD, strenuous, arduous, laborious, tough, onerous, burdensome, demanding, punishing, gruelling, back-breaking, exhausting, tiring, fatiguing, wearisome; informal hellish, killing, no picnic; archaic toilsome. **2** *she found maths very difficult* HARD, complicated, complex, involved, impenetrable, unfathomable, over/above one's head, beyond one, puzzling, baffling, perplexing, confusing, mystifying; problematic, intricate, knotty, thorny, ticklish. **3** *a difficult child* TROUBLESOME, tiresome, trying, exasperating, awkward, demanding, perverse, contrary, recalcitrant, unmanageable, obstreperous, unaccommodating, unhelpful, uncooperative, disobliging; hard to please, fussy, finicky; formal refractory. **4** *you've come at a difficult time* INCONVENIENT, awkward, inopportune, unfavourable, unfortunate, inappropriate, unsuitable, untimely, ill-timed. **5** *the family have been through very difficult times* BAD, tough, grim, dark, black, hard, adverse, distressing; straitened, hard-pressed.
– OPPOSITES easy, simple, accommodating.
difficulty • noun **1** *the difficulty of balancing motherhood with a career* STRAIN, trouble, problems, toil, struggle, laboriousness, arduousness; informal hassle, stress. **2** *practical difficulties* PROBLEM, complication, snag, hitch, pitfall, handicap, impediment, hindrance, obstacle, hurdle, stumbling block, obstruction, barrier; informal fly in the ointment, headache, hiccup; Brit. informal spanner in the works. **3** *Charles got into difficulties* TROUBLE, predicament, plight, hard times, dire straits; quandary, dilemma; informal deep water, a fix, a jam, a spot, a scrape, a stew, a hole, a pickle.
– OPPOSITES ease.
diffidence • noun SHYNESS, bashfulness, modesty, self-effacement, meekness, unassertiveness, timidity, humility, hesitancy, reticence, insecurity, self-doubt, uncertainty, self-consciousness.
diffident • adjective SHY, bashful, modest, self-effacing, unassuming, meek, unconfident, unassertive, timid, timorous, humble, shrinking, reticent, hesitant, insecure, self-doubting, doubtful, uncertain, unsure, self-conscious; informal mousy.
– OPPOSITES confident.
diffuse • verb *such ideas were diffused widely in the 1970s* SPREAD, spread around, send out, disseminate, scatter, disperse, distribute, put about, circulate, communicate, purvey, propagate, transmit, broadcast, promulgate.
• adjective **1** *a diffuse community centred on the church* SPREAD OUT, scattered. **2** *a diffuse narrative* VERBOSE, wordy, prolix, long-winded, long-drawn-out, discursive, rambling, wandering, meandering, maundering, digressive, circuitous, roundabout, circumlocutory, periphrastic; Brit. informal waffly.
diffusion • noun SPREAD, dissemination, scattering, dispersal, distribution, circulation, propagation, transmission, broadcasting, promulgation.
dig • verb **1** *she began to dig the heavy clay soil* TURN OVER, work, break up; till, harrow, plough. **2** *he took a spade and dug a hole* EXCAVATE, dig out, quarry, hollow out, scoop out, gouge out; cut, bore, tunnel, burrow, mine. **3** *the bodies were hastily dug up* EXHUME, disinter, unearth. **4** *Winnie dug her elbow into his ribs* POKE, prod, jab, stab, shove, ram, push, thrust, drive. **5** *he'd been dig-*

digerati /dijəraati/ ● plural noun informal people with expertise in information technology.
– ORIGIN blend of DIGITAL and LITERATI.

digest ● verb /dījest, di-/ **1** break down (food) in the stomach and intestines into substances that can be absorbed by the body. **2** Chemistry treat (a substance) with heat, enzymes, or a solvent to break it down. **3** reflect on and assimilate (information). ● noun /dījest/ **1** a compilation or summary of material or information. **2** Chemistry a substance or mixture obtained by digestion.
– DERIVATIVES **digestible** adjective.
– ORIGIN Latin *digerere* 'distribute, dissolve, digest'.

digestif /dījestif, deezhesteef/ ● noun a drink taken before or after a meal in order to aid the digestion.
– ORIGIN French, 'digestive'.

digestion ● noun **1** the process of digesting. **2** a person's capacity to digest food.

digestive ● adjective relating to the process of digesting food. ● noun **1** a food or medicine that aids the digestion of food. **2** Brit. a round semi-sweet biscuit made with wholemeal flour.

digger ● noun **1** a person, animal, or large machine that digs earth. **2** Austral./NZ informal a friendly form of address for a man.

diggings ● plural noun a site that has been excavated.

dight /dīt/ ● adjective archaic clothed or equipped. ● verb **1** literary make ready; prepare. **2** Scottish & N. English wipe clean or dry.
– ORIGIN from archaic *dight* 'order, deal with', from Latin *dictare* 'dictate'.

digit /dijit/ ● noun **1** any of the numerals from 0 to 9, especially when forming part of a number. **2** a finger or thumb.
– ORIGIN Latin *digitus* 'finger, toe'; sense 1 arose from the practice of counting on the fingers.

digital ● adjective **1** of or relating to information represented as digits using particular values of a physical quantity such as voltage or magnetic polarization. **2** (of a clock or watch) showing the time by means of displayed digits. **3** of or relating to a finger or fingers.
– DERIVATIVES **digitally** adverb.

digital audiotape ● noun magnetic tape used to make digital recordings.

digitalis /dijitayliss/ ● noun a drug prepared from foxglove leaves, containing substances that stimulate the heart muscle.
– ORIGIN from the Latin genus name of the foxglove, from *digitalis herba* 'plant relating to the finger' (with reference to the shape of the flowers).

digitalize (also **digitalise**) ● verb another term for DIGITIZE.
– DERIVATIVES **digitalization** noun.

digitigrade /dijitigrayd/ ● adjective Zoology walking on the toes and not touching the ground with the heels, in the way that dogs, cats, and certain other mammals walk. Compare with PLANTIGRADE.
– ORIGIN from Latin *digitus* 'finger, toe' + *-gradus* '-walking'.

digitize (also **digitise**) ● verb convert (pictures or sound) into a digital form that can be processed by a computer.
– DERIVATIVES **digitization** noun **digitizer** noun.

dignified ● adjective having or showing dignity.

dignify ● verb (**dignifies**, **dignified**) cause to be or appear impressive or worthy of respect.
– ORIGIN Latin *dignificare*, from *dignus* 'worthy'.

dignitary /dignitri/ ● noun (pl. **dignitaries**) a person holding high rank or office.

dignity ● noun (pl. **dignities**) **1** the state or quality of being worthy of respect. **2** a composed or serious manner. **3** a sense of pride in oneself.
– PHRASES **stand on one's dignity** insist on being treated with respect.
– ORIGIN Latin *dignitas*, from *dignus* 'worthy'.

digraph /dīgraaf/ ● noun a combination of two letters representing one sound, as in *ph*.

digress /dīgress/ ● verb leave the main subject temporarily in speech or writing.
– DERIVATIVES **digression** noun **digressive** adjective.
– ORIGIN Latin *digredi* 'step away'.

dihedral /dīheedrəl/ ● adjective having or contained by two plane faces. ● noun **1** an angle formed by two plane faces. **2** Aeronautics upward inclination of an aircraft's wing.

dike[1] ● noun variant spelling of DYKE[1].

dike[2] ● noun variant spelling of DYKE[2].

diktat /diktat/ ● noun a decree imposed by someone in power without popular consent.
– ORIGIN German.

dilapidated /dilappidaytid/ ● adjective in a state of disrepair or ruin.
– DERIVATIVES **dilapidation** noun.
– ORIGIN from Latin *dilapidare* 'demolish' (literally 'scatter as if throwing stones').

dilatation /dīlətaysh'n/ ● noun chiefly Medicine & Physiology the action of dilating a vessel or opening or the process of becoming dilated.

dilatation and curettage ● noun a surgical procedure involving dilatation of the cervix and curettage (scraping) of the uterus.

dilate /dīlayt/ ● verb **1** make or become wider, larger, or more open. **2** (**dilate on**) speak or write at length on.
– DERIVATIVES **dilation** noun.
– ORIGIN Latin *dilatare* 'spread out'.

dilator ● noun **1** (also **dilator muscle**) Anatomy a muscle whose contraction dilates an organ or aperture. **2** a surgical instrument for dilating a tube or cavity in the body.

dilatory /dillətri/ ● adjective **1** slow to act. **2** intended to cause delay.
– DERIVATIVES **dilatoriness** noun.
– ORIGIN Latin *dilatorius*, from *dilator* 'delayer'.

Thesaurus

ging into my past DELVE, probe, search, inquire, look, investigate, research, examine, scrutinize, check up on; *informal* check out. **6** *I dug up some disturbing information* UNCOVER, discover, find (out), unearth, dredge up, root out, ferret out, turn up, reveal, bring to light, expose. **7** *(informal, dated) I dig talking with him.* See ENJOY verb sense 1.
● noun **1** *a dig in the ribs* POKE, prod, jab, stab, shove, push. **2** *(informal) they're always making digs at each other* SNIDE REMARK, cutting remark, jibe, jeer, taunt, sneer, insult, barb, insinuation; *informal* wisecrack, crack, put-down.

digest ● verb *Liz digested this information* ASSIMILATE, absorb, take in, understand, comprehend, grasp; consider, think about, reflect on, ponder, contemplate, mull over.
● noun *a digest of their findings* SUMMARY, synopsis, abstract, precis, résumé, summation; compilation; *N. Amer. informal* wrap-up.

digit ● noun **1** *the door code has ten digits* NUMERAL, number, figure, integer. **2** *our frozen digits* FINGER, thumb, toe; extremity.

dignified ● adjective STATELY, noble, courtly, majestic, distinguished, proud, august, lofty, exalted, regal, lordly, imposing, impressive, grand; solemn, serious, grave, formal, proper, ceremonious, decorous, reserved, composed, sedate.

dignify ● verb ENNOBLE, enhance, distinguish, add distinction to, honour, grace, exalt, magnify, glorify, elevate.

dignitary ● noun WORTHY, personage, grandee, VIP, notable, notability, pillar of society, luminary, leading light, big name; *informal* heavyweight, bigwig, top brass, top dog, big gun, big shot, big noise, big cheese, big chief, supremo; *N. Amer. informal* big wheel, big kahuna, big enchilada, top banana.

dignity ● noun **1** *the dignity of the Crown* STATELINESS, nobility, majesty, regality, courtliness, augustness, loftiness, lordliness, grandeur; solemnity, gravity, gravitas, formality, decorum, propriety, sedateness. **2** *he had lost his dignity* SELF-RESPECT, pride, self-esteem, self-worth, amour propre. **3** *Cnut promised dignities to the noblemen* HIGH RANK, high standing, high station, status, elevation, eminence, honour, glory, greatness.

digress ● verb DEVIATE, go off at a tangent, get off the subject, get sidetracked, lose the thread, diverge, turn aside/away, depart, drift, stray, wander.

digression ● noun DEVIATION, detour, diversion, departure, divergence, excursus; aside, incidental remark.

digs ● plural noun *(informal)* LODGINGS, rooms, accommodation, living quarters; bedsit, flat, house, home; *informal* pad, place; *formal* abode, dwelling, dwelling place, residence, domicile, habitation.

dilapidated ● adjective RUN DOWN, tumbledown, ramshackle, broken-down, in disrepair, shabby, battered, rickety, shaky, unsound, crumbling, in ruins, ruined, decayed, decaying, decrepit; neglected, uncared-for, untended, the worse for wear, falling to pieces, falling apart, gone to rack and ruin, gone to seed.

dilate ● verb **1** *her nostrils dilated* ENLARGE, widen, expand, distend. **2** *Diane dilated on the joys of her married life* EXPATIATE, expound, enlarge, elaborate, speak/write at length.
– OPPOSITES contract.

d

dildo ● noun (pl. **dildos** or **dildoes**) an object shaped like an erect penis, used for sexual stimulation.
– ORIGIN of unknown origin.
dilemma /dilemmə, di-/ ● noun **1** a situation in which a difficult choice has to be made between two alternatives, especially when a decision either way will bring undesirable consequences. **2** informal a difficult situation or problem.
– ORIGIN Greek, from *di-* 'twice' + *lēmma* 'premise'.
dilettante /dillitanti/ ● noun (pl. **dilettanti** /dillitanti/ or **dilettantes**) a person who dabbles in a subject for enjoyment but without serious study.
– DERIVATIVES **dilettantish** adjective **dilettantism** noun.
– ORIGIN Italian, 'person loving the arts'.
diligence[1] /dillijənss/ ● noun care and conscientiousness in one's work.
diligence[2] /dillijənss/ ● noun historical a public stagecoach.
– ORIGIN French, from *carrosse de diligence* 'coach of speed'.
diligent ● adjective careful and conscientious in a task or duties.
– DERIVATIVES **diligently** adverb.
– ORIGIN from Latin *diligere* 'love, take delight in'.
dill[1] ● noun an aromatic herb with yellow flowers, used in cookery or for medicinal purposes.
– ORIGIN Old English.
dill[2] ● noun Austral./NZ informal a naive or foolish person.
– ORIGIN probably from dated *dilly* 'odd, foolish'.
dill pickle ● noun pickled cucumber flavoured with dill.
dillybag ● noun Austral. an Aboriginal bag or basket made from woven grass or fibre.
– ORIGIN from an Aboriginal word meaning 'coarse grass or reeds' + BAG.
dilly-dally ● verb (**dilly-dallies**, **dilly-dallied**) informal dawdle or vacillate.
– ORIGIN reduplication of DALLY.
dilophosaurus /dīlōfəsawrəss/ ● noun a large bipedal dinosaur of the early Jurassic period, with two long crests on the head.
– ORIGIN from Greek *dilophos* 'two-crested' + *sauros* 'lizard'.
diluent /dilyooənt/ technical ● noun a substance used to dilute something. ● adjective acting to cause dilution.
dilute /dīlyōōt/ ● verb **1** make (a liquid) thinner or weaker by adding water or another solvent. **2** weaken by modifying or adding other elements. ● adjective /also dīlyōōt/ **1** (of a liquid) diluted. **2** Chemistry (of a solution) having a relatively low concentration of solute.
– DERIVATIVES **diluter** noun **dilution** noun **dilutive** adjective.
– ORIGIN Latin *diluere* 'wash away, dissolve'.
dim ● adjective (**dimmer**, **dimmest**) **1** (of a light or illuminated object) not shining brightly or clearly. **2** made difficult to see by darkness, shade, or distance. **3** (of the eyes) not able to see clearly. **4** not clearly remembered. **5** informal stupid or slow to understand. ● verb (**dimmed**, **dimming**) make or become dim.
– PHRASES **take a dim view of** regard with disapproval.
– DERIVATIVES **dimly** adverb **dimness** noun.
– ORIGIN Old English.
dime /dīm/ ● noun N. Amer. a ten-cent coin.
– PHRASES **a dime a dozen** informal very common and of little value.
– ORIGIN Old French *disme*, from Latin *decima pars* 'tenth part'.
dimension /dīmensh'n, di-/ ● noun **1** a measurable extent, such as length, breadth, or height. **2** an aspect or feature.
– DERIVATIVES **dimensional** adjective.
– ORIGIN Latin, from *dimetiri* 'measure out'.
dimer /dīmər/ ● noun Chemistry a molecule or molecular complex consisting of two identical molecules linked together.
– DERIVATIVES **dimeric** adjective **dimerize** verb.
– ORIGIN from DI-, on the pattern of *polymer*.
dime store ● noun N. Amer. a shop selling cheap merchandise.
dimetrodon /dīmeetrədon/ ● noun a large fossil carnivorous mammal-like reptile of the Permian period, with long spines on its back supporting a sail-like crest.
– ORIGIN Latin, from *di-* 'twice' + Greek *metron* 'measure' + *odous* 'tooth'.
diminish ● verb make or become less.
– PHRASES **(the law of) diminishing returns** the principle that as expenditure or investment increases each further increase produces a proportionately smaller return.
– ORIGIN Latin *deminuere* 'lessen'.
diminished responsibility ● noun English Law an unbalanced mental state considered as grounds to reduce a charge of murder to that of manslaughter.
diminuendo /diminyooendō/ ● adverb & adjective Music with a decrease in loudness.
– ORIGIN Italian, 'diminishing'.
diminution /diminyōōsh'n/ ● noun a reduction.
diminutive /diminyootiv/ ● adjective **1** extremely or unusually

Thesaurus

dilatory ● adjective **1** *he had been dilatory in appointing a solicitor* SLOW, tardy, unhurried, sluggish, sluggardly, snail-like, tortoise-like, lazy. **2** *dilatory procedural tactics* DELAYING, stalling, temporizing, procrastinating, time-wasting, Fabian.
– OPPOSITES fast.
dilemma ● noun QUANDARY, predicament, catch-22, vicious circle, plight, mess, muddle; difficulty, problem, trouble, perplexity, confusion, conflict; *informal* no-win situation, fix, tight spot/corner; *Brit. informal* sticky wicket.
– PHRASES **on the horns of a dilemma** BETWEEN THE DEVIL AND THE DEEP BLUE SEA, between Scylla and Charybdis; *informal* between a rock and a hard place.
dilettante ● noun DABBLER, amateur, non-professional, non-specialist, layman, layperson.
– OPPOSITES professional.
diligence ● noun CONSCIENTIOUSNESS, assiduousness, assiduity, hard work, application, concentration, effort, care, industriousness, rigour, meticulousness, thoroughness; perseverance, persistence, tenacity, dedication, commitment, tirelessness, indefatigability, doggedness.
diligent ● adjective INDUSTRIOUS, hard-working, assiduous, conscientious, particular, punctilious, meticulous, painstaking, rigorous, careful, thorough, sedulous, earnest; persevering, persistent, tenacious, zealous, dedicated, committed, unflagging, untiring, tireless, indefatigable, dogged; *archaic* laborious.
– OPPOSITES lazy.
dilly-dally ● verb *(informal)* WASTE TIME, dally, dawdle, loiter, linger, take one's time, delay, temporize, stall, procrastinate, pussyfoot around, drag one's feet; dither, hesitate, falter, vacillate, waver; *Brit.* haver, hum and haw; *informal* shilly-shally, let the grass grow under one's feet; *archaic* tarry.
– OPPOSITES hurry.
dilute ● verb **1** *strong bleach can be diluted with water* MAKE WEAKER, weaken, water down; thin out, thin; doctor, adulterate; *informal* cut. **2** *the original plans have been diluted* WEAKEN, moderate, tone down, water down.
● adjective *a dilute acid.* See DILUTED.
diluted ● adjective WEAK, dilute, thin, watered down, watery; adulterated.
– OPPOSITES concentrated.
dim ● adjective **1** *the dim light* FAINT, weak, feeble, soft, pale, dull, subdued, muted, wishy-washy. **2** *long dim corridors* DARK, badly lit, ill-lit, dingy, dismal, gloomy, murky; *poetic/literary* tenebrous. **3** *a dim figure* INDISTINCT, ill-defined, unclear, vague, shadowy, nebulous, obscured, blurred, blurry, fuzzy. **4** *dim memories* VAGUE, imprecise, imperfect, unclear, indistinct, sketchy, hazy, blurred, shadowy. **5** *(informal) I'm awfully dim.* See STUPID sense 1. **6** *their prospects for the future looked dim* GLOOMY, unpromising, unfavourable, discouraging, disheartening, depressing, dispiriting, hopeless.
– OPPOSITES bright, distinct, encouraging.
● verb **1** *the lights were dimmed* TURN DOWN, lower, dip, soften, subdue, mute; *poetic/literary* bedim. **2** *my memories have not dimmed with time* FADE, become vague, dwindle, blur. **3** *the fighting dimmed hopes of peace* DIMINISH, reduce, lessen, weaken, undermine.
– OPPOSITES brighten, sharpen, intensify.
dimension ● noun **1** *the dimensions of the room* SIZE, measurements, proportions, extent; length, width, breadth, depth, area, volume, capacity; footage, acreage. **2** *the dimension of the problem* SIZE, scale, extent, scope, magnitude; importance, significance. **3** *the cultural dimensions of the problem* ASPECT, feature, element, facet, side.
diminish ● verb **1** *the pain will gradually diminish* DECREASE, lessen, decline, reduce, subside, die down, abate, dwindle, fade, slacken off, moderate, let up, ebb, wane, recede, die away/out, peter out; *archaic* remit. **2** *new legislation diminished the courts' authority* REDUCE, decrease, lessen, curtail, cut, cut down/back, constrict, restrict, limit, curb, check; weaken, blunt, erode, undermine, sap. **3** *she lost no opportunity to diminish him* BELITTLE, disparage, deni-

small. **2** (of a word, name, or suffix) implying smallness (e.g. *-let* in *booklet*). • **noun** a shortened form of a name, typically used informally.
– DERIVATIVES **diminutively** adverb **diminutiveness** noun.
– ORIGIN Latin *diminutivus*, from *deminuere* 'lessen'.
dimity /dimmiti/ • **noun** a hard-wearing cotton fabric woven with stripes or checks.
– ORIGIN Greek *dimitos*, from *di-* 'twice' + *mitos* 'warp thread'.
dimmer • **noun** (also **dimmer switch**) a device for varying the brightness of an electric light.
dimorphic /dīmorfik/ • **adjective** chiefly Biology occurring in or representing two distinct forms.
– DERIVATIVES **dimorphism** noun.
– ORIGIN from Greek *dimorphos*, from *morphē* 'form'.
dimple • **noun 1** a small depression formed in the fleshy part of the cheeks when one smiles. **2** any small depression in a surface. • **verb** produce a dimple or dimples in the surface of.
– DERIVATIVES **dimply** adjective.
– ORIGIN Germanic.
dim sum /dim sum/ (also **dim sim** /dim sim/) • **noun** a Chinese dish of small dumplings containing various fillings.
– ORIGIN from the Chinese words for 'dot' and 'heart'.
dimwit • **noun** informal a stupid or silly person.
– DERIVATIVES **dim-witted** adjective.
DIN • **noun** any of a series of international technical standards, used especially to designate electrical connections and film speeds.
– ORIGIN acronym from German *Deutsche Industrie-Norm* 'German Industrial Standard'.
din • **noun** a prolonged loud and unpleasant noise. • **verb** (**dinned**, **dinning**) (**din into**) instil (information) into by constant repetition.
– ORIGIN Old English.
dinar /deenaar/ • **noun 1** the basic monetary unit of the states of Yugoslavia. **2** the basic monetary unit of certain countries of the Middle East and North Africa.
– ORIGIN Turkish and Serbo-Croat, from Latin *denarius* 'containing ten'.
dine • **verb 1** eat dinner. **2** (**dine out on**) regularly entertain friends with (a particular anecdote).
– ORIGIN Old French *disner*, probably from *desjëuner* 'to break fast'.
diner • **noun 1** a person who dines. **2** a dining car on a train. **3** N. Amer. a small roadside restaurant.
dinette /dīnet/ • **noun** a small room or part of a room used for eating meals.
ding • **verb** make the metallic ringing sound of a bell.
dingbat • **noun** informal **1** N. Amer. & Austral./NZ a stupid or eccentric person. **2** (**dingbats**) Austral./NZ delusions or feelings of unease.
– ORIGIN origin uncertain.
ding-dong • **noun** Brit. **1** the sound of a bell ringing with simple alternate chimes. **2** informal a fierce argument or fight. • **adjective** (of a contest) evenly matched and intensely fought.
dinghy /dinggi, dingi/ • **noun** (pl. **dinghies**) **1** a small open boat with a mast and sails, for recreation or racing. **2** a small inflatable rubber boat.
– ORIGIN originally denoting a rowing boat in India: from Hindi.
dingle • **noun** literary or dialect a deep wooded valley.
– ORIGIN of unknown origin.
dingo /dinggō/ • **noun** (pl. **dingoes** or **dingos**) a wild or semi-domesticated Australian dog with a sandy-coloured coat.
– ORIGIN from an Aboriginal language.
dingy /dinji/ • **adjective** (**dingier**, **dingiest**) gloomy and drab.
– DERIVATIVES **dingily** adverb **dinginess** noun.
– ORIGIN perhaps from an Old English word meaning 'dung'.
dining car • **noun** a railway carriage equipped as a restaurant.
dinkum /dingkəm/ • **adjective** Austral./NZ informal genuine.
– PHRASES **fair dinkum** used to emphasize that or query whether something is genuine or true.
– ORIGIN of unknown origin.
dinkum oil • **noun** Austral./NZ informal the honest truth.
dinky • **adjective** (**dinkier**, **dinkiest**) Brit. informal attractively small and neat.
– ORIGIN from Scots and northern English dialect *dink* 'neat, trim'.
dinner • **noun 1** the main meal of the day, taken either around midday or in the evening. **2** a formal evening meal.
– ORIGIN Old French *disner* 'to dine' (used as a noun).
dinner jacket • **noun** a man's short jacket without tails, worn with a bow tie for formal evening occasions.
dinner lady • **noun** a woman who supervises children at mealtimes in a school.
dinosaur /dīnəsawr/ • **noun 1** an extinct reptile of the Mesozoic era, of which there were many kinds including large bipedal and quadrupedal forms. **2** a thing that is outdated or has become obsolete.
– ORIGIN from Greek *deinos* 'terrible' + *sauros* 'lizard'.
dint • **noun** an impression or hollow in a surface; a dent.
– PHRASES **by dint of** by means of.
– ORIGIN Old English, 'a blow with a weapon'.
diocese /dīəsiss/ • **noun** (pl. **dioceses** /dīəseez, -seeziz/) a district under the pastoral care of a bishop in the Christian Church.
– DERIVATIVES **diocesan** adjective /dīossis'n/.
– ORIGIN Latin *dioecesis* 'governor's jurisdiction, diocese', from Greek *dioikein* 'keep house, administer'.
diode /dīōd/ • **noun** Electronics **1** a semiconductor device with two terminals, typically allowing the flow of current in one direction only. **2** a thermionic valve with two electrodes.
– ORIGIN from DI- + a shortened form of ELECTRODE.
dioecious /dīeeshəss/ • **adjective** Biology (of a plant or invertebrate animal) having the male and female reproductive organs in separate individuals. Compare with MONOECIOUS.
– ORIGIN from DI- + Greek *-oikos* 'house'.
Dionysiac /dīənissiak/ (also **Dionysian** /dīənissiən/) • **adjective 1** relating to Dionysus, the Greek god of fertility in nature and later of wine, associated with ecstatic religious rites. **2** uninhibited and emotional; frenzied.
dioptre /dīoptə/ (US **diopter**) • **noun** a unit of refractive power, equal to the reciprocal of the focal length (in metres) of a given

d

Thesaurus

grate, defame, deprecate, run down; decry, demean, cheapen, devalue; *formal* derogate.
– OPPOSITES increase.
diminution • **noun** REDUCTION, decrease, lessening, decline, dwindling, moderation, fading, weakening, ebb.
diminutive • **adjective** TINY, small, little, petite, elfin, minute, miniature, mini, minuscule, compact, pocket, toy, midget, undersized, short; *Scottish* wee; *informal* teeny, weeny, teeny-weeny, teensy-weensy, itty-bitty, itsy-bitsy, tiddly, dinky, baby, pint-sized, knee-high to a grasshopper; *Brit. informal* titchy; *N. Amer. informal* little-bitty.
– OPPOSITES enormous.
dimple • **noun** INDENTATION, hollow, cleft, dint.
dimwit • **noun** *(informal)*. See FOOL noun sense 1.
dim-witted • **adjective** *(informal)*. See STUPID senses 1, 2.
din • **noun** *he shouted above the din* NOISE, racket, rumpus, cacophony, babel, hubbub, tumult, uproar, commotion, clangour, clatter; shouting, yelling, screaming, caterwauling, clamour, outcry; *Scottish & N. English* stramash; *informal* hullabaloo; *Brit. informal* row.
– OPPOSITES silence.
• **verb 1** *she had had the evils of drink dinned into her* INSTIL, inculcate, drive, drum, hammer, drill, ingrain; indoctrinate, brainwash. **2** *the sound dinning in my ears* BLARE, blast, clang, clatter, crash, clamour.
dine • **verb 1** *we dined at a restaurant* HAVE DINNER, have supper, eat; *dated* sup, break bread. **2** *they dined on lobster* EAT, feed on, feast on, banquet on, partake of; *informal* tuck into.
dingle • **noun** *(poetic/literary)* VALLEY, dale, vale, hollow; *Brit.* dene; *Scottish* glen, strath; *poetic/literary* dell.
dingy • **adjective** GLOOMY, dark, dull, badly/poorly lit, murky, dim, dismal, dreary, drab, sombre, grim, cheerless; dirty, grimy, shabby, faded, worn, dowdy, seedy, run down.
– OPPOSITES bright.
dinky • **adjective** *(Brit. informal)* SMALL, little, petite, dainty, neat, diminutive, mini, miniature; sweet, cute, dear, adorable; *Scottish* wee; *informal* teeny, teeny-weeny, teensy-weensy; *N. Amer. informal* little-bitty.
dinner • **noun** EVENING MEAL, supper, main meal; lunch; feast, banquet, dinner party; *Brit.* tea; *informal* spread, blowout; *Brit. informal* nosh-up, slap-up meal; *formal* repast.
– RELATED TERMS prandial.
dint • **noun** DENT, indentation, hollow, depression, dip, dimple, cleft, pit.
– PHRASES **by dint of** BY MEANS OF, by virtue of, on account of, as a result of, as a consequence of, owing to, on the strength of, due

lens.
– ORIGIN French, from Greek *di-* 'through' + *optos* 'visible'.
dioptric • adjective of or relating to the refraction of light.
– DERIVATIVES **dioptrics** plural noun.
diorama /dīəraamə/ • noun **1** a model representing a scene with three-dimensional figures against a painted background. **2** chiefly historical a scenic painting, viewed through a peephole, in which changes in colour and direction of illumination simulate changes in the weather and time of day.
– ORIGIN French, from DIA-, on the pattern of *panorama*.
diorite /dīərīt/ • noun Geology a speckled, coarse-grained igneous rock.
– DERIVATIVES **dioritic** adjective.
– ORIGIN French, from Greek *diorizein* 'distinguish'.
dioxide /dīoksīd/ • noun Chemistry an oxide containing two atoms of oxygen in its molecule or empirical formula.
dioxin /dīoksin/ • noun a highly toxic organic compound produced as a by-product in some manufacturing processes.
Dip. • abbreviation diploma.
dip • verb (**dipped**, **dipping**) **1** (**dip in/into**) put or lower briefly in or into. **2** sink, drop, or slope downwards. **3** (of a level or amount) temporarily become lower or smaller. **4** lower or move downwards. **5** Brit. lower the beam of (a vehicle's headlights). **6** (**dip into**) put a hand or implement into (a bag or container) to take something out. **7** (**dip into**) spend from (one's financial resources). **8** (**dip out**) Austral./NZ informal fail. • noun **1** an act of dipping. **2** a thick sauce in which pieces of food are dipped before eating. **3** a brief swim. **4** a brief downward slope followed by an upward one.
– ORIGIN Old English, related to DEEP.
diphtheria /diptheeriə/ • noun a serious bacterial disease causing inflammation of the mucous membranes, especially in the throat.
– ORIGIN Greek *diphthera* 'skin, hide' (referring to the false membrane that forms in the throat).
diphthong /difthong/ • noun a sound formed by the combination of two vowels in a single syllable (as in *coin*).
– ORIGIN Greek *diphthongos*, from *di-* 'twice' + *phthongos* 'sound'.
diplodocus /diploddəkəss/ • noun a huge herbivorous dinosaur of the late Jurassic period, with a long slender neck and tail.
– ORIGIN from Greek *diplous* 'double' + *dokos* 'wooden beam'.
diploid /dipployd/ • adjective Genetics (of a cell or nucleus) containing two complete sets of chromosomes, one from each parent. Compare with HAPLOID.
– ORIGIN from Greek *diplous* 'double'.
diploma • noun a certificate awarded by an educational establishment for passing an examination or completing a course of study.
– ORIGIN originally in the sense 'state paper': from Greek, 'folded paper', from *diplous* 'double'.
diplomacy • noun **1** the profession, activity, or skill of managing international relations. **2** skill and tact in dealing with people.
– ORIGIN French *diplomatie*, from Greek *diplōma* (see DIPLOMA).
diplomat • noun an official representing a country abroad.
diplomatic • adjective **1** concerning diplomacy. **2** tactful.
– DERIVATIVES **diplomatically** adverb.
diplomatic bag • noun chiefly Brit. a container in which official mail is sent to or from an embassy, which is not subject to customs inspection.
diplomatic corps • noun the body of diplomats representing other countries in a particular state.
diplomatic immunity • noun the exemption from certain laws granted to diplomats by the state in which they are working.
dipole /dīpōl/ • noun **1** Physics a pair of equal and oppositely charged or magnetized poles separated by a distance. **2** an aerial consisting of a horizontal metal rod with a connecting wire at its centre.
– DERIVATIVES **dipolar** adjective.
dipper • noun **1** a short-tailed songbird able to dive into fast-flowing streams to feed. **2** a ladle.
dippy • adjective (**dippier**, **dippiest**) informal foolish or eccentric.
– ORIGIN of unknown origin.
dipsomania /dipsəmayniə/ • noun alcoholism.
– DERIVATIVES **dipsomaniac** noun.
– ORIGIN from Greek *dipsa* 'thirst'.
dipstick • noun **1** a graduated rod for measuring the depth of a liquid, especially oil in an engine. **2** informal a stupid or inept person.
dipteran /diptərən/ • noun Entomology an insect of the order that comprises the two-winged or true flies. • adjective relating to this order of insects.
– DERIVATIVES **dipterous** adjective.
– ORIGIN from Greek *dipteros* 'two-winged'.
diptych /diptik/ • noun a painting on two hinged wooden panels, typically forming an altarpiece.
– ORIGIN Greek *diptukha* 'pair of writing tablets', from *diptukhos* 'folded in two'.
dire • adjective **1** extremely serious or urgent. **2** informal of a very poor quality.
– DERIVATIVES **direly** adverb **direness** noun.
– ORIGIN Latin *dirus* 'fearful, threatening'.
direct /direkt, dī-/ • adjective **1** going from one place to another without changing direction or stopping. **2** without intervening factors or intermediaries. **3** straightforward; frank. **4** clear; unambiguous. **5** (of descent) proceeding in continuous succession from parent to child. • adverb in a direct way or by a direct route. • verb **1** control the operations of. **2** aim (something) in a particular direction. **3** tell or show (someone) the way. **4** supervise and control (a film, play, or other production). **5** give an order to.
– DERIVATIVES **directness** noun.
– ORIGIN Latin *directus*, from *dirigere*, from *regere* 'put straight'.
direct action • noun the use of public forms of protest rather

Thesaurus

to, thanks to, by; *formal* by reason of.
diocese • noun BISHOPRIC, see.
dip • verb **1** *he dipped a rag in the water* IMMERSE, submerge, plunge, duck, dunk, lower, sink. **2** *the sun dipped below the horizon* SINK, set, drop, go/drop down, fall, descend; disappear, vanish. **3** *the president's popularity has dipped* DECREASE, fall, drop, fall off, decline, diminish, dwindle, slump, plummet, plunge; *informal* hit the floor. **4** *the road dipped* SLOPE DOWN, descend, go down; drop away, fall, sink. **5** *he dipped his headlights* DIM, LOWER, turn down. **6** *you might have to dip into your savings* DRAW ON, use, make use of, have recourse to, spend. **7** *an interesting book to dip into* BROWSE THROUGH, skim through, look through, flick through, glance at, peruse, run one's eye over.
– OPPOSITES rise, increase.
• noun **1** *a relaxing dip in the pool* SWIM, bathe; paddle. **2** *give the fish a ten-minute dip in a salt bath* IMMERSION, plunge, ducking, dunking. **3** *chicken satay with peanut dip* SAUCE, relish, dressing. **4** *the hedge at the bottom of the dip* SLOPE, incline, decline, descent; hollow, concavity, depression, basin, indentation. **5** *a dip in sales* DECREASE, fall, drop, downturn, decline, falling-off, slump, reduction, diminution, ebb.
diplomacy • noun **1** *diplomacy failed to win them independence* STATESMANSHIP, statecraft, negotiation(s), discussion(s), talks, dialogue; international relations, foreign affairs. **2** *Jack's quiet diplomacy* TACT, tactfulness, sensitivity, discretion, subtlety, finesse, delicacy, savoir faire, politeness, thoughtfulness, care, judiciousness, prudence.
diplomat • noun AMBASSADOR, attaché, consul, chargé d'affaires, envoy, emissary, plenipotentiary; *archaic* legate.
diplomatic • adjective **1** *diplomatic activity* AMBASSADORIAL, consular, foreign-office. **2** *he tried to be diplomatic* TACTFUL, sensitive, subtle, delicate, polite, discreet, thoughtful, careful, judicious, prudent, politic, clever, skilful.
– OPPOSITES tactless.
dire • adjective **1** *the dire economic situation* TERRIBLE, dreadful, appalling, frightful, awful, atrocious, grim, alarming; grave, serious, disastrous, ruinous, hopeless, irretrievable, wretched, desperate, parlous; *formal* grievous. **2** *he was in dire need of help* URGENT, desperate, pressing, crying, sore, grave, serious, extreme, acute, drastic. **3** *dire warnings of fuel shortages* OMINOUS, gloomy, grim, dismal, unpropitious, inauspicious, unfavourable, pessimistic. **4** *(informal) the concert was dire*. See AWFUL sense 2.
direct • adjective **1** *the most direct route* STRAIGHT, undeviating, unswerving; shortest, quickest. **2** *a direct flight* NON-STOP, unbroken, uninterrupted, through. **3** *he is very direct* FRANK, candid, straightforward, honest, open, blunt, plain-spoken, outspoken, forthright, downright, no-nonsense, matter-of-fact, not afraid to call a spade a spade; *informal* upfront. **4** *direct contact with the president* FACE TO

than negotiation to achieve one's aims.

direct current ● noun an electric current flowing in one direction only. Compare with ALTERNATING CURRENT.

direct debit ● noun Brit. an arrangement made with a bank that allows a third party to transfer money from a person's account.

direction /direksh'n, dī-/ ● noun **1** a course along which someone or something moves, or which leads to a destination. **2** a point to or from which a person or thing moves or faces. **3** the action of directing or managing people. **4** (**directions**) instructions on how to reach a destination or how to do something.
– DERIVATIVES **directional** adjective **directionless** adjective.

directive ● noun an official or authoritative instruction. ● adjective involving the direction of operations.

directly ● adverb **1** in a direct manner. **2** exactly in a specified position. **3** immediately. ● conjunction Brit. as soon as.

direct mail ● noun unsolicited commercial literature mailed to prospective customers.

direct object ● noun a noun phrase denoting a person or thing that is the recipient of the action of a transitive verb (e.g. *the dog* in *Jeremy fed the dog*).

director ● noun **1** a person who is in charge of a department, organization, or activity. **2** a member of the managing board of a business. **3** a person who directs a film, play, etc.
– DERIVATIVES **directorial** adjective **directorship** noun.

directorate ● noun **1** the board of directors of a company. **2** a section of a government department in charge of a particular activity.

director-general ● noun (pl. **directors-general**) chiefly Brit. the chief executive of a large organization.

directory ● noun (pl. **directories**) a book listing individuals or organizations with details such as addresses and telephone numbers.

directory enquiries ● plural noun (usu. treated as sing.) a telephone service used to find out someone's telephone number.

direct speech ● noun the reporting of speech by repeating the actual words of a speaker, for example *'I'm going', she said.* Contrasted with REPORTED SPEECH.

direct tax ● noun a tax, such as income tax, which is levied on the income or profits of the person who pays it.

dirge /durj/ ● noun **1** a lament for the dead, especially one forming part of a funeral rite. **2** a mournful song, piece of music, or sound.
– ORIGIN from Latin *dirige!* 'direct!', the first word of a psalm used in the Latin Office for the Dead.

dirham /durham/ ● noun the basic monetary unit of Morocco and the United Arab Emirates.
– ORIGIN Arabic, from Greek *drakhmē* 'drachma'.

dirigible /dirrijib'l/ ● noun an airship.
– ORIGIN from Latin *dirigere* 'to direct'.

dirigisme /dirizhiz'm/ ● noun state control of economic and social matters.
– DERIVATIVES **dirigiste** adjective.
– ORIGIN French, from *diriger* 'to direct'.

dirk /durk/ ● noun a short dagger of a kind formerly carried by Scottish Highlanders.
– ORIGIN of unknown origin.

dirndl /durnd'l/ ● noun **1** (also **dirndl skirt**) a full, wide skirt gathered into a tight waistband. **2** a woman's dress with a dirndl skirt and a close-fitting bodice.
– ORIGIN German dialect, 'little girl'.

dirt ● noun **1** a substance that causes uncleanliness. **2** loose soil or earth. **3** informal excrement. **4** informal scandalous or sordid information or material.
– ORIGIN Old Norse, 'excrement'.

dirt bike ● noun a motorcycle designed for use on rough terrain, especially in scrambling.

dirt cheap ● adjective & adverb extremely cheap.

dirt poor ● adjective & adverb extremely poor.

dirt track ● noun a racing track made of earth or rolled cinders.

dirty ● adjective (**dirtier**, **dirtiest**) **1** covered or marked with dirt; not clean. **2** lewd; obscene. **3** dishonest; dishonourable. **4** (of weather) rough and unpleasant. ● adverb Brit. informal used for emphasis: *a dirty great slab of stone.* ● verb (**dirties**, **dirtied**) make dirty.
– PHRASES **do the dirty on** Brit. informal cheat or betray. **get one's hands dirty** (or **dirty one's hands**) do manual, menial, or other hard work. **play dirty** informal act in a dishonest or unfair way.
– DERIVATIVES **dirtily** adverb **dirtiness** noun.

dirty look ● noun informal a look expressing disapproval, disgust,

Thesaurus

FACE, personal, head-on, immediate, first-hand, tête-à-tête. **5** *a direct quotation* VERBATIM, word for word, to the letter, faithful, exact, precise, accurate, correct. **6** *the direct opposite* EXACT, absolute, complete, diametrical.

● verb **1** *an economic elite directed the nation's affairs* MANAGE, govern, run, administer, control, conduct, handle, be in charge/control of, preside over, lead, head, rule, be at the helm of; supervise, superintend, oversee, regulate, orchestrate, coordinate; *informal* run the show, call the shots/tune, be in the driving seat. **2** *was that remark directed at me?* AIM AT, target at, address to, intend for, mean for, design for. **3** *a man in uniform directed them to the hall* GIVE DIRECTIONS, show the way, guide, lead, conduct, accompany, usher, escort. **4** *the judge directed the jury to return a not guilty verdict* INSTRUCT, tell, command, order, charge, require; *poetic/literary* bid.

direction ● noun **1** *a northerly direction* WAY, route, course, line, run, bearing, orientation. **2** *the newspaper's political direction* ORIENTATION, inclination, leaning, tendency, bent, bias, preference; drift, tack, attitude, tone, tenor, mood, current, trend. **3** *his direction of the project* ADMINISTRATION, management, conduct, handling, running, supervision, superintendence, regulation, orchestration; control, command, rule, leadership, guidance. **4** *explicit directions about nursing care* INSTRUCTION, order, command, prescription, rule, regulation, requirement.

directive ● noun INSTRUCTION, direction, command, order, charge, injunction, prescription, rule, ruling, regulation, law, dictate, decree, dictum, edict, mandate, fiat; *formal* ordinance.

directly ● adverb **1** *they flew directly to New York* STRAIGHT, right, as the crow flies, by a direct route. **2** *I went directly after breakfast* IMMEDIATELY, at once, instantly, right away, straight away, post-haste, without delay, without hesitation, forthwith; quickly, speedily, promptly; *informal* pronto. **3** *the houses directly opposite* EXACTLY, right, immediately; diametrically; *informal* bang. **4** *she spoke simply and directly* FRANKLY, candidly, openly, bluntly, forthrightly, without beating around the bush.

director ● noun ADMINISTRATOR, manager, chairman, chairwoman, chairperson, chair, head, chief, principal, leader, governor, president; managing director, MD, chief executive, CEO; supervisor, controller, overseer; *informal* boss, kingpin, top dog, gaffer, head honcho, numero uno; *N. Amer. informal* Mister Big.

directory ● noun INDEX, list, listing, register, catalogue, record, archive, inventory.

dirge ● noun ELEGY, lament, threnody, requiem, dead march; *Irish* keen; *Irish & Scottish* coronach.

dirt ● noun **1** *his face was streaked with dirt* GRIME, filth; dust, soot, smut; muck, mud, mire, sludge, slime, ooze, dross; smudges, stains; *informal* crud, yuck, grunge; *Brit. informal* grot, gunge. **2** *the packed dirt of the road* EARTH, soil, loam, clay, silt; ground. **3** *(informal) dog dirt.* See EXCREMENT. **4** *(informal) they tried to dig up dirt on the President* SCANDAL, gossip, revelations, rumour(s); information.

dirty ● adjective **1** *a dirty sweatshirt* | *dirty water* SOILED, grimy, grubby, filthy, mucky, stained, unwashed, greasy, smeared, smeary, spotted, smudged, cloudy, muddy, dusty, sooty; unclean, sullied, impure, tarnished, polluted, contaminated, defiled, foul, unhygienic, insanitary, unsanitary; *informal* cruddy, yucky, icky; *Brit. informal* manky, gungy, grotty; *poetic/literary* befouled, besmirched, begrimed. **2** *a dirty joke* INDECENT, obscene, rude, naughty, vulgar, smutty, coarse, crude, filthy, bawdy, suggestive, ribald, racy, salacious, risqué, offensive, off colour, lewd, pornographic, explicit, X-rated; *informal* blue; *euphemistic* adult. **3** *dirty tricks* DISHONEST, deceitful, unscrupulous, dishonourable, unsporting, ungentlemanly, below the belt, unfair, unethical, unprincipled; crooked, double-dealing, underhand, sly, crafty, devious, sneaky; *Brit. informal* out of order, not cricket. **4** *(informal) a dirty cheat* DESPICABLE, contemptible, hateful, vile, low, mean, unworthy, worthless, beyond contempt, sordid; *informal* rotten; *archaic* scurvy. **5** *a dirty look* MALEVOLENT, resentful, hostile, black, dark; angry, cross, indignant, annoyed, disapproving; *informal* peeved. **6** *dirty weather* UNPLEASANT, nasty, foul, inclement, bad; rough, stormy, squally, gusty, windy, blowy, rainy; murky, overcast, louring.
– OPPOSITES clean, innocent, honourable, pleasant.

● verb *the dog had dirtied her dress* SOIL, stain, muddy, blacken, mess up, mark, spatter, bespatter, smudge, smear, splatter; sully,

or anger.

dirty old man ● noun informal an older man who is sexually interested in younger women or girls.

dirty weekend ● noun Brit. informal a weekend spent away, especially in secret, with a lover.

dirty word ● noun **1** an offensive or indecent word. **2** a reference to something regarded with dislike or disapproval.

dirty work ● noun unpleasant or dishonest activities that are delegated to someone else.

d

dis /diss/ ● verb (also **diss**) (**dissed**, **dissing**) informal, chiefly US speak disrespectfully to or of. ● noun disrespectful talk.

dis- /diss/ ● prefix **1** expressing negation: *disadvantage*. **2** denoting reversal or absence of an action or state: *discharge*. **3** denoting removal, separation, or expulsion: *disbar*. **4** expressing completeness or intensification of an action: *disgruntled*.
– ORIGIN Latin.

disability ● noun (pl. **disabilities**) **1** a physical or mental condition that limits a person's movements, senses, or activities. **2** a disadvantage or handicap.

disable ● verb **1** (of a disease, injury, or accident) limit (someone) in their movements, senses, or activities. **2** put out of action.
– DERIVATIVES **disablement** noun.

disabled ● adjective having a physical or mental disability.
– USAGE **Disabled** is the standard term for people with physical or mental disabilities, and should be used rather than outmoded, now sometimes offensive, terms such as **crippled**.

disabuse /dissəbyo͞oz/ ● verb persuade (someone) that an idea or belief is mistaken.

disaccharide /dīsakkərīd/ ● noun Chemistry a sugar whose molecule can be broken down to give two simple sugar molecules.

disadvantage ● noun an unfavourable circumstance or condition. ● verb **1** put in an unfavourable position. **2** (**disadvantaged**) in socially or economically deprived circumstances.
– DERIVATIVES **disadvantageous** adjective.

disaffected ● adjective discontented through having lost one's feelings of loyalty or commitment.
– DERIVATIVES **disaffection** noun.

disagree ● verb (**disagrees**, **disagreed**, **disagreeing**) **1** have a different opinion. **2** be inconsistent. **3** (**disagree with**) make slightly unwell.
– DERIVATIVES **disagreement** noun.

disagreeable ● adjective **1** unpleasant. **2** unfriendly and bad-tempered.
– DERIVATIVES **disagreeably** adverb.

disallow ● verb declare invalid.
– DERIVATIVES **disallowance** noun.

disambiguate ● verb remove uncertainty of meaning from.
– DERIVATIVES **disambiguation** noun.

disappear ● verb **1** cease to be visible. **2** cease to exist or be in use. **3** (of a person) go missing or be killed.
– DERIVATIVES **disappearance** noun.

disappoint ● verb **1** fail to fulfil the hopes or expectations of. **2** prevent (hopes or expectations) from being realized.
– DERIVATIVES **disappointing** adjective **disappointment** noun.
– ORIGIN originally in the sense 'deprive of a position'; from Old French *desappointer*.

disappointed ● adjective sad or displeased because one's hopes or expectations have not been fulfilled.
– DERIVATIVES **disappointedly** adverb.

Thesaurus

pollute, foul, defile; *poetic/literary* befoul, besmirch, begrime.
– OPPOSITES clean.

disability ● noun HANDICAP, disablement, incapacity, impairment, infirmity, defect, abnormality; condition, disorder, affliction.

disable ● verb **1** *an injury that could disable somebody for life* INCAPACITATE, put out of action, debilitate; handicap, cripple, lame, maim, immobilize, paralyse. **2** *the bomb squad disabled the device* DEACTIVATE, defuse, disarm. **3** *he was disabled from holding public office* DISQUALIFY, prevent, preclude.

disabled ● adjective HANDICAPPED, incapacitated; debilitated, infirm, out of action; crippled, lame, paralysed, immobilized, bedridden; *euphemistic* physically challenged, differently abled.
– OPPOSITES able-bodied.

disabuse ● verb DISILLUSION, set straight, open someone's eyes, correct, enlighten, disenchant, shatter someone's illusions.

disadvantage ● noun DRAWBACK, snag, downside, stumbling block, fly in the ointment, catch, hindrance, obstacle, impediment; flaw, defect, weakness, fault, handicap, con, trouble, difficulty, problem, complication, nuisance; *Brit.* disbenefit; *informal* minus, spanner in the works.
– OPPOSITES benefit.

disadvantaged ● adjective DEPRIVED, underprivileged, depressed, in need, needy, poor, impoverished, indigent, hard up; *Brit.* on the breadline.

disadvantageous ● adjective UNFAVOURABLE, adverse, unfortunate, unlucky, bad; detrimental, prejudicial, deleterious, harmful, damaging, injurious, hurtful; inconvenient, inopportune, ill-timed, untimely, inexpedient.

disaffected ● adjective DISSATISFIED, disgruntled, discontented, malcontent, frustrated, alienated; disloyal, rebellious, mutinous, seditious, dissident, up in arms; hostile, antagonistic, unfriendly.
– OPPOSITES contented.

disagree ● verb **1** *no one was willing to disagree with him* TAKE ISSUE, challenge, contradict, oppose; be at variance/odds, not see eye to eye, differ, dissent, be in dispute, debate, argue, quarrel, wrangle, clash, be at loggerheads, cross swords, lock horns; *formal* gainsay. **2** *their accounts disagree on details* DIFFER, be dissimilar, be different, vary, diverge; contradict each other, conflict, clash, contrast. **3** *the spicy food disagreed with her* MAKE ILL, make unwell, nauseate, sicken, upset.

disagreeable ● adjective **1** *a disagreeable smell* UNPLEASANT, displeasing, nasty, offensive, off-putting, obnoxious, objectionable, horrible, horrid, dreadful, frightful, abominable, odious, repugnant, repulsive, repellent, revolting, disgusting, foul, vile, nauseating, sickening, unpalatable. **2** *a disagreeable man* BAD-TEMPERED, ill-tempered, curmudgeonly, cross, crabbed, irritable, grumpy, peevish, sullen, prickly; unfriendly, unpleasant, nasty, mean, mean-spirited, rude, surly, discourteous, impolite, brusque, abrupt, churlish, disobliging.
– OPPOSITES pleasant.

disagreement ● noun **1** *there was some disagreement over possible solutions* DISSENT, dispute, difference of opinion, variance, controversy, disaccord, discord, contention, division. **2** *a heated disagreement* ARGUMENT, debate, quarrel, wrangle, squabble, falling-out, altercation, dispute, disputation, war of words, contretemps; *informal* tiff, barney, set-to, spat, ding-dong; *Brit. informal* row; *Scottish informal* rammy. **3** *the disagreement between the results of the two assessments* DIFFERENCE, dissimilarity, variation, variance, discrepancy, disparity, divergence, deviation, nonconformity; incompatibility, contradiction, conflict, clash, contrast; *formal* dissimilitude.

disallow ● verb REJECT, refuse, dismiss, say no to; ban, bar, block, debar, forbid, prohibit; cancel, invalidate, overrule, quash, overturn, countermand, reverse, throw out, set aside; *informal* give the thumbs down to.

disappear ● verb **1** *by 4 o'clock the mist had disappeared* VANISH, pass from sight, be lost to view/sight, recede from view; fade (away), melt away, clear, dissolve, disperse, evaporate, dematerialize; *poetic/literary* evanesce. **2** *this way of life has disappeared* DIE OUT, die, cease to exist, come to an end, end, pass away, pass into oblivion, perish, vanish.
– OPPOSITES materialize.

disappoint ● verb **1** *I'm sorry to have disappointed you* LET DOWN, fail, dissatisfy, dash someone's hopes; upset, dismay, sadden, disenchant, disillusion, shatter someone's illusions, disabuse. **2** *his hopes were disappointed* THWART, frustrate, foil, dash, put a/the damper on; *informal* throw cold water on.
– OPPOSITES fulfil.

disappointed ● adjective UPSET, saddened, let down, cast down, disheartened, downhearted, downcast, depressed, dispirited, discouraged, despondent, dismayed, crestfallen, distressed, chagrined; disenchanted, disillusioned; displeased, discontented, dissatisfied, frustrated, disgruntled; *informal* choked, miffed, cut up; *Brit. informal* gutted, as sick as a parrot.
– OPPOSITES pleased.

disappointing ● adjective REGRETTABLE, unfortunate, sorry, discouraging, disheartening, dispiriting, depressing, dismaying, upsetting, saddening; dissatisfactory, unsatisfactory; *informal* not all it's cracked up to be.

disappointment ● noun **1** *she tried to hide her disappointment* SADNESS, regret, dismay, sorrow; dispiritedness, despondency, distress, chagrin; disenchantment, disillusionment; displeasure, dissatisfaction, disgruntlement. **2** *the trip was a bit of a disappointment* LET-DOWN, non-event, anticlimax; *Brit.* damp squib; *informal*

disapprobation /dissaprəbaysh'n/ ● noun strong disapproval.
disapprove ● verb have or express an unfavourable opinion.
– DERIVATIVES **disapproval** noun **disapproving** adjective.
disarm ● verb **1** take a weapon or weapons away from. **2** (of a country or force) give up or reduce its armed forces or weapons. **3** remove the fuse from (a bomb). **4** allay the hostility or suspicions of; win over.
disarmament /disaarməmənt/ ● noun the reduction or withdrawal of military forces and weapons.
disarming ● adjective **1** allaying suspicion or hostility. **2** captivating; charming.
– DERIVATIVES **disarmingly** adverb.
disarrange ● verb make untidy or disordered.
disarray ● noun a state of disorganization or untidiness. ● verb throw into a state of disarray.
disassemble ● verb take to pieces.
– DERIVATIVES **disassembly** noun.
disassociate ● verb another term for DISSOCIATE.
– DERIVATIVES **disassociation** noun.
disaster ● noun **1** a sudden accident or a natural catastrophe that causes great damage or loss of life. **2** an event or fact leading to ruin or failure.
– ORIGIN Italian *disastro* 'ill-starred event', from Latin *astrum* 'star'.
disastrous ● adjective **1** causing great damage. **2** informal highly unsuccessful.
– DERIVATIVES **disastrously** adverb.
disavow ● verb deny any responsibility or support for.
– DERIVATIVES **disavowal** noun.
disband ● verb (with reference to an organized group) break up or cause to break up.
disbar ● verb (**disbarred**, **disbarring**) **1** expel (a barrister) from the Bar. **2** exclude.
– DERIVATIVES **disbarment** noun.
disbelief ● noun **1** inability or refusal to accept that something is true or real. **2** lack of faith.
disbelieve ● verb **1** be unable to believe. **2** have no religious faith.
– DERIVATIVES **disbeliever** noun.
disbenefit ● noun Brit. a disadvantage.
disburden ● verb relieve of a burden or responsibility.
disburse /disburss/ ● verb pay out (money from a fund).
– DERIVATIVES **disbursal** noun **disbursement** noun.
– ORIGIN Old French *desbourser*, from *bourse* 'purse'.
disc (US also **disk**) ● noun **1** a flat, thin, round object. **2** (**disk**) an information storage device for a computer, on which data is stored either magnetically or optically. **3** a layer of cartilage separating vertebrae in the spine. **4** dated a gramophone record.
– ORIGIN Greek *diskos* 'discus'.
discard ● verb /diskaard/ get rid of as no longer useful or desirable. ● noun /diskaard/ a discarded item.
– DERIVATIVES **discardable** /diskaardəb'l/ adjective.
– ORIGIN originally in the sense 'reject (a playing card)'; from DIS- + CARD[1].
disc brake ● noun a type of vehicle brake employing the friction of pads against a disc attached to the wheel.
discern /disern/ ● verb **1** recognize or find out. **2** distinguish with difficulty by sight or with the other senses.
– DERIVATIVES **discernible** adjective.
– ORIGIN Latin *discernere*, from *cernere* 'to separate'.
discerning ● adjective having or showing good judgement.
– DERIVATIVES **discernment** noun.

Thesaurus

washout, lead balloon.
– OPPOSITES satisfaction.
disapprobation ● noun. See DISAPPROVAL.
disapproval ● noun DISAPPROBATION, objection, dislike; dissatisfaction, disfavour, displeasure, distaste, exception; criticism, censure, condemnation, denunciation, deprecation; *informal* the thumbs down.
disapprove ● verb **1** *he disapproved of gamblers* OBJECT TO, have a poor opinion of, look down one's nose at, take exception to, dislike, take a dim view of, look askance at, frown on, be against, not believe in; deplore, criticize, censure, condemn, denounce, decry, deprecate. **2** *the board disapproved the plan* REJECT, veto, refuse, turn down, disallow, throw out, dismiss, rule against; *informal* give the thumbs down to.
disapproving ● adjective REPROACHFUL, reproving, critical, censorious, condemnatory, disparaging, denigratory, deprecatory, unfavourable; dissatisfied, displeased, hostile.
disarm ● verb **1** *the UN must disarm the country* DEMILITARIZE, demobilize. **2** *the militia refused to disarm* LAY DOWN ONE'S ARMS, demilitarize; *poetic/literary* turn swords into ploughshares. **3** *police disarmed the bomb* DEFUSE, disable, deactivate, put out of action, make harmless. **4** *the warmth in his voice disarmed her* WIN OVER, charm, persuade, thaw; mollify, appease, placate, pacify, conciliate, propitiate.
disarmament ● noun DEMILITARIZATION, demobilization, decommissioning; arms reduction, arms limitation, arms control; the zero option.
disarming ● adjective WINNING, charming, irresistible, persuasive, beguiling; conciliatory, mollifying.
disarrange ● verb DISORDER, throw into disarray/disorder, put out of place, disorganize, disturb, displace; mess up, make untidy, make a mess of, jumble, mix up, muddle, turn upside-down, scatter; dishevel, tousle, rumple; *informal* turn topsy-turvy, make a shambles of; *N. Amer. informal* muss up.
disarray ● noun *the room was in disarray* DISORDER, confusion, chaos, untidiness, disorganization, dishevelment, mess, muddle, clutter, jumble, tangle, hotchpotch, shambles.
– OPPOSITES tidiness.
● verb *her clothes were disarrayed*. See DISARRANGE.
disassemble ● verb DISMANTLE, take apart, take to pieces, take to bits, deconstruct, break up, strip down.
disaster ● noun **1** *a railway disaster* CATASTROPHE, calamity, cataclysm, tragedy, act of God, holocaust; accident. **2** *a string of personal disasters* MISFORTUNE, mishap, misadventure, mischance, setback, reversal, stroke of bad luck, blow. **3** *(informal) the film was a disaster* FAILURE, fiasco, catastrophe, debacle; *informal* flop, dud, washout, dead loss.
– OPPOSITES success.
disastrous ● adjective CATASTROPHIC, calamitous, cataclysmic, tragic; devastating, ruinous, harmful, dire, terrible, awful, shocking, appalling, dreadful; black, dark, unfortunate, unlucky, ill-fated, ill-starred, inauspicious; *formal* grievous.
disavow ● verb DENY, disclaim, disown, wash one's hands of, repudiate, reject, renounce.
disavowal ● noun DENIAL, rejection, repudiation, renunciation, disclaimer.
disband ● verb BREAK UP, disperse, demobilize, dissolve, scatter, separate, go separate ways, part company.
– OPPOSITES assemble.
disbelief ● noun **1** *she stared at him in disbelief* INCREDULITY, incredulousness, scepticism, doubt, doubtfulness, dubiousness; cynicism, suspicion, distrust, mistrust; *formal* dubiety. **2** *I'll burn in hell for disbelief* ATHEISM, unbelief, godlessness, irreligion, agnosticism, nihilism.
disbelieve ● verb NOT BELIEVE, give no credence to, discredit, discount, doubt, distrust, mistrust, be incredulous, be unconvinced; reject, repudiate, question, challenge; *informal* take with a pinch of salt.
disbeliever ● noun UNBELIEVER, non-believer, atheist, irreligionist, nihilist; sceptic, doubter, agnostic, doubting Thomas, cynic; *rare* nullifidian.
disbelieving ● adjective INCREDULOUS, doubtful, dubious, unconvinced; distrustful, mistrustful, suspicious, cynical, sceptical.
disburden ● verb RELIEVE, free, liberate, unburden, disencumber, discharge, excuse, absolve.
disburse ● verb PAY OUT, spend, expend, dole out, dish out, hand out, part with, donate, give; *informal* fork out, shell out, lay out; *Brit. informal* stump up; *N. Amer. informal* ante up, pony up.
disc, disk ● noun **1** *the sun was a huge scarlet disc* CIRCLE, round, saucer, discus, ring. **2** *computer disks* DISKETTE, floppy disk, floppy; hard disk; CD-ROM. **3** *(dated) an old T-Rex disc* RECORD, gramophone record, album, LP, vinyl.
discard ● verb DISPOSE OF, throw away/out, get rid of, toss out, jettison, scrap, dispense with, cast aside/off, throw on the scrap heap; reject, repudiate, abandon, drop, have done with, shed; *informal* chuck (away/out), dump, ditch, bin, junk, get shut of; *Brit. informal* get shot of; *N. Amer. informal* trash.
– OPPOSITES keep.
discern ● verb PERCEIVE, make out, pick out, detect, recognize, notice, observe, see, spot; identify, determine, distinguish; *poetic/literary* descry, espy.
discernible ● adjective VISIBLE, detectable, noticeable, perceptible,

d

discharge ● verb /dischaarj/ **1** dismiss or allow to leave. **2** emit or send out (a liquid, gas, or other substance). **3** fire (a gun or missile). **4** do all that is required to fulfil (a responsibility). **5** release from a contract or obligation. **6** Physics release or neutralize the electric charge of). ● noun /dischaarj, dischaarj/ **1** the action of discharging. **2** a substance that has been discharged. **3** a flow of electricity through the air or other gas.
– DERIVATIVES **discharger** noun.
– ORIGIN Old French *descharger*, from Latin *discarricare* 'unload'.
disciple /disīp'l/ ● noun **1** a personal follower of Christ during his life, especially one of the twelve Apostles. **2** a follower or pupil of a teacher, leader, or philosophy.
– DERIVATIVES **discipleship** noun.
– ORIGIN Latin *discipulus* 'learner', from *discere* 'learn'.
disciplinarian ● noun a person who enforces firm discipline.
discipline /dissiplin/ ● noun **1** the practice of training people to obey rules or a code of behaviour. **2** controlled behaviour resulting from such training. **3** a branch of knowledge, especially one studied in higher education. ● verb **1** train in obedience or self-control by punishment or imposing rules. **2** punish or rebuke formally for an offence. **3** (**disciplined**) behaving in a controlled way.
– DERIVATIVES **disciplinary** adjective.
– ORIGIN Latin *disciplina* 'instruction, knowledge'.
disc jockey ● noun a person who introduces and plays recorded popular music on radio or at a disco.
disclaim ● verb **1** refuse to acknowledge. **2** Law renounce a legal claim to (a property or title).
disclaimer ● noun a statement disclaiming something, especially responsibility.
disclose ● verb **1** make (secret or new information) known. **2** expose to view.
– DERIVATIVES **discloser** noun.
disclosure ● noun **1** the action of disclosing information. **2** a fact, especially a secret, that is disclosed.
disco ● noun (pl. **discos**) informal **1** a club or party at which people dance to pop music. **2** (also **disco music**) soul-influenced, melodic pop music with a regular bass beat.
discography /diskogrəfi/ ● noun (pl. **discographies**) **1** a descriptive catalogue of musical recordings, particularly those of a particular performer or composer. **2** the study of musical recordings and compilation of descriptive catalogues.
– DERIVATIVES **discographer** noun.
discoid /diskoyd/ ● adjective shaped like a disc.
– DERIVATIVES **discoidal** adjective.
discolour (US **discolor**) ● verb become or cause to become stained, yellowed, or otherwise changed in colour.
– DERIVATIVES **discoloration** (also **discolouration**) noun.
discombobulate /diskəmbobyoolayt/ ● verb humorous, chiefly N. Amer. disconcert or confuse.
– ORIGIN probably based on DISCOMPOSE or DISCOMFIT.
discomfit /diskumfit/ ● verb (**discomfited**, **discomfiting**) make uneasy or embarrassed.
– DERIVATIVES **discomfiture** noun.
– ORIGIN originally in the sense 'defeat in battle': from Old French *desconfire*, from Latin *conficere* 'put together'.
discomfort ● noun **1** slight pain. **2** slight anxiety or embarrassment. ● verb cause discomfort to.

Thesaurus

observable, distinguishable, recognizable, identifiable; apparent, evident, distinct, appreciable, clear, obvious, manifest, conspicuous.
discerning ● adjective DISCRIMINATING, judicious, shrewd, clever, astute, intelligent, sharp, selective, sophisticated, tasteful, sensitive, perceptive, percipient, perspicacious, wise, aware, knowing.
discharge ● verb **1** *he was discharged from the RAF* DISMISS, eject, expel, throw out, give someone notice, make redundant; release, let go; Military cashier; informal sack, give someone the sack, fire, boot out, give someone the boot, turf out, give someone their cards, give someone their marching orders, give someone the push. **2** *he was discharged from prison* RELEASE, free, set free, let go, liberate, let out. **3** *oil is routinely discharged from ships* SEND OUT, release, eject, let out, pour out, void, give off. **4** *the swelling will burst and discharge pus* EMIT, exude, ooze, leak. **5** *he accidentally discharged a pistol* FIRE, shoot, let off; set off, loose off, trigger, explode, detonate. **6** *the ferry was discharging passengers* UNLOAD, offload, put off; remove; archaic unlade. **7** *they discharged their duties efficiently* CARRY OUT, perform, execute, conduct, do; fulfil, accomplish, achieve, complete. **8** *the executor must discharge the funeral expenses* PAY, pay off, settle, clear, honour, meet, liquidate, defray, make good; informal square.
– OPPOSITES recruit, imprison, absorb.
● noun **1** *his discharge from the service* DISMISSAL, release, removal, ejection, expulsion, congé; Military cashiering; informal the sack, the boot. **2** *her discharge from prison* RELEASE, liberation. **3** *a discharge of diesel oil into the river* LEAK, leakage, emission, release, flow. **4** *a watery discharge from the eyes* EMISSION, secretion, excretion, seepage, suppuration; pus, matter; Medicine exudate. **5** *a single discharge of his gun* SHOT, firing, blast; explosion, detonation. **6** *the discharge of their duties* CARRYING OUT, performance, performing, execution, conduct; fulfilment, accomplishment, completion. **7** *the discharge of all debts* PAYMENT, repayment, settlement, clearance, meeting, liquidation, defrayal.
disciple ● noun **1** *the disciples of Jesus* APOSTLE, follower. **2** *a disciple of Rousseau* FOLLOWER, adherent, believer, admirer, devotee, acolyte, votary; pupil, student, learner; upholder, supporter, advocate, proponent, apologist.
disciplinarian ● noun MARTINET, hard taskmaster, authoritarian, stickler for discipline; tyrant, despot; N. Amer. ramrod; informal slave-driver.
discipline ● noun **1** *a lack of proper parental discipline* CONTROL, training, teaching, instruction, regulation, direction, order, authority, rule, strictness, a firm hand; routine, regimen, drill, drilling. **2** *he was able to maintain discipline among his men* GOOD BEHAVIOUR, orderliness, control, obedience; self-control, self-discipline, self-government, self-restraint. **3** *sociology is a fairly new discipline* FIELD (OF STUDY), branch of knowledge, subject, area; speciality, specialty.
● verb **1** *she had disciplined herself to ignore the pain* TRAIN, drill, teach, school, coach; regiment. **2** *she learned to discipline her emotions* CONTROL, restrain, regulate, govern, keep in check, check, curb, keep a tight rein on, rein in, bridle, tame, bring into line. **3** *he was disciplined by the management* PUNISH, penalize, bring to book; reprimand, rebuke, reprove, chastise, upbraid; informal dress down, give someone a dressing-down, rap over the knuckles, give someone a roasting; Brit. informal carpet; formal castigate.
disclaim ● verb **1** *the school disclaimed responsibility for his death* DENY, refuse to accept/acknowledge, reject, wash one's hands of. **2** (Law) *the earl disclaimed his title* RENOUNCE, relinquish, resign, give up, abandon.
– OPPOSITES accept.
disclose ● verb **1** *the information must not be disclosed to anyone* REVEAL, make known, divulge, tell, impart, communicate, pass on, vouchsafe; release, make public, broadcast, publish, report, unveil; leak, betray, let slip, let drop, give away; informal let on, blab, spill the beans, let the cat out of the bag; Brit. informal blow the gaff; archaic discover, unbosom. **2** *exploratory surgery disclosed an aneurysm* UNCOVER, reveal, show, bring to light.
– OPPOSITES conceal.
disclosure ● noun **1** *she was embarrassed by this unexpected disclosure* REVELATION, declaration, announcement, news, report; exposé, leak. **2** *the disclosure of official information* PUBLISHING, broadcasting; revelation, communication, release, uncovering, unveiling, exposure; leakage.
discoloration ● noun STAIN, mark, patch, soiling, streak, spot, blotch, tarnishing; blemish, flaw, defect, bruise, contusion; birthmark, naevus; liver spot, age spot; informal splodge, splotch; Medicine ecchymosis.
discolour ● verb STAIN, mark, soil, dirty, streak, smear, spot, tarnish, sully, spoil, mar, blemish; blacken, char; fade, bleach.
discoloured ● adjective STAINED, marked, spotted, dirty, soiled, tarnished, blackened; bleached, faded, yellowed.
discomfit ● verb EMBARRASS, abash, disconcert, nonplus, discompose, discomfort, take aback, set someone back on their heels, unsettle, unnerve, put someone off their stroke, ruffle, confuse, fluster, agitate, disorientate, upset, disturb, perturb, distress; chagrin, mortify; informal faze, rattle; N. Amer. informal discombobulate.
discomfiture ● noun EMBARRASSMENT, unease, uneasiness, awkwardness, discomfort, discomposure, abashment, confusion, agitation, nervousness, disorientation, perturbation, distress; chagrin, mortification, shame, humiliation; N. Amer. informal discombobulation.
discomfort ● noun **1** *abdominal discomfort* PAIN, aches and pains, soreness, tenderness, irritation, stiffness; ache, twinge, pang,

discommode /diskəmōd/ ● verb formal cause trouble or inconvenience to.
– DERIVATIVES **discommodious** adjective.
– ORIGIN obsolete French *discommoder*, variant of *incommoder* 'incommode'.
discompose ● verb disturb or agitate.
– DERIVATIVES **discomposure** noun.
disconcert /diskənsert/ ● verb disturb the composure of.
– DERIVATIVES **disconcerted** adjective **disconcerting** adjective.
– ORIGIN obsolete French *desconcerter*, from *concerter* 'bring together'.
disconnect ● verb **1** break the connection of or between. **2** detach (an electrical device) from a power supply.
– DERIVATIVES **disconnection** noun.
disconnected ● adjective (of speech, writing, or thought) lacking a logical sequence.
disconsolate /diskonsələt/ ● adjective unable to be comforted or consoled; very unhappy.
– DERIVATIVES **disconsolately** adverb.
discontent ● noun lack of contentment or satisfaction.
– DERIVATIVES **discontented** adjective **discontentment** noun.
discontinue ● verb (**discontinues**, **discontinued**, **discontinuing**) stop doing, providing, or making.
– DERIVATIVES **discontinuation** noun.
discontinuous ● adjective having intervals or gaps; not continuous.
– DERIVATIVES **discontinuity** noun.
discord ● noun /diskord/ **1** lack of agreement or harmony. **2** Music lack of harmony between notes sounding together. **3** Music a chord regarded as displeasing or requiring resolution by another.
– DERIVATIVES **discordance** noun **discordancy** noun **discordant** adjective **discordantly** adverb.
– ORIGIN from Latin *discors* 'discordant', from *cor* 'heart'.
discotheque /diskətek/ ● noun another term for DISCO (in sense 1).
– ORIGIN French (originally meaning 'record library'), on the pattern of *bibliothèque* 'library'.
discount ● noun /diskownt/ a deduction from the usual cost of something. ● verb /diskownt/ **1** deduct a discount from (the usual price of something). **2** disregard as lacking credibility or significance. **3** Finance buy or sell (a bill of exchange) before its due date at a discount.
– DERIVATIVES **discounter** /diskowntər/ noun.
discountenance ● verb **1** refuse to approve of. **2** disturb the composure of.
discount house ● noun Brit. a company that discounts bills of exchange.
discount rate ● noun Finance **1** a minimum interest rate set by the US Federal Reserve for lending to other banks. **2** a rate used for discounting bills of exchange.
discourage ● verb **1** cause a loss of confidence or enthusiasm in. **2** prevent or try to prevent by showing disapproval or creating difficulties. **3** (**discourage from**) persuade (someone) against (an action).
– DERIVATIVES **discouragement** noun **discouraging** adjective.
– ORIGIN Old French *descouragier*, from *corage* 'courage'.
discourse ● noun /diskorss/ **1** written or spoken communica-

d

Thesaurus

throb, cramp; *Brit. informal* gyp. **2** *the discomforts of life at sea* INCONVENIENCE, difficulty, bother, nuisance, vexation, drawback, disadvantage, trouble, problem, trial, tribulation, hardship; *informal* hassle. **3** *Ruth flushed and Thomas noticed her discomfort* EMBARRASSMENT, discomfiture, unease, uneasiness, awkwardness, discomposure, confusion, nervousness, flusteredness, perturbation, distress, anxiety; chagrin, mortification, shame, humiliation.
● verb *his purpose was to discomfort the Prime Minister.* See DISCOMFIT.
discomposure ● noun AGITATION, discomfiture, discomfort, uneasiness, unease, confusion, disorientation, perturbation, distress, nervousness; anxiety, worry, consternation, disquiet, disquietude; embarrassment, abashment, chagrin, loss of face; *N. Amer. informal* discombobulation.
disconcert ● verb UNSETTLE, nonplus, discomfit, throw/catch off balance, take aback, rattle, set someone back on their heels, unnerve, disorient, perturb, disturb, perplex, confuse, bewilder, baffle, fluster, ruffle, shake, upset, agitate, worry, dismay, discountenance; surprise, take by surprise, startle, put someone off (their stroke/stride), distract; *informal* throw, faze; *N. Amer. informal* discombobulate.
disconcerting ● adjective UNSETTLING, unnerving, discomfiting, disturbing, perturbing, troubling, upsetting, worrying, alarming, distracting, off-putting; confusing, bewildering, perplexing.
disconnect ● verb **1** *the trucks were disconnected from the train* DETACH, disengage, uncouple, decouple, unhook, unhitch, undo, unfasten, unyoke. **2** *she felt as if she had been disconnected from the real world* SEPARATE, cut off, divorce, sever, isolate, divide, part, disengage, dissociate, remove. **3** *an engineer disconnected the appliance* DEACTIVATE, shut off, turn off, switch off, unplug.
– OPPOSITES attach.
disconnected ● adjective **1** *a world that seemed disconnected from reality* DETACHED, separate, separated, divorced, cut off, isolated, dissociated, disengaged; apart. **2** *a disconnected narrative* DISJOINTED, incoherent, garbled, confused, jumbled, mixed up, rambling, wandering, disorganized, uncoordinated, ill-thought-out.
disconsolate ● adjective SAD, unhappy, doleful, woebegone, dejected, downcast, downhearted, despondent, dispirited, crestfallen, cast down, depressed, down, fed up, disappointed, disheartened, discouraged, demoralized, low-spirited, forlorn, in the doldrums, melancholy, miserable, long-faced, glum, gloomy; *informal* blue, choked, down in the mouth, down in the dumps; *poetic/literary* dolorous.
– OPPOSITES cheerful.
discontent ● noun DISSATISFACTION, disaffection, discontentment, discontentedness, disgruntlement, grievances, unhappiness, displeasure, bad feelings, resentment, envy; restlessness, unrest, uneasiness, unease, frustration, irritation, annoyance; *informal* a chip on one's shoulder.
– OPPOSITES satisfaction.
discontented ● adjective DISSATISFIED, disgruntled, fed up, disaffected, discontent, malcontent, unhappy, aggrieved, displeased, resentful, envious; restless, frustrated, irritated, annoyed; *informal* fed up to the (back) teeth, browned off, hacked off; *Brit. informal* cheesed off, brassed off; *N. Amer. informal* teed off, ticked off.
– OPPOSITES satisfied.
discontinue ● verb STOP, end, terminate, put an end to, put a stop to, wind up, finish, call a halt to, cancel, drop, abandon, dispense with, do away with, get rid of, axe, abolish; suspend, interrupt, break off, withdraw; *informal* cut, pull the plug on, scrap, knock something on the head.
discontinuity ● noun DISCONNECTEDNESS, disconnection, break, disruption, interruption, disjointedness.
discontinuous ● adjective INTERMITTENT, sporadic, broken, fitful, interrupted, on and off, disrupted, erratic, disconnected.
discord ● noun **1** *stress resulting from family discord* STRIFE, conflict, friction, hostility, antagonism, antipathy, enmity, bad feeling, ill feeling, bad blood, argument, quarrelling, squabbling, bickering, wrangling, feuding, contention, disagreement, dissension, dispute, difference of opinion, disunity, division, opposition. **2** *the music faded in discord* DISSONANCE, discordance, disharmony, cacophony, jangling.
– OPPOSITES accord, harmony.
discordant ● adjective **1** *the messages from Washington and London were discordant* DIFFERENT, in disagreement, at variance, at odds, divergent, discrepant, contradictory, contrary, in conflict, conflicting, opposite, opposed, opposing, clashing; incompatible, inconsistent, irreconcilable. **2** *discordant sounds* INHARMONIOUS, tuneless, off-key, dissonant, harsh, jarring, grating, jangling, jangly, strident, shrill, screeching, screechy, cacophonous; sharp, flat.
– OPPOSITES harmonious.
discount ● noun *students get a 10 per cent discount* REDUCTION, deduction, markdown, price cut, cut, concession; rebate.
● verb **1** *I'd heard rumours, but discounted them* DISREGARD, pay no attention to, take no notice of, take no account of, dismiss, ignore, overlook, disbelieve, reject; *informal* take with a pinch of salt, pooh-pooh. **2** *the RRP is discounted in many stores* REDUCE, mark down, cut, lower; *informal* knock down. **3** *top Paris hotels discounted 20 per cent off published room rates* DEDUCT, take off, rebate; *informal* knock off, slash.
– OPPOSITES believe, increase.
discountenance ● verb **1** *she was not discountenanced by the accusation* DISCONCERT, discomfit, unsettle, nonplus, throw/catch off balance, take aback, unnerve, disorient, perturb, disturb, perplex, fluster, ruffle, shake, upset, agitate, worry, dismay, discompose,

tion or debate. **2** a formal discussion of a topic in speech or writing. ● verb /diskorss/ **1** speak or write authoritatively about a topic. **2** engage in conversation.
– ORIGIN Latin *discursus* 'running to and fro', from *discurrere* 'run away'.
discourteous ● adjective rude and lacking consideration for others.
– DERIVATIVES **discourteously** adverb **discourteousness** noun.
discourtesy ● noun (pl. **discourtesies**) **1** rude and inconsiderate behaviour. **2** an impolite act or remark.

d

discover ● verb **1** find unexpectedly or in the course of a search. **2** become aware of (a fact or situation). **3** be the first to find or observe (a place, substance, or scientific phenomenon).
– DERIVATIVES **discoverable** adjective **discoverer** noun.
discovery ● noun (pl. **discoveries**) **1** the action or process of discovering or being discovered. **2** a person or thing discovered. **3** Law the compulsory disclosure of documents relevant to an action.
discredit ● verb (**discredited**, **discrediting**) **1** harm the good reputation of. **2** cause (an idea or piece of evidence) to seem false or unreliable. ● noun loss or lack of reputation.
– DERIVATIVES **discreditable** adjective.
discreet /diskreet/ ● adjective (**discreeter**, **discreetest**) careful not to attract attention or give offence.
– DERIVATIVES **discreetly** adverb.
– USAGE The words **discrete** and **discreet** are often confused. **Discrete** means 'separate' (*a discrete unit*), while **discreet** means 'careful and prudent'.
– ORIGIN Old French *discret*, from Latin *discretus* 'separate'.
discrepancy /diskreppənsi/ ● noun (pl. **discrepancies**) an illogical or surprising lack of compatibility between facts.
– DERIVATIVES **discrepant** adjective.
– ORIGIN Latin *discrepantia*, from *discrepare* 'be discordant'.
discrete /diskreet/ ● adjective individually separate and distinct.
– DERIVATIVES **discretely** adverb **discreteness** noun.
– ORIGIN Latin *discretus* 'separate': compare with DISCREET.
discretion ● noun **1** the quality of being discreet. **2** the freedom to decide what should be done in a particular situation.
– PHRASES **discretion is the better part of valour** proverb it's better to avoid a dangerous situation than to confront it.
– DERIVATIVES **discretionary** adjective.
– ORIGIN Latin, 'separation' (later 'discernment'), from *discernere* (see DISCERN).
discretionary income ● noun income remaining after deduction of taxes, social security charges, and basic living costs.
discriminable ● adjective able to be discriminated; distinguishable.
– DERIVATIVES **discriminably** adverb.
discriminate /diskrimminayt/ ● verb **1** recognize a distinction. **2** make an unjust distinction in the treatment of different categories of people, especially on the grounds of race, sex, or age.
– DERIVATIVES **discriminative** adjective.
– ORIGIN Latin *discriminare* 'distinguish between'.
discriminating ● adjective having or showing good taste or

Thesaurus

abash; *informal* throw, faze, rattle; *N. Amer. informal* discombobulate. **2** *a family environment in which alcohol consumption is discountenanced* DISAPPROVE OF, frown on, take a dim view of, object to.
discourage ● verb **1** *we want to discourage children from smoking* DETER, dissuade, disincline, put off, talk out of; advise against, urge against. **2** *she was discouraged by his hostile tone* DISHEARTEN, dispirit, demoralize, cast down, depress, disappoint, dash someone's hopes; put off, unnerve, daunt, intimidate, cow, crush. **3** *he sought to discourage further conversation* PREVENT, stop, put a stop to, avert, fend off, stave off, ward off; inhibit, hinder, check, curb, put a damper on, throw cold water on.
– OPPOSITES encourage.
discouraged ● adjective DISHEARTENED, dispirited, demoralized, deflated, disappointed, let down, disconsolate, despondent, fed up, dejected, cast down, downcast, depressed, crestfallen, dismayed, low-spirited, gloomy, glum, pessimistic, unenthusiastic; put off, daunted, intimidated, cowed, crushed; *informal* down in the mouth, down in the dumps, unenthused; *archaic* chap-fallen.
discouraging ● adjective DEPRESSING, demoralizing, disheartening, dispiriting, disappointing, gloomy, off-putting; unfavourable, unpromising, inauspicious.
– OPPOSITES encouraging.
discourse ● noun **1** *they prolonged their discourse outside the door* DISCUSSION, conversation, talk, dialogue, conference, debate, consultation; parley, powwow, chat; *informal* confab; *formal* confabulation, colloquy; *archaic* converse. **2** *a discourse on critical theory* ESSAY, treatise, dissertation, paper, study, critique, monograph, disquisition, tract; lecture, address, speech, oration; sermon, homily.
● verb **1** *he discoursed at length on his favourite topic* HOLD FORTH, expatiate, pontificate; talk, give a talk, give a speech, lecture, sermonize, preach; *informal* spout, sound off; *formal* perorate. **2** *Edward was discoursing with his friends* CONVERSE, talk, speak, debate, confer, consult, parley, chat; *formal* confabulate.
discourteous ● adjective RUDE, impolite, ill-mannered, bad-mannered, disrespectful, uncivil, unmannerly, unchivalrous, ungentlemanly, unladylike, ill-bred, churlish, boorish, crass, ungracious, graceless, uncouth; insolent, impudent, cheeky, audacious, presumptuous; curt, brusque, blunt, offhand, unceremonious, short, sharp; *informal* ignorant; *archaic* malapert.
– OPPOSITES polite.
discourtesy ● noun RUDENESS, impoliteness, ill manners, bad manners, incivility, disrespect, ungraciousness, churlishness, boorishness, ill breeding, uncouthness, crassness; insolence, impudence, impertinence; curtness, brusqueness, abruptness.
discover ● verb **1** *firemen discovered a body in the debris* FIND, locate, come across/upon, stumble on, chance on, light on, bring to light, uncover, unearth, turn up; track down, run to earth, run to ground. **2** *eventually, I discovered the truth* FIND OUT, learn, realize, recognize, see, ascertain, work out, fathom out, dig up/out, ferret out, root out; *informal* figure out, tumble to; *Brit. informal* twig, rumble, suss out; *N. Amer. informal* dope out. **3** *scientists discovered a new way of dating fossil crustaceans* HIT ON, come up with, invent, originate, devise, design, contrive, conceive of; pioneer, develop.
discoverer ● noun ORIGINATOR, inventor, creator, deviser, designer; pioneer.
discovery ● noun **1** *the discovery of the body* FINDING, location, uncovering, unearthing. **2** *the discovery that she was pregnant* REALIZATION, recognition; revelation, disclosure. **3** *the discovery of new drugs* INVENTION, origination, devising; pioneering. **4** *he failed to take out a patent on his discoveries* FIND, finding; invention, breakthrough, innovation.
discredit ● verb **1** *an attempt to discredit him and his company* BRING INTO DISREPUTE, disgrace, dishonour, damage the reputation of, blacken the name of, put/show in a bad light, reflect badly on, compromise, stigmatize, smear, tarnish, taint; *N. Amer.* slur. **2** *that theory has been discredited* DISPROVE, invalidate, explode, drive a coach and horses through, refute; *informal* debunk, shoot full of holes, blow sky-high; *formal* confute.
● noun **1** *crimes which brought discredit on the administration* DISHONOUR, disrepute, disgrace, shame, humiliation, ignominy, infamy, notoriety; censure, blame, reproach, opprobrium; stigma; *dated* disesteem. **2** *the ships were a discredit to the country* DISGRACE, source of shame, reproach, blot on the escutcheon.
– OPPOSITES honour, glory.
discreditable ● adjective DISHONOURABLE, reprehensible, shameful, deplorable, disgraceful, disreputable, blameworthy, ignoble, shabby, objectionable, regrettable, unacceptable, unworthy.
– OPPOSITES praiseworthy.
discreet ● adjective **1** *discreet enquiries* CAREFUL, circumspect, cautious, wary, chary, guarded; tactful, diplomatic, prudent, judicious, strategic, politic, delicate, sensitive, kid-glove; *informal* softly-softly. **2** *discreet lighting* UNOBTRUSIVE, inconspicuous, subtle, low-key, understated, subdued, muted, soft, restrained.
discrepancy ● noun DIFFERENCE, disparity, variance, variation, deviation, divergence, disagreement, inconsistency, dissimilarity, mismatch, discordance, incompatibility, conflict; *formal* dissimilitude.
– OPPOSITES correspondence.
discrete ● adjective SEPARATE, distinct, individual, detached, unattached, disconnected, discontinuous, disjunct, disjoined.
– OPPOSITES connected.
discretion ● noun **1** *you can rely on his discretion* CIRCUMSPECTION, carefulness, caution, wariness, chariness, guardedness; TACT, tactfulness, diplomacy, delicacy, sensitivity, prudence, judiciousness. **2** *honorary fellowships awarded at the discretion of the council* CHOICE, option, preference, disposition, volition; pleasure, liking, wish, will, inclination, desire.

judgement.
discrimination • noun **1** the action of discriminating against people. **2** recognition of the difference between one thing and another. **3** good judgement or taste.
discriminatory • adjective showing discrimination or prejudice.
discursive /diskursiv/ • adjective **1** digressing from subject to subject. **2** relating to discourse or modes of discourse.
– DERIVATIVES **discursively** adverb **discursiveness** noun.
– ORIGIN Latin *discursivus*, from *discurrere* (see DISCOURSE).
discus • noun (pl. **discuses**) a heavy thick-centred disc thrown by an athlete, in ancient Greek games or in modern field events.
– ORIGIN Greek *diskos*; related to DISC and DISH.
discuss • verb **1** talk about so as to reach a decision. **2** talk or write about (a topic) in detail.
– DERIVATIVES **discussable** adjective.
– ORIGIN Latin *discutere* 'dash to pieces' (later 'investigate').
discussant • noun a person who takes part in a discussion, especially a pre-arranged one.
discussion • noun **1** the action or process of discussing something. **2** a conversation or debate about a topic. **3** a detailed treatment of a topic in speech or writing.
disdain • noun the feeling that someone or something is unworthy of one's consideration or respect. • verb consider with disdain.
– ORIGIN Old French *desdeign*, from Latin *dedignari* 'consider unworthy'.
disdainful • adjective showing contempt or lack of respect.
– DERIVATIVES **disdainfully** adverb **disdainfulness** noun.
disease • noun a disorder of structure or function in a human, animal, or plant, especially one that produces specific symptoms.
– DERIVATIVES **diseased** adjective.
– ORIGIN Old French *desaise* 'lack of ease'.
diseconomy • noun (pl. **diseconomies**) an economic disadvantage such as an increase in cost arising from an increase in the size of an organization.
disembark • verb leave a ship, aircraft, or train.
– DERIVATIVES **disembarkation** noun.
disembarrass • verb (**disembarrass oneself of/from**) free oneself of (a burden or nuisance).
disembodied • adjective **1** separated from or existing without the body. **2** (of a sound) lacking any obvious physical source.
– DERIVATIVES **disembodiment** noun **disembody** verb.
disembowel • verb (**disembowelled**, **disembowelling**; US **disemboweled**, **disemboweling**) cut open and remove the internal organs of.
– DERIVATIVES **disembowelment** noun.
disempower • verb make less powerful or confident.
– DERIVATIVES **disempowerment** noun.
disenchant • verb make disillusioned.
– DERIVATIVES **disenchanting** adjective **disenchantment** noun.
disenfranchise • verb **1** deprive of the right to vote. **2** deprive of a right or privilege.
– DERIVATIVES **disenfranchisement** noun.
disengage • verb **1** separate, release, or detach. **2** remove (troops) from an area of conflict. **3** (**disengaged**) emotionally detached; uninvolved.
– DERIVATIVES **disengagement** noun.
disentangle • verb free from entanglement; untwist.
disequilibrium • noun a loss or lack of equilibrium, especially

d

Thesaurus

discretionary • adjective OPTIONAL, voluntary, at one's discretion, elective; *Law* permissive.
– OPPOSITES compulsory.
discriminate • verb **1** *he cannot discriminate between fact and opinion* DIFFERENTIATE, distinguish, draw a distinction, tell the difference, tell apart; separate, separate the sheep from the goats, separate the wheat from the chaff. **2** *existing employment policies discriminate against women* BE BIASED, be prejudiced; treat differently, treat unfairly, put at a disadvantage, disfavour; victimize.
discriminating • adjective DISCERNING, perceptive, astute, shrewd, judicious, perspicacious, insightful, keen; selective, fastidious, tasteful, refined, sensitive, cultivated, cultured, artistic, aesthetic.
– OPPOSITES indiscriminate.
discrimination • noun **1** *racial discrimination* PREJUDICE, bias, bigotry, intolerance, narrow-mindedness, unfairness, inequity, favouritism, one-sidedness, partisanship; sexism, chauvinism, racism, racialism, anti-Semitism, heterosexism, ageism, classism; positive discrimination; *(in S. Africa, historical)* apartheid. **2** *a man with no discrimination* DISCERNMENT, judgement, perception, perceptiveness, perspicacity, acumen, astuteness, shrewdness, judiciousness, insight; selectivity, (good) taste, fastidiousness, refinement, sensitivity, cultivation, culture.
– OPPOSITES impartiality.
discriminatory • adjective PREJUDICIAL, biased, prejudiced, preferential, unfair, unjust, invidious, inequitable, weighted, one-sided, partisan; sexist, chauvinistic, chauvinist, racist, racialist, anti-Semitic, ageist, classist.
– OPPOSITES impartial.
discursive • adjective **1** *dull, discursive prose* RAMBLING, digressive, meandering, wandering, maundering, diffuse, long, lengthy, wordy, verbose, long-winded, prolix; circuitous, roundabout, circumlocutory; *Brit. informal* waffly. **2** *an elegant discursive style* FLUENT, flowing, fluid, eloquent, expansive.
– OPPOSITES concise, terse.
discuss • verb **1** *I discussed the matter with my wife* TALK OVER, talk about, talk through, converse about, debate, confer about, deliberate about, chew over, consider, weigh up, consider the pros and cons of, thrash out; *informal* kick around/about, bat around/about. **2** *chapter three discusses this topic in detail* EXAMINE, explore, study, analyse, go into, deal with, treat, consider, concern itself with, tackle.
discussion • noun **1** *a long discussion with her husband* CONVERSATION, talk, dialogue, discourse, conference, debate, exchange of views, consultation, deliberation; powwow, chat, tête-à-tête, heart-to-heart; negotiations, parley; *informal* confab, chit-chat, rap; *N. Amer. informal* skull session, bull session; *formal* confabulation, colloquy; *archaic* converse. **2** *the book's candid discussion of sexual matters* EXAMINATION, exploration, analysis, study; treatment, consideration.
disdain • noun *she looked at him with disdain* CONTEMPT, scorn, scornfulness, contemptuousness, derision, disrespect; disparagement, condescension, superciliousness, hauteur, haughtiness, arrogance, snobbishness, indifference, dismissiveness; distaste, dislike, disgust; *archaic* despite.
– OPPOSITES respect.
• verb **1** *she disdained such vulgar exhibitionism* SCORN, deride, pour scorn on, regard with contempt, sneer at, sniff at, curl one's lip at, look down one's nose at, look down on; despise; *informal* turn up one's nose at, pooh-pooh; *archaic* contemn. **2** *she disdained his invitation* SPURN, reject, refuse, rebuff, disregard, ignore, snub; decline, turn down, brush aside.
disdainful • adjective CONTEMPTUOUS, scornful, derisive, sneering, withering, slighting, disparaging, disrespectful, condescending, patronizing, supercilious, haughty, superior, arrogant, proud, snobbish, lordly, aloof, indifferent, dismissive; *informal* high and mighty, hoity-toity, sniffy, snotty; *archaic* contumelious.
– OPPOSITES respectful.
disease • noun ILLNESS, sickness, ill health; infection, ailment, malady, disorder, complaint, affliction, condition, indisposition, upset, problem, trouble, infirmity, disability, defect, abnormality; pestilence, plague, cancer, canker, blight; *informal* bug, virus; *Brit. informal* lurgy; *dated* contagion.
– RELATED TERMS pathological.
diseased • adjective UNHEALTHY, ill, sick, unwell, ailing, sickly, unsound; infected, septic, contaminated, blighted, rotten, bad, abnormal.
disembark • verb GET OFF, step off, leave, pile out; go ashore, debark, detrain; land, arrive; *Brit.* alight; *N. Amer.* deplane.
disembodied • adjective BODILESS, incorporeal, discarnate, spiritual; intangible, insubstantial, impalpable; ghostly, spectral, phantom, wraithlike.
disembowel • verb GUT, draw, remove the guts from; *formal* eviscerate.
disenchanted • adjective DISILLUSIONED, disappointed, disabused, let down, fed up, dissatisfied, discontented; cynical, soured, jaundiced, sick, out of love, indifferent.
disenchantment • noun DISILLUSIONMENT, disappointment, dissatisfaction, discontent, discontentedness, rude awakening; cynicism.
disengage • verb **1** *I disengaged his hand from mine* REMOVE, detach, disentangle, extricate, separate, release, free, loosen, loose, disconnect, unfasten, unclasp, uncouple, undo, unhook, unhitch,

in relation to supply, demand, and prices.

disestablish • verb deprive (an organization, especially a national Church) of its official status.

– DERIVATIVES **disestablishment** noun.

disfavour (US **disfavor**) • noun **1** disapproval or dislike. **2** the state of being disliked. • verb regard or treat with disfavour.

disfigure • verb spoil the appearance of.

– DERIVATIVES **disfiguration** noun **disfigurement** noun.

disgorge • verb **1** cause to pour out; discharge. **2** bring up or vomit (food). **3** yield or give up (funds, especially when dishonestly acquired).

– ORIGIN Old French *desgorger*, from *gorge* 'throat'.

disgrace • noun **1** loss of reputation as the result of a dishonourable action. **2** a person or thing regarded as shameful and unacceptable. • verb bring disgrace on.

– ORIGIN Italian *disgrazia*, from Latin *gratia* 'grace'.

disgraceful • adjective shockingly unacceptable.

– DERIVATIVES **disgracefully** adverb.

disgruntled • adjective angry or dissatisfied.

– DERIVATIVES **disgruntlement** noun.

– ORIGIN from dialect *gruntle* 'utter little grunts, grumble'.

disguise • verb **1** alter in appearance or nature so as to conceal the identity of. **2** hide the nature or existence of (a feeling or situation). • noun a means of disguising one's identity.

– ORIGIN Old French *desguisier*.

disgust • noun strong revulsion or profound indignation. • verb cause disgust in.

– DERIVATIVES **disgusted** adjective **disgustedly** adverb.

– ORIGIN French *desgoust* or Italian *disgusto*, from Latin *gustus* 'taste'.

disgusting • adjective arousing revulsion or strong indignation.

– DERIVATIVES **disgustingly** adverb **disgustingness** noun.

dish • noun **1** a shallow container for cooking or serving food. **2** (**the dishes**) all the items used in the preparation, serving, and eating of a meal. **3** a particular variety of food served as part of a meal. **4** a shallow, concave receptacle. **5** informal a sexually attractive person. • verb **1** (**dish out/up**) put (food) on to a plate or plates before a meal. **2** (**dish out**) dispense in a casual or indiscriminate way. **3** N. Amer. informal gossip.

– PHRASES **dish the dirt** informal reveal or spread scandal or gossip.

– ORIGIN Latin *discus* 'disc or plate', from Greek *diskos* 'discus'.

disharmony • noun lack of harmony.

– DERIVATIVES **disharmonious** adjective **disharmoniously** adverb.

dishearten • verb cause to lose determination or confidence.

– DERIVATIVES **disheartening** adjective.

dishevelled /dishevv'ld/ (US **disheveled**) • adjective (of a person's hair, clothes, or appearance) untidy; disordered.

– DERIVATIVES **dishevelment** noun.

– ORIGIN originally in the sense 'having the hair uncovered': from

Thesaurus

untie, unyoke, disentwine. **2** *American forces disengaged from the country* WITHDRAW, leave, pull out of, quit, retreat from.

– OPPOSITES attach, enter.

disentangle • verb **1** *Allen was disentangling a coil of rope* UNTANGLE, unravel, untwist, unwind, undo, untie, straighten out, smooth out; comb, card. **2** *he disentangled his fingers from her hair* EXTRICATE, extract, free, remove, disengage, untwine, disentwine, release, loosen, detach, unfasten, unclasp, disconnect.

disfavour • noun DISAPPROVAL, disapprobation; dislike, displeasure, distaste, dissatisfaction, low opinion; *dated* disesteem; *archaic* disrelish.

disfigure • verb MAR, spoil, deface, scar, blemish, uglify; damage, injure, impair, blight, mutilate, deform, maim, ruin; vandalize.

– OPPOSITES adorn.

disfigurement • noun **1** *the disfigurement of Victorian buildings* DEFACEMENT, spoiling, scarring, uglification, mutilation, damage, vandalizing, ruin. **2** *a permanent facial disfigurement* BLEMISH, flaw, defect, imperfection, discoloration, blotch; scar, pockmark; deformity, malformation, abnormality, injury, wound.

disgorge • verb **1** *the combine disgorged a stream of grain* POUR OUT, discharge, eject, throw out, emit, expel, spit out, spew out, belch forth, spout; vomit, regurgitate. **2** *they were made to disgorge all the profits* SURRENDER, relinquish, hand over, give up, turn over, yield.

disgrace • noun **1** *he brought disgrace on the family* DISHONOUR, shame, discredit, ignominy, degradation, disrepute, ill-repute, infamy, scandal, stigma, opprobrium, obloquy, condemnation, vilification, contempt, disrespect; humiliation, embarrassment, loss of face; *Austral.* strife; *dated* disesteem. **2** *the unemployment figures are a disgrace* SCANDAL, outrage; discredit, reproach, affront, insult; stain, blemish, blot, blot on the escutcheon, black mark; *informal* crime, sin.

– OPPOSITES honour.

• verb **1** *you have disgraced the family name* BRING SHAME ON, shame, dishonour, discredit, bring into disrepute, degrade, debase, defame, stigmatize, taint, sully, tarnish, besmirch, stain, blacken, drag through the mud/mire. **2** *he was publicly disgraced* DISCREDIT, dishonour, stigmatize; humiliate, cause to lose face, chasten, humble, demean, put someone in their place, take down a peg or two, cut down to size.

– OPPOSITES honour.

– PHRASES **in disgrace** OUT OF FAVOUR, unpopular, in bad odour, under a cloud, disgraced; *informal* in someone's bad/black books, in the doghouse; *NZ informal* in the dogbox.

disgraceful • adjective SHAMEFUL, shocking, scandalous, deplorable, despicable, contemptible, beyond contempt, beyond the pale, dishonourable, discreditable, reprehensible, base, mean, low, blameworthy, unworthy, ignoble, shabby, inglorious, outrageous, abominable, atrocious, appalling, dreadful, terrible, disgusting, shameless, vile, odious, monstrous, heinous, iniquitous, unspeakable, loathsome, sordid, nefarious; *archaic* scurvy.

– OPPOSITES admirable.

disgruntled • adjective DISSATISFIED, discontented, aggrieved, resentful, fed up, displeased, unhappy, disappointed, disaffected; angry, irate, annoyed, cross, exasperated, indignant, vexed, irritated, piqued, irked, put out; *informal* peeved, miffed, aggravated, hacked off, browned off, riled, peed off, hot under the collar, in a huff; *Brit. informal* cheesed off, shirty, narked; *N. Amer. informal* sore, teed off, ticked off.

disguise • verb *his controlled voice disguised his true feelings* CAMOUFLAGE, conceal, hide, cover up, dissemble, mask, screen, shroud, veil, cloak; paper over, gloss over, put up a smokescreen.

– OPPOSITES expose.

– PHRASES **disguise oneself as** DRESS UP AS, pretend to be, pass oneself of as, impersonate, pose as; *formal* personate.

disguised • adjective IN DISGUISE, camouflaged; incognito, under cover.

disgust • noun *a look of disgust* REVULSION, repugnance, aversion, distaste, nausea, abhorrence, loathing, detestation, odium, horror; contempt, outrage; *archaic* disrelish.

– OPPOSITES delight.

• verb **1** *the hospital food disgusted me* REVOLT, repel, repulse, sicken, nauseate, turn someone's stomach, make someone's gorge rise; *informal* turn off; *N. Amer. informal* gross out. **2** *Toby's behaviour disgusted her* OUTRAGE, shock, horrify, appal, scandalize, offend.

disgusting • adjective **1** *the food was disgusting* REVOLTING, repellent, repulsive, sickening, nauseating, stomach-churning, stomach-turning, off-putting, unpalatable, distasteful, foul, nasty; *N. Amer.* vomitous; *informal* yucky, icky, gross, sick-making. **2** *I find racism disgusting* ABHORRENT, loathsome, offensive, appalling, outrageous, objectionable, shocking, horrifying, scandalous, monstrous, unspeakable, shameful, vile, odious, obnoxious, detestable, hateful, sickening, contemptible, despicable, deplorable, abominable, beyond the pale; *informal* gross, ghastly, sick.

– OPPOSITES delicious, appealing.

dish • noun **1** *a china dish* BOWL, plate, platter, salver, paten; container, receptacle; *archaic* trencher, charger; *historical* porringer. **2** *vegetarian dishes* RECIPE, meal, course; (**dishes**) food, fare. **3** (*informal*) *she's quite a dish*. See BEAUTY sense 2.

– PHRASES **dish something out** DISTRIBUTE, dispense, issue, hand out/round, give out, pass out/round; deal out, dole out, share out, allocate, allot, apportion. **dish something up** SERVE (UP), spoon out, ladle out, scoop out.

disharmony • noun DISCORD, friction, strife, conflict, hostility, acrimony, bad blood, bad feeling, enmity, dissension, disagreement, feuding, quarrelling; disunity, division, divisiveness.

dishearten • verb DISCOURAGE, dispirit, demoralize, cast down, depress, disappoint, dismay, dash someone's hopes; put off, deter, unnerve, daunt, intimidate, cow, crush.

– OPPOSITES encourage.

disheartened • adjective DISCOURAGED, dispirited, demoralized, deflated, disappointed, let down, disconsolate, despondent, fed up, dejected, cast down, downcast, depressed, crestfallen, dismayed, low-spirited, gloomy, glum, pessimistic, unenthusiastic; daunted,

Old French *deschevele*, from Latin *capillus* 'hair'.

dishonest • adjective not honest, trustworthy, or sincere.
– DERIVATIVES **dishonestly** adverb **dishonesty** noun.

dishonour (US **dishonor**) • noun a state of shame or disgrace. • verb **1** bring dishonour to. **2** fail to honour (an agreement, cheque, etc.).

dishonourable (US **dishonorable**) • adjective bringing shame or disgrace.
– DERIVATIVES **dishonourably** adverb.

dishonourable discharge • noun dismissal from the armed forces as a result of criminal or morally unacceptable actions.

dishwasher • noun **1** a machine for washing dishes automatically. **2** a person employed to wash dishes.

dishy • adjective (**dishier**, **dishiest**) informal, chiefly Brit. sexually attractive.

disillusion • noun disappointment from discovering that something is not as good as one believed it to be. • verb cause to experience disillusion.
– DERIVATIVES **disillusioned** adjective **disillusionment** noun.

disincentive • noun a factor that discourages a particular action.

disinclination • noun a reluctance to do something.

disinclined • adjective reluctant; unwilling.

disinfect • verb make clean and free from infection, especially with a chemical disinfectant.
– DERIVATIVES **disinfection** noun.

disinfectant • noun a chemical liquid that destroys bacteria. • adjective causing disinfection.

disinflation • noun Economics reduction in the rate of inflation.
– DERIVATIVES **disinflationary** adjective.

disinformation • noun information which is intended to mislead.

disingenuous /dissinjenyooəss/ • adjective not candid or sincere, especially in feigning ignorance.
– DERIVATIVES **disingenuously** adverb **disingenuousness** noun.

disinherit • verb (**disinherited**, **disinheriting**) dispossess of or bar from an inheritance.
– DERIVATIVES **disinheritance** noun.

disintegrate • verb **1** break up into small parts as a result of impact or decay. **2** lose strength or cohesion.
– DERIVATIVES **disintegrative** adjective **disintegrator** noun.

disintegration • noun **1** the process of disintegrating. **2** Physics a process in which a nucleus or other subatomic particle emits a smaller particle or divides into smaller particles.

disinter /dissinter/ • verb (**disinterred**, **disinterring**) dig up (something buried).
– DERIVATIVES **disinterment** noun.

disinterest • noun **1** impartiality. **2** lack of interest.

disinterested • adjective **1** not influenced by considerations of personal advantage; impartial. **2** having or feeling no interest.
– DERIVATIVES **disinterestedly** adverb **disinterestedness** noun.
– USAGE There is a difference between **disinterested** and **uninterested**. **Disinterested** primarily means 'impartial', while **uninterested** means 'not interested'.

disintermediation • noun Economics reduction in the use of intermediaries between producers and consumers, e.g. by involvement in the securities market directly rather than through a bank.

disinvest • verb withdraw or reduce an investment.
– DERIVATIVES **disinvestment** noun.

disjoint • verb disturb the cohesion or organization of.

disjointed • adjective lacking a coherent sequence or connection.
– DERIVATIVES **disjointedly** adverb **disjointedness** noun.

Thesaurus

intimidated, cowed, crushed; *informal* down in the mouth, down in the dumps, unenthused; *archaic* chap-fallen.

dishevelled • adjective UNTIDY, unkempt, scruffy, messy, in a mess, disordered, disarranged, rumpled, bedraggled; uncombed, tousled, tangled, tangly, knotted, knotty, shaggy, straggly, windswept, wind-blown, wild; slovenly, slatternly, blowsy, frowzy; *informal* ratty; *N. Amer. informal* mussed (up); *archaic* draggle-tailed.
– OPPOSITES tidy.

dishonest • adjective FRAUDULENT, corrupt, swindling, cheating, double-dealing; underhand, crafty, cunning, devious, treacherous, unfair, unjust, dirty, unethical, immoral, dishonourable, untrustworthy, unscrupulous, unprincipled, amoral; criminal, illegal, unlawful; false, untruthful, deceitful, deceiving, lying, mendacious; *informal* crooked, shady, tricky, sharp, shifty; *Brit. informal* bent, dodgy; *Austral./NZ informal* shonky; *poetic/literary* perfidious.

dishonesty • noun FRAUD, fraudulence, sharp practice, corruption, cheating, chicanery, double-dealing, deceit, deception, duplicity, lying, falseness, falsity, falsehood, untruthfulness; craft, cunning, trickery, artifice, underhandedness, subterfuge, skulduggery, treachery, untrustworthiness, unscrupulousness, criminality, misconduct; *informal* crookedness, dirty tricks, shenanigans; *Brit. informal* jiggery-pokery; *poetic/literary* perfidy.
– OPPOSITES probity.

dishonour • noun *the incident brought dishonour upon the police profession* DISGRACE, shame, discredit, humiliation, degradation, ignominy, scandal, infamy, disrepute, ill repute, loss of face, disfavour, ill favour, debasement, opprobrium, obloquy; stigma; *dated* disesteem.
• verb *his family name has been dishonoured* DISGRACE, shame, discredit, bring into disrepute, humiliate, degrade, debase, lower, cheapen, drag down, drag through the mud, blacken the name of, give a bad name to; sully, stain, taint, besmirch, smear, mar, blot, stigmatize.

dishonourable • adjective DISGRACEFUL, shameful, disreputable, discreditable, degrading, ignominious, ignoble, blameworthy, contemptible, despicable, reprehensible, shabby, shoddy, sordid, sorry, base, low, improper, unseemly, unworthy; unprincipled, unscrupulous, corrupt, untrustworthy, treacherous, traitorous; *informal* shady, dirty; *poetic/literary* perfidious; *archaic* scurvy.

disillusion • verb DISABUSE, enlighten, set straight, open someone's eyes; disenchant, shatter someone's illusions, disappoint, make sadder and wiser.
– OPPOSITES deceive.

disillusioned • adjective DISENCHANTED, disabused, disappointed, let down, discouraged; cynical, sour, negative, world-weary.

disincentive • noun DETERRENT, discouragement, damper, brake, curb, check, restraint, inhibitor; obstacle, impediment, hindrance, obstruction, block, barrier.

disinclination • noun RELUCTANCE, unwillingness, lack of enthusiasm, indisposition, hesitancy; aversion, dislike, distaste; objection, demur, resistance, opposition; *archaic* disrelish.
– OPPOSITES enthusiasm.

disinclined • adjective RELUCTANT, unwilling, unenthusiastic, unprepared, indisposed, ill-disposed, not in the mood, hesitant; loath, averse, antipathetic, resistant, opposed.
– OPPOSITES willing.

disinfect • verb STERILIZE, sanitize, clean, cleanse, purify, decontaminate; fumigate.
– OPPOSITES contaminate.

disinfectant • noun ANTISEPTIC, bactericide, germicide, sterilizer, cleanser, decontaminant; fumigant.

disingenuous • adjective INSINCERE, dishonest, untruthful, false, deceitful, duplicitous, lying, mendacious; hypocritical; *archaic* hollow-hearted.

disinherit • verb CUT SOMEONE OUT OF ONE'S WILL, cut off, dispossess; disown, repudiate, reject, cast off/aside, wash one's hands of, have nothing more to do with, turn one's back on; *informal* cut off without a penny.

disintegrate • verb BREAK UP, break apart, fall apart, fall to pieces, fragment, fracture, shatter, splinter; explode, blow up, blow apart, fly apart; crumble, deteriorate, decay, decompose, rot, moulder, perish, dissolve, collapse, go to rack and ruin, degenerate; *informal* bust, be smashed to smithereens.

disinter • verb EXHUME, unearth, dig up, disentomb.

disinterest • noun **1** *scholarly disinterest* IMPARTIALITY, neutrality, objectivity, detachment, disinterestedness, lack of bias, lack of prejudice; open-mindedness, fairness, fair-mindedeness, equity, balance, even-handedness. **2** *he looked at us with complete disinterest* INDIFFERENCE, lack of interest, unconcern, impassivity; boredom, apathy.
– OPPOSITES bias.

disinterested • adjective **1** *disinterested advice* UNBIASED, unprejudiced, impartial, neutral, non-partisan, detached, uninvolved, objective, dispassionate, impersonal, clinical; open-minded, fair, just, equitable, balanced, even-handed, with no axe to grind, without fear or favour. **2** *he looked at her with disinterested eyes* UNINTERESTED, indifferent, incurious, unconcerned, unmoved, unresponsive, impassive, passive, detached, unenthusiastic, lukewarm, bored, apathetic; *informal* couldn't-care-less.

disjointed • adjective UNCONNECTED, disconnected, disunited, dis-

disjunction • noun a lack of correspondence or consistency.

disjunctive • adjective **1** lacking connection. **2** Grammar (of a conjunction) expressing a choice between two mutually exclusive possibilities, for example *or* in *she asked if he was going or staying.*

disk • noun variant spelling in the US and in computing contexts of DISC.

disk drive • noun a device which allows a computer to read from and write on to computer disks.

diskette • noun another term for FLOPPY.

dislike • verb feel distaste for or hostility towards. • noun **1** a feeling of distaste or hostility. **2** a thing that is disliked.
– DERIVATIVES **dislikable** (also **dislikeable**) adjective.

dislocate • verb **1** displace (a bone) from its proper position in a joint. **2** put out of order; disrupt.

dislocation • noun the process of dislocating or state of being dislocated.

dislodge • verb remove from a fixed position.
– DERIVATIVES **dislodgement** noun.

disloyal • adjective not loyal or faithful.
– DERIVATIVES **disloyally** adverb **disloyalty** noun.

dismal • adjective **1** causing or showing gloom or depression. **2** informal pitifully or disgracefully bad.
– DERIVATIVES **dismally** adverb.
– ORIGIN from obsolete *dismals*, the two days in each month which in medieval times were believed to be unlucky, from Old French *dis mal*, from Latin *dies mali* 'evil days'.

dismantle • verb take to pieces.
– DERIVATIVES **dismantlement** noun **dismantler** noun.
– ORIGIN Old French *desmanteler*, from *manteler* 'fortify'.

dismast • verb break or force down the mast or masts of (a ship).

dismay • noun discouragement and distress. • verb cause to feel dismay.
– ORIGIN Old French, related to MAY.

dismember • verb **1** tear or cut the limbs from. **2** divide up (a territory or organization).
– DERIVATIVES **dismembered** adjective **dismemberment** noun.
– ORIGIN Old French *desmembrer*, from Latin *membrum* 'limb'.

dismiss • verb **1** order or allow to leave; send away. **2** discharge from employment. **3** regard as unworthy of consideration. **4** Law refuse further hearing to (a case). **5** Cricket end the innings of (a batsman or side).
– DERIVATIVES **dismissal** noun **dismissible** adjective.
– ORIGIN Latin *dimittere* 'send away'.

dismissive • adjective feeling or showing that something is unworthy of serious consideration.
– DERIVATIVES **dismissively** adverb **dismissiveness** noun.

dismount • verb **1** alight from a horse or bicycle. **2** remove (something) from its support.

disobedient • adjective failing or refusing to be obedient.
– DERIVATIVES **disobedience** noun **disobediently** adverb.

disobey • verb fail or refuse to obey.
– DERIVATIVES **disobeyer** noun.

disobliging • adjective unwilling to help or cooperate.

disorder • noun **1** a lack of order; confusion. **2** the disruption of peaceful and law-abiding behaviour. **3** Medicine a disruption of normal physical or mental functions. • verb bring disorder to.

Thesaurus

continuous, fragmented, disorganized, disordered, muddled, mixed up, jumbled, garbled, incoherent, confused; rambling, wandering.

dislike • verb *a man she had always disliked* FIND DISTASTEFUL, regard with distaste, be averse to, have an aversion to, have no liking/taste for, disapprove of, object to, take exception to; hate, detest, loathe, abhor, despise, be unable to bear/stand, shrink from, shudder at, find repellent; *informal* be unable to stomach; *formal* abominate; *archaic* disrelish.
• noun *she viewed the other woman with dislike* DISTASTE, aversion, disfavour, disapproval, disapprobation, enmity, animosity, hostility, antipathy, antagonism; hate, hatred, detestation, loathing, disgust, repugnance, abhorrence, disdain, contempt; *archaic* disrelish.

dislocate • verb **1** *she dislocated her hip* PUT OUT OF JOINT; *informal* put out; *Medicine* luxate. **2** *trade was dislocated by a famine* DISRUPT, disturb, throw into disarray, throw into confusion, play havoc with, interfere with, disorganize, upset; *informal* mess up.

dislodge • verb **1** *replace any stones you dislodge* DISPLACE, knock out of place/position, move, shift; knock over, upset. **2** *economic sanctions failed to dislodge the dictator* REMOVE, force out, drive out, oust, eject, get rid of, evict, unseat, depose, topple, drum out; *informal* kick out, boot out; *Brit. informal* turf out.

disloyal • adjective UNFAITHFUL, faithless, false, false-hearted, untrue, inconstant, untrustworthy, unreliable, undependable, fickle; treacherous, traitorous, subversive, seditious, unpatriotic, two-faced, double-dealing, double-crossing, deceitful; dissident, renegade; adulterous; *informal* back-stabbing, two-timing; *poetic/literary* perfidious; *archaic* hollow-hearted.

disloyalty • noun UNFAITHFULNESS, infidelity, inconstancy, faithlessness, fickleness, unreliability, untrustworthiness, betrayal, falseness; duplicity, double-dealing, treachery, treason, subversion, sedition, dissidence; adultery; *informal* back-stabbing, two-timing; *poetic/literary* perfidy, perfidiousness.

dismal • adjective **1** *a dismal look* GLOOMY, glum, melancholy, morose, doleful, woebegone, forlorn, dejected, depressed, dispirited, downcast, despondent, disconsolate, miserable, sad, unhappy, sorrowful, desolate, wretched; *informal* blue, fed up, down in the dumps/mouth; *poetic/literary* dolorous. **2** *a dismal hall* DINGY, dim, dark, gloomy, dreary, drab, dull, bleak, cheerless, depressing, uninviting, unwelcoming. **3** *(informal) a dismal performance.* See POOR sense 2.
– OPPOSITES cheerful, bright.

dismantle • verb TAKE APART, take to pieces/bits, pull apart, pull to pieces, disassemble, break up, strip (down); knock down, pull down, demolish.
– OPPOSITES assemble, build.

dismay • verb *he was dismayed by the change in his friend* APPAL, horrify, shock, shake (up); disconcert, take aback, alarm, unnerve, unsettle, throw off balance, discompose; disturb, upset, distress; *informal* rattle, faze, knock sideways; *Brit. informal* knock for six.
– OPPOSITES encourage, please.
• noun *they greeted his decision with dismay* ALARM, shock, surprise, consternation, concern, perturbation, disquiet, discomposure, distress.
– OPPOSITES pleasure, relief.

dismember • verb DISJOINT, joint; pull apart, cut up, chop up, butcher.

dismiss • verb **1** *the president dismissed five ministers* GIVE SOMEONE THEIR NOTICE, get rid of, discharge; lay off, make redundant; *informal* sack, give someone the sack, fire, boot out, give someone the boot/elbow/push, give someone their marching orders, show someone the door; *Brit. informal* give someone their cards; *Military* cashier. **2** *the guards were dismissed* SEND AWAY, let go; disband, dissolve, discharge. **3** *he dismissed all morbid thoughts* BANISH, set aside, disregard, brush off, shrug off, put out of one's mind; reject, deny, repudiate, spurn.
– OPPOSITES engage.

dismissal • noun **1** *the threat of dismissal* ONE'S NOTICE, discharge; redundancy, laying off; *informal* the sack, sacking, firing, the push, the boot, the axe, the elbow, one's marching orders; *Brit. informal* one's cards, the chop; *Military* cashiering. **2** *a condescending dismissal* REJECTION, repudiation, repulse, non-acceptance.
– OPPOSITES recruitment.

dismissive • adjective CONTEMPTUOUS, disdainful, scornful, sneering, snide, disparaging, negative; *informal* sniffy.
– OPPOSITES admiring.

dismount • verb **1** *the cyclist dismounted* ALIGHT, get off/down. **2** *the horse dismounted the trooper* UNSEAT, dislodge, throw, unhorse.

disobedient • adjective INSUBORDINATE, unruly, wayward, badly behaved, naughty, delinquent, disruptive, troublesome, rebellious, defiant, mutinous, recalcitrant, uncooperative, wilful, intractable, obstreperous; *Brit. informal* bolshie; *archaic* contumacious.

disobey • verb DEFY, go against, flout, contravene, infringe, transgress, violate; disregard, ignore, pay no heed to.

disobliging • adjective UNHELPFUL, uncooperative, unaccommodating, unamenable, unreasonable, awkward, difficult; discourteous, uncivil, unfriendly.
– OPPOSITES helpful.

disorder • noun **1** *he hates disorder* UNTIDINESS, disorderliness, mess, disarray, chaos, confusion; clutter, jumble; a muddle, a shambles. **2** *incidents of public disorder* UNREST, disturbance, disruption, upheaval, turmoil, mayhem, pandemonium; violence, fighting, rioting, lawlessness, anarchy; breach of the peace, fra-

disorderly ● adjective **1** lacking organization; untidy. **2** involving a breakdown of peaceful and law-abiding behaviour.
– DERIVATIVES **disorderliness** noun.

disorderly conduct ● noun Law unruly behaviour constituting a minor offence.

disorganized (also **disorganised**) ● adjective **1** not properly planned and controlled. **2** not able to plan one's activities efficiently.
– DERIVATIVES **disorganization** noun.

disorient ● verb chiefly N. Amer. another term for DISORIENTATE.

disorientate ● verb cause (someone) to lose their sense of direction or feel confused.
– DERIVATIVES **disorientated** adjective **disorientation** noun.

disown ● verb refuse to acknowledge any connection with.

disparage /disparrij/ ● verb regard or represent as being of little worth; scorn.
– DERIVATIVES **disparagement** noun **disparaging** adjective.
– ORIGIN Old French *desparagier* 'marry someone of unequal rank', from Latin *par* 'equal'.

disparate /dispərət/ ● adjective **1** essentially different in kind; not able to be compared. **2** containing elements very different from one another: *a culturally disparate country*.
– DERIVATIVES **disparately** adverb **disparateness** noun.
– ORIGIN from Latin *disparare* 'to separate'.

disparity ● noun (pl. **disparities**) a great difference.

dispassionate ● adjective not influenced by strong emotion; rational and impartial.
– DERIVATIVES **dispassion** noun **dispassionately** adverb.

dispatch (also **despatch**) ● verb **1** send off to a destination or for a purpose. **2** deal with (a task or problem) quickly and efficiently. **3** kill. ● noun **1** the action or an instance of dispatching. **2** an official report on the latest situation in state or military affairs. **3** a report sent in from abroad by a journalist. **4** promptness and efficiency: *proceed with dispatch*.
– DERIVATIVES **dispatcher** noun.
– ORIGIN Italian *dispacciare* or Spanish *despachar* 'expedite'.

dispatch box ● noun **1** (also **dispatch case**) a container for state or military dispatches. **2** (**the Dispatch Box**) a box in the House of Commons next to which ministers stand when speaking.

dispatch rider ● noun a messenger who delivers urgent business documents or military dispatches.

dispel ● verb (**dispelled**, **dispelling**) make (a doubt, feeling, or belief) disappear.
– ORIGIN Latin *dispellere* 'drive apart'.

dispensable ● adjective able to be replaced or done without.

dispensary ● noun (pl. **dispensaries**) **1** a room where medicines are prepared and provided. **2** a clinic provided by public or charitable funds.

dispensation ● noun **1** exemption from a rule or usual requirement. **2** a religious or political system prevailing at a particular time. **3** the action of dispensing.
– DERIVATIVES **dispensational** adjective.

dispense ● verb **1** distribute to a number of people. **2** (of a chemist) supply (medicine) according to a doctor's prescription. **3** (of a machine or container) supply or release (a product). **4** (**dispense with**) get rid of or manage without.
– DERIVATIVES **dispenser** noun.
– ORIGIN Latin *dispensare* 'continue to weigh out or disburse', from *pendere* 'weigh'.

Thesaurus

cas, rumpus, melee; *Law, dated* affray; *informal* aggro. **3** *a blood disorder* DISEASE, infection, complaint, condition, affliction, malady, sickness, illness, ailment, infirmity, irregularity.
– OPPOSITES tidiness, peace.

disordered ● adjective **1** *her grey hair was disordered* UNTIDY, unkempt, messy, in a mess; disorganized, chaotic, confused, jumbled, muddled; *N. Amer. informal* mussed (up); *Brit. informal* shambolic. **2** *a disordered digestive system* DYSFUNCTIONAL, disturbed, unsettled, unbalanced, upset, poorly.

disorderly ● adjective **1** *a disorderly desk* UNTIDY, disorganized, messy, cluttered; in disarray, in a mess, in a jumble, in a muddle, at sixes and sevens; *informal* like a bomb's hit it, higgledy-piggledy; *Brit. informal* shambolic. **2** *disorderly behaviour* UNRULY, boisterous, rough, rowdy, wild, riotous; disruptive, troublesome, undisciplined, lawless, unmanageable, uncontrollable, out of hand, out of control.
– OPPOSITES tidy, peaceful.

disorganized ● adjective **1** *a disorganized tool box* DISORDERLY, disordered, unorganized, jumbled, muddled, untidy, messy, chaotic, topsy-turvy, haphazard; in disorder, in disarray, in a mess, in a muddle, in a shambles; *informal* higgledy-piggledy; *Brit. informal* shambolic. **2** *muddled and disorganized* UNMETHODICAL, unsystematic, undisciplined, badly organized, inefficient; haphazard, careless, slapdash; *informal* sloppy, hit-or-miss.
– OPPOSITES orderly.

disorientated, disoriented ● adjective CONFUSED, bewildered, (all) at sea; lost, adrift, off-course, having lost one's bearings; *informal* not knowing whether one is coming or going; *archaic* mazed.

disown ● verb REJECT, cast off/aside, abandon, renounce, deny; turn one's back on, wash one's hands of, have nothing more to do with; *poetic/literary* forsake.

disparage ● verb BELITTLE, denigrate, deprecate, play down, trivialize, make light of, undervalue, underrate; ridicule, deride, mock, scorn, scoff at, sneer at; run down, defame, discredit, speak badly of, cast aspersions on, impugn, vilify, traduce, criticize; *N. Amer.* slur; *informal* do down, pick holes in, knock, slam, pan, bad-mouth, pooh-pooh; *Brit. informal* rubbish, slate; *formal* calumniate, derogate.
– OPPOSITES praise, overrate.

disparaging ● adjective DEROGATORY, deprecatory, denigratory, belittling; critical, scathing, negative, unfavourable, uncomplimentary, uncharitable; contemptuous, scornful, snide, disdainful; *informal* bitchy, catty; *archaic* contumelious.
– OPPOSITES complimentary.

disparate ● adjective CONTRASTING, different, differing, dissimilar, unalike, poles apart; varying, various, diverse, diversified, heterogeneous, distinct, separate, divergent; *poetic/literary* divers.
– OPPOSITES homogen(e)ous.

disparity ● noun DISCREPANCY, inconsistency, imbalance; variance, variation, divergence, gap, gulf; difference, dissimilarity, contrast; *formal* dissimilitude.
– OPPOSITES similarity.

dispassionate ● adjective **1** *a calm, dispassionate manner* UNEMOTIONAL, emotionless, impassive, cool, calm, {cool, calm, and collected}, unruffled, unperturbed, composed, self-possessed, self-controlled, unexcitable; *informal* laid-back. **2** *a dispassionate analysis* OBJECTIVE, detached, neutral, disinterested, impartial, non-partisan, unbiased, unprejudiced; scientific, analytical.
– OPPOSITES emotional, biased.

dispatch ● verb **1** *all the messages were dispatched* SEND (OFF), post, mail, forward, transmit. **2** *the business was dispatched in the morning* DEAL WITH, finish, conclude, settle, discharge, perform; expedite, push through; *informal* make short work of. **3** *the good guy dispatched a host of villains* KILL, put to death, take/end the life of; slaughter, butcher, massacre, wipe out, exterminate, eliminate; murder, assassinate, execute; *informal* bump off, do in, do away with, top, take out, blow away; *N. Amer. informal* ice, rub out, waste; *poetic/literary* slay.
● noun **1** *goods ready for dispatch* SENDING, posting, mailing. **2** *efficiency and dispatch* PROMPTNESS, speed, speediness, swiftness, rapidity, briskness, haste, hastiness; *poetic/literary* fleetness, celerity; *formal* expedition. **3** *the latest dispatch from the front* COMMUNICATION, communiqué, bulletin, report, statement, letter, message; news, intelligence; *informal* memo, info, low-down; *poetic/literary* tidings. **4** *the capture and dispatch of the wolf* KILLING, slaughter, massacre, extermination, elimination; murder, assassination, execution; *poetic/literary* slaying.

dispel ● verb BANISH, eliminate, drive away/off, get rid of; relieve, allay, ease, quell.

dispensable ● adjective EXPENDABLE, disposable, replaceable, inessential, non-essential; unnecessary, redundant, superfluous, surplus to requirements.

dispensation ● noun **1** *the dispensation of supplies* DISTRIBUTION, supply, supplying, issue, issuing, handing out, doling out, dishing out, sharing out, dividing out; division, allocation, allotment, apportionment. **2** *the dispensation of justice* ADMINISTRATION, administering, delivery, discharge, dealing out, meting out. **3** *dispensation from National Insurance contributions* EXEMPTION, immunity, exception, exoneration, reprieve, remission; *informal* a let-off. **4** *the new constitutional dispensation* SYSTEM, order, arrangement, organization.

dispense ● verb **1** *servants dispensed the drinks* DISTRIBUTE, pass round, hand out, dole out, dish out, share out; allocate, supply, allot, apportion. **2** *the soldiers dispensed summary justice* ADMINIS-

dispersant • noun a liquid or gas used to disperse small particles in a medium.

disperse • verb **1** go or distribute in different directions or over a wide area. **2** thin out and eventually disappear. **3** Physics divide (light) into constituents of different wavelengths.
– DERIVATIVES **dispersal** noun **disperser** noun **dispersible** adjective **dispersive** adjective.
– ORIGIN Latin *dispergere* 'scatter widely'.

dispersion • noun **1** the action or process of dispersing or the state of being dispersed. **2** (**the dispersion**) another term for DIASPORA.

d

dispirit • verb cause to lose enthusiasm or hope.
– DERIVATIVES **dispiritedly** adverb **dispiritedness** noun **dispiriting** adjective.

displace • verb **1** shift from the proper or usual position. **2** take over the place, position, or role of. **3** (especially of war or natural disaster) force (someone) to leave their home.

displacement • noun **1** the action or process of displacing. **2** the amount by which a thing is moved from a position. **3** the volume or weight of water displaced by a floating ship, used as a measure of the ship's size. **4** Psychoanalysis the unconscious transfer of an intense emotion from one object to another.

display • verb **1** put on show in a noticeable and attractive way. **2** show (data or an image) on a screen. **3** give a conspicuous demonstration of (a quality, emotion, or skill). **4** (of a male animal) engage in behaviour intended to attract a mate. • noun **1** a performance, show, or event for public entertainment. **2** a collection of objects being displayed. **3** the action or an instance of displaying. **4** an electronic device for displaying data.
– ORIGIN Old French *despleier*, from Latin *displicare* 'scatter, disperse'.

displease • verb annoy or upset.
– DERIVATIVES **displeased** adjective **displeasing** adjective.

displeasure • noun a feeling of annoyance or dissatisfaction.

disport • verb (**disport oneself**) enjoy oneself unrestrainedly; frolic.
– ORIGIN Old French *desporter* 'carry away'.

disposable • adjective **1** (of an article) intended to be used once and then thrown away. **2** (of financial assets) readily available for the owner's use as required. • noun a disposable article.
– DERIVATIVES **disposability** noun.

disposable income • noun income remaining after deduction of taxes and social security charges, available to be spent or saved as one wishes.

disposal • noun the action or process of disposing.
– PHRASES **at one's disposal** available for one to use whenever or however one wishes.

dispose • verb **1** (**dispose of**) get rid of. **2** arrange in a particular position. **3** give, sell, or transfer (money or assets). **4** incline (someone) towards a particular activity or frame of mind.
– DERIVATIVES **disposer** noun.
– ORIGIN Old French *disposer*, from Latin *disponere* 'arrange'.

disposed • adjective **1** inclined to do or feel something. **2** having a specified attitude to or towards.

disposition • noun **1** a person's inherent qualities of character. **2** an inclination or tendency. **3** the action or result of arranging people or things in a particular way.

dispossess • verb **1** deprive of land or property. **2** (in sport) deprive (a player) of the ball.
– DERIVATIVES **dispossession** noun.

disproof • noun evidence that something is untrue.

disproportion • noun a lack of proportion.

Thesaurus

TER, deliver, issue, discharge, deal out, mete out. **3** *dispensing medicines* PREPARE, make up; supply, provide, sell. **4** *the pope dispensed him from his impediment* EXEMPT, excuse, except, release, let off, reprieve, absolve.
– PHRASES **dispense with 1** *let's dispense with the formalities* WAIVE, omit, drop, leave out, forgo; do away with; *informal* give something a miss. **2** *he dispensed with his crutches* GET RID OF, throw away/out, dispose of, discard; manage without, cope without; *informal* ditch, scrap, dump, chuck out/away, get shut of; *Brit. informal* get shot of.

disperse • verb **1** *the crowd began to disperse | police dispersed the demonstrators* BREAK UP, split up, disband, scatter, leave, go their separate ways; drive away/off, chase away. **2** *the fog finally dispersed* DISSIPATE, dissolve, melt away, fade away, clear, lift. **3** *seeds dispersed by birds* SCATTER, disseminate, distribute, spread, broadcast.
– OPPOSITES assemble, gather.

dispirited • adjective DISHEARTENED, discouraged, demoralized, downcast, low, low-spirited, dejected, downhearted, depressed, disconsolate; *informal* fed up; *Brit. informal* cheesed off.
– OPPOSITES heartened.

dispiriting • adjective DISHEARTENING, depressing, discouraging, daunting, demoralizing.

displace • verb **1** *roof tiles displaced by gales* DISLODGE, dislocate, move, shift, reposition; move out of place, knock out of place/position. **2** *the minister was displaced* DEPOSE, dislodge, unseat, remove (from office), dismiss, eject, oust, expel, force out, drive out; overthrow, topple, bring down; *informal* boot out, give someone the boot, show someone the door; *Brit. informal* turf out; *dated* out. **3** *English displaced the local language* REPLACE, take the place of, supplant, supersede.
– OPPOSITES replace, reinstate.

display • noun **1** *a display of dolls and puppets | a motorcycle display* EXHIBITION, exposition, array, arrangement, presentation, demonstration; spectacle, show, parade, pageant. **2** *they vied to outdo each other in display* OSTENTATION, ostentatiousness, showiness, extravagance, flamboyance, lavishness, splendour; *informal* swank, flashiness, glitziness. **3** *his display of concern* MANIFESTATION, expression, show.
• verb **1** *the Crown Jewels are displayed in London* EXHIBIT, show, put on show/view; arrange, array, present, lay out, set out. **2** *the play displays his many theatrical talents* SHOW OFF, parade, flaunt, reveal; publicize, make known, call/draw attention to; *informal* hype. **3** *she displayed a vein of sharp humour* MANIFEST, show evidence of, reveal; demonstrate, show; *formal* evince.
– OPPOSITES conceal.

displease • verb ANNOY, irritate, anger, irk, vex, pique, gall, nettle; put out, upset; *informal* aggravate, peeve, needle, bug, rile, miff, hack off; *N. Amer. informal* tee off, tick off.

displeasure • noun ANNOYANCE, irritation, crossness, anger, vexation, pique, rancour; dissatisfaction, discontent, discontentedness, discontentment, disgruntlement, disapproval; *informal* aggravation.
– OPPOSITES satisfaction.

disposable • adjective **1** *disposable plates* THROWAWAY, expendable, one-use. **2** *disposable income* AVAILABLE, usable, spendable.

disposal • noun **1** *rubbish ready for disposal* THROWING AWAY, discarding, jettisoning, scrapping; *informal* dumping, ditching, chucking (out/away). **2** *we have twenty copies for disposal* DISTRIBUTION, handing out, giving out/away, allotment, allocation. **3** *the disposal of the troops in two lines* ARRANGEMENT, arranging, positioning, placement, lining up, disposition, grouping; *Military* dressing.
– PHRASES **at someone's disposal** FOR USE BY, in reserve for, in the hands of, in the possession of.

dispose • verb **1** *he disposed his attendants in a circle* ARRANGE, place, put, position, array, set up, form; marshal, gather, group; *Military* dress. **2** *the experience disposed him to be more charitable* INCLINE, encourage, persuade, predispose, make willing, prompt, lead, motivate; sway, influence.
– PHRASES **dispose of 1** *the waste was disposed of* THROW AWAY/OUT, get rid of, discard, jettison, scrap; *informal* dump, ditch, chuck (out/away), get shut of; *Brit. informal* get shot of; *N. Amer. informal* trash. **2** *he had disposed of all his assets* PART WITH, give away, hand over, deliver up, transfer; sell, auction; *informal* get shut of; *Brit. informal* get shot of. **3** (*informal*) *she disposed of a fourth cake*. See CONSUME sense 1. **4** (*informal*) *he robbed her and then disposed of her*. See KILL verb sense 1.

disposed • adjective **1** *they are philanthropically disposed* INCLINED, predisposed, minded. **2** *we are not disposed to argue* WILLING, inclined, prepared, ready, minded, in the mood. **3** *he was disposed to be cruel* LIABLE, apt, inclined, likely, predisposed, prone, tending; capable of.

disposition • noun **1** *a nervous disposition* TEMPERAMENT, nature, character, constitution, make-up, mentality. **2** *his disposition to clemency* INCLINATION, tendency, proneness, propensity, proclivity. **3** *the disposition of the armed forces* ARRANGEMENT, positioning, placement, configuration; set-up, line-up, layout, array; marshalling, mustering, grouping; *Military* dressing. **4** (*Law*) *the disposition of the company's property* DISTRIBUTION, disposal, allocation, transfer; sale, auction.
– PHRASES **at someone's disposition** AT THE DISPOSAL OF, for use by, in reserve for, in the hands of, in the possession of.

– DERIVATIVES **disproportional** adjective **disproportionally** adverb.
disproportionate • adjective too large or too small in comparison with something else.
– DERIVATIVES **disproportionately** adverb.
disprove • verb prove to be false.
– DERIVATIVES **disprovable** adjective.
disputable • adjective open to debate.
disputation • noun debate or argument.
– DERIVATIVES **disputative** adjective.
disputatious • adjective **1** fond of argument. **2** (of an argument or situation) motivated by or causing strong opinions.
– DERIVATIVES **disputatiously** adverb **disputatiousness** noun.
dispute • verb /dispyōōt/ **1** argue about. **2** question the truth or validity of (a statement or fact). **3** compete for; battle to win. • noun /dispyōōt, dispyōōt/ **1** an argument. **2** a disagreement between management and employees that leads to industrial action.
– DERIVATIVES **disputant** noun.
– ORIGIN Latin *disputare* 'to estimate'.
disqualify • verb (**disqualifies, disqualified**) **1** pronounce ineligible for an office or activity because of an offence or infringement. **2** (of a feature or characteristic) make unsuitable for an office or activity.
– DERIVATIVES **disqualification** noun.
disquiet • noun a feeling of anxiety. • verb make anxious.
– DERIVATIVES **disquieting** adjective **disquietude** noun.
disquisition /diskwizish'n/ • noun a long or complex discussion of a topic in speech or writing.
– ORIGIN Latin, 'investigation', from *quaerere* 'seek'.
disregard • verb pay no attention to. • noun the action of disregarding or the state of being disregarded.
disrepair • noun a poor condition due to neglect.
disreputable • adjective not respectable in appearance or character.
disrepute • noun the state of being held in low public esteem.
disrespect • noun lack of respect or courtesy. • verb informal, chiefly N. Amer. show a lack of respect for.
– DERIVATIVES **disrespectful** adjective **disrespectfully** adverb.
disrobe • verb **1** undress. **2** take off official regalia or vestments.
disrupt • verb interrupt or disturb (an activity or process).
– DERIVATIVES **disrupter** (also **disruptor**) noun **disruption** noun **disruptive** adjective.
– ORIGIN Latin *disrumpere* 'break apart'.
diss • verb variant spelling of DIS.
dissatisfaction • noun lack of satisfaction.
dissatisfied • adjective not content or happy.
dissatisfy • verb (**dissatisfies, dissatisfied**) fail to satisfy or give pleasure to.
dissect /disekt/ • verb **1** methodically cut up (a body, part, or plant) in order to study its internal parts. **2** analyse in great detail. **3** (**dissected**) technical divided into separate parts.
– DERIVATIVES **dissection** noun **dissector** noun.
– ORIGIN Latin *dissecare* 'cut up'.

d

Thesaurus

dispossess • verb DIVEST, strip, rob, cheat out of, deprive; *informal* do out of; *archaic* reave.
disproportionate • adjective OUT OF PROPORTION TO, not appropriate to, not commensurate with, relatively too large/small for; inordinate, unreasonable, excessive, undue.
disprove • verb REFUTE, prove false, rebut, falsify, debunk, negate, invalidate, contradict, confound, controvert, negative, discredit; *informal* shoot full of holes, blow out of the water; *formal* confute, gainsay.
disputable • adjective DEBATABLE, open to debate/question, arguable, contestable, moot, questionable, doubtful, controvertible; *informal* iffy.
disputation • noun DEBATE, discussion, dispute, argument, arguing, altercation, dissension, disagreement, controversy; polemics.
dispute • noun **1** *a subject of dispute* DEBATE, discussion, disputation, argument, controversy, disagreement, quarrelling, dissension, conflict, friction, strife, discord. **2** *they have settled their dispute* QUARREL, argument, altercation, squabble, falling-out, disagreement, difference of opinion, clash, wrangle; *informal* tiff, spat, scrap; *Brit. informal* row, barney, ding-dong; *N. Amer. informal* rhubarb; *archaic* broil.
– OPPOSITES agreement.
• verb **1** *George disputed with him* DEBATE, discuss, exchange views; quarrel, argue, disagree, clash, fall out, wrangle, bicker, squabble; *informal* have words, have a tiff/spat; *archaic* altercate. **2** *they disputed his proposals* CHALLENGE, contest, question, call into question, impugn, quibble over, contradict, controvert, argue about, disagree with, take issue with; *formal* gainsay.
– OPPOSITES accept.
disqualified • adjective BANNED, barred, debarred; ineligible.
– OPPOSITES allowed.
disquiet • noun *grave public disquiet* UNEASE, uneasiness, worry, anxiety, anxiousness, concern, disquietude; perturbation, consternation, upset, malaise, angst; agitation, restlessness, fretfulness; *informal* jitteriness.
– OPPOSITES calm.
• verb *I was disquieted by the news* PERTURB, agitate, upset, disturb, unnerve, unsettle, discompose, disconcert; make uneasy, worry, make anxious; trouble, concern, make fretful, make restless.
disquisition • noun ESSAY, dissertation, treatise, paper, tract, article; discussion, lecture, address, presentation, speech, talk.
disregard • verb *Annie disregarded the remark* IGNORE, take no notice of, pay no attention/heed to; overlook, turn a blind eye to, turn a deaf ear to, shut one's eyes to, gloss over, brush off/aside, shrug off.
– OPPOSITES heed.
• noun *blithe disregard for the rules* INDIFFERENCE, non-observance, inattention, heedlessness, neglect.
– OPPOSITES attention.
disrepair • noun DILAPIDATION, decrepitude, shabbiness, ricketiness, collapse, ruin; abandonment, neglect, disuse.
disreputable • adjective **1** *he fell into disreputable company* OF BAD REPUTATION, infamous, notorious, louche; dishonourable, dishonest, untrustworthy, unwholesome, villainous, corrupt, immoral; unsavoury, slippery, seedy, sleazy; *informal* crooked, shady, shifty; *Brit. informal* dodgy. **2** *filthy and disreputable* SCRUFFY, shabby, down at heel, seedy, untidy, unkempt, dishevelled.
– OPPOSITES respectable, smart.
disrepute • noun DISGRACE, shame, dishonour, infamy, notoriety, ignominy, bad reputation; humiliation, discredit, ill repute, low esteem, opprobrium, obloquy.
– OPPOSITES honour.
disrespect • noun **1** *disrespect for authority* CONTEMPT, lack of respect, scorn, disregard, disdain. **2** *he meant no disrespect to anybody* DISCOURTESY, rudeness, impoliteness, incivility, ill/bad manners; insolence, impudence, impertinence.
– OPPOSITES esteem.
disrespectful • adjective DISCOURTEOUS, rude, impolite, uncivil, ill-mannered, bad-mannered; insolent, impudent, impertinent, cheeky, flippant, insubordinate.
– OPPOSITES polite.
disrobe • verb UNDRESS, strip, take off one's clothes, remove one's clothes; *Brit. informal* peel off.
disrupt • verb **1** *the strike disrupted public transport* THROW INTO CONFUSION/DISORDER/DISARRAY, cause confusion/turmoil in, play havoc with; disturb, interfere with, upset, unsettle; obstruct, impede, hold up, delay, interrupt, suspend; *Brit. informal* throw a spanner in the works of; *N. Amer. informal* throw a monkey wrench in the works of. **2** *the explosion disrupted the walls of the crater* DISTORT, damage, buckle, warp; shatter; *poetic/literary* sunder.
disruptive • adjective TROUBLESOME, unruly, badly behaved, rowdy, disorderly, undisciplined, wild; unmanageable, uncontrollable, uncooperative, out of control/hand, obstreperous, truculent; *formal* refractory.
– OPPOSITES well behaved.
dissatisfaction • noun DISCONTENT, discontentment, disaffection, disquiet, unhappiness, malaise, disgruntlement, vexation, annoyance, irritation, anger; disapproval, disapprobation, disfavour, displeasure.
dissatisfied • adjective DISCONTENTED, malcontent, unsatisfied, disappointed, disaffected, unhappy, displeased; disgruntled, aggrieved, vexed, annoyed, irritated, angry, exasperated, fed up; *informal* cheesed off; *Brit. informal* brassed off.
– OPPOSITES contented.
dissect • verb **1** *the body was dissected* ANATOMIZE, cut up/open, dismember; vivisect. **2** *the text of the gospels was dissected* ANALYSE, examine, study, scrutinize, pore over, investigate, go over with a fine-tooth comb.
dissection • noun **1** *the dissection of corpses* CUTTING UP/OPEN, dismemberment; autopsy, post-mortem, necropsy, anatomy, vivisec-

d

dissemble • verb hide or disguise one's true motives or feelings.
– DERIVATIVES **dissembler** noun.
– ORIGIN Latin *dissimulare* 'disguise, conceal'.
disseminate • verb spread widely.
– DERIVATIVES **dissemination** noun **disseminator** noun.
– ORIGIN Latin *disseminare* 'scatter', from *semen* 'seed'.
dissension • noun disagreement that leads to discord.
– ORIGIN Latin, from *dissentire* 'differ in sentiment'.
dissent • verb **1** express disagreement with a prevailing or official view. **2** disagree with the doctrine of an established or orthodox Church. • noun the holding or expression of a dissenting view.
– ORIGIN Latin *dissentire* 'differ in sentiment'.
dissenter • noun **1** a person who dissents. **2** (**Dissenter**) Brit. historical a member of a non-established Church; a Nonconformist.
dissentient /disenshʼnt/ • adjective in opposition to a majority or official opinion. • noun a dissenter.
dissertation • noun a long essay, especially one written for a university degree or diploma.
– ORIGIN Latin, from *dissertare* 'continue to discuss'.
disservice • noun a harmful action.
dissident • noun a person who opposes official policy. • adjective in opposition to official policy.
– DERIVATIVES **dissidence** noun.
– ORIGIN from Latin *dissidere* 'sit apart, disagree'.
dissimilar • adjective not similar; different.
– DERIVATIVES **dissimilarity** noun **dissimilarly** adverb.
dissimulate • verb hide or disguise one's thoughts or feelings.
– DERIVATIVES **dissimulation** noun **dissimulator** noun.
– ORIGIN Latin *dissimulare* 'to conceal'.
dissipate • verb **1** be or cause to be dispelled or dispersed. **2** waste (money, energy, or resources).
– DERIVATIVES **dissipative** adjective **dissipator** (also **dissipater**) noun.
– ORIGIN Latin *dissipare* 'scatter'.
dissipated • adjective overindulgent in sensual pleasures.
dissipation • noun **1** dissipated living. **2** the action of dissipating.
dissociate • verb **1** disconnect or separate. **2** (**dissociate oneself from**) declare that one is not connected with (someone or something).
– DERIVATIVES **dissociation** noun **dissociative** adjective.
– ORIGIN Latin *dissociare* 'separate'.
dissoluble • adjective able to be dissolved, loosened, or disconnected.
dissolute /dissəloot/ • adjective overindulgent in sensual pleasures.
– ORIGIN Latin *dissolutus* 'disconnected, loose', from *dissolvere* 'dissolve'.
dissolution • noun **1** the formal closing down or ending of an assembly, official body, or agreement. **2** the action or process of dissolving. **3** disintegration; decomposition. **4** debauched living; dissipation.
dissolve • verb **1** (with reference to a solid) become or cause to become incorporated into a liquid so as to form a solution.

Thesaurus

tion. **2** *a thorough dissection of their policies* ANALYSIS, examination, study, scrutiny, scrutinization, investigation; evaluation, assessment.
dissemble • verb DISSIMULATE, pretend, feign, act, masquerade, sham, fake, bluff, posture, hide one's feelings, put on a false front.
dissembler • noun LIAR, dissimulator; humbug, bluffer, fraud, impostor, actor, hoaxer, charlatan.
disseminate • verb SPREAD, circulate, distribute, disperse, promulgate, propagate, publicize, communicate, pass on, put about, make known.
dissension • noun DISAGREEMENT, difference of opinion, dispute, dissent, conflict, friction, strife, discord, antagonism; argument, debate, controversy, disputation, contention.
dissent • verb *two members dissented* DIFFER, disagree, demur, fail to agree, be at variance/odds, take issue; decline/refuse to support, protest, object, dispute, challenge, quibble.
– OPPOSITES agree, accept.
• noun *murmurs of dissent* DISAGREEMENT, difference of opinion, argument, dispute; disapproval, objection, protest, opposition, defiance; conflict, friction, strife.
– OPPOSITES agreement.
dissenter • noun DISSIDENT, dissentient, objector, protester, disputant; rebel, renegade, maverick, independent; apostate, heretic.
dissentient • adjective *dissentient voices* DISSENTING, dissident, disagreeing, differing, discordant, contradicting, contrary, anti-; opposing, objecting, protesting, complaining, rebellious, revolutionary; nonconformist, recusant, unorthodox, heterodox, heretical.
• noun *a dissentient spoke up.* See DISSENTER.
dissertation • noun ESSAY, thesis, treatise, paper, study, discourse, disquisition, tract, monograph.
disservice • noun UNKINDNESS, bad/ill turn, disfavour; injury, harm, hurt, damage, wrong, injustice.
– OPPOSITES favour.
dissidence • noun DISAGREEMENT, dissent, discord, discontent; opposition, resistance, protest, sedition.
dissident • noun *a jailed dissident* DISSENTER, objector, protester; rebel, revolutionary, recusant, subversive, agitator, insurgent, insurrectionist, refusenik.
– OPPOSITES conformist.
• adjective *dissident intellectuals* DISSENTIENT, dissenting, disagreeing; opposing, objecting, protesting, rebellious, rebelling, revolutionary, recusant, nonconformist.
– OPPOSITES conforming.
dissimilar • adjective DIFFERENT, differing, unalike, variant, diverse, divergent, heterogeneous, disparate, unrelated, distinct, contrasting; *poetic/literary* divers.
dissimilarity • noun DIFFERENCE(S), variance, diversity, heterogeneity, disparateness, disparity, distinctness, contrast, nonuniformity, divergence; *formal* dissimilitude.
dissimilitude • noun *(formal).* See DISSIMILARITY.
dissimulate • verb PRETEND, deceive, feign, act, dissemble, masquerade, pose, posture, sham, fake, bluff, hide one's feelings, be dishonest, put on a false front, lie.
dissimulation • noun PRETENCE, dissembling, deceit, dishonesty, duplicity, lying, guile, subterfuge, feigning, shamming, faking, bluff, bluffing, posturing, hypocrisy.
dissipate • verb **1** *his anger dissipated* DISAPPEAR, vanish, evaporate, dissolve, melt away, melt into thin air, be dispelled; disperse, scatter; *poetic/literary* evanesce. **2** *he dissipated his fortune* SQUANDER, fritter (away), misspend, waste, be prodigal with, spend like water, spend recklessly/freely; expend, use up, consume, run through, go through; *informal* blow, splurge.
dissipated • adjective DISSOLUTE, debauched, decadent, intemperate, profligate, self-indulgent, wild, depraved; licentious, promiscuous; drunken.
– OPPOSITES ascetic.
dissipation • noun **1** *drunken dissipation* DEBAUCHERY, decadence, dissoluteness, dissolution, intemperance, excess, profligacy, self-indulgence, wildness; depravity, degeneracy; licentiousness, promiscuity; drunkenness. **2** *the dissipation of our mineral wealth* SQUANDERING, frittering (away), waste, misspending; expenditure, draining, depletion.
– OPPOSITES asceticism.
dissociate • verb *the word 'spiritual' has become dissociated from religion* SEPARATE, detach, disconnect, sever, cut off, divorce; isolate, alienate.
– OPPOSITES relate.
– PHRASES **dissociate oneself from 1** *he dissociated himself from the Church of England* BREAK AWAY FROM, end relations with, sever connections with; withdraw from, quit, leave, disaffiliate from, resign from, pull out of, drop out of, defect from. **2** *he dissociated himself from the statement* DISOWN, reject, disagree with, distance oneself from.
dissociation • noun SEPARATION, disconnection, detachment, severance, divorce, split; segregation, division; *poetic/literary* sundering.
– OPPOSITES union.
dissolute • adjective DISSIPATED, debauched, decadent, intemperate, profligate, self-indulgent, wild, depraved; licentious, promiscuous; drunken.
– OPPOSITES ascetic.
dissolution • noun **1** *the dissolution of parliament* CESSATION, conclusion, end, ending, termination, winding up/down, discontinuation, suspension, disbanding; prorogation, recess. **2** *the dissolution of a polymer in a solvent* DISSOLVING, liquefaction, melting, deliquescence; breaking up, decomposition, disintegration. **3** *the dissolution of the empire* DISINTEGRATION, breaking up; decay, col-

2 (with reference to an assembly or body) close down, dismiss, or annul. 3 (**dissolve into/in**) subside uncontrollably into (an expression of strong feelings).
– DERIVATIVES **dissolvable** adjective.
– ORIGIN Latin *dissolvere*, from *solvere* 'loosen or solve'.

dissonant • adjective 1 Music sounding harsh or discordant. 2 unsuitable in combination; clashing.
– DERIVATIVES **dissonance** noun **dissonantly** adverb.
– ORIGIN from Latin *dissonare* 'be discordant', from *sonare* 'to sound'.

dissuade /diswayd/ • verb (**dissuade from**) persuade or advise not to do.
– DERIVATIVES **dissuasion** noun **dissuasive** adjective.
– ORIGIN Latin *dissuadere*, from *suadere* 'advise, persuade'.

distaff • noun 1 a stick or spindle on to which wool or flax is wound for spinning. 2 (before another noun) denoting the female side or members of a family. Compare with SPEAR (in sense 3).
– ORIGIN Old English.

distal • adjective chiefly Anatomy situated away from the centre of the body or an area or from the point of attachment. The opposite of PROXIMAL.
– DERIVATIVES **distally** adverb.
– ORIGIN from DISTANT, on the pattern of words such as *dorsal*.

distance • noun 1 the length of the space between two points. 2 the condition of being far off; remoteness. 3 a far-off point or place. 4 an interval of time or relation. 5 the full length or time of a race or other contest. 6 Brit. Horse Racing a space of more than twenty lengths between two finishers in a race. 7 aloofness. • verb 1 make distant. 2 (**distance oneself from**) dissociate or separate oneself from.
– PHRASES **go the distance** continue to participate until the scheduled end of a contest.
– ORIGIN Latin *distantia*, from *distare* 'stand apart'.

distance learning • noun a method of studying in which lectures are broadcast and lessons are conducted by correspondence.

distant • adjective 1 far away in space or time. 2 at a specified distance. 3 remote or far apart in resemblance or relationship: *a distant acquaintance*. 4 aloof or reserved. 5 remote; abstracted: *the distant look in his eyes*.
– DERIVATIVES **distantly** adverb.

distaste • noun dislike or aversion.
– DERIVATIVES **distasteful** adjective **distastefully** adverb **distastefulness** noun.

distemper[1] • noun a kind of paint having a base of glue or size, used on walls. • verb paint with distemper.
– ORIGIN from Latin *distemperare* 'soak'.

distemper[2] • noun a disease of some animals, especially dogs, spread by a virus and causing fever.
– ORIGIN originally in the sense 'upset, derange': from Latin *distemperare* 'soak, mix in the wrong proportions'.

distend • verb swell because of internal pressure.
– DERIVATIVES **distended** adjective **distensibility** noun **distensible** adjective **distension** noun.
– ORIGIN Latin *distendere*, from *tendere* 'to stretch'.

distil (US **distill**) • verb (**distilled**, **distilling**) 1 purify (a liquid) by heating it so that it vaporizes, then cooling and condensing the vapour and collecting the resulting liquid. 2 make (spirits) in this way. 3 extract the essential meaning of.
– DERIVATIVES **distillate** noun **distillation** noun.
– ORIGIN Latin *distillare*, from *stilla* 'a drop'.

distiller • noun a person or company that manufactures spirits.

distillery • noun (pl. **distilleries**) a place where spirits are manufactured.

distinct • adjective 1 recognizably different or individual. 2 able to be perceived clearly by the senses.
– DERIVATIVES **distinctly** adverb **distinctness** noun.
– ORIGIN Latin *distinctus*, from *distinguere* 'distinguish'.

distinction • noun 1 a marked difference or contrast. 2 the action of distinguishing. 3 outstanding excellence. 4 a special honour or recognition.

distinctive • adjective individually characteristic; distinct from others of its kind.
– DERIVATIVES **distinctively** adverb **distinctiveness** noun.

d

Thesaurus

lapse, demise, extinction. 4 *a life of dissolution*. See DISSIPATION sense 1.

dissolve • verb 1 *sugar dissolves in water* GO INTO SOLUTION, break down; liquefy, deliquesce, disintegrate. 2 *his hopes dissolved* DISAPPEAR, vanish, melt away, evaporate, disperse, dissipate, disintegrate; dwindle, fade (away), wither; poetic/literary evanesce. 3 *the crowd dissolved* DISPERSE, disband, break up, scatter, go in different directions. 4 *the assembly was dissolved* DISBAND, disestablish, bring to an end, end, terminate, discontinue, close down, wind up/down, suspend; prorogue, adjourn. 5 *their marriage was dissolved* ANNUL, nullify, void, invalidate, overturn, revoke.
– PHRASES **dissolve into/in** BURST INTO, break (down) into, be overcome with.

dissonant • adjective 1 *dissonant sounds* INHARMONIOUS, discordant, unmelodious, atonal, off-key, cacophonous. 2 *harmonious and dissonant colours* INCONGRUOUS, anomalous, clashing; disparate, different, dissimilar.
– OPPOSITES harmonious.

dissuade • verb DISCOURAGE, deter, prevent, divert, stop; talk out of, persuade against, advise against, argue out of.
– OPPOSITES encourage.

distance • noun 1 *they measured the distance* INTERVAL, space, span, gap, extent; length, width, breadth, depth; range, reach. 2 *our perception of distance* REMOTENESS; closeness. 3 *a mix of warmth and distance* ALOOFNESS, remoteness, detachment, unfriendliness; reserve, reticence, restraint, formality; informal standoffishness.
• verb *he distanced himself from her* WITHDRAW, detach, separate, dissociate, isolate, put at a distance.
– PHRASES **in the distance** FAR AWAY/OFF, afar, just in view; on the horizon; archaic yonder.

distant • adjective 1 *distant parts of the world* FARAWAY, far-off, far-flung, remote, out of the way, outlying. 2 *the distant past* LONG AGO, bygone, olden; ancient, prehistoric; poetic/literary of yore. 3 *half a mile distant* AWAY, off, apart. 4 *a distant memory* VAGUE, faint, dim, indistinct, unclear, indefinite, sketchy, hazy. 5 *a distant family connection* REMOTE, indirect, slight. 6 *father was always distant* ALOOF, reserved, remote, detached, unapproachable; withdrawn, reticent, taciturn, uncommunicative, undemonstrative, unforthcoming, unresponsive, unfriendly; informal standoffish. 7 *a distant look in his eyes* DISTRACTED, absent-minded, faraway, detached, distrait, vague.
– OPPOSITES near, close, recent.

distaste • noun DISLIKE, aversion, disinclination, disapproval, disapprobation, disdain, repugnance, hatred, loathing; archaic disrelish.
– OPPOSITES liking.

distasteful • adjective 1 *distasteful behaviour* UNPLEASANT, disagreeable, displeasing, undesirable; objectionable, offensive, unsavoury, unpalatable, obnoxious; disgusting, repellent, repulsive, revolting, repugnant, abhorrent, loathsome, vile. 2 *their eggs are distasteful to predators* UNPALATABLE, unsavoury, unappetizing, inedible, disgusting.
– OPPOSITES agreeable, tasty.

distended • adjective SWOLLEN, bloated, dilated, engorged, enlarged, inflated, expanded, extended, bulging, protuberant.

distil • verb 1 *the water was distilled* PURIFY, refine, filter, treat, process; evaporate and condense. 2 *oil distilled from marjoram* EXTRACT, press out, squeeze out, express. 3 *whisky is distilled from barley* BREW, ferment. 4 *the solvent is distilled to leave the oil* BOIL DOWN, reduce, concentrate, condense; purify, refine.

distinct • adjective 1 *two distinct categories* DISCRETE, separate, different, unconnected; precise, specific, distinctive, contrasting. 2 *the tail has distinct black tips* CLEAR, well defined, unmistakable, easily distinguishable; recognizable, visible, obvious, pronounced, prominent, striking.
– OPPOSITES overlapping, indefinite.

distinction • noun 1 *class distinctions* DIFFERENCE, contrast, dissimilarity, variance, variation; division, differentiation, dividing line, gulf, gap; formal dissimilitude. 2 *a painter of distinction* IMPORTANCE, significance, note, consequence; renown, fame, celebrity, prominence, eminence, pre-eminence, repute, reputation; merit, worth, greatness, excellence, quality. 3 *he had served with distinction* HONOUR, credit, excellence, merit.
– OPPOSITES similarity, mediocrity.

distinctive • adjective DISTINGUISHING, characteristic, typical, individual, particular, peculiar, unique, exclusive, special.
– OPPOSITES common.

distinctly • adverb 1 *there's something distinctly odd about him* DECIDEDLY, markedly, definitely; clearly, noticeably, obviously,

distinguish ● verb **1** recognize, show, or treat as different. **2** manage to discern (something barely perceptible). **3** be an identifying characteristic of. **4** (**distinguish oneself**) make oneself worthy of respect.
– DERIVATIVES **distinguishable** adjective.
– ORIGIN Latin *distinguere*, from *stinguere* 'put out'.
distinguished ● adjective **1** dignified in appearance. **2** successful and commanding great respect.
distort ● verb **1** pull or twist out of shape. **2** give a misleading account of. **3** change the form of (an electrical signal or sound wave) during transmission or amplification.
– DERIVATIVES **distorted** adjective **distortion** noun.
– ORIGIN Latin *distorquere* 'twist apart'.
distract ● verb **1** prevent (someone) from giving their full attention to something. **2** divert (attention) from something.
– DERIVATIVES **distracted** adjective **distracting** adjective.
– ORIGIN Latin *distrahere* 'draw apart'.
distraction ● noun **1** a thing that diverts attention. **2** a thing offering entertainment. **3** mental agitation.
distrain ● verb Law impose distraint on.
– ORIGIN Old French *destreindre*, from Latin *distringere* 'stretch apart'.
distraint /distraynt/ ● noun Law the seizure of someone's property in order to obtain payment of rent or other money owed.
distrait /distray/ ● adjective (fem. **distraite** /distrayt/) distracted; absent-minded.
– ORIGIN French, from Old French *destrait* 'distracted'.
distraught ● adjective very worried and upset.
– ORIGIN alteration of obsolete adjective *distract*, from Latin *distractus* 'pulled apart'.
distress ● noun **1** extreme anxiety or suffering. **2** the state of a ship or aircraft when in danger or difficulty. **3** Medicine a state of physical strain, especially difficulty in breathing. **4** Law another term for DISTRAINT. ● verb **1** cause distress to. **2** give (furniture, leather, etc.) simulated marks of age and wear.
– DERIVATIVES **distressed** adjective **distressful** adjective **distressing** adjective.
– ORIGIN Old French *destresce*, from Latin *distringere* 'stretch apart'.
distributary /distribyootəri/ ● noun (pl. **distributaries**) a branch of a river that does not return to the main stream after leaving it, as in a delta.
distribute ● verb **1** hand or share out to a number of recipients. **2** (**be distributed**) be spread over an area. **3** supply (goods) to retailers.
– DERIVATIVES **distributable** adjective.
– ORIGIN Latin *distribuere* 'divide up'.
distributed system ● noun Computing a number of independent computers linked by a network.
distribution ● noun **1** the action of distributing. **2** the way in which something is distributed among a group or over an area.
– DERIVATIVES **distributional** adjective.
distributive ● adjective **1** relating to the processes of distribution or things that are distributed. **2** Grammar (of a determiner or pronoun) referring to each individual of a class, not to the class collectively, e.g. *each*, *either*.
– DERIVATIVES **distributively** adverb.
distributor ● noun **1** an agent who supplies goods to retailers. **2** a device in a petrol engine for passing electric current to each spark plug in turn.
district ● noun **1** an area of a town or region, especially one regarded as a unit because of a particular characteristic. **2** Brit. a division of a county or region that elects its own councillors.
– ORIGIN Latin *districtus* '(territory of) jurisdiction', from *distringere* 'draw apart'.
district attorney ● noun (in the US) a public official who acts as prosecutor for the state or the federal government in court in a particular district.
district nurse ● noun (in the UK) a nurse who treats patients in their homes, operating within a particular district.
distrust ● noun lack of trust. ● verb have little trust in; regard with suspicion.
– DERIVATIVES **distrustful** adjective **distrustfully** adverb.
disturb ● verb **1** interfere with the normal arrangement or func-

Thesaurus

plainly, evidently, unmistakably, manifestly, patently; *Brit. informal* dead. **2** *Laura spoke quite distinctly* CLEARLY, plainly, intelligibly, audibly, unambiguously.
distinguish ● verb **1** *distinguishing reality from fantasy* DIFFERENTIATE, tell apart, discriminate between, tell the difference between. **2** *he could distinguish shapes in the dark* DISCERN, see, perceive, make out; detect, recognize, identify; *poetic/literary* descry, espy. **3** *this is what distinguishes history from other disciplines* SEPARATE, set apart, make distinctive, make different; single out, mark off, characterize.
– PHRASES **distinguish oneself** ATTAIN DISTINCTION, be successful, bring fame/honour to oneself, become famous.
distinguishable ● adjective DISCERNIBLE, recognizable, identifiable, detectable.
distinguished ● adjective EMINENT, famous, renowned, prominent, well known; esteemed, respected, illustrious, acclaimed, celebrated, great; notable, important, influential.
– OPPOSITES unknown, obscure.
distinguishing ● adjective DISTINCTIVE, differentiating, characteristic, typical, peculiar, singular, unique.
distorted ● adjective **1** *a distorted face* TWISTED, warped, contorted, buckled, deformed, malformed, misshapen, disfigured, crooked, awry, out of shape. **2** *a distorted version* MISREPRESENTED, perverted, twisted, falsified, misreported, misstated, garbled, inaccurate; biased, prejudiced, slanted, coloured, loaded, weighted, altered, changed.
distract ● verb DIVERT, sidetrack, draw away, disturb, put off.
distracted ● adjective PREOCCUPIED, inattentive, vague, abstracted, distrait, absent-minded, faraway, in a world of one's own; bemused, confused, bewildered; troubled, harassed, worried; *informal* miles away, not with it.
– OPPOSITES attentive.
distracting ● adjective DISTURBING, unsettling, intrusive, disconcerting, bothersome, off-putting.
distraction ● noun **1** *a distraction from the real issues* DIVERSION, interruption, disturbance, interference, hindrance. **2** *frivolous distractions* AMUSEMENT, entertainment, diversion, recreation, leisure pursuit, divertissement. **3** *he was driven to distraction* FRENZY, hysteria, mental distress, madness, insanity, mania; agitation, perturbation.
distrait, fem. **distraite** ● adjective DISTRACTED, preoccupied, absorbed, abstracted, distant, faraway; absent-minded, vague, inattentive, in a brown study, wool-gathering, with one's head in the clouds, in a world of one's own; *informal* miles away, not with it.
– OPPOSITES alert.
distraught ● adjective WORRIED, upset, distressed, fraught; overcome, overwrought, beside oneself, out of one's mind, desperate, hysterical, worked up, at one's wits' end; *informal* in a state.
distress ● noun **1** *she concealed her distress* ANGUISH, suffering, pain, agony, torment, heartache, heartbreak; misery, wretchedness, sorrow, grief, woe, sadness, unhappiness, desolation, despair. **2** *a ship in distress* DANGER, peril, difficulty, trouble, jeopardy, risk. **3** *the poor in distress* HARDSHIP, adversity, poverty, deprivation, privation, destitution, indigence, impoverishment, penury, need, dire straits.
– OPPOSITES happiness, safety, prosperity.
● verb *he was distressed by the trial* CAUSE ANGUISH/SUFFERING TO, pain, upset, make miserable; trouble, worry, bother, perturb, disturb, disquiet, agitate, harrow, torment; *informal* cut up.
– OPPOSITES calm, please.
distressing ● adjective UPSETTING, worrying, disturbing, disquieting, painful, traumatic, agonizing, harrowing; sad, saddening, heartbreaking, heart-rending.
– OPPOSITES comforting.
distribute ● verb **1** *the were proceeds distributed among his creditors* GIVE OUT, deal out, dole out, dish out, hand out/round; allocate, allot, apportion, share out, divide out/up, parcel out. **2** *the newsletter is distributed free* CIRCULATE, issue, hand out, deliver. **3** *a hundred and thirty different species are distributed worldwide* DISPERSE, scatter, spread.
– OPPOSITES collect.
distribution ● noun **1** *the distribution of charity* GIVING OUT, dealing out, doling out, handing out/round, issue, issuing, dispensation; allocation, allotment, apportioning, sharing out, dividing up/out, parcelling out. **2** *the geographical distribution of plants* DISPERSAL, dissemination, spread; placement, position, location, disposition. **3** *centres of food distribution* SUPPLY, supplying, delivery, transport, transportation. **4** *the statistical distribution of the problem* FREQUENCY, prevalence, incidence, commonness.

tioning of. **2** interrupt the sleep, relaxation, or privacy of. **3** make anxious.
– DERIVATIVES **disturbing** adjective.
– ORIGIN Latin *disturbare*, from *turbare* 'disturb'.
disturbance • noun **1** the action of disturbing or the process of being disturbed. **2** a breakdown of peaceful behaviour; a riot.
disturbed • adjective suffering from emotional or psychological problems.
disunited • adjective lacking unity.
– DERIVATIVES **disunity** noun.
disuse • noun the state of not being used; neglect.
– DERIVATIVES **disused** adjective.
disyllable /dīsilləb'l, di-/ • noun Poetry a word or metrical foot consisting of two syllables.
– DERIVATIVES **disyllabic** adjective
– ORIGIN from Greek *disullabos* 'of two syllables'.
ditch • noun a narrow channel dug to hold or carry water. • verb **1** provide with a ditch. **2** (with reference to an aircraft) bring or come down in a forced landing on the sea. **3** informal get rid of; give up.
– DERIVATIVES **ditcher** noun.
– ORIGIN Old English, related to DYKE[1].
dither • verb be indecisive. • noun informal **1** indecisive behaviour. **2** a state of agitation.
– DERIVATIVES **ditherer** noun **dithery** adjective.
– ORIGIN variant of dialect *didder*; related to DODDER[1].
dithyramb /dithiram/ • noun **1** a wildly ecstatic choral hymn of ancient Greece, especially one dedicated to the god Dionysus. **2** a passionate or inflated speech or text.
– DERIVATIVES **dithyrambic** adjective.
– ORIGIN Greek *dithurambos*.
ditsy • adjective variant spelling of DITZY.
ditto • noun **1** the same thing again (used in lists and often indicated by a ditto mark). **2** (also **ditto mark**) a symbol consisting of two apostrophes (") representing a repetition.
– ORIGIN originally meaning 'in the aforesaid month': from Italian *detto* 'said'.
ditty • noun (pl. **ditties**) a short simple song.
– ORIGIN Old French *dite* 'composition', from Latin *dictare* 'to dictate'.
ditz • noun N. Amer. informal a scatterbrained person.
ditzy (also **ditsy**) • adjective N. Amer. informal silly or scatterbrained.
– DERIVATIVES **ditziness** noun.
– ORIGIN of unknown origin.
diuretic /dīyoorettik/ Medicine • adjective causing increased passing of urine. • noun a diuretic drug.
– ORIGIN Greek *diourētikos*, from *diourein* 'urinate'.
diurnal /dīurn'l/ • adjective **1** of or during the daytime. **2** daily; of each day.
– DERIVATIVES **diurnally** adverb.
– ORIGIN Latin *diurnalis*, from *dies* 'day'.
diva /deevə/ • noun a celebrated female opera singer.
– ORIGIN Latin, 'goddess'.
Divali • noun variant spelling of DIWALI.
divan /divan/ • noun **1** a bed consisting of a base and mattress but no footboard or headboard. **2** a long, low sofa without a back or arms.
– ORIGIN originally denoting a legislative body, council chamber, or court in the Middle East: from Persian, 'bench, court'.
dive • verb (past and past part. **dived**; US also **dove** /dōv/) **1** plunge head first and with arms outstretched into water. **2** go to a deeper level in water. **3** swim under water using breathing equipment. **4** plunge steeply downwards through the air. **5** move quickly or suddenly in a downward direction or under cover. **6** Soccer deliberately fall as if fouled in order to deceive the referee. • noun **1** an act or instance of diving. **2** informal a disreputable nightclub or bar.
– ORIGIN Old English, related to DEEP and DIP.
dive-bomb • verb bomb (a target) while diving steeply in an aircraft.
– DERIVATIVES **dive-bomber** noun.
diver • noun **1** a person who dives under water as a sport or as part of their work. **2** a large diving waterbird with a straight pointed bill.
diverge • verb **1** (of a road, route, or line) separate from another route and go in a different direction. **2** (of an opinion or approach) differ. **3** (**diverge from**) depart from (a set course or standard).
– DERIVATIVES **divergence** noun **diverging** adjective.
– ORIGIN Latin *divergere*, from *vergere* 'to turn or incline'.

d

Thesaurus

district • noun NEIGHBOURHOOD, area, region, locality, locale, community, quarter, sector, zone, territory; administrative division, ward, parish; *informal* neck of the woods.
distrust • noun *the general distrust of authority* MISTRUST, suspicion, wariness, chariness, leeriness, lack of trust, lack of confidence; scepticism, doubt, doubtfulness, cynicism; misgivings, qualms, disbelief; *formal* dubiety.
• verb *Louise distrusted him* MISTRUST, be suspicious of, be wary/chary of, be leery of, regard with suspicion, suspect; be sceptical of, have doubts about, doubt, be unsure of/about, have misgivings about, wonder about, disbelieve (in).
disturb • verb **1** *somewhere where we won't be disturbed* INTERRUPT, intrude on, butt in on, barge in on; distract, disrupt, bother, trouble, pester, harass; *informal* hassle. **2** *don't disturb his papers* DISARRANGE, muddle, rearrange, disorganize, disorder, mix up, interfere with, throw into disorder/confusion, turn upside down. **3** *waters disturbed by winds* AGITATE, churn up, stir up; *poetic/literary* roil. **4** *he wasn't disturbed by the allegations* PERTURB, trouble, concern, worry, upset; agitate, fluster, discomfit, disconcert, dismay, distress, discompose, unsettle, ruffle.
disturbance • noun **1** *a disturbance to local residents* DISRUPTION, distraction, interference; bother, trouble, inconvenience, upset, annoyance, irritation, intrusion, harassment; *informal* hassle. **2** *disturbances among the peasantry* RIOT, fracas, upheaval, brawl, street fight, melee, free-for-all, ruckus, rumpus; *Law, dated* affray; *informal* ruction. **3** *emotional disturbance* TROUBLE, perturbation, distress, worry, upset, agitation, discomposure, discomfiture; neurosis, illness, sickness, disorder, complaint.
disturbed • adjective **1** *disturbed sleep* DISRUPTED, interrupted, fitful, intermittent, broken. **2** *disturbed children* TROUBLED, distressed, upset, distraught; unbalanced, unstable, disordered, dysfunctional, maladjusted, neurotic, unhinged; *informal* screwed up, mixed up.
disturbing • adjective WORRYING, perturbing, troubling, upsetting; distressing, discomfiting, disconcerting, disquieting, unsettling, dismaying, alarming, frightening.
disunion • noun BREAKING UP, separation, dissolution, partition.
– OPPOSITES federation.
disunite • verb BREAK UP, separate, divide, split up, partition, dismantle; *poetic/literary* sunder.
– OPPOSITES unify.
disunity • noun DISAGREEMENT, dissent, dissension, argument, arguing, quarrelling, feuding; conflict, strife, friction, discord.
disuse • noun NON-USE, non-employment, lack of use; neglect, abandonment, desertion, obsolescence; *formal* desuetude.
disused • adjective UNUSED, no longer in use, unemployed, idle; abandoned, deserted, vacated, unoccupied, uninhabited.
ditch • noun *she rescued an animal from a ditch* TRENCH, trough, channel, dyke, drain, gutter, gully, watercourse, conduit; *Archaeology* fosse.
• verb **1** *they started ditching the coastal areas* DIG A DITCH IN, trench, excavate, drain. **2** *(informal) she ditched her old curtains.* See THROW SOMETHING AWAY sense 1 at THROW. **3** *(informal) she ditched her husband.* See THROW SOMEONE OVER at THROW.
dither • verb HESITATE, falter, waver, vacillate, change one's mind, be in two minds, be indecisive, be undecided; *Brit.* haver; *informal* shilly-shally, dilly-dally.
diurnal • adjective DAILY, everyday, quotidian, occurring every/each day.
divan • noun SETTEE, sofa, couch; sofa bed; *Brit.* put-you-up; *N. Amer.* studio couch.
dive • verb **1** *they dived into the clear water | the plane was diving towards the ground* PLUNGE, nosedive, jump head first, bellyflop; plummet, fall, drop, pitch. **2** *the islanders dive for oysters* SWIM UNDER WATER; snorkel, scuba dive. **3** *they dived for cover* LEAP, jump, lunge, launch oneself, throw oneself, go headlong, duck.
• noun **1** *a dive into the pool* PLUNGE, nosedive, jump, bellyflop; plummet, fall, drop, swoop, pitch. **2** *a sideways dive* LUNGE, spring, jump, leap. **3** *(informal) John got into a fight in some dive* SLEAZY BAR/NIGHTCLUB, seedy bar/nightclub, drinking den; *informal* drinking joint.
diverge • verb **1** *the two roads diverged* SEPARATE, part, fork, divide, split, bifurcate, go in different directions. **2** *areas where our views diverge* DIFFER, be different, be dissimilar; disagree, be at

divergent ● adjective diverging.
– DERIVATIVES **divergently** adverb.
divers /dīvərz/ ● adjective literary of varying types.
diverse /dīverss/ ● adjective widely varied.
– DERIVATIVES **diversely** adverb.
– ORIGIN Latin *diversus* 'diverse', from *divertere* (see DIVERT).
diversify ● verb (**diversifies**, **diversified**) **1** make or become more diverse. **2** (of a company) enlarge or vary its range of products or field of operation.
– DERIVATIVES **diversification** noun.

d

diversion ● noun **1** an instance of diverting. **2** Brit. an alternative route for use when the usual road is closed. **3** something intended to distract attention. **4** a recreation or pastime.
– DERIVATIVES **diversionary** adjective.
diversity ● noun (pl. **diversities**) **1** the state of being diverse. **2** a diverse range; a variety.
divert /dīvert, di-/ ● verb **1** cause to change course or take a different route. **2** reallocate (a resource) to a different purpose. **3** draw the attention of; distract or entertain.
– DERIVATIVES **diverting** adjective.
– ORIGIN Latin *divertere* 'turn in separate ways'.
diverticula plural of DIVERTICULUM.
diverticulitis /dīvertikyoolītiss/ ● noun Medicine inflammation of a diverticulum, causing pain and disturbance of bowel function.
diverticulum /dīvertikyooləm/ ● noun (pl. **diverticula** /dīvertikyoolə/) Anatomy & Zoology **1** a blind tube leading from a cavity or passage. **2** Medicine an abnormal sac or pouch formed in the wall of the alimentary tract.
– ORIGIN Latin *deverticulum* 'byway'.
divertimento /divertimentō, divair-/ ● noun (pl. **divertimenti** /divertimenti, divair-/ or **divertimentos**) Music a light and entertaining composition.
– ORIGIN Italian, 'diversion'.
divertissement /divertissmənt, divairteesmon/ ● noun **1** a minor entertainment. **2** Ballet a short discrete dance within a ballet.
– ORIGIN French, from Latin *divertere* 'turn in separate ways'.
divest /dīvest/ ● verb (**divest of**) **1** deprive or dispossess (someone or something) of. **2** free or rid of.
– ORIGIN Old French *desvestir*, from Latin *vestire* 'clothe'.
divestiture (also **divesture**) ● noun another term for DIVESTMENT.
divestment ● noun the action or process of selling off subsidiary business interests or investments.
divi ● noun (pl. **divis**) variant spelling of DIVVY.
divide ● verb **1** separate into parts. **2** distribute or share out. **3** disagree or cause to disagree. **4** form a boundary between. **5** Mathematics find how many times (a number) contains another. **6** Mathematics (of a number) be susceptible of division without a remainder. **7** (of a legislative assembly) separate or be separated into two groups for voting. ● noun a wide divergence between two groups: *the North-South divide*.
– PHRASES **divide and rule** (or **conquer**) maintain control over opponents by encouraging a disunity that makes their opposition ineffective.
– DERIVATIVES **divided** adjective.
– ORIGIN Latin *dividere* 'force apart, remove'.
dividend ● noun **1** a sum of money that is divided among a number of people, such as the part of a company's profits paid to its shareholders or the winnings from a football pool. **2** (**dividends**) benefits from an action or policy. **3** Mathematics a number to be divided by another number.
– ORIGIN Latin *dividendum* 'something to be divided'.
divider ● noun **1** (also **room divider**) a screen or piece of furniture that divides a room into two parts. **2** (**dividers**) a measuring compass, especially one with a screw for making fine adjustments.
divination ● noun the practice of seeking knowledge of the future or the unknown by supernatural means.
– DERIVATIVES **divinatory** adjective.
divine[1] ● adjective (**diviner**, **divinest**) **1** of, from, or like God or a god. **2** informal excellent. ● noun **1** dated a cleric or theologian. **2** (**the Divine**) providence or God.
– DERIVATIVES **divinely** adverb.
– ORIGIN Latin *divinus*, from *divus* 'godlike'.
divine[2] ● verb **1** discover by guesswork or intuition. **2** have supernatural insight into (the future). **3** discover (water) by dowsing.
– DERIVATIVES **diviner** noun.
– ORIGIN Old French *deviner* 'predict', from Latin *divinus* (see DIVINE[1]).
diving bell ● noun an open-bottomed chamber supplied with

Thesaurus

variance/odds, conflict, clash. **3** *he diverged from his text* DEVIATE, digress, depart, veer, stray; stray from the point, get off the subject.
– OPPOSITES converge, agree.
divergence ● noun **1** *the divergence of the human and ape lineages* SEPARATION, dividing, parting, forking, bifurcation. **2** *a marked political divergence* DIFFERENCE, dissimilarity, variance, disparity; disagreement, incompatibility, mismatch; *formal* dissimilitude. **3** *divergence from standard behaviour* DEVIATION, digression, departure, shift, straying; variation, change, alteration.
divergent ● adjective DIFFERING, varying, different, dissimilar, unalike, disparate, contrasting, contrastive; conflicting, incompatible, contradictory, at odds, at variance.
– OPPOSITES similar.
divers ● adjective (*poetic/literary*) SEVERAL, many, numerous, multiple, manifold, multifarious, multitudinous; sundry, miscellaneous, assorted, various; *poetic/literary* myriad.
diverse ● adjective VARIOUS, sundry, manifold, multiple; varied, varying, miscellaneous, assorted, mixed, diversified, divergent, heterogeneous, a mixed bag of; different, differing, distinct, unlike, dissimilar; *poetic/literary* divers, myriad.
diversify ● verb **1** *farmers looking for ways to diversify* BRANCH OUT, expand, extend operations. **2** *a plan aimed at diversifying the economy* VARY, bring variety to; modify, alter, change, transform; expand, enlarge.
diversion ● noun **1** *the diversion of 19 rivers* RE-ROUTING, redirection, deflection, deviation, divergence. **2** *traffic diversions* DETOUR, deviation, alternative route. **3** *the noise created a diversion* DISTRACTION, disturbance, smokescreen. **4** *a city full of diversions* ENTERTAINMENT, amusement, pastime, delight, divertissement; fun, recreation, rest and relaxation, pleasure; *informal* R and R; *dated* sport.
diversity ● noun VARIETY, miscellany, assortment, mixture, mix, melange, range, array, multiplicity; variation, variance, diverseness, diversification, heterogeneity, difference, contrast; *formal* dissimilitude.
– OPPOSITES uniformity.
divert ● verb **1** *a plan to divert Siberia's rivers* RE-ROUTE, redirect, change the course of, deflect, channel. **2** *he diverted her from her studies* DISTRACT, sidetrack, disturb, draw away, be a distraction, put off. **3** *the story diverted them* AMUSE, entertain, distract, delight, enchant, interest, fascinate, absorb, engross, rivet, grip, hold the attention of.
diverting ● adjective ENTERTAINING, amusing, enjoyable, pleasing, agreeable, delightful, appealing; interesting, fascinating, intriguing, absorbing, riveting, compelling; humorous, funny, witty, comical.
– OPPOSITES boring.
divest ● verb DEPRIVE, strip, dispossess, rob, cheat/trick out of; *archaic* reave.
divide ● verb **1** *he divided his kingdom into four* SPLIT (UP), cut up, carve up; dissect, bisect, halve, quarter; *poetic/literary* sunder. **2** *a curtain divided her cabin from the galley* SEPARATE, segregate, partition, screen off, section off, split off. **3** *the stairs divide at the mezzanine* DIVERGE, separate, part, branch (off), fork, split (in two), bifurcate. **4** *Jack divided up the cash* SHARE OUT, allocate, allot, apportion, portion out, ration out, parcel out, deal out, dole out, dish out, distribute, dispense; *informal* divvy up. **5** *he aimed to divide his opponents* DISUNITE, drive apart, break up, split up, set at variance/odds; separate, isolate, estrange, alienate; *poetic/literary* tear asunder. **6** *living things are divided into three categories* CLASSIFY, sort (out), categorize, order, group, grade, rank.
– RELATED TERMS schizo-.
– OPPOSITES unify, join, converge.
● noun *the sectarian divide* BREACH, gulf, gap, split; borderline, boundary, dividing line.
dividend ● noun **1** *an annual dividend* SHARE, portion, premium, return, gain, profit; *informal* cut, rake-off; *Brit. informal* divvy. **2** *the research will produce dividends in the future* BENEFIT, advantage, gain; bonus, extra, plus.
divination ● noun FORTUNE TELLING, divining, prophecy, prediction, soothsaying, augury; clairvoyance, second sight.

air, in which a person can be let down under water.
diving board ● noun a board projecting over a swimming pool or other body of water, from which people dive or jump in.
diving suit ● noun a watertight suit, typically with a helmet and an air supply, worn for working or exploring deep under water.
divining rod ● noun a stick or rod used for dowsing.
divinity ● noun (pl. **divinities**) **1** the state or quality of being divine. **2** a divine being. **3** (**the Divinity**) God. **4** the study of religion; theology.
divisible ● adjective **1** capable of being divided. **2** Mathematics (of a number) containing another number a number of times without a remainder.
– DERIVATIVES **divisibility** noun.
division ● noun **1** the action or process of dividing. **2** each of the parts into which something is divided. **3** a major unit or section of an organization. **4** a number of teams or competitors grouped together in a sport for competitive purposes. **5** a partition that divides two groups or things.
– PHRASES **division of labour** the assignment of different parts of a manufacturing process or task to different people.
– DERIVATIVES **divisional** adjective.
division bell ● noun a bell rung in the British Parliament to announce an imminent division for voting.
division sign ● noun the sign ÷, placed between two numbers showing that the first is to be divided by the second, as in *6 ÷ 3 = 2*.
divisive /divīsiv/ ● adjective causing disagreement or hostility.
– DERIVATIVES **divisively** adverb **divisiveness** noun.
divisor ● noun Mathematics a number by which another number is to be divided.
divorce ● noun the legal dissolution of a marriage. ● verb **1** legally dissolve one's marriage with. **2** (**divorce from**) detach or dissociate (something) from.
– ORIGIN Old French, from Latin *divertere* 'divert'.
divorcee /divorsee/ ● noun (US masc. **divorcé**, fem. **divorcée** /divorsay/) a divorced person.
– ORIGIN French *divorcé(e)* 'divorced man (or woman)'.
divot /divvət/ ● noun a piece of turf cut out of the ground, especially by a golf club in making a stroke.
– ORIGIN of unknown origin.
divulge /dīvulj, di-/ ● verb make known (private or sensitive information).
– ORIGIN Latin *divulgare* 'publish widely'.
divvy informal ● noun (also **divi**) (pl. **divvies**) Brit. a dividend or share, especially of profits earned by a cooperative. ● verb (**divvies**, **divvied**) share out.
Diwali /diwaali/ (also **Divali**) ● noun a Hindu festival with lights, held in October and November to celebrate the end of the monsoon.
– ORIGIN Sanskrit, 'row of lights'.
Dixie ● noun an informal name for the Southern states of the US.
– ORIGIN of unknown origin.
dixie ● noun (pl. **dixies**) a large iron cooking pot used especially by campers or soldiers.
– ORIGIN Persian, 'small pot'.
Dixieland ● noun a kind of jazz with a strong two-beat rhythm and collective improvisation.
DIY ● noun chiefly Brit. the activity of decorating and making repairs in the home oneself rather than employing a professional.
– DERIVATIVES **DIY'er** noun.
– ORIGIN abbreviation of DO-IT-YOURSELF.
dizzy ● adjective (**dizzier**, **dizziest**) **1** having a sensation of spinning around and losing one's balance. **2** informal (of a woman) silly but attractive. ● verb (**dizzies**, **dizzied**) cause to feel unsteady, confused, or amazed.
– PHRASES **the dizzy heights** informal a position of great importance in a particular field.
– DERIVATIVES **dizzily** adverb **dizziness** noun.
– ORIGIN Old English, 'foolish'.
DJ[1] ● noun **1** a disc jockey. **2** a person who uses samples of recorded music to make techno or rap music.
DJ[2] ● abbreviation Brit. dinner jacket.
djellaba /jelləbə/ (also **djellabah** or **jellaba**) ● noun a loose woollen hooded cloak of a kind traditionally worn by Arabs.
– ORIGIN Arabic.
Djiboutian /jibōōtiən/ ● noun a person from Djibouti, a country on the north-east coast of Africa. ● adjective relating to Djibouti.
djinn ● noun variant spelling of JINN.
dl ● abbreviation decilitre(s).
DLitt ● abbreviation Doctor of Letters.
– ORIGIN Latin *Doctor Litterarum*.
D-lock ● noun a mechanism used to secure a bicycle or motorbike, consisting of a metal U-shaped bar and crosspiece.
DM (also **D-mark**) ● abbreviation Deutschmark.
dm ● abbreviation decimetre(s).
DMA ● abbreviation Computing direct memory access.
DMs ● abbreviation Dr Martens (shoes or boots).
DMus ● abbreviation Doctor of Music.
DNA ● noun Biochemistry deoxyribonucleic acid, a substance which is present in the cell nuclei of nearly all living organisms and is the carrier of genetic information.
DNA fingerprinting (also **DNA profiling**) ● noun another term for GENETIC FINGERPRINTING.
D notice ● noun Brit. a government notice requiring news editors not to publicize certain sensitive information.
– ORIGIN *D* for *defence*.
do[1] ● verb (**does**; past **did**; past part. **done**) **1** perform or carry out (an action). **2** achieve or complete (a specified target). **3** act or

d

Thesaurus

– RELATED TERMS mantic, -mancy.
divine[1] ● adjective **1** *a divine being* GODLY, angelic, seraphic, saintly, beatific; heavenly, celestial, holy. **2** *divine worship* RELIGIOUS, holy, sacred, sanctified, consecrated, blessed, devotional. **3** *(informal) divine food.* See LOVELY sense 3.
– OPPOSITES mortal.
● noun (dated) *puritan divines* THEOLOGIAN, clergyman, clergywoman, member of the clergy, churchman, churchwoman, cleric, minister, man/woman of the cloth, preacher, priest; *informal* reverend.
divine[2] ● verb **1** *Fergus divined how afraid she was* GUESS, surmise, conjecture, deduce, infer; discern, intuit, perceive, recognize, see, realize, appreciate, understand, grasp, comprehend; *informal* figure (out), savvy; *Brit. informal* twig, suss. **2** *they divined that this was an auspicious day* FORETELL, predict, prophesy, forecast, foresee, prognosticate; *rare* vaticinate. **3** *he divined water supplies* DOWSE, find by dowsing.
diviner ● noun FORTUNE TELLER, clairvoyant, crystal-gazer, psychic, seer, soothsayer, prognosticator, prophesier, oracle, sibyl; *rare* vaticinator.
divinity ● noun **1** *they denied Christ's divinity* DIVINE NATURE, divineness, godliness, deity, godhead, holiness. **2** *the study of divinity* THEOLOGY, religious studies, religion, scripture. **3** *a female divinity* DEITY, god, goddess, divine/supreme being.
division ● noun **1** *the division of the island | cell division* DIVIDING (UP), breaking up, break-up, carving up, splitting, dissection, bisection; partitioning, separation, segregation. **2** *the division of his estates* SHARING OUT, dividing up, parcelling out, dishing out, allocation, allotment, apportionment; splitting up, carving up; *informal* divvying up. **3** *the division between nomadic and urban cultures* DIVIDING LINE, divide, boundary, borderline, border, demarcation line. **4** *each class is divided into nine divisions* SECTION, subsection, subdivision, category, class, group, grouping, set, family. **5** *an independent division of the executive* DEPARTMENT, branch, arm, wing, sector, section, subsection, subdivision, subsidiary. **6** *the causes of social division* DISUNITY, disunion, conflict, discord, disagreement, dissension, disaffection, estrangement, alienation, isolation.
divisive ● adjective ALIENATING, estranging, isolating, schismatic.
– OPPOSITES unifying.
divorce ● noun **1** *she wants a divorce* DISSOLUTION, annulment, (official/judicial) separation. **2** *a growing divorce between the church and people* SEPARATION, division, split, disunity, estrangement, alienation; schism, gulf, chasm.
– OPPOSITES marriage, unity.
● verb **1** *her parents have divorced* DISSOLVE ONE'S MARRIAGE, annul one's marriage, end one's marriage, get a divorce. **2** *religion cannot be divorced from morality* SEPARATE, disconnect, divide, dissociate, detach, isolate, alienate, set apart, cut off.
divulge ● verb DISCLOSE, reveal, tell, communicate, pass on, publish, broadcast, proclaim; expose, uncover, make public, give away, let slip; *informal* spill the beans about, let on about.
– OPPOSITES conceal.
dizzy ● adjective **1** *she felt dizzy* GIDDY, light-headed, faint, unsteady, shaky, muzzy, wobbly; *informal* woozy. **2** *dizzy heights* CAUSING DIZZI-

progress in a specified way. **4** work on (something) to bring it to a required state. **5** have a specified result or effect on: *the walk will do me good.* **6** work at for a living or take as one's subject of study: *what does she do?* **7** make or provide. **8** be suitable or acceptable: *he'll do.* **9** (**be/have done with**) give up concern for; have finished with. **10** informal regularly take (a narcotic drug). ● auxiliary verb **1** used before a verb in questions and negative statements. **2** used to refer back to a verb already mentioned: *he looks better than he did before.* **3** used in negative or positive commands, or to give emphasis to a positive verb: *do sit down.* ● noun (pl. **dos** or **do's**) informal, chiefly Brit. a party or other social event.

d

– PHRASES **be done up** be dressed elaborately. **do away with** informal put an end to; kill. **do for 1** informal defeat, ruin, or kill. **2** suffice for. **do one's head in** Brit. informal make one extremely angry or agitated. **do in** informal **1** kill. **2** tire out. **do or die** persist, even if death is the result. **do out of** informal unfairly deprive of. **dos and don'ts** rules of behaviour. **do time** informal spend a period of time in prison. **do up 1** fasten, wrap, or arrange. **2** informal renovate or redecorate. **do with** informal **1** (**can/could do with**) would find useful or would like. **2** (**can't/won't be doing with**) Brit. be unwilling to tolerate.
– DERIVATIVES **doable** adjective (informal) **doer** noun.
– ORIGIN Old English.

do² ● noun variant spelling of DOH.

do. ● abbreviation ditto.

DOA ● abbreviation dead on arrival.

dob ● verb (**dobbed**, **dobbing**) Austral./NZ informal inform against.
– ORIGIN figurative use of dialect *dob* 'put down abruptly', later 'throw at a target'.

Dobermann /dōbərmən/ (also **Dobermann pinscher** /pinshər/, chiefly N. Amer. also **Doberman**) ● noun a large breed of dog with powerful jaws, typically black with tan markings.
– ORIGIN named after the 19th-century German dog-breeder Ludwig *Dobermann* (+ German *Pinscher* 'terrier').

dobra /dobrə/ ● noun the basic monetary unit of São Tomé and Principe, equal to 100 centavos.
– ORIGIN Portuguese, 'doubloon'.

dobro /dobrō/ ● noun (pl. **dobros**) trademark a type of acoustic guitar with steel resonating discs inside the body under the bridge.
– ORIGIN from *Do(pěra) Bro(thers)*, the Czech-American inventors of the instrument.

doc ● abbreviation informal doctor.

docent /dōsənt/ ● noun **1** (in certain US and European universities) a member of the teaching staff immediately below professor in rank. **2** a person who acts as a guide in a museum, art gallery, or zoo.
– ORIGIN from Latin *docere* 'teach'.

docile ● adjective ready to accept control or instruction; submissive.
– DERIVATIVES **docilely** adverb **docility** noun.
– ORIGIN Latin *docilis*, from *docere* 'teach'.

dock¹ ● noun **1** an enclosed area of water in a port for the loading, unloading, and repair of ships. **2** (also **loading dock**) a platform for loading trucks or goods trains. ● verb **1** (with reference to a ship) come or bring into a dock. **2** (of a spacecraft) join with a space station or another spacecraft in space. **3** attach (a piece of equipment) to another.
– ORIGIN Dutch or Low German *docke*.

dock² ● noun the enclosure in a criminal court where a defendant stands or sits.
– ORIGIN probably related to Flemish *dok* 'chicken coop, rabbit hutch'.

dock³ ● noun a weed with broad leaves, popularly used to relieve nettle stings.
– ORIGIN Old English.

dock⁴ ● verb **1** deduct (money or a point in a score). **2** cut short (an animal's tail).
– ORIGIN originally in the sense 'the solid part of an animal's tail': perhaps related to a Frisian word meaning 'bunch, ball (of string)' and German *Docke* 'doll'.

docker ● noun a person employed in a port to load and unload ships.

docket ● noun Brit. a document accompanying a consignment of goods that lists its contents, certifies payment of duty, or entitles the holder to delivery. ● verb (**docketed**, **docketing**) mark (a consignment or package) with a docket.
– ORIGIN originally referring to a short abstract or summary: perhaps from DOCK⁴.

docking station ● noun a device to which a portable computer is connected so that it can be used like a desktop computer.

dockland ● noun (also **docklands**) the area containing a city's docks.

Thesaurus

NESS, causing giddiness, vertiginous. **3** *(informal) a dizzy blond.* See EMPTY-HEADED.

do ● verb **1** *she does most of the manual work* CARRY OUT, undertake, discharge, execute, perform, accomplish, achieve; bring about, engineer; *informal* pull off; *formal* effectuate. **2** *they can do as they please* ACT, behave, conduct oneself, acquit oneself; *formal* comport oneself. **3** *regular coffee will do* SUFFICE, be adequate, be satisfactory, fill/fit the bill, serve one's purpose, meet one's needs. **4** *the boys will do the dinner* PREPARE, make, get ready, see to, arrange, organize, be responsible for, be in charge of; *informal* fix. **5** *the company are doing a new range | a portrait I am doing* MAKE, create, produce, turn out, design, manufacture; paint, draw, sketch; *informal* knock up/off. **6** *each room was done in a different colour* DECORATE, furnish, ornament, deck out, trick out; *informal* do up. **7** *her maid did her hair* STYLE, arrange, adjust; brush, comb, wash, dry, cut; *informal* fix. **8** *I am doing a show to raise money* PUT ON, present, produce; perform in, act in, take part in, participate in. **9** *you've done me a favour* GRANT, pay, render, give. **10** *show me how to do these equations* WORK OUT, figure out, calculate; solve, resolve. **11** *she's doing archaeology* STUDY, read, learn, take a course in. **12** *what does he do?* HAVE AS A JOB, have as a profession, be employed at, earn a living at. **13** *he is doing well at college* GET ON/ALONG, progress, fare, manage, cope; succeed, prosper. **14** *he was doing 80mph* DRIVE AT, travel at, move at. **15** *the cyclists do 30 miles per day* TRAVEL (OVER), journey, cover, traverse, achieve, notch up, log; *informal* chalk up. **16** *(informal) we're doing Scotland this summer* VISIT, tour, sightsee in.
● noun *(Brit. informal) he invited us to a grand do* PARTY, reception, gathering, celebration, function, social event/occasion, social, soirée; *informal* bash, shindig; *Brit. informal* knees-up, beanfeast, bunfight; *Austral./NZ informal* rage, jollo.
– PHRASES **do away with 1** *they want to do away with the old customs* ABOLISH, get rid of, discard, remove, eliminate, discontinue, stop, end, terminate, put an end/stop to, dispense with, drop, abandon, give up; *informal* scrap, ditch, dump. **2** *(informal) she tried to do away with her husband.* See KILL verb sense 1. **do someone/something down** *(informal)* BELITTLE, disparage, denigrate, run down, deprecate, cast aspersions on, discredit, vilify, defame, criticize, malign; *N. Amer.* slur; *informal* have a go at, hit out at, knock, slam, pan, bad-mouth; *Brit. informal* rubbish, slag off. **do someone/something in** *(informal)* **1** *the poor devil's been done in.* See KILL verb sense 1. **2** *the long walk home did me in* WEAR OUT, tire out, exhaust, fatigue, weary, overtire, drain; *informal* shatter, take it out of; *Brit. informal* knacker. **3** *I did my back in* INJURE, hurt, damage. **do something out** *(Brit. informal)* DECORATE, furnish, ornament, deck out, trick out; *informal* do up. **do someone out of something** *(informal)* SWINDLE OUT OF, cheat out of, trick out of, deprive of; *informal* con out of, diddle out of. **do something up 1** *she did her bootlace up* FASTEN, tie (up), lace, knot; make fast, secure. **2** *(informal) he's had his house done up* RENOVATE, refurbish, refit, redecorate, decorate, revamp, make over, modernize, improve, spruce up, smarten up; *informal* give something a facelift; *N. Amer. informal* rehab. **do without** FORGO, dispense with, abstain from, refrain from, eschew, give up, cut out, renounce, manage without; *formal* forswear.

docile ● adjective COMPLIANT, obedient, pliant, dutiful, submissive, deferential, unassertive, cooperative, amenable, accommodating, biddable, malleable.
– OPPOSITES disobedient, wilful.

dock¹ ● noun *his boat was moored at the dock* HARBOUR, marina, port, anchorage; wharf, quay, pier, jetty, landing stage.
● verb *the ship docked* MOOR, berth, put in, tie up, anchor.

dock² ● verb **1** *they docked the money from his salary* DEDUCT, subtract, remove, debit, take off/away; *informal* knock off. **2** *workers had their pay docked* REDUCE, cut, decrease. **3** *the dog's tail was docked* CUT OFF, cut short, shorten, crop, lop; remove, amputate, detach, sever, chop off, take off.

docket *(Brit.)* ● noun *a docket for every transaction* DOCUMENT, chit, coupon, voucher, certificate, counterfoil, bill, receipt; *Brit. informal* chitty.

dockyard ● noun an area with docks and equipment for repairing and maintaining ships.

doctor ● noun **1** a person who is qualified to practise medicine. **2** (**Doctor**) a person who holds the highest university degree. **3** Austral./NZ informal a cook on board a ship or in a camp or station. ● verb **1** change in order to deceive; falsify. **2** adulterate (a food or drink) with a harmful or potent ingredient. **3** Brit. remove the sexual organs of (an animal) so that it cannot reproduce.
– PHRASES **go for the doctor** Austral./NZ informal make an all-out effort. **what the doctor ordered** informal something beneficial or desirable.
– ORIGIN Latin, 'teacher'.

doctoral ● adjective relating to a doctorate.

doctorate ● noun the highest degree awarded by a university faculty.

Doctor of Philosophy ● noun a person holding a doctorate in any subject except law, medicine, or sometimes theology.

doctrinaire /doktrinair/ ● adjective seeking to impose a doctrine without compromise.
– ORIGIN French.

doctrine /**dok**trin/ ● noun a set of beliefs or principles held and taught by a Church, political party, or other group.
– DERIVATIVES **doctrinal** /**dok**trin'l, doktrīn'l/ adjective **doctrinally** adverb.
– ORIGIN Latin *doctrina* 'teaching, learning'.

docudrama ● noun a dramatized film based on real events and incorporating documentary features.

document ● noun /**dok**yoomənt/ a piece of written, printed, or electronic matter that provides information or evidence. ● verb /**dok**yooment/ record in written or other form.
– ORIGIN Latin *documentum* 'lesson, proof', from *docere* 'teach'.

documentary ● adjective **1** consisting of documents and other material providing a factual account. **2** using film, photographs, and sound recordings of real events. ● noun (pl. **documentaries**) a documentary film or television or radio programme.

documentation ● noun **1** the documents required in the provision of information or evidence. **2** written specifications or instructions.

docusoap ● noun a documentary following people in a particular occupation or location over a period of time.

DOD ● abbreviation (in the US) Department of Defense.

dodder[1] ● verb be slow and unsteady.
– DERIVATIVES **dodderer** noun **doddering** adjective **doddery** adjective.
– ORIGIN variant of obsolete dialect *dadder*; related to DITHER.

dodder[2] ● noun a parasitic climbing plant with leafless stems that are attached to the host plant by means of suckers.
– ORIGIN related to Low German *doder*, *dodder*, High German *toter*.

doddle ● noun Brit. informal a very easy task.
– ORIGIN of unknown origin.

dodecagon /dōdekkəgən/ ● noun a plane figure with twelve straight sides and angles.

dodecahedron /dōdekkəheedrən/ ● noun (pl. **dodecahedra** /dōdekkəheedrə/ or **dodecahedrons**) a three-dimensional shape having twelve plane faces.
– ORIGIN Greek *dōdekaedron*, from *dōdekaedros* 'twelve-faced'.

dodge ● verb **1** avoid by a sudden quick movement. **2** cunningly avoid doing or paying. ● noun **1** an act or instance of dodging. **2** informal a cunning trick, especially one used to avoid something.
– ORIGIN of unknown origin.

dodgem ● noun a small electrically powered car with rubber bumpers, driven within an enclosure at a funfair with the aim of bumping other such cars.
– ORIGIN US proprietary name (as *Dodg'em*), from *dodge them*.

dodger ● noun informal a person who evades something that is required of them: *a tax dodger*.

dodgy ● adjective (**dodgier**, **dodgiest**) Brit. informal **1** dishonest. **2** risky. **3** not good or reliable.

dodo /dōdō/ ● noun (pl. **dodos** or **dodoes**) a large extinct flightless bird found on Mauritius until the end of the 17th century.
– PHRASES **as dead as a dodo** utterly dead or finished.
– ORIGIN Portuguese *doudo* 'simpleton' (because the birds were tame and easy to catch).

DoE ● abbreviation (in the UK) Department of the Environment.

doe ● noun **1** a female roe or fallow deer or reindeer. **2** a female hare, rabbit, rat, ferret, or kangaroo.
– ORIGIN Old English.

doe-eyed ● adjective having large gentle dark eyes.

does third person singular present of DO[1].

doesn't ● contraction does not.

doff ● verb remove (an item of clothing, especially a hat).
– ORIGIN contraction of *do off*.

dog ● noun **1** a domesticated carnivorous mammal with a barking or howling voice and an acute sense of smell. **2** a wild animal resembling this, in particular any member of the dog family (Canidae), which includes the wolf, fox, coyote, jackal, and other species. **3** the male of such an animal. **4** (**the dogs**) Brit. informal greyhound racing. **5** informal, derogatory an unattractive woman. **6** informal a contemptible man. **7** informal, dated a person of a specified kind: *you lucky dog!* ● verb (**dogged**, **dogging**) **1** follow closely and persistently. **2** (of a problem) cause continual trouble for.
– PHRASES **a dog in the manger** a person who prevents others from having things that they do not need themselves. [ORIGIN alluding to the fable of the dog that lay in a manger to prevent the ox and horse from eating the hay.] **a dog's dinner** (or **breakfast**) Brit. informal a mess. **every dog has his** (or **its**) **day** proverb everyone will have good luck or success at some point in

d

Thesaurus

● verb *docket the package* DOCUMENT, record, register; label, tag, tab, mark.

doctor ● noun *Tim went to see a doctor* PHYSICIAN, medical practitioner, clinician; general practitioner, GP, consultant, registrar, medical officer, MO; *Brit.* house officer, houseman; *N. Amer.* intern, extern; *informal* doc, medic, medico; *Brit. informal* quack.
● verb **1** *(informal) he doctored their wounds* TREAT, medicate, cure, heal; tend, attend to, minister to, care for, nurse. **2** *he doctored Stephen's drinks* ADULTERATE, contaminate, tamper with, lace; *informal* spike, dope. **3** *the reports have been doctored* FALSIFY, tamper with, interfere with, alter, change; forge, fake; *informal* cook; *Brit. informal* fiddle (with).

doctrinaire ● adjective DOGMATIC, rigid, inflexible, uncompromising; authoritarian, intolerant, fanatical, zealous, extreme.

doctrine ● noun CREED, credo, dogma, belief, teaching, ideology; tenet, maxim, canon, principle, precept.

document ● noun *their solicitor drew up a document* (OFFICIAL/LEGAL) PAPER, certificate, deed, contract, legal agreement; *Law* instrument, indenture.
● verb *many aspects of school life have been documented* RECORD, register, report, log, chronicle, archive, put on record, write down; detail, note, describe.

documentary ● adjective **1** *a film based on documentary evidence* RECORDED, documented, registered, written, chronicled, archived, on record/paper, in writing. **2** *a documentary film* FACTUAL, non-fictional.
● noun *a documentary about rural England* FACTUAL FILM/PROGRAMME; programme, film, broadcast.

dodder ● verb TOTTER, teeter, toddle, hobble, shuffle, shamble, falter.

doddery ● adjective TOTTERING, tottery, staggering, shuffling, shambling, faltering, shaky, unsteady, wobbly; feeble, frail, weak.

dodge ● verb **1** *she dodged into a telephone booth* DART, bolt, dive, lunge, leap, spring. **2** *he could easily dodge the two coppers* ELUDE, evade, avoid, escape, run away from, lose, shake (off); *informal* give someone the slip. **3** *the minister tried to dodge the debate* AVOID, evade, get out of, back out of, sidestep; *N. Amer.* end-run; *informal* duck, wriggle out of; *Austral./NZ informal* duck-shove.
● noun **1** *a dodge to the right* DART, bolt, dive, lunge, leap, spring. **2** *a clever dodge | a tax dodge* RUSE, ploy, scheme, tactic, stratagem, subterfuge, trick, hoax, wile, cheat, deception, blind; swindle, fraud; *informal* scam, con (trick); *Brit. informal* wheeze; *N. Amer. informal* bunco, grift; *Austral. informal* lurk, rort.

dodgy ● adjective *(Brit. informal)* **1** *a dodgy second-hand car salesman.* See DISHONEST. **2** *the champagne was dodgy* SECOND-RATE, third-rate, substandard, low-quality; awful, terrible, dreadful, dire; *N. Amer.* cheapjack; *informal* not up to much, woeful; *Brit. informal* ropy, grotty.

doer ● noun **1** *the doer of unspeakable deeds* PERFORMER, perpetrator, executor, accomplisher, agent. **2** *Daniel is a thinker more than a doer* WORKER, organizer, man/woman of action; *informal* mover and shaker, busy bee.

doff ● verb TAKE OFF, remove, strip off, pull off; raise, lift, tip; *dated*

their lives. **go to the dogs** informal deteriorate badly. **you can't teach an old dog new tricks** proverb you cannot make people change their ways. **why keep a dog and bark yourself?** proverb why pay someone to work for you and then do the work yourself?
– DERIVATIVES **dogdom** noun **doggish** adjective.
– ORIGIN Old English.
dog cart • noun a two-wheeled cart for driving in, with cross seats back to back.
dog collar • noun **1** a collar for a dog. **2** informal a clerical collar.

d

dog days • plural noun chiefly literary the hottest period of the year (reckoned in antiquity from the heliacal rising of Sirius, the Dog Star).
doge /dōj/ • noun historical the chief magistrate of Venice or Genoa.
– ORIGIN Italian *doze*, from Latin *dux* 'leader'.
dog-eared • adjective having worn or battered corners.
dog-end • noun informal **1** a cigarette end. **2** the last and least pleasing part of something.
dogfight • noun **1** a close combat between military aircraft. **2** a ferocious struggle or fight.
– DERIVATIVES **dogfighting** noun.
dogfish • noun a small bottom-dwelling shark with a long tail.
dogged /doggid/ • adjective very persistent.
– DERIVATIVES **doggedly** adverb **doggedness** noun.
doggerel /doggərəl/ • noun **1** comic verse composed in irregular rhythm. **2** badly written verse.
– ORIGIN apparently from DOG (used contemptuously).
doggie • noun variant spelling of DOGGY.
doggo • adverb (in phrase **lie doggo**) Brit. informal, dated remain motionless and quiet to escape detection.
– ORIGIN origin uncertain.
doggone /doggon/ N. Amer. informal • adjective damned. • verb damn (used to express surprise or irritation).
– ORIGIN probably from *dog on it*, euphemism for *God damn it*.
doggy • adjective **1** of or like a dog. **2** fond of dogs.
doggy bag • noun a bag used to take home leftover food from a restaurant, supposedly for one's dog.
doggy-paddle • noun an elementary swimming stroke resembling that of a dog.
doghouse • noun N. Amer. a dog's kennel.
– PHRASES **in the doghouse** informal in disgrace or disfavour.
dog-leg • noun a sharp bend.
dogma • noun an inflexible principle or set of principles laid down by an authority.
– ORIGIN Greek, 'opinion', from *dokein* 'seem good, think'.
dogmatic • adjective inclined to impose dogma; firmly asserting personal opinions as true.
– DERIVATIVES **dogmatically** adverb **dogmatism** noun **dogmatist** noun.
do-gooder • noun a well-meaning but unrealistic or interfering person.
dog rose • noun a delicately scented wild rose with pink or white flowers.
dogsbody • noun (pl. **dogsbodies**) Brit. informal a person who is given boring, menial tasks.
Dog Star • noun Sirius, the brightest star in the sky.
– ORIGIN so named as it appears to follow at the heels of Orion (the hunter).
dog-tired • adjective extremely tired.
dog-tooth • noun **1** Architecture a small pointed moulding forming one of a series radiating from a raised centre. **2** (also **dogstooth**) a small check pattern with notched corners.
dogwatch • noun either of two short watches on a ship (4–6 or 6–8 p.m.).
dogwood • noun a flowering shrub or small tree with red stems, colourful berries, and hard wood.
– ORIGIN so named because the wood was formerly used to make 'dogs' (i.e. skewers).
DoH • abbreviation (in the UK) Department of Health.
doh /dō/ (also **do**) • noun Music the first note of a major scale, coming before 'ray'.
– ORIGIN Italian *do*, an arbitrarily chosen syllable.
doily • noun (pl. **doilies**) a small ornamental mat made of lace or paper.
– ORIGIN from *Doiley* or *Doyley*, a 17th-century London draper.
doing • noun **1** (also **doings**) the activities in which someone engages. **2** (treated as sing. or pl.) informal, chiefly Brit. things whose name one has forgotten. **3** (**doings**) informal excrement.
do-it-yourself • noun full form of DIY.
dojo /dōjō/ • noun (pl. **dojos**) a place in which judo and other martial arts are practised.
– ORIGIN from the Japanese words for 'way, pursuit' and 'a place'.
Dolby /dolbi/ • noun trademark **1** a noise-reduction system used in tape recording. **2** an electronic system providing stereophonic sound for cinemas and televisions.
– ORIGIN named after the American engineer Ray M. *Dolby* (born 1933).
dolce far niente /dolchay faar nientay/ • noun pleasant idleness.
– ORIGIN Italian, 'sweet doing nothing'.
Dolcelatte /dolchəlaatay/ • noun trademark a kind of soft creamy blue-veined cheese from Italy.
– ORIGIN Italian, 'sweet milk'.
dolce vita /dolchay veetə/ • noun a life of pleasure and luxury.
– ORIGIN Italian 'sweet life'.
doldrums /doldrəmz/ • plural noun (**the doldrums**) **1** a state of stagnation or depression. **2** a region of the Atlantic Ocean with calms, sudden storms, and light unpredictable winds.
– ORIGIN perhaps from DULL.
dole • noun (often in phrase **on the dole**) Brit. informal benefit paid by the state to the unemployed. • verb (**dole out**) distribute.
– ORIGIN Old English, 'division, portion, or share'; related to DEAL[1].
doleful • adjective **1** sorrowful. **2** causing grief or misfortune.
– DERIVATIVES **dolefully** adverb.
– ORIGIN from Old French *doel* 'mourning', from Latin *dolere* 'grieve'.

Thesaurus

divest oneself of.
– OPPOSITES don.
dog • noun **1** *she went for a walk with her dog* HOUND, canine, mongrel; pup, puppy; *informal* doggy, pooch; *Austral. informal* bitzer. **2** *(informal) you black-hearted dog!* See SCOUNDREL. **3** *(informal, dated) you're a lucky dog!* See FELLOW sense 1.
• verb **1** *they dogged him the length of the country* PURSUE, follow, track, trail, shadow, hound; *informal* tail. **2** *the scheme was dogged by bad weather* PLAGUE, beset, bedevil, beleaguer, blight, trouble.
dogged • adjective TENACIOUS, determined, resolute, resolved, purposeful, persistent, persevering, single-minded, tireless; strong-willed, steadfast, staunch; *formal* pertinacious.
– OPPOSITES half-hearted.
dogma • noun TEACHING, belief, tenet, principle, precept, maxim, article of faith, canon; creed, credo, set of beliefs, doctrine, ideology.
dogmatic • adjective OPINIONATED, peremptory, assertive, insistent, emphatic, adamant, doctrinaire, authoritarian, imperious, dictatorial, uncompromising, unyielding, inflexible, rigid.
dogsbody • noun *(Brit. informal)* DRUDGE, menial (worker), factotum, servant, slave, lackey, minion, man/girl Friday; *informal* gofer; *Brit. informal* skivvy; *N. Amer. informal* peon; *archaic* scullion.
doing • noun **1** *the doing of the act constitutes the offence* PERFORMANCE, performing, carrying out, execution, implementation, implementing, achievement, accomplishment, realization, completion; *formal* effectuation. **2** *an account of his doings in Paris* EXPLOIT, activity, act, action, deed, feat, achievement, accomplishment; *informal* caper. **3** *that would take some doing* EFFORT, exertion, (hard) work, application, labour, toil, struggle. **4** *(Brit. informal) the drawer where he kept the doings* THING, so-and so; *informal* whatsit, whatnot, doodah, thingummy, thingamajig, thingamabob, what's-its-name, what-d'you-call-it, oojamaflip, oojah; *Brit. informal* gubbins; *N. Amer. informal* doohickey, doojigger, dingus.
doldrums • plural noun *winter doldrums* DEPRESSION, melancholy, gloom, gloominess, downheartedness, dejection, despondency, low spirits, despair; inertia, apathy, listlessness; *N. Amer.* blahs; *informal* blues.
– PHRASES **in the doldrums** INACTIVE, quiet, slow, slack, sluggish, stagnant.
dole • noun **1** *(dated) the customary dole was a tumblerful of rice* HANDOUT, charity; gift, donation; *historical* alms. **2** *(Brit. informal) he was on the dole* (UNEMPLOYMENT/STATE) BENEFIT, benefit payments, social security, welfare.
– PHRASES **dole something out** DEAL OUT, share out, divide up, allocate, allot, distribute, dispense, hand out, give out, dish out/up; *informal* divvy up.

dolerite /dollərīt/ ● **noun** Geology a dark igneous rock typically occurring in dykes and sills.
– ORIGIN from Greek *doleros* 'deceptive' (because it resembles diorite).

doll ● **noun 1** a small model of a human figure, used as a child's toy. **2** informal an attractive young woman. ● **verb** (**doll up**) informal dress (someone) smartly and attractively.
– ORIGIN from the given name *Dorothy*.

dollar ● **noun** the basic monetary unit of the US, Canada, Australia, and certain countries in the Pacific, Caribbean, SE Asia, Africa, and South America.
– ORIGIN German *Thaler*, short for *Joachimsthaler*, a coin from the silver-mine of *Joachimsthal* ('Joachim's valley'), now *Jáchymov* in the Czech Republic.

dollar sign (also **dollar mark**) ● **noun** the sign $, representing a dollar.

dollop informal ● **noun** a shapeless mass or lump, especially of soft food. ● **verb** (**dolloped**, **dolloping**) add or serve out in large shapeless quantities.
– ORIGIN perhaps Scandinavian.

doll's house (N. Amer. also **dollhouse**) ● **noun** a miniature toy house for dolls.

dolly ● **noun** (pl. **dollies**) **1** informal, dated an attractive young woman. **2** a small platform on wheels for holding heavy objects, typically film cameras.

dolly bird ● **noun** Brit. informal, dated an attractive and fashionable young woman.

dolma /dolmə/ ● **noun** (pl. **dolmas** or **dolmades** /dolmaadez/) a Greek and Turkish dish of spiced rice and meat wrapped in vine or cabbage leaves.
– ORIGIN Turkish, from *dolmak* 'fill, be filled'.

dolman sleeve /dolmən/ ● **noun** a loose sleeve cut in one piece with the body of a garment.
– ORIGIN *dolman* from Turkish *dolama, dolaman* 'open robe'.

dolmen /dolmen/ ● **noun** a megalithic tomb with a large flat stone laid on upright ones.
– ORIGIN Cornish, 'hole of a stone'.

dolomite /dolləmīt/ ● **noun** a mineral or sedimentary rock consisting chiefly of a carbonate of calcium and magnesium.
– DERIVATIVES **dolomitic** adjective.
– ORIGIN named after the French geologist *Dolomieu* (1750–1801).

dolorous /dollərəss/ ● **adjective** literary feeling great sorrow or distress.
– DERIVATIVES **dolorously** adverb.

dolour /dollər/ (US **dolor**) ● **noun** literary a state of great sorrow or distress.
– ORIGIN Latin *dolor* 'pain, grief'.

dolphin ● **noun** a small gregarious toothed whale with a beak-like snout and a curved fin on the back.
– ORIGIN Old French *dauphin*, from Greek *delphin*.

dolphinarium /dolfinairiəm/ ● **noun** (pl. **dolphinariums** or **dolphinaria**) an aquarium in which dolphins are kept and trained for public entertainment.

dolt /dōlt/ ● **noun** a stupid person.
– DERIVATIVES **doltish** adjective.
– ORIGIN perhaps a variant of *dulled*, from DULL.

Dom /dom/ ● **noun** a title prefixed to the names of some Roman Catholic dignitaries and Benedictine and Carthusian monks.
– ORIGIN from Latin *dominus* 'master'.

-dom ● **suffix** forming nouns: **1** denoting a state or condition: *freedom*. **2** denoting status: *earldom*. **3** denoting a domain. **4** denoting a class of people: *officialdom*.
– ORIGIN Old English, 'decree, judgement'.

domain /dəmayn/ ● **noun 1** an area controlled by a ruler or government. **2** a sphere of activity or knowledge. **3** Computing a distinct subset of the Internet with addresses sharing a common suffix.
– ORIGIN French *domaine*, from Old French *demeine* 'belonging to a lord' (see DEMESNE).

dome ● **noun 1** a rounded vault forming the roof of a building, typically with a circular base. **2** a sports stadium or other building with a domed roof. **3** informal the top of the head.
– DERIVATIVES **domed** adjective **domical** adjective.
– ORIGIN Italian *duomo* 'cathedral, dome', from Latin *domus* 'house'.

domestic ● **adjective 1** relating to a home or family affairs or relations. **2** of or for use in the home. **3** fond of family life and running a home. **4** (of an animal) tame and kept by humans. **5** existing or occurring within a country; not foreign. ● **noun 1** (also **domestic worker** or **domestic help**) a person employed to do domestic tasks. **2** informal a violent quarrel between family members.
– DERIVATIVES **domestically** adverb.
– ORIGIN Latin *domesticus*, from *domus* 'house'.

domesticate ● **verb 1** tame (an animal) and keep it as a pet or for farm produce. **2** cultivate (a plant) for food.
– DERIVATIVES **domestication** noun.

domesticity ● **noun** home or family life.

domestic science ● **noun** dated home economics.

domicile /dommisil, -sil/ ● **noun** formal or Law **1** the country in which a person has permanent residence. **2** chiefly N. Amer. a person's home. ● **verb** (**be domiciled**) formal or Law **1** treat a specified country as a permanent home. **2** chiefly N. Amer. reside; be based.
– ORIGIN Latin *domicilium* 'dwelling', from *domus* 'home'.

domiciliary /dommisilliəri/ ● **adjective** concerned with or occurring in someone's home.

dominance ● **noun 1** power and influence over others. **2** Genetics the property of being dominant.

dominant ● **adjective 1** most important, powerful, or influential. **2** (of a high place or object) overlooking others. **3** Genetics (of a heritable characteristic) controlled by a gene that is expressed in offspring even when inherited from only one parent. Compare with RECESSIVE. ● **noun** Genetics a dominant trait or gene.
– DERIVATIVES **dominantly** adverb.

dominate ● **verb 1** have a commanding or controlling influence over. **2** (of something tall or high) overlook.

Thesaurus

doleful ● **adjective** MOURNFUL, woeful, sorrowful, sad, unhappy, depressed, gloomy, morose, melancholy, miserable, forlorn, wretched, woebegone, despondent, dejected, disconsolate, downcast, crestfallen, downhearted; *informal* blue, down in the mouth/dumps; *poetic/literary* dolorous, heartsick.

doll ● **noun 1** *the child was hugging a doll* FIGURE, figurine, model; toy, plaything; *informal* dolly. **2** *(informal) she was quite a doll.* See BEAUTY sense 2.
– PHRASES **doll oneself up** *(informal)* DRESS UP; *informal* get/do oneself up, dress up to the nines, put on one's glad rags; *Brit. informal* tart oneself up.

dollop ● **noun** *(informal)* BLOB, gobbet, lump, ball; *informal* glob; *Brit. informal* gob, wodge.

dolorous ● **adjective** *(poetic/literary)*. See DOLEFUL.

dolour ● **noun** *(poetic/literary)*. See MISERY sense 1.

dolt ● **noun.** See IDIOT.

doltish ● **adjective.** See STUPID sense 1.

domain ● **noun 1** *they extended their domain* REALM, kingdom, empire, dominion, province, territory, land. **2** *the domain of art* FIELD, area, sphere, discipline, province, world.

dome ● **noun** CUPOLA, vault, arched roof.

domestic ● **adjective 1** *domestic commitments* FAMILY, home, household. **2** *she was not at all domestic* HOUSEWIFELY, domesticated, homely. **3** *small domestic animals* DOMESTICATED, tame, pet, household. **4** *the domestic car industry* NATIONAL, state, home, internal. **5** *domestic plants* NATIVE, indigenous.
● **noun** *the cleaning was undertaken by domestics* SERVANT, domestic worker/help, home help, maid, housemaid, cleaner, housekeeper; *Brit. dated* charwoman, charlady, char; *Brit. informal* daily (help).

domesticated ● **adjective 1** *domesticated animals* TAME, tamed, pet, domestic, trained. **2** *domesticated crops* CULTIVATED, naturalized. **3** *I'm quite domesticated really* HOUSEWIFELY, home-loving, homely.
– OPPOSITES wild.

domicile *(formal)* ● **noun** *changes of domicile* RESIDENCE, home, house, address, residency, lodging, accommodation; *informal* digs; *formal* dwelling (place), abode, habitation.
● **verb** *he is now domiciled in Australia* SETTLE, live, make one's home, take up residence; move to, emigrate to.

dominance ● **noun** SUPREMACY, superiority, ascendancy, preeminence, predominance, domination, dominion, mastery, power, authority, rule, command, control, sway; *poetic/literary* puissance.

dominant ● **adjective 1** *the dominant classes* PRESIDING, ruling, governing, controlling, commanding, ascendant, supreme, authoritative. **2** *he has a dominant personality* ASSERTIVE, authoritative, forceful, domineering, commanding, controlling, pushy; *dated* pushful. **3** *the dominant issues in psychology* MAIN, principal,

– DERIVATIVES **domination** noun **dominator** noun.
– ORIGIN Latin *dominari* 'rule, govern', from *dominus* 'lord, master'.

dominatrix /domminaytriks/ ● noun (pl. **dominatrices** /domminaytriseez/ or **dominatrixes**) a dominating woman, especially in sadomasochistic practices.
– ORIGIN Latin.

domineering ● adjective arrogant and overbearing.
– ORIGIN from Dutch *dominieren*, from Latin *dominari* 'rule, govern'.

d

Dominican[1] /dəminnikən/ ● noun a member of the order of preaching friars founded by St Dominic, or of a similar religious order for women. ● adjective relating to St Dominic or the Dominicans.

Dominican[2] /dəminnikən/ ● noun a person from the Dominican Republic in the Caribbean. ● adjective relating to the Dominican Republic.

Dominican[3] /dommineekən, dəminnikən/ ● noun a person from the Caribbean island of Dominica. ● adjective relating to the island of Dominica.

dominion ● noun **1** sovereignty; control. **2** the territory of a sovereign or government. **3** (**Dominion**) historical a self-governing territory of the British Commonwealth.
– ORIGIN Latin *dominium*, from *dominus* 'lord, master'.

domino ● noun (pl. **dominoes**) **1** any of 28 small oblong pieces marked with 0–6 pips in each half. **2** (**dominoes**) (treated as sing.) the game played with such pieces.
– ORIGIN probably from Latin *dominus* 'lord, master'.

domino effect ● noun the hypothetical influence of political events in one country upon its neighbours.

don[1] ● noun **1** a university teacher, especially a senior member of a college at Oxford or Cambridge. **2** (**Don**) a Spanish title prefixed to a male forename. **3** N. Amer. informal a high-ranking member of the Mafia.
– ORIGIN Spanish, from Latin *dominus* 'lord, master'.

don[2] ● verb (**donned**, **donning**) put on (an item of clothing).
– ORIGIN contraction of *do on*.

donate ● verb **1** give (money or goods) to a good cause. **2** allow the removal of (blood or an organ) from one's body for transfusion or transplantation.
– DERIVATIVES **donator** noun.

donation ● noun something that is given to a charity.
– ORIGIN Latin, from *donare* 'give'.

done past participle of DO[1]. ● adjective **1** (of food) cooked thoroughly. **2** no longer happening or existing. **3** informal socially acceptable: *the done thing*. ● exclamation (in response to an offer) accepted.
– PHRASES **done for** informal in serious trouble. **done in** informal extremely tired.

donee /dōnee/ ● noun a person who receives a gift.

doner kebab /donnə, dōnə/ ● noun a Turkish dish consisting of spiced lamb cooked on a spit and served in slices.
– ORIGIN from Turkish *döner* 'rotating' and *kebap* 'roast meat'.

dong[1] ● verb (of a bell) make a deep resonant sound. ● noun a deep resonant sound.

dong[2] ● noun the basic monetary unit of Vietnam, equal to 100 xu.
– ORIGIN Vietnamese, 'coin'.

donga /donggə/ ● noun **1** S. African a dry watercourse. **2** Austral. a makeshift shelter.
– ORIGIN from Xhosa and Zulu.

dongle /dongg'l/ ● noun Computing an electronic device which must be attached to a computer in order for protected software to be used.
– ORIGIN an arbitrary formation.

donjon /donjən, dun-/ ● noun **1** the great tower or innermost keep of a castle. **2** archaic a dungeon.
– ORIGIN from DUNGEON.

Don Juan /don jōōən, waan/ ● noun a seducer of women.
– ORIGIN from the name of a legendary Spanish nobleman.

donkey ● noun (pl. **donkeys**) **1** a domesticated hoofed mammal of the horse family with long ears and a braying call. **2** informal a foolish person.
– PHRASES **donkey's years** informal a very long time. **talk the hind leg off a donkey** Brit. informal talk incessantly.
– ORIGIN perhaps from DUN[1], or from the given name *Duncan*.

donkey engine ● noun a small auxiliary engine.

donkey jacket ● noun Brit. a heavy jacket with a patch of waterproof material across the shoulders.

donkey work ● noun informal the laborious part of a job.

donna /donnə/ ● noun **1** an Italian, Spanish, or Portuguese lady. **2** (**Donna**) a courtesy title prefixed to the forename of such a lady.
– ORIGIN Latin *domina* 'mistress'.

donnish ● adjective resembling a college don, particularly in having a pedantic manner.

donor ● noun **1** a person who donates. **2** a substance, molecule, etc. which provides electrons for a physical or chemical process.
– ORIGIN Old French *doneur*, from Latin *donare* 'give'.

donor card ● noun a card consenting to the use of one's organs for transplant surgery in the event of one's death.

Thesaurus

prime, premier, chief, foremost, primary, predominant, paramount, prominent; central, key, crucial, core; *informal* number-one.
– OPPOSITES subservient.

dominate ● verb **1** *the Russians dominated Iran in the nineteenth century* CONTROL, influence, exercise control over, command, be in command of, be in charge of, rule, govern, direct, have ascendancy over, have mastery over; *informal* head up, be in the driver's seat, be at the helm, rule the roost; *Brit. informal* wear the trousers; *N. Amer. informal* have someone in one's hip pocket; *poetic/literary* sway. **2** *the Puritan work ethic still dominates* PREDOMINATE, prevail, reign, be prevalent, be paramount, be pre-eminent. **3** *the village is dominated by the viaduct* OVERLOOK, command, tower above/over, loom over.

domination ● noun RULE, government, sovereignty, control, command, authority, power, dominion, dominance, mastery, supremacy, superiority, ascendancy, sway.

domineer ● verb BROWBEAT, bully, intimidate, push around/about, order about/around, lord it over; dictate to, be overbearing, have under one's thumb, rule with a rod of iron; *informal* boss about/around, walk all over.

domineering ● adjective OVERBEARING, authoritarian, imperious, high-handed, autocratic; masterful, dictatorial, despotic, oppressive, iron-fisted, strict, harsh; *informal* bossy.

dominion ● noun **1** *France had dominion over Laos* SUPREMACY, ascendancy, dominance, domination, superiority, predominance, pre-eminence, hegemony, authority, mastery, control, command, power, sway, rule, government, jurisdiction, sovereignty, suzerainty. **2** *a British dominion* DEPENDENCY, colony, protectorate, territory, province, possession; *historical* tributary.

don[1] ● noun *an Oxford don* UNIVERSITY TEACHER, (university) lecturer, fellow, professor, reader, academic, scholar.

don[2] ● verb *he donned an overcoat* PUT ON, get dressed in, dress (oneself) in, get into, slip into/on.

donate ● verb GIVE, give/make a donation of, contribute, make a contribution of, gift, subscribe, grant, bestow; *informal* chip in, pitch in; *Brit. informal* stump up; *N. Amer. informal* kick in.

donation ● noun GIFT, contribution, subscription, present, handout, grant, offering; charity; *formal* benefaction; *historical* alms.

done ● adjective **1** *the job is done* FINISHED, ended, concluded, complete, completed, accomplished, achieved, fulfilled, discharged, executed; *informal* wrapped up, sewn up, polished off. **2** *is the meat done?* COOKED (THROUGH), ready. **3** *those days are done* OVER (AND DONE WITH), at an end, finished, ended, concluded, terminated, no more, dead, gone, in the past. **4** *(informal) that's just not done* PROPER, seemly, decent, respectable, right, correct, in order, fitting, appropriate, acceptable, the done thing.
– OPPOSITES incomplete, underdone, ongoing.
● exclamation *Done!* AGREED, all right, very well; *informal* you're on, OK, okey-dokey; *Brit. informal* righto, righty-ho.
– PHRASES **be/have done with** BE/HAVE FINISHED WITH, be through with, want no more to do with. **done for** *(informal)* RUINED, finished, destroyed, undone, doomed, lost; *informal* washed-up. **done in** *(informal)*. See EXHAUSTED sense 1.

Don Juan ● noun WOMANIZER, philanderer, Casanova, Lothario, flirt, ladies' man, playboy, seducer, rake, roué, libertine; *informal* skirt-chaser, ladykiller, wolf.

donkey ● noun **1** *the cart was drawn by a donkey* ASS, jackass, jenny; mule, hinny; *Brit. informal* moke. **2** *(informal) you silly donkey!* See FOOL noun sense 1.
– RELATED TERMS asinine.

donnish ● adjective SCHOLARLY, studious, academic, bookish, intellectual, learned, highbrow; *informal* egghead; *dated* lettered.

don't ● contraction do not.
donut ● noun US spelling of DOUGHNUT.
doodah /do͞odaa/ (N. Amer. **doodad** /do͞odad/) ● noun informal an object that the speaker cannot name precisely.
– ORIGIN perhaps from the refrain of the song *Camptown Races*.
doodle ● verb scribble absent-mindedly. ● noun a drawing made absent-mindedly.
– DERIVATIVES **doodler** noun.
– ORIGIN from Low German *dudeldopp* 'simpleton'.
doodlebug ● noun Brit. informal a V-1 bomb.
doo-doo ● noun a child's word for excrement.
doofus /do͞ofəss/ (also **dufus**) ● noun (pl. **doofuses**) N. Amer. informal a stupid person.
– ORIGIN perhaps from GOOF, or from Scots *doof* 'dolt'.
doolally /do͞olali/ ● adjective informal temporarily insane.
– ORIGIN from Indian army slang *doolally tap*, from *Deolali* (a town near Bombay) + Urdu *tap* 'fever'.
doom ● noun death, destruction, or another terrible fate. ● verb condemn to certain destruction or failure.
– DERIVATIVES **doomy** adjective.
– ORIGIN Old English, 'statute, judgement'.
doomsayer ● noun a person who predicts disaster.
– DERIVATIVES **doomsaying** noun.
doomsday ● noun **1** the last day of the world's existence. **2** (in religious belief) the day of the Last Judgement.
doomster ● noun a doomsayer.
doona /do͞onə/ ● noun Austral. trademark a quilt or duvet.
– ORIGIN perhaps from Swedish *dun* 'down'.
door ● noun **1** a movable barrier at the entrance to a building, room, or vehicle, or in the framework of a cupboard. **2** the distance from one building in a row to another: *he lived two doors away*.
– PHRASES **lay at someone's door** blame someone for. **out of doors** in or into the open air.
– DERIVATIVES **doored** adjective.
– ORIGIN Old English.
doorbell ● noun a bell in a building which can be rung by visitors outside.
do-or-die ● adjective showing or requiring a determination not to be deterred.
door furniture ● noun the handles, lock, and other fixtures on a door.
doorkeeper ● noun a person on duty at the entrance to a building.
doorman ● noun a man who is on duty at the entrance to a large building.
doormat ● noun **1** a mat placed in a doorway for wiping the shoes. **2** informal a submissive person.
doornail ● noun (in phrase **dead as a doornail**) quite dead.
doorstep ● noun **1** a step leading up to the outer door of a house. **2** Brit. informal a thick sandwich or slice. ● verb (**doorstepped**, **doorstepping**) Brit. informal **1** (of a journalist) wait uninvited outside the home of (someone) for an interview or photograph. **2** go from door to door selling or canvassing.
doorstop (also **doorstopper**) ● noun an object that keeps a door open or in place.
doo-wop /do͞owop/ ● noun a style of pop music involving close harmony vocals and nonsense phrases.
– ORIGIN imitative.
dopamine /dōpəmeen/ ● noun Biochemistry a compound which exists in the body as a neurotransmitter and as a precursor of other substances including adrenalin.
– ORIGIN from *dopa* (a related substance) + AMINE; *dopa* is an acronym of *dihydroxyphenylalanine*.
dopant /dōpənt/ ● noun Electronics a substance used to produce a desired electrical characteristic in a semiconductor.
– ORIGIN from DOPE.
dope ● noun **1** informal an illegal drug, especially cannabis or (US) heroin. **2** a drug used to enhance the performance of an athlete, racehorse, or greyhound. **3** informal a stupid person. **4** informal information. ● verb **1** administer dope to (a racehorse, greyhound, or athlete). **2** (**be doped up**) informal be heavily under the influence of drugs.
– DERIVATIVES **doper** noun.
– ORIGIN originally in the sense 'thick liquid': from Dutch *doop* 'sauce'.
dopey (also **dopy**) ● adjective (**dopier**, **dopiest**) informal **1** stupefied by sleep or a drug. **2** idiotic.
– DERIVATIVES **dopily** adverb **dopiness** noun.
doppelgänger /dopp'lgengər/ ● noun an apparition or double of a living person.
– ORIGIN German, 'double-goer'.
Doppler effect /doplər/ (also **Doppler shift**) ● noun Physics an increase (or decrease) in the apparent frequency of sound, light, or other waves as the source and the observer move towards (or away from) each other.
– ORIGIN named after the Austrian physicist Johann Christian *Doppler* (1803–53).
dorado /dəraadō/ ● noun (pl. **dorados**) a large edible fish of warm seas, with bright coloration.
– ORIGIN Spanish, 'gilded'.
Dorian /doriən/ ● noun a member of a people speaking the Doric dialect of Greek, thought to have entered Greece from the north *c*.1100 BC. ● adjective relating to the Dorians or to Doris in central Greece.
Doric /dorrik/ ● adjective relating to a classical order of architecture characterized by a plain column and a square abacus.
dork ● noun informal a socially inept person.
– ORIGIN perhaps a variant of DIRK, influenced by DICK[1].
dorm ● noun informal a dormitory.
dormant ● adjective **1** (of an animal) in or as if in a deep sleep. **2** (of a plant or bud) alive but not growing. **3** (of a volcano) temporarily inactive.
– DERIVATIVES **dormancy** noun.
– ORIGIN Old French, 'sleeping', from Latin *dormire* 'to sleep'.
dormer (also **dormer window**) ● noun a window set vertically into a sloping roof.
– ORIGIN originally denoting the window of a dormitory or bedroom: from Old French *dormir* 'to sleep'.
dormitory ● noun (pl. **dormitories**) **1** a bedroom for a number of people in an institution. **2** (before another noun) denoting a small town or suburb from which people travel to work in a nearby city.
– ORIGIN Latin *dormitorium*, from *dormire* 'to sleep'.
dormouse ● noun (pl. **dormice**) an agile mouse-like rodent with a bushy tail.
– ORIGIN of unknown origin, but associated with Latin *dormire* 'to sleep'.
dorsal ● adjective Anatomy, Zoology, & Botany on or relating to the upper side or back. Compare with VENTRAL.
– DERIVATIVES **dorsally** adverb.
– ORIGIN Latin *dorsalis*, from *dorsum* 'back'.
dory /dori/ ● noun (pl. **dories**) a narrow marine fish with a large mouth.
– ORIGIN French *dorée* 'gilded', from Latin *aurum* 'gold'.
DOS ● abbreviation Computing disk operating system.
dosage ● noun the size of a dose of medicine or radiation.
dose ● noun **1** a quantity of a medicine or drug taken at one

Thesaurus

donor ● noun GIVER, contributor, benefactor, benefactress, subscriber; supporter, backer, patron, sponsor; *informal* angel.
doom ● noun **1** *his impending doom* DESTRUCTION, downfall, ruin, ruination; extinction, annihilation, death. **2** *(archaic) the day of doom* JUDGEMENT DAY, the Last Judgement, doomsday, Armageddon.
● verb *we were doomed to fail* DESTINE, fate, predestine, preordain, foredoom, mean; condemn, sentence.
doomed ● adjective ILL-FATED, ill-starred, cursed, jinxed, foredoomed, damned; *poetic/literary* star-crossed.
door ● noun DOORWAY, portal, opening, entrance, entry, exit.
– PHRASES **out of doors** OUTSIDE, outdoors, in/into the open air, alfresco.
doorkeeper ● noun DOORMAN, commissionaire, concierge.
dope ● noun *(informal)* **1** *he was caught smuggling dope* (ILLEGAL) DRUGS, narcotics; cannabis, heroin. **2** *what a dope!* See FOOL noun sense 1. **3** *they had plenty of dope on Mr Dixon.* See INTELLIGENCE sense 2.
● verb **1** *the horse was doped* DRUG, administer drugs/narcotics to, tamper with, interfere with; sedate; *Brit. informal* nobble. **2** *they doped his drink* ADD DRUGS TO, tamper with, adulterate, contaminate, lace; *informal* spike, doctor.
dopey ● adjective *(informal)* STUPEFIED, confused, muddled, befuddled, disorientated, groggy, muzzy; *informal* woozy, not with it.
– OPPOSITES alert.
dormant ● adjective ASLEEP, sleeping, resting; INACTIVE, passive,

time. **2** an amount of ionizing radiation received or absorbed at one time. **3** informal a venereal infection. ● **verb** administer a dose to.
– PHRASES **like a dose of salts** Brit. informal very fast and efficiently. [ORIGIN from the use of Epsom salts as a laxative.]
– ORIGIN Greek *dosis* 'gift', from *didonai* 'give'.
dosh ● **noun** Brit. informal money.
– ORIGIN of unknown origin.
do-si-do /dōzidō, -si-/ (also **do-se-do**) ● **noun** (pl. **do-si-dos**) (in country dancing) a figure in which two dancers pass round each other back to back.
– ORIGIN from French *dos-à-dos* 'back to back'.
dosimeter /dōsimmitər/ ● **noun** a device used to measure an absorbed dose of ionizing radiation.
– DERIVATIVES **dosimetry** noun.
doss Brit. informal ● **verb 1** sleep in rough or improvised conditions. **2** spend time idly. ● **noun 1** archaic a bed in a cheap lodging house. **2** an easy task giving time for idling.
– DERIVATIVES **dosser** noun.
– ORIGIN perhaps related to Latin *dorsum* 'back'.
dosshouse ● **noun** Brit. informal a cheap lodging house for homeless people.
dossier /dossiər, -iay/ ● **noun** a collection of documents about a person or subject.
– ORIGIN French, denoting a bundle of papers with a label on the back, from *dos* 'back'.
dost /dust/ archaic second person singular present of DO[1].
DoT ● **abbreviation** (in the UK and Canada) Department of Transport.
dot ● **noun 1** a small round mark or spot. **2** Music a dot used to denote the lengthening of a note or rest by half, or to indicate staccato. **3** the shorter signal of the two used in Morse code. ● **verb** (**dotted, dotting**) **1** mark with a dot or dots. **2** scatter over (an area).
– PHRASES **dot the i's and cross the t's** informal ensure that all details are correct. **on the dot** informal exactly on time. **the year dot** Brit. informal a very long time ago.
– ORIGIN Old English, 'head of a boil'.
dotage /dōtij/ ● **noun** the period of life in which a person is old and weak.
– ORIGIN from DOTE + -AGE.
dotard /dōtəd/ ● **noun** an old person, especially one who is weak or senile.
dot-com ● **noun** a company that conducts its business on the Internet.
– ORIGIN from '.com' in an Internet address, indicating a commercial site.
dote ● **verb** (**dote on/upon**) be extremely and uncritically fond of.
– DERIVATIVES **doting** adjective.
– ORIGIN related to Dutch *doten* 'be silly'.
doth /duth/ archaic third person singular present of DO[1].
dot matrix ● **noun** a grid of dots which are filled selectively to produce an image.
dotterel ● **noun** a small migratory plover.
– ORIGIN from DOTE (from the bird's tameness).
dottle ● **noun** a remnant of tobacco left in a pipe after smoking.
– ORIGIN from DOT.
dotty ● **adjective** (**dottier, dottiest**) informal, chiefly Brit. slightly mad or eccentric.
– DERIVATIVES **dottily** adverb **dottiness** noun.
– ORIGIN perhaps from obsolete *dote* 'simpleton, fool'.
double ● **adjective 1** consisting of two equal, identical, or similar parts or things. **2** having twice the usual size, quantity, or strength: *a double brandy.* **3** designed to be used by two people. **4** having two different roles or interpretations: *she began a double life.* **5** (of a flower) having more than one circle of petals. ● **predeterminer** twice as much or as many. ● **adverb** at or to twice the amount or extent. ● **noun 1** a thing which is twice as large as usual or is made up of two parts. **2** a person who looks exactly like another. **3** (**doubles**) a game involving sides made up of two players. **4** Brit. (**the double**) the winning of two sporting trophies in the same season. **5** Darts a hit on the ring enclosed by the two outer circles of a dartboard, scoring double. ● **pronoun** an amount twice as large as usual. ● **verb 1** make or become double. **2** fold or bend over on itself. **3** (**double up**) bend over or curl up with pain or laughter. **4** (**double (up) as**) be used in or play another, different role. **5** (**double back**) go back in the direction one has come.
– PHRASES **at the double** very fast.
– DERIVATIVES **doubleness** noun **doubler** noun **doubly** adverb.
– ORIGIN Latin *duplus*, from *duo* 'two'.
double act ● **noun** a performance involving two people.
double agent ● **noun** an agent who pretends to act as a spy for one country while in fact acting for its enemy.
double-barrelled ● **adjective 1** (of a gun) having two barrels. **2** Brit. (of a surname) having two parts joined by a hyphen.
double bass ● **noun** the largest and lowest-pitched instrument of the violin family.
double bind ● **noun** a dilemma.
double-blind ● **adjective** (of a test or trial) in which information which may influence the behaviour of the tester or subject is withheld.
double bluff ● **noun** an action or statement intended to appear as a bluff, but which is in fact genuine.
double boiler ● **noun** a saucepan with an upper compartment heated by boiling water in the lower one.
double bond ● **noun** a chemical bond in which two pairs of electrons are shared between two atoms.
double-book ● **verb** inadvertently reserve (something) for two different customers at the same time.
double-breasted ● **adjective** (of a jacket or coat) having a large overlap at the front and two rows of buttons.
double-check ● **verb** check again.
double chin ● **noun** a roll of flesh below a person's chin.
– DERIVATIVES **double-chinned** adjective.
double cream ● **noun** Brit. thick cream containing a high proportion of milk fat.

Thesaurus

inert, latent, quiescent.
– OPPOSITES awake, active.
dose ● **noun** MEASURE, portion, dosage, drench; *informal* hit.
dossier ● **noun** FILE, report, case history; account, notes, document(s), documentation, data, information, evidence.
dot ● **noun** *a pattern of tiny dots* SPOT, speck, fleck, speckle; full stop, decimal point.
● **verb 1** *spots of rain dotted his shirt* SPOT, fleck, mark, stipple, freckle, sprinkle; *poetic/literary* bestrew, besprinkle. **2** *restaurants are dotted around the site* SCATTER, pepper, sprinkle, strew; spread, disperse, distribute.
– PHRASES **on the dot** *(informal)* PRECISELY, exactly, sharp, prompt, dead on, on the stroke of ——; *informal* bang on; *N. Amer. informal* on the button, on the nose.
dotage ● **noun** DECLINING YEARS, winter/autumn of one's life; advanced years, old age; *poetic/literary* eld.
dote ● **verb**
– PHRASES **dote on** ADORE, love dearly, be devoted to, idolize, treasure, cherish, worship, hold dear; indulge, spoil, pamper.
doting ● **adjective** ADORING, loving, besotted, infatuated; affectionate, fond, devoted, caring.
dotty ● **adjective** *(informal).* See MAD sense 1.
double ● **adjective 1** *a double garage | double yellow lines* DUAL, duplex, twin, binary, duplicate, in pairs, coupled, twofold. **2** *a double helping* DOUBLED, twofold. **3** *a double meaning* AMBIGUOUS, equivocal, dual, two-edged, double-edged, ambivalent, cryptic, enigmatic. **4** *a double life* DECEITFUL, double-dealing, two-faced, dual; hypocritical, false, duplicitous, insincere, deceiving, dissembling, dishonest.
– RELATED TERMS di-, diplo-.
– OPPOSITES single, unambiguous.
● **adverb** *we had to pay double* TWICE (OVER), twice the amount, doubly.
● **noun 1** *if it's not her, it's her double* LOOKALIKE, twin, clone, duplicate, exact likeness, replica, copy, facsimile, Doppelgänger; *informal* spitting image, dead ringer, dead spit. **2** *she used a double for the stunts* STAND-IN, substitute.
● **verb 1** *they doubled his salary* MULTIPLY BY TWO, increase twofold. **2** *the bottom sheet had been doubled up* FOLD (BACK/UP/DOWN/OVER/UNDER), turn back/up/down/over/under, tuck back/up/down/under. **3** *the kitchen doubles as a dining room* FUNCTION, do, (also) serve.
– PHRASES **at/on the double** VERY QUICKLY, as fast as one's legs can carry one, at a run, at a gallop, fast, swiftly, rapidly, speedily, at (full) speed, at full tilt, as fast as possible; *informal* double quick, like (greased) lightning, like the wind, like a scalded cat, like a

double-cross ● verb betray (a person one is supposedly helping).
double-dealing ● noun deceitful behaviour. ● adjective acting deceitfully.
double-decker ● noun something, especially a bus, with two levels.
double Dutch ● noun Brit. informal incomprehensible language.
double-edged ● adjective **1** (of a blade) having two cutting edges. **2** having two contradictory aspects or possible outcomes.
double entendre /dŏob'l ONTONdrə/ ● noun (pl. **double entendres** pronunc. same) a word or phrase open to two interpretations, one of which is usually indecent.
– ORIGIN from obsolete French, 'double understanding'.
double-entry ● adjective relating to a system of bookkeeping in which each transaction is entered as a debit in one account and a credit in another.
double exposure ● noun the repeated exposure of a photographic plate or film.
double fault ● noun Tennis an instance of two consecutive faults in serving, forfeiting a point.
double figures ● plural noun a number between 10 and 99.
double first ● noun Brit. a university degree with first-class honours in two subjects or examinations.
double glazing ● noun windows having two layers of glass with a space between them, designed to reduce heat loss and exclude noise.
– DERIVATIVES **double-glaze** verb.
Double Gloucester ● noun a hard cheese originally made in Gloucestershire.
– ORIGIN so named because the curd is milled twice.
double-header ● noun **1** a train pulled by two locomotives. **2** chiefly N. Amer. a sporting event in which two games are played in succession at the same venue.
double helix ● noun a pair of parallel helices intertwined about a common axis, especially that in the structure of DNA.
double jeopardy ● noun Law the prosecution of a person twice for the same offence.
double-jointed ● adjective (of a person) having unusually flexible joints.
double negative ● noun Grammar **1** a negative statement containing two negative elements (e.g. *didn't say nothing*), regarded as incorrect in standard English. **2** a positive statement in which two negative elements are used to produce the positive force, e.g. *there is not nothing to worry about!*
double pneumonia ● noun pneumonia affecting both lungs.
doublespeak ● noun deliberately ambiguous or obscure language.
– ORIGIN coined by George Orwell (see DOUBLETHINK).
double standard ● noun a rule or principle applied unfairly in different ways to different people.
doublet ● noun **1** a man's short close-fitting padded jacket, worn from the 14th to the 17th century. **2** either of a pair of similar things.
– ORIGIN Old French, 'something folded', from *double* 'double'.
double take ● noun a delayed reaction to something unexpected, immediately following one's first reaction.
doublethink ● noun the acceptance of contrary opinions or beliefs at the same time.
– ORIGIN coined by George Orwell in his novel *Nineteen Eighty-Four* (1949).
double time ● noun a rate of pay equal to double the standard rate.
double vision ● noun the perception of two overlapping images of a single scene.
double whammy ● noun informal a twofold blow or setback.
doubloon /dubloon/ ● noun historical a Spanish gold coin.
– ORIGIN Spanish *doblón*, from *doble* 'double' (because the coin was worth double the value of another former Spanish coin, the pistole).
doubt ● noun a feeling of uncertainty. ● verb **1** feel uncertain about. **2** question the truth of.
– PHRASES **no doubt** certainly; probably.
– DERIVATIVES **doubter** noun **doubting** adjective.
– ORIGIN Old French *doute*, from Latin *dubitare* 'hesitate', from *dubius* 'doubtful'.
doubtful ● adjective **1** uncertain. **2** not known with certainty. **3** improbable.
– DERIVATIVES **doubtfully** adverb **doubtfulness** noun.
doubting Thomas ● noun a person who refuses to believe something without proof.
– ORIGIN with biblical allusion to the apostle Thomas (Gospel of John, Chapter 20).
doubtless ● adverb very probably.
– DERIVATIVES **doubtlessly** adverb.
douceur /dōōsör/ ● noun a bribe.
– ORIGIN French, 'sweetness'.
douche /dōōsh/ ● noun **1** a shower of water. **2** a jet of liquid applied to part of the body for cleansing or medicinal purposes. **3** a device for washing out the vagina as a contraceptive measure. ● verb **1** spray or shower with water. **2** use a contraceptive douche.

d

Thesaurus

bat out of hell; *Brit. informal* like the clappers, at a rate of knots; *N. Amer. informal* lickety-split.
double-cross ● verb BETRAY, cheat, defraud, trick, hoodwink, mislead, deceive, swindle, be disloyal to, be unfaithful to, play false; *informal* do the dirty on, sell down the river.
double-dealing ● noun DUPLICITY, treachery, betrayal, double-crossing, unfaithfulness, untrustworthiness, infidelity, bad faith, disloyalty, breach of trust, fraud, underhandedness, cheating, dishonesty, deceit, deceitfulness, deception, falseness; *informal* crookedness.
– OPPOSITES honesty.
double entendre ● noun AMBIGUITY, double meaning, innuendo, play on words.
doubly ● adverb TWICE AS, in double measure, even more, especially, extra.
doubt ● noun **1** *there was some doubt as to the caller's identity* UNCERTAINTY, unsureness, indecision, hesitation, dubiousness, suspicion, confusion; queries, questions; *formal* dubiety. **2** *a weak leader racked by doubt* INDECISION, hesitation, uncertainty, insecurity, unease, uneasiness, apprehension; hesitancy, vacillation, irresolution. **3** *there is doubt about their motives* SCEPTICISM, distrust, mistrust, doubtfulness, suspicion, cynicism, uneasiness, apprehension, wariness, chariness, leeriness; reservations, misgivings, suspicions; *formal* dubiety.
– OPPOSITES certainty, conviction.
● verb **1** *they doubted my story* DISBELIEVE, distrust, mistrust, suspect, have doubts about, be suspicious of, have misgivings about, feel uneasy about, feel apprehensive about, query, question, challenge. **2** *I doubt whether he will come* THINK SOMETHING UNLIKELY, have (one's) doubts about, question, query, be dubious. **3** *stop doubting and believe!* BE UNDECIDED, have doubts, be irresolute, be ambivalent, be doubtful, be unsure, be uncertain, be in two minds, hesitate, shilly-shally, waver, vacillate.
– OPPOSITES trust.
– PHRASES **in doubt 1** *the issue was in doubt* DOUBTFUL, uncertain, open to question, unconfirmed, unknown, undecided, unresolved, in the balance, up in the air; *informal* iffy. **2** *if you are in doubt, ask for advice* IRRESOLUTE, hesitant, vacillating, dithering, wavering, ambivalent; doubtful, unsure, uncertain, in two minds, shilly-shallying, undecided, in a quandary/dilemma; *informal* sitting on the fence. **no doubt** DOUBTLESS, undoubtedly, indubitably, doubtlessly, without (a) doubt; unquestionably, undeniably, incontrovertibly, irrefutably; unequivocally, clearly, plainly, obviously, patently.
doubter ● noun SCEPTIC, doubting Thomas, non-believer, unbeliever, disbeliever, cynic, scoffer, questioner, challenger, dissenter.
– OPPOSITES believer.
doubtful ● adjective **1** *I was doubtful about going alone* IRRESOLUTE, hesitant, vacillating, dithering, wavering, in doubt, unsure, uncertain, in two minds, shilly-shallying, undecided, in a quandary/dilemma, blowing hot and cold. **2** *it is doubtful whether he will come* IN DOUBT, uncertain, open to question, unsure, unconfirmed, not definite, unknown, undecided, unresolved, debatable, in the balance, up in the air; *informal* iffy. **3** *the whole trip is looking rather doubtful* UNLIKELY, improbable, dubious, impossible. **4** *they are doubtful of the methods used* DISTRUSTFUL, mistrustful, suspicious, wary, chary, leery, apprehensive; sceptical, unsure, ambivalent, dubious, cynical. **5** *this decision is of doubtful validity* QUESTIONABLE, arguable, debatable, controversial, contentious; *informal* iffy; *Brit. informal* dodgy.
– OPPOSITES confident, certain, probable, trusting.

– ORIGIN French, from Italian *doccia* 'conduit pipe'.

dough ● noun **1** a thick mixture of flour and liquid, for baking into bread or pastry. **2** informal money.
– DERIVATIVES **doughy** adjective (**doughier**, **doughiest**).
– ORIGIN Old English.

doughnut (also US **donut**) ● noun a small fried cake or ring of sweetened dough.

doughty /dowti/ ● adjective (**doughtier**, **doughtiest**) archaic or humorous brave and resolute.
– ORIGIN Old English.

Douglas fir ● noun a tall, slender conifer valued for its wood.
– ORIGIN named after the Scottish botanist and explorer David *Douglas* (1798–1834).

doula /do͞olə/ ● noun a woman who gives support, help, and advice to another woman during pregnancy and during and after the birth.
– ORIGIN modern Greek.

dour /do͞oər, dowər/ ● adjective very severe, stern, or gloomy.
– DERIVATIVES **dourly** adverb **dourness** noun.
– ORIGIN probably from Scottish Gaelic, 'dull, obstinate, stupid'.

douse /dowz/ (also **dowse**) ● verb **1** drench with liquid. **2** extinguish (a fire or light).
– ORIGIN perhaps imitative, influenced by SOUSE, or perhaps from dialect *douse* 'strike, beat'.

dove[1] /duv/ ● noun **1** a stocky bird with a small head, short legs, and a cooing voice, very similar to but generally smaller than a pigeon. **2** a person who advocates conciliatory policies.
– DERIVATIVES **dovish** adjective.
– ORIGIN Old Norse.

dove[2] /dōv/ chiefly N. Amer. past of DIVE.

dovecote /duvkot/ (also **dovecot**) ● noun a shelter with nest holes for domesticated pigeons.

Dover sole ● noun a marine flatfish which is highly valued as food.

dovetail ● noun a joint formed by interlocking tenons and mortises. ● verb **1** join by means of a dovetail. **2** fit together easily or conveniently.

dowager /dowəjər/ ● noun **1** a widow with a title or property derived from her late husband. **2** informal a dignified elderly woman.
– ORIGIN Old French *douagiere*, from *douer* 'endow', from Latin *dos* 'dowry'.

dowdy ● adjective (**dowdier**, **dowdiest**) (especially of a woman) unfashionable and dull in appearance.
– DERIVATIVES **dowdily** adverb **dowdiness** noun.

dowel ● noun a headless peg used for holding together components. ● verb (**dowelled**, **dowelling**; US **doweled**, **doweling**) fasten with a dowel.
– ORIGIN perhaps Low German.

dowelling (US **doweling**) ● noun cylindrical rods for cutting into dowels.

dower ● noun **1** a widow's share for life of her husband's estate. **2** archaic a dowry.
– ORIGIN Old French *douaire*, from Latin *dotare* 'endow', from *dos* 'dowry'.

Dow Jones index /dowjōnz/ ● noun an index of figures indicating the relative price of shares on the New York Stock Exchange.
– ORIGIN named after the American financial news agency *Dow Jones & Co, Inc.*

down[1] ● adverb **1** towards or in a lower place or position. **2** to or at a lower level or value. **3** so as to lie flush or flat. **4** in or into a weaker or worse position, mood, or condition. **5** to a smaller amount or size, or a simpler or more basic state. **6** in or into writing. **7** from an earlier to a later point in time or order. **8** (of a computer system) out of action. **9** away from a central place or the north. **10** (**down with ——**) expressing strong dislike. **11** (with reference to partial payment of a sum) made initially. **12** (of sailing) with the current or the wind. ● preposition **1** from a higher to a lower point of. **2** at a point further along the course of. **3** throughout (a period of time). **4** along the course or extent of. **5** informal at or to (a place). ● adjective **1** directed or moving towards a lower place or position. **2** unhappy. **3** (of a computer system) out of action. ● verb informal **1** knock or bring to the ground. **2** consume (a drink).
– PHRASES **be** (or **have a**) **down on** informal feel hostile towards. **be down to 1** be attributable to (a factor). **2** be left with only (the specified amount). **down in the mouth** informal unhappy. **down on one's luck** informal having a period of bad luck. **down tools** Brit. informal stop work.
– ORIGIN Old English.

down[2] ● noun **1** soft fine feathers forming the covering of a young bird or an insulating layer below the contour feathers of an adult bird, used for stuffing cushions and quilts. **2** fine soft hairs.
– ORIGIN Old Norse.

down[3] ● noun **1** a gently rolling hill. **2** (**the Downs**) ridges of undulating chalk and limestone hills in southern England.
– ORIGIN Old English.

down and out ● adjective destitute. ● noun (**down-and-out**) a destitute person.

down at heel ● adjective **1** (of a shoe) with the heel worn down. **2** shabby or impoverished.

downbeat ● adjective **1** pessimistic; gloomy. **2** understated.

Thesaurus

doubtless ● adverb UNDOUBTEDLY, indubitably, doubtlessly, no doubt; unquestionably, indisputably, undeniably, incontrovertibly, irrefutably; certainly, surely, of course, indeed.

doughty ● adjective *(archaic)* FEARLESS, dauntless, determined, resolute, indomitable, intrepid, plucky, spirited, bold, valiant, brave, stout-hearted, courageous; *informal* gutsy, spunky, feisty.

dour ● adjective STERN, unsmiling, unfriendly, severe, forbidding, gruff, surly, grim, sullen, solemn, austere, stony.
– OPPOSITES cheerful, friendly.

douse ● verb **1** *a mob doused the thieves with petrol* DRENCH, soak, saturate, wet, splash, slosh. **2** *a guard doused the flames* EXTINGUISH, put out, quench, smother, dampen down.

dovetail ● verb **1** *the ends of the logs were dovetailed* JOINT, join, fit together, splice, mortise, tenon. **2** *this will dovetail well with the division's existing activities* FIT IN, go together, be consistent, match, conform, harmonize, be in tune, correspond; *informal* square; *N. Amer. informal* jibe.

dowdy ● adjective UNFASHIONABLE, frumpy, old-fashioned, inelegant, shabby, scruffy, frowzy; *Brit. informal* mumsy; *Austral./NZ informal* daggy.
– OPPOSITES fashionable.

down[1] ● adverb **1** *they went down in the lift* TOWARDS A LOWER POSITION, downwards, downstairs. **2** *she fell down* TO THE GROUND/FLOOR, over.
– OPPOSITES up.
● preposition **1** *the lift plunged down the shaft* TO A LOWER POSITION IN, to the bottom of. **2** *I walked down the street* ALONG, to the other end of, from one end of —— to the other. **3** *down the years* THROUGHOUT, through, during.
● adjective **1** *I'm feeling a bit down* DEPRESSED, sad, unhappy, melancholy, miserable, wretched, sorrowful, gloomy, dejected, downhearted, despondent, dispirited, low; *informal* blue, down in the dumps/mouth, fed up. **2** *the computer is down* NOT WORKING, inoperative, malfunctioning, out of order, broken; not in service, out of action, out of commission; *informal* conked out, bust, (gone) kaput; *N. Amer. informal* on the fritz.
– OPPOSITES elated, working.
● verb *(informal)* **1** *he struck Slater, downing him* KNOCK DOWN/OVER, knock to the ground, bring down, topple; *informal* deck, floor, flatten. **2** *he downed his beer* DRINK (UP/DOWN), gulp (down), guzzle, quaff, drain, toss off, slug, finish off; *informal* sink, knock back, put away; *N. Amer. informal* scarf (down/up), snarf (down/up).
● noun **1** *the ups and downs of running a business* SETBACKS, upsets, reverses, reversals, mishaps, vicissitudes; *informal* glitches. **2** *(informal) he's having a bit of a down* FIT OF DEPRESSION; *informal* the blues, the dumps, a low; *N. Amer. informal* the blahs.
– PHRASES **have a down on** *(informal)* DISAPPROVE OF, be against, feel antagonism to, be hostile to, feel ill will towards; *informal* have it in for, be down on.

down[2] ● noun *goose down* SOFT FEATHERS, fine hair; fluff, fuzz, floss, lint.

down and out ● adjective DESTITUTE, poverty-stricken, impoverished, penniless, insolvent, impecunious; needy, in straitened circumstances, distressed, badly off; homeless, on the streets, vagrant, sleeping rough; *informal* hard up, (flat) broke, strapped (for cash), without a brass farthing, without two pennies to rub together; *Brit. informal* stony broke, skint; *N. Amer. informal* without a red cent, on skid row.
– OPPOSITES wealthy.
● noun (**down-and-out**) POOR PERSON, pauper, indigent; beggar,

● noun Music an accented beat, usually the first of the bar.
downcast ● adjective 1 (of eyes) looking downwards. 2 feeling despondent.
downer ● noun informal 1 a depressant or tranquillizing drug. 2 something dispiriting or depressing.
downfall ● noun a loss of power, prosperity, or status.
downgrade ● verb reduce to a lower grade, rank, or level of importance.
downhearted ● adjective discouraged; dejected.
downhill ● adverb & adjective /downhil/ 1 towards the bottom of a slope. 2 into a steadily worsening situation. ● noun /downhil/ 1 a downward slope. 2 Skiing a downhill race.
downland ● noun gently rolling hill country.
downlink ● noun a telecommunications link for signals coming to the earth from a satellite, spacecraft, or aircraft.
download Computing ● verb copy (data) from one computer system to another or to a disk. ● noun the act or process of downloading.
– DERIVATIVES **downloadable** adjective.
downmarket ● adjective & adverb chiefly Brit. towards or relating to the cheaper or less prestigious sector of the market.
down payment ● noun an initial payment made when buying on credit.
downpipe ● noun Brit. a pipe to carry rainwater from a roof to a drain or to ground level.
downplay ● verb make (something) appear less important than it really is.
downpour ● noun a heavy fall of rain.
downright ● adjective utter; complete. ● adverb to an extreme degree; thoroughly.
downriver ● adverb & adjective towards or situated at a point nearer the mouth of a river.
downscale N. Amer. ● verb reduce in size or extent. ● adjective at the lower end of a scale; downmarket.
downshift ● verb chiefly N. Amer. 1 change to a lower gear. 2 change to a less stressful lifestyle.
downside ● noun the negative aspect of something.
downsize ● verb chiefly N. Amer. 1 make smaller. 2 (of a company) shed staff.
Down's syndrome ● noun Medicine a congenital disorder causing intellectual impairment and physical abnormalities.
– USAGE **Down's syndrome** is the accepted term in modern use, and former terms such as **mongol** and **mongolism**, which are likely to cause offence, should be avoided.
– ORIGIN named after the English physician John L. H. *Down* (1828–96).
downstage ● adjective & adverb at or towards the front of a stage.
downstairs ● adverb & adjective down a flight of stairs; on or to a lower floor. ● noun the ground floor or lower floors of a building.
downstream ● adverb & adjective situated or moving in the direction in which a stream or river flows.
down time ● noun time during which a computer or other machine is out of action.
down-to-earth ● adjective practical and realistic.
downtown chiefly N. Amer. ● adjective & adverb of, in, or towards the central area of a city. ● noun a downtown area.
– DERIVATIVES **downtowner** noun.
downtrodden ● adjective oppressed or treated badly by people in power.
downturn ● noun a decline in economic or other activity.
down under informal ● adverb in or to Australia or New Zealand. ● noun Australia and New Zealand.
downward ● adverb (also **downwards**) towards a lower point or level. ● adjective moving towards a lower point or level.
– DERIVATIVES **downwardly** adverb.
downwind ● adverb & adjective in the direction in which the wind is blowing.
downy ● adjective (**downier**, **downiest**) covered with fine soft hair or feathers.
dowry /dowri/ ● noun (pl. **dowries**) property or money brought by a bride to her husband on their marriage.
– ORIGIN Old French *dowarie*, from Latin *dotare* 'endow' (see DOWER).
dowse[1] /dowz/ ● verb search for underground water or minerals with a pointer which is supposedly moved by unseen influences.
– DERIVATIVES **dowser** noun.
– ORIGIN of unknown origin.
dowse[2] ● verb variant spelling of DOUSE.
doxology /doksolləji/ ● noun (pl. **doxologies**) a liturgical for-

d

Thesaurus

homeless person, vagrant, tramp, drifter, derelict, vagabond; *N. Amer.* hobo; *Austral.* bagman; *informal* have-not, dosser, bag lady; *N. Amer. informal* bum.
down at heel ● adjective 1 *the resort looks down at heel* RUN DOWN, dilapidated, neglected, uncared-for; seedy, insalubrious, squalid, slummy, wretched; *informal* scruffy, scuzzy; *Brit. informal* grotty; *N. Amer. informal* shacky. 2 *a down-at-heel labourer* SCRUFFY, shabby, ragged, tattered, mangy, sorry; unkempt, bedraggled, dishevelled, ungroomed, seedy, untidy, slovenly; *informal* tatty, scuzzy, grungy; *Brit. informal* grotty; *N. Amer. informal* raggedy.
– OPPOSITES smart.
downbeat ● adjective 1 *the mood is decidedly downbeat* PESSIMISTIC, gloomy, negative, defeatist, cynical, bleak, fatalistic, dark, black; despairing, despondent, depressed, dejected, demoralized, hopeless, melancholy, glum. 2 *his downbeat joviality* RELAXED, easygoing, easy, casual, informal, nonchalant, insouciant; low-key, subtle, unostentatious, cool; *informal* laid-back.
downcast ● adjective DESPONDENT, disheartened, discouraged, dispirited, downhearted, crestfallen, down, low, disconsolate, despairing; sad, melancholy, gloomy, glum, morose, doleful, dismal, woebegone, miserable, depressed, dejected; *informal* blue, down in the mouth, down in the dumps.
– OPPOSITES elated.
downfall ● noun UNDOING, ruin, ruination; defeat, conquest, deposition, overthrow; nemesis, destruction, annihilation, elimination; end, collapse, fall, crash, failure; debasement, degradation, disgrace; Waterloo.
– OPPOSITES rise.
downgrade ● verb 1 *plans to downgrade three workers* DEMOTE, lower, reduce/lower in rank; relegate. 2 *I won't downgrade their achievement* DISPARAGE, denigrate, detract from, run down, belittle; *informal* bad-mouth.
– OPPOSITES promote, praise.
downhearted ● adjective DESPONDENT, disheartened, discouraged, dispirited, downcast, crestfallen, down, low, disconsolate, wretched; melancholy, gloomy, glum, morose, doleful, dismal, woebegone, miserable, depressed, dejected, sorrowful, sad; *informal* blue, down in the mouth, down in the dumps.
– OPPOSITES elated.
downmarket ● adjective *(Brit.)* CHEAP, cheap and nasty, inferior; low-class, lowbrow, unsophisticated, rough, insalubrious; *informal* tacky, rubbishy, dumbed down.
downpour ● noun RAINSTORM, cloudburst, deluge; thunderstorm; torrential/pouring rain.
downright ● adjective 1 *downright lies* COMPLETE, total, absolute, utter, thorough, out-and-out, outright, sheer, arrant, pure, real, veritable, categorical, unmitigated, unadulterated, unalloyed, unequivocal; *Brit. informal* proper. 2 *her downright attitude* FRANK, straightforward, direct, blunt, plain-spoken, forthright, uninhibited, unreserved; no-nonsense, matter-of-fact, bluff, undiplomatic; explicit, clear, plain, unequivocal, unambiguous; honest, candid, open, sincere; *informal* upfront.
● adverb *that's downright dangerous* THOROUGHLY, utterly, positively, profoundly, really, completely, totally, entirely; unquestionably, undeniably, in every respect, through and through; *informal* plain.
downside ● noun DRAWBACK, disadvantage, snag, stumbling block, catch, pitfall, fly in the ointment; handicap, limitation, trouble, difficulty, problem, complication, nuisance; hindrance; weak spot/point; *informal* minus, flip side.
– OPPOSITES advantage.
down-to-earth ● adjective PRACTICAL, sensible, realistic, matter-of-fact, responsible, reasonable, rational, logical, balanced, sober, pragmatic, level-headed, commonsensical, sane.
– OPPOSITES idealistic.
downtrodden ● adjective OPPRESSED, subjugated, persecuted, repressed, tyrannized, crushed, enslaved, exploited, victimized, bullied; disadvantaged, underprivileged, powerless, helpless; abused, maltreated.
downward ● adjective DESCENDING, downhill, falling, sinking, dipping; earthbound, earthward.
downy ● adjective SOFT, velvety, smooth, fleecy, fluffy, fuzzy, fea-

d

mula of praise to God.
– ORIGIN Greek *doxologia*, from *doxa* 'appearance, glory'.

doxy ● noun (pl. **doxies**) archaic **1** a lover or mistress. **2** a prostitute.
– ORIGIN of unknown origin.

doyen /doyən, dwaajan/ ● noun (fem. **doyenne** /doyen, dwaajen/) the most respected or prominent person in a particular field.
– ORIGIN Old French *deien* (see DEAN).

doze ● verb sleep lightly. ● noun a short light sleep.
– ORIGIN perhaps related to Danish *døse* 'make drowsy'.

dozen ● noun (pl. same) a group or set of twelve.
– PHRASES **talk nineteen to the dozen** Brit. talk quickly and incessantly.
– DERIVATIVES **dozenth** adjective.
– ORIGIN Old French *dozeine*, from Latin *duodecim* 'twelve'.

dozer ● noun informal short for BULLDOZER.

dozy ● adjective (**dozier**, **doziest**) **1** feeling drowsy and lazy. **2** Brit. informal not alert; stupid.
– DERIVATIVES **dozily** adverb **doziness** noun.

DP ● abbreviation data processing.

dpc ● abbreviation damp-proof course.

DPhil ● abbreviation Doctor of Philosophy.

DPP ● abbreviation (in the UK) Director of Public Prosecutions.

Dr ● abbreviation **1** debit. [ORIGIN formerly representing *debtor*.] **2** (as a title) Doctor.

dr. ● abbreviation **1** drachma(s). **2** dram(s).

drab[1] ● adjective (**drabber**, **drabbest**) drearily dull. ● noun a dull light brown colour.
– DERIVATIVES **drably** adverb **drabness** noun.
– ORIGIN probably from Old French *drap* 'cloth' (see DRAPE).

drab[2] ● noun archaic a slovenly woman or a prostitute.
– ORIGIN perhaps related to Low German *drabbe* 'mire' and Dutch *drab* 'dregs'.

drachm /dram/ ● noun historical **1** a unit of weight equivalent to 60 grains or one eighth of an ounce. **2** (also **fluid drachm**) a liquid measure equivalent to 60 minims or one eighth of a fluid ounce.
– ORIGIN originally denoting the ancient Greek drachma: from Greek *drakhmē*.

drachma /drakmə/ ● noun (pl. **drachmas** or **drachmae** /**drak**mee/) **1** the basic monetary unit of Greece. **2** a silver coin of ancient Greece.
– ORIGIN Greek *drakhmē*, an Attic weight and coin.

draconian /drəkōniən, dray-/ ● adjective (of laws) excessively harsh.
– ORIGIN named after the Athenian legislator *Draco* (7th century BC).

draft ● noun **1** a preliminary version of a piece of writing. **2** a plan or sketch. **3** a written order to pay a specified sum. **4** (**the draft**) chiefly US compulsory recruitment for military service. **5** US spelling of DRAUGHT. ● verb **1** prepare a preliminary version of (a text). **2** select (a person or group) and bring them somewhere for a purpose. **3** US conscript for military service.
– DERIVATIVES **drafter** noun.
– ORIGIN phonetic spelling of DRAUGHT.

draftee ● noun chiefly US a person conscripted for military service.

draftsman ● noun **1** a person who drafts legal documents. **2** chiefly N. Amer. variant spelling of DRAUGHTSMAN.

drafty ● adjective US spelling of DRAUGHTY.

drag ● verb (**dragged**, **dragging**) **1** pull along forcefully, roughly, or with difficulty. **2** trail along the ground. **3** take (someone) somewhere, despite their reluctance. **4** (of time) pass slowly. **5** (**drag out**) protract (something) unnecessarily. **6** (**drag up**) informal deliberately mention (something unwelcome). **7** move (an image) across a computer screen using a mouse. **8** search the bottom of (a body of water) with grapnels or nets. **9** (**drag on**) informal inhale the smoke from (a cigarette). ● noun **1** the action of dragging. **2** the longitudinal retarding force exerted by air or other fluid surrounding a moving object. **3** informal a boring or tiresome person or thing. **4** informal women's clothing worn by a man. **5** informal an act of inhaling smoke from a cigarette. **6** a strong-smelling lure drawn before hounds as a substitute for a fox.
– PHRASES **drag one's feet 1** walk wearily or with difficulty. **2** be slow or reluctant to act.
– ORIGIN Old English or Old Norse.

dragée /draazhay/ ● noun **1** a sweet consisting of a centre covered with a coating, such as a sugared almond. **2** a small silver ball for decorating a cake.
– ORIGIN French, from Old French *dragie* (see DREDGE[2]).

draggle ● verb **1** make dirty or wet by trailing on the ground. **2** hang untidily. **3** archaic trail behind others.
– ORIGIN from DRAG.

dragnet ● noun **1** a net drawn through water or across ground to trap fish or game. **2** a systematic search for criminals.

dragoman /draggəmən/ ● noun (pl. **dragomans** or **dragomen**) an interpreter or guide in a country speaking Arabic, Turkish, or Persian.
– ORIGIN Arabic, 'interpreter'.

dragon ● noun **1** a mythical monster like a giant reptile, typically able to breathe out fire. **2** derogatory a fierce and intimidating woman.
– PHRASES **chase the dragon** informal smoke heroin.
– ORIGIN Greek *drakōn* 'serpent'.

dragonfly ● noun a fast-flying long-bodied insect with two pairs of large transparent wings.

dragoon /drəgōōn/ ● noun **1** a member of any of several British cavalry regiments. **2** historical a mounted infantryman armed with a carbine. ● verb coerce into doing something.
– ORIGIN originally denoting a kind of carbine or musket, thought of as breathing fire: from French *dragon* 'dragon'.

drag queen ● noun informal a man who ostentatiously dresses up in women's clothes, especially in an entertainment.

drag race ● noun a short race between two cars as a test of acceleration.
– DERIVATIVES **drag racer** noun **drag racing** noun.

Thesaurus

thery, furry, woolly, silky.

dowry ● noun MARRIAGE SETTLEMENT, (marriage) portion; *archaic* dot.

doze ● verb CATNAP, nap, drowse, sleep lightly, rest; *informal* snooze, snatch forty winks, get some shut-eye; *Brit. informal* kip; *N. Amer. informal* catch some Zs; *poetic/literary* slumber.
● noun CATNAP, nap, siesta, light sleep, drowse, rest; *informal* snooze, forty winks; *Brit. informal* kip, zizz; *poetic/literary* slumber.
– PHRASES **doze off** FALL ASLEEP, go to sleep, drop off; *informal* nod off, drift off; *N. Amer. informal* sack out, zone out.

dozy ● adjective DROWSY, sleepy, half asleep, heavy-eyed, somnolent; lethargic, listless, enervated, inactive, languid, weary, tired, fatigued; *N. Amer.* logy; *informal* dopey, yawny.

drab ● adjective **1** *a drab interior* COLOURLESS, grey, dull, washed out, muted, lacklustre; dingy, dreary, dismal, cheerless, gloomy, sombre. **2** *a drab existence* UNINTERESTING, dull, boring, tedious, monotonous, dry, dreary; unexciting, unimaginative, uninspiring, insipid, lacklustre, flat, stale, wishy-washy, colourless; lame, tired, sterile, anaemic, barren, tame; middle-of-the-road, run-of-the-mill, mediocre, nondescript, characterless, mundane, unremarkable, humdrum.
– OPPOSITES bright, cheerful, interesting.

draconian ● adjective HARSH, severe, strict, extreme, drastic, stringent, tough; cruel, oppressive, ruthless, relentless, punitive; authoritarian, despotic, tyrannical, repressive; *Brit.* swingeing.
– OPPOSITES lenient.

draft ● noun **1** *the draft of his speech* PRELIMINARY VERSION, rough outline, plan, skeleton, abstract; main points, bare bones. **2** *a draft of the building* PLAN, blueprint, design, diagram, drawing, sketch, map, layout, representation. **3** *a banker's draft* CHEQUE, order, money order, bill of exchange, postal order.

drag ● verb **1** *she dragged the chair backwards* HAUL, pull, tug, heave, lug, draw; trail, trawl, tow; *informal* yank. **2** *the day dragged* BECOME TEDIOUS, pass slowly, creep along, hang heavy, wear on, go on too long, go on and on.
● noun **1** *the drag of the air brakes* PULL, resistance, tug. **2** *(informal) work can be a drag* BORE, nuisance, bother, trouble, pest, annoyance, trial, vexation; *informal* pain (in the neck), bind, headache, hassle.
– PHRASES **drag on** PERSIST, continue, go on, carry on, extend, run on, be protracted, endure, prevail. **drag something out** PROLONG, protract, draw out, spin out, string out, extend, lengthen, carry on, keep going, continue.

dragoon ● noun *(historical) the dragoons charged* CAVALRYMAN, mounted soldier; *historical* knight, chevalier, hussar; *archaic* cavalier.
● verb *he dragooned his friends into participating* COERCE, pressure, pressurize, press, push; force, compel, impel; hound, harass,

dragster ● noun a car used in drag races.
drain ● verb **1** cause the liquid in (something) to run out. **2** (of liquid) run off or out. **3** become dry as liquid runs off. **4** deprive of strength or resources. **5** drink the entire contents of. ● noun **1** a channel or pipe carrying off surplus liquid. **2** a thing that uses up a resource or one's strength.
– PHRASES **go down the drain** informal be totally wasted. **laugh like a drain** Brit. informal laugh raucously.
– ORIGIN Old English.
drainage ● noun **1** the action or process of draining. **2** a system of drains.
drainer ● noun **1** a rack used to hold draining crockery. **2** a draining board.
draining board ● noun Brit. a sloping grooved surface on which crockery is left to drain into an adjacent sink.
drainpipe ● noun **1** a pipe for carrying off rainwater from a building. **2** (**drainpipes** or **drainpipe trousers**) trousers with very narrow legs.
drake ● noun a male duck.
– ORIGIN Germanic.
Dralon /draylon/ ● noun trademark, chiefly Brit. a synthetic textile made from acrylic fibre.
– ORIGIN on the pattern of *nylon*.
DRAM ● abbreviation Electronics dynamic random-access memory.
dram[1] ● noun **1** chiefly Scottish a small drink of spirits. **2** another term for DRACHM.
– ORIGIN Latin *dragma*, from Greek *drakhmē* 'drachma'.
dram[2] /draam/ ● noun the basic monetary unit of Armenia, equal to 100 luma.
drama ● noun **1** a play. **2** plays as a genre. **3** an exciting series of events.
– ORIGIN Greek *drama*, from *dran* 'do, act'.
dramatic ● adjective **1** relating to drama. **2** sudden and striking: *a dramatic increase.* **3** exciting or impressive. **4** intended to create an effect; theatrical.
– DERIVATIVES **dramatically** adverb.
dramatics ● plural noun **1** the study or practice of acting in and producing plays. **2** theatrically exaggerated behaviour.
dramatis personae /drammətiss pərsōnī/ ● plural noun the characters of a play, novel, or narrative.
– ORIGIN Latin, 'persons of the drama'.
dramatist ● noun a person who writes plays.
dramatize (also **dramatise**) ● verb **1** present (a novel, event, etc.) as a play. **2** exaggerate the excitement or seriousness of.
– DERIVATIVES **dramatization** noun.
dramaturgy /drammәturji/ ● noun the theory and practice of dramatic composition.
– DERIVATIVES **dramaturgic** adjective **dramaturgical** adjective.
Drambuie /drambyōoi/ ● noun trademark a sweet Scotch whisky liqueur.
– ORIGIN from Scottish Gaelic *dram buidheach* 'satisfying drink'.
drank past of DRINK.
drape ● verb arrange (cloth or clothing) loosely on or round something. ● noun **1** (**drapes**) long curtains. **2** the way in which a garment or fabric hangs.
– ORIGIN back-formation from DRAPERY.
draper ● noun Brit. dated a person who sells textile fabrics.
drapery ● noun (pl. **draperies**) cloth, curtains, or clothing hanging in loose folds.
– ORIGIN Old French *draperie*, from *drap* 'cloth'.
drastic ● adjective having a strong or far-reaching effect.
– DERIVATIVES **drastically** adverb.
– ORIGIN Greek *drastikos*, from *dran* 'do'.
drat ● exclamation used to express mild annoyance.
– DERIVATIVES **dratted** adjective.
– ORIGIN shortening of *od rat*, a euphemism for *God rot*.
draught (US **draft**) ● noun **1** a current of cool air in a room or confined space. **2** a single act of drinking or inhaling. **3** literary or archaic a quantity of a liquid with medicinal properties: *a sleeping draught.* **4** the depth of water needed to float a particular ship. **5** the drawing in of a fishing net. ● verb variant spelling of DRAFT. ● adjective **1** denoting beer served from a cask rather than from a bottle or can. **2** denoting an animal used for pulling heavy loads.
– ORIGIN Old Norse.
draughtboard ● noun Brit. a square chequered board of sixty-four squares, used for playing draughts.
draughts ● noun Brit. a game played on a chequered board by two players with pieces which are moved diagonally.
– ORIGIN from DRAUGHT in the obsolete sense 'move' (in chess).
draughtsman (or **draughtswoman**) ● noun **1** a person who makes detailed technical plans or drawings. **2** an artist skilled in drawing. **3** variant spelling of DRAFTSMAN.
– DERIVATIVES **draughtsmanship** noun.
draughty (US **drafty**) ● adjective (**draughtier**, **draughtiest**) uncomfortable because of draughts of cold air.
Dravidian /drәviddiәn/ ● noun **1** a family of languages spoken in southern India and Sri Lanka, including Tamil and Kannada. **2** a member of any of the peoples speaking these languages. ● adjective relating to Dravidian or Dravidians.
– ORIGIN Sanskrit, 'relating to the Tamils'.
draw ● verb (past **drew**; past part. **drawn**) **1** produce (a picture or diagram) by making lines and marks on paper. **2** produce (a line) on a surface. **3** pull or drag (a vehicle) so as to make it fol-

Thesaurus

nag, harry, badger, goad, pester; browbeat, bludgeon, bully, twist someone's arm, strong-arm; *informal* railroad.
drain ● verb **1** *a valve for draining the tank* EMPTY (OUT), void, clear (out), evacuate, unload. **2** *drain off any surplus liquid* DRAW OFF, extract, withdraw, remove, siphon off, pour out, pour off; milk, bleed, tap, void, filter, discharge. **3** *the water drained away to the sea* FLOW, pour, trickle, stream, run, rush, gush, flood, surge; leak, ooze, seep, dribble, issue, filter, bleed, leach. **4** *more people would just drain our resources* USE UP, exhaust, deplete, consume, expend, get through, sap, strain, tax; milk, bleed. **5** *he drained his drink* DRINK (UP/DOWN), gulp (down), guzzle, quaff, down, imbibe, sup, swallow, finish off, toss off, slug; *informal* sink, swig, swill (down), polish off, knock back, put away.
– OPPOSITES fill.
● noun **1** *the drain filled with water* SEWER, channel, conduit, ditch, culvert, duct, pipe, gutter, trough; sluice, spillway, race, flume, chute. **2** *a drain on the battery* STRAIN, pressure, burden, load, tax, demand.
dram ● noun DRINK, nip, tot, sip, drop, finger, splash, little, spot, taste.
drama ● noun **1** *a television drama* PLAY, show, piece, theatrical work, dramatization. **2** *he is studying drama* ACTING, the theatre, the stage, the performing arts, dramatic art, stagecraft. **3** *she liked to create a drama* INCIDENT, scene, spectacle, crisis; excitement, thrill, sensation; disturbance, row, commotion, turmoil; dramatics, theatrics.
dramatic ● adjective **1** *dramatic art* THEATRICAL, theatric, thespian, stage, dramaturgical; *formal* histrionic. **2** *a dramatic increase* CONSIDERABLE, substantial, sizeable, goodly, fair, marked, noticeable, measurable, perceptible, obvious, appreciable; significant, notable, noteworthy, remarkable, extraordinary, exceptional, phenomenal; *informal* tidy. **3** *there were dramatic scenes in the city* EXCITING, stirring, action-packed, sensational, spectacular; startling, unexpected, tense, gripping, riveting, fascinating, thrilling, hair-raising; rousing, lively, electrifying, impassioned, moving. **4** *dramatic headlands* STRIKING, impressive, imposing, spectacular, breathtaking, dazzling, sensational, awesome, awe-inspiring, remarkable, outstanding, incredible, phenomenal. **5** *a dramatic gesture* EXAGGERATED, theatrical, ostentatious, actressy, stagy, showy, melodramatic, overdone, histrionic, affected, mannered, artificial; *informal* hammy, ham, campy.
– OPPOSITES insignificant, boring.
dramatist ● noun PLAYWRIGHT, writer, scriptwriter, screenwriter, scenarist, dramaturge.
dramatize ● verb **1** *the novel was dramatized for television* TURN INTO A PLAY/FILM, adapt for the stage/screen. **2** *the tabloids dramatized the event* EXAGGERATE, overdo, overstate, hyperbolize, magnify, amplify, inflate; sensationalize, embroider, colour, aggrandize, embellish, elaborate; *informal* blow up (out of all proportion).
drape ● verb **1** *she draped a shawl round her* WRAP, wind, swathe, sling, hang. **2** *the chair was draped with blankets* COVER, envelop, swathe, shroud, deck, festoon, overlay, cloak, wind, enfold, sheathe. **3** *he draped one leg over the arm of his chair* DANGLE, hang, suspend, droop, drop.
drastic ● adjective EXTREME, serious, desperate, radical, far-reaching, momentous, substantial; heavy, severe, harsh, rigorous; oppressive, draconian.
– OPPOSITES moderate.
draught ● noun **1** *the draught made Robyn shiver* CURRENT OF AIR, rush of air; waft, wind, breeze, gust, puff, blast; *informal* blow. **2** *a*

low behind. **4** pull or move in a specified direction. **5** pull (curtains) shut or open. **6** arrive at a point in time: *the campaign drew to a close.* **7** extract from a container or receptacle: *he drew his gun.* **8** take in (a breath). **9** be the cause of (a specified response). **10** attract to a place or an event. **11** induce to reveal or do something. **12** reach (a conclusion) by deduction or inference. **13** (**draw on**) suck smoke from (a cigarette or pipe). **14** finish (a contest or game) with an even score. ● **noun 1** an act of selecting names randomly, for prizes, sporting fixtures, etc. **2** a game or match that ends with the scores even. **3** a person or thing that is very attractive or interesting. **4** an act of inhaling smoke from a cigarette. **5** Cricket a game which is left incomplete for lack of time. Compare with TIE.

d

– PHRASES **draw someone's fire** attract hostile criticism away from a more important target. **draw in** (of successive days) become shorter because of the changing seasons. **draw the line at** set a limit of what one is willing to do or accept. **draw on** (of a period of time) pass by and approach its end. **draw out 1** make (something) last longer. **2** persuade to be more talkative. **draw up 1** come to a halt. **2** prepare (a plan or document) in detail.

– ORIGIN Old English, related to DRAUGHT.

drawback ● **noun** a disadvantage or problem.

drawbridge ● **noun** a bridge which is hinged at one end so that it can be raised.

drawcord ● **noun** another term for DRAWSTRING.

drawee /drawee/ ● **noun** the person or organization who has to pay a draft or bill.

drawer ● **noun 1** /draw/ a lidless storage compartment made to slide horizontally in and out of a desk or chest. **2** (**drawers**) /drawz/ dated or humorous knickers or underpants. **3** /drawər/ a person who draws something. **4** /drawər/ the person who writes a cheque.

drawing ● **noun 1** a monochrome picture or diagram made with a pencil, pen, or crayon rather than paint. **2** the art or skill of making such pictures.

drawing board ● **noun** a board on which paper can be spread for artists or designers to work on.

– PHRASES **back to the drawing board** a plan has failed and a new one is needed.

drawing pin ● **noun** Brit. a short flat-headed pin for fastening paper to a surface.

drawing room ● **noun** a room in a large private house in which guests can be received.

– ORIGIN abbreviation of *withdrawing-room* 'a room to withdraw to'.

drawl ● **verb** speak in a slow, lazy way with prolonged vowel sounds. ● **noun** a drawling accent.

– ORIGIN from Low German or Dutch *dralen* 'delay, linger'.

drawn past participle of DRAW. ● **adjective** looking strained from illness or exhaustion.

drawn-out ● **adjective** lasting longer than is necessary.

drawstring ● **noun** a string in the seam of a garment or bag, which can be pulled to tighten or close it.

dray ● **noun** a low truck or cart without sides, for delivering barrels or other heavy loads.

– ORIGIN perhaps from an Old English word meaning 'dragnet'; related to DRAW.

dread ● **verb** anticipate with great apprehension or fear. ● **noun** great fear or apprehension. ● **adjective** greatly feared; dreadful.

– DERIVATIVES **dreaded** adjective.

– ORIGIN Old English.

dreadful ● **adjective 1** extremely bad or serious. **2** used for emphasis: *a dreadful flirt.*

– DERIVATIVES **dreadfully** adverb.

dreadlocks ● **plural noun** a Rastafarian hairstyle in which the hair is twisted into tight braids or ringlets.

– DERIVATIVES **dreadlocked** adjective.

dreadnought ● **noun** historical a type of battleship of the early 20th century, equipped entirely with large-calibre guns.

– ORIGIN named after Britain's HMS *Dreadnought*, completed 1906.

Thesaurus

deep draught of beer GULP, drink, swallow, mouthful, slug; *informal* swig, swill.

draw ● **verb 1** *he drew the house* SKETCH, make a drawing (of), delineate, outline, draft, rough out, illustrate, render, represent, trace; portray, depict. **2** *she drew her chair in to the table* PULL, haul, drag, tug, heave, lug, trail, tow; *informal* yank. **3** *the train drew into the station* MOVE, go, come, proceed, progress, travel, advance, pass, drive; inch, roll, glide, cruise; forge, sweep; back. **4** *she drew the curtains* CLOSE, shut, pull to, lower; open, part, pull back, pull open, fling open, raise. **5** *he drew some fluid off the knee joint* DRAIN, extract, withdraw, remove, suck, pump, siphon, milk, bleed, tap. **6** *he drew his gun* PULL OUT, take out, produce, fish out, extract, withdraw; unsheathe. **7** *I drew £50 out of the bank* WITHDRAW, take out. **8** *while I draw breath* BREATHE IN, inhale, inspire, respire. **9** *she was drawing huge audiences* ATTRACT, interest, win, capture, catch, engage, lure, entice; absorb, occupy, rivet, engross, fascinate, mesmerize, spellbind, captivate, enthral, grip. **10** *what conclusion can we draw?* DEDUCE, infer, conclude, derive, gather, glean.

● **noun 1** *she won the Christmas draw* RAFFLE, lottery, sweepstake, sweep, tombola, ballot; *N. Amer.* lotto. **2** *the match ended in a draw* TIE, dead heat, stalemate. **3** *the draw of central London* ATTRACTION, lure, allure, pull, appeal, glamour, enticement, temptation, charm, seduction, fascination, magnetism.

– PHRASES **draw on** CALL ON, have recourse to, avail oneself of, turn to, look to, fall back on, rely on, exploit, use, employ, utilize, bring into play. **draw something out 1** *he drew out a gun.* See DRAW verb sense 6. **2** *they always drew their parting out* PROLONG, protract, drag out, spin out, string out, extend, lengthen. **draw someone out** ENCOURAGE TO TALK, put at ease. **draw up** STOP, pull up, halt, come to a standstill, brake, park; arrive. **draw something up 1** *we drew up a list* COMPOSE, formulate, frame, write down, draft, prepare, think up, devise, work out; create, invent, design. **2** *he drew up his forces in battle array* ARRANGE, marshal, muster, assemble, group, order, range, rank, line up, dispose, position, array.

drawback ● **noun** DISADVANTAGE, snag, downside, stumbling block, catch, hitch, pitfall, fly in the ointment; weak spot/point, weakness, imperfection; handicap, limitation, trouble, difficulty, problem, complication; hindrance, obstacle, impediment, obstruction, inconvenience, discouragement, deterrent; *informal* minus, hiccup; *Brit. informal* spanner in the works.

– OPPOSITES benefit.

drawing ● **noun** SKETCH, picture, illustration, representation, portrayal, delineation, depiction, composition, study; diagram, outline, design, plan.

– RELATED TERMS graphic.

drawl ● **verb** SAY SLOWLY, speak slowly; drone.

drawn ● **adjective** *she looked pale and drawn* PINCHED, haggard, drained, wan, hollow-cheeked; fatigued, tired, exhausted; tense, stressed, strained, worried, anxious, harassed, fraught; *informal* hassled.

dread ● **verb** *I used to dread going to school* FEAR, be afraid of, worry about, be anxious about, have forebodings about; be terrified by, tremble/shudder at, shrink from, quail from, flinch from; *informal* get cold feet about.

● **noun** *she was filled with dread* FEAR, apprehension, trepidation, anxiety, worry, concern, foreboding, disquiet, unease, angst; fright, panic, alarm; terror, horror; *informal* the jitters, the heebie-jeebies.

– OPPOSITES confidence.

● **adjective** *a dread secret* AWFUL, frightful, terrible, horrible, dreadful; feared, frightening, alarming, terrifying, dire, dreaded.

dreadful ● **adjective 1** *a dreadful accident* TERRIBLE, frightful, horrible, grim, awful, dire; horrifying, alarming, shocking, distressing, appalling, harrowing; ghastly, fearful, horrendous; tragic, calamitous; *formal* grievous. **2** *a dreadful meal* UNPLEASANT, disagreeable, nasty; frightful, shocking, awful, abysmal, atrocious, disgraceful, deplorable, very bad, repugnant; poor, inadequate, inferior, unsatisfactory, distasteful; *informal* pathetic, woeful, crummy, rotten, sorry, third-rate, lousy, ropy, God-awful; *Brit. informal* duff, chronic, rubbish. **3** *you're a dreadful flirt* OUTRAGEOUS, shocking; inordinate, immoderate, unrestrained.

– OPPOSITES pleasant, agreeable.

dreadfully ● **adverb 1** *I'm dreadfully hungry* EXTREMELY, very, really, exceedingly, tremendously, exceptionally, extraordinarily; decidedly, most, particularly; *N. English* right; *informal* terrifically, terribly, desperately, awfully, devilishly, mega, seriously, majorly; *Brit. informal* jolly, ever so, dead, well; *N. Amer. informal* real, mighty, awful; *informal, dated* frightfully. **2** *she missed James dreadfully* VERY MUCH, much, lots, a lot, a great deal, intensely, desperately. **3** *the company performed dreadfully* TERRIBLY, awfully, very badly, atro-

dream ● noun **1** a series of thoughts, images, and sensations occurring in a person's mind during sleep. **2** a cherished ambition or ideal; a fantasy. **3** informal someone or something perceived as wonderful or perfect. ● verb (past and past part. **dreamed** /dreemd/ or **dreamt** /dremt/) **1** experience dreams during sleep. **2** indulge in daydreams or fantasies. **3** contemplate the possibility of: *I never dreamed she'd take offence.* **4** (**dream up**) imagine or invent.
– PHRASES **like a dream** informal very easily or successfully.
– DERIVATIVES **dreamer** noun **dreamless** adjective.
– ORIGIN Germanic.
dreamboat ● noun informal a very attractive person, especially a man.
dreamscape ● noun a scene with the strangeness or mystery characteristic of dreams.
dreamy ● adjective (**dreamier**, **dreamiest**) **1** dreamlike; pleasantly distracting or unreal. **2** given to daydreaming.
– DERIVATIVES **dreamily** adverb **dreaminess** noun.
dreary ● adjective (**drearier**, **dreariest**) dull, bleak, and depressing.
– DERIVATIVES **drearily** adverb **dreariness** noun.
– ORIGIN Old English, 'gory, cruel, melancholy'.
dreck /drek/ ● noun informal rubbish.
– ORIGIN Yiddish, 'filth, dregs'.
dredge[1] ● verb **1** clean out the bed of (a harbour, river, etc.) with a dredge. **2** bring up or remove with a dredge. **3** (**dredge up**) bring (something unwelcome and forgotten) to people's attention. ● noun an apparatus for bringing up objects or mud from a river or seabed by scooping or dragging.
– DERIVATIVES **dredger** noun.
– ORIGIN perhaps related to Dutch *dregghe* 'grappling hook'.
dredge[2] ● verb sprinkle (food) with sugar or other powdered substance.
– ORIGIN from obsolete *dredge* 'sweet confection, mixture of spices', from Old French *dragie*.
dregs ● noun **1** the remnants of a liquid left in a container, together with any sediment. **2** the most worthless parts: *the dregs of society.*
– ORIGIN probably Scandinavian.
drench ● verb **1** wet thoroughly; soak. **2** cover liberally with something. **3** forcibly give a liquid medicine to (an animal). ● noun a dose of medicine administered to an animal.
– ORIGIN Old English, related to DRINK.
dress ● verb **1** (also **get dressed**) put on one's clothes. **2** put clothes on (someone). **3** wear clothes in a particular way or of a particular type: *she dresses well.* **4** decorate or arrange in an artistic or attractive way. **5** clean, treat, or apply a dressing to (a wound). **6** clean and prepare (food) for cooking or eating. **7** add a dressing to (a salad). **8** apply fertilizer to. **9** treat or smooth the surface of (leather, fabric, or stone). ● noun **1** a one-piece garment for a woman or girl that covers the body and extends down over the legs. **2** clothing of a specified kind. **3** (before another noun) (of clothing) formal or ceremonial: *a dress suit.*
– PHRASES **dress down** informal **1** reprimand. **2** wear informal clothes. **dressed to kill** informal wearing glamorous clothes intended to create a striking impression. **dress up** dress in smart or formal clothes, or in a special costume.
– ORIGIN Old French *dresser* 'arrange, prepare', from Latin *directus* 'direct, straight'.
dressage /dressaazh/ ● noun the art of riding and training horses so as to develop obedience, flexibility, and balance.
– ORIGIN French, 'training'.
dress circle ● noun the first level of seats above the ground floor in a theatre.
dresser[1] ● noun **1** a sideboard with shelves above for storing and displaying crockery. **2** N. Amer. a dressing table or chest of drawers.
– ORIGIN originally denoting a sideboard or table on which food was prepared.
dresser[2] ● noun **1** a person who dresses in a specified way: *a*

d

Thesaurus

ciously, appallingly, abominably, poorly; *informal* abysmally, pitifully, diabolically.
dream ● noun **1** *I awoke from my dreams* REM sleep; nightmare; vision, fantasy, hallucination. **2** *she went around in a dream* DAYDREAM, reverie, trance, daze, stupor, haze; *Scottish* dwam. **3** *he realized his childhood dream* AMBITION, aspiration, hope; goal, aim, objective, grail, intention, intent, target; desire, wish, yearning; daydream, fantasy, pipe dream. **4** *he's an absolute dream* DELIGHT, joy, marvel, wonder, gem, treasure; beauty, vision.
● verb **1** *she dreamed of her own funeral* HAVE A DREAM, have a nightmare. **2** *I dreamt of making the Olympic team* FANTASIZE ABOUT, daydream about; WISH FOR, hope for, long for, yearn for, hanker after, set one's heart on; aspire to, aim for, set one's sights on. **3** *she's always dreaming* DAYDREAM, be in a trance, be lost in thought, be preoccupied, be abstracted, stare into space, be in cloud cuckoo land; muse. **4** *I wouldn't dream of being late* THINK, consider, contemplate, conceive.
● adjective *his dream home* IDEAL, perfect, fantasy.
– PHRASES **dream something up** THINK UP, invent, concoct, devise, hatch, contrive, create, work out, come up with; *informal* cook up.
dreamer ● noun FANTASIST, daydreamer; romantic, sentimentalist, idealist, wishful thinker, Don Quixote; Utopian, visionary.
– OPPOSITES realist.
dreamland ● noun **1** *I drift off to dreamland* SLEEP; *humorous* the land of Nod. **2** *they must be living in dreamland* THE LAND OF MAKE-BELIEVE, fairyland, cloud cuckoo land; paradise, Utopia, heaven, Shangri-La.
dreamlike ● adjective UNREAL, illusory, imaginary, unsubstantial, chimerical, ethereal, phantasmagorical, trance-like; surreal; nightmarish, Kafkaesque; hazy, shadowy, faint, indistinct, unclear; *poetic/literary* illusive.
dreamy ● adjective **1** *a dreamy expression* DAYDREAMING, dreaming; pensive, thoughtful, reflective, meditative, ruminative; lost in thought, preoccupied, distracted, rapt, inattentive, woolgathering, vague, absorbed, absent-minded, with one's head in the clouds, in a world of one's own; *informal* miles away. **2** *he was dreamy as a child* IDEALISTIC, romantic, starry-eyed, impractical, unrealistic, Utopian, quixotic; *Brit. informal* airy-fairy. **3** *a dreamy recollection* DREAMLIKE, vague, dim, hazy, shadowy, faint, indistinct, unclear. **4** *(informal) the prince was really dreamy* ATTRACTIVE, handsome, good-looking; appealing, lovely, delightful; *informal* heavenly, divine, gorgeous, hot, cute.
– OPPOSITES alert, practical, clear, ugly.
dreary ● adjective **1** *a dreary day at school* DULL, drab, uninteresting, flat, tedious, wearisome, boring, unexciting, unstimulating, uninspiring, soul-destroying; humdrum, monotonous, uneventful, unremarkable, featureless. **2** *she thought of dreary things* SAD, miserable, depressing, gloomy, sombre, grave, mournful, melancholic, joyless, cheerless. **3** *a dreary day* GLOOMY, dismal, dull, dark, dingy, murky, overcast; depressing, sombre.
– OPPOSITES exciting, cheerful, bright.
dregs ● plural noun **1** *the dregs from a bottle of wine* SEDIMENT, deposit, residue, accumulation, sludge, lees, grounds, settlings; remains; *technical* residuum; *archaic* grouts. **2** *the dregs of humanity* SCUM, refuse, riff-raff, outcasts, deadbeats; the underclass, the untouchables, the lowest of the low, the great unwashed, the hoi polloi; *informal* trash, dossers.
drench ● verb SOAK, saturate, wet through, permeate, douse, souse; drown, swamp, inundate, flood; steep, bathe.
dress ● verb **1** *he dressed quickly* PUT ON CLOTHES, clothe oneself, get dressed. **2** *she was dressed in a suit* CLOTHE, attire, garb, deck out, trick out/up, costume, array, robe; *informal* get up, doll up; *archaic* apparel. **3** *they dress for dinner every day* WEAR FORMAL CLOTHES, wear evening dress, dress up. **4** *she enjoyed dressing the tree* DECORATE, trim, deck, adorn, ornament, embellish, beautify, prettify; festoon, garland, garnish. **5** *they dressed his wounds* BANDAGE, cover, bind, wrap, swathe. **6** *she had to dress the chickens* PREPARE, get ready; clean. **7** *the field was dressed with manure* FERTILIZE, enrich, manure, mulch, compost, top-dress. **8** *he dressed Michelle's hair* STYLE, groom, arrange, do; comb, brush; preen, primp; *informal* fix. **9** *(Military) the battalion dressed its ranks* LINE UP, align, straighten, arrange, order, dispose; fall in.
● noun **1** *a long blue dress* FROCK, gown, robe, shift. **2** *full evening dress* CLOTHES, clothing, garments, attire; costume, outfit, ensemble, garb, turnout; *informal* gear, get-up, togs, duds, glad rags; *Brit. informal* clobber; *N. Amer. informal* threads; *formal* apparel; *archaic* raiment.
– RELATED TERMS sartorial.
– PHRASES **dress down** DRESS INFORMALLY, dress casually; *informal* slob around. **dress someone down** *(informal).* See REPRIMAND verb. **dress up 1** *Angela loved dressing up* DRESS SMARTLY, dress formally, wear evening dress; *informal* doll oneself up, put on one's glad rags. **2** *Hugh dressed up as Santa Claus* DISGUISE ONESELF, dress; put on fancy dress, put on a costume. **dress something up** PRES-

d

snappy dresser. **2** a person who looks after theatrical costumes.

dressing ● noun **1** a sauce for salads, usually consisting of oil and vinegar with herbs or other flavourings. **2** N. Amer. stuffing. **3** a piece of material placed on a wound to protect it. **4** size or stiffening used in the finishing of fabrics. **5** a fertilizer spread over land.

dressing-down ● noun informal a severe reprimand.

dressing gown ● noun a long loose robe worn after getting out of bed or bathing.

dressing room ● noun **1** a room in which actors or other performers change clothes. **2** a small room attached to a bedroom for storing clothes.

dressing table ● noun a table with a mirror and drawers, used while dressing or applying make-up.

dressmaker ● noun a person who makes women's clothes.

dress rehearsal ● noun a final rehearsal in which everything is done as it would be in a real performance.

dress sense ● noun a good instinct for selecting clothes.

dress shirt ● noun **1** a man's white shirt worn with a bow tie and a dinner jacket on formal occasions. **2** N. Amer. a shirt suitable for wearing with a tie.

dressy ● adjective (**dressier**, **dressiest**) (of clothes) suitable for a smart or formal occasion.

drew past of DRAW.

drey /dray/ ● noun (pl. **dreys**) a squirrel's nest of twigs in a tree.
– ORIGIN of unknown origin.

dribble ● verb **1** (of a liquid) fall slowly in drops or a thin stream. **2** allow saliva to run from the mouth. **3** (in sport) take (the ball) forward with slight touches or (in basketball) by continuous bouncing. ● noun **1** a thin stream of liquid. **2** (in sport) an act of dribbling.
– DERIVATIVES **dribbler** noun **dribbly** adjective.
– ORIGIN originally in sense 'shoot an arrow short or wide of its target': from obsolete *drib*, variant of DRIP.

driblet ● noun **1** a thin stream or small drop of liquid. **2** a small or insignificant amount.

dribs and drabs ● plural noun (in phrase **in dribs and drabs**) informal in small scattered or sporadic amounts.

dried past and past participle of DRY.

drier[1] ● noun variant spelling of DRYER.

drier[2] ● adjective comparative of DRY.

drift ● verb **1** be carried slowly by a current of air or water. **2** walk or move slowly or casually. **3** (of snow, leaves, etc.) be blown into heaps by the wind. ● noun **1** a continuous slow movement from one place to another. **2** the general intention or meaning of someone's remarks: *he got her drift.* **3** a large mass of snow, leaves, etc. piled up by the wind. **4** deviation from a course because of currents or winds. **5** Geology deposits left by retreating ice sheets. **6** S. African a ford.
– ORIGIN Old Norse, 'snowdrift, something driven'; related to DRIVE.

drifter ● noun **1** a person who is continually moving from place to place, without any fixed home or job. **2** a fishing boat equipped with a drift net.

drift net ● noun a large fishing net kept upright by weights at the bottom and floats at the top and allowed to drift in the sea.

driftwood ● noun pieces of wood floating on the sea or washed ashore.

drill[1] ● noun **1** a tool or machine used for boring holes. **2** training in military exercises. **3** instruction by means of repeated exercises. **4** (**the drill**) informal the correct or recognized procedure. ● verb **1** bore (a hole) with a drill. **2** subject to military training or other intensive instruction. **3** informal hit hard so as to travel in a straight line.
– DERIVATIVES **driller** noun.
– ORIGIN from Dutch *drillen* 'bore, turn in a circle'.

drill[2] ● noun **1** a machine which makes small furrows, sows seed in them, and then covers the sown seed. **2** a small furrow made by such a machine. ● verb sow with a drill.
– ORIGIN perhaps from DRILL[1].

drill[3] ● noun a West African baboon with a naked blue or purple rump.
– ORIGIN probably a local word; compare with MANDRILL.

drill[4] ● noun a coarse twilled cotton or linen fabric.
– ORIGIN abbreviation of earlier *drilling*, from Latin *trilix* 'triple-twilled'.

drily /drīli/ (also **dryly**) ● adverb **1** in a matter-of-fact or ironically humorous way. **2** in a dry way or condition.

drink ● verb (past **drank**; past part. **drunk**) **1** take (a liquid) into the mouth and swallow. **2** consume alcohol, especially to excess. **3** (**drink in**) watch or listen eagerly to. ● noun **1** a liquid consumed as refreshment or nourishment. **2** a quantity of liquid swallowed at one time. **3** the habitual or excessive consumption of alcohol. **4** (**the drink**) informal the sea.
– PHRASES **drink someone's health** (or **drink to someone**) express good wishes for someone by raising one's glass and drinking a small amount. **I'll drink to that** expressing agreement or approval. **in drink** when intoxicated.
– DERIVATIVES **drinkable** adjective.
– ORIGIN Old English.

Thesaurus

ENT, represent, portray, depict, characterize; embellish, enhance, touch up, embroider.

dressing ● noun **1** *salad dressing* SAUCE, relish, condiment, dip. **2** *they put fresh dressings on her burns* BANDAGE, covering, plaster, gauze, lint, compress. **3** *a soil dressing* FERTILIZER, mulch; manure, compost, dung, bonemeal, fishmeal, guano; top-dressing.

dressmaker ● noun TAILOR, seamstress, needlewoman; outfitter, costumier, clothier; couturier, designer; *dated* modiste.
– RELATED TERMS sartorial.

dressy ● adjective SMART, formal; elaborate, ornate; stylish, elegant, chic, fashionable; *informal* snappy, snazzy, natty, trendy.
– OPPOSITES casual.

dribble ● verb **1** *the baby started to dribble* DROOL, slaver, slobber, salivate, drivel; *Scottish & Irish* slabber. **2** *rainwater dribbled down her face* TRICKLE, drip, fall, drizzle; ooze, seep.
● noun **1** *there was dribble on his chin* SALIVA, spittle, spit, slaver, slobber, drool. **2** *a dribble of sweat* TRICKLE, drip, driblet, stream, drizzle; drop, splash.

dried ● adjective DEHYDRATED, desiccated, dry, dried up, moistureless.

drift ● verb **1** *his raft drifted down the river* BE CARRIED, be borne; float, bob, waft, meander. **2** *the guests drifted away* WANDER, meander, stray, potter, dawdle; *Brit. informal* mooch. **3** *don't allow your attention to drift* STRAY, digress, deviate, diverge, veer, get sidetracked. **4** *snow drifted over the path* PILE UP, bank up, heap up, accumulate, gather, amass.
● noun **1** *a drift from the country to urban areas* MOVEMENT, shift, flow, transfer, relocation, gravitation. **2** *the pilot had not noticed any drift* DEVIATION, digression. **3** *he caught the drift of her thoughts* GIST, essence, meaning, sense, substance, significance; thrust, import, tenor; implication, intention; direction, course. **4** *a drift of deep snow* PILE, heap, bank, mound, mass, accumulation.

drifter ● noun WANDERER, traveller, transient, roamer, tramp, vagabond, vagrant; *N. Amer.* hobo.

drill ● noun **1** *a hydraulic drill* DRILLING TOOL, boring tool, auger, (brace and) bit, gimlet, awl, bradawl. **2** *they learned military discipline and drill* TRAINING, instruction, coaching, teaching; (physical) exercises, workout; *informal* square-bashing. **3** *Estelle knew the drill* PROCEDURE, routine, practice, regimen, programme, schedule; method, system.
● verb **1** *drill the piece of wood* BORE A HOLE IN, make a hole in; bore, pierce, puncture, perforate. **2** *a sergeant drilling new recruits* TRAIN, instruct, coach, teach, discipline; exercise, put someone through their paces. **3** *his mother had drilled politeness into him* INSTIL, hammer, drive, drum, din, implant, ingrain; teach, indoctrinate, brainwash.

drink ● verb **1** *she drank her coffee* SWALLOW, gulp down, quaff, guzzle, sup; imbibe, sip, consume; drain, toss off, slug; *informal* swig, down, knock back, put away, neck, sink, swill. **2** *he never drank* DRINK ALCOHOL, tipple, indulge; carouse; *informal* hit the bottle, booze, knock a few back, have one over the eight, get tanked up, go on a bender; *Brit. informal* bevvy; *N. Amer. informal* bend one's elbow. **3** *let's drink to success* TOAST, salute.
● noun **1** *he took a sip of his drink* BEVERAGE, liquid refreshment; dram, bracer, nightcap, nip, tot; pint; *Brit. informal* bevvy; *humorous* libation; *archaic* potation. **2** *she turned to drink* ALCOHOL, (intoxicating) liquor, alcoholic drink; *informal* booze, hooch, the hard stuff, firewater, rotgut, moonshine, the bottle, the sauce, grog, Dutch courage. **3** *she took a drink of her wine* SWALLOW, gulp, sip, draught, slug; *informal* swig, swill. **4** *a drink of orange juice* GLASS, cup, mug. **5** *(informal) he fell into the drink* THE SEA, the ocean, the water; *informal* the briny, Davy Jones's locker; *poetic/literary* the deep.
– PHRASES **drink something in** ABSORB, assimilate, digest, ingest,

drink-driving ● noun Brit. the crime of driving a vehicle with an excess of alcohol in the blood.
drinker ● noun **1** a person who drinks. **2** a container from which an animal can drink.
drinking chocolate ● noun a mixture of cocoa powder, milk solids, and sugar added to hot water to make a chocolate drink.
drinking fountain ● noun a device producing a small jet of water for drinking.
drip ● verb (**dripped**, **dripping**) fall or let fall in small drops of liquid. ● noun **1** a small drop of a liquid. **2** an apparatus which slowly passes fluid, nutrients, or drugs into a patient's body intravenously. **3** informal a weak and ineffectual person. **4** Architecture a projection which is channelled to prevent rain from running down the wall below.
– ORIGIN Old English, related to DROP.
drip-dry ● verb (of fabric or a garment) become dry without forming creases when hung up after washing. ● adjective capable of drip-drying.
drip-feed ● verb introduce (fluid) drop by drop. ● noun (**drip feed**) a device for introducing fluid drop by drop.
dripping ● noun Brit. fat that has melted and dripped from roasting meat. ● adjective extremely wet.
drippy ● adjective (**drippier**, **drippiest**) **1** informal weak, ineffectual, or sloppily sentimental. **2** tending to drip.
– DERIVATIVES **drippily** adverb **drippiness** noun.
dripstone ● noun **1** Architecture a moulding over a door or window which deflects rain. **2** Geology rock formed from dripping water, e.g. as stalactites and stalagmites.
drive ● verb (past **drove**; past part. **driven**) **1** operate and control (a motor vehicle). **2** convey in a motor vehicle. **3** propel or carry along in a specified direction. **4** urge (animals or people) to move in a specified direction. **5** compel to act in a particular way. **6** provide the energy to keep (an engine or machine) in motion. ● noun **1** a trip or journey in a car. **2** (also **driveway**) a short private road leading to a house. **3** an innate, biologically determined urge. **4** an organized effort to achieve a particular purpose. **5** determination and ambition. **6** the transmission of power to machinery or to the wheels of a vehicle. **7** Brit. a large organized gathering for playing a game: *a whist drive.*
– PHRASES **what someone is driving at** the point that someone is attempting to make.
– DERIVATIVES **drivable** (also **driveable**) adjective.
– ORIGIN Old English.
drive-by ● adjective chiefly N. Amer. (of a shooting) carried out from a passing vehicle.
drive-in ● adjective chiefly N. Amer. (of a cinema, restaurant, etc.) that one can visit without leaving one's car.
drivel /drivv'l/ ● noun nonsense. ● verb (**drivelled**, **drivelling**; US **driveled**, **driveling**) **1** talk nonsense. **2** archaic let saliva or mucus flow from the mouth or nose.
– ORIGIN Old English.
driven past participle of DRIVE.
driver ● noun **1** a person or thing that drives something. **2** a flat-faced golf club used for driving.
– PHRASES **in the driver's seat** in control.
– DERIVATIVES **driverless** adjective.
driveshaft ● noun a rotating shaft which transmits torque in an engine.
drivetrain ● noun the system in a motor vehicle which connects the transmission to the drive axles.
driving ● adjective **1** having a controlling influence: *the driving force behind the plan.* **2** being blown by the wind with great force: *driving rain.*
– PHRASES **in the driving seat** in control.
driving range ● noun an area where golfers can practise drives.
drizzle ● noun light rain falling in very fine drops. ● verb **1** (**it drizzles, it is drizzling**, etc.) rain lightly. **2** Cookery pour a thin stream of (a liquid ingredient) over a dish.
– DERIVATIVES **drizzly** adjective.
– ORIGIN probably from an Old English word meaning 'to fall'.
drogue /drōg/ ● noun a device towed behind a boat or aircraft to reduce speed or improve stability, or as an aerial target for gunnery practice.
– ORIGIN originally a term for a board attached to a harpoon line, used to slow down or mark the position of a whale: perhaps related to DRAG.
drogue parachute ● noun a small parachute used as a brake or to pull out a larger parachute.
droid /droyd/ ● noun (in science fiction) a robot.
– ORIGIN shortening of ANDROID.
droit de seigneur /drwaa də senyör/ ● noun the alleged right of a medieval feudal lord to have sexual intercourse with a vassal's bride on her wedding night.
– ORIGIN French, 'lord's right'.
droll /drōl/ ● adjective amusing in a strange or quaint way.
– DERIVATIVES **drollery** noun **drollness** noun **drolly** /drōl-li/ adverb.
– ORIGIN French, perhaps from Dutch *drolle* 'imp, goblin'.
dromaeosaur /drōmiəsawr/ ● noun a carnivorous bipedal dinosaur of a group including deinonychus and the velociraptors.
– ORIGIN from Greek *dromaios* 'swift-running' + *sauros* 'lizard'.
-drome ● combining form **1** denoting a place for running or racing: *velodrome.* **2** denoting something that proceeds in a certain way: *palindrome.*
– ORIGIN from Greek *dromos* 'running'.
dromedary /drommidəri/ ● noun (pl. **dromedaries**) an Arabian camel, with one hump.

d

Thesaurus

take in; be rapt in, be lost in, be fascinated by, pay close attention to.
drinkable ● adjective FIT TO DRINK, palatable; pure, clean, safe, unpolluted, untainted, uncontaminated; *formal* potable.
drinker ● noun DRUNKARD, drunk, inebriate, imbiber, tippler, sot; alcoholic, dipsomaniac, alcohol-abuser; *informal* boozer, soak, lush, wino, alky, sponge, barfly; *Austral./NZ informal* hophead; *archaic* toper.
– OPPOSITES teetotaller.
drip ● verb **1** *there was a tap dripping* DRIBBLE, drop, leak. **2** *sweat dripped from his chin* DROP, dribble, trickle, drizzle, run, splash, plop; leak, emanate, issue.
● noun **1** *a bucket to catch the drips* DROP, dribble, spot, trickle, splash. **2** *(informal) that drip who fancies you* WEAKLING, ninny, milksop, namby-pamby, crybaby, softie, doormat; *informal* wimp, weed, sissy, wuss; *Brit. informal* wet, big girl's blouse; *N. Amer. informal* candy-ass, pantywaist, pussy.
drive ● verb **1** *I can't drive a car* OPERATE, handle, manage; pilot, steer. **2** *he drove to the police station* TRAVEL BY CAR, motor. **3** *I'll drive you to the airport* CHAUFFEUR, run, give someone a lift, take, ferry, transport, convey, carry. **4** *the engine drives the front wheels* POWER, propel, move, push. **5** *he drove a nail into the boot* HAMMER, screw, ram, sink, plunge, thrust, propel, knock. **6** *she drove her cattle to market* IMPEL, urge; herd, round-up, shepherd. **7** *a desperate mother driven to crime* FORCE, compel, prompt, precipitate; oblige, coerce, pressure, goad, spur, prod. **8** *he drove his staff extremely hard* WORK, push, tax, exert.
● noun **1** *an afternoon drive* EXCURSION, outing, trip, jaunt, tour; ride, run, journey; *informal* spin. **2** *the house has a long drive* DRIVEWAY, approach, access road. **3** *sexual drive* URGE, appetite, desire, need; impulse, instinct. **4** *she lacked the drive to succeed* MOTIVATION, ambition, single-mindedness, will power, dedication, doggedness, tenacity; enthusiasm, zeal, commitment, aggression, spirit; energy, vigour, verve, vitality, pep; *informal* get-up-and-go. **5** *an anti-corruption drive* CAMPAIGN, crusade, movement, effort, push, appeal. **6** *(Brit.) a whist drive* TOURNAMENT, competition, contest, event, match.
– PHRASES **drive at** SUGGEST, imply, hint at, allude to, intimate, insinuate, indicate; refer to, mean, intend; *informal* get at.
drivel ● noun *he was talking complete drivel* NONSENSE, twaddle, claptrap, balderdash, gibberish, rubbish, mumbo-jumbo; *N. Amer.* garbage; *informal* rot, poppycock, phooey, piffle, tripe, bosh, bull, hogwash, baloney; *Brit. informal* cobblers, codswallop, waffle, tosh, double Dutch; *N. Amer. informal* flapdoodle, bushwa; *informal, dated* tommyrot, bunkum.
● verb *you always drivel on* TALK NONSENSE, talk rubbish, babble, ramble, gibber, blather, blether, prattle, gabble; *Brit. informal* waffle, witter.
driver ● verb MOTORIST, chauffeur; pilot, operator.
drizzle ● noun **1** *they shivered in the drizzle* FINE RAIN, light shower, spray; *N. English* mizzle. **2** *a drizzle of sour cream* TRICKLE, dribble, drip, stream, rivulet; sprinkle, sprinkling.
● verb **1** *it's beginning to drizzle* RAIN LIGHTLY, shower, spot; *Brit.* spit; *N. English* mizzle; *N. Amer.* sprinkle. **2** *drizzle the cream over the jelly* TRICKLE, drip, dribble, pour, splash, sprinkle.
droll ● adjective FUNNY, humorous, amusing, comic, comical, mirthful, hilarious; clownish, farcical, zany, quirky; jocular, light-

– ORIGIN from Latin *dromedarius camelus* 'swift camel', from Greek *dromas* 'runner'.

drone ● verb **1** make a continuous low humming sound. **2** speak tediously and at length. ● noun **1** a low continuous humming sound. **2** a pipe (especially in a set of bagpipes) or string used to sound a continuous note of low pitch. **3** a male bee which does no work in a colony but can fertilize a queen. **4** an idler. **5** a remote-controlled pilotless aircraft.
– ORIGIN Old English, 'male bee'.

d

drongo /drɒnggō/ ● noun (pl. **drongos** or **drongoes**) **1** a long-tailed, crested songbird with glossy black plumage, found in Africa, southern Asia, and Australia. **2** informal, chiefly Austral./NZ a stupid or incompetent person.
– ORIGIN from Malagasy (the language of Madagascar); sense 2 is said to be from the name of a very unsuccessful Australian racehorse of the 1920s.

drool ● verb **1** drop saliva uncontrollably from the mouth. **2** (often **drool over**) informal show excessive pleasure or desire. ● noun saliva falling from the mouth.
– ORIGIN contraction of DRIVEL.

droop ● verb **1** bend or hang downwards limply. **2** sag down from weariness or dejection. ● noun an act or instance of drooping.
– ORIGIN Old Norse, 'hang the head'; related to DRIP and DROP.

droopy ● adjective (**droopier**, **droopiest**) **1** hanging down limply; drooping. **2** lacking strength or spirit.
– DERIVATIVES **droopily** adverb **droopiness** noun.

drop ● verb (**dropped**, **dropping**) **1** fall or cause to fall. **2** sink to the ground. **3** make or become lower, weaker, or less. **4** abandon or discontinue. **5** (often **drop off**) set down or unload (a passenger or goods). **6** place or leave (something) without ceremony. **7** informal collapse from exhaustion. **8** lose (a point, a match, etc.). **9** mention casually. **10** (of an animal) give birth to. ● noun **1** a small round or pear-shaped portion of liquid. **2** an instance of falling or dropping. **3** a small drink, especially of alcohol. **4** an abrupt fall or slope. **5** informal a delivery. **6** a sweet or lozenge.
– PHRASES **at the drop of a hat** informal without delay or good reason. **drop back/behind** fall back or get left behind. **drop by/in** visit informally and briefly. **drop a clanger** Brit. informal make an embarrassing or foolish mistake. **drop a curtsy** Brit. make a curtsy. **drop dead** die suddenly and unexpectedly. **drop one's guard** abandon a previously watchful attitude. **a drop in the ocean** a very small amount compared with what is needed. **drop a line** informal send (someone) a note or letter. **drop off** fall asleep, especially without intending to. **drop out 1** cease to participate. **2** pursue an alternative lifestyle.
– ORIGIN Old English, related to DRIP and DROOP.

drop cloth ● noun **1** (also **drop curtain**) a curtain or painted cloth lowered vertically on to a theatre stage. **2** N. Amer. a dust sheet.

drop-dead ● adjective informal used to emphasize attractiveness: *drop-dead gorgeous*.

drop goal ● noun Rugby a goal scored by drop-kicking the ball over the crossbar.

drop handlebars ● plural noun handlebars with the handles bent below the rest of the bar, used especially on racing cycles.

drophead ● noun Brit. a convertible car.

drop kick ● noun (chiefly in rugby) a kick made by dropping the ball and kicking it as it bounces.

droplet ● noun a very small drop of a liquid.

drop-off ● noun **1** a decline or decrease. **2** chiefly N. Amer. a sheer downward slope.

dropout ● noun **1** a person who has dropped out of society or a course of study. **2** Rugby the restarting of play with a drop kick.

dropper ● noun a short glass tube with a rubber bulb at one end, for measuring out drops of liquid.

droppings ● plural noun the excrement of animals.

drop scone ● noun a small thick pancake made by dropping batter on to a heated surface.

drop shot ● noun (in tennis or squash) a softly hit shot which drops abruptly to the ground.

drop shoulder ● noun a style of shoulder on a garment cut with the seam positioned on the upper arm rather than the shoulder.

dropsy /drɒpsi/ ● noun old-fashioned or less technical term for OEDEMA.
– DERIVATIVES **dropsical** adjective.
– ORIGIN shortening of obsolete *hydropsy*, from Greek *hudōr* 'water'.

drop tank ● noun an external fuel tank on an aircraft which can be jettisoned when empty.

drop waist ● noun a style of waistline with the seam positioned at the hips rather than the waist.

Thesaurus

hearted, facetious, witty, whimsical, wry, tongue-in-cheek; *informal* waggish, wacky, side-splitting, rib-tickling.
– OPPOSITES serious.

drone ● verb **1** *a plane droned overhead* HUM, buzz, whirr, vibrate, murmur, rumble, purr. **2** *he droned on about right and wrong* SPEAK BORINGLY, go on and on, talk at length; intone, pontificate; *informal* spout, sound off, jaw, spiel, speechify.
● noun **1** *the drone of aircraft taking off* HUM, buzz, whirr, vibration, murmur, purr. **2** *drones supported by tax-payers' money* HANGER-ON, parasite, leech, passenger; idler, loafer, layabout, good-for-nothing, do-nothing; *informal* lazybones, scrounger, sponger, cadger, freeloader, bloodsucker, waster, slacker.

drool ● verb *his mouth was drooling* SALIVATE, dribble, slaver, slobber; *Scottish & Irish* slabber.
● noun *a fine trickle of drool* SALIVA, spit, spittle, dribble, slaver, slobber.

droop ● verb **1** *the dog's tail is drooping* HANG (DOWN), dangle, sag, flop; wilt, sink, slump, drop, drape. **2** *his eyelids were drooping* CLOSE, shut, fall. **3** *the news made her droop* BE DESPONDENT, lose heart, give up hope, become dispirited, become dejected; flag, languish, wilt.

droopy ● adjective HANGING (DOWN), dangling, falling, dropping, draped; bent, bowed, stooping; sagging, flopping, wilting.

drop ● verb **1** *Eric dropped the box* LET FALL, let go of, lose one's grip on; release, unhand, relinquish. **2** *water drops from the cave roof* DRIP, fall, dribble, trickle, run, plop, leak. **3** *a plane dropped out of the sky* FALL, descend, plunge, plummet, dive, nosedive, tumble, pitch. **4** *she dropped to her knees* FALL, sink, collapse, slump, tumble. **5** *(informal) I was dropping with exhaustion* COLLAPSE, faint, pass out, black out, swoon, keel over; *informal* flake out, conk out. **6** *the track dropped from the ridge* SLOPE DOWNWARDS, slant downwards, descend, go down, fall away, sink, dip. **7** *the exchange rate dropped* DECREASE, lessen, reduce, diminish, depreciate; fall, decline, dwindle, sink, slump, plunge, plummet. **8** *pupils can drop history if they wish* GIVE UP, finish with, withdraw from; discontinue, end, stop, cease, halt; abandon, forgo, relinquish, dispense with, have done with; *informal* pack in, quit. **9** *he was dropped from the team* EXCLUDE, discard, expel, oust, throw out, leave out; dismiss, discharge, let go; *informal* boot out, kick out, turf out. **10** *he dropped his unsuitable friends* ABANDON, desert, throw over; renounce, disown, turn one's back on, wash one's hands of; reject, give up, cast off; neglect, shun; *poetic/literary* forsake. **11** *he dropped all reference to compensation* OMIT, leave out, eliminate, take out, miss out, delete, cut, erase. **12** *the taxi dropped her off* DELIVER, bring, take, convey, carry, transport; leave, unload. **13** *drop the gun on the ground* PUT, place, deposit, set, lay, leave; *informal* pop, plonk. **14** *she dropped names* MENTION, refer to, hint at; bring up, raise, broach, introduce; show off. **15** *the team has yet to drop a point* LOSE, concede, give away.
– OPPOSITES lift, rise, increase, keep, win.
● noun **1** *a drop of water* DROPLET, blob, globule, bead, bubble, tear, dot; *informal* glob. **2** *it needs a drop of oil* SMALL AMOUNT, little, bit, dash, spot; dribble, driblet, sprinkle, trickle, splash; dab, speck, smattering, sprinkling, modicum; *informal* smidgen, tad. **3** *an acid drop* SWEET, lozenge, pastille, bonbon; *N. Amer.* candy. **4** *a small drop in profits* DECREASE, reduction, decline, fall-off, downturn, slump; cut, cutback, curtailment; depreciation. **5** *I walked to the edge of the drop* CLIFF, abyss, chasm, gorge, gully, precipice; slope, descent, incline. **6** *the hangman measured her for the drop* HANGING, gibbeting; execution; *informal* stringing up.
– OPPOSITES increase.
– PHRASES **drop back/behind** FALL BACK/BEHIND, get left behind, lag behind; straggle, linger, dawdle, dally, hang back, loiter, bring/take up the rear; *informal* dilly-dally. **drop off 1** *trade dropped off sharply.* See DROP verb sense 7. **2** *she kept dropping off* FALL ASLEEP, doze (off), nap, catnap, drowse; *informal* nod off, drift off, snooze, take forty winks. **drop out of** *he dropped out of his studies.* See DROP verb sense 8.

dropout ● noun NONCONFORMIST, hippy, beatnik, bohemian, free spirit, rebel; idler, layabout, loafer; *informal* oddball, deadbeat,

drop zone ● noun a designated area into which troops or supplies are dropped by parachute.

droshky /droshki/ ● noun (pl. **droshkies**) a low four-wheeled open carriage of a kind formerly used in Russia.
– ORIGIN Russian *drozhki* 'little wagon'.

drosophila /drəsoffilə/ ● noun a fruit fly of a kind used extensively in genetic research.
– ORIGIN from Greek *drosos* 'dew, moisture' + *philos* 'loving'.

dross ● noun **1** rubbish. **2** scum on the surface of molten metal.
– ORIGIN Old English.

drought /drowt/ ● noun a prolonged period of abnormally low rainfall; a shortage of water.
– ORIGIN Old English, 'dryness'.

drove[1] past of DRIVE.

drove[2] ● noun **1** a flock of animals being driven. **2** a large number of people doing the same thing: *tourists arrived in droves.* ● verb historical drive (livestock) to market.
– DERIVATIVES **drover** noun.
– ORIGIN Old English.

drown ● verb **1** die or kill through submersion in water. **2** submerge or flood (an area). **3** (usu. **drown out**) make inaudible by being much louder.
– PHRASES **drown one's sorrows** forget one's problems by getting drunk.
– ORIGIN related to an Old Norse word meaning 'be drowned'.

drowse /drowz/ ● verb be half asleep; doze. ● noun an instance or state of drowsing.

drowsy ● adjective (**drowsier**, **drowsiest**) sleepy and lethargic.
– DERIVATIVES **drowsily** adverb **drowsiness** noun.
– ORIGIN probably from an Old English word meaning 'be languid or slow'; related to DREARY.

drub ● verb (**drubbed**, **drubbing**) **1** hit or beat repeatedly. **2** informal defeat thoroughly.
– DERIVATIVES **drubbing** noun.
– ORIGIN originally with reference to the punishment of bastinado: probably from Arabic.

drudge ● noun a person made to do hard, menial, or dull work.
– ORIGIN of unknown origin; perhaps related to DRAG.

drudgery ● noun hard, menial, or dull work.

drug ● noun **1** a medicine or other substance which has a marked effect when taken into the body. **2** a substance with narcotic or stimulant effects. ● verb (**drugged**, **drugging**) make (someone) unconscious or stupefied by administering a drug.
– ORIGIN Old French *drogue*, perhaps from Dutch *droge vate* 'dry vats'.

drugget /druggit/ ● noun a floor covering made of a coarse woven fabric.
– ORIGIN French *droguet*, from *drogue* in the sense 'poor-quality article'.

druggist ● noun chiefly N. Amer. a pharmacist or retailer of medicinal drugs.

druggy informal ● adjective caused by or involving drugs. ● noun (also **druggie**) (pl. **druggies**) a drug addict.

drugstore ● noun N. Amer. a pharmacy which also sells toiletries and other articles.

Druid /droōid/ ● noun a priest, magician, or soothsayer in the ancient Celtic religion.
– DERIVATIVES **Druidic** adjective **Druidical** adjective **Druidism** noun.
– ORIGIN Gaulish (the language of the ancient Gauls); related to Irish *draoidh* 'magician, sorcerer'.

drum ● noun **1** a percussion instrument with a skin stretched across a rounded frame, sounded by being struck with sticks or the hands. **2** a cylindrical object or part, especially a container. **3** a sound made by or resembling that of a drum. **4** Austral./NZ informal a piece of reliable inside information. ● verb (**drummed**, **drumming**) **1** play on a drum. **2** make a continuous rhythmic noise. **3** (**drum into**) instruct someone in (something) by prolonged repetition. **4** (**drum out**) expel (someone) from somewhere in disgrace. **5** (**drum up**) attempt to obtain (something) by canvassing or soliciting.
– ORIGIN from Dutch or Low German *tromme*, of imitative origin.

drum and bass ● noun a type of dance music consisting largely of electronic drums and bass.

drumbeat ● noun a stroke or pattern of strokes on a drum.

drumfire ● noun heavy continuous rapid artillery fire.

drumhead ● noun the membrane or skin of a drum. ● adjective (of a trial) summary, as carried out by an army in the field.

drum kit ● noun a set of drums, cymbals, and other percussion instruments.

drumlin /drumlin/ ● noun Geology a mound or small hill consisting of compacted boulder clay moulded by glacial action.
– ORIGIN probably from *drum* 'long narrow hill', from Scottish Gaelic and Irish *druim* 'ridge'.

drum major ● noun **1** a non-commissioned officer commanding regimental drummers. **2** the male leader of a marching band.

drum majorette ● noun **1** the female leader of a marching band. **2** a female member of such a band.

drummer ● noun a person who plays a drum or drums.

drum roll ● noun a rapid succession of drumbeats.

drumstick ● noun **1** a stick used for beating a drum. **2** the

d

Thesaurus

waster.

droppings ● plural noun EXCREMENT, excreta, faeces, stools, dung, ordure, manure; *informal* pooh.

dross ● noun RUBBISH, junk; debris, chaff, detritus, flotsam and jetsam; *N. Amer.* garbage, trash; *informal* dreck.

drought ● noun DRY SPELL, lack of rain, shortage of water.

drove ● noun **1** *a drove of cattle* HERD, flock, pack. **2** *they came in droves* CROWD, swarm, horde, multitude, mob, throng, host, mass, army, herd.

drown ● verb **1** *he nearly drowned* SUFFOCATE IN WATER, inhale water; go to a watery grave. **2** *the valleys were drowned* FLOOD, submerge, immerse, inundate, deluge, swamp, engulf. **3** *his voice was drowned out by the footsteps* MAKE INAUDIBLE, overpower, overwhelm, override; muffle, deaden, stifle, extinguish.

drowse ● verb *they like to drowse in the sun* DOZE, nap, catnap, rest; *informal* snooze, get forty winks, get some shut-eye; *Brit. informal* kip; *N. Amer. informal* catch some Zs.
● noun *she had been woken from her drowse* DOZE, light sleep, nap, catnap, rest; *informal* snooze, forty winks, shut-eye; *Brit. informal* kip.

drowsy ● adjective **1** *the tablet made her drowsy* SLEEPY, dozy, heavy-eyed, groggy, somnolent; tired, weary, fatigued, exhausted, yawning, nodding; lethargic, sluggish, torpid, listless, languid; *informal* snoozy, dopey, yawny, dead beat, all in, dog-tired; *Brit. informal* knackered. **2** *a drowsy afternoon* SOPORIFIC, sleep-inducing, sleepy, somniferous; narcotic, sedative, tranquillizing; lulling, soothing.
– OPPOSITES alert, invigorating.

drubbing ● noun **1** *I gave him a good drubbing* BEATING, thrashing, walloping, thumping, battering, pounding, pummelling, slapping, punching, pelting; *informal* hammering, licking, clobbering, belting, bashing, pasting, tanning, hiding, kicking. **2** *(informal) Scotland's 3-0 drubbing by France.* See DEFEAT noun sense 1.

drudge ● noun *a household drudge* MENIAL WORKER, slave, lackey, servant, labourer, worker, maid/man of all work; *informal* dogsbody, gofer, runner; *Brit. informal* skivvy; *Brit. dated* charwoman, charlady, char.
● verb *(archaic) he drudged in the fields.* See TOIL verb sense 1.

drudgery ● noun HARD WORK, menial work, donkey work, toil, labour; chores; *informal* skivvying; *Brit. informal* graft; *Austral./NZ informal* (hard) yakka.

drug ● noun **1** *drugs prescribed by doctors* MEDICINE, medication, medicament; remedy, cure, antidote. **2** *they began to suspect that she was taking drugs* NARCOTIC, stimulant, hallucinogen; *informal* dope, gear, downer, upper.
● verb **1** *he was drugged* ANAESTHETIZE, narcotize; poison; knock out, stupefy; *informal* dope. **2** *she drugged his coffee* ADD DRUGS TO, tamper with, adulterate, contaminate, lace, poison; *informal* dope, spike, doctor.

drugged ● adjective STUPEFIED, insensible, befuddled; delirious, hallucinating, narcotized; anaesthetized, knocked out; *informal* stoned, high (as a kite), doped, tripping, spaced out, wasted, wrecked, off one's head.
– OPPOSITES sober.

drum ● noun **1** *the beat of a drum* percussion instrument; bongo, tom-tom, snare drum, kettledrum; *historical* tambour. **2** *the steady drum of raindrops* BEAT, rhythm, patter, tap, pounding, thump, thud, rattle, pitter-patter, pit-a-pat, rat-a-tat, thrum. **3** *a drum of radioactive waste* CANISTER, barrel, cylinder, tank, bin, can; container.
● verb **1** *she drummed her fingers on the desk* TAP, beat, rap, thud, thump; tattoo, thrum. **2** *the rules were drummed into us at school* INSTIL, drive, din, hammer, drill, drub, implant, ingrain, inculcate.
– PHRASES **drum someone out** EXPEL, dismiss, throw out, oust; drive out, get rid of; exclude, banish; *informal* give someone the boot, boot out, kick out, give someone their marching orders,

lower joint of the leg of a cooked fowl.

drunk past part. of DRINK. ● adjective affected by alcohol to the extent of losing control of one's faculties or behaviour. ● noun a person who is drunk or who habitually drinks to excess.
– PHRASES **drunk and disorderly** creating a public disturbance under the influence of alcohol.

drupe /dro͞op/ ● noun Botany a fleshy fruit with thin skin and a central stone, e.g. a plum or olive.
– ORIGIN Latin *drupa* 'overripe olive'.

d

drupel /dro͞op'l/ (also **drupelet** /dro͞oplit/) ● noun Botany any of the small individual drupes forming a fleshy aggregate fruit such as a raspberry.

dry ● adjective (**drier**, **driest**) **1** free from moisture or liquid. **2** not yielding water, oil, or milk. **3** without grease or other moisturizer or lubricator. **4** dully factual. **5** unemotional or undemonstrative. **6** (of humour) subtle and expressed in a matter-of-fact way. **7** (of wine) not sweet. **8** prohibiting the sale or consumption of alcoholic drink. ● verb (**dries**, **dried**) **1** make or become dry. **2** preserve by evaporating the moisture from. **3** (**dry up**) (of a supply or flow) decrease and stop. **4** (**dry up**) informal cease talking. **5** (**dry out**) informal overcome alcoholism. ● noun (pl. **dries** or **drys**) **1** (**the dry**) a dry place. **2** Brit. a Conservative politician (especially in the 1980s) in favour of strict monetarist policies.
– DERIVATIVES **dryness** noun.
– ORIGIN Old English.

dryad /drīad/ ● noun (in folklore and Greek mythology) a nymph inhabiting a tree or wood.
– ORIGIN Greek *druas*, from *drus* 'tree'.

dry cell (also **dry battery**) ● noun an electric cell (or battery) in which the electrolyte is absorbed in a solid to form a paste.

dry-clean ● verb clean (a garment) with an organic solvent.

dry dock ● noun a dock which can be drained of water to allow repair of a ship's hull.

dryer (also **drier**) ● noun a machine or device for drying something, especially the hair or laundry.

dry fly ● noun an artificial fishing fly which floats lightly on the water.

dry goods ● plural noun **1** solid commodities traded in bulk, e.g. tea or sugar. **2** chiefly N. Amer. drapery and haberdashery.

dry ice ● noun **1** solid carbon dioxide. **2** white mist produced with this as a theatrical effect.

dryly ● adverb variant spelling of DRILY.

dry measure ● noun a measure of volume for dry goods.

dry rot ● noun a fungus causing decay of wood in poorly ventilated conditions.

dry run ● noun informal a rehearsal of a performance or procedure.

dry-shod ● adjective & adverb without wetting one's shoes.

dry slope (also **dry ski slope**) ● noun an artificial ski slope.

drystone ● adjective Brit. (of a stone wall) built without using mortar.

drysuit ● noun a waterproof rubber suit for water sports, under which warm clothes can be worn.

drywall ● noun N. Amer. plasterboard.

DSC ● abbreviation (in the UK) Distinguished Service Cross.

DSc ● abbreviation Doctor of Science.

DSM ● abbreviation (in the UK) Distinguished Service Medal.

DSO ● abbreviation (in the UK) Distinguished Service Order.

DSP ● abbreviation digital signal processor or processing.

DSS ● abbreviation (in the UK) Department of Social Security.

DTI ● abbreviation (in the UK) Department of Trade and Industry.

DTP ● abbreviation desktop publishing.

DTp ● abbreviation (in the UK) Department of Transport.

DTs ● plural noun informal delirium tremens.

dual ● adjective consisting of two parts, elements, or aspects.
– DERIVATIVES **dualize** (also **dualise**) verb **dually** adverb.
– ORIGIN Latin *dualis*, from *duo* 'two'.

dual carriageway ● noun Brit. a road consisting of two or more lanes in each direction, with a dividing strip separating the two directions.

dualism ● noun **1** division into two opposed or contrasted aspects, such as good and evil or mind and matter. **2** duality.
– DERIVATIVES **dualist** noun & adjective **dualistic** adjective.

duality ● noun (pl. **dualities**) **1** the quality or condition of being dual. **2** an opposition or contrast between two concepts or aspects.

dub[1] ● verb (**dubbed**, **dubbing**) **1** give an unofficial name or nickname to. **2** knight (someone) by the ritual touching of the shoulder with a sword. **3** smear (leather) with grease.
– ORIGIN Old French *adober* 'equip with armour'.

dub[2] ● verb (**dubbed**, **dubbing**) **1** provide (a film) with a soundtrack in a different language from the original. **2** add (sound effects or music) to a film or a recording. **3** make a copy of (a recording). ● noun **1** an instance of dubbing sound effects or music. **2** a style of popular music originating from the remixing of recorded music (especially reggae).
– ORIGIN abbreviation of DOUBLE.

dubbin /dubbin/ Brit. ● noun prepared grease used for softening and waterproofing leather. ● verb (**dubbined**, **dubbining**) apply

Thesaurus

give someone the push, show someone the door, send packing; *Military* cashier. **drum something up** ROUND UP, gather, collect; summon, attract; canvass, solicit, petition.

drunk ● adjective INTOXICATED, inebriated, drunken, incapable, tipsy, the worse for drink, under the influence; *informal* tight, merry, in one's cups, three sheets to the wind, pie-eyed, plastered, smashed, wrecked, wasted, sloshed, soused, sozzled, blotto, stewed, pickled, tanked (up), off one's face, out of one's head, ratted; *Brit. informal* legless, bevvied, paralytic, Brahms and Liszt, half cut, out of it, bladdered, trolleyed, squiffy, tiddly; *N. Amer. informal* loaded, trashed, juiced, sauced, out of one's gourd, in the bag, zoned; *euphemistic* tired and emotional; *informal, dated* lit up.
– OPPOSITES sober.
● noun DRUNKARD, inebriate, drinker, tippler, imbiber, sot; heavy drinker, problem drinker, alcoholic, dipsomaniac; *informal* boozer, soak, lush, wino, alky, sponge, barfly, tosspot; *Austral./NZ informal* hophead, metho; *archaic* toper.
– OPPOSITES teetotaller.

drunken ● adjective **1** *a drunken driver*. See DRUNK adjective. **2** *a drunken all-night party* DEBAUCHED, dissipated, carousing, roistering, intemperate, unrestrained, uninhibited, abandoned; bacchanalian, bacchic; *informal* boozy.

drunkenness ● noun INTOXICATION, inebriation, insobriety, tipsiness; intemperance, overindulgence, debauchery; heavy drinking, alcoholism, alcohol abuse, dipsomania.

dry ● adjective **1** *the dry desert* ARID, parched, droughty, scorched, baked; waterless, moistureless, rainless; dehydrated, desiccated, thirsty, bone dry. **2** *dry leaves* PARCHED, dried, withered, shrivelled, wilted, wizened; crisp, crispy, brittle; dehydrated, desiccated. **3** *the hamburgers were dry* HARD, stale, old, past its best; off. **4** *a dry well* WATERLESS, empty. **5** *I'm really dry* THIRSTY, dehydrated; *informal* parched, gasping. **6** *it was dry work* THIRSTY, thirst-making; hot; strenuous, arduous. **7** *dry toast* UNBUTTERED, butterless, plain. **8** *the dry facts* BARE, simple, basic, fundamental, stark, bald, hard, straightforward. **9** *a dry debate* DULL, uninteresting, boring, unexciting, tedious, tiresome, wearisome, dreary, monotonous; unimaginative, sterile, flat, bland, lacklustre, stodgy, prosaic, humdrum, mundane; *informal* deadly. **10** *a dry sense of humour* WRY, subtle, laconic, sharp; ironic, sardonic, sarcastic, cynical; satirical, mocking, droll; *informal* waggish; *Brit. informal* sarky. **11** *a dry response to his cordial advance* UNEMOTIONAL, indifferent, impassive, cool, cold, emotionless; reserved, restrained, impersonal, formal, stiff, wooden. **12** *this is a dry state* TEETOTAL, prohibitionist, alcohol-free, non-drinking, abstinent, sober; *informal* on the wagon. **13** *dry white wine* CRISP, sharp, piquant, tart, bitter.
– OPPOSITES wet, moist, fresh, lively, emotional, sweet.
● verb **1** *the sun dried the ground* PARCH, scorch, bake; dehydrate, desiccate, dehumidify. **2** *dry the leaves completely* DEHYDRATE, desiccate; wither, shrivel. **3** *he dried the dishes* TOWEL, rub; mop up, blot up, soak up, absorb. **4** *she dried her eyes* WIPE, rub, dab. **5** *methods of drying meat* DESICCATE, dehydrate; preserve, cure, smoke.
– OPPOSITES moisten.
– PHRASES **dry out** GIVE UP DRINKING, give up alcohol, become teetotal, take the pledge; *informal* go on the wagon. **dry up 1** *(informal) he dried up and didn't say another thing* STOP SPEAKING, stop talking, fall silent, shut up; forget one's words. **2** *investment may dry up* DWINDLE, subside, peter out, wane, taper off, ebb, come to a halt/end, run out, give out, disappear, vanish.

dual ● adjective DOUBLE, twofold, binary; duplicate, twin, matching, paired, coupled.
– OPPOSITES single.

dub ● verb **1** *he was dubbed 'the world's sexiest man'* NICKNAME, call, name, label, christen, term, tag, entitle, style; designate, charac-

dubbin to (leather).
– ORIGIN from DUB[1] (sense 3).
dubiety /dyoobīəti/ ● noun formal uncertainty.
dubious /dyoobiəss/ ● adjective **1** hesitating or doubting. **2** not to be relied upon. **3** of questionable value; suspect.
– DERIVATIVES **dubiously** adverb **dubiousness** noun.
– ORIGIN Latin *dubiosus*, from *dubium* 'a doubt'.
dubnium /dubniəm/ ● noun a very unstable chemical element made by high-energy atomic collisions.
– ORIGIN from *Dubna* in Russia, site of the Joint Nuclear Institute.
Dubonnet /dyoobonnay/ ● noun trademark a sweet French red wine.
– ORIGIN from the name of a family of French wine merchants.
ducal /dyook'l/ ● adjective relating to a duke or dukedom.
ducat /dukkət/ ● noun **1** a gold coin formerly current in most European countries. **2** (**ducats**) informal money.
– ORIGIN Italian *ducato*, originally referring to a silver coin minted by the Duke of Apulia in 1190.
duchess ● noun **1** the wife or widow of a duke. **2** a woman holding a rank equivalent to duke.
– ORIGIN Old French, from Latin *ducissa*, from *dux* 'duke'.
duchesse /dooshess, duchiss/ ● noun **1** (also **duchesse satin**) a soft, heavy, glossy kind of satin. **2** a chaise longue resembling two armchairs linked by a stool. **3** a dressing table with a pivoting mirror.
– ORIGIN French, 'duchess'.
duchesse potatoes ● plural noun mashed potatoes mixed with egg yolk, piped into small shapes and baked.
duchy /duchi/ ● noun (pl. **duchies**) the territory of a duke or duchess.
– ORIGIN Old French *duche*, from Latin *dux* 'leader'.
duck[1] ● noun (pl. same or **ducks**) **1** a waterbird with a broad blunt bill, short legs, webbed feet, and a waddling gait. **2** the female of such a bird. Contrasted with DRAKE. **3** (also **ducks**) Brit. informal an affectionate form of address.
– PHRASES **like water off a duck's back** (of a critical remark) having no effect.
– ORIGIN Old English, related to DUCK[2] (expressing the notion of 'diving bird').
duck[2] ● verb **1** lower the head or body quickly to avoid a blow or missile or so as not to be seen. **2** push (someone) under water. **3** informal evade (an unwelcome duty). ● noun a quick lowering of the head.
– PHRASES **duck and dive** informal use one's ingenuity to deal with or evade a situation.
– DERIVATIVES **ducker** noun.
– ORIGIN Germanic, related to DUCK[1].
duck[3] ● noun Cricket a batsman's score of nought.
– PHRASES **break one's duck** score the first run of one's innings.
– ORIGIN short for *duck's egg*, used for the figure 0.
duck[4] ● noun **1** a strong untwilled linen or cotton fabric, used for work clothes and sails. **2** (**ducks**) trousers made from such a fabric.
– ORIGIN Dutch *doek* 'linen'.
duckbill ● noun an animal with jaws resembling a duck's bill, e.g. a platypus.
duck-billed platypus ● noun see PLATYPUS.
duckboards ● plural noun wooden slats joined together to form a path over muddy ground.
ducking stool ● noun historical a chair fastened to the end of a pole, used to plunge offenders into a pond or river as a punishment.
duckling ● noun a young duck.
ducks and drakes ● noun a game of throwing flat stones so that they skim along the surface of water.
– ORIGIN from the movement of the stone over the water.
duck's arse (US **duck's ass**) ● noun informal a man's hairstyle in which the hair is slicked back on both sides and tapered at the nape.
duck soup ● noun N. Amer. informal an easy task.
duckwalk ● verb walk in a squatting posture.
duckweed ● noun a tiny aquatic flowering plant that floats in large quantities on still water.
ducky informal ● noun Brit. a friendly form of address. ● adjective chiefly N. Amer. delightful.
duct ● noun **1** a tube or passageway for air, cables, etc. **2** a vessel in the body for conveying lymph or glandular secretions. ● verb convey through a duct.
– DERIVATIVES **ducting** noun.
– ORIGIN Latin *ductus* 'leading, aqueduct', from *ducere* 'lead'.
ductile /duktīl/ ● adjective **1** (of a metal) able to be drawn out into a thin wire. **2** able to be deformed without losing toughness.
– DERIVATIVES **ductility** noun.
ductless ● adjective Anatomy (of a gland) secreting directly into the bloodstream (e.g. an endocrine gland).
duct tape ● noun N. Amer. strong cloth-backed waterproof adhesive tape.
– ORIGIN originally used for repairing leaks in ducted systems.
dud informal ● noun **1** a thing that fails to work properly. **2** (**duds**) clothes. ● adjective failing to work or meet a standard.
– ORIGIN of unknown origin.
dude /dyood, dood/ ● noun N. Amer. informal **1** a man. **2** a dandy.
– ORIGIN probably from German dialect *Dude* 'fool'.
dude ranch ● noun (in the western US) a cattle ranch converted to a holiday centre for tourists.
dudgeon /dujən/ ● noun (often in phrase **in high dudgeon**) deep resentment.
– ORIGIN of unknown origin.
due ● adjective **1** owing or payable. **2** expected at or planned for a certain time. **3** (often **due to**) merited; fitting. **4** at a point where something is owed or merited: *he was due for a rise.* **5** proper; appropriate: *due process of law.* ● noun **1** (**one's due**/**dues**) a person's right. **2** (**dues**) fees. ● adverb (with reference to a point of the compass) directly.
– PHRASES **due to 1** caused by. **2** because of. **give someone their due** be fair to someone. **in due course** at the appropriate time. **pay one's dues** fulfil one's obligations.
– USAGE **Due to** in the sense 'because of' has been condemned as incorrect on the grounds that **due** is an adjective and should not be used in a prepositional phrase. However, this use is now common and is regarded as part of standard English.
– ORIGIN Old French *deu* 'owed', from Latin *debere* 'owe'.

d

Thesaurus

terize, nominate; *formal* denominate. **2** *she dubbed a new knight* KNIGHT, invest.
dubiety ● noun (*formal*) DOUBTFULNESS, uncertainty, unsureness, incertitude; ambiguity, ambivalence, confusion; hesitancy, doubt.
dubious ● adjective **1** *I was rather dubious about the idea* DOUBTFUL, uncertain, unsure, hesitant; undecided, indefinite, unresolved, up in the air; vacillating, irresolute; sceptical, suspicious; *informal* iffy. **2** *a dubious businessman* SUSPICIOUS, suspect, untrustworthy, unreliable, questionable; *informal* shady, fishy; *Brit. informal* dodgy.
– OPPOSITES certain, trustworthy.
duck ● verb **1** *he ducked behind the wall* BOB DOWN, bend (down), stoop (down), crouch (down), squat (down), hunch down, hunker down; cower, cringe. **2** *she was ducked in the river* DIP, dunk, plunge, immerse, submerge, lower, sink. **3** (*informal*) *they cannot duck the issue forever* SHIRK, dodge, evade, avoid, elude, escape, back out of, shun, eschew, sidestep, bypass, circumvent; *informal* cop out of, get out of, wriggle out of, funk; *Austral./NZ informal* duck-shove.
duct ● noun TUBE, channel, canal, vessel; conduit, culvert; pipe, pipeline, outlet, inlet, flue, shaft, vent; *Anatomy* ductus, ductule.
ductile ● adjective **1** *ductile metals* PLIABLE, pliant, flexible, supple, plastic, tensile; soft, malleable, workable, bendable; *informal* bendy. **2** *a way to make people ductile* DOCILE, obedient, submissive, meek, mild, lamblike; willing, accommodating, amenable, cooperative, compliant, malleable, tractable, biddable, persuadable.
– OPPOSITES brittle, intransigent.
dud (*informal*) ● noun *their new product is a dud* FAILURE, flop, letdown, disappointment; *Brit.* damp squib; *informal* washout, lemon, no-hoper, non-starter, dead loss, lead balloon; *N. Amer. informal* clinker.
– OPPOSITES success.
● adjective **1** *a dud typewriter* DEFECTIVE, faulty, unsound, inoperative, broken, malfunctioning; *informal* bust, busted, kaput, conked out; *Brit. informal* duff, knackered. **2** *a dud £50 note* COUNTERFEIT, fraudulent, forged, fake, faked, false, bogus; invalid, worthless; *informal* phoney.
– OPPOSITES sound, genuine.
dudgeon ● noun
– PHRASES **in high dudgeon** INDIGNANTLY, resentfully, angrily, furiously; in a temper, in anger, with displeasure; *informal* in a huff, in

d

duel ● noun **1** historical a pre-arranged contest with deadly weapons between two people to settle a point of honour. **2** a contest between two parties. ● verb (**duelled**, **duelling**; US **dueled**, **dueling**) fight a duel.
– DERIVATIVES **dueller** (US **dueler**) noun **duellist** (US **duelist**) noun.
– ORIGIN Latin *duellum*, literary form of *bellum* 'war'.
duenna /doo͞ennə/ ● noun an older woman acting as a governess and chaperone to girls in a Spanish family.
– ORIGIN Spanish, from Latin *domina* 'lady, mistress'.
duet ● noun **1** a performance by two singers, instrumentalists, or dancers. **2** a musical composition for two performers. ● verb (**duetted**, **duetting**) perform a duet.
– ORIGIN Italian *duetto*, from *duo* 'duet'.
duff[1] ● noun a flour pudding boiled or steamed in a cloth bag.
– ORIGIN northern English form of DOUGH.
duff[2] ● adjective Brit. informal worthless or false.
– ORIGIN of unknown origin.
duff[3] ● verb informal **1** (**duff up**) Brit. beat (someone) up. **2** Austral. steal and alter brands on (cattle). **3** Golf mishit (a shot).
– ORIGIN sense 1 of uncertain origin; senses 2 and 3 probably from DUFFER.
duff[4] ● noun N. Amer. informal a person's buttocks.
– ORIGIN of unknown origin.
duff[5] ● noun (in phrase **up the duff**) Brit. informal pregnant.
– ORIGIN perhaps related to DUFF[1].
duffel (also **duffle**) ● noun **1** a coarse woollen cloth with a thick nap. **2** N. Amer. sporting or camping equipment.
– ORIGIN from *Duffel*, the name of a town in Belgium where the cloth was originally made.
duffel bag ● noun a cylindrical canvas bag closed by a drawstring.
duffel coat ● noun a hooded coat made of duffel, typically fastened with toggles.
duffer[1] ● noun informal an incompetent or stupid person.
– ORIGIN from Scots *dowfart* 'stupid person'.
duffer[2] ● noun Austral. informal a person who steals and alters the brands on cattle.
– ORIGIN of unknown origin.
dug[1] past and past participle of DIG.
dug[2] ● noun the udder, teat, or nipple of a female animal.
– ORIGIN perhaps Old Norse.
dugong /doo͝gong/ ● noun (pl. same or **dugongs**) a sea cow found in the Indian Ocean.
– ORIGIN Malay.
dugout ● noun **1** a trench that is roofed over as a shelter for troops. **2** an underground air-raid or nuclear shelter. **3** a low shelter at the side of a sports field for a team's coaches and substitutes. **4** (also **dugout canoe**) a canoe made from a hollowed tree trunk.
duiker /dīkər/ ● noun (pl. same or **duikers**) a small African antelope.
– ORIGIN Dutch, 'diver' (from the antelope's habit of plunging through bushes when pursued).
du jour /doo zhoo͝r/ ● adjective informal enjoying great but probably short-lived popularity: *black comedy is the genre du jour*.
– ORIGIN French, 'of the day'.
duke ● noun **1** a male holding the highest hereditary title in the British and certain other peerages. **2** chiefly historical (in parts of Europe) a male ruler of a small independent state. **3** (**dukes**) informal fists.
– PHRASES **duke it out** N. Amer. informal fight it out.
– DERIVATIVES **dukedom** noun.
– ORIGIN Old French *duc*, from Latin *dux* 'leader'; sense 3 is from rhyming slang *Duke of Yorks* 'forks' (= fingers).
DUKW /duk/ ● noun an amphibious transport vehicle used by the Allies during the Second World War.
– ORIGIN a combination of factory-applied letters referring to features of the vehicle.
dulcet /dulsit/ ● adjective often ironic (of a sound) sweet and soothing.
– ORIGIN Old French *doucet*, from Latin *dulcis* 'sweet'.
dulcimer /dulsimər/ ● noun a musical instrument with strings of graduated length struck with hand-held hammers.
– ORIGIN Old French *doulcemer*, probably from Latin *dulce melos* 'sweet melody'.
dull ● adjective **1** lacking interest or excitement. **2** lacking brightness or sheen. **3** (of the weather) overcast. **4** slow to understand; rather unintelligent. **5** indistinctly felt or heard. ● verb make or become dull.
– DERIVATIVES **dullness** (also **dulness**) noun **dully** /dul-li/ adverb.
– ORIGIN Old English, 'stupid'.
dullard /dullərd/ ● noun a slow or stupid person.
duly ● adverb in accordance with what is required, appropriate, or expected.

Thesaurus

a paddy, as cross as two sticks, seeing red; *Brit. informal, dated* in a bate, in a wax.
due ● adjective **1** *their fees were due* OWING, owed, payable; outstanding, overdue, unpaid, unsettled, undischarged; *N. Amer.* delinquent. **2** *the chancellor's statement is due today* EXPECTED, anticipated, scheduled for, awaited; required. **3** *the respect due to a great artist* DESERVED BY, merited by, warranted by; appropriate to, fit for, fitting for, right for, proper to. **4** *he drove without due care* PROPER, correct, rightful, suitable, appropriate, apt; adequate, sufficient, enough, satisfactory, requisite.
● noun **1** *he attracts more criticism than is his due* RIGHTFUL TREATMENT, fair treatment, just punishment; right, entitlement; just deserts; *informal* comeuppance. **2** *members have paid their dues* FEE, subscription, charge; payment, contribution.
● adverb *he hiked due north* DIRECTLY, straight, exactly, precisely, dead.
– PHRASES **due to 1** *her death was due to an infection* ATTRIBUTABLE TO, caused by, ascribed to, because of, put down to. **2** *the train was cancelled due to staff shortages* BECAUSE OF, owing to, on account of, as a consequence of, as a result of, thanks to, in view of; *formal* by reason of.
duel ● noun **1** *he was killed in a duel* MANO-A-MANO, single combat; fight, confrontation, head-to-head; *informal* face-off, shoot-out; *archaic* rencounter. **2** *a snooker duel* CONTEST, match, game, meet, encounter.
● verb *they duelled with swords* FIGHT A DUEL, fight, battle, combat, contend.
duff ● adjective *(Brit. informal)*. See BAD sense 1.
duffer ● noun *(informal)*. See DUNCE.
dulcet ● adjective SWEET, soothing, mellow, honeyed, mellifluous, euphonious, pleasant, agreeable; melodious, melodic, lilting, lyrical, silvery, golden.
– OPPOSITES harsh.
dull ● adjective **1** *a dull novel* UNINTERESTING, boring, tedious, monotonous, unrelieved, unvaried, unimaginative, uneventful; characterless, featureless, colourless, lifeless, insipid, unexciting, uninspiring, unstimulating, jejune, flat, bland, dry, stale, tired, banal, lacklustre, stodgy, dreary, humdrum, mundane; mind-numbing, soul-destroying, wearisome, tiring, tiresome, irksome; *informal* deadly, not up to much; *Brit. informal* samey; *N. Amer. informal* dullsville. **2** *a dull morning* OVERCAST, cloudy, gloomy, dark, dismal, dreary, sombre, grey, murky, sunless. **3** *dull colours* DRAB, dreary, sombre, dark, subdued, muted, lacklustre, faded, washed out, muddy. **4** *a dull sound* MUFFLED, muted, quiet, soft, faint, indistinct; stifled, suppressed. **5** *the chisel became dull* BLUNT, unsharpened, edgeless, worn down. **6** *a rather dull child* UNINTELLIGENT, stupid, slow, witless, vacuous, empty-headed, brainless, mindless, foolish, idiotic; *informal* dense, dim, moronic, cretinous, half-witted, thick, dumb, dopey, dozy, bovine, slow on the uptake, wooden-headed, fat-headed. **7** *her cold made her feel dull* SLUGGISH, lethargic, enervated, listless, languid, torpid, slow, sleepy, drowsy, weary, tired, fatigued; apathetic; *informal* dozy, dopey, yawny.
– OPPOSITES interesting, bright, loud, resonant, sharp, clever.
● verb **1** *the pain was dulled by drugs* LESSEN, decrease, diminish, reduce, dampen, blunt, deaden, allay, ease, soothe, assuage, alleviate. **2** *sleep dulled her mind* NUMB, benumb, deaden, desensitize, stupefy, daze. **3** *the leaves are dulled by mildew* FADE, bleach, decolorize, decolour, etiolate. **4** *rain dulled the sky* DARKEN, blacken, dim, veil, obscure, shadow, fog. **5** *the sombre atmosphere dulled her spirit* DAMPEN, lower, depress, crush, sap, extinguish, smother, stifle.
– OPPOSITES intensify, enliven, enhance, brighten.
dullard ● noun IDIOT, fool, stupid person, simpleton, ignoramus, oaf, dunce, dolt; *informal* duffer, moron, cretin, imbecile, nincompoop, dope, chump, nitwit, dimwit, birdbrain, pea-brain, numbskull, fathead, dumbo, dum-dum, donkey; *Brit. informal* wally, berk, divvy; *N. Amer. informal* doofus, goof, bozo, dummy; *Austral./NZ informal* galah.
duly ● adverb **1** *the document was duly signed* PROPERLY, correctly,

dumb ● adjective **1** unable to speak; lacking the power of speech. **2** temporarily unable or unwilling to speak. **3** informal, chiefly N. Amer. stupid. **4** (of a computer terminal) having no independent processing capability. ● verb **1** (**dumb down**) N. Amer. informal make or become less intellectually challenging. **2** literary silence.
– DERIVATIVES **dumbly** adverb **dumbness** noun.
– USAGE Avoid **dumb** in the sense meaning 'not able to speak', as it likely to cause offence; use alternatives such as **speech-impaired**.
– ORIGIN Old English.
dumb-bell ● noun **1** a short bar with a weight at each end, used for exercise or muscle-building. **2** informal a stupid person.
– ORIGIN originally denoting an object similar to that used to ring a church bell (but without the bell, so 'dumb').
dumbfound (also **dumfound**) ● verb astonish greatly.
– ORIGIN blend of DUMB and CONFOUND.
dumbo ● noun (pl. **dumbos**) informal a stupid person.
dumbshow ● noun **1** gestures used to convey something without speech. **2** (especially in English drama of the 16th and 17th centuries) a part of a play acted in mime.
dumbstruck ● adjective so shocked or surprised as to be unable to speak.
dumb waiter ● noun **1** a small lift for carrying food and crockery between floors. **2** Brit. a movable table, typically with revolving shelves, used in a dining room.
dumdum (also **dumdum bullet**) ● noun a kind of soft-nosed bullet that expands on impact and inflicts laceration.
– ORIGIN from *Dum Dum*, name of a town and arsenal near Calcutta, India, where they were first produced.
dum-dum ● noun informal a stupid person.
dummy ● noun (pl. **dummies**) **1** a model or replica of a human being. **2** an object designed to resemble and serve as a substitute for the real one. **3** Brit. a rubber or plastic teat for a baby to suck on. **4** (in sport) a feigned pass or kick. **5** informal, chiefly N. Amer. a stupid person. ● verb (**dummies, dummied**) feign a pass or kick.
– PHRASES **sell someone a dummy** deceive an opponent by feigning a pass or kick.
– ORIGIN originally 'a person who cannot speak', later 'an imaginary fourth player in whist': from DUMB.
dummy run ● noun a practice or trial.
dump ● noun **1** a site for depositing rubbish or waste. **2** a heap of rubbish left at a dump. **3** informal an unpleasant or dreary place. **4** Military a temporary store of weaponry or provisions. **5** Computing an act of dumping stored data. ● verb **1** deposit or dispose of (rubbish or something unwanted). **2** put down (something) firmly and carelessly. **3** informal abandon (someone). **4** Computing copy (stored data) to a different location. **5** send (goods) to a foreign market for sale at a low price.
– ORIGIN perhaps from Old Norse; in later use partly imitative.
dumper ● noun **1** a person or thing that dumps something. **2** (also **dumper truck**) Brit. a truck with a body that tilts or opens at the back for unloading.
dumpling ● noun **1** a small savoury ball of dough boiled in water or in a stew. **2** a pudding consisting of fruit enclosed in a sweet dough and baked.
– ORIGIN apparently from the obsolete adjective *dump* 'of the consistency of dough'.
dumps ● plural noun (in phrase (**down**) **in the dumps**) informal depressed or unhappy.
– ORIGIN originally as *dump* in the sense 'a dazed or puzzled state': probably a figurative use of Dutch *domp* 'haze, mist'.
dumpster ● noun N. Amer. a rubbish skip.
– ORIGIN originally *Dempster Dumpster*, a proprietary name given by the American manufacturers, Dempster Brothers of Tennessee.
dump truck ● noun N. Amer. a dumper truck.
dumpy ● adjective (**dumpier, dumpiest**) short and stout.
dun[1] ● adjective of a dull greyish-brown colour. ● noun **1** a dull greyish-brown colour. **2** a horse with a sandy coat and a dark side stripe.
– ORIGIN Old English, probably related to DUSK.
dun[2] ● verb (**dunned, dunning**) make persistent demands on (someone) for payment of a debt.
– ORIGIN perhaps from obsolete *Dunkirk privateer* (with connotations of piratical demands), or from the name of Joe *Dun*, a well-known bailiff.
dunce ● noun a person who is slow at learning.
– ORIGIN originally a name for a follower of the 13th-century Scottish theologian John *Duns* Scotus, whose followers were ridiculed by humanists and reformers as enemies of learning.
dunce's cap ● noun a paper cone formerly put on the head of a dunce at school as a mark of disgrace.
Dundee cake ● noun a rich fruit cake decorated with almonds.
dunderhead ● noun informal a stupid person.
– DERIVATIVES **dunderheaded** adjective.
– ORIGIN perhaps from obsolete Scots *dunder, dunner* 'resounding noise'.
dune ● noun a mound or ridge of sand formed by the wind, especially on the sea coast or in a desert.
– ORIGIN Dutch, related to DOWN[3].
dung ● noun manure.

d

Thesaurus

appropriately, suitably, fittingly. **2** *he duly arrived to collect Alice* AT THE RIGHT TIME, on time, punctually.
dumb ● adjective **1** *she stood dumb while he shouted* MUTE, speechless, tongue-tied, silent, at a loss for words; taciturn, uncommunicative, untalkative, tight-lipped, close-mouthed; *informal* mum. **2** *(informal) he is not as dumb as you'd think* STUPID, unintelligent, ignorant, dense, brainless, mindless, foolish, slow, dull, simple, empty-headed, vacuous, vapid, idiotic, half-baked, imbecilic, bovine; *informal* thick, dim, moronic, cretinous, dopey, dozy, thickheaded, wooden-headed, fat-headed, birdbrained, pea-brained; *Brit. informal* daft.
– OPPOSITES clever.
dumbfound ● verb ASTONISH, astound, amaze, stagger, surprise, startle, stun, confound, stupefy, daze, nonplus, take aback, stop someone in their tracks, strike dumb, leave open-mouthed, leave aghast; *informal* flabbergast, floor, knock sideways, bowl over; *Brit. informal* knock for six.
dumbfounded ● adjective ASTONISHED, astounded, amazed, staggered, surprised, startled, stunned, confounded, nonplussed, stupefied, dazed, dumbstruck, open-mouthed, speechless, thunderstruck; taken aback, disconcerted; *informal* flabbergasted, flummoxed; *Brit. informal* gobsmacked.
dummy ● noun **1** *a shop-window dummy* MANNEQUIN, model, figure. **2** *the book is just a dummy* MOCK-UP, imitation, likeness, lookalike, representation, substitute, sample; replica, reproduction; counterfeit, sham, fake, forgery; *informal* dupe. **3** *(informal) you're a dummy.* See IDIOT.
● adjective *a dummy attack on the airfield* SIMULATED, feigned, pretended, practice, trial, mock, make-believe; *informal* pretend, phoney.
– OPPOSITES real.
dump ● noun **1** *take the rubbish to the dump* TIP, rubbish dump, rubbish heap, dumping ground; dustheap, slag heap. **2** *(informal) the house is a dump* HOVEL, shack, slum; mess; *informal* hole, pigsty.
● verb **1** *he dumped his bag on the table* PUT DOWN, set down, deposit, place, shove, unload; drop, throw down; *informal* stick, park, plonk; *Brit. informal* bung; *N. Amer. informal* plunk. **2** *they will dump asbestos at the site* DISPOSE OF, get rid of, throw away/out, discard, bin, jettison; *informal* ditch, junk. **3** *(informal) he dumped her* ABANDON, desert, leave, jilt, break up with, finish with, throw over; *informal* walk out on, rat on, drop, ditch, chuck, give someone the elbow; *Brit. informal* give someone the big E.
dumps ● plural noun
– PHRASES **down in the dumps** *(informal)* UNHAPPY, sad, depressed, gloomy, glum, melancholy, miserable, dejected, despondent, dispirited, downhearted, downcast, down, low, heavy-hearted, dismal, desolate; tearful, upset; *informal* blue, down in the mouth, fed up.
dumpy ● adjective SHORT, squat, stubby; PLUMP, stout, chubby, chunky, portly, fat, bulky; *informal* tubby, roly-poly, pudgy, porky; *Brit. informal* podgy.
– OPPOSITES tall, slender.
dun[1] ● adjective *a dun cow* GREYISH-BROWN, brownish, mousy, muddy, khaki, umber.
dun[2] ● verb *you can't dun me for her debts* IMPORTUNE, press, plague, pester, nag, harass, hound, badger; *informal* hassle, bug; *N. English informal* mither.
dunce ● noun FOOL, idiot, stupid person, simpleton, ignoramus, dullard; *informal* dummy, dumbo, clot, thickhead, nitwit, dimwit, halfwit, moron, cretin, imbecile, dope, duffer, booby, chump, numbskull, nincompoop, fathead, airhead, birdbrain, pea-brain, ninny, ass; *Brit. informal* wally, berk, divvy; *N. Amer. informal* doofus,

d

– ORIGIN Old English.
dungaree /dunggəree/ ● noun **1** (**dungarees**) a garment consisting of trousers with a bib held up by straps over the shoulders. **2** a kind of coarse Indian calico.
– ORIGIN Hindi.
dung beetle ● noun a beetle whose larvae feed on dung, especially a scarab.
dungeon ● noun a strong underground prison cell, especially in a castle.
– ORIGIN Old French, probably originally with the sense 'lord's tower', from Latin *dominus* 'lord'.
dunghill ● noun a heap of dung or refuse, especially in a farmyard.
dungworm ● noun an earthworm found in dung or compost, used by anglers as bait.
dunk ● verb **1** dip (bread or other food) into a drink or soup before eating it. **2** immerse in water. **3** Basketball score a field goal by shooting the ball down through the basket with the hands above the rim. ● noun Basketball a goal scored by dunking.
– ORIGIN German *tunken* 'dip or plunge'.
dunlin /dunlin/ ● noun (pl. same or **dunlins**) a sandpiper with a downcurved bill and (in winter) greyish-brown upper parts.
– ORIGIN probably from DUN[1] + -LING.
dunnage /dunnij/ ● noun **1** loose wood, matting, or similar material used to keep a cargo in position in a ship's hold. **2** informal baggage.
– ORIGIN of unknown origin.
dunnart /dunnaart/ ● noun a mouse-like marsupial with a pointed snout and prominent eyes, found in Australia and New Guinea.
– ORIGIN from an Aboriginal language.
dunnock /dunnək/ ● noun a small songbird with a dark grey head and a reddish-brown back.
– ORIGIN apparently from DUN[1].
dunny /dunni/ ● noun (pl. **dunnies**) Austral./NZ informal a toilet.
– ORIGIN probably from DUNG (the original sense) + archaic slang *ken* 'house'.
duo ● noun (pl. **duos**) **1** a pair of people or things, especially in music or entertainment. **2** Music a duet.
– ORIGIN Latin, 'two'.
duodecimal /dyoo-ōdessim'l/ ● adjective relating to a system of counting or numerical notation that has twelve as a base.
– ORIGIN Latin *duodecimus* 'twelfth'.
duodecimo /dyoo-ōdessimō/ ● noun (pl. **duodecimos**) a size of book page that results from folding each printed sheet into twelve leaves (twenty-four pages).
duodenum /dyooədeenəm/ ● noun (pl. **duodenums** or **duodena** /dyooədeenə/) the first part of the small intestine immediately beyond the stomach.
– DERIVATIVES **duodenal** adjective.
– ORIGIN Latin, from *duodeni* 'in twelves', its length being equivalent to the breadth of approximately twelve fingers.
duologue /dyooəlog/ ● noun a play or part of a play with speaking roles for only two actors.
duopoly /dyooopрəli/ ● noun (pl. **duopolies**) a situation in which two suppliers dominate a market.
dupe ● verb deceive; trick. ● noun a victim of deception.
– DERIVATIVES **duper** noun.
– ORIGIN French dialect *dupe* 'hoopoe', from the bird's supposedly stupid appearance.
dupion /dyoopiən/ ● noun a rough silk fabric woven from the threads of double cocoons.
– ORIGIN French *doupion*, from Italian *doppio* 'double'.
duple /dyoop'l/ ● adjective Music (of rhythm) based on two main beats to the bar.
– ORIGIN Latin *duplus*, from *duo* 'two'.
duplex /dyoopleks/ ● noun **1** N. Amer. a residential building divided into two apartments. **2** N. Amer. & Austral. a semi-detached house. ● adjective having two parts.
– ORIGIN Latin, from *duplicare* 'double'.
duplicate ● adjective /dyooplikət/ **1** exactly like something else. **2** having two corresponding parts. **3** twice the number or quantity. ● noun /dyooplikət/ one of two or more identical things. ● verb /dyooplikayt/ **1** make or be an exact copy of. **2** multiply by two. **3** do (something) again unnecessarily.
– DERIVATIVES **duplication** noun.
– ORIGIN Latin *duplicare*, from *duo* 'two' + *plicare* 'to fold'.
duplicator ● noun a machine for copying something.
duplicitous ● adjective deceitful.
duplicity /dyooplissiti/ ● noun deceitfulness.
duppy /duppi/ ● noun (pl. **duppies**) W. Indian a malevolent spirit or ghost.
– ORIGIN probably West African.
durable ● adjective **1** hard-wearing. **2** (of goods) not for immediate consumption and so able to be kept.
– DERIVATIVES **durability** noun **durably** adverb.
– ORIGIN Latin *durabilis*, from *durare* 'to last'.
dura mater /dyoorə maytər/ ● noun Anatomy the tough outermost membrane enveloping the brain and spinal cord.
– ORIGIN Latin, 'hard mother'.
durance ● noun archaic imprisonment.
– ORIGIN originally in the sense 'continuance': from Old French, from Latin *durare* 'to last'.
duration ● noun the time during which something continues.
– PHRASES **for the duration** informal for a very long time.
– DERIVATIVES **durational** adjective.
– ORIGIN Latin, from *durare* 'to last'.
durbar /durbaar/ ● noun historical **1** the court of an Indian ruler. **2** a public reception held by an Indian prince or a British governor or viceroy in India.
– ORIGIN Persian, 'court'.
duress /dyooress/ ● noun threats or violence used to coerce a person into doing something: *confessions extracted under duress.*
– ORIGIN originally in the sense 'harshness, cruel treatment': from Latin *durus* 'hard'.
Durex ● noun (pl. same) Brit. trademark a contraceptive sheath.
– ORIGIN name invented by the manufacturers, probably from Latin *durare* 'to last'.
durian /doorіən/ ● noun a tropical fruit containing a creamy pulp with a fetid smell but agreeable taste.
– ORIGIN Malay.
during ● preposition **1** throughout the course or duration of. **2** at a particular point in the course of.

Thesaurus

goof, schmuck, bozo, lummox; *Austral./NZ informal* galah.
– OPPOSITES genius.
dune ● noun BANK, mound, hillock, hummock, knoll, ridge, heap, drift.
dung ● noun MANURE, muck; excrement, faeces, droppings, ordure, cowpats.
dungeon ● noun UNDERGROUND PRISON, oubliette; cell, jail, lock-up.
dupe ● verb *they were duped by a con man* DECEIVE, trick, hoodwink, hoax, swindle, defraud, cheat, double-cross; gull, mislead, take in, fool, inveigle; *informal* con, do, rip off, diddle, shaft, bilk, rook, pull the wool over someone's eyes, pull a fast one on, sell a pup to; *N. Amer. informal* sucker, snooker; *Austral. informal* pull a swifty on.
● noun *an innocent dupe in her game* VICTIM, gull, pawn, puppet, instrument; fool, innocent; *informal* sucker, stooge, sitting duck, muggins, fall guy; *Brit. informal* mug; *N. Amer. informal* pigeon, patsy, sap.
duplicate ● noun *a duplicate of the invoice* COPY, carbon copy, photocopy, facsimile, mimeograph, reprint; replica, reproduction, clone; *informal* dupe; *trademark* Xerox, photostat.
● adjective *duplicate keys* MATCHING, identical, twin, corresponding, equivalent.
● verb **1** *she will duplicate the newsletter* COPY, photocopy, photostat, xerox, mimeograph, reproduce, replicate, reprint, run off. **2** *a feat difficult to duplicate* REPEAT, do again, redo, replicate.
duplicity ● noun DECEITFULNESS, deceit, deception, double-dealing, underhandedness, dishonesty, fraud, fraudulence, sharp practice, chicanery, trickery, subterfuge, skulduggery, treachery; *informal* crookedness, shadiness, dirty tricks, shenanigans, monkey business; *poetic/literary* perfidy.
– OPPOSITES honesty.
durability ● noun IMPERISHABILITY, durableness, longevity; resilience, strength, sturdiness, toughness, robustness.
– OPPOSITES fragility.
durable ● adjective **1** *durable carpets* HARD-WEARING, long-lasting, heavy-duty, tough, resistant, imperishable, indestructible, strong, sturdy. **2** *a durable peace* LASTING, long-lasting, long-term, enduring, persistent, abiding; stable, secure, firm, deep-rooted, permanent, undying, everlasting.
– OPPOSITES delicate, short-lived.
duration ● noun FULL LENGTH, time, time span, time scale, period,

– ORIGIN from obsolete *dure* 'last, endure', from Latin *durare* 'to last'.

durum wheat /dyoorəm/ ● noun a kind of hard wheat grown in arid regions, yielding flour that is used to make pasta.
– ORIGIN Latin, from *durus* 'hard'.

dusk ● noun the darker stage of twilight.
– ORIGIN Old English, 'dark, swarthy'.

dusky ● adjective (**duskier**, **duskiest**) darkish in colour.
– DERIVATIVES **duskily** adverb **duskiness** noun.

dust ● noun **1** fine, dry powder consisting of tiny particles of earth or waste matter. **2** any material in the form of tiny particles: *coal dust.* **3** an act of dusting. ● verb **1** remove dust from the surface of. **2** cover lightly with a powdered substance. **3** (**dust down/off**) bring (something) out for use again after a long period of neglect.
– PHRASES **not see someone for dust** find that a person has made a hasty departure. **when the dust settles** when things quieten down.
– ORIGIN Old English.

dust bath ● noun a bird's rolling in dust to clean its feathers.

dustbin ● noun Brit. a large container for household refuse.

dust bowl ● noun an area where vegetation has been lost and soil reduced to dust and eroded.

dustcart ● noun Brit. a vehicle used for collecting household refuse.

dust cover ● noun a dust jacket or dust sheet.

dust devil ● noun a small whirlwind visible as a column of dust and debris.

duster ● noun Brit. a cloth for dusting furniture.

dust jacket ● noun a removable paper cover on a book.

dustman ● noun Brit. a man employed to remove household refuse from dustbins.

dustpan ● noun a flat hand-held receptacle into which dust and waste can be swept.

dust sheet ● noun Brit. a large sheet for covering furniture to protect it from dust or while decorating.

dust storm ● noun a strong wind carrying clouds of fine dust and sand.

dust-up ● noun informal a fight or quarrel.

dusty ● adjective (**dustier**, **dustiest**) **1** covered with or resembling dust. **2** staid and uninteresting.
– DERIVATIVES **dustily** adverb **dustiness** noun.

dusty answer ● noun Brit. a curt and unhelpful reply.

Dutch ● adjective relating to the Netherlands or its language. ● noun the Germanic language of the Netherlands.
– PHRASES **go Dutch** share the cost of a meal equally.
– ORIGIN Dutch *dutsch* 'Dutch, Netherlandish, German'.

dutch ● noun (usu. **one's old dutch**) Brit. informal (among cockneys) one's wife.
– ORIGIN abbreviation of DUCHESS.

Dutch auction ● noun a method of selling in which the price is reduced until a buyer is found.

Dutch barn ● noun Brit. a farm building comprising a curved roof set on an open frame, used to cover hay.

Dutch cap ● noun **1** a woman's lace cap with triangular flaps on each side, worn as part of Dutch traditional dress. **2** see CAP (sense 7).

Dutch courage ● noun confidence gained from drinking alcohol.

Dutch elm disease ● noun a disease of elm trees, caused by a fungus and spread by bark beetles.

Dutch hoe ● noun a hoe used with a pushing action just under the surface of the soil.

Dutch oven ● noun **1** a covered earthenware or cast-iron container for cooking casseroles. **2** chiefly historical a large metal box serving as a simple oven, heated by being placed under or next to hot coals.

Dutch uncle ● noun informal, chiefly N. Amer. a person giving firm but benevolent advice.

dutiable /dyōōtiəb'l/ ● adjective liable to customs or other duties.

dutiful ● adjective conscientiously fulfilling one's duty.
– DERIVATIVES **dutifully** adverb.

duty ● noun (pl. **duties**) **1** a moral or legal obligation. **2** a task required as part of one's job. **3** a payment levied on the import, export, manufacture, or sale of goods. **4** Brit. a payment levied on the transfer of property, for licences, and for the legal recognition of documents.
– PHRASES **on** (or **off**) **duty** engaged (or not engaged) in one's regular work.
– ORIGIN Old French *duete*, from *deu* 'owed, due'.

duty-bound ● adjective morally or legally obliged.

duty-free ● adjective & adverb exempt from payment of duty.

duvet /dōōvay/ ● noun chiefly Brit. a soft thick quilt used instead of an upper sheet and blankets.
– ORIGIN French, 'down'.

DVD ● abbreviation digital versatile disc.

DVLA ● abbreviation Driver and Vehicle Licensing Agency.

dwarf ● noun (pl. **dwarfs** or **dwarves**) **1** a member of a mythical race of short, stocky human-like creatures. **2** an abnormally small person. **3** (before another noun) (of an animal or plant) much smaller than is usual for its type or species. **4** (also **dwarf star**) Astronomy a star of relatively small size and low luminosity. ● verb cause to seem small in comparison.
– DERIVATIVES **dwarfish** adjective.
– USAGE In the sense 'an abnormally small person', **dwarf** is normally considered offensive. However, there is no accepted alternative, since terms such as **person of restricted growth** have gained little currency.
– ORIGIN Old English.

dwarfism ● noun unusually low stature or small size.

dweeb ● noun N. Amer. informal a boring, studious, or socially inept

Thesaurus

term, span, fullness, length, extent, continuation.

duress ● noun COERCION, compulsion, force, pressure, intimidation, constraint; threats; *informal* arm-twisting.

during ● conjunction THROUGHOUT, through, in, in the course of, for the time of.

dusk ● noun TWILIGHT, nightfall, sunset, sundown, evening, close of day; semi-darkness, gloom, murkiness; *poetic/literary* gloaming, eventide.
– OPPOSITES dawn.

dusky ● adjective **1** *the dusky countryside* SHADOWY, dark, dim, gloomy, murky, shady; unlit, unilluminated; sunless, moonless. **2** *(dated) a dusky maiden* DARK-SKINNED, dark, olive-skinned, swarthy, ebony, black; tanned, bronzed, brown.
– OPPOSITES bright, fair.

dust ● noun **1** *the desk was covered in dust* DIRT, grime, filth, smut, soot; fine powder. **2** *they fought in the dust* EARTH, soil, dirt; ground.
● verb **1** *she dusted her mantelpiece* WIPE, clean, brush, sweep, mop. **2** *dust the cake with icing sugar* SPRINKLE, scatter, powder, dredge, sift, cover, strew.

dust-up ● noun *(informal)*. See SCRAP² noun.

dusty ● adjective **1** *the floor was dusty* DIRTY, grimy, grubby, unclean, soiled, mucky, sooty; undusted; *informal* grungy, cruddy; *Brit. informal* grotty. **2** *dusty sandstone* POWDERY, crumbly, chalky, friable; granular, gritty, sandy. **3** *a dusty pink* MUTED, dull, faded, pale, pastel, subtle; greyish, darkish, dirty. **4** *(Brit.) a dusty answer* CURT, abrupt, terse, brusque, blunt, short, sharp, tart, gruff, offhand; *informal* snippy, snappy.
– OPPOSITES clean, bright.

dutiful ● adjective CONSCIENTIOUS, responsible, dedicated, devoted, attentive; obedient, compliant, submissive, biddable; deferential, reverent, reverential, respectful, good.
– OPPOSITES remiss.

duty ● noun **1** *she was free of any duty* RESPONSIBILITY, obligation, commitment; allegiance, loyalty, faithfulness, fidelity, homage. **2** *it was his duty to attend the king* JOB, task, assignment, mission, function, charge, place, role, responsibility, obligation; *dated* office. **3** *the duty was raised on alcohol* TAX, levy, tariff, excise, toll, fee, payment, rate; dues.
– PHRASES **off duty** NOT WORKING, at leisure, on holiday, on leave, off (work), free. **on duty** WORKING, at work, busy, occupied, engaged; *informal* on the job, tied up.

dwarf ● noun **1** person of restricted growth, small person, short person; midget, pygmy, manikin. **2** *the wizard captured the dwarf* GNOME, goblin, hobgoblin, troll, imp, elf, brownie, leprechaun.
● adjective *dwarf conifers* MINIATURE, small, little, tiny, toy, pocket, diminutive, baby, pygmy, stunted, undersized, undersize; *Scottish* wee; *informal* mini, teeny, teeny-weeny, itsy-bitsy, tiddly, pint-sized; *Brit. informal* titchy; *N. Amer. informal* little-bitty.
– OPPOSITES giant.
● verb **1** *the buildings dwarf the trees* DOMINATE, tower over, loom over, overshadow, overtop. **2** *her progress was dwarfed by her sis-*

person.
– ORIGIN perhaps a blend of DWARF and *feeb* 'a feeble-minded person'.
dwell ● verb (past and past part. **dwelt** or **dwelled**) **1** formal live in or at a place. **2** (**dwell on/upon**) think, speak, or write at length about.
– DERIVATIVES **dweller** noun.
– ORIGIN Old English.
dwelling (also **dwelling place**) ● noun formal a house or other place of residence.
d
dwindle ● verb diminish gradually.
– ORIGIN from Scots and dialect *dwine* 'fade away'.
Dy ● symbol the chemical element dysprosium.
dyad /dīad/ ● noun technical something consisting of two elements or parts.
– DERIVATIVES **dyadic** adjective.
– ORIGIN from Latin *dyas*, from Greek *duo* 'two'.
Dyak /dīak/ ● noun & adjective variant spelling of DAYAK.
dybbuk /dibbŏŏk/ ● noun (pl. **dybbuks** or **dybbukim** /dibbŏŏkim/) (in Jewish folklore) a malevolent wandering spirit able to possess the body of a living person.
– ORIGIN Yiddish, from a Hebrew word meaning 'cling'.
dye ● noun a natural or synthetic substance used to colour something. ● verb (**dyeing**) make (something) a specified colour with dye.
– PHRASES **dyed in the wool** unchanging in a particular belief. [ORIGIN with allusion to the fact that yarn was dyed when raw, producing a more even and permanent colour.]
– DERIVATIVES **dyer** noun.
– ORIGIN Old English.
dyestuff ● noun a substance used as or yielding a dye.
dying present participle of DIE[1].
dyke[1] (also **dike**) ● noun **1** an embankment built to prevent flooding from the sea. **2** an earthwork serving as a boundary or defence: *Offa's Dyke*. **3** a ditch or watercourse. **4** Geology an intrusion of igneous rock cutting across existing strata. Compare with SILL. ● verb provide (land) with a dyke to prevent flooding.
– ORIGIN Old Norse, related to DITCH.
dyke[2] (also **dike**) ● noun informal a lesbian.
– DERIVATIVES **dykey** adjective.
– ORIGIN earlier as *bulldyke*: of unknown origin.
dynamic ● adjective **1** (of a process or system) characterized by constant change or activity. **2** full of energy and new ideas. **3** Physics relating to forces producing motion. Often contrasted with STATIC. **4** Music relating to the volume of sound produced by an instrument or voice. ● noun **1** an energizing or motive force. **2** Music another term for DYNAMICS (in sense 3).
– DERIVATIVES **dynamical** adjective **dynamically** adverb.
– ORIGIN Greek *dunamikos*, from *dunamis* 'power'.
dynamic equilibrium ● noun a state of balance between continuing processes.
dynamic range ● noun the range of sound intensity that occurs in a piece of music or that can be satisfactorily handled by a piece of equipment.
dynamics ● plural noun **1** (treated as sing.) the branch of mechanics concerned with the motion of bodies under the action of forces. **2** the forces which stimulate development or change within a system or process. **3** Music the varying levels of volume of sound in a musical performance.
dynamism ● noun the quality of being dynamic.
dynamite ● noun **1** a high explosive consisting of nitroglycerine mixed with an absorbent material. **2** informal an extremely impressive or potentially dangerous person or thing. ● verb blow up with dynamite.
– ORIGIN from Greek *dunamis* 'power'.
dynamo ● noun (pl. **dynamos**) chiefly Brit. a machine for converting mechanical energy into electrical energy by rotating conducting coils in a magnetic field.
– ORIGIN abbreviation of *dynamo-electric machine*.
dynamometer /dīnəmommitər/ ● noun an instrument which measures the power output of an engine.
dynast /dinnast, dī-/ ● noun a member of a dynasty, especially a hereditary ruler.
dynasty /dinnəsti/ ● noun (pl. **dynasties**) **1** a line of hereditary rulers. **2** a succession of powerful or prominent people from the same family.
– DERIVATIVES **dynastic** adjective **dynastically** adverb.
– ORIGIN Greek *dunasteia* 'lordship', from *dunasthai* 'be able'.
dyne /dīn/ ● noun Physics a unit of force that, acting on a mass of one gram, increases its velocity by one centimetre per second every second along the direction in which it acts.
– ORIGIN from Greek *dunamis* 'force, power'.
dynode /dīnōd/ ● noun Electronics an intermediate electrode which emits additional electrons in a photomultiplier or similar amplifying device.
– ORIGIN from Greek *dunamis* 'power'.
dys- /diss/ ● combining form bad; difficult (used especially in medical terms): *dyspepsia*.
– ORIGIN from Greek *dus-*.
dysentery /dissəntri/ ● noun a disease in which the intestines are infected, resulting in severe diarrhoea with blood and mucus in the faeces.
– ORIGIN Greek *dusenteria*, from *dusenteros* 'afflicted in the bowels'.
dysfunctional ● adjective **1** not operating normally or properly. **2** unable to deal adequately with normal social relations.
– DERIVATIVES **dysfunction** noun **dysfunctionally** adverb.
dyskinesia /diskineeziə, -kī-/ ● noun Medicine abnormality or impairment of voluntary movement.
– ORIGIN from Greek *kinēsis* 'motion'.
dyslexia /disleksiə/ ● noun a disorder involving difficulty in learning to read or interpret words, letters, and other symbols.
– DERIVATIVES **dyslexic** adjective & noun.
– ORIGIN from Greek *lexis* 'speech' (apparently by confusion of Greek *legein* 'to speak' and Latin *legere* 'to read').
dysmenorrhoea /dismenəreeə/ (US **dysmenorrhea**) ● noun Medicine painful menstruation.
dyspepsia /dispepsiə/ ● noun indigestion.

Thesaurus

ter's success OVERSHADOW, outshine, surpass, exceed, outclass, outstrip, outdo, top, trump, transcend; diminish, minimize.
dwell ● verb *(formal) gypsies dwell in these caves* RESIDE, live, be settled, be housed, lodge, stay; *informal* put up; *formal* abide, be domiciled.
– PHRASES **dwell on** LINGER OVER, mull over, muse on, brood about/over, think about; be preoccupied by, be obsessed by, eat one's heart out over; harp on about, discuss at length.
dwelling ● noun *(formal)* RESIDENCE, home, house, accommodation, lodging place; lodgings, quarters, rooms; *informal* place, pad, digs; *formal* abode, domicile, habitation.
dwindle ● verb **1** *the population dwindled* DIMINISH, decrease, reduce, lessen, shrink; fall off, tail off, drop, fall, slump, plummet; disappear, vanish, die out; *informal* nosedive. **2** *her career dwindled* DECLINE, deteriorate, fail, slip, slide, fade, go downhill, go to rack and ruin; *informal* go to pot, go to the dogs, hit the skids, go down the toilet; *Austral./NZ informal* go to the pack.
– OPPOSITES increase, flourish.
dye ● noun *a blue dye* COLOURANT, colouring, colour, dyestuff, pigment, tint, stain, wash.
● verb *the gloves were dyed* COLOUR, tint, pigment, stain, wash.
dyed-in-the-wool ● adjective INVETERATE, confirmed, entrenched, established, long-standing, deep-rooted, diehard; complete, absolute, thorough, thoroughgoing, out-and-out, true blue; firm, unshakeable, staunch, steadfast, committed, devoted, dedicated, loyal, unswerving; *N. Amer.* full-bore; *informal* deep-dyed, card-carrying.
dying ● adjective **1** *his dying aunt* TERMINALLY ILL, at death's door, on one's deathbed, near death, fading fast, expiring, moribund, not long for this world, in extremis; *informal* on one's last legs, having one foot in the grave. **2** *a dying art form* DECLINING, vanishing, fading, ebbing, waning; *informal* on the way out. **3** *her dying words* FINAL, last; deathbed.
– OPPOSITES thriving, first.
● noun *he took her dying very hard* DEATH, demise, passing, loss of life, quietus; *formal* decease; *archaic* expiry.
dynamic ● adjective ENERGETIC, spirited, active, lively, zestful, vital, vigorous, forceful, powerful, positive; high-powered, aggressive, bold, enterprising; magnetic, passionate, fiery, high-octane; *informal* go-getting, peppy, full of get-up-and-go, full of vim and vigour, gutsy, spunky, feisty, go-ahead.
– OPPOSITES half-hearted.
dynamism ● noun ENERGY, spirit, liveliness, zestfulness, vitality, vigour, forcefulness, power, potency, positivity; aggression, drive, ambition, enterprise; magnetism, passion, fire; *informal* pep, get-up-and-go, vim and vigour, guts, feistiness.

– ORIGIN Greek *duspepsia*, from *duspeptos* 'difficult to digest'.
dyspeptic ● adjective **1** relating to or suffering from dyspepsia. **2** irritable.
dysphasia /disfayziə/ ● noun a disorder marked by difficulty in using language coherently, due to brain disease or damage.
– DERIVATIVES **dysphasic** adjective.
– ORIGIN from Greek *phatos* 'spoken'.
dysphoria /disforiə/ ● noun a state of unease or general dissatisfaction.
– DERIVATIVES **dysphoric** adjective.
– ORIGIN Greek *dusphoria*, from *dusphoros* 'hard to bear'.
dysplasia /displayziə/ ● noun the enlargement of an organ or tissue by the proliferation of abnormal cells.
– DERIVATIVES **dysplastic** adjective.
– ORIGIN from Greek *plasis* 'formation'.
dyspnoea /dispneeə/ (US **dyspnea**) ● noun difficult or laboured breathing.
– DERIVATIVES **dyspnoeic** adjective.
– ORIGIN Greek *duspnoia*, from *pnoē* 'breathing'.
dyspraxia /dispraksiə/ ● noun a disorder of the brain in childhood causing difficulty in activities requiring coordination and movement.
– ORIGIN from Greek *dus-* 'bad or difficult' + *praxis* 'action'.
dysprosium /disprōziəm/ ● noun a soft silvery-white metallic chemical element of the lanthanide series.
– ORIGIN from Greek *dusprositos* 'hard to get at'.
dysthymia /disthīmiə/ ● noun persistent mild depression.
– DERIVATIVES **dysthymic** adjective.
– ORIGIN Greek *dusthumia*.
dystopia /distōpiə/ ● noun an imaginary place or society in which everything is bad.
– DERIVATIVES **dystopian** adjective & noun.
– ORIGIN from DYS- + UTOPIA.
dystrophy /distrəfi/ ● noun Medicine a disorder in which an organ or tissue of the body wastes away. See also MUSCULAR DYSTROPHY.
– DERIVATIVES **dystrophic** adjective.
– ORIGIN from Greek *-trophia* 'nourishment'.

d

Thesaurus

dynasty ● noun BLOODLINE, line, ancestral line, lineage, house, family, ancestry, descent, succession, genealogy, family tree; regime, rule, reign, empire, sovereignty.
dyspeptic ● adjective BAD-TEMPERED, short-tempered, irritable, snappish, testy, tetchy, touchy, crabby, crotchety, grouchy, cantankerous, peevish, cross, disagreeable, waspish, prickly; *informal* snappy, on a short fuse; *Brit. informal* stroppy, ratty, eggy, like a bear with a sore head; *N. Amer. informal* cranky, ornery.

Ee

E[1] (also **e**) • noun (pl. **Es** or **E's**) **1** the fifth letter of the alphabet. **2** denoting the fifth in a set. **3** Music the third note of the diatonic scale of C major.

E[2] • abbreviation **1** East or Eastern. **2** informal the drug Ecstasy or a tablet of Ecstasy. **3** Physics energy. **4** denoting products, in particular food additives, which comply with EU regulations.

each • determiner & pronoun every one of two or more people or things, regarded and identified separately. • adverb to, for, or by every one of a group.
– PHRASES **each and every** every single.
– ORIGIN Old English.

each other • pronoun the other one or ones.

each-way • adjective & adverb Brit. (of a bet) backing a horse or other competitor either to win or to finish in the first three.

eager • adjective **1** strongly wanting to do or have. **2** keenly expectant or interested.
– DERIVATIVES **eagerly** adverb **eagerness** noun.
– ORIGIN originally also in the sense 'pungent, sour': from Old French *aigre* 'keen', from Latin *acer* 'sharp, pungent'.

eagle • noun a large keen-sighted bird of prey with a massive hooked bill and long broad wings.
– DERIVATIVES **eaglet** noun.
– ORIGIN Old French *aigle*, from Latin *aquila*.

eagle-eyed • adjective sharp sighted and keenly observant.

eagle owl • noun a very large owl with ear tufts and a deep hoot.

ear[1] • noun **1** the organ of hearing and balance in humans and other vertebrates. **2** the fleshy external part of this organ. **3** (in other animals) an organ sensitive to sound. **4** an ability to recognize and appreciate music or language. **5** willingness to listen and pay attention: *a sympathetic ear*.
– PHRASES **be all ears** informal be listening attentively. **one's ears are burning** one is subconsciously aware of being talked about. **have someone's ear** have access to and power to persuade or influence someone. **have** (or **keep**) **an ear to the ground** be well informed about events and trends. **be out on one's ear** informal be dismissed ignominiously. **up to one's ears in** informal very busy with.
– DERIVATIVES **eared** adjective.
– ORIGIN Old English.

ear[2] • noun the seed-bearing head or spike of a cereal plant.
– ORIGIN Old English.

earache • noun pain inside the ear.

earbashing • noun informal a lengthy and reproachful speech.

eardrum • noun the membrane of the middle ear, which vibrates in response to sound waves.

earful • noun informal a prolonged reprimand.

earhole • noun the external opening of the ear.

earl • noun a British nobleman ranking above a viscount and below a marquess.
– DERIVATIVES **earldom** noun.
– ORIGIN Old English.

Earl Grey • noun a kind of China tea flavoured with bergamot.
– ORIGIN probably named after the 2nd *Earl Grey* (1764–1845), said to have been given the recipe by a Chinese mandarin.

ear lobe • noun the soft, rounded fleshy part at the lower edge of the external ear.

early • adjective (**earlier**, **earliest**) & adverb **1** before the usual or expected time. **2** of or at the beginning of a particular time, period, or sequence.
– PHRASES **at the earliest** not before the time or date specified. **early bird** humorous a person who rises or arrives early. **the early bird catches the worm** proverb the person who takes the earliest opportunity to do something will gain the advantage over others. **early** (or **earlier**) **on** at an early (or earlier) stage. **it's early days** informal, chiefly Brit. it is too soon to be sure how a situation will develop.
– DERIVATIVES **earliness** noun.
– ORIGIN Old English.

Early English • adjective denoting a style of English Gothic architecture typical of the late 12th and 13th centuries, characterized by pointed arches and narrow pointed windows.

early music • noun medieval, Renaissance, and early baroque music, especially as revived and played on period instruments.

earmark • noun **1** a mark on the ear of a domesticated animal indicating ownership or identity. **2** an identifying feature. • verb **1** apply an earmark to. **2** (**be earmarked**) be designated for a particular purpose.

earmuffs • plural noun a pair of soft fabric coverings, connected by a band, worn over the ears to protect them from cold or noise.

earn • verb **1** obtain (money) in return for labour or services. **2** gain as the reward for hard work or merit. **3** (of capital invested) gain (money) as interest or profit.
– DERIVATIVES **earner** noun.
– ORIGIN Old English.

earned income • noun money derived from paid work as opposed to profit from investments.

Thesaurus

each • pronoun *there are 5000 books and each must be cleaned* EVERY ONE, each one, each and every one, all, the whole lot.
• determiner *he visited each month* EVERY, each and every, every single.
• adverb *they gave a tenner each* APIECE, per person, per capita, from each, individually, respectively, severally.

eager • adjective **1** *small eager faces* KEEN, enthusiastic, avid, fervent, ardent, motivated, wholehearted, dedicated, committed, earnest; *informal* mad keen, (as) keen as mustard. **2** *we were eager for news* ANXIOUS, impatient, longing, yearning, wishing, hoping, hopeful; desirous of, hankering after; on the edge of one's seat, on tenterhooks; *informal* itching, gagging, dying.
– OPPOSITES apathetic.

eagerness • noun KEENNESS, enthusiasm, avidity, fervour, zeal, wholeheartedness, earnestness, commitment, dedication; impatience, desire, longing, yearning, hunger, appetite, ambition; *informal* yen.

ear • noun **1** *an infection of the ear* inner ear, middle ear, outer ear. **2** *he had the ear of the president* ATTENTION, notice, heed, regard, consideration. **3** *he has an ear for a good song* APPRECIATION, discrimination, perception.
– RELATED TERMS aural, auricular.
– PHRASES **play it by ear** IMPROVISE, extemporize, ad lib; make it up as one goes along, think on one's feet; *informal* busk it, wing it.

early • adjective **1** *early copies of the book* ADVANCE, forward; initial, preliminary, first; pilot, trial. **2** *an early death* UNTIMELY, premature, unseasonable, before time. **3** *early man* PRIMITIVE, ancient, prehistoric, primeval; *poetic/literary* of yore. **4** *an early official statement* PROMPT, timely, quick, speedy, rapid, fast.
– OPPOSITES late, modern, overdue.
• adverb **1** *Rachel has to get up early* IN THE EARLY MORNING; at dawn, at daybreak, at cockcrow, with the lark. **2** *they hoped to leave school early* BEFORE THE USUAL TIME; prematurely, too soon, ahead of time, ahead of schedule.
– OPPOSITES late.

earmark • verb *the cash had been earmarked for the firm* SET ASIDE, keep (back), reserve; designate, assign, mark; allocate, allot, devote, pledge, give over.
• noun *he has all the earmarks of a leader* CHARACTERISTICS, attribute, feature, hallmark, quality.

earn • verb **1** *they earned £20,000* BE PAID, take home, gross; receive, get, make, obtain, collect, bring in; *informal* pocket, bank, rake in, net, bag. **2** *he has earned their trust* DESERVE, merit, warrant, justify, be worthy of; gain, win, secure, establish, obtain, procure,

earnest[1] /ernist/ ● adjective intensely serious.
– PHRASES **in earnest** with sincere and serious intention.
– DERIVATIVES **earnestly** adverb **earnestness** noun.
– ORIGIN Old English.
earnest[2] /ernist/ ● noun a sign or promise of what is to come.
– ORIGIN originally as *ernes* 'instalment paid to confirm a contract': from Old French *erres*, from Latin *arrabo* 'a pledge'.
earnings ● plural noun money or income earned.
earphone ● noun an electrical device worn on the ear to receive radio or telephone communications or to listen to a radio or tape recorder.
earpiece ● noun the part of a telephone, radio receiver, or other aural device that is applied to the ear during use.
ear-piercing ● adjective loud and shrill. ● noun the piercing of the lobes or edges of the ears to allow the wearing of earrings.
earplug ● noun a piece of wax, cotton wool, etc., placed in the ear as protection against noise or water.
earring ● noun a piece of jewellery worn on the lobe or edge of the ear.
earshot ● noun the range or distance over which one can hear or be heard.
ear-splitting ● adjective extremely loud.
earth ● noun **1** (also **Earth**) the planet on which we live. **2** the substance of the land surface; soil. **3** Brit. electrical connection to the ground, regarded as having zero electrical potential. **4** the underground lair of a badger or fox. **5** one of the four elements (air, earth, fire, and water) in ancient and medieval philosophy and in astrology. ● verb **1** Brit. connect (an electrical device) to earth. **2** Hunting (of a fox) run to its earth.
– PHRASES **come back** (or **down**) **to earth** return to reality. **the earth** chiefly Brit. a very large amount: *her hat cost the earth.* **go to earth** go into hiding. **on earth** used for emphasis: *what on earth are you doing?*
– DERIVATIVES **earthward** adjective & adverb **earthwards** adverb.
– ORIGIN Old English.
earthbound ● adjective **1** confined to the earth or earthly things. **2** moving towards the earth.
earth closet ● noun Brit. a basic type of toilet with dry earth used to cover excrement.
earthen ● adjective **1** made of compressed earth. **2** (of a pot) made of baked or fired clay.
earthenware ● noun pottery made of fired clay.
earthling ● noun (in science fiction) an inhabitant of the earth.
earthly ● adjective **1** relating to the earth or human life on the earth. **2** material; worldly. **3** informal used for emphasis; *there was no earthly reason to rush.*
– DERIVATIVES **earthliness** noun.
earth mother ● noun (in mythology and primitive religion) a goddess symbolizing fertility and the source of life.
earthquake ● noun a sudden violent shaking of the ground as a result of movements within the earth's crust.
earth sciences ● plural noun the branches of science concerned with the physical constitution of the earth and its atmosphere.
earth-shattering ● adjective informal very important or shocking.
earthwork ● noun a large artificial bank of soil, especially one made as a defence in ancient times.
earthworm ● noun a burrowing segmented worm that lives in the soil.
earthy ● adjective (**earthier**, **earthiest**) **1** resembling or suggestive of soil. **2** direct and uninhibited, especially about sexual subjects or bodily functions.
– DERIVATIVES **earthily** adverb **earthiness** noun.
ear trumpet ● noun a trumpet-shaped device formerly used as a hearing aid.
earwax ● noun the protective yellow waxy substance secreted in the passage of the outer ear.
earwig ● noun a small elongated insect with a pair of terminal appendages that resemble pincers. ● verb (**earwigged**, **earwigging**) informal eavesdrop.
– ORIGIN Old English, from *ēare* 'ear' + *wicga* 'earwig'; the insect was once thought to crawl into the human ear.
ease ● noun **1** absence of difficulty or effort. **2** freedom from worries or problems. ● verb **1** make or become less serious or severe. **2** move carefully or gradually. **3** (**ease off**/**up**) do something with more moderation. **4** (of share prices, interest rates, etc.) decrease in value or amount.
– PHRASES **at** (**one's**) **ease 1** relaxed. **2** (**at ease**) Military in a relaxed attitude with the feet apart and the hands behind the back.
– DERIVATIVES **easeful** adjective (literary).
– ORIGIN Old French *aise*, from Latin *adjacere* 'lie close by'.
easel /eez'l/ ● noun a wooden frame on legs for holding an artist's work in progress.
– ORIGIN Dutch *ezel* 'ass'.
easement /eezmənt/ ● noun **1** Law a right to cross or otherwise use another's land for a specified purpose. **2** literary comfort or peace.
easily ● adverb **1** without difficulty or effort. **2** without doubt. **3** very probably.

e

Thesaurus

get, acquire; *informal* clinch.
– OPPOSITES lose.
earnest[1] ● adjective **1** *he is dreadfully earnest* SERIOUS, solemn, grave, sober, humourless, staid, intense; committed, dedicated, keen, diligent, zealous; thoughtful, cerebral, deep, profound. **2** *earnest prayer* DEVOUT, heartfelt, wholehearted, sincere, impassioned, fervent, ardent, intense, urgent.
– OPPOSITES frivolous, half-hearted.
– PHRASES **in earnest 1** *we are in earnest about stopping burglaries* SERIOUS, sincere, wholehearted, genuine; committed, firm, resolute, determined. **2** *he started writing in earnest* ZEALOUSLY, purposefully, determinedly, resolutely; passionately, wholeheartedly.
earnest[2] ● noun *an earnest of a good harvest* SIGN, token, promise, guarantee, pledge, assurance; security, surety, deposit.
earnestly ● adverb SERIOUSLY, solemnly, gravely, intently; sincerely, resolutely, firmly, ardently, fervently, eagerly.
earnings ● plural noun INCOME, wages, salary, stipend, pay, payment, fees; revenue, yield, profit, takings, proceeds, dividends, return, remuneration.
earth ● noun **1** *the moon orbits the earth* WORLD, globe, planet. **2** *a trembling of the earth* LAND, ground, terra firma; floor. **3** *he ploughed the earth* SOIL, clay, loam; dirt, sod, turf; ground. **4** *the fox's earth* DEN, lair, sett, burrow, warren, hole; retreat, shelter, hideout, hideaway; *informal* hidey-hole.
– RELATED TERMS terrestrial, telluric.
earthenware ● noun POTTERY, crockery, stoneware; china, porcelain; pots.
earthly ● adjective **1** *the earthly environment* TERRESTRIAL, telluric. **2** *the promise of earthly delights* WORLDLY, temporal, mortal, human; material; carnal, fleshly, bodily, physical, corporeal, sensual. **3** *(informal) there is no earthly explanation for this* FEASIBLE, possible, likely, conceivable, imaginable.
– OPPOSITES extraterrestrial, heavenly.
earthquake ● noun (EARTH) TREMOR, shock, foreshock, aftershock, convulsion; *informal* quake, shake, trembler.
– RELATED TERMS seismic.
earthy ● adjective **1** *an earthy smell* SOIL-LIKE, dirt-like. **2** *the earthy Calvinistic tradition* DOWN-TO-EARTH, unsophisticated, unrefined, simple, plain, unpretentious, natural. **3** *Emma's earthy language* BAWDY, ribald, off colour, racy, rude, vulgar, lewd, crude, foul, coarse, uncouth, unseemly, indelicate, indecent, obscene; *informal* blue, locker-room, X-rated; *Brit. informal* fruity, near the knuckle.
ease ● noun **1** *he defeated them all with ease* EFFORTLESSNESS, no trouble, simplicity; deftness, adroitness, proficiency, mastery. **2** *his ease of manner* NATURALNESS, casualness, informality, amiability, affability; unconcern, composure, nonchalance, insouciance. **3** *he couldn't find any ease* PEACE, calm, tranquillity, serenity; repose, restfulness, quiet, security, comfort. **4** *a life of ease* AFFLUENCE, wealth, prosperity, luxury, plenty; comfort, contentment, enjoyment, well-being.
– OPPOSITES difficulty, formality, trouble, hardship.
● verb **1** *the alcohol eased his pain* RELIEVE, alleviate, mitigate, soothe, palliate, moderate, dull, deaden, numb; reduce, lighten, diminish. **2** *the rain eased off* ABATE, subside, die down, let up, slacken off, diminish, lessen, peter out, relent, come to an end. **3** *work helped to ease her mind* CALM, quieten, pacify, soothe, comfort, console; hearten, gladden, uplift, encourage. **4** *we want to ease their adjustment* FACILITATE, expedite, assist, help, aid, advance, further, forward, simplify. **5** *he eased out the cork* GUIDE, manoeuvre, inch, edge; slide, slip, squeeze.
– OPPOSITES aggravate, worsen, hinder.
– PHRASES **at ease/at one's ease** RELAXED, calm, serene, tranquil, unworried, contented, content, happy; comfortable.
easily ● adverb **1** *I overcame this problem easily* EFFORTLESSLY, com-

east ● noun (**the east**) **1** the direction towards the point of the horizon where the sun rises at the equinoxes, on the right-hand side of a person facing north. **2** the eastern part of a country, region, or town. **3** (**the East**) the regions or countries lying to the east of Europe, especially China, Japan, and India. **4** (**the East**) historical the former communist states of eastern Europe. ● adjective **1** lying towards, near, or facing the east. **2** (of a wind) blowing from the east. ● adverb to or towards the east.
– DERIVATIVES **eastbound** adjective & adverb.
– ORIGIN Old English.

Easter (also **Easter Day** or **Easter Sunday**) ● noun the festival of the Christian Church celebrating the resurrection of Christ, held (in the Western Church) on the first Sunday after the first full moon following the northern spring equinox.
– ORIGIN Old English, related to EAST.

e

Easter egg ● noun a chocolate egg or decorated hard-boiled egg given as a gift at Easter.

easterly ● adjective & adverb **1** in an eastward position or direction. **2** (of a wind) blowing from the east. ● noun a wind blowing from the east.

eastern ● adjective **1** situated in, directed towards, or facing the east. **2** (**Eastern**) coming from or characteristic of the regions to the east of Europe.
– DERIVATIVES **easternmost** adjective.

Eastern Church (also **Eastern Orthodox Church**) ● noun **1** another name for ORTHODOX CHURCH. **2** any of the Christian Churches originating in eastern Europe and the Middle East.

easterner ● noun a person from the east of a region or country.

Eastertide ● noun the Easter period.

East Indian ● adjective **1** relating to the islands of SE Asia. **2** archaic relating to the whole of SE Asia to the east of and including India.

easting ● noun **1** distance travelled or measured eastward. **2** a figure or line representing eastward distance on a map.

east-north-east ● noun the direction or compass point midway between east and north-east.

east-south-east ● noun the direction or compass point midway between east and south-east.

eastward ● adjective in an easterly direction. ● adverb (also **eastwards**) towards the east.
– DERIVATIVES **eastwardly** adjective & adverb.

easy ● adjective (**easier**, **easiest**) **1** achieved without great effort; presenting few difficulties. **2** free from worry or problems. **3** lacking anxiety or awkwardness. **4** informal, derogatory willingly responsive to sexual advances. ● exclamation be careful!
– PHRASES **easy on the eye** (or **ear**) informal pleasant to look at (or listen to). **go** (or **be**) **easy on** informal refrain from being harsh with or critical of. **take it easy 1** proceed calmly. **2** make no unnecessary effort.
– DERIVATIVES **easiness** noun.

easy chair ● noun a large, comfortable chair, typically an armchair.

easy-going ● adjective relaxed and open-minded.

easy listening ● noun popular music that is tuneful and undemanding.

easy street ● noun informal a state of financial comfort or security.

eat ● verb (past **ate** /et, ayt/; past part. **eaten**) **1** put (food) into the mouth and chew and swallow it. **2** (**eat out** or **in**) have a meal in a restaurant (or at home). **3** (**eat something away** or **eat away at/into**) gradually erode or destroy something. **4** (**eat up**) use (resources) in very large quantities. ● noun (**eats**) informal light food or snacks.
– PHRASES **eat one's heart out** suffer from longing for something unattainable. **eat one's words** retract what one has said. **I'll eat my hat** informal said to indicate that one thinks something is extremely unlikely to happen. **what's eating you** (or **him** etc.)**?** informal what is worrying or annoying you (or him etc.)?
– DERIVATIVES **eater** noun.
– ORIGIN Old English.

eatable ● adjective fit to be consumed as food. ● noun (**eatables**) items of food.

eatery ● noun (pl. **eateries**) informal a restaurant or cafe.

eating apple ● noun an apple suitable for eating raw.

eau de cologne /ō də kəlōn/ ● noun (pl. **eaux de cologne** pronunc. same) a toilet water with a strong, characteristic scent.
– ORIGIN French, 'water of Cologne'.

eau de Nil /ō də neel/ ● noun a pale greenish colour.
– ORIGIN French, 'water of the Nile'.

eau de toilette /ō də twaalet/ ● noun (pl. **eaux de toilette** pronunc. same) a dilute form of perfume.
– ORIGIN French, 'toilet water'.

eau de vie /ō də vee/ ● noun (pl. **eaux de vie** pronunc. same) brandy.
– ORIGIN French, 'water of life'.

eaves ● plural noun the part of a roof that meets or overhangs the walls of a building.
– ORIGIN Old English.

eavesdrop ● verb (**eavesdropped**, **eavesdropping**) secretly listen to a conversation.
– DERIVATIVES **eavesdropper** noun.
– ORIGIN from obsolete *eavesdrop* 'the ground on to which water drips from the eaves'.

ebb ● noun the movement of the tide out to sea. ● verb **1** (of tidewater) move away from the land; recede. **2** (often **ebb away**) (of an emotion or quality) gradually lessen or reduce.
– PHRASES **at a low ebb** in a poor state.
– ORIGIN Old English.

E-boat ● noun a German torpedo boat used in the Second World War.

Thesaurus

fortably, simply; with ease, without difficulty, without a hitch, smoothly; skilfully, deftly, smartly; *informal* no sweat. **2** *he's easily the best* UNDOUBTEDLY, without doubt, without question, indisputably, undeniably, definitely, certainly, clearly, obviously, patently; by far, far and away, by a mile.

east ● adjective EASTERN, easterly, oriental.

easy ● adjective **1** *the task was very easy* UNCOMPLICATED, undemanding, unchallenging, effortless, painless, trouble-free, facile, simple, straightforward, elementary, plain sailing; *informal* easy as pie, a piece of cake, child's play, kids' stuff, a cinch, no sweat, a doddle, a breeze; *Brit. informal* easy-peasy; *N. Amer. informal* duck soup, a snap; *dated* a snip. **2** *easy babies* DOCILE, manageable, amenable, tractable, compliant, pliant, acquiescent, obliging, cooperative, easy-going. **3** *an easy target* VULNERABLE, susceptible, defenceless; naive, gullible, trusting. **4** *Vic's easy manner* NATURAL, casual, informal, unceremonious, unreserved, uninhibited, unaffected, easy-going, amiable, affable, genial, good-humoured; carefree, nonchalant, unconcerned; *informal* laid-back. **5** *an easy life* CALM, tranquil, serene, quiet, peaceful, untroubled, contented, relaxed, comfortable, secure, safe; *informal* cushy. **6** *an easy pace* LEISURELY, unhurried, comfortable, undemanding, easy-going, gentle, sedate, moderate, steady. **7** *(informal) people think she's easy* PROMISCUOUS, free with one's favours, unchaste, loose, wanton, abandoned, licentious, debauched; *informal* sluttish, whorish, tarty; *N. Amer. informal* roundheeled.
– OPPOSITES difficult, demanding, formal, chaste.

easy-going ● adjective RELAXED, even-tempered, placid, mellow, mild, happy-go-lucky, carefree, free and easy, nonchalant, insouciant, imperturbable; amiable, considerate, undemanding, patient, tolerant, lenient, broad-minded, understanding; good-natured, pleasant, agreeable; *informal* laid-back, unflappable.
– OPPOSITES intolerant.

eat ● verb **1** *we ate a hearty breakfast* CONSUME, devour, ingest, partake of; gobble (up/down), bolt (down), wolf (down); swallow, chew, munch, chomp; *informal* guzzle, nosh, put away, tuck into, demolish, dispose of, polish off, get stuck into, pig out on, get outside of; *Brit. informal* scoff, gollop; *N. Amer. informal* scarf, snarf. **2** *we ate at a local restaurant* HAVE A MEAL, consume food, feed, snack; breakfast, lunch, dine; feast, banquet; *informal* graze, nosh. **3** *acidic water can eat away at pipes* ERODE, corrode, wear away/down/through, burn through, consume, dissolve, disintegrate, crumble, decay; damage, destroy.

eatable ● adjective EDIBLE, palatable, digestible; fit to eat, fit for consumption.

eats ● plural noun *(informal)* FOOD, sustenance, nourishment, fare; eatables, snacks, titbits; *informal* nosh, grub, chow; *Brit. informal* scoff, tuck; *N. Amer. informal* chuck.

eavesdrop ● verb LISTEN IN, spy; monitor, tap, wiretap, record, overhear; *informal* snoop, bug.

ebb ● verb **1** *the tide ebbed* RECEDE, go out, retreat, flow back, fall back/away, subside. **2** *his courage began to ebb* DIMINISH, dwindle, wane, fade away, peter out, decline, flag, let up, decrease, weaken, disappear.
– OPPOSITES increase.

– ORIGIN from *E*- for *enemy*.

Ebola fever /eebōlə/ ● noun an infectious and generally fatal viral disease marked by fever and severe internal bleeding.
– ORIGIN named after a river in the Democratic Republic of Congo.

ebonite ● noun another term for VULCANITE.

ebonize (also **ebonise**) ● verb make (wood or furniture) look like ebony.

ebony /ebbəni/ ● noun **1** heavy blackish or very dark brown wood from a tree of tropical and warm regions. **2** a very dark brown or black colour.
– ORIGIN Greek *ebenos* 'ebony tree'.

ebullient /ibulliənt/ ● adjective **1** cheerful and full of energy. **2** archaic or literary boiling or agitated as if boiling.
– DERIVATIVES **ebullience** noun **ebulliently** adverb.
– ORIGIN from Latin *ebullire* 'boil up'.

EC ● abbreviation **1** East Central (London postal district). **2** European Commission. **3** European Community.

eccentric /iksentrik/ ● adjective **1** unconventional and slightly strange. **2** technical not placed centrally or not having its axis placed centrally. **3** technical (of an orbit) not circular, especially to a marked degree. ● noun **1** an eccentric person. **2** a cam or other part mounted eccentrically on a revolving shaft in order to transform rotation into backward-and-forward motion.
– DERIVATIVES **eccentrically** adverb **eccentricity** noun.
– ORIGIN Greek *ekkentros*, from *ek* 'out of' + *kentron* 'centre'.

Eccles cake ● noun Brit. a round flat cake of sweetened pastry filled with currants.
– ORIGIN named after the town of *Eccles* near Manchester.

ecclesiastic formal ● noun a priest or clergyman. ● adjective ecclesiastical.

ecclesiastical ● adjective relating to the Christian Church or its clergy.
– DERIVATIVES **ecclesiastically** adverb.
– ORIGIN Greek *ekklēsiastikos*, from *ekklēsiastēs* 'member of an assembly'.

ecclesiology /ikleeziolləji/ ● noun **1** the study of churches. **2** theology as applied to the nature and structure of the Christian Church.
– DERIVATIVES **ecclesiological** adjective **ecclesiologist** noun.

eccrine /ekrīn, -krin/ ● adjective Physiology relating to or denoting multicellular glands which do not lose cytoplasm in their secretions, especially the sweat glands.
– ORIGIN from Greek *ekkrinein* 'secrete'.

ecdysis /ekdīsiss/ ● noun Zoology the process of shedding the old skin (in reptiles) or casting off the outer cuticle (in insects and other arthropods).
– DERIVATIVES **ecdysial** /ekdizziəl/ adjective.
– ORIGIN Greek *ekdusis*, from *ekduein* 'put off'.

ECG ● abbreviation electrocardiogram or electrocardiograph.

echelon /eshəlon/ ● noun **1** a level or rank in an organization, profession, or society. **2** Military a formation of troops, ships, etc. in parallel rows with the end of each row projecting further than the one in front.
– ORIGIN French *échelon*, from *échelle* 'ladder'.

echidna /ikidnə/ ● noun (pl. **echidnas** or **echidnae**) a spiny egg-laying mammal with a long snout and claws, native to Australia and New Guinea.
– ORIGIN Greek *ekhidna* 'viper'.

echinoderm /ikīnəderm, ekkin-/ ● noun Zoology a marine invertebrate of a large group (the phylum Echinodermata) including starfishes, sea urchins, and sea cucumbers.
– ORIGIN from Greek *ekhinos* 'hedgehog, sea urchin' + *derma* 'skin'.

echo ● noun (pl. **echoes**) **1** a sound caused by the reflection of sound waves from a surface back to the listener. **2** a reflected radio or radar beam. **3** something suggestive of or parallel to something else. ● verb (**echoes**, **echoed**) **1** (of a sound) reverberate or be repeated after the original sound has stopped. **2** have a continued significance or influence. **3** repeat (someone's words or opinions).
– DERIVATIVES **echoer** noun **echoey** adjective **echoless** adjective.
– ORIGIN Greek *ēkhō*.

echocardiography /ekkōkaardiogreəfi/ ● noun Medicine the use of ultrasound waves to investigate the action of the heart.
– DERIVATIVES **echocardiogram** noun **echocardiograph** noun **echocardiographic** adjective.

echo chamber ● noun an enclosed space for producing echoes.

echogram ● noun a recording of depth or distance under water made by an echo sounder.

echograph ● noun an instrument for recording echograms.

echoic /ekōik/ ● adjective **1** of or like an echo. **2** representing a sound by imitation; onomatopoeic.
– DERIVATIVES **echoically** adverb.

echolocation /ekkōlōkaysh'n/ ● noun the location of objects by reflected sound, in particular as used by animals such as dolphins and bats.

echo sounder ● noun a device for determining the depth of the seabed or detecting objects in water by measuring the time taken for echoes to return to the listener.

echt /ekht/ ● adjective authentic and typical.
– ORIGIN German.

eclair /iklayr/ ● noun a small, soft, long cake of choux pastry filled with cream and topped with chocolate icing.
– ORIGIN French, 'lightning'.

eclampsia /iklampsiə/ ● noun Medicine a condition in which one or more convulsions occur in a pregnant woman suffering from high blood pressure, often followed by coma.
– DERIVATIVES **eclamptic** adjective.
– ORIGIN Greek *eklampsis* 'sudden development'.

éclat /ayklaa/ ● noun a conspicuously brilliant or successful effect.
– ORIGIN French, from *éclater* 'burst out'.

eclectic /iklektik/ ● adjective deriving ideas or style from a

Thesaurus

● noun **1** *the ebb of the tide* RECEDING, retreat, subsiding. **2** *the ebb of the fighting* ABATEMENT, subsiding, easing, dying down, de-escalation, decrease, decline, diminution.

ebony ● adjective BLACK, jet black, pitch black, coal black, sable, inky, sooty, raven, dark.

ebullience ● noun EXUBERANCE, buoyancy, cheerfulness, cheeriness, merriment, jollity, sunniness, jauntiness, light-heartedness, high spirits, elation, euphoria, jubilation; animation, sparkle, vivacity, enthusiasm, perkiness; *informal* bubbliness, chirpiness, bounciness, pep.

ebullient ● adjective EXUBERANT, buoyant, cheerful, joyful, cheery, merry, jolly, sunny, jaunty, light-hearted, elated; animated, sparkling, vivacious, irrepressible; *informal* bubbly, bouncy, peppy, upbeat, chirpy, smiley, full of beans; *dated* gay.
– OPPOSITES depressed.

eccentric ● adjective *eccentric behaviour* UNCONVENTIONAL, uncommon, abnormal, irregular, aberrant, anomalous, odd, queer, strange, peculiar, weird, bizarre, outlandish, freakish, extraordinary; idiosyncratic, quirky, nonconformist, outré; *informal* way out, offbeat, freaky, oddball, wacky, cranky; *Brit. informal* rum; *N. Amer. informal* kooky, wacko.
– OPPOSITES conventional.
● noun *he was something of an eccentric* ODDITY, odd fellow, character, individualist, individual, free spirit; misfit; *informal* oddball, queer fish, weirdo, freak, nut, head case, crank; *Brit. informal* one-off, odd bod, nutter; *N. Amer. informal* wacko, screwball.

eccentricity ● noun UNCONVENTIONALITY, singularity, oddness, strangeness, weirdness, quirkiness, freakishness; peculiarity, foible, idiosyncrasy, caprice, whimsy, quirk; *informal* nuttiness, screwiness, freakiness; *N. Amer. informal* kookiness.

ecclesiastic ● noun *a high ecclesiastic* CLERGYMAN, clergywoman, priest, churchman/woman, man/woman of the cloth, man/woman of God, cleric, minister, preacher, chaplain, father; bishop, vicar, rector, parson, curate, deacon; *Scottish* kirkman; *N. Amer.* dominie; *informal* reverend, padre, Holy Joe, Bible-basher.
● adjective *ecclesiastic law*. See ECCLESIASTICAL.

ecclesiastical ● adjective PRIESTLY, ministerial, clerical, ecclesiastic, canonical, sacerdotal; church, churchly, religious, spiritual, holy, divine; *informal* churchy.

echelon ● noun LEVEL, rank, grade, step, rung, tier, position, order.

echo ● noun **1** *a faint echo of my shout* REVERBERATION, reflection, ringing, repetition, repeat. **2** *the scene she described was an echo of the photograph* DUPLICATE, copy, replica, imitation, mirror image, double, match, parallel; *informal* lookalike, spitting image, dead ringer. **3** *an echo of their love* TRACE, vestige, remnant, ghost, memory, recollection, remembrance; reminder, sign, mark, token, indication, suggestion, hint; evidence.
● verb **1** *his laughter echoed round the room* REVERBERATE, resonate, resound, reflect, ring, vibrate. **2** *Bill echoed Rex's words* REPEAT,

broad and varied range of sources. • noun an eclectic person.
– DERIVATIVES **eclectically** adverb **eclecticism** noun.
– ORIGIN Greek *eklektikos*, from *eklegein* 'pick out'.

eclipse /iklips/ • noun **1** an obscuring of the light from one celestial body by the passage of another between it and the observer or between it and its source of illumination. **2** a sudden loss of significance, power, or prominence. • verb **1** (of a celestial body) obscure the light from or to (another body). **2** deprive of significance, power, or prominence.
– ORIGIN Greek *ekleipsis*, from *ekleipein* 'fail to appear, be eclipsed'.

eclipse plumage • noun a male duck's plumage during a moult, with distinctive markings obscured.

e

ecliptic /ikliptik/ Astronomy • noun a great circle on the celestial sphere representing the sun's apparent path during the year, so called because lunar and solar eclipses can only occur when the moon crosses it. • adjective of eclipses or the ecliptic.

eclogue /eklog/ • noun a short pastoral poem, especially one in the form of a dialogue.
– ORIGIN Greek *eklogē* 'selection'.

ECM • abbreviation electronic countermeasures.

eco- /eekō/ • combining form representing ECOLOGY.

eco-friendly • adjective not harmful to the environment.

eco-labelling • noun the use of labels to identify products conforming to recognized environmental standards.
– DERIVATIVES **eco-label** noun.

E. coli /kōlī/ • noun the bacterium *Escherichia coli*, commonly found in the intestines of humans and other animals, some strains of which can cause severe food poisoning.

ecology /ikolləji/ • noun the branch of biology concerned with the relations of organisms to one another and to their physical surroundings.
– DERIVATIVES **ecological** adjective **ecologically** adverb **ecologist** noun.
– ORIGIN from Greek *oikos* 'house' .

e-commerce • noun commercial transactions conducted electronically on the Internet.

econometrics /ikonnəmetriks/ • plural noun (treated as sing.) the branch of economics concerned with the use of mathematical methods (especially statistics) in describing economic systems.
– DERIVATIVES **econometric** adjective **econometrician** noun **econometrist** noun.

economic /eekənommik, ek-/ • adjective **1** relating to economics or the economy. **2** justified in terms of profitability.

economical • adjective **1** giving good value or return in relation to the resources used or money spent. **2** sparing in the use of resources or money.
– PHRASES **economical with the truth** euphemistic lying or deliberately withholding information.
– DERIVATIVES **economically** adverb.

economic rationalism • noun Austral. a policy of promoting efficiency and productivity in a free market system by privatization, deregulation, and reduced government spending.

economics • plural noun (often treated as sing.) the branch of knowledge concerned with the production, consumption, and transfer of wealth.

economist • noun an expert in economics.

economize (also **economise**) • verb spend less; be economical.
– DERIVATIVES **economizer** noun.

economy • noun (pl. **economies**) **1** the state of a country or region in terms of the production and consumption of goods and services and the supply of money. **2** careful management of available resources. **3** a financial saving. **4** (also **economy class**) the cheapest class of air or rail travel. **5** (before another noun) offering good value for money: *an economy pack.*
– PHRASES **economy of scale** a proportionate saving in costs gained by an increased level of production.
– ORIGIN Greek *oikonomia* 'household management'.

ecosphere • noun a region in which life exists or could exist; the biosphere.

ecosystem • noun a biological community of interacting organisms and their physical environment.

ecotourism • noun tourism directed towards unspoiled natural environments and intended to support conservation efforts.
– DERIVATIVES **ecotour** noun & verb **ecotourist** noun.

ecotype • noun Botany & Zoology a distinct form or race of a plant or animal species occupying a particular habitat.

eco-warrior /eekōworriər/ • noun a person actively involved in protecting the environment from damage.

ecru /aykroo/ • noun the light cream or beige colour of unbleached linen.
– ORIGIN French, 'unbleached'.

ecstasy /ekstəsi/ • noun (pl. **ecstasies**) **1** an overwhelming feeling of great happiness or joyful excitement. **2** an emotional or religious frenzy or trancelike state. **3** (**Ecstasy**) an illegal amphetamine-based synthetic drug with euphoric effects.
– ORIGIN from Greek *ekstasis* 'standing outside oneself'.

ecstatic /ikstattik/ • adjective feeling or characterized by ecstasy. • noun a person who is subject to mystical experiences.
– DERIVATIVES **ecstatically** adverb.

ECT • abbreviation electroconvulsive therapy.

ecto- • combining form outer; external: *ectoderm.*
– ORIGIN from Greek *ektos* 'outside'.

ectomorph /ektōmorf/ • noun Physiology a person with a lean and delicate build of body. Compare with ENDOMORPH and MESOMORPH.
– DERIVATIVES **ectomorphic** adjective.
– ORIGIN from *ectodermal* (the ectoderm being the layer of the embryo giving rise to these physical characteristics).

-ectomy • combining form denoting surgical removal of a specified part of the body: *appendectomy.*
– ORIGIN from Greek *ektomē* 'excision'.

ectopic /ektopik/ • adjective Medicine in an abnormal place or position.
– ORIGIN from Greek *ektopos* 'out of place'.

ectopic pregnancy • noun a pregnancy in which the fetus develops outside the womb, typically in a Fallopian tube.

ectoplasm /ektōplaz'm/ • noun a viscous substance that sup-

Thesaurus

restate, reiterate; copy, imitate, parrot, mimic; reproduce, recite, quote, regurgitate; *informal* recap.

éclat • noun STYLE, flamboyance, confidence, elan, dash, flair, vigour, gusto, verve, zest, sparkle, brio, panache, dynamism, spirit; *informal* pizzazz, pep, oomph.

eclectic • adjective WIDE-RANGING, broad-based, extensive, comprehensive, encyclopedic; varied, diverse, catholic, all-embracing, multifaceted, multifarious, heterogeneous, miscellaneous, assorted.

eclipse • noun **1** *the eclipse of the sun* BLOTTING OUT, blocking, covering, obscuring, concealing, darkening; *Astronomy* occultation. **2** *the eclipse of the empire* DECLINE, fall, failure, decay, deterioration, degeneration, weakening, collapse.
• verb **1** *the sun was eclipsed by the moon* BLOT OUT, block, cover, obscure, hide, conceal, obliterate, darken; shade; *Astronomy* occult. **2** *the system was eclipsed by new methods* OUTSHINE, overshadow, surpass, exceed, outclass, outstrip, outdo, top, trump, transcend, upstage.

economic • adjective **1** *economic reform* FINANCIAL, monetary, budgetary, fiscal; commercial. **2** *the firm cannot remain economic* PROFITABLE, moneymaking, lucrative, remunerative, fruitful, productive; solvent, viable, cost-effective. **3** *an economic alternative to carpeting* CHEAP, inexpensive, low-cost, budget, economy, economical, cut-price, discount, bargain.
– OPPOSITES unprofitable, expensive.

economical • adjective **1** *an economical car* CHEAP, inexpensive, low-cost, budget, economy, economic; cut-price, discount, bargain. **2** *a very economical shopper* THRIFTY, provident, prudent, sensible, frugal, sparing, abstemious; mean, parsimonious, penny-pinching, miserly; *N. Amer.* forehanded; *informal* stingy.
– OPPOSITES expensive, spendthrift.

economize • verb SAVE (MONEY), cut costs; cut back, make cutbacks, retrench, budget, make economies, be thrifty, be frugal, scrimp, cut corners, tighten one's belt, draw in one's horns, watch the/your pennies.

economy • noun **1** *the nation's economy* WEALTH, (financial) resources; financial system, financial management. **2** *one can combine good living with economy* THRIFT, thriftiness, providence, prudence, careful budgeting, economizing, saving, scrimping, restraint, frugality, abstemiousness; *N. Amer.* forehandedness.
– OPPOSITES extravagance.

ecstasy • noun RAPTURE, bliss, elation, euphoria, transports, rhapsodies; joy, jubilation, exultation.
– OPPOSITES misery.

ecstatic • adjective ENRAPTURED, elated, in raptures, euphoric, rapturous, joyful, overjoyed, blissful; on cloud nine, in seventh

posedly exudes from the body of a medium during a spiritualistic trance and forms the material for the manifestation of spirits.
– DERIVATIVES **ectoplasmic** adjective.

ecu /ekyoo, ay-/ (also **ECU**) ● noun (pl. same or **ecus**) former term for EURO.
– ORIGIN acronym from *European currency unit*.

Ecuadorean /ekwədoriən/ (also **Ecuadorian**) ● noun a person from Ecuador. ● adjective relating to Ecuador.

ecumenical /eekyoomennik'l, ek-/ ● adjective **1** representing a number of different Christian Churches. **2** promoting or relating to unity among the world's Christian Churches.
– DERIVATIVES **ecumenically** adverb.
– ORIGIN Greek *oikoumenikos*, from *oikoumenē* 'the inhabited earth'.

ecumenism /ikyoomәniz'm/ ● noun the principle or aim of promoting unity among the world's Christian Churches.

eczema /eksimə/ ● noun a condition in which patches of skin become rough and inflamed, causing itching and bleeding.
– DERIVATIVES **eczematous** /ekseemətəss/ adjective.
– ORIGIN Greek *ekzema*, from *ekzein* 'boil over, break out'.

-ed[1] ● suffix forming adjectives: **1** (added to nouns) having; possessing; affected by: *talented*. **2** from phrases consisting of adjective and noun: *bad-tempered*.
– ORIGIN Old English.

-ed[2] ● suffix forming: **1** the past tense and past participle of weak verbs: *landed*. **2** participial adjectives: *wounded*.

Edam /eedam/ ● noun a round pale yellow cheese with a red wax coating.
– ORIGIN from *Edam* in the Netherlands, where it is made.

eddo /eddō/ ● noun (pl. **eddoes**) a taro corm or plant of a West Indian variety with many edible cormlets.
– ORIGIN West African.

eddy ● noun (pl. **eddies**) a circular movement of water causing a small whirlpool. ● verb (**eddies, eddied**) (of water, air, smoke, etc.) move in a circular way.
– ORIGIN probably related to an Old English prefix meaning 'again, back'.

edelweiss /ayd'lvīss/ ● noun a mountain plant which has woolly white bracts around its small flowers and downy grey-green leaves.
– ORIGIN German, from *edel* 'noble' + *weiss* 'white'.

edema ● noun US spelling of OEDEMA.

Eden /eed'n/ ● noun **1** (also **Garden of Eden**) the place where Adam and Eve lived in the biblical account of the Creation. **2** a place or state of unspoilt happiness or beauty.
– ORIGIN Hebrew.

edentate /eedentayt/ ● noun Zoology a mammal of a group having no incisor or canine teeth, including the anteaters, sloths, and armadillos.
– ORIGIN from Latin *edentare* 'make toothless'.

edge ● noun **1** the outside limit of an object, area, or surface. **2** the line along which two surfaces of a solid meet. **3** the sharpened side of a blade. **4** an intense or striking quality. **5** a quality or factor which gives superiority over close rivals. ● verb **1** provide with an edge or border. **2** move or cause to move carefully or furtively.
– PHRASES **on edge** tense, nervous, or irritable. **set someone's teeth on edge** (of a sound or taste) cause intense discomfort or irritation to someone.
– DERIVATIVES **edged** adjective **edgeless** adjective **edger** noun.
– ORIGIN Old English, 'sharpened side of a blade'.

edgeways (also **edgewise**) ● adverb with the edge uppermost or towards the viewer.
– PHRASES **get a word in edgeways** manage to break into a lively conversation.

edging ● noun something forming an edge or border.

edgy ● adjective (**edgier, edgiest**) tense, nervous, or irritable.
– DERIVATIVES **edgily** adverb **edginess** noun.

EDI ● abbreviation electronic data interchange.

edible ● adjective fit to be eaten. ● noun (**edibles**) items of food.
– DERIVATIVES **edibility** noun.
– ORIGIN Latin *edibilis*, from *edere* 'eat'.

edict /eedikt/ ● noun an official order or proclamation.
– ORIGIN Latin *edictum* 'something proclaimed', from *dicere* 'say, tell'.

edifice /eddifiss/ ● noun **1** a large, imposing building. **2** a complex abstract or conceptual system.
– ORIGIN Latin *aedificium*, from *aedis* 'dwelling' + *facere* 'make'.

edify /eddifī/ ● verb (**edifies, edified**) instruct or improve morally or intellectually.
– DERIVATIVES **edification** noun **edifying** adjective.
– ORIGIN Latin *aedificare* 'build'.

edit ● verb (**edited, editing**) **1** prepare (written material) for publication by correcting, condensing, or otherwise modifying it. **2** prepare and arrange material for (a recording or broadcast). **3** (**edit out**) remove (material) in preparing a recording or broadcast. **4** be editor of (a newspaper or magazine). ● noun a change or correction made as a result of editing.
– DERIVATIVES **editable** adjective.
– ORIGIN from EDITOR, reinforced by French *éditer* 'to edit'.

edition ● noun **1** a particular form or version of a published text. **2** the total number of copies of a book, newspaper, etc. issued at one time. **3** a particular version or instance of a regular programme or broadcast.
– ORIGIN Latin, from *edere* 'put out'.

editor ● noun **1** a person who is in charge of a newspaper, magazine, or multi-author book. **2** a person who commissions written texts for publication. **3** a person who prepares texts or recorded material for publication or broadcasting.
– DERIVATIVES **editorship** noun.
– ORIGIN Latin, from *edere* 'put out'.

Thesaurus

heaven, beside oneself with joy, jumping for joy, delighted, thrilled, exultant; *informal* over the moon, on top of the world, blissed out.

ecumenical ● adjective NON-DENOMINATIONAL, universal, catholic, all-embracing, all-inclusive.
– OPPOSITES denominational.

eddy ● noun *small eddies at the river's edge* SWIRL, whirlpool, vortex, maelstrom.
● verb *cold air eddied around her* SWIRL, whirl, spiral, wind, circulate, twist; flow, ripple, stream, surge, billow.

edge ● noun **1** *the edge of the lake* BORDER, boundary, extremity, fringe, margin, side; lip, rim, brim, brink, verge; perimeter, circumference, periphery, limits, bounds. **2** *she had an edge in her voice* SHARPNESS, severity, bite, sting, asperity, acerbity, acidity, trenchancy; sarcasm, acrimony, malice, spite, venom. **3** *they have an edge over their rivals* ADVANTAGE, lead, head start, the whip hand, the upper hand; superiority, dominance, ascendancy, supremacy, primacy.
– OPPOSITES middle, disadvantage.
● verb **1** *poplars edged the orchard* BORDER, fringe, verge, skirt; surround, enclose, encircle, circle, encompass, bound. **2** *a frock edged with lace* TRIM, pipe, band, decorate, finish; border, fringe; bind, hem. **3** *he edged closer to the fire* CREEP, inch, work one's way, pick one's way, ease oneself; sidle, steal, slink.
– PHRASES **on edge** TENSE, nervous, edgy, anxious, apprehensive, uneasy, unsettled; twitchy, jumpy, nervy, keyed up, restive, skittish, neurotic, insecure; *informal* uptight, wired; *Brit. informal* strung up.

edgy ● adjective TENSE, nervous, on edge, anxious, apprehensive, uneasy, unsettled; twitchy, jumpy, nervy, keyed up, restive, skittish, neurotic, insecure; irritable, touchy, tetchy, testy, crotchety, prickly; *informal* uptight, wired, snappy; *Brit. informal* strung up.
– OPPOSITES calm.

edible ● adjective SAFE TO EAT, fit for human consumption, wholesome; consumable, digestible, palatable; *formal* comestible.

edict ● noun DECREE, order, command, commandment, mandate, proclamation, pronouncement, dictate, fiat, promulgation; law, statute, act, bill, ruling, injunction; *formal* ordinance.

edification ● noun EDUCATION, instruction, tuition, teaching, training, tutelage, guidance; enlightenment, cultivation, information; improvement, development.

edifice ● noun BUILDING, structure, construction, erection, pile, complex; property, development, premises.

edify ● verb EDUCATE, instruct, teach, school, tutor, train, guide; enlighten, inform, cultivate, develop, improve, better.

edit ● verb **1** *she edited the text* CORRECT, check, copy-edit, improve, emend, polish; modify, adapt, revise, rewrite, reword, rework, redraft; shorten, condense, cut, abridge; *informal* clean up. **2** *this volume was edited by a consultant* SELECT, choose, assemble, organize, put together. **3** *he edited The Times* BE THE EDITOR OF, direct, run, manage, head, lead, supervise, oversee, preside over; *informal* be the boss of.

editorial ● adjective relating to the commissioning or preparing of material for publication. ● noun a newspaper article giving an opinion on a topical issue.
– DERIVATIVES **editorialist** noun **editorially** adverb.

editorialize (also **editorialise**) ● verb (of a newspaper or editor) express opinions rather than just report news.

editress (also **editrix**) ● noun dated or humorous a female editor.

educate /edyookayt/ ● verb **1** give intellectual, moral, and social instruction to. **2** give training in or information on a particular subject.
– DERIVATIVES **educable** adjective **educative** adjective **educator** noun.
– ORIGIN Latin *educare* 'lead out'.

educated guess ● noun a guess based on knowledge and experience.

education ● noun **1** the process of educating or being educated. **2** the theory and practice of teaching. **3** information about or training in a particular subject. **4** (**an education**) informal an enlightening experience.
– DERIVATIVES **educational** adjective **educationalist** noun **educationally** adverb **educationist** noun.

educe /idyoōss/ ● verb formal **1** bring out or develop (something latent or potential). **2** infer from data.
– DERIVATIVES **eduction** noun.
– ORIGIN Latin *educere* 'lead out'.

Edwardian /edwawrdiən/ ● adjective relating to the reign of King Edward VII (1901–10). ● noun a person who lived during this period.

-ee ● suffix forming nouns: **1** denoting the person affected directly or indirectly by the action of a verb: *employee*. **2** denoting a person described as or concerned with: *absentee*. **3** denoting an object of relatively smaller size: *bootee*.
– ORIGIN Old French *-é*; some forms are anglicized modern French nouns (e.g. *refugee* from *réfugié*).

EEC ● abbreviation European Economic Community.

EEG ● abbreviation electroencephalogram or electroencephalograph.

eel ● noun a snake-like fish with a slender elongated body and poorly developed fins.
– DERIVATIVES **eel-like** adjective **eely** adjective.
– ORIGIN Old English.

eelgrass ● noun **1** a marine plant with long ribbon-like leaves. **2** a submerged aquatic plant with narrow, grass-like leaves.

eelworm ● noun a small soil nematode that can become a serious pest of crops and ornamental plants.

e'er /air/ ● adverb literary form of EVER.

-eer ● suffix **1** denoting a person concerned with or engaged in an activity: *auctioneer*. **2** denoting concern or involvement with an activity: *electioneer*.
– ORIGIN French *-ier*.

eerie /eeri/ ● adjective (**eerier**, **eeriest**) strange and frightening.
– DERIVATIVES **eerily** adverb **eeriness** noun.
– ORIGIN originally northern English and Scots in the sense 'fearful': probably from Old English, 'cowardly'.

EFA ● abbreviation essential fatty acid.

eff ● noun & verb Brit. used as a euphemism for 'fuck'.
– PHRASES **eff and blind** informal swear. [ORIGIN *blind* from its use in expletives such as *blind me* (or *blimey*).]
– DERIVATIVES **effing** adjective & adverb.

efface /ifayss/ ● verb **1** erase (a mark) from a surface. **2** (**efface oneself**) make oneself appear insignificant or inconspicuous.
– DERIVATIVES **effacement** noun.
– ORIGIN originally in the sense 'pardon or be absolved from (an offence)': from French *effacer*, from *face* 'face'.

effect ● noun **1** a change which is a result or consequence of an action or other cause. **2** the state of being or becoming operative. **3** the extent to which something succeeds or is operative: *wind power can be used to great effect*. **4** (**effects**) personal belongings. **5** (**effects**) the lighting, sound, or scenery used in a play or film. **6** Physics a physical phenomenon, typically named after its discoverer. ● verb cause to happen; bring about.
– PHRASES **for effect** in order to impress people. **in effect** in practice, even if not formally acknowledged. **to that effect** having that general result, purpose, or meaning.
– USAGE On the confusion of **effect** and **affect**, see the note at AFFECT[1].
– ORIGIN Latin *effectus*, from *efficere* 'accomplish'.

effective ● adjective **1** producing a desired or intended result. **2** (of a law or policy) operative. **3** existing in fact, though not formally acknowledged as such.
– DERIVATIVES **effectively** adverb **effectiveness** noun **effectivity** noun.

effectual /ifektyooəl/ ● adjective **1** effective. **2** Law (of a legal document) valid or binding.

Thesaurus

edition ● noun ISSUE, number, volume, impression, publication; version, revision.

educate ● verb TEACH, school, tutor, instruct, coach, train, drill; guide, inform, enlighten, edify; inculcate, indoctrinate.

educated ● adjective INFORMED, literate, schooled, tutored, well read, learned, knowledgeable, enlightened; intellectual, academic, erudite, scholarly, cultivated, cultured; dated lettered.

education ● noun **1** *the education of young children* TEACHING, schooling, tuition, tutoring, instruction, coaching, training, tutelage, guidance; indoctrination, inculcation, enlightenment, edification. **2** *a woman of some education* LEARNING, knowledge, literacy, scholarship, enlightenment.
– RELATED TERMS pedagogic.

educational ● adjective **1** *an educational establishment* ACADEMIC, scholastic, school, learning, teaching, pedagogic, tuitional, instructional. **2** *an educational experience* INSTRUCTIVE, instructional, educative, informative, illuminating, pedagogic, enlightening, edifying, didactic, heuristic.

educative ● adjective. See EDUCATIONAL sense 2.

educator ● noun TEACHER, tutor, instructor, schoolteacher, schoolmaster, schoolmistress; educationalist, educationist; lecturer, professor; guide, mentor, guru; N. Amer. informal schoolmarm; Brit. informal beak; formal pedagogue; archaic schoolman.

eerie ● adjective UNCANNY, sinister, ghostly, unnatural, unearthly, supernatural, other-worldly; strange, abnormal, odd, weird, freakish; frightening, spine-chilling, hair-raising, blood-curdling, terrifying; informal creepy, scary, spooky, freaky.

efface ● verb **1** *the words were effaced by the rain* ERASE, eradicate, expunge, blot out, rub out, wipe out, remove, eliminate; delete, cancel, obliterate, blank out. **2** *he attempted to efface himself* MAKE ONESELF INCONSPICUOUS, keep out of sight, keep out of the limelight, lie low, keep a low profile, withdraw.

effect ● noun **1** *the effect of these changes* RESULT, consequence, upshot, outcome, out-turn, repercussions, ramifications; end result, conclusion, culmination, corollary, concomitant, aftermath; fruit(s), product, by-product; informal pay-off; Medicine sequela. **2** *the effect of the drug* IMPACT, action, effectiveness, influence; power, potency, strength; success; formal efficacy. **3** *with effect from tomorrow* FORCE, operation, enforcement, implementation, effectiveness; validity, lawfulness, legality, legitimacy. **4** *some words to that effect* SENSE, meaning, theme, drift, import, intent, intention, tenor, significance, message; gist, essence, spirit. **5** *the dead man's effects* BELONGINGS, possessions, (worldly) goods, chattels; property, paraphernalia; informal gear, tackle, things, stuff, bits and pieces; Brit. informal clobber.
– OPPOSITES cause.
● verb *they effected many changes* ACHIEVE, accomplish, carry out, realize, manage, bring off, execute, conduct, engineer, perform, do, perpetrate, discharge, complete, consummate; cause, bring about, create, produce, make; provoke, occasion, generate, engender, actuate, initiate; formal effectuate.
– PHRASES **in effect** REALLY, in reality, in truth, in (actual) fact, effectively, essentially, in essence, practically, to all intents and purposes, all but, as good as, more or less, almost, nearly, just about; informal pretty much; poetic/literary well nigh, nigh on. **take effect 1** *these measures will take effect in May* COME INTO FORCE, come into operation, begin, become valid, become law, apply, be applied. **2** *the drug started to take effect* WORK, act, be effective, produce results.

effective ● adjective **1** *an effective treatment* SUCCESSFUL, effectual, potent, powerful; helpful, beneficial, advantageous, valuable, useful; formal efficacious. **2** *a more effective argument* CONVINCING, compelling, strong, forceful, potent, weighty, sound, valid; impressive, persuasive, plausible, credible, authoritative; logical, reasonable, lucid, coherent, cogent, eloquent; formal efficacious. **3** *the new law will be effective next week* OPERATIVE, in force, in effect; valid, official, lawful, legal, binding; Law effectual. **4** *Korea was under effective Japanese control* VIRTUAL, practical, essential, actual, implicit, tacit.
– OPPOSITES weak, invalid, theoretical.

– DERIVATIVES **effectuality** noun **effectually** adverb **effectualness** noun.

effeminate /ifemminit/ ● adjective (of a man) having characteristics regarded as typical of a woman.
– DERIVATIVES **effeminacy** noun **effeminately** adverb.
– ORIGIN from Latin *effeminare* 'make feminine'.

effendi /efendi/ ● noun (pl. **effendis**) a man of high education or social standing in an eastern Mediterranean or Arab country.
– ORIGIN Turkish *efendi*, from Greek *authentēs* 'lord, master'.

efferent /effərənt/ Physiology ● adjective referring to the conduction of nerve impulses or blood outwards or away from something. The opposite of AFFERENT. ● noun an efferent nerve fibre or blood vessel.
– ORIGIN from Latin *efferre* 'carry out'.

effervescent ● adjective **1** (of a liquid) giving off bubbles; fizzy. **2** vivacious and enthusiastic.
– DERIVATIVES **effervesce** verb **effervescence** noun.
– ORIGIN from Latin *effervescere* 'boil up'.

effete /ifeet/ ● adjective **1** affected, over-refined, and ineffectual. **2** having lost vitality; worn out.
– DERIVATIVES **effetely** adverb **effeteness** noun.
– ORIGIN Latin *effetus* 'worn out by bearing young'; related to FETUS.

efficacious /effikayshəss/ ● adjective formal effective.
– DERIVATIVES **efficaciously** adverb **efficaciousness** noun.
– ORIGIN from Latin *efficere* 'accomplish'.

efficacy /effikəsi/ ● noun formal the ability to produce a desired or intended result.

efficiency ● noun (pl. **efficiencies**) **1** the state or quality of being efficient. **2** an action intended to achieve efficiency.

efficient ● adjective working productively with minimum wasted effort or expense.
– DERIVATIVES **efficiently** adverb.
– ORIGIN from Latin *efficere* 'accomplish'.

effigy /effiji/ ● noun (pl. **effigies**) a sculpture or model of a person.
– ORIGIN Latin *effigies*, from *effingere* 'to fashion'.

effloresce /efloress/ ● verb **1** (of a substance) lose moisture and turn to a fine powder on exposure to air. **2** (of salts) come to the surface of brickwork or other material and crystallize. **3** reach an optimum stage of development.
– DERIVATIVES **efflorescence** noun **efflorescent** adjective.
– ORIGIN Latin *efflorescere*, from *florescere* 'begin to bloom'.

effluence /effloōənss/ ● noun **1** a substance that flows out. **2** the action of flowing out.
– ORIGIN from Latin *effluere* 'flow out'.

effluent ● noun liquid waste or sewage discharged into a river or the sea.

effluvium /iflōōviəm/ ● noun (pl. **effluvia** /iflōōviə/) an unpleasant or harmful odour or discharge.
– ORIGIN Latin.

effort ● noun **1** a vigorous or determined attempt. **2** strenuous physical or mental exertion.
– DERIVATIVES **effortful** adjective.
– ORIGIN French, from Latin *ex-* 'out' + *fortis* 'strong'.

effortless ● adjective done or achieved without effort; natural and easy.
– DERIVATIVES **effortlessly** adverb **effortlessness** noun.

effrontery /ifruntəri/ ● noun insolence or impertinence.
– ORIGIN French *effronterie*, from Latin *effrons* 'shameless, barefaced', from *frons* 'forehead'.

effulgent /ifuljənt/ ● adjective literary shining brightly.
– DERIVATIVES **effulgence** noun **effulgently** adverb.
– ORIGIN from Latin *effulgere*.

effusion ● noun **1** an instance of giving off a liquid, light, or smell. **2** Medicine an escape of fluid into a body cavity. **3** an instance of unrestrained speech or writing.
– DERIVATIVES **effuse** verb.
– ORIGIN Latin, from *effundere* 'pour out'.

effusive ● adjective expressing gratitude, pleasure, or approval in an unrestrained manner.
– DERIVATIVES **effusively** adverb **effusiveness** noun.

EFL ● abbreviation English as a foreign language.

eft /eft/ ● noun **1** dialect a newt. **2** Zoology the juvenile stage of a

e

Thesaurus

effectiveness ● noun SUCCESS, productiveness, potency, power; benefit, advantage, value, virtue, usefulness; *formal* efficacy.

effectual ● adjective **1** *effectual political action* EFFECTIVE, successful, productive, constructive; worthwhile, helpful, beneficial, advantageous, valuable, useful; *formal* efficacious. **2** (*Law*) *an effectual document* VALID, authentic, bona fide, genuine, official; lawful, legal, legitimate, (legally) binding, contractual.

effeminate ● adjective WOMANISH, effete, foppish, mincing; *informal* camp, campy, limp-wristed.
– OPPOSITES manly.

effervesce ● verb **1** *heat the mixture until it effervesces* FIZZ, sparkle, bubble; froth, foam. **2** *managers must effervesce with praise* SPARKLE, be vivacious, be animated, be ebullient, be exuberant, be bubbly, be effervescent.

effervescence ● noun **1** *wines of uniform effervescence* FIZZ, fizziness, sparkle, gassiness, carbonation, aeration, bubbliness. **2** *his cheeky effervescence* VIVACITY, liveliness, animation, high spirits, ebullience, exuberance, buoyancy, sparkle, gaiety, jollity, cheerfulness, perkiness, breeziness, enthusiasm, irrepressibility, vitality, zest, energy, dynamism; *informal* pep, bounce.

effervescent ● adjective **1** *an effervescent drink* FIZZY, sparkling, carbonated, aerated, gassy, bubbly; mousseux, pétillant, spumante. **2** *effervescent young people* VIVACIOUS, lively, animated, high-spirited, bubbly, ebullient, buoyant, sparkling, scintillating, light-hearted, jaunty, happy, jolly, cheery, cheerful, perky, sunny, enthusiastic, irrepressible, vital, zestful, energetic, dynamic; *informal* bright-eyed and bushy-tailed, peppy, bouncy, upbeat, chirpy, full of beans.
– OPPOSITES still, depressed.

effete ● adjective **1** *effete trendies* AFFECTED, pretentious, precious, mannered, over-refined; ineffectual; *informal* la-di-da, pseud; *Brit. informal* poncey. **2** *an effete young man* EFFEMINATE, unmanly, girlish, feminine; soft, timid, cowardly, lily-livered, spineless, pusillanimous; *informal* sissy, wimpish, wimpy. **3** *the fabric of society is effete* WEAK, enfeebled, enervated, worn out, exhausted, finished, drained, spent, powerless, ineffectual.
– OPPOSITES manly, powerful.

efficacious ● adjective (*formal*) EFFECTIVE, effectual, successful, productive, constructive, potent; helpful, beneficial, advantageous, valuable, useful.

efficacy ● noun (*formal*) EFFECTIVENESS, success, productiveness, potency, power; benefit, advantage, value, virtue, usefulness.

efficiency ● noun **1** *we need reforms to bring efficiency* ORGANIZATION, order, orderliness, regulation, coherence; productivity, effectiveness. **2** *I compliment you on your efficiency* COMPETENCE, capability, ability, proficiency, adeptness, expertise, professionalism, skill, effectiveness.

efficient ● adjective **1** *efficient techniques* ORGANIZED, methodical, systematic, logical, orderly, businesslike, streamlined, productive, effective, cost-effective. **2** *an efficient secretary* COMPETENT, capable, able, proficient, adept, skilful, skilled, effective, productive, organized, businesslike.
– OPPOSITES disorganized, incompetent.

effigy ● noun STATUE, statuette, sculpture, model, dummy, figurine; guy; likeness, image; bust.

effluent ● noun (LIQUID) WASTE, sewage, effluvium, outflow, discharge, emission.

effort ● noun **1** *they made an effort to work together* ATTEMPT, try, endeavour; *informal* crack, shot, stab, bash; *formal* essay. **2** *his score was a fine effort* ACHIEVEMENT, accomplishment, attainment, result, feat; undertaking, enterprise, work; triumph, success, coup. **3** *the job requires little effort* EXERTION, energy, work, endeavour, application, labour, power, muscle, toil, strain; *informal* sweat, elbow grease; *Brit. informal* graft; *Austral./NZ informal* (hard) yakka.

effortless ● adjective EASY, undemanding, unchallenging, painless, simple, uncomplicated, straightforward, elementary; fluent, natural; *informal* as easy as pie, child's play, kids' stuff, a cinch, no sweat, a doddle, a breeze; *Brit. informal* easy-peasy; *N. Amer. informal* duck soup, a snap.
– OPPOSITES difficult.

effrontery ● noun IMPUDENCE, impertinence, cheek, insolence, cockiness, audacity, temerity, presumption, nerve, gall, shamelessness, impoliteness, disrespect, bad manners; *informal* brass (neck), face, chutzpah; *Brit. informal* sauce; *N. Amer. informal* sass.

effusion ● noun **1** *an effusion of poisonous gas* OUTFLOW, outpouring, rush, current, flood, deluge, emission, discharge, emanation; spurt, surge, jet, stream, torrent, gush, flow. **2** *reporters' flamboyant effusions* OUTBURST, outpouring, gushing; wordiness, verbiage.

effusive ● adjective GUSHING, gushy, unrestrained, extravagant, ful-

newt.
– ORIGIN Old English.
EFTA • abbreviation European Free Trade Association.
e.g. • abbreviation for example.
– ORIGIN from Latin *exempli gratia* 'for the sake of example'.
egalitarian /igalitairiən/ • adjective in accordance with the principle that all people are equal and deserve equal rights and opportunities. • noun an egalitarian person.
– DERIVATIVES **egalitarianism** noun.
– ORIGIN French *égalitaire*, from Latin *aequalis* 'equal'.
egg[1] • noun **1** an oval or round object laid by a female bird, reptile, fish, or invertebrate and containing an ovum which if fertilized can develop into a new organism. **2** an infertile egg of the domestic hen, used for food. **3** Biology the female reproductive cell in animals and plants; an ovum. **4** informal, dated a person of a specified kind: *you're a good egg.*
– PHRASES **don't put all your eggs in one basket** proverb don't risk everything on the success of one venture. **kill the goose that lays the golden eggs** destroy a reliable and valuable source of income. [ORIGIN with allusion to one of Aesop's fables.] **with egg on one's face** informal appearing foolish or ridiculous.
– DERIVATIVES **eggy** adjective.
– ORIGIN Old English.
egg[2] • verb (**egg on**) urge or encourage to do something foolish or risky.
– ORIGIN Old Norse, 'incite'.
egg custard • noun a custard made with milk and eggs, typically sweetened and baked.
egghead • noun informal a very academic or studious person.
egg-nog (Brit. also **egg-flip**) • noun a drink consisting of wine or other alcohol mixed with beaten egg and milk.
eggplant • noun chiefly N. Amer. another term for AUBERGINE.
eggshell • noun **1** the thin, hard, fragile outer layer of an egg. **2** (before another noun) (of china) extremely thin and delicate. **3** (before another noun) denoting an oil-based paint that dries with a slight sheen.
egg white • noun the clear, viscous substance round the yolk of an egg that turns white when cooked or beaten.
eglantine /egləntīn/ • noun another term for SWEETBRIAR.
– ORIGIN Old French, from Latin *acus* 'needle' or *aculeus* 'prickle'.
EGM • abbreviation extraordinary general meeting.
ego /eegō, egō/ • noun (pl. **egos**) **1** a person's sense of self-esteem or self-importance. **2** Psychoanalysis the part of the mind that mediates between the conscious and the unconscious and is responsible for the interpretation of reality and the development of a sense of self. Compare with ID and SUPEREGO.
– ORIGIN Latin, 'I'.
egocentric • adjective self-centred. • noun an egocentric person.
– DERIVATIVES **egocentrically** adverb **egocentricity** noun **egocentrism** noun.
egoism • noun **1** an ethical theory that treats self-interest as the foundation of morality. **2** another term for EGOTISM.
– DERIVATIVES **egoist** noun **egoistic** adjective **egoistical** adjective.
egomania • noun obsessive egotism.
– DERIVATIVES **egomaniac** noun **egomaniacal** adjective.
egotism • noun the quality of being excessively conceited or absorbed in oneself.
– DERIVATIVES **egotist** noun **egotistic** adjective **egotistical** adjective.
ego trip • noun informal something done as a result of an undue sense of self-importance.
egregious /igreejəss/ • adjective **1** outstandingly bad. **2** archaic remarkably good.
– DERIVATIVES **egregiously** adverb **egregiousness** noun.
– ORIGIN Latin *egregius* 'illustrious' (literally 'standing out from the flock'), from *grex* 'flock'.
egress /eegress/ • noun formal **1** the action of going out of or leaving a place. **2** a way out.
– DERIVATIVES **egression** noun.
– ORIGIN from Latin *egressus*, from *egredi* 'go out'.
egret /eegrit/ • noun a heron with mainly white plumage, having long plumes in the breeding season.
– ORIGIN Old French *aigrette*, from the Germanic base of HERON.
Egyptian • noun **1** a person from Egypt. **2** the Afro-Asiatic language used in ancient Egypt, represented in its oldest stages by hieroglyphic inscriptions. • adjective relating to Egypt.
Egyptology /eejiptolləji/ • noun the study of the language, history, and culture of ancient Egypt.
– DERIVATIVES **Egyptological** adjective **Egyptologist** noun.
Eid /eed/ (also **Id**) • noun **1** (in full **Eid ul-Fitr** /eed ŏŏl feetrə/) the Muslim festival marking the end of the fast of Ramadan. **2** (in full **Eid ul-Adha** /eed ŏŏl aadə/) the festival marking the culmination of the annual pilgrimage to Mecca.
– ORIGIN Arabic, 'feast'.
eider /īdə/ • noun (pl. same or **eiders**) **1** (also **eider duck**) a northern sea duck, the male of which has mainly black-and-white plumage. **2** (also **eider down**) small, soft feathers from the breast of the female eider duck.
– ORIGIN Old Norse.
eiderdown • noun chiefly Brit. a quilt filled with down (originally from the eider) or some other soft material.
eidetic /īdettik/ • adjective Psychology relating to mental images having unusual vividness and detail.
– DERIVATIVES **eidetically** adverb.
– ORIGIN Greek *eidētikos*, from *eidos* 'form'.
eight • cardinal number **1** one more than seven; 8. (Roman numeral: **viii** or **VIII**.) **2** an eight-oared rowing boat or its crew.
– PHRASES **have one over the eight** Brit. informal have one drink too many. **pieces of eight** historical Spanish dollars, equivalent to eight reals.
– ORIGIN Old English.
eighteen • cardinal number one more than seventeen; 18. (Roman numeral: **xviii** or **XVIII**.)
– DERIVATIVES **eighteenth** ordinal number.
eighth • ordinal number constituting number eight in a sequence; 8th.
– DERIVATIVES **eighthly** adverb.
eighth note • noun Music, chiefly N. Amer. a quaver.
eights • plural noun a race for eight-oared rowing boats.
eightsome reel • noun a lively Scottish dance for eight people.
eighty • cardinal number (pl. **eighties**) ten less than ninety; 80. (Roman numeral: **lxxx** or **LXXX**.)
– DERIVATIVES **eightieth** ordinal number.
einsteinium /īnstīniəm/ • noun an unstable radioactive chemical element made by high-energy atomic collisions.
– ORIGIN named after the German-born physicist Albert *Einstein*

Thesaurus

some, demonstrative, lavish, enthusiastic, lyrical; expansive, wordy, verbose; *informal* over the top, OTT.
– OPPOSITES restrained.
egg • noun OVUM; gamete, germ cell; (**eggs**) roe, spawn, seed.
– RELATED TERMS ovoid.
– PHRASES **egg someone on** URGE, goad, incite, provoke, push, drive, prod, prompt, induce, impel, spur on; encourage, exhort, motivate, galvanize.
egghead • noun *(informal)* INTELLECTUAL, thinker, academic, scholar, sage; bookworm, highbrow; expert, genius, Einstein, mastermind; *informal* brain, whizz; *Brit. informal* brainbox, boffin; *N. Amer. informal* brainiac, rocket scientist.
– OPPOSITES dunce.
ego • noun SELF-ESTEEM, self-importance, self-worth, self-respect, self-image, self-confidence.
egocentric • adjective SELF-CENTRED, egomaniacal, self-interested, selfish, self-seeking, self-absorbed, self-obsessed; narcissistic, vain, self-important.
– OPPOSITES altruistic.
egotism, egoism • noun SELF-CENTREDNESS, egomania, egocentricity, self-interest, selfishness, self-seeking, self-serving, self-regard, self-obsession; self-love, narcissism, self-admiration, vanity, conceit, self-importance; boastfulness.
egotist, egoist • noun SELF-SEEKER, egocentric, egomaniac, narcissist; boaster, brag, braggart; *informal* swank, show-off, big-head; *N. Amer. informal* showboat.
egotistic, egoistic • adjective SELF-CENTRED, selfish, egocentric, egomaniacal, self-interested, self-seeking, self-absorbed, self-obsessed; narcissistic, vain, conceited, self-important; boastful.
egregious • adjective SHOCKING, appalling, terrible, awful, horrendous, frightful, atrocious, abominable, abhorrent, outrageous; monstrous, heinous, dire, unspeakable, shameful, unforgivable, intolerable, dreadful; *formal* grievous.
– OPPOSITES marvellous.
egress • noun **1** *the egress from the gallery was blocked* EXIT, way out, escape route. **2** *a means of egress* DEPARTURE, exit, withdrawal, retreat, exodus; escape; vacation.
– OPPOSITES entrance.

(1879–1955).

eirenic /īrennik, -ree-/ (also **irenic**) ● adjective formal aiming or aimed at peace.
– ORIGIN from Greek *eirēnē* 'peace'.

eisteddfod /īstethvod/ ● noun (pl. **eisteddfods** or **eisteddfodau** /īstethvədī/) a competitive festival of music and poetry in Wales.
– ORIGIN Welsh, 'session'.

either /īthər, ee-/ ● conjunction & adverb **1** used before the first of two (or occasionally more) alternatives specified (the other being introduced by 'or'). **2** (adverb) used to indicate a similarity or link with a statement just made: *You don't like him, do you? I don't either.* **3** for that matter; moreover. ● determiner & pronoun **1** one or the other of two people or things. **2** each of two.
– ORIGIN Old English, related to AYE[2] and WHETHER.

ejaculate ● verb /ijakyoolayt/ **1** (of a man or male animal) eject semen from the penis at the moment of orgasm. **2** dated say something quickly and suddenly. ● noun /ijakyoolət/ semen that has been ejaculated.
– DERIVATIVES **ejaculation** noun **ejaculator** noun **ejaculatory** /ijakyoolətri/ adjective.
– ORIGIN Latin *ejaculari* 'dart out', from *iacere* 'to throw'.

eject ● verb **1** force or throw out violently or suddenly. **2** (of a pilot) escape from an aircraft by means of an ejection seat. **3** compel (someone) to leave a place.
– DERIVATIVES **ejection** noun **ejector** noun.
– ORIGIN Latin *eicere* 'throw out', from *jacere* 'to throw'.

ejection seat (also **ejector seat**) ● noun an aircraft seat that can propel its occupant from the craft in an emergency.

eke[1] /eek/ ● verb (**eke out**) **1** use or consume frugally. **2** make (a living) with difficulty.
– ORIGIN Old English, 'increase'.

eke[2] /eek/ ● adverb archaic term for ALSO.
– ORIGIN Old English.

elaborate ● adjective /ilabbərət/ involving many carefully arranged parts; detailed and complicated. ● verb /ilabbərayt/ **1** develop or present in detail. **2** (**elaborate on**) add more detail to (something already said).
– DERIVATIVES **elaborately** adverb **elaborateness** noun **elaboration** noun **elaborative** adjective.
– ORIGIN from Latin *elaborare* 'work out'.

elan /ilan/ ● noun energy and flair.
– ORIGIN French, from *élancer* 'to dart'.

eland /eelənd/ ● noun a spiral-horned African antelope, the largest of the antelopes.
– ORIGIN Dutch, 'elk'.

elapse ● verb (of time) pass.
– ORIGIN Latin *elabi* 'slip away'.

elastane /ilastayn/ ● noun an elastic polyurethane material, used for close-fitting clothing.

elastic /ilastik/ ● adjective **1** able to resume normal shape spontaneously after being stretched or squeezed. **2** flexible and adaptable. ● noun cord, tape, or fabric which returns to its original length or shape after being stretched.
– DERIVATIVES **elastically** adverb **elasticity** /illastissiti/ noun **elasticize** (also **elasticise**) verb.
– ORIGIN Greek *elastikos* 'propulsive'.

elasticated ● adjective chiefly Brit. (of a garment or material) made elastic by the insertion of rubber thread or tape.

elastic band ● noun a rubber band.

elastin /ilastin/ ● noun Biochemistry an elastic, fibrous protein found in connective tissue.

elastomer /ilastəmər/ ● noun a natural or synthetic polymer having elastic properties, e.g. rubber.
– DERIVATIVES **elastomeric** adjective.

Elastoplast /ilastəplast, -plaast/ ● noun trademark adhesive sticking plaster for covering cuts and wounds.

elated /ilaytid/ ● adjective extremely happy and excited.
– DERIVATIVES **elatedly** adverb **elatedness** noun **elation** noun.
– ORIGIN Latin *elatus* 'raised', from *efferre* 'to raise'.

elbow ● noun **1** the joint between the forearm and the upper arm. **2** a piece of piping or something similar bent through an angle. ● verb **1** strike with one's elbow. **2** push roughly away. **3** (often **elbow one's way**) move by pushing past people with one's elbows.
– PHRASES **give someone the elbow** informal summarily reject or dismiss someone. **up to one's elbows in** informal deeply involved in.
– ORIGIN Old English.

elbow grease ● noun informal hard physical work, especially vigorous polishing or cleaning.

elbow room ● noun informal adequate space to move or work in.

e

Thesaurus

eight ● cardinal number OCTET, eightsome, octuplets; *technical* octad.
– RELATED TERMS octo-.

ejaculate ● verb **1** EMIT SEMEN, climax, orgasm; *informal* come. **2** *the sperm is ejaculated* EMIT, eject, discharge, release, expel, disgorge; shoot out, squirt out, spurt out. **3** *(dated) 'What?' he ejaculated* EXCLAIM, cry out, call out, yell, blurt out, come out with.

ejaculation ● noun **1** *the ejaculation of fluid* EMISSION, ejection, discharge, release, expulsion. **2** *premature ejaculation* EMISSION OF SEMEN, climax, orgasm. **3** *(dated) the conversation consisted of ejaculations* EXCLAMATION, interjection; call, shout, yell.

eject ● verb **1** *the volcano ejected ash* EMIT, spew out, discharge, give off, send out, belch, vent; expel, release, disgorge, spout, vomit, throw up. **2** *the pilot had time to eject* BAIL OUT, escape, get out. **3** *they were ejected from the hall* EXPEL, throw out, turn out, cast out, remove, oust; evict, banish; *informal* chuck out, kick out, turf out, boot out; *N. Amer. informal* give someone the bum's rush. **4** *he was ejected from the job* DISMISS, remove, discharge, oust, expel, axe, throw out, force out, drive out; *informal* sack, fire, send packing, boot out, chuck out, kick out, give someone their marching orders, give someone the push, show someone the door; *Brit. informal* give someone their cards, turf out; *Military* cashier.
– OPPOSITES admit, appoint.

ejection ● noun **1** *the ejection of electrons* EMISSION, discharge, expulsion, release; elimination. **2** *their ejection from the ground* EXPULSION, removal; eviction, banishment, exile. **3** *his ejection from office* DISMISSAL, removal, discharge, expulsion; *informal* the sack, the boot, the push, the (old) heave-ho, the bullet; *Brit. informal* the chop.

eke ● verb *I had to eke out my remaining funds* HUSBAND, use sparingly, be thrifty with, be frugal with, be sparing with, use economically; *informal* go easy on.
– OPPOSITES squander.
– PHRASES **eke out a living** SUBSIST, survive, get by, scrape by, make ends meet, keep body and soul together, keep the wolf from the door, keep one's head above water.

elaborate ● adjective **1** *an elaborate plan* COMPLICATED, complex, intricate, involved; detailed, painstaking, careful; tortuous, convoluted, serpentine, Byzantine. **2** *an elaborate plasterwork ceiling* ORNATE, decorated, embellished, adorned, ornamented, fancy, fussy, busy, ostentatious, extravagant, showy, baroque, rococo, florid, wedding-cake.
– OPPOSITES simple, plain.
● verb *both sides refused to elaborate on their reasons* EXPAND ON, enlarge on, add to, flesh out, put flesh on the bones of, add detail to, expatiate on; develop, fill out, embellish, embroider, enhance, amplify.

elan ● noun FLAIR, style, panache, confidence, dash, éclat; energy, vigour, vitality, liveliness, brio, esprit, animation, vivacity, zest, verve, spirit, pep, sparkle, enthusiasm, gusto, eagerness, feeling, fire; *informal* pizzazz, zing, zip, vim, oomph.

elapse ● verb PASS, go by/past, wear on, slip by/away/past, roll by/past, slide by/past, steal by/past, tick by/past.

elastic ● adjective **1** *elastic material* STRETCHY, elasticated, stretchable, springy, flexible, pliant, pliable, supple, yielding, plastic, resilient. **2** *an elastic concept of nationality* ADAPTABLE, flexible, adjustable, accommodating, variable, fluid, versatile.
– OPPOSITES rigid.

elasticity ● noun **1** *the skin's natural elasticity* STRETCHINESS, flexibility, pliancy, suppleness, plasticity, resilience, springiness; *informal* give. **2** *the elasticity of the term* ADAPTABILITY, flexibility, adjustability, fluidity, versatility.

elated ● adjective THRILLED, delighted, overjoyed, ecstatic, euphoric, very happy, joyous, gleeful, jubilant, beside oneself, exultant, rapturous, in raptures, walking on air, on cloud nine/seven, in seventh heaven, jumping for joy, in transports of delight; *informal* on top of the world, over the moon, on a high, tickled pink; *Austral. informal* wrapped.
– OPPOSITES miserable.

elation ● noun EUPHORIA, ecstasy, happiness, delight, transports of delight, joy, joyousness, glee, jubilation, exultation, bliss, rapture.

elbow ● verb *he elbowed his way through the crowd* PUSH, shove, force, shoulder, jostle, barge, muscle, bulldoze.

elbow room ● noun ROOM TO MANOEUVRE, room, space, breathing

elder[1] • adjective (of one or more out of a group of people) of a greater age. • noun **1** (**one's elder**) a person of greater age than oneself. **2** a leader or senior figure in a tribe. **3** an official or minister in certain Protestant Churches.
– ORIGIN Old English, related to OLD.
elder[2] • noun a small tree or shrub with white flowers and bluish-black or red berries.
– ORIGIN Old English.
elderberry • noun the berry of the elder, used for making jelly or wine.
elderflower • noun the flower of the elder, used to make wines and cordials.
elderly • adjective old or ageing.
– DERIVATIVES **elderliness** noun.
elder statesman • noun an experienced and respected politician or other public figure.
eldest • adjective (of one out of a group of people) oldest.
El Dorado /el dəraadō/ (also **eldorado**) • noun (pl. **El Dorados**) a place of great abundance and wealth.
– ORIGIN Spanish, 'the gilded one', the name of a country or city formerly believed to exist in South America.
eldritch /eldrich/ • adjective weird and sinister or ghostly.
– ORIGIN originally Scots: perhaps related to ELF.
elecampane /ellikampayn/ • noun a plant with yellow daisy-like flowers and bitter aromatic roots that are used in herbal medicine.
– ORIGIN from Latin *enula* 'helenium' (a plant of the daisy family) + *campana*, probably meaning 'of the fields'.
elect • verb **1** choose (someone) to hold public office or another position by voting. **2** opt for or choose to do something. • adjective **1** chosen or singled out. **2** elected to a position but not yet in office: *the President Elect.*
– DERIVATIVES **electable** adjective.
– ORIGIN Latin *eligere* 'pick out'.
election • noun **1** a formal procedure whereby a person is elected, especially to a public office. **2** the action of electing or fact of being elected.
electioneering • noun the action of campaigning to be elected to public office.
elective • adjective **1** relating to or appointed by election. **2** (of a course of study, treatment, etc.) selected by the person concerned; not compulsory. • noun chiefly N. Amer. an optional course of study.
– DERIVATIVES **electively** adverb.
elector • noun **1** a person who has the right to vote in an election. **2** (in the US) a member of the electoral college. **3** historical a German prince entitled to take part in the election of the Holy Roman Emperor.
– DERIVATIVES **electorship** noun.
electoral • adjective relating to elections or electors.
– DERIVATIVES **electorally** adverb.
electoral college • noun **1** a body of electors chosen or appointed by a larger group. **2** (in the US) a body of people representing the states of the US, who formally cast votes for the election of the President and Vice-President.
electoral roll (also **electoral register**) • noun an official list of the people in a district who are entitled to vote in an election.
electorate /ilektərət/ • noun **1** the body of people in a country or area who are entitled to vote in an election. **2** Austral./NZ the area represented by one Member of Parliament. **3** historical the office or territories of a German elector.
electric • adjective **1** of, worked by, or producing electricity. **2** thrillingly exciting. • noun (**electrics**) Brit. the system of electric wiring and parts in a house or vehicle.
– DERIVATIVES **electrically** adverb.
– ORIGIN from Greek *ēlektron* 'amber' (because rubbing amber causes electrostatic phenomena).
electrical • adjective concerned with, operating by, or producing electricity. • noun (**electricals**) electrical equipment or circuitry.
electric blanket • noun an electrically wired blanket used for heating a bed.
electric blue • noun a steely or brilliant light blue.
electric chair • noun a chair in which convicted criminals are executed by electrocution.
electric eel • noun a large eel-like freshwater fish of South America, which uses pulses of electricity to kill prey, assist in navigation, and for defence.
electric eye • noun informal a photoelectric cell operating a relay when the beam of light illuminating it is obscured.
electric fence • noun a fence through which an electric current can be passed, giving an electric shock to any person or animal touching it.
electric guitar • noun a guitar with a built-in pickup which converts sound vibrations into electrical signals for amplification.
electrician • noun a person who installs and maintains electrical equipment.
electricity • noun **1** a form of energy resulting from the existence of charged particles (such as electrons or protons), either statically as an accumulation of charge or dynamically as a current. **2** the supply of electric current to a building for heating, lighting, etc. **3** thrilling excitement.
electric shock • noun a sudden discharge of electricity through a part of the body.
electric storm • noun a thunderstorm or other violent disturbance of the electrical condition of the atmosphere.
electrify • verb (**electrifies, electrified**) **1** charge with electricity. **2** convert to the use of electrical power. **3** (**electrifying**) causing thrilled admiration or excitement.
– DERIVATIVES **electrification** noun **electrifier** noun.
electrocardiography /ilektrōkaardiogrəfi/ • noun the measurement and recording of activity in the heart using electrodes placed on the skin.
– DERIVATIVES **electrocardiogram** noun **electrocardiograph** noun **electrocardiographic** adjective.
electroconvulsive • adjective relating to or denoting the treatment of mental illness by applying electric shocks to the brain.
electrocute • verb injure or kill by electric shock.
– DERIVATIVES **electrocution** noun.
electrode /ilektrōd/ • noun a conductor through which electricity enters or leaves something.
– ORIGIN from ELECTRIC + Greek *hodos* 'way', on the pattern of *anode* and *cathode*.
electrodynamics • plural noun (usu. treated as sing.) the branch of mechanics concerned with the interaction of electric currents

Thesaurus

space, Lebensraum, scope, freedom, play, free rein, licence, latitude, leeway.
elder • adjective *his elder brother* OLDER, senior, big.
• noun *the church elders* LEADER, senior figure, patriarch, father.
elderly • adjective *her elderly mother* AGED, old, advanced in years, ageing, long in the tooth, past one's prime; grey-haired, grey-bearded, grizzled, hoary; in one's dotage, decrepit, doddering, doddery, senescent; *informal* getting on, past it, over the hill, no spring chicken.
– OPPOSITES youthful.
• noun (**the elderly**) OLD PEOPLE, senior citizens, (old-age) pensioners, OAPs, retired people; geriatrics; *N. Amer.* seniors, retirees, golden agers; *informal* (golden) oldies, wrinklies; *N. Amer. informal* oldsters, woopies.
elect • verb **1** *a new president was elected* VOTE FOR, VOTE IN, return, cast one's vote for; choose, pick, select. **2** *she elected to stay behind* CHOOSE, decide, opt, vote.
• adjective *the president elect* FUTURE, -to-be, designate, chosen, elected, coming, next, appointed, presumptive.
• noun (**the elect**) THE CHOSEN, the elite, the favoured; the crème de la crème.
election • noun BALLOT, vote, popular vote; poll; *Brit.* by-election; *US* primary.
– RELATED TERMS psephology.
electioneer • verb CAMPAIGN, canvass, go on the hustings, doorstep; *Brit. informal* go out on the knocker.
elector • noun VOTER, member of the electorate, constituent; selector.
electric • adjective **1** *an electric kettle* ELECTRIC-POWERED, electrically operated, mains-operated, battery-operated. **2** *the atmosphere was electric* EXCITING, charged, electrifying, thrilling, heady, dramatic, intoxicating, dynamic, stimulating, galvanizing, rousing, stirring, moving; tense, knife-edge, explosive, volatile.
electricity • noun POWER, electric power, energy, current, static; *Brit.* mains; *Canadian* hydro; *Brit. informal* leccy; *historical* galvanism.
electrify • verb EXCITE, thrill, stimulate, arouse, rouse, inspire, stir (up), exhilarate, intoxicate, galvanize, move, fire (with enthusiasm), fire someone's imagination, invigorate, animate; startle,

with magnetic or electric fields.
– DERIVATIVES **electrodynamic** adjective.
electroencephalography /ilektrōenseffəlogrəfi, -keff-/ ● noun the measurement and recording of electrical activity in the brain.
– DERIVATIVES **electroencephalogram** noun **electroencephalograph** noun.
electrolyse /ilektrəlīz/ (US **electrolyze**) ● verb subject to electrolysis.
– DERIVATIVES **electrolyser** noun.
electrolysis /ilektrollisiss/ ● noun **1** chemical decomposition produced by passing an electric current through a conducting liquid. **2** the breaking up and removal of hair roots or small blemishes on the skin by means of an electric current.
– DERIVATIVES **electrolytic** /ilektrəlittik/ adjective.
electrolyte /ilektrəlīt/ ● noun **1** a liquid or gel which contains ions and can be decomposed by electrolysis, e.g. that present in a battery. **2** Physiology the ionic constituents of cells, blood, etc.
– ORIGIN from Greek *lutos* 'released'.
electromagnet ● noun a metal core made into a magnet by the passage of electric current through a surrounding coil.
electromagnetic ● adjective relating to the interrelation of electric currents or fields and magnetic fields.
– DERIVATIVES **electromagnetically** adverb **electromagnetism** noun.
electromagnetic radiation ● noun a kind of radiation including visible light, radio waves, gamma rays, and X-rays, in which electric and magnetic fields vary simultaneously.
electrometer /illektrommitər/ ● noun an instrument for measuring electrical potential without drawing any current from the circuit.
electromotive /ilektrəmōtiv/ ● adjective tending to produce an electric current.
electromotive force ● noun a difference in potential that tends to give rise to an electric current.
electromyography /ilektrōmīogrəfi/ ● noun the recording of the electrical activity of muscle tissue by means of electrodes.
– DERIVATIVES **electromyogram** noun **electromyograph** noun **electromyographic** adjective.
electron ● noun Physics a stable negatively charged subatomic particle with a mass 1,836 times less than that of the proton, found in all atoms and acting as the primary carrier of electricity in solids.
electron gun ● noun a device for producing a narrow stream of electrons from a heated cathode.
electronic ● adjective **1** having components such as microchips and transistors that control and direct electric currents. **2** relating to electrons or electronics. **3** relating to or carried out by means of a computer or other electronic device: *electronic shopping*.
– DERIVATIVES **electronically** adverb.
electronic flash ● noun Photography a flash from a gas-discharge tube.
electronic mail ● noun another term for EMAIL.
electronic publishing ● noun the issuing of texts in machine-readable form rather than on paper.
electronics ● plural noun **1** (usu. treated as sing.) the branch of physics and technology concerned with the behaviour and movement of electrons, especially in semiconductors and gases. **2** (treated as pl.) circuits or devices using transistors, microchips, etc.
electron microscope ● noun a microscope with high magnification and resolution, employing electron beams in place of light.
electronvolt ● noun a unit of energy equal to the work done on an electron in accelerating it through a potential difference of one volt.
electrophoresis /ilektrōfəreesiss/ ● noun Physics & Chemistry the movement of charged particles in a fluid or gel under the influence of an electric field.
– DERIVATIVES **electrophoretic** adjective.
– ORIGIN from Greek *phorēsis* 'being carried'.
electroplate /ilektrəplayt/ ● verb coat (a metal object) by electrolytic deposition with another metal. ● noun electroplated articles.
– DERIVATIVES **electroplater** noun **electroplating** noun.
electroscope ● noun an instrument for detecting and measuring electric charge.
electroshock ● adjective another term for ELECTROCONVULSIVE.
electrostatic ● adjective relating to stationary electric charges or fields as opposed to electric currents.
– DERIVATIVES **electrostatics** plural noun.
electrosurgery ● noun surgery using a high-frequency electric current to cut tissue.
– DERIVATIVES **electrosurgical** adjective.
electrotechnology ● noun the technological application of electricity.
– DERIVATIVES **electrotechnical** adjective.
electrotherapy ● noun the use of electric currents passed through the body to treat paralysis and other disorders.
electrum /ilektrəm/ ● noun an alloy of gold with at least 20 per cent of silver, used for jewellery.
– ORIGIN Greek *ēlektron* 'amber, electrum'.
eleemosynary /elli-eemossinəri/ ● adjective formal charitable.
– ORIGIN from Greek *eleēmosunē* 'compassion'.
elegant ● adjective **1** graceful and stylish. **2** pleasingly ingenious and simple.
– DERIVATIVES **elegance** noun **elegantly** adverb.
– ORIGIN Latin *elegans* 'discriminating'; related to ELECT.
elegiac /ellijīək/ ● adjective **1** relating to or characteristic of an elegy. **2** wistfully mournful.
– DERIVATIVES **elegiacally** adverb.
elegize /ellijīz/ (also **elegise**) ● verb write in a wistfully mournful way.
elegy /elliji/ ● noun (pl. **elegies**) a mournful poem, typically a lament for the dead.
– ORIGIN Greek *elegos* 'mournful poem'.
element ● noun **1** a basic constituent part. **2** (also **chemical element**) each of more than one hundred substances that cannot be chemically interconverted or broken down. **3** any of the four substances (earth, water, air, and fire) regarded as the fundamental constituents of the world in ancient and medieval philosophy. **4** a trace: *an element of danger.* **5** a distinct group within a larger group: *right-wing elements in the army.* **6** (**the elements**) the weather, especially bad weather. **7** one's natural or preferred environment. **8** a part in an electric device consisting of a wire through which an electric current is passed to provide heat.
– ORIGIN Latin *elementum* 'principle, rudiment'.
elemental /elliment'l/ ● adjective **1** fundamental. **2** of or resembling the powerful and primitive forces of nature: *elemental hatred.* **3** relating to or of the nature of a chemical element.

Thesaurus

jolt, shock; *N. Amer.* light a fire under; *informal* give someone a buzz, give someone a kick; *N. Amer. informal* give someone a charge.
elegance ● noun **1** *he was attracted by her elegance* STYLE, stylishness, grace, gracefulness, taste, tastefulness, sophistication; refinement, dignity, beauty, poise, charm, culture; suaveness, urbanity, panache. **2** *the elegance of the idea* NEATNESS, simplicity; ingenuity, cleverness, inventiveness.
elegant ● adjective **1** *an elegant black outfit* STYLISH, graceful, tasteful, sophisticated, classic, chic, smart, fashionable, modish; refined, dignified, poised, beautiful, lovely, charming, artistic, aesthetic; cultivated, polished, cultured; dashing, debonair, suave, urbane. **2** *an elegant solution* NEAT, simple, effective; ingenious, clever, deft, intelligent, inventive.
– OPPOSITES gauche.
elegiac ● adjective MOURNFUL, melancholic, melancholy, plaintive, sorrowful, sad, lamenting, doleful; funereal, dirgelike; nostalgic, valedictory, poignant; *poetic/literary* dolorous.
– OPPOSITES cheerful.
elegy ● noun LAMENT, requiem, funeral poem/song, threnody, dirge, plaint; *Irish* keen; *Irish & Scottish* coronach.
element ● noun **1** *an essential element of the local community* COMPONENT, constituent, part, section, portion, piece, segment, bit; aspect, factor, feature, facet, ingredient, strand, detail, point; member, unit, module, item. **2** *there is an element of truth in this stereotype* TRACE, touch, hint, smattering, soupçon. **3** (**elements**) *the elements of political science* BASICS, essentials, principles, first principles; foundations, fundamentals, rudiments; *informal* nuts and bolts, ABC. **4** *I braved the elements* THE WEATHER, the climate, meteorological conditions, atmospheric conditions; the wind, the rain.
elemental ● adjective **1** *the elemental principles of accountancy* BASIC, primary, fundamental, essential, root, underlying; rudi-

elementary ● adjective **1** relating to the most rudimentary aspects of a subject. **2** straightforward and uncomplicated. **3** not decomposable into elements or other primary constituents.
– DERIVATIVES **elementarily** adverb.
elementary school ● noun a primary school, especially (N. Amer.) for the first six or eight grades.
elephant ● noun (pl. same or **elephants**) a very large plant-eating mammal with a trunk, long curved tusks, and large ears, native to Africa and southern Asia.
– DERIVATIVES **elephantoid** /ellifantoyd/ adjective.
– ORIGIN Greek *elephas* 'ivory, elephant'.
elephantiasis /ellifəntīəsiss/ ● noun Medicine a condition in which a limb becomes grossly enlarged due to obstruction of the lymphatic vessels, especially by nematode parasites.
elephantine /ellifantīn/ ● adjective resembling or characteristic of an elephant, especially in being large or clumsy.
elevate /ellivayt/ ● verb **1** lift to a higher position. **2** raise to a higher level or status.
– ORIGIN Latin *elevare* 'to raise'.
elevated ● adjective of a high intellectual or moral level.
elevation ● noun **1** the action of elevating or the fact of being elevated. **2** height above a given level, especially sea level. **3** the angle of something with the horizontal. **4** a particular side of a building. **5** a scale drawing showing the vertical projection of one side of a building.
– DERIVATIVES **elevational** adjective.
elevator ● noun **1** North American term for LIFT (in sense 1). **2** a machine consisting of an endless belt with scoops attached, used for raising grain. **3** N. Amer. a tall building used for storing grain.
eleven ● cardinal number **1** one more than ten; 11. (Roman numeral: **xi** or **XI**.) **2** a sports team of eleven players.
– DERIVATIVES **elevenfold** adjective & adverb.
– ORIGIN Old English, from the base of ONE + a second element occurring also in TWELVE.
eleven-plus ● noun (in the UK, especially formerly) an examination taken at the age of 11–12 to determine the type of secondary school a child should enter.
elevenses ● plural noun Brit. informal a break for light refreshments taken at about eleven o'clock in the morning.
eleventh ● ordinal number constituting number eleven in a sequence; 11th.
– PHRASES **the eleventh hour** the latest possible moment.
elf ● noun (pl. **elves**) a supernatural creature of folk tales, represented as a small, delicate human figure with pointed ears and a capricious nature.
– DERIVATIVES **elfish** adjective **elven** adjective (literary) **elvish** adjective.
– ORIGIN Old English.
elfin ● adjective of or resembling an elf, especially in being small and delicate.
elicit /ilissit/ ● verb (**elicited**, **eliciting**) evoke or draw out (a response or reaction).
– DERIVATIVES **elicitation** noun **elicitor** noun.
– ORIGIN Latin *elicere* 'draw out by trickery'.
elide /ilīd/ ● verb **1** omit (a sound or syllable) when speaking. **2** join together; merge.
– ORIGIN Latin *elidere* 'crush out'.
eligible /ellijib'l/ ● adjective **1** satisfying the conditions to do or receive something: *you may be eligible for a refund.* **2** desirable or suitable as a spouse.
– DERIVATIVES **eligibility** noun.
– ORIGIN Latin *eligibilis*, from *eligere* 'choose, select'.
eliminate /ilimminayt/ ● verb **1** completely remove or get rid of. **2** reject or exclude from consideration or further participation.
– DERIVATIVES **elimination** noun **eliminator** noun.
– ORIGIN Latin *eliminare* 'turn out of doors'.
elision /ilizh'n/ ● noun **1** the omission of a sound or syllable in speech. **2** the action of joining or merging.
– ORIGIN Latin, from *elidere* 'crush out'.
elite /ileet/ ● noun **1** a group of people regarded as the best in a particular society or organization. **2** a size of letter in typewriting, with 12 characters to the inch (about 4.7 to the centimetre).
– ORIGIN French, 'selection, choice'.
elitism ● noun **1** the belief that a society or system should be run by an elite. **2** the superior attitude or behaviour associated with an elite.
– DERIVATIVES **elitist** adjective & noun.
elixir /ilikseer/ ● noun a magical or medicinal potion, especially (in former times) either one supposedly able to change metals into gold or (also called **elixir of life**) supposedly able to prolong life indefinitely.
– ORIGIN Arabic, from Greek *xērion* 'powder for drying wounds'.
Elizabethan /ilizzəbeethən/ ● adjective relating to or characteristic of the reign of Queen Elizabeth I (1558–1603). ● noun a person, especially a writer, of the Elizabethan age.
elk /elk/ ● noun (pl. same or **elks**) **1** a large northern deer with palmate antlers and a growth of skin hanging from the neck. **2** North American term for WAPITI.
– ORIGIN probably Old English.
ell ● noun a former measure of length used mainly for textiles, normally 45 inches in England and 37 inches in Scotland.
– ORIGIN Old English, related to Latin *ulna* (see ULNA); the measure was originally linked to the length of the human arm or forearm.
ellipse /ilips/ ● noun a regular oval shape, traced by a point moving in a plane so that the sum of its distances from two other points is constant, or resulting when a cone is cut by an oblique plane which does not intersect the base.
ellipsis /ilipsiss/ ● noun (pl. **ellipses** /ilipseez/) **1** the omission

Thesaurus

mentary. **2** *elemental forces* NATURAL, atmospheric, meteorological, environmental.
elementary ● adjective **1** *an elementary astronomy course* BASIC, rudimentary, fundamental; preparatory, introductory, initiatory. **2** *a lot of the work is elementary* EASY, simple, straightforward, uncomplicated, undemanding, painless, child's play, plain sailing; *informal* as easy as falling off a log, as easy as pie, as easy as ABC, a piece of cake, no sweat, kids' stuff; *Brit. informal* easy-peasy.
– OPPOSITES advanced, difficult.
elephantine ● adjective ENORMOUS, huge, gigantic, very big, massive, giant, immense, tremendous, colossal, mammoth, gargantuan, vast, prodigious, monumental, titanic; hulking, bulky, heavy, weighty, ponderous, lumbering; *informal* jumbo, whopping, humongous, monster; *Brit. informal* whacking, ginormous.
– OPPOSITES tiny.
elevate ● verb **1** *we need a breeze to elevate the kite* RAISE, lift (up), raise up/aloft, upraise; hoist, hike up, haul up. **2** *he was elevated to Secretary of State* PROMOTE, upgrade, advance, move up, raise, prefer; ennoble, exalt, aggrandize; *informal* kick upstairs, move up the ladder.
– OPPOSITES lower, demote.
elevated ● adjective **1** *an elevated motorway* RAISED, upraised, high up, aloft; overhead. **2** *elevated language* LOFTY, grand, exalted, fine, sublime; inflated, pompous, bombastic, orotund. **3** *the gentry's elevated status* HIGH, higher, high-ranking, of high standing, lofty, superior, exalted, eminent; grand, noble.
– OPPOSITES lowly.
elevation ● noun **1** *his elevation to the peerage* PROMOTION, upgrading, advancement, advance, preferment, aggrandizement; ennoblement; *informal* step up the ladder, kick upstairs. **2** *1500 to 3,00 metres in elevation* ALTITUDE, height. **3** *elevations in excess of 3000 metres* HEIGHT, hill, mountain, mount; *formal* eminence. **4** *elevation of thought* GRANDEUR, greatness, nobility, loftiness, majesty, sublimity.
elf ● noun PIXIE, fairy, sprite, imp, brownie; dwarf, gnome, goblin, hobgoblin; leprechaun, puck, troll.
elfin ● adjective ELFLIKE, elfish, elvish, pixie-like; puckish, impish, playful, mischievous; dainty, delicate, small, petite, slight, little, tiny, diminutive.
elicit ● verb OBTAIN, draw out, extract, bring out, evoke, call forth, bring forth, induce, prompt, generate, engender, trigger, provoke; *formal* educe.
eligible ● adjective **1** *those people eligible to vote* ENTITLED, permitted, allowed, qualified, able. **2** *an eligible bachelor* DESIRABLE, suitable; available, single, unmarried, unattached, unwed.
eliminate ● verb **1** *a policy that would eliminate inflation* REMOVE, get rid of, put an end to, do away with, end, stop, terminate, eradicate, destroy, annihilate, stamp out, wipe out, extinguish; *informal* knock something on the head. **2** *he was eliminated from the title race* KNOCK OUT, beat; exclude, rule out, disqualify.
elite ● noun BEST, pick, cream, crème de la crème, flower, nonpareil, elect; high society, jet set, beautiful people, beau monde, haut monde; aristocracy, nobility, upper class; *N. Amer.* four hundred.
– OPPOSITES dregs.

of words from speech or writing. **2** a set of dots indicating such an omission.
– ORIGIN Greek *elleipsis*, from *elleipein* 'leave out'.

ellipsoid /ilipsoyd/ ● noun a symmetrical three-dimensional figure with a circular cross-section when viewed along one axis and elliptical cross-sections when viewed along the other axes.
– DERIVATIVES **ellipsoidal** adjective.

elliptic ● adjective relating to or having the form of an ellipse.
– DERIVATIVES **ellipticity** noun.

elliptical ● adjective **1** another term for ELLIPTIC. **2** (of speech or text) using or involving ellipsis, especially so as to be difficult to understand.
– DERIVATIVES **elliptically** adverb.

elm ● noun a tall deciduous tree with rough serrated leaves.
– ORIGIN Old English.

El Niño /el neenjō/ ● noun (pl. **El Niños**) an irregularly occurring and complex cycle of climatic changes affecting the Pacific region.
– ORIGIN Spanish, 'the Christ child', so called because the characteristic sign of an El Niño is the appearance of unusually warm, nutrient-poor water off northern Peru and Ecuador around Christmas time.

elocution /elləkyo͞osh'n/ ● noun **1** the skill of clear and expressive speech, especially of distinct pronunciation and articulation. **2** a particular style of speaking.
– DERIVATIVES **elocutionist** noun.
– ORIGIN Latin, from *eloqui* 'speak out'.

elongate /eelonggayt/ ● verb make or become longer.
– DERIVATIVES **elongation** noun.
– ORIGIN originally in the sense 'move away': from Latin *elongare* 'place at a distance'.

elope ● verb run away secretly in order to get married.
– DERIVATIVES **elopement** noun.
– ORIGIN Old French *aloper*.

eloquence /elləkwənss/ ● noun fluent or persuasive speaking or writing.
– ORIGIN Latin *eloquentia*, from *eloqui* 'speak out'.

eloquent ● adjective **1** showing eloquence. **2** clearly indicative or expressive.
– DERIVATIVES **eloquently** adverb.

else ● adverb **1** in addition; besides. **2** different; instead.
– PHRASES **or else 1** used to introduce the second of two alternatives. **2** in circumstances different from those mentioned; otherwise.
– ORIGIN Old English.

elsewhere ● adverb in, at, or to some other place or other places. ● pronoun some other place.

ELT ● abbreviation English language teaching.

elucidate /ilo͞osidayt, -lyo͞o-/ ● verb make clear; explain.
– DERIVATIVES **elucidation** noun **elucidatory** adjective.
– ORIGIN Latin *elucidare* 'make clear'.

elude /ilo͞od, ilyo͞od/ ● verb **1** evade or escape adroitly from. **2** fail to be attained or understood by: *the logic of this eluded her*.
– ORIGIN Latin *eludere*, from *ludere* 'to play'.

elusive ● adjective **1** difficult to find, catch, or achieve. **2** difficult to remember.
– DERIVATIVES **elusively** adverb **elusiveness** noun.
– ORIGIN from Latin *eludere* 'elude'.

elver /elvər/ ● noun a young eel.
– ORIGIN variant of dialect *eel-fare* 'the passage of young eels up a river', from FARE in its original sense 'a journey'.

elves plural of ELF.

Elysian /ilizziən/ ● adjective **1** relating to Elysium or the Elysian Fields, the place in Greek mythology where heroes were conveyed after death. **2** of or like paradise.

em ● noun Printing **1** a unit for measuring the width of printed matter, equal to the height of the type size being used. **2** a unit of measurement equal to twelve points.
– ORIGIN the letter *M*, since it is approximately this width.

em- ● prefix variant spelling of EN-[1], EN-[2] assimilated before *b*, *p* (as in *emblazon*, *emplacement*).

emaciated /imaysiaytid/ ● adjective abnormally thin and weak.
– DERIVATIVES **emaciation** noun.
– ORIGIN from Latin *emaciare* 'make thin'.

email ● noun the sending of messages by electronic means from one computer user to one or more recipients via a network. ● verb mail or send using email.
– DERIVATIVES **emailer** noun.
– ORIGIN abbreviation of *electronic mail*.

emalangeni plural of LILANGENI.

emanate /emmənayt/ ● verb **1** (**emanate from**) issue or spread out from (a source). **2** give out or emit: *he emanated a brooding air*.
– ORIGIN Latin *emanare* 'flow out'.

emanation ● noun **1** something which emanates from a source. **2** (in various mystical traditions) a being or force which is a manifestation of God. **3** the action or process of emanating.

emancipate /imansipayt/ ● verb **1** set free, especially from legal, social, or political restrictions. **2** free from slavery.
– DERIVATIVES **emancipation** noun **emancipator** noun **emancipatory** adjective.

Thesaurus

elixir ● noun POTION, concoction, brew, philtre, decoction, mixture; medicine, tincture; extract, essence, concentrate, distillate, distillation; *poetic/literary* draught; *archaic* potation.

elliptical ● adjective **1** *an elliptical shape* OVAL, egg-shaped, elliptic, ovate, ovoid, oviform, ellipsoidal; *Botany* obovate. **2** *elliptical phraseology* CRYPTIC, abstruse, ambiguous, obscure, oblique, Delphic; terse, concise, succinct, compact, economic, laconic, sparing.

elocution ● noun PRONUNCIATION, enunciation, articulation, diction, speech, intonation, vocalization, modulation; phrasing, delivery, public speaking.

elongate ● verb **1** *an exercise that elongates the muscles* LENGTHEN, extend, stretch (out). **2** *the high notes were elongated* PROLONG, protract, draw out, sustain.
– OPPOSITES shorten.

eloquence ● noun FLUENCY, articulacy, articulateness, expressiveness, silver tongue, persuasiveness, forcefulness, power, potency, effectiveness; oratory, rhetoric, grandiloquence, magniloquence; *informal* gift of the gab, way with words, blarney.

eloquent ● adjective **1** *an eloquent speaker* FLUENT, articulate, expressive, silver-tongued; persuasive, strong, forceful, powerful, potent, well expressed, effective, lucid, vivid, graphic; smooth-tongued, glib. **2** *her glance was more eloquent than words* EXPRESSIVE, meaningful, suggestive, revealing, telling, significant, indicative.
– OPPOSITES inarticulate.

elsewhere ● adverb SOMEWHERE ELSE, in/at/to another place, in/at/to a different place, hence; not here, not present, absent, away, abroad, out.
– OPPOSITES here.

elucidate ● verb EXPLAIN, make clear, illuminate, throw/shed light on, clarify, clear up, sort out, unravel, spell out; interpret, explicate; gloss.
– OPPOSITES confuse.

elucidation ● noun EXPLANATION, clarification, illumination; interpretation, explication; gloss.

elude ● verb EVADE, avoid, get away from, dodge, escape from, run (away) from; lose, shake off, give the slip to, slip away from, throw off the scent; *informal* slip through someone's fingers, slip through the net; *archaic* bilk.

elusive ● adjective **1** *her elusive husband* DIFFICULT TO FIND; evasive, slippery; *informal* always on the move. **2** *an elusive quality* INDEFINABLE, intangible, impalpable, unanalysable; fugitive; ambiguous.

Elysian ● adjective HEAVENLY, paradisal, paradisiacal, celestial, superlunary, divine; *poetic/literary* empyrean.

Elysium ● noun *(Greek Mythology)* HEAVEN, paradise, the Elysian fields; eternity, the afterlife, the next world, the hereafter; *Scandinavian Mythology* Valhalla; *Classical Mythology* the Islands of the Blessed; *Arthurian Legend* Avalon.

emaciated ● adjective THIN, skeletal, bony, gaunt, wasted, thin as a rake; scrawny, skinny, scraggy, skin and bones, raw-boned, stick-like; starved, underfed, undernourished, underweight, half-starved; cadaverous, shrivelled, shrunken, withered; *informal* anorexic, like a bag of bones.
– OPPOSITES fat.

emanate ● verb **1** *warmth emanated from the fireplace* ISSUE, spread, radiate, be sent forth/out. **2** *the proposals emanated from a committee* ORIGINATE, stem, derive, proceed, spring, issue, emerge, flow, come. **3** *he emanated an air of power* EXUDE, emit, radiate, give off/out, send out/forth.

emanation ● noun **1** *an emanation of his tortured personality* PRODUCT, consequence, result, fruit. **2** *radon gas emanation* DIS-

– ORIGIN Latin *emancipare* 'transfer as property', from *mancipium* 'slave'.

emasculate /imaskyoolayt/ ● verb **1** make weaker or less effective. **2** deprive (a man) of his male role or identity.
– DERIVATIVES **emasculation** noun.
– ORIGIN Latin *emasculare* 'castrate'.

embalm /imbaam/ ● verb preserve (a corpse) from decay, originally with spices and now usually by injection of a preservative.
– DERIVATIVES **embalmer** noun.
– ORIGIN Old French *embaumer*, from *baume* 'balm'.

embankment ● noun **1** a wall or bank built to prevent flooding by a river. **2** a bank of earth or stone built to carry a road or railway over an area of low ground.

e

embargo /embaargō/ ● noun (pl. **embargoes**) **1** an official ban, especially on trade or other commercial activity with a particular country. **2** historical an order of a state forbidding foreign ships to enter, or any ships to leave, its ports. ● verb (**embargoes, embargoed**) impose an embargo on.
– ORIGIN Spanish, from *embargar* 'to arrest'.

embark ● verb **1** go on board a ship or aircraft. **2** (**embark on/upon**) begin (a new project or course of action).
– DERIVATIVES **embarkation** noun.
– ORIGIN French *embarquer*, from *barque* 'bark, ship'.

embarras de richesses /onbaraa də reeshess/ (also **embarras de choix** /onbaraa də shwaa/) ● noun more options or resources than one knows what to do with.
– ORIGIN French, 'embarrassment of riches (or choice)'.

embarrass /imbarrəss/ ● verb **1** cause to feel awkward, self-conscious, or ashamed. **2** (**be embarrassed**) be caused financial difficulties.
– DERIVATIVES **embarrassed** adjective **embarrassing** adjective **embarrassment** noun.
– ORIGIN French *embarrasser*, probably from Portuguese *embaraçar*, from *baraço* 'halter'.

embassy ● noun (pl. **embassies**) **1** the official residence or offices of an ambassador. **2** chiefly historical a deputation sent by one state to another.
– ORIGIN Old French *ambasse*, from Latin *ambactus* 'servant' (related to AMBASSADOR).

embattled ● adjective **1** prepared for battle, especially because surrounded by enemy forces. **2** beset by difficulties: *the embattled Chancellor*. **3** fortified; having battlements.

embed (also **imbed**) ● verb (**embedded, embedding**) **1** fix firmly and deeply in a surrounding mass. **2** implant (an idea or feeling).
– DERIVATIVES **embedment** noun.

embellish ● verb **1** make more attractive; decorate. **2** add extra details to (a story or account) for interest.
– DERIVATIVES **embellisher** noun **embellishment** noun.
– ORIGIN Old French *embellir*, from *bel* 'handsome'.

ember /embər/ ● noun a small piece of burning wood or coal in a dying fire.
– ORIGIN Old English.

Ember day ● noun any of a number of days reserved for fasting and prayer in the Western Christian Church.
– ORIGIN Old English, perhaps from *ymbryne* 'period'.

embezzle ● verb steal or misappropriate (money placed in one's trust or under one's control).
– DERIVATIVES **embezzlement** noun **embezzler** noun.
– ORIGIN Old French *embesiler*, from *besiler* 'destroy, maltreat'.

embitter ● verb make bitter or resentful.

emblazon /imblayz'n/ ● verb **1** (usu. **be emblazoned**) conspicuously display (a design) on something. **2** depict (a heraldic device) on something.

emblem /embləm/ ● noun **1** a heraldic device or symbolic object as a distinctive badge of a nation, organization, or family. **2** a symbol or symbolic representation.
– DERIVATIVES **emblematic** adjective.
– ORIGIN Greek *emblēma* 'insertion'.

Thesaurus

CHARGE, emission, radiation, effusion, outflow, outpouring, flow, leak; *technical* efflux.

emancipate ● verb FREE, liberate, set free, release, deliver, discharge; unchain, unfetter, unshackle, untie, unyoke; *historical* manumit; *rare* disenthral.
– OPPOSITES enslave.

emancipated ● adjective LIBERATED, independent, unconstrained, uninhibited; free.

emasculate ● verb **1** *an Act which emasculated the House of Lords* WEAKEN, enfeeble, debilitate, erode, undermine, cripple; remove the sting from, pull the teeth of; *informal* water down. **2** *(archaic) young cocks should be emasculated at three months.* See CASTRATE.

embalm ● verb **1** *his body had been embalmed* PRESERVE, mummify, lay out. **2** *the poem ought to embalm his memory* PRESERVE, conserve, enshrine, immortalize.

embankment ● noun BANK, mound, ridge, earthwork, causeway, barrier, levee, dam, dyke.

embargo ● noun *an embargo on oil sales* BAN, bar, prohibition, stoppage, interdict, proscription, veto, moratorium; restriction, restraint, block, barrier, impediment, obstruction; boycott.
● verb *arms sales were embargoed* BAN, bar, prohibit, stop, interdict, debar, proscribe, outlaw; restrict, restrain, block, obstruct; boycott.
– OPPOSITES allow.

embark ● verb **1** *he embarked at Dover* BOARD SHIP, go on board, go aboard, take ship; emplane; *informal* hop on, jump on; *dated* ship. **2** *he embarked on a new career* BEGIN, start, commence, undertake, set about, take up, turn one's hand to, get down to; enter into, venture into, launch into, plunge into, engage in, settle down to; *informal* get cracking on, get going on, have a go/crack/shot at.

embarrass ● verb MORTIFY, shame, put someone to shame, humiliate, abash, chagrin, make uncomfortable, make self-conscious; discomfit, disconcert, discompose, upset, discountenance, distress; *informal* show up.

embarrassed ● adjective MORTIFIED, red-faced, blushing, abashed, shamed, ashamed, shamefaced, humiliated, chagrined, awkward, self-conscious, uncomfortable, not knowing where to look, sheepish; discomfited, disconcerted, upset, discomposed, flustered, agitated, discountenanced, distressed; shy, bashful, tongue-tied; *informal* with egg on one's face, wishing the earth would swallow one up.

embarrassing ● adjective HUMILIATING, shaming, shameful, mortifying, ignominious; awkward, uncomfortable, compromising; disconcerting, discomfiting, upsetting, distressing; *informal* blush-making, cringeworthy, cringe-making, toe-curling.

embarrassment ● noun **1** *he was scarlet with embarrassment* MORTIFICATION, humiliation, shame, shamefacedness, chagrin, awkwardness, self-consciousness, sheepishness, discomfort, discomfiture, discomposure, agitation, distress; ignominy; shyness, bashfulness. **2** *his current financial embarrassment* DIFFICULTY, predicament, plight, problem, mess; *informal* bind, jam, pickle, fix, scrape. **3** *an embarrassment of riches* SURPLUS, excess, overabundance, superabundance, glut, surfeit, superfluity; abundance, profusion, plethora.

embassy ● noun **1** *the Italian embassy* CONSULATE, legation, ministry. **2** *(historical) Charles sent an embassy to the Lombards* ENVOY, representative, delegate, emissary; delegation, deputation, legation, (diplomatic) mission; *archaic* embassage, legate.

embed, imbed ● verb IMPLANT, plant, set, fix, lodge, root, insert, place; sink, drive in, hammer in, ram in.

embellish ● verb **1** *weapons embellished with precious metal* DECORATE, adorn, ornament; beautify, enhance, grace; trim, garnish, gild; deck, bedeck, festoon, emblazon; *poetic/literary* bejewel, bedizen. **2** *the legend was embellished by an American academic* ELABORATE, embroider, expand on, exaggerate.

embellishment ● noun **1** *architectural embellishments* DECORATION, ornamentation, adornment; beautification, enhancement, trimming, trim, garnishing, gilding. **2** *we wanted the truth, not romantic embellishments* ELABORATION, addition, exaggeration.

ember ● noun GLOWING COAL, live coal; cinder; (**embers**) ashes, residue.

embezzle ● verb MISAPPROPRIATE, steal, thieve, pilfer, purloin, appropriate, abstract, defraud someone of, siphon off, pocket, help oneself to; put one's hand in the till; *informal* rob, rip off, skim, line one's pockets; *Brit. informal* pinch, nick, half-inch; *formal* peculate.

embezzlement ● noun MISAPPROPRIATION, theft, stealing, robbery, thieving, pilfering, purloining, pilferage, appropriation, swindling; fraud, larceny; *formal* peculation.

embittered ● adjective BITTER, resentful, sour, rancorous, jaundiced, aggrieved, grudge-bearing, frustrated, dissatisfied, alienated, disaffected.

emblazon ● verb **1** *shirts emblazoned with the company name* ADORN, decorate, ornament, embellish; inscribe. **2** *a flag with a*

emblematize /emblemmətīz/ (also **emblematise**) ● verb formal serve as an emblem of.

embody ● verb (**embodies**, **embodied**) **1** give a tangible or visible form to (an idea or quality). **2** include or contain as a constituent part.
– DERIVATIVES **embodiment** noun.

embolden ● verb give courage or confidence to.

embolism /embəliz'm/ ● noun Medicine obstruction of an artery, typically by a clot of blood or an air bubble.
– ORIGIN Greek *embolismos*, from *emballein* 'insert'.

embolus /embələss/ ● noun (pl. **emboli** /embəlee/) a blood clot, air bubble, fatty deposit, or other object obstructing a blood vessel.
– DERIVATIVES **embolic** adjective.
– ORIGIN originally denoting the plunger of a syringe: from Greek *embolos* 'peg, stopper'.

embonpoint /ONbONpwaN/ ● noun plumpness or fleshiness, especially with reference to a woman's bosom.
– ORIGIN from French *en bon point* 'in good condition'.

emboss ● verb carve a design in relief on.
– DERIVATIVES **embosser** noun.
– ORIGIN from obsolete French *embosser*, from *boce* 'protuberance'.

embrace ● verb **1** hold closely in one's arms, especially as a sign of affection. **2** include or contain. **3** accept or support (a belief or change) willingly. ● noun an act of embracing.
– DERIVATIVES **embraceable** adjective.
– ORIGIN Old French *embracer*, from Latin *bracchium* 'arm'.

embrasure /imbrayzhər/ ● noun **1** an opening in a wall or parapet, used for shooting through. **2** an opening or recess around a window or door forming an enlargement of the area from the inside.
– ORIGIN French, from obsolete *embraser* 'widen an opening'.

embrocation /embrəkaysh'n/ ● noun a liquid medication rubbed on the body to relieve pain from sprains and strains.
– ORIGIN Latin, from Greek *embrokhē* 'lotion'.

embroider ● verb **1** sew decorative needlework patterns on. **2** add fictitious or exaggerated details to.
– DERIVATIVES **embroiderer** noun.
– ORIGIN Old French *enbrouder*.

embroidery ● noun (pl. **embroideries**) **1** the art or pastime of embroidering. **2** embroidered cloth.

embroil ● verb involve deeply in a conflict or difficult situation.
– DERIVATIVES **embroilment** noun.
– ORIGIN French *embrouiller* 'to muddle'.

embryo /embriō/ ● noun (pl. **embryos**) **1** an unborn or unhatched offspring in the process of development, especially an unborn human in the first eight weeks from conception. Compare with FETUS. **2** the part of a seed which develops into a new plant.
– PHRASES **in embryo** at a rudimentary stage.
– DERIVATIVES **embryonal** /embriən'l/ adjective.
– ORIGIN Greek *embruon* 'fetus'.

embryology /embriolləji/ ● noun the branch of biology and medicine concerned with the study of embryos.
– DERIVATIVES **embryological** adjective **embryologist** noun.

embryonic /embrionnik/ ● adjective **1** relating to an embryo. **2** in or at a rudimentary stage.

emcee /emsee/ N. Amer. informal ● noun a master of ceremonies. ● verb (**emcees**, **emceed**, **emceeing**) act as a master of ceremonies for or at.
– ORIGIN representing the pronunciation of MC.

emend /imend/ ● verb correct and revise (a text).
– DERIVATIVES **emendation** noun.
– USAGE The words **emend** and **amend** both derive from Latin *emendare* 'to correct' and have similar, but not identical, meanings in English. **Emend** means 'correct and revise (a text)', while **amend** means 'make minor improvements to (a document, rule, or proposal)'.
– ORIGIN Latin *emendare*, from *menda* 'a fault'.

emerald ● noun **1** a bright green gem variety of beryl. **2** a bright green colour.
– ORIGIN Old French *esmeraud*, from Greek *smaragdos*.

emerge ● verb **1** become gradually visible or apparent. **2** (of facts) become known. **3** recover from or survive a difficult period.
– DERIVATIVES **emergence** noun.
– ORIGIN Latin *emergere*, from *mergere* 'to dip'.

emergency ● noun (pl. **emergencies**) **1** a serious, unexpected, and potentially dangerous situation requiring immediate action. **2** (before another noun) arising from or used in an emergency: *an emergency exit*. **3** N. Amer. the casualty department in a hospital.
– ORIGIN Latin *emergentia*, from *emergere* 'emerge'.

e

Thesaurus

hammer and sickle emblazoned on it DISPLAY, depict, show.

emblem ● noun SYMBOL, representation, token, image, figure, mark, sign; crest, badge, device, insignia, stamp, seal, heraldic device, coat of arms, shield; logo, trademark.

emblematic, emblematical ● adjective **1** *a situation emblematic of the industrialized twentieth century* SYMBOLIC, representative, demonstrative, suggestive, indicative. **2** *emblematic works of art* ALLEGORICAL, symbolic, metaphorical, parabolic, figurative.

embodiment ● noun PERSONIFICATION, incarnation, realization, manifestation, expression, representation, actualization, symbol, symbolization; paradigm, epitome, paragon, soul, model; type, essence, quintessence, exemplification, example, exemplar, ideal; formal reification.

embody ● verb **1** *Gradgrind embodies the spirit of industrial capitalism* PERSONIFY, realize, manifest, symbolize, represent, express, concretize, incarnate, epitomize, stand for, typify, exemplify; formal reify. **2** *the changes in law embodied in the Children Act* INCORPORATE, include, contain, encompass; assimilate, consolidate, integrate, organize, systematize; combine.

embolden ● verb FORTIFY, make brave/braver, encourage, hearten, strengthen, brace, stiffen the resolve of, lift the morale of; rouse, stir, stimulate, cheer, rally, fire, animate, inspirit, invigorate; informal buck up.
– OPPOSITES dishearten.

embrace ● verb **1** *he embraced her warmly* HUG, take/hold in one's arms, hold, cuddle, clasp to one's bosom, clasp, squeeze, clutch; caress; enfold, enclasp, encircle, envelop, entwine oneself around; informal canoodle, smooch; poetic/literary embosom. **2** *most western European countries have embraced the concept* WELCOME, welcome with open arms, accept, take up, take to one's heart, adopt; espouse, support, back, champion. **3** *the faculty embraces a wide range of departments* INCLUDE, take in, comprise, contain, incorporate, encompass, cover, involve, embody, subsume, comprehend.
● noun *a fond embrace* HUG, cuddle, squeeze, clinch, caress; bear hug.

embrocation ● noun OINTMENT, lotion, cream, rub, salve, emollient, liniment, balm, unguent.

embroider ● verb **1** *a cushion embroidered with a pattern of golden keys* SEW, stitch; DECORATE, adorn, ornament, embellish. **2** *she embroidered her stories with colourful detail* ELABORATE, embellish, enlarge on, exaggerate, touch up, dress up, gild, colour; informal jazz up.

embroidery ● noun **1** *the girls were taught embroidery* NEEDLEWORK, needlepoint, needlecraft, sewing, tatting, crewel work, tapestry. **2** *fanciful embroidery of the facts* ELABORATION, embellishment, adornment, ornamentation, colouring, enhancement; exaggeration, overstatement, hyperbole.

embroil ● verb INVOLVE, entangle, ensnare, enmesh, catch up, mix up, bog down, mire.

embryo ● noun **1** *a human embryo* FETUS, fertilized egg, unborn child/baby. **2** *the embryo of a capitalist economy* GERM, nucleus, seed; rudimentary version, rudiments, basics, beginning, start.

embryonic ● adjective **1** *an embryonic chick* FETAL, unborn, unhatched. **2** *an embryonic pro-democracy movement* RUDIMENTARY, undeveloped, unformed, immature, incomplete, incipient, inchoate; fledgling, budding, nascent, emerging, developing, early, germinal.
– OPPOSITES mature.

emend ● verb CORRECT, rectify, repair, fix; improve, enhance, polish, refine, amend; edit, rewrite, revise, copy-edit, subedit, redraft, recast, rephrase, reword, rework, alter, change, modify; rare redact.

emerge ● verb **1** *a policeman emerged from the alley* COME OUT, appear, come into view, become visible, surface, materialize, manifest oneself, issue, come forth. **2** *several unexpected facts emerged* BECOME KNOWN, become apparent, be revealed, come to light, come out, turn up, transpire, unfold, turn out, prove to be the case.

emergence ● noun APPEARANCE, arrival, coming, materialization; advent, inception, dawn, birth, origination, start, development, rise.

emergent ● adjective in the process of coming into being.
emeritus /imerritəss/ ● adjective having retired but allowed to retain a title as an honour: *an emeritus professor*.
– ORIGIN Latin, from *emereri* 'earn one's discharge by service'.
emery /emməri/ ● noun a greyish-black form of corundum, used in powdered form as an abrasive.
– ORIGIN Old French *esmeri*, from Greek *smuris* 'polishing powder'.
emery board ● noun a strip of thin wood or card coated with emery or another abrasive and used as a nail file.
emetic /imettik/ ● adjective (of a substance) causing vomiting. ● noun an emetic substance.
– ORIGIN Greek *emetikos*, from *emein* 'to vomit'.
EMF ● abbreviation **1** electromagnetic field(s). **2** (**emf**) electromotive force.
-emia ● combining form US spelling of -AEMIA.
emigrant ● noun a person who emigrates.
emigrate /emmigrayt/ ● verb leave one's own country in order to settle permanently in another.
– DERIVATIVES **emigration** noun.
– ORIGIN Latin *emigrare*, from *migrare* 'migrate'.
émigré /emmigray/ ● noun a person who has emigrated, especially for political reasons.
– ORIGIN French.
eminence /emminənss/ ● noun **1** acknowledged superiority within a particular sphere. **2** an important or distinguished person. **3** (**His/Your Eminence**) a title given to a Roman Catholic cardinal. **4** formal or literary a piece of rising ground.
– ORIGIN Latin *eminentia*, from *eminere* 'jut, project'.
éminence grise /ayminoNS greez/ ● noun (pl. **éminences grises** pronunc. same) a person who exercises power or influence without holding an official position.
– ORIGIN French, 'grey eminence'; the term was originally applied to Cardinal Richelieu's grey-cloaked private secretary, Père Joseph (1577–1638).
eminent ● adjective **1** respected; distinguished. **2** outstanding or conspicuous: *the eminent reasonableness of their claim*.
– DERIVATIVES **eminently** adverb.
emir /emeer/ (also **amir**) ● noun a title of various Muslim (mainly Arab) rulers.
– ORIGIN originally denoting a male descendant of Muhammad: from Arabic, 'commander'.
emirate /emmirət/ ● noun the rank, lands, or reign of an emir.
emissary /emmisəri/ ● noun (pl. **emissaries**) a person sent as a diplomatic representative on a special mission.
– ORIGIN Latin *emissarius* 'scout, spy', from *emittere* 'emit'.
emission /imish'n/ ● noun **1** the action of emitting something, especially heat, light, gas, or radiation. **2** a substance which is emitted.
emit ● verb (**emitted**, **emitting**) **1** discharge; send forth or give out. **2** make (a sound).
– DERIVATIVES **emitter** noun.
– ORIGIN Latin *emittere*, from *mittere* 'send'.
Emmental /emməntaal/ (also **Emmenthal**) ● noun a kind of hard Swiss cheese with holes in it, similar to Gruyère.
– ORIGIN German, the name of a valley in Switzerland where the cheese was originally made.
Emmy ● noun (pl. **Emmys**) (in the US) a statuette awarded annually to an outstanding television programme or performer.
– ORIGIN said to be from *Immy*, short for *image orthicon tube* (a kind of television camera tube).
emollient /imolliənt/ ● adjective **1** having the quality of softening or soothing the skin. **2** attempting to avoid confrontation or anger; calming. ● noun an emollient substance.
– DERIVATIVES **emollience** noun.
– ORIGIN from Latin *emollire* 'make soft'.
emolument /imoljoomənt/ ● noun formal a salary, fee, or benefit from employment or office.
– ORIGIN Latin *emolumentum* (originally probably meaning 'payment for grinding corn'), from *molere* 'grind'.
emote /imōt/ ● verb portray emotion in an exaggerated way.
– ORIGIN back-formation from EMOTION.
emoticon /imōtikon/ ● noun a representation of a facial expression such as a smile, formed with keyboard characters and used in electronic communications to convey the writer's feelings.
– ORIGIN blend of EMOTION and ICON.
emotion ● noun **1** a strong feeling, such as joy or anger. **2** instinctive feeling as distinguished from reasoning or knowledge.
– DERIVATIVES **emotionless** adjective.
– ORIGIN originally denoting a public disturbance: from French, from Latin *emovere* 'disturb'.
emotional ● adjective **1** relating to the emotions. **2** arousing or showing emotion. **3** easily affected by or readily displaying emotion.
– DERIVATIVES **emotionalism** noun **emotionality** noun **emotionalize** (also **emotionalise**) verb **emotionally** adverb.
emotive ● adjective arousing intense feeling.

Thesaurus

emergency ● noun *a military emergency* CRISIS, urgent situation, extremity, exigency; accident, disaster, catastrophe, calamity; difficulty, plight, predicament, danger; *informal* panic stations.
● adjective **1** *an emergency meeting* URGENT, crisis; impromptu, extraordinary. **2** *emergency supplies* RESERVE, standby, back-up, fallback, in reserve.
emergent ● adjective EMERGING, developing, rising, dawning, budding, embryonic, infant, fledgling, nascent, incipient.
emigrate ● verb MOVE ABROAD, move overseas, leave one's country, migrate; relocate, resettle; defect.
– OPPOSITES immigrate.
emigration ● noun MOVING ABROAD, moving overseas, expatriation, migration; exodus, diaspora; relocation, resettling; defection.
eminence ● noun **1** *his eminence as a scientist* FAME, celebrity, illustriousness, distinction, renown, pre-eminence, notability, greatness, prestige, importance, reputation, repute, note; prominence, superiority, stature, standing. **2** *various legal eminences* IMPORTANT PERSON, dignitary, luminary, worthy, grandee, notable, notability, personage, leading light, VIP; *informal* somebody, someone, big shot, big noise, big gun, heavyweight. **3** *(formal) the hotel's eminence above the sea* ELEVATION, height, rise.
eminent ● adjective **1** *an eminent man of letters* ILLUSTRIOUS, distinguished, renowned, esteemed, pre-eminent, notable, noteworthy, great, prestigious, important, influential, outstanding, noted, of note; famous, celebrated, prominent, well known, lionized, acclaimed, exalted, revered, august, venerable. **2** *the eminent reasonableness of their claims* OBVIOUS, clear, conspicuous, marked, singular, signal; total, complete, utter, absolute, thorough, perfect, downright, sheer.
– OPPOSITES unknown.
eminently ● adverb VERY, greatly, highly, exceedingly, extremely, particularly, exceptionally, supremely, uniquely; obviously, clearly, conspicuously, markedly, singularly, signally, outstandingly, strikingly, notably, surpassingly; totally, completely, utterly, absolutely, thoroughly, perfectly, downright.
emissary ● noun ENVOY, ambassador, delegate, attaché, consul, plenipotentiary; agent, representative, deputy; messenger, courier; nuncio; *archaic* legate.
emission ● noun DISCHARGE, release, outpouring, outflow, outrush, leak, excretion, secretion, ejection; emanation, radiation, effusion, ejaculation, disgorgement, issuance.
emit ● verb **1** *the hydrocarbons emitted from vehicle exhausts* DISCHARGE, release, give out/off, pour out, send forth, throw out, void, vent, issue; leak, ooze, excrete, disgorge, secrete, eject, ejaculate; spout, belch, spew out; emanate, radiate, exude. **2** *he emitted a loud cry* UTTER, voice, let out, produce, give vent to, come out with, vocalize.
– OPPOSITES absorb.
emollient ● adjective **1** *a rich emollient shampoo* MOISTURIZING, soothing, softening. **2** *an emollient response* CONCILIATORY, conciliating, appeasing, soothing, calming, pacifying, assuaging, placating, mollifying, propitiatory.
● noun *she applied an emollient* MOISTURIZER, cream, lotion, oil, rub, salve, unguent, balm; *technical* humectant.
emolument ● noun *(formal)* SALARY, pay, payment, wage(s), earnings, allowance, stipend, honorarium, reward, premium; fee, charge, consideration; income, profit, gain, return.
emotion ● noun **1** *she was good at hiding her emotions* FEELING, sentiment; reaction, response. **2** *overcome by emotion, she turned away* PASSION, strength of feeling, warmth of feeling. **3** *responses based purely on emotion* INSTINCT, intuition, gut feeling; sentiment, the heart.
emotional ● adjective **1** *an emotional young man* PASSIONATE, hot-blooded, ardent, fervent, excitable, temperamental, melodramatic, tempestuous; demonstrative, responsive, tender, loving, feeling, sentimental, sensitive. **2** *he paid an emotional tribute to his wife*

– DERIVATIVES **emotively** adverb **emotivity** /eemōtivviti/ noun.
empanada /empənaadə/ • noun a pastry turnover filled with savoury ingredients and baked or fried, typical of South American cooking.
– ORIGIN Spanish, from *empanar* 'roll in pastry'.
empanel • verb variant spelling of IMPANEL.
empathize (also **empathise**) • verb understand and share the feelings of another.
empathy /empəthi/ • noun the ability to empathize.
– DERIVATIVES **empathetic** adjective **empathic** /empathik/ adjective.
– ORIGIN Greek *empatheia*, from *pathos* 'feeling'.
emperor • noun the ruler of an empire.
– ORIGIN Latin *imperator* 'military commander', from *imperare* 'to command'.
emperor penguin • noun the largest kind of penguin, which breeds in the Antarctic and has a yellow patch on each side of the head.
emphasis /emfəsiss/ • noun (pl. **emphases** /emfəseez/) **1** special importance, value, or prominence given to something. **2** stress laid on a word or words in speaking.
– ORIGIN Greek, originally in the sense 'appearance, show', later denoting a figure of speech in which more is implied than said.
emphasize (also **emphasise**) • verb give special importance or prominence to.
emphatic • adjective **1** showing or giving emphasis. **2** definite and clear: *an emphatic win.*
– DERIVATIVES **emphatically** adverb.
emphysema /emfiseemə/ (also **pulmonary emphysema**) • noun Medicine a condition in which the air sacs of the lungs are damaged and enlarged, causing breathlessness.
– ORIGIN Greek *emphusēma*, from *emphusan* 'puff up'.
empire • noun **1** an extensive group of states ruled over by a single monarch or ruling authority. **2** supreme political power. **3** a large commercial organization under the control of one person or group. • adjective (**Empire**) denoting a neoclassical style of furniture and dress fashionable chiefly during the First Empire (1804–15) in France.
– ORIGIN Latin *imperium*, from *imperare* 'to command'.
empire line • noun a style of women's clothing characterized by a waistline cut just under the bust and a low neckline, first popular during the First Empire in France.
empirical (also **empiric**) • adjective based on observation or experience rather than theory or pure logic.
– DERIVATIVES **empirically** adverb.
– ORIGIN Greek *empeirikos*, from *empeiria* 'experience'.
empiricism /empirrisiz'm/ • noun Philosophy the theory that all knowledge is derived from experience and observation.
– DERIVATIVES **empiricist** noun & adjective.
emplacement • noun a structure or platform where a gun is placed for firing.
employ • verb **1** give work to (someone) and pay them for it. **2** make use of. **3** keep occupied.
– PHRASES **in the employ of** employed by.
– DERIVATIVES **employability** noun **employable** adjective.
– ORIGIN Old French *employer*, from Latin *implicare* 'involve, imply'.
employee • noun a person employed for wages or salary.
employer • noun a person or organization that employs people.
employment • noun **1** the action of employing or the state of being employed. **2** a person's work or profession.
emporium /emporiəm/ • noun (pl. **emporia** /emporiə/ or **emporiums**) a large store selling a wide variety of goods.
– ORIGIN Greek *emporion*, from *emporos* 'merchant'.
empower • verb **1** give authority or power to; authorize. **2** give strength and confidence to.
– DERIVATIVES **empowerment** noun.
empress /empriss/ • noun **1** a female emperor. **2** the wife or widow of an emperor.
empty • adjective (**emptier, emptiest**) **1** containing nothing; not filled or occupied. **2** having no meaning or likelihood of

e

Thesaurus

POIGNANT, moving, touching, affecting, powerful, stirring, emotive, heart-rending, heart-warming, impassioned, dramatic; haunting, pathetic, sentimental; *informal* tear-jerking.
– OPPOSITES unfeeling.
emotionless • adjective UNEMOTIONAL, unfeeling, dispassionate, passionless, unexpressive, cool, cold, cold-blooded, impassive, indifferent, detached, remote, aloof; toneless, flat, dead, expressionless, blank, wooden, stony, deadpan, vacant.
emotive • adjective CONTROVERSIAL, contentious, inflammatory; sensitive, delicate, difficult, problematic, touchy, awkward.
empathize • verb IDENTIFY, sympathize, be in sympathy, understand, share someone's feelings, be in tune; be on the same wavelength as, talk the same language as; relate to, feel for, have insight into; *informal* put oneself in someone else's shoes.
emperor • noun RULER, sovereign, king, monarch, potentate; *historical* tsar, kaiser, mikado.
– RELATED TERMS imperial.
emphasis • noun **1** *the curriculum gave more emphasis to reading and writing* PROMINENCE, importance, significance, value; stress, weight, accent, attention, priority, pre-eminence, urgency, force. **2** *the emphasis is on the word 'little'* STRESS, accent, accentuation, weight, prominence; beat; *Prosody* ictus.
emphasize • verb STRESS, underline, highlight, focus attention on, point up, lay stress on, draw attention to, spotlight, foreground, play up, make a point of; bring to the fore, insist on, belabour; accent, accentuate, underscore; *informal* press home, rub it in.
– OPPOSITES understate.
emphatic • adjective **1** *an emphatic denial* VEHEMENT, firm, wholehearted, forceful, forcible, energetic, vigorous, direct, assertive, insistent; certain, definite, out-and-out, one hundred per cent; decided, determined, categorical, unqualified, unconditional, unequivocal, unambiguous, absolute, explicit, downright, outright, clear. **2** *an emphatic victory* CONCLUSIVE, decisive, decided, unmistakable; resounding, telling; *informal* thumping, thundering.
– OPPOSITES hesitant, narrow.
empire • noun **1** *the Ottoman Empire* KINGDOM, realm, domain, territory; commonwealth; power, world power, superpower. **2** *a worldwide shipping empire* ORGANIZATION, corporation, multinational, conglomerate, consortium, company, business, firm, operation. **3** *his dream of empire* POWER, rule, ascendancy, supremacy, command, control, authority, sway, dominance, domination, dominion.
– RELATED TERMS imperial.
empirical • adjective EXPERIENTIAL, practical, heuristic, first-hand, hands-on; observed, seen.
– OPPOSITES theoretical.
employ • verb **1** *she employed a chauffeur* HIRE, engage, recruit, take on, secure the services of, sign up, sign, put on the payroll, enrol, appoint; retain; indenture, apprentice. **2** *Sam was employed in carving a stone figure* OCCUPY, engage, involve, keep busy, tie up; absorb, engross, immerse. **3** *the team employed subtle psychological tactics* USE, utilize, make use of, avail oneself of; apply, exercise, practise, put into practice, exert, bring into play, bring to bear; draw on, resort to, turn to, have recourse to.
– OPPOSITES dismiss.
employed • adjective WORKING, in work, in employment, holding down a job; earning, waged, breadwinning.
employee • noun WORKER, member of staff; blue-collar worker, white-collar worker, workman, labourer, (hired) hand; wage-earner, breadwinner; (**employees**) personnel, staff, workforce; *informal* liveware.
employer • noun **1** *his employer gave him a glowing reference* MANAGER, manageress, proprietor, director, head man, head woman; *informal* boss, boss man, skipper; *Brit. informal* gaffer, governor, guv'nor; *N. Amer. informal* padrone, sachem. **2** *the largest private sector employer in Sheffield* FIRM, company, business, organization, manufacturer.
employment • noun **1** *she found employment as a clerk* WORK, labour, service; job, post, position, situation, occupation, profession, trade, métier, business, line, line of work, calling, vocation, craft, pursuit; *archaic* employ. **2** *the employment of children* HIRING, hire, engagement, taking on; apprenticing. **3** *the employment of nuclear weapons* USE, utilization, application, exercise.
emporium • noun SHOP, store, outlet, retail outlet; department store, chain store, supermarket, hypermarket, superstore, megastore; establishment.
empower • verb **1** *the act empowered Henry to punish heretics* AUTHORIZE, entitle, permit, allow, license, sanction, warrant, commission, delegate, qualify, enable, equip. **2** *movements to empower the poor* EMANCIPATE, unshackle, set free, liberate.
– OPPOSITES forbid.
empress • noun RULER, sovereign, queen, monarch, potentate; *historical* tsarina.

fulfilment: *an empty threat.* **3** having no value or purpose. ● verb (**empties**, **emptied**) **1** make or become empty. **2** discharge (the contents) from a container. **3** (of a river) flow into the sea or a lake. ● noun (pl. **empties**) informal a bottle or glass left empty of its contents.
– PHRASES **be running on empty** have exhausted all of one's resources. **empty vessels make most noise** (or **sound**) proverb those with least wisdom or knowledge are always the most talkative.
– DERIVATIVES **emptily** adverb **emptiness** noun.
– ORIGIN Old English, 'at leisure, empty'.
empty-handed ● adjective having failed to obtain or achieve what one wanted.
empty-headed ● adjective unintelligent and foolish.
empty nester ● noun informal, chiefly N. Amer. a parent whose children have grown up and left home.
empyema /empīeemə/ ● noun (pl. **empyemata** /empīeemətə/ or **empyemas**) Medicine the collection of pus in a body cavity, especially in the chest.
– ORIGIN from Greek *empuein* 'suppurate'.
empyrean /empīreeən, empirriən/ literary ● noun (**the empyrean**) heaven or the sky. ● adjective relating to heaven.
– ORIGIN Greek *empurios* (used by the ancients to refer to the highest part of heaven, thought to be the realm of pure fire), from *pur* 'fire'.
em rule ● noun Brit. a long dash used in punctuation, roughly the width of the letter *M*.
EMS ● abbreviation European Monetary System.
EMU ● abbreviation Economic and Monetary Union.
emu ● noun a large flightless fast-running Australian bird similar to an ostrich.
– ORIGIN Portuguese *ema*.
emulate /emyoolayt/ ● verb try to equal or surpass, typically by imitation.
– DERIVATIVES **emulation** noun **emulative** adjective **emulator** noun.
– ORIGIN Latin *aemulari* 'to rival or equal'.
emulsifier ● noun a substance that stabilizes an emulsion, especially an additive used to stabilize processed foods.
emulsify /imulsifī/ ● verb (**emulsifies**, **emulsified**) make into or become an emulsion.
– DERIVATIVES **emulsifiable** adjective **emulsification** noun.
emulsion ● noun **1** a fine dispersion of minute droplets of one liquid in another in which it is not soluble or miscible. **2** a type of paint consisting of pigment bound in a synthetic resin which forms an emulsion with water. **3** a light-sensitive coating for photographic films and plates, containing crystals of a silver compound dispersed in a medium such as gelatin.
– ORIGIN originally denoting a milky liquid made by crushing almonds in water: from Latin, from *emulgere* 'milk out'.
en ● noun Printing a unit of measurement equal to half an em.
– ORIGIN the letter *N*, since it is approximately this width.
en-[1] (also **em-**) ● prefix forming verbs: **1** (added to nouns) meaning 'put into or on': *engulf.* **2** (added to nouns and adjectives) meaning 'bring into the condition of': *enliven.* **3** (added to verbs) meaning 'in, into, or on' or as an intensifier: *ensnare | entangle.*
– ORIGIN French, from Latin *in-*.
en-[2] (also **em-**) ● prefix within; inside: *enthusiasm.*
– ORIGIN Greek.
-en[1] ● suffix forming verbs from adjectives or nouns denoting the development or intensification of a state or quality: *widen.*
– ORIGIN Old English.
-en[2] ● suffix (also **-n**) forming adjectives from nouns: **1** made or consisting of: *earthen.* **2** resembling: *golden.*
– ORIGIN Old English.
-en[3] (also **-n**) ● suffix forming past participles of strong verbs: **1** as a regular inflection: *spoken.* **2** as an adjective: *mistaken.*
– ORIGIN Old English.
enable ● verb **1** provide with the ability or means to do something. **2** make possible.
– DERIVATIVES **enablement** noun **enabler** noun.
enact ● verb **1** make (a bill or other proposal) law. **2** act out (a role or play).
– DERIVATIVES **enactor** noun.
enactment ● noun **1** the process of enacting. **2** a law that has been passed.
enamel ● noun **1** a coloured opaque glassy substance applied to metal, glass, or pottery for decorative or protective purposes. **2** the hard glossy substance that covers the crown of a tooth. **3** a paint that dries to give a smooth, hard coat. ● verb (**enamelled**, **enamelling**; US **enameled**, **enameling**) (usu. as adj. **enamelled**) coat or decorate with enamel.
– DERIVATIVES **enameller** noun.
– ORIGIN Old French *enamailler*, from *amail* 'enamel'.
enamour /inammər/ (US **enamor**) ● verb (**be enamoured of/with/by**) be filled with love or admiration for.
– ORIGIN Old French *enamourer*, from *amour* 'love'.
enantiomer /inantiəmər/ ● noun Chemistry each of a pair of molecules that are mirror images of each other.
– DERIVATIVES **enantiomeric** adjective.
– ORIGIN from Greek *enantios* 'opposite'.
en bloc /on blok/ ● adverb all together or all at once.
– ORIGIN French.
encamp ● verb settle in or establish a camp.
encampment ● noun **1** a place where a camp is set up. **2** a prehistoric enclosed or fortified site, especially an Iron Age hill fort.
encapsulate /inkapsyoolayt/ ● verb **1** enclose in or as if in a capsule. **2** express concisely and succinctly.
– DERIVATIVES **encapsulation** noun.

Thesaurus

emptiness ● noun *she had filled an emptiness in his life* VOID, vacuum, empty space, vacuity, gap, vacancy, hole.
empty ● adjective **1** *an empty house* VACANT, unoccupied, uninhabited, untenanted, bare, desolate, deserted, abandoned; clear, free. **2** *an empty threat* MEANINGLESS, hollow, idle, vain, futile, worthless, useless, insubstantial, ineffective, ineffectual. **3** *without her my life is empty* FUTILE, pointless, purposeless, worthless, meaningless, valueless, of no value, useless, of no use, aimless, senseless, hollow, barren, insignificant, inconsequential, trivial. **4** *his eyes were empty* BLANK, expressionless, vacant, deadpan, wooden, stony, impassive, absent, glazed, fixed, lifeless, emotionless, unresponsive.
– OPPOSITES full, serious, worthwhile.
● verb **1** *I emptied the dishwasher* UNLOAD, unpack, void; clear, evacuate; archaic unlade. **2** *he emptied out the contents of the case* REMOVE, take out, extract, tip out, pour out.
– OPPOSITES fill.
empty-headed ● adjective STUPID, foolish, silly, unintelligent, idiotic, brainless, witless, vacuous, vapid, feather-brained, bird-brained, scatterbrained, scatty, thoughtless; informal half-witted, dumb, dim, airheaded, brain-dead, dippy, dizzy, dopey, dozy, soft in the head, slow on the uptake; Brit. informal daft; N. Amer. informal ditsy, dumb-ass.
– OPPOSITES intelligent.
empyrean (poetic/literary) ● adjective *the empyrean regions* HEAVENLY, celestial, ethereal; upper.
● noun (**the empyrean**) HEAVEN, the heavens, the sky, the upper regions, the stratosphere; poetic/literary the ether, the wide blue yonder, the firmament, the welkin.
emulate ● verb IMITATE, copy, mirror, echo, follow, model oneself on, take a leaf out of someone's book; match, equal, parallel, be on a par with, be in the same league as, come close to; compete with, contend with, rival, surpass.
enable ● verb ALLOW, permit, let, give the means to, equip, empower, make able, fit; authorize, entitle, qualify; formal capacitate.
– OPPOSITES prevent.
enact ● verb **1** *the Bill was enacted in 1963* PASS, make law, legislate; approve, ratify, sanction, authorize; impose, lay down. **2** *members of the church enacted a nativity play* ACT OUT, act, perform, appear in, stage, mount, put on, present.
– OPPOSITES repeal.
enactment ● noun **1** *the enactment of a Bill of Rights* PASSING; ratification, sanction, approval, authorization; imposition. **2** *parliamentary enactments* ACT, law, by-law, ruling, rule, regulation, statute, measure; N. Amer. formal ordinance; (**enactments**) legislation. **3** *the enactment of the play* ACTING, performing, performance, staging, presentation.
enamoured ● adjective IN LOVE, infatuated, besotted, smitten, captivated, enchanted, fascinated, bewitched, beguiled; keen on, taken with; informal mad about, crazy about, wild about, bowled over by, struck on, sweet on, carrying a torch for; poetic/literary ensorcelled by.
encampment ● noun CAMP, military camp, bivouac, cantonment; campsite, camping ground; tents.

encase (also **incase**) ● verb enclose or cover in a case or close-fitting surround.
– DERIVATIVES **encasement** noun.

encash ● verb Brit. convert (a cheque, bond, etc.) into money.
– DERIVATIVES **encashment** noun.

encaustic /enkawstik/ ● adjective (in painting and ceramics) decorated with coloured clays or pigments mixed with hot wax, which are burnt in as an inlay. ● noun the art or process of encaustic painting.
– ORIGIN Greek *enkaustikos*, from *enkaiein* 'burn in'.

-ence ● suffix forming nouns: **1** denoting a quality: *impertinence.* **2** denoting an action or its result: *reference.*
– ORIGIN Latin *-entia, -antia.*

encephalitis /enseffəlītiss, enkeff-/ ● noun inflammation of the brain.
– DERIVATIVES **encephalitic** adjective.
– ORIGIN from Greek *enkephalos* 'brain'.

encephalography /enseffəlogrəfi, enkeff-/ ● noun any of various techniques for recording the structure or electrical activity of the brain.
– DERIVATIVES **encephalogram** /enseffəlōgram, enkeff-/ noun **encephalograph** noun.

encephalomyelitis /enseffəlōmīəlītiss, enkeff-/ ● noun Medicine inflammation of the brain and spinal cord, typically due to acute infection with a virus.

encephalopathy /enseffəloppəthi, enkeff-/ ● noun (pl. **encephalopathies**) a disease in which the functioning of the brain is affected, especially by viral infection or toxins in the blood.

enchant ● verb **1** delight; charm. **2** put under a spell.
– DERIVATIVES **enchanter** noun **enchantment** noun **enchantress** noun.
– ORIGIN French *enchanter*, from Latin *cantare* 'sing'.

enchanting ● adjective delightfully charming or attractive.
– DERIVATIVES **enchantingly** adverb.

enchilada /enchilaadə/ ● noun a tortilla filled with meat or cheese and served with chilli sauce.
– ORIGIN Latin American Spanish, from *enchilar* 'season with chilli'.

encipher ● verb convert into a coded form.
– DERIVATIVES **encipherment** noun.

encircle ● verb form a circle around; surround.
– DERIVATIVES **encirclement** noun.

enclave /enklayv/ ● noun **1** a portion of territory surrounded by a larger territory whose inhabitants are culturally or ethnically distinct. **2** a group that is different in character from those surrounding it: *a male enclave.*
– ORIGIN from Old French *enclaver* 'enclose', from Latin *clavis* 'key'.

enclose (also **inclose**) ● verb **1** surround or close off on all sides. **2** place in an envelope together with a letter.
– ORIGIN Old French *enclore*, from Latin *includere* 'shut in'.

enclosure /inklōzhər/ (also **inclosure**) ● noun **1** an area that is enclosed by a fence, wall, or other barrier. **2** a document or object placed in an envelope together with a letter.

encode ● verb convert into a coded form.
– DERIVATIVES **encoder** noun.

encomium /enkōmiəm/ ● noun (pl. **encomiums** or **encomia**) formal a speech or piece of writing expressing praise.
– ORIGIN Greek *enkōmion* 'eulogy'.

encompass /inkumpəss/ ● verb **1** surround and have or hold within. **2** include comprehensively.

encore /ongkor/ ● noun a repeated or additional performance of an item at the end of a concert, as called for by an audience. ● exclamation again! (as called by an audience at the end of a concert) ● verb call for (an encore).
– ORIGIN French, 'still, again'.

encounter ● verb unexpectedly meet or be faced with. ● noun **1** an unexpected or casual meeting. **2** a confrontation or difficult struggle.
– ORIGIN originally in the sense 'meet as an adversary': from Old French *encontrer*, from Latin *contra* 'against'.

encourage ● verb **1** give support, confidence, or hope to. **2** help or stimulate the development of.
– DERIVATIVES **encouragement** noun **encourager** noun **encouraging** adjective.
– ORIGIN French *encourager*, from *corage* 'courage'.

encroach ● verb **1** (**encroach on/upon**) gradually intrude on (a person's territory, rights, etc.). **2** advance gradually beyond expected or acceptable limits: *the sea has encroached all round the coast.*
– DERIVATIVES **encroachment** noun.

e

Thesaurus

encapsulate ● verb **1** *their conclusions are encapsulated in one sentence* SUMMARIZE, sum up, give the gist of, put in a nutshell; capture, express. **2** *seeds encapsulated in resin* ENCLOSE, encase, contain, envelop, enfold, sheath, cocoon, surround.

enchant ● verb CAPTIVATE, charm, delight, enrapture, entrance, enthral, beguile, bewitch, spellbind, fascinate, hypnotize, mesmerize, rivet, grip, transfix; *informal* bowl someone over.
– OPPOSITES bore.

enchanter ● noun WIZARD, witch, sorcerer, warlock, magician, necromancer, magus; witch doctor, medicine man, shaman; *archaic* mage; *rare* thaumaturge.

enchanting ● adjective CAPTIVATING, charming, delightful, bewitching, beguiling, adorable, lovely, attractive, appealing, engaging, winning, fetching, winsome, alluring, disarming, irresistible, fascinating; *dated* taking.

enchantment ● noun **1** *a race of giants skilled in enchantment* MAGIC, witchcraft, sorcery, wizardry, necromancy; charms, spells, incantations; *N. Amer.* mojo; *rare* thaumaturgy. **2** *the enchantment of the garden by moonlight* ALLURE, delight, charm, beauty, attractiveness, appeal, fascination, irresistibility, magnetism, pull, draw, lure. **3** *being with him was sheer enchantment* BLISS, ecstasy, heaven, rapture, joy.

enchantress ● noun WITCH, sorceress, magician, fairy; Circe, siren.

encircle ● verb SURROUND, enclose, circle, girdle, ring, encompass; close in, shut in, fence in, wall in, hem in, confine; *poetic/literary* gird, engirdle.

enclose ● verb **1** *tall trees enclosed the garden* SURROUND, circle, ring, girdle, encompass, encircle; confine, close in, shut in, fence in, wall in, hedge in, hem in; *poetic/literary* gird, engirdle. **2** *please enclose a stamped addressed envelope* INCLUDE, insert, put in; send.

enclosure ● noun PADDOCK, fold, pen, compound, stockade, ring, yard; sty, coop; *N. Amer.* corral.

encomium ● noun (*formal*) EULOGY, panegyric, paean, accolade, tribute, testimonial; praise, acclaim, acclamation, homage; *formal* laudation.

encompass ● verb **1** *the monument is encompassed by Hunsbury Park* CONTAIN, have within; surround, enclose, encircle. **2** *debates encompassing a vast range of subjects* COVER, embrace, include, incorporate, take in, contain, comprise, involve, deal with; *formal* comprehend.

encounter ● verb **1** *I encountered a girl I used to know* MEET, meet by chance, run into, come across/upon, stumble across/on, chance on, happen on; *informal* bump into; *archaic* run against, rencounter. **2** *we encountered a slight problem* EXPERIENCE, run into, come up against, face, be faced with, confront.
● noun **1** *an unexpected encounter* MEETING, chance meeting; *archaic* rencounter. **2** *a violent encounter between police and demonstrators* BATTLE, fight, clash, confrontation, struggle, skirmish, engagement; *informal* run-in, set-to, dust-up, scrap.

encourage ● verb **1** *the players were encouraged by the crowd's response* HEARTEN, cheer, buoy up, uplift, inspire, motivate, spur on, stir, stir up, fire up, stimulate, invigorate, vitalize, revitalize, embolden, fortify, rally; *informal* buck up, pep up, give a shot in the arm to. **2** *she had encouraged him to go* PERSUADE, coax, urge, press, push, pressure, pressurize, prod, goad, egg on, prompt, influence, sway. **3** *the Government was keen to encourage local businesses* SUPPORT, back, champion, promote, further, foster, nurture, cultivate, strengthen, stimulate; help, assist, aid, boost, fuel.
– OPPOSITES discourage, dissuade, hinder.

encouragement ● noun **1** *she needed a bit of encouragement* HEARTENING, cheering up, inspiration, motivation, stimulation, fortification; morale-boosting; *informal* a shot in the arm. **2** *they required no encouragement to get back to work* PERSUASION, coaxing, urging, pressure, pressurization, prodding, prompting; spur, goad, inducement, incentive, bait, motive; *informal* carrot. **3** *the encouragement of foreign investment* SUPPORT, backing, championship, championing, sponsoring, promotion, furtherance, furthering, fostering, nurture, cultivation; help, assistance; *N. Amer.* boosterism.

encouraging ● adjective **1** *an encouraging start* PROMISING, hopeful, auspicious, propitious, favourable, bright, rosy; heartening,

– ORIGIN Old French *encrochier* 'seize'.
en croute /ON kroot/ • adjective & adverb in a pastry crust.
– ORIGIN French.
encrust (also **incrust**) • verb cover with a hard crust.
– DERIVATIVES **encrustation** noun.
encrypt /enkript/ • verb convert into code.
– DERIVATIVES **encryption** noun.
– ORIGIN from Greek *kruptos* 'hidden'.
encumber /inkumbər/ • verb be a burden or impediment to.
– ORIGIN Old French *encombrer* 'block up', from *combre* 'river barrage'.
encumbrance • noun **1** a burden or impediment. **2** Law a mortgage or other charge on property or assets.
-ency • suffix forming nouns denoting a quality or state: *efficiency*.
– ORIGIN Latin *-entia*.
encyclical /ensiklik'l/ • noun a letter sent by the pope to all bishops of the Roman Catholic Church.
– ORIGIN from Greek *enkuklios* 'circular, general'.
encyclopedia /ensīklәpeediә/ (also **encyclopaedia**) • noun a book or set of books giving information on many subjects or on many aspects of one subject, typically arranged alphabetically.
– ORIGIN pseudo-Greek *enkuklopaideia*, for *enkuklios paideia* 'all-round education'.
encyclopedic /ensīklәpeedik/ (also **encyclopaedic**) • adjective **1** comprehensive: *an encyclopedic knowledge*. **2** relating to encyclopedias or information suitable for an encyclopedia.
encyclopedist (also **encyclopaedist**) • noun a person who writes, edits, or contributes to an encyclopedia.
end • noun **1** the final part of something. **2** the furthest or most extreme part. **3** a termination of a state or situation: *they called for an end to violence*. **4** a person's death or downfall. **5** a goal or desired result. **6** a part or share of an activity: *your end of the deal*. **7** a small piece that is left after use. **8** the part of a sports field or court defended by one team or player. • verb **1** come or bring to an end; finish. **2** (**end in**) have as its result. **3** (**end up**) eventually reach or come to a particular state or place.
– PHRASES **at the end of the day** informal, chiefly Brit. when everything is taken into consideration. **be the end** informal be the limit of what one can tolerate. **end it all** commit suicide. **the end of the road** (or **line**) the point beyond which progress or survival cannot continue. **the end of one's tether** having no patience or energy left. **end on** situated on or viewed from the end. **end to end** in a row with the ends touching or close together. **in the end** eventually. **keep** (or **hold**) **one's end up** informal perform well in a difficult or competitive situation. **make** (**both**) **ends meet** earn just enough money to live on. **no end** informal very much. **no end of** informal a vast number or amount of. **on end 1** continuously. **2** upright. **the sharp end** informal the most challenging and risky part of an activity.
– ORIGIN Old English.
endanger • verb put in danger.
– DERIVATIVES **endangerment** noun.
endangered • adjective in danger of extinction.
endear /indeer/ • verb cause to be loved or liked.
endearing • adjective inspiring love or affection.
– DERIVATIVES **endearingly** adverb.
endearment • noun **1** love or affection. **2** a word or phrase expressing this.
endeavour /indevvәr/ (US **endeavor**) • verb try hard to do or achieve something. • noun **1** an earnest attempt to achieve something. **2** earnest and industrious effort.
– ORIGIN from the obsolete phrase *put oneself in devoir* 'do one's utmost' (from archaic *devoir* 'one's duty').
endemic /endemmik/ • adjective **1** (of a disease or condition) regularly found among particular people or in a certain area. **2** (of a plant or animal) native or restricted to a certain area.
– DERIVATIVES **endemicity** /endimissiti/ noun **endemism** /endimiz'm/ noun.
– ORIGIN Greek *endēmios* 'native'.
endgame • noun the final stage of a game such as chess or bridge, when few pieces or cards remain.
ending • noun an end or final part.
endive /endīv, -div/ • noun **1** a plant with bitter curly or smooth leaves, eaten in salads. **2** (also **Belgian endive**) N. Amer. a chicory crown.
– ORIGIN Old French, from Greek *entubon*.

Thesaurus

reassuring, cheering, comforting, welcome, pleasing, gratifying. **2** *my parents were very encouraging* SUPPORTIVE, understanding, helpful; positive, responsive, enthusiastic.
encroach • verb INTRUDE, trespass, impinge, obtrude, impose oneself, invade, infiltrate, interrupt, infringe, violate, interfere with, disturb; tread/step on someone's toes; *informal* horn in on, muscle in on; *archaic* entrench on.
encroachment • noun INTRUSION, trespass, invasion, infiltration, incursion, obtrusion, infringement, impingement.
encumber • verb **1** *her movements were encumbered by her heavy skirts* HAMPER, hinder, obstruct, impede, cramp, inhibit, restrict, limit, constrain, restrain, bog down, retard, slow (down); inconvenience, disadvantage, handicap. **2** *they are encumbered with debt* BURDEN, load, weigh down, saddle; overwhelm, tax, stress, strain, overload, overburden; *Brit. informal* lumber.
encumbrance • noun **1** *he found the equipment a great encumbrance* HINDRANCE, obstruction, obstacle, impediment, constraint, handicap, inconvenience, nuisance, disadvantage, drawback; *poetic/literary* trammel; *archaic* cumber. **2** *she knew she was an encumbrance to him* BURDEN, responsibility, obligation, liability, weight, load, stress, strain, pressure, trouble, worry; millstone, albatross, cross to bear.
encyclopedic • adjective COMPREHENSIVE, complete, thorough, thoroughgoing, full, exhaustive, in-depth, wide-ranging, all-inclusive, all-embracing, all-encompassing, universal, vast; *formal* compendious.
end • noun **1** *the end of the road* EXTREMITY, furthermost part, limit; margin, edge, border, boundary, periphery; point, tip, tail end; *N. Amer.* tag end. **2** *the end of the novel* CONCLUSION, termination, ending, finish, close, resolution, climax, finale, culmination, denouement; epilogue, coda, peroration. **3** *a cigarette end* BUTT, stub, stump, remnant; *informal* fag end, dog end. **4** *wealth is a means and not an end in itself* AIM, goal, purpose, objective, object, holy grail, target; intention, intent, design, motive; aspiration, wish, desire, ambition. **5** *the commercial end of the business* ASPECT, side, section, area, field, part, share, portion, segment, province. **6** *his end might come at any time* DEATH, dying, demise, passing, expiry, quietus; doom, extinction, annihilation, extermination, destruction; downfall, ruin, ruination, Waterloo; *informal* curtains; *formal* decease.
– OPPOSITES beginning.
• verb **1** *the show ended with a wedding scene* FINISH, conclude, terminate, come to an end, draw to a close, close, stop, cease; culminate, climax. build up to, lead up to, come to a head. **2** *she ended their relationship* BREAK OFF, call off, bring to an end, put an end to, stop, finish, terminate, discontinue; dissolve, cancel, annul.
– OPPOSITES begin.
endanger • verb IMPERIL, jeopardize, risk, put at risk, put in danger; threaten, pose a threat to, be a danger to, be detrimental to, damage, injure, harm; *archaic* peril.
endearing • adjective LOVABLE, adorable, cute, sweet, dear, delightful, lovely, charming, appealing, attractive, engaging, winning, captivating, enchanting, beguiling, winsome; *dated* taking.
endearment • noun **1** *his murmured endearments* TERM OF AFFECTION, term of endearment, pet name; (**endearments**) sweet nothings, sweet talk. **2** *he spoke to her without endearment* AFFECTION, fondness, tenderness, feeling, sentiment, warmth, love, liking, care.
endeavour • verb *the company endeavoured to expand its activities* TRY, attempt, seek, undertake, aspire, aim, set out; strive, struggle, labour, toil, work, exert oneself, apply oneself, do one's best, do one's utmost, give one's all, be at pains; *informal* have a go/shot/stab, give something one's best shot, do one's damnedest, go all out, bend over backwards; *formal* essay.
• noun **1** *an endeavour to build a more buoyant economy* ATTEMPT, try, bid, effort, venture; *informal* go, crack, shot, stab, bash; *formal* essay. **2** *several days of endeavour* EFFORT, exertion, striving, struggling, labouring, struggle, labour, hard work, application, industry; pains; *informal* sweat, {blood, sweat, and tears}, elbow grease; *Brit. informal* graft; *Austral./NZ informal* (hard) yakka; *poetic/literary* travail. **3** *an extremely unwise endeavour* UNDERTAKING, enterprise, venture, exercise, activity, exploit, deed, act, action, move; scheme, plan, project; *informal* caper.
ending • noun END, finish, close, closing, conclusion, resolution, summing-up, denouement, finale; cessation, stopping, termin-

endless ● adjective **1** having or seeming to have no end or limit. **2** innumerable. **3** (of a belt, chain, or tape) having the ends joined to allow for continuous action.
– DERIVATIVES **endlessly** adverb **endlessness** noun.
endmost ● adjective nearest to the end.
endo- ● combining form internal; within: *endoderm.*
– ORIGIN from Greek *endon* 'within'.
endocarditis /endōkaarditiss/ ● noun Medicine inflammation of the membrane lining the interior of the heart.
endocrine /endōkrīn, -krin/ ● adjective (of a gland) secreting hormones or other products directly into the blood.
– ORIGIN from Greek *krinein* 'sift'.
endocrinology /endōkrinolləji/ ● noun the branch of physiology and medicine concerned with endocrine glands and hormones.
– DERIVATIVES **endocrinologist** noun.
endogenous /endojinəss/ ● adjective technical relating to an internal cause or origin. Often contrasted with EXOGENOUS.
– DERIVATIVES **endogenously** adverb.
endometriosis /endōmeetriōsiss/ ● noun Medicine a condition in which endometrial tissue proliferates in other parts of the body, causing pelvic pain.
endometrium /endōmeetriəm/ ● noun the mucous membrane lining the womb.
– DERIVATIVES **endometrial** adjective.
– ORIGIN from Greek *mētra* 'womb'.
endomorph /endōmorf/ ● noun a person with a soft round build of body and a high proportion of fat tissue. Compare with ECTOMORPH and MESOMORPH.
– DERIVATIVES **endomorphic** adjective.
– ORIGIN from *endodermal* (the endoderm being the layer of the embryo giving rise to these physical characteristics).
endorphin /endorfin/ ● noun any of a group of hormones secreted within the brain and nervous system and causing an analgesic effect.
– ORIGIN blend of ENDOGENOUS and MORPHINE.
endorse /indorss/ (US & Law also **indorse**) ● verb **1** declare one's public approval of. **2** sign (a cheque or bill of exchange) on the back to specify another as the payee or to accept responsibility for paying it. **3** Brit. enter an endorsement on (a driving licence).
– DERIVATIVES **endorsable** adjective **endorsee** noun **endorser** noun.
– ORIGIN Latin *indorsare,* from *dorsum* 'back'.
endorsement (chiefly US also **indorsement**) ● noun **1** an act or the action of endorsing. **2** (in the UK) a note on a driving licence recording the penalty points incurred for a driving offence. **3** a clause in an insurance policy detailing an exemption from or change in cover.
endoscope /endəskōp/ ● noun an instrument which can be introduced into the body to view its internal parts.
– DERIVATIVES **endoscopic** adjective **endoscopically** adverb **endoscopist** noun **endoscopy** noun.
endoskeleton ● noun an internal skeleton, such as that of vertebrates. Compare with EXOSKELETON.
endosperm ● noun Botany the part of a seed which acts as a food store for the developing plant embryo.
endothelium /endōtheeliəm/ ● noun the layer of cells lining the blood vessels, heart, and other organs and cavities of the body.
– ORIGIN Latin, from Greek *thēlē* 'nipple'.
endothermic ● adjective **1** Chemistry (of a reaction) accompanied by the absorption of heat. The opposite of EXOTHERMIC. **2** Zoology (of an animal) dependent on the internal generation of heat.
endow /indow/ ● verb **1** give or bequeath an income or property to. **2** (usu. **be endowed with**) provide with a quality, ability, or asset. **3** establish (a university post, annual prize, etc.) by donating funds.
– DERIVATIVES **endower** noun.
– ORIGIN Old French *endouer,* from Latin *dotare* 'endow'.
endowment ● noun **1** the action of endowing. **2** a quality or ability with which a person is endowed. **3** an income or form of property endowed. **4** (before another noun) denoting a form of life insurance involving payment of a fixed sum to the insured person on a specified date, or to their estate should they die before this date.
endowment mortgage ● noun Brit. a mortgage linked to an endowment insurance policy which is intended to repay the capital sum on maturity.
endpaper ● noun a leaf of paper at the beginning or end of a book, fixed to the inside of the cover.
endue /indyōō/ (also **indue**) ● verb (**endues, endued, enduing**) literary (usu. **be endued with**) endow with a quality or ability.
– ORIGIN Old French *enduire,* partly from Latin *inducere* 'lead in', reinforced by the sense of Latin *induere* 'put on clothes'.
endurance ● noun **1** the fact or power of enduring something painful and prolonged. **2** the capacity of something to last or to withstand wear and tear.
endure /indyoor/ ● verb **1** suffer (something painful and prolonged) patiently. **2** tolerate. **3** remain in existence.
– DERIVATIVES **endurable** adjective.
– ORIGIN Latin *indurare* 'harden'.
enduro /indyoorō/ ● noun (pl. **enduros**) a long-distance race for motor vehicles or bicycles over rough terrain, designed to test endurance.
end-user ● noun the person who uses a particular product.
endways (also **endwise**) ● adverb **1** with its end facing upwards, forwards, or towards the viewer. **2** end to end.
ENE ● abbreviation east-north-east.
-ene ● suffix **1** denoting an inhabitant: *Nazarene.* **2** Chemistry forming names of unsaturated hydrocarbons containing a double bond: *benzene.*

e

Thesaurus

ation, discontinuation.
– OPPOSITES beginning.
endless ● adjective **1** *a woman with endless energy* UNLIMITED, limitless, infinite, inexhaustible, boundless, unbounded, untold, immeasurable, measureless, incalculable; abundant, abounding, great; ceaseless, unceasing, unending, without end, everlasting, constant, continuous, continual, interminable, unfading, unfailing, perpetual, eternal, enduring, lasting. **2** *as children we played endless games* COUNTLESS, innumerable, untold, legion, numberless, unnumbered, numerous, very many, manifold, multitudinous, multifarious; a great number of, infinite numbers of, a multitude of; *informal* umpteen, no end of, loads of, stacks of, heaps of, masses of, oodles of, scads of, zillions of; *N. Amer. informal* gazillions of; *poetic/literary* myriad, divers.
– OPPOSITES limited, few.
endorse ● verb SUPPORT, back, agree with, approve (of), favour, subscribe to, recommend, champion, stick up for, uphold, affirm, sanction; *informal* throw one's weight behind.
– OPPOSITES oppose.
endorsement ● noun SUPPORT, backing, approval, seal of approval, agreement, recommendation, championship, patronage, affirmation, sanction.
endow ● verb **1** *Henry II endowed a hospital for poor pilgrims* FINANCE, fund, pay for, subsidize, support financially, settle money on; establish, found, set up, institute. **2** *nature endowed the human race with intelligence* PROVIDE, supply, furnish, equip, invest, favour, bless, grace, gift; give, bestow; *poetic/literary* endue.
endowment ● noun **1** *the endowment of a Chair of Botany* FUNDING, financing, subsidizing; establishment, foundation, institution. **2** *a generous endowment* BEQUEST, legacy, inheritance; gift, present, grant, award, donation, contribution, subsidy, settlement; *formal* benefaction. **3** *his natural endowments* QUALITY, characteristic, feature, attribute, facility, faculty, ability, talent, gift, strength, aptitude, capability, capacity.
endurable ● adjective BEARABLE, tolerable, supportable, manageable, sustainable.
– OPPOSITES unbearable.
endurance ● noun **1** *she pushed him beyond the limit of his endurance* TOLERATION, tolerance, sufferance, forbearance, patience, acceptance, resignation, stoicism. **2** *the race is a test of endurance* STAMINA, staying power, fortitude, perseverance, persistence, tenacity, doggedness, grit, indefatigability, resolution, determination; *informal* stickability; *formal* pertinacity.
endure ● verb **1** *he endured years of pain* UNDERGO, go through, live through, experience, meet, encounter; cope with, deal with, face, suffer, tolerate, put up with, brave, bear, withstand, sustain, weather; *Scottish* thole. **2** *I cannot endure such behaviour* TOLERATE, bear, put up with, suffer, take; *informal* hack, stand for, stomach, swallow, abide, hold with; *Brit. informal* stick, wear, be doing with; *formal* brook. **3** *God's love will endure for ever* LAST, live, live on, go on, survive, abide, continue, persist, remain, stay.
– OPPOSITES fade.
enduring ● adjective LASTING, long-lasting, abiding, durable, continuing, persisting, eternal, perennial, permanent, unending,

– ORIGIN Greek *-ēnos*.

enema /ennimə/ ● **noun** (pl. **enemas** or **enemata** /inemmətə/) a procedure in which fluid is injected into the rectum, typically to expel its contents.

– ORIGIN Greek, from *enienai* 'send or put in'.

enemy ● **noun** (pl. **enemies**) **1** a person who is actively opposed or hostile to someone or something. **2** (**the enemy**) (treated as sing. or pl.) a hostile nation or its armed forces in time of war. **3** a thing that damages or opposes something: *routine is the enemy of art.*

– ORIGIN Old French *enemi*, from Latin *inimicus*, from *in-* 'not' + *amicus* 'friend'.

energetic ● **adjective 1** showing or involving great energy or activity. **2** Physics relating to energy.

– DERIVATIVES **energetically** adverb.

– ORIGIN originally meaning 'powerfully effective': from Greek *energein* 'operate, work in or upon'.

energy ● **noun** (pl. **energies**) **1** the strength and vitality required for sustained activity. **2** (**energies**) a person's physical and mental powers as applied to a particular activity. **3** power derived from physical or chemical resources to provide light and heat or to work machines. **4** Physics the property of matter and radiation which is manifest as a capacity to perform work.

– DERIVATIVES **energize** (also **energise**) verb.

– ORIGIN Greek *energeia*, from *ergon* 'work'.

enervate /ennərvayt/ ● **verb** cause to feel drained of energy.

– DERIVATIVES **enervation** noun.

– ORIGIN Latin *enervare* 'weaken (by extraction of the sinews)', from *nervus* 'sinew'.

en famille /ON fameey/ ● **adverb 1** with one's family. **2** as or like a family; informally.

– ORIGIN French, 'in family'.

enfant terrible /ONFON tereeblə/ ● **noun** (pl. **enfants terribles** pronunc. same) a person who behaves in an unconventional or controversial way.

– ORIGIN French, 'terrible child'.

enfeeble ● **verb** weaken.

– DERIVATIVES **enfeeblement** noun.

enfilade /enfilayd/ ● **noun 1** a volley of gunfire directed along a line from end to end. **2** a suite of rooms with doorways in line with each other. ● **verb** direct an enfilade at.

– ORIGIN originally denoting a military post commanding the length of a line: from French, from *enfiler* 'thread on a string'.

enfold ● **verb** surround; envelop.

enforce ● **verb 1** compel compliance with (a law, rule, or obligation). **2** cause to happen by necessity or force.

– DERIVATIVES **enforceable** adjective **enforced** adjective **enforcement** noun **enforcer** noun.

enfranchise /infranchīz/ ● **verb 1** give the right to vote to. **2** historical free (a slave).

– DERIVATIVES **enfranchisement** noun.

engage ● **verb 1** attract or involve (someone's interest or attention). **2** (**engage in/with**) participate or become involved in. **3** chiefly Brit. employ or hire. **4** enter into a contract to do. **5** enter into combat with. **6** (with reference to a part of a machine or engine) move into position so as to come into operation.

– ORIGIN originally in the sense 'pawn or pledge': from French *engager*, ultimately from GAGE[1].

engagé /ONgazhay/ ● **adjective** (of a writer or artist) morally committed to a particular cause.

– ORIGIN French.

engaged ● **adjective 1** busy; occupied. **2** Brit. (of a telephone line) unavailable because already in use. **3** having formally agreed to marry.

engagement ● **noun 1** a formal agreement to get married. **2** an appointment. **3** the action of engaging or being engaged. **4** a fight or battle between armed forces.

Thesaurus

everlasting; constant, stable, steady, steadfast, fixed, firm, unwavering, unfaltering, unchanging.

– OPPOSITES short-lived.

enemy ● **noun** OPPONENT, adversary, rival, antagonist, combatant, challenger, competitor, opposer, opposition, competition, other side; *poetic/literary* foe.

– OPPOSITES ally.

energetic ● **adjective 1** *an energetic woman* ACTIVE, lively, dynamic, zestful, spirited, animated, vital, vibrant, bouncy, bubbly, exuberant, perky, frisky, sprightly, tireless, indefatigable, enthusiastic; *informal* peppy, sparky, feisty, full of beans, full of the joys of spring, bright-eyed and bushy-tailed. **2** *energetic exercises* VIGOROUS, strenuous, brisk; hard, arduous, demanding, taxing, tough, rigorous. **3** *an energetic advertising campaign* FORCEFUL, vigorous, high-powered, all-out, determined, bold, powerful, potent; intensive, hard-hitting, pulling no punches, aggressive, high-octane; *informal* punchy, in-your-face.

– OPPOSITES lethargic, gentle, half-hearted.

energize ● **verb 1** *people are energized by his ideas* ENLIVEN, liven up, animate, vitalize, invigorate, perk up, excite, electrify, stimulate, stir up, fire up, rouse, motivate, move, drive, spur on, encourage, galvanize; *informal* pep up, buck up, give a shot in the arm to. **2** *floor sensors energized by standing passengers* ACTIVATE, trigger, trip, operate, actuate, switch on, turn on, start, start up, power.

energy ● **noun** VITALITY, vigour, life, liveliness, animation, vivacity, spirit, spiritedness, verve, enthusiasm, zest, vibrancy, spark, sparkle, effervescence, exuberance, buoyancy, sprightliness; strength, stamina, forcefulness, power, dynamism, drive; fire, passion, ardour, zeal; *informal* zip, zing, pep, pizzazz, punch, bounce, oomph, go, get-up-and-go, vim and vigour; *N. Amer. informal* feistiness.

enervate ● **verb** EXHAUST, tire, fatigue, weary, wear out, devitalize, drain, sap, weaken, enfeeble, debilitate, incapacitate, prostrate; *informal* knock out, do in, shatter, fag out; *Brit. informal* knacker.

– OPPOSITES invigorate.

enervation ● **noun** FATIGUE, exhaustion, tiredness, weariness, lassitude, weakness, feebleness, debilitation, indisposition, prostration.

enfeeble ● **verb** WEAKEN, debilitate, incapacitate, indispose, lay low; drain, sap, exhaust, tire, fatigue, devitalize.

– OPPOSITES strengthen.

enfold ● **verb 1** *the summit was enfolded in white cloud* ENVELOP, engulf, sheathe, swathe, swaddle, cocoon, shroud, veil, cloak, drape, cover; surround, enclose, encase, encircle; *poetic/literary* enshroud, mantle. **2** *he enfolded her in his arms* CLASP, hold, fold, wrap, squeeze, clutch, gather; embrace, hug, cuddle; *poetic/literary* embosom.

enforce ● **verb 1** *the sheriff enforced the law* IMPOSE, apply, administer, implement, bring to bear, discharge, execute, prosecute. **2** *they cannot enforce cooperation between the parties* FORCE, compel, coerce, exact, extort; *archaic* constrain.

enforced ● **adjective** COMPULSORY, obligatory, mandatory, involuntary, forced, imposed, required, requisite, stipulated, prescribed, contractual, binding, necessary, unavoidable, inescapable.

– OPPOSITES voluntary.

enfranchise ● **verb 1** *women over thirty were enfranchised in 1918* GIVE THE VOTE TO, give/grant suffrage to. **2** (*historical*) *he enfranchised his slaves* EMANCIPATE, liberate, free, set free, release; unchain, unyoke, unfetter, unshackle; *historical* manumit.

engage ● **verb 1** *tasks which engage children's interest* CAPTURE, catch, arrest, grab, draw, attract, gain, win, hold, grip, captivate, engross, absorb, occupy. **2** *he engaged a nursemaid* EMPLOY, hire, recruit, take on, secure the services of, put on the payroll, enrol, appoint. **3** (*dated*) *she engaged a room in the boarding house* BOOK, reserve; rent, hire; *formal* bespeak. **4** *he engaged to pay them £10,000* CONTRACT, promise, agree, pledge, vow, covenant, commit oneself, bind oneself, undertake, enter into an agreement. **5** *the chance to engage in many social activities* PARTICIPATE IN, take part in, join in, become involved in, go in for, partake in/of, share in, play a part/role in; have a hand in, be a party to, enter into. **6** *infantry units engaged the enemy* FIGHT, do battle with, wage war on/against, attack, take on, set upon, clash with, skirmish with; encounter, meet.

– OPPOSITES lose, dismiss.

engaged ● **adjective 1** *he's otherwise engaged* BUSY, occupied, unavailable; *informal* tied up. **2** *she's engaged to an American guy* promised/pledged in marriage; attached; *informal* spoken for; *dated* betrothed; *poetic/literary* affianced; *archaic* plighted, espoused.

– OPPOSITES free, unattached.

engagement ● **noun 1** *they broke off their engagement* MARRIAGE CONTRACT; *dated* betrothal; *archaic* espousal. **2** *a business engagement* APPOINTMENT, meeting, arrangement, commitment; date, assignation, rendezvous; *poetic/literary* tryst. **3** *Britain's continued engagement in open trading* PARTICIPATION, involvement, association. **4** *his engagement as a curate* EMPLOYMENT, appointment; work, job, post,

engaging ● adjective charming and attractive.
– DERIVATIVES **engagingly** adverb.

engender /injendər/ ● verb give rise to.
– ORIGIN Old French *engendrer*, from Latin *generare* 'beget'.

engine ● noun **1** a machine with moving parts that converts power into motion. **2** (also **railway engine**) a locomotive. **3** historical a mechanical device or instrument, especially one used in warfare: *a siege engine.*
– DERIVATIVES **-engined** adjective **engineless** adjective.
– ORIGIN originally in the sense 'ingenuity, cunning': from Latin *ingenium* 'talent, device', from *gignere* 'beget'.

engineer ● noun **1** a person qualified in engineering. **2** a person who maintains or controls an engine or machine. **3** a person who skilfully originates something. ● verb **1** design and build. **2** contrive to bring about.

engineering ● noun the branch of science and technology concerned with the design, building, and use of engines, machines, and structures.

English ● noun the language of England, now used in many varieties throughout the world. ● adjective relating to England.
– DERIVATIVES **Englishness** noun.
– ORIGIN Old English, related to ANGLE.

English breakfast ● noun a substantial cooked breakfast, typically including bacon and eggs.

Englishman (or **Englishwoman**) ● noun a person from England.
– PHRASES **an Englishman's home is his castle** Brit. proverb an English person's home is a place where they may do as they please.

English muffin ● noun North American term for MUFFIN (in sense 1).

English rose ● noun an attractive English girl with a delicate, fair-skinned complexion.

engorge /ingorj/ ● verb (often **be engorged**) swell or cause to swell with blood, water, etc.
– DERIVATIVES **engorgement** noun.
– ORIGIN originally in the sense 'gorge oneself': from Old French *engorgier* 'feed to excess'.

engraft (also **ingraft**) ● verb another term for GRAFT[1].
– DERIVATIVES **engraftment** noun.

engrain ● verb variant spelling of INGRAIN.

engrained ● adjective variant spelling of INGRAINED.

engrave ● verb **1** cut or carve (a text or design) on a hard surface. **2** cut or carve a text or design on. **3** (**be engraved on** or **in**) be permanently fixed in (one's mind).
– DERIVATIVES **engraver** noun.
– ORIGIN from EN-[1] + GRAVE[3].

engraving ● noun **1** a print made from an engraved plate, block, or other surface. **2** the process or art of cutting or carving a design on a hard surface, especially so as to make a print.

engross /ingrōss/ ● verb **1** (often **be engrossed in**) absorb all the attention of. **2** Law produce (a legal document) in its final or definitive form.
– ORIGIN sense 1 is from Latin *in grosso* 'wholesale'; sense 2 is from Latin *ingrossare* 'write in large letters'.

engrossment ● noun Law the final version of a legal document, eventually becoming the original deed.

engulf ● verb (of a natural force) sweep over so as to completely surround or cover.
– DERIVATIVES **engulfment** noun.

enhance /inhaans/ ● verb increase the quality, value, or extent of.
– DERIVATIVES **enhancement** noun **enhancer** noun.
– ORIGIN originally in the sense 'elevate': from Old French *enhauncer*, from Latin *altus* 'high'.

enharmonic /enhaarmonnik/ ● adjective Music **1** relating to notes which are the same in pitch though bearing different names (e.g. F sharp and G flat). **2** of or having intervals smaller than a semitone.

enigma /inigmə/ ● noun a mysterious or puzzling person or thing.
– DERIVATIVES **enigmatic** adjective **enigmatical** adjective **enigmatically** adverb.
– ORIGIN Greek *ainigma* 'riddle'.

enjoin ● verb **1** instruct or urge to do. **2** (**enjoin from**) Law prohibit (someone) from performing (an action) by an injunction.
– ORIGIN Old French *enjoindre*, from Latin *injungere* 'join, attach, impose'.

enjoy ● verb **1** take pleasure in. **2** (**enjoy oneself**) have a pleasant time. **3** possess and benefit from: *these professions enjoy high status.*
– DERIVATIVES **enjoyment** noun.
– ORIGIN Old French *enjoier* 'give joy to' or *enjoïr* 'enjoy'.

enjoyable ● adjective giving delight or pleasure.

Thesaurus

situation. **5** *the first engagement of the war* BATTLE, fight, clash, confrontation, encounter, conflict, skirmish; warfare, action, combat, hostilities; *informal* dogfight.

engaging ● adjective CHARMING, appealing, attractive, pretty, delightful, lovely, pleasing, pleasant, agreeable, likeable, lovable, sweet, winning, winsome, fetching, captivating, enchanting, bewitching; *Scottish & N. English* bonny; *dated* taking; *archaic* comely, fair.
– OPPOSITES unappealing.

engender ● verb **1** *his works engendered considerable controversy* CAUSE, be the cause of, give rise to, bring about, occasion, lead to, result in, produce, create, generate, arouse, rouse, inspire, provoke, kindle, trigger, spark, stir up, whip up, induce, incite, instigate, foment; *poetic/literary* beget, enkindle. **2** *(archaic) he engendered six children* FATHER, sire, bring into the world, spawn, breed; *poetic/literary* beget.

engine ● noun **1** *a car engine* MOTOR, machine, mechanism. **2** *the main engine of change* CAUSE, agent, instrument, originator, initiator, generator. **3** *(historical) engines of war* DEVICE, contraption, apparatus, machine, appliance, mechanism, implement, instrument, tool.

engineer ● noun **1** *a structural engineer* designer, planner, builder. **2** *the ship's engineer* OPERATOR, driver, controller. **3** *the prime engineer of the approach* ORIGINATOR, deviser, designer, architect, inventor, developer, creator; mastermind.
● verb *he engineered a takeover deal* BRING ABOUT, arrange, pull off, bring off, contrive, manoeuvre, manipulate, negotiate, organize, orchestrate, choreograph, mount, stage, mastermind, originate, manage, stage-manage, coordinate, control, superintend, direct, conduct; *informal* wangle.

England ● noun *Brit. informal* Blighty; *Austral./NZ informal* Old Dart; *poetic/literary* Albion.

engrained ● adjective. See INGRAINED.

engrave ● verb **1** *my name was engraved on the ring* CARVE, inscribe, cut (in), incise, chisel, chase, score, notch, etch, imprint, impress. **2** *the image was engraved in his memory* FIX, set, imprint, stamp, brand, impress, embed, etch.

engraving ● noun ETCHING, print, impression, lithograph; plate, dry point, woodcut, linocut.

engross ● verb ABSORB, engage, rivet, grip, hold, interest, involve, occupy, preoccupy; fascinate, captivate, enthral, intrigue.

engrossed ● adjective ABSORBED, involved, interested, occupied, preoccupied, immersed, caught up, riveted, gripped, rapt, fascinated, intent, captivated, enthralled, intrigued.

engrossing ● adjective ABSORBING, interesting, riveting, gripping, captivating, compelling, compulsive, fascinating, intriguing, enthralling; *informal* unputdownable.

engulf ● verb INUNDATE, flood, deluge, immerse, swamp, swallow up, submerge; bury, envelop, overwhelm.

enhance ● verb INCREASE, add to, intensify, heighten, magnify, amplify, inflate, strengthen, build up, supplement, augment, boost, raise, lift, elevate, exalt; improve, enrich, complement.
– OPPOSITES diminish.

enigma ● noun MYSTERY, puzzle, riddle, conundrum, paradox, problem; a closed book; *informal* poser.

enigmatic ● adjective MYSTERIOUS, inscrutable, puzzling, mystifying, baffling, perplexing, impenetrable, unfathomable, sphinxlike, Delphic, oracular; cryptic, elliptical, ambiguous, equivocal, paradoxical, obscure, oblique, secret.

enjoin ● verb URGE, encourage, admonish, press; instruct, direct, require, order, command, tell, call on, demand, charge; *formal* adjure; *poetic/literary* bid.

enjoy ● verb **1** *he enjoys playing the piano* LIKE, love, be fond of, be entertained by, take pleasure in, be keen on, delight in, appreciate, relish, revel in, adore, lap up, savour, luxuriate in, bask in; *informal* get a kick out of, get a thrill out of, get a buzz out of, go a bundle on. **2** *she had always enjoyed good health* BENEFIT FROM, have the benefit of; be blessed with, be favoured with, be endowed with, be possessed of, possess, own, boast.
– OPPOSITES dislike, lack.

– DERIVATIVES **enjoyability** noun **enjoyably** adverb.

enlarge • verb **1** make or become bigger. **2** (**enlarge on/upon**) speak or write about in greater detail.

– DERIVATIVES **enlarger** noun.

enlargement • noun **1** the action of enlarging or the state of being enlarged. **2** a photograph that is larger than the original negative or than an earlier print.

enlighten • verb **1** give greater knowledge and understanding to. **2** (**enlightened**) rational, tolerant, and well-informed.

enlightenment • noun **1** the action of enlightening or the state of being enlightened. **2** (**the Enlightenment**) a European intellectual movement of the late 17th and 18th centuries emphasizing reason and individualism rather than tradition.

e

enlist • verb **1** enrol or be enrolled in the armed services. **2** engage (a person or their help).

– DERIVATIVES **enlistment** noun.

enlisted man • noun US a member of the armed forces below the rank of officer.

enliven • verb **1** make more interesting or appealing. **2** make more cheerful or animated.

en masse /ON mass/ • adverb all together.

– ORIGIN French, 'in a mass'.

enmesh • verb (usu. **be enmeshed in**) entangle.

– DERIVATIVES **enmeshment** noun.

enmity • noun (pl. **enmities**) the state of being an enemy; hostility.

– ORIGIN Old French *enemistie*, from Latin *inimicus* 'enemy'.

ennoble • verb **1** give a noble rank or title to. **2** give greater dignity to; elevate.

– DERIVATIVES **ennoblement** noun.

ennui /onwee/ • noun listlessness and dissatisfaction arising from boredom.

– ORIGIN French, from the same Latin base as ANNOY.

enology • noun US spelling of OENOLOGY.

enormity • noun (pl. **enormities**) **1** (**the enormity of**) the extreme seriousness or extent of (something bad). **2** great size or scale: *the enormity of Einstein's intellect.* **3** a grave crime or sin.

– USAGE **Enormity** is not related to **enormous** and originally meant 'a crime or deviation from morality'. For this reason some people object to its use in modern English as a synonym for *hugeness.*

– ORIGIN Latin *enormitas*, from *norma* 'pattern, standard'.

enormous • adjective very large.

– DERIVATIVES **enormously** adverb **enormousness** noun.

enough • determiner & pronoun as much or as many as is necessary or desirable. • adverb **1** to the required degree or extent. **2** to a moderate degree.

– PHRASES **enough is as good as a feast** proverb moderation is more satisfying than excess. **enough is enough** no more will be tolerated. **enough said** all is understood and there is no need to say more.

– ORIGIN Old English.

en passant /ON pasON/ • adverb by the way.

– ORIGIN French, 'in passing'.

enquire • verb **1** ask for information. **2** (**enquire after**) ask about the health and well-being of. **3** (**enquire into**) investigate.

Thesaurus

– PHRASES **enjoy oneself** HAVE FUN, have a good time, have the time of one's life; make merry, celebrate, revel; *informal* party, have a ball, have a whale of a time, whoop it up, let one's hair down.

enjoyable • adjective ENTERTAINING, amusing, diverting, delightful, to one's liking, pleasant, congenial, convivial, lovely, fine, good, great, agreeable, pleasurable, delicious, delectable, satisfying, gratifying; marvellous, wonderful, magnificent, splendid; *informal* super, fantastic, fabulous, fab, terrific, grand, magic; *Brit. informal* brilliant, brill, smashing.

enjoyment • noun PLEASURE, fun, entertainment, amusement, diversion, recreation, relaxation; delight, happiness, merriment, joy, gaiety, jollity; satisfaction, gratification, liking, relish, gusto; *humorous* delectation; *dated* sport.

enlarge • verb **1** *they enlarged the scope of their research* EXTEND, expand, grow, add to, amplify, augment, magnify, build up, supplement; widen, broaden, stretch, lengthen; elongate, deepen, thicken. **2** *the lymph glands had enlarged* SWELL, distend, bloat, bulge, dilate, tumefy, blow up, puff up, balloon. **3** *he enlarged on this subject* ELABORATE ON, expand on, add to, build on, flesh out, put flesh on the bones of, add detail to, expatiate on; develop, fill out, embellish, embroider.

– OPPOSITES reduce, shrink.

enlargement • noun EXPANSION, extension, growth, amplification, augmentation, addition, magnification, widening, broadening, lengthening; elongation, deepening, thickening; swelling, distension, dilation, tumefaction.

enlighten • verb INFORM, tell, make aware, open someone's eyes, notify, illuminate, apprise, brief, update, bring up to date; disabuse, set straight; *informal* put in the picture, clue in, fill in, put wise, bring up to speed.

enlightened • adjective INFORMED, well informed, aware, sophisticated, advanced, developed, liberal, open-minded, broad-minded, educated, knowledgeable, wise; civilized, refined, cultured, cultivated.

– OPPOSITES benighted.

enlightenment • noun INSIGHT, understanding, awareness, wisdom, education, learning, knowledge; illumination, awakening, instruction, teaching; sophistication, advancement, development, open-mindedness, broad-mindedness; culture, refinement, cultivation, civilization.

enlist • verb **1** *he enlisted in the Royal Engineers* JOIN UP, join, enrol in, sign up for, volunteer for; *Brit. archaic* take the King's shilling. **2** *he was enlisted in the army* RECRUIT, call up, enrol, sign up; conscript; *US* draft, induct; *archaic* levy. **3** *he enlisted the help of a friend* OBTAIN, engage, secure, win, get, procure.

enliven • verb **1** *a meeting enlivened by her wit and vivacity* LIVEN UP, spice up, add spice to, ginger up, vitalize, leaven; *informal* perk up, pep up. **2** *the visit had enlivened my mother* CHEER UP, brighten up, liven up, raise someone's spirits, uplift, gladden, buoy up, animate, vivify, vitalize, invigorate, restore, revive, refresh, stimulate, rouse, boost, exhilarate; *N. Amer.* light a fire under; *informal* perk up, buck up, pep up.

en masse • adverb (ALL) TOGETHER, as a group, as one, en bloc, as a whole, in a body, wholesale.

enmesh • verb EMBROIL, entangle, ensnare, snare, trap, entrap, ensnarl, involve, catch up, mix up, bog down, mire.

enmity • noun HOSTILITY, animosity, antagonism, friction, antipathy, animus, acrimony, bitterness, rancour, resentment, aversion, ill feeling, bad feeling, ill will, bad blood, hatred, hate, loathing, odium; malice, spite, spitefulness, venom, malevolence; *Brit. informal* needle.

– OPPOSITES friendship.

ennoble • verb DIGNIFY, honour, exalt, elevate, raise, enhance, add dignity to, distinguish; magnify, glorify, aggrandize.

– OPPOSITES demean.

ennui • noun BOREDOM, tedium, listlessness, lethargy, lassitude, languor, weariness, enervation; malaise, dissatisfaction, melancholy, world-weariness, depression, Weltschmerz.

enormity • noun **1** *the enormity of the task* IMMENSITY, hugeness; size, extent, magnitude, greatness. **2** *the enormity of his crimes* WICKEDNESS, evil, vileness, baseness, depravity; outrageousness, monstrousness, hideousness, heinousness, horror, atrocity; villainy, cruelty, inhumanity, mercilessness, brutality, savagery, viciousness. **3** *the enormities of the regime* OUTRAGE, horror, evil, atrocity, barbarity, abomination, monstrosity, obscenity, iniquity; crime, sin, violation, wrong, offence, disgrace, injustice, abuse.

enormous • adjective HUGE, vast, immense, gigantic, very big, great, giant, massive, colossal, mammoth, tremendous, mighty, monumental, epic, prodigious, mountainous, titanic, towering, elephantine, king-size(d), gargantuan; *informal* mega, monster, whopping (great), humongous, jumbo, astronomical; *Brit. informal* whacking (great), ginormous.

– OPPOSITES tiny.

enormously • adverb **1** *an enormously important factor* VERY, extremely, really, exceedingly, exceptionally, tremendously, immensely, hugely; singularly, particularly, eminently; *informal* terrifically, awfully, terribly, seriously, desperately, ultra, damn, damned; *Brit. informal* ever so, well, dead, jolly; *N. Amer. informal* real, mighty, darned; *informal, dated* frightfully. **2** *prices vary enormously* CONSIDERABLY, greatly, very much, a great deal, a lot.

– OPPOSITES slightly.

enough • determiner *they had enough food* SUFFICIENT, adequate, ample, the necessary; *informal* plenty of.

– OPPOSITES insufficient.

• pronoun *there's enough for everyone* SUFFICIENT, plenty, a sufficient amount, an adequate amount, as much as necessary; a sufficiency, an ample supply; one's fill.

– DERIVATIVES **enquirer** noun **enquiring** adjective.
– ORIGIN Latin *inquirere*, from *quaerere* 'seek'.
enquiry ● noun (pl. **enquiries**) **1** an act of asking for information. **2** an official investigation.
enrage ● verb make very angry.
– DERIVATIVES **enraged** adjective.
enrapture ● verb give intense pleasure to.
– DERIVATIVES **enrapt** adjective.
enrich ● verb **1** improve the quality or value of. **2** make wealthy or wealthier.
– DERIVATIVES **enrichment** noun.
enriched uranium ● noun uranium containing an increased proportion of the fissile isotope U-235.
enrobe ● verb formal dress in a robe or vestment.
enrol /inrōl/ (US **enroll**) ● verb (**enrolled**, **enrolling**) officially register or recruit as a member or student.
– ORIGIN Old French *enroller*, from *rolle* 'a roll': names were originally written on a roll of parchment.
enrolment (US **enrollment**) ● noun **1** the action of enrolling or being enrolled. **2** N. Amer. the number of people enrolled at a school or college.
en route /on ro͞ot/ ● adverb on the way.
– ORIGIN French.
en rule ● noun Brit. a short dash, the width of an en, used in punctuation.
ensconce /inskonss/ ● verb establish in a comfortable, safe, or secret place.
– ORIGIN originally in the senses 'fortify' and 'shelter with a fortification': from archaic *sconce*, denoting a small fort or earthwork, from High German *schanze* 'brushwood'.
ensemble /onsomb'l/ ● noun **1** a group of musicians, actors, or dancers who perform together. **2** a passage for a whole choir or group of instruments. **3** a group of items viewed as a whole, in particular a set of clothes worn together.
– ORIGIN French, from Latin *simul* 'at the same time'.
enshrine ● verb **1** place (a revered or precious object) in an appropriate receptacle. **2** preserve (a right, tradition, or idea) in a form that ensures it will be respected.
– DERIVATIVES **enshrinement** noun.
enshroud /inshrowd/ ● verb literary envelop completely and hide from view.
ensign /ensīn/ ● noun **1** a flag, especially a military or naval one indicating nationality. **2** the lowest rank of commissioned officer in the US and some other navies, above chief warrant officer and below lieutenant. **3** historical a standard-bearer.
– ORIGIN Old French *enseigne*, from Latin *insignia* (see INSIGNIA).
enslave ● verb **1** make (someone) a slave. **2** cause (someone) to lose freedom of choice or action.
– DERIVATIVES **enslavement** noun **enslaver** noun.
ensnare ● verb catch in or as in a trap.
– DERIVATIVES **ensnarement** noun.
ensue ● verb (**ensues**, **ensued**, **ensuing**) happen or occur afterwards or as a result.
– ORIGIN Old French *ensivre*, from Latin *sequi* 'follow'.
en suite /on sweet/ ● adjective & adverb Brit. (of a bathroom) immediately adjoining a bedroom and forming a single unit.
– ORIGIN French, 'in sequence'.
ensure /inshoor/ ● verb **1** make certain that (something) will occur or be so. **2** (**ensure against**) make sure that (a problem) does not occur.
– ORIGIN Old French *enseurer*, earlier form of *assurer* 'assure'.
ENT ● abbreviation ear, nose, and throat (as a department in a hospital).
-ent ● suffix **1** (forming adjectives) denoting a state or an occurrence of action: *convenient*. **2** (forming nouns) denoting an agent: *coefficient*.
– ORIGIN Latin.
entablature /intablәchәr/ ● noun Architecture the upper part of a classical building supported by columns or a colonnade, comprising the architrave, frieze, and cornice.
– ORIGIN Italian *intavolatura* 'boarding'.
entail ● verb **1** involve (something) as an inevitable part or consequence. **2** Law settle the inheritance of (property) over a number of generations so that it remains within a family. ● noun Law an instance of entailing property.
– DERIVATIVES **entailment** noun.
– ORIGIN from Old French *taille* (see TAIL[2]).
entangle ● verb (usu. **be entangled in/with**) **1** cause to become tangled. **2** involve in complicated circumstances.
– DERIVATIVES **entanglement** noun.

e

Thesaurus

en passant ● adverb IN PASSING, incidentally, by the way, parenthetically, while on the subject, apropos.
enquire, inquire ● verb **1** *I enquired about part-time training courses* ASK, make enquiries, question someone, request information. **2** *the commission is to enquire into alleged illegal payments* INVESTIGATE, conduct an enquiry, probe, look into; research, examine, explore, delve into; *informal* check out.
enquiring, inquiring ● adjective INQUISITIVE, curious, interested, questioning, probing, searching; investigative.
enquiry, inquiry ● noun **1** *telephone enquiries* QUESTION, query. **2** *an enquiry into alleged security leaks* INVESTIGATION, probe, examination, exploration; inquest, hearing.
enrage ● verb ANGER, infuriate, incense, madden, inflame; antagonize, provoke, exasperate; *informal* drive mad/crazy, drive up the wall, make someone see red, make someone's blood boil, make someone's hackles rise, get someone's back up, get someone's dander up; *N. Amer. informal* burn up.
– OPPOSITES placate.
enraged ● adjective FURIOUS, infuriated, very angry, irate, incensed, raging, incandescent, fuming, ranting, raving, seething, beside oneself; *informal* mad, hopping mad, wild, livid, boiling, apoplectic, hot under the collar, foaming at the mouth, steamed up, in a paddy, fit to be tied; *poetic/literary* wrathful.
– OPPOSITES calm.
enrapture ● verb DELIGHT, enchant, captivate, charm, enthral, entrance, bewitch, beguile, transport, thrill, excite, exhilarate, intoxicate, take someone's breath away; *informal* bowl someone over, blow someone's mind; *poetic/literary* ravish.
enrich ● verb ENHANCE, improve, better, add to, augment; supplement, complement; boost, elevate, raise, lift, refine.
– OPPOSITES spoil.
enrol ● verb **1** *they both enrolled for the course* REGISTER, sign on/up, put one's name down, apply, volunteer; matriculate; enter, join. **2** *280 new members were enrolled* ACCEPT, admit, take on, register, sign on/up, recruit, engage; matriculate; impanel.
en route ● adverb ON THE WAY, in transit, during the journey, along/on the road, on the move; coming, going, proceeding, travelling.
ensconce ● verb *she ensconced herself in a huge leather armchair* SETTLE, install, plant, position, seat, sit, sit down; establish; *informal* park, plonk.
ensemble ● noun **1** *a Bulgarian folk ensemble* GROUP, band; company, troupe, cast, chorus, corps; *informal* combo. **2** *the buildings present a charming provincial ensemble* WHOLE, entity, unit, body, set, combination, composite, package; sum, total, totality, entirety, aggregate. **3** *a pink and black ensemble* OUTFIT, costume, suit; separates, coordinates; *informal* get-up.
enshrine ● verb *the following rights should be enshrined in the treaty* SET DOWN, set out, spell out, express, lay down, set in stone, embody, realize, manifest, incorporate, represent, contain, include, preserve, treasure, immortalize, cherish.
enshroud ● verb (*poetic/literary*) ENVELOP, shroud, swathe, veil, cloak, cloud, enfold, surround, bury; cover, conceal, obscure, blot out, hide, mask; *poetic/literary* mantle.
ensign ● noun FLAG, standard, colour(s), banner, pennant, pennon, streamer, banderole.
enslavement ● noun SLAVERY, servitude, bondage, forced labour; exploitation, oppression, bonds, chains, fetters, shackles, yoke; *historical* thraldom.
– OPPOSITES liberation.
ensnare ● verb CAPTURE, catch, trap, entrap, snare, net; entangle, embroil, enmesh.
ensue ● verb RESULT, follow, be consequent on, develop, proceed, succeed, emerge, stem, arise, derive, issue; occur, happen, take place, come next/after, transpire, supervene; *formal* eventuate; *poetic/literary* come to pass, befall.
ensure ● verb **1** *ensure that the surface is completely clean* MAKE SURE, make certain, see to it; check, confirm, establish, verify. **2** *legislation to ensure equal opportunities for all* SECURE, guarantee, assure, certify, set the seal on, clinch.
entail ● verb INVOLVE, necessitate, require, need, demand, call for; mean, imply; cause, produce, result in, lead to, give rise to, occasion.
entangle ● verb **1** *their parachutes became entangled* TWIST, inter-

entente /ONTONT kordiaal/ (also **entente cordiale**) ● noun a friendly understanding or informal alliance between states or factions.
– ORIGIN from French *entente cordiale* 'friendly understanding'.
enter ● verb **1** come or go into. **2** (often **enter into/on/upon**) begin to be involved in or do. **3** join (an institution or profession). **4** register as a competitor or participant in. **5** (**enter into**) undertake to bind oneself by (an agreement) **6** record (information) in a book, computer, etc.
– ORIGIN Old French *entrer*, from Latin *intra* 'within'.
enteric /enterrik/ ● adjective relating to or occurring in the intestines.
– ORIGIN Greek *enterikos*, from *enteron* 'intestine'.
enteric fever ● noun typhoid or paratyphoid.
enteritis /entərītiss/ ● noun Medicine inflammation of the intestine, especially the small intestine, usually accompanied by diarrhoea.
enterprise ● noun **1** a project or undertaking, especially a bold one. **2** bold resourcefulness. **3** a business or company.
– ORIGIN Old French, 'something undertaken', from Latin *prehendere* 'to take'.
enterprising ● adjective showing initiative and resourcefulness.
– DERIVATIVES **enterprisingly** adverb.
entertain ● verb **1** provide with amusement or enjoyment. **2** show hospitality to. **3** give attention or consideration to.
– ORIGIN originally in the sense 'maintain, continue': from French *entretenir*, from Latin *tenere* 'to hold'.
entertainer ● noun a person, such as a singer or comedian, whose job is to entertain others.
entertaining ● adjective providing amusement or enjoyment.
– DERIVATIVES **entertainingly** adverb.
entertainment ● noun **1** the action of entertaining or being entertained. **2** an event, performance, or activity designed to entertain others.
enthral /inthrawl/ (US **enthrall**) ● verb (**enthralled, enthralling**) **1** fascinate (someone) and hold their attention. **2** (also **inthrall**) archaic enslave.
– DERIVATIVES **enthralment** (US **enthrallment**) noun.
enthrone ● verb ceremonially install (a monarch or bishop) on a throne.
– DERIVATIVES **enthronement** noun.
enthuse /inthyo͞oz/ ● verb **1** (often **enthuse over**) express one's great enthusiasm for something. **2** make enthusiastic.
enthusiasm ● noun **1** intense enjoyment, interest, or approval. **2** an object of such feelings. **3** archaic, derogatory religious fervour supposedly resulting directly from divine inspiration.
– ORIGIN Greek *enthousiasmos*, from *enthous* 'possessed by a god'.
enthusiast ● noun **1** a person who is full of enthusiasm for something. **2** archaic, derogatory a person with intense and visionary Christian views.
enthusiastic ● adjective having or showing great enthusiasm.
– DERIVATIVES **enthusiastically** adverb.
entice /intīss/ ● verb attract by offering pleasure or advantage.
– DERIVATIVES **enticement** noun **enticer** noun **enticing** adjective.
– ORIGIN Old French *enticier*, probably from a base meaning 'set on fire'.
entire /intīr/ ● adjective **1** with no part left out; whole. **2** not broken, damaged, or decayed. **3** without qualification; absolute.
– ORIGIN Old French *entier*, from Latin *integer* 'untouched, whole'.

Thesaurus

twine, entwine, tangle, ravel, snarl, knot, coil, mat. **2** *the fish are easily entangled in fine nets* CATCH, capture, trap, snare, ensnare, entrap, enmesh. **3** *he was entangled in a lawsuit* INVOLVE, implicate, embroil, mix up, catch up, bog down, mire.
entanglement ● noun **1** *their entanglement in the war* INVOLVEMENT, embroilment. **2** *romantic entanglements* AFFAIR, relationship, love affair, romance, amour, fling, dalliance, liaison, involvement, intrigue; complication.
entente ● noun UNDERSTANDING, agreement, arrangement, entente cordiale, settlement, deal; alliance, treaty, pact, accord, convention, concordat.
enter ● verb **1** *police entered the house* GO IN/INTO, come in/into, get in/into, set foot in, cross the threshold of, gain access to. **2** *a bullet entered his chest* PENETRATE, pierce, puncture, perforate; *poetic/literary* transpierce. **3** *he entered politics in 1979* GET INVOLVED IN, join, throw oneself into, engage in, embark on, take up; participate in, take part in, play a part/role in, contribute to. **4** *the planning entered a new phase* REACH, move into, get to, begin, start, commence. **5** *they entered the Army at eighteen* JOIN, become a member of, enrol in/for, enlist in, volunteer for, sign up for; take up. **6** *she entered a cookery competition* GO IN FOR, put one's name down for, register for, enrol for, sign on/up for; compete in, take part in, participate in. **7** *the cashier entered the details in a ledger* RECORD, write, set down, put down, take down, note, jot down; put on record, minute, register, log. **8** *please enter your password* KEY (IN), type (in), tap in. **9** *(Law) he entered a plea of guilty* SUBMIT, register, lodge, record, file, put forward, present.
– OPPOSITES leave.
enterprise ● noun **1** *a joint enterprise* UNDERTAKING, endeavour, venture, exercise, activity, operation, task, business, proceeding; project, scheme, plan, programme, campaign. **2** *a woman with enterprise* INITIATIVE, resourcefulness, entrepreneurialism, imagination, ingenuity, inventiveness, originality, creativity; quick-wittedness, native wit, cleverness; enthusiasm, dynamism, drive, ambition, energy; boldness, daring, courage; *informal* gumption, get-up-and-go, oomph. **3** *a profit-making enterprise* BUSINESS, company, firm, venture, organization, operation, concern, corporation, establishment, partnership; *informal* outfit, set-up.
enterprising ● adjective RESOURCEFUL, entrepreneurial, imaginative, ingenious, inventive, creative; quick-witted, clever, bright, sharp, sharp-witted; enthusiastic, dynamic, ambitious, energetic; bold, daring, courageous, adventurous; *informal* go-ahead.
– OPPOSITES unimaginative.
entertain ● verb **1** *he wrote stories to entertain them* AMUSE, divert, delight, please, charm, cheer, interest; engage, occupy, absorb, engross. **2** *he entertains foreign visitors* RECEIVE, play host/hostess to, invite (round/over), throw a party for; wine and dine, feast, cater for, feed, treat, welcome, fête. **3** *we don't entertain much* RECEIVE GUESTS, have people round/over, have company, hold/throw a party. **4** *I would never entertain such an idea* CONSIDER, give consideration to, contemplate, think about, give thought to; countenance, tolerate, support; *formal* brook.
– OPPOSITES bore, reject.
entertainer ● noun PERFORMER, artiste, artist.
entertaining ● adjective DELIGHTFUL, enjoyable, diverting, amusing, pleasing, agreeable, appealing, engaging, interesting, fascinating, absorbing, compelling; humorous, funny, comical; *informal* fun.
entertainment ● noun **1** *he read for entertainment* AMUSEMENT, pleasure, leisure, recreation, relaxation, fun, enjoyment, interest, diversion; *N. Amer. informal* rec. **2** *an entertainment for the emperor* SHOW, performance, presentation, production, spectacle, extravaganza.
enthral ● verb CAPTIVATE, charm, enchant, bewitch, fascinate, beguile, entrance, delight; win, ensnare, absorb, engross, rivet, grip, transfix, hypnotize, mesmerize, spellbind.
– OPPOSITES bore.
enthralling ● adjective FASCINATING, entrancing, enchanting, bewitching, captivating, charming, beguiling, delightful; absorbing, engrossing, compelling, riveting, gripping, exciting, spellbinding; *informal* unputdownable.
enthuse ● verb **1** *I enthused about the idea* RAVE, be enthusiastic, gush, wax lyrical, be effusive, get all worked up, rhapsodize; praise to the skies; *informal* go wild/mad/crazy; *N. Amer. informal* ballyhoo. **2** *he enthuses people* MOTIVATE, inspire, stimulate, encourage, spur (on), galvanize, rouse, excite, stir (up), fire, inspirit.
enthusiasm ● noun **1** *she worked with enthusiasm* EAGERNESS, keenness, ardour, fervour, passion, zeal, zest, gusto, energy, verve, vigour, vehemence, fire, spirit, avidity; wholeheartedness, commitment, willingness, devotion, earnestness; *informal* get-up-and-go. **2** *they put their enthusiasms to good use* INTEREST, passion, obsession, mania; inclination, preference, penchant, predilection, fancy; pastime, hobby, recreation, pursuit.
– OPPOSITES apathy.
enthusiast ● noun FAN, devotee, aficionado, lover, admirer, follower; expert, connoisseur, authority, pundit; *informal* buff, freak, fanatic, nut, fiend, addict, maniac.
enthusiastic ● adjective EAGER, keen, avid, ardent, fervent, passionate, zealous, vehement; excited, wholehearted, committed, devoted, fanatical, earnest.
entice ● verb TEMPT, lure, attract, appeal to; invite, persuade, convince, beguile, coax, woo; seduce, lead on; *informal* sweet-talk.
enticement ● noun LURE, temptation, allure, attraction, appeal, draw, pull, bait; charm, seduction, fascination; *informal* come-on.

entirely ● adverb **1** wholly; completely. **2** solely.

entirety ● noun (**the entirety**) the whole.
– PHRASES **in its entirety** as a whole.

entitle ● verb **1** give (someone) a right to do or have. **2** give a title to (a book, play, etc.).
– DERIVATIVES **entitlement** noun.

entity /entiti/ ● noun (pl. **entities**) a thing with distinct and independent existence.
– ORIGIN French *entité*, from Latin *ens* 'being'.

entomb ● verb **1** place in a tomb. **2** bury in or under something.
– DERIVATIVES **entombment** noun.

entomology /entəmolləji/ ● noun the branch of zoology concerned with the study of insects.
– DERIVATIVES **entomological** adjective **entomologist** noun.
– ORIGIN from Greek *entomon* 'insect', from *entomos* 'cut up, segmented'.

entourage /ontooraazh/ ● noun a group of people attending or surrounding an important person.
– ORIGIN French, from *entourer* 'to surround'.

entr'acte /ontrakt/ ● noun **1** an interval between two acts of a play or opera. **2** a piece of music or a dance performed during such an interval.
– ORIGIN French, from *entre* 'between' + *acte* 'act'.

entrails ● plural noun a person's or animal's intestines or internal organs.
– ORIGIN Latin *intralia* 'internal things'.

entrain ● verb board or put on board a train.

entrammel /intramm'l/ ● verb (**entrammelled**, **entrammelling**; US **entrammeled**, **entrammeling**) literary entangle or trap.

entrance[1] /entrənss/ ● noun **1** an opening that allows access to a place. **2** an act of entering. **3** the right, means, or opportunity to enter.

entrance[2] /intraanss/ ● verb **1** fill with wonder and delight. **2** cast a spell on.
– DERIVATIVES **entrancement** noun **entrancing** adjective.

entrant ● noun a person who enters, joins, or takes part in something.

entrap ● verb (**entrapped**, **entrapping**) **1** catch in a trap. **2** (of a police officer) deceive (someone) into committing a crime in order to secure their prosecution.
– DERIVATIVES **entrapment** noun.

en travesti /on travestee/ ● adverb & adjective dressed as a member of the opposite sex, especially for a theatrical role.
– ORIGIN French, '(dressed) in disguise'.

entreat ● verb **1** ask (someone) earnestly or anxiously. **2** ask earnestly or anxiously for.
– ORIGIN Old French *entraitier*, from Latin *tractare* 'to handle'.

entreaty ● noun (pl. **entreaties**) an earnest or humble request.

entrechat /ontrəshaa/ ● noun Ballet a vertical jump during which the dancer repeatedly crosses the feet and beats them together.
– ORIGIN French, from Italian *capriola intrecciata* 'complicated caper'.

entrecôte /ontrəkōt/ ● noun a boned steak cut off the sirloin.
– ORIGIN French, from *entre* 'between' + *côte* 'rib'.

entrée /ontray/ ● noun **1** the main course of a meal. **2** Brit. a dish served between the fish and meat courses at a formal dinner. **3** right of entry.
– ORIGIN French.

entrench ● verb **1** establish (something) so firmly that change is difficult. **2** establish (a military force, camp, etc.) in trenches or other fortified positions.
– DERIVATIVES **entrenchment** noun.

entre nous /ontrə noo/ ● adverb between ourselves.
– ORIGIN French.

entrepôt /ontrəpō/ ● noun a port or other place which acts as a centre for import and export.
– ORIGIN French, from *entreposer* 'to store'.

entrepreneur /ontrəprənör/ ● noun a person who sets up a business or businesses.
– DERIVATIVES **entrepreneurial** /ontrəprənöriəl, -nyooriəl/ adjective **entrepreneurialism** noun **entrepreneurially** adverb **entrepreneurism** noun.
– ORIGIN French, from *entreprendre* 'undertake'.

entropy /entrəpi/ ● noun Physics a thermodynamic quantity expressing the unavailability of a system's thermal energy for conversion into mechanical work, often interpreted as the degree of disorder or randomness in the system.

Thesaurus

enticing ● adjective TEMPTING, alluring, attractive, appealing, inviting, seductive, beguiling, charming; magnetic, irresistible.

entire ● adjective **1** *I devoted my entire life to him* WHOLE, complete, total, full; undivided. **2** *only one of the gates is entire* INTACT, unbroken, undamaged, unimpaired, unscathed, unspoiled, perfect, in one piece. **3** *they are in entire agreement* ABSOLUTE, total, utter, out-and-out, thorough, wholehearted; unqualified, unreserved, outright.
– OPPOSITES partial, broken.

entirely ● adverb **1** *that's entirely out of the question* ABSOLUTELY, completely, totally, wholly, utterly, quite; altogether, in every respect, thoroughly, downright, one hundred per cent. **2** *a gift entirely for charitable purposes* SOLELY, only, exclusively, purely, merely, just, alone.

entirety ● noun WHOLE, total, aggregate, totality, sum total.
– OPPOSITES part.
– PHRASES **in its entirety** COMPLETELY, entirely, totally, fully, wholly; in every respect, in every way, one hundred per cent, all the way, every inch, to the hilt, to the core.

entitle ● verb **1** *this pass entitles you to visit the museum* QUALIFY, make eligible, authorize, allow, permit; enable, empower. **2** *a chapter entitled 'Comedy and Tragedy'* TITLE, name, call, label, designate, dub; formal denominate.

entitlement ● noun **1** *their entitlement to benefits* RIGHT, prerogative, claim; permission, dispensation, privilege. **2** *your holiday entitlement* ALLOWANCE, allocation, quota, ration, limit.

entity ● noun **1** *a single entity* BEING, creature, individual, organism, life form; person; body, object, article, thing. **2** *the distinction between entity and nonentity* EXISTENCE, being; life, living, animation; substance, essence, reality, actuality.

entomb ● verb INTER, lay to rest, bury; informal plant; poetic/literary inhume, sepulchre.

entourage ● noun RETINUE, escort, cortège, train, suite; court, staff, bodyguard; attendants, companions, retainers.

entrails ● plural noun INTESTINES, bowels, guts, viscera, internal organs, vital organs; offal; informal insides, innards.

entrance[1] ● noun **1** *the main entrance* ENTRY, way in, access, ingress, approach; door, portal, gate; opening, mouth; entrance hall, foyer, lobby, porch; N. Amer. entryway. **2** *the entrance of Mrs Knight* APPEARANCE, arrival, entry, ingress, coming. **3** *he was refused entrance* ADMISSION, admittance, (right of) entry, access, ingress.
– OPPOSITES exit, departure.

entrance[2] ● verb **1** *I was entranced by her beauty* ENCHANT, bewitch, beguile, captivate, mesmerize, hypnotize, spellbind; enthral, engross, absorb, fascinate; stun, overpower, electrify; charm, delight; informal bowl over, knock out. **2** *Orpheus entranced the wild beasts* CAST A SPELL ON, bewitch, hex, spellbind, hypnotize, mesmerize.

entrant ● noun **1** *university entrants* NEW MEMBER, new arrival, beginner, newcomer, fresher, freshman, recruit; novice, neophyte; N. Amer. tenderfoot, greenhorn; informal rookie. **2** *a prize will be awarded to the best entrant* COMPETITOR, contestant, contender, participant; candidate, applicant.

entrap ● verb **1** *fishing lines can entrap wildlife* TRAP, snare, ensnare, entangle, enmesh; catch, capture. **2** *he was entrapped by an undercover policeman* ENTICE, lure, inveigle; bait, decoy, trap; lead on, trick, deceive, dupe, hoodwink; informal set up, frame; Brit. informal fit up.

entreat ● verb IMPLORE, beg, plead with, pray, ask, request; bid, enjoin, appeal to, call on, petition, solicit; poetic/literary beseech.

entreaty ● noun PLEA, appeal, request, petition; suit, application, claim; solicitation, supplication; prayer.

entrée ● noun **1** *there are a dozen entrées on the menu* MAIN COURSE, main dish. **2** *an excellent entrée into the profession* (MEANS OF) ENTRY, entrance, ingress; route, path, avenue, way, key, passport.

entrench, intrench ● verb ESTABLISH, settle, lodge, set, root, install, plant, embed, seat; informal dig in.

entrenched, intrenched ● adjective INGRAINED, established, confirmed, fixed, firm, deep-seated, deep-rooted; unshakeable, indelible, ineradicable, inexorable.

entre nous ● adverb BETWEEN OURSELVES, between us, between you and me, in confidence, confidentially, privately, off the record; informal between you and me and the gatepost.

entrepreneur ● noun BUSINESSMAN/WOMAN, enterpriser, speculator, tycoon, magnate, mogul; dealer, trader; promoter, impresario;

– DERIVATIVES **entropic** /entroppik/ adjective.
– ORIGIN from Greek *tropē* 'transformation'.
entrust ● verb **1** (**entrust with**) assign a responsibility to. **2** (**entrust to**) put (something) into someone's care.
entry ● noun (pl. **entries**) **1** an act or the action of entering. **2** an opening through which one may enter, e.g. a door. **3** the right, means, or opportunity to enter. **4** an item entered in a list, account book, reference book, etc. **5** a person who enters a competition.
entryism ● noun the infiltration of a political party by members of another group, to subvert its policies or objectives.
– DERIVATIVES **entryist** noun.
entry-level ● adjective suitable for a beginner or first-time user.
entryphone ● noun Brit. trademark a type of intercom at the entrance to a building by which visitors may identify themselves.
entwine ● verb wind or twist together.
E-number ● noun Brit. a code number preceded by the letter E, given to food additives numbered in accordance with EU directives.
enumerate /inyoōmərayt/ ● verb **1** mention one by one. **2** formal establish the number of.
– DERIVATIVES **enumerable** adjective **enumeration** noun **enumerative** adjective.
– ORIGIN Latin *enumerare* 'count out'.
enumerator ● noun a person employed in taking a census of the population.
enunciate /inunsiayt/ ● verb **1** say or pronounce clearly. **2** set out precisely or definitely.
– DERIVATIVES **enunciation** noun **enunciator** noun.
– ORIGIN Latin *enuntiare* 'announce clearly'.
enuresis /enyooreesiss/ ● noun involuntary urination, especially by children at night.
– DERIVATIVES **enuretic** adjective.
– ORIGIN Latin, from Greek *enourein* 'urinate in'.
envelop /invelləp/ ● verb (**enveloped**, **enveloping**) wrap up, cover, or surround completely.
– DERIVATIVES **envelopment** noun.
– ORIGIN Old French *envoluper*, related to DEVELOP.
envelope /envəlōp, on-/ ● noun **1** a flat paper container with a sealable flap, used to enclose a letter or document. **2** a covering or containing structure or layer. **3** the outer housing of a vacuum tube, electric light, etc. **4** the structure within a balloon or non-rigid airship containing the gas.
– PHRASES **push the (edge of the) envelope** informal approach or extend the limits of what is possible. [ORIGIN originally aviation slang, relating to graphs of aerodynamic performance.]
– ORIGIN from French *envelopper* 'envelop'.
envenom ● verb poison by biting or stinging.
enviable /enviəb'l/ ● adjective arousing or likely to arouse envy.
– DERIVATIVES **enviably** adverb.
envious ● adjective feeling or showing envy.
– DERIVATIVES **enviously** adverb.
environment ● noun **1** the surroundings or conditions in which a person, animal, or plant lives or operates. **2** (**the environment**) the natural world, especially as affected by human activity. **3** Computing the overall structure within which a user, computer, or program operates.
– DERIVATIVES **environmental** adjective **environmentally** adverb.
environmentalist ● noun **1** a person who is concerned with the protection of the environment. **2** a person who considers that environment has the primary influence on the development of a person or group.
– DERIVATIVES **environmentalism** noun.
environs ● plural noun the surrounding area or district.
– ORIGIN French, plural of *environ* 'surroundings'.
envisage /invizzij/ ● verb **1** regard or conceive of as a possibility. **2** form a mental picture of.
– ORIGIN French *envisager*, from *visage* 'face'.
envision ● verb visualize; envisage.
envoi /envoy/ (also **envoy**) ● noun archaic an author's concluding words.
– ORIGIN Old French, from *envoyer* 'send'
envoy /envoy/ ● noun **1** a messenger or representative, especially one on a diplomatic mission. **2** (also **envoy extraordinary**) a minister plenipotentiary, ranking below ambassador and above chargé d'affaires.
– ORIGIN from French *envoyé* 'sent'.
envy ● noun (pl. **envies**) **1** discontented or resentful longing aroused by another's possessions, qualities, or luck. **2** (**the envy of**) a person or thing that inspires such a feeling. ● verb (**envies**, **envied**) feel envy of.
– ORIGIN Old French *envie*, from Latin *invidia* 'hostility, ill will'; related to INVIDIOUS.
enwrap ● verb (**enwrapped**, **enwrapping**) wrap; envelop.

Thesaurus

informal wheeler-dealer, whizz-kid, mover and shaker, go-getter, high-flyer.
entrust ● verb **1** *he was entrusted with the task* CHARGE, invest, endow; burden, encumber, saddle. **2** *the powers entrusted to the Home Secretary* ASSIGN, confer on, bestow on, vest in, consign; delegate, depute, devolve; give, grant, vouchsafe. **3** *she entrusted them to the hospital* HAND OVER, give custody of, turn over, commit, consign, deliver; *formal* commend.
entry ● noun **1** *my moment of entry* APPEARANCE, arrival, entrance, ingress, coming. **2** *the entry to the flats* ENTRANCE, way in, access, ingress, approach; door, portal, gate; entrance hall, foyer, lobby; *N. Amer.* entryway. **3** *he was refused entry* ADMISSION, admittance, entrance, access, ingress. **4** *entries in the cash book* ITEM, record, note, listing; memo, memorandum; account. **5** *data entry* RECORDING, archiving, logging, documentation, capture. **6** *we must pick a winner from the entries* CONTESTANT, competitor, contender, entrant, participant; candidate, applicant; submission, entry form, application.
– OPPOSITES departure, exit.
entwine ● verb WIND ROUND, twist round, coil round; weave, intertwine, interlace, interweave; entangle, tangle; twine, braid, plait, knit.
enumerate ● verb **1** *he enumerated four objectives* LIST, itemize, set out, give; cite, name, specify, identify, spell out, detail, particularize. **2** *(formal) they enumerated hospital readmission rates* CALCULATE, compute, count, add up, tally, total, number, quantify; reckon, work out; *Brit.* tot up.
enunciate ● verb **1** *she enunciated each word slowly* PRONOUNCE, articulate; say, speak, utter, voice, vocalize, sound, mouth. **2** *a document enunciating the policy* EXPRESS, state, put into words, declare, profess, set forth, assert, affirm; put forward, air, proclaim.
envelop ● verb SURROUND, cover, enfold, engulf, encircle, encompass, cocoon, sheathe, swathe, enclose; cloak, screen, shield, veil, shroud.
envelope ● noun WRAPPER, wrapping, sleeve, cover, covering, casing.
envenom ● verb **1** *(archaic) the arrows are envenomed* POISON. **2** *incidents which envenom international relations* EMBITTER, sour, poison, jaundice, taint; antagonize.
enviable ● adjective DESIRABLE, desired, favoured, sought-after, admirable, covetable, attractive; fortunate, lucky; *informal* to die for.
envious ● adjective JEALOUS, covetous, desirous; grudging, begrudging, resentful; bitter, green-eyed.
environ ● verb *(formal)* SURROUND, encircle, enclose, ring, envelop.
environment ● noun **1** *birds from many environments* HABITAT, territory, domain; surroundings, conditions. **2** *the hospital environment* SITUATION, SETTING, milieu, background, backdrop, scene, location; context, framework; sphere, world, realm; ambience, atmosphere. **3** *the impact of pesticides on the environment* THE NATURAL WORLD, nature, the earth, the ecosystem, the biosphere, Mother Nature; wildlife, flora and fauna, the countryside.
environmentalist ● noun CONSERVATIONIST, preservationist, ecologist, nature-lover; *informal* ecofreak, tree hugger.
environs ● plural noun SURROUNDINGS, surrounding area, vicinity; locality, neighbourhood, district, region; precincts; *N. Amer.* vicinage.
envisage ● verb **1** *it was envisaged that the hospital would open soon* FORESEE, predict, forecast, anticipate, expect, think likely. **2** *I cannot envisage what the future holds* IMAGINE, contemplate, visualize, envision, picture; conceive of, think of.
envision ● verb VISUALIZE, imagine, envisage, picture; conceive of, think of, see; intend, mean.
envoy ● noun AMBASSADOR, emissary, diplomat, consul, attaché, chargé d'affaires, plenipotentiary; nuncio; representative, delegate, proxy, surrogate, liaison, spokesperson; agent, intermediary, mediator; *informal* go-between; *historical* legate.
envy ● noun **1** *a pang of envy* JEALOUSY, covetousness; resentment, bitterness, discontent; the green-eyed monster. **2** *the firm is the envy of Europe* FINEST, best, pride, top, cream, jewel, flower, leading light, the crème de la crème.

Enzed /enzed/ • **noun** Austral./NZ informal New Zealand or a New Zealander.
– DERIVATIVES **Enzedder** noun.
– ORIGIN representing a pronunciation of the initials *NZ*.
enzyme /enzīm/ • **noun** a substance produced by a living organism and acting as a catalyst to promote a specific biochemical reaction.
– DERIVATIVES **enzymatic** adjective **enzymic** adjective.
– ORIGIN from modern Greek *enzumos* 'leavened'.
EOC • **abbreviation** (in the UK) Equal Opportunities Commission.
Eocene /eeəseen/ • **adjective** Geology relating to the second epoch of the Tertiary period (between the Palaeocene and Oligocene epochs, 56.5 to 35.4 million years ago).
– ORIGIN from Greek *ēōs* 'dawn' + *kainos* 'new'.
eolian • **adjective** US spelling of AEOLIAN.
eon • **noun** US and technical spelling of AEON.
EP • **abbreviation 1** (of a record or compact disc) extended-play. **2** European Parliament.
ep- • **prefix** variant spelling of EPI- shortened before a vowel or *h*.
épater /aypattay/ • **verb** (in phrase **épater les bourgeois**) shock people regarded as conventional or complacent.
– ORIGIN French.
epaulette /eppəlet/ (US also **epaulet**) • **noun** an ornamental shoulder piece on a military uniform.
– ORIGIN French, 'little shoulder'.
épée /aypay, eppay/ • **noun** a sharp-pointed duelling sword, used, with the end blunted, in fencing.
– ORIGIN French, 'sword'.
ephedrine /effədrin/ • **noun** a drug which causes constriction of the blood vessels and widening of the bronchial passages and is used to relieve asthma and hay fever.
– ORIGIN from *ephedra*, an evergreen plant which is the source of the drug.
ephemera /ifemmərə/ • **plural noun** items of short-lived interest or usefulness, especially those that later acquire value to collectors.
– ORIGIN Greek, 'things lasting only a day'.
ephemeral • **adjective** lasting or living for a very short time.
– DERIVATIVES **ephemerality** noun **ephemerally** adverb.
epi- (also **ep-**) • **prefix 1** upon: *epigraph*. **2** above: *epidermis*. **3** in addition: *epiphenomenon*.
– ORIGIN from Greek *epi*.
epic • **noun 1** a long poem describing the deeds of heroic or legendary figures or the past history of a nation. **2** a long film, book, etc. portraying heroic deeds or covering an extended period of time. • **adjective 1** relating to or characteristic of an epic. **2** heroic or grand in scale or character.
– DERIVATIVES **epical** adjective **epically** adverb.
– ORIGIN from Greek *epikos*, from *epos* 'word, song'.
epicanthic fold • **noun** a fold of skin from the upper eyelid covering the inner angle of the eye, typical in many peoples of eastern Asia.
epicene /eppiseen/ • **adjective 1** having characteristics of both sexes or no characteristics of either sex. **2** effete.
– ORIGIN Greek *epikoinos*, from *koinos* 'common'.
epicentre (US **epicenter**) • **noun** the point on the earth's surface vertically above the focus of an earthquake.
epicure /eppikyoor/ • **noun** a person who takes particular pleasure in fine food and drink.
– ORIGIN from *Epicurus* (see EPICUREAN).
Epicurean /eppikyooreeən/ • **noun 1** a follower of the Greek philosopher Epicurus (341–270 BC), who taught that pleasure, particularly mental pleasure, was the highest good. **2** (**epicurean**) an epicure. • **adjective 1** relating to Epicurus or his ideas. **2** (**epicurean**) relating to or suitable for an epicure.
– DERIVATIVES **Epicureanism** noun.
epicycle /eppisīk'l/ • **noun** Geometry a small circle whose centre moves round the circumference of a larger one.
– DERIVATIVES **epicyclic** adjective.
epidemic • **noun 1** a widespread occurrence of an infectious disease in a community at a particular time. **2** a sudden, widespread occurrence of something undesirable. • **adjective** relating to or of the nature of an epidemic.
– ORIGIN Greek *epidēmia*, from *epi* 'upon' + *dēmos* 'the people'.
epidemiology /eppideemiolləji/ • **noun** the study of the incidence and distribution of diseases and other factors relating to health.
– DERIVATIVES **epidemiological** adjective **epidemiologist** noun.
epidermis /eppidermiss/ • **noun 1** the surface layer of an animal's skin, overlying the dermis. **2** the outer layer of tissue in a plant.
– DERIVATIVES **epidermal** adjective.
– ORIGIN Greek, from *derma* 'skin'.
epidiascope /eppidīəskōp/ • **noun** an optical projector capable of giving images of both opaque and transparent objects.
epididymis /eppididdimiss/ • **noun** (pl. **epididymides** /eppididimmideez/) Anatomy a duct behind the testis, along which sperm passes to the vas deferens.
– ORIGIN Greek *epididumis*, from *didumos* 'testicle'.
epidural /eppidyoorəl/ • **adjective** on or around the dura mater of the spinal cord. • **noun** an anaesthetic introduced into the space around the dura mater, used especially in childbirth.
epifauna • **noun** Ecology animals living on the bed of a body of water or on other submerged surfaces. Compare with INFAUNA.
epigenetic /eppijinettik/ • **adjective** Biology resulting from external rather than genetic influences.
epiglottis /eppiglottiss/ • **noun** a flap of cartilage at the root of the tongue, which is depressed during swallowing to cover the opening of the windpipe.
– ORIGIN Greek, from *glōtta* 'tongue'.
epigone /eppigōn/ • **noun** (pl. **epigones** or **epigoni** /ipiggənī/) a less distinguished follower or imitator.
– ORIGIN from Greek *epigonoi* 'those born afterwards'.
epigram /eppigram/ • **noun 1** a concise and witty saying or remark. **2** a short witty poem.
– DERIVATIVES **epigrammatic** adjective.
– ORIGIN Greek *epigramma*, from *gramma* 'writing'.
epigraph /eppigraaf/ • **noun 1** an inscription on a building, statue, or coin. **2** a short quotation or saying introducing a book or chapter.
– ORIGIN from Greek *epigraphein* 'write on'.
epigraphy /ipigrəfi/ • **noun** the study of ancient inscriptions.
– DERIVATIVES **epigraphic** adjective.
epilation /eppilaysh'n/ • **noun** the removal of hair by the roots.
– DERIVATIVES **epilator** noun.
– ORIGIN from French *épiler*, from Latin *pilus* 'strand of hair'.
epilepsy /eppilepsi/ • **noun** a disorder marked by sudden recurrent episodes of sensory disturbance, loss of consciousness, or

Thesaurus

• **verb 1** *I admired and envied her* BE ENVIOUS OF, be jealous of; begrudge, be resentful of. **2** *we envied her lifestyle* COVET, desire, aspire to, wish for, want, long for, yearn for, hanker after, crave.
ephemeral • **adjective** TRANSITORY, transient, fleeting, passing, short-lived, momentary, brief, short; temporary, impermanent, short-term; fly-by-night.
– OPPOSITES permanent.
epic • **noun 1** *the epics of Homer* HEROIC POEM; story, saga, legend, romance, chronicle, myth, fable, tale. **2** *a big Hollywood epic* long film; informal blockbuster.
• **adjective 1** *a traditional epic poem* HEROIC, long, grand, monumental, Homeric, Miltonian. **2** *their epic journey* AMBITIOUS, heroic, grand, great, Herculean; very long, monumental.
epicene • **adjective 1** *a sort of epicene beauty* SEXLESS, asexual, neuter; androgynous. **2** *he gave an epicene titter* EFFEMINATE, unmanly, unmasculine, girly, girlish; informal camp, campy.
– OPPOSITES macho.
epicure • **noun** GOURMET, gastronome, gourmand, connoisseur; informal foodie.
epicurean • **noun** HEDONIST, sensualist, pleasure-seeker, sybarite, voluptuary, bon viveur; epicure, gourmet, gastronome, connoisseur, gourmand.
• **adjective** HEDONISTIC, sensualist, pleasure-seeking, self-indulgent, sybaritic, voluptuary, lotus-eating; decadent, unrestrained, extravagant, intemperate, immoderate; gluttonous, gourmandizing.
epidemic • **noun 1** *an epidemic of typhoid* OUTBREAK, plague, pandemic, epizootic. **2** *a joyriding epidemic* SPATE, rash, wave, eruption, outbreak, craze; flood, torrent; upsurge, upturn, increase, growth, rise.
• **adjective** *the craze is now epidemic* RIFE, rampant, widespread, wide-ranging, extensive, pervasive; global, universal, ubiquitous; endemic, pandemic, epizootic.
epigram • **noun** WITTICISM, quip, jest, pun, bon mot; saying, maxim, adage, aphorism, apophthegm, epigraph; informal one-liner, wisecrack, (old) chestnut.
epigrammatic • **adjective** CONCISE, succinct, pithy, aphoristic; in-

convulsions.
– DERIVATIVES **epileptic** adjective & noun.
– ORIGIN Greek *epilēpsia*, from *epilambanein* 'seize, attack'.

epilogue /eppilog/ (US also **epilog**) • noun a section or speech at the end of a book or play serving as a comment on or conclusion to what has happened.
– ORIGIN Greek *epilogos*, from *logos* 'speech'.

epiphany /ipiffəni/ • noun (pl. **epiphanies**) **1** (**Epiphany**) the manifestation of Christ to the Magi (Gospel of Matthew, chapter 2). **2** (**Epiphany**) the festival commemorating this, on 6 January. **3** a moment of sudden and great revelation.
– DERIVATIVES **epiphanic** adjective.
– ORIGIN from Greek *epiphainein* 'reveal'.

e

epiphenomenon /eppifinomminən/ • noun (pl. **epiphenomena** /eppifinomminə/) **1** Medicine a secondary symptom, occurring simultaneously with a disease or condition but not directly related to it. **2** a mental state regarded as a by-product of brain activity.

epiphyte /eppifīt/ • noun a plant that grows on a tree or other plant but is not a parasite.
– DERIVATIVES **epiphytic** /eppifittik/ adjective.
– ORIGIN from Greek *epi* 'upon' + *phuton* 'plant'.

episcopacy /ipiskəpəsi/ • noun (pl. **episcopacies**) **1** government of a Church by bishops. **2** (**the episcopacy**) the bishops of a region or church collectively.

episcopal /ipiskəp'l/ • adjective **1** of a bishop or bishops. **2** (of a Church) governed by or having bishops.
– DERIVATIVES **episcopally** adverb.
– ORIGIN from Latin *episcopus* 'bishop', from Greek *episkopos* 'overseer'.

Episcopal Church • noun the Anglican Church in Scotland and the US, with elected bishops.

episcopalian /ipiskəpaylian/ • adjective **1** of or advocating government of a Church by bishops. **2** of or belonging to an episcopal Church. • noun **1** an advocate of government of a Church by bishops. **2** (**Episcopalian**) a member of the Episcopal Church.
– DERIVATIVES **episcopalianism** noun.

episcopate /ipiskəpət/ • noun **1** the office or term of office of a bishop. **2** (**the episcopate**) the bishops of a church or region collectively.

episiotomy /ipisiottəmi/ • noun (pl. **episiotomies**) a surgical cut made at the opening of the vagina during childbirth, to aid a difficult delivery.
– ORIGIN from Greek *epision* 'pubic region'.

episode • noun **1** an event or a group of events occurring as part of a sequence. **2** each of the separate instalments into which a serialized story or programme is divided.
– ORIGIN Greek *epeisodion*, from *epeisodios* 'coming in besides'.

episodic /eppisoddik/ • adjective **1** occurring as or presented in episodes. **2** occurring at irregular intervals.
– DERIVATIVES **episodically** adverb.

epistemology /ipistimolləji/ • noun the branch of philosophy that deals with knowledge, especially with regard to its methods, validity, and scope.
– DERIVATIVES **epistemic** adjective **epistemological** adjective **epistemologist** noun.
– ORIGIN from Greek *epistēmē* 'knowledge'.

epistle /ipiss'l/ • noun **1** formal or humorous a letter. **2** (**Epistle**) a book of the New Testament in the form of a letter from an Apostle.
– ORIGIN Greek *epistolē*, from *epistellein* 'send news'.

epistolary /ipistələri/ • adjective **1** relating to the writing of letters. **2** (of a literary work) in the form of letters.

epitaph /eppitaaf/ • noun words written in memory of a person who has died, especially as an inscription on a tombstone.
– ORIGIN Greek *epitaphion* 'funeral oration', from *ephitaphios* 'over or at a tomb'.

epithalamium /eppithəlaymiəm/ • noun (pl. **epithalamiums** or **epithalamia**) a song or poem celebrating a marriage.
– ORIGIN Latin, from Greek *epi* 'upon' + *thalamos* 'bridal chamber'.

epithelium /eppitheeliəm/ • noun (pl. **epithelia** /eppitheeliə/) Anatomy the thin tissue forming the outer layer of the body's surface and lining the alimentary canal and other hollow structures.
– ORIGIN Latin, from Greek *thēlē* 'teat'.

epithet /eppithet/ • noun a word or phrase expressing a quality or attribute of the person or thing mentioned.
– ORIGIN Greek *epitheton*, from *epitithenai* 'add'.

epitome /ipittəmi/ • noun **1** (**the epitome of**) a perfect example of (a quality or type). **2** a summary of a written work.
– ORIGIN Greek, from *epitemnein* 'abridge'.

epitomize (also **epitomise**) • verb **1** be a perfect example of. **2** archaic summarize (a written work).

e pluribus unum /ay plooribōōss yōōnōōm/ • noun one out of many (the motto of the US).
– ORIGIN Latin.

epoch /eepok/ • noun **1** a period of time marked by particular events or characteristics. **2** the beginning of a period of history. **3** Geology a division of time that is a subdivision of a period and is itself subdivided into ages.
– DERIVATIVES **epochal** adjective.
– ORIGIN Greek *epokhē* 'stoppage, fixed point of time'.

epoch-making • adjective significant; historic.

eponym /eppənim/ • noun **1** a word or name derived from the name of a person. **2** a person after whom a discovery, invention, place, etc. is named.

eponymous /iponniməss/ • adjective **1** (of a person) giving their name to something. **2** (of a thing) named after a particular person.
– ORIGIN Greek *epōnumos*, from *onoma* 'name'.

epoxide /ipoksīd/ • noun Chemistry an organic compound whose molecule contains a three-membered ring involving an oxygen atom and two carbon atoms.

epoxy /ipoksi/ (also **epoxy resin**) • noun (pl. **epoxies**) an adhesive, plastic, paint, etc. made from synthetic polymers containing epoxide groups.

EPROM /eeprom/ • noun Computing a read-only memory whose contents can be erased and reprogrammed using special means.
– ORIGIN from *erasable programmable ROM*.

epsilon /epsilon, epsīlon/ • noun the fifth letter of the Greek alphabet (E, ε), transliterated as 'e'.
– ORIGIN Greek, 'bare or simple E', from *psilos* 'bare'.

Epsom salts • plural noun crystals of hydrated magnesium sulphate used as a laxative.
– ORIGIN named after the town of *Epsom* in Surrey, where the salts were first found occurring naturally.

equable /ekwəb'l/ • adjective **1** calm and even-tempered. **2** not varying or fluctuating greatly.
– DERIVATIVES **equability** noun **equably** adverb.
– ORIGIN Latin *aequabilis*, from *aequare* 'make equal'.

Thesaurus

cisive, short and sweet; witty, clever, quick-witted, piquant, sharp; *informal* snappy.
– OPPOSITES expansive.

epilogue • noun AFTERWORD, postscript, PS, coda, codicil, appendix, tailpiece, supplement, addendum, postlude, rider, back matter; conclusion.
– OPPOSITES prologue.

episode • noun **1** *the best episode of his career* INCIDENT, event, occurrence, happening; occasion, interlude, chapter, experience, adventure, exploit; matter, affair, thing. **2** *the final episode of the series* INSTALMENT, chapter, passage; part, portion, section, component; programme, show. **3** *an episode of illness* PERIOD, spell, bout, attack, phase; *informal* dose.

episodic • adjective **1** *episodic wheezing* INTERMITTENT, sporadic, periodic, fitful, irregular, spasmodic, occasional. **2** *an episodic account of the war* IN EPISODES, in instalments, in sections, in parts.
– OPPOSITES continuous.

epistle • noun *(formal)* LETTER, missive, communication, dispatch, note, line; correspondence, news.

epitaph • noun ELEGY, commemoration, obituary; inscription, legend.

epithet • noun SOBRIQUET, nickname, byname, title, name, label, tag; description, designation; *informal* moniker, handle; *formal* appellation, denomination.

epitome • noun **1** *he was the epitome of respectability* PERSONIFICATION, embodiment, incarnation, paragon; essence, quintessence, archetype, paradigm, typification; exemplar, model, soul, example; height. **2** *an epitome of a larger work* SUMMARY, abstract, synopsis, precis, résumé, outline, digest, summation; abridgement, abbreviation, condensation.

epitomize • verb **1** *the town epitomizes the pioneer spirit* EMBODY, encapsulate, typify, exemplify, represent, manifest, symbolize, il-

equal ● adjective **1** being the same in quantity, size, degree, value, or status. **2** evenly or fairly balanced: *an equal contest.* **3** (**equal to**) having the ability or resources to meet (a challenge). ● noun a person or thing that is equal to another. ● verb (**equalled**, **equalling**; US **equaled**, **equaling**) **1** be equal or equivalent to. **2** match or rival.
– ORIGIN Latin *aequalis*, from *aequus* 'even, level, equal'.
equality ● noun the state of being equal.
equalize (also **equalise**) ● verb **1** make or become equal. **2** level the score in a match by scoring a goal.
– DERIVATIVES **equalization** noun.
equalizer (also **equaliser**) ● noun **1** a thing that has an equalizing effect. **2** a goal that levels the score in a match.
equally ● adverb **1** in an equal manner. **2** in amounts or parts that are equal. **3** to an equal degree.
– USAGE The construction **equally as**, as in *follow-up discussion is equally as important* should be avoided: just use either **equally** or **as** alone.
equals sign (also **equal sign**) ● noun the symbol =.
equanimity /ekwənimmiti, ee-/ ● noun calmness; composure.
– DERIVATIVES **equanimous** /ikwannimǝss, ee-/ adjective.
– ORIGIN Latin *aequanimitas*, from *aequus* 'equal' + *animus* 'mind'.
equate /ikwayt/ ● verb (often **equate to/with**) **1** consider (one thing) as equal or equivalent to another. **2** be or cause to be the same as or equivalent to.
equation /ikwayzh'n/ ● noun **1** the process of equating one thing with another. **2** Mathematics a statement that the values of two mathematical expressions are equal (indicated by the sign =). **3** Chemistry a symbolic representation of the changes which occur in a chemical reaction.
equator /ikwaytər/ ● noun **1** a notional line around the earth equidistant from the poles, dividing the earth into northern and southern hemispheres. **2** Astronomy short for CELESTIAL EQUATOR.
– ORIGIN Latin *aequator*, in the phrase *circulus aequator diei et noctis* 'circle equalizing day and night'.
equatorial /ekwətoriəl/ ● adjective of, at, or near the equator.
– DERIVATIVES **equatorially** adverb.
equerry /ekwəri, ikwerri/ ● noun (pl. **equerries**) **1** an officer of the British royal household who attends members of the royal family. **2** historical an officer of the household of a prince or noble who had charge over the stables.
– ORIGIN Old French *esquierie* 'company of squires, prince's stables'.
equestrian /ikwestriən/ ● adjective **1** relating to horse riding. **2** depicting or representing a person on horseback. ● noun (fem. **equestrienne** /ikwestrien/) a person on horseback.
– ORIGIN Latin *equester*, from *eques* 'horseman, knight', from *equus* 'horse'.
equestrianism ● noun the skill or sport of horse riding.
equi- /eekwi, ekwi/ ● combining form equal; equally: *equidistant.*
– ORIGIN from Latin *aequus* 'equal'.
equiangular ● adjective having equal angles.
equidistant ● adjective at equal distances.
– DERIVATIVES **equidistance** noun **equidistantly** adverb.
equilateral /eekwilattərəl, ekwi-/ ● adjective having all its sides of the same length.
equilibrate /ikwillibrayt, eekwilībrayt/ ● verb bring into or maintain a state of equilibrium.
– DERIVATIVES **equilibration** noun.
equilibrist /ikwillibrist/ ● noun chiefly archaic an acrobat, especially a tightrope walker.
equilibrium /eekwilibriəm, ekwi-/ ● noun (pl. **equilibria** /eekwilibriə, ekwi-/) **1** a state in which opposing forces or influences are balanced. **2** the state of being physically balanced. **3** a calm state of mind.
– ORIGIN Latin *aequilibrium*, from *libra* 'balance'.
equine /ekwīn/ ● adjective **1** relating to horses or other members of the horse family. **2** resembling a horse. ● noun a horse or other member of the horse family.
– ORIGIN Latin *equinus*, from *equus* 'horse'.
equinoctial /eekwinoksh'l, ekwi-/ ● adjective **1** relating to or at the time of the equinox. **2** at or near the equator. ● noun (also **equinoctial line**) another term for CELESTIAL EQUATOR.
equinoctial point ● noun either of two points at which the ecliptic cuts the celestial equator.
equinoctial year ● noun another term for SOLAR YEAR.
equinox /eekwinoks, ek-/ ● noun the time or date (twice each year, about 22 September and 20 March) at which the sun crosses the celestial equator and when day and night are of equal length.
– ORIGIN Latin *aequinoctium*, from *aequus* 'equal' + *nox* 'night'.
equip ● verb (**equipped**, **equipping**) **1** supply with the items

e

Thesaurus

lustrate, sum up; personify; *formal* reify. **2** (*archaic*) *we will epitomize the pamphlet.* See SUMMARIZE.
epoch ● noun ERA, age, period, time, span, stage; aeon.
equable ● adjective **1** *an equable man* EVEN-TEMPERED, calm, composed, collected, self-possessed, relaxed, easy-going; nonchalant, insouciant, mellow, mild, tranquil, placid, stable, level-headed; imperturbable, unexcitable, untroubled, well balanced; *informal* unflappable, together, laid-back. **2** *an equable climate* STABLE, constant, uniform, unvarying, consistent, unchanging, changeless; moderate, temperate.
– OPPOSITES temperamental, extreme.
equal ● adjective **1** *lines of equal length* IDENTICAL, uniform, alike, like, the same, equivalent; matching, comparable, similar, corresponding. **2** *fares equal to a fortnight's wages* EQUIVALENT, identical, amounting; proportionate to, commensurate with, on a par with. **3** *equal treatment before the law* UNBIASED, impartial, non-partisan, fair, just, equitable; unprejudiced, non-discriminatory, egalitarian; neutral, objective, disinterested. **4** *an equal contest* EVENLY MATCHED, even, balanced, level; on a par, on an equal footing; *informal* fifty-fifty, level pegging, neck and neck.
– OPPOSITES different, discriminatory.
● noun *they did not treat him as their equal* EQUIVALENT, peer, fellow, coequal, like; counterpart, match, parallel.
● verb **1** *two plus two equals four* BE EQUAL TO, be equivalent to, be the same as; come to, amount to, make, total, add up to. **2** *he equalled the world record* MATCH, reach, parallel, be level with, measure up to. **3** *the fable equals that of any other poet* BE AS GOOD AS, be a match for, measure up to, equate with; be in the same league as, rival, compete with.
– PHRASES **equal to** CAPABLE OF, fit for, up to, good/strong enough for; suitable for, suited to, appropriate for; *informal* having what it takes.
equality ● noun **1** *we promote equality for women* FAIRNESS, equal rights, equal opportunities, equitability, egalitarianism; impartiality, even-handedness; justice. **2** *equality between supply and demand* PARITY, similarity, comparability, correspondence; likeness, resemblance; uniformity, evenness, balance, equilibrium, consistency, agreement, congruence, symmetry.
equalize ● verb **1** *attempts to equalize their earnings* MAKE EQUAL, make even, even out/up, level, regularize, standardize, balance, square, match; bring into line. **2** *Villa equalized in the second half* LEVEL THE SCORE, draw.
equanimity ● noun COMPOSURE, calm, level-headedness, self-possession, cool-headedness, presence of mind; serenity, tranquillity, phlegm, imperturbability, equilibrium; poise, assurance, self-confidence, aplomb, sangfroid, nerve; *informal* cool.
– OPPOSITES anxiety.
equate ● verb **1** *he equates criticism with treachery* IDENTIFY, compare, bracket, class, associate, connect, link, relate, ally. **2** *the rent equates to £24 per square foot* CORRESPOND, be equivalent, amount; equal. **3** *moves to equate supply and demand* EQUALIZE, balance, even out/up, level, square, tally, match; make equal, make even, make equivalent.
equation ● noun **1** *a quadratic equation* MATHEMATICAL PROBLEM, sum, calculation, question. **2** *the equation of success with riches* IDENTIFICATION, association, connection, matching; equivalence, correspondence, agreement, comparison. **3** *other factors came into the equation* SITUATION, problem, case, question; quandary, predicament.
equatorial ● adjective TROPICAL, hot, humid, sultry.
– OPPOSITES polar.
equestrian ● adjective *an equestrian statue* ON HORSEBACK, mounted, riding.
● noun *tracks for equestrians* (HORSE) RIDER, horseman, horsewoman, jockey.
equilibrium ● noun **1** *the equilibrium of the economy* BALANCE, symmetry, equipoise, parity, equality; stability. **2** *his equilibrium was never shaken* COMPOSURE, calm, equanimity, sangfroid; level-headedness, cool-headedness, imperturbability, poise, presence of mind; self-possession, self-command; impassivity, placidity, tran-

needed for a purpose. **2** prepare (someone) mentally for a situation or task.
– ORIGIN French *équiper*, probably from an Old Norse word meaning 'to man a ship'.
equipage /ekwipij/ ● **noun** **1** archaic equipment. **2** historical a carriage and horses with attendants.
equipment ● **noun** **1** the items needed for a particular purpose. **2** the process of supplying these items.
equipoise /ekwipoyz/ ● **noun** **1** balance of forces or interests. **2** a counterbalance or balancing force.
equitable /ekwitəb'l/ ● **adjective** **1** fair and impartial. **2** Law valid in equity as distinct from law.
– DERIVATIVES **equitably** adverb.
equitation /ekwitaysh'n/ ● **noun** formal the art and practice of horse riding.
– ORIGIN Latin, from *equitare* 'ride a horse'.
equity /ekwiti/ ● **noun** (pl. **equities**) **1** the quality of being fair and impartial. **2** Law a branch of law that developed alongside common law in order to remedy some of its defects in fairness and justice. **3** the value of a mortgaged property after deduction of charges against it. **4** the value of the shares issued by a company. **5** (**equities**) stocks and shares that carry no fixed interest.
– ORIGIN Latin *aequitas*, from *aequus* 'equal'.
equivalent /ikwivvələnt/ ● **adjective** (often **equivalent to**) **1** equal in value, amount, function, meaning, etc. **2** having the same or a similar effect. ● **noun** a person or thing that is equivalent to another.
– DERIVATIVES **equivalence** noun **equivalency** noun **equivalently** adverb.
– ORIGIN from Latin *aequivalere* 'be of equal worth'.
equivocal /ikwivvək'l/ ● **adjective** unclear in meaning or intention; ambiguous.
– DERIVATIVES **equivocally** adverb.
– ORIGIN from Latin *aequus* 'equal' + *vocare* 'to call'.
equivocate /ikwivvəkayt/ ● **verb** use ambiguous or evasive language.
– DERIVATIVES **equivocation** noun.
ER ● **abbreviation** **1** Queen Elizabeth. [ORIGIN from Latin *Elizabetha Regina*.] **2** N. Amer. emergency room.
Er ● **symbol** the chemical element erbium.
-er[1] ● **suffix** **1** denoting a person or thing that performs a specified action or activity: *farmer*. **2** denoting a person or thing that has a specified attribute or form: *two-wheeler*. **3** denoting a person concerned with a specified thing: *milliner*. **4** denoting a person belonging to a specified place or group: *city-dweller*.
– ORIGIN Old English.
-er[2] ● **suffix** forming the comparative of adjectives (as in *bigger*) and adverbs (as in *faster*).
– ORIGIN Old English.
-er[3] ● **suffix** forming nouns used informally, usually by distortion of the root word: *footer*.
– ORIGIN originally Rugby School slang, later adopted at Oxford University.
era /eerə/ ● **noun** **1** a long and distinct period of history. **2** Geology a major division of time that is a subdivision of an aeon and is itself subdivided into periods.
– ORIGIN Latin *aera*, denoting a number used as a basis of reckoning, plural of *aes* 'money, counter'.
eradicate /iraddikayt/ ● **verb** remove or destroy completely.
– DERIVATIVES **eradication** noun **eradicator** noun.
– ORIGIN Latin *eradicare* 'tear up by the roots', from *radix* 'root'.
erase /irayz/ ● **verb** rub out or obliterate; remove all traces of.
– DERIVATIVES **erasable** adjective **erasure** noun.
– ORIGIN Latin *eradere* 'scrape away'.
eraser ● **noun** a piece of rubber or plastic used to rub out something written.
erbium /erbiəm/ ● **noun** a soft silvery-white metallic chemical element of the lanthanide series.
– ORIGIN named after *Ytterby* in Sweden (see YTTERBIUM).
ere /air/ ● **preposition & conjunction** literary or archaic before (in time).
– ORIGIN Old English.
erect ● **adjective** **1** rigidly upright or straight. **2** (of a body part) enlarged and rigid, especially in sexual excitement. ● **verb** **1** construct (a building, wall, etc.). **2** create or establish (a theory or system).
– DERIVATIVES **erectly** adverb **erectness** noun **erector** noun.
– ORIGIN from Latin *erigere* 'set up'.
erectile /irektīl/ ● **adjective** able to become erect.
erection ● **noun** **1** the action of erecting. **2** a building or other upright structure. **3** an erect state of the penis.
eremite /errimīt/ ● **noun** archaic a Christian hermit.
– DERIVATIVES **eremitic** adjective **eremitical** adjective.
– ORIGIN Latin *eremita* 'hermit'.
erg /erg/ ● **noun** Physics a unit of work or energy, equal to the work done by a force of one dyne when its point of application moves one centimetre in the direction of action of the force.
– ORIGIN from Greek *ergon* 'work'.
ergo /ergō/ ● **adverb** therefore.

Thesaurus

quillity, serenity; *informal* cool.
– OPPOSITES imbalance, agitation.
equip ● **verb** **1** *the boat was equipped with a flare gun* PROVIDE, furnish, supply, issue, kit out, stock, provision, arm, endow. **2** *the course will equip them for the workplace* PREPARE, qualify, suit.
equipment ● **noun** APPARATUS, paraphernalia, articles, appliances, impedimenta; tools, utensils, implements, instruments, hardware, gadgets, gadgetry; stuff, things; kit, tackle; resources, supplies; trappings, appurtenances, accoutrements; *informal* gear; *Military* materiel, baggage.
equipoise ● **noun** **1** *an equipoise of power* EQUILIBRIUM, balance, evenness, symmetry, parity, equality, equity; stability. **2** *an equipoise to imbalances in savings* COUNTERWEIGHT, counterbalance, counterpoise, balance; stabilizer.
– OPPOSITES imbalance.
equitable ● **adjective** FAIR, just, impartial, even-handed, unbiased, unprejudiced, egalitarian; disinterested, objective, neutral, non-partisan, open-minded; *informal* fair and square.
– OPPOSITES unfair.
equity ● **noun** **1** *the equity of Finnish society* FAIRNESS, justness, impartiality, egalitarianism; objectivity, balance, open-mindedness. **2** *he owns 25% of the equity in the property* VALUE, worth; ownership, rights, proprietorship.
equivalence ● **noun** EQUALITY, sameness, interchangeability, comparability, correspondence; uniformity, similarity, likeness, nearness.
equivalent ● **adjective** *a degree or equivalent qualification* EQUAL, identical; similar, parallel, analogous, comparable, corresponding, commensurate; approximate, near.
● **noun** *Denmark's equivalent of the Daily Mirror* COUNTERPART, parallel, alternative, match, analogue, twin, opposite number; equal, peer.
equivocal ● **adjective** AMBIGUOUS, indefinite, non-committal, vague, imprecise, inexact, inexplicit, hazy; unclear, cryptic, enigmatic; ambivalent, uncertain, unsure, indecisive.
– OPPOSITES definite.
equivocate ● **verb** PREVARICATE, be evasive, be non-committal, be vague, be ambiguous, dodge the issue, beat about the bush, hedge one's bets, pussyfoot around; vacillate, shilly-shally, waver; temporize, hesitate, stall; *Brit.* hum and haw; *informal* sit on the fence, duck the issue; *rare* tergiversate.
era ● **noun** EPOCH, age, period, time, span, aeon; generation.
eradicate ● **verb** ELIMINATE, get rid of, remove, obliterate; exterminate, destroy, annihilate, kill, wipe out; abolish, stamp out, extinguish, quash; erase, efface, excise, expunge.
erase ● **verb** **1** *they erased his name from all lists* DELETE, rub out, wipe off, blot out, blank out, cancel; efface, expunge, excise, remove, obliterate, eliminate. **2** *the old differences in style were erased* DESTROY, wipe out, obliterate, eradicate, abolish, stamp out, quash.
erect ● **adjective** **1** *she held her body erect* UPRIGHT, straight, vertical, perpendicular; standing. **2** *an erect penis* ENGORGED, enlarged, swollen, tumescent; hard, stiff. **3** *the dog's fur was erect* BRISTLING, standing on end, upright.
– OPPOSITES bent, flaccid, flat.
● **verb** **1** *the bridge was erected in 1973* BUILD, construct, put up; assemble, put together, fabricate. **2** *the party that erected the welfare state* ESTABLISH, form, set up, found, institute, initiate, create, organize.
– OPPOSITES demolish, dismantle, lower.
erection ● **noun** **1** *the erection of a house* CONSTRUCTION, building, assembly, fabrication, elevation. **2** *a bleak concrete erection* BUILDING, structure, edifice, construction, pile. **3** ERECT PENIS, phallus; tumescence, tumidity.

– ORIGIN Latin.
ergocalciferol /ergōkalsiffərol/ ● noun another term for CALCIFEROL.
– ORIGIN blend of ERGOT and CALCIFEROL.
ergonomic /ergənommik/ ● adjective **1** relating to ergonomics. **2** designed to be conducive to efficient use.
– DERIVATIVES **ergonomist** noun.
ergonomics ● plural noun (treated as sing.) the study of people's efficiency in their working environment.
– ORIGIN from Greek *ergon* 'work', on the pattern of *economics*.
ergot /ergət/ ● noun a disease of rye and other cereals, caused by a fungus.
– ORIGIN French, from Old French *argot* 'cock's spur' (because of the appearance produced by the disease).
ergotism /ergətiz'm/ ● noun poisoning produced by eating food affected by ergot, which produces a number of toxic compounds.
erica /errikə/ ● noun a plant of a large genus including the heaths.
– ORIGIN Greek *ereikē*.
ericaceous /errikayshəss/ ● adjective Botany **1** relating to plants of the heather family (Ericaceae). **2** (of compost) suitable for heathers and other lime-hating plants.
Erin /errin, eerin/ ● noun archaic or literary Ireland.
– ORIGIN Irish.
Erinys /erinnis/ ● noun (pl. **Erinyes** /erini-eez/) (in Greek mythology) a Fury.
– ORIGIN Greek.
Eritrean /erritrayən/ ● noun a person from the independent state of Eritrea in NE Africa. ● adjective relating to Eritrea.
erk /erk/ ● noun Brit. informal a male member of the RAF of the lowest rank.
– ORIGIN of unknown origin.
erl-king /erl king/ ● noun (in Germanic mythology) a bearded giant or goblin believed to lure little children to the land of death.
– ORIGIN German *Erlkönig* 'alder-king', a mistranslation of Danish *ellerkonge* 'king of the elves'.
ERM ● abbreviation Exchange Rate Mechanism.
ermine /ermin/ ● noun (pl. same or **ermines**) **1** a stoat. **2** the white winter fur of the stoat, used for trimming the ceremonial robes of judges or peers.
– ORIGIN Old French *hermine*, probably from Latin *mus Armenius* 'Armenian mouse'.
Ernie /erni/ ● noun (in the UK) the computer that randomly selects the prize-winning numbers of Premium Bonds.
– ORIGIN from *electronic random number indicator equipment*.
erode /irōd/ ● verb **1** gradually wear or be worn away. **2** gradually destroy (an abstract quality or state).
– DERIVATIVES **erodible** adjective.
– ORIGIN Latin *erodere*, from *rodere* 'gnaw'.
erogenous /irojinəss/ ● adjective (of a part of the body) sensitive to sexual stimulation.
– ORIGIN from EROS.
Eros /eeross/ ● noun sexual love or desire.
– ORIGIN Greek, 'sexual love' (also the name of the god of love in Greek mythology).
erosion /irōzh'n/ ● noun the process or result of eroding or being eroded.
– DERIVATIVES **erosional** adjective **erosive** adjective.
erotic /irottik/ ● adjective relating to or tending to arouse sexual desire or excitement.
– DERIVATIVES **erotically** adverb.
– ORIGIN Greek *erōtikos*, from *erōs* 'sexual love'.
erotica ● plural noun (treated as sing. or pl.) erotic literature or art.
eroticism ● noun **1** the quality or character or being erotic. **2** sexual desire or excitement.
eroticize (also **eroticise**) ● verb give erotic qualities to.
– DERIVATIVES **eroticization** noun.
erotism /errətiz'm/ ● noun sexual desire or excitement.
erotogenic /irottəjennik/ ● adjective another term for EROGENOUS.
erotomania /irottōmayniə/ ● noun **1** excessive sexual desire. **2** a delusion in which a person believes that another person is in love with them.
– DERIVATIVES **erotomaniac** noun.
err /er/ ● verb **1** be mistaken or incorrect. **2** do wrong.
– PHRASES **err on the side of** display more rather than less of (a specified quality) in one's actions. **to err is human, to forgive divine** proverb it is human nature to make mistakes oneself while finding it hard to forgive others.
– ORIGIN Latin *errare* 'to stray'.
errand ● noun a short journey made to deliver or collect something, especially on someone else's behalf.
– PHRASES **errand of mercy** a journey or mission carried out to help someone in difficulty or danger.
– ORIGIN Old English, 'message, mission'.
errant /errənt/ ● adjective **1** straying from the accepted course or standards. **2** archaic or literary travelling in search of adventure.
– DERIVATIVES **errantry** noun.
– ORIGIN sense 1 from Latin *errare* 'err'; sense 2 from Old French, 'travelling', from Latin *iterare*.
erratic /irattik/ ● adjective not even or regular in pattern or movement.
– DERIVATIVES **erratically** adverb **erraticism** noun.
erratum /eraatəm/ ● noun (pl. **errata**) **1** an error in printing or writing. **2** (**errata**) a list of corrected errors added to a publication.
– ORIGIN Latin, 'error'.
erroneous /irōniəss/ ● adjective wrong; incorrect.
– DERIVATIVES **erroneously** adverb.
– ORIGIN Latin *erroneus*, from *errare* 'to stray, err'.
error ● noun **1** a mistake. **2** the state of being wrong in conduct or judgement. **3** technical a measure of the estimated difference between the observed or calculated value of a quantity and its true value.
– PHRASES **see the error of one's ways** acknowledge one's wrongdoing.
– ORIGIN Latin, from *errare* 'to stray, err'.

e

Thesaurus

eremite ● noun *(archaic)* HERMIT, recluse, solitary, ascetic; *historical* anchorite, anchoress.
ergo ● adverb THEREFORE, consequently, so, as a result, hence, thus, accordingly, for that reason, that being the case, on that account; *formal* whence; *archaic* wherefore.
erode ● verb WEAR AWAY/DOWN, abrade, grind down, crumble; weather; eat away at, dissolve, corrode, rot, decay; undermine, weaken, deteriorate, destroy.
erosion ● noun WEARING AWAY, abrasion, attrition; weathering; dissolution, corrosion, decay; deterioration, disintegration, destruction; *rare* detrition.
erotic ● adjective SEXUALLY AROUSING, sexually stimulating, titillating, suggestive; pornographic, sexually explicit, lewd, smutty, hard-core, soft-core, dirty, racy, risqué, ribald, naughty; sexual, sexy, sensual, amatory; seductive, alluring, tantalizing; *informal* blue, X-rated, steamy, raunchy; *euphemistic* adult.
err ● verb **1** *the judge had erred* MAKE A MISTAKE, be wrong, be in error, be mistaken, blunder, be incorrect, miscalculate, get it wrong; *informal* slip up, screw up, foul up, goof, make a boo-boo, bark up the wrong tree, get the wrong end of the stick; *Brit. informal* boob. **2** *she struck them when they erred* MISBEHAVE, be bad, be naughty, get up to mischief, cause trouble; sin, transgress, lapse; clown about/around, fool about/around, act the goat; *informal* mess about/around, act up; *Brit. informal* play up.
errand ● noun TASK, job, chore, assignment; collection, delivery; mission, undertaking.
errant ● adjective **1** *he fined the errant councillors* OFFENDING, guilty, culpable, misbehaving, delinquent, lawbreaking; troublesome, unruly, disobedient. **2** *(archaic) a knight errant* TRAVELLING, wandering, itinerant, roaming, roving, voyaging.
– OPPOSITES innocent.
erratic ● adjective UNPREDICTABLE, inconsistent, changeable, variable, inconstant, irregular, fitful, unstable, turbulent, unsettled, changing, varying, fluctuating, mutable; unreliable, undependable, volatile, mercurial, capricious, fickle, temperamental, moody.
– OPPOSITES consistent.
erring ● adjective OFFENDING, guilty, culpable, misbehaving, errant, delinquent, lawbreaking, aberrant, deviant.
erroneous ● adjective WRONG, incorrect, mistaken, in error, inaccurate, untrue, false, fallacious; unsound, specious, faulty, flawed; *informal* off beam, way out, full of holes.
– OPPOSITES correct.
error ● noun MISTAKE, inaccuracy, miscalculation, blunder, over-

e

ersatz /ersats, air-/ ● **adjective** **1** (of a product) made or used as an inferior substitute for something else. **2** not real or genuine: *ersatz emotion.*
– ORIGIN German, 'replacement'.
Erse /erss/ ● **noun** the Scottish or Irish Gaelic language.
– ORIGIN early Scots form of IRISH.
erst /erst/ ● **adverb** archaic long ago; formerly.
– ORIGIN Old English, related to ERE.
erstwhile ● **adjective** former. ● **adverb** archaic formerly.
eructation /eeruktaysh'n/ ● **noun** formal a belch.
– ORIGIN Latin, from *ructare* 'belch'.
erudite /erroodīt/ ● **adjective** having or showing knowledge or learning.
– DERIVATIVES **eruditely** adverb **erudition** noun.
– ORIGIN Latin *eruditus*, from *erudire* 'instruct, train'.
erupt ● **verb** **1** (of a volcano) forcefully eject lava, rocks, ash, or gases. **2** break out suddenly. **3** give vent to feelings in a sudden and noisy way. **4** (of a spot, rash, etc.) suddenly appear on the skin.
– DERIVATIVES **eruptive** adjective.
– ORIGIN Latin *erumpere* 'break out'.
eruption ● **noun** an act or the action or erupting.
-ery (also **-ry**) ● **suffix** forming nouns: **1** denoting a class or kind: *greenery.* **2** denoting an occupation, a state or condition, or behaviour: *archery.* **3** denoting a place set aside for an activity or a grouping of things, animals, etc.: *rookery.*
– ORIGIN from Latin *-arius* and *-ator.*
erysipelas /errisippiləss/ ● **noun** a skin disease caused by a streptococcus and characterized by large raised red patches on the face and legs.
– ORIGIN Greek *erusipelas*; perhaps related to *eruthros* 'red' and *pella* 'skin'.
erythema /erritheemə/ ● **noun** superficial reddening of the skin caused by dilation of the blood capillaries.
– ORIGIN Greek *eruthēma*, from *eruthros* 'red'.
erythrocyte /irithrōsīt/ ● **noun** a red blood cell, containing the pigment haemoglobin and transporting oxygen to the tissues.
Es ● **symbol** the chemical element einsteinium.
ESA ● **abbreviation** **1** (in the UK) Environmentally Sensitive Area. **2** European Space Agency.
escalade /eskəlayd/ ● **noun** historical the scaling of fortified walls using ladders, as a form of military attack.
– ORIGIN French, from Latin *scalare* 'to scale, climb'.
escalate /eskəlayt/ ● **verb** **1** increase rapidly. **2** become more intense or serious.
– DERIVATIVES **escalation** noun.
– ORIGIN originally in the sense 'travel on an escalator': from ESCALATOR.
escalator ● **noun** a moving staircase consisting of a circulating belt of steps driven by a motor.
– ORIGIN from ESCALADE, on the pattern of *elevator.*
escallonia /eskəlōniə/ ● **noun** an evergreen South American shrub with pink or white flowers.
– ORIGIN named after the 18th-century Spanish traveller *Escallon*, who discovered the plants.
escalope /iskaləp/ (also **escallop**) ● **noun** a thin slice of coated and fried meat, especially veal.
– ORIGIN Old French, 'shell'.
escapade /eskəpayd/ ● **noun** an incident involving daring and adventure.
escape ● **verb** **1** break free from confinement or control. **2** elude or get free from (someone). **3** succeed in eluding (something dangerous or undesirable). **4** fail to be noticed or remembered by. ● **noun** **1** an act of escaping. **2** a means of escaping. **3** (also **escape key**) Computing a key which interrupts the current operation or converts subsequent characters to a control sequence.
– DERIVATIVES **escapable** adjective **escapee** noun **escaper** noun.
– ORIGIN Old French *eschaper*, from Latin *ex-* 'out' + *cappa* 'cloak'.
escape clause ● **noun** a clause in a contract which specifies the conditions under which one party can be freed from an obligation.
escapement /iskaypmənt/ ● **noun** **1** a mechanism in a clock or watch that connects and regulates the motive power. **2** a mechanism in a typewriter that shifts the carriage a small fixed amount to the left after a key is pressed and released. **3** the part of the mechanism in a piano that enables the hammer to fall back as soon as it has struck the string.
escape wheel ● **noun** a toothed wheel in the escapement of a watch or clock.
escapism ● **noun** the seeking of distraction from reality by engaging in entertainment or fantasy.
– DERIVATIVES **escapist** noun & adjective.
escapologist /eskəpolləjist/ ● **noun** an entertainer who specializes in breaking free from ropes, handcuffs, and chains.
– DERIVATIVES **escapology** noun.
escargot /eskaargō/ ● **noun** an edible snail.
– ORIGIN French.
escarpment /iskaarpmənt/ ● **noun** a long, steep slope at the edge of a plateau or separating areas of land at different heights.
– ORIGIN French *escarpement*, from Italian *scarpa* 'slope'.
eschatology /eskətolləji/ ● **noun** the part of theology concerned with death, judgement, and destiny.

Thesaurus

sight; fallacy, misconception, delusion; misprint, erratum; *informal* slip-up, bloomer, boo-boo; *Brit. informal* boob.
– PHRASES **in error** WRONGLY, by mistake, mistakenly, incorrectly; accidentally, by accident, inadvertently, unintentionally, by chance.
ersatz ● **adjective** ARTIFICIAL, substitute, imitation, synthetic, fake, false, mock, simulated; pseudo, sham, bogus, spurious, counterfeit; manufactured, man-made; *informal* phoney.
– OPPOSITES genuine.
erstwhile ● **adjective** FORMER, old, past, one-time, sometime, ex-, late, then; previous; *formal* quondam.
– OPPOSITES present.
erudite ● **adjective** LEARNED, scholarly, educated, knowledgeable, well read, well informed, intellectual; intelligent, clever, academic, literary; bookish, highbrow, cerebral; *informal* brainy; *dated* lettered.
– OPPOSITES ignorant.
erupt ● **verb** **1** *the volcano erupted* EMIT LAVA, become active, flare up; explode. **2** *lava was erupted* EMIT, discharge, eject, expel, spew out, pour out, disgorge. **3** *fighting erupted* BREAK OUT, flare up, start suddenly; ensue, arise, happen. **4** *a boil erupted on her temple* APPEAR, break out, flare up, come to a head, emerge.
eruption ● **noun** **1** *a volcanic eruption* DISCHARGE, ejection, emission; explosion. **2** *an eruption of violence* OUTBREAK, flare-up, upsurge, outburst, breakout, explosion; wave, spate. **3** *a skin eruption* RASH, outbreak, inflammation.
escalate ● **verb** **1** *prices have escalated* INCREASE RAPIDLY, soar, rocket, shoot up, mount, spiral, climb, go up; *informal* go through the roof, skyrocket. **2** *the dispute escalated* GROW, develop, mushroom, increase, heighten, intensify, accelerate.
– OPPOSITES plunge, shrink.
escalation ● **noun** **1** *an escalation in oil prices* INCREASE, rise, hike, growth, leap, upsurge, upturn, climb. **2** *an escalation of the conflict* INTENSIFICATION, aggravation, exacerbation, magnification, amplification, augmentation; expansion, build-up; deterioration.
escapade ● **noun** EXPLOIT, stunt, caper, antic(s), spree; adventure, venture, mission; deed, feat, trial, experience; incident, occurrence, event.
escape ● **verb** **1** *he escaped from prison* RUN AWAY/OFF, get out, break out, break free, make a break for it, bolt, flee, take flight, make off, take off, abscond, take to one's heels, make one's getaway, make a run for it; disappear, vanish, slip away, sneak away; *informal* cut and run, skedaddle, scarper, vamoose, do a vanishing act, fly the coop, take French leave, leg it; *Brit. informal* do a bunk, do a runner; *N. Amer. informal* go on the lam. **2** *he escaped his pursuers* GET AWAY FROM, escape from, elude, avoid, dodge, shake off; *informal* give someone the slip. **3** *they escaped injury* AVOID, evade, dodge, elude, miss, cheat, sidestep, circumvent, steer clear of; shirk; *informal* duck. **4** *lethal gas escaped* LEAK (OUT), seep (out), discharge, emanate, issue, flow (out), pour (out), gush (out), spurt (out), spew (out).
● **noun** **1** *his escape from prison* GETAWAY, breakout, bolt, flight; disappearance, vanishing act; *Brit. informal* flit; *informal, dated* spring. **2** *a narrow escape from death* AVOIDANCE OF, evasion of, circumvention of. **3** *a gas escape* LEAK, leakage, spill, seepage, discharge, emanation, outflow, outpouring; gush, stream, spurt. **4** *an escape from boredom* DISTRACTION, diversion.
escapee ● **noun** RUNAWAY, escaper, absconder; jailbreaker, fugitive; truant; deserter, defector.
escapism ● **noun** FANTASY, fantasizing, daydreaming, daydreams,

– DERIVATIVES **eschatological** adjective **eschatologist** noun.
– ORIGIN from Greek *eskhatos* 'last'.
escheat /isscheet/ • noun chiefly historical the reversion of property to the state, or (in feudal law) to a lord, on the owner's dying without legal heirs.
– ORIGIN Old French *eschete*, from Latin *excidere* 'fall away'.
eschew /isschōō/ • verb abstain from.
– DERIVATIVES **eschewal** noun.
– ORIGIN Old French *eschiver*, related to SHY[1].
escort • noun /eskort/ **1** a person, vehicle, or group accompanying another to provide protection or as a mark of rank. **2** a person who accompanies a member of the opposite sex to a social event. • verb /iskort/ accompany as an escort.
– ORIGIN French *escorte*, from Italian *scorta* 'conducted, guided'.
escritoire /eskritwaar/ • noun a small writing desk with drawers and compartments.
– ORIGIN French, from Latin *scriptorium* 'room for writing'.
escrow /eskrō/ • noun Law **1** a bond, deed, or deposit kept by a third party until a specified condition has been fulfilled. **2** the state of being kept in this way.
– ORIGIN Old French *escroe* 'scrap, scroll'; related to SHRED.
escudo /eskyōōdō/ • noun (pl. **escudos**) the basic monetary unit of Portugal and Cape Verde, equal to 100 centavos.
– ORIGIN Portuguese, from Latin *scutum* 'shield'.
esculent /eskyoolənt/ • adjective formal fit to be eaten.
– ORIGIN Latin *esculentus*, from *esca* 'food'.
escutcheon /iskuchən/ • noun **1** a shield or emblem bearing a coat of arms. **2** a flat piece of metal framing a keyhole, door handle, or light switch.
– PHRASES **a blot on one's escutcheon** a stain on one's reputation or character.
– ORIGIN Old French *escuchon*, from Latin *scutum* 'shield'.
ESE • abbreviation east-south-east.
-ese • suffix forming adjectives and nouns: **1** denoting an inhabitant or language of a country or city: *Chinese*. **2** often derogatory (especially with reference to language) denoting character or style: *journalese*.
– ORIGIN from Latin *-ensis*.
esker /eskər/ • noun Geology a long winding ridge of sediment deposited by meltwater from a retreating glacier or ice sheet.
– ORIGIN Irish *eiscir*.
Eskimo • noun (pl. same or **Eskimos**) **1** a member of a people inhabiting northern Canada, Alaska, Greenland, and eastern Siberia. **2** either of the two main languages of this people (Inuit and Yupik). • adjective relating to the Eskimos or their languages.
– USAGE The word **Eskimo** is now regarded by some as offensive: the peoples inhabiting the regions from NW Canada to western Greenland prefer to call themselves **Inuit**. The term **Eskimo**, however, is the only term that covers both the Inuit and the Yupik, and is still widely used.
– ORIGIN an Algonquian word, perhaps in the sense 'people speaking a different language'.
ESL • abbreviation English as a second language.
ESN • abbreviation electronic serial number.
ESOL • abbreviation English for speakers of other languages.
esophagus etc. • noun US spelling of OESOPHAGUS etc.
esoteric /essəterrik, eesə-/ • adjective intended for or understood by only a small number of people with a specialized knowledge.
– DERIVATIVES **esoterically** adverb **esotericism** noun **esotericist** noun.
– ORIGIN Greek *esōterikos*, from *esō* 'within'.
esoterica /essəterrikə, eesə-/ • plural noun esoteric subjects or publications.
ESP • abbreviation extrasensory perception.
espadrille /espədril/ • noun a light canvas shoe with a plaited fibre sole.
– ORIGIN French, from Provençal *espart* 'esparto'.
espalier /ispaliər/ • noun a fruit tree or ornamental shrub whose branches are trained to grow flat against a wall. • verb train (a tree or shrub) in such a way.
– ORIGIN French, from Italian *spalliera*, from Latin *spatula* 'small spathe'.
esparto /espaartō/ (also **esparto grass**) • noun (pl. **espartos**) a coarse grass native to Spain and North Africa, used to make ropes, wickerwork, and paper.
– ORIGIN Spanish, from Greek *sparton* 'rope'.
especial • adjective **1** notable; special. **2** for or belonging chiefly to one person or thing.
– ORIGIN Latin *specialis* 'special'.
especially • adverb **1** in particular. **2** to a great extent; very much.
– USAGE The words **especially** and **specially** are not interchangeable, although both can mean 'particularly'. Only **especially** means 'in particular', as in *he despised them all, especially Thomas*, and only **specially** means 'for a special purpose', as in *the car was specially made for the occasion*.
Esperanto /espərantō/ • noun an artificial language devised in 1887 as an international medium of communication.
– DERIVATIVES **Esperantist** noun.
– ORIGIN from *Dr Esperanto*, a pen name of the inventor of the language, Polish physician Ludwik L. Zamenhof; the literal sense is 'one who hopes'.
espionage /espiənaazh/ • noun the practice of spying or of using spies.
– ORIGIN French, from *espion* 'a spy'.
esplanade /espləṉayd/ • noun a long, open, level area, typically beside the sea, along which people may walk for pleasure.
– ORIGIN French, from Latin *explanatus* 'levelled'.
espousal /ispowz'l/ • noun the action of espousing.
espouse /ispowz/ • verb adopt or support (a cause, belief, or way of life).
– ORIGIN Old French *espouser*, from Latin *sponsus* 'betrothed'.
espresso /espressō/ (also **expresso**) • noun (pl. **espressos**) strong black coffee made by forcing steam through ground coffee beans.
– ORIGIN from Italian *caffè espresso* 'pressed out coffee'.
esprit /espree/ • noun liveliness.
– ORIGIN French, from Latin *spiritus* 'spirit'.
esprit de corps /espree də **kor**/ • noun a feeling of pride and loyalty uniting the members of a group.
– ORIGIN French, 'spirit of the body'.
espy /ispī/ • verb (**espies, espied**) literary catch sight of.

e

Thesaurus

reverie; imagination, flight(s) of fancy, pipe dreams, wishful thinking, wool-gathering; *informal* pie in the sky.
– OPPOSITES realism.
eschew • verb ABSTAIN FROM, refrain from, give up, forgo, shun, renounce, steer clear of, have nothing to do with, fight shy of; relinquish, reject, disavow, abandon, spurn, wash one's hands of, drop; *informal* kick, pack in; *Brit. informal* jack in; *formal* forswear, abjure.
escort • noun **1** *a police escort* GUARD, bodyguard, protector, minder, custodian; attendant, chaperone; entourage, retinue, cortège; protection, defence, convoy. **2** *her escort for the evening* COMPANION, partner; *informal* date. **3** *an agency dealing with escorts* PAID COMPANION, hostess, geisha; gigolo.
• verb **1** *he was escorted home by the police* CONDUCT, accompany, guide, usher, shepherd, take. **2** *he escorted her in to dinner* ACCOMPANY, partner, take, bring.
esoteric • adjective ABSTRUSE, obscure, arcane, recherché, rarefied, recondite, abstract; enigmatic, inscrutable, cryptic, Delphic; complex, complicated, incomprehensible, opaque, impenetrable, mysterious.
especial • adjective **1** *especial care is required* PARTICULAR, (extra) special, superior, exceptional, extraordinary; unusual, out of the ordinary, uncommon, remarkable, singular. **2** *her especial brand of charm* DISTINCTIVE, individual, special, particular, distinct, peculiar, personal, own, unique, specific.
especially • adverb **1** *work poured in, especially from Kent* MAINLY, mostly, chiefly, principally, largely; substantially, particularly, primarily, generally, usually, typically. **2** *a committee especially for the purpose* EXPRESSLY, specially, specifically, exclusively, just, particularly, explicitly. **3** *he is especially talented* EXCEPTIONALLY, particularly, specially, very, extremely, singularly, distinctly, unusually, extraordinarily, uncommonly, uniquely, remarkably, outstandingly, really; *informal* seriously, majorly; *Brit. informal* jolly, dead, well.
espionage • noun SPYING, infiltration; eavesdropping, surveillance, reconnaissance, intelligence.
espousal • noun ADOPTION, embracing, acceptance; support, championship, encouragement, defence; sponsorship, promotion, endorsement, advocacy, approval.
espouse • verb ADOPT, embrace, take up, accept, welcome; sup-

– ORIGIN Old French *espier*.
Esq. ● abbreviation Esquire.
-esque ● suffix (forming adjectives) in the style of: *Kafkaesque*.
– ORIGIN French, from Latin *-iscus*.
Esquimau ● noun (pl. **Esquimaux**) archaic spelling of ESKIMO.
esquire /iskwīr/ ● noun **1** (**Esquire**) Brit. a polite title appended to a man's name when no other title is used. **2** historical a young nobleman who acted as an attendant to a knight.
– ORIGIN Old French *esquier*, from Latin *scutarius* 'shield-bearer'.
-ess ● suffix forming nouns denoting female gender: *abbess*.
– USAGE In modern English, feminine forms (e.g. **poetess**, **authoress**) are likely to be regarded as old-fashioned or sexist and should be avoided in favour of the 'neutral' base form (e.g. **poet**, **author**).
– ORIGIN French *-esse*, from Greek *-issa*.
essay ● noun /essay/ **1** a piece of writing on a particular subject. **2** formal an attempt or effort. ● verb /esay/ formal attempt.
– DERIVATIVES **essayist** noun **essayistic** adjective.
– ORIGIN Old French *essai* 'trial'; the verb is an alteration of ASSAY.
essence ● noun **1** the intrinsic nature of something; the quality which determines something's character. **2** an extract or concentrate obtained from a plant or other substance and used for flavouring or scent.
– PHRASES **in essence** basically; fundamentally. **of the essence** critically important.
– ORIGIN Latin *essentia*, from *esse* 'be'.
essential ● adjective **1** fundamental; central. **2** absolutely necessary. ● noun (**essentials**) **1** the fundamental elements. **2** things that are absolutely necessary.
– DERIVATIVES **essentially** adverb.
essential oil ● noun a natural oil extracted from a plant.
EST ● abbreviation Eastern Standard Time.
est. ● abbreviation **1** established. **2** estimated.
-est ● suffix forming the superlative of adjectives (such as *shortest*) and of adverbs (such as *soonest*).
– ORIGIN Old English.
establish ● verb **1** set up on a firm or permanent basis. **2** initiate or bring about. **3** (**be established**) be settled or accepted in a particular place or role. **4** show to be true or certain by determining the facts. **5** (**established**) recognized by the state as the national Church or religion. **6** (of a plant) take root and grow.
– DERIVATIVES **establisher** noun
– ORIGIN Old French *establir*, from Latin *stabilire* 'make firm'.
establishment ● noun **1** the action of establishing or being established. **2** a business organization, public institution, or household. **3** (**the Establishment**) a group in a society exercising power and influence over matters of policy or opinion, and seen as resisting change.
establishmentarian /istablishməntairiən/ ● adjective advocating or relating to the principle of an established Church. ● noun a person advocating this.
estate ● noun **1** a property consisting of a large house and extensive grounds. **2** Brit. an area of land and modern buildings developed for residential, industrial, or commercial purposes. **3** a property where crops such as coffee or rubber are cultivated or where wine is produced. **4** a person's money and property in its entirety at the time of their death. **5** (also **estate of the realm**) (in Britain) one of the three groups constituting Parliament, now the Lords spiritual (the heads of the Church), the Lords temporal (the peerage), and the Commons. **6** archaic or literary a particular state, period, or condition in life. **7** Brit. an estate car.
– ORIGIN Old French *estat*, from Latin *status* 'state, condition'.
estate agency ● noun chiefly Brit. a business that sells and rents out buildings and land for clients.
– DERIVATIVES **estate agent** noun.
estate car ● noun Brit. a car incorporating a large carrying area behind the seats and an extra door at the rear.
estate duty ● noun Brit. a former death duty levied on property.
esteem ● noun respect and admiration. ● verb **1** respect and admire. **2** formal consider; deem.
– ORIGIN Latin *aestimare* 'to estimate'.
ester /estər/ ● noun Chemistry an organic compound made by replacing the hydrogen of an acid by an alkyl or other organic group.
esthetic etc. ● adjective US spelling of AESTHETIC etc.
estimable ● adjective worthy of great respect.
– DERIVATIVES **estimably** adverb.
estimate ● noun /estimət/ **1** an approximate calculation. **2** a written statement indicating the likely price that will be charged for specified work. **3** a judgement or appraisal. ● verb

Thesaurus

port, back, champion, favour, prefer, encourage; promote, endorse, advocate.
– OPPOSITES reject.
espy ● verb *(poetic/literary)* CATCH SIGHT OF, glimpse, see, spot, spy, notice, observe, discern, pick out, detect; *poetic/literary* behold, descry.
essay ● noun **1** *he wrote an essay* ARTICLE, composition, study, paper, dissertation, thesis, discourse, treatise, disquisition, monograph; commentary, critique; *N. Amer.* theme. **2** *(formal) his first essay in telecommunications* ATTEMPT, effort, endeavour, try, venture, trial, experiment, undertaking.
● verb *(formal) many essayed to travel that way* ATTEMPT, try, strive, venture, endeavour, seek, undertake.
essence ● noun **1** *the very essence of economics* QUINTESSENCE, soul, spirit, nature; core, heart, crux, nucleus, substance; principle, fundamental quality, sum and substance, reality, actuality; *informal* nitty-gritty. **2** *essence of ginger* EXTRACT, concentrate, distillate, elixir, decoction, juice, tincture; scent, perfume, oil.
– PHRASES **in essence** ESSENTIALLY, basically, fundamentally, primarily, principally, chiefly, predominantly, substantially; above all, first and foremost; effectively, virtually, to all intents and purposes; intrinsically, inherently. **of the essence.** See ESSENTIAL adjective sense 1.
essential ● adjective **1** *it is essential to remove the paint* CRUCIAL, necessary, key, vital, indispensable, important, all-important, of the essence, critical, imperative, mandatory, compulsory, obligatory; urgent, pressing, paramount, pre-eminent, high-priority. **2** *the essential simplicity of his style* BASIC, inherent, fundamental, quintessential, intrinsic, underlying, characteristic, innate, primary, elementary, elemental; central, pivotal, vital. **3** *the essential English gentleman* IDEAL, absolute, complete, perfect, quintessential.
– OPPOSITES unimportant, optional, secondary.
● noun **1** *an essential for broadcasters* NECESSITY, prerequisite, requisite, requirement, need; condition, precondition, stipulation; sine qua non; *informal* must. **2** *the essentials of the job* FUNDAMENTALS, basics, rudiments, first principles, foundations, bedrock; essence, basis, core, kernel, crux, sine qua non; *informal* nitty-gritty, brass tacks, nuts and bolts.
establish ● verb **1** *they established an office in Moscow* SET UP, start, initiate, institute, form, found, create, inaugurate; build, construct, install. **2** *evidence to establish his guilt* PROVE, demonstrate, show, indicate, signal, exhibit, manifest, attest to, evidence, determine, confirm, verify, certify, substantiate.
established ● adjective **1** *established practice* ACCEPTED, traditional, orthodox, habitual, set, fixed, official; usual, customary, common, normal, general, prevailing, accustomed, familiar, expected, routine, typical, conventional, standard. **2** *an established composer* WELL KNOWN, recognized, esteemed, respected, famous, prominent, noted, renowned.
establishment ● noun **1** *the establishment of a democracy* FOUNDATION, institution, formation, inception, creation, installation; inauguration, start, initiation. **2** *a dressmaking establishment* BUSINESS, firm, company, concern, enterprise, venture, organization, operation; factory, plant, shop, office, practice; *informal* outfit, setup. **3** *educational establishments* INSTITUTION, place, premises, foundation, institute. **4** *they dare to poke fun at the Establishment* THE AUTHORITIES, the powers that be, the system, the ruling class; *informal* Big Brother.
estate ● noun **1** *the Balmoral estate* PROPERTY, grounds, garden(s), park, parkland, land(s), landholding, manor, territory. **2** *a housing estate* AREA, site, development, complex. **3** *a coffee estate* PLANTATION, farm, holding; forest, vineyard; *N. Amer.* ranch. **4** *he left an estate worth £610,000* ASSETS, capital, wealth, riches, holdings, fortune; property, effects, possessions, belongings; *Law* goods and chattels. **5** *(archaic) the estate of matrimony* STATE, condition, situation, position, circumstance.
estate agent ● noun PROPERTY AGENT; *Brit.* house agent; *N. Amer.* realtor.
esteem ● noun *she was held in high esteem* RESPECT, admiration, acclaim, approbation, appreciation, favour, recognition, honour, reverence; estimation, regard, opinion.
● verb **1** *such ceramics are highly esteemed* RESPECT, ADMIRE, value,

/estimayt/ form an estimate of.
– DERIVATIVES **estimation** noun **estimator** noun.
– ORIGIN Latin *aestimare* 'determine, appraise'.
Estonian • noun a person from Estonia. • adjective relating to Estonia.
estop /istop/ • verb (**estopped, estopping**) Law bar or preclude by estoppel.
– ORIGIN Old French *estopper* 'stop up, impede', from Latin *stuppa* 'tow, oakum'.
estoppel /istopp'l/ • noun Law the principle by which a person cannot assert something contrary to their previous statements or to a relevant judicial determination.
estradiol • noun US spelling of OESTRADIOL.
estrange • verb **1** cause to feel less close or friendly. **2** (**estranged**) (of a husband or wife) no longer living with their spouse.
– DERIVATIVES **estrangement** noun.
– ORIGIN Old French *estranger*, from Latin *extraneare* 'treat as a stranger'.
estrogen etc. • noun US spelling of OESTROGEN etc.
estrus etc. • noun US spelling of OESTRUS etc.
estuary /estyoori/ • noun (pl. **estuaries**) the tidal mouth of a large river.
– DERIVATIVES **estuarine** /estyoorin/ adjective.
– ORIGIN Latin *aestuarium* 'tidal part of a shore', from *aestus* 'tide'.
Estuary English • noun (in the UK) a type of accent containing features of both received pronunciation and London speech.
esurient /isyooriənt/ • adjective archaic or humorous hungry or greedy.
– ORIGIN from Latin *esurire* 'be hungry'.
ET • abbreviation **1** (in North America) Eastern time. **2** extraterrestrial.
-et • suffix forming nouns which were originally diminutives: *baronet.*
– ORIGIN Old French *-et, -ete.*
ETA /ee-tee-ay/ • abbreviation estimated time of arrival.
eta /eetə/ • noun the seventh letter of the Greek alphabet (Η, η), transliterated as 'e' or 'ē'.
– ORIGIN Greek.
e-tailer • noun a retailer who sells goods via electronic transactions on the Internet.
et al. /et al/ • abbreviation and others.
– ORIGIN Latin *et alii.*
etc. • abbreviation et cetera.
et cetera /etsettrə/ (also **etcetera**) • adverb and other similar things; and so on. • noun (**et ceteras**) unspecified extra items.
– ORIGIN Latin, from *et* 'and' and *cetera* 'the rest'.
etch • verb **1** engrave (metal, glass, or stone) by drawing on a protective layer with a needle, and then covering it with acid to attack the exposed parts. **2** (of an acid or other solvent) corrode the surface of. **3** cut (a text or design) on a surface. **4** cause to be clearly defined: *etched in the memory.*
– DERIVATIVES **etcher** noun.
– ORIGIN Dutch *etsen*, from German *ätzen.*
etching • noun **1** the art or process of etching. **2** a print produced by etching.
eternal • adjective **1** lasting or existing forever. **2** valid for all time: *eternal truths.*
– PHRASES **the Eternal City** the city of Rome. **eternal triangle** a relationship between three people involving sexual rivalry.
– DERIVATIVES **eternally** adverb.
– ORIGIN Latin *aeternalis*, from *aevum* 'age'.
eternity • noun (pl. **eternities**) **1** infinite or unending time. **2** Theology endless life after death. **3** (**an eternity**) informal an undesirably long period of time.
ethane /eethayn/ • noun Chemistry a flammable hydrocarbon gas of the alkane series, present in petroleum and natural gas.
– ORIGIN from ETHER.
ethanol /ethənol/ • noun systematic chemical name for ETHYL ALCOHOL (see ALCOHOL).
ether /eethər/ • noun **1** (also **diethyl ether**) a volatile, highly flammable liquid used as an anaesthetic and as a solvent. **2** Chemistry any organic compound with an oxygen atom linking two alkyl groups. **3** (also **aether**) chiefly literary the clear sky; the upper regions of air. **4** (also **aether**) Physics, historical a substance formerly thought to permeate all space.
– DERIVATIVES **etheric** adjective.
– ORIGIN Greek *aithēr* 'upper air', from *aithein* 'burn, shine'.
ethereal /itheeriəl/ (also **etherial**) • adjective **1** extremely delicate and light. **2** heavenly or spiritual.
– DERIVATIVES **ethereality** noun **ethereally** adverb.
Ethernet • noun Computing a system for connecting a number of computer systems to form a local area network.
– ORIGIN blend of ETHER and NETWORK.
ethic • noun a set of moral principles.
– ORIGIN Latin *ethice*, from Greek *hē ēthikē tekhnē* 'the science of morals'.
ethical • adjective **1** relating to moral principles or the branch of knowledge concerned with these. **2** morally correct. **3** (of a medicine) available only on prescription.
– DERIVATIVES **ethically** adverb.
ethics • plural noun **1** the moral principles governing or

Thesaurus

regard, acclaim, appreciate, like, prize, treasure, favour, revere. **2** (formal) *I would esteem it a favour if you could speak to him.* See DEEM.
estimate • verb **1** *estimate the cost* CALCULATE ROUGHLY, approximate, guess; evaluate, judge, gauge, reckon, rate, determine; informal guesstimate. **2** *we estimate it to be worth £50,000* CONSIDER, believe, reckon, deem, judge, rate, gauge; formal opine.
• noun **1** *an estimate of the cost* ROUGH CALCULATION, approximation, estimation, rough guess; costing, quotation, valuation, evaluation; informal guesstimate. **2** *his estimate of Paul's integrity* EVALUATION, estimation, judgement, rating, appraisal, opinion, view.
estimation • noun **1** *an estimation of economic growth* ESTIMATE, approximation, rough calculation, rough guess, evaluation; informal guesstimate. **2** *he rated highly in Carl's estimation* ASSESSMENT, evaluation, judgement; esteem, opinion, view.
estrange • verb ALIENATE, antagonize, turn away, drive away, distance; sever, set at odds with, drive a wedge between.
estrangement • noun ALIENATION, antagonism, antipathy, disaffection, hostility, unfriendliness; variance, difference; parting, separation, divorce, break-up, split, breach, schism.
estuary • noun (RIVER) MOUTH, firth; delta.
et cetera • adverb AND SO ON, and so forth, and the rest, and/or the like, and suchlike, among others, et al., etc.; informal and what have you, and whatnot.
etch • verb **1** *the metal is etched with acid* CORRODE, burn into; mark. **2** *a stone etched with tiny designs* ENGRAVE, carve, inscribe, incise, chase, score, print, mark.
etching • noun ENGRAVING, print, impression, block, plate; woodcut, linocut.
eternal • adjective **1** *eternal happiness* EVERLASTING, never-ending, endless, perpetual, undying, immortal, abiding, permanent, enduring, infinite, boundless, timeless. **2** *eternal vigilance* CONSTANT, continual, continuous, perpetual, persistent, sustained, unremitting, relentless, unrelieved, uninterrupted, unbroken, never-ending, non-stop, round-the-clock, endless, ceaseless.
– OPPOSITES transient, intermittent.
eternally • adverb **1** *I shall be eternally grateful* FOREVER, permanently, perpetually, (for) evermore, for ever and ever, for eternity, in perpetuity, enduringly; N. Amer. forevermore; informal until doomsday, until the cows come home; archaic for aye. **2** *the tenants complain eternally* CONSTANTLY, continually, continuously, always, all the time, persistently, repeatedly, regularly; day and night, non-stop; endlessly, incessantly, perpetually; interminably, relentlessly; informal 24-7.
eternity • noun **1** *the memory will remain for eternity* EVER, all time, perpetuity. **2** (Theology) *souls destined for eternity* THE AFTERLIFE, everlasting life, life after death, the hereafter, the afterworld, the next world; heaven, paradise, immortality. **3** (informal) *I waited an eternity for you* A LONG TIME, an age, ages, a lifetime; hours, years, aeons; forever; informal donkey's years, a month of Sundays; Brit. informal yonks.
ethereal • adjective **1** *her ethereal beauty* DELICATE, exquisite, dainty, elegant, graceful; fragile, airy, fine, subtle. **2** *theologians discuss ethereal ideas* CELESTIAL, heavenly, spiritual, other-worldly, paradisal, Elysian.
– OPPOSITES substantial, earthly.
ethical • adjective **1** *an ethical dilemma* MORAL, social, behavioural. **2** *an ethical investment policy* MORALLY CORRECT, right-minded, principled, irreproachable; righteous, high-minded, virtuous, good, moral; clean, lawful, just, honourable, reputable, respectable,

influencing conduct. **2** the branch of knowledge concerned with moral principles.
– DERIVATIVES **ethicist** noun.

Ethiopian ● noun a person from Ethiopia. ● adjective relating to Ethiopia.

ethnic ● adjective **1** relating to a group of people having a common national or cultural tradition. **2** referring to origin by birth rather than by present nationality: *ethnic Albanians.* **3** relating to a non-Western cultural tradition: *ethnic music.*
– DERIVATIVES **ethnically** adverb **ethnicity** noun.
– ORIGIN Greek *ethnikos* 'heathen', from *ethnos* 'nation'.

ethnic cleansing ● noun the mass expulsion or killing of members of an ethnic or religious group in an area by those of another.

e

ethnic minority ● noun a group within a community which differs ethnically from the main population.

ethnocentric ● adjective evaluating other cultures according to the preconceptions of one's own.
– DERIVATIVES **ethnocentrically** adverb **ethnocentricity** noun **ethnocentrism** noun.

ethnography ● noun the scientific description of peoples and cultures.
– DERIVATIVES **ethnographer** noun **ethnographic** adjective.

ethnology /ethnolləji/ ● noun the study of the characteristics of different peoples and the differences and relationships between them.
– DERIVATIVES **ethnologic** adjective **ethnological** adjective **ethnologist** noun.

ethology /eetholləji/ ● noun **1** the science of animal behaviour. **2** the study of human behaviour from a biological perspective.
– DERIVATIVES **ethological** adjective **ethologist** noun.
– ORIGIN Greek *ēthologia*, from *ēthos* 'nature, disposition'.

ethos /eethoss/ ● noun the characteristic spirit of a culture, era, or community.
– ORIGIN Greek *ēthos* 'nature, disposition'.

ethyl /ethīl/ ● noun Chemistry the alkyl radical $-C_2H_5$, derived from ethane.
– ORIGIN German, from *Äther* 'ether'.

ethyl alcohol ● noun another term for ALCOHOL (in sense 1).

ethylene /ethileen/ ● noun Chemistry a flammable hydrocarbon gas of the alkene series, present in natural gas and coal gas.

ethylene glycol ● noun Chemistry a colourless viscous liquid used in antifreeze and in wood preservatives.

etiolated /eetiəlaytid/ ● adjective (of a plant) pale and weak due to a lack of light.
– ORIGIN from French *étieuler* 'grow into haulm'.

etiology ● noun US spelling of AETIOLOGY.

etiquette /ettiket/ ● noun the code of polite behaviour in a society.
– ORIGIN French, 'list of ceremonial observances of a court', also 'label, etiquette', from Old French *estiquette* (see TICKET).

Etruscan /itruskən/ ● noun **1** a person from Etruria, an ancient Italian state that was at its height *c.*500 BC. **2** the language of Etruria. ● adjective relating to Etruria.
– ORIGIN from Latin *Etruscus.*

et seq. ● adverb and what follows (used in page references).
– ORIGIN from Latin *et sequens* 'and the following'.

-ette ● suffix forming nouns: **1** denoting small size: *kitchenette.* **2** denoting an imitation or substitute: *leatherette.* **3** denoting female gender: *suffragette.*
– ORIGIN Old French.

étude /aytyōōd/ ● noun a short musical composition or exercise.
– ORIGIN French, 'study'.

etymology /ettimolləji/ ● noun (pl. **etymologies**) an account of the origins and the developments in meaning of a word.
– DERIVATIVES **etymological** adjective **etymologically** adverb **etymologist** noun.
– ORIGIN Greek *etumologia*, from *etumos* 'true'.

etymon /ettimon/ ● noun a word or form from which a later word is derived.
– ORIGIN Greek *etumon*, from *etumos* 'true'.

EU ● abbreviation European Union.

Eu ● symbol the chemical element europium.

eucalyptus /yōōkəliptəss/ (also **eucalypt**) ● noun (pl. **eucalyptuses** or **eucalypti** /yōōkəliptī/) **1** an evergreen Australasian tree valued for its wood, oil, gum, and resin. **2** the oil from eucalyptus leaves, used for its medicinal properties.
– ORIGIN Latin, from Greek *eu* 'well' + *kaluptos* 'covered', because the unopened flower is protected by a cap.

Eucharist /yōōkərist/ ● noun **1** the Christian ceremony commemorating the Last Supper, in which consecrated bread and wine are consumed. **2** the consecrated elements, especially the bread.
– DERIVATIVES **Eucharistic** adjective.
– ORIGIN Greek *eukharistia* 'thanksgiving', from *eu* 'well' + *kharizesthai* 'offer graciously'.

euchre /yōōkər/ ● noun a card game played with the thirty-two highest cards, the aim being to win at least three of the five tricks played. ● verb **1** (in euchre) prevent (another player) from taking three tricks. **2** N. Amer. informal deceive or outwit.
– ORIGIN German dialect *Juckerspiel.*

Euclidean /yōōkliddiən/ ● adjective (of systems of geometry) obeying the postulates of the Greek mathematician Euclid (*c.* 300 BC), in particular that only one line through a given point can be parallel to a given line.

eugenics /yōōjenniks/ ● plural noun the science of using controlled breeding to increase the occurrence of desirable heritable characteristics in a population.
– DERIVATIVES **eugenic** adjective **eugenicist** noun & adjective.
– ORIGIN from Greek *eu* 'well' + *genēs* 'born'.

eukaryote /yōōkariōt/ ● noun Biology an organism consisting of a cell or cells in which the genetic material is DNA in the form of chromosomes contained within a distinct nucleus (that is, all living organisms other than the bacteria and archaea). Compare with PROKARYOTE.
– DERIVATIVES **eukaryotic** adjective.
– ORIGIN from Greek *eu* 'well' + *karuon* 'kernel'.

eulogize /yōōləjīz/ (also **eulogise**) ● verb praise highly.
– DERIVATIVES **eulogist** noun **eulogistic** adjective.

eulogy /yōōləji/ ● noun (pl. **eulogies**) a speech or piece of writing that praises someone highly.
– ORIGIN Greek *eulogia* 'praise'.

eunuch /yōōnək/ ● noun a man who has been castrated.
– ORIGIN Greek *eunoukhos* 'bedroom guard' (eunuchs were formerly employed to guard the women's living areas at an oriental court).

euonymus /yōōonniməss/ ● noun a shrub or small tree noted for its autumn colours and bright fruit.
– ORIGIN Greek *euōnumos* 'having an auspicious or honoured name'.

euphemism /yōōfəmiz'm/ ● noun a mild or less direct word substituted for one that is harsh or blunt when referring to something unpleasant or embarrassing.
– DERIVATIVES **euphemistic** adjective **euphemistically** adverb.
– ORIGIN Greek *euphēmismos*, from *eu* 'well' + *phēmē* 'speaking'.

euphonious /yōōfōniəss/ ● adjective sounding pleasant.
– DERIVATIVES **euphoniously** adverb.

euphonium /yōōfōniəm/ ● noun a brass musical instrument re-

Thesaurus

noble, worthy; praiseworthy, commendable, admirable, laudable; whiter than white, saintly, impeccable; *informal* squeaky clean.

ethics ● plural noun MORAL CODE, morals, morality, values, rights and wrongs, principles, ideals, standards (of behaviour), virtues.

ethnic ● adjective RACIAL, race-related, ethnological; cultural, national, tribal, ancestral, traditional.

ethos ● noun SPIRIT, character, atmosphere, climate, mood, feeling, tenor, essence; disposition, rationale, morality, moral code, principles, standards, ethics.

etiquette ● noun PROTOCOL, manners, accepted behaviour, rules of conduct, decorum, good form; courtesy, propriety, formalities, niceties, punctilios; custom, convention; *informal* the done thing; *formal* politesse.

etymology ● noun DERIVATION, word history, development, origin, source.

eulogize ● verb EXTOL, acclaim, sing the praises of, praise to the skies, wax lyrical about, rhapsodize about, rave about, enthuse about; *N. Amer. informal* ballyhoo.
– OPPOSITES criticize.

eulogy ● noun ACCOLADE, panegyric, paean, tribute, compliment, commendation; praise, acclaim; plaudits, bouquets; *formal* encomium.
– OPPOSITES attack.

euphemism ● noun POLITE TERM, indirect term, substitute, alternative, understatement, genteelism.

euphemistic ● adjective POLITE, substitute, mild, understated, in-

sembling a small tuba.
– ORIGIN from Greek *euphōnos* 'having a pleasing sound'.
euphony /yōōfəni/ • noun (pl. **euphonies**) **1** the quality of being pleasing to the ear. **2** the tendency to make phonetic change for ease of pronunciation.
– DERIVATIVES **euphonic** adjective.
euphorbia /yōōforbiə/ • noun a plant of a genus that comprises the spurges.
– ORIGIN named after *Euphorbus*, Greek physician to the reputed discoverer of the plant, Juba II of Mauretania (1st century BC).
euphoria /yōōforiə/ • noun a feeling of intense happiness.
– DERIVATIVES **euphoric** adjective **euphorically** adverb.
– ORIGIN Greek, from *euphoros* 'borne well, healthy'.
Eurasian • adjective **1** of mixed European (or European-American) and Asian parentage. **2** relating to Eurasia. • noun a person of Eurasian parentage.
eureka /yooreekə/ • exclamation a cry of joy or satisfaction when one finds or discovers something. • noun an alloy of copper and nickel used for electrical filament and resistance wire.
– ORIGIN Greek *heurēka* 'I have found it', said to have been uttered by Archimedes (died 212 BC) when he hit upon a method of determining the purity of gold.
Euro • adjective informal European, especially concerned with the European Union. • noun (**euro**) the single European currency, introduced in the European Union in 1999.
Eurobond • noun an international bond issued in Europe or elsewhere outside the country in whose currency its value is stated.
Eurocentric • adjective implicitly regarding European culture as pre-eminent.
– DERIVATIVES **Eurocentrism** noun.
Eurocrat • noun informal, chiefly derogatory a bureaucrat in the administration of the European Union.
Eurodollar • noun a US dollar held in Europe or elsewhere outside the US.
Euroland (also **Eurozone**) • noun the economic region formed by the member countries of the European Union that have adopted the euro.
European • noun **1** a person from Europe. **2** a person who is white or of European parentage. • adjective relating to Europe or the European Union.
– DERIVATIVES **Europeanism** noun **Europeanize** (also **Europeanise**) verb.
European Union • noun an economic and political association of certain European countries as a unit with internal free trade and common external tariffs.
europium /yoorōpiəm/ • noun a soft silvery-white metallic element of the lanthanide series.
– ORIGIN from *Europe*.
Euro-sceptic • noun a person who is opposed to increasing the powers of the European Union.
– DERIVATIVES **Euro-scepticism** noun.
Eurotrash • noun informal rich European socialites, especially those living in the United States.
Euskara /yōōsskərə/ • noun the Basque language.
– ORIGIN the name in Basque.
Eustachian tube /yōōstaysh'n/ • noun Anatomy a narrow passage leading from the pharynx to the cavity of the middle ear, permitting the equalization of pressure on each side of the eardrum.
– ORIGIN named after the Italian anatomist Bartolomeo *Eustachio* (died 1574).
eustasy /yōōstəsi/ • noun a change of sea level throughout the world, caused typically by movements of parts of the earth's crust or melting of glaciers.
– DERIVATIVES **eustatic** adjective.
– ORIGIN from Greek *eu* 'well' + *statikos* 'static'.
eutectic /yōōtektik/ • adjective Chemistry (of a mixture of two substances) having a distinct melting point which is lower than the melting points of the separate constituents.
– ORIGIN Greek *eutēktos* 'easily melting'.
euthanasia /yōōthənayziə/ • noun the painless killing of a patient suffering from an incurable disease or in an irreversible coma.
– ORIGIN from Greek *eu* 'well' + *thanatos* 'death'.
eutrophic /yōōtrōfik, -troff-/ • adjective Ecology (of a body of water) rich in nutrients and so supporting a dense plant population.
– DERIVATIVES **eutrophication** noun.
– ORIGIN from Greek *eu* 'well' + *trephein* 'nourish'.
EVA • abbreviation ethyl vinyl acetate.
evacuate • verb **1** remove from a place of danger to a safer place. **2** leave (a dangerous place). **3** technical remove air, water, or other contents from (a container). **4** empty (the bowels or another bodily organ).
– DERIVATIVES **evacuation** noun.
– ORIGIN Latin *evacuare*, from *vacuus* 'empty'.
evacuee • noun a person evacuated from a place of danger.
evade • verb **1** escape or avoid, especially by cunning or trickery. **2** avoid giving a direct answer to (a question). **3** escape paying (tax or duty), especially by illegitimate presentation of one's finances.
– DERIVATIVES **evader** noun.
– ORIGIN Latin *evadere* from *vadere* 'go'.
evaluate • verb **1** form an idea of the amount or value of; assess. **2** Mathematics find a numerical expression or equivalent for (a formula, function, etc.).
– DERIVATIVES **evaluation** noun **evaluative** adjective **evaluator** noun.
evanescent • adjective chiefly literary quickly fading from sight, memory, or existence.
– DERIVATIVES **evanesce** verb **evanescence** noun.
– ORIGIN from Latin *evanescere* 'disappear'.
evangelical • adjective **1** of or according to the teaching of the gospel or Christianity. **2** relating to a tradition within Protestant Christianity emphasizing Biblical authority and personal conversion. **3** fervent in advocating something. • noun a member of the evangelical tradition in the Christian Church.
– DERIVATIVES **evangelicalism** noun **evangelically** adverb.
– ORIGIN from Greek *euangelos* 'bringing good news'.
evangelist • noun **1** a person who seeks to convert others to

e

Thesaurus

direct, neutral, evasive; diplomatic, inoffensive, genteel.
euphonious • adjective PLEASANT-SOUNDING, sweet-sounding, mellow, mellifluous, dulcet, sweet, honeyed, lyrical, silvery, golden, lilting, soothing; harmonious, melodious; *informal* easy on the ear.
– OPPOSITES cacophonous.
euphoria • noun ELATION, happiness, joy, delight, glee; excitement, exhilaration, jubilation, exultation; ecstasy, bliss, rapture.
– OPPOSITES misery.
euphoric • adjective ELATED, happy, joyful, delighted, gleeful; excited, exhilarated, jubilant, exultant; ecstatic, blissful, rapturous, transported, on cloud nine, in seventh heaven; *informal* on the top of the world, over the moon, on a high.
euthanasia • noun MERCY KILLING, assisted suicide.
evacuate • verb **1** *local residents were evacuated* REMOVE, clear, move out, take away. **2** *they evacuated the bombed town* LEAVE, vacate, abandon, desert, move out of, quit, withdraw from, retreat from, decamp from, flee, depart from, escape from. **3** *police evacuated the area* CLEAR, empty, depopulate. **4** *patients couldn't evacuate their bowels* EMPTY (OUT), void, open, move, purge; defecate. **5** *he evacuated the contents of his stomach* EXPEL, eject, discharge, excrete, void, empty (out).
evacuation • noun **1** *the evacuation of civilians* REMOVAL, clearance, shifting; eviction, deportation. **2** *the evacuation of military bases* CLEARANCE, depopulation; abandonment, vacation, desertion. **3** *involuntary evacuation of the bowels* EMPTYING (OUT), voidance, opening, purging; defecation. **4** *dysenteric evacuations* BOWEL MOVEMENT/MOTION, stools, excrement, excreta, faeces, waste.
evade • verb **1** *they evaded the guards* ELUDE, avoid, dodge, escape (from), steer clear of, keep at arm's length, sidestep; lose, leave behind, shake off; *N. Amer.* end-run; *informal* give someone the slip. **2** *he evaded the question* AVOID, dodge, sidestep, bypass, hedge, fence, skirt round, fudge, be evasive about; *informal* duck, cop out of.
– OPPOSITES confront.
evaluate • verb ASSESS, judge, gauge, rate, estimate, appraise, analyse, weigh up, get the measure of; *informal* size up, check out.
evaluation • noun ASSESSMENT, appraisal, judgement, gauging, rating, estimation, consideration, analysis.
evanescent • adjective (*poetic/literary*) VANISHING, fading, evaporating, melting away, disappearing; ephemeral, fleeting, short-lived, short-term, transitory, transient, fugitive, temporary.
– OPPOSITES permanent.
evangelical • adjective **1** *evangelical Christianity* SCRIPTURAL, biblical; fundamentalist, orthodox. **2** *an evangelical preacher* EVANGEL-

the Christian faith. **2** the writer of one of the four Gospels. **3** a passionate advocate of something.
– DERIVATIVES **evangelism** noun **evangelistic** adjective.
evangelize (also **evangelise**) ● verb **1** convert or seek to convert (someone) to Christianity. **2** preach the gospel.
– DERIVATIVES **evangelization** noun.
evaporate ● verb **1** turn from liquid into vapour. **2** cease to exist: *my goodwill evaporated.*
– DERIVATIVES **evaporation** noun **evaporative** adjective **evaporator** noun.
– ORIGIN Latin *evaporare*, from *vapor* 'steam, vapour'.
evaporated milk ● noun thick sweetened milk that has had some of the liquid removed by evaporation.
evasion ● noun the action or an instance of evading.
evasive ● adjective **1** tending to avoid commitment or self-revelation. **2** directed towards avoidance or escape: *evasive action.*
– DERIVATIVES **evasively** adverb **evasiveness** noun.
eve ● noun **1** the day or period of time immediately before an event or occasion. **2** chiefly literary evening.
– ORIGIN short form of EVEN².
even¹ ● adjective **1** flat and smooth; level. **2** equal in number, amount, or value. **3** having little variation in quality; regular. **4** equally balanced: *the match was even.* **5** (of a person's temper or disposition) placid; calm. **6** (of a number) divisible by two without a remainder. ● verb make or become even. ● adverb used for emphasis: *he knows even less than I do.*
– PHRASES **even as** at the very same time as. **even if** despite the possibility that. **even now** (or **then**) **1** now (or then) as well as before. **2** in spite of what has (or had) happened. **3** at this (or that) very moment. **even so** nevertheless. **even though** despite the fact that.
– DERIVATIVES **evenly** adverb **evenness** noun.
– ORIGIN Old English.
even² ● noun archaic or literary evening.
– ORIGIN Old English.
even-handed ● adjective fair and impartial.
– DERIVATIVES **even-handedly** adverb **even-handedness** noun.
evening ● noun the period of time at the end of the day. ● adverb (**evenings**) informal in the evening; every evening.
– ORIGIN Old English.
evening primrose ● noun a plant with pale yellow flowers that open in the evening, used for a medicinal oil.
evening star ● noun (**the evening star**) the planet Venus, seen shining in the western sky after sunset.
even money ● noun (in betting) odds offering an equal chance of winning or losing.
evens ● plural noun Brit. even money.
evensong ● noun (especially in the Anglican Church) a service of evening prayers, psalms, and canticles.
event ● noun **1** a thing that happens or takes place. **2** a public or social occasion. **3** each of several contests making up a sports competition.
– PHRASES **in any event** (or **at all events**) whatever happens or may have happened. **in the event 1** as it turned out. **2** (**in the event of/that**) if the specified thing happens.
– DERIVATIVES **eventless** adjective.
– ORIGIN Latin *eventus*, from *evenire* 'result, happen'.
eventer ● noun Brit. a horse or rider that takes part in eventing.
eventful ● adjective marked by interesting or exciting events.
event horizon ● noun Astronomy a notional boundary around a black hole beyond which no light or other radiation can escape.
eventide ● noun archaic or literary evening.
eventing ● noun an equestrian sport in which competitors must take part in each of several contests.
eventual ● adjective occurring at the end of or resulting from a process or period of time.
– DERIVATIVES **eventually** adverb.
eventuality ● noun (pl. **eventualities**) a possible event or outcome.

Thesaurus

ISTIC, evangelizing, missionary, crusading, propagandist, propagandizing, proselytizing.
evangelist ● noun PREACHER, missionary, gospeller, proselytizer, crusader, propagandist.
evangelistic ● adjective. See EVANGELICAL sense 2.
evangelize ● verb CONVERT, proselytize, redeem, save, preach to, recruit; act as a missionary, crusade, campaign.
evaporate ● verb **1** *the water evaporated* VAPORIZE, become vapour, volatilize; dry up. **2** *the rock salt is washed and evaporated* DRY OUT, dehydrate, desiccate, dehumidify. **3** *the feeling has evaporated* END, pass (away), fizzle out, peter out, wear off, vanish, fade, disappear, melt away.
– OPPOSITES condense, wet, materialize.
evasion ● noun **1** *the evasion of immigration control* AVOIDANCE, elusion, circumvention, dodging, sidestepping. **2** *she grew tired of all the evasion* PREVARICATION, evasiveness, beating about the bush, hedging, pussyfooting, equivocation, vagueness, temporization; *Brit.* humming and hawing; *rare* tergiversation.
evasive ● adjective EQUIVOCAL, prevaricating, elusive, ambiguous, non-committal, vague, inexplicit, unclear; roundabout, indirect; *informal* cagey.
eve ● noun **1** *the eve of the election* DAY BEFORE, evening before, night before; the run-up to. **2** (*poetic/literary*) *a winter's eve* EVENING, night; *poetic/literary* eventide.
– OPPOSITES morning.
even ● adjective **1** *an even surface* FLAT, smooth, uniform, featureless; unbroken, undamaged; level, plane. **2** *an even temperature* UNIFORM, constant, steady, stable, consistent, unvarying, unchanging, regular. **3** *they all have an even chance* EQUAL, the same, identical, like, alike, similar, comparable, parallel. **4** *the score was even* LEVEL, drawn, tied, all square, balanced; neck and neck; *Brit.* level pegging; *informal* even-steven(s). **5** *an even disposition* EVEN-TEMPERED, balanced, stable, equable, placid, calm, composed, poised, cool, relaxed, easy, imperturbable, unexcitable, unruffled, untroubled; *informal* together, laid-back, unflappable.
– OPPOSITES bumpy, irregular, unequal, moody.
● verb **1** *the canal bottom was evened out* FLATTEN, level (off/out), smooth (off/out), plane; make uniform, make regular. **2** *the union wants to even up our wages* EQUALIZE, make equal, level up, balance, square; standardize, regularize.
● adverb **1** *it got even colder* STILL, yet, more, all the more. **2** *even the best hitters missed the ball* SURPRISINGLY, unexpectedly, paradoxically. **3** *she is afraid, even ashamed, to ask for help* INDEED, you could say, veritably, in truth, actually, or rather, nay. **4** *she couldn't even afford food* SO MUCH AS.
– PHRASES **even as** WHILE, whilst, as, just as, at the very time that, during the time that. **even so** NEVERTHELESS, nonetheless, all the same, just the same, anyway, anyhow, still, yet, however, notwithstanding, despite that, in spite of that, for all that, be that as it may, in any event, at any rate. **get even** HAVE ONE'S REVENGE, avenge oneself, take vengeance, even the score, settle the score, hit back, give as good as one gets, pay someone back, repay someone, reciprocate, retaliate, take reprisals, exact retribution; give someone their just deserts; *informal* get one's own back, give someone a taste of their own medicine, settle someone's hash; *poetic/literary* be revenged.
even-handed ● adjective FAIR, just, equitable, impartial, unbiased, unprejudiced, non-partisan, non-discriminatory; disinterested, detached, objective, neutral.
– OPPOSITES biased.
evening ● noun NIGHT, late afternoon, end of day, close of day; twilight, dusk, nightfall, sunset, sundown; *poetic/literary* eve, eventide.
event ● noun **1** *an annual event* OCCURRENCE, happening, proceeding, incident, affair, circumstance, occasion, phenomenon; function, gathering; *informal* bash, do. **2** *the team lost the event* COMPETITION, contest, tournament, round, heat, match, fixture; race, game, bout.
– PHRASES **in any event/at all events** REGARDLESS, whatever happens, come what may, no matter what, at any rate, in any case, anyhow, anyway, even so, still, nevertheless, nonetheless; *N. Amer. informal* anyways. **in the event** AS IT TURNED OUT, as it happened, in the end; as a result, as a consequence.
even-tempered ● adjective SERENE, calm, composed, tranquil, relaxed, easy-going, mellow, unworried, untroubled, unruffled, imperturbable, placid, equable, stable, level-headed; *informal* laid-back, unflappable, together.
– OPPOSITES excitable.
eventful ● adjective BUSY, action-packed, full, lively, active, hectic, strenuous; momentous, significant, important, historic, consequential, fateful.
– OPPOSITES dull.
eventual ● adjective FINAL, ultimate, concluding, closing, end; resulting, ensuing, consequent, subsequent.
eventuality ● noun EVENT, incident, occurrence, happening, devel-

eventuate • verb formal **1** occur as a result. **2** (**eventuate in**) lead to as a result.

ever • adverb **1** at any time. **2** used in comparisons for emphasis: *better than ever*. **3** always. **4** increasingly; constantly: *ever larger sums*. **5** used for emphasis in questions expressing astonishment: *why ever did you do it?*

– PHRASES **ever and anon** archaic occasionally. **ever so** (or **such**) Brit. informal very; very much.

– ORIGIN Old English.

evergreen • adjective **1** (of a plant) retaining green leaves throughout the year. Often contrasted with DECIDUOUS. **2** having an enduring freshness or success. • noun an evergreen plant.

everlasting • adjective lasting forever or a very long time. • noun a flower that retains its shape and colour after being dried.

– DERIVATIVES **everlastingly** adverb.

evermore • adverb archaic or literary always; forever.

evert /ivert/ • verb technical turn inside out.

– DERIVATIVES **eversion** noun.

– ORIGIN Latin *evertere*, from *vertere* 'to turn'.

every • determiner **1** used to refer to all the individual members of a set without exception. **2** used to indicate something happening at specified intervals: *every thirty minutes*. **3** all possible; the utmost: *every effort was made*.

– PHRASES **every bit as** (in comparisons) quite as. **every now and again** (or **every so often**) occasionally. **every other** each alternate in a series. **every which way** informal **1** in all directions. **2** by all available means.

everybody • pronoun every person.

everyday • adjective **1** daily. **2** commonplace.

Everyman • noun an ordinary or typical human being.

everyone • pronoun every person.

every one • pronoun each one.

everything • pronoun **1** all things, or all the things of a group or class. **2** the most important thing or aspect: *money isn't everything*. **3** the current situation; life in general.

everywhere • adverb **1** in or to all places. **2** very common or widely distributed.

evict • verb expel (someone) from a property, especially with the support of the law.

– DERIVATIVES **eviction** noun.

– ORIGIN from Latin *evincere* 'overcome, defeat'.

evidence • noun **1** information or signs indicating whether a belief or proposition is true or valid. **2** Law information used to establish facts in a legal investigation or admissible as testimony in a law court. • verb be or show evidence of.

– PHRASES **in evidence** noticeable; conspicuous. **turn King's** (or **Queen's** or US **state's**) **evidence** Law (of a criminal) give information in court against one's partners in order to receive a less severe punishment.

– ORIGIN Latin *evidentia*, from *evidens* 'obvious to the mind or eye'.

evident • adjective plain or obvious.

– DERIVATIVES **evidently** adverb.

evidential • adjective formal of or providing evidence.

evil • adjective **1** deeply immoral and malevolent. **2** embodying or associated with the devil. **3** extremely unpleasant: *an evil smell*. • noun **1** extreme wickedness and depravity, especially when regarded as a supernatural force. **2** something harmful or undesirable.

– PHRASES **the evil eye** a gaze superstitiously believed to cause material harm. **the Evil One** archaic the Devil. **speak evil of**

e

Thesaurus

opment, phenomenon, situation, circumstance, case, contingency, chance, likelihood, possibility, probability; outcome, result.

eventually • adverb IN THE END, in due course, by and by, in time, after some time, after a bit, finally, at last; ultimately, in the long run, at the end of the day, one day, some day, sometime, sooner or later.

eventuate • verb (formal) **1** *you never know what might eventuate*. See HAPPEN sense 1. **2** *the fight eventuated in his death* RESULT IN, end in, lead to, give rise to, bring about, cause.

ever • adverb **1** *the best I've ever done* AT ANY TIME, at any point, on any occasion, under any circumstances, on any account; up till now, until now. **2** *he was ever the optimist* ALWAYS, forever, eternally, until hell freezes over; informal until the twelfth of never, until the cows come home, until doomsday. **3** *an ever increasing rate of crime* CONTINUALLY, constantly, always, endlessly, perpetually, incessantly, unremittingly. **4** *will she ever learn?* AT ALL, in any way.

– PHRASES **ever so** (Brit. informal) VERY, extremely, exceedingly, especially, immensely, particularly, really, truly; N. English right; informal awfully, terribly, desperately, mega, ultra; Brit. informal well, dead, jolly; N. Amer. informal real, mighty, awful.

everlasting • adjective **1** *everlasting love* ETERNAL, endless, never-ending, perpetual, undying, abiding, enduring, infinite, boundless, timeless. **2** *his everlasting complaints* CONSTANT, continual, continuous, persistent, relentless, unrelieved, uninterrupted, unabating, endless, interminable, never-ending, non-stop, incessant.

– OPPOSITES transient, occasional.

evermore • adverb ALWAYS, forever, ever, for always, for all time, until hell freezes over, eternally, in perpetuity; ever after, henceforth; Brit. for evermore, forever more; N. Amer. forevermore; informal until the cows come home, until the twelfth of never.

every • determiner **1** *he exercised every day* EACH, each and every, every single. **2** *we make every effort to satisfy our clients* ALL POSSIBLE, the utmost.

everybody • pronoun EVERYONE, every person, each person, all, one and all, all and sundry, the whole world, the public; informal {every Tom, Dick, and Harry}, every man jack, every mother's son.

everyday • adjective **1** *the everyday demands of a baby* DAILY, day-to-day, quotidian. **2** *everyday drugs like aspirin* COMMONPLACE, ordinary, common, usual, regular, familiar, conventional, run-of-the-mill, standard, stock; household, domestic; Brit. common or garden; informal bog-standard.

– OPPOSITES unusual.

everyone • pronoun EVERYBODY, every person, each person, all, one and all, all and sundry, the whole world, the public; informal {every Tom, Dick, and Harry}, every man jack, every mother's son.

everything • pronoun EACH ITEM, each thing, every single thing, the (whole) lot; all; informal the whole caboodle, the whole shebang; N. Amer. informal the whole ball of wax.

– OPPOSITES nothing.

everywhere • adverb ALL OVER, all around, in every nook and cranny, far and wide, near and far, high and low, {here, there, and everywhere}; throughout the land, the world over, worldwide; informal all over the place; Brit. informal all over the shop; N. Amer. informal all over the map.

– OPPOSITES nowhere.

evict • verb EXPEL, eject, oust, remove, dislodge, turn out, throw out, drive out; dispossess, expropriate; informal chuck out, kick out, boot out, bounce, give someone the (old) heave-ho, throw someone out on their ear; Brit. informal turf out; N. Amer. informal give someone the bum's rush; dated out.

eviction • noun EXPULSION, ejection, ousting, removal, dislodgement, displacement, banishment; dispossession, expropriation; Law ouster.

evidence • noun **1** *they found evidence of his plotting* PROOF, confirmation, verification, substantiation, corroboration, affirmation, attestation. **2** *the court accepted her evidence* TESTIMONY, statement, attestation, declaration, avowal, submission, claim, contention, allegation; Law deposition, representation, affidavit. **3** *evidence of a struggle* SIGNS, indications, pointers, marks, traces, suggestions, hints; manifestation.
• verb *the rise of racism is evidenced here* INDICATE, show, reveal, display, exhibit, manifest; testify to, confirm, prove, substantiate, endorse, bear out; formal evince.

– OPPOSITES disprove.

– PHRASES **in evidence** NOTICEABLE, conspicuous, obvious, perceptible, visible, on view, plain to see; palpable, tangible, unmistakable, undisguised, prominent, striking, glaring; informal as plain as the nose on your face, sticking out like a sore thumb, sticking out a mile, staring someone in the face.

evident • adjective OBVIOUS, apparent, noticeable, conspicuous, perceptible, visible, discernible, clear, plain, manifest, patent; palpable, tangible, distinct, pronounced, marked, striking, glaring, blatant; unmistakable, indisputable; informal as plain as the nose on your face, sticking out like a sore thumb, sticking out a mile, as clear as day.

evidently • adverb **1** *he was evidently dismayed* OBVIOUSLY, clearly, plainly, visibly, manifestly, patently, distinctly, markedly; unmistakably, undeniably, undoubtedly, as sure as eggs is eggs. **2** *evi-*

slander.
– DERIVATIVES **evilly** adverb **evilness** noun.
– ORIGIN Old English.
evil-doer ● noun a person who commits evil deeds.
evince ● verb formal reveal the presence of; indicate (a quality or feeling).
– ORIGIN Latin *evincere* 'overcome, defeat'.
eviscerate /ivissərayt/ ● verb formal disembowel.
– DERIVATIVES **evisceration** noun.
– ORIGIN Latin *eviscerare*, from *viscera* 'internal organs'.
evocative /ivokkətiv/ ● adjective evoking strong images, memories, or feelings.
evoke /ivōk/ ● verb **1** bring or recall to the conscious mind. **2** obtain (a response). **3** invoke (a spirit or deity).
– DERIVATIVES **evocation** noun.
– ORIGIN Latin *evocare*, from *vocare* 'to call'.
evolution ● noun **1** the process by which different kinds of living organism are believed to have developed, especially by natural selection. **2** gradual development. **3** Chemistry the giving off of a gaseous product or of heat. **4** a pattern of movements or manoeuvres.
– DERIVATIVES **evolutionarily** adverb **evolutionary** adjective.
– ORIGIN Latin, 'unrolling', from *evolvere* (see EVOLVE).
evolutionist ● noun a person who believes in the theories of evolution and natural selection.
– DERIVATIVES **evolutionism** noun.
evolve ● verb **1** develop gradually. **2** (of an organism or biological feature) develop over successive generations by evolution. **3** Chemistry give off (gas or heat).
– ORIGIN Latin *evolvere*, from *volvere* 'to roll'.
ewe ● noun a female sheep.
– ORIGIN Old English.
ewer /yoōər/ ● noun a large jug with a wide mouth.
– ORIGIN Old French *aiguiere*, from Latin *aquarius* 'of water'.
ex[1] ● preposition (of goods) sold direct from.
ex[2] ● noun informal a former husband, wife, or partner in a relationship.
ex-[1] (also **e-**; **ef-** before *f*) ● prefix **1** out: *exclude.* **2** upward: *extol.* **3** thoroughly: *excruciate.* **4** referring to removal or release: *excommunicate.* **5** forming verbs which indicate inducement of a state: *exasperate.* **6** referring to a former state: *ex-husband.*
– ORIGIN Latin *ex* 'out of'.
ex-[2] ● prefix out: *exodus.*
– ORIGIN Greek *ex* 'out of'.
exa- ● combining form denoting a factor of one million million million (10^{18}).
– ORIGIN from *(h)exa-* (see HEXA-).
exacerbate /igzassərbayt/ ● verb make (something bad) worse.
– DERIVATIVES **exacerbation** noun.
– ORIGIN Latin *exacerbare* 'make harsh'.
exact ● adjective **1** not approximated in any way; precise. **2** accurate or correct in all details: *an exact replica.* **3** tending to be accurate about minor details. ● verb **1** demand and obtain (something) from someone. **2** inflict (revenge) on someone.
– DERIVATIVES **exactitude** noun **exactness** noun.
– ORIGIN from Latin *exigere* 'complete, ascertain, enforce'.
exacting ● adjective making great demands on one's endurance or skill.
exaction ● noun formal **1** the action of exacting something, especially a payment. **2** a sum of money exacted.
exactly ● adverb **1** in exact terms. **2** used to confirm or agree with what has just been said.
exaggerate ● verb **1** represent as being greater than in reality. **2** (**exaggerated**) enlarged or altered beyond normal proportions.
– DERIVATIVES **exaggeratedly** adverb **exaggeration** noun.
– ORIGIN Latin *exaggerare* 'heap up'.
exalt ● verb **1** praise or regard highly. **2** raise to a higher rank or position.
– ORIGIN Latin *exaltare*, from *altus* 'high'.

Thesaurus

dently, she believed herself superior SEEMINGLY, apparently, as far as one can tell, from all appearances, on the face of it; it seems (that), it appears (that).
evil ● adjective **1** *an evil deed* WICKED, bad, wrong, immoral, sinful, foul, vile, dishonourable, corrupt, iniquitous, depraved, villainous, nefarious, vicious, malicious; malevolent, sinister, demonic, devilish, diabolical, fiendish, dark; monstrous, shocking, despicable, atrocious, heinous, odious, contemptible, horrible, execrable; *informal* low-down, dirty. **2** *an evil spirit* HARMFUL, hurtful, injurious, detrimental, deleterious, inimical, bad, mischievous, pernicious, malignant, malign, baleful; destructive, ruinous. **3** *evil weather* UNPLEASANT, disagreeable, nasty, horrible, foul, filthy, vile, inclement.
– OPPOSITES good, beneficial, pleasant.
● noun **1** *the evil in our midst* WICKEDNESS, bad, badness, wrongdoing, sin, immorality, vice, iniquity, degeneracy, corruption, depravity, villainy, nefariousness, malevolence; *formal* turpitude. **2** *nothing but evil would ensue* HARM, pain, misery, sorrow, suffering, trouble, disaster, misfortune, catastrophe, affliction, woe, hardship. **3** *the evils of war* ABOMINATION, atrocity, obscenity, outrage, enormity, crime, monstrosity, barbarity.
evince ● verb *(formal)* REVEAL, show, make plain, manifest, indicate, display, exhibit, demonstrate, evidence, attest to; convey, communicate, proclaim, bespeak.
– OPPOSITES conceal.
eviscerate ● verb *(formal)* DISEMBOWEL, gut, draw, dress.
evocative ● adjective REMINISCENT, suggestive, redolent; expressive, vivid, graphic, powerful, haunting, moving, poignant.
evoke ● verb BRING TO MIND, put one in mind of, conjure up, summon (up), invoke, elicit, induce, kindle, stimulate, stir up, awaken, arouse; recall, echo, capture.
evolution ● noun **1** *the evolution of Bolshevism* DEVELOPMENT, advancement, growth, rise, progress, expansion, evolvement; transformation, adaptation, modification, revision. **2** *his interest in evolution* DARWINISM, natural selection.
evolve ● verb DEVELOP, progress, advance; mature, grow, expand, spread; alter, change, transform, adapt, metamorphose; *humorous* transmogrify.
exacerbate ● verb AGGRAVATE, worsen, inflame, compound; intensify, increase, heighten, magnify, add to, amplify, augment; *informal* add fuel to the fire/flames.
– OPPOSITES reduce.
exact ● adjective **1** *an exact description* PRECISE, accurate, correct, faithful, close, true; literal, strict, faultless, perfect, impeccable; explicit, detailed, minute, meticulous, thorough; *informal* on the nail, on the mark; *Brit. informal* spot on, bang on; *N. Amer. informal* on the money, on the button. **2** *an exact manager* CAREFUL, meticulous, painstaking, punctilious, conscientious, scrupulous, exacting; methodical, organized, orderly.
– OPPOSITES inaccurate, careless.
● verb **1** *she exacted high standards from them* DEMAND, require, insist on, request, impose, expect; extract, compel, force, squeeze. **2** *they exacted a terrible vengeance on him* INFLICT, impose, administer, apply.
exacting ● adjective **1** *an exacting training routine* DEMANDING, stringent, testing, challenging, onerous, arduous, laborious, taxing, gruelling, punishing, hard, tough. **2** *an exacting boss* STRICT, stern, firm, demanding, tough, harsh; inflexible, uncompromising, unyielding, unsparing.
– OPPOSITES easy, easy-going.
exactly ● adverb **1** *it's exactly as I expected it to be* PRECISELY, entirely, absolutely, completely, totally, just, quite, in every way, in every respect, one hundred per cent, every inch, to the hilt; *informal* to a T; *N. Amer. informal* on the money. **2** *write the quotation out exactly* ACCURATELY, precisely, correctly, unerringly, faultlessly, perfectly; verbatim, word for word, letter for letter, to the letter, faithfully.
● exclamation *'She escaped?' 'Exactly.'* PRECISELY, yes, that's right, just so, quite (so), indeed, absolutely; *informal* you got it.
– PHRASES **not exactly** BY NO MEANS, not at all, in no way, certainly not; not really.
exaggerate ● verb OVERSTATE, overemphasize, overestimate, magnify, amplify, aggrandize, inflate; embellish, embroider, elaborate, overplay, dramatize; hyperbolize, stretch the truth; *Brit.* overpitch; *informal* lay it on thick, make a mountain out of a molehill, blow out of all proportion, make a big thing of.
– OPPOSITES understate.
exaggerated ● adjective OVERSTATED, inflated, magnified, amplified, aggrandized, excessive; hyperbolic, elaborate, overdone, overplayed, over-dramatized, highly coloured, melodramatic, sensational; *informal* over the top, OTT.
exaggeration ● noun OVERSTATEMENT, overemphasis, magnification, amplification, aggrandizement; dramatization, elaboration, embellishment, embroidery, hyperbole, overkill, gilding

exaltation ● noun **1** extreme happiness. **2** the action of exalting.

exalted ● adjective **1** at a high level. **2** (of an idea) noble; lofty. **3** extremely happy.

exam ● noun short for EXAMINATION (in sense 2).

examination ● noun **1** a detailed inspection or investigation. **2** a formal test of knowledge or proficiency in a subject or skill. **3** the action of examining.

examine ● verb **1** inspect closely to determine the nature or condition of. **2** test the knowledge or proficiency of. **3** *Law* formally question (a defendant or witness) in court.
– DERIVATIVES **examinee** noun **examiner** noun.
– ORIGIN Latin *examinare* 'weigh, test'.

example ● noun **1** a thing characteristic of its kind or illustrating a general rule. **2** a person or thing regarded in terms of their fitness to be imitated.
– PHRASES **for example** by way of illustration. **make an example of** punish as a warning to others.
– ORIGIN Latin *exemplum*, from *eximere* 'take out'.

exasperate /igzaaspərayt/ ● verb irritate intensely.
– DERIVATIVES **exasperated** adjective **exasperating** adjective **exasperation** noun.
– ORIGIN Latin *exasperare* 'irritate to anger'.

ex cathedra /eks kətheedrə/ ● adverb & adjective with the full authority of office (especially that of the Pope).
– ORIGIN Latin, 'from the teacher's chair'.

excavate ● verb **1** make (a hole or channel) by digging. **2** extract (material) from the ground by digging. **3** carefully remove earth from (an area) in order to find buried remains.
– DERIVATIVES **excavation** noun **excavator** noun.
– ORIGIN Latin *excavare* 'hollow out'.

exceed ● verb **1** be greater in number or size than. **2** go beyond what is stipulated by (a set limit). **3** surpass.
– ORIGIN Latin *excedere*, from *cedere* 'go'.

exceedingly ● adverb **1** extremely. **2** *archaic* to a great extent.

excel ● verb (**excelled**, **excelling**) **1** be exceptionally good at an activity or subject. **2** (**excel oneself**) perform exceptionally well.
– ORIGIN Latin *excellere*, from *celsus* 'lofty'.

excellence ● noun the quality of being excellent.

Excellency ● noun (pl. **Excellencies**) (**His**, **Your**, etc. **Excellency**) a title or form of address for certain high officials of state, especially ambassadors, or of the Roman Catholic Church.

excellent ● adjective extremely good; outstanding.

except ● preposition not including; other than. ● conjunction used before a statement that forms an exception to one just made. ● verb exclude: *present company excepted.*
– ORIGIN from Latin *excipere* 'take out'.

excepting ● preposition except for; apart from.

e

Thesaurus

the lily.

exalt ● verb **1** *they exalted their hero* EXTOL, praise, acclaim, esteem; pay homage to, revere, venerate, worship, lionize, idolize, look up to; *informal* put on a pedestal; *formal* laud. **2** *this power exalts the peasant* ELEVATE, promote, raise, advance, upgrade, ennoble, dignify, aggrandize. **3** *his works exalt the emotions* UPLIFT, elevate, inspire, excite, stimulate, enliven, exhilarate.
– OPPOSITES disparage, lower, depress.

exaltation ● noun **1** *a heart full of exaltation* ELATION, joy, rapture, ecstasy, bliss, happiness, delight, gladness. **2** *their exaltation of Shakespeare* PRAISE, extolment, acclamation, reverence, veneration, worship, adoration, idolization, lionization; *formal* laudation. **3** *the exaltation of Jesus to God's right hand* ELEVATION, rise, promotion, advancement, ennoblement.

exalted ● adjective **1** *his exalted office* HIGH, high-ranking, elevated, superior, lofty, eminent, prestigious, illustrious, distinguished, esteemed. **2** *his exalted aims* NOBLE, lofty, high-minded, elevated; inflated, pretentious. **3** *she felt spiritually exalted* ELATED, exultant, jubilant, joyful, rapturous, ecstatic, blissful, transported, happy, exuberant, exhilarated; *informal* high.

exam ● noun TEST, examination, assessment; paper, oral, practical; *Brit.* viva (voce); *N. Amer.* quiz.

examination ● noun **1** *artefacts spread out for examination* SCRUTINY, inspection, perusal, study, investigation, consideration, analysis, appraisal, evaluation. **2** *a medical examination* INSPECTION, check-up, assessment, appraisal; probe, test, scan; *informal* once-over, overhaul. **3** *a school examination* TEST, exam, assessment; paper, oral, practical; *Brit.* viva (voce); *N. Amer.* quiz. **4** *(Law) the examination of witnesses* INTERROGATION, questioning, cross-examination, inquisition.

examine ● verb **1** *they examined the bank records* INSPECT, scrutinize, investigate, look at, study, scan, sift, probe, appraise, analyse, review, survey; *informal* check out. **2** *students were examined after a year* TEST, quiz, question; assess, appraise. **3** *(Law) name the witnesses to be examined* INTERROGATE, question, quiz, cross-examine; catechize, give the third degree to, probe, sound out; *informal* grill, pump.

examiner ● noun TESTER, questioner, interviewer, assessor, appraiser, marker, inspector; auditor, analyst; adjudicator, judge, scrutineer.

example ● noun **1** *a fine example of Chinese porcelain* SPECIMEN, sample, exemplar, exemplification, instance, case, illustration. **2** *we must follow their example* PRECEDENT, lead, model, pattern, exemplar, ideal, standard; role model. **3** *he was hanged as an example to others* WARNING, caution, lesson, deterrent, admonition; moral.
– PHRASES **for example** FOR INSTANCE, e.g., by way of illustration, such as, as, like; in particular, namely, viz.

exasperate ● verb INFURIATE, incense, anger, annoy, irritate, madden, enrage, antagonize, provoke, irk, vex, get on someone's nerves, ruffle someone's feathers; *Brit.* rub up the wrong way; *informal* aggravate, rile, bug, needle, hack off, get up someone's nose, get someone's back up, get someone's goat, give someone the hump; *Brit. informal* nark, wind up, get on someone's wick; *N. Amer. informal* tee off, tick off.
– OPPOSITES please.

exasperating ● adjective INFURIATING, annoying, irritating, maddening, provoking, irksome, vexatious, trying, displeasing; *informal* aggravating.

exasperation ● noun IRRITATION, annoyance, vexation, anger, fury, rage, ill humour, crossness, tetchiness, testiness; disgruntlement, discontent, displeasure; *informal* aggravation.

excavate ● verb **1** *she excavated a narrow tunnel* DIG (OUT), bore, hollow out, scoop out; burrow, tunnel, sink, gouge. **2** *numerous artefacts have been excavated* UNEARTH, dig up, uncover, reveal; disinter, exhume.

excavation ● noun **1** *the excavation of a grave* UNEARTHING, digging up; disinterment, exhumation. **2** *the excavation of a moat* DIGGING, hollowing out, boring, channelling. **3** *implements found in the excavations* HOLE, pit, trench, trough; archaeological site.

exceed ● verb **1** *the cost will exceed £400* BE MORE THAN, be greater than, be over, go beyond, overreach, top. **2** *Brazil exceeds America in fertile land* SURPASS, outdo, outstrip, outshine, outclass, transcend, top, beat, better, eclipse, overshadow; *informal* best, leave standing, be head and shoulders above.

exceeding *(archaic)* ● adjective *his exceeding kindness* GREAT, considerable, exceptional, tremendous, immense, extreme, supreme, outstanding.
● adverb *the Lord has been exceeding gracious.* See EXCEEDINGLY.

exceedingly ● adverb EXTREMELY, exceptionally, especially, tremendously, very, really, truly, most; *informal* terribly, awfully, seriously, mega, ultra; *Brit. informal* ever so, well, dead, jolly; *N. Amer. informal* real, mighty; *archaic* exceeding.

excel ● verb **1** *he excelled at football* SHINE, be excellent, be outstanding, be skilful, be talented, be pre-eminent, reign supreme; stand out, be the best, be unparalleled, be unequalled, be second to none, be unsurpassed. **2** *she excelled him in her work* SURPASS, outdo, outshine, outclass, outstrip, beat, top, transcend, better, pass, eclipse, overshadow; *informal* best, be head and shoulders above, be a cut above.

excellence ● noun DISTINCTION, quality, superiority, brilliance, greatness, merit, calibre, eminence, pre-eminence, supremacy, peerlessness; skill, talent, virtuosity, accomplishment, mastery.

excellent ● adjective VERY GOOD, superb, outstanding, exceptional, marvellous, wonderful; pre-eminent, perfect, matchless, peerless, supreme, first-rate, first-class, superlative, splendid, fine; *informal* A1, ace, great, terrific, tremendous, fantastic, fabulous, fab, top-notch, class, awesome, magic, wicked, cool, out of this world; *Brit. informal* brilliant, brill, smashing; *Austral. informal* bonzer; *informal, dated* spiffing, capital.
– OPPOSITES inferior.

except ● preposition *every day except Monday* EXCLUDING, not including, excepting, omitting, not counting, but, besides, apart from, aside from, barring, bar, other than, saving; with the exception

exception ● noun **1** a person or thing that is excepted or that does not follow a rule. **2** the action of excepting or the state of being excepted.
– PHRASES **the exception proves the rule** proverb the fact that some cases do not follow a rule proves that the rule applies in all other cases. **take exception to** object strongly to; be offended by.
exceptionable ● adjective formal open to objection; causing disapproval or offence.
exceptional ● adjective **1** unusual; not typical. **2** unusually good.
– DERIVATIVES **exceptionally** adverb.
excerpt ● noun /eksert/ a short extract from a film or piece of music or writing. ● verb /ikserpt/ take (a short extract) from a text.
– ORIGIN from Latin *excerpere* 'pluck out'.
excess /iksess, eksess/ ● noun **1** an amount that is more than necessary, permitted, or desirable. **2** lack of moderation, especially in eating or drinking. **3** (**excesses**) outrageous or immoderate behaviour. **4** Brit. a part of an insurance claim to be paid by the insured. ● adjective usu. /eksess/ **1** exceeding a prescribed or desirable amount. **2** Brit. required as extra payment.
– ORIGIN Latin *excessus*, from *excedere* 'surpass'.
excess baggage ● noun luggage weighing more than the limit allowed on an aircraft, liable to an extra charge.
excessive ● adjective more than is necessary, normal, or desirable.
– DERIVATIVES **excessively** adverb **excessiveness** noun.
exchange ● verb give something and receive something else in return. ● noun **1** an act or the action of exchanging. **2** a short conversation or argument. **3** the giving of money for its equivalent in the currency of another country. **4** a building or institution used for the trading of commodities. **5** a set of equipment that connects telephone lines during a call.
– DERIVATIVES **exchangeable** adjective **exchanger** noun.
– ORIGIN Old French *eschangier*, from *changer* (see CHANGE).
exchange rate ● noun the value of one currency for the purpose of conversion to another.
exchequer /ikschekkər/ ● noun **1** a royal or national treasury. **2** (**Exchequer**) Brit. the account at the Bank of England into which tax receipts and other public monies are paid.
– ORIGIN Old French *eschequier*, from Latin *scaccarium* 'chessboard'; modern senses derive from the chequered tablecloth on which accounts were kept by means of counters.
excise[1] /eksīz/ ● noun a tax levied on certain goods, commodities, and licences.
– ORIGIN Dutch *excijs*.
excise[2] /iksīz/ ● verb **1** cut out surgically. **2** remove (a section) from a text or piece of music.
– DERIVATIVES **excision** noun.
– ORIGIN Latin *excidere* 'cut out'.
excised ● adjective (of goods) having excise charged on them.
exciseman ● noun Brit. historical an official who collected excise duty and prevented smuggling.
excitable ● adjective easily excited.
– DERIVATIVES **excitability** noun **excitably** adverb.
excite ● verb **1** cause strong feelings of enthusiasm and eagerness in. **2** arouse sexually. **3** give rise to (a feeling or reaction). **4** produce a state of increased energy or activity in (a physical or biological system).
– DERIVATIVES **excitation** noun **excitatory** adjective (chiefly Physiology) **excited** adjective.
– ORIGIN Latin *excitare*, from *exciere* 'call out'.
excitement ● noun **1** a feeling of great enthusiasm and eagerness. **2** something that arouses such a feeling. **3** sexual arousal.
exciting ● adjective causing excitement.

Thesaurus

of; *informal* outside of; *formal* save.
– OPPOSITES including.
● verb *you're all crooks, present company excepted* EXCLUDE, omit, leave out, count out, disregard.
– OPPOSITES include.
exception ● noun *this case is an exception* ANOMALY, irregularity, deviation, special case, peculiarity, abnormality, oddity; misfit; *informal* freak.
– PHRASES **take exception** OBJECT, take offence, take umbrage, demur, disagree; resent, argue against, protest against, oppose, complain about; *informal* kick up a fuss, kick up a stink. **with the exception of.** See EXCEPT preposition.
exceptionable ● adjective *(formal)*. See OBJECTIONABLE.
exceptional ● adjective **1** *the drought was exceptional* UNUSUAL, uncommon, abnormal, atypical, extraordinary, out of the ordinary, rare, unprecedented, unexpected, surprising; strange, odd, freakish, anomalous, peculiar; *Brit.* out of the common; *informal* weird, freaky, something else. **2** *her exceptional ability* OUTSTANDING, extraordinary, remarkable, special, excellent, phenomenal, prodigious; unequalled, unparalleled, unsurpassed, peerless, matchless, first-rate, first-class; *informal* A1, top-notch.
– OPPOSITES normal, average.
exceptionally ● adverb **1** *it was exceptionally cold* UNUSUALLY, uncommonly, abnormally, atypically, extraordinarily, unexpectedly, surprisingly; strangely, oddly; *informal* weirdly, freakily. **2** *an exceptionally acute mind* EXCEEDINGLY, outstandingly, extraordinarily, remarkably, especially, phenomenally, prodigiously.
excerpt ● noun EXTRACT, part, section, piece, portion, snippet, clip, bit; reading, citation, quotation, quote, line, passage; *N. Amer.* cite.
excess ● noun **1** *an excess of calcium in the bloodstream* SURPLUS, surfeit, overabundance, superabundance, superfluity, glut; too much. **2** *the excess is turned into fat* REMAINDER, rest, residue; leftovers, remnants; surplus, extra, difference. **3** *a life of excess* OVERINDULGENCE, intemperance, immoderation, profligacy, lavishness, extravagance, decadence, self-indulgence.
– OPPOSITES lack, restraint.
● adjective *excess skin oils* SURPLUS, superfluous, redundant, unwanted, unneeded, excessive; extra.
– PHRASES **in excess of** MORE THAN, over, above, upwards of, beyond.
excessive ● adjective **1** *excessive alcohol consumption* IMMODERATE, intemperate, imprudent, overindulgent, unrestrained, uncontrolled, lavish, extravagant; superfluous. **2** *the cost is excessive* EXORBITANT, extortionate, unreasonable, outrageous, undue, uncalled for, extreme, inordinate, unwarranted, disproportionate, too much; *informal* over the top, OTT.
excessively ● adverb INORDINATELY, unduly, unnecessarily, unreasonably, ridiculously, overly; very, extremely, exceedingly, exceptionally, impossibly; immoderately, intemperately, too much.
exchange ● noun **1** *the exchange of ideas* INTERCHANGE, trade, trading, swapping, traffic, trafficking; *archaic* truck. **2** *a broker on the exchange* STOCK EXCHANGE, money market, bourse. **3** *an acrimonious exchange* CONVERSATION, dialogue, chat, talk, discussion; debate, argument, altercation; *Brit. informal* confab, row, barney; *formal* confabulation, colloquy.
● verb *we exchanged shirts* TRADE, swap, switch, change, interchange; *archaic* truck.
– PHRASES **exchange blows** FIGHT, brawl, scuffle, tussle, engage in fisticuffs; *informal* scrap, have a set-to; *Brit. informal* have a punch-up. **exchange words** ARGUE, quarrel, squabble, cross swords, have an argument/disagreement; *informal* have a slanging match.
excise[1] ● noun *the excise on spirits* DUTY, tax, levy, tariff.
excise[2] ● verb **1** *the tumours were excised* CUT OUT/OFF/AWAY, take out, extract, remove; *technical* resect. **2** *all unnecessary detail should be excised* DELETE, cross out/through, strike out, score out, cancel, put a line through; erase; *Computing, informal* kill; *Printing* dele.
excitable ● adjective TEMPERAMENTAL, mercurial, volatile, emotional, sensitive, highly strung, unstable, nervous, tense, edgy, jumpy, twitchy, uneasy, neurotic; *informal* uptight, wired.
– OPPOSITES placid.
excite ● verb **1** *the prospect of a holiday excited me* THRILL, exhilarate, animate, enliven, rouse, stir, stimulate, galvanize, electrify, inspirit; *informal* buck up, pep up, ginger up, give someone a buzz/kick; *N. Amer. informal* give someone a charge. **2** *she wore a chiffon nightgown to excite him* AROUSE (SEXUALLY), stimulate, titillate, inflame; *informal* turn someone on, get someone going, float someone's boat. **3** *his clothes excited envy* PROVOKE, stir up, rouse, arouse, kindle, trigger (off), spark off, incite, cause; *poetic/literary* enkindle.
– OPPOSITES bore, depress.
excited ● adjective **1** *they were excited about the prospect* THRILLED, exhilarated, animated, enlivened, electrified; enraptured, intoxicated, feverish, enthusiastic; *informal* high (as a kite), fired up. **2** (SEXUALLY) AROUSED, stimulated, titillated, inflamed; *informal* turned on, hot, horny, sexed up; *Brit. informal* randy; *N. Amer. informal* squirrelly.
excitement ● noun **1** *the excitement of seeing a leopard in the wild* THRILL, pleasure, delight, joy; *informal* kick, buzz; *N. Amer. informal*

– DERIVATIVES **excitingly** adverb.

exclaim • verb cry out suddenly, especially in surprise, anger, or pain.
– DERIVATIVES **exclamation** noun **exclamatory** adjective.
– ORIGIN Latin *exclamare*, from *clamare* 'to shout'.

exclamation mark (N. Amer. **exclamation point**) • noun a punctuation mark (!) indicating an exclamation.

exclosure /iksklōzhər/ • noun Forestry an area from which unwanted animals are excluded.

exclude • verb **1** deny access to; keep out. **2** remove from consideration. **3** prevent the occurrence of. **4** expel (a pupil) from a school.
– DERIVATIVES **excludable** adjective **excluder** noun.
– ORIGIN Latin *excludere*, from *claudere* 'to shut'.

excluding • preposition not taking into account; except.

exclusion • noun the process of excluding or state of being excluded.
– DERIVATIVES **exclusionary** adjective.

exclusive • adjective **1** excluding or not admitting other things. **2** restricted to the person, group, or area concerned. **3** high-class and expensive; select. **4** not published or broadcast elsewhere. • noun an exclusive story or broadcast.
– DERIVATIVES **exclusively** adverb **exclusiveness** noun **exclusivity** noun.
– ORIGIN Latin *exclusivus*, from *excludere* 'exclude'.

excommunicate • verb /ekskəmyōōnikayt/ officially exclude from the sacraments and services of the Christian Church. • adjective /ekskəmyōōnikət/ excommunicated. • noun /ekskəmyōōnikət/ an excommunicated person.
– DERIVATIVES **excommunication** noun.
– ORIGIN Latin *excommunicare*, from *communis* 'common to all'.

ex-con • noun informal an ex-convict.

excoriate /ikskoriayt/ • verb **1** chiefly Medicine damage or remove part of the surface of (the skin). **2** formal censure or criticize severely.
– DERIVATIVES **excoriation** noun.
– ORIGIN Latin *excoriare* 'to skin'.

excrement /ekskrimənt/ • noun faeces.
– DERIVATIVES **excremental** adjective.
– ORIGIN Latin *excrementum*, from *excernere* 'sift out'.

excrescence /ikskress'nss/ • noun **1** an abnormal outgrowth on a body or plant. **2** an unattractive addition or feature.
– ORIGIN Latin *excrescentia*, from *excrescere* 'grow out'.

excreta /ikskreetə/ • noun waste discharged from the body, especially faeces and urine.
– ORIGIN Latin.

excrete • verb expel (a substance, especially a product of metabolism) as waste.
– DERIVATIVES **excretion** noun **excretory** adjective.
– ORIGIN Latin *excernere* 'sift out'.

excruciating • adjective **1** intensely painful. **2** very embarrassing, awkward, or tedious.
– DERIVATIVES **excruciatingly** adverb.
– ORIGIN from Latin *excruciare* 'torment', from *crux* 'a cross'.

exculpate /ekskulpayt/ • verb formal show or declare to be not guilty of wrongdoing.
– DERIVATIVES **exculpation** noun **exculpatory** adjective.
– ORIGIN Latin *exculpare* 'free from blame'.

excursion • noun a short journey or trip, especially one taken for leisure.
– DERIVATIVES **excursionist** noun.
– ORIGIN Latin, from *excurrere* 'run out'.

excursus /ikskursəss/ • noun (pl. same or **excursuses**) **1** a detailed discussion of a particular point in a book. **2** a digression in a written text.
– ORIGIN Latin, 'excursion'.

excuse • verb /ikskyōōz/ **1** seek or serve to justify (a fault or offence). **2** release from a duty or requirement. **3** forgive (a fault or a person committing one). **4** (used in polite formulas) allow (someone) to leave a room or gathering. **5** (**excuse oneself**) say politely that one is leaving. • noun /ikskyōōss/ **1** a defence or justification of a fault or offence. **2** something said to conceal the real reason for an action. **3** (**an excuse for**) informal a poor or inadequate example of.
– PHRASES **excuse me 1** a polite apology. **2** chiefly N. Amer. used to ask someone to repeat what they have just said.
– DERIVATIVES **excusable** adjective **excusably** adverb.
– ORIGIN Latin *excusare* 'to free from blame'.

ex-directory • adjective Brit. (of a telephone number) not listed in a telephone directory at the wish of the subscriber.

exec • noun informal an executive.

execrable /eksikrəb'l/ • adjective extremely bad or unpleasant.
– DERIVATIVES **execrably** adverb.
– ORIGIN Latin *execrabilis*, from *exsecrari* 'curse'.

e

Thesaurus

charge. **2** *excitement in her eyes* EXHILARATION, elation, animation, enthusiasm, eagerness, anticipation, feverishness; *informal* pep, vim, zing. **3** (SEXUAL) AROUSAL, passion, stimulation, titillation.

exciting • adjective **1** *an exciting story* THRILLING, exhilarating, stirring, rousing, stimulating, intoxicating, electrifying, invigorating; gripping, compelling, powerful, dramatic. **2** (SEXUALLY) AROUSING, (sexually) stimulating, titillating, erotic, sexual, sexy; *informal* raunchy, steamy.

exclaim • verb CRY (OUT), declare, blurt out; call (out), shout, yell; *dated* ejaculate.

exclamation • noun CRY, call, shout, yell, interjection; *dated* ejaculation.

exclude • verb **1** *women were excluded from many scientific societies* KEEP OUT, deny access to, shut out, debar, disbar, bar, ban, prohibit. **2** *the clause excluded any judicial review* ELIMINATE, rule out, preclude; *formal* except. **3** *the price excludes postage* BE EXCLUSIVE OF, not include. **4** *he excluded his name from the list* LEAVE OUT, omit, miss out.
– OPPOSITES admit, include.

exclusion • noun **1** *the exclusion of women from the society* BARRING, keeping out, debarment, debarring, disbarring, banning, prohibition. **2** *the exclusion of other factors* ELIMINATION, ruling out, precluding. **3** *the exclusion of pupils* EXPULSION, ejection, throwing out; suspension.
– OPPOSITES acceptance, inclusion, admission.

exclusive • adjective **1** *an exclusive club* SELECT, chic, high-class, elite, fashionable, stylish, elegant, premier, grade A; expensive; *Brit.* upmarket; *N. Amer.* high-toned; *informal* posh, ritzy, classy; *Brit. informal* swish; *N. Amer. informal* tony. **2** *a room for your exclusive use* SOLE, unshared, unique, only, individual, personal, private. **3** *prices exclusive of VAT* NOT INCLUDING, excluding, leaving out, omitting, excepting. **4** *mutually exclusive alternatives* INCOMPATIBLE, irreconcilable.
– OPPOSITES inclusive.
• noun *a six-page exclusive* SCOOP, exposé, special, coup.

excoriate • verb **1** *(Medicine) the skin had been excoriated* ABRADE, rub away/raw, scrape, scratch, chafe; strip away, skin. **2** *(formal) he was excoriated in the press.* See CRITICIZE.

excrement • noun FAECES, excreta, stools, droppings; waste matter, ordure, dung; *informal* pooh, doings; *Brit. informal* cack, whoopsies, jobbies; *N. Amer. informal* poop.
– RELATED TERMS copro-, scato-.

excrescence • noun **1** *an excrescence on his leg* GROWTH, lump, swelling, nodule, outgrowth. **2** *the new buildings were an excrescence* EYESORE, blot on the landscape, monstrosity.

excrete • verb EXPEL, pass, void, discharge, eject, evacuate; defecate, urinate.
– OPPOSITES ingest.

excruciating • adjective AGONIZING, severe, acute, intense, violent, racking, searing, piercing, stabbing, raging; unbearable, unendurable; *informal* splitting, killing.

excursion • noun TRIP, outing, jaunt, expedition, journey, tour; day trip/out, drive, run, ride; *informal* junket, spin.

excusable • adjective FORGIVABLE, pardonable, defensible, justifiable; venial.
– OPPOSITES unforgivable.

excuse • verb **1** *eventually she excused him* FORGIVE, pardon, absolve, exonerate, acquit; *informal* let someone off (the hook); *formal* exculpate. **2** *such conduct can never be excused* JUSTIFY, defend, condone, vindicate; forgive, overlook, disregard, ignore, tolerate, sanction. **3** *she has been excused from her duties* LET OFF, release, relieve, exempt, absolve, free.
– OPPOSITES punish, blame, condemn.
• noun **1** *that's no excuse for stealing* JUSTIFICATION, defence, reason, explanation, mitigating circumstances, mitigation, vindication. **2** *an excuse to get away* PRETEXT, ostensible reason, pretence; *Brit.* get-out; *informal* story, alibi. **3** *(informal) that pathetic excuse for a man!* TRAVESTY OF, poor specimen of; *informal* apology for.

execrable • adjective APPALLING, awful, dreadful, terrible, frightful, atrocious, lamentable, egregious; disgusting, deplorable, disgrace-

e

execrate /eksikrayt/ ● verb **1** feel or express great loathing for. **2** archaic curse; swear.
– DERIVATIVES **execration** noun.
– ORIGIN Latin *exsecrari* 'curse'.
execute ● verb **1** carry out or put into effect (a plan, order, etc.). **2** carry out a sentence of death on (a condemned person). **3** perform (an activity or manoeuvre). **4** Law make (a legal instrument) valid by signing or sealing it. **5** Law carry out (a judicial sentence, the terms of a will, or other order). **6** Computing run (a file or program).
– DERIVATIVES **executable** adjective **execution** noun.
– ORIGIN Latin *executare*, from *exsequi* 'follow up, carry out, punish'.
executioner ● noun an official who executes condemned criminals.
executive /igzekyootiv/ ● adjective having the power to execute plans, actions, or laws. ● noun **1** a person with senior managerial responsibility in a business organization. **2** (**the executive**) the branch of a government responsible for executing plans, actions, or laws. **3** an executive committee within an organization.
– DERIVATIVES **executively** adverb.
executor /igzekyootər/ ● noun Law a person appointed by a testator to carry out the terms of their will.
executrix /igzekyootriks/ ● noun (pl. **executrices** /igzekyootriseez/ or **executrixes**) Law a female executor.
exegesis /eksijeesiss/ ● noun (pl. **exegeses** /eksijeeseez/) critical explanation or interpretation of a text, especially of scripture.
– DERIVATIVES **exegetic** adjective **exegetical** adjective.
– ORIGIN Greek, from *exēgeisthai* 'interpret'.
exegete /eksijeet/ ● noun a person who interprets text, especially of scripture.
exemplar /igzemplər/ ● noun a person or thing serving as a typical example or appropriate model.
– ORIGIN Latin *exemplarium*, from *exemplum* 'example'.
exemplary ● adjective **1** serving as a desirable model; very good. **2** (of a punishment) serving as a warning.
exemplify /igzemplifī/ ● verb (**exemplifies**, **exemplified**) be or give a typical example of.
– DERIVATIVES **exemplification** noun.
exemplum /igzempləm/ ● noun (pl. **exempla**) an example or model, especially a moralizing or illustrative story.
– ORIGIN Latin.
exempt /igzempt/ ● adjective free from an obligation or liability imposed on others. ● verb make exempt.
– DERIVATIVES **exemption** noun.
– ORIGIN Latin *exemptus* 'taken out, freed'.
exequies /eksikwiz/ ● plural noun (sing. **exequy**) formal funeral rites.
– ORIGIN Latin *exsequiae*, from *exsequi* 'follow after'.
exercise ● noun **1** activity requiring physical effort carried out for the sake of health and fitness. **2** a task set to practise or test a skill. **3** an activity carried out for a specific purpose: *a public relations exercise.* **4** (**exercises**) military drills or training manoeuvres. **5** the application of a faculty, right, or process: *the exercise of authority.* ● verb **1** use or apply (a faculty, right, or process). **2** take or subject to exercise. **3** worry or perplex.
– DERIVATIVES **exercisable** adjective **exerciser** noun.
– ORIGIN Latin *exercitium*, from *exercere* 'keep busy, practise'.
exercise bike ● noun a stationary piece of exercise equipment resembling an ordinary bicycle.
exercise book ● noun Brit. a booklet with blank pages for students to write in.
exert /igzert/ ● verb **1** apply or bring to bear (a force, influence, or quality). **2** (**exert oneself**) make a physical or mental effort.
– DERIVATIVES **exertion** noun.
– ORIGIN Latin *exserere* 'put forth'.
exeunt /eksiunt/ ● verb (as a stage direction) (actors) leave the stage.
– ORIGIN Latin, 'they go out'.
exfoliant ● noun a cosmetic for exfoliating the skin.
exfoliate /eksfōliayt/ ● verb **1** shed or be shed from a surface in scales or layers. **2** wash or rub (the skin) with a granular substance to remove dead cells.
– DERIVATIVES **exfoliation** noun **exfoliative** adjective **exfoliator** noun.
– ORIGIN Latin *exfoliare* 'strip of leaves'.
ex gratia /eks grayshə/ ● adverb & adjective (with reference to

Thesaurus

ful, reprehensible, abhorrent, loathsome, odious, hateful, vile; *informal* abysmal, diabolical, lousy, God-awful; *Brit. informal* chronic, shocking.
– OPPOSITES admirable.
execrate ● verb **1** *the men were execrated as corrupt* REVILE, denounce, decry, condemn, vilify; detest, loathe, abhor, despise; *formal* abominate, excoriate. **2** *(archaic) he execrated aloud.* See SWEAR sense 3.
execute ● verb **1** *he was convicted and executed* PUT TO DEATH, kill; hang, behead, guillotine, electrocute, shoot, put before a firing squad; *N. Amer.* send to the (electric) chair; *informal* string up; *N. Amer. informal* fry. **2** *the corporation executed a series of financial deals* CARRY OUT, accomplish, bring off/about, achieve, complete, engineer; *informal* pull off; *formal* effectuate. **3** *a well-executed act* PERFORM, present, render; stage.
execution ● noun **1** *the execution of the plan* IMPLEMENTATION, carrying out, accomplishment, bringing off/about, engineering, attainment, realization. **2** *the execution of the play* PERFORMANCE, presentation, rendition, rendering, staging. **3** *thousands were sentenced to execution* CAPITAL PUNISHMENT, the death penalty; the gibbet, the gallows, the noose, the rope, the scaffold, the guillotine, the firing squad; *N. Amer.* the (electric) chair.
executioner ● noun HANGMAN, official killer; *historical* headsman.
executive ● adjective *executive powers* ADMINISTRATIVE, decision-making, managerial; law-making.
● noun **1** *top-level bank executives* CHIEF, head, director, senior official, senior manager, CEO, chief executive officer; *informal* boss, exec, suit. **2** *the executive has increased in number* ADMINISTRATION, management, directorate; government, legislative body.
exegesis ● noun INTERPRETATION, explanation, exposition, explication.
exemplar ● noun EPITOME, perfect example, model, paragon, ideal, exemplification, textbook example, embodiment, essence, quintessence.
exemplary ● adjective **1** *her exemplary behaviour* PERFECT, ideal, model, faultless, flawless, impeccable, irreproachable; excellent, outstanding, admirable, commendable, laudable, above/beyond reproach. **2** *exemplary jail sentences* SERVING AS A DETERRENT, cautionary, warning, admonitory; *rare* monitory. **3** *her works are exemplary of certain feminist arguments* TYPICAL, characteristic, representative, illustrative.
– OPPOSITES deplorable.
exemplify ● verb **1** *this story exemplifies current trends* TYPIFY, epitomize, be a typical example of, be representative of, symbolize. **2** *he exemplified his point with an anecdote* ILLUSTRATE, give an example of, demonstrate.
exempt ● adjective *they are exempt from all charges* FREE, not liable/subject, exempted, excepted, excused, absolved.
– OPPOSITES subject to.
● verb *he had been exempted from military service* EXCUSE, free, release, exclude, give/grant immunity, spare, absolve; *informal* let off (the hook); *N. Amer. informal* grandfather.
exemption ● noun IMMUNITY, exception, dispensation, indemnity, exclusion, freedom, release, relief, absolution; *informal* let-off.
exercise ● noun **1** *exercise improves your heart* PHYSICAL ACTIVITY, a workout, working-out; gymnastics, sports, games, physical education, PE, physical training, PT, aerobics, jogging, running; *Brit. informal* physical jerks. **2** *translation exercises* TASK, piece of work, problem, assignment; *Music* étude. **3** *the exercise of professional skill* USE, utilization, employment; practice, application. **4** *military exercises* MANOEUVRES, operations; war games.
● verb **1** *she exercised every day* WORK OUT, do exercises, train; *informal* pump iron. **2** *he must learn to exercise patience* USE, employ, make use of, utilize; practise, apply. **3** *the problem continued to exercise him* WORRY, trouble, concern, make anxious, bother, disturb, perturb, distress, preoccupy, prey on someone's mind, make uneasy; *informal* bug, do someone's head in.
exert ● verb **1** *he exerted considerable pressure on me* BRING TO BEAR, apply, exercise, employ, use, utilize, deploy. **2** *he had been exerting himself* MAKE AN/EVERY EFFORT, try hard, strive, endeavour, do one's best/utmost, give one's all, push oneself, drive oneself, work hard; *informal* go all out, pull out all the stops, bend/lean over backwards, do one's damnedest, move heaven and earth, work one's socks off; *N. Amer. informal* do one's darnedest, bust one's chops; *Austral. informal* go for the doctor.
exertion ● noun **1** *she was panting with the exertion* EFFORT,

payment) done from a sense of moral obligation rather than because of any legal requirement.
– ORIGIN Latin, 'from favour'.

exhale ● verb **1** breathe out. **2** give off (vapour or fumes).
– DERIVATIVES **exhalation** noun.
– ORIGIN Latin *exhalare*, from *halare* 'breathe'.

exhaust ● verb **1** tire out completely. **2** use up (resources or reserves) completely. **3** explore (a subject) thoroughly. **4** expel (gas or steam) from an engine or other machine. ● noun **1** waste gases or air expelled from an engine or other machine. **2** the system through which such gases are expelled.
– DERIVATIVES **exhauster** noun **exhaustible** adjective **exhausting** adjective.
– ORIGIN Latin *exhaurire* 'drain out'.

exhaustion ● noun the action of exhausting or the state of being exhausted.

exhaustive ● adjective fully comprehensive.
– DERIVATIVES **exhaustively** adverb **exhaustiveness** noun.

exhibit ● verb **1** publicly display (an item) in an art gallery or museum. **2** show (a quality). **3** show as a sign or symptom. ● noun **1** an object or collection of objects on display in an art gallery or museum. **2** Law a document or other object produced in a court as evidence. **3** N. Amer. an exhibition.
– DERIVATIVES **exhibitor** noun.
– ORIGIN Latin *exhibere* 'hold out'.

exhibition ● noun **1** a public display of items in an art gallery or museum. **2** a display or demonstration of a skill or quality.
– PHRASES **make an exhibition of oneself** behave very foolishly in public.

exhibitionism ● noun **1** extravagant behaviour that is intended to attract attention to oneself. **2** Psychiatry a mental condition characterized by the compulsion to display one's genitals in public.
– DERIVATIVES **exhibitionist** noun **exhibitionistic** adjective.

exhilarate ● verb cause to feel very happy or animated.
– DERIVATIVES **exhilaratingly** adverb **exhilaration** noun.
– ORIGIN Latin *exhilarare* 'make cheerful'.

exhort /igzort/ ● verb strongly encourage or urge (someone) to do something.
– DERIVATIVES **exhortation** noun.
– ORIGIN Latin *exhortari*, from *hortari* 'encourage'.

exhume /igzyōōm/ ● verb dig out (something buried, especially a corpse) from the ground.
– DERIVATIVES **exhumation** noun.
– ORIGIN Latin *exhumare*, from *humus* 'ground'.

exigency /eksijənsi/ (also **exigence**) ● noun (pl. **exigencies**) urgent need or demand.
– ORIGIN Latin *exigentia*, from *exigere* 'complete, ascertain, enforce'.

exigent /eksijənt/ ● adjective formal pressing; demanding.

exiguous /igzigyooəss/ ● adjective formal very small.
– ORIGIN Latin *exiguus* 'scanty'.

exile ● noun **1** the state of being barred from one's native country. **2** a person who lives in exile. ● verb expel and bar (someone) from their native country.
– ORIGIN Latin *exilium* 'banishment'.

exilic /ekzillik/ ● adjective relating to a period of exile.

exist ● verb **1** have objective reality or being. **2** live, especially under adverse conditions. **3** be found: *two conflicting stereotypes exist.*

existence ● noun **1** the fact or state of existing. **2** a way of living.
– ORIGIN Latin *existentia*, from *exsistere* 'come into being'.

existent ● adjective existing.

existential /egzistensh'l/ ● adjective **1** relating to existence. **2** Philosophy concerned with existentialism.
– DERIVATIVES **existentially** adverb.

existentialism ● noun a philosophical theory which emphasizes the existence of the individual person as a free and responsible agent.

e

Thesaurus

strain, struggle, toil, endeavour, hard work, labour; Brit. informal graft; Austral./NZ informal yakka; poetic/literary travail. **2** *the exertion of pressure* USE, application, exercise, employment, utilization.

exhale ● verb **1** *she exhaled her cigarette smoke* BREATHE OUT, blow out, puff out. **2** *the jungle exhaled mists of early morning* GIVE OFF, emanate, send forth, emit.
– OPPOSITES inhale.

exhaust ● verb **1** *the effort had exhausted him* TIRE (OUT), wear out, overtire, fatigue, weary, drain, run someone into the ground; informal do in, take it out of one, wipe out, knock out, shatter; Brit. informal knacker; N. Amer. informal poop, tucker out. **2** *the country has exhausted its reserves* USE UP, run through, go through, consume, finish, deplete, spend, empty, drain; informal blow. **3** *we've exhausted the subject* TREAT THOROUGHLY, do to death, study in great detail.
– OPPOSITES invigorate, replenish.

exhausted ● adjective **1** *I'm exhausted* TIRED OUT, worn out, weary, dog-tired, bone-tired, ready to drop, drained, fatigued, enervated; informal done in, all in, dead beat, shattered, bushed, knocked out, wiped out, bushwhacked; Brit. informal knackered, whacked (out), jiggered; N. Amer. informal pooped, tuckered out, fried, whipped; Austral./NZ informal stonkered. **2** *exhausted reserves* USED UP, consumed, finished, spent, depleted; empty, drained.

exhausting ● adjective TIRING, wearying, taxing, fatiguing, wearing, enervating, draining; arduous, strenuous, onerous, demanding, gruelling; informal killing, murderous; Brit. informal knackering.

exhaustion ● noun **1** *sheer exhaustion forced Paul to give up* EXTREME TIREDNESS, overtiredness, fatigue, weariness. **2** *the exhaustion of fuel reserves* CONSUMPTION, depletion, using up, expenditure; draining, emptying.

exhaustive ● adjective COMPREHENSIVE, all-inclusive, complete, full, encyclopedic, thorough, in-depth; detailed, meticulous, painstaking.
– OPPOSITES perfunctory.

exhibit ● verb **1** *the paintings were exhibited at Sotheby's* PUT ON DISPLAY/SHOW, display, show, put on public view, showcase; set out, lay out, array, arrange. **2** *Luke exhibited signs of jealousy* SHOW, reveal, display, manifest; express, indicate, demonstrate, present; formal evince.
● noun **1** *an exhibit at the British Museum* OBJECT ON DISPLAY, item, piece. **2** (N. Amer.) *people flocked to the exhibit in record numbers.* See EXHIBITION sense 1.

exhibition ● noun **1** *an exhibition of French sculpture* (PUBLIC) DISPLAY, show, showing, presentation, demonstration, exposition, showcase; N. Amer. exhibit. **2** *a convincing exhibition of concern* DISPLAY, show, demonstration, manifestation, expression.

exhibitionist ● noun POSTURER, poser, self-publicist; extrovert; informal show-off; N. Amer. informal showboat.

exhilarate ● verb THRILL, excite, intoxicate, elate, delight, enliven, animate, invigorate, energize, stimulate; informal give someone a thrill/buzz; N. Amer. informal give someone a charge.

exhilaration ● noun ELATION, euphoria, exultation, exaltation, joy, happiness, delight, joyousness, jubilation, rapture, ecstasy.

exhort ● verb URGE, encourage, call on, enjoin, charge, press; bid, appeal to, entreat, implore; formal adjure; poetic/literary beseech.

exhortation ● noun **1** *no amount of exhortation had any effect* URGING, encouragement, persuasion, pressure; admonishment, warning. **2** *the government's exhortations* ENTREATY, appeal, call, charge, injunction; admonition, warning.

exhume ● verb DISINTER, dig up, disentomb.
– OPPOSITES bury.

exigency ● noun **1** *the exigencies of the continuing war* NEED, demand, requirement, necessity. **2** *financial exigency* URGENCY, crisis, difficulty, pressure.

exiguous ● adjective (formal) MEAGRE, inadequate, insufficient, small, scanty, paltry, negligible, modest, deficient, miserly, niggardly, beggarly; informal measly, stingy, piddling.
– OPPOSITES ample, generous.

exile ● noun **1** *his exile from the land of his birth* BANISHMENT, expulsion, expatriation, deportation. **2** *political exiles* ÉMIGRÉ, expatriate; displaced person, DP, refugee, deportee; informal expat.
● verb *he was exiled from his country* EXPEL, banish, expatriate, deport, drive out, throw out, outlaw.

exist ● verb **1** *animals existing in the distant past* LIVE, be alive, be living; be, have being, have existence. **2** *the liberal climate that existed during his presidency* PREVAIL, occur, be found, be in existence; be the case. **3** *she had to exist on a low income* SURVIVE, subsist, live, support oneself; manage, make do, get by, scrape by, make ends meet.

existence ● noun **1** *the industry's continued existence* ACTUALITY, being, existing, reality; survival, continuation. **2** *her suburban existence* WAY OF LIFE/LIVING, life, lifestyle. **3** (archaic) *malevolent existences* BEING, entity, creation.
– PHRASES **in existence 1** *there are several million unidentified species in existence* ALIVE, existing, extant, existent. **2** *the only copy*

– DERIVATIVES **existentialist** noun & adjective.
exit ● noun **1** a way out of a building, room, or passenger vehicle. **2** an act of leaving. **3** a place for traffic to leave a major road or roundabout. ● verb (**exited**, **exiting**) **1** go out of or leave a place. **2** Computing terminate a process or program.
– ORIGIN Latin, 'he or she goes out', from *exire* 'go out'.
exit poll ● noun a poll of people leaving a polling station, asking how they voted.
ex libris /eks leebriss/ ● adverb used as an inscription on a bookplate to show the name of the book's owner.
– ORIGIN Latin, 'out of the books or library (of someone)'.
ex nihilo /eks nīhilō/ ● adverb formal out of nothing.
– ORIGIN Latin.
exo- ● prefix external; from outside: *exoskeleton.*
– ORIGIN Greek *exō* 'outside'.
exobiology ● noun the branch of science concerned with the possibility and likely nature of life on other planets or in space.
– DERIVATIVES **exobiologist** noun.
exocrine /eksōkrīn, -krin/ ● adjective (of a gland) secreting hormones or other products through ducts rather than directly into the blood.
– ORIGIN from Greek *krinein* 'sift'.
exodus ● noun a mass departure of people, especially emigrants.
– ORIGIN Greek *exodos*, from *hodos* 'way'.
ex officio /eks əfishiō/ ● adverb & adjective by virtue of one's position or status.
– ORIGIN from Latin *ex* 'out of, from' + *officium* 'duty'.
exogenous /eksojinəss/ ● adjective relating to external factors. Often contrasted with ENDOGENOUS.
– DERIVATIVES **exogenously** adverb.
exon /ekson/ ● noun Biochemistry a segment of a DNA or RNA molecule containing information coding for a protein or peptide sequence. Compare with INTRON.
– ORIGIN from *expressed* (see EXPRESS[1]).
exonerate /igzonnərayt/ ● verb **1** officially absolve from blame. **2** (**exonerate from**) release (someone) from (a duty or obligation).
– DERIVATIVES **exoneration** noun.
– ORIGIN Latin *exonerare* 'free from a burden'.
exoplanet /eksōplannit/ ● noun a planet which orbits a star outside the solar system.
exorbitant /igzorbitənt/ ● adjective (of a price or amount charged) unreasonably high.
– DERIVATIVES **exorbitance** noun **exorbitantly** adverb.
– ORIGIN from Latin *exorbitare* 'go off the track'.
exorcize /eksorsīz/ (also **exorcise**) ● verb drive out (a supposed evil spirit) from a person or place.
– DERIVATIVES **exorcism** noun **exorcist** noun.
– ORIGIN Greek *exorkizein*, from *horkos* 'oath'.
exoskeleton ● noun Zoology the rigid external covering of the body in insects and some other invertebrate animals.
exothermic /eksōthermik/ ● adjective Chemistry (of a reaction) accompanied by the release of heat. The opposite of ENDOTHERMIC.
exotic /igzottik/ ● adjective **1** originating in or characteristic of a distant foreign country. **2** strikingly colourful or unusual. ● noun an exotic plant or animal.
– DERIVATIVES **exotically** adverb **exoticism** noun.
– ORIGIN Greek *exōtikos* 'foreign'.
exotica /igzottikə/ ● plural noun objects considered exotic.
expand /ikspand/ ● verb **1** make or become larger or more extensive. **2** (**expand on**) give a fuller version or account of. **3** become less reserved.
– DERIVATIVES **expandable** adjective **expander** noun **expansible** adjective.
– ORIGIN Latin *expandere* 'spread out'.
expanded ● adjective **1** denoting materials which have a light cellular structure. **2** denoting sheet metal slit and stretched into a mesh, used to reinforce concrete and other brittle materials. **3** relatively broad in shape.
expanse ● noun **1** a wide continuous area of something, typically land or sea. **2** the distance to which something expands or can be expanded.
expansion ● noun **1** the action or an instance of expanding. **2** extension of a state's territory by encroachment on that of other nations.
– DERIVATIVES **expansionary** adjective.
expansionism ● noun the policy of territorial expansion.
– DERIVATIVES **expansionist** noun & adjective.
expansion joint ● noun a joint that makes allowance for thermal expansion of the parts joined without distortion.
expansive ● adjective **1** covering a wide area; extensive. **2** relaxed, genial, and communicative. **3** tending towards territorial expansion.
– DERIVATIVES **expansively** adverb **expansiveness** noun.
expansivity ● noun the amount a material expands or contracts per unit length due to a one-degree change in temperature.
ex parte /eks paartay/ ● adjective & adverb Law with respect to or in the interests of one side only.
– ORIGIN Latin, 'from a side'.
expat ● noun & adjective informal short for EXPATRIATE.
expatiate /ikspayshiayt/ ● verb (usu. **expatiate on**) speak or write at length or in detail.

Thesaurus

still in existence SURVIVING, remaining, undestroyed, in circulation.
existent ● adjective IN EXISTENCE, alive, existing, living, extant; surviving, remaining, undestroyed.
exit ● noun **1** *the fire exit* WAY OUT, door, egress, escape route; doorway, gate, gateway, portal. **2** *take the second exit* TURNING, turn-off, turn; *N. Amer.* turnout. **3** *his sudden exit* DEPARTURE, leaving, withdrawal, going, decamping, retreat; flight, exodus, escape.
– OPPOSITES entrance, arrival.
● verb *the doctor had just exited* LEAVE, go (out), depart, withdraw, retreat.
– OPPOSITES enter.
exodus ● noun MASS DEPARTURE, withdrawal, evacuation, leaving; migration, emigration; flight, escape, fleeing.
exonerate ● verb **1** *the inquiry exonerated them* ABSOLVE, clear, acquit, find innocent, discharge; *formal* exculpate. **2** *the pope exonerated the king from his oath* RELEASE, discharge, free, liberate; excuse, exempt, except, dispense; *informal* let off.
– OPPOSITES convict.
exorbitant ● adjective EXTORTIONATE, excessively high, excessive, prohibitive, outrageous, unreasonable, inflated, unconscionable, huge, enormous; *Brit.* over the odds; *informal* steep, stiff, over the top, a rip-off; *Brit. informal* daylight robbery.
– OPPOSITES reasonable.
exorcize ● verb **1** *exorcizing an spirit* DRIVE OUT, cast out, expel. **2** *they exorcized the house* PURIFY, cleanse, purge; *rare* lustrate.
exordium ● noun (*formal*) INTRODUCTION, opening, preface, prelude, foreword, preamble, prologue; *informal* intro; *formal* proem, prolegomenon.
– OPPOSITES conclusion.
exotic ● adjective **1** *exotic birds* FOREIGN, non-native, tropical. **2** *exotic places* FOREIGN, faraway, far-off, far-flung, distant. **3** *Linda's exotic appearance* STRIKING, colourful, eye-catching; unusual, unconventional, out of the ordinary, foreign-looking, extravagant, outlandish; *informal* offbeat, off the wall.
– OPPOSITES native, nearby, conventional.
expand ● verb **1** *metals expand when heated* INCREASE IN SIZE, become larger, enlarge; swell, dilate, inflate; lengthen, stretch, thicken, fill out; *rare* intumesce. **2** *the company is expanding | he is expanding his business* GROW, become/make larger, become/make bigger, increase in size/scope; extend, augment, broaden, widen, develop, diversify, build up; branch out, spread, proliferate. **3** *the minister expanded on the proposals* ELABORATE ON, enlarge on, go into detail about, flesh out, develop, expatiate on. **4** *she expanded and flourished* RELAX, unbend, become relaxed, grow friendlier, loosen up.
– OPPOSITES shrink, contract.
expanse ● noun AREA, stretch, sweep, tract, swathe, belt, region; sea, carpet, blanket, sheet.
expansion ● noun **1** *expansion and contraction* ENLARGEMENT, increase in size, swelling, dilation; lengthening, elongation, stretching, thickening. **2** *the expansion of the company* GROWTH, increase in size, enlargement, extension, development; spread, proliferation, multiplication. **3** *an expansion of a lecture given last year* ELABORATION, enlargement, amplification, development.
– OPPOSITES contraction.
expansive ● adjective **1** *expansive moorland* EXTENSIVE, sweeping, rolling. **2** *expansive coverage* WIDE-RANGING, extensive, broad, wide, comprehensive, thorough. **3** *Cara became engagingly expansive*

– DERIVATIVES **expatiation** noun.
– ORIGIN Latin *exspatiari* 'move beyond one's usual bounds'.
expatriate ● noun /ekspatriət/ a person who lives outside their native country. ● adjective living outside one's native country. ● verb /ekspatriayt/ settle abroad.
– DERIVATIVES **expatriation** noun.
– ORIGIN Latin *expatriare*, from *patria* 'native country'.
expect ● verb **1** regard as likely to happen. **2** regard (someone) as likely to do or be something. **3** believe that (someone) will arrive soon. **4** require as appropriate or rightfully due. **5** (**be expecting**) informal be pregnant.
– DERIVATIVES **expectable** adjective.
– ORIGIN Latin *exspectare* 'look out for'.
expectancy ● noun (pl. **expectancies**) **1** hope or anticipation that something will happen. **2** something expected.
expectant ● adjective **1** hoping or anticipating that something is about to happen. **2** (of a woman) pregnant.
– DERIVATIVES **expectantly** adverb.
expectation ● noun **1** belief that something will happen or be the case. **2** a thing that is expected to happen.
expectorant ● noun a medicine which promotes the secretion of sputum by the air passages, used to treat coughs.
expectorate /ikspektərayt/ ● verb cough or spit out (phlegm) from the throat or lungs.
– DERIVATIVES **expectoration** noun.
– ORIGIN Latin *expectorare* 'expel from the chest'.
expedient /ikspeediənt/ ● adjective **1** advantageous. **2** advisable on practical rather than moral grounds. ● noun a means of attaining an end.
– DERIVATIVES **expedience** noun **expediency** noun **expediently** adverb.
– ORIGIN Latin, from *expedire* (see EXPEDITE).
expedite /ekspidīt/ ● verb cause to happen sooner or be accomplished more quickly.
– DERIVATIVES **expediter** (also **expeditor**) noun.
– ORIGIN Latin *expedire* 'extricate (originally by freeing the feet), put in order', from *pes* 'foot'.
expedition ● noun **1** a journey undertaken by a group of people with a particular purpose. **2** formal promptness or speed in doing something.
– DERIVATIVES **expeditionary** adjective.
expeditious /ekspidishəss/ ● adjective quick and efficient.
– DERIVATIVES **expeditiously** adverb **expeditiousness** noun.
expel ● verb (**expelled**, **expelling**) **1** force or drive out. **2** force (a pupil) to leave a school.
– DERIVATIVES **expellable** adjective **expellee** noun **expeller** noun.
– ORIGIN Latin *expellere*, from *pellere* 'to drive'.
expend ● verb spend or use up (a resource).
– ORIGIN Latin *expendere*, from *pendere* 'weigh, pay'.
expendable ● adjective **1** suitable to be used once only; not worth preserving. **2** able to be sacrificed because of little significance when compared to an overall purpose.
– DERIVATIVES **expendability** noun **expendably** adverb.
expenditure /ikspendichər/ ● noun **1** the action of spending funds. **2** the amount of money spent.
expense ● noun **1** the cost incurred in or required for something. **2** (**expenses**) specific costs incurred in the performance of a job or task. **3** something on which money must be spent.
– PHRASES **at the expense of 1** paid for by. **2** to the detriment of.
– ORIGIN Old French, from Latin *expendere* 'weigh or pay out'.
expense account ● noun an arrangement under which money spent in the course of business is later reimbursed by one's employer.
expensive ● adjective costing a lot of money.
– DERIVATIVES **expensively** adverb **expensiveness** noun.
experience ● noun **1** practical contact with and observation of facts or events. **2** knowledge or skill acquired over time. **3** an event or occurrence which leaves an impression on one. ● verb

e

Thesaurus

COMMUNICATIVE, forthcoming, sociable, friendly, outgoing, affable, chatty, talkative, garrulous, loquacious, voluble.
expatiate ● verb SPEAK/WRITE AT LENGTH, go into detail, expound, dwell, dilate, expand, enlarge, elaborate; *formal* perorate.
expatriate ● noun *expatriates working overseas* EMIGRANT, non-native, émigré, (economic) migrant; *informal* expat.
– OPPOSITES national.
● adjective *expatriate workers* EMIGRANT, living abroad, non-native, émigré; *informal* expat.
– OPPOSITES indigenous.
● verb **1** *he was not tempted to expatriate himself* SETTLE ABROAD, live abroad. **2** *he was expatriated* EXILE, deport, banish, expel.
expect ● verb **1** *I expect she'll be late* SUPPOSE, presume, think, believe, imagine, assume, surmise; *informal* guess, reckon; *N. Amer. informal* figure. **2** *I'm expecting a letter | a 10 per cent rise was expected* ANTICIPATE, await, look for, hope for, look forward to; contemplate, bargain for/on, bank on; predict, forecast, envisage, envision. **3** *we expect total loyalty* REQUIRE, ask for, call for, want, insist on, demand.
expectancy ● noun **1** *feverish expectancy* ANTICIPATION, expectation, eagerness, excitement. **2** *life expectancy* LIKELIHOOD, probability, outlook, prospect.
expectant ● adjective **1** *expectant fans* EAGER, excited, agog, waiting with bated breath, hopeful; in suspense, on tenterhooks. **2** *an expectant mother* PREGNANT; *informal* expecting, in the family way, preggers; *Brit. informal* up the duff/spout, in the (pudding) club; *technical* gravid; *archaic* with child, in a delicate/interesting condition.
expectation ● noun **1** *her expectations were unrealistic* SUPPOSITION, assumption, presumption, conjecture, surmise, calculation, prediction. **2** *tense with expectation* ANTICIPATION, expectancy, eagerness, excitement, suspense.
expecting ● adjective *(informal) his wife's expecting again.* See EXPECTANT sense 2.
expedient ● adjective *a politically expedient strategy* CONVENIENT, advantageous, in one's own interests, useful, of use, beneficial, of benefit, helpful; practical, pragmatic, politic, prudent, wise, judicious, sensible.
● noun *a temporary expedient* MEASURE, means, method, stratagem, scheme, plan, move, tactic, manoeuvre, device, contrivance, ploy, machination, dodge; *Austral. informal* lurk.
expedite ● verb SPEED UP, accelerate, hurry, hasten, step up, quicken, precipitate, dispatch; advance, facilitate, ease, make easier, further, promote, aid, push through, urge on, boost, stimulate, spur on, help along.
– OPPOSITES delay.
expedition ● noun **1** *an expedition to the South Pole* JOURNEY, voyage, tour, odyssey; exploration, safari, trek, hike. **2** *(informal) a shopping expedition* TRIP, excursion, outing, jaunt. **3** *all members of the expedition* GROUP, team, party, crew, band, squad. **4** *(formal) use all expedition possible* SPEED, haste, swiftness, quickness, rapidity, briskness; *poetic/literary* fleetness, celerity.
expeditious ● adjective SPEEDY, swift, quick, rapid, fast, brisk, efficient; prompt, punctual, immediate, instant; *poetic/literary* fleet.
– OPPOSITES slow.
expel ● verb **1** *she was expelled from her party* THROW OUT, bar, ban, debar, drum out, oust, remove, get rid of, dismiss; *Military* cashier; *informal* chuck out, sling out, kick/boot out; *Brit. informal* turf out; *N. Amer. informal* give someone the bum's rush; *dated* out. **2** *he was expelled from the country* BANISH, exile, deport, evict, expatriate, drive out, throw out. **3** *Dolly expelled a hiss* LET OUT, discharge, eject, issue, send forth.
– OPPOSITES admit.
expend ● verb **1** *they had already expended $75,000* SPEND, pay out, disburse, dole out, dish out, get through, waste, fritter (away), dissipate; *informal* fork out, shell out, lay out, cough up, blow, splurge; *Brit. informal* splash out, stump up; *N. Amer. informal* ante up. **2** *children expend a lot of energy* USE (UP), utilize, consume, eat up, deplete, get through.
– OPPOSITES save, conserve.
expendable ● adjective **1** *an accountant decided he was expendable* DISPENSABLE, replaceable, non-essential, inessential, unnecessary, not required, superfluous, disposable. **2** *an expendable satellite launcher* DISPOSABLE, throwaway, one-use, single-use.
– OPPOSITES indispensable.
expenditure ● noun **1** *the expenditure of funds* SPENDING, paying out, outlay, disbursement, doling out, waste, wasting, frittering (away), dissipation. **2** *reducing public expenditure* OUTGOINGS, costs, payments, expenses, overheads, spending.
– OPPOSITES saving, income.
expense ● noun **1** *Nigel resented the expense* COST, price, charge, outlay, fee, tariff, levy, payment; *informal, humorous* damage. **2** *regular expenses* OUTGOING, payment, outlay, expenditure, charge, bill, overhead. **3** *pollution controls come at the expense of jobs* SACRIFICE, cost, loss.
expensive ● adjective COSTLY, dear, high-priced, overpriced, exorbitant, extortionate; *informal* steep, pricey, costing an arm and a

1 encounter or undergo (an event or occurrence). **2** feel (an emotion).
– ORIGIN Latin *experientia*, from *experiri* 'try'.

experienced ● adjective having knowledge or skill in a particular field gained over time.

experiential /ikspeeriensh'l/ ● adjective involving or based on experience and observation.
– DERIVATIVES **experientially** adverb.

experiment ● noun **1** a scientific procedure undertaken to make a discovery, test a hypothesis, or demonstrate a known fact. **2** a course of action tentatively adopted without being sure of the outcome. ● verb **1** perform a scientific experiment. **2** try out new things.
– DERIVATIVES **experimentation** noun **experimenter** noun.
– ORIGIN Latin *experimentum*, from *experiri* 'try'.

e

experimental ● adjective **1** based on untested ideas or techniques and not yet established or finalized. **2** of or relating to scientific experiments. **3** (of art, music, etc.) radically new and innovative.
– DERIVATIVES **experimentalism** noun **experimentalist** noun **experimentally** adverb.

expert ● noun a person who is very knowledgeable about or skilful in a particular area. ● adjective having or involving such knowledge or skill.
– DERIVATIVES **expertly** adverb **expertness** noun.
– ORIGIN Latin *expertus*, from *experiri* 'try'.

expertise /eksperteez/ ● noun great skill or knowledge in a particular field.

expiate /ekspiayt/ ● verb atone for (guilt or sin).
– DERIVATIVES **expiable** adjective **expiation** noun **expiator** noun **expiatory** /ekspiətəri/ adjective.
– ORIGIN Latin *expiare* 'appease by sacrifice', from *pius* 'pious'.

expire /ikspīr/ ● verb **1** (of a document or agreement) come to the end of the period of validity. **2** (of a period of time) come to an end. **3** (of a person) die. **4** technical exhale (air) from the lungs.
– DERIVATIVES **expiration** noun **expiratory** adjective **expiry** noun.
– ORIGIN Latin *exspirare* 'breathe out'.

explain ● verb **1** make clear by giving a detailed description. **2** give a reason or justification for. **3** (**explain oneself**) excuse or justify one's motives or conduct. **4** (**explain away**) minimize the significance of (something awkward) by giving an excuse or justification.
– DERIVATIVES **explainable** adjective **explainer** noun **explanation** noun.
– ORIGIN Latin *explanare*, from *planus* 'plain'.

explanatory /iksplanətri/ ● adjective serving to explain something.
– DERIVATIVES **explanatorily** adverb.

expletive /ikspleetiv/ ● noun an oath or swear word.
– ORIGIN originally denoting a word used to fill out a sentence: from Latin *expletivus*, from *explere* 'fill out'.

explicable /iksplikkəb'l, eksplik-/ ● adjective able to be explained or accounted for.
– ORIGIN from Latin *explicare* 'unfold'.

explicate /eksplikayt/ ● verb **1** analyse and develop (an idea or principle) in detail. **2** analyse (a literary work) in order to reveal its meaning.
– DERIVATIVES **explication** noun **explicative** /eksplikkətiv, eksplik-/ adjective **explicator** noun **explicatory** /eksplikkətri/ adjective.
– ORIGIN Latin *explicare* 'unfold'.

explicit /iksplissit/ ● adjective **1** clear and detailed, with no room for confusion or doubt. **2** graphically describing or representing sexual activity.
– DERIVATIVES **explicitly** adverb **explicitness** noun.
– ORIGIN from Latin *explicare* 'unfold'.

explode ● verb **1** burst or shatter violently as a result of rapid

Thesaurus

leg, costing the earth, costing a bomb.
– OPPOSITES cheap, economical.

experience ● noun **1** *qualifications and experience* SKILL, (practical) knowledge, understanding; background, record, history; maturity, worldliness, sophistication; *informal* know-how. **2** *an enjoyable experience* INCIDENT, occurrence, event, happening, episode; adventure, exploit, escapade. **3** *his first experience of business* INVOLVEMENT IN, participation in, contact with, acquaintance with, exposure to, observation of, awareness of, insight into.
● verb *some policemen experience harassment* UNDERGO, encounter, meet, come into contact with, come across, come up against, face, be faced with.

experienced ● adjective **1** *an experienced pilot* KNOWLEDGEABLE, skilful, skilled, expert, accomplished, adept, adroit, master, consummate; proficient, trained, competent, capable, well trained, well versed; seasoned, practised, mature, veteran. **2** *she deluded herself that she was experienced* WORLDLY (WISE), sophisticated, suave, urbane, mature, knowing; *informal* streetwise.
– OPPOSITES novice, naive.

experiment ● noun **1** *carrying out experiments* TEST, investigation, trial, examination, observation; assessment, evaluation, appraisal, analysis, study. **2** *these results have been established by experiment* RESEARCH, experimentation, observation, analysis, testing.
– RELATED TERMS empirical.
● verb *they experimented with new ideas* CONDUCT EXPERIMENTS, carry out trials/tests, conduct research; test, trial, do tests on, try out, assess, appraise, evaluate.

experimental ● adjective **1** *the experimental stage* EXPLORATORY, investigational, trial, test, pilot; speculative, conjectural, hypothetical, tentative, preliminary, untested, untried. **2** *experimental music* INNOVATIVE, innovatory, new, original, radical, avant-garde, alternative, unorthodox, unconventional, left-field; *informal* way-out.

expert ● noun *he is an expert in kendo* SPECIALIST, authority, pundit; adept, maestro, virtuoso, (past) master, wizard; connoisseur, aficionado; *informal* ace, buff, pro, whizz, hotshot; *Brit. informal* dab hand; *N. Amer. informal* maven, crackerjack.
● adjective *an expert chess player* SKILFUL, skilled, adept, accomplished, talented, fine; master, masterly, brilliant, virtuoso, magnificent, outstanding, great, exceptional, excellent, first-class, first-rate, superb; proficient, good, able, capable, experienced, practised, knowledgeable; *informal* wizard, ace, crack, mean.
– OPPOSITES incompetent.

expertise ● noun SKILL, skilfulness, expertness, prowess, proficiency, competence; knowledge, mastery, ability, aptitude, facility, capability; *informal* know-how.

expiate ● verb ATONE FOR, make amends for, make up for, do penance for, pay for, redress, redeem, offset, make good.

expire ● verb **1** *my contract has expired* RUN OUT, become invalid, become void, lapse; END, finish, stop, come to an end, terminate. **2** *the spot where he expired* DIE, pass away/on, breathe one's last; *informal* kick the bucket, bite the dust, croak, buy it; *Brit. informal* snuff it, peg out, pop one's clogs; *archaic* decease, depart this life. **3** (*technical*) *afterwards the breath is expired* BREATHE OUT, exhale, blow out, expel.

expiry ● noun **1** *the expiry of the lease* LAPSE, expiration. **2** *the expiry of his term of office* END, finish, termination, conclusion. **3** (*archaic*) *the sad expiry of their friend* DEATH, demise, passing (away/on), dying; *formal* decease.

explain ● verb **1** *a technician explained the procedure* DESCRIBE, give an explanation of, make clear/intelligible, spell out, put into words; elucidate, expound, explicate, clarify, throw light on; gloss, interpret. **2** *nothing could explain his new-found wealth* ACCOUNT FOR, give an explanation for, give a reason for; justify, give a justification for, give an excuse for, vindicate, legitimize.

explanation ● noun **1** *an explanation of the ideas contained in the essay* CLARIFICATION, simplification; description, report, statement; elucidation, exposition, expounding, explication; gloss, interpretation, commentary, exegesis. **2** *I owe you an explanation* ACCOUNT, reason; justification, excuse, alibi, defence, vindication.

explanatory ● adjective EXPLAINING, descriptive, describing, illustrative, illuminative, elucidatory.

expletive ● noun SWEAR WORD, oath, curse, obscenity, profanity, four-letter word, dirty word; *informal* cuss word, cuss; *formal* imprecation; (**expletives**) bad language, foul language, strong language, swearing.

explicable ● adjective EXPLAINABLE, understandable, comprehensible, accountable, intelligible, interpretable.

explicate ● verb EXPLAIN, make explicit, clarify, make plain/clear, spell out; interpret, elucidate, expound, illuminate, throw light on.

explicit ● adjective **1** *explicit instructions* CLEAR, plain, straightforward, crystal clear, easily understandable; precise, exact, specific, unequivocal, unambiguous; detailed, comprehensive, exhaustive. **2** *sexually explicit material* UNCENSORED, graphic, candid, full-

combustion or excessive internal pressure. **2** suddenly give expression to violent emotion. **3** increase suddenly in number or extent. **4** show (a belief or theory) to be false or unfounded. **5** (**exploded**) (of a diagram) showing parts or components of something in the normal relative positions but slightly separated from each other.
– DERIVATIVES **exploder** noun.
– ORIGIN originally in the sense 'reject scornfully': from Latin *explodere* 'drive out by clapping, hiss off the stage', from *plaudere* 'to clap'.
exploit ● verb /iksployt/ **1** make good use of (a resource). **2** make use of unfairly; benefit unjustly from the work of. ● noun /eksployt/ a bold or daring feat.
– DERIVATIVES **exploitable** adjective **exploitation** noun **exploitative** adjective **exploiter** noun **exploitive** adjective.
– ORIGIN originally in the sense 'success, progress': from Old French *esploit*, from Latin *explicare* 'unfold'.
explore ● verb **1** travel through (an unfamiliar area) in order to learn about it. **2** inquire into or discuss in detail. **3** evaluate (a new option or possibility). **4** examine or scrutinize by searching through or touching.
– DERIVATIVES **exploration** noun **explorative** adjective **exploratory** adjective **explorer** noun.
– ORIGIN Latin *explorare* 'search out', from *plorare* 'utter a cry'.
explosion ● noun an act or instance of exploding.
explosive ● adjective **1** able or likely to explode. **2** likely to cause an eruption of anger or controversy. **3** (of an increase) sudden and dramatic. ● noun a substance which can be made to explode.
– DERIVATIVES **explosively** adverb **explosiveness** noun.
exponent /ikspōnənt/ ● noun **1** a promoter of an idea or theory. **2** a person who does a particular thing skilfully. **3** Mathematics the power to which a given quantity is raised (e.g. 3 in $2^3 = 2 \times 2 \times 2$).
– ORIGIN Latin, from *exponere* 'present, explain'.
exponential /ekspənensh'l/ ● adjective **1** (of an increase) becoming more and more rapid. **2** Mathematics of or expressed by a mathematical exponent.
– DERIVATIVES **exponentially** adverb.
export ● verb /iksport/ **1** send (goods or services) to another country for sale. **2** spread or introduce (ideas or customs) to another country. ● noun /eksport/ **1** the exporting of goods or services. **2** an exported commodity, article, or service.
– DERIVATIVES **exportability** noun **exportable** adjective **exportation** noun **exporter** noun.
– ORIGIN Latin *exportare*, from *portare* 'carry'.
expose ● verb **1** uncover and make visible. **2** reveal the true nature of. **3** (**exposed**) unprotected from the weather. **4** (**expose to**) make vulnerable to. **5** subject (photographic film) to light. **6** (**expose oneself**) publicly and indecently display one's genitals.
– DERIVATIVES **exposer** noun.
– ORIGIN Latin *exponere* 'present, explain', but influenced by *expositus* 'put or set out' and Old French *poser* 'to place'.
exposé /ikspōzay/ ● noun a report in the media that reveals something discreditable.
– ORIGIN French, 'shown, set out'.
exposition ● noun **1** a comprehensive description and explanation of a theory. **2** a large public exhibition of art or trade goods. **3** Music the part of a movement in which the principal themes are first presented.
– DERIVATIVES **expositional** adjective.
– ORIGIN Latin, from *exponere* 'present, explain'.
expositor /ikspozzitər/ ● noun a person or thing that explains complicated ideas or theories.
– DERIVATIVES **expository** adjective.

e

Thesaurus

frontal.
– OPPOSITES vague.
explode ● verb **1** *a bomb has exploded* BLOW UP, detonate, go off, burst (apart), fly apart. **2** *exploding the first atomic device* DETONATE, set off, let off, discharge. **3** *he exploded in anger* LOSE ONE'S TEMPER, blow up, get angry, become enraged; *informal* fly off the handle, hit the roof, blow one's cool/top, go wild, go bananas, see red, go off the deep end; *Brit. informal* go spare, go crackers; *N. Amer. informal* blow one's lid/stack. **4** *the city's exploding population* INCREASE SUDDENLY/RAPIDLY, mushroom, snowball, escalate, multiply, burgeon, rocket. **5** *exploding the myths about men* DISPROVE, refute, rebut, invalidate, negate, negative, controvert, repudiate, discredit, debunk, belie, give the lie to; *informal* shoot full of holes, blow out of the water; *formal* confute.
– OPPOSITES defuse.
exploit ● verb **1** *we should exploit this new technology* UTILIZE, use, make use of, turn/put to good use, make the most of, capitalize on, benefit from; *informal* cash in on. **2** *exploiting the workers* TAKE ADVANTAGE OF, abuse, impose on, treat unfairly, misuse, ill-treat; *informal* walk (all) over, take for a ride, rip off.
● noun *his exploits brought him notoriety* FEAT, deed, act, adventure, stunt, escapade; achievement, accomplishment, attainment; *informal* lark, caper.
exploitation ● noun **1** *the exploitation of mineral resources* UTILIZATION, use, making use of, making the most of, capitalization on; *informal* cashing in on. **2** *the exploitation of the poor* TAKING ADVANTAGE, abuse, misuse, ill-treatment, unfair treatment, oppression.
exploration ● noun **1** *the exploration of space* INVESTIGATION, study, survey, research, inspection, examination, scrutiny, observation; consideration, analysis, review. **2** *explorations into the mountains* EXPEDITION, trip, journey, voyage; *archaic* peregrination; (**explorations**) travels.
exploratory ● adjective INVESTIGATIVE, investigational, explorative, probing, fact-finding; experimental, trial, test, preliminary, provisional.
explore ● verb **1** *they explored all the possibilities* INVESTIGATE, look into, consider; examine, research, survey, scrutinize, study, review, go over with a fine-tooth comb; *informal* check out. **2** *exploring Iceland's north-west* TRAVEL OVER, tour, range over; survey, take a look at, inspect, investigate, reconnoitre; *informal* recce, give something a/the once-over.
explorer ● noun TRAVELLER, discoverer, voyager, adventurer; surveyor, scout, prospector.
explosion ● noun **1** *Edward heard the explosion* DETONATION, eruption, blowing up; bang, blast, boom. **2** *an explosion of anger* OUTBURST, flare-up, outbreak, eruption, storm, rush, surge; fit, paroxysm, attack. **3** *the explosion of human populations* SUDDEN/RAPID INCREASE, mushrooming, snowballing, escalation, multiplication, burgeoning, rocketing.
explosive ● adjective **1** *explosive gases* VOLATILE, inflammable, flammable, combustible, incendiary. **2** *Marco's explosive temper* FIERY, stormy, violent, volatile, angry, passionate, tempestuous, turbulent, touchy, irascible, hot-headed, short-tempered. **3** *an explosive situation* TENSE, (highly) charged, overwrought; dangerous, perilous, hazardous, sensitive, delicate, unstable, volatile. **4** *explosive population growth* SUDDEN, dramatic, rapid; mushrooming, snowballing, escalating, rocketing, accelerating.
● noun *stocks of explosives* BOMB, incendiary (device).
exponent ● noun **1** *an exponent of free-trade policies* ADVOCATE, supporter, proponent, upholder, backer, defender, champion; promoter, propagandist, campaigner, fighter, crusader, enthusiast, apologist. **2** *a karate exponent* PRACTITIONER, performer, player.
– OPPOSITES critic, opponent.
export ● verb **1** *exporting raw materials* SELL OVERSEAS/ABROAD, send overseas/abroad, trade internationally. **2** *he is trying to export his ideas to America* TRANSMIT, spread, disseminate, circulate, communicate, pass on; *poetic/literary* bruit about/abroad.
– OPPOSITES import.
expose ● verb **1** *at low tide the sands are exposed* REVEAL, uncover, lay bare. **2** *he was exposed to asbestos* MAKE VULNERABLE, subject, lay open, put at risk, put in jeopardy. **3** *they were exposed to liberal ideas* INTRODUCE TO, bring into contact with, make aware of, familiarize with, acquaint with. **4** *he was exposed as a liar* UNCOVER, reveal, unveil, unmask, detect, find out; discover, bring to light, bring into the open, make known; denounce, condemn; *informal* spill the beans on, blow the whistle on.
– OPPOSITES cover.
– PHRASES **expose oneself** DISPLAY/REVEAL ONE'S GENITALIA; *informal* flash.
exposé ● noun REVELATION, disclosure, exposure; report, feature, piece, column; *informal* scoop.
– OPPOSITES cover-up.
exposed ● adjective UNPROTECTED, unsheltered, open to the elements/weather; vulnerable, defenceless, undefended, pregnable.
– OPPOSITES sheltered.
exposition ● noun **1** *a lucid exposition* EXPLANATION, description, elucidation, explication, interpretation; account, commentary, ap-

ex post facto /eks pōst faktō/ • **adjective & adverb** with retrospective action or force.
– ORIGIN from Latin *ex postfacto* 'in the light of subsequent events'.
expostulate /ikspossty oolayt/ • **verb** express strong disapproval or disagreement.
– DERIVATIVES **expostulation** noun **expostulatory** /iksposs-tyoolətri/ adjective.
– ORIGIN Latin *expostulare* 'demand'.
exposure • **noun 1** the state of being exposed to something harmful. **2** a physical condition resulting from being exposed to severe weather conditions. **3** the action of exposing a photographic film. **4** the quantity of light reaching a photographic film, as determined by shutter speed and lens aperture. **5** the revelation of something secret. **6** the publicizing of information or an event.
expound • **verb** present and explain (a theory or idea) systematically.
– DERIVATIVES **expounder** noun.
– ORIGIN Latin *exponere* 'present, explain'.
express[1] /ikspress/ • **verb 1** convey (a thought or feeling) in words or by gestures and conduct. **2** squeeze out (liquid or air).
– DERIVATIVES **expresser** noun **expressible** adjective.
– ORIGIN Old French *expresser*, from Latin *pressare* 'to press'.
express[2] /ikspress/ • **adjective 1** operating at high speed. **2** denoting a service in which deliveries are made by a special messenger. • **adverb** by express train or delivery service. • **noun 1** (also **express train**) a train that stops at few stations and so travels quickly. **2** a special delivery service. • **verb** send by express messenger or delivery.
– ORIGIN extension of EXPRESS[3].
express[3] /ikspress, ekspress/ • **adjective 1** stated explicitly. **2** specifically identified to the exclusion of anything else.
– DERIVATIVES **expressly** adverb.
– ORIGIN Latin *expressus* 'distinctly presented', from *exprimere* 'press out, express'.
expression • **noun 1** the action of expressing. **2** the look on someone's face. **3** a word or phrase expressing an idea. **4** Mathematics a collection of symbols expressing a quantity.
– DERIVATIVES **expressional** adjective **expressionless** adjective.
expressionism • **noun** a style in art, music, or drama in which the artist or writer seeks to express the inner world of emotion rather than external reality.
– DERIVATIVES **expressionist** noun & adjective **expressionistic** adjective.
expressive • **adjective 1** effectively conveying thought or feeling. **2** (**expressive of**) conveying (a quality or idea).
– DERIVATIVES **expressively** adverb **expressiveness** noun **expressivity** noun.
expresso • **noun** variant spelling of ESPRESSO.
expressway • **noun** chiefly N. Amer. an urban motorway.
expropriate /eksprōpriayt/ • **verb** (of the state) take (property) from its owner for public use or benefit.
– DERIVATIVES **expropriation** noun **expropriator** noun.
– ORIGIN Latin *expropriare*, from *proprium* 'property'.
expulsion • **noun** the action of expelling.
– DERIVATIVES **expulsive** adjective.
– ORIGIN Latin, from *expellere* 'drive out'.
expunge /ikspunj/ • **verb** obliterate or remove completely.
– DERIVATIVES **expungement** noun **expunger** noun.
– ORIGIN Latin *expungere* 'mark for deletion by means of points', from *pungere* 'to prick'.
expurgate /ekspergayt/ • **verb** remove matter regarded as obscene or unsuitable from (a text or account).
– DERIVATIVES **expurgation** noun **expurgator** noun **expurgatory** /ekspergətri/ adjective.
– ORIGIN Latin *expurgare* 'cleanse thoroughly'.
exquisite /ekskwizit/ • **adjective 1** of great beauty and delicacy.

Thesaurus

praisal, assessment, discussion, exegesis. **2** *the exposition will feature 200 exhibits* EXHIBITION, (trade) fair, display, show, presentation, demonstration; *N. Amer.* exhibit.
expository • **adjective** EXPLANATORY, descriptive, describing, elucidatory, explicatory, explicative, interpretative, exegetic.
expostulate • **verb** REMONSTRATE, disagree, argue, take issue, protest, reason, express disagreement, raise objections.
exposure • **noun 1** *the exposure of the lizard's vivid blue tongue* REVEALING, revelation, uncovering, baring, laying bare. **2** *exposure to harmful chemicals* SUBJECTION, vulnerability, laying open. **3** *suffering from exposure* FROSTBITE, cold, hypothermia. **4** *exposure to great literature* INTRODUCTION TO, experience of, contact with, familiarity with, acquaintance with, awareness of. **5** *the exposure of a banking scandal* UNCOVERING, revelation, disclosure, unveiling, unmasking, discovery, detection; denunciation, condemnation. **6** *we're getting a lot of exposure* PUBLICITY, publicizing, advertising, public interest/attention, media interest/attention; *informal* hype. **7** *the exposure is perfect* OUTLOOK, aspect, view; position, setting, location.
expound • **verb 1** *he expounded his theories* PRESENT, put forward, set forth, propose, propound; explain, give an explanation of, detail, spell out, describe. **2** *a treatise expounding Paul's teachings* EXPLAIN, interpret, explicate, elucidate; comment on, give a commentary on.
– PHRASES **expound on** ELABORATE ON, expand on, expatiate on, discuss at length.
express[1] • **verb 1** *community leaders expressed their anger* COMMUNICATE, convey, indicate, show, demonstrate, reveal, make manifest, put across/over, get across/over; articulate, put into words, utter, voice, give voice to; state, assert, proclaim, profess, air, make public, give vent to; *formal* evince. **2** *all the juice is expressed* SQUEEZE OUT, press out, extract.
– PHRASES **express oneself** COMMUNICATE ONE'S THOUGHTS/OPINIONS/VIEWS, put thoughts into words, speak one's mind, say what's on one's mind.
express[2] • **adjective** *an express bus* RAPID, swift, fast, quick, speedy, high-speed; non-stop, direct.
– OPPOSITES slow.
• **noun** *an overnight express* EXPRESS TRAIN, fast train, direct train.
express[3] • **adjective 1** *express reference to confidential matters* EXPLICIT, clear, direct, obvious, plain, distinct, unambiguous, unequivocal; specific, precise, crystal clear, certain, categorical. **2** *one express purpose* SOLE, specific, particular, exclusive, specified, fixed.
– OPPOSITES implied.
expression • **noun 1** *the free expression of opposition views* UTTERANCE, uttering, voicing, pronouncement, declaration, articulation, assertion, setting forth; dissemination, circulation, communication, spreading, promulgation. **2** *an expression of sympathy* INDICATION, demonstration, show, exhibition, token; communication, illustration, revelation. **3** *an expression of harassed fatigue* LOOK, appearance, air, manner, countenance, mien. **4** *a time-worn expression* IDIOM, phrase, idiomatic expression; proverb, saying, adage, maxim, axiom, aphorism, saw, motto, platitude, cliché. **5** *these pieces are very different in expression* EMOTION, feeling, spirit, passion, intensity; style, intonation, tone. **6** *essential oils obtained by expression* SQUEEZING, pressing, extraction, extracting.
expressionless • **adjective 1** *his face was expressionless* INSCRUTABLE, deadpan, poker-faced; blank, vacant, emotionless, unemotional, inexpressive; glazed, stony, wooden, impassive. **2** *a flat, expressionless tone* DULL, dry, toneless, monotonous, boring, tedious, flat, wooden, unmodulated, unvarying, devoid of feeling/emotion.
– OPPOSITES expressive, lively.
expressive • **adjective 1** *an expressive shrug* ELOQUENT, meaningful, demonstrative, suggestive. **2** *an expressive song* EMOTIONAL, full of emotion/feeling, passionate, poignant, moving, stirring, evocative, powerful, emotionally charged. **3** *his diction is very expressive of his Englishness* INDICATIVE, demonstrative, demonstrating, showing, suggesting.
– OPPOSITES expressionless, unemotional.
expressly • **adverb 1** *he was expressly forbidden to discuss the matter* EXPLICITLY, clearly, directly, plainly, distinctly, unambiguously, unequivocally; specifically, categorically, pointedly, emphatically. **2** *a machine expressly built for spraying paint* SOLELY, specifically, particularly, specially, exclusively, just, only, explicitly.
expropriate • **verb** SEIZE, take (away/over), appropriate, take possession of, requisition, commandeer, claim, acquire, sequestrate, confiscate; *Law* distrain.
expulsion • **noun 1** *expulsion from the party* REMOVAL, debarment, dismissal, exclusion, discharge, ejection, drumming out. **2** *the expulsion of bodily wastes* DISCHARGE, ejection, excretion, voiding, evacuation, elimination, passing.
– OPPOSITES admission.
expunge • **verb** ERASE, remove, delete, rub out, wipe out, efface;

2 highly refined: *exquisite taste.* **3** intensely felt; acute.
– DERIVATIVES **exquisitely** adverb **exquisiteness** noun.
– ORIGIN originally in the sense 'precise': from Latin *exquirere* 'seek out'.

ex-serviceman (or **ex-servicewoman**) ● noun chiefly Brit. a former member of the armed forces.

extant /ekstant/ ● adjective still in existence.
– ORIGIN Latin, from *exstare* 'be visible or prominent'.

extemporaneous /ikstempərayniəss/ ● adjective another term for EXTEMPORARY.
– DERIVATIVES **extemporaneously** adverb **extemporaneousness** noun.

extemporary /ikstempərəri/ ● adjective spoken or done without preparation.
– DERIVATIVES **extemporarily** adverb **extemporariness** noun.
– ORIGIN from EXTEMPORE.

extempore /ikstempəri/ ● adjective & adverb spoken or done without preparation.
– ORIGIN from Latin *ex tempore* 'on the spur of the moment' (literally 'out of the time').

extemporize /ikstempərīz/ (also **extemporise**) ● verb improvise.
– DERIVATIVES **extemporization** noun.

extend ● verb **1** make larger in area. **2** cause to last longer. **3** occupy a specified area or continue for a specified distance. **4** hold out (one's hand or another part of one's body) towards someone. **5** offer; make available.
– DERIVATIVES **extendability** noun **extendable** adjective **extendibility** noun **extendible** adjective **extensibility** noun **extensible** adjective.
– ORIGIN Latin *extendere* 'stretch out'.

extended family ● noun a family which extends beyond the nuclear family to include relatives living close by.

extender ● noun **1** a person or thing that extends something. **2** a substance added to a liquid or soft product to increase its bulk.

extensile /ikstensīl/ ● adjective capable of being extended.

extension ● noun **1** the action or process of extending. **2** a part added to a building to enlarge it. **3** an additional period of time. **4** (also **extension lead** or **cable**) an additional length of electric cable which can be plugged into a fixed socket and terminates in a further socket. **5** a subsidiary telephone, especially one with its own additional number on a line leading from a main switchboard.
– DERIVATIVES **extensional** adjective.
– ORIGIN Latin, from *extendere* 'stretch out'.

extensive ● adjective **1** covering a large area. **2** large in amount or scale.
– DERIVATIVES **extensively** adverb **extensiveness** noun.

extensor /ikstensər/ ● noun Anatomy a muscle whose contraction extends a limb or other part of the body.

extent ● noun **1** the area covered by something. **2** size or scale. **3** the degree to which something is the case: *everyone compromises to some extent.*
– ORIGIN Old French *extente*, from Latin *extendere* 'stretch out'.

extenuate /ikstenyooayt/ ● verb **1** (usu. as adj. **extenuating**) lessen the seriousness of (an offence) by referring to a factor that helps excuse it. **2** (**extenuated**) literary thin.
– DERIVATIVES **extenuation** noun **extenuatory** /ikstenyooətəri/ adjective.
– ORIGIN Latin *extenuare* 'make thin'.

exterior ● adjective **1** forming, situated on, or relating to the outside. ● noun the outer surface or structure of something.
– DERIVATIVES **exteriorly** adverb.
– ORIGIN Latin, from *exter* 'outer'.

exterminate /iksterminayt/ ● verb destroy completely; eradicate.
– DERIVATIVES **extermination** noun **exterminator** noun **exterminatory** /iksterminətəri/ adjective.
– ORIGIN originally in the sense 'drive out': from Latin *exterminare*, from *terminus* 'boundary'.

external ● adjective **1** belonging to, situated on, or forming the outside. **2** coming or derived from a source outside the subject affected. **3** coming from or relating to another country or institution. ● noun (**externals**) outward features.
– DERIVATIVES **externally** adverb.
– ORIGIN Latin, from *exter* 'outer'.

external ear ● noun the parts of the ear outside the eardrum,

e

Thesaurus

cross out, strike out, blot out, blank out; destroy, obliterate, eradicate, eliminate.

expurgate ● verb CENSOR, bowdlerize, blue-pencil, cut, edit; clean up, sanitize, make acceptable, make palatable, water down.

exquisite ● adjective **1** *exquisite antique glass* BEAUTIFUL, lovely, elegant, fine; magnificent, superb, excellent, wonderful, well-crafted, well-made, perfect; delicate, fragile, dainty, subtle. **2** *exquisite taste* DISCRIMINATING, discerning, sensitive, selective, fastidious; refined, cultivated, cultured, educated. **3** *exquisite agony* INTENSE, acute, keen, piercing, sharp, severe, racking, excruciating, agonizing, harrowing, searing; unbearable, unendurable.
● noun *(dated) even among these snappy dressers, he was an exquisite* DANDY, fop, glamour boy; *informal* dude, snappy dresser, natty dresser; *informal, dated* swell, blade; *dated* beau.

extant ● adjective STILL EXISTING, in existence, existent, surviving, remaining, undestroyed.

extemporary, extemporaneous ● adjective *an extemporaneous address.* See EXTEMPORE.

extempore ● adjective *an extempore speech* IMPROMPTU, spontaneous, unscripted, ad lib, extemporary, extemporaneous; improvised, unrehearsed, unplanned, unprepared, off the top of one's head; *informal* off-the-cuff; *formal* ad libitum.
– OPPOSITES rehearsed.
● adverb *he was speaking extempore* SPONTANEOUSLY, extemporaneously, ad lib, without preparation, without rehearsal, off the top of one's head; *informal* off the cuff; *formal* ad libitum.

extemporize ● verb IMPROVISE, ad lib, play it by ear, think on one's feet, do something off the top of one's head; *informal* busk it, wing it, do something off the cuff.

extend ● verb **1** *he attempted to extend his dominions* EXPAND, enlarge, increase, make larger/bigger; lengthen, widen, broaden. **2** *the garden extends down to the road* CONTINUE, carry on, run on, stretch (out), reach, lead. **3** *we have extended our range of services* WIDEN, expand, broaden; augment, supplement, increase, add to, enhance, develop. **4** *extending the life of parliament* PROLONG, lengthen, increase; stretch out, protract, spin out, string out. **5** *extend your arms and legs* STRETCH OUT, spread out, reach out, straighten out. **6** *he extended a hand in greeting* HOLD OUT, reach out, hold forth; offer, give, outstretch, proffer. **7** *we wish to extend our thanks to Mr Bayes* OFFER, proffer, give, grant, bestow, accord.
– OPPOSITES reduce, narrow, shorten.
– PHRASES **extend to** INCLUDE, take in, incorporate, encompass.

extended ● adjective PROLONGED, protracted, long-lasting, long-drawn-out, spun out, dragged out, strung out, lengthy, long.

extension ● noun **1** *they are planning a new extension* ADDITION, add-on, adjunct, annexe, wing, supplementary building; *N. Amer.* ell. **2** *an extension of knowledge* EXPANSION, increase, enlargement, widening, broadening, deepening; augmentation, enhancement, development, growth, continuation. **3** *an extension of opening hours* PROLONGATION, lengthening, increase. **4** *I need an extension of time* POSTPONEMENT, deferral, delay, more/extra time.

extensive ● adjective **1** *a mansion with extensive grounds* LARGE, large-scale, sizeable, substantial, considerable, ample, expansive, great, vast. **2** *extensive knowledge* COMPREHENSIVE, thorough, exhaustive; broad, wide, wide-ranging, catholic.

extent ● noun **1** *two acres in extent* AREA, size, expanse, length; proportions, dimensions. **2** *the full extent of her father's illness* DEGREE, scale, level, magnitude, scope; size, breadth, width, reach, range.

extenuate ● verb EXCUSE, make allowances/excuses for, mitigate, palliate, defend, vindicate, justify; diminish, lessen, moderate, qualify, play down.

extenuating ● adjective MITIGATING, excusing, exonerative, palliating, palliative, justifying, justificatory, vindicating; *formal* exculpatory.

exterior ● adjective *the exterior walls* OUTER, outside, outermost, outward, external.
– RELATED TERMS ecto-, exo-.
– OPPOSITES interior.
● noun *the exterior of the building* OUTSIDE, outer surface, external surface, outward appearance, facade.

exterminate ● verb KILL, put to death, take/end the life of, dispatch; slaughter, butcher, massacre, wipe out, eliminate, eradicate, annihilate; murder, assassinate, execute; *informal* do away with, bump off, do in, top, take out, blow away; *N. Amer. informal* ice, rub out, waste; *poetic/literary* slay.

especially the pinna.

externalize (also **externalise**) ● verb **1** give external existence or concrete form to. **2** express (a thought or feeling) in words or actions.

– DERIVATIVES **externalization** noun.

extinct ● adjective **1** (of a species or other large group) having no living members. **2** no longer in existence. **3** (of a volcano) not having erupted in recorded history.

– ORIGIN originally in the sense 'no longer alight': from Latin *exstinguere* 'extinguish'.

extinction ● noun the state or process of being or becoming extinct.

extinguish ● verb **1** put out (a fire or light). **2** put an end to. **3** cancel (a debt) by full payment. **4** Law render (a right or obligation) void.

– DERIVATIVES **extinguishable** adjective **extinguisher** noun **extinguishment** noun (Law).

– ORIGIN Latin *exstinguere*, from *stinguere* 'quench'.

extirpate /ekstərpayt/ ● verb search out and destroy completely.

– DERIVATIVES **extirpation** noun **extirpator** noun.

– ORIGIN Latin *exstirpare*, from *stirps* 'a stem'.

extol /ikstōl/ ● verb (**extolled**, **extolling**) praise enthusiastically.

– DERIVATIVES **extoller** noun **extolment** noun.

– ORIGIN Latin *extollere*, from *tollere* 'raise'.

extort /ikstort/ ● verb obtain by force, threats, or other unfair means.

– DERIVATIVES **extorter** noun **extortion** noun **extortioner** noun **extortionist** noun **extortive** adjective.

– ORIGIN Latin *extorquere*, from *torquere* 'twist'.

extortionate /ikstorshənət/ ● adjective **1** (of a price) much too high. **2** using or given to extortion.

– DERIVATIVES **extortionately** adverb.

extra ● adjective added to an existing or usual amount or number. ● adverb **1** to a greater extent than usual. **2** in addition. ● noun **1** an item for which an extra charge is made. **2** an extra item. **3** a person engaged temporarily to take part in a crowd scene in a film or play.

– ORIGIN probably a shortening of EXTRAORDINARY.

extra- ● prefix **1** outside; beyond: *extramarital*. **2** beyond the scope of: *extra-curricular*.

– ORIGIN Latin *extra* 'outside'.

extract ● verb /ikstrakt/ **1** remove with care or effort. **2** obtain (money, information, etc.) from someone unwilling to give it. **3** obtain (a substance or resource) from something by a special method. **4** select (a passage from a text, film, or piece of music) for quotation, performance, or reproduction. ● noun /ekstrakt/ **1** a short passage taken from a text, film, or piece of music. **2** a preparation containing the active ingredient of a substance in concentrated form.

– DERIVATIVES **extractability** noun **extractable** adjective **extractive** adjective.

– ORIGIN Latin *extrahere* 'draw out'.

extraction ● noun **1** the action of extracting. **2** the ethnic origin of someone's family.

extractor ● noun **1** a machine or device used to extract something. **2** (before another noun) denoting a fan or other device for extracting odours and stale air.

extra-curricular ● adjective (of an activity at a school or college) pursued in addition to the normal curriculum.

extradite /ekstrədīt/ ● verb hand over (a person accused or convicted of committing a crime in a foreign state) to the jurisdiction of that state.

– DERIVATIVES **extraditable** adjective **extradition** noun.

– ORIGIN from French *extradition*, from *tradition* 'delivery'.

extramarital /ekstrəmarrit'l/ ● adjective (especially of sexual relations) occurring outside marriage.

– DERIVATIVES **extramaritally** adverb.

extramural /ekstrəmyoorəl/ ● adjective **1** Brit. (of a course of study) arranged for people who are not full-time members of a university or other educational establishment. **2** outside the walls or boundaries of a town or city.

– DERIVATIVES **extramurally** adverb.

– ORIGIN from Latin *extra muros* 'outside the walls'.

extraneous /ikstrayniəss/ ● adjective **1** irrelevant or unrelated

Thesaurus

extermination ● noun KILLING, murder, assassination, putting to death, execution, dispatch, slaughter, massacre, liquidation, elimination, eradication, annihilation; *poetic/literary* slaying.

external ● adjective **1** *an external wall* OUTER, outside, outermost, outward, exterior. **2** *an external examiner* OUTSIDE, independent, non-resident, from elsewhere.

– RELATED TERMS ecto-, exo-.

– OPPOSITES internal, in-house.

extinct ● adjective **1** *an extinct species* VANISHED, lost, died out, no longer existing, no longer extant, wiped out, destroyed, gone. **2** *an extinct volcano* INACTIVE.

– OPPOSITES extant, dormant.

extinction ● noun DYING OUT, disappearance, vanishing; extermination, destruction, elimination, eradication, annihilation.

extinguish ● verb **1** *the fire was extinguished* DOUSE, put out, stamp out, smother, beat out, dampen down. **2** *all hope was extinguished* DESTROY, end, finish off, put an end to, bring to an end, terminate, remove, annihilate, wipe out, erase, eliminate, eradicate, obliterate; *informal* take out, rub out.

– OPPOSITES light.

extirpate ● verb WEED OUT, destroy, eradicate, stamp out, root out, wipe out, eliminate, suppress, crush, put down, put an end to, get rid of.

extol ● verb PRAISE ENTHUSIASTICALLY, go into raptures about/over, wax lyrical about, sing the praises of, praise to the skies, acclaim, eulogize, rhapsodize over, rave about, enthuse about/over; *informal* go wild about, go on about; *N. Amer. informal* ballyhoo; *formal* laud; *archaic* panegyrize.

– OPPOSITES criticize.

extort ● verb OBTAIN BY FORCE, obtain by threat(s), blackmail someone for, extract, exact, wring, wrest, screw, squeeze; *N. Amer. & Austral. informal* put the bite on someone for.

extortion ● noun DEMANDING MONEY WITH MENACES, blackmail, extraction; *N. Amer. informal* shakedown; *formal* exaction.

extortionate ● adjective **1** *extortionate prices* EXORBITANT, excessively high, excessive, outrageous, unreasonable, inordinate, inflated; *informal* over the top, OTT. **2** *an extortionate clause* GRASPING, bloodsucking, avaricious, greedy; exacting, harsh, severe, oppressive; *informal* money-grubbing.

extortionist ● noun RACKETEER, extortioner, extorter, blackmailer; *informal* bloodsucker.

extra ● adjective *extra income* ADDITIONAL, more, added, supplementary, further, auxiliary, ancillary, subsidiary, secondary.

● adverb **1** *working extra hard* EXCEPTIONALLY, particularly, specially, especially, very, extremely; unusually, extraordinarily, uncommonly, remarkably, outstandingly, amazingly, incredibly, really; *informal* seriously, mucho, awfully, terribly; *Brit.* jolly, dead, well; *informal, dated* frightfully. **2** *postage is charged extra* IN ADDITION, additionally, as well, also, too, besides, on top (of that); *archaic* withal.

● noun **1** *an optional extra* ADDITION, supplement, adjunct, addendum, add-on. **2** *a film extra* WALK-ON, supernumerary, spear-carrier.

extract ● verb **1** *he extracted the cassette* TAKE OUT, draw out, pull out, remove, withdraw; free, release, extricate. **2** *extracting money* WREST, exact, wring, screw, squeeze, obtain by force, obtain by threat(s), extort, blackmail someone for; *N. Amer. & Austral. informal* put the bite on someone for. **3** *the roots are crushed to extract the juice* SQUEEZE OUT, express, press out, obtain. **4** *the table is extracted from the report* EXCERPT, select, reproduce, copy, take. **5** *ideas extracted from a variety of theories* DERIVE, develop, evolve, deduce, infer, obtain; *formal* educe.

– OPPOSITES insert.

● noun **1** *an extract from his article* EXCERPT, passage, citation, quotation; (**excerpts**) analects. **2** *an extract of the ginseng root* DECOCTION, distillation, distillate, abstraction, concentrate, essence, juice.

extraction ● noun **1** *the extraction of gall bladder stones* REMOVAL, taking out, drawing out, pulling out, withdrawal; freeing, release, extrication. **2** *the extraction of grape juice* SQUEEZING, expressing, pressing, obtaining. **3** *a man of Irish extraction* DESCENT, ancestry, parentage, ancestors, family, antecedents; lineage, line, origin, derivation, birth; genealogy, heredity, stock, pedigree, blood, bloodline; roots, origins.

– OPPOSITES insertion.

extradite ● verb **1** *the government extradited him to Germany* DEPORT, send back, send home, repatriate. **2** *the government attempted to extradite suspects from Belgium* HAVE SOMEONE DEPORTED, have

to the subject. **2** of external origin.
– DERIVATIVES **extraneously** adverb **extraneousness** noun.
– ORIGIN Latin *extraneus*.
extranet ● noun an Intranet that can be partially accessed by authorized outside users.
extraordinaire /ikstrordinair/ ● adjective outstanding in a particular capacity: *a gardener extraordinaire*.
– ORIGIN French.
extraordinary /ikstrordinəri/ ● adjective **1** very unusual or remarkable. **2** (of a meeting) specially convened rather than being one of a regular series. **3** (of an official) specially employed: *Ambassador Extraordinary*.
– DERIVATIVES **extraordinarily** adverb **extraordinariness** noun.
– ORIGIN Latin *extraordinarius*, from *extra ordinem* 'outside the normal course of events'.
extrapolate /ikstrappəlayt/ ● verb **1** extend the application of (a method, conclusion, etc.) to different or larger groups. **2** extend (a graph) by inferring unknown values from trends in the known data.
– DERIVATIVES **extrapolation** noun **extrapolative** adjective **extrapolator** noun.
– ORIGIN from EXTRA- + a shortened form of INTERPOLATE.
extrasensory perception /ekstrəsensəri/ ● noun the supposed faculty of perceiving things by means other than the known senses, e.g. by telepathy.
extraterrestrial /ekstrətərestriəl/ ● adjective of or from outside the earth or its atmosphere. ● noun a hypothetical or fictional being from outer space.
extra time ● noun chiefly Brit. (in sport) a further period of play added on to a game if the scores are equal.
extravagant /ikstravvəgənt/ ● adjective **1** lacking restraint in spending money or using resources. **2** costing a great deal. **3** exceeding what is reasonable or appropriate: *extravagant claims*.
– DERIVATIVES **extravagance** noun **extravagancy** noun **extravagantly** adverb.
– ORIGIN originally in the sense 'unusual, unsuitable': from Latin *extravagari* 'diverge greatly'.
extravaganza /ikstravvəganzə/ ● noun an elaborate and spectacular entertainment.
– ORIGIN Italian *estravaganza* 'extravagance'.
extra virgin ● adjective denoting a particularly fine grade of olive oil made from the first pressing of the olives.
extreme ● adjective **1** to the highest degree; very great. **2** highly unusual; exceptional. **3** very severe or serious. **4** not moderate, especially politically. **5** furthest from the centre or a given point. **6** (of a sport) performed in a hazardous environment. ● noun **1** either of two abstract things that are as different from each other as possible. **2** the most extreme degree: *extremes of temperature*.
– DERIVATIVES **extremely** adverb **extremeness** noun.
– ORIGIN Latin *extremus* 'outermost, utmost'.
extreme unction ● noun (in the Roman Catholic Church) a former name for the sacrament of anointing of the sick, especially when administered to the dying.
extremist ● noun a person who holds extreme political or religious views.
– DERIVATIVES **extremism** noun.
extremity /ikstremmiti/ ● noun (pl. **extremities**) **1** the furthest point or limit. **2** (**extremities**) the hands and feet. **3** severity or seriousness. **4** extreme adversity.
extricate /ekstrikayt/ ● verb free from a constraint or difficulty.
– DERIVATIVES **extrication** noun.
– ORIGIN Latin *extricare* 'unravel', from *tricae* 'perplexities'.
extrinsic /ikstrinsik/ ● adjective not essential or inherent.
– DERIVATIVES **extrinsically** adverb.
– ORIGIN Latin *extrinsecus* 'outward'.
extrovert /ekstrəvert/ ● noun **1** an outgoing, socially confident person. **2** Psychology a person predominantly concerned with external things or objective considerations. ● adjective of or characteristic of an extrovert.

e

Thesaurus

someone sent home, bring back.
extradition ● noun DEPORTATION, repatriation, expulsion.
extraneous ● adjective **1** *extraneous considerations* IRRELEVANT, immaterial, beside the point, unrelated, unconnected, inapposite, inapplicable. **2** *extraneous noise* EXTERNAL, outside, exterior.
extraordinary ● adjective **1** *an extraordinary coincidence* REMARKABLE, exceptional, amazing, astonishing, astounding, sensational, stunning, incredible, unbelievable, phenomenal; striking, outstanding, momentous, impressive, singular, memorable, unforgettable, unique, noteworthy; out of the ordinary, unusual, uncommon, rare, surprising; *informal* fantastic, terrific, tremendous, stupendous, awesome; *poetic/literary* wondrous. **2** *extraordinary speed* VERY GREAT, tremendous, enormous, immense, prodigious, stupendous, monumental; *informal* almighty.
extravagance ● noun **1** *a fit of extravagance* PROFLIGACY, unthriftiness, improvidence, wastefulness, prodigality, lavishness. **2** *the costliest brands are an extravagance* LUXURY, indulgence, self-indulgence, treat, extra, non-essential. **3** *the extravagance of the decor* ORNATENESS, elaborateness, embellishment, ornamentation; ostentation, over-elaborateness. **4** *the extravagance of his compliments* EXCESSIVENESS, exaggeration, outrageousness, immoderation, excess.
extravagant ● adjective **1** *an extravagant lifestyle* SPENDTHRIFT, profligate, unthrifty, improvident, wasteful, prodigal, lavish. **2** *extravagant gifts* EXPENSIVE, costly, dear, high-priced, high-cost; valuable, precious; *informal* pricey, costing the earth, costing a bomb. **3** *extravagant prices* EXORBITANT, extortionate, excessive, high, unreasonable. **4** *extravagant praise* EXCESSIVE, immoderate, exaggerated, gushing, unrestrained, effusive, fulsome. **5** *decorated in an extravagant style* ORNATE, elaborate, decorated, ornamented, fancy; over-elaborate, ostentatious, exaggerated, baroque, rococo; *informal* flash, flashy.
– OPPOSITES thrifty, cheap, plain.
extravaganza ● noun SPECTACULAR, display, spectacle, show, pageant.
extreme ● adjective **1** *extreme danger* UTMOST, very great, greatest (possible), maximum, maximal, highest, supreme, great, acute, enormous, severe, high, exceptional, extraordinary. **2** *extreme measures* DRASTIC, serious, desperate, dire, radical, far-reaching, momentous, consequential; heavy, sharp, severe, austere, harsh, tough, strict, rigorous, oppressive, draconian; *Brit.* swingeing. **3** *extreme views* RADICAL, extremist, immoderate, fanatical, revolutionary, rebel, subversive, militant. **4** *extreme sports* DANGEROUS, hazardous, risky, high-risk, adventurous. **5** *the extreme north-west* FURTHEST, farthest, furthermost, farthermost, very, utmost; *archaic* outmost.
– RELATED TERMS ultra-.
– OPPOSITES slight, moderate.
● noun **1** *the two extremes* OPPOSITE, antithesis, side of the coin, (opposite) pole, antipode. **2** *this attitude is taken to its extreme in the following quote* LIMIT, extremity, highest/greatest degree, maximum, height, top, zenith, peak.
– PHRASES **in the extreme.** See EXTREMELY.
extremely ● adverb VERY, exceedingly, exceptionally, especially, extraordinarily, in the extreme, tremendously, immensely, vastly, hugely, intensely, acutely, singularly, uncommonly, unusually, decidedly, particularly, supremely, highly, remarkably, really, truly, mightily; *informal* terrifically, awfully, fearfully, terribly, devilishly, majorly, seriously, mega, ultra, damn, damned; *Brit. informal* ever so, well, hellish, dead, jolly; *N. Amer. informal* real, mighty, awful, darned; *informal, dated* devilish, frightfully; *archaic* exceeding.
– OPPOSITES slightly.
extremist ● noun FANATIC, radical, zealot, fundamentalist, hardliner, militant, activist; *informal* ultra.
– OPPOSITES moderate.
extremity ● noun **1** *the eastern extremity* LIMIT, end, edge, side, farthest point, boundary, border, frontier; perimeter, periphery, margin; *poetic/literary* bourn, marge. **2** *she lost feeling in her extremities* HANDS AND FEET, fingers and toes, limbs. **3** *the extremity of the violence* INTENSITY, magnitude, acuteness, ferocity, vehemence, fierceness, violence, severity, seriousness, strength, power, powerfulness, vigour, force, forcefulness. **4** *in extremity he will send for her* DIRE STRAITS, trouble, difficulty, hard times, hardship, adversity, misfortune, distress; crisis, emergency, disaster, catastrophe, calamity; predicament, plight, mess, dilemma; *informal* fix, pickle, jam, spot, bind, scrape, hole, sticky situation, hot/deep water.
extricate ● verb EXTRACT, free, release, disentangle, get out, remove, withdraw, disengage; *informal* get someone/oneself off the hook.
extrinsic ● adjective EXTERNAL, extraneous, exterior, outside, out-

– DERIVATIVES **extroversion** noun **extroverted** adjective.
– ORIGIN from *extro-* (variant of EXTRA-) + Latin *vertere* 'to turn'.

extrude /ikstrōōd/ ● verb **1** thrust or force out. **2** shape (a material such as metal or plastic) by forcing it through a die.
– DERIVATIVES **extrudable** adjective **extrusion** noun.
– ORIGIN Latin *extrudere*, from *trudere* 'to thrust'.

extrusive ● adjective Geology referring to rock that has been extruded at the earth's surface as lava or other volcanic deposits.

exuberant /igzyōōbərənt/ ● adjective **1** lively and cheerful. **2** growing profusely.
– DERIVATIVES **exuberance** noun **exuberantly** adverb.
– ORIGIN from Latin *exuberare* 'be abundantly fruitful'.

e

exude /igzyōōd/ ● verb **1** discharge or be discharged slowly and steadily. **2** display (an emotion or quality) strongly and openly.
– DERIVATIVES **exudate** noun **exudation** noun **exudative** adjective.
– ORIGIN Latin *exsudare*, from *sudare* 'to sweat'.

exult ● verb show or feel triumphant elation.
– DERIVATIVES **exultancy** noun **exultant** adjective **exultantly** adverb **exultation** noun **exulting** adjective.
– ORIGIN Latin *exsultare*, from *exsilire* 'leap up'.

exurb /eksurb/ ● noun N. Amer. a prosperous area beyond a city's suburbs.
– DERIVATIVES **exurban** adjective.
– ORIGIN (as *exurban*): from Latin *ex* 'out of' + URBAN, on the model of *suburban*.

ex-voto /eks vōtō/ ● noun (pl. **ex-votos**) an offering given in order to fulfil a vow.
– ORIGIN from Latin *ex voto* 'from a vow'.

eye ● noun **1** the organ of sight in humans and animals. **2** a rounded eye-like marking on an animal or bird. **3** a round, dark spot on a potato from which a new shoot grows. **4** the small hole in a needle through which the thread is passed. **5** a small metal loop into which a hook is fitted as a fastener on a garment. **6** Nautical a loop at the top end of a shroud or stay rope. **7** the calm region at the centre of a storm. **8** used to refer to a person's opinion or feelings: *to European eyes, the city seems overcrowded.* ● verb (**eyeing** or **eying**) **1** look at closely or with interest. **2** (**eye up**) informal look at (someone) in a way that reveals a sexual interest.
– PHRASES **be all eyes** be watching eagerly and attentively. **close one's eyes to** refuse to acknowledge (something unpleasant). **an eye for an eye and a tooth for a tooth** retaliation in kind is the appropriate way to deal with an offence or crime. [ORIGIN with biblical allusion to the Book of Exodus, chapter 21.] **give someone the eye** informal look at someone with sexual interest. **have an eye for** be able to recognize and judge wisely. **have** (or **keep**) **one's eye on 1** keep under careful observation. **2** (**have one's eye on**) aim to acquire. **have** (or **with**) **an eye to** have (or having) as one's objective. **have eyes in the back of one's head** know what is going on around one even when one cannot see it. **keep an eye on** keep under careful observation. **keep an eye out** (or **open**) look out for something. **keep one's eyes open** (or **peeled** or Brit. **skinned**) watch out for something. **make eyes at** look at in a way that indicates sexual interest. **one in the eye for** a disappointment or setback for. **only have eyes for** be exclusively interested in. **open someone's eyes** cause someone to realize something. **see eye to eye** be in full agreement. **a twinkle** (or **gleam**) **in someone's eye** something that is as yet no more than an idea or dream. **up to one's eyes** informal extremely busy. **what the eye doesn't see, the heart doesn't grieve over** proverb if someone is unaware of an unpleasant fact or situation they can't be troubled by it. **with one's eyes open** fully aware of possible difficulties.
– DERIVATIVES **eyed** adjective.
– ORIGIN Old English.

eyeball ● noun the round part of the eye of a vertebrate, within the eyelids and socket. ● verb informal, chiefly N. Amer. stare at closely.
– PHRASES **eyeball to eyeball** face to face with someone, especially in an aggressive way.

eyebath ● noun chiefly Brit. a small container used for applying cleansing solutions to the eye.

eyebright ● noun a small white-flowered plant, traditionally used as a remedy for eye problems.

eyebrow ● noun the strip of hair growing on the ridge above a person's eye socket.
– PHRASES **raise one's eyebrows** (or **an eyebrow**) show surprise or mild disapproval.

eye-catching ● adjective immediately appealing or noticeable.

Thesaurus

ward.
– OPPOSITES intrinsic.

extrovert ● noun *like most extroverts he was a good dancer* OUTGOING PERSON, sociable person, socializer, life and soul of the party.
– OPPOSITES introvert.
● adjective *his extrovert personality* OUTGOING, extroverted, sociable, gregarious, genial, affable, friendly, unreserved.
– OPPOSITES introverted.

extrude ● verb FORCE OUT, thrust out, express, eject, expel, release, emit.

exuberant ● adjective **1** *exuberant guests dancing on the terrace* EBULLIENT, buoyant, cheerful, jaunty, light-hearted, high-spirited, exhilarated, excited, elated, exultant, euphoric, joyful, cheery, merry, jubilant, vivacious, enthusiastic, irrepressible, energetic, animated, full of life, lively, vigorous; *informal* bubbly, bouncy, chipper, chirpy, full of beans; *poetic/literary* blithe, blithesome. **2** *an exuberant coating of mosses* LUXURIANT, lush, rich, dense, thick, abundant, profuse, plentiful, prolific. **3** *an exuberant welcome* EFFUSIVE, extravagant, fulsome, expansive, gushing, gushy, demonstrative.
– OPPOSITES gloomy, restrained.

exude ● verb **1** *milkweed exudes a milky sap* GIVE OFF/OUT, discharge, release, emit, issue; ooze, weep, secrete, excrete. **2** *slime exudes from the fungus* OOZE, seep, issue, escape, discharge, flow, leak. **3** *he exuded self-confidence* EMANATE, radiate, ooze, emit; display, show, exhibit, manifest, transmit, embody.

exult ● verb **1** *her opponents exulted when she left* REJOICE, be joyful, be happy, be delighted, be elated, be ecstatic, be overjoyed, be cock-a-hoop, be jubilant, be rapturous, be in raptures, be thrilled, jump for joy, be on cloud nine, be in seventh heaven; celebrate, cheer; *informal* be over the moon, be on top of the world; *Austral. informal* be wrapped; *poetic/literary* joy; *archaic* jubilate. **2** *he exulted in his triumph* REJOICE AT/IN, take delight in, find/take pleasure in, find joy in, enjoy, revel in, glory in, delight in, relish, savour; be/feel proud of, congratulate oneself on; *archaic* pique oneself on/in.
– OPPOSITES sorrow.

exultant ● adjective JUBILANT, thrilled, triumphant, delighted, exhilarated, happy, overjoyed, joyous, joyful, gleeful, cock-a-hoop, excited, rejoicing, ecstatic, euphoric, elated, rapturous, in raptures, enraptured, on cloud nine/seven, in seventh heaven; *informal* over the moon; *N. Amer. informal* wigged out.

exultation ● noun JUBILATION, rejoicing, happiness, pleasure, joy, gladness, delight, glee, elation, cheer, euphoria, exhilaration, delirium, ecstasy, rapture, exuberance.

eye ● noun **1** *he rubbed his eyes* EYEBALL; *informal* peeper; *poetic/literary* orb. **2** *sharp eyes* EYESIGHT, vision, sight, powers of observation, (visual) perception. **3** *an eye for a bargain* APPRECIATION, awareness, alertness, perception, consciousness, feeling, instinct, intuition, nose. **4** *his watchful eye* WATCH, observance, gaze, stare, regard; observation, surveillance, vigilance, contemplation, scrutiny. **5** *to desert was despicable in their eyes* OPINION, (way of) thinking, mind, view, viewpoint, attitude, standpoint, perspective, belief, judgement, assessment, analysis, estimation. **6** *the eye of a needle* HOLE, opening, aperture, eyelet, slit, slot. **7** *the eye of the storm* CENTRE, middle, heart, core, hub, thick.
– RELATED TERMS ocular, ophthalmic.
● verb **1** *he eyed the stranger suspiciously* LOOK AT, observe, view, gaze at, stare at, regard, contemplate, survey, scrutinize, consider, glance at; watch, keep an eye on, keep under observation; *informal* have/take a gander at, check out, size up; *Brit. informal* have/take a butcher's at, have/take a dekko at, have/take a shufti at, clock; *N. Amer. informal* eyeball; *poetic/literary* behold. **2** *eyeing young women in the street* OGLE, leer at, stare at, make eyes at; *informal* eye up, give someone the glad eye; *Brit. informal* gawp at, gawk at; *Austral./NZ informal* perv on.
– PHRASES **clap/lay/set eyes on** *(informal)* SEE, observe, notice, spot, spy, catch sight of, glimpse, catch/get a glimpse of; *poetic/literary* behold, espy, descry. **see eye to eye** AGREE, concur, be in agreement, be of the same mind/opinion, be in accord, think as one; be on the same wavelength, get on/along. **up to one's eyes** *(informal)* VERY BUSY, fully occupied; overloaded, overburdened, overworked, under pressure, hard-pressed, rushed/run off one's feet; *informal* pushed, up against it.

eyeful • noun informal **1** a long steady look. **2** an eye-catching person or thing.

eyeglass • noun **1** a single lens for correcting or assisting defective eyesight, especially a monocle. **2** (**eyeglasses**) chiefly N. Amer. another term for GLASSES.

eyelash • noun each of the short hairs growing on the edges of the eyelids.

eyelet • noun **1** a small round hole made in leather or cloth, used for threading a lace, string, or rope through. **2** a metal ring reinforcing such a hole.
– ORIGIN Old French *oillet*, from *oil* 'eye', from Latin *oculus*.

eyelid • noun each of the upper and lower folds of skin which cover the eye when closed.

eyeliner • noun a cosmetic applied as a line round the eyes.

eye-opener • noun informal an unexpected revelation.
– DERIVATIVES **eye-opening** adjective.

eyepatch • noun a patch worn to protect an injured eye.

eyepiece • noun the lens that is closest to the eye in a microscope or other optical instrument.

eye-popping • adjective informal astonishingly large or blatant.

eyeshade • noun a translucent visor used to protect the eyes from strong light.

eyeshadow • noun a coloured cosmetic applied to the eyelids or to the skin around the eyes.

eyesight • noun a person's ability to see.

eye socket • noun the cavity in the skull which encloses an eyeball with its surrounding muscles.

eyesore • noun a thing that is very ugly.

eye tooth • noun a canine tooth, especially one in the upper jaw.
– PHRASES **give one's eye teeth for** (or **to be** or **to do**) do anything in order to have or to be or do.

eyewash • noun **1** cleansing lotion for a person's eye. **2** informal nonsense.

eyewitness • noun a person who has seen something happen and so can give a first-hand description of it.

eyrie /eeri, iri/ (US also **aerie**) • noun a large nest of an eagle or other bird of prey, typically built high in a tree or on a cliff.
– ORIGIN probably from Old French *aire*, from Latin *area* 'level piece of ground', later 'nest of a bird of prey'.

eyrir /ireer/ • noun (pl. **aurar** /awraar/) a monetary unit of Iceland, equal to one hundredth of a krona.
– ORIGIN Icelandic, probably from Latin *aureus* 'golden, a gold coin'.

e

Thesaurus

eye-catching • adjective STRIKING, arresting, conspicuous, dramatic, impressive, spectacular, breathtaking, dazzling, amazing, stunning, sensational, remarkable, distinctive, unusual, out of the ordinary.

eyeful • noun *(informal)* **1** *did you get an eyeful of that?* LOOK, peep, peek, glimpse, view, gaze, glance, sight; *informal* gander, squint; *Brit. informal* dekko, shufti, butcher's; *Austral./NZ informal* geek, squiz. **2** *she was quite an eyeful* BEAUTIFUL SIGHT, vision, picture, dream, sensation, beauty, dazzler; *informal* stunner, looker, knockout, sight for sore eyes, bombshell, dish, cracker, good-looker; *Brit. informal* smasher.

eyelash • noun LASH; *Anatomy* cilium.

eyesight • noun SIGHT, vision, faculty of sight, ability to see, (visual) perception.

eyesore • noun UGLY SIGHT, blot (on the landscape), mess, scar, blight, disfigurement, blemish, monstrosity; *informal* sight.

eyewitness • noun OBSERVER, onlooker, witness, bystander, spectator, watcher, viewer, passer-by; *poetic/literary* beholder.

Ff

F[1] (also **f**) ● noun (pl. **Fs** or **F's**) **1** the sixth letter of the alphabet. **2** denoting the next item after E in a set. **3** Music the fourth note of the diatonic scale of C major.

F[2] ● abbreviation **1** Fahrenheit. **2** farad(s). **3** (in racing results) favourite. **4** female. **5** Brit. fine (used in describing grades of pencil lead). **6** Franc(s). ● symbol **1** the chemical element fluorine. **2** Physics force.

f ● abbreviation **1** Grammar feminine. **2** (in textual references) folio. **3** Music forte. **4** (in racing results) furlong(s). ● symbol **1** focal length. **2** Mathematics a function of a specified variable. **3** Electronics frequency.

FA ● abbreviation (in the UK) Football Association.

fa ● noun variant spelling of FAH.

fab ● adjective informal fabulous; wonderful.

Fabian /faybiən/ ● noun a member or supporter of the Fabian Society, an organization of socialists aiming to achieve socialism by non-revolutionary methods. ● adjective **1** relating to the Fabians. **2** employing cautious delaying tactics to wear out an enemy.
– DERIVATIVES **Fabianism** noun **Fabianist** noun.
– ORIGIN from the name of the Roman general Quintus *Fabius* Maximus Verrucosus (died 203 BC), known for his delaying tactics.

fable ● noun **1** a short story with a moral, typically featuring animals as characters. **2** a supernatural story incorporating elements of myth and legend. **3** myth and legend.
– DERIVATIVES **fabler** noun.
– ORIGIN Old French, from Latin *fabula* 'story'.

fabled ● adjective **1** famous. **2** mythical or imaginary.

fabric ● noun **1** material produced by weaving or knitting textile fibres; cloth. **2** a structure or framework, especially the walls, floor, and roof of a building. **3** the essential structure of a system or organization.
– ORIGIN Latin *fabrica* 'something skilfully produced'.

fabricate ● verb **1** invent, typically with deceitful intent. **2** construct or manufacture (an industrial product).
– DERIVATIVES **fabrication** noun **fabricator** noun.
– ORIGIN Latin *fabricare* 'manufacture'.

fabulate /fabyoolayt/ ● verb tell invented stories.
– DERIVATIVES **fabulation** noun.
– ORIGIN Latin *fabulari* 'narrate as a fable'.

fabulist ● noun **1** a person who composes fables. **2** a liar.

fabulous ● adjective **1** great; extraordinary. **2** informal wonderful. **3** mythical.
– DERIVATIVES **fabulously** adverb **fabulousness** noun.
– ORIGIN Latin *fabulosus* 'celebrated in fable', from *fabula* 'story'.

facade /fəsaad/ ● noun **1** the face of a building, especially the front. **2** a deceptive outward appearance.
– ORIGIN French, from *face* 'face'.

face ● noun **1** the front part of a person's head from the forehead to the chin, or the corresponding part in an animal. **2** an expression on someone's face. **3** the surface of a thing, especially one presented to the view or with a particular function. **4** a vertical or sloping side of a mountain or cliff. **5** an aspect: *the unacceptable face of social drinking.* ● verb **1** be positioned with the face or front towards or in a specified direction. **2** confront and deal with. **3** have (a difficult event or situation) in prospect. **4** (**face off**) chiefly N. Amer. take up an attitude of confrontation. **5** cover the surface of (something) with a layer of a different material.
– PHRASES **someone's face fits** Brit. someone has the necessary qualities for something. **face the music** be confronted with the unpleasant consequences of one's actions. **face to face** close together and looking directly at one another. **in the face of** when confronted with. **lose** (or **save**) **face** incur (or avoid) humiliation. **on the face of it** apparently. **set one's face against** resist with determination. **to one's face** openly in one's presence.
– DERIVATIVES **-faced** adjective.
– ORIGIN Old French, from Latin *facies* 'form, appearance, face'.

Thesaurus

fable ● noun **1** *the fable of the wary fox* MORAL TALE, parable, apologue, allegory. **2** *the fables of ancient Greece* MYTH, legend, saga, epic, folk tale, folk story, fairy tale, mythos, mythus; folklore, mythology. **3** *it's a fable that I have a taste for fancy restaurants* FALSEHOOD, fib, fabrication, made-up story, invention, fiction, falsification, fairy story/tale, cock-and-bull story; lie, untruth, half-truth, exaggeration; story, rumour, myth; informal tall story; Brit. informal porky (pie).

fabled ● adjective **1** *a fabled god-giant of Irish myth* LEGENDARY, mythical, mythic, mythological, fabulous, folkloric, fairy-tale; fictitious, imaginary, imagined, made up. **2** *the fabled quality of French wine* CELEBRATED, renowned, famed, famous, well known, prized, noted, notable, acclaimed, esteemed, prestigious, of repute, of high standing.

fabric ● noun **1** *the finest silk fabric* CLOTH, material, textile, tissue. **2** *the fabric of the building* STRUCTURE, framework, frame, form, composition, construction, foundations.

fabricate ● verb **1** *he fabricated research data* FALSIFY, fake, counterfeit; invent, make up. **2** *fabricating a pack of lies* CONCOCT, make up, dream up, invent, trump up; informal cook up. **3** *you will have to fabricate an exhaust system* MAKE, create, manufacture, produce; construct, build, assemble, put together, form, fashion.

fabrication ● noun **1** *the story was a complete fabrication* INVENTION, concoction, (piece of) fiction, falsification, lie, untruth, falsehood, fib, myth, made-up story, fairy story/tale, cock-and-bull story; white lie, half-truth, exaggeration; informal tall story, whopper; Brit. informal porky (pie). **2** *the lintels are galvanized after fabrication* MANUFACTURE, creation, production; construction, building, assembly, forming, fashioning.

fabulous ● adjective **1** *fabulous salaries* TREMENDOUS, stupendous, prodigious, phenomenal, remarkable, exceptional; astounding, amazing, fantastic, breathtaking, staggering, unthinkable, unimaginable, incredible, unbelievable, unheard of, untold, undreamed of, beyond one's wildest dreams; informal mind-boggling, mind-blowing. **2** (informal) *we had a fabulous time.* See EXCELLENT. **3** *a fabulous horse-like beast* MYTHICAL, legendary, mythic, mythological, fabled, folkloric, fairy-tale; fictitious, imaginary, imagined, made up.

facade ● noun **1** *a half-timbered facade* FRONT, frontage, face, elevation, exterior, outside. **2** *a facade of bonhomie* SHOW, front, appearance, pretence, simulation, affectation, semblance, illusion, act, masquerade, charade, mask, cloak, veil, veneer.

face ● noun **1** *a beautiful face* COUNTENANCE, physiognomy, features; informal mug; Brit. informal mush, dial, clock, phiz, boat race; N. Amer. informal puss, pan; poetic/literary visage; archaic front. **2** *her face grew sad* (FACIAL) EXPRESSION, look, appearance, air, manner, bearing, countenance, mien. **3** *he made a face at the sourness of the drink* GRIMACE, scowl, wry face, wince, frown, glower, pout, moue. **4** *a cube has six faces* SIDE, aspect, flank, surface, plane, facet, wall, elevation. **5** *a watch face* DIAL, display. **6** *changing the face of the industry* (OUTWARD) APPEARANCE, aspect, nature, image. **7** *he put on a brave face* FRONT, show, display, act, appearance, facade, exterior, mask, masquerade, pretence, pose, veneer. **8** *criticism should never cause the recipient to lose face* RESPECT, honour, esteem, regard, admiration, approbation, acclaim, approval, favour, appreciation, popularity, prestige, standing, status, dignity; self-respect, self-esteem. **9** (informal) *they had the face to upbraid others.* See EFFRONTERY.
– RELATED TERMS facial.
● verb **1** *the hotel faces the sea* LOOK OUT ON, front on to, look towards, be facing, look over/across, overlook, give on to, be opposite (to). **2** *you'll just have to face facts* ACCEPT, become reconciled

facecloth ● noun **1** (Brit. also **face flannel**) a small towelling cloth for washing one's face. **2** smooth-surfaced woollen cloth.

faceless ● adjective remote and impersonal.
– DERIVATIVES **facelessness** noun.

facelift ● noun a cosmetic surgical operation to remove unwanted wrinkles by tightening the skin of the face.

face mask ● noun **1** a protective mask covering the face or part of the face. **2** a face pack.

face-off ● noun **1** chiefly N. Amer. a direct confrontation. **2** Ice Hockey the start of play.

face pack ● noun chiefly Brit. a cosmetic preparation spread over the face to improve the skin.

face paint ● noun bold-coloured paint used to decorate the face.

face-saving ● adjective preserving one's reputation or dignity.

facet /fassit/ ● noun **1** one side of something many-sided, especially of a cut gem. **2** an aspect: *different facets of the truth.*
– DERIVATIVES **faceted** adjective.
– ORIGIN French *facette* 'little face'.

facetious /fəseeshəss/ ● adjective trivially or inappropriately humorous.
– DERIVATIVES **facetiously** adverb **facetiousness** noun.
– ORIGIN French *facétieux*, from Latin *facetia* 'jest'.

face value ● noun **1** the value printed or depicted on a coin, postage stamp, etc. **2** the apparent value or nature of something.

faceworker ● noun a miner who works at the coalface.

facia ● noun chiefly Brit. variant spelling of FASCIA.

facial /faysh'l/ ● adjective of or affecting the face. ● noun a beauty treatment for the face.
– DERIVATIVES **facially** adverb.

facile /fassīl/ ● adjective **1** ignoring the complexities of an issue; superficial. **2** (of an achievement) easily accomplished.
– DERIVATIVES **facilely** adverb **facileness** noun.
– ORIGIN Latin *facilis* 'easy'.

facilitate /fəsillitayt/ ● verb make easy or easier.
– DERIVATIVES **facilitation** noun **facilitative** adjective **facilitator** noun **facilitatory** adjective.
– ORIGIN French *faciliter*, from Latin *facilis* 'easy'.

facility ● noun (pl. **facilities**) **1** a building, service, or piece of equipment provided for a particular purpose. **2** a natural ability to do something well and easily.

facing ● noun **1** a piece of material attached to the edge of a garment at the neck, armhole, etc. and turned inside, used to strengthen the edge. **2** an outer layer covering the surface of a wall. ● adjective positioned so as to face.

facsimile /faksimmili/ ● noun an exact copy. ● verb (**facsimiled**, **facsimileing**) make a copy of.
– ORIGIN from Latin *fac!* 'make!' and *simile*, from *similis* 'like'.

fact ● noun **1** a thing that is indisputably the case. **2** (**facts**) information used as evidence or as part of a report.
– PHRASES **before** (or **after**) **the fact** Law before (or after) the committing of a crime. **a fact of life** something that must be accepted, even if unpalatable. **the facts of life** information about sexual matters. **in (point of) fact** in reality.
– ORIGIN originally meaning 'an act', later 'a crime': from Latin *factum*, from *facere* 'do'.

faction[1] ● noun a small dissenting group within a larger one.
– DERIVATIVES **factional** adjective **factionalism** noun **factionally** adverb.
– ORIGIN originally in the sense 'doing, making': from Latin *facere* 'do, make'.

faction[2] ● noun a literary and cinematic genre in which real events are used as a basis for a fictional narrative or dramatization.
– ORIGIN blend of FACT and FICTION.

factious /fakshəss/ ● adjective relating or inclined to dissension.
– DERIVATIVES **factiously** adverb **factiousness** noun.
– ORIGIN Latin *factiosus*, from *facere* 'do, make'.

factitious /faktishəss/ ● adjective artificial; contrived.
– DERIVATIVES **factitiously** adverb **factitiousness** noun.
– ORIGIN Latin *facticius* 'made by art'.

factoid ● noun **1** an item of unreliable information that is re-

f

Thesaurus

to, get used to, become accustomed to, adjust to, acclimatize oneself to; learn to live with, cope with, deal with, come to terms with, become resigned to. **3** *he faces a humiliating rejection* BE CONFRONTED BY, be faced with, encounter, experience, come into contact with, come up against. **4** *the problems facing our police force* BESET, worry, distress, trouble, bother, confront; harass, oppress, vex, irritate, exasperate, strain, stress, tax; torment, plague, blight, bedevil, curse; formal discommode. **5** *he faced the challenge boldly* BRAVE, face up to, encounter, meet (head-on), confront; oppose, resist, withstand. **6** *a wall faced with flint* COVER, clad, veneer, overlay, surface, dress, put a facing on, laminate, coat, line.
– PHRASES **face to face** FACING (EACH OTHER), opposite (each other), across from each other. **on the face of it** OSTENSIBLY, to all appearances, to all intents and purposes, at first glance, on the surface, superficially; apparently, seemingly, outwardly, it seems (that), it would seem (that), it appears (that), it would appear (that), as far as one can see/tell, by all accounts.

facelift ● noun **1** *she's planning to have a facelift* COSMETIC SURGERY, plastic surgery. **2** (informal) *the theatre is reopening after a facelift* RENOVATION, redecoration, refurbishment, revamp, revamping, makeover, reconditioning, overhauling, modernization, restoration, repair, redevelopment, rebuilding, reconstruction, refit.

facet ● noun **1** *the many facets of the gem* SURFACE, face, side, plane. **2** *other facets of his character* ASPECT, feature, side, dimension, characteristic, detail, point, ingredient, strand; component, constituent, element.

facetious ● adjective FLIPPANT, flip, glib, frivolous, tongue-in-cheek, joking, jokey, jocular, playful, sportive, teasing, mischievous; witty, amusing, funny, droll, comic, comical, light-hearted; formal jocose.
– OPPOSITES serious.

facile ● adjective **1** *a facile explanation* SIMPLISTIC, superficial, oversimplified; shallow, glib, jejune, naive; N. Amer. dime-store. **2** *he achieved a facile victory* EFFORTLESS, easy, undemanding, unexacting, painless, trouble-free; Brit. informal easy-peasy.

facilitate ● verb MAKE EASY/EASIER, ease, make possible, make smooth/smoother, smooth the way for; enable, assist, help (along), aid, oil the wheels of, expedite, speed up, accelerate, forward, advance, promote, further, encourage.
– OPPOSITES impede.

facility ● noun **1** *car-parking facilities* PROVISION, space, means, potential, equipment. **2** *the camera has a zoom facility* POSSIBILITY, feature. **3** *a wealth of local facilities* AMENITY, resource, service, advantage, convenience, benefit. **4** *a medical facility* ESTABLISHMENT, centre, place, station, location, premises, site, post, base; informal joint, outfit, set-up. **5** *his facility for drawing* APTITUDE, talent, gift, flair, bent, skill, knack, genius; ability, proficiency, competence, capability, capacity, faculty; expertness, adeptness, prowess, mastery, artistry. **6** *I was turning out poetry with facility* EASE, effortlessness, no difficulty, no trouble, facileness; deftness, adroitness, dexterity, proficiency, mastery.

facing ● noun **1** *green velvet facings* COVERING, trimming, lining, interfacing. **2** *brick facing on a concrete core* CLADDING, veneer, skin, surface, facade, front, coating, covering, dressing, overlay, lamination, plating; N. Amer. siding.

facsimile ● noun COPY, reproduction, duplicate, photocopy, mimeograph, replica, likeness, carbon copy, print, reprint, offprint, autotype; fax, telefax; trademark Xerox, photostat.
– OPPOSITES original.

fact ● noun **1** *it is a fact that the water is polluted* REALITY, actuality, certainty; truth, verity, gospel. **2** *every fact was double-checked* DETAIL, piece of information, particular, item, specific, element, point, factor, feature, characteristic, ingredient, circumstance, aspect, facet; (**facts**) information. **3** *an accessory after the fact* EVENT, happening, occurrence, incident, act, deed.
– OPPOSITES lie, fiction.
– PHRASES **in fact** ACTUALLY, in actuality, in actual fact, really, in reality, in point of fact, as a matter of fact, in truth, to tell the truth; archaic in sooth, verily.

faction ● noun **1** *a faction of the Liberal Party* CLIQUE, coterie, caucus, cabal, bloc, camp, group, grouping, sector, section, wing, arm, branch, set; ginger group, pressure group. **2** *the council was split by faction* INFIGHTING, dissension, dissent, dispute, discord, strife, conflict, friction, argument, disagreement, controversy, quarrelling, wrangling, bickering, squabbling, disharmony, disunity, schism.

factious ● adjective DIVIDED, split, schismatic, discordant, conflicting, argumentative, disagreeing, disputatious, quarrelling, quarrelsome, clashing, warring, at loggerheads, at odds, rebellious, mutinous.
– OPPOSITES harmonious.

peated so often that it becomes accepted as fact. **2** N. Amer. a brief or trivial item of information.

factor • noun **1** a circumstance, fact, or influence that contributes to a result. **2** Mathematics a number or quantity that when multiplied with another produces a given number or expression. **3** Physiology any of a number of substances in the blood which are involved in coagulation. **4** Biology a gene that determines a hereditary characteristic. **5** a business or land agent. • verb (**factor in/out**) include (or exclude) as relevant when making a decision.
– ORIGIN originally in the sense 'doer': from Latin *facere* 'do'.

factorial Mathematics • noun the product of an integer and all the integers below it, e.g. 4 × 3 × 2 × 1 (*factorial 4*, denoted by *4!* and equal to 24). • adjective relating to a factor or factorial.
– DERIVATIVES **factorially** adverb.

factorize (also **factorise**) • verb Mathematics resolve or be resolvable into factors.
– DERIVATIVES **factorization** noun.

factor VIII (also **factor eight**) • noun Physiology a blood protein involved in clotting, a deficiency of which causes one of the main forms of haemophilia.

factory • noun (pl. **factories**) a building where goods are manufactured or assembled chiefly by machine.
– ORIGIN Latin *factorium* 'oil press'.

factory farming • noun a system of rearing poultry, pigs, or cattle indoors intensively and under strictly controlled conditions.

factory floor • noun the workers in a company or industry, rather than the management.

factotum /faktōtəm/ • noun (pl. **factotums**) an employee who does all kinds of work.
– ORIGIN from Latin *fac!* 'do!' + *totum* 'the whole thing'.

factual /faktyooəl/ • adjective based on or concerned with fact or facts.
– DERIVATIVES **factuality** noun **factually** adverb **factualness** noun.

faculty • noun (pl. **faculties**) **1** an inherent mental or physical power. **2** an aptitude or talent. **3** chiefly Brit. a group of university departments concerned with a major division of knowledge. **4** N. Amer. the teaching or research staff of a university or college.
– ORIGIN Latin *facultas*, from *facilis* 'easy'.

fad • noun **1** a craze. **2** an idiosyncrasy or arbitrary like or dislike.
– DERIVATIVES **faddish** adjective **faddism** noun **faddist** noun.
– ORIGIN probably from FIDDLE-FADDLE.

faddy • adjective (**faddier**, **faddiest**) Brit. having many likes and dislikes about food; fussy.
– DERIVATIVES **faddily** adverb **faddiness** noun.

fade • verb **1** gradually grow faint and disappear. **2** lose or cause to lose colour. **3** (with reference to a film or video image or recorded sound) increase or decrease in clarity or volume. • noun an act or instance of fading.
– ORIGIN Old French *fader*, from *fade* 'dull, insipid'.

fader • noun a device for varying the volume of sound, the intensity of light, or the gain on a video or audio signal.

fado /faadō/ • noun (pl. **fados**) a type of popular Portuguese song, usually with a melancholy theme.
– ORIGIN Portuguese, 'fate'.

faeces /feeseez/ (US **feces**) • plural noun waste matter remaining after food has been digested, discharged from the bowels.
– DERIVATIVES **faecal** /feek'l/ adjective.
– ORIGIN Latin, plural of *faex* 'dregs'.

faerie /fairi/ (also **faery**) • noun archaic or literary fairyland.
– ORIGIN introduced as a pseudo-archaic variant of *fairy* by the English poet Edmund Spenser in his romance the *Faerie Queene* (1590).

Faeroese • noun & adjective variant spelling of FAROESE.

faff Brit. informal • verb bustle ineffectually. • noun ineffectual activity.
– ORIGIN originally dialect in the sense 'blow in puffs', describing the wind.

fag[1] Brit. informal • noun **1** a tiring or unwelcome task. **2** a junior pupil at a public school who does minor chores for a senior pupil. • verb (**fagged**, **fagging**) **1** work hard. **2** (of a public-school pupil) act as a fag. **3** (**fagged out**) exhausted.
– ORIGIN of unknown origin.

fag[2] • noun N. Amer. informal, derogatory a male homosexual.
– DERIVATIVES **faggy** adjective.
– ORIGIN short for FAGGOT (in sense 3).

fag[3] • noun Brit. informal a cigarette.
– ORIGIN from FAG END.

fag end • noun informal, chiefly Brit. **1** a cigarette end. **2** a useless remnant.
– ORIGIN from obsolete *fag* 'a flap'.

faggot /faggət/ • noun **1** Brit. a ball of seasoned chopped liver, baked or fried. **2** (US **fagot**) a bundle of sticks bound together as fuel. **3** N. Amer. informal, derogatory a male homosexual.
– DERIVATIVES **faggoty** adjective.
– ORIGIN Old French *fagot*, from Greek *phakelos* 'bundle'.

faggoting (US **fagoting**) • noun embroidery in which threads

Thesaurus

factitious • adjective BOGUS, fake, specious, false, counterfeit, fraudulent, spurious, sham, mock, feigned, affected, pretended, contrived, engineered; *informal* phoney, pseudo, pretend; *Brit. informal* cod.
– OPPOSITES genuine.

factor • noun ELEMENT, part, component, ingredient, strand, constituent, point, detail, item, feature, facet, aspect, characteristic, consideration, influence, circumstance.

factory • noun WORKS, plant, yard, mill, industrial unit; workshop, shop; *archaic* manufactory.

factotum • noun ODD-JOB MAN, handyman, man/maid of all work, jack of all trades, man/girl Friday; *Austral.* knockabout; *informal* (Mr) Fixit.

factual • adjective TRUTHFUL, true, accurate, authentic, historical, genuine, fact-based; true-to-life, correct, exact, honest, faithful, literal, verbatim, word for word, unbiased, objective, unvarnished; *formal* veridical.
– OPPOSITES fictitious.

faculty • noun **1** *the faculty of speech* POWER, capability, capacity, facility, wherewithal, means; (**faculties**) senses, wits, reason, intelligence. **2** *an unusual faculty for unearthing contributors* ABILITY, proficiency, competence, capability, potential, capacity, facility; aptitude, talent, gift, flair, bent, skill, knack, genius; expertise, expertness, adeptness, adroitness, dexterity, prowess, mastery, artistry. **3** *the arts faculty* DEPARTMENT, school, division, section. **4** *the vicar introduced certain ornaments without the faculty to do so* AUTHORIZATION, authority, power, right, permission, consent, leave, sanction, licence, dispensation, assent, acquiescence, agreement, approval, endorsement, clearance; *informal* the go-ahead, the thumbs up, the OK, the green light, say-so.

fad • noun CRAZE, vogue, trend, fashion, mode, enthusiasm, passion, obsession, mania, rage, compulsion, fixation, fetish, fancy, whim, fascination; *informal* thing.

faddy • adjective (*Brit. informal*) FUSSY, finicky, faddish, overparticular, over-fastidious, dainty; *informal* picky, pernickety; *N. Amer. informal* persnickety; *archaic* nice.

fade • verb **1** *the paintwork has faded* BECOME PALE, become bleached, become washed out, lose colour, discolour; grow dull, grow dim, lose lustre. **2** *sunlight had faded the picture* BLEACH, wash out, make pale, blanch, whiten. **3** *remove the flower heads as they fade* WITHER, wilt, droop, shrivel, die. **4** *the afternoon light began to fade* (GROW) DIM, grow faint, fail, dwindle, die away, wane, disappear, vanish, decline, melt away; *poetic/literary* evanesce. **5** *the Communist movement was fading away* DECLINE, die out, diminish, deteriorate, decay, crumble, collapse, fail, fall, sink, slump, go downhill; *informal* go to pot, go to the dogs; *archaic* retrograde.
– OPPOSITES brighten, increase.

faeces • plural noun EXCREMENT, bodily waste, waste matter, ordure, dung, manure; excreta, stools, droppings; dirt, filth, muck, mess, night soil; *informal* pooh, doo-doo, doings, turds; *Brit. informal* cack, whoopsies, jobbies; *N. Amer. informal* poop.
– RELATED TERMS copro-.

fag[1] (*Brit. informal*) • noun *it's too much of a fag!* CHORE, slog, grind, bother, bore; *informal* pain, sweat.
• verb *we fagged away all day* TOIL, slave, slog, labour, grind, work hard; *informal* work one's socks off; *Brit. informal* graft; *Austral./NZ informal* bullock; *poetic/literary* travail.
– PHRASES **fag someone out** EXHAUST, tire (out), wear out, fatigue, overtire, weary; *informal* do in, wipe out, knock out, shatter; *Brit. informal* knacker; *N. Amer. informal* poop, tucker out.

fag[2] • noun (*Brit. informal*) *he was smoking a fag* CIGARETTE, filter tip, king-size; *informal* ciggy, cig, smoke, cancer stick, coffin nail; *Brit. informal* snout, roll-up.

fagged • adjective (*Brit. informal*) EXHAUSTED, tired (out), worn out, fa-

are fastened together in bundles.

fah (also **fa**) ● noun Music the fourth note of a major scale, coming after 'me' and before 'soh'.
– ORIGIN the first syllable of *famuli*, taken from a Latin hymn.

Fahr. ● abbreviation Fahrenheit.

Fahrenheit /farrənhīt/ ● adjective of or denoting a scale of temperature on which water freezes at 32° and boils at 212°.
– ORIGIN named after the German physicist Gabriel Daniel *Fahrenheit* (1686–1736).

faience /fiONSS/ ● noun glazed ceramic ware, in particular decorated tin-glazed earthenware of the type which includes delftware.
– ORIGIN originally denoting pottery made at Faenza in Italy: from *Faïence*, the French name for *Faenza*.

fail ● verb **1** be unsuccessful in an undertaking. **2** be unable to meet the standards set by (a test). **3** judge (a candidate in an examination or test) not to have passed. **4** neglect to do. **5** disappoint expectations: *chaos has failed to materialize.* **6** stop working properly. **7** become weaker or less good. **8** go out of business. **9** desert or let down. ● noun a mark which is not high enough to pass an examination or test.
– PHRASES **without fail** whatever happens.
– ORIGIN Old French *faillir*, from Latin *fallere* 'deceive'.

failing ● noun a weakness in a person's character. ● preposition if not.

fail-safe ● adjective **1** causing machinery to revert to a safe condition in the event of a breakdown. **2** unlikely or unable to fail.

failure ● noun **1** lack of success. **2** an unsuccessful person or thing. **3** the omission of expected or required action. **4** an instance or the state of not functioning.

fain archaic ● adjective **1** pleased or willing under the circumstances. **2** obliged. ● adverb gladly.
– ORIGIN Old English, 'happy'; related to FAWN².

faint ● adjective **1** (of a sight, smell, or sound) barely perceptible. **2** (of a hope, chance, or idea) slight. **3** close to losing consciousness. ● verb briefly lose consciousness because of an insufficient supply of oxygen to the brain. ● noun a sudden loss of consciousness.
– DERIVATIVES **faintly** adverb **faintness** noun.
– ORIGIN Old French, from Latin *fingere* 'mould, contrive'; related to FEIGN.

faint heart ● noun a person who has a timid or reserved nature.
– PHRASES **faint heart never won fair lady** proverb timidity will prevent you from achieving your objective.
– DERIVATIVES **faint-hearted** adjective.

fair¹ ● adjective **1** just or appropriate in the circumstances. **2** treating people equally. **3** considerable in size or amount. **4** moderately good. **5** (of hair or complexion) light; blonde. **6** (of weather) fine and dry. **7** Austral./NZ informal complete. **8** archaic beautiful. ● adverb **1** in a fair manner. **2** dialect to a high degree.
– PHRASES **all's fair in love and war** proverb in certain highly charged situations, any method of achieving your objective is justifiable. **fair and square 1** with absolute accuracy. **2** honestly and straightforwardly. **fair dinkum** see DINKUM. **fair dos** Brit. informal used as a request for just treatment or an acceptance that it has been given. **fair enough** informal that is reasonable or acceptable. **the fair sex** (also **the fairer sex**) dated or humorous women. **fair's fair** informal used as a request for just treatment or an assertion that an arrangement is just. **it's a fair cop** informal an admission that the speaker has been caught doing wrong and deserves punishment.
– DERIVATIVES **fairish** adjective **fairness** noun.
– ORIGIN Old English.

fair² ● noun **1** a gathering of stalls and amusements for public entertainment. **2** a periodic gathering for the sale of goods. **3** an exhibition to promote particular products.
– ORIGIN Latin *feria*, from *feriae* 'holy days' (on which fairs were often held).

fair copy ● noun written or printed matter transcribed or repro-

Thesaurus

tigued, weary, drained, washed out; *informal* done in, all in, dead beat, dead on one's feet, shattered, bushed; *Brit. informal* knackered; *N. Amer. informal* tuckered, pooped.

fail ● verb **1** *the enterprise had failed* BE UNSUCCESSFUL, not succeed, fall through, fall flat, collapse, founder, backfire, meet with disaster, come to nothing/naught; *informal* flop, bomb. **2** *he failed his examination* BE UNSUCCESSFUL IN, not pass; not make the grade; *informal* flunk. **3** *his friends had failed him* LET DOWN, disappoint; desert, abandon, betray, be disloyal to; *poetic/literary* forsake. **4** *the crops failed* BE DEFICIENT, be insufficient, be inadequate; wither. **5** *the daylight failed* FADE, dim, die away, wane, disappear, vanish. **6** *the ventilation system failed* BREAK (DOWN), stop working, cut out, crash; malfunction, go wrong, develop a fault; *informal* conk out, go on the blink; *Brit. informal* pack up, play up. **7** *Ceri's health was failing* DETERIORATE, degenerate, decline, fade, wane, ebb. **8** *900 businesses are failing a week* COLLAPSE, crash, go under, go bankrupt, go into receivership, go into liquidation, cease trading, be wound up; *informal* fold, flop, go bust, go broke, go to the wall.
– OPPOSITES succeed, pass, thrive, work.
– PHRASES **without fail** WITHOUT EXCEPTION, unfailingly, regularly, invariably, predictably, conscientiously, religiously, whatever happened.

failing ● noun *Jeanne accepted him despite his failings* FAULT, shortcoming, weakness, imperfection, defect, flaw, frailty, foible, idiosyncrasy, vice.
– OPPOSITES strength.
● preposition *failing financial assistance, you will be bankrupt* IN THE ABSENCE OF, lacking, notwithstanding.

failure ● noun **1** *the failure of the assassination attempt* LACK OF SUCCESS, non-fulfilment, defeat, collapse, foundering. **2** *all his schemes had been a failure* FIASCO, debacle, catastrophe, disaster; *informal* flop, washout, dead loss; *N. Amer. informal* snafu, clinker. **3** *she was regarded as a failure* LOSER, underachiever, ne'er-do-well, disappointment; *informal* no-hoper, dead loss. **4** *a failure in duty* NEGLIGENCE, remissness, dereliction; omission, oversight. **5** *a crop failure* INADEQUACY, insufficiency, deficiency. **6** *the failure of the camera* BREAKING DOWN, breakdown, malfunction; crash. **7** *company failures* COLLAPSE, crash, bankruptcy, insolvency, liquidation, closure.
– OPPOSITES success.

faint ● adjective **1** *a faint mark* INDISTINCT, vague, unclear, indefinite, ill-defined, imperceptible, unobtrusive; pale, light, faded. **2** *a faint cry* QUIET, muted, muffled, stifled; feeble, weak, whispered, murmured, indistinct; low, soft, gentle. **3** *a faint possibility* SLIGHT, slender, slim, small, tiny, negligible, remote, vague, unlikely, improbable; *informal* minuscule. **4** *faint praise* UNENTHUSIASTIC, half-hearted, weak, feeble. **5** *I suddenly felt faint* DIZZY, giddy, light-headed, unsteady; *informal* woozy.
– OPPOSITES clear, loud, strong.
● verb *she thought he would faint* PASS OUT, lose consciousness, black out, keel over, swoon; *informal* flake out, conk out, zonk out, go out like a light.
● noun *a dead faint* BLACKOUT, fainting fit, loss of consciousness, swoon; *Medicine* syncope.

faint-hearted ● adjective TIMID, timorous, nervous, nervy, easily scared, fearful, afraid; cowardly, craven, spineless, pusillanimous, lily-livered; *informal* chicken-hearted, yellow-bellied, gutless, sissy, wimpy, wimpish; *archaic* recreant.
– OPPOSITES brave.

faintly ● adverb **1** *Maria called his name faintly* INDISTINCTLY, softly, gently, weakly; in a whisper, in a murmur, in a low voice. **2** *he looked faintly bewildered* SLIGHTLY, vaguely, somewhat, quite, fairly, rather, a little, a bit, a touch, a shade; *informal* sort of, kind of.
– OPPOSITES loudly, extremely.

fair¹ ● adjective **1** *the courts were generally fair* JUST, equitable, honest, upright, honourable, trustworthy; impartial, unbiased, unprejudiced, non-partisan, neutral, even-handed; lawful, legal, legitimate; *informal* legit, on the level; *N. Amer. informal* on the up and up. **2** *fair weather* FINE, dry, bright, clear, sunny, cloudless; warm, balmy, clement, benign, pleasant. **3** *fair winds* FAVOURABLE, advantageous, benign; on one's side, in one's favour. **4** *fair hair* BLOND(E), yellowish, golden, flaxen, light, light brown, tow-coloured, ash blonde; fair-haired, light-haired, golden-haired. **5** *fair skin* PALE, light, light-coloured, white, creamy. **6** (*archaic*) *the fair maiden's heart.* See BEAUTIFUL. **7** *a fair achievement* REASONABLE, passable, tolerable, satisfactory, acceptable, respectable, decent, all right, good enough, pretty good, not bad, average, middling; *informal* OK, so-so.
– OPPOSITES inclement, unfavourable, dark.
– PHRASES **fair and square** HONESTLY, fairly, without cheating, without foul play, by the book; lawfully, legally, legitimately; *informal* on the level; *N. Amer. informal* on the up and up.

fair² ● noun **1** *a country fair* FÊTE, gala, festival, carnival. **2** *an antiques fair* MARKET, bazaar, mart, exchange, sale; *archaic* emporium.

duced after final correction.
fair game ● noun a person or thing that is considered a reasonable target for criticism or exploitation.
fairground ● noun an outdoor area where a fair is held.
fairing[1] ● noun an external metal or plastic structure added to increase streamlining on a high-performance vehicle, boat, or aircraft.
fairing[2] ● noun Brit. archaic a small present bought at a fair.
Fair Isle ● noun a traditional multicoloured geometric design used in woollen knitwear.
– ORIGIN *Fair Isle* in the Shetlands, where the design was first devised.
fairly ● adverb **1** with justice. **2** moderately. **3** actually; positively: *he fairly snarled at me.*
fair-minded ● adjective impartial; just.
fair play ● noun respect for the rules or equal treatment of all concerned.
fair trade ● noun trade in which fair prices are paid to producers in developing countries.
fairway ● noun **1** the part of a golf course between a tee and a green. **2** a navigable channel in a river or harbour.
fair-weather friend ● noun a person who stops being a friend in times of difficulty.
fairy ● noun (pl. **fairies**) **1** a small imaginary being of human form that has magical powers. **2** informal, derogatory a male homosexual.
– ORIGIN Old French *faerie* 'fairyland', from *fae* 'a fairy', from Latin *fata* 'the Fates'.
fairy cake ● noun Brit. a small iced sponge cake.
fairy floss ● noun Austral. candyfloss.
fairy godmother ● noun a female character in fairy stories who brings unexpected good fortune to the hero or heroine.
fairyland ● noun the imaginary home of fairies.
fairy lights ● plural noun chiefly Brit. small coloured electric lights used for decoration, especially on a Christmas tree.
fairy ring ● noun a ring of grass that is darker in colour than the surrounding grass due to the growth of certain fungi, once believed to have been caused by fairies dancing.
fairy story ● noun **1** a children's tale about magical and imaginary beings and lands. **2** an untrue account.
fairy tale ● noun **1** a fairy story. **2** (before another noun) magical or idealized: *a fairy-tale romance.*
fait accompli /fayt ə**kom**pli/ ● noun a thing that has been done or decided and cannot now be altered.
– ORIGIN French, 'accomplished fact'.
faith ● noun **1** complete trust or confidence. **2** strong belief in a religion. **3** a system of religious belief.
– ORIGIN Old French *feid*, from Latin *fides*.
faithful ● adjective **1** remaining loyal and steadfast. **2** remaining sexually loyal to a lover or spouse. **3** true to the facts or the original. ● noun (**the faithful**) the believers in a particular religion.
– DERIVATIVES **faithfulness** noun.
faithfully ● adverb in a faithful manner.
– PHRASES **yours faithfully** chiefly Brit. a formula for ending a formal letter in which the recipient is not addressed by name.
faith healing ● noun healing achieved by religious faith and prayer, rather than by medical treatment.
faithless ● adjective **1** disloyal, especially to a spouse or lover. **2** without religious faith.
– DERIVATIVES **faithlessly** adverb **faithlessness** noun.
fajitas /fə**hee**təz/ ● plural noun a dish of Mexican origin consisting of strips of spiced meat with vegetables and cheese, wrapped in a soft tortilla.
– ORIGIN Mexican Spanish, 'little strips'.
fake ● adjective not genuine; counterfeit. ● noun a person or thing that is not genuine. ● verb **1** forge or counterfeit. **2** pretend to feel or suffer from (an emotion or illness).
– DERIVATIVES **faker** noun **fakery** noun.
– ORIGIN origin uncertain.
fakir /**fay**keer, fə**keer**/ ● noun a Muslim (or, loosely, a Hindu) religious ascetic who lives solely on alms.
– ORIGIN Arabic, 'needy man'.
falafel /fə**laff**'l/ (also **felafel**) ● noun a Middle Eastern dish of spiced mashed chickpeas formed into balls and deep-fried.
– ORIGIN Arabic, 'pepper'.
falciparum /fal**sip**pərəm/ ● noun the most severe form of malaria, caused by the parasitic protozoan *Plasmodium falciparum*.
– ORIGIN from Latin *falx* 'sickle' + *-parum* 'bearing'.
falcon /**fawl**kən/ ● noun **1** a fast-flying bird of prey with long pointed wings and a notched beak. **2** Falconry the female of such a bird, especially a peregrine. Compare with TERCEL.
– ORIGIN Old French *faucon*, from Latin *falx* 'scythe'.
falconer ● noun a person who keeps, trains, or hunts with falcons or other birds of prey.
falconry ● noun the keeping and training of falcons or other birds of prey; the sport of hunting with such birds.
falderal /**fal**dəral/ ● noun variant spelling of FOLDEROL.
fall ● verb (past **fell**; past part. **fallen**) **1** move rapidly and without control from a higher to a lower level. **2** collapse to the ground. **3** (**fall off**) become detached and drop to the ground. **4** hang

Thesaurus

3 *a new art fair* EXHIBITION, display, show, presentation, exposition; *N. Amer.* exhibit.
fairly ● adverb **1** *all pupils were treated fairly* JUSTLY, equitably, impartially, without bias, without prejudice, even-handedly; lawfully, legally, legitimately, by the book; equally, the same. **2** *the pipes are in fairly good condition* REASONABLY, passably, tolerably, adequately, moderately, quite, relatively, comparatively; *informal* pretty, kind of, sort of. **3** *he fairly hauled her along the street* POSITIVELY, really, veritably, simply, actually, absolutely; practically, almost, nearly, all but; *informal* plain.
fair-minded ● adjective FAIR, just, even-handed, equitable, impartial, non-partisan, unbiased, unprejudiced; honest, honourable, trustworthy, upright, decent; *informal* on the level; *N. Amer. informal* on the up and up.
fairy ● noun SPRITE, pixie, elf, imp, brownie, puck, leprechaun, pishogue, nixie; *poetic/literary* faerie, fay.
fairy tale, fairy story ● noun **1** *the film was inspired by a fairy tale* FOLK TALE, folk story, traditional story, myth, legend, fantasy, fable. **2** *she accused him of telling fairy tales* (WHITE) LIE, fib, half-truth, untruth, falsehood, (tall) story, fabrication, invention, piece of fiction; *informal* whopper, cock-and-bull story; *Brit. informal* porky (pie).
faith ● noun **1** *he justified his boss's faith in him* TRUST, belief, confidence, conviction; optimism, hopefulness, hope. **2** *she gave her life for her faith* RELIGION, church, sect, denomination, (religious) persuasion, (religious) belief, ideology, creed, teaching, doctrine.
– OPPOSITES mistrust.
– PHRASES **break faith with** BE DISLOYAL TO, be unfaithful to, be untrue to, betray, play someone false, break one's promise to, fail, let down; double-cross, deceive, cheat, stab in the back; *informal* do the dirty on. **keep faith with** BE LOYAL TO, be faithful to, be true to, stand by, stick by, keep one's promise to.
faithful ● adjective **1** *his faithful assistant* LOYAL, constant, true, devoted, true-blue, unswerving, staunch, steadfast, dedicated, committed; trusty, trustworthy, dependable, reliable. **2** *a faithful copy* ACCURATE, precise, exact, errorless, unerring, faultless, true, close, strict; realistic, authentic; *informal* on the mark, on the nail; *Brit. informal* spot on, bang on; *N. Amer. informal* on the money.
– OPPOSITES inaccurate.
faithless ● adjective **1** *her faithless lover* UNFAITHFUL, disloyal, inconstant, false, untrue, adulterous, traitorous; fickle, flighty, untrustworthy, unreliable, undependable; deceitful, two-faced, double-crossing; *informal* cheating, two-timing, back-stabbing; *poetic/literary* perfidious. **2** *the natives were faithless* UNBELIEVING, non-believing, irreligious, disbelieving, agnostic, atheistic; pagan, heathen; *rare* nullifidian.
fake ● noun **1** *the sculpture was a fake* FORGERY, counterfeit, copy, pirate(d) copy, sham, fraud, hoax, imitation, mock-up, dummy, reproduction; *informal* phoney, rip-off, dupe. **2** *that doctor is a fake* CHARLATAN, quack, mountebank, sham, fraud, humbug, impostor, hoaxer, cheat, (confidence) trickster, fraudster; *informal* phoney, con man, con artist.
● adjective **1** *fake banknotes* COUNTERFEIT, forged, fraudulent, sham, imitation, pirate(d), false, bogus; invalid; *informal* phoney, dud. **2** *fake diamonds* IMITATION, artificial, synthetic, simulated, reproduction, replica, ersatz, man-made, dummy, false, mock, bogus; *informal* pretend, phoney, pseudo. **3** *a fake accent* FEIGNED, faked, put-on, assumed, invented, affected, pseudo; unconvincing, artificial, mock; *informal* phoney, pseud; *Brit. informal* cod.
– OPPOSITES genuine, authentic.
● verb **1** *the certificate was faked* FORGE, counterfeit, falsify, mock

down. **5** (of someone's face) show dismay or disappointment. **6** be captured or defeated. **7** decrease. **8** pass into a specified state: *she fell silent.* **9** occur. **10** be classified in the way specified: *canals fall within the Minister's brief.* **11** (**fall to**) become the duty of. ● noun **1** an act of falling. **2** a downward difference in height between parts of a surface. **3** a thing which falls or has fallen. **4** a waterfall or cascade. **5** a decrease. **6** a defeat or downfall. **7** N. Amer. autumn.

– PHRASES **fall about** Brit. informal laugh uncontrollably. **fall apart** (or **to pieces**) informal lose one's capacity to cope. **fall back** retreat. **fall back on** have recourse to when in difficulty. **fall for** informal **1** fall in love with. **2** be deceived by. **fall foul** (or chiefly N. Amer. **afoul**) **of** come into conflict with. **fall in** (or **into**) **line** conform. **fall into place** begin to make sense. **fall in with** **1** meet by chance and become involved with. **2** agree to. **fall on** (or **upon**) **1** attack fiercely or unexpectedly. **2** (of someone's eyes or gaze) be directed towards. **3** (of a burden or duty) be borne or incurred by. **fall out** have an argument. **fall over oneself to do** informal be excessively eager to do. **fall short** (**of**) **1** (of a missile) fail to reach its target. **2** be deficient or inadequate. **fall through** fail. **take the fall** N. Amer. informal receive blame or punishment, typically in the place of another.

– ORIGIN Old English.

fallacy /faləsi/ ● noun (pl. **fallacies**) **1** a mistaken belief. **2** a failure in reasoning which makes an argument invalid.

– DERIVATIVES **fallacious** adjective.

– ORIGIN Latin *fallacia*, from *fallere* 'deceive'.

fallback ● noun **1** an alternative plan for use in an emergency. **2** a reduction.

fallen past participle of FALL. ● adjective **1** dated (of a woman) regarded as having lost her honour through engaging in an extramarital sexual relationship. **2** killed in battle.

fallen angel ● noun (in Christian, Jewish, and Muslim tradition) an angel who rebelled against God and was cast out of heaven.

faller ● noun **1** Brit. a person or thing that falls, especially a horse that falls during a race. **2** N. Amer. a person who fells trees for a living.

fall guy ● noun informal a scapegoat.

fallible /falib'l/ ● adjective capable of making mistakes or being wrong.

– DERIVATIVES **fallibility** noun **fallibly** adverb.

– ORIGIN Latin *fallibilis*, from *fallere* 'deceive'.

falling-out ● noun a quarrel.

falling star ● noun a meteor or shooting star.

fall line ● noun **1** (**the fall line**) Skiing the route leading straight down any particular part of a slope. **2** a narrow zone marking the geological boundary between an upland region and a plain, distinguished by the occurrence of falls where rivers cross it.

fall-off (also **falling-off**) ● noun a decrease.

Fallopian tube /fəlōpiən/ ● noun Anatomy (in a female mammal) either of a pair of tubes along which eggs travel from the ovaries to the uterus.

– ORIGIN named after the Italian anatomist Gabriello *Fallopio* (1523–62).

fallout ● noun **1** radioactive particles dispersed over a wide area after a nuclear explosion. **2** the adverse results of a situation.

fallow[1] ● adjective **1** (of farmland) ploughed and harrowed but

f

Thesaurus

up, copy, pirate, reproduce, replicate; doctor, alter, tamper with. **2** *he faked a yawn* FEIGN, pretend, simulate, put on, make-believe, affect.

fall ● verb **1** *bombs began to fall* DROP, descend, come down, go down; plummet, plunge, sink, dive, tumble; cascade. **2** *he tripped and fell* TOPPLE OVER, tumble over, keel over, fall down/over, go head over heels, go headlong, collapse, take a spill, pitch forward; trip (over), stumble, slip; *informal* come a cropper; *Brit. informal* go for six. **3** *the river began to fall* SUBSIDE, recede, ebb, flow back, fall away, go down, sink. **4** *inflation will fall* DECREASE, decline, diminish, fall off, drop off, lessen, dwindle; plummet, plunge, slump, sink; depreciate, cheapen, devalue; *informal* go through the floor, nosedive, take a header, crash. **5** *the Mogul empire fell* DECLINE, deteriorate, degenerate, go downhill, go to rack and ruin; decay, wither, fade, fail; *informal* go to the dogs, go to pot, go down the toilet; *Austral./NZ informal* go to the pack. **6** *those who fell in the war* DIE, perish, lose one's life, be killed, be slain, be lost, meet one's death; *informal* bite the dust, croak, buy it; *Brit. informal* snuff it; *archaic* decease. **7** *the town fell to the barbarians* SURRENDER, yield, submit, give in, capitulate, succumb; be taken by, be defeated by, be conquered by, be overwhelmed by. **8** *Easter falls on 23rd April* OCCUR, take place, happen, come about; arise; *poetic/literary* come to pass. **9** *night fell* COME, arrive, appear, arise, materialize. **10** *she fell ill* BECOME, grow, get, turn. **11** *more tasks may fall to him* BE THE RESPONSIBILITY OF, be the duty of, be borne by, be one's job; come someone's way.

– OPPOSITES rise, flood, increase, flourish.

● noun **1** *an accidental fall* TUMBLE, trip, spill, topple, slip; collapse; *informal* nosedive, header, cropper. **2** *a fall in sales* DECLINE, fall-off, drop, decrease, cut, dip, reduction, downswing; plummet, plunge, slump; *informal* nosedive, crash. **3** *the fall of the Roman Empire* DOWNFALL, collapse, ruin, ruination, failure, decline, deterioration, degeneration; destruction, overthrow, demise. **4** *the fall of the city* SURRENDER, capitulation, yielding, submission; defeat. **5** *a steep fall down to the ocean* DESCENT, declivity, slope, slant, incline; *N. Amer.* downgrade. **6** *the fall of man* SIN, wrongdoing, transgression, error, offence, lapse, fall from grace. **7** *rafting trips below the falls* WATERFALL, cascade, cataract; rapids, white water.

– OPPOSITES increase, rise, ascent.

– PHRASES **fall apart** FALL/COME TO PIECES, fall/come to bits, come apart (at the seams); disintegrate, fragment, break up, break apart, crumble, decay, perish; *informal* bust. **fall asleep** DOZE OFF, drop off, go to sleep; *informal* nod off, go off, drift off, crash (out), flake out, conk out, go out like a light; *N. Amer. informal* sack out. **fall away** SLOPE (DOWN), slant down, go down, drop (away), descend, dip, sink, plunge. **fall back** RETREAT, withdraw, back off, draw back, pull back, pull away, move away. **fall back on** RESORT TO, turn to, look to, call on, have recourse to; rely on, depend on, lean on. **fall behind** **1** *the other walkers fell behind* LAG (BEHIND), trail (behind), be left behind, drop back, bring up the rear; straggle, dally, dawdle, hang back. **2** *they fell behind on their payments* GET INTO DEBT, get into arrears, default, be in the red. **fall down** **1** *I spin round till I fall down.* See FALL verb sense 2. **2** *his work fell down in some areas* FAIL, be unsuccessful, not succeed, not make the grade, fall short, fall flat, disappoint; miss the mark; *informal* come a cropper, flop. **fall for** (*informal*) **1** *she fell for John* FALL IN LOVE WITH, become infatuated with, lose one's heart to, take a fancy to, be smitten by, be attracted to; *informal* fancy, have the hots for. **2** *she won't fall for that trick* BE DECEIVED BY, be duped by, be fooled by, be taken in by, believe, trust, be convinced by; *informal* go for, buy, swallow (hook, line, and sinker). **fall in** **1** *the roof fell in* COLLAPSE, cave in, crash in, fall down; give way, crumble, disintegrate. **2** *the troops fell in* GET IN FORMATION, get in line, line up, take one's position; *Military* dress. **fall in with** **1** *he fell in with a bad crowd* GET INVOLVED WITH, take up with, join up with, go around with, string along with, make friends with; *informal* hang out/about with. **2** *he won't fall in with their demands* COMPLY WITH, go along with, support, cooperate with, obey, yield to, submit to, bow to, defer to, adhere to, conform to; agree to, agree with, accept, concur with. **fall off.** See FALL verb sense 4. **fall on** ATTACK, assail, assault, fly at, set about, set upon; pounce upon, ambush, surprise, rush, storm, charge; *informal* jump, lay into, pitch into, beat someone up; *Brit. informal* have a go at. **fall out** **1** *let's not fall out* QUARREL, argue, row, fight, squabble, bicker, have words, disagree, be at odds, clash, wrangle, cross swords, lock horns, be at loggerheads, be at each other's throats; *informal* scrap, argufy, argy-bargy. **2** *the soldiers fell out* MOVE OUT OF FORMATION, move out of line; stand at ease. **fall short of** FAIL TO MEET, fail to reach, fail to live up to; be deficient, be inadequate, be insufficient, be wanting, be lacking, disappoint; *informal* not come up to scratch. **fall through** FAIL, be unsuccessful, come to nothing, miscarry, abort, go awry, collapse, founder, come to grief; *informal* fizzle out, flop, fold, come a cropper.

fallacious ● adjective ERRONEOUS, false, untrue, wrong, incorrect, flawed, inaccurate, mistaken, misinformed, misguided; specious, spurious, bogus, fictitious, fabricated, made up; groundless, unfounded, unproven, unsupported, uncorroborated; *informal* phoney, full of holes, off beam.

– OPPOSITES correct.

fallacy ● noun MISCONCEPTION, misbelief, delusion, mistaken impression, misapprehension, misinterpretation, misconstruction, error, mistake; untruth, inconsistency, myth.

fallen ● adjective **1** *fallen heroes* DEAD, perished, killed, slain, slaughtered, murdered; lost, late, lamented, departed, gone; *formal* deceased; *rare* demised. **2** (*dated*) *fallen women* IMMORAL, loose, promiscuous, unchaste, sinful, impure, sullied, tainted, dishonoured, ruined.

left for a period without being sown. **2** characterized by inactivity. **3** (of a sow) not pregnant. ● **noun** a piece of fallow land.
– DERIVATIVES **fallowness** noun.
– ORIGIN Old English.
fallow[2] ● **noun** a pale brown or reddish yellow colour.
– ORIGIN Old English.
fallow deer ● **noun** a deer with branched antlers, having a white-spotted reddish-brown coat in summer.
false ● **adjective** **1** not in accordance with the truth or facts. **2** invalid or illegal. **3** deliberately intended to deceive. **4** artificial. **5** not actually so; illusory: *a false sense of security*. **6** disloyal.
– DERIVATIVES **falsely** adverb **falseness** noun **falsity** noun.
– ORIGIN from Latin *falsum* 'fraud', from *fallere* 'deceive'.
false acacia ● **noun** a North American tree with clusters of fragrant white flowers.
false alarm ● **noun** a warning given about something that fails to take place.
false dawn ● **noun** a transient light which precedes the rising of the sun by about an hour, commonly seen in Eastern countries.
false economy ● **noun** an apparent financial saving that in fact leads to greater expenditure.
falsehood ● **noun** **1** the state of being untrue. **2** a lie.
false memory ● **noun** an apparent recollection of an event which did not actually occur, especially one of childhood sexual abuse arising from suggestion during psychoanalysis.
false move ● **noun** an unwise action with potentially dangerous consequences.
false pretences ● **plural noun** behaviour intended to deceive.
false start ● **noun** an invalid start to a race.
false step ● **noun** **1** a slip or stumble. **2** a mistake.
falsetto /fawlsettō/ ● **noun** (pl. **falsettos**) a method of voice production used by male singers, especially tenors, to sing notes higher than their normal range.
– ORIGIN Italian, from *falso* 'false'.
falsies ● **plural noun** informal **1** pads of material used to increase the apparent size of the breasts. **2** false eyelashes.
falsify /fawlsifī/ ● **verb** (**falsifies**, **falsified**) **1** alter (information or evidence) so as to mislead. **2** prove (a statement or theory) to be false.
– DERIVATIVES **falsifiable** adjective **falsification** noun.
Falstaffian /fawlstaafiən/ ● **adjective** of or resembling Shakespeare's character Sir John Falstaff in being fat, jolly, and debauched.
falter /fawltər/ ● **verb** **1** lose strength or momentum. **2** move or speak hesitantly.
– DERIVATIVES **falterer** noun **faltering** adjective.
– ORIGIN perhaps from FOLD[1] (which was occasionally used of the faltering of the legs or tongue).
fame ● **noun** the state of being famous.
famed ● **adjective** famous; well known.
familiar ● **adjective** **1** well known through long or close association. **2** frequently encountered; common. **3** (**familiar with**) having a good knowledge of. **4** in close friendship. **5** inappropriately intimate or informal. ● **noun** **1** (also **familiar spirit**) a spirit supposedly attending and obeying a witch. **2** a close friend or associate.
– PHRASES **familiarity breeds contempt** proverb extensive knowledge of or close association with someone or something leads to a loss of respect for them or it.
– DERIVATIVES **familiarity** noun (pl. **familiarities**) **familiarly** adverb.
– ORIGIN Latin *familiaris*, from *familia* 'household servants, family'.
familiarize (also **familiarise**) ● **verb** **1** (**familiarize with**) make (someone) familiar with. **2** make better known or easier to understand.
– DERIVATIVES **familiarization** noun.
family ● **noun** (pl. **families**) **1** a group consisting of two parents and their children living together as a unit. **2** a group of people related by blood or marriage. **3** the children of a person or couple. **4** all the descendants of a common ancestor. **5** all the languages derived from a particular early language. **6** a group united by a significant shared characteristic. **7** Biology a principal taxonomic category ranking above genus and below order. ● **adjective** designed to be suitable for children as well as adults.
– PHRASES **in the family way** informal pregnant.
– DERIVATIVES **familial** adjective.
– ORIGIN Latin *familia* 'household servants, family', from *famulus*

Thesaurus

fallible ● **adjective** ERROR-PRONE, errant, liable to err, open to error; imperfect, flawed, weak.
fallow ● **adjective** **1** *fallow farmland* UNCULTIVATED, unploughed, untilled, unplanted, unsown; unused, dormant, resting, empty, bare. **2** *a fallow trading period* INACTIVE, dormant, quiet, slack, slow, stagnant; barren, unproductive.
– OPPOSITES cultivated, busy.
false ● **adjective** **1** *a false report* INCORRECT, untrue, wrong, erroneous, fallacious, flawed, distorted, inaccurate, imprecise; untruthful, fictitious, concocted, fabricated, invented, made up, trumped up, unfounded, spurious; counterfeit, forged, fraudulent. **2** *a false friend* FAITHLESS, unfaithful, disloyal, untrue, inconstant, treacherous, traitorous, two-faced, double-crossing, deceitful, dishonest, duplicitous, untrustworthy, unreliable; untruthful; *informal* cheating, two-timing, back-stabbing; *poetic/literary* perfidious. **3** *false pearls* FAKE, artificial, imitation, synthetic, simulated, reproduction, replica, ersatz, man-made, dummy, mock; *informal* phoney, pretend, pseudo.
– OPPOSITES correct, truthful, faithful, genuine.
falsehood ● **noun** **1** *a downright falsehood* LIE, untruth, fib, falsification, fabrication, invention, fiction, story, cock and bull story, fairy story, fairy tale, flight of fancy; half truth; *informal* tall story, tall tale, whopper; *Brit. informal* porky (pie); *humorous* terminological inexactitude. **2** *he accused me of falsehood* LYING, mendacity, untruthfulness, fibbing, fabrication, invention, perjury, telling stories; deceit, deception, pretence, artifice, double-crossing, treachery; *poetic/literary* perfidy.
– OPPOSITES truth, honesty.
falsify ● **verb** **1** *she falsified the accounts* FORGE, fake, counterfeit, fabricate; alter, change, doctor, tamper with, fudge, manipulate, adulterate, corrupt, misrepresent, misreport, distort, warp, embellish, embroider. **2** *the theory is falsified by the evidence* DISPROVE, refute, rebut, deny, debunk, negate, negative, invalidate, contradict, controvert, confound, demolish, discredit; *informal* shoot full of holes, blow out of the water; *formal* confute, gainsay.
falsity ● **noun** UNTRUTHFULNESS, untruth, fallaciousness, falseness, falsehood, fictitiousness, inaccuracy; mendacity, fabrication, dishonesty, deceit.
falter ● **verb** **1** *the government faltered* HESITATE, delay, drag one's feet, stall; waver, vacillate, be indecisive, be irresolute, blow hot and cold; *Brit.* haver, hum and haw; *informal* sit on the fence, dilly-dally, shilly-shally. **2** *she faltered over his name* STAMMER, stutter, stumble; hesitate, flounder.
fame ● **noun** RENOWN, celebrity, stardom, popularity, prominence; note, distinction, esteem, importance, account, consequence, greatness, eminence, prestige, stature, repute; notoriety, infamy.
– OPPOSITES obscurity.
famed ● **adjective** FAMOUS, celebrated, well known, prominent, noted, notable, renowned, respected, esteemed, acclaimed; notorious, infamous.
familiar ● **adjective** **1** *a familiar task* WELL KNOWN, recognized, accustomed; common, commonplace, everyday, day-to-day, ordinary, habitual, usual, customary, routine, standard, stock, mundane, run-of-the-mill; *poetic/literary* wonted. **2** *are you familiar with the subject?* ACQUAINTED, conversant, versed, knowledgeable, well informed; skilled, proficient; at home with, no stranger to, au fait with, au courant with; *informal* well up on, in the know about, genned up on, clued up on. **3** *a familiar atmosphere* INFORMAL, casual, relaxed, easy, comfortable; friendly, unceremonious, unreserved, open, natural, unpretentious. **4** *he is too familiar with the teachers* OVERFAMILIAR, presumptuous, disrespectful, forward, bold, impudent, impertinent.
– OPPOSITES formal.
familiarity ● **noun** **1** *he wants greater familiarity with politics* ACQUAINTANCE WITH, awareness of, experience of, insight into, conversancy with, conversance with; knowledge of, understanding of, comprehension of, grasp of, skill in, proficiency in. **2** *she was affronted by his familiarity* OVERFAMILIARITY, presumption, presumptuousness, forwardness, boldness, audacity, cheek, impudence, impertinence, disrespect; liberties. **3** *our familiarity allows us to tease each other* CLOSENESS, intimacy, attachment, affinity, friendliness, friendship, amity; *informal* chumminess, palliness; *Brit. informal* mateyness.
familiarize ● **verb** *I will familiarize them with the text* MAKE CONVERSANT, make familiar, acquaint; accustom to, habituate to, instruct in, teach in, educate in, school in, prime in, introduce to;

'servant'.

family credit ● noun (in the UK) a regular payment by the state to a family with an income below a certain level.

family name ● noun a surname.

family planning ● noun the control of the number of children in a family and the intervals between their births by means of contraception.

family tree ● noun a diagram showing the relationship between people in several generations of a family.

family values ● plural noun values supposedly characteristic of a traditional family unit, typically those of high moral standards and discipline.

famine /fammin/ ● noun **1** extreme scarcity of food. **2** archaic hunger.
– ORIGIN Old French, from *faim* 'hunger', from Latin *fames*.

famish ● verb archaic reduce or be reduced to extreme hunger.
– ORIGIN Old French *afamer*, from Latin *fames* 'hunger'.

famished ● adjective informal extremely hungry.

famous ● adjective **1** known about by many people. **2** informal magnificent.
– DERIVATIVES **famously** adverb **famousness** noun.
– ORIGIN Latin *famosus*, from *fama* 'fame'.

fan[1] ● noun **1** an apparatus with rotating blades that creates a current of air for cooling or ventilation. **2** a hand-held device, typically folding and circular, that is waved so as to cool the user. ● verb (**fanned**, **fanning**) **1** cool by waving something to create a current of air. **2** (of an air current) increase the strength of (a fire). **3** cause (a belief or emotion) to become stronger. **4** (**fan out**) spread out from a central point to cover a wide area.
– ORIGIN Latin *vannus* 'winnowing fan'.

fan[2] ● noun a person who has a strong interest in or admiration for a particular sport, art form, or famous person.
– DERIVATIVES **fandom** noun.
– ORIGIN abbreviation of FANATIC.

fanatic ● noun **1** a person filled with excessive zeal, especially for an extreme political or religious cause. **2** informal a person with an obsessive enthusiasm for a pastime or hobby. ● adjective filled with or expressing excessive zeal.
– DERIVATIVES **fanatical** adjective **fanatically** adverb **fanaticism** noun.
– ORIGIN from Latin *fanaticus* 'of a temple, inspired by a god', from *fanum* 'temple'.

fan belt ● noun (in a motor-vehicle engine) a belt that drives the radiator fan and usually also the dynamo or alternator.

fancier ● noun a person who has a special interest in or breeds a particular animal.

fanciful ● adjective **1** over-imaginative and unrealistic. **2** existing only in the imagination. **3** highly ornamental or imaginative in design.
– DERIVATIVES **fancifully** adverb **fancifulness** noun.

fan club ● noun an organized group of fans of a famous person or team.

fancy ● verb (**fancies**, **fancied**) **1** Brit. informal feel a desire for. **2** Brit. informal find sexually attractive. **3** regard as a likely winner. **4** imagine. **5** used to express surprise: *fancy that!* ● adjective (**fancier**, **fanciest**) elaborate or highly decorated. ● noun (pl. **fancies**) **1** a superficial or transient feeling of attraction. **2** the faculty of imagination. **3** an unfounded or tentative belief or idea. **4** (also **fancy cake**) a small iced cake or biscuit.
– PHRASES **take someone's fancy** appeal to someone. **take a fancy to** become fond of, especially without an obvious reason.
– DERIVATIVES **fanciable** adjective (informal) **fancily** adverb **fanciness** noun.
– ORIGIN contraction of FANTASY.

fancy dress ● noun a costume worn to make someone look like a famous person, fictional character, or an animal.

fancy-free ● adjective without emotional commitments.

fancy man ● noun informal, often derogatory a woman's lover.

fancy woman ● noun informal, often derogatory a married man's mistress.

fandango /fandanggō/ ● noun (pl. **fandangoes** or **fandangos**) a lively Spanish dance for two people, typically accompanied by castanets or tambourine.
– ORIGIN Spanish.

fanfare ● noun **1** a short ceremonial tune or flourish played on brass instruments. **2** an elaborate welcome or introduction.
– ORIGIN French.

f

Thesaurus

informal gen up on, clue up on, put in the picture about, give the gen about, give the low-down on, fill in on.

family ● noun **1** *I met his family* RELATIVES, relations, (next of) kin, kinsfolk, kindred, one's (own) flesh and blood, nearest and dearest, people, connections; extended family; clan, tribe; informal folks. **2** *he had the right kind of family* ANCESTRY, parentage, pedigree, genealogy, background, family tree, descent, lineage, bloodline, blood, extraction, stock; forebears, forefathers, antecedents, roots, origins. **3** *she is married with a family* CHILDREN, little ones, youngsters; offspring, progeny, descendants, scions, heirs; brood; Law issue; informal kids, kiddies, tots. **4** *the weaver bird family* TAXONOMIC GROUP, order, class, genus, species; stock, strain, line; Zoology phylum.

family tree ● noun ANCESTRY, genealogy, descent, lineage, line, bloodline, pedigree, background, extraction, derivation; family, dynasty, house; forebears, forefathers, antecedents, roots, origins.

famine ● noun **1** *a nation threatened by famine* SCARCITY OF FOOD, food shortages. **2** *the cotton famine* SHORTAGE, scarcity, lack, dearth, deficiency, insufficiency, shortfall, scantiness, paucity, poverty, drought.
– OPPOSITES plenty.

famished ● adjective (informal) RAVENOUS, hungry, starving, starved, empty, unfed; informal peckish.
– OPPOSITES full.

famous ● adjective WELL KNOWN, prominent, famed, popular; renowned, noted, eminent, distinguished, esteemed, celebrated, respected; of distinction, of repute; illustrious, acclaimed, great, legendary, lionized; notorious, infamous.
– OPPOSITES unknown.

fan[1] ● noun *a ceiling fan* AIR-COOLER, air conditioner, ventilator, blower, aerator.
● verb **1** *she fanned her face* COOL, aerate, ventilate; freshen, refresh. **2** *they fanned public fears* INTENSIFY, increase, agitate, inflame, exacerbate; stimulate, stir up, whip up, fuel, kindle, spark, arouse. **3** *the police squad fanned out* SPREAD, branch; outspread.

fan[2] ● noun *a basketball fan* ENTHUSIAST, devotee, admirer, lover; supporter, follower, disciple, adherent, zealot; expert, connoisseur, aficionado; informal buff, fiend, freak, nut, addict, fanatic, groupie; N. Amer. informal jock.

fanatic ● noun **1** *a religious fanatic* ZEALOT, extremist, militant, dogmatist, devotee, adherent; sectarian, bigot, partisan, radical, diehard, ultra; informal maniac. **2** (informal) *a keep-fit fanatic*. See FAN[2].

fanatical ● adjective **1** *they are fanatical about their faith* ZEALOUS, extremist, extreme, militant, dogmatic, radical, diehard; intolerant, single-minded, blinkered, inflexible, uncompromising. **2** *he was fanatical about tidiness* ENTHUSIASTIC, eager, keen, fervent, ardent, passionate; obsessive, obsessed, fixated, compulsive; informal wild, gung-ho, nuts, crazy; Brit. informal potty.

fancier ● noun *a pigeon fancier* ENTHUSIAST, lover, hobbyist; expert, connoisseur, aficionado; breeder; informal buff.

fanciful ● adjective **1** *a fanciful story* FANTASTIC, far-fetched, unbelievable, extravagant; ridiculous, absurd, preposterous; imaginary, made-up, make-believe, mythical, fabulous; informal tall, hard to swallow. **2** *a fanciful girl* IMAGINATIVE, inventive; whimsical, impractical, dreamy, quixotic; out of touch with reality, in a world of one's own. **3** *a fanciful building* ORNATE, exotic, fancy, imaginative, extravagant, fantastic; curious, bizarre, eccentric, unusual.
– OPPOSITES literal, practical.

fancy ● verb **1** (Brit. informal) *I fancied a change of scene* WISH FOR, want, desire; long for, yearn for, crave, thirst for, hanker after, dream of, covet; informal have a yen for; archaic be desirous of. **2** (Brit. informal) *she fancied him* BE ATTRACTED TO, find attractive, be infatuated with, be taken with, desire; lust after, burn for; informal have a crush on, have the hots for, be crazy about, have a thing about, have a soft spot for, carry a torch for. **3** *I fancied I could see lights* THINK, imagine, believe, be of the opinion, be under the impression; informal reckon.
● adjective *fancy clothes* ELABORATE, ornate, ornamental, decorative, adorned, embellished, intricate; ostentatious, showy, flamboyant; luxurious, lavish, extravagant, expensive; informal flash, flashy, jazzy, ritzy, snazzy, posh, classy; Brit. informal swish.
– OPPOSITES plain.
● noun **1** *his fancy to own a farm* DESIRE, urge, wish; inclination, whim, impulse, notion, whimsy; yearning, longing, hankering,

fang ● noun **1** a large sharp tooth, especially a canine tooth of a dog or wolf. **2** a tooth with which a snake injects poison. **3** the biting mouthpart of a spider.
– DERIVATIVES **fanged** adjective.
– ORIGIN from Old Norse, 'capture, grasp'.
fankle /fangk'l/ ● verb Scottish entangle.
– ORIGIN from Scots *fank* 'coil of rope'.
fanlight ● noun a small window, typically semicircular, over a door or another window.
fanny ● noun (pl. **fannies**) **1** Brit. vulgar slang a woman's genitals. **2** N. Amer. informal a person's bottom.
– ORIGIN of unknown origin.
Fanny Adams (also **sweet Fanny Adams**) ● noun Brit. informal nothing at all.
– ORIGIN originally a nautical term for tinned meat or stew (a reference to the name of a murder victim *c.*1870), now often understood as a euphemism for *fuck all.*

f

fantabulous /fantabyooləss/ ● adjective informal excellent; wonderful.
– ORIGIN blend of FANTASTIC and FABULOUS.
fantail ● noun **1** a fan-shaped tail or end. **2** a domestic pigeon of a broad-tailed variety.
– DERIVATIVES **fan-tailed** adjective.
fantasia /fantayziə, fantəzeeə/ ● noun **1** a musical or other composition with a free form and often an improvisatory style. **2** a musical composition based on several familiar tunes.
– ORIGIN Italian, 'fantasy'.
fantasize (also **fantasise**) ● verb indulge in daydreaming or speculation about something desired.
– DERIVATIVES **fantasist** noun.
fantastic ● adjective **1** imaginative or fanciful; remote from reality. **2** informal extraordinarily good or attractive.
– DERIVATIVES **fantastical** adjective **fantastically** adverb.
fantasy ● noun (pl. **fantasies**) **1** the imagining of improbable or impossible things. **2** an idea with no basis in reality. **3** a genre of imaginative fiction involving magic and adventure.
– ORIGIN Greek *phantasia* 'imagination, appearance', from *phantazein* 'make visible'.
fanzine /fanzeen/ ● noun a magazine for fans of a particular team, performer, or genre.
– ORIGIN blend of FAN² and MAGAZINE.
FAO ● abbreviation for the attention of.
FAQ ● abbreviation Computing frequently asked questions.
far ● adverb (**further**, **furthest** or **farther**, **farthest**) **1** at, to, or by a great distance. **2** over a long way in space or time. **3** by a great deal. ● adjective **1** situated at a great distance in space or time. **2** distant from the centre; extreme. **3** more distant than another object of the same kind: *the far corner.*
– PHRASES **as far as 1** for as great a distance as. **2** to the extent that. **be a far cry from** be very different to. **by far** by a great amount. **far and away** by a very large amount. **far and wide** over a large area. **far be it from** (or **for**) **me to** used to express reluctance. **far gone 1** in a bad or worsening state. **2** advanced in time. **go far 1** achieve a great deal. **2** be worth or amount to much. **go too far** exceed the limits of what is reasonable or acceptable. (**in**) **so far as** (or **that**) to the extent that.
– ORIGIN Old English.
farad /farrəd/ ● noun the unit of electrical capacitance in the SI system, equal to a capacitance in which one coulomb of charge causes a potential difference of one volt.
– ORIGIN from the name of the English physicist Michael *Faraday* (1791–1867).
faraway ● adjective **1** distant in space or time. **2** seeming remote; dreamy: *a faraway look.*
farce ● noun **1** a comic dramatic work or genre using buffoonery and horseplay and typically including ludicrously improbable situations. **2** an absurd event.
– ORIGIN French, 'stuffing' (from the former practice of 'stuffing' comic interludes into religious plays).
farceur /faarsör/ ● noun a writer of or performer in farces.
– ORIGIN French.
farcical ● adjective resembling farce; absurd or ridiculous.
– DERIVATIVES **farcically** adverb.
fardel /faard'l/ ● noun archaic a bundle.
– ORIGIN Old French.
fare ● noun **1** the money a passenger on public transport has to pay. **2** a range of food. ● verb **1** perform in a specified way in a particular situation or period. **2** archaic travel.

Thesaurus

craving; *informal* yen, itch. **2** *I've a fancy they want to be alone* IDEA, notion, thought, supposition, opinion, belief, impression, understanding; feeling, suspicion, hunch, inkling.
fanfare ● noun **1** *a fanfare announced her arrival* TRUMPET CALL, flourish, fanfaronade; *archaic* trump. **2** *the project was greeted with great fanfare* FUSS, commotion, show, display, ostentation, flashiness, pageantry, splendour; *informal* ballyhoo, hype, pizzazz, razzle-dazzle, glitz.
fantasize ● verb DAYDREAM, dream, muse, make-believe, pretend, imagine; build castles in the air, build castles in Spain, live in a dream world.
fantastic ● adjective **1** *a fantastic notion* FANCIFUL, extravagant, extraordinary, irrational, wild, absurd, far-fetched, nonsensical, incredible, unbelievable, unthinkable, implausible, improbable, unlikely, doubtful, dubious; strange, peculiar, odd, queer, weird, eccentric, whimsical, capricious; visionary, romantic; *informal* crazy, cock-eyed, off the wall. **2** *his fantastic accuracy* TREMENDOUS, remarkable, great, terrific, impressive, outstanding, phenomenal. **3** *fantastic shapes* STRANGE, weird, bizarre, outlandish, queer, peculiar, grotesque, freakish, surreal, exotic; elaborate, ornate, intricate. **4** *(informal) a fantastic car* MARVELLOUS, wonderful, sensational, outstanding, superb, excellent, first-rate, first-class, dazzling, out of this world, breathtaking; *informal* great, terrific, fabulous, fab, mega, super, ace, magic, cracking, cool, wicked, awesome; *Brit. informal* brilliant, brill, smashing; *Austral./NZ informal* bonzer; *Brit. informal, dated* spiffing.
– OPPOSITES rational, ordinary.
fantasy ● noun **1** *a mix of fantasy and realism* IMAGINATION, fancy, invention, make-believe; creativity, vision; daydreaming, reverie. **2** *his fantasy about being famous* DREAM, daydream, pipe dream, fanciful notion, wish; fond hope, chimera, delusion, illusion; *informal* pie in the sky.
– OPPOSITES realism.
far ● adverb **1** *we are far from the palace* A LONG WAY, a great distance, a good way; afar. **2** *her charm far outweighs any flaws* MUCH, considerably, markedly, immeasurably, greatly, significantly, substantially, appreciably, noticeably; to a great extent, by a long way, by far, by a mile, easily.
– OPPOSITES near.
● adjective **1** *far places* DISTANT, faraway, far-off, remote, out of the way, far-flung, outlying. **2** *the far side of the campus* FURTHER, more distant; opposite.
– OPPOSITES near.
– PHRASES **by far** BY A GREAT AMOUNT, by a good deal, by a long way, by a mile, far and away; undoubtedly, without doubt, without question, positively, absolutely, easily; significantly, substantially, appreciably, much; *Brit.* by a long chalk. **far and away.** See BY FAR. **far and near** EVERYWHERE, {here, there, and everywhere}, all over (the world), throughout the land, worldwide; *informal* all over the place; *Brit. informal* all over the shop; *N. Amer. informal* all over the map. **far and wide.** See FAR AND NEAR. **far from** *staff were far from happy* NOT, not at all, nowhere near; the opposite of. **go far** BE SUCCESSFUL, succeed, prosper, flourish, thrive, get on (in the world), make good, set the world on fire; *informal* make a name for oneself, make one's mark, go places, do all right for oneself, find a place in the sun. **go too far** GO OVER THE TOP, go to extremes, go overboard. **so far 1** *nobody has noticed so far* UNTIL NOW, up to now, up to this point, as yet, thus far, hitherto, up to the present, to date. **2** *his liberalism only extends so far* TO A CERTAIN EXTENT, up to a point, to a degree, within reason, within limits.
faraway ● adjective **1** *faraway places* DISTANT, far off, far, remote, far-flung, outlying; obscure, out of the way, off the beaten track. **2** *a faraway look in her eyes* DREAMY, daydreaming, abstracted, absent-minded, distracted, preoccupied, vague; lost in thought, somewhere else, not with us, in a world of one's own; *informal* miles away.
– OPPOSITES nearby.
farce ● noun **1** *the stories approach farce* SLAPSTICK (COMEDY), burlesque, vaudeville, buffoonery. **2** *the trial was a farce* MOCKERY, travesty, absurdity, sham, pretence, masquerade, charade, joke, waste of time; *informal* shambles.
– OPPOSITES tragedy.
farcical ● adjective **1** *the idea is farcical* RIDICULOUS, preposterous, ludicrous, absurd, laughable, risible, nonsensical; senseless, pointless, useless; silly, foolish, idiotic, stupid, hare-brained; *informal* crazy; *Brit. informal* barmy, daft. **2** *farcical goings-on* MADCAP,

– ORIGIN Old English.
Far East ● noun China, Japan, and other countries of east Asia.
– DERIVATIVES **Far Eastern** adjective.
farewell ● exclamation archaic goodbye. ● noun an act of parting or of marking someone's departure.
farfalle /faarfalay/ ● plural noun small pieces of pasta shaped like bows or butterflies' wings.
– ORIGIN Italian, 'butterflies'.
far-fetched ● adjective unconvincing; implausible.
far-flung ● adjective distant or remote.
farina /fəreenə/ ● noun flour or meal made of cereal grains, nuts, or starchy roots.
– DERIVATIVES **farinaceous** /farrinayshəss/ adjective.
– ORIGIN Latin, from *far* 'corn'.
farl ● noun a thin Scottish cake of oatmeal or flour.
– ORIGIN from obsolete *fardel* 'quarter', contraction of *fourth deal*.
farm ● noun **1** an area of land and its buildings used for growing crops and rearing animals. **2** a farmhouse. **3** an establishment for breeding or growing something, or devoted to a particular thing: *a fish farm*. ● verb **1** make one's living by growing crops or keeping livestock. **2** use (land) for this purpose. **3** breed or grow (a type of livestock or crop) commercially. **4** (**farm out**) send out or subcontract (work) to others.
– DERIVATIVES **farming** noun.
– ORIGIN originally denoting a fixed annual amount payable as rent or tax, later land leased for farming: from Old French *ferme*, from Latin *firmare* 'fix, settle'.
farmer ● noun a person who owns or manages a farm.
farmhand ● noun a worker on a farm.
farmhouse ● noun a house attached to a farm.
farmstead ● noun a farm and its buildings.
farmyard ● noun a yard or enclosure attached to a farmhouse. ● adjective (of manners or language) coarse.
faro /fairō/ ● noun a gambling card game in which players bet on the order in which the cards will appear.
– ORIGIN French *pharaon* 'pharaoh', said to have been the name of the king of hearts.
Faroese /fairōeez/ (also **Faeroese**) ● noun (pl. same) **1** a person from the Faroe Islands. **2** the language of the Faroe Islands.
farouche /fəroosh/ ● adjective sullen or shy in company.
– ORIGIN Old French *forache*, from Latin *foras* 'out of doors'.
far out ● adjective informal **1** unconventional or avant-garde. **2** informal, dated excellent.
farrago /fəraagō/ ● noun (pl. **farragos** or US **farragoes**) a confused mixture.
– ORIGIN Latin, 'mixed fodder', from *far* 'corn'.
far-reaching ● adjective having important and extensive effects or implications.
farrier /farriər/ ● noun a smith who shoes horses.
– DERIVATIVES **farriery** noun.
– ORIGIN Old French *ferrier*, from Latin *ferrum* 'iron, horseshoe'.
farrow ● noun a litter of pigs. ● verb (of a sow) give birth to (piglets).
– ORIGIN Old English, 'young pig'.
far-seeing ● adjective having shrewd judgement and foresight.
Farsi /faarsee/ ● noun the modern form of the Persian language, spoken in Iran.
– ORIGIN from the Persian word for 'Persia'.
far-sighted ● adjective **1** far-seeing. **2** N. Amer. long-sighted.
fart informal ● verb **1** emit wind from the anus. **2** (**fart about/around**) waste time on silly or trivial things. ● noun **1** an emission of wind from the anus. **2** a boring or contemptible person.
– ORIGIN Old English.
farther ● adverb & adjective variant form of FURTHER.
– USAGE On the difference in use between **farther** and **further**, see the note at FURTHER.
farthermost ● adjective variant form of FURTHERMOST.
farthest ● adjective & adverb variant form of FURTHEST.
farthing ● noun **1** a former monetary unit and coin of the UK, equal to a quarter of an old penny. **2** the least possible amount: *she didn't care a farthing*.
– ORIGIN Old English, 'fourth'.
farthingale /farrthinggayl/ ● noun historical a hooped petticoat or circular pad of fabric around the hips, formerly worn under women's skirts to extend and shape them.
– ORIGIN French *verdugale*, from Spanish *verdugo* 'rod, stick'.
fartlek /faartlek/ ● noun Athletics a system of training for distance runners in which the terrain and pace are continually varied.
– ORIGIN Swedish, from *fart* 'speed' + *lek* 'play'.
fasces /fasseez/ ● plural noun historical a bundle of rods with a projecting axe blade, a symbol of a magistrate's power in ancient Rome.
– ORIGIN Latin, from *fascis* 'bundle'.
fascia (Brit. also **facia** except in sense 5) ● noun **1** /fayshə/ a board covering the ends of rafters or other fittings. **2** a signboard on a shopfront. **3** chiefly Brit. the dashboard of a motor vehicle. **4** (in classical architecture) a long flat surface between mouldings on an architrave. **5** /fashə/ (pl. **fasciae** /fashi-ee/) Anatomy a thin sheath of fibrous tissue enclosing a muscle or other organ.
– DERIVATIVES **fascial** adjective.
– ORIGIN Latin, 'band, door frame'.
fascicle /fassik'l/ ● noun a separately published instalment of a book.
– ORIGIN Latin *fasciculus* 'little bundle'.
fascinate ● verb irresistibly attract the interest of.
– DERIVATIVES **fascinating** adjective **fascinatingly** adverb **fascination** noun.
– ORIGIN Latin *fascinare* 'bewitch', from *fascinum* 'spell, witchcraft'.

f

Thesaurus

zany, slapstick, comic, comical, clownish, amusing; hilarious, uproarious; *informal* wacky.
fare ● noun **1** *we paid the fare* TICKET PRICE, transport cost; price, cost, charge, fee, toll, tariff. **2** *the taxi picked up a fare* PASSENGER, traveller, customer; *Brit. informal* punter. **3** *they eat simple fare* FOOD, meals, sustenance, nourishment, nutriment, foodstuffs, provender, eatables, provisions; cooking, cuisine; diet, table; *informal* grub, nosh, eats, chow; *Brit. informal* scoff; *formal* comestibles, victuals.
● verb *how are you faring?* GET ON, get along, cope, manage, do, muddle through/along, survive; *informal* make out.
farewell ● exclamation *farewell, Patrick!* GOODBYE, so long, adieu; au revoir, ciao; *informal* bye, bye-bye, cheerio, see you (later), later(s); *Brit. informal* ta-ta, cheers; *informal, dated* toodle-oo, toodle-pip.
● noun *an emotional farewell* GOODBYE, valediction, adieu; leave-taking, parting, departure; send-off.
far-fetched ● adjective IMPROBABLE, unlikely, implausible, unconvincing, dubious, doubtful, incredible, unbelievable, unthinkable; contrived, fanciful, unrealistic, ridiculous, absurd, preposterous; *informal* hard to swallow, fishy.
– OPPOSITES likely.
farm ● noun *a farm of 100 acres* SMALLHOLDING, farmstead, plantation, estate; farmland; *Brit.* grange, croft; *Scottish* steading; *N. Amer.* ranch; *Austral./NZ* station.
● verb **1** *he farmed locally* BE A FARMER, cultivate the land, work the land; rear livestock. **2** *they farm the land* CULTIVATE, till, work, plough, dig, plant. **3** *the family farms sheep* BREED, rear, keep, raise, tend.
– PHRASES **farm something out** CONTRACT OUT, outsource, subcontract, delegate.
farmer ● noun AGRICULTURALIST, agronomist, smallholder, grazier; farmhand; *Brit.* crofter; *N. Amer.* rancher; *historical* yeoman.
farming ● noun AGRICULTURE, cultivation, land management, farm management; husbandry; agriscience, agronomy, agribusiness; *Brit.* crofting.
far out ● adjective *(informal)*. See UNCONVENTIONAL.
farrago ● noun HOTCHPOTCH, mishmash, ragbag, pot-pourri, jumble, mess, confusion, melange, gallimaufry, hash, assortment, miscellany, mixture, conglomeration, medley; *N. Amer.* hodgepodge.
far-reaching ● adjective EXTENSIVE, wide-ranging, comprehensive, widespread, all-embracing, overarching, across the board, sweeping, blanket, wholesale; important, significant, radical, major, consequential.
– OPPOSITES limited.
far-sighted ● adjective PRESCIENT, visionary, percipient, shrewd, discerning, judicious, canny, prudent.
farther ● adverb & adjective. See FURTHER.
farthest ● adjective. See FURTHEST.
fascinate ● verb INTEREST, captivate, engross, absorb, enchant, enthral, entrance, transfix, rivet, mesmerize, engage, compel; lure, tempt, entice, draw; charm, attract, intrigue, divert, entertain.
– OPPOSITES bore.

fascism /fashiz'm/ ● noun **1** an authoritarian and nationalistic right-wing system of government. **2** extreme right-wing, authoritarian, or intolerant views or practice.
– DERIVATIVES **fascist** noun & adjective **fascistic** adjective.
– ORIGIN Italian *fascismo*, from *fascio* 'bundle, political group', from Latin *fascis* 'bundle'.
fash ● verb (**fash oneself**) Scottish feel upset or worried.
– ORIGIN French *fascher*, from Latin *fastus* 'disdain, contempt'.
fashion ● noun **1** a popular trend, especially in dress. **2** the production and marketing of new styles of clothing and cosmetics. **3** a manner of doing something. ● verb make into a particular form or article.
– PHRASES **after a fashion** to a certain extent but not perfectly. **in** (or **out of**) **fashion** fashionable (or unfashionable).
– ORIGIN Old French *façon*, from Latin *facere* 'do, make'.
fashionable ● adjective characteristic of or influenced by a current popular trend or style.
– DERIVATIVES **fashionability** noun **fashionably** adverb.
fashionista /fashənisstə/ ● noun informal **1** a designer of haute couture. **2** a devoted follower of fashion.
fashion victim ● noun informal a person who follows popular fashions slavishly.
fast[1] ● adjective **1** moving or capable of moving at high speed. **2** taking place or acting rapidly. **3** (of a clock or watch) ahead of the correct time. **4** firmly fixed or attached. **5** (of a dye) not fading in light or when washed. **6** (of photographic film) needing only a short exposure. **7** involving exciting or shocking activities. ● adverb **1** at high speed. **2** within a short time. **3** so as to be hard to move; firmly or securely. **4** so as to be hard to wake.
– PHRASES **pull a fast one** informal try to gain an unfair advantage.
– ORIGIN Old English.
fast[2] ● verb abstain from food or drink, especially as a religious observance. ● noun an act or period of fasting.
– ORIGIN Old English.
fastback ● noun a car with a rear that slopes continuously down to the bumper.
fast breeder ● noun a breeder reactor in which the neutrons causing fission are not slowed by any moderator.
fasten ● verb **1** close or do up securely. **2** fix or hold in place. **3** (**fasten on/upon**) single out and concentrate on. **4** (**fasten off**) secure the end of (a thread) with stitches or a knot.
– DERIVATIVES **fastener** noun **fastening** noun.
– ORIGIN Old English, 'make sure, confirm'.
fast food ● noun cooked food sold in snack bars and restaurants as a quick meal.
fast forward ● noun a control on a tape or video player for advancing the tape rapidly. ● verb (**fast-forward**) advance (a tape) with such a control.
fastidious /fastiddiəss/ ● adjective **1** very attentive to accuracy and detail. **2** very concerned about matters of cleanliness.
– DERIVATIVES **fastidiously** adverb **fastidiousness** noun.
– ORIGIN originally in the sense 'disagreeable, distasteful': from Latin *fastidium* 'loathing'.
fastigiate /fastijiət/ ● adjective Botany (of a tree) having the branches more or less parallel to the main stem.
– ORIGIN from Latin *fastigium* 'tapering point, gable'.
fastness ● noun **1** a secure place well protected by natural features. **2** the ability of a dye to maintain its colour.
fast-talk ● verb informal, chiefly N. Amer. pressurize into doing something using rapid or misleading speech.
fast track ● noun a rapid route or method. ● verb (**fast-track**)

Thesaurus

fascinating ● adjective INTERESTING, captivating, engrossing, absorbing, enchanting, enthralling, spellbinding, riveting, engaging, compelling, compulsive, gripping, thrilling; alluring, tempting, irresistible; charming, attractive, intriguing, diverting, entertaining.
fascination ● noun INTEREST, preoccupation, passion, obsession, compulsion; allure, lure, charm, attraction, intrigue, appeal, pull, draw.
fascism ● noun AUTHORITARIANISM, totalitarianism, dictatorship, despotism, autocracy; Nazism, rightism; nationalism, xenophobia, racism, anti-Semitism, jingoism, isolationism; neo-fascism, neo-Nazism.
fascist ● noun *he was branded a fascist* AUTHORITARIAN, totalitarian, autocrat, extreme right-winger, rightist; Nazi, blackshirt; nationalist, xenophobe, racist, anti-Semite, jingoist; neo-fascist, neo-Nazi.
– OPPOSITES liberal.
● adjective *a fascist regime* AUTHORITARIAN, totalitarian, dictatorial, despotic, autocratic, undemocratic, illiberal; Nazi, extreme right-wing, rightist, militarist; nationalist(ic), xenophobic, racist, jingoistic.
– OPPOSITES democratic.
fashion ● noun **1** *the fashion for tight clothes* VOGUE, trend, craze, rage, mania, fad; style, look; tendency, convention, custom, practice; *informal* thing. **2** *the world of fashion* CLOTHES, clothing design, couture; *informal* the rag trade. **3** *it needs to be run in a sensible fashion* MANNER, way, method, mode, style; system, approach.
● verb *the model was fashioned from lead* CONSTRUCT, build, make, manufacture, fabricate, contrive; cast, shape, form, mould, sculpt; forge, hew.
– PHRASES **after a fashion** TO A CERTAIN EXTENT, in a way, somehow (or other), in a manner of speaking, in its way. **in fashion** FASHIONABLE, in vogue, up to date, up to the minute, all the rage, chic, à la mode; *informal* trendy, with it, cool, in, the in thing, hot, big, hip, happening, now, sharp, groovy; *N. Amer.* tony, fly; *Brit. informal, dated* all the go. **out of fashion** UNFASHIONABLE, old-fashioned, out of date, outdated, dated, outmoded, behind the times; unstylish, unpopular, passé, démodé; *informal* old hat, out, square, out of the ark.
fashionable ● adjective IN VOGUE, voguish, in fashion, popular, (bang) up to date, up to the minute, modern, all the rage, modish, à la mode, trendsetting; stylish, chic; *informal* trendy, classy, with it, cool, in, the in thing, hot, big, hip, happening, now, sharp, groovy, snazzy; *N. Amer. informal* tony, fly; *Brit. informal, dated* all the go.
fast[1] ● adjective **1** *a fast pace* SPEEDY, quick, swift, rapid; fast-moving, high-speed, turbo, sporty; accelerated, express, blistering, breakneck, pell-mell; hasty, hurried; *informal* nippy, zippy, scorching, blinding, supersonic; *Brit. informal* cracking; *poetic/literary* fleet. **2** *he held the door fast* SECURE, fastened, tight, firm, closed, shut, to; immovable, unbudgeable. **3** *a fast colour* INDELIBLE, lasting, permanent, stable. **4** *fast friends* LOYAL, devoted, faithful, firm, steadfast, staunch, true, boon, bosom, inseparable; constant, enduring, unswerving. **5** *a fast woman* PROMISCUOUS, licentious, dissolute, debauched, impure, unchaste, wanton, abandoned, of easy virtue; sluttish, whorish; intemperate, immoderate, shameless, sinful, immoral; *informal* easy, tarty; *Brit. informal* slaggy; *N. Amer. informal* roundheeled; *dated* loose.
– OPPOSITES slow, loose, temporary, chaste.
● adverb **1** *she drove fast* QUICKLY, rapidly, swiftly, speedily, briskly, at speed, at full tilt; hastily, hurriedly, in a hurry, post-haste, pell-mell; like a shot, like a flash, on the double, at the speed of light; *informal* double quick, p.d.q. (pretty damn quick), nippily, like (greased) lightning, hell for leather, like mad, like the wind, like a scalded cat, like a bat out of hell; *Brit. informal* like the clappers, at a rate of knots, like billy-o; *N. Amer. informal* lickety-split; *poetic/literary* apace. **2** *his wheels were stuck fast* SECURELY, firmly, immovably, fixedly. **3** *he's fast asleep* DEEPLY, sound, completely. **4** *she lived fast and dangerously* WILDLY, dissolutely, intemperately, immoderately, recklessly, self-indulgently, extravagantly.
– OPPOSITES slowly.
fast[2] ● verb *we must fast and pray* EAT NOTHING, abstain from food, refrain from eating, go without food, go hungry, starve oneself; go on hunger strike.
– OPPOSITES eat.
● noun *a five-day fast* PERIOD OF FASTING, period of abstinence; hunger strike; diet.
– OPPOSITES feast.
fasten ● verb **1** *he fastened the door* BOLT, lock, secure, make fast, chain, seal. **2** *they fastened splints to his leg* ATTACH, fix, affix, clip, pin, tack; stick, bond, join. **3** *he fastened his horse to a tree* TIE (UP), bind, tether, truss, fetter, lash, hitch, anchor, strap, rope. **4** *the dress fastens at the front* BUTTON (UP), zip (up), do up, close. **5** *his gaze fastened on me* FOCUS, fix, be riveted, concentrate, zero in, zoom in, direct at. **6** *blame had been fastened on some nutter* ASCRIBE TO, attribute to, assign to, chalk up to; pin on, lay at the door of. **7** *critics fastened on the end of the report* SINGLE OUT, concentrate on, focus on, pick out, fix on, seize on.
– OPPOSITES unlock, remove, open, untie, undo.
fastidious ● adjective SCRUPULOUS, punctilious, painstaking, meticulous; perfectionist, fussy, finicky, over-particular; critical, overcritical, hypercritical, hard to please, exacting, demanding;

accelerate the development or progress of.

fat • noun **1** a natural oily substance in animal bodies, deposited under the skin or around certain organs. **2** such a substance, or a similar one made from plants, used in cooking. **3** Chemistry any of a group of solid natural esters of glycerol and various fatty acids, the main constituents of animal and vegetable fat. • adjective (**fatter**, **fattest**) **1** (of a person or animal) having much excess fat. **2** (of food) containing much fat. **3** informal substantial: *fat profits*. **4** informal very little: *fat chance*.
– PHRASES **kill the fatted calf** produce one's best food to celebrate, especially at a prodigal's return. [ORIGIN with biblical allusion to the Gospel of Luke, chapter 15.] **live off the fat of the land** have the best of everything.
– DERIVATIVES **fatless** adjective **fatly** adverb **fatness** noun **fattish** adjective.
– ORIGIN Old English.

fatal • adjective **1** causing death. **2** leading to failure or disaster.
– DERIVATIVES **fatally** adverb.
– ORIGIN Latin *fatalis*, from *fatum* (see FATE).

fatalism • noun **1** the belief that all events are predetermined and inevitable. **2** a submissive attitude to events.
– DERIVATIVES **fatalist** noun **fatalistic** adjective.

fatality • noun (pl. **fatalities**) **1** an occurrence of death by accident, in war, or from disease. **2** helplessness in the face of fate.

fat cat • noun derogatory a wealthy and powerful businessperson or politician.

fate • noun **1** the development of events outside a person's control, regarded as predetermined. **2** the course or inevitable outcome of a person's life. **3** (**the Fates**) Greek & Roman Mythology the three goddesses (Clotho, Lachesis, and Atropos) who preside over the birth and life of humans. • verb (**be fated**) be destined to happen or act in a particular way.
– PHRASES **seal someone's fate** make it inevitable that something unpleasant will happen to someone.
– ORIGIN Latin *fatum* 'that which has been spoken', from *fari* 'speak'.

fateful • adjective having far-reaching and typically disastrous consequences.
– DERIVATIVES **fatefully** adverb **fatefulness** noun.

fathead • noun informal a stupid person.

father • noun **1** a male parent. **2** an important figure in the origin and early history of something: *Pasteur, the father of microbiology*. **3** literary a male ancestor. **4** (often as a title or form of address) a priest. **5** (**the Father**) (in Christian belief) the first person of the Trinity; God. • verb be the father of.
– PHRASES **how's your father** Brit. informal sexual intercourse.
– DERIVATIVES **fatherhood** noun **fatherless** adjective.
– ORIGIN Old English.

Father Christmas • noun an imaginary being said to bring presents for children on the night before Christmas Day.

father-in-law • noun (pl. **fathers-in-law**) the father of one's husband or wife.

fatherland • noun a person's native country.

fatherly • adjective referring to a father, especially in being protective and affectionate.
– DERIVATIVES **fatherliness** noun.

Father's Day • noun a day of the year on which fathers are honoured with gifts and greetings cards (in the US and Britain usually the third Sunday in June).

fathom • noun a unit of length equal to six feet (1.8 metres), used in measuring the depth of water. • verb **1** understand after much thought: *I can't fathom him out*. **2** measure the depth of.
– DERIVATIVES **fathomable** adjective **fathomless** adjective.
– ORIGIN Old English, 'something which embraces' (the original measurement was based on the span of a person's outstretched arms).

fatigue • noun **1** extreme tiredness. **2** brittleness in metal or other materials caused by repeated stress. **3** (**fatigues**) loose-fitting clothing of a sort worn by soldiers. **4** (**fatigues**) menial non-military tasks performed by a soldier. • verb (**fatigues**, **fatigued**, **fatiguing**) cause to suffer fatigue.
– ORIGIN from Latin *fatigare* 'tire out', from *ad fatim* 'to bursting, to excess'.

fatso • noun (pl. **fatsoes**) informal, derogatory a fat person.

fatten • verb make or become fat or fatter.

fatty • adjective (**fattier**, **fattiest**) **1** containing a large amount of fat. **2** Medicine involving abnormal deposition of fat. • noun (pl. **fatties**) informal a fat person.

f

Thesaurus

informal pernickety, nit-picking, choosy, picky; *N. Amer. informal* persnickety.
– OPPOSITES lax.

fat • adjective **1** *a fat man* PLUMP, stout, overweight, large, chubby, portly, flabby, paunchy, pot-bellied, beer-bellied, meaty, of ample proportions; obese, corpulent, gross, fleshy; *informal* tubby, roly-poly, beefy, porky, blubbery, chunky; *Brit. informal* podgy, fubsy; *archaic* pursy. **2** *fat bacon* FATTY, greasy, oily, oleaginous; *formal* pinguid. **3** *a fat book* THICK, big, chunky, substantial; long. **4** *(informal) a fat salary* LARGE, substantial, sizeable, considerable; generous, lucrative.
– OPPOSITES thin, lean, small, good.
• noun **1** *whale fat* BLUBBER, fatty tissue, adipose tissue. **2** *he was running to fat* FATNESS, plumpness, stoutness, chubbiness, tubbiness, portliness, podginess, flabbiness; obesity, corpulence; *informal* flab, blubber. **3** *eggs in sizzling fat* COOKING OIL, grease; lard, suet, butter, margarine.

fatal • adjective **1** *a fatal disease* DEADLY, lethal, mortal, death-dealing; terminal, incurable, untreatable, inoperable, malignant; *poetic/literary* deathly. **2** *a fatal mistake* DISASTROUS, devastating, ruinous, catastrophic, calamitous, dire; costly; *formal* grievous.
– OPPOSITES harmless, beneficial.

fatalism • noun PASSIVE ACCEPTANCE, resignation, stoicism; fate.

fatality • noun DEATH, casualty, mortality, victim; fatal accident.

fate • noun **1** *what has fate in store for me?* DESTINY, providence, the stars, chance, luck, serendipity, fortune, kismet, karma. **2** *my fate was in their hands* FUTURE, destiny, outcome, end, lot. **3** *a similar fate would befall other killers* DEATH, demise, end; retribution, sentence. **4** *the Fates will decide* the weird sisters, the Parcae, the Moirai.
• verb *his daughter was fated to face the same problem* BE PREDESTINED, be preordained, be destined, be meant, be doomed; be sure, be certain, be bound, be guaranteed.

fateful • adjective **1** *that fateful day* DECISIVE, critical, crucial, pivotal; momentous, important, key, significant, historic, portentous. **2** *the fateful defeat of 1402* DISASTROUS, ruinous, calamitous, devastating, tragic, terrible.
– OPPOSITES unimportant.

father • noun **1** *his mother and father* MALE PARENT, patriarch, paterfamilias; *informal* dad, daddy, pop, pa, old man; *Brit. informal, dated* pater. **2** *(poetic/literary) the religion of my fathers* ANCESTOR, forefather, forebear, predecessor, antecedent, progenitor, primogenitor. **3** *the father of democracy* ORIGINATOR, initiator, founder, inventor, creator, maker, author, architect. **4** *the city fathers* LEADER, elder, patriarch, official. **5** *our heavenly Father* GOD, Lord (God). **6** *pray for me, Father* PRIEST, pastor, parson, clergyman, cleric, minister, preacher; *informal* reverend, padre.
– RELATED TERMS paternal, patri-.
– OPPOSITES child, mother, descendant.
• verb **1** *he fathered six children* BE THE FATHER OF, sire, bring into the world, spawn, breed; *poetic/literary* beget; *archaic* engender. **2** *he fathered a strand of applied economics* ESTABLISH, institute, originate, initiate, invent, found, create.

fatherland • noun NATIVE LAND, native country, homeland, mother country, motherland, land of one's birth.

fatherly • adjective PATERNAL, fatherlike; protective, supportive, encouraging, affectionate, caring, sympathetic, indulgent.

fathom • verb **1** *Charlie tried to fathom her expression* UNDERSTAND, comprehend, work out, make sense of, grasp, divine, puzzle out, get to the bottom of; interpret, decipher, decode; *informal* make head or tail of, tumble to, crack; *Brit. informal* twig, suss (out), savvy. **2** *fathoming the ocean* MEASURE THE DEPTH OF, sound, plumb; gauge, estimate.

fatigue • noun **1** *his face was grey with fatigue* TIREDNESS, weariness, exhaustion, enervation, prostration. **2** *(Military) kitchen fatigues* MENIAL WORK, drudgery, chores; *informal* skivvying.
– OPPOSITES energy.
• verb *the troops were fatigued* TIRE (OUT), exhaust, wear out, drain, weary, wash out, overtire, prostrate, enervate; *informal* knock out, take it out of, do in, fag out, whack, poop, shatter, bush, wear to a frazzle; *Brit. informal* knacker.
– OPPOSITES invigorate.

fatness • noun PLUMPNESS, stoutness, heaviness, chubbiness, portliness, rotundity, flabbiness, paunchiness; obesity, corpulence; *informal* tubbiness, podginess.
– OPPOSITES thinness.

– DERIVATIVES **fattiness** noun.
fatty acid • noun Chemistry an organic acid whose molecule contains a hydrocarbon chain.
fatuous • adjective silly and pointless.
– DERIVATIVES **fatuity** noun (pl. **fatuities**) **fatuously** adverb **fatuousness** noun.
– ORIGIN Latin *fatuus* 'foolish'.
fatwa /fatwaa/ • noun an authoritative ruling on a point of Islamic law.
– ORIGIN from Arabic, 'decide a point of law'.
faucet /fawsit/ • noun chiefly N. Amer. a tap.
– ORIGIN Old French *fausset*, from Provençal *falsar* 'to bore'.
fault • noun **1** an unattractive or unsatisfactory feature; a defect or mistake. **2** responsibility for an accident or misfortune. **3** (in tennis) a service that infringes the rules. **4** Geology an extended break in a rock formation, marked by the relative displacement and discontinuity of strata. • verb **1** criticize for inadequacy or mistakes. **2** (**be faulted**) Geology be broken by a fault or faults.
– PHRASES **find fault** make an adverse criticism or objection, especially unfairly. —— **to a fault** displaying the specified quality to an excessive extent.
– DERIVATIVES **faultless** adjective **faultlessly** adverb.
– ORIGIN from Latin *fallere* 'deceive'.
faulty • adjective (**faultier**, **faultiest**) having or displaying faults.
– DERIVATIVES **faultily** adverb **faultiness** noun.
faun /fawn/ • noun Roman Mythology a lustful rural god represented as a man with a goat's horns, ears, legs, and tail.
– ORIGIN from the name of the pastoral god *Faunus*.
fauna /fawnə/ • noun the animals of a particular region, habitat, or geological period. Compare with FLORA.
– DERIVATIVES **faunal** adjective.
– ORIGIN Latin, from *Fauna*, a rural goddess and the sister of *Faunus* (see FAUN).
Faustian /fowstiən/ • adjective relating to the German astronomer and necromancer Johann Faust (died *c.*1540), reputed to have sold his soul to the Devil.
faute de mieux /fōt də myö/ • adverb for want of a better alternative.
– ORIGIN French.
Fauve /fōv/ • noun a member of a group of early 20th-century French painters who favoured a vivid expressionistic use of colour.
– DERIVATIVES **fauvism** noun **fauvist** noun & adjective.
– ORIGIN French, 'wild beast', with reference to a remark by the art critic Louis Vauxcelles in 1905.
faux /fō/ • adjective made in imitation; artificial.
– ORIGIN French, 'false'.
faux pas /fō paa/ • noun (pl. same) a social blunder.
– ORIGIN French, 'false step'.
fava bean /faavə/ • noun North American term for BROAD BEAN.
– ORIGIN from Latin *faba* 'bean'.
favela /favellə/ • noun (in Brazil) a shack or shanty town.
– ORIGIN Portuguese.
favour (US **favor**) • noun **1** approval or liking. **2** an act of kindness beyond what is due or usual. **3** overgenerous preferential treatment. **4** (**one's favours**) dated a woman's consent to a man having sexual intercourse with her. **5** archaic a thing such as a badge that is worn as a mark of favour or support. • verb **1** regard or treat with favour. **2** work to the advantage of. **3** (**favour with**) give (something desired) to. **4** informal resemble (a relative) in facial features.
– PHRASES **in favour of 1** to be replaced by. **2** in support or to the advantage of.
– ORIGIN Latin *favor*, from *favere* 'show kindness to'.
favourable (US **favorable**) • adjective **1** expressing approval or consent. **2** to the advantage of someone or something. **3** suggesting a good outcome.
– DERIVATIVES **favourably** adverb.
favourite (US **favorite**) • adjective preferred to all others of the same kind. • noun **1** a favourite person or thing. **2** the competitor thought most likely to win.
favouritism (US **favoritism**) • noun the unfair favouring of one

Thesaurus

fatten • verb **1** *fattening livestock* MAKE FAT/FATTER, feed (up), build up. **2** *we're sending her home to fatten up* PUT ON WEIGHT, gain weight, get heavier, grow fatter, fill out.
fatty • adjective GREASY, oily, fat, oleaginous.
– OPPOSITES lean.
fatuous • adjective SILLY, foolish, stupid, inane, idiotic, vacuous, asinine; pointless, senseless, ridiculous, ludicrous, absurd; *informal* dumb, gormless; *Brit. informal* daft.
– OPPOSITES sensible.
fault • noun **1** *he has his faults* DEFECT, failing, imperfection, flaw, blemish, shortcoming, weakness, frailty, foible, vice. **2** *engineers have located the fault* DEFECT, flaw, imperfection, bug; error, mistake, inaccuracy; *informal* glitch, gremlin. **3** *it was not my fault* RESPONSIBILITY, liability, culpability, blameworthiness, guilt. **4** *don't blame one child for another's faults* MISDEED, wrongdoing, offence, misdemeanour, misconduct, indiscretion, peccadillo, transgression.
– OPPOSITES merit, strength.
• verb *you couldn't fault any of the players* FIND FAULT WITH, criticize, attack, censure, condemn, reproach; complain about, quibble about, moan about; *informal* knock, slam, gripe about, beef about, pick holes in; *Brit. informal* slag off, have a go at, slate.
– PHRASES **at fault** TO BLAME, blameworthy, culpable; responsible, guilty, in the wrong. **to a fault** EXCESSIVELY, unduly, immoderately, overly, needlessly.
fault-finding • noun CRITICISM, captiousness, cavilling, quibbling; complaining, grumbling, carping, moaning; *informal* griping, grousing, bellyaching.
– OPPOSITES praise.
faultless • adjective PERFECT, flawless, without fault, error-free, impeccable, accurate, precise, exact, correct, exemplary.
– OPPOSITES flawed.
faulty • adjective **1** *a faulty electric blanket* MALFUNCTIONING, broken, damaged, defective, not working, out of order; *informal* on the blink, acting up, kaput, bust; *Brit. informal* knackered, playing up, duff; *N. Amer. informal* on the fritz. **2** *her logic is faulty* DEFECTIVE, flawed, unsound, inaccurate, incorrect, erroneous, fallacious, wrong.
– RELATED TERMS dys-.
– OPPOSITES working, sound.
faux pas • noun GAFFE, blunder, mistake, indiscretion, impropriety, solecism; *informal* boo-boo; *Brit. informal* boob; *N. Amer. informal* blooper.
favour • noun **1** *will you do me a favour?* GOOD TURN, service, good deed, (act of) kindness, courtesy. **2** *she looked on him with favour* APPROVAL, approbation, goodwill, kindness, benevolence. **3** *they showed favour to one of the players* FAVOURITISM, bias, partiality, partisanship. **4** *you shall receive the king's favour* PATRONAGE, backing, support, assistance. **5** *(archaic) you shall wear my favours* RIBBON, rosette, badge, token; keepsake, souvenir, memento.
– OPPOSITES disservice, disapproval.
• verb **1** *the party favours electoral reform* ADVOCATE, recommend, approve of, be in favour of, support, back, champion; campaign for, stand up for, press for, lobby for, promote; *informal* plug, push for. **2** *Robyn favours loose clothes* PREFER, go (in) for, choose, opt for, select, pick, plump for, be partial to, like. **3** *father always favoured George* SHOW FAVOURITISM TOWARDS, have a bias towards, think more highly of. **4** *the conditions favoured the other team* BENEFIT, be to the advantage of, help, assist, aid, be of service to, do someone a favour. **5** *he favoured Lucy with a smile* OBLIGE, honour, gratify, humour, indulge. **6** *(informal) Travis favours our father* RESEMBLE, look like, be similar to, bear a resemblance to, remind one of, take after; *informal* be the spitting image of, be a dead ringer for.
– OPPOSITES oppose, dislike, hinder.
– PHRASES **in favour of** ON THE SIDE OF, pro, (all) for, giving support to, approving of, sympathetic to.
favourable • adjective **1** *a favourable assessment of his ability* APPROVING, commendatory, complimentary, flattering, glowing, enthusiastic; good, pleasing, positive; *informal* rave. **2** *conditions are favourable* ADVANTAGEOUS, beneficial, in one's favour, good, right, suitable, fitting, appropriate; propitious, auspicious, promising, encouraging. **3** *a favourable reply* POSITIVE, affirmative, assenting, agreeing, approving; encouraging, reassuring.
– OPPOSITES critical, disadvantageous, negative.
favourably • adverb POSITIVELY, approvingly, sympathetically, enthusiastically, appreciatively.
favoured • adjective PREFERRED, favourite, recommended, chosen, choice.
favourite • adjective *his favourite aunt* BEST-LOVED, most-liked, favoured, dearest; preferred, chosen, choice.
• noun **1** *Brutus was Caesar's favourite* (FIRST) CHOICE, pick, prefer-

person or group at the expense of another.

fawn[1] ● noun **1** a young deer in its first year. **2** a light brown colour.
– ORIGIN Old French *faon*, from Latin *fetus* 'offspring'.

fawn[2] ● verb **1** give a servile display of exaggerated flattery or affection. **2** (of an animal, especially a dog) show slavish devotion.
– DERIVATIVES **fawning** adjective.
– ORIGIN Old English, 'make or be glad'; related to FAIN.

fax ● noun **1** an exact copy of a document made by electronic scanning and transmitted by telecommunications links. **2** the production or transmission of documents in this way. **3** (also **fax machine**) a machine for transmitting and receiving such documents. ● verb **1** send (a document) by fax. **2** contact by fax.
– ORIGIN abbreviation of FACSIMILE.

fay ● noun literary a fairy.
– ORIGIN Old French *fae*, from Latin *fatum* (see FATE).

fayre ● noun pseudo-archaic spelling of FAIR[2].

faze ● verb informal disturb or disconcert.
– ORIGIN from dialect *feeze* 'drive off', from Old English.

FBI ● abbreviation (in the US) Federal Bureau of Investigation.

FC ● abbreviation Football Club.

FCO ● abbreviation (in the UK) Foreign and Commonwealth Office.

FDA ● abbreviation (in the US) Food and Drug Administration.

FE ● abbreviation (in the UK) further education.

Fe ● symbol the chemical element iron.
– ORIGIN from Latin *ferrum*.

fealty /feeəlti/ ● noun historical a feudal tenant's or vassal's sworn loyalty to a lord.
– ORIGIN Old French *feaulte* from Latin *fidelitas* 'fidelity'.

fear ● noun **1** an unpleasant emotion caused by the threat of danger, pain, or harm. **2** the likelihood of something unwelcome happening. ● verb **1** be afraid of. **2** (**fear for**) be anxious about. **3** archaic regard (God) with reverence and awe.
– PHRASES **no fear** Brit. informal used as an emphatic expression of denial or refusal. **put the fear of God in** (or **into**) make very frightened. **without fear or favour** impartially.
– DERIVATIVES **fearless** adjective **fearlessly** adverb **fearlessness** noun.
– ORIGIN Old English, 'danger'.

fearful ● adjective **1** showing or causing fear. **2** informal very great.
– DERIVATIVES **fearfully** adverb **fearfulness** noun.

fearsome ● adjective frightening, especially in appearance.
– DERIVATIVES **fearsomely** adverb.

feart ● adjective Scottish afraid.

feasible ● adjective **1** possible and practical to achieve easily or conveniently. **2** informal likely.
– DERIVATIVES **feasibility** noun **feasibly** adverb.
– USAGE In formal contexts, the use of **feasible** to mean 'likely' or 'probable' should be avoided. This sense, although it has been in use since the 17th century, is regarded as incorrect because it does not relate to the French and Latin origins of the word.
– ORIGIN Old French *faisible*, from Latin *facere* 'do, make'.

feast ● noun **1** a large meal, especially a celebratory one. **2** an annual religious celebration. **3** a day dedicated to a particular saint. ● verb **1** have a feast. **2** (**feast on**) eat large quantities of.
– PHRASES **feast one's eyes on** gaze at with pleasure.
– DERIVATIVES **feaster** noun.
– ORIGIN Latin *festa*, from *festus* 'joyous'.

feast day ● noun a day on which an annual Christian celebration is held.

feat ● noun an achievement requiring great courage, skill, or strength.
– ORIGIN Old French *fait*, from Latin *factum* 'fact'.

feather ● noun any of the flat appendages growing from a bird's skin, consisting of a partly hollow horny shaft fringed with vanes of barbs. ● verb **1** rotate the blades of (a propeller) to less-

f

Thesaurus

ence, pet, darling, the apple of one's eye; *informal* blue-eyed boy, golden boy; *N. Amer. informal* fair-haired boy. **2** *the favourite fell at the first fence* EXPECTED WINNER, front runner.

favouritism ● noun PARTIALITY, partisanship, unfair preference, preferential treatment, favour, prejudice, bias, inequality, unfairness, discrimination.

fawn[1] ● adjective *a fawn carpet* BEIGE, yellowish-brown, pale brown, buff, sand, oatmeal, café au lait, camel, ecru, taupe, stone, mushroom.

fawn[2] ● verb *they were fawning over the President* BE OBSEQUIOUS TO, be sycophantic to, curry favour with, pay court to, play up to, crawl to, ingratiate oneself with, dance attendance on; *informal* suck up to, make up to, be all over; *Austral./NZ informal* smoodge to.

fawning ● adjective OBSEQUIOUS, servile, sycophantic, flattering, ingratiating, unctuous, oleaginous, grovelling, crawling; *informal* bootlicking, smarmy.

fear ● noun **1** *she felt fear at entering the house* TERROR, fright, fearfulness, horror, alarm, panic, agitation, trepidation, dread, consternation, dismay, distress; anxiety, worry, angst, unease, uneasiness, apprehension, apprehensiveness, nervousness, nerves, perturbation, foreboding; *informal* the creeps, the willies, the heebie-jeebies, jitteriness, twitchiness, butterflies (in the stomach), (blue) funk. **2** *she overcame her fears* PHOBIA, aversion, antipathy, dread, bugbear, bogey, nightmare, horror, terror; anxiety, neurosis; *informal* hang-up. **3** *(archaic) the love and fear of God* AWE, wonder, wonderment; reverence, veneration, respect. **4** *there's no fear of me leaving you alone* LIKELIHOOD, likeliness, prospect, possibility, chance, probability; risk, danger.
● verb **1** *she feared her husband* BE AFRAID OF, be fearful of, be scared of, be apprehensive of, dread, live in fear of, be terrified of; be anxious about, worry about, feel apprehensive about. **2** *he fears heights* HAVE A PHOBIA ABOUT, have a horror of, take fright at. **3** *he feared to tell them* BE TOO AFRAID, be too scared, hesitate, dare not. **4** *they feared for his health* WORRY ABOUT, feel anxious about, feel concerned about, have anxieties about. **5** *(archaic) all who fear the Lord* STAND IN AWE OF, revere, reverence, venerate, respect. **6** *I fear that you may be right* SUSPECT, have a (sneaking) suspicion, be inclined to think, be afraid, have a hunch, think it likely.

fearful ● adjective **1** *they are fearful of being overheard* AFRAID, frightened, scared (stiff), scared to death, terrified, petrified; alarmed, panicky, nervy, nervous, tense, apprehensive, uneasy, worried (sick), anxious; *informal* jittery, jumpy; *Brit. informal* in a (blue) funk; *archaic* afeared, affrighted. **2** *the guards were fearful* NERVOUS, trembling, quaking, cowed, daunted; timid, timorous, faint-hearted; *Brit.* nervy; *informal* jittery, jumpy, twitchy, keyed up, in a cold sweat, a bundle of nerves, like a cat on a hot tin roof; *Brit. informal* having kittens, like a cat on hot bricks; *N. Amer. informal* spooky. **3** *a fearful accident* TERRIBLE, dreadful, awful, appalling, frightful, ghastly, horrific, horrible, horrifying, horrendous, terribly bad, shocking, atrocious, abominable, hideous, monstrous, gruesome. **4** *(informal) he was in a fearful hurry* (VERY) GREAT, extreme, real, dreadful; *informal* terrible.

fearfully ● adverb **1** *she opened the door fearfully* APPREHENSIVELY, uneasily, nervously, timidly, timorously, hesitantly, with one's heart in one's mouth. **2** *(informal) Stephanie looked fearfully glamorous* EXTREMELY, exceedingly, exceptionally, remarkably, uncommonly, extraordinarily, tremendously, incredibly, very, really; *Scottish* unco; *informal* awfully, terribly, dreadfully; *Brit.* well, ever so, dead; *N. Amer. informal* real, mighty, awful; *dated* frightfully.

fearless ● adjective BOLD, brave, courageous, intrepid, valiant, valorous, gallant, plucky, lionhearted, heroic, daring, audacious, indomitable, doughty; unafraid, undaunted, unflinching; *informal* gutsy, spunky, ballsy, feisty.
– OPPOSITES timid, cowardly.

fearsome ● adjective FRIGHTENING, horrifying, terrifying, menacing, chilling, spine-chilling, hair-raising, alarming, unnerving, daunting, formidable, forbidding, dismaying, disquieting, disturbing; *informal* scary.

feasible ● adjective PRACTICABLE, practical, workable, achievable, attainable, realizable, viable, realistic, sensible, reasonable, within reason; suitable, possible, expedient, constructive; *informal* doable.
– OPPOSITES impractical.

feast ● noun **1** *a wedding feast* BANQUET, celebration meal, lavish dinner; treat, entertainment; revels, festivities; *informal* blowout, spread; *Brit. informal* nosh-up, beanfeast, bunfight, beano, slap-up meal. **2** *the feast of St Stephen* (RELIGIOUS) FESTIVAL, feast day, saint's day, holy day, holiday. **3** *a feast for the eyes* TREAT, delight, joy, pleasure.
● verb **1** *they feasted on lobster* GORGE ON, dine on, eat one's fill of, overindulge in, binge on; eat, devour, consume, partake of; *informal* stuff one's face with, stuff oneself with, pig oneself on, pig out on. **2** *they feasted the deputation* HOLD A BANQUET FOR, throw a feast/party for, wine and dine, entertain lavishly, regale, treat, fête.

feat ● noun ACHIEVEMENT, accomplishment, attainment, coup, tri-

en the air or water resistance. **2** (**feathered**) covered or decorated with feathers.
– PHRASES **a feather in one's cap** an achievement to be proud of. **feather one's nest** make money illicitly and at someone else's expense.
– DERIVATIVES **feathery** adjective.
– ORIGIN Old English.
feather bed ● noun a bed with a mattress stuffed with feathers. ● verb (**feather-bed**) provide with excessively favourable economic or working conditions.
feather-brained ● adjective silly or absent-minded.
feathering ● noun **1** a bird's plumage. **2** the feathers of an arrow. **3** feather-like markings or structure.
featherweight ● noun **1** a weight in boxing intermediate between bantamweight and lightweight. **2** a person or thing not worth serious consideration.

f

feature ● noun **1** a distinctive attribute or aspect. **2** a part of the face, such as the mouth, making a significant contribution to its overall appearance. **3** a newspaper or magazine article or a broadcast programme devoted to a particular topic. **4** (also **feature film**) a full-length film intended as the main item in a cinema programme. ● verb **1** have as a feature. **2** have as an important actor or participant. **3** be a feature of; take an important part in.
– DERIVATIVES **featured** adjective **featureless** adjective.
– ORIGIN Old French *faiture* 'form', from Latin *factura*, from *frangere* 'to break'.
Feb. ● abbreviation February.
febrifuge /febrifyōōj/ ● noun a medicine used to reduce fever.
– ORIGIN French, from Latin *febris* 'fever' + *fugare* 'drive away'.
febrile /feebrīl/ ● adjective **1** having or showing the symptoms of a fever. **2** having or showing a great deal of nervous excitement.
– ORIGIN Latin *febrilis*, from *febris* 'fever'.
February /febrooəri, febyooəri/ ● noun (pl. **Februaries**) the second month of the year.
– ORIGIN Latin *februarius*, from *februa*, the name of a purification feast held in this month.
feces ● noun US spelling of FAECES.
feckless ● adjective **1** ineffectual; feeble. **2** unthinking and irresponsible.
– DERIVATIVES **fecklessly** adverb **fecklessness** noun.
– ORIGIN from Scots and northern English dialect *feck*, from *effeck*, variant of EFFECT.
feculent /fekyoolənt/ ● adjective of or containing dirt, sediment, or waste matter.
– ORIGIN Latin *faeculentus*, from *faex* 'dregs'.
fecund /fekənd, feek-/ ● adjective highly fertile; able to produce offspring.
– DERIVATIVES **fecundity** noun.
– ORIGIN Latin *fecundus*.
fecundate ● verb **1** archaic fertilize. **2** literary make fruitful.
– DERIVATIVES **fecundation** noun.
Fed ● noun US informal a member of the FBI or other federal agent or official.
fed past and past participle of FEED.
federal ● adjective **1** referring to a system of government in which several states form a unity but remain independent in internal affairs. **2** referring to the central government as distinguished from the separate units constituting a federation. **3** (**Federal**) US historical of the Northern States in the Civil War.
– DERIVATIVES **federalism** noun **federalist** noun & adjective **federally** adverb.
– ORIGIN from Latin *foedus* 'league, covenant'.
Federal Reserve ● noun (in the US) the banking authority that performs the functions of a central bank.
federate ● verb /feddərayt/ (of a number of states or organizations) organize or be organized on a federal basis. ● adjective /feddərət/ relating to such an arrangement.
federation ● noun **1** a federal group of states. **2** an organization within which smaller divisions have some internal autonomy. **3** the action of federating.
fedora /fidorə/ ● noun a soft felt hat with a curled brim and the crown creased lengthways.
– ORIGIN from *Fédora* (1882), a drama written by the French dramatist Victorien Sardou.
fed up ● adjective informal annoyed or bored.
fee ● noun **1** a payment made in exchange for advice or services. **2** a charge made for a privilege such as admission.
– ORIGIN originally denoting an estate held on condition of feudal service: from Old French *feu*, from Latin *feodum*; related to FEUDAL, FIEF.
feeble ● adjective (**feebler**, **feeblest**) **1** lacking physical or mental strength. **2** failing to convince or impress: *a feeble excuse.*
– DERIVATIVES **feebleness** noun **feebly** adverb.
– ORIGIN Old French *fieble*, from Latin *flebilis* 'lamentable', from *flere* 'weep'.
feeble-minded ● adjective **1** foolish; stupid. **2** dated having less than average intelligence.
feed ● verb (past and past part. **fed**) **1** give food to. **2** provide an adequate supply of food for. **3** eat. **4** (**feed on/off**) derive regular nourishment from (a particular substance). **5** supply with material, power, water, etc. **6** pass gradually through a confined space. **7** prompt (an actor) with (a line). ● noun **1** an act of feeding or of being fed. **2** food for domestic animals. **3** a device or pipe for supplying material to a machine. **4** the supply of raw material to a machine or device.
– ORIGIN Old English, related to FOOD.

Thesaurus

umph; undertaking, enterprise, venture, operation, exercise, endeavour, effort, performance, exploit.
feather ● noun PLUME, quill, flight feather, tail feather; *Ornithology* covert, plumule; (**feathers**) plumage, feathering, down.
feature ● noun **1** *a typical feature of French music* CHARACTERISTIC, attribute, quality, property, trait, hallmark, trademark; aspect, facet, factor, ingredient, component, element, theme; peculiarity, idiosyncrasy, quirk. **2** *her delicate features* FACE, countenance, physiognomy; *informal* mug, kisser; *Brit. informal* mush, phiz; *N. Amer. informal* puss, pan; *poetic/literary* visage, lineaments. **3** *she made a feature of her garden sculptures* CENTREPIECE, (special) attraction, highlight, focal point, focus (of attention). **4** *a series of short features* ARTICLE, piece, item, report, story, column, review, commentary, write-up.
● verb **1** *Radio Ulster is featuring a week of live concerts* PRESENT, promote, make a feature of, give prominence to, focus attention on, spotlight, highlight. **2** *she is to feature in a major advertising campaign* STAR, appear, participate, play a part.
febrile ● adjective FEVERISH, hot, burning, flushed, sweating; *informal* having a temperature; *rare* pyretic.
feckless ● adjective USELESS, worthless, incompetent, inept, good-for-nothing, ne'er-do-well; lazy, idle, slothful, indolent, shiftless; *informal* no-good, no-account.
fecund ● adjective FERTILE, fruitful, productive, high-yielding; rich, lush, flourishing, thriving; *formal* fructuous.
– OPPOSITES barren.
federal ● adjective CONFEDERATE, federated, federative; combined, allied, united, amalgamated, integrated.
federate ● verb CONFEDERATE, combine, unite, unify, merge, amalgamate, integrate, join (up), band together, team up.
federation ● noun CONFEDERATION, confederacy, federacy, league; combination, alliance, coalition, union, syndicate, guild, consortium, partnership, cooperative, association, amalgamation.
fee ● noun PAYMENT, wage, salary, allowance; price, cost, charge, tariff, rate, amount, sum, figure; (**fees**) remuneration, dues, earnings, pay, *formal* emolument.
feeble ● adjective **1** *he was very old and feeble* WEAK, weakly, weakened, frail, infirm, delicate, sickly, ailing, unwell, poorly, enfeebled, enervated, debilitated, incapacitated, decrepit. **2** *a feeble argument* INEFFECTIVE, ineffectual, inadequate, unconvincing, implausible, unsatisfactory, poor, weak, flimsy. **3** *he's too feeble to stand up to his boss* COWARDLY, craven, faint-hearted, spineless, spiritless, lily-livered; timid, timorous, fearful, unassertive, weak, ineffectual; *informal* wimpy, sissy, sissified, gutless, chicken; *Brit. informal* wet. **4** *a feeble light* FAINT, dim, weak, pale, soft, subdued, muted.
– OPPOSITES strong, brave.
feeble-minded ● adjective **1** *don't be so feeble-minded* STUPID, idiotic, imbecilic, foolish, witless, doltish, empty-headed, vacuous; *informal* half-witted, moronic, dumb, dim, dopey, dozy, dotty, dippy; *Brit. informal* daft. **2** *(dated) the segregation of the feeble-minded* HAVING LEARNING DIFFICULTIES, having special (educational) needs, backward, simple, slow, (mentally) retarded; *dated* educationally subnormal, ESN; *informal* mental.
– OPPOSITES clever, gifted.
feed ● verb **1** *a large family to feed* GIVE FOOD TO, provide (food) for,

feedback ● noun **1** information given in response to a product, performance etc., used as a basis for improvement. **2** the modification or control of a process or system by its results or effects. **3** the return of a fraction of the output of an amplifier, microphone, or other device to the input, causing distortion or a whistling sound.

feeder ● noun **1** a person or animal that eats a particular food or in a particular manner. **2** a thing that feeds or supplies something. **3** a road or rail route linking outlying districts with a main system.

feeding frenzy ● noun **1** an aggressive and competitive group attack on prey by a number of sharks or piranhas. **2** an episode of frantic competition for something.

feedstock ● noun raw material to supply a machine or industrial process.

feel ● verb (past and past part. **felt**) **1** perceive, examine, or search by touch. **2** be aware of through physical sensation. **3** give a sensation of a particular quality when touched: *the wool feels soft.* **4** experience (an emotion or sensation). **5** be emotionally affected by. **6** have a belief, attitude, or impression. **7** consider oneself. **8** (**feel up to**) have the strength or energy to. ● noun **1** an act of feeling. **2** the sense of touch. **3** a sensation given by something when touched. **4** an impression given by something.
– PHRASES **get a feel for** become accustomed to. **have a feel for** have a sensitive appreciation or understanding of. **make oneself** (or **one's presence**) **felt** have a noticeable effect.
– ORIGIN Old English.

feeler ● noun **1** an animal organ such as an antenna that is used for testing things by touch. **2** a tentative proposal intended to ascertain someone's attitude or opinion.

feeler gauge ● noun a gauge consisting of a number of thin blades for measuring narrow gaps or clearances.

feel-good ● adjective informal causing a feeling of happiness and well-being: *a feel-good movie.*

feeling ● noun **1** an emotional state or reaction. **2** (**feelings**) emotional responses or tendencies to respond. **3** strong emotion. **4** the capacity to feel. **5** the sensation of touching or being touched. **6** a belief or opinion. **7** (**feeling for**) a sensitivity to or intuitive understanding of. ● adjective showing emotion or sensitivity.
– DERIVATIVES **feelingly** adverb.

fee simple ● noun (pl. **fees simple**) Law a permanent and absolute tenure of an estate in land with freedom to dispose of it at will.

feet plural of FOOT.

feign ● verb pretend to be affected by (a feeling, state, or injury).
– ORIGIN Old French *feindre*, from Latin *fingere* 'mould, contrive'.

feint[1] /faynt/ ● noun a deceptive or pretended attacking movement, especially in boxing or fencing. ● verb make a feint.
– ORIGIN French *feinte*, from *feindre* 'feign'.

feint[2] /faynt/ ● adjective denoting paper printed with faint lines as a guide for handwriting.
– ORIGIN variant of FAINT.

feisty /fīsti/ ● adjective (**feistier**, **feistiest**) informal **1** spirited and exuberant. **2** touchy and aggressive.
– DERIVATIVES **feistily** adverb **feistiness** noun.
– ORIGIN from obsolete *feist* 'small dog', from *fisting cur* or *hound*, a derogatory term for a lapdog, from *fist* 'break wind'.

felafel /fəlaff'l/ ● noun variant spelling of FALAFEL.

Feldenkrais method /feldənkrīss/ ● noun a system designed to promote bodily and mental well-being through exercises designed to improve flexibility and coordination.
– ORIGIN named after the Russian-born physicist and mechanical engineer Moshe *Feldenkrais* (1904–84).

feldspar /feldspaar/ (also **felspar**) ● noun a pale rock-forming silicate mineral.
– ORIGIN German *Feldspat* 'field spar'.

felicitations ● plural noun congratulations.

felicitous /fəlissitəss/ ● adjective well chosen or appropriate.
– DERIVATIVES **felicitously** adverb.

felicity ● noun (pl. **felicities**) **1** complete happiness. **2** the ability to express oneself appropriately. **3** a felicitous feature of a work of literature or art.
– ORIGIN Latin *felicitas*, from *felix* 'happy'.

feline /feelīn/ ● adjective referring to a cat or cats. ● noun a cat or other animal of the cat family.

f

Thesaurus

cater for, cook for; suckle, breastfeed, bottle-feed; dated victual. **2** *the baby spends all day feeding* EAT, consume food, have a meal, snack; informal nosh, graze. **3** *too many cows feeding in a small area* GRAZE, browse, crop, pasture. **4** *the birds feed on a varied diet* LIVE ON/OFF, exist on, subsist on, eat, consume. **5** *feeding one's self-esteem* STRENGTHEN, fortify, support, bolster, reinforce, boost, fuel, encourage. **6** *she fed secrets to the Russians* SUPPLY, provide, give, deliver, furnish, issue.
● noun **1** *feed for goats and sheep* FODDER, food, forage, pasturage, herbage, provender; formal comestibles. **2** (informal) *they halted for their feed* MEAL, lunch, dinner, supper; Brit. tea; informal nosh; Brit. informal scoff; formal repast.

feel ● verb **1** *she felt the fabric* TOUCH, stroke, caress, fondle, finger, thumb, handle. **2** *she felt a breeze on her back* PERCEIVE, sense, detect, discern, notice, be aware of, be conscious of. **3** *the patient does not feel pain* EXPERIENCE, undergo, go through, bear, endure, suffer. **4** *he felt his way towards the door* GROPE, fumble, scrabble, pick. **5** *feel the temperature of the water* TEST, try (out), assess. **6** *he feels that he should go to the meeting* BELIEVE, think, consider (it right), be of the opinion, hold, maintain, judge; informal reckon, figure. **7** *I feel that he is only biding his time* SENSE, have a (funny) feeling, get the impression, have a hunch, intuit. **8** *the air feels damp* SEEM, appear, strike one as.
● noun **1** *the divers worked by feel* (SENSE OF) TOUCH, tactile sense, feeling (one's way). **2** *the feel of the paper* TEXTURE, surface, finish; weight, thickness, consistency, quality. **3** *the feel of a room* ATMOSPHERE, ambience, aura, mood, feeling, air, impression, character, tenor, spirit, flavour; informal vibrations, vibes. **4** *a feel for languages* APTITUDE, knack, flair, bent, talent, gift, faculty, ability.
– PHRASES **feel for** SYMPATHIZE WITH, be sorry for, pity, feel pity for, feel sympathy for, feel compassion for, be moved by; commiserate with, condole with. **feel like** WANT, would like, wish for, desire, fancy, feel in need of, long for; informal yen for, be dying for.

feeler ● noun **1** *the fish has two feelers on its head* ANTENNA, tentacle, tactile/sensory organ; Zoology antennule. **2** *the minister put out feelers* TENTATIVE ENQUIRY/PROPOSAL, advance, approach, overture, probe.

feeling ● noun **1** *assess the fabric by feeling* (SENSE OF) TOUCH, feel, tactile sense, using one's hands. **2** *a feeling of nausea* SENSATION, sense, consciousness. **3** *I had a feeling that I would win* (SNEAKING) SUSPICION, notion, inkling, hunch, funny feeling, feeling in one's bones, fancy, idea; presentiment, premonition; informal gut feeling. **4** *the strength of her feeling* LOVE, affection, fondness, tenderness, warmth, warmness, emotion, sentiment; passion, ardour, desire. **5** *out of touch with public feeling* SENTIMENT, emotion; opinion, attitude, belief, ideas, views. **6** *a rush of feeling* COMPASSION, sympathy, empathy, fellow feeling, concern, solicitude, solicitousness, tenderness, (brotherly) love; pity, sorrow, commiseration. **7** *he had hurt her feelings* SENSIBILITIES, sensitivities, self-esteem, pride. **8** *my feeling is that it is true* OPINION, belief, view, impression, intuition, instinct, hunch, estimation, guess. **9** *a feeling of peace* ATMOSPHERE, ambience, aura, air, feel, mood, impression, spirit, quality, flavour; informal vibrations, vibes. **10** *a remarkable feeling for language* APTITUDE, knack, flair, bent, talent, gift, faculty, ability.
● adjective *a feeling man* SENSITIVE, warm, warm-hearted, tender, tender-hearted, caring, sympathetic, compassionate, understanding, thoughtful.

feign ● verb **1** *she lay still and feigned sleep* SIMULATE, fake, sham, affect, give the appearance of, make a pretence of. **2** *he's not really ill, he's only feigning* PRETEND, put it on, fake, sham, bluff, masquerade, play-act; informal kid.

feigned ● adjective PRETENDED, simulated, affected, artificial, insincere, put-on, fake, false, sham; informal pretend, phoney.
– OPPOSITES sincere.

feint ● noun BLUFF, blind, ruse, deception, subterfuge, hoax, trick, ploy, device, dodge, sham, pretence, cover, smokescreen, distraction, contrivance; informal red herring.

felicitations ● plural noun CONGRATULATIONS, good/best wishes, (kind) regards, blessings, compliments, respects.

felicitous ● adjective **1** *his nickname was particularly felicitous* APT, well chosen, fitting, suitable, appropriate, apposite, pertinent, germane, relevant. **2** *the room's only felicitous feature* FAVOURABLE, advantageous, good, pleasing.
– OPPOSITES inappropriate, unfortunate.

felicity ● noun **1** *domestic felicity* HAPPINESS, joy, joyfulness, joyousness, bliss, delight, cheerfulness; contentedness, satisfaction, pleasure. **2** *David expressed his feelings with his customary felicity*

– ORIGIN Latin *felinus*, from *feles* 'cat'.
fell[1] past of FALL.
fell[2] ● verb **1** cut down (a tree). **2** knock down. **3** stitch down (the edge of a seam) to lie flat.
– DERIVATIVES **feller** noun.
– ORIGIN Old English, related to FALL.
fell[3] ● noun a hill or stretch of high moorland, especially in northern England.
– ORIGIN Old Norse, 'hill'.
fell[4] ● adjective literary of terrible evil or ferocity.
– PHRASES **in** (or **at**) **one fell swoop** all in one go. [ORIGIN from Shakespeare's *Macbeth* (IV. iii. 219).]
– ORIGIN Old French *fel*, from *felon* 'wicked, a wicked person'.
fellatio /fəlayshiō/ ● noun oral stimulation of a man's penis.
– DERIVATIVES **fellate** verb.
– ORIGIN Latin, from *fellare* 'to suck'.
felloes /fellōz/ (also **fellies** /felliz/) ● plural noun the outer rim of a wheel, to which the spokes are fixed.
– ORIGIN Old English.
fellow ● noun **1** informal a man or boy. **2** a person in the same position or otherwise associated with another. **3** a thing of the same kind as or otherwise associated with another. **4** a member of a learned society. **5** Brit. an incorporated senior member of a college. ● adjective sharing a particular activity, quality, or condition: *a fellow sufferer*.
– ORIGIN Old English, 'a person who lays down money in a joint enterprise', from Old Norse, 'property, money'.
fellow feeling ● noun sympathy based on shared experiences.
fellowship ● noun **1** friendliness and companionship based on shared interests. **2** a group of people meeting to pursue a shared interest or aim. **3** the status of a fellow of a college or society.
fellow-traveller ● noun a non-member of the Communist Party who nevertheless sympathizes with its policies.
– DERIVATIVES **fellow-travelling** adjective.
felon /fellən/ ● noun a person who has committed a felony.
– ORIGIN Old French, 'wicked, a wicked person', from Latin *fello*.
felony ● noun (pl. **felonies**) a crime, typically one involving violence, regarded in the US and other judicial systems as more serious than a misdemeanour.
– DERIVATIVES **felonious** adjective **feloniously** adverb.
felsic /felsik/ ● adjective referring to a group of light-coloured minerals including feldspar and quartz. Often contrasted with MAFIC.
– ORIGIN from FELDSPAR + SILICA.
felspar /felspaar/ ● noun variant spelling of FELDSPAR.
felt[1] ● noun cloth made by rolling and pressing wool or another suitable textile accompanied by the application of moisture or heat, which causes the fibres to mat together. ● verb **1** mat together or become matted. **2** cover with felt.
– ORIGIN Old English, related to FILTER.
felt[2] past and past participle of FEEL.
felt-tip pen (also **felt-tipped pen**) ● noun a pen with a writing point made of felt or tightly packed fibres.
felucca /felukkə/ ● noun a small boat propelled by oars or sails, used on the Nile and formerly more widely in the Mediterranean region.
– ORIGIN Arabic.
female ● adjective **1** referring to the sex that can bear offspring or produce eggs. **2** relating to or characteristic of women or female animals. **3** (of a plant or flower) having a pistil but no stamens. **4** (of a fitting) manufactured hollow so that a corresponding male part can be inserted. ● noun a female person, animal, or plant.
– DERIVATIVES **femaleness** noun.
– ORIGIN Latin *femella*, from *femina* 'a woman'.
female circumcision ● noun (among some peoples) the action or practice of cutting off the clitoris and sometimes the labia of girls or young women.
feminine ● adjective **1** having qualities traditionally associated with women, especially delicacy and prettiness. **2** female. **3** Grammar referring to a gender of nouns and adjectives, conventionally regarded as female. ● noun (**the feminine**) the female sex or gender.
– DERIVATIVES **femininely** adverb **femininity** noun.
– ORIGIN Latin *femininus*, from *femina* 'woman'.
feminism ● noun the advocacy of women's rights on the grounds of sexual equality.
– DERIVATIVES **feminist** noun & adjective.
feminize (also **feminise**) ● verb make more feminine or female.
– DERIVATIVES **feminization** noun.
femme /fem/ (also **fem**) ● noun informal a lesbian who takes a traditionally feminine sexual role.
– ORIGIN French, 'woman'.
femme fatale /fam fətaal/ ● noun (pl. **femmes fatales** pronunc. same) an attractive and seductive woman.
– ORIGIN French, 'disastrous woman'.
femto- ● combining form denoting a factor of one thousand million millionth (10^{-15}).
– ORIGIN from Danish or Norwegian *femten* 'fifteen'.
femur /feemər/ ● noun (pl. **femurs** or **femora** /femmərə/) Anatomy the bone of the thigh or upper hindlimb.
– DERIVATIVES **femoral** adjective,
– ORIGIN Latin, 'thigh'.
fen[1] ● noun **1** a low and marshy or frequently flooded area of land. **2** (**the Fens**) flat low-lying areas of Lincolnshire, Cambridgeshire, and Norfolk, formerly marshland but now largely drained.
– DERIVATIVES **fenny** adjective.
– ORIGIN Old English.
fen[2] ● noun (pl. same) a monetary unit of China, equal to one hundredth of a yuan.
– ORIGIN Chinese, 'a hundredth part'.
fence ● noun **1** a barrier enclosing an area, typically consisting

Thesaurus

ELOQUENCE, aptness, appropriateness, suitability, suitableness, applicability, fitness, relevance, pertinence.
– OPPOSITES unhappiness, inappropriateness.
feline ● adjective *she moved with feline grace* CATLIKE, graceful, sleek, sinuous.
● noun *her pet feline* CAT, kitten; *informal* puss, pussy (cat); *Brit. informal* moggie, mog; *archaic* grimalkin.
fell[1] ● verb **1** *all the dead sycamores had to be felled* CUT DOWN, chop down, hack down, saw down, clear. **2** *she felled him with one punch* KNOCK DOWN/OVER, knock to the ground, strike down, bring down, bring to the ground, prostrate; knock out, knock unconscious; *informal* deck, floor, flatten, down, lay out, KO; *Brit. informal* knock for six.
fell[2] ● adjective *(poetic/literary) a fell intent* MURDEROUS, savage, violent, vicious, fierce, ferocious, barbarous, barbaric, monstrous, cruel, ruthless; *archaic* sanguinary.
– PHRASES **at/in one fell swoop** ALL AT ONCE, together, at the same time, in one go.
fellow ● noun **1** *(informal) he's a decent sort of fellow* MAN, boy; person, individual, soul; *informal* guy, geezer, lad, fella, character, customer, devil, bastard; *Brit. informal* chap, bloke; *N. Amer. informal* dude, hombre; *Austral./NZ informal* digger; *informal, dated* body, dog, cove. **2** *(informal) she longed to have a fellow* BOYFRIEND, lover. **3** *he exchanged glances with his fellows* COMPANION, friend, comrade, partner, associate, co-worker, colleague; *informal* chum, pal, buddy; *Brit. informal* mate. **4** *some peasants were wealthier than their fellows* PEER, equal, contemporary, confrère; *archaic* compeer.
– PHRASES **fellow feeling** SYMPATHY, empathy, feeling, compassion, care, concern, solicitude, solicitousness, warmth, tenderness, (brotherly) love; pity, sorrow, commiseration.
fellowship ● noun **1** *a community bound together in fellowship* COMPANIONSHIP, companionability, sociability, comradeship, camaraderie, friendship, mutual support; togetherness, solidarity; *informal* chumminess, palliness; *Brit. informal* mateyness. **2** *the church fellowship* ASSOCIATION, society, club, league, union, guild, affiliation, alliance, fraternity, brotherhood, sorority, sodality.
female ● adjective *typical female attributes* FEMININE, womanly, ladylike; *archaic* feminal.
● noun *the author was a female.* See WOMAN sense 1.
– RELATED TERMS gynaeco-.
– OPPOSITES male.
feminine ● adjective **1** *a very feminine young woman* WOMANLY, ladylike, girlish, girly; *archaic* feminal. **2** *he seemed slightly feminine* EFFEMINATE, womanish, unmanly, effete; *informal* sissy, wimpy, limp-wristed.
– OPPOSITES masculine, manly.
femininity ● noun WOMANLINESS, feminineness, womanly/feminine qualities.
feminism ● noun THE WOMEN'S MOVEMENT, the feminist movement, women's liberation, female emancipation, women's rights; *informal*

of posts connected by wire, wood, etc. **2** a large upright obstacle in steeplechasing, showjumping, or cross-country. **3** informal a dealer in stolen goods. **4** a guard or guide on a plane or other tool. • **verb 1** surround or protect with a fence. **2** informal deal in (stolen goods). **3** practise the sport of fencing.
– PHRASES **sit on the fence** informal avoid making a decision or commitment.
– DERIVATIVES **fencer** noun.
– ORIGIN shortening of DEFENCE.

fencing • **noun 1** the sport of fighting with blunted swords in order to score points. **2** a series of fences. **3** material for making fences.

fend • **verb 1** (**fend for oneself**) look after and provide for oneself. **2** (**fend off**) defend oneself from (an attack or attacker).
– ORIGIN shortening of DEFEND.

fender • **noun 1** a low frame bordering a fireplace to keep in falling coals. **2** a cushioning device hung over a ship's side to protect it against impact. **3** N. Amer. the mudguard or area around the wheel well of a vehicle.

fenestration /fennistraysh'n/ • **noun 1** Architecture the arrangement of windows in a building. **2** Medicine a surgical operation in which a new opening is formed in the labyrinth of the inner ear to improve hearing.
– ORIGIN Latin, from *fenestra* 'window'.

feng shui /fəng shway/ • **noun** (in Chinese thought) a system of laws considered to govern spatial arrangement in relation to the flow of energy, and whose effects are taken into account when designing buildings.
– ORIGIN from the Chinese words for 'wind' and 'water'.

Fenian /feeniən/ • **noun 1** a member of the Irish Republican Brotherhood, a 19th-century revolutionary nationalist organization. **2** informal, offensive (chiefly in Northern Ireland) a Protestant name for a Catholic.
– ORIGIN from an Old Irish name of an ancient Irish people.

fennel /fenn'l/ • **noun** an aromatic yellow-flowered plant, with feathery leaves used as herbs or eaten as a vegetable.
– ORIGIN Latin *faeniculum*, from *faenum* 'hay'.

fenugreek /fenyoogreek/ • **noun** a white-flowered plant of the pea family, with aromatic seeds that are used as a spice.
– ORIGIN from Latin *faenum graecum* 'Greek hay' (the Romans used the dried plant as fodder).

feral /feerəl, ferrəl/ • **adjective 1** (of an animal or plant) in a wild state, especially after having been domesticated. **2** resembling a wild animal.
– ORIGIN from Latin *fera* 'wild animal'.

Fermat's last theorem • **noun** Mathematics the theorem (proved in 1995) that if n is an integer greater than 2, the equation $x^n + y^n = z^n$ has no positive integral solutions.
– ORIGIN named after the French mathematician Pierre de *Fermat* (1601–65).

ferment • **verb** /fərment/ **1** undergo or cause to undergo fermentation. **2** stir up (disorder). • **noun** /ferment/ **1** agitation and social unrest. **2** dated a fermenting agent or enzyme.
– DERIVATIVES **fermentable** adjective **fermenter** noun.
– ORIGIN from Latin *fermentum* 'yeast', from *fervere* 'to boil'.

fermentation • **noun** the chemical breakdown of a substance by bacteria, yeasts, or other micro-organisms, especially that involved in the making of beers, wines, and spirits.
– DERIVATIVES **fermentative** adjective.

fermion /fermion/ • **noun** Physics a subatomic particle, such as a nucleon, which has a spin of a half integer.
– ORIGIN named after the Italian physicist Enrico *Fermi* (1901–54).

fermium /fermiəm/ • **noun** an unstable radioactive chemical element made by high-energy atomic collisions.

fern • **noun** (pl. same or **ferns**) a flowerless plant which has feathery or leafy fronds and reproduces by spores released from the undersides of the fronds.
– DERIVATIVES **fernery** noun (pl. **ferneries**) **ferny** adjective.
– ORIGIN Old English.

ferocious • **adjective 1** savagely fierce, cruel, or violent. **2** informal very great; extreme.
– DERIVATIVES **ferociously** adverb **ferociousness** noun **ferocity** noun.
– ORIGIN from Latin *ferox* 'fierce'.

-ferous (usu. **-iferous**) • **combining form** having, bearing, or containing (a specified thing): *Carboniferous*.
– ORIGIN from Latin *-fer* 'producing'.

ferret /ferrit/ • **noun 1** a domesticated albino or brown polecat, used for catching rabbits. **2** informal a search. • **verb** (**ferreted**, **ferreting**) **1** hunt with ferrets. **2** search for something in a place or container. **3** (**ferret out**) investigate assiduously.
– DERIVATIVES **ferreter** noun **ferrety** adjective.
– ORIGIN Old French *fuiret*, from Latin *fur* 'thief'.

ferric /ferrik/ • **adjective** Chemistry of iron with a valency of three.
– ORIGIN from Latin *ferrum* 'iron'.

Ferris wheel • **noun** a fairground ride consisting of a giant vertical revolving wheel with passenger cars suspended on its outer edge.
– ORIGIN named after the American engineer George W. G. *Ferris* (1859–96).

ferrite /ferrīt/ • **noun** a magnetic oxide of iron and one or more other metals.

ferroconcrete • **noun** concrete reinforced with steel.

ferroelectric • **adjective** Physics displaying or denoting permanent electric polarization which varies in strength with the applied electric field.
– DERIVATIVES **ferroelectricity** noun.

ferromagnetism • **noun** Physics strong, persistent magnetism of

Thesaurus

women's lib.

femme fatale • **noun** SEDUCTRESS, temptress, siren; *informal* vamp.

fen • **noun** MARSH, marshland, salt marsh, fenland, wetland, (peat) bog, swamp, swampland; *N. Amer.* moor.

fence • **noun 1** *a gap in the fence* BARRIER, paling, railing, enclosure, barricade, stockade, palisade. **2** *(informal) a fence dealing mainly in jewellery* RECEIVER (OF STOLEN GOODS), dealer.
• **verb 1** *they fenced off many acres* ENCLOSE, surround, circumscribe, encircle, circle, encompass; *poetic/literary* engirdle; *archaic* compass. **2** *he fenced in his chickens* CONFINE, pen in, coop up, shut in/up, separate off; enclose, surround; *N. Amer.* corral. **3** *he fences as a hobby* FIGHT WITH SWORDS, sword-fight. **4** *the man fenced but Jim persisted* BE EVASIVE, be vague, be non-committal, equivocate, prevaricate, stall, vacillate, hedge, pussyfoot around, sidestep the issue; *informal* duck the question/issue, shilly-shally; *Brit. informal* waffle; *rare* palter.
– PHRASES **(sitting) on the fence** *(informal)* UNDECIDED, uncommitted, uncertain, unsure, vacillating, wavering, dithering, hesitant, doubtful, ambivalent, in two minds, in a quandary; neutral, impartial, non-partisan, open-minded; *Brit.* humming and hawing.

fend • **verb** *they were unable to fend off the invasion* WARD OFF, head off, stave off, hold off, repel, repulse, resist, fight off, defend oneself against, prevent, stop, block, intercept, hold back.
– PHRASES **fend for oneself** TAKE CARE OF ONESELF, look after oneself, provide for oneself, shift for oneself, manage by oneself, cope alone, stand on one's own two feet.

feral • **adjective 1** *feral dogs* WILD, untamed, undomesticated, untrained. **2** *a feral snarl* FIERCE, ferocious, vicious, savage, predatory, menacing, bloodthirsty.
– OPPOSITES tame, pet.

ferment • **verb 1** *the beer continues to ferment* UNDERGO FERMENTATION, brew; effervesce, fizz, foam, froth. **2** *an environment that ferments disorder* CAUSE, bring about, give rise to, generate, engender, spawn, instigate, provoke, incite, excite, stir up, whip up, foment; *poetic/literary* beget, enkindle.
• **noun 1** *a ferment of revolutionary upheaval* FEVER, furore, frenzy, tumult, storm, rumpus; turmoil, upheaval, unrest, disquiet, uproar, agitation, turbulence, disruption, confusion, disorder, chaos, mayhem; *informal* kerfuffle, hoo-ha, to-do; *Brit. informal* aggro. **2** *(dated) the action of a ferment* FERMENTING AGENT/SUBSTANCE, enzyme; yeast, bacteria, leaven.

ferocious • **adjective 1** *ferocious animals* FIERCE, savage, wild, predatory, aggressive, dangerous. **2** *a ferocious attack* BRUTAL, vicious, violent, bloody, barbaric, savage, sadistic, ruthless, cruel, merciless, bloodthirsty, murderous; *poetic/literary* fell; *archaic* sanguinary. **3** *(informal) a ferocious headache* INTENSE, strong, powerful, fierce, severe, extreme, acute, unbearable; *informal* hellish.
– OPPOSITES gentle, mild.

ferocity • **noun** SAVAGERY, brutality, barbarity, fierceness, violence, bloodthirstiness, murderousness; ruthlessness, cruelty, pitilessness, mercilessness, heartlessness.

ferret • **verb 1** *she ferreted in her handbag* RUMMAGE, feel about/around, grope around, forage around, fish about/around, poke about/around; search through, hunt through, rifle through; *Austral./NZ informal* fossick through. **2** *ferreting out misdemeanours* UNEARTH, uncover, discover, detect, search out, bring to light,

the kind possessed by iron.
– DERIVATIVES **ferromagnetic** adjective.

ferrous /ferrəss/ ● adjective **1** (chiefly of metals) containing iron. **2** Chemistry of iron with a valency of two.

ferruginous /fəro͞ojinəss/ ● adjective **1** containing iron oxides or rust. **2** rust-coloured.
– ORIGIN from Latin *ferrugo* 'rust, dark red'.

ferrule /ferro͞ol/ ● noun **1** a ring or cap which strengthens the end of a handle, stick, or tube. **2** a metal band strengthening or forming a joint.
– ORIGIN Old French *virelle*, from Latin *viriae* 'bracelets'.

ferry ● noun (pl. **ferries**) a boat or ship for conveying passengers and goods, especially as a regular service. ● verb (**ferries, ferried**) convey by ferry or other transport, especially on short, regular trips.
– DERIVATIVES **ferryman** noun.
– ORIGIN Old Norse, related to FARE.

f

fertile ● adjective **1** (of soil or land) producing or capable of producing abundant vegetation or crops. **2** (of a person, animal, or plant) able to conceive young or produce seed. **3** productive in generating new ideas.
– DERIVATIVES **fertility** noun.
– ORIGIN Latin *fertilis*, from *ferre* 'to bear'.

fertilize (also **fertilise**) ● verb **1** cause (an egg, female animal, or plant) to develop a new individual by introducing male reproductive material. **2** add fertilizer to (soil or land).
– DERIVATIVES **fertilization** noun.

fertilizer (also **fertiliser**) ● noun a chemical or natural substance added to soil to increase its fertility.

fervent /ferv'nt/ ● adjective intensely passionate.
– DERIVATIVES **fervency** noun **fervently** adverb.
– ORIGIN from Latin *fervere* 'boil'.

fervid ● adjective intensely or excessively enthusiastic.
– DERIVATIVES **fervidly** adverb.
– ORIGIN Latin *fervidus*, from *fervere* 'to boil'.

fervour (US **fervor**) ● noun intense and passionate feeling.

fescue /fesky͞o/ ● noun a narrow-leaved grass, some kinds of which are valuable for pasture and fodder.
– ORIGIN Old French *festu*, from Latin *festuca* 'stalk, straw'.

festal ● adjective relating to a festival; festive.
– ORIGIN from Latin *festa* 'feast'.

fester ● verb **1** (of a wound or sore) become septic. **2** (of food or rubbish) become rotten. **3** (of a negative feeling or a problem) intensify, especially through neglect. **4** deteriorate physically and mentally in isolated inactivity.
– ORIGIN from Old French *festre*, from Latin *fistula* 'reed, fistula'.

festival ● noun **1** a day or period of celebration, typically for religious reasons. **2** an organized series of concerts, films, etc.
– ORIGIN Latin *festivalis*, from *festa* 'feast'.

festive ● adjective **1** relating to a festival. **2** jovially celebratory.
– DERIVATIVES **festively** adverb **festiveness** noun.

festivity ● noun (pl. **festivities**) **1** joyful and exuberant celebration. **2** (**festivities**) celebratory activities or events.

festoon /festo͞on/ ● noun **1** an ornamental chain or garland of flowers, leaves, or ribbons, hung in a curve. **2** a carved or moulded ornament representing a festoon. ● verb decorate with festoons or other decorations.
– ORIGIN Italian *festone* 'festive ornament'.

Festschrift /festshrift/ ● noun (pl. **Festschriften** or **Festschrifts**) a collection of writings published in honour of a scholar.
– ORIGIN German, from *Fest* 'celebration' + *Schrift* 'writing'.

feta /fettə/ (also **feta cheese**) ● noun a white salty Greek cheese made from the milk of ewes or goats.
– ORIGIN modern Greek *pheta*.

fetal /feet'l/ ● adjective **1** relating to a fetus. **2** referring to a posture characteristic of a fetus, with the limbs folded in front of the body.

fetch ● verb **1** go for and bring back. **2** cause to come to a place. **3** achieve (a particular price) when sold. **4** (**fetch up**) informal arrive or come to rest. **5** informal inflict (a blow) on. **6** archaic bring forth (blood or tears). ● noun an act of fetching.
– PHRASES **fetch and carry** run backwards and forwards bringing things to someone in a servile way.
– DERIVATIVES **fetcher** noun.
– ORIGIN Old English.

fetching ● adjective attractive.
– DERIVATIVES **fetchingly** adverb.

fête /fayt/ ● noun **1** Brit. an outdoor public function to raise funds for a charity or institution, typically involving entertainment and the sale of goods. **2** chiefly N. Amer. a celebration or festival. ● verb honour or entertain lavishly.
– ORIGIN French, from Latin *festa* 'a feast'.

fetid /fettid, feetid/ (also **foetid**) ● adjective smelling very un-

Thesaurus

track down, dig up, root out, nose out; *informal* get wise to; *Brit. informal* rumble.

ferry ● noun *the ferry from Dover to Calais* PASSENGER BOAT/SHIP, ferry boat, car ferry; ship, boat, vessel; *dated* packet (boat).
● verb **1** *ferrying passengers to and from the Continent* TRANSPORT, convey, carry, ship, run, take, bring, shuttle. **2** *the boat ferried hourly across the river* GO BACK AND FORTH, shuttle, run.

fertile ● adjective **1** *the soil is fertile* FECUND, fruitful, productive, high-yielding, rich, lush; *formal* fructuous. **2** *fertile couples* ABLE TO CONCEIVE, able to have children; *technical* fecund. **3** *a fertile brain* IMAGINATIVE, inventive, innovative, creative, visionary, original, ingenious; productive, prolific.
– OPPOSITES barren.

fertilization ● noun CONCEPTION, impregnation, insemination; pollination, propagation.

fertilize ● verb **1** *the field was fertilized* ADD FERTILIZER TO, feed, mulch, compost, manure, dress, top-dress. **2** *these orchids are fertilized by insects* POLLINATE, cross-pollinate, cross-fertilize.

fertilizer ● noun MANURE, plant food, compost, dressing, top dressing, dung.

fervent ● adjective IMPASSIONED, passionate, intense, vehement, ardent, sincere, fervid, heartfelt; enthusiastic, zealous, fanatical, wholehearted, avid, eager, keen, committed, dedicated, devout; *informal* mad keen; *poetic/literary* perfervid.
– OPPOSITES apathetic.

fervid ● adjective FERVENT, ardent, passionate, impassioned, intense, vehement, wholehearted, heartfelt, sincere, earnest; *poetic/literary* perfervid.

fervour ● noun PASSION, ardour, intensity, zeal, vehemence, emotion, warmth, earnestness, avidity, eagerness, keenness, enthusiasm, excitement, animation, vigour, energy, fire, spirit, zest, fervency, ardency.

fester ● verb **1** *his deep wound festered* SUPPURATE, become septic, form pus, weep; *Medicine* maturate, be purulent; *archaic* rankle. **2** *rubbish festered* ROT, moulder, decay, decompose, putrefy, go bad/off, spoil, deteriorate. **3** *their resentment festered* RANKLE, eat/gnaw away at one's mind, brew, smoulder.

festival ● noun **1** *the town's autumn festival* FÊTE, fair, gala (day), carnival, fiesta, jamboree, celebrations, festivities, eisteddfod. **2** *fasting precedes the festival* HOLY DAY, feast day, saint's day, commemoration, day of observance.

festive ● adjective JOLLY, merry, joyous, joyful, happy, jovial, light-hearted, cheerful, jubilant, convivial, high-spirited, mirthful, uproarious; celebratory, holiday, carnival; Christmassy; *archaic* festal.

festivity ● noun **1** *food plays an important part in the festivities* CELEBRATION, festival, entertainment, party, jamboree; merrymaking, feasting, revelry, jollification; revels, fun and games; *informal* bash, shindig, shindy; *Brit. informal* rave-up, knees-up, beanfeast, bunfight, beano. **2** *the festivity of the Last Night of the Proms* JOLLITY, merriment, gaiety, cheerfulness, cheer, joyfulness, jubilance, conviviality, high spirits, revelry.

festoon ● noun *festoons of paper flowers* GARLAND, chain, lei, swathe, swag, loop.
● verb *the room was festooned with streamers* DECORATE, adorn, ornament, trim, deck (out), hang, loop, drape, swathe, garland, wreathe, bedeck; *informal* do up/out, get up, trick out; *poetic/literary* bedizen, furbelow.

fetch ● verb **1** *he went to fetch a doctor* (GO AND) GET, go for, call for, summon, pick up, collect, bring, carry, convey, transport. **2** *the land could fetch a million pounds* SELL FOR, bring in, raise, realize, yield, make, command, cost, be priced at; *informal* go for, set one back, pull in; *Brit. informal* knock someone back.
– PHRASES **fetch up** (*informal*) *the boat fetched up on a remote island* END UP, finish up, turn up, appear, materialize, find itself; *informal* wind up, show up.

fetching ● adjective ATTRACTIVE, appealing, sweet, pretty, lovely, delightful, charming, prepossessing, captivating, enchanting, irresistible; *Scottish & N. English* bonny; *informal* divine, heavenly; *Brit. informal* fit, smashing; *archaic* comely, fair.

pleasant.
– ORIGIN Latin *fetidus*, from *fetere* 'to stink'.

fetish • noun **1** an inanimate object worshipped for its supposed magical powers. **2** a form of sexual desire in which gratification is focused abnormally on an object, part of the body, or activity. **3** a course of action to which one has an excessive and irrational commitment.
– DERIVATIVES **fetishism** noun **fetishist** noun **fetishistic** adjective **fetishization** (also **-isation**) noun **fetishize** (also **fetishise**) verb.
– ORIGIN French *fétiche*, from Latin *facticius* 'made by art'.

fetlock • noun a joint of a horse's or other quadruped's leg between the knee and the hoof.
– ORIGIN Germanic, related to FOOT.

fetor /feetər/ • noun a strong, foul smell.
– ORIGIN Latin, from *fetere* 'to stink'.

fetter • noun **1** a chain or shackle placed around a prisoner's ankles. **2** a restraint or check. • verb **1** restrain with fetters. **2** (**be fettered**) be restricted.
– ORIGIN Old English.

fettle • noun condition: *in fine fettle.*
– ORIGIN Old English, 'strip of material'.

fettuccine /fettoocheeni/ (also **fettucini**) • plural noun pasta made in ribbons.
– ORIGIN Italian, 'little ribbons'.

fetus /feetəss/ (Brit. (in non-technical use) also **foetus**) • noun (pl. **fetuses**) an unborn or unhatched offspring of a mammal, in particular an unborn human more than eight weeks after conception.
– ORIGIN Latin, 'pregnancy, childbirth, offspring'.

feud • noun **1** a prolonged and bitter quarrel or dispute. **2** a state of prolonged mutual hostility and violence. • verb take part in a feud.
– ORIGIN Old French *feide* 'hostility'.

feudal • adjective relating or referring to feudalism.
– ORIGIN Latin *feudalis*, from *feodum* 'fee'.

feudalism • noun the dominant social system in medieval Europe, in which the nobility held lands from the Crown in exchange for military service, and vassals were tenants of and protected by the nobles.

feuilleton /föiton/ • noun a part of a newspaper or magazine devoted to fiction, criticism, or light literature.
– ORIGIN French, *feuillet* 'little leaf'.

fever • noun **1** an abnormally high body temperature, usually accompanied by shivering, headache, and in severe instances, delirium. **2** a state of nervous excitement or agitation.
– DERIVATIVES **feverish** adjective **feverishly** adverb **feverishness** noun.
– ORIGIN Old French *fievre* or Latin *febris*.

fevered • adjective **1** having or showing the symptoms of fever. **2** nervously excited or agitated: *my fevered imagination.*

feverfew • noun an aromatic plant with feathery leaves and daisy-like flowers, used as a herbal remedy for headaches.
– ORIGIN Latin *febrifuga*, from *febris* 'fever' + *fugare* 'drive away'.

fever pitch • noun a state of extreme excitement.

few • determiner, pronoun, & adjective **1** (**a few**) a small number of. **2** not many. • noun (**the few**) a select minority.
– PHRASES **few and far between** scarce. **a good few** Brit. a fairly large number of. **no fewer than** a surprisingly large number of. **not a few** a considerable number. **quite a few** a fairly large number. **some few** some but not many.
– USAGE **Fewer**, the comparative form of **few**, should be used with plural nouns, as in *there are fewer people here today*; use **less** with nouns denoting things that cannot be counted, as in *there is less blossom on this tree*. The use of **less** with a plural noun (*less people*) is incorrect in standard English.
– ORIGIN Old English.

fey • adjective **1** unworldly and vague. **2** having clairvoyant powers.
– ORIGIN Old English.

fez • noun (pl. **fezzes**) a flat-topped conical red hat, worn by men in some Muslim countries.
– ORIGIN Turkish *fes*, named after the city of *Fez* in Morocco.

ff • abbreviation Music fortissimo.

ff. • abbreviation **1** folios. **2** following pages.

fiancé /fionsay/ • noun (fem. **fiancée** pronunc. same) a person to whom another is engaged to be married.
– ORIGIN French, from *fiancer* 'betroth'.

fiasco /fiaskō/ • noun (pl. **fiascos**) a ludicrous or humiliating failure.
– ORIGIN Italian, 'bottle, flask', used in the phrase *far fiasco*, literally 'make a bottle', figuratively 'fail in a performance'.

fiat /fiat/ • noun an official order or authorization.
– ORIGIN Latin, 'let it be done'.

fib • noun a trivial lie. • verb (**fibbed, fibbing**) tell a fib.
– DERIVATIVES **fibber** noun.
– ORIGIN perhaps from obsolete *fible-fable* 'nonsense', a reduplication of FABLE.

fiber etc. • noun US spelling of FIBRE etc.

Fibonacci series • noun Mathematics a series of numbers in which each number (**Fibonacci number**) is the sum of the two preceding numbers (e.g. the series 1, 1, 2, 3, 5, 8, etc.).
– ORIGIN named after the Italian mathematician Leonardo *Fibo-*

f

Thesaurus

fête • noun (*Brit.*) GALA (DAY), bazaar, fair, festival, fiesta, jubilee, carnival; fund-raiser, charity event.

fetid • adjective STINKING, smelly, foul-smelling, malodorous, reeking, pungent, acrid, high, rank, foul, noxious; *Brit. informal* niffy, pongy, whiffy, humming; *N. Amer. informal* funky; *poetic/literary* noisome, miasmic, miasmal.
– OPPOSITES fragrant.

fetish • noun **1** *he developed a rubber fetish* FIXATION, obsession, compulsion, mania; weakness, fancy, fascination, fad; *informal* thing, hang-up. **2** *an African fetish* JUJU, talisman, charm, amulet; totem, idol, image, effigy; *archaic* periapt.

fetter • verb **1** *the captive was fettered* SHACKLE, manacle, handcuff, clap in irons, put in chains, chain (up); *informal* cuff; *poetic/literary* enfetter. **2** *these obligations fetter the company's powers* RESTRICT, restrain, constrain, limit; hinder, hamper, impede, obstruct, hamstring, inhibit, check, curb, trammel.

fetters • plural noun SHACKLES, manacles, handcuffs, irons, leg-irons, chains, restraints; *informal* cuffs, bracelets; *historical* bilboes.

fettle • noun SHAPE, trim, (physical) fitness, (state of) health; condition, form, (state of) repair, (working) order; *Brit. informal* nick.

fetus • noun EMBRYO, fertilized egg, unborn baby/child.

feud • noun *tribal feuds* VENDETTA, conflict; rivalry, hostility, enmity, strife, discord; quarrel, argument, falling-out.
• verb *he feuded with his teammates* QUARREL, fight, argue, bicker, squabble, fall out, dispute, clash, differ, be at odds; *informal* scrap.

fever • noun **1** *he developed fever* FEVERISHNESS, high temperature, febrility; *Medicine* pyrexia; *informal* temperature. **2** *a fever of excitement* FERMENT, frenzy, furore; ecstasy, rapture. **3** *World Cup fever* EXCITEMENT, frenzy, agitation, passion.
– RELATED TERMS febrile.

fevered • adjective **1** *her fevered brow* FEVERISH, febrile, hot, burning; *rare* pyretic. **2** *a fevered imagination* EXCITED, agitated, frenzied, overwrought, fervid.

feverish • adjective **1** *she's really feverish* FEBRILE, fevered, hot, burning; *informal* having a temperature; *rare* pyretic. **2** *feverish excitement* FRENZIED, frenetic, hectic, agitated, excited, restless, nervous, worked up, overwrought, frantic, furious, hysterical, wild, uncontrolled, unrestrained.

few • determiner *police are revealing few details* NOT MANY, hardly any, scarcely any; a small number of, a small amount of, one or two, a handful of; little.
– OPPOSITES many.
• adjective *comforts here are few* SCARCE, scant, meagre, insufficient, in short supply; thin on the ground, few and far between, infrequent, uncommon, rare.
– OPPOSITES plentiful.
– PHRASES **a few** *only a few are prepared to speak up* A SMALL NUMBER, a handful, one or two, a couple, two or three; not many, hardly any.

fiancée, masc. **fiancé** • noun BETROTHED, wife-to-be, husband-to-be, bride-to-be, future wife/husband, prospective spouse; *informal* intended.

fiasco • noun FAILURE, disaster, catastrophe, debacle, shambles, farce, mess, wreck; *informal* flop, washout; *Brit. informal* cock-up; *N. Amer. informal* snafu; *Austral./NZ informal* fizzer.
– OPPOSITES success.

fiat • noun DECREE, edict, order, command, commandment, injunction, proclamation, mandate, dictum, diktat.

fib • noun *you're telling a fib* LIE, untruth, falsehood, made-up story, invention, fabrication, deception, (piece of) fiction; (little) white lie, half-truth; *informal* tall story/tale, whopper; *Brit. informal* porky (pie).

nacci (*c.*1170–*c.*1250).

fibre (US **fiber**) ● noun **1** a thread or filament from which a plant or animal tissue, mineral substance, or textile is formed. **2** a substance formed of fibres. **3** dietary material containing substances such as cellulose, that are resistant to the action of digestive enzymes. **4** strength of character: *moral fibre.*
– ORIGIN Latin *fibra* 'fibre, entrails'.

fibreboard (US **fiberboard**) ● noun a building material made of wood or other plant fibres compressed into boards.

fibreglass (US **fiberglass**) ● noun **1** a reinforced plastic material composed of glass fibres embedded in a resin matrix. **2** a textile fabric made from woven glass filaments.

fibre optics ● plural noun (treated as sing.) the use of thin flexible transparent fibres to transmit light signals, chiefly for telecommunications or for internal inspection of the body.
– DERIVATIVES **fibre-optic** adjective.

f

fibrescope (US **fiberscope**) ● noun a fibre-optic device for viewing inaccessible internal structures, especially in the human body.

fibril /fībril/ ● noun technical a small or slender fibre.
– DERIVATIVES **fibrillar** adjective **fibrillary** adjective.
– ORIGIN Latin *fibrilla* 'little fibre'.

fibrillate /fibrilayt, fī-/ ● verb **1** (of a muscle, especially in the heart) make a quivering movement due to uncoordinated contraction of the individual fibrils. **2** (with reference to a fibre) split up or break into fibrils.
– DERIVATIVES **fibrillation** noun.

fibrin /fībrin/ ● noun Biochemistry an insoluble protein formed as a fibrous mesh during the clotting of blood.
– DERIVATIVES **fibrinoid** adjective **fibrinous** adjective.

fibroblast /fībrōblast/ ● noun Physiology a cell in connective tissue which produces collagen and other fibres.

fibroid ● adjective referring to fibres or fibrous tissue. ● noun Medicine a benign tumour of muscular and fibrous tissues, typically developing in the wall of the womb.

fibroma /fībrōmə/ ● noun (pl. **fibromas** or **fibromata** /fībrōmətə/) Medicine a benign fibrous tumour of connective tissue.

fibrosis /fībrōsiss/ ● noun Medicine the thickening and scarring of connective tissue, usually as a result of injury.
– DERIVATIVES **fibrotic** adjective.

fibrous ● adjective consisting of or characterized by fibres.

fibula /fibyoolə/ ● noun (pl. **fibulae** /fibyoolee/ or **fibulas**) Anatomy the outer and usually smaller of the two bones between the knee and the ankle, parallel with the tibia.
– ORIGIN Latin, 'brooch', because the shape it makes with the tibia resembles a clasp.

-fic (usu. as **-ific**) ● suffix (forming adjectives) producing; making: *prolific.*
– ORIGIN Latin *-ficus*, from *facere* 'do, make'.

fichu /feeshōō/ ● noun a small triangular shawl, worn round a woman's shoulders and neck.
– ORIGIN French, from *ficher* 'to fix, pin'.

fickle ● adjective changeable, especially as regards one's loyalties.
– DERIVATIVES **fickleness** noun.
– ORIGIN Old English, 'deceitful'.

fiction ● noun **1** prose literature, especially novels, describing imaginary events and people. **2** invention as opposed to fact. **3** a false belief or statement, accepted as true for the sake of convenience.
– DERIVATIVES **fictional** adjective **fictionality** noun **fictionalize** (also **fictionalise**) verb **fictionally** adverb **fictionist** noun.
– ORIGIN Latin, from *fingere* 'form, contrive'.

fictitious /fiktishəss/ ● adjective **1** not real or true, being imaginary or invented. **2** referring to the characters and events found in fiction.
– DERIVATIVES **fictitiously** adverb **fictitiousness** noun.

fictive ● adjective creating or created by imagination.
– DERIVATIVES **fictiveness** noun.

ficus /feekəss/ ● noun (pl. same) a tropical tree, shrub, or climbing plant belonging to a genus that includes the figs and the rubber plant.
– ORIGIN Latin, 'fig, fig tree'.

fiddle ● noun **1** informal a violin. **2** informal, chiefly Brit. an act of fraud or cheating. **3** informal an unnecessarily intricate or awkward task. ● verb informal **1** touch or fidget with something restlessly or nervously. **2** chiefly Brit. falsify (figures, data, or records).
– PHRASES **fiddle while Rome burns** be concerned with trivial matters while ignoring the serious events going on around one. **fit as a fiddle** in very good health. **play second fiddle to** take a subordinate role to.
– DERIVATIVES **fiddler** noun (informal).
– ORIGIN Old English *fithele* 'violin', from Latin *vitulari* 'celebrate a festival'.

fiddle-de-dee ● noun dated nonsense.

fiddle-faddle ● noun trivial matters; nonsense.

fiddler crab ● noun a small amphibious crab, the males of which have one greatly enlarged claw.

fiddlesticks ● exclamation informal nonsense.

fiddling ● adjective informal annoyingly trivial.

fiddly ● adjective (**fiddlier**, **fiddliest**) Brit. informal complicated and awkward to do or use.

fideism /fīdi-iz'm/ ● noun the doctrine that knowledge depends on faith or revelation.
– ORIGIN from Latin *fides* 'faith'.

fidelity /fidelliti/ ● noun **1** continuing faithfulness to a person, cause, or belief. **2** the degree of exactness with which something is copied or reproduced.
– ORIGIN from Latin *fidelis* 'faithful'.

fidget /fijit/ ● verb (**fidgeted**, **fidgeting**) make small movements through nervousness or impatience. ● noun **1** a person who fidgets. **2** (**fidgets**) mental or physical restlessness.
– DERIVATIVES **fidgety** adjective.
– ORIGIN from obsolete or dialect *fidge* 'to twitch'.

fiducial /fidyōōsh'l/ ● adjective technical (of a point or line) used as

Thesaurus

– OPPOSITES truth.
● verb *she had bunked off school, fibbing about a sore throat* LIE, tell a fib, tell a lie, invent a story, make up a story; *informal* kid.

fibre ● noun **1** *fibres from the murderer's jumper* THREAD, strand, filament; *technical* fibril. **2** *natural fibres* MATERIAL, cloth, fabric. **3** *a man with no fibre.* See MORAL FIBRE. **4** *fibre in the diet* ROUGHAGE, bulk.

fickle ● adjective CAPRICIOUS, changeable, variable, volatile, mercurial; inconstant, undependable, unsteady, unfaithful, faithless, flighty, giddy, skittish; *technical* labile; *poetic/literary* mutable.
– OPPOSITES constant.

fiction ● noun **1** *the traditions of British fiction* NOVELS, stories, creative writing, prose literature. **2** *the president dismissed the allegation as absolute fiction* FABRICATION, invention, lies, fibs, untruth, falsehood, fantasy, nonsense.
– OPPOSITES fact.

fictional ● adjective FICTITIOUS, invented, imaginary, made up, make-believe, unreal, fabricated, mythical.
– OPPOSITES real.

fictitious ● adjective **1** *a fictitious name* FALSE, fake, fabricated, sham; bogus, spurious, assumed, affected, adopted, feigned, invented, made up; *informal* pretend, phoney. **2** *a fictitious character.* See FICTIONAL.
– OPPOSITES genuine.

fiddle (*informal*) ● noun **1** *she played the fiddle* VIOLIN, viola. **2** *a VAT fiddle* FRAUD, swindle, confidence trick; *informal* racket, con trick, flimflam.
● verb **1** *he fiddled with a beer mat* FIDGET, play, toy, twiddle, fuss, fool about/around; finger, thumb, handle; *informal* mess about/around; *Brit. informal* muck about/around. **2** *he fiddled with the dials* ADJUST, tinker, play about/around, meddle, interfere. **3** *fiddling the figures* FALSIFY, manipulate, massage, rig, distort, misrepresent, doctor, alter, tamper with, interfere with; *informal* fix, flimflam, cook (the books).

fiddling ● adjective (*informal*) TRIVIAL, petty, trifling, insignificant, unimportant, inconsequential, negligible, paltry, footling, minor, small, incidental, of little/no account; *informal* piddling, piffling.

fidelity ● noun **1** *fidelity to her husband* FAITHFULNESS, loyalty, constancy; true-heartedness, trustworthiness, dependability, reliability; *formal* troth. **2** *fidelity to your king* LOYALTY, allegiance, obedience, constancy, homage; *historical* fealty. **3** *the fidelity of the reproduction* ACCURACY, exactness, precision, preciseness, correctness; strictness, closeness, faithfulness, authenticity.
– OPPOSITES disloyalty.

fidget ● verb **1** *the audience began to fidget* MOVE RESTLESSLY, wriggle, squirm, twitch, jiggle, shuffle, be agitated; *informal* be jittery. **2** *she fidgeted with her scarf* PLAY, fuss, toy, twiddle, fool about/around; *informal* fiddle, mess about/around. **3** *she seemed to*

a fixed basis of comparison.
– ORIGIN from Latin *fiducia* 'trust, confidence'.
fiduciary /fidyo͞oshəri/ • adjective Law involving trust, especially with regard to the relationship between a trustee and a beneficiary. • noun (pl. **fiduciaries**) a trustee.
fie /fī/ • exclamation archaic used to express disgust or outrage.
– ORIGIN Latin *fi*, an exclamation of disgust at a stench.
fief /feef/ • noun **1** historical an estate of land held on condition of feudal service. **2** a person's sphere of operation or control.
– DERIVATIVES **fiefdom** noun.
– ORIGIN Old French, variant of *feu* 'fee'.
field • noun **1** an area of open land, especially one planted with crops or pasture. **2** a piece of land used for a sport or game. **3** a subject of study or sphere of activity. **4** a region or space with a particular property: *a magnetic field.* **5** a space or range within which objects are visible from a particular viewpoint or through a piece of apparatus: *field of view.* **6** (**the field**) all the participants in a contest or sport. **7** archaic a battle. • verb **1** chiefly Cricket & Baseball attempt to catch or stop the ball and return it after it has been hit. **2** select to play in a game or to stand in an election. **3** try to deal with (a question, problem, etc.). • adjective **1** carried out or working in the natural environment, rather than in a laboratory or office. **2** (of military equipment) light and mobile for use on campaign.
– PHRASES **hold the field** remain the most important. **in the field** **1** engaged in combat or manoeuvres. **2** engaged in fieldwork. **play the field** informal indulge in a series of casual sexual relationships. **take the field** (of a team) go on to a field to begin a game.
– DERIVATIVES **fielder** noun.
– ORIGIN Old English.
fieldcraft • noun the techniques involved in living in or making military or scientific observations in the field.
field day • noun an opportunity for action or success, especially at the expense of others.
field events • plural noun athletic sports other than races, such as throwing and jumping events.
fieldfare • noun a large grey-headed northern thrush.
– ORIGIN probably from archaic sense of FARE 'to travel'.
field glasses • plural noun binoculars for outdoor use.
field hockey • noun hockey played on grass or a hard pitch, as opposed to ice hockey.
field hospital • noun a temporary hospital set up near a battlefield.
field marshal • noun the highest rank of officer in the British army.
field mouse • noun a common dark brown mouse with a long tail and large eyes.
field mushroom • noun the common edible mushroom.
field officer • noun a major, lieutenant colonel, or colonel.
field sports • plural noun outdoor sports, especially hunting, shooting, and fishing.
fieldstone • noun stone used in its natural form.
field test • noun (also **field trial**) a test carried out in the environment in which a product is to be used. • verb (**field-test**) subject to a field test.
fieldwork • noun practical work conducted by a researcher in the field.
fiend /feend/ • noun **1** an evil spirit or demon. **2** a very wicked or cruel person. **3** informal an enthusiast or devotee: *an exercise fiend.*
– ORIGIN Old English, 'an enemy, the devil'.
fiendish • adjective **1** extremely cruel or unpleasant. **2** extremely difficult.
– DERIVATIVES **fiendishly** adverb **fiendishness** noun.
fierce • adjective **1** violent or aggressive; ferocious. **2** intense. **3** (of a mechanism) having a powerful abruptness of action.
– DERIVATIVES **fiercely** adverb **fierceness** noun.
– ORIGIN Latin *ferus* 'untamed'.
fiery • adjective (**fierier**, **fieriest**) **1** resembling or consisting of fire. **2** quick-tempered or passionate.
– DERIVATIVES **fierily** adverb **fieriness** noun.
fiesta /fiestə/ • noun **1** (in Spanish-speaking countries) a religious festival. **2** a festive occasion.
– ORIGIN Spanish, from Latin *festum* 'feast'.
FIFA /feefə/ • abbreviation Fédération Internationale de Football Association, the international governing body of soccer.
fife • noun a small shrill flute used with the drum in military bands.
– ORIGIN German *Pfeife* 'pipe'
fifteen • cardinal number **1** one more than fourteen; 15. (Roman numeral: **xv** or **XV**.) **2** a team of fifteen players, especially in rugby.
– DERIVATIVES **fifteenth** ordinal number.
– ORIGIN Old English.
fifth • ordinal number **1** constituting number five in a sequence; 5th. **2** (**a fifth/one fifth**) each of five equal parts into which something is or may be divided. **3** Music an interval spanning five consecutive notes in a diatonic scale, in particular (also **perfect fifth**) an interval of three tones and a semitone.
– PHRASES **take the fifth** (in the US) exercise the right guaranteed by the Fifth Amendment to the Constitution to refuse to answer questions in order to avoid incriminating oneself.
– DERIVATIVES **fifthly** adverb.
fifth column • noun a group within a country at war who are working for its enemies.
– DERIVATIVES **fifth columnist** noun.
– ORIGIN from the Spanish Civil War, when General Mola, leading four columns of troops towards Madrid, declared that he had a fifth column inside the city.
fifty • cardinal number (pl. **fifties**) ten less than sixty; 50. (Roman numeral: **l** or **L**.)

Thesaurus

fidget him MAKE UNEASY, worry, agitate, bother, upset, ruffle.
• noun **1** *his convulsive fidgets* TWITCH, wriggle, squirm, jiggle, shuffle, tic, spasm. **2** *what a fidget you are!* RESTLESS PERSON, bundle of nerves. **3** *that woman gives me the fidgets* RESTLESSNESS, nervousness, fidgetiness; *informal* the jitters, twitchiness.
fidgety • adjective RESTLESS, restive, on edge, uneasy, nervous, nervy, keyed up, anxious, agitated; *informal* jittery, twitchy.
field • noun **1** *a large ploughed field* MEADOW, pasture, paddock, grassland, pastureland, sward; *poetic/literary* lea, mead; *archaic* glebe. **2** *a football field* PITCH, ground, sports field, playing field, recreation ground. **3** *the field of biotechnology* AREA, sphere, discipline, province, department, domain, sector, branch, subject; *informal* bailiwick. **4** *your field of vision* SCOPE, range, sweep, reach, extent. **5** *she is well ahead of the field* COMPETITORS, entrants, competition; applicants, candidates, possibles.
• verb **1** *he was fielding* ACT AS A FIELDER, play in outfield. **2** *she fielded the ball* CATCH, stop, retrieve; return, throw back. **3** *fielding an ineligible player* PUT IN THE TEAM, send out, play, put up. **4** *they can field an army of about one million* DEPLOY, position, range, dispose. **5** *he fielded some awkward questions* DEAL WITH, handle, cope with, answer, reply to, respond to.
• adjective **1** *field experience* PRACTICAL, hands-on, applied, experiential, empirical. **2** *field artillery* MOBILE, portable, transportable, movable, manoeuvrable, light.
– OPPOSITES theoretical.
fiend • noun **1** *a fiend had taken possession of him* DEMON, devil, evil spirit, bogie, cacodemon; *informal* spook. **2** *a fiend bent on global evil-doing* BRUTE, beast, villain, barbarian, monster, ogre, sadist, evil-doer; *informal* swine. **3** *(informal) a drug fiend* ADDICT, abuser, user; *informal* junkie, ——head/freak. **4** *(informal) I'm a fiend for Mexican food* ENTHUSIAST, maniac; devotee, fan, lover; *informal* fanatic, addict, buff, freak, nut.
fiendish • adjective **1** *a fiendish torturer* WICKED, cruel, vicious, evil, malevolent, villainous; brutal, savage, barbaric, barbarous, inhuman, murderous, ruthless, merciless; *dated* dastardly. **2** *a fiendish plot* CUNNING, clever, ingenious, crafty, canny, wily, devious, shrewd; *informal* foxy, sneaky. **3** *a fiendish puzzle* DIFFICULT, complex, challenging, complicated, intricate, involved, knotty, thorny.
fierce • adjective **1** *a fierce black mastiff* FEROCIOUS, savage, vicious, aggressive. **2** *fierce competition* AGGRESSIVE, cut-throat, competitive; keen, intense, strong, relentless. **3** *fierce, murderous jealousy* INTENSE, powerful, vehement, passionate, impassioned, fervent, fervid, ardent. **4** *a fierce wind* POWERFUL, strong, violent, forceful; stormy, blustery, gusty, tempestuous. **5** *a fierce pain* SEVERE, extreme, intense, acute, awful, dreadful; excruciating, agonizing, piercing.
– OPPOSITES gentle, mild.
fiery • adjective **1** *fiery breath* BURNING, blazing, flaming; on fire, ablaze; *poetic/literary* afire. **2** *a fiery red* BRIGHT, brilliant, vivid, intense, deep, rich. **3** *her fiery spirit* PASSIONATE, impassioned, ardent, fervent, fervid, spirited; quick-tempered, volatile, explosive,

– DERIVATIVES **fiftieth** ordinal number.
– ORIGIN Old English.
fifty-fifty ● adjective & adverb with equal shares or chances.
fig[1] ● noun a soft pear-shaped fruit with sweet dark flesh and many small seeds.
– PHRASES **not give** (or **care**) **a fig** not care at all.
– ORIGIN Old French *figue* from Latin *ficus*.
fig[2] ● noun (in phrase **full fig**) informal the complete set of clothes appropriate to a particular occasion or profession.
– ORIGIN from obsolete *feague* 'whip', later 'liven up'.
fight ● verb (past and past part. **fought**) **1** take part in a violent struggle involving physical force or weapons. **2** engage in (a war or contest). **3** quarrel or argue. **4** (**fight off**) defend oneself against an attack by. **5** struggle to overcome, eliminate, or prevent. **6** (**fight for**) try very hard to obtain or do. ● noun an act of fighting.
– PHRASES **fight fire with fire** use the weapons or tactics of one's opponent, even if one finds them distasteful. **fight or flight** the instinctive physiological response to a threatening situation, which readies one either to resist forcibly or to run away. **fight shy of** avoid through unwillingness. **fight one's way** move forward with difficulty.
– ORIGIN Old English.
fightback ● noun Brit. a rally or recovery.
fighter ● noun **1** a person or animal that fights. **2** a fast military aircraft designed for attacking other aircraft.
fighting chance ● noun a possibility of success if great effort is made.
fighting fit ● adjective in excellent health.
fig leaf ● noun a leaf of a fig tree used to conceal the genitals in paintings and sculpture.
– ORIGIN with reference to the story of Adam and Eve in the Bible, who made clothes out of fig leaves after becoming aware of their nakedness.
figment /figmənt/ ● noun a thing believed to be real but existing only in the imagination.
– ORIGIN Latin *figmentum*, related to *fingere* 'form, contrive.'
figural /figyoorəl/ ● adjective another term for FIGURATIVE.
figuration /figgəraysh'n/ ● noun **1** ornamentation using designs. **2** Music use of florid counterpoint. **3** allegorical representation.
figurative ● adjective **1** not using words literally; metaphorical. **2** Art representing forms that are recognizably derived from life.
– DERIVATIVES **figuratively** adverb **figurativeness** noun.
figure ● noun **1** a number or numerical symbol. **2** an amount of money. **3** a person's bodily shape, especially that of a woman. **4** a person seen indistinctly. **5** an artistic representation of a human or animal form. **6** a shape defined by one or more lines. **7** a diagram or illustrative drawing. **8** Music a short succession of notes producing a single impression. ● verb **1** be a significant part of or contributor to something. **2** calculate arithmetically. **3** (**figure out**) informal reach an understanding of. **4** informal, chiefly N. Amer. be perfectly understandable: *that figures!* **5** (**figure on**) N. Amer. informal count or rely on something happening or being the case. **6** informal, chiefly N. Amer. think; consider. **7** represent in a diagram or picture.
– ORIGIN Latin *figura* 'figure, form'.
figurehead ● noun **1** a carved bust or full-length figure set at the prow of an old-fashioned sailing ship. **2** a nominal leader without real power.

Thesaurus

aggressive, determined, resolute.
fiesta ● noun FESTIVAL, carnival, holiday, celebration, party.
fight ● verb **1** *two men were fighting* BRAWL, exchange blows, attack/assault each other, hit/punch each other; struggle, grapple, wrestle; *informal* scrap, have a dust-up, have a set-to; *Brit. informal* have a punch-up; *N. Amer. informal* rough-house; *Austral./NZ informal* stoush, go the knuckle. **2** *he fought in the First World War* (DO) BATTLE, go to war, take up arms, be a soldier; engage, meet, clash, skirmish. **3** *a war fought for freedom* ENGAGE IN, wage, conduct, prosecute, undertake. **4** *they are always fighting* QUARREL, argue, row, bicker, squabble, fall out, have a row/fight, wrangle, be at odds, disagree, differ, have words, bandy words, be at each other's throats, be at loggerheads; *informal* scrap; *archaic* altercate. **5** *fighting against wage reductions* CAMPAIGN, strive, battle, struggle, contend, crusade, agitate, lobby, push, press. **6** *they will fight the decision* OPPOSE, contest, contend with, confront, challenge, combat, dispute, quarrel with, argue against/with, strive against, struggle against. **7** *Donaldson fought the urge to put his tongue out* REPRESS, restrain, suppress, stifle, smother, hold back, fight back, keep in check, curb, control, rein in, choke back; *informal* keep the lid on, cork up.
● noun **1** *a fight outside a club* BRAWL, fracas, melee, rumpus, skirmish, sparring match, struggle, scuffle, altercation, scrum, clash, disturbance; fisticuffs; *informal* scrap, dust-up, set-to, shindy, shindig; *Brit. informal* punch-up, bust-up, ruck; *N. Amer. informal* rough house, brannigan; *Austral./NZ informal* stoush; *Law, dated* affray; *rare* broil. **2** *a heavyweight fight* BOXING MATCH, bout, match. **3** *Britain's fight against Germany* BATTLE, engagement, clash, conflict, struggle; war, campaign, crusade, action, hostilities. **4** *a fight with my girlfriend* ARGUMENT, quarrel, squabble, row, wrangle, disagreement, falling-out, contretemps, altercation, dispute; *informal* tiff, spat, scrap, slanging match; *Brit. informal* barney, ding-dong, bust-up. **5** *their fight for control of the company* STRUGGLE, battle, campaign, push, effort. **6** *she had no fight left in her* WILL TO RESIST, resistance, spirit, courage, pluck, pluckiness, grit, strength, backbone, determination, resolution, resolve, resoluteness, aggression, aggressiveness; *informal* guts, spunk; *Brit. informal* bottle; *N. Amer. informal* sand, moxie.
– PHRASES **fight back 1** *use your pent-up anger to fight back* RETALIATE, counter-attack, strike back, hit back, respond, reciprocate, return fire, give tit for tat; *formal* requite something. **2** *she fought back tears.* See FIGHT verb sense 7. **fight someone/something off** REPEL, repulse, beat off/back, ward off, fend off, keep/hold at bay, drive away/back, force back. **fight shy of** FLINCH FROM, demur from, recoil from; have scruples about, have misgivings about, have qualms about, be averse to, be chary of, be loath to, be reluctant to, be disinclined to, be afraid to, hesitate to, baulk at; *informal* boggle at; *archaic* disrelish.
fightback ● noun *(Brit.)* COUNTER-ATTACK, counter-offensive; rally, recovery; *informal* comeback.
fighter ● noun **1** *a guerrilla fighter* SOLDIER, fighting man/woman, warrior, combatant, serviceman, servicewoman, trooper; *Brit. informal* squaddie; *archaic* man-at-arms. **2** *the fighter was knocked to the ground* BOXER, pugilist, prizefighter; wrestler; *informal* scrapper, pug. **3** *enemy fighters* WARPLANE, armed aircraft.
fighting ● adjective *a fighting man* VIOLENT, combative, aggressive, pugnacious, truculent, belligerent, bellicose.
– OPPOSITES peaceful.
● noun *200 were injured in the fighting* VIOLENCE, hostilities, conflict, action, combat; warfare, war, battles, skirmishing, rioting; *Law, dated* affray.
– OPPOSITES peace.
figment ● noun INVENTION, creation, fabrication; hallucination, illusion, delusion, fancy, vision.
figurative ● adjective METAPHORICAL, non-literal, symbolic, allegorical, representative, emblematic.
– OPPOSITES literal.
figure ● noun **1** *the production figure* STATISTIC, number, quantity, amount, level, total, sum; (**figures**) data, information. **2** *the second figure was 9* DIGIT, numeral, numerical symbol. **3** *he can't put a figure on it* PRICE, cost, amount, value, valuation. **4** *I'm good at figures* ARITHMETIC, mathematics, sums, calculations, computation, numbers; *Brit. informal* maths; *N. Amer. informal* math. **5** *her petite figure* PHYSIQUE, build, frame, body, proportions, shape, form. **6** *a dark figure emerged* SILHOUETTE, outline, shape, form. **7** *a figure of authority* PERSON, personage, individual, man, woman, character, personality; representative, embodiment, personification, epitome. **8** *life-size figures* HUMAN REPRESENTATION, effigy. **9** *geometrical figures* SHAPE, pattern, design, motif. **10** *see figure 4* DIAGRAM, illustration, drawing, picture, plate.
● verb **1** *a beast figuring in Egyptian legend* FEATURE, appear, be featured, be mentioned, be referred to, have prominence. **2** *a way to figure the values* CALCULATE, work out, total, reckon, compute, determine, assess, put a figure on; *Brit.* tot up. **3** *(informal) I figured that I didn't have a chance* SUPPOSE, think, believe, consider, expect, take it, suspect, sense; assume, dare say, conclude, take it as read, presume, deduce, infer, gather; *N. Amer.* guess. **4** *(informal) 'Rosemary's away.' 'That figures.'* MAKE SENSE, stand to reason, seem reasonable, be understandable, be to be expected, be logical, follow, ring true.
– PHRASES **figure on** *(N. Amer. informal)* PLAN ON, count on, rely on, bank on, bargain on, depend on, pin one's hopes on; anticipate, expect to. **figure something out** *(informal) he tried to figure out how to switch on the lamp* WORK OUT, fathom, puzzle out, decipher, as-

figure of speech ● noun a word or phrase used in a non-literal sense for rhetorical or vivid effect.
figure skating ● noun the sport of skating in prescribed patterns from a stationary position.
figurine /figyooreen/ ● noun a small statue of a human form.
– ORIGIN Italian *figurina* 'small figure'.
Fijian /feejeeən/ ● noun a person from Fiji, a country in the South Pacific consisting of some 840 islands. ● adjective relating to Fiji.
filagree ● noun variant spelling of FILIGREE.
filament /filləmənt/ ● noun **1** a slender thread-like object or fibre. **2** a metal wire in an electric light bulb, which glows white-hot when an electric current is passed through it. **3** Botany the slender part of a stamen that supports the anther.
– DERIVATIVES **filamentary** adjective **filamentous** adjective.
– ORIGIN Latin *filamentum*, from *filare* 'to spin'.
filariasis /filairiaysiss, fillərīəsiss/ ● noun a disease caused by infestation with parasitic nematode worms, transmitted by biting flies and mosquitoes in the tropics.
– ORIGIN from Latin *Filaria*, former name of a genus of nematodes, from *filum* 'thread'.
filbert ● noun a cultivated oval hazelnut.
– ORIGIN from French *noix de filbert* (so named because it is ripe about 20 August, the feast day of St *Philibert*).
filch ● verb informal pilfer; steal.
– ORIGIN of unknown origin.
file[1] ● noun **1** a folder or box for keeping loose papers together and in order. **2** Computing a collection of data or programs stored under a single identifying name. **3** a line of people or things one behind another. **4** Military a small detachment of men. **5** Chess a row of squares on a chessboard running away from the player toward the opponent. ● verb **1** place in a file. **2** submit (a legal document, application, or charge) to be officially placed on record. **3** walk one behind the other.
– DERIVATIVES **filing** noun.
– ORIGIN French *fil* 'a thread', from Latin *filum*.
file[2] ● noun a tool with a roughened surface or surfaces, used for smoothing or shaping a hard material. ● verb smooth or shape with a file.
– ORIGIN Old English.
filet mignon /feelay meenyon/ ● noun a small tender piece of beef from the end of the undercut.
– ORIGIN French, 'dainty fillet'.
filial /filliəl/ ● adjective relating to or due from a son or daughter.
– DERIVATIVES **filially** adverb.
– ORIGIN Latin *filialis*, from *filius* 'son', *filia* 'daughter'.
filibuster /fillibustər/ ● noun prolonged speaking which obstructs progress in a legislative assembly. ● verb obstruct legislation with a filibuster.
– ORIGIN French *flibustier*, first applied to pirates who pillaged the Spanish colonies in the West Indies, influenced by Spanish *filibustero*; ultimately from Dutch *vrijbuiter* 'freebooter'.
filicide /fillisīd/ ● noun **1** the killing of one's son or daughter. **2** a person who does this.
– ORIGIN from Latin *filius* 'son', *filia* 'daughter'.
filigree /filligree/ (also **filagree**) ● noun delicate ornamental work of fine gold, silver, or copper wire.
– DERIVATIVES **filigreed** adjective.
– ORIGIN from Latin *filum* 'thread' + *granum* 'seed'.
filing cabinet ● noun a large piece of office furniture with deep drawers for storing files.
filings ● plural noun small particles rubbed off by a file.
Filipino /fillipeenō/ ● noun (pl. **Filipinos**; fem. **Filipina**, pl. **Filipinas**) **1** a person from the Philippines. **2** the national language of the Philippines. ● adjective relating to Filipinos or their language.
– ORIGIN Spanish, from *las Islas Filipinas* 'the Philippine Islands'.
fill ● verb **1** make or become full. **2** block up (a hole, gap, etc.). **3** appoint a person to hold (a vacant post). **4** hold and perform the duties of (a position or role). **5** occupy (time). ● noun (**one's fill**) as much as one wants or can bear.
– PHRASES **fill in 1** make (a hole) completely full of material. **2** complete (a form) by adding information. **3** inform more fully of a matter. **4** act as a substitute. **fill out 1** put on weight. **2** chiefly N. Amer. fill in (a form). **fill someone's shoes** (or **boots**) informal take over someone's role and fulfil it satisfactorily.
– ORIGIN Old English, related to FULL[1].
filler[1] ● noun **1** something used to fill a gap or cavity, or to increase bulk. **2** an item serving only to fill space or time.
filler[2] /filör/ ● noun (pl. same) a monetary unit of Hungary, equal to one hundredth of a forint.
– ORIGIN Hungarian.
filler cap ● noun a cap closing the pipe leading to the petrol tank of a motor vehicle.
fillet ● noun **1** a fleshy boneless piece of meat from near the loins or the ribs of an animal. **2** a boned side of a fish. **3** a band or ribbon binding the hair. **4** Architecture a narrow flat band separating two mouldings. ● verb (**filleted**, **filleting**) **1** remove the bones from (a fish). **2** cut into fillets.
– ORIGIN Old French *filet* 'thread', from Latin *filum*.
filling ● noun a quantity or piece of material that fills or is used to fill something. ● adjective (of food) leaving one with a pleasantly satiated feeling.
filling station ● noun a petrol station.
fillip /fillip/ ● noun a stimulus or boost.
– ORIGIN from an archaic sense of the word meaning 'a flick with the fingers'.
filly ● noun (pl. **fillies**) **1** a young female horse, especially one less than four years old. **2** humorous a lively girl or young woman.
– ORIGIN Old Norse, related to FOAL.

Thesaurus

certain, make sense of, think through, get to the bottom of; understand, comprehend, see, grasp, get the hang of, get the drift of; *informal* twig, crack; *Brit. informal* suss out.
filament ● noun FIBRE, thread, strand; *technical* fibril.
file[1] ● noun **1** *he opened the file* FOLDER, portfolio, binder, document case. **2** *we have files on all the major companies* DOSSIER, document, record, report; data, information, documentation, annals, archives. **3** *the computer file was searched* DATA, document, text.
● verb **1** *file the documents correctly* CATEGORIZE, classify, organize, put in place/order, order, arrange, catalogue, record, store, archive. **2** *Debbie has filed for divorce* APPLY, register, ask. **3** *two women have filed a civil suit against him* BRING, press, lodge, place; *formal* prefer.
file[2] ● noun *a file of boys* LINE, column, row, string, chain, procession; *Brit. informal* crocodile.
● verb *we filed out into the car park* WALK IN A LINE, march, parade, troop.
file[3] ● verb *she filed her nails* SMOOTH, buff, rub (down), polish, shape; scrape, abrade, rasp, sandpaper.
filial ● adjective DUTIFUL, devoted, compliant, respectful, affectionate, loving.
filibuster ● noun *many hours in committee are characterized by filibuster* DELAYING TACTICS, stonewalling, procrastination, obstruction.
● verb *the opposition are filibustering* WASTE TIME, stall, play for time, stonewall, procrastinate, buy time, employ delaying tactics.
filigree ● noun TRACERY, fretwork, latticework, scrollwork, lacework.
fill ● verb **1** *he filled a bowl with cereal* MAKE/BECOME FULL, fill up, fill to the brim, top up, charge. **2** *guests filled the parlour* CROWD INTO, throng, pack (into), occupy, squeeze into, cram (into); overcrowd, overfill. **3** *he began filling his shelves* STOCK, pack, load, supply, replenish, restock, refill. **4** *fill all the holes with a wood-repair compound* BLOCK UP, stop (up), plug, seal, caulk. **5** *the perfume filled the room* PERVADE, permeate, suffuse, be diffused through, penetrate, infuse, perfuse. **6** *he was going to fill a government post* OCCUPY, hold, take up; *informal* hold down. **7** *we had just filled a big order* CARRY OUT, complete, fulfil, execute, discharge; *formal* effectuate.
– OPPOSITES empty.
– PHRASES **fill in** SUBSTITUTE, deputize, stand in, cover, take over, act as stand-in, take the place of; *informal* sub, step into someone's shoes/boots; *N. Amer. informal* pinch-hit. **fill someone in** INFORM OF, advise of, tell about, acquaint with, apprise of, brief on, update with; *informal* put in the picture about, bring up to speed on. **fill something in** COMPLETE, answer, fill up; *N. Amer.* fill out. **fill out** GROW FATTER, become plumper, flesh out, put on weight, get heavier. **fill something out 1** *this account needs to be filled out* EXPAND, enlarge, add to, elaborate on, flesh out; supplement, extend, develop, amplify. **2** *(N. Amer.) he filled out the application forms.* See FILL SOMETHING IN.
filling ● noun *filling for cushions* STUFFING, padding, wadding, filler.
● adjective *a filling meal* SUBSTANTIAL, hearty, ample, abundant, satisfying, square; heavy, stodgy.

film ● noun **1** a thin flexible strip of plastic or other material coated with light-sensitive emulsion for exposure in a camera. **2** a story or event recorded by a camera as a series of moving images and shown in a cinema or on television. **3** motion pictures considered as an art or industry. **4** material in the form of a very thin flexible sheet. **5** a thin layer covering a surface. ● verb **1** make a film of; record on film. **2** become covered with a thin film.
– ORIGIN Old English, 'membrane'.
filmic ● adjective of or relating to films or cinematography.
film noir /film nwaar/ ● noun a style of film marked by a mood of pessimism, fatalism, and menace.
– ORIGIN French, 'black film'.
filmography ● noun (pl. **filmographies**) a list of films by one director or actor, or on one subject.
film star ● noun a well-known film actor or actress.
filmstrip ● noun a series of transparencies in a strip for projection.
filmy ● adjective (**filmier**, **filmiest**) **1** thin and translucent. **2** covered with a thin film.
– DERIVATIVES **filminess** noun.
filo /feelō/ (also **phyllo**) ● noun a kind of flaky pastry stretched into very thin sheets, used especially in eastern Mediterranean cookery.
– ORIGIN modern Greek *phullo* 'leaf'.
Filofax /fīlōfaks/ ● noun trademark a loose-leaf notebook for recording appointments, addresses, and notes.
– ORIGIN representing a colloquial pronunciation of *file of facts*.
filovirus /fīlōvīrəss/ ● noun a filamentous RNA virus of a group which causes severe haemorrhagic fevers.
fils[1] /feess/ ● noun used after a surname to distinguish a son from a father of the same name.
– ORIGIN French, 'son'.
fils[2] /filss/ ● noun (pl. same) a monetary unit of Iraq, Bahrain, Jordan, Kuwait, and Yemen, equal to one hundredth of a riyal in Yemen and one thousandth of a dinar elsewhere.
– ORIGIN Arabic.
filter ● noun **1** a porous device for removing solid particles from a liquid or gas passed through it. **2** a screen, plate, or layer which absorbs some of the light passing through it. **3** Brit. an arrangement at a junction whereby vehicles may turn while traffic waiting to go straight ahead is stopped by a red light. ● verb **1** pass through a filter. **2** (often **filter in/out/through**) move gradually through something or in a specified direction. **3** (of information) gradually become known.
– DERIVATIVES **filterable** adjective **filtration** noun.
– ORIGIN Latin *filtrum* 'felt used as a filter'.
filter-feeder ● noun an aquatic animal which feeds by filtering out plankton or nutrients suspended in the water.
filter tip ● noun a filter attached to a cigarette for removing impurities from the inhaled smoke.
filth ● noun **1** disgusting dirt. **2** obscene and offensive language or printed material. **3** (**the filth**) Brit. informal, derogatory the police.
– ORIGIN Old English, related to FOUL.
filthy ● adjective (**filthier**, **filthiest**) **1** disgustingly dirty. **2** obscene and offensive. **3** informal very unpleasant or disagreeable: *filthy weather*. ● adverb informal extremely: *filthy rich*.
– DERIVATIVES **filthily** adverb **filthiness** noun.
filtrate ● noun a liquid which has passed through a filter.
fin ● noun **1** an external organ on the body of a fish or other aquatic animal, used for propelling, steering, and balancing. **2** an underwater swimmer's flipper. **3** a projection on an aircraft, rocket, or car, for providing aerodynamic stability.
– DERIVATIVES **finned** adjective.
– ORIGIN Old English.
finagle /finayg'l/ ● verb N. Amer. informal obtain or act dishonestly or deviously.
– DERIVATIVES **finagler** noun.
– ORIGIN from dialect *fainaigue* 'cheat'.
final ● adjective **1** coming at the end of a series. **2** reached as the outcome of a process. **3** allowing no further doubt or dispute. ● noun **1** the last game in a tournament, which will decide the overall winner. **2** (**finals**) a series of games constituting the final stage of a competition. **3** (**finals**) Brit. a series of examinations at the end of a degree course.
– ORIGIN Latin *finalis*, from *finis* 'end'.
finale /finaali/ ● noun the last part of a piece of music, an entertainment, or a public event.
– ORIGIN Italian.
finalist ● noun **1** a participant in a final or finals. **2** a student taking finals.
finality ● noun the fact or quality of being final.
finalize (also **finalise**) ● verb **1** complete (a transaction) after discussion of the terms. **2** produce or agree on a finished version of.
– DERIVATIVES **finalization** noun.
finally ● adverb **1** after a long time and much difficulty or delay. **2** as a final point or reason.

Thesaurus

fillip ● noun STIMULUS, stimulation, boost, incentive, impetus; tonic, spur, push, aid, help; *informal* shot in the arm.
film ● noun **1** *a film of sweat* LAYER, coat, coating, covering, cover, sheet, patina, overlay. **2** *Emma was watching a film* MOVIE, picture, feature (film), motion picture; *informal* flick, pic, talkie; *dated* moving picture. **3** *she would like to work in film* CINEMA, movies, the pictures.
– RELATED TERMS cinematic.
● verb **1** *he immediately filmed the next scene* RECORD (ON FILM), shoot, capture on film, video. **2** *his eyes had filmed over* CLOUD, mist, haze; become blurred, blur; *archaic* blear.
film star ● noun (FILM) ACTOR/ACTRESS, movie star, leading man/woman, leading lady, lead; celebrity, star, starlet, superstar; *informal* celeb; *informal, dated* matinee idol.
filmy ● adjective DIAPHANOUS, transparent, see-through, translucent, sheer, gossamer; delicate, fine, light, thin, silky.
– OPPOSITES thick, opaque.
filter ● noun *a carbon filter* STRAINER, sifter; sieve, riddle; gauze, netting.
● verb **1** *the farmers filter the water* SIEVE, strain, sift, filtrate, riddle; clarify, purify, refine, treat. **2** *the rain had filtered through her jacket* SEEP, percolate, leak, trickle, ooze.
filth ● noun **1** *stagnant pools of filth* DIRT, muck, grime, mud, mire, sludge, slime, ooze; excrement, excreta, dung, manure, ordure, sewage; rubbish, refuse, dross; pollution, contamination, filthiness, uncleanness, foulness; *N. Amer.* garbage, trash; *informal* crud, grunge; *Brit. informal* grot, gunge. **2** *I felt sick after reading that filth* PORNOGRAPHY, pornographic literature/films, dirty books, smut, obscenity, indecency; *informal* porn, porno.
filthy ● adjective **1** *the room was filthy* DIRTY, mucky, grimy, muddy, slimy, unclean; foul, squalid, sordid, nasty, soiled, sullied; polluted, contaminated, unhygienic, unsanitary; *informal* cruddy, grungy; *Brit. informal* grotty; *poetic/literary* besmirched. **2** *his face was filthy* UNWASHED, unclean, dirty, grimy, smeared, grubby, muddy, mucky, black, blackened, stained; *poetic/literary* begrimed. **3** *filthy jokes* OBSCENE, indecent, dirty, smutty, rude, improper, coarse, bawdy, vulgar, lewd, racy, off colour, earthy, ribald, risqué, 'adult', pornographic, explicit; *informal* blue, porn, porno, X-rated; *N. Amer. informal* raw. **4** *you filthy brute!* DESPICABLE, contemptible, nasty, low, base, mean, vile, obnoxious; *informal* dirty (rotten), low-down, no-good. **5** *he was in a filthy mood* BAD, foul, bad-tempered, ill-tempered, irritable, grumpy, grouchy, cross, fractious, peevish; *informal* snappish, snappy; *Brit. informal* shirty, stroppy, narky, ratty; *N. Amer. informal* cranky, ornery.
– OPPOSITES clean.
● adverb *filthy rich* VERY, extremely, tremendously, immensely, remarkably, excessively, exceedingly; *informal* stinking, awfully, terribly, seriously, mega, ultra, damn.
final ● adjective **1** *the final year of study* LAST, closing, concluding, finishing, end, terminating, ultimate, eventual. **2** *their decisions are final* IRREVOCABLE, unalterable, absolute, conclusive, irrefutable, incontrovertible, indisputable, unchallengeable, binding.
– OPPOSITES first, provisional.
● noun *the FA Cup final* DECIDER, final game/match.
– OPPOSITES qualifier.
finale ● noun CLIMAX, culmination; end, ending, finish, close, conclusion, termination; denouement, last act, final scene.
– OPPOSITES beginning.
finality ● noun CONCLUSIVENESS, decisiveness, decision, definiteness, definitiveness, certainty, certitude; irrevocability, irrefutability, incontrovertibility.
finalize ● verb CONCLUDE, complete, clinch, settle, work out, secure, wrap up, wind up, put the finishing touches to; reach an agreement on, agree on, come to terms on; *informal* sew up.
finally ● adverb **1** *she finally got her man to the altar* EVENTUALLY, ultimately, in the end, after a long time, at (long) last; in the long

final solution ● noun the Nazi policy (1941–5) of exterminating Jews.

finance /finanss, fī-/ ● noun **1** the management of large amounts of money, especially by governments or large companies. **2** monetary support for an enterprise. **3** (**finances**) monetary resources. ● verb provide funding for.
– ORIGIN Old French, from *finer* 'settle a debt'.

finance company (also **finance house**) ● noun a company concerned primarily with providing money, e.g. for hire-purchase transactions.

financial ● adjective **1** relating to finance. **2** Austral./NZ informal possessing money.
– DERIVATIVES **financially** adverb.

financial year ● noun a year as reckoned for taxing or accounting purposes, especially the British tax year reckoned from 6 April.

financier /finansiər/ ● noun a person engaged in managing the finances of governments or other large organizations.
– ORIGIN French.

finch ● noun a seed-eating songbird of a large group including the chaffinch, goldfinch, linnet, etc.
– ORIGIN Old English.

find ● verb (past and past part. **found**) **1** discover by chance or deliberately. **2** recognize or discover to be present or to be the case. **3** ascertain by research or calculation. **4** Law (of a court) officially declare to be the case. **5** (**find against** or **for**) Law (of a court) make a decision against (or in favour of). **6** reach or arrive at by a natural or normal process: *water finds its own level.* ● noun a valuable or interesting discovery.
– PHRASES **find one's feet** establish oneself in a particular field. **find out 1** discover (information, a fact, etc). **2** detect (someone) in a crime or lie.
– DERIVATIVES **findable** adjective.
– ORIGIN Old English.

finder ● noun **1** a person who finds someone or something. **2** a small telescope attached to a large one to locate an object for observation. **3** a viewfinder.
– PHRASES **finders keepers** (**losers weepers**) informal whoever finds something is entitled to keep it.

fin de siècle /faɴ də syeklə/ ● adjective relating to or characteristic of the end of a century, especially the 19th century.
– ORIGIN French, 'end of century'.

finding ● noun a conclusion reached as a result of an inquiry, investigation, or trial.

fine[1] ● adjective **1** of very high quality. **2** satisfactory. **3** in good health and feeling well. **4** (of the weather) bright and clear. **5** (of a thread, filament, or hair) thin. **6** of delicate or intricate workmanship. **7** (of speech or writing) impressive but ultimately insincere: *fine words.* ● adverb informal in a satisfactory or pleasing manner. ● verb **1** clarify (beer or wine) by causing the precipitation of sediment. **2** (usu. **fine down**) make thinner.
– PHRASES **cut it fine** allow a very small margin of time. **fine feathers make fine birds** proverb beautiful clothes or an eye-catching appearance make a person appear similarly beautiful or impressive. **one's finest hour** the time of one's greatest success. **fine words butter no parsnips** proverb nothing is achieved by empty promises or flattery. **have down to a fine art** achieve a high level of skill in (something) through experience. **not to put too fine a point on it** to speak bluntly. **one fine day** at some unspecified time.
– DERIVATIVES **finely** adverb **fineness** noun.
– ORIGIN Old French *fin*, from Latin *finire* 'finish'.

fine[2] ● noun a sum of money exacted as a penalty by a court of law or other authority. ● verb punish by a fine.
– DERIVATIVES **fineable** adjective.
– ORIGIN Old French *fin* 'end, payment', from Latin *finis* 'end'.

fine art ● noun art intended to be appreciated primarily or solely for its aesthetic content.

f

Thesaurus

run, in the fullness of time. **2** *finally, wrap the ribbon round the edge* LASTLY, last, in conclusion, to conclude, to end. **3** *this should finally dispel that common misconception* CONCLUSIVELY, irrevocably, decisively, definitively, for ever, for good, once and for all.

finance ● noun **1** *he knows about finance* FINANCIAL AFFAIRS, money matters, fiscal matters, economics, money management, commerce, business, investment. **2** *short-term finance* FUNDS, assets, money, capital, resources, cash, reserves, revenue, income; funding, backing, sponsorship.
● verb *the project was financed by grants* FUND, pay for, back, capitalize, endow, subsidize, invest in; underwrite, guarantee, sponsor, support; *N. Amer. informal* bankroll.

financial ● adjective MONETARY, money, economic, pecuniary, fiscal, banking, commercial, business, investment.

financier ● noun INVESTOR, speculator, banker, capitalist, industrialist, businessman, businesswoman, stockbroker; *informal* money man.

find ● verb **1** *I found the book I wanted* LOCATE, spot, pinpoint, unearth, obtain; search out, nose out, track down, root out; come across/upon, run across/into, chance on, light on, happen on, stumble on, encounter; *informal* bump into; *poetic/literary* espy, descry. **2** *they have found a cure for rabies* DISCOVER, invent, come up with, hit on. **3** *the police found her purse* RETRIEVE, recover, get back, regain, repossess. **4** *I hope you find peace* OBTAIN, acquire, get, procure, come by, secure, gain, earn, achieve, attain. **5** *I found the courage to speak* SUMMON (UP), gather, muster (up), screw up, call up. **6** *caffeine is found in coffee and tea* BE (PRESENT), occur, exist, be existent, appear. **7** *you'll find that it's a lively area* DISCOVER, become aware, realize, observe, notice, note, perceive, learn. **8** *I find their decision strange* CONSIDER, think, believe to be, feel to be, look on as, view as, see as, judge, deem, regard as. **9** *he was found guilty* JUDGE, adjudge, adjudicate, deem, rule, declare, pronounce. **10** *her barb found its mark* ARRIVE AT, reach, attain, achieve; hit, strike.
– OPPOSITES lose.
● noun **1** *an archaeological find* DISCOVERY, acquisition, asset. **2** *this table is a real find* GOOD BUY, bargain; godsend, boon.
– PHRASES **find out** DISCOVER, become aware, learn, detect, discern, perceive, observe, notice, note, get/come to know, realize; bring to light, reveal, expose, unearth, disclose; *informal* figure out, cotton on, catch on, tumble, get wise, savvy; *Brit. informal* twig, rumble, suss.

finding ● noun **1** *the finding of the leak* DISCOVERY, location, locating, detection, detecting, uncovering. **2** *the tribunal's findings* CONCLUSION, decision, verdict, pronouncement, judgement, ruling, rule, decree, order, recommendation; *Law* determination; *N. Amer.* resolve.

fine[1] ● adjective **1** *fine wines* EXCELLENT, first-class, first-rate, great, exceptional, outstanding, quality, superior, splendid, magnificent, exquisite, choice, select, prime, supreme, superb, wonderful, superlative, of high quality, second to none; *informal* A1, top-notch, splendiferous. **2** *a fine lady* WORTHY, admirable, praiseworthy, laudable, estimable, upright, upstanding, respectable. **3** *the initiative is fine, but it's not enough on its own* ALL RIGHT, acceptable, suitable, good (enough), passable, satisfactory, adequate, reasonable, tolerable; *informal* OK. **4** *I feel fine* IN GOOD HEALTH, well, healthy, all right, (fighting) fit, as fit as a fiddle/flea, blooming, thriving, in good shape/condition, in fine fettle; *informal* OK, in the pink. **5** *a fine day* FAIR, dry, bright, clear, sunny, without a cloud in the sky, warm, balmy, summery. **6** *a fine old house* IMPRESSIVE, imposing, striking, splendid, grand, majestic, magnificent, stately. **7** *fine clothes* ELEGANT, stylish, expensive, smart, chic, fashionable; fancy, sumptuous, lavish, opulent; *informal* flashy, swanky, ritzy, plush. **8** *a fine mind* KEEN, quick, alert, sharp, bright, brilliant, astute, clever, intelligent, perspicacious. **9** *fine china* DELICATE, fragile, dainty. **10** *fine hair* THIN, light, delicate, wispy, flyaway. **11** *a fine point* SHARP, keen, acute, sharpened, razor-sharp. **12** *fine material* SHEER, light, lightweight, thin, flimsy; diaphanous, filmy, gossamer, silky, transparent, translucent, see-through. **13** *a fine gold chain* PURE, sterling, solid, unmixed, unblended, one hundred per cent. **14** *fine sand* FINE-GRAINED, powdery, powdered, ground, crushed; *technical* comminuted; *archaic* pulverulent. **15** *fine detailed work* INTRICATE, delicate, detailed, elaborate, dainty, meticulous. **16** *a fine distinction* SUBTLE, ultra-fine, nice, hair-splitting. **17** *people's finer feelings* ELEVATED, lofty, exalted; refined, sensitive, cultivated, cultured, civilized, sophisticated. **18** *fine taste* DISCERNING, discriminating, refined, cultivated, cultured, critical.
– OPPOSITES poor, unsatisfactory, ill, inclement, thick, coarse.
● adverb *(informal) you're doing fine* WELL, all right, not badly, satisfactorily, adequately, nicely, tolerably; *informal* OK, good.
– OPPOSITES badly.
● verb **1** *it can be fined right down to the required shape* THIN, make/become thin, narrow, taper, attenuate. **2** *additives for fining wine* CLARIFY, clear, purify, refine, filter.

fine[2] ● noun *heavy fines* (FINANCIAL) PENALTY, sanction, fee, charge; *for-*

fine print ● noun another term for SMALL PRINT.
finery /fīnəri/ ● noun showy clothes or decoration.
fines herbes /feenz airb/ ● plural noun mixed herbs used in cooking.
– ORIGIN French, 'fine herbs'.
fine-spun ● adjective (especially of fabric) fine or delicate in texture.
finesse ● noun **1** refinement and delicacy. **2** subtle skill in handling or manipulating people or situations. **3** (in bridge and whist) an attempt to win a trick with a card that is not a certain winner. ● verb **1** do in a subtle and delicate manner. **2** slyly attempt to avoid blame when dealing with (a situation). **3** play (a card) as a finesse.
– ORIGIN French, related to FINE[1].
fine-tooth comb (also **fine-toothed comb**) ● noun (in phrase **with a fine-tooth comb**) with a very thorough search or analysis.
fine-tune ● verb make small adjustments to in order to achieve the best performance.
finger ● noun **1** each of the four slender jointed parts attached to either hand (or five, if the thumb is included). **2** a measure of liquor in a glass, based on the breadth of a finger. **3** an object with the long, narrow shape of a finger. ● verb **1** touch or feel with the fingers. **2** identify or choose for a particular purpose. **3** informal, chiefly N. Amer. inform on. **4** Music play (a passage) with a particular sequence of positions of the fingers.
– PHRASES **be all fingers and thumbs** Brit. informal be clumsy. **burn one's fingers** suffer unpleasant consequences as a result of one's actions. **have a finger in the pie** be involved in a matter. **have one's finger on the pulse** be aware of the latest trends. **lay a finger on** touch (someone), especially with the intention of harming them. **pull one's finger out** Brit. informal cease prevaricating and start to act. **put the finger on** informal inform on. **put one's finger on** identify exactly. **snap** (or **click**) **one's fingers** make a sharp clicking sound by bending the middle finger against the thumb and suddenly releasing it.
– DERIVATIVES **fingered** adjective **fingerless** adjective.
– ORIGIN Old English.
fingerboard ● noun a flat strip on the neck of a stringed instrument, against which the strings are pressed in order to vary the pitch.
finger bowl ● noun a small bowl holding water for rinsing the fingers at a meal.
finger food ● noun food that can conveniently be eaten with the fingers.
fingering ● noun a manner or technique of using the fingers to play a musical instrument.
fingernail ● noun the nail on the upper surface of the tip of each finger.
finger paint ● noun thick paint designed to be applied with the fingers, used especially by young children.
fingerpick ● verb play (a guitar or similar instrument) using the fingernails or plectrums worn on the fingertips.
fingerplate ● noun a piece of metal or porcelain fixed to a door above the handle to prevent fingermarks on the door itself.
fingerpost ● noun a post at a road junction from which signs project in the direction of the place indicated.
fingerprint ● noun a mark made on a surface by a person's fingertip, useful for purposes of identification. ● verb record the fingerprints of.
fingerstall ● noun a cover to protect a finger.
fingertip ● adjective using or operated by the fingers.
– PHRASES **at one's fingertips** (especially of information) readily available.
finial /finniəl/ ● noun **1** a distinctive section or ornament at the highest point of a roof, pinnacle, or similar structure. **2** an ornament at the top, end, or corner of an object.
– ORIGIN from Latin *finis* 'end'.
finical /finnik'l/ ● adjective finicky.
– DERIVATIVES **finically** adverb.
finicky ● adjective **1** fussy. **2** excessively detailed or elaborate.
– DERIVATIVES **finickiness** noun.
fining ● noun a substance used for clarifying beer or wine.
finis /feeniss/ ● noun the end (printed at the end of a book or shown at the end of a film).
– ORIGIN Latin.
finish ● verb **1** bring or come to an end. **2** consume or get through the whole or the remainder of (food or drink). **3** (**finish with**) have nothing more to do with. **4** reach the end of a race or other sporting competition. **5** (**finish up**) chiefly Brit. end by doing something or being in a particular position. **6** (**finish off**) kill or comprehensively defeat. **7** complete the manufacture or decoration of (something) by giving it an attractive surface appearance. ● noun **1** an end or final stage. **2** the place at which a race or competition ends. **3** the manner in which a manufactured article is finished.
– PHRASES **a fight to the finish** a fight or contest which ends only with the complete defeat of one of the participants.
– DERIVATIVES **finisher** noun.
– ORIGIN Latin *finire*, from *finis* 'end'.
finishing school ● noun a private college where girls are prepared for entry into fashionable society.
finishing touch ● noun a final detail completing and enhancing a piece of work.
finite /fīnīt/ ● adjective limited in size or extent.
– DERIVATIVES **finitely** adverb **finiteness** noun.
– ORIGIN Latin *finitus* 'finished'.
finito /fineetō/ ● adjective informal finished.

Thesaurus

mal mulct; *Brit. historical* amercement.
● verb *they were fined for breaking environmental laws* PENALIZE, impose a fine on, charge; *formal* mulct; *Brit. historical* amerce.
finery ● noun REGALIA, best clothes, (Sunday) best; *informal* glad rags, best bib and tucker.
finesse ● noun **1** *masterly finesse* SKILL, skilfulness, expertise, subtlety, flair, panache, elan, polish, artistry, virtuosity, mastery. **2** *a modicum of finesse* TACT, tactfulness, discretion, diplomacy, delicacy, sensitivity, perceptiveness, savoir faire. **3** *a clever finesse* WINNING MOVE, trick, stratagem, ruse, manoeuvre, artifice, machination.
finger ● noun *he wagged his finger at her* DIGIT, thumb, index finger, forefinger; *informal* pinkie.
– RELATED TERMS digital.
● verb **1** *she fingered her brooch uneasily* TOUCH, feel, handle, stroke, rub, caress, fondle, toy with, play (about/around) with, fiddle with. **2** *(N. Amer. informal) no one fingered the culprit* IDENTIFY, recognize, pick out, spot; inform on, point the finger at; *informal* rat on, squeal on, tell on, blow the whistle on, snitch on, peach on; *Brit. informal* grass on.
finicky ● adjective FUSSY, fastidious, punctilious, over-particular, difficult, exacting, demanding; *informal* picky, choosy, pernickety; *N. Amer. informal* persnickety; *archaic* nice.
finish ● verb **1** *Mrs Porter had just finished the task* COMPLETE, end, conclude, stop, cease, terminate, bring to a conclusion/end/close, wind up; crown, cap, round off, put the finishing touches to; accomplish, discharge, carry out, do, get done, fulfil; *informal* wrap up, sew up, polish off. **2** *Sarah has finished school* LEAVE, give up, drop; stop, discontinue, have done with, complete; *informal* pack in, quit. **3** *Hitch finished his dinner* CONSUME, eat, devour, drink, finish off, polish off, gulp (down); use (up), exhaust, empty, drain, get through, run through; *informal* down. **4** *the programme has finished* END, come to an end, stop, conclude, come to a conclusion/end/close, cease. **5** *some items were finished in a black lacquer* VARNISH, lacquer, veneer, coat, stain, wax, shellac, enamel, glaze.
– OPPOSITES start, begin, continue.
● noun **1** *the finish of filming* END, ending, completion, conclusion, close, closing, cessation, termination; final part/stage, finale, denouement; *informal* sewing up, polishing off. **2** *a gallop to the finish* FINISHING LINE/POST, tape. **3** *an antiquated paint finish* VENEER, lacquer, lamination, glaze, coating, covering; surface, texture.
– OPPOSITES start, beginning.
– PHRASES **finish someone/something off 1** *the executioners finished them off* KILL, take/end the life of, execute, terminate, exterminate, liquidate, get rid of; *informal* wipe out, do in, bump off, take out, dispose of, do away with; *N. Amer. informal* ice, rub out, waste. **2** *financial difficulties finished off the business* OVERWHELM, overcome, defeat, get the better of, worst, bring down; *informal* drive to the wall, best.
finished ● adjective **1** *the finished job* COMPLETED, concluded, terminated, over (and done with), at an end; accomplished, executed, discharged, fulfilled, done; *informal* wrapped up, sewn up, polished off; *formal* effectuated. **2** *a finished performance* ACCOMPLISHED, polished, flawless, faultless, perfect; expert, proficient, masterly, impeccable, virtuoso, skilful, skilled, professional. **3** *he*

– ORIGIN Italian.

fink N. Amer. informal • noun **1** an unpleasant or contemptible person. **2** an informer. • verb **1** (**fink on**) inform on. **2** (**fink out**) back out of a responsibility.
– ORIGIN of unknown origin.

Finn • noun a person from Finland.

finnan haddock /finnən/ • noun haddock cured with the smoke of green wood, turf, or peat.
– ORIGIN from the Scottish fishing village of *Findon*.

Finnish • noun the language of the Finns. • adjective relating to the Finns or their language.

fino /feenō/ • noun (pl. **finos**) a light-coloured dry sherry.
– ORIGIN Spanish, 'fine'.

fiord • noun variant spelling of FJORD.

fir • noun an evergreen coniferous tree with upright cones and flat needle-shaped leaves.
– ORIGIN probably Old Norse.

fir cone • noun chiefly Brit. the dry fruit of a fir tree or other conifer.

fire • noun **1** the state of burning, in which substances combine chemically with oxygen from the air and give out bright light, heat, and smoke. **2** an instance of destructive burning. **3** wood or coal burnt in a hearth or stove for heating or cooking. **4** (also **electric fire** or **gas fire**) Brit. a domestic heating appliance that uses electricity (or gas) as fuel. **5** a burning sensation. **6** passionate emotion or enthusiasm. **7** the firing of guns. **8** strong criticism. **9** one of the four elements (air, earth, fire, and water) in ancient and medieval philosophy and in astrology. • verb **1** propel (a bullet or projectile) from a gun or other weapon. **2** direct a rapid succession of (questions or statements) towards someone. **3** informal dismiss from a job. **4** supply (a furnace, power station, etc.) with fuel. **5** set fire to. **6** stimulate (the imagination or an emotion). **7** (**fire up**) fill with enthusiasm. **8** bake or dry (pottery, bricks, etc.) in a kiln.
– PHRASES **catch fire** begin to burn. **fire away** informal go ahead. **fire and brimstone** the supposed torments of hell. **firing on all (four) cylinders** functioning at a peak level. **go through fire (and water)** face any peril. **on fire 1** burning. **2** very excited. **set fire to** (or **set on fire**) cause to burn. **set the world on fire** do something remarkable or sensational. **under fire 1** being shot at. **2** being rigorously criticized.
– ORIGIN Old English.

fire alarm • noun a device making a loud noise that gives warning of a fire.

firearm • noun a rifle, pistol, or other portable gun.

fireball • noun **1** a ball of flame or fire. **2** a large bright meteor. **3** an energetic or hot-tempered person.

fire blanket • noun a sheet of flexible material used to smother a fire.

fireblight • noun a serious disease of fruit trees and other plants spread by bacteria, which gives leaves a scorched appearance.

firebomb • noun a bomb designed to cause a fire. • verb attack with a firebomb.

firebrand • noun a fervent supporter of a particular cause, especially one who incites unrest.

firebreak • noun an obstacle to the spread of fire, e.g. a strip of open space in a forest.

firebrick • noun a brick capable of withstanding intense heat, used especially to line furnaces and fireplaces.

fire brigade • noun chiefly Brit. an organized body of people trained and employed to extinguish fires.

firebug • noun informal an arsonist.

fireclay • noun clay capable of withstanding high temperatures, used for making firebricks.

firecracker • noun a loud, explosive firework.

firedamp • noun methane, especially as forming an explosive mixture with air in coal mines.

firedog • noun each of a pair of decorative metal supports for wood burning in a fireplace.

fire door • noun a fire-resistant door to prevent the spread of fire.

fire drill • noun a practice of the emergency procedures to be used in case of fire.

fire-eater • noun an entertainer who appears to eat fire.

fire engine • noun a vehicle carrying firefighters and their equipment.

fire escape • noun a staircase or other apparatus used for escaping from a building where there is a fire.

fire extinguisher • noun a portable device that discharges a jet of liquid, foam, or gas to extinguish a fire.

firefight • noun Military a battle using guns rather than bombs or other weapons.

firefighter • noun a person whose job is to extinguish fires.

firefly • noun a soft-bodied beetle which glows in the dark.

fireguard • noun a protective screen or grid placed in front of an open fire.

firehouse • noun N. Amer. a fire station.

fire irons • plural noun tongs, a poker, and a shovel for tending a domestic fire.

firelighter • noun Brit. a piece of flammable material used to help start a fire.

fireman • noun a male firefighter.

fireplace • noun a partially enclosed space at the base of a chimney for a domestic fire.

firepower • noun the destructive capacity of guns, missiles, or a military force.

fire practice • noun Brit. a fire drill.

fireproof • adjective able to withstand fire or great heat. • verb make fireproof.

fire-raiser • noun Brit. an arsonist.

fire sale • noun **1** a sale of goods remaining after a fire. **2** a sale of goods or assets at a very low price.

fire screen • noun **1** a fireguard. **2** an ornamental screen placed in front of a fireplace when the fire is unlit.

fireside • noun the area round a fireplace, especially as considered to be the focus of domestic life.

fireside chat • noun an informal and intimate conversation.

fire station • noun the headquarters of a fire brigade.

firestorm • noun a very intense and destructive fire, fanned by strong currents of air drawn in from the surrounding area.

firetrap • noun a building without proper provision for escape in case of fire.

firewall • noun **1** a wall or partition designed to stop the spread of fire. **2** Computing a part of a computer system or network which is designed to block unauthorized access while permitting outward communication.

firewater • noun informal strong alcoholic liquor.

fireweed • noun rosebay willowherb.
– ORIGIN so called from its tendency to grow on burnt land.

f

Thesaurus

was finished RUINED, defeated, beaten, wrecked, doomed, bankrupt, broken; *informal* washed up, through.
– OPPOSITES incomplete.

finite • adjective LIMITED, restricted, determinate, fixed.

fire • noun **1** *a fire broke out* BLAZE, conflagration, inferno; flames, burning, combustion. **2** *an electric fire* HEATER, radiator, convector. **3** *he lacked fire* DYNAMISM, energy, vigour, animation, vitality, vibrancy, exuberance, zest, elan; passion, ardour, zeal, spirit, verve, vivacity, vivaciousness; enthusiasm, eagerness, gusto, fervour, fervency; *informal* pep, vim, go, get-up-and-go, oomph. **4** *rapid machine-gun fire* GUNFIRE, firing, flak, bombardment. **5** *they directed their fire at the prime minister* CRITICISM, censure, condemnation, denunciation, opprobrium, admonishments, brickbats, flak; hostility, antagonism, animosity.
– RELATED TERMS pyro-.
• verb **1** *howitzers firing shells* LAUNCH, shoot, discharge, let fly with. **2** *someone fired a gun* SHOOT, discharge, let off, set off. **3** *(informal) he was fired* DISMISS, discharge, give someone their notice, lay off, let go, get rid of, axe, cashier; *informal* sack, give someone the sack, boot out, give someone the boot/bullet, give someone the elbow/push, give someone their marching orders; *Brit. informal* give someone their cards. **4** *the engine fired* START, get started, get going. **5** *I fired the straw* LIGHT, ignite, set fire to, set on fire, set alight, set ablaze; *informal* torch; *poetic/literary* enkindle, inflame. **6** *the stories fired my imagination* STIMULATE, stir up, excite, awaken, arouse, rouse, inflame, animate, inspire, motivate.
– PHRASES **catch fire** IGNITE, catch light, burst into flames, go up in flames. **on fire 1** *the restaurant was on fire* BURNING, alight, ablaze, blazing, aflame, in flames; *poetic/literary* afire. **2** *she was on fire with passion* ARDENT, passionate, fervent, excited, eager, enthusiastic.

firearm • noun GUN, weapon; *informal* shooter; *N. Amer. informal* piece, rod, shooting iron.

firebrand • noun RADICAL, revolutionary, agitator, rabble-rouser, incendiary, subversive, troublemaker.

firewood • noun wood that is burnt as fuel.
firework • noun **1** a device containing combustible chemicals that is ignited to produce spectacular effects and explosions. **2** (**fireworks**) an outburst of anger or a display of brilliance.
firing line • noun **1** the front line of troops in a battle. **2** a position where one is subject to criticism or blame.
firing squad • noun a group of soldiers detailed to shoot a condemned person.
firkin /furkin/ • noun chiefly historical a small cask used chiefly for liquids, butter, or fish.
– ORIGIN probably from Dutch *vierde* 'fourth' (a firkin originally contained a quarter of a barrel).
firm[1] • adjective **1** having an unyielding surface or structure. **2** solidly in place and stable. **3** having steady power or strength: *a firm grip.* **4** showing resolute determination. **5** fixed or definite: *firm plans.* • verb **1** make firm. **2** (often **firm up**) make (an agreement or plan) explicit and definite. • adverb in a resolute and determined manner.
– PHRASES **be on firm ground** be sure of one's facts or secure in one's position. **a firm hand** strict discipline or control.
– DERIVATIVES **firmly** adverb **firmness** noun.
– ORIGIN Latin *firmus.*
firm[2] • noun a company or business partnership.
– ORIGIN originally denoting a signature, later the name under which the business of a firm was transacted: from Latin *firmare* 'confirm by signature, settle'.
firmament /furməmənt/ • noun literary the heavens; the sky.
– ORIGIN Latin *firmamentum,* from *firmare* 'fix, settle'.
firmware • noun Computing permanent software programmed into a read-only memory.
first • ordinal number **1** coming before all others in time or order; earliest; 1st. **2** before doing something else specified or implied. **3** foremost in position, rank, or importance. **4** informal something never previously achieved or occurring. **5** Brit. a place in the top grade in an examination for a degree.
– PHRASES **at first** at the beginning. **first and foremost** more than anything else. **first and last** fundamentally. **first of all 1** before doing anything else. **2** most importantly. **first off** informal, chiefly N. Amer. as a first point. **first past the post 1** winning a race by being the first to reach the finishing line. **2** Brit. (of an electoral system) in which a candidate or party is selected by achievement of a simple majority. **first thing** early in the morning; before anything else. **first things first** important matters should be dealt with before other things. **first up** informal first of all. **in the first place 1** as the first consideration or point. **2** at the beginning; to begin with. **of the first order** (or **magnitude**) excellent or considerable of its kind.
– ORIGIN Old English.
first aid • noun help given to a sick or injured person until full medical treatment is available.
firstborn • noun the first child to be born to someone.
first class • noun **1** a set of people or things grouped together as the best. **2** the best accommodation in an aircraft, train, or ship. **3** Brit. the highest division in the results of the examinations for a university degree. • adjective & adverb (**first-class**) relating to the first class.
first-day cover • noun an envelope bearing one or more stamps postmarked on their day of issue.
first-degree • adjective **1** (of burns) affecting only the surface of the skin and causing reddening. **2** Law, chiefly N. Amer. (of crime, especially murder) in the most serious category.
– PHRASES **first-degree relative** a person's parent, sibling, or child.
first-foot • verb be the first person to cross someone's threshold in the New Year. • noun the first person to cross a threshold in such a way.
– DERIVATIVES **first-footer** noun.
first fruits • plural noun **1** the first agricultural produce of a season. **2** the initial results of an enterprise or endeavour.
first-hand • adjective & adverb from the original source or personal experience; direct: *first-hand knowledge.*
– PHRASES **at first hand** directly or from personal experience.
first lady • noun the wife of the President of the US or other head of state.
first lieutenant • noun a rank of officer in the US army or air force, above second lieutenant and below captain.
firstly • adverb in the first place; first.
first mate • noun the officer second in command to the master of a merchant ship.
first name • noun a personal name given to someone at birth or baptism and used before a family name.
– PHRASES **on first-name terms** having a friendly and informal relationship.
first night • noun the first public performance of a play or show.
first officer • noun **1** the first mate on a merchant ship. **2** the second in command to the captain on an aircraft.
first person • noun the form of a pronoun or verb used to refer to oneself, or to a group including oneself.
first principles • plural noun the fundamental concepts or assumptions on which a theory, system, or method is based.
first-rate • adjective of the best class, quality, or condition; excellent.
first reading • noun the first presentation of a bill to a legislative assembly, to permit its introduction.
first refusal • noun the privilege of deciding whether to accept or reject something before it is offered to others.
first school • noun Brit. a school for children from five to nine years old.
first strike • noun an opening attack with nuclear weapons.

Thesaurus

fireproof • adjective NON-FLAMMABLE, incombustible, fire resistant, flame resistant, flame retardant, heatproof.
– OPPOSITES inflammable.
fireworks • plural noun **1** *firework displays* PYROTECHNICS, feux d'artifice. **2** *his stubbornness has produced some fireworks* UPROAR, trouble, mayhem, fuss; tantrums, hysterics.
firm[1] • adjective **1** *the ground is fairly firm* HARD, solid, unyielding, resistant; solidified, hardened, compacted, compressed, dense, stiff, rigid, frozen, set. **2** *firm foundations* SECURE, secured, stable, steady, strong, fixed, fast, set, taut, tight; immovable, irremovable, stationary, motionless. **3** *a firm handshake* STRONG, vigorous, sturdy, forceful. **4** *I was very firm about what I wanted | a firm supporter* RESOLUTE, determined, decided, resolved, steadfast; adamant, emphatic, insistent, single-minded, in earnest, wholehearted; unfaltering, unwavering, unflinching, unswerving, unbending; hard-line, committed, dyed-in-the-wool. **5** *firm friends* CLOSE, good, boon, intimate, inseparable, dear, special, fast; constant, devoted, loving, faithful, long-standing, steady, steadfast. **6** *firm plans* DEFINITE, fixed, settled, decided, established, confirmed, agreed; unalterable, unchangeable, irreversible.
– OPPOSITES soft, unstable, limp, indefinite.
firm[2] • noun *an accountancy firm* COMPANY, business, concern, enterprise, organization, corporation, conglomerate, office, bureau, agency, consortium; *informal* outfit, set-up.
firmament • noun *(poetic/literary)* THE SKY, heaven; the heavens, the skies; *poetic/literary* the empyrean, the welkin.
first • adjective **1** *the first chapter* EARLIEST, initial, opening, introductory. **2** *first principles* FUNDAMENTAL, basic, rudimentary, primary; key, cardinal, central, chief, vital, essential. **3** *our first priority* FOREMOST, principal, highest, greatest, paramount, top, uppermost, prime, chief, leading, main, major; overriding, predominant, prevailing, central, core, dominant; *informal* number-one. **4** *first prize* TOP, best, prime, premier, winner's, winning.
– OPPOSITES last, closing.
• adverb **1** *the room they had first entered* AT FIRST, to begin with, first of all, at the outset, initially. **2** *she would eat first* BEFORE ANYTHING ELSE, first and foremost, now. **3** *she wouldn't go—she'd die first!* IN PREFERENCE, sooner, rather.
• noun **1** *from the first, surrealism was theatrical* THE (VERY) BEGINNING, the start, the outset, the commencement; *informal* the word go, the off. **2** *(informal) it was a first for both of us* NOVELTY, new/first experience.
first-class • adjective SUPERIOR, first-rate, high-quality, top-quality, high-grade, five-star; prime, premier, premium, grade A, best, finest, select, exclusive, excellent, superb; *informal* tip-top, A1, topnotch.
– OPPOSITES poor.
first-hand • adjective DIRECT, immediate, personal, hands-on, experiential, empirical.
– OPPOSITES vicarious, indirect.
first name • noun FORENAME, Christian name, given name.
– OPPOSITES surname.
first-rate • adjective TOP-QUALITY, high-quality, top-grade, first-class, second to none, fine; superlative, excellent, superb, outstanding,

First World ● noun the industrialized capitalist countries of western Europe, North America, Japan, Australia, and New Zealand.

firth ● noun a narrow inlet of the sea.
– ORIGIN Old Norse.

fiscal /fisk'l/ ● adjective **1** relating to government revenue, especially taxes. **2** chiefly N. Amer. relating to financial matters.
– DERIVATIVES **fiscally** adverb.
– ORIGIN Latin *fiscalis*, from *fiscus* 'rush basket, purse, treasury'.

fiscal year ● noun North American term for FINANCIAL YEAR.

fish[1] ● noun (pl. same or **fishes**) **1** a limbless cold-blooded animal with a backbone, gills and fins, living wholly in water. **2** the flesh of fish as food. **3** informal a person who is strange in a specified way: *he's a cold fish.* ● verb **1** catch fish with a net or hook and line. **2** (**fish out**) pull or take out of water or a receptacle. **3** grope or feel for something concealed. **4** (**fish for**) try subtly or deviously to obtain (a response or information).
– PHRASES **all's fish that comes to the net** proverb you can or should take advantage of anything that comes your way. **a big fish** an important person. **a big fish in a small pond** a person who is important only within a small community. **a fish out of water** a person who feels out of place in their surroundings. **have other** (or **bigger**) **fish to fry** have more important matters to attend to.
– DERIVATIVES **fishing** noun.
– USAGE The normal plural of **fish** is **fish**, as in *he caught two huge fish*; however the older form **fishes** is still used when referring to different kinds of fish: *freshwater fishes of the British Isles.*
– ORIGIN Old English.

fish[2] ● noun **1** (also **fishplate**) a flat connecting or strengthening piece fixed across a joint, e.g. in railway track. **2** a long curved piece of wood lashed to a ship's damaged mast or spar as a temporary repair. ● verb join, strengthen, or mend with a fish.
– ORIGIN probably from French *fiche*, from *ficher* 'to fix'.

fishbowl ● noun a round glass bowl for keeping pet fish in.

fish cake ● noun a patty of shredded fish and mashed potato.

fisher ● noun **1** a large brown marten found in North American woodland. **2** archaic a fisherman.

fisherfolk ● plural noun people who catch fish for a living.

fisherman ● noun a person who catches fish for a living or for sport.

fishery ● noun (pl. **fisheries**) **1** a place where fish are reared, or caught in numbers. **2** the occupation or industry of catching or rearing fish.

fisheye ● noun a very wide-angle lens with a field of vision covering up to 180°, the scale being reduced towards the edges.

fish finger ● noun Brit. a small oblong piece of flaked or minced fish coated in batter or breadcrumbs.

fishing line ● noun a long thread of silk or nylon attached to a baited hook and used for catching fish.

fishing rod ● noun a long, tapering rod to which a fishing line is attached.

fish kettle ● noun an oval pan for boiling fish.

fish knife ● noun a blunt knife with a broad blade used for eating or serving fish.

fishmeal ● noun ground dried fish used as fertilizer or animal feed.

fishmonger ● noun a person or shop that sells fish for food.

fishnet ● noun an open mesh fabric resembling a fishing net.

fish slice ● noun Brit. a kitchen utensil with a broad flat blade for lifting fish and fried foods.

fishtail ● noun a thing resembling a fish's tail in shape or movement. ● verb travel with a side-to-side motion.

fishwife ● noun a coarse-mannered woman who is prone to shouting.

fishy ● adjective (**fishier**, **fishiest**) **1** referring to or resembling a fish or fish. **2** informal arousing feelings of doubt or suspicion.
– DERIVATIVES **fishily** adverb **fishiness** noun.

fissile /fissīl/ ● adjective **1** (of an atom or element) able to undergo nuclear fission. **2** (chiefly of rock) easily split.
– ORIGIN Latin *fissilis*, from *findere* 'split, crack'.

fission /fish'n/ ● noun **1** the action of splitting or being split into two or more parts. **2** a reaction in which an atomic nucleus splits in two, releasing much energy. **3** Biology reproduction by means of cell division. ● verb undergo fission.
– DERIVATIVES **fissionable** adjective.

fission bomb ● noun an atom bomb.

fissiparous /fisippərəss/ ● adjective inclined to cause or undergo fission.
– DERIVATIVES **fissiparousness** noun.
– ORIGIN from Latin *fissus* 'split', on the pattern of *viviparous.*

fissure /fishər/ ● noun a long, narrow crack. ● verb split; crack.
– ORIGIN Latin *fissura*, from *findere* 'to split'.

fist ● noun a person's hand when the fingers are bent in towards the palm and held there tightly.
– PHRASES **make a —— fist of** informal do something to the specified degree of success.
– DERIVATIVES **fisted** adjective **fistful** noun.
– ORIGIN Old English.

fisticuffs ● plural noun fighting with the fists.

fistula /fistyoolə/ ● noun (pl. **fistulas** or **fistulae** /fistyoolee/) Medicine an abnormal or surgically made passage between a hollow or tubular organ and the body surface, or between two hollow or tubular organs.
– ORIGIN Latin, 'pipe, flute, fistula'.

fit[1] ● adjective (**fitter**, **fittest**) **1** of a suitable quality, standard, or type to meet the required purpose. **2** in good health, especially through regular physical exercise. **3** (**fit to do**) informal on the point of doing. **4** Brit. informal sexually attractive. ● verb (**fitted** (US also **fit**), **fitting**) **1** be of the right shape and size for. **2** be or make able to occupy a particular position, place, or period of time. **3** fix into place. **4** (often **be fitted with**) provide with a particular component or article. **5** join together to form a whole. **6** be or make suitable for. **7** (usu. **be fitted for**) try clothing on (someone) in order to make or alter it to the correct size. ● noun the way in which something fits.
– PHRASES **fit in 1** be compatible or in harmony. **2** (also **fit into**) constitute part of a particular situation or larger structure. **fit out** (or **up**) provide with necessary items. **fit to be tied** informal very angry. **fit up** Brit. informal incriminate (someone) by falsifying evidence against them. **see** (or **think**) **fit** consider it correct or acceptable.
– DERIVATIVES **fitness** noun **fitter** noun **fitly** adverb.
– ORIGIN of unknown origin.

fit[2] ● noun **1** a sudden attack of convulsions. **2** a sudden attack of coughing, fainting, etc. **3** a sudden burst of intense feeling or activity.
– PHRASES **in** (or **by**) **fits and starts** with irregular bursts of activity.
– ORIGIN Old English, 'conflict'.

fitful ● adjective active or occurring intermittently; not regular or

f

Thesaurus

exceptional, exemplary, marvellous, magnificent, splendid; *informal* tip-top, top-notch, ace, A1, super, great, terrific, tremendous, fantastic; *Brit. informal* top-hole, smashing; *informal, dated* capital.

fiscal ● adjective TAX, budgetary; financial, economic, monetary, money.

fish ● verb **1** *some people were fishing in the lake* GO FISHING, angle, trawl. **2** *she fished for her purse* SEARCH, delve, look, hunt; grope, fumble, ferret (about/around), root about/around, rummage (about/around/round). **3** *I'm not fishing for compliments* TRY TO GET, seek to obtain, solicit, angle, aim, hope, be after, cast about/around/round.
– PHRASES **fish someone/something out** PULL OUT, haul out, remove, extricate, extract, retrieve; rescue from, save from.

fisherman ● noun ANGLER, rod; *archaic* fisher.

fishing ● noun ANGLING, trawling, catching fish.

fishy ● adjective **1** *a fishy smell* FISHLIKE, piscine. **2** *round fishy eyes* EXPRESSIONLESS, inexpressive, vacant, lacklustre, glassy. **3** *(informal) there was something fishy going on* SUSPICIOUS, questionable, dubious, doubtful, suspect; odd, queer, peculiar, strange; *informal* funny, shady, crooked, bent; *Brit. informal* dodgy; *Austral./NZ informal* shonky.

fission ● noun SPLITTING, division, dividing, rupture, breaking, severance.
– OPPOSITES fusion.

fissure ● noun OPENING, crevice, crack, cleft, breach, crevasse, chasm; break, fracture, fault, rift, rupture, split.

fist ● noun CLENCHED HAND; *informal* duke, meat hook; *Brit. informal* bunch of fives.

fit[1] ● adjective **1** *fit for human habitation | he is a fit subject for such a book* SUITABLE, good enough; relevant, pertinent, apt, appropriate, suited, apposite, fitting; *archaic* meet. **2** *is he fit to look after a child?* COMPETENT, able, capable; ready, prepared, qualified, trained, equipped. **3** *(informal) you look fit to commit murder!* READY,

steady.

– DERIVATIVES **fitfully** adverb **fitfulness** noun.

fitment ● noun chiefly Brit. a fixed item of furniture or piece of equipment.

fitted ● adjective **1** made to fill a space or to cover something closely. **2** chiefly Brit. (of a room) equipped with matching units of furniture. **3** attached to or provided with a particular component or article. **4** (**fitted for/to do**) being fit for or to do.

fitting ● noun **1** an attachment. **2** (**fittings**) items which are fixed in a building but can be removed when the owner moves. **3** an occasion when one tries on a garment that is being made or altered. ● adjective appropriate; right or proper.

– DERIVATIVES **fittingly** adverb **fittingness** noun.

fitting room ● noun a room in a shop where one can try on clothes before purchase.

five ● cardinal number one more than four; 5. (Roman numeral: **v** or **V**.)

– DERIVATIVES **fivefold** adjective & adverb.

– ORIGIN Old English.

five-and-dime (also **five-and-dime store** or **five-and-ten**) ● noun N. Amer. a shop selling a wide variety of inexpensive goods.

five-a-side ● noun a form of soccer with five players in each team.

five o'clock shadow ● noun a slight growth of beard visible on a man's chin several hours after he has shaved.

fiver ● noun **1** Brit. informal a five-pound note. **2** N. Amer. a five-dollar bill.

fives ● plural noun (treated as sing.) a game in which a ball is hit with a gloved hand or a bat against a wall.

– ORIGIN plural of FIVE; the significance is unknown.

five-spice ● noun a blend of five powdered spices, typically fennel seeds, cinnamon, cloves, star anise, and peppercorns, used in Chinese cuisine.

fix ● verb **1** attach or position securely. **2** repair or restore. **3** decide or settle on. **4** make arrangements for. **5** make unchanging, constant or permanent. **6** (**fix on**) direct or be directed unwaveringly toward. **7** informal deviously influence the outcome of. **8** informal take an injection of a narcotic drug. **9** informal, chiefly N. Amer. provide with food or drink. ● noun **1** an act of fixing. **2** informal a difficult or awkward situation. **3** informal a dose of a narcotic drug to which one is addicted.

– PHRASES **fix up 1** arrange or organize. **2** informal provide with something. **get a fix on** determine the position, nature, or facts of.

– DERIVATIVES **fixable** adjective **fixer** noun.

– ORIGIN Latin *fixus* 'fixed', from *figere* 'fix, fasten'.

fixate /fiksayt/ ● verb **1** (often **be fixated on**) cause to be obsessively interested in. **2** direct one's eyes towards.

fixation ● noun **1** the action of fixating or the state of being fixated. **2** an obsessive interest in or feeling about someone or something. **3** the process by which some plants and micro-organisms combine chemically with gaseous nitrogen or carbon dioxide to form non-gaseous compounds.

fixative /fiksətiv/ ● noun a substance used to fix, protect, or stabilize something. ● adjective (of a substance) used as a fixative.

fixed ● adjective **1** fastened securely in position. **2** predetermined or inflexibly held. **3** (**fixed for**) informal situated with regard to: *how are you fixed for money?*

– DERIVATIVES **fixedly** adverb **fixedness** noun.

Thesaurus

prepared, all set, in a fit state, likely, about; *informal* psyched up. **4** *he looked tanned and fit* HEALTHY, well, in good health, in (good) shape, in (good) trim, in good condition, fighting fit, as fit as a fiddle/flea; athletic, muscular, strong, robust, hale and hearty.

– OPPOSITES unsuitable, incapable, unwell.

● verb **1** *my overcoat should fit you* BE THE RIGHT/CORRECT SIZE (FOR), be big/small enough (for), fit like a glove. **2** *have your carpets fitted professionally* LAY, put in place/position, position, place, fix. **3** *cameras fitted with a backlight button* EQUIP, provide, supply, fit out, furnish. **4** *concrete slabs were fitted together* JOIN, connect, put together, piece together, attach, unite, link. **5** *a sentence that fits his crimes* BE APPROPRIATE TO, suit, match, correspond to, tally with, go with, accord with, correlate to, be congruous with, be congruent with, be consonant with. **6** *an MSc fits you for a professional career* QUALIFY, prepare, make ready, train, groom.

● noun *the degree of fit between a school's philosophy and practice* CORRELATION, correspondence, agreement, consistency, equivalence, match, similarity, compatibility, concurrence.

– PHRASES **fit in** CONFORM, be in harmony, blend in, be in line, be assimilated into. **fit someone/something out/up** EQUIP, provide, supply, furnish, kit out, rig out. **fit someone up** (*Brit. informal*) FALSELY INCRIMINATE; *informal* frame, set up.

fit[2] ● noun **1** *an epileptic fit* CONVULSION, spasm, paroxysm, seizure, attack; *Medicine* ictus. **2** *a fit of the giggles* OUTBREAK, outburst, attack, bout, spell. **3** *my mother would have a fit if she knew* TANTRUM, fit of temper, outburst of anger/rage, frenzy; *informal* paddy, stress; *N. Amer. informal* blowout; *formal* boutade.

– PHRASES **in/by fits and starts** SPASMODICALLY, intermittently, sporadically, erratically, irregularly, fitfully, haphazardly.

fitful ● adjective INTERMITTENT, sporadic, spasmodic, broken, disturbed, disrupted, patchy, irregular, uneven, unsettled.

fitness ● noun **1** *polo requires tremendous fitness* GOOD HEALTH, strength, robustness, vigour, athleticism, toughness, physical fitness, muscularity; good condition, good shape, well-being. **2** *his fitness for active service* SUITABILITY, capability, competence, ability, aptitude; readiness, preparedness, eligibility.

fitted ● adjective **1** *a fitted sheet* SHAPED, contoured, fitting tightly/well. **2** *a fitted wardrobe* BUILT-IN, integral, integrated, fixed. **3** *he wasn't fitted for the job* (WELL) SUITED, right, suitable; equipped, fit; *informal* cut out.

fitting ● noun **1** *a light fitting* ATTACHMENT, connection, part, piece, component, accessory. **2** *bathroom fittings* FURNISHINGS, furniture, fixtures, fitments, equipment, appointments, appurtenances. **3** *the fitting of catalytic converters* INSTALLATION, installing, putting in, fixing.

● adjective *a fitting conclusion* APT, appropriate, suitable, apposite; fit, proper, right, seemly, correct; *archaic* meet.

– OPPOSITES unsuitable.

five ● cardinal number QUINTET, fivesome; quintuplets; *technical* pentad.

– RELATED TERMS quin-, quinque-, penta-.

fix ● verb **1** *signs were fixed to lamp posts* FASTEN, attach, affix, secure; join, connect, couple, link; install, implant, embed; stick, glue, pin, nail, screw, bolt, clamp, clip. **2** *his words are fixed in my memory* STICK, lodge, embed. **3** *his eyes were fixed on the ground* FOCUS, direct, level, point, train. **4** *techniques of fixing audience's attention* ATTRACT, draw; hold, grip, engage, captivate, rivet. **5** *he fixed my washing machine* REPAIR, mend, put right, put to rights, get working, restore (to working order); overhaul, service, renovate, recondition. **6** *James fixed it for his parents to watch the show from the wings* ARRANGE, organize, contrive, manage, engineer; *informal* swing, wangle. **7** (*informal*) *Laura was fixing her hair* ARRANGE, put in order, adjust; style, groom, comb, brush; *informal* do. **8** (*informal*) *Chris will fix supper* PREPARE, cook, make, get; *informal* rustle up; *Brit. informal* knock up. **9** *let's fix a date for the meeting* DECIDE ON, select, choose, resolve on; determine, settle, set, arrange, establish, allot; designate, name, appoint, specify. **10** *chemicals are used to fix the dye* MAKE PERMANENT, make fast, set. **11** (*informal*) *the fight was fixed* RIG, arrange fraudulently; tamper with, influence; *informal* fiddle. **12** (*informal*) *don't tell anybody, or I'll fix you!* GET ONE'S REVENGE ON, avenge oneself on, get even with, get back at, take reprisals against, punish, deal with; *informal* get one's own back on, sort someone out, settle someone's hash. **13** (*informal*) *a place where they can fix* INJECT DRUGS, take drugs; *informal* shoot up, mainline. **14** *the cat has been fixed* CASTRATE, neuter, geld, spay, desex, sterilize; *N. Amer. & Austral.* alter; *Brit. informal* doctor; *archaic* emasculate.

– OPPOSITES remove.

● noun (*informal*) **1** *they are in a bit of a fix* PREDICAMENT, plight, difficulty, awkward situation, corner, tight spot; mess, mare's nest, dire straits; *informal* pickle, jam, hole, scrape, bind, sticky situation. **2** *he needed his fix* DOSE; *informal* hit. **3** *a quick fix for the coal industry* SOLUTION, answer, resolution, way out, remedy, cure; *informal* magic bullet. **4** *the result was a complete fix* FRAUD, swindle, trick, charade, sham; *informal* set-up, fiddle.

– PHRASES **fix someone up** (*informal*) PROVIDE, supply, furnish. **fix something up** ORGANIZE, arrange, make arrangements for, fix, sort out.

fixated ● adjective OBSESSED, preoccupied, obsessive; focussed, keen, gripped, engrossed, immersed, wrapped up, enthusiastic, fanatical; *informal* hooked, wild, nuts, crazy; *Brit. informal* potty.

fixation ● noun OBSESSION, preoccupation, mania, addiction, compulsion; *informal* thing, bug, craze, fad.

fixed ● adjective **1** *there are fixed ropes on the rock face* FASTENED, secure, fast, firm; riveted, moored, anchored. **2** *a fixed period of*

fixed assets ● plural noun assets which are purchased for long-term use and are not likely to be converted quickly into cash, such as land, buildings, and equipment. Compare with CURRENT ASSETS.

fixed charge ● noun a liability to a creditor which relates to specific assets of a company. Compare with FLOATING CHARGE.

fixed odds ● plural noun betting odds that are predetermined, as opposed to a pool system or a starting price.

fixed-wing ● adjective (of aircraft) of the conventional type as opposed to those with rotating wings, such as helicopters.

fixing ● noun **1** the action of fixing. **2** (**fixings**) Brit. screws, bolts, etc. used to fix or assemble building material, furniture, or equipment.

fixity ● noun the state of being unchanging or permanent.

fixture /fikschər/ ● noun **1** a piece of equipment or furniture which is fixed in position in a building or vehicle. **2** (**fixtures**) articles attached to a house or land and considered legally part of it so that they normally remain in place when an owner moves. **3** Brit. a sporting event which takes place on a particular date. **4** informal a person or thing that has become established in a particular place.

fizgig /fizgig/ ● noun **1** archaic a silly or flirtatious young woman. **2** Austral. informal a police informer.
– ORIGIN probably from FIZZ + obsolete *gig* 'flighty girl'.

fizz ● verb **1** (of a liquid) produce bubbles of gas and make a hissing sound. **2** make a buzzing or crackling sound. ● noun **1** the action or sound of fizzing. **2** informal an effervescent drink, especially sparkling wine. **3** exuberance.
– ORIGIN imitative.

fizzer ● noun informal **1** Brit. an outstandingly lively or excellent thing. **2** Austral./NZ a failure or fiasco.

fizzle ● verb **1** make a feeble hissing or spluttering sound. **2** (**fizzle out**) end or fail in a weak or disappointing way. ● noun an instance of fizzling.
– ORIGIN probably imitative.

fizzog ● noun variant of PHIZ.

fizzy ● adjective (**fizzier**, **fizziest**) **1** (of a drink) effervescent. **2** exuberant.
– DERIVATIVES **fizzily** adverb **fizziness** noun.

fjord /fyord/ (also **fiord**) ● noun a long, narrow, deep inlet of the sea between high cliffs, found predominantly in Norway.
– ORIGIN Norwegian.

FL ● abbreviation Florida.

fl. ● abbreviation **1** floruit. **2** fluid.

flab ● noun informal soft, loose flesh on a person's body; fat.

flabbergast /flabbərgaast/ ● verb informal surprise greatly.
– DERIVATIVES **flabbergasted** adjective.
– ORIGIN of unknown origin.

flabby ● adjective (**flabbier**, **flabbiest**) **1** (of a part of a person's body) soft, loose, and fleshy. **2** not tightly controlled and therefore ineffective.
– DERIVATIVES **flabbily** adverb **flabbiness** noun.
– ORIGIN alteration of earlier *flappy*.

flaccid /flaksid, flassid/ ● adjective soft and limp.
– DERIVATIVES **flaccidity** noun **flaccidly** adverb.
– ORIGIN French *flaccide*, from Latin *flaccus* 'flabby'.

flack[1] N. Amer. informal ● noun a publicity agent. ● verb publicize or promote.
– ORIGIN of unknown origin.

flack[2] ● noun variant spelling of FLAK.

flag[1] ● noun **1** an oblong piece of cloth that is raised on or attached to a pole and used as an emblem or marker. **2** a device or symbol resembling a flag, used as a marker. **3** a small paper badge given to people who donate to a charity appeal. ● verb (**flagged**, **flagging**) **1** mark for attention. **2** direct or alert by waving a flag or using hand signals. **3** (**flag down**) signal to (a driver) to stop.
– PHRASES **fly the flag 1** (of a ship) be registered in a particular country and sail under its flag. **2** represent one's country or demonstrate one's affiliation with a party or organization. **put the flags out** celebrate.
– ORIGIN perhaps from obsolete *flag* 'drooping', of unknown origin.

flag[2] ● noun a flat rectangular or square stone slab, used for paving.
– DERIVATIVES **flagged** adjective.
– ORIGIN probably Scandinavian.

flag[3] ● noun a plant with long sword-shaped leaves, especially an iris.
– ORIGIN of unknown origin.

flag[4] ● verb (**flagged**, **flagging**) **1** become tired or less enthusiastic. **2** (**flagging**) becoming weaker or less dynamic.
– ORIGIN related to obsolete *flag* 'drooping'.

flag day ● noun Brit. a day on which money is collected in the street for a charity and contributors are given flags to wear.

flagellant /flajələnt/ ● noun a person who subjects themselves to flagellation.

flagellate[1] /flajəlayt/ ● verb flog, either as a religious discipline or for sexual gratification.
– DERIVATIVES **flagellation** noun.
– ORIGIN Latin *flagellare* 'whip'.

flagellate[2] /flajələt/ Zoology ● noun any of a large group of protozoans that have one or more flagella used for swimming. ● adjective having one or more flagella.

flagellum /fləjelləm/ ● noun (pl. **flagella**) Biology a microscopic whip-like appendage which enables many protozoans, bacteria,

f

Thesaurus

time PREDETERMINED, set, established, arranged, specified, decided, agreed, determined, confirmed, prescribed, definite, defined, explicit, precise.

fixture ● noun **1** *fixtures and fittings* FIXED APPLIANCE, installation, unit. **2** *(Brit.) their first fixture of the season* MATCH, race, game, competition, contest, sporting event.

fizz ● verb **1** *the mixture fizzed like mad* EFFERVESCE, sparkle, bubble, froth; *poetic/literary* spume. **2** *all the screens were fizzing* CRACKLE, buzz, hiss, fizzle, crepitate.
● noun **1** *the fizz in champagne* EFFERVESCENCE, sparkle, fizziness, bubbles, bubbliness, gassiness, carbonation, froth. **2** *(informal) they all had another glass of fizz* SPARKLING WINE, champagne; *informal* bubbly, champers, sparkler. **3** *their set is a little lacking in fizz* EBULLIENCE, exuberance, liveliness, life, vivacity, animation, vigour, energy, verve, dash, spirit, sparkle, zest; *informal* pizzazz, pep, zip, oomph. **4** *the fizz of the static* CRACKLE, crackling, buzz, buzzing, hiss, hissing, white noise; *poetic/literary* susurration.

fizzle ● verb *the loudspeaker fizzled* CRACKLE, buzz, hiss, fizz, crepitate.
● noun **1** *electric fizzle.* See FIZZ noun sense 4. **2** *the whole thing turned out to be a fizzle* FAILURE, fiasco, debacle, disaster; *Brit.* damp squib; *informal* flop, washout, let-down, dead loss; *N. Amer. informal* snafu.
– PHRASES **fizzle out** PETER OUT, die off, ease off, cool off; tail off, wither away.

fizzy ● adjective EFFERVESCENT, sparkling, carbonated, gassy, bubbly, frothy; mousseux, pétillant, spumante, frizzante.
– OPPOSITES still, flat.

flab ● noun *(informal)* FAT, excessive weight, fatness, plumpness; paunch, pot belly, beer gut.

flabbergast ● verb *(informal).* See ASTONISH.

flabbiness ● noun FAT, fatness, fleshiness, plumpness, chubbiness, portliness, obesity, corpulence; softness, looseness, flaccidity, droopiness, sag; *informal* flab, tubbiness.

flabby ● adjective **1** *his flabby stomach* SOFT, loose, flaccid, slack, untoned, drooping, sagging. **2** *a flabby woman* FAT, fleshy, overweight, plump, chubby, portly, rotund, broad in the beam, of ample proportions, obese, corpulent; *informal* tubby, roly-poly, well covered, well upholstered.
– OPPOSITES firm, thin.

flaccid ● adjective **1** *your muscles are sagging, they're flaccid* SOFT, loose, flabby, slack, lax; drooping, sagging. **2** *his play seemed flaccid* LACKLUSTRE, lifeless, listless, uninspiring, unanimated, tame.
– OPPOSITES firm, spirited.

flag[1] ● noun *the Irish flag* BANNER, standard, ensign, pennant, banderole, streamer, jack, gonfalon; colours; *Brit.* pendant.
– RELATED TERMS vexillary.
● verb *flag the misspelt words* INDICATE, identify, point out, mark, label, tag.
– PHRASES **flag someone/something down** HAIL, wave down, signal to stop, stop, halt.

flag[2] ● noun *stone flags.* See FLAGSTONE.

flag[3] ● verb **1** *they were flagging towards the finish* TIRE, grow tired/weary, weaken, grow weak, wilt, droop. **2** *my energy flags in the afternoon* FADE, decline, wane, ebb, diminish, decrease, lessen, dwindle; wither, melt away, peter out, die away/down.
– OPPOSITES revive.

and spermatozoa to swim.
– ORIGIN Latin, 'little whip'.
flageolet[1] /flajəlet/ ● noun **1** a very small flute-like instrument resembling a recorder. **2** a tin whistle.
– ORIGIN French, from Provençal *flaujol*.
flageolet[2] /flajəlay/ ● noun a small variety of French kidney bean.
– ORIGIN French, from Latin *phaseolus* 'bean'.
flagitious /fləjishəss/ ● adjective extremely and criminally wicked.
– ORIGIN Latin *flagitiosus*, from *flagitium* 'shameful crime'.
flagon /flaggən/ ● **1** noun a large container for serving or consuming drinks. **2** a large bottle in which wine or cider is sold, typically holding 1.13 litres (about 2 pints).
– ORIGIN Old French *flacon*, from Latin *flasco*.
flagpole ● noun a pole used for flying a flag.
flagrant /flaygrənt/ ● adjective conspicuous; blatant.
– DERIVATIVES **flagrancy** noun **flagrantly** adverb.
– ORIGIN from Latin *flagrare* 'blaze'.
flagship ● noun **1** the ship in a fleet which carries the commanding admiral. **2** the best or most important thing owned or produced by an organization.
flagstaff ● noun a flagpole.
flagstone ● noun a flat square or rectangular stone slab, used for paving.
flail /flayl/ ● noun a tool or machine with a swinging action, used for threshing. ● verb **1** swing or wave wildly. **2** (**flail around/about**) flounder; struggle.
– ORIGIN Latin *flagellum* 'little whip'.
flair ● noun **1** a natural ability or talent. **2** stylishness.
– ORIGIN French, from *flairer* 'to smell'.
flak (also **flack**) ● noun **1** anti-aircraft fire. **2** strong criticism.
– ORIGIN abbreviation of German *Fliegerabwehrkanone* 'aviator-defence gun'.
flake[1] ● noun **1** a small, flat, very thin piece of something. **2** N. Amer. informal a crazy or eccentric person. ● verb **1** come away from a surface in flakes. **2** split into flakes.
– ORIGIN probably Germanic.
flake[2] ● verb (**flake out**) informal fall asleep or drop from exhaustion.
– ORIGIN variant of obsolete *flack* and the verb FLAG[4].
flak jacket ● noun a sleeveless jacket made of heavy fabric reinforced with metal, worn as protection against bullets and shrapnel.
flaky ● adjective (**flakier**, **flakiest**) **1** breaking or separating easily into flakes. **2** N. Amer. informal crazy or eccentric.
– DERIVATIVES **flakiness** noun.
flaky pastry ● noun pastry consisting of a number of thin layers.
flambé /flombay/ ● adjective (after a noun) (of food) covered with spirits and set alight briefly. ● verb (**flambés**, **flambéed**, **flambéing**) cover (food) with spirits and set it alight briefly.
– ORIGIN French, 'singed'.
flambeau /flambō/ ● noun (pl. **flambeaus** or **flambeaux** /flambōz/) **1** a flaming torch. **2** a branched candlestick.
– ORIGIN French, from *flambe* 'a flame'.
flamboyant /flamboyənt/ ● adjective **1** conspicuously and confidently exuberant. **2** brightly coloured and showy.
– DERIVATIVES **flamboyance** noun **flamboyantly** adverb.
– ORIGIN French, 'flaming, blazing'.
flame ● noun **1** a hot glowing body of ignited gas produced by something on fire. **2** something thought of as burning fiercely or able to be extinguished: *the flame of hope.* **3** a brilliant orange-red colour. ● verb **1** give off flames. **2** apply a flame to; set alight. **3** (of an intense emotion) appear suddenly and fiercely. **4** (of a person's face) become red with embarrassment or anger. **5** Computing, informal send abusive or acrimonious email messages to.
– PHRASES **old flame** informal a former lover.
– ORIGIN Latin *flamma*.
flamenco /fləmengkō/ ● noun a spirited style of Spanish guitar music accompanied by singing and dancing.
– ORIGIN Spanish, 'like a gypsy' (literally 'Fleming'), from Dutch *Vlaminc*.
flameproof ● adjective **1** (of fabric) treated so as to be non-flammable. **2** (of cookware) able to be used either in an oven or on a hob.
flame-thrower ● noun a weapon that sprays out burning fuel.
flaming ● adjective **1** emitting flames. **2** very hot. **3** of a brilliant orange-red colour. **4** (especially of an argument) passionate. **5** informal expressing annoyance: *that flaming dog.*
flamingo /fləminggō/ ● noun (pl. **flamingos** or **flamingoes**) a wading bird with mainly pink or scarlet plumage and a long neck and legs.
– ORIGIN Spanish *flamengo*, earlier form of *flamenco*; associated, because of its colour, with Latin *flamma* 'a flame'.
flammable /flamməb'l/ ● adjective easily set on fire.
– DERIVATIVES **flammability** noun.
– USAGE The words **flammable** and **inflammable** have the same meaning. It is, however, safer to use **flammable** to avoid ambi-

Thesaurus

flagellate ● verb FLOG, whip, beat, scourge, lash, birch, strap, belt, cane, thrash, horsewhip, tan/whip someone's hide, give someone a hiding.
flagon ● noun JUG, vessel, bottle, carafe, flask, decanter, tankard, ewer, pitcher.
flagrant ● adjective BLATANT, glaring, obvious, overt, conspicuous, barefaced, shameless, brazen, undisguised, unconcealed; outrageous, scandalous, shocking, disgraceful, dreadful, terrible, gross.
flagstone ● noun PAVING SLAB, paving stone, slab, flag, sett.
flail ● verb **1** *he fell headlong, his arms flailing* WAVE, swing, thrash about, flap about. **2** *I was flailing about in the water* FLOUNDER, struggle, thrash, writhe, splash. **3** *he flailed their shoulders with his cane* THRASH, beat, strike, flog, whip, lash, scourge, cane; *informal* wallop, whack.
flair ● noun **1** *a flair for publicity* APTITUDE, talent, gift, instinct, (natural) ability, facility, skill, bent, feel. **2** *she dressed with flair* STYLE, stylishness, panache, dash, elan, poise, elegance; (good) taste, discernment, discrimination; *informal* class.
flak ● noun **1** *my aircraft had been damaged by flak* ANTI-AIRCRAFT FIRE, shelling, gunfire; bombardment, barrage, salvo, volley. **2** *he has come in for a lot of flak* CRITICISM, censure, disapproval, disapprobation, hostility, complaints; opprobrium, obloquy, calumny, calumniation, vilification, abuse, brickbats; *Brit. informal* stick, verbal; *formal* castigation, excoriation.
flake[1] ● noun *flakes of pastry* SLIVER, wafer, shaving, paring; chip, scale, spillikin; fragment, scrap, shred; *technical* lamina.
● verb *the paint was flaking* PEEL (OFF), chip, blister, come off (in layers).
flake[2] ● verb
– PHRASES **flake out** *(informal) she flaked out in her chair* FALL ASLEEP, go to sleep, drop off; collapse, faint, pass out, lose consciousness, black out, swoon; *informal* conk out, nod off; *N. Amer. informal* sack out, zone out.
flaky ● adjective FLAKING, peeling, scaly, blistering, scabrous.
flamboyant ● adjective **1** *her flamboyant personality* OSTENTATIOUS, exuberant, confident, lively, animated, vibrant, vivacious. **2** *a flamboyant cravat* COLOURFUL, brightly coloured, bright, vibrant, vivid; dazzling, eye-catching, bold; showy, gaudy, garish, lurid, loud; *informal* jazzy, flashy; *dated* gay. **3** *a flamboyant architectural style* ELABORATE, ornate, fancy; baroque, rococo.
– OPPOSITES restrained.
flame ● noun **1** *a sheet of flames* FIRE, blaze, conflagration, inferno. **2** *the flames of her anger* PASSION, warmth, ardour, fervour, fervency, fire, intensity. **3** *(informal) an old flame* SWEETHEART, boyfriend, girlfriend, lover, partner; *informal* steady; *dated* beau.
● verb **1** *logs crackled and flamed* BURN, blaze, be ablaze, be alight, be on fire, be in flames, be aflame. **2** *pour the whisky over the lobster and flame it* IGNITE, light, set light to, set fire to, set on fire, set alight, touch off; *informal* set/put a match to. **3** *Erica's cheeks flamed* BECOME RED, go red, blush, flush, redden, colour, grow pink/crimson/scarlet, glow.
– OPPOSITES extinguish.
– PHRASES **in flames** ON FIRE, burning, alight, flaming, blazing, ignited; *poetic/literary* afire.
flameproof ● adjective NON-FLAMMABLE, non-inflammable, flame-resistant, fire-resistant, flame-retardant, uninflammable.
– OPPOSITES flammable.
flaming ● adjective **1** *a flaming bonfire* BLAZING, ablaze, burning, on fire, in flames, aflame; *poetic/literary* afire. **2** *flaming hair* BRIGHT, brilliant, vivid; red, reddish-orange, ginger. **3** *a flaming row* FURIOUS, violent, vehement, frenzied, angry, passionate. **4** *in a flaming temper* FURIOUS, enraged, fuming, seething, incensed, infuriated, angry, raging; *informal* livid; *poetic/literary* wrathful. **5** *(informal) where's that flaming ambulance?* WRETCHED; *informal* damned,

guity, as the *in-* prefix of **inflammable** can give the impression that the word means 'non-flammable'.

flan ● noun a baked dish consisting of an open-topped pastry case with a savoury or sweet filling.
– ORIGIN Old French *flaon*, from Latin *flado*.

flâneur /flanör/ ● noun (pl. **flâneurs** pronunc. same) a man about town who strolls around and observes society.
– ORIGIN French, from *flâner* 'saunter, lounge'.

flange /flanj/ ● noun a projecting rim or piece.
– DERIVATIVES **flanged** adjective.
– ORIGIN perhaps from Old French *flanchir* 'to bend'.

flank ● noun **1** the side of a person's or animal's body between the ribs and the hip. **2** the side of something such as a building or mountain. **3** the left or right side of a body of people. ● verb be situated on each or on one side of.
– ORIGIN Old French *flanc*.

flanker ● noun **1** Rugby a wing forward. **2** American Football an offensive back who is positioned to the outside of an end. **3** Military a fortification to the side of a force or position.

flannel ● noun **1** a kind of soft-woven woollen or cotton fabric. **2** (**flannels**) men's trousers made of woollen flannel. **3** Brit. a small piece of towelling for washing oneself. **4** Brit. informal empty or flattering talk used to avoid dealing with a difficult subject. ● verb (**flannelled**, **flannelling**; US also **flanneled**, **flanneling**) informal, chiefly Brit. use empty or flattering talk to avoid dealing with a difficult subject.
– ORIGIN probably from Welsh *gwlanen* 'woollen article'.

flannelette /flannəlet/ ● noun a napped cotton fabric resembling flannel.

flap ● verb (**flapped**, **flapping**) **1** move or be moved up and down or from side to side. **2** (**flap at**) strike at with a light blow, a cloth, etc. **3** informal be agitated. ● noun **1** a piece of something attached on one side only, that covers an opening. **2** a hinged or sliding section of an aircraft wing, used to control lift. **3** a single flapping movement. **4** informal a panic.
– DERIVATIVES **flappy** adjective.
– ORIGIN probably imitative.

flapjack ● noun **1** Brit. a soft, thick biscuit made from oats and butter. **2** N. Amer. a pancake.
– ORIGIN from FLAP (in the dialect sense 'toss a pancake') + JACK[1].

flapper ● noun informal a fashionable and unconventional young woman of the 1920s.

flare ● noun **1** a sudden brief burst of flame or light. **2** a device producing a very bright flame as a signal or marker. **3** a gradual widening towards the hem of a garment. **4** (**flares**) trousers of which the legs widen from the knees down. ● verb **1** burn, shine, or be revealed with a sudden intensity. **2** (**flare up**) suddenly become intense, angry, or violent. **3** gradually become wider at one end.
– ORIGIN of unknown origin.

flarepath ● noun an area illuminated to enable an aircraft to land or take off.

flash ● verb **1** shine or cause to shine with a bright but brief or intermittent light. **2** move, pass, or send swiftly in a particular direction: *the scenery flashed by*. **3** display or be displayed briefly or repeatedly. **4** informal display conspicuously so as to impress: *they flash their money about*. **5** informal (of a man) show one's genitals in public. ● noun **1** a sudden brief burst of bright light. **2** a camera attachment that produces a flash of light, for taking photographs in poor light. **3** a sudden or brief manifestation or occurrence: *a flash of inspiration*. **4** a bright patch of colour. **5** Brit. a coloured patch of cloth worn on a uniform as a distinguishing emblem. ● adjective informal ostentatiously stylish or expensive.
– PHRASES **flash in the pan** a sudden but brief success. [ORIGIN with allusion to the priming of a firearm, the flash arising from an explosion of gunpowder within the lock.] **in a flash** very quickly.
– DERIVATIVES **flasher** noun.
– ORIGIN originally in the sense 'splash water about': probably imitative.

flashback ● noun **1** a scene in a film or novel set in a time earlier than the main story. **2** a sudden vivid memory of a past event.

flashboard ● noun a board used for sending more water from a mill dam into a mill race.

flashbulb ● noun a bulb for a flashgun.

flashcard ● noun a card containing a clear display of a word or words, used in teaching reading.

flash flood ● noun a sudden local flood resulting from extreme rainfall.

flashgun ● noun a device which gives a brief flash of intense light, used for taking photographs in poor light.

flashing ● noun a strip of metal used to seal the junction of a roof with another surface.

flashlight ● noun **1** an electric torch with a strong beam. **2** a flashgun.

flash memory ● noun Computing memory that retains data in the absence of a power supply.

flashover ● noun **1** a high-voltage electric short circuit. **2** an instance of a fire spreading very rapidly through the air because of intense heat.

flashpoint ● noun **1** a point or place at which anger or violence flares up. **2** Chemistry the temperature at which a flammable

f

Thesaurus

damnable, blasted, blessed, confounded; *Brit. informal* flipping, blinking, blooming, bleeding, effing; *Brit. informal, dated* bally, ruddy; *dated* cursed, accursed.

flammable ● adjective INFLAMMABLE, burnable, combustible.

flank ● noun **1** *the horse's flanks* SIDE, haunch, quarter, thigh. **2** *the southern flank of the Eighth Army* SIDE, wing; face, aspect.
● verb *the garden is flanked by two rivers* EDGE, bound, line, border, fringe.

flannel ● noun **1** *(Brit.) she dabbed her face with a flannel* FACECLOTH, cloth; *N. Amer.* washcloth, washrag; *Austral.* washer. **2** *(Brit. informal) don't accept any flannel from salespeople* SMOOTH TALK, flattery, blarney, blandishments, honeyed words; prevarication, equivocation, evasion, doublespeak; *informal* spiel, soft soap, sweet talk, baloney, hot air; *Brit. informal* waffle; *Austral./NZ informal* guyver.
● verb *(Brit. informal) she can tell if you're flannelling* USE FLATTERY, talk blarney; prevaricate, equivocate, be evasive, blather, stall; *Brit.* hum and haw; *informal* soft-soap, sweet-talk; *Brit. informal* waffle; *N. Amer. informal* fast-talk; *rare* tergiversate.

flap ● verb **1** *the mallards flapped their wings* BEAT, flutter, agitate, wave, wag, swing. **2** *the flag flapped in the breeze* FLUTTER, fly, blow, swing, sway, ripple, stir. **3** *(informal) a deliberate ploy to make us flap* PANIC, go into a panic, become flustered, be agitated, fuss; *informal* be in a state, be in a tizzy.
● noun **1** *pockets with buttoned flaps* FOLD, overlap, covering; lappet. **2** *a few flaps of the wing* FLUTTER, fluttering, beat, beating, waving. **3** *(informal) I'm in a frightful flap* PANIC, fluster; *informal* state, dither, twitter, blue funk, stew, tizzy; *N. Amer. informal* twit. **4** *(informal) she created a flap with her controversial statement* FUSS, commotion, stir, hubbub, storm, uproar; controversy, brouhaha, furore; *informal* to-do, ballyhoo, hoo-ha, kerfuffle.

flare ● noun **1** *the flare of the match* BLAZE, flash, dazzle, burst, flicker. **2** *a flare set off by the crew* DISTRESS SIGNAL, rocket, Very light, beacon, light, signal. **3** *a flare of anger* BURST, rush, eruption, explosion, spasm, access.
● verb **1** *the match flared* BLAZE, flash, flare up, flame, burn; glow, flicker. **2** *her nostrils flared* SPREAD, broaden, widen; dilate.
– PHRASES **flare up 1** *the wooden houses flared up like matchsticks* BURN, blaze, go up in flames. **2** *his injury has flared up again* RECUR, reoccur, reappear; break out, start suddenly, erupt. **3** *I flared up at him* LOSE ONE'S TEMPER, become enraged, fly into a temper, go berserk; *informal* blow one's top, fly off the handle, go mad, go bananas, hit the roof, go up the wall, go off the deep end, lose one's rag, flip (one's lid), explode, have a fit; *Brit. informal* go spare, go crackers, do one's nut; *N. Amer. informal* flip one's wig, blow one's lid/stack, have a conniption fit.

flash ● verb **1** *a torch flashed* LIGHT UP, shine, flare, blaze, gleam, glint, sparkle, burn; blink, wink, flicker, shimmer, twinkle, glimmer, glisten, scintillate; *poetic/literary* glister, coruscate. **2** *(informal) he was flashing his money about* SHOW OFF, flaunt, flourish, display, parade. **3** *(informal) he flashed at me* EXPOSE ONESELF, commit indecent exposure. **4** *racing cars flashed past* ZOOM, streak, tear, shoot, dash, dart, fly, whistle, hurtle, rush, bolt, race, speed, career, whizz, whoosh, buzz; *informal* belt, zap; *Brit. informal* bomb, bucket; *N. Amer. informal* barrel.
● noun **1** *a flash of light* FLARE, blaze, burst; gleam, glint, sparkle, flicker, shimmer, twinkle, glimmer. **2** *a basic uniform with no flashes* EMBLEM, insignia, badge; stripe, bar, chevron. **3** *a sudden flash of inspiration* BURST, outburst, wave, rush, surge, flush.
● adjective *(informal) a flash sports car*. See FLASHY.
– PHRASES **in/like a flash** INSTANTLY, suddenly, abruptly, immediate-

compound gives off sufficient vapour to ignite in air.

flashy ● adjective (**flashier**, **flashiest**) ostentatiously stylish.

– DERIVATIVES **flashily** adverb **flashiness** noun.

flask ● noun **1** a narrow-necked conical or spherical bottle. **2** Brit. a vacuum flask. **3** a hip flask. **4** (also **nuclear flask**) a lead-lined container for radioactive nuclear waste.

– ORIGIN Latin *flasca* 'cask or bottle'.

flat[1] ● adjective (**flatter**, **flattest**) **1** having a level and even surface. **2** not sloping. **3** with a level surface and little height or depth: *a flat cap.* **4** (of shoes) without high heels. **5** lacking vitality or interest: *a flat voice.* **6** (of a sparkling drink) having lost its effervescence. **7** (of something kept inflated) having lost some or all of its air. **8** Brit. (of a battery) having exhausted its charge. **9** (of a fee, charge, or price) unvarying; fixed. **10** (of a negative statement) definite and firm: *a flat denial.* **11** (of musical sound) below true or normal pitch. **12** (after a noun) (of a note or key) lower by a semitone than a specified note or key. ● adverb **1** in or to a horizontal position. **2** so as to become level and even. **3** informal completely; absolutely: *she turned him down flat.* **4** emphasizing the speed of an action: *in ten minutes flat.* ● noun **1** the flat part of something. **2** (**flats**) an area of low level ground, especially near water. **3** informal a flat tyre. **4** (**the Flat**) Brit. flat racing. **5** an upright section of stage scenery. **6** a musical note lowered a semitone below natural pitch. **7** the sign (♭) indicating this.

– PHRASES **fall flat** fail to produce the intended effect. **flat out** as fast or as hard as possible. **on the flat 1** on level ground as opposed to uphill. **2** (**on the Flat**) (of a horse race) on a course without jumps.

– DERIVATIVES **flatly** adverb **flatness** noun **flattish** adjective.

– ORIGIN Old Norse.

flat[2] ● noun chiefly Brit. a set of rooms comprising an individual place of residence within a larger building. ● verb (**flatted**, **flatting**) Austral./NZ live in or share a flat.

– PHRASES **go flatting** Austral./NZ leave one's family home to live in a flat.

– DERIVATIVES **flatlet** noun.

– ORIGIN alteration of obsolete *flet* 'floor, dwelling'; related to FLAT[1].

flatbed ● noun **1** (before another noun) denoting a vehicle with a flat load-carrying area. **2** Computing a scanner, plotter, or other device which keeps paper flat during use.

flat feet ● plural noun feet with arches that are lower than usual.

flat file ● noun Computing a file having no internal hierarchy.

flatfish ● noun a marine fish, such as a plaice or sole, that swims on its side with both eyes on the upper side of its flattened body.

flat-footed ● adjective **1** having flat feet. **2** informal clumsy.

flat iron ● noun historical an iron heated on a hotplate or fire.

flatline ● verb informal die.

– DERIVATIVES **flatliner** noun.

– ORIGIN with reference to the continuous straight line displayed on a heart monitor when a person dies.

flatmate ● noun Brit. a person with whom one shares a flat.

flat-pack ● noun (before another noun) denoting furniture or equipment that is sold in pieces and assembled by the buyer.

flat race ● noun a horse race over a course with no jumps, as opposed to a steeplechase or hurdles.

flatten ● verb **1** make or become flat or flatter. **2** informal knock down.

– DERIVATIVES **flattener** noun.

flatter ● verb **1** praise or compliment insincerely, especially to further one's own interests. **2** (usu. **be flattered**) cause to feel honoured and pleased. **3** (**flatter oneself**) believe something favourable about oneself, especially something unfounded. **4** (of clothing or a colour) make attractive. **5** (often as adj. **flattering**) give an unrealistically favourable impression of: *a rather flattering picture.*

– DERIVATIVES **flatterer** noun.

flattery ● noun (pl. **flatteries**) excessive and insincere praise.

– ORIGIN Old French *flaterie*, from *flater* 'stroke, flatter'.

flattie (also **flatty**) ● noun (pl. **flatties**) informal a flat-heeled shoe.

flatulent /flatyoolənt/ ● adjective suffering from or marked by an accumulation of gas in the alimentary canal.

– DERIVATIVES **flatulence** noun.

flatus /flaytəss/ ● noun formal gas in or from the stomach or intestines.

– ORIGIN Latin, 'blowing', from *flare* 'to blow'.

flatware ● noun **1** items of crockery such as plates and saucers. **2** N. Amer. domestic cutlery.

Thesaurus

ly, all of a sudden; quickly, rapidly, swiftly, speedily; in an instant/moment, in a (split) second, in a trice, in the blink of an eye; *informal* in a jiffy, before you can say Jack Robinson.

flashy ● adjective OSTENTATIOUS, showy, flamboyant, conspicuous, extravagant, expensive; vulgar, tasteless, brash, lurid, garish, obtrusive, loud, gaudy; *informal* snazzy, fancy, swanky, flash, jazzy, glitzy.

– OPPOSITES understated.

flask ● noun BOTTLE, container; hip flask, vacuum flask; *trademark* Thermos.

flat[1] ● adjective **1** *a flat surface* LEVEL, horizontal; smooth, even, uniform, regular, plane. **2** *the sea was flat* CALM, still, pacific, glassy, undisturbed, without waves, like a millpond. **3** *a flat wooden box* SHALLOW, low-sided. **4** *flat sandals* LOW, low-heeled, without heels. **5** *his voice was flat* MONOTONOUS, toneless, droning, boring, dull, tedious, uninteresting, unexciting, soporific; bland, dreary, colourless, featureless, emotionless, expressionless, lifeless, spiritless, lacklustre. **6** *he felt flat and weary* DEPRESSED, dejected, dispirited, despondent, downhearted, disheartened, low, low-spirited, down, unhappy, blue; without energy, enervated, sapped, weary, tired out, worn out, exhausted, drained; *informal* down in the mouth/dumps. **7** *the market was flat* SLOW, inactive, sluggish, slack, quiet, depressed. **8** *(Brit.) a flat battery* EXPIRED, dead, finished, used up, run out. **9** *a flat tyre* DEFLATED, punctured, burst. **10** *a flat fee* FIXED, set, regular, unchanging, unvarying, invariable. **11** *a flat denial* OUTRIGHT, direct, absolute, definite, positive, straight, plain, explicit; firm, resolute, adamant, assertive, emphatic, categorical, unconditional, unqualified, unequivocal.

– OPPOSITES vertical, uneven.

● adverb **1** *she lay down flat on the floor* STRETCHED OUT, outstretched, spreadeagled, prone, sprawling, supine, prostrate, recumbent. **2** *(informal) she turned me down flat* OUTRIGHT, absolutely, firmly, resolutely, adamantly, emphatically, insistently, categorically, unconditionally, unequivocally.

– PHRASES **flat out** HARD, as hard as possible, for all one's worth, to the full/limit, all out; at full speed, as fast as possible, at full tilt; *informal* like crazy, like mad, like the wind, like a bomb; *Brit. informal* like billy-o, like the clappers.

flat[2] ● noun *a two-bedroom flat* APARTMENT, set of rooms, penthouse; rooms; *Austral.* home unit; *N. Amer. informal* crib.

flatten ● verb **1** *Tom flattened the crumpled paper* MAKE/BECOME FLAT, make/become even, smooth (out/off), level (out/off). **2** *the cows flattened the grass* COMPRESS, press down, crush, squash, compact, trample. **3** *tornadoes can flatten buildings in seconds* DEMOLISH, raze (to the ground), tear down, knock down, destroy, wreck, devastate, obliterate; *N. Amer. informal* total. **4** *(informal) Flynn flattened him with a single punch* KNOCK DOWN/OVER, knock to the ground, fell, prostrate; *informal* floor, deck; *Brit. informal* knock for six. **5** *I flattened a drunken heckler* HUMILIATE, crush, quash, squash, take down a peg or two, put someone in their place; *informal* put down, cut down to size.

flatter ● verb **1** *it amused him to flatter her* COMPLIMENT, praise, express admiration for, say nice things about, pay court to, fawn on; cajole, humour, flannel, blarney; *informal* sweet-talk, soft-soap, butter up, play up to; *formal* laud. **2** *I was flattered to be asked* HONOUR, gratify, please, delight; *informal* tickle pink. **3** *a hairstyle that flattered her* SUIT, become, look good on, go well with; *informal* do something for.

– OPPOSITES insult, offend.

flatterer ● noun SYCOPHANT, groveller, fawner, lackey; *informal* crawler, toady, bootlicker, yes man, lickspittle; *formal* encomiast.

flattering ● adjective **1** *flattering remarks* COMPLIMENTARY, praising, favourable, commending, admiring, applauding, appreciative; honeyed, sugary, cajoling, flannelling, silver-tongued, honey-tongued; fawning, obsequious, ingratiating, servile, sycophantic; *informal* sweet-talking, soft-soaping, crawling, boot-licking; *formal* encomiastic. **2** *it was very flattering to be nominated* PLEASING, gratifying, honouring, gladdening. **3** *her most flattering dress* BECOMING, enhancing.

flattery ● noun PRAISE, adulation, compliments, blandishments, honeyed words; fawning, blarney, cajolery; *informal* sweet talk, soft soap, buttering up, toadying; *Brit. informal* flannel; *formal* laudation.

flatulence ● noun **1** *medications that help with flatulence* (INTESTINAL) GAS, wind; *informal* farting; *formal* flatus. **2** *the flatulence of his*

flatworm ● noun a worm of a large group (the phylum Platyhelminthes) which includes the parasitic flukes and tapeworms, distinguished by a simple flattened body lacking blood vessels.

flaunt ● verb display ostentatiously.
– USAGE It is a common error to use **flaunt** when **flout** is intended. **Flaunt** means 'display ostentatiously', while **flout** means 'openly disregard (a rule or convention)'.
– ORIGIN of unknown origin.

flautist /flawtist/ ● noun a flute player.
– ORIGIN Italian *flautista*, from *flauto* 'flute'.

flavonoid /flayvənoyd/ ● noun Chemistry any of a class of compounds including several white or yellow plant pigments.
– ORIGIN from Latin *flavus* 'yellow'.

flavour (US **flavor**) ● noun **1** the distinctive taste of a food or drink. **2** a quality reminiscent of something specified: *balconies gave the building a Spanish flavour.* **3** chiefly N. Amer. a flavouring. **4** Physics a property of quarks with values designated up, down, charmed, strange, top, and bottom. ● verb give flavour to.
– PHRASES **flavour of the month** a person or thing that is currently popular.
– DERIVATIVES **flavourful** adjective **flavourless** adjective **flavoursome** adjective.
– ORIGIN Old French *flaor* 'a smell', perhaps from a blend of Latin *flatus* 'blowing' and *foetor* 'stench'.

flavouring (US **flavoring**) ● noun a substance used to enhance the flavour of a food or drink.

flaw ● noun **1** a blemish or imperfection. **2** a fundamental weakness or error. ● verb (usu. **be flawed**) mar or weaken.
– DERIVATIVES **flawless** adjective **flawlessly** adverb.
– ORIGIN originally in the sense 'a snowflake', later 'a fragment': perhaps from an Old Norse word meaning 'stone slab'.

flax ● noun **1** a blue-flowered herbaceous plant that is cultivated for its seed (linseed) and for textile fibre made from its stalks. **2** textile fibre obtained from this plant.
– ORIGIN Old English.

flaxen ● adjective **1** literary (especially of hair) of the pale yellow colour of dressed flax. **2** of flax.

flaxseed ● noun another term for LINSEED.

flay ● verb **1** strip the skin from (a body or carcass). **2** whip or beat harshly. **3** criticize harshly.
– DERIVATIVES **flayer** noun.
– ORIGIN Old English.

flea ● noun a small wingless jumping insect which feeds on the blood of mammals and birds.
– PHRASES (as) **fit as a flea** in very good health. **a flea in one's ear** a sharp reproof.
– ORIGIN Old English.

flea-bitten ● adjective **1** bitten by or infested with fleas. **2** dilapidated or disreputable.

flea collar ● noun a collar for a cat or dog that is impregnated with insecticide to kill or deter fleas.

fleadh /flaa/ ● noun a festival of Irish or Celtic music, dancing, and culture.
– ORIGIN from Irish *fleadh ceoil* 'music festival'.

flea market ● noun a street market selling second-hand goods.

fleapit ● noun chiefly Brit. a dingy, dirty place, especially a run-down cinema.

fleck ● noun **1** a very small patch of colour or light. **2** a small particle. ● verb (usu. **be flecked**) mark or dot with flecks.
– ORIGIN perhaps from Old Norse, or from Low German, Dutch *vlecke*.

fled past and past participle of FLEE.

fledge /flej/ ● verb **1** (of a young bird) develop wing feathers that are large enough for flight. **2** bring up (a young bird) until its wing feathers are developed enough for flight.
– ORIGIN from Old English, 'ready to fly'; related to FLY[1].

fledged ● adjective **1** (of a young bird) having wing feathers that are large enough for flight. **2** having just taken on the role specified: *a newly fledged Detective Inspector.*

fledgling (also **fledgeling**) ● noun **1** a young bird that has just fledged. **2** (before another noun) new and inexperienced: *fledgling democracies.*

flee ● verb (**flees**, **fleeing**; past and past part. **fled**) run away.
– ORIGIN Old English.

fleece ● noun **1** the wool coat of a sheep. **2** a soft, warm fabric with a pile, or a garment made from this. ● verb informal defraud, especially by overcharging.
– DERIVATIVES **fleeced** adjective **fleecy** adjective.
– ORIGIN Old English.

fleer /fleeər/ ● verb literary laugh impudently or jeeringly. ● noun archaic an impudent or jeering look or speech.
– ORIGIN probably Scandinavian.

fleet[1] ● noun **1** a group of ships sailing together. **2** (**the fleet**) a country's navy. **3** a number of vehicles or aircraft operating together.
– ORIGIN Old English, related to FLEET[3].

fleet[2] ● adjective fast and nimble.
– DERIVATIVES **fleetly** adverb **fleetness** noun.
– ORIGIN probably from Old Norse and related to FLEET[3].

fleet[3] ● verb literary move or pass quickly.
– ORIGIN Old English, 'float, swim'; related to FLIT and FLOAT.

f

Thesaurus

latest recordings POMPOSITY, pompousness, pretension, pretentiousness, grandiloquence, bombast, turgidity.

flaunt ● verb SHOW OFF, display ostentatiously, make a (great) show of, put on show/display, parade; brag about, crow about, vaunt; *informal* flash.

flavour ● noun **1** *the flavour of prosciutto* TASTE, savour, tang. **2** *salami can give extra flavour* FLAVOURING, seasoning, tastiness, tang, relish, bite, piquancy, pungency, spice, spiciness, zest; *informal* zing, zip. **3** *a strong international flavour* CHARACTER, quality, feel, feeling, ambience, atmosphere, aura, air, mood, tone; spirit, essence, nature. **4** *this excerpt will give a flavour of the report* IMPRESSION, suggestion, hint, taste.
– RELATED TERMS gustative, gustatory.
● verb *spices for flavouring food* ADD FLAVOUR TO, add flavouring to, season, spice (up), add piquancy to, ginger up, enrich; *informal* pep up.
– PHRASES **flavour of the month** ALL THE RAGE, the latest thing, the fashion, in vogue, very popular; *informal* hot, in; *Brit. informal, dated* all the go.

flavouring ● noun **1** *this cheese is often combined with other flavourings* SEASONING, spice, herb, additive; condiment, dressing. **2** *vanilla flavouring* ESSENCE, extract, concentrate, distillate.

flaw ● noun DEFECT, blemish, fault, imperfection, deficiency, weakness, weak spot/point, inadequacy, shortcoming, limitation, failing, foible; *Computing* bug; *informal* glitch.
– OPPOSITES strength.

flawed ● adjective **1** *a flawed mirror* FAULTY, defective, unsound, imperfect; broken, cracked, torn, scratched, deformed, distorted, warped, buckled; *Brit. informal* duff. **2** *the findings were flawed* UNSOUND, defective, faulty, distorted, inaccurate, incorrect, erroneous, imprecise, fallacious, misleading.
– OPPOSITES flawless, sound.

flawless ● adjective PERFECT, unblemished, unmarked, unimpaired; whole, intact, sound, unbroken, undamaged, mint, pristine; impeccable, immaculate, consummate, accurate, correct, faultless, error-free, unerring; exemplary, model, ideal, copybook.
– OPPOSITES flawed.

flay ● verb **1** *the saint was flayed alive* SKIN, strip the skin off; *Medicine* excoriate. **2** *he flayed his critics.* See CRITICIZE.

fleck ● noun *flecks of pale blue* SPOT, mark, dot, speck, speckle, freckle, patch, smudge, streak, blotch, dab; *informal* splosh, splodge; *rare* macula.
● verb *the deer's flanks were flecked with white* SPOT, mark, dot, speckle, bespeckle, freckle, stipple, stud, bestud, blotch, mottle, streak, splash, spatter, bespatter, scatter, sprinkle; *Scottish & Irish* slabber; *informal* splosh, splodge.

fledgling ● noun *a woodpecker fledgling* CHICK, baby bird, nestling.
● adjective *fledgling industries* EMERGING, emergent, sunrise, dawning, embryonic, infant, nascent; developing, in the making, budding, up-and-coming, rising.
– OPPOSITES declining, mature.

flee ● verb **1** *she fled to her room* RUN (AWAY/OFF), run for it, make a run for it, take flight, be gone, make off, take off, take to one's heels, make a break for it, bolt, beat a (hasty) retreat, make a quick exit, make one's getaway, escape; *informal* beat it, clear off/out, vamoose, skedaddle, split, leg it, turn tail, scram; *Brit. informal* scarper; *N. Amer. informal* light out, bug out, cut out, peel out; *Austral. informal* shoot through; *archaic* fly. **2** *they fled the country* RUN AWAY FROM, leave hastily, escape from; *informal* skip; *archaic* fly.

fleece ● noun *a sheep's fleece* WOOL, coat.
● verb (*informal*) *we were fleeced by a ticket tout.* See SWINDLE verb.

fleecy ● adjective FLUFFY, woolly, downy, soft, fuzzy, furry, velvety,

fleeting ● adjective lasting for a very short time.
– DERIVATIVES **fleetingly** adverb.

Fleming /flemming/ ● noun **1** a Flemish person. **2** a member of the Flemish-speaking people inhabiting northern and western Belgium. Compare with WALLOON.
– ORIGIN Old English.

Flemish /flemmish/ ● noun **1** (**the Flemish**) the people of Flanders, a region divided between Belgium, France, and the Netherlands. **2** the Dutch language as spoken in Flanders. ● adjective relating to the Flemish people or language.
– ORIGIN Dutch *Vlāmisch*.

flense /flenz/ ● verb slice the skin or fat from (a carcass, especially that of a whale).
– DERIVATIVES **flenser** noun.
– ORIGIN Danish *flensa*.

flesh ● noun **1** the soft substance in the body consisting of muscle tissue and fat. **2** the edible pulpy part of a fruit or vegetable. **3** the surface of the human body with reference to its appearance or sensory properties. **4** (**the flesh**) the physicality of the human body as contrasted with the mind or the soul: *pleasures of the flesh*. ● verb (**flesh out**) make more substantial or detailed.
– PHRASES **go the way of all flesh** die or come to an end. **in the flesh** in person or (of a thing) in its actual state. **make someone's flesh creep** (or **crawl**) cause someone to feel fear, horror, or disgust.
– DERIVATIVES **fleshless** adjective.
– ORIGIN Old English.

fleshly ● adjective (**fleshlier**, **fleshliest**) relating to the body; sensual.

fleshpots ● plural noun places providing a hedonistic experience.
– ORIGIN with biblical allusion to the *fleshpots of Egypt* (mentioned in the Book of Exodus).

flesh wound ● noun a wound that breaks the skin but does not damage bones or vital organs.

fleshy ● adjective (**fleshier**, **fleshiest**) **1** having a substantial amount of flesh; plump. **2** (of plant or fruit tissue) soft and thick. **3** resembling flesh.
– DERIVATIVES **fleshiness** noun.

fleur-de-lis /flör də lee/ (also **fleur-de-lys**) ● noun (pl. **fleurs-de-lis** pronunc. same) Art & Heraldry a stylized lily composed of three petals bound together near their bases.
– ORIGIN Old French *flour de lys* 'flower of the lily'.

flew past of FLY[1].

flex[1] ● verb **1** bend (a limb or joint). **2** contract or tense (a muscle). **3** warp or bend and then revert to shape.
– ORIGIN Latin *flectere* 'to bend'.

flex[2] ● noun chiefly Brit. a flexible insulated cable used for carrying electric current to an appliance.
– ORIGIN abbreviation of FLEXIBLE.

flexecutive /fleksekyootiv/ ● noun a professional whose use of information technology allows them to be flexible in where and when they work.

flexible ● adjective **1** capable of bending easily without breaking. **2** able to change or be changed to respond to different circumstances.
– DERIVATIVES **flexibility** noun **flexibly** adverb.

flexion /fleksh'n/ (also **flection**) ● noun the action of bending or the condition of being bent.

flexitime (N. Amer. also **flextime**) ● noun a system allowing some flexibility as to when workers put in their allotted hours.

flexor /fleksər/ ● noun a muscle whose contraction bends a limb or other part of the body.

flexuous /fleksyooəss/ ● adjective full of bends and curves.

flibbertigibbet /flibbərtijibbət/ ● noun a frivolous and restless person.
– ORIGIN probably imitative of idle chatter.

flick ● noun **1** a sudden sharp movement up and down or from side to side. **2** the sudden release of a finger or thumb held bent against another finger. **3** informal a cinema film. **4** informal (**the flicks**) the cinema. ● verb **1** make or cause to make a sudden sharp movement. **2** propel with a flick of the fingers. **3** (**flick through**) look quickly through (a book or a collection of papers).
– ORIGIN symbolic.

flicker ● verb **1** shine or burn unsteadily and intermittently. **2** (of a feeling) be briefly perceptible. **3** make small, quick movements. ● noun **1** a flickering movement or light. **2** a brief and transient occurrence of a feeling.
– ORIGIN Old English, 'to flutter'.

flick knife ● noun Brit. a knife with a blade that springs out from the handle when a button is pressed.

flier ● noun variant spelling of FLYER.

flight ● noun **1** the action or process of flying. **2** a journey made in an aircraft or in space. **3** the path of a projectile through the air. **4** a series of steps between floors or levels. **5** the action or an act of fleeing: *the enemy were in flight*. **6** an uninhibited mental journey: *a flight of fancy*. **7** a flock of birds flying to-

Thesaurus

shaggy; *technical* floccose, pilose.
– OPPOSITES coarse.

fleet[1] ● noun *the fleet set sail* NAVY, naval force, (naval) task force, armada, flotilla, squadron, convoy.

fleet[2] ● adjective *(poetic/literary) as fleet as a greyhound* NIMBLE, agile, lithe, lissom, acrobatic, supple, light-footed, light on one's feet, spry, sprightly; quick, fast, swift, rapid, speedy, brisk, smart; *informal* nippy, zippy, twinkle-toed.

fleeting ● adjective BRIEF, short, short-lived, quick, momentary, cursory, transient, ephemeral, fugitive, passing, transitory; *poetic/literary* evanescent.
– OPPOSITES lasting.

flesh ● noun **1** *you need more flesh on your bones* MUSCLE, meat, tissue, brawn; *informal* beef. **2** *she carries too much flesh* FAT, weight; *Anatomy* adipose tissue; *informal* blubber, flab. **3** *a fruit with juicy flesh* PULP, soft part, marrow, meat. **4** *the pleasures of the flesh* THE BODY, human nature, physicality, carnality, animality; sensuality, sexuality.
– RELATED TERMS carn-.
– PHRASES **one's (own) flesh and blood** FAMILY, relative(s), relation(s), blood relation(s), kin, kinsfolk, kinsman, kinsmen, kinswoman, kinswomen, kindred, nearest and dearest, people; *informal* folks. **flesh out** PUT ON WEIGHT, gain weight, get heavier, grow fat/fatter, fatten up, get fat, fill out. **flesh something out** EXPAND (ON), elaborate on, add to, build on, add flesh to, put flesh on (the bones of), add detail to, expatiate on, supplement, reinforce, augment, fill out, enlarge on. **in the flesh** IN PERSON, before one's (very) eyes, in front of one; in real life, live; physically, bodily, in bodily/human form, incarnate.

fleshly ● adjective CARNAL, physical, animal, bestial; sexual, sensual, erotic, lustful.
– OPPOSITES spiritual.

fleshy ● adjective PLUMP, chubby, portly, fat, obese, overweight, stout, corpulent, paunchy, well padded, well covered, well upholstered, rotund; *informal* tubby, pudgy, beefy, porky, roly-poly, blubbery; *Brit. informal* podgy, fubsy; *N. Amer. informal* corn-fed; *Austral./NZ* nuggety; *rare* abdominous.
– OPPOSITES thin.

flex[1] ● verb **1** *you must flex your elbow* BEND, crook, hook, cock, angle, double up. **2** *Rachel flexed her cramped muscles* TIGHTEN, tauten, tense (up), tension, contract.
– OPPOSITES straighten, relax.

flex[2] ● noun *(Brit.) an electric flex* CABLE, wire, lead; *N. Amer.* cord.

flexibility ● noun **1** *the flexibility of wood* PLIABILITY, suppleness, pliancy, plasticity; elasticity, stretchiness, springiness, spring, resilience, bounce; *informal* give. **2** *the flexibility of an endowment loan* ADAPTABILITY, adjustability, variability, versatility, open-endedness, freedom, latitude. **3** *the flexibility shown by the local authority* WILLINGNESS TO COMPROMISE, accommodation, amenability, cooperation, tolerance.
– OPPOSITES rigidity, inflexibility, intransigence.

flexible ● adjective **1** *flexible tubing* PLIABLE, supple, bendable, pliant, plastic; elastic, stretchy, whippy, springy, resilient, bouncy; *informal* bendy; *archaic* flexile. **2** *a flexible arrangement* ADAPTABLE, adjustable, variable, versatile, open-ended, open, free. **3** *the need to be flexible towards tenants* ACCOMMODATING, amenable, willing to compromise, cooperative, tolerant, easy-going.
– OPPOSITES rigid, inflexible, intransigent.

flick ● noun *a flick of the wrist* JERK, snap, flip, whisk.
● verb **1** *he flicked the switch* CLICK, snap, flip, jerk. **2** *the horse flicked its tail* SWISH, twitch, wave, wag, waggle, shake.
– PHRASES **flick through** THUMB (THROUGH), leaf through, flip through, skim through, scan, look through, browse through, dip into, glance at/through, peruse, run one's eye over.

flicker ● verb **1** *the lights flickered* GLIMMER, glint, flare, dance, gutter; twinkle, sparkle, blink, wink, flash, scintillate; *poetic/literary*

gether. **8** an RAF or USAF unit of about six aircraft operating together. **9** the tail of an arrow or dart.
– PHRASES **in full flight** having gained optimum momentum. **take flight 1** (of a bird) take off and fly. **2** flee.
– ORIGIN Old English; related to FLY[1].
flight deck • noun **1** the cockpit of a large aircraft. **2** the deck of an aircraft carrier, used as a runway.
flight feather • noun any of the large primary or secondary feathers in a bird's wing, supporting it in flight.
flightless • adjective (of a bird or insect) naturally unable to fly.
– DERIVATIVES **flightlessness** noun.
flight lieutenant • noun a rank of officer in the RAF, above flying officer and below squadron leader.
flight path • noun the course of an aircraft or spacecraft.
flight recorder • noun an electronic device in an aircraft that records technical details during a flight, used in the event of an accident to discover its cause.
flight sergeant • noun a rank of non-commissioned officer in the RAF, above sergeant and below warrant officer.
flighty • adjective (**flightier**, **flightiest**) frivolous and fickle.
– DERIVATIVES **flightiness** noun.
flimflam informal • noun **1** insincere and unconvincing talk. **2** a confidence trick. • verb (**flimflammed**, **flimflamming**) swindle with a confidence trick.
– ORIGIN symbolic reduplication.
flimsy • adjective (**flimsier**, **flimsiest**) **1** weak and insubstantial. **2** (of clothing) light and thin. **3** (of a pretext or account) weak; unconvincing. • noun (pl. **flimsies**) Brit. **1** very thin paper. **2** a copy of a document, made on very thin paper.
– DERIVATIVES **flimsily** adverb **flimsiness** noun.
– ORIGIN probably from FLIMFLAM.
flinch • verb **1** make a quick, nervous movement as an instinctive reaction to fear or pain. **2** (**flinch from**) avoid through fear or anxiety. • noun an act of flinching.
– ORIGIN originally in the sense 'slink or sneak off': from Old French *flenchir* 'turn aside'.
flinders • plural noun small fragments or splinters.
– ORIGIN probably Scandinavian.
fling • verb (past and past part. **flung**) **1** throw forcefully; hurl. **2** (**fling oneself into**) wholeheartedly engage in (an activity or enterprise). **3** move with speed: *he flung away to his study.* **4** (**fling on/off**) put on or take off (clothes) carelessly and rapidly. • noun **1** a short period of enjoyment or wild behaviour. **2** a short sexual relationship. **3** a Highland fling.
– DERIVATIVES **flinger** noun.
– ORIGIN perhaps related to an Old Norse word meaning 'flog'.
flint • noun **1** a hard grey rock consisting of nearly pure silica, occurring chiefly as nodules in chalk. **2** a piece of this rock. **3** a piece of flint or an alloy used with steel to produce an igniting spark, especially in a cigarette lighter.
– ORIGIN Old English.
flintlock • noun an old-fashioned type of gun fired by a spark from a flint.
flinty • adjective (**flintier**, **flintiest**) **1** of, containing, or resembling flint. **2** grim and unyielding: *a flinty stare.*
– DERIVATIVES **flintily** adverb **flintiness** noun.
flip • verb (**flipped**, **flipping**) **1** turn over with a quick, smooth movement. **2** move, push, or throw with a sudden sharp movement: *he flipped a switch.* **3** toss (something, especially a coin) so as to turn over in the air. **4** informal suddenly become deranged or very angry. • noun a flipping action or movement. • adjective flippant. • exclamation informal used to express mild annoyance.
– PHRASES **flip one's lid** informal suddenly become deranged or lose one's self-control.
– ORIGIN probably a contraction of FILLIP.
flip chart • noun a very large pad of paper bound so that pages can be turned over at the top, used on a stand at presentations.
flip-flop • noun **1** a light sandal with a thong that passes between the big and second toes. **2** Electronics a switching circuit which works by changing between two stable states. • verb move with a flapping sound or motion.
flippant • adjective not showing the proper seriousness or respect.
– DERIVATIVES **flippancy** noun **flippantly** adverb.
– ORIGIN originally in senses 'nimble' and 'talkative': from FLIP.
flipper • noun **1** a broad, flat limb without fingers, used for swimming by sea animals such as seals and turtles. **2** a flat rubber attachment worn on the foot for underwater swimming. **3** a pivoted arm in a pinball machine.
flipping • adjective informal, chiefly Brit. used for emphasis or to express mild annoyance.
flip side • noun informal **1** the B-side of a pop single. **2** the reverse or unwelcome aspect of a situation.
flirt • verb **1** behave playfully in a sexually enticing manner. **2** (**flirt with**) experiment casually with (an idea or activity). **3** (**flirt with**) deliberately risk (danger or death). • noun a person who habitually flirts.
– DERIVATIVES **flirtation** noun **flirtatious** adjective **flirty** adjective (**flirtier**, **flirtiest**).
– ORIGIN originally in the senses 'strike sharply' and 'sneer at': apparently symbolic.

Thesaurus

glister, coruscate. **2** *his eyelids flickered* FLUTTER, quiver, tremble, shiver, shudder, spasm, jerk, twitch.
flight • noun **1** *the history of flight* AVIATION, flying, air transport, aerial navigation, aeronautics. **2** *a charter flight to Rome* PLANE TRIP/JOURNEY, air trip/journey, trip/journey by air. **3** *the flight of a cricket ball* TRAJECTORY, path through the air, track, orbit. **4** *a flight of birds* FLOCK, skein, covey, swarm, cloud. **5** *his headlong flight from home* ESCAPE, getaway, hasty departure, exit, exodus, decamping, breakout, bolt, disappearance; Brit. informal flit. **6** *a flight of stairs* STAIRCASE, set of steps/stairs.
– PHRASES **put someone to flight** CHASE AWAY/OFF, drive back/away/off/out, scatter (to the four winds), disperse, repel, repulse, rout, stampede, scare off; Brit. see off; informal send packing. **take flight** FLEE, run (away/off), run for it, make a run for it, be gone, make off, take off, take to one's heels, make a break for it, bolt, beat a (hasty) retreat, make a quick exit, make one's getaway, escape; informal beat it, clear off/out, vamoose, skedaddle, split, leg it, turn tail, scram; Brit. informal scarper; N. Amer. informal light out, bug out, cut out, peel out; Austral. informal shoot through; archaic fly.
flighty • adjective FICKLE, inconstant, mercurial, whimsical, capricious, skittish, volatile, impulsive; irresponsible, giddy, reckless, wild, careless, thoughtless.
– OPPOSITES steady, responsible.
flimsy • adjective **1** *a flimsy building* INSUBSTANTIAL, fragile, breakable, frail, shaky, unstable, wobbly, tottery, rickety, ramshackle, makeshift; jerry-built, badly built, shoddy, gimcrack. **2** *a flimsy garment* THIN, light, fine, filmy, floaty, diaphanous, sheer, delicate, insubstantial, wispy, gossamer, gauzy. **3** *flimsy evidence* WEAK, feeble, poor, inadequate, insufficient, thin, unsubstantial, unconvincing, implausible, unsatisfactory.
– OPPOSITES sturdy, thick, sound.
flinch • verb **1** *he flinched at the noise* WINCE, start, shudder, quiver, jerk, shy. **2** *he never flinched from his duty* SHRINK FROM, recoil from, shy away from, swerve from, demur from; dodge, evade, avoid, duck, baulk at, jib at, quail at, fight shy of.
fling • verb *he flung the axe into the river* THROW, toss, sling, hurl, cast, pitch, lob; informal chuck, heave, bung, buzz; dated shy.
• noun **1** *a birthday fling* GOOD TIME, spree, bit of fun, night on the town; fun and games, revels, larks; informal binge. **2** *she had a brief fling with him* AFFAIR, love affair, relationship, romance, affaire (de cœur), amour, flirtation, dalliance, liaison, entanglement, involvement, attachment.
flip • verb **1** *the wave flipped the dinghy over | the plane flipped on to its back* OVERTURN, turn over, tip over, roll (over), upturn, capsize; upend, invert, knock over; keel over, topple over, turn turtle; archaic overset. **2** *he flipped the key through the air* THROW, flick, toss, fling, sling, pitch, cast, spin, lob; informal chuck, bung; dated shy. **3** *I flipped the transmitter switch* FLICK, click, snap.
– PHRASES **flip through** THUMB (THROUGH), leaf through, flick through, skim through, scan, look through, browse through, dip into, glance at/through, peruse, run one's eye over.
flippancy • noun FRIVOLITY, levity, facetiousness; disrespect, irreverence, cheek, impudence, impertinence; Brit. informal sauce; N. Amer. informal sassiness; dated waggery.
– OPPOSITES seriousness, respect.
flippant • adjective FRIVOLOUS, facetious, tongue-in-cheek; disrespectful, irreverent, cheeky, impudent, impertinent; informal flip, saucy, waggish; N. Amer. informal sassy.
– OPPOSITES serious, respectful.
flirt • verb **1** *it amused him to flirt with her* TRIFLE WITH, toy with, tease, lead on. **2** *those conservatives who flirted with fascism* DAB-

f

flit • verb (**flitted**, **flitting**) **1** move swiftly and lightly. **2** chiefly Scottish & N. English move house or leave one's home, especially in secrecy. • noun Brit. informal an act of leaving one's home in secrecy.
– ORIGIN Old Norse, related to FLEET[3].
flitch /flich/ • noun **1** a slab of wood cut from a tree trunk. **2** chiefly dialect a side of bacon.
– ORIGIN Old English.
flitter • verb move quickly in a random manner.
– ORIGIN from FLIT.
float • verb **1** rest on the surface of a liquid without sinking. **2** move slowly, hover, or be suspended in a liquid or the air. **3** put forward (an idea) as a suggestion or test of reactions. **4** (usu. as adj. **floating**) remain unsettled in one's opinions, where one lives, etc. **5** offer the shares of (a company) for sale on the stock market for the first time. **6** (with reference to a currency) fluctuate or allow to fluctuate freely in value. • noun **1** a hollow or lightweight object or device designed to float on water, for example one attached to a fishing line signalling the bite of a fish. **2** a floating device which forms part of a valve apparatus controlling a flow of water. **3** Brit. a small vehicle powered by electricity: *a milk float*. **4** a platform mounted on a truck and carrying a display in a procession. **5** Brit. a sum of money available for minor expenses or to provide change. **6** a hand tool with a rectangular blade used for smoothing plaster.
– PHRASES **float someone's boat** informal appeal to or excite someone.
– DERIVATIVES **floater** noun.
– ORIGIN Old English, related to FLEET[3].
floatation • noun variant spelling of FLOTATION.
floating charge • noun a liability to a creditor which relates to the company's assets as a whole. Compare with FIXED CHARGE.
floating-point • noun (before another noun) Computing denoting a mode of representing numbers as two sequences of bits, one representing the digits in the number and the other an exponent which determines the position of the radix point.
floating rib • noun any of the lower ribs which are not attached directly to the breastbone.
floating voter • noun a person who does not consistently vote for the same party.
floatplane • noun a seaplane.
float valve • noun a ball valve.
floaty • adjective chiefly Brit. (especially of a woman's garment or a fabric) light and flimsy.
floccinaucinihilipilification /floksinawsinihilpillifi**kay**sh'n/ • noun the action or habit of estimating something as worthless.
– ORIGIN from Latin *flocci, nauci, nihili, pili* (words meaning 'at little value').
flocculate /**flok**yoolayt/ • verb technical form or cause to form into small clumps or masses.
– DERIVATIVES **flocculation** noun.
– ORIGIN from Latin *flocculus* 'small tuft of wool'.
flocculent /**flok**yoolǝnt/ • adjective **1** having or resembling tufts of wool. **2** having a loosely clumped texture.
flock[1] • noun **1** a number of birds moving or resting together. **2** a number of domestic animals, especially sheep, that are kept together. **3** (**a flock/flocks**) a large number or crowd. **4** a Christian congregation under the charge of a particular minister. • verb congregate or move in a flock.
– ORIGIN Old English.
flock[2] • noun **1** a soft material for stuffing cushions and quilts, made of wool refuse or torn-up cloth. **2** powdered wool or cloth, used in making flock wallpaper. **3** a lock or tuft of wool or cotton.
– ORIGIN Latin *floccus*.
flock wallpaper • noun wallpaper with a raised flock pattern.
floe /flō/ • noun a sheet of floating ice.
– ORIGIN probably from Norwegian *flo* 'layer'.
flog • verb (**flogged**, **flogging**) **1** beat with a whip or stick as a punishment. **2** Brit. informal sell or offer for sale. **3** informal focus on or promote to excess.
– PHRASES **flog a dead horse** waste energy on a lost cause or unalterable situation.
– DERIVATIVES **flogger** noun.
– ORIGIN perhaps imitative, or from Latin *flagellare* 'to whip'.
flokati /flo**kaa**ti/ • noun (pl. **flokatis**) a Greek woven woollen rug with a thick loose pile.
– ORIGIN modern Greek *phlokatē* 'peasant's blanket'.
flood • noun **1** an overflow of a large amount of water over dry land. **2** (**the Flood**) the biblical flood brought by God upon the earth because of the wickedness of the human race. **3** an overwhelming quantity of things or people appearing at once. **4** an outpouring of tears or emotion. **5** the inflow of the tide. **6** a floodlight. • verb **1** cover or become covered with water in a flood. **2** (of a river) become swollen and overflow its banks. **3** arrive in or overwhelm with very large numbers. **4** fill or suffuse completely: *she flooded the room with light*. **5** overfill the carburettor of (an engine) with petrol.
– ORIGIN Old English, related to FLOW.
floodgate • noun **1** a gate that can be opened or closed to admit or exclude water, especially the lower gate of a lock. **2** (**the floodgates**) last restraints holding back a powerful outpouring.
floodlight • noun a large, powerful light used to illuminate a stage, sports ground, etc. • verb (past and past part. **floodlit**) (usu. as adj. **floodlit**) illuminate with floodlights.
flood plain • noun an area of low-lying ground adjacent to a river that is subject to flooding.
flood tide • noun an incoming tide.
floor • noun **1** the lower surface of a room. **2** a storey of a building. **3** the bottom of the sea, a cave, etc. **4** a minimum level of prices or wages. **5** (**the floor**) the part of a legislative assembly in which members sit and from which they speak. **6** (**the floor**)

Thesaurus

BLE IN, toy with, trifle with, amuse oneself with, play with, tinker with, dip into, scratch the surface of. **3** *he is flirting with danger* DICE WITH, court, risk, not fear.
• noun *Anna was quite a flirt* TEASE, trifler, philanderer, coquette, heartbreaker; archaic fizgig.
flirtation • noun COQUETRY, teasing, trifling.
flirtatious • adjective COQUETTISH, flirty, kittenish, teasing.
flit • verb DART, dance, skip, play, dash, trip, flutter, bob, bounce.
float • verb **1** *oil floats on water* STAY AFLOAT, stay on the surface, be buoyant, be buoyed up. **2** *the balloon floated in the air* HOVER, levitate, be suspended, hang, defy gravity. **3** *a cloud floated across the moon* DRIFT, glide, sail, slip, slide, waft. **4** *he has just floated that idea* SUGGEST, put forward, come up with, submit, moot, propose, advance, test the popularity of; informal run something up the flagpole (to see who salutes). **5** *the company was floated on the Stock Exchange* LAUNCH, get going, get off the ground, offer, sell, introduce.
– OPPOSITES sink, rush, withdraw.
floating • adjective **1** *floating seaweed* BUOYANT, on the surface, afloat, drifting. **2** *floating gas balloons* HOVERING, levitating, suspended, hanging, defying gravity. **3** *floating voters* UNCOMMITTED, undecided, in two minds, torn, split, uncertain, unsure, wavering, vacillating, blowing hot and cold, indecisive, undeclared; informal sitting on the fence. **4** *a floating population* UNSETTLED, transient, temporary, variable, fluctuating; migrant, wandering, nomadic, on the move, migratory, travelling, drifting, roving, roaming, itinerant, vagabond. **5** *a floating exchange rate* VARIABLE, changeable, changing, fluid, fluctuating.
– OPPOSITES sunken, grounded, committed, settled, fixed.
flock • noun **1** *a flock of sheep* HERD, drove. **2** *a flock of birds* FLIGHT, congregation, covey, clutch. **3** *flocks of people* CROWD, throng, horde, mob, rabble, mass, multitude, host, army, pack, swarm, sea; informal gaggle.
• verb **1** *people flocked around Jesus* GATHER, collect, congregate, assemble, converge, mass, crowd, throng, cluster, swarm; formal foregather. **2** *tourists flock to the place* STREAM, go in large numbers, swarm, crowd, troop.
flog • verb **1** *the thief was flogged* WHIP, scourge, flagellate, lash, birch, switch, cane, thrash, beat, tan/whip someone's hide. **2** (Brit. informal) *he is flogging his old car* SELL, put on sale, put up for sale, offer for sale, trade in, deal in, peddle; informal push.
flood • noun **1** *a flood warning* INUNDATION, swamping, deluge; torrent, overflow, flash flood, freshet; Brit. spate. **2** *a flood of tears* OUTPOURING, torrent, rush, stream, gush, surge, cascade. **3** *a flood of complaints* SUCCESSION, series, string, chain; barrage, volley, battery; avalanche, torrent, stream, tide, spate, storm, shower, cascade.
– OPPOSITES trickle.
• verb **1** *the whole town was flooded* INUNDATE, swamp, deluge, immerse, submerge, drown, engulf. **2** *the river could flood* OVERFLOW, burst its banks, brim over, run over. **3** *imports are flooding the domestic market* GLUT, swamp, saturate, oversupply. **4** *refugees*

the right to speak in an assembly: *other speakers have the floor*. ● verb **1** provide with a floor. **2** informal knock to the ground. **3** informal baffle completely.
– DERIVATIVES **flooring** noun.
– ORIGIN Old English.
floorboard ● noun a long plank making up part of a wooden floor.
floor manager ● noun **1** the stage manager of a television production. **2** a supervisor of shop assistants in a large store.
floor show ● noun an entertainment presented on the floor of a nightclub or restaurant.
floozy (also **floozie**) ● noun (pl. **floozies**) informal a disreputable or promiscuous girl or woman.
– ORIGIN perhaps related to FLOSSY or to dialect *floosy* 'fluffy'.
flop ● verb (**flopped**, **flopping**) **1** hang or swing loosely. **2** sit or lie down heavily and clumsily. **3** informal fail totally. ● noun **1** a heavy and clumsy fall. **2** informal a total failure.
– ORIGIN variant of FLAP.
flophouse ● noun informal, chiefly N. Amer. a dosshouse.
floppy ● adjective (**floppier**, **floppiest**) tending to flop; not firm or rigid. ● noun (pl. **floppies**) (also **floppy disk**) Computing a flexible removable magnetic disk used for storing data.
– DERIVATIVES **floppily** adverb **floppiness** noun.
flora ● noun (pl. **floras** or **florae**) **1** the plants of a particular region, habitat, or geological period. Compare with FAUNA. **2** the symbiotic bacteria occurring naturally in the intestines: *the gut flora*.
– ORIGIN Latin *flos* 'flower'.
floral ● adjective **1** of or decorated with flowers. **2** Botany of flora or floras.
– DERIVATIVES **florally** adverb.
Florentine /florrəntīn/ ● adjective **1** relating to the city of Florence in Italy. **2** (**florentine** /florrənteen/) (after a noun) (of a dish) served on a bed of spinach: *eggs florentine*. ● noun **1** a person from Florence. **2** a biscuit consisting mainly of nuts and preserved fruit, coated on one side with chocolate.
florescence /floress'nss/ ● noun the process of flowering.
– ORIGIN Latin *florescentia*, from *florescere* 'begin to flower'.
floret /florrit/ ● noun **1** one of the small flowers making up a composite flower head. **2** one of the flowering stems making up a head of cauliflower or broccoli.
– ORIGIN from Latin *flos* 'flower' + -ET[1].
floribunda /florribundə/ ● noun a plant, especially a rose, which bears dense clusters of flowers.
– ORIGIN Latin, from *floribundus* 'freely flowering'.
floriculture /florikulchər/ ● noun the cultivation of flowers.
– DERIVATIVES **floriculturist** noun.
florid /florrid/ ● adjective **1** having a red or flushed complexion. **2** elaborately or excessively ornate or intricate: *florid prose*.
– DERIVATIVES **floridity** noun **floridly** adverb **floridness** noun.
– ORIGIN Latin *floridus*, from *flos* 'flower'.
floriferous /floriffərəss/ ● adjective producing many flowers.
florin /florrin/ ● noun **1** a former British coin worth two shillings. **2** an English gold coin of the 14th century, worth six shillings and eight old pence. **3** a Dutch guilder.
– ORIGIN Italian *fiorino* 'little flower' (originally referring to a Florentine coin bearing a fleur-de-lis).
florist ● noun a person who sells and arranges cut flowers.
– DERIVATIVES **floristry** noun.
floruit /florroo-it/ ● verb used to indicate when a historical figure lived, worked, or was most active.
– ORIGIN Latin, 'he or she flourished'.
floss ● noun **1** the rough silk enveloping a silkworm's cocoon. **2** untwisted silk fibres used in embroidery. **3** (also **dental floss**) a soft thread used to clean between the teeth. ● verb clean between (one's teeth) with dental floss.
– ORIGIN Old French *flosche* 'down, nap of velvet'.
flossy ● adjective (**flossier**, **flossiest**) **1** of or like floss. **2** N. Amer. informal excessively showy.
flotation /flōtaysh'n/ (also **floatation**) ● noun **1** the action of floating or capacity to float. **2** the process of offering a company's shares for sale on the stock market for the first time.
flotation tank ● noun a lightproof, soundproof tank of salt water in which a person floats as a form of deep relaxation.
flotilla /flətillə/ ● noun a small fleet of ships or boats.
– ORIGIN Spanish, 'small fleet'.
flotsam /flotsəm/ ● noun wreckage found floating on the sea. Compare with JETSAM.
– PHRASES **flotsam and jetsam** useless or discarded objects.
– ORIGIN Old French *floteson*, from *floter* 'to float'.
flounce[1] ● verb move in an exaggeratedly impatient or angry manner. ● noun an exaggerated action expressing annoyance or impatience.
– ORIGIN perhaps related to Norwegian *flunsa* 'hurry', or perhaps symbolic, like *bounce*.
flounce[2] ● noun a wide ornamental strip of material gathered and sewn to a skirt or dress; a frill.
– DERIVATIVES **flounced** adjective **flouncy** adjective.
– ORIGIN from an alteration of obsolete *frounce* 'a fold or pleat', from Old French *fronce*.
flounder[1] ● verb **1** stagger clumsily in mud or water. **2** have trouble doing or understanding something.
– USAGE On the confusion of **flounder** and **founder**, see the note at FOUNDER[3].
– ORIGIN perhaps a blend of FOUNDER[3] and BLUNDER.
flounder[2] ● noun a small flatfish of shallow coastal waters.
– ORIGIN Old French *flondre*.
flour ● noun a powder obtained by grinding grain, used to make bread, cakes, and pastry. ● verb sprinkle with flour.
– ORIGIN a specific use of FLOWER in the sense 'the best part', used originally to mean 'the finest quality of ground wheat'.
flourish ● verb **1** grow or develop in a healthy or vigorous way. **2** be working or at the height of one's career during a specified period. **3** wave about dramatically. ● noun **1** a bold or extravagant gesture or action. **2** an ornamental flowing curve in handwriting or scrollwork. **3** an ornate musical passage. **4** a fanfare played by brass instruments.

f

Thesaurus

flooded in POUR, stream, flow, surge, swarm, pile, crowd.
– OPPOSITES trickle.
floor ● noun **1** *he sat on the floor* GROUND, flooring. **2** *the second floor* STOREY, level, deck, tier.
● verb **1** *(informal) he floored his attacker* KNOCK DOWN, knock over, bring down, fell, prostrate; *informal* lay out. **2** *(informal) the question floored him* BAFFLE, defeat, confound, perplex, puzzle, nonplus, mystify; *informal* beat, flummox, stump, fox, make someone scratch their head; *N. Amer. informal* buffalo; *archaic* pose.
flop ● verb **1** *he flopped into a chair* COLLAPSE, slump, crumple, subside, sink, drop. **2** *his hair flopped over his eyes* HANG (DOWN), dangle, droop, sag, loll. **3** *(informal) the play flopped* BE UNSUCCESSFUL, fail, not work, fall flat, founder, misfire, backfire, be a disappointment, do badly, lose money, be a disaster; *informal* bomb, go to the wall, come a cropper, bite the dust, blow up in someone's face; *N. Amer. informal* tank.
– OPPOSITES succeed.
● noun *(informal) the play was a flop* FAILURE, disaster, debacle, catastrophe, loser; *Brit.* damp squib; *informal* flopperoo, washout, also-ran, dog, lemon, non-starter; *N. Amer. informal* clinker.
– OPPOSITES success.
floppy ● adjective LIMP, flaccid, slack, flabby, relaxed; drooping, droopy; loose, flowing.
– OPPOSITES erect, stiff.
florid ● adjective **1** *a florid complexion* RUDDY, red, red-faced, rosy, rosy-cheeked, pink; flushed, blushing, high-coloured; *archaic* sanguine. **2** *florid plasterwork* ORNATE, fancy, elaborate, embellished, curlicued, extravagant, flamboyant, baroque, rococo, fussy, busy. **3** *florid English* FLOWERY, flamboyant, high-flown, high-sounding, grandiloquent, ornate, fancy, bombastic, elaborate, turgid, pleonastic; *informal* highfalutin; *rare* fustian.
– OPPOSITES pale, plain.
flotsam ● noun WRECKAGE, lost cargo, floating remains; rubbish, debris, detritus, waste, dross, refuse, scrap; *N. Amer.* trash, garbage; *informal* dreck, junk; *Brit. informal* grot.
flounce[1] ● verb *she flounced off to her room* STORM, stride angrily, sweep, stomp, stamp, march, strut, stalk.
flounce[2] ● noun *a lace flounce* FRILL, ruffle, ruff, peplum, jabot, furbelow, ruche.
flounder ● verb **1** *people were floundering in the water* STRUGGLE, thrash, flail, twist and turn, splash, stagger, stumble, lurch, blunder, squirm, writhe. **2** *she floundered, not knowing quite what to say* STRUGGLE MENTALLY, be out of one's depth, have difficulty, be confounded, be confused; *informal* scratch one's head, be flummoxed, be clueless, be foxed, be fazed, be floored, be beaten. **3** *more firms are floundering* STRUGGLE FINANCIALLY, be in dire

– ORIGIN Old French *florir*, from Latin *flos* 'a flower'.
floury ● adjective **1** covered with flour. **2** (of a potato) having a soft, fluffy texture when cooked.
flout /flowt/ ● verb **1** openly disregard (a rule, law, or convention). **2** archaic mock; scoff.
– USAGE On the confusion of **flout** and **flaunt**, see the note at FLAUNT.
– ORIGIN perhaps from Dutch *fluiten* 'whistle, play the flute, hiss derisively'.
flow ● verb **1** move steadily and continuously in a current or stream. **2** move or issue forth steadily and freely: *people flowed into the courtyard.* **3** (often as adj. **flowing**) hang loosely and elegantly. **4** (of the sea or a tidal river) move towards the land; rise. **5** (of a solid) undergo a permanent change of shape under stress, without melting. ● noun **1** the action or process of flowing. **2** a steady, continuous stream. **3** the rise of a tide or a river.
– PHRASES **go with the flow** informal be relaxed and accept a situation. **in full flow** talking or performing fluently and enthusiastically.
– ORIGIN Old English, related to FLOOD.
flow chart (also **flow diagram**) ● noun a diagram of a sequence of operations or functions making up a complex process or computer program.
flower ● noun **1** the seed-bearing part of a plant, consisting of reproductive organs typically surrounded by brightly coloured petals and green sepals. **2** (often in phrase **in flower**) the state or period in which a plant's flowers have developed and opened. **3** (**the flower of**) the best of (a group). ● verb **1** produce flowers. **2** be in or reach a peak of development.
– DERIVATIVES **flowerer** noun **flowerless** adjective.
– ORIGIN Old French *flour*, *flor*, from Latin *flos*.
flowered ● adjective **1** having a floral design. **2** (in combination) bearing flowers: *yellow-flowered japonica.*
flower head ● noun a compact mass of flowers at the top of a stem, especially a dense flat cluster of florets.
flowerpot ● noun an earthenware or plastic container in which to grow a plant.
flower power ● noun the promotion by hippies of peace and love as means of changing the world.
flowers of sulphur ● noun (treated as sing.) Chemistry a fine yellow powdered form of sulphur produced by sublimation.
flowery ● adjective **1** full of, decorated with, or resembling flowers. **2** (of speech or writing) elaborate.
flown past participle of FLY[1].
flowsheet ● noun a flow chart.
flu ● noun influenza or any similar, milder infection.
flub N. Amer. informal ● verb (**flubbed**, **flubbing**) botch or bungle. ● noun a blunder.
– ORIGIN of unknown origin.
fluctuate /fluktyooayt/ ● verb rise and fall irregularly in number or amount.
– DERIVATIVES **fluctuation** noun.
– ORIGIN Latin *fluctuare* 'undulate', from *fluere* 'to flow'.
flue /floo/ ● noun **1** a duct in a chimney for smoke and waste gases. **2** a pipe or passage for conveying heat.
– ORIGIN of unknown origin.
fluence /flooənss/ ● noun Brit. informal magical or hypnotic power.
– ORIGIN shortening of INFLUENCE.
fluent /flooənt/ ● adjective **1** speaking or writing in an articulate and natural manner. **2** (of a language) used easily and accurately. **3** smoothly graceful and easy: *a runner in fluent motion.* **4** able to flow freely; fluid.
– DERIVATIVES **fluency** noun **fluently** adverb.
– ORIGIN from Latin *fluere* 'to flow'.
fluff ● noun **1** soft fibres accumulated in small light clumps. **2** the soft fur or feathers of a young mammal or bird. **3** trivial or superficial entertainment or writing. **4** informal a mistake. ● verb **1** (usu. **fluff up**) make fuller and softer by shaking or patting. **2** informal fail to accomplish properly: *he fluffed his only line.*
– ORIGIN probably a dialect alteration of earlier *flue* 'down, nap, fluff', apparently from Flemish *vluwe.*
fluffy ● adjective (**fluffier**, **fluffiest**) **1** of, like, or covered with fluff. **2** (of food) light in texture. **3** informal frivolous, silly, or vague.
– DERIVATIVES **fluffily** adverb **fluffiness** noun.
flugelhorn /floog'lhorn/ ● noun a valved brass musical instrument like a cornet but with a broader tone.
– ORIGIN German, from *Flügel* 'wing' + *Horn* 'horn'.
fluid ● noun a substance, such as a liquid or gas, that has no fixed shape and yields easily to external pressure. ● adjective

f

Thesaurus

straits, face financial ruin, be in difficulties, face bankruptcy/insolvency.
– OPPOSITES prosper.
flourish ● verb **1** *ferns flourish in the shade* GROW, thrive, prosper, do well, burgeon, increase, multiply, proliferate; spring up, shoot up, bloom, blossom, bear fruit, burst forth, run riot. **2** *the arts flourished* THRIVE, prosper, bloom, be in good health, be vigorous, be in its heyday; progress, make progress, advance, make headway, develop, improve; evolve, make strides, move forward (in leaps and bounds), expand; *informal* be in the pink, go places, go great guns, get somewhere. **3** *he flourished the sword at them* BRANDISH, wave, shake, wield; swing, twirl, swish; display, exhibit, flaunt, show off.
– OPPOSITES die, wither, decline.
flout ● verb DEFY, refuse to obey, disobey, break, violate, fail to comply with, fail to observe, contravene, infringe, breach, commit a breach of, transgress against; ignore, disregard; *informal* cock a snook at.
– OPPOSITES observe.
flow ● verb **1** *the water flowed down the channel* RUN, course, glide, drift, circulate; trickle, seep, ooze, dribble, drip, drizzle, spill; stream, swirl, surge, sweep, gush, cascade, pour, roll, rush. **2** *many questions flow from today's announcement* RESULT, proceed, arise, follow, ensue, derive, stem, accrue; originate, emanate, spring, emerge; be caused by, be brought about by, be produced by, be consequent on.
● noun *a good flow of water* MOVEMENT, motion, current, flux, circulation; trickle, ooze, percolation, drip; stream, swirl, surge, gush, rush, spate, tide.
flower ● noun **1** *blue flowers* BLOOM, blossom, floweret, floret. **2** *the flower of the nation's youth* BEST, finest, pick, choice, cream, the crème de la crème, elite.
– RELATED TERMS floral, flor-.
– OPPOSITES dregs.
flowery ● adjective **1** *flowery fabrics* FLORAL, flower-patterned. **2** *flowery language* FLORID, flamboyant, ornate, fancy, convoluted; high-flown, high-sounding, magniloquent, grandiloquent, baroque, orotund, overblown, pleonastic; *informal* highfalutin, purple; *rare* fustian.
– OPPOSITES plain.
flowing ● adjective **1** *long flowing hair* LOOSE, free, unconfined, draping. **2** *the new model will have soft, flowing lines* SLEEK, streamlined, aerodynamic, smooth, clean; elegant, graceful; *technical* faired. **3** *he writes in an easy, flowing style* FLUENT, fluid, free-flowing, effortless, easy, natural, smooth.
– OPPOSITES stiff, curly, jagged, halting.
fluctuate ● verb VARY, change, differ, shift, alter, waver, swing, oscillate, alternation, rise and fall, go up and down, see-saw, yo-yo, be unstable.
fluctuation ● noun VARIATION, change, shift, alteration, swing, movement, oscillation, alternation, rise and fall, see-sawing, yo-yoing, instability, unsteadiness.
– OPPOSITES stability.
flue ● noun DUCT, tube, shaft, vent, pipe, passage, channel, conduit; funnel, chimney, smokestack.
fluent ● adjective **1** *a fluent speech* ARTICULATE, eloquent, expressive, communicative, coherent, cogent, illuminating, vivid. **2** *fluent in French* ARTICULATE; (**be fluent in**) have a (good) command of. **3** *a very fluent running style* FREE-FLOWING, smooth, effortless, easy, natural, fluid; graceful, elegant; regular, rhythmic.
– OPPOSITES inarticulate, jerky.
fluff ● noun **1** *fluff on her sleeve* FUZZ, lint, dust; *N. Amer.* dustballs, dust bunnies. **2** *(informal) he only made a few fluffs* MISTAKE, error, slip, slip of the tongue; wrong note; *informal* slip-up; *formal* lapsus linguae.
● verb *(informal) Penney fluffed the shot | he fluffed his only line* BUNGLE, make a mess of, fumble, miss, deliver badly, muddle up, forget; *informal* mess up, make a hash of, make a botch of, foul up, bitch up, screw up, louse up; *Brit. informal* make a muck of, make a pig's ear of, cock up, make a Horlicks of; *N. Amer. informal* flub, goof up.
– OPPOSITES succeed in.

1 able to flow easily. **2** not settled or stable. **3** smoothly elegant or graceful.
– DERIVATIVES **fluidity** noun **fluidly** adverb.
– ORIGIN from Latin *fluidus*, from *fluere* 'to flow'.
fluid mechanics ● noun (treated as sing.) the study of forces and flow within fluids.
fluid ounce ● noun **1** Brit. a unit of capacity equal to one twentieth of a pint (approximately 0.028 litre). **2** (also **fluidounce**) US a unit of capacity equal to one sixteenth of a US pint (approximately 0.03 litre).
fluke[1] ● noun a lucky chance occurrence. ● verb achieve by luck rather than skill.
– DERIVATIVES **fluky** (also **flukey**) adjective.
– ORIGIN perhaps a dialect word.
fluke[2] ● noun **1** a parasitic flatworm which typically has suckers and hooks for attachment to the host. **2** chiefly dialect or N. Amer. a flounder or other flatfish.
– ORIGIN Old English.
fluke[3] ● noun **1** a broad triangular plate on the arm of an anchor. **2** either of the lobes of a whale's tail.
– ORIGIN perhaps from FLUKE[2] (because of the shape).
flume /flo͞om/ ● noun **1** an artificial channel conveying water, typically used for transporting logs. **2** a water slide or chute at a swimming pool or amusement park.
– ORIGIN Latin *flumen* 'river', from *fluere* 'to flow'.
flummery /flummәri/ ● noun (pl. **flummeries**) **1** empty talk or compliments. **2** a sweet dish made with beaten eggs and sugar.
– ORIGIN Welsh *llymru*.
flummox /flummәks/ ● verb informal perplex; bewilder.
– ORIGIN probably dialect.
flump ● verb fall, sit, or throw down heavily. ● noun a heavy fall.
– ORIGIN imitative.
flung past and past participle of FLING.
flunk ● verb informal, chiefly N. Amer. **1** fail to reach the required standard in (an examination). **2** (**flunk out**) fail utterly and leave or be dismissed from school or college.
– ORIGIN perhaps related to FUNK[1] or to US *flink* 'be a coward'.
flunkey (also **flunky**) ● noun (pl. **flunkeys** or **flunkies**) chiefly derogatory **1** a liveried manservant or footman. **2** a person who performs menial tasks.
– ORIGIN perhaps from FLANK in the sense 'a person who stands at one's flank'.
fluoresce /flooress/ ● verb shine or glow brightly due to fluorescence.
fluorescence ● noun **1** light emitted by a substance when it is exposed to radiation such as ultraviolet light or X-rays. **2** the property of emitting light in this way.
– ORIGIN from FLUORSPAR (which fluoresces), on the pattern of *opalescence*.
fluorescent ● adjective **1** having or showing fluorescence. **2** (of lighting) based on fluorescence from a substance illuminated by ultraviolet light. **3** vividly colourful.
fluorescent screen ● noun a transparent screen coated with fluorescent material to show images from X-rays.
fluoridate /flooridayt/ ● verb add traces of fluorides to (something, especially a water supply).
– DERIVATIVES **fluoridation** noun.
fluoride /floorīd/ ● noun **1** Chemistry a compound of fluorine with another element or group. **2** sodium fluoride or another fluorine-containing salt added to water supplies or toothpaste to reduce tooth decay.
fluorinate /floorinayt/ ● verb **1** Chemistry introduce fluorine into (a compound). **2** another term for FLUORIDATE.
– DERIVATIVES **fluorination** noun.
fluorine /floorin/ ● noun a poisonous, extremely reactive, pale yellow gaseous chemical element.
– ORIGIN from *fluor* (see FLUORSPAR).
fluorite ● noun a mineral form of calcium fluoride.
fluorocarbon ● noun Chemistry a compound formed by replacing one or more of the hydrogen atoms in a hydrocarbon with fluorine atoms.
fluoroscope ● noun an instrument with a fluorescent screen used for viewing X-ray images without taking and developing X-ray photographs.
– DERIVATIVES **fluoroscopic** adjective **fluoroscopy** noun.
fluorspar /floorspaar/ ● noun another term for FLUORITE.
– ORIGIN from Latin *fluor* 'a flow' (formerly used in English to mean 'fluorspar, a flow, a flux') + SPAR[3].
flurried ● adjective agitated, nervous, or anxious.
flurry ● noun (pl. **flurries**) **1** a small swirling mass of snow, leaves, etc. moved by a sudden gust of wind. **2** a sudden short spell of commotion or excitement. **3** a number of things arriving suddenly and simultaneously. ● verb (**flurries**, **flurried**) move in an agitated or excited way.
– ORIGIN from obsolete *flurr* 'fly up, flutter', probably influenced by HURRY.
flush[1] ● verb **1** (of a person's skin or face) become red and hot, typically through illness or emotion. **2** glow or cause to glow with warm colour or light. **3** (**be flushed with**) be excited or elated by. **4** cleanse (something, especially a toilet) by passing large quantities of water through it. **5** remove or dispose of by flushing with water. **6** drive (a bird or animal, especially a game bird) from cover. **7** force into the open: *their task was to flush out the rebels.* ● noun **1** a reddening of the face or skin. **2** a sudden rush of intense emotion. **3** a period of freshness and vigour: *the first flush of youth.* **4** an act of flushing.
– DERIVATIVES **flusher** noun.
– ORIGIN originally in the sense 'spring or fly up': symbolic.
flush[2] ● adjective **1** completely level or even with another surface. **2** informal having plenty of money. ● verb fill in (a joint) level with a surface.
– ORIGIN originally in the sense 'perfect, lacking nothing': probably related to FLUSH[1].
flush[3] ● noun (in poker or brag) a hand of cards all of the same suit.
– ORIGIN French *flux* (formerly *flus*), from Latin *fluxus* 'flux'.

Thesaurus

fluffy ● adjective FLEECY, woolly, fuzzy, hairy, feathery, downy, furry; soft.
– OPPOSITES rough.
fluid ● noun *the fluid seeps up the tube* LIQUID, watery substance, solution; GAS, gaseous substance, vapour.
– OPPOSITES solid.
● adjective **1** *a fluid substance* FREE-FLOWING; liquid, liquefied, melted, molten, runny, running; gaseous, gassy. **2** *his plans were still fluid* ADAPTABLE, flexible, adjustable, open-ended, open, open to change, changeable, variable. **3** *the fluid state of affairs* FLUCTUATING, changeable, subject/likely to change, (ever-)shifting, inconstant; unstable, unsettled, turbulent, volatile, mercurial, protean. **4** *he stood up in one fluid movement* SMOOTH, fluent, flowing, effortless, easy, continuous; graceful, elegant.
– OPPOSITES solid, firm, static, jerky.
fluke ● noun CHANCE, coincidence, accident, twist of fate; piece of luck, stroke of good luck/fortune.
fluky ● adjective LUCKY, fortunate, providential, timely, opportune, serendipitous, expedient, heaven-sent, auspicious, propitious, felicitous; chance, fortuitous, accidental, unintended; Brit. informal jammy.
– OPPOSITES planned.
flummox ● verb (informal) BAFFLE, perplex, puzzle, bewilder, mystify, bemuse, confuse, confound, nonplus; informal faze, stump, beat, fox, make someone scratch their head, be all Greek to, floor; N. Amer. informal discombobulate, buffalo.
flunkey ● noun **1** *a flunkey brought us drinks* LIVERIED SERVANT, lackey, steward, butler, footman, valet, attendant, page. **2** *government flunkeys searched his offices* MINION, lackey, hireling, subordinate, underling, servant; creature, instrument, cat's paw; informal stooge, gofer; Brit. informal poodle, dogsbody, skivvy.
flurried ● adjective AGITATED, flustered, ruffled, in a panic, worked up, beside oneself, overwrought, perturbed, frantic; informal in a flap, in a state, in a twitter, in a fluster, in a dither, all of a dither, all of a lather, in a tizz/tizzy, in a tiz-woz; Brit. informal in a (flat) spin, having kittens; N. Amer. informal in a twit.
– OPPOSITES calm.
flurry ● noun **1** *a flurry of snow* SWIRL, whirl, eddy, billow, shower, gust. **2** *a flurry of activity* BURST, outbreak, spurt, fit, spell, bout, rash, eruption; (**flurry of excitement**) fuss, stir, bustle, hubbub, commotion, disturbance, furore; informal to-do, flap. **3** *a flurry of imports* SPATE, wave, flood, deluge, torrent, stream, tide, avalanche; series, succession, string, outbreak, rash, explosion, run, rush.
– OPPOSITES dearth, trickle.
● verb *snow flurried through the door* SWIRL, whirl, eddy, billow, gust, blast, blow, rush.
flush[1] ● verb **1** *she flushed in embarrassment* BLUSH, redden, go

fluster ● verb (often as adj. **flustered**) make (someone) agitated or confused. ● noun a flustered state.
– ORIGIN originally in the sense 'make slightly drunk': perhaps Scandinavian.

flute ● noun **1** a high-pitched wind instrument consisting of a tube with holes along it, usually held horizontally so that the breath can be directed against a fixed edge. **2** Architecture an ornamental vertical groove in a column. **3** a tall, narrow wine glass. ● verb **1** speak in a melodious way. **2** make grooves in.
– DERIVATIVES **fluting** noun **fluty** (also **flutey**) adjective.
– ORIGIN Old French *flahute*, probably from Provençal *flaüt*, perhaps a blend of *flaujol* 'flageolet' + *laüt* 'lute'.

flutist ● noun US term for FLAUTIST.

flutter ● verb **1** fly unsteadily by flapping the wings quickly and lightly. **2** move or fall with a light irregular motion. **3** (of a pulse or heartbeat) beat feebly or irregularly. ● noun **1** an act or instance of fluttering. **2** a state of tremulous excitement. **3** Brit. informal a small bet. **4** Electronics rapid variation in the pitch or amplitude of a signal, especially of recorded sound. Compare with WOW[2].
– DERIVATIVES **fluttery** adjective.
– ORIGIN Old English, related to FLEET[3].

fluvial /flo͞oviəl/ ● adjective chiefly Geology of or found in a river.
– ORIGIN Latin *fluvialis*, from *fluvius* 'river'.

flux /fluks/ ● noun **1** continuous change. **2** the action or an instance of flowing. **3** Medicine an abnormal discharge of blood or other matter from or within the body. **4** Physics the total amount of radiation, or of electric or magnetic field lines, passing through an area. **5** a substance mixed with a solid to lower the melting point, especially in soldering or smelting. ● verb treat (a metal object) with a flux to promote melting.
– ORIGIN Latin *fluxus*, from *fluere* 'to flow'.

fly[1] ● verb (**flies**; past **flew**; past part. **flown**) **1** (of a winged creature or aircraft) move through the air under control. **2** control the flight of or convey in (an aircraft). **3** move or be hurled quickly through the air. **4** go or move quickly. **5** wave or flutter in the wind. **6** (of a flag) be displayed on a flagpole. **7** (**fly into**) suddenly go into (a rage or other strong emotion). **8** (**fly at**) attack verbally or physically. **9** archaic flee. ● noun (pl. **flies**) **1** (Brit. also **flies**) an opening at the crotch of a pair of trousers, closed with a zip or buttons. **2** a flap of material covering the opening of a tent. **3** (**the flies**) the space over the stage in a theatre.
– PHRASES **fly in the face of** be openly at variance with (what is usual or expected). **fly a kite** informal try something out to test public opinion. **fly off the handle** informal lose one's temper suddenly.
– DERIVATIVES **flyable** adjective.
– ORIGIN Old English, related to FLY[2].

fly[2] ● noun (pl. **flies**) **1** a flying insect of a large order characterized by a single pair of transparent wings and sucking or piercing mouthparts. **2** used in names of other flying insects, e.g. **dragonfly**. **3** a fishing bait consisting of a mayfly or other natural or artificial flying insect.
– PHRASES **a fly in the ointment** a minor irritation that spoils the enjoyment of something. **fly on the wall** an unnoticed observer. **there are no flies on ——** the person specified is quick and astute.
– ORIGIN Old English, related to FLY[1].

fly[3] ● adjective (**flyer**, **flyest**) informal **1** Brit. knowing and clever; worldly-wise. **2** N. Amer. stylish and fashionable.
– ORIGIN of unknown origin.

fly agaric ● noun a poisonous toadstool which has a red cap with fluffy white spots.

flyaway ● adjective (of hair) fine and difficult to control.

flyblown ● adjective contaminated by contact with flies and their eggs and larvae.

fly-by-night ● adjective unreliable or untrustworthy, especially in business or financial matters.

fly-by-wire ● adjective a semi-automatic, computer-regulated system for controlling an aircraft or spacecraft.

Thesaurus

pink, go red, go crimson, go scarlet, colour (up); *archaic* mantle. **2** *fruit helps to flush toxins from the body* RINSE, wash, sluice, swill, cleanse, clean; *Brit. informal* sloosh. **3** *they flushed out the snipers* DRIVE, chase, force, dislodge, expel, frighten, scare.
– OPPOSITES pale.
● noun **1** *a flush crept over her face* BLUSH, reddening, high colour, colour, rosiness, pinkness, ruddiness, bloom. **2** *the first flush of manhood* BLOOM, glow, freshness, radiance, vigour, rush.
– OPPOSITES paleness.

flush[2] ● adjective (*informal*) **1** *the company was flush with cash* WELL SUPPLIED, well provided, well stocked, replete, overflowing, bursting, brimful, brimming, loaded, overloaded, stuffed, teeming, swarming, thick, solid; full of, abounding in, rich in, abundant in; *informal* awash, jam-packed, chock-full of; *Austral./NZ informal* chocker. **2** *the years when cash was flush* PLENTIFUL, abundant, in abundance, copious, ample, profuse, superabundant; *informal* a gogo, galore; *poetic/literary* plenteous, bounteous.
– OPPOSITES lacking, low (on).

flushed ● adjective **1** *flushed faces* RED, pink, ruddy, glowing, reddish, pinkish, rosy, florid, high-coloured, healthy-looking, aglow, burning, feverish; blushing, red-faced, embarrassed, shamefaced. **2** *flushed with success* ELATED, excited, thrilled, exhilarated, happy, delighted, overjoyed, joyous, gleeful, jubilant, exultant, ecstatic, euphoric, rapturous; *informal* blissed out, over the moon, high, on a high; *N. Amer. informal* wigged out.
– OPPOSITES pale, dismayed.

fluster ● verb *she was flustered by his presence* UNSETTLE, make nervous, unnerve, agitate, ruffle, upset, bother, put on edge, disquiet, disturb, worry, perturb, disconcert, confuse, throw off balance, confound, nonplus; *informal* rattle, faze, put into a flap, throw into a tizzy; *Brit. informal* send into a spin; *N. Amer. informal* discombobulate.
– OPPOSITES calm.
● noun *I was in a terrible fluster* STATE OF AGITATION, state of anxiety, nervous state, panic, frenzy, fret; *informal* dither, flap, tizz, tizzy, tiz-woz, twitter, state, sweat; *N. Amer. informal* twit.
– OPPOSITES state of calm.

fluted ● adjective GROOVED, channelled, furrowed, ribbed, corrugated, ridged.
– OPPOSITES smooth, plain.

flutter ● verb **1** *butterflies fluttered around* FLIT, hover, flitter, dance. **2** *a tern was fluttering its wings* FLAP, move up and down, beat, quiver, agitate, vibrate. **3** *she fluttered her eyelashes* FLICKER, bat. **4** *flags fluttered* FLAP, wave, ripple, undulate, quiver; fly. **5** *her heart fluttered* BEAT WEAKLY/IRREGULARLY, palpitate, miss/skip a beat, quiver, go pit-a-pat; *Medicine* exhibit arrhythmia; *rare* quop.
● noun **1** *the flutter of wings* BEATING, flapping, quivering, agitation, vibrating. **2** *a flutter of dark eyelashes* FLICKER, bat. **3** *the flutter of the flags* FLAPPING, waving, rippling. **4** *a flutter of nervousness* TREMOR, wave, rush, surge, flash, stab, flush, tremble, quiver, shiver, frisson, chill, thrill, tingle, shudder, ripple, flicker. **5** (*Brit. informal*) *he enjoys a flutter on the horses* BET, wager, gamble; *Brit. informal* punt.

flux ● noun CONTINUOUS CHANGE, changeability, variability, inconstancy, fluidity, instability, unsteadiness, fluctuation, variation, shift, movement, oscillation, alternation, rise and fall, see-sawing, yo-yoing.
– OPPOSITES stability.

fly[1] ● verb **1** *a bird flew overhead* TRAVEL THROUGH THE AIR, wing its way, wing, glide, soar, wheel; hover, hang; take wing, take to the air, mount. **2** *they flew to Paris* TRAVEL BY PLANE/AIR, jet. **3** *military planes flew in food supplies* TRANSPORT BY PLANE/AIR, airlift, lift, jet. **4** *he could fly a plane* PILOT, operate, control, manoeuvre, steer. **5** *the ship was flying a quarantine flag* DISPLAY, show, exhibit; have hoisted, have run up. **6** *flags flew in the town* FLUTTER, flap, wave. **7** *doesn't time fly?* GO QUICKLY, fly by/past, pass swiftly, slip past, rush past. **8** *the runners flew by.* See SPEED verb sense 1. **9** (*archaic*) *the beaten army had to fly.* See FLEE sense 1. **10** (*dated*) *they had to fly the country.* See FLEE sense 2.
– PHRASES **fly at** *Robbie flew at him, fists clenched* ATTACK, assault, pounce on, set upon, set about, weigh into, let fly at, turn on, round on, lash out at, hit out at, belabour, fall on; *informal* lay into, tear into, lace into, sail into, pitch into, wade into, let someone have it, jump; *Brit. informal* have a go at; *N. Amer. informal* light into. **let fly.** See LET.

fly[2] ● adjective (*Brit. informal*) *she's fly enough not to get conned* SHREWD, sharp, astute, acute, canny, worldly-wise, knowing, clever; *informal* streetwise, not born yesterday, smart, no fool, nobody's fool; *Brit. informal* suss, knowing how many beans make five; *Scottish & N. English informal* pawky.
– OPPOSITES naive.

fly-by-night ● adjective UNRELIABLE, undependable, untrustworthy, disreputable; DISHONEST, deceitful, dubious, unscrupulous; *informal* iffy, shady, shifty, slippery, crooked; *Brit. informal* dodgy, bent;

flycatcher • noun a perching bird that catches flying insects.
flyer (also **flier**) • noun **1** a person or thing that flies. **2** informal a fast-moving person or thing. **3** a small handbill advertising an event or product. **4** a flying start.
fly-fishing • noun the sport of fishing using a rod and an artificial fly as bait.
fly half • noun Rugby another term for STAND-OFF HALF.
flying • adjective **1** moving through or fluttering in the air. **2** hasty; brief: *a flying visit.*
– PHRASES **with flying colours** with distinction.
flying boat • noun a large seaplane that lands with its fuselage in the water.
flying bomb • noun a small pilotless aircraft with an explosive warhead.
flying buttress • noun Architecture a buttress slanting from a separate column, typically forming an arch with the wall it supports.
flying doctor • noun (in Australia) a doctor who travels by aircraft to visit patients in remote areas.
flying fish • noun a fish of warm seas which leaps out of the water and uses its wing-like pectoral fins to glide for some distance.
flying fox • noun a large fruit bat with a foxlike face, found in Madagascar, SE Asia, and northern Australia.
flying officer • noun a rank of commissioned officer in the RAF, above pilot officer and below flight lieutenant.
flying picket • noun Brit. a person who travels to picket a workplace where there is an industrial dispute.
flying saucer • noun a disc-shaped flying craft supposedly piloted by aliens.
flying squad noun • noun Brit. a division of a police force which is capable of reaching an incident quickly.
flying start • noun **1** a start of a race in which the competitors are already moving at speed as they pass the starting point. **2** a good beginning giving an advantage over competitors.
flyleaf • noun (pl. **flyleaves**) a blank page at the beginning or end of a book.
flyover • noun chiefly Brit. a bridge carrying one road or railway line over another.
flypaper • noun sticky, poison-treated strips of paper that are hung indoors to catch and kill flies.
fly-past • noun Brit. a ceremonial flight of aircraft past a person or a place.
fly-post • verb Brit. put up (advertising posters) in unauthorized places.
fly-poster • noun Brit. **1** an advertising poster put up in an unauthorized place. **2** a person who fly-posts.
flysheet • noun **1** Brit. a fabric cover pitched over a tent to give extra protection against bad weather. **2** a tract or circular of two or four pages.
flyspeck • noun **1** a tiny stain made by the excrement of an insect. **2** something contemptibly small or insignificant: *a flyspeck of a town.*
fly-tip • verb Brit. illegally dump waste.
flyweight • noun a weight in boxing and other sports intermediate between light flyweight and bantamweight.
flywheel • noun a heavy revolving wheel in a machine which is used to increase momentum and thereby provide greater stability or a reserve of available power.
FM • abbreviation **1** Field Marshal. **2** frequency modulation.
Fm • symbol the chemical element fermium.
fm • abbreviation fathom(s).
f-number • noun the ratio of the focal length of a camera lens to the diameter of the aperture being used for a particular shot.
FO • abbreviation Foreign Office.
foal • noun a young horse or related animal. • verb (of a mare) give birth to a foal.
– ORIGIN Old English, related to FILLY.
foam • noun **1** a mass of small bubbles formed on or in liquid. **2** a liquid preparation containing many small bubbles: *shaving foam.* **3** a lightweight form of rubber or plastic made by solidifying foam. • verb form or produce foam.
– PHRASES **foam at the mouth** informal be very angry.
– DERIVATIVES **foamy** adjective.
– ORIGIN Old English.
fob[1] • noun **1** a chain attached to a watch for carrying in a waistcoat or waistband pocket. **2** (also **fob pocket**) a small pocket for carrying a watch. **3** a tab on a key ring.
– ORIGIN probably related to German dialect *Fuppe* 'pocket'.
fob[2] • verb (**fobbed**, **fobbing**) **1** (**fob off**) try to deceive (someone) into accepting excuses or something inferior. **2** (**fob off on**) give (something) inferior to.
– ORIGIN perhaps related to German *foppen* 'deceive, banter', or to FOP.
fob watch • noun a pocket watch.
focaccia /fəkachə/ • noun a type of flat Italian bread made with olive oil and flavoured with herbs.
– ORIGIN Italian.
focal /fōk'l/ • adjective relating to a focus, especially the focus of a lens.
focal length • noun the distance between the centre of a lens or curved mirror and its focus.
focal point • noun **1** the point at which rays or waves meet after reflection or refraction, or the point from which diverging rays or waves appear to proceed. **2** the centre of interest or activity.
fo'c's'le /fōks'l/ • noun variant spelling of FORECASTLE.
focus /fōkəss/ • noun (pl. **focuses** or **foci** /fōsī/) **1** the centre of interest or activity. **2** the state or quality of having or producing clear visual definition: *his face is out of focus.* **3** the point at which an object must be situated with respect to a lens or mirror for an image of the object to be well defined. **4** a focal point. **5** an act of focusing on something. **6** the point of origin of an earthquake. Compare with EPICENTRE. **7** Geometry one of the fixed points from which the distances to any point of an ellipse, parabola, or other curve are connected by a linear relation. • verb (**focused**, **focusing** or **focussed**, **focussing**) **1** adapt to the prevailing level of light and become able to see clearly. **2** adjust the focus of (a telescope, camera, etc.). **3** (with reference to rays or waves) meet or cause to meet at a single point. **4** (**focus on**) pay particular attention to.
– DERIVATIVES **focuser** noun.
– ORIGIN Latin, 'domestic hearth'.
focus group • noun a group of people assembled to assess a new product, political campaign, television series, etc.
fodder • noun **1** food for cattle and other livestock. **2** a person

Thesaurus

Austral./NZ informal shonky.
– OPPOSITES reliable, honest.
flyer, flier • noun **1** *frequent flyers* AIR TRAVELLER, air passenger, airline customer. **2** *flyers killed in the war* PILOT, airman, airwoman; *N. Amer. informal* jock; *dated* aviator, aeronaut. **3** *flyers promoting a new sandwich bar* HANDBILL, bill, handout, leaflet, circular, advertisement; *N. Amer.* dodger.
flying • adjective **1** *a flying beetle* WINGED; AIRBORNE, in the air, in flight. **2** *a flying visit* BRIEF, short, lightning, fleeting, hasty, rushed, hurried, quick, whistle-stop, cursory, perfunctory; *informal* quickie.
– OPPOSITES long.
foam • noun *the white foam on the huge, breaking waves* FROTH, spume, surf, spindrift; fizz, effervescence, bubbles, head; lather, suds.
• verb *the water foamed* FROTH, spume; fizz, effervesce, bubble; lather; ferment, rise; boil, seethe, simmer.
foamy • adjective FROTHY, foaming, spumy, bubbly, aerated, bubbling; sudsy; whipped, whisked.
fob • verb
– PHRASES **fob someone off** *I wasn't going to be fobbed off with excuses* PUT OFF, stall, give someone the runaround, deceive; placate, appease. **fob something off on** *he fobbed off the chairmanship on Clifford* IMPOSE, palm off, unload, dump, get rid of, foist, offload; saddle someone with something, land someone with something, lumber someone with something.
focus • noun **1** *schools are a focus of community life* CENTRE, focal point, central point, centre of attention, hub, pivot, nucleus, heart, cornerstone, linchpin, cynosure. **2** *the focus is on helping people* EMPHASIS, accent, priority, attention, concentration. **3** *the main focus of this chapter* SUBJECT, theme, concern, subject matter, topic, issue, thesis, point, thread; substance, essence, gist, matter. **4** *the resulting light beams are brought to a focus at the eyepiece* FOCAL POINT, point of convergence.
• verb **1** *he focused his binoculars on the tower* BRING INTO FOCUS; aim, point, turn. **2** *the investigation will focus on areas of social need* CONCENTRATE, centre, zero in, zoom in; address itself to, pay attention to, pinpoint, revolve around, have as its starting point.

or thing regarded only as material to satisfy a need: *young people ending up as factory fodder*.
– ORIGIN Old English, related to FOOD.

foe ● noun formal or literary an enemy or opponent.
– ORIGIN from Old English, 'hostile'; related to FEUD.

foehn ● noun variant spelling of FÖHN.

foetid ● adjective variant spelling of FETID.

foetus ● noun variant spelling of FETUS (chiefly in British non-technical use).
– DERIVATIVES **foetal** adjective.

fog ● noun **1** a thick cloud of tiny water droplets suspended in the atmosphere at or near the earth's surface which obscures or restricts visibility. **2** a state or cause of perplexity or confusion. **3** Photography cloudiness obscuring the image on a developed negative or print. ● verb (**fogged**, **fogging**) **1** cover or become covered with steam. **2** bewilder or confuse. **3** Photography make (a film, negative, or print) obscure or cloudy.
– ORIGIN perhaps a back-formation from FOGGY.

f

fogey /fōgi/ (also **fogy**) ● noun (pl. **fogeys** or **fogies**) a very old-fashioned or conservative person.
– DERIVATIVES **fogeydom** noun **fogeyish** adjective **fogeyism** noun.
– ORIGIN related to earlier slang *fogram*, of unknown origin.

foggy ● adjective (**foggier**, **foggiest**) **1** full of or accompanied by fog. **2** confused.
– PHRASES **not have the foggiest (idea)** informal, chiefly Brit. have no idea at all.
– ORIGIN perhaps from *fog* 'grass which grows in a field after a crop of hay has been cut', perhaps from Norwegian *fogg*.

foghorn ● noun a device making a loud, deep sound as a warning to ships in fog.

fogy ● noun variant spelling of FOGEY.

föhn /fōn/ (also **foehn**) ● noun a hot southerly wind on the northern slopes of the Alps.
– ORIGIN German, from Latin *ventus Favonius* 'mild west wind', *Favonius* being the Roman personification of the west or west wind.

foible /foyb'l/ ● noun a minor weakness or eccentricity.
– ORIGIN French, obsolete form of Old French *fieble* 'feeble'.

foie gras /fwaa graa/ ● noun short for PÂTÉ DE FOIE GRAS.

foil[1] ● verb prevent the success of.
– ORIGIN originally in the sense 'trample down': perhaps from Old French *fouler* 'to full cloth, trample', from Latin *fullo* 'fuller'.

foil[2] ● noun **1** metal hammered or rolled into a thin flexible sheet. **2** a person or thing that contrasts with and so enhances the qualities of another.
– ORIGIN Latin *folium* 'leaf'.

foil[3] ● noun a light, blunt-edged fencing sword with a button on its point.
– ORIGIN of unknown origin.

foist /foyst/ ● verb (**foist on**) impose (an unwelcome person or thing) on.
– ORIGIN originally in the sense 'dishonestly manipulate a dice': from Dutch dialect *vuisten* 'take in the hand'.

fold[1] ● verb **1** bend (something) over on itself so that one part of it covers another. **2** (often as adj. **folding**) be able to be folded into a flatter shape. **3** use (a soft or flexible material) to cover or wrap something in. **4** affectionately clasp in one's arms. **5** informal (of a company) cease trading as a result of financial problems. **6** (**fold in/into**) mix (an ingredient) gently with (another ingredient). ● noun **1** a folded part or thing. **2** a line or crease produced by folding. **3** chiefly Brit. a slight hill or hollow. **4** Geology a bend or curvature of strata.
– PHRASES **fold one's arms** bring one's arms together and cross them over one's chest.
– DERIVATIVES **foldable** adjective.
– ORIGIN Old English.

fold[2] ● noun **1** a pen or enclosure for livestock, especially sheep. **2** (**the fold**) a group or community with shared aims and values.
– ORIGIN Old English.

-fold ● suffix forming adjectives and adverbs from cardinal numbers: **1** in an amount multiplied by: *threefold*. **2** consisting of so many parts or facets: *twofold*.
– ORIGIN Old English, related to FOLD[1].

folder ● noun **1** a folding cover or wallet for storing loose papers. **2** Computing a directory containing related files or documents.

folderol /foldərol/ (also **falderal**) ● noun **1** trivial or nonsensical fuss. **2** a showy but useless item.
– ORIGIN from a meaningless refrain in old songs.

folding money ● noun informal money in the form of notes.

foley ● noun (before a noun) chiefly US relating to the addition of sound effects after the shooting of a film.
– ORIGIN named after the inventor of the editing process.

foliage /fōli-ij/ ● noun leaves of plants collectively.
– ORIGIN Old French *feuillage*, from Latin *folium* 'leaf'.

foliar /fōliər/ ● adjective technical relating to leaves.

foliate ● adjective /fōliət/ decorated with leaves or a leaf-like pattern. ● verb /fōliayt/ **1** decorate with leaves or a leaf-like pattern. **2** (**foliated**) chiefly Geology consisting of thin sheets of laminae.

folic acid /fōlik/ ● noun a vitamin of the B complex found especially in leafy green vegetables, liver, and kidney.
– DERIVATIVES **folate** noun.
– ORIGIN from Latin *folium* 'leaf'.

folie à deux /folli a dö/ ● noun (pl. **folies à deux**) delusion or mental illness shared by two people in close association.
– ORIGIN French, 'shared madness'.

folie de grandeur /folli də groNdör/ ● noun delusions of grandeur.
– ORIGIN French.

folio /fōliō/ ● noun (pl. **folios**) **1** a sheet of paper folded once to form two leaves (four pages) of a book. **2** a book made up of such sheets. **3** an individual leaf of paper numbered on the

Thesaurus

– PHRASES **in focus** SHARP, crisp, distinct, clear, well defined, well focused. **out of focus** BLURRED, unfocused, indistinct, blurry, fuzzy, hazy, misty, cloudy, lacking definition, nebulous.

foe ● noun (*poetic/literary*) ENEMY, adversary, opponent, rival, antagonist, combatant, challenger, competitor, opposer, opposition, competition, other side.
– OPPOSITES friend.

fog ● noun MIST, smog, murk, haze, haar; *N. English* (sea) fret; *informal* pea-souper; *poetic/literary* brume, fume.
● verb **1** *the windscreen fogged up | his breath fogged the glass* STEAM UP, mist over, cloud over, film over, make/become misty. **2** *his brain was fogged with sleep* MUDDLE, daze, stupefy, fuddle, befuddle, bewilder, confuse, befog; *poetic/literary* bedim, becloud.

foggy ● adjective **1** *the weather was foggy* MISTY, smoggy, hazy, murky. **2** *she was foggy with sleep | a foggy memory* MUDDLED, fuddled, befuddled, confused, bewildered, dazed, stupefied, numb, groggy, fuzzy, bleary; dark, dim, hazy, shadowy, cloudy, blurred, obscure, vague, indistinct, unclear; *informal* dopey, woolly, woozy, out of it.
– OPPOSITES clear.

foible ● noun WEAKNESS, failing, shortcoming, flaw, imperfection, blemish, fault, defect, limitation; quirk, kink, idiosyncrasy, eccentricity, peculiarity.
– OPPOSITES strength.

foil[1] ● verb *their escape attempt was foiled* THWART, frustrate, counter, baulk, impede, obstruct, hamper, hinder, snooker, cripple, scotch, derail, smash; stop, block, prevent, defeat; *informal* do for, put paid to, stymie, cook someone's goose; *Brit. informal* scupper, nobble, queer, put the mockers on.
– OPPOSITES assist.

foil[2] ● noun *the wine was a perfect foil to pasta* CONTRAST, complement, antithesis, relief.

foist ● verb IMPOSE, force, thrust, offload, unload, dump, palm off, fob off; pass off, get rid of; saddle someone with, land someone with, lumber someone with.

fold[1] ● verb **1** *I folded the cloth* DOUBLE (OVER/UP), crease, turn under/up/over, bend; tuck, gather, pleat. **2** *fold the cream into the chocolate mixture* MIX, blend, stir gently. **3** *he folded her in his arms* ENFOLD, wrap, envelop; take, gather, clasp, squeeze, clutch; embrace, hug, cuddle, cradle. **4** *(informal) the firm folded last year* FAIL, collapse, founder; go bankrupt, become insolvent, cease trading, go into receivership, go into liquidation, be wound up, be closed (down), be shut (down); *informal* crash, go bust, go broke, go under, go to the wall, go belly up.
● noun *there was a fold in the paper* CREASE, knife-edge; wrinkle, crinkle, pucker, furrow; pleat, gather.

fold[2] ● noun **1** *the sheep were in their fold* ENCLOSURE, pen, paddock, pound, compound, ring; *N. Amer.* corral. **2** *Lloyd George returned to the Liberal fold* COMMUNITY, group, body, company, mass, throng, flock, congregation, assembly.

front side only. **4** the page number in a printed book.
– ORIGIN Latin, used to mean 'on leaf (as specified)', from *folium* 'leaf'.

folk /fōk/ ● plural noun **1** (also **folks**) informal people in general. **2** (**one's folks**) informal one's family, especially one's parents. **3** (also **folk music**) traditional music of unknown authorship, transmitted orally. **4** (before another noun) originating from the beliefs, culture, and customs of ordinary people: *folk wisdom.*
– ORIGIN Old English.

folk dance ● noun a traditional dance associated with a particular people or area.

folk etymology ● noun **1** a popular but mistaken account of the origin of a word or phrase. **2** the process by which the form of an unfamiliar or foreign word is adapted to a more familiar form through popular usage.

folkie ● noun informal a singer, player, or fan of folk music.

folkish ● adjective **1** characteristic of ordinary people or traditional culture. **2** resembling folk music.

folklore ● noun the traditional beliefs, stories, and customs of a community, passed on by word of mouth.
– DERIVATIVES **folkloric** adjective **folklorist** noun.

folk memory ● noun a body of recollections or legends that persists among a people.

folksy ● adjective (**folksier**, **folksiest**) traditional and homely, especially in an artificial way.
– DERIVATIVES **folksiness** noun.

folk tale ● noun a traditional story originally transmitted orally.

folky ● adjective (**folkier**, **folkiest**) resembling or characteristic of folk music.

follicle /follik'l/ ● noun a small glandular cavity or pouch, especially that in which the root of a hair develops.
– DERIVATIVES **follicular** /folikyoolər/ adjective.
– ORIGIN Latin *folliculus* 'little bag'.

follow ● verb **1** move or travel behind. **2** go after (someone) so as to observe or monitor them. **3** go along (a route or path). **4** come after in time or order. **5** be a logical consequence. **6** (also **follow on from**) occur as a result of. **7** act according to (an instruction or precept). **8** act according to the lead or example of. **9** take an interest in or pay close attention to. **10** understand the meaning of. **11** practise or undertake (a career or course of action). **12** (**follow through**) continue (an action or task) to its conclusion. **13** (**follow up**) pursue or investigate further.
– PHRASES **follow one's nose 1** trust to one's instincts. **2** go straight ahead. **follow on** (of a cricket team) be required to bat again immediately after failing to reach a certain score in their first innings. **follow suit 1** conform to another's actions. **2** (in bridge, whist, and other card games) play a card of the suit led.
– ORIGIN Old English.

follower ● noun **1** a person who follows. **2** a supporter, fan, or disciple.

following ● preposition coming after or as a result of. ● noun a body of supporters or admirers. ● adjective **1** next in time or order. **2** about to be mentioned: *the following information.*

follow-the-leader (also **follow-my-leader**) ● noun a children's game in which the participants must copy the actions and words of a person acting as leader.

follow-through ● noun the continuing of an action or task to its conclusion.

follow-up ● noun **1** an activity carried out to monitor or further develop earlier work. **2** a work that follows or builds on an earlier work.

folly ● noun (pl. **follies**) **1** foolishness. **2** a foolish act or idea. **3** an ornamental building with no practical purpose, especially a tower or mock-Gothic ruin.
– ORIGIN Old French *folie* 'madness'.

foment /fōment/ ● verb **1** instigate or stir up (revolution or strife). **2** archaic bathe (a part of the body) with warm or medicated lotions.
– DERIVATIVES **fomentation** noun.
– ORIGIN Latin *fomentare*, from *fomentum* 'poultice, lotion'.

fond ● adjective **1** (**fond of**) having an affection or liking for. **2** affectionate; loving: *fond memories.* **3** (of a hope or belief) foolishly optimistic; naive.
– DERIVATIVES **fondly** adverb **fondness** noun.
– ORIGIN from obsolete *fon* 'a fool, be foolish', of unknown origin.

fondant /fondənt/ ● noun **1** a thick paste made of sugar and water, used in making sweets and icing cakes. **2** a sweet made of fondant.

f

Thesaurus

folder ● noun FILE, binder, ring binder, portfolio, document case, envelope, sleeve, wallet.

foliage ● noun LEAVES, leafage; greenery, vegetation, verdure.

folk ● noun (*informal*) **1** *the local folk* PEOPLE, individuals, {men, women, and children}, (living) souls, mortals; citizenry, inhabitants, residents, populace, population; *informal* peeps; *formal* denizens. **2** *my folks came from the north* RELATIVES, relations, blood relations, family, nearest and dearest, people, kinsfolk, kinsmen, kinswomen, kin, kith and kin, kindred, flesh and blood.

folklore ● noun MYTHOLOGY, lore, oral history, tradition, folk tradition; legends, fables, myths, folk tales, folk stories, old wives' tales; mythos.

follow ● verb **1** *we'll let the others follow* COME BEHIND, come after, go behind, go after, walk behind. **2** *he was expected to follow his father in the business* TAKE THE PLACE OF, replace, succeed, take over from; *informal* step into someone's shoes, fill someone's shoes/boots. **3** *people used to follow the band around* ACCOMPANY, go along with, go around with, travel with, escort, attend, trail around with, string along with; *informal* tag along with. **4** *the KGB man followed her everywhere* SHADOW, trail, stalk, track, dog, hound; *informal* tail. **5** *do follow the instructions* OBEY, comply with, conform to, adhere to, stick to, keep to, act in accordance with, abide by, observe, heed, pay attention to. **6** *penalties may follow from such behaviour* RESULT, arise, be a consequence of, be caused by, be brought about by, be a result of, come after, develop, ensue, emanate, issue, proceed, spring, flow, originate, stem. **7** *I couldn't follow what he said* UNDERSTAND, comprehend, apprehend, take in, grasp, fathom, appreciate, see; *informal* make head or tail of, get, figure out, savvy, get one's head around, get one's mind around, get the drift of; *Brit. informal* suss out. **8** *he followed his master in his poetic style* IMITATE, copy, mimic, ape, reproduce, mirror, echo; emulate, take as a pattern, take as an example, take as a model, adopt the style of, model oneself on, take a leaf out of someone's book. **9** *he follows Manchester United* BE A FAN OF, be a supporter of, support, be a follower of, be an admirer of, be a devotee of, be devoted to.
– OPPOSITES lead, flout, misunderstand.
– PHRASES **follow something through** COMPLETE, bring to completion, see something through; continue with, carry on with, keep on with, keep going with, stay with; *informal* stick something out. **follow something up** INVESTIGATE, research, look into, dig into, delve into, make enquiries into, enquire about, ask questions about, pursue, chase up; *informal* check out; *N. Amer. informal* scope out.

follower ● noun **1** *the president's closest followers* ACOLYTE, assistant, attendant, companion, henchman, minion, lackey, servant; *informal* hanger-on, sidekick; *archaic* liegeman. **2** *a follower of Caravaggio* IMITATOR, emulator, copier, mimic; pupil, disciple; *informal* copycat. **3** *a follower of Christ* DISCIPLE, apostle, supporter, defender, champion; believer, worshipper. **4** *followers of Scottish football* FAN, enthusiast, admirer, devotee, lover, supporter, adherent; *N. Amer. informal* rooter.
– OPPOSITES leader, opponent.

following ● noun *his devoted following* ADMIRERS, supporters, backers, fans, adherents, devotees, advocates, patrons, public, audience, circle, retinue, train.
– OPPOSITES opposition.
● adjective **1** *the following day* NEXT, ensuing, succeeding, subsequent. **2** *the following questions* below, further on, underneath; these; *formal* hereunder, hereinafter.
– OPPOSITES preceding, aforementioned.

folly ● noun FOOLISHNESS, foolhardiness, stupidity, idiocy, lunacy, madness, rashness, recklessness, imprudence, injudiciousness, irresponsibility, thoughtlessness, indiscretion; *informal* craziness; *Brit. informal* daftness.
– OPPOSITES wisdom.

foment ● verb INSTIGATE, incite, provoke, agitate, excite, stir up, whip up, encourage, urge, fan the flames of.

fond ● adjective **1** *she was fond of dancing* KEEN ON, partial to, addicted to, enthusiastic about, passionate about; attached to, attracted to, enamoured of, in love with, having a soft spot for; *informal* into, hooked on, gone on, sweet on, struck on. **2** *his fond father* ADORING, devoted, doting, loving, caring, affectionate, warm, tender, kind, attentive. **3** *a fond hope* UNREALISTIC, naive, foolish,

– ORIGIN French, 'melting'.

fondle ● verb stroke or caress lovingly or erotically. ● noun an act of fondling.

– DERIVATIVES **fondler** noun.

– ORIGIN back-formation from obsolete *fondling* 'much-loved or petted person', from FOND.

fondue /fondyo͞o/ ● noun a dish in which small pieces of food are dipped into melted cheese, a hot sauce, or a hot cooking medium such as oil.

– ORIGIN French, 'melted'.

fons et origo /fonz et orrigō/ ● noun the source and origin of something.

– ORIGIN Latin.

font[1] ● noun a receptacle in a church for the water used in baptism.

– ORIGIN Latin *fons* 'spring, fountain'.

font[2] (Brit. also **fount**) ● noun Printing a set of type of a particular face and size.

– ORIGIN originally denoting casting or founding: from French *fonte*, from *fondre* 'to melt'.

fontanelle /fontənel/ (US **fontanel**) ● noun a soft area between the bones of the cranium in an infant or fetus, where the sutures are not yet fully formed.

– ORIGIN originally denoting a hollow of the skin between muscles: from Old French, 'little fountain'.

fontina /fonteenə/ ● noun a pale yellow Italian cheese.

– ORIGIN Italian.

food ● noun any nutritious substance that people or animals eat or drink or that plants absorb to maintain life and growth.

– PHRASES **food for thought** something that warrants serious consideration.

– ORIGIN Old English, related to FODDER.

food chain ● noun a series of organisms each dependent on the next as a source of food.

foodie (also **foody**) ● noun (pl. **foodies**) informal a person with a strong interest in food; a gourmet.

food poisoning ● noun illness caused by bacteria or other toxins in food, typically with vomiting and diarrhoea.

foodstuff ● noun a substance suitable for consumption as food.

fool[1] ● noun **1** a person who acts unwisely. **2** historical a jester or clown. ● verb **1** trick or deceive. **2** (**fool about/around**) act in a joking or frivolous way. **3** (**fool around**) N. Amer. engage in casual or extramarital sexual activity. ● adjective N. Amer. informal foolish or silly.

– PHRASES **a fool and his money are soon parted** proverb a foolish person spends money carelessly and will soon be penniless. **fools rush in where angels fear to tread** proverb people without good sense or judgement will have no hesitation in tackling a situation that even the wisest would avoid. **there's no fool like an old fool** proverb the foolish behaviour of an older person seems especially foolish as they are expected to think and act more sensibly than a younger one.

– DERIVATIVES **foolery** noun.

– ORIGIN Old French *fol* 'fool, foolish', from Latin *follis* 'bellows, windbag', by extension 'empty-headed person'.

fool[2] ● noun chiefly Brit. a cold dessert made of puréed fruit mixed or served with cream or custard.

– ORIGIN perhaps from FOOL[1].

foolhardy ● adjective (**foolhardier**, **foolhardiest**) recklessly bold or rash.

– DERIVATIVES **foolhardily** adverb **foolhardiness** noun.

– ORIGIN Old French *folhardi*, from *fol* 'foolish' + *hardi* 'emboldened'.

foolish ● adjective lacking good sense or judgement; silly or unwise.

– DERIVATIVES **foolishly** adverb **foolishness** noun.

foolproof ● adjective incapable of going wrong or being misused.

foolscap /fo͞olskap/ ● noun Brit. a size of paper, about 330 × 200 (or 400) mm.

– ORIGIN said to be named from a former watermark representing a fool's cap.

fool's errand ● noun a task or activity that has no hope of success.

fool's gold ● noun a brassy yellow mineral that can be mistaken for gold, especially pyrite.

fool's paradise ● noun a state of happiness based on not knowing about or ignoring potential trouble.

foot ● noun (pl. **feet**) **1** the lower extremity of the leg below the

Thesaurus

over-optimistic, deluded, delusory, absurd, vain, Panglossian.

– OPPOSITES indifferent, unfeeling, realistic.

fondle ● verb CARESS, stroke, pat, pet, finger, tickle, play with; maul, molest; *informal* paw, grope, feel up, touch up, cop a feel of.

fondness ● noun **1** *they look at each other with such fondness* AFFECTION, love, liking, warmth, tenderness, kindness, devotion, endearment, attachment, friendliness. **2** *a fondness for spicy food* LIKING, love, taste, partiality, keenness, inclination, penchant, predilection, relish, passion, appetite; weakness, soft spot; *informal* thing, yen.

– OPPOSITES hatred.

food ● noun **1** *French food* NOURISHMENT, sustenance, nutriment, fare, bread, daily bread; cooking, cuisine; foodstuffs, edibles, provender, refreshments, meals, provisions, rations; solids; *informal* eats, eatables, nosh, grub, chow, nibbles; *Brit. informal* scoff, tuck; *N. Amer. informal* chuck; *formal* comestibles; *poetic/literary* viands; *dated* victuals; *archaic* commons, meat, aliment. **2** *food for the cattle* FODDER, feed, provender, forage.

– RELATED TERMS alimentary, culinary.

foodie ● noun *(informal)* GOURMET, epicure, gastronome, gourmand.

fool ● noun **1** *you've acted like a complete fool* IDIOT, ass, halfwit, blockhead, dunce, dolt, dullard, simpleton, clod; *informal* dope, ninny, nincompoop, chump, dimwit, coot, goon, dumbo, dummy, dum-dum, fathead, numbskull, dunderhead, pudding-head, thickhead, airhead, lamebrain, cretin, moron, imbecile, pea-brain, birdbrain, jerk, nerd, dipstick, donkey, noodle; *Brit. informal* nit, nitwit, twit, clot, goat, plonker, berk, prat, pillock, wally, git, dork, twerp, charlie, mug; *Scottish informal* nyaff, balloon, sumph, gowk; *N. Amer. informal* schmuck, bozo, boob, turkey, schlepper, chowderhead, dumbhead, goofball, goof, goofus, galoot, lummox, klutz, putz, schlemiel, sap, meatball; *Austral./NZ informal* drongo, dill, alec, galah, boofhead. **2** *she made a fool of me* LAUGHING STOCK, dupe, butt, gull; *informal* stooge, sucker, mug, fall guy; *N. Amer. informal* sap. **3** *(historical) the fool in King James's court* JESTER, court jester, clown, buffoon, joker, zany, merry andrew; wearer of the motley.

● verb **1** *he'd been fooled by a schoolboy* DECEIVE, trick, hoax, dupe, take in, mislead, delude, hoodwink, bluff, gull; swindle, defraud, cheat, double-cross; *informal* con, bamboozle, pull a fast one on, take for a ride, pull the wool over someone's eyes, put one over on, have on, diddle, fiddle, rip off, do, sting, shaft; *Brit. informal* sell a pup to; *N. Amer. informal* sucker, snooker, stiff, euchre, hornswoggle; *Austral. informal* pull a swifty on; *poetic/literary* cozen. **2** *I'm not fooling, I promise* PRETEND, make believe, feign, put on an act, act, sham, fake; joke, jest; *informal* kid; *Brit. informal* have someone on.

– PHRASES **fool around 1** *someone's been fooling around with the controls* FIDDLE, play (about/around), toy, trifle, meddle, tamper, interfere, monkey about/around; *informal* mess about/around; *Brit. informal* muck about/around. **2** *(N. Amer. informal) my husband's been fooling around* PHILANDER, womanize, flirt, have an affair, commit adultery; *informal* play around, mess about/around, carry on, play the field, sleep around; *Brit. informal* play away.

foolery ● noun CLOWNING, fooling, tomfoolery, buffoonery, silliness, foolishness, stupidity, idiocy; antics, capers; *informal* larking around, larks, shenanigans; *Brit. informal* monkey tricks; *N. Amer. informal* didoes; *archaic* harlequinade.

foolhardy ● adjective RECKLESS, rash, irresponsible, impulsive, hot-headed, impetuous, daredevil, devil-may-care, death-or-glory, madcap, hare-brained, precipitate, hasty, overhasty; *poetic/literary* temerarious.

– OPPOSITES prudent.

foolish ● adjective STUPID, silly, idiotic, witless, brainless, mindless, unintelligent, thoughtless, half-baked, imprudent, incautious, injudicious, unwise; ill-advised, ill-considered, impolitic, rash, reckless, foolhardy; *informal* dumb, dim, dim-witted, half-witted, gormless, hare-brained, crackbrained, pea-brained, wooden-headed; *Brit. informal* barmy, daft; *Scottish & N. English informal* glaikit; *N. Amer. informal* dumb-ass, chowderheaded.

– OPPOSITES sensible, wise.

foolishness ● noun FOLLY, stupidity, idiocy, imbecility, silliness, inanity, thoughtlessness, imprudence, injudiciousness, lack of caution/foresight/sense, irresponsibility, indiscretion, foolhardiness, rashness, recklessness; *Brit. informal* daftness.

– OPPOSITES sense, wisdom.

foolproof ● adjective INFALLIBLE, dependable, reliable, trustworthy, certain, sure, guaranteed, safe, sound, tried and tested; water-

ankle, on which a person walks. **2** the base or bottom of something vertical. **3** the end of a bed where the occupant's feet normally rest. **4** a unit of linear measure equal to 12 inches (30.48 cm). **5** Poetry a group of syllables constituting a metrical unit. ● verb **1** informal pay (a bill). **2** (**foot it**) cover a distance on foot.
– PHRASES **feet of clay** a flaw or weakness in a person otherwise revered. **fleet of foot** able to walk or move swiftly. **get** (or **start**) **off on the right** (or **wrong**) **foot** make a good (or bad) start at something. **have** (or **keep**) **one's feet on the ground** be (or remain) practical and sensible. **have** (or **get**) **a foot in the door** have (or gain) a first introduction to a profession or organization. **have one foot in the grave** humorous be very old or ill. **land** (or **fall**) **on one's feet** have good luck or success. **on** (or **by**) **foot** walking rather than using a car or other transport. **put one's best foot forward** begin with as much effort and determination as possible. **put one's foot down** informal **1** adopt a firm policy when faced with opposition or disobedience. **2** Brit. accelerate a motor vehicle by pressing the accelerator pedal. **put one's foot in it** informal say or do something tactless or embarrassing. **put a foot wrong** make a mistake: *he never put a foot wrong with his hosts.* **under one's feet** in one's way. **under foot** on the ground.
– DERIVATIVES **footless** adjective.
– ORIGIN Old English.

footage ● noun **1** a length of film made for cinema or television. **2** size or length measured in feet.

foot-and-mouth disease ● noun a contagious viral disease of cattle and sheep, causing ulceration of the hoofs and around the mouth.

football ● noun **1** any of a number of forms of team game involving kicking a ball, in particular (in the UK) soccer or (in the US) American football. **2** a large inflated ball used in such a game.
– DERIVATIVES **footballer** noun.

footbrake ● noun a foot-operated brake lever in a motor vehicle.

footbridge ● noun a bridge for pedestrians.

footer[1] /fŏŏtər/ ● noun **1** a person or thing of a specified number of feet in length or height: *a six-footer.* **2** a kick of a football performed with a specified foot: *a low left-footer.* **3** variant of FOOTY. **4** a line of text appearing at the foot of each page of a book or document.

footer[2] /fŏŏtər/ ● verb Scottish fiddle about.
– ORIGIN variant of obsolete *foutre* 'worthless thing', from Old French *foutre* 'have sexual intercourse with'.

footfall ● noun **1** the sound of a footstep or footsteps. **2** the number of people entering a shop or shopping area in a given time.

foot fault ● noun (in tennis, squash, etc.) an infringement of the rules made by overstepping the baseline when serving.

foothill ● noun a low hill at the base of a mountain or mountain range.

foothold ● noun **1** a place where one can lodge a foot to give secure support while climbing. **2** a secure position from which further progress may be made.

footie ● noun variant spelling of FOOTY.

footing ● noun **1** (**one's footing**) a secure grip with one's feet. **2** the basis on which something is established or operates. **3** the foundations of a wall, usually with a course of brickwork wider than the base of the wall.

footle /fŏŏt'l/ ● verb chiefly Brit. engage in fruitless activity; mess about.
– ORIGIN perhaps from FOOTER[2].

footlights ● plural noun a row of spotlights along the front of a stage at the level of the actors' feet.

footling /fŏŏtling/ ● adjective trivial and irritating.

footloose ● adjective free to go where one likes and do as one pleases.

footman ● noun a liveried servant whose duties include admitting visitors and waiting at table.

footmark ● noun a footprint.

footnote ● noun an additional piece of information printed at the bottom of a page.

footpad ● noun historical a highwayman operating on foot rather than riding a horse.

footpath ● noun a path for people to walk along, especially a right of way in the countryside.

footplate ● noun chiefly Brit. the platform for the crew in the cab of a locomotive.

footprint ● noun the impression left by a foot or shoe on the ground.

footsie /fŏŏtsi/ ● noun (usu. in phrase **play footsie**) informal the action of touching someone's feet lightly with one's own as a playful expression of romantic interest.

footslog ● verb (**footslogged**, **footslogging**) laboriously walk or march for a long distance. ● noun a long and exhausting walk or march.
– DERIVATIVES **footslogger** noun.

foot soldier ● noun **1** a soldier who fights on foot. **2** a low-ranking person who nevertheless does valuable work.

footsore ● adjective having sore feet from much walking.

footstep ● noun a step taken in walking, especially as heard by another person.
– PHRASES **follow** (or **tread**) **in someone's footsteps** do as another person did before.

footstool ● noun a low stool for resting the feet on when sitting.

footwear ● noun shoes, boots, and other coverings for the feet.

footwell ● noun a space for the feet in front of a seat in a vehicle.

footwork ● noun the manner in which one moves one's feet in dancing and sport.

footy (also **footie** or **footer**) ● noun Brit. informal term for FOOTBALL (in sense 1).

fop ● noun a man who is excessively concerned with his clothes and appearance.
– DERIVATIVES **foppery** noun **foppish** adjective **foppishly** adverb **foppishness** noun.
– ORIGIN originally in the sense 'fool'.

for ● preposition **1** in favour of. **2** affecting or with regard to. **3** on behalf of or to the benefit of. **4** having as a purpose or function. **5** having as a reason or cause. **6** having as a destination. **7** representing. **8** in exchange for. **9** in relation to the expected norm of. **10** indicating the extent of (a distance) or the length of (a period of time). **11** indicating an occasion in a series. ● conjunction literary because; since.
– PHRASES **be for it** Brit. informal be about to be punished or get into trouble. **oh for ——** I long for ——.
– ORIGIN Old English, related to FORE.

for- ● prefix **1** denoting prohibition: *forbid.* **2** denoting abstention, neglect, or renunciation: *forgive.* **3** used as an intensifier: *forlorn.*
– ORIGIN Old English.

fora plural of FORUM (in sense 3).

forage /forrij/ ● verb **1** search for food or provisions. **2** obtain (food) by searching. ● noun **1** food for horses and cattle. **2** an act

Thesaurus

tight, airtight, flawless, perfect; *informal* sure-fire; *formal* efficacious.
– OPPOSITES flawed.

foot ● noun **1** *my feet hurt* *informal* tootsies, trotters, plates of meat; *N. Amer. informal* dogs. **2** *the animal's foot* paw, hoof, trotter, pad. **3** *the foot of the hill* BOTTOM, base, lowest part; end; foundation.
– RELATED TERMS pedi-, -pod(e).
– PHRASES **foot the bill** *(informal)* PAY (THE BILL), settle up; *informal* pick up the tab, cough up, fork out, shell out, come across; *N. Amer. informal* pick up the check.

football ● noun *(Brit.)* SOCCER, Association Football.

footing ● noun **1** *Jenny lost her footing* FOOTHOLD, toehold, grip, purchase. **2** *a solid financial footing* BASIS, base, foundation. **3** *on an equal footing* STANDING, status, position; condition, arrangement, basis; relationship, terms.

footling ● adjective TRIVIAL, trifling, petty, insignificant, inconsequential, unimportant, minor, small, time-wasting; *informal* piddling, piffling, fiddling.
– OPPOSITES important, large.

footnote ● noun NOTE, marginal note, annotation, comment, gloss; aside, incidental remark, digression.

footprint ● noun FOOTMARK, footstep, mark, impression; pug, slot; (**footprints**) track(s), spoor.

footstep ● noun **1** *he heard a footstep* FOOTFALL, step, tread, stomp, stamp. **2** *footsteps in the sand* FOOTPRINT, footmark, mark, impression; (**footsteps**) track(s), spoor.

footwear ● noun BOOTS AND SHOES, footgear.

fop ● noun DANDY, poseur, man about town; *informal* snappy dresser, natty dresser, trendy; *informal, dated* swell; *dated* beau; *archaic* coxcomb, popinjay.

foppish ● adjective DANDYISH, dandified, dapper, dressy; affected,

of foraging.
– DERIVATIVES **forager** noun.
– ORIGIN Old French *fourrager*, from *fuerre* 'straw'.
forage cap ● noun a soldier's peaked cap.
foramen /fəraymen/ ● noun (pl. **foramina** /fərammınə/) Anatomy an opening, hole, or passage, especially in a bone.
– ORIGIN Latin.
foraminifera /forrəminnifərə/ ● plural noun (sing. **foraminifer**) Zoology single-celled planktonic animals with a perforated chalky shell.
forasmuch as ● conjunction archaic because; since.
foray /forray/ ● noun **1** a sudden attack or incursion into enemy territory. **2** a brief but spirited attempt to become involved in a new activity. ● verb make or go on a foray.
– DERIVATIVES **forayer** noun.
– ORIGIN from Old French *forrier* 'forager'.

f

forbade (also **forbad**) past of FORBID.
forbear[1] /forbair/ ● verb (past **forbore**; past part. **forborne**) refrain from doing something.
– ORIGIN Old English.
forbear[2] /forbair/ ● noun variant spelling of FOREBEAR.
forbearance ● noun **1** patient self-control and restraint. **2** tolerance.
forbearing ● adjective patient and restrained.
forbid /forbid/ ● verb (**forbidding**; past **forbade** /forbad, -bayd/ or **forbad**; past part. **forbidden**) **1** refuse to allow. **2** order not to do.
– PHRASES **the forbidden degrees** the number of steps of descent from the same ancestor that bar two related people from marrying. **forbidden fruit** a thing that is desired all the more because it is not allowed. [ORIGIN with biblical allusion to the Book of Genesis, chapter 2.] **God** (or **Heaven**) **forbid** expressing a fervent wish that something does not happen.
– ORIGIN Old English.
forbidding ● adjective unfriendly or threatening.
– DERIVATIVES **forbiddingly** adverb.
forbore past of FORBEAR[1].
forborne past participle of FORBEAR[1].
force ● noun **1** physical strength or energy as an attribute of action or movement. **2** Physics an influence tending to change the motion of a body or produce motion or stress in a stationary body. **3** coercion backed by the use or threat of violence. **4** mental or moral strength or power. **5** a person or thing regarded as exerting power or influence. **6** an organized body of military personnel, police, or workers. **7** (**the forces**) Brit. informal the army, navy, and air force. ● verb **1** make a way through or into by force. **2** push into a specified position using force. **3** achieve or bring about by effort. **4** make (someone) do something against their will. **5** (**force on/upon**) impose (something) on. **6** artificially hasten the development or maturity of (a plant).
– PHRASES **force someone's hand** make someone do something. **force the issue** compel the making of a decision. **in force 1** in great strength or numbers. **2** (**in/into force**) in or into effect.
– DERIVATIVES **forceable** adjective **forcer** noun.
– ORIGIN Old French, from Latin *fortis* 'strong'.
forced landing ● noun the abrupt landing of an aircraft in an emergency.
– DERIVATIVES **force-land** verb.
forced march ● noun a fast march by soldiers over a long distance.
force-feed ● verb force to eat food.
force field ● noun (chiefly in science fiction) an invisible barrier of force.
forceful ● adjective powerful, assertive, or vigorous.
– DERIVATIVES **forcefully** adverb **forcefulness** noun.
force majeure /forss mazhör/ ● noun **1** Law unforeseeable circumstances that prevent someone from fulfilling a contract. **2** superior strength.
– ORIGIN French.
forcemeat ● noun a mixture of meat or vegetables chopped and seasoned for use as a stuffing or garnish.
forceps /forseps/ ● plural noun **1** a pair of pincers used in surgery or in a laboratory. **2** a large instrument of such a type with broad blades, used to assist in the delivery of a baby.
– ORIGIN Latin, 'tongs, pincers'.
forcible ● adjective done by force.
– DERIVATIVES **forcibly** adverb.
ford ● noun a shallow place in a river or stream where it can be crossed. ● verb cross at a ford.
– DERIVATIVES **fordable** adjective **fordless** adjective.
– ORIGIN Old English, related to FARE.
fore ● adjective situated or placed in front. ● noun the front part of something, especially a ship. ● exclamation called out as a warning to people in the path of a golf ball.
– PHRASES **to the fore** in or to a conspicuous or leading position.

Thesaurus

preening, vain; effeminate, girly, niminy-piminy, mincing; *informal* natty, sissy, camp, campy; *Brit. informal* poncey.
forage ● verb HUNT, search, look, rummage (about/around/round), ferret (about/around), root about/around, scratch about/around, nose around/about/round, scavenge; *Brit. informal* rootle around.
● noun **1** *forage for the horses* FODDER, feed, food, provender. **2** *a nightly forage for food* HUNT, search, look, quest, rummage, scavenge.
foray ● noun RAID, attack, assault, incursion, swoop, strike, onslaught, sortie, sally, push, thrust; *archaic* onset.
forbear ● verb REFRAIN, abstain, desist, keep, restrain oneself, stop oneself, hold back, withhold; resist the temptation to; eschew, avoid, decline to.
– OPPOSITES persist.
forbearance ● noun TOLERANCE, patience, resignation, endurance, fortitude, stoicism; leniency, clemency, indulgence; restraint, self-restraint, self-control.
forbearing ● adjective PATIENT, tolerant, easy-going, lenient, clement, forgiving, understanding, accommodating, indulgent; long-suffering, resigned, stoic; restrained, self-controlled.
– OPPOSITES impatient, intolerant.
forbid ● verb PROHIBIT, ban, outlaw, make illegal, veto, proscribe, disallow, embargo, bar, debar, interdict; *Law* enjoin, restrain.
– OPPOSITES permit.
forbidding ● adjective **1** *a forbidding manner* HOSTILE, unwelcoming, unfriendly, off-putting, unsympathetic, unapproachable, grim, stern, hard, tough, frosty. **2** *the dark castle looked forbidding* THREATENING, ominous, menacing, sinister, brooding, daunting, fearsome, frightening, chilling, disturbing, disquieting.
– OPPOSITES friendly, inviting.
force ● noun **1** *he pushed with all his force* STRENGTH, power, energy, might, effort, exertion; impact, pressure, weight, impetus. **2** *they used force to achieve their aims* COERCION, compulsion, constraint, duress, oppression, harassment, intimidation, threats; *informal* arm-twisting. **3** *the force of the argument* COGENCY, weight, effectiveness, soundness, validity, strength, power, significance, influence, authority; *informal* punch; *formal* efficacy. **4** *a force for good* AGENCY, power, influence, instrument, vehicle, means. **5** *a peace-keeping force* BODY, body of people, group, outfit, party, team; detachment, unit, squad; *informal* bunch.
– OPPOSITES weakness.
● verb **1** *he was forced to pay* COMPEL, coerce, make, constrain, oblige, impel, drive, pressurize, pressure, press, push, press-gang, bully, dragoon, bludgeon; *informal* put the screws on, lean on, twist someone's arm. **2** *the door had to be forced* BREAK OPEN, burst open, knock down, smash down, kick in. **3** *water was forced through a hole* PROPEL, push, thrust, shove, drive, press, pump. **4** *they forced a confession out of the kids* EXTRACT, elicit, exact, extort, wrest, wring, drag, screw, squeeze.
– PHRASES **in force 1** *the law is now in force* EFFECTIVE, in operation, operative, operational, in action, valid. **2** *her fans were out in force* IN GREAT NUMBERS, in hordes, in full strength.
forced ● adjective **1** *forced entry* VIOLENT, forcible. **2** *forced repatriation* ENFORCED, compulsory, obligatory, mandatory, involuntary, imposed, required, stipulated, dictated, ordained, prescribed. **3** *a forced smile* STRAINED, unnatural, artificial, false, feigned, simulated, contrived, laboured, stilted, studied, mannered, affected, unconvincing, insincere, hollow; *informal* phony, pretend, put on.
– OPPOSITES voluntary, natural.
forceful ● adjective **1** *a forceful personality* DYNAMIC, energetic, assertive, authoritative, vigorous, powerful, strong, pushy, driving, determined, insistent, commanding, dominant, domineering; *informal* bossy, in-your-face, go-ahead, feisty. **2** *a forceful argument* COGENT, convincing, compelling, strong, powerful, potent, weighty, effective, well founded, telling, persuasive, irresistible, eloquent, coherent.
– OPPOSITES weak, submissive, unconvincing.
forcible ● adjective **1** *forcible entry* FORCED, violent. **2** *forcible repat-*

– ORIGIN Old English.
fore- • combining form **1** (added to verbs) in front: *foreshorten.* **2** in advance: *forebode.* **3** (added to nouns) situated in front of: *forecourt.* **4** the front part of: *forebrain.* **5** preceding: *forefather.*
fore and aft • adverb **1** at the front and rear. **2** backwards and forwards. • adjective **1** backwards and forwards. **2** (of a sail or rigging) set lengthwise, not on the yards.
forearm[1] /foraarm/ • noun the part of a person's arm extending from the elbow to the wrist or the fingertips.
forearm[2] /foraarm/ • verb (**be forearmed**) be prepared in advance for danger or attack.
forebear (also **forbear**) • noun an ancestor.
– ORIGIN from FORE + *bear*, variant of obsolete *beer* 'someone who exists'.
forebode • verb archaic or literary act as an advance warning of (something bad).
foreboding • noun fearful apprehension. • adjective ominous.
– DERIVATIVES **forebodingly** adverb.
forebrain • noun Anatomy the front part of the brain.
forecast • verb (past and past part. **forecast** or **forecasted**) predict or estimate (a future event or trend). • noun a prediction or estimate, especially of the weather or a financial trend.
– DERIVATIVES **forecaster** noun.
forecastle /fōks'l/ (also **fo'c's'le**) • noun the forward part of a ship below the deck, traditionally used as the crew's living quarters.
foreclose • verb **1** take possession of a mortgaged property as a result of defaults in mortgage payments. **2** rule out or prevent.
– DERIVATIVES **foreclosure** noun.
– ORIGIN originally in the sense 'bar from escaping', 'shut out': from Old French *forclore* 'shut out'.
forecourt • noun **1** an open area in front of a large building or petrol station. **2** Tennis the part of the court between the service line and the net.
foredoom • verb (**be foredoomed**) be condemned beforehand to certain failure.
forefather (or **foremother**) • noun an ancestor.
forefinger • noun the finger next to the thumb.
forefoot • noun (pl. **forefeet**) each of the two front feet of a four-footed animal.
forefront • noun the leading position or place.
foregather (also **forgather**) • verb formal assemble or gather together.
forego[1] • verb variant spelling of FORGO.
forego[2] • verb (**foregoes**; past **forewent**; past part. **foregone**) archaic precede in place or time.
foregoing • adjective previously mentioned.
foregone past participle of FOREGO[2]. • adjective archaic past.
– PHRASES **a foregone conclusion** an easily predictable result.
foreground • noun **1** the part of a view or image nearest to the observer. **2** the most prominent or important position.
forehand • noun (in tennis and other racket sports) a stroke played with the palm of the hand facing in the direction of the stroke.
– DERIVATIVES **forehanded** adjective.
forehead /forhed, forrid/ • noun the part of the face above the eyebrows.
foreign /forrin/ • adjective **1** of, from, in, or characteristic of a country or language other than one's own. **2** dealing with or relating to other countries. **3** coming or introduced from outside. **4** (**foreign to**) strange and unfamiliar to. **5** (**foreign to**) not belonging to or characteristic of.
– DERIVATIVES **foreignness** noun.
– ORIGIN Old French *forein, forain*, from Latin *foras, foris* 'outside'.
Foreign and Commonwealth Office (also **Foreign Office**) • noun the British government department dealing with foreign affairs.
foreign body • noun a piece of extraneous matter in the body.
foreigner • noun **1** a person from a foreign country. **2** informal a stranger or outsider.
foreign exchange • noun the currency of other countries.
Foreign Legion • noun a military formation of the French army composed chiefly of non-Frenchmen and originally founded to fight France's colonial wars.
Foreign Secretary • noun (in the UK) the government minister who heads the Foreign and Commonwealth Office.
foreknowledge • noun awareness of something before it happens or exists.
foreland • noun **1** an area of land in front of a particular feature. **2** a cape or promontory.
forelock • noun a lock of hair growing just above the forehead.
– PHRASES **touch** (or **tug**) **one's forelock** raise a hand to one's forehead in deference to a person of higher social rank.
foreman (or **forewoman**) • noun **1** a worker who supervises other workers. **2** (in a law court) a person who presides over a jury and speaks on its behalf.
foremast • noun the mast of a ship nearest the bow.
foremost • adjective the most prominent in rank, importance, or position. • adverb in the first place.
forename • noun another term for FIRST NAME.
forenoon • noun N. Amer. or Nautical the morning.
forensic /fərensik/ • adjective **1** relating to or denoting the application of scientific methods to the investigation of crime. **2** of or relating to courts of law. • noun (**forensics**) forensic tests or techniques.
– DERIVATIVES **forensically** adverb.
– ORIGIN Latin *forensis* 'in open court, public', from *forum* 'what is out of doors'.
forensic medicine • noun the application of medical know-

Thesaurus

riation. See FORCED sense 2. **3** *a forcible argument.* See FORCEFUL sense 2.
forebear • noun ANCESTOR, forefather, antecedent, progenitor, primogenitor.
– OPPOSITES descendant.
forebode • verb (*poetic/literary*) PRESAGE, augur, portend, herald, warn of, forewarn of, foreshadow, be an omen of, indicate, signify, signal, promise, threaten, spell, denote; *poetic/literary* betoken, foretoken.
foreboding • noun **1** *a feeling of foreboding* APPREHENSION, anxiety, trepidation, disquiet, unease, uneasiness, misgiving, suspicion, worry, fear, fearfulness, dread, alarm; *informal* the willies, the heebie-jeebies, the jitters. **2** *their forebodings proved justified* PREMONITION, presentiment, bad feeling, sneaking suspicion, funny feeling, intuition; *archaic* presage.
– OPPOSITES calm.
forecast • verb *they forecast record profits* PREDICT, prophesy, prognosticate, foretell, foresee, forewarn of.
• noun *a gloomy forecast* PREDICTION, prophecy, forewarning, prognostication, augury, divination, prognosis.
forefather • noun FOREBEAR, ancestor, antecedent, progenitor, primogenitor.
– OPPOSITES descendant.
forefront • noun VANGUARD, van, spearhead, head, lead, front, fore, front line, cutting edge.
– OPPOSITES rear, background.
forego • verb. See FORGO.
foregoing • adjective PRECEDING, aforesaid, aforementioned, previously mentioned, earlier, above; previous, prior, antecedent.
– OPPOSITES following.
foregone • adjective
– PHRASES **a foregone conclusion** CERTAINTY, inevitability, matter of course, predictable result; *informal* sure thing; *Brit. informal* cert, dead cert.
foreground • noun **1** *the foreground of the picture* FRONT, fore. **2** *in the foreground of the political drama* FOREFRONT, vanguard, van, spearhead, head, lead, front, fore, front line, cutting edge.
forehead • noun BROW, temple.
– RELATED TERMS frontal, metopic.
foreign • adjective **1** *foreign branches of UK banks* OVERSEAS, exotic, distant, external, alien, non-native. **2** *the concept is very foreign to us* UNFAMILIAR, unknown, unheard of, strange, alien; novel, new.
– RELATED TERMS xeno-.
– OPPOSITES domestic, native, familiar.
foreigner • noun ALIEN, non-native, stranger, outsider; immigrant, settler, newcomer, incomer.
– OPPOSITES native.
foreman, forewoman • noun SUPERVISOR, overseer, superintendent, team leader; foreperson; *Brit.* chargehand, captain, ganger; *Scottish* grieve; *N. Amer. informal* ramrod, straw boss; *Austral. informal* pannikin boss; *Mining* overman.
foremost • adjective LEADING, principal, premier, prime, top, top-level, greatest, best, supreme, pre-eminent, outstanding, most important, most prominent, most influential, most illustrious, most

ledge to the investigation of crime, particularly in establishing the causes of injury or death.

foreordain /forordayn/ ● verb (of God or fate) appoint or decree beforehand.

foreplay ● noun sexual activity that precedes intercourse.

forequarters ● plural noun the front legs and adjoining parts of a four-legged animal.

forerun ● verb (**forerunning**; past **foreran**; past part. **forerun**) literary go before or indicate the coming of.

forerunner ● noun **1** a precursor. **2** archaic an advance messenger.

foresail /forsayl, fors'l/ ● noun the principal sail on a foremast.

foresee ● verb (**foresees**, **foreseeing**; past **foresaw**; past part. **foreseen**) be aware of beforehand; predict.

– DERIVATIVES **foreseeable** adjective **foreseeably** adverb **foreseer** noun.

foreshadow ● verb be a warning or indication of.

f

foresheet ● noun Nautical **1** a rope by which the lee corner of a foresail is kept in place. **2** (**foresheets**) the inner part of the bows.

foreshore ● noun the part of a shore between high- and low-water marks, or between the water and cultivated or developed land.

foreshorten ● verb **1** represent as having less depth or distance than in reality, so as to convey an effect of perspective. **2** shorten or reduce in time or scale.

foresight ● noun **1** ability to predict the future. **2** the application of care and attention to the likely outcome of something or to future needs. **3** the front sight of a gun.

– DERIVATIVES **foresighted** adjective.

foreskin ● noun the retractable roll of skin covering the end of the penis.

forest ● noun **1** a large area covered with trees and undergrowth. **2** historical an area, typically owned by the sovereign and partly wooded, kept for hunting and having its own laws. **3** a mass of vertical or tangled objects. ● verb plant with trees.

– DERIVATIVES **forestation** noun.

– ORIGIN from Latin *forestis silva* 'outside wood', from *foris* 'outside'.

forestall /forstawl/ ● verb **1** prevent or obstruct (something anticipated) by taking advance action. **2** anticipate and prevent the action of.

– DERIVATIVES **forestaller** noun **forestalment** noun.

– ORIGIN from Old English, 'an ambush'.

forestay /forstay/ ● noun a rope supporting a ship's foremast, running from its top to the deck at the bow.

forester ● noun **1** a person in charge of a forest or skilled in forestry. **2** chiefly archaic a person or animal living in a forest.

forestry ● noun **1** the science or practice of planting, managing, and caring for forests. **2** forests.

foretaste ● noun a sample or suggestion of something that lies ahead.

foretell ● verb (past and past part. **foretold**) predict.

– DERIVATIVES **foreteller** noun.

forethought ● noun careful consideration of what will be necessary or may happen in the future.

foretoken ● verb /fortōkən/ literary be a sign of. ● noun /fortōkən/ a sign of something to come.

foretold past and past participle of FORETELL.

foretop ● noun a platform around the head of the lower section of a sailing ship's foremast.

forever ● adverb **1** (also **for ever**) for all future time. **2** a very long time. **3** continually.

forewarn ● verb warn in advance.

– PHRASES **forewarned is forearmed** proverb prior knowledge of possible dangers or problems gives one a tactical advantage.

forewent past of FOREGO[1], FOREGO[2].

foreword ● noun a short introduction to a book.

forex ● abbreviation foreign exchange.

forfeit /forfit/ ● verb (**forfeited**, **forfeiting**) **1** lose or be deprived of (property or a right or privilege) as a penalty for wrongdoing. **2** lose or give up as a necessary consequence. ● noun **1** a fine or penalty for wrongdoing. **2** Law a forfeited right, privilege, or item of property. **3** (**forfeits**) a game in which trivial penalties are exacted for minor misdemeanours. ● adjective lost or surrendered as a forfeit.

– DERIVATIVES **forfeitable** adjective **forfeiter** noun **forfeiture** noun.

– ORIGIN originally denoting a crime or transgression: from Old French *forfet*, *forfait*, from *forfaire* 'transgress'.

forfend /forfend/ ● verb **1** archaic prevent or ward off (something evil or unpleasant). **2** US protect by precautionary measures.

– PHRASES **God** (or **Heaven**) **forfend** archaic or humorous used to express dismay at the thought of something.

forgather ● verb variant spelling of FOREGATHER.

Thesaurus

notable; *N. Amer.* ranking; *informal* number-one.

– OPPOSITES minor.

foreordained ● adjective PREDETERMINED, preordained, ordained, predestined, destined, fated.

forerunner ● noun **1** *archosaurs were the forerunners of dinosaurs* PREDECESSOR, precursor, antecedent, ancestor, forebear; prototype. **2** *headache may be the forerunner of other complaints* PRELUDE, herald, harbinger, precursor, sign, signal, indication, warning.

– OPPOSITES descendant.

foresee ● verb ANTICIPATE, predict, forecast, expect, envisage, envision, see; foretell, prophesy, prognosticate; *poetic/literary* foreknow; *Scottish* spae.

foreshadow ● verb SIGNAL, indicate, signify, mean, be a sign of, suggest, herald, be a harbinger of, warn of, portend, prefigure, presage, promise, point to, anticipate; *informal* spell; *poetic/literary* forebode, foretoken, betoken; *archaic* foreshow.

foresight ● noun FORETHOUGHT, planning, far-sightedness, vision, anticipation, prudence, care, caution, precaution, readiness, preparedness; *N. Amer.* forehandedness.

– OPPOSITES hindsight.

forest ● noun WOOD(S), woodland, trees, plantation; jungle; *archaic* greenwood.

– RELATED TERMS sylvan.

forestall ● verb PRE-EMPT, get in before, steal a march on; anticipate, second-guess; nip in the bud, thwart, frustrate, foil, stave off, ward off, fend off, avert, preclude, obviate, prevent; *informal* beat someone to it.

forestry ● noun FOREST MANAGEMENT, tree growing, agroforestry; *technical* arboriculture, silviculture.

foretaste ● noun SAMPLE, taster, taste, preview, specimen, example; indication, suggestion, hint, whiff; warning, forewarning, omen; *informal* try-out.

foretell ● verb **1** *the locals can foretell a storm* PREDICT, forecast, prophesy, prognosticate; foresee, anticipate, envisage, envision, see; *Scottish* spae. **2** *dreams can foretell the future* INDICATE, foreshadow, prefigure, anticipate, warn of, point to, signal, portend, augur, presage, be an omen of; *poetic/literary* forebode, foretoken, betoken; *archaic* foreshow.

forethought ● noun ANTICIPATION, planning, forward planning, provision, precaution, prudence, care, caution; foresight, far-sightedness, vision.

– OPPOSITES impulse, recklessness.

forever ● adverb **1** *their love would last forever* FOR ALWAYS, evermore, for ever and ever, for good, for all time, until the end of time, until hell freezes over, eternally; *Brit.* for evermore; *N. Amer.* forevermore; *informal* until the cows come home, until doomsday, until kingdom come; *archaic* for aye. **2** *he was forever banging into things* ALWAYS, continually, constantly, perpetually, incessantly, endlessly, persistently, repeatedly, regularly; non-stop, day and night, {morning, noon, and night}; all the time, the entire time; *Scottish* aye; *informal* 24-7.

– OPPOSITES never, occasionally.

forewarn ● verb WARN, warn in advance, give advance warning, give fair warning, give notice, apprise, inform; alert, caution, put someone on their guard; *informal* tip off; *Brit. informal* tip someone the wink.

forewarning ● noun OMEN, sign, indication, portent, presage, warning, harbinger, foreshadowing, augury, signal, promise, threat, straw in the wind, writing on the wall, hint; *poetic/literary* foretoken.

foreword ● noun PREFACE, introduction, prologue, preamble; *informal* intro; *formal* exordium, prolegomenon, proem.

– OPPOSITES conclusion.

forfeit ● verb *latecomers will forfeit their places* LOSE, be deprived of, surrender, relinquish, sacrifice, give up, yield, renounce, forgo; *informal* pass up, lose out on.

– OPPOSITES retain.

● noun *they are liable to a forfeit* PENALTY, sanction, punishment, penance; fine; confiscation, loss, relinquishment, forfeiture, surrender; *Law* sequestration.

forgave past of FORGIVE.
forge[1] ● verb **1** make or shape (a metal object) by heating and hammering the metal. **2** create. **3** produce a fraudulent copy or imitation of (a banknote, work of art, signature, etc.). ● noun **1** a blacksmith's workshop. **2** a furnace or hearth for melting or refining metal.
– DERIVATIVES **forgeable** adjective **forger** noun.
– ORIGIN Old French *forger*, from Latin *fabricare* 'fabricate'.
forge[2] ● verb **1** move forward gradually or steadily. **2** (**forge ahead**) make progress.
– ORIGIN perhaps from a pronunciation of FORCE.
forgery ● noun (pl. **forgeries**) **1** the action of forging a banknote, work of art, signature, etc. **2** a forged or copied item.
forget ● verb (**forgetting**; past **forgot**; past part. **forgotten** or chiefly US **forgot**) **1** fail to remember. **2** inadvertently neglect to do something. **3** cease to think of. **4** (**forget oneself**) neglect to behave appropriately.
– DERIVATIVES **forgettable** adjective **forgetter** noun.
– ORIGIN Old English.
forgetful ● adjective apt or likely not to remember.
– DERIVATIVES **forgetfully** adverb **forgetfulness** noun.
forget-me-not ● noun a low-growing plant of the borage family with bright blue flowers.
– ORIGIN translating the Old French name *ne m'oubliez mye*; said to ensure that the wearer of the flower would never be forgotten by a lover.
forgive ● verb (past **forgave**; past part. **forgiven**) **1** stop feeling angry or resentful towards (someone) for an offence or mistake. **2** excuse (an offence, flaw, or mistake).
– DERIVATIVES **forgivable** adjective **forgiver** noun **forgiving** adjective.
– ORIGIN Old English.
forgiveness ● noun the action of forgiving or the state of being forgiven.
forgo (also **forego**) ● verb (**forgoes**; past **forwent**; past part. **forgone**) go without (something desirable).
– ORIGIN Old English.
forgot past of FORGET.
forgotten past participle of FORGET.
forint /forrint/ ● noun the basic monetary unit of Hungary, equal to 100 filler.
– ORIGIN Hungarian, from Italian *fiorino* (see FLORIN).
fork ● noun **1** an implement with two or more prongs used for lifting or holding food. **2** a pronged farm or garden tool used for digging or lifting. **3** each of a pair of supports in which a bicycle or motorcycle wheel revolves. **4** the point where a road, path, or river divides into two parts. **5** either of two such parts. ● verb **1** divide into two parts. **2** take one route or the other at a fork. **3** dig or lift with a fork. **4** (**fork out/up**) (or N. Amer. **fork over**) informal pay money for something, especially reluctantly.
– ORIGIN Latin *furca* 'pitchfork, forked stick'.
forked ● adjective having a divided or pronged end.
forked lightning ● noun lightning that is visible in the form of a zigzag or branching line across the sky.
forklift truck ● noun a vehicle with a pronged device in front for lifting and carrying heavy loads.
forlorn /fəlorn/ ● adjective **1** pitifully sad and lonely. **2** unlikely to succeed or be fulfilled.
– PHRASES **forlorn hope** a persistent or desperate hope that is unlikely to be fulfilled. [ORIGIN from Dutch *verloren hoop* 'lost troop', originally denoting a band of soldiers picked to begin an attack, many of whom would not survive.]
– DERIVATIVES **forlornly** adverb **forlornness** noun.
– ORIGIN Old English, 'depraved, lost'.
form ● noun **1** visible shape or configuration. **2** a way in which a thing exists or appears. **3** a type or variety. **4** the customary or correct method or procedure. **5** a printed document with blank spaces for information to be inserted. **6** chiefly Brit. a class or year in a school. **7** the state of a sports player with regard to their current standard of play. **8** details of previous performances by a racehorse or greyhound. **9** a person's mood and

Thesaurus

forfeiture ● noun CONFISCATION, loss; relinquishment, giving up, surrender, sacrifice; *Law* sequestration; *historical* attainder.
forge[1] ● verb **1** *a smith forged swords* HAMMER OUT, beat into shape, fashion. **2** *they forged a partnership* BUILD, construct, form, create, establish, set up. **3** *he forged her signature* FAKE, falsify, counterfeit, copy, imitate, reproduce, replicate, simulate; *informal* pirate.
forge[2] ● verb *they forged through swamps* ADVANCE STEADILY, advance gradually, press on, push on, soldier on, march on, push forward, make progress, make headway.
– PHRASES **forge ahead** ADVANCE RAPIDLY, progress quickly, make rapid progress, increase speed, put a spurt on.
forged ● adjective FAKE, faked, false, counterfeit, imitation, copied, pirate(d); sham, bogus; *informal* phoney, dud.
– OPPOSITES genuine.
forger ● noun COUNTERFEITER, faker, copyist, imitator, pirate.
forgery ● noun **1** *guilty of forgery* COUNTERFEITING, falsification, faking, copying, pirating. **2** *the painting was a forgery* FAKE, counterfeit, fraud, sham, imitation, replica, copy, pirate copy; *informal* phoney.
forget ● verb **1** *he forgot where he was* FAIL TO REMEMBER, fail to recall, fail to think of. **2** *I never forget my briefcase* LEAVE BEHIND, fail to take/bring. **3** *I forgot to close the door* NEGLECT, fail, omit. **4** *you can forget that idea* STOP THINKING ABOUT, put out of one's mind, shut out, blank out, pay no heed to, not worry about, ignore, overlook, take no notice of.
– OPPOSITES remember.
– PHRASES **forget oneself** MISBEHAVE, behave badly, be naughty, be disobedient, get up to mischief, get up to no good; be badmannered, be rude; *informal* carry on, act up.
forgetful ● adjective **1** *I'm so forgetful these days* ABSENT-MINDED, amnesic, amnesiac, vague, disorganized, dreamy, abstracted, with a mind/memory like a sieve; *informal* scatterbrained, scatty. **2** *forgetful of the time* HEEDLESS, careless, unmindful; inattentive to, negligent about, oblivious to, unconcerned about, indifferent to, not bothered about.
– OPPOSITES reliable, heedful.
forgetfulness ● noun **1** *his excuse was forgetfulness* ABSENT-MINDEDNESS, amnesia, poor memory, a lapse of memory, vagueness, abstraction; *informal* scattiness. **2** *a forgetfulness of God* NEGLECT, heedlessness, carelessness, disregard; inattention, obliviousness, lack of concern, indifference.
– OPPOSITES reliability, heed.
forgivable ● adjective PARDONABLE, excusable, condonable, understandable, tolerable, permissible, allowable, justifiable.
forgive ● verb **1** *she would not forgive him* PARDON, excuse, exonerate, absolve; make allowances for, feel no resentment/malice towards, harbour no grudge against, bury the hatchet with; let bygones be bygones; *informal* let off (the hook); *formal* exculpate. **2** *you must forgive his rude conduct* EXCUSE, overlook, disregard, ignore, pass over, make allowances for, allow; turn a blind eye to, turn a deaf ear to, wink at, blink at, indulge, tolerate.
– OPPOSITES blame, resent, punish.
forgiveness ● noun PARDON, absolution, exoneration, remission, dispensation, indulgence, clemency, mercy; reprieve, amnesty; *informal* let-off; *archaic* shrift.
– OPPOSITES mercilessness, punishment.
forgiving ● adjective MERCIFUL, lenient, compassionate, magnanimous, humane, soft-hearted, forbearing, tolerant, indulgent, understanding.
– OPPOSITES merciless, vindictive.
forgo, forego ● verb DO WITHOUT, go without, give up, waive, renounce, surrender, relinquish, part with, drop, sacrifice, abstain from, refrain from, eschew, cut out; *informal* swear off; *formal* forswear, abjure.
– OPPOSITES keep.
forgotten ● adjective UNREMEMBERED, out of mind, gone clean out of someone's mind, past recollection, beyond/past recall, consigned to oblivion; left behind; neglected, overlooked, ignored, disregarded, unrecognized.
– OPPOSITES remembered.
fork ● verb SPLIT, branch (off), divide, subdivide, separate, part, diverge, go in different directions, bifurcate; *technical* furcate, divaricate, ramify.
forked ● adjective SPLIT, branching, branched, bifurcate(d), Y-shaped, V-shaped, pronged, divided; *technical* divaricate.
– OPPOSITES straight.
forlorn ● adjective **1** *he sounded forlorn* UNHAPPY, sad, miserable, sorrowful, dejected, despondent, disconsolate, wretched, abject, down, downcast, dispirited, downhearted, crestfallen, depressed, melancholy, gloomy, glum, mournful, despairing, doleful, woebegone; *informal* blue, down in the mouth, down in the dumps, fed up; *rare* lachrymose. **2** *a forlorn garden* DESOLATE, deserted, abandoned, forsaken, forgotten, neglected. **3** *a forlorn attempt* HOPELESS, with no chance of success; useless, futile, pointless, purposeless, vain,

state of health: *she was on good form.* **10** Brit. a long bench without a back. ● **verb 1** bring together parts to create. **2** go to make up. **3** establish or develop. **4** make or be made into a certain form.
– PHRASES **in** (or Brit. **on**) **form** playing or performing well. **off** (or Brit. **out of**) **form** not playing or performing well.
– DERIVATIVES **formable** adjective **formless** adjective.
– ORIGIN Latin *forma* 'a mould or form'.
formal ● **adjective 1** done in accordance with rules of convention or etiquette. **2** officially recognized: *a formal complaint.* **3** of or concerned with outward form rather than content. **4** (of language) characterized by the use of studied grammatical structure and conservative vocabulary. **5** (especially of a garden) arranged in a precise or symmetrical manner.
– DERIVATIVES **formally** adverb.
formaldehyde /formal**dih**id/ ● **noun** Chemistry a colourless pungent gas derived from methanol, used in solution as a preservative for biological specimens.
– ORIGIN blend of FORMIC ACID and ALDEHYDE.
formalin /**for**məlin/ ● **noun** a solution of formaldehyde in water.
formalism ● **noun 1** excessive adherence to prescribed forms. **2** concern with form rather than content in artistic creation. **3** a description in formal mathematical or logical terms.
– DERIVATIVES **formalist** noun.
formality ● **noun** (pl. **formalities**) **1** the rigid observance of rules or convention. **2** a thing done simply to comply with convention or regulations. **3** (**a formality**) a thing done or occurring as a matter of course; an inevitability.
formalize (also **formalise**) ● **verb 1** give legal or official status to. **2** give a definite form to.
– DERIVATIVES **formalization** noun.
format ● **noun 1** the way in which something is arranged or presented. **2** the shape, size, and presentation of a book, document, etc. **3** the medium in which a sound recording is made available: *LP and CD formats.* **4** Computing a defined structure for the processing, storage, or display of data. ● **verb** (**formatted, formatting**) (especially in computing) arrange or put into a format.
– ORIGIN from Latin *formatus liber* 'shaped book'.
formation ● **noun 1** the action of forming or the process of being formed. **2** a structure or arrangement. **3** a formal arrangement of aircraft in flight or troops.
– DERIVATIVES **formational** adjective.
formative ● **adjective** serving to form something, especially having a profound influence on a person's development.
– DERIVATIVES **formatively** adverb.
former[1] ● **adjective 1** having been previously. **2** of or occurring in the past. **3** (**the former**) denoting the first of two things mentioned.
– ORIGIN Old English.
former[2] ● **noun 1** a person or thing that forms something. **2** Brit. a person in a particular school year: *a fifth-former.*
formerly ● **adverb** in the past.
Formica /for**mī**kə/ ● **noun** trademark a hard durable plastic laminate used for worktops, cupboard doors, etc.
– ORIGIN of unknown origin.
formic acid /**for**mik/ ● **noun** Chemistry an irritant acid present in the fluid emitted by some ants.
– ORIGIN *formic* from Latin *formica* 'ant'.
formication /formi**kay**sh'n/ ● **noun** a sensation like that of insects crawling over the skin.
– ORIGIN Latin, from *formicare* 'crawl like an ant'.
formidable /**for**midəb'l/ ● **adjective** inspiring fear or respect through being impressively large, powerful, or capable.

Thesaurus

unavailing, nugatory; *archaic* bootless.
– OPPOSITES happy, busy, cared for, hopeful, sure-fire.
form ● **noun 1** *the general form of the landscape | form is less important than content* SHAPE, configuration, formation, structure, construction, arrangement, appearance, exterior, outline, format, layout, design. **2** *the human form* BODY, shape, figure, stature, build, frame, physique, anatomy; *informal* vital statistics. **3** *the infection takes different forms* MANIFESTATION, appearance, embodiment, incarnation, semblance, shape, guise. **4** *sponsorship is a form of advertising* KIND, sort, type, class, classification, category, variety, genre, brand, style; species, genus, family. **5** *put the mixture into a form* MOULD, cast, shape, matrix, die. **6** *what is the form here?* ETIQUETTE, social practice, custom, usage, use, modus operandi, habit, wont, protocol, procedure, rules, convention, tradition, fashion, style; *formal* praxis. **7** *you have to fill in a form* QUESTIONNAIRE, document, coupon, tear-off slip, paper. **8** *what form is your daughter in?* CLASS, year; *N. Amer.* grade. **9** *in top form* FITNESS, condition, fettle, shape, trim, health; *Brit. informal* nick. **10** *(Brit.) a wooden form* BENCH, pew, stall.
– OPPOSITES content.
● **verb 1** *the pads are formed from mild steel* MAKE, construct, build, manufacture, fabricate, assemble, put together; create, produce, concoct, devise, contrive, frame, fashion, shape. **2** *he formed a plan* FORMULATE, devise, conceive, work out, think up, lay, draw up, put together, produce, fashion, concoct, forge, hatch, develop; *informal* dream up. **3** *they plan to form a company* SET UP, establish, found, launch, float, create, bring into being, institute, start, get going, initiate, bring about, inaugurate. **4** *a mist was forming* MATERIALIZE, come into being/existence, crystallize, emerge, spring up, develop; take shape, appear, loom, show up, become visible. **5** *the horse may form bad habits* ACQUIRE, develop, get, pick up, contract, slip into, get into. **6** *his men formed themselves into an arrowhead* ARRANGE, draw up, line up, assemble, organize, sort, order, range, array, dispose, marshal, deploy. **7** *the parts of society form an integrated whole* COMPRISE, make, make up, constitute, compose, add up to. **8** *the city formed a natural meeting point* CONSTITUTE, serve as, act as, function as, perform the function of, do duty for, make. **9** *natural objects are most important in forming the mind of the child* DEVELOP, mould, shape, train, teach, instruct, educate, school, drill, discipline, prime, prepare, guide, direct, inform, enlighten, inculcate, indoctrinate, edify.
– OPPOSITES dissolve, disappear, break.
– PHRASES **good form** GOOD MANNERS, manners, polite behaviour, correct behaviour, convention, etiquette, protocol; *informal* the done thing.
formal ● **adjective 1** *a formal dinner* CEREMONIAL, ceremonious, ritualistic, ritual, conventional, traditional; stately, courtly, solemn, dignified; elaborate, ornate, dressy. **2** *a very formal manner* ALOOF, reserved, remote, detached, unapproachable; stiff, prim, stuffy, staid, ceremonious, correct, proper, decorous, conventional, precise, exact, punctilious, unbending, inflexible, strait-laced; *informal* stand-offish. **3** *a formal garden* SYMMETRICAL, regular, orderly, arranged, methodical, systematic. **4** *formal permission* OFFICIAL, legal, authorized, approved, validated, certified, endorsed, documented, sanctioned, licensed, recognized, authoritative. **5** *formal education* CONVENTIONAL, mainstream; school, institutional.
– OPPOSITES informal, casual, colloquial, unofficial.
formality ● **noun 1** *the formality of the occasion* CEREMONY, ceremoniousness, ritual, conventionality, red tape, protocol, decorum; stateliness, courtliness, solemnity. **2** *his formality was off-putting* ALOOFNESS, reserve, remoteness, detachment, unapproachability; stiffness, primness, stuffiness, staidness, correctness, decorum, punctiliousness, inflexibility; *informal* stand-offishness. **3** *we keep the formalities to a minimum* OFFICIAL PROCEDURE, bureaucracy, red tape, paperwork. **4** *the medical examination is just a formality* ROUTINE, routine practice, normal procedure. **5** *promotion looks a formality* MATTER OF COURSE, foregone conclusion, inevitability, certainty; *informal* sure thing.
– OPPOSITES informality.
format ● **noun** DESIGN, style, presentation, appearance, look; form, shape, size; arrangement, plan, structure, scheme, composition, configuration.
formation ● **noun 1** *the formation of the island's sand ridges* EMERGENCE, coming into being, genesis, development, evolution, origination, shaping. **2** *the formation of a new government* ESTABLISHMENT, setting up, start, initiation, institution, foundation, inception, creation, inauguration, launch, flotation. **3** *the aircraft were flying in tight formation* CONFIGURATION, arrangement, pattern, array, alignment, positioning, disposition, order.
– OPPOSITES destruction, disappearance, dissolution.
formative ● **adjective 1** *at a formative stage* DEVELOPMENTAL, developing, growing, malleable, impressionable, susceptible. **2** *a formative influence* DETERMINING, controlling, influential, guiding, decisive, forming, shaping, determinative.
former ● **adjective 1** *the former bishop* ONE-TIME, erstwhile, sometime, ex-, late; PREVIOUS, foregoing, preceding, earlier, prior, past, last. **2** *in former times* EARLIER, old, past, bygone, olden, long-ago, gone by, long past, of old; *poetic/literary* of yore. **3** *the former view* FIRST-MENTIONED, first.
– OPPOSITES future, next, latter.

– DERIVATIVES **formidably** adverb.
– ORIGIN Latin *formidabilis*, from *formidare* 'to fear'.
formula /formyoolə/ ● noun (pl. **formulae** /formyoolee/ (in senses 1 and 2) or **formulas**) **1** a mathematical relationship or rule expressed in symbols. **2** (also **chemical formula**) a set of chemical symbols showing the elements present in a compound and their relative proportions. **3** a fixed form of words, as used conventionally or in particular contexts. **4** a method or procedure for achieving something. **5** (before another noun) denoting a rule or style followed without originality: *a formula fantasy film*. **6** a list of ingredients with which something is made. **7** an infant's liquid food preparation based on cow's milk or soya protein. **8** a classification of racing car: *formula one*.
– ORIGIN Latin, 'small shape or mould'.
formulaic /formyoolayik/ ● adjective **1** constituting or containing a set form of words. **2** produced in accordance with a slavishly followed rule or style: *much romantic fiction is formulaic*.
– DERIVATIVES **formulaically** adverb.
formulary /formyoolәri/ ● noun (pl. **formularies**) **1** a collection of set forms, especially for use in religious ceremonies. **2** an official list giving details of prescribable medicines.
– ORIGIN French *formulaire* 'book of formulae'.
formulate /formyoolayt/ ● verb **1** create or prepare methodically. **2** express (an idea) in a concise or systematic way.
– DERIVATIVES **formulator** noun.
formulation ● noun **1** the action of formulating. **2** a material or mixture prepared according to a formula.
fornicate ● verb formal or humorous have sexual intercourse with someone one is not married to.
– DERIVATIVES **fornication** noun **fornicator** noun.
– ORIGIN Latin, from *fornix* 'vaulted chamber', later 'brothel'.
forsake ● verb (past **forsook**; past part. **forsaken**) chiefly literary **1** abandon. **2** renounce or give up.
– ORIGIN Old English.
forsooth /fәrsoōth/ ● adverb archaic or humorous indeed.
forswear ● verb (past **forswore**; past part. **forsworn**) formal **1** agree to give up or do without. **2** (**forswear oneself/be forsworn**) commit perjury.
forsythia /forsīthiә/ ● noun an ornamental shrub whose bright yellow flowers appear in early spring before its leaves.
– ORIGIN named after the Scottish botanist William *Forsyth* (1737–1804).
fort ● noun a fortified building or strategic position.
– PHRASES **hold the fort** take responsibility for something temporarily.
– ORIGIN from Latin *fortis* 'strong'.
forte[1] /fortay/ ● noun a thing at which someone excels.
– ORIGIN French, 'strong'.
forte[2] /fortay/ ● adverb & adjective Music loud or loudly.
– ORIGIN Italian, 'strong, loud'.
Fortean /fortiәn/ ● adjective relating to paranormal phenomena.
– DERIVATIVES **Forteana** plural noun.
– ORIGIN from the name of the American student of paranormal phenomena Charles H. *Fort* (1874–1932).
fortepiano /fortaypiannō/ ● noun (pl. **fortepianos**) Music a piano, especially of the kind made in the 18th and early 19th centuries.
– ORIGIN from FORTE[2] + PIANO[2].
forte piano /fortay pyaanō/ ● adverb & adjective Music loud or loudly and then immediately soft.
forth ● adverb chiefly archaic **1** out from a starting point and forwards or into view. **2** onwards in time.
– PHRASES **and so forth** and so on.
– ORIGIN Old English.
forthcoming ● adjective **1** about to happen or appear. **2** ready or made available when required: *help was not forthcoming*. **3** willing to divulge information.
– DERIVATIVES **forthcomingness** noun.
forthright ● adjective direct and outspoken.
– DERIVATIVES **forthrightly** adverb **forthrightness** noun.
– ORIGIN Old English.
forthwith ● adverb without delay.
fortify /fortifī/ ● verb (**fortifies, fortified**) **1** provide with defensive works as protection against attack. **2** invigorate or encourage. **3** add spirits to (wine) to make port, sherry, etc. **4** increase the nutritive value of (food) by adding vitamins.
– DERIVATIVES **fortifiable** adjective **fortification** noun **fortifier** noun.
– ORIGIN Latin *fortificare*, from *fortis* 'strong'.

Thesaurus

formerly ● adverb PREVIOUSLY, earlier, before, until now/then, hitherto, née, once, once upon a time, at one time, in the past; *formal* heretofore.
formidable ● adjective **1** *a formidable curved dagger* INTIMIDATING, forbidding, daunting, alarming, frightening, disturbing, disquieting, brooding, awesome, fearsome, ominous, foreboding, sinister, menacing, threatening, dangerous. **2** *a formidable task* ONEROUS, arduous, taxing, difficult, hard, heavy, laborious, burdensome, strenuous, back-breaking, uphill, Herculean, monumental, colossal; demanding, tough, challenging, exacting; *formal* exigent; *archaic* toilsome. **3** *a formidable pianist* CAPABLE, able, proficient, adept, adroit, accomplished, seasoned, skilful, skilled, gifted, talented, masterly, virtuoso, expert, knowledgeable, qualified; impressive, powerful, mighty, terrific, tremendous, great, complete, redoubtable; *informal* mean, wicked, deadly, nifty, crack, ace, wizard, magic; *N. Amer. informal* crackerjack.
– OPPOSITES pleasant-looking, comforting, easy, poor, weak.
formless ● adjective SHAPELESS, amorphous, unshaped, indeterminate; structureless, unstructured.
– OPPOSITES shaped, definite.
formula ● noun **1** *a legal formula* FORM OF WORDS, set expression, phrase, saying, aphorism. **2** *a peace formula* RECIPE, prescription, blueprint, plan, method, procedure, technique, system. **3** *a formula for removing grease* PREPARATION, concoction, mixture, compound, creation, substance.
formulate ● verb **1** *the miners formulated a plan* DEVISE, conceive, work out, think up, lay, draw up, put together, form, produce, fashion, concoct, contrive, forge, hatch, prepare, develop; *informal* dream up. **2** *this is how Marx formulated his question* EXPRESS, phrase, word, put into words, frame, couch, put, articulate, convey, say, state, utter.
fornication ● noun *(formal)* EXTRAMARITAL SEX, extramarital relations, adultery, infidelity, unfaithfulness, cuckoldry; *informal* hanky-panky, a bit on the side.
forsake ● verb *(poetic/literary)* **1** *he forsook his wife* ABANDON, desert, leave, leave high and dry, turn one's back on, cast aside, break (up) with; jilt, strand, leave stranded, leave in the lurch, throw over; *informal* walk out on, run out on, dump, ditch. **2** *I won't forsake my vegetarian principles* RENOUNCE, abandon, relinquish, dispense with, disclaim, disown, disavow, discard, wash one's hands of; give up, drop, jettison, do away with, axe; *informal* ditch, scrap, scrub, junk; *formal* forswear.
– OPPOSITES keep to, adopt.
forswear ● verb *(formal)* RENOUNCE, relinquish, reject, forgo, disavow, abandon, deny, repudiate, give up, wash one's hands of; eschew, abstain from, refrain from; *informal* kick, pack in, quit, swear off; *Law* disaffirm; *poetic/literary* forsake; *formal* abjure, abnegate.
– OPPOSITES adhere to, persist with, take up.
fort ● noun FORTRESS, castle, citadel, blockhouse, burg; stronghold, redoubt, fortification, bastion; fastness.
forte ● noun STRENGTH, strong point, speciality, strong suit, talent, special ability, skill, bent, gift, métier; *informal* thing.
– OPPOSITES weakness.
forth ● adverb **1** *smoke billowed forth* OUT, outside, away, off, ahead, forward, into view; into existence. **2** *from that day forth* ONWARDS, onward, on, forward; for ever, into eternity; until now.
forthcoming ● adjective **1** *forthcoming events* IMMINENT, impending, coming, upcoming, approaching, future; close, (close) at hand, in store, in the wind, in the air, in the offing, in the pipeline, on the horizon, on the way, on us, about to happen. **2** *no reply was forthcoming* AVAILABLE, ready, at hand, accessible, obtainable, at someone's disposal, on offer; obtained, given, vouchsafed to someone; *informal* up for grabs, on tap. **3** *he was not very forthcoming about himself* COMMUNICATIVE, talkative, chatty, loquacious, vocal; expansive, expressive, unreserved, uninhibited, outgoing, frank, open, candid; *informal* gabby.
– OPPOSITES past, current, unavailable, uncommunicative.
forthright ● adjective FRANK, direct, straightforward, honest, candid, open, sincere, straight, blunt, plain-spoken, outspoken, no-nonsense, bluff, matter-of-fact, to the point; *informal* upfront.
– OPPOSITES secretive, evasive.
forthwith ● adverb IMMEDIATELY, at once, instantly, directly, right away, straight away, post-haste, without delay, without hesitation; quickly, speedily, promptly; *informal* pronto.
– OPPOSITES sometime.

fortissimo /fortissimō/ ● **adverb & adjective** Music very loud or loudly.
– ORIGIN Italian, from Latin *fortissimus* 'very strong'.
fortitude /fortityo͞od/ ● **noun** courage and strength in bearing pain or trouble.
– ORIGIN Latin *fortitudo*, from *fortis* 'strong'.
fortnight ● **noun** chiefly Brit. a period of two weeks.
– ORIGIN Old English, 'fourteen nights'.
fortnightly chiefly Brit. ● **adjective** happening or produced every two weeks. ● **adverb** every two weeks. ● **noun** (pl. **fortnightlies**) a magazine issued every two weeks.
fortress ● **noun** a military stronghold, especially a strongly fortified town fit for a large garrison.
– ORIGIN Old French *forteresse* 'strong place', from Latin *fortis* 'strong'.
fortuitous /fortyo͞oitəss/ ● **adjective** **1** happening by chance rather than design. **2** happening by a lucky chance; fortunate.
– DERIVATIVES **fortuitously** adverb **fortuitousness** noun **fortuity** noun (pl. **fortuities**).
– ORIGIN Latin *fortuitus*, from *forte* 'by chance'.
fortunate ● **adjective** **1** favoured by or involving good luck. **2** auspicious or favourable.
fortunately ● **adverb** it is fortunate that.
fortune ● **noun** **1** chance as an arbitrary force affecting human affairs. **2** luck, especially good luck. **3** (**fortunes**) the success or failure of a person or enterprise. **4** a large amount of money or assets.
– PHRASES **fortune favours the brave** proverb a successful person is often one who is willing to take risks. **a small fortune** informal a large amount of money. **tell someone's fortune** make predictions about a person's future by palmistry or similar divining methods.
– ORIGIN Latin *Fortuna*, the name of a goddess personifying luck or chance.
fortune-teller ● **noun** a person who tells people's fortunes.
– DERIVATIVES **fortune-telling** noun.
forty ● **cardinal number** (pl. **forties**) **1** ten less than fifty; 40. (Roman numeral: **xl** or **XL**.) **2** (**the Forties**) the central North Sea between Scotland and southern Norway, so called from its prevailing depth of forty fathoms or more.
– PHRASES **forty winks** informal a short daytime sleep.
– DERIVATIVES **fortieth** ordinal number.
– ORIGIN Old English.
forty-five ● **noun** a gramophone record played at 45 rpm.
forum /forəm/ ● **noun** (pl. **forums**) **1** a meeting or medium for an exchange of views. **2** chiefly N. Amer. a court or tribunal. **3** (pl. **fora**) (in ancient Roman cities) a public square or marketplace used for judicial and other business.
– ORIGIN Latin, 'what is out of doors'.
forward ● **adverb** (also **forwards**) **1** in the direction that one is facing or travelling. **2** onward so as to make progress. **3** ahead in time. **4** in or near the front of a ship or aircraft. ● **adjective** **1** towards the direction that one is facing or travelling. **2** relating to the future. **3** bold or over-familiar in manner. **4** further advanced than expected or required. **5** situated in or near the front of a ship or aircraft. ● **noun** an attacking player in football, hockey, or other sports. ● **verb** **1** send (a letter) on to a further destination. **2** dispatch; send. **3** promote.
– DERIVATIVES **forwarder** noun **forwardly** adverb **forwardness** noun.
– ORIGIN Old English.
forward-looking ● **adjective** favouring innovation; progressive.
forwent past of FORGO.
fosse /foss/ ● **noun** Archaeology a long trench or ditch.
– ORIGIN Latin *fossa*.
fossick /fossik/ ● **verb** Austral./NZ informal **1** rummage; search. **2** search for gold in abandoned workings.
– DERIVATIVES **fossicker** noun.
– ORIGIN probably from the English dialect sense 'obtain by asking'.
fossil /foss'l/ ● **noun** **1** the remains or impression of a prehis-

Thesaurus

fortification ● **noun** **1** RAMPART, wall, defence, bulwark, palisade, stockade, redoubt, earthwork, bastion, parapet, barricade.
fortify ● **verb** **1** *the knights fortified their citadel* BUILD DEFENCES ROUND, strengthen, secure, protect. **2** *the wall had been fortifed* STRENGTHEN, reinforce, toughen, consolidate, bolster, shore up, brace, buttress. **3** *I'll have a drink to fortify me* INVIGORATE, strengthen, energize, enliven, liven up, animate, vitalize, rejuvenate, restore, revive, refresh; informal pep up, buck up, give a shot in the arm to.
– OPPOSITES weaken, sedate, subdue.
fortitude ● **noun** COURAGE, bravery, endurance, resilience, mettle, moral fibre, strength of mind, strength of character, strong-mindedness, backbone, spirit, grit, doughtiness, steadfastness; informal guts; Brit. informal bottle.
– OPPOSITES faint-heartedness.
fortress ● **noun** FORT, castle, citadel, blockhouse, burg; stronghold, redoubt, fortification, bastion; fastness.
fortuitous ● **adjective** **1** *a fortuitous resemblance* CHANCE, adventitious, unexpected, unanticipated, unpredictable, unforeseen, unlooked-for, serendipitous, casual, incidental, coincidental, random, accidental, inadvertent, unintentional, unintended, unplanned, unpremeditated. **2** *United were saved by a fortuitous penalty* LUCKY, fluky, fortunate, providential, advantageous, timely, opportune, serendipitous, heaven-sent; Brit. informal jammy.
– OPPOSITES predictable, unlucky.
fortunate ● **adjective** **1** *he was fortunate that the punishment was so slight* LUCKY, favoured, blessed, blessed with good luck, in luck, having a charmed life, charmed; informal sitting pretty; Brit. informal jammy. **2** *in a fortunate position* FAVOURABLE, advantageous, providential, auspicious, welcome, heaven-sent, beneficial, propitious, fortuitous, opportune, happy, felicitous. **3** *the society gives generously to less fortunate people* WEALTHY, rich, affluent, prosperous, well off, moneyed, well-to-do, well heeled, opulent, comfortable; favoured, privileged.
– OPPOSITES unfortunate, unfavourable, underprivileged.
fortunately ● **adverb** LUCKILY, by good luck, by good fortune, as luck would have it, propitiously; mercifully, thankfully; thank goodness, thank God, thank heavens, thank the stars.
fortune ● **noun** **1** *fortune favoured him* CHANCE, accident, coincidence, serendipity, destiny, fortuity, providence; N. Amer. happenstance. **2** *a change of fortune* LUCK, fate, destiny, predestination, the stars, serendipity, karma, kismet, lot. **3** *an upswing in Sheffield's fortunes* CIRCUMSTANCES, state of affairs, condition, position, situation; plight, predicament. **4** *he made his fortune in steel* WEALTH, riches, substance, property, assets, resources, means, possessions, treasure, estate. **5** *this dress cost a fortune* HUGE AMOUNT, vast sum, king's ransom, millions, billions; informal small fortune, packet, mint, bundle, pile, wad, pretty penny, arm and a leg, tidy sum, killing, big money; Brit. informal bomb, loadsamoney, shedloads; N. Amer. informal big bucks, gazillions.
– OPPOSITES pittance.
fortune teller ● **noun** CLAIRVOYANT, crystal-gazer, psychic, prophet, seer, oracle, soothsayer, augur, diviner, sibyl; palmist, palm-reader; Scottish spaewife.
forum ● **noun** **1** *forums were held for staff to air grievances* MEETING, assembly, gathering, rally, conference, seminar, convention, symposium, colloquium; N. Amer. caucus; informal get-together; formal colloquy. **2** *a forum for discussion* SETTING, place, scene, context, stage, framework, backdrop; medium, means, apparatus, auspices. **3** *the Roman forum* PUBLIC MEETING PLACE, marketplace, agora.
forward ● **adverb** **1** *the traffic moved forward* AHEAD, forwards, onwards, onward, on, further. **2** *the winner stepped forward* TOWARDS THE FRONT, out, forth, into view. **3** *from that day forward* ONWARD, onwards, on, forth; for ever, into eternity; until now.
– OPPOSITES backwards.
● **adjective** **1** *in a forward direction* MOVING FORWARDS, moving ahead, onward, advancing, progressing, progressive. **2** *the fortress served as the Austrian army's forward base against the Russians* FRONT, advance, foremost, head, leading, frontal. **3** *forward planning* FUTURE, forward-looking, for the future, prospective. **4** *the girls seemed very forward* BOLD, BRAZEN, brazen-faced, barefaced, brash, shameless, immodest, audacious, daring, presumptuous, familiar, overfamiliar, pert; informal brass-necked, fresh.
– OPPOSITES backward, rear, shy, late.
● **verb** **1** *my mother forwarded me your letter* SEND ON, post on, redirect, readdress, pass on. **2** *the goods were forwarded by sea* SEND, dispatch, transmit, carry, convey, deliver, ship. **3** *Sir William forwarded his plan* ADVANCE, further, promote, assist, carry forward, hasten, hurry along, expedite, accelerate, speed up.
forward-looking ● **adjective** PROGRESSIVE, enlightened, dynamic, pushing, bold, enterprising, ambitious, pioneering, innovative, modern, avant-garde, positive, reforming, radical; informal go-ahead, go-getting.

toric plant or animal embedded in rock and preserved in petrified form. **2** humorous an antiquated person or thing.
– DERIVATIVES **fossiliferous** adjective **fossilization** (also **fossilisation**) noun **fossilize** (also **fossilise**) verb.
– ORIGIN French *fossile*, from Latin *fossilis* 'dug up'.
fossil fuel ● noun a natural fuel such as coal or gas, formed in the geological past from the remains of living organisms.
foster ● verb **1** promote the development of. **2** bring up (a child that is not one's own by birth). **3** Brit. assign (a child) to be fostered.
– DERIVATIVES **fosterage** noun **fosterer** noun.
– ORIGIN Old English, 'feed, nourish'; related to FOOD.
fought past and past participle of FIGHT.
foul ● adjective **1** having an offensive smell or taste; causing disgust. **2** very disagreeable or unpleasant. **3** morally offensive; wicked or obscene. **4** done contrary to the rules of a sport. **5** polluted or contaminated. **6** (**foul with**) clogged or choked with. ● noun **1** (in sport) an unfair or invalid piece of play. **2** a collision or entanglement in riding, rowing, or running. ● verb **1** make foul; pollute. **2** (of an animal) dirty with excrement. **3** (in sport) commit a foul against. **4** (**foul up**) make a mistake with; spoil. **5** (of a ship) collide with or interfere with the passage of (another). **6** cause (a cable, anchor, etc.) to become entangled or jammed.
– DERIVATIVES **foully** adverb **foulness** noun.
– ORIGIN Old English.
foulard /fo͞olaard/ ● noun a thin, soft material of silk or silk and cotton.
– ORIGIN French.
foul-mouthed ● adjective habitually using bad language.
foul play ● noun **1** unfair play in a game or sport. **2** criminal or violent activity, especially murder.
found[1] past and past participle of FIND.
found[2] ● verb **1** establish (an institution or organization). **2** (**be founded on/upon**) be based on (a particular principle or concept).
– ORIGIN Old French *fonder*, from Latin *fundus* 'bottom, base'.
found[3] ● verb **1** melt and mould (metal). **2** fuse (materials) to make glass. **3** make by founding.
– ORIGIN French *fondre*, from Latin *fundere* 'melt, pour'.
foundation ● noun **1** the lowest load-bearing part of a building, typically below ground level. **2** an underlying basis or principle. **3** justification or reason: *there was no foundation for the claim.* **4** the action of founding an institution or organization. **5** an institution so established. **6** a cream or powder applied to the face as a base for other make-up.
– DERIVATIVES **foundational** adjective.
foundation course ● noun Brit. a preparatory course taken at some colleges and universities, either in a wide range of subjects or in one subject at a basic level.
foundation garment ● noun a woman's supportive undergarment, such as a corset.
foundation stone ● noun a stone laid with ceremony to celebrate the founding of a building.
founder[1] ● noun a person who founds an institution or settlement.
founder[2] ● noun the owner or operator of a foundry.
founder[3] ● verb **1** (of a ship) fill with water and sink. **2** (of a plan or undertaking) fail. **3** (of a horse) stumble or fall.
– USAGE The words **founder** and **flounder** are often confused. In its general use, **founder** means 'fail or come to nothing', while **flounder** means 'struggle; be in a state of confusion'.
– ORIGIN Old French *fondrer* 'submerge, collapse', from Latin *fundus* 'bottom, base'.
founding father ● noun **1** a founder. **2** (**Founding Father**) a member of the convention that drew up the constitution of the US in 1787.
foundling ● noun an infant that has been abandoned by its parents and is discovered and cared for by others.
foundry ● noun (pl. **foundries**) a workshop or factory for casting metal.
fount[1] ● noun **1** a source of a desirable quality. **2** literary a spring or fountain.
– ORIGIN from FOUNTAIN.

f

Thesaurus

– OPPOSITES backward-looking.
forwards ● adverb. See FORWARD adverb.
fossil ● noun PETRIFIED REMAINS, petrified impression, remnant, relic; *Geology* reliquiae.
fossilized ● adjective **1** *fossilized remains* petrified, ossified. **2** *a fossilized idea* ARCHAIC, antiquated, antediluvian, old-fashioned, quaint, outdated, outmoded, behind the times, anachronistic, stuck in time; *informal* prehistoric.
foster ● verb **1** *he fostered the arts* ENCOURAGE, promote, further, stimulate, advance, forward, cultivate, nurture, strengthen, enrich; help, aid, abet, assist, contribute to, support, back. **2** *they started fostering children* BRING UP, rear, raise, care for, take care of, look after, nurture, provide for; mother, parent.
– OPPOSITES neglect, suppress.
foul ● adjective **1** *a foul stench* DISGUSTING, revolting, repulsive, repugnant, abhorrent, loathsome, offensive, sickening, nauseating, nauseous, stomach-churning, stomach-turning, distasteful, obnoxious, objectionable, odious, noxious; *N. Amer.* vomitous; *informal* ghastly, gruesome, gross, putrid, yucky, skanky, sick-making; *Brit. informal* beastly; *Austral. informal* on the nose; *poetic/literary* miasmic, noisome, mephitic. **2** *a foul mess* DIRTY, filthy, mucky, grimy, grubby, muddy, muddied, unclean, unwashed; squalid, sordid, soiled, sullied, scummy; rotten, defiled, decaying, putrid, putrefied, smelly, fetid; *informal* cruddy, yucky, icky; *Brit. informal* manky, gungy, grotty; *rare* feculent. **3** *he had been foul to her* UNKIND, malicious, mean, nasty, unpleasant, unfriendly, spiteful, cruel, vicious, base, malevolent, despicable, contemptible; *informal* horrible, horrid, rotten; *Brit. informal* beastly. **4** *foul weather* INCLEMENT, unpleasant, disagreeable, bad; rough, stormy, squally, gusty, windy, blustery, blowy, wild, rainy, wet; *Brit. informal* filthy. **5** *foul drinking water* CONTAMINATED, polluted, infected, tainted, impure, filthy, dirty, unclean; *rare* feculent. **6** *a foul deed* EVIL, wicked, bad, wrong, immoral, sinful, vile, dishonourable, corrupt, iniquitous, depraved, villainous, nefarious, vicious, malicious; malevolent, sinister, demonic, devilish, diabolical, fiendish, dark; monstrous, shocking, despicable, atrocious, heinous, odious, contemptible, horrible, execrable; *informal* low-down, dirty. **7** *foul language* VULGAR, crude, coarse, filthy, dirty, obscene, indecent, indelicate, naughty, suggestive, smutty, lewd, ribald, salacious, scatological, offensive, abusive; *informal* blue. **8** *a foul tackle* UNFAIR, illegal, unsporting, unsportsmanlike, below the belt, dirty.
– OPPOSITES pleasant, kind, fair, clean, righteous, mild, fair.
● verb **1** *the river had been fouled with waste* DIRTY, infect, pollute, contaminate, poison, taint, sully, soil, stain, blacken, muddy, splash, spatter, smear, blight, defile, make filthy. **2** *the vessel had fouled her nets* TANGLE UP, entangle, snarl, catch, entwine, enmesh, twist.
– OPPOSITES clean up, disentangle.
foul-mouthed ● adjective VULGAR, crude, coarse; obscene, rude, smutty, dirty, filthy, indecent, indelicate, offensive, lewd, X-rated, scatological, foul, abusive; *informal* blue.
found ● verb **1** *he founded his company in 1989* ESTABLISH, set up, start, begin, get going, institute, inaugurate, launch, float, form, create, bring into being, originate, develop. **2** *they founded a new city* BUILD, construct, erect, put up; plan, lay plans for. **3** *their relationship was founded on trust* BASE, build, construct; ground in, root in; rest, hinge, depend.
– OPPOSITES dissolve, liquidate, abandon, demolish.
foundation ● noun **1** *the foundations of a wall* FOOTING, foot, base, substructure, underpinning; bottom, bedrock, substratum. **2** *the report has a scientific foundation* BASIS, starting point, base, point of departure, beginning, premise; principles, fundamentals, rudiments; cornerstone, core, heart, thrust, essence, kernel. **3** *there was no foundation for the claim* JUSTIFICATION, grounds, defence, reason, rationale, cause, basis, motive, excuse, call, pretext, provocation. **4** *an educational foundation* ENDOWED INSTITUTION, charitable body, funding agency, source of funds.
founder[1] ● noun *the founder of modern physics* ORIGINATOR, creator, (founding) father, prime mover, architect, engineer, designer, developer, pioneer, author, planner, inventor, mastermind; *poetic/literary* begetter.
founder[2] ● verb **1** *the ship foundered* SINK, go to the bottom, go down, be lost at sea; *informal* go to Davy Jones's locker. **2** *the scheme foundered* FAIL, be unsuccessful, not succeed, fall through, fall flat, collapse, backfire, meet with disaster, come to nothing/naught; *informal* flop, bomb. **3** *their horses foundered in the river bed* STUMBLE, trip, trip up, lose one's balance, lose/miss one's footing, slip, stagger, lurch, totter, fall, tumble, topple, sprawl, collapse.
– OPPOSITES succeed.

fount[2] ● noun Brit. variant spelling of FONT[2].
fountain ● noun **1** an ornamental structure in a pool or lake from which a jet of water is pumped into the air. **2** literary a natural spring of water. **3** a source of something desirable. ● verb spurt or cascade like a fountain.
– ORIGIN Old French *fontaine*, from Latin *fons* 'a spring'.
fountainhead ● noun an original source.
fountain pen ● noun a pen with a reservoir or cartridge from which ink flows continuously to the nib.
four ● cardinal number **1** one more than three; 4. (Roman numeral: **iv** or **IV**.) **2** Cricket a hit that reaches the boundary after first striking the ground, scoring four runs. **3** a four-oared rowing boat or its crew.
– DERIVATIVES **fourfold** adjective & adverb.
– ORIGIN Old English.
four-dimensional ● adjective having the three dimensions of space (length, breadth, and depth) plus time.
four-eyes ● noun informal, derogatory a person who wears glasses.
Fourier series ● noun Mathematics an infinite series of trigonometric functions used to represent a given periodic function.
– ORIGIN named after the French mathematician Jean B. J. *Fourier* (1768–1830).
four-in-hand ● noun a vehicle with four horses driven by one person.
four-leaf clover (also **four-leaved clover**) ● noun a clover leaf with four lobes, thought to bring good luck.
four-letter word ● noun any of several short words regarded as coarse or offensive.
four-poster (also **four-poster bed**) ● noun a canopied bed with a post at each corner.
fourscore ● cardinal number archaic eighty.
foursome ● noun a group of four people.
four-square ● adjective **1** (of a building) having a square shape and solid appearance. **2** firm and resolute. ● adverb **1** squarely and solidly. **2** firmly and resolutely.
four-stroke ● adjective (of an internal-combustion engine) having a cycle of four strokes (intake, compression, combustion, and exhaust).
fourteen ● cardinal number one more than thirteen; 14. (Roman numeral: **xiv** or **XIV**.)
– DERIVATIVES **fourteenth** ordinal number.
fourth ● ordinal number **1** constituting number four in a sequence; 4th. **2** (**a fourth/one fourth**) chiefly N. Amer. a quarter. **3** Music an interval spanning four consecutive notes in a diatonic scale, in particular an interval of two tones and a semitone.
– PHRASES **the fourth estate** the press; journalism.
– DERIVATIVES **fourthly** adverb.
fourth dimension ● noun time regarded as a dimension analogous to the three linear dimensions.
Fourth World ● noun those countries and communities considered to be the poorest and most underdeveloped of the Third World.
four-wheel drive ● noun a transmission system which provides power directly to all four wheels of a vehicle.
fovea /fōviə/ ● noun (pl. **foveae** /fōvi-ee/) Anatomy a small depression in the retina of the eye where vision is sharpest.
– DERIVATIVES **foveal** adjective.
– ORIGIN Latin, 'small pit'.
fowl ● noun (pl. same or **fowls**) **1** (also **domestic fowl**) a domesticated bird derived from a junglefowl and kept for its eggs or flesh; a cock or hen. **2** any domesticated bird, e.g. a turkey or duck. **3** birds collectively, especially as the quarry of hunters.
– DERIVATIVES **fowler** noun **fowling** noun.
– ORIGIN Old English, related to FLY[1].
fox ● noun **1** an animal of the dog family with a pointed muzzle, bushy tail, and a reddish coat. **2** informal a cunning or sly person. **3** N. Amer. informal a sexually attractive woman. ● verb informal baffle or deceive.
– ORIGIN Old English.
foxed ● adjective (of the paper of old books or prints) discoloured with brown spots.
– DERIVATIVES **foxing** noun.
foxglove ● noun a tall plant with erect spikes of typically pinkish-purple flowers shaped like the fingers of gloves.
foxhole ● noun a hole in the ground used by troops as a shelter against enemy fire or as a firing point.
foxhound ● noun a breed of dog with smooth hair and drooping ears, trained to hunt foxes in packs.
fox-hunting ● noun the sport of hunting a fox across country with a pack of hounds, carried out by a group of people on foot and horseback.
foxtail ● noun a common meadow grass with soft brush-like flowering spikes.
fox terrier ● noun a short- or wire-haired breed of terrier originally used for unearthing foxes.
foxtrot ● noun a ballroom dance having an uneven rhythm with alternation of slow and quick steps. ● verb (**foxtrotted**, **foxtrotting**) dance the foxtrot.
foxy ● adjective (**foxier**, **foxiest**) **1** resembling or likened to a fox. **2** informal cunning or sly. **3** N. Amer. informal (of a woman) sexually attractive.
– DERIVATIVES **foxily** adverb **foxiness** noun.
foyer /foyay/ ● noun a large entrance hall in a hotel or theatre.
– ORIGIN originally denoting the centre of attention or activity: from French, 'hearth, home'.
Fr ● abbreviation Father (as a courtesy title of priests).
– ORIGIN from French *frère* 'brother'.
fr. ● abbreviation franc(s).
Fra /fraa/ ● noun a prefixed title given to an Italian monk or friar.
– ORIGIN Italian, from *frate* 'brother'.
fracas /frakaa/ ● noun (pl. same or /frakaaz/ or US **fracases** /frakəsiz/) a noisy disturbance or quarrel.
– ORIGIN French, from Italian *fracassare* 'make an uproar'.
fractal /frakt'l/ Mathematics ● noun a curve or geometrical figure, each part of which has the same statistical character as the whole. ● adjective relating to or of the nature of a fractal or fractals.
– ORIGIN French, from Latin *frangere* 'break'.
fraction /fraksh'n/ ● noun **1** a numerical quantity that is not a whole number (e.g. ½, 0.5). **2** a small or tiny part, amount, or proportion. **3** Chemistry each of the portions into which a mixture may be separated according to a physical property such as boiling point or solubility.
– ORIGIN Latin, from *frangere* 'to break'.
fractional ● adjective **1** relating to or expressed as a fraction. **2** small or tiny in amount. **3** Chemistry relating to or denoting the separation of a mixture into fractions.
– DERIVATIVES **fractionally** adverb.
fractionalize (also **fractionalise**) ● verb divide into separate groups or parts.
fractionate ● verb chiefly Chemistry divide into fractions or components.
– DERIVATIVES **fractionation** noun.
fractious /frakshəss/ ● adjective **1** easily irritated. **2** difficult to control.
– DERIVATIVES **fractiously** adverb **fractiousness** noun.
– ORIGIN from FRACTION, probably on the pattern of *faction, factious*.
fracture ● noun **1** the cracking or breaking of a hard object or

Thesaurus

foundling ● noun ABANDONED INFANT, waif, stray, orphan, outcast; *archaic* wastrel.
fountain ● noun **1** *a fountain of water* JET, spray, spout, spurt, well, fount, cascade. **2** *a fountain of knowledge* SOURCE, fount, well; reservoir, fund, mass, mine.
four ● cardinal number QUARTET, foursome, tetralogy, quadruplets; *technical* tetrad; *rare* quadrumvirate.
– RELATED TERMS quadri-, tetra-.
foxy ● adjective *(informal)* CRAFTY, wily, artful, guileful, devious, sly, scheming, designing, calculating, Machiavellian; shrewd, astute, clever, canny; deceitful, deceptive, duplicitous; *archaic* subtle.
foyer ● noun ENTRANCE HALL, hall, hallway, entrance, entry, porch, reception area, atrium, concourse, lobby; *N. Amer.* entryway.
fracas ● noun DISTURBANCE, brawl, melee, rumpus, skirmish, struggle, scuffle, scrum, clash, fisticuffs, altercation; *informal* scrap, dust-up, set-to, shindy, shindig; *Brit. informal* punch-up, bust-up, ruck; *N. Amer. informal* rough house, brannigan; *Austral./NZ informal* stoush; *Law, dated* affray.
fraction ● noun **1** *a fraction of the population* PART, subdivision, division, portion, segment, slice, section, sector; proportion, percentage, ratio, measure. **2** *only a fraction of the collection* TINY PART, fragment, snippet, snatch, smattering, selection. **3** *he moved a fraction closer* TINY AMOUNT, little, bit, touch, soupçon, trifle, mite, shade, jot; *informal* smidgen, smidge, tad.

material. **2** a crack or break, especially in a bone or layer of rock. ● verb **1** break or cause to break. **2** (of a group or organization) break up or fragment.
– ORIGIN Latin *fractura*, from *frangere* 'to break'.

fragile ● adjective **1** easily broken or damaged. **2** delicate and vulnerable.
– DERIVATIVES **fragilely** adverb **fragility** noun.
– ORIGIN originally in the sense 'morally weak': from Latin *fragilis*, from *frangere* 'to break'.

fragment ● noun /fragmənt/ **1** a small part broken off or detached. **2** an isolated or incomplete part: *a fragment of conversation.* ● verb /fragment/ break or cause to break into fragments.
– DERIVATIVES **fragmentary** adjective.
– ORIGIN Latin *fragmentum*, from *frangere* 'to break'.

fragmentation ● noun the process of breaking or the state of being broken into fragments.

fragmentation bomb (or **fragmentation grenade**) ● noun a bomb (or grenade) designed to break into small fragments as it explodes.

fragrance /fraygrənss/ ● noun **1** a pleasant, sweet smell. **2** a perfume or aftershave.
– DERIVATIVES **fragranced** adjective.

fragrant ● adjective having a pleasant, sweet smell.
– DERIVATIVES **fragrantly** adverb.
– ORIGIN Latin, from *fragrare* 'smell sweet'.

frail ● adjective **1** weak and delicate. **2** easily damaged or broken.
– DERIVATIVES **frailly** adverb **frailness** noun.
– ORIGIN Old French *fraile*, from Latin *fragilis* 'fragile'.

frailty ● noun (pl. **frailties**) **1** the condition of being frail. **2** weakness in character or morals.

frame ● noun **1** a rigid structure surrounding a picture, door, etc. **2** (**frames**) a metal or plastic structure holding the lenses of a pair of glasses. **3** the rigid supporting structure of a vehicle, piece of furniture, or other object. **4** a person's body with reference to its size or build: *her slim frame.* **5** the underlying structure of a system, concept, or text. **6** a single complete picture in a series forming a cinema or video film. **7** the triangular structure for positioning the red balls in snooker. **8** a single game of snooker. ● verb **1** place (a picture or photograph) in a frame. **2** surround so as to create a sharp or attractive image. **3** formulate or construct. **4** informal produce false incriminating evidence against (an innocent person).
– PHRASES **be in** (or **out of**) **the frame 1** be (or not be) eligible. **2** be wanted (or not wanted) by the police. **frame of mind** a particular mood.
– DERIVATIVES **framed** adjective **frameless** adjective **framer** noun **framing** noun.
– ORIGIN Old English, 'be useful', later 'prepare timber for building'.

frame house ● noun chiefly N. Amer. a house constructed from a wooden frame covered with timber boards.

frame of reference ● noun **1** a set of criteria in relation to which judgements can be made. **2** a system of geometrical axes in relation to which size, position, or motion can be defined.

frame saw ● noun a saw with a thin blade kept rigid by being stretched in a frame.

frame tent ● noun chiefly Brit. a tent supported by a tall frame, giving it nearly perpendicular sides and standing headroom throughout.

frame-up ● noun informal a conspiracy to incriminate someone falsely.

framework ● noun a supporting or underlying structure.

franc /frangk/ ● noun the basic monetary unit of France, Belgium, Switzerland, Luxembourg, and several other countries, equal to 100 centimes.
– ORIGIN Old French, from Latin *Francorum Rex* 'king of the Franks', the inscription on 14th-century gold coins.

franchise /franchīz/ ● noun **1** an authorization granted by a government or company to an individual or group enabling them to carry out specified commercial activities. **2** a business or service granted such a franchise. **3** the right to vote in public elections. **4** N. Amer. an authorization given by a professional league to own a sports team. **5** N. Amer. informal a team granted such a franchise. ● verb **1** grant a franchise to. **2** grant a franchise for (goods or a service).
– DERIVATIVES **franchisee** noun **franchiser** (also **franchisor**) noun.
– ORIGIN originally denoting a grant of legal immunity: from Old French, from *franc* 'free'.

Franciscan /fransiskən/ ● noun a monk or nun of a Christian

f

Thesaurus

– OPPOSITES whole.

fractious ● adjective **1** *fractious children* GRUMPY, bad-tempered, irascible, irritable, crotchety, grouchy, cantankerous, short-tempered, tetchy, testy, curmudgeonly, ill-tempered, ill-humoured, peevish, cross, pettish, waspish, crabbed, crabby, crusty, prickly, touchy; informal snappish, snappy, chippy; Brit. informal shirty, stroppy, narky, ratty; N. Amer. informal cranky, ornery; Austral./NZ informal snaky. **2** *the fractious parliamentary party* WAYWARD, unruly, uncontrollable, unmanageable, out of hand, obstreperous, difficult, headstrong, recalcitrant, intractable; disobedient, insubordinate, disruptive, disorderly, undisciplined; contrary, wilful; formal refractory; archaic contumacious.
– OPPOSITES contented, affable, dutiful.

fracture ● noun **1** *the risk of vertebral fracture* BREAKING, breakage, cracking, fragmentation, splintering, rupture. **2** *tiny fractures in the rock* CRACK, split, fissure, crevice, break, rupture, breach, rift, cleft, chink, interstice; crazing.
● verb *the glass may fracture under pressure* BREAK, crack, shatter, splinter, split, rupture; informal bust.

fragile ● adjective **1** *fragile porcelain* BREAKABLE, easily broken; delicate, dainty, fine, flimsy; eggshell; formal frangible. **2** *the fragile ceasefire* TENUOUS, shaky, insecure, unreliable, vulnerable, flimsy. **3** *she is still very fragile* WEAK, delicate, frail, debilitated; ill, unwell, ailing, poorly, sickly, infirm, enfeebled.
– OPPOSITES strong, durable, robust.

fragment ● noun **1** *meteorite fragments* PIECE, bit, particle, speck; chip, shard, sliver, splinter; shaving, paring, snippet, scrap, offcut, flake, shred, wisp, morsel; Scottish skelf. **2** *a fragment of conversation* SNATCH, snippet, scrap, bit.
● verb *explosions caused the chalk to fragment* BREAK UP, break, break into pieces, crack open/apart, shatter, splinter, fracture; disintegrate, fall to pieces, fall apart.

fragmentary ● adjective INCOMPLETE, fragmented, disconnected, disjointed, broken, discontinuous, piecemeal, scrappy, bitty, sketchy, uneven, patchy.

fragrance ● noun **1** *the fragrance of spring flowers* SWEET SMELL, scent, perfume, bouquet; aroma, redolence, nose. **2** *a bottle of fragrance* PERFUME, scent, eau de toilette, toilet water; eau de cologne, cologne; aftershave.

fragrant ● adjective SWEET-SCENTED, sweet-smelling, scented, perfumed, aromatic, perfumy; poetic/literary redolent.
– OPPOSITES smelly.

frail ● adjective **1** *a frail old lady* WEAK, delicate, feeble, enfeebled, debilitated; infirm, ill, ailing, unwell, sickly, poorly, in poor health. **2** *a frail structure* FRAGILE, breakable, easily damaged, delicate, flimsy, insubstantial, unsteady, unstable, rickety; formal frangible.
– OPPOSITES strong, robust.

frailty ● noun **1** *the frailty of old age* INFIRMITY, weakness, enfeeblement, debility; fragility, delicacy; ill health, sickliness. **2** *his many frailties* WEAKNESS, fallibility; weak point, flaw, imperfection, defect, failing, fault, shortcoming, deficiency, inadequacy, limitation.
– OPPOSITES strength.

frame ● noun **1** *a tubular metal frame* FRAMEWORK, structure, substructure, skeleton, chassis, shell, casing, body, bodywork; support, scaffolding, foundation. **2** *his tall, slender frame* BODY, figure, form, shape, physique, build, size, proportions. **3** *a photograph frame* SETTING, mount, mounting.
● verb **1** *he had the picture framed* MOUNT, set in a frame. **2** *the legislators who frame the regulations* FORMULATE, draw up, draft, plan, shape, compose, put together, form, devise, create, establish, conceive, think up, originate; informal dream up.
– PHRASES **frame of mind** MOOD, state of mind, humour, temper, disposition.

frame-up ● noun (informal) CONSPIRACY, plot; trick, trap, entrapment; informal put-up job, fit-up, set-up.

framework ● noun **1** *a metal framework* FRAME, substructure, structure, skeleton, chassis, shell, body, bodywork; support, scaffolding, foundation. **2** *the framework of society* STRUCTURE, shape, fabric, order, scheme, system, organization, construction, configuration, composition; informal make-up.

franchise ● noun **1** *the extension of the franchise to women* SUFFRAGE, the vote, the right to vote, voting rights, enfranchisement.

religious order following the rule of the Italian monk St Francis of Assisi (*c.*1181–1226). ● **adjective** of St Francis or the Franciscans.

francium /fransiəm/ ● **noun** an unstable radioactive chemical element of the alkali-metal group.
– ORIGIN from the country *France*.

Franco- (also **franco-**) ● **combining form 1** French; French and ...: *francophone*. **2** relating to France: *Francophile*.
– ORIGIN from Latin *Francus* 'Frank'.

Francoist ● **noun** a supporter of the Spanish dictator General Francisco Franco (1892–1975) or his policies. ● **adjective** relating to Franco's regime or policies.
– DERIVATIVES **Francoism** noun.

francolin /frangkōlin/ ● **noun** a large game bird resembling a partridge, native to Africa and South Asia.
– ORIGIN Italian *francolino*.

f

Francophile ● **noun** a person who is fond of or greatly admires France or the French.

francophone /frangkəfōn/ ● **adjective** French-speaking. ● **noun** a French-speaking person.

frangible /franjib'l/ ● **adjective** fragile; brittle.
– ORIGIN Latin *frangibilis*, from *frangere* 'to break'.

frangipane /franjipayn/ ● **noun** an almond-flavoured cream or paste.
– ORIGIN originally denoting the frangipani plant, which was used to flavour frangipane.

frangipani /franjipaani/ ● **noun** (pl. **frangipanis**) **1** a tropical American tree or shrub with clusters of fragrant white, pink, or yellow flowers. **2** perfume obtained from this plant.
– ORIGIN named after the Marquis Muzio *Frangipani*, a 16th-century Italian nobleman who invented a perfume for scenting gloves.

franglais /fronglay/ ● **noun** a blend of French and English, either French that makes excessive use of English expressions, or unidiomatic French spoken by an English person.
– ORIGIN coined in French, from a blend of *français* 'French' and *anglais* 'English'.

Frank ● **noun** a member of a Germanic people that conquered Gaul in the 6th century.
– DERIVATIVES **Frankish** adjective & noun.
– ORIGIN Old English *Franca*, perhaps from the name of a weapon and related to *franca* 'javelin'; also related to FRENCH.

frank[1] ● **adjective 1** honest and direct, especially when dealing with unpleasant matters. **2** open or undisguised: *frank admiration*.
– DERIVATIVES **frankness** noun.
– ORIGIN originally in the sense 'free': from Latin *francus* 'free', from *Francus* 'Frank' (only Franks had full freedom in Frankish Gaul).

frank[2] ● **verb 1** stamp an official mark on (a letter or parcel) to indicate that postage has been paid or does not need to be paid. **2** historical sign (a letter or parcel) to ensure delivery free of charge. ● **noun** a franking mark or signature on a letter or parcel.
– DERIVATIVES **franker** noun **franking** noun.
– ORIGIN from FRANK[1], an early sense being 'free of obligation'.

Frankenfood /frangkənfōōd/ ● **noun** derogatory a food that contains genetically modified ingredients.
– ORIGIN from FRANKENSTEIN.

Frankenstein /frangkənstīn/ (also **Frankenstein's monster**) ● **noun** a thing that becomes terrifying or destructive to its maker.
– ORIGIN from Victor *Frankenstein*, a character in a novel (1818) by Mary Shelley, who creates a manlike monster which eventually destroys him.

frankfurter ● **noun** a seasoned smoked sausage made of beef and pork.
– ORIGIN from German *Frankfurter Wurst* 'Frankfurt sausage'.

frankincense /frangkinsenss/ ● **noun** an aromatic gum resin obtained from an African tree and burnt as incense.
– ORIGIN from Old French *franc encens* 'high-quality incense'.

franklin ● **noun** a landowner of free but not noble birth in the 14th and 15th centuries in England.
– ORIGIN from Latin *francalis* 'held without dues', from *francus* 'free'.

frankly ● **adverb 1** in a frank manner. **2** to be frank.

frantic ● **adjective 1** distraught with fear, anxiety, etc. **2** done in a hurried and chaotic way.
– DERIVATIVES **frantically** adverb **franticness** noun.
– ORIGIN Old French *frenetique* 'violently mad', from Greek *phrenitis* (see FRENETIC).

frappé /frappay/ ● **adjective** (of a drink) iced or chilled. ● **noun** a drink served with ice or frozen to a slushy consistency.
– ORIGIN French.

Frascati /fraskaati/ ● **noun** a white wine produced in the Frascati region of Italy.

frass /frass/ ● **noun 1** powdery refuse produced by wood-boring insects. **2** the excrement of insect larvae.
– ORIGIN German, from *fressen* 'devour'.

fraternal /frətern'l/ ● **adjective 1** of or like a brother; brotherly. **2** of or denoting a fraternity. **3** (of twins) developed from separate ova and therefore not identical.
– DERIVATIVES **fraternalism** noun **fraternally** adverb.
– ORIGIN Latin *fraternalis*, from *frater* 'brother'.

fraternity /frəterniti/ ● **noun** (pl. **fraternities**) **1** a group of people sharing a common profession or interests. **2** N. Amer. a male students' society in a university or college. **3** a religious or masonic society or guild. **4** friendship and mutual support within a group.

fraternize /frattərnīz/ (also **fraternise**) ● **verb** (usu. **fraternize with**) be on friendly terms.
– DERIVATIVES **fraternization** noun.

fratricide /fratrisīd/ ● **noun 1** the killing of one's brother or sister. **2** the accidental killing of one's own forces in war.
– DERIVATIVES **fratricidal** adjective.
– ORIGIN from Latin *frater* 'brother' + -CIDE.

Frau /frow/ ● **noun** (pl. **Frauen** /frowən/) a title or form of address for a married or widowed German woman.
– ORIGIN German.

fraud /frawd/ ● **noun 1** wrongful or criminal deception intended to result in financial or personal gain. **2** a person intending or thing intended to deceive.
– DERIVATIVES **fraudster** noun.
– ORIGIN Old French *fraude*, from Latin *fraus* 'deceit, injury'.

Thesaurus

2 *the company lost its TV franchise* WARRANT, charter, licence, permit, authorization, permission, sanction.

frank[1] ● **adjective 1** *he was quite frank with me* CANDID, direct, forthright, plain, plain-spoken, straight, straightforward, straight from the shoulder, explicit, to the point, matter-of-fact; open, honest, truthful, sincere; outspoken, bluff, blunt, unsparing, not afraid to call a spade a spade; *informal* upfront. **2** *she looked at Sam with frank admiration* OPEN, undisguised, unconcealed, naked, unmistakable, clear, obvious, transparent, patent, manifest, evident, perceptible, palpable; blatant, barefaced, flagrant.
– OPPOSITES evasive.

frank[2] ● **verb** *the envelope had not been franked* STAMP, postmark; imprint, print, mark.

frankly ● **adverb 1** *frankly, I'm not very interested* TO BE FRANK, to be honest, to tell you the truth, to be truthful, in all honesty, as it happens. **2** *he stated the case quite frankly* CANDIDLY, directly, plainly, straightforwardly, straight from the shoulder, forthrightly, openly, honestly, without beating about the bush, without mincing one's words, without prevarication, point-blank; bluntly, outspokenly, with no holds barred.

frantic ● **adjective** PANIC-STRICKEN, panic-struck, panicky, beside oneself, at one's wits' end, distraught, overwrought, worked up, agitated, distressed; frenzied, wild, frenetic, fraught, feverish, hysterical, desperate; *informal* in a state, in a tizzy/tizz, wound up, het up, in a flap, tearing one's hair out; *Brit. informal* having kittens, in a flat spin.
– OPPOSITES calm.

fraternity ● **noun 1** *a spirit of fraternity* BROTHERHOOD, fellowship, kinship, friendship, (mutual) support, solidarity, community, union, togetherness; sisterhood. **2** *the teaching fraternity* PROFESSION, body of workers; band, group, set, circle. **3** *(N. Amer.) a college fraternity* SOCIETY, club, association; group, set.

fraternize ● **verb** ASSOCIATE, mix, consort, socialize, keep company, rub shoulders; *N. Amer.* rub elbows; *informal* hang around/round, hang out, run around, knock about/around, hobnob, be thick with.

fraud ● **noun 1** *he was arrested for fraud* FRAUDULENCE, sharp practice, cheating, swindling, embezzlement, deceit, deception, double-dealing, chicanery. **2** *social security frauds* SWINDLE, racket, deception, trick, cheat, hoax; *informal* scam, con, con trick, rip-off,

fraudulent /frawdyoolənt/ ● adjective **1** done by or involving fraud. **2** deceitful or dishonest.
– DERIVATIVES **fraudulence** noun **fraudulently** adverb.
fraught /frawt/ ● adjective **1** (**fraught with**) filled with (something undesirable). **2** causing or affected by anxiety or stress.
– ORIGIN from obsolete *fraught* 'load with cargo', from Dutch *vracht* 'ship's cargo'; related to FREIGHT.
Fräulein /froylīn/ ● noun a title or form of address for a young German woman.
– ORIGIN German, from FRAU.
fray[1] ● verb **1** (of a fabric, rope, or cord) unravel or become worn at the edge. **2** (of a person's nerves or temper) show the effects of strain.
– ORIGIN Old French *freiier*, from Latin *fricare* 'to rub'.
fray[2] ● noun (**the fray**) **1** a situation of intense competitive activity. **2** a battle or fight.
– ORIGIN from Old French *afrayer* 'disturb, startle'.
frazzle informal ● verb **1** (**frazzled**) completely exhausted. **2** cause to shrivel up with burning. ● noun (**a frazzle**) **1** an exhausted state. **2** a charred or burnt state.
– ORIGIN originally dialect: perhaps a blend of FRAY[1] and obsolete *fazle* 'ravel out'.
freak ● noun **1** (also **freak of nature**) a person, animal, or plant which is abnormal or deformed. **2** a very unusual and unexpected event. **3** informal a person who is obsessed with a particular activity or interest: *a fitness freak*. ● verb (usu. **freak out**) informal behave or cause to behave in a wild and irrational way.
– DERIVATIVES **freakish** adjective.
– ORIGIN probably from a dialect word.
freaky ● adjective (**freakier**, **freakiest**) informal very odd or strange.
– DERIVATIVES **freakily** adverb **freakiness** noun.
freckle ● noun a small light brown spot on the skin, caused and made more pronounced by exposure to the sun. ● verb cover or become covered with freckles.
– DERIVATIVES **freckly** adjective.
– ORIGIN Old Norse.
free ● adjective (**freer**, **freest**) **1** not under the control or in the power of another. **2** permitted to take a specified action. **3** not or no longer confined, obstructed, or fixed. **4** not subject to engagements or obligations. **5** not occupied or in use. **6** (**free of/from**) not subject to or affected by. **7** available without charge. **8** generous or lavish. **9** frank and unrestrained. **10** not subject to the normal conventions; improvised. **11** (of a translation or interpretation) conveying only the broad sense; not literal. ● adverb without cost or payment. ● verb (**frees**, **freed**, **freeing**) **1** make free; release. **2** make available.
– PHRASES **free and easy** informal and relaxed. **a free hand** freedom to act completely as one wishes. **a free ride** a situation in which someone benefits without having to make a fair contribution. **the free world** the non-communist countries of the world, as formerly opposed to the Soviet bloc. **make free with** treat without ceremony or proper respect.
– DERIVATIVES **freeness** noun.
– ORIGIN Old English, related to FRIEND.
free association ● noun a psychoanalytic technique for investigating the unconscious mind, in which the analyst puts forward key words or images in order to prompt spontaneous words and thoughts from the subject.
freebase ● noun cocaine that has been purified by heating with ether, taken by inhaling the fumes or smoking the residue. ● verb take (cocaine) in such a way.
freebie ● noun informal a thing given free of charge.
freeboard ● noun the height of a ship's side between the waterline and the deck.
freebooter ● noun a pirate or lawless adventurer.
– DERIVATIVES **freeboot** verb.
– ORIGIN Dutch *vrijbuiter*, from *vrij* 'free' + *buit* 'booty'.
freeborn ● adjective not born in slavery.
Free Church ● noun a Christian Church which has dissented

f

Thesaurus

sting, gyp, diddle, fiddle; *N. Amer. informal* bunco, hustle, grift. **3** *they exposed him as a fraud* IMPOSTOR, fake, sham, charlatan, quack, mountebank; swindler, fraudster, racketeer, cheat, confidence trickster; *informal* phoney, con man, con artist.
fraudulent ● adjective DISHONEST, cheating, swindling, corrupt, criminal, illegal, unlawful, illicit; deceitful, double-dealing, duplicitous, dishonourable, unscrupulous, unprincipled; *informal* crooked, shady, dirty; *Brit. informal* bent, dodgy; *Austral./NZ informal* shonky.
– OPPOSITES honest.
fraught ● adjective **1** *their world is fraught with danger* FULL OF, filled with, rife with; attended by, accompanied by. **2** *she sounded a bit fraught* ANXIOUS, worried, stressed, upset, distraught, overwrought, worked up, agitated, distressed, distracted, desperate, frantic, panic-stricken, panic-struck, panicky; beside oneself, at one's wits' end, at the end of one's tether; *informal* wound up, in a state, in a flap, in a cold sweat, tearing one's hair out; *Brit. informal* having kittens, in a flat spin.
fray[1] ● verb **1** *cheap fabric soon frays* UNRAVEL, wear, wear thin, wear out/through, become worn. **2** *her nerves were frayed* STRAIN, tax, overtax, put on edge.
fray[2] ● noun *two men started the fray* BATTLE, fight, engagement, conflict, clash, skirmish, altercation, tussle, struggle, scuffle, melee, brawl; *informal* scrap, dust-up, set-to; *Brit. informal* punch-up, bust-up; *Scottish informal* rammy; *Law, dated* affray.
frayed ● adjective **1** *a frayed shirt collar* WORN, well worn, threadbare, tattered, ragged, holey, moth-eaten, in holes, the worse for wear; *informal* tatty; *N. Amer. informal* raggedy. **2** *his frayed nerves* STRAINED, fraught, tense, edgy, stressed.
freak ● noun **1** *a genetically engineered freak* ABERRATION, abnormality, irregularity, oddity; monster, monstrosity, mutant; freak of nature. **2** *the accident was a complete freak* ANOMALY, aberration, rarity, oddity, unusual occurrence; fluke, twist of fate. **3** *(informal) they were dismissed as a bunch of freaks* ODDITY, eccentric, misfit; crank, lunatic; *informal* oddball, weirdo, nutcase, nut; *Brit. informal* nutter; *N. Amer. informal* wacko, kook. **4** *(informal) a fitness freak* ENTHUSIAST, fan, devotee, lover, aficionado; *informal* fiend, nut, fanatic, addict, maniac.
● adjective *a freak storm | a freak result* UNUSUAL, anomalous, aberrant, atypical, unrepresentative, irregular, fluky, exceptional, unaccountable, bizarre, queer, peculiar, odd, freakish; unpredictable, unforeseeable, unexpected, unanticipated, surprising; rare, singular, isolated.
– OPPOSITES normal.
● verb *(informal) he freaked out* GO CRAZY, go mad, go out of one's mind, go to pieces, crack, snap, lose control; panic, become hysterical; *informal* lose it, lose one's cool, crack up; *N. Amer. informal* go ape, go postal.
freakish ● adjective *freakish weather*. See FREAK adjective.
freaky ● adjective *(informal)*. See ODD senses 1, 2.
free ● adjective **1** *admission is free* WITHOUT CHARGE, free of charge, for nothing; complimentary, gratis, for free, on the house. **2** *she was free of any pressures* UNENCUMBERED BY, unaffected by, clear of, without, rid of; exempt from, not liable to, safe from, immune to, excused of; *informal* sans, minus. **3** *I'm free this afternoon* UNOCCUPIED, not busy, available, between appointments; off duty, off work, off, on holiday, on leave; at leisure, with time on one's hands, with time to spare. **4** *the bathroom's free now* VACANT, empty, available, unoccupied, not taken, not in use. **5** *a citizen of a proud free nation* INDEPENDENT, self-governing, self-governed, self-ruling, self-determining, non-aligned, sovereign, autonomous; democratic. **6** *the killer is still free* ON THE LOOSE, at liberty, at large; loose, unconfined, unbound, untied, unchained, untethered, unshackled, unfettered, unrestrained. **7** *you are free to leave* ABLE TO, in a position to, capable of; ALLOWED, permitted. **8** *the free flow of water* UNIMPEDED, unobstructed, unrestricted, unhampered, clear, open, unblocked. **9** *she was free with her money* GENEROUS, liberal, open-handed, unstinting, bountiful; lavish, extravagant, prodigal. **10** *his free and hearty manner* FRANK, open, candid, direct, plain-spoken; unrestrained, unconstrained, free and easy, uninhibited.
– OPPOSITES busy, occupied, captive, mean.
● verb **1** *three of the hostages were freed* RELEASE, set free, let go, liberate, discharge, deliver; set loose, let loose, turn loose, untie, unchain, unfetter, unshackle, unleash; *poetic/literary* disenthral; *historical* manumit. **2** *the victims were freed by firefighters* EXTRICATE, release, get out, pull out, pull free; rescue, set free. **3** *they wish to be freed from all legal ties* EXEMPT, except, excuse, relieve, unburden, disburden.
– OPPOSITES confine, trap.
– PHRASES **free and easy** EASY-GOING, relaxed, casual, informal, unceremonious, unforced, natural, open, spontaneous, uninhibited, friendly; tolerant, liberal; *informal* laid-back. **a free hand** FREE REIN, carte blanche, freedom, liberty, licence, latitude, leeway.

or seceded from an established Church.

freedom • noun **1** the power or right to act, speak, or think freely. **2** the state of being free. **3** (**freedom from**) exemption or immunity from. **4** unrestricted use of something: *the dog had the freedom of the house.* **5** a special privilege or right of access, especially that of full citizenship of a particular city given to a public figure as an honour.

freedom fighter • noun a person who takes part in a revolutionary struggle.

free enterprise • noun an economic system in which private business operates in competition and largely free of state control.

free fall • noun **1** downward movement under the force of gravity. **2** rapid descent or decline without means of stopping. • verb (**free-fall**) move under the force of gravity; fall rapidly.

free-for-all • noun a disorganized or unrestricted situation or event in which everyone may take part, especially a fight or discussion.

free-form • adjective not conforming to a regular or formal structure.

freehand • adjective & adverb done manually without the aid of instruments such as rulers.

free-handed • adjective generous, especially with money.

freehold • noun **1** permanent and absolute tenure of land or property with freedom to dispose of it at will. **2** chiefly Brit. a piece of land or property held by such tenure.
– DERIVATIVES **freeholder** noun.

free house • noun Brit. a public house not controlled by a brewery and therefore not restricted to selling particular brands of beer or liquor.

free kick • noun (in soccer and rugby) an unimpeded kick of the stationary ball awarded for a foul or infringement by the opposing team.

freelance /freelaanss/ • adjective self-employed and hired to work for different companies on particular assignments. • adverb earning one's living in such a way. • noun (also **freelancer**) a freelance worker. • verb earn one's living as a freelance.
– ORIGIN originally denoting a mercenary in medieval Europe: from FREE + LANCE.

freeloader • noun informal a person who takes advantage of others' generosity without giving anything in return.
– DERIVATIVES **freeload** verb.

free love • noun the practice of having sexual relations without fidelity to one partner.

freely • adverb **1** not under the control of another. **2** without restriction or interference. **3** in abundant amounts. **4** openly and honestly. **5** willingly and readily.

freeman • noun **1** a person who has been given the freedom of a city or borough. **2** historical a person who is not a slave or serf.

free market • noun an economic system in which prices are determined by unrestricted competition between privately owned businesses.

Freemason • noun a member of an international order established for mutual help and fellowship, which holds elaborate secret ceremonies.
– DERIVATIVES **Freemasonry** noun.

free pardon • noun an unconditional remission of the legal consequences of an offence or conviction.

free port • noun **1** a port open to all traders. **2** a port area where goods in transit are exempt from customs duty.

free radical • noun Chemistry a molecule (typically highly reactive) with an unpaired electron.

free-range • adjective (of livestock or their produce) kept or produced in natural conditions, where the animals have freedom of movement.

freesia /freeziə/ • noun a small plant with fragrant, colourful, tubular flowers, native to southern Africa.
– ORIGIN named after the 19th-century German physician Friedrich H. T. *Freese.*

free-standing • adjective not attached to or supported by another structure.

free state • noun historical a state of the US in which slavery did not exist.

freestyle • noun denoting a contest, race, or type of sport in which there are few restrictions on the style or technique that competitors employ.

freethinker • noun a person who questions or rejects accepted opinions, especially those concerning religious belief.

free trade • noun international trade left to its natural course without tariffs, quotas, or other restrictions.

free verse • noun poetry that does not rhyme or have a regular rhythm.

free vote • noun chiefly Brit. a parliamentary division in which members vote independently of party policy.

freeway • noun N. Amer. **1** a dual-carriageway main road. **2** a toll-free highway.

freewheel • noun a bicycle wheel which is able to revolve freely when no power is being applied to the pedals. • verb **1** coast on a bicycle without using the pedals. **2** (**freewheeling**) cheerily unconcerned.
– DERIVATIVES **freewheeler** noun.

free will • noun the power to act without the constraints of necessity or fate; the ability to act at one's own discretion.

freeze • verb (past **froze**; past part. **frozen**) **1** (with reference to a liquid) turn or be turned into ice or another solid as a result of extreme cold. **2** become or cause to become blocked or rigid with ice. **3** be or cause to be very cold. **4** store at a very low temperature as a means of preservation. **5** become suddenly motionless or paralysed with fear or shock. **6** (of a computer screen) suddenly become locked. **7** keep or stop at a fixed level or in a fixed state. **8** (**freeze out**) informal cause (someone) to feel excluded by being hostile or obstructive. • noun **1** an act of freezing. **2** informal a period of very cold weather.
– DERIVATIVES **freezable** adjective.
– ORIGIN Old English.

freeze-dry • verb preserve by rapid freezing followed by subjection to a high vacuum which removes ice by sublimation.

freeze-frame • noun **1** a single frame forming a motionless image from a film or videotape. **2** the facility or process of stop-

Thesaurus

freebooter • noun PIRATE, marauder, raider; bandit, robber; adventurer, swashbuckler; *historical* privateer; *archaic* buccaneer, corsair.

freedom • noun **1** *a desperate bid for freedom* LIBERTY, liberation, release, deliverance, delivery, discharge; *poetic/literary* disenthralment; *historical* manumission. **2** *national revolution was the only path to freedom* INDEPENDENCE, self-government, self-determination, self rule, home rule, sovereignty, non-alignment, autonomy; democracy. **3** *freedom from local political accountability* EXEMPTION, immunity, dispensation; impunity. **4** *patients have more freedom to choose who treats them* RIGHT, entitlement, privilege, prerogative; scope, latitude, leeway, flexibility, space, breathing space, room, elbow room; licence, leave, free rein, a free hand, carte blanche.
– OPPOSITES captivity, subjection, liability.

free-for-all • noun BRAWL, fight, scuffle, tussle, struggle, confrontation, clash, altercation, fray, fracas, melee, rumpus, disturbance; breach of the peace; *informal* dust-up, scrap, set-to, shindy; *Brit. informal* punch-up, bust-up, barney; *Scottish informal* rammy; *Law, dated* affray.

freely • adverb **1** *may I speak freely?* OPENLY, candidly, frankly, directly, without constraint, without inhibition; truthfully, honestly, without beating about the bush, without mincing one's words, without prevarication. **2** *they gave their time and labour freely* VOLUNTARILY, willingly, readily; of one's own volition, of one's own accord, of one's own free will, without compulsion.

freethinker • noun NONCONFORMIST, individualist, independent, maverick; agnostic, atheist, non-believer, unbeliever.
– OPPOSITES conformist.

free will • noun SELF-DETERMINATION, freedom of choice, autonomy, liberty, independence.
– PHRASES **of one's own free will** VOLUNTARILY, willingly, readily, freely, without reluctance, without compulsion, of one's own accord, of one's own volition, of one's own choosing.

freeze • verb **1** *the stream had frozen* ICE OVER, ice up, solidify. **2** *the campers stifled in summer and froze in winter* BE VERY COLD, be numb with cold, turn blue with cold, shiver, be chilled to the bone/marrow. **3** *she froze in horror* STOP DEAD, stop in one's tracks, stop, stand (stock) still, go rigid, become motionless, become paralysed. **4** *the prices of basic foodstuffs were frozen* FIX, hold, peg, set; limit, restrict, cap, confine, regulate; hold/keep down.
– OPPOSITES thaw.
– PHRASES **freeze someone out** *(informal)* EXCLUDE, leave out, shut out, cut out, ignore, ostracize, spurn, snub, shun, cut, cut dead,

ping a film or videotape to obtain a freeze-frame.

freezer • noun a refrigerated cabinet or room for preserving food at very low temperatures.

freezing • adjective **1** having a temperature below 0°C. **2** informal very cold. **3** (of fog or rain) consisting of droplets which freeze rapidly on contact with a surface. • noun the freezing point of water (0°C).

freezing point • noun the temperature at which a liquid turns into a solid when cooled.

freight /frayt/ • noun **1** transport of goods in bulk by truck, train, ship, or aircraft. **2** goods transported by freight. • verb **1** transport by freight. **2** (**be freighted with**) be laden or burdened with.
– ORIGIN Dutch and Low German *vrecht*, from *vracht* 'ship's cargo'.

freightage • noun **1** the carrying of goods in bulk. **2** goods carried in bulk; freight.

freighter • noun **1** a large ship or aircraft designed to carry freight. **2** a person who loads, receives, or forwards goods for transport.

French • adjective relating to France or its people or language. • noun the language of France, also used in parts of Belgium, Switzerland, and Canada, in certain countries in Africa and the Caribbean, and elsewhere.
– PHRASES **excuse** (or **pardon**) **my French** informal used to apologize for swearing.
– DERIVATIVES **Frenchness** noun.
– ORIGIN Old English, related to FRANK.

French bean • noun Brit. a bean plant of which many varieties are commercially cultivated for food.

French bread • noun white bread in a long, crisp loaf.

French Canadian • noun a Canadian whose native language is French. • adjective relating to French Canadians.

French chalk • noun a kind of steatite used for marking cloth and removing grease.

French cricket • noun an informal game resembling cricket, in which a soft ball is bowled at the batter's legs.

French dressing • noun a salad dressing of vinegar, oil, and seasonings.

French fries • plural noun chiefly N. Amer. potatoes deep-fried in thin strips; chips.

French horn • noun a brass instrument with a coiled tube, valves, and a wide bell.

Frenchify • verb (**Frenchifies**, **Frenchified**) often derogatory make French in form or character.

French kiss • noun a kiss with contact between tongues.
– DERIVATIVES **French kissing** noun.

French knickers • plural noun women's loose-fitting, wide-legged underpants.

French leave • noun informal, dated absence from work or duty without permission.
– ORIGIN said to derive from the French custom of leaving a function without saying goodbye to the host.

French letter • noun Brit. informal, dated a condom.

Frenchman • noun a man who is French by birth or descent.

French polish • noun shellac polish that produces a high gloss on wood. • verb (**french-polish**) treat (wood) with French polish.

French stick • noun a loaf of French bread.

French toast • noun **1** bread coated in egg and milk and fried. **2** Brit. bread buttered on one side and toasted on the other.

French window • noun each of a pair of glazed doors in an outside wall.

Frenchwoman • noun a woman who is French by birth or descent.

Frenchy (also **Frenchie**) informal, chiefly derogatory • adjective French in character. • noun (pl. **Frenchies**) a French person.

frenetic /frənettik/ • adjective fast and energetic in a rather wild and uncontrolled way.
– DERIVATIVES **frenetically** adverb **freneticism** noun.
– ORIGIN Old French *frenetique* 'violently mad', from Greek *phrenitis* 'delirium'.

frenzy • noun (pl. **frenzies**) a state or period of uncontrolled excitement or wild behaviour.
– DERIVATIVES **frenzied** adjective **frenziedly** adverb.
– ORIGIN Latin *phrenesia*, from Greek *phrēn* 'mind'.

frequency • noun (pl. **frequencies**) **1** the rate at which something occurs over a particular period or in a given sample. **2** the fact or state of being frequent. **3** the rate per second of a vibration constituting a wave, e.g. sound, light, or radio waves. **4** the particular waveband at which radio signals are broadcast or transmitted.

frequency modulation • noun the modulation of a wave by varying its frequency, used as a means of broadcasting an audio signal by radio.

frequent • adjective /freekwənt/ **1** occurring or done many times at short intervals. **2** doing something often; habitual. • verb /frikwent/ visit (a place) often or habitually.
– DERIVATIVES **frequenter** noun **frequently** adverb.
– ORIGIN Latin *frequens* 'crowded, frequent'.

fresco /freskō/ • noun (pl. **frescoes** or **frescos**) a painting done on wet plaster on a wall or ceiling, in which the colours become fixed as the plaster dries.
– DERIVATIVES **frescoed** adjective.
– ORIGIN Italian, 'cool, fresh'.

fresh • adjective **1** not previously known or used; new or different. **2** (of food) recently made or obtained; not preserved. **3** recently created and not faded or impaired: *the memory was fresh in their minds.* **4** (of water) not salty. **5** (of the wind) cool and fairly strong. **6** pleasantly clean, invigorating, and cool: *fresh air.* **7** full of energy and vigour. **8** informal presumptuous or impudent. • adverb newly; recently.
– DERIVATIVES **freshly** adverb **freshness** noun.
– ORIGIN Old English, 'not salt, fit for drinking'.

Thesaurus

turn one's back on, cold-shoulder, give someone the cold shoulder, leave out in the cold; *Brit.* send to Coventry; *Brit. informal* blank.

freezing • adjective **1** *a freezing wind* BITTER, bitterly cold, icy, chill, frosty, glacial, wintry, sub-zero; raw, biting, piercing, penetrating, cutting, numbing; arctic, polar, Siberian. **2** *you must be freezing* FROZEN, extremely cold, numb with cold, chilled to the bone/marrow, frozen stiff, shivery, shivering; *informal* frozen to death.
– OPPOSITES balmy, hot.

freight • noun **1** *freight carried by rail* GOODS, cargo, freightage; load, consignment, delivery, shipment; merchandise. **2** *the importance of air freight* TRANSPORTATION, transport, conveyance, freightage, carriage, portage, haulage.

frenetic • adjective FRANTIC, wild, frenzied, hectic, fraught, feverish, fevered, mad, manic, hyperactive, energetic, intense, fast and furious, turbulent, tumultuous.
– OPPOSITES calm.

frenzied • adjective FRANTIC, wild, frenetic, hectic, fraught, feverish, fevered, mad, crazed, manic, intense, furious, uncontrolled, out of control.
– OPPOSITES calm.

frenzy • noun **1** *the crowd worked themselves into a state of frenzy* HYSTERIA, madness, mania, dementedness, delirium, feverishness, fever, wildness, agitation, turmoil, tumult; wild excitement, euphoria, elation, ecstasy. **2** *a frenzy of anger* FIT, paroxysm, spasm, bout.

frequency • noun RATE OF OCCURRENCE, incidence, amount, commonness, prevalence; *Statistics* distribution.

frequent • adjective **1** *frequent bouts of chest infection* RECURRENT, recurring, repeated, periodic, continual, one after another, successive; many, numerous, lots of, several. **2** *a frequent business traveller* HABITUAL, regular.
– OPPOSITES occasional.
• verb *he frequented chic supper clubs* VISIT, patronize, spend time in, visit regularly, be a regular visitor to, haunt; *informal* hang out at.

frequenter • noun HABITUÉ, patron, regular, regular visitor, regular customer, regular client, familiar face.

frequently • adverb REGULARLY, often, very often, all the time, habitually, customarily, routinely; many times, many a time, lots of times, again and again, time and again, over and over again, repeatedly, recurrently, continually; *N. Amer.* oftentimes; *poetic/literary* oft, oft-times.

fresh • adjective **1** *fresh fruit* NEWLY PICKED, garden-fresh, crisp, unwilted; raw, natural, unprocessed. **2** *a fresh sheet of paper* CLEAN, blank, empty, clear, white; unused, new, pristine, unmarked, untouched. **3** *a fresh approach* NEW, recent, latest, up-to-date, modern, modernistic, ultra-modern, newfangled; original, novel, different, innovative, unusual, unconventional, unorthodox; radical, revolutionary; *informal* offbeat. **4** *fresh recruits* YOUNG,

freshen ● verb **1** make or become fresh. **2** chiefly N. Amer. top up (a drink).
fresher ● noun Brit. informal a first-year student at college or university.
freshet ● noun **1** the flood of a river from heavy rain or melted snow. **2** a rush of fresh water flowing into the sea.
– ORIGIN probably from Old French *freschete*, from *freis* 'fresh'.
freshman ● noun a first-year student at university or (N. Amer.) at high school.
freshwater ● adjective of or found in fresh water; not of the sea.
fret[1] ● verb (**fretted**, **fretting**) **1** be constantly or visibly anxious. **2** gradually wear away by rubbing or gnawing. ● noun chiefly Brit. a state of anxiety.
– ORIGIN Old English, 'devour, consume'.
fret[2] ● noun Art & Architecture an ornamental design of vertical and horizontal lines. ● verb (**fretted**, **fretting**) decorate with fretwork.
– ORIGIN Old French *frete* 'trelliswork'.
fret[3] ● noun each of a sequence of ridges on the fingerboard of some stringed instruments, used for fixing the positions of the fingers. ● verb (**fretted**, **fretting**) **1** provide with frets. **2** play (a note) while pressing against a fret.
– DERIVATIVES **fretless** adjective.
– ORIGIN of unknown origin.
fretful ● adjective anxious or irritated.
– DERIVATIVES **fretfully** adverb **fretfulness** noun.
fretsaw ● noun a saw with a narrow blade for cutting designs in thin wood or metal.
fretwork ● noun ornamental design done with a fretsaw.
Freudian ● adjective **1** relating to or influenced by the Austrian psychotherapist Sigmund Freud (1856–1939) and his methods of psychoanalysis. **2** susceptible to analysis in terms of unconscious thoughts or desires: *a Freudian slip*. ● noun a follower of Freud or his methods.
– DERIVATIVES **Freudianism** noun.
Fri. ● abbreviation Friday.
friable /frīəb'l/ ● adjective easily crumbled.
– DERIVATIVES **friability** noun.
– ORIGIN Latin *friabilis*, from *friare* 'to crumble'.
friar ● noun a member of any of certain religious orders of men, especially the four mendicant orders (Augustinians, Carmelites, Dominicans, and Franciscans).
– ORIGIN Old French *frere*, from Latin *frater* 'brother'.
friary ● noun (pl. **friaries**) a building or community occupied by or consisting of friars.
fricassée /frikkəsee/ ● noun a dish of stewed or fried pieces of meat served in a thick white sauce.
– DERIVATIVES **fricasséed** adjective.
– ORIGIN French, from *fricasser* 'cut up and cook in a sauce'.
fricative /frikkətiv/ ● adjective Phonetics referring to a type of consonant (e.g. *f* and *th*) made by the friction of breath in a narrow opening.
– ORIGIN Latin *fricativus*, from *fricare* 'to rub'.
friction ● noun **1** the resistance that one surface or object encounters when moving over another. **2** the action of one surface or object rubbing against another. **3** conflict or disagreement.
– DERIVATIVES **frictional** adjective **frictionless** adjective.
– ORIGIN Latin, from *fricare* 'to rub'.
Friday ● noun the day of the week before Saturday and following Thursday. ● adverb **1** chiefly N. Amer. on Friday. **2** (**Fridays**) on Fridays; each Friday.
– ORIGIN Old English, named after the Germanic goddess *Frigga*.
fridge ● noun a refrigerator.
fridge-freezer ● noun chiefly Brit. an upright unit comprising a separate refrigerator and freezer.
fried past and past participle of FRY[1].
friend ● noun **1** a person with whom one has a bond of mutual affection, typically one exclusive of sexual or family relations. **2** a familiar or helpful thing. **3** a person who supports a particular cause or organization. **4** (**Friend**) a Quaker.
– PHRASES **a friend in need is a friend indeed** proverb a person who helps at a difficult time is a person to be relied upon.
– DERIVATIVES **friendless** adjective **friendship** noun.
– ORIGIN Old English, related to FREE.
friendly ● adjective (**friendlier**, **friendliest**) **1** kind and pleasant;

Thesaurus

youthful; new, inexperienced, naive, untrained, unqualified, untried, raw; *informal* wet behind the ears. **5** *he felt fresh and happy to be alive* REFRESHED, rested, restored, revived; (as) fresh as a daisy, energetic, vigorous, invigorated, full of vim and vigour, lively, vibrant, spry, sprightly, bright, alert, perky; *informal* full of beans, raring to go, bright-eyed and bushy-tailed, chirpy, chipper. **6** *her fresh complexion* HEALTHY, healthy-looking, clear, bright, youthful, blooming, glowing, unblemished; fair, rosy, rosy-cheeked, pink, ruddy. **7** *the night air was fresh* COOL, crisp, refreshing, invigorating, tonic; pure, clean, clear, uncontaminated, untainted. **8** *a fresh wind* CHILLY, chill, cool, cold, brisk, bracing, invigorating; strong; *informal* nippy; *Brit. informal* parky. **9** *(informal) that young man has been getting a little too fresh* IMPUDENT, impertinent, insolent, presumptuous, forward, cheeky, disrespectful, rude, brazen, shameless, pert, bold, (as) bold as brass; *informal* brass-necked, lippy, mouthy, saucy; *N. Amer. informal* sassy.
– OPPOSITES stale, old, tired, warm.
freshen ● verb **1** *the cold water freshened him* REFRESH, revitalize, restore, revive, wake up, rouse, enliven, liven up, energize, brace, invigorate; *informal* buck up, pep up. **2** *he opened a window to freshen the room* VENTILATE, air, aerate, oxygenate; deodorize, purify, cleanse; refresh, cool. **3** *she went to freshen up before dinner* HAVE A WASH, wash oneself, bathe, shower; tidy oneself (up), spruce oneself up, smarten oneself up, groom oneself, primp oneself; *N. Amer.* wash up; *informal* titivate oneself, do oneself up, doll oneself up; *Brit. informal* tart oneself up; *formal or humorous* perform one's ablutions. **4** *(N. Amer.) the waitress freshened their coffee* REFILL, top up, fill up, replenish.
freshman, freshwoman ● noun FIRST YEAR STUDENT, undergraduate; newcomer, new recruit, starter, probationer; beginner, learner, novice; *N. Amer.* tenderfoot; *informal* undergrad, rookie; *Brit. informal* fresher; *N. Amer. informal* greenhorn.
fret ● verb **1** *she was fretting about Jonathan* WORRY, be anxious, feel uneasy, be distressed, be upset, upset oneself, concern oneself; agonize, sigh, pine, brood, eat one's heart out. **2** *his absence began to fret her* TROUBLE, bother, concern, perturb, disturb, disquiet, disconcert, distress, upset, alarm, panic, agitate; *informal* eat away at.
fretful ● adjective DISTRESSED, upset, miserable, unsettled, uneasy, ill at ease, uncomfortable, edgy, agitated, worked up, tense, stressed, restive, fidgety; querulous, irritable, cross, fractious, peevish, petulant, out of sorts, bad-tempered, irascible, grumpy, crotchety, captious, testy, tetchy; *N. Amer. informal* cranky; *informal* het up, uptight, twitchy, crabby.
friable ● adjective CRUMBLY, easily crumbled, powdery, dusty, chalky, soft; dry, crisp, brittle.
friar ● noun MONK, brother, religious, coenobite, contemplative; prior, abbot.
friction ● noun **1** *a lubrication system which reduces friction* ABRASION, rubbing, chafing, grating, rasping, scraping; resistance, drag. **2** *there was considerable friction between father and son* DISCORD, strife, conflict, disagreement, dissension, dissent, opposition, contention, dispute, disputation, arguing, argument, quarrelling, bickering, squabbling, wrangling, fighting, feuding, rivalry; hostility, animosity, antipathy, enmity, antagonism, resentment, acrimony, bitterness, bad feeling, ill feeling, ill will, bad blood.
– OPPOSITES harmony.
friend ● noun **1** *a close friend* COMPANION, boon companion, bosom friend, best friend, intimate, confidante, confidant, familiar, soul mate, alter ego, second self, playmate, playfellow, classmate, schoolmate, workmate; ally, associate; sister, brother; *informal* pal, chum, sidekick, crony, main man; *Brit. informal* mate, china, mucker; *N. English informal* marrow, marra; *N. Amer. informal* buddy, amigo, compadre, homeboy; *archaic* compeer. **2** *the friends of the Royal Botanic Garden* PATRON, backer, supporter, benefactor, benefactress, sponsor; well-wisher, defender, champion; *informal* angel.
– OPPOSITES enemy.
friendless ● adjective ALONE, all alone, by oneself, solitary, lonely, with no one to turn to, lone, without friends, companionless, unbefriended, unpopular, unwanted, unloved, abandoned, rejected, forsaken, shunned, spurned, forlorn; *N. Amer.* lonesome.
– OPPOSITES popular.
friendliness ● noun AFFABILITY, amiability, geniality, congeniality, bonhomie, cordiality, good nature, good humour, warmth, affection, affectionateness, demonstrativeness, conviviality, joviality, companionability, sociability, gregariousness, camaraderie, neighbourliness, hospitableness, approachability, accessibility,

of or like a friend. **2** (in combination) not harmful to a specified thing: *environment-friendly.* **3** favourable or serviceable. **4** Military of or allied with one's own forces. ● noun (pl. **friendlies**) Brit. a game or match not forming part of a serious competition.
– DERIVATIVES **friendlily** adverb **friendliness** noun.

friendly fire ● noun Military weapon fire coming from one's own side that causes accidental injury or death to one's own forces.

friendly society ● noun (in the UK) a mutual association providing sickness benefits, life assurance, and pensions.

Friesian /freezhən/ ● noun Brit. an animal of a black-and-white breed of dairy cattle originally from Friesland in the Netherlands.

frieze /freez/ ● noun **1** a broad horizontal band of sculpted or painted decoration. **2** Architecture the part of an entablature between the architrave and the cornice.
– ORIGIN Latin *frisium,* from *Phrygium opus* 'work of Phrygia'.

frig ● verb (**frigged, frigging**) vulgar slang **1** have sexual intercourse with. **2** masturbate.
– ORIGIN originally in sense 'move restlessly', later 'rub, chafe': of unknown origin.

frigate /friggət/ ● noun **1** a warship with a mixed armament, generally lighter than a destroyer. **2** historical a sailing warship of a size just below that of a ship of the line.
– ORIGIN Italian *fregata.*

frigate bird ● noun a predatory tropical seabird with a deeply forked tail and a long hooked bill.

fright ● noun **1** a sudden intense feeling of fear. **2** an experience causing fright; a shock.
– PHRASES **look a fright** informal look ridiculous or grotesque. **take fright** suddenly become frightened.
– ORIGIN Old English.

frighten ● verb **1** make afraid. **2** (**frighten off**) drive away by fear.
– DERIVATIVES **frightened** adjective **frightening** adjective **frighteningly** adverb.

frightener ● noun a frightening person or thing.
– PHRASES **put the frighteners on** Brit. informal threaten or intimidate.

frightful ● adjective **1** very unpleasant, serious, or shocking. **2** informal terrible; awful.
– DERIVATIVES **frightfully** adverb **frightfulness** noun.

fright wig ● noun a wig with the hair arranged sticking out, as worn by a clown.

frigid /frijid/ ● adjective **1** very cold. **2** (of a woman) unable to be sexually aroused. **3** stiff or formal in style.
– DERIVATIVES **frigidity** noun **frigidly** adverb.
– ORIGIN Latin *frigidus,* from *frigere* 'be cold'.

frigid zone ● noun each of the two areas of the earth respectively north of the Arctic Circle and south of the Antarctic Circle.

frill ● noun **1** a strip of gathered or pleated material used as a decorative edging. **2** a frill-like fringe of feathers, hair, skin, etc. on a bird, reptile, or other animal. **3** (**frills**) unnecessary extra features or embellishments.
– DERIVATIVES **frilled** adjective **frilly** adjective.
– ORIGIN from or related to Flemish *frul.*

fringe ● noun **1** a border of threads, tassels, or twists, used to edge clothing or material. **2** chiefly Brit. the front part of someone's hair, cut so as to hang over the forehead. **3** a natural border of hair or fibres in an animal or plant. **4** the outer part of something. **5** (before another noun) not part of the mainstream: *fringe theatre.* ● verb provide with or form a fringe.
– DERIVATIVES **fringing** noun **fringy** adjective.
– ORIGIN Old French *frenge,* from Latin *fimbria* 'fibres, shreds'.

fringe benefit ● noun an additional benefit.

frippery ● noun (pl. **fripperies**) **1** showy or unnecessary ornament. **2** a tawdry or frivolous thing.

Thesaurus

openness, kindness, kindliness, sympathy, amenability, benevolence.

friendly ● adjective **1** *a friendly woman* AFFABLE, amiable, genial, congenial, cordial, warm, affectionate, demonstrative, convivial, companionable, sociable, gregarious, outgoing, clubbable, comradely, neighbourly, hospitable, approachable, easy to get on with, accessible, communicative, open, unreserved, easy-going, good-natured, kindly, benign, amenable, agreeable, obliging, sympathetic, well disposed, benevolent; *Scottish* couthy; *informal* chummy, pally, clubby; *Brit. informal* matey; *N. Amer. informal* buddy-buddy. **2** *friendly conversation* AMICABLE, congenial, cordial, pleasant, easy, relaxed, casual, informal, unceremonious; close, intimate, familiar. **3** *a friendly wind swept the boat to the shore* FAVOURABLE, advantageous, helpful; lucky, providential.
– OPPOSITES hostile.

friendship ● noun **1** *lasting friendships* RELATIONSHIP, close relationship, attachment, mutual attachment, association, bond, tie, link, union. **2** *old ties of love and friendship* AMITY, camaraderie, friendliness, comradeship, companionship, fellowship, fellow feeling, closeness, affinity, rapport, understanding, harmony, unity; intimacy, mutual affection.
– OPPOSITES enmity.

fright ● noun **1** *she was paralysed with fright* FEAR, fearfulness, terror, horror, alarm, panic, dread, trepidation, dismay, nervousness, apprehension, apprehensiveness, perturbation, disquiet; *informal* jitteriness, twitchiness. **2** *the experience gave everyone a fright* SCARE, shock, surprise, turn, jolt, start; the shivers, the shakes; *informal* the jitters, the heebie-jeebies, the willies, the creeps, the collywobbles, a cold sweat; *Brit. informal* the (screaming) abdabs, butterflies (in one's stomach). **3** *(informal) she looked an absolute fright* UGLY SIGHT, eyesore, monstrosity; *informal* mess, sight, state, blot on the landscape.

frighten ● verb SCARE, startle, alarm, terrify, petrify, shock, chill, panic, shake, disturb, dismay, unnerve, unman, intimidate, terrorize, cow, daunt; strike terror into, put the fear of God into, chill someone to the bone/marrow, make someone's blood run cold; *informal* scare the living daylights out of, scare stiff, scare someone out of their wits, scare witless, scare to death, scare the pants off, spook, make someone's hair stand on end, throw into a blue funk, make someone jump out of their skin; *Brit. informal* put the wind up, give someone the heebie-jeebies, make someone's hair curl; *Irish informal* scare the bejesus out of; *archaic* affright.

frightening ● adjective TERRIFYING, horrifying, alarming, startling, chilling, spine-chilling, hair-raising, blood-curdling, disturbing, unnerving, intimidating, daunting, dismaying, upsetting, harrowing, traumatic; eerie, sinister, fearsome, nightmarish, macabre, menacing; *Scottish* eldritch; *informal* scary, spooky, creepy, hairy.

frightful ● adjective **1** *a frightful accident* HORRIBLE, horrific, ghastly, horrendous, serious, awful, dreadful, terrible, nasty, grim, dire, unspeakable; alarming, shocking, terrifying, harrowing, appalling, fearful; hideous, gruesome, grisly; *informal* horrid; *formal* grievous. **2** *(informal) a frightful racket* AWFUL, very bad, terrible, dreadful, appalling, ghastly, abominable; unpleasant, disagreeable, lamentable, deplorable, insufferable, unbearable; *informal* God-awful; *Brit. informal* beastly.

frigid ● adjective **1** *a frigid January night* VERY COLD, bitterly cold, bitter, freezing, frozen, frosty, icy, gelid, chilly, chill, wintry, bleak, sub-zero, arctic, Siberian, polar, glacial; *informal* nippy; *Brit. informal* parky. **2** *frigid politeness* STIFF, formal, stony, wooden, unemotional, passionless, unfeeling, indifferent, unresponsive, unenthusiastic, austere, distant, aloof, remote, reserved, unapproachable; frosty, cold, icy, cool, unsmiling, forbidding, unfriendly, unwelcoming, hostile; *informal* offish, stand-offish.
– OPPOSITES hot, friendly.

frill ● noun **1** *a full skirt with a wide frill* RUFFLE, flounce, ruff, furbelow, jabot, peplum, ruche, ruching, fringe; *archaic* purfle. **2** *a comfortable flat with no frills* OSTENTATION, ornamentation, decoration, embellishment, fanciness, fuss, chichi, gilding, excess; trimmings, extras, additions, non-essentials, luxuries, extravagances, superfluities.

frilly ● adjective RUFFLED, flounced, frilled, crimped, ruched, trimmed, lacy, frothy; fancy, ornate.

fringe ● noun **1** *the city's northern fringe* PERIMETER, periphery, border, borderline, margin, rim, outer edge, edge, extremity, limit; outer limits, limits, borders, bounds, outskirts, marches; *poetic/literary* marge, bourn. **2** *blue curtains with a yellow fringe* EDGING, edge, border, trimming, frill, flounce, ruffle; tassels; *archaic* purfle.
– OPPOSITES middle.
● adjective *fringe theatre* UNCONVENTIONAL, unorthodox, alternative, avant-garde, experimental, innovative, left-field, innovatory, radical, extreme; peripheral; off Broadway; *informal* offbeat, way out.
– OPPOSITES mainstream.
● verb **1** *a robe of gold, fringed with black velvet* TRIM, edge, hem, border, bind, braid; decorate, adorn, ornament, embellish, finish; *archaic* purfle. **2** *the lake is fringed by a belt of trees* BORDER, edge, bound, skirt, line, surround, enclose, encircle, circle, girdle, encompass, ring; *poetic/literary* gird.

– ORIGIN Old French *freperie* 'second-hand clothes', from *frepe* 'rag'.
frisbee • noun trademark a plastic disc designed for skimming through the air as an outdoor game.
– ORIGIN said to be named after the pie tins of the *Frisbie* bakery in Connecticut.
frisée /freezay/ • noun a kind of endive with curled leaves.
– ORIGIN French, from *chicorée frisée* 'curly endive'.
Frisian /freezhən, fri-/ • noun **1** a person from Frisia or Friesland in the Netherlands. **2** the Germanic language spoken in northern parts of the Netherlands and adjacent islands. • adjective relating to Frisia or Friesland.
frisk • verb **1** pass the hands over (someone) in a search for hidden weapons or drugs. **2** skip or move playfully; frolic. • noun **1** a search by frisking. **2** a playful skip or leap.
– ORIGIN Old French *frisque* 'alert, lively'.
frisky • adjective (**friskier, friskiest**) playful and full of energy.
frisson /freesson/ • noun a sudden strong feeling of excitement or fear; a thrill.
– ORIGIN French.
fritillary /fritilləri/ • noun **1** a plant with hanging bell-like flowers. **2** a butterfly with orange-brown wings chequered with black.
– ORIGIN Latin *fritillaria*, from *fritillus* 'dice-box' (probably with reference to the chequered corolla of the snake's head fritillary).
frittata /fritaatə/ • noun an Italian dish made with fried beaten eggs, resembling a Spanish omelette.
– ORIGIN Italian, from *fritto* 'fried'.
fritter[1] • verb (**fritter away**) waste (time, money, or energy) on trifling matters.
– ORIGIN from obsolete *fitter* 'break into fragments'.
fritter[2] • noun a piece of fruit, vegetable, or meat that is coated in batter and deep-fried.
– ORIGIN Old French *friture*, from Latin *frigere* 'fry'.
fritto misto /frittō mistō/ • noun a dish of various foods deep-fried in batter.
– ORIGIN Italian, 'mixed fry'.
frivolous • adjective **1** not having any serious purpose or value. **2** (of a person) carefree and superficial.
– DERIVATIVES **frivolity** noun **frivolously** adverb **frivolousness** noun.
– ORIGIN Latin *frivolus* 'silly, trifling'.
frizz • verb (of hair) form into a mass of tight curls. • noun a mass of tightly curled hair.
– ORIGIN French *friser*.
frizzle[1] • verb fry until crisp or burnt.
– ORIGIN from FRY[1], probably influenced by SIZZLE.
frizzle[2] • verb form (hair) into tight curls. • noun a tight curl in hair.
– ORIGIN from FRIZZ.
frizzy • adjective (**frizzier, frizziest**) formed of a mass of small, tight, wiry curls.
– DERIVATIVES **frizziness** noun.
fro • adverb see TO AND FRO.
– ORIGIN Old Norse.
frock • noun **1** chiefly Brit. a woman's or girl's dress. **2** a loose outer garment, in particular a long gown with flowing sleeves worn by monks, priests, or clergy.
– ORIGIN Old French *froc*.
frock coat • noun a man's double-breasted, long-skirted coat, now worn chiefly on formal occasions.
frog[1] • noun **1** a tailless amphibian with a short squat body and very long hind legs for leaping. **2** (**Frog**) informal, derogatory a French person.
– PHRASES **have a frog in one's throat** informal lose one's voice or find it hard to speak because of hoarseness.
– DERIVATIVES **froggy** adjective **froglet** noun.
– ORIGIN Old English: sense 2 is partly from alliteration with *French* and partly from the reputation of the French for eating frogs' legs.
frog[2] • noun **1** a thing used to hold or fasten something. **2** an ornamental coat fastener consisting of a spindle-shaped button and a loop.
– ORIGIN perhaps a use of FROG[1], influenced by Italian *forchetta* or French *fourchette* 'small fork', because of the shape.
frog[3] • noun an elastic horny pad in the sole of a horse's hoof.
– ORIGIN perhaps from FROG[1]; perhaps also influenced by Italian *forchetta* or French *fourchette* (see FROG[2]).
froghopper • noun a jumping, plant-sucking bug, the larva of which produces cuckoo spit.
frogman • noun a diver equipped with a rubber suit, flippers, and breathing equipment.
frogmarch • verb force (someone) to walk forward by pinning their arms from behind.
frogspawn • noun a mass of frogs' eggs surrounded by transparent jelly.
froideur /frwadör/ • noun coolness or reserve between people.
– ORIGIN French, from *froid* 'cold'.
frolic • verb (**frolicked, frolicking**) play or move about in a cheerful and lively way. • noun a playful action or movement.
– DERIVATIVES **frolicker** noun.
– ORIGIN from Dutch *vrolijk* 'merry, cheerful'.
frolicsome • adjective literary lively and playful.
from • preposition **1** indicating the point in space or time at which a journey, process, or action starts. **2** indicating source or provenance. **3** indicating the starting point of a range. **4** indicating separation, removal, or prevention. **5** indicating a cause. **6** indicating a difference.
– PHRASES **from time to time** occasionally.
– ORIGIN Old English.
fromage blanc /frommaazh BLON/ • noun a type of soft French cheese having a creamy sour taste.
– ORIGIN French, 'white cheese'.
fromage frais /frommaazh fray/ • noun a type of smooth soft

Thesaurus

fringe benefit • noun EXTRA, added extra, additional benefit, privilege; *informal* perk; *formal* perquisite.
frippery • noun **1** *a functional building with not a hint of frippery* OSTENTATION, showiness, embellishment, ornamentation, ornament, adornment, decoration, trimming, gilding, prettification, gingerbread; finery; *informal* bells and whistles. **2** *stalls full of fripperies* TRINKET, bauble, knick-knack, gewgaw, gimcrack, bibelot, ornament, novelty, trifle; *N. Amer.* kickshaw; *archaic* gaud.
frisk • verb **1** *the spaniels frisked around my ankles* FROLIC, gambol, cavort, caper, cut capers, scamper, skip, dance, romp, trip, prance, leap, spring, hop, jump, bounce. **2** *the officer frisked him* SEARCH, body-search, check.
frisky • adjective LIVELY, bouncy, bubbly, perky, active, energetic, animated, zestful, full of vim and vigour; playful, coltish, skittish, spirited, high-spirited, in high spirits, exuberant; *informal* full of beans, sparky, zippy, peppy, bright-eyed and bushy-tailed; *poetic/literary* frolicsome.
fritter • verb SQUANDER, waste, misuse, misspend, dissipate; overspend, spend like water, be prodigal with, run through, get through; *informal* blow, splurge, pour/chuck something down the drain; *Brit. informal, dated* blue.
– OPPOSITES save.
frivolity • noun LIGHT-HEARTEDNESS, levity, joking, jocularity, gaiety, fun, frivolousness, silliness, foolishness, flightiness, skittishness; superficiality, shallowness, vacuity, empty-headedness.
frivolous • adjective **1** *a frivolous girl* SKITTISH, flighty, giddy, silly, foolish, superficial, shallow, light-minded, irresponsible, thoughtless, feather-brained, empty-headed, pea-brained, birdbrained, vacuous, vapid; *informal* dizzy, dippy; *N. Amer. informal* ditsy. **2** *frivolous remarks* FLIPPANT, glib, facetious, joking, jokey, light-hearted; fatuous, inane, senseless, thoughtless; *informal* flip. **3** *new rules to stop frivolous lawsuits* TIME-WASTING, pointless, trivial, trifling, minor, petty, insignificant, unimportant.
– OPPOSITES sensible, serious.
frizzle[1] • verb *a hamburger frizzled in the pan* SIZZLE, crackle, fizz, hiss, spit, sputter, crack, snap; fry, cook.
frizzle[2] • verb *their hair was powdered and frizzled* CURL, coil, crimp, crinkle, kink, wave, frizz.
– OPPOSITES straighten.
frizzy • adjective CURLY, curled, corkscrew, ringlety, crimped, crinkly, kinky, frizzed; permed; *N. Amer. informal* nappy.
– OPPOSITES straight.
frock • noun DRESS, gown, robe, shift; garment, costume.
frolic • verb *children frolicked on the sand* PLAY, amuse oneself, romp, disport oneself, frisk, gambol, cavort, caper, cut capers, scamper, skip, dance, prance, leap about; *dated* sport.
• noun *the youngsters enjoyed their frolic* ANTIC, caper, game, romp, escapade; (**frolics**) fun (and games), high jinks, merrymaking, amusement, skylarking.
frolicsome • adjective (*poetic/literary*) PLAYFUL, frisky, fun-loving,

fresh cheese.
– ORIGIN French, 'fresh cheese'.
frond ● noun the leaf or leaf-like part of a palm, fern, or similar plant.
– ORIGIN Latin *frons* 'leaf'.
front ● noun **1** the side or part of an object that presents itself to view or that is normally seen first. **2** the position directly ahead. **3** the forward-facing part of a person's body. **4** any face of a building, especially that of the main entrance: *the west front of the Cathedral.* **5** the foremost line of an armed force; the furthest position that an army has reached. **6** Meteorology the boundary of an advancing mass of air. **7** a particular situation or sphere of operation: *good news on the jobs front.* **8** an organized political group. **9** a deceptive appearance or mode of behaviour. **10** a person or organization serving as a cover for subversive activities. **11** boldness and confidence of manner. ● adjective of or at the front. ● verb **1** have the front facing towards. **2** place or be placed at the front of. **3** provide with a front or facing. **4** lead or be at the forefront of. **5** present or host (a television or radio programme). **6** act as a front for.
– PHRASES **front of house 1** the parts of a theatre in front of the proscenium arch. **2** the business of a theatre that concerns the audience, such as ticket sales. **in front of** in the presence of.
– DERIVATIVES **frontward** adjective & adverb **frontwards** adverb.
– ORIGIN Latin *frons* 'forehead, front'.
frontage ● noun **1** the facade of a building. **2** a strip or extent of land abutting on a street or waterway.
frontal ● adjective **1** of or at the front. **2** relating to the forehead or front part of the skull.
– DERIVATIVES **frontally** adverb.
frontal lobe ● noun each of the paired lobes of the brain lying immediately behind the forehead.
front bench ● noun (in the UK) the foremost seats in the House of Commons, occupied by the members of the cabinet and shadow cabinet.
– DERIVATIVES **frontbencher** noun.
front-end ● adjective **1** relating to the front, especially of a vehicle. **2** informal (of money) paid or charged at the beginning of a transaction. **3** Computing (of a device or program) directly accessed by the user and allowing access to further devices or programs. ● noun Computing the front-end part of a computer or program.
frontier ● noun **1** a border separating two countries. **2** the extreme limit of settled land beyond which lies wilderness. **3** the extreme limit of understanding or achievement in a particular area.
– ORIGIN Old French *frontiere*, from Latin *frons* 'front'.
frontiersman (or **frontierswoman**) ● noun a man (or woman) living in the region of a frontier.
frontispiece /fruntispeess/ ● noun an illustration facing the title page of a book.
– ORIGIN Latin *frontispicium* 'facade'.
front line ● noun the military line or part of an army that is closest to the enemy.
frontman ● noun a person who acts as a front, in particular the leader of a band or the representative of an illegal organization.
front-runner ● noun the contestant that is leading in a race or other competition.
front-wheel drive ● noun a transmission system that provides power to the front wheels of a motor vehicle.
frost ● noun **1** a deposit of white ice crystals formed on surfaces when the temperature falls below freezing. **2** a period of cold weather when frost forms. ● verb **1** cover or be covered with or as if with frost; freeze. **2** N. Amer. decorate with icing.
– ORIGIN Old English, related to FREEZE.
frostbite ● noun injury to body tissues, especially the nose, fingers, or toes, caused by exposure to extreme cold.
frosted ● adjective **1** covered with or as if with frost. **2** (of glass) having a translucent textured surface so that it is difficult to see through.
frosting ● noun **1** N. Amer. icing. **2** a roughened matt finish on otherwise shiny material.
frosty ● adjective (**frostier**, **frostiest**) **1** (of the weather) very cold with frost forming on surfaces. **2** cold and unfriendly.
– DERIVATIVES **frostily** adverb **frostiness** noun.
froth ● noun **1** a mass of small bubbles in liquid caused by agitation, fermentation, or salivating. **2** impure matter that rises to the surface of liquid. **3** worthless or insubstantial talk, ideas, or activities. ● verb form, produce, or contain froth.
– DERIVATIVES **frothily** adverb **frothy** adjective.
– ORIGIN Old Norse.
frottage /frotaazh/ ● noun **1** Art the technique or process of taking a rubbing from an uneven surface to form the basis of a work of art. **2** the practice of rubbing against the clothed body of another person to obtain sexual gratification.
– ORIGIN French, 'rubbing, friction'.
frou-frou /froofroo/ ● noun **1** a rustling noise made by someone walking in a dress. **2** frills or other ornamentation: *a little frou-frou skirt.*
– ORIGIN French.
froward /frōərd/ ● adjective archaic (of a person) difficult to deal with; contrary.
– ORIGIN Old English, 'leading away from, away'.
frown ● verb **1** furrow one's brows in an expression indicating disapproval, displeasure, or concentration. **2** (**frown on/upon**) disapprove of. ● noun an expression of this type.
– DERIVATIVES **frowning** adjective.
– ORIGIN Old French *froignier*, from *froigne* 'surly look'.
frowst /frowst/ informal, chiefly Brit. ● noun a warm stuffy atmosphere in a room. ● verb lounge about in such an atmosphere.
frowsty ● adjective (**frostier**, **frowstiest**) Brit. having a stale,

f

Thesaurus

jolly, merry, gleeful, light-hearted, exuberant, high-spirited, spirited, lively, perky, skittish, coltish, kittenish; mischievous, impish, roguish; *informal* peppy, zippy, full of beans.
front ● noun **1** *the front of the boat* FORE, foremost part, forepart, anterior, forefront, nose, head; bow, prow; foreground. **2** *a shop front* FRONTAGE, face, facing, facade; window. **3** *battlefield surgeons who work at the front* FRONT LINE, firing line, vanguard, van; trenches. **4** *the front of the queue* HEAD, beginning, start, top, lead. **5** *she kept up a brave front* APPEARANCE, air, face, manner, demeanour, bearing, pose, exterior, veneer, (outward) show, act, pretence, affectation. **6** *the shop was a front for his real business* COVER, cover-up, false front, blind, disguise, facade, mask, cloak, screen, smokescreen, camouflage. **7** *he's got a lot of front* SELF-CONFIDENCE, boldness, forwardness, pushiness, audacity, temerity, presumption, presumptuousness, cockiness, daring; *informal* nerve, face, neck, brass neck.
– OPPOSITES rear, back.
● adjective *the front runners* LEADING, lead, first, foremost; in first place.
– OPPOSITES last.
● verb *the houses fronted on a reservoir* OVERLOOK, look out on/over, face (towards), lie opposite (to); have a view of, command a view of.
– PHRASES **in front** AHEAD, to/at the fore, at the head, up ahead, in the vanguard, in the van, in the lead, leading, coming first; at the head of the queue; *informal* up front.
frontier ● noun BORDER, boundary, borderline, dividing line, demarcation line; perimeter, limit, edge, rim; marches, bounds.
frost ● noun **1** *hedges covered with frost* ICE CRYSTALS, ice, rime, verglas; hoar frost, ground frost, black frost; *informal* Jack Frost; *archaic* hoar. **2** *there was frost in his tone* COLDNESS, coolness, frostiness, ice, iciness, frigidity; hostility, unfriendliness, stiffness; *informal* stand-offishness.
frosty ● adjective **1** *a frosty morning* FREEZING, cold, icy-cold, bitter, bitterly cold, chill, wintry, frigid, glacial, arctic; frozen, icy, gelid; *informal* nippy; *Brit. informal* parky; *poetic/literary* frore, rimy. **2** *her frosty gaze* COLD, frigid, icy, glacial, unfriendly, inhospitable, unwelcoming, forbidding, hostile, stony, stern, hard.
froth ● noun *the froth on top of the beer* FOAM, head; bubbles, frothiness, fizz, effervescence; lather, suds; scum; *poetic/literary* spume.
● verb *the liquid frothed up* BUBBLE, fizz, effervesce, foam, lather; churn, seethe; *poetic/literary* spume.
frothy ● adjective **1** *a frothy liquid* FOAMING, foamy, bubbling, bubbly, fizzy, sparkling, effervescent, gassy, carbonated; sudsy; *poetic/literary* spumy, spumous. **2** *a frothy pink evening dress* FRILLY, flouncy, lacy. **3** *a frothy woman's magazine* LIGHTWEIGHT, light, superficial, shallow, slight, insubstantial; trivial, trifling, frivolous.
frown ● verb **1** *she frowned at him* SCOWL, glower, glare, lour, make a face, look daggers, give someone a black look; knit/furrow one's brows; *informal* give someone a dirty look. **2** *public displays of affection were frowned on* DISAPPROVE OF, view with disfavour, dis-

warm, and stuffy atmosphere.
– ORIGIN variant of FROWZY.
frowzy /frowzy/ (also **frowsy**) ● adjective (**frowzier**, **frowziest**) scruffy, dingy, and neglected in appearance.
– ORIGIN of unknown origin.
froze past of FREEZE.
frozen past participle of FREEZE.
FRS ● abbreviation (in the UK) Fellow of the Royal Society.
fructify /fruktifī/ ● verb (**fructifies**, **fructified**) **1** formal make or become fruitful. **2** bear fruit.
– ORIGIN Latin *fructificare*, from *fructus* 'fruit'.
fructose /fruktōz/ ● noun Chemistry a simple sugar found chiefly in honey and fruit.
– ORIGIN from Latin *fructus* 'fruit'.
frugal /froog'l/ ● adjective sparing or economical as regards money or food.
– DERIVATIVES **frugality** noun **frugally** adverb.
– ORIGIN Latin *frugalis*, from *frux* 'fruit'.
frugivore /froojivor/ ● noun Zoology an animal that feeds on fruit.
– DERIVATIVES **frugivorous** adjective.
– ORIGIN from Latin *frux* 'fruit'.
fruit ● noun **1** the sweet and fleshy product of a tree or other plant that contains seed and can be eaten as food. **2** Botany the seed-bearing structure of a plant, e.g. an acorn. **3** the result or reward of work or activity. **4** informal, derogatory, chiefly N. Amer. a male homosexual. ● verb produce fruit.
– PHRASES **bear fruit** have good results.
– ORIGIN Latin *fructus* 'enjoyment of produce, harvest', from *frui* 'enjoy'.
fruitarian ● noun a person who eats only fruit.
– DERIVATIVES **fruitarianism** noun.
fruit bat ● noun a large bat which feeds chiefly on fruit or nectar.
fruitcake ● noun **1** a cake containing dried fruit and nuts. **2** informal an eccentric or mad person.
fruit cocktail ● noun a finely chopped fruit salad, commercially produced in tins.
fruiterer ● noun chiefly Brit. a retailer of fruit.
fruit fly ● noun a small fly which feeds on fruit in both its adult and larval stages.
fruitful ● adjective **1** producing much fruit; fertile. **2** producing good results; productive.
– DERIVATIVES **fruitfully** adverb **fruitfulness** noun.
fruiting body ● noun Botany the spore-producing organ of a fungus, often seen as a toadstool.
fruition /frooish'n/ ● noun **1** the realization or fulfilment of a plan. **2** literary the state or action of producing fruit.
– ORIGIN Latin from *frui* 'enjoy'.
fruitless ● adjective **1** failing to achieve the desired results; unproductive. **2** not producing fruit.
– DERIVATIVES **fruitlessly** adverb **fruitlessness** noun.
fruitlet ● noun an immature or small fruit.
fruit machine ● noun Brit. a coin-operated gambling machine that generates combinations of symbols (typically representing fruit), certain combinations winning money for the player.
fruit salad ● noun a mixture of different types of chopped fruit served in syrup or juice.
fruit sugar ● noun another term for FRUCTOSE.
fruity ● adjective (**fruitier**, **fruitiest**) **1** of, resembling, or containing fruit. **2** (of a voice) mellow, deep, and rich. **3** Brit. informal sexually suggestive.
– DERIVATIVES **fruitiness** noun.
frump ● noun an unattractive woman who wears dowdy old-fashioned clothes.
– DERIVATIVES **frumpy** adjective.
– ORIGIN originally denoting a mocking speech or action, later sulkiness: probably from Dutch *verrompelen* 'wrinkle'.
frustrate ● verb **1** prevent (a plan or action) from progressing or succeeding. **2** prevent (someone) from doing or achieving something. **3** cause to feel dissatisfied or unfulfilled.
– DERIVATIVES **frustrated** adjective **frustrating** adjective **frustration** noun.
– ORIGIN Latin *frustrare* 'disappoint', from *frustra* 'in vain'.
fry[1] ● verb (**fries**, **fried**) **1** cook or be cooked in hot fat or oil. **2** informal (of a person) burn or overheat. ● noun (pl. **fries**) **1** a fried dish or meal. **2** (**fries**) N. Amer. short for FRENCH FRIES.
– ORIGIN Old French *frire*, from Latin *frigere*.
fry[2] ● plural noun young fish, especially when newly hatched.
– ORIGIN Old Norse.
fryer ● noun a large, deep container for frying food.
frying pan (also **frypan**) ● noun a shallow pan with a long handle, used for frying food.
– PHRASES **out of the frying pan into the fire** from a bad situ-

Thesaurus

like, look askance at, not take kindly to, take a dim view of, take exception to, object to, have a low opinion of.
– OPPOSITES smile.
frowsty ● adjective *(Brit.)* STUFFY, airless, unventilated, fusty, close, muggy, stifling; stale, musty, smelly; *N. Amer.* funky.
– OPPOSITES airy.
frowzy ● adjective **1** *a frowzy old biddy* SCRUFFY, unkempt, untidy, messy, dishevelled, slovenly, slatternly, bedraggled, down at heel, badly dressed, dowdy; *N. Amer. informal* raggedy. **2** *a frowzy room* DINGY, gloomy, dull, drab, dark, dim; stuffy, close, musty, stale, stifling; shabby, seedy, run down; *Brit.* frowsty, fuggy.
frozen ● adjective **1** *the frozen ground* ICY, ice-covered, ice-bound, frosty, frosted, gelid; frozen solid, hard, (as) hard as iron; *poetic/literary* rimy. **2** *his hands were frozen* FREEZING, icy, very cold, chilled to the bone/marrow, numb, numbed, frozen stiff; *informal* frozen to death.
– OPPOSITES boiling.
frugal ● adjective **1** *a hard-working, frugal man* THRIFTY, economical, careful, cautious, prudent, provident, unwasteful, sparing, scrimping; abstemious, abstinent, austere, self-denying, ascetic, monkish, spartan; parsimonious, miserly, niggardly, cheese-paring, penny-pinching, close-fisted; *N. Amer.* forehanded; *informal* tight-fisted, tight, stingy. **2** *their frugal breakfast* MEAGRE, scanty, scant, paltry, skimpy; plain, simple, spartan, inexpensive, cheap, economical.
– OPPOSITES extravagant, lavish.
fruit ● noun *the fruits of their labours* REWARD, benefit, profit, product, return, yield, legacy, issue; result, outcome, upshot, consequence, effect.
fruitful ● adjective **1** *a fruitful tree* FERTILE, fecund, prolific, high-yielding; fruit-bearing, fruiting. **2** *fruitful discussions* PRODUCTIVE, constructive, useful, of use, worthwhile, helpful, beneficial, valuable, rewarding, profitable, advantageous, gainful, successful, effective, effectual, well spent.
– OPPOSITES barren, futile.
fruition ● noun FULFILMENT, realization, actualization, materialization, achievement, attainment, accomplishment, resolution; success, completion, consummation, conclusion, close, finish, perfection, maturity, maturation, ripening, ripeness; implementation, execution, performance.
fruitless ● adjective FUTILE, vain, in vain, to no avail, to no effect, idle; pointless, useless, worthless, wasted, hollow; ineffectual, ineffective, inefficacious; unproductive, unrewarding, profitless, unsuccessful, unavailing, barren, for naught; abortive; *archaic* bootless.
– OPPOSITES productive.
fruity ● adjective **1** *his fruity voice* DEEP, rich, resonant, full, mellow, clear, strong, vibrant. **2** *(Brit. informal) a fruity story* BAWDY, racy, risqué, naughty, spicy, earthy, ribald, suggestive, titillating; rude, indelicate, vulgar, indecent, improper, dirty, smutty, coarse, off colour; *N. Amer.* gamy; *euphemistic* adult; *informal* blue, near the knuckle, nudge-nudge, raunchy; *Brit. informal* saucy.
frumpy ● adjective DOWDY, frumpish, unfashionable, old-fashioned; drab, dull, shabby, scruffy; *Brit. informal* mumsy.
– OPPOSITES fashionable.
frustrate ● verb **1** *his plans were frustrated* THWART, defeat, foil, block, stop, put a stop to, counter, spoil, check, baulk, disappoint, forestall, dash, scotch, quash, crush, derail, snooker; obstruct, impede, hamper, hinder, hamstring, stand in the way of, spike someone's guns; *informal* stymie, foul up, screw up, put the kibosh on, banjax, do for; *Brit. informal* scupper. **2** *the delays frustrated him* EXASPERATE, infuriate, annoy, anger, vex, irritate, irk, try someone's patience; disappoint, discontent, dissatisfy, discourage, dishearten, dispirit; *informal* aggravate, bug, miff, hack off.
– OPPOSITES help, facilitate.
frustration ● noun **1** *he clenched his fists in frustration* EXASPERATION, annoyance, anger, vexation, irritation; disappointment, dissatisfaction, discontentment, discontent; *informal* aggravation. **2** *the frustration of his attempts to introduce changes* THWARTING, defeat, prevention, foiling, blocking, spoiling, circumvention, forestall-

ation to one that is worse.

fry-up • noun Brit. informal a dish or meal of fried food.

f-stop • noun Photography a camera setting corresponding to a particular f-number.

ft • abbreviation foot or feet.

FTP • abbreviation Computing file transfer protocol, a standard for the exchange of program and data files across a network.

FTSE index (also **FT index**) • noun a figure (published by the *Financial Times*) indicating the relative prices of shares on the London Stock Exchange.
– ORIGIN abbreviation of *Financial Times Stock Exchange*.

fuchsia /fyo͞oshə/ • noun **1** an ornamental shrub with drooping tubular flowers that are typically of two contrasting colours. **2** a vivid purplish-red colour.
– ORIGIN named after the German botanist Leonhard *Fuchs* (1501–66).

fuck vulgar slang • verb **1** have sexual intercourse with. **2** damage or ruin. • noun an act of sexual intercourse. • exclamation a strong expression of annoyance or contempt.
– PHRASES **fuck about** (or **around**) spend time doing unimportant or trivial things. **fuck all** Brit. absolutely nothing. **fuck off** go away. **fuck up 1** damage or confuse emotionally. **2** do badly or ineptly.
– DERIVATIVES **fucker** noun.
– ORIGIN Germanic.

fucus /fyo͞okəss/ • noun (pl. **fuci** /fyo͞osī/) a seaweed of a large genus of brown algae having flat leathery fronds.
– DERIVATIVES **fucoid** adjective & noun.
– ORIGIN Latin, 'rock lichen, red dye, rouge', from Greek *phukos* 'seaweed'.

fuddled • adjective confused or stupefied, especially with alcohol.
– ORIGIN of unknown origin.

fuddy-duddy • noun (pl. **fuddy-duddies**) informal a person who is very old-fashioned and pompous.
– ORIGIN of unknown origin.

fudge • noun **1** a soft sweet made from sugar, butter, and milk or cream. **2** (before another noun) chiefly N. Amer. rich chocolate, used as a sauce or a filling for cakes. **3** an attempt to fudge an issue. • verb **1** present in a vague way, especially to mislead. **2** manipulate (facts or figures) so as to present a desired picture.
– ORIGIN probably from obsolete *fadge* 'to fit'.

fuehrer • noun variant spelling of FÜHRER.

fuel • noun **1** material such as coal, gas, or oil that is burned to produce heat or power. **2** food, drink, or drugs as a source of energy. **3** something that acts to inflame argument or intense emotion. • verb (**fuelled**, **fuelling**; US **fueled**, **fueling**) **1** supply or power with fuel. **2** sustain or inflame.
– ORIGIN Old French *fouaille*, from Latin *focus* 'hearth'.

fuel cell • noun a cell producing an electric current direct from a chemical reaction.

fuel injection • noun the direct introduction of fuel under pressure into the combustion units of an internal-combustion engine.
– DERIVATIVES **fuel-injected** adjective.

fug • noun Brit. informal a warm, stuffy atmosphere.
– DERIVATIVES **fuggy** adjective.
– ORIGIN of unknown origin.

fugal /fyo͞og'l/ • adjective relating to a fugue.

fugitive • noun a person who has escaped from captivity or is in hiding. • adjective quick to disappear; fleeting.
– ORIGIN Latin *fugitivus*, from *fugere* 'flee'.

fugu /fo͞ogo͞o/ • noun a pufferfish that is eaten as a Japanese delicacy, after some highly poisonous parts have been removed.
– ORIGIN Japanese.

fugue /fyo͞og/ • noun **1** Music a contrapuntal composition in which a short melody or phrase is introduced by one part and successively taken up by others. **2** Psychiatry loss of awareness of one's identity, often coupled with flight from one's usual environment.
– ORIGIN Latin *fuga* 'flight'.

führer /fyoorer/ (also **fuehrer**) • noun the title assumed by Hitler as leader of Germany.
– ORIGIN German, 'leader'.

-ful • suffix **1** (forming adjectives from nouns) full of; having the qualities of: *sorrowful*. **2** forming adjectives from adjectives or from Latin stems with little change of sense: *grateful*. **3** (forming adjectives from verbs) apt to; able to; accustomed to: *forgetful*. **4** forming nouns denoting the amount needed to fill the specified container: *bucketful*.

fulcrum /fo͝olkrəm/ • noun (pl. **fulcra** /fo͝olkrə/ or **fulcrums**) the point against which a lever is placed to get a purchase, or on which it turns or is supported.
– ORIGIN Latin, 'post of a couch', from *fulcire* 'prop up'.

fulfil (US **fulfill**) • verb (**fulfilled**, **fulfilling**) **1** achieve or realize (something desired, promised, or predicted). **2** satisfy or meet (a requirement or condition). **3** (**fulfil oneself**) gain happiness or satisfaction by fully achieving one's potential.
– DERIVATIVES **fulfilled** adjective **fulfilling** adjective.
– ORIGIN Old English, 'fill up, make full'.

fulfilment (US **fulfillment**) • noun **1** satisfaction or happiness as a result of fully developing one's abilities or character. **2** the action of fulfilling.

full[1] • adjective **1** containing or holding as much or as many as possible; having no empty space. **2** (**full of**) having a large number or quantity of. **3** not lacking or omitting anything; complete. **4** (**full of**) unable to stop talking or thinking about. **5** plump or rounded. **6** (of flavour, sound, or colour) strong, rich, or intense. • adverb **1** straight; directly. **2** very.
– PHRASES **full of oneself** very self-satisfied and with an exaggerated sense of self-worth. **full on 1** running at or providing maximum power or capacity. **2** so as to make a direct or significant impact. **full out** with maximum effort or power. **full steam** (or **speed**) **ahead** proceeding with as much speed or energy as

f

Thesaurus

ing, disappointment, derailment; obstruction, hampering, hindering; failure, collapse.

fuddled • adjective STUPEFIED, addled, befuddled, confused, muddled, bewildered, dazed, stunned, muzzy, groggy, foggy, fuzzy, vague, disorientated, disoriented, all at sea; *informal* dopey, woozy, woolly-minded, fazed, not with it; *N. Amer. informal* discombobulated.

fuddy-duddy • noun (*informal*) (OLD) FOGY, conservative, traditionalist, conformist; fossil, dinosaur, troglodyte; *Brit.* museum piece; *informal* stick-in-the-mud, square, stuffed shirt, dodo.

fudge • verb **1** *the minister tried to fudge the issue* EVADE, avoid, dodge, skirt, duck, gloss over; hedge, prevaricate, vacillate, be non-committal, stall, beat about the bush, equivocate; *Brit.* hum and haw; *informal* cop out, sit on the fence; *rare* tergiversate. **2** *the government has been fudging figures* ADJUST, manipulate, massage, put a spin on, juggle, misrepresent, misreport, bend; tamper with, tinker with, interfere with, doctor, falsify, distort; *informal* cook, fiddle with.
• noun *the latest proposals are a fudge* COMPROMISE, cover-up; spin, casuistry, sophistry; *informal* cop-out.

fuel • noun **1** *the car ran out of fuel* PETROL, diesel; power source; *N. Amer.* gasoline, gas. **2** *she added more fuel to the fire* FIREWOOD, wood, kindling, logs; coal, coke, anthracite; oil, paraffin, kerosene; heat source. **3** *we all need fuel to keep our bodies going* NOURISHMENT, food, sustenance, nutriment, nutrition. **4** *his antics added fuel to the Republican cause* ENCOURAGEMENT, ammunition, stimulus, incentive; provocation, goading.
• verb **1** *power stations fuelled by low-grade coal* POWER, fire, charge. **2** *the rumours fuelled anxiety among opposition backbenchers* FAN, feed, stoke up, inflame, intensify, stimulate, encourage, provoke, incite, whip up; sustain, keep alive.

fug • noun (*Brit. informal*) STUFFINESS, fustiness, frowstiness, staleness, stuffy atmosphere.

fuggy • adjective (*Brit. informal*) STUFFY, smoky, close, muggy, stale, fusty, unventilated, airless, stifling, heavy.
– OPPOSITES airy.

fugitive • noun *a hunted fugitive* ESCAPEE, runaway, deserter, absconder; refugee.
• adjective **1** *a fugitive criminal* ESCAPED, runaway, on the run, on the loose, at large; wanted; *informal* AWOL; *N. Amer. informal* on the lam. **2** *the fugitive nature of life* FLEETING, transient, transitory, ephemeral, fading, momentary, short-lived, short, brief, passing, impermanent, here today and gone tomorrow; *poetic/literary* evanescent.

fulfil • verb **1** *he fulfilled a lifelong ambition to visit Israel* ACHIEVE, attain, realize, actualize, make happen, succeed in, bring to completion, bring to fruition, satisfy. **2** *she failed to fulfil her duties* CARRY OUT, perform, accomplish, execute, do, discharge, conduct; complete, finish, conclude, perfect. **3** *they fulfilled the criteria* MEET, satisfy, comply with, conform to, fill, answer.

fulfilled • adjective SATISFIED, content, contented, happy, pleased;

possible. **full up** filled to capacity. **to the full** to the greatest possible extent.
– ORIGIN Old English.
full[2] ● verb clean, shrink, and felt (cloth) by heat, pressure, and moisture.
– ORIGIN probably from FULLER, influenced by Old French *fouler* 'press hard upon'.
fullback ● noun a player in a defensive position near the goal in a ball game such as soccer.
full-blooded ● adjective **1** of unmixed ancestry. **2** vigorous and wholehearted.
full-blown ● adjective fully developed; complete.
full board ● noun Brit. provision of accommodation and all meals at a hotel or guest house.
full-bodied ● adjective rich and satisfying in flavour or sound.
full bore ● adverb at full speed or maximum capacity. ● adjective **1** denoting firearms of relatively large calibre. **2** complete; thoroughgoing.
full dress ● noun clothes worn on very formal occasions. ● adjective formal and serious.
fuller ● noun a person whose occupation is fulling cloth.
– ORIGIN Old English *fullere*, from Latin *fullo*.
fullerene /fŏŏlləreen/ ● noun Chemistry a form of carbon having a molecule consisting of a large spheroidal cage of atoms.
– ORIGIN contraction of *buckminsterfullerene* (the first known example, named after the American architect Richard Buckminster Fuller, 1895–1983).
fuller's earth ● noun a type of clay used in fulling cloth and as an adsorbent.
full face ● adverb with all the face visible; facing directly at someone or something. ● adjective **1** showing all of the face. **2** covering all of the face.
full-fledged ● adjective North American term for FULLY FLEDGED.
full-frontal ● adjective with full exposure of the front of the body.
full house ● noun **1** a theatre or meeting that is filled to capacity. **2** a poker hand with three of a kind and a pair. **3** a winning card at bingo.
full marks ● plural noun the maximum award in an examination or assessment.
full moon ● noun the phase of the moon in which its whole disc is illuminated.
full-motion video ● noun digital video data that is transmitted or stored on video discs for real-time reproduction on a computer or other multimedia system.
fullness (also **fulness**) ● noun **1** the state of being full. **2** richness or abundance.
– PHRASES **in the fullness of time** after a due length of time has elapsed.
full-scale ● adjective **1** (of a model or representation) of the same size as the thing represented. **2** unrestricted in extent or intensity: *a full-scale invasion.*
full stop ● noun a punctuation mark (.) used at the end of a sentence or an abbreviation.
full-time ● adjective occupying the whole of the time available. ● adverb on a full-time basis. ● noun (**full time**) the end of a sports match.
– DERIVATIVES **full-timer** noun.
fully ● adverb **1** completely or entirely. **2** no less or fewer than: *fully 65 per cent.*
-fully ● suffix forming adverbs corresponding to adjectives ending in *-ful* (such as *sorrowfully* corresponding to *sorrowful*).
fully fashioned ● adjective (of women's clothing) shaped and seamed to fit the body.
fully fledged ● adjective **1** with fully developed wing feathers and able to fly. **2** Brit. completely developed or established; of full status.
fulmar /fŏŏlmər/ ● noun a gull-sized grey and white northern seabird of the petrel family.
– ORIGIN from Old Norse, 'stinking gull' (because of its habit of regurgitating its stomach contents when disturbed).
fulminant /fulminənt/ ● adjective Medicine (of a disease or symptom) severe and sudden in onset.
– ORIGIN from Latin *fulminare* 'strike with lightning'.
fulminate ● verb **1** express vehement protest. **2** literary explode violently or flash like lightning. **3** (of a disease or symptom) develop suddenly and severely.
– ORIGIN Latin *fulminare* 'strike with lightning', from *fulmen* 'lightning'.
fulmination ● noun an expression of vehement protest.

Thesaurus

serene, placid, untroubled, at ease, at peace.
– OPPOSITES discontented.
full ● adjective **1** *her glass was full* FILLED, filled up, filled to capacity, filled to the brim, brimming, brimful. **2** *streets full of people* CROWDED, packed, crammed, congested; teeming, swarming, thick, thronged, overcrowded, overrun; abounding, bursting, overflowing; *informal* jam-packed, wall-to-wall, stuffed, chock-a-block, chock-full, bursting at the seams, packed to the gunwales, awash. **3** *all the seats were full* OCCUPIED, taken, in use, unavailable. **4** *I'm full* REPLETE, full up, satisfied, well fed, sated, satiated, surfeited; gorged, glutted; *informal* stuffed. **5** *she'd had a full life* EVENTFUL, interesting, exciting, lively, action-packed, busy, energetic, active. **6** *a full list of available facilities* COMPREHENSIVE, thorough, exhaustive, all-inclusive, all-encompassing, all-embracing, in depth; complete, entire, whole, unabridged, uncut. **7** *a fire engine driven at full speed* MAXIMUM, top, greatest, highest. **8** *she had a full figure* PLUMP, well rounded, rounded, buxom, shapely, ample, curvaceous, voluptuous, womanly, Junoesque; *informal* busty, curvy, well upholstered, well endowed; *N. Amer. informal* zaftig. **9** *a full skirt* LOOSE-FITTING, loose, baggy, voluminous, roomy, capacious, billowing. **10** *his full baritone voice* RESONANT, rich, sonorous, deep, vibrant, full-bodied, strong, fruity, clear. **11** *the full flavour of a Bordeaux* RICH, intense, full-bodied, strong, deep.
– OPPOSITES empty, hungry, selective, thin.
● adverb **1** *she looked full into his face* DIRECTLY, right, straight, squarely, square, dead, point-blank; *informal* bang, slap (bang), plumb. **2** *you knew full well I was leaving* VERY, perfectly, quite; *informal* darn, damn, damned; *Brit. informal* jolly, bloody; *N. Amer. informal* darned.
– PHRASES **in full** IN ITS ENTIRETY, in toto, in total, unabridged, uncut. **to the full** FULLY, thoroughly, completely, to the utmost, to the limit, to the maximum, for all one's worth.
full-blooded ● adjective *a full-blooded price war* UNCOMPROMISING, all-out, out and out, committed, vigorous, strenuous, intense; unrestrained, uncontrolled, unbridled, hard-hitting, pulling no punches.
– OPPOSITES half-hearted.
full-blown ● adjective FULLY DEVELOPED, full-scale, full-blooded, fully fledged, complete, total, thorough, entire; advanced.
full-bodied ● adjective FULL-FLAVOURED, flavourful, flavoursome, full of flavour, rich, mellow, fruity, robust, strong, well-matured.
– OPPOSITES tasteless.
full-grown ● adjective ADULT, mature, grown-up, of age; fully grown, fully developed, fully fledged, in one's prime, in full bloom, ripe.
fullness ● noun **1** *the fullness of the information they provide* COMPREHENSIVENESS, completeness, thoroughness, exhaustiveness, all-inclusiveness. **2** *the fullness of her body* PLUMPNESS, roundedness, roundness, shapeliness, curvaceousness, voluptuousness, womanliness; *informal* curviness. **3** *the recording has a fullness and warmth* RESONANCE, richness, intensity, depth, vibrancy, strength, clarity.
– PHRASES **in the fullness of time** IN DUE COURSE, when the time is ripe, eventually, in time, in time to come, one day, some day, sooner or later; ultimately, finally, in the end.
full-scale ● adjective **1** *a full-scale model* FULL-SIZE, unreduced. **2** *a full-scale public inquiry* THOROUGH, comprehensive, extensive, exhaustive, complete, all-out, all-encompassing, all-inclusive, all-embracing, thoroughgoing, wide-ranging, sweeping, in-depth, far-reaching.
fully ● adverb **1** *I fully agree with him* COMPLETELY, entirely, wholly, totally, quite, utterly, perfectly, altogether, thoroughly, in all respects, in every respect, without reservation, without exception, to the hilt. **2** *fully two minutes must have passed* AT LEAST, no less than, no fewer than, easily, without exaggeration.
– OPPOSITES partly, nearly.
fully fledged ● adjective TRAINED, qualified, proficient, experienced; mature, fully developed, full grown; *Brit.* time-served.
fulminate ● verb PROTEST, rail, rage, rant, thunder, storm, vociferate, declaim, inveigh, speak out, make/take a stand; denounce, decry, condemn, criticize, censure, disparage, attack, execrate, arraign; *informal* mouth off about, kick up a stink about; *formal* excoriate.

fulness ● noun variant spelling of FULLNESS.

fulsome ● adjective **1** complimentary or flattering to an excessive degree. **2** of large size or quantity; generous or abundant: *fulsome details.*
– DERIVATIVES **fulsomely** adverb **fulsomeness** noun.
– USAGE Although the earliest sense of **fulsome** was 'abundant', this is now regarded by many as incorrect; the correct meaning today is said to be 'excessively flattering'. This gives rise to ambiguity: the possibility that while for one speaker **fulsome praise** will be a genuine compliment, for others it will be interpreted as an insult.

fumarole /fyo͞omərōl/ ● noun an opening in or near a volcano, through which hot sulphurous gases emerge.
– ORIGIN Latin *fumariolum* 'vent, hole for smoke'.

fumble ● verb **1** use the hands clumsily while doing or handling something. **2** (of the hands) do or handle something clumsily. **3** (**fumble about/around**) move about clumsily using the hands to find one's way. **4** express oneself or deal with something clumsily or nervously. **5** (in ball games) fail to catch or field (the ball) cleanly. ● noun an act of fumbling.
– DERIVATIVES **fumbler** noun **fumbling** adjective.
– ORIGIN Low German *fommeln* or Dutch *fommelen.*

fume ● noun a gas or vapour that smells strongly or is dangerous to inhale. ● verb **1** emit fumes. **2** expose (something, especially wood) to ammonia fumes in order to produce dark tints. **3** feel great anger.
– DERIVATIVES **fuming** adjective **fumy** adjective.
– ORIGIN Latin *fumus* 'smoke'.

fumigate ● verb disinfect or purify with the fumes of certain chemicals.
– DERIVATIVES **fumigant** noun **fumigation** noun **fumigator** noun.
– ORIGIN Latin *fumigare*, from *fumus* 'smoke'.

fumitory /fyo͞omitəri/ ● noun a plant with small tubular pink or white flowers and greyish leaves.
– ORIGIN Old French *fumeterre*, from Latin *fumus terrae* 'smoke of the earth' (because of its greyish leaves).

fun ● noun **1** light-hearted pleasure or amusement. **2** a source of this. **3** playfulness or good humour. ● adjective informal enjoyable.
– PHRASES **make fun of** tease or laugh at in a mocking way.
– ORIGIN from obsolete *fun* 'to cheat or hoax', of unknown origin.

function ● noun **1** an activity that is natural to or the purpose of a person or thing. **2** a large or formal social event or ceremony. **3** a computer operation corresponding to a single instruction from the user. **4** Mathematics a relation or expression involving one or more variables. **5** a variable quantity regarded as depending on another variable; a consequence: *depreciation is a function of time.* ● verb **1** work or operate in a proper or particular way. **2** (**function as**) fulfil the purpose or task of.
– DERIVATIVES **functionless** adjective.
– ORIGIN French *fonction*, from Latin *fungi* 'perform'.

functional ● adjective **1** of, relating to, or having a function. **2** designed to be practical and useful, rather than attractive. **3** working or operating. **4** (of a disease) affecting the operation rather than the structure of an organ.
– DERIVATIVES **functionality** noun **functionally** adverb.

functional food ● noun a food containing health-giving additives.

functionalism ● noun the theory that the design of an object should be governed by function rather than aesthetics.
– DERIVATIVES **functionalist** noun & adjective.

functionary ● noun (pl. **functionaries**) an official.

function key ● noun Computing a key on a computer keyboard to which software can assign a particular function.

fund ● noun **1** a sum of money saved or made available for a purpose. **2** (**funds**) financial resources. **3** a large stock. ● verb provide with a fund.
– DERIVATIVES **funding** noun.
– ORIGIN Latin *fundus* 'bottom, piece of landed property'.

fundament ● noun **1** the foundation or basis of something. **2** humorous a person's bottom.

f

Thesaurus

fulmination ● noun PROTEST, objection, complaint, rant, tirade, diatribe, harangue, invective, railing, obloquy; denunciation, condemnation, criticism, censure, attack, broadside, brickbats; *formal* excoriation; *poetic/literary* philippic.

fulsome ● adjective EXCESSIVE, extravagant, overdone, immoderate, inordinate, over-appreciative, flattering, adulatory, fawning, unctuous, ingratiating, cloying, saccharine; enthusiastic, effusive, rapturous, glowing, gushing, profuse, generous, lavish; *informal* over the top, OTT, smarmy.

fumble ● verb **1** *he fumbled for his keys* GROPE, fish, search blindly, scrabble around. **2** *he fumbled about in the dark* STUMBLE, blunder, flounder, lumber, stagger, totter, lurch; feel one's way, grope one's way. **3** *the keeper fumbled the ball* MISS, drop, mishandle; misfield. **4** *he fumbled his lines* MESS UP, make a mess of, bungle, mismanage, mishandle, spoil; *informal* make a hash of, fluff, botch, muff; *Brit. informal* cock up; *N. Amer. informal* flub.
● noun *a fumble from the goalkeeper* SLIP, mistake, error, gaffe; *informal* slip-up, boo-boo; *Brit. informal* cock-up, boob.

fume ● noun **1** *a fire giving off toxic fumes* SMOKE, vapour, gas, effluvium; exhaust; pollution. **2** *stale wine fumes* SMELL, odour, stink, reek, stench; *Brit. informal* pong, niff; *Scottish informal* guff; *N. Amer. informal* funk; *poetic/literary* miasma.
● verb **1** *fragments of lava were fuming and sizzling* EMIT SMOKE, emit gas, smoke; *archaic* reek. **2** *Ella was still fuming at his arrogance* BE FURIOUS, be enraged, be very angry, seethe, be livid, be incensed, be worked up, boil, be beside oneself, spit; rage, rant and rave; *informal* be hot under the collar, be steamed up, foam at the mouth, see red.

fumigate ● verb DISINFECT, purify, sterilize, sanitize, decontaminate, cleanse, clean out.

fun ● noun **1** *I joined in with the fun* ENJOYMENT, entertainment, amusement, pleasure; jollification, merrymaking; recreation, diversion, leisure, relaxation; good time, great time; *informal* R and R (rest and recreation), living it up, a ball, beer and skittles. **2** *she's full of fun* MERRIMENT, cheerfulness, cheeriness, jollity, joviality, jocularity, high spirits, gaiety, mirth, laughter, hilarity, glee, gladness, light-heartedness, levity. **3** *he became a figure of fun* RIDICULE, derision, mockery, laughter, scorn, contempt, jeering, sneering, jibing, teasing, taunting.
– OPPOSITES boredom, misery.
● adjective *(informal) a fun evening* ENJOYABLE, entertaining, amusing, diverting, pleasurable, pleasing, agreeable, interesting.
– OPPOSITES boring.
– PHRASES **in fun** PLAYFUL, in jest, as a joke, tongue in cheek, light-hearted, for a laugh, to tease, teasing. **make fun of** TEASE, poke fun at, chaff, rag; ridicule, mock, laugh at, taunt, jeer at, scoff at, deride; parody, lampoon, caricature, satirize; *informal* take the mickey out of, rib, kid, have on, pull someone's leg, send up; *Brit. informal* wind up; *N. Amer. informal* goof on, rag on, razz.

function ● noun **1** *the main function of the machine* PURPOSE, task, use, role. **2** *my function was to select and train the recruits* RESPONSIBILITY, duty, role, concern, province, activity, assignment, obligation, charge; task, job, mission, undertaking, commission; capacity, post, situation, office, occupation, employment, business. **3** *a function attended by local dignitaries* SOCIAL EVENT, party, social occasion, affair, gathering, reception, soirée, jamboree, gala; *N. Amer.* levee; *informal* do, bash, shindig; *Brit. informal* jolly, beanfeast.
● verb **1** *the electrical system had ceased to function* WORK, go, run, be in working/running order, operate, be operative. **2** *the museum functions as an educational and study centre* ACT, serve, operate; perform, work, play the role of, do duty as.

functional ● adjective **1** *a small functional kitchen* PRACTICAL, useful, utilitarian, utility, workaday, serviceable; minimalist, plain, simple, basic, modest, unadorned, unostentatious, no-frills, without frills; impersonal, characterless, soulless, institutional, clinical. **2** *the machine is now fully functional* WORKING, in working order, functioning, in service, in use; going, running, operative, operating, in operation, in commission, in action; *informal* up and running.
– OPPOSITES impractical.

functionary ● noun OFFICIAL, office-holder, public servant, civil servant, bureaucrat, administrator, apparatchik; *Brit.* jack-in-office.

fund ● noun **1** *an emergency fund for refugees* COLLECTION, kitty, reserve, pool, purse; endowment, foundation, trust, grant, investment; savings, nest egg; *informal* stash. **2** *I was very short of funds* MONEY, cash, ready money; wealth, means, assets, resources, savings, capital, reserves, the wherewithal; *informal* dough, bread, loot, dosh, the ready; *Brit. informal* lolly, spondulicks. **3** *his fund of stories* STOCK, store, supply, accumulation, collection, bank, pool; mine, reservoir, storehouse, treasury, treasure house, hoard, repository.
● verb *the agency was funded by the Treasury* FINANCE, pay for, back, capitalize, sponsor, put up the money for, subsidize, under-

– ORIGIN Latin *fundamentum*, from *fundare* 'to found'.
fundamental ● adjective of or serving as a foundation or core; of central importance. ● noun a central or primary rule or principle.
– DERIVATIVES **fundamentally** adverb.
fundamentalism ● noun **1** a form of Protestant Christianity which upholds belief in the strict and literal interpretation of the Bible. **2** the strict maintenance of the ancient or fundamental doctrines of any religion or ideology.
– DERIVATIVES **fundamentalist** noun & adjective.
fundamental note ● noun Music the lowest note of a chord.
fundholding ● noun (in the UK) a former system of state funding in which a general practitioner controls their own budget for the purchase of hospital services.
– DERIVATIVES **fundholder** noun.
fundie /fundi/ (also **fundi**) ● noun (pl. **fundies** or **fundis**) informal a religious fundamentalist.

f

fund-raiser ● noun **1** a person engaged in seeking financial support for an organization or cause. **2** an event held to generate such financial support.
– DERIVATIVES **fund-raising** noun.
funeral ● noun a ceremony in which a dead person is buried or cremated.
– PHRASES **it's one's funeral** informal it is one's own responsibility (used to imply that an undesirable outcome is possible).
– ORIGIN Latin *funeralia*, from *funus* 'funeral, death, corpse'.
funeral director ● noun an undertaker.
funeral parlour (also **funeral home**) ● noun an establishment where the dead are prepared for burial or cremation.
funerary /fyoonərəri, -nəri/ ● adjective relating to a funeral or the commemoration of the dead.
funereal /fyooneeriəl/ ● adjective having the sombre character appropriate to a funeral.
funfair ● noun chiefly Brit. a fair consisting of rides, sideshows, and other amusements.
fungi plural of FUNGUS.
fungible /funjib'l/ ● adjective Law (of goods contracted for without an individual specimen being specified) interchangeable with other identical items.
– ORIGIN from Latin *fungi* 'perform, enjoy'.
fungicide /funjisīd/ ● noun a chemical that destroys fungus.
– DERIVATIVES **fungicidal** adjective.
fungus /funggəss/ ● noun (pl. **fungi** /funggī/) any of a large group of spore-producing organisms which feed on organic matter and include moulds, yeast, mushrooms, and toadstools.
– DERIVATIVES **fungal** adjective **fungoid** adjective.
– ORIGIN Latin, perhaps from Greek *spongos* 'sponge'.
funicular /fyoonikjələr/ ● adjective (of a railway on a steep slope) operated by cable with ascending and descending cars counterbalanced. ● noun a funicular railway.
– ORIGIN from Latin *funiculus* 'little rope'.
funk[1] informal ● noun (also **blue funk**) a state of panic or depression. ● verb avoid out of fear.
– ORIGIN perhaps from FUNK[2] in the informal sense 'tobacco smoke', or from obsolete Flemish *fonck* 'disturbance, agitation'.
funk[2] ● noun a style of popular dance music of US black origin, having a strong rhythm that typically accentuates the first beat in the bar.
– ORIGIN perhaps from French dialect *funkier* 'blow smoke on'.
funkster ● noun informal a performer or fan of funk music.
funky ● adjective (**funkier**, **funkiest**) informal **1** (of music) having a strong dance rhythm. **2** unconventionally modern and stylish.
– DERIVATIVES **funkily** adverb **funkiness** noun.
funnel ● noun **1** a utensil that is wide at the top and narrow at the bottom, used for guiding liquid or powder into a small opening. **2** a metal chimney on a ship or steam engine. ● verb (**funnelled**, **funnelling**; US **funneled**, **funneling**) guide or move through or as if through a funnel.
– ORIGIN Provençal *fonilh*, from Latin *fundibulum*, from *infundere* 'pour into'.
funnel-web spider ● noun a dangerously venomous Australian spider that builds a funnel-shaped web.
funny ● adjective (**funnier**, **funniest**) **1** causing laughter or amusement. **2** strange; peculiar. **3** arousing suspicion. **4** informal slightly unwell; out of sorts. ● noun (**funnies**) informal **1** amusing jokes. **2** N. Amer. the comic strips in newspapers.
– DERIVATIVES **funnily** adverb **funniness** noun.
funny bone ● noun informal the part of the elbow over which the ulnar nerve passes, which may cause numbness and pain if knocked.
funny farm ● noun informal a psychiatric hospital.
funny man ● noun a professional clown or comedian.
funny money ● noun informal currency that is forged or otherwise worthless.
fun run ● noun informal an uncompetitive run for sponsored runners, held in support of a charity.
funster ● noun informal a joker.
fur ● noun **1** the short, soft hair of certain animals. **2** the skin of an animal with fur on it, used in making garments. **3** a coat made from fur. **4** Brit. a coating formed by hard water on the inside surface of a pipe, kettle, etc. **5** a coating formed on the tongue as a symptom of sickness. ● verb (**furred**, **furring**) Brit. coat or clog with a deposit.
– PHRASES **the fur will fly** informal there will be a dramatic argument.
– DERIVATIVES **furred** adjective.
– ORIGIN from Old French *forrer* 'to line, sheathe', from *forre* 'sheath'.

Thesaurus

write, endow, support, maintain; *informal* foot the bill for, pick up the tab for; *N. Amer. informal* bankroll, stake.
fundamental ● adjective BASIC, underlying, core, foundational, rudimentary, elemental, elementary, basal, root; primary, prime, cardinal, first, principal, chief, key, central, vital, essential, important, indispensable, necessary, crucial, pivotal, critical; structural, organic, constitutional, inherent, intrinsic.
– OPPOSITES secondary, unimportant.
fundamentally ● adverb *she was, fundamentally, a good person* ESSENTIALLY, in essence, basically, at heart, at bottom, deep down, au fond; primarily, above all, first and foremost, first of all; *informal* at the end of the day, when all is said and done, when you get right down to it.
fundamentals ● plural noun BASICS, essentials, rudiments, foundations, basic principles, first principles, preliminaries; crux, crux of the matter, heart of the matter, essence, core, heart, base, bedrock; *informal* nuts and bolts, nitty-gritty, brass tacks, ABC.
funeral ● noun **1** *he'd attended a funeral* BURIAL, interment, entombment, committal, inhumation, laying to rest; cremation; obsequies, last offices; *formal* exequies; *archaic* sepulture. **2** *(informal) remember, it was you who asked—it's your funeral* RESPONSIBILITY, problem, worry, concern, business, affair; *informal* headache; *Brit. informal* lookout.
funereal ● adjective **1** *the funereal atmosphere* SOMBRE, gloomy, mournful, melancholy, lugubrious, sepulchral, miserable, doleful, woeful, sad, sorrowful, cheerless, joyless, bleak, dismal, depressing, dreary; grave, solemn, serious; *poetic/literary* dolorous. **2** *funereal colours* DARK, black, drab.
– OPPOSITES cheerful.
fungus ● noun MUSHROOM, toadstool; mould, mildew, rust; *Biology* saprophyte.
– RELATED TERMS myco-
funk *(informal)* ● noun **1** *he put us all into a funk* PANIC, state of fear, fluster; *informal* cold sweat, state, stew, flap, tizzy, tizz; *Brit. informal* blue funk, heebie-jeebies; *N. Amer. informal* twit.
● verb *I'm certain he funked it* AVOID, evade, dodge, run away from, baulk at, flinch from; *informal* chicken out of, duck out of, wriggle out of, cop out of, get out of.
funnel ● noun **1** *fluid was poured through the funnel* TUBE, pipe, channel, conduit. **2** *smoke poured from the ship's funnels* CHIMNEY, flue, vent.
● verb *the money was funnelled back into Europe* CHANNEL, feed, direct, convey, move, pass; pour, filter.
funny ● adjective **1** *a very funny film* AMUSING, humorous, witty, comic, comical, droll, facetious, jocular, jokey; hilarious, hysterical, riotous, uproarious; entertaining, diverting, sparkling, scintillating; silly, farcical, slapstick; *informal* side-splitting, rib-tickling, laugh-a-minute, wacky, zany, waggish, off the wall, a scream, rich, priceless; *informal, dated* killing. **2** *a funny coincidence* STRANGE, peculiar, odd, queer, weird, bizarre, curious, freakish, freak, quirky; mysterious, mystifying, puzzling, perplexing; unusual, uncommon, anomalous, irregular, abnormal, exceptional, singular, out of the ordinary, extraordinary; *Brit. informal, dated* rum. **3** *there's something funny about him* SUSPICIOUS, suspect, dubious, untrustworthy, questionable; *informal* shady, fishy; *Brit. informal* dodgy.

furbelow ● noun **1** a flounce on a skirt or petticoat. **2** (**furbelows**) showy trimmings.
– ORIGIN French *falbala* 'trimming, flounce'.
furious ● adjective **1** extremely angry. **2** full of energy or intensity.
– DERIVATIVES **furiously** adverb.
– ORIGIN Latin *furiosus*, from *furia* 'fury'.
furl ● verb roll or fold up neatly and securely.
– DERIVATIVES **furled** adjective.
– ORIGIN French *ferler*, from Old French *fer, ferm* 'firm' + *lier* 'bind'.
furlong ● noun an eighth of a mile, 220 yards.
– ORIGIN from the Old English words for 'furrow + 'long' (originally denoting the length of a furrow in a common field).
furlough /furlō/ ● noun leave of absence, especially from military duty. ● verb US grant furlough to.
– ORIGIN Dutch *verlof*.
furnace ● noun **1** an enclosed chamber in which material can be heated to very high temperatures. **2** a very hot place.
– ORIGIN Latin *fornax*, from *fornus* 'oven'.
furnish ● verb **1** provide (a room or building) with furniture and fittings. **2** (**furnish with**) supply with (equipment or information). **3** be a source of; provide.
– DERIVATIVES **furnished** adjective **furnisher** noun.
– ORIGIN Old French *furnir*.
furnishing ● noun **1** (**furnishings**) furniture and fittings in a room or building. **2** denoting fabrics used for curtains or upholstery: *furnishing fabrics*.
furniture ● noun **1** the movable articles that are used to make a room or building suitable for living or working in, such as tables, chairs, or desks. **2** the small accessories or fittings that are required for a particular task or function: *door furniture*.
– PHRASES **a part of the furniture** informal a person or thing that has become so familiar as to be unnoticed.
– ORIGIN French *fourniture*, from *fournir* 'to furnish'.
furore /fyoorori/ (US **furor** /fyooror/) ● noun an outbreak of public anger or excitement.
– ORIGIN Italian, from Latin *furere* 'be mad, rage'.
furphy /furfi/ ● noun (pl. **furphies**) Austral. informal a far-fetched rumour.
– ORIGIN from the name painted on water and sanitary carts manufactured by the *Furphy* family of Shepparton, Victoria.
furrier /furriər/ ● noun a person who prepares or deals in furs.
furrow ● noun **1** a long, narrow trench made in the ground by a plough. **2** a rut or groove. **3** a deep wrinkle on a person's face. ● verb **1** make a furrow in. **2** mark or be marked with furrows.
– ORIGIN Old English.
furry ● adjective (**furrier**, **furriest**) covered with or resembling fur.
– DERIVATIVES **furriness** noun.
fur seal ● noun a gregarious eared seal whose thick underside fur is used commercially as sealskin.
further used as comparative of FAR. ● adverb (also **farther**) **1** at, to, or by a greater distance. **2** over a greater expanse of space or time. **3** beyond the point already reached. **4** at or to a more advanced or desirable stage. **5** in addition; also. ● adjective **1** (also **farther**) more distant in space. **2** additional. ● verb help the progress or development of.
– PHRASES **further to** formal following on from (used especially at the beginning of a letter).
– USAGE Is there any difference between **further** and **farther**? In the sense 'at, to, or by a greater distance' they may be used interchangeably: *she moved further down the train* and *she moved farther down the train* are both correct. However **further** is a much commoner word, and in addition it is used in certain abstract contexts, for example in references to time, in which it would be unusual to substitute **farther**, e.g. *have you anything further to say?; without further delay*.
– ORIGIN Old English, related to FORTH.
furtherance ● noun the advancement of a scheme or interest.
further education ● noun Brit. education below degree level for people above school age.
furthermore ● adverb in addition; besides.
furthermost (also **farthermost**) ● adjective at the greatest distance from a central point or implicit standpoint.
furthest (also **farthest**) used as superlative of FAR. ● adjective **1** situated at the greatest distance. **2** covering the greatest area or distance. ● adverb **1** at or by the greatest distance. **2** over the greatest distance or area. **3** to the most extreme or advanced point.
furtive ● adjective characterized by guilty or evasive secrecy; stealthy.
– DERIVATIVES **furtively** adverb **furtiveness** noun.
– ORIGIN Latin *furtivus*, from *furtum* 'theft'.
fury ● noun (pl. **furies**) **1** extreme anger. **2** extreme strength or violence in an action or a natural phenomenon. **2** (**Fury**) Greek Mythology a spirit of punishment, often represented as one of three goddesses.
– PHRASES **like fury** informal with great energy or effort.
– ORIGIN Latin *furia*, from *furere* 'be mad, rage'.

f

Thesaurus

– OPPOSITES serious, unsurprising, trustworthy.
fur ● noun HAIR, wool; coat, fleece, pelt; *Zoology* pelage.
furious ● adjective **1** *he was furious when he learned about it* ENRAGED, infuriated, very angry, irate, incensed, raging, incandescent, fuming, ranting, raving, seething, beside oneself, outraged; *informal* mad, hopping mad, wild, livid, boiling, apoplectic, hot under the collar, on the warpath, foaming at the mouth, steamed up, in a paddy, fit to be tied; *poetic/literary* wrathful. **2** *a furious debate* HEATED, hot, passionate, fiery, 'lively'; fierce, vehement, violent, wild, tumultuous, turbulent, tempestuous, stormy.
– OPPOSITES calm.
furnish ● verb **1** *the bedrooms are elegantly furnished* FIT OUT, provide with furniture, appoint, outfit; *Brit. informal* do out. **2** *grooms furnished us with horses for our journey* SUPPLY, provide, equip, provision, issue, kit out, present, give, offer, afford, purvey, bestow; *informal* fix up.
furniture ● noun FURNISHINGS, fittings, fitments, movables, appointments, effects; *Law* chattels; *informal* stuff, things.
furore ● noun COMMOTION, uproar, outcry, fuss, upset, brouhaha, palaver, pother, tempest, agitation, pandemonium, disturbance, hubbub, rumpus, tumult, turmoil; stir, excitement; *informal* song and dance, to-do, hoo-ha, hullabaloo, ballyhoo, flap, stink, kerfuffle; *Brit. informal* carry-on.
furrow ● noun **1** *furrows in a ploughed fields* GROOVE, trench, rut, trough, channel, hollow. **2** *the furrows on either side of her mouth* WRINKLE, line, crease, crinkle, crow's foot, corrugation.
● verb *his brow furrowed* WRINKLE, crease, line, crinkle, pucker, screw up, scrunch up, corrugate.
furry ● adjective COVERED WITH FUR, hairy, downy, fleecy, soft, fluffy, fuzzy, woolly.
further ● adverb *further, it gave him an excellent excuse not to attend* FURTHERMORE, moreover, what's more, also, additionally, in addition, besides, as well, too, to boot, on top of that, over and above that, into the bargain, by the same token; *archaic* withal.
● adjective **1** *the further side of the field* MORE DISTANT, more remote, remoter, further away/off, farther (away/off); far, other, opposite. **2** *further information* ADDITIONAL, more, extra, supplementary, supplemental, other; new, fresh.
● verb *an attempt to further his career* PROMOTE, advance, forward, develop, facilitate, aid, assist, help, help along, lend a hand to, abet; expedite, hasten, speed up, accelerate, step up, spur on, oil the wheels of, give a push to, boost, encourage, cultivate, nurture, foster.
– OPPOSITES impede.
furtherance ● noun PROMOTION, furthering, advancement, forwarding, development, facilitation, aiding, assisting, helping, abetting; hastening, acceleration, boosting, encouragement, cultivation, nurturing, fostering.
– OPPOSITES hindrance.
furthermore ● adverb MOREOVER, further, what's more, also, additionally, in addition, besides, as well, too, to boot, on top of that, over and above that, into the bargain, by the same token; *archaic* withal.
furthest ● adjective MOST DISTANT, most remote, remotest, furthest/farthest away, farthest, furthermost, farthermost; outlying, outer, outermost, extreme, uttermost, ultimate; *archaic* outmost.
– OPPOSITES nearest.
furtive ● adjective SECRETIVE, secret, surreptitious, clandestine, hidden, covert, conspiratorial, cloak-and-dagger, hole-and-corner, backstairs, hugger-mugger; sly, sneaky, under-the-table; sidelong, sideways, oblique, indirect; *informal* hush-hush, shifty.
– OPPOSITES open.
fury ● noun **1** *she exploded with fury* RAGE, anger, wrath, outrage,

furze ● noun another term for GORSE.
– ORIGIN Old English.
fuse[1] ● verb **1** join, blend, or coalesce to form a single entity. **2** melt (a material or object) with intense heat, so as to join it with something else. **3** Brit. (with reference to an electrical appliance) stop or cause to stop working when a fuse melts. **4** provide (a circuit or electrical appliance) with a fuse. ● noun a safety device consisting of a strip of wire that melts and breaks an electric circuit if the current exceeds a safe level.
– ORIGIN from Latin *fundere* 'pour, melt'.
fuse[2] (also **fuze**) ● noun **1** a length of material along which a small flame moves to explode a bomb or firework. **2** a device in a bomb that controls the timing of the explosion. ● verb fit a fuse to (a bomb).
– ORIGIN Latin *fusus* 'spindle'.
fuse box ● noun a box or board housing the fuses for circuits in a building.

f

fuselage /fyoozəlaazh/ ● noun the main body of an aircraft.
– ORIGIN French, from *fuseler* 'shape into a spindle'.
fusible ● adjective able to be fused or melted easily.
fusil /fyoozil/ ● noun historical a light musket.
– ORIGIN originally denoting a flint: from French, from Latin *focus* 'hearth, fire'.
Fusilier /fyoozileer/ ● noun a member of any of several British regiments formerly armed with fusils.
fusillade /fyoozilayd/ ● noun a series of shots fired at the same time or in rapid succession.
– ORIGIN French.
fusilli /fyoozeeli/ ● plural noun pasta pieces in the form of short spirals.
– ORIGIN Italian, 'little spindles'.
fusion ● noun **1** the process or result of fusing. **2** a reaction in which light atomic nuclei fuse to form a heavier nucleus, releasing much energy. **3** music that is a mixture of different styles, especially jazz and rock.
– DERIVATIVES **fusionist** noun.
– ORIGIN Latin, from *fundere* 'pour, melt'.
fuss ● noun **1** a display of unnecessary or excessive excitement, activity, or interest. **2** a protest or complaint. ● verb **1** show unnecessary or excessive concern about something. **2** Brit. disturb or bother. **3** treat with excessive attention or affection.
– PHRASES **not be fussed** Brit. informal not have strong feelings about something.
– ORIGIN perhaps Anglo-Irish.
fusspot ● noun informal a fussy person.
fussy ● adjective (**fussier**, **fussiest**) **1** fastidious about one's requirements and hard to please. **2** full of unnecessary detail or decoration.
– DERIVATIVES **fussily** adverb **fussiness** noun.
fustian /fustiən/ ● noun a thick, hard-wearing twilled cloth.
– ORIGIN from Latin *pannus fustaneus* 'cloth from *Fostat*', a suburb of Cairo.
fusty ● adjective (**fustier**, **fustiest**) **1** smelling stale, damp, or stuffy. **2** old-fashioned.
– DERIVATIVES **fustiness** noun.
– ORIGIN Old French *fuste* 'smelling of the cask'.
futile ● adjective producing no useful result; pointless.
– DERIVATIVES **futilely** adverb **futility** noun.
– ORIGIN Latin *futilis* 'leaky, futile'.
futon /footon/ ● noun a padded unsprung mattress originating in Japan, that can be rolled up.
– ORIGIN Japanese.
future ● noun **1** (**the future**) time that is still to come. **2** events or conditions occurring or existing in that time. **3** a prospect of success or happiness: *I might have a future as an artist.* **4** Grammar a tense of verbs expressing events that have not yet happened. **5** (**futures**) contracts for assets bought at agreed prices but delivered and paid for later. ● adjective **1** existing or occurring in the future. **2** planned or destined to hold a specified position: *his future wife.* **3** Grammar (of a tense) expressing an event yet to happen.
– PHRASES **in future** from now onwards.
– ORIGIN from Latin *futurus* 'going to be'.
future perfect ● noun Grammar a tense of verbs expressing expected completion in the future, in English exemplified by *will have done.*
future-proof ● adjective (of a product) unlikely to become obsolete.
future shock ● noun a state of distress or disorientation due to rapid social or technological change.
Futurism ● noun an artistic movement launched in Italy in 1909, which strongly rejected traditional forms and embraced modern technology.
futurist ● noun **1** (**Futurist**) an adherent of Futurism. **2** a person who studies the future and makes predictions about it. ● adjective **1** (**Futurist**) relating to Futurism or the Futurists. **2** relating to a vision of the future.
futuristic ● adjective **1** having or involving very modern technology or design. **2** (of a film or book) set in the future.
– DERIVATIVES **futuristically** adverb.

Thesaurus

spleen, temper; crossness, indignation, umbrage, annoyance, exasperation; *poetic/literary* ire, choler. **2** *the fury of the storm* FIERCENESS, ferocity, violence, turbulence, tempestuousness, savagery; severity, intensity, vehemence, force, forcefulness, power, strength. **3** *she turned on Mother like a fury* VIRAGO, hellcat, termagant, spitfire, vixen, shrew, harridan, dragon, gorgon; (**Furies**) *Greek Mythology* Eumenides.
– OPPOSITES good humour, mildness.
fuse ● verb **1** *a band which fuses rap with rock* COMBINE, amalgamate, put together, join, unite, marry, blend, merge, meld, mingle, integrate, intermix, intermingle, synthesize; coalesce, compound, alloy; *technical* admix; *poetic/literary* commingle. **2** *metal fused to a base of coloured glass* BOND, stick, bind, weld, solder; melt, smelt. **3** *(Brit.) a light had fused* SHORT-CIRCUIT, stop working, trip; *informal* go, blow.
– OPPOSITES separate.
fusillade ● noun SALVO, volley, barrage, bombardment, cannonade, battery, burst, blast, hail, shower, rain, stream; *historical* broadside.
fusion ● noun BLEND, blending, combination, amalgamation, joining, union, marrying, bonding, merging, melding, mingling, integration, intermixture, intermingling, synthesis; coalescence.
fuss ● noun **1** *what's all the fuss about?* ADO, excitement, agitation, pother, stir, commotion, confusion, disturbance, brouhaha, uproar, furore, palaver, storm in a teacup, much ado about nothing; bother, fluster, flurry, bustle; *informal* hoo-ha, to-do, ballyhoo, song and dance, performance, pantomime, kerfuffle; *Brit. informal* carry-on; *N. Amer. informal* fuss and feathers. **2** *they settled in with very little fuss* BOTHER, trouble, inconvenience, effort, exertion, labour; *informal* hassle. **3** *he didn't put up a fuss* PROTEST, complaint, objection, grumble, grouse; *informal* gripe.
● verb *he was still fussing about his clothes* WORRY, fret, be anxious, be agitated, make a big thing out of; make a mountain out of a molehill; *informal* flap, be in a tizzy, be in a stew, make a meal of.
fussy ● adjective **1** *he's very fussy about what he eats* FINICKY, particular, over-particular, fastidious, discriminating, selective, dainty; hard to please, difficult, exacting, demanding; faddish; *informal* pernickety, choosy, picky, old womanish; *Brit. informal* faddy; *N. Amer. informal* persnickety. **2** *a fussy, frilly bridal gown* OVERELABORATE, over-decorated, ornate, fancy, overdone; busy, cluttered.
fusty ● adjective **1** *the room smelt fusty* STALE, musty, dusty; stuffy, airless, unventilated; damp, mildewed, mildewy; *Brit.* frowsty. **2** *a fusty conservative* OLD-FASHIONED, out of date, outdated, behind the times, antediluvian, backward-looking; fogeyish; *informal* square, out of the ark.
– OPPOSITES fresh.
futile ● adjective FRUITLESS, vain, pointless, useless, ineffectual, ineffective, inefficacious, to no effect, of no use, in vain, to no avail, unavailing; unsuccessful, failed, thwarted; unproductive, barren, unprofitable, abortive; impotent, hollow, empty, forlorn, idle, hopeless; *archaic* bootless.
– OPPOSITES useful.
futility ● noun FRUITLESSNESS, pointlessness, uselessness, vanity, ineffectiveness, inefficacy; failure, barrenness, unprofitability; impotence, hollowness, emptiness, forlornness, hopelessness; *archaic* bootlessness.
future ● noun **1** *his plans for the future* TIME TO COME, time ahead; what lies ahead, coming times. **2** *she knew her future lay in acting* DESTINY, fate, fortune; prospects, expectations, chances.
– OPPOSITES past.
● adjective **1** *a future date* LATER, to come, following, ensuing, succeeding, subsequent, coming. **2** *his future wife* TO BE, destined; intended, planned, prospective.

futurity /fyootyooriti/ ● noun (pl. **futurities**) **1** the future time. **2** a future event.

futurology ● noun systematic forecasting of the future based on present trends.
– DERIVATIVES **futurologist** noun.

fuze ● noun variant spelling of FUSE².

fuzz¹ ● noun **1** a frizzy mass of hair or fibre. **2** a blurred image. ● verb make or become fuzzy.
– DERIVATIVES **fuzzed** adjective.
– ORIGIN probably Low German or Dutch.

fuzz² ● noun (**the fuzz**) informal the police.
– ORIGIN of unknown origin.

fuzzy ● adjective (**fuzzier, fuzziest**) **1** having a frizzy texture or appearance. **2** indistinct or vague. **3** Computing & Logic referring to a form of set theory and logic in which predicates may have degrees of applicability, rather than simply being true or false.
– PHRASES **warm and fuzzy** N. Amer. informal sentimental.
– DERIVATIVES **fuzzily** adverb **fuzziness** noun.

fuzzy logic ● noun a form of logic in which predicates can have fractional values rather than simply being true or false.

F-word ● noun euphemistic the word 'fuck'.

FX ● abbreviation visual or sound effects.
– ORIGIN from the pronunciation of the two syllables of *effects*.

-fy ● suffix **1** (added to nouns) forming verbs denoting making or producing: *speechify*. **2** denoting transformation or the process of making into: *petrify*. **3** forming verbs denoting the making of a state defined by an adjective: *falsify*. **4** forming verbs expressing a causative sense: *horrify*.
– ORIGIN from Latin *-ficare*, from *facere* 'do, make'.

FYI ● abbreviation for your information.

f

Thesaurus

– PHRASES **in future** FROM NOW ON, after this, in the future, from this day forward, hence, henceforward, subsequently, in time to come; *formal* hereafter.

fuzz¹ ● noun *the soft fuzz on his cheeks* HAIR, down; fur, fluff.

fuzz² ● noun *(informal) we'd better call the fuzz.* See POLICE noun.

fuzzy ● adjective **1** *her fuzzy hair* FRIZZY, fluffy, woolly; downy, soft; *N. Amer. informal* nappy. **2** *a fuzzy picture* BLURRY, blurred, indistinct, unclear, bleary, misty, distorted, out of focus, unfocused, lacking definition, nebulous; ill-defined, indefinite, vague, hazy, imprecise, inexact, loose, woolly. **3** *my mind was fuzzy* CONFUSED, muddled, addled, fuddled, befuddled, groggy, disoriented, disorientated, mixed up, fazed, foggy, dizzy, stupefied, benumbed.

Gg

G[1] (also **g**) • noun (pl. **Gs** or **G's**) **1** the seventh letter of the alphabet. **2** denoting the next item after F in a set. **3** Music the fifth note in the diatonic scale of C major.

G[2] • abbreviation **1** giga- (10^9). **2** N. Amer. informal grand (a thousand dollars). **3** the force exerted by the earth's gravitational field. • symbol Physics the gravitational constant (6.67×10^{-11} N m^2 kg^{-2}).

g • abbreviation **1** Chemistry gas. **2** gram(s). • symbol Physics the acceleration due to gravity (9.81 m s^{-2}).

G7 • abbreviation Group of Seven.

GA • abbreviation Georgia.

Ga • symbol the chemical element gallium.

gab informal • verb (**gabbed**, **gabbing**) talk at length. • noun talk; chatter.
– PHRASES **the gift of the gab** the ability to speak with eloquence and fluency.
– DERIVATIVES **gabby** adjective (**gabbier**, **gabbiest**).
– ORIGIN from GOB[1].

gabardine • noun variant spelling of GABERDINE.

gabble • verb talk rapidly and unintelligibly. • noun rapid, unintelligible talk.
– DERIVATIVES **gabbler** noun.
– ORIGIN Dutch *gabbelen.*

gabbro /gabrō/ • noun (pl. **gabbros**) a dark, coarse-grained igneous rock of crystalline texture.
– DERIVATIVES **gabbroic** adjective.
– ORIGIN Italian, from Latin *glaber* 'smooth'.

gaberdine /gabbərdeen/ • noun **1** a smooth, durable twill-woven worsted or cotton cloth. **2** Brit. a raincoat made of gaberdine.
– ORIGIN Old French *gauvardine*, perhaps from High German *wallevart* 'pilgrimage' and originally 'a garment worn by a pilgrim'.

gable • noun **1** the triangular upper part of a wall at the end of a ridged roof. **2** a gable-shaped canopy over a window or door.
– DERIVATIVES **gabled** adjective.
– ORIGIN Old Norse.

Gabonese /gaabəneez/ • noun (pl. same) a person from Gabon, a country in West Africa. • adjective relating to Gabon.

gad • verb (**gadded**, **gadding**) (**gad about/around**) informal go around from one place to another seeking pleasure and entertainment.
– ORIGIN from obsolete *gadling* 'wanderer, vagabond', from Germanic.

gadabout • noun informal a person who gads about.

Gadarene /gaddəreen/ • adjective involving or engaged in a headlong or disastrous rush.
– ORIGIN Greek *Gadarēnos* 'inhabitant of *Gadara*', with reference to the story in the Gospel of Matthew of the swine that rushed down a steep cliff into the sea and drowned.

gadfly • noun **1** a fly that bites livestock, especially a horsefly, warble fly, or botfly. **2** an annoying and provocative person.
– ORIGIN from GAD, or obsolete *gad* 'goad, spike', from Old Norse.

gadget • noun a small mechanical device or tool.
– DERIVATIVES **gadgetry** noun.
– ORIGIN probably from French *gâchette* 'lock mechanism' or from French dialect *gagée* 'tool'.

gadolinium /gaddəlinniəm/ • noun a soft silvery-white metallic chemical element of the lanthanide series.
– ORIGIN from *gadolinite* (a rare mineral containing the element), named after the Finnish mineralogist Johan *Gadolin* (1760–1852).

gadroon /gədroon/ • noun a decorative curved edging on silverware, wood, etc.
– DERIVATIVES **gadrooned** adjective **gadrooning** noun.
– ORIGIN French *godron*, probably related to *goder* 'to pucker'.

gadzooks /gadzooks/ • exclamation archaic expressing surprise or annoyance.
– ORIGIN alteration of *God's hooks*, i.e. the nails by which Christ was fastened to the cross.

Gael /gayl/ • noun a Gaelic-speaking person.
– ORIGIN Scottish Gaelic *Gaidheal.*

Gaelic /gaylik, galik/ • noun **1** (also **Scottish Gaelic**) a Celtic language spoken in western Scotland, brought from Ireland in the 5th and 6th centuries AD. **2** (also **Irish Gaelic**) another term for IRISH (the language). • adjective relating to the Celtic languages and their speakers.

Gaelic coffee • noun coffee served with cream and whisky.

gaff[1] • noun **1** a stick with a hook or barbed spear, for landing large fish. **2** Sailing a spar to which the head of a fore-and-aft sail is bent. • verb seize or impale (a fish) with a gaff.
– ORIGIN Provençal *gaf* 'hook'; related to GAFFE.

gaff[2] • noun (in phrase **blow the gaff**) Brit. informal reveal a plot or secret.
– ORIGIN of unknown origin.

gaff[3] • noun Brit. informal a person's house, flat, or shop.
– ORIGIN of unknown origin.

gaffe /gaf/ (also **gaff**) • noun an embarrassing blunder.
– ORIGIN French, 'boathook', in colloquial use 'blunder'.

gaffer • noun Brit. **1** informal an old man. **2** informal a boss. **3** the chief electrician in a film or television production unit.
– ORIGIN probably a contraction of GODFATHER.

gaffer tape • noun strong cloth-backed waterproof adhesive tape.

gag[1] • noun **1** a piece of cloth put in or over a person's mouth to prevent them from speaking. **2** a restriction on free speech. • verb (**gagged**, **gagging**) **1** put a gag on. **2** choke or retch.
– ORIGIN perhaps imitative of a person choking.

gag[2] • noun a joke or funny story or act. • verb tell jokes.
– ORIGIN of unknown origin.

Thesaurus

gab *(informal)* • verb *they were all gabbing away like crazy* CHATTER, chitter-chatter, chat, talk, gossip, gabble, babble, prattle, jabber, blather, blab; *informal* yak, yackety-yak, yabber, yatter, yammer, blabber, blah-blah, jaw, gas, shoot one's mouth off; *Brit. informal* witter, rabbit, chunter, natter; *N. Amer. informal* run off at the mouth.
– PHRASES **the gift of the gab** ELOQUENCE, fluency, expressiveness, a silver tongue; persuasiveness; *informal* a way with words, blarney.

gabble • verb *he gabbled on in a panicky way* JABBER, babble, prattle, rattle, blabber, gibber, blab, drivel, twitter, splutter; *Brit. informal* waffle, chunter, witter.
• noun *the boozy gabble of the crowd* JABBERING, babbling, chattering, gibbering, babble, chatter, rambling; *Brit. informal* waffle, waffling, chuntering, wittering.

gabby • adjective *(informal)*. See TALKATIVE.

gad • verb *(informal) she's been gadding about in Italy,* FLIT AROUND, run around, travel around, roam (around); *informal* gallivant; *Brit. informal* swan about.

gadabout • noun *(informal)* PLEASURE-SEEKER; traveller, globetrotter, wanderer, drifter, bird of passage; *informal* gallivanter.

gadget • noun APPLIANCE, apparatus, instrument, implement, tool, utensil, contrivance, contraption, machine, mechanism, device, labour-saving device, convenience, invention; *informal* gizmo, gimmick, widget, mod con.

gaffe • noun BLUNDER, mistake, error, slip, faux pas, indiscretion, impropriety, miscalculation, gaucherie, solecism; *informal* slip-up, howler, boo-boo, boner, fluff; *Brit. informal* boob, bloomer, clanger; *N. Amer. informal* blooper, goof.

gaffer • noun *(Brit. informal)* **1** *being the gaffer's gone to her head* MANAGER, manageress, foreman, forewoman, overseer, supervisor, superintendent; *informal* boss, boss man, head honcho, numero uno, number one, kingpin, top dog, big chief, skipper; *Brit. informal* governor, guv'nor; *N. Amer. informal* padrone, sachem, big kahuna.

gaga /gaagaa/ ● **adjective** informal rambling in speech or thought; senile or slightly mad.
– ORIGIN French.
gage[1] /gayj/ archaic ● **noun 1** a valued object deposited as a guarantee of good faith. **2** a glove or other object thrown down as a challenge to fight. ● **verb** offer as a gage.
– ORIGIN Old French; related to WAGE and WED.
gage[2] ● **noun & verb** variant spelling of GAUGE.
gage[3] /gayj/ ● **noun** another term for GREENGAGE.
– ORIGIN after the English botanist Sir William *Gage* (1657–1727).
gaggle ● **noun 1** a flock of geese. **2** informal a disorderly group of people.
– ORIGIN imitative of the noise that a goose makes.
Gaia /gīə/ ● **noun** the earth viewed as a vast self-regulating organism.
– ORIGIN coined by the English scientist James Lovelock (b.1919) from the name of the Greek goddess *Gaia*.
gaiety (US also **gayety**) ● **noun** (pl. **gaieties**) **1** the state or quality of being light-hearted and cheerful. **2** merrymaking; festivity.
– ORIGIN French *gaieté*.
gaijin /gījin/ ● **noun** (pl. same) (in Japan) a foreigner.
– ORIGIN Japanese, from *gaikoku* 'foreign country' + *jin* 'person'.
gaillardia /gaylaardiə/ ● **noun** an American plant of the daisy family, cultivated for its bright red and yellow flowers.
– ORIGIN named in memory of the 18th-century French amateur botanist *Gaillard* de Marentonneau.
gaily ● **adverb 1** in a light-hearted and cheerful manner. **2** without thinking of the consequences. **3** with a bright appearance.
gain ● **verb 1** obtain or secure. **2** reach or arrive at. **3** (**gain on**) come closer to (a person or thing pursued). **4** increase the amount or rate of (weight, speed, etc.). **5** increase in value. **6** (**gain in**) improve or advance in (some respect). **7** (of a clock or watch) become fast. ● **noun 1** a thing that is gained. **2** an increase in wealth or resources.
– DERIVATIVES **gainable** adjective **gainer** noun.
– ORIGIN originally in the sense 'booty': from Old French *gaignier* 'to gain'.
gainful ● **adjective** serving to increase wealth or resources.
– DERIVATIVES **gainfully** adverb **gainfulness** noun.
gainsay /gaynsay/ ● **verb** (past and past part. **gainsaid**) formal deny or contradict; speak against.
– DERIVATIVES **gainsayer** noun.
– ORIGIN from obsolete *gain-* 'against' + SAY.
gait /gayt/ ● **noun 1** a person's manner of walking. **2** the paces of a horse or dog.
– ORIGIN from GATE[2].
gaiter ● **noun 1** a covering of cloth or leather for the ankle and lower leg. **2** chiefly US a shoe or overshoe extending to the ankle or above.
– DERIVATIVES **gaitered** adjective.
– ORIGIN French *guêtre*.
gal ● **noun** informal, chiefly N. Amer. a girl or young woman.
gal. ● **abbreviation** gallon(s).
gala /gaalə, gaylə/ ● **noun 1** a festive entertainment or performance. **2** Brit. a special sports event, especially a swimming competition.
– ORIGIN originally in the sense 'showy dress': from Old French *gale* 'rejoicing'.
galactic /gəlaktik/ ● **adjective 1** relating to a galaxy or galaxies. **2** Astronomy measured relative to the galactic equator.
galactic equator ● **noun** Astronomy the great circle of the celestial sphere passing as closely as possible through the densest parts of the Milky Way.
galactose /gəlaktōz/ ● **noun** Chemistry a simple sugar which is a constituent of lactose and some other compound sugars.
– ORIGIN from Greek *galaktos* 'milk'.
galago /gəlaygō/ ● **noun** (pl. **galagos**) another term for BUSHBABY.
– ORIGIN Latin genus name.
galangal /galəngg'l/ (also **galingale**) ● **noun** an Asian plant of the ginger family, the rhizome of which is used in cookery and herbal medicine.
– ORIGIN Old French *galingale*, from Arabic, perhaps from a Chinese word denoting ginger from a particular district in Guangdong Province, China.
galant /gəlant/ ● **adjective** relating to or denoting a light and elegant style of 18th-century music.
– ORIGIN French and German (see GALLANT).
galantine /galənteen/ ● **noun** a dish of cooked meat or fish served cold in aspic.
– ORIGIN originally in the sense 'sauce for fish': from Latin *galatina*.
Galatian /gəlaysh'n/ ● **noun** an inhabitant of Galatia, an ancient region of Asia Minor. ● **adjective** relating to Galatia.
galaxy ● **noun** (pl. **galaxies**) **1** a system of millions or billions of stars, together with gas and dust, held together by gravitational attraction. **2** (**the Galaxy**) the galaxy of which the solar system is a part; the Milky Way. **3** a large and impressive group of people or things.
– ORIGIN from Greek *galaxias kuklos* 'milky vault' (referring to the Milky Way), from *gala* 'milk'.
gale ● **noun 1** a very strong wind. **2** an outburst of laughter.

Thesaurus

2 *an old gaffer* OLD MAN, elderly man, senior citizen, pensioner, OAP; *informal* old boy, old codger, old-timer, greybeard, grandad, wrinkly; *Brit. informal* buffer.
gag[1] ● **verb 1** *a dirty rag was used to gag her mouth* STOP UP, block, plug, stifle, smother, muffle. **2** *the government tried to gag its critics* SILENCE, muzzle, mute, muffle, suppress, stifle; censor, curb, check, restrain, fetter, shackle, restrict. **3** *the stench made her gag* RETCH, heave, dry-heave; *informal* keck.
● **noun** *his scream was muffled by the gag* MUZZLE, tie, restraint.
gag[2] ● **noun** *he told a few gags* JOKE, jest, witticism, quip, pun, play on words, double entendre; *informal* crack, wisecrack, one-liner, funny.
gaiety ● **noun 1** *I was struck by her gaiety* CHEERFULNESS, light-heartedness, happiness, merriment, glee, gladness, joy, joie de vivre, joyfulness, joyousness, delight, high spirits, good spirits, good humour, cheeriness, jollity, mirth, joviality, exuberance, elation; liveliness, vivacity, animation, effervescence, sprightliness, zest, zestfulness; *informal* chirpiness, bounce, pep; *poetic/literary* blitheness. **2** *the hotel restaurant was a scene of gaiety* MERRYMAKING, festivity, fun, fun and games, frolics, revelry, jollification, celebration, pleasure; *informal* partying.
– OPPOSITES misery.
gaily ● **adverb 1** *she skipped gaily along the path* MERRILY, cheerfully, cheerily, happily, joyfully, joyously, light-heartedly, blithely, jauntily, gleefully. **2** *gaily painted boats* BRIGHTLY, colourfully, brilliantly. **3** *she plunged gaily into speculation on the stock market* HEEDLESSLY, unthinkingly, thoughtlessly, without thinking, carelessly; casually, nonchalantly, airily, breezily, lightly.
gain ● **verb 1** *he gained a scholarship to the college* OBTAIN, get, secure, acquire, come by, procure, attain, achieve, earn, win, capture, clinch, pick up, carry off, reap; *informal* land, net, bag, scoop, wangle, swing, walk away/off with. **2** *they stood to gain from the deal* PROFIT, make money, reap benefits, benefit, do well out of; *informal* make a killing, milk. **3** *she had gained weight* PUT ON, increase in. **4** *the others were gaining on us* CATCH UP WITH/ON, catch someone up, catch, close in on, near. **5** *we gained the ridge* REACH, arrive at, get to, come to, make, attain, set foot on; *informal* hit.
– OPPOSITES lose.
● **noun 1** *his gain from the deal* PROFIT, advantage, benefit, reward; percentage, takings, yield, return, winnings, receipts, proceeds, dividend, interest; *informal* pickings, cut, take, rake-off, slice of the cake; *Brit. informal* whack. **2** *a price gain of 7.5 per cent* INCREASE, rise, increment, augmentation, addition.
– OPPOSITES loss, decrease.
– PHRASES **gain time** PLAY FOR TIME, stall, procrastinate, delay, temporize, hold back, hang back, hang fire, dally, drag one's feet.
gainful ● **adjective** PROFITABLE, paid, well paid, remunerative, lucrative, moneymaking; rewarding, fruitful, worthwhile, useful, productive, constructive, beneficial, advantageous, valuable.
gainsay ● **verb** *(formal)* DENY, dispute, disagree with, argue with, dissent from, contradict, repudiate, challenge, oppose, contest, counter, controvert, refute, rebut; *formal* confute.
– OPPOSITES confirm.
gait ● **noun** WALK, step, stride, pace, tread, way of walking; bearing, carriage; *Brit.* deportment; *formal* comportment.
gala ● **noun** *the annual summer gala* FÊTE, fair, festival, carnival, pageant, jubilee, jamboree, party, garden party, celebration; festivities.
● **adjective** *a gala occasion* FESTIVE, celebratory, merry, joyous, joyful; diverting, entertaining, enjoyable, spectacular.
galaxy ● **noun 1** *a distant galaxy* STAR SYSTEM, solar system, constellation; stars, heavens. **2** *a galaxy of the rock world's biggest*

– ORIGIN perhaps related to an Old Norse word meaning 'mad, frantic'.

galena /gəleenə/ ● noun a metallic grey or black mineral consisting of lead sulphide.

– ORIGIN Latin, 'lead ore'.

Galilean[1] /galilayən/ ● adjective relating to the Italian astronomer and physicist Galileo Galilei (1564–1642) or his methods.

Galilean[2] /galileeən/ ● noun a person from Galilee, the region of ancient Palestine associated with the ministry of Jesus and now part of Israel. ● adjective relating to Galilee.

galingale /galinggayl/ ● noun **1** (also **English** or **sweet galingale**) a sedge with an aromatic rhizome, formerly used in perfumes. **2** variant spelling of GALANGAL.

– ORIGIN from GALANGAL.

gall[1] /gawl/ ● noun **1** bold and impudent behaviour. **2** bitterness or cruelty. **3** an animal's gall bladder. **4** archaic the contents of the gall bladder; bile.

– ORIGIN Old English.

gall[2] /gawl/ ● noun **1** annoyance; irritation. **2** a sore on the skin made by chafing. ● verb **1** annoy; irritate. **2** make sore by chafing.

– DERIVATIVES **galling** adjective.

– ORIGIN Old English.

gall[3] /gawl/ ● noun an abnormal growth formed in response to the presence of insect larvae, mites, or fungi on plants and trees.

– ORIGIN Latin *galla*.

gall. ● abbreviation gallon(s).

gallant /galənt/ ● adjective **1** brave; heroic. **2** /gəlant/ (of a man) charming; chivalrous. **3** archaic of fine appearance; grand. ● noun /gəlant/ archaic a man who is charmingly attentive to women.

– DERIVATIVES **gallantly** adverb.

– ORIGIN originally in the sense 'finely dressed': from Old French *galant*, from *galer* 'have fun, make a show'.

gallantry ● noun (pl. **gallantries**) **1** courageous behaviour. **2** polite attention or respect given by men to women.

gall bladder ● noun a small sac-shaped organ beneath the liver, in which bile is stored.

galleon ● noun historical a large square-rigged sailing ship with three or more decks and masts.

– ORIGIN French *galion* or Spanish *galeón*.

galleria /galəreeə/ ● noun an arcade of small shops.

– ORIGIN Italian, 'gallery'.

gallery ● noun (pl. **galleries**) **1** a room or building for the display or sale of works of art. **2** a balcony or upper floor projecting from a back or side wall inside a hall or church. **3** the highest balcony in a theatre, having the cheapest seats. **4** (**the gallery**) a group of spectators. **5** a long room or passage forming a portico or colonnade. **6** a horizontal underground passage in a mine.

– PHRASES **play to the gallery** aim to attract popular attention.

– DERIVATIVES **galleried** adjective.

– ORIGIN Italian *galleria* 'gallery', formerly also 'church porch', from Latin *galeria*.

galley ● noun (pl. **galleys**) **1** historical a low, flat ship with one or more sails and up to three banks of oars, often manned by slaves or criminals. **2** a narrow kitchen in a ship or aircraft. **3** (also **galley proof**) a printer's proof in the form of long single-column strips.

– ORIGIN Greek *galaia*; sense 3 is from French *galée* denoting an oblong tray for holding set-up type.

galliard /galiaard/ ● noun historical a lively dance in triple time for two people.

– ORIGIN originally in the senses 'valiant, sturdy' and 'lively, brisk': from Old French *gaillard* 'valiant'.

Gallic /galik/ ● adjective **1** of or characteristic of France or the French. **2** of or relating to the Gauls.

– DERIVATIVES **Gallicize** (also **Gallicise**) verb.

– ORIGIN Latin *Gallicus*, from *Gallus* 'a Gaul'.

Gallicism /galisiz'm/ ● noun a French word or idiom adopted in another language.

gallimaufry /galimawfri/ ● noun a jumble or medley.

– ORIGIN archaic French *galimafrée* 'unappetizing dish'.

gallimimus /galimīməss/ ● noun (pl. **gallimimuses**) an ostrich-like dinosaur of the late Cretaceous period.

– ORIGIN from Latin *galli* 'of a cockerel' + *mimus* 'mime, pretence'.

gallium /galiəm/ ● noun a soft, silvery-white metallic chemical element which melts just above normal room temperature.

– ORIGIN from Latin *Gallia* 'France' or *gallus* 'cock'; named by the French chemist Paul-Émile *Lecoq de Boisbaudran* (1838–1912).

gallivant /galivant/ ● verb informal go from place to place seeking pleasure and entertainment.

– ORIGIN perhaps from GALLANT.

gallon /galən/ ● noun **1** a unit of volume for liquid measure equal to eight pints: in Britain (also **imperial gallon**), equivalent to 4.55 litres; in the US, equivalent to 3.79 litres. **2** (**gallons**) informal large quantities.

– ORIGIN Old French *galon*, from Latin *galleta* 'pail, liquid measure'.

gallop ● noun **1** the fastest pace of a horse or other quadruped, with all the feet off the ground together in each stride. **2** a ride on a horse at a gallop. ● verb (**galloped**, **galloping**) **1** go or

Thesaurus

stars HOST, multitude, array, gathering, assemblage, assembly, throng, crowd, company, flock, group.

gale ● noun **1** *a howling gale* STRONG WIND, high wind, hurricane, tornado, cyclone, whirlwind; storm, squall, tempest, typhoon; *N. Amer.* windstorm; *informal* burster, buster. **2** *gales of laughter* PEAL, howl, hoot, shriek, scream, roar; outburst, burst, fit, paroxysm, explosion.

gall[1] ● noun **1** *she had the gall to ask for money* EFFRONTERY, impudence, impertinence, cheek, cheekiness, insolence, audacity, temerity, presumption, cockiness, nerve, shamelessness, disrespect, bad manners; *informal* brass neck, face, chutzpah; *Brit. informal* sauce; *N. Amer. informal* sass. **2** *scholarly gall was poured on this work* BITTERNESS, resentment, rancour, bile, spleen, malice, spite, spitefulness, malignity, venom, vitriol, poison.

gall[2] ● noun **1** *this was a gall that she frequently had to endure* IRRITATION, irritant, annoyance, vexation, nuisance, provocation, bother, torment, plague, thorn in one's side/flesh; *informal* aggravation, pain, pain in the neck, bore, headache, hassle; *N. Amer. informal* pain in the butt. **2** *a bay horse with a gall on its side* SORE, ulcer, ulceration; abrasion, scrape, scratch, graze, chafe.

● verb **1** *it galled him to have to sit in silence* IRRITATE, annoy, vex, anger, infuriate, exasperate, irk, pique, nettle, put out, displease, antagonize, get on someone's nerves, make someone's hackles rise; *Brit.* rub up the wrong way; *informal* aggravate, peeve, miff, rile, needle, get (to), bug, hack off, get up someone's nose, get someone's goat, get/put someone's back up, get someone's dander up, drive mad/crazy, drive round the bend/twist, drive up the wall; *Brit. informal* wind up, nark, get on someone's wick, give someone the hump; *N. Amer. informal* tee off, tick off, rankle; *informal, dated* give someone the pip. **2** *the straps galled their shoulders* CHAFE, abrade, rub (against), rub raw, scrape, graze, skin, scratch, rasp, bark.

gallant ● adjective **1** *his gallant countrymen* BRAVE, courageous, valiant, valorous, bold, plucky, daring, fearless, intrepid, heroic, lionhearted, stout-hearted, doughty, mettlesome, death-or-glory, dauntless, undaunted, unflinching, unafraid; *informal* gutsy, spunky. **2** *her gallant companion* CHIVALROUS, gentlemanly, honourable, courteous, polite, mannerly, attentive, respectful, gracious, considerate, thoughtful.

– OPPOSITES cowardly, discourteous.

● noun *(archaic)* **1** *a young gallant in red and white silks* MAN ABOUT TOWN, ladies' man, man of the world, dandy, fop; *informal* ladykiller; *informal, dated* gay dog, blade, swell, blood; *archaic* coxcomb. **2** *her amorous gallant* SUITOR, wooer, admirer; sweetheart, lover, love, beloved, boyfriend, young man; *poetic/literary* swain; *dated* beau.

gallantry ● noun **1** *he received medals for gallantry* BRAVERY, courage, courageousness, valour, pluck, pluckiness, nerve, daring, boldness, fearlessness, dauntlessness, intrepidity, heroism, stout-heartedness, mettle, grit; *informal* guts, spunk; *Brit. informal* bottle; *N. Amer. informal* moxie. **2** *she acknowledged his selfless gallantry* CHIVALRY, chivalrousness, gentlemanliness, courtesy, courteousness, politeness, good manners, attentiveness, graciousness, respectfulness, respect, considerateness.

gallery ● noun **1** *the National Gallery* ART GALLERY, museum; exhibition room, display room. **2** *they sat up in the gallery* BALCONY, circle, upper circle; *informal* gods. **3** *a long gallery with doors along each side* PASSAGE, passageway, corridor, walkway, arcade.

galling ● adjective ANNOYING, irritating, vexing, vexatious, infuriating, maddening, irksome, provoking, exasperating, trying, tiresome, troublesome, bothersome, displeasing, disagreeable; *informal*

cause to go at the pace of a gallop. **2** proceed at great speed.
– DERIVATIVES **galloper** noun.
– ORIGIN Old French *galoper*; related to WALLOP.

gallows ● plural noun (usu. treated as sing.) **1** a structure consisting of two uprights and a crosspiece, used for hanging a person. **2** (**the gallows**) execution by hanging.
– ORIGIN Old English.

gallows humour ● noun grim and ironical humour in a desperate or hopeless situation.

gallstone /gawlstōn/ ● noun a small, hard crystalline mass formed abnormally in the gall bladder or bile ducts from bile pigments, cholesterol, and calcium salts.

Gallup poll /galəp/ ● noun trademark an assessment of public opinion by the questioning of a representative sample, used in forecasting voting results in an election.
– ORIGIN named after the American statistician George H. *Gallup* (1901–84).

galoot /gəloot/ ● noun N. Amer. & Scottish informal a clumsy or stupid person.
– ORIGIN originally in nautical use meaning 'an inexperienced marine': of unknown origin.

galore ● adjective in abundance: *there were prizes galore.*
– ORIGIN from Irish *go leor* 'to sufficiency'.

galosh /gəlosh/ ● noun a waterproof rubber overshoe.
– ORIGIN originally denoting a type of clog: from Latin *gallica solea* 'Gallic shoe'.

galumph /gəlumf/ ● verb informal move in a clumsy, ponderous, or noisy manner.
– ORIGIN originally in the sense 'prance in triumph': coined by Lewis Carroll in *Through the Looking Glass*; perhaps a blend of GALLOP and TRIUMPH.

galvanic /galvannik/ ● adjective **1** relating to or involving electric currents produced by chemical action. **2** sudden and dramatic.
– DERIVATIVES **galvanically** adverb.
– ORIGIN French *galvanique*, from the name of the Italian physiologist Luigi *Galvani* (1737–98), known for his discovery of the twitching of frogs' legs in an electric field.

galvanize /galvənīz/ (also **galvanise**) ● verb **1** shock or excite into action. **2** (**galvanized**) (of iron or steel) coated with a protective layer of zinc.
– DERIVATIVES **galvanization** noun **galvanizer** noun.
– ORIGIN originally in the sense 'stimulate by electricity': from French *galvaniser* (see GALVANIC).

galvanometer /galvənommitər/ ● noun an instrument for detecting and measuring small electric currents.
– DERIVATIVES **galvanometric** adjective.

Gamay /gammay/ ● noun a variety of black wine grape native to the Beaujolais district of France.
– ORIGIN from the name of a hamlet in Burgundy, eastern France.

Gambian /gambiən/ ● noun a person from Gambia, a country in West Africa. ● adjective relating to Gambia.

gambit ● noun **1** an action or remark calculated to gain an advantage. **2** (in chess) an opening move in which a player makes a sacrifice for the sake of some compensating advantage.
– ORIGIN Italian *gambetto* 'tripping up'.

gamble ● verb **1** play games of chance for money; bet. **2** bet (a sum of money). **3** take risky action in the hope of a desired result. ● noun **1** an act of gambling. **2** a risky undertaking.
– DERIVATIVES **gambler** noun.
– ORIGIN from obsolete *gamel* 'play games', or from the verb GAME[1].

gamboge /gambōzh/ ● noun a gum resin produced by certain East Asian trees, used as a yellow pigment and in medicine as a purgative.
– ORIGIN Latin *gambaugium*, from *Cambodia*.

gambol ● verb (**gambolled**, **gambolling**; US **gamboled**, **gamboling**) run or jump about playfully. ● noun an act of gambolling.
– ORIGIN Italian *gambata* 'trip up'.

gambrel /gambrəl/ ● noun **1** a roof having a shallower slope above a steeper one on each side. **2** Brit. a hipped roof with a small gable forming the upper part of each end.
– ORIGIN Old French *gamberel*, from *gambier* 'forked stick'.

game[1] ● noun **1** an activity engaged in for amusement. **2** a form of competitive activity or sport played according to rules. **3** a complete episode or period of play, ending in a final result. **4** a single portion of play, forming a scoring unit within a game. **5** (**games**) a meeting for sporting contests. **6** the equipment used in playing a board game, computer game, etc. **7** a type of activity or business regarded as a game. **8** a secret plan or trick. **9** wild mammals or birds hunted for sport or food. ● adjective eager and willing to do something new or challenging: *they were game for anything.* ● verb play at games of chance for money.
– PHRASES **ahead of the game** ahead of one's competitors or peers. **beat someone at their own game** use someone's own methods to outdo them. **the game is up** the deception or crime is revealed or foiled. **on the game** Brit. informal working as a prostitute. **play the game** behave in a fair or honourable way; abide by the rules.
– DERIVATIVES **gamely** adverb **gameness** noun **gamester** noun.
– ORIGIN Old English, 'amusement, fun'.

game[2] ● adjective (of a person's leg) lame.
– ORIGIN originally dialect: of unknown origin.

game bird ● noun **1** a bird shot for sport or food. **2** a bird of a large group that includes pheasants, grouse, quails, guineafowl, etc.

game fish ● noun (pl. same) a fish caught by anglers for sport, especially (in fresh water) salmon and trout and (in the sea) marlins, sharks, bass, and mackerel. Compare with COARSE FISH.

g

Thesaurus

aggravating.

gallivant ● verb FLIT, jaunt, run; roam, wander, travel, rove; informal gad.

gallop ● verb *Paul galloped across the clearing* RUSH, race, run, sprint, bolt, dart, dash, career, charge, shoot, hurtle, hare, fly, speed, zoom, streak; informal tear, belt, pelt, scoot, zip, whip, hotfoot it, leg it; Brit. informal bomb, go like the clappers; N. Amer. informal barrel.
– OPPOSITES amble.

gallows ● plural noun **1** *the wooden gallows* GIBBET, scaffold, gallows tree, Tyburn tree. **2** *they were condemned to the gallows* HANGING, being hanged, the noose, the rope, the gibbet, the scaffold, execution; informal the drop.

galore ● adjective APLENTY, in abundance, in profusion, in great quantities, in large numbers, by the dozen; to spare; everywhere, all over (the place); informal a gogo, by the truckload; Brit. informal by the shedload.

galvanize ● verb JOLT, shock, startle, impel, stir, spur, prod, urge, motivate, stimulate, electrify, excite, rouse, arouse, awaken; invigorate, fire, animate, vitalize, energize, exhilarate, thrill, dynamize, inspire; N. Amer. light a fire under; informal give someone a shot in the arm.

gambit ● noun STRATAGEM, scheme, plan, tactic, manoeuvre, move, course/line of action, device; machination, ruse, trick, ploy; Brit. informal wheeze, wangle.

gamble ● verb **1** *he started to gamble more often* BET, place/lay a bet on something, stake money on something, back the horses, game; informal play the ponies; Brit. informal punt, have a flutter. **2** *investors are gambling that the pound will fall* TAKE A CHANCE, take a risk; N. Amer. take a flier; informal stick one's neck out, go out on a limb; Brit. informal chance one's arm.
● noun **1** *his grandfather enjoyed a gamble* BET, wager, speculation; game of chance; Brit. informal flutter, punt. **2** *I took a gamble and it paid off* RISK, chance, hazard, leap in the dark; pig in a poke, pot luck.

gambol ● verb FROLIC, frisk, cavort, caper, skip, dance, romp, prance, leap, hop, jump, spring, bound; play; dated sport.

game ● noun **1** *the children invented a new game* PASTIME, diversion, entertainment, amusement, distraction, divertissement, recreation, sport, activity. **2** *the club haven't lost a game all season* MATCH, contest, fixture, tie, tournament; cup tie, final, cup final, play-off. **3** *we were only playing a game on him* PRACTICAL JOKE, prank, jest, trick, hoax; informal lark. **4** *he's in the banking game* BUSINESS, profession, occupation, trade, industry, line, line of work/business; informal racket. **5** *I spoiled his little game* SCHEME, plot, ploy, stratagem, strategy, gambit, cunning plan, tactics; trick, device, manoeuvre, wile, dodge, ruse, machination, contrivance, subterfuge; informal scam; Brit. informal wheeze; archaic shift. **6** *he hunted game in Africa* WILD ANIMALS, wild fowl, big game.
● adjective **1** *they weren't game enough to join in* BRAVE, courageous, plucky, bold, daring, intrepid, valiant, stout-hearted, mettlesome; fearless, dauntless, undaunted, unflinching; informal gutsy, spunky. **2** *I need a bit of help—are you game?* WILLING, prepared, ready, disposed, of a mind; eager, keen, enthusiastic.

gamekeeper ● noun a person employed to breed and protect game for a large estate.
gamelan /gamməlan/ ● noun a traditional instrumental ensemble in Java and Bali, including many bronze percussion instruments.
– ORIGIN Javanese.
game plan ● noun a planned strategy in sport, politics, or business.
game point ● noun (in tennis and other sports) a point which if won by a player or side will also win them the game.
gamer ● noun **1** a participant in a computer or role-playing game. **2** N. Amer. (especially in sporting contexts) a person known for consistently making a strong effort.
game show ● noun a programme on television in which people compete to win prizes.
gamesmanship ● noun the art of winning games by using ploys and tactics to gain a psychological advantage.
– DERIVATIVES **gamesman** noun.
gamete /gammeet/ ● noun Biology a mature haploid male or female germ cell which is able to unite with another of the opposite sex in sexual reproduction to form a zygote.
– DERIVATIVES **gametic** /gəmettik/ adjective.
– ORIGIN Greek *gametē* 'wife', *gametēs* 'husband', from *gamos* 'marriage'.
game theory ● noun the mathematical study of strategies for dealing with competitive situations where the outcome of a participant's choice of action depends critically on the actions of other participants.
gametophyte /gəmeetəfīt/ ● noun Botany (in the life cycle of plants with alternating generations, e.g. ferns) the gamete-producing phase (typically haploid), which produces the zygote.
gamey ● adjective variant spelling of GAMY.
gamine /gameen/ ● noun a girl with a mischievous, boyish charm. ● adjective characteristic of a gamine.
– ORIGIN French.
gamma /gammə/ ● noun **1** the third letter of the Greek alphabet (Γ, γ), transliterated as 'g'. **2** Brit. a third-class mark given for a piece of work. **3** (before another noun) relating to gamma rays.
– ORIGIN Greek.
gamma globulin ● noun Biochemistry a mixture of blood plasma proteins, mainly immunoglobulins, often given to boost immunity.
gamma rays (also **gamma radiation**) ● plural noun penetrating electromagnetic radiation of shorter wavelength than X-rays.
gammon ● noun **1** ham which has been cured like bacon. **2** the bottom piece of a side of bacon, including a hind leg.
– ORIGIN Old French *gambon*, from *gambe* 'leg'.
gammy ● adjective Brit. informal (especially of a leg) unable to function normally because of injury or chronic pain.
– ORIGIN dialect form of GAME².
gamut /gammət/ ● noun **1** the complete range or scope of something. **2** Music a complete scale of musical notes; the compass or range of a voice or instrument. **3** historical a scale consisting of seven overlapping hexachords, containing all the recognized notes used in medieval music. **4** historical the lowest note in this scale.
– PHRASES **run the gamut** experience, display, or perform the complete range of something.
– ORIGIN from Latin *gamma ut* (in sense 4): the Greek letter Γ (gamma) was used for bass G, with *ut* indicating that it was the first note in the lowest of the hexachords.
gamy (also **gamey**) ● adjective (**gamier**, **gamiest**) **1** (of meat) having the strong flavour or smell of game when it is high. **2** chiefly N. Amer. racy or risqué.
– DERIVATIVES **gamily** adverb **gaminess** noun.
gander /gandər/ ● noun **1** a male goose. **2** informal a look or glance.
– ORIGIN Old English, related to GANNET.
gang¹ ● noun **1** an organized group of criminals or disorderly young people. **2** informal a group of people who regularly meet and do things together. **3** an organized group of people doing manual work. **4** a set of switches, sockets, or other devices grouped together. ● verb **1** (**gang together**) form a group or gang. **2** (**gang up**) join together in opposition to someone. **3** arrange (electrical devices or machines) together to work in coordination.
– ORIGIN Old Norse, 'gait, course, going'; related to GANG².
gang² ● verb Scottish go; proceed.
– ORIGIN Old English, related to GO¹.
gang bang ● noun informal **1** a gang rape. **2** a sexual orgy. **3** N. Amer. an instance of violence involving members of a criminal gang.
– DERIVATIVES **gang-bang** verb **gang banger** noun.
gangbuster ● noun informal **1** a police officer engaged in breaking up criminal gangs. **2** (before another noun) N. Amer. very successful.
– PHRASES **go** (or **like**) **gangbusters** N. Amer. with great vigour or success.
ganger ● noun Brit. the foreman of a gang of labourers.
gangling (also **gangly**) ● adjective (of a person) tall, thin, and awkward.
– ORIGIN from GANG².
ganglion /gangglіən/ ● noun (pl. **ganglia** or **ganglions**) Anatomy & Medicine **1** a structure containing a number of nerve cells, often forming a swelling on a nerve fibre. **2** a well-defined mass of grey matter within the central nervous system. **3** an abnormal benign swelling on a tendon sheath.
– DERIVATIVES **ganglionic** adjective.
– ORIGIN Greek, 'tumour on or near sinews or tendons'.
gangplank ● noun a movable plank used to board or disembark from a ship or boat.
gang rape ● noun the rape of one person by a group of other people.
gangrene /ganggreen/ ● noun Medicine localized death and decomposition of body tissue, resulting from either obstructed circulation or bacterial infection. ● verb become affected with gangrene.
– DERIVATIVES **gangrenous** /ganggrinəss/ adjective.
– ORIGIN Greek *gangraina*.
gangsta ● noun N. Amer. black slang a gang member.
gangster ● noun a member of an organized gang of violent criminals.
– DERIVATIVES **gangsterism** noun.
gangway ● noun **1** a raised platform or walkway providing a passage. **2** a movable bridge linking a ship to the shore. **3** Brit. a passage between rows of seats in an auditorium, aircraft, etc. ● exclamation make way!
ganja /ganjə/ ● noun cannabis.
– ORIGIN Hindi.
gannet /gannit/ ● noun **1** a large seabird with mainly white plumage, catching fish by plunge-diving. **2** Brit. informal a greedy person.
– ORIGIN Old English, related to GANDER.
gantlet /gantlit/ ● noun US spelling of GAUNTLET².
gantry ● noun (pl. **gantries**) a bridge-like overhead structure supporting equipment such as a crane or railway signals.
– ORIGIN originally denoting a wooden stand for barrels: probably from GALLON + TREE.
gaol ● noun Brit. variant spelling of JAIL.
gap ● noun **1** a break or hole in an object or between two ob-

Thesaurus

● verb *they were drinking and gaming all evening* GAMBLE, bet, place/lay bets.
gamine ● adjective BOYISH, mischievous, playful; appealing, engaging, cute, charming.
gamut ● noun RANGE, spectrum, span, scope, sweep, compass, area, breadth, reach, extent, catalogue, scale; variety.
gang ● noun **1** *a gang of teenagers* BAND, group, crowd, pack, horde, throng, mob, herd, swarm, troop, cluster; company, gathering; *informal* posse, bunch, gaggle, load. **2** *(informal) John was one of our gang* CIRCLE, social circle, social set, group, clique, in-crowd, coterie, lot, ring; *informal* crew. **3** *a gang of workmen* CREW, team, group, squad, shift, detachment, unit.
● verb *they all ganged up to put me down* CONSPIRE, cooperate, work together, act together, combine, join forces, team up, get together, unite, ally.
gangling, gangly ● adjective LANKY, rangy, tall, thin, skinny, spindly, stringy, bony, angular, scrawny, spare; awkward, uncoordinated, ungainly, gawky, inelegant, graceless, ungraceful; *dated* spindle-shanked.
– OPPOSITES squat.
gangster ● noun HOODLUM, gang member, racketeer, robber, ruffian, thug, tough, villain, lawbreaker, criminal; gunman, terrorist; Mafioso; *informal* mobster, crook, hit man; *N. Amer. informal* hood; *dated* desperado.

jects. **2** a space, interval, or break.
– DERIVATIVES **gapped** adjective **gappy** adjective.
– ORIGIN Old Norse, 'chasm'; related to GAPE.
gape ● verb **1** be or become wide open. **2** stare with one's mouth open wide in amazement or wonder. ● noun **1** a wide opening. **2** an open-mouthed stare. **3** a widely open mouth or beak.
– DERIVATIVES **gaper** noun.
– ORIGIN Old Norse, related to GAP.
gap year ● noun a period, typically an academic year, taken by a student as a break from education between leaving school and starting a university or college course.
gar ● noun the freshwater garfish of North America.
garage /garraaj, garrij/ ● noun **1** a building for housing a motor vehicle or vehicles. **2** an establishment which sells fuel or which repairs and sells motor vehicles. ● verb put or keep (a motor vehicle) in a garage.
– ORIGIN French, from *garer* 'to shelter'.
garage sale ● noun chiefly N. Amer. a sale of unwanted goods held in a garage or front garden.
garam masala /gurrəm məsaalə/ ● noun a spice mixture used in Indian cookery.
– ORIGIN Urdu, 'pungent spice'.
garb ● noun clothing or dress of a distinctive kind. ● verb (usu. **be garbed**) dress in distinctive clothes.
– ORIGIN French, from Italian *garbo* 'elegance'; related to GEAR.
garbage ● noun chiefly N. Amer. **1** domestic rubbish or waste. **2** something worthless or meaningless.
– ORIGIN originally in the sense 'offal': from Old French.
garbanzo /gaarbanzō/ ● noun (pl. **garbanzos**) N. Amer. a chick-pea.
– ORIGIN Spanish.
garble ● verb reproduce (a message or transmission) in a confused and distorted way. ● noun a garbled account or transmission.
– DERIVATIVES **garbler** noun.
– ORIGIN originally in the sense 'sift out, cleanse': from an Arabic word meaning 'sift'.
garçon /gaarsoN/ ● noun a waiter in a French restaurant.
– ORIGIN French, 'boy'.
Garda /gaardə/ ● noun **1** the state police force of the Irish Republic. **2** (pl. **Gardai** /gaardi/) a member of the Irish police force.
– ORIGIN from Irish *Garda Siochána* 'Civic Guard'.
garden ● noun **1** chiefly Brit. a piece of ground adjoining a house, typically cultivated to provide a lawn and flowerbeds. **2** (**gardens**) ornamental grounds laid out for public enjoyment. ● verb cultivate or work in a garden.
– DERIVATIVES **gardener** noun.
– ORIGIN Old French *jardin*; related to YARD[2].
garden centre ● noun an establishment where plants and gardening equipment are sold.
garden city ● noun a new town built on a plan incorporating open space and greenery.
gardenia /gaardeeniə/ ● noun a tree or shrub of warm climates, with large fragrant white or yellow flowers.
– ORIGIN named in honour of the Scottish naturalist Dr Alexander *Garden* (1730–91).
garden party ● noun a social event held on a lawn in a garden.
garden suburb ● noun Brit. a suburb set in rural surroundings or incorporating much landscaping.
garden-variety ● adjective N. Amer. of the usual or ordinary type; commonplace.
garderobe /gaardrōb/ ● noun **1** a toilet in a medieval building. **2** a wardrobe or storeroom in a medieval building.
– ORIGIN French, from *garder* 'to keep' + *robe* 'robe, dress'; related to WARDROBE.
garfish ● noun **1** a long, slender marine fish with beak-like jaws and sharp teeth. **2** N. Amer. a similar freshwater fish.
– ORIGIN from Old English *gār* 'spear' + FISH[1].
garganey /gaargəni/ ● noun (pl. same or **garganeys**) a small duck, the male of which has a brown head with a white stripe from the eye to the neck.
– ORIGIN Italian dialect *garganei*.
gargantuan /gaargantyooən/ ● adjective enormous.
– ORIGIN from *Gargantua*, a voracious giant in Rabelais' book of the same name (1534).
gargle ● verb wash one's mouth and throat with a liquid that is kept in motion by breathing through it with a gurgling sound. ● noun **1** an act of gargling. **2** a liquid used for gargling.
– ORIGIN French *gargouiller* 'gurgle, bubble', from Old French *gargouille* 'throat' (see GARGOYLE).
gargoyle /gaargoyl/ ● noun a grotesque carved human or animal face or figure projecting from the gutter of a building, usually as a spout to carry water clear of a wall.
– ORIGIN Old French *gargouille* 'throat', also 'gargoyle'.
garibaldi /garribawldi/ ● noun (pl. **garibaldis**) Brit. a thin biscuit containing a compressed layer of currants.
– ORIGIN named after the Italian patriot Giuseppe *Garibaldi* (1807–82).
garish /gairish/ ● adjective obtrusively bright and showy; lurid.
– DERIVATIVES **garishly** adverb **garishness** noun.
– ORIGIN of unknown origin.
garland ● noun **1** a wreath of flowers and leaves, worn on the head or hung as a decoration. **2** a prize or distinction. **3** archaic a literary anthology. ● verb adorn or crown with a garland.
– ORIGIN Old French *garlande*.
garlic ● noun the strong-smelling pungent-tasting bulb of a plant of the onion family, used as a flavouring in cookery.

Thesaurus

gaol ● noun *(Brit.)*. See JAIL.
gaoler ● noun *(Brit.)*. See JAILER.
gap ● noun **1** *a gap in the shutters* OPENING, aperture, space, breach, chink, slit, slot, vent, crack, crevice, cranny, cavity, hole, orifice, interstice, perforation, break, fracture, rift, rent, fissure, cleft, divide. **2** *a gap between meetings* PAUSE, intermission, interval, interlude, break, breathing space, breather, respite, hiatus; *N. Amer.* recess. **3** *a gap in our records* OMISSION, blank, lacuna, void, vacuity. **4** *the gap between rich and poor* CHASM, gulf, rift, split, separation, breach; contrast, difference, disparity, divergence, imbalance.
gape ● verb **1** *she gaped at him in astonishment* STARE, stare open-mouthed, stare in wonder, goggle, gaze, ogle; *informal* rubberneck; *Brit. informal* gawk, gawp. **2** *a leather jerkin which gaped at every seam* OPEN WIDE, open up, yawn; part, split.
gaping ● adjective *a gaping hole* CAVERNOUS, yawning, wide, broad; vast, huge, enormous, immense, extensive.
garb ● noun *men and women in riding garb* CLOTHES, clothing, garments, attire, dress, costume, outfit, wear, uniform, livery, regalia; *informal* gear, get-up, togs, rig-out, duds; *Brit. informal* clobber; *formal* apparel; *archaic* raiment, habiliment, vestments.
● verb *both men were garbed in black* DRESS, clothe, attire, fit out, turn out, deck (out), kit out, costume, robe; *informal* get up; *archaic* apparel.
garbage *(N. Amer.)* ● noun **1** *the garbage is taken to landfill sites* RUBBISH, refuse, waste, detritus, litter, junk, scrap; scraps, scourings, leftovers, remains, slops; *N. Amer.* trash; *Austral./NZ* mullock. **2** *most of what he says is garbage* RUBBISH, nonsense, balderdash, claptrap, twaddle, blather; dross; *informal* hogwash, baloney, tripe, bilge, bull, bunk, poppycock, rot, bosh, piffle, dreck; *Brit. informal* tosh, codswallop, cobblers, stuff and nonsense; *informal, dated* tommyrot, bunkum.
garble ● verb MIX UP, muddle, jumble, confuse, obscure, distort; misstate, misquote, misreport, misrepresent, mistranslate, misinterpret, misconstrue, twist.
garden ● noun cottage garden, flower garden, rock garden, walled garden, knot garden; vegetable garden, kitchen garden, potager; (**gardens**) park, estate, grounds.
– RELATED TERMS horticultural.
– PHRASES **lead someone up the garden path** *(informal)* DECEIVE, mislead, delude, hoodwink, dupe, trick, entrap, beguile, take in, fool, pull the wool over someone's eyes, gull; *informal* con, pull a fast one on, string along, take for a ride, put one over on.
gargantuan ● adjective HUGE, enormous, vast, gigantic, very big, giant, massive, colossal, mammoth, immense, mighty, monumental, mountainous, titanic, towering, tremendous, elephantine, king-size(d), prodigious; *informal* mega, monster, whopping, humongous, jumbo; *Brit. informal* whacking, ginormous.
– OPPOSITES tiny.
garish ● adjective GAUDY, lurid, loud, over-bright, harsh, glaring, violent, showy, glittering, brassy, brash; tasteless, in bad taste, vulgar, unattractive, bilious; *informal* flash, flashy, tacky.
– OPPOSITES drab.
garland ● noun *a garland of flowers* FESTOON, lei, wreath, ring, circle, swag; coronet, crown, coronal, chaplet, fillet.
● verb *gardens garlanded with coloured lights* FESTOON, wreathe,

– DERIVATIVES **garlicky** adjective.
– ORIGIN Old English, from *gār* 'spear' (because the shape of a clove resembles the head of a spear) + *lēac* 'leek'.
garment ● noun an item of clothing.
– ORIGIN Old French *garnement* 'equipment', from *garnir* (see GARNISH).
garner ● verb **1** gather or collect. **2** archaic store; deposit. ● noun archaic a storehouse for corn; a granary.
– ORIGIN Old French *gernier*, from Latin *granarium* 'granary'.
garnet /gaarnit/ ● noun a deep red semi-precious stone.
– ORIGIN perhaps from Latin *granatum*, as in *pomum granatum* 'pomegranate' (literally 'apple having many seeds'), because the garnet is similar in colour to the pulp of the fruit.
garnish ● verb **1** decorate (something, especially food). **2** Law serve notice on (a third party) for the purpose of legally seizing money belonging to a debtor or defendant. **3** Law seize (money, especially part of a person's salary) to settle a debt or claim. ● noun a decoration for food.
– ORIGIN originally in the sense 'equip, arm': from Old French *garnir*; related to WARN.
garniture /gaarnichər/ ● noun a set of decorative vases.
– ORIGIN French, from *garnir* 'to garnish'.
garotte ● verb & noun variant spelling of GARROTTE.
garret ● noun a top-floor or attic room.
– ORIGIN originally in the sense 'watchtower': from Old French *garite*, from *garir* (see GARRISON).
garrison ● noun a body of troops stationed in a fortress or town to defend it. ● verb provide (a place) with a garrison.
– ORIGIN originally in the sense 'safety, means of protection': from Old French *garison*, from *garir* 'defend, provide'.
garrotte /gərot/ (also **garotte**; US **garrote**) ● verb kill by strangulation. ● noun a wire, cord, or apparatus used for garrotting.
– ORIGIN Spanish *garrote* 'cudgel, garrotte'.
garrulous /garrooləss/ ● adjective excessively talkative.
– DERIVATIVES **garrulity** /gərōōliti/ noun **garrulously** adverb **garrulousness** noun.
– ORIGIN Latin *garrulus*, from *garrire* 'to chatter, prattle'.
garter ● noun **1** a band worn around the leg to keep up a stocking or sock. **2** N. Amer. a suspender for a sock or stocking.
– DERIVATIVES **gartered** adjective.
– ORIGIN Old French *gartier*, from *garet* 'bend of the knee, calf of the leg'.
garter snake ● noun **1** a common, harmless North American snake with well-defined longitudinal stripes. **2** a venomous burrowing African snake, typically dark with lighter bands.
garter stitch ● noun knitting in which all of the rows are knitted in plain stitch, rather than alternating with purl rows.
garth ● noun **1** Brit. an open space surrounded by cloisters. **2** archaic a yard or garden.
– ORIGIN Old Norse, related to YARD².
gas ● noun (pl. **gases** or chiefly US **gasses**) **1** an air-like fluid substance which expands freely to fill any space available, irrespective of its quantity. **2** a flammable substance of this type used as a fuel. **3** a gaseous anaesthetic such as nitrous oxide, used in dentistry. **4** (**a gas**) informal an entertaining or amusing person or thing. **5** N. Amer. informal gasoline. **6** chiefly N. Amer. flatulence. **7** Mining an explosive mixture of firedamp with air. ● verb (**gases, gassed, gassing**) **1** attack with, expose to, or kill with gas. **2** N. Amer. informal fill the tank of (a motor vehicle) with petrol. **3** informal talk idly; chatter.
– DERIVATIVES **gasification** noun **gasify** verb **gasser** noun.
– ORIGIN invented by the Belgian chemist J. B. van Helmont (1577–1644) to denote an occult principle which he believed to exist in all matter; suggested by Greek *khaos* 'chaos'.
gasbag ● noun informal a person who talks idly and excessively.
gas chamber ● noun an airtight room that can be filled with poisonous gas to kill people or animals.
Gascon /gaskən/ ● noun a person from Gascony, a region in SW France.
– ORIGIN Old French, from Latin *Vasco*; related to BASQUE.
gaseous /gassiəss, gaysiəss/ ● adjective relating to or having the characteristics of a gas.
– DERIVATIVES **gaseousness** noun.
gash ● noun a long, deep slash, cut, or wound. ● verb make a gash in.
– ORIGIN from Old French *garcer* 'to chap, crack', perhaps from Greek *kharassein* 'sharpen, scratch, engrave'.
gasket /gaskit/ ● noun a sheet or ring of rubber or other material sealing the junction between two surfaces in an engine or other device.
– ORIGIN originally denoting a cord securing a furled sail to the yard of a sailing ship: perhaps from French *garcette* 'thin rope' (originally 'little girl').
gaslight ● noun light from lamps in which an incandescent mantle is heated by a jet of burning gas.
– DERIVATIVES **gaslit** adjective.
gas mask ● noun a protective mask used to cover the face as a defence against poison gas.
gasoline (also **gasolene**) ● noun N. Amer. petrol.
gasometer ● noun a large tank in which gas for use as fuel is stored before being distributed to consumers.
gasp ● verb **1** catch one's breath with an open mouth, from pain, breathlessness, or astonishment. **2** (**gasp for**) strain to obtain (air) by gasping. **3** (**be gasping for**) informal be desperate to have. ● noun a convulsive catching of breath.
– PHRASES **the last gasp** the point of exhaustion, death, or completion.
– ORIGIN Old Norse, 'to yawn'.
gasper ● noun Brit. informal, dated a cigarette.
gas-permeable ● adjective (of a contact lens) allowing the diffusion of gases into and out of the cornea.
gassy ● adjective (**gassier, gassiest**) **1** resembling or full of gas. **2** informal verbose; idly chattering.
– DERIVATIVES **gassiness** noun.
gastrectomy /gastrektəmi/ ● noun (pl. **gastrectomies**) surgical removal of a part or the whole of the stomach.

Thesaurus

swathe, hang; adorn, ornament, embellish, decorate, deck, trim, dress, bedeck, array; *poetic/literary* bedizen, caparison.
garment ● noun ITEM OF CLOTHING, article of clothing; (**garments**) clothes, clothing, dress, garb, outfit, costume, attire; *informal* get-up, rig-out, gear, togs, duds; *N. Amer. informal* threads; *formal* apparel.
garner ● verb *Edward garnered ideas from his travels* GATHER, collect, accumulate, amass, get together, assemble.
● noun *(archaic) the malt went into a garner* GRANARY, silo, storehouse, store, storeroom, depository.
garnish ● verb *garnish the dish with chopped parsley* DECORATE, adorn, ornament, trim, dress, embellish; enhance, grace, beautify, prettify, add the finishing touch to.
● noun *keep a few sprigs for a garnish* DECORATION, adornment, trim, trimming, ornament, ornamentation, embellishment, enhancement, finishing touch; *Cookery* chiffonade.
garret ● noun ATTIC, loft, roof space, cock loft, mansard.
garrison ● noun **1** *the English garrison had been burned alive* TROOPS, militia, soldiers, forces; armed force, military detachment, unit, platoon, brigade, squadron, battalion, corps. **2** *forces from three garrisons* FORTRESS, fort, fortification, stronghold, citadel, camp, encampment, cantonment, command post, base, station; barracks.
● verb **1** *French infantry garrisoned the town* DEFEND, guard, protect, barricade, shield, secure; man, occupy. **2** *troops were garrisoned in various regions* STATION, post, put on duty, deploy, assign, install; base, site, place, position; billet.
garrulity ● noun TALKATIVENESS, garrulousness, loquacity, loquaciousness, volubility, verbosity, verboseness, long-windedness, wordiness, chattiness, effusiveness; *informal* the gift of the gab; *Brit. informal* wittering; *rare* logorrhoea.
garrulous ● adjective **1** *a garrulous old man* TALKATIVE, loquacious, voluble, verbose, chatty, chattering, gossipy; effusive, expansive, forthcoming, conversational, communicative; *informal* mouthy, gabby, gassy, windy, having the gift of the gab, having kissed the Blarney Stone; *Brit. informal* able to talk the hind legs off a donkey. **2** *his garrulous reminiscences* LONG-WINDED, wordy, verbose, prolix, long, lengthy, rambling, wandering, maundering, meandering, digressive, diffuse, discursive; gossipy, chatty; *informal* windy, gassy.
– OPPOSITES taciturn, concise.
gash ● noun *a gash on his forehead* LACERATION, cut, wound, injury, slash, tear, incision; slit, split, rip, rent; scratch, scrape, graze, abrasion; *Medicine* lesion.
● verb *he gashed his hand on some broken glass* LACERATE, cut (open), wound, injure, hurt, slash, tear, gouge, puncture, slit, split, rend; scratch, scrape, graze, abrade.
gasp ● verb **1** *I gasped in surprise* CATCH ONE'S BREATH, draw in one's breath, gulp; exclaim, cry (out). **2** *he collapsed on the ground, gasping* PANT, puff, puff and pant, puff and blow, wheeze,

gastric ● adjective of the stomach.
– ORIGIN from Greek *gastēr* 'stomach'.
gastric flu ● noun a short-lived stomach disorder of unknown cause, popularly attributed to a virus.
gastric juice ● noun an acid fluid secreted by the stomach glands and active in promoting digestion.
gastritis /gastrītiss/ ● noun Medicine inflammation of the lining of the stomach.
gastro-enteritis ● noun inflammation of the stomach and intestines, typically resulting from bacterial toxins or viral infection and causing vomiting and diarrhoea.
gastroenterology /gastrōentərolləji/ ● noun the branch of medicine which deals with disorders of the stomach and intestines.
– DERIVATIVES **gastroenterological** adjective **gastroenterologist** noun.
– ORIGIN from Greek *gastēr* 'stomach' and *enteron* 'intestine'.
gastrointestinal /gastrōintestin'l/ ● adjective of or relating to the stomach and the intestines.
gastronome /gastrənōm/ ● noun a gourmet.
gastronomy /gastronnəmi/ ● noun the practice or art of choosing, cooking, and eating good food.
– DERIVATIVES **gastronomic** adjective.
– ORIGIN Greek *gastronomia*, from *gastēr* 'stomach'.
gastropod /gastrəpod/ ● noun Zoology any of a large class of molluscs including snails, slugs, and whelks.
– ORIGIN from Greek *gastēr* 'stomach' + *pous* 'foot'.
gastroscope ● noun an optical instrument used for inspecting the interior of the stomach.
– DERIVATIVES **gastroscopic** adjective **gastroscopy** noun.
gas turbine ● noun a turbine driven by expanding hot gases produced by burning fuel, as in a jet engine.
gasworks ● plural noun (treated as sing.) a place where gas is manufactured and processed.
gat archaic past of GET.
gate[1] ● noun **1** a hinged barrier used to close an opening in a wall, fence, or hedge. **2** an exit from an airport building to an aircraft. **3** a hinged or sliding barrier for controlling the flow of water. **4** the number of people who pay to enter a sports ground for an event. **5** an electric circuit with an output which depends on the combination of several inputs. ● verb Brit. confine (a pupil or student) to school or college.
– PHRASES **get** (or **be given**) **the gate** N. Amer. informal be dismissed from a job.
– DERIVATIVES **gated** adjective.
– ORIGIN Old English.
gate[2] ● noun Brit. (in place names) a street.
– ORIGIN Old Norse.
gateau /gattō/ ● noun (pl. **gateaus** or **gateaux** /gattōz/) chiefly Brit. a rich cake, typically one containing layers of cream or fruit.
– ORIGIN French.
gatecrash ● verb enter (a party) without an invitation or ticket.
– DERIVATIVES **gatecrasher** noun.
gatefold ● noun an oversized page in a book or magazine folded to the same size as the other pages but intended to be opened out for reading.
gatehouse ● noun **1** a house standing by the gateway to a country estate. **2** historical a room over a city or palace gate, often used as a prison.
gatekeeper ● noun an attendant at a gate.
gateleg table ● noun a table with hinged legs that may be swung out from the centre to support folding leaves.
– DERIVATIVES **gatelegged** adjective.
gatepost ● noun a post on which a gate is hinged or against which it shuts.
gateway ● noun **1** an opening that can be closed by a gate. **2** a frame or arch built around or over a gate. **3** Computing a device used to connect two different networks, especially a connection to the Internet.
gather ● verb **1** come or bring together; assemble or accumulate. **2** harvest (a crop). **3** collect plants, fruits, etc., for food. **4** draw together or towards oneself. **5** develop a higher degree of: *the movement is gathering pace.* **6** infer; understand. **7** pull and hold together (fabric) in a series of folds by drawing thread through it. ● noun (**gathers**) a series of folds in fabric, formed by gathering.
– PHRASES **gather way** (of a ship) begin to move.
– DERIVATIVES **gatherer** noun.
– ORIGIN Old English, related to TOGETHER.
gathering ● noun an assembly of people.
Gatling gun ● noun an early type of machine gun, with clustered barrels.
– ORIGIN named after the American inventor Richard J. *Gatling* (1818–1903).
gauche /gōsh/ ● adjective socially awkward or unsophisticated.
– DERIVATIVES **gauchely** adverb **gaucheness** noun.
– ORIGIN French, 'left'.
gaucherie /gōshəri/ ● noun awkward or unsophisticated ways.
– ORIGIN French.
gaucho /gowchō/ ● noun (pl. **gauchos**) a cowboy from the South American pampas.
– ORIGIN Latin American Spanish, probably from an American Indian language, meaning 'friend'.
gaudy[1] ● adjective (**gaudier**, **gaudiest**) extravagantly or tastelessly bright or showy.
– DERIVATIVES **gaudily** adverb **gaudiness** noun.
– ORIGIN probably from Old French *gaudir* 'rejoice', from Latin *gaudere*.
gaudy[2] ● noun (pl. **gaudies**) Brit. a celebratory dinner or entertainment held by a college for old members.
– ORIGIN from Latin *gaudium* 'joy' or from *gaude* 'rejoice!'.
gauge /gayj/ (chiefly US also **gage**) ● noun **1** an instrument that measures and gives a visual display of the amount, level, or contents of something. **2** the thickness, size, or capacity of a wire, sheet, tube, bullet, etc., especially as a standard measure. **3** the distance between the rails of a line of railway track. ● verb **1** estimate or determine the amount or level of. **2** judge or assess (a situation, mood, etc.). **3** measure the dimensions of with a gauge. **4** (**gauged**) made in standard dimensions.
– DERIVATIVES **gaugeable** adjective **gauger** noun.
– ORIGIN Old French.
Gaul /gawl/ ● noun a person from the ancient European region

g

Thesaurus

breathe hard, choke, fight for breath.
● noun *a gasp of dismay* DRAWING-IN OF BREATH, gulp; exclamation, cry; dated ejaculation.
gastric ● adjective *gastric pain* STOMACH, intestinal, enteric, duodenal, coeliac, abdominal, ventral.
gate ● noun **1** *heavy wooden gates* BARRIER, wicket gate, lychgate, five-barred gate, turnstile; Brit. kissing gate. **2** *she went through the gate* GATEWAY, doorway, entrance, exit, egress, opening; door, portal; N. Amer. entryway.
gather ● verb **1** *we gathered in the hotel lobby* CONGREGATE, assemble, meet, collect, come/get together, convene, muster, rally, converge; cluster together, crowd, mass, flock together; formal foregather. **2** *he gathered his family together* SUMMON, call together, bring together, assemble, convene, rally, round up, muster, marshal. **3** *knick-knacks she had gathered over the years* COLLECT, accumulate, amass, garner, accrue; store, stockpile, hoard, put by/away, lay by/in; informal stash away, squirrel away. **4** *they gathered corn from the fields* HARVEST, reap, crop; pick, pluck; collect. **5** *the show soon gathered a fanatical following* ATTRACT, draw, pull, pull in, collect, pick up. **6** *I gather he's a keen footballer* UNDERSTAND, be given to understand, believe, be led to believe, think, conclude, deduce, infer, assume, take it, surmise, fancy; hear, hear tell, learn, discover. **7** *he gathered her to his chest* CLASP, clutch, pull, embrace, enfold, hold, hug, cuddle, squeeze; poetic/literary embosom; archaic strain. **8** *his tunic was gathered at the waist* PLEAT, shirr, pucker, tuck, fold, ruffle.
– OPPOSITES disperse.
gathering ● noun **1** *she rose to address the gathering* ASSEMBLY, meeting, convention, rally, turnout, congress, convocation, conclave, council, synod, forum; congregation, audience, crowd, group, throng, mass, multitude; informal get-together; formal concourse. **2** *the gathering of data for a future book* COLLECTING, collection, garnering, amassing, accumulation, accrual, cumulation, building up.
gauche ● adjective AWKWARD, gawky, inelegant, graceless, ungraceful, ungainly, maladroit, inept; lacking in social grace(s), unsophisticated, uncultured, uncultivated, unrefined, raw, inexperienced, unworldly.
– OPPOSITES elegant, sophisticated.
gaudy ● adjective GARISH, lurid, loud, over-bright, glaring, harsh,

of Gaul.
– ORIGIN Latin *Gallus*, probably of Celtic origin.
Gauleiter /gowlītər/ ● **noun 1** historical an official governing a district under Nazi rule. **2** an overbearing official.
– ORIGIN German, from *Gau* 'administrative district' + *Leiter* 'leader'.
Gaulish ● **noun** the Celtic language of the ancient Gauls. ● **adjective** relating to the ancient Gauls.
Gaullism /gōliz'm/ ● **noun** the principles and policies of the French statesman Charles de Gaulle (1890–1970), characterized by conservatism, nationalism, and advocacy of centralized government.
– DERIVATIVES **Gaullist** noun & adjective.
gaunt ● **adjective 1** lean and haggard, especially through suffering, hunger, or age. **2** (of a place) grim or desolate in appearance.
– DERIVATIVES **gauntly** adverb **gauntness** noun.
– ORIGIN of unknown origin.
gauntlet[1] ● **noun 1** a stout glove with a long loose wrist. **2** a glove worn as part of medieval armour, made of leather with protective steel plates.
– PHRASES **take up** (or **throw down**) **the gauntlet** accept (or issue) a challenge. [ORIGIN from the medieval custom of issuing a challenge by throwing one's gauntlet to the ground; whoever picked it up was deemed to have accepted the challenge.]
– ORIGIN Old French *gantelet*, from *gant* 'glove'.
gauntlet[2] (US also **gantlet**) ● **noun** (in phrase **run the gauntlet**) **1** go through an intimidating crowd, place, or experience in order to reach a goal. **2** historical undergo the military punishment of receiving blows while running between two rows of men with sticks.
– ORIGIN alteration of *gantlope*, from Swedish *gata* 'lane' + *lopp* 'course', associated with GAUNTLET[1].
gauss /gowss/ ● **noun** (pl. same or **gausses**) a unit of magnetic flux density, equal to one ten-thousandth of a tesla.
– ORIGIN named after the German mathematician Karl Friedrich *Gauss* (1777–1855).
gauze /gawz/ ● **noun 1** a thin transparent fabric. **2** Medicine thin, loosely woven cloth used for dressing and swabbing wounds. **3** (also **wire gauze**) a very fine wire mesh.
– DERIVATIVES **gauzy** adjective.
– ORIGIN French *gaze*.
gave past of GIVE.
gavel /gavv'l/ ● **noun** a small hammer with which an auctioneer, judge, etc., hits a surface to call for attention or order. ● **verb** (**gavelled**, **gavelling**; US **gaveled**, **gaveling**) bring to order by use of a gavel.
– ORIGIN originally denoting a stonemason's mallet: of unknown origin.
gavial /gayviəl/ ● **noun** variant spelling of GHARIAL.
gavotte /gəvot/ ● **noun** a medium-paced French dance, popular in the 18th century.
– ORIGIN Provençal *gavoto* 'dance of the mountain people', from *Gavot* 'a native of the Alps'.
gawk informal ● **verb** stare openly and stupidly. ● **noun** an awkward or shy person.
– DERIVATIVES **gawker** noun **gawkish** adjective.
– ORIGIN perhaps related to obsolete *gaw* 'to gaze', from an Old Norse word meaning 'heed'.
gawky ● **adjective** (**gawkier**, **gawkiest**) nervously awkward and ungainly.
– DERIVATIVES **gawkily** adverb **gawkiness** noun.
gawp ● **verb** Brit. informal stare openly in a stupid or rude manner.
– DERIVATIVES **gawper** noun.
– ORIGIN perhaps an alteration of GAPE.
gay ● **adjective** (**gayer**, **gayest**) **1** (especially of a man) homosexual. **2** relating to homosexuals. **3** dated light-hearted and carefree. **4** dated brightly coloured; showy. ● **noun** a homosexual person, especially a man.
– DERIVATIVES **gayness** noun.
– USAGE **Gay** is now a standard term for 'homosexual', and is the term preferred by homosexual men to describe themselves. As a result, it is now very difficult to use **gay** in its earlier meanings 'carefree' or 'bright and showy' without arousing a sense of double entendre. **Gay** in its modern sense typically refers to men, **lesbian** being the standard term for homosexual women.
– ORIGIN Old French *gai*.
gaydar ● **noun** informal a homosexual person's ability to identify another person as homosexual by interpreting subtle signals conveyed by their appearance, interests, etc.
– ORIGIN from GAY + RADAR.
gayety ● **noun** US variant spelling of GAIETY.
gaze ● **verb** look steadily and intently. ● **noun** a steady intent look.
– DERIVATIVES **gazer** noun.
– ORIGIN perhaps related to obsolete *gaw* (see GAWK).
gazebo /gəzeebō/ ● **noun** (pl. **gazebos** or **gazeboes**) a summer house or similar structure offering a wide view of the surrounding area.
– ORIGIN perhaps humorously from GAZE, in imitation of Latin future tenses ending in *-ebo*.
gazelle ● **noun** a small slender antelope with curved horns and white underparts.
– ORIGIN French, probably from Arabic.
gazette ● **noun** a journal or newspaper, especially the official journal of an organization or institution. ● **verb** Brit. announce or publish in an official gazette.
– ORIGIN from Venetian *gazeta de la novità* 'a halfpennyworth of news' (with reference to a news-sheet sold for a *gazeta*, a Venetian coin of small value).

Thesaurus

violent, showy, glittering, brassy, ostentatious; tasteless, in bad taste, vulgar, unattractive, bilious; *informal* flash, flashy, tacky.
– OPPOSITES drab, tasteful.
gauge ● **noun 1** *the temperature gauge* MEASURING DEVICE, measuring instrument, meter, measure; indicator, dial, scale, display. **2** *exports are an important gauge of economic activity* MEASURE, indicator, barometer, point of reference, guide, guideline, touchstone, yardstick, benchmark, criterion, test, litmus test. **3** *guitar strings of a different gauge* SIZE, diameter, thickness, width, breadth; measure, capacity, magnitude; bore, calibre.
● **verb 1** *astronomers can gauge the star's intrinsic brightness* MEASURE, calculate, compute, work out, determine, ascertain; count, weigh, quantify, put a figure on. **2** *it is difficult to gauge how effective the ban was* ASSESS, evaluate, determine, estimate, form an opinion of, appraise, weigh up, get the measure of, judge, guess; *informal* guesstimate, size up.
gaunt ● **adjective 1** *a gaunt, greying man* HAGGARD, drawn, thin, lean, skinny, spindly, spare, bony, angular, raw-boned, pinched, hollow-cheeked, scrawny, scraggy, as thin as a rake, cadaverous, skeletal, emaciated, skin-and-bones; wasted, withered; *informal* like a bag of bones; *dated* spindle-shanked; *archaic* starveling. **2** *the gaunt ruin of Pendragon Castle* BLEAK, stark, desolate, bare, gloomy, dismal, sombre, grim, stern, harsh, forbidding, uninviting, cheerless.
– OPPOSITES plump.
gauzy ● **adjective** TRANSLUCENT, transparent, sheer, see-through, fine, delicate, flimsy, filmy, gossamer-like, diaphanous, chiffony, wispy, thin, light, insubstantial; *Brit.* floaty.
– OPPOSITES opaque, thick.
gawk ● **verb** *(informal)* GAPE, goggle, gaze, ogle, stare, stare open-mouthed; *informal* rubberneck; *Brit. informal* gawp.
gawky ● **adjective** AWKWARD, ungainly, gangling, gauche, maladroit, clumsy, inelegant, uncoordinated, graceless, ungraceful; unsophisticated, unconfident.
– OPPOSITES graceful.
gay ● **adjective 1** *gay men and women* HOMOSEXUAL, lesbian; *informal* queer, camp, pink, swinging the other way, homo, dykey; *Brit. informal* bent, poofy. **2** *(dated) her children all looked chubby and gay* CHEERFUL, cheery, merry, jolly, light-hearted, carefree, jovial, glad, happy, in good/high spirits, joyful, elated, exuberant, animated, lively, sprightly, vivacious, buoyant, bouncy, bubbly, perky, effervescent, playful; *informal* chirpy. **3** *(dated) they were having a gay old time* JOLLY, merry, hilarious, amusing, uproarious, rollicking, entertaining, enjoyable, convivial; festive. **4** *(dated) gay checked curtains* BRIGHT, brightly coloured, vivid, brilliant, vibrant; richly coloured, many-coloured, multicoloured; flamboyant, showy, gaudy.
– OPPOSITES heterosexual, gloomy.
● **noun** *in Denmark gays can marry in church* HOMOSEXUAL, lesbian; *informal* queer, homo, queen, friend of Dorothy, pansy, nancy, dyke, les, lezzy, butch, femme; *Brit. informal* poof, ponce, woofter.
gaze ● **verb** *he gazed at her* STARE, look fixedly, gape, goggle, eye, look, study, scrutinize, take a good look; ogle, leer; *informal* gawk, rubberneck; *Brit. informal* gawp; *N. Amer. informal* eyeball.

gazetteer /gazziteer/ ● noun a geographical index or dictionary.
– ORIGIN originally in the sense 'journalist' (for whom such an index was provided): from Italian *gazzettiere*, from *gazzetta* 'gazette'.

gazillion /gəzillyən/ (also **kazillion**) ● cardinal number N. Amer. informal a very large number or quantity.
– ORIGIN fanciful formation on the pattern of *billion* and *million*.

gazpacho /gəspachō/ ● noun (pl. **gazpachos**) a cold Spanish soup made from tomatoes, peppers, and other salad vegetables.
– ORIGIN Spanish.

gazump /gəzump/ ● verb Brit. informal deprive (someone whose offer to purchase a house has already been accepted) from proceeding with the purchase by offering or accepting a higher figure.
– DERIVATIVES **gazumper** noun.
– ORIGIN originally in the sense 'swindle': from Yiddish, 'overcharge'.

GB ● abbreviation **1** Great Britain. **2** (also **Gb**) Computing gigabyte(s).

GBE ● abbreviation Knight or Dame Grand Cross of the Order of the British Empire.

GBH ● abbreviation Brit. grievous bodily harm.

GC ● abbreviation George Cross.

GCB ● abbreviation Knight or Dame Grand Cross of the Order of the Bath.

GCE ● abbreviation General Certificate of Education.

GCHQ ● abbreviation Government Communications Headquarters.

GCMG ● abbreviation Knight or Dame Grand Cross of the Order of St Michael and St George.

GCSE ● abbreviation (in the UK except Scotland) General Certificate of Secondary Education (the lower of the two main levels of the GCE examination).

GCVO ● abbreviation Knight or Dame Grand Cross of the Royal Victorian Order.

Gd ● symbol the chemical element gadolinium.

GDP ● abbreviation gross domestic product.

GDR ● abbreviation historical German Democratic Republic.

Ge ● symbol the chemical element germanium.

gean /jeen/ ● noun the wild or sweet cherry.
– ORIGIN Old French *guine*.

gear ● noun **1** a toothed wheel that works with others to alter the relation between the speed of an engine and the speed of the driven parts (e.g. wheels). **2** a particular setting of engaged gears. **3** informal apparatus, equipment, or clothing. ● verb **1** design or adjust gears to give a specified speed or power output. **2** (often **gear up**) make ready; equip or prepare. **3** (**gear down** or **up**) change to a lower (or higher) gear.
– PHRASES **in** (or **out of**) **gear** with a gear (or no gear) engaged.
– ORIGIN Scandinavian.

gearbox ● noun a set of gears with its casing, especially in a motor vehicle; the transmission.

gear lever (also **gearstick**) ● noun Brit. a lever used to engage or change gear in a motor vehicle.

gear shift ● noun chiefly N. Amer. a gear lever.

gearwheel ● noun **1** a toothed wheel in a set of gears. **2** (on a bicycle) a cogwheel driven directly by the chain.

gecko /gekkō/ ● noun (pl. **geckos** or **geckoes**) a nocturnal lizard with adhesive pads on the feet, found in warm regions.
– ORIGIN from a Malay word imitative of its cry.

gee[1] (also **gee whiz**) ● exclamation informal, chiefly N. Amer. a mild expression of surprise, enthusiasm, or sympathy.
– ORIGIN perhaps an abbreviation of JESUS.

gee[2] ● exclamation (**gee up**) a command to a horse to go faster. ● verb (**gees**, **geed**, **geeing**) (**gee up**) command (a horse) to go faster.
– ORIGIN of unknown origin.

gee-gee ● noun Brit. informal a child's word for a horse.
– ORIGIN reduplication of GEE[2].

geek /geek/ ● noun informal, chiefly N. Amer. **1** an unfashionable or socially inept person. **2** an obsessive enthusiast.
– DERIVATIVES **geeky** adjective.
– ORIGIN from the related English dialect word *geck* 'fool'.

geese plural of GOOSE.

Ge'ez /geeez/ ● noun an ancient Semitic language of Ethiopia, which survives as the liturgical language of the Ethiopian Orthodox Church.

geezer /geezər/ ● noun informal a man.
– ORIGIN representing a dialect pronunciation of earlier *guiser* 'mummer'.

gefilte fish /gəfiltə/ ● noun a dish of stewed or baked stuffed fish, or of fish cakes boiled in a fish or vegetable broth.
– ORIGIN Yiddish, 'stuffed fish'.

Geiger counter ● noun a device for measuring radioactivity by detecting and counting ionizing particles.
– ORIGIN named after the German physicist Hans *Geiger* (1882–1945).

geisha /gayshə/ ● noun (pl. same or **geishas**) a Japanese hostess trained to entertain men with conversation, dance, and song.
– ORIGIN Japanese, 'entertainer'.

gel[1] /jel/ ● noun **1** a jelly-like substance containing a cosmetic, medicinal, or other preparation. **2** Chemistry a semi-solid colloidal suspension of a solid dispersed in a liquid. ● verb (**gelled**, **gelling**) **1** Chemistry form into a gel. **2** smooth (one's hair) with gel.
– ORIGIN from GELATIN.

gel[2] /jel/ ● verb variant spelling of JELL.

gelatin /jellətin/ (also **gelatine** /jelləteen/) ● noun **1** a virtually colourless and tasteless water-soluble protein prepared from collagen and used in food preparation, in photographic processing, and for making glue. **2** a high explosive consisting chiefly of a gel of nitroglycerine with added cellulose nitrate.
– DERIVATIVES **gelatinize** (also **gelatinise**) verb **gelatinous** adjective.
– ORIGIN French *gélatine*, from Latin *gelata* 'frozen'; related to JELLY.

geld ● verb castrate (a male animal).
– ORIGIN from an Old Norse word meaning 'barren'.

gelding ● noun a castrated animal, especially a male horse.

gelid /jellid/ ● adjective icy; extremely cold.
– ORIGIN Latin *gelidus*, from *gelu* 'frost, intense cold'.

gelignite /jellignīt/ ● noun a high explosive made from a gel of nitroglycerine and nitrocellulose in a base of wood pulp and sodium or potassium nitrate, used particularly for blasting rock.
– ORIGIN probably from GELATIN + Latin *lignis* 'wood'.

gelt /gelt/ ● noun informal money.
– ORIGIN German *Geld*.

gem ● noun **1** a precious or semi-precious stone, especially one that has been cut and polished. **2** an outstanding person or thing.
– ORIGIN Latin *gemma* 'bud, jewel'.

Gemini /jemminī/ ● noun **1** Astronomy a northern constellation (the Twins), said to represent the twins Castor and Pollux. **2** Astrology the third sign of the zodiac, which the sun enters about 21 May.

g

Thesaurus

● noun *his piercing gaze* STARE, fixed look, gape; regard, inspection, scrutiny.

gazebo ● noun SUMMER HOUSE, pavilion, belvedere; arbour, bower.

gazette ● noun NEWSPAPER, paper, journal, periodical, organ, news-sheet, newsletter, bulletin; *informal* rag.

gear ● noun (*informal*) **1** *his fishing gear* EQUIPMENT, apparatus, paraphernalia, articles, appliances, impedimenta; tools, utensils, implements, instruments, gadgets; stuff, things; kit, rig, tackle, odds and ends, bits and pieces, bits and bobs; trappings, appurtenances, accoutrements, regalia; *Brit. informal* clobber, gubbins, odds and sods; *archaic* equipage. **2** *I'll go back to my hotel and pick up my gear* BELONGINGS, possessions, effects, personal effects, property, paraphernalia, odds and ends, bits and pieces, bits and bobs, bags, baggage; *Law* chattels; *informal* things, stuff, kit; *Brit. informal* clobber. **3** *the best designer gear* CLOTHES, clothing, garments, outfits, attire, garb; dress, wear; *informal* togs, duds, get-up; *Brit. informal* clobber, kit; *N. Amer. informal* threads; *formal* apparel.

gel, jell ● verb **1** *leave the mixture to gel* SET, stiffen, solidify, thicken, harden; cake, congeal, coagulate, clot. **2** *things started to gel very quickly* TAKE SHAPE, fall into place, come together, take form, work out; crystallize.

gelatinous ● adjective JELLY-LIKE, glutinous, viscous, viscid, mucilaginous, ropy, sticky, gluey, gummy, slimy; *informal* gooey, gunky.

geld ● verb CASTRATE, neuter, desex, fix; *N. Amer. & Austral.* alter; *Brit. informal* doctor.

gelid ● adjective FROZEN, freezing, icy, glacial, frosty, wintry, snowy; arctic, polar, Siberian.

gem ● noun **1** *rubies and other gems* JEWEL, precious stone, semi-precious stone, stone; solitaire, brilliant, cabochon; *archaic* bijou. **2** *the gem of the collection* BEST, finest, pride, prize, treasure,

– DERIVATIVES **Geminian** /jemmineeən/ noun & adjective.
– ORIGIN Latin, 'twins'.
gemsbok /gemzbok/ • **noun** a large African antelope with distinctive black-and-white head markings and long straight horns.
– ORIGIN Dutch, 'chamois'.
gemstone • **noun** a gem used in a piece of jewellery.
gemütlich /gəmōōtlikh/ • **adjective** pleasant and cheerful.
– ORIGIN German.
Gemütlichkeit /gəmōōtlikhkit/ • **noun** geniality; friendliness.
– ORIGIN German.
gen /jen/ Brit. informal • **noun** information. • **verb** (**genned**, **genning**) (**gen up**) provide with or obtain information.
– ORIGIN originally in military use: perhaps from *general information.*
-gen • **combining form 1** Chemistry denoting a substance that produces something: *allergen.* **2** Botany denoting a substance or plant that is produced.
– ORIGIN from Greek *genēs* '-born, of a specified kind'.

g

gendarme /zhondaarm/ • **noun** a paramilitary police officer in French-speaking countries.
– ORIGIN French, from *gens d'armes* 'men of arms'.
gendarmerie /zhondaarməri/ • **noun 1** a force of gendarmes. **2** the headquarters of such a force.
gender • **noun 1** Grammar a class (usually masculine, feminine, common, or neuter) into which nouns and pronouns are placed in some languages. **2** the state of being male or female (with reference to social or cultural differences). **3** the members of one or other sex.
– DERIVATIVES **gendered** adjective.
– USAGE The words **gender** and **sex** both have the sense 'the state of being male or female', but they are typically used in slightly different ways: **sex** tends to refer to biological differences, while **gender** tends to refer to cultural or social ones.
– ORIGIN Old French *gendre,* from Latin *genus* 'birth, family, nation'.
gene /jeen/ • **noun** Biology a distinct sequence of DNA forming part of a chromosome, by which offspring inherit characteristics from a parent.
– ORIGIN German *Gen,* from *Pangen,* a supposed ultimate unit of heredity, from Greek *pan-* 'all' + *genos* 'race, kind, offspring'.
genealogy /jeeniələji/ • **noun** (pl. **genealogies**) **1** a line of descent traced continuously from an ancestor. **2** the study of lines of descent.
– DERIVATIVES **genealogical** /jeeniəlojik'l/ adjective **genealogist** noun.
– ORIGIN Greek *genealogia,* from *genea* 'race, generation' + *logos* 'account'.
gene pool • **noun** the stock of different genes in an interbreeding population.
genera plural of GENUS.
general • **adjective 1** affecting or concerning all or most people or things; not specialized or limited. **2** involving only the main features or elements and disregarding exceptions; overall. **3** chief or principal: *the general manager.* • **noun 1** a commander of an army, or an army officer ranking above lieutenant general. **2** short for LIEUTENANT GENERAL or MAJOR GENERAL.
– PHRASES **in general 1** usually; mainly. **2** as a whole.
– ORIGIN Latin *generalis,* from *genus* 'class, race, kind'.
general anaesthetic • **noun** an anaesthetic that affects the whole body and causes a loss of consciousness.
general election • **noun** the election of representatives to a legislature from constituencies throughout the country.
generalissimo /jennərəlissimō/ • **noun** (pl. **generalissimos**) the commander of a combined military force consisting of army, navy, and air force units.
– ORIGIN from Italian, 'having greatest authority'.
generalist • **noun** a person competent in several different fields or activities.
generality • **noun** (pl. **generalities**) **1** a statement or principle having general rather than specific validity or force. **2** the quality or state of being general. **3** (**the generality**) the majority.
generalize (also **generalise**) • **verb 1** make a general or broad statement by inferring from specific cases. **2** make more common or more widely applicable. **3** (**generalized**) Medicine (of a disease) affecting much or all of the body; not localized.
– DERIVATIVES **generalizable** adjective **generalization** noun **generalizer** noun.
generally • **adverb 1** in most cases. **2** without regard to particulars or exceptions. **3** widely.
general meeting • **noun** a meeting open to all members of an organization.
general practitioner • **noun** a community doctor who treats patients with minor or chronic illnesses.
– DERIVATIVES **general practice** noun.
general-purpose • **adjective** having a range of potential uses or functions.
general staff • **noun** the staff assisting a military commander.
general strike • **noun** a strike of workers in all or most industries.
generate • **verb 1** cause to arise or come about. **2** produce (energy, especially electricity).
– DERIVATIVES **generable** adjective.
– ORIGIN Latin *generare* 'create', from *genus* 'stock, race'.
generation • **noun 1** all of the people born and living at about the same time, regarded collectively. **2** the average period in which children grow up and have children of their own (usually reckoned as about thirty years). **3** a set of members of a family regarded as a single stage in descent. **4** the action of producing or generating. **5** the propagation of living organisms; procreation.
– DERIVATIVES **generational** adjective.
generation gap • **noun** a difference in attitudes between people of different generations, leading to lack of understanding.
Generation X • **noun** the generation born between the mid 1960s and the mid 1970s, perceived as being disaffected and dir-

Thesaurus

flower, pearl, the jewel in the crown; pick, choice, cream, the crème de la crème, elite, acme; *informal* one in a million, the bee's knees.
genealogy • **noun** LINEAGE, line (of descent), family tree, bloodline; pedigree, ancestry, extraction, heritage, parentage, birth, family, dynasty, house, stock, blood, roots.
general • **adjective 1** *this is suitable for general use* WIDESPREAD, common, extensive, universal, wide, popular, public, mainstream; established, conventional, traditional, orthodox, accepted. **2** *a general pay increase* COMPREHENSIVE, overall, across the board, blanket, umbrella, mass, wholesale, sweeping, broad-ranging, inclusive, company-wide; universal, global, worldwide, nationwide. **3** *general knowledge* MISCELLANEOUS, mixed, assorted, diversified, composite, heterogeneous. **4** *the general practice* USUAL, customary, habitual, traditional, normal, conventional, typical, standard, regular; familiar, accepted, prevailing, routine, run-of-the-mill, established, everyday, ordinary, common. **5** *a general description* BROAD, imprecise, inexact, rough, loose, approximate, unspecific, vague, woolly, indefinite; *N. Amer. informal* ballpark.
– OPPOSITES restricted, localized, specialist, exceptional, detailed.
generality • **noun 1** *the debate has moved on from generalities* GENERALIZATION, general statement, general principle, sweeping statement; abstraction, extrapolation. **2** *the generality of this principle* UNIVERSALITY, comprehensiveness, all-inclusiveness, broadness. **3** *the generality of people are kind* MAJORITY, greater part/number, best/better part; bulk, mass, preponderance, predominance; most.
– OPPOSITES specific, minority.
generally • **adverb 1** *summers were generally hot* NORMALLY, in general, as a rule, by and large, more often than not, almost always, mainly, mostly, for the most part, predominantly, on the whole; usually, habitually, customarily, typically, ordinarily, commonly. **2** *France was moving generally to the left* OVERALL, in general terms, generally speaking, all in all, broadly, on average, basically, effectively. **3** *the method was generally accepted* WIDELY, commonly, extensively, universally, popularly.
generate • **verb 1** *moves to generate extra business* CAUSE, give rise to, lead to, result in, bring about, create, make, produce, engender, spawn, precipitate, prompt, provoke, trigger, spark off, stir up, induce, promote, foster. **2** *the male most likely to generate offspring* PROCREATE, breed, father, sire, spawn, create, produce, have; *poetic/literary* beget; *archaic* engender.
generation • **noun 1** *people of the same generation* AGE, age group, peer group. **2** *generations ago* AGES, years, aeons, a long time, an eternity; *informal* donkey's years; *Brit. informal* yonks. **3** *the next generation of computers* CROP, batch, wave, range. **4** *the gener-*

ectionless.
– DERIVATIVES **Generation Xer** noun.
generative ● adjective relating to or capable of production or reproduction.
generator ● noun **1** a person or thing that generates. **2** a dynamo or similar machine for converting mechanical energy into electricity.
generic /jinerrik/ ● adjective **1** referring to a class or group; not specific. **2** (of goods) having no brand name. **3** Biology relating to a genus.
– DERIVATIVES **generically** adverb.
– ORIGIN from Latin *genus* 'stock, race'.
generous ● adjective **1** freely giving more than is necessary or expected. **2** kind towards others. **3** larger or more plentiful than is usual.
– DERIVATIVES **generosity** noun **generously** adverb.
– ORIGIN originally in the sense 'of noble birth': from Latin *generosus* 'noble, magnanimous'.
genesis /jennisiss/ ● noun **1** the origin or mode of formation of something. **2** (**Genesis**) the first book of the Bible, which includes the story of the creation of the world.
– ORIGIN Greek, 'generation, creation', from *gignesthai* 'be born or produced'.
gene therapy ● noun the introduction of normal genes into cells in place of missing or defective ones in order to correct genetic disorders.
genetic ● adjective **1** relating to genes or heredity. **2** relating to genetics. **3** relating to origin, or arising from a common origin.
– DERIVATIVES **genetical** adjective **genetically** adverb.
– ORIGIN from GENESIS.
genetically modified ● adjective (of an organism) containing genetic material that has been artificially altered so as to produce a desired characteristic.
genetic code ● noun the means by which DNA and RNA molecules carry genetic information.
genetic engineering ● noun the deliberate modification of an organism by manipulating its genetic material.
genetic fingerprinting (also **genetic profiling**) ● noun the analysis of DNA from samples of body tissues or fluids in order to identify individuals.
genetic pollution ● noun the spread of altered genes from genetically engineered organisms to other, non-engineered organisms.
genetics ● plural noun **1** (treated as sing.) the study of heredity and the variation of inherited characteristics. **2** (treated as sing. or pl.) the genetic properties or features of an organism.
– DERIVATIVES **geneticist** noun.
genial ● adjective **1** friendly and cheerful. **2** literary (of weather) pleasantly mild and warm.
– DERIVATIVES **geniality** noun **genially** adverb.
– ORIGIN Latin *genialis* 'nuptial, productive', from *genius* (see GENIUS).
-genic ● combining form **1** producing or produced by: *carcinogenic*. **2** well suited to: *photogenic*.
– ORIGIN from -GEN + -IC.
genie /jeeni/ ● noun (pl. **genii** /jeeni-ī/ or **genies**) (in Arabian folklore) a jinn or spirit, especially one capable of granting wishes when summoned.
– ORIGIN originally denoting a guardian or protective spirit: from Latin *genius* (see GENIUS).
genii plural of GENIE, GENIUS.
genital ● adjective referring to the human or animal reproductive organs. ● noun (**genitals**) a person or animal's external reproductive organs.
– ORIGIN Latin *genitalis*, from *gignere* 'beget'.
genitalia /jennitayliə/ ● plural noun formal or technical the genitals.
– ORIGIN Latin.
genitive Grammar ● adjective denoting a case indicating possession or close association. ● noun a word in the genitive case.
– ORIGIN from Latin *genitivus casus* 'case of production or origin', from *gignere* 'beget'.
genito-urinary ● adjective chiefly Medicine relating to the genital and urinary organs.
genius /jeeniəss/ ● noun (pl. **geniuses**) **1** exceptional intellectual or creative power or other natural ability. **2** an exceptionally intelligent or able person. **3** (pl. **genii** /jeeni-ī/) (in some mythologies) a spirit associated with a person, place, or institution. **4** the prevalent character or spirit of a nation, period, etc.
– ORIGIN Latin, also in the sense 'spirit present at one's birth', from *gignere* 'beget'.
genlock ● noun a device for synchronizing two different video signals, or between a video signal and a computer or audio signal, enabling video images and computer graphics to be mixed.
– ORIGIN from GENERATOR + LOCK[1].
genoa /jennōə/ (also **genoa jib**) ● noun Sailing a large jib or foresail whose foot extends aft of the mast, used especially on racing yachts.
– ORIGIN named after the Italian city of *Genoa*.
genocide /jennəsīd/ ● noun the deliberate killing of a very large number of people from a particular ethnic group or nation.
– DERIVATIVES **genocidal** adjective.
– ORIGIN from Greek *genos* 'race' + -CIDE.
genome /jeenōm/ ● noun Biology **1** the haploid set of chromosomes of an organism. **2** the complete set of genetic material of an organism.
– DERIVATIVES **genomic** adjective.
– ORIGIN blend of GENE and CHROMOSOME.
genotype /jeenətīp/ ● noun Biology the genetic constitution of an individual organism. Often contrasted with PHENOTYPE.
– DERIVATIVES **genotypic** adjective.
-genous ● combining form **1** producing; inducing: *erogenous*. **2** originating in: *endogenous*.
– ORIGIN from -GEN + -OUS.

g

Thesaurus

ation of novel ideas CREATION, production, initiation, origination, inception, inspiration. **5** *human generation* PROCREATION, reproduction, breeding; creation.
generic ● adjective **1** *a generic term for two separate offences* GENERAL, common, collective, non-specific, inclusive, umbrella, all-encompassing, broad, comprehensive, blanket. **2** *generic drugs are cheaper than branded ones* UNBRANDED, non-proprietary, untrademarked.
– OPPOSITES specific.
generosity ● noun **1** *the generosity of our host* LIBERALITY, lavishness, magnanimity, munificence, open-handedness, free-handedness, unselfishness; kindness, benevolence, altruism, charity, big-heartedness, goodness; poetic/literary bounteousness. **2** *the generosity of the food portions* ABUNDANCE, plentifulness, copiousness, lavishness, liberality, largeness.
generous ● adjective **1** *she is generous with money* LIBERAL, lavish, magnanimous, munificent, giving, open-handed, free-handed, bountiful, unselfish, ungrudging, free, indulgent, prodigal; poetic/literary bounteous. **2** *it was generous of them to offer* MAGNANIMOUS, kind, benevolent, altruistic, charitable, noble, big-hearted, honourable, good; unselfish, self-sacrificing. **3** *a generous amount of fabric* LAVISH, plentiful, copious, ample, liberal, large, great, abundant, profuse, bumper, opulent, prolific; informal a gogo, galore.
– OPPOSITES mean, selfish, meagre.
genesis ● noun **1** *the hatred had its genesis in something dark* ORIGIN, source, root, beginning, start. **2** *the genesis of neurosis* FORMATION, development, evolution, emergence, inception, origination, creation, formulation, propagation.
genial ● adjective FRIENDLY, affable, cordial, amiable, warm, easygoing, approachable, sympathetic; good-natured, good-humoured, cheerful; neighbourly, hospitable, companionable, comradely, sociable, convivial, outgoing, gregarious; informal chummy, pally; Brit. informal matey.
– OPPOSITES unfriendly.
genitals ● plural noun PRIVATE PARTS, genitalia, sexual organs, reproductive organs, pudenda; crotch, groin; informal naughty bits, privates; euphemistic nether regions.
genius ● noun **1** *the world knew of his genius* BRILLIANCE, intelligence, intellect, ability, cleverness, brains, erudition, wisdom, fine mind; artistry, flair. **2** *he has a genius for organization* TALENT, gift, flair, aptitude, facility, knack, bent, ability, expertise, capacity, faculty; strength, forte, brilliance, skill, artistry. **3** *he is a genius* BRILLIANT PERSON, gifted person, mastermind, Einstein, intellectual, great intellect, brain; prodigy; informal egghead, bright spark; Brit. informal brainbox, clever clogs; N. Amer. informal brainiac, rocket scientist.
– OPPOSITES stupidity, dunce.
genocide ● noun MASS MURDER, mass homicide, massacre; annihilation, extermination, elimination, liquidation, eradication, deci-

genre /zhonrə/ ● noun **1** a style or category of art or literature. **2** (before another noun) denoting a style of painting depicting scenes from ordinary life.
– ORIGIN French, 'a kind', from Latin *genus* 'birth, family, nation'.
gent ● noun informal **1** a gentleman. **2** (**the Gents**) Brit. a men's public toilet.
genteel ● adjective affectedly polite and refined.
– DERIVATIVES **genteelly** adverb.
– ORIGIN French *gentil* 'well-born'.
gentian /jensh'n/ ● noun a plant of temperate and mountainous regions with violet or blue trumpet-shaped flowers.
– ORIGIN allegedly named after *Gentius*, king of Illyria, who discovered the plant's medicinal properties.
gentian violet ● noun a synthetic violet dye used as an antiseptic.
Gentile /jentīl/ ● adjective not Jewish. ● noun a person who is not Jewish.
– ORIGIN Latin *gentilis* 'of a family or nation, of the same clan', from *gens*, 'family, race'.
gentility ● noun socially superior or genteel character or behaviour.
– ORIGIN from Old French *gentil* 'high-born, noble' (see GENTLE).
gentle ● adjective (**gentler, gentlest**) **1** mild or kind; not rough or violent. **2** not harsh or severe. **3** archaic noble or courteous.
– DERIVATIVES **gentleness** noun **gently** adverb.
– ORIGIN Old French *gentil* 'high-born, noble', from Latin *gens* 'family, race'.
gentlefolk ● plural noun archaic people of noble birth or good social position.
gentleman ● noun **1** a courteous or honourable man. **2** a man of good social position, especially one of wealth and leisure. **3** (in polite or formal use) a man.
– DERIVATIVES **gentlemanly** adjective.
gentleman's agreement ● noun an arrangement which is based on trust rather than being legally binding.
gentlewoman ● noun archaic a woman of noble birth or good social standing.
gentrify ● verb (**gentrifies, gentrified**) renovate and improve (a house or district) so that it conforms to middle-class taste.
– DERIVATIVES **gentrification** noun **gentrifier** noun.
gentry ● noun (**the gentry**) people of good social position, specifically the class next below the nobility.
– ORIGIN Old French *genterie*, from *gentil* 'high-born, noble'.
genuflect /jenyooflekt/ ● verb lower one's body briefly by bending one knee to the ground in worship or as a sign of respect.
– DERIVATIVES **genuflection** noun.
– ORIGIN Latin *genuflectere*, from *genu* 'knee' + *flectere* 'to bend'.
genuine ● adjective **1** truly what it is said to be; authentic. **2** sincere; honest.
– DERIVATIVES **genuinely** adverb **genuineness** noun.
– ORIGIN Latin *genuinus*, from *genu* 'knee' (with reference to the ancient Roman custom of a father acknowledging paternity of a newborn child by placing it on his knee).
genus /jeenəss/ ● noun (pl. **genera** /jennərə/) **1** Biology a principal taxonomic category that ranks above species and below family, denoted by a capitalized Latin name, e.g. *Leo*. **2** a class of things which have common characteristics.
– ORIGIN Latin, 'birth, race, stock'.
-geny ● combining form denoting the mode by which something develops or is produced: *ontogeny*.
– ORIGIN Greek *-geneia*, from the root of *gignomai* 'be born, become' and *genos* 'a kind'.
geo- /jeeō/ ● combining form relating to the earth: *geocentric*.
– ORIGIN from Greek *gē* 'earth'.
geocentric ● adjective **1** having or representing the earth as the centre, as in former astronomical systems. Compare with HELIOCENTRIC. **2** Astronomy measured from or considered in relation to the centre of the earth.
geochemistry ● noun the study of the chemical composition of the earth and its rocks and minerals.
– DERIVATIVES **geochemical** adjective **geochemist** noun.
geode /jeeōd/ ● noun **1** a small cavity in rock lined with crystals or other mineral matter. **2** a rock containing such a cavity.
– ORIGIN from Greek *geōdēs* 'earthy'.
geodesic /jeeōdeezik/ ● adjective **1** referring to the shortest possible line between two points on a sphere or other curved surface. **2** (of a dome) constructed from struts which follow geodesic lines and form an open framework of triangles and polygons.
geodesy /jioddisi/ ● noun the branch of mathematics concerned with the shape and area of the earth or large portions of it.
– DERIVATIVES **geodesist** noun.
– ORIGIN Greek *geōdaisia*, from *gē* 'earth' + *daiein* 'to divide'.
geodetic /jiōdettik/ ● adjective relating to geodesy, especially as applied to land surveying.
geographical ● adjective relating to geography.
– DERIVATIVES **geographic** adjective **geographically** adverb.
geographical mile ● noun a distance equal to one minute of longitude or latitude at the equator (about 1,850 metres).
geography ● noun **1** the study of the physical features of the earth and of human activity as it relates to these. **2** the relative arrangement of places and physical features.
– DERIVATIVES **geographer** noun.
geology ● noun **1** the science which deals with the physical structure and substance of the earth. **2** the geological features of a district.
– DERIVATIVES **geologic** adjective **geological** adjective **geologically** adverb **geologist** noun.
geomagnetism ● noun the branch of geology concerned with the magnetic properties of the earth.
– DERIVATIVES **geomagnetic** adjective.
geomancy /jeeōmansi/ ● noun **1** the art of siting buildings auspiciously. **2** divination from the configuration of a handful of earth or random dots.
– DERIVATIVES **geomantic** adjective.
geometric /jiəmetrik/ ● adjective **1** relating to geometry. **2** (of a design) characterized by or decorated with regular lines and shapes.
– DERIVATIVES **geometrical** adjective **geometrically** adverb.
geometric mean ● noun the central number in a geometric progression (e.g. 9 in 3, 9, 27), also calculable as the nth root of a product of n numbers.
geometric progression (also **geometric series**) ● noun a sequence of numbers with a constant ratio between each number and the one before (e.g. 1, 3, 9, 27, 81).
geometry /jiommitri/ ● noun (pl. **geometries**) **1** the branch of mathematics concerned with the properties and relations of

Thesaurus

mation, butchery, bloodletting; pogrom, ethnic cleansing, holocaust.
genre ● noun CATEGORY, class, classification, group, set, list; type, sort, kind, variety, style, model, school, stamp, cast, ilk.
genteel ● adjective REFINED, respectable, decorous, mannerly, well mannered, courteous, polite, proper, correct, seemly; well bred, cultured, sophisticated, ladylike, gentlemanly, dignified, gracious; affected; Brit. informal posh.
– OPPOSITES uncouth.
gentility ● noun SOCIAL SUPERIORITY, respectability, punctiliousness, decorum, good manners, politeness, civility, courtesy, correctness; refinement, distinction, breeding, sophistication; graciousness, affectation, ostentation.
gentle ● adjective **1** *his manner was gentle* KIND, tender, sympathetic, considerate, understanding, compassionate, benevolent, good-natured; humane, lenient, merciful, clement; mild, placid, serene, sweet-tempered. **2** *a gentle breeze* LIGHT, soft. **3** *a gentle slope* GRADUAL, slight, easy. **4** (archaic) *a woman of gentle birth*. See NOBLE adjective sense 1.
– OPPOSITES brutal, strong, steep, low.
gentleman ● noun MAN; nobleman, honnête homme; informal gent; archaic cavalier.
gentlemanly ● adjective CHIVALROUS, gallant, honourable, noble, courteous, civil, mannerly, polite, gracious, considerate, thoughtful; well bred, cultivated, cultured, refined, suave, urbane.
– OPPOSITES rude.
gentry ● noun UPPER CLASSES, privileged classes, elite, high society, haut monde, smart set; establishment; informal upper crust, top drawer; Brit. informal nobs, toffs.
genuine ● adjective **1** *a genuine Picasso* AUTHENTIC, real, actual, original, bona fide, true, veritable; attested, undisputed; informal pukka, the real McCoy, the real thing, kosher; Austral./NZ informal dinkum. **2** *a very genuine person* SINCERE, honest, truthful, straightforward, direct, frank, candid, open; artless, natural, unaffected; informal straight, upfront, on the level; N. Amer. informal on the up and up.
– OPPOSITES bogus, insincere.
genus ● noun **1** (Biology) *a large genus of plants* subdivision, div-

points, lines, surfaces, and solids. **2** the shape and relative arrangement of the parts of something.
– DERIVATIVES **geometrician** noun.
– ORIGIN Greek, from *gē* 'earth' + *-metrēs* 'measurer'.
geomorphology /jeeōmorfolləji/ ● noun the study of the physical features of the surface of the earth and their relation to its geological structures.
– DERIVATIVES **geomorphological** adjective **geomorphologist** noun.
geophysics ● plural noun (treated as sing.) the physics of the earth.
– DERIVATIVES **geophysical** adjective **geophysicist** noun.
geopolitics ● plural noun (treated as sing. or pl.) politics, especially international relations, as influenced by geographical factors.
– DERIVATIVES **geopolitical** adjective.
Geordie ● noun Brit. informal a person from Tyneside.
– ORIGIN from the given name *George*.
georgette /jorjet/ ● noun a thin silk or crêpe dress material.
– ORIGIN named after the French dressmaker *Georgette* de la Plante (fl. *c.*1900).
Georgian[1] ● adjective **1** relating to or characteristic of the reigns of the British Kings George I–IV (1714–1830). **2** relating to British neoclassical architecture of this period.
Georgian[2] ● noun **1** a person from the country of Georgia. **2** the official language of Georgia. ● adjective relating to Georgians or Georgian.
geostationary ● adjective (of an artificial satellite) orbiting in such a way that it appears to be stationary above a fixed point on the earth's surface.
geosynchronous /jeeōsingkrənəss/ ● adjective another term for SYNCHRONOUS (in sense 2).
geothermal ● adjective relating to or produced by the internal heat of the earth.
geranium ● noun **1** a herbaceous plant or small shrub of a genus that comprises the cranesbills. **2** (in general use) a cultivated pelargonium.
– ORIGIN Greek *geranion*, from *geranos* 'crane'.
gerbera /jerbərə/ ● noun a tropical plant of the daisy family, with large brightly coloured flowers.
– ORIGIN named after the German naturalist Traugott *Gerber* (died 1743).
gerbil ● noun a burrowing mouse-like desert rodent.
– ORIGIN Latin *gerbillus* 'little jerboa'.
geriatric /jerriatrik/ ● adjective **1** relating to old people. **2** informal decrepit or out of date. ● noun an old person, especially one receiving special care.
– ORIGIN from Greek *gēras* 'old age' + *iatros* 'doctor'.
geriatrics ● plural noun (treated as sing. or pl.) the branch of medicine or social science concerned with the health and care of old people.
– DERIVATIVES **geriatrician** noun.
germ ● noun **1** a micro-organism, especially one which causes disease. **2** a portion of an organism capable of developing into a new one or part of one. **3** an initial stage from which something may develop: *the germ of an idea*.
– ORIGIN Latin *germen* 'seed, sprout'.
German ● noun **1** a person from Germany. **2** the language of Germany, Austria, and parts of Switzerland. ● adjective relating to Germany or German.
– DERIVATIVES **Germanize** (also **Germanise**) verb.
germane /jermayn/ ● adjective relevant to a subject under consideration.
– ORIGIN Latin *germanus* 'genuine, of the same parents'.
Germanic ● adjective **1** referring to the branch of the Indo-European language family that includes English, German, Dutch, Frisian, and the Scandinavian languages. **2** referring to the peoples of ancient northern and western Europe speaking such languages. **3** characteristic of Germans or Germany. ● noun **1** the Germanic languages collectively. **2** the unrecorded ancient language from which these developed.
germanium /jermayniəm/ ● noun a grey crystalline element with semiconducting properties, resembling silicon.
– ORIGIN from Latin *Germanus* 'German'.
German measles ● plural noun (usu. treated as sing.) another term for RUBELLA.
German shepherd ● noun a large breed of dog often used as guard dogs or for police work; an Alsatian.
German silver ● noun a white alloy of nickel, zinc, and copper.
germ cell ● noun Biology a gamete, or an embryonic cell with the potential of developing into one.
germicide ● noun a substance which destroys harmful micro-organisms.
– DERIVATIVES **germicidal** adjective.
germinal ● adjective **1** relating to a germ cell or embryo. **2** in the earliest stage of development. **3** providing material for future development.
– ORIGIN from Latin *germen* 'sprout, seed'.
germinate ● verb (of a seed or spore) begin to grow and put out shoots after a period of dormancy.
– DERIVATIVES **germination** noun.
– ORIGIN Latin *germinare* 'sprout forth, bud', from *germen* 'sprout, seed'.
germ warfare ● noun the use of disease-spreading micro-organisms as a military weapon.
Geronimo /jəronnimō/ ● exclamation used to express exhilaration when leaping or moving quickly.
– ORIGIN adopted as a slogan by American paratroopers, by association with the Apache chief *Geronimo* (*c.*1829–1909).
gerontic /jərontik/ ● adjective technical or literary relating to old age.
– ORIGIN from Greek *gerōn* 'old man'.
gerontocracy /jerrəntokrəsi/ ● noun **1** a state, society, or group governed by old people. **2** government based on rule by old people.
– DERIVATIVES **gerontocrat** noun **gerontocratic** adjective.
gerontology /jerrəntolləji/ ● noun the scientific study of old age and old people.
– DERIVATIVES **gerontological** adjective **gerontologist** noun.
gerrymander ● verb manipulate the boundaries of (an electoral constituency) so as to favour one party or class.
– ORIGIN from the name of Governor Elbridge *Gerry* of Massachusetts + SALAMANDER, from the supposed similarity between a salamander and the shape of a new voting district created when he was in office (1812), which was felt to favour his party.
gerund /jerrənd/ ● noun Grammar a verb form which functions as a noun, in English ending in *-ing* (e.g. *asking* in *do you mind my asking you?*).
– ORIGIN Latin *gerundum*, from *gerere* 'do'.
gesso /jessō/ ● noun a hard compound of plaster of Paris or whiting in glue, used in sculpture.
– ORIGIN Italian, from Greek *gupsos* 'gypsum'.
gestalt /gəstaalt/ ● noun Psychology an organized whole that is perceived as more than the sum of its parts.
– ORIGIN German, 'form, shape'.
Gestapo /gəstaapō/ ● noun the German secret police under Nazi rule.
– ORIGIN German, from *Geheime Staatspolizei* 'secret state police'.
gestation ● noun **1** the process of carrying or the state of being carried in the womb between conception and birth. **2** the development of a plan or idea over a period of time.
– DERIVATIVES **gestate** verb.
– ORIGIN Latin, from *gestare* 'carry, carry in the womb'.
gesticulate /jestikyoolayt/ ● verb gesture dramatically in place of or to emphasize speech.
– DERIVATIVES **gesticulation** noun.
– ORIGIN Latin *gesticulari*, from *gestus* 'action'.
gesture ● noun **1** a movement of part of the body to express an

g

Thesaurus

ision, group, subfamily. **2** *a new genus of music* TYPE, sort, kind, genre, style, variety, category, class; breed, brand, family, stamp, cast, ilk.
germ ● noun **1** *this detergent kills germs* MICROBE, micro-organism, bacillus, bacterium, virus; *informal* bug. **2** *a fertilized germ* EMBRYO, bud; seed, spore, ovule; egg, ovum. **3** *the germ of an idea* START, beginning(s), seed, embryo, bud, root, rudiment; origin, source, potential; core, nucleus, kernel, essence.
germane ● adjective RELEVANT, pertinent, applicable, apposite, material; apropos, to the point, appropriate, apt, fitting, suitable; connected, related, akin; *formal* ad rem.
– OPPOSITES irrelevant.
germinate ● verb **1** *the grain is allowed to germinate* SPROUT, shoot (up), bud; develop, grow, spring up; *dated* vegetate. **2** *the idea began to germinate* DEVELOP, take root, grow, emerge, evolve, mature, expand, advance, progress.
gestation ● noun **1** *a gestation of thirty days* PREGNANCY, incubation; development, maturation. **2** *the law underwent a period of gestation* DEVELOPMENT, evolution, formation, origination.
gesticulate ● verb GESTURE, signal, motion, wave, sign.

idea or meaning. **2** an action performed to convey one's feelings or intentions. **3** an action performed for show in the knowledge that it will have no effect. ● **verb** make a gesture.

– DERIVATIVES **gestural** adjective.

– ORIGIN Latin *gestura*, from *gerere* 'bear, wield, perform'.

get ● **verb** (**getting**; past **got**; past part. **got**, N. Amer. or archaic **gotten**) **1** come to have or hold; receive. **2** succeed in attaining, achieving, or experiencing; obtain. **3** experience, suffer, or be afflicted with. **4** move in order to pick up, deal with, or bring. **5** bring or come into a specified state or condition. **6** catch, apprehend, or thwart. **7** come or go eventually or with some difficulty. **8** move or come into a specified position or state. **9** tend to meet with or find. **10** travel by or catch (a form of transport). **11** begin to be or do something, especially gradually or by chance. **12** strike or wound. **13** informal punish, injure, or kill. **14** used with past participle to form the passive mood.

– PHRASES **get across** manage to communicate (an idea) clearly. **get at 1** reach or gain access to. **2** informal imply. **3** Brit. informal criticize subtly and repeatedly. **get away** escape. **get away with** escape blame or punishment for. **get back at** take revenge on. **get by** manage with difficulty to live or accomplish something. **get down** N. Amer. informal dance energetically. **get down to** begin to do or give serious attention to. **get off 1** informal escape a punishment. **2** go to sleep. **3** (**get off with**) Brit. informal have a sexual encounter with. **get on 1** manage or make progress with a task. **2** chiefly Brit. have a friendly relationship. **3** (**be getting on**) informal be old or comparatively old. **get out of** contrive to avoid or escape. **get over 1** recover from (an ailment or an unpleasant experience). **2** manage to communicate (an idea or theory). **3** promptly complete (an unpleasant but necessary task). **4** overcome (a difficulty). **get one's own back** informal have one's revenge. **get round** chiefly Brit. **1** coax or persuade (someone) to do or allow something. **2** deal successfully with (a problem). **get round to** chiefly Brit. deal with (a task) in due course. **get through 1** pass or endure (a difficult experience or period). **2** chiefly Brit. use up (a large amount or number of something). **3** make contact by telephone. **4** succeed in communicating with someone. **getting on for** chiefly Brit. almost (a specified time, age, or amount). **get to** informal annoy or upset by persistent action. **get together** gather or assemble socially or to cooperate. **get up 1** rise from bed after sleeping. **2** (of wind or the sea) become strong or agitated. **get up to** Brit. informal be involved in (something illicit or surprising).

– ORIGIN Old Norse, 'obtain, beget, guess'.

g

Thesaurus

gesticulation ● **noun** GESTURING, gesture, hand movement, signals, signs; wave, indication; body language.

gesture ● **noun 1** *a gesture of surrender* SIGNAL, sign, motion, indication, gesticulation. **2** *a symbolic gesture* ACTION, act, deed, move. ● **verb** *he gestured to her* SIGNAL, motion, gesticulate, wave, indicate, give a sign.

get ● **verb 1** *where did you get that hat?* ACQUIRE, obtain, come by, receive, gain, earn, win, come into, take possession of, be given; buy, purchase, procure, secure; gather, collect, pick up, hook, net, land; achieve, attain; *informal* get one's hands on, get one's mitts on, get hold of, grab, bag, score. **2** *I got your letter* RECEIVE, be sent, be in receipt of, be given. **3** *your tea's getting cold* BECOME, grow, turn, go. **4** *get the children from school* FETCH, collect, go for, call for, pick up, bring, deliver, convey, ferry, transport. **5** *the chairman gets £650,000 a year* EARN, be paid, take home, bring in, make, receive, collect, gross; *informal* pocket, bank, rake in, net, bag. **6** *have the police got their man?* APPREHEND, catch, arrest, capture, seize; take prisoner, take into custody, detain, put in jail, put behind bars, imprison, incarcerate; *informal* collar, grab, nab, nail, run in, pinch, bust, pick up, pull in, do, feel someone's collar; *Brit. informal* nick. **7** *I got a taxi* TRAVEL BY/ON/IN; take, catch, use. **8** *she got flu* SUCCUMB TO, develop, go/come down with, sicken for, fall victim to, be struck down with, be afflicted by/with; become infected with, catch, contract, fall ill with, be taken ill with; *Brit.* go down with; *informal* take ill with; *N. Amer. informal* take sick with. **9** *I got a pain in my arm* EXPERIENCE, suffer, be afflicted with, sustain, feel, have. **10** *I got him on the radio* CONTACT, get in touch with, communicate with, make contact with, reach; phone, call, radio; speak to, talk to; *Brit.* get on to; *informal* get hold of. **11** *I didn't get what he said* HEAR, discern, distinguish, make out, perceive, follow, take in. **12** *I don't get the joke* UNDERSTAND, comprehend, grasp, see, fathom, follow, perceive, apprehend, unravel, decipher; *informal* get the drift of, catch on to, latch on to, figure out; *Brit. informal* twig, suss. **13** *we got there early* ARRIVE, reach, come, make it, turn up, appear, come on the scene, approach, enter, present oneself, come along, materialize, show one's face; *informal* show (up), roll in/up, blow in. **14** *we got her to go* PERSUADE, induce, prevail on, influence; wheedle into, talk into, cajole into. **15** *I'd like to get to meet him* CONTRIVE, arrange, find a way, manage; succeed in, organize; *informal* work it, fix it. **16** *I'll get supper* PREPARE, get ready, cook, make, assemble, muster, concoct; *informal* fix, rustle up; *Brit. informal* knock up. **17** *(informal) I'll get him for that* TAKE REVENGE ON, exact/wreak revenge on, get one's revenge on, avenge oneself on, take vengeance on, get even with, pay back, get back at, exact retribution on, give someone their just deserts; *Brit. informal* get one's own back on. **18** *He scratched his head. 'You've got me there.'* BAFFLE, nonplus, perplex, puzzle, bewilder, mystify, bemuse, confuse, confound; *informal* flummox, faze, stump, beat, fox; *N. Amer. informal* discombobulate. **19** *what gets me is how neurotic she is* ANNOY, irritate, exasperate, anger, irk, vex, provoke, incense, infuriate, madden, try someone's patience, ruffle someone's feathers; *informal* aggravate, peeve, miff, rile, get to, needle, hack off, get someone's back up, get on someone's nerves, get up someone's nose, get someone's goat, drive mad, make someone see red; *Brit. informal* wind up, nark, get someone's wick; *N. Amer. informal* tee off, tick off.

– OPPOSITES give, send, take, leave.

– PHRASES **get about** MOVE ABOUT, move around, travel. **get something across** COMMUNICATE, get over, impart, convey, transmit, make clear, express. **get ahead** PROSPER, flourish, thrive, do well; succeed, make it, advance, get on in the world, go up in the world, make good, become rich; *informal* go places, get somewhere, make the big time. **get along 1** *does he get along with his family?* BE FRIENDLY, be compatible, get on; agree, see eye to eye, concur, be in accord; *informal* hit it off, be on the same wavelength. **2** *he was getting along well at school* FARE, manage, progress, advance, get on, get by, do, cope; succeed. **get around** TRAVEL, circulate, socialize, do the rounds. **get at 1** *it's difficult to get at the pipes* ACCESS, get to, reach, touch. **2** *he had been got at by enemy agents* CORRUPT, suborn, influence, bribe, buy off, pay off; *informal* fix, square; *Brit. informal* nobble. **3** *(informal) what are you getting at?* IMPLY, suggest, intimate, insinuate, hint, mean, drive at, allude to. **4** *(Brit. informal) I don't like being got at* CRITICIZE, pick on, find fault with, nag; BULLY, victimize, persecute, discriminate against. **get away** ESCAPE, run away/off, break out, break free, break loose, bolt, flee, take flight, make off, take off, decamp, abscond, make a run for it; slip away, sneak away; *informal* cut and run, skedaddle, do a disappearing act, scarper, leg it; *Brit. informal* do a bunk, do a runner. **get away with** ESCAPE BLAME FOR, escape punishment for. **get back** RETURN, come home, come back. **get something back** RETRIEVE, regain, win back, recover, recoup, reclaim, repossess, recapture, redeem; find (again), trace. **get back at** TAKE REVENGE ON, exact/wreak revenge on, avenge oneself on, take vengeance on, get even with, pay back, retaliate on/against, exact retribution on, give someone their just deserts; *Brit. informal* get one's own back on. **get someone down** DEPRESS, sadden, make unhappy, make gloomy, dispirit, dishearten, demoralize, discourage, crush, weigh down, oppress; upset, distress, grieve, haunt, harrow; *informal* give someone the blues, make someone fed up. **get by** MANAGE, cope, survive, exist, subsist, muddle through/along, scrape by, make ends meet, make do, keep the wolf from the door; *informal* make out. **get off 1** *Sally got off the bus* ALIGHT (FROM), step off, dismount (from), descend (from), disembark (from), leave, exit. **2** *(informal) he was arrested but got off* ESCAPE PUNISHMENT, be acquitted, be absolved, be cleared, be exonerated. **get on 1** *we got on the train* BOARD, enter, step aboard, climb on, mount, ascend, catch; *informal* hop on, jump on. **2** *how are you getting on?* FARE, manage, progress, get along, do, cope, get by, survive, muddle through/along; succeed, prosper; *informal* make out. **3** *he got on with his job* CONTINUE, proceed, go ahead, carry on, go on, press on, persist, persevere; keep at; *informal* stick with/at. **4** *we don't get on.* See GET ALONG sense 1. **get out 1** *the prisoners got out.* See GET AWAY. **2** *the news got out* BECOME KNOWN, become common knowledge, come to light, emerge, transpire; come out, be uncovered, be revealed, be divulged, be disclosed, be reported, be released, leak out. **get out of** *he tried to get out of paying any compensation* EVADE, dodge, shirk, avoid, escape, sidestep; *informal* duck (out of), wriggle out of, cop out of, funk; *Brit. informal* skive off; *N. Amer. informal* cut; *Austral./NZ informal* duck-shove. **get over** *I have just got over flu* RECOVER FROM, recuperate from, get better after, shrug off, sur-

getaway ● noun an escape or quick departure, especially after committing a crime.
get-together ● noun an informal gathering.
get-up ● noun informal a style or arrangement of dress, especially an elaborate or unusual one.
gewgaw /gyo͞ogaw/ ● noun a showy thing, especially one that is useless or worthless.
– ORIGIN of unknown origin.
Gewürztraminer /gəvoortstramminər/ ● noun a variety of white wine grape grown mainly in Alsace, Austria, and the Rhine valley.
– ORIGIN German, from *Gewürz* 'spice' + *Traminer*, a white wine grape grown in Germany and Alsace.
geyser /geezər/ ● noun **1** a hot spring in which water intermittently boils, sending a tall column of water and steam into the air. **2** Brit. a gas-fired water heater.
– ORIGIN from the name of a particular spring in Iceland.
Ghanaian /gaanayən/ ● noun a person from Ghana. ● adjective relating to Ghana.
gharial /gairiəl/ (also **gavial**) ● noun a large fish-eating crocodile with a long narrow snout.
– ORIGIN Hindi.
ghastly ● adjective (**ghastlier**, **ghastliest**) **1** causing great horror or fear. **2** deathly white or pallid. **3** informal very unpleasant.
– DERIVATIVES **ghastliness** noun.
– ORIGIN from obsolete *gast* 'terrify', from Old English; related to and influenced in spelling by GHOST.
ghat /gaat/ ● noun **1** (in the Indian subcontinent) a flight of steps leading down to a river. **2** (in the Indian subcontinent) a mountain pass.
– ORIGIN Hindi.
GHB ● abbreviation (sodium) gamma-hydroxybutyrate, a designer drug with anaesthetic properties.
ghee /gee/ ● noun clarified butter used in Indian cooking.
– ORIGIN from Sanskrit, 'sprinkled'.
Gheg /geg/ ● noun (pl. same or **Ghegs**) **1** a member of one of the two main ethnic groups of Albania, living mainly in the north of the country. Compare with TOSK. **2** the dialect of Albanian spoken by this people.
– ORIGIN Albanian *Geg*.
gherkin /gerkin/ ● noun a small pickled cucumber.
– ORIGIN Dutch *gurkje*, from Greek *angourion* 'cucumber'.
ghetto /gettō/ ● noun (pl. **ghettos** or **ghettoes**) **1** a part of a city, especially a slum area, occupied by a minority group. **2** historical the Jewish quarter in a city.
– DERIVATIVES **ghettoize** (also **ghettoise**) verb.
– ORIGIN perhaps from Italian *getto* 'foundry' (because the first ghetto was established on the site of a foundry in Venice), or from Italian *borghetto* 'small borough'.
ghetto blaster ● noun informal a large portable radio and cassette or CD player.
Ghibelline /gibbilīn/ ● noun a member of one of the two great political factions in Italian medieval politics, traditionally supporting the Holy Roman emperor against the Pope and his supporters, the Guelphs.
– ORIGIN Italian *Ghibellino*, perhaps from German *Waiblingen*, an estate belonging to Hohenstaufen emperors.
ghillie ● noun variant spelling of GILLIE.
ghost ● noun **1** an apparition of a dead person which is believed to appear to the living. **2** a faint trace: *the ghost of a smile.* **3** a faint secondary image produced by a fault in an optical system or on a cathode ray screen. ● verb act as ghost writer of.
– PHRASES **give up the ghost** die or stop functioning.
– ORIGIN Old English, 'spirit, soul'.
ghosting ● noun the appearance of a secondary image on a television or other display screen.
ghostly ● adjective (**ghostlier**, **ghostliest**) of or like a ghost; eerie and unnatural.
ghost town ● noun a town with few or no remaining inhabitants.
ghost train ● noun a miniature train at a funfair that travels through a dark tunnel in which there are eerie effects.
ghost writer ● noun a person employed to write material for another person, who is the named author.
– DERIVATIVES **ghost-write** verb.
ghoul /go͞ol/ ● noun **1** an evil spirit or phantom, especially one supposed to rob graves and feed on dead bodies. **2** a person morbidly interested in death or disaster.
– DERIVATIVES **ghoulish** adjective **ghoulishly** adverb **ghoulishness** noun.
– ORIGIN Arabic, denoting a desert demon believed to rob graves and devour corpses.
GHQ ● abbreviation General Headquarters.
GI ● noun (pl. **GIs**) a private soldier in the US army.
– ORIGIN originally denoting equipment supplied to US forces: abbreviation of *government* (or *general*) *issue*.
giant ● noun **1** an imaginary or mythical being of human form but superhuman size. **2** an abnormally tall or large person, animal, or plant. **3** Astronomy a star of relatively great size and luminosity. ● adjective of very great size or force; gigantic.
– DERIVATIVES **giantess** noun.
– ORIGIN Old French *geant*, from Greek *gigas*.
giant-killer ● noun a person or team that defeats a seemingly much more powerful opponent.
– DERIVATIVES **giant-killing** noun.
giardiasis /jiaardīəsiss/ ● noun infection of the intestine with a flagellate protozoan.
– ORIGIN named after the French biologist Alfred M. *Giard*

g

Thesaurus

vive. **get something over.** See GET SOMETHING ACROSS. **get round someone** CAJOLE, persuade, wheedle, coax, prevail on, win over, bring round, sway, beguile, charm, inveigle, influence, woo; *informal* sweet-talk, soft-soap, butter up, twist someone's arm. **get together 1** *get together the best writers* COLLECT, gather, assemble, bring together, rally, muster, marshal, congregate, convene, amass; *formal* convoke. **2** *we must get together soon* MEET (UP), rendezvous, see each other, socialize. **get up** GET OUT OF BED, rise, stir, rouse oneself; *informal* surface, show signs of life; *formal* arise. **get someone up** *(informal)* DRESS, clothe, attire, garb, fit out, turn out, deck (out), trick out/up, costume, array, robe; *informal* doll up; *archaic* apparel.
getaway ● noun ESCAPE, breakout, bolt for freedom, flight; disappearance, vanishing act; *Brit. informal* flit.
get-together ● noun PARTY, gathering, meeting, social event; *informal* do, bash; *Brit. informal* rave-up, knees-up, jolly, bunfight, beano.
get-up ● noun *(informal)* OUTFIT, clothes, costume, ensemble, suit, clothing, dress, attire, garments, garb; *informal* gear, togs, duds; *Brit. informal* clobber, rig-out; *N. Amer. informal* threads; *formal* apparel.
get-up-and-go ● noun *(informal)* DRIVE, initiative, enterprise, enthusiasm, eagerness, ambition, motivation, dynamism, energy, gusto, vigour, vitality, verve, fire, fervour, zeal, commitment, spirit; *informal* gumption, oomph, vim, pep.
– OPPOSITES apathy.
ghastly ● adjective **1** *a ghastly stabbing* TERRIBLE, frightful, horrible, grim, awful, dire; frightening, terrifying, horrifying, alarming; distressing, shocking, appalling, harrowing; dreadful, horrendous, monstrous, gruesome, grisly. **2** *(informal) a ghastly building* UNPLEASANT, objectionable, disagreeable, distasteful, awful, terrible, dreadful, frightful, detestable, insufferable, vile; *informal* horrible, horrid. **3** *he felt positively ghastly* ILL, unwell, peaky, poorly; sick, queasy, nauseous; *Brit.* off colour; *informal* rough, lousy, rotten, terrible, awful, dreadful; *Brit. informal* grotty, ropy; *Scottish informal* peely-wally; *Austral./NZ informal* crook. **4** *a ghastly pallor* PALE, white, pallid, pasty, wan, bloodless, peaky, ashen, grey, waxy, blanched, drained, pinched, green, sickly; *informal* like death warmed up.
– OPPOSITES pleasant, charming, fine, healthy.
ghost ● noun **1** *his ghost haunts the crypt* SPECTRE, phantom, wraith, spirit, presence; apparition; *informal* spook. **2** *the ghost of a smile* TRACE, hint, suggestion, impression, suspicion, tinge; glimmer, semblance, shadow, whisper.
ghostly ● adjective SPECTRAL, ghostlike, phantom, wraithlike, phantasmal, phantasmic; unearthly, unnatural, supernatural; insubstantial, shadowy; eerie, weird, uncanny; frightening, spine-chilling, hair-raising, blood-curdling, terrifying, chilling, sinister; *informal* creepy, scary, spooky.
ghoulish ● adjective MACABRE, grisly, gruesome, grotesque, ghastly; unhealthy, horrible, unwholesome.
giant ● noun COLOSSUS, man mountain, behemoth, Brobdingnagian, mammoth, monster; *informal* jumbo.
– OPPOSITES dwarf.
● adjective *a giant vacuum cleaner* HUGE, colossal, massive, enormous, gigantic, very big, mammoth, vast, immense, monumental, mountainous, titanic, towering, elephantine, king-size(d), gargantuan, Brobdingnagian; substantial, hefty; *informal* mega, monster,

(1846–1908).

gibber /jibbər/ • verb speak rapidly and unintelligibly, typically through fear or shock.
– DERIVATIVES **gibbering** adjective.
– ORIGIN imitative.

gibberish /jibbərish/ • noun unintelligible or meaningless speech or writing; nonsense.

gibbet /jibbit/ historical • noun **1** a gallows. **2** an upright post with an arm on which the bodies of executed criminals were left hanging as a warning to others. • verb (**gibbeted**, **gibbeting**) hang up on a gibbet or execute by hanging.
– ORIGIN Old French *gibet* 'little staff, cudgel, or gallows'.

gibbon • noun a small tree-dwelling ape with long, powerful arms, native to the forests of SE Asia.
– ORIGIN French, from an Indian dialect word.

gibbous /gibbəss/ • adjective (of the moon) having the illuminated part greater than a semicircle and less than a circle.
– ORIGIN Latin *gibbosus*, from *gibbus* 'hump'.

gibe /jīb/ • noun & verb variant spelling of JIBE[1].

g

giblets /jiblits/ • plural noun the liver, heart, gizzard, and neck of a chicken or other fowl, usually removed before the bird is cooked.
– ORIGIN Old French *gibelet* 'game bird stew', probably from *gibier* 'game hunted for sport'.

Gibraltarian /jibrawltairiən/ • noun a person from Gibraltar. • adjective relating to Gibraltar.

giddy • adjective (**giddier**, **giddiest**) **1** having or causing a sensation of whirling and a tendency to fall or stagger; dizzy. **2** excitable and frivolous. • verb (**giddies**, **giddied**) make (someone) feel excited to the point of disorientation.
– DERIVATIVES **giddily** adverb **giddiness** noun.
– ORIGIN Old English, 'insane' (literally 'possessed by a god').

giddy-up • exclamation said to induce a horse to start moving or go faster.
– ORIGIN reproducing a pronunciation of *get up*.

GIF • noun Computing **1** a popular format for image files, with built-in data compression. **2** (also **gif**) a file in this format.
– ORIGIN acronym from *graphic interchange format*.

gift • noun **1** a thing given willingly to someone without payment; a present. **2** a natural ability or talent. **3** informal a very easy task or unmissable opportunity. • verb **1** give as a gift, especially formally. **2** (**gift with**) endow (someone) with (an ability or talent). **3** (**gifted**) having exceptional talent or ability.
– PHRASES **don't look a gift horse in the mouth** proverb don't find fault with something that you have discovered or been given.
– DERIVATIVES **giftedness** adjective.
– ORIGIN Old Norse, related to GIVE.

gift token (also **gift voucher**) • noun Brit. a voucher given as a gift which is exchangeable for goods.

gift wrap • noun decorative paper for wrapping gifts. • verb (**gift-wrap**) wrap (a gift) in decorative paper.

gig[1] /gig/ • noun **1** chiefly historical a light two-wheeled carriage pulled by one horse. **2** a light, fast, narrow boat adapted for rowing or sailing.
– ORIGIN apparently from obsolete *gig* 'a flighty girl'.

gig[2] /gig/ informal • noun a live performance by a musician or other performer. • verb (**gigged**, **gigging**) perform a gig or gigs.
– ORIGIN of unknown origin.

giga- /giggə, jiggə/ • combining form **1** denoting a factor of one thousand million (10^9). **2** Computing denoting a factor of 2^{30}.
– ORIGIN from Greek *gigas* 'giant'.

gigabyte /giggəbīt, jigg-/ • noun Computing a unit of information equal to one thousand million (10^9) or (strictly) 2^{30} bytes.

gigaflop • noun Computing a unit of computing speed equal to one thousand million floating-point operations per second.

gigantic • adjective of very great size or extent.
– DERIVATIVES **gigantically** adverb.
– ORIGIN from Latin *gigas* 'giant'.

gigantism • noun chiefly Biology unusual or abnormal largeness.

giggle • verb laugh lightly in a nervous, affected, or silly manner. • noun **1** a laugh of such a kind. **2** informal an amusing person or thing.
– DERIVATIVES **giggler** noun **giggly** adjective.
– ORIGIN imitative.

GIGO /gīgō/ • abbreviation chiefly Computing garbage in, garbage out.

gigolo /jiggəlō/ • noun (pl. **gigolos**) **1** a young man paid by an older woman to be her escort or lover. **2** a professional male dancing partner.
– ORIGIN French, formed as the masculine of *gigole* 'dance hall woman', from colloquial *gigue* 'leg'.

gigot /jiggət/ • noun a leg of mutton or lamb.
– ORIGIN French, from colloquial *gigue* 'leg'.

gild • verb **1** cover thinly with gold. **2** (**gilded**) wealthy and privileged: *gilded youth.*
– PHRASES **gild the lily** try to improve what is already beautiful or excellent. [ORIGIN misquotation of a line from Shakespeare's *King John* VI. ii.]
– DERIVATIVES **gilder** noun **gilding** noun.
– ORIGIN Old English, related to GOLD.

gilded cage • noun a luxurious but restrictive environment.

gilet /jilay/ • noun (pl. **gilets** pronunc. same) a light sleeveless padded jacket.
– ORIGIN French, 'waistcoat', from Turkish.

gill[1] /gil/ • noun **1** the paired respiratory organ of fishes and some amphibians. **2** the vertical plates on the underside of mushrooms and many toadstools. **3** (**gills**) the wattles or dewlap of a fowl. • verb gut or clean (a fish).
– PHRASES **green about the gills** sickly-looking. **to the gills** until completely full.
– DERIVATIVES **gilled** adjective.
– ORIGIN Old Norse.

gill[2] /jil/ • noun a unit of liquid measure, equal to a quarter of a pint.
– ORIGIN Old French *gille* 'measure or container for wine', from Latin *gillo* 'water pot'.

gill[3] /gil/ • noun chiefly N. English **1** a deep ravine, especially a

Thesaurus

whopping, humongous, jumbo, hulking, bumper; *Brit. informal* ginormous.
– OPPOSITES miniature.

gibber • verb PRATTLE, babble, ramble, drivel, jabber, gabble, burble, twitter, flannel, mutter, mumble; *informal* yammer, blabber, jibber-jabber, blather, blether; *Brit. informal* witter, chunter.

gibberish • noun NONSENSE, rubbish, balderdash, blather, blether; *informal* drivel, gobbledegook, mumbo-jumbo, tripe, hogwash, baloney, bilge, bosh, bull, bunk, guff, eyewash, piffle, twaddle, poppycock; *Brit. informal* cobblers, codswallop, double Dutch, tosh, cack; *N. Amer. informal* garbage, blathers, applesauce.

gibe • noun & verb. See JIBE.

giddiness • noun DIZZINESS, light-headedness; faintness, unsteadiness, shakiness, wobbliness; *informal* wooziness, legs like jelly.

giddy • adjective **1** *she felt giddy* DIZZY, light-headed, faint, weak, vertiginous; unsteady, shaky, wobbly, reeling; *informal* woozy. **2** *she was young and giddy* FLIGHTY, silly, frivolous, skittish, irresponsible, flippant, whimsical, capricious; feather-brained, scatty, thoughtless, heedless, carefree; *informal* dippy; *N. Amer. informal* ditsy.
– OPPOSITES steady, sensible.

gift • noun **1** *he gave the staff a gift* PRESENT, handout, donation, offering, bestowal, bonus, award, endowment; tip, gratuity, baksheesh; largesse; *informal* prezzie, freebie, perk; *formal* benefaction. **2** *a gift for melody* TALENT, flair, aptitude, facility, knack, bent, ability, expertise, capacity, capability, faculty; endowment, strength, genius, brilliance, skill, artistry.
• verb *he gifted a composition to the orchestra* PRESENT, give, bestow, confer, donate, endow, award, accord, grant; hand over, make over.

gifted • adjective TALENTED, skilful, skilled, accomplished, expert, consummate, master(ly), first-rate, able, apt, adept, proficient; intelligent, clever, bright, brilliant; precocious; *informal* crack, top-notch, ace.
– OPPOSITES inept.

gigantic • adjective HUGE, enormous, vast, extensive, very big, very large, giant, massive, colossal, mammoth, immense, monumental, mountainous, titanic, towering, elephantine, king-size(d), gargantuan; *informal* mega, monster, whopping, humongous, jumbo, hulking, bumper; *Brit. informal* ginormous.
– OPPOSITES tiny.

giggle • verb *he giggled at the picture* TITTER, snigger, snicker, teehee, chuckle, chortle, laugh.
• noun *she suppressed a giggle* TITTER, snigger, snicker, tee-hee, chuckle, chortle, laugh.

gigolo • noun PLAYBOY, (male) escort; admirer, lover; *informal* fancy man; *Brit. informal* toy boy.

gild • verb **1** *a gilded weathercock* COVER WITH GOLD, paint gold. **2** *he tends to gild the truth* ELABORATE, embellish, embroider; cam-

wooded one. **2** a narrow mountain stream.
– ORIGIN Old Norse, 'deep glen'.
gillie /gilli/ (also **ghillie**) ● noun (in Scotland) an attendant on a hunting or fishing expedition.
– ORIGIN Scottish Gaelic *gille* 'lad, servant'.
gillyflower /jilliflowr/ (also **gilliflower**) ● noun any of a number of fragrant flowers, such as the wallflower or white stock.
– ORIGIN Old French *gilofre, girofle*, from Greek *karuophullon*, from *karuon* 'nut' + *phullon* 'leaf'.
gilt[1] ● adjective covered thinly with gold leaf or gold paint. ● noun **1** gold leaf or gold paint applied in a thin layer to a surface. **2** (**gilts**) fixed-interest loan securities issued by the UK government.
– ORIGIN archaic past participle of GILD.
gilt[2] ● noun a young sow.
– ORIGIN Old Norse.
gilt-edged ● adjective referring to stocks or securities (such as gilts) that are regarded as extremely reliable investments.
gimbal /jimb'l/ (also **gimbals**) ● noun a device for keeping an instrument such as a compass horizontal in a moving vessel or aircraft.
– DERIVATIVES **gimballed** adjective.
– ORIGIN obsolete *gemel* 'twin, hinge', from Old French *gemel* 'twin'.
gimcrack /jimkrak/ ● adjective showy but flimsy or poorly made. ● noun a cheap and showy ornament.
– DERIVATIVES **gimcrackery** noun.
– ORIGIN of unknown origin.
gimlet /gimlit/ ● noun a small T-shaped tool with a screw-tip for boring holes.
– ORIGIN Old French *guimbelet* 'little drill'.
gimmick ● noun a trick or device intended to attract attention rather than fulfil a useful purpose.
– DERIVATIVES **gimmickry** noun **gimmicky** adjective.
– ORIGIN originally in sense 'piece of magicians' apparatus': of unknown origin.
gimp[1] /gimp/ ● noun **1** twisted, reinforced material used as upholstery trimming. **2** (in lacemaking) coarser thread forming the outline of the design. **3** fishing line made of silk bound with wire.
– ORIGIN Dutch.
gimp[2] /gimp/ N. Amer. informal, derogatory ● noun **1** a physically handicapped or lame person. **2** a feeble or contemptible person. ● verb limp; hobble.
– DERIVATIVES **gimpy** adjective.
– ORIGIN of unknown origin.
gin[1] ● noun **1** a clear alcoholic spirit distilled from grain or malt and flavoured with juniper berries. **2** (also **gin rummy**) a form of the card game rummy.
– ORIGIN abbreviation of *genever*, a kind of Dutch gin, from Latin *juniperus* (gin being flavoured with juniper berries).
gin[2] ● noun **1** a machine for separating cotton from its seeds. **2** a machine for raising and moving heavy weights. **3** a trap for catching small game. ● verb (**ginned**, **ginning**) treat (cotton) in a gin.
– ORIGIN Old French *engin* 'engine'.
ginger ● noun **1** a hot, fragrant spice made from the rhizome of a SE Asian plant resembling bamboo. **2** a light reddish-yellow colour. **3** spirit; mettle. ● verb **1** flavour with ginger. **2** (**ginger up**) stimulate or enliven.
– DERIVATIVES **gingery** adjective.
– ORIGIN Latin *gingiber*, from Dravidian.
ginger ale (also **ginger beer**) ● noun an effervescent, typically non-alcoholic drink flavoured with ginger.
gingerbread ● noun cake made with treacle or syrup and flavoured with ginger.
– PHRASES **take the gilt off the gingerbread** make something no longer attractive or desirable.
ginger group ● noun chiefly Brit. a highly active faction within a party or movement that presses for stronger action on a particular issue.
gingerly ● adverb in a careful or cautious manner. ● adjective showing great care or caution.
– ORIGIN perhaps from Old French *gensor* 'delicate', from Latin *genitus* 'well-born'.
gingham /gingəm/ ● noun lightweight plain-woven cotton cloth, typically checked.
– ORIGIN from a Malay word meaning 'striped'.
gingival /jinjīv'l/ ● adjective Medicine concerned with the gums.
– ORIGIN from Latin *gingiva* 'gum'.
gingivitis /jinjivītiss/ ● noun Medicine inflammation of the gums.
ginkgo /ginkgō/ (also **gingko**) /gingkō/ ● noun (pl. **ginkgos** or **ginkgoes**) a deciduous Chinese tree with fan-shaped leaves and yellow flowers.
– ORIGIN Chinese.
ginormous ● adjective Brit. informal extremely large.
– ORIGIN blend of GIANT and ENORMOUS.
ginseng /jinseng/ ● noun the tuber of an east Asian and North American plant, credited with various tonic and medicinal properties.
– ORIGIN from Chinese 'man' + the name of a kind of herb (because of the supposed resemblance of the forked root to a person).
gip ● noun variant spelling of GYP[1].
gipsy ● noun variant spelling of GYPSY.
giraffe ● noun (pl. same or **giraffes**) a large mammal with a very long neck and forelegs, the tallest living animal.
– ORIGIN French *girafe*, from Arabic.
gird ● verb (past and past part. **girded** or **girt**) literary **1** encircle or secure with a belt or band. **2** (often in phrase **gird one's loins**) prepare and strengthen oneself for what is to come.
– ORIGIN Old English, related to GIRDLE[1] and GIRTH.
girder ● noun a large metal beam used in building bridges and large buildings.
– ORIGIN from GIRD in the archaic sense 'brace, strengthen'.
girdle[1] ● noun **1** a belt or cord worn round the waist. **2** a woman's elasticated corset extending from waist to thigh. ● verb encircle with a girdle or belt.
– ORIGIN Old English, related to GIRD and GIRTH.
girdle[2] ● noun Scottish and northern English term for GRIDDLE.
girl ● noun **1** a female child. **2** a young or relatively young woman. **3** a person's girlfriend. **4** dated a female servant.
– DERIVATIVES **girlhood** noun **girlish** adjective **girlishly** adverb.
– ORIGIN originally denoting a child or young person of either sex: perhaps related to Low German *gör* 'child'.
girlfriend ● noun **1** a person's regular female companion in a romantic or sexual relationship. **2** chiefly N. Amer. a woman's female friend.
Girl Guide ● noun a member of the Guides Association.
girlie ● noun (also **girly**) (pl. **girlies**) informal a girl or young woman. ● adjective **1** (usu. **girly**) often derogatory like or characteristic of a girl. **2** depicting nude or partially nude young women

Thesaurus

ouflage, disguise, dress up, colour, exaggerate, expand on; *informal* jazz up.
gimcrack ● adjective SHODDY, jerry-built, flimsy, insubstantial, thrown together, makeshift; inferior, poor-quality, second-rate, cheap, cheapjack, tawdry, kitschy, trashy; *informal* tacky, junky, rubbishy.
gimmick ● noun PUBLICITY DEVICE, stunt, contrivance, scheme, stratagem, ploy; *informal* shtick.
gingerly ● adverb CAUTIOUSLY, carefully, with care, warily, charily, circumspectly, delicately; heedfully, watchfully, vigilantly, attentively; hesitantly, timidly.
– OPPOSITES recklessly.
gird ● verb (*poetic/literary*) **1** *Sir Hector girded on his sword* FASTEN, belt, bind, tie. **2** *the island was girded by rocks* SURROUND, enclose, encircle, circle, encompass, border, bound, edge, skirt, fringe; close in, confine. **3** *they girded themselves for war* PREPARE, get ready, gear up; nerve, steel, galvanize, brace, fortify; *informal* psych oneself up.
girdle ● noun **1** *a diamond-studded girdle* BELT, sash, cummerbund, waistband, strap, band, girth, cord. **2** *her stockings were held up by her girdle* CORSET, corselet, foundation garment, panty girdle; truss.
● verb *a large garden girdled the house* SURROUND, enclose, encircle, circle, encompass, circumscribe, border, bound, skirt, edge; *poetic/literary* gird.
girl ● noun **1** *a five-year-old girl* FEMALE CHILD, daughter; schoolgirl; *Scottish & N. English* lass, lassie; *derogatory* chit. See also CHILD. **2** *a tall dark girl* YOUNG WOMAN, young lady, miss, mademoiselle; *Scottish* lass, lassie; *Irish* colleen; *informal* chick, girlie, filly; *Brit. informal* bird, bint; *N. Amer. informal* gal, broad, dame, jane, babe; *Austral./NZ informal* sheila; *poetic/literary* maid, damsel; *archaic* wench. **3** *his girl left him.* See GIRLFRIEND.

in erotic poses: *girlie magazines*.
Girl Scout • noun a girl belonging to the Scout Association.
giro • noun (pl. **giros**) **1** a system of electronic credit transfer involving banks, post offices, and public utilities. **2** a cheque or payment by giro, especially a social security payment.
– ORIGIN Italian, 'circulation (of money)'.
girt past participle of GIRD.
girth • noun **1** the measurement around the middle of something, especially a person's waist. **2** a band attached to a saddle and fastened around a horse's belly.
– ORIGIN Old Norse.
gist /jist/ • noun the substance or essence of a speech or text.
– ORIGIN Old French, 'he, she, or it lies', from the legal phrase *cest action gist* 'this action lies', denoting there were sufficient grounds to proceed.
git • noun Brit. informal an unpleasant or contemptible person.
– ORIGIN variant of GET in the informal or dialect noun sense 'a stupid or unpleasant person'.
give • verb (past **gave**; past part. **given**) **1** freely transfer the possession of; cause to receive or have. **2** yield as a product or result. **3** carry out (an action). **4** cause to experience or suffer. **5** state or put forward (information or argument). **6** present (an appearance or impression). **7** (**give off/out**) emit (odour, vapour, etc). **8** produce (a sound). **9** alter in shape under pressure rather than resist or break. **10** concede or yield (something) as valid or deserved in respect of (someone). • noun capacity to bend or alter in shape under pressure.
– PHRASES **give oneself airs** act pretentiously or snobbishly. **give and take** mutual concessions and compromises. **give away 1** reveal (something secret or concealed). **2** (in sport) concede (a goal or advantage) to the opposition. **give the game** (or **show**) **away** inadvertently reveal something secret. **give in** cease fighting or arguing. **give or take ——** informal to within a specified amount. **give out** be completely used up or broken. **give rise to** cause or induce to happen. **give up 1** cease making an effort; resign oneself to failure. **2** stop the habitual doing or consuming of (something). **3** deliver (a wanted person) to authority.
– DERIVATIVES **giver** noun.
– ORIGIN Old English.
giveaway • noun informal **1** something given free, especially for promotional purposes. **2** something that makes an inadvertent revelation.
given past participle of GIVE. • adjective **1** specified or stated. **2** (**given to**) inclined or disposed to. • preposition taking into account. • noun an established fact or situation.
given name • noun another term for FIRST NAME.
gizmo • noun (pl. **gizmos**) informal a gadget, especially one the speaker cannot name.
– ORIGIN of unknown origin.
gizzard • noun **1** a muscular, thick-walled part of a bird's stomach for grinding food, typically with grit. **2** a muscular stomach of some fish, insects, molluscs, and other invertebrates.
– ORIGIN Old French, from Latin *gigeria* 'cooked entrails of fowl'.
GLA • abbreviation gamma linolenic acid.
glacé /glassay/ • adjective **1** (of fruit) having a glossy surface due to preservation in sugar. **2** (of cloth or leather) smooth and highly polished.
– ORIGIN French, 'iced'.
glacé icing • noun icing made with icing sugar and water.
glacial /glaysh'l/ • adjective **1** relating to ice, especially in the form of glaciers. **2** extremely cold or unfriendly; icy.
– DERIVATIVES **glacially** adverb.
– ORIGIN Latin *glacialis* 'icy', from *glacies* 'ice'.
glacial period • noun a period in the earth's history when ice sheets were unusually extensive; an ice age.
glaciated /glaysiaytid/ • adjective covered or having been covered by glaciers or ice sheets.
glaciation • noun Geology **1** the condition or result of being glaciated. **2** a glacial period.
glacier /glassiər, glay-/ • noun a slowly moving mass of ice formed by the accumulation of snow on mountains or near the poles.
– ORIGIN French, from *glace* 'ice'.
glaciology • noun the study of glaciers.
– DERIVATIVES **glaciological** adjective **glaciologist** noun.
glad • adjective (**gladder**, **gladdest**) **1** pleased; delighted. **2** (often **glad of**) grateful. **3** causing happiness.
– DERIVATIVES **gladly** adverb **gladness** noun.
– ORIGIN Old English, 'bright, shining'.
gladden • verb make glad.
glade • noun an open space in a wood or forest.

g

Thesaurus

girlfriend • noun SWEETHEART, lover, partner, significant other, girl, woman; fiancée; *informal* steady; *Brit. informal* bird; *N. Amer. informal* squeeze; *dated* lady (friend), lady love, betrothed; *archaic* leman.
girlish • adjective GIRLY, youthful, childlike, childish, immature; feminine.
girth • noun **1** *a tree ten feet in girth* CIRCUMFERENCE, perimeter; width, breadth. **2** *he tied the towel around his girth* STOMACH, midriff, middle, abdomen, belly, gut; *informal* tummy, tum. **3** *a horse's girth N. Amer.* cinch.
gist • noun ESSENCE, substance, central theme, heart of the matter, nub, kernel, marrow, meat, burden, crux; thrust, drift, sense, meaning, significance, import; *informal* nitty-gritty.
give • verb **1** *he gave them £2000* PRESENT WITH, provide with, supply with, furnish with, let someone have; hand (over), offer, proffer; award, grant, bestow, accord, confer, make over; donate, contribute, put up. **2** *can I give him a message?* CONVEY, pass on, impart, communicate, transmit; send, deliver, relay; tell. **3** *a baby given into their care* ENTRUST, commit, consign, assign; *formal* commend. **4** *he gave his life for them* SACRIFICE, give up, relinquish; devote, dedicate. **5** *he gave her time to think* ALLOW, permit, grant, accord; offer. **6** *this leaflet gives our opening times* SHOW, display, set out, indicate, detail, list. **7** *they gave no further trouble* CAUSE, make, create, occasion. **8** *garlic gives flavour* PRODUCE, yield, afford, impart, lend. **9** *he gave a party* ORGANIZE, arrange, lay on, throw, host, hold, have, provide. **10** *Dominic gave a bow* PERFORM, execute, make, do. **11** *she gave a shout* UTTER, let out, emit, produce, make. **12** *he gave Harry a beating* ADMINISTER, deliver, deal, inflict, impose. **13** *the door gave* GIVE WAY, cave in, collapse, break, fall apart; bend, buckle.
– OPPOSITES receive, take.
• noun *there isn't enough give in the jacket* ELASTICITY, flexibility, stretch, stretchiness; slack, play.
– PHRASES **give someone away** BETRAY, inform on; *informal* split on, rat on, peach on, do the dirty on, blow the whistle on, sell down the river; *Brit. informal* grass on, shop; *N. Amer. informal* rat out, finger; *Austral./NZ informal* dob on; *English Law* turn Queen's/King's evidence. **give something away** REVEAL, disclose, divulge, let slip, leak, let out. **give in** CAPITULATE, concede defeat, admit defeat, give up, surrender, yield, submit, back down, give way, defer, relent, throw in the towel/sponge. **give something off/out** EMIT, produce, send out, throw out; discharge, release, exude, vent. **give out** RUN OUT, be used up, be consumed, be exhausted, be depleted; fail, flag; dry up. **give something out** DISTRIBUTE, issue, hand out, pass round, dispense; dole out, dish out, mete out; allocate, allot, share out. **give up.** See GIVE IN. **give something up** STOP, cease, discontinue, desist from, abstain from, cut out, renounce, forgo; resign from, stand down from; *informal* quit, kick, swear off, leave off, pack in, lay off; *Brit. informal* jack in.
give and take • noun COMPROMISE, concession; cooperation, reciprocity, teamwork, interplay.
given • adjective **1** *a given number of years* SPECIFIED, stated, designated, set, particular, specific; prescribed, agreed, appointed, prearranged, predetermined. **2** *she was given to fits of temper* PRONE, liable, inclined, disposed, predisposed, apt, likely.
– OPPOSITES unspecified.
• preposition *given the issue's complexity , a summary is difficult* CONSIDERING, in view of, bearing in mind, in the light of; assuming.
• noun *his aggression is taken as a given* ESTABLISHED FACT, reality, certainty.
giver • noun DONOR, contributor, donator, benefactor, benefactress, provider; supporter, backer, patron, sponsor, subscriber.
glacial • adjective **1** *glacial conditions* FREEZING, cold, icy, ice-cold, sub-zero, frozen, gelid, wintry; arctic, polar, Siberian; bitter, biting, raw, chill. **2** *Polly's tone was glacial* UNFRIENDLY, hostile, unwelcoming; frosty, icy, cold, chilly.
– OPPOSITES tropical, hot, friendly.
glad • adjective **1** *I'm really glad you're coming* PLEASED, happy, delighted, thrilled, overjoyed, cock-a-hoop, elated, gleeful; gratified, grateful, thankful; *informal* tickled pink, over the moon; *Brit. informal* chuffed; *N. English informal* made up; *Austral. informal* wrapped. **2** *I'd be glad to help* WILLING, eager, happy, pleased, delighted; ready, pre-

– ORIGIN of unknown origin.
glad-hand chiefly N. Amer. ● **verb** (especially of a politician) greet or welcome warmly. ● **noun** (**glad hand**) a warm and hearty greeting or welcome.
– DERIVATIVES **glad-hander** noun.
gladiator ● **noun** (in ancient Rome) a man trained to fight with weapons against other men or wild animals in an arena.
– DERIVATIVES **gladiatorial** adjective.
– ORIGIN Latin, from *gladius* 'sword'.
gladiolus /gladdiōləss/ ● **noun** (pl. **gladioli** /gladdiōlī/ or **gladioluses**) a plant with sword-shaped leaves and spikes of brightly coloured flowers.
– ORIGIN Latin, from *gladius* 'sword'.
glad rags ● **plural noun** informal clothes for a party or special occasion.
Gladstone bag ● **noun** a bag like a briefcase having two equal compartments joined by a hinge.
– ORIGIN named after the British Liberal statesman W. E. *Gladstone* (1809–98).
Glagolitic /glaggəlittik/ ● **adjective** referring to an alphabet based on Greek minuscules, formerly used in writing some Slavic languages.
– ORIGIN Latin *glagoliticus*, from a word in a former Slavic language meaning 'word'.
Glam. ● **abbreviation** Glamorgan.
glam informal ● **adjective** glamorous. ● **noun** glamour. ● **verb** (**glammed**, **glamming**) (**glam up**) make oneself look glamorous.
glamorize (also **glamorise**) ● **verb** make (something) seem glamorous or desirable, especially spuriously so.
– DERIVATIVES **glamorization** noun.
glamorous ● **adjective** having glamour.
– DERIVATIVES **glamorously** adverb.
glamour (US also **glamor**) ● **noun** an attractive and exciting quality.
– ORIGIN originally in the sense 'enchantment, magic': alteration of GRAMMAR, with reference to the occult practices associated with learning in medieval times.
glam rock ● **noun** a style of rock music characterized by male performers wearing exaggeratedly flamboyant clothes and make-up.
glance ● **verb** **1** take a brief or hurried look. **2** strike at an angle and bounce off obliquely. ● **noun** a brief or hurried look.
– DERIVATIVES **glancing** adjective.
– ORIGIN Old French *glacier* 'to slip', from *glace* 'ice'.
gland ● **noun** **1** an organ of the body which secretes particular chemical substances. **2** a lymph node.
– ORIGIN from Latin *glandulae* 'throat glands'.
glanders /glandərz/ ● **plural noun** (usu. treated as sing.) a contagious disease that affects horses, characterized by swellings below the jaw and mucous discharge from the nostrils.
– ORIGIN from Old French *glandre*, from Latin *glandulae* 'throat glands'.
glandular ● **adjective** relating to or affecting a gland or glands.
glandular fever ● **noun** an infectious viral disease characterized by swelling of the lymph glands and prolonged lassitude.
glans /glanz/ ● **noun** (pl. **glandes** /glandeez/) Anatomy the rounded part forming the end of the penis or clitoris.
– ORIGIN Latin, 'acorn'.
glare ● **verb** **1** stare in an angry or fierce way. **2** shine with a strong or dazzling light. **3** (**glaring**) highly obvious or conspicuous. ● **noun** **1** a fierce or angry stare. **2** strong and dazzling light.
– DERIVATIVES **glaringly** adverb **glary** adjective.
– ORIGIN from Dutch and Low German *glaren* 'to gleam or glare'.
glasnost /glaznost/ ● **noun** (in the former Soviet Union) the policy or practice of more open government.
– ORIGIN Russian *glasnost'* 'the fact of being public, openness'.
glass ● **noun** **1** a hard, brittle, usually transparent or translucent substance made by fusing sand with soda and lime. **2** a drinking container made of glass. **3** chiefly Brit. a mirror. **4** a lens or optical instrument, in particular a monocle or a magnifying lens. ● **verb** cover or enclose with glass.
– PHRASES **people (who live) in glass houses shouldn't throw stones** proverb you shouldn't criticize others when you have similar faults of your own.
– DERIVATIVES **glassful** noun **glassware** noun.
– ORIGIN Old English.
glass-blowing ● **noun** the craft of making glassware by blowing semi-molten glass through a long tube.
glass ceiling ● **noun** an unacknowledged barrier to advancement in a profession, especially affecting women and members of minorities.
glasses ● **plural noun** a pair of lenses set in a frame that rests on the nose and ears, used to correct defective eyesight.
glass fibre ● **noun** chiefly Brit. a strong plastic or other material containing embedded glass filaments for reinforcement.
glasshouse ● **noun** Brit. **1** a greenhouse. **2** military slang a place of detention.
glasspaper ● **noun** paper covered with powdered glass, used for smoothing and polishing.
glass wool ● **noun** glass in the form of fine fibres used for packing and insulation.
glassy ● **adjective** (**glassier**, **glassiest**) **1** of or resembling glass. **2** (of a person's eyes or expression) showing no interest or animation.
– DERIVATIVES **glassily** adverb.
Glaswegian /glazweejən/ ● **noun** a native of Glasgow. ● **adjective**

g

Thesaurus

pared. **3** *glad tidings* PLEASING, welcome, happy, joyful, cheering, heartening, gratifying; *poetic/literary* gladsome.
– OPPOSITES dismayed, reluctant, distressing.
gladden ● **verb** DELIGHT, please, make happy, elate; cheer (up), hearten, buoy up, give someone a lift, uplift; gratify; *informal* give someone a kick, tickle someone pink, buck up.
– OPPOSITES sadden.
gladly ● **adverb** WITH PLEASURE, happily, cheerfully; willingly, readily, eagerly, freely, ungrudgingly; *archaic* fain, lief.
glamorous ● **adjective** **1** *a glamorous woman* BEAUTIFUL, attractive, lovely, bewitching, enchanting, beguiling; elegant, chic, stylish, fashionable; charming, charismatic, appealing, alluring, seductive; *informal* classy, glam. **2** *a glamorous lifestyle* EXCITING, thrilling, stimulating; dazzling, glittering, glossy, colourful, exotic; *informal* ritzy, glitzy, jet-setting.
– OPPOSITES dowdy, dull.
glamour ● **noun** **1** *she had undeniable glamour* BEAUTY, allure, attractiveness; elegance, chic, style; charisma, charm, magnetism, desirability. **2** *the glamour of show business* ALLURE, attraction, fascination, charm, magic, romance, mystique, exoticism, spell; excitement, thrill; glitter, the bright lights; *informal* glitz, glam.
glance ● **verb** **1** *Rachel glanced at him* LOOK BRIEFLY, look quickly, peek, peep; glimpse; *Scottish* keek; *informal* have a gander; *Brit. informal* take a dekko, have a shufti, have a butcher's; *Austral./NZ informal* squiz. **2** *I glanced through the report* READ QUICKLY, scan, skim, leaf, flick, flip, thumb, browse; dip into. **3** *a bullet glanced off the ice* RICOCHET, rebound, be deflected, bounce; graze, clip. **4** *sunlight glanced off her hair* REFLECT, flash, gleam, glint, glitter, glisten, glimmer, shimmer.
● **noun** **1** *a glance at his watch* PEEK, peep, brief look, quick look, glimpse; *Scottish* keek; *informal* gander; *Brit. informal* dekko, shufti, butcher's; *Austral./NZ informal* squiz, geek.
– PHRASES **at first glance** ON THE FACE OF IT, on the surface, at first sight, to the casual eye, to all appearances; apparently, seemingly, outwardly, superficially, it would seem, it appears, as far as one can see/tell, by all accounts.
glare ● **verb** **1** *she glared at him* SCOWL, glower, stare angrily, look daggers, frown, lour, give someone a black look, look threateningly; *informal* give someone a dirty look. **2** *the sun glared out of the sky* BLAZE, beam, shine brightly, be dazzling, be blinding.
● **noun** **1** *a cold glare* SCOWL, glower, angry stare, frown, black look, threatening look; *informal* dirty look. **2** *the harsh glare of the lights* BLAZE, dazzle, shine, beam; radiance, brilliance, luminescence.
glaring ● **adjective** **1** *glaring lights* DAZZLING, blinding, blazing, strong, bright, harsh. **2** *a glaring omission* OBVIOUS, conspicuous, unmistakable, inescapable, unmissable, striking; flagrant, blatant, outrageous, gross; overt, patent, transparent, manifest; *informal* standing/sticking out like a sore thumb.
– OPPOSITES soft, minor.
glass ● **noun** **1** *a glass of water* TUMBLER, drinking vessel; flute, schooner, balloon, goblet, chalice. **2** *we sell china and glass* GLASSWARE, crystal, crystalware. **3** (*Brit.*) *she looked in the glass* MIRROR, looking glass.
– RELATED TERMS vitreous.
glasses ● **plural noun** SPECTACLES; *N. Amer.* eyeglasses; *informal* specs.

relating to Glasgow.

glaucoma /glawkōmə/ ● noun Medicine a condition of increased pressure within the eyeball, causing gradual loss of sight.
– ORIGIN Greek *glaukōma*, from *glaukos* 'bluish green or grey' (because of the grey-green haze in the pupil).

glaucous /glawkəss/ ● adjective technical or literary **1** of a dull greyish-green or blue colour. **2** covered with a powdery bloom like that on grapes.
– ORIGIN Greek *glaukos*.

glaze ● verb **1** fit panes of glass into (a window frame or similar structure). **2** enclose or cover with glass. **3** cover with a glaze. **4** (often **glaze over**) lose brightness and animation. ● noun **1** a glass-like substance fused on to the surface of pottery to form an impervious decorative coating. **2** a thin topcoat of transparent paint used to modify the tone of an underlying colour. **3** a liquid such as milk or beaten egg, used to form a smooth shiny coating on food.
– DERIVATIVES **glazer** noun **glazing** noun.
– ORIGIN from GLASS.

g

glazier /glayziər/ ● noun a person whose trade is fitting glass into windows and doors.

gleam ● verb shine brightly, especially with reflected light. ● noun **1** a faint or brief light. **2** a brief or faint show of a quality or emotion.
– PHRASES **a gleam in someone's eye** see EYE.
– DERIVATIVES **gleaming** adjective.
– ORIGIN Old English.

glean ● verb **1** collect gradually from various sources. **2** historical gather (leftover grain) after a harvest.
– DERIVATIVES **gleaner** noun.
– ORIGIN Latin *glennare*.

gleanings ● plural noun things gleaned from various sources rather than acquired as a whole.

glebe /gleeb/ ● noun historical a piece of land serving as part of a clergyman's benefice and providing income.
– ORIGIN Latin *gleba* 'clod, land, soil'.

glee ● noun **1** great delight. **2** a song for men's voices in three or more parts.
– ORIGIN Old English, 'entertainment, music, fun'.

gleeful ● adjective exuberantly or triumphantly joyful.
– DERIVATIVES **gleefully** adverb.

glen ● noun a narrow valley, especially in Scotland or Ireland.
– ORIGIN Scottish Gaelic and Irish *gleann*.

glib ● adjective (**glibber**, **glibbest**) articulate and voluble but insincere and shallow.
– DERIVATIVES **glibly** adverb **glibness** noun.
– ORIGIN Germanic.

glide ● verb **1** move with a smooth, quiet, continuous motion. **2** fly without power or in a glider. ● noun an instance of gliding.
– DERIVATIVES **gliding** noun.
– ORIGIN Old English.

glide path ● noun an aircraft's line of descent to land.

glider ● noun **1** a light aircraft designed to fly without using an engine. **2** a person or thing that glides.

glimmer ● verb shine faintly with a wavering light. ● noun **1** a faint or wavering light. **2** a faint sign of a feeling or quality: *a glimmer of hope.*
– DERIVATIVES **glimmering** adjective & noun.
– ORIGIN probably Scandinavian.

glimpse ● noun a momentary or partial view. ● verb see briefly or partially.
– ORIGIN originally in the sense 'shine faintly': probably Germanic, related to GLIMMER.

glint ● verb give out or reflect small flashes of light. ● noun a small flash of light, especially a reflected one.
– ORIGIN originally in the sense 'move quickly or obliquely': variant of dialect *glent*, probably Scandinavian.

glissade /glisaad, -sayd/ ● noun **1** a slide down a steep slope of snow or ice, typically on the feet with the support of an ice axe. **2** Ballet a gliding movement. ● verb perform or move by means of a glissade.
– ORIGIN Fench, from *glisser* 'to slip, slide'.

glissando /glisandō/ ● noun (pl. **glissandi** /glisandi/ or **glissandos**) Music a continuous slide upwards or downwards between two notes.
– ORIGIN Italian, from French *glisser* 'to slip, slide'.

glisten ● verb (of something wet or greasy) shine or sparkle. ● noun a sparkling light reflected from something wet.
– ORIGIN Old English.

glister /glistər/ literary ● verb sparkle; glitter. ● noun a sparkle.
– ORIGIN probably from Low German *glistern* or Dutch *glisteren*.

glitch ● noun informal **1** a sudden malfunction or irregularity of equipment. **2** an unexpected setback in a plan.
– ORIGIN of unknown origin.

glitter ● verb **1** shine with a bright, shimmering reflected light. **2** (**glittering**) impressively successful or glamorous: *a glittering career.* ● noun **1** bright, shimmering reflected light. **2** tiny pieces of sparkling material used for decoration. **3** an attractive but superficial quality.
– PHRASES **all that glitters is not gold** proverb the attractive external appearance of something is not a reliable indication of its true nature.
– DERIVATIVES **glittery** adjective.
– ORIGIN Old Norse.

Thesaurus

glasshouse ● noun GREENHOUSE, hothouse, conservatory.

glassy ● adjective **1** *the glassy surface of the lake* SMOOTH, mirror-like, gleaming, shiny, glossy, polished, vitreous; slippery, icy; clear, transparent, translucent; calm, still, flat. **2** *a glassy stare* EXPRESSIONLESS, glazed, blank, vacant, fixed, motionless; emotionless, impassive, lifeless, wooden, vacuous.
– OPPOSITES rough, expressive.

glaze ● verb **1** *the pots are glazed when dry* VARNISH, enamel, lacquer, japan, shellac, paint; gloss. **2** *pastry glazed with caramel* COVER, coat; ice, frost. **3** *his eyes glazed over* BECOME GLASSY, go blank; mist over, film over.
● noun **1** *pottery with a blue glaze* VARNISH, enamel, lacquer, finish, coating; lustre, shine, gloss. **2** *a cake with an apricot glaze* COATING, topping; icing, frosting.

gleam ● verb SHINE, glimmer, glint, glitter, shimmer, sparkle, twinkle, flicker, wink, glisten, flash; poetic/literary glister.
● noun **1** *a gleam of light* GLIMMER, glint, shimmer, twinkle, sparkle, flicker, flash; beam, ray, shaft. **2** *the gleam of brass* SHINE, lustre, gloss, sheen; glint, glitter, glimmer, sparkle; brilliance, radiance, glow; poetic/literary glister. **3** *a gleam of hope* GLIMMER, flicker, ray, spark, trace, suggestion, hint, sign.

glean ● verb OBTAIN, get, take, draw, derive, extract, cull, garner, gather; learn, find out.

glee ● noun DELIGHT, pleasure, happiness, joy, gladness, elation, euphoria; amusement, mirth, merriment; excitement, gaiety, exuberance; triumph, jubilation, relish, satisfaction, gratification.
– OPPOSITES disappointment.

gleeful ● adjective DELIGHTED, pleased, joyful, happy, glad, overjoyed, elated, euphoric; amused, mirthful, merry, exuberant; cock-a-hoop, jubilant; informal over the moon.

glib ● adjective SLICK, pat, plausible; smooth-talking, fast-talking, silver-tongued, smooth, urbane, having kissed the Blarney Stone; disingenuous, insincere, facile, shallow, superficial, flippant; informal flip, sweet-talking.
– OPPOSITES sincere.

glide ● verb **1** *a gondola glided past* SLIDE, slip, sail, float, drift, flow; coast, freewheel, roll; skim, skate. **2** *seagulls gliding over the waves* SOAR, wheel, plane; fly. **3** *he glided out of the door* SLIP, steal, slink.

glimmer ● verb *moonlight glimmered on the lawn* GLEAM, shine, glint, flicker, shimmer, glisten, glow, twinkle, sparkle, glitter, wink, flash; poetic/literary glister.
● noun **1** *a glimmer of light* GLEAM, glint, flicker, shimmer, glow, twinkle, sparkle, flash, ray. **2** *a glimmer of hope* GLEAM, flicker, ray, trace, sign, suggestion, hint.

glimpse ● noun *a glimpse of her face* BRIEF LOOK, quick look; glance, peek, peep; sight, sighting.
● verb *he glimpsed a figure* CATCH SIGHT OF, notice, discern, spot, spy, sight, pick out, make out; Brit. informal clock; poetic/literary espy, descry.

glint ● verb *the diamond glinted* SHINE, gleam, catch the light, glitter, sparkle, twinkle, wink, glimmer, shimmer, glisten, flash; poetic/literary glister.
● noun *the glint of the silver* GLITTER, gleam, sparkle, twinkle, glimmer, flash.

glisten ● verb SHINE, sparkle, twinkle, glint, glitter, glimmer, shimmer, wink, flash; poetic/literary glister.

glitter ● verb *crystal glittered in the candlelight* SHINE, sparkle, twinkle, glint, gleam, shimmer, glimmer, wink, flash, catch the light; poetic/literary glister.

glitterati /glittəraati/ ● plural noun informal fashionable people involved in show business or some other glamorous activity.
– ORIGIN blend of GLITTER and LITERATI.
glitz ● noun informal extravagant but superficial display.
– DERIVATIVES **glitzy** adjective.
– ORIGIN from GLITTER, suggested by RITZY.
gloaming ● noun (**the gloaming**) literary twilight; dusk.
– ORIGIN Old English, related to GLOW.
gloat ● verb contemplate one's own success or another's misfortune with smugness or malignant pleasure. ● noun an act of gloating.
– DERIVATIVES **gloater** noun **gloating** adjective & noun.
– ORIGIN originally in the sense 'give a sideways or furtive look': of uncertain origin.
glob ● noun informal a lump of a semi-liquid substance.
– ORIGIN perhaps a blend of BLOB and GOB[2].
global ● adjective **1** relating to the whole world; worldwide. **2** relating to or embracing the whole of something, or of a group of things. **3** Computing operating or applying through the whole of a file or program.
– DERIVATIVES **globalist** noun **globalize** (also **globalise**) verb **globally** adverb.
global village ● noun the world considered as a single community linked by telecommunications.
global warming ● noun the gradual increase in the overall temperature of the earth's atmosphere due to the greenhouse effect caused by increased levels of carbon dioxide, CFCs, and other pollutants.
globe ● noun **1** a spherical or rounded object. **2** (**the globe**) the earth. **3** a spherical representation of the earth with a map on the surface.
– DERIVATIVES **globose** adjective.
– ORIGIN Latin *globus*.
globetrotter ● noun informal a person who travels widely.
– DERIVATIVES **globetrotting** noun & adjective.
globular ● adjective **1** globe-shaped; spherical. **2** composed of globules.
globule ● noun a small round particle of a substance; a drop.
– ORIGIN Latin *globulus* 'little globe'.
globulin /globyoolin/ ● noun Biochemistry any of a group of simple proteins found in blood serum and soluble in salt solution.
glockenspiel /glokkənspeel, -shpeel/ ● noun a musical percussion instrument containing tuned metal pieces which are struck with small hammers.
– ORIGIN German, 'bell play'.
gloom ● noun **1** partial or total darkness. **2** a state of depression or despondency.
– ORIGIN of unknown origin.
gloomy ● adjective (**gloomier**, **gloomiest**) **1** dark or poorly lit, especially so as to cause fear or depression. **2** causing or feeling depression or despondency.
– DERIVATIVES **gloomily** adverb **gloominess** noun.
gloop ● noun informal sloppy or sticky semi-fluid matter.
– DERIVATIVES **gloopy** adjective.
– ORIGIN symbolic.
glorify ● verb (**glorifies**, **glorified**) **1** describe or represent as admirable, especially unjustifiably or undeservedly. **2** (**glorified**) represented as or appearing more elevated or special than is the case: *a glorified courier*. **3** praise and worship (God).
– DERIVATIVES **glorification** noun.
glorious ● adjective **1** having or bringing glory. **2** strikingly beautiful or impressive.
– DERIVATIVES **gloriously** adverb **gloriousness** noun.
glory ● noun (pl. **glories**) **1** high renown or honour won by notable achievements. **2** magnificence; great beauty. **3** a very beautiful or impressive thing. **4** worship and thanksgiving offered to God. ● verb (**glory in**) **1** take great pride or pleasure in. **2** exult in unpleasantly or boastfully.
– PHRASES **in one's glory** informal in a state of extreme joy or exaltation.
– ORIGIN Latin *gloria*.
glory box ● noun Austral./NZ a box in which a woman stores clothes and household items in preparation for marriage.
glory hole ● noun informal an untidy room or cupboard used for storage.
Glos. ● abbreviation Gloucestershire.
gloss[1] ● noun **1** the shine on a smooth surface. **2** (also **gloss paint**) a type of paint which dries to a bright shiny surface. **3** a superficially attractive appearance or impression. ● verb **1** give a glossy appearance to. **2** (**gloss over**) try to conceal or pass over by mentioning briefly or misleadingly.
– ORIGIN of unknown origin.
gloss[2] ● noun a translation or explanation of a word, phrase, or passage. ● verb provide a gloss for.
– ORIGIN alteration of GLOZE, suggested by Latin *glossa* 'explanation of a difficult word'.

g

Thesaurus

● noun **1** *the glitter of light on the water* SPARKLE, twinkle, glint, gleam, shimmer, glimmer, flicker, flash; brilliance, luminescence. **2** *the glitter of show business* GLAMOUR, excitement, thrills, attraction, appeal; dazzle; *informal* razzle-dazzle, razzmatazz, glitz, ritziness.
gloat ● verb DELIGHT, relish, take great pleasure, revel, rejoice, glory, exult, triumph, crow; boast, brag, be smug, congratulate oneself, preen oneself, pat oneself on the back; rub one's hands together; *informal* rub it in.
global ● adjective **1** *the global economy* WORLDWIDE, international, world, intercontinental. **2** *a global view of the problem* COMPREHENSIVE, overall, general, all-inclusive, all-encompassing, encyclopedic, universal, blanket; broad, far-reaching, extensive, sweeping.
globe ● noun **1** *every corner of the globe* WORLD, earth, planet. **2** *the sun is a globe* SPHERE, orb, ball, spheroid, round.
globular ● adjective SPHERICAL, spheric, spheroidal, round, globe-shaped, ball-shaped, orb-shaped, rounded, bulbous.
globule ● noun DROPLET, drop, bead, tear, ball, bubble, pearl; *informal* blob, glob.
gloom ● noun **1** *she peered into the gloom* DARKNESS, dark, dimness, blackness, murkiness, shadows, shade; dusk, twilight, gloaming. **2** *his gloom deepened* DESPONDENCY, depression, dejection, downheartedness, melancholy, melancholia, unhappiness, sadness, glumness, gloominess, misery, sorrow, woe, wretchedness; despair, pessimism, hopelessness; *informal* the blues, the dumps.
– OPPOSITES light, happiness.
gloomy ● adjective **1** *a gloomy room* DARK, shadowy, sunless, dim, sombre, dingy, dismal, dreary, murky, unwelcoming, cheerless, comfortless, funereal; *poetic/literary* Stygian. **2** *Joanna looked gloomy* DESPONDENT, downcast, downhearted, dejected, dispirited, disheartened, discouraged, demoralized, crestfallen; depressed, desolate, low, sad, unhappy, glum, melancholy, miserable, fed up, woebegone, mournful, forlorn, morose; *informal* blue, down in the mouth, down in the dumps. **3** *gloomy forecasts about the economy* PESSIMISTIC, depressing, downbeat, disheartening, disappointing; unfavourable, bleak, bad, black, sombre, grim, cheerless, hopeless.
– OPPOSITES bright, cheerful, optimistic.
glorify ● verb **1** *they gather to glorify God* PRAISE, extol, exalt, worship, revere, reverence, venerate, pay homage to, honour, adore, thank, give thanks to; *formal* laud; *archaic* magnify. **2** *a poem to glorify the memory of the dead* ENNOBLE, exalt, elevate, dignify, enhance, augment, promote; praise, celebrate, honour, extol, lionize, acclaim, applaud, hail; glamorize, idealize, romanticize, enshrine, immortalize; *formal* laud.
– OPPOSITES dishonour.
glorious ● adjective **1** *a glorious victory* ILLUSTRIOUS, celebrated, famous, acclaimed, distinguished, honoured; outstanding, great, magnificent, noble, triumphant. **2** *glorious views* WONDERFUL, marvellous, magnificent, superb, sublime, spectacular, lovely, fine, delightful; *informal* super, great, stunning, fantastic, terrific, tremendous, sensational, heavenly, divine, gorgeous, fabulous, fab, awesome, ace; *informal, dated* capital, spiffing; *Brit. informal* smashing; *poetic/literary* wondrous, beauteous.
– OPPOSITES undistinguished, horrid.
glory ● noun **1** *a sport that won him glory* RENOWN, fame, prestige, honour, distinction, kudos, eminence, acclaim, praise; celebrity, recognition, reputation; *informal* bouquets. **2** *glory be to God* PRAISE, worship, adoration, veneration, honour, reverence, exaltation, extolment, homage, thanksgiving, thanks. **3** *a house restored to its former glory* MAGNIFICENCE, splendour, resplendence, grandeur, majesty, greatness, nobility; opulence, beauty, elegance. **4** *the glories of Vermont* WONDER, beauty, delight, marvel, phenomenon; sight, spectacle.
– OPPOSITES shame, obscurity, modesty.
● verb *we gloried in our independence* TAKE PLEASURE IN, revel in, rejoice in, delight in; relish, savour; congratulate oneself on, be proud of; boast about; *informal* get a kick out of, get a thrill out of.

glossary ● noun (pl. **glossaries**) an alphabetical list of words relating to a specific subject, text, or dialect, with explanations.
– ORIGIN Latin *glossarium*, from *glossa* 'explanation of a difficult word'.

glossolalia /glossəlayliə/ ● noun the phenomenon of apparently speaking in an unknown language during religious worship, regarded as a gift of the Holy Spirit.
– DERIVATIVES **glossolalic** adjective.
– ORIGIN from Greek *glōssa* 'language, tongue' + *lalia* 'speech'.

glossy ● adjective (**glossier**, **glossiest**) **1** shiny and smooth. **2** superficially attractive and stylish. ● noun (pl. **glossies**) informal a magazine printed on glossy paper with many colour photographs.
– DERIVATIVES **glossily** adverb **glossiness** noun.

glottal ● adjective of or produced by the glottis.

glottal stop ● noun a consonant formed by the audible release of the airstream after complete closure of the glottis.

glottis /glottiss/ ● noun the part of the larynx consisting of the vocal cords and the slit-like opening between them.
– ORIGIN Greek, from *glōtta*, variant of *glōssa* 'tongue'.

g

glove ● noun **1** a covering for the hand having separate parts for each finger and the thumb. **2** a padded protective covering for the hand used in boxing and other sports.
– PHRASES **fit like a glove** (of clothes) fit exactly.
– DERIVATIVES **gloved** adjective.
– ORIGIN Old English.

glovebox ● noun **1** a glove compartment. **2** a closed chamber with sealed-in gloves for handling radioactive or other hazardous material.

glove compartment ● noun a small recess for storage in the dashboard of a motor vehicle.

glove puppet ● noun chiefly Brit. a cloth puppet fitted on the hand and worked by the fingers.

glover ● noun a maker of gloves.

glow ● verb **1** give out steady light without flame. **2** have an intense colour and a slight radiance. **3** convey deep pleasure through one's expression and bearing. ● noun **1** a steady radiance of light or heat. **2** a feeling or appearance of warmth. **3** a strong feeling of pleasure or well-being.
– ORIGIN Old English.

glower /glowr/ ● verb have an angry or sullen look on one's face; scowl. ● noun an angry or sullen look.
– ORIGIN perhaps a Scots variant of dialect *glore*, or from obsolete *glow* 'to stare', both possibly Scandinavian.

glowing ● adjective expressing great praise: *a glowing report*.
– DERIVATIVES **glowingly** adverb.

glow-worm ● noun a soft-bodied beetle whose larvalike wingless female emits light to attract males.

gloxinia /gloksinniə/ ● noun a tropical American plant with large, velvety, bell-shaped flowers.
– ORIGIN named after the 18th-century German botanist Benjamin P. *Gloxin*.

gloze /glōz/ ● verb archaic **1** (often **gloze over**) conceal or pass over; explain away. **2** use ingratiating or fawning language.
– ORIGIN from Old French *glose* 'a gloss, comment', from Latin *glossa* 'explanation of a difficult word'.

glucose /glōōkōz/ ● noun a simple sugar which is an important energy source in living organisms and is a component of many carbohydrates.
– ORIGIN Greek *gleukos* 'sweet wine'.

glue ● noun an adhesive substance used for sticking objects or materials together. ● verb (**glues**, **glued**, **gluing** or **glueing**) **1** fasten or join with glue. **2** (**be glued to**) informal be paying very close attention to.
– DERIVATIVES **gluey** adjective.
– ORIGIN Latin *glus*, from *gluten* 'glue'.

glue ear ● noun blocking of the Eustachian tube by mucus, occurring especially in children and causing impaired hearing.

glue-sniffing ● noun the practice of inhaling intoxicating fumes from the solvents in adhesives.

glug informal ● verb (**glugged**, **glugging**) pour or drink (liquid) with a hollow gurgling sound. ● noun a hollow gurgling sound.
– DERIVATIVES **gluggable** adjective.
– ORIGIN imitative.

glum ● adjective (**glummer**, **glummest**) dejected; morose.
– DERIVATIVES **glumly** adverb.
– ORIGIN related to dialect *glum* 'to frown', variant of GLOOM.

gluon /glōōon/ ● noun Physics a hypothetical massless particle believed to transmit the force binding quarks together.
– ORIGIN from GLUE.

glut ● noun an excessively abundant supply. ● verb (**glutted**, **glutting**) supply or fill to excess.
– ORIGIN probably from Latin *gluttire* 'to swallow'; related to GLUTTON.

glutamate /glōōtəmayt/ ● noun Biochemistry a salt or ester of an amino acid (**glutamic acid**) which is a constituent of many proteins.
– ORIGIN from *glutamic acid*, from GLUTEN + AMINE.

glutamine /glōōtəmeen/ ● noun Biochemistry an amino acid which is a constituent of most proteins.

gluten /glōōt'n/ ● noun a protein present in cereal grains, especially wheat, which is responsible for the elastic texture of dough.
– ORIGIN Latin, 'glue'.

gluteus /glōōtiəss/ ● noun (pl. **glutei** /glōōti-ī/) any of three muscles in each buttock which move the thigh.

Thesaurus

gloss[1] ● noun **1** *the gloss of her hair* SHINE, sheen, lustre, gleam, patina, brilliance, shimmer. **2** *beneath the gloss of success* FACADE, veneer, surface, show, camouflage, disguise, mask, smokescreen; window dressing.
● verb **1** *she glossed her lips* MAKE GLOSSY, shine; glaze, polish, burnish. **2** *he tried to gloss over his problems* CONCEAL, cover up, hide, disguise, mask, veil; shrug off, brush aside, play down, minimize, understate, make light of; informal brush under the carpet.

gloss[2] ● noun *glosses in the margin* EXPLANATION, interpretation, exegesis, explication, elucidation; annotation, note, footnote, commentary, comment; translation; historical scholium.
● verb *difficult words are glossed in a footnote* EXPLAIN, interpret, explicate, elucidate; annotate; translate, paraphrase.

glossy ● adjective **1** *a glossy wooden floor* SHINY, gleaming, lustrous, brilliant, shimmering, glistening, satiny, sheeny, smooth, glassy; polished, lacquered, glazed. **2** *a glossy magazine* EXPENSIVE, high-quality; stylish, fashionable, glamorous; attractive, artistic; Brit. upmarket, coffee-table; informal classy, ritzy, glitzy.
– OPPOSITES dull, cheap.

glove ● noun MITTEN, mitt, gauntlet.

glow ● verb **1** *lights glowed from the windows* SHINE, radiate, gleam, glimmer, flicker, flare; luminesce. **2** *a fire glowed in the hearth* RADIATE HEAT, smoulder, burn. **3** *she glowed with embarrassment* FLUSH, blush, redden, colour (up), go pink, go scarlet; burn. **4** *she glowed with pride* TINGLE, thrill; beam.
● noun **1** *the glow of the fire* RADIANCE, light, shine, gleam, glimmer, incandescence, luminescence; warmth, heat. **2** *a glow spread over her face* FLUSH, blush, rosiness, pinkness, redness, high colour; bloom, radiance. **3** *a warm glow deep inside her* HAPPINESS, contentment, pleasure, satisfaction.
– OPPOSITES pallor.

glower ● verb *she glowered at him* SCOWL, glare, look daggers, frown, lour, give a someone black look; informal give someone a dirty look.
● noun *the glower on his face* SCOWL, glare, frown, black look; informal dirty look.

glowing ● adjective **1** *glowing coals* BRIGHT, shining, radiant, glimmering, flickering, twinkling, incandescent, luminous, luminescent; lit (up), lighted, illuminated, ablaze; aglow, smouldering. **2** *his glowing cheeks* ROSY, pink, red, flushed, blushing; radiant, blooming, ruddy, florid; hot, burning. **3** *glowing colours* VIVID, vibrant, bright, brilliant, rich, intense, strong, radiant, warm. **4** *a glowing report* COMPLIMENTARY, favourable, enthusiastic, commendatory, admiring, lionizing, rapturous, rhapsodic, adulatory; fulsome; informal rave.

glue ● noun *a tube of glue* ADHESIVE, fixative, gum, paste, cement; epoxy (resin), size; N. Amer. mucilage; N. Amer. informal stickum.
● verb **1** *the planks were glued together* STICK, gum, paste; affix, fix, cement. **2** (informal) *she was glued to the television* BE RIVETED TO, be gripped by, be hypnotized by, be mesmerized by.

glum ● adjective GLOOMY, downcast, downhearted, dejected, despondent, crestfallen, disheartened; depressed, desolate, unhappy, doleful, melancholy, miserable, woebegone, mournful, forlorn, fed up, in the doldrums, morose; informal blue, down in the mouth, down in the dumps.
– OPPOSITES cheerful.

glut ● noun *a glut of cars* SURPLUS, excess, surfeit, superfluity, overabundance, superabundance, oversupply, plethora.

– DERIVATIVES **gluteal** adjective.
– ORIGIN Greek *gloutos* 'buttock'.
glutinous /glōōtinəss/ ● adjective **1** like glue in texture; sticky. **2** excessively sentimental; sickly: *glutinous ballads.*
– DERIVATIVES **glutinously** adverb.
– ORIGIN Latin *glutinosus*, from *gluten* 'glue'.
glutton ● noun **1** an excessively greedy eater. **2** a person with a great eagerness or capacity for something: *a glutton for adventure.*
– PHRASES **a glutton for punishment** a person who is always eager to undertake unpleasant tasks.
– DERIVATIVES **gluttonous** adjective.
– ORIGIN Latin *glutto*, related to *gluttire* 'to swallow' and *gluttus* 'greedy'.
gluttony ● noun habitual greed or excess in eating.
glycerine /glissəreen/ (US **glycerin**) ● noun another term for GLYCEROL.
– ORIGIN French *glycerin*, from Greek *glukeros* 'sweet'
glycerol /glissərol/ ● noun a colourless, sweet, viscous liquid formed as a by-product in soap manufacture, used as an emollient and laxative.
glycine /glīseen/ ● noun Biochemistry the simplest naturally occurring amino acid, a constituent of most proteins.
– ORIGIN from Greek *glukus* 'sweet'.
glycogen /glīkəjən/ ● noun a substance deposited in bodily tissues as a store of carbohydrates.
glycol /glīkol/ ● noun short for ETHYLENE GLYCOL.
– ORIGIN from GLYCERINE.
glycolysis /glīkollisiss/ ● noun Biochemistry the breakdown of glucose by enzymes, releasing energy.
– DERIVATIVES **glycolytic** /glīkəlittik/ adjective.
glycoprotein /glīkōprōteen/ ● noun any of a class of proteins which have carbohydrate groups attached to the polypeptide chain.
glycoside /glīkəsīd/ ● noun Biochemistry a compound formed from a simple sugar and another compound by replacement of a hydroxyl group in the sugar molecule.
glyph /glif/ ● noun **1** a hieroglyphic character; a pictograph or sculptured symbol. **2** Architecture an ornamental carved groove or channel, as on a Greek frieze. **3** Computing a small graphic symbol.
– ORIGIN Greek *gluphē* 'carving'.
glyphosate /glīfosfayt/ ● noun a synthetic compound which is a non-selective systemic herbicide.
GM ● abbreviation **1** general manager. **2** genetically modified. **3** George Medal. **4** (of a school) grant-maintained.
gm ● abbreviation gram(s).
G-man ● noun informal **1** US an FBI agent. **2** Irish a political detective.
– ORIGIN probably an abbreviation of *Government man.*
GMO ● abbreviation genetically modified organism.
GMT ● abbreviation Greenwich Mean Time.
gn ● abbreviation guinea(s).
gnarled ● adjective knobbly, rough, and twisted, especially with age.
– ORIGIN variant of *knarled*, from obsolete *knarre* 'rugged rock or stone'.
gnarly ● adjective (**gnarlier**, **gnarliest**) **1** gnarled. **2** N. Amer. informal dangerous, challenging, or unpleasant.
gnash /nash/ ● verb grind (one's teeth) together, especially as a sign of anger.
– ORIGIN perhaps related to a Old Norse word meaning 'a gnashing of teeth'.
gnashers ● plural noun Brit. informal teeth.
gnat /nat/ ● noun a small two-winged fly resembling a mosquito.
– ORIGIN Old English.
gnaw /naw/ ● verb **1** bite at or nibble persistently. **2** cause persistent anxiety or pain.
– DERIVATIVES **gnawingly** adverb.
– ORIGIN Old English, ultimately imitative.
gneiss /nīss/ ● noun a metamorphic rock with a banded or foliated structure, typically consisting of feldspar, quartz, and mica.
– ORIGIN German, from High German *gneisto* 'spark' (because of the rock's sheen).
gnocchi /nyokki/ ● plural noun (in Italian cooking) small dumplings made from potato, semolina, or flour.
– ORIGIN Italian, plural of *gnocco*, alteration of *nocchio* 'knot in wood'.
gnome ● noun **1** a legendary dwarfish creature supposed to guard the earth's treasures underground. **2** a small garden ornament in the form of a bearded man with a pointed hat. **3** informal a person having secret or sinister influence, especially in financial matters: *the gnomes of Zurich.*
– DERIVATIVES **gnomish** adjective.
– ORIGIN Latin *gnomus*, a word used by the Swiss physician Paracelsus (*c.*1493–1541) as a synonym of *Pygmaeus* 'pygmy'.
gnomic /nōmik/ ● adjective **1** in the form of short, pithy maxims or aphorisms. **2** enigmatic; ambiguous.
– DERIVATIVES **gnomically** adverb.
– ORIGIN from Greek *gnōmē* 'thought, opinion'
gnomon /nōmon/ ● noun the projecting piece on a sundial that shows the time by its shadow.
– ORIGIN Grek *gnōmōn* 'indicator, carpenter's square'.
gnosis /nōsiss/ ● noun knowledge of spiritual mysteries.
– ORIGIN Greek, 'knowledge'.
gnostic /nostik/ ● adjective **1** relating to knowledge, especially esoteric mystical knowledge. **2** (**Gnostic**) relating to Gnosticism. ● noun (**Gnostic**) an adherent of Gnosticism.
– ORIGIN Greek *gnōstikos*, from *gnōstos* 'known'.
Gnosticism /nostisiz'm/ ● noun a heretical movement of the 2nd-century Christian Church, teaching that esoteric knowledge (gnosis) of the supreme divine being enabled the redemption of the human spirit.
GNP ● abbreviation gross national product.
gnu /nōō/ ● noun a large African antelope with a long head and a beard and mane.
– ORIGIN from Khoikhoi and San, perhaps imitative of the sound made by the animal when alarmed.
GNVQ ● abbreviation General National Vocational Qualification.
go[1] ● verb (**goes**, **going**; past **went**; past part. **gone**) **1** move to or from a place. **2** pass into or be in a specified state: *her mind went blank.* **3** (**go to/into**) enter into a specified state or course of action: *go to sleep.* **4** lie or extend in a certain direction. **5** come to an end; cease to exist. **6** disappear or be used up. **7** (of time) pass. **8** pass time in a particular way: *they went for months without talking.* **9** engage in a specified activity. **10** have a particular outcome. **11** (**be going to be/do**) used to express a future tense. **12** function or operate. **13** be harmonious or matching. **14** be acceptable or permitted: *anything goes.* **15** fit into or be regularly kept in a particular place. **16** make a specified sound. **17** informal say. **18** (**go by/under**) be known or called by (a specified name). ● noun (pl. **goes**) informal **1** an attempt: *give it a go.* **2** a turn to do or use something. **3** Brit. informal a single item, action, or spell of activity: *it costs ten quid a go.* **4** spirit or energy. **5** Brit. vigorous activity.
– PHRASES **go about** begin or carry on work at. **go along with** agree to. **go at** energetically attack or tackle. **go back on** fail to keep (a promise). **go down 1** be defeated in a contest. **2** be recorded or remembered in a particular way. **3** obtain a specified reaction: *the show went down well.* **go for 1** decide on. **2** attempt to gain. **3** attack. **4** apply to. **go halves** (or **shares**) share something equally. **go in for 1** enter (a contest) as a competitor. **2** like or habitually take part in. **going!, gone!** an auc-

g

Thesaurus

– OPPOSITES dearth.
● verb *the factories are glutted* CRAM FULL, overfill, overload, oversupply, saturate, flood, inundate, deluge, swamp; *informal* stuff.
glutinous ● adjective STICKY, viscous, viscid, tacky, gluey, gummy, treacly; adhesive; *informal* gooey, gloopy, cloggy; *N. Amer. informal* gloppy.
glutton ● noun GOURMAND, overeater, big eater, gorger, gobbler; *informal* (greedy) pig, gannet, greedy guts, gutbucket, guzzler.
gluttonous ● adjective GREEDY, gourmandizing, voracious, insatiable, wolfish; *informal* piggish, piggy.
gluttony ● noun GREED, greediness, overeating, gourmandism, gourmandizing, voracity, insatiability; *informal* piggishness.
gnarled ● adjective **1** *a gnarled tree trunk* KNOBBLY, knotty, knotted, gnarly, lumpy, bumpy, nodular; twisted, bent, crooked, distorted, contorted. **2** *gnarled hands* TWISTED, bent, misshapen; arthritic; rough, wrinkled, wizened.
gnash ● verb GRIND, grate, rasp, grit.
gnaw ● verb **1** *the dog gnawed at a bone* CHEW, champ, chomp, bite, munch, crunch; nibble, worry. **2** *the pressures are gnawing away their independence* ERODE, wear away, wear down, eat away (at);

tioneer's announcement that bidding is closing or closed. **go into 1** investigate or enquire into. **2** (of a whole number) be capable of dividing another, typically without a remainder. **go off 1** (of a gun or bomb) explode or fire. **2** chiefly Brit. (of food) begin to decompose. **3** informal, chiefly Brit. begin to dislike. **go on 1** continue or persevere. **2** take place. **3** proceed to do. **go out 1** be extinguished. **2** (of the tide) ebb. **3** carry on a regular romantic relationship with someone. **go over 1** examine or check the details of. **2** be received in a specified way. **go round** chiefly Brit. (chiefly US also **go around**) be sufficient to supply everybody present. **go through 1** undergo (a difficult experience). **2** examine carefully. **3** use up or spend. **go under** become bankrupt. **go with 1** give one's consent or agreement to. **2** have a romantic or sexual relationship with. **go without** suffer lack or deprivation. **have a go at** chiefly Brit. attack or criticize. **have —— going for one** informal be in one's favour or to one's advantage. **make a go of** informal be successful in. **no go** informal impossible, hopeless, or forbidden. **on the go** informal very active or busy. **to go** chiefly N. Amer. (of food or drink from a restaurant or cafe) to be eaten or drunk off the premises. **what goes around comes around** proverb the consequences of one's actions will have to be dealt with eventually.

– ORIGIN Old English; the form *went* was originally the past tense of WEND.

go² ● noun a Japanese board game of territorial possession and capture.

– ORIGIN Japanese.

goad /gōd/ ● noun **1** a spiked stick used for driving cattle. **2** a thing that stimulates someone into action. ● verb **1** provoke to action. **2** urge on with a goad.

– ORIGIN Old English.

go-ahead informal ● noun (**the go-ahead**) permission to proceed. ● adjective enterprising and ambitious.

goal ● noun **1** (in soccer, rugby, etc.) a pair of posts linked by a

g

Thesaurus

consume, devour. **3** *the doubts gnawed at her* NAG, plague, torment, torture, trouble, distress, worry, haunt, oppress, burden, hang over, bother, fret; niggle.

go ● verb **1** *he's gone into town* MOVE, proceed, make one's way, advance, progress, pass; walk, travel, journey; poetic/literary betake oneself. **2** *the road goes to London* EXTEND, stretch, reach; lead. **3** *the money will go to charity* BE GIVEN, be donated, be granted, be presented, be awarded; be devoted; be handed (over). **4** *it's time to go* LEAVE, depart, take oneself off, go away, withdraw, absent oneself, make an exit, exit; set off, start out, get under way, be on one's way; decamp, retreat, retire, make off, clear out, run off/away, flee; Brit. make a move; informal make tracks, push off, beat it, take off, skedaddle, scram, split, scoot; Brit. informal sling one's hook. **5** *three years went past* PASS, elapse, slip by/past, roll by/past, tick away; fly by/past. **6** *a golden age that has gone for good* DISAPPEAR, vanish, be no more, be over, run its course, fade away; finish, end, cease. **7** *all our money had gone* BE USED UP, be spent, be exhausted, be consumed, be drained, be depleted. **8** *I'd like to see my grandchildren before I go* DIE, pass away, pass on, lose one's life, expire, breathe one's last, perish, go to meet one's maker; informal give up the ghost, kick the bucket, croak, buy it, turn up one's toes; Brit. informal snuff it, pop one's clogs; N. Amer. informal bite the big one, buy the farm; archaic decease, depart this life. **9** *the bridge went suddenly* COLLAPSE, give way, fall down, cave in, crumble, disintegrate. **10** *his hair had gone grey* BECOME, get, turn, grow. **11** *he heard the bell go* MAKE A SOUND, sound, reverberate, resound; ring, chime, peal, toll, clang. **12** *everything went well* TURN OUT, work out, develop, come out; result, end (up); informal pan out. **13** *those colours don't go* MATCH, be harmonious, harmonize, blend, be suited, be complementary, coordinate, be compatible. **14** *my car won't go* FUNCTION, work, run, operate. **15** *where does the cutlery go?* BELONG, be kept, be found, be located, be situated. **16** *this all goes to prove my point* CONTRIBUTE, help, serve; incline, tend.

– OPPOSITES arrive, come, return, clash.

● noun (informal) **1** *his second go* ATTEMPT, try, effort, bid, endeavour; informal shot, stab, crack, bash, whirl, whack; formal essay. **2** *he has plenty of go in him* ENERGY, vigour, vitality, life, liveliness, spirit, verve, enthusiasm, zest, vibrancy, sparkle; stamina, dynamism, drive, push, determination; informal pep, punch, oomph, get-up-and-go.

– PHRASES **go about** SET ABOUT, begin, embark on, start, commence, address oneself to, get down to, get to work on, get going on, undertake; approach, tackle, attack; informal get cracking on/with. **go along with** AGREE TO/WITH, fall in with, comply with, cooperate with, acquiesce in, assent to, follow; submit to, yield to, defer to. **go away.** See GO verb sense 4. **go back on** RENEGE ON, break, fail to honour, default on, repudiate, retract; do an about-face; informal cop out (of), rat on. **go by** *we have to go by his decision* OBEY, abide by, comply with, keep to, conform to, follow, heed, defer to, respect. **go down 1** *the ship went down* SINK, founder, go under. **2** *interest rates are going down* DECREASE, get lower, fall, drop, decline; plummet, plunge, slump. **3** *they went down in the first leg* LOSE, be beaten, be defeated, come to grief. **4** *his name will go down in history* BE REMEMBERED, be recorded, be commemorated, be immortalized. **go down with** (Brit.) FALL ILL WITH, get, develop, contract, pick up, succumb to, fall victim to, be struck down with, become infected with. **go far** BE SUCCESSFUL, succeed, be a success, do well, get on, get somewhere, get ahead, make good; informal make a name for oneself, make one's mark. **go for 1** *I went for the tuna* CHOOSE, pick, opt for, select, plump for, decide on. **2** *the man went for her* ATTACK, assault, hit, strike, beat up, assail, set upon, rush at, lash out at; informal lay into, rough up; Brit. informal have a go at, duff up; N. Amer. informal beat up on. **3** *he goes for older women* BE ATTRACTED TO, like, fancy; prefer, favour, choose; informal have a thing about. **go in for** TAKE PART IN, participate in, engage in, get involved in, join in, enter into, undertake; practise, pursue; espouse, adopt, embrace. **go into** INVESTIGATE, examine, enquire into, look into, research, probe, explore, delve into; consider, review, analyse. **go off 1** *the bomb went off* EXPLODE, detonate, blow up. **2** (Brit.) *the milk's gone off* GO BAD, go stale, go sour, turn, spoil, go rancid; decompose, go mouldy. **go on 1** *the lecture went on for hours* LAST, continue, carry on, run on, proceed; endure, persist; take. **2** *she went on about the sea* TALK AT LENGTH, ramble, rattle on, chatter, prattle, gabble, blether, blather, twitter; informal gab, yak, yabber, yatter; Brit. informal witter, rabbit, natter, waffle, chunter; N. Amer. informal run off at the mouth. **3** *I'm not sure what went on* HAPPEN, take place, occur, transpire; N. Amer. informal go down; poetic/literary come to pass, betide; archaic hap. **go out 1** *the lights went out* BE TURNED OFF, be extinguished; stop burning. **2** *he's going out with Kate* SEE, take out, be someone's boyfriend/girlfriend, be involved with; informal date, go steady with, go with; N. Amer. informal, dated step out with; dated court, woo. **go over 1** *go over the figures* EXAMINE, study, scrutinize, inspect, look at/over, scan, check; analyse, appraise, review. **2** *we are going over our lines* REHEARSE, practise, read through, run through. **go round 1** *the wheels were going round* SPIN, revolve, turn, rotate, whirl. **2** *a nasty rumour going round* BE SPREAD, be circulated, be put about, circulate, pass round, be broadcast. **go through 1** *the terrible things she has gone through* UNDERGO, experience, face, suffer, be subjected to, live through, endure, brave, bear, tolerate, withstand, put up with, cope with, weather. **2** *he went through hundreds of pounds* SPEND, use up, run through, get through, expend, deplete; waste, squander, fritter away. **3** *he went through Susie's bag* SEARCH, look, hunt, rummage, rifle; informal frisk. **4** *I have to go through the report* EXAMINE, study, scrutinize, inspect, look over, scan, check; analyse, appraise, review. **5** *the deal has gone through* BE COMPLETED, be concluded, be brought off; be approved, be signed, be rubber-stamped. **go under** GO BANKRUPT, cease trading, go into receivership, go into liquidation, become insolvent, be liquidated, be wound up, be shut (down); fail; informal go broke, go to the wall, go belly up, fold. **go without 1** *I went without breakfast* ABSTAIN FROM, refrain from, forgo, do without, deny oneself. **2** *the children did not go without* BE DEPRIVED, be in want, go short, go hungry, be in need.

goad ● noun **1** *he applied his goad to the cows* PROD, spike, staff, crook, rod. **2** *a goad to political change* STIMULUS, incentive, encouragement, inducement, fillip, spur, prod, prompt; motive, motivation.

● verb *we were goaded into action* PROVOKE, spur, prod, egg on, hound, badger, incite, rouse, stir, move, stimulate, motivate, prompt, induce, encourage, urge, inspire; impel, pressure, pressurize, dragoon.

go-ahead (informal) ● noun *they gave the go-ahead for the scheme* PERMISSION, consent, leave, licence, dispensation, warrant, clearance; authorization, assent, agreement, approval, endorsement, sanction, blessing, the nod; informal the thumbs up, the OK, the green light.

● adjective *go-ahead companies* ENTERPRISING, resourceful, innovative, ingenious, original, creative; progressive, pioneering, mod-

crossbar and forming a space into or over which the ball has to be sent to score. **2** an instance of sending the ball into or over a goal. **3** an aim or desired result.
– DERIVATIVES **goalless** adjective.
– ORIGIN of unknown origin.
goal average ● noun Soccer the ratio of the numbers of goals scored for and against a team in a series of matches.
goal difference ● noun Soccer the difference between the number of goals scored for and against a team in a series of matches.
goalie ● noun informal a goalkeeper.
goalkeeper ● noun a player in soccer or field hockey whose special role is to stop the ball from entering the goal.
goal kick ● noun **1** Soccer a free kick taken by the defending side after attackers send the ball over the byline. **2** Rugby an attempt to kick a goal.
goal line ● noun a line across a football or hockey field on which the goal is placed or which acts as the boundary beyond which a try or touchdown is scored.
goalpost ● noun either of the two upright posts of a goal.
– PHRASES **move the goalposts** unfairly alter the conditions or rules of a procedure during its course.
goat ● noun **1** a hardy domesticated mammal that has backward-curving horns and (in the male) a beard. **2** a wild mammal related to this, such as the ibex. **3** informal a lecherous man. **4** Brit. informal a stupid person.
– PHRASES **get someone's goat** informal irritate someone.
– DERIVATIVES **goatish** adjective **goaty** adjective.
– ORIGIN Old English.
goat-antelope ● noun a mammal of a group including the chamois and musk ox, with characteristics of both goats and antelopes.
goatee /gōtee/ ● noun a small pointed beard like that of a goat.
– DERIVATIVES **goateed** adjective.
goatherd ● noun a person who tends goats.
gob[1] ● noun informal, chiefly Brit. a person's mouth.
– ORIGIN perhaps from Scottish Gaelic.
gob[2] informal ● noun **1** a lump or clot of a slimy or viscous substance. **2** (**gobs of**) N. Amer. a lot of. ● verb (**gobbed, gobbing**) Brit. spit.
– ORIGIN Old French *gobe* 'mouthful, lump', from *gober* 'to swallow, gulp'.
gobbet /gobbit/ ● noun a piece or lump of flesh, food, or other matter.
– ORIGIN Old French *gobet* 'little lump or mouthful'.
gobble[1] ● verb (often **gobble up**) **1** eat hurriedly and noisily. **2** use a large amount of (something) very quickly.
– DERIVATIVES **gobbler** noun.
– ORIGIN probably from GOB[2].
gobble[2] ● verb (of a turkeycock) make a characteristic swallowing sound in the throat.
– DERIVATIVES **gobbler** noun.
– ORIGIN imitative, perhaps influenced by GOBBLE[1].
gobbledegook /gobb'ldigōōk/ (also **gobbledygook**) ● noun informal pompous or unintelligible jargon.
– ORIGIN probably imitating a turkey's gobble.
go-between ● noun an intermediary or negotiator.
goblet ● noun **1** a drinking glass with a foot and a stem. **2** Brit. a receptacle forming part of a liquidizer.
– ORIGIN Old French *gobelet* 'little cup'.
goblin ● noun a mischievous, ugly, dwarf-like creature of folklore.
– ORIGIN Old French *gobelin*, possibly related to German *Kobold* (denoting a spirit who haunts houses or lives underground) or to Greek *kobalos* 'mischievous goblin'.
gobshite /gobshīt/ ● noun vulgar slang, chiefly Irish a stupid or incompetent person.
– ORIGIN perhaps from *gob*, dialect variant of GAB, + SHITE.
gobsmacked ● adjective Brit. informal utterly astonished.
– DERIVATIVES **gobsmacking** adjective.
gobstopper ● noun chiefly Brit. a large, hard spherical sweet.
goby /gōbi/ ● noun (pl. **gobies**) a small marine fish, typically with a sucker on the underside.
– ORIGIN Greek *kōbios*.
go-cart ● noun **1** variant spelling of GO-KART. **2** a handcart. **3** a pushchair.
God ● noun **1** (in Christianity and other monotheistic religions) the creator and supreme ruler of the universe. **2** (**god**) a superhuman being or spirit worshipped as having power over nature and human fortunes. **3** (**god**) a greatly admired or influential person. **4** (**the gods**) informal the gallery in a theatre. ● exclamation used to express surprise, anger, etc. or for emphasis.
– PHRASES **God the Father, Son, and Holy Ghost** (in Christian doctrine) the persons of the Trinity. **God Save the Queen** (or **King**) the British national anthem.
– DERIVATIVES **godhood** noun **godlike** adjective **godward** adjective & adverb.
– ORIGIN Old English.
God-awful ● adjective informal extremely bad or unpleasant.
godchild ● noun (pl. **godchildren**) a person in relation to a godparent.
god-daughter ● noun a female godchild.
goddess ● noun **1** a female deity. **2** a woman who is adored, especially for her beauty.
godet /gōday/ ● noun a triangular piece of material inserted in a garment to make it flared or for ornamentation.
– ORIGIN French.
godetia /gōdeeshə/ ● noun a North American plant with showy lilac to red flowers.
– ORIGIN named after the Swiss botanist Charles H. *Godet* (1797–1879).
godfather ● noun **1** a male godparent. **2** the male head of an illegal organization, especially a leader of the American Mafia.
God-fearing ● adjective earnestly religious.
godforsaken ● adjective lacking any merit or attraction.
godhead ● noun **1** (**the Godhead**) God. **2** divine nature.
godless ● adjective **1** not believing in a god or God. **2** profane; wicked.
– DERIVATIVES **godlessness** noun.
godly ● adjective (**godlier, godliest**) devoutly religious; pious.

g

Thesaurus

ern, forward-looking, enlightened; enthusiastic, ambitious, entrepreneurial, high-powered; bold, daring, audacious, adventurous, dynamic; *informal* go-getting.
goal ● noun OBJECTIVE, aim, end, target, design, intention, intent, plan, purpose; (holy) grail; ambition, aspiration, wish, dream, desire, hope.
goat ● noun **1** *a herd of goats* billy (goat), nanny (goat), kid. **2** *(Brit. informal) she's always playing the goat.* See FOOL noun sense 1. **3** *(informal) be careful of that old goat* LECHER, libertine, womanizer, seducer, Don Juan, Casanova, Lothario, Romeo; pervert, debauchee, rake; *informal* lech, dirty old man, ladykiller.
– RELATED TERMS caprine.
gobble ● verb GUZZLE, bolt, gulp, devour, wolf, cram, gorge (oneself) on; *informal* tuck into, put away, demolish, polish off, shovel down, stuff one's face (with), pig oneself (on); *Brit. informal* scoff, gollop, shift; *N. Amer. informal* scarf (down/up).
gobbledegook ● noun *(informal)* GIBBERISH, claptrap, nonsense, rubbish, balderdash, mumbo-jumbo, blather, blether; *N. Amer.* garbage; *informal* drivel, tripe, hogwash, baloney, bilge, bosh, bull, bunk, guff, eyewash, piffle, twaddle, poppycock, phooey, hooey; *Brit. informal* cobblers, codswallop, double Dutch, tosh; *N. Amer. informal* bushwa, applesauce.
go-between ● noun INTERMEDIARY, middleman, agent, broker, liaison, linkman, contact; negotiator, interceder, intercessor, mediator.
goblet ● noun WINE GLASS, chalice; glass, beaker, tumbler, cup.
goblin ● noun HOBGOBLIN, gnome, dwarf, troll, imp, elf, brownie, fairy, pixie, leprechaun.
god ● noun **1** *a gift from God* THE LORD, the Almighty, the Creator, the Maker, the Godhead; Allah, Jehovah, Yahweh; (God) the Father, (God) the Son, the Holy Ghost/Spirit, the Holy Trinity. **2** *sacrifices to appease the gods* DEITY, goddess, divine being, celestial being, divinity, immortal, avatar. **3** *wooden gods* IDOL, graven image, icon, totem, talisman, fetish, juju.
godforsaken ● adjective WRETCHED, miserable, dreary, dismal, depressing, grim, cheerless, bleak, desolate, gloomy; deserted, neglected, isolated, remote, backward; *Brit. informal* grotty.
– OPPOSITES charming.
godless ● adjective **1** *a godless society* ATHEISTIC, unbelieving, agnostic, sceptical, heretical, faithless, irreligious, ungodly, unholy, impious, profane; infidel, heathen, idolatrous, pagan; satanic, devilish. **2** *godless pleasures* IMMORAL, wicked, sinful, wrong, evil, bad, iniquitous, corrupt; irreligious, sacrilegious, profane, blasphemous, impious; depraved, degenerate, debauched, perverted,

– DERIVATIVES **godliness** noun.
godmother ● noun a female godparent.
godown /gōdown/ ● noun (in east Asia, especially India) a warehouse.
– ORIGIN Portuguese *gudão*, from Tamil.
godparent ● noun a person who presents a child at baptism and promises to take responsibility for their religious education.
godsend ● noun something very helpful or opportune.
God's gift ● noun chiefly ironic the best possible person or thing.
godson ● noun a male godchild.
Godspeed ● exclamation dated an expression of good wishes to a person starting a journey.
godwit ● noun a large, long-legged wader with a long bill.
– ORIGIN of unknown origin.
goer ● noun **1** a person who regularly attends a specified place or event: *a theatre-goer*. **2** informal a person or thing that goes. **3** informal a sexually unrestrained woman.
goes third person singular present of GO[1].

g

gofer /gōfər/ (also **gopher**) ● noun informal, chiefly N. Amer. a person who runs errands; a dogsbody.
– ORIGIN from *go for* (i.e. go and fetch).
goffer /gōffər/ ● verb (usu. as adj. **goffered**) crimp or flute (a lace edge or frill) with heated irons. ● noun an iron used for goffering.
– ORIGIN French *gaufrer* 'stamp with a patterned tool', from Low German *wāfel* 'waffle'.
go-getter ● noun informal an aggressively enterprising person.
– DERIVATIVES **go-getting** adjective.
goggle ● verb **1** look with wide open eyes. **2** (of the eyes) protrude or open wide. ● noun (**goggles**) close-fitting protective glasses with side shields.
– ORIGIN probably symbolic of oscillating movement.
goggle-box ● noun Brit. informal a television set.
goggle-eyed ● adjective having wide-open eyes, especially through astonishment.
go-go ● adjective **1** denoting an unrestrained and erotic style of dancing to popular music. **2** assertively dynamic.
going ● noun **1** the condition of the ground viewed in terms of suitability for horse racing or walking. **2** conditions for, or progress in, an endeavour. ● adjective **1** chiefly Brit. existing or available: *any jobs going?* **2** (of a price) acceptable or current.
going concern ● noun a thriving business.
going-over ● noun informal **1** a thorough cleaning or inspection. **2** a beating.
goings-on ● plural noun informal activities of a suspect or unusual nature.
goitre /goytər/ (US **goiter**) ● noun a swelling of the neck resulting from enlargement of the thyroid gland.
– DERIVATIVES **goitrous** adjective.
– ORIGIN French, or from Old French *goitron* 'gullet', both from Latin *guttur* 'throat'.
go-kart (also **go-cart**) ● noun a small racing car with a lightweight or skeleton body.
gold ● noun **1** a yellow precious metal, used in jewellery and decoration and as a monetary medium. **2** a deep lustrous yellow or yellow-brown colour. **3** coins or articles made of gold. **4** wealth.
– PHRASES **pot** (or **crock**) **of gold** a large but distant or imaginary reward. [ORIGIN with allusion to the story of a crock of gold supposedly to be found at the end of a rainbow.]
– ORIGIN Old English.
goldcrest ● noun a very small warbler with a yellow or orange crest.
gold-digger ● noun informal a woman who forms relationships with men purely for financial gain.
gold disc ● noun a framed golden disc awarded to a recording artist or group for sales exceeding a specified figure.
gold dust ● noun **1** fine particles of gold. **2** something rare and very valuable.
golden ● adjective **1** made of or resembling gold. **2** (of a period) very happy and prosperous. **3** excellent: *a golden opportunity*.
– DERIVATIVES **goldenly** adverb.
golden age ● noun **1** an idyllic, often imaginary past time of peace, prosperity, and happiness. **2** the period when a specified art or activity is at its peak.
golden boy (or **golden girl**) ● noun informal a very popular or successful young man or woman.
Golden Delicious ● noun a variety of dessert apple with a greenish-yellow skin.
golden eagle ● noun a large eagle with yellow-tipped head feathers.
goldeneye ● noun (pl. same or **goldeneyes**) a northern diving duck, the male of which has a dark head with a white cheek patch and yellow eyes.
golden goose ● noun a continuing source of wealth or profit that may be exhausted if it is misused.
golden handcuffs ● plural noun informal benefits provided by an employer to discourage an employee from working elsewhere.
golden handshake ● noun informal a payment given to someone who is made redundant or retires early.
golden jubilee ● noun the fiftieth anniversary of a significant event.
golden mean ● noun the ideal moderate position between two extremes.
golden oldie ● noun informal **1** an old song of enduring popularity. **2** a person who is no longer young but is still successful.
golden parachute ● noun informal a payment guaranteed to a company executive should they be dismissed as a result of a merger or takeover.
golden retriever ● noun a breed of retriever with a thick golden-coloured coat.
goldenrod ● noun a plant with tall spikes of small bright yellow flowers.
golden rule ● noun a basic principle which should always be followed.
golden syrup ● noun Brit. a pale treacle.
golden wedding ● noun the fiftieth anniversary of a wedding.
goldfield ● noun a district in which gold is found as a mineral.
goldfinch ● noun a brightly coloured finch with a yellow patch on each wing.
goldfish ● noun a small reddish-golden carp popular in ponds and aquaria.
goldfish bowl ● noun chiefly Brit. **1** a spherical glass container for goldfish. **2** a place or situation lacking privacy.
gold leaf ● noun gold beaten into a very thin sheet, used in gilding.
gold medal ● noun a medal made of or coloured gold, awarded for first place in a race or competition.
gold mine ● noun **1** a place where gold is mined. **2** a source of

Thesaurus

decadent; impure.
– OPPOSITES religious, virtuous.
godlike ● adjective DIVINE, godly, superhuman; angelic, seraphic; spiritual, heavenly, celestial; sacred, holy, saintly.
godly ● adjective RELIGIOUS, devout, pious, reverent, believing, God-fearing, saintly, holy, prayerful, churchgoing.
– OPPOSITES irreligious.
godsend ● noun BOON, blessing, bonus, plus, benefit, advantage, help, aid, asset; stroke of luck; informal perk; formal perquisite.
– OPPOSITES curse.
goggle ● verb STARE, gape, gaze, ogle; informal gawk, rubberneck; Brit. informal gawp.
going-over ● noun (informal) **1** *his work was subjected to a going-over* EXAMINATION, inspection, investigation, probe, check-up; assessment, review, analysis, appraisal, critique; informal once-over. **2** *the flat needs a going-over* CLEAN, dust, mop, scrub; informal vacuum, once-over. **3** *the thugs gave him a going-over* BEATING, thrashing, thumping, pummelling, battering, pelting; assault, attack; informal doing-over, belting, bashing, pasting, walloping, clobbering, hiding.
goings-on ● plural noun (informal) EVENTS, happenings, affairs, business; mischief, misbehaviour, misconduct, funny business; informal monkey business, hanky-panky, shenanigans; Brit. informal jiggery-pokery, carry-on; N. Amer. informal monkeyshines.
gold ● noun *she won the gold* GOLD MEDAL, first prize.
– RELATED TERMS auric, aurous.
golden ● adjective **1** *her golden hair* BLOND(E), yellow, fair, flaxen, tow-coloured. **2** *a golden time* SUCCESSFUL, prosperous, flourishing, thriving; favourable, providential, lucky, fortunate; happy, joyful, glorious. **3** *a golden opportunity* EXCELLENT, fine, superb, splendid; special, unique; favourable, opportune, promising, bright, full of promise; advantageous, profitable, valuable, providential. **4** *the golden girl of tennis* FAVOURITE, favoured, popular, admired, beloved, pet; acclaimed, applauded, praised; brilliant, consummate,

great wealth or valuable resources.

gold plate ● noun **1** a thin layer of gold applied as a coating to another metal. **2** plates, dishes, etc. made of or plated with gold. ● verb (**gold-plate**) cover with gold plate.

gold reserve ● noun a quantity of gold held by a central bank to support the issue of currency.

gold rush ● noun a rapid movement of people to a newly discovered goldfield.

goldsmith ● noun a person who makes gold articles.

gold standard ● noun historical the system by which the value of a currency was defined in terms of gold.

golem /gōləm/ ● noun **1** (in Jewish legend) a clay figure brought to life by magic. **2** an automaton or robot.

– ORIGIN Hebrew, 'shapeless mass'.

golf ● noun a game played on an outdoor course, the aim of which is to strike a small, hard ball with a club into a series of small holes with the fewest possible strokes. ● verb (usu. as noun **golfing**) play golf.

– DERIVATIVES **golfer** noun.

– ORIGIN perhaps related to Dutch *kolf* 'club, bat'.

golf ball ● noun **1** a ball used in golf. **2** (**golfball**) a small metal globe used in some electric typewriters to carry the type.

golf club ● noun see CLUB² (sense 2).

golliwog ● noun a soft doll with a black face and fuzzy hair.

– ORIGIN from *Golliwogg*, the name of a doll character in books by the US writer Bertha Upton (died 1912).

golly¹ ● exclamation informal used to express surprise or delight.

– ORIGIN euphemism for GOD.

golly² ● noun (pl. **gollies**) Brit. informal a golliwog.

-gon ● combining form in nouns denoting plane figures with a specified number of angles and sides: *hexagon*.

– ORIGIN from Greek *-gōnos* '-angled'.

gonad /gōnad/ ● noun a bodily organ that produces gametes; a testis or ovary.

– DERIVATIVES **gonadal** /gōnayd'l/ adjective.

– ORIGIN Latin *gonades*, plural of *gonas*, from Greek *gonē* 'generation, seed'.

gonadotrophin /gōnadōtrōfin/ (also **gonadotropin** /gōnadōtrōpin/) ● noun any of a group of hormones secreted by the pituitary which stimulate the activity of the gonads.

gondola /gondələ/ ● noun **1** a light flat-bottomed boat used on Venetian canals, having a high point at each end and worked by one oar at the stern. **2** a cabin on a ski lift, or suspended from an airship or balloon.

– ORIGIN Venetian Italian.

gondolier /gondəleer/ ● noun a person who propels and steers a gondola.

gone past participle of GO¹. ● adjective **1** no longer present or in existence. **2** informal in a trance or stupor, especially through alcohol or drugs. **3** informal having reached a specified time in a pregnancy: *four months gone.* ● preposition Brit. **1** (of time) past. **2** (of age) older than.

– PHRASES **be gone on** informal be infatuated with.

goner /gonnər/ ● noun informal a person or thing that is doomed or cannot be saved.

gong ● noun **1** a metal disc with a turned rim, giving a resonant note when struck. **2** Brit. informal a medal or decoration. ● verb sound a gong or make a sound like that of a gong.

– ORIGIN Malay.

gonna ● contraction informal going to.

gonorrhoea /gonnəreeə/ (US **gonorrhea**) ● noun a venereal disease involving inflammatory discharge from the urethra or vagina.

– ORIGIN Greek *gonorrhoia*, from *gonos* 'semen' + *rhoia* 'flux'.

gonzo ● adjective informal, chiefly N. Amer. **1** of or associated with journalism of an exaggerated, subjective, and fictionalized style. **2** bizarre or crazy.

– ORIGIN perhaps from Italian *gonzo* 'foolish' or Spanish *ganso* 'goose, fool'.

goo ● noun informal **1** a sticky or slimy substance. **2** sickly sentiment.

– ORIGIN perhaps from *burgoo*, a nautical slang term for porridge, from a Persian word meaning 'bruised grain'.

good ● adjective (**better**, **best**) **1** to be desired or approved of. **2** having the required qualities; of a high standard. **3** morally right; virtuous. **4** well behaved. **5** enjoyable or satisfying. **6** appropriate. **7** (**good for**) beneficial to. **8** thorough. **9** at least. ● noun **1** that which is morally right or beneficial. **2** (**goods**) merchandise or possessions. **3** (**goods**) Brit. freight.

– PHRASES **as good as** very nearly ——. **be —— to the good** have a specified net profit or advantage. **come up with** (or **deliver**) **the goods** informal do what is expected or required. **do good 1** act virtuously, especially by helping others. **2** be helpful or beneficial. **for good** forever. **the Good Book** the Bible. **good for** (or **on**) **you!** well done! **the Good Shepherd** a name for Jesus. **a good word** words in recommendation or defence of a person. **in good time 1** with no risk of being late. **2** (also **all in good time**) in due course but without haste. **make good 1** compensate for (loss, damage, or expense). **2** fulfil (a promise or claim). **3** be successful. **take something in good part** not be offended.

– ORIGIN Old English.

Thesaurus

gifted; *informal* blue-eyed; *formal* lauded.

– OPPOSITES dark, unhappy.

gone ● adjective **1** *I wasn't gone long* AWAY, absent, off, out; missing, unavailable. **2** *those days are gone* PAST, over (and done with), no more, done, finished, ended; forgotten, dead and buried. **3** *the milk's all gone* USED UP, consumed, finished, spent, depleted; at an end. **4** *an aunt of mine, long since gone* DEAD, expired, departed, no more, passed on/away; late, lost, lamented; perished, fallen; defunct, extinct; *informal* six feet under, pushing up daisies; *formal* deceased; *euphemistic* with God, asleep, at peace.

– OPPOSITES present, here, alive.

goo ● noun *(informal)* STICKY SUBSTANCE, ooze, sludge, muck; *informal* gunk, crud, gloop; *Brit. informal* gunge; *N. Amer. informal* glop.

good ● adjective **1** *a good product* FINE, superior, quality; excellent, superb, outstanding, magnificent, exceptional, marvellous, wonderful, first-rate, first-class, sterling; satisfactory, acceptable, up to scratch, up to standard, not bad, all right; *informal* great, OK, A1, ace, terrific, fantastic, fabulous, fab, top-notch, class, awesome, wicked; *informal, dated* capital; *Brit. informal* smashing, brilliant, brill; *Austral. informal* beaut, bonzer; *Brit. informal, dated* spiffing, top hole. **2** *a good person* VIRTUOUS, righteous, upright, upstanding, moral, ethical, high-minded, principled; exemplary, law-abiding, irreproachable, blameless, guiltless, unimpeachable, honourable, scrupulous, reputable, decent, respectable, noble, trustworthy; meritorious, praiseworthy, admirable; whiter than white, saintly, saintlike, angelic; *informal* squeaky clean. **3** *the children are good at school* WELL BEHAVED, obedient, dutiful, polite, courteous, respectful, deferential, compliant. **4** *a good thing to do* RIGHT, correct, proper, decorous, seemly; appropriate, fitting, apt, suitable; convenient, expedient, favourable, opportune, felicitous, timely. **5** *a good driver* CAPABLE, able, proficient, adept, adroit, accomplished, skilful, skilled, talented, masterly, expert; *informal* great, mean, wicked, nifty, ace; *N. Amer. informal* crackerjack. **6** *a good friend* CLOSE, intimate, dear, bosom, special, best, firm, valued, treasured; loving, devoted, loyal, faithful, constant, reliable, dependable, trustworthy, trusty, true, unfailing, staunch. **7** *the dogs are in good condition* HEALTHY, fine, sound, tip-top, hale and hearty, fit, robust, sturdy, strong, vigorous. **8** *a good time was had by all* ENJOYABLE, pleasant, agreeable, pleasurable, delightful, great, nice, lovely; amusing, diverting, jolly, merry, lively; *informal* super, fantastic, fabulous, fab, terrific, grand; *Brit. informal* brilliant, brill, smashing; *N. Amer. informal* peachy, ducky; *Austral./NZ informal* beaut, bonzer. **9** *it was good of you to come* KIND, kind-hearted, good-hearted, generous, charitable, magnanimous, gracious; altruistic, unselfish, selfless. **10** *a good time to call* CONVENIENT, suitable, appropriate, fitting, fit; opportune, timely, favourable, advantageous, expedient, felicitous, happy, providential. **11** *milk is good for you* WHOLESOME, healthy, healthful, nourishing, nutritious, nutritional, beneficial, salubrious. **12** *are these eggs good?* EDIBLE, safe to eat, fit for human consumption; fresh, wholesome, consumable; *formal* comestible. **13** *good food* DELICIOUS, tasty, mouthwatering, appetizing, flavoursome, flavourful, delectable, toothsome, palatable; succulent, luscious; *informal* scrumptious, delish, scrummy, yummy; *Brit. informal* moreish; *N. Amer. informal* finger-licking, nummy. **14** *a good reason* VALID, genuine, authentic, legitimate, sound, bona fide; convincing, persuasive, telling, potent, cogent, compelling. **15** *we waited a good hour* WHOLE, full, entire, complete, solid. **16** *a good number of them* CONSIDERABLE, sizeable, substantial, appreciable, significant; goodly, fair, reasonable; plentiful, abundant, great, large, generous; *informal* tidy. **17** *wear your good clothes* BEST, smart, smartest, finest, nicest; special, party, Sunday, formal, dressy. **18** *good weather* FINE, fair, dry;

goodbye (US also **goodby**) ● exclamation used to express good wishes when parting or ending a conversation. ● noun (pl. **goodbyes**; US also **goodbys**) an instance of saying 'goodbye'; a parting.
– ORIGIN contraction of *God be with you!*
good faith ● noun honesty or sincerity of intention.
good form ● noun behaviour complying with social conventions.
good-for-nothing ● adjective worthless. ● noun a worthless person.
Good Friday ● noun the Friday before Easter Sunday, on which the Crucifixion of Christ is commemorated in the Christian Church.
good-hearted ● adjective kind and well meaning.
good-humoured ● adjective genial or cheerful.
goodie ● noun variant spelling of GOODY.
goodish ● adjective **1** fairly good. **2** fairly large.
good-looking ● adjective attractive.
goodly ● adjective (**goodlier**, **goodliest**) **1** considerable in size or quantity. **2** archaic attractive, excellent, or virtuous.
good natured ● adjective kind and unselfish.
goodness ● noun **1** the quality of being good. **2** the nutritious element of food. ● exclamation (as a substitution for 'God') expressing surprise, anger, etc.
goods and chattels ● plural noun all kinds of personal possessions.
good-tempered ● adjective not easily irritated or made angry.
good-time ● adjective recklessly pursuing pleasure.
goodwill ● noun **1** friendly or helpful feelings or attitude. **2** the established reputation of a business regarded as a quantifiable asset.
good works ● plural noun charitable acts.
goody ● noun (also **goodie**) (pl. **goodies**) informal **1** Brit. a good or favoured person, especially a hero in a story or film. **2** (**goodies**) tasty things to eat. ● exclamation expressing childish delight.
goody-goody informal ● noun a smugly virtuous person. ● adjective smugly virtuous.
gooey ● adjective (**gooier**, **gooiest**) informal **1** soft and sticky. **2** mawkishly sentimental.
– DERIVATIVES **gooeyness** noun.
goof informal, chiefly N. Amer. ● noun **1** a mistake. **2** a foolish or stupid person. ● verb **1** fool around. **2** make a mistake.
– ORIGIN of unknown origin.
goofy ● adjective (**goofier**, **goofiest**) informal **1** chiefly N. Amer. foolish; harmlessly eccentric. **2** having protruding or crooked front teeth.
– DERIVATIVES **goofily** adverb **goofiness** noun.
goog ● noun Austral./NZ informal an egg.
– PHRASES **(as) full as a goog** very drunk.
– ORIGIN from Scottish dialect *goggie*, a child's word for an egg.
googly ● noun (pl. **googlies**) Cricket an off break bowled with an apparent leg-break action.

Thesaurus

bright, clear, sunny, cloudless; calm, windless; warm, mild, balmy, clement, pleasant, nice.
– OPPOSITES bad, wicked, naughty, poor, terrible, inconvenient, small, scruffy.
● noun **1** *issues of good and evil* VIRTUE, righteousness, goodness, morality, integrity, rectitude; honesty, truth, honour, probity; propriety, worthiness, merit; blamelessness, purity. **2** *it's all for your good* BENEFIT, advantage, profit, gain, interest, welfare, well-being; enjoyment, comfort, ease, convenience; help, aid, assistance, service; behalf.
– OPPOSITES wickedness, disadvantage.
● exclamation *good, that's settled* FINE, very well, all right, right, right then, yes, agreed; informal okay, OK, okey-dokey, roger; Brit. informal righto, righty-ho.
– PHRASES **for good** *those days are gone for good* FOREVER, permanently, for always, (for) evermore, for ever and ever, for eternity, until hell freezes over, never to return; N. Amer. forevermore; informal for keeps, until doomsday, until the cows come home; archaic for aye. **in good part** *she took the joke in good part* GOOD-NATUREDLY, good-humouredly, without offence, amicably, favourably, tolerantly, indulgently, cheerfully, well. **make good** SUCCEED, be successful, be a success, do well, get ahead, reach the top; prosper, flourish, thrive; informal make it, make the grade, make a name for oneself, make one's mark, get somewhere, arrive. **make something good 1** *he promised to make good any damage* REPAIR, mend, fix, put right, see to; restore, remedy, rectify. **2** *they made good their escape* EFFECT, conduct, perform, implement, execute, carry out; achieve, accomplish, succeed in, realize, attain, engineer, bring about, bring off. **3** *he will make good his promise* FULFIL, carry out, implement, discharge, honour, redeem; keep, observe, abide by, comply with, stick to, heed, follow, be bound by, live up to, stand by, adhere to.
goodbye ● exclamation FAREWELL, adieu, au revoir, ciao, auf Wiedersehen, adios; Austral./NZ hooray; informal bye, bye-bye, so long, see you (later), later(s); Brit. informal cheers, cheerio, ta-ta; N. English informal ta-ra; informal, dated toodle-oo, toodle-pip.
good-for-nothing ● adjective *a good-for-nothing layabout* USELESS, worthless, incompetent, inefficient, inept, ne'er-do-well; lazy, idle, slothful, indolent, shiftless; informal no-good, lousy.
– OPPOSITES worthy.
● noun *lazy good-for-nothings* NE'ER-DO-WELL, layabout, do-nothing, idler, loafer, lounger, sluggard, shirker; informal waster, slacker, lazybones, couch potato; Brit. informal skiver.
good-humoured ● adjective GENIAL, affable, cordial, friendly, amiable, easy-going, approachable, good-natured, cheerful, cheery; companionable, comradely, sociable, convivial, company-loving; informal chummy, pally; Brit. informal matey; N. Amer. informal clubby.
– OPPOSITES grumpy.
good-looking ● adjective ATTRACTIVE, beautiful, pretty, handsome, lovely, stunning, striking, arresting, gorgeous, prepossessing, fetching, captivating, bewitching, beguiling, engaging, charming, enchanting, appealing, delightful; sexy, seductive, alluring, tantalizing, irresistible, ravishing, desirable; Scottish & N. English bonny; informal fanciable, tasty, hot, easy on the eye, drop-dead gorgeous; Brit. informal fit; N. Amer. informal cute, foxy; Austral./NZ informal spunky; poetic/literary beauteous; archaic comely, fair.
– OPPOSITES ugly.
goodly ● adjective LARGE, largish, sizeable, substantial, considerable, respectable, significant, decent, generous, handsome; informal tidy, serious.
– OPPOSITES paltry.
good-natured ● adjective WARM-HEARTED, friendly, amiable; neighbourly, benevolent, kind, kind-hearted, generous, unselfish, considerate, thoughtful, obliging, helpful, supportive, charitable; understanding, sympathetic, easy-going, accommodating; Brit. informal decent.
– OPPOSITES malicious.
goodness ● noun **1** *he had some goodness in him* VIRTUE, good, righteousness, morality, integrity, rectitude; honesty, truth, truthfulness, honour, probity; propriety, decency, respectability, nobility, worthiness, worth, merit, trustworthiness; blamelessness, purity. **2** *God's goodness towards us* KINDNESS, kindliness, tender-heartedness, humanity, mildness, benevolence, graciousness; tenderness, warmth, affection, love, goodwill; sympathy, compassion, care, concern, understanding, tolerance, generosity, charity, leniency, clemency, magnanimity. **3** *slow cooking retains the food's goodness* NUTRITIONAL VALUE, nutrients, wholesomeness, nourishment.
goods ● plural noun **1** *he dispatched the goods* MERCHANDISE, wares, stock, commodities, produce, products, articles; imports, exports. **2** *the dead man's goods* PROPERTY, possessions, effects, chattels, valuables; informal things, stuff, junk, gear, kit, bits and pieces; Brit. informal clobber. **3** (Brit.) *most goods went by train* FREIGHT, cargo; load, consignment, delivery, shipment.
good-tempered ● adjective EQUABLE, even-tempered, imperturbable; unruffled, unflustered, untroubled, well balanced; easy-going, mellow, mild, calm, relaxed, cool, at ease; placid, stable, level-headed; cheerful, upbeat; informal unflappable, laid-back.
– OPPOSITES moody.
goodwill ● noun BENEVOLENCE, compassion, goodness, kindness, consideration, charity; cooperation, collaboration; friendliness, thoughtfulness, decency, amity, sympathy, understanding, neighbourliness.
– OPPOSITES hostility.
goody-goody ● adjective (informal) SELF-RIGHTEOUS, sanctimonious, pious; prim and proper, strait-laced, prudish, priggish, puritanical, moralistic; informal starchy, square.
gooey ● adjective (informal) **1** *a gooey mess* STICKY, viscous, viscid; gluey, tacky, gummy, treacly, syrupy; Brit. claggy; informal gloopy, gungy, icky; N. Amer. informal gloppy. **2** *a gooey film* SENTIMENTAL, mawkish, cloying, sickly, saccharine, sugary, syrupy; romantic; Brit. twee; informal slushy, sloppy, mushy, schmaltzy, lovey-dovey,

– ORIGIN of unknown origin.
gook[1] /gŏŏk/ ● **noun** N. Amer. informal, offensive a person of SE Asian descent.
– ORIGIN of unknown origin.
gook[2] /gŏŏk/ ● **noun** informal a sloppy wet or viscous substance.
– ORIGIN variant of GUCK.
goolie (also **gooly**) ● **noun** (pl. **goolies**) Brit. informal a testicle.
– ORIGIN perhaps related to a Hindi word meaning 'bullet, ball, pill'.
goon ● **noun** informal **1** a foolish or eccentric person. **2** chiefly N. Amer. a ruffian or thug.
– ORIGIN perhaps from dialect *gooney* 'stupid person'; later influenced by the American cartoon character 'Alice the *Goon*'.
goosander /gŏŏsandər/ ● **noun** (pl. same or **goosanders**) a large merganser (diving duck), the male of which has a dark green head and whitish underparts.
– ORIGIN probably from GOOSE + *-ander* as in dialect *bergander* 'shelduck'.
goose ● **noun** (pl. **geese**) **1** a large waterbird with a long neck, short legs, webbed feet, and a short, broad bill. **2** the female of such a bird. **3** informal a foolish person. ● **verb** informal poke (someone) in the bottom.
– ORIGIN Old English.
gooseberry ● **noun** (pl. **gooseberries**) **1** a round edible yellowish-green berry with a hairy skin, growing on a thorny shrub. **2** Brit. informal a third person in the company of two lovers, who would prefer to be alone.
– ORIGIN the first element perhaps from GOOSE, or perhaps from Old French *groseille*.
goose egg ● **noun** N. Amer. informal a zero score in a game.
gooseflesh ● **noun** a pimply state of the skin with the hairs erect, produced by cold or fright.
goose pimples ● **plural noun** gooseflesh.
goose step ● **noun** a military marching step in which the legs are not bent at the knee. ● **verb** (**goose-step**) march with such a step.
GOP ● **abbreviation** informal Grand Old Party (a name for the US Republican Party).
gopher /gōfər/ ● **noun** **1** (also **pocket gopher**) a burrowing American rodent with pouches on its cheeks. **2** N. Amer. informal a ground squirrel. **3** variant spelling of GOFER.
– ORIGIN perhaps from Canadian French *gaufre* 'honeycomb' (because the gopher 'honeycombs' the ground with its burrows).
gopik /gōpik/ ● **noun** (pl. same or **gopiks**) a monetary unit of Azerbaijan, equal to one hundredth of a manat.
gorblimey ● **exclamation** Brit. informal an expression of surprise or indignation.
– ORIGIN alteration of *God blind me*.
Gordian knot /gordiən/ ● **noun** (in phrase **cut the Gordian knot**) solve a difficult problem in a direct or forceful way.
– ORIGIN from the legendary knot tied by *Gordius*, king of Gordium, and cut through by Alexander the Great in response to the prophecy that whoever untied it would rule Asia.
Gordon Bennett ● **exclamation** expressing surprise, incredulity, or exasperation.
– ORIGIN probably an alteration of GORBLIMEY, after the American publisher and sports sponsor James *Gordon Bennett* (1841–1918).
gore[1] ● **noun** blood that has been shed, especially as a result of violence.
– ORIGIN Old English, 'dung, dirt'.
gore[2] ● **verb** (of an animal such as a bull) pierce or stab with a horn or tusk.
– ORIGIN of unknown origin.
gore[3] ● **noun** a triangular or tapering piece of material used in making a garment, sail, or umbrella. ● **verb** (usu. as adj. **gored**) shape with a gore or gores.
– ORIGIN Old English, 'triangular piece of land'.
Gore-tex /gorteks/ ● **noun** trademark a breathable waterproof fabric used in outdoor clothing.
gorge ● **noun** **1** a steep, narrow valley or ravine. **2** archaic the contents of the stomach. ● **verb** eat a large amount greedily.
– PHRASES **one's gorge rises** one is sickened or disgusted.
– DERIVATIVES **gorger** noun.
– ORIGIN originally in the sense 'throat': from Old French, 'throat', from Latin *gurges* 'whirlpool'.
gorgeous ● **adjective** **1** beautiful; very attractive. **2** informal very pleasant.
– DERIVATIVES **gorgeously** adverb **gorgeousness** noun.
– ORIGIN Old French *gorgias* 'fine, elegant'.
gorget /gorjit/ ● **noun** **1** historical an article of clothing or piece of armour covering the throat. **2** a patch of colour on the throat of a bird or other animal.
– ORIGIN Old French *gorgete*, from *gorge* 'throat'.
gorgio /gorjiō/ ● **noun** (pl. **gorgios**) the gypsy name for a non-gypsy.
– ORIGIN Romany.
gorgon /gorgən/ ● **noun** **1** Greek Mythology each of three sisters with snakes for hair, who had the power to turn anyone who looked at them to stone. **2** a fierce, frightening, or repulsive woman.
– ORIGIN Greek *Gorgō*, from *gorgos* 'terrible'.
Gorgonzola /gorgənzōlə/ ● **noun** a rich, strong-flavoured Italian cheese with bluish-green veins.
– ORIGIN named after the Italian village of *Gorgonzola*.
gorilla ● **noun** **1** a powerfully built great ape of central Africa, the largest living primate. **2** informal a heavily built aggressive-looking man.
– ORIGIN Greek, representing an alleged African word for a wild or hairy person.
gormless ● **adjective** Brit. informal stupid or slow-witted.
– DERIVATIVES **gormlessly** adverb **gormlessness** noun.
– ORIGIN from dialect *gaum* 'understanding', from an Old Norse word meaning 'care, heed'.
gorse ● **noun** a yellow-flowered shrub, the leaves of which have the form of spines.
– ORIGIN Old English.
gory ● **adjective** (**gorier, goriest**) **1** involving violence and bloodshed. **2** covered in blood.
– PHRASES **the gory details** humorous explicit details.
– DERIVATIVES **goriness** noun.
gosh ● **exclamation** informal used to express surprise or give emphasis.
– ORIGIN euphemism for GOD.
goshawk /goss-hawk/ ● **noun** a short-winged hawk resembling a large sparrowhawk.
– ORIGIN Old English, 'goose-hawk'.
gosling ● **noun** a young goose.
– ORIGIN Old Norse.

g

Thesaurus

cheesy, corny, sick-making; *Brit. informal* soppy; *N. Amer. informal* cornball, sappy.
goose ● **noun** gander, gosling.
gore[1] ● **noun** *the film's gratuitous gore* BLOOD, bloodiness; bloodshed, slaughter, carnage, butchery.
gore[2] ● **verb** *he was gored by a bull* PIERCE, stab, stick, impale, spear, horn.
gorge ● **noun** *the river runs through a gorge* RAVINE, canyon, gully, defile, couloir; chasm, gulf; *N. English* clough, gill; *N. Amer.* gulch, coulee.
● **verb** **1** *they gorged themselves on cakes* STUFF, cram, fill; glut, satiate, overindulge, overfill; *informal* pig. **2** *vultures gorged on the flesh* DEVOUR, guzzle, gobble, gulp (down), wolf; *informal* tuck into, demolish, polish off, scoff (down), down, stuff one's face (with); *Brit. informal* gollop; *N. Amer. informal* scarf (down/up).
gorgeous ● **adjective** **1** *a gorgeous girl* GOOD-LOOKING, attractive, beautiful, pretty, handsome, lovely, stunning, striking, arresting, prepossessing, fetching, captivating, bewitching, charming, enchanting, appealing, delightful; sexy, seductive, alluring, tantalizing, irresistible, ravishing, desirable; *Scottish & N. English* bonny; *informal* fanciable, tasty, hot, easy on the eye, drop-dead gorgeous; *Brit. informal* fit; *N. Amer. informal* cute, foxy; *Austral./NZ informal* spunky; *poetic/literary* beauteous; *archaic* comely, fair. **2** *a gorgeous view* SPECTACULAR, splendid, superb, wonderful, grand, impressive, awe-inspiring, awesome, amazing, stunning, breathtaking, incredible; *informal* sensational, fabulous, fantastic. **3** *gorgeous uniforms* RESPLENDENT, magnificent, sumptuous, luxurious, elegant, opulent; dazzling, brilliant. **4** *(informal) gorgeous weather* EXCELLENT, marvellous, superb, very good, first-rate, first-class, wonderful, magnificent, splendid; *informal* great, glorious, terrific, fantastic, fabulous, fab, ace; *Brit. informal* smashing, brilliant, brill; *Austral./NZ informal* bonzer.
– OPPOSITES ugly, drab, terrible.
gory ● **adjective** **1** *a gory ritual slaughter* GRISLY, gruesome, violent, bloody, brutal, savage; ghastly, frightful, horrid, fearful, hideous, macabre, horrible, horrific; shocking, appalling, monstrous, un-

go-slow • noun chiefly Brit. a form of industrial action in which work is delayed or slowed down.

gospel • noun **1** the teachings of Christ. **2** (**Gospel**) the record of Christ's life and teaching in the first four books of the New Testament. **3** (**Gospel**) each of these books. **4** (also **gospel truth**) something absolutely true. **5** (also **gospel music**) a fervent style of black American evangelical religious singing.
– ORIGIN Old English, 'good news'.

gospeller (US **gospeler**) • noun **1** a zealous preacher. **2** the reader of the Gospel in a Communion service.

gossamer • noun a fine, filmy substance consisting of cobwebs spun by small spiders. • adjective very fine and insubstantial.
– ORIGIN apparently from GOOSE + SUMMER, perhaps from the time of year around St Martin's day (11 November) when geese were eaten and gossamer is often seen.

gossip • noun **1** casual conversation or unsubstantiated reports about other people. **2** chiefly derogatory a person who likes talking about other people's private lives. • verb (**gossiped**, **gossiping**) engage in gossip.
– DERIVATIVES **gossiper** noun **gossipy** adjective.
– ORIGIN Old English, originally in the sense 'godfather or godmother', later 'a close friend, a person with whom one gossips'; related to SIB.

g

gossip column • noun a section of a newspaper devoted to gossip about well-known people.

got past and past participle of GET.

Goth /goth/ • noun **1** a member of a Germanic people that invaded the Roman Empire between the 3rd and 5th centuries. **2** (**goth**) a style of rock music typically having apocalyptic or mystical lyrics. **3** a member of a subculture favouring black clothing and goth music.
– ORIGIN Greek *Gothoi*, from Gothic.

Gothic • adjective **1** relating to the ancient Goths or their extinct language. **2** of the style of architecture prevalent in western Europe in the 12th–16th centuries, characterized by pointed arches and elaborate tracery. **3** portentously gloomy or horrifying. **4** (of lettering) derived from the angular style of handwriting with broad vertical downstrokes used in medieval western Europe. • noun **1** the language of the Goths. **2** Gothic architecture.
– DERIVATIVES **Gothicism** noun.

gothic novel • noun an English genre of fiction popular in the 18th to early 19th centuries, characterized by an atmosphere of mystery and horror.

gotten N. Amer. past participle of GET.
– USAGE The form **gotten** is not used in British English but is very common in North American English, though even there it is often regarded as non-standard.

gouache /goōaash/ • noun **1** a method of painting using opaque pigments ground in water and thickened with a glue-like substance. **2** paint of this kind.
– ORIGIN French, from Italian *guazzo*.

Gouda /gowdə/ • noun a flat round Dutch cheese with a yellow rind.
– ORIGIN originally made in *Gouda* in the Netherlands.

gouge /gowj/ • verb **1** make (a rough hole or indentation) in a surface. **2** (**gouge out**) cut or force out roughly or brutally. • noun **1** a chisel with a concave blade. **2** an indentation or groove made by gouging.
– DERIVATIVES **gouger** noun.
– ORIGIN Old French, from Latin *gubia*, *gulbia*.

goujons /goōjənz/ • plural noun Brit. deep-fried strips of chicken or fish.
– ORIGIN French *goujon* 'gudgeon'.

goulash /goōlash/ • noun a rich Hungarian stew of meat and vegetables, flavoured with paprika.
– ORIGIN from Hungarian *gulyás* 'herdsman' + *hús* 'meat'.

gourami /gooraami/ • noun (pl. same or **gouramis**) an Asian fish of a large group including many kinds popular in aquaria.
– ORIGIN Malay.

gourd /goord/ • noun **1** the large hard-skinned fleshy fruit of a climbing or trailing plant. **2** a container made from the hollowed and dried skin of a gourd.
– ORIGIN Old French *gourde*, from Latin *cucurbita*.

gourde • noun the basic monetary unit of Haiti, equal to 100 centimes.
– ORIGIN formerly the Franco-American name for a dollar: from French, 'stupid, dull, heavy'.

gourmand /goormand/ • noun **1** a person who enjoys eating, sometimes to excess. **2** a connoisseur of good food; a gourmet.
– ORIGIN Old French.

gourmandize (also **gourmandise**) • verb indulge in good eating; eat greedily. • noun appreciation or consumption of good food.

gourmet /goormay/ • noun **1** a connoisseur of good food. **2** (before another noun) suitable for a gourmet: *a gourmet meal.*
– ORIGIN French, originally 'wine taster', influenced by GOURMAND.

gout /gowt/ • noun **1** a disease in which defective metabolism of uric acid causes arthritis, especially in the smaller bones of the feet. **2** literary a drop or spot.
– DERIVATIVES **gouty** adjective.
– ORIGIN Latin *gutta* 'drop' (because gout was believed to be caused by the dropping of diseased matter from the blood into the joints).

govern • verb **1** conduct the policy and affairs of (a state, organization, or people). **2** control or influence. **3** constitute a rule, standard, or principle for. **4** Grammar (of a word) require that (another word or group of words) be in a particular case.
– DERIVATIVES **governability** noun **governable** adjective.
– ORIGIN Old French *governer*, from Greek *kubernan* 'to steer'.

governance • noun the action or manner of governing.

governess • noun a woman employed to teach children in a private household.
– DERIVATIVES **governessy** adjective.

governing body • noun a group of people who govern an institution in partnership with the managers.

government • noun **1** (treated as sing. or pl.) the governing body of a state. **2** the system by which a state or community is governed. **3** the action or manner of governing a state, organization, or people.
– DERIVATIVES **governmental** adjective.

Government House • noun Brit. the official residence of a gov-

Thesaurus

speakable; *informal* blood-and-guts, sick-making. **2** *gory pieces of flesh* BLOODY, bloodstained, bloodsoaked.

gospel • noun **1** *the Gospel was spread by missionaries* CHRISTIAN TEACHING, Christian doctrine, Christ's teaching; the word of God, the New Testament. **2** *don't treat this as gospel* THE TRUTH; fact, actual fact, reality, actuality, factuality, the case, a certainty. **3** *his gospel of non-violence* DOCTRINE, dogma, teaching, principle, ethic, creed, credo, ideology, ideal; belief, tenet, canon.

gossamer • noun *her dress swirled like gossamer* COBWEBS; silk, gauze, chiffon.
• adjective *a gossamer veil* GAUZY, gossamery, fine, diaphanous, delicate, filmy, floaty, chiffony, cobwebby, wispy, thin, light, insubstantial, flimsy; translucent, transparent, see-through, sheer.

gossip • noun **1** *tell me all the gossip* TITTLE-TATTLE, tattle, rumour(s), whispers, canards, titbits; scandal, hearsay; *informal* dirt, buzz; *Brit. informal* goss; *N. Amer. informal* scuttlebutt. **2** *they went for a gossip* CHAT, talk, conversation, chatter, heart-to-heart, tête-à-tête, blether, blather; discussion, dialogue; *informal* chit-chat, jaw, gas, confab, goss; *Brit. informal* natter, chinwag; *N. Amer. informal* gabfest; *Austral./NZ informal* yarn; *formal* confabulation. **3** *she's such a gossip* SCANDALMONGER, gossipmonger, tattler, busybody, muckraker.
• verb **1** *she gossiped about his wife* SPREAD RUMOURS, spread gossip, tittle-tattle, tattle, talk, whisper, tell tales; *informal* dish the dirt. **2** *people sat around gossiping* CHAT, talk, converse, speak to each other, discuss things; *informal* gas, chew the fat, chew the rag, jaw, yak, yap; *Brit. informal* natter, chinwag; *N. Amer. informal* shoot the breeze, shoot the bull; *formal* confabulate.

gouge • verb SCOOP OUT, hollow out, excavate; cut (out), dig (out), scrape (out), scratch (out).

gourmand • noun GLUTTON, overeater, big eater, gobbler, gorger; *informal* (greedy) pig, gannet, greedy guts, gutbucket, guzzler.

gourmet • noun GASTRONOME, epicure, epicurean; connoisseur; *informal* foodie.

govern • verb **1** *he governs the province* RULE, preside over, reign over, control, be in charge of, command, lead, dominate; run, head, administer, manage, regulate, oversee, supervise; *informal* be in the driving seat. **2** *the rules governing social behaviour* DETERMINE, decide, control, regulate, direct, rule, dictate, shape; affect, influence, sway, act on, mould, modify, impact on.

governess • noun TUTOR, instructress, duenna; teacher.

government • noun **1** *the government announced cuts* ADMINISTRATION, executive, regime, authority, powers that be, directorate,

ernor.

government securities ● plural noun bonds or other promissory certificates issued by the government.

governor ● noun **1** an official appointed to govern a town or region. **2** the elected executive head of a US state. **3** the representative of the British Crown in a colony or in a Commonwealth state that regards the monarch as head of state. **4** the head of a public institution. **5** a member of a governing body. **6** Brit. informal the person in authority. **7** a device automatically regulating the supply of fuel, steam, or water to a machine.
– DERIVATIVES **governorate** noun **governorship** noun.

Governor General ● noun (pl. **Governors General**) the chief representative of the Crown in a Commonwealth country of which the British monarch is head of state.

gown ● noun **1** a long dress worn on formal occasions. **2** a protective garment worn in hospital by surgical staff or patients. **3** a loose cloak indicating one's profession or status, worn by a lawyer, teacher, academic, or university student. **4** the members of a university as distinct from the residents of a town. ● verb (**be gowned**) be dressed in a gown.
– ORIGIN Old French *goune*, from Latin *gunna* 'fur garment'.

goy /goy/ ● noun (pl. **goyim** /goyim/ or **goys**) informal, offensive a Jewish name for a non-Jew.
– DERIVATIVES **goyish** adjective.
– ORIGIN Hebrew, 'people, nation'.

GP ● abbreviation **1** general practitioner. **2** Grand Prix.

gr. ● abbreviation **1** grain(s). **2** gram(s). **3** gross.

grab ● verb (**grabbed**, **grabbing**) **1** seize suddenly and roughly. **2** informal obtain quickly or opportunistically. **3** informal impress: *how does that grab you?* ● noun **1** a quick sudden attempt to seize. **2** a mechanical device for gripping, lifting, and moving loads.
– PHRASES **up for grabs** informal available.
– DERIVATIVES **grabber** noun.
– ORIGIN Low German and Dutch *grabben*.

grab bag ● noun N. Amer. **1** a lucky dip in which wrapped items are chosen blindly from a bag. **2** an assortment of items in a sealed bag which one buys or is given without knowing what the contents are.

grace ● noun **1** elegance of movement. **2** courteous good will: *she had the grace to look sheepish.* **3** (**graces**) attractive qualities or behaviour: *a horrible character with no saving graces.* **4** (in Christian belief) the free and unearned favour of God. **5** a person's favour. **6** a period officially allowed for fulfilment of an obligation. **7** a short prayer of thanks said before or after a meal. **8** (**His**, **Her**, or **Your Grace**) used as forms of description or address for a duke, duchess, or archbishop. ● verb **1** lend honour to by one's presence. **2** be an attractive presence in or on.
– PHRASES **be in someone's good** (or **bad**) **graces** be regarded by someone with favour (or disfavour). **the (Three) Graces** Greek Mythology three beautiful goddesses, daughters of Zeus, believed to personify and bestow charm, grace, and beauty. **with good** (or **bad**) **grace** in a willing (or reluctant) manner.
– ORIGIN Latin *gratia*, from *gratus* 'pleasing, thankful'.

grace and favour ● adjective Brit. (of accommodation) occupied by permission of a sovereign or government.

graceful ● adjective having or showing grace or elegance.
– DERIVATIVES **gracefully** adverb **gracefulness** noun.

graceless ● adjective lacking grace, elegance, or charm.
– DERIVATIVES **gracelessly** adverb **gracelessness** noun.

grace note ● noun Music an extra note added as an embellishment and not essential to the harmony or melody.

gracious ● adjective **1** courteous, kind, and pleasant. **2** showing the elegance and comfort associated with high social status or wealth. **3** (in Christian belief) showing divine grace. ● exclamation expressing polite surprise.
– DERIVATIVES **graciously** adverb **graciousness** noun.

grackle ● noun **1** a songbird of the American blackbird family, the male of which is shiny black with a blue-green sheen. **2** an Asian mynah or starling with mainly black plumage.
– ORIGIN Latin *graculus* 'jackdaw'.

gradation ● noun **1** a scale of successive changes, stages, or degrees. **2** a stage in a such a scale.
– DERIVATIVES **gradational** adjective.

grade ● noun **1** a specified level of rank, quality, proficiency, or value. **2** a mark indicating the quality of a student's work. **3** N. Amer. (with specifying ordinal number) those pupils in a school who are grouped by age or ability for teaching at a particular level for a year. ● verb **1** arrange in or allocate to grades. **2** pass gradually from one level to another. **3** N. Amer. give a grade to (a student or their work). **4** reduce (a road) to an easy gradient.
– PHRASES **make the grade** informal succeed.
– ORIGIN Latin *gradus* 'step'.

grade crossing ● noun N. Amer. a level crossing.

grader ● noun **1** a person or thing that grades. **2** (in combination) N.

g

Thesaurus

council, leadership; cabinet, ministry; *informal* top brass. **2** *they help him in the government of the country* RULE, running, leadership, control, administration, regulation, management, supervision.

governor ● noun LEADER, ruler, chief, head; premier, president, viceroy, chancellor; administrator, principal, director, chairman/woman, chair, superintendent, commissioner, controller; *informal* boss.

gown ● noun DRESS, frock, shift, robe.

grab ● verb **1** *Dot grabbed his arm* SEIZE, grasp, snatch, take hold of, grip, clasp, clutch; take. **2** *(informal) I'll grab another drink* OBTAIN, acquire, get; buy, purchase, procure, secure, snap up; gather, collect; achieve, attain; *informal* get one's hands on, get one's mitts on, get hold of, bag, score, nab.
● noun *she made a grab for his gun* LUNGE, snatch.
– PHRASES **up for grabs** *(informal)* AVAILABLE, obtainable, to be had, for the taking; for sale, on the market; *informal* for the asking, on tap, gettable.

grace ● noun **1** *the grace of a ballerina* ELEGANCE, poise, gracefulness, finesse; suppleness, agility, nimbleness, light-footedness. **2** *he had the grace to look sheepish* COURTESY, decency, (good) manners, politeness, decorum, respect, tact. **3** *he fell from grace* FAVOUR, approval, approbation, acceptance, esteem, regard, respect; goodwill. **4** *he lived there by grace of the king* FAVOUR, goodwill, generosity, kindness, indulgence; *formal* benefaction. **5** *they have five days' grace to decide* DEFERMENT, deferral, postponement, suspension, adjournment, delay, pause; respite, stay, moratorium, reprieve. **6** *say grace* PRAYER OF THANKS, thanksgiving, blessing, benediction.
– OPPOSITES inelegance, effrontery, disfavour.
● verb **1** *the occasion was graced by the prince* DIGNIFY, distinguish, honour, favour; enhance, ennoble, glorify, elevate, aggrandize, upgrade. **2** *a mosaic graced the floor* ADORN, embellish, decorate, ornament, enhance; beautify, prettify, enrich, bedeck.

graceful ● adjective ELEGANT, fluid, fluent, natural, neat; agile, supple, nimble, light-footed.

graceless ● adjective GAUCHE, maladroit, inept, awkward, unsure, unpolished, unsophisticated, uncultured, unrefined; clumsy, ungainly, ungraceful, inelegant, uncoordinated, gawky, gangling, bumbling; tactless, thoughtless, inconsiderate; *informal* cack-handed, ham-fisted.

gracious ● adjective **1** *a gracious hostess* COURTEOUS, polite, civil, chivalrous, well mannered, mannerly, decorous; tactful, diplomatic; kind, benevolent, considerate, thoughtful, obliging, accommodating, indulgent, magnanimous; friendly, amiable, cordial, hospitable. **2** *gracious colonial buildings* ELEGANT, stylish, tasteful, graceful; comfortable, luxurious, sumptuous, opulent, grand, high-class; *informal* swanky, plush. **3** *God's gracious intervention* MERCIFUL, compassionate, kind; forgiving, lenient, clement, forbearing, humane, tender-hearted, sympathetic; indulgent, generous, magnanimous, benign, benevolent.
– OPPOSITES rude, crude, cruel.

gradation ● noun **1** *a gradation of ability* RANGE, scale, spectrum, compass, span; progression, hierarchy, ladder, pecking order. **2** *each pay band has a number of gradations* LEVEL, grade, rank, position, status, stage, standard, echelon, rung, step, notch; class, stratum, group, grouping, set.

grade ● noun **1** *hotels within the same grade* CATEGORY, class, classification, grouping, group, set, bracket. **2** *his job is of the lowest grade* RANK, level, echelon, standing, position, class, status, order; step, rung, stratum, tier. **3** *the best grades in the school* MARK, score; assessment, evaluation, appraisal. **4** *(N. Amer.) the fifth grade* YEAR, form, class.
● verb **1** *eggs are graded by size* CLASSIFY, class, categorize, bracket, sort, group, arrange, pigeonhole; rank, evaluate, rate, value. **2** *(N. Amer.) the essays have been graded* ASSESS, mark, score, judge, evaluate, appraise. **3** *the colours grade into one another* PASS, shade, merge, blend.

Amer. a pupil of a specified grade in a school.

grade school ● noun N. Amer. elementary school.

gradient /graydiənt/ ● noun **1** a sloping part of a road or railway. **2** the degree of a slope, expressed as change of height divided by distance travelled. **3** Physics a change in the magnitude of a property (e.g. temperature) observed in passing from one point or moment to another.
– ORIGIN from GRADE.

gradual ● adjective **1** taking place in stages over an extended period. **2** (of a slope) not steep or abrupt.
– DERIVATIVES **gradually** adverb **gradualness** noun.
– ORIGIN Latin *gradualis*, from *gradus* 'step'.

gradualism ● noun a policy or theory of gradual rather than sudden change.
– DERIVATIVES **gradualist** noun.

graduand /gradyooand/ ● noun Brit. a person who is about to receive an academic degree.

graduate ● noun /gradyooət/ a person who has been awarded a first academic degree, or (N. Amer.) a high-school diploma. ● verb /gradyooayt/ **1** successfully complete a degree, course, or (N. Amer.) high school. **2** (**graduate to**) move up to (something more advanced). **3** arrange or mark out in gradations. **4** change gradually.
– DERIVATIVES **graduation** noun.
– ORIGIN from Latin *graduare* 'take a degree', from *gradus* 'degree, step'.

graduate school ● noun N. Amer. a department of a university for advanced work by graduates.

Graeco- /greekō/ (also **Greco-**) ● combining form Greek; Greek and ...: *Graeco-Roman*.
– ORIGIN Latin *Graecus* 'Greek'.

graffiti /grəfeeti/ ● plural noun (sing. **graffito** /grəfeetō/) (treated as sing. or pl.) unauthorized writing or drawings on a surface in a public place. ● verb write or draw graffiti on.
– DERIVATIVES **graffitist** noun.
– USAGE In Italian the word **graffiti** is a plural noun and its singular form is **graffito**. In modern English, however, **graffiti** is generally treated as if it were a mass noun (with a singular verb), similar to a word like **writing**.
– ORIGIN Italian, from *graffio* 'a scratch'.

graft[1] ● noun **1** a shoot from one plant inserted into a slit cut into another to form a new growth. **2** a piece of living bodily tissue that is transplanted surgically to replace diseased or damaged tissue. **3** an operation in which tissue is transplanted. ● verb **1** insert or transplant as a graft. **2** incorporate in or attach to something else, especially inappropriately.
– ORIGIN Old French *grafe*, from Greek *graphion* 'writing implement' (with reference to the tapered tip of the plant shoot).

graft[2] Brit. informal ● noun hard work. ● verb work hard.
– DERIVATIVES **grafter** noun.
– ORIGIN perhaps related to the phrase *spade's graft* 'the amount of earth that one stroke of a spade will move'.

graft[3] informal ● noun bribery and other corrupt measures pursued for gain in politics or business. ● verb make money by graft.
– DERIVATIVES **grafter** noun.
– ORIGIN of unknown origin.

graham ● adjective N. Amer. denoting wholewheat flour, or biscuits or bread made from this.
– ORIGIN named after the American advocate of dietary reform Sylvester *Graham* (1794–1851).

Grail (also **Holy Grail**) ● noun (in medieval legend) the cup or platter used by Christ at the Last Supper and in which Joseph of Arimathea received Christ's blood, especially as the object of quests by knights.
– ORIGIN Old French *graal*, from Latin *gradalis* 'dish'.

grain ● noun **1** wheat or other cultivated cereal used as food. **2** a single seed or fruit of a cereal. **3** a small, hard particle of a substance such as sand. **4** the smallest unit of weight in the troy and avoirdupois systems, equal to 1/5760 of a pound troy and 1/7000 of a pound avoirdupois (approximately 0.0648 grams). **5** the smallest possible amount: *there wasn't a grain of truth in it*. **6** the longitudinal arrangement of fibres, particles, or layers in wood, paper, rock, etc. **7** the texture resulting from the grain of wood, rock, etc. **8** a grainy appearance of a photograph or negative. ● verb **1** give a rough surface or texture to. **2** form into grains.
– PHRASES **against the grain** contrary to one's nature or instinct.
– DERIVATIVES **grainer** noun **grainless** adjective.
– ORIGIN Old French, from Latin *granum*; sense 4 arose because the weight was originally equivalent to that of a grain of wheat.

grainy ● adjective (**grainier**, **grainiest**) **1** granular. **2** (of a photograph) showing visible grains of emulsion. **3** (of wood) having prominent grain.
– DERIVATIVES **graininess** noun.

gram (Brit. also **gramme**) ● noun a metric unit of mass equal to one thousandth of a kilogram.
– ORIGIN French *gramme*, from Greek *gramma* 'a small weight'.

-gram ● combining form forming nouns denoting something written or recorded: *anagram*.
– ORIGIN from Greek *gramma* 'thing written, letter of the alphabet'.

graminivorous /gramminivvərəss/ ● adjective Zoology (of an animal) feeding on grass.
– ORIGIN from Latin *gramen* 'grass'.

grammar ● noun **1** the whole system and structure of a language or of languages in general, usually taken as consisting of syntax and morphology. **2** knowledge and use of the rules or principles of grammar: *bad grammar*. **3** a book on grammar. **4** the basic elements of an area of knowledge or skill.
– ORIGIN from Greek *grammatikē tekhnē* 'art of letters', from *gramma* 'letter of the alphabet'.

grammarian /grəmairiən/ ● noun a person who studies and writes about grammar.

grammar school ● noun **1** (in the UK, especially formerly) a state secondary school to which pupils are admitted on the basis of ability. **2** US another term for ELEMENTARY SCHOOL.

grammatical /grəmattik'l/ ● adjective **1** relating to grammar. **2** in accordance with the rules of grammar.
– DERIVATIVES **grammaticality** noun **grammatically** adverb.

gramme ● noun variant spelling of GRAM.

Thesaurus

– PHRASES **make the grade** (*informal*) COME UP TO STANDARD, come up to scratch, qualify, pass, pass muster, measure up; succeed, win through; *informal* be up to snuff, cut it, cut the mustard.

gradient ● noun **1** *a steep gradient* SLOPE, incline, hill, rise, ramp, bank; acclivity, declivity; *N. Amer.* grade. **2** *the gradient of the line* STEEPNESS, angle, slant, slope, inclination.

gradual ● adjective **1** *a gradual transition* SLOW, measured, unhurried, cautious; piecemeal, step-by-step, little-by-little, bit-by-bit; progressive, continuous, systematic, steady. **2** *a gradual slope* GENTLE, moderate, slight, easy.
– OPPOSITES abrupt, steep.

gradually ● adverb SLOWLY, slowly but surely, cautiously, gently, gingerly; piecemeal, little by little, bit by bit, inch by inch, by degrees; progressively, systematically; regularly, steadily.

graduate ● verb **1** *he wants to teach when he graduates* QUALIFY, pass one's exams, get one's degree, complete one's studies. **2** *she wants to graduate to serious drama* PROGRESS, advance, move up. **3** *a proposal to graduate income tax* RANK, grade, order, group, classify, categorize. **4** *a thermometer graduated in Fahrenheit* CALIBRATE, mark off, measure out, grade.

graft[1] ● noun **1** *grafts may die from lack of water* SCION, cutting, shoot, offshoot, bud, sprout, sprig. **2** *a skin graft* TRANSPLANT, implant.
● verb **1** *graft a bud onto the stem* AFFIX, join, insert, splice. **2** *tissue is grafted on to the cornea* TRANSPLANT, implant. **3** *a mansion grafted on to a farmhouse* ATTACH, add, join.

graft[2] (*Brit. informal*) ● noun *hard graft*. See WORK noun sense 1.
● verb *they often graft for each other*. See WORK verb sense 1.

graft[3] ● noun (*informal*) *sweeping measures to curb official graft* CORRUPTION, bribery, subornation, dishonesty, deceit, fraud, unlawful practices, illegal means; *N. Amer.* payola; *informal* palm-greasing, hush money, kickbacks, crookedness, sharp practices.
– OPPOSITES honesty.

grain ● noun **1** *the local farmers grow grain* CEREAL, cereal crops. **2** *a grain of corn* KERNEL, seed, grist. **3** *grains of sand* GRANULE, particle, speck, mote, mite; bit, piece; scrap, crumb, fragment, morsel. **4** *a grain of truth* TRACE, hint, tinge, suggestion, shadow; bit, soupçon; scintilla, ounce, iota, jot, whit, scrap, shred; *informal* smidgen, smidge, tad. **5** *the grain of the timber* TEXTURE, surface, finish; weave, pattern.

grammar ● noun SYNTAX, rules of language, morphology; linguistics.

Grammy • noun (pl. **Grammys** or **Grammies**) an annual award given by the American National Academy of Recording Arts and Sciences for achievement in the record industry.
– ORIGIN blend of GRAMOPHONE and EMMY.
gramophone • noun dated, chiefly Brit. a record player.
– ORIGIN formed by inversion of elements of *phonogram* 'sound recording'.
gramophone record • noun fuller form of RECORD (in sense 3).
grampa (also **gramps, grampy**) • noun dialect or informal one's grandfather.
grampus /grampəss/ • noun (pl. **grampuses**) a killer whale or other cetacean of the dolphin family.
– ORIGIN alteration (by association with GRAND) of Old French *grapois*, from Latin *crassus piscis* 'fat fish'.
gran • noun informal, chiefly Brit. one's grandmother.
granadilla /grannədillə/ (also **grenadilla** /gren-/) • noun a passion fruit.
– ORIGIN Spanish, 'little pomegranate'.
granary • noun (pl. **granaries**) **1** a storehouse for threshed grain. **2** a region supplying large quantities of corn.
– ORIGIN Latin *granarium*.
granary bread • noun Brit. trademark a type of brown bread containing whole grains of wheat.
grand • adjective **1** magnificent and imposing. **2** large, ambitious, or impressive in scope or scale. **3** of the highest importance or rank. **4** dignified, noble, or proud. **5** informal excellent. **6** Law (of a crime) serious. Compare with PETTY (in sense 4). **7** (in combination) (in names of family relationships) denoting one generation removed in ascent or descent. • noun **1** (pl. same) informal a thousand dollars or pounds. **2** a grand piano.
– DERIVATIVES **grandly** adverb **grandness** noun.
– ORIGIN Latin *grandis* 'full-grown, great'.
grandad (also **granddad**) • noun **1** informal one's grandfather. **2** (before another noun) (of a shirt) having a collar in the form of a narrow upright band.
grandam /grandam/ (also **grandame**) • noun archaic term for GRANDMOTHER.
– ORIGIN Old French *graund dame*.
grandchild • noun a child of one's son or daughter.
granddaughter • noun a daughter of one's son or daughter.
grand duchess • noun **1** the wife or widow of a grand duke. **2** a woman holding the rank of grand duke in her own right.
grand duchy • noun a territory ruled by a grand duke or duchess.
grand duke • noun **1** a prince or nobleman ruling over a territory in certain European countries. **2** historical a son (or son's son) of a Russian tsar.
grande dame /grond daam/ • noun a woman who is influential within a particular sphere.
– ORIGIN French, 'grand lady'.
grandee /grandee/ • noun **1** a Spanish or Portuguese nobleman of the highest rank. **2** a high-ranking or eminent man.
– ORIGIN from Spanish and Portuguese *grande* 'grand'.
grandeur /grandyər/ • noun **1** splendour and impressiveness. **2** high rank or social importance.
grandfather • noun **1** the father of one's father or mother. **2** a founder or originator.
grandfather clock • noun a clock in a tall free-standing wooden case, driven by weights.
Grand Guignol /gron geenyol/ • noun a dramatic entertainment of a sensational or horrific nature, originally as performed at the Grand Guignol theatre in Paris.
– ORIGIN *Guignol* was the bloodthirsty chief character in a French puppet show resembling Punch and Judy.
grandiflora /grandiflorə/ • adjective (of a cultivated plant) bearing large flowers.
– ORIGIN from Latin *grandis* 'great' + *flos* 'flower'.
grandiloquent /grandilləkwənt/ • adjective pompous or extravagant in language, style, or manner.
– DERIVATIVES **grandiloquence** noun **grandiloquently** adverb.
– ORIGIN Latin *grandiloquus* 'grand-speaking'.
grandiose /grandiōss/ • adjective **1** impressive or magnificent, especially pretentiously so. **2** conceived on a very ambitious scale.
– DERIVATIVES **grandiosely** adverb **grandiosity** noun.
– ORIGIN Italian *grandioso*, from *grande* 'grand'.
grand jury • noun US Law a jury selected to examine the validity of an accusation prior to trial.
grand larceny • noun Law (in many US states and formerly in Britain) theft of personal property having a value above a specified amount.
grandma • noun informal one's grandmother.
grand mal /gron mal/ • noun a serious form of epilepsy with muscle spasms and prolonged loss of consciousness. Compare with PETIT MAL.
– ORIGIN French, 'great sickness'.
Grand Marnier /gron maarniay/ • noun trademark an orange-flavoured cognac-based liqueur.
– ORIGIN French.
grand master • noun **1** (also **grandmaster**) a chess player of the highest class. **2** (**Grand Master**) the head of an order of chivalry or of Freemasons.
grandmother • noun the mother of one's father or mother.
– PHRASES **teach one's grandmother to suck eggs** presume to advise a more experienced person.
grandmother clock • noun a clock similar to a grandfather clock but about two thirds the size.
Grand National • noun an annual steeplechase held at Aintree, Liverpool.
grand opera • noun an opera on a serious theme in which the entire libretto is sung.
grandpa • noun informal one's grandfather.
grandparent • noun a grandmother or grandfather.
grand piano • noun a large, full-toned piano which has the body, strings, and soundboard arranged horizontally and is supported by three legs.
Grand Prix /gron pree/ • noun (pl. **Grands Prix** pronunc. same) a race forming part of a motor-racing or motorcycling world championship.
– ORIGIN French, 'great or chief prize'.
grandsire • noun archaic term for GRANDFATHER.
grand slam • noun **1** the winning of each of a group of major

Thesaurus

grammatical • adjective **1** *the grammatical structure of a sentence* SYNTACTIC, morphological; linguistic. **2** *a grammatical sentence* WELL FORMED, correct, proper; acceptable, allowable.
grand • adjective **1** *a grand hotel* MAGNIFICENT, imposing, impressive, awe-inspiring, splendid, resplendent, majestic, monumental; palatial, stately, large; luxurious, sumptuous, lavish, opulent; *Brit.* upmarket; *N. Amer.* upscale; *informal* fancy, posh, plush, classy, swanky; *Brit. informal* swish. **2** *a grand scheme* AMBITIOUS, bold, epic, big, extravagant. **3** *a grand old lady* AUGUST, distinguished, illustrious, eminent, esteemed, honoured, venerable, dignified, respectable; pre-eminent, prominent, notable, renowned, celebrated, famous; aristocratic, noble, regal, blue-blooded, high-born, patrician; *informal* upper-crust; *Brit. informal* posh, upmarket. **4** *a grand total of £2,000* COMPLETE, comprehensive, all-inclusive, inclusive; final. **5** *the grand staircase* MAIN, principal, central, prime; biggest, largest. **6** *(informal) you're doing a grand job* EXCELLENT, very good, marvellous, splendid, first-class, first-rate, wonderful, outstanding, sterling, fine; *informal* superb, terrific, great, super, ace; *Brit. informal* smashing, brilliant, brill.
– OPPOSITES inferior, humble, minor, poor.
• noun *(informal) a cheque for ten grand* THOUSAND POUNDS/DOLLARS; *informal* thou, K; *N. Amer. informal* G, gee.
grandeur • noun SPLENDOUR, magnificence, impressiveness, glory, resplendence, majesty, greatness; stateliness, pomp, ceremony.
grandfather • noun **1** *his grandfather lives here informal* grandad, grandpa, gramps, grampy, grandaddy. **2** *the grandfather of modern liberalism* FOUNDER, inventor, originator, creator, initiator; father, founding father, pioneer. **3** *our Victorian grandfathers* FOREFATHER, forebear, ancestor, progenitor, antecedent.
• verb *(N. Amer. informal) some smokers have been grandfathered* EXEMPT, excuse, free, exclude, grant immunity, spare, absolve; *informal* let off (the hook).
grandiloquent • adjective POMPOUS, bombastic, magniloquent, pretentious, ostentatious, high-flown, orotund, florid, flowery; overwrought, overblown, overdone; *informal* highfalutin, purple.
– OPPOSITES understated.
grandiose • adjective **1** *the court's grandiose facade* MAGNIFICENT, impressive, grand, imposing, awe-inspiring, splendid, resplendent, majestic, glorious, elaborate; palatial, stately, luxurious, opulent; *informal* plush, swanky, flash. **2** *a grandiose plan* AMBITIOUS, bold, overambitious, extravagant, high-flown, flamboyant; *informal* over the top, OTT.

championships or matches in a particular sport in the same year. **2** Bridge the bidding and winning of all thirteen tricks.
grandson • noun the son of one's son or daughter.
grandstand • noun the main stand at a racecourse or sports ground.
grandstand finish • noun a close or exciting finish to a race or competition.
grand total • noun the final amount after everything is added up.
grand tour • noun a cultural tour of Europe formerly undertaken by upper-class young men.
grange • noun Brit. **1** a country house with farm buildings attached. **2** archaic a barn.
– ORIGIN Old French, from Latin *granica villa* 'grain house or farm'.
graniferous /grəniffərəss/ • adjective Botany producing grain or a grain-like seed.
granita /graneetə/ • noun (pl. **granite** /graneetay/) a coarse Italian-style water ice.
– ORIGIN Italian.
g
granite /grannit/ • noun a very hard rock consisting mainly of quartz, mica, and feldspar.
– DERIVATIVES **granitic** adjective.
– ORIGIN from Italian *granito* 'grained'.
granivorous /grənivvərəss/ • adjective (of an animal) feeding on grain.
– DERIVATIVES **granivore** noun.
granny (also **grannie**) • noun (pl. **grannies**) informal one's grandmother.
granny bond • noun Brit. informal a form of index-linked National Savings certificate, originally available only to pensioners.
granny flat • noun informal a part of a house made into self-contained accommodation suitable for an elderly relative.
granny glasses • plural noun informal round metal-rimmed glasses.
granny knot • noun a reef knot with the ends crossed the wrong way and therefore liable to slip.
Granny Smith • noun a bright green variety of apple with crisp sharp-flavoured flesh, originating in Australia.
– ORIGIN named after Maria Ann (*Granny*) *Smith* (*c.*1801–1870), who first produced such apples.
granola /grənōlə/ • noun N. Amer. a kind of breakfast cereal resembling muesli.
grant • verb **1** agree to give or allow (something requested) to. **2** give (something) formally or legally to. **3** agree or admit to (someone) that (something) is true. • noun **1** a sum of money given by a government or public body for a particular purpose. **2** the action of granting something. **3** Law a legal conveyance or formal conferment.
– PHRASES **take for granted 1** fail to appreciate through over-familiarity. **2** assume that (something) is true.
– DERIVATIVES **grantee** noun **granter** noun **grantor** noun.
– ORIGIN Old French *granter* 'consent to support', from Latin *credere* 'entrust'.
grant aid • noun Brit. financial assistance granted by central government to local government or an institution.
granted • adverb admittedly; it is true. • conjunction (**granted that**) even assuming that.
grant-in-aid • noun (pl. **grants-in-aid**) a grant given to local government, an institution, or a particular scholar.
grant-maintained • adjective Brit. (of a school) funded by central rather than local government, and self-governing.
gran turismo /gran toorizmō/ • noun (pl. **gran turismos**) a high-performance model of car.
– ORIGIN Italian, 'great touring'.
granular • adjective **1** resembling or consisting of granules. **2** having a roughened surface or structure.
– DERIVATIVES **granularity** noun.
granulated • adjective **1** in the form of granules. **2** chiefly Biology having a roughened surface.
– DERIVATIVES **granulation** noun.
granule /granyōōl/ • noun a small compact particle of a substance.
– ORIGIN Latin *granulum* 'little grain'.
grape • noun **1** a green, purple, or black berry growing in clusters on a vine, eaten as fruit and used in making wine. **2** (**the grape**) informal wine.
– DERIVATIVES **grapey** adjective.
– ORIGIN Old French, 'bunch of grapes', probably from *grap* 'hook' (used in harvesting grapes).
grapefruit • noun (pl. same) a large round yellow citrus fruit with an acid juicy pulp.
– ORIGIN from GRAPE + FRUIT, probably because the fruits grow in clusters.
grape hyacinth • noun a small plant with clusters of small globular blue flowers.
grapeshot • noun historical ammunition consisting of a number of small iron balls fired together from a cannon.
grapevine • noun **1** a vine bearing grapes. **2** (**the grapevine**) informal the circulation of rumours and unofficial information.
graph • noun a diagram showing the relation between variable quantities, typically of two variables measured along a pair of lines at right angles. • verb plot or trace on a graph.
– ORIGIN abbreviation of *graphic formula*.
-graph • combining form **1** in nouns denoting something written or drawn in a specified way: *autograph*. **2** in nouns denoting an instrument that records: *seismograph*.
– ORIGIN from Greek *graphos* 'written, writing'.
graphic • adjective **1** relating to visual art, especially involving drawing, engraving, or lettering. **2** giving vividly explicit detail. **3** of or in the form of a graph. • noun Computing a visual image displayed on a screen or stored as data.
– DERIVATIVES **graphically** adverb.
– ORIGIN Greek *graphikos*, from *graphē* 'writing, drawing'.
graphical • adjective **1** of or in the form of a graph. **2** relating to visual art or computer graphics.
– DERIVATIVES **graphically** adverb.
graphical user interface • noun Computing a visual way of interacting with a computer using items such as windows and icons.
graphic arts • plural noun visual arts based on the use of line and tone rather than three-dimensional work or the use of colour.
graphic design • noun the art of combining text and pictures in advertisements, magazines, or books.
graphic equalizer • noun a device for controlling the strength and quality of selected frequency bands.
graphic novel • noun a novel in comic-strip format.
graphics • plural noun (usu. treated as sing.) **1** products of the graphic arts, especially commercial design or illustration. **2** the use of diagrams in calculation and design.
graphite • noun a grey form of carbon used as a solid lubricant and as pencil lead.
– DERIVATIVES **graphitic** adjective.
– ORIGIN from Greek *graphein* 'write' (because of its use in pencils).
graphology • noun **1** the study of handwriting, especially as used to infer a person's character. **2** Linguistics the study of writ-

Thesaurus

– OPPOSITES humble, modest.
grandmother • noun *informal* grandma, granny, gran, nan, nanna.
grant • verb **1** *he granted them leave of absence* ALLOW, accord, permit, afford, vouchsafe. **2** *he granted them £20,000* GIVE, award, bestow on, confer on, present with, provide with, endow with, supply with. **3** *I grant that the difference is not absolute* ADMIT, accept, concede, yield, allow, appreciate, recognize, acknowledge, confess; agree.
– OPPOSITES refuse, deny.
• noun *a grant from the council* ENDOWMENT, subvention, award, donation, bursary, allowance, subsidy, contribution, handout, allocation, gift; scholarship.
granular • adjective POWDER, powdered, powdery, grainy, granulated, gritty.
granulated • adjective POWDERED, crushed, crumbed, ground, minced, grated, pulverized.
granule • noun GRAIN, particle, fragment, bit, crumb, morsel, mote, speck.
graph • noun *use graphs to analyse your data* CHART, diagram; histogram, bar chart, pie chart, scatter diagram.
• verb *we graphed the new prices* PLOT, trace, draw up, delineate.
graphic • adjective **1** *a graphic representation of language* VISUAL, symbolic, pictorial, illustrative, diagrammatic; drawn, written. **2** *a graphic account* VIVID, explicit, expressive, detailed; uninhibited, powerful, colourful, rich, lurid, shocking; realistic, descriptive, illustrative; telling, effective.

ten and printed symbols and of writing systems.
– DERIVATIVES **graphological** adjective **graphologist** noun.
– ORIGIN from Greek *graphē* 'writing'.
graph paper • noun paper printed with a network of small squares to assist the drawing of graphs or other diagrams.
-graphy • combining form in nouns denoting: **1** a descriptive science: *geography*. **2** a technique of producing images: *radiography*. **3** a style or method of writing or drawing: *calligraphy*. **4** writing about (a specified subject): *hagiography*. **5** a written or printed list: *filmography*.
– DERIVATIVES **-graphic** combining form.
– ORIGIN from or suggested by Greek *-graphia* 'writing'.
grapnel /grapnəl/ • noun **1** a grappling hook. **2** a small anchor with several flukes.
– ORIGIN Old French *grapon*, related to GRAPE.
grappa /grappə/ • noun a brandy distilled from the fermented residue of grapes after they have been pressed in winemaking.
– ORIGIN Italian, 'grape stalk'.
grapple • verb **1** engage in a close fight or struggle without weapons. **2** (**grapple with**) struggle to deal with or understand. **3** archaic seize with a grapnel. • noun **1** an act of grappling. **2** a grapnel.
– DERIVATIVES **grappler** noun.
– ORIGIN from Old French *grapil* 'small hook'; related to GRAPE.
grappling hook (also **grappling iron**) • noun a device with iron claws, attached to a rope and used for dragging or grasping.
graptolite /graptəlīt/ • noun an extinct planktonic invertebrate animal of the Palaeozoic era.
– ORIGIN from Greek *graptos* 'marked with letters': so named because impressions left on hard shales resemble slate pencil marks.
grasp /graasp/ • verb **1** seize and hold firmly. **2** comprehend fully. • noun **1** a firm grip. **2** a person's capacity to attain or understand something.
– DERIVATIVES **graspable** adjective **grasper** noun.
– ORIGIN perhaps related to GROPE.
grasping • adjective greedy.
grass • noun **1** vegetation consisting of short plants with long narrow leaves, growing wild or cultivated on lawns and pasture. **2** ground covered with grass. **3** informal cannabis. **4** Brit. informal a police informer. • verb **1** cover with grass. **2** (often **grass on**) Brit. informal inform the police of someone's criminal activity or plans.
– PHRASES **at grass** grazing. **the grass is always greener on the other side of the fence** proverb other people's lives or situations always seem better than your own. **not let the grass grow under one's feet** not delay in taking action. **put out to grass 1** put (an animal) out to graze. **2** informal force (someone) to retire.
– ORIGIN Old English, related to GREEN and GROW; sense 4 is perhaps related to 19th-century rhyming slang *grasshopper* 'copper'.
grasshopper • noun a plant-eating insect with long hind legs which are used for jumping and for producing a chirping sound.
grass roots • plural noun the most basic level of an activity or organization.
grass skirt • noun a skirt made of long grass and leaves, worn by female dancers from some Pacific islands.
grass snake • noun a harmless grey-green snake with a yellowish band around the neck.
grass widow • noun a woman whose husband is away often or for a prolonged period.
– ORIGIN originally denoting an unmarried woman with a child: perhaps from the idea of a couple having lain on the grass instead of in bed.
grassy • adjective (**grassier**, **grassiest**) covered with or resembling grass.
grate[1] • verb **1** reduce (food) to small shreds by rubbing it on a grater. **2** make an unpleasant rasping sound. **3** (often **grate on**) have an irritating effect.
– ORIGIN Old French *grater*.
grate[2] • noun **1** the recess of a fireplace or furnace. **2** a metal frame confining fuel in a fireplace or furnace.
– ORIGIN Old French, from Latin *cratis* 'hurdle'.
grateful • adjective feeling or showing gratitude.
– DERIVATIVES **gratefully** adverb.
– ORIGIN from obsolete *grate* 'pleasing, thankful', from Latin *gratus*.
grater • noun a device having a surface covered with sharp-edged holes, used for grating food.
graticule /grattikyōōl/ • noun a network of fine lines for use as a measuring scale or an aid in locating objects, e.g. in an eyepiece or on an oscilloscope screen.
– ORIGIN Latin *graticula* 'a little grating'.
gratify • verb (**gratifies**, **gratified**) **1** give pleasure or satisfaction. **2** indulge or satisfy (a desire).
– DERIVATIVES **gratification** noun **gratifier** noun **gratifying** adjective.
– ORIGIN Latin *gratificari* 'give or do as a favour', from *gratus* 'pleasing, thankful'.
gratin /gratan/ • noun a dish with a light browned crust of breadcrumbs or melted cheese.
– ORIGIN French, from *gratter*, earlier *grater* 'to grate'.
gratiné /grattinay/ • adjective (after a noun) another term for AU GRATIN.
– ORIGIN French.
grating[1] • adjective **1** sounding harsh and unpleasant. **2** irritating.
– DERIVATIVES **gratingly** adverb.
grating[2] • noun **1** a framework of parallel or crossed bars that prevents access through an opening. **2** Optics a set of equally spaced parallel wires or ruled lines, used to produce spectra by diffraction.

Thesaurus

– OPPOSITES vague.
• noun *(Computing) this printer's good enough for graphics* PICTURE, illustration, image; diagram, graph, chart.
grapple • verb **1** *the policemen grappled with him* WRESTLE, struggle, tussle; brawl, fight, scuffle, battle. **2** *he grappled his prey* SEIZE, grab, catch (hold of), take hold of, grasp. **3** *she is grappling with the problems of exile* TACKLE, confront, face, deal with, cope with, get to grips with; apply oneself to, devote oneself to.
grasp • verb **1** *she grasped his hands* GRIP, clutch, clasp, hold, clench; catch, seize, grab, snatch, latch on to. **2** *everybody grasped the important points* UNDERSTAND, comprehend, follow, take in, perceive, see, apprehend, assimilate, absorb; *informal* get, catch on to, figure out, get one's head around, take on board; *Brit. informal* twig, suss (out). **3** *he grasped the opportunity* TAKE ADVANTAGE OF, act on; seize, leap at, snatch, jump at, pounce on.
– OPPOSITES release, overlook.
• noun **1** *his grasp on her hand* GRIP, hold; clutch, clasp, clench. **2** *his domineering mother's grasp* CONTROL, power, clutches, command, domination, rule, tyranny. **3** *a prize lay within their grasp* REACH, scope, power, limits, range; sights. **4** *your grasp of history* UNDERSTANDING, comprehension, perception, apprehension, awareness, grip, knowledge; mastery, command.
grasping • adjective AVARICIOUS, acquisitive, greedy, rapacious, mercenary, materialistic; mean, miserly, parsimonious, niggardly, hoarding, selfish, possessive, close; *informal* tight-fisted, tight, stingy, money-grubbing; *N. Amer. informal* cheap, grabby.
grass • noun **1** *he sat down on the grass* TURF, sod; lawn, green. **2** *(informal) they smoked grass.* See CANNABIS. **3** *(Brit. informal) few clubs were without a grass* INFORMER, mole, stool pigeon; *informal* snitch, snout, whistle-blower, rat; *Brit. informal* supergrass, nark; *N. Amer. informal* fink, stoolie.
• verb **1** *the hill is completely grassed* GRASS OVER, turf. **2** *(Brit. informal) he grassed on the robbers* INFORM, tell; give away, betray, sell out; *informal* split, blow the whistle, rat, peach, squeal, do the dirty, stitch up, sell down the river; *Brit. informal* shop; *N. Amer. informal* finger; *Austral./NZ informal* dob, pimp.
grate • verb **1** *she grated the cheese* SHRED, pulverize, mince, grind, granulate, crush, crumble. **2** *her bones grated together* GRIND, rub, rasp, scrape, jar, grit, creak. **3** *the tune grates slightly* IRRITATE, set someone's teeth on edge, jar; annoy, nettle, chafe, fret; *informal* aggravate, get on someone's nerves, get under someone's skin, get someone's goat.
grateful • adjective THANKFUL, appreciative; indebted, obliged, obligated, in your debt, beholden.
gratification • noun SATISFACTION, fulfilment, indulgence, relief, appeasement; pleasure, enjoyment, relish.
gratify • verb **1** *it gratified him to be seen with her* PLEASE, gladden, make happy, delight, make someone feel good, satisfy; *informal* tickle pink, give someone a kick, buck up. **2** *he gratified his desires* SATISFY, fulfil, indulge, comply with, pander to, cater to, give

gratis /graatiss/ ● adverb & adjective free of charge.
– ORIGIN Latin, from *gratia* 'grace, kindness'.
gratitude ● noun thankfulness; appreciation of kindness.
– ORIGIN Latin *gratitudo*, from *gratus* 'pleasing, thankful'.
gratuitous /grətyoo͞itəss/ ● adjective 1 uncalled for. 2 free of charge.
– DERIVATIVES **gratuitously** adverb **gratuitousness** noun.
– ORIGIN Latin *gratuitus* 'given freely, spontaneous'.
gratuity /grətyoo͞iti/ ● noun (pl. **gratuities**) 1 formal a tip given to a waiter, porter, etc. 2 Brit. a sum of money paid to an employee at the end of a period of employment.
– ORIGIN Latin *gratuitas* 'gift'.
gravadlax /gravvədlaks/ ● noun variant spelling of GRAVLAX.
gravamen /grəvaymen/ ● noun (pl. **gravamina** /grəvaymina/) chiefly Law the essence or most serious part of a complaint or accusation.
– ORIGIN Latin, 'physical inconvenience'.
grave[1] ● noun 1 a hole dug in the ground to receive a coffin or corpse. 2 (**the grave**) death.
– PHRASES **dig one's own grave** do something foolish which causes one's downfall. **turn in one's grave** (of a dead person) be likely to have been angry or distressed about something had they been alive.
– ORIGIN Old English.
grave[2] ● adjective 1 giving cause for alarm or concern. 2 solemn.
– DERIVATIVES **gravely** adverb **graveness** noun.
– ORIGIN Old French, from Latin *gravis* 'heavy, serious'.
grave[3] ● verb (past part. **graven** or **graved**) 1 archaic engrave on a surface. 2 literary fix indelibly in the mind.
– ORIGIN Old English, 'dig'; related to GRAVE[1] and GROOVE.
grave accent /graav/ ● noun a mark (`) placed over a vowel in some languages to indicate a feature such as altered sound quality.
– ORIGIN French *grave* 'heavy, serious'.
gravel ● noun a loose mixture of small stones and coarse sand, used for paths and roads. ● verb (**gravelled**, **gravelling**; US **graveled**, **graveling**) cover with gravel.
– ORIGIN Old French, from *grave* 'shore'.
gravelly ● adjective 1 resembling, containing, or consisting of gravel. 2 (of a voice) deep and rough-sounding.
graven image ● noun a carved figure of a god used as an idol.
– ORIGIN with biblical allusion to the Book of Exodus, chapter 20.
graver ● noun 1 a burin or other engraving tool. 2 archaic an engraver.
Graves /graav/ ● noun a red or white wine from Graves, a district of SW France.
gravestone ● noun an inscribed headstone marking a grave.
graveyard ● noun a burial ground beside a church.
graveyard shift ● noun informal, chiefly N. Amer. a work shift that runs from midnight to 8 a.m.
gravid /gravvid/ ● adjective 1 technical pregnant. 2 literary full of meaning or a specified quality.
– ORIGIN Latin *gravidus* 'laden, pregnant'.
gravimeter /grəvimmitər/ ● noun an instrument for measuring the force of gravity at different places.
gravimetric /gravvimetrik/ ● adjective 1 relating to the measurement of weight. 2 relating to the measurement of gravity.
– DERIVATIVES **gravimetry** /grəvimmitri/ noun.
gravitas /gravvitass/ ● noun dignity or solemnity of manner.
– ORIGIN Latin, from *gravis* 'serious'.
gravitate /gravvitayt/ ● verb 1 be drawn towards to a place, person, or thing. 2 Physics move, or tend to move, towards a centre of gravity.
gravitation ● noun 1 movement, or a tendency to move, towards a centre of gravity. 2 Physics gravity.
– DERIVATIVES **gravitational** adjective **gravitationally** adverb.
gravitational constant ● noun Physics the constant in Newton's law of gravitation relating gravity to the masses and separation of particles, equal to 6.67×10^{-11} N m^2 kg^{-2}.
gravity ● noun 1 the force that attracts a body towards the centre of the earth, or towards any other physical body having mass. 2 extreme importance or seriousness. 3 solemnity of manner.
– ORIGIN Latin *gravitas* 'weight, seriousness'.
gravlax /gravlaks/ (also **gravadlax**) ● noun a Scandinavian dish of dry-cured salmon marinated in herbs.
– ORIGIN Swedish, from *grav* 'trench' + *lax* 'salmon' (from the former practice of burying the salmon in salt in a hole in the ground).
gravure /grəvyoor/ ● noun short for PHOTOGRAVURE.
gravy ● noun (pl. **gravies**) 1 the fat and juices that come out of meat during cooking. 2 a sauce made from these juices together with stock and other ingredients. 3 informal unearned or unexpected money.
– ORIGIN perhaps from a misreading (as *gravé*) of Old French *grané*, probably from *grain* 'spice'.
gravy boat ● noun a long narrow jug used for serving gravy.
gravy train ● noun informal a situation in which someone can easily make a lot of money.
gray[1] ● noun Physics the SI unit of the absorbed dose of ionizing radiation, corresponding to one joule per kilogram.
– ORIGIN named after the English radiobiologist Louis H. *Gray* (1905–65).
gray[2] ● adjective US spelling of GREY.
grayling ● noun an edible silvery-grey freshwater fish with horizontal violet stripes.
graze[1] ● verb 1 (of cattle, sheep, etc.) eat grass in a field. 2 informal eat frequent snacks at irregular intervals.
– DERIVATIVES **grazer** noun.
– ORIGIN Old English, related to GRASS.
graze[2] ● verb 1 scrape and break the skin on (part of the body). 2 touch or scrape (something) lightly in passing. ● noun a

Thesaurus

in to, satiate, feed, accommodate.
– OPPOSITES displease, frustrate.
grating[1] ● adjective 1 *the chair made a grating noise* SCRAPING, scratching, grinding, rasping, jarring. 2 *a grating voice* HARSH, raucous, strident, piercing, shrill, screechy; discordant, cacophonous; hoarse, rough, gravelly. 3 *it's written in grating language* IRRITATING, annoying, infuriating, irksome, maddening, displeasing, tiresome; jarring, discordant, inharmonious, unsuitable, inappropriate; *informal* aggravating.
– OPPOSITES harmonious, pleasing, appropriate.
grating[2] ● noun *a strong iron grating* GRID, grate, grille, lattice, trellis, mesh.
gratis ● adverb FREE (OF CHARGE), without charge, for nothing, at no cost, on the house, for free.
gratitude ● noun GRATEFULNESS, thankfulness, thanks, appreciation, indebtedness; recognition, acknowledgement, credit.
gratuitous ● adjective 1 *gratuitous violence* UNJUSTIFIED, uncalled for, unwarranted, unprovoked, undue; indefensible, unjustifiable; needless, unnecessary, inessential, unmerited, groundless, senseless, wanton, indiscriminate; excessive, immoderate, inordinate, inappropriate. 2 *they offer gratuitous advice* FREE, gratis, complimentary, voluntary, unpaid; free of charge, for nothing; *Law* pro bono (publico); *informal* for free, on the house; *Brit. informal* buckshee.
– OPPOSITES necessary, paid.
gratuity ● noun *(formal)* TIP, pourboire, baksheesh, gift, present, donation, reward, handout; bonus, extra; *informal* perk; *formal* perquisite.
grave[1] ● noun *she left flowers at his grave* BURYING PLACE, tomb, sepulchre, vault, burial chamber, mausoleum, crypt; last resting place.
grave[2] ● adjective 1 *a grave matter* SERIOUS, important, weighty, profound, significant, momentous; critical, acute, urgent, pressing; dire, terrible, awful, dreadful; *formal* exigent. 2 *Jackie looked grave* SOLEMN, serious, sober, unsmiling, grim, sombre; severe, stern, dour.
– OPPOSITES trivial, cheerful.
gravel ● noun SHINGLE, grit, pebbles, stones.
gravelly ● adjective 1 *a gravelly beach* SHINGLY, pebbly, stony, gritty. 2 *his gravelly voice* HUSKY, gruff, throaty, deep, croaky, rasping, grating, harsh, rough.
gravestone ● noun HEADSTONE, tombstone, stone, monument, memorial.
graveyard ● noun CEMETERY, churchyard, burial ground, necropolis; *informal* boneyard; *historical* potter's field; *archaic* God's acre.
gravitas ● noun DIGNITY, seriousness, solemnity, gravity, sobriety.
– OPPOSITES frivolity.
gravitate ● verb MOVE, head, drift, be drawn, be attracted; tend, lean, incline.
gravity ● noun 1 *the gravity of the situation* SERIOUSNESS, importance, significance, weight, consequence, magnitude; acuteness, urgency, exigence; awfulness, dreadfulness; *formal* moment. 2 *the gravity of his demeanour* SOLEMNITY, seriousness, sombreness, so-

superficial injury caused by grazing the skin.
– ORIGIN perhaps a specific use of GRAZE[1].
grazier /grayziər/ ● noun a person who rears or fattens cattle or sheep for market.
grazing ● noun grassland suitable for use as pasture.
grease ● noun **1** a thick oily substance, especially one used as a lubricant. **2** animal fat used or produced in cooking. ● verb smear or lubricate with grease.
– PHRASES **grease the palm of** informal bribe. **like greased lightning** informal extremely rapidly.
– ORIGIN Old French *graisse*, from Latin *crassus* 'thick, fat'.
grease gun ● noun a device for pumping grease under pressure to a particular point.
grease monkey ● noun informal a mechanic.
greasepaint ● noun a waxy substance used as make-up by actors.
greaseproof ● adjective impermeable to grease.
greaser ● noun **1** a motor mechanic or unskilled engineer on a ship. **2** informal a long-haired young man belonging to a motorcycle gang. **3** US informal, offensive a Hispanic American, especially a Mexican.
greasy ● adjective (**greasier**, **greasiest**) **1** covered with or resembling grease. **2** effusively polite in a repellently insincere way.
– DERIVATIVES **greasily** adverb **greasiness** noun.
greasy spoon ● noun informal a cheap cafe or restaurant serving fried foods.
great ● adjective **1** of an extent, amount, or intensity considerably above average. **2** of ability, quality, or eminence considerably above average. **3** informal excellent. **4** most important: *the great thing is the challenge.* **5** particularly deserving a specified description: *I was a great fan of Hank's.* **6** (**Greater**) (of a city) including adjacent urban areas. **7** (in combination) (in names of family relationships) referring to one degree further removed upwards or downwards: *a great-great-grandfather.* ● noun **1** a distinguished person. **2** (**Greats**) the honours course in classics, philosophy, and ancient history at Oxford University. ● adverb informal very well.
– PHRASES **Great Scott!** expressing surprise or amazement. [ORIGIN arbitrary euphemism for *Great God!*]
– DERIVATIVES **greatness** noun.
– ORIGIN Old English.
great ape ● noun a large ape of a family closely related to humans, including the gorilla and chimpanzees.
great-aunt ● noun an aunt of one's father or mother.
great circle ● noun a circle on the surface of a sphere which lies in a plane passing through the sphere's centre, especially as representing the shortest path between two given points on the sphere.
greatcoat ● noun a long heavy overcoat.
Great Dane ● noun a dog of a very large, powerful, short-haired breed.
greatly ● adverb very much.
great-nephew ● noun a son of one's nephew or niece.
great-niece ● noun a daughter of one's nephew or niece.
great-uncle ● noun an uncle of one's mother or father.
Great War ● noun the First World War.
greave ● noun historical a piece of armour for the shin.
– ORIGIN Old French *greve* 'shin, greave'.
grebe /greeb/ ● noun a diving waterbird with a long neck, lobed toes, and a very short tail.
– ORIGIN French.
Grecian ● adjective relating to ancient Greece, especially its architecture.
Grecian nose ● noun a straight nose that continues the line of the forehead without a dip.
greed ● noun intense and selfish desire for food, wealth, or power.
greedy ● adjective (**greedier**, **greediest**) having or showing greed.
– DERIVATIVES **greedily** adverb **greediness** noun.
– ORIGIN Old English.
Greek ● noun **1** a person from Greece. **2** the ancient or modern language of Greece. ● adjective relating to Greece.
– PHRASES **beware** (or **fear**) **the Greeks bearing gifts** proverb if a rival or enemy shows one generosity or kindness, one should be suspicious of their motives. [ORIGIN with allusion to the warning given by Laocoön to the Trojans in Virgil's *Aeneid*, against admitting the wooden horse to Troy.] **it's all Greek to me** informal I can't understand it at all.

g

Thesaurus

briety, soberness, severity, grimness, humourlessness, dourness; gloominess.
graze[1] ● verb *the deer grazed* FEED, eat, crop, nibble, browse.
graze[2] ● verb **1** *he grazed his knuckles on the box* SCRAPE, abrade, skin, scratch, chafe, bark, scuff, rasp; cut, nick. **2** *his shot grazed the far post* TOUCH, brush, shave, skim, kiss, scrape, clip, glance off.
● noun *grazes on the skin* SCRATCH, scrape, abrasion, cut; Medicine trauma.
grease ● noun **1** *guns packed in grease* OIL, lubricant, lubricator, lubrication. **2** *the kitchen was filmed with grease* FAT, oil, cooking oil, animal fat; lard, suet. **3** *his hair was smothered with grease* GEL, lotion, cream; trademark Brylcreem.
● verb *grease a baking dish* LUBRICATE, oil, smear with oil.
greasy ● adjective **1** *a greasy supper* FATTY, oily, buttery, oleaginous; formal pinguid. **2** *greasy hair* OILY. **3** *the pitch was very greasy* SLIPPERY, slick, slimy, slithery, oily; informal slippy, skiddy. **4** *a greasy little man* INGRATIATING, obsequious, sycophantic, fawning, grovelling, toadying; effusive, gushing, gushy; unctuous, oily; informal smarmy, slimy, bootlicking, sucky.
– OPPOSITES lean, dry.
great ● adjective **1** *they showed great interest* CONSIDERABLE, substantial, significant, appreciable, special, serious; exceptional, extraordinary. **2** *a great expanse of water* LARGE, big, extensive, expansive, broad, wide, sizeable, ample; vast, immense, huge, enormous, massive; informal humongous, whopping; Brit. informal ginormous. **3** *a great big house* VERY, extremely, exceedingly, exceptionally, especially, really; informal dirty. **4** *you great fool!* ABSOLUTE, total, utter, out-and-out, downright, thoroughgoing, complete; perfect, positive, prize, sheer, arrant, unqualified, consummate, veritable; informal thundering; Brit. informal right, proper. **5** *great writers* PROMINENT, eminent, important, distinguished, illustrious, celebrated, honoured, acclaimed, admired, esteemed, revered, renowned, notable, famous, famed, well known; leading, top, major, principal, first-rate, matchless, peerless, star. **6** *the country is now a great power* POWERFUL, dominant, influential, strong, potent, formidable, redoubtable; leading, important, foremost, major, chief, principal. **7** *a great castle* MAGNIFICENT, imposing, impressive, awe-inspiring, grand, splendid, majestic, sumptuous, resplendent. **8** *a great sportsman* EXPERT, skilful, skilled, adept, accomplished, talented, fine, masterly, master, brilliant, virtuoso, marvellous, outstanding, first class, superb; informal crack, ace, A1, class. **9** *a great fan of rugby* ENTHUSIASTIC, eager, keen, zealous, devoted, ardent, fanatical, passionate, dedicated, committed. **10** (informal) *we had a great time* ENJOYABLE, delightful, lovely, pleasant, congenial; exciting, thrilling; excellent, marvellous, wonderful, fine, splendid; informal terrific, fantastic, fabulous, fab, super, grand, cool; Brit. informal smashing, brilliant, brill; Austral./NZ informal bonzer, beaut; Brit. informal, dated spiffing; N. Amer. informal, dated swell.
– OPPOSITES little, small, minor, modest, poor, unenthusiastic, bad.
greatly ● adverb VERY MUCH, considerably, substantially, appreciably, significantly, markedly, sizeably, seriously, materially, profoundly; enormously, vastly, immensely, tremendously, mightily, abundantly, extremely, exceedingly; informal plenty, majorly.
– OPPOSITES slightly.
greatness ● noun **1** *a woman destined for greatness* EMINENCE, distinction, illustriousness, repute, high standing; importance, significance; celebrity, fame, prominence, renown. **2** *his greatness as a writer* BRILLIANCE, genius, prowess, talent, expertise, mastery, artistry, virtuosity, skill, proficiency; flair, finesse; calibre, distinction.
greed, greediness ● noun **1** *human greed* AVARICE, cupidity, acquisitiveness, covetousness, rapacity; materialism, mercenariness, Mammonism; informal money-grubbing, money-grabbing. **2** *her mouth watered with greed* GLUTTONY, hunger, voracity, insatiability; gourmandism, overeating, self-indulgence; informal piggishness. **3** *their greed for power* DESIRE, appetite, hunger, thirst, craving, longing, yearning, hankering; avidity, eagerness; informal yen, itch.
– OPPOSITES generosity, temperance, indifference.
greedy ● adjective **1** *a greedy eater* GLUTTONOUS, ravenous, voracious, intemperate, self-indulgent, insatiable, wolfish; informal piggish, piggy. **2** *a greedy millionaire* AVARICIOUS, acquisitive, covetous, grasping, materialistic, mercenary, possessive; informal

– ORIGIN Greek *Graikoi*, which according to Aristotle was the prehistoric name of the Hellenes.

Greek coffee • noun very strong black coffee served with the fine grounds in it.

Greek cross • noun a cross of which all four arms are of equal length.

Greek Orthodox Church • noun the Eastern Orthodox Church which uses the Byzantine rite in Greek, in particular the national Church of Greece.

green • adjective **1** of the colour between blue and yellow in the spectrum; coloured like grass. **2** covered with grass or other vegetation. **3** (**Green**) concerned with or supporting protection of the environment. **4** (of a plant or fruit) young or unripe. **5** in an untreated or original state; not cured, seasoned, fired, etc. **6** inexperienced or naive. **7** pale and sickly-looking. • noun **1** green colour, pigment, or material. **2** a piece of common grassy land, especially in the centre of a village. **3** an area of smooth, very short grass immediately surrounding a hole on a golf course. **4** (**greens**) green vegetables. **5** (**Green**) a member or supporter of an environmentalist group or party. • verb **1** make or become green. **2** make less harmful to the environment.

– DERIVATIVES **greenish** adjective **greenness** noun.

– ORIGIN Old English, related to GRASS and GROW.

greenback • noun US informal a dollar.

green belt • noun an area of open land around a city, on which building is restricted.

Green Beret • noun informal a British commando or a member of the US Army Special Forces.

green card • noun **1** (in the UK) an international insurance document for motorists. **2** (in the US) a permit allowing a foreign national to live and work permanently in the US.

greenery • noun green foliage or vegetation.

green-eyed monster • noun (**the green-eyed monster**) informal, humorous jealousy personified.

– ORIGIN from Shakespeare's *Othello*.

greenfield • adjective (of a site) previously undeveloped.

greenfinch • noun a large finch with green and yellow plumage.

green fingers • plural noun Brit. informal natural ability in growing plants.

greenfly • noun chiefly Brit. a green aphid.

greengage • noun a sweet greenish fruit resembling a small plum.

– ORIGIN named after the English botanist Sir William *Gage* (1657–1727).

greengrocer • noun Brit. a retailer of fruit and vegetables.

– DERIVATIVES **greengrocery** noun.

greenhorn • noun informal, chiefly N. Amer. an inexperienced or naive person.

greenhouse • noun a glass building in which plants that need protection from cold weather are grown.

greenhouse effect • noun the trapping of the sun's warmth in a planet's lower atmosphere, due to the greater transparency of the atmosphere to visible radiation from the sun than to infrared radiation emitted from the planet's surface.

greenhouse gas • noun a gas, such as carbon dioxide, that contributes to the greenhouse effect by absorbing infrared.

Greenlander • noun a person from Greenland.

green light • noun **1** a green traffic light giving permission to proceed. **2** permission to go ahead with a project.

green man • noun historical a man dressed up in greenery to represent a wild man of the woods or seasonal fertility.

Green Paper • noun (in the UK) a preliminary report of government proposals published to stimulate discussion.

green pepper • noun the mild-flavoured unripe fruit of a sweet pepper.

green plover • noun Brit. the lapwing.

green pound • noun the exchange rate for the pound applied to payments for agricultural produce in the EU.

green revolution • noun a large increase in crop production in developing countries achieved by the use of artificial fertilizers, pesticides, and high-yield crop varieties.

green room • noun a room in a theatre or studio in which performers can relax when they are not performing.

greensand • noun Geology a greenish kind of sandstone.

greenshank • noun a large grey and white sandpiper with long greenish legs.

greenstick fracture • noun a fracture of the bone, occurring typically in children, in which one side of the bone is broken and the other only bent.

greenstone • noun **1** Geology a greenish igneous rock containing feldspar and hornblende. **2** chiefly NZ a variety of jade.

greensward /greenswawrd/ • noun archaic or literary grass-covered ground.

green tea • noun tea made from unfermented leaves, produced mainly in China and Japan.

green thumb • noun North American term for GREEN FINGERS.

greenware • noun unfired pottery.

Greenwich Mean Time • noun the mean solar time at the Greenwich meridian, used as the standard time in a zone that includes the British Isles.

– ORIGIN from *Greenwich* in London, former site of the Royal Observatory.

Greenwich meridian • noun the meridian of zero longitude, passing through Greenwich.

greenwood • noun archaic a wood or forest in leaf, especially as a refuge for medieval outlaws.

greet[1] • verb **1** give a word or sign of welcome when meeting (someone). **2** receive or acknowledge in a specified way. **3** (of a sight or sound) become apparent to (a person arriving somewhere).

– DERIVATIVES **greeter** noun.

– ORIGIN Old English.

greet[2] • verb Scottish weep; cry.

– ORIGIN Old English.

greeting • noun **1** a word or sign of welcome or recognition. **2** (usu. **greetings**) a formal expression of goodwill.

greetings card (N. Amer. **greeting card**) • noun a decorative card sent to convey good wishes.

gregarious /grigairiəss/ • adjective **1** fond of company; sociable. **2** (of animals) living in flocks or colonies.

– DERIVATIVES **gregariously** adverb **gregariousness** noun.

– ORIGIN Latin *gregarius*, from *grex* 'a flock'.

Thesaurus

money-grubbing, money-grabbing; *N. Amer. informal* grabby. **3** *she is greedy for a title* EAGER, avid, hungry, craving, longing, yearning, hankering; impatient, anxious; *informal* dying, itching, gagging.

green • adjective **1** *a green scarf* viridescent; olive green, pea green, emerald green, lime green, bottle green, Lincoln green, sea green, eau de Nil; *poetic/literary* virescent, glaucous. **2** *a green island* VERDANT, grassy, leafy, verdurous. **3** *he promotes Green issues* ENVIRONMENTAL, ecological, conservation, eco-. **4** *a green alternative to diesel* ENVIRONMENTALLY FRIENDLY, non-polluting; ozone-friendly. **5** *green bananas* UNRIPE, immature. **6** *green timber* UNSEASONED, not aged, unfinished; pliable, supple. **7** *green bacon* RAW, fresh, unsmoked, uncured. **8** *the new lieutenant was very green* INEXPERIENCED, unversed, callow, immature; new, raw, unseasoned, untried; inexpert, untrained, unqualified, ignorant; simple, unsophisticated, unpolished; naive, innocent, ingenuous, credulous, gullible, unworldly; *informal* wet behind the ears, born yesterday. **9** *he went green* PALE, wan, pallid, ashen, ashen-faced, pasty, pasty-faced, grey, whitish, washed out, whey-faced, waxen, waxy, blanched, drained, pinched, sallow; sickly, nauseous, ill, sick, unhealthy.

– OPPOSITES barren, dry, cured, experienced, ruddy.

• noun **1** *a canopy of green over the road* FOLIAGE, greenery, plants, leaves, leafage, vegetation. **2** *a village green* LAWN, common, grassy area, sward. **3** *they had roast beef and greens* VEGETABLES, leaf vegetables; *informal* veg, veggies. **4** *Greens are against multinational companies* ENVIRONMENTALIST, conservationist, preservationist, nature-lover, eco-activist.

greenery • noun FOLIAGE, vegetation, plants, green, leaves, leafage, undergrowth, plant life, flora, herbage, verdure.

greenhorn • noun *(N. Amer. informal).* See NOVICE sense 1.

greenhouse • noun HOTHOUSE, glasshouse, conservatory.

greet • verb **1** *she greeted Hank cheerily* SAY HELLO TO, address, salute, hail, halloo; welcome, meet, receive. **2** *the decision was greeted with outrage* RECEIVE, acknowledge, respond to, react to, take.

greeting • noun **1** *he shouted a greeting* HELLO, salute, salutation, address; welcome; acknowledgement. **2** *birthday greetings* BEST WISHES, good wishes, congratulations, felicitations; compliments, regards, respects.

– OPPOSITES farewell.

gregarious • adjective **1** *he was fun-loving and gregarious* SOCI-

Gregorian calendar /grigoriən/ ● noun the modified form of the Julian calendar introduced in 1582 by Pope Gregory XIII, and still used today.
Gregorian chant ● noun medieval church plainsong.
– ORIGIN named after St *Gregory* the Great (*c.*540–604).
gremlin ● noun a mischievous sprite regarded as responsible for unexplained mechanical or electrical faults.
– ORIGIN a Second World War term: perhaps suggested by GOBLIN.
Grenache /grənash/ ● noun a variety of black wine grape native to the Languedoc-Roussillon region of France.
– ORIGIN French.
grenade /grənayd/ ● noun a small bomb thrown by hand or launched mechanically.
– ORIGIN from Old French *pome grenate* 'pomegranate', also the original sense in English; the bomb was regarded as resembling a pomegranate.
Grenadian /grənaydiən/ ● noun a person from the Caribbean country of Grenada. ● adjective relating to Grenada.
grenadier /grennədeer/ ● noun **1** historical a soldier armed with grenades. **2** (**Grenadiers** or **Grenadier Guards**) the first regiment of the royal household infantry.
grenadilla /grennədillə/ ● noun variant spelling of GRANADILLA.
grenadine /grennədeen/ ● noun a sweet cordial made in France from pomegranates.
– ORIGIN French.
grew past of GROW.
grey (US **gray**) ● adjective **1** of a colour intermediate between black and white, as of ashes or lead. **2** (of hair) turning grey or white with age. **3** (of the weather) cloudy and dull; without sun. **4** dull and nondescript: *grey, faceless men.* **5** not accounted for in official statistics: *the grey economy.* ● noun grey colour or pigment. ● verb (especially of hair) become grey with age.
– DERIVATIVES **greyish** adjective **greyly** adverb **greyness** noun.
– ORIGIN Old English.
grey area ● noun an ill-defined area of activity that does not readily conform to an existing category or set of rules.
greybeard ● noun humorous or derogatory an old man.
Grey Friar ● noun a friar of the Franciscan order (who wear grey habits).
greyhound ● noun a swift, slender breed of dog used in racing and coursing.
– ORIGIN Old English, related to an Old Norse word meaning 'bitch'.
greylag ● noun a large goose with mainly grey plumage, the ancestor of the domestic goose.
– ORIGIN probably from dialect *lag* 'goose'.
grey matter ● noun **1** the darker tissue of the brain and spinal cord. **2** informal intelligence.
grey seal ● noun a large North Atlantic seal with a spotted greyish coat.
grey squirrel ● noun a tree squirrel with mainly grey fur, native to eastern North America and introduced to Britain and elsewhere.
gricer /grīsər/ ● noun Brit. informal a trainspotter.
– ORIGIN perhaps a humorous representation of an upper-class pronunciation of *grouser* 'grouse-shooter'.
grid ● noun **1** a framework of spaced bars that are parallel to or cross each other. **2** a network of lines that cross each other to form a series of squares or rectangles. **3** a network of cables or pipes for distributing power, especially high-voltage electricity. **4** a pattern of lines marking the starting places on a motor-racing track. ● verb put into or set out as a grid.
– ORIGIN from GRIDIRON.
griddle ● noun a circular iron plate that is heated and used for cooking food. ● verb cook on a griddle.
– ORIGIN Old French *gredil*, from Latin *craticula* 'small hurdle'.
gridiron /griddīrn/ ● noun **1** a frame of parallel metal bars used for grilling meat or fish over an open fire. **2** a grid pattern, especially of streets. **3** a field for American football, marked with regularly spaced parallel lines. **4** N. Amer. the game of American football.
– ORIGIN alteration of obsolete *gredile* 'griddle', by association with *iron*.
gridlock ● noun a traffic jam affecting a whole network of intersecting streets.
– DERIVATIVES **gridlocked** adjective.
grief ● noun **1** intense sorrow, especially caused by someone's death. **2** informal trouble or annoyance.
– PHRASES **come to grief** have an accident; meet with disaster. **good grief!** an exclamation of surprise or alarm.
– ORIGIN Old French, from *grever* 'to burden'.
grievance ● noun a real or imagined cause for complaint.
grieve ● verb **1** suffer grief. **2** cause great distress to.
– DERIVATIVES **griever** noun.
– ORIGIN Old French *grever* 'burden, encumber', from Latin *gravis* 'heavy, serious'.
grievous ● adjective formal (of something bad) very severe or serious.
– DERIVATIVES **grievously** adverb **grievousness** noun.
grievous bodily harm ● noun Law serious physical injury inflicted on a person by the deliberate action of another, considered more serious than actual bodily harm.
griffin (also **gryphon** or **griffon**) ● noun a mythical creature with the head and wings of an eagle and the body of a lion.
– ORIGIN Old French *grifoun*, from Greek *grups.*
griffon /griff'n/ ● noun **1** a dog of a small terrier-like breed. **2** a large vulture with predominantly pale brown plumage. **3** variant spelling of GRIFFIN.
– ORIGIN variant of GRIFFIN.
grig ● noun dialect **1** a small eel. **2** a grasshopper or cricket.

g

Thesaurus

ABLE, company-loving, convivial, companionable, outgoing, friendly, affable, amiable, genial, warm, comradely, clubbable; *Scottish* couthy; *informal* chummy, pally; *Brit. informal* matey. **2** *gregarious fish* SOCIAL, living in groups.
– OPPOSITES unsociable.
grey ● adjective **1** *a grey suit* silvery, silver-grey, gunmetal, slate, charcoal, smoky. **2** *his grey hair* WHITE, silver, hoary. **3** *a grey day* CLOUDY, overcast, dull, sunless, gloomy, dreary, dismal, sombre, bleak, murky. **4** *her face looked grey* ASHEN, wan, pale, pasty, pallid, colourless, bloodless, white, waxen; sickly, peaky, drained, drawn, deathly. **5** *the grey daily routine* CHARACTERLESS, colourless, nondescript, unremarkable, insipid, jejune, flat, bland, dry, stale; dull, uninteresting, boring, tedious, monotonous. **6** *a grey area* AMBIGUOUS, doubtful, unclear, uncertain, indefinite, open to question, debatable. **7** *the grey economy* UNOFFICIAL, informal, irregular, back-door.
– OPPOSITES sunny, ruddy, lively, certain.
● verb *the population greyed* AGE, grow old, mature.
grid ● noun **1** *a metal grid* GRATING, mesh, grille, gauze, lattice. **2** *the grid of streets* NETWORK, matrix, reticulation.
grief ● noun **1** *he was overcome with grief* SORROW, misery, sadness, anguish, pain, distress, heartache, heartbreak, agony, torment, affliction, suffering, woe, desolation, dejection, despair; mourning, mournfulness, bereavement, lamentation; *poetic/literary* dolour, dole. **2** *(informal) the police gave me loads of grief* TROUBLE, annoyance, bother, irritation, vexation, harassment; *informal* aggravation, aggro, hassle.
– OPPOSITES joy.
– PHRASES **come to grief** FAIL, meet with disaster, miscarry, go wrong, go awry, fall through, fall flat, founder, come to nothing, come to naught; *informal* come unstuck, come a cropper, flop, go phut; *Brit. informal* go pear-shaped.
grief-stricken ● adjective SORROWFUL, sorrowing, miserable, sad, heartbroken, broken-hearted, anguished, pained, distressed, tormented, suffering, woeful, doleful, desolate, despairing, devastated, upset, inconsolable, wretched; mourning, grieving, mournful, bereaved, lamenting; *poetic/literary* dolorous, heartsick.
– OPPOSITES joyful.
grievance ● noun **1** *social and economic grievances* INJUSTICE, wrong, injury, ill, unfairness; affront, insult, indignity. **2** *students voiced their grievances* COMPLAINT, criticism, objection, grumble, grouse; ill feeling, bad feeling, resentment, bitterness, pique; *informal* gripe, whinge, moan, grouch, niggle, beef, bone to pick.
grieve ● verb **1** *she grieved for her father* MOURN, lament, sorrow, be sorrowful; cry, sob, weep, shed tears, keen, weep and wail, beat one's breast. **2** *it grieved me to leave her* SADDEN, upset, distress, pain, hurt, wound, break someone's heart, make someone's heart bleed.
– OPPOSITES rejoice, please.
grievous *(formal)* ● adjective **1** *his death was a grievous blow* SERIOUS, severe, grave, bad, critical, dreadful, terrible, awful, crushing, calamitous; painful, agonizing, traumatic, wounding, damaging, injurious; sharp, acute. **2** *a grievous sin* HEINOUS, grave, deplorable, shocking, appalling, atrocious, gross, dreadful, egre-

– ORIGIN of unknown origin.

grill ● noun Brit. **1** a device on a cooker that radiates heat downwards for cooking food. **2** a gridiron used for cooking food on an open fire. **3** a dish of food cooked using a grill. **4** a restaurant serving grilled food. **5** variant form of GRILLE. ● verb **1** cook with a grill. **2** informal subject to intense questioning or interrogation.

– ORIGIN Old French *graille* 'grille', from Latin *craticula* 'small hurdle'; related to CRATE, GRATE², and GRIDDLE.

grille (also **grill**) ● noun a grating or screen of metal bars or wires.

– ORIGIN French.

grilse /griss/ ● noun a salmon that has returned to fresh water after a single winter at sea.

– ORIGIN of unknown origin.

grim ● adjective (**grimmer**, **grimmest**) **1** very serious or gloomy; forbidding. **2** horrifying, depressing, or unappealing.

– PHRASES **like** (or **for**) **grim death** with great determination.

– DERIVATIVES **grimly** adverb **grimness** noun.

– ORIGIN Old English.

g

grimace /grimməss/ ● noun an ugly, twisted expression on a person's face, expressing disgust, pain, or wry amusement. ● verb make a grimace.

– ORIGIN French, from Spanish *grima* 'fright'.

grimalkin /grimalkin/ ● noun archaic **1** a cat. **2** a spiteful old woman.

– ORIGIN from GREY + *Malkin* (familiar form of the given name *Matilda*).

grime ● noun dirt ingrained on a surface. ● verb blacken or make dirty with grime.

– ORIGIN Low German and Dutch.

grimoire /grimwaar/ ● noun a book of magic spells and invocations.

– ORIGIN French, alteration of *grammaire* 'grammar'.

grimy ● adjective (**grimier**, **grimiest**) covered with or characterized by grime.

– DERIVATIVES **grimily** adverb **griminess** noun.

grin ● verb (**grinned**, **grinning**) **1** smile broadly. **2** grimace grotesquely in a way that reveals the teeth. ● noun a smile or grimace produced by grinning.

– PHRASES **grin and bear it** suffer pain or misfortune in a stoical manner.

– ORIGIN Old English.

grind ● verb (past and past part. **ground**) **1** reduce to small particles or powder by crushing. **2** sharpen, smooth, or produce by crushing or friction. **3** rub together or move gratingly. **4** (**grind down**) wear (someone) down with harsh treatment. **5** (**grind out**) produce (something) slowly and laboriously. **6** (**grinding**) oppressive and seemingly endless: *grinding poverty.* **7** (often **grind away**) work or study hard. **8** informal (of a dancer) rotate the hips. ● noun **1** an act or process of grinding. **2** hard dull work: *the daily grind.*

– PHRASES **grind to a halt** (or **come to a grinding halt**) stop laboriously and noisily.

– DERIVATIVES **grinder** noun **grindingly** adverb.

– ORIGIN Old English.

grindstone ● noun **1** a thick revolving disc of abrasive material used for sharpening or polishing metal objects. **2** a millstone.

– PHRASES **keep one's nose to the grindstone** work hard and continuously.

gringo /gringgō/ ● noun (pl. **gringos**) informal (in Latin America) a white English-speaking person.

– ORIGIN Spanish, 'foreign, foreigner, or gibberish'.

griot /greeō/ ● noun a West African travelling poet, musician, and storyteller.

– ORIGIN French, perhaps from Portuguese *criado*.

grip ● verb (**gripped**, **gripping**) **1** take and keep a firm hold of; grasp tightly. **2** deeply affect or afflict. **3** hold the attention or interest of. ● noun **1** a firm hold. **2** intellectual understanding. **3** a part or attachment by which something is held in the hand. **4** a travelling bag. **5** a stage hand in a theatre. **6** a member of a camera crew responsible for moving and setting up equipment.

– PHRASES **come** (or **get**) **to grips with 1** engage in combat with. **2** begin to deal with or understand. **lose one's grip** become unable to understand or control one's situation.

– DERIVATIVES **gripper** noun **gripping** adjective.

– ORIGIN Old English.

gripe ● verb **1** informal express a trivial complaint; grumble. **2** affect with stomach or intestinal pain. ● noun **1** informal a trivial complaint. **2** pain in the stomach or intestines; colic.

– ORIGIN Old English, 'grasp, clutch'; related to GRIP and GROPE.

gripe water ● noun Brit. trademark a solution given to babies for

Thesaurus

gious, iniquitous.

– OPPOSITES slight, trivial.

grim ● adjective **1** *his grim expression* STERN, forbidding, uninviting, unsmiling, dour, formidable, harsh, steely, flinty, stony; cross, churlish, crabbed, surly, sour, ill-tempered; fierce, ferocious, threatening, menacing, implacable, ruthless, merciless. **2** *grim humour* BLACK, dark, mirthless, bleak, cynical. **3** *the asylum holds some grim secrets* DREADFUL, dire, ghastly, horrible, horrendous, horrid, terrible, awful, appalling, frightful, shocking, unspeakable, grisly, gruesome, hideous, macabre; depressing, distressing, upsetting, worrying, unpleasant. **4** *a grim little hovel* BLEAK, dreary, dismal, dingy, wretched, miserable, depressing, cheerless, comfortless, joyless, gloomy, uninviting; informal God-awful. **5** *grim determination* RESOLUTE, determined, firm, decided, steadfast, dead set; obstinate, stubborn, obdurate, unyielding, uncompromising, unshakeable, intractable, unrelenting, relentless, dogged, tenacious.

– OPPOSITES amiable, pleasant.

grimace ● noun *his mouth twisted into a grimace* SCOWL, frown, sneer; face.

● verb *Nina grimaced at Joe* SCOWL, frown, sneer, glower, lour; make a face, make faces, pull a face; Brit. gurn.

– OPPOSITES smile.

grime ● noun *her skirt was smeared with grime* DIRT, smut, soot, dust, mud, filth, mire; informal muck, yuck, crud; Brit. informal grot, gunge.

● verb *concrete grimed by diesel exhaust* BLACKEN, dirty, stain, soil; poetic/literary begrime, besmirch.

grimy ● adjective DIRTY, grubby, mucky, soiled, stained, smeared, filthy, smutty, sooty, dusty, muddy; informal yucky, cruddy; Brit. informal manky, grotty, gungy; Austral./NZ scungy; poetic/literary besmirched, begrimed.

– OPPOSITES clean.

grin ● verb *he grinned at her* SMILE, smile broadly, beam, smile from ear to ear, grin like a Cheshire cat; smirk; informal be all smiles.

● noun *a silly grin* SMILE, broad smile; smirk.

– OPPOSITES frown, scowl.

grind ● verb **1** *the sandstone is ground into powder* CRUSH, pound, pulverize, mill, granulate, crumble, smash, press; technical triturate, comminute; archaic levigate, bray. **2** *a knife being ground on a wheel* SHARPEN, whet, hone, file, strop; smooth, polish, sand, sandpaper. **3** *one tectonic plate grinds against another* RUB, grate, scrape, rasp.

● noun *the daily grind* DRUDGERY, toil, hard work, labour, donkey work, exertion, chores, slog; informal fag, sweat; poetic/literary travail.

– PHRASES **grind away** LABOUR, toil, work hard, slave (away), work one's fingers to the bone, work like a Trojan, work like a dog; informal slog, plug away, beaver away, work one's socks off; Brit. informal graft; poetic/literary travail; archaic drudge. **grind someone down** OPPRESS, crush, persecute, tyrannize, ill-treat, maltreat.

grip ● verb **1** *she gripped the edge of the table* GRASP, clutch, hold, clasp, take hold of, clench, grab, seize, cling to; squeeze, press. **2** *Harry was gripped by a sneezing fit* AFFLICT, affect, take over, beset, rack, convulse. **3** *we were gripped by the drama* ENGROSS, enthral, absorb, rivet, spellbind, hold spellbound, bewitch, fascinate, hold, mesmerize, enrapture; interest.

– OPPOSITES release.

● noun **1** *a tight grip* GRASP, hold. **2** *the wheels lost their grip on the road* TRACTION, purchase, friction, adhesion, resistance. **3** *he was in the grip of an obsession* CONTROL, power, hold, stranglehold, clutches, command, mastery, influence. **4** *I had a pretty good grip on the situation* UNDERSTANDING, comprehension, grasp, perception, awareness, apprehension, conception; formal cognizance. **5** *a leather grip* TRAVELLING BAG, bag, holdall, overnight bag, flight bag, kitbag, Gladstone bag.

– PHRASES **come/get to grips with** DEAL WITH, cope with, handle, grasp, grasp the nettle of, tackle, undertake, take on, grapple with, face, face up to, confront.

gripe (informal) ● verb *he's always griping about something* COMPLAIN, grumble, grouse, protest, whine, bleat; informal moan, bellyache, beef, bitch, whinge; Brit. informal chunter; N. Amer. informal kvetch.

the relief of colic, wind, and indigestion.

grisaille /grizīl/ ● noun a method of painting in grey monochrome, typically to imitate sculpture.
– ORIGIN French, from *gris* 'grey'.

gris-gris /greegree/ ● noun (pl. same) **1** an African or Caribbean charm or amulet. **2** the use of such charms, especially in voodoo.
– ORIGIN French, of West African origin.

grisly /grizli/ ● adjective (**grislier**, **grisliest**) causing horror or revulsion.
– DERIVATIVES **grisliness** noun.
– ORIGIN Old English.

grissini /griseeni/ ● plural noun thin, crisp Italian breadsticks.
– ORIGIN Italian.

grist ● noun **1** corn that is ground to make flour. **2** malt crushed to make mash for brewing.
– PHRASES **grist to the mill** useful experience or knowledge.
– ORIGIN Old English, 'grinding'.

gristle /griss'l/ ● noun cartilage, especially when found as tough inedible tissue in meat.
– DERIVATIVES **gristly** adjective.
– ORIGIN Old English.

grit ● noun **1** small loose particles of stone or sand. **2** (also **gritstone**) a coarse sandstone. **3** courage and resolve. ● verb (**gritted**, **gritting**) **1** clench (the teeth), especially in order to keep one's resolve. **2** spread grit on (an icy road).
– DERIVATIVES **gritter** noun.
– ORIGIN Old English.

grits ● plural noun US coarsely ground maize kernels, served boiled with water or milk.
– ORIGIN Old English, 'bran, mill dust'.

gritty ● adjective (**grittier**, **grittiest**) **1** containing or covered with grit. **2** showing courage and resolve. **3** tough and uncompromising: *a gritty look at urban life.*
– DERIVATIVES **grittily** adverb **grittiness** noun.

grizzle ● verb informal, chiefly Brit. (of a child) cry or whimper fretfully.
– ORIGIN of unknown origin.

grizzled ● adjective having grey or grey-streaked hair.
– ORIGIN from Old French *gris* 'grey'.

grizzly bear ● noun a large variety of brown bear often having white-tipped fur, native to western North America.
– ORIGIN *grizzly* from GRIZZLED.

groan ● verb **1** make a deep inarticulate sound of pain or despair. **2** make a low creaking sound when pressure or weight is applied. **3** (**groan beneath/under**) be burdened by. ● noun a groaning sound.
– DERIVATIVES **groaner** noun.
– ORIGIN Old English.

groat ● noun historical an English silver coin worth four old pence.
– ORIGIN from Dutch *groot* or Low German *grōte* 'great, thick', hence 'thick penny'.

groats ● plural noun hulled or crushed grain, especially oats.
– ORIGIN Old English, related to GRIT and GRITS.

grocer ● noun a person who sells food and small household goods.
– ORIGIN originally in the sense 'a person who sold things by the gross': from Old French *grossier*, from Latin *grossus* 'gross'.

grocery ● noun (pl. **groceries**) **1** a grocer's shop or business. **2** (**groceries**) items of food sold in a grocer's shop or supermarket.

grockle ● noun Brit. informal, derogatory a holidaymaker, especially one in the West Country.
– ORIGIN an invented word, originally a fantastic creature in a children's comic, popularized by the film *The System* (1962).

grog ● noun **1** spirits (originally rum) mixed with water. **2** informal alcoholic drink.
– ORIGIN said to be from *Old Grog*, the reputed nickname (because of his grogram cloak) of Admiral Vernon (1684–1757), who ordered diluted (instead of neat) rum to be served out to sailors.

groggy ● adjective (**groggier**, **groggiest**) dazed and unsteady after intoxication, sleep, etc.
– DERIVATIVES **groggily** adverb **grogginess** noun.

grogram /grogrəm/ ● noun a coarse fabric made of silk, often combined with mohair or wool and stiffened with gum.
– ORIGIN from French *gros grain* 'coarse grain'.

groin[1] ● noun **1** the area between the abdomen and the thigh on either side of the body. **2** informal the region of the genitals. **3** Architecture a curved edge formed by two intersecting vaults.
– ORIGIN perhaps from an Old English word meaning 'depression, abyss'.

groin[2] ● noun US spelling of GROYNE.

grommet /grommit/ ● noun **1** a protective eyelet in a hole that a rope or cable passes through. **2** a tube surgically implanted in the eardrum to drain fluid from the middle ear.
– ORIGIN originally in sense 'circle of rope used as a fastening': from obsolete French *gourmer* 'to curb'.

groom ● verb **1** brush and clean the coat of (a horse or dog). **2** give a neat and tidy appearance to. **3** prepare or train for a particular purpose or activity. ● noun **1** a person employed to take care of horses. **2** a bridegroom.
– ORIGIN originally in the sense 'boy', later 'man, male servant': of unknown origin.

groove ● noun **1** a long, narrow cut or depression in a hard material. **2** a spiral track cut in a gramophone record, into which the stylus fits. **3** an established routine or habit. **4** informal a rhythmic pattern in popular or jazz music. ● verb **1** make a groove or grooves in. **2** informal dance to or play popular or jazz music.
– PHRASES **in the groove** informal **1** performing confidently. **2** en-

g

Thesaurus

● noun *employees' gripes* COMPLAINT, grumble, grouse, grievance, objection; cavil, quibble, niggle; *informal* moan, beef, whinge; *N. Amer. informal* kvetch.

gripping ● adjective ENGROSSING, enthralling, absorbing, riveting, captivating, spellbinding, bewitching, fascinating, compulsive, compelling, mesmerizing; thrilling, exciting, action-packed, dramatic, stimulating; *informal* unputdownable, page-turning.
– OPPOSITES boring.

grisly ● adjective GRUESOME, ghastly, frightful, horrid, horrifying, fearful, hideous, macabre, spine-chilling, horrible, horrendous, grim, awful, dire, dreadful, terrible, horrific, shocking, appalling, abominable, loathsome, abhorrent, odious, monstrous, unspeakable, disgusting, repulsive, repugnant, revolting, repellent, sickening; *informal* sick-making, gross; *archaic* disgustful.

gristly ● adjective STRINGY, sinewy, fibrous; tough, leathery, chewy.

grit ● noun **1** *the grit from the paths* GRAVEL, pebbles, stones, shingle, sand; dust, dirt. **2** *the true grit of a seasoned campaigner* COURAGE, bravery, pluck, mettle, backbone, spirit, strength of character, strength of will, moral fibre, steel, nerve, fortitude, toughness, hardiness, resolve, resolution, determination, tenacity, perseverance, endurance; *informal* guts, spunk; *Brit. informal* bottle.
● verb *Gina gritted her teeth* CLENCH, clamp together, shut tightly; grind, gnash.

gritty ● adjective **1** *a gritty floor* SANDY, gravelly, pebbly, stony; powdery, dusty. **2** *a gritty performance* COURAGEOUS, brave, plucky, mettlesome, stout-hearted, valiant, bold, spirited, intrepid, tough, determined, resolute, purposeful, dogged, tenacious; *informal* gutsy, spunky.

grizzle ● verb *(Brit. informal)* CRY, whimper, mewl, snivel, sob, wail; *Scottish* greet.

grizzled ● adjective GREY, greying, silver, silvery, snowy, white, salt-and-pepper; grey-haired, hoary.

groan ● verb **1** *she groaned and rubbed her stomach* MOAN, whimper, cry, call out. **2** *they were groaning about the management* COMPLAIN, grumble, grouse; *informal* moan, niggle, beef, bellyache, bitch, whinge, gripe. **3** *the old wooden door groaned* CREAK, squeak; grate, rasp.
● noun **1** *a groan of anguish* MOAN, cry, whimper. **2** *their moans and groans* COMPLAINT, grumble, grouse, objection, protest, grievance; *informal* grouch, moan, beef, whinge; *informal* gripe. **3** *the groan of the elevator* CREAKING, creak, squeak, grating, grinding.

groggy ● adjective DAZED, muzzy, stupefied, in a stupor, befuddled, fuddled, disoriented, disorientated, dizzy, punch-drunk, shaky, unsteady, wobbly, weak, faint; *informal* dopey, woozy, not with it.

groin ● noun CROTCH, crutch, genitals.
– RELATED TERMS inguinal.

groom ● verb **1** *she groomed her pony* CURRY, brush, comb, clean, rub down. **2** *his dark hair was carefully groomed* BRUSH, comb, arrange, do; tidy, spruce up, smarten up, preen, primp; *informal* fix. **3** *they were groomed for stardom* PREPARE, prime, ready, condition, tailor; coach, train, instruct, drill, teach, school.
● noun **1** *a groom took his horse* STABLE HAND, stableman, stable lad,

joying oneself, especially by dancing.
– DERIVATIVES **grooved** adjective.
– ORIGIN Dutch *groeve* 'furrow, pit'; related to GRAVE[1].
groovy ● adjective (**groovier**, **grooviest**) informal, dated or humorous fashionable and exciting.
– DERIVATIVES **groovily** adverb **grooviness** noun.
grope ● verb **1** feel about or search blindly or uncertainly with the hands. **2** informal feel or fondle (someone) for sexual pleasure, especially against their will. ● noun informal an act of groping someone.
– ORIGIN Old English, related to GRIPE.
groper[1] ● noun a person who gropes.
groper[2] ● noun chiefly Austral./NZ variant spelling of GROUPER.
grosbeak /grōsbeek/ ● noun a finch or related songbird with a stout conical bill and brightly coloured plumage.
– ORIGIN from French *gros* 'big, fat' + *bec* 'beak'.
groschen /grōshən/ ● noun (pl. same) a monetary unit of Austria, equal to one hundredth of a schilling.
– ORIGIN German, from Latin *denarius grossus* 'thick penny'; compare with GROAT.
g
grosgrain /grōgrayn/ ● noun a heavy ribbed fabric, typically of silk or rayon.
– ORIGIN French, 'coarse grain'.
gros point /grō pwan/ ● noun a type of needlepoint embroidery consisting of stitches crossing two or more threads of the canvas in each direction.
– ORIGIN French, 'large stitch'.
gross ● adjective **1** unattractively large or bloated. **2** vulgar; unrefined. **3** informal very unpleasant; repulsive. **4** complete; blatant: *a gross exaggeration.* **5** (of income, profit, or interest) without deduction of tax or other contributions; total. Often contrasted with NET[2]. **6** (of weight) including contents or other variable items; overall. ● adverb without tax or other contributions having been deducted. ● verb **1** produce or earn (an amount of money) as gross profit or income. **2** (**gross up**) add deductions such as tax to (a net amount). **3** (**gross out**) informal, chiefly N. Amer. disgust (someone) with repulsive behaviour or appearance. ● noun **1** (pl. same) an amount equal to twelve dozen; 144. **2** (pl. **grosses**) a gross profit or income.
– DERIVATIVES **grossly** adverb **grossness** noun.
– ORIGIN Old French *gros* 'large', from Latin *grossus*; sense 1 of the noun is from French *grosse douzaine* 'large dozen'.
gross domestic product ● noun the total value of goods produced and services provided within a country during one year.
gross national product ● noun the total value of goods produced and services provided by a country during one year, equal to the gross domestic product plus the net income from foreign investments.
grosz /grawss/ ● noun (pl. **groszy** or **grosze**) a monetary unit of Poland, equal to one hundredth of a zloty.
– ORIGIN Polish.
grot[1] ● noun Brit. informal something unpleasant, dirty, or of poor quality; rubbish.
– ORIGIN from GROTTY.
grot[2] ● noun literary a grotto.
grotesque /grōtesk/ ● adjective **1** comically or repulsively ugly or distorted. **2** shockingly incongruous or inappropriate. ● noun **1** a grotesque figure or image. **2** a style of decorative painting or sculpture consisting of the interweaving of human and animal forms with flowers and foliage.
– DERIVATIVES **grotesquely** adverb **grotesqueness** noun.
– ORIGIN Italian *grottesca*, from *opera* or *pittura grottesca* 'work or painting resembling that found in a grotto'.
grotesquerie /grōteskəri/ ● noun (pl. **grotesqueries**) grotesque quality or things.
grotto ● noun (pl. **grottoes** or **grottos**) a small picturesque cave, especially an artificial one in a park or garden.
– ORIGIN Italian *grotta*, from Greek *kruptē* 'vault'.
grotty ● adjective (**grottier**, **grottiest**) Brit. informal **1** unpleasant and of poor quality. **2** unwell.
– DERIVATIVES **grottiness** noun.
– ORIGIN from GROTESQUE.
grouch /growch/ informal ● noun **1** a habitually grumpy person. **2** a complaint or grumble. ● verb complain ill-temperedly; grumble.
– ORIGIN from Old French *grouchier* 'to grumble, murmur'.
grouchy ● adjective (**grouchier**, **grouchiest**) irritable and bad-tempered; grumpy.
– DERIVATIVES **grouchily** adverb **grouchiness** noun.
ground[1] ● noun **1** the solid surface of the earth. **2** land of a specified kind: *marshy ground.* **3** an area of land or sea with a specified use: *fishing grounds.* **4** (**grounds**) an area of enclosed land surrounding a large house. **5** (**grounds**) factors forming a basis for action or the justification for a belief. **6** a prepared surface to which paint or other decoration is applied. **7** (**grounds**) solid particles, especially of coffee, which form a residue. **8** N. Amer. electrical connection to the earth. ● verb **1** prohibit or prevent (a pilot or aircraft) from flying. **2** run (a ship) aground. **3** (usu. **be grounded in/on**) give a firm theoretical or practical basis to. **4** place on the ground or touch the ground with. **5** informal, chiefly N. Amer. (of a parent) refuse to allow (a child) to go out socially, as a punishment. **6** N. Amer. connect (an electrical device) with the ground.
– PHRASES **be thick** (or **thin**) **on the ground** exist in large (or small) numbers or amounts. **break new ground** be innovative. **gain ground 1** become more popular or accepted. **2** (usu. **gain ground on**) get closer to someone being pursued. **get off the ground** start happening or functioning successfully. **give** (or **lose**) **ground** retreat or lose one's advantage. **go to ground** (of a fox or other animal) enter its earth or burrow. **hold** (or **stand**) **one's ground** not retreat or lose one's advantage. **on the ground** in a place where real, practical work is done. **on one's own ground** in one's own territory or area of knowledge. **work** (or **run**) **oneself into the ground** exhaust oneself by working or running very hard.
– ORIGIN Old English.

Thesaurus

stable boy, stable girl; *historical* equerry. **2** *the bride and groom* BRIDEGROOM; newly-married man, newly-wed.
groove ● noun FURROW, channel, trench, trough, canal, gouge, hollow, indentation, rut, gutter, cutting, cut, fissure; *Carpentry* rebate.
grooved ● adjective FURROWED, fluted, corrugated, ribbed, ridged.
grope ● verb **1** *she groped for her glasses* FUMBLE, scrabble, fish, ferret, rummage, feel, search, hunt; *Brit. informal* rootle. **2** *(informal) one of the men started groping her* FONDLE, touch; *informal* paw, maul, feel up, touch up.
gross ● adjective **1** *the man was pale and gross* OBESE, corpulent, overweight, fat, big, large, fleshy, flabby, portly, bloated; *informal* porky, pudgy, tubby, blubbery, roly-poly; *Brit. informal* podgy, fubsy. **2** *men of gross natures* BOORISH, coarse, vulgar, loutish, oafish, thuggish, brutish, philistine, uncouth, crass, common, unrefined, unsophisticated, uncultured, uncultivated; *informal* cloddish; *Brit. informal* yobbish. **3** *(informal) the place smelled gross* DISGUSTING, repellent, repulsive, abhorrent, loathsome, foul, nasty, obnoxious, sickening, nauseating, stomach-churning, unpalatable; *N. Amer.* vomitous; *informal* yucky, icky, sick-making, gut-churning; *archaic* disgustful. **4** *a gross distortion of the truth* FLAGRANT, blatant, glaring, obvious, overt, naked, barefaced, shameless, brazen, audacious, brass-necked, undisguised, unconcealed, patent, transparent, manifest, palpable; out and out, utter, complete. **5** *their gross income* TOTAL, whole, entire, complete, full, overall, combined, aggregate; before deductions, before tax.
– OPPOSITES slender, refined, pleasant, net.
● verb *he grosses over a million dollars a month* EARN, make, bring in, take, get, receive, collect; *informal* rake in.
grotesque ● adjective **1** *a grotesque creature* MALFORMED, deformed, misshapen, misproportioned, distorted, twisted, gnarled, mangled, mutilated; ugly, unsightly, monstrous, hideous, freakish, unnatural, abnormal, strange, odd, peculiar; *informal* weird, freaky. **2** *grotesque mismanagement of funds* OUTRAGEOUS, monstrous, shocking, appalling, preposterous; ridiculous, ludicrous, farcical, unbelievable, incredible.
– OPPOSITES normal.
grotto ● noun CAVE, cavern, hollow; pothole, underground chamber.
grouch *(informal)* ● noun *an ill-mannered grouch* GRUMBLER, complainer, moaner; *informal* grump, sourpuss, crosspatch, whinger; *Brit. informal* misery, bear with a sore head; *N. Amer. informal* sorehead, kvetch.
● verb *there's not a lot to grouch about* GRUMBLE, complain, grouse, whine, bleat, carp, cavil; *informal* moan, whinge, gripe, beef, bellyache, bitch, sound off; *Brit. informal* chunter; *N. Amer. informal* kvetch.
grouchy ● adjective GRUMPY, cross, irritable, bad-tempered, crotchety, crabby, crabbed, cantankerous, curmudgeonly, testy,

ground² past and past participle of GRIND.
groundbait ● noun Brit. bait thrown into the water while fishing.
ground-breaking ● adjective innovative; pioneering.
ground control ● noun (treated as sing. or pl.) the personnel and equipment that monitor and direct the flight and landing of aircraft or spacecraft.
ground elder ● noun a common weed with leaves that resemble those of the elder and spreading underground stems.
ground floor ● noun Brit. the floor of a building at ground level.
ground frost ● noun Brit. frost formed on the surface of the ground or in the top layer of soil.
ground glass ● noun **1** glass with a smooth ground surface that makes it non-transparent. **2** glass ground into an abrasive powder.
groundhog ● noun North American term for WOODCHUCK.
grounding ● noun basic training or instruction in a subject.
ground ivy ● noun a creeping plant with bluish-purple flowers.
groundless ● adjective not based on any good reason.
groundling ● noun a spectator or reader of inferior taste.
– ORIGIN originally a member of the part of a theatre audience that stood in the pit beneath the stage: with reference to Shakespeare's *Hamlet* III. ii. 11.
groundmass ● noun Geology the compact, finer-grained material in which the crystals are embedded in a porphyritic rock.
groundnut ● noun another term for PEANUT.
ground rent ● noun Brit. rent paid by the owner of a building to the owner of the land on which it is built.
ground rule ● noun a basic principle established to govern action or procedure.
groundsel /grownsʼl/ ● noun a plant of the daisy family with small yellow flowers.
– ORIGIN Old English, probably from two words meaning 'pus' + 'to swallow' (with reference to its use in poultices).
groundsheet ● noun a waterproof sheet spread on the ground inside a tent.
groundsman (N. Amer. **groundskeeper**) ● noun Brit. a person who maintains a sports ground or the grounds of a large building.
ground speed ● noun an aircraft's speed relative to the ground.
ground squirrel ● noun a burrowing squirrel of a large group including the chipmunks.
groundswell /growndswel/ ● noun **1** a large swell in the sea. **2** a build-up of opinion in a large section of the population.
groundwater ● noun water held underground in the soil or in pores and crevices in rock.
groundwork ● noun preliminary or basic work.
ground zero ● noun the point on the earth's surface directly below an exploding nuclear bomb.
group ● noun (treated as sing. or pl.) **1** a number of people or things located, gathered, or classed together. **2** a number of musicians who play popular music together. **3** a division of an air force. **4** Chemistry a set of elements occupying a column in the periodic table and having broadly similar properties. **5** Chemistry a combination of atoms having a recognizable identity in a number of compounds. ● verb place in or form a group or groups.
– DERIVATIVES **grouping** noun.
– ORIGIN Italian *gruppo*; related to CROP.
group captain ● noun a rank of officer in the RAF, above wing commander and below air commodore.
grouper (chiefly Austral./NZ also **groper**) ● noun a large heavy-bodied fish found in warm seas.
– ORIGIN Portuguese *garoupa*, probably from a local term in South America.
groupie ● noun informal a young woman who follows a pop group or celebrity, especially in the hope of a sexual relationship with them.
group therapy ● noun a form of psychiatric therapy in which patients meet to discuss their problems.
groupware ● noun Computing software designed to facilitate collective working by a number of different users.
grouse¹ ● noun (pl. same) a medium-sized game bird with a plump body and feathered legs.
– ORIGIN perhaps related to Latin *gruta* or to Old French *grue* 'crane'.
grouse² ● verb complain pettily; grumble. ● noun a grumble or complaint.
– ORIGIN of unknown origin.
grout /growt/ ● noun a mortar or paste for filling crevices, especially the gaps between wall or floor tiles. ● verb fill in with grout.
– ORIGIN perhaps from GROUTS or related to French dialect *grouter* 'grout a wall'.
grouts /growts/ ● plural noun archaic sediment; dregs; grounds.
– ORIGIN Old English, related to GRITS and GROATS.
grove ● noun a small wood, orchard, or group of trees.
– ORIGIN Old English.
grovel ● verb (**grovelled**, **grovelling**; US **groveled**, **groveling**) **1** crouch or crawl abjectly on the ground. **2** act obsequiously to obtain forgiveness or favour.
– DERIVATIVES **groveller** noun.
– ORIGIN from an Old Norse word meaning 'face downwards'.
grow ● verb (past **grew**; past part. **grown**) **1** (of a living thing) undergo natural development by increasing in size and chan-

g

Thesaurus

tetchy, huffy, snappish, waspish, prickly; *informal* snappy; *Brit. informal* narky, ratty, like a bear with a sore head, whingy; *N. Amer. informal* cranky, soreheaded; *informal, dated* miffy.
ground ● noun **1** *she collapsed on the ground* FLOOR, earth, terra firma; flooring; *informal* deck. **2** *the soggy ground* EARTH, soil, dirt, clay, loam, turf, clod, sod; land, terrain. **3** *the team's home ground* STADIUM, pitch, field, arena, track; *N. Amer.* bowl; *Brit. informal* park. **4** *the mansion's grounds* ESTATE, gardens, lawns, park, parkland, land, acres, property, surroundings, holding, territory; *archaic* demesne. **5** *grounds for dismissal* REASON, cause, basis, base, foundation, justification, rationale, argument, premise, occasion, excuse, pretext, motive, motivation. **6** *coffee grounds* SEDIMENT, precipitate, settlings, dregs, lees, deposit, residue; *archaic* grouts.
● verb **1** *the boat grounded on a mud bank* RUN AGROUND, run ashore, beach, land. **2** *an assertion grounded on results of several studies* BASE, found, establish, root, build, construct, form. **3** *they were grounded in classics and history* INSTRUCT, coach, teach, tutor, educate, school, train, drill, prime, prepare; familiarize with, acquaint with.
groundless ● adjective BASELESS, without basis, without foundation, ill-founded, unfounded, unsupported, uncorroborated, unproven, empty, idle, unsubstantiated, unwarranted, unjustified, unjustifiable, without cause, without reason, without justification, unreasonable, irrational, illogical, misguided.
groundwork ● noun PRELIMINARY WORK, preliminaries, preparations, spadework, legwork, donkey work; planning, arrangements, organization, homework; basics, essentials, fundamentals, underpinning, foundation.
group ● noun **1** *the exhibits were divided into three distinct groups* CATEGORY, class, classification, grouping, set, lot, batch, bracket, type, sort, kind, variety, family, species, genus, breed; grade, grading, rank, status. **2** *a group of tourists* CROWD, party, body, band, company, gathering, congregation, assembly, collection, cluster, flock, pack, troop, gang; *informal* bunch. **3** *a coup attempt by a group within the parliament* FACTION, division, section, clique, coterie, circle, set, ring, camp, bloc, caucus, cabal, fringe movement, splinter group. **4** *the women's group* ASSOCIATION, club, society, league, guild, circle, union. **5** *a small group of trees* CLUSTER, knot, collection, mass, clump. **6** *a local folk group* BAND, ensemble, act; *informal* line-up, combo, outfit.
● verb **1** *patients were grouped according to their symptoms* CATEGORIZE, classify, class, catalogue, sort, bracket, pigeonhole, grade, rate, rank. **2** *wooden chairs were grouped round the table* PLACE, arrange, assemble, organize, range, line up, dispose. **3** *the two parties grouped together* UNITE, join together/up, team up, join forces, get together, ally, form an alliance, affiliate, combine; collaborate, work together, pull together, cooperate.
grouse ● verb *she groused about the food* GRUMBLE, complain, protest, whine, bleat, carp, cavil, make a fuss; *informal* moan, bellyache, gripe, beef, bitch, grouch, whinge, sound off; *Brit. informal* chunter, create; *N. Amer. informal* kvetch.
● noun *our biggest grouse was about the noise* GRUMBLE, complaint, grievance, objection, cavil, quibble; *informal* moan, beef, gripe, grouch.
grove ● noun COPSE, wood, thicket, coppice; orchard, plantation; *Brit.* spinney; *archaic* hurst, holt.
grovel ● verb **1** *George grovelled at his feet* PROSTRATE ONESELF, lie, kneel, cringe. **2** *she was not going to grovel to him* BE OBSEQUIOUS, fawn on, kowtow, bow and scrape, toady, truckle, abase oneself, humble oneself; curry favour with, flatter, dance attendance on,

ging physically. **2** (of a plant) germinate and develop. **3** become larger or greater over a period of time; increase. **4** become gradually or increasingly: *we grew braver.* **5** (**grow up**) advance to maturity; become an adult. **6** (**grow out of** or **into**) become too large (or large enough) to wear. **7** (**grow on**) become gradually more appealing to.
– DERIVATIVES **grower** noun.
– ORIGIN Old English, related to GRASS and GREEN.

growbag • noun Brit. a bag containing potting compost, in which plants such as tomatoes can be grown.

growing pains • plural noun **1** pains occurring in the limbs of young children. **2** difficulties experienced in the early stages of an enterprise.

growl • verb **1** (especially of a dog) make a low guttural sound of hostility in the throat. **2** say something in a low grating voice. **3** make a low or harsh rumbling sound. • noun a growling sound.
– ORIGIN probably imitative.

growler • noun **1** a person or thing that growls. **2** a small iceberg.

g

grown past participle of GROW.

grown-up • adjective adult. • noun informal an adult.

growth • noun **1** the process of growing. **2** something that has grown or is growing. **3** a tumour or other abnormal formation.

growth hormone • noun a hormone which stimulates growth in animal or plant cells.

growth industry • noun an industry that is developing particularly rapidly.

growth ring • noun a concentric layer of wood, shell, or bone developed during a regular period of growth.

growth stock • noun a company stock that tends to increase in capital value rather than yield high income.

groyne (US **groin**) • noun a low wall or barrier built out into the sea from a beach to prevent erosion and drifting.
– ORIGIN from dialect *groin* 'snout', from Latin *grunium* 'pig's snout'.

GRP • abbreviation glass-reinforced plastic.

grub • noun **1** the larva of an insect, especially a beetle. **2** informal food. • verb (**grubbed**, **grubbing**) **1** dig shallowly in soil. **2** (**grub up**) dig (something) up. **3** (often **grub about/around**) search or work clumsily and unmethodically.
– DERIVATIVES **grubber** noun.
– ORIGIN perhaps related to Dutch *grobbelen*, also to GRAVE[1].

grubby • adjective (**grubbier**, **grubbiest**) **1** dirty; grimy. **2** disreputable; sordid.
– DERIVATIVES **grubbily** adverb **grubbiness** noun.

grub screw • noun Brit. a small headless screw.

Grub Street • noun the world or class of impoverished journalists and writers.
– ORIGIN the former name of a London street inhabited by such authors in the 17th century.

grudge • noun a persistent feeling of ill will or resentment resulting from a past insult or injury. • verb **1** be resentfully unwilling to grant or allow (something). **2** feel resentful that (someone) has achieved (something).
– DERIVATIVES **grudging** adjective.
– ORIGIN variant of obsolete *grutch* 'murmur, grumble'; related to GROUCH.

gruel • noun a thin liquid food of oatmeal or other meal boiled in milk or water.
– ORIGIN Old French.

gruelling (US **grueling**) • adjective extremely tiring and demanding.
– DERIVATIVES **gruellingly** adverb.
– ORIGIN from obsolete *gruel* 'exhaust, punish', from *get one's gruel* 'receive one's punishment'.

gruesome • adjective **1** causing repulsion or horror; grisly. **2** informal extremely unpleasant.
– DERIVATIVES **gruesomely** adverb **gruesomeness** noun.
– ORIGIN from Scottish *grue* 'to feel horror, shudder'.

gruff • adjective **1** (of a voice) rough and low in pitch. **2** abrupt or taciturn in manner.
– DERIVATIVES **gruffly** adverb **gruffness** noun.
– ORIGIN from Flemish and Dutch *grof* 'coarse, rude'.

grumble • verb **1** complain or protest in a bad-tempered but muted way. **2** make a low rumbling sound. **3** (**grumbling**) (of an internal organ) giving intermittent discomfort. • noun an instance of grumbling; a complaint.
– DERIVATIVES **grumbler** noun.
– ORIGIN from obsolete *grumme*, probably of Germanic origin.

Thesaurus

make up to, play up to, ingratiate oneself with; *informal* crawl, creep, suck up to, lick someone's boots.

grow • verb **1** *the boys had grown* GET BIGGER, get taller, get larger, increase in size. **2** *sales and profits continue to grow* INCREASE, swell, multiply, snowball, mushroom, balloon, build up, mount up, pile up; *informal* skyrocket. **3** *flowers grew among the rocks* SPROUT, germinate, shoot up, spring up, develop, bud, burst forth, bloom, flourish, thrive, run riot. **4** *he grew vegetables* CULTIVATE, produce, propagate, raise, rear, nurture, tend; farm. **5** *the family business grew* EXPAND, extend, develop, progress, make progress; flourish, thrive, burgeon, prosper, succeed, boom. **6** *the fable grew from an ancient Indian source* ORIGINATE, stem, spring, arise, emerge, issue; develop, evolve. **7** *Leonora grew bored* BECOME, get, turn, begin to feel.
– OPPOSITES shrink, decline.

growl • verb SNARL, bark, yap, bay.

grown-up • noun *(informal) children and grown-ups* ADULT, (grown) woman, (grown) man, mature woman, mature man.
– OPPOSITES child.
• adjective *she has two grown-up daughters* ADULT, mature, of age; fully grown, full-grown, fully developed.

growth • noun **1** *population growth* INCREASE, expansion, augmentation, proliferation, multiplication, enlargement, mushrooming, snowballing, rise, escalation, build-up. **2** *the growth of plants* DEVELOPMENT, maturation, growing, germination, sprouting; blooming. **3** *the marked growth of local enterprises* EXPANSION, extension, development, progress, advance, advancement, headway, spread; rise, success, boom, upturn, upswing. **4** *a growth on his jaw* TUMOUR, malignancy, cancer; lump, excrescence, outgrowth, swelling, nodule; cyst, polyp.
– OPPOSITES decrease, decline.

grub • noun **1** *a small black grub* LARVA; maggot; caterpillar. **2** *(informal) pub grub.* See FOOD sense 1.
• verb **1** *kids grubbing around in the dirt* DIG, poke, scratch. **2** *they grubbed up the old trees* DIG UP, unearth, uproot, root up/out, pull up/out, tear out. **3** *he began grubbing about in the bin* RUMMAGE, search, hunt, delve, dig, scrabble, ferret, root, rifle, fish, poke; *Brit. informal* rootle; *Austral./NZ informal* fossick through.

grubby • adjective DIRTY, grimy, filthy, mucky, unwashed, stained, soiled, smeared, spotted, muddy, dusty, sooty; unhygienic, insanitary; *informal* cruddy, yucky; *Brit. informal* manky, grotty, gungy; *poetic/literary* befouled, begrimed.
– OPPOSITES clean.

grudge • noun *a former employee with a grudge* GRIEVANCE, resentment, bitterness, rancour, pique, umbrage, dissatisfaction, disgruntlement, bad feelings, hard feelings, ill feelings, ill will, animosity, antipathy, antagonism, enmity, animus; *informal* a chip on one's shoulder.
• verb **1** *he grudged the time that the meetings involved* BEGRUDGE, resent, feel aggrieved about, be resentful of, mind, object to, take exception to. **2** *I don't grudge you your success* ENVY, begrudge, resent, be jealous of, be envious of, be resentful of.

grudging • adjective RELUCTANT, unwilling, forced, half-hearted, unenthusiastic, hesitant; begrudging, resentful.
– OPPOSITES eager.

gruelling • adjective EXHAUSTING, tiring, fatiguing, wearying, taxing, draining, debilitating; demanding, exacting, difficult, hard, arduous, strenuous, laborious, back-breaking, harsh, severe, stiff, punishing, crippling; *informal* killing, murderous, hellish; *Brit. informal* knackering.

gruesome • adjective GRISLY, ghastly, frightful, horrid, horrifying, hideous, horrible, horrendous, grim, awful, dire, dreadful, terrible, horrific, shocking, appalling, disgusting, repulsive, repugnant, revolting, repellent, sickening; loathsome, abhorrent, odious, monstrous, unspeakable; *informal* sick, sick-making, gross; *archaic* disgustful.
– OPPOSITES pleasant.

gruff • adjective **1** *a gruff reply* | *his gruff exterior* ABRUPT, brusque, curt, short, blunt, bluff, no-nonsense; laconic, taciturn; surly, churlish, grumpy, crotchety, crabby, crabbed, cross, bad-tempered, short-tempered, ill-natured, crusty, tetchy, bearish, ungracious, unceremonious; *informal* grouchy. **2** *a gruff voice* ROUGH, guttural, throaty, gravelly, husky, croaking, rasping, raspy, growly, hoarse, harsh; low, thick.

grump informal ● noun **1** a grumpy person. **2** a fit of sulking. ● verb act in a sulky, grumbling manner.
– ORIGIN imitative of sounds expressing displeasure.
grumpy ● adjective (**grumpier**, **grumpiest**) bad-tempered and sulky.
– DERIVATIVES **grumpily** adverb **grumpiness** noun.
grunge ● noun **1** chiefly N. Amer. grime; dirt. **2** a style of rock music characterized by a raucous guitar sound and lazy vocal delivery. **3** a casual style of fashion including loose, layered clothing and ripped jeans.
– DERIVATIVES **grungy** adjective.
– ORIGIN originally as *grungy*: perhaps suggested by GRUBBY and DINGY.
grunt ● verb **1** (of an animal, especially a pig) make a low, short guttural sound. **2** make a low inarticulate sound to express effort or indicate assent. ● noun **1** a grunting sound. **2** informal, chiefly N. Amer. a low-ranking soldier or worker.
– DERIVATIVES **grunter** noun
– ORIGIN Old English; sense 2 of the noun is an alteration of *ground*, from *ground man* (with reference to unskilled railway work).
Gruyère /grooyair/ ● noun a firm, tangy Swiss cheese.
– ORIGIN named after *Gruyère*, a district in Switzerland.
gryphon ● noun variant spelling of GRIFFIN.
GSM ● abbreviation Global System (or Standard) for Mobile.
gsm ● abbreviation grams per square metre.
GSOH ● abbreviation good sense of humour.
G-spot ● noun a sensitive area of the anterior wall of the vagina believed by some to be highly erogenous.
– ORIGIN originally as *Gräfenberg spot*, from *Gräfenberg* and Dickinson, who first described it in 1944.
GST ● abbreviation (in New Zealand and Canada) Goods and Services Tax.
G-string ● noun a skimpy undergarment covering the genitals, consisting of a narrow strip of cloth attached to a waistband.
G-suit ● noun a garment with inflatable pressurized pouches, worn by fighter pilots and astronauts to enable them to withstand high gravitational forces.
– ORIGIN abbreviation of *gravity*-suit.
GT ● noun a high-performance car.
– ORIGIN abbreviation of GRAN TURISMO.
gîte /zheet/ ● noun a small furnished holiday house in France.
– ORIGIN French, from Old French *giste*.
GTi ● noun a GT car with a fuel-injected engine.
guacamole /gwakkəmōlay/ ● noun a dish of mashed avocado mixed with chilli peppers, tomatoes, etc.
– ORIGIN Nahuatl, 'avocado sauce'.
Guadeloupian /gwaadəloopiən/ ● noun a person from Guadeloupe, a group of islands in the Lesser Antilles. ● adjective relating to Guadeloupe.
guanaco /gwənaakō/ ● noun (pl. **guanacos**) a wild mammal native to the Andes of South America, similar to the domestic llama.
– ORIGIN Quechua.
guanine /gwaaneen/ ● noun Biochemistry a compound that occurs in guano and fish scales, and is one of the four constituent bases of nucleic acids.
guano /gwaanō/ ● noun (pl. **guanos**) **1** the excrement of seabirds. **2** an artificial fertilizer resembling natural guano.
– ORIGIN Quechua (a language of Peru and neighbouring countries), 'dung'.
Guarani /gwaarənee/ ● noun (pl. same) **1** a member of an American Indian people of Paraguay and adjacent regions. **2** the language of this people. **3** (**guarani**) the basic monetary unit of Paraguay, equal to 100 centimos.
– ORIGIN Spanish.
guarantee ● noun **1** a formal assurance that certain conditions will be fulfilled, especially that a product will be of a specified quality. **2** something that makes an outcome certain. **3** variant spelling of GUARANTY. **4** less common term for GUARANTOR. ● verb (**guarantees**, **guaranteed**, **guaranteeing**) **1** provide a guarantee for something. **2** promise with certainty. **3** provide financial security for; underwrite.
– ORIGIN perhaps from Spanish *garante*; related to WARRANT.
guarantor /garrəntor/ ● noun a person or organization that gives or acts as a guarantee.
guaranty /garrənti/ (also **guarantee**) ● noun (pl. **guaranties**) **1** an undertaking to answer for the payment of a debt or for the performance of an obligation by another person liable in the first instance. **2** a thing serving as security for such an undertaking.
guard ● verb **1** watch over in order to protect or control. **2** (**guard against**) take precautions against. ● noun **1** a person, especially a soldier, who guards or keeps watch. **2** (treated as sing. or pl.) a body of soldiers guarding a place or person. **3** (**Guards**) the household troops of the British army. **4** a defensive posture adopted in a fight. **5** (often in phrase **off** or **on guard**) a state of vigilance. **6** a device worn or fitted to prevent injury or damage. **7** Brit. an official who rides on and is in general charge of a train. **8** N. Amer. a prison warder.
– PHRASES **guard of honour** a group of soldiers ceremonially welcoming an important visitor.
– ORIGIN Old French *garder*, related to WARD.
guarded ● adjective cautious and having possible reservations.
– DERIVATIVES **guardedly** adverb.
guard hair ● noun long, coarse hair forming an animal's outer fur.
guardhouse (also **guardroom**) ● noun a building used to accommodate a military guard or to detain military prisoners.
guardian ● noun **1** a defender, protector, or keeper. **2** a person legally responsible for someone unable to manage their own affairs, especially a child whose parents have died.
– DERIVATIVES **guardianship** noun.
– ORIGIN Old French *garden*.

Thesaurus

– OPPOSITES friendly, soft.
grumble ● verb *they grumbled about the disruption* COMPLAIN, grouse, whine, mutter, bleat, carp, cavil, protest, make a fuss; *informal* moan, bellyache, beef, bitch, grouch, whinge, sound off; *Brit. informal* gripe, chunter, create; *N. English informal* mither; *N. Amer. informal* kvetch.
● noun *his customers' grumbles* COMPLAINT, grouse, grievance, protest, cavil, quibble, criticism; *informal* grouch, moan, whinge, beef, bitch, gripe.
grumpy ● adjective BAD-TEMPERED, ill-tempered, short-tempered, crotchety, crabby, crabbed, tetchy, testy, waspish, prickly, touchy, irritable, irascible, crusty, cantankerous, curmudgeonly, bearish, surly, churlish, ill-natured, ill-humoured, peevish, cross, fractious, disagreeable, pettish; *informal* grouchy, snappy, snappish; *Brit. informal* shirty, stroppy, narky, ratty, eggy, like a bear with a sore head; *N. Amer. informal* cranky, ornery, soreheaded; *informal, dated* miffy.
– OPPOSITES good-humoured.
guarantee ● noun **1** *all repairs have a one-year guarantee* WARRANTY, warrant. **2** *a guarantee that the hospital will stay open* PROMISE, assurance, word (of honour), pledge, vow, oath, bond, commitment, covenant. **3** *banks usually demand a personal guarantee for loans* COLLATERAL, security, surety, guaranty, earnest.
● verb **1** *he agreed to guarantee the loan* UNDERWRITE, put up collateral for. **2** *can you guarantee he wasn't involved?* PROMISE, swear, swear to the fact, pledge, vow, undertake, give one's word, give an assurance, give an undertaking, take an oath, cross one's heart (and hope to die); *archaic* plight.
guard ● verb **1** *infantry guarded the barricaded bridge* PROTECT, stand guard over, watch over, keep an eye on; cover, patrol, police, defend, shield, safeguard, keep safe, secure. **2** *the prisoners were guarded by armed men* KEEP UNDER SURVEILLANCE, keep under guard, keep watch over, mind. **3** *forest wardens must guard against poachers* BEWARE OF, keep watch for, be alert to, keep an eye out for, be on the alert/lookout for.
● noun **1** *border guards* SENTRY, sentinel, security guard, nightwatchman; protector, defender, guardian; lookout, watch; garrison; *archaic* watchman. **2** *her prison guard* WARDER, warden, keeper; jailer; *informal* screw; *archaic* turnkey. **3** *he let his guard slip and they escaped* VIGILANCE, vigil, watch, surveillance, watchfulness, caution, heed, attention, care, wariness. **4** *a metal guard* SAFETY GUARD, safety device, protective device, shield, screen, fender; bumper, buffer.
– PHRASES **off (one's) guard** UNPREPARED, unready, inattentive, unwary, with one's defences down, cold, unsuspecting; *informal* napping, asleep at the wheel, on the hop. **on one's guard** VIGILANT, alert, on the alert, wary, watchful, cautious, careful, heedful, chary, circumspect, on the lookout, on the qui vive, on one's toes, prepared, ready, wideawake, attentive, observant, keeping one's eyes peeled; *informal* keeping a weather eye out.

guardian angel • noun a spirit believed to watch over and protect a person or place.

guardsman • noun **1** (in the UK) a soldier of a regiment of Guards. **2** (in the US) a member of the National Guard.

guard's van • noun Brit. a carriage or wagon occupied by the guard on a train.

guar gum /gwaar/ • noun a gum used in the food and paper industries, obtained from the seeds of an African and Asian bean plant.
– ORIGIN Hindi.

Guatemalan /gwaatəmaalən/ • noun a person from Guatemala in Central America. • adjective relating to Guatemala.

guava /gwaavə/ • noun a tropical American fruit with pink juicy flesh.
– ORIGIN probably from Taino (an extinct Caribbean language).

gubbins • plural noun Brit. informal **1** (treated as sing. or pl.) miscellaneous items; paraphernalia. **2** (treated as sing.) a gadget.
– ORIGIN originally in the sense 'fragments': from obsolete *gobbon* 'piece, slice, gob', from Old French.

g

gubernatorial /goobərnətoriəl/ • adjective relating to a governor, particularly of a US state.
– ORIGIN from Latin *gubernator* 'governor'.

guck • noun N. Amer. informal a slimy, dirty, or otherwise unpleasant substance.
– ORIGIN possibly a blend of GOO and MUCK.

gudgeon[1] /gujən/ • noun a small freshwater fish often used as bait by anglers.
– ORIGIN Old French *goujon*, from Latin *gobius* 'goby'.

gudgeon[2] /gujən/ • noun **1** a pivot or spindle on which something swings or rotates. **2** the tubular part of a hinge into which the pin fits. **3** a socket at the stern of a boat, into which the rudder is fitted. **4** a pin holding two blocks of stone together.
– ORIGIN Old French *goujon*, from *gouge* 'chisel'.

gudgeon pin • noun a pin holding a piston rod and a connecting rod together.

guelder rose /geldər/ • noun a shrub with flattened heads of fragrant creamy-white flowers followed by translucent red berries.
– ORIGIN from Dutch *geldersche roos* 'rose of *Gelderland*' (a province of the Netherlands).

Guelph /gwelf/ • noun **1** a member of one of two great factions in Italian medieval politics, traditionally supporting the Pope against the Holy Roman emperor and his supporters, the Ghibellines. **2** a member of a German princely family from which the British royal house is descended.
– ORIGIN Italian *Guelfo*, from High German *Welf*, the name of the founder of the Guelph political faction.

guerdon /gerd'n/ archaic • noun a reward or recompense. • verb give a reward to.
– ORIGIN Old French, related to Latin *donum* 'gift'.

Guernsey /gernzi/ • noun (pl. **Guernseys**) **1** a breed of dairy cattle from Guernsey in the Channel Islands, noted for producing rich, creamy milk. **2** (**guernsey**) a thick sweater made from oiled wool. **3** (**guernsey**) Austral. a football shirt.

guerrilla /gərillə/ (also **guerilla**) • noun a member of a small independent group fighting against the government or regular forces.
– ORIGIN Spanish, 'little war'.

guess • verb **1** estimate or suppose (something) without sufficient information to be sure of being correct. **2** correctly estimate or conjecture. **3** (**I guess**) informal, chiefly N. Amer. I suppose. • noun an estimate or conjecture.
– DERIVATIVES **guesser** noun.
– ORIGIN perhaps from Dutch *gissen*; probably related to GET.

guesstimate (also **guestimate**) informal • noun /gestimət/ an estimate based on a mixture of guesswork and calculation. • verb /gestimayt/ estimate in such a way.

guesswork • noun the process or results of guessing.

guest • noun **1** a person invited to visit someone's home or take part in a function. **2** a visiting performer invited to take part in an entertainment. **3** a person staying at a hotel or boarding house. • verb informal appear as a guest.
– PHRASES **be my guest** informal please do! **guest of honour** the most important guest at an occasion.
– ORIGIN Old Norse.

guest beer • noun Brit. a draught beer offered temporarily or in addition to those produced by the parent brewery.

guest house • noun a private house offering accommodation to paying guests.

guest worker • noun a person with temporary permission to work in another country.

guff • noun **1** informal trivial or worthless talk or ideas. **2** Scottish an unpleasant smell.
– ORIGIN imitative.

guffaw /gəfaw/ • noun a loud and boisterous laugh. • verb laugh in such a way.
– ORIGIN imitative.

GUI • abbreviation Computing graphical user interface.

guidance • noun **1** advice or information aimed at resolving a problem or difficulty. **2** the directing of the motion or position of something.

guide • noun **1** a person who advises or shows the way to others. **2** a directing principle or standard. **3** a book providing information on a subject. **4** a structure or marking which directs the motion or positioning of something. **5** (**Guide**) a member of the Guides Association, a girls' organization corresponding to the Scouts. • verb **1** show or indicate the way to. **2** direct the motion, positioning, or course of. **3** (**guided**) directed by remote control or internal equipment: *a guided missile.*
– ORIGIN Old French, related to WIT[2].

guidebook • noun a book of information about a place for vis-

Thesaurus

guarded • adjective CAUTIOUS, careful, circumspect, wary, chary, on one's guard, reluctant, non-committal, reticent, restrained, reserved; *informal* cagey.

guardian • noun PROTECTOR, defender, preserver, custodian, warden, guard, keeper; conservator, curator, caretaker, steward, trustee.
– RELATED TERMS tutelary.

guerrilla • noun FREEDOM FIGHTER, irregular, member of the resistance, partisan; rebel, radical, revolutionary, revolutionist; terrorist.

guess • verb **1** *he guessed she was about 40* ESTIMATE, hazard a guess, reckon, gauge, judge, calculate; hypothesize, postulate, predict, speculate, conjecture, surmise; *informal* guesstimate. **2** (*informal*) *I guess I owe you an apology* SUPPOSE, think, imagine, expect, suspect, dare say; *informal* reckon, figure.
• noun *my guess was right* HYPOTHESIS, theory, prediction, postulation, conjecture, surmise, estimate, belief, opinion, reckoning, judgement, supposition, speculation, suspicion, impression, feeling; *informal* guesstimate.

guesswork • noun GUESSING, conjecture, surmise, supposition, assumptions, presumptions, speculation, hypothesizing, theorizing, prediction; approximations, rough calculations; hunches; *informal* guesstimates.

guest • noun **1** *I have two guests coming to dinner* VISITOR, caller; company; *archaic* visitant. **2** *hotel guests* RESIDENT, boarder, lodger, paying guest, PG; patron, client; *N. Amer.* roomer.
– OPPOSITES host.

guest house • noun BOARDING HOUSE, bed and breakfast, B&B, hotel; pension, pensione.

guff • noun (*informal*). See NONSENSE sense 1.

guffaw • verb ROAR WITH LAUGHTER, laugh heartily/loudly, roar, bellow, cackle; *informal* laugh like a drain.

guidance • noun **1** *she looked to her father for guidance* ADVICE, counsel, direction, instruction, enlightenment, information; recommendations, suggestions, tips, hints, pointers, guidelines. **2** *work continued under the guidance of a project supervisor* DIRECTION, control, leadership, management, supervision, superintendence, charge; handling, conduct, running, overseeing.

guide • noun **1** *our guide took us back to the hotel* ESCORT, attendant, courier, cicerone, dragoman; usher; chaperone. **2** *he is my inspiration and my guide* ADVISER, mentor, counsellor; guru. **3** *the light acted as a guide for shipping* POINTER, marker, indicator, signpost, mark, landmark; guiding light, sign, signal, beacon. **4** *the techniques outlined are meant as a guide* MODEL, pattern, blueprint, template, example, exemplar; standard, touchstone, measure, benchmark, yardstick, gauge. **5** *a pocket guide of Paris* GUIDEBOOK, travelogue, vade mecum; companion, handbook, directory, A to Z; *informal* bible.
• verb **1** *he guided her to her seat* LEAD, lead the way, conduct, show, show someone the way, usher, shepherd, direct, steer, pilot, escort, accompany, attend; see, take, help, assist. **2** *the chairman must guide the meeting* DIRECT, steer, control, manage,

itors or tourists.

guide dog ● noun a dog that has been trained to lead a blind person.

guideline ● noun a general rule, principle, or piece of advice.

Guider ● noun an adult leader in the Guides Association.

guild ● noun **1** a medieval association of craftsmen or merchants. **2** an association of people for a common purpose.
– ORIGIN Old English, related to YIELD.

guilder /gildər/ ● noun (pl. same or **guilders**) **1** the basic monetary unit of the Netherlands, equal to 100 cents. **2** historical a gold or silver coin formerly used in the Netherlands, Germany, and Austria.
– ORIGIN Dutch, from *gulden* 'golden'.

guildhall ● noun **1** the meeting place of a guild or corporation. **2** Brit. a town hall. **3** (**the Guildhall**) the hall of the Corporation of the City of London.

guile /gīl/ ● noun sly or cunning intelligence.
– DERIVATIVES **guileful** adjective.
– ORIGIN Old French, related to WILE.

guileless ● adjective lacking guile; innocent and without deception.
– DERIVATIVES **guilelessly** adverb.

guillemot /gillimot/ ● noun an auk with a narrow pointed bill, typically nesting on cliff ledges.
– ORIGIN French, from *Guillaume* 'William'.

guillotine /gillәteen/ ● noun **1** a machine with a heavy blade sliding vertically in grooves, used for beheading people. **2** a device with a descending or sliding blade used for cutting paper or sheet metal. **3** Brit. (in parliament) a procedure used to limit discussion of a legislative bill by fixing times at which various parts of it must be voted on. ● verb **1** execute by guillotine. **2** Brit. (in parliament) apply a guillotine to (a bill or debate).
– ORIGIN named after the French physician Joseph-Ignace *Guillotin* (1738–1814), who recommended its use for executions in 1789.

guilt ● noun **1** the fact of having committed an offence or crime. **2** a feeling of having done something wrong or failed in an obligation.
– ORIGIN Old English.

guiltless ● adjective **1** having no guilt; innocent. **2** (**guiltless of**) lacking.
– DERIVATIVES **guiltlessly** adverb.

guilt trip ● noun informal a feeling of guilt, especially when self-indulgent or unjustified.

guilty ● adjective (**guiltier**, **guiltiest**) **1** (often **guilty of**) responsible for a specified wrongdoing, fault, or error. **2** having or showing a feeling of guilt.
– DERIVATIVES **guiltily** adverb **guiltiness** noun.

guinea /ginni/ ● noun Brit. **1** the sum of £1.05 (21 shillings in pre-decimal currency), used mainly for determining professional fees and auction prices. **2** a former British gold coin with a value of 21 shillings.
– ORIGIN named after *Guinea* in West Africa (the source of the gold from which the first guineas were minted).

guineafowl ● noun (pl. same) a large African game bird with slate-coloured, white-spotted plumage.

Guinean /ginniən/ ● noun a person from Guinea, a country on the west coast of Africa. ● adjective relating to Guinea.

guinea pig ● noun **1** a tailless South American cavy, domesticated as a pet or laboratory animal. **2** a person or thing used as a subject for experiment.

guipure /gipyoor/ ● noun heavy lace consisting of embroidered motifs held together by large connecting stitches.
– ORIGIN French, from *guiper* 'cover with silk'.

guise /gīz/ ● noun an external form, appearance, or manner of presentation.
– ORIGIN Old French, related to WISE².

guitar ● noun a stringed musical instrument with six (or occasionally twelve) strings, played by plucking or strumming with the fingers or a plectrum.
– DERIVATIVES **guitarist** noun.
– ORIGIN Spanish *guitarra*, from Greek *kithara*, denoting an instrument similar to the lyre.

Gujarati /gŏŏjəraati/ (also **Gujerati**) ● noun (pl. **Gujaratis**) **1** a person from the Indian state of Gujarat. **2** the language of the Gujaratis. ● adjective relating to the Gujaratis or their language.

Gulag /gōōlag/ ● noun (**the Gulag**) a system of harsh labour camps maintained in the Soviet Union 1930–1955.
– ORIGIN Russian, from *G(lavnoe) u(pravlenie ispravitel'no-trudovykh) lag(ereĭ)* 'Chief Administration for Corrective Labour Camps'.

gulch /gulch/ ● noun N. Amer. a narrow, steep-sided ravine.
– ORIGIN perhaps from dialect *gulch* 'to swallow'.

gulden ● noun (pl. same or **guldens**) another term for GUILDER.
– ORIGIN from Dutch and German, 'golden'.

gules /gyōōlz/ ● noun red, as a conventional heraldic colour.
– ORIGIN Old French *goles* 'throats', from Latin *gula*, used to denote pieces of red-dyed fur used as a neck ornament.

gulf ● noun **1** a deep inlet of the sea almost surrounded by land, with a narrow mouth. **2** a deep ravine, chasm, or abyss. **3** a substantial difference between two people, concepts, or situations.
– ORIGIN Italian *golfo*, from Greek *kolpos* 'bosom, gulf'.

Gulf War syndrome ● noun an unexplained medical condition affecting some veterans of the 1991 Gulf War, causing fatigue, chronic headaches, and skin and respiratory disorders.

gull¹ ● noun a long-winged seabird having white plumage with a grey or black back.
– ORIGIN Celtic.

gull² ● verb fool or deceive (someone). ● noun a person who is fooled or deceived.
– ORIGIN of unknown origin.

g

Thesaurus

command, lead, conduct, run, be in charge of, have control of, govern, preside over, superintend, supervise, oversee; handle, regulate. **3** *he was always there to guide me* ADVISE, counsel, give advice to, direct, give direction to.

guidebook ● noun GUIDE, travel guide, travelogue, vade mecum; companion, handbook, directory, A to Z; *informal* bible.

guideline ● noun RECOMMENDATION, instruction, direction, suggestion, advice; regulation, rule, principle, guiding principle; standard, criterion, measure, gauge, yardstick, benchmark, touchstone; procedure, parameter.

guild ● noun ASSOCIATION, society, union, league, organization, company, cooperative, fellowship, club, order, lodge, brotherhood, fraternity, sisterhood, sorority.

guile ● noun CUNNING, craftiness, craft, artfulness, art, artifice, wiliness, slyness, deviousness; wiles, ploys, schemes, stratagems, manoeuvres, subterfuges, tricks, ruses; deception, deceit, duplicity, underhandedness, double-dealing, trickery.
– OPPOSITES honesty.

guileless ● adjective ARTLESS, ingenuous, naive, open, genuine, natural, simple, childlike, innocent, unsophisticated, unworldly, unsuspicious, trustful, trusting; honest, truthful, sincere, straightforward.
– OPPOSITES scheming.

guilt ● noun **1** *the proof of his guilt* CULPABILITY, guiltiness, blameworthiness; wrongdoing, wrong, criminality, misconduct, sin. **2** *a terrible feeling of guilt* SELF-REPROACH, self-condemnation, shame, a guilty conscience, pangs of conscience; remorse, remorsefulness, regret, contrition, contriteness, compunction.
– OPPOSITES innocence.

guiltless ● adjective INNOCENT, blameless, not to blame, without fault, above reproach, above suspicion, in the clear, unimpeachable, irreproachable, faultless, sinless, spotless, immaculate, unsullied, uncorrupted, undefiled, untainted, unblemished, untarnished, impeccable; *informal* squeaky clean, whiter than white, as pure as the driven snow.
– OPPOSITES guilty.

guilty ● adjective **1** *the guilty party* CULPABLE, to blame, at fault, in the wrong, blameworthy, responsible; erring, errant, delinquent, offending, sinful, criminal; *archaic* peccant. **2** *I still feel guilty about it* ASHAMED, guilt-ridden, conscience-stricken, remorseful, sorry, contrite, repentant, penitent, regretful, rueful, abashed, shamefaced, sheepish, hangdog; in sackcloth and ashes.
– OPPOSITES innocent, unrepentant.

guise ● noun **1** *the god appeared in the guise of a swan* LIKENESS, outward appearance, appearance, semblance, form, shape, image; disguise. **2** *additional sums paid under the guise of consultancy fees* PRETENCE, disguise, front, facade, cover, blind, screen, smokescreen.

gulf ● noun **1** *our ship sailed into the gulf* INLET, bay, creek, bight, cove, fjord, estuary, sound, arm of the sea; *Scottish* firth, frith. **2** *the ice gave way and a gulf widened slowly* HOLE, crevasse, fissure, cleft, split, rift, pit, cavity, chasm, abyss, void; ravine,

Gullah /gullə/ ● noun **1** a member of a black people living on the coast of South Carolina and nearby islands. **2** the Creole language of this people, having an English base with West African elements.
– ORIGIN perhaps a shortening of *Angola*, or from *Gola*, a people of Liberia and Sierra Leone.
gullet ● noun the passage by which food passes from the mouth to the stomach; the oesophagus.
– ORIGIN Old French *goulet* 'little throat'.
gullible ● adjective easily persuaded to believe something; credulous.
– DERIVATIVES **gullibility** noun **gullibly** adverb.
– ORIGIN from GULL².
gull-wing ● noun (of a door on a car or aircraft) opening upwards.
gully ● noun (pl. **gullies**) **1** (also **gulley**) a water-worn ravine. **2** (also **gulley**) a gutter or drain. **3** Cricket a fielding position on the off side between point and the slips.
– ORIGIN originally in the sense 'gullet': from French *goulet* (see GULLET).

g

gulp ● verb **1** swallow (drink or food) quickly or in large mouthfuls. **2** swallow with difficulty in response to strong emotion.
● noun **1** an act of gulping. **2** a large mouthful of liquid hastily drunk.
– ORIGIN probably from Dutch *gulpen*, of imitative origin.
gum¹ ● noun **1** a thick sticky substance produced by some trees and shrubs. **2** glue used for sticking paper or other light materials together. **3** chewing gum or bubble gum. **4** a firm, jelly-like sweet. ● verb (**gummed**, **gumming**) **1** cover or fasten with gum or glue. **2** (**gum up**) clog up (a mechanism) and prevent it from working properly.
– ORIGIN Old French *gomme*, from Greek *kommi*, from Egyptian.
gum² ● noun the firm area of flesh around the roots of the teeth in the upper or lower jaw.
– ORIGIN Old English.
gum³ ● noun (in phrase **by gum!**) chiefly N. English an exclamation used for emphasis.
– ORIGIN euphemistic alteration of *God*.
gum arabic ● noun a gum produced by some kinds of acacia and used as glue and in incense.
gumbo ● noun (pl. **gumbos**) N. Amer. **1** okra, especially the gelatinous pods used in cooking. **2** (in Cajun cooking) a spicy chicken or seafood soup thickened with okra or rice.
– ORIGIN Angolan.
gumboil ● noun a small swelling formed on the gum over an abscess at the root of a tooth.
gumboot ● noun a long rubber boot; a wellington.
gumdrop ● noun a firm, jelly-like sweet.
gummy¹ ● adjective (**gummier**, **gummiest**) viscous; sticky.
– DERIVATIVES **gumminess** noun.
gummy² ● adjective (**gummier**, **gummiest**) toothless: *a gummy grin.*
– DERIVATIVES **gummily** adverb.
gumption /gumpsh'n/ ● noun informal shrewd initiative and resourcefulness.
– ORIGIN of unknown origin.
gum resin ● noun a plant secretion consisting of resin mixed with gum.
gumshield ● noun a pad or plate used by a sports player to protect the teeth and gums.
gumshoe ● noun N. Amer. informal a detective.
– ORIGIN from *gumshoes* in the sense 'sneakers', suggesting stealth.
gum tree ● noun a tree that produces gum, especially a eucalyptus.
– PHRASES **up a gum tree** Brit. informal in a predicament.
gun ● noun **1** a weapon incorporating a metal tube from which bullets or shells are propelled by explosive force. **2** a device for discharging something (e.g. grease) in a required direction. **3** N. Amer. a gunman: *a hired gun.* ● verb (**gunned**, **gunning**) **1** (**gun down**) shoot with a gun. **2** (**gun for**) aggressively pursue or act against. **3** informal cause (an engine) to race.
– PHRASES **go great guns** informal proceed forcefully or successfully. **jump the gun** informal act before the proper or appropriate time. **stick to one's guns** informal refuse to compromise or change.
– ORIGIN perhaps from a familiar form of the Scandinavian name *Gunnhildr*, from *gunnr* + *hildr*, both meaning 'war'.
gunboat ● noun a small ship armed with guns.
gunboat diplomacy ● noun foreign policy supported by the use or threat of military force.
gun carriage ● noun a wheeled support for a piece of artillery.
guncotton ● noun an explosive made by steeping cotton or wood pulp in a mixture of nitric and sulphuric acids.
gun dog ● noun a dog trained to retrieve game that has been shot.
gunge Brit. informal ● noun sticky, viscous, and unpleasantly messy material. ● verb (**gunged**, **gungeing**) (**gunge up**) clog or obstruct with gunge.
– DERIVATIVES **gungy** adjective.
– ORIGIN perhaps suggested by GOO and GUNK.
gung-ho /gunghō/ ● adjective unthinkingly enthusiastic and eager, especially about taking part in fighting or warfare.
– ORIGIN from a Chinese word taken to mean 'work together' and adopted as a slogan by US Marines.
gunk ● noun informal unpleasantly sticky or messy matter.
– ORIGIN the proprietary name of a US detergent.
gunman ● noun a man who uses a gun to commit a crime or terrorist act.
gunmetal ● noun **1** a grey corrosion-resistant form of bronze containing zinc. **2** a dull bluish-grey colour.
gunnel¹ /gunn'l/ ● noun an elongated marine fish with a dorsal fin running along most of the back.
– ORIGIN of unknown origin.
gunnel² ● noun variant spelling of GUNWALE.
gunner ● noun **1** a person who operates a gun. **2** a British artil-

Thesaurus

gorge, canyon, gully. **3** *a growing gulf between rich and poor* DIVIDE, division, separation, gap, breach, rift, split, chasm, abyss; difference, contrast, polarity.
gull ● verb HOODWINK, fool, dupe, deceive, delude, hoax, trick, mislead, lead on, take in, swindle, cheat, double-cross; *informal* pull the wool over someone's eyes, pull a fast one on, put one over on, sell a pup to, bamboozle, con, do; *N. Amer. informal* sucker, snooker; *Austral. informal* pull a swifty on; *poetic/literary* cozen.
gullet ● noun OESOPHAGUS, throat, maw, pharynx; crop, craw; *archaic* throttle, gorge.
gullible ● adjective CREDULOUS, naive, over-trusting, over-trustful, easily deceived, easily taken in, exploitable, dupable, impressionable, unsuspecting, unsuspicious, unwary, ingenuous, innocent, inexperienced, unworldly, green; *informal* wet behind the ears, born yesterday.
– OPPOSITES suspicious.
gully ● noun **1** *a steep icy gully* RAVINE, canyon, gorge, pass, defile, couloir; *S. English* chine; *N. English* clough, gill; *N. Amer.* gulch, coulee. **2** *water runs from the drainpipe into a gully* CHANNEL, conduit, trench, ditch, drain, culvert, cut, gutter.
gulp ● verb **1** *she gulped her juice* SWALLOW, quaff, swill down, down; *informal* swig, knock back. **2** *he gulped down the rest of his meal* GOBBLE, guzzle, devour, bolt, wolf, cram, stuff; *informal* put away, demolish, polish off, shovel down; *Brit. informal* scoff. **3** *Jenny gulped back her tears* CHOKE BACK, fight back, hold back/in, suppress, stifle, smother.
– OPPOSITES sip.
● noun *a gulp of cold beer* MOUTHFUL, swallow, draught; *informal* swig.
gum ● noun *photographs stuck down with gum* GLUE, adhesive, fixative, paste, epoxy resin; *N. Amer.* mucilage.
● verb *the receipts were gummed into a book* STICK, glue, paste; fix, affix, attach, fasten.
– PHRASES **gum something up** CLOG (UP), choke (up), stop up, plug; obstruct; *informal* bung up; *Brit. informal* gunge up; *technical* occlude.
gummy ● adjective STICKY, tacky, gluey, adhesive, resinous, viscous, viscid, glutinous, mucilaginous; *informal* gooey.
gumption ● noun *(informal)* INITIATIVE, resourcefulness, enterprise, ingenuity, imagination; astuteness, shrewdness, acumen, sense, common sense, wit, mother wit, native wit, practicality; spirit, backbone, pluck, mettle, nerve, courage; *informal* get-up-and-go, spunk, oomph, nous, savvy, horse sense; *N. Amer. informal* smarts.
gun ● noun FIREARM, pistol, revolver, rifle, shotgun, automatic, handgun, machine gun; weapon; *informal* shooter; *N. Amer. informal* piece, shooting iron.
gunfire ● noun GUNSHOTS, shots, shooting, firing, sniping; artillery fire, strafing, shelling.
gunman ● noun ARMED ROBBER, gangster, terrorist; sniper,

lery soldier (an official term for a private).

gunnery ● noun the design, manufacture, or firing of heavy guns.

gunplay ● noun chiefly N. Amer. the use of guns.

gunpoint ● noun (in phrase **at gunpoint**) while threatening or being threatened with a gun.

gunpowder ● noun **1** an explosive consisting of a powdered mixture of saltpetre, sulphur, and charcoal. **2** a fine green China tea, the leaves of which are rolled up into pellets.

gunrunner ● noun a person engaged in the illegal sale or importing of firearms.
– DERIVATIVES **gunrunning** noun.

gunsel /guns'l/ ● noun US informal **1** a criminal carrying a gun. **2** dated a homosexual youth.
– ORIGIN Yiddish, 'little goose'; influenced by GUN.

gunship ● noun a heavily armed helicopter.

gun-shy ● adjective (especially of a hunting dog) alarmed at the sound of a gun.

gunsight ● noun a device on a gun enabling it to be aimed accurately.

gunslinger ● noun informal a man who carries a gun.

gunsmith ● noun a person who makes and sells small firearms.

gunwale /gunn'l/ (also **gunnel**) ● noun the upper edge or planking of the side of a boat.
– PHRASES **to the gunwales** informal so as to be almost overflowing.
– ORIGIN from GUN + WALE (because it was formerly used to support guns).

gunyah /gunyə/ ● noun Austral. an Aboriginal bush hut.
– ORIGIN from an Aboriginal word.

guppy /guppi/ ● noun (pl. **guppies**) a small freshwater fish native to tropical America, widely kept in aquaria.
– ORIGIN named after the Trinidadian clergyman R. J. Lechmere *Guppy* (1836–1916), who sent the first specimen to the British Museum.

gurdwara /gurdwaarə/ ● noun a Sikh place of worship.
– ORIGIN from Sanskrit words meaning 'teacher' and 'door'.

gurgle ● verb make or move with a hollow bubbling sound. ● noun a gurgling sound.
– ORIGIN imitative, or from Latin *gurgulio* 'gullet'.

Gurkha /gurkə/ ● noun **1** a member of any of several Nepalese peoples noted for their military prowess. **2** a member of a regiment in the British army established for Nepalese recruits.
– ORIGIN a Nepalese place name.

gurn /gurn/ (also **girn**) ● verb Brit. pull a grotesque face.
– ORIGIN dialect variant of GRIN.

gurnard /gurnərd/ ● noun a small coastal fish with three finger-like pectoral rays with which it searches for food and walks on the seabed.
– ORIGIN Old French *gornart* 'grunter', from Latin *grundire*, *grunnire* 'to grunt'.

gurney ● noun (pl. **gurneys**) chiefly N. Amer. a wheeled stretcher for transporting hospital patients.
– ORIGIN apparently named after J. T. *Gurney* of Boston, Massachusetts, patentee of a new cab design in 1883.

guru /gōōrōō/ ● noun **1** a Hindu spiritual teacher. **2** each of the ten first leaders of the Sikh religion. **3** an influential teacher or popular expert: *a management guru*.
– ORIGIN from Sanskrit, 'weighty, grave'.

gush ● verb **1** send out or flow in a rapid and plentiful stream. **2** speak or write effusively. ● noun **1** a rapid and plentiful stream. **2** effusiveness.
– DERIVATIVES **gushing** adjective.
– ORIGIN probably imitative.

gusher ● noun **1** an oil well from which oil flows profusely without being pumped. **2** an effusive person.

gushy ● adjective (**gushier**, **gushiest**) excessively effusive.

gusset /gussit/ ● noun **1** a piece of material sewn into a garment to strengthen or enlarge a part of it, e.g. the crotch of an undergarment. **2** a bracket strengthening an angle of a structure.
– ORIGIN Old French *gousset* 'small pod or shell'.

gust ● noun **1** a brief, strong rush of wind. **2** a burst of rain, sound, emotion, etc. ● verb blow in gusts.
– DERIVATIVES **gusty** adjective.
– ORIGIN Old Norse.

gustation /gustaysh'n/ ● noun formal the action or faculty of tasting.
– DERIVATIVES **gustatory** /gustaytəri, gustətəri/ adjective.
– ORIGIN Latin, from *gustare* 'to taste'.

gusto ● noun enjoyment or vigour.
– ORIGIN Italian, from Latin *gustus* 'taste'.

gut ● noun **1** the stomach or belly. **2** Medicine & Biology the intestine. **3** (**guts**) entrails that have been removed or exposed. **4** (**guts**) the internal parts or essence of something. **5** (**guts**) informal courage and determination. **6** (before another noun) informal instinctive: *a gut feeling*. **7** fibre from the intestines of animals, used for violin or racket strings. ● verb (**gutted**, **gutting**) **1** take out the internal organs of (a fish or other animal) before cooking. **2** remove or destroy the internal parts of.
– PHRASES **bust a gut** informal make a strenuous effort. **hate someone's guts** informal dislike someone intensely. **have someone's guts for garters** informal, humorous used as a threat of punishment.
– ORIGIN Old English.

gutless ● adjective informal lacking courage or determination.
– DERIVATIVES **gutlessly** adverb **gutlessness** noun.

gutsy ● adjective (**gutsier**, **gutsiest**) informal **1** showing courage and determination. **2** strongly flavoured. **3** greedy.
– DERIVATIVES **gutsiness** noun.

g

Thesaurus

gunfighter; assassin, murderer, killer; *informal* hit man, hired gun, gunslinger, mobster; *N. Amer. informal* shootist, hood.

gurgle ● verb *the water swirled and gurgled* BABBLE, burble, tinkle, bubble, ripple, murmur, purl, splash; *poetic/literary* plash.
● noun *the gurgle of a small brook* BABBLING, tinkling, bubbling, rippling, trickling, murmur, murmuring, purling, splashing; *poetic/literary* plashing.

guru ● noun **1** *a Hindu guru and mystic* SPIRITUAL TEACHER, teacher, tutor, sage, mentor, spiritual leader, leader, master; *Hinduism* swami, Maharishi. **2** *a management guru* EXPERT, authority, pundit, leading light, master, specialist; *informal* whizz.
– OPPOSITES disciple.

gush ● verb **1** *water gushed through the weir* SURGE, burst, spout, spurt, jet, stream, rush, pour, spill, well out, cascade, flood; flow, run, issue; *Brit. informal* sloosh. **2** *everyone gushed about the script* ENTHUSE, rave, be enthusiastic, be effusive, rhapsodize, go into raptures, wax lyrical, praise to the skies; *informal* go mad/wild/crazy, go over the top; *N. Amer. informal* ballyhoo.
● noun *a gush of water* SURGE, stream, spurt, jet, spout, outpouring, outflow, burst, rush, cascade, flood, torrent; *technical* efflux.

gushing, gushy ● adjective EFFUSIVE, enthusiastic, over-enthusiastic, unrestrained, extravagant, fulsome, lavish, rhapsodic, lyrical; *informal* over the top, OTT, laid on with a trowel.
– OPPOSITES restrained.

gust ● noun **1** *a sudden gust of wind* FLURRY, blast, puff, blow, rush; squall. **2** *gusts of laughter* OUTBURST, burst, eruption, fit, paroxysm; gale, peal, howl, hoot, shriek, roar.
● verb *the wind gusted around the chimneys* BLOW, bluster, flurry, roar.

gusto ● noun ENTHUSIASM, relish, appetite, enjoyment, delight, glee, pleasure, satisfaction, appreciation, liking; zest, zeal, fervour, verve, keenness, avidity.
– OPPOSITES apathy, distaste.

gusty ● adjective BLUSTERY, windy, breezy; squally, stormy, tempestuous, wild, turbulent; *informal* blowy.
– OPPOSITES calm.

gut ● noun **1** *he had an ache in his gut* STOMACH, belly, abdomen, solar plexus; intestines, bowels; *informal* tummy, tum, insides, innards. **2** *fish heads and guts* ENTRAILS; intestines, viscera; offal; *informal* insides, innards; *Brit. archaic* numbles. **3** *(informal) Nicola had the guts to say what she felt* COURAGE, bravery, backbone, nerve, pluck, spirit, boldness, audacity, daring, grit, fearlessness, toughness, determination; *informal* spunk; *Brit. informal* bottle; *N. Amer. informal* moxie.
– RELATED TERMS visceral, enteric.
● adjective *(informal) a gut feeling* INSTINCTIVE, instinctual, intuitive, deep-seated; knee-jerk, automatic, involuntary, spontaneous, unthinking.
● verb **1** *clean, scale, and gut the sardines* REMOVE THE GUTS FROM, disembowel, draw; *formal* eviscerate. **2** *the church was gutted by fire* DEVASTATE, destroy, demolish, wipe out, lay waste, ravage, consume, ruin, wreck.

gutless ● adjective *(informal)*. See COWARDLY.

gutsy ● adjective *(informal)* BRAVE, courageous, plucky, bold, daring,

gutta-percha /guttəperchə/ ● **noun** the hard tough coagulated latex of certain Malaysian trees, resembling rubber.
– ORIGIN Malay.
gutted ● **adjective** Brit. informal bitterly disappointed or upset.
gutter ● **noun 1** a shallow trough beneath the edge of a roof, or a channel at the side of a street, for carrying off rainwater. **2** (**the gutter**) a very poor or squalid environment. **3** technical a groove or channel for flowing liquid. ● **verb 1** (of a flame) flicker and burn unsteadily. **2** archaic channel or furrow with streams, tears, etc.
– ORIGIN Old French *gotiere*, from Latin *gutta* 'a drop'.
guttering ● **noun** chiefly Brit. the gutters of a building.
gutter press ● **noun** chiefly Brit. newspapers engaging in sensational journalism.
guttersnipe ● **noun** a street urchin.
guttural /guttərəl/ ● **adjective 1** (of a speech sound) produced in the throat. **2** (of speech) characterized by guttural sounds. ● **noun** a guttural consonant (e.g. *k*, *g*).
– DERIVATIVES **gutturally** adverb.
– ORIGIN Latin *gutturalis*, from *guttur* 'throat'.
guv (also **guv'nor**) ● **noun** Brit. informal (as a form of address) sir.
guy[1] ● **noun 1** informal a man. **2** (**guys**) N. Amer. informal people of either sex. **3** Brit. a figure representing the Catholic conspirator Guy Fawkes, burnt on a bonfire on 5 November to commemorate a plot to blow up Parliament in 1605. ● **verb** ridicule.
guy[2] ● **noun** a rope or line fixed to the ground to secure a tent. ● **verb** secure with a guy or guys.
– ORIGIN probably Low German.
Guyanese /gīəneez/ ● **noun** (pl. same) a person from Guyana, a country on the NE coast of South America. ● **adjective** relating to Guyana.
Guy Fawkes Night ● **noun** another term for BONFIRE NIGHT.
guzzle ● **verb** eat or drink greedily.
– DERIVATIVES **guzzler** noun.
– ORIGIN perhaps from Old French *gosillier* 'chatter, vomit'.
Gy ● **abbreviation** Physics gray(s).
gybe /jīb/ (US **jibe**) Sailing ● **verb 1** change course by swinging the sail across a following wind. **2** (of a sail or boom) swing across the wind. ● **noun** an act of gybing.
– ORIGIN from obsolete Dutch *gijben*.
gym ● **noun** informal **1** a gymnasium. **2** gymnastics.
gymkhana /jimkaanə/ ● **noun** an event comprising competitions on horseback, typically for children.
– ORIGIN Urdu, 'racket court'.
gymnasium /jimnayziəm/ ● **noun** (pl. **gymnasiums** or **gymnasia** /jimnayziə/) a hall or building equipped for gymnastics and other physical exercise.
– ORIGIN Latin, from Greek *gumnasion*, from *gumnazein* 'exercise naked'.
gymnast ● **noun** a person trained in gymnastics.
gymnastics ● **plural noun** (also treated as sing.) **1** exercises involving physical agility, flexibility, and coordination, especially tumbling and acrobatic feats. **2** physical or mental agility or skill: *vocal gymnastics*.
– DERIVATIVES **gymnastic** adjective.
gymnosperm /jimnōsperm/ ● **noun** a plant of a large group that have seeds unprotected by an ovary or fruit, including conifers and cycads. Compare with ANGIOSPERM.
– ORIGIN from Greek *gumnos* 'naked'.
gymslip ● **noun** Brit. dated a sleeveless belted tunic reaching from the shoulder to the knee, worn by schoolgirls doing physical education.
gynaecology /gīnikolləji/ (US **gynecology**) ● **noun** the branch of physiology and medicine concerned with the functions and diseases specific to women and girls, especially those affecting the reproductive system.
– DERIVATIVES **gynaecological** adjective **gynaecologically** adverb **gynaecologist** noun.
– ORIGIN from Greek *gunē* 'woman, female'.
gynophobia /gīnəfōbiə/ ● **noun** extreme or irrational fear of women.
– DERIVATIVES **gynophobic** adjective.
gyp[1] /jip/ (also **gip**) ● **noun** Brit. informal pain or discomfort.
– ORIGIN perhaps from *gee-up* (see GEE[2]).
gyp[2] /jip/ informal ● **verb** (**gypped**, **gypping**) cheat or swindle. ● **noun** a swindle.
– ORIGIN of unknown origin.
gypsophila /jipsoffilə/ ● **noun** a garden plant with small pink or white flowers.
– ORIGIN Latin, from Greek *gupsos* 'chalk, gypsum' + *philos* 'loving'.
gypsum /jipsəm/ ● **noun** a soft white or grey mineral used to make plaster of Paris and in the building industry.
– ORIGIN Latin, from Greek *gupsos* 'chalk'.
gypsy (also **gipsy**) ● **noun** (pl. **gypsies**) a member of a travelling people with dark skin and hair, speaking the Romany language.
– DERIVATIVES **gypsyish** adjective.
– ORIGIN originally *gipcyan*, short for EGYPTIAN (because gypsies were believed to have come from Egypt).
gyrate ● **verb 1** move in a circle or spiral. **2** dance in a wild or suggestive manner.
– DERIVATIVES **gyration** noun **gyrator** noun.
– ORIGIN Latin *gyrare* 'revolve', from Greek *guros* 'a ring'.
gyratory /jīraytəri/ ● **adjective** involving circular or spiral motion. ● **noun** (pl. **gyratories**) a traffic system requiring the circular movement of traffic.
gyre /jīr/ ● **verb** literary whirl; gyrate. ● **noun** a spiral or vortex.
– ORIGIN Latin *gyrare*, from Greek *guros* 'a ring'.
gyrfalcon /jurfawlkən/ ● **noun** a large arctic falcon, with mainly grey or white plumage.
– ORIGIN probably related to High German *gēr* 'spear'.
gyro /jīrō/ ● **noun** (pl. **gyros**) a gyroscope or gyrocompass.
gyrocompass ● **noun** a compass in which the direction of true north is maintained by a gyroscope rather than magnetism.
– ORIGIN from Greek *guros* 'a ring'.
gyrocopter ● **noun** a small single-seater autogiro.
gyroscope ● **noun** a device, used to provide stability or maintain a fixed orientation, consisting of a wheel or disc spinning rapidly about an axis which is itself free to alter in direction.
– DERIVATIVES **gyroscopic** adjective.
gyve /jīv, gīv/ ● **noun** archaic a fetter or shackle.
– ORIGIN of unknown origin.

Thesaurus

fearless, adventurous, audacious, valiant, intrepid, heroic, lionhearted, undaunted, unflinching, unshrinking, unafraid, dauntless, indomitable, doughty, stout-hearted; spirited, determined, resolute, death-or-glory; *informal* spunky, ballsy, have-a-go.
gutter ● **noun** DRAIN, sluice, sluiceway, culvert, spillway, sewer; channel, conduit, pipe; trough, trench, ditch, furrow, cut.
guttersnipe ● **noun** URCHIN, ragamuffin, waif, stray; *dated* gamin; *archaic* mudlark, street Arab.
guttural ● **adjective** THROATY, husky, gruff, gravelly, growly, growling, croaky, croaking, harsh, rough, rasping, raspy; deep, low, thick.
guy ● **noun** *(informal) he's a handsome guy* MAN, fellow, gentleman; youth, boy; *informal* lad, fella, geezer, gent; *Brit. informal* chap, bloke; *N. Amer. informal* dude, hombre; *Brit. informal, dated* cove.
● **verb** *she guyed him about his weight* MAKE FUN OF, poke fun at, laugh at, mock, ridicule, jeer at, scoff at; satirize, lampoon; *informal* send up, take the mickey out of; *N. Amer. informal* goof on.
guzzle ● **verb 1** *he guzzled his burger* GOBBLE, bolt, wolf, devour; *informal* tuck into, put away, pack away, demolish, polish off, stuff one's face with, pig oneself on, shovel down; *Brit. informal* scoff, shift; *N. Amer. informal* snarf down/up, scarf down/up. **2** *she guzzled down the orange juice* GULP DOWN, swallow, quaff, down, swill; *informal* knock back, swig, slug down.
gypsy, gipsy ● **noun** ROMANY, Rom, chal, gitano, gitana, tzigane; traveller, nomad, rover, roamer, wanderer; *dialect* didicoi; *Brit. derogatory* tinker.
gyrate ● **verb** ROTATE, revolve, wheel, turn round, whirl, circle, pirouette, twirl, swirl, spin, swivel.

Hh

H[1] (also **h**) ● noun (pl. **Hs** or **H's**) **1** the eighth letter of the alphabet. **2** denoting the next after G in a set.
H[2] ● abbreviation **1** (of a pencil lead) hard. **2** height. **3** Physics henry(s). ● symbol the chemical element hydrogen.
h ● abbreviation **1** (in measuring the height of horses) hand(s). **2** hour(s). **3** Brit. (with reference to sporting fixtures) home.
ha ● abbreviation hectare(s).
habdabs ● plural noun variant spelling of ABDABS.
habeas corpus /haybiəss **kor**pəss/ ● noun Law a writ requiring a person to be brought before a judge or into court, especially to investigate the lawfulness of their detention.
– ORIGIN Latin, 'you shall have the body (in court)'.
haberdasher /**hab**bərdashər/ ● noun **1** Brit. a dealer in dressmaking and sewing goods. **2** N. Amer. a dealer in men's clothing.
– DERIVATIVES **haberdashery** noun.
– ORIGIN probably from Old French *hapertas*, perhaps the name of a fabric.
habergeon /**hab**bərjən/ ● noun historical a sleeveless coat of mail or scale armour.
– ORIGIN Old French *haubergeon*, from *hauberc* 'hauberk'.
habiliment /hə**bil**limənt/ ● noun archaic clothing.
– ORIGIN Old French *habillement*, from Latin *habilis* 'able'.
habit ● noun **1** a settled or regular tendency or practice. **2** informal an addiction to drugs. **3** general shape or mode of growth, especially of a plant or mineral. **4** a long, loose garment worn by a member of a religious order. ● verb archaic dress.
– ORIGIN Latin *habitus* 'condition, appearance', from *habere* 'have, consist of'.
habitable ● adjective suitable to live in.
– DERIVATIVES **habitability** noun.
– ORIGIN Latin *habitabilis*, from *habitare* 'possess, inhabit'.
habitant ● noun **1** /abbi**ton**/ an early French settler in Canada or Louisiana. **2** /**hab**bit'nt/ archaic an inhabitant.
habitat ● noun the natural home or environment of an organism.
– ORIGIN Latin, 'it inhabits'.
habitation ● noun **1** the state or process of inhabiting. **2** formal a house or home.
habit-forming ● adjective (of a drug) addictive.
habitual /hə**bit**yooəl/ ● adjective **1** done constantly or as a habit. **2** regular; usual.
– DERIVATIVES **habitually** adverb.
habituate ● verb chiefly Zoology make or become accustomed to something.
– DERIVATIVES **habituation** noun.
habitué /hə**bit**yooay/ ● noun a resident of or frequent visitor to a place.
– ORIGIN French, 'accustomed'.
haboob /hə**boob**/ ● noun (especially in Sudan) a violent and oppressive summer wind bringing sand from the desert.
– ORIGIN from Arabic, 'blowing furiously'.
háček /**ha**check/ ● noun a diacritic mark (ˇ) placed over a letter to modify the sound in Slavic and other languages.
– ORIGIN Czech, 'little hook'.
hachures /ha**shyoorz**/ ● plural noun parallel lines used on maps to shade in hills, their closeness indicating steepness of gradient.
– DERIVATIVES **hachured** adjective.
– ORIGIN French, from *hacher* (see HATCH[3]).
hacienda /hassi**en**də/ ● noun (in Spanish-speaking countries) a large estate with a house.
– ORIGIN Spanish, from Latin *facienda* 'things to be done'.
hack[1] ● verb **1** cut with rough or heavy blows. **2** kick wildly or roughly. **3** use a computer to gain unauthorized access to data. **4** (**hack it**) informal manage; cope. **5** (**hack off**) informal annoy. ● noun **1** a rough cut or blow. **2** a tool for rough striking or cutting.
– DERIVATIVES **hacker** noun.
– ORIGIN Old English.
hack[2] ● noun **1** a writer producing dull, unoriginal work. **2** a horse for ordinary riding, or one that is inferior or let out for hire. **3** a ride on a horse. **4** N. Amer. a taxi. ● verb ride a horse.
– DERIVATIVES **hackery** noun.
– ORIGIN abbreviation of HACKNEY.
hacking cough ● noun a dry, frequent cough.
hacking jacket ● noun a riding jacket with slits at the side or back.
hackle ● noun **1** (**hackles**) hairs along an animal's back which rise when it is angry or alarmed. **2** a long, narrow feather on the neck or saddle of a domestic cock or other bird. **3** a steel comb for dressing flax.
– PHRASES **make someone's hackles rise** make someone angry

Thesaurus

habit ● noun **1** *it was his habit to go for a run every morning* CUSTOM, practice, routine, wont, pattern, convention, way, norm, tradition, matter of course, rule, usage. **2** *her many irritating habits* MANNERISM, way, quirk, foible, trick, trait, idiosyncrasy, peculiarity, singularity, oddity, eccentricity, feature; tendency, propensity, inclination, bent, proclivity, disposition, predisposition. **3** *a scientific habit of mind* DISPOSITION, temperament, character, nature, make-up, constitution, frame of mind, bent. **4** *(informal) his cocaine habit* ADDICTION, dependence, dependency, craving, fixation, compulsion, obsession, weakness; *informal* monkey on one's back; *N. Amer. informal* jones. **5** *a monk's habit* GARMENTS, dress, garb, clothes, clothing, attire, outfit, costume; *informal* gear; *formal* apparel.
– PHRASES **in the habit of** ACCUSTOMED TO, used to, given to, wont to, inclined to.
habitable ● adjective FIT TO LIVE IN, inhabitable, fit to occupy, in good repair, liveable-in; *formal* tenantable.
habitat ● noun NATURAL ENVIRONMENT, natural surroundings, home, domain, haunt; *formal* habitation.
habitation ● noun **1** *a house fit for human habitation* OCCUPANCY, occupation, residence, residency, living in, tenancy; *archaic* inhabitancy. **2** *(formal) his main habitation* RESIDENCE, place of residence, house, home, seat, lodging place, billet, quarters, living quarters, rooms, accommodation; *informal* pad, digs; *formal* dwelling, dwelling place, abode, domicile.
habitual ● adjective **1** *her father's habitual complaints* CONSTANT, persistent, continual, continuous, perpetual, non-stop, recurrent, repeated, frequent; interminable, incessant, ceaseless, endless, never-ending; *informal* eternal. **2** *habitual drinkers* INVETERATE, confirmed, compulsive, obsessive, incorrigible, hardened, ingrained, dyed-in-the-wool, chronic, regular; addicted; *informal* pathological. **3** *his habitual secretiveness* CUSTOMARY, accustomed, regular, usual, normal, set, fixed, established, routine, common, ordinary, familiar, traditional, typical, general, characteristic, standard, time-honoured; *poetic/literary* wonted.
– OPPOSITES occasional, unaccustomed.
habituate ● verb ACCUSTOM, make used, familiarize, adapt, adjust, attune, acclimatize, acculturate, condition; inure, harden; *N. Amer.* acclimate.
habitué ● noun FREQUENT VISITOR, regular visitor/customer/client, familiar face, regular, patron, frequenter, haunter.
hack[1] ● verb *I hacked the padlock off* CUT, chop, hew, lop, saw; slash.
– PHRASES **hack it** *(informal)* COPE, manage, get on/by, carry on, muddle along/through, come through; stand it, tolerate it, bear it, endure it, put up with it; *informal* handle it, abide it, stick it; *Brit. informal* be doing with it. **hack someone off** *(informal)*. See ANNOY.
hack[2] ● noun **1** *a tabloid hack* JOURNALIST, reporter, newspaperman, newspaperwoman, writer, Grub Street writer; *informal* journo, scribbler, hackette; *archaic* penny-a-liner. **2** *office hacks*

or indignant.

– ORIGIN variant of obsolete *hatchel*, from Germanic.

hackney ● noun (pl. **hackneys**) chiefly historical **1** a light horse with a high-stepping trot, used in harness. **2** a horse-drawn vehicle kept for hire.

– ORIGIN probably from *Hackney* in East London, where horses were pastured.

hackney carriage ● noun Brit. the official term for a taxi.

hackneyed ● adjective (of a phrase or idea) unoriginal and trite.

– ORIGIN from the obsolete verb *hackney* 'use a horse for general purposes', later 'make commonplace by overuse'.

hacksaw ● noun a saw with a narrow blade set in a frame, used for cutting metal.

had past and past participle of HAVE.

haddock ● noun (pl. same) a silvery-grey fish of North Atlantic coastal waters, popular as a food fish.

– ORIGIN Old French *hadoc*.

Hades /haydeez/ ● noun **1** Greek Mythology the underworld; the abode of the spirits of the dead. **2** informal hell.

– ORIGIN Greek *Haidēs*, a name of Pluto, the god of the dead.

Hadith /hadeeth/ ● noun (pl. same or **Hadiths**) a collection of Islamic traditions containing sayings of the prophet Muhammad.

– ORIGIN Arabic, 'tradition'.

h

hadn't ● contraction had not.

hadron /hadron/ ● noun Physics a subatomic particle that can take part in the strong interaction, such as a baryon or meson.

– ORIGIN from Greek *hadros* 'bulky'.

hadst archaic second person singular past of HAVE.

haemal /heem'l/ (US **hemal**) ● adjective **1** Physiology relating to the blood. **2** Zoology situated on the same side of the body as the heart and major blood vessels.

– ORIGIN from Greek *haima* 'blood'.

haematite /heemətīt/ (US **hematite**) ● noun a reddish-black mineral consisting of ferric oxide.

– ORIGIN from Greek *haimatitēs lithos* 'blood-like stone'.

haematology /heemətolləji/ (US **hematology**) ● noun the study of the physiology of the blood.

– DERIVATIVES **haematological** adjective **haematologist** noun.

haematoma /heemətōmə/ (US **hematoma**) ● noun (pl. **haematomas** or **haematomata** /heemətōmətə/) Medicine a solid swelling of clotted blood within the tissues.

haemoglobin /heeməglōbin/ (US **hemoglobin**) ● noun a red protein containing iron, responsible for transporting oxygen in the blood of vertebrates.

– ORIGIN a contracted form of *haematoglobulin*, in the same sense.

haemophilia /heeməfilliə/ (US **hemophilia**) ● noun a medical condition in which the ability of the blood to clot is severely reduced, causing severe bleeding from even a slight injury.

– DERIVATIVES **haemophilic** adjective.

haemophiliac (US **hemophiliac**) ● noun a person suffering from haemophilia.

haemorrhage /hemmərij/ (US **hemorrhage**) ● noun **1** an escape of blood from a ruptured blood vessel. **2** a damaging loss of something valuable. ● verb **1** suffer a haemorrhage. **2** expend in large amounts, seemingly uncontrollably: *the business was haemorrhaging cash.*

– ORIGIN Greek *haimorrhagia*, from *haima* 'blood' + *rhēgnunai* 'burst'.

haemorrhoid /hemməroydz/ (US **hemorrhoid**) ● noun a swollen vein or group of veins (piles) in the region of the anus.

– ORIGIN from Greek *haimorrhoides phlebes* 'bleeding veins'.

haemostasis /heemōstaysiss/ (US **hemostasis**) ● noun Medicine the stopping of a flow of blood.

– DERIVATIVES **haemostatic** adjective.

haere mai /hīrə mī/ ● exclamation a Maori greeting.

– ORIGIN Maori, 'come hither'.

hafiz /haafeez/ ● noun a Muslim who knows the Koran by heart.

– ORIGIN Arabic, 'guardian'.

hafnium /hafniəm/ ● noun a hard silver-grey metal resembling zirconium.

– ORIGIN from *Hafnia*, the Latin form of *Havn*, a former name of Copenhagen.

haft /haaft/ ● noun the handle of a knife, axe, or spear. ● verb provide with a haft.

– ORIGIN Old English, related to HEAVE.

hag[1] ● noun **1** an ugly old woman. **2** a witch.

– DERIVATIVES **haggish** adjective.

– ORIGIN perhaps from Old English.

hag[2] ● noun Scottish & N. English a soft place on a moor or a firm place in a bog.

– ORIGIN Old Norse, 'gap'.

hagfish ● noun a primitive jawless marine fish with a slimy eel-like body and a rasping tongue used for feeding on dead or dying fish.

haggard ● adjective **1** looking exhausted and unwell. **2** (of a hawk) caught and trained as an adult.

– ORIGIN French *hagard*, perhaps related to HEDGE.

haggis ● noun (pl. same) a Scottish dish consisting of seasoned sheep's or calf's offal mixed with suet and oatmeal, boiled in a bag traditionally made from the animal's stomach.

– ORIGIN probably from earlier *hag* 'hack, hew', from Old Norse.

haggle ● verb dispute or bargain persistently, especially over a price. ● noun a period of haggling.

– DERIVATIVES **haggler** noun.

– ORIGIN originally in the sense 'hack, mangle': from Old Norse.

hagiographer /haggiogrəfər/ ● noun **1** a writer of the lives of the saints. **2** a writer of a biography that idealizes its subject.

– ORIGIN from Greek *hagios* 'holy'.

hagiography /haggiogrəfi/ ● noun **1** the writing of the lives of saints. **2** a biography idealizing its subject.

– DERIVATIVES **hagiographic** adjective **hagiographical** adjective.

hagiolatry /haggiollətri/ ● noun the worship of saints.

hagiology /haggiolləji/ ● noun literature concerned with the lives and legends of saints.

– DERIVATIVES **hagiological** adjective **hagiologist** noun.

hag-ridden ● adjective afflicted by nightmares or anxieties.

ha-ha ● noun a ditch with a wall on its inner side below ground level, forming a boundary to a park or garden without interrupting the view.

– ORIGIN said to be from the cry of surprise uttered on encountering such an obstacle.

haiku /hīkoo/ ● noun (pl. same or **haikus**) a Japanese poem of seventeen syllables, in three lines of five, seven, and five.

– ORIGIN Japanese, contraction of a phrase meaning 'light verse'.

hail[1] ● noun **1** pellets of frozen rain falling in showers from cumulonimbus clouds. **2** a large number of things hurled forcefully through the air. ● verb (**it hails, it is hailing**, etc.) hail falls.

– ORIGIN Old English.

hail[2] ● verb **1** call out to (someone) to attract attention. **2** acclaim enthusiastically: *he has been hailed as the new James Dean.* **3** (**hail from**) have one's home or origins in. ● exclamation archaic expressing greeting or acclaim.

– PHRASES **within hail** within earshot.

Thesaurus

DRUDGE, menial, menial worker, factotum; *informal* dogsbody, gofer; *Brit. informal* skivvy. **3** *a riding-school hack* HORSE, pony; *informal* nag; *N. Amer. informal* plug; *Austral./NZ informal* moke.

hackles ● plural noun

– PHRASES **make someone's hackles rise** ANNOY, irritate, exasperate, anger, incense, infuriate, irk, nettle, vex, put out, provoke, gall, antagonize, get on someone's nerves, ruffle someone's feathers, rankle with; *Brit.* rub up the wrong way; *informal* aggravate, peeve, needle, rile, make someone see red, make someone's blood boil, hack off, get someone's back up, get someone's goat, get up someone's nose, get someone's dander up, bug, miff; *Brit. informal* wind up, nark, get on someone's wick; *N. Amer. informal* tee off, tick off, burn up; *informal, dated* give someone the pip.

hackneyed ● adjective OVERUSED, overworked, overdone, worn out, time-worn, platitudinous, vapid, stale, tired, threadbare; trite, banal, hack, clichéd, hoary, commonplace, common, ordinary, stock, conventional, stereotyped, predictable; unimaginative, unoriginal, uninspired, prosaic, dull, boring, pedestrian, run-of-the-mill, routine; *informal* old hat, corny, played out.

– OPPOSITES original.

Hades ● noun. See HELL sense 1.

haft ● noun HANDLE, shaft, hilt, butt, stock, grip, handgrip, helve, shank.

hag ● noun CRONE, old woman, gorgon; *informal* witch, crow, cow, old bag, old boot; *archaic* beldam.

haggard ● adjective DRAWN, tired, exhausted, drained, careworn, unwell, unhealthy, spent, washed out, rundown; gaunt, pinched, peaked, peaky, hollow-cheeked, hollow-eyed, thin, emaciated, wasted, cadaverous; pale, wan, grey, ashen.

– OPPOSITES healthy.

– ORIGIN from obsolete *hail* 'healthy', related to HALE[1] and WHOLE.

hail-fellow-well-met ● adjective showing excessive familiarity.

Hail Mary ● noun (pl. **Hail Marys**) a prayer to the Virgin Mary used chiefly by Roman Catholics.

hailstone ● noun a pellet of hail.

hair ● noun **1** any of the fine thread-like strands growing from the skin of mammals and other animals, or from the epidermis of a plant. **2** strands of hair collectively, especially on a person's head. **3** a very small quantity or extent.

– PHRASES **hair of the dog** informal an alcoholic drink taken to cure a hangover. [ORIGIN from *hair of the dog that bit you*, formerly recommended as a remedy for the bite of a mad dog.] **a hair's breadth** a very small margin. **in** (or **out of**) **someone's hair** informal burdening (or ceasing to burden) someone. **keep your hair on!** Brit. informal stay calm. **let one's hair down** informal behave wildly or uninhibitedly. **make someone's hair stand on end** alarm someone. **not turn a hair** remain apparently unmoved. **split hairs** make overfine distinctions.

– DERIVATIVES **haired** adjective **hairless** adjective.

– ORIGIN Old English.

hairball ● noun a ball of hair which collects in the stomach of an animal as a result of the animal licking its coat.

hairband ● noun a band for securing or tying back one's hair.

hairbrush ● noun a brush for smoothing one's hair.

haircut ● noun **1** the style in which someone's hair is cut. **2** an act of cutting someone's hair.

hairdo ● noun (pl. **hairdos**) informal the style of a person's hair.

hairdresser ● noun a person who cuts and styles hair.

– DERIVATIVES **hairdressing** noun.

hairdryer (also **hairdrier**) ● noun an electrical device for drying the hair with warm air.

hairgrip ● noun Brit. a flat hairpin with the ends close together.

hairline ● noun **1** the edge of a person's hair. **2** (before another noun) very thin or fine: *a hairline fracture.*

hairnet ● noun a fine mesh for confining the hair.

hairpiece ● noun a patch or bunch of false hair used to augment a person's natural hair.

hairpin ● noun a U-shaped pin for fastening the hair.

hairpin bend ● noun Brit. a sharp U-shaped bend in a road.

hair-raising ● adjective extremely alarming, astonishing, or frightening.

hair shirt ● noun a shirt made of stiff cloth woven from horsehair, formerly worn by penitents and ascetics.

hairslide ● noun Brit. a clip for keeping a woman's hair in position.

hair-splitting ● noun the making of overfine distinctions.

hairspray ● noun a solution sprayed on to hair to keep it in place.

hairspring ● noun a slender flat coiled spring regulating the movement of the balance wheel in a watch.

hairstyle ● noun a way in which someone's hair is cut or arranged.

– DERIVATIVES **hairstyling** noun **hairstylist** noun.

hair trigger ● noun a firearm trigger set for release at the slightest pressure.

hairy ● adjective (**hairier**, **hairiest**) **1** covered with or resembling hair. **2** informal alarming and difficult.

– DERIVATIVES **hairiness** noun.

Haitian /haysh'n/ ● noun a person from Haiti. ● adjective relating to Haiti.

haji /haji/ (also **hajji**) ● noun (pl. **hajis**) a Muslim who has been to Mecca as a pilgrim.

– ORIGIN Arabic.

hajj /haj/ (also **haj**) ● noun the pilgrimage to Mecca which all Muslims are expected to make at least once.

– ORIGIN Arabic, 'pilgrimage'.

haka /haakə/ ● noun a ceremonial Maori war dance involving chanting.

– ORIGIN Maori.

hake ● noun a large-headed elongated food fish with long jaws and strong teeth.

– ORIGIN perhaps from Old English, 'hook'.

halal /həlaal/ ● adjective (of meat) prepared as prescribed by Muslim law.

– ORIGIN Arabic, 'according to religious law'.

halala /həlaalə/ ● noun (pl. same or **halalas**) a monetary unit of Saudi Arabia, equal to one hundredth of a rial.

– ORIGIN Arabic.

halberd /halbərd/ (also **halbert**) ● noun historical a combined spear and battleaxe.

– ORIGIN High German *helmbarde*, from *helm* 'handle' + *barde* 'hatchet'.

halberdier /halbərdeer/ ● noun historical a man armed with a halberd.

halcyon /halsiən/ ● adjective (of a past time) idyllically happy and peaceful: *halcyon days.*

– ORIGIN originally denoting a mythical bird (usually identified with a species of kingfisher) said to breed in a nest floating at sea, charming the wind and waves into calm: from Greek *alkuōn* 'kingfisher'.

hale[1] ● adjective (of an old person) strong and healthy.

– ORIGIN Old English, 'whole'.

hale[2] ● verb archaic haul.

– ORIGIN Old French *haler*.

Thesaurus

haggle ● verb BARTER, bargain, negotiate, dicker, quibble, wrangle; beat someone down, drive a hard bargain; *archaic* chaffer.

hail[1] ● verb **1** *a friend hailed him from the upper deck* CALL OUT TO, shout to, halloo, address; greet, say hello to, salute. **2** *he hailed a cab* FLAG DOWN, wave down, signal to. **3** *critics hailed the film as a masterpiece* ACCLAIM, praise, applaud, rave about, extol, eulogize, hymn, lionize, sing the praises of, make much of, glorify, cheer, salute, toast; *N. Amer. informal* ballyhoo; *black English* big up; *formal* laud. **4** *Rick hails from Australia* COME FROM, be from, be a native of, have one's roots in.

hail[2] ● noun *a hail of bullets* BARRAGE, volley, shower, rain, torrent, burst, stream, storm, avalanche, onslaught; bombardment, cannonade, battery, blast, salvo; *historical* broadside.

● verb *tons of dust hailed down on us* BEAT, shower, rain, fall, pour; pelt, pepper, batter, bombard, assail.

hail-fellow-well-met ● adjective CONVIVIAL, sociable, outgoing, gregarious, companionable, friendly, genial, affable, amiable, congenial, agreeable, good-humoured; extrovert, uninhibited; *Scottish* couthy; *informal* backslapping, chummy, pally, clubbable, clubby, buddy-buddy; *Brit. informal* matey.

– OPPOSITES unsociable.

hair ● noun **1** *her thick black hair* HEAD OF HAIR, shock of hair, mane, mop; locks, tresses, curls, ringlets. **2** *I like your hair* HAIRSTYLE, haircut, cut, coiffure; *informal* hairdo, do, coif. **3** *a dog with short, blue-grey hair* FUR, wool; coat, fleece, pelt; mane.

– RELATED TERMS tricho-.

– PHRASES **a hair's breadth** THE NARROWEST OF MARGINS, a narrow margin, the skin of one's teeth, a split second, a nose; *informal* a whisker. **let one's hair down** *(informal)* ENJOY ONESELF, have a good time, have fun, make merry, let oneself go; *informal* have a ball, whoop it up, paint the town red, live it up, have a whale of a time, let it all hang out. **make someone's hair stand on end** HORRIFY, shock, appal, scandalize, stun; make someone's blood run cold; *informal* make someone's hair curl. **split hairs** QUIBBLE, cavil, carp, niggle, chop logic; *informal* nit-pick; *archaic* pettifog.

hairdo ● noun *(informal).* See HAIRSTYLE.

hairdresser ● noun HAIRSTYLIST, stylist, coiffeur, coiffeuse; barber; *informal* crimper.

hairless ● adjective BALD, bald-headed; shaven, shaved, shorn, clean-shaven, beardless, smooth, smooth-faced, depilated; tonsured; *informal* baldy; *technical* glabrous; *archaic* bald-pated.

– OPPOSITES hairy.

hairpiece ● noun WIG, toupee, periwig; merkin; *informal* rug.

hair-raising ● adjective TERRIFYING, frightening, petrifying, alarming, chilling, horrifying, shocking, spine-chilling, blood-curdling, fearsome, nightmarish; eerie, sinister, weird, ghostly, unearthly; *Scottish* eldritch; *informal* hairy, spooky, scary, creepy.

hair-splitting ● adjective PEDANTIC, pettifogging; quibbling, niggling, cavilling, carping, critical, overcritical, hypercritical; *informal* nit-picking, pernickety, picky; *N. Amer. informal* persnickety.

hairstyle ● noun HAIRCUT, cut, style, hair, coiffure; *informal* hairdo, do, coif.

hairy ● adjective **1** *animals with hairy coats* SHAGGY, bushy, long-haired; woolly, furry, fleecy, fuzzy; *Botany & Zoology* pilose. **2** *his hairy face* BEARDED, bewhiskered, moustachioed; unshaven, stubbly, bristly; hirsute. **3** *(informal) a hairy situation* RISKY, dangerous, perilous, hazardous, touch-and-go; tricky, ticklish, difficult, awkward; *informal* dicey, sticky; *Brit. informal* dodgy.

– OPPOSITES hairless, short-haired.

halcyon ● adjective HAPPY, golden, idyllic, palmy, carefree, blissful,

haler /haaləR/ ● noun (pl. same or **haleru** /haaləroo/) a monetary unit of the Czech Republic and Slovakia, equal to one hundredth of a koruna.
– ORIGIN Czech *haléř*, from *Schwäbisch Hall*, a German town where coins were minted.

half ● noun (pl. **halves**) **1** either of two equal or corresponding parts into which something is or can be divided. **2** either of two equal periods into which a match or performance is divided. **3** Brit. informal half a pint of beer. **4** informal a half-price fare or ticket. **5** a halfback. ● predeterminer & pronoun an amount equal to a half. ● adjective forming a half. ● adverb **1** to the extent of half. **2** partly: *half-cooked.*
– PHRASES **at half mast 1** (of a flag) flown halfway down its mast, as a mark of respect for a person who has died. **2** humorous (of clothing) in a lower position than normal. **half a chance** informal the slightest opportunity. **half past one (two,** etc.) thirty minutes after one (two, etc.) o'clock. **not do things by halves** do things thoroughly or extravagantly. **not half 1** not nearly. **2** informal not at all. **3** Brit. informal to an extreme degree. **too —— by half** excessively ——.
– ORIGIN Old English.

half-and-half ● adverb & adjective in equal parts.

half-arsed ● adjective vulgar slang incompetent or inadequate.

halfback ● noun a player in a ball game whose position is between the forwards and fullbacks.

half-baked ● adjective incompetently planned or considered.

half binding ● noun a type of bookbinding in which the spine and corners are bound in a different material to the rest of the cover.

half blood ● noun **1** the relationship between people having one parent in common. **2** a person related to another in this way. **3** offensive a half-breed.

half board ● noun Brit. provision of bed, breakfast, and a main meal at a hotel or guest house.

half-breed ● noun offensive a person of mixed race.

half-brother (or **half-sister**) ● noun a brother (or sister) with whom one has only one parent in common.

half-caste ● noun offensive a person of mixed race.

half-century ● noun **1** a period of fifty years. **2** a score of fifty in cricket.

half-cock ● noun the partly raised position of the cock of a gun.
– PHRASES **at half-cock 1** (of a gun) with the cock partly raised. **2** when only partly ready.
– DERIVATIVES **half-cocked** adjective.

half-crown (also **half a crown**) ● noun a former British coin and monetary unit equal to two shillings and sixpence (12½p).

half-cut ● adjective Brit. informal drunk.

half-dozen (also **half a dozen**) ● noun a group of six.

half-hardy ● adjective (of a plant) able to grow outdoors except in severe frost.

half-hearted ● adjective without enthusiasm or energy.
– DERIVATIVES **half-heartedly** adverb **half-heartedness** noun.

half hitch ● noun a knot formed by passing the end of a rope round its standing part and then through the loop.

half holiday ● noun a half day taken as a holiday, especially at school.

half-hour ● noun **1** (also **half an hour**) a period of thirty minutes. **2** a point in time thirty minutes after a full hour of the clock.
– DERIVATIVES **half-hourly** adjective & adverb.

half-hunter ● noun a pocket watch with a small opening in the cover allowing one to read the approximate time.

half-inch ● verb Brit. informal steal.
– ORIGIN rhyming slang for 'pinch'.

half landing ● noun Brit. a landing where a flight of stairs turns through 180 degrees.

half-life ● noun the time taken for something to decrease by half, in particular the radioactivity of an isotope.

half-light ● noun dim light, as at dusk.

half measure ● noun an inadequate action or policy.

half-moon ● noun **1** the moon when only half its surface is visible from the earth. **2** a semicircular or crescent-shaped object.

half nelson ● noun see NELSON.

half note ● noun Music, chiefly N. Amer. a minim.

halfpenny /haypni/ (also **ha'penny**) ● noun (pl. **halfpennies** (for separate coins); **halfpence** (for a sum of money) /hayp'nss/) a former British coin equal to half an old or new penny.

halfpennyworth /haypəth, haypniwəth/ (also **ha'p'orth**) ● noun Brit. **1** as much as could be bought for a halfpenny. **2** (**ha'p'orth**) informal a negligible amount: *he's never been a ha'p'orth of bother.*
– PHRASES **don't spoil the ship for a ha'p'orth of tar** proverb don't risk the failure of a large project by trying to economize on trivial things. [ORIGIN referring to the use of tar to keep flies off sores on sheep (from dialect pronunciation of *sheep* as *ship*).]

half-pie ● adjective NZ informal imperfect; mediocre.
– ORIGIN *pie* perhaps derives from a Maori word meaning 'good'.

half relief ● noun a method of moulding, carving, or stamping a design in which figures project to half their true proportions.

half-term ● noun Brit. a short holiday halfway through a school term.

half-timbered ● adjective having walls with a timber frame and a brick or plaster filling.

half-time ● noun (in sport) a short interval between two halves of a match.

half-title ● noun the title of a book, printed on the right-hand page before the title page.

half-tone ● noun **1** a reproduction of an image in which the tones of grey or colour are produced by variously sized dots. **2** Music, chiefly N. Amer. a semitone.

half-track ● noun a vehicle with wheels at the front and caterpillar tracks at the rear.

half-truth ● noun a statement conveying only part of the truth.

half-volley ● noun (in sport) a strike or kick of the ball immediately after it bounces.

halfway ● adverb & adjective **1** at or to a point equidistant between two others. **2** (as adverb) to some extent: *halfway decent.*

halfway house ● noun **1** the halfway point in a progression. **2** a compromise. **3** a centre for rehabilitating former prisoners or psychiatric patients.

halfwit ● noun informal a stupid person.
– DERIVATIVES **half-witted** adjective.

half-yearly ● adjective & adverb at intervals of six months.

halibut ● noun (pl. same) a large marine flatfish, used as food.
– ORIGIN from obsolete *haly* 'holy' + *butt* 'flatfish' (because it was

Thesaurus

joyful, joyous, contented; flourishing, thriving, prosperous, successful; serene, calm, tranquil, peaceful.

hale ● adjective HEALTHY, fit, fighting fit, well, in good health, bursting with health, in fine fettle, as fit as a fiddle/flea; strong, robust, vigorous, hardy, sturdy, hearty, lusty, able-bodied; *informal* in the pink, as right as rain.
– OPPOSITES unwell.

half ● adjective *a half grapefruit* HALVED, divided in two.
– OPPOSITES whole.
● adverb **1** *half-cooked chicken* PARTIALLY, partly, incompletely, inadequately, insufficiently; slightly, in part, part. **2** *I'm half inclined to believe you* TO A CERTAIN EXTENT/DEGREE, to some extent/degree, (up) to a point, in part, partly, in some measure.
– OPPOSITES fully.

half-baked ● adjective **1** *half-baked theories* ILL-CONCEIVED, hare-brained, ill-judged, impractical, unrealistic, unworkable, ridiculous, absurd; *informal* crazy, crackpot, cock-eyed. **2** *her half-baked young nephew* FOOLISH, stupid, silly, idiotic, simple-minded, feeble-minded, empty-headed, feather-brained, feather-headed, brainless, witless, unintelligent, ignorant; *informal* dim, dopey, dumb, thick, half-witted, dim-witted, birdbrained; *Brit. informal* gormless, daft, divvy, dozy.
– OPPOSITES sensible.

half-hearted ● adjective UNENTHUSIASTIC, lukewarm, tepid, cool, apathetic, indifferent, uninterested, unconcerned, languid, listless; perfunctory, cursory, superficial, desultory, feeble, lacklustre.
– OPPOSITES enthusiastic.

halfway ● adjective *the halfway point* MIDWAY, middle, mid, central, centre, intermediate; *Anatomy* medial, mesial.
● adverb **1** *he stopped halfway down the passage* MIDWAY, in the middle, in the centre; part of the way, part-way. **2** *he seemed halfway friendly* TO SOME EXTENT/DEGREE, in some measure, relatively, comparatively, moderately, somewhat, (up) to a point; just about, almost, nearly.
– PHRASES **meet someone halfway** COMPROMISE, come to terms, reach an agreement, make a deal, make concessions, find the middle ground, strike a balance; give and take.

often eaten on holy days).

halide /haylīd/ ● **noun** Chemistry a binary compound of a halogen with another element or group: *silver halide.*

halite /halīt/ ● **noun** sodium chloride as a mineral; rock salt.
– ORIGIN from Greek *hals* 'salt'.

halitosis /halitōsiss/ ● **noun** unpleasant-smelling breath.
– ORIGIN from Latin *halitus* 'breath'.

hall ● **noun 1** the room or space just inside the front entrance of a house. **2** a large room for meetings, concerts, etc. **3** (also **hall of residence**) chiefly Brit. a university building in which students live. **4** the dining room of a college, university, or school. **5** Brit. a large country house. **6** the principal living room of a medieval house. **7** N. Amer. a passage in a building.
– ORIGIN Old English.

hallelujah /halilooyə/ (also **alleluia**) ● **exclamation** God be praised. ● **noun** an utterance of the word 'hallelujah'.
– ORIGIN Hebrew, 'praise ye the Lord'.

hallmark ● **noun 1** a mark stamped on articles of gold, silver, or platinum by the British assay offices, certifying purity. **2** a distinctive feature, especially of excellence. ● **verb** stamp with a hallmark.
– ORIGIN from *Goldsmiths' Hall* in London, where articles were tested and stamped.

hallo ● **exclamation** variant spelling of HELLO.

Hall of Fame ● **noun** chiefly N. Amer. the group of people who have excelled in a particular sphere.

halloo ● **exclamation** used to incite dogs to the chase during a hunt.
– ORIGIN probably from Old French *haloer* 'pursue or urge on with shouts'.

hallow /halō/ ● **verb 1** make holy; consecrate. **2** honour as holy. **3** (**hallowed**) greatly revered. ● **noun** archaic a saint or holy person.
– ORIGIN Old English, related to HOLY.

Halloween (also **Hallowe'en**) ● **noun** the night of 31 October, the eve of All Saints' Day.
– ORIGIN contraction of *All Hallow Even* (see HALLOW, EVEN²).

hallucinate /həloosinayt/ ● **verb** experience a seemingly real perception of something not actually present.
– DERIVATIVES **hallucination** noun **hallucinator** noun **hallucinatory** adjective.
– ORIGIN Latin *hallucinari* 'go astray in thought', from Greek *alussein* 'be uneasy or distraught'.

hallucinogen /həloosinnəjən/ ● **noun** a drug causing hallucinations.
– DERIVATIVES **hallucinogenic** adjective.

hallway ● **noun** another term for HALL (in sense 1).

halo /haylō/ ● **noun** (pl. **haloes** or **halos**) **1** (in a painting) a circle of light surrounding the head of a holy person. **2** a circle of light round the sun or moon caused by refraction through ice crystals in the atmosphere. ● **verb** (**haloes, haloed**) surround with or as if with a halo.
– ORIGIN Greek *halōs* 'disc of the sun or moon'.

halogen /haləjən/ ● **noun 1** Chemistry any of the group of reactive, non-metallic elements fluorine, chlorine, bromine, iodine, and astatine. **2** (before another noun) using a filament surrounded by halogen vapour: *a halogen bulb.*
– ORIGIN from Greek *hals* 'salt'.

halon /haylon/ ● **noun** any of a number of unreactive gaseous compounds of carbon with halogens, used in fire extinguishers.
– ORIGIN from HALOGEN.

halt¹ ● **verb** bring or come to an abrupt stop. ● **noun 1** a suspension of movement or activity. **2** Brit. a minor stopping place on a railway line.
– PHRASES **call a halt** order a stop.
– ORIGIN German *halten* 'to hold'.

halt² archaic ● **adjective** lame. ● **verb** walk with a limp.
– ORIGIN Old English.

halter ● **noun 1** a rope or strap placed around the head of an animal and used to lead or tether it. **2** archaic a noose for hanging a person. **3** a strap passing behind the neck by which the bodice of a sleeveless dress or top is held in place. ● **verb** put a halter on (an animal).
– ORIGIN Old English, related to HELVE.

halter neck ● **noun** a style of neckline incorporating a halter.

halting ● **adjective** slow and hesitant.
– DERIVATIVES **haltingly** adverb.

halva /halvə/ (also **halvah**) ● **noun** a Middle Eastern sweet made of sesame flour and honey.
– ORIGIN Arabic and Persian, 'sweetmeat'.

halve ● **verb 1** divide into two parts of equal size. **2** reduce or be reduced by half.

halves plural of HALF.

halyard /halyərd/ ● **noun** a rope used for raising and lowering a sail, yard, or flag on a ship.
– ORIGIN from HALE².

ham¹ ● **noun 1** meat from the upper part of a pig's leg salted and dried or smoked. **2** (**hams**) the back of the thigh or the thighs and buttocks.
– ORIGIN from a Germanic word meaning 'be crooked'.

ham² ● **noun 1** an inexpert or unsubtle actor or piece of acting. **2** (also **radio ham**) informal an amateur radio operator. ● **verb** (**hammed, hamming**) informal overact.
– ORIGIN perhaps from the first syllable of AMATEUR.

hamadryad /hammədrīad/ ● **noun** Greek & Roman Mythology a nymph who lives in a tree and dies when it dies.
– ORIGIN Greek *Hamadruas*, from *hama* 'together' + *drus* 'tree'.

hamburger ● **noun** a small flat cake of minced beef, fried or grilled and typically served in a bread roll.
– ORIGIN German, from the city of *Hamburg* in Germany.

ham-fisted ● **adjective** informal clumsy; awkward.

ham-handed ● **adjective** another term for HAM-FISTED.
– DERIVATIVES **ham-handedly** adverb.

hamlet ● **noun** a small village, especially (in Britain) one without a church.
– ORIGIN Old French *hamelet*, from *hamel* 'little village'.

hammer ● **noun 1** a tool consisting of a heavy metal head mounted at the end of a handle, used for breaking things and driving in nails. **2** an auctioneer's mallet, tapped to indicate a sale. **3** a part of a mechanism that hits another, e.g. one explod-

Thesaurus

halfwit ● **noun** *(informal).* See FOOL noun sense 1.

half-witted ● **adjective** *(informal).* See STUPID senses 1, 2.

hall ● **noun 1** *hang your coat in the hall* ENTRANCE HALL, hallway, entry, entrance, lobby, foyer, vestibule; atrium, concourse; passageway, passage, corridor; *N. Amer.* entryway. **2** *the village hall* ASSEMBLY ROOM, meeting room, chamber; auditorium, concert hall, theatre.

hallmark ● **noun 1** *the hallmark on silver* ASSAY MARK, official mark, stamp of authenticity. **2** *the tiny bubbles are the hallmark of fine champagnes* MARK, distinctive feature, distinctive characteristic, sign, sure sign, telltale sign, badge, stamp, trademark, indication, indicator.

halloo ● **verb** CALL OUT, shout, cry out, yell, bawl, bellow, roar, whoop; hail, greet; *informal* holler, yoo-hoo, cooee.

hallowed ● **adjective** HOLY, sacred, consecrated, sanctified, blessed; revered, venerated, honoured, sacrosanct, worshipped, divine, inviolable.

hallucinate ● **verb** HAVE HALLUCINATIONS, see things, be delirious, fantasize; *informal* trip, see pink elephants.

hallucination ● **noun** DELUSION, illusion, figment of the imagination, vision, apparition, mirage, chimera, fantasy; (**hallucinations**) delirium, phantasmagoria; *informal* trip, pink elephants.

halo ● **noun** RING OF LIGHT, nimbus, aureole, glory, crown of light, corona; *technical* halation; *rare* gloriole.

halt ● **verb 1** *Len halted and turned round* STOP, come to a halt, come to a stop, come to a standstill; pull up, draw up. **2** *a further strike has halted production* STOP, bring to a stop, put a stop to, bring to an end, put an end to, terminate, end, wind up; suspend, break off, arrest; impede, check, curb, stem, staunch, block, stall, hold back; *informal* pull the plug on, put the kibosh on.
– OPPOSITES start, continue.
● **noun 1** *the car drew to a halt* STOP, standstill. **2** *a halt in production* STOPPAGE, stopping, discontinuation, break, suspension, pause, interval, interruption, hiatus; cessation, termination, close, end.

halter ● **noun** HARNESS, head collar, bridle; *N. Amer.* headstall.

halting ● **adjective 1** *a halting conversation | halting English* HESITANT, faltering, hesitating, stumbling, stammering, stuttering; broken, imperfect. **2** *his halting gait* UNSTEADY, awkward, faltering, stumbling, limping, hobbling.
– OPPOSITES fluent.

ham-fisted ● **adjective** CLUMSY, bungling, incompetent, amateurish, inept, unskilful, inexpert, maladroit, gauche, awkward, inefficient, bumbling, useless; *informal* cack-handed, ham-handed; *Brit.*

ing the charge in a gun. **4** a heavy metal ball attached to a wire for throwing in an athletic contest. ● **verb 1** hit or beat repeatedly with or as with a hammer. **2** (**hammer away**) work hard and persistently. **3** (**hammer in/into**) instil (something) forcefully or repeatedly. **4** (**hammer out**) laboriously work out (the details of a plan or agreement). **5** (**hammer out**) play (a tune) loudly and unskilfully, especially on the piano. **6** informal utterly defeat.
– PHRASES **come** (or **go**) **under the hammer** be sold at an auction. **hammer and tongs** informal enthusiastically or vehemently: *they fought hammer and tongs.*
– ORIGIN Old English.

hammer and sickle ● **noun** the symbols of the industrial worker and the peasant used as the emblem of the former USSR and of international communism.

hammer beam ● **noun** a short wooden beam projecting from a wall to support a principal rafter or one end of an arch.

hammer drill ● **noun** a power drill that delivers a rapid succession of blows.

hammerhead ● **noun** a shark with flattened blade-like extensions on either side of the head.

hammerlock ● **noun** an armlock in which a person's arm is bent up behind their back.

h

hammer toe ● **noun** a toe that is bent permanently downwards, typically as a result of pressure from footwear.

hammock ● **noun** a wide strip of canvas or rope mesh suspended by two ends, used as a bed.
– ORIGIN from Taino (an extinct Caribbean language).

Hammond organ ● **noun** trademark a type of electronic organ.
– ORIGIN named after the American mechanical engineer Laurens *Hammond* (1895–1973).

hammy ● **adjective** (**hammier, hammiest**) informal (of acting or an actor) exaggerated or over-theatrical.

hamper[1] ● **noun 1** a basket with a carrying handle and a hinged lid, used for food, cutlery, etc. on a picnic. **2** Brit. a box containing food and drink for a special occasion.
– ORIGIN Old French *hanaper* 'case for a goblet', from *hanap* 'goblet'.

hamper[2] ● **verb** hinder or impede the movement or progress of.
– ORIGIN perhaps related to German *hemmen* 'restrain'.

hamster ● **noun** a burrowing rodent with a short tail and large cheek pouches, native to Europe and North Asia.
– ORIGIN High German *hamustro* 'corn-weevil'.

hamstring ● **noun 1** any of five tendons at the back of a person's knee. **2** the great tendon at the back of a quadruped's hock. ● **verb** (past and past part. **hamstrung**) **1** cripple by cutting the hamstrings. **2** severely restrict; thwart.
– ORIGIN from HAM[1] + STRING.

Han /han/ ● **noun 1** the Chinese dynasty that ruled almost continuously from 206 BC until AD 220. **2** the dominant ethnic group in China.

hand ● **noun 1** the end part of the arm beyond the wrist. **2** (before another noun) operated by or held in the hand. **3** (before another noun or in combination) done or made manually. **4** a pointer on a clock or watch indicating the passing of units of time. **5** (**hands**) a person's power or control: *taking the law into their own hands.* **6** an active role. **7** help in doing something. **8** a person engaging in manual labour. **9** informal a round of applause. **10** the set of cards dealt to a player in a card game. **11** a person's handwriting or workmanship. **12** a pledge of marriage by a woman. **13** a unit of measurement of a horse's height, equal to 4 inches (10.16 cm). [ORIGIN denoting the breadth of a hand.] ● **verb 1** give to. **2** hold the hand of, in order to assist.
– PHRASES **at hand** near; readily accessible. **by hand** by a person and not a machine. **get** (or **keep**) **one's hand in** become (or remain) practised in something. **hand down 1** pass (something) on to a successor. **2** announce formally or publicly. **hand in glove** in close association. **hand in hand** closely associated; together. **hand out** distribute among a group. (**from**) **hand to mouth** satisfying only one's immediate needs because of lack of money. **hands down** easily and decisively. **hands-off** not involving or requiring direct intervention. **hands-on** involving or offering active participation. **have to hand it to someone** informal used to acknowledge the merit or achievement of someone. **in hand 1** in progress; requiring immediate attention. **2** ready for use if required. **in safe hands** protected by someone trustworthy. **make** (or **lose** or **spend**) **money hand over fist** informal make (or lose or spend) money very rapidly. **many hands make light work** proverb a task is soon accomplished if several people help. **on hand 1** present and available. **2** needing to be dealt with. **on someone's hands 1** under the responsibility of the person specified. **2** at someone's disposal. **on the one** (or **the other**) **hand** used to present factors for (and against). **out of hand 1** not under control. **2** without taking time to think. **to hand** within easy reach. **turn one's hand to** undertake (an activity different from one's usual occupation). **wait on someone hand and foot** attend to someone's needs or requests, especially when excessive.
– ORIGIN Old English.

handbag ● **noun** Brit. a small bag used by a woman to carry

Thesaurus

informal all fingers and thumbs.
– OPPOSITES expert.

hammer ● **noun** *a hammer and chisel* mallet, beetle, gavel, sledgehammer.
● **verb 1** *the alloy is hammered into a circular shape* BEAT, forge, shape, form, mould, fashion, make. **2** *Sally hammered at the door* BATTER, pummel, beat, bang, pound; strike, hit, knock on, thump on; cudgel, bludgeon, club; *informal* bash, wallop, clobber, whack, thwack. **3** *they hammered away at their non-smoking campaign* WORK HARD, labour, slog away, plod away, grind away, slave away, work like a Trojan, work like a dog, keep one's nose to the grindstone; persist with, persevere with, press on with; *informal* stick at, peg away, beaver away, plug away, work one's socks off, soldier on; *Brit. informal* graft away. **4** *anti-racism had been hammered into her* DRUM, instil, inculcate, knock, drive, din; drive home to, impress upon; ingrain. **5** *(informal) he got hammered for an honest mistake.* See CHASTISE sense 1. **6** *(informal) we've hammered them twice this season.* See TROUNCE.
– PHRASES **hammer something out** THRASH OUT, work out, agree on, sort out, decide on, bring about, effect, produce, broker, negotiate, reach an agreement on.

hamper[1] ● **noun** *a picnic hamper* BASKET, pannier, wickerwork basket; box, container, holder.

hamper[2] ● **verb** *the search was hampered by fog* HINDER, obstruct, impede, inhibit, retard, baulk, thwart, foil, curb, delay, set back, slow down, hold up, interfere with; restrict, constrain, trammel, block, check, curtail, frustrate, cramp, bridle, handicap, cripple, hamstring, shackle, fetter; *informal* stymie; *Brit. informal* throw a spanner in the works of; *N. Amer. informal* bork, throw a monkey wrench in the works of.
– OPPOSITES help.

hamstring ● **verb 1** *cattle were killed or hamstrung* CRIPPLE, lame, disable, incapacitate. **2** *manufacturing companies were hamstrung by the economic chaos* HANDICAP, constrain, restrict, cripple, shackle, fetter, encumber, block, frustrate; hamper, hinder, obstruct, impede, trammel, inhibit, baulk, thwart, foil; *informal* stymie; *N. Amer. informal* bork.
– OPPOSITES help.

hand ● **noun 1** *big, strong hands* palm, fist; *informal* paw, mitt, duke, hook, meat hook; *Zoology* manus. **2** *the clock's second hand* POINTER, indicator, needle, arrow, marker. **3** *the frontier posts remained in government hands* CONTROL, power, charge, authority; command, responsibility, guardianship, management, care, supervision, jurisdiction; possession, keeping, custody; clutches, grasp, thrall; disposal; *informal* say-so. **4** *let me give you a hand* HELP, a helping hand, assistance, aid, support, succour, relief; a good turn, a favour. **5** *(informal) his fans gave him a big hand* ROUND OF APPLAUSE, clap, handclap, ovation, standing ovation; applause, handclapping. **6** *a document written in his own hand* HANDWRITING, writing, script, calligraphy. **7** *a factory hand* WORKER, factory worker, manual worker, unskilled worker, blue-collar worker, workman, labourer, operative, hired hand, roustabout; *N. Amer.* peon; *Austral./NZ* rouseabout.
– RELATED TERMS manual.
– OPPOSITES foot.
● **verb 1** *he handed each man a glass* PASS, give, reach, let someone have, throw, toss; present to; *informal* chuck, bung. **2** *he handed him into a carriage* ASSIST, help, give someone a hand; guide.
– PHRASES **at hand 1** *keep the manual close at hand* READILY AVAILABLE, available, handy, to hand, within reach, accessible, close (by), near, nearby, at the ready, at one's fingertips, at one's disposal, convenient; *informal* get-at-able. **2** *the time for starting the campaign is at hand* IMMINENT, approaching, coming, about to happen, on the horizon; impending. **hand something down** PASS ON,

everyday personal items.

handball ● noun **1** a game similar to fives, in which the ball is hit with the hand in a walled court. **2** Soccer illegal touching of the ball with the hand or arm.

handbill ● noun a small printed advertisement or other notice distributed by hand.

handbook ● noun a book giving information such as basic facts or instructions.

handbrake ● noun a brake operated by hand, used to hold an already stationary vehicle.

handcraft ● verb (**handcrafted**) made skilfully by hand. ● noun another term for HANDICRAFT.

handcuff ● noun (**handcuffs**) a pair of lockable linked metal rings for securing a prisoner's wrists. ● verb put handcuffs on.

handful ● noun **1** a quantity that fills the hand. **2** a small number or amount. **3** informal a person who is difficult to deal with or control.

hand grenade ● noun a hand-thrown grenade.

handgun ● noun a gun designed for use by one hand, chiefly either a pistol or a revolver.

handhold ● noun something for a hand to grip on.

handicap ● noun **1** a condition that markedly restricts a person's ability to function physically, mentally, or socially. **2** a disadvantage imposed on a superior competitor in sports such as golf and horse racing in order to make the chances more equal. **3** the extra weight given as a handicap to a racehorse or other competitor. **4** the number of strokes by which a golfer normally exceeds par for a course. ● verb (**handicapped**, **handicapping**) act as a handicap to; place at a disadvantage.

– ORIGIN from the phrase *hand in cap*, a game in which players showed acceptance or rejection of a disputed object's valuation by bringing their hands either full or empty out of a cap in which forfeit money had been deposited. In the 18th century a similar practice was used to signify agreement or disagreement with an allocation of additional weight to be carried in horse races.

handicapped ● adjective having a handicap.

– USAGE In the middle decades of the 20th century **handicapped** was the standard term used in reference to people with physical and mental disabilities. However by the 1980s it had been superseded, in British English, by **disabled**. It is now regarded as dated, if not actually offensive.

handicraft ● noun **1** a particular skill of making decorative domestic or other objects by hand. **2** an object made using a skill of this kind.

handiwork ● noun **1** (**one's handiwork**) something that one has made or done. **2** the making of things by hand.

handkerchief /hangkərchif/ ● noun (pl. **handkerchiefs** or **handkerchieves**) a square of cotton or other material for wiping one's nose.

handle ● verb **1** feel or manipulate with the hands. **2** manage or cope with. **3** deal with. **4** control or manage commercially. **5** (**handle oneself**) conduct oneself. **6** (of a vehicle) respond in a specified way when being driven: *the new model does not handle well.* ● noun **1** the part by which a thing is held, carried, or controlled. **2** a means of understanding, controlling, or approaching a person or situation. **3** informal the name of a person or place.

– DERIVATIVES **handled** adjective **handling** noun.

handlebar (also **handlebars**) ● noun the steering bar of a bicycle, motorbike, or other similar vehicle.

handlebar moustache ● noun a wide, thick moustache with the ends curving slightly upwards.

handler ● noun **1** a person who handles a particular type of article or commodity. **2** a person who trains or has charge of an animal. **3** a person who trains or manages another person.

handmade ● adjective made by hand rather than machine.

handmaid ● noun **1** archaic a female servant. **2** a subservient partner or element.

handmaiden ● noun another term for HANDMAID.

hand-me-down ● noun a garment or other item that has been passed on from another person.

handout ● noun **1** an amount of money or other aid given to a needy person or organization. **2** a piece of printed information provided free of charge, especially to accompany a lecture.

handover ● noun chiefly Brit. an act of handing something over.

h

Thesaurus

pass down; bequeath, will, leave, make over, give, gift, transfer; *Law* demise, devise. **hand in glove** IN CLOSE COLLABORATION, in close association, in close cooperation, very closely, in partnership, in league, in collusion; *informal* in cahoots. **hand something on** GIVE, pass, hand, transfer, grant, cede, surrender, relinquish, yield; part with, let go of; bequeath, will, leave. **hand something out** DISTRIBUTE, hand round, give out/round, pass out/round, share out, dole out, dish out, deal out, mete out, issue, dispense; allocate, allot, apportion, disburse; circulate, disseminate. **hand something over** YIELD, give, give up, pass, grant, entrust, surrender, relinquish, cede, turn over, deliver up, forfeit, sacrifice. **hands down** EASILY, effortlessly, with ease, with no trouble, without effort; *informal* by a mile, no sweat. **to hand** READILY AVAILABLE, available, handy, at hand, within reach, accessible, ready, close (by), near, nearby, at the ready, at one's fingertips, at one's disposal, convenient; *informal* get-at-able. **try one's hand** HAVE A GO, make an attempt, have a shot; attempt, try, try out, give something a try; *informal* have a stab, have a bash, give something a whirl; *formal* essay.

handbag ● noun BAG, shoulder bag, clutch bag, evening bag, pochette; *N. Amer.* purse, pocketbook; *historical* reticule.

handbill ● noun NOTICE, advertisement, flyer, leaflet, circular, handout, pamphlet, brochure; *N. Amer.* dodger; *informal* ad; *Brit. informal* advert.

handbook ● noun MANUAL, instructions, instruction manual, ABC, A to Z; almanac, companion, directory, compendium; guide, guidebook, vade mecum.

handcuff ● verb MANACLE, shackle, fetter; restrain, clap/put someone in irons; *informal* cuff.

handcuffs ● plural noun MANACLES, shackles, irons, fetters, bonds, restraints; *informal* cuffs, bracelets; *archaic* darbies, gyves.

handful ● noun **1** *a handful of British firms* A FEW, a small number, a small amount, a small quantity, one or two, some, not many, a scattering, a trickle. **2** *(informal) the child is a real handful* NUISANCE, problem, bother, irritant, thorn in someone's flesh/side; *informal* pest, headache, pain, pain in the neck/backside; *Scottish informal* nyaff, skelf; *N. Amer. informal* pain in the butt.

handgun ● noun PISTOL, revolver, gun, side arm, six-shooter, thirty-eight, derringer; *N. Amer. informal* piece, shooting iron, Saturday night special, rod; *trademark* Colt.

handicap ● noun **1** *a visual handicap* DISABILITY, physical/mental abnormality, defect, impairment, affliction, deficiency. **2** *a handicap to the competitiveness of the industry* IMPEDIMENT, hindrance, obstacle, barrier, bar, obstruction, encumbrance, constraint, restriction, check, block, curb; disadvantage, drawback, stumbling block, difficulty, shortcoming, limitation; ball and chain, albatross, millstone round someone's neck; *poetic/literary* trammel.

– OPPOSITES benefit, advantage.

● verb *lack of funding handicapped the research* HAMPER, impede, hinder, impair, hamstring; restrict, check, obstruct, block, curb, bridle, hold back, constrain, trammel, limit, encumber; *informal* stymie; *N. Amer. informal* bork.

– OPPOSITES help.

handicapped ● adjective DISABLED, incapacitated, disadvantaged; infirm, invalid; *euphemistic* physically challenged, differently abled.

handicraft ● noun CRAFT, handiwork, craftwork; craftsmanship, workmanship, artisanship, art, skill.

handiwork ● noun *jewellery which is the handiwork of Chinese smiths* CREATION, product, work, achievement; handicraft, craft, craftwork.

handkerchief ● noun pocket handkerchief, tissue, paper handkerchief; *trademark* Kleenex; *informal* hanky, nose rag, snot rag; *poetic/literary* kerchief.

handle ● verb **1** *the equipment must be handled with care* HOLD, pick up, grasp, grip, lift; feel, touch, finger; *informal* paw. **2** *a car which is easy to handle* CONTROL, drive, steer, operate, manoeuvre, manipulate. **3** *she handled the job formidably* DEAL WITH, manage, tackle, take care of, take charge of, attend to, see to, sort out, apply oneself to, take in hand. **4** *the advertising company that is handling the account* ADMINISTER, manage, control, conduct, direct, guide, supervise, oversee, be in charge of, take care of, look after. **5** *the traders handled goods manufactured in the Rhineland* TRADE IN, deal in, buy, sell, supply, peddle, traffic in, purvey, hawk, tout, market.

● noun *the knife's handle* HAFT, shank, stock, shaft, grip, handgrip, hilt, helve, butt; knob.

hand-me-down ● adjective SECOND-HAND, used, nearly new, handed-down, passed-on, cast-off, worn, old, pre-owned; *Brit. informal*

hand-pick • verb select carefully.
handprint • noun the mark left by the impression of a hand.
handset • noun **1** the part of a telephone that is held up to speak into and listen to. **2** a hand-held control device for a piece of electronic equipment.
handshake • noun an act of shaking a person's hand.
– DERIVATIVES **handshaking** noun.
handsome • adjective (**handsomer, handsomest**) **1** (of a man) good-looking. **2** (of a woman) striking and imposing rather than conventionally pretty. **3** (of a thing) well made, imposing, and of obvious quality. **4** (of an amount) substantial; sizeable.
– PHRASES **handsome is as handsome does** proverb character and behaviour are more important than appearance.
– DERIVATIVES **handsomely** adverb **handsomeness** noun.
– ORIGIN originally in the sense 'easy to handle or use', later 'apt, clever': from HAND + -SOME[1].
handspring • noun a jump through the air on to one's hands followed by another on to one's feet.
handstand • noun an act of balancing upside down on one's hands.
hand-to-hand • adjective (of fighting) at close quarters.
handwriting • noun **1** writing with a pen or pencil rather than by typing or printing. **2** a person's particular style of writing.
handwritten • adjective written with a pen, pencil, or other hand-held implement.
handy • adjective (**handier, handiest**) **1** convenient to handle or use; useful. **2** ready to hand. **3** placed or occurring conveniently. **4** skilful.
– DERIVATIVES **handily** adverb **handiness** noun.
handyman • noun a person employed to do general decorating or domestic repairs.
hang • verb (past and past part. **hung** except in sense 2) **1** suspend or be suspended from above with the lower part not attached. **2** (past and past part. **hanged**) kill or be killed by tying a rope attached from above around the neck and removing the support from beneath the feet (used as a form of capital punishment). **3** attach so as to allow free movement about the point of attachment: *hanging a door*. **4** (of fabric or a garment) fall or drape in a specified way. **5** attach (meat or game) to a hook and leave it until dry, tender, or high. **6** remain static in the air. **7** be present or imminent, especially oppressively. **8** paste (wallpaper) to a wall. • noun the way in which something hangs or is hung. • exclamation dated used in expressions as a mild oath.
– PHRASES **get the hang of** informal learn how to operate or do. **hang around** informal **1** loiter; wait around. **2** (**hang around with**) associate with. **hang back** remain behind. **hang fire** delay or be delayed in taking action. **hang on 1** hold tightly. **2** informal wait for a short time. **3** be contingent or dependent on. **4** listen closely to. **hang out** informal spend time relaxing or enjoying oneself. **hang up** end a telephone conversation by cutting the connection. **let it all hang out** informal be very relaxed or uninhibited.
– USAGE In modern English **hang** has two past tense and past participle forms: **hanged** and **hung**. Sometime after the 16th century **hung** replaced the earlier form **hanged** in general contexts, as in *they hung out the washing*, while **hanged** was, as it still is, retained for use in reference to execution by hanging, as in *the prisoner was hanged*.
– ORIGIN Old English.
hangar /hangər/ • noun a large building with extensive floor area, typically for housing aircraft.
– ORIGIN French, probably from Germanic words meaning 'hamlet' and 'enclosure'.
hangdog • adjective having a dejected or guilty appearance.
hanger • noun **1** a person who hangs something. **2** (also **coat hanger**) a shaped piece of wood, plastic, or metal with a hook at the top, for hanging clothes from a rail.
hanger-on • noun (pl. **hangers-on**) a person who associates sycophantically with another person.
hang-glider • noun an unpowered flying apparatus for a single person, consisting of a frame with a fabric aerofoil stretched over it from which the operator is suspended.
– DERIVATIVES **hang-glide** verb **hang-gliding** noun.
hangi /hangi, haangi/ • noun NZ **1** a pit in which food is cooked on heated stones. **2** the food or meal cooked in such a pit.
– ORIGIN Maori.
hanging • noun **1** the practice of hanging condemned people as a form of capital punishment. **2** a decorative piece of fabric hung on the wall of a room or around a bed. • adjective suspended in the air.
hanging valley • noun a valley which is cut across by a deeper valley or a cliff.
hangman • noun an executioner who hangs condemned people.
hangnail • noun a piece of torn skin at the root of a fingernail.

Thesaurus

reach-me-down.
– OPPOSITES new.
handout • noun **1** *she existed on handouts* CHARITY, aid, benefit, financial support, donations, subsidies; historical alms. **2** *a xeroxed handout* LEAFLET, pamphlet, brochure; handbill, flyer, notice, circular, mailshot.
hand-picked • adjective SPECIALLY CHOSEN, selected, invited; select, elite; choice.
handsome • adjective **1** *a handsome man* GOOD-LOOKING, attractive, personable, striking; informal hunky, dishy, tasty, fanciable; Brit. informal fit; N. Amer. informal cute; Austral./NZ informal spunky. **2** *a handsome woman of 30* STRIKING, imposing, prepossessing, elegant, stately, dignified, statuesque, good-looking, attractive, personable. **3** *a handsome profit* SUBSTANTIAL, considerable, sizeable, princely, large, big, ample, bumper; informal tidy, whopping, not to be sneezed at; Brit. informal whacking, ginormous.
– OPPOSITES ugly, meagre.
handwriting • noun WRITING, script, hand, pen; penmanship, calligraphy, chirography; informal scrawl, scribble.
handy • adjective **1** *a handy reference tool* USEFUL, convenient, practical, easy-to-use, well-designed, user-friendly, user-oriented, helpful, functional, serviceable. **2** *keep your credit card handy* READILY AVAILABLE, available, at hand, to hand, near at hand, within reach, accessible, ready, close (by), near, nearby, at the ready, at one's fingertips; informal get-at-able. **3** *he's handy with a needle* SKILFUL, skilled, dexterous, deft, nimble-fingered, adroit, able, adept, proficient, capable; good with one's hands; informal nifty.
– OPPOSITES inconvenient, inept.
handyman • noun ODD-JOB MAN, odd-jobber, factotum, jack of all trades, man of all work; DIY'er; informal Mr Fixit.
hang • verb **1** *lights hung from the trees* BE SUSPENDED, hang down, be pendent, dangle, swing, sway; archaic depend. **2** *hang your pictures at eye level* PUT UP, fix, attach, affix, fasten, post, display, suspend, pin up, nail up. **3** *the room was hung with streamers* DECORATE, adorn, drape, festoon, deck out, trick out, bedeck, array, garland, swathe, cover, ornament; poetic/literary bedizen. **4** *he was hanged for murder* HANG BY THE NECK, send to the gallows; informal string up. **5** *a pall of smoke hung over the city* HOVER, float, drift, be suspended. **6** *the threat of budget cuts is hanging over us* BE IMMINENT, threaten, be close, be impending, impend, loom, be on the horizon.
– PHRASES **hang about** (Brit. informal). See HANG AROUND. **hang around/round** (informal) **1** *they spent their time hanging around in bars* LOITER, linger, wait around, waste time, kill time, mark time, while away the/one's time, kick/cool one's heels, twiddle one's thumbs; frequent, be a regular visitor to, haunt; informal hang out in. **2** *hang about, what's this?* See HANG ON sense 4. **3** *she's hanging around with a bunch of hippies* ASSOCIATE, mix, keep company, socialize, fraternize, consort, rub shoulders; N. Amer. rub elbows; informal hang out, run around, knock about/around, be thick, hobnob. **hang fire** DELAY, hang back, hold back, hold on, stall, pause; procrastinate, vacillate, adopt Fabian tactics; informal hang about/around, sit tight, hold one's horses. **hang on 1** *he hung on to her coat* HOLD ON, hold fast, grip, clutch, grasp, hold tightly, cling. **2** *her future hung on his decision* DEPEND ON, be dependent on, turn on, hinge on, rest on, be contingent on, be determined by, be decided by. **3** *I'll hang on as long as I can* PERSEVERE, hold out, hold on, go on, carry on, keep on, keep going, keep at it, continue, persist, stay with it, struggle on, plod on, plough on; informal soldier on, stick at it, stick it out, hang in there. **4** (informal) *hang on, let me think* WAIT, wait a minute, hold on, stop; hold the line; informal hold your horses, sit tight; Brit. informal hang about.
hangdog • adjective SHAMEFACED, sheepish, abashed, ashamed, guilty-looking, abject, cowed, dejected, downcast, crestfallen, woebegone, disconsolate.
– OPPOSITES unabashed.
hanger-on • noun FOLLOWER, flunkey, toady, camp follower, sycophant, parasite, leech; henchman, minion, lackey, vassal, dependant, retainer; acolyte; N. Amer. cohort; informal groupie, sponger, freeloader, passenger, sidekick.

– ORIGIN alteration of *agnail* 'painful swelling around a nail', from Old English; influenced by HANG.

hang-out ● noun informal a place one lives in or frequently visits.

hangover ● noun **1** a severe headache or other after-effects caused by drinking an excess of alcohol. **2** a thing that has survived from the past.

hang-up ● noun informal an emotional problem or inhibition.

hank ● noun a coil or skein of wool, hair, or other material.
– ORIGIN Old Norse.

hanker ● verb (**hanker after/for/to do**) feel a strong desire for or to do.
– ORIGIN probably related to HANG.

hanky (also **hankie**) ● noun (pl. **hankies**) informal a handkerchief.

hanky-panky ● noun informal, humorous behaviour considered improper but not seriously so.
– ORIGIN perhaps an alteration of 'hokey-pokey' (see HOKEY-COKEY).

Hanoverian /hannəveeriən/ ● adjective relating to the royal house of Hanover, who ruled as monarchs in Britain from 1714 to 1901.

Hansard /hansaard/ ● noun the official verbatim record of debates in the British, Canadian, Australian, or New Zealand parliament.
– ORIGIN named after the English printer Thomas C. *Hansard* (1776–1833).

Hansen's disease ● noun another term for LEPROSY.
– ORIGIN named after the Norwegian physician Gerhard H. A. *Hansen* (1841–1912).

hansom /hansəm/ (also **hansom cab**) ● noun historical a two-wheeled horse-drawn cab with space for two inside, with the driver seated behind.
– ORIGIN named after the English architect Joseph A. *Hansom* (1803–82), who patented it.

hantavirus /hantəvīrəss/ ● noun a virus of a kind carried by rodents and causing various diseases characterized by fever and haemorrhaging.
– ORIGIN from *Hantaan* (a river in Korea where the virus was first isolated).

Hants ● abbreviation Hampshire.

Hanukkah /hannəkə/ (also **Chanukkah**) ● noun an eight-day Jewish festival of lights held in December, commemorating the rededication of the Jewish Temple in Jerusalem.
– ORIGIN Hebrew, 'consecration'.

hap ● noun archaic luck; fortune.
– ORIGIN Old Norse.

hapax legomenon /happaks ligomminon/ ● noun (pl. **hapax legomena** /happaks ligomminə/) a term of which only one instance of use is recorded.
– ORIGIN from Greek, 'a thing said once'.

ha'penny ● noun variant spelling of HALFPENNY.

haphazard ● adjective lacking order or organization.
– DERIVATIVES **haphazardly** adverb.

hapless ● adjective unlucky; unfortunate.
– DERIVATIVES **haplessly** adverb.

haplography /haplografi/ ● noun the inadvertent omission of a repeated letter or letters in writing (e.g. writing *philogy* for *philology*).

haploid /haployd/ ● adjective Genetics (of a cell or nucleus) having a single set of unpaired chromosomes. Compare with DIPLOID.

happen ● verb **1** take place; occur. **2** come about by chance. **3** (**happen on**) come across by chance. **4** chance to do something or come about. **5** (**happen to**) be experienced by. **6** (**happen to**) become of.
– PHRASES **as it happens** actually; as a matter of fact.
– ORIGIN from HAP.

happening ● noun **1** an event or occurrence. **2** a partly improvised or spontaneous artistic or theatrical performance. ● adjective informal fashionable.

happenstance ● noun chiefly N. Amer. coincidence.
– ORIGIN blend of HAPPEN and CIRCUMSTANCE.

happy ● adjective (**happier, happiest**) **1** feeling or showing pleasure or contentment. **2** willing to do something. **3** fortunate and convenient: *a happy coincidence.* **4** (in combination) informal inclined to use a specified thing excessively or at random: *trigger-happy.*
– DERIVATIVES **happily** adverb **happiness** noun.
– ORIGIN from HAP.

happy-go-lucky ● adjective cheerfully unconcerned about the future.

happy hour ● noun a period of the day when drinks are sold at

h

Thesaurus

hanging ● noun *silk wall hangings* DRAPE, curtain; drapery.
● adjective *hanging fronds of honeysuckle* PENDENT, dangling, trailing, tumbling; suspended.

hang-out ● noun *(informal)* HAUNT, stamping ground, favourite spot, meeting place; den, refuge, retreat; *N. Amer.* stomping ground.

hang-up ● noun *(informal)* NEUROSIS, phobia, preoccupation, fixation, obsession, idée fixe; inhibition, mental block, psychological block, block, difficulty; *informal* complex, thing.

hank ● noun COIL, skein, length, roll, loop, twist, piece; lock, ringlet, curl.

hanker ● verb YEARN, long, crave, desire, wish, want, hunger, thirst, lust, ache, pant, be eager, be desperate, be eating one's heart out; fancy, pine for, have one's heart set on; *informal* be dying, have a yen, itch.

hankering ● noun LONGING, yearning, craving, desire, wish, hunger, thirst, urge, ache, lust, appetite, fancy; *informal* yen, itch; *archaic* appetency.
– OPPOSITES aversion.

hanky-panky ● noun *(informal)* GOINGS-ON, funny business, mischief, misbehaviour, misconduct, chicanery, dishonesty, deception, deceit, trickery, intrigue, skulduggery, subterfuge, machinations; infidelity, unfaithfulness, adultery; *informal* monkey business, shenanigans, carryings-on; *Brit. informal* jiggery-pokery.

haphazard ● adjective RANDOM, unplanned, unsystematic, unmethodical, disorganized, disorderly, irregular, indiscriminate, chaotic, hit-and-miss, arbitrary, aimless, careless, casual, slapdash, slipshod; chance, accidental; *informal* higgledy-piggledy.
– OPPOSITES methodical.

hapless ● adjective UNFORTUNATE, unlucky, luckless, out of luck, ill-starred, ill-fated, jinxed, cursed, doomed; unhappy, forlorn, wretched, miserable, woebegone; *informal* down on one's luck; *poetic/literary* star-crossed.
– OPPOSITES lucky.

happen ● verb **1** *remember what happened last time he was here* OCCUR, take place, come about; ensue, result, transpire, materialize, arise, crop up, come up, present itself, supervene; *N. Amer. informal* go down; *formal* eventuate; *poetic/literary* come to pass, betide; *archaic* hap. **2** *I wonder what happened to Susie?* BECOME OF; *poetic/literary* befall, betide. **3** *they happened to be in London* CHANCE, have the good/bad luck. **4** *he happened on a linnet's nest* DISCOVER, find, find by chance, come across, chance on, stumble on, hit on.

happening ● noun *bizarre happenings* OCCURRENCE, event, incident, proceeding, affair, circumstance, phenomenon, episode, experience, occasion, development, eventuality.
● adjective *(informal) a happening nightspot* FASHIONABLE, modern, popular, new, latest, up to date, up to the minute, in fashion, in vogue, le dernier cri; *informal* trendy, funky, hot, cool, with it, hip, in, big, now, groovy; *N. Amer. informal* kicky, tony.
– OPPOSITES old-fashioned.

happily ● adverb **1** *he smiled happily* CONTENTEDLY, cheerfully, cheerily, merrily, delightedly, joyfully, joyously, gaily, gleefully. **2** *I will happily do as you ask* GLADLY, willingly, readily, freely, cheerfully, ungrudgingly, with pleasure; *archaic* fain. **3** *happily, we are living in enlightened times* FORTUNATELY, luckily, thankfully, mercifully, by good luck, by good fortune, as luck would have it; thank goodness, thank God, thank heavens, thank the stars.

happiness ● noun PLEASURE, contentment, satisfaction, cheerfulness, merriment, gaiety, joy, joyfulness, joviality, jollity, glee, delight, good spirits, light-heartedness, well-being, enjoyment; exuberance, exhilaration, elation, ecstasy, jubilation, rapture, bliss, blissfulness, euphoria, transports of delight.

happy ● adjective **1** *Melissa looked happy and excited* CHEERFUL, cheery, merry, joyful, jovial, jolly, jocular, gleeful, carefree, untroubled, delighted, smiling, beaming, grinning, in good spirits, in a good mood, light-hearted, pleased, contented, content, satisfied, gratified, buoyant, radiant, sunny, blithe, joyous, beatific; thrilled, elated, exhilarated, ecstatic, blissful, euphoric, overjoyed, exultant, rapturous, in seventh heaven, on cloud nine, walking on air, jumping for joy, cock-a-hoop, jubilant; *informal* chirpy, over the moon, on top of the world, as happy as a sandboy, tickled pink, like a dog with two tails, as pleased as Punch, on a high; *Brit. informal* chuffed, as happy as Larry; *N. English informal* made up; *N. Amer. informal* as happy as a clam; *Austral. informal* wrapped; *formal* jocund; *dated* gay. **2** *we will be happy to advise you* GLAD, pleased, delighted; willing, ready, disposed. **3** *a happy coincidence* FORTUNATE, lucky, favourable, advantageous, opportune,

reduced prices in a bar or other establishment.

happy hunting ground ● noun a place where success or enjoyment is obtained.
– ORIGIN referring to the optimistic hope of American Indians for good hunting grounds in the afterlife.

hapten /haptən/ ● noun Physiology a small molecule which, when combined with a protein, can induce the production of antibodies.
– ORIGIN from Greek *haptein* 'fasten'.

haptic /haptik/ ● adjective technical relating to the sense of touch.
– ORIGIN Greek *haptikos* 'able to touch or grasp'.

hara-kiri /harrəkirri/ ● noun ritual suicide by disembowelment with a sword, formerly practised in Japan by samurai.
– ORIGIN from the Japanese words for 'belly' + 'cutting'.

haram /haaraam/ ● adjective forbidden or proscribed by Islamic law.
– ORIGIN Arabic.

harangue /hərang/ ● verb criticize at length in an aggressive manner. ● noun a forceful and aggressive speech.
– ORIGIN Latin *harenga*.

harass /harrəss, hərass/ ● verb **1** torment (someone) by subjecting them to constant interference or intimidation. **2** make repeated small-scale attacks on (an enemy) in order to wear down resistance.
– DERIVATIVES **harasser** noun **harassment** noun.
– USAGE The word **harass** is pronounced either with the stress on the **har-** or with the stress on the **-rass**; the first pronunciation, which is the older one, is considered by some people to be the only correct one, especially in British English.
– ORIGIN French *harasser*, from *harer* 'set a dog on'.

harbinger /haarbinjer/ ● noun a person or thing that announces or signals the approach of something.
– ORIGIN originally denoting a person who provides or goes ahead to find lodging: from Old French *herbergere*, from an obsolete Low German dialect word meaning 'shelter for an army, lodging'.

harbour (US **harbor**) ● noun a place on the coast where ships may moor in shelter. ● verb **1** keep (a thought or feeling) secretly in one's mind. **2** give a refuge or shelter to. **3** carry the germs of (a disease).
– ORIGIN Old English, 'shelter'.

hard ● adjective **1** solid, firm, and rigid; not easily broken, bent, or pierced. **2** requiring or demonstrating a great deal of endurance or effort; difficult. **3** (of a person) not showing any signs of weakness; tough. **4** (of information or a subject of study) concerned with precise and verifiable facts. **5** harsh or unpleasant to the senses. **6** done with a great deal of force or strength. **7** (of liquor) strongly alcoholic. **8** (of a drug) potent and addictive. **9** (of pornography) highly obscene and explicit. **10** denoting an extreme faction within a political party. **11** (of water) containing mineral salts. ● adverb **1** with a great deal of effort or force. **2** so as to be solid or firm. **3** to the fullest extent possible.
– PHRASES **be hard put (to it)** find it very difficult. **hard and fast** (of a rule or distinction) fixed and definitive. **hard at it** informal busily working. **hard done by** Brit. harshly or unfairly treated. **hard feelings** feelings of resentment. **hard going** difficult to understand or enjoy. **hard luck** (or **lines**) Brit. informal used to express sympathy or commiserations. **hard of hearing** not able to hear well. **hard on** (or **upon**) following soon after. **hard up** informal short of money. **play hard to get** informal deliberately adopt an uninterested attitude. **put the hard word on** Austral./NZ informal ask a favour of.
– DERIVATIVES **hardish** adjective **hardness** noun.
– ORIGIN Old English.

hardback ● noun a book bound in stiff covers.

Thesaurus

timely, well-timed, convenient.
– OPPOSITES sad, unwilling, unfortunate.

happy-go-lucky ● adjective EASY-GOING, carefree, casual, free and easy, devil-may-care, blithe, nonchalant, insouciant, blasé, unconcerned, untroubled, unworried, light-hearted; *informal* laid-back.
– OPPOSITES anxious.

harangue ● noun *a ten-minute harangue* TIRADE, diatribe, lecture, polemic, rant, fulmination, broadside, attack, onslaught; criticism, condemnation, censure, admonition; declamation, speech; *informal* blast; *poetic/literary* philippic.
● verb *he harangued his erstwhile colleagues* RANT AT, hold forth to, lecture, shout at; berate, criticize, attack; *informal* earbash, sound off at, mouth off at.

harass ● verb **1** *council tenants who harass their neighbours* PERSECUTE, intimidate, hound, harry, plague, torment, bedevil, pressurize; pester, bother, worry, disturb, trouble, provoke, stress; *informal* hassle, bug, give someone a hard time; *N. English informal* mither; *N. Amer. informal* devil, ride. **2** *they were sent to harass the enemy flanks* HARRY, attack, beleaguer, set upon, assail.

harassed ● adjective STRESSED, strained, worn out, hard-pressed, careworn, worried, troubled, beleaguered, under pressure, at the end of one's tether; *N. Amer.* at the end of one's rope; *informal* hassled.
– OPPOSITES carefree.

harassment ● noun PERSECUTION, intimidation, pressure, pressurization, force, coercion; *informal* hassle.

harbinger ● noun HERALD, sign, indication, signal, portent, omen, augury, forewarning, presage; forerunner, precursor, messenger; *poetic/literary* foretoken.

harbour ● noun **1** *a picturesque harbour* PORT, dock, haven, marina; mooring, moorage, anchorage, harbourage; waterfront. **2** *a safe harbour for me* REFUGE, haven, safe haven, shelter, sanctuary, retreat, place of safety, port in a storm.
● verb **1** *he is harbouring a dangerous criminal* SHELTER, conceal, hide, shield, protect, give sanctuary to; take in, put up, accommodate, house. **2** *Rose had harboured a grudge against him* BEAR, nurse, nurture, cherish, entertain, foster, hold on to, cling to.

hard ● adjective **1** *hard ground* FIRM, solid, rigid, stiff, resistant, unbreakable, inflexible, impenetrable, unyielding, solidified, hardened, compact, compacted, dense, close-packed, compressed; steely, tough, strong, stony, rock-like, flinty, as hard as iron, as hard as stone; frozen; *poetic/literary* adamantine. **2** *hard physical work* ARDUOUS, strenuous, tiring, fatiguing, exhausting, wearying, back-breaking, gruelling, heavy, laborious; difficult, taxing, exacting, testing, challenging, demanding, punishing, tough, formidable, onerous, rigorous, uphill, Herculean; *informal* murderous, killing, hellish; *Brit. informal* knackering; *formal* exigent; *archaic* toilsome. **3** *hard workers* DILIGENT, hard-working, industrious, sedulous, assiduous, conscientious, energetic, keen, enthusiastic, zealous, earnest, persevering, persistent, unflagging, untiring, indefatigable; studious. **4** *a hard problem* DIFFICULT, puzzling, perplexing, baffling, bewildering, mystifying, knotty, thorny, problematic, complicated, complex, intricate, involved; insoluble, unfathomable, impenetrable, incomprehensible, unanswerable. **5** *times are hard* HARSH, grim, difficult, bad, bleak, dire, tough, austere, unpleasant, uncomfortable, straitened, spartan; dark, distressing, painful, awful. **6** *a hard taskmaster* STRICT, harsh, firm, severe, stern, tough, rigorous, demanding, exacting; callous, unkind, unsympathetic, cold, heartless, hard-hearted, unfeeling; intransigent, unbending, uncompromising, inflexible, implacable, stubborn, obdurate, unyielding, unrelenting, unsparing, grim, ruthless, merciless, pitiless, cruel; standing no nonsense, ruling with a rod of iron. **7** *a hard winter* BITTERLY COLD, cold, bitter, harsh, severe, bleak, freezing, icy, icy-cold, arctic. **8** *a hard blow* FORCEFUL, heavy, strong, sharp, smart, violent, powerful, vigorous, mighty, hefty, tremendous. **9** *hard facts* RELIABLE, definite, true, confirmed, substantiated, undeniable, indisputable, unquestionable, verifiable. **10** *hard liquor* ALCOHOLIC, strong, intoxicating, potent; *formal* spirituous. **11** *hard drugs* ADDICTIVE, habit-forming; strong, harmful.
– OPPOSITES soft, easy lazy, gentle.
● adverb **1** *George pushed her hard* FORCEFULLY, forcibly, roughly, powerfully, strongly, heavily, sharply, vigorously, energetically, with all one's might, with might and main. **2** *they worked hard* DILIGENTLY, industriously, assiduously, conscientiously, sedulously, busily, enthusiastically, energetically, doggedly, steadily; *informal* like mad, like crazy; *Brit. informal* like billy-o. **3** *this prosperity has been hard won* WITH DIFFICULTY, with effort, after a struggle, painfully, laboriously. **4** *her death hit him hard* SEVERELY, badly, acutely, deeply, keenly, seriously, profoundly, gravely; *formal* grievously. **5** *it was raining hard* HEAVILY, strongly, in torrents, in sheets, cats and dogs; steadily. **6** *my mother looked hard at me* CLOSELY, attentively, intently, critically, carefully, keenly, searchingly, earnestly, sharply.
– PHRASES **hard and fast** DEFINITE, fixed, set, strict, rigid, binding, clear-cut, cast-iron; inflexible, immutable, unchangeable, incontestable. **hard by** CLOSE TO, right by, beside, near (to), nearby, not far from, a stone's throw from, on the doorstep of; *informal* within

hardbitten • adjective tough and cynical.
hardboard • noun stiff board made of compressed and treated wood pulp.
hard-boiled • adjective **1** (of an egg) boiled until solid. **2** informal (of a person) tough and cynical.
hard cash • noun negotiable coins and banknotes as opposed to other forms of payment.
hard copy • noun a printed version on paper of data held in a computer.
hard core • noun **1** the most committed or doctrinaire members of a group. **2** popular music that is experimental in nature and typically characterized by high volume and aggressive presentation. **3** pornography of a very explicit kind. **4** Brit. broken bricks and rubble used as a filling or foundation in building.
hardcover • adjective & noun chiefly N. Amer. another term for HARDBACK.
hard disk (also **hard drive**) • noun Computing a rigid non-removable magnetic disk with a large data storage capacity.
harden • verb make or become hard or harder.
– DERIVATIVES **hardened** adjective **hardener** noun.
hard hat • noun a rigid protective helmet, as worn by factory and building workers.
hard-headed • adjective tough and realistic.
– DERIVATIVES **hard-headedly** adverb **hard-headedness** noun.
hard-hearted • adjective unfeeling.
– DERIVATIVES **hard-heartedly** adverb **hard-heartedness** noun.
hardihood • noun dated boldness; daring.
hard labour • noun heavy manual work as a punishment.
hard line • noun an uncompromising adherence to a firm policy. • adjective uncompromising; strict.
– DERIVATIVES **hardliner** noun.
hardly • adverb **1** scarcely; barely. **2** only with great difficulty. **3** no or not (suggesting surprise at or disagreement with a statement).
hard-nosed • adjective informal realistic and tough-minded.
hard-on • noun vulgar slang an erection of the penis.
hard palate • noun the bony front part of the palate.
hardpan • noun a hardened layer, occurring in or below the soil, that resists penetration by water and plant roots.
hard-pressed • adjective **1** closely pursued. **2** in difficulties.
hard rock • noun highly amplified rock music with a heavy beat.
hard sell • noun a policy or technique of aggressive selling or advertising.
hardship • noun severe suffering or privation.
hard shoulder • noun Brit. a hardened strip alongside a motorway for use in an emergency.
hardstanding • noun Brit. ground surfaced with a hard material for parking vehicles on.
hard tack • noun archaic hard dry bread or biscuit, especially as rations for sailors or soldiers.
hardtop • noun a motor vehicle with a rigid roof which in some cases is detachable.
hardware • noun **1** heavy military equipment such as tanks and missiles. **2** the machines, wiring, and other physical components of a computer. **3** tools, implements, and other items used in the home and in activities such as gardening.
hard-wired • adjective Electronics involving permanently connected circuits rather than software.
hardwood • noun the wood from a broadleaved tree as distinguished from that of conifers.
hardy • adjective (**hardier**, **hardiest**) **1** capable of enduring difficult conditions; robust. **2** (of a plant) able to survive outside during winter.
– DERIVATIVES **hardily** adverb **hardiness** noun.
– ORIGIN Old French *hardi*, from *hardir* 'become bold'.

Thesaurus

spitting distance of, {a hop, skip, and jump away from}. **hard feelings** RESENTMENT, animosity, ill feeling, ill will, bitterness, bad blood, resentfulness, rancour, malice, acrimony, antagonism, antipathy, animus, friction, anger, hostility, hate, hatred. **hard up** *(informal)* POOR, short of money, badly off, impoverished, impecunious, in reduced circumstances, unable to make ends meet; penniless, destitute, poverty-stricken; *informal* broke, strapped (for cash); *Brit. informal* skint.
hardbitten • adjective HARDENED, tough, cynical, unsentimental, hard-headed, case-hardened, as hard as nails; *informal* hard-nosed, hard-boiled.
– OPPOSITES sentimental.
hard-boiled • adjective *(informal) a hard-boiled undercover agent.* See HARDBITTEN.
hard-core • adjective DIEHARD, staunch, dedicated, committed, steadfast, dyed-in-the-wool, long-standing; hard-line, extreme, entrenched, radical, intransigent, uncompromising, rigid; *informal* deep-dyed.
harden • verb **1** *this glue will harden in four hours* SOLIDIFY, set, congeal, clot, coagulate, stiffen, thicken, cake, inspissate; freeze, crystallize; ossify, petrify. **2** *their suffering had hardened them* TOUGHEN, desensitize, inure, case-harden, harden someone's heart; deaden, numb, benumb, anaesthetize; brutalize.
– OPPOSITES liquefy, soften.
hardened • adjective **1** *he was hardened to the violence he had seen* INURED, desensitized, deadened; accustomed, habituated, acclimatized, used. **2** *a hardened criminal* INVETERATE, seasoned, habitual, chronic, compulsive, confirmed, dyed-in-the-wool; incorrigible, incurable, irredeemable, unregenerate. **3** *the silos are hardened against air attack* STRENGTHENED, fortified, reinforced, toughened.
hard-headed • adjective UNSENTIMENTAL, practical, pragmatic, businesslike, realistic, sensible, rational, clear-thinking, cool-headed, down-to-earth, matter-of-fact, no-nonsense, with one's/both feet on the ground; tough, hardbitten; shrewd, astute, sharp, sharp-witted; *informal* hard-nosed, hard-boiled.
– OPPOSITES idealistic.
hard-hearted • adjective UNFEELING, heartless, cold, hard, callous, unsympathetic, uncaring, unloving, unconcerned, indifferent, unmoved, unkind, uncharitable, unemotional, cold-hearted, cold-blooded, mean-spirited, stony-hearted, having a heart of stone, as hard as nails, cruel.
– OPPOSITES compassionate.
hard-hitting • adjective UNCOMPROMISING, blunt, forthright, frank, honest, direct, tough; critical, unsparing, strongly worded, straight-talking, pulling no punches, not mincing one's words, not beating about the bush.
hardihood • noun BRAVERY, courage, pluck, valour, intrepidity, nerve, daring, fearlessness, audacity, boldness, dauntlessness, stout-heartedness, heroism; backbone, grit, spine, spirit, mettle; *informal* guts, spunk; *Brit. informal* bottle; *N. Amer. informal* moxie.
– OPPOSITES timidity.
hardiness • noun ROBUSTNESS, strength, toughness, ruggedness, sturdiness, resilience, stamina, vigour; healthiness, good health.
– OPPOSITES frailty.
hard-line • adjective UNCOMPROMISING, strict, extreme, tough, diehard, inflexible, intransigent, intractable, unyielding, single-minded, not giving an inch.
– OPPOSITES moderate.
hardly • adverb *we hardly know each other* SCARCELY, barely, only just, slightly.
hard-nosed • adjective *(informal)* TOUGH-MINDED, unsentimental, no-nonsense, hard-headed, hardbitten, pragmatic, realistic, down-to-earth, practical, rational, shrewd, astute, businesslike; *informal* hard-boiled.
– OPPOSITES sentimental.
hard-pressed • adjective **1** *the hard-pressed infantry* UNDER ATTACK, hotly pursued, harried. **2** *the hard-pressed construction industry* IN DIFFICULTIES, under pressure, troubled, beleaguered, harassed, with one's back to/against the wall, in a tight corner, in a tight spot, between a rock and a hard place; overburdened, overworked, overloaded, rushed off one's feet; *informal* pushed, up against it.
hardship • noun PRIVATION, deprivation, destitution, poverty, austerity, penury, want, need, neediness, impecuniousness; misfortune, distress, suffering, affliction, trouble, pain, misery, wretchedness, tribulation, adversity, trials, trials and tribulations, dire straits; *poetic/literary* travails.
– OPPOSITES prosperity, ease.
hardware • noun EQUIPMENT, apparatus, gear, paraphernalia, tackle, kit, machinery; tools, articles, implements, instruments, appliances.
hard-wearing • adjective DURABLE, strong, tough, resilient, lasting, long-lasting, made to last, stout, well made, rugged, heavy-duty.
– OPPOSITES flimsy.
hard-working • adjective DILIGENT, industrious, conscientious, assiduous, sedulous, painstaking, persevering, unflagging, untiring, tireless, indefatigable, studious; keen, enthusiastic, zealous, busy,

hare ● noun a fast-running, long-eared mammal resembling a large rabbit, with very long hind legs. ● verb run with great speed.
– PHRASES **run with the hare and hunt with the hounds** Brit. try to remain on good terms with both sides in a conflict.
– ORIGIN Old English.

harebell ● noun a plant with slender stems and pale blue bell-shaped flowers.

hare-brained ● adjective rash; ill-judged.

Hare Krishna /haari krishnə/ ● noun a member of the International Society for Krishna Consciousness, a religious sect based on the worship of the Hindu god Krishna.
– ORIGIN Sanskrit, 'O Vishnu Krishna', a devotional chant.

harelip ● noun another term for CLEFT LIP.
– DERIVATIVES **harelipped** adjective.
– USAGE Use of the word **harelip** can cause offence and should be avoided; use **cleft lip** instead.
– ORIGIN from a perceived resemblance to the mouth of a hare.

harem /haareem, haareem/ ● noun **1** the separate part of a Muslim household reserved for women. **2** the wives and concubines collectively of a polygamous man. **3** a group of female animals sharing a single mate.
– ORIGIN Arabic, 'prohibited place'.

h

haricot /harrikō/ ● noun a variety of French bean with small white seeds, which can be dried and used as a vegetable.
– ORIGIN French, perhaps from Aztec *ayacotli*.

harissa /arrissə, hərissə/ ● noun a hot sauce or paste used in North African cuisine, made from chilli peppers, paprika, and olive oil.
– ORIGIN Arabic.

hark ● verb **1** literary listen. **2** (**hark at**) informal used to draw attention to an ill-advised or foolish remark or action. **3** (**hark back**) recall an earlier period.
– ORIGIN Germanic.

harken ● verb variant spelling of HEARKEN.

harlequin /haarlikwin/ ● noun (**Harlequin**) a mute character in traditional pantomime, typically masked and dressed in a diamond-patterned costume. ● adjective in varied colours; variegated.
– ORIGIN French, from earlier *Herlequin*, the leader of a legendary troop of demon horsemen.

harlequinade /haarlikwinayd/ ● noun **1** historical the section of a traditional pantomime in which Harlequin played a leading role. **2** dated a piece of buffoonery.

harlot ● noun archaic a prostitute or promiscuous woman.
– DERIVATIVES **harlotry** noun.
– ORIGIN Old French, 'young man, knave'.

harm ● noun **1** physical injury, especially that which is deliberately inflicted. **2** material damage. **3** actual or potential ill effect. ● verb **1** physically injure. **2** have an adverse effect on.
– PHRASES **out of harm's way** in a safe place.
– ORIGIN Old English.

harmattan /haarmatt'n/ ● noun a very dry, dusty easterly or north-easterly wind on the West African coast, occurring from December to February.
– ORIGIN Akan.

harmful ● adjective causing or likely to cause harm.
– DERIVATIVES **harmfully** adverb **harmfulness** noun.

harmless ● adjective not able or likely to cause harm.
– DERIVATIVES **harmlessly** adverb **harmlessness** noun.

harmonic /haarmonnik/ ● adjective **1** relating to or characterized by harmony. **2** Music relating to or denoting a harmonic or harmonics. ● noun Music an overtone accompanying a fundamental tone at a fixed interval, produced by vibration of a string, column of air, etc. in any of certain fractions of its length.
– DERIVATIVES **harmonically** adverb.

harmonica ● noun a small rectangular wind instrument with a row of metal reeds capable of producing different notes.

harmonic progression ● noun **1** Music a series of chord changes forming the underlying harmony of a piece of music. **2** Mathematics a sequence of quantities whose reciprocals are in arithmetical progression (e.g. 1, ⅓, ⅕, ⅐, etc.).

harmonious ● adjective **1** tuneful; not discordant. **2** forming a pleasing or consistent whole. **3** free from conflict.
– DERIVATIVES **harmoniously** adverb **harmoniousness** noun.

harmonium ● noun a keyboard instrument in which the notes are produced by air driven through metal reeds by foot-operated bellows.
– ORIGIN from Greek *harmonios* 'harmonious'.

harmonize (also **harmonise**) ● verb **1** Music add notes to (a melody) to produce harmony. **2** make or be harmonious.
– DERIVATIVES **harmonization** noun.

harmony ● noun (pl. **harmonies**) **1** the combination of simultaneously sounded musical notes to produce chords and chord progressions having a pleasing effect. **2** the quality of forming a pleasing and consistent whole. **3** agreement or concord.

Thesaurus

with one's shoulder to the wheel, with one's nose to the grindstone.
– OPPOSITES lazy.

hardy ● adjective ROBUST, healthy, fit, strong, sturdy, tough, rugged, hearty, lusty, vigorous, hale and hearty, fit as a fiddle, fighting fit, in fine fettle, in good health, in good condition; *Brit.* in rude health; *dated* stalwart.
– OPPOSITES delicate.

hare-brained ● adjective **1** *a hare-brained scheme* ILL-JUDGED, rash, foolish, foolhardy, reckless, madcap, wild, silly, stupid, ridiculous, absurd, idiotic, asinine, imprudent, impracticable, unworkable, unrealistic, unconsidered, half-baked, ill-thought-out, ill-advised, ill-conceived; *informal* crackpot, crackbrained, cock-eyed, crazy; *Brit. informal* daft, barmy. **2** *a hare-brained young girl* FOOLISH, silly, idiotic, unintelligent, empty-headed, scatterbrained, feather-brained, birdbrained, pea-brained, brainless, giddy; *informal* dippy, dizzy, dopey, dotty, airheaded.
– OPPOSITES sensible, intelligent.

harem ● noun SERAGLIO, zenana; *historical* gynaeceum.

hark ● verb *(poetic/literary) hark, I hear a warning note* LISTEN, lend an ear, pay attention, attend, mark; *archaic* hearken, give ear.
– PHRASES **hark back to** RECALL, call/bring to mind, evoke, put one in mind of.

harlequin ● noun JESTER, joker, merry andrew.
● adjective *a harlequin pattern* MULTICOLOURED, many-coloured, colourful, particoloured, many-hued, rainbow, varicoloured, variegated, jazzy, kaleidoscopic, psychedelic, polychromatic, chequered; *archaic* motley.

harlot ● noun *(archaic)* PROSTITUTE, whore, fille de joie, call girl; promiscuous woman, slut; *informal* tart, pro, member of the oldest profession; *Brit. informal* scrubber, slag, slapper; *N. Amer. informal* hooker, hustler, tramp, roundheel; *dated* streetwalker, hussy, woman of the streets, woman of the night, scarlet woman, loose woman, fallen woman, cocotte, wanton; *archaic* strumpet, courtesan, trollop, doxy, drab, trull.

harm ● noun **1** *the voltage is not sufficient to cause harm* INJURY, hurt, pain, trauma; damage, impairment, mischief. **2** *I can't see any harm in it* EVIL, wrong, ill, wickedness, iniquity, sin.
– OPPOSITES benefit.
● verb **1** *he's never harmed anybody in his life* INJURE, hurt, wound, lay a finger on, maltreat, mistreat, misuse, ill-treat, ill-use, abuse, molest. **2** *this could harm his World Cup prospects* DAMAGE, spoil, mar, do mischief to, impair.

harmful ● adjective DAMAGING, injurious, detrimental, dangerous, deleterious, unfavourable, negative, disadvantageous, unhealthy, unwholesome, hurtful, baleful, destructive; noxious, hazardous, poisonous, toxic, deadly, lethal; bad, evil, malign, malignant, malevolent, corrupting, subversive, pernicious.
– OPPOSITES beneficial.

harmless ● adjective **1** *a harmless substance* SAFE, innocuous, benign, gentle, mild, wholesome, non-toxic, non-poisonous, non-irritant; non-addictive. **2** *he seems harmless enough* INOFFENSIVE, innocuous, unobjectionable, unexceptionable.
– OPPOSITES dangerous.

harmonious ● adjective **1** *harmonious music* TUNEFUL, melodious, melodic, sweet-sounding, mellifluous, dulcet, lyrical; euphonious, euphonic, harmonic, polyphonic; *informal* easy on the ear. **2** *their harmonious relationship* FRIENDLY, amicable, cordial, amiable, congenial, easy, peaceful, peaceable, cooperative; compatible, sympathetic, united, attuned, in harmony, in rapport, in tune, in accord, of one mind, seeing eye to eye. **3** *a harmonious blend of traditional and modern* CONGRUOUS, coordinated, balanced, in proportion, compatible, well matched, well balanced.
– OPPOSITES discordant, hostile, incongruous.

harmonize ● verb **1** *colours which harmonize in a pleasing way* COORDINATE, go together, match, blend, mix, balance, tone in; be compatible, be harmonious, suit each other, set each other off. **2** *the need to harmonize tax laws across Europe* COORDINATE, sys-

– ORIGIN Latin *harmonia* 'joining, concord', from Greek *harmos* 'joint'.

harness ● noun **1** a set of straps and fittings by which a horse or other draught animal is fastened to a cart, plough, etc. and is controlled by its driver. **2** a similar arrangement of straps, as for fastening a parachute to a person's body or for restraining a young child. ● verb **1** fit with a harness. **2** control and make use of (resources).

– PHRASES **in harness 1** (of an animal) used for draught work. **2** in the routine of daily work.

– ORIGIN Old French *harneis* 'military equipment', from Old Norse.

harp ● noun a musical instrument consisting of a frame supporting a graduated series of parallel strings, played by plucking with the fingers. ● verb (**harp on**) talk or write persistently and tediously on a particular topic.

– DERIVATIVES **harper** noun **harpist** noun.

– ORIGIN Old English.

harpoon ● noun a barbed spear-like missile attached to a long rope and thrown by hand or fired from a gun, used for catching whales and other large sea creatures. ● verb spear with a harpoon.

– DERIVATIVES **harpooner** noun.

– ORIGIN French *harpon*, from Greek *harpē* 'sickle'.

harpsichord ● noun a keyboard instrument similar in shape to a grand piano, with horizontal strings plucked by points operated by depressing the keys.

– DERIVATIVES **harpsichordist** noun.

– ORIGIN from Latin *harpa* 'harp' + *chorda* 'string'.

harpy ● noun (pl. **harpies**) **1** Greek & Roman Mythology a rapacious monster usually depicted with a woman's head and body and a bird's wings and claws. **2** a grasping, unscrupulous woman.

– ORIGIN Greek *harpuiai* 'snatchers'.

harquebus /haarkwibəss/ (also **arquebus**) ● noun historical an early type of portable gun supported on a tripod or a forked rest.

– ORIGIN French *harquebuse*, from Low German *hake* 'hook' + *busse* 'gun'.

harridan ● noun a strict, bossy, or belligerent old woman.

– ORIGIN perhaps from French *haridelle* 'old horse'.

harrier[1] ● noun a person who harries others.

harrier[2] ● noun a hound of a breed used for hunting hares.

– ORIGIN from HARE.

harrier[3] ● noun a long-winged, slender-bodied bird of prey with low hunting flight.

– ORIGIN from an obsolete variant of HARRY.

Harris tweed ● noun trademark handwoven tweed made traditionally on the island of Lewis and Harris in Scotland.

harrow ● noun an implement consisting of a heavy frame set with teeth which is dragged over ploughed land to break up or spread the soil. ● verb **1** draw a harrow over. **2** (**harrowing**) very distressing.

– ORIGIN Old Norse.

harrumph ● verb **1** clear the throat noisily. **2** grumpily express dissatisfaction.

– ORIGIN imitative.

harry ● verb (**harries**, **harried**) **1** persistently carry out attacks on (an enemy). **2** persistently harass.

– ORIGIN Old English.

harsh ● adjective **1** unpleasantly rough or jarring to the senses. **2** cruel or severe. **3** (of climate or conditions) difficult to survive in; hostile.

– DERIVATIVES **harshen** verb **harshly** adverb **harshness** noun.

– ORIGIN Low German *harsch* 'rough', from *haer* 'hair'.

hart ● noun an adult male deer, especially a red deer over five years old.

– ORIGIN Old English.

hartebeest /haartibeest/ ● noun a large African antelope with a long head and sloping back.

– ORIGIN from Dutch *hert* 'hart' + *beest* 'beast'.

harum-scarum ● adjective reckless; impetuous.

– ORIGIN from HARE and SCARE.

harvest ● noun **1** the process or period of gathering in crops. **2** the season's yield or crop. ● verb gather as a harvest.

– DERIVATIVES **harvestable** adjective **harvester** noun.

– ORIGIN Old English, 'autumn'.

harvest home ● noun **1** the gathering in of the final part of the year's harvest. **2** a festival marking the end of the harvest period.

harvestman ● noun an arachnid with a globular body and very long thin legs.

harvest moon ● noun the full moon that is seen closest to the time of the autumn equinox.

harvest mouse ● noun a small mouse with a prehensile tail,

h

Thesaurus

tematize, correlate, integrate, synchronize, make consistent, bring in line, bring in tune.

– OPPOSITES clash.

harmony ● noun **1** *musical harmony* EUPHONY, polyphony; tunefulness, melodiousness, mellifluousness. **2** *the harmony of the whole structure* BALANCE, symmetry, congruity, consonance, coordination, compatibility. **3** *the villagers live together in harmony* ACCORD, agreement, peace, peacefulness, amity, amicability, friendship, fellowship, cooperation, understanding, consensus, unity, sympathy, rapport, like-mindedness; unison, union, concert, oneness, synthesis; formal concord.

– OPPOSITES dissonance, disagreement.

harness ● noun *a horse's harness* TACK, tackle, equipment; trappings; yoke; archaic equipage.

● verb **1** *he harnessed his horse* HITCH UP, put in harness, yoke, couple. **2** *attempts to harness solar energy* CONTROL, exploit, utilize, use, employ, make use of, put to use; channel, mobilize, apply, capitalize on.

harp ● noun lyre, aeolian harp, wind harp, Jew's harp, Celtic harp, clarsach, triple harp, Welsh harp; historical trigon.

– PHRASES **harp on about** KEEP ON ABOUT, go on about, keep talking about, dwell on, make an issue of; labour the point.

harpoon ● noun SPEAR, trident, dart, barb, gaff, leister.

harridan ● noun SHREW, termagant, virago, harpy, vixen, nag, hag, crone, dragon, ogress; fishwife, hellcat, she-devil, gorgon; martinet, tartar; informal old bag, old bat, old cow, bitch, battleaxe, witch; archaic scold.

harried ● adjective HARASSED, beleaguered, flustered, agitated, bothered, vexed, beset, plagued; informal hassled, up against it.

harrow ● verb DISTRESS, trouble, bother, afflict, grieve, torment, pain, hurt, mortify.

– OPPOSITES comfort.

harrowing ● adjective DISTRESSING, distressful, traumatic, upsetting; shocking, disturbing, painful, haunting, appalling, horrifying.

harry ● verb **1** *they harried the retreating enemy* ATTACK, assail, assault; charge, rush, strike, set upon; bombard, shell, strafe. **2** *the government was harried by a new lobby* HARASS, hound, pressurize, bedevil, torment, pester, bother, worry, badger, nag, plague; informal hassle, bug, lean on, give someone a hard time, get on someone's back.

harsh ● adjective **1** *a harsh voice* GRATING, jarring, rasping, strident, raucous, brassy, discordant, unharmonious, unmelodious; screeching, shrill; rough, coarse, hoarse, gruff, croaky. **2** *harsh colours* GLARING, bright, dazzling; loud, garish, gaudy, lurid, bold. **3** *his harsh rule over them* CRUEL, savage, barbarous, despotic, dictatorial, tyrannical, tyrannous; ruthless, merciless, pitiless, relentless, unmerciful; severe, strict, intolerant, illiberal; hard-hearted, heartless, unkind, inhuman, inhumane. **4** *they took harsh measures to end the crisis* SEVERE, stringent, firm, stiff, hard, stern, rigorous, grim, uncompromising; punitive, cruel, brutal. **5** *harsh words* RUDE, discourteous, uncivil, impolite; unfriendly, sharp, bitter, abusive, unkind, disparaging; abrupt, brusque, curt, gruff, short, surly, offhand. **6** *harsh conditions* AUSTERE, grim, spartan, hard, comfortless, inhospitable, stark, bleak, desolate. **7** *a harsh winter* HARD, severe, cold, bitter, bleak, freezing, icy; arctic, polar, Siberian. **8** *harsh cream cleaners* ABRASIVE, strong, caustic; coarse, rough.

– OPPOSITES soft, subdued, kind, friendly, comfortable, balmy, mild.

harum-scarum ● adjective RECKLESS, impetuous, impulsive, imprudent, rash, wild; daredevil, madcap, hot-headed, hare-brained, foolhardy, incautious, careless, heedless; informal devil-may-care; poetic/literary temerarious.

– OPPOSITES cautious.

harvest ● noun **1** *we all helped with the harvest* HARVESTING, reaping, picking, collecting; formal ingathering. **2** *a poor harvest* YIELD, crop, vintage; fruits, produce. **3** *the experiment yielded a meagre harvest* RETURN, result, fruits; product, output, effect; consequence.

● verb **1** *he harvested the wheat* GATHER (IN), bring in, reap, pick, collect; formal ingather. **2** *he harvested many honours* ACQUIRE, ob-

nesting among the stalks of growing cereals.
has third person singular present of HAVE.
has-been ● noun informal a person or thing that is outmoded or no longer significant.
hash[1] ● noun **1** a dish of diced cooked meat reheated with potatoes. **2** a jumble; a mess. ● verb make or chop into a hash.
– PHRASES **make a hash of** informal make a mess of. **settle someone's hash** informal deal with and subdue someone in no uncertain manner.
– ORIGIN French *hacher*, from *hache* 'axe'.
hash[2] ● noun informal short for HASHISH.
hash[3] ● noun the symbol #.
– ORIGIN probably an alteration of HATCH[3].
hash browns ● plural noun chiefly N. Amer. a dish of chopped and fried cooked potatoes.
hashish /hasheesh/ ● noun cannabis.
– ORIGIN Arabic, 'dry herb, powdered hemp leaves'.
Hasid /hassid/ (also **Chasid**, **Chassid**, or **Hassid**) ● noun (pl. **Hasidim**) an adherent of Hasidism.
– DERIVATIVES **Hasidic** /hasiddik/ adjective.
– ORIGIN from Hebrew, 'pious'.
Hasidism /hassidiz'm/ (also **Chasidism**, **Chassidism**, or **Hassidism**) ● noun a mystical Jewish movement founded in Poland in the 18th century, represented today by fundamentalist communities in Israel and New York.
haslet /hazlit/ ● noun chiefly Brit. a cold meat consisting of chopped and compressed pork offal.
– ORIGIN Old French *hastelet*, from *haste* 'roast meat, spit'.
hasn't ● contraction has not.
hasp ● noun a slotted hinged metal plate that forms part of a fastening for a door or lid and is fitted over a metal loop and secured by a pin or padlock.
– ORIGIN Old English.
Hassid ● noun variant spelling of HASID.
Hassidism ● noun variant spelling of HASIDISM.
hassium /hassiəm/ ● noun a very unstable chemical element made by high-energy atomic collisions.
– ORIGIN from *Hassias*, the Latin name for the German state of *Hesse*.
hassle informal ● noun **1** irritating inconvenience. **2** deliberate harassment. ● verb harass; pester.
– ORIGIN originally a dialect word meaning 'hack or saw at', of unknown origin.
hassock ● noun chiefly Brit. a cushion for kneeling on in church.
– ORIGIN Old English, 'clump of grass in marshy ground'.
hast archaic second person singular present of HAVE.
haste ● noun excessive speed or urgency of action.
– PHRASES **more haste, less speed** proverb you make better progress with a task if you don't try to do it too quickly.
– ORIGIN Old French.
hasten ● verb **1** be quick to do something; move quickly. **2** cause to happen sooner than anticipated.
hasty ● adjective (**hastier**, **hastiest**) done or acting with haste; hurried.
– DERIVATIVES **hastily** adverb **hastiness** noun.
hat ● noun a shaped covering for the head, typically with a brim and a crown.
– PHRASES **keep something under one's hat** keep something a secret. **pass the hat round** (or N. Amer. **pass the hat**) collect contributions of money. **pick out of a hat** select at random. **take one's hat off to** used to express admiration or praise for. **talk through one's hat** informal talk foolishly or ignorantly. **throw one's hat into the ring** express willingness to take up a challenge.
– DERIVATIVES **hatful** noun **hatless** adjective **hatted** adjective.
– ORIGIN Old English, related to HOOD[1].
hatband ● noun a decorative ribbon encircling a hat, held in position above the brim.
hatch[1] ● noun **1** a small opening in a floor, wall, or roof allowing access from one area to another. **2** a door in an aircraft, spacecraft, or submarine.
– PHRASES **down the hatch** informal used as a toast.
– ORIGIN Old English, denoting the lower half of a divided door.
hatch[2] ● verb **1** (with reference to a young bird, fish, or reptile) emerge or cause to emerge from its egg. **2** (of an egg) open and produce a young animal. **3** conspire to devise (a plot or plan). ● noun a newly hatched brood.
– ORIGIN of unknown origin.
hatch[3] ● verb (in technical drawing) shade with closely drawn parallel lines.
– DERIVATIVES **hatching** noun.
– ORIGIN Old French *hacher*, from *hache* 'axe'.
hatchback ● noun a car with a door across the full width at the back end that opens upwards to provide easy access for loading.
hatchery ● noun (pl. **hatcheries**) an establishment where fish or poultry eggs are hatched.
hatchet ● noun a small axe with a short handle for use in one hand.
– PHRASES **bury the hatchet** end a quarrel or conflict. [ORIGIN in allusion to an American Indian custom.]
– ORIGIN Old French *hachette* 'little axe', from Latin *hapia* 'axe'.
hatchet-faced ● adjective informal sharp-featured and grim-looking.
hatchet job ● noun informal a fierce verbal or written attack.
hatchet man ● noun informal **1** a person employed to carry out controversial or disagreeable tasks. **2** a harsh critic.
hatchling ● noun a newly hatched young animal.

Thesaurus

tain, gain, get, earn; accumulate, amass, gather, collect; *informal* land, net, bag, scoop.
hash[1] ● noun *a whole hash of excuses* MIXTURE, assortment, variety, array, mix, miscellany, selection, medley, mishmash, hotchpotch, ragbag, gallimaufry, pot-pourri; *N. Amer.* hodgepodge.
– PHRASES **make a hash of** *(informal)* BUNGLE, fluff, mess up, make a mess of; mismanage, mishandle, ruin, wreck; *informal* botch, muff, muck up, foul up, screw up, blow; *Brit. informal* make a pig's ear of, cock up; *N. Amer. informal* flub.
hash[2] ● noun *(informal) she smokes a lot of hash.* See CANNABIS.
hassle *(informal)* ● noun **1** *parking is such a hassle* INCONVENIENCE, bother, nuisance, problem, trouble, struggle, difficulty, annoyance, irritation, thorn in one's flesh/side, fuss; *informal* aggravation, aggro, stress, headache, pain (in the neck). **2** *(N. Amer.) she got into a hassle with that guy.* See QUARREL noun.
● verb *they were hassling him to pay up* HARASS, pester, nag, keep on at, badger, hound, harry, chivvy, bother, torment, plague; *informal* bug, give someone a hard time, get on someone's back, breathe down someone's neck; *N. English informal* mither.
hassled ● adjective *(informal)* HARASSED, stressed (out), harried, frayed, agitated, flustered; beleaguered, hounded, plagued, bothered, beset, tormented; under pressure, hot and bothered; *informal* up against it.
– OPPOSITES calm.
haste ● noun *working with feverish haste* SPEED, hastiness, hurriedness, swiftness, rapidity, quickness, briskness; *formal* expedition.
– OPPOSITES delay.
– PHRASES **in haste** QUICKLY, rapidly, fast, speedily, with urgency, in a rush, in a hurry.
hasten ● verb **1** *we hastened back home* HURRY, rush, dash, race, fly, shoot; scurry, scramble, dart, bolt, sprint, run, gallop; go fast, go quickly, go like lightning, go hell for leather; *informal* tear, hare, pelt, scoot, zip, zoom, belt, hotfoot it, leg it; *Brit. informal* bomb, bucket; *N. Amer. informal* hightail, barrel. **2** *chemicals can hasten ageing* SPEED UP, accelerate, quicken, precipitate, advance, hurry on, step up, spur on; facilitate, aid, assist, boost.
– OPPOSITES dawdle, delay.
hastily ● adverb **1** *Meg retreated hastily* QUICKLY, hurriedly, fast, swiftly, rapidly, speedily, briskly, without delay, post-haste; with all speed, as fast as possible, at breakneck speed, at a run, hotfoot, on the double; *informal* double quick, p.d.q. (pretty damn quick), nippily, like (greased) lightning, like the wind, like a scalded cat, like a bat out of hell; *Brit. informal* at a rate of knots, like the clappers; *N. Amer. informal* lickety-split. **2** *an agreement was hastily drawn up* HURRIEDLY, speedily, quickly; on the spur of the moment, prematurely.
hasty ● adjective **1** *hasty steps* QUICK, hurried, fast, swift, rapid, speedy, brisk; *poetic/literary* fleet. **2** *hasty decisions* RASH, impetuous, impulsive, reckless, precipitate, spur-of-the-moment, premature, unconsidered, unthinking; *poetic/literary* temerarious.
– OPPOSITES slow, considered.
hat ● noun CAP, beret, bonnet; *Brit. informal* titfer.
hatch ● verb **1** *the duck hatched her eggs* INCUBATE, brood, sit on. **2** *the plot that you hatched up last night* DEVISE, conceive, concoct, brew, invent, plan, design, formulate; think up, dream up; *informal*

hatchway • noun an opening or hatch, especially in a ship's deck.

hate • verb feel intense dislike for or a strong aversion towards. • noun **1** intense dislike; strong aversion. **2** informal a disliked person or thing. **3** (before a noun) denoting hostile actions motivated by intense dislike or prejudice: *a hate campaign.*
– DERIVATIVES **hatable** (also **hateable**) adjective **hater** noun.
– ORIGIN Old English.

hateful • adjective arousing or deserving of hatred.
– DERIVATIVES **hatefully** adverb **hatefulness** noun.

hath archaic third person singular present of HAVE.

hatha yoga /hathə yōgə/ • noun a system of physical exercises and breathing control used in yoga.
– ORIGIN *hatha* from Sanskrit, 'force'.

hatred • noun intense hate.

hatter • noun a person who makes and sells hats.
– PHRASES **(as) mad as a hatter** informal completely insane. [ORIGIN with allusion to the effects of mercury poisoning from the use of mercurous nitrate in the manufacture of felt hats.]

hat-trick • noun three successes of the same kind, especially (in soccer) a player scoring three goals in a game or (in cricket) a bowler taking three wickets with successive balls.
– ORIGIN referring originally to the club presentation of a new hat to a bowler taking a hat-trick.

hauberk /hawberk/ • noun historical a full-length coat of mail.
– ORIGIN Old French *hauberc.*

haughty • adjective (**haughtier**, **haughtiest**) arrogantly superior and disdainful.
– DERIVATIVES **haughtily** adverb **haughtiness** noun.
– ORIGIN Old French *hault* 'high' from Latin *altus.*

haul • verb **1** pull or drag with effort or force. **2** transport in a truck or cart. • noun **1** a quantity of something obtained, especially illegally. **2** a number of fish caught at one time. **3** a distance to be travelled.
– PHRASES **haul over the coals** see COAL.
– DERIVATIVES **hauler** noun.
– ORIGIN originally in the nautical sense 'trim sails for sailing closer to the wind': variant of HALE[2].

haulage • noun the commercial transport of goods.

haulier • noun Brit. a person or company employed in the commercial transport of goods by road.

haulm /hawm/ • noun **1** a stalk or stem. **2** the stalks or stems of peas, beans, or potatoes collectively.
– ORIGIN Old English.

haunch • noun **1** the buttock and thigh considered together, in a human or animal. **2** the leg and loin of an animal, as food.
– ORIGIN Old French *hanche.*

haunt • verb **1** (of a ghost) manifest itself regularly at (a place). **2** (of a person) frequent (a place). **3** be persistently and disturbingly present in the mind. • noun a place frequented by a specified person: *a favourite haunt of pickpockets.*
– DERIVATIVES **haunter** noun.
– ORIGIN Old French *hanter.*

haunted • adjective **1** (of a place) frequented by a ghost. **2** having or showing signs of mental anguish.

haunting • adjective poignant; evocative.
– DERIVATIVES **hauntingly** adverb.

hausfrau /howssfrow/ • noun a German housewife, especially with reference to orderliness and efficiency.
– ORIGIN German, from *Haus* 'house' + *Frau* 'woman, wife'.

hautboy /(h)ōboy/ • noun archaic form of OBOE.
– ORIGIN French *hautbois,* from *haut* 'high' + *bois* 'wood'.

haute couture /ōt kootyoor/ • noun the designing and making of high-quality clothes by leading fashion houses.
– ORIGIN French, 'high dressmaking'.

haute cuisine /ōt kwizeen/ • noun high-quality cooking following the style of traditional French cuisine.
– ORIGIN French, 'high cookery'.

hauteur /ōtör/ • noun proud haughtiness of manner.
– ORIGIN French, from *haut* 'high'.

Havana • noun a cigar made in Cuba or from Cuban tobacco.
– ORIGIN named after *Havana,* the capital of Cuba.

have • verb (**has**; past and past part. **had**) **1** possess, own, or hold. **2** experience; undergo: *have difficulty.* **3** be able to make use of. **4** (**have to**) be obliged to; must. **5** perform the action indicated by the noun specified: *he had a look round.* **6** demonstrate (a personal attribute). **7** suffer from (an illness or disability). **8** cause to be in a particular state. **9** cause to be done for one by someone else. **10** place, hold, or keep in a particular position. **11** be the recipient or host of. **12** eat or drink. **13** (**not have**) refuse to tolerate. **14** (**be had**) informal be cheated or deceived. • auxiliary verb used with a past participle to form the perfect, pluperfect, and future perfect tenses, and the conditional mood. • noun (usu. in phrase **the haves and the have-nots**) informal people with plenty of money.
– PHRASES **have had it** informal **1** be beyond repair or revival. **2** be unable to tolerate any longer. **have (got) it in for** informal behave in a hostile way towards. **have it out** informal attempt to resolve a dispute by confrontation. **have on** Brit. informal try to make (someone) believe something untrue, especially as a joke. **have up** Brit. informal bring before a court to answer for an alleged offence.

h

Thesaurus

cook up.

hatchet • noun AXE, cleaver, mattock, tomahawk; *Brit.* chopper.

hate • verb **1** *they hate each other* LOATHE, detest, despise, dislike, abhor, execrate; be repelled by, be unable to bear/stand, find intolerable, recoil from, shrink from; *formal* abominate; *archaic* disrelish. **2** *I hate to bother you* BE SORRY, be reluctant, be loath, be unwilling, be disinclined; regret, dislike.
– OPPOSITES love.
• noun **1** *feelings of hate* HATRED, loathing, detestation, dislike, distaste, abhorrence, abomination, execration, aversion; hostility, enmity, animosity, antipathy, revulsion, disgust, contempt, odium; *archaic* disrelish. **2** *(informal) his pet hate is filling in forms* BUGBEAR, bane, bête noire, bogey, aversion, thorn in one's flesh/side; *N. Amer.* bugaboo.
– OPPOSITES love.

hateful • adjective DETESTABLE, horrible, horrid, unpleasant, awful, nasty, disagreeable, despicable, objectionable, insufferable, revolting, loathsome, abhorrent, abominable, execrable, odious, disgusting, distasteful, obnoxious, offensive, vile, heinous; *informal* ghastly; *Brit. informal* beastly, God-awful.
– OPPOSITES delightful.

hatred • noun LOATHING, hate, detestation, dislike, distaste, abhorrence, abomination, execration; aversion, hostility, ill will, ill feeling, enmity, animosity, antipathy; revulsion, disgust, contempt, odium; *archaic* disrelish.

haughtiness • noun ARROGANCE, conceit, pride, hubris, hauteur, vanity, self-importance, pomposity, condescension, disdain, contempt; snobbishness, snobbery, superciliousness; *informal* snootiness.
– OPPOSITES modesty.

haughty • adjective PROUD, arrogant, vain, conceited, snobbish, superior, self-important, pompous, supercilious, condescending, patronizing; scornful, contemptuous, disdainful; full of oneself, above oneself; *informal* stuck-up, snooty, hoity-toity, uppity, uppish, big-headed, high and mighty, la-di-da; *Brit. informal* toffee-nosed; *N. Amer. informal* chesty.
– OPPOSITES humble.

haul • verb **1** *she hauled the basket along* DRAG, pull, tug, heave, lug, hump, draw, tow; *informal* yank. **2** *a contract to haul coal* TRANSPORT, convey, carry, ship, ferry, move, shift.
• noun *the thieves abandoned their haul* BOOTY, loot, plunder; spoils, stolen goods, ill-gotten gains; *informal* swag, boodle.

haunches • plural noun RUMP, hindquarters, rear (end), seat; buttocks, thighs, derrière; *Brit.* bottom; *Anatomy* nates; *informal* behind, backside; *Brit. informal* bum, botty; *N. Amer. informal* butt, fanny, tush, heinie; *humorous* fundament, posterior, stern.

haunt • verb **1** *a ghost haunts this house* APPEAR IN, materialize in; visit. **2** *he haunts street markets* FREQUENT, patronize, visit regularly; loiter in, linger in; *informal* hang out in. **3** *the sight haunted me for years* TORMENT, disturb, trouble, worry, plague, burden, beset, beleaguer; prey on, weigh on, gnaw at, nag at, weigh heavily on, obsess; *informal* bug.
• noun *a favourite haunt of artists,* STAMPING GROUND, meeting place; territory, domain, resort, retreat, spot; *N. Amer.* stomping ground; *informal* hang-out; *Brit. informal* patch.

haunted • adjective **1** *a haunted house* POSSESSED, cursed; ghostly, eerie; *informal* spooky, scary. **2** *his haunted eyes* TORMENTED, anguished, troubled, tortured, worried, disturbed.

haunting • adjective EVOCATIVE, emotive, affecting, moving, touching, stirring, powerful; poignant, nostalgic, wistful; memorable, unforgettable, indelible.

hauteur • noun HAUGHTINESS, superciliousness, arrogance, pride,

– ORIGIN Old English.
have-a-go ● adjective Brit. informal (of a member of the public) intervening to stop a criminal during the course of a crime.
haven ● noun **1** a place of safety or refuge. **2** a harbour or small port.
– ORIGIN Old English.
have-nots ● plural noun informal economically disadvantaged people.
haven't ● contraction have not.
haver /hayvər/ ● verb **1** Scottish talk foolishly; babble. **2** Brit. act in an indecisive manner.
– ORIGIN of unknown origin.
haversack ● noun a small, stout bag carried on the back or over the shoulder.
– ORIGIN obsolete German *Habersack*, denoting a bag used to carry oats as horse feed, from dialect *Haber* 'oats' + *Sack* 'sack, bag'.
havoc ● noun **1** widespread destruction. **2** great confusion or disorder.
– PHRASES **play havoc with** completely disrupt.
– ORIGIN Old French *havot*; the word was originally used in the phrase *cry havoc* 'give an army the order *havoc*', which was the signal for plundering.
h
haw[1] ● noun the red fruit of the hawthorn.
– ORIGIN Old English.
haw[2] ● verb see **hum and haw** at HUM.
Hawaiian ● noun **1** a person from Hawaii. **2** the language of Hawaii. ● adjective relating to Hawaii.
hawfinch ● noun a large finch with a massive bill for cracking open cherry stones and other hard seeds.
– ORIGIN from HAW[1] + FINCH.
hawk[1] ● noun **1** a fast-flying bird of prey with broad rounded wings and a long tail. **2** any bird used in falconry. **3** a person who advocates an aggressive foreign policy. ● verb hunt game with a trained hawk.
– DERIVATIVES **hawkish** adjective.
– ORIGIN Old English.
hawk[2] ● verb carry about and offer (goods) for sale in the street.
– ORIGIN probably from HAWKER.
hawk[3] ● verb **1** clear the throat noisily. **2** (**hawk up**) bring (phlegm) up from the throat.
– ORIGIN probably imitative.
hawker ● noun a person who travels about selling goods.
– ORIGIN probably from Low German or Dutch and related to HUCKSTER.
hawkmoth ● noun a large swift-flying moth with a stout body and narrow forewings, typically feeding on nectar while hovering.
hawksbeard ● noun a plant which resembles a dandelion but has a branched stem with several flowers.
hawkweed ● noun a plant with yellow dandelion-like flower heads.
– ORIGIN Old English.
hawser /hawzər/ ● noun a thick rope or cable for mooring or towing a ship.
– ORIGIN from Old French *haucier* 'to hoist', from Latin *altus* 'high'.
hawthorn ● noun a thorny shrub or tree with white, pink, or red blossom and small dark red fruits (haws).
– ORIGIN Old English, probably with the literal meaning 'hedge thorn'.
hay ● noun grass that has been mown and dried for use as fodder.
– PHRASES **hit the hay** informal go to bed. **make hay** (**while the sun shines**) make good use of an opportunity while it lasts.
– DERIVATIVES **haying** noun.
– ORIGIN Old English, related to HEW.
haycock ● noun a conical heap of hay left in the field to dry.
hay fever ● noun an allergy caused by pollen or dust in which the mucous membranes of the eyes and nose are inflamed, causing sneezing and watery eyes.
hayloft ● noun a loft over a stable used for storing hay or straw.
haymaker ● noun **1** a person who is involved in making hay. **2** an apparatus for shaking and drying hay. **3** informal a forceful blow.
– DERIVATIVES **haymaking** noun.
hayrick ● noun a haystack.
hayride ● noun chiefly N. Amer. a ride or other activity undertaken

Thesaurus

conceit, snobbery, snobbishness, superiority, self-importance; disdain, condescension; airs and graces; *informal* snootiness, uppishness; *Brit. informal* side.
have ● verb **1** *he had a new car* POSSESS, own, be in possession of, be the owner of; be blessed with, boast, enjoy; keep, retain, hold, occupy. **2** *the flat has five rooms* COMPRISE, consist of, contain, include, incorporate, be composed of, be made up of; encompass; *formal* comprehend. **3** *they had tea together* EAT, consume, devour, partake of; drink, imbibe, quaff; *informal* demolish, dispose of, put away, get outside of, scoff (down); sink, knock back; *N. Amer. informal* scarf (down/up). **4** *she had a letter from Mark* RECEIVE, get, be given, be sent, obtain, acquire, come by, take receipt of. **5** *we've decided to have a party* ORGANIZE, arrange, hold, give, host, throw, put on, lay on, set up, fix up. **6** *she's going to have a baby* GIVE BIRTH TO, bear, be delivered of, bring into the world; *informal* drop; *archaic* be brought to bed of, beget. **7** *we are having guests for dinner* ENTERTAIN, be host to, cater for, receive; invite round/over, ask round/over, wine and dine; accommodate, put up. **8** *he had trouble finding the restaurant* EXPERIENCE, encounter, face, meet, find, run into, go through, undergo. **9** *I have a headache* BE SUFFERING FROM, be afflicted by, be affected by, be troubled with; *informal* be a martyr to. **10** *I had a good time* EXPERIENCE; enjoy. **11** *many of them have doubts* HARBOUR, entertain, feel, nurse, nurture, sustain, maintain. **12** *he had little patience* MANIFEST, show, display, exhibit, demonstrate. **13** *he had them throw Chris out* MAKE, ask to, request to, get to, tell to, require to, induce to, prevail upon someone to; order to, command to, direct to, force to. **14** *I can't have you insulting me* TOLERATE, endure, bear, support, accept, put up with, go along with, take, countenance; permit to, allow to; *informal* stand, abide, stomach; *Brit. informal* stick, be doing with; *formal* brook. **15** *I have to get up at six* MUST, be obliged to, be required to, be compelled to, be forced to, be bound to. **16** (*informal*) *I realized I'd been had* TRICK, fool, deceive, cheat, dupe, take in, hoodwink, swindle; *informal* do, con, diddle, rip off, shaft; *N. Amer. informal* sucker, snooker.
– OPPOSITES send, give, visit.
– PHRASES **have done with** HAVE FINISHED WITH, be done with, be through with, want no more to do with; have given up, have turned one's back on, have washed one's hands of, have no more truck with. **have had it** (*informal*) **1** *they admit that they've had it* HAVE NO CHANCE, have no hope, have failed, be finished, be defeated, have lost; *informal* have flopped, have come a cropper. **2** *if you tell anyone, you've had it* BE IN TROUBLE, be in for a scolding; *informal* be for the high jump, be in hot water, be in (deep) shtook; *Brit. informal* be for it. **have nothing on someone** (*informal*) HAVE NO EVIDENCE AGAINST, know nothing bad about, know nothing incriminating about. **have someone on** (*Brit. informal*) PLAY A TRICK ON, play a joke on, joke with, trick, tease, rag, make a monkey (out) of, pull someone's leg; *informal* kid, rib, take for a ride, lead up the garden path; *Brit. informal* wind up; *N. Amer. informal* put on. **have something on 1** *she had a blue dress on* BE WEARING, be dressed in, be clothed in, be attired in, be decked out in, be robed in. **2** (*Brit.*) *I have got a lot on at the moment* BE COMMITTED TO, have arranged, have planned, have organized, have fixed up, have on the agenda.
haven ● noun **1** *they stopped in a small haven* ANCHORAGE, harbour, harbourage, port, moorage, mooring; road, roadstead; cove, inlet, bay. **2** *a safe haven* REFUGE, retreat, shelter, sanctuary, asylum; port in a storm, oasis, sanctum.
haversack ● noun KNAPSACK, rucksack, backpack, pack.
havoc ● noun **1** *the hurricane caused havoc* DEVASTATION, destruction, damage, desolation, ruination, ruin; disaster, catastrophe. **2** *hyperactive children create havoc* DISORDER, chaos, disruption, mayhem, bedlam, pandemonium, turmoil, tumult, uproar; commotion, furore; *N. Amer.* a three-ring circus; *informal* hullabaloo.
hawk ● verb PEDDLE, sell, tout, vend, trade in, traffic in, push; *Brit. informal* flog.
hawker ● noun PEDLAR, trader, seller, dealer, purveyor, vendor, huckster, door-to-door salesman, travelling salesman; *Brit.* barrow boy, tout; *informal* pusher.
hawk-eyed ● adjective VIGILANT, observant, alert, sharp-eyed, keen-eyed, eagle-eyed; on the alert, on the lookout, with one's eyes skinned/peeled; *informal* beady-eyed, not missing a trick, on the ball.
– OPPOSITES inattentive.
hay ● noun FORAGE, dried grass, herbage, silage, fodder, straw.
– PHRASES **make hay while the sun shines** make the most of an

for pleasure (originally a ride taken in a wagon carrying hay).

hayseed ● noun **1** grass seed obtained from hay. **2** informal, chiefly N. Amer. a simple, unsophisticated country person.

haystack ● noun a large packed pile of hay.

haywire ● adjective informal erratic; out of control.
– ORIGIN from HAY + WIRE, from the use of hay-baling wire in makeshift repairs.

hazard ● noun **1** a danger or risk. **2** a permanent feature of a golf course which presents an obstruction. **3** literary chance; probability. **4** a gambling game using two dice. ● verb **1** venture to say. **2** put at risk of being lost or harmed.
– ORIGIN Old French *hasard*, from Persian or Turkish, 'dice'.

hazard lights ● plural noun flashing indicator lights on a vehicle, used to warn that the vehicle is stationary or unexpectedly slow.

hazardous ● adjective risky; dangerous.
– DERIVATIVES **hazardously** adverb **hazardousness** noun.

haze[1] ● noun **1** a slight obscuration of the lower atmosphere, typically caused by fine particles of dust, pollutants, etc. **2** a state of obscurity or confusion.
– ORIGIN probably from HAZY.

haze[2] ● verb N. Amer. torment or harass (a new student or recruit) by subjection to strenuous, humiliating, or dangerous tasks.
– ORIGIN Scots and dialect in the sense 'frighten, scold, or beat'.

hazel ● noun **1** a shrub or small tree bearing prominent catkins in spring and edible nuts in autumn. **2** a rich reddish-brown colour.
– ORIGIN Old English.

hazelnut ● noun the round brown edible hard-shelled nut of the hazel.

hazy ● adjective (**hazier**, **haziest**) **1** covered by a haze. **2** vague, indistinct, or ill-defined.
– DERIVATIVES **hazily** adverb **haziness** noun.
– ORIGIN of unknown origin.

HB ● abbreviation **1** half board. **2** (also **hb**) hardback. **3** hard black (as a medium grade of pencil lead).

H-bomb ● noun short for HYDROGEN BOMB.

h & c ● abbreviation Brit. hot and cold (water).

HC ● abbreviation **1** (in the UK) House of Commons. **2** hydrocarbon.

HDTV ● abbreviation high-definition television.

HE ● abbreviation high explosive.

He ● symbol the chemical element helium.

he ● pronoun (third person sing.) **1** used to refer to a man, boy, or male animal previously mentioned or easily identified. **2** used to refer to a person or animal of unspecified sex (in modern use, now largely replaced by 'he or she' or 'they'). **3** any person (in modern use, now largely replaced by 'anyone' or 'the person'). ● noun a male; a man.
– USAGE Until recently, **he** was used to refer to a person of unspecified sex; this use is now regarded as dated and sexist. A solution has been to use **he or she**, but this can be long-winded if used repeatedly. Use of **they** as an alternative to **he** (as in *everyone needs to feel that they matter*) has been in use since the 18th century, in contexts where it occurs after an indefinite pronoun such as **everyone** or **someone**, and it is now becoming more and more accepted both in speech and in writing.
– ORIGIN Old English.

head ● noun **1** the upper part of the human body, or the front or upper part of the body of an animal, containing the brain, mouth, and sense organs. **2** a person in charge; a director or leader. **3** the front, forward, or upper part or end of something. **4** the cutting or operational end of a tool or mechanism. **5** a person considered as a numerical unit. **6** (treated as pl.) a number of cattle or game as specified: *seventy head of cattle.* **7** a compact mass of leaves or flowers at the top of a stem. **8** a component in an audio, video, or information system by which information is transferred from an electrical signal to the recording medium, or vice versa. **9** the flattened or knobbed end of a nail, pin, screw, or match. **10** the source of a river or stream. **11** the foam on top of a glass of beer. **12** (**heads**) the side of a coin bearing the image of a head. **13** pressure of water or steam in an engine or other confined space: *a good head of steam.* ● adjective chief; principal. ● verb **1** be or act as the head of. **2** give a title or heading to. **3** move in a specified direction. **4** (**head off**) intercept and turn aside. **5** Soccer shoot or pass (the ball) with the head.
– PHRASES **be banging one's head against a brick wall** be doggedly attempting the impossible. **come to a head** reach a crisis. **get one's head down** Brit. informal **1** sleep. **2** concentrate on the task in hand. **give someone his** (or **her**) **head** allow someone complete freedom of action. **go to someone's head 1** (of alcohol) make someone slightly drunk. **2** (of success) make someone conceited. **a head for** an aptitude for or tolerance of. **—— one's head off** informal talk, laugh, shout, etc. unrestrainedly. **head over heels 1** turning over completely in forward motion, as in a somersault. **2** madly in love. **a head start** an advantage granted or gained at the beginning. **keep one's head** remain calm. **keep one's head above water** avoid succumbing to difficulties. **lose one's head** lose self-control; panic. **make head or tail of** understand at all. **off** (or **out of**) **one's head** informal crazy. **off the top of one's head** without careful thought or investigation. **over someone's head 1** (also **above someone's head**) beyond someone's ability to understand. **2** without consultation or involvement. **turn someone's head** make someone conceited.
– DERIVATIVES **headed** adjective **headless** adjective.
– ORIGIN Old English.

headache ● noun **1** a continuous pain in the head. **2** informal

Thesaurus

opportunity, take advantage of something, strike while the iron is hot, seize the day, carpe diem.

haywire ● adjective *(informal)* OUT OF CONTROL, erratic, faulty, malfunctioning, out of order; chaotic, confused, disorganized, disordered, topsy-turvy; *informal* on the blink; *Brit. informal* up the spout, shambolic.

hazard ● noun **1** *the hazards of radiation* DANGER, risk, peril, threat, menace; problem, pitfall. **2** *(poetic/literary) the laws of hazard* CHANCE, probability, fortuity, luck, fate, destiny, fortune, providence.
● verb **1** *he hazarded a guess* VENTURE, advance, put forward, volunteer; conjecture, speculate, surmise; *formal* opine. **2** *it's too risky to hazard money on* RISK, jeopardize, gamble, stake, bet, chance; endanger, imperil.

hazardous ● adjective RISKY, dangerous, unsafe, perilous, precarious, fraught with danger; unpredictable, uncertain, chancy, high-risk, insecure, touch-and-go; *informal* dicey, hairy; *Brit. informal* dodgy.
– OPPOSITES safe, certain.

haze ● noun **1** *a thick haze on the sea* MIST, fog, cloud; smoke, vapour, steam. **2** *a haze of euphoria* BLUR, daze, confusion, muddle, befuddlement.

hazy ● adjective **1** *a hazy day* MISTY, foggy, cloudy, overcast; smoggy, murky. **2** *hazy memories* VAGUE, indistinct, unclear, faint, dim, nebulous, shadowy, blurred, fuzzy, confused.

head ● noun **1** *her head hit the wall* skull, cranium, crown; *informal* nut, noodle, noggin, dome; *Brit. informal* bonce; *informal, dated* conk, noddle. **2** *he had to use his head* BRAIN(S), brainpower, intellect, intelligence; wit(s), wisdom, mind, sense, reasoning, common sense; *informal* nous, savvy, grey matter; *Brit. informal* loaf; *N. Amer. informal* smarts. **3** *she had a good head for business* APTITUDE, faculty, talent, gift, capacity, ability; mind, brain. **4** *the head of the church* LEADER, chief, controller, governor, superintendent, headman; commander, captain; director, manager; principal, president, premier; *informal* boss, boss man, kingpin, top dog, Mr Big, skipper, numero uno, head honcho; *Brit. informal* gaffer, guv'nor; *N. Amer. informal* sachem, big kahuna. **5** *the head of the queue* FRONT, beginning, start, fore, forefront; top. **6** *the head of the river* SOURCE, origin, well head, headspring, headwater; *poetic/literary* wellspring. **7** *beer with a head* FROTH, foam, bubbles, spume, fizz, effervescence; suds.
– OPPOSITES back, mouth.
● adjective *the head waiter* CHIEF, principal, leading, main, first, prime, premier, top, highest, supreme, top-ranking; *N. Amer.* ranking; *informal* top-notch.
– OPPOSITES subordinate.
● verb **1** *the procession was headed by the mayor* LEAD, be at the front of; be first, lead the way. **2** *a team headed by a line manager* COMMAND, control, lead, run, manage, direct, supervise, superintend, oversee, preside over, rule, govern, captain; *informal* be the boss of. **3** *he was heading for the exit* MOVE TOWARDS, make for, aim for, go in the direction of, be bound for, make a beeline for; set out for, start out for.
– PHRASES **at the head of** IN CHARGE OF, controlling, commanding,

something that causes worry or trouble.
– DERIVATIVES **headachy** adjective.

headage • noun the number of animals held as stock on a farm.

headband • noun a band of fabric worn around the head as a decoration or to keep the hair off the face.

headbanger • noun informal a fan or performer of heavy metal music.

headbanging • noun violent rhythmic shaking of the head by fans of heavy metal music.

headboard • noun an upright panel at the head of a bed.

headbutt • verb attack (someone) using a forceful thrust with the head. • noun an act of headbutting.

head case • noun informal a mentally ill or unstable person.

headcount • noun a count of the number of people present or available.

headdress • noun an ornamental covering for the head.

header • noun **1** Soccer a shot or pass made with the head. **2** informal a headlong fall or dive. **3** a brick or stone laid at right angles to the face of a wall. **4** (also **header tank**) a raised tank of water maintaining pressure in a plumbing system. **5** a line or block of text appearing at the top of each page of a book or document.

head first • adjective & adverb **1** with the head in front of the rest of the body. **2** without sufficient forethought.

h

headgear • noun hats, helmets, and other items worn on the head.

headhunt • verb **1** (as noun **headhunting**) the practice among some peoples of collecting the heads of dead enemies as trophies. **2** identify and approach (someone employed elsewhere) to fill a business position.
– DERIVATIVES **headhunter** noun.

heading • noun **1** a title at the head of a page or section of a book. **2** a direction or bearing. **3** the top of a curtain extending above the hooks or wire by which it is suspended. **4** a horizontal passage made in preparation for building a tunnel.

headland • noun a narrow piece of land projecting into the sea.

headlight (also **headlamp**) • noun a powerful light at the front of a motor vehicle or railway engine.

headline • noun **1** a heading at the top of an article or page in a newspaper or magazine. **2** (**the headlines**) a summary of the most important items of news. • verb **1** provide with a headline. **2** appear as the star performer at (a concert).
– DERIVATIVES **headliner** noun.

headlock • noun a method of restraining someone by holding an arm firmly around their head.

headlong • adverb & adjective **1** with the head foremost. **2** in a rush; with reckless haste.

head louse • noun a louse which infests the hair of the human head.

headman • noun the chief or leader of a tribe.

headmaster • noun chiefly Brit. a male head teacher.

headmistress • noun chiefly Brit. a female head teacher.

head of state • noun the chief public representative of a country, who may also be the head of government.

head-on • adjective & adverb **1** with or involving the front of a vehicle. **2** with or involving direct confrontation.

headphones • plural noun a pair of earphones joined by a band placed over the head.

headpiece • noun a device worn on the head.

headquarter • verb (**be headquartered**) have headquarters at a specified place.

headquarters • noun (treated as sing. or pl.) **1** the managerial and administrative centre of an organization. **2** the premises of a military commander and their staff.

headrest • noun a padded support for the head on the back of a seat or chair.

headroom • noun the space between the top of a vehicle or a person's head and the ceiling or other structure above.

headscarf • noun (pl. **headscarves**) a square of fabric worn as a covering for the head.

headset • noun a set of headphones with a microphone attached.

headship • noun **1** the position of leader or chief. **2** chiefly Brit. the position of head teacher in a school.

headshrinker • noun informal, chiefly N. Amer. a psychiatrist.

headstone • noun an inscribed stone slab set up at the head of a grave.

headstrong • adjective obstinate and determined.

head teacher • noun the teacher in charge of a school.

head-to-head • adjective & adverb involving two parties confronting each other.

head-turning • adjective extremely noticeable or attractive.

headwater • noun a tributary stream of a river close to or forming part of its source.

headway • noun forward movement or progress.

headwind • noun a wind blowing from directly in front.

headword • noun a word which begins a separate entry in a reference work.

headwork • noun mental effort.

heady • adjective (**headier**, **headiest**) **1** (of alcohol) potent; in-

Thesaurus

leading, managing, running, directing, supervising, overseeing; at the wheel of, at the helm of. **come to a head** REACH A CRISIS, come to a climax, reach a critical point, reach a crossroads; informal come to the crunch. **go to someone's head 1** *the wine has gone to my head* INTOXICATE, befuddle, make drunk; informal make woozy; formal inebriate. **2** *her victory went to her head* MAKE CONCEITED, make someone full of themselves, puff someone up. **head someone/something off 1** *he went to head off the cars* INTERCEPT, divert, deflect, redirect, re-route, draw away, turn away. **2** *they headed off a row* FORESTALL, avert, ward off, fend off, stave off, hold off, nip in the bud, keep at bay; prevent, avoid, stop. **keep one's head** KEEP/STAY CALM, keep one's self-control, maintain one's composure; informal keep one's cool, keep one's shirt on. **lose one's head** LOSE CONTROL, lose one's composure, lose one's equilibrium, go to pieces; panic, get flustered, get confused, get hysterical; informal lose one's cool, freak out, crack up; Brit. informal go into a (flat) spin, throw a wobbly.

headache • noun **1** *I've got a splitting headache* PAIN IN THE HEAD, sore head, migraine; neuralgia; informal head. **2** (informal) *their behaviour was a headache for Mr Jones* NUISANCE, trouble, problem, bother, bugbear, pest, worry, inconvenience, vexation, irritant, thorn in one's flesh; informal aggravation, hassle, pain (in the neck), bind.

head case • noun (informal) MANIAC, lunatic, madman, madwoman; informal loony, nut, nutcase, fruitcake, crank, crackpot; Brit. informal nutter; N. Amer. informal screwball, crazy, kook, wacko; N. Amer. & Austral./NZ informal dingbat.

head first • adjective & adverb **1** *she dived head first into the water* HEADLONG, on one's head. **2** *don't plunge head first into a relationship* WITHOUT THINKING, without forethought, precipitously, impetuously, rashly, recklessly, heedlessly, hastily, headlong.
– OPPOSITES cautiously.

heading • noun **1** *chapter headings* TITLE, caption, legend, subtitle, sub-heading, rubric, headline. **2** *this topic falls under four main headings* CATEGORY, division, classification, class, section, group, grouping, subject, topic.

headland • noun CAPE, promontory, point, head, foreland, peninsula, ness, bluff; Scottish mull.

headlong • adverb **1** *he fell headlong into the tent* HEAD FIRST, on one's head. **2** *she rushed headlong to join the craze* WITHOUT THINKING, without forethought, precipitously, impetuously, rashly, recklessly, carelessly, heedlessly, hastily.
– OPPOSITES cautiously.
• adjective *a headlong dash* BREAKNECK, whirlwind; reckless, precipitate, precipitous, hasty, careless, heedless.
– OPPOSITES cautious.

headman • noun CHIEF, chieftain, leader, ruler, head, overlord, master, commander; lord, potentate; N. Amer. sachem.
– OPPOSITES underling.

head-on • adjective **1** *a head-on collision* DIRECT, front-to-front. **2** *a head-on confrontation* DIRECT, face to face, eyeball to eyeball, personal.

headquarters • plural noun HEAD OFFICE, main office, HQ, base, nerve centre, mission control, command post.

headstone • noun GRAVESTONE, tombstone, stone, monument, memorial.

headstrong • adjective WILFUL, strong-willed, stubborn, obstinate, unyielding, obdurate; contrary, perverse, wayward, unruly; formal refractory.
– OPPOSITES tractable.

head teacher • noun HEAD, headmaster, headmistress, principal, director, president, governor; Brit. master.

headway • noun
– PHRASES **make headway** MAKE PROGRESS, progress, make strides,

toxicating. **2** having a strong or exhilarating effect.
– DERIVATIVES **headily** adverb.
heal ● verb **1** make or become sound or healthy again. **2** put right (an undesirable situation).
– DERIVATIVES **healer** noun.
– ORIGIN Old English, related to WHOLE.
heal-all ● noun **1** a universal remedy; a panacea. **2** any of a number of medicinal plants, especially roseroot and self-heal.
health ● noun **1** the state of being free from illness or injury. **2** a person's mental or physical condition.
– ORIGIN Old English, related to WHOLE.
health centre ● noun an establishment housing local medical services or the practice of a group of doctors.
health farm ● noun a residential establishment where people seek improved health by dieting, exercise, and treatment.
health food ● noun natural food that is thought to have health-giving qualities.
healthful ● adjective having or conducive to good health.
– DERIVATIVES **healthfully** adverb **healthfulness** noun.
health service ● noun a public service providing medical care.
health visitor ● noun Brit. a nurse who visits the homes of the chronically ill or parents with very young children.
healthy ● adjective (**healthier**, **healthiest**) **1** having or promoting good health. **2** normal, sensible, or desirable: *a healthy balance*. **3** of a very satisfactory size or amount: *a healthy profit*.
– DERIVATIVES **healthily** adverb **healthiness** noun.
heap ● noun **1** a pile of a substance or of a number of objects. **2** informal a large amount or number: *heaps of room*. **3** informal an untidy or dilapidated place or vehicle. ● verb **1** put in or form a heap. **2** (**heap with**) load copiously with. **3** (**heap on**) bestow liberally on: *the press heaped abuse on him*.
– ORIGIN Old English.
hear ● verb (past and past part. **heard**) **1** perceive (a sound) with the ear. **2** be told or informed of. **3** (**have heard of**) be aware of the existence of. **4** (**hear from**) receive a letter or phone call from. **5** listen or pay attention to. **6** Law listen to and judge (a case or plaintiff).
– PHRASES **hear! hear!** used to express wholehearted agreement with something said in a speech. **will** (or **would**) **not hear of** will (or would) not allow or agree to.
– DERIVATIVES **hearable** adjective **hearer** noun.
– ORIGIN Old English.
hearing ● noun **1** the faculty of perceiving sounds. **2** the range within which sounds may be heard; earshot. **3** an opportunity to state one's case: *a fair hearing*. **4** an act of listening to evidence, especially a trial before a judge without a jury.
hearing aid ● noun a small amplifying device worn on the ear by a partially deaf person.
hearken /haarkən/ (also **harken**) ● verb (usu. **hearken to**) archaic listen.
– ORIGIN Old English, probably related to HARK.
hearsay ● noun information which cannot be adequately substantiated; rumour.
hearse /herss/ ● noun a vehicle for conveying the coffin at a funeral.
– ORIGIN originally denoting a latticework canopy placed over the coffin of an important person in church: from Old French *herce* 'harrow, frame', from Latin *hirpex* 'rake'.
heart ● noun **1** a hollow muscular organ that pumps the blood through the circulatory system by rhythmic contraction and dilation. **2** the central, innermost, or vital part: *the heart of the city*. **3** a person's feeling of or capacity for love or compassion. **4** mood or feeling: *a change of heart*. **5** courage or enthusiasm. **6** a symbolic representation of a heart with two equal curves meeting at a point at the bottom and a cusp at the top. **7** (**hearts**) one of the four suits in a pack of playing cards, denoted by a red symbol of a heart.
– PHRASES **after one's own heart** sharing one's tastes. **at heart** in one's real nature, in contrast to how one may appear. **break someone's heart** overwhelm someone with sadness. **by heart** from memory. **close** (or **dear**) **to one's heart** of deep interest and concern to one. **from the** (or **the bottom of one's**) **heart** with sincere feeling. **have a heart** be merciful. **have a heart of gold** have a generous or compassionate nature. **have one's heart in one's mouth** be greatly alarmed or apprehensive. **have one's heart in the right place** be sincere or well intentioned. **one's heart's desire** something that one greatly wishes for. **one's heartstrings** used in reference to one's deepest feelings of love or compassion. **in one's heart of hearts** in one's innermost feelings. **take to heart** take (criticism) seriously and be affected by it. **wear one's heart on one's sleeve** make one's feelings apparent.
– ORIGIN Old English.
heartache ● noun emotional anguish or grief.

h

Thesaurus

gain ground, advance, proceed, move, get ahead, come along, take shape.
heady ● adjective **1** *heady wine* POTENT, intoxicating, strong; alcoholic, vinous; *formal* spirituous. **2** *the heady days of my youth* EXHILARATING, exciting, thrilling, stimulating, invigorating, electrifying, rousing; *informal* mind-blowing.
heal ● verb **1** *he heals sick people* MAKE BETTER, make well, cure, treat, restore to health. **2** *his knee had healed* GET BETTER, get well, be cured, recover, mend, improve. **3** *time will heal the pain of grief* ALLEVIATE, ease, assuage, palliate, relieve, help, lessen, mitigate, attenuate, allay. **4** *we tried to heal the rift* PUT RIGHT, set right, repair, remedy, resolve, correct, settle; conciliate, reconcile, harmonize; *informal* patch up.
– OPPOSITES aggravate, worsen.
healing ● adjective CURATIVE, therapeutic, medicinal, remedial, corrective, reparative; restorative, tonic, health-giving, healthful, beneficial.
– OPPOSITES harmful.
health ● noun **1** *he was restored to health* WELL-BEING, healthiness, fitness, good condition, good shape, fine fettle; strength, vigour. **2** *bad health forced him to retire* PHYSICAL STATE, physical shape, condition, constitution.
– OPPOSITES illness.
healthful ● adjective HEALTHY, health-giving, beneficial, good for one, salubrious; wholesome, nourishing, nutritious.
– OPPOSITES unhealthy.
healthy ● adjective **1** *a healthy baby* WELL, in good health, fine, fit, in good trim, in good shape, in fine fettle, in tip-top condition; blooming, thriving, hardy, robust, strong, vigorous, fighting fit, fit as a fiddle, the picture of health; *Brit.* in rude health; *informal* OK, in the pink, right as rain. **2** *a healthy diet* HEALTH-GIVING, healthful, good for one; wholesome, nutritious, nourishing; beneficial, salubrious.
– OPPOSITES ill, unwholesome.
heap ● noun **1** *a heap of boxes* PILE, stack, mound, mountain, mass, quantity, load, lot, jumble; collection, accumulation, assemblage, store, hoard. **2** (*informal*) *we have heaps of room* A LOT, a fair amount, much, plenty, a good deal, a great deal, an abundance, a wealth, a profusion; (a great) many, a large number, numerous, scores; *informal* hundreds, thousands, millions; a load, loads, loadsa, a pile, piles, oodles, stacks, lots, masses, scads, reams, wads, pots, oceans, miles, tons, zillions; *Brit. informal* a shedload, lashings.
● verb *she heaped logs on the fire* PILE (UP), stack (up), make a mound of.
– PHRASES **heap something on/upon** *they heaped praise on her* SHOWER ON, lavish on, load on; bestow on, confer on, give, grant, vouchsafe, favour with.
hear ● verb **1** *she can't hear* PERCEIVE SOUND; have hearing. **2** *she could hear men's voices* PERCEIVE, make out, discern, catch, get, apprehend; overhear. **3** *they heard that I had moved* BE INFORMED, be told, find out, discover, learn, gather, glean, ascertain, get word, get wind. **4** *a jury heard the case* TRY, judge; adjudicate (on), adjudge, pass judgement on.
hearing ● noun **1** *acute hearing* ABILITY TO HEAR, auditory perception, sense of hearing, aural faculty. **2** *she moved out of hearing* EARSHOT, hearing distance, hearing range, auditory range. **3** *I had a fair hearing* CHANCE TO SPEAK, opportunity to be heard; interview, audience. **4** *he gave evidence at the hearing* TRIAL, court case, inquiry, inquest, tribunal; investigation, inquisition.
– RELATED TERMS acoustic, auditory, aural.
hearsay ● noun RUMOUR, gossip, tittle-tattle, tattle, idle talk; stories, tales, on dit; *informal* the grapevine; *Brit. informal* goss; *N. Amer. informal* scuttlebutt.
heart ● noun **1** *his heart stopped beating* *informal* ticker. **2** *he poured out his heart* EMOTIONS, feelings, sentiments; soul, mind, bosom, breast; love, affection, passion. **3** *he has no heart* COMPASSION, sympathy, humanity, feeling(s), fellow feeling, brotherly love, tenderness, empathy, understanding; kindness, goodwill. **4** *they may lose heart* ENTHUSIASM, keenness, eagerness, spirit, determination,

heart attack ● noun a sudden occurrence of coronary thrombosis.
heartbeat ● noun **1** a pulsation of the heart. **2** an animating force or influence. **3** a very brief moment of time: *I'd go there in a heartbeat.*
– PHRASES **a heartbeat away** very close.
heartbreak ● noun overwhelming distress.
– DERIVATIVES **heartbreaker** noun **heartbreaking** adjective **heartbroken** adjective.
heartburn ● noun a form of indigestion felt as a burning sensation in the chest, caused by acid regurgitation into the oesophagus.
hearten ● verb make more cheerful or confident.
– DERIVATIVES **heartening** adjective.
heart failure ● noun severe failure of the heart to function properly, especially as a cause of death.
heartfelt ● adjective deeply and strongly felt; sincere.
hearth /haarth/ ● noun **1** the floor or surround of a fireplace (often used as a symbol of domestic comfort). **2** the base or lower part of a furnace, where molten metal collects.
– ORIGIN Old English.
hearthrug ● noun a rug laid in front of a fireplace.
hearthstone ● noun a flat stone forming a hearth.
heartily ● adverb **1** in a hearty manner. **2** very: *I'm heartily sick of them.*
heartland ● noun the central or most important part of a country or area.
heartless ● adjective completely lacking in feeling or consideration.
– DERIVATIVES **heartlessly** adverb **heartlessness** noun.
heart-lung machine ● noun a machine that temporarily takes over the functions of the heart and lungs, especially during heart surgery.
heart-rending ● adjective very sad or distressing.
heart-searching ● noun thorough examination of one's feelings and motives.
heartsease /haartseez/ ● noun a wild pansy with purple and yellow flowers, source of most garden varieties.
heartsick (also **heartsore**) ● adjective chiefly literary despondent from grief or loss of love.
heart-stopping ● adjective very exciting.
heart-throb ● noun informal a man whom women find very attractive.
heart-to-heart ● adjective (of a conversation) intimate and personal.
heart-warming ● adjective emotionally rewarding or uplifting.
heartwood ● noun the dense inner part of a tree trunk, yielding the hardest wood.
hearty ● adjective (**heartier**, **heartiest**) **1** enthusiastic and friendly. **2** strong and healthy. **3** (of a feeling or opinion) heartfelt. **4** (of a meal) wholesome and substantial.
– DERIVATIVES **heartiness** noun.
heat ● noun **1** the quality of being hot; high temperature. **2** heat seen as a form of energy arising from the random motion of molecules. **3** a source or level of heat for cooking. **4** intensity of feeling, especially of anger or excitement. **5** (**the heat**) informal intensive and unwelcome pressure: *the heat is on.* **6** a preliminary round in a race or contest. ● verb **1** make or become hot or

Thesaurus

resolve, purpose, courage, nerve, will power, fortitude; *informal* guts, spunk; *Brit. informal* bottle. **5** *the heart of the city* CENTRE, middle, hub, core, nucleus, eye, bosom. **6** *the heart of the matter* ESSENCE, crux, core, nub, root, gist, meat, marrow, pith, substance, kernel; *informal* nitty-gritty.
– RELATED TERMS cardiac, coronary.
– OPPOSITES edge.
– PHRASES **after one's own heart** LIKE-MINDED, of the same mind, kindred, compatible, congenial, sharing one's tastes; *informal* on the same wavelength. **at heart** DEEP DOWN, basically, fundamentally, essentially, in essence, intrinsically; really, actually, truly, in fact; *informal* when you get right down to it. **(off) by heart** FROM MEMORY, off pat, by rote, word for word, verbatim, parrot-fashion, word-perfect. **do one's heart good** CHEER (UP), please, gladden, make one happy, delight, hearten, gratify, make one feel good, give one a lift; *informal* give someone a buzz, tickle someone pink, buck up. **eat one's heart out** PINE, long, ache, brood, mope, fret, sigh, sorrow, yearn, agonize; grieve, mourn, lament. **from the (bottom of one's) heart** SINCERELY, earnestly, fervently, passionately, truly, genuinely, heartily, with all sincerity. **give/lose one's heart to** FALL IN LOVE WITH, fall for, be smitten by; *informal* fall head over heels for, be swept off one's feet by, develop a crush on. **have a change of heart** CHANGE ONE'S MIND, change one's tune, have second thoughts, have a rethink, think again, think twice; *informal* get cold feet. **have a heart** BE COMPASSIONATE, be kind, be merciful, be lenient, be sympathetic, be considerate, have mercy. **heart and soul** WHOLEHEARTEDLY, enthusiastically, eagerly, zealously; absolutely, completely, entirely, fully, utterly, to the hilt, one hundred per cent. **take heart** BE ENCOURAGED, be heartened, be comforted; cheer up, brighten up, perk up, liven up, revive; *informal* buck up. **with one's heart in one's mouth** IN ALARM, in fear, fearfully, apprehensively, on edge, with trepidation, in suspense, in a cold sweat, with bated breath, on tenterhooks; *informal* with butterflies in one's stomach, in a state, in a stew, in a sweat; *Brit. informal* having kittens; *N. Amer. informal* in a twit.
heartache ● noun ANGUISH, grief, suffering, distress, unhappiness, misery, sorrow, sadness, heartbreak, pain, hurt, agony, angst, despondency, despair, woe, desolation.
– OPPOSITES happiness.
heartbreak ● noun. See HEARTACHE.
heartbreaking ● adjective DISTRESSING, upsetting, disturbing, heart-rending, sad, tragic, painful, traumatic, agonizing, harrowing; pitiful, poignant, plaintive, moving, tear-jerking.
– OPPOSITES comforting.
heartbroken ● adjective ANGUISHED, devastated, broken-hearted, heavy-hearted, grieving, grief-stricken, inconsolable, crushed, shattered, desolate, despairing; upset, distressed, miserable, sorrowful, sad, downcast, disconsolate, crestfallen, despondent; *informal* choked, down in the mouth, down in the dumps, cut up.
heartburn ● noun INDIGESTION, dyspepsia, pyrosis.
hearten ● verb CHEER (UP), encourage, raise someone's spirits, boost, buoy up, perk up, ginger up, inspirit, uplift, elate; comfort, reassure; *informal* buck up, pep up.
heartfelt ● adjective SINCERE, genuine, from the heart; earnest, profound, deep, wholehearted, ardent, fervent, passionate, enthusiastic, eager; honest, bona fide.
– OPPOSITES insincere.
heartily ● adverb **1** *we heartily welcome the changes* WHOLEHEARTEDLY, sincerely, genuinely, warmly, profoundly, with all one's heart; eagerly, enthusiastically, earnestly, ardently. **2** *they were heartily sick of her* VERY, extremely, thoroughly, completely, absolutely, really, exceedingly, immensely, most, downright; *N. Amer.* quite; *informal* right, seriously; *Brit. informal* jolly, dead, well; *N. Amer. informal* real, mighty.
heartless ● adjective UNFEELING, unsympathetic, unkind, uncaring, unconcerned, insensitive, inconsiderate, hard-hearted, stony-hearted, cold-hearted, mean-spirited; cold, callous, cruel, merciless, pitiless, inhuman.
– OPPOSITES compassionate.
heart-rending ● adjective DISTRESSING, upsetting, disturbing, heartbreaking, sad, tragic, painful, traumatic, harrowing; pitiful, poignant, plaintive, moving, tear-jerking.
heartsick ● adjective *(poetic/literary)* DESPONDENT, dejected, depressed, desolate, downcast, forlorn, unhappy, sad, upset, miserable, wretched, woebegone, inconsolable, grieving, grief-stricken, heavy-hearted, broken-hearted.
– OPPOSITES happy.
heart-throb ● noun *(informal)* IDOL, pin-up, star, superstar, hero; *informal* dreamboat.
heart-to-heart ● adjective *a heart-to-heart chat* INTIMATE, personal, man-to-man, woman-to-woman; candid, honest, truthful, sincere. ● noun *they had a long heart-to-heart* PRIVATE CONVERSATION, tête-à-tête, one-to-one, head-to-head; chat, talk, word; *informal* confab, chinwag; *Brit. informal* natter.
heart-warming ● adjective TOUCHING, moving, heartening, stirring, uplifting, pleasing, cheering, gladdening, encouraging, gratifying.
– OPPOSITES distressing.
hearty ● adjective **1** *a hearty character* EXUBERANT, jovial, ebullient, cheerful, uninhibited, effusive, lively, loud, animated, vivacious, energetic, spirited, dynamic, enthusiastic, eager; warm, cordial, friendly, affable, amiable, good natured. **2** *hearty congratulations* WHOLEHEARTED, heartfelt, sincere, genuine, real, true; earnest, fervent, ardent, enthusiastic. **3** *a hearty woman of sixty-five* ROBUST, healthy, hardy, fit, flourishing, blooming, fighting fit, fit as a fiddle; vigorous, sturdy, strong; *Brit.* in rude health; *informal* full of

warm. **2** (**heat up**) become more intense and exciting. **3** (**heated**) inflamed with passion or conviction: *a heated argument.*
– PHRASES **if you can't stand the heat, get out of the kitchen** proverb if you can't cope with the pressures of a situation, you should leave others to deal with it rather than complaining. **in the heat of the moment** while temporarily angry or excited and without stopping for thought. **on heat** (of a female mammal) in the receptive period of the sexual cycle; in oestrus.
– DERIVATIVES **heatedly** adverb.
– ORIGIN Old English, related to HOT.

heater ● noun **1** a device for heating something. **2** N. Amer. informal, dated a gun.

heath ● noun **1** chiefly Brit. an area of open uncultivated land, typically on sandy soil and covered with heather, gorse, and coarse grasses. **2** a dwarf shrub with small leathery leaves and small pink or purple bell-shaped flowers, characteristic of heaths and moors.
– DERIVATIVES **heathy** adjective.
– ORIGIN Old English.

heathen /heeth̲ən/ ● noun derogatory a person who does not belong to a widely held religion (especially Christianity, Judaism, or Islam) as regarded by those who do. ● adjective relating to heathens.
– DERIVATIVES **heathendom** noun **heathenish** adjective **heathenism** noun.
– ORIGIN Old English, probably from a Germanic word meaning 'inhabiting open country, savage'; related to HEATH.

heather ● noun a purple-flowered heath typical of moors and heaths.
– DERIVATIVES **heathery** adjective.
– ORIGIN Old English.

Heath Robinson ● adjective Brit. ingeniously or ridiculously over-complicated in design or construction.
– ORIGIN named after the English cartoonist William *Heath Robinson* (1872–1944).

heating ● noun equipment or devices used to provide heat, especially to a building.

heat-seeking ● adjective (of a missile) able to detect and home in on infrared radiation emitted by a target.

heatstroke ● noun a feverish condition caused by failure of the body's temperature-regulating mechanism when exposed to excessively high temperatures.

heat treatment ● noun the use of heat for therapeutic purposes in medicine or to modify the properties of a material, especially in metallurgy.

heatwave ● noun a prolonged period of abnormally hot weather.

heave ● verb (past and past part. **heaved** or chiefly Nautical **hove**) **1** lift or haul with great effort. **2** produce (a sigh) noisily. **3** informal throw (something heavy). **4** rise and fall rhythmically or spasmodically. **5** try to vomit; retch. **6** (**heave to**) Nautical come to a stop. ● noun an act of heaving.
– PHRASES **heave in sight** (or **into view**) Nautical come into view.
– DERIVATIVES **heaver** noun.
– ORIGIN Old English.

heave-ho ● exclamation a cry emitted with an action that requires physical effort. ● noun (**the heave-ho**) informal dismissal.

heaven ● noun **1** a place regarded in various religions as the abode of God or the gods and of the good after death, often depicted as being above the sky. **2** (**the heavens**) literary the sky. **3** informal a place or state of supreme bliss. **4** (also **heavens**) used in exclamations as a substitute for 'God'.
– PHRASES **the heavens open** it suddenly starts to rain very heavily. **in seventh heaven** in a state of ecstasy. **move heaven and earth to do** make extraordinary efforts to do.
– DERIVATIVES **heavenward** adjective & adverb **heavenwards** adverb.
– ORIGIN Old English.

heavenly ● adjective **1** of heaven; divine. **2** relating to the sky. **3** informal very pleasing; wonderful.

heavenly body ● noun a planet, star, or other celestial body.

heavenly host ● noun a literary or biblical term for the angels.

heaven-sent ● adjective occurring at a very favourable time.

heaving ● adjective Brit. informal extremely crowded.

Thesaurus

vim. **4** *a hearty meal* SUBSTANTIAL, large, ample, sizeable, filling, generous, square, solid; healthy.
– OPPOSITES introverted, half-hearted, frail, light.

heat ● noun **1** *a plant sensitive to heat* WARMTH, hotness, warmness, high temperature; hot weather, warm weather, sultriness, mugginess, humidity; heatwave, hot spell. **2** *he took the heat out of the dispute* PASSION, intensity, vehemence, warmth, fervour, fervency, ardency; enthusiasm, excitement, agitation; anger, fury.
– RELATED TERMS thermal.
– OPPOSITES cold, apathy.
● verb **1** *the food was heated* WARM (UP), heat up, make hot, make warm; reheat, cook; Brit. informal hot up. **2** *the pipes expand as they heat up* BECOME HOT, become warm, get hotter, get warmer, increase in temperature; Brit. informal hot up. **3** *he calmed down as quickly as he had heated up* BECOME IMPASSIONED, become excited, become animated; get angry, become enraged.
– OPPOSITES cool.

heated ● adjective **1** *a heated swimming pool* MADE WARM, made hot, warmed up; reheated; hot, piping hot. **2** *a heated argument* VEHEMENT, passionate, impassioned, animated, spirited, 'lively', intense, fiery; angry, bitter, furious, fierce, stormy, tempestuous. **3** *Robert grew heated as he spoke of the risks* EXCITED, animated, inflamed, worked up, wound up, keyed up; informal het up, in a state.

heater ● noun RADIATOR, convector, fire, brazier, warmer.

heath ● noun (Brit.) MOOR, heathland, moorland, scrub; common land.

heathen ● noun **1** *bringing Christianity to the heathens* PAGAN, infidel, idolater, idolatress; unbeliever, non-believer, disbeliever, atheist, agnostic, sceptic, heretic; archaic paynim. **2** *heathens who spoil good whisky with ice* PHILISTINE, boor, oaf, ignoramus, lout, yahoo, vulgarian, plebeian; informal pleb, peasant, oik.
– OPPOSITES believer.
● adjective *a heathen practice* PAGAN, infidel, idolatrous, heathenish; unbelieving, non-believing, atheistic, agnostic, heretical, faithless, godless, irreligious, ungodly, unholy; barbarian, barbarous, uncivilized, uncultured, primitive, ignorant, philistine.

heave ● verb **1** *she heaved the sofa backwards* HAUL, pull, lug, drag, draw, tug, heft; informal hump, yank. **2** (informal) *she heaved a brick at him* THROW, fling, cast, toss, hurl, lob, pitch; informal chuck, sling; Brit. informal bung; N. English & Austral. informal hoy; NZ informal bish. **3** *he heaved a sigh of relief* LET OUT, breathe, give, sigh; emit, utter. **4** *the sea heaved* RISE AND FALL, roll, swell, surge, churn, seethe, swirl. **5** *she heaved into the sink* RETCH, gag; vomit, bring up, cough up; Brit. be sick; N. Amer. get sick; informal throw up, puke, chunder, chuck up, hurl, spew; Brit. informal sick up; Scottish informal boke; N. Amer. informal barf, upchuck.

heaven ● noun **1** *the good will have a place in heaven* PARADISE, nirvana, Zion; the hereafter, the next world, the next life, the afterworld; Elysium, the Elysian Fields, Valhalla; poetic/literary the empyrean. **2** *a good book is my idea of heaven* BLISS, ecstasy, rapture, contentment, happiness, delight, joy, seventh heaven; paradise, Utopia, nirvana. **3** *he observed the heavens* THE SKY, the skies, the upper atmosphere, the stratosphere; poetic/literary the firmament, the vault of heaven, the blue, the (wide) blue yonder, the welkin, the empyrean, the azure, the upper regions, the sphere.
– RELATED TERMS celestial.
– OPPOSITES hell, misery.
– PHRASES **in seventh heaven** ECSTATIC, euphoric, thrilled, elated, delighted, overjoyed, on cloud nine, walking on air, jubilant, rapturous, jumping for joy, transported, delirious, blissful; informal over the moon, on top of the world, on a high, tickled pink, as pleased as Punch, cock-a-hoop, as happy as a sandboy; Brit. informal as happy as Larry; N. Amer. informal as happy as a clam; Austral. informal wrapped. **move heaven and earth** TRY ONE'S HARDEST, do one's best, do one's utmost, do all one can, give one's all, spare no effort, put oneself out; strive, exert oneself, work hard; informal bend over backwards, do one's damnedest, go all out, bust a gut.

heavenly ● adjective **1** *heavenly choirs* DIVINE, holy, celestial; angelic, seraphic, cherubic; poetic/literary empyrean. **2** *heavenly constellations* CELESTIAL, cosmic, stellar; planetary; extraterrestrial, superterrestrial. **3** (informal) *a heavenly morning* DELIGHTFUL, wonderful, glorious, perfect, excellent, sublime, idyllic, first-class, first-rate; blissful, pleasurable, enjoyable; exquisite, beautiful, lovely, gorgeous, enchanting; informal divine, super, great, fantastic, fabulous, terrific.
– OPPOSITES mortal, infernal, terrestrial, dreadful.

heaven-sent ● adjective AUSPICIOUS, providential, propitious, felicitous, opportune, golden, favourable, advantageous, serendipit-

heavy ● adjective (**heavier**, **heaviest**) **1** of great weight; difficult to lift or move. **2** of great density; thick or substantial. **3** of more than the usual size, amount, or force. **4** doing something to excess: *a heavy smoker*. **5** striking or falling with force: *a heavy blow*. **6** not delicate or graceful; coarse or slow. **7** needing much physical effort. **8** hard to endure. **9** very important or serious. **10** informal strict, harsh, or difficult to deal with: *things were getting heavy*. **11** (of music, especially rock) having a strong bass component and a forceful rhythm. **12** (of ground) muddy or full of clay. ● noun (pl. **heavies**) **1** something large or heavy of its kind. **2** informal a large, strong man, especially one hired for protection. **3** informal an important person.
– PHRASES **heavy going** a person or situation that is difficult or boring to deal with.
– DERIVATIVES **heavily** adverb **heaviness** noun **heavyish** adjective.
– ORIGIN Old English, related to HEAVE.

heavy cream ● noun N. Amer. double cream.

heavy-duty ● adjective designed to withstand demanding use or wear.

heavy-handed ● adjective clumsy, insensitive, or overly forceful.

heavy-hearted ● adjective depressed or melancholy.

heavy horse ● noun a large, strong, heavily built horse of a type used for draught work.

heavy hydrogen ● noun another term for DEUTERIUM.

heavy industry ● noun the manufacture of large, heavy articles and materials in bulk.

heavy metal ● noun **1** a metal of relatively high density, or of high relative atomic weight. **2** a type of highly amplified harsh-sounding rock music with a strong beat.

heavy petting ● noun erotic contact between two people involving stimulation of the genitals but stopping short of intercourse.

heavy water ● noun water in which the hydrogen in the molecules is partly or wholly replaced by the isotope deuterium, used especially in nuclear reactors.

heavyweight ● noun **1** a weight in boxing and other sports, typically the heaviest category. **2** informal an important or influential person. ● adjective **1** of above-average weight. **2** informal serious, important, or influential.

hebdomadal /hebdommәd'l/ ● adjective formal weekly.
– ORIGIN from Greek *hebdomas* 'the number seven, seven days'.

hebe /heebi/ ● noun an evergreen flowering shrub with spikes of mauve, pink, or white flowers, native to New Zealand.
– ORIGIN named after the Greek goddess *Hebe*, cup-bearer of the gods.

hebetude /hebbityo͞od/ ● noun literary the state of being dull or lethargic.
– ORIGIN Latin *hebetudo*, from *hebes* 'blunt'.

Hebraic /hibrayik/ ● adjective of Hebrew or the Hebrews.

Hebraist /heebrayist/ ● noun a scholar of the Hebrew language.

Hebrew /heebro͞o/ ● noun **1** a member of an ancient people living in what is now Israel and Palestine, who established the kingdoms of Israel and Judah. **2** the Semitic language of the Hebrews, in its ancient or modern form. **3** old-fashioned and sometimes offensive term for JEW.
– ORIGIN Greek *Hebraios*, from a Hebrew word understood to mean 'one from the other side (of the river)'.

Hebrew Bible ● noun the sacred writings of Judaism, called by Christians the Old Testament.

Hebridean /hebrideeәn/ ● noun a person from the Hebrides off the NW coast of Scotland. ● adjective relating to the Hebrides.

hecatomb /hekkәto͞om/ ● noun (in ancient Greece or Rome) a great public sacrifice, originally of a hundred oxen.
– ORIGIN Greek *hekatombē*, from *hekaton* 'hundred' + *bous* 'ox'.

heck ● exclamation used for emphasis, or to express surprise, annoyance, etc.
– ORIGIN euphemistic alteration of HELL.

heckle ● verb interrupt (a public speaker) with derisive comments or abuse. ● noun an instance of heckling.
– DERIVATIVES **heckler** noun.
– ORIGIN originally in the sense 'dress (flax or hemp) with a comb to split and straighten the fibres': from a dialect form of HACKLE.

hectare /hektair/ (abbrev.: **ha**) ● noun a metric unit of square measure, equal to 10,000 square metres (2.471 acres).
– DERIVATIVES **hectarage** noun.
– ORIGIN from Greek *hekaton* 'hundred' + ARE².

hectic ● adjective full of incessant or frantic activity.
– DERIVATIVES **hectically** adverb.
– ORIGIN Greek *hektikos* 'habitual'.

hecto- ● combining form a hundred: *hectometre*.
– ORIGIN French, from Greek *hekaton* 'hundred'.

hectogram (also **hectogramme**) ● noun a metric unit of mass equal to one hundred grams.

Thesaurus

ous, lucky, happy, good, fortunate.
– OPPOSITES inopportune.

heavily ● adverb **1** *Dad walked heavily* LABORIOUSLY, slowly, ponderously, woodenly, stiffly; with difficulty, painfully, awkwardly, clumsily. **2** *we were heavily defeated* DECISIVELY, conclusively, roundly, soundly; utterly, completely, thoroughly. **3** *he drank heavily* EXCESSIVELY, to excess, immoderately, copiously, inordinately, intemperately, a great deal, too much, overmuch. **4** *the area is heavily planted with trees* DENSELY, closely, thickly. **5** *I became heavily involved* DEEPLY, very, extremely, greatly, exceedingly, tremendously, profoundly; informal terribly, seriously; Brit. informal jolly, ever so.
– OPPOSITES easily, narrowly, moderately.

heavy ● adjective **1** *a heavy box* WEIGHTY, hefty, substantial, ponderous; solid, dense, leaden; burdensome; informal hulking, weighing a ton. **2** *a heavy man* OVERWEIGHT, fat, obese, corpulent, large, bulky, stout, stocky, portly, plump, paunchy, fleshy; informal hulking, tubby, beefy, porky; Brit. informal podgy. **3** *a heavy blow to the head* FORCEFUL, hard, strong, violent, powerful, vigorous, mighty, hefty, sharp, smart, severe. **4** *a gardener did the heavy work for me* ARDUOUS, hard, physical, laborious, difficult, strenuous, demanding, tough, onerous, back-breaking, gruelling; archaic toilsome. **5** *a heavy burden of responsibility* ONEROUS, burdensome, demanding, challenging, difficult, formidable, weighty; worrisome, stressful, trying, crushing, oppressive. **6** *heavy fog* DENSE, thick, soupy, murky, impenetrable. **7** *a heavy sky* OVERCAST, cloudy, clouded, grey, dull, gloomy, murky, dark, black, stormy, leaden, louring. **8** *heavy rain* TORRENTIAL, relentless, copious, teeming, severe. **9** *heavy soil* CLAY, clayey, muddy, sticky, wet; Brit. claggy; informal cloggy. **10** *a heavy fine* SIZEABLE, hefty, substantial, colossal, big, considerable; stiff; informal tidy, whopping, steep, astronomical. **11** *heavy seas* TEMPESTUOUS, turbulent, rough, wild, stormy, choppy, squally. **12** *heavy fighting* INTENSE, fierce, vigorous, relentless, all-out, severe, serious. **13** *a heavy drinker* IMMODERATE, excessive, intemperate, overindulgent, unrestrained, uncontrolled. **14** *a heavy meal* SUBSTANTIAL, filling, hearty, large, big, ample, sizeable, generous, square, solid. **15** *their diet is heavy on vegetables* ABOUNDING IN, abundant in, lavish with, profuse with, unstinting with, using a lot of. **16** *he felt heavy and very tired* LETHARGIC, listless, sluggish, torpid, languid, apathetic. **17** *a heavy heart* SAD, sorrowful, melancholy, gloomy, downcast, downhearted, heartbroken, dejected, disconsolate, demoralized, despondent, depressed, crestfallen, desolate, down; informal blue; poetic/literary dolorous. **18** *these poems are rather heavy* TEDIOUS, difficult, dull, dry, serious, heavy going, dreary, boring, turgid, uninteresting; informal deadly. **19** *branches heavy with blossoms* LADEN, loaded, covered, filled, groaning, bursting, teeming, abounding. **20** *a heavy crop* BOUNTIFUL, plentiful, abundant, large, bumper, rich, copious, considerable, sizeable, profuse; informal whopping; poetic/literary plenteous. **21** *he has heavy features* COARSE, rough, rough-hewn, unrefined; rugged, craggy.
– OPPOSITES light, thin, gentle, easy, bright, friable, small, calm, moderate, energetic, cheerful, meagre, delicate.

heavy-handed ● adjective **1** *they are heavy-handed with the equipment* CLUMSY, awkward, maladroit, unhandy, inept, unskilful; informal ham-handed, ham-fisted, cack-handed; Brit. informal all (fingers and) thumbs. **2** *heavy-handed policing* INSENSITIVE, oppressive, overbearing, high-handed, harsh, stern, severe, tyrannical, despotic, ruthless, merciless; tactless, undiplomatic, inept.
– OPPOSITES dexterous, sensitive.

heavy-hearted ● adjective MELANCHOLY, sad, sorrowful, mournful, gloomy, depressed, desolate, despondent, dejected, downhearted, downcast, crestfallen, disconsolate, glum, miserable, wretched, dismal, morose, woeful, woebegone, doleful, unhappy; informal down in the dumps, down in the mouth, blue; poetic/literary dolorous.
– OPPOSITES cheerful.

heckle ● verb JEER, taunt, jibe at, shout down, boo, hiss, harass; Brit. & Austral./NZ barrack; informal give someone a hard time.
– OPPOSITES cheer.

hectolitre /hektōleetər/ (US **hectoliter**) ● noun a metric unit of capacity equal to one hundred litres.
hectometre /hektōmeetər/ (US **hectometer**) ● noun a metric unit of length equal to one hundred metres.
hector /hektər/ ● verb talk to in a bullying or intimidating way.
– DERIVATIVES **hectoring** adjective.
– ORIGIN originally denoting a hero, later a braggart or bully: from the Trojan warrior *Hector* in Homer's *Iliad*.
he'd ● contraction **1** he had. **2** he would.
hedge ● noun **1** a fence or boundary formed by closely growing bushes or shrubs. **2** a contract entered into or asset held as a protection against possible financial loss. **3** a word or phrase used to allow for additional possibilities or to avoid over-precise commitment, for example *etc.* ● verb **1** surround with a hedge. **2** limit or qualify by conditions or exceptions. **3** avoid making a definite statement or commitment. **4** protect (an investor or investment) against loss by making compensating contracts or transactions.
– PHRASES **hedge one's bets** avoid committing oneself when faced with a difficult choice.
– DERIVATIVES **hedger** noun.
– ORIGIN Old English.
hedgehog ● noun a small nocturnal insect-eating mammal with a spiny coat, able to roll itself into a ball for defence.
hedge-hop ● verb fly an aircraft at a very low altitude.
hedgerow ● noun a hedge of wild shrubs and occasional trees bordering a field.
hedge sparrow ● noun another term for DUNNOCK.
hedging ● noun **1** the planting or trimming of hedges. **2** bushes and shrubs planted to form hedges.
hedonism /heedəniz'm/ ● noun **1** the pursuit of pleasure; sensual self-indulgence. **2** Philosophy the theory that pleasure (in the sense of the satisfaction of desires) is the highest good and proper aim of human life.
– DERIVATIVES **hedonist** noun **hedonistic** adjective.
– ORIGIN from Greek *hēdonē* 'pleasure'.
-hedron ● combining form (pl. **-hedra** or **-hedrons**) forming nouns denoting geometrical solids having faces of various numbers or shapes: *decahedron* | *rhombohedron*.
– DERIVATIVES **-hedral** combining form in corresponding adjectives.
– ORIGIN from Greek *hedra* 'seat, base'.
heebie-jeebies ● plural noun (**the heebie-jeebies**) informal a state of nervous fear or anxiety.
– ORIGIN of unknown origin.
heed ● verb pay attention to. ● noun (usually **pay** (or **take**) **heed**) careful attention.
– DERIVATIVES **heedful** adjective.
– ORIGIN Old English.
heedless ● adjective showing a reckless lack of care or attention.
– DERIVATIVES **heedlessly** adverb **heedlessness** noun.
hee-haw ● noun the loud, harsh cry of a donkey or mule. ● verb make such a cry.
heel[1] ● noun **1** the back part of the foot below the ankle. **2** the part of a shoe or boot supporting the heel. **3** the part of the palm of the hand next to the wrist. **4** informal, dated a contemptible person. ● exclamation a command to a dog to walk close behind its owner. ● verb fit or renew a heel on (a shoe or boot).
– PHRASES **at** (or **on**) **the heels of** following closely after. **bring to heel** bring under control. **cool** (or Brit. **kick**) **one's heels** be kept waiting. **take to one's heels** run away. **turn** (**on one's**) **heel** turn sharply.
– DERIVATIVES **heeled** adjective **heelless** adjective.
– ORIGIN Old English, related to HOCK[1].
heel[2] ● verb (of a ship) lean over owing to the pressure of wind or an uneven load. ● noun an instance of heeling, or the amount that a ship heels.
– ORIGIN from obsolete *heeld*, *hield* 'incline', from Germanic.
heel[3] ● verb (**heel in**) set (a plant) in the ground and cover its roots; plant temporarily.
– ORIGIN Old English, 'cover, hide'.
heelball ● noun a mixture of hard wax and lampblack used by shoemakers for polishing or in brass rubbing.
heft ● verb **1** lift or carry (something heavy). **2** lift or hold (something) to test its weight.
– ORIGIN probably from HEAVE, on the pattern of words such as *cleft*.
hefty ● adjective (**heftier**, **heftiest**) **1** large, heavy, and powerful. **2** (of a number or amount) considerable.
– DERIVATIVES **heftily** adverb.
Hegelian /haygeeliən, higay-/ ● adjective relating to the German philosopher Georg Hegel (1770–1831) or his philosophy of objective idealism. ● noun a follower of Hegel.
– DERIVATIVES **Hegelianism** noun.
hegemony /hijemməni, higemm-/ ● noun dominance, especially by one state or social group over others.

h

Thesaurus

hectic ● adjective FRANTIC, frenetic, frenzied, feverish, manic, busy, active, fast and furious; lively, brisk, bustling, buzzing.
– OPPOSITES leisurely.
hector ● verb BULLY, intimidate, browbeat, harass, torment, plague; coerce, pressurize, strong-arm; threaten, menace; *informal* bulldoze; *N. Amer. informal* bullyrag.
hedge ● noun **1** *high hedges* HEDGEROW, bushes, fence; windbreak; *Brit.* quickset. **2** *an excellent hedge against a fall in sterling* SAFEGUARD, protection, shield, screen, guard, buffer, cushion; insurance, security. **3** *his analysis is full of hedges* EQUIVOCATION, evasion, fudge, quibble, qualification; temporizing, uncertainty, prevarication, vagueness.
● verb **1** *fields hedged with hawthorn* SURROUND, enclose, encircle, ring, border, edge, bound. **2** *she was hedged in by her education* CONFINE, restrict, limit, hinder, obstruct, impede, constrain, trap; hem in. **3** *he hedged at every new question* PREVARICATE, equivocate, vacillate, quibble, hesitate, stall, dodge the issue, be noncommittal, be evasive, be vague, beat about the bush, pussyfoot around, mince one's words; *Brit.* hum and haw; *informal* sit on the fence, duck the question. **4** *the company hedged its position on the market* SAFEGUARD, protect, shield, guard, cushion; cover, insure.
hedonism ● noun SELF-INDULGENCE, pleasure-seeking, self-gratification, lotus-eating, sybaritism; intemperance, immoderation, extravagance, luxury, high living.
– OPPOSITES self-restraint.
hedonist ● noun SYBARITE, sensualist, voluptuary, pleasure-seeker, bon viveur, bon vivant; epicure, gastronome.
– OPPOSITES ascetic.
hedonistic ● adjective SELF-INDULGENT, pleasure-seeking, sybaritic, lotus-eating, epicurean; unrestrained, intemperate, immoderate, extravagant, decadent.
heed ● verb *heed the warnings* PAY ATTENTION TO, take notice of, take note of, pay heed to, attend to, listen to; bear in mind, be mindful of, mind, mark, consider, take into account, follow, obey, adhere to, abide by, observe, take to heart, be alert to.
– OPPOSITES disregard.
● noun *he paid no heed* ATTENTION, notice, note, regard; consideration, thought, care.
heedful ● adjective ATTENTIVE, careful, mindful, cautious, prudent, circumspect; alert, aware, wary, chary, watchful, vigilant, on guard, on the alert.
heedless ● adjective UNMINDFUL, taking no notice, paying no heed, unheeding, disregardful, neglectful, oblivious, inattentive, blind, deaf; incautious, imprudent, rash, reckless, foolhardy, improvident, unwary.
heel[1] ● noun **1** *shoes with low heels* heel piece; wedge, stiletto. **2** *the heel of a loaf* TAIL END, end, crust, remnant, remainder, remains. **3** (*informal, dated*) *you're such a heel* SCOUNDREL, rogue, rascal, reprobate, miscreant; *informal* beast, rat, louse, swine, snake, scumbag, stinker; *Brit. informal, dated* rotter, bounder, blighter; *dated* cad, blackguard.
– PHRASES **take to one's heels** RUN AWAY, run off, make a run for it, take flight, take off, make a break for it, flee, make one's getaway, escape; *informal* beat it, clear off, vamoose, skedaddle, split, cut and run, leg it, hotfoot it, show a clean pair of heels, scram; *Brit. informal* do a runner, scarper, do a bunk; *N. Amer. informal* light out, bug out; *Austral. informal* shoot through.
heel[2] ● verb *the ship heeled to starboard* LEAN OVER, list, careen, tilt, tip, incline, keel over.
heft ● verb LIFT (UP), raise (up), heave, hoist, haul; carry, lug, tote; *informal* cart, hump.
hefty ● adjective **1** *a hefty young man* BURLY, heavy, sturdy, strapping, bulky, brawny, husky, strong, muscular, large, big, solid, well built; portly, stout; *informal* hulking, hunky, beefy. **2** *a hefty kick* POWERFUL, violent, hard, forceful, heavy, mighty. **3** *hefty loads of timber* HEAVY, weighty, bulky, big, large, substantial, massive, ponderous; unwieldy, cumbersome, burdensome; *informal* hulking. **4** *a hefty fine* SUBSTANTIAL, sizeable, considerable, stiff, extortion-

– DERIVATIVES **hegemonic** adjective.
– ORIGIN Greek *hēgemonia*, from *hēgemōn* 'leader'.
Hegira /hejirə/ (also **Hejira** or **Hijra**) ● **noun 1** Muhammad's departure from Mecca to Medina in AD 622, marking the consolidation of the first Muslim community. **2** the Muslim era reckoned from this date.
– ORIGIN Arabic, 'departure'.
heifer /heffər/ ● **noun** a cow that has not borne a calf, or has borne only one calf.
– ORIGIN Old English.
heigh-ho /hayhō/ ● **exclamation** informal expressing boredom, resignation, or jollity.
height ● **noun 1** the measurement of someone or something from head to foot or from base to top. **2** the distance of something above ground or sea level. **3** the quality of being tall or high. **4** a high place or area. **5** the most intense part or period: *the height of the attack.* **6** an extreme instance or example: *the height of folly.*
– ORIGIN Old English, related to HIGH.
heighten ● **verb 1** make higher. **2** make or become more intense.
heinous /haynəss, heenəss/ ● **adjective** utterly abhorrent and wicked: *a heinous crime.*
– DERIVATIVES **heinously** adverb **heinousness** noun.
– ORIGIN Old French *haineus*, from *hair* 'to hate'.
heir /air/ ● **noun 1** a person legally entitled to the property or rank of another on that person's death. **2** a person who continues the work of a predecessor.
– DERIVATIVES **heirship** noun.
– ORIGIN Old French, from Latin *heres*.
heir apparent ● **noun** (pl. **heirs apparent**) **1** an heir whose claim cannot be set aside by the birth of another heir. **2** a person who is most likely to succeed to the place of another.
heiress ● **noun** a female heir, especially to vast wealth.
heirloom ● **noun** a valuable object that has belonged to a family for several generations.
– ORIGIN from HEIR + LOOM[1] (in the former senses 'tool, heirloom').
heir presumptive ● **noun** (pl. **heirs presumptive**) an heir whose claim may be set aside by the birth of another heir.
heist /hīst/ informal, chiefly N. Amer. ● **noun** a robbery. ● **verb** steal.
– ORIGIN from a local pronunciation of HOIST.
Hejira ● **noun** variant spelling of HEGIRA.
held past and past participle of HOLD[1].
Heldentenor /heldəntennor/ ● **noun** a powerful tenor voice suitable for heroic roles in opera.
– ORIGIN German, 'hero tenor'.
helical /hellik'l/ ● **adjective** having the shape or form of a helix; spiral.
– DERIVATIVES **helically** adverb.
helices plural of HELIX.
helichrysum /hellikrīsəm/ ● **noun** a plant of the daisy family, with flowers retaining their shape and colour when dried.
– ORIGIN Latin, from Greek *helix* 'spiral' + *khrusos* 'gold'.
helicopter ● **noun** a type of aircraft deriving both lift and propulsion from one or two sets of horizontally revolving rotors.
– ORIGIN French *hélicoptère*, from Greek *helix* 'spiral' + *pteron* 'wing'.
heliocentric ● **adjective 1** having or representing the sun as the centre, as in the accepted astronomical model of the solar system. Compare with GEOCENTRIC. **2** Astronomy measured from or considered in relation to the centre of the sun.
– ORIGIN from Greek *hēlios* 'sun'.
heliograph ● **noun 1** a signalling device by which sunlight is reflected in flashes from a movable mirror. **2** a message sent by heliograph. **3** a telescopic apparatus for photographing the sun.
– DERIVATIVES **heliographic** adjective.
heliosphere ● **noun** the region of space, encompassing the solar system, in which the solar wind has a significant influence.
– DERIVATIVES **heliospheric** adjective.
heliotrope /heeliətrōp/ ● **noun** a plant of the borage family, grown for its fragrant purple or blue flowers.
– ORIGIN Greek *hēliotropion* 'plant turning its flowers towards the sun', from *hēlios* 'sun' + *trepein* 'to turn'.
helipad ● **noun** a landing and take-off area for helicopters.
heliport ● **noun** an airport or landing place for helicopters.
heli-skiing ● **noun** skiing in which the skier is taken up the mountain by helicopter.
helium /heeliəm/ ● **noun** an inert gaseous chemical element, the lightest member of the noble gas series.
– ORIGIN from Greek *hēlios* 'sun', because before it was discovered on the earth its existence had been proposed to explain lines in the sun's spectrum.
helix /heeliks/ ● **noun** (pl. **helices** /heeliseez/) an object with a three-dimensional spiral shape like that of a wire wound uniformly in a single layer around a cylinder or cone.
– ORIGIN Greek.
hell ● **noun 1** a place regarded in various religions as a spiritual realm of evil and suffering, often depicted as a place of perpetual fire beneath the earth to which the wicked are sent after death. **2** a state or place of great suffering. ● **exclamation** used to express annoyance or surprise or for emphasis.
– PHRASES **all hell breaks** (or **is let**) **loose** informal suddenly there is pandemonium. **come hell or high water** whatever difficulties may occur. **for the hell of it** informal just for fun. **get** (or **give**) **hell** informal receive (or give) a severe reprimand. **hell hath no fury like a woman scorned** proverb a woman rejected by a man can be ferociously angry and vindictive. **hell for leather** as fast as possible. **hell's bells** informal an exclamation of annoyance or anger. **like hell** informal very fast, much, hard, etc. **not a hope in hell** informal no chance at all. **play hell** (or **merry hell**) informal create havoc or cause damage. **the road to hell is paved with good intentions** proverb promises and plans must be put into action, otherwise they are useless. **there will be hell to pay** informal serious trouble will result. **until hell freezes over** forever.
– DERIVATIVES **hellward** adverb & adjective.
– ORIGIN Old English.
he'll ● **contraction** he shall or he will.

Thesaurus

ate, large, excessive; *informal* steep, astronomical, whopping.
– OPPOSITES slight, feeble, light, small.
hegemony ● **noun** LEADERSHIP, dominance, dominion, supremacy, authority, mastery, control, power, sway, rule, sovereignty.
height ● **noun 1** *the height of the wall* HIGHNESS, tallness, extent upwards, vertical measurement, elevation, stature, altitude. **2** *the mountain heights* SUMMIT, top, peak, crest, crown, tip, cap, pinnacle, apex, brow, ridge. **3** *the height of their fame* HIGHEST POINT, crowning moment, peak, acme, zenith, apogee, pinnacle, climax, high water mark. **4** *the height of bad manners* EPITOME, acme, zenith, quintessence, very limit; ultimate, utmost. **5** *he is terrified of heights* HIGH PLACES, high ground; precipices, cliffs.
– OPPOSITES width, nadir.
heighten ● **verb 1** *the roof had to be heightened* MAKE HIGHER, raise, lift (up), elevate. **2** *her pleasure was heightened by guilt* INTENSIFY, increase, enhance, add to, augment, boost, strengthen, deepen, magnify, amplify, reinforce.
– OPPOSITES lower, reduce.
heinous ● **adjective** ODIOUS, wicked, evil, atrocious, monstrous, abominable, detestable, contemptible, reprehensible, despicable, egregious, horrific, terrible, awful, abhorrent, loathsome, hideous, unspeakable, execrable; iniquitous, villainous, beyond the pale.
– OPPOSITES admirable.
heir, heiress ● **noun** SUCCESSOR, next in line, inheritor, beneficiary, legatee; descendant, scion; *Law* devisee; *English Law* coparcener; *Scottish Law* heritor.
helix ● **noun** SPIRAL, coil, corkscrew, curl, twist, gyre, whorl, convolution.
hell ● **noun 1** *they feared hell* THE NETHERWORLD, the Inferno, the infernal regions, the abyss; eternal damnation, perdition; hellfire, fire and brimstone; Hades, Acheron, Gehenna, Tophet, Sheol; *poetic/literary* the pit. **2** *he made her life hell* A MISERY, torture, agony, a torment, a nightmare, an ordeal; anguish, wretchedness, woe.
– RELATED TERMS infernal.
– OPPOSITES heaven, paradise.
– PHRASES **give someone hell** *(informal)* **1** *when I found out I gave him hell* REPRIMAND SEVERELY, rebuke, admonish, chastise, chide, upbraid, reprove, scold, berate, remonstrate with, reprehend, take to task, lambaste; read someone the Riot Act, give someone a piece of one's mind, haul over the coals; *informal* tell off, dress down, give someone an earful, give someone a roasting, rap over the knuckles, let someone have it, bawl out, come down hard on, lay into, blast; *Brit. informal* tick off, have a go at, carpet, give someone a rollicking, give someone a mouthful, tear someone off a strip, give someone what for; *N. Amer. informal* chew out; *formal* casti-

hell-bent • adjective determined to achieve something at all costs.
hellcat • noun a spiteful, violent woman.
hellebore /hellibor/ • noun a poisonous winter-flowering plant with large white, green, or purplish flowers.
– ORIGIN Greek *helleboros*.
helleborine /hellibəreen/ • noun an orchid with greenish, white, or pink flowers, growing chiefly in woodland.
– ORIGIN Greek *helleborinē*, a plant like hellebore.
Hellene /helleen/ • noun a Greek.
– ORIGIN named after *Hellen*, son of Deucalion, who was held in Greek mythology to be the ancestor of all the Greeks.
Hellenic /helennik, heleenik/ • adjective **1** Greek. **2** relating to Iron Age and Classical Greek culture. • noun the Greek language.
Hellenism • noun **1** the national character or culture of Greece, especially ancient Greece. **2** the study or imitation of ancient Greek culture.
– DERIVATIVES **Hellenist** noun **Hellenize** (also **Hellenise**) verb.
Hellenistic • adjective relating to Greek culture from the death of Alexander the Great (323BC) to the defeat of Cleopatra and Mark Antony by Octavian in 31BC.
hellfire • noun the fire regarded as existing in hell.
hellhole • noun an oppressive or unbearable place.
hellhound • noun a demon in the form of a dog.
hellish • adjective **1** of or like hell. **2** informal extremely difficult or unpleasant. • adverb Brit. informal very; extremely.
– DERIVATIVES **hellishly** adverb **hellishness** noun.
hello (also **hallo** or **hullo**) • exclamation **1** used as a greeting or to begin a telephone conversation. **2** Brit. used to express surprise or to attract someone's attention.
– ORIGIN related to archaic *holla*, from French *ho* 'ho!' + *là* 'there'.
hellraiser • noun a person who causes trouble by violent, drunken, or outrageous behaviour.
Hell's Angel • noun a member of a gang of male motorcycle enthusiasts notorious for lawless behaviour.
helm[1] • noun **1** a tiller or wheel for steering a ship or boat. **2** (**the helm**) a position of leadership. • verb **1** steer (a boat or ship). **2** manage the running of.
– ORIGIN Old English, probably related to HELVE.
helm[2] • noun archaic a helmet.
– ORIGIN Old English, related to HELMET.
helmet • noun a hard or padded protective hat.
– DERIVATIVES **helmeted** adjective.
– ORIGIN Old French, 'little helmet'; related to HELM[2].
helminth /helminth/ • noun a parasitic worm; a fluke, tapeworm, or nematode.
– DERIVATIVES **helminthic** adjective **helminthology** noun.
– ORIGIN Greek *helmins* 'intestinal worm'.
helmsman • noun a person who steers a boat.
helot /hellət/ • noun **1** a member of a class of serfs in ancient Sparta, intermediate in status between slaves and citizens. **2** a serf or slave.
– ORIGIN Greek *Heilōtes*, traditionally taken as referring to inhabitants of *Helos*, an ancient Greek town whose inhabitants were enslaved.
help • verb **1** make it easier for (someone) to do something. **2** improve (a situation or problem). **3** (**help someone to**) serve someone with (food or drink). **4** (**help oneself**) take something without permission. **5** (**can/could not help**) cannot or could not refrain from. • noun **1** assistance or a source of assistance. **2** a domestic servant or employee.
– PHRASES **so help me (God)** used to emphasize that one means what one is saying. **there is no help for it** there is no way of avoiding a situation.
– DERIVATIVES **helper** noun.
– ORIGIN Old English.
helpful • adjective **1** giving or ready to give help. **2** useful.
– DERIVATIVES **helpfully** adverb **helpfulness** noun.
helping • noun a portion of food served to one person at one time.
helpless • adjective **1** unable to defend oneself or to act without help. **2** uncontrollable.
– DERIVATIVES **helplessly** adverb **helplessness** noun.
helpline • noun a telephone service providing help with

h

Thesaurus

gate. **2** *she gave me hell when I was her junior* HARASS, hound, plague, harry, bother, trouble, bully, intimidate, pick on, victimize, terrorize; *informal* hassle, give someone a hard time. **hell for leather** VERY FAST, very quickly, rapidly, speedily, swiftly, hurriedly, at full tilt, at full pelt, headlong, hotfoot, post-haste, helter-skelter, at the speed of light, at breakneck speed; *informal* like a bat out of hell, like the wind, like greased lightning, like a bomb; *Brit. informal* like the clappers, at a rate of knots; *N. Amer. informal* lickety-split. **raise hell** *(informal)* **1** *they were hollering and raising hell* CAUSE A DISTURBANCE, cause a commotion, be noisy, run riot, run wild, go on the rampage, be out of control; *informal* raise the roof. **2** *he raised hell with the planners* REMONSTRATE, expostulate, be angry, be furious; argue; *informal* kick up a fuss, kick up a stink.
hell-bent • adjective INTENT, bent, determined, (dead) set, insistent, fixed, resolved; single-minded, fixated.
– OPPOSITES half-hearted.
hellish • adjective **1** *the hellish face of Death* INFERNAL, Hadean; diabolical, fiendish, satanic, demonic; evil, wicked. **2** *(informal) a hellish week* HORRIBLE, rotten, awful, terrible, dreadful, ghastly, horrid, vile, foul, appalling, atrocious, horrendous, frightful; difficult, unpleasant, nasty, disagreeable; stressful, taxing, tough, hard, frustrating, fraught, traumatic, gruelling; *informal* murderous, lousy; *Brit. informal* beastly; *N. Amer. informal* hellacious.
– OPPOSITES angelic, wonderful.
• adverb *(Brit. informal) it's hellish hard work* EXTREMELY, very, exceedingly, exceptionally, tremendously, immensely, intensely, unusually, decidedly, particularly, really, truly, mightily; most, so; *N. English* right; *informal* terrifically, awfully, fearfully, terribly, devilishly, majorly, seriously, ultra, oh-so, damn, damned; *Brit. informal* ever so, well, bloody, dead; *N. Amer. informal* real, mighty, awful; *informal, dated* devilish; *archaic* exceeding.
– OPPOSITES moderately.
helm • noun *he took the helm* TILLER, wheel; steering gear, rudder.
– PHRASES **at the helm** IN CHARGE, in command, in control, responsible, in authority, at the wheel, in the driving seat, in the saddle; *informal* holding the reins, running the show, calling the shots.
help • verb **1** *can you help me please?* ASSIST, aid, lend a (helping) hand to, give assistance to, come to the aid of; be of service to, be of use to; do someone a favour, do someone a service, do someone a good turn, bail someone out, come to the rescue, give someone a leg up; rally round, pitch in; *informal* get someone out of a tight spot, save someone's bacon, save someone's skin. **2** *this credit card helps cancer research* SUPPORT, contribute to, give money to, donate to; promote, boost, back; further the interests of; *N. Amer. informal* bankroll. **3** *sore throats are helped by lozenges* RELIEVE, soothe, ease, alleviate, make better, improve, assuage, lessen; remedy, cure, heal.
– OPPOSITES hinder, impede, worsen.
• noun **1** *this could be of help to you* ASSISTANCE, aid, a helping hand, support, succour, advice, guidance; benefit, use, advantage, service, comfort; *informal* a shot in the arm. **2** *he sought help for his eczema* RELIEF, alleviation, improvement, assuagement, healing; a remedy, a cure, a restorative. **3** *they treated the help badly* DOMESTIC WORKER, domestic servant, cleaner, cleaning lady, home help, maid, housemaid, hired help, helper; *Brit. informal* daily (woman), skivvy, Mrs Mop; *Brit. dated* charwoman, charlady, char.
– PHRASES **cannot help** *he could not help laughing* BE UNABLE TO STOP, be unable to refrain from, be unable to keep from. **help oneself to** STEAL, take, appropriate, 'borrow', 'liberate', pocket, purloin, commandeer; *informal* swipe, nab, filch, snaffle, walk off with, run off with; *Brit. informal* nick, pinch, whip, knock off.
helper • noun ASSISTANT, aide, helpmate, helpmeet, deputy, auxiliary, second, right-hand man/woman, attendant, acolyte; co-worker, workmate, teammate, associate, colleague, partner; *informal* sidekick.
helpful • adjective **1** *the staff are helpful* OBLIGING, eager to please, kind, accommodating, supportive, cooperative; sympathetic, neighbourly, charitable. **2** *we found your comments helpful* USEFUL, of use, beneficial, valuable, profitable, fruitful, advantageous, worthwhile, constructive; informative, instructive. **3** *a helpful new tool* HANDY, useful, convenient, practical, easy-to-use, functional, serviceable; *informal* neat, nifty.
– OPPOSITES unsympathetic, useless, inconvenient.
helping • noun PORTION, serving, piece, slice, share, ration, allocation; *informal* dollop.
helpless • adjective DEPENDENT, incapable, powerless, impotent, weak; defenceless, vulnerable, exposed, unprotected, open to at-

problems.
helpmate (also **helpmeet**) ● noun a helpful companion or partner.
– ORIGIN from an erroneous reading of a passage in the Book of Genesis (chapter 2), where Adam's future wife is described as 'an help meet for him' (i.e. a suitable helper for him).
helter-skelter ● adjective & adverb in disorderly haste or confusion. ● noun Brit. a tall spiral slide winding around a tower at a fair.
– ORIGIN perhaps symbolic of running feet or from obsolete *skelte* 'hasten'.
helve /helv/ ● noun the handle of a weapon or tool.
– ORIGIN Old English, related to HALTER.
Helvetian (also **Helvetic**) ● adjective Swiss. ● noun a person from Switzerland.
– ORIGIN from Latin *Helvetia* 'Switzerland'.
hem[1] ● noun the edge of a piece of cloth or clothing which has been turned under and sewn. ● verb (**hemmed**, **hemming**) **1** turn under and sew the edge of. **2** (**hem in**) surround and restrict the space or movement of.
– ORIGIN Old English.
hem[2] ● exclamation expressing the sound made when coughing or clearing the throat to attract attention or show hesitation.
– PHRASES **hem and haw** another way of saying **hum and haw** (see HUM).
– ORIGIN imitative.
hemal etc. ● adjective US spelling of HAEMAL etc.
he-man ● noun informal a very well-built, masculine man.
hemi- ● prefix half: *hemisphere*.
– ORIGIN Greek *hēmi-*.
-hemia ● combining form US spelling of -AEMIA.
hemidemisemiquaver /hemmidemmi**semm**ikwayvər/ ● noun Music, chiefly Brit. a note with the time value of half a demisemiquaver.
hemiparesis /hemmipəreesiss/ ● noun another term for HEMIPLEGIA.
hemiplegia /hemmi**plee**jə/ ● noun paralysis of one side of the body.
– DERIVATIVES **hemiplegic** noun & adjective.
hemisphere ● noun **1** a half of a sphere. **2** a half of the earth, usually as divided into northern and southern halves by the equator, or into western and eastern halves by an imaginary line passing through the poles. **3** (also **cerebral hemisphere**) each of the two parts of the cerebrum (left and right) in the brain of a vertebrate.
– DERIVATIVES **hemispheric** adjective **hemispherical** adjective.
hemline ● noun the level of the lower edge of a garment such as a skirt or coat.
hemlock ● noun **1** a highly poisonous plant of the parsley family, with fern-like leaves and small white flowers. **2** a sedative or poison obtained from hemlock.
– ORIGIN Old English.
hemp ● noun **1** (also **Indian hemp**) the cannabis plant. **2** the fibre of this plant, extracted from the stem and used to make rope, strong fabrics, paper, etc. **3** the drug cannabis.
– ORIGIN Old English.
hen ● noun **1** a female bird, especially of a domestic fowl. **2** (**hens**) domestic fowls of either sex.
– PHRASES **as rare** (or **scarce**) **as hen's teeth** extremely rare.
– ORIGIN Old English.
henbane /**hen**bayn/ ● noun a poisonous plant of the nightshade family, with sticky hairy leaves and an unpleasant smell.
hence ● adverb **1** as a consequence; for this reason. **2** from now; in the future. **3** (also **from hence**) archaic from here.
– ORIGIN Old English.
henceforth (also **henceforward**) ● adverb from this or that time on.
henchman ● noun **1** chiefly derogatory a faithful supporter or aide, especially one prepared to engage in underhand practices. **2** historical a squire or page attending a prince or noble.
– ORIGIN from Old English *hengest* 'male horse' + MAN, the original sense being probably 'a groom'.
hendeca- /hendekkə, hen**dek**kə/ ● combining form eleven; having eleven: *hendecagon*.
– ORIGIN Greek *hendeka* 'eleven'.
hendecagon /hen**dek**kəgən/ ● noun a plane figure with eleven straight sides and angles.
hendiadys /hen**dī**ədiss/ ● noun the expression of a single idea by two words connected with 'and', e.g. *nice and warm*, when one could be used to modify the other, as in *nicely warm*.
– ORIGIN from Greek *hen dia duoin* 'one thing by two'.
henge /henj/ ● noun a prehistoric monument consisting of a circle of stone or wooden uprights.
– ORIGIN back-formation from *Stonehenge*, such a monument in Wiltshire, from two Old English words meaning 'stone' + 'to hang'.
henna ● noun the powdered leaves of a tropical shrub, used as a reddish-brown dye to colour the hair and decorate the body. ● verb (**hennas**, **hennaed**, **hennaing**) dye with henna.
– ORIGIN Arabic.
hen night ● noun Brit. informal a celebration held for a woman who is about to get married, attended only by women.
hen party ● noun informal a social gathering of women.
henpeck ● verb (usu. as adj. **henpecked**) (of a woman) continually criticize and order about (her husband).
henry ● noun (pl. **henries** or **henrys**) Physics the unit of inductance in the SI system.
– ORIGIN named after the American physicist Joseph *Henry* (1797–1878).
heparin /**hep**pərin/ ● noun a compound occurring in the liver and other tissues which prevents blood coagulation, used as an anticoagulant in the treatment of thrombosis.
– ORIGIN from Greek *hēpar* 'liver'.
hepatic /hi**pat**tik/ ● adjective relating to the liver.
– ORIGIN Greek *hēpatikos*, from *hēpar* 'liver'.
hepatitis /heppə**tī**tiss/ ● noun a disease in which the liver becomes inflamed and there is jaundice and other symptoms, mainly spread by a series of viruses (**hepatitis A**, **B**, and **C**) transmitted in blood or food.
hepcat ● noun informal, dated a stylish or fashionable person.
– ORIGIN from *hep* (variant of HIP[3]) + *cat* (informal term for a man, especially among jazz enthusiasts).
hepta- ● combining form seven; having seven: *heptathlon*.
– ORIGIN Greek *hepta* 'seven'.
heptagon /**hep**təgən/ ● noun a plane figure with seven straight sides and angles.
heptahedron /heptə**hee**drən/ ● noun (pl. **heptahedra** or **heptahedrons**) a solid figure with seven plane faces.

Thesaurus

tack; paralysed, disabled.
– OPPOSITES independent.
helpmate, helpmeet ● noun HELPER, assistant, attendant; supporter, friend, companion; spouse, partner, mate, husband, wife.
helter-skelter ● adverb *they ran helter-skelter down the hill* HEADLONG, pell-mell, hotfoot, post-haste, hastily, hurriedly, at full pelt, at full tilt, hell for leather; recklessly, precipitately, heedlessly, wildly; *informal* like a bat out of hell, like the wind, like greased lightning, like a bomb; *Brit. informal* like the clappers, at a rate of knots; *N. Amer. informal* lickety-split.
● adjective *a helter-skelter collection of houses* DISORDERED, disorderly, chaotic, muddled, jumbled, untidy, haphazard, disorganized, topsy-turvy; *informal* higgledy-piggledy; *Brit. informal* shambolic.
– OPPOSITES orderly.
hem ● noun *the hem of her dress* EDGE, edging, border, trim, trimming.
● verb *Nan taught me to hem skirts* EDGE, trim.
– PHRASES **hem someone/something in 1** *a bay hemmed in by pine trees* SURROUND, border, edge, encircle, circle, ring, enclose, skirt, fringe, encompass. **2** *we were hemmed in by the rules* RESTRICT, confine, trap, hedge in, fence in; constrain, restrain, limit, curb, check.
he-man ● noun *(informal)* MUSCLEMAN, strongman, macho man, iron man; Hercules, Samson, Tarzan; *informal* hunk, tough guy, beefcake, bruiser.
– OPPOSITES wimp.
hence ● adverb CONSEQUENTLY, as a consequence, for this reason, therefore, ergo, thus, so, accordingly, as a result, because of that, that being so.
henceforth, henceforward ● adverb FROM NOW ON, as of now, in (the) future, hence, subsequently, from this day on, from this day forth; *formal* hereafter.
henchman ● noun RIGHT-HAND MAN, assistant, aide, helper; underling, minion, man Friday, lackey, flunkey, stooge; bodyguard, minder; *informal* sidekick, crony, heavy.
henpecked ● adjective BROWBEATEN, downtrodden, bullied, domin-

heptathlon /heptathlən/ • **noun** an athletic contest for women that consists of seven separate events.
– DERIVATIVES **heptathlete** noun.
– ORIGIN from HEPTA- + Greek *athlon* 'contest'.

her • **pronoun** (third person sing.) **1** used as the object of a verb or preposition to refer to a female person or animal previously mentioned. **2** referring to a ship, country, or other inanimate thing regarded as female. • **possessive determiner 1** belonging to or associated with a female person or animal previously mentioned. **2** (**Her**) used in titles.
– PHRASES **her indoors** Brit. informal, humorous one's wife.
– ORIGIN Old English.

herald • **noun 1** historical a person who carried official messages, made proclamations, and oversaw tournaments. **2** a person or thing viewed as a sign that something is about to happen. **3** an official employed to oversee state ceremonial, precedence, and the use of armorial bearings. **4** (in the UK) an official of the College of Arms ranking above a pursuivant. • **verb 1** signal the imminence of. **2** announce or proclaim.
– ORIGIN Old French *herault*.

heraldic /heraldik/ • **adjective** relating to heraldry.
– DERIVATIVES **heraldically** adverb.

heraldry • **noun 1** the system by which coats of arms and other armorial bearings are devised, described, and regulated. **2** armorial bearings or other heraldic symbols.
– DERIVATIVES **heraldist** noun.

herb • **noun 1** any plant with leaves, seeds, or flowers used for flavouring, food, medicine, or perfume. **2** Botany any seed-bearing plant which does not have a woody stem and dies down to the ground after flowering.
– DERIVATIVES **herby** adjective.
– ORIGIN Latin *herba* 'grass, green crops, herb'.

herbaceous /herbayshəss/ • **adjective** relating to herbs (in the botanical sense).

herbaceous border • **noun** a garden border containing mainly perennial flowering plants.

herbage • **noun** herbaceous plants, especially grass used for grazing.

herbal • **adjective** relating to or made from herbs, especially those used in cooking and medicine. • **noun** a book that describes herbs and their culinary and medicinal properties.

herbalism • **noun** the study or practice of the medicinal and therapeutic use of plants.

herbalist • **noun 1** a practitioner of herbalism. **2** a dealer in medicinal herbs.

herbarium /herbairiəm/ • **noun** (pl. **herbaria** /herbairiə/) a systematically arranged collection of dried plants.

herbed • **adjective** cooked or flavoured with herbs.

herbicide /herbisīd/ • **noun** a toxic substance used to destroy unwanted vegetation.

herbivore /herbivor/ • **noun** an animal that feeds on plants.
– DERIVATIVES **herbivorous** /herbivvərəss/ adjective.

Herculean /herkyooleeən, herkyōōliən/ • **adjective** requiring or having great strength or effort.
– ORIGIN named after the Roman and Greek mythological hero *Hercules* (famed for his strength).

Hercynian /hersinniən/ • **adjective** Geology denoting a major mountain-forming period in western Europe, eastern North America, and the Andes, in the Upper Palaeozoic era.
– ORIGIN from Latin *Hercynia silva*, the ancient name of an area of forested mountains in central Germany.

herd • **noun 1** a large group of animals, especially hoofed mammals, that live or are kept together. **2** derogatory a large group or class of people. • **verb 1** move in a large group. **2** keep or look after (livestock).
– DERIVATIVES **herder** noun.
– ORIGIN Old English.

herd instinct • **noun** an inclination to behave or think like the majority.

herdsman • **noun** the owner or keeper of a herd of domesticated animals.

here • **adverb 1** in, at, or to this place or position. **2** (usu. **here is/are**) used when introducing or handing over something or someone. **3** used when indicating a time, point, or situation that has arrived or is happening. • **exclamation** used to attract someone's attention.
– PHRASES **here and now** at the present time. **here and there** in various places. **here goes** said to indicate that one is about to start something difficult or exciting. **here's to** used to wish health or success before drinking. **neither here nor there** of no importance or relevance.
– ORIGIN Old English.

hereabouts (also **hereabout**) • **adverb** near this place.

hereafter • **adverb** formal **1** from now on or at some time in the future. **2** after death. • **noun** (**the hereafter**) life after death.

hereby • **adverb** formal as a result of this.

hereditary /hireddit ri/ • **adjective 1** conferred by, based on, or relating to inheritance. **2** (of a characteristic or disease) able to be passed on genetically from parents to their offspring or descendants.
– DERIVATIVES **hereditarily** adverb.

heredity /hireddit i/ • **noun 1** the passing on of physical or mental characteristics genetically from one generation to another. **2** inheritance of a title, office, or right.
– ORIGIN Latin *hereditas* 'heirship', from *heres* 'heir'.

Hereford /herrifərd/ • **noun** an animal of a breed of red and white beef cattle.
– ORIGIN from *Hereford* in west central England.

herein • **adverb** formal in this document, book, or matter.

hereinafter • **adverb** formal further on in this document.

h

Thesaurus

ated, subjugated, oppressed, intimidated; meek, timid, cringing; *informal* under someone's thumb, led by the nose.
– OPPOSITES domineering.

herald • **noun 1** *(historical) a herald announced the armistice* MESSENGER, courier; proclaimer, announcer, crier. **2** *the first herald of spring* HARBINGER, sign, indicator, indication, signal, prelude, portent, omen; forerunner, precursor; *poetic/literary* foretoken.
• **verb 1** *shouts heralded their approach* PROCLAIM, announce, broadcast, publicize, declare, trumpet, blazon, advertise. **2** *the speech heralded a policy change* SIGNAL, indicate, announce, spell, presage, augur, portend, promise, foretell; usher in, pave the way for, be a harbinger of; *poetic/literary* foretoken, betoken.

Herculean • **adjective 1** *a Herculean task* ARDUOUS, gruelling, laborious, back-breaking, onerous, strenuous, difficult, formidable, hard, tough, huge, massive, uphill; demanding, exhausting, taxing; *archaic* toilsome. **2** *his Herculean build* STRONG, muscular, muscly, powerful, robust, solid, strapping, brawny, burly; *informal* hunky, beefy, hulking.
– OPPOSITES easy, puny.

herd • **noun 1** *a herd of cows* drove, flock, pack, fold; group, collection. **2** *a herd of actors* CROWD, group, bunch, horde, mob, host, pack, multitude, throng, swarm, company. **3** *(derogatory) they consider themselves above the herd* THE COMMON PEOPLE, the masses, the rank and file, the crowd, the commonality, the commonalty, the plebeians; the hoi polloi, the mob, the proletariat, the rabble, the riff-raff, the great unwashed; *informal* the proles, the plebs.
• **verb 1** *we herded the sheep into the pen* DRIVE, shepherd, guide; round up, gather, collect. **2** *we all herded into the room* CROWD, pack, flock; cluster, huddle. **3** *they herd reindeer* TEND, look after, keep, watch (over), mind, guard.

herdsman, herdswoman • **noun** STOCKMAN, herder, drover, cattleman, cowherd, cowhand, cowman, cowboy, rancher, shepherd; *N. Amer.* ranchero; *N. Amer. informal* cowpuncher, cowpoke; *archaic* herd.

here • **adverb 1** *they lived here* AT/IN THIS PLACE, at/in this spot, at/in this location. **2** *I am here now* PRESENT, in attendance, attending, at hand; available. **3** *come here tomorrow* TO THIS PLACE, to this spot, to this location, over here, nearer, closer; *poetic/literary* hither. **4** *here is your opportunity* NOW, at this moment, at this point (in time), at this juncture, at this stage.
– OPPOSITES absent.
– PHRASES **here and there 1** *clumps of heather here and there* IN VARIOUS PLACES, in different places; at random. **2** *they darted here and there* HITHER AND THITHER, around, about, to and fro, back and forth, in all directions.

hereafter • **adverb** *(formal) nothing I say hereafter is intended to offend* FROM NOW ON, after this, as of now, from this moment forth, from this day forth, from this day forward, subsequently, in (the) future, hence, henceforth, henceforward; *formal* hereinafter.
• **noun** *our preparation for the hereafter* LIFE AFTER DEATH, the afterlife, the afterworld, the next world; eternity, heaven, paradise.

hereditary • **adjective 1** *a hereditary right* INHERITED; bequeathed, willed, handed-down, passed-down, passed-on, transferred; ancestral, family, familial. **2** *a hereditary disease* GENETIC, genetical, congenital, inborn, inherited, inbred, innate; in the family, in the

hereof • adverb formal of this document.
heresiarch /hereeziaark/ • noun the founder of a heresy or the leader of a heretical sect.
heresy /herrisi/ • noun (pl. **heresies**) **1** belief or opinion contrary to orthodox religious (especially Christian) doctrine. **2** opinion profoundly at odds with what is generally accepted.
– ORIGIN Greek *hairesis* 'choice, sect'.
heretic /herritik/ • noun a person believing in or practising heresy.
– DERIVATIVES **heretical** /hirettik'l/ adjective **heretically** adverb.
hereto • adverb formal to this matter or document.
heretofore • adverb formal before now.
hereunder • adverb formal **1** as provided for under the terms of this document. **2** further on in this document.
hereupon • adverb archaic after or as a result of this.
herewith • adverb formal with this letter.
heritable • adjective able to be inherited.
– DERIVATIVES **heritability** noun **heritably** adverb.
heritage • noun **1** property that is or may be inherited; an inheritance. **2** valued things such as historic buildings that have been passed down from previous generations. **3** (before another noun) relating to things of historic or cultural value that are worthy of preservation.
– ORIGIN Old French, from *heriter* 'inherit'.
heritor • noun a person who inherits.
hermaphrodite /hermafrədīt/ • noun **1** a person or animal having both male and female sex organs or other sexual characteristics. **2** Botany a plant having stamens and pistils in the same flower.
– DERIVATIVES **hermaphroditic** adjective **hermaphroditism** noun.
– ORIGIN Greek *hermaphroditos*, originally the name of the son of Hermes and Aphrodite who became joined in one body with the nymph Salmacis.
hermeneutic /herminyōōtik/ • adjective concerning interpretation, especially of the Bible or literary texts.
– DERIVATIVES **hermeneutical** adjective.
– ORIGIN Greek *hermēneutikos*, from *hermēneuein* 'interpret'.
hermeneutics • plural noun (usu. treated as sing.) the branch of knowledge that deals with interpretation, especially of the Bible or literary texts.
hermetic /hermettik/ • adjective **1** (of a seal or closure) complete and airtight. **2** insulated or protected from outside influences. **3** esoteric or cryptic: *hermetic poems.*
– DERIVATIVES **hermetically** adverb **hermeticism** noun.
– ORIGIN from Latin *Hermes Trismegistus* 'thrice-greatest Hermes', the legendary founder of alchemy and astrology identified with the Greek god Hermes.
hermit • noun **1** a person living in solitude as a religious discipline. **2** a reclusive or solitary person.
– DERIVATIVES **hermitic** adjective.
– ORIGIN Greek *erēmitēs*, from *erēmos* 'solitary'.
hermitage • noun the home of a hermit, especially when small and remote.
hermit crab • noun a crab with a soft abdomen, which lives in a cast-off mollusc shell for protection.
hernia /herniə/ • noun (pl. **hernias** or **herniae** /herni-ee/) a condition in which part of an organ (typically the intestine) is displaced and protrudes through the wall of the cavity containing it.
– DERIVATIVES **herniated** adjective **herniation** noun.
– ORIGIN Latin.
hero • noun (pl. **heroes**) **1** a person, typically a man, who is admired for their courage or outstanding achievements. **2** the chief male character in a book, play, or film. **3** (in mythology and folklore) a person of superhuman qualities.
– ORIGIN Greek *hērōs*.
heroic • adjective **1** of or like a hero or heroine; very brave. **2** grand or grandiose in scale or intention: *pyramids on a heroic scale.* • noun (**heroics**) behaviour or talk that is bold or dramatic.
– DERIVATIVES **heroically** adverb.
heroic couplet • noun (in verse) a pair of rhyming iambic pentameters.
heroin • noun a highly addictive painkilling drug derived from morphine, often used illicitly as a narcotic.
– ORIGIN German, from Latin *heros* 'hero' (because of its effects on the user's self-esteem).
heroine • noun **1** a woman admired for her courage or outstanding achievements. **2** the chief female character in a book, play, or film.
heroism • noun great bravery.
heron • noun a large fish-eating wading bird with long legs, a long neck, and a long pointed bill.
– ORIGIN Old French.
heronry • noun (pl. **heronries**) a breeding colony of herons, typically in a group of trees.
hero worship • noun excessive admiration for someone. • verb (**hero-worship**) admire excessively.
herpes /herpeez/ • noun a disease caused by a virus, affecting the skin (often with blisters) or the nervous system.
– DERIVATIVES **herpetic** adjective.
– ORIGIN Greek *herpēs* 'shingles, creeping', from *herpein* 'to creep'.
herpes simplex • noun a form of herpes which can produce cold sores, genital inflammation, or conjunctivitis.
herpes zoster /herpeez zostər/ • noun medical name for SHINGLES.
– ORIGIN Greek *zōstēr* 'girdle, shingles'.
herpetology /herpitolləji/ • noun the branch of zoology concerned with reptiles and amphibians.
– DERIVATIVES **herpetological** adjective **herpetologist** noun.
– ORIGIN from Greek *herpeton* 'creeping thing', from *herpein* 'to creep'.
Herr /hair/ • noun (pl. **Herren** /herrən/) a title or form of ad-

Thesaurus

blood, in the genes.
heredity • noun CONGENITAL TRAITS, genetic make-up, genes; ancestry, descent, extraction, parentage.
heresy • noun DISSENSION, dissent, nonconformity, heterodoxy, unorthodoxy, apostasy, blasphemy, freethinking; agnosticism, atheism, non-belief; idolatry, paganism.
heretic • noun DISSENTER, nonconformist, apostate, freethinker, iconoclast; agnostic, atheist, non-believer, unbeliever, idolater, idolatress, pagan, heathen; *archaic* paynim.
– OPPOSITES conformist, believer.
heritage • noun **1** *they stole his heritage* INHERITANCE, birthright, patrimony; legacy, bequest; *Law, dated* hereditament. **2** *Europe's cultural heritage* TRADITION, history, past, background; culture, customs. **3** *his Greek heritage* ANCESTRY, lineage, descent, extraction, parentage, roots, background, heredity.
hermaphrodite • noun ANDROGYNE, intersex, epicene; *Biology* bisexual, gynandromorph.
• adjective *hermaphrodite creatures* ANDROGYNOUS, intersex, hermaphroditic, hermaphroditical, epicene; *Biology* bisexual, gynandrous, gynandromorphic.
hermetic • adjective AIRTIGHT, tight, sealed; watertight, waterproof.
hermit • noun RECLUSE, solitary, loner, ascetic; *historical* anchorite, anchoress; *archaic* eremite.
hermitage • noun RETREAT, refuge, hideaway, hideout, shelter; *informal* hidey-hole.
hero • noun **1** *a war hero* BRAVE MAN, man of courage, man of the hour, lionheart, warrior; champion, victor, conqueror. **2** *a football hero* STAR, superstar, megastar, idol, celebrity, luminary; ideal, paragon, shining example; favourite, darling; *informal* celeb. **3** *the hero of the film is a young pianist* MALE PROTAGONIST, principal male character/role, starring role, star part; male lead, lead (actor), leading man.
– OPPOSITES coward, loser, villain.
heroic • adjective **1** *heroic rescuers* BRAVE, courageous, valiant, valorous, lionhearted, intrepid, bold, fearless, daring, audacious; unafraid, undaunted, dauntless, doughty, plucky, stout-hearted, mettlesome; gallant, chivalrous, noble; *informal* gutsy, spunky. **2** *obelisks on a heroic scale* PRODIGIOUS, grand, enormous, huge, massive, titanic, colossal, monumental; epic; *informal* mega.
heroine • noun **1** *she's a heroine—she saved my baby* BRAVE WOMAN, hero, woman of courage, woman of the hour; victor, winner, conqueror. **2** *the literary heroine of Moscow* STAR, superstar, megastar, idol, celebrity, luminary; ideal, paragon, shining example; favourite, darling; *informal* celeb. **3** *the film's heroine* FEMALE PROTAGONIST, principal female character/role; female lead, lead (actress), leading lady; prima donna, diva.
heroism • noun BRAVERY, courage, valour, intrepidity, boldness, daring, audacity, fearlessness, dauntlessness, pluck, stout-heartedness, lionheartedness; backbone, spine, grit, spirit, mettle; gallantry, chivalry; *informal* guts, spunk; *Brit. informal* bottle; *N. Amer.*

dress used of or to a German-speaking man, corresponding to *Mr* and also used before a rank or occupation.
– ORIGIN from High German *hērro* 'more exalted'.
Herrenvolk /herrənfolk/ ● noun the German nation as considered by the Nazis to be innately superior to others.
– ORIGIN German, 'master race'.
herring ● noun a silvery fish which is most abundant in coastal waters and is an important food fish.
– ORIGIN Old English.
herringbone ● noun a zigzag pattern consisting of columns of short parallel lines, with all the lines in one column sloping one way and all the lines in the next column sloping the other way.
herring gull ● noun a common northern gull with grey black-tipped wings.
hers ● possessive pronoun used to refer to a thing or things belonging to or associated with a female person or animal previously mentioned.
herself ● pronoun (third person sing.) **1** (reflexive) used as the object of a verb or preposition to refer to a female person or animal previously mentioned as the subject of the clause. **2** (emphatic) she or her personally.
Herts. /haarts/ ● abbreviation Hertfordshire.
hertz /herts/ ● noun (pl. same) the SI unit of frequency, equal to one cycle per second.
– ORIGIN named after the German physicist H. R. *Hertz* (1857–94).
Herzegovinian /hertsəgovvinyən/ ● noun a person from Herzegovina, the southern part of Bosnia–Herzegovina. ● adjective relating to Herzegovina.
he's ● contraction **1** he is. **2** he has.
hesitant ● adjective slow to act or speak through indecision or reluctance.
– DERIVATIVES **hesitance** noun **hesitancy** noun **hesitantly** adverb.
hesitate ● verb **1** pause in indecision. **2** be reluctant to do something.
– PHRASES **he who hesitates is lost** proverb delay or vacillation may have unfortunate consequences.
– DERIVATIVES **hesitation** noun.
– ORIGIN Latin *haesitare* 'stick fast, leave undecided'.
hessian ● noun a strong, coarse fabric made from hemp or jute, used especially for sacks and in upholstery.
– ORIGIN from *Hesse*, a state of western Germany.
hetero- ● combining form other; different: *heterosexual*.
– ORIGIN from Greek **heteros** 'other'.
heterocyclic /hetərōsiklik/ ● adjective Chemistry (of a compound) whose molecule contains a ring of atoms of at least two elements (one of which is generally carbon).
heterodox /hettərədoks/ ● adjective not conforming with orthodox standards or beliefs.
– DERIVATIVES **heterodoxy** noun.
– ORIGIN from Greek *doxa* 'opinion'.
heterodyne /hettərədīn/ ● adjective (usu. before another noun) Electronics a radio receiver or other circuit which produces a lower frequency signal by combining two almost equal high frequencies: *a heterodyne receiver*.
– DERIVATIVES **heterodyning** noun.
– ORIGIN from HETERO- + *-dyne*, from Greek *dunamis* 'power'.
heterogeneous /hettərəjeeniəss/ ● adjective diverse in character or content: *a heterogeneous collection*.
– DERIVATIVES **heterogeneity** /hettərəjəneeəti/ noun **heterogeneously** adverb.
– ORIGIN from Greek *heteros* 'other' + *genos* 'a kind'.
heteromorphic /hettərōmorfik/ ● adjective Biology occurring in two or more different forms, especially at different stages in the life cycle.
– DERIVATIVES **heteromorph** noun **heteromorphism** noun.
heterosexism ● noun discrimination or prejudice against homosexuals on the assumption that heterosexuality is the norm.
– DERIVATIVES **heterosexist** adjective.
heterosexual ● adjective **1** sexually attracted to the opposite sex. **2** involving or characterized by such sexual attraction. ● noun a heterosexual person.
– DERIVATIVES **heterosexuality** noun **heterosexually** adverb.
het up ● adjective informal angry and agitated.
– ORIGIN from dialect *het* 'heated, hot'.
heuristic /hyooristik/ ● adjective **1** enabling a person to discover or learn something for themselves. **2** Computing proceeding to a solution by trial and error or by rules that are only loosely defined. ● noun **1** (**heuristics**) (usu. treated as sing.) the study and use of heuristic techniques. **2** a heuristic process or method.
– DERIVATIVES **heuristically** adverb.
– ORIGIN from Greek *heuriskein* 'to find'.
hew /hyoo/ ● verb (past part. **hewn** or **hewed**) **1** chop or cut (wood, coal, etc.) with an axe, pick, or other tool. **2** (usu. **be hewn**) make or shape by hewing a hard material.
– ORIGIN Old English.
hewer ● noun dated a person who hews something, especially a miner who cuts coal from a seam.
– PHRASES **hewers of wood and drawers of water** menial drudges. [ORIGIN with biblical allusion to the Book of Joshua, chapter 9.]
hex chiefly N. Amer. ● verb cast a spell on. ● noun **1** a magic spell. **2** a witch.
– ORIGIN German *hexen*.
hexa- (also **hex-** before a vowel) ● combining form six; having six: *hexagon*.
– ORIGIN from Greek *hex* 'six'.
hexadecimal /heksədessim'l/ ● adjective Computing relating to or using a system of numerical notation that has 16 rather than 10 as its base.
hexagon /heksəgən/ ● noun a plane figure with six straight sides and angles.
– DERIVATIVES **hexagonal** adjective.
hexagram ● noun a six-pointed star formed by two intersecting equilateral triangles.
hexahedron /heksəheedrən/ ● noun (pl. **hexahedra** or **hexahedrons**) a solid figure with six plane faces.
– DERIVATIVES **hexahedral** adjective.
hexameter /heksammitər/ ● noun a line of verse consisting of six metrical feet.
hexane ● noun Chemistry a colourless liquid hydrocarbon of the alkane series, present in petroleum spirit.
– ORIGIN from HEXA- 'six' (denoting six carbon atoms).
hexose /heksōz/ ● noun any of the class of simple sugars whose molecules contain six carbon atoms (e.g. glucose).
hey ● exclamation used to attract attention or to express surprise, interest, etc.
heyday ● noun (**one's heyday**) the period of one's greatest success, activity, or vigour.

Thesaurus

informal moxie.
hero-worship ● noun IDOLIZATION, adulation, admiration, lionization, idealization, worship, adoration, veneration.
hesitancy ● noun. See HESITATION.
hesitant ● adjective **1** *she is hesitant about buying* UNCERTAIN, undecided, unsure, doubtful, dubious, sceptical; tentative, nervous, reluctant; indecisive, irresolute, hesitating, dithering, vacillating, blowing hot and cold; ambivalent, in two minds; *Brit.* havering, humming and hawing; *informal* iffy. **2** *a hesitant child* LACKING CONFIDENCE, diffident, timid, shy, bashful, insecure.
– OPPOSITES certain, decisive, confident.
hesitate ● verb **1** *she hesitated, unsure of what to say* PAUSE, delay, wait, shilly-shally, dither, stall, temporize; be in two minds, be uncertain, be unsure, be doubtful, be indecisive, equivocate, vacillate, waver, blow hot and cold, have second thoughts; *Brit.* haver, hum and haw; *informal* dilly-dally. **2** *don't hesitate to contact me* BE RELUCTANT, be unwilling, be disinclined, scruple; have misgivings about, have qualms about, shrink from, demur from, think twice about, baulk at.
hesitation ● noun HESITANCY, hesitance, uncertainty, unsureness, doubt, doubtfulness, dubiousness; irresolution, irresoluteness, indecision, indecisiveness; equivocation, vacillation, second thoughts; dithering, stalling, temporization, delay; reluctance, disinclination, unease, ambivalence; *formal* dubiety.
heterodox ● adjective UNORTHODOX, nonconformist, dissenting, dissident, rebellious, renegade; heretical, blasphemous, apostate, sceptical.
– OPPOSITES orthodox.
heterogeneous ● adjective DIVERSE, varied, varying, miscellaneous, assorted, mixed, sundry, disparate, different, differing, unrelated; motley; *poetic/literary* divers.
– OPPOSITES homogeneous.
heterosexual ● adjective *informal* STRAIGHT, hetero, het.
– OPPOSITES homosexual, gay.

– ORIGIN originally an exclamation of joy or surprise.
HF ● abbreviation Physics high frequency.
Hf ● symbol the chemical element hafnium.
HFC ● abbreviation hydrofluorocarbon.
Hg ● symbol the chemical element mercury.
– ORIGIN abbreviation of Latin *hydrargyrum.*
hg ● abbreviation hectogram(s).
HGV ● abbreviation Brit. heavy goods vehicle.
HH ● abbreviation extra hard (as a grade of pencil lead).
H-hour ● noun the time of day at which an attack or other military operation is scheduled to begin.
– ORIGIN from *H* (for *hour*) + HOUR.
HI ● abbreviation Hawaii.
hi ● exclamation informal used as a friendly greeting.
hiatus /hīaytəss/ ● noun (pl. **hiatuses**) a pause or gap in continuity.
– ORIGIN Latin, 'gaping'.
hiatus hernia (also **hiatal hernia**) ● noun the protrusion of an organ (usually the stomach) through the oesophageal opening in the diaphragm.
Hib ● noun a bacterium that causes infant meningitis.
– ORIGIN acronym from *Haemophilus influenzae type B.*
hibachi /hibachi/ ● noun (pl. **hibachis**) **1** a portable cooking apparatus similar to a small barbecue. **2** (in Japan) a large earthenware pan or brazier in which charcoal is burnt to provide indoor heating.
– ORIGIN Japanese (also *hi-hachi*), from *hi* 'fire' + *hachi* 'bowl, pot'.
hibernate ● verb (of an animal or plant) spend the winter in a dormant state.
– DERIVATIVES **hibernation** noun **hibernator** noun.
– ORIGIN Latin *hibernare*, from *hiberna* 'winter quarters'.
Hibernian /hībernian/ ● adjective Irish (now chiefly used in names). ● noun an Irish person (now chiefly used in names).
– ORIGIN Latin *Hibernia*, from Celtic.
hibiscus /hibiskəss/ ● noun a plant of the mallow family with large brightly coloured flowers.
– ORIGIN Greek *hibiskos* 'marsh mallow'.
hiccup (also **hiccough** (pronounced same)) ● noun **1** an involuntary spasm of the diaphragm and respiratory organs, with a sudden closure of the glottis and a characteristic gulping sound. **2** a minor difficulty or setback. ● verb (**hiccuped, hiccuping**) make the sound of a hiccup or series of hiccups.
– DERIVATIVES **hiccupy** adjective.
– ORIGIN imitative; the form *hiccough* arose by association with COUGH.
hick ● noun informal, chiefly N. Amer. an unsophisticated country-dweller.
– ORIGIN familiar form of the given name *Richard.*
hickey ● noun (pl. **hickeys**) **1** N. Amer. informal a gadget. **2** a blemish in printing. **3** N. Amer. informal a love bite.
– ORIGIN of unknown origin.
hickory ● noun **1** a chiefly North American tree which yields tough, heavy wood and bears edible nuts. **2** a stick made of hickory wood.
– ORIGIN from *pohickery*, the local Virginian name, from Algonquian.
hid past of HIDE[1].
hidden past participle of HIDE[1].
– DERIVATIVES **hiddenness** noun.
hidden agenda ● noun an ulterior motive or undivulged plan.
hidden reserves ● plural noun a company's funds that are not declared on its balance sheet.
hide[1] ● verb (past **hid**; past part. **hidden**) **1** put or keep out of sight. **2** conceal oneself. **3** keep secret. ● noun Brit. a camouflaged shelter used to observe wildlife at close quarters.
– PHRASES **hide one's light under a bushel** keep quiet about one's talents or accomplishments. [ORIGIN with biblical allusion to the Gospel of Matthew, chapter 15.]
– DERIVATIVES **hider** noun.
– ORIGIN Old English.
hide[2] ● noun the skin of an animal, especially when tanned or dressed.
– PHRASES **neither hide nor hair of** not the slightest trace of. **save one's hide** escape from difficulty. **tan** (or **whip**) **someone's hide** beat or flog someone.
– DERIVATIVES **hided** adjective.
– ORIGIN Old English.
hide-and-seek ● noun a children's game in which one or more players hide and the other or others have to look for them.
hideaway ● noun a hiding place, especially as a retreat from others.
hidebound ● adjective constrained by tradition or convention; narrow-minded.
– ORIGIN originally referring to malnourished cattle, later to emaciated human beings, hence the sense 'narrow in outlook': from HIDE[2] + BOUND[4].
hideous ● adjective **1** extremely ugly. **2** extremely unpleasant.
– DERIVATIVES **hideously** adverb **hideousness** noun.
– ORIGIN Old French *hidos, hideus*, from *hide* 'fear'.
hideout ● noun a hiding place, especially one used by someone who has broken the law.
hidey-hole (also **hidy-hole**) ● noun informal a hiding place.
hiding[1] ● noun informal **1** a physical beating. **2** a severe defeat.
– PHRASES **be on a hiding to nothing** Brit. be unlikely to succeed.
– ORIGIN from HIDE[2].
hiding[2] ● noun the action of hiding or the state of being hidden.
hie /hī/ ● verb (**hies, hied, hieing** or **hying**) archaic go quickly.
– ORIGIN Old English, 'strive, pant'.
hierarch /hīəraark/ ● noun a chief priest, archbishop, or other

Thesaurus

hew ● verb CHOP, hack, cut, lop, axe, cleave; fell; carve, shape, fashion, sculpt, model.
heyday ● noun PRIME, peak, height, pinnacle, acme, zenith; day, time, bloom; prime of life, salad days.
hiatus ● noun PAUSE, break, gap, lacuna, interval, intermission, interlude, interruption, suspension, lull, respite, time out; *N. Amer.* recess; *informal* breather, let-up.
hibernate ● verb LIE DORMANT, lie torpid, sleep; overwinter.
hidden ● adjective **1** *a hidden camera* CONCEALED, secret, invisible, unseen, out of sight; camouflaged, disguised, masked. **2** *a hidden meaning* OBSCURE, unclear, concealed, indistinct, indefinite, vague, unfathomable, inexplicable; cryptic, mysterious, secret, covert, abstruse, arcane; ulterior, deep, subliminal, coded.
– OPPOSITES visible, obvious.
hide[1] ● verb **1** *he hid the money* CONCEAL, secrete, put out of sight; camouflage; lock up, stow away, cache; *informal* stash. **2** *they hid in an air vent* CONCEAL ONESELF, secrete oneself, hide out, take cover, keep out of sight; lie low, go to ground, go to earth; *informal* hole up; *Brit. informal, dated* lie doggo. **3** *clouds hid the moon* OBSCURE, block out, blot out, obstruct, cloud, shroud, veil, blanket, envelop, eclipse. **4** *he could not hide his dislike* CONCEAL, keep secret, cover up, keep dark, keep quiet about, hush up, bottle up, suppress; disguise, mask, camouflage; *informal* keep under one's hat, keep a/the lid on.
– OPPOSITES flaunt, reveal.
hide[2] ● noun *the hide should be tanned quickly* SKIN, pelt, coat; leather.
hideaway ● noun RETREAT, refuge, hiding place, hideout, den, bolt-hole, shelter, sanctuary, sanctum; hermitage; *informal* hidey-hole.
hidebound ● adjective CONSERVATIVE, reactionary, conventional, orthodox; fundamentalist, diehard, hard-line, dyed-in-the-wool, set in one's ways; narrow-minded, small-minded, intolerant, uncompromising, rigid; prejudiced, bigoted; *Brit.* blimpish.
– OPPOSITES liberal.
hideous ● adjective **1** *a hideous smile* UGLY, repulsive, repellent, unsightly, revolting, gruesome, grotesque, monstrous, ghastly, reptilian; *informal* as ugly as sin. **2** *hideous cases of torture* HORRIFIC, terrible, appalling, awful, dreadful, frightful, horrible, horrendous, horrifying, shocking, sickening, gruesome, ghastly, unspeakable, abhorrent, monstrous, heinous, abominable, foul, vile, odious, execrable.
– OPPOSITES beautiful, pleasant.
hideout ● noun HIDING PLACE, hideaway, retreat, refuge, shelter, bolt-hole, safe house, sanctuary, sanctum; *informal* hidey-hole.
hiding[1] ● noun (*informal*) *they gave him a hiding* BEATING, battering, thrashing, thumping, drubbing, pelting; flogging, whipping, caning, birching; *informal* licking, belting, bashing, pasting, walloping, clobbering, tanning.
hiding[2] ● noun
– PHRASES **in hiding** *the fugitive is in hiding* HIDDEN, concealed, lying low, gone to ground, gone to earth, in a safe house; *Brit. informal, dated* lying doggo.
hiding place ● noun HIDEAWAY, hideout, retreat, refuge, shelter,

leader.

hierarchy /hīəraarki/ ● noun (pl. **hierarchies**) **1** a ranking system ordered according to status or authority. **2** an arrangement according to relative importance or inclusiveness. **3** (**the hierarchy**) the clergy of the Catholic Church or of an episcopal Church. **4** Theology the traditional system of orders of angels and other heavenly beings.
– DERIVATIVES **hierarchic** adjective **hierarchical** adjective **hierarchize** (also **hierarchise**) verb.
– ORIGIN Greek *hierarkhia*, from *hierarkhēs* 'sacred ruler'.

hieratic /hīərattik/ ● adjective of or concerning priests.
– DERIVATIVES **hieratically** adverb.
– ORIGIN Greek *hieratikos*, from *hierasthai* 'be a priest'.

hieroglyph /hīrəglif/ ● noun a stylized picture of an object representing a word, syllable, or sound, as found in ancient Egyptian and certain other writing systems.

hieroglyphic ● noun (**hieroglyphics**) writing consisting of hieroglyphs. ● adjective of or written in hieroglyphs.
– DERIVATIVES **hieroglyphical** adjective.
– ORIGIN Greek *hierogluphikos*, from *hieros* 'sacred' + *gluphē* 'carving'.

hierophant /hīrəfant/ ● noun a person, especially a priest, who interprets sacred or esoteric mysteries.
– DERIVATIVES **hierophantic** adjective.
– ORIGIN Greek *hierophantēs*, from *hieros* 'sacred' + *phainein* 'show'.

hi-fi informal ● adjective relating to the reproduction of high fidelity sound. ● noun (pl. **hi-fis**) a set of equipment for high-fidelity sound reproduction.

higgledy-piggledy informal ● adverb & adjective in confusion or disorder.
– ORIGIN probably with reference to the irregular herding together of pigs.

high ● adjective **1** of great vertical extent. **2** of a specified height. **3** far above ground or sea level. **4** extending above the normal level. **5** great in amount, value, size, or intensity. **6** (of a period or movement) at its peak. **7** great in rank or status. **8** morally or culturally superior. **9** (of a sound or note) having a frequency at the upper end of the auditory range. **10** informal euphoric, especially from the effects of drugs or alcohol. **11** (of food) strong-smelling because beginning to go bad. **12** (of game) slightly decomposed and so ready to cook. ● noun **1** a high point, level, or figure. **2** an anticyclone. **3** informal a state of euphoria. **4** informal, chiefly N. Amer. high school. ● adverb **1** at or to a high or specified level or position. **2** at a high price. **3** (of a sound) at or to a high pitch.
– PHRASES **from on high** from heaven or another remote authority. **high and dry 1** stranded by the sea as it retreats. **2** without resources. **high and low** in many different places. **high and mighty** informal arrogant. **the high ground** a position of superiority. **a high old time** informal a most enjoyable time. **it is high time that ——** it is past the time when something should have happened or been done. **on one's high horse** informal behaving arrogantly or pompously. **run high 1** (of a river) be full and close to overflowing, with a strong current. **2** (of feelings) be intense.
– ORIGIN Old English.

high altar ● noun the chief altar of a church.

highball N. Amer. ● noun a long drink consisting of a spirit and a mixer such as soda, served with ice. ● verb informal travel fast.

highboy ● noun N. Amer. a tall chest of drawers on legs.

highbrow ● adjective intellectual or rarefied in taste.

high chair ● noun a small chair with long legs for a baby or small child, fitted with a tray and used at mealtimes.

High Church ● noun a tradition within the Anglican Church emphasizing ritual, priestly authority, sacraments, and historical continuity with Catholic Christianity.

high colour ● noun a flushed complexion.

high command ● noun the commander-in-chief and associated senior staff of an army, navy, or air force.

h

Thesaurus

sanctuary, sanctum, bolt-hole, safe house; *informal* hidey-hole.

hie ● verb *(archaic)*. See HURRY verb sense 1.

hierarchy ● noun PECKING ORDER, ranking, grading, ladder, scale.

hieroglyphic ● noun **1** *hieroglyphics on a stone monument* SYMBOLS, signs, ciphers, code; cryptograms. **2** *notebooks filled with hieroglyphics* SCRIBBLE, scrawl, illegible writing; shorthand.
● adjective **1** *hieroglyphic brass ornamentation* SYMBOLIC, stylized, emblematic. **2** *hieroglyphic handwriting* ILLEGIBLE, indecipherable, unreadable, scribbled, scrawled.

higgledy-piggledy *(informal)* ● adjective *a higgledy-piggledy pile of papers* DISORDERED, disorderly, disorganized, untidy, messy, chaotic, jumbled, muddled, confused, unsystematic, irregular; out of order, in disarray, in a mess, in a muddle, haphazard; *informal* all over the place; *Brit. informal* shambolic.
– OPPOSITES tidy.
● adverb *the cars were parked higgledy-piggledy* IN DISORDER, in a muddle, in a jumble, in disarray, untidily, haphazardly, anyhow; *informal* all over the place, topsy-turvy, every which way, any old how; *Brit. informal* all over the shop; *N. Amer. informal* all over the map, all over the lot.

high ● adjective **1** *a high mountain* TALL, lofty, towering, elevated, giant, big; multi-storey, high-rise. **2** *a high position in the government* HIGH-RANKING, high-level, leading, top, top-level, prominent, pre-eminent, foremost, senior; influential, powerful, important, elevated, prime, premier, exalted; *N. Amer.* ranking; *informal* top-notch. **3** *high principles* HIGH-MINDED, noble, lofty, moral, ethical, honourable, admirable, upright, honest, virtuous, righteous. **4** *high prices* INFLATED, excessive, unreasonable, expensive, dear, costly, exorbitant, extortionate, prohibitive; *Brit.* over the odds; *informal* steep, stiff, pricey. **5** *high standards* EXCELLENT, outstanding, exemplary, exceptional, admirable, fine, good, first-class, first-rate, superior, superlative, superb; impeccable, irreproachable, unimpeachable, perfect, flawless; *informal* A1, top-notch. **6** *high winds* STRONG, powerful, violent, intense, extreme, forceful, stiff; blustery, gusty, squally, tempestuous, turbulent. **7** *the high life* LUXURIOUS, lavish, extravagant, grand, opulent; sybaritic, hedonistic; *Brit.* upmarket; *N. Amer.* upscale; *informal* fancy, classy, swanky. **8** *I have a high opinion of you* FAVOURABLE, good, positive, approving, admiring, complimentary, commendatory, flattering, glowing, adulatory, rapturous. **9** *a high note* HIGH-PITCHED, high-frequency; soprano, treble, falsetto, shrill, sharp, piercing, penetrating. **10** *(informal) they are high on drugs* INTOXICATED, inebriated, drugged, stupefied, befuddled, delirious, hallucinating; *informal* high as a kite, stoned, tripping, hyped up, spaced out, wasted, wrecked, off one's head. **11** *the partridges were high* GAMY, smelly, strong-smelling; stinking, reeking, rank, malodorous, bad, off, rotting; *Brit. informal* pongy, niffy, whiffy; *N. Amer. informal* funky.
– OPPOSITES short, lowly, amoral, cheap, low, light, abstemious, unfavourable, deep, sober, fresh.
● noun *prices were at a rare high* HIGH LEVEL, high point, peak, high water mark; pinnacle, zenith, acme, height.
– OPPOSITES low.
● adverb *a jet flew high overhead* AT GREAT HEIGHT, high up, far up, way up, at altitude; in the air, in the sky, on high, aloft, overhead.
– OPPOSITES low.
– PHRASES **high and dry** DESTITUTE, bereft, helpless, in the lurch, in difficulties; abandoned, stranded, marooned. **high and low** EVERYWHERE, all over, all around, far and wide, {here, there, and everywhere}, extensively, thoroughly, widely, in every nook and cranny; *informal* all over the place; *Brit. informal* all over the shop; *N. Amer. informal* all over the map. **high and mighty** *(informal)* SELF-IMPORTANT, condescending, patronizing, disdainful, supercilious, superior, snobbish, snobby, haughty, conceited, above oneself; *informal* stuck-up, snooty, hoity-toity, la-di-da, uppity; *Brit. informal* toffee-nosed. **on a high** *(informal)* ECSTATIC, euphoric, delirious, elated, thrilled, overjoyed, beside oneself, walking on air, on cloud nine, in seventh heaven, jumping for joy, in raptures, exultant, jubilant; excited, overexcited; *informal* blissed out, over the moon, on top of the world; *Austral./NZ informal* wrapped.

high-born ● adjective NOBLE, aristocratic, well born, titled, patrician, blue-blooded, upper-class; *informal* upper-crust, top-drawer; *Brit. informal* posh; *archaic* gentle.
– OPPOSITES lowly.

highbrow ● adjective *his work has a highbrow following* INTELLECTUAL, scholarly, bookish, academic, educated, donnish, bluestocking; sophisticated, erudite, learned; *informal* brainy, egghead.
– OPPOSITES lowbrow.
● noun *highbrows who hate pop music* INTELLECTUAL, scholar, academic, bluestocking, bookish person, thinker; *informal* egghead, brain, bookworm; *Brit. informal* brainbox, boffin; *N. Amer. informal* brainiac.

high-class ● adjective SUPERIOR, upper-class, first-rate; excellent, select, elite, choice, premier, top, top-flight; luxurious, de luxe,

high commission • noun an embassy of one Commonwealth country in another.
– DERIVATIVES **high commissioner** noun.
high court • noun **1** a supreme court of justice. **2** (in full **High Court of Justice**) (in England and Wales) the court of unlimited civil jurisdiction forming part of the Supreme Court. **3** (in full **High Court of Justiciary**) the supreme criminal court of Scotland.
high day • noun Brit. the day of a religious festival.
– PHRASES **high days and holidays** informal special occasions.
Higher • noun (in Scotland) the more advanced of the two main levels of the Scottish Certificate of Education. Compare with ORDINARY GRADE.
higher animals • plural noun mammals and other vertebrates, regarded as having relatively advanced characteristics.
higher court • noun Law a court that can overrule the decision of another.
higher education • noun education provided at universities or similar educational establishments, to degree level or equivalent.
higher mathematics • plural noun the more advanced aspects of mathematics, such as number theory and topology.
higher plants • plural noun vascular plants, regarded as having relatively advanced characteristics.
highest common factor • noun the highest number that can be divided exactly into each of two or more numbers.
high explosive • noun a powerful chemical explosive of the kind used in shells and bombs.
highfalutin /hīfəlo͞otin/ (also **highfaluting** /hīfəlo͞oting/) • adjective informal pompous or pretentious.
– ORIGIN perhaps from HIGH + *fluting*.
high fashion • noun another term for HAUTE COUTURE.
high fidelity • noun the reproduction of sound with little distortion.
high finance • noun financial transactions involving large sums.
high five • noun a gesture of celebration or greeting in which two people slap each other's palms with their arms raised.
high-flown • adjective (especially of language) extravagant or grandiose.
high-flyer (also **high-flier**) • noun a very successful person.
high frequency • noun (in radio) a frequency of 3–30 megahertz.
high gear • noun a gear that causes a wheeled vehicle to move fast.
High German • noun the standard literary and spoken form of German, originally used in the highlands in the south of Germany.
high-handed • adjective domineering or inconsiderate.
high hat • noun **1** a top hat. **2** N. Amer. informal a snobbish or supercilious person.
high-impact • adjective **1** (of plastic or a similar substance) able to withstand great impact without breaking. **2** denoting extremely strenuous aerobic exercises.
high jinks • plural noun boisterous fun.
high jump • noun (**the high jump**) an athletic event in which competitors jump as high as possible over a bar of adjustable height.
– PHRASES **be for the high jump** Brit. informal be about to be severely reprimanded.
– DERIVATIVES **high jumper** noun.
highland • noun (also **highlands**) **1** an area of high or mountainous land. **2** (**the Highlands**) the mountainous northern part of Scotland.
– DERIVATIVES **highlander** noun **highlandman** noun.
Highland cattle • plural noun a shaggy-haired breed of cattle with long, curved, widely spaced horns.
Highland dress • noun the kilt and other clothing in the traditional style of the Scottish Highlands.
Highland fling • noun a vigorous solo Scottish dance consisting of a series of complex steps.
high-level • adjective **1** of relatively high importance. **2** Computing denoting a programming language that has instructions resembling an existing language such as English.
high life • noun an extravagant social life as enjoyed by the wealthy.
highlight • noun **1** an outstanding part of an event or period of time. **2** a bright or reflective area in a painting, picture, or design. **3** (**highlights**) bright tints in the hair, produced by bleaching or dyeing. • verb **1** draw attention to. **2** mark with a highlighter. **3** create highlights in (hair).
highlighter • noun **1** a broad marker pen used to overlay transparent fluorescent colour on a part of a text or plan. **2** a cosmetic used to emphasize the cheekbones or other features.
highly • adverb **1** to a high degree or level. **2** favourably.
highly strung • adjective Brit. very nervous and easily upset.
High Mass • noun a Roman Catholic or Anglo-Catholic mass with full ceremonial, including music and incense.
high-minded • adjective having strong moral principles.
highness • noun **1** (**His**, **Your**, etc. **Highness**) a title given to a person of royal rank, or used in addressing them. **2** the state of being high.
high-octane • adjective **1** denoting petrol having a high octane number and thus good anti-knock properties. **2** powerful or dynamic.
high-powered • adjective informal (of a person) dynamic and forceful.
high priest • noun **1** a chief priest of a non-Christian religion, especially of historic Judaism. **2** (also **high priestess**) the leader of a cult or movement.

Thesaurus

high-quality, top-quality; *Brit.* upmarket; *informal* top-notch, top-drawer, A1, classy, posh.
highfalutin • adjective *(informal).* See PRETENTIOUS.
high-flown • adjective GRAND, extravagant, elaborate, flowery, ornate, overblown, overdone, overwrought, grandiloquent, magniloquent, grandiose, inflated, affected, pretentious, turgid; *informal* windy, purple, highfalutin, la-di-da.
– OPPOSITES plain.
high-handed • adjective IMPERIOUS, arbitrary, peremptory, arrogant, haughty, domineering, pushy, overbearing, heavy-handed, lordly; inflexible, rigid; autocratic, authoritarian, dictatorial, tyrannical; *informal* bossy, high and mighty.
– OPPOSITES liberal.
high jinks • plural noun ANTICS, pranks, larks, escapades, stunts, practical jokes, tricks; fun (and games), skylarking, mischief, horseplay, tomfoolery, clowning; *informal* shenanigans, capers, monkey business; *Brit. informal* monkey tricks.
highland • noun UPLANDS, highlands, mountains, hills, heights, moors; upland, tableland, plateau; *Brit.* wolds.
highlight • noun *the highlight of his career* HIGH POINT, high spot, best part, climax, peak, pinnacle, height, acme, zenith, summit, crowning moment, high water mark.
– OPPOSITES nadir.
• verb *he has highlighted shortcomings in the plan* SPOTLIGHT, call attention to, focus on, underline, feature, play up, show up, bring out, accentuate, accent, give prominence to, zero in on, stress, emphasize.
highly • adverb **1** *a highly dangerous substance* VERY, extremely, exceedingly, particularly, most, really, thoroughly, decidedly, distinctly, exceptionally, immensely, inordinately, singularly, extraordinarily; *N. English* right; *informal* terrifically, awfully, terribly, majorly, seriously, desperately, mega, ultra, oh-so, damn, damned; *Brit. informal* ever so, well, dead, jolly; *N. Amer. informal* real, mighty, awful; *dated* frightfully. **2** *he was highly regarded* FAVOURABLY, well, appreciatively, admiringly, approvingly, positively, glowingly, enthusiastically.
– OPPOSITES slightly, unfavourably.
highly strung • adjective NERVOUS, nervy, excitable, temperamental, sensitive, unstable; brittle, on edge, edgy, jumpy, restless, anxious, tense, stressed, overwrought, neurotic; *informal* uptight, twitchy, wired, wound up, het up.
– OPPOSITES easy-going.
high-minded • adjective HIGH-PRINCIPLED, principled, honourable, moral, upright, upstanding, right-minded, noble, good, honest, decent, ethical, righteous, virtuous, worthy, idealistic.
– OPPOSITES unprincipled.
high-pitched • adjective HIGH, high-frequency, shrill, sharp, piping, piercing; soprano, treble, falsetto.
– OPPOSITES deep.
high-powered • adjective DYNAMIC, ambitious, energetic, assertive, enterprising, vigorous; forceful, aggressive, pushy, high-octane; *informal* go-ahead, go-getting; *N. Amer. informal* go-go.
high-pressure • adjective FORCEFUL, insistent, persistent, pushy; intensive, high-powered, aggressive, coercive, compelling, thrust-

high relief ● noun see RELIEF (sense 8).
high-rise ● adjective (of a building) having many storeys.
high road ● noun **1** a main road. **2** N. Amer. a morally superior approach.
high roller ● noun informal, chiefly N. Amer. a person who gambles or spends large sums of money.
high school ● noun **1** N. Amer. a secondary school. **2** (in the UK except Scotland) used chiefly in names of grammar schools or independent fee-paying secondary schools.
high seas ● plural noun (**the high seas**) the open ocean, especially that not within any country's jurisdiction.
high season ● noun Brit. the most popular time of year for a holiday, when prices are highest.
high sheriff ● noun see SHERIFF.
high sign ● noun N. Amer. informal a surreptitious gesture indicating a warning or that all is well.
high spirits ● plural noun lively and cheerful behaviour or mood.
– DERIVATIVES **high-spirited** adjective.
high spot ● noun the most enjoyable or significant part of an experience or period of time.
high street ● noun Brit. **1** the main street of a town. **2** (before another noun) (**high-street**) (of retail goods) catering to the needs of the ordinary public: *high-street fashion*.
hight /hīt/ ● adjective archaic or literary named.
– ORIGIN Old English.
high table ● noun Brit. a table in a dining hall at which high-ranking people, such as the fellows of a college, sit.
hightail ● verb informal, chiefly N. Amer. move or travel fast.
high tea ● noun Brit. a meal eaten in the late afternoon or early evening, typically consisting of a cooked dish and tea.
high-tech (also **hi-tech**) ● adjective **1** employing, requiring, or involved in high technology. **2** (of architecture and interior design) employing a functional style and industrial materials, such as steel and plastic.
high technology ● noun advanced technological development, especially in electronics.
high-tensile ● adjective (of metal) very strong under tension.
high tide ● noun the state of the tide when at its highest level.
high-top ● adjective denoting a soft-soled sports shoe with a laced upper that extends above the ankle. ● noun (**high-tops**) a pair of such shoes.
high treason ● noun see TREASON.
high water ● noun high tide.
high-water mark ● noun the level reached by the sea at high tide, or by a lake or river in time of flood.
highway ● noun **1** chiefly N. Amer. a main road. **2** (chiefly in official use) a public road.
highwayman ● noun historical a man, typically on horseback, who held up and robbed travellers.
high wire ● noun a high tightrope.
hijack ● verb **1** illegally seize control of (an aircraft, ship, etc.) while it is in transit. **2** take over (something) and use it for a different purpose. ● noun an instance of hijacking.
– DERIVATIVES **hijacker** noun.
– ORIGIN of unknown origin.
Hijra /hijrə/ ● noun variant spelling of HEGIRA.
hijra /hijrə/ ● noun Indian a transvestite or eunuch.
– ORIGIN Hindi.
hike ● noun **1** a long walk or walking tour. **2** a sharp increase, especially in price. ● verb **1** go on a hike. **2** pull or lift up (clothing). **3** increase (a price) sharply.
– PHRASES **take a hike** informal, chiefly N. Amer. go away.
– DERIVATIVES **hiker** noun.
– ORIGIN of unknown origin.
hilarious /hilairiəss/ ● adjective extremely funny or merry.
– DERIVATIVES **hilariously** adverb **hilarity** noun.
– ORIGIN Greek *hilaros* 'cheerful'.
hill ● noun a naturally raised area of land, not as high or craggy as a mountain.
– PHRASES **over the hill** informal old and past one's best.
– ORIGIN Old English.
hillbilly ● noun (pl. **hillbillies**) N. Amer. informal, chiefly derogatory an unsophisticated country person, originally one from the Appalachians.
– ORIGIN from HILL + *Billy* (familiar form of the given name *William*).
hill fort ● noun a fort built on a hill, in particular an Iron Age system of defensive banks and ditches.
hillock ● noun a small hill or mound.
– DERIVATIVES **hillocky** adjective.
hill station ● noun a town in the low mountains of the Indian subcontinent, popular as a holiday resort during the hot season.
hillwalking ● noun the pastime of walking in hilly country.
hilly ● adjective (**hillier**, **hilliest**) having many hills.
– DERIVATIVES **hilliness** noun.
hilt ● noun the handle of a sword, dagger, or knife.
– PHRASES **to the hilt** completely.
– ORIGIN Old English.
him ● pronoun (third person sing.) used as the object of a verb or preposition to refer to a male person or animal previously mentioned.
– ORIGIN Old English.
Himalayan ● adjective relating to the Himalayas, a mountain system in southern Asia.
himself ● pronoun (third person sing.) **1** (reflexive) used as the object of a verb or preposition to refer to a male person or animal previously mentioned as the subject of the clause. **2** (emphatic) he or him personally.

h

Thesaurus

ing, not taking no for an answer.
high-priced ● adjective EXPENSIVE, costly, dear; overpriced, exorbitant, extortionate; *Brit.* over the odds; *informal* pricey, steep, stiff.
high-sounding ● adjective GRAND, high-flown, extravagant, elaborate, flowery, ornate, overblown, overdone, overwrought, grandiloquent, magniloquent, grandiose, inflated, affected, pretentious, turgid; *informal* windy, purple, highfalutin, la-di-da.
– OPPOSITES plain.
high-speed ● adjective FAST, quick, rapid, speedy, swift, breakneck, lightning, brisk; express, non-stop, whistle-stop; *informal* nippy, zippy, supersonic; *poetic/literary* fleet.
– OPPOSITES slow.
high-spirited ● adjective LIVELY, spirited, full of fun, fun-loving, animated, zestful, bouncy, bubbly, sparkling, vivacious, buoyant, cheerful, joyful, exuberant, ebullient, jaunty, irrepressible; *informal* chirpy, peppy, sparky, bright and breezy, full of beans; *poetic/literary* frolicsome.
high spirits ● plural noun LIVELINESS, vitality, spirit, zest, energy, bounce, sparkle, vivacity, buoyancy, cheerfulness, good humour, joy, joyfulness, exuberance, ebullience, joie de vivre; *informal* pep, zing.
highwayman ● noun *(historical)* BANDIT, robber, outlaw, ruffian, marauder, raider; *historical* footpad; *poetic/literary* brigand.
hijack ● verb COMMANDEER, seize, take over; skyjack; appropriate, expropriate, confiscate; *informal* snatch.
hike ● noun *a five-mile hike* WALK, trek, tramp, trudge, slog, footslog, march; ramble; *Brit. informal* yomp.
● verb *they hiked across the moors* WALK, trek, tramp, trudge, slog, footslog, march; ramble; *informal* hoof it, leg it; *Brit. informal* yomp.
– PHRASES **hike something up 1** *Roy hiked up his trousers* HITCH UP, pull up, hoist, lift, raise; *informal* yank up. **2** *they hiked up the price* INCREASE, raise, up, put up, mark up, push up, inflate; *informal* jack up, bump up.
hilarious ● adjective **1** *a hilarious story* VERY FUNNY, hysterically funny, hysterical, uproarious, riotous, farcical, rib-tickling; humorous, comic, amusing, entertaining; *informal* side-splitting, priceless, a scream, a hoot. **2** *a hilarious evening* AMUSING, entertaining, animated, high-spirited, lively, funny, merry, jolly, mirthful, cheerful, uproarious, boisterous; *informal* wacky.
– OPPOSITES sad, serious.
hilarity ● noun AMUSEMENT, mirth, laughter, merriment, lightheartedness, levity, fun, humour, jocularity, jollity, gaiety, delight, glee, exuberance, high spirits; comedy.
hill ● noun **1** *the top of the hill* HIGH GROUND, prominence, hillock, foothill, hillside, rise, mound, mount, knoll, hummock, tor, tump, fell, pike, mesa; bank, ridge, slope, incline, gradient; (**hills**) heights, downs; *Geology* drumlin; *Scottish & Irish* drum; *Scottish* brae; *formal* eminence. **2** *a hill of rubbish* HEAP, pile, stack, mound, mountain, mass; *Scottish, Irish, & N. English* rickle.
hillock ● noun MOUND, small hill, prominence, elevation, rise, knoll, hummock, hump, tump, dune; bank, ridge; *N. English* howe; *N. Amer.* knob; *formal* eminence.
hilt ● noun HANDLE, haft, handgrip, grip, shaft, shank, stock, helve.
– PHRASES **to the hilt** COMPLETELY, fully, wholly, totally, entirely, ut-

hind[1] ● adjective situated at the back.
– ORIGIN perhaps from Old English, 'behind'.
hind[2] ● noun a female deer.
– ORIGIN Old English.
hinder[1] /hindər/ ● verb delay or impede.
– ORIGIN Old English, 'damage'; related to BEHIND.
hinder[2] /hīndər/ ● adjective situated at or towards the back.
– ORIGIN perhaps from Old English, 'backward'.
Hindi /hindi/ ● noun a language of northern India derived from Sanskrit. ● adjective relating to Hindi.
– ORIGIN Urdu, from a word meaning 'India'.
hindmost ● adjective furthest back.
hindquarters ● plural noun the hind legs and adjoining parts of a four-legged animal.
hindrance /hindrənss/ ● noun a thing that hinders.
hindsight ● noun understanding of a situation or event after it has happened.
Hindu /hindoo/ ● noun (pl. **Hindus**) a follower of Hinduism. ● adjective relating to Hinduism.
– ORIGIN Urdu, from a word meaning 'India'.
Hinduism ● noun a major religious and cultural tradition of the Indian subcontinent, including belief in reincarnation and the worship of a large number of gods and goddesses.
– DERIVATIVES **Hinduize** (also **Hinduise**) verb.
Hindustani /hindoostaani/ ● noun **1** a group of mutually intelligible languages and dialects spoken in NW India, principally Hindi and Urdu. **2** the Delhi dialect of Hindi, widely used throughout India as a lingua franca. ● adjective relating to the culture of NW India.
hinge ● noun a movable joint or mechanism by which a door, gate, or lid opens and closes or which connects linked objects. ● verb (**hingeing** or **hinging**) **1** attach or join with a hinge. **2** (**hinge on**) depend entirely on.
– ORIGIN related to HANG.
hinky ● adjective (**hinkier**, **hinkiest**) US informal dishonest or suspect.
– ORIGIN of obscure origin.
hinny ● noun (pl. **hinnies**) the offspring of a female donkey and a male horse.
– ORIGIN Greek *hinnos*.
hint ● noun **1** a slight or indirect indication. **2** a very small trace. **3** a small piece of practical information. ● verb **1** indicate indirectly. **2** (**hint at**) be a slight indication of.
– ORIGIN originally in the sense 'occasion, opportunity': apparently from an Old English word meaning 'grasp'; related to HUNT.
hinterland /hintərland/ ● noun **1** the remote areas of a country, away from the coast and major rivers. **2** the area around or beyond a major town or port.
– ORIGIN German, from *hinter* 'behind' + *Land* 'land'.
hip[1] ● noun **1** a projection of the pelvis and upper thigh bone on each side of the body. **2** (**hips**) the circumference of the body at the buttocks. **3** the edge formed where two sloping sides of a roof meet.
– DERIVATIVES **hipped** adjective.
– ORIGIN Old English, related to HOP[1].
hip[2] ● noun the fruit of a rose.
– ORIGIN Old English.
hip[3] ● adjective (**hipper**, **hippest**) informal **1** fashionable. **2** (**hip to**) aware of or informed about.
– DERIVATIVES **hipness** noun.
– ORIGIN of unknown origin.
hip[4] ● exclamation introducing a communal cheer.
– ORIGIN of unknown origin.
hip bath ● noun a bath shaped to sit rather than lie down in.
hip bone ● noun a large bone forming the main part of the pelvis on each side of the body.
hip flask ● noun a small flask for spirits, carried in a hip pocket.
hip hop ● noun a style of popular music of US black and Hispanic origin, featuring rap with an electronic backing.
– ORIGIN probably from HIP[3].
hippie ● noun & adjective variant spelling of HIPPY[1].
hippo ● noun (pl. same or **hippos**) informal term for HIPPOPOTAMUS.
hippocampus /hippəkampəss/ ● noun (pl. **hippocampi** /hippəkampī/) Anatomy a curving strand of tissue lying deep within the cerebral cortex in each hemisphere of the brain, that functions in the feeling and expression of emotions and in memory.
– ORIGIN Greek *hippokampos*, from *hippos* 'horse' + *kampos* 'sea monster'.
Hippocratic oath /hippəkrattik/ ● noun a former oath taken by those beginning medical practice to observe a code of professional behaviour (parts of which are still used in some medical schools).
– ORIGIN with reference to *Hippocrates*, a Greek physician of the 5th century BC.
hippodrome /hippədrōm/ ● noun **1** a theatre or concert hall. **2** (in ancient Greece or Rome) a course for chariot or horse races.
– ORIGIN Greek *hippodromos*, from *hippos* 'horse' + *dromos* 'race, course'.
hippopotamus /hippəpottəməss/ ● noun (pl. **hippopotamuses** or **hippopotami** /hippəpottəmī/) a large African mammal with a thick skin and massive jaws, living partly on land and partly in water.
– ORIGIN Greek *hippopotamos*, from *hippos ho potamios*, 'river horse'.
hippy[1] (also **hippie**) ● noun (pl. **hippies**) (especially in the 1960s) a young person associated with a subculture which advocated peace and free love and adopted an unconventional appearance.
– DERIVATIVES **hippiedom** noun **hippiness** noun **hippyish** adjective.
– ORIGIN from HIP[3].
hippy[2] ● adjective (of a woman) having large hips.
hipster[1] Brit. ● adjective (of a garment) having the waistline at the hips rather than the waist. ● noun (**hipsters**) trousers with such a waistline.
– ORIGIN from HIP[1].
hipster[2] ● noun informal a person who follows the latest trends and fashions.
– ORIGIN from HIP[3].
hire ● verb **1** chiefly Brit. obtain the temporary use of (something) in return for payment. **2** (**hire out**) grant the temporary use of (something) in return for payment. **3** employ for wages. **4** obtain the temporary services of (someone) to do a particular job. ● noun **1** the action of hiring. **2** N. Amer. a recently recruited em-

Thesaurus

terly, unreservedly, unconditionally, in every respect, in all respects, one hundred per cent, every inch, to the full, to the maximum extent, all the way, body and soul, heart and soul.
hind ● adjective BACK, rear, hinder, hindmost, posterior.
– OPPOSITES fore, front.
hinder ● verb HAMPER, obstruct, impede, inhibit, retard, baulk, thwart, foil, curb, delay, arrest, interfere with, set back, slow down, hold back, hold up, stop, halt; restrict, restrain, constrain, block, check, curtail, frustrate, cramp, handicap, cripple, hamstring; *informal* stymie; *Brit. informal* throw a spanner in the works.
– OPPOSITES facilitate.
hindmost ● adjective FURTHEST BACK, last, rear, rearmost, end, endmost, final, tail.
– OPPOSITES leading.
hindrance ● noun IMPEDIMENT, obstacle, barrier, bar, obstruction, handicap, block, hurdle, restraint, restriction, limitation, encumbrance; complication, delay, drawback, setback, difficulty, inconvenience, snag, catch, hitch, stumbling block; *informal* fly in the ointment, hiccup, facer; *Brit. informal* spanner in the works.
– OPPOSITES help.
hinge ● verb *our future hinges on the election* DEPEND, hang, rest, turn, centre, be contingent, be dependent, be conditional; be determined by, be decided by, revolve around.
hint ● noun **1** *a hint that he would leave* CLUE, inkling, suggestion, indication, indicator, sign, signal, pointer, intimation, insinuation, innuendo, mention, whisper. **2** *handy hints about painting* TIP, suggestion, pointer, clue, guideline, recommendation; advice, help; *informal* how-to, wrinkle. **3** *a hint of mint* TRACE, touch, suspicion, suggestion, dash, soupçon, tinge, modicum, whiff, taste, undertone; *informal* smidgen, tad.
● verb *what are you hinting at?* IMPLY, insinuate, intimate, suggest, indicate, signal; allude to, refer to, drive at, mean; *informal* get at.
hinterland ● noun THE BACKWOODS, a backwater, the wilds, the bush, the back of beyond; *Austral./NZ* the outback, the backblocks, the booay; *informal* the sticks, the middle of nowhere; *N. Amer. informal* the boondocks, the tall timbers.
hip ● adjective *(informal)*. See FASHIONABLE.
hippy ● noun FLOWER CHILD, bohemian, dropout, free spirit, noncon-

ployee.
– PHRASES **for** (or **on**) **hire** available to be hired.
– DERIVATIVES **hireable** (US also **hirable**) adjective **hirer** noun.
– ORIGIN Old English.
hired gun ● noun N. Amer. informal **1** an expert brought in to resolve legal or financial problems or disputes. **2** a lobbyist on behalf of others. **3** a bodyguard. **4** a mercenary or hired assassin.
hireling ● noun chiefly derogatory a person who is hired, especially for morally dubious or illegal work.
hire purchase ● noun Brit. a system by which someone pays for a thing in regular instalments while having the use of it.
hirsute /hursyo͞ot/ ● adjective having abundant hair on the face or body; hairy.
– DERIVATIVES **hirsuteness** noun.
– ORIGIN Latin *hirsutus*.
hirsutism ● noun Medicine abnormal growth of hair on a woman's face and body.
his ● possessive determiner **1** belonging to or associated with a male person or animal previously mentioned. **2** (**His**) used in titles. ● possessive pronoun used to refer to a thing belonging to or associated with a male person or animal previously mentioned.
– ORIGIN Old English.
Hispanic /hispannik/ ● adjective relating to Spain or the Spanish-speaking countries of Central and South America. ● noun a Spanish-speaking person, especially one of Latin American descent, living in the US.
– DERIVATIVES **Hispanicize** (also **Hispanicise**) verb.
– ORIGIN Latin *Hispanicus*, from *Hispania* 'Spain'.
Hispanist /hispənist/ (also **Hispanicist** /hispannisist/) ● noun an expert in Hispanic language and culture.
Hispano- /hispannō/ ● combining form Spanish; Spanish and .... *Hispano-Argentine.*
hiss ● verb **1** make a sharp sibilant sound as of the letter *s*, often as a sign of disapproval or derision. **2** whisper something in an urgent or angry way. ● noun **1** a hissing sound. **2** electrical interference at audio frequencies.
– ORIGIN imitative.
histamine /histəmeen/ ● noun a compound which is released by cells in response to injury and in allergic and inflammatory reactions, causing muscle contraction and capillary dilation.
– DERIVATIVES **histaminic** adjective.
– ORIGIN from Greek *histos* 'web, tissue' and AMINE.
histidine /histideen/ ● noun Biochemistry an amino acid which is a constituent of most proteins and is essential in the human diet.
– ORIGIN from Greek *histos* 'web, tissue'.
histology /histolləji/ ● noun the branch of biology concerned with the microscopic structure of tissues.
– DERIVATIVES **histological** adjective **histologist** noun.
histopathology ● noun the branch of medicine concerned with the changes in tissues caused by disease.
– DERIVATIVES **histopathological** adjective **histopathologist** noun.
historian ● noun an expert in history.
historic ● adjective **1** famous or important in history, or potentially so. **2** Grammar (of a tense) used in relating past events.
historical ● adjective **1** of or concerning history. **2** belonging to or set in the past. **3** (of the study of a subject) based on an analysis of its development over a period.
– DERIVATIVES **historically** adverb.
historicism ● noun **1** the theory that social and cultural phenomena are determined by history. **2** (in art and architecture) excessive regard for past styles.
– DERIVATIVES **historicist** noun **historicize** (also **historicise**) verb.
historicity /histərissiti/ ● noun historical authenticity.
historic present ● noun Grammar the present tense used instead of the past in vivid narrative.
historiography /historiogrəfi/ ● noun **1** the study of the writing of history and of written histories. **2** the writing of history.
– DERIVATIVES **historiographer** noun **historiographic** adjective **historiographical** adjective.
history ● noun (pl. **histories**) **1** the study of past events. **2** the past considered as a whole. **3** the past events connected with someone or something. **4** a continuous record of past events or trends.
– PHRASES **be history** informal be dismissed or dead; be finished. **the rest is history** the events succeeding those already related are so well known that they need not be recounted again.
– ORIGIN Greek *historia* 'narrative, history', from *histōr* 'learned, wise man'.
histrionic /histrionnik/ ● adjective **1** overly theatrical or melodramatic. **2** formal of or concerning actors or acting. ● noun (**histrionics**) dramatized behaviour designed to attract attention.
– DERIVATIVES **histrionically** adverb.
– ORIGIN Latin *histrionicus*, from *histrio* 'actor'.
hit ● verb (**hitting**; past and past part. **hit**) **1** direct a blow at (someone or something) with one's hand or a tool or weapon. **2** propel (a ball) with a bat, racket, etc. **3** accidentally strike (part of one's body) against something. **4** (of a moving object or body) come into contact with (someone or something stationary) quickly and forcefully. **5** strike (a target). **6** cause harm or distress to. **7** (**hit out**) make a strongly worded criticism or attack. **8** informal reach or arrive at. **9** be suddenly and vividly realized by: *it hit me that I was successful.* **10** (**hit on**) suddenly discover or think of. ● noun **1** an instance of hitting or being hit. **2** a successful and popular film, pop record, person, etc. **3** Computing an instance of identifying an item of data which matches the requirements of a search. **4** informal, chiefly N. Amer. a murder carried out by a criminal organization. **5** informal a dose of a narcotic drug.
– PHRASES **hit-and-miss** done or occurring at random. **hit-and-run** denoting a road accident from which the driver responsible escapes rapidly without lending assistance. **hit someone below the belt 1** Boxing give one's opponent an illegal low blow. **2** behave unfairly towards someone. **hit someone for six** Brit. affect someone very severely. [ORIGIN with allusion to a forceful hit that scores six runs in cricket.] **hit the ground running** informal start something new at a fast pace and with enthusiasm. **hit it off** informal be naturally friendly or well suited. **hit the nail on the head** find exactly the right answer. **hit-or-miss** as likely to be unsuccessful as successful. **hit the road** (or N. Amer. **trail**) informal set out on a journey.
– DERIVATIVES **hitter** noun.
– ORIGIN Old Norse, 'come upon, meet with'.

Thesaurus

formist.
hips ● plural noun PELVIS, hindquarters, haunches, thighs.
– RELATED TERMS sciatic.
hire ● verb **1** *we hired a car* RENT, lease, charter. **2** *they hire labour in line with demand* EMPLOY, engage, recruit, appoint, take on, sign up, enrol, commission, enlist.
– OPPOSITES dismiss.
● noun *the hire of the machine* RENTAL, rent, hiring, lease, leasing, charter.
hire purchase ● noun INSTALMENT PLAN, deferred payment, HP, credit, finance, easy terms; *Brit. informal* the never-never.
hirsute ● adjective HAIRY, shaggy, bushy, hair-covered; woolly, furry, fleecy, fuzzy; bearded, unshaven, bristly.
hiss ● verb **1** *the escaping gas hissed* FIZZ, fizzle, whistle, wheeze; *rare* sibilate. **2** *the audience hissed* JEER, catcall, whistle, hoot; scoff, jibe.
● noun **1** *the hiss of the steam* FIZZ, fizzing, whistle, hissing, sibilance, wheeze; *rare* sibilation. **2** *the speaker received hisses* JEER, catcall, whistle; abuse, scoffing, taunting, derision.
historian ● noun CHRONICLER, annalist, archivist, recorder; historiographer, antiquarian, chronologist.
historic ● adjective SIGNIFICANT, notable, important, momentous, consequential, memorable, unforgettable, remarkable; famous, famed, celebrated, renowned; landmark, ground-breaking, epoch-making, red-letter, earth-shattering.
– OPPOSITES insignificant.
historical ● adjective **1** *historical evidence* DOCUMENTED, recorded, chronicled, archival; authentic, factual, actual, true. **2** *historical figures* PAST, bygone, ancient, old, former; *poetic/literary* of yore.
– OPPOSITES contemporary.
history ● noun **1** *my interest in history* THE PAST, former times, historical events, the olden days, the old days, bygone days, yesterday, antiquity; *poetic/literary* days of yore, yesteryear. **2** *a history of the Civil War* CHRONICLE, archive, record, report, narrative, account, study, tale; memoir. **3** *she gave details of her history* BACKGROUND, past, life story, experiences; antecedents.
histrionic ● adjective MELODRAMATIC, theatrical, dramatic, exaggerated, actressy, stagy, showy, affected, artificial, overacted, overdone; *informal* hammy, ham, camp.
histrionics ● plural noun DRAMATICS, theatricals, theatrics, tan-

hitch • verb **1** move into a different position with a jerk. **2** fasten or tether with a rope. **3** informal travel or obtain (a lift) by hitch-hiking. • noun **1** a temporary difficulty. **2** a knot of a kind used to fasten one thing temporarily to another. **3** informal an act of hitch-hiking. **4** N. Amer. informal a period of service.
– PHRASES **get hitched** informal get married. **hitch one's wagon to a star** try to succeed by forming a relationship with a successful person.
– ORIGIN of unknown origin.

hitcher • noun a hitch-hiker.

hitch-hike • verb travel by getting free lifts in passing vehicles. • noun a journey made by hitch-hiking.
– DERIVATIVES **hitch-hiker** noun.

hither • adverb archaic or literary to or towards this place.
– ORIGIN Old English.

hither and thither (also **hither and yon**) • adverb to and fro.

hitherto • adverb until the point in time under discussion.

Hitlerian /hitleeriən/ • adjective relating to or characteristic of the Austrian-born Nazi leader and Chancellor of Germany Adolf Hitler (1889–1945).

hit list • noun a list of people to be killed for criminal or political reasons.

hit man • noun informal a hired assassin.

hit parade • noun dated a weekly listing of the current best-selling pop records.

Hittite /hittīt/ • noun **1** a member of an ancient people who established an empire in Asia Minor and Syria *c.*1700–1200 BC. **2** the language of the Hittites, the oldest Indo-European language. • adjective relating to the Hittites.

HIV • abbreviation human immunodeficiency virus, a retrovirus which causes Aids.

hive • noun **1** a beehive. **2** a place full of people working hard. • verb **1** place (bees) in a hive. **2** (**hive off**) chiefly Brit. transfer (part of a business) to new ownership.
– ORIGIN Old English.

hives • plural noun (treated as sing. or pl.) another term for URTICARIA.
– ORIGIN of unknown origin.

HIV-positive • adjective having had a positive result in a blood test for HIV.

HK • abbreviation Hong Kong.

HL • abbreviation (in the UK) House of Lords.

hl • abbreviation hectolitre or hectolitres.

HM • abbreviation (in the UK) Her (or His) Majesty or Majesty's.

hm • abbreviation hectometre or hectometres.

HMG • abbreviation (in the UK) Her or His Majesty's Government.

HMI • abbreviation historical (in the UK) Her or His Majesty's Inspector (of Schools).

HMS • abbreviation Her or His Majesty's Ship.

HMSO • abbreviation (in the UK) Her or His Majesty's Stationery Office, which publishes government documents and legislation.

HNC • abbreviation (in the UK) Higher National Certificate.

HND • abbreviation (in the UK) Higher National Diploma.

Ho • symbol the chemical element holmium.

hoagie /hōgi/ • noun (pl. **hoagies**) chiefly N. Amer. a sandwich made of a long roll filled with meat, cheese, and salad.
– ORIGIN of unknown origin.

hoar /hor/ archaic or literary • adjective grey or grey-haired. • noun hoar frost.
– ORIGIN Old English.

hoard • noun **1** a store of money or valued objects. **2** an amassed store of useful information. • verb amass and hide or store away.
– DERIVATIVES **hoarder** noun.
– ORIGIN Old English.

hoarding • noun Brit. **1** a large board used to display advertisements. **2** a temporary board fence around a building site.
– ORIGIN from obsolete *hoard* in the same sense, probably from Old French *hourd*.

hoar frost • noun a greyish-white feathery deposit of frost.

hoarse • adjective (of a voice) rough and harsh.
– DERIVATIVES **hoarsely** adverb **hoarsen** verb **hoarseness** noun.
– ORIGIN Old English.

hoary • adjective (**hoarier**, **hoariest**) **1** greyish-white. **2** having grey hair; aged. **3** old and trite.
– DERIVATIVES **hoarily** adverb **hoariness** noun.

hoax • noun a humorous or malicious deception. • verb deceive

Thesaurus

trums; affectation, staginess, artificiality.

hit • verb **1** *she hit her child* STRIKE, slap, smack, cuff, punch, thump, swat; beat, thrash, batter, belabour, pound, welt, pummel, box someone's ears; whip, flog, cane; *informal* whack, wallop, bash, biff, bop, lam, clout, clip, clobber, sock, swipe, crown, beat the living daylights out of, give someone a (good) hiding, belt, tan, lay into, let someone have it, deck, floor; *Brit. informal* stick one on, dot, slosh; *N. Amer. informal* slug, boff; *Austral./NZ informal* dong; *poetic/literary* smite. **2** *a car hit the barrier* CRASH INTO, run into, smash into, smack into, knock into, bump into, cannon into, plough into, collide with, meet head-on; *N. Amer.* impact. **3** *the tragedy hit her hard* DEVASTATE, affect badly, hurt, harm, leave a mark on; upset, shatter, crush, shock, overwhelm, traumatize; *informal* knock sideways, knock the stuffing out of; *Brit. informal* knock for six. **4** *(informal) spending will hit £1,800 million* REACH, touch, arrive at, rise to, climb to. **5** *it hit me that I had forgotten* OCCUR TO, strike, dawn on, come to; enter one's head, cross one's mind, come to mind, spring to mind.
• noun **1** *he received a hit from behind* BLOW, thump, punch, knock, bang, box, cuff, slap, smack, tap, crack, stroke, welt; impact, collision, bump, crash; *informal* whack, thwack, wallop, bash, belt, biff, clout, sock, swipe, clip; *Brit. informal* slosh; *N. Amer. informal* boff, slug; *Austral./NZ* dong. **2** *a hit at his friend's religion* JIBE, taunt, jeer, sneer, barb; *informal* dig, crack, wisecrack, put-down. **3** *he directed many big hits* SUCCESS, box-office success, sell-out, winner, triumph, sensation; best-seller; *informal* smash (hit), knockout, crowd-puller, wow, biggie; *Brit. informal* smasher.
– OPPOSITES compliment, failure.
– PHRASES **hit back** RETALIATE, respond, reply, react, counter, defend oneself. **hit home** HAVE THE INTENDED EFFECT, strike home, hit the mark, register, be understood, get through, sink in. **hit it off** *(informal)* GET ON (WELL), get along, be friends, be friendly, be compatible, feel a rapport, see eye to eye, take to each other, warm to each other; *informal* click, get on like a house on fire, be on the same wavelength. **hit on/upon** DISCOVER, come up with, think of, conceive of, dream up, work out, invent, create, devise, design, pioneer; uncover, stumble on, chance on, light on, come upon. **hit out at** CRITICIZE, attack, censure, denounce, condemn, lambaste, pillory, rail against, inveigh against, arraign, cast aspersions on, pour scorn on, disparage, denigrate, give a bad press to, run down; *informal* knock, pan, slam, hammer, lay into, pull to pieces, pick holes in; *Brit. informal* slag off, slate, rubbish; *N. Amer. informal* pummel, trash; *formal* excoriate.

hitch • verb **1** *she hitched the blanket around her* PULL, jerk, hike, lift, raise; *informal* yank. **2** *Tom hitched the pony to his cart* HARNESS, yoke, couple, fasten, connect, attach, tether. **3** *(informal) they hitched to college* HITCH-HIKE; *informal* thumb a lift, hitch a lift.
• noun *it went without a hitch* PROBLEM, difficulty, snag, setback, hindrance, obstacle, obstruction, complication, impediment, barrier, stumbling block; hold-up, interruption, delay; *informal* headache, glitch, hiccup.

hither • adverb *(poetic/literary)* HERE, to this place, to here, over here, near, nearer, close, closer.

hitherto • adverb PREVIOUSLY, formerly, earlier, before, beforehand; so far, thus far, to date, as yet, until now, until then, till now, till then, up to now, up to then; *formal* heretofore.

hit-or-miss, hit-and-miss • adjective ERRATIC, haphazard, disorganized, undisciplined, unmethodical, uneven; careless, slapdash, slipshod, casual, cursory, lackadaisical, perfunctory, random, aimless, undirected, indiscriminate; *informal* sloppy, slap-happy.
– OPPOSITES meticulous.

hoard • noun *a secret hoard of gold* CACHE, stockpile, stock, store, collection, supply, reserve, reservoir, fund, accumulation; treasure house, treasure trove; *informal* stash.
• verb *they hoarded rations* STOCKPILE, store (up), stock up on, put aside, put by, lay by, lay up, set aside, stow away, buy up; cache, amass, collect, save, gather, garner, accumulate, squirrel away, put aside for a rainy day; *informal* stash away, salt away.
– OPPOSITES squander.

hoarse • adjective ROUGH, harsh, croaky, throaty, gruff, husky, guttural, gravelly, growly, grating, rasping.
– OPPOSITES mellow, clear.

hoary • adjective **1** *hoary cobwebs* GREYISH-WHITE, grey, white, silver, silvery; frosty; *poetic/literary* rimy. **2** *a hoary ancient* GREY-HAIRED, white-haired, silver-haired, grizzled; elderly, aged, old, long in the tooth; *informal* getting on, over the hill. **3** *a hoary old adage* TRITE, hackneyed, clichéd, banal, commonplace, predictable, overused, stale, time-worn, tired, unimaginative, unoriginal, uninspired; *in-*

with a hoax.
– DERIVATIVES **hoaxer** noun.
– ORIGIN probably a contraction of obsolete *hocus* 'trickery', from HOCUS-POCUS.

hob • noun Brit. **1** the flat top part of a cooker, with hotplates or burners. **2** a flat metal shelf at the side of a fireplace, used for heating pans. **3** a machine tool for cutting gears or screw threads.
– ORIGIN alteration of HUB.

hobbit • noun a member of an imaginary race similar to humans, of small size and with hairy feet.
– ORIGIN invented by the British writer J. R. R. Tolkien (1892–1973), and said by him to mean 'hole-dweller'.

hobble • verb **1** walk awkwardly, typically because of pain. **2** strap together the legs of (a horse) to prevent it straying. **3** be or cause a problem for. • noun **1** an awkward way of walking. **2** a rope or strap for hobbling a horse.
– DERIVATIVES **hobbler** noun.
– ORIGIN probably related to Dutch *hobbelen* 'rock from side to side'.

hobbledehoy /hobb'ldihoy/ • noun informal, dated a clumsy or awkward youth.
– ORIGIN of unknown origin.

hobble skirt • noun a skirt so narrow at the hem as to impede walking, popular in the 1910s.

hobby[1] • noun (pl. **hobbies**) **1** an activity followed regularly for pleasure. **2** historical a very early type of bicycle propelled by the pressure of the rider's feet against the ground.
– ORIGIN originally in the sense 'small horse', later 'toy horse or hobby horse': from a familiar form of the given name *Robin*.

hobby[2] • noun (pl. **hobbies**) a small migratory falcon which hunts birds and insects in flight.
– ORIGIN Old French *hobet* 'little falcon'.

hobby horse • noun **1** a child's toy consisting of a stick with a model of a horse's head at one end. **2** a rocking horse. **3** a person's favourite topic of conversation.

hobbyist • noun a person with a particular hobby.

hobgoblin • noun a mischievous imp.
– ORIGIN from *hob*, familiar form of the names *Robin* and *Robert*, used in the sense 'country fellow'.

hobnail • noun **1** a short heavy-headed nail used to reinforce the soles of boots. **2** a blunt projection, especially in cut or moulded glassware.
– DERIVATIVES **hobnailed** adjective.
– ORIGIN from HOB + NAIL.

hobnob • verb (**hobnobbed**, **hobnobbing**) informal mix socially, especially with those of higher social status.
– ORIGIN originally in the sense 'drink together, drink each other's health': from obsolete *hob or nob*, or *hob and nob*, probably meaning 'give and take'.

hobo • noun (pl. **hoboes** or **hobos**) N. Amer. a vagrant.
– ORIGIN of unknown origin.

Hobson's choice • noun a choice of taking what is offered or nothing at all.
– ORIGIN named after Thomas *Hobson* (1554–1631), a carrier who hired out horses, making the customer take the one nearest the door or none at all.

hock[1] • noun **1** the joint in the hind leg of a four-legged animal, between the knee and the fetlock. **2** a knuckle of pork or ham.
– ORIGIN variant of an Old English word meaning 'heel'.

hock[2] • noun Brit. a dry white wine from the German Rhineland.
– ORIGIN from German *Hochheimer Wein* 'wine from Hochheim'.

hock[3] • verb informal pawn (an object).
– PHRASES **in hock 1** having been pawned. **2** in debt.
– ORIGIN from Dutch *hok* 'hutch, prison, debt'.

hockey[1] /hokki/ • noun a game played between two teams of eleven players each, using hooked sticks to drive a small hard ball towards a goal.
– ORIGIN of unknown origin.

hockey[2] /okki/ • noun variant spelling of OCHE.

hocus-pocus • noun **1** meaningless talk used to deceive. **2** a form of words used by a conjuror.
– ORIGIN from *hax pax max Deus adimax*, a pseudo-Latin phrase used as a magic formula by conjurors.

hod • noun **1** a builder's V-shaped open trough attached to a short pole, used for carrying bricks. **2** a coal scuttle.
– ORIGIN Old French *hotte* 'pannier'.

hodgepodge • noun N. Amer. variant of HOTCHPOTCH.

Hodgkin's disease • noun a malignant disease of lymphatic tissues typically causing enlargement of the lymph nodes, liver, and spleen.
– ORIGIN named after the English physician Thomas *Hodgkin* (1798–1866).

hoe • noun a long-handled gardening tool with a thin metal blade, used mainly for cutting through weeds at their roots. • verb (**hoes**, **hoed**, **hoeing**) **1** use a hoe to turn (earth) or cut through (weeds). **2** (**hoe in**) Austral./NZ informal eat eagerly. **3** (**hoe into**) Austral./NZ informal attack or criticize.
– DERIVATIVES **hoer** noun.
– ORIGIN Old French *houe*; related to HEW.

hoedown • noun N. Amer. a lively folk dance.

hog • noun **1** a pig, especially a castrated male reared for slaughter. **2** informal a greedy person. • verb (**hogged**, **hogging**) informal take or hoard selfishly.
– PHRASES **go the whole hog** informal do something completely or thoroughly.
– DERIVATIVES **hogger** noun **hoggery** noun **hoggish** adjective.
– ORIGIN Old English.

hogback (also **hog's back**) • noun a long steep hill or mountain ridge.

hogget • noun **1** Brit. a yearling sheep. **2** NZ a lamb between weaning and first shearing.

Hogmanay /hogmənay, hogmənay/ • noun (in Scotland) New Year's Eve.
– ORIGIN perhaps from Old French *aguillanneuf* 'last day of the year, new year's gift'.

hogshead • noun **1** a large cask. **2** a measure of liquid volume equal to 52.5 imperial gallons (63 US gallons, 238.7 litres) for wine or 54 imperial gallons (64 US gallons, 245.5 litres) for beer.

hog-tie • verb N. Amer. **1** secure (a person or animal) by fastening the hands and feet or all four feet together. **2** impede.

hogwash • noun informal nonsense.
– ORIGIN originally meaning 'kitchen swill for pigs'.

hogweed • noun a large white-flowered weed of the parsley family, formerly used as forage for pigs.

hoick Brit. informal • verb lift or pull with a jerk. • noun a jerky pull.
– ORIGIN perhaps from HIKE.

hoi polloi /hoy pəloy/ • plural noun derogatory the common people.
– ORIGIN Greek, 'the many'.

h

Thesaurus

formal old hat, corny; *N. Amer. informal* cornball.
– OPPOSITES young, original.

hoax • noun *the call was a hoax* PRACTICAL JOKE, joke, jest, prank, trick; ruse, deception, fraud, bluff, humbug, confidence trick; *informal* con, spoof, scam.
• verb *the DJ hoaxed his listeners* PLAY A (PRACTICAL) JOKE ON, play a prank on, trick, fool; deceive, hoodwink, delude, dupe, take in, lead on, bluff, gull, humbug; *informal* con, kid, have on, pull a fast one on, put one over on, take for a ride, lead up the garden path; *N. Amer. informal* sucker, snooker.

hoaxer • noun (PRACTICAL) JOKER, prankster, trickster; fraudster, hoodwinker, swindler; *informal* spoofer, con man.

hobble • verb LIMP, walk with difficulty, move unsteadily, walk haltingly; shamble, totter, dodder, stagger, stumble; *Scottish* hirple.

hobby • noun PASTIME, leisure activity, leisure pursuit; sideline, diversion, avocation; recreation, entertainment, amusement, enthusiasm.

hobgoblin • noun GOBLIN, imp, sprite, elf, brownie, pixie, leprechaun, gnome; *Scottish* kelpie.

hobnob • verb *(informal)* ASSOCIATE, mix, fraternize, socialize, keep company, spend time, go around, mingle, consort, rub shoulders; *N. Amer.* rub elbows; *informal* hang around/round/out, knock about/around, be thick with.

hocus-pocus • noun JARGON, mumbo-jumbo, argle-bargle, gibberish, balderdash, claptrap, nonsense, rubbish, twaddle, garbage; *informal* gobbledegook, double Dutch, hokum; *N. Amer. informal* flapdoodle; *informal, dated* bunkum.

hodgepodge • noun *(N. Amer.)* See HOTCHPOTCH.

hog • noun PIG, sow, swine, porker, piglet, boar; *informal* piggy.
• verb *(informal) he hogged the limelight* MONOPOLIZE, dominate, take over, corner, control.
– OPPOSITES share.

hogwash • noun *(informal).* See NONSENSE sense 1.

hoi polloi • noun *(derogatory)* THE MASSES, the common people, the

hoisin sauce /hoyzin/ ● noun a sweet, spicy dark red sauce made from soya beans, used in Chinese cooking.
– ORIGIN *hoisin* from two Cantonese words meaning 'sea' + 'fresh'.

hoist ● verb **1** raise by means of ropes and pulleys. **2** haul or lift up. ● noun **1** an act of hoisting. **2** an apparatus for hoisting. **3** the part of a flag nearest the staff. **4** a group of flags raised as a signal.
– PHRASES **hoist one's flag** (of an admiral) take up command. **hoist the flag** stake one's claim to territory by displaying a flag.
– DERIVATIVES **hoister** noun.
– ORIGIN probably from Dutch *hijsen* or Low German *hiesen*.

hoity-toity ● adjective informal haughty.
– ORIGIN originally in the sense 'frolicsome, flighty': from obsolete *hoit* 'indulge in riotous mirth'.

hokey ● adjective (**hokier, hokiest**) N. Amer. informal excessively sentimental or contrived.
– DERIVATIVES **hokeyness** (also **hokiness**) noun.
– ORIGIN from HOKUM.

hokey-cokey (US **hokey-pokey**) ● noun a communal song and dance performed in a circle, involving synchronized shaking of each limb in turn.
– ORIGIN perhaps from HOCUS-POCUS.

h

hoki /hōki/ ● noun an edible marine fish found off the southern coasts of New Zealand.
– ORIGIN Maori.

hokum /hōkəm/ ● noun informal **1** nonsense. **2** trite or sentimental material in a film, book, etc.
– ORIGIN of unknown origin.

hold[1] ● verb (past and past part. **held**) **1** grasp, carry, or support. **2** keep or detain. **3** have in one's possession. **4** contain or be capable of containing. **5** have or occupy (a job or position). **6** have (a belief or opinion). **7** stay or cause to stay at a certain value or level. **8** (**hold to**) adhere or cause to adhere to (a commitment). **9** continue to follow (a course). **10** arrange and take part in (a meeting or conversation). **11** (**hold in**) regard (someone or something) with (a specified feeling). **12** N. Amer. informal refrain from adding or using. ● noun **1** an act or manner of grasping someone or something. **2** a handhold. **3** a degree of power or control.
– PHRASES **get hold of 1** grasp. **2** informal find or contact. **hold against** allow (a past action) to have a negative influence on one's attitude towards. **hold back** hesitate. **hold down** informal succeed in keeping (a job). **hold fast 1** remain tightly secured. **2** continue to adhere to a principle. **hold forth** talk at length or tediously. **hold good** (or **true**) remain true or valid. **hold it** informal wait or stop doing something. **hold off 1** resist (an attacker or challenge). **2** postpone (an action or decision). **3** (of bad weather) fail to occur. **hold on 1** wait; stop. **2** keep going in difficult circumstances. **hold out 1** resist difficult circumstances. **2** continue to be sufficient. **hold out for** continue to demand. **hold over 1** postpone. **2** use (information) to threaten. **hold up 1** delay the progress of. **2** rob using the threat of violence. **3** present as an example. **4** remain strong or vigorous. **no holds barred 1** (in wrestling) with no restrictions on the kinds of holds that are used. **2** without rules or restrictions. **on hold 1** waiting to be connected by telephone. **2** pending. **take hold** start to have an effect.
– DERIVATIVES **holder** noun.
– ORIGIN Old English.

hold[2] ● noun a storage space in the lower part of a ship or aircraft.
– ORIGIN from HOLE; the *-d* was added by association with HOLD[1].

holdall ● noun Brit. a large bag with handles and a shoulder

Thesaurus

populace, the public, the multitude, the rank and file, the lower orders, the commonality, the commonalty, the third estate, the plebeians, the proletariat; the mob, the herd, the rabble, the riff-raff, the great unwashed; *informal* the plebs, the proles.

hoist ● verb *we hoisted the mainsail* RAISE, lift (up), haul up, heave up, jack up, hike up, winch up, pull up, upraise, uplift, elevate, erect.
– OPPOSITES lower.
● noun *a mechanical hoist* LIFTING GEAR, crane, winch, block and tackle, pulley, windlass, derrick.

hoity-toity ● adjective *(informal)* SNOBBISH, snobby, haughty, disdainful, conceited, proud, arrogant, supercilious, superior, imperious, above oneself, self-important; *informal* high and mighty, snooty, uppity, uppish, la-di-da; *Brit. informal* toffee-nosed.

hold ● verb **1** *she held a suitcase* CLASP, clutch, grasp, grip, clench, cling to, hold on to; carry, bear. **2** *I wanted to hold her* EMBRACE, hug, clasp, cradle, enfold, squeeze, fold in one's arms. **3** *do you hold a driving licence?* POSSESS, have, own, bear, carry, have to one's name. **4** *the branch held my weight* SUPPORT, bear, carry, take, keep up, sustain, prop up, shore up. **5** *the police were holding him* DETAIN, hold in custody, imprison, lock up, put behind bars, put in prison, put in jail, incarcerate, keep under lock and key, confine, intern; *informal* put away, put inside. **6** *try to hold the audience's attention* MAINTAIN, keep, occupy, engross, absorb, interest, captivate, fascinate, enthral, rivet; engage, catch, capture, arrest. **7** *he held a senior post* OCCUPY, have, fill; *informal* hold down. **8** *the tank held 250 gallons* TAKE, contain, accommodate, fit; have a capacity of, have room for. **9** *the court held that there was no evidence* MAINTAIN, consider, take the view, believe, think, feel, deem, be of the opinion; judge, rule, decide; *informal* reckon; *formal* opine. **10** *let's hope the weather holds* PERSIST, continue, carry on, go on, hold out, keep up, last, endure, stay, remain. **11** *the offer still holds* BE AVAILABLE, be valid, hold good, stand, apply, remain, exist, be the case, be in force, be in effect. **12** *they held a meeting* CONVENE, call, summon; conduct, have, organize, run; *formal* convoke.
– OPPOSITES release, lose, end.
● noun **1** *she kept a hold on my hand* GRIP, grasp, clasp, clutch. **2** *Tom had a hold over his father* INFLUENCE, power, control, dominance, authority, leverage, sway, mastery. **3** *the military tightened their hold on the capital* CONTROL, grip, power, stranglehold, dominion, authority.
– PHRASES **get hold of** *(informal)* **1** *I just can't get hold of saffron* OBTAIN, acquire, get, find, come by, pick up, procure; buy, purchase; *informal* get one's hands on. **2** *I'll try to get hold of Mark* CONTACT, get in touch with, communicate with, make contact with, reach, notify; phone, call, speak to, talk to; *Brit.* ring (up), get on to. **hold back** HESITATE, pause, stop oneself, desist, forbear. **hold someone back** HINDER, hamper, impede, obstruct, check, curb, block, thwart, baulk, hamstring, restrain, frustrate, stand in someone's way. **hold something back 1** *Jane held back the tears* SUPPRESS, fight back, choke back, stifle, smother, subdue, rein in, repress, curb, control, keep a tight rein on; *informal* keep a/the lid on. **2** *don't hold anything back from me* WITHHOLD, hide, conceal, keep secret, keep hidden, keep quiet about, hush up; *informal* sit on, keep under one's hat. **hold someone/something dear** CHERISH, treasure, prize, appreciate, value highly, care for/about, set great store by; *informal* put on a pedestal. **hold someone down** OPPRESS, repress, suppress, subdue, subjugate, keep down, keep under, tyrannize, dominate. **hold something down 1** *they will hold down inflation* KEEP DOWN, keep low, freeze, fix. **2** *(informal) she held down two jobs* OCCUPY, hold, have, do, fill. **hold forth** SPEAK AT LENGTH, talk at length, go on, sound off; declaim, spout, pontificate, orate, preach, sermonize; *informal* speechify, preachify, drone on. **hold off** *the rain held off* STAY AWAY, keep off. **hold something off** RESIST, repel, repulse, rebuff, parry, deflect, fend off, stave off, ward off, keep at bay. **hold on 1** *hold on a minute* WAIT (A MINUTE), just a moment, just a second; stay here, stay put; hold the line; *informal* hang on, sit tight, hold your horses; *Brit. informal* hang about. **2** *if only they could hold on a while* KEEP GOING, persevere, survive, last, continue, struggle on, carry on, go on, hold out, see it through, stay the course; *informal* soldier on, stick at it, hang in there. **hold on to 1** *he held on to the chair* CLUTCH, hold, hang on to, clasp, grasp, grip, cling to. **2** *they can't hold on to their staff* RETAIN, keep, hang on to. **hold one's own.** See OWN. **hold out 1** *we held out against the attacks* RESIST, withstand, hold off, fight off, fend off, keep off, keep at bay, stand up to, stand firm against. **2** *our supplies will hold out* LAST, remain, be extant, continue. **hold something out** EXTEND, proffer, offer, present; outstretch, reach out, stretch out, put out. **hold something over** POSTPONE, put off, put back, delay, defer, suspend, shelve, hold in abeyance; *N. Amer.* put over, table, take a rain check on; *informal* put on ice, put on the back burner, put in cold storage, mothball. **hold up** *the argument doesn't hold up* BE CONVINCING, be logical, hold water, bear examination, be sound. **hold something up 1** *they held up the trophy* DISPLAY, hold aloft, exhibit, show (off), flourish, brandish; *informal* flash. **2** *concrete pillars hold up the bridge* SUPPORT, hold, bear, carry, take, keep up, prop up, shore up, buttress. **3** *our flight was held up for hours* DELAY, detain, make late, set back, keep back, retard, slow up. **4** *a lack of cash has held up progress* OBSTRUCT, impede, hinder, hamper, inhibit,

strap.

holding • noun **1** an area of land held by lease. **2** (**holdings**) financial assets owned by a person or organization.

holding company • noun a company created to buy shares in other companies, which it then controls.

holding pattern • noun the flight path maintained by an aircraft awaiting permission to land.

hold-up • noun **1** a cause of delay. **2** a robbery conducted with the threat of violence. **3** a stocking held up by an elasticated top.

hole • noun **1** a hollow space in a solid object or surface. **2** an opening or gap in or passing through something. **3** a cavity on a golf course into which the ball is directed. **4** informal a small, awkward, or unpleasant place or situation. • verb **1** make a hole or holes in. **2** Golf hit (the ball) into a hole. **3** (**hole up**) informal hide oneself.
– PHRASES **hole-and-corner** secret. **hole-in-one** (pl. **holes-in-one**) Golf a shot that enters the hole from the tee. **make a hole in** use a significant amount of.
– DERIVATIVES **holey** adjective.
– ORIGIN Old English.

hole in the heart • noun a congenital defect in the wall between the chambers of the heart, resulting in inadequate circulation of oxygenated blood.

hole in the wall • noun informal **1** Brit. an automatic cash dispenser installed in an outside wall. **2** a small dingy place.

holiday chiefly Brit. • noun **1** an extended period of recreation, especially away from home. **2** a day of festivity or recreation when no work is done. • verb spend a holiday.
– ORIGIN Old English, 'holy day'.

holiday camp • noun Brit. a camp for holidaymakers with accommodation and entertainments.

holidaymaker • noun Brit. a tourist.

holier-than-thou • adjective offensively self-righteous.

holiness • noun **1** the state of being holy. **2** (**His/Your Holiness**) the title of the Pope, Orthodox patriarchs, and the Dalai Lama.

holism /hōliz'm/ • noun Medicine the treating of the whole person, taking into account mental and social factors, rather than just the symptoms of a disease.
– DERIVATIVES **holistic** adjective.
– ORIGIN from Greek *holos* 'whole'.

hollandaise sauce /holləndayz/ • noun a creamy sauce for fish, made of butter, egg yolks, and vinegar.
– ORIGIN French *hollandais* 'Dutch'.

holler informal • verb give a loud shout. • noun a loud shout.
– ORIGIN related to HALLOO.

hollow • adjective **1** having a hole or empty space inside. **2** concave. **3** (of a sound) echoing. **4** lacking significance or sincerity. • noun **1** a hole or depression. **2** a small valley. • verb (usu. **hollow out**) **1** make hollow. **2** form by hollowing.
– PHRASES **beat hollow** defeat thoroughly.
– DERIVATIVES **hollowly** adverb **hollowness** noun.
– ORIGIN Old English, 'cave'; related to HOLE.

holly • noun an evergreen shrub with prickly dark green leaves and red berries.
– ORIGIN Old English.

hollyhock • noun a tall plant of the mallow family, with large showy flowers.
– ORIGIN from HOLY + obsolete *hock* 'mallow'.

holmium /hōlmiəm/ • noun a soft silvery-white metallic element.
– ORIGIN from *Holmia*, Latinized form of *Stockholm*, the capital of Sweden (because holmium and related minerals are found there).

holm oak • noun an evergreen oak with dark green glossy leaves.
– ORIGIN from dialect *hollin*, from Old English, 'holly'.

holo- • combining form whole; complete: *holocaust.*
– ORIGIN from Greek *holos* 'whole'.

holocaust /holləkawst/ • noun **1** destruction or slaughter on a mass scale. **2** (**the Holocaust**) the mass murder of Jews under the German Nazi regime in World War II.
– ORIGIN from Greek *kaustos* 'burnt'.

h

Thesaurus

baulk, thwart, curb, hamstring, frustrate, foil, interfere with, stop; *informal* stymie; *Brit. informal* throw a spanner in the works of. **5** *a raider held up the bank* ROB; *informal* stick up, mug. **hold water.** See WATER. **hold with** APPROVE OF, agree with, be in favour of, endorse, accept, countenance, support, subscribe to, give one's blessing to, take kindly to; *informal* stand for; *Brit. informal* be doing with.

holder • noun **1** *a knife holder* CONTAINER, receptacle, case, casing, cover, covering, housing, sheath; stand, rest, rack. **2** *a British passport holder* BEARER, owner, possessor, keeper; custodian.

holdings • plural noun ASSETS, funds, capital, resources, savings, investments, securities, equities, bonds, stocks and shares, reserves; property, possessions.

hold-up • noun **1** *I ran into a series of hold-ups* DELAY, setback, hitch, snag, difficulty, problem, trouble; traffic jam, tailback, gridlock; *informal* snarl-up, glitch, hiccup. **2** *a bank hold-up* (ARMED) ROBBERY, (armed) raid; theft, burglary, mugging; *informal* stick-up; *N. Amer. informal* heist.

hole • noun **1** *a hole in the roof* OPENING, aperture, gap, space, orifice, vent, chink, breach; crack, leak, rift, rupture; puncture, perforation, cut, split, gash, slit, crevice, fissure. **2** *a hole in the ground* PIT, ditch, trench, cavity, crater, depression, hollow; well, borehole, excavation, dugout; cave, cavern, pothole. **3** *the badger's hole* BURROW, lair, den, earth, sett; retreat, shelter. **4** *there are holes in their argument* FLAW, fault, defect, weakness, shortcoming, inconsistency, discrepancy, loophole; error, mistake. **5** (*informal*) *I was living in a real hole* HOVEL, slum, shack, mess; *informal* dump, dive, pigsty, tip. **6** (*informal*) *they steal when they are in a hole* PREDICAMENT, difficult situation, awkward situation, (tight) corner, quandary, dilemma; crisis, emergency, difficulty, trouble, plight, dire straits; *informal* fix, jam, bind, (tight) spot, pickle, sticky situation, hot water; *Brit. informal* spot of bother.
• verb *a fuel tank was holed by the attack* PUNCTURE, perforate, pierce, penetrate, rupture, split, rent, lacerate, gash.
– PHRASES **hole up 1** *the bears hole up in winter* HIBERNATE, lie dormant. **2** (*informal*) *the snipers holed up in a farmhouse* HIDE (OUT), conceal oneself, secrete oneself, shelter, take cover, lie low, go to ground, go to earth; *Brit. informal, dated* lie doggo. **pick holes in** (*informal*). See CRITICIZE.

hole-and-corner • adjective SECRET, secretive, clandestine, covert, furtive, surreptitious; underhand, devious, stealthy, sneaky, backstairs, hugger-mugger, cloak-and-dagger, under-the-counter; *informal* hush-hush.

holiday • noun **1** *a ten-day holiday* VACATION, break, rest, recess; time off, time out, leave, furlough, sabbatical; trip, tour, journey, voyage; *informal* hols, vac; *formal* sojourn. **2** *the twenty-fourth of May is a holiday* PUBLIC HOLIDAY, bank holiday, festival, feast day, fête, fiesta, celebration, anniversary, jubilee; saint's day, holy day.

holier-than-thou • adjective SANCTIMONIOUS, self-righteous, smug, self-satisfied; priggish, pious, pietistic, Pharisaic; *informal* goody-goody, preachy.
– OPPOSITES humble.

holler (*informal*) • verb *he hollers when he wants feeding* SHOUT, yell, cry (out), vociferate, call (out), roar, bellow, bawl, bark, howl; boom, thunder.
– OPPOSITES whisper.
• noun *a euphoric holler* SHOUT, cry, yell, roar, bellow, bawl, howl; whoop.
– OPPOSITES whisper.

hollow • adjective **1** *each fibre has a hollow core* EMPTY, void, unfilled, vacant. **2** *hollow cheeks* SUNKEN, deep-set, concave, depressed, indented. **3** *a hollow voice* DULL, low, flat, toneless, expressionless; muffled, muted. **4** *a hollow victory* MEANINGLESS, empty, valueless, worthless, useless, pyrrhic, futile, fruitless, profitless, pointless. **5** *a hollow promise* INSINCERE, hypocritical, feigned, false, sham, deceitful, cynical, spurious, untrue, two-faced; *informal* phoney, pretend.
– OPPOSITES solid, worthwhile, sincere.
• noun **1** *a hollow under the tree* HOLE, pit, cavity, crater, trough, cave, cavern; depression, indentation, dip; niche, nook, cranny, recess. **2** *the village lay in a hollow* VALLEY, vale, dale; *Brit.* dene, combe; *N. English* clough; *Scottish* glen, strath; *poetic/literary* dell.
• verb *a tunnel hollowed out of a mountain* GOUGE, scoop, dig, cut; excavate, channel.
– PHRASES **beat someone hollow** TROUNCE, defeat utterly, crush, rout, overwhelm, outclass; *informal* annihilate, drub, hammer, clobber, thrash, lick, paste, crucify, slaughter, massacre, flatten, demolish, destroy, walk over, wipe the floor with, make mincemeat of; *Brit. informal* stuff; *N. Amer. informal* shellac, cream, skunk.

holocaust • noun CATACLYSM, disaster, catastrophe; destruction,

Holocene /holləseen/ ● adjective Geology relating to or denoting the present epoch (from about 10,000 years ago, following the Pleistocene).
– ORIGIN French, from Greek *kainos* 'new'.
hologram /holləgram/ ● noun **1** a three-dimensional image formed by the interference of light beams from a laser or other coherent light source. **2** a photograph of an interference pattern which, when suitably illuminated, produces a three-dimensional image.
– DERIVATIVES **holographic** adjective **holography** noun.
holograph /holləgraaf/ ● noun a manuscript handwritten by its author.
hols ● plural noun Brit. informal holidays.
holster /hōlstər/ ● noun a holder for carrying a handgun, typically worn on a belt or under the arm. ● verb put (a gun) into its holster.
– ORIGIN of unknown origin.
holt /hōlt/ ● noun the den of an otter.
– ORIGIN from HOLD[1].
holy ● adjective (**holier**, **holiest**) **1** dedicated to God or a religious purpose. **2** morally and spiritually excellent and to be revered.
– ORIGIN Old English, related to WHOLE.
holy day ● noun a religious festival.
Holy Father ● noun the Pope.
holy of holies ● noun **1** historical the inner chamber of the sanctuary in the Jewish Temple in Jerusalem. **2** a place regarded as most sacred or special.
holy orders ● plural noun see ORDER (in sense 10 of the noun).
Holy Roman Empire ● noun the western part of the Roman empire, as revived by Charlemagne in 800.
Holy Scripture ● noun the Bible.
Holy See ● noun the papacy or the papal court.
Holy Spirit (or **Holy Ghost**) ● noun (in Christianity) the third person of the Trinity; God as spiritually active in the world.
holy war ● noun a war waged in support of a religious cause.
holy water ● noun water blessed by a priest and used in religious ceremonies.
Holy Week ● noun the week before Easter.
Holy Writ ● noun sacred writings collectively, especially the Bible.
homage /hommij/ ● noun honour or respect shown publicly.
– ORIGIN Old French, from Latin *homo* 'man'; in medieval times the word denoted the ceremony by which a vassal declared himself to be his feudal lord's 'man'.
hombre /ombray/ ● noun informal, chiefly N. Amer. a man.
– ORIGIN Spanish.
homburg /homburg/ ● noun a man's felt hat having a narrow curled brim and a lengthwise indentation in the crown.
– ORIGIN named after the German town of *Homburg*, where such hats were first worn.
home ● noun **1** the place where one lives. **2** an institution for people needing professional care. **3** a place where something flourishes or from which it originated. **4** the finishing point in a race. **5** (in games) the place where a player is free from attack. ● adjective **1** relating to one's home. **2** made, done, or intended for use in the home. **3** relating to one's own country. **4** (in sport) denoting a team's own ground. ● adverb **1** to or at one's home. **2** to the end or conclusion of something. **3** to the intended or correct position. ● verb **1** (of an animal) return by instinct to its territory. **2** (**home in on**) move or be aimed towards.
– PHRASES **at home 1** comfortable and at ease. **2** ready to receive visitors. **bring home to** make aware of the significance of. **close to home** (of a remark) uncomfortably accurate. **drive** (or **hammer**) **home** stress forcefully. **hit** (or **strike**) **home 1** (of words) have the intended effect. **2** (of the significance of a situation) be fully realized. **home and dry** chiefly Brit. having achieved one's objective. **home is where the heart is** proverb your home will always be the place for which you feel the deepest affection, no matter where you are.
– DERIVATIVES **homeless** adjective **homelessness** noun.
– ORIGIN Old English.
homeboy (or **homegirl**) ● noun US & S. African informal a person from one's own town or neighbourhood.
home brew ● noun beer or other alcoholic drink brewed at home.
homecoming ● noun an instance of returning home.
home economics ● plural noun (often treated as sing.) the study of cookery and household management.
home farm ● noun Brit. & S. African a farm on an estate that provides produce for the estate owner.
home-grown ● adjective grown or produced in one's own garden or country.
Home Guard ● noun the British volunteer force organized in 1940 to defend the UK against invasion.
home help ● noun Brit. a person employed to help with domestic work.
homeland ● noun **1** a person's native land. **2** an autonomous state occupied by a particular people. **3** historical any of ten partially self-governing areas in South Africa designated for indigenous African peoples.
homely ● adjective (**homelier**, **homeliest**) **1** simple but comfortable. **2** unsophisticated. **3** N. Amer. unattractive.
– DERIVATIVES **homeliness** noun.

Thesaurus

devastation, annihilation; massacre, slaughter, mass murder, carnage, butchery; genocide, ethnic cleansing.
holy ● adjective **1** *holy men* SAINTLY, godly, saintlike, pious, pietistic, religious, devout, God-fearing, spiritual; righteous, good, virtuous, sinless, pure; canonized, beatified, ordained. **2** *a Jewish holy place* SACRED, consecrated, hallowed, sanctified, venerated, revered, divine, religious, blessed, dedicated.
– OPPOSITES sinful, irreligious, cursed.
homage ● noun RESPECT, honour, reverence, worship, admiration, esteem, adulation, acclaim; tribute, acknowledgement, recognition; accolade, panegyric, paean, salute.
– PHRASES **pay homage to** HONOUR, acclaim, applaud, salute, praise, commend, pay tribute to, take one's hat off to; *formal* laud.
home ● noun **1** *they fled their homes* RESIDENCE, place of residence, house, flat, apartment, bungalow, cottage; accommodation, property, quarters, lodgings, rooms; a roof over one's head; address, place; *informal* pad, digs, semi; *formal* domicile, abode, dwelling (place), habitation. **2** *I am far from my home* HOMELAND, native land, home town, birthplace, roots, fatherland, motherland, mother country, country of origin, the old country. **3** *a home for the elderly* INSTITUTION, nursing home, retirement home, rest home, children's home; hospice, shelter, refuge, retreat, asylum, hostel. **4** *the home of fine wines* DOMAIN, realm, origin, source, cradle, fount, fountainhead.
● adjective **1** *the UK home market* DOMESTIC, internal, local, national, interior. **2** *home produce* HOME-MADE, home-grown, local, family.
– OPPOSITES foreign, international.
– PHRASES **at home 1** *I was at home all day* IN, in one's house, present, available, indoors, inside, here. **2** *she felt very much at home* AT EASE, comfortable, relaxed, content; in one's element. **3** *he is at home with mathematics* CONFIDENT WITH, conversant with, proficient in; used to, familiar with, au fait with, au courant with, skilled in, experienced in, well versed in; *informal* well up on. **4** *she was not at home to friends* ENTERTAINING, receiving; playing host to. **bring something home to someone** MAKE SOMEONE REALIZE, make someone understand, make someone aware, make something clear to someone; drive home, press home, impress upon someone, draw attention to, focus attention on, underline, highlight, spotlight, emphasize, stress. **hit home.** See HIT. **home in on** FOCUS ON, concentrate on, zero in on, centre on, fix on; highlight, spotlight, underline, pinpoint; *informal* zoom in on. **nothing to write home about** *(informal)* UNEXCEPTIONAL, mediocre, ordinary, commonplace, indifferent, average, middle-of-the-road, run-of-the-mill; tolerable, passable, adequate, fair; *informal* OK, so-so, bog-standard, (plain) vanilla, no great shakes, not so hot, not up to much; *Brit. informal* common or garden; *N. Amer. informal* ornery.
homeland ● noun NATIVE LAND, country of origin, home, fatherland, motherland, mother country, land of one's fathers, the old country.
homeless ● adjective *homeless people* OF NO FIXED ABODE, without a roof over one's head, on the streets, vagrant, sleeping rough; destitute, down and out.
● noun *charities for the homeless* PEOPLE OF NO FIXED ABODE, vagrants, down-and-outs, tramps, vagabonds, itinerants, transients, migrants, derelicts, drifters; *N. Amer.* hoboes; *Austral.* bagmen; *informal* bag ladies; *Brit. informal* dossers; *N. Amer. informal* bums.
homely ● adjective **1** *a homely atmosphere* COSY, homelike, homey, comfortable, snug, welcoming, friendly, congenial, intimate, warm, hospitable, informal, relaxed, pleasant, cheerful; *informal* comfy. **2** *homely pursuits* UNSOPHISTICATED, everyday, ordinary, do-

home-made ● adjective made at home.
homemaker ● noun a person who manages a home.
home movie ● noun a film made in the home or in a domestic setting by an amateur.
Home Office ● noun the British government department dealing with law and order, immigration, etc. in England and Wales.
homeopath /hōmiəpath, homm-/ (also **homoeopath**) ● noun a person who practises homeopathy.
homeopathy /hōmioppəthi, hommi-/ (also **homoeopathy**) ● noun a system of complementary medicine in which disease is treated by minute doses of natural substances that in large quantities would produce symptoms of the disease.
– DERIVATIVES **homeopathic** adjective.
– ORIGIN from Greek *homoios* 'like' + *patheia* 'suffering, feeling'.
homeostasis /hōmiəstaysiss, homm-/ (also **homoeostasis**) ● noun (pl. **homeostases** /hōmiəstayseez, homm-/) the maintenance of a stable equilibrium, especially through physiological processes.
– DERIVATIVES **homeostatic** adjective.
– ORIGIN from Greek *homoios* 'like' + *stasis* 'stoppage, standing'.
homeotherm /hommiətherm/ (also **homoiotherm**) ● noun Zoology an organism that maintains a constant body temperature by means of its metabolic activity; a warm-blooded organism. Often contrasted with POIKILOTHERM.
– DERIVATIVES **homeothermic** adjective.
– ORIGIN from Greek *homoios* 'like' + *thermē* 'heat'.
home page ● noun Computing an individual's or organization's introductory document on the World Wide Web.
home plate ● noun Baseball the five-sided flat white rubber base which must be touched in scoring a run.
Homeric /hōmerrik/ ● adjective of, or in the style of, the ancient Greek poet Homer (8th century BC) or the epic poems ascribed to him.
home rule ● noun the government of a place by its own citizens.
home run ● noun Baseball a hit that allows the batter to make a complete circuit of the bases.
Home Secretary ● noun (in the UK) the Secretary of State in charge of the Home Office.
homesick ● adjective feeling upset because one is missing one's home.
homespun ● adjective **1** simple and unsophisticated. **2** (of cloth or yarn) made or spun at home. ● noun cloth of this type.
homestead ● noun **1** a house with surrounding land and outbuildings. **2** N. Amer. historical an area of land (usually 160 acres) granted to a settler as a home. **3** (in South Africa) a hut or cluster of huts occupied by one family or clan.
– DERIVATIVES **homesteader** noun **homesteading** noun.
home straight (also **home stretch**) ● noun the concluding stretch of a racecourse.
home truth ● noun an unpleasant fact about oneself.
home unit ● noun Austral./NZ a flat that is one of several in a building.
homeward ● adverb (also **homewards**) towards home. ● adjective going or leading towards home.
homework ● noun **1** school work that a pupil is required to do at home. **2** preparation for an event or situation. **3** paid work done in one's own home, especially piecework.
homeworker ● noun a person who works from home.
homey (also **homy**) ● adjective (**homier**, **homiest**) **1** comfortable and cosy. **2** unsophisticated. ● noun variant of HOMIE.
– DERIVATIVES **homeyness** (also **hominess**) noun.
homicide ● noun murder.
– DERIVATIVES **homicidal** adjective.
– ORIGIN Old French, from Latin *homo* 'man' + -CIDE.
homie (also **homey**) ● noun (pl. **homies** or **homeys**) informal, chiefly US a homeboy or homegirl.
homiletic /hommilettik/ ● adjective of or like a homily. ● noun (**homiletics**) (usu. treated as sing.) the art of preaching or writing sermons.
homily /hommili/ ● noun (pl. **homilies**) **1** a talk on a religious subject, intended to be spiritually uplifting rather than giving doctrinal instruction. **2** a tedious moralizing talk.
– DERIVATIVES **homilist** noun.
– ORIGIN Greek *homilia* 'discourse', from *homilos* 'crowd'.
homing ● adjective **1** (of a pigeon or other animal) able to return home from a great distance. **2** (of a weapon) able to find and hit a target electronically.
hominid /homminid/ ● noun Zoology a member of a family of primates which includes humans and their fossil ancestors.
– ORIGIN from Latin *homo* 'man'.
hominoid ● noun Zoology a primate of a group (superfamily Hominoidea) that includes humans, their fossil ancestors, and the great apes.
hominy /hommini/ ● noun US coarsely ground maize used to make grits.
– ORIGIN Algonquian.
Homo /hōmō, hommō/ ● noun the genus of primates of which modern humans (*Homo sapiens*) are the present-day representatives.
– ORIGIN Latin, 'man'.
homo /hōmō/ informal, chiefly derogatory ● noun (pl. **homos**) a homosexual man. ● adjective homosexual.
homo- ● combining form **1** same: *homogeneous.* **2** relating to homosexual love: *homoerotic.*
– ORIGIN from Greek *homos* 'same'.
homoeopath ● noun variant spelling of HOMEOPATH.
homoeopathy ● noun variant spelling of HOMEOPATHY.
homoeostasis ● noun variant spelling of HOMEOSTASIS.
homoerotic /hōmōirottik, homm-/ ● adjective concerning or arousing sexual desire centred on a person of the same sex.
– DERIVATIVES **homoeroticism** noun.
homogeneous /hommәjeeniəss/ ● adjective **1** of the same kind. **2** consisting of parts all of the same kind.
– DERIVATIVES **homogeneity** /hommәjineiti/ noun **homogeneously** adverb **homogeneousness** noun.
– ORIGIN Greek *homogenēs*, from *homos* 'same' + *genos* 'race, kind'.
homogenize (also **homogenise**) ● verb **1** make homogeneous. **2** subject (milk) to a process in which the fat droplets are emulsified and the cream does not separate.
– DERIVATIVES **homogenization** noun **homogenizer** noun.
homograph ● noun each of two or more words having the same spelling but different meanings and origins.
– DERIVATIVES **homographic** adjective.
homoiotherm /hommoyətherm/ ● noun variant spelling of HOMEOTHERM.
homolog ● noun US spelling of HOMOLOGUE.
homologate /həmolləgayt/ ● verb **1** formal agree with or ap-

h

Thesaurus

mestic, simple, modest, unpretentious, unassuming; homespun, folksy. **3** (N. Amer.) *she's rather homely* UNATTRACTIVE, plain, unprepossessing, unlovely, ill-favoured, ugly; informal not much to look at; Brit. informal no oil painting.
– OPPOSITES uncomfortable, formal, sophisticated, attractive.
homespun ● adjective UNSOPHISTICATED, simple, plain, unpolished, unrefined, rustic, folksy; coarse, rough, crude, rudimentary.
– OPPOSITES sophisticated.
homey ● adjective **1** *the house is homey yet elegant* COSY, homelike, homely, comfortable, snug, welcoming, informal, relaxed, intimate, warm, pleasant, cheerful; informal comfy. **2** *peasant life was simple and homey* UNSOPHISTICATED, homely, unrefined, unpretentious, plain, simple, modest.
– OPPOSITES uncomfortable, formal, sophisticated.
homicidal ● adjective MURDEROUS, violent, brutal, savage, ferocious, vicious, bloody, bloodthirsty, barbarous, barbaric; deadly, lethal, mortal, death-dealing; poetic/literary fell; archaic sanguinary.
homicide ● noun **1** *he was charged with homicide* MURDER, killing, slaughter, butchery, massacre; assassination, execution, extermination; patricide, matricide, infanticide; poetic/literary slaying. **2** (dated) *a convicted homicide* KILLER, assassin, serial killer, butcher, slaughterer; patricide, matricide, infanticide; informal hit man, hired gun; dated cut-throat; poetic/literary slayer.
homily ● noun SERMON, lecture, discourse, address, lesson, talk, speech, oration.
homogeneous ● adjective **1** *a homogeneous group* UNIFORM, identical, unvaried, consistent, undistinguishable; alike, similar, (much) the same, all of a piece; informal much of a muchness. **2** *we have to compete with homogeneous products* SIMILAR, comparable, equivalent, like, analogous, corresponding, parallel, matching, related; formal cognate.
– OPPOSITES different.
homogenize ● verb MAKE UNIFORM, make similar, unite, integrate, fuse, merge, blend, meld, coalesce, amalgamate, combine.

prove of. **2** approve (a vehicle or engine) for sale or for a class of racing.
– DERIVATIVES **homologation** noun.
– ORIGIN Latin *homologare* 'agree', from Greek *homologein* 'confess'.
homologous /həmolləgəss/ ● adjective **1** having the same relation, relative position, or structure. **2** Biology (of organs) similar in position, structure, and evolutionary origin.
– DERIVATIVES **homologize** (also **homologise**) verb **homology** noun.
– ORIGIN Greek *homologos* 'agreeing, consistent', from *homos* 'same' + *logos* 'ratio, proportion'.
homologue /homməlog/ (US **homolog**) ● noun technical a homologous thing.
homomorphic ● adjective technical of the same or similar form.
– DERIVATIVES **homomorphically** adverb.
– ORIGIN from Greek *morphē* 'form'.
homonym /hommənim/ ● noun each of two or more words having the same spelling or pronunciation but different meanings and origins.
– DERIVATIVES **homonymic** adjective **homonymous** adjective **homonymy** /həmonnimi/ noun.
– ORIGIN Greek *homōnumos* 'having the same name', from *homos* 'same' + *onoma* 'name'.

h

homophobia ● noun an extreme and irrational aversion to homosexuality and homosexuals.
– DERIVATIVES **homophobe** noun **homophobic** adjective.
homophone ● noun each of two or more words having the same pronunciation but different meanings, origins, or spelling (e.g. *new* and *knew*).
– ORIGIN from Greek *phōnē* 'sound, voice'.
homophonic ● adjective **1** Music characterized by the movement of accompanying parts in the same rhythm as the melody. **2** another term for HOMOPHONOUS.
– DERIVATIVES **homophonically** adverb.
homophonous /həmoffənəss/ ● adjective **1** (of music) homophonic. **2** (of a word or words) having the same pronunciation as another but different meaning, origin, or spelling.
– DERIVATIVES **homophony** noun.
Homo sapiens /hōmō sappi-enz/ ● noun the primate species to which modern humans belong.
– ORIGIN Latin, 'wise man'.
homosexual ● adjective feeling or involving sexual attraction to people of one's own sex. ● noun a homosexual person.
– DERIVATIVES **homosexuality** noun **homosexually** adverb.
homunculus /həmungkyooləss/ (also **homuncule** /həmungkyoōl/) ● noun (pl. **homunculi** /həmungkyooli/ or **homuncules**) a very small human or human-like creature.
– ORIGIN Latin, 'little man'.
homy ● adjective variant spelling of HOMEY.
Hon ● abbreviation **1** (in official job titles) Honorary. **2** (in titles of the British nobility, members of parliament, and (in the US) judges) Honourable.
honcho /honchō/ informal ● noun (pl. **honchos**) a leader. ● verb (**honchoes**, **honchoed**) N. Amer. be in charge of.
– ORIGIN Japanese, 'group leader'.
Honduran /hondyoorən/ ● noun a person from Honduras, a country in Central America. ● adjective relating to Honduras.
hone ● verb **1** sharpen with a whetstone. **2** make sharper or more focused or efficient. ● noun a whetstone.
– ORIGIN Old English, 'stone'.
honest ● adjective **1** free of deceit; truthful and sincere. **2** fairly earned: *an honest living*. **3** simple and unpretentious. ● adverb informal genuinely; really.
– PHRASES **make an honest woman of** dated or humorous (of a man) marry (a woman) with whom he is having a sexual relationship.
– ORIGIN Latin *honestus*, from *honor* 'honour'.
honestly ● adverb **1** in an honest way. **2** really (used for emphasis).
honest-to-God informal ● adjective genuine; real. ● adverb genuinely; really.
honest-to-goodness ● adjective genuine and straightforward.
honesty ● noun **1** the quality of being honest. **2** a plant with purple or white flowers and round, flat, translucent seed pods. [ORIGIN so named from its seed pods, translucency symbolizing lack of deceit.]
– PHRASES **honesty is the best policy** proverb there are often practical as well as moral reasons for being honest.
honey ● noun (pl. **honeys**) **1** a sweet, sticky yellowish-brown fluid made by bees from flower nectar. **2** chiefly N. Amer. darling; sweetheart. **3** informal an excellent example: *it's a honey of a movie.*
– ORIGIN Old English.
honeybee ● noun the common bee.
honeycomb ● noun **1** a structure of hexagonal cells of wax, made by bees to store honey and eggs. **2** a structure of linked cavities. ● verb fill with cavities or tunnels.
honeydew ● noun a sweet, sticky substance excreted by aphids.
honeydew melon ● noun a melon of a variety with smooth pale skin and sweet green flesh.
honeyed ● adjective **1** containing or coated with honey. **2** having a warm yellow colour. **3** soothing and soft: *honeyed words.*
honeymoon ● noun **1** a holiday taken by a newly married couple. **2** an initial period of enthusiasm or goodwill. ● verb spend a honeymoon.
– DERIVATIVES **honeymooner** noun.
– ORIGIN originally referring to affection waning like the moon, later denoting the first month after marriage.
honeypot ● noun **1** a container for honey. **2** a place to which many people are attracted.
honeysuckle ● noun a climbing shrub with fragrant yellow and pink flowers.
honeytrap ● noun a stratagem in which an attractive person entices another person into unwittingly revealing information.
hongi /hongi/ ● noun NZ the traditional Maori greeting in which people press their noses together.
– ORIGIN Maori.
honk ● noun **1** the cry of a goose. **2** the sound of a car horn. ● verb **1** make or cause to make a honk.
– ORIGIN imitative.
honky ● noun (pl. **honkies**) N. Amer. informal, derogatory (among black people) a white person.
– ORIGIN of unknown origin.

Thesaurus

– OPPOSITES diversify.
homogenous ● adjective. See HOMOGENEOUS.
homologous ● adjective SIMILAR, comparable, equivalent, like, analogous, corresponding, correspondent, parallel, matching, related, congruent; formal cognate.
– OPPOSITES different.
homosexual ● adjective GAY, lesbian; informal queer, camp, pink, swinging the other way, homo, dykey; Brit. informal bent, poofy.
– OPPOSITES heterosexual.
● noun GAY, lesbian; informal queer, homo, queen, friend of Dorothy, pansy, nancy, dyke, les, lezzy, butch, femme; Brit. informal poof, ponce, woofter.
– OPPOSITES heterosexual.
hone ● verb SHARPEN, whet, strop, grind, file.
– OPPOSITES blunt.
honest ● adjective **1** *an honest man* UPRIGHT, honourable, moral, ethical, principled, righteous, right-minded, respectable; virtuous, good, decent, law-abiding, high-minded, upstanding, incorruptible, truthful, trustworthy, trusty, reliable, conscientious, scrupulous, reputable; informal on the level. **2** *I haven't been honest with you* TRUTHFUL, sincere, candid, frank, open, forthright, straight; straightforward, plain-speaking, matter-of-fact; informal upfront. **3** *an honest mistake* GENUINE, real, authentic, actual, true, bona fide, legitimate, fair and square; informal legit, kosher, on the level, honest-to-goodness.
– OPPOSITES unscrupulous, insincere.
honestly ● adverb **1** *he earned the money honestly* FAIRLY, lawfully, legally, legitimately, honourably, decently, ethically, in good faith, by the book; informal on the level. **2** *we honestly believe this is for the best* SINCERELY, genuinely, truthfully, truly, wholeheartedly; really, actually, to be honest, to tell you the truth, to be frank, in all honesty, in all sincerity; informal Scouts' honour.
honesty ● noun **1** *I can attest to his honesty* INTEGRITY, uprightness, honourableness, honour, morality, morals, ethics, (high) principles, righteousness, right-mindedness; virtue, goodness, probity, high-mindedness, fairness, incorruptibility, truthfulness, trustworthiness, reliability, dependability. **2** *they spoke with honesty about their fears* SINCERITY, candour, frankness, directness, truthfulness, truth, openness, straightforwardness.
honeyed ● adjective SWEET, sugary, saccharine, pleasant,

honky-tonk ● noun informal **1** chiefly N. Amer. a cheap or disreputable bar or club. **2** ragtime piano music.
– ORIGIN of unknown origin.
honor ● noun & verb US spelling of HONOUR.
honorable ● adjective US spelling of HONOURABLE.
honorarium /onnərairiəm/ ● noun (pl. **honorariums** or **honoraria** /onnərairiə/) a payment for professional services which are given nominally without charge.
– ORIGIN Latin, denoting a gift made on being admitted to public office.
honorary ● adjective **1** (of a title or position) conferred as an honour. **2** Brit. (of an office or its holder) unpaid.
honorific ● adjective given as a mark of respect.
honour (US **honor**) ● noun **1** high respect. **2** pride and pleasure from being shown respect. **3** a clear sense of what is morally right. **4** a person or thing that brings credit. **5** a thing conferred as a distinction. **6** (**honours**) a course of degree studies more specialized than for an ordinary pass. **7** (**His, Your,** etc. **Honour**) a title of respect for a circuit judge. **8** dated a woman's chastity. **9** Bridge an ace, king, queen, jack, or ten. ● verb **1** regard with great respect. **2** pay public respect to. **3** fulfil (an obligation) or keep (an agreement). **4** grace; privilege: *the Princess honoured the ball with her presence.*
– PHRASES **do the honours** informal perform a social duty for others, especially serve food or drink. **in honour of** as an expression of respect for. **on one's honour** under a moral obligation. **there's honour among thieves** proverb dishonest people may have certain standards of behaviour which they will respect.
– ORIGIN Latin *honor.*
honourable (US **honorable**) ● adjective **1** bringing or worthy of honour. **2** (**Honourable**) a title given to certain high officials, members of the nobility, and MPs.
– DERIVATIVES **honourably** adverb.
honourable mention ● noun a commendation for a candidate in an examination or competition not awarded a prize.
honours list ● noun a list of people to be awarded honours.
honour system ● noun a system of payment or examinations which relies on the honesty of those concerned.
hooch /hooch/ (also **hootch**) ● noun informal alcoholic liquor, especially inferior or illicit whisky.
– ORIGIN abbreviation of *Hoochinoo*, an Alaskan Indian people who made liquor.
hood[1] ● noun **1** a covering for the head and neck with an opening for the face. **2** Brit. a folding waterproof cover of a vehicle or pram. **3** N. Amer. the bonnet of a vehicle. **4** a protective canopy. ● verb put a hood on or over.
– DERIVATIVES **hooded** adjective.
– ORIGIN Old English, related to HAT.
hood[2] ● noun informal, chiefly N. Amer. a gangster or violent criminal.
– ORIGIN abbreviation of HOODLUM.
hood[3] ● noun informal, chiefly US a neighbourhood.
-hood ● suffix forming nouns: **1** denoting a condition or quality: *womanhood.* **2** denoting a collection or group: *brotherhood.*
– ORIGIN Old English, originally a noun meaning 'person, condition, quality'.
hoodlum /hoodləm/ ● noun a hooligan or gangster.
– ORIGIN of unknown origin.
hoodoo ● noun **1** voodoo. **2** a run or cause of bad luck. ● verb (**hoodoos, hoodooed**) bring bad luck to.
– ORIGIN originally an alternative US word for VOODOO.
hoodwink ● verb deceive or trick.
– ORIGIN originally in the sense 'to blindfold': from HOOD[1] + an obsolete sense of WINK 'close the eyes'.
hooey ● noun informal nonsense.
– ORIGIN of unknown origin.
hoof ● noun (pl. **hoofs** or **hooves**) the horny part of the foot of a horse, cow, etc. ● verb informal **1** kick (a ball) powerfully. **2** (**hoof it**) go on foot. **3** (**hoof it**) dance.
– PHRASES **on the hoof 1** (of livestock) not yet slaughtered. **2** informal without great thought or preparation.
– DERIVATIVES **hoofed** adjective.
– ORIGIN Old English.
hoofer ● noun informal a professional dancer.
hoo-ha ● noun informal a commotion.
– ORIGIN of unknown origin.
hook ● noun **1** a piece of curved metal or other material for catching hold of things or hanging things on. **2** a thing designed to catch people's attention. **3** a catchy passage in a song. **4** a curved cutting instrument. **5** a short swinging punch made with the elbow bent and rigid. ● verb **1** be or become attached or fastened with a hook. **2** (**hook up**) link or be linked to electronic equipment. **3** bend into the shape of a hook. **4** catch with a hook. **5** (**be hooked**) informal be captivated or addicted. **6** (in cricket or golf) hit (the ball) in a curving path.
– PHRASES **by hook or by crook** by any possible means. **get one's hooks into** informal get hold of. **hook, line, and sinker** entirely. **off the hook 1** informal no longer in trouble. **2** (of a telephone receiver) not on its rest. **sling one's hook** Brit. informal leave.
– ORIGIN Old English.
hookah /hookə/ ● noun an oriental tobacco pipe with a long,

h

Thesaurus

flattering, adulatory, unctuous; dulcet, soothing, soft, mellow, mellifluous.
– OPPOSITES harsh.
honorarium ● noun FEE, payment, consideration, allowance; remuneration, pay, expenses, compensation, recompense, reward; *formal* emolument.
honorary ● adjective **1** *an honorary doctorate* TITULAR, nominal, in name only, unofficial, token. **2** *(Brit.) an honorary treasurer* UNPAID, unsalaried, voluntary, volunteer; *N. Amer.* pro bono (publico).
honour ● noun **1** *a man of honour* INTEGRITY, honesty, uprightness, ethics, morals, morality, (high) principles, righteousness, high-mindedness; virtue, goodness, decency, probity, scrupulousness, worth, fairness, justness, trustworthiness, reliability, dependability. **2** *a mark of honour* DISTINCTION, privilege, glory, kudos, cachet, prestige, merit, credit; importance, illustriousness, notability; respect, esteem, approbation. **3** *our honour is at stake* REPUTATION, (good) name, character, repute, image, kudos, standing, stature, status. **4** *he was welcomed with honour* ACCLAIM, acclamation, applause, accolades, tributes, compliments, salutes, bouquets; homage, praise, glory, reverence, adulation, exaltation. **5** *she had the honour of meeting the Queen* PRIVILEGE, pleasure, pride, joy; compliment, favour. **6** *military honours* ACCOLADE, award, reward, prize, decoration, distinction, medal, ribbon, star, laurel; *Military, informal* fruit salad; *Brit. informal* gong. **7** *(dated) she died defending her honour* CHASTITY, virginity, maidenhead, purity, innocence, modesty; *informal* cherry; *archaic* virtue, maidenhood.
– OPPOSITES unscrupulousness, shame.
● verb **1** *we should honour our parents* ESTEEM, respect, admire, defer to, look up to; appreciate, value, cherish; reverence, revere, venerate, worship; *informal* put on a pedestal. **2** *they were honoured at a special ceremony* APPLAUD, acclaim, praise, salute, recognize, celebrate, commemorate, commend, hail, lionize, exalt, eulogize, pay homage to, pay tribute to, sing the praises of; *formal* laud. **3** *he honoured the contract* FULFIL, observe, keep, obey, heed, follow, carry out, discharge, implement, execute, effect; keep to, abide by, adhere to, comply with, conform to, be true to, live up to. **4** *the cheque was not honoured* ACCEPT, take, clear, pass, cash; *Brit.* encash.
– OPPOSITES disgrace, criticize, disobey.
honourable ● adjective **1** *an honourable man* HONEST, moral, ethical, principled, righteous, right-minded; decent, respectable, virtuous, good, upstanding, upright, worthy, noble, fair, just, truthful, trustworthy, trusty, law-abiding, reliable, reputable, dependable. **2** *an honourable career* ILLUSTRIOUS, distinguished, eminent, great, glorious, prestigious, noble, creditable.
– OPPOSITES crooked, deplorable.
hoodlum ● noun HOOLIGAN, thug, lout, delinquent, tearaway, vandal, ruffian; gangster, mobster, criminal, Mafioso; *Austral.* larrikin; *informal* tough, bruiser, roughneck, heavy, hit man; *Brit. informal* yob, yobbo, bovver boy, lager lout; *N. Amer. informal* hood.
hoodoo ● noun WITCHCRAFT, magic, black magic, sorcery, wizardry, devilry, voodoo, necromancy; *N. Amer.* mojo.
hoodwink ● verb DECEIVE, trick, dupe, outwit, fool, delude, cheat, take in, hoax, mislead, lead on, defraud, double-cross, swindle, gull; *informal* con, bamboozle, do, have, sting, gyp, diddle, shaft, rip off, lead up the garden path, pull a fast one on, put one over on, take for a ride, pull the wool over someone's eyes; *N. Amer. informal* sucker, snooker; *Austral. informal* pull a swifty on; *poetic/literary* cozen.
hoof ● noun trotter, foot; *Zoology* ungula.
hook ● noun **1** *she hung her jacket on the hook* PEG. **2** *the dress has six hooks* FASTENER, fastening, catch, clasp, hasp, clip, pin. **3** *I had a fish on the end of my hook* FISH-HOOK, barb, snare. **4** *a right hook*

flexible tube which draws the smoke through water in a bowl.
– ORIGIN Urdu, from Arabic, 'casket, jar'.
hook and eye ● noun a small metal hook and loop used to fasten a garment.
hooked ● adjective having or resembling a hook or hooks.
hooker ● noun **1** Rugby the player in the middle of the front row of the scrum. **2** informal, chiefly N. Amer. a prostitute.
hookey (also **hooky**) ● noun (in phrase **play hookey**) N. Amer. informal play truant.
– ORIGIN of unknown origin.
hook nose ● noun an aquiline nose.
hook-up ● noun a connection to mains electricity, a communications system, etc.
hookworm ● noun a parasitic worm which inhabits the intestines and feeds by attaching itself with hook-like mouthparts.
hooligan ● noun a violent young troublemaker.
– DERIVATIVES **hooliganism** noun.
– ORIGIN possibly from *Hooligan*, the surname of a fictional rowdy Irish family in a music-hall song of the 1890s.
hoon Austral./NZ informal ● noun a lout. ● verb behave like a lout.
– ORIGIN of unknown origin.
hoop ● noun **1** a rigid circular band. **2** a large ring used as a toy or for circus performers to jump through. **3** chiefly Brit. a metal arch through which the balls are hit in croquet. **4** a contrasting horizontal band on a sports shirt or cap. ● verb bind or encircle with hoops.
– PHRASES **put someone** (or **go**) **through hoops** make someone undergo (or be made to undergo) a gruelling test.
– DERIVATIVES **hooped** adjective.
– ORIGIN Old English.
hoopla /hōōplaa/ ● noun **1** Brit. a game in which rings are thrown in an attempt to encircle a prize. **2** informal unnecessary fuss.
hoopoe /hōōpōō/ ● noun a salmon-pink bird with a long downcurved bill, a large crest, and black-and-white wings and tail.
– ORIGIN Latin *upupa*, imitative of the bird's call.
hooray ● exclamation **1** hurrah. **2** Austral./NZ goodbye.
Hooray Henry ● noun (pl. **Hooray Henrys** or **Hooray Henries**) Brit. informal a lively but ineffectual young upper-class man.
hoot ● noun **1** a low musical sound made by owls or a similar sound made by a horn, siren, etc. **2** a shout expressing scorn or disapproval. **3** an outburst of laughter. **4** (**a hoot**) informal an amusing person or thing. ● verb make or cause to make a hoot.
– PHRASES **not care** (or **give**) **a hoot** (or **two hoots**) informal not care at all.
– ORIGIN perhaps imitative.
hootch ● noun variant spelling of HOOCH.
hootenanny /hōōt'nanni/ ● noun (pl. **hootenannies**) informal, chiefly US an informal gathering with folk music.
– ORIGIN originally denoting a gadget: of unknown origin.
hooter ● noun **1** Brit. a siren, steam whistle, or horn. **2** informal a person's nose.
Hoover Brit. ● noun trademark a vacuum cleaner. ● verb (**hoover**) clean with a vacuum cleaner.
– ORIGIN named after the American industrialist William H. *Hoover* (1849–1942).
hooves plural of HOOF.
hop[1] ● verb (**hopped**, **hopping**) **1** move by jumping on one foot. **2** (of a bird or animal) move by jumping with two or all feet at once. **3** jump over or on to. **4** informal move or go quickly. **5** (**hop it**) Brit. informal go away. ● noun **1** a hopping movement. **2** a short journey or distance.
– PHRASES **hopping mad** informal extremely angry. **hop, skip** (or **step**), **and jump 1** old-fashioned term for TRIPLE JUMP. **2** informal a short distance. **on the hop** Brit. informal **1** unprepared. **2** busy.
– ORIGIN Old English.
hop[2] ● noun **1** a climbing plant whose dried flowers (**hops**) are used in brewing to give a bitter flavour. **2** (**hops**) Austral./NZ informal beer. ● verb (**hopped**, **hopping**) flavour with hops.
– DERIVATIVES **hoppy** adjective.
– ORIGIN from Low German or Dutch.
hope ● noun **1** a feeling of expectation and desire for something to happen. **2** a person or thing that gives cause for hope. ● verb **1** expect and want something to happen. **2** intend if possible to do something.
– PHRASES **hope against hope** cling to a mere possibility. **hope springs eternal in the human breast** proverb it is human nature to always find fresh cause for optimism. **not a** (or **some**) **hope** informal no chance at all.
– DERIVATIVES **hoper** noun.
– ORIGIN Old English.
hope chest ● noun N. Amer. a chest in which household linen is stored by a woman in preparation for marriage.
hopeful ● adjective feeling or inspiring hope. ● noun a person likely or hoping to succeed.
– DERIVATIVES **hopefulness** noun.
hopefully ● adverb **1** in a hopeful manner. **2** it is to be hoped

Thesaurus

to the chin PUNCH, blow, hit, cuff, thump, smack; *Scottish & N. English* skelp; *informal* belt, bop, biff, sock, clout, whack, wallop, slug; *N. Amer. informal* boff.
● verb **1** *they hooked baskets onto the ladder* ATTACH, hitch, fasten, fix, secure, clasp. **2** *he hooked his thumbs in his belt* CURL, bend, crook, loop, curve. **3** *he hooked a 24 lb pike* CATCH, land, net, take, bag, snare, trap.
– PHRASES **by hook or by crook** BY ANY MEANS, somehow (or other), no matter how, in one way or another, by fair means or foul. **hook, line, and sinker** COMPLETELY, totally, utterly, entirely, wholly, absolutely, through and through, one hundred per cent, {lock, stock, and barrel}. **off the hook** *(informal)* OUT OF TROUBLE, in the clear, free; acquitted, cleared, reprieved, exonerated, absolved; *informal* let off.
hooked ● adjective **1** *a hooked nose* CURVED, hook-shaped, hook-like, aquiline, bent, angular; *Biology* falcate, falciform, uncinate. **2** *(informal) they are hooked on cocaine* ADDICTED TO, dependent on; *informal* using; *N. Amer. informal* have a jones for. **3** *(informal) he is hooked on crosswords* KEEN ON, enthusiastic about, addicted to, obsessed with, fixated on, fanatical about; *informal* mad about, crazy about, wild about, nuts about; *Brit. informal* potty about.
– OPPOSITES straight.
hooligan ● noun HOODLUM, thug, lout, delinquent, tearaway, vandal, ruffian, troublemaker; *Austral.* larrikin; *informal* tough, rough, bruiser, roughneck; *Brit. informal* yob, yobbo, bovver boy, lager lout; *Scottish informal* ned.
hoop ● noun RING, band, circle, circlet, loop; *technical* annulus.
hoot ● noun **1** *the hoot of an owl* SCREECH, shriek, call, cry; tu-whit tu-whoo. **2** *the hoot of a horn* BEEP, honk, toot, blast, blare. **3** *hoots of derision* SHOUT, yell, cry, howl, shriek, whoop, whistle; boo, hiss, jeer, catcall. **4** *(informal) your mum's a real hoot* AMUSING PERSON, character, clown; *informal* scream, laugh, card, case, one, riot, giggle, barrel of laughs; *informal, dated* caution.
● verb **1** *an owl hooted* SCREECH, shriek, cry, call; tu-whit tu-whoo. **2** *a car horn hooted* BEEP, honk, toot, blare, blast, sound. **3** *they hooted in disgust* SHOUT, yell, cry, howl, shriek, whistle; boo, hiss, jeer, catcall.
– PHRASES **give a hoot** *(informal)* CARE, be concerned, mind, be interested, be bothered, get worked up; *informal* give a damn, give a rap, give a monkey's.
hop ● verb **1** *he hopped along the road* JUMP, bound, spring, bounce, skip, jig, leap; prance, dance, frolic, gambol. **2** *(informal) she hopped over the Atlantic* GO, dash; travel; *informal* pop, whip; *Brit. informal* nip.
● noun **1** *the rabbit had a hop around* JUMP, bound, bounce, prance, leap, spring, gambol. **2** *a short hop by taxi* JOURNEY, distance, ride, drive, run, trip; flight. **3** *(informal) come to the hop on Saturday* DANCE, social, party, disco; *informal* bash, bop, shindig, do; *Brit. informal* rave-up, knees-up.
– PHRASES **on the hop** *(Brit. informal)* **1** *he was caught on the hop* UNPREPARED, unready, off guard, unawares, by surprise, with one's defences down; *informal* napping; *Brit. informal* with one's trousers down. **2** *we were always kept on the hop* BUSY, occupied, employed, working, at work, on the job; rushed off one's feet; *informal* on the go.
hope ● noun **1** *I had high hopes* ASPIRATION, desire, wish, expectation, ambition, aim, plan; dream, daydream, pipe dream. **2** *a life filled with hope* HOPEFULNESS, optimism, expectation, expectancy; confidence, faith, trust, belief, conviction, assurance; promise.
– OPPOSITES pessimism.
● verb **1** *he's hoping for a medal* EXPECT, anticipate, look for, be hopeful of, pin one's hopes on, want; wish for, dream of. **2** *we're hoping to address the issue* AIM, intend, be looking, have the intention, have in mind, plan, aspire.
hopeful ● adjective **1** *he remained hopeful* OPTIMISTIC, full of hope, confident, positive, buoyant, sanguine, bullish, cheerful; *informal* upbeat. **2** *hopeful signs* PROMISING, encouraging, heartening, re-

that.

– USAGE The traditional sense of **hopefully** is 'in a hopeful manner'. In the 20th century a new use arose, with the meaning 'it is to be hoped that'. Although this newer use is now very much the dominant one, it is regarded by some people as incorrect.

hopeless ● adjective **1** feeling or causing despair. **2** inadequate; incompetent.
– DERIVATIVES **hopelessly** adverb **hopelessness** noun.

Hopi /hōpi/ ● noun (pl. same or **Hopis**) **1** a member of an American Indian people living chiefly in NE Arizona. **2** the language of this people.
– ORIGIN Hopi.

hoplite /hoplīt/ ● noun a heavily armed foot soldier of ancient Greece.
– ORIGIN Greek *hoplitēs*, from *hoplon* 'weapon'.

hopper ● noun **1** a tapering container that discharges its contents at the bottom. **2** a person or thing that hops.

hopsack ● noun a coarse clothing fabric of a loose weave.

hopscotch ● noun a children's game of hopping into and over squares marked on the ground to retrieve a marker.
– ORIGIN from HOP[1] + SCOTCH in the sense 'put and end to, stop', reflecting the pattern of hopping and stopping characteristic of the game.

horde ● noun **1** chiefly derogatory a large group of people. **2** an army or tribe of nomadic warriors.
– ORIGIN Polish *horda*, from Turkish *ordu* 'royal camp'.

horehound /horhownd/ ● noun a plant of the mint family, traditionally used as a medicinal herb.
– ORIGIN Old English, related to HOAR.

horizon ● noun **1** the line at which the earth's surface and the sky appear to meet. **2** the limit of a person's mental perception, experience, or interest. **3** Geology & Archaeology a layer or level with particular characteristics or representing a particular period.
– PHRASES **on the horizon** imminent.
– ORIGIN from Greek *horizōn* 'limiting'.

horizontal ● adjective parallel to the plane of the horizon; at right angles to the vertical. ● noun a horizontal line, plane or structure.
– DERIVATIVES **horizontality** noun **horizontally** adverb.

hormone ● noun a substance produced by a living thing and transported in tissue fluids to specific cells or tissues to stimulate them into action.
– DERIVATIVES **hormonal** adjective.
– ORIGIN Greek *hormōn* 'setting in motion'.

hormone replacement therapy ● noun treatment with certain hormones to alleviate menopausal symptoms or osteoporosis.

horn ● noun **1** a hard bony outgrowth, often curved and pointed, found in pairs on the heads of cattle, sheep, and other animals. **2** the substance of which horns are composed. **3** a wind instrument, now usually of brass, conical in shape or wound into a spiral. **4** an instrument sounding a warning or other signal. **5** a pointed projection or extremity. ● verb **1** butt or gore with the horns. **2** (**horn in**) informal interfere.
– PHRASES **blow** (or **toot**) **one's own horn** N. Amer. informal boast about oneself or one's achievements. **draw** (or **pull**) **in one's horns** become less assertive or ambitious. **on the horns of a dilemma** faced with a decision involving equally unfavourable alternatives.
– DERIVATIVES **horned** adjective.
– ORIGIN Old English.

hornbeam ● noun a deciduous tree with hard pale wood.
– ORIGIN so named because of the tree's hard wood.

hornbill ● noun a tropical bird with a horn-like structure on its large curved bill.

hornblende /hornblend/ ● noun a dark brown, black, or green mineral present in many rocks.
– ORIGIN German, from *Horn* 'horn' + *Blende*, denoting a zinc ore.

hornet ● noun a kind of large wasp, typically red and yellow or red and black.
– PHRASES **stir up a hornets' nest** provoke opposition or difficulties.
– ORIGIN Old English.

horn of plenty ● noun a cornucopia.

hornpipe ● noun **1** a lively solo dance traditionally performed by sailors. **2** a piece of music for such a dance.
– ORIGIN originally denoting a wind instrument made of horn, played to accompany dancing: from HORN + PIPE.

horn-rimmed ● adjective (of glasses) having rims made of horn or a similar substance.

hornswoggle /hornswogg'l/ ● verb N. Amer. informal outwit by cheating or deception.
– ORIGIN of unknown origin.

horny ● adjective (**hornier**, **horniest**) **1** of or like horn. **2** hard and rough. **3** informal sexually aroused or arousing.
– DERIVATIVES **horniness** noun.

horology /hərolləji/ ● noun **1** the study and measurement of time. **2** the art of making clocks and watches.
– DERIVATIVES **horological** adjective **horologist** noun.
– ORIGIN from Greek *hōra* 'time'.

horoscope ● noun a forecast of a person's future based on the relative positions of the stars and planets at the time of their birth.
– ORIGIN Greek *hōroskopos*, from *hōra* 'time' + *skopos* 'observer'.

horrendous ● adjective extremely unpleasant or horrifying.
– DERIVATIVES **horrendously** adverb.
– ORIGIN Latin *horrendus*, from *horrere* (see HORROR).

horrible ● adjective **1** causing or likely to cause horror. **2** informal very unpleasant.
– DERIVATIVES **horribly** adverb.

horrid ● adjective **1** causing horror. **2** informal very unpleasant.
– DERIVATIVES **horridly** adverb **horridness** noun.

horrific ● adjective causing horror.

h

Thesaurus

assuring, auspicious, favourable, optimistic, propitious, bright, rosy.

hopefully ● adverb **1** *he rode on hopefully* OPTIMISTICALLY, full of hope, confidently, buoyantly, sanguinely; expectantly. **2** *hopefully it should finish soon* ALL BEING WELL, if all goes well, God willing, with luck; most likely, probably; conceivably, feasibly; *informal* touch wood, fingers crossed.

hopeless ● adjective **1** *her hopeless appeal* DESPAIRING, desperate, wretched, forlorn, pessimistic, defeatist, resigned; dejected, downhearted, despondent, demoralized. **2** *a hopeless case* IRREMEDIABLE, beyond hope, lost, beyond repair, irreparable, irreversible; past cure, incurable; impossible, no-win, futile, forlorn, unworkable, impracticable; *archaic* bootless. **3** *Joseph was hopeless at maths* BAD, poor, awful, terrible, dreadful, appalling, atrocious; inferior, incompetent, unskilled; *informal* pathetic, useless, lousy, rotten; *Brit. informal* duff, rubbish.

hopelessly ● adverb **1** *she began to cry hopelessly* DESPAIRINGLY, in despair, in distress, desperately; dejectedly, downheartedly, despondently, wretchedly, miserably, forlornly. **2** *she was hopelessly lost* UTTERLY, completely, irretrievably, impossibly; extremely, very, desperately, totally; *informal* terribly, dreadfully.

horde ● noun CROWD, mob, pack, gang, troop, army, swarm, mass; throng, multitude, host, band, flock; *informal* crew, tribe, load.

horizon ● noun **1** *the sun rose above the horizon* SKYLINE. **2** *she wanted to broaden her horizons* OUTLOOK, perspective, perception; range of experience, scope, ambit, orbit.
– PHRASES **on the horizon** IMMINENT, impending, close, near, approaching, coming, forthcoming, in prospect, at hand, on the way, about to happen, upon us, in the offing, in the pipeline, in the air, just around the corner; brewing, looming, threatening, menacing; *informal* on the cards.

horizontal ● adjective **1** *a horizontal surface* level, flat, plane, smooth, even; straight, parallel. **2** *she was stretched horizontal on a sunbed* FLAT, supine, prone, prostrate.
– OPPOSITES vertical.

horny ● adjective *(informal)* (SEXUALLY) AROUSED, excited, stimulated, titillated, inflamed; *informal* turned on, hot, sexed up; *Brit. informal* randy.

horrendous ● adjective. See HORRIBLE sense 1.

horrible ● adjective **1** *a horrible murder* DREADFUL, awful, terrible, shocking, appalling, horrifying, horrific, horrendous, grisly, ghastly, gruesome, harrowing, heinous, vile, unspeakable; nightmarish, macabre, spine-chilling; loathsome, monstrous, abhorrent, hateful, execrable, abominable, atrocious, sickening. **2** *(informal) a horrible little man* NASTY, horrid, disagreeable, unpleasant, awful, dreadful, terrible, appalling, horrendous, foul, repulsive, repellent, ghastly; obnoxious, hateful, odious, objectionable, insufferable, vile, loathsome, abhorrent; *informal* frightful, God-awful; *Brit. informal* beastly.
– OPPOSITES pleasant, agreeable.

– DERIVATIVES **horrifically** adverb.
horrify ● verb (**horrifies, horrified**) fill with horror.
– DERIVATIVES **horrified** adjective **horrifying** adjective.
– ORIGIN Latin *horrificare*.
horror ● noun **1** an intense feeling of fear, shock, or disgust. **2** a thing causing such a feeling. **3** intense dismay. **4** informal a bad or mischievous person, especially a child.
– ORIGIN Latin, from *horrere* 'shudder, (of hair) stand on end'.
hors de combat /or də KONbaa/ ● adjective out of action due to injury or damage.
– ORIGIN French, 'out of the fight'.
hors d'oeuvre /or dörv/ ● noun (pl. same or **hors d'oeuvres** pronunc. same or /or **dörvz**/) a savoury appetizer.
– ORIGIN French, 'outside the work'.
horse ● noun **1** a large four-legged mammal with a flowing mane and tail, used for riding and for pulling heavy loads. **2** an adult male horse, as opposed to a mare or colt. **3** (treated as sing. or pl.) cavalry. **4** a frame or structure on which something is mounted or supported: *a clothes horse.* ● verb **1** (**horse around/about**) informal fool about.
– PHRASES **don't change horses in midstream** proverb choose a sensible moment to change your mind. **from the horse's mouth** from an authoritative source. **hold one's horses** informal wait a moment. **horses for courses** Brit. proverb different people are suited to different things or situations. **you can lead a horse to water but you can't make him drink** proverb you can give someone an opportunity, but you can't force them to take it.
– ORIGIN Old English.
horseback ● noun (in phrase **on horseback**) & adjective mounted on a horse.
horsebox ● noun Brit. a motorized vehicle or a trailer for transporting one or more horses.
horse chestnut ● noun **1** a large deciduous tree producing nuts (conkers) enclosed in a spiny case. **2** a conker.
– ORIGIN horse chestnuts are said to have been an Eastern remedy for chest diseases in horses.
horseflesh ● noun horses considered collectively.
horsefly ● noun a large fly that inflicts painful bites on horses and other large mammals.
Horse Guards ● plural noun the mounted squadrons provided from the Household Cavalry for ceremonial duties.
horsehair ● noun hair from the mane or tail of a horse, used in furniture for padding.
horse latitudes ● plural noun a belt of calm air and sea occurring in both the northern and southern hemispheres between the trade winds and the westerlies.
– ORIGIN origin uncertain.
horse laugh ● noun a loud, coarse laugh.
horseman (or **horsewoman**) ● noun a rider on horseback, especially a skilled one.
– DERIVATIVES **horsemanship** noun.
horseplay ● noun rough, boisterous play.
horsepower ● noun (pl. same) an imperial unit of power equal to 550 foot-pounds per second (about 750 watts), especially as a measurement of engine power.
horseradish ● noun a plant grown for its pungent root which is often made into a sauce.
horse sense ● noun informal common sense.
horseshoe ● noun an iron shoe for a horse in the form of an extended circular arc.
horsetail ● noun a flowerless plant with a jointed stem carrying whorls of narrow leaves.
horse-trading ● noun informal hard and shrewd bargaining.
horsewhip ● noun a long whip used for driving and controlling horses. ● verb (**horsewhipped, horsewhipping**) beat with such a whip.
horsey (also **horsy**) ● adjective **1** of or resembling a horse. **2** devoted to horses or horse racing.
horst /horst/ ● noun Geology a raised elongated block of the earth's crust lying between two faults.
– ORIGIN German, 'heap'.
hortatory /hortətəri/ ● adjective formal intended to exhort someone to do something.
– ORIGIN Latin *hortatorius*, from *hortari* 'exhort'.
horticulture /hortikulchər/ ● noun the art or practice of garden cultivation and management.
– DERIVATIVES **horticultural** adjective **horticulturalist** noun **horticulturist** noun.
– ORIGIN from Latin *hortus* 'garden'.
hosanna (also **hosannah**) ● noun & exclamation a biblical cry of praise or joy.
– ORIGIN Greek, from a Hebrew phrase meaning 'save, we pray'.
hose ● noun **1** (Brit. also **hosepipe**) a flexible tube conveying water. **2** (treated as pl.) stockings, socks, and tights. ● verb water or spray with a hose.
– ORIGIN Old English.
hosier /hōziər/ ● noun a manufacturer or seller of hosiery.
hosiery ● noun stockings, socks, and tights collectively.
hospice ● noun **1** a home providing care for the sick or terminally ill. **2** archaic a lodging for travellers, especially one run by a religious order.
– ORIGIN French, from Latin *hospitium*, from *hospes* 'host'.
hospitable ● adjective **1** showing or inclined to show hospitality. **2** (of an environment) pleasant and favourable for living in.
– DERIVATIVES **hospitably** adverb.
hospital ● noun **1** an institution providing medical and surgical treatment and nursing care for sick or injured people. **2** historical a hospice, especially one run by the Knights Hospitallers.
– ORIGIN Latin *hospitale*, from *hospes* 'host, guest'.

Thesaurus

horrid ● adjective **1** *horrid apparitions.* See HORRIBLE sense 1. **2** *(informal) the teachers were horrid.* See HORRIBLE sense 2.
horrific ● adjective DREADFUL, horrendous, horrible, frightful, awful, terrible, atrocious; horrifying, shocking, appalling, harrowing, gruesome; hideous, grisly, ghastly, unspeakable, monstrous, nightmarish, sickening.
horrify ● verb **1** *she horrified us with ghastly tales* FRIGHTEN, scare, terrify, petrify, alarm, panic, terrorize, fill with fear, scare someone out of their wits, frighten the living daylights out of, make someone's hair stand on end, make someone's blood run cold; *informal* scare the pants off; *Brit. informal* put the wind up; *N. Amer. informal* spook; *archaic* affright. **2** *he was horrified by her remarks* SHOCK, appal, outrage, scandalize, offend; disgust, revolt, nauseate, sicken.
horror ● noun **1** *children screamed in horror* TERROR, fear, fright, alarm, panic; dread, trepidation. **2** *to her horror she found herself alone* DISMAY, consternation, perturbation, alarm, distress; disgust, outrage, shock. **3** *the horror of the tragedy* AWFULNESS, frightfulness, savagery, barbarity, hideousness; atrocity, outrage. **4** *(informal) he's a little horror* RASCAL, devil, imp, monkey; *informal* terror, scamp, scallywag, tyke; *Brit. informal* perisher; *N. Amer. informal* varmint.
– OPPOSITES delight, satisfaction.
– PHRASES **have a horror of** HATE, detest, loathe, abhor; *formal* abominate.
horror-struck, horror-stricken ● adjective HORRIFIED, terrified, petrified, frightened, afraid, fearful, scared, panic-stricken, scared/frightened to death, scared witless; *informal* scared stiff.
horse ● noun MOUNT, charger, cob, nag, hack; pony, foal, yearling, colt, stallion, gelding, mare, filly; *N. Amer.* bronco; *Austral./NZ* moke, yarraman; *informal* gee-gee; *archaic* steed.
– RELATED TERMS equine.
– PHRASES **horse around/about** *(informal)* FOOL AROUND/ABOUT, play the fool, act the clown, clown about/around, monkey about/around; *informal* mess about/around, lark about/around; *Brit. informal* muck about/around; *dated* play the giddy goat.
horseman, horsewoman ● noun RIDER, equestrian, jockey; cavalryman, trooper; *historical* hussar, dragoon; *archaic* cavalier.
horseplay ● noun TOMFOOLERY, fooling around, foolish behaviour, clowning, buffoonery; pranks, antics, high jinks; *informal* shenanigans, monkey business; *Brit. informal* monkey tricks.
horse sense ● noun *(informal).* See COMMON SENSE.
horticulture ● noun GARDENING, floriculture, arboriculture, agriculture, cultivation.
hosanna ● noun SHOUT OF PRAISE, alleluia, hurrah, hurray, cheer, paean; *formal* laudation.
hose ● noun **1** *a garden hose* PIPE, piping, tube, tubing, duct, outlet, pipeline, siphon. **2** *her hose had laddered.* See HOSIERY.
hosiery ● noun STOCKINGS, tights, stay-ups, nylons, hose; socks; *N. Amer.* pantyhose.
hospitable ● adjective WELCOMING, friendly, congenial, genial, sociable, convivial, cordial; gracious, well disposed, amenable, helpful, obliging, accommodating, neighbourly, warm, kind, generous, bountiful.

hospital corners ● plural noun overlapping folds used to tuck sheets neatly and securely under the mattress at the corners.
hospitality ● noun the friendly and generous treatment of guests or strangers.
hospitalize (also **hospitalise**) ● verb admit or cause (someone) to be admitted to hospital for treatment.
– DERIVATIVES **hospitalization** noun.
hospitaller (US **hospitaler**) ● noun a member of a charitable religious order.
hospital trust ● noun a UK National Health Service hospital which has opted to withdraw from local authority control and be managed by a trust instead.
host[1] ● noun **1** a person who receives or entertains guests. **2** the presenter of a television or radio programme. **3** a person, place, or organization that holds and organizes an event to which others are invited. **4** often humorous the landlord or landlady of a pub: *mine host raised his glass.* **5** Biology an animal or plant on or in which a parasite lives. **6** the recipient of transplanted tissue or a transplanted organ. ● verb act as host at (an event) or for (a television or radio programme).
– ORIGIN Old French *hoste*, from Latin *hospes* 'host, guest'.
host[2] ● noun (**a host/hosts of**) a large number of.
– ORIGIN Latin *hostis* 'stranger, enemy', later 'army'.
host[3] ● noun (**the Host**) the bread consecrated in the Eucharist.
– ORIGIN Latin *hostia* 'victim'.
hosta /hɒstə/ ● noun a shade-tolerant plant with ornamental foliage.
– ORIGIN named after the Austrian physician Nicolaus T. *Host* (1761–1834).
hostage ● noun a person seized or held in order to induce others to comply with a demand or condition.
– PHRASES **a hostage to fortune** an act or remark regarded as unwise because it invites trouble in the future.
– ORIGIN Old French, from Latin *obsidatus* 'the state of being a hostage', from *obses* 'hostage'.
hostel ● noun an establishment which provides cheap food and lodging for a specific group of people.
– ORIGIN Old French, from Latin *hospitale* (see HOSPITAL).
hostelling (US **hosteling**) ● noun the practice of staying in youth hostels when travelling.
– DERIVATIVES **hosteller** noun.
hostelry ● noun (pl. **hostelries**) archaic or humorous an inn or pub.
– ORIGIN Old French *hostelerie* from *hostelier* 'innkeeper'.
hostess ● noun **1** a female host. **2** a woman employed to welcome and entertain customers at a nightclub or bar. **3** a stewardess on an aircraft, train, etc.
hostile ● adjective **1** antagonistic; opposed. **2** of or belonging to a military enemy. **3** (of a takeover bid) opposed by the company to be bought.
– DERIVATIVES **hostilely** adverb **hostility** noun (pl. **hostilities**).
– ORIGIN Latin *hostilis*, from *hostis* 'stranger, enemy'.
hot ● adjective (**hotter**, **hottest**) **1** having a high temperature. **2** feeling or producing an uncomfortable sensation of heat. **3** feeling or showing intense excitement, anger, lust, or other emotion. **4** informal currently popular, fashionable, or interesting. **5** informal (of goods) stolen and difficult to dispose of because easily identifiable. **6** (often **hot on**) informal very knowledgeable or skilful. **7** (**hot on**) informal strict about. ● verb (**hotted**, **hotting**) (**hot up**) Brit. informal become or make more intense or exciting.
– PHRASES **go hot and cold** experience a sudden feeling of fear or shock. **have the hots for** informal be sexually attracted to. **hot under the collar** informal angry or resentful. **in hot water** informal in trouble or disgrace. **make it** (or **things**) **hot for** informal stir up trouble for.
– DERIVATIVES **hotly** adverb **hotness** noun.
– ORIGIN Old English.
hot air ● noun informal empty or boastful talk.
hotbed ● noun **1** a bed of earth heated by fermenting manure, for raising or forcing plants. **2** an environment promoting the growth of an activity or trend.
hot-blooded ● adjective lustful; passionate.
hot button ● noun N. Amer. informal an issue that is highly charged emotionally or politically.
hotchpotch (N. Amer. **hodgepodge**) ● noun a confused mixture.
– ORIGIN Old French *hochepot*, from *hocher* 'to shake' + *pot* 'pot'.
hot cross bun ● noun a bun marked with a cross, traditionally eaten on Good Friday.
hot-desking ● noun the allocation of desks to office workers when they are required or on a rota system.
hot dog ● noun a hot sausage served in a long, soft roll. ● exclam-

h

Thesaurus

hospital ● noun INFIRMARY, sanatorium, hospice, medical centre, health centre, clinic; *Brit.* cottage hospital; *Military* field hospital.
hospitality ● noun **1** *he is renowned for his hospitality* FRIENDLINESS, hospitableness, warm reception, helpfulness, neighbourliness, warmth, kindness, congeniality, geniality, cordiality, amenability, generosity. **2** *corporate hospitality* entertainment; catering, food.
host[1] ● noun **1** *the host greeted the guests* PARTY-GIVER, hostess, entertainer. **2** *the host of a TV series* PRESENTER, compère, anchor, anchorman, anchorwoman, announcer.
– OPPOSITES guest.
● verb **1** *the Queen hosted a dinner* GIVE, have, hold, throw, put on, provide, arrange, organize. **2** *the show is hosted by Angus* PRESENT, introduce, compère, front, anchor.
host[2] ● noun **1** *a host of memories* MULTITUDE, lot, abundance, wealth, profusion; *informal* load, heap, mass, pile, ton; *Brit. informal* shedload; *poetic/literary* myriad. **2** *a host of film stars* CROWD, throng, flock, herd, swarm, horde, mob, army, legion; assemblage, gathering.
hostage ● noun CAPTIVE, prisoner, detainee, internee.
hostel ● noun CHEAP HOTEL, YMCA, YWCA, bed and breakfast, B&B, boarding house, guest house, pension.
hostile ● adjective **1** *a hostile attack* UNFRIENDLY, unkind, bitter, unsympathetic, malicious, vicious, rancorous, venomous; antagonistic, aggressive, confrontational, belligerent, truculent. **2** *hostile climatic conditions* UNFAVOURABLE, adverse, bad, harsh, grim, hard, tough, inhospitable, forbidding. **3** *they are hostile to the idea* OPPOSED, averse, antagonistic, ill-disposed, unsympathetic, antipathetic; opposing, against; *informal* anti, down on.
– OPPOSITES friendly, favourable.
hostility ● noun **1** *he glared at her with hostility* ANTAGONISM, unfriendliness, malevolence, malice, unkindness, rancour, venom, hatred; aggression, belligerence. **2** *their hostility to the present regime* OPPOSITION, antagonism, animosity, antipathy, ill will, ill feeling, resentment, aversion, enmity. **3** *a cessation of hostilities* FIGHTING, (armed) conflict, combat, warfare, war, bloodshed, violence.
hot ● adjective **1** *hot food* HEATED, piping (hot), sizzling, steaming, roasting, boiling (hot), searing, scorching, scalding, red-hot. **2** *a hot day* VERY WARM, balmy, summery, tropical, scorching, searing, blistering; sweltering, torrid, sultry, humid, muggy, close; *informal* boiling, baking, roasting. **3** *she felt very hot* FEVERISH, fevered, febrile; burning, flushed. **4** *a hot chilli* SPICY, spiced, highly seasoned, peppery, fiery, strong; piquant, pungent, aromatic. **5** *the competition was too hot* FIERCE, intense, keen, competitive, cutthroat, dog-eat-dog, ruthless, aggressive, strong. **6** *(informal) the hottest story in Fleet Street* NEW, fresh, recent, late, up to date, up to the minute; just out, hot off the press. **7** *(informal) this band is hot* POPULAR, in demand, sought-after, in favour; fashionable, in vogue, all the rage; *informal* big, in, now, hip, trendy, cool. **8** *(informal) she is hot on local history* KNOWLEDGEABLE ABOUT, well informed about, au fait with, up on, well versed in, au courant with; *informal* clued up about, genned up about. **9** *(informal) hot goods* STOLEN, illegally obtained, illegal, illicit, unlawful; smuggled, bootleg, contraband; *Brit. informal* dodgy.
– OPPOSITES cold, chilly, mild, dispassionate, weak, old, lawful.
– PHRASES **blow hot and cold** VACILLATE, dither, shilly-shally, waver, be indecisive, change one's mind, be undecided, be uncertain, be unsure; *Brit.* haver, hum and haw; *Scottish* swither. **hot on the heels of** CLOSE BEHIND, directly after, right after, straight after, hard on the heels of, following closely. **hot under the collar** *(informal)*. See ANGRY sense 1. **make it/things hot for someone** *(informal)* HARASS, hound, plague, badger, harry; bully, intimidate, pick on, persecute, victimize, terrorize; *N. Amer.* devil; *informal* hassle, give someone a hard time, get on someone's back.
hot air ● noun *(informal)* NONSENSE, rubbish, garbage, empty talk, wind, blather, claptrap, drivel, balderdash, gibberish; pomposity, bombast; *informal* guff, bosh, hogwash, poppycock, bilge, twaddle; *Brit. informal* cobblers, codswallop, tosh; *N. Amer. informal* flapdoodle.
hotbed ● noun *a hotbed of crime* BREEDING GROUND, den, cradle, nest.
hot-blooded ● adjective PASSIONATE, amorous, amatory, ardent, lustful, libidinous, lecherous, sexy; *informal* horny, randy.
– OPPOSITES cold.
hotchpotch ● noun MIXTURE, mix, mixed bag, assortment, random

ation N. Amer. informal used to express enthusiastic approval. ● verb (hotdog) (hotdogged, hotdogging) N. Amer. informal perform stunts.

hotel ● noun an establishment providing accommodation and meals for travellers and tourists.
– ORIGIN French *hôtel*, from Old French *hostel* (see HOSTEL).

hotelier ● noun a person who owns or manages a hotel.

hot flush (also **hot flash**) ● noun a sudden feeling of feverish heat, often as a symptom of the menopause.

hotfoot ● adverb in eager haste. ● verb (**hotfoot it**) informal hurry eagerly.

hothead ● noun an impetuous or quick-tempered person.
– DERIVATIVES **hot-headed** adjective.

hothouse ● noun 1 a heated greenhouse. 2 an environment that encourages rapid growth or development. ● verb educate (a child) to a higher level than is usual for their age.

hot key ● noun Computing a key or combination of keys providing quick access to a function within a program.

hotline ● noun a direct telephone line set up for a specific purpose.

hot pants ● plural noun women's tight, brief shorts.

hotplate ● noun a flat heated metal or ceramic surface on an electric cooker.

h

hotpot (also **Lancashire hotpot**) ● noun Brit. a casserole of meat and vegetables with a covering layer of sliced potato.

hot potato ● noun informal a controversial and awkward issue.

hot rod ● noun a motor vehicle that has been specially modified to give it extra power and speed. ● verb (**hot-rod**) 1 modify (a vehicle or other device) to make it faster or more powerful. 2 drive a hot rod.
– DERIVATIVES **hot-rodder** noun.

hot seat ● noun (**the hot seat**) informal 1 the position of a person who carries full responsibility for something. 2 chiefly N. Amer. the electric chair.

hot shoe ● noun Photography a socket on a camera with direct electrical contacts for an attached flashgun or other accessory.

hotshot ● noun informal an important or exceptionally able person.

hot spot ● noun 1 a small area with a relatively high temperature. 2 a place of significant activity or danger.

hot stuff ● noun informal 1 a person or thing of outstanding talent or interest. 2 a sexually exciting person, book, etc.

hot-tempered ● adjective easily angered.

Hottentot /hott'ntot/ ● noun & adjective used to refer to the Khoikhoi peoples of South Africa and Namibia.
– USAGE The word **Hottentot** is now regarded as offensive with reference to people (where **Khoikhoi** or, specifically, **Nama**, are the standard terms) but is still standard when used in the names of some animals and plants.
– ORIGIN Dutch, perhaps a repetitive formula in a Khoikhoi dancing song, transferred by Dutch sailors to the people themselves, or from German *hotteren-totteren* 'stutter' (with reference to their click language).

hot ticket ● noun informal a person or thing that is much in demand.

hot tub ● noun a large tub filled with hot aerated water, used for recreation or physical therapy.

hot-water bottle (US also **hot-water bag**) ● noun a flat, oblong rubber container that is filled with hot water and used for warming a bed or part of the body.

hot-wire ● verb informal start the engine of (a vehicle) by bypassing the ignition switch.

Houdini /hoodeeni/ ● noun a person skilled at escaping from desperate situations.
– ORIGIN named after the American magician and escape artist Harry *Houdini* (Erik Weisz) (1874–1926).

hound ● noun 1 a dog of a breed used for hunting. 2 a person who pursues something eagerly: *a publicity hound.* ● verb harass or pursue relentlessly.
– ORIGIN Old English.

houndstooth ● noun a large check pattern with notched corners.

hour ● noun 1 a period of time equal to a twenty-fourth part of a day and night; 60 minutes. 2 a time of day specified as an exact number of hours from midnight or midday. 3 a period set aside for a particular purpose or activity. 4 a point in time.
– PHRASES **on the hour** 1 at an exact hour, or on each hour, of the day or night. 2 after a period of one hour.
– ORIGIN Greek *hōra* 'season, hour'.

hourglass ● noun a device with two connected glass bulbs containing sand that takes an hour to fall from the upper to the lower bulb. ● adjective shaped like an hourglass.

houri /hoori/ ● noun (pl. **houris**) 1 a beautiful young woman. 2 one of the virgin companions of the faithful in the Muslim Paradise.
– ORIGIN from an Arabic word meaning 'having eyes with a marked contrast of black and white'.

hourly ● adjective 1 done or occurring every hour. 2 reckoned hour by hour. ● adverb 1 every hour. 2 by the hour.

house ● noun /howss/ 1 a building for human habitation. 2 a building in which animals live or in which things are kept: *a reptile house.* 3 a building devoted to a particular activity: *a house of prayer.* 4 a firm or institution: *a fashion house.* 5 a religious community that occupies a particular building. 6 chiefly Brit. a body of pupils living in the same building at a boarding school. 7 a legislative or deliberative assembly. 8 (**the House**) (in the UK) the House of Commons or Lords; (in the US) the House of Representatives. 9 a dynasty. 10 (also **house music**) a style of fast popular dance music. 11 Astrology a twelfth division of the celestial sphere. ● adjective 1 (of an animal or plant) kept in, frequenting, or infesting buildings. 2 relating to medical staff resident at a hospital. 3 relating to a firm, institution, or society. ● verb /howz/ 1 provide with shelter or accommodation. 2 provide space for. 3 enclose or encase.
– PHRASES **get on like a house on fire** informal have a very good and friendly relationship. **a house divided cannot stand** proverb a group or organization weakened by internal disagreements will be unable to withstand external pressures. **keep house** run a household. **on the house** at the management's expense. **put one's house in order** make necessary reforms.
– DERIVATIVES **houseful** noun.
– ORIGIN Old English.

Thesaurus

collection, jumble, ragbag, miscellany, medley, pot-pourri; melange, mishmash, farrago, gallimaufry; *N. Amer.* hodgepodge.

hotel ● noun INN, motel, boarding house, guest house, bed and breakfast, B&B, hostel; pension, auberge.

hotfoot ● adverb HASTILY, hurriedly, speedily, quickly, fast, rapidly, swiftly, without delay; at top speed, at full tilt, headlong, posthaste, pell-mell, helter-skelter; *informal* like the wind, like greased lightning, like blazes; *Brit. informal* like the clappers, like billy-o; *N. Amer. informal* lickety-split.
– OPPOSITES slowly.
– PHRASES **hotfoot it** *(informal)* HURRY, dash, run, race, sprint, bolt, dart, career, charge, shoot, hurtle, hare, fly, speed, zoom, streak; *informal* tear, belt, pelt, scoot, clip, leg it, go like a bat out of hell; *Brit. informal* bomb; *N. Amer. informal* hightail it.

hot-headed ● adjective IMPETUOUS, impulsive, headstrong, reckless, rash, irresponsible, foolhardy, madcap; excitable, volatile, fiery, hot-tempered, quick-tempered, harum-scarum.

hothouse ● noun GREENHOUSE, glasshouse, conservatory, orangery, vinery, winter garden.
● adjective *the school has a hothouse atmosphere* INTENSE, oppressive, stifling; overprotected, pampered, shielded.

hotly ● adverb 1 *the rumours were hotly denied* VEHEMENTLY, vigorously, strenuously, fiercely, passionately, heatedly; angrily, indignantly. 2 *he was hotly pursued by Boris* CLOSELY, swiftly, quickly, hotfoot; eagerly, enthusiastically.
– OPPOSITES calmly.

hot-tempered ● adjective IRASCIBLE, quick-tempered, short-tempered, irritable, fiery, bad-tempered; touchy, volatile, testy, tetchy, fractious, prickly, peppery; *informal* snappish, snappy, chippy, on a short fuse; *Brit. informal* narky, ratty, like a bear with a sore head; *N. Amer. informal* soreheaded.
– OPPOSITES easy-going.

hound ● noun 1 (HUNTING) DOG, canine, mongrel, cur; *informal* doggy, pooch, mutt; *Austral./NZ informal* mong, bitzer. 2 *(informal, dated) you monstrous hound!* See SCOUNDREL.
● verb 1 *she was hounded by the press* PURSUE, chase, follow, shadow, be hot on someone's heels, hunt (down), stalk, track, trail; harass, persecute, harry, pester, bother, badger, torment, bedevil; *informal* hassle, bug, give someone a hard time; *N. Amer. informal* devil. 2 *they hounded him out of office* FORCE, drive, pressure, pressurize, push, urge, coerce, impel, dragoon, strong-arm; nag, bully, browbeat, chivvy; *informal* bulldoze, railroad; *Brit. informal*

house arrest • noun the state of being kept as a prisoner in one's own house.
houseboat • noun a boat which is fitted for use as a dwelling.
housebound • adjective unable to leave one's house, often due to illness or old age.
houseboy • noun a boy or man employed to undertake domestic duties.
housebreaking • noun the action of breaking into a building, especially in daytime, to commit a crime.
– DERIVATIVES **housebreaker** noun.
housecoat • noun a woman's long, loose robe for informal wear around the house.
housefather (or **housemother**) • noun a person in charge of and living in a boarding school house or children's home.
housefly • noun a common small fly occurring in and around human habitation.
household • noun a house and its occupants regarded as a unit.
– DERIVATIVES **householder** noun.
Household Cavalry • noun the two cavalry regiments of the British army responsible for guarding the monarch.
household name (also **household word**) • noun a famous person or thing.
household troops • plural noun (in the UK) troops nominally employed to guard the sovereign.
house-hunting • noun the process of seeking a house to buy or rent.
– DERIVATIVES **house-hunter** noun.
house husband • noun a man who lives with a partner and carries out the household duties traditionally done by a housewife.
housekeeper • noun a person, typically a woman, employed to manage a household.
– DERIVATIVES **housekeeping** noun.
houseleek • noun a succulent plant with rosettes of fleshy leaves and small pink flowers, growing on walls and roofs.
house lights • plural noun the lights in the auditorium of a theatre.
housemaid • noun a female domestic employee who cleans rooms.
housemaid's knee • noun inflammation of the fluid-filled cavity covering the kneecap, often due to excessive kneeling.
houseman • noun 1 Brit. a house officer. 2 N. Amer. a houseboy.
house martin • noun a black-and-white bird of the swallow family, nesting on buildings.
housemaster (or **housemistress**) • noun a teacher in charge of a house at a boarding school.
house mouse • noun a greyish-brown mouse found abundantly as a scavenger in human dwellings.
House of Commons • noun the elected chamber of Parliament in the UK.
house officer • noun Brit. a recent medical graduate receiving supervised training in a hospital and acting as an assistant physician or surgeon.
house of God • noun a place of religious worship.
house of ill fame (also **house of ill repute**) • noun archaic or humorous a brothel.
House of Keys • noun the elected chamber of Tynwald, the parliament of the Isle of Man.
House of Lords • 1 noun the chamber of Parliament in the UK composed of peers and bishops. 2 a committee of specially qualified members of this chamber, appointed as the ultimate judicial appeal court of England and Wales.
House of Representatives • noun the lower house of the US Congress.
house-proud • adjective attentive to, or preoccupied with, the care and appearance of one's home.
houseroom • noun space or accommodation in one's house.
– PHRASES **not give something houseroom** Brit. be unwilling to have or consider something.
house-sit • verb live in and look after a house while its owner is away.
– DERIVATIVES **house-sitter** noun.
Houses of Parliament • plural noun the Houses of Lords and Commons in the UK regarded together.
house sparrow • noun a common brown and grey sparrow that nests in the eaves and roofs of houses.
house style • noun a company's preferred manner of presentation and layout of written material.
house-to-house • adjective performed at or taken to each house in turn.
house-train • verb chiefly Brit. train (a pet) to excrete outside the house.
house-warming • noun a party celebrating a move to a new home.
housewife • noun (pl. **housewives**) a married woman whose main occupation is caring for her family and running the household.
– DERIVATIVES **housewifely** adjective **housewifery** noun.
housework • noun regular work done in housekeeping, such as cleaning and cooking.
housey-housey • noun Brit. old-fashioned term for BINGO.
housing • noun 1 houses and flats considered collectively. 2 the provision of accommodation. 3 a rigid casing for a piece of equipment. 4 a groove cut in a piece of wood to allow another piece to be attached to it.
housing estate • noun Brit. a residential area planned and built as a unit.
hove chiefly Nautical past tense of HEAVE.
hovel • noun a small squalid or poorly constructed dwelling.
– ORIGIN of unknown origin.
hover • verb 1 remain in one place in the air. 2 linger close at hand in an uncertain manner. 3 remain at or near a particular level or in an intermediate state. • noun an act of hovering.
– DERIVATIVES **hoverer** noun.
– ORIGIN of unknown origin.
hovercraft • noun (pl. same) a vehicle or craft that travels over land or water on a cushion of air.
hoverfly • noun a fly which hovers in the air and feeds on the nectar of flowers.
hoverport • noun a terminal for hovercraft.
how[1] • adverb 1 in what way or by what means. 2 in what condition or health. 3 to what extent or degree. 4 the way in which.
– PHRASES **and how!** informal very much so. **how about?** would you like? **the how and why** the methods and reasons for doing

h

Thesaurus

bounce; *N. Amer. informal* hustle.
house • noun 1 *an estate of 200 houses* RESIDENCE, home, place of residence; homestead; a roof over one's head; *formal* habitation, dwelling (place), abode, domicile. 2 *you'll wake the whole house!* HOUSEHOLD, family, clan, tribe; *informal* brood. 3 *the house of Stewart* FAMILY, clan, tribe; dynasty, line, bloodline, lineage, ancestry, family tree. 4 *a printing house* FIRM, business, company, corporation, enterprise, establishment, institution, concern, organization, operation; *informal* outfit, set-up. 5 *the country's upper house* LEGISLATIVE ASSEMBLY, legislative body, chamber, council, parliament, congress, senate, diet. 6 *the house applauded* AUDIENCE, crowd, spectators, viewers; congregation; gallery, stalls; *Brit. informal* punters.
• verb 1 *they can house twelve employees* ACCOMMODATE, provide accommodation for, give someone a roof over their head, lodge, quarter, board, billet, take in, sleep, put up; harbour, shelter. 2 *this panel houses the main switch* CONTAIN, hold, store; cover, protect, enclose.
– PHRASES **on the house** FREE (OF CHARGE), without charge, at no cost, for nothing, gratis; courtesy, complimentary; *informal* for free; *N. Amer. informal* comp.
household • noun *the household was asleep* FAMILY, house, occupants; clan, tribe; *informal* brood.
• adjective *household goods* DOMESTIC, family; everyday, workaday.
householder • noun HOMEOWNER, owner, occupant, resident; tenant, leaseholder; proprietor, landlady, landlord, freeholder; *Brit.* occupier, owner-occupier.
housekeeping • noun HOUSEHOLD MANAGEMENT, domestic work, home-making, housewifery; home economics; *Brit.* housecraft.
houseman • noun *(Brit.)* JUNIOR DOCTOR, house doctor, newly qualified doctor; *Brit.* house officer; *N. Amer.* intern, resident.
house-trained • adjective *(Brit.)* DOMESTICATED, trained; *N. Amer.* housebroken.
housing • noun 1 *they invested in housing* HOUSES, homes, residences, buildings; accommodation, living quarters; *formal* dwellings, dwelling places, habitations. 2 *the housing for the antennae* CASING, covering, case, cover, holder, sheath, jacket, shell, capsule.
hovel • noun SHACK, slum, shanty, hut; *informal* dump, hole.
hover • verb 1 *helicopters hovered overhead* BE SUSPENDED, be poised, hang, levitate; fly. 2 *she hovered anxiously nearby* LINGER,

something. **how do you do?** a formal greeting. **how many** what number. **how much** what amount or price. **how now?** archaic what is the meaning of this? **how's that?** Cricket is the batsman out or not? (said to an umpire).
– ORIGIN Old English.
how² ● **exclamation** a greeting attributed to North American Indians.
– ORIGIN from a North American Indian word.
howbeit ● **adverb** archaic nevertheless.
howdah /howdə/ ● **noun** a seat for riding on the back of an elephant, usually having a canopy.
– ORIGIN Urdu, from Arabic, 'litter'.
howdy ● **exclamation** N. Amer. an informal friendly greeting.
– ORIGIN alternative of *how d'ye*.
how-d'ye-do (also **how-de-do**) ● **noun** informal an awkward or annoying situation.
however ● **adverb 1** used to introduce a statement contrasting with a previous one. **2** in whatever way. **3** to whatever extent.
howitzer /howitsər/ ● **noun** a short gun for firing shells at a high angle.
– ORIGIN Dutch *houwitser*, from Czech *houfnice* 'catapult'.
howk /howk/ ● **verb** chiefly Scottish dig out or up.
– ORIGIN related to HOLE.
howl ● **noun 1** a long doleful cry uttered by an animal. **2** a loud cry of pain, amusement, etc. ● **verb** make a howling sound.
– ORIGIN probably imitative.
howler ● **noun** informal a ludicrous mistake.
howling ● **adjective** informal great: *a howling success.*
howsoever formal or archaic ● **adverb** to whatever extent. ● **conjunction** in whatever way.
howzat ● **exclamation** Cricket shortened form of **how's that** (see HOW¹).
hoy ● **exclamation** used to attract someone's attention. ● **noun** Austral. a game resembling bingo, using playing cards.
hoya /hoyə/ ● **noun** an evergreen climbing shrub with ornamental foliage and waxy flowers, native to SE Asia and the Pacific.
– ORIGIN named after the English gardener Thomas *Hoy* (*c.*1750–*c.*1821).
hoyden /hoyd'n/ ● **noun** dated a boisterous girl.
– DERIVATIVES **hoydenish** adjective.
– ORIGIN probably from Dutch *heiden*, denoting a rude man; related to HEATHEN.
h.p. (also **HP**) ● **abbreviation 1** high pressure. **2** Brit. hire purchase. **3** horsepower.
HQ ● **abbreviation** headquarters.
hr ● **abbreviation** hour.
HRH ● **abbreviation** Brit. Her (or His) Royal Highness.
HRT ● **abbreviation** hormone replacement therapy.
Hs ● **symbol** the chemical element hassium.
HST ● **abbreviation** (in the UK) high-speed train.
HTML ● **noun** Computing Hypertext Mark-up Language.
HTTP ● **abbreviation** Computing Hypertext Transport (or Transfer) Protocol.
hub ● **noun 1** the central part of a wheel, rotating on or with the axle. **2** the centre of an activity, region, or network.
– ORIGIN related to HOB.
hubbub ● **noun 1** a chaotic din caused by a crowd. **2** a busy, noisy situation.
– ORIGIN perhaps Irish.
hubby ● **noun** (pl. **hubbies**) informal a husband.
hubcap ● **noun** a cover for the hub of a motor vehicle's wheel.
hubris /hyo͞obriss/ ● **noun** excessive pride or self-confidence.
– DERIVATIVES **hubristic** adjective.
– ORIGIN Greek, originally denoting presumption towards or defiance of the gods, leading to nemesis.
huckleberry ● **noun** the soft edible blue-black fruit of a low-growing North American plant of the heath family.
– ORIGIN probably originally a dialect name for the bilberry, from *huckle* 'hip, haunch' (because of the plant's jointed stems).
huckster ● **noun 1** a person who sells small items, either door-to-door or from a stall. **2** N. Amer. a person who uses aggressive selling techniques. ● **verb** chiefly N. Amer. **1** promote or sell aggressively. **2** bargain.
– DERIVATIVES **hucksterism** noun.
– ORIGIN probably Low German.
huddle ● **verb 1** crowd together. **2** curl one's body into a small space. ● **noun** a number of people or things crowded together.
– ORIGIN originally in the sense 'conceal': perhaps Low German.
hue ● **noun 1** a colour or shade. **2** technical the attribute of a colour, dependent on its dominant wavelength, by virtue of which it is discernible as red, green, etc. **3** aspect: *men of all political hues.*
– ORIGIN Old English.
hue and cry ● **noun** a loud clamour or public outcry.
– ORIGIN from an Old French legal phrase *hu e cri*, 'outcry and cry'.
huff ● **verb** (often **huff and puff**) **1** exhale noisily. **2** show one's annoyance in an obvious way. ● **noun** a fit of petty annoyance.
– ORIGIN imitative.
huffy ● **adjective** (**huffier**, **huffiest**) easily offended.
– DERIVATIVES **huffily** adverb **huffiness** noun.
hug ● **verb** (**hugged**, **hugging**) **1** squeeze or hold tightly in one's arms. **2** keep close to: *a few craft hugged the shore.* ● **noun** an act of hugging.
– DERIVATIVES **huggable** adjective.
– ORIGIN probably Scandinavian.

Thesaurus

loiter, wait about; *informal* hang around, stick around; *Brit. informal* hang about.
however ● **adverb 1** *however, gaining weight is not inevitable* NEVERTHELESS, nonetheless, but, still, yet, though, although, even so, for all that, despite that, in spite of that; anyway, anyhow, be that as it may, having said that, notwithstanding; *informal* still and all. **2** *however you look at it* IN WHATEVER WAY, regardless of how, no matter how.
howl ● **noun 1** *the howl of a wolf* BAYING, howling, bay, cry, yowl, bark, yelp. **2** *a howl of anguish* WAIL, cry, yell, yelp, yowl; bellow, roar, shout, shriek, scream, screech.
● **verb 1** *dogs howled in the distance* BAY, cry, yowl, bark, yelp. **2** *a baby started to howl* WAIL, cry, yell, yowl, bawl, bellow, shriek, scream, screech, caterwaul; *informal* holler. **3** *we howled with laughter* LAUGH, guffaw, roar; be creased up, be doubled up, split one's sides; *informal* fall about, crack up, be in stitches, be rolling in the aisles.
howler ● **noun** *(informal)* MISTAKE, error, blunder, fault, gaffe, slip; *informal* slip-up, boo-boo, botch, clanger; *Brit. informal* boob; *N. Amer. informal* blooper.
hub ● **noun 1** *the hub of the wheel* PIVOT, axis, fulcrum, centre, middle. **2** *the hub of family life* CENTRE, core, heart, focus, focal point, nucleus, kernel, nerve centre.
– OPPOSITES periphery.
hubbub ● **noun 1** *her voice was lost in the hubbub* NOISE, din, racket, commotion, clamour, cacophony, babel, rumpus; *Brit. informal* row. **2** *she fought through the hubbub* CONFUSION, chaos, pandemonium, bedlam, mayhem, disorder, turmoil, tumult, fracas, hurly-burly.
hubris ● **noun** ARROGANCE, conceit, haughtiness, hauteur, pride, self-importance, pomposity, superciliousness, superiority; *informal* big-headedness.
– OPPOSITES humility.
huckster ● **noun** TRADER, dealer, seller, purveyor, vendor, salesman, pedlar, hawker; *informal* pusher.
huddle ● **verb 1** *they huddled together* CROWD, cluster, gather, bunch, throng, flock, herd, collect, group, congregate; press, pack, squeeze. **2** *he huddled beneath the sheets* CURL UP, snuggle, nestle, hunch up.
– OPPOSITES disperse.
● **noun 1** *a huddle of passengers* CROWD, cluster, bunch, knot, group, throng, flock, press, pack; collection, assemblage; *informal* gaggle. **2** *the team went into a huddle* CONSULTATION, discussion, debate, talk, parley, meeting, conference; *informal* confab, powwow.
hue ● **noun 1** *paints in a variety of hues* COLOUR, shade, tone, tint. **2** *men of all political hues* COMPLEXION, type, kind, sort, cast, stamp, character, nature.
hue and cry ● **noun** COMMOTION, outcry, uproar, fuss, clamour, storm, stir, furore, ruckus, brouhaha, palaver, rumpus; *informal* hoo-ha, hullabaloo, ballyhoo, kerfuffle, to-do, song and dance, *Brit. informal* row, stink.
huff ● **noun** BAD MOOD, sulk, fit of pique, pet; temper, tantrum, rage; *informal* grump; *Brit. informal* strop, paddy; *N. Amer. informal* snit; *Brit. informal, dated* bate, wax.
huffy ● **adjective** IRRITABLE, irritated, annoyed, cross, grumpy, bad-tempered, crotchety, crabby, cantankerous, moody, petulant, sullen, surly; touchy, testy, tetchy, snappish; *informal* snappy, cranky; *Brit. informal* narky, miffed, ratty, eggy, shirty, like a bear with a

huge • adjective (**huger**, **hugest**) extremely large.
– DERIVATIVES **hugely** adverb **hugeness** noun.
– ORIGIN shortening of Old French *ahuge*, of unknown origin.
hugger-mugger • adjective **1** confused. **2** secret. • noun **1** confusion. **2** secrecy.
– ORIGIN probably related to HUDDLE and to dialect *mucker* 'hoard money, conceal'.
Huguenot /hyoogənō/ • noun a French Protestant of the 16th–17th centuries.
– ORIGIN French, alternative (by association with the name of a mayor of Geneva, Besançon *Hugues*) of *eiguenot*, from Swiss German *Eidgenoss* 'confederate'.
hui /hooi/ • noun (pl. **huis** or **huies**) NZ a large social or ceremonial gathering.
– ORIGIN Maori.
hula /hoolə/ (also **hula-hula**) • noun a dance performed by Hawaiian women, characterized by undulating hips and symbolic gestures.
– ORIGIN Hawaiian.
hula hoop (also US trademark **Hula-Hoop**) • noun a large hoop spun round the body by gyrating the hips.
hulk • noun **1** an old ship stripped of fittings and permanently moored. **2** a large or clumsy person or thing.
– ORIGIN Old English, 'fast ship'.
hulking • adjective informal very large or clumsy.
hull[1] • noun the main body of a ship or other vessel, including the bottom, sides and deck but not the superstructure, engines, and other fittings.
– DERIVATIVES **hulled** adjective.
– ORIGIN perhaps the same word as HULL[2], or related to HOLD[2].
hull[2] • noun **1** the outer covering of a fruit or seed. **2** the green calyx of a strawberry or raspberry. • verb remove the hulls from.
– ORIGIN Old English.
hullabaloo • noun informal a commotion or uproar.
– ORIGIN reduplication of *hallo, hullo*, etc.
hullo • exclamation variant spelling of HELLO.
hum • verb (**hummed**, **humming**) **1** make a low, steady continuous sound like that of a bee. **2** sing with closed lips. **3** informal be in a state of great activity. **4** Brit. informal smell unpleasant. • noun a low, steady continuous sound.
– PHRASES **hum and haw** (or **ha**) Brit. be indecisive.
– DERIVATIVES **hummable** adjective **hummer** noun.
– ORIGIN imitative.
human • adjective **1** of, relating to, or characteristic of humankind. **2** showing the better qualities of humankind, such as sensitivity. • noun a human being.
– DERIVATIVES **humanly** adverb **humanness** noun.
– ORIGIN Latin *humanus*, from *homo* 'man, human being'.
human being • noun a man, woman, or child of the species *Homo sapiens*.
humane /hoomayn/ • adjective **1** having or showing compassion or benevolence. **2** formal (of a branch of learning) intended to civilize.
– DERIVATIVES **humanely** adverb **humaneness** noun.
human interest • noun the aspect of a news story concerned with the experiences or emotions of individuals.
humanism • noun **1** a rationalistic system of thought attaching prime importance to human rather than divine or supernatural matters. **2** a Renaissance cultural movement which turned away from medieval scholasticism and revived interest in ancient Greek and Roman thought.
– DERIVATIVES **humanist** noun & adjective **humanistic** adjective.
humanitarian /hyoomannitairiən/ • adjective concerned with or seeking to promote human welfare. • noun a humanitarian person.
– DERIVATIVES **humanitarianism** noun.
humanity • noun (pl. **humanities**) **1** humankind. **2** the condition of being human. **3** compassion or benevolence. **4** (**humanities**) learning or literature concerned with human culture.

h

Thesaurus

sore head; *N. Amer. informal* soreheaded.
hug • verb **1** *they hugged each other* EMBRACE, cuddle, squeeze, clasp, clutch, cling to, hold close, hold tight, take someone in one's arms, clasp someone to one's bosom; *poetic/literary* embosom. **2** *our route hugged the coastline* FOLLOW CLOSELY, keep close to, stay near to, follow the course of. **3** *we hugged the comforting thought* CLING TO, hold on to, cherish, harbour, nurse, foster, retain, keep in mind.
• noun *there were hugs as we left* EMBRACE, cuddle, squeeze, bear hug, clinch.
huge • adjective ENORMOUS, vast, immense, large, big, great, massive, colossal, prodigious, gigantic, gargantuan, mammoth, monumental; giant, towering, elephantine, mountainous, titanic; epic, Herculean, Brobdingnagian; *informal* jumbo, mega, monster, whopping, humongous, hulking, bumper, astronomical; *Brit. informal* ginormous.
– OPPOSITES tiny.
hugely • adverb VERY, extremely, exceedingly, most, really, particularly, tremendously, greatly, decidedly, exceptionally, immensely, inordinately, extraordinarily, vastly; very much, to a great extent; *N. English* right; *informal* terrifically, awfully, terribly, majorly, seriously, mega, ultra, oh-so, damn, damned; *Brit. informal* ever so, well, dead, jolly; *N. Amer. informal* real, mighty, awful; *informal, dated* devilish, frightfully; *archaic* exceeding.
hugger-mugger • adjective **1** *at home, all was hugger-mugger* DISORDERLY, confused, disorganized, chaotic, muddled, haphazard, in a mess, in disarray, topsy-turvy; *informal* higgledy-piggledy; *Brit. informal* shambolic. **2** *hugger-mugger dealings* CLANDESTINE, secret, covert, furtive, cloak-and-dagger, hole-and-corner, sneaky, sly, underhand; undercover, underground; *informal* hush-hush.
– OPPOSITES orderly, overt.
hulk • noun **1** *the rusting hulks of ships* WRECK, shipwreck, ruin, derelict; shell, skeleton, hull. **2** *a great hulk of a man* GIANT, lump; oaf; *informal* clodhopper, ape, gorilla; *N. Amer. informal* lummox.
hulking • adjective *(informal)* LARGE, big, heavy, sturdy, burly, brawny, hefty, strapping; bulky, weighty, massive, ponderous; clumsy, awkward, ungainly, lumbering, lumpish, oafish; *informal* hunky, beefy, clodhopping.
– OPPOSITES small.
hull[1] • noun *the ship's hull* FRAMEWORK, body, shell, frame, skeleton, structure.
hull[2] • noun *seed hulls* SHELL, husk, pod, case, covering, integument, shuck; *Botany* pericarp, legume.
• verb *the bird uses its beak to hull seeds* SHELL, husk, peel, pare, skin, shuck; *technical* decorticate.
hullabaloo • noun *(informal)* FUSS, commotion, hue and cry, uproar, outcry, clamour, storm, furore, hubbub, ruckus, brouhaha; pandemonium, mayhem, tumult, turmoil, hurly-burly; *informal* hoo-ha, to-do, kerfuffle, song and dance; *Brit. informal* carry-on, row, stink.
hum • verb **1** *the engine was humming* PURR, drone, murmur, buzz, thrum, whirr, throb, vibrate; *poetic/literary* bombinate. **2** *she hummed a tune* sing, croon, murmur, drone. **3** *the workshops are humming* BE BUSY, be active, be lively, buzz, bustle, be a hive of activity, throb. **4** *(Brit. informal) this stuff really hums.* See REEK verb.
• noun *a low hum of conversation* MURMUR, drone, purr, buzz; *poetic/literary* bombination.
– PHRASES **hum and haw** *(Brit.)* HESITATE, dither, vacillate, be indecisive, equivocate, prevaricate, waver, blow hot and cold; *Brit.* haver; *Scottish* swither; *informal* shilly-shally.
human • adjective **1** *the human race* anthropoid. **2** *they're only human* MORTAL, flesh and blood; fallible, weak, frail, imperfect, vulnerable, susceptible, erring, error-prone; physical, bodily, fleshly. **3** *the human side of politics* COMPASSIONATE, humane, kind, considerate, understanding, sympathetic, tolerant; approachable, accessible.
– OPPOSITES infallible.
• noun *the link between humans and animals* PERSON, human being, personage, mortal, member of the human race; man, woman; individual, (living) soul, being; Homo sapiens; earthling.
humane • adjective COMPASSIONATE, kind, considerate, understanding, sympathetic, tolerant; lenient, forbearing, forgiving, merciful, mild, tender, clement, benign, humanitarian, benevolent, charitable.
– OPPOSITES cruel.
humanitarian • adjective **1** *a humanitarian act* COMPASSIONATE, humane; unselfish, altruistic, generous, magnanimous, benevolent, merciful, kind, sympathetic. **2** *a humanitarian organization* CHARITABLE, philanthropic, public-spirited, socially concerned, welfare.
– OPPOSITES selfish.
• noun PHILANTHROPIST, altruist, benefactor, social reformer, good Samaritan; do-gooder; *archaic* philanthrope.
humanities • plural noun (LIBERAL) ARTS, literature; classics, classical studies, classical literature.

humanize (also **humanise**) ● verb **1** make more humane. **2** give a human character to.
– DERIVATIVES **humanization** noun.
humankind ● noun human beings considered collectively.
human nature ● noun the general characteristics, feelings, and traits of people.
humanoid /hyōōmənoyd/ ● adjective having human characteristics. ● noun a humanoid being.
human rights ● plural noun rights which are believed to belong justifiably to every person.
humble ● adjective (**humbler**, **humblest**) **1** having or showing a modest or low estimate of one's own importance. **2** of low rank. **3** of modest pretensions or dimensions: *humble beginnings*. ● verb lower in dignity or importance.
– PHRASES **eat humble pie** make a humble apology and accept humiliation. [ORIGIN *humble pie* is from a pun based on archaic *umbles* 'offal', considered inferior food.]
– DERIVATIVES **humbly** adverb.
– ORIGIN Latin *humilis* 'low, lowly', from *humus* 'ground'.
humblebee ● noun dated another term for BUMBLEBEE.
– ORIGIN probably from Low German *hummel* 'to buzz' + *bē* 'bee'.
humbug ● noun **1** deceptive or false talk or behaviour. **2** a hypocrite. **3** Brit. a boiled peppermint sweet. ● verb (**humbugged**, **humbugging**) deceive; trick.
– DERIVATIVES **humbuggery** noun.
– ORIGIN of unknown origin.
humdinger /humdingər/ ● noun informal a remarkable or outstanding person or thing of its kind.
– ORIGIN of unknown origin.
humdrum ● adjective dull or monotonous. ● noun monotonous routine.
– ORIGIN probably a reduplication of HUM.
humectant /hyoomektənt/ ● adjective retaining or preserving moisture. ● noun a substance used to reduce the loss of moisture.
– ORIGIN from Latin *humectare* 'moisten'.
humerus /hyōōmərəss/ ● noun (pl. **humeri** /hyōōmərī/) Anatomy the bone of the upper arm or forelimb, between the shoulder and the elbow.
– DERIVATIVES **humeral** adjective.
– ORIGIN Latin, 'shoulder'.
humid /hyōōmid/ ● adjective marked by a high level of water vapour in the atmosphere.
– DERIVATIVES **humidly** adverb **humidity** noun.
– ORIGIN Latin *humidus*, from *humere* 'be moist'.
humidify ● verb (**humidifies**, **humidified**) (often as adj. **humidified**) increase the level of moisture in air.
– DERIVATIVES **humidification** noun **humidifier** noun.
humidor /hyōōmidor/ ● noun an airtight container for keeping cigars or tobacco moist.
humiliate ● verb injure the dignity and self-respect of.
– DERIVATIVES **humiliating** adjective **humiliation** noun **humiliator** noun.
– ORIGIN Latin *humiliare* 'make humble'.
humility ● noun a humble view of one's own importance.
hummingbird ● noun a small long-billed tropical American bird able to hover by beating its wings extremely fast.
hummock ● noun a hillock or mound.
– DERIVATIVES **hummocky** adjective.
– ORIGIN of unknown origin.
hummus /hōōməss/ ● noun a thick Middle Eastern dip made from ground chickpeas and sesame seeds.
– USAGE Because there are a number of ways in which the original Arabic word may be transliterated into English, there are a number of different English spellings: **hummus**, **houmous**, **hoummos**, and **humous** are all commonly used, and all are acceptable. **Hummus** is, however, the most widespread.
– ORIGIN Arabic.
humongous /hyoomunggəss/ (also **humungous**) ● adjective informal enormous.
– ORIGIN perhaps from HUGE and MONSTROUS.
humor ● noun US spelling of HUMOUR.
humoral /hyōōmərəl/ ● adjective Medicine of or relating to the body fluids.
– ORIGIN Latin *humoralis*, from *humor* 'moisture'.
humoresque /hyōōməresk/ ● noun a short, lively piece of music.
– ORIGIN German *Humoreske*, from *Humor* 'humour'.
humorist ● noun a humorous writer, performer, or artist.
humorous ● adjective **1** causing amusement. **2** having or showing a sense of humour.
– DERIVATIVES **humorously** adverb **humorousness** noun.
humour (US **humor**) ● noun **1** the quality of being amusing or comic. **2** a state of mind: *her good humour vanished*. **3** (also

h

Thesaurus

humanity ● noun **1** *humanity evolved from the apes* HUMANKIND, mankind, man, people, the human race; Homo sapiens. **2** *the humanity of Christ* HUMAN NATURE, humanness, mortality. **3** *he praised them for their humanity* COMPASSION, brotherly love, fellow feeling, humaneness, kindness, consideration, understanding, sympathy, tolerance; leniency, mercy, mercifulness, pity, tenderness; benevolence, charity.
humanize ● verb CIVILIZE, improve, better; educate, enlighten, instruct; sophisticate, socialize, refine, polish; formal edify.
humankind ● noun THE HUMAN RACE, the human species, humanity, human beings, mankind, man, people, mortals; Homo sapiens.
humble ● adjective **1** *her bearing was humble* MEEK, deferential, respectful, submissive, self-effacing, unassertive; unpresuming, modest, unassuming, self-deprecating; Scottish mim. **2** *a humble background* LOWLY, working-class, lower-class, poor, undistinguished, mean, ignoble, low-born; common, ordinary, simple, inferior, unremarkable, insignificant, inconsequential; informal plebby. **3** *my humble abode* MODEST, plain, simple, ordinary, unostentatious, unpretentious.
– OPPOSITES proud, noble, grand.
● verb **1** *he humbled himself to ask for help* HUMILIATE, abase, demean, lower, degrade, debase; mortify, shame, eat humble pie; take someone down a peg or two; informal cut down to size, settle someone's hash; N. Amer. informal make someone eat crow. **2** *Wales were humbled at by Romania* DEFEAT, beat, trounce, rout, overwhelm, get the better of, bring to one's knees; informal lick, clobber, slaughter, massacre, crucify, walk all over; N. Amer. informal shellac, cream.
humbug ● noun **1** *that is sheer humbug* HYPOCRISY, hypocritical talk, sanctimoniousness, posturing, cant, empty talk; insincerity, dishonesty, falseness, deceit, deception, fraud. **2** *you see what a humbug I am?* HYPOCRITE, fraud, fake, plaster saint; charlatan, cheat, deceiver, dissembler; informal phoney; poetic/literary whited sepulchre.
● verb *Dave is easily humbugged* DECEIVE, trick, delude, mislead, fool, hoodwink, dupe, take in, beguile, bamboozle, gull; informal con, kid, have on, put one over on someone.
humdrum ● adjective MUNDANE, dull, dreary, boring, tedious, monotonous, prosaic; unexciting, uninteresting, uneventful, unvaried, unremarkable; routine, ordinary, everyday, day-to-day, quotidian, run-of-the-mill, commonplace, workaday, pedestrian; informal (plain) vanilla.
– OPPOSITES remarkable, exciting.
humid ● adjective MUGGY, close, sultry, sticky, steamy, oppressive, airless, stifling, suffocating, stuffy, clammy, heavy.
– OPPOSITES fresh.
humiliate ● verb EMBARRASS, mortify, humble, shame, put to shame, disgrace; discomfit, chasten, abash, deflate, crush, squash; abase, debase, demean, degrade; cause to feel small, cause to lose face, take down a peg or two; informal show up, put down, cut down to size, settle someone's hash; N. Amer. informal make someone eat crow.
humiliating ● adjective EMBARRASSING, mortifying, humbling, ignominious, inglorious, shameful; discreditable, undignified, chastening, demeaning, degrading, deflating.
humiliation ● noun EMBARRASSMENT, mortification, shame, indignity, ignominy, disgrace, dishonour, degradation, discredit, obloquy, opprobrium; loss of pride, loss of face; blow to one's pride, slap in the face, kick in the teeth.
– OPPOSITES honour.
humility ● noun MODESTY, humbleness, meekness, diffidence, unassertiveness; lack of pride, lack of vanity.
– OPPOSITES pride.
hummock ● noun HILLOCK, hump, mound, knoll, tump, prominence, elevation, rise, dune; N. Amer. knob; formal eminence.
humorist ● noun COMIC WRITER, wit, wag; comic, funny man/woman, comedian, comedienne, joker, jokester; clown.
humorous ● adjective AMUSING, funny, comic, comical, entertaining, diverting, witty, jocular, light-hearted, tongue-in-cheek, wry; hilarious, uproarious, riotous, zany, farcical, droll; informal price-

cardinal humour) historical each of four fluids of the body (blood, phlegm, yellow bile or choler, and black bile or melancholy), formerly believed to determine a person's physical and mental qualities. ● verb comply with the wishes or whims of.
– PHRASES **out of humour** in a bad mood.
– DERIVATIVES **humourless** adjective.
– ORIGIN originally in the sense 'bodily fluid', surviving in *aqueous humour* and *vitreous humour*: from Latin *humor* 'moisture'.

hump ● noun **1** a rounded protuberance found on the back of a camel or other animal or as an abnormality on a person's back. **2** a rounded raised mass of earth or land. ● verb **1** informal lift or carry with difficulty. **2** make hump-shaped. **3** vulgar slang have sexual intercourse with.
– PHRASES **get the hump** Brit. informal become annoyed or sulky. **over the hump** informal past the most difficult part of something.
– DERIVATIVES **humped** adjective **humpless** adjective **humpy** adjective.
– ORIGIN probably related to Low German *humpe* 'hump'.

humpback ● noun another term for HUNCHBACK.
– DERIVATIVES **humpbacked** adjective.

humpback bridge ● noun Brit. a small road bridge with a steep ascent and descent.

humungous ● adjective variant spelling of HUMONGOUS.

humus /hyōōməss/ ● noun the organic component of soil, formed by the decomposition of leaves and other plant material.
– DERIVATIVES **humic** adjective.
– ORIGIN Latin, 'soil'.

Hun ● noun **1** a member of an Asiatic people who invaded Europe in the 4th–5th centuries. **2** informal, derogatory a German (especially in military contexts during the First and Second World Wars).
– ORIGIN Greek *Hounnoi*.

hunch ● verb raise (one's shoulders) and bend the top of one's body forward. ● noun a feeling or guess based on intuition.
– ORIGIN originally meaning 'push, shove': of unknown origin.

hunchback ● noun **1** a deformed back in the shape of a hump, often caused by collapse of a vertebra. **2** often offensive a person with such a deformity.
– DERIVATIVES **hunchbacked** adjective.

hundred ● cardinal number **1** ten more than ninety; 100. (Roman numeral: **c** or **C**.) **2** (**hundreds**) informal an unspecified large number. **3** used to express whole hours in the twenty-four-hour system. ● noun Brit. historical a subdivision of a county or shire, having its own court.
– PHRASES **a** (or **one**) **hundred per cent 1** entirely. **2** informal completely fit and healthy: *she didn't feel one hundred per cent.* **3** informal maximum effort and commitment.
– DERIVATIVES **hundredfold** adjective & adverb **hundredth** ordinal number.
– ORIGIN Old English.

hundreds and thousands ● plural noun Brit. tiny sugar beads of varying colours used for decorating cakes and desserts.

hundredweight ● noun (pl. same or **hundredweights**) **1** (also **long hundredweight**) Brit. a unit of weight equal to 112 lb (about 50.8 kg). **2** (also **short hundredweight**) US a unit of weight equal to 100 lb (about 45.4 kg). **3** (also **metric hundredweight**) a unit of weight equal to 50 kg.

hung past and past participle of HANG. ● adjective **1** having no political party with an overall majority: *a hung parliament.* **2** (of a jury) unable to agree on a verdict. **3** (**hung up**) informal emotionally confused or disturbed.

Hungarian /hunggairiən/ ● noun **1** a person from Hungary. **2** the official language of Hungary. ● adjective relating to Hungary.

hunger ● noun **1** a feeling of discomfort or weakness caused by lack of food, coupled with the desire to eat. **2** a strong desire. ● verb (**hunger after/for**) have a strong desire for.
– ORIGIN Old English.

hunger strike ● noun a prolonged refusal to eat, carried out as a protest by a prisoner.

hung-over ● adjective suffering from a hangover.

hungry ● adjective (**hungrier**, **hungriest**) **1** feeling or showing hunger. **2** (often **hungry for**) having a strong desire.
– DERIVATIVES **hungrily** adverb **hungriness** noun.

hunk ● noun **1** a large piece cut or broken from something larger. **2** informal a sexually attractive man.
– DERIVATIVES **hunky** adjective.
– ORIGIN probably Dutch or Low German.

hunker ● verb **1** squat or crouch down low. **2** (**hunker down**) apply oneself seriously to a task.
– ORIGIN probably related to German *hocken*.

hunkers ● plural noun informal haunches.
– ORIGIN from HUNKER.

hunky-dory ● adjective informal excellent.
– ORIGIN *hunky* from Dutch *honk* 'home' (in games); the origin of *dory* is unknown.

hunt ● verb **1** pursue and kill (a wild animal) for sport or food. **2** (also **hunt for** or **after**) try to find by diligent searching. **3** (**hunt down**) pursue and capture (someone). **4** (**hunted**) appearing alarmed or harassed as if being hunted. **5** (of a device) undergo a cyclic variation in its working speed. ● noun **1** an act or the process of hunting. **2** an association of people who meet regularly to hunt animals as a sport.
– DERIVATIVES **hunting** noun.
– ORIGIN Old English.

hunter ● noun **1** a person or animal that hunts. **2** a watch with a

h

Thesaurus

less, side-splitting, rib-tickling, a scream, a hoot, a barrel of laughs, waggish; *informal, dated* killing.
– OPPOSITES serious.

humour ● noun **1** *the humour of the situation* COMEDY, comical aspect, funny side, funniness, hilarity; absurdity, ludicrousness, drollness; satire, irony. **2** *the stories are spiced up with humour* JOKES, jests, jesting, quips, witticisms, funny remarks, puns; wit, wittiness, comedy, drollery; *informal* gags, wisecracks, cracks, waggishness, one-liners. **3** *his good humour was infectious* MOOD, temper, disposition, temperament, state of mind; spirits.
● verb *she was always humouring him* INDULGE, accommodate, pander to, cater to, yield to, give way to, give in to, go along with; pamper, spoil, overindulge, mollify, placate, gratify, satisfy.

humourless ● adjective SERIOUS, solemn, sober, sombre, grave, grim, dour, unsmiling, stony-faced; gloomy, glum, sad, melancholy, dismal, joyless, cheerless, lugubrious; boring, tedious, dull, dry.
– OPPOSITES jovial.

hump ● noun *a hump at the base of the spine* PROTUBERANCE, prominence, lump, bump, knob, protrusion, projection, bulge, swelling, hunch; growth, outgrowth.
● verb **1** *he humped his body to avoid a blow* ARCH, hunch, bend, bow, curve. **2** *(informal) he humped boxes up the stairs* HEAVE, carry, lug, lift, hoist, heft, tote; *informal* schlep.
– OPPOSITES straighten.
– PHRASES **give someone the hump** *(Brit. informal)*. See ANNOY.

hunch ● verb **1** *he hunched his shoulders* ARCH, curve, hump, bow. **2** *I hunched up as small as I could* CROUCH, huddle, curl; hunker down, bend, stoop, squat.
– OPPOSITES straighten.
● noun **1** *the hunch on his back* PROTUBERANCE, hump, lump, bump, knob, protrusion, prominence, bulge, swelling; growth, outgrowth. **2** *my hunch is that he'll be back* FEELING, feeling in one's bones, guess, suspicion, impression, inkling, idea, notion, fancy, intuition; *informal* gut feeling.

hundred ● cardinal number century; *informal* ton.
– RELATED TERMS centenary, centennial, centi-, hecto-.

hunger ● noun **1** *she was faint with hunger* LACK OF FOOD, hungriness, ravenousness, emptiness; starvation, malnutrition, malnourishment, undernourishment. **2** *a hunger for news* DESIRE, craving, longing, yearning, hankering, appetite, thirst; want, need; *informal* itch, yen.
– PHRASES **hunger after/for** DESIRE, crave; long for, yearn for, pine for, ache for, hanker after, thirst for, lust for; want, need; *informal* have a yen for, itch for, be dying for, be gagging for.

hungry ● adjective **1** *I was really hungry* RAVENOUS, empty, in need of food, hollow, faint from hunger; starving, starved; malnourished, undernourished, underfed; *informal* peckish, famished, able to eat a horse; *archaic* esurient. **2** *they are hungry for success* EAGER, keen, avid, longing, yearning, aching, greedy; craving, desirous of, hankering after; *informal* itching, dying, gagging, hot.
– OPPOSITES full.

hunk ● noun **1** *a hunk of bread* CHUNK, wedge, block, slab, lump, square, gobbet; *Brit. informal* wodge. **2** *(informal) he's such a hunk* MUSCLEMAN, strongman, macho man, iron man, Hercules; *informal* tough guy, he-man, beefcake, stud; *N. Amer. informal* studmuffin.
– OPPOSITES wimp.

hunt ● verb **1** *they hunted deer* CHASE, stalk, pursue, course, run

hinged cover protecting the glass.
– DERIVATIVES **huntress** noun.

hunter-gatherer ● noun a member of a nomadic people who live chiefly by hunting and fishing, and harvesting wild food.

hunter's moon ● noun the first full moon after a harvest moon.

hunting crop (also **hunting whip**) ● noun a short rigid riding whip with a handle at right angles to the stock and a long leather thong, used chiefly in hunting.

hunting ground ● noun a place likely to be a fruitful source of something desired or sought.

Huntington's disease ● noun a hereditary disease marked by degeneration of brain cells, causing chorea and progressive dementia.
– ORIGIN named after the American neurologist George *Huntington* (1851–1916).

hunt saboteur ● noun a person who attempts to disrupt a hunt.

huntsman ● noun **1** a person who hunts. **2** a hunt official in charge of hounds.

hurdle ● noun **1** one of a series of upright frames which athletes in a race must jump over. **2** (**hurdles**) a hurdle race. **3** an obstacle or difficulty. **4** a portable rectangular frame used as a temporary fence. ● verb **1** run in a hurdle race. **2** jump over (a hurdle or other obstacle) while running. **3** enclose or fence off with hurdles.
– DERIVATIVES **hurdler** noun.
– ORIGIN Old English.

h

hurdy-gurdy /hurdigurdi/ ● noun (pl. **hurdy-gurdies**) **1** a musical instrument with a droning sound played by turning a handle, with keys worked by the other hand. **2** informal a barrel organ.
– ORIGIN probably imitative of the instrument's sound.

hurl ● verb **1** throw or impel with great force. **2** utter (abuse) vehemently. ● noun Scottish informal a ride in a vehicle.
– ORIGIN probably imitative, but influenced by Low German *hurreln*.

hurley ● noun **1** a stick used in the game of hurling. **2** another term for HURLING.
– ORIGIN from HURL.

hurling ● noun an Irish game resembling hockey, played with a shorter stick with a broader oval blade.

hurly-burly ● noun busy, boisterous activity.
– ORIGIN from HURL.

Huron /hyooron/ ● noun (pl. same or **Hurons**) a member of a confederation of native North American peoples formerly living in the region east of Lake Huron.
– ORIGIN French, 'having hair standing in bristles on the head', from Old French *hure* 'head of a wild boar'.

hurrah (also **hooray, hurray**) ● exclamation used to express joy or approval.
– ORIGIN alteration of HUZZA.

hurricane ● noun a storm with a violent wind, in particular a tropical cyclone in the Caribbean.
– ORIGIN Spanish *huracán*, probably from a word in an extinct Caribbean language meaning 'god of the storm'.

hurricane lamp ● noun an oil lamp with a glass chimney, designed to protect the flame even in high winds.

hurry ● verb (**hurries**, **hurried**) move or act quickly or more quickly. ● noun great haste; urgency.
– PHRASES **in a hurry 1** rushed; in a rushed manner. **2** informal easily; readily: *you won't forget that in a hurry.*
– DERIVATIVES **hurried** adjective **hurriedly** adverb.
– ORIGIN imitative.

hurt ● verb (past and past part. **hurt**) **1** cause or feel physical pain or injury. **2** cause or feel mental pain or distress. ● noun injury or pain; harm.
– ORIGIN Old French *hurter* 'to strike'.

hurtful ● adjective causing mental pain or distress.
– DERIVATIVES **hurtfully** adverb.

hurtle ● verb move or cause to move at great speed, often in a wildly uncontrolled manner.
– ORIGIN originally in the sense 'strike against': from HURT.

husband ● noun a married man considered in relation to his wife. ● verb use (resources) economically.

Thesaurus

down; track, trail, follow, shadow; *informal* tail. **2** *police are hunting for her* SEARCH, look (high and low), scour the area; seek, try to find; cast about/around/round, rummage (about/around/round), root about/around, fish about/around.
● noun **1** *the thrill of the hunt* CHASE, pursuit. **2** *police have stepped up their hunt* SEARCH, look, quest.

hunted ● adjective HARASSED, persecuted, harried, hounded, beleaguered, troubled, stressed, tormented; careworn, haggard; distraught, desperate; *informal* hassled.
– OPPOSITES carefree.

hunter ● noun HUNTSMAN, huntswoman, stalker, trapper, woodsman; nimrod; predator.

hunting ● noun BLOOD SPORTS, field sports, coursing, fox-hunting; trapping; the chase.

hurdle ● noun **1** *his leg hit a hurdle* FENCE, jump, barrier, barricade, bar, railing, rail. **2** *the final hurdle to overcome* OBSTACLE, difficulty, problem, barrier, bar, snag, stumbling block, impediment, obstruction, complication, hindrance; *informal* headache, fly in the ointment; *Brit. informal* spanner in the works.

hurl ● verb THROW, toss, fling, pitch, cast, lob, bowl, launch, catapult; project, propel, let fly; *informal* chuck, heave, sling, buzz, bung; *N. Amer. informal* peg; *Austral. & N. English informal* hoy; *NZ informal* bish; *dated* shy.

hurly-burly ● noun BUSTLE, hustle and bustle, hubbub, confusion, disorder, uproar, tumult, pandemonium, mayhem, rumpus; *informal* hoo-ha, hullabaloo, ballyhoo, kerfuffle.
– OPPOSITES calm, order.

hurricane ● noun CYCLONE, typhoon, tornado, storm, tempest, windstorm, whirlwind; *N. Amer. informal* twister; *Austral.* willy-willy.

hurried ● adjective **1** *hurried glances* QUICK, fast, swift, rapid, speedy, brisk, hasty; cursory, perfunctory, brief, short, fleeting, passing, superficial. **2** *a hurried decision* HASTY, rushed, speedy, quick; impetuous, impulsive, precipitate, precipitous, rash, incautious, imprudent, spur-of-the-moment.
– OPPOSITES slow, considered.

hurriedly ● adverb HASTILY, speedily, quickly, fast, rapidly, swiftly, briskly; without delay, at top speed, at full tilt, at the double; headlong, hotfoot, post-haste; *informal* like the wind, like greased lightning, in double quick time; *Brit. informal* like the clappers, at a rate of knots, like billy-o; *N. Amer. informal* lickety-split.

hurry ● verb **1** *hurry or you'll be late* BE QUICK, hurry up, hasten, speed up, press on, push on; run, dash, rush, race, fly; scurry, scramble, scuttle, sprint; *informal* get a move on, step on it, get cracking, get moving, shake a leg, tear, hare, zip, zoom, hotfoot it, leg it; *Brit. informal* shift, get one's skates on, stir one's stumps; *N. Amer. informal* get the lead out, get a wiggle on; *dated* make haste; *archaic* hie. **2** *she hurried him out* HUSTLE, hasten, push, urge, drive, spur, goad, prod; *informal* gee up.
– OPPOSITES dawdle, delay.
● noun *in all the hurry, we forgot* RUSH, haste, flurry, hustle and bustle, confusion, commotion, hubbub, turmoil; race, scramble, scurry.

hurt ● verb **1** *my back hurts* BE PAINFUL, be sore, be tender, cause pain, cause discomfort; ache, smart, sting, burn, throb; *informal* be killing; *Brit. informal* be playing up. **2** *Dad hurt his leg* INJURE, wound, damage, disable, incapacitate, maim, mutilate; bruise, cut, gash, graze, scrape, scratch, lacerate. **3** *his words hurt her* DISTRESS, pain, wound, sting, upset, sadden, devastate, grieve, mortify; cut to the quick. **4** *high interest rates are hurting the economy* HARM, damage, be detrimental to, weaken, blight, impede, jeopardize, undermine, ruin, wreck, sabotage, cripple.
– OPPOSITES heal, comfort, benefit.
● noun **1** *falling properly minimizes hurt* HARM, injury, wounding, pain, suffering, discomfort, soreness; aching, smarting, stinging, throbbing. **2** *all the hurt he had caused* DISTRESS, pain, suffering, grief, misery, anguish, trauma, woe, upset, sadness, sorrow; harm, damage, trouble.
– OPPOSITES joy.
● adjective **1** *my hurt hand* INJURED, wounded, bruised, grazed, cut, gashed, sore, painful, aching, smarting, throbbing. **2** *Anne's hurt expression* PAINED, distressed, anguished, upset, sad, mortified, offended; *informal* miffed, peeved, sore.
– OPPOSITES pleased.

hurtful ● adjective **1** *hurtful words* UPSETTING, distressing, wounding, painful; unkind, cruel, nasty, mean, malicious, spiteful; cutting, barbed; *informal* catty, bitchy. **2** *this is hurtful to the interests of women* DETRIMENTAL, harmful, damaging, injurious, disadvantageous, unfavourable, prejudicial, deleterious, ruinous.

hurtle ● verb SPEED, rush, run, race, bolt, dash, career, whizz, zoom, charge, shoot, streak, gallop, hare, fly, scurry, go like the

– DERIVATIVES **husbandless** adjective **husbandly** adjective.
– ORIGIN original senses included 'steward of a household' and 'farmer': from Old Norse.
husbandman • noun archaic a farmer.
husbandry • noun **1** the care, cultivation, and breeding of crops and animals. **2** management and conservation of resources.
hush • verb **1** make or become quiet. **2** (**hush up**) suppress public mention of. • noun a silence.
– ORIGIN from obsolete *husht* 'silent', 'be quiet!'
hush-hush • adjective informal highly secret or confidential.
hush money • noun informal money paid to someone to prevent them from disclosing information.
husk • noun **1** the dry outer covering of some fruits or seeds. **2** a dry or rough discarded outer layer. • verb remove the husk from.
– ORIGIN probably from Low German *hūske* 'sheath', 'little house'.
husky[1] • adjective (**huskier**, **huskiest**) **1** sounding low-pitched and slightly hoarse. **2** strong; hefty.
– DERIVATIVES **huskily** adverb **huskiness** noun.
husky[2] • noun (pl. **huskies**) a powerful dog of a breed with a thick double coat, used in the Arctic for pulling sledges.
– ORIGIN from a North American dialect word meaning 'Eskimo'.
huss /huss/ • noun Brit. a dogfish.
– ORIGIN of unknown origin.
hussar /hoozaar/ • noun historical (except in titles) a soldier in a light cavalry regiment which adopted a dress uniform modelled on that of the Hungarian light horsemen of the 15th century.
– ORIGIN Hungarian *huszár*, from Italian *corsaro* 'corsair'.
hussy • noun (pl. **hussies**) dated or humorous a promiscuous or immoral girl or woman.
– ORIGIN contraction of HOUSEWIFE.
hustings • noun (treated as pl. or sing.) **1** a meeting at which candidates in an election address potential voters. **2** (**the hustings**) political campaigning; electioneering.
– ORIGIN Old Norse, 'household assembly held by a leader', from *hús* 'house' + *thing* 'assembly, parliament'.
hustle • verb **1** push roughly; jostle. **2** informal, chiefly N. Amer. obtain illicitly or by forceful action or persuasion. **3** (**hustle into**) informal coerce or pressure into. **4** N. Amer. informal engage in prostitution. • noun **1** busy movement and activity. **2** N. Amer. informal a fraud or swindle.
– DERIVATIVES **hustler** noun.
– ORIGIN Dutch *hutselen* 'shake, toss'.
hut • noun a small single-storey building of simple or crude construction.
– ORIGIN High German *hütte*.
hutch • noun a box or cage for keeping rabbits or other small domesticated animals.
– ORIGIN originally in the sense 'storage chest': from Old French *huche*, from Latin *hutica*.
Hutu /hōōtōō/ • noun (pl. same or **Hutus** or **Bahutu** /bəhōōtōō/) a member of a people forming the majority population in Rwanda and Burundi.
– ORIGIN a local name.
huzza /həzaa/ (also **huzzah**) • exclamation archaic used to express approval or delight.
– ORIGIN perhaps used originally as a sailor's cry when hauling.
hwyl /hōōil/ • noun (in Welsh use) a stirring, emotional feeling.
– ORIGIN Welsh.
hyacinth /hīəsinth/ • noun **1** a plant with a spike of bell-shaped fragrant flowers. **2** another term for JACINTH.
– ORIGIN named after *Hyacinthus* in Greek mythology: Hyacinthus was a youth loved by the god Apollo but accidentally killed by him, from whose blood Apollo caused a flower to grow.
hyaena • noun variant spelling of HYENA.
hyaline /hīəlin, -leen/ • adjective Anatomy & Zoology **1** glassy and translucent in appearance. **2** relating to or consisting of hyalin, a clear substance produced by the degeneration of certain body tissues.
– ORIGIN Greek *hualinos*, from *hualos* 'glass'.
hyalite /hīəlīt/ • noun a translucent, colourless variety of opal.
– ORIGIN from Greek *hualos* 'glass'.
hyaluronic acid /hīəlyooronnik/ • noun a viscous fluid carbohydrate present in connective tissue, synovial fluid, and the humours of the eye.
– ORIGIN from a blend of *hyaloid* 'glassy' (from Greek *hualoeidēs* 'like glass') and *uronic acid*.
hybrid /hībrid/ • noun **1** the offspring of two plants or animals of different species or varieties, such as a mule. **2** a thing made by combining two different elements.
– DERIVATIVES **hybridity** noun.
– ORIGIN Latin *hybrida* 'offspring of a tame sow and wild boar, child of a freeman and slave, etc.'
hybridize (also **hybridise**) • verb cross-breed to produce hybrids.
– DERIVATIVES **hybridization** noun.
hybrid vigour • noun Genetics the tendency of a cross-bred individual to show qualities superior to those of both parents.
hydra • noun a minute freshwater invertebrate animal with a stalk-like tubular body and a ring of tentacles around the mouth.

h

Thesaurus

wind; *informal* belt, pelt, tear, scoot, go like a bat out of hell; *Brit. informal* bomb, bucket, go like the clappers; *N. Amer. informal* hightail, barrel.
husband • noun SPOUSE, partner, mate, consort, man, helpmate, helpmeet; groom, bridegroom; *informal* hubby, old man, one's better half; *Brit. informal* other half.
• verb *oil reserves should be husbanded* CONSERVE, preserve, save, safeguard, save for a rainy day, put aside, put by, lay in, reserve, stockpile, hoard; use economically, use sparingly, be frugal with.
– OPPOSITES squander.
husbandry • noun **1** *farmers have new methods of husbandry* FARM MANAGEMENT, land management, farming, agriculture, agronomy; cultivation; animal husbandry. **2** *the careful husbandry of their resources* CONSERVATION, management; economy, thrift, thriftiness, frugality.
hush • verb **1** *he tried to hush her* SILENCE, quieten (down), shush; gag, muzzle; *informal* shut up. **2** *the crowd hushed* FALL SILENT, stop talking, quieten down; *informal* pipe down, shut up. **3** *they hushed up the dangers* KEEP SECRET, conceal, hide, suppress, cover up, keep dark, keep quiet about; obscure, veil, sweep under the carpet; *informal* sit on, keep under one's hat.
– OPPOSITES disclose.
• exclamation *Hush! Someone will hear you* BE QUIET, keep quiet, quieten down, be silent, stop talking, hold your tongue; *informal* shut up, shut your mouth, shut your face, shut your trap, button your lip, pipe down, put a sock in it, give it a rest, save it, not another word; *Brit. informal* shut your gob.
• noun *a hush descended* SILENCE, quiet, quietness; stillness, peace, peacefulness, calm, tranquillity.
– OPPOSITES noise.
hush-hush • adjective *(informal)*. See SECRET adjective sense 1.
husk • noun SHELL, hull, pod, case, covering, integument, shuck; *Botany* pericarp, legume.
husky • adjective **1** *a husky voice* THROATY, gruff, gravelly, hoarse, croaky, rough, guttural, harsh, rasping, raspy. **2** *Paddy was a husky guy* STRONG, muscular, muscly, muscle-bound, brawny, hefty, burly, hulking, chunky, strapping, thickset, solid, powerful, heavy, robust, sturdy, Herculean, well built; *informal* beefy, hunky.
– OPPOSITES shrill, soft, puny.
hussy • noun *(dated)* MINX, coquette, tease, seductress, Lolita, Jezebel; slut, loose woman; *informal* floozie, tart, vamp; *Brit. informal* scrubber, slapper, slag; *N. Amer. informal* tramp; *dated* trollop; *archaic* jade, strumpet.
hustle • verb **1** *they were hustled as they went* JOSTLE, shove, push, bump, knock, nudge, elbow, shoulder. **2** *I was hustled away* MANHANDLE, push, shove, thrust, frogmarch; rush, hurry, whisk; *informal* bundle. **3** *(informal) don't be hustled into anything* COERCE, force, pressure, pressurize, badger, pester, hound, nag, goad, prod; browbeat, bulldoze, steamroller, dragoon; *informal* railroad, fast-talk.
– PHRASES **hustle and bustle** HURLY-BURLY, bustle, tumult, hubbub, activity, action, liveliness, animation, excitement, agitation, flurry, whirl; *informal* toing and froing, comings and goings, ballyhoo, hoo-ha, hullabaloo.
hut • noun SHACK, shanty, (log) cabin, shelter, shed, lean-to; hovel; *Scottish* bothy, shieling; *N. Amer.* cabana.
hybrid • noun *a hybrid between a brown and albino mouse* CROSS, cross-breed, mixed-breed, half-breed, half-blood; mixture, blend, amalgamation, combination, composite, fusion.
• adjective *hybrid roses* COMPOSITE, cross-bred, interbred, mongrel; mixed, compound, blended.

– ORIGIN named after the *Hydra* of Greek mythology, a many-headed snake whose heads regrew as they were cut off: the hydra is so named because, if cut into pieces, each section can grow into a whole animal.
hydrangea /hīdraynjə/ ● noun a shrub with large white, blue, or pink flowers, native to Asia and America.
– ORIGIN from Greek *hudro-* 'water' + *angeion* 'vessel' (from the cup shape of its seed capsule).
hydrant /hīdrənt/ ● noun a water pipe with a nozzle to which a fire hose can be attached.
hydrate ● noun /hīdrayt/ Chemistry a compound in which water molecules are chemically bound to another compound or an element. ● verb /hīdrayt/ cause to absorb or combine with water.
– DERIVATIVES **hydration** noun.
hydraulic /hīdrollik/ ● adjective **1** relating to a liquid moving in a confined space under pressure. **2** relating to the science of hydraulics. **3** (of cement) hardening under water.
– DERIVATIVES **hydraulically** adverb.
– ORIGIN Greek *hudraulikos*, from *hudro-* 'water' + *aulos* 'pipe'.
hydraulics ● plural noun (usu. treated as sing.) the branch of science and technology concerned with the conveyance of liquids through pipes and channels.
hydride /hīdrīd/ ● noun Chemistry a binary compound of hydrogen with a metal.
hydro ● noun (pl. **hydros**) **1** Brit. a hotel or clinic originally providing hydropathic treatment. **2** a hydroelectric power plant.
hydro- (also **hydr-**) ● combining form **1** water; relating to water: *hydraulic*. **2** Medicine affected with an accumulation of serous fluid: *hydrocephalus*. **3** Chemistry combined with hydrogen: *hydrocarbon*.
– ORIGIN from Greek *hudōr* 'water'.
hydrocarbon ● noun a compound of hydrogen and carbon, such as any of those which are the chief components of petroleum and natural gas.
hydrocephalus /hīdrəseffələss, -keff-/ ● noun a condition in which fluid accumulates in the brain.
– DERIVATIVES **hydrocephalic** adjective **hydrocephaly** noun.
– ORIGIN from Greek *hudro-* 'water' + *kephalē* 'head'.
hydrochloric acid ● noun a strongly acidic solution of the gas hydrogen chloride.
hydrochloride ● noun a compound of an organic base with hydrochloric acid.
hydrocortisone ● noun a steroid hormone produced by the adrenal cortex, used medicinally to treat inflammation and rheumatism.
hydrocyanic acid /hīdrōsīannik/ ● noun a highly poisonous acidic solution of hydrogen cyanide.
hydrodynamics ● plural noun (treated as sing.) the science of the forces acting on or exerted by fluids (especially liquids).
– DERIVATIVES **hydrodynamic** adjective.
hydroelectric ● adjective relating to the generation of electricity using flowing water to drive a turbine which powers a generator.
– DERIVATIVES **hydroelectricity** noun.
hydrofoil ● noun **1** a boat fitted with structures (known as foils) which lift the hull clear of the water at speed. **2** each of the foils of such a craft.
hydrogen /hīdrəjən/ ● noun a colourless, odourless, highly flammable gas which is the lightest of the chemical elements.
hydrogenate /hīdrojinayt/ ● verb charge with or cause to combine with hydrogen.
– DERIVATIVES **hydrogenation** noun.
hydrogen bomb ● noun a nuclear bomb whose destructive power comes from the fusion of isotopes of hydrogen (deuterium and tritium).
hydrogen bond ● noun Chemistry a weak chemical bond resulting from electrostatic attraction between a proton in one molecule and an electronegative atom in another.
hydrogen cyanide ● noun a highly poisonous gas or volatile liquid with an odour of bitter almonds, made by the action of acids on cyanides.
hydrogen peroxide ● noun a colourless viscous liquid used in some disinfectants and bleaches.
hydrogen sulphide ● noun a colourless poisonous gas with a smell of bad eggs, made by the action of acids on sulphides.
hydrogeology ● noun the branch of geology concerned with underground or surface water.
– DERIVATIVES **hydrogeological** adjective **hydrogeologist** noun.
hydrography /hīdrografi/ ● noun the science of surveying and charting bodies of water.
– DERIVATIVES **hydrographer** noun **hydrographic** adjective.
hydroid /hīdroyd/ ● noun Zoology an aquatic invertebrate animal of an order which includes the hydras and many corals.
hydrology ● noun the science of the properties and distribution of water on the earth's surface.
– DERIVATIVES **hydrologic** adjective **hydrological** adjective **hydrologist** noun.
hydrolyse /hīdrəlīz/ (also **hydrolyze**) ● verb Chemistry break down (a compound) by chemical reaction with water.
hydrolysis /hīdrollisiss/ ● noun Chemistry the chemical breakdown of a compound due to reaction with water.
– DERIVATIVES **hydrolytic** adjective.
hydromassage ● noun massage using jets of water.
hydromechanics ● plural noun (treated as sing.) the mechanics of liquids; hydrodynamics.
– DERIVATIVES **hydromechanical** adjective.
hydrometer /hīdrommitər/ ● noun an instrument for measuring the density of liquids.
– DERIVATIVES **hydrometric** adjective **hydrometry** noun.
hydropathy /hīdroppəthi/ ● noun the treatment of illness through the use of water, either internally or externally.
– DERIVATIVES **hydropathic** adjective **hydropathist** noun.
hydrophilic /hīdrəfillik/ ● adjective having a tendency to mix with, dissolve in, or be wetted by water.
hydrophobia ● noun **1** extreme or irrational fear of water, especially as a symptom of rabies. **2** rabies.
hydrophobic ● adjective **1** tending to repel or fail to mix with water. **2** of or suffering from hydrophobia.
hydrophone ● noun a microphone which detects sound waves under water.
hydroplane ● noun **1** a light, fast motor boat. **2** a fin-like attachment which enables a moving submarine to rise or fall in the water. **3** US a seaplane. ● verb chiefly N. Amer. another term for AQUAPLANE.
hydroponics /hīdrəponniks/ ● plural noun (treated as sing.) the growing of plants in sand, gravel, or liquid, with added nutrients but without soil.
– DERIVATIVES **hydroponic** adjective **hydroponically** adverb.
– ORIGIN from Greek *hudōr* 'water' + *ponos* 'labour'.
hydrosphere ● noun the seas, lakes, and other waters of the earth's surface, considered collectively.
hydrostatic ● adjective relating to the equilibrium of liquids and the pressure exerted by liquid at rest.
– DERIVATIVES **hydrostatics** plural noun.
hydrotherapy ● noun **1** the therapeutic use of exercises in a pool. **2** another term for HYDROPATHY.
– DERIVATIVES **hydrotherapist** noun.
hydrothermal ● adjective relating to the action of heated water in the earth's crust.
– DERIVATIVES **hydrothermally** adverb.
hydrothermal vent ● noun an opening in the sea floor out of which heated mineral-rich water flows.
hydrous ● adjective containing water.
hydroxide ● noun a compound containing the hydroxide ion OH^- or the group –OH.
hydroxyl /hīdroksīl/ ● noun Chemistry the radical –OH, present in alcohols and many other organic compounds.
hyena (also **hyaena**) ● noun a doglike carnivorous African mammal with long forelimbs and an erect mane.
– ORIGIN Greek *huaina* 'female pig' (probably because of the resemblance of the hyena's mane to a hog's bristles).
hygiene ● noun conditions or practices that help to maintain health and prevent disease, especially cleanliness.
– ORIGIN from Greek *hugieinē tekhnē* 'art of health', from *hugiēs* 'healthy'.
hygienic ● adjective promoting or conducive to hygiene; sanitary.
– DERIVATIVES **hygienically** adverb.
hygienist ● noun a specialist in the promotion of hygiene.

Thesaurus

hybridize ● verb CROSS-BREED, cross, interbreed, cross-fertilize, cross-pollinate; mix, blend, combine, amalgamate.

hygiene ● noun CLEANLINESS, sanitation, sterility, purity, disinfection; public health, environmental health.

hygrometer /hīgrommitər/ ● noun an instrument for measuring humidity.
– DERIVATIVES **hygrometric** adjective **hygrometry** noun.
– ORIGIN from Greek *hugros* 'wet'.
hygroscope /hīgrəskōp/ ● noun an instrument which indicates (though does not necessarily measure) the humidity of the air.
hygroscopic ● adjective tending to absorb moisture from the air.
– DERIVATIVES **hygroscopically** adverb.
hying present participle of HIE.
hymen /hīmən/ ● noun a membrane which partially closes the opening of the vagina and whose presence is traditionally taken to be a mark of virginity.
– ORIGIN Greek *humēn* 'membrane'.
hymeneal /hīmineeəl/ ● adjective literary of or concerning marriage.
– ORIGIN from *Hymen*, the Greek god of marriage.
hymenopteran /hīmənoptərən/ ● noun an insect of a large group (the order Hymenoptera) including the bees, wasps, and ants, having four transparent wings.
– DERIVATIVES **hymenopterous** adjective.
– ORIGIN from Greek *humenopteros* 'membrane-winged'.
hymn ● noun a religious song of praise, especially a Christian song in praise of God. ● verb praise or celebrate.
– ORIGIN Greek *humnos* 'ode or song in praise'.
hymnal /himn'l/ ● noun a book of hymns. ● adjective relating to hymns.
hymnary /himnəri/ ● noun (pl. **hymnaries**) another term for HYMNAL.
hymnody /himnədi/ ● noun the singing or composition of hymns.
– ORIGIN Greek *humnōidia*, from *humnos* 'hymn' + *ōidē* 'song'.
hyoid /hīoyd/ ● noun a U-shaped bone in the neck which supports the tongue. ● adjective relating to this bone.
– ORIGIN from Greek *huoeidēs* 'shaped like the letter upsilon (υ)'.
hyoscine /hīəseen/ ● noun a poisonous substance found in plants and used to prevent motion sickness and as a preoperative medication for examination of the eye.
– ORIGIN from Greek *huoskamos* 'henbane'.
hype[1] informal ● noun **1** extravagant or intensive publicity or promotion. **2** a deception or hoax. ● verb promote or publicize intensively or extravagantly.
– ORIGIN originally in the sense 'short-change, cheat': of unknown origin.
hype[2] ● verb (**be hyped up**) informal be stimulated or excited.
– ORIGIN originally in sense 'hypodermic needle, drug addict': abbreviation of HYPODERMIC.
hyper ● adjective informal hyperactive or unusually energetic.
hyper- ● prefix **1** over; beyond; above: *hypersonic*. **2** excessively; above normal: *hyperthyroidism*.
– ORIGIN from Greek *huper* 'over, beyond'.
hyperactive ● adjective abnormally or extremely active.
– DERIVATIVES **hyperactivity** noun.
hyperaemia /hīpəreemiə/ (US **hyperemia**) ● noun Medicine an excess of blood in an organ or other part of the body.
hyperbaric /hīpərbarrik/ ● adjective (of gas) at a pressure greater than normal.
– ORIGIN from Greek *baros* 'heavy'.
hyperbola /hīperbələ/ ● noun (pl. **hyperbolas** or **hyperbolae** /hīperbəlee/) a symmetrical open curve formed by the intersection of a cone with a plane at a smaller angle with its axis than the side of the cone.
– ORIGIN Latin, from Greek *huperbolē* (see HYPERBOLE).
hyperbole /hīperbəli/ ● noun deliberate exaggeration, not meant to be taken literally.
– DERIVATIVES **hyperbolical** adjective **hyperbolically** adverb.
– ORIGIN Greek *huperbolē* 'excess', from *ballein* 'to throw'.
hyperbolic /hīpərbollik/ ● adjective **1** (of language) deliberately exaggerated. **2** relating to a hyperbola.
hyperborean /hīpərboreeən/ literary ● noun **1** an inhabitant of the extreme north. **2** (**Hyperborean**) Greek Mythology a member of a race worshipping Apollo and living in a land of sunshine beyond the north wind. ● adjective relating to the extreme north.
– ORIGIN from Greek *huper* 'beyond' + *boreas* 'north wind'.
hypercritical ● adjective excessively and unreasonably critical.
hyperdrive ● noun (in science fiction) a supposed propulsion system for travel in hyperspace.
hyperglycaemia /hīpərglīseemiə/ (US **hyperglycemia**) ● noun an excess of glucose in the bloodstream, often associated with diabetes mellitus.
– DERIVATIVES **hyperglycaemic** adjective.
hypericum /hīperrikəm/ ● noun a yellow-flowered plant of a family that includes St John's wort and rose of Sharon.
– ORIGIN Greek *hupereikon*, from *huper* 'over' + *ereikē* 'heath'.
hyperinflation ● noun monetary inflation occurring at a very high rate.
hyperkinesis /hīpərkineesiss, -kī-/ (also **hyperkinesia**) ● noun **1** Medicine muscle spasm. **2** Psychiatry a disorder of children marked by hyperactivity and inability to concentrate.
– DERIVATIVES **hyperkinetic** adjective.
hyperlink ● noun Computing a link from a hypertext document to another location, activated by clicking on a highlighted word or image.
hyperlipaemia /hīpərlipeemiə/ (US **hyperlipemia**) ● noun Medicine an abnormally high concentration of fats or lipids in the blood.
hypermarket ● noun chiefly Brit. a very large supermarket.
hypermedia ● noun Computing an extension to hypertext providing multimedia facilities, such as sound and video.
hyperreal ● adjective **1** exaggerated in comparison to reality. **2** (of art) extremely realistic in detail.
hypersensitive ● adjective abnormally or excessively sensitive.
hypersonic ● adjective **1** relating to speeds of more than five times the speed of sound (Mach 5). **2** relating to sound frequencies above about a thousand million hertz.
hyperspace ● noun **1** space of more than three dimensions. **2** (in science fiction) a notional space–time continuum in which it is possible to travel faster than light.
hypertension ● noun abnormally high blood pressure.
– DERIVATIVES **hypertensive** adjective.
hypertext ● noun Computing a system allowing extensive cross-referencing between related sections of text.
hyperthermia /hīpərthermiə/ ● noun the condition of having a body temperature greatly above normal.
hyperthyroidism /hīpərthīroydiz'm/ ● noun overactivity of the thyroid gland, resulting in a rapid heartbeat and an increased rate of metabolism.
– DERIVATIVES **hyperthyroid** adjective.
hypertonic /hīpərtonnik/ ● adjective **1** having a higher osmotic pressure than a particular fluid. **2** having abnormally high muscle tone.
– DERIVATIVES **hypertonia** noun.
hypertrophy /hīpertrəfi/ ● noun enlargement of an organ or tissue resulting from an increase in size of its cells.
– DERIVATIVES **hypertrophic** adjective **hypertrophied** adjective.
– ORIGIN from Greek *-trophia* 'nourishment'.
hyperventilate ● verb **1** breathe at an abnormally rapid rate. **2** be or become overexcited.
– DERIVATIVES **hyperventilation** noun.
hypha /hīfə/ ● noun (pl. **hyphae** /hīfi/) Botany each of the branching filaments that make up the mycelium of a fungus.
– ORIGIN Greek *huphē* 'web'.
hyphen /hīfən/ ● noun the sign (-) used to join words to indicate that they have a combined meaning or that they are grammatically linked, or to indicate word division at the end of a line.
– ORIGIN from Greek *huphen* 'together'.

h

Thesaurus

hygienic ● adjective SANITARY, clean, germ-free, disinfected, sterilized, sterile, antiseptic, aseptic, unpolluted, uncontaminated, salubrious, healthy, wholesome; *informal* squeaky clean.
– OPPOSITES insanitary.
hymn ● noun RELIGIOUS SONG, song of praise, anthem, canticle, chorale, psalm, carol; spiritual.
hype (*informal*) ● noun *her work relies on hype and headlines* PUBLICITY, advertising, promotion, marketing, propaganda, exposure; *informal* plugging, ballyhoo; *Brit. informal* puff.
● verb *a stunt to hype a new product* PUBLICIZE, advertise, promote, push, puff, boost, merchandise, build up, bang the drum for; *informal* plug.
hyperbole ● noun EXAGGERATION, overstatement, magnification, embroidery, embellishment, excess, overkill; *informal* purple prose, puffery.
– OPPOSITES understatement.
hypercritical ● adjective OVERCRITICAL, fault-finding, hair-splitting, carping, cavilling, captious, niggling, quibbling, pedantic, petti-

hyphenate ● verb write or separate with a hyphen.
– DERIVATIVES **hyphenation** noun.
hypnagogic /hipnəgojik/ (also **hypnogogic**) ● adjective relating to the state immediately before falling asleep.
– ORIGIN from Greek *hupnos* 'sleep' + *agōgos* 'leading'.
hypnosis ● noun the induction of a state of consciousness in which a person loses the power of voluntary action and is highly responsive to suggestion or direction.
– ORIGIN from Greek *hupnos* 'sleep'.
hypnotherapy ● noun the use of hypnosis as a therapeutic technique.
– DERIVATIVES **hypnotherapist** noun.
hypnotic ● adjective **1** of, producing, or relating to hypnosis. **2** having a compelling or soporific effect. **3** (of a drug) sleep-inducing. ● noun a sleep-inducing drug.
– DERIVATIVES **hypnotically** adverb.
hypnotism ● noun the study or practice of hypnosis.
– DERIVATIVES **hypnotist** noun.
hypnotize (also **hypnotise**) ● verb produce a state of hypnosis in.
hypo[1] ● noun Photography the chemical sodium thiosulphate (formerly called hyposulphite) used as a photographic fixer.
hypo[2] ● noun (pl. **hypos**) informal a hypodermic.
hypo[3] ● noun (pl. **hypos**) informal an attack of hypoglycaemia.
hypo- (also **hyp-**) ● prefix **1** under: *hypodermic*. **2** below normal: *hypoglycaemia*. **3** slightly: *hypomanic*.
– ORIGIN from Greek *hupo* 'under'.
hypo-allergenic ● adjective unlikely to cause an allergic reaction.
hypocaust /hīpəkawst/ ● noun an ancient Roman heating system, comprising a hollow space under the floor into which hot air was directed.
– ORIGIN Greek *hupokauston* 'place heated from below'.
hypochlorite /hīpəklorīt/ ● noun a salt of a weak acid (**hypochlorous acid**) formed when chlorine dissolves in cold water.
hypochondria /hīpəkondriə/ ● noun abnormal chronic anxiety about one's health.
– ORIGIN Greek *hupokhondria*, denoting the soft body area below the ribs, originally thought to be the seat of melancholy.
hypochondriac ● noun a person who is abnormally anxious about their health. ● adjective (also **hypochondriacal**) related to or affected by hypochondria.
hypocoristic /hīpəkəristik/ ● adjective used as a pet name or diminutive form of a name.
– ORIGIN Greek *hupokorisma*, from *hupokorizesthai* 'play the child'.
hypocotyl /hīpəkottil/ ● noun Botany the part of the stem of an embryo plant between the stalks of the cotyledons and the root.
– ORIGIN from HYPO- + COTYLEDON.
hypocrisy ● noun (pl. **hypocrisies**) the practice of claiming to have higher standards or beliefs than is the case.
– ORIGIN Greek *hupokrisis* 'acting of a theatrical part'.
hypocrite ● noun a person who is given to hypocrisy.
– DERIVATIVES **hypocritical** adjective **hypocritically** adverb.
hypodermic ● adjective **1** relating to the region immediately beneath the skin. **2** (of a needle or syringe) used to inject beneath the skin. ● noun a hypodermic syringe or injection.
– DERIVATIVES **hypodermically** adverb.
– ORIGIN from Greek *derma* 'skin'.
hypoglycaemia /hīpōglīseemiə/ (US **hypoglycemia**) ● noun deficiency of glucose in the bloodstream.
– DERIVATIVES **hypoglycaemic** adjective.
hypomania ● noun a mild form of mania, marked by elation and hyperactivity.
– DERIVATIVES **hypomanic** adjective.
hypostasize (also **hypostasise**) ● verb formal treat or represent as concrete reality.
hypostyle /hīpōstīl/ ● adjective having a roof supported by pillars. ● noun a building having such a roof.
– ORIGIN from Greek *hupo* 'under' + *stulos* 'column'.
hypotension ● noun abnormally low blood pressure.
– DERIVATIVES **hypotensive** adjective.
hypotenuse /hīpottənyōoz/ ● noun the longest side of a right-angled triangle, opposite the right angle.
– ORIGIN from Greek *hupoteinousa grammē* 'subtending line'.
hypothalamus /hīpəthaləməss/ ● noun (pl. **hypothalami** /hīpəthaləmi/) a region of the forebrain below the thalamus, controlling body temperature, thirst, and hunger, and involved in sleep and emotional activity.
– DERIVATIVES **hypothalamic** adjective.
hypothecate /hīpothikayt/ ● verb pledge (money) by law to a specific purpose.
– DERIVATIVES **hypothecation** noun.
– ORIGIN Latin *hypothecare* 'give as a pledge'.
hypothermia /hīpəthermiə/ ● noun the condition of having an abnormally low body temperature.
– ORIGIN from Greek *thermē* 'heat'.
hypothesis /hīpothisiss/ ● noun (pl. **hypotheses** /hīpothiseez/) **1** a supposition made on the basis of limited evidence as a starting point for further investigation. **2** Philosophy a proposition made as a basis for reasoning.
– ORIGIN Greek *hupothesis* 'foundation'.
hypothesize (also **hypothesise**) ● verb put forward as a hypothesis.
hypothetical /hīpəthettik'l/ ● adjective **1** of, based on, or serving as a hypothesis. **2** supposed but not necessarily real or true.
– DERIVATIVES **hypothetically** adverb.
hypothyroidism ● noun abnormally low activity of the thyroid gland, resulting in retarded growth and mental development.
– DERIVATIVES **hypothyroid** adjective.
hypoventilation ● noun breathing at an abnormally slow rate.
hypoxia /hīpoksiə/ ● noun deficiency in the amount of oxygen reaching the tissues.
– DERIVATIVES **hypoxic** adjective.
hypsilophodont /hipsəloffədont/ ● noun a small swift-running bipedal dinosaur of the late Jurassic and Cretaceous periods.
– ORIGIN from Greek *hupsilophos* 'high-crested' + *odous* 'tooth'.
hyrax /hīraks/ ● noun a small short-tailed herbivorous mammal, found in Africa and Arabia.
– ORIGIN Greek *hurax* 'shrew-mouse'.
hyssop /hissəp/ ● noun **1** a small bushy aromatic plant whose leaves are used in cookery and herbal medicine. **2** (in biblical use) a wild shrub whose twigs were used in ancient Jewish rites of purification.
– ORIGIN Greek *hyssōpos*, of Semitic origin.
hysterectomy /histərektəmi/ ● noun (pl. **hysterectomies**) a surgical operation to remove all or part of the womb.
– ORIGIN from Greek *hustera* 'womb'.
hysteresis /histəreesiss/ ● noun Physics the phenomenon by

Thesaurus

fogging, fussy, finicky; *informal* picky, nit-picking, pernickety; *N. Amer. informal* persnickety; *archaic* nice.
hypnosis ● noun MESMERISM, hypnotism, hypnotic suggestion, auto-suggestion.
hypnotic ● adjective MESMERIZING, mesmeric, spellbinding, entrancing, bewitching, irresistible, compelling; soporific, sedative, numbing; *Medicine* stupefacient.
hypnotism ● noun MESMERISM, hypnosis, hypnotic suggestion, auto-suggestion.
hypnotize ● verb **1** *he had been hypnotized* MESMERIZE, put into a trance. **2** *they were hypnotized by the dancers* ENTRANCE, spellbind, enthral, transfix, captivate, bewitch, enrapture, grip, rivet, absorb, magnetize.
hypochondria ● noun VALETUDINARIANISM, imagined ill health, health obsession; neurosis; *technical* hypochondriasis.
hypochondriac ● noun *a hypochondriac who depends on her pills* VALETUDINARIAN, valetudinary; neurotic. ● adjective *her hypochondriac husband* VALETUDINARIAN, valetudinary, hypochondriacal, malingering, health-obsessed, neurotic.
hypocrisy ● noun SANCTIMONIOUSNESS, sanctimony, pietism, piousness, false virtue, cant, posturing, speciousness, empty talk; insincerity, falseness, deceit, dishonesty, dissimulation, duplicity; *informal* phoneyness.
– OPPOSITES sincerity.
hypocrite ● noun SANCTIMONIOUS PERSON, pietist, plaster saint, humbug, pretender, deceiver, dissembler; *informal* phoney; *poetic/literary* whited sepulchre.
hypocritical ● adjective SANCTIMONIOUS, pious, pietistic, self-righteous, holier-than-thou, superior; insincere, specious, false; deceitful, dishonest, dissembling, two-faced; *informal* phoney.
hypodermic ● noun NEEDLE, syringe; *informal* hype, spike.
hypothesis ● noun THEORY, theorem, thesis, conjecture, supposition, postulation, postulate, proposition, premise, assumption; notion, concept, idea.

which the value of a physical property lags behind changes in the effect causing it, especially that involving magnetic induction and a magnetizing force.
– ORIGIN Greek *husterēsis* 'shortcoming'.

hysteria ● noun **1** a psychological disorder whose symptoms include volatile emotions and attention-seeking behaviour. **2** exaggerated or uncontrollable emotion or excitement.

hysteric ● noun **1** (**hysterics**) informal wildly emotional behaviour. **2** (**hysterics**) informal uncontrollable laughter. **3** a person suffering from hysteria. ● adjective hysterical.
– ORIGIN Greek *husterikos* 'of the womb', from *hustera* 'womb' (hysteria being thought to be associated with the womb).

hysterical ● adjective **1** associated with or suffering from hysteria. **2** wildly uncontrolled. **3** informal extremely funny.
– DERIVATIVES **hysterically** adverb.

Hz ● abbreviation hertz.

Thesaurus

hypothetical ● adjective THEORETICAL, speculative, conjectured, notional, suppositional, supposed, assumed; academic.
– OPPOSITES actual.

hysteria ● noun FRENZY, feverishness, hysterics, fit of madness, derangement, mania; panic, alarm, distress; *Brit. informal* the screaming abdabs.
– OPPOSITES calm.

hysterical ● adjective **1** *Janet became hysterical* OVERWROUGHT, overemotional, out of control, frenzied, frantic, wild, feverish; beside oneself, driven to distraction, agitated, berserk, manic, delirious, unhinged, deranged, out of one's mind, raving; *informal* in a state. **2** *(informal) her attempts to dance were hysterical* HILARIOUS, uproarious, very funny, very amusing, comical, farcical; *informal* hysterically funny, side-splitting, rib-tickling, a scream, a hoot, a barrel of laughs; *dated* killing.

hysterics ● plural noun *(informal)* **1** *a fit of hysterics* HYSTERIA, wildness, feverishness, irrationality, frenzy, loss of control, delirium, derangement, mania; *Brit. informal* the screaming abdabs. **2** *the girls collapsed in hysterics* FITS OF LAUGHTER, gales of laughter, uncontrollable laughter, convulsions, fits; *informal* stitches.

Ii

I[1] (also **i**) ● noun (pl. **Is** or **I's**) **1** the ninth letter of the alphabet. **2** denoting the next after H in a set. **3** the Roman numeral for one.

I[2] ● pronoun (first person sing.) used by a speaker to refer to himself or herself.
– ORIGIN Old English.

I[3] ● abbreviation (**I.**) Island(s) or Isle(s). ● symbol the chemical element iodine.

IA ● abbreviation Iowa.

IAEA ● abbreviation International Atomic Energy Agency.

iambic /īambik/ Poetry ● adjective of or using iambuses. ● noun (**iambics**) verse using iambuses.

iambus /īambəss/ (also **iamb**) ● noun (pl. **iambuses** or **iambi** /īambī/) Poetry a metrical foot consisting of one short (or unstressed) syllable followed by one long (or stressed) syllable.
– ORIGIN Greek *iambos* 'iambus, lampoon' (because the iambic meter was first used by Greek satirists).

-ian ● suffix forming adjectives and nouns such as *antediluvian* and *Bostonian*.
– ORIGIN from French *-ien* or Latin *-ianus*.

-iasis ● suffix variant form of -ASIS.

IATA /īaatə/ ● abbreviation International Air Transport Association.

iatrogenic /īatrəjennik/ ● adjective (of illness) caused by medical treatment.

IB ● abbreviation International Baccalaureate.

IBA ● abbreviation Independent Broadcasting Authority.

I-beam ● noun a girder which has the shape of a capital I when viewed in section.

Iberian ● adjective relating to Iberia (the peninsula that consists of modern Spain and Portugal). ● noun a person from Iberia.

ibex /ībeks/ ● noun (pl. **ibexes**) a wild mountain goat with long, thick ridged horns.
– ORIGIN Latin.

IBF ● abbreviation International Boxing Federation.

ibid. /ibid/ ● adverb in the same source (referring to a previously cited work).
– ORIGIN abbreviation of Latin *ibidem* 'in the same place'.

ibis /ībiss/ ● noun (pl. **ibises**) a large wading bird with a long downcurved bill, long neck, and long legs.
– ORIGIN Greek.

Ibizan /ibeethən/ ● noun a person from Ibiza, the westernmost of the Balearic Islands. ● adjective relating to Ibiza.

-ible ● suffix forming adjectives: **1** able to be: *defensible*. **2** suitable for being: *edible*. **3** causing: *horrible*.
– DERIVATIVES **-ibility** suffix **-ibly** suffix.
– ORIGIN Latin *-ibilis*.

IBM ● abbreviation International Business Machines.

IBS ● abbreviation irritable bowel syndrome.

ibuprofen /ībyooprōfen/ ● noun a synthetic compound used as a pain-killer and anti-inflammatory drug.
– ORIGIN from elements of the chemical name *2-(4-isobutylphenyl) propionic acid*.

IC ● abbreviation integrated circuit.

i/c ● abbreviation **1** in charge of. **2** in command.

-ic ● suffix **1** forming adjectives such as *Islamic, terrific*. **2** forming nouns such as *lyric, mechanic*. **3** Chemistry denoting an element in a higher valency: *ferric*. Compare with -OUS.
– ORIGIN from Latin *-icus* or Greek *-ikos*.

-ical ● suffix forming adjectives: **1** corresponding to nouns or adjectives usually ending in *-ic* (such as *comical* corresponding to *comic*). **2** corresponding to nouns ending in *-y* (such as *pathological* corresponding to *pathology*).
– DERIVATIVES **-ically** suffix.

ICBM ● abbreviation intercontinental ballistic missile.

ICC ● abbreviation International Cricket Council.

ice ● noun **1** frozen water, a brittle transparent crystalline solid. **2** chiefly Brit. an ice cream or water ice. **3** informal diamonds. ● verb **1** decorate with icing. **2** (usu. **ice up/over**) become covered or blocked with ice. **3** N. Amer. informal clinch (a victory or deal). **4** N. Amer. informal kill.
– PHRASES **break the ice** start conversation at the beginning of a social gathering or between strangers. **on thin ice** in a precarious or risky situation.
– DERIVATIVES **iced** adjective.
– ORIGIN Old English.

-ice ● suffix forming nouns such as *police* and *justice*.
– ORIGIN from Latin *-itia, -itius, -itium*.

ice age ● noun a period when ice sheets were unusually extensive across the earth's surface, in particular during the Pleistocene period.

ice axe ● noun a small axe used by climbers for cutting footholds in ice.

ice beer ● noun a type of strong lager matured at a low temperature after the main fermentation is complete.

iceberg ● noun a large mass of ice floating in the sea.
– PHRASES **the tip of the iceberg** the small perceptible part of a much larger situation or problem.
– ORIGIN Dutch *ijsberg*, from *ijs* 'ice' + *berg* 'hill'.

iceberg lettuce ● noun a kind of lettuce having a dense round head of crisp pale leaves.

icebox ● noun **1** a chilled container for keeping food cold. **2** Brit. a compartment in a refrigerator for making and storing ice. **3** US dated a refrigerator.

ice-breaker ● noun a ship designed for breaking a channel through ice.

ice cap ● noun a permanent covering of ice over a large area, especially on the polar region of a planet.

ice cream ● noun a semi-soft frozen dessert made with sweetened and flavoured milk fat.

ice dancing ● noun a form of ice skating incorporating choreographed dance moves based on ballroom dances.

ice field ● noun a large permanent expanse of ice, especially in polar regions.

ice hockey ● noun a form of hockey played on an ice rink between two teams of six skaters.

ice house ● noun a building for storing ice.

Icelander ● noun a person from Iceland.

Icelandic /īslandik/ ● noun the language of Iceland. ● adjective relating to Iceland or its language.

ice lolly (also **iced lolly**) ● noun Brit. a piece of flavoured water ice or ice cream on a stick.

Iceni /īseenī, -ni/ ● plural noun a tribe of ancient Britons inhabiting an area of SE England, whose queen was Boudicca (Boadicea).
– ORIGIN Latin.

ice pack ● noun a bag filled with ice and applied to the body to reduce swelling or lower temperature.

ice pick ● noun a small pick used by climbers or for breaking ice.

Thesaurus

ice ● noun **1** *a lake covered with ice* FROZEN WATER, icicles; black ice, verglas, frost, rime; *N. Amer.* glaze. **2** *assorted ices* ICE CREAM, water ice, sorbet; *N. Amer.* sherbet. **3** *the ice in her voice* COLDNESS, coolness, frostiness, iciness; hostility, unfriendliness.
– RELATED TERMS gelid, glacial.
● verb **1** *the lake has iced over* FREEZE (OVER), turn into ice, harden, solidify. **2** *I'll ice the drinks* COOL, chill, refrigerate. **3** *she had iced the cake* COVER WITH ICING, glaze; *N. Amer.* frost.
– OPPOSITES thaw, heat.
– PHRASES **on ice** *(informal)* PUT TO ONE SIDE, deferred, postponed; *informal* on the back burner, in cold storage.

ice-cold ● adjective ICY, freezing, glacial, gelid, sub-zero, frozen,

ice skate ● noun a boot with a blade attached to the sole, used for skating on ice. ● verb (**ice-skate**) skate on ice as a sport or pastime.
– DERIVATIVES **ice skater** noun **ice skating** noun.
I Ching /ee ching/ ● noun an ancient Chinese manual of divination based on eight symbolic trigrams and sixty-four hexagrams, interpreted in terms of the principles of yin and yang.
– ORIGIN Chinese, 'book of changes'.
ichneumon /iknyo͞omən/ ● noun 1 a slender parasitic wasp which deposits its eggs in or on the larvae of other insects. 2 the Egyptian mongoose.
– ORIGIN Greek *ikhneumōn* 'tracker'.
ichor /īkor/ ● noun 1 Greek Mythology the fluid said to flow like blood in the veins of the gods. 2 archaic a watery discharge from a wound.
– ORIGIN Greek *ikhōr*.
ichthyology /ikthiolləji/ ● noun the branch of zoology concerned with fishes.
– DERIVATIVES **ichthyological** adjective **ichthyologist** noun.
– ORIGIN from Greek *ikhthus* 'fish'.
ichthyosaur /ikthiəsor/ (also **ichthyosaurus** /ikthiəsorəss/) ● noun a fossil marine reptile with a long pointed head, four flippers, and a vertical tail.
ICI ● abbreviation Imperial Chemical Industries.
-ician ● suffix (forming nouns) denoting a person involved in a particular subject: *statistician*.
– ORIGIN from French *-icien*.
icicle ● noun a hanging, tapering piece of ice formed by the freezing of dripping water.
– ORIGIN from ICE + dialect *ickle* 'icicle', from Old English.
icing ● noun a mixture of sugar with liquid or fat, used as a coating or filling for cakes or biscuits.
– PHRASES **the icing on the cake** an attractive but inessential addition or enhancement.
icing sugar ● noun chiefly Brit. finely powdered sugar used to make icing.
icky ● adjective informal, chiefly N. Amer. 1 unpleasantly sticky. 2 distastefully sentimental.
– ORIGIN perhaps related to SICK[1] or to the child's word *ickle* 'little'.
icon /īkon/ ● noun 1 (also **ikon**) a devotional painting of Christ or another holy figure, typically on wood, venerated in the Byzantine and other Eastern Churches. 2 a person regarded with particular admiration or as a representative symbol. 3 Computing a symbol or graphic representation on a VDU screen of a program, option, or window.
– ORIGIN Greek *eikōn* 'image'.
iconic ● adjective relating to or of the nature of an icon.
– DERIVATIVES **iconically** adverb.
iconify ● verb (**iconifies**, **iconified**) Computing reduce (a window on a VDU screen) to an icon.
iconoclast /ikonnəklast/ ● noun 1 a person who attacks cherished beliefs or institutions. 2 a person who destroys images used in religious worship, especially one belonging to a movement opposing such images in the Byzantine Church during the 8th and 9th century.
– DERIVATIVES **iconoclasm** noun **iconoclastic** adjective.
– ORIGIN from Greek *eikōn* 'image, likeness' + *klan* 'to break'.
iconography /īkənogrəfi/ ● noun 1 the use or study of images or symbols in visual arts. 2 the visual images associated with a person or movement. 3 the illustration of a subject by drawings or figures.
– DERIVATIVES **iconographer** noun **iconographic** adjective.
iconostasis /īkənostəsiss/ ● noun (pl. **iconostases** /īkənostəseez/) a screen bearing icons, separating the sanctuary of many Eastern churches from the nave.
– ORIGIN from Greek *eikōn* 'image' + *stasis* 'standing'.
icosahedron /īkossəheedrən/ ● noun (pl. **icosahedra** or **icosahedrons**) a three-dimensional shape having twenty plane faces, in particular a regular solid figure with twenty equal triangular faces.
– DERIVATIVES **icosahedral** adjective.
– ORIGIN from Greek *eikosaedros* 'twenty-faced'.
-ics ● suffix (forming nouns) denoting a subject of study or branch of knowledge, or a field of activity: *politics*.
– ORIGIN from Latin *-ica* or Greek *-ika* (plural forms).
icy ● adjective (**icier**, **iciest**) 1 covered with or consisting of ice. 2 very cold. 3 very unfriendly or hostile.
– DERIVATIVES **icily** adverb **iciness** noun.
ID ● abbreviation 1 identification or identity. 2 Idaho.
Id ● noun variant spelling of EID.
I'd ● contraction 1 I had. 2 I should or I would.
id /id/ ● noun Psychoanalysis the part of the mind in which innate instinctive impulses and primary processes are manifest. Compare with EGO and SUPEREGO.
– ORIGIN Latin, 'that'.
id. ● abbreviation idem.
-ide ● suffix Chemistry forming nouns: 1 denoting binary compounds: *chloride*. 2 denoting groups of elements: *lanthanide*.
idea ● noun 1 a thought or suggestion about a possible course of action. 2 a mental impression. 3 a belief. 4 (**the idea**) the aim or purpose.
– ORIGIN Greek, 'form, pattern'.
ideal ● adjective 1 most suitable; perfect. 2 desirable or perfect but existing only in the imagination. ● noun 1 a person or thing regarded as perfect. 2 a principle to be aimed for; a standard of perfection.
– DERIVATIVES **ideally** adverb.
idealism ● noun 1 the practice of forming or pursuing ideals, especially unrealistically. 2 (in art or literature) the representation of things in ideal form.
– DERIVATIVES **idealist** noun **idealistic** adjective **idealistically** adverb.
idealize (also **idealise**) ● verb regard or represent as perfect or better than in reality.
– DERIVATIVES **idealization** noun.
idée fixe /eeday feeks/ ● noun (pl. **idées fixes** pronunc. same) an

i

Thesaurus

wintry; arctic, polar, Siberian; bitter, biting, raw, chilly; *poetic/literary* frore, rimy.
– OPPOSITES hot.
icing ● noun GLAZE, sugar paste; *N. Amer.* frosting.
icon ● noun IMAGE, idol, portrait, representation, symbol; figure, statue.
iconoclast ● noun CRITIC, sceptic; heretic, unbeliever, dissident, dissenter; rebel, renegade, mutineer.
icy ● adjective 1 *icy roads* FROSTY, frozen (over), iced over, icebound, ice-covered, iced up; slippery; *poetic/literary* rimy. 2 *an icy wind* FREEZING, chill, chilly, biting, bitter, raw, arctic, glacial, Siberian, polar, gelid. 3 *an icy voice* UNFRIENDLY, hostile, forbidding; cold, cool, chilly, frigid, frosty, glacial, gelid; haughty, stern, hard.
idea ● noun 1 *the idea of death scares her* CONCEPT, notion, conception, thought; image, visualization; hypothesis, postulation. 2 *our idea is to open a new shop* PLAN, scheme, design, proposal, proposition, suggestion; aim, intention, objective, object, goal, target. 3 *Liz had other ideas on the subject* THOUGHT, theory, view, opinion, feeling, belief, conclusion. 4 *I had an idea that it might happen* SENSE, feeling, suspicion, fancy, inkling, hunch, theory, notion, impression. 5 *an idea of the cost* ESTIMATE, estimation, approximation, guess, conjecture, rough calculation; *informal* guesstimate.
ideal ● adjective 1 *ideal flying weather* PERFECT, best possible, consummate, supreme, flawless, faultless, exemplary, classic, model, ultimate, quintessential. 2 *an ideal concept* ABSTRACT, theoretical, conceptual, notional; hypothetical, speculative, conjectural, suppositional. 3 *an ideal world* UNATTAINABLE, unachievable, impracticable; unreal, fictitious, hypothetical, theoretical, ivory-towered, imaginary, idealized, Utopian, fairy-tale.
– OPPOSITES bad, concrete, real.
● noun 1 *she tried to be his ideal* PERFECTION, paragon, epitome, ne plus ultra, nonpareil, dream; *informal* one in a million, the tops, the bee's knees. 2 *an ideal to aim at* MODEL, pattern, exemplar, example, paradigm, archetype; yardstick. 3 *liberal ideals* PRINCIPLE, standard, value, belief, conviction, persuasion; (**ideals**) morals, morality, ethics, ideology, creed.
idealist ● noun UTOPIAN, visionary, fantasist, romantic, dreamer, daydreamer; Walter Mitty, Don Quixote; *N. Amer.* fantast.
– OPPOSITES realist.
idealistic ● adjective UTOPIAN, visionary, romantic, quixotic, dreamy, unrealistic, impractical.
idealize ● verb ROMANTICIZE, be unrealistic about, look at something through rose-tinted spectacles, paint a rosy picture of, glamorize.
ideally ● adverb IN A PERFECT WORLD; preferably, if possible, for preference, by choice, as a matter of choice, (much) rather; all things

obsession.
– ORIGIN French, 'fixed idea'.
idem /iddem, īdem/ ● adverb used in citations to indicate an author or word that has just been mentioned.
– ORIGIN Latin, 'the same'.
identical ● adjective **1** exactly alike or the same. **2** (of twins) developed from a single fertilized ovum, and therefore of the same sex and usually very similar in appearance.
– DERIVATIVES **identically** adverb.
– ORIGIN Latin *identicus*, from *identitas* (see IDENTITY).
identification ● noun **1** the action or process of identifying or the fact of being identified. **2** an official document or other proof of one's identity.
identify ● verb (**identifies**, **identified**) **1** establish the identity of. **2** recognize or select by analysis. **3** (**identify with**) regard oneself as sharing the same characteristics or thinking as (someone else). **4** (**identify with**) associate (someone or something) closely with.
– DERIVATIVES **identifiable** adjective **identifiably** adverb **identifier** noun.
identikit ● noun trademark a picture of a person sought by the police, reconstructed from typical facial features according to witnesses' descriptions. ● adjective often derogatory very typical and ordinary; having few unique features.
identity ● noun (pl. **identities**) **1** the fact of being who or what a person or thing is. **2** the characteristics determining this. **3** a close similarity or affinity. **4** Mathematics an equation expressing the equality of two expressions for all values of the variables, e.g. $(x + 1)^2 = x^2 + 2x + 1$.
– ORIGIN Latin *identitas*, from *idem* 'same'.
identity operation ● noun Mathematics a transformation that leaves an object unchanged.
identity parade ● noun Brit. a group of people assembled so that an eyewitness may identify a suspect for a crime from among them.
ideogram /iddiəgram, īdiə-/ ● noun a character symbolizing the idea of a thing without indicating the sounds used to say it (e.g. a numeral).
ideograph /iddiəgraaf, īdiə-/ ● noun another term for IDEOGRAM.
– DERIVATIVES **ideographic** adjective.
ideologue /iddiəlog, īdiə-/ ● noun a person who follows an ideology in a dogmatic or uncompromising way.
ideology /īdiolləji/ ● noun (pl. **ideologies**) **1** a system of ideas and ideals forming the basis of an economic or political theory. **2** the set of beliefs characteristic of a social group or individual.
– DERIVATIVES **ideological** adjective **ideologically** adverb **ideologist** noun.
– ORIGIN from Greek *idea* 'form' + *-logos* (denoting discourse or compilation).
ides /īdz/ ● plural noun (in the ancient Roman calendar) a day falling roughly in the middle of each month, from which other dates were calculated.
– ORIGIN Latin *idus* (plural).
idiocy ● noun (pl. **idiocies**) extremely stupid behaviour.
idiolect /iddiəlekt/ ● noun the speech habits peculiar to a particular person.
– ORIGIN from Greek *idios* 'own, distinct' + *-lect* as in *dialect*.
idiom ● noun **1** a group of words whose meaning cannot be deduced from those of the individual words (e.g. *over the moon*). **2** a form of expression natural to a language, person, or group. **3** a characteristic mode of expression in music or art.
– ORIGIN Greek *idiōma* 'private property'.
idiomatic ● adjective **1** using or relating to expressions that are natural to a native speaker. **2** appropriate to the style of art or music associated with a particular period or person.
– DERIVATIVES **idiomatically** adverb.
idiosyncrasy /iddiəsingkrəsi/ ● noun (pl. **idiosyncrasies**) **1** a way of behaving or thinking peculiar to an individual. **2** a distinctive characteristic of a thing.
– ORIGIN Greek *idiosunkrasia*, from *idios* 'own' + *sun* 'with' + *krasis* 'mixture'.
idiosyncratic /iddiəsingkrattik/ ● adjective characterized by idiosyncrasy; peculiar or individual.
– DERIVATIVES **idiosyncratically** adverb.
idiot ● noun **1** a stupid person. **2** Medicine, archaic a mentally handicapped person.
– ORIGIN Greek *idiōtēs* 'layman, ignorant person', from *idios* 'own'.
idiotic ● adjective very stupid or foolish.

Thesaurus

being equal, theoretically, hypothetically, in theory, in principle, on paper.
idée fixe ● noun OBSESSION, fixation, (consuming) passion, mania, compulsion, preoccupation, infatuation, addiction, fetish; phobia, complex, neurosis; *informal* bee in one's bonnet, hang-up, thing.
identical ● adjective **1** *identical badges* SIMILAR, (exactly) the same, indistinguishable, uniform, twin, interchangeable, undifferentiated, homogeneous, of a piece, cut from the same cloth; alike, like, matching, like (two) peas in a pod; *informal* much of a muchness. **2** *I used the identical technique* THE (VERY) SAME, the selfsame, the very, one and the same; aforementioned, aforesaid, aforenamed, above, above-stated; foregoing, preceding.
– OPPOSITES different.
identifiable ● adjective DISTINGUISHABLE, recognizable, known; noticeable, perceptible, discernible, appreciable, detectable, observable, perceivable, visible; distinct, marked, conspicuous, unmistakable, clear.
– OPPOSITES unrecognizable.
identification ● noun **1** *the identification of the suspect* RECOGNITION, singling out, pinpointing, naming; discerning, distinguishing; *informal* fingering. **2** *early identification of problems* DETERMINATION, establishment, ascertainment, discovery, diagnosis, divination; verification, confirmation. **3** *may I see your identification?* ID, (identity/identification) papers, bona fides, documents, credentials; ID card, identity card, pass, badge, warrant, licence, permit, passport. **4** *the identification of the party with high taxes* ASSOCIATION, link, linkage, connection, bracketing. **5** *his identification with the music* EMPATHY, rapport, unity, togetherness, bond, sympathy, understanding.
identify ● verb **1** *Gail identified her attacker* RECOGNIZE, single out, pick out, spot, point out, pinpoint, put one's finger on, put a name to, name, know; discern, distinguish; remember, recall, recollect; *informal* finger. **2** *I identified four problem areas* DETERMINE, establish, ascertain, make out, diagnose, discern, distinguish; verify, confirm; *informal* figure out, get a fix on. **3** *we identify sport with glamour* ASSOCIATE, link, connect, relate, bracket, couple; mention in the same breath as, set side by side with. **4** *Peter identifies with the hero* EMPATHIZE, be in tune, have a rapport, feel at one, sympathize; be on the same wavelength as, speak the same language as; understand, relate to, feel for. **5** *they identify him with this painter of the same name* EQUATE WITH, identify as, consider to be, regard as being the same as.
identity ● noun **1** *the identity of the owner* NAME; specification. **2** *she was afraid of losing her identity* INDIVIDUALITY, self, selfhood; personality, character, originality, distinctiveness, singularity, uniqueness. **3** *a case of mistaken identity* IDENTIFICATION, recognition, naming, singling out. **4** *we share an identity of interests* CONGRUITY, congruence, sameness, oneness, interchangeability; likeness, uniformity, similarity, closeness, accordance, alignment.
ideology ● noun BELIEFS, ideas, ideals, principles, ethics, morals; doctrine, creed, credo, teaching, theory; tenets, canon(s); conviction(s), persuasion.
idiocy ● noun STUPIDITY, folly, foolishness, foolhardiness; madness, insanity, lunacy; silliness, brainlessness, thoughtlessness, senselessness, irresponsibility, imprudence, ineptitude, inanity, absurdity, ludicrousness, fatuousness; *informal* craziness; *Brit. informal* daftness.
– OPPOSITES sense.
idiom ● noun **1** *a rather dated idiom* EXPRESSION, phrase, turn of phrase, locution. **2** *the poet's idiom is terse* LANGUAGE, mode of expression, style, speech, locution, usage, phraseology, phrasing, vocabulary, parlance, jargon, patter; *informal* lingo.
idiomatic ● adjective VERNACULAR, colloquial, everyday, conversational; natural, grammatical, correct.
idiosyncrasy ● noun PECULIARITY, oddity, eccentricity, mannerism, quirk, whim, vagary, caprice, kink; fetish, foible, crotchet, habit, characteristic; individuality; unconventionality, unorthodoxy; *archaic* megrim, freak.
idiosyncratic ● adjective DISTINCTIVE, individual, individualistic, characteristic, peculiar, typical, special, specific, unique, personal; eccentric, unconventional, irregular, anomalous, odd, quirky, queer, strange, weird, bizarre, freakish; *informal* freaky.
idiot ● noun FOOL, ass, halfwit, blockhead, dunce, dolt, ignoramus, simpleton; *informal* dope, ninny, nincompoop, chump, dimwit,

– DERIVATIVES **idiotically** adverb.

idiot savant /iddiō savon/ ● noun (pl. **idiot savants** or **idiots savants** pronunc. same) a mentally handicapped person who displays brilliance in a specific area, especially one involving memory.
– ORIGIN French, 'knowledgeable idiot'.

idle ● adjective (**idler, idlest**) **1** avoiding work; lazy. **2** not working or in use. **3** having no purpose or basis: *idle threats.* ● verb **1** spend time doing nothing. **2** (of an engine) run slowly while disconnected from a load or out of gear.
– DERIVATIVES **idleness** noun **idler** noun **idly** adverb.
– ORIGIN Old English, 'empty, useless'.

idol ● noun **1** an image or representation of a god used as an object of worship. **2** a person who is greatly admired: *a soccer idol.*
– ORIGIN Greek *eidōlon*, from *eidos* 'form'.

idolatry ● noun **1** worship of idols. **2** adulation.
– DERIVATIVES **idolater** noun **idolatrous** adjective.
– ORIGIN from Greek *eidōlon* 'idol' + *-latreia* 'worship'.

idolize (also **idolise**) ● verb revere or love greatly or excessively: *he idolized his mother.*
– DERIVATIVES **idolization** noun.

idyll /iddil/ ● noun **1** a blissful or peaceful period or situation. **2** a short description in verse or prose of a picturesque pastoral scene or incident.
– ORIGIN Greek *eidullion* 'little form'.

idyllic ● adjective extremely happy, peaceful, or picturesque.
– DERIVATIVES **idyllically** adverb.

i.e. ● abbreviation that is to say.
– ORIGIN from Latin *id est* 'that is'.

IF ● abbreviation intermediate frequency.

if ● conjunction **1** introducing a conditional clause; on the condition or supposition that. **2** despite the possibility or fact that. **3** whether. **4** every time that; whenever. **5** expressing a polite request or tentative opinion. **6** expressing surprise or regret. ● noun a condition or supposition.
– PHRASES **if anything** used to suggest tentatively that something may be the case. **if only** even if for no other reason than. **if so** if that is the case.
– USAGE **If** and **whether** are more or less interchangeable in sentences like *I'll see if he left an address* and *I'll see whether he left an address*, although **whether** is more formal and more suitable for written use.
– ORIGIN Old English.

iffy ● adjective (**iffier, iffiest**) informal **1** doubtful. **2** of doubtful quality or legality.

igloo ● noun a dome-shaped Eskimo house, typically built from blocks of solid snow.
– ORIGIN Inuit, 'house'.

igneous /igniəss/ ● adjective Geology (of rock) having solidified from lava or magma.
– ORIGIN from Latin *ignis* 'fire'.

ignite /ignīt/ ● verb **1** catch fire or set on fire. **2** provoke or inflame (an emotion or situation).
– ORIGIN Latin *ignire*, from *ignis* 'fire'.

igniter ● noun **1** a device for igniting a fuel mixture in an engine. **2** a device for causing an electric arc.

ignition ● noun **1** the action of igniting or the state of being ignited. **2** the process of starting the combustion of fuel in the cylinders of an internal-combustion engine.

ignoble ● adjective (**ignobler, ignoblest**) **1** not honourable. **2** of humble origin or social status.
– DERIVATIVES **ignobly** adverb.
– ORIGIN Latin *ignobilis*, from *in-* 'not' + *gnobilis* 'noble'.

ignominious /ignəminniəss/ ● adjective deserving or causing public disgrace or shame.
– DERIVATIVES **ignominiously** adverb.
– ORIGIN Latin *ignominiosus*, from *in-* 'not' + a variant of *nomen* 'name'.

ignominy /ignəmini/ ● noun public shame or disgrace.

i

Thesaurus

dumbo, dummy, loon, dork, jackass, bonehead, fathead, numbskull, dunderhead, thickhead, woodenhead, airhead, pinhead, lamebrain, cretin, moron, imbecile, pea-brain, birdbrain, jerk, nerd, donkey; *Brit. informal* nit, nitwit, twit, clot, plonker, berk, prat, pillock, wally, divvy, twerp, charlie; *Scottish informal* nyaff, balloon; *N. Amer. informal* schmuck, bozo, turkey, chowderhead, dingbat; *Austral./NZ informal* drongo, dill, alec, galah.
– OPPOSITES genius.

idiotic ● adjective STUPID, silly, foolish, witless, brainless, mindless, thoughtless, unintelligent; imprudent, unwise, ill-advised, ill-considered, half-baked, foolhardy; absurd, senseless, pointless, nonsensical, inane, fatuous, ridiculous; *informal* dumb, dim, dim-witted, half-witted, dopey, gormless, hare-brained, pea-brained, wooden-headed, thickheaded; *Brit. informal* barmy, daft; *Scottish & N. English informal* glaikit; *N. Amer. informal* dumb-ass.

idle ● adjective **1** *an idle fellow* LAZY, indolent, slothful, work-shy, shiftless, inactive, sluggish, lethargic, listless; slack, lax, lackadaisical, good-for-nothing; *informal* bone idle. **2** *I was bored with being idle* UNEMPLOYED, jobless, out of work, redundant, between jobs, workless, unwaged, unoccupied; *Brit. informal* on the dole, 'resting'. **3** *they left the machine idle* INACTIVE, unused, unoccupied, unemployed, disused; out of action, inoperative, out of service. **4** *their idle hours* UNOCCUPIED, spare, empty, vacant, unfilled, available. **5** *idle remarks* FRIVOLOUS, trivial, trifling, minor, petty, lightweight, shallow, superficial, insignificant, unimportant, worthless, paltry, niggling, peripheral, inane, fatuous; unnecessary, time-wasting. **6** *idle threats* EMPTY, meaningless, pointless, worthless, vain, insubstantial, futile, ineffective, ineffectual; groundless, baseless.
– OPPOSITES industrious, employed, working, busy, serious.
● verb **1** *Lily idled on the window seat* DO NOTHING, be inactive, vegetate, take it easy, mark time, kick one's heels, twiddle one's thumbs, kill time, languish, laze, lounge, loll, loaf, slouch; *informal* hang around, veg out; *Brit. informal* hang about; *N. Amer. informal* bum around, lollygag. **2** *Rob idled along the pavement* SAUNTER, stroll, dawdle, drift, potter, amble, maunder, wander, straggle; *informal* mosey, tootle; *Brit. informal* pootle, mooch. **3** *he let the engine idle* TICK OVER.

idler ● noun LOAFER, layabout, good-for-nothing, ne'er-do-well, lounger, shirker, sluggard; *informal* skiver, waster, slacker, slowcoach, slob, lazybones; *N. Amer. informal* slowpoke; *poetic/literary* wastrel.
– OPPOSITES workaholic.

idol ● noun **1** *an idol in a shrine* ICON, effigy, statue, figure, figurine, fetish, totem; graven image, false god, golden calf. **2** *the pop world's latest idol* HERO, heroine, star, superstar, icon, celebrity; favourite, darling; *informal* pin-up, heart throb, blue-eyed boy/girl, golden boy/girl.

idolatry ● noun **1** *he preached against idolatry* IDOL WORSHIP, fetishism, iconolatry; paganism, heathenism. **2** *our idolatry of art* IDOLIZATION, fetishization, worship, adulation, adoration, reverence, glorification, lionization, hero-worshipping.

idolize ● verb HERO-WORSHIP, worship, revere, venerate, deify, lionize; stand in awe of, reverence, look up to, admire, exalt; *informal* put on a pedestal.

idyll ● noun **1** *an idyll unspoilt by machines* PERFECT TIME, ideal time, moment of bliss; paradise, heaven (on earth), Shangri-La, Utopia; *poetic/literary* Arcadia. **2** *the poem began as a two-part idyll* PASTORAL, eclogue, georgic, rural poem.

idyllic ● adjective PERFECT, wonderful, blissful, halcyon, happy; ideal, idealized; heavenly, paradisal, Utopian, Elysian; peaceful, picturesque; *poetic/literary* Arcadian.

if ● conjunction **1** *if the weather is fine, we can walk* ON CONDITION THAT, provided (that), providing (that), presuming (that), supposing (that), assuming (that), as long as, given that, in the event that. **2** *if I go out she gets nasty* WHENEVER, every time. **3** *I wonder if he noticed* WHETHER, whether or not. **4** *a useful, if unintended innovation* ALTHOUGH, albeit, but, yet, whilst; even though, despite being.
● noun *there is one if in all this* UNCERTAINTY, doubt; condition, stipulation, provision, proviso, constraint, precondition, requirement, specification, restriction.

iffy ● adjective (*informal*) **1** *the windscreen's a bit iffy, but it's a good car* SUBSTANDARD, second-rate, low-grade, low-quality; doubtful, dubious, questionable; *informal* not up to much; *Brit. informal* dodgy, ropy. **2** *that date is a bit iffy* TENTATIVE, undecided, unsettled, unsure, unresolved, in doubt; *informal* up in the air.

ignite ● verb **1** *he got to safety moments before the petrol ignited* CATCH FIRE, burst into flames; be set off, explode. **2** *a cigarette ignited the fumes* LIGHT, set fire to, set on fire, set alight, kindle, touch off; *informal* set/put a match to. **3** *the campaign failed to ignite voter interest* AROUSE, kindle, trigger, spark, instigate, excite, provoke, stimulate, stir up, whip up, incite, fuel.
– OPPOSITES go out, extinguish.

ignoble ● adjective DISHONOURABLE, unworthy, base, shameful, con-

ignoramus /ignəraymәss/ ● noun (pl. **ignoramuses**) an ignorant or stupid person.
– ORIGIN originally a formula uttered by a grand jury about an indictment considered to be backed by insufficient evidence to bring before a petty jury: from Latin, 'we do not know' (in legal use 'we take no notice of it').
ignorance ● noun lack of knowledge or information.
ignorant ● adjective **1** lacking knowledge or awareness in general. **2** (often **ignorant of**) uninformed about or unaware of a specific subject or fact. **3** informal rude; discourteous.
– DERIVATIVES **ignorantly** adverb.
– ORIGIN from Latin *ignorare* 'not know'.
ignore ● verb **1** disregard intentionally. **2** fail to consider (something significant).
– ORIGIN Latin *ignorare* 'not know'.
iguana /igwaanə/ ● noun a large lizard with a spiny crest along the back.
– ORIGIN Arawak.
iguanodon /igwaanədon/ ● noun a large herbivorous dinosaur with a broad stiff tail and the thumb developed into a spike.
– ORIGIN from IGUANA + Greek *odous* 'tooth' (because its teeth resemble those of the iguana).
IHS ● abbreviation Jesus.
– ORIGIN from Greek ΙΗΣ as an abbreviation of *Iēsous* 'Jesus'.
ikat /ikat/ ● noun fabric made using an Indonesian technique in which threads are tie-dyed before weaving.
– ORIGIN from Malay, 'fasten, tie'.
ikebana /ikkibaanə/ ● noun the art of Japanese flower arrangement.
– ORIGIN Japanese, 'living flowers'.
ikon ● noun variant spelling of ICON (in sense 1).
IL ● abbreviation Illinois.
il- ● prefix variant spelling of IN-¹, IN-² before *l*.
-il (also **-ile**) ● suffix forming adjectives and nouns such as *civil*.
– ORIGIN from Latin *-ilis*.
ileum /illiəm/ ● noun (pl. **ilea**) Anatomy the third portion of the small intestine, between the jejunum and the caecum.
– ORIGIN Latin, variant of ILIUM.
ilex /ileks/ ● noun **1** the holm oak. **2** a tree or shrub of a family that includes holly.
– ORIGIN Latin.
iliac /illiak/ ● adjective relating to the ilium or the nearby regions of the lower body.
ilium /illiəm/ ● noun (pl. **ilia**) the large broad bone forming the upper part of each half of the pelvis.
– ORIGIN Latin, singular of *ilia* 'flanks, entrails'.
ilk ● noun **1** a type: *fascists, racists, and others of that ilk.* **2** (**of that ilk**) Scottish, chiefly archaic of the place or estate of the same name.
– ORIGIN Old English, related to ALIKE.
I'll ● contraction I shall; I will.
ill ● adjective **1** not in full health; unwell. **2** poor in quality. **3** harmful, hostile, or unfavourable. ● adverb **1** badly, wrongly, or imperfectly: *ill-chosen.* **2** only with difficulty. ● noun **1** a problem or misfortune. **2** evil or harm.
– PHRASES **ill at ease** uncomfortable or embarrassed.
– ORIGIN Old Norse, 'evil, difficult'.
ill-advised ● adjective unwise or badly thought out.
ill-assorted ● adjective not well matched.
ill-bred ● adjective badly brought up or rude.

Thesaurus

temptible, despicable, shabby, sordid; improper, unprincipled, discreditable.
ignominious ● adjective HUMILIATING, undignified, embarrassing, ignoble, inglorious.
– OPPOSITES glorious.
ignominy ● noun SHAME, humiliation, embarrassment; disgrace, dishonour, discredit, degradation, scandal, infamy, indignity, ignobility, loss of face.
ignoramus ● noun FOOL, ass, halfwit, blockhead, dunce, simpleton; *informal* dope, ninny, nincompoop, chump, dimwit, imbecile, moron, dumbo, dummy, fathead, numbskull, thickhead, woodenhead, airhead, birdbrain; *Brit. informal* nit, nitwit, twit, clot, plonker, berk, divvy; *Scottish informal* balloon; *N. Amer. informal* schmuck, bozo, turkey; *Austral./NZ informal* drongo.
ignorance ● noun **1** *his ignorance of economics* INCOMPREHENSION, unawareness, unconsciousness, unfamiliarity, inexperience, innocence, lack of knowledge; *informal* cluelessness; *poetic/literary* nescience. **2** *their attitudes are based on ignorance* LACK OF KNOWLEDGE, lack of education; unenlightenment, benightedness; lack of intelligence, stupidity, foolishness, idiocy.
– OPPOSITES knowledge, education.
ignorant ● adjective **1** *an ignorant country girl* UNEDUCATED, unknowledgeable, untaught, unschooled, untutored, untrained, illiterate, unlettered, unlearned, unread, uninformed, unenlightened, benighted; inexperienced, unworldly, unsophisticated; *informal* pig-ignorant, thick. **2** *they were ignorant of working-class life* WITHOUT KNOWLEDGE, unaware, unconscious, unfamiliar, unacquainted, uninformed, in the dark, unenlightened, unconversant, inexperienced, naive, innocent, green; *informal* clueless; *poetic/literary* nescient. **3** (*informal*) *she could be so ignorant!* See IMPOLITE.
– OPPOSITES educated, knowledgeable.
ignore ● verb **1** *he ignored the customers* DISREGARD, take no notice of, pay no attention to, pay no heed to; turn a blind eye to, turn a deaf ear to. **2** *he was ignored by the countess* SNUB, slight, spurn, shun, look right through, cold-shoulder, freeze out; *Brit.* send to Coventry; *informal* give someone the brush-off, cut (dead); *Brit. informal* blank. **3** *doctors ignored her husband's instructions* SET ASIDE, pay no attention to, take no account of; break, contravene, fail to comply with, fail to observe, disregard, disobey, breach, defy, flout.
– OPPOSITES acknowledge, obey.
ilk ● noun TYPE, sort, class, category, group, set, bracket, genre, vintage, make, model, brand, stamp, variety.
ill ● adjective **1** *she was feeling rather ill* UNWELL, sick, not (very) well, ailing, poorly, sickly, peaky, indisposed, infirm; out of sorts, not oneself, under/below par, bad, in a bad way; bedridden, invalided, on the sick list, valetudinarian; queasy, nauseous, nauseated; *Brit.* off colour; *informal* under the weather, laid up, lousy, rough; *Brit. informal* ropy, grotty; *Austral./NZ informal* crook; *Brit. informal, dated* queer. **2** *the ill effects of smoking* HARMFUL, damaging, detrimental, deleterious, adverse, injurious, hurtful, destructive, pernicious, dangerous; unhealthy, unwholesome, poisonous, noxious; *poetic/literary* malefic, maleficent, nocuous; *archaic* baneful. **3** *ill feeling* HOSTILE, antagonistic, acrimonious, inimical, antipathetic; unfriendly, unsympathetic; resentful, spiteful, malicious, vindictive, malevolent, bitter. **4** *an ill omen* UNLUCKY, adverse, unfavourable, unfortunate, unpropitious, inauspicious, unpromising, infelicitous, ominous, sinister; *poetic/literary* direful. **5** *ill manners* RUDE, discourteous, impolite; impertinent, insolent, impudent, uncivil, disrespectful; *informal* ignorant. **6** *ill management* BAD, poor, unsatisfactory, incompetent, deficient, defective, inexpert.
– OPPOSITES well, healthy, beneficial, auspicious, polite.
● noun **1** *the ills of society* PROBLEMS, troubles, difficulties, misfortunes, trials, tribulations; worries, anxieties, concerns; *informal* headaches, hassles. **2** *he wished them no ill* HARM, hurt, injury, damage, pain, trouble, misfortune, suffering, distress. **3** *the body's ills* ILLNESSES, ailments, disorders, complaints, afflictions, sicknesses, diseases, maladies, infirmities.
● adverb **1** *such behaviour ill became the king* POORLY, badly, imperfectly. **2** *the look on her face boded ill* UNFAVOURABLY, adversely, badly, inauspiciously. **3** *he can ill afford the loss of income* BARELY, scarcely, hardly, only just, just possibly. **4** *things are going ill* BADLY, adversely, unsuccessfully, unfavourably; unfortunately, unluckily, inauspiciously. **5** *we are ill prepared* INADEQUATELY, unsatisfactorily, insufficiently, imperfectly, poorly, badly.
– OPPOSITES well, auspiciously, satisfactorily.
– PHRASES **ill at ease** AWKWARD, uneasy, uncomfortable, embarrassed, self-conscious, out of place, inhibited, gauche; restless, restive, fidgety, discomfited, worried, anxious, on edge, edgy, nervous, tense; *informal* twitchy, jittery; *N. Amer. informal* discombobulated, antsy. **speak ill of** DENIGRATE, disparage, criticize, be critical of, speak badly of, be malicious about, blacken the name of, run down, insult, abuse, attack, revile, malign, vilify; *N. Amer.* slur; *informal* bad-mouth, bitch about, pull to pieces; *Brit. informal* rubbish, slate, slag off; *formal* derogate; *rare* asperse.
ill-advised ● adjective UNWISE, injudicious, misguided, imprudent, ill-considered, ill-judged; foolhardy, hare-brained, rash, reckless; *informal* crazy, crackpot.
– OPPOSITES judicious.
ill-assorted ● adjective MISMATCHED, ill-matched, incongruous, incompatible; dissimilar, unalike, varied, disparate.
ill-bred ● adjective ILL-MANNERED, bad-mannered, rude, impolite, discourteous, uncivil; boorish, churlish, loutish, vulgar, coarse,

ill-disposed • adjective unfriendly or unsympathetic.
illegal • adjective contrary to or forbidden by law.
– DERIVATIVES **illegality** noun **illegally** adverb.
– USAGE Both **illegal** and **unlawful** can mean 'contrary to or forbidden by law', but **unlawful** has a broader meaning 'not permitted by rules': thus handball in soccer is **unlawful**, but not **illegal**.
illegible /ilejib'l/ • adjective not clear enough to be read.
– DERIVATIVES **illegibility** noun **illegibly** adverb.
illegitimate /illijittimət/ • adjective **1** not in accordance with the law or accepted standards. **2** (of a child) born of parents not lawfully married to each other.
– DERIVATIVES **illegitimacy** noun **illegitimately** adverb.
ill fame • noun dated disrepute.
ill-fated • adjective destined to fail or have bad luck.
ill-favoured (US **ill-favored**) • adjective unattractive or offensive.
ill-gotten • adjective acquired by illegal or unfair means.
ill humour • noun irritability or bad temper.
illiberal • adjective opposed to liberal principles.
– DERIVATIVES **illiberality** noun **illiberally** adverb.
illicit • adjective forbidden by law, rules, or custom.
– DERIVATIVES **illicitly** adverb.
– ORIGIN Latin *illicitus*, from *in-* 'not' + *licitus* 'allowed'.
illimitable • adjective limitless.
– DERIVATIVES **illimitably** adverb.
illiterate /illittərət/ • adjective **1** unable to read or write. **2** ignorant in a particular subject or activity; *politically illiterate*.
– DERIVATIVES **illiteracy** noun **illiterately** adverb.
ill-natured • adjective bad-tempered and churlish.
illness • noun a disease or period of sickness.
illogical • adjective lacking sense or sound reasoning.
– DERIVATIVES **illogicality** noun (pl. **illogicalities**) **illogically** adverb.
ill-omened • adjective accompanied by bad omens.
ill-starred • adjective unlucky.
ill-tempered • adjective irritable or morose.
ill-treat • verb act cruelly towards.
illuminance /ilōōminənss/ • noun Physics the amount of luminous flux per unit area.
illuminate /ilōōminayt/ • verb **1** light up. **2** help to clarify or

Thesaurus

crass, uncouth, uncivilized, ungentlemanly, indecorous, unseemly; *informal* ignorant; *Brit. informal* yobbish.
ill-considered • adjective RASH, ill-advised, ill-judged, injudicious, imprudent, unwise, hasty; misjudged, ill-conceived, badly thought out, hare-brained; *poetic/literary* temerarious.
– OPPOSITES judicious.
ill-defined • adjective VAGUE, indistinct, unclear, imprecise; blurred, fuzzy, hazy, woolly.
ill-disposed • adjective HOSTILE, antagonistic, unfriendly, unsympathetic, antipathetic, inimical, unfavourable, averse, at odds; *informal* anti.
– OPPOSITES friendly.
illegal • adjective UNLAWFUL, illicit, illegitimate, criminal, felonious; unlicensed, unauthorized, unsanctioned; outlawed, banned, forbidden, prohibited, proscribed; contraband, black-market, bootleg; *Law* malfeasant; *informal* crooked, shady; *Brit. informal* bent, dodgy.
– OPPOSITES lawful, legitimate.
illegible • adjective UNREADABLE, indecipherable, unintelligible; scrawled, scribbled, crabbed.
illegitimate • adjective **1** *illegitimate share trading* ILLEGAL, unlawful, illicit, criminal, felonious; unlicensed, unauthorized, unsanctioned; outlawed, banned, forbidden, prohibited, proscribed; fraudulent, corrupt, dishonest; *Law* malfeasant; *informal* crooked, shady; *Brit. informal* bent, dodgy. **2** *an illegitimate child* BORN OUT OF WEDLOCK; *dated* born on the wrong side of the blanket, unfathered; *archaic* bastard, natural, misbegotten, baseborn, spurious, nameless.
– OPPOSITES legal, lawful.
ill-fated • adjective DOOMED, blighted, damned, cursed, ill-starred, jinxed; *poetic/literary* star-crossed.
ill-favoured • adjective UNATTRACTIVE, plain, ugly; *N. Amer.* homely; *informal* not much to look at; *Austral./NZ informal* drack.
– OPPOSITES attractive.
ill-founded • adjective BASELESS, groundless, without foundation, unjustified; questionable, misinformed, misguided.
ill humour • noun BAD MOOD, bad temper, irritability, irascibility, cantankerousness, peevishness, petulance, pettishness, pique, crabbiness, testiness, tetchiness, fractiousness, snappishness, waspishness, touchiness, moodiness, sullenness, sulkiness, surliness, annoyance, anger, crossness.
ill-humoured • adjective BAD-TEMPERED, ill-tempered, short-tempered, in a (bad) mood, cross; irritable, irascible, tetchy, testy, crotchety, touchy, cantankerous, curmudgeonly, peevish, fractious, waspish, prickly, pettish; grumpy, grouchy, crabbed, crabby, splenetic, dyspeptic, choleric; *informal* snappish, snappy, chippy, on a short fuse; *Brit. informal* shirty, stroppy, ratty, like a bear with a sore head; *N. Amer. informal* cranky, ornery, peckish; *Austral./NZ informal* snaky; *informal, dated* waxy, miffy.
– OPPOSITES amiable.
illiberal • adjective INTOLERANT, unenlightened, reactionary, conservative, undemocratic, authoritarian, repressive, totalitarian, despotic, tyrannical, oppressive.
illicit • adjective **1** *illicit drugs* ILLEGAL, unlawful, illegitimate, criminal, felonious; outlawed, banned, forbidden, prohibited, proscribed; unlicensed, unauthorized, unsanctioned; contraband, black-market, bootleg; *Law* malfeasant. **2** *an illicit love affair* TABOO, forbidden, impermissible, unacceptable, haram, tapu; secret, clandestine.
– OPPOSITES lawful, legal.
illimitable • adjective LIMITLESS, unlimited, unbounded; endless, unending, never-ending, infinite, immeasurable.
illiteracy • noun **1** *illiteracy was widespread* ILLITERATENESS, inability to read or write. **2** *economic illiteracy* IGNORANCE, unawareness, inexperience, unenlightenment, lack of knowledge/education; *poetic/literary* nescience.
illiterate • adjective **1** *an illiterate peasant* UNABLE TO READ OR WRITE, unlettered. **2** *politically illiterate* IGNORANT, unknowledgeable, uneducated, unschooled, untutored, untrained, uninstructed, uninformed; *poetic/literary* nescient.
ill-judged • adjective ILL-CONSIDERED, ill-thought-out; unwise, imprudent, incautious, injudicious, misguided, ill-advised, impolitic, inexpedient; rash, hasty, thoughtless, careless, reckless.
– OPPOSITES judicious.
ill-mannered • adjective BAD-MANNERED, rude, impolite, discourteous, uncivil, abusive; insolent, impertinent, impudent, cheeky, presumptuous, disrespectful; badly behaved, ill-behaved, loutish, oafish, uncouth, uncivilized, ill-bred; *informal* ignorant.
– OPPOSITES polite.
ill-natured • adjective MEAN, nasty, spiteful, malicious, disagreeable; ill-tempered, bad-tempered, moody, irritable, irascible, surly, sullen, peevish, petulant, fractious, crabbed, crabby, tetchy, testy, grouchy.
illness • noun SICKNESS, disease, ailment, complaint, malady, affliction, infection, indisposition; ill health, poor health, infirmity; *informal* bug, virus; *Brit. informal* lurgy; *Austral. informal* wog; *dated* contagion.
– RELATED TERMS -pathy.
– OPPOSITES good health.
illogical • adjective IRRATIONAL, unreasonable, unsound, unreasoned, unjustifiable; incorrect, erroneous, invalid, spurious, faulty, flawed, fallacious, unscientific; specious, sophistic, casuistic; absurd, preposterous, untenable; *informal* off beam, way out.
ill-starred • adjective ILL-FATED, doomed, blighted, ill-omened, damned, cursed, jinxed; unlucky, luckless, unfortunate, hapless; *poetic/literary* star-crossed.
– OPPOSITES blessed.
ill temper • noun BAD MOOD, irritation, vexation, exasperation, indignation, huff, moodiness, pet, pique; anger, crossness, bad temper; irritability, irascibility, peevishness, tetchiness, testiness; *informal* grump; *Brit. informal* paddy, strop; *N. Amer. informal* blowout, hissy fit; *Brit. informal, dated* bate, wax.
ill-tempered • adjective BAD-TEMPERED, short-tempered, ill-humoured, moody; in a (bad) mood, cross, irritable, irascible, tetchy, testy, crotchety, touchy, cantankerous, curmudgeonly, peevish, fractious, waspish, prickly, pettish; grumpy, grouchy, crabbed, crabby, splenetic, dyspeptic, choleric; *informal* snappish, snappy, chippy, on a short fuse; *Brit. informal* shirty, stroppy, ratty; *N. Amer. informal* cranky, ornery, peckish; *Austral./NZ informal* snaky; *informal, dated* waxy, miffy.
ill-timed • adjective UNTIMELY, mistimed, badly timed; premature, early, hasty, inopportune.
– OPPOSITES timely.
ill-treat • verb ABUSE, mistreat, maltreat, ill-use, misuse; manhandle, handle roughly, molest; harm, injure, damage; *informal* knock about/around.
– OPPOSITES pamper.

explain. **3** decorate (a page or initial letter in a manuscript) with gold, silver, or coloured designs.
– DERIVATIVES **illuminative** adjective **illuminator** noun.
– ORIGIN Latin *illuminare* 'illuminate', from *lumen* 'light'.

illuminati /iloominaati/ • plural noun people claiming to possess special enlightenment or knowledge.
– ORIGIN plural of Italian *illuminato* or Latin *illuminatus* 'enlightened'.

illumination • noun **1** lighting or light. **2** (**illuminations**) lights used in decorating a building or other structure. **3** the action or process of illuminating.

illumine • verb literary light up; illuminate.

ill-use • verb ill-treat.

illusion /iloozh'n/ • noun **1** a false or unreal perception or belief. **2** a deceptive appearance or impression.
– ORIGIN Latin, from *illudere* 'to mock'.

illusionism • noun the use of perspective in art to give a three-dimensional appearance.
– DERIVATIVES **illusionistic** adjective.

illusionist • noun a magician or conjuror.

illusive /iloosiv/ • adjective chiefly literary deceptive; illusory.

illusory /iloosəri/ • adjective apparently real but not actually so; deceptive.
– DERIVATIVES **illusorily** adverb.

illustrate • verb **1** provide (a book or periodical) with pictures. **2** make clear by using examples, charts, etc. **3** serve as an example of.
– DERIVATIVES **illustrator** noun.
– ORIGIN Latin *illustrare* 'light up'.

illustration • noun **1** a picture illustrating a book or periodical. **2** the action or fact of illustrating. **3** an illustrative example.
– DERIVATIVES **illustrational** adjective.

illustrative • adjective serving as an example or explanation.
– DERIVATIVES **illustratively** adverb.

illustrious /ilustriəss/ • adjective famous and admired for past achievements.
– DERIVATIVES **illustriousness** noun.
– ORIGIN Latin *illustris* 'clear, bright'.

ill will • noun animosity.

illywhacker /illiwakkər/ • noun Austral. informal a small-time confidence trickster.
– ORIGIN of unknown origin.

I'm • contraction I am.

im- • prefix variant spelling of IN-[1], IN-[2] assimilated before *b*, *m*, *p* (as in *imbibe*, *impart*).

image • noun **1** a representation of the external form of a person or thing in art. **2** a visible impression obtained by a camera, displayed on a video screen, or produced by reflection or refraction. **3** the general impression that a person, organization, or product presents to the public. **4** a picture in the mind. **5** a simile or metaphor. **6** a person or thing closely resembling another. **7** likeness. **8** (in biblical use) an idol. • verb make or form an image of.
– DERIVATIVES **imageless** adjective.
– ORIGIN Latin *imago*; related to IMITATE.

imager • noun an electronic or other device which records images.

imagery • noun **1** figurative language, especially in a literary work. **2** visual symbolism. **3** visual images collectively.

imaginable • adjective possible to be thought of or believed.
– DERIVATIVES **imaginably** adverb.

imaginary • adjective **1** existing only in the imagination. **2** Mathematics expressed in terms of the square root of -1 (represented by *i* or *j*): *imaginary numbers.*
– DERIVATIVES **imaginarily** adverb.

imagination • noun **1** the faculty or action of forming ideas or images in the mind. **2** the ability of the mind to be creative or resourceful.

Thesaurus

ill-treatment • noun ABUSE, mistreatment, maltreatment, ill use, ill usage, misuse; manhandling, rough treatment.

illuminate • verb **1** *the bundle was illuminated by the torch* LIGHT (UP), throw light on, brighten, shine on; poetic/literary illumine. **2** *the manuscripts were illuminated* DECORATE, illustrate, embellish, adorn, ornament. **3** *documents often illuminate people's thought processes* CLARIFY, elucidate, explain, reveal, shed light on, give insight into.
– OPPOSITES darken, conceal.

illuminating • adjective INFORMATIVE, enlightening, revealing, explanatory, instructive, helpful, educational.

illumination • noun **1** *a floodlamp provided illumination* LIGHT, lighting, radiance, gleam, glow, glare; shining, gleaming, glowing; poetic/literary illumining, irradiance, lucency, lambency, effulgence, refulgence. **2** *the illumination of a manuscript* DECORATION, illustration, embellishment, adornment, ornamentation. **3** *these books give illumination on the subject* CLARIFICATION, elucidation, explanation, revelation, explication. **4** *moments of real illumination* ENLIGHTENMENT, insight, understanding, awareness; learning, education, edification.

illusion • noun **1** *he had destroyed her illusions* DELUSION, misapprehension, misconception, false impression; fantasy, fancy, dream, chimera. **2** *the lighting increases the illusion of depth* APPEARANCE, impression, semblance. **3** *it's just an illusion* MIRAGE, hallucination, apparition, figment of the imagination, trick of the light. **4** *magical illusions* (MAGIC) TRICK, conjuring trick; (**illusions**) magic, conjuring, sleight of hand, legerdemain.

illusory • adjective DELUSORY, delusive; illusionary, imagined, imaginary, fanciful, fancied, unreal; sham, false, fallacious, fake, bogus, mistaken, erroneous, misguided, untrue.
– OPPOSITES genuine.

illustrate • verb **1** *the photographs that illustrate the book* DECORATE, adorn, ornament, accompany; add pictures/drawings to, provide artwork for. **2** *this can be illustrated through a brief example* EXPLAIN, elucidate, clarify, make plain, demonstrate, show, emphasize; informal get across/over. **3** *his wit was illustrated by his remark to Lucy* EXEMPLIFY, show, demonstrate, display, represent.

illustrated • adjective WITH ILLUSTRATIONS, with pictures, with drawings, pictorial.

illustration • noun **1** *the illustrations in children's books* PICTURE, drawing, sketch, figure, plate, print. **2** *by way of illustration* EXEMPLIFICATION, demonstration, showing; example, typical case, case in point, analogy. **3** *a career in illustration* ARTWORK, (graphic) design; ornamentation, decoration, embellishment.

illustrative • adjective EXEMPLIFYING, explanatory, elucidatory, elucidative, explicative, expository, illuminative, exegetic.

illustrious • adjective EMINENT, distinguished, acclaimed, notable, noteworthy, prominent, pre-eminent, foremost, leading, important, influential; renowned, famous, famed, well known, celebrated; esteemed, honoured, respected, venerable, august, highly regarded, well thought of, of distinction.
– OPPOSITES unknown.

ill will • noun ANIMOSITY, hostility, enmity, acrimony, animus, hatred, hate, loathing, antipathy; ill feeling, bad blood, antagonism, unfriendliness, dislike; spite, spitefulness, resentment, hard feelings, bitterness; archaic disrelish.
– OPPOSITES goodwill.

image • noun **1** *an image of the Madonna* LIKENESS, resemblance; depiction, portrayal, representation; statue, statuette, sculpture, bust, effigy; painting, picture, portrait, drawing, sketch. **2** *images of the planet Neptune* PICTURE, photograph, snapshot, photo. **3** *he contemplated his image in the mirror* REFLECTION, mirror image, likeness. **4** *the image of this country as democratic* CONCEPTION, impression, idea, perception, notion; mental picture, vision. **5** *biblical images* SIMILE, metaphor, metonymy; figure of speech, trope, turn of phrase. **6** *his heart-throb image* PUBLIC PERCEPTION, persona, profile, face, front, facade, mask, guise. **7** *I'm the image of my grandfather* DOUBLE, living image, lookalike, clone, copy, twin, duplicate, exact likeness, mirror-image; informal spitting image, dead ringer; archaic similitude. **8** *a graven image* IDOL, icon, fetish, totem.
– RELATED TERMS icono-.
• verb *she imaged imposing castles* ENVISAGE, envision, imagine, picture, see in one's mind's eye.

imaginable • adjective THINKABLE, conceivable, supposable, believable, credible, creditable; possible, plausible, feasible; rare cogitable.

imaginary • adjective UNREAL, non-existent, fictional, fictitious, pretend, make-believe, mythical, fanciful, illusory; made-up, dreamed-up, invented, fancied; archaic visionary.
– OPPOSITES real.

imagination • noun **1** *a vivid imagination* CREATIVE POWER, fancy; informal mind's eye. **2** *you need imagination in dealing with these problems* CREATIVITY, imaginativeness, creativeness; vision, inspiration, inventiveness, invention, resourcefulness, ingenuity; originality, innovation, innovativeness. **3** *the album captured the*

imaginative ● adjective having or showing creativity or inventiveness.
– DERIVATIVES **imaginatively** adverb **imaginativeness** noun.
imagine ● verb **1** form a mental image or concept of. **2** believe (something unreal) to exist. **3** suppose or assume.
– DERIVATIVES **imaginer** noun.
– ORIGIN from Latin *imaginare* 'form an image of' and *imaginari* 'picture to oneself', both from *imago* 'image'.
imaginings ● plural noun thoughts or fantasies.
imagism /immijiz'm/ ● noun a movement in early 20th-century English and American poetry which sought clarity of expression through the use of precise images.
– DERIVATIVES **imagist** noun **imagistic** adjective.
imago /imaygō/ ● noun (pl. **imagos** or **imagines** /imayjineez/) the final and fully developed adult stage of an insect.
– ORIGIN Latin, 'image'.
imam /imaam/ ● noun **1** the person who leads prayers in a mosque. **2** (**Imam**) a title of various Muslim leaders, especially of one succeeding Muhammad as leader of Shiite Islam.
– DERIVATIVES **imamate** noun.
– ORIGIN Arabic, 'leader'.
IMAX /īmaks/ ● noun trademark a cinematographic technique which produces an image approximately ten times larger than that from standard 35 mm film.
– ORIGIN from *i-* (probably representing a pronunciation of EYE) + *max* (short for MAXIMUM).
imbalance ● noun a lack of proportion or balance.
imbecile /imbiseel/ ● noun informal a stupid person. ● adjective stupid.
– DERIVATIVES **imbecilic** adjective **imbecility** noun (pl. **imbecilities**).
– ORIGIN originally in the sense 'physically weak': from Latin *imbecillus* 'without a supporting staff'.
imbed ● verb variant spelling of EMBED.
imbibe /imbīb/ formal or humorous ● verb **1** drink (alcohol). **2** absorb (ideas or knowledge).
– DERIVATIVES **imbiber** noun.
– ORIGIN Latin *imbibere*, from *bibere* 'to drink'.
imbricate /imbrikət/ (also **imbricated**) ● adjective technical arranged in an overlapping manner like roof tiles.
– DERIVATIVES **imbrication** noun.
– ORIGIN from Latin *imbricare* 'cover with roof tiles'.
imbroglio /imbrōliō/ ● noun (pl. **imbroglios**) a very confused or complicated situation.
– ORIGIN Italian, from *imbrogliare* 'confuse'.
imbue /imbyoō/ ● verb (**imbues**, **imbued**, **imbuing**) (often **be imbued with**) fill with a feeling or quality.
– ORIGIN originally in the sense 'saturate': from Latin *imbuere* 'moisten'.
IMF ● abbreviation International Monetary Fund.
IMHO ● abbreviation in my humble opinion.
imitate ● verb **1** follow as a model. **2** copy (a person's speech or mannerisms), especially for comic effect. **3** reproduce; simulate: *synthetic fabrics that imitate silk*.
– DERIVATIVES **imitable** adjective **imitator** noun.
– ORIGIN Latin *imitari*, related to *imago* 'image'.
imitation ● noun **1** the action of imitating. **2** a copy.
– PHRASES **imitation is the sincerest form of flattery** proverb copying someone or something is an implicit way of paying them a compliment.
imitative /immitətiv/ ● adjective **1** following a model. **2** (of a word) reproducing a natural sound (e.g. *fizz*) or pronounced in a way thought to correspond to the appearance or character of the object or action described (e.g. *blob*).
– DERIVATIVES **imitatively** adverb.
immaculate ● adjective **1** perfectly clean, neat, or tidy. **2** free from flaws or mistakes. **3** Catholic Theology free from sin.
– DERIVATIVES **immaculacy** noun **immaculately** adverb.
– ORIGIN Latin *immaculatus*, from *in-* 'not' + *maculatus* 'stained'.
Immaculate Conception ● noun **1** (in the Roman Catholic Church) the doctrine that God preserved the Virgin Mary from the taint of original sin from the moment she was conceived. **2** the feast commemorating the Immaculate Conception on December 8th.
immanent /immənənt/ ● adjective **1** present within; inherent. **2** (of God) permanently pervading the universe.
– DERIVATIVES **immanence** noun.
– ORIGIN from Latin *immanere* 'remain within'.
immaterial ● adjective **1** unimportant under the circumstances; irrelevant. **2** spiritual rather than physical.
– DERIVATIVES **immateriality** noun.
immature ● adjective **1** not fully developed. **2** having or showing emotional or intellectual development appropriate to someone

i

Thesaurus

public's imagination INTEREST, fascination, attention, passion, curiosity.
imaginative ● adjective CREATIVE, visionary, inspired, inventive, resourceful, ingenious; original, innovative, innovatory, unorthodox, unconventional; fanciful, whimsical.
imagine ● verb **1** *one can imagine the cloud-capped castle* VISUALIZE, envisage, envision, picture, see in the mind's eye; dream up, think up/of, conceive. **2** *I imagine he was at home* ASSUME, presume, expect, take it (as read), presuppose; suppose, think (it likely), dare say, surmise, believe, be of the view; *N. Amer.* figure; *informal* guess, reckon; *formal* opine.
imbalance ● noun DISPARITY, variance, variation, polarity, contrast, lack of harmony; gulf, breach, gap.
imbed ● verb. See EMBED.
imbibe ● verb (*formal*) **1** *they'd imbibed too much whisky* DRINK, consume, quaff, guzzle, gulp (down); *informal* knock back, down, sink. **2** *he had imbibed liberally* DRINK (ALCOHOL), take strong drink, tipple; *informal* booze, knock a few back; *N. Amer. informal* bend one's elbow; *archaic* tope. **3** *imbibing local history* ASSIMILATE, absorb, soak up, take in, drink in, learn, acquire, grasp, pick up, familiarize oneself with.
imbroglio ● noun **1** *a political imbroglio* COMPLICATED SITUATION, complication, problem, difficulty, predicament, trouble, entanglement, confusion, muddle, mess; *informal* bind, jam, pickle, fix, corner, hole. **2** (*archaic*) *an imbroglio of papers* JUMBLE, muddle, mess, clutter, hotchpotch, mishmash; *N. Amer.* hodgepodge.
imbue ● verb PERMEATE, saturate, diffuse, suffuse, pervade; impregnate, inject, inculcate, ingrain, inspire; fill.
imitate ● verb **1** *other artists have imitated his style* EMULATE, copy, model oneself on, follow, echo, parrot; *informal* rip off. **2** *he imitated Winston Churchill* MIMIC, do an impression of, impersonate, ape; parody, caricature, burlesque, travesty; *informal* take off, send up; *N. Amer. informal* make like; *formal* personate; *archaic* monkey. **3** *the tombs imitated houses* RESEMBLE, look like, be like; echo, mirror; bring to mind, remind one of.
imitation ● noun **1** *an imitation of a sailor's hat* COPY, simulation, reproduction, replica. **2** *learning by imitation* EMULATION, copying, echoing, parroting. **3** *a perfect imitation of Francis* IMPERSONATION, impression, parody, mockery, caricature, burlesque, travesty, lampoon, pastiche; mimicry, mimicking, imitating, aping; *informal* send-up, take-off, spoof.
● adjective *imitation ivory* ARTIFICIAL, synthetic, simulated, man-made, manufactured, ersatz, substitute; mock, sham, fake, bogus; *informal* pseudo, phoney.
– OPPOSITES real, genuine.
imitative ● adjective **1** *imitative crime* SIMILAR, like, mimicking; *informal* copycat. **2** *I found the film empty and imitative* DERIVATIVE, unoriginal, unimaginative, uninspired, plagiarized, plagiaristic; clichéd, hackneyed, stale, trite, banal; *informal* cribbed, old hat. **3** *imitative words* ONOMATOPOEIC, echoic.
imitator ● noun **1** *the show's success has sparked off many imitators* COPIER, copyist, emulator, follower, mimic, plagiarist, ape, parrot; *informal* copycat. **2** *an Elvis imitator* IMPERSONATOR, impressionist, mimicker; parodist, caricaturist, lampooner.
immaculate ● adjective **1** *an immaculate white shirt* CLEAN, spotless, pristine, unsoiled, unstained, unsullied; shining, shiny, gleaming; neat, tidy, spick and span; *informal* squeaky clean. **2** *immaculate condition* PERFECT, pristine, mint; flawless, faultless, unblemished, unspoiled, undamaged; excellent, impeccable; *informal* tip-top, A1. **3** *his immaculate record* UNBLEMISHED, spotless, impeccable, unsullied, undefiled, untarnished, stainless; *informal* squeaky clean.
– OPPOSITES dirty, damaged.
immanent ● adjective **1** *the protection of liberties immanent in the constitution* INHERENT, intrinsic, innate, latent, essential, fundamental, basic. **2** *God is immanent in His creation* PERVASIVE, pervading, permeating; omnipresent.
immaterial ● adjective **1** *the difference in our ages was immaterial* IRRELEVANT, unimportant, inconsequential, insignificant, of no matter/moment, of little account, beside the point, neither here nor there. **2** *the immaterial soul* INTANGIBLE, incorporeal, bodiless, disembodied, impalpable, ethereal, insubstantial; spiritual, un-

younger.
– DERIVATIVES **immaturely** adverb **immaturity** noun.
immeasurable • adjective too large or extreme to measure.
– DERIVATIVES **immeasurably** adverb.
immediate • adjective **1** occurring or done at once. **2** nearest in time, space, or relationship. **3** most urgent; current. **4** without an intervening medium or agency; direct: *a coronary was the immediate cause of death.*
– DERIVATIVES **immediacy** noun.
– ORIGIN Latin *immediatus*, from *in-* 'not' + *mediatus* 'intervening'.
immediately • adverb **1** at once. **2** very close in time, space, or relationship. • conjunction chiefly Brit. as soon as.
immemorial • adjective existing from before what can be remembered or found in records: *from time immemorial.*
– DERIVATIVES **immemorially** adverb.
immense • adjective extremely large or great.
– DERIVATIVES **immensity** noun.
– ORIGIN Latin *immensus* 'immeasurable'.
immensely • adverb to a great extent; extremely.
immerse • verb **1** dip or submerge in a liquid. **2** (**immerse oneself** or **be immersed**) involve oneself deeply in an activity or interest.
– ORIGIN Latin *immergere* 'dip into'.
immersion • noun **1** the action of immersing or the state of being immersed. **2** deep involvement.
immersion heater • noun an electric heating element that is positioned in the liquid to be heated, typically in a domestic hot-water tank.
immersive • adjective (of a computer display) generating a three-dimensional image which appears to surround the user.
immigrant • noun a person who comes to live permanently in a foreign country.
immigrate • verb come to live permanently in a foreign country.
– DERIVATIVES **immigration** noun.
– ORIGIN Latin *immigrare.*
imminent • adjective about to happen.
– DERIVATIVES **imminence** noun **imminently** adverb.
– ORIGIN from Latin *imminere* 'overhang, impend'.
immiscible /imissib'l/ • adjective (of liquids) not forming a homogeneous mixture when added together.
immobile • adjective **1** not moving. **2** incapable of moving or being moved.
– DERIVATIVES **immobility** noun.
immobilize (also **immobilise**) • verb **1** prevent from moving or operating as normal. **2** restrict the movements of (a limb or patient) to allow healing.
– DERIVATIVES **immobilization** noun **immobilizer** noun.
immoderate • adjective lacking moderation; excessive.
– DERIVATIVES **immoderately** adverb **immoderation** noun.
immodest • adjective not humble, decent, or decorous.
– DERIVATIVES **immodestly** adverb **immodesty** noun.
immolate /imməlayt/ • verb kill or offer as a sacrifice, especially by burning.
– DERIVATIVES **immolation** noun.
– ORIGIN Latin *immolare* 'sprinkle with sacrificial meal', from *mola* 'meal'.
immoral • adjective not conforming to accepted standards of morality.
– DERIVATIVES **immorality** noun (pl. **immoralities**) **immorally** adverb.
immoral earnings • plural noun earnings from prostitution.
immortal /imort'l/ • adjective **1** living forever. **2** deserving to be

i

Thesaurus

earthly, supernatural.
– OPPOSITES significant, physical.
immature • adjective **1** *an immature Stilton* UNRIPE, not mature, unmellowed; undeveloped, unformed, unfinished. **2** *an extremely immature girl* CHILDISH, babyish, infantile, juvenile, puerile, jejune, callow, green, inexperienced, unsophisticated, unworldly, naive; *informal* wet behind the ears.
– OPPOSITES ripe.
immeasurable • adjective INCALCULABLE, inestimable, innumerable, untold; limitless, boundless, unbounded, unlimited, illimitable, infinite, endless, never-ending, interminable, inexhaustible; vast, immense, great, abundant; *informal* no end of; *poetic/literary* myriad.
immediate • adjective **1** *the UN called for immediate action* INSTANT, instantaneous, prompt, swift, speedy, rapid, quick, expeditious; sudden, hurried, hasty, precipitate; *informal* snappy; *poetic/literary* rathe. **2** *their immediate concerns* CURRENT, present, existing, actual; urgent, pressing. **3** *the immediate past* RECENT, not long past, just gone; occurring recently. **4** *our immediate neighbours* NEAREST, near, close, closest, next-door; adjacent, adjoining. **5** *the immediate cause of death* DIRECT, primary.
– OPPOSITES delayed, distant.
immediately • adverb **1** *it was necessary to make a decision immediately* STRAIGHT AWAY, at once, right away, instantly, now, directly, promptly, forthwith, this/that (very) minute, this/that instant, there and then, here and now, without delay, without further ado, post-haste; quickly, as fast as possible, speedily, as soon as possible, a.s.a.p.; *informal* pronto, in double-quick time, pretty damn quick, p.d.q., toot sweet; *archaic* instanter, forthright. **2** *I sat immediately behind him* DIRECTLY, right, exactly, precisely, squarely, just, dead; *informal* slap bang; *N. Amer. informal* smack dab.
immemorial • adjective ANCIENT, (very) old, age-old, antediluvian, timeless, archaic, long-standing, time-worn, time-honoured; traditional; *poetic/literary* of yore.
immense • adjective HUGE, vast, massive, enormous, gigantic, colossal, great, very large/big, monumental, towering, tremendous; giant, elephantine, monstrous, mammoth, titanic, king-sized; *informal* mega, monster, whopping (great), thumping (great), humongous, jumbo; *Brit. informal* whacking (great), ginormous.
– OPPOSITES tiny.
immensely • adverb EXTREMELY, very, exceedingly, exceptionally, extraordinarily, tremendously, hugely, singularly, distinctly, outstandingly, uncommonly, unusually, decidedly, particularly, eminently, supremely, highly, remarkably, really, truly, mightily, thoroughly, in the extreme; *informal* terrifically, awfully, fearfully, terribly, devilishly, seriously, mega, damn, damned; *Brit. informal* ever so, well, bloody, hellish, dead, jolly; *N. Amer. informal* real, mighty, powerful, awful, darned; *informal, dated* devilish, frightfully; *archaic* exceeding.
– OPPOSITES slightly.
immerse • verb **1** *litmus paper turns red on being immersed in acid* SUBMERGE, dip, dunk, duck, sink; soak, drench, saturate, wet. **2** *new Christians were immersed in the river* BAPTIZE, christen; *informal, dated* dip; *rare* lustrate. **3** *Elliot was immersed in his work* ABSORB, engross, occupy, engage, involve, bury; busy, employ, preoccupy; *informal* lose oneself in.
immigrant • noun NEWCOMER, settler, incomer, migrant, emigrant; non-native, foreigner, alien.
– OPPOSITES native.
imminent • adjective IMPENDING, close (at hand), near, (fast) approaching, coming, forthcoming, on the way, in the offing, in the pipeline, on the horizon, in the air/wind, expected, anticipated, brewing, looming; *informal* on the cards.
immobile • adjective **1** *she sat immobile for a long time* MOTIONLESS, without moving, still, stock-still, static, stationary; rooted to the spot, rigid, frozen, transfixed, like a statue, not moving a muscle. **2** *she dreaded being immobile* UNABLE TO MOVE, immobilized; paralysed, crippled.
– OPPOSITES moving.
immobilize • verb PUT OUT OF ACTION, disable, make inoperative, inactivate, deactivate, paralyse, cripple; bring to a standstill, halt, stop; clamp, wheel-clamp.
immoderate • adjective EXCESSIVE, heavy, intemperate, unrestrained, unrestricted, uncontrolled, unlimited, unbridled, uncurbed, overindulgent, imprudent, reckless; undue, inordinate, unreasonable, unjustified, unwarranted, uncalled for, outrageous; extravagant, lavish, prodigal, profligate.
immodest • adjective INDECOROUS, improper, indecent, indelicate, immoral; forward, bold, brazen, impudent, shameless, loose, wanton; *informal* fresh, cheeky, saucy.
immolate • verb SACRIFICE, offer up; kill, slaughter, burn.
immoral • adjective UNETHICAL, bad, morally wrong, wrongful, wicked, evil, unprincipled, unscrupulous, dishonourable, dishonest, unconscionable, iniquitous, disreputable, corrupt, depraved, vile, villainous, nefarious, base, miscreant; sinful, impure, unchaste, unvirtuous, shameless, degenerate, debauched, dissolute, reprobate, lewd, licentious, wanton, promiscuous; *informal* shady, low-down; *Brit. informal* dodgy, crooked.
– OPPOSITES ethical, chaste.
immorality • noun WICKEDNESS, immoral behaviour, badness, evil,

remembered forever. ● **noun 1** an immortal being, especially a god of ancient Greece or Rome. **2** a person of enduring fame.
– DERIVATIVES **immortality** noun **immortalize** (also **immortalise**) verb.

immortelle /immortel/ ● **noun** another term for EVERLASTING.
– ORIGIN French, 'everlasting'.

immovable (also **immoveable**) ● **adjective 1** not able to be moved or changed. **2** Law (of property) consisting of land, buildings, or other permanent items.
– DERIVATIVES **immovability** noun **immovably** adverb.

immune ● **adjective 1** resistant to a particular infection owing to the presence of specific antibodies or sensitized white blood cells. **2** relating to such resistance: *the immune system.* **3** exempt from an obligation or penalty. **4** (often **immune to**) not susceptible.
– ORIGIN Latin *immunis* 'exempt from public service or charge', from *in-* 'not' + *munis* 'ready for service'.

immune response ● **noun** the reaction of the cells and fluids of the body to the presence of an antigen.

immunity ● **noun** (pl. **immunities**) **1** the ability of an organism to resist a particular infection. **2** exemption from an obligation or penalty.

immunize (also **immunise**) ● **verb** make immune to infection, typically by inoculation.
– DERIVATIVES **immunization** noun.

immunoblotting /imyoonōblotting/ ● **noun** a technique for analysing or identifying proteins in a mixture, involving separation by electrophoresis followed by staining with antibodies.

immunodeficiency ● **noun** reduced ability of the immune system to protect the body from infection.

immunoglobulin /imyoonōglobyoolin/ ● **noun** any of a class of blood proteins which function as antibodies.

immunology ● **noun** the branch of medicine and biology concerned with immunity.
– DERIVATIVES **immunologic** adjective **immunological** adjective **immunologist** noun.

immunosuppression ● **noun** suppression of an individual's immune response, especially as induced to help the survival of an organ after a transplant operation.
– DERIVATIVES **immunosuppressant** noun **immunosuppressed** adjective.

immunosuppressive ● **adjective** (chiefly of drugs) partially or completely suppressing the immune response of an individual. ● **noun** an immunosuppressive drug.

immunotherapy ● **noun** the prevention or treatment of disease with substances that stimulate the immune response.

immure /imyoor/ ● **verb** (usu. **be immured**) confine or imprison.
– DERIVATIVES **immurement** noun.
– ORIGIN Latin *immurare*, from *murus* 'wall'.

immutable /imyōōtəb'l/ ● **adjective** unchanging or unchangeable.
– DERIVATIVES **immutability** noun **immutably** adverb.

imp ● **noun 1** a small, mischievous devil or sprite. **2** a mischievous child.
– ORIGIN originally denoting a descendant, later an evil person (regarded as a child of the devil): from an Old English word meaning 'young shoot', from Greek *emphuein* 'to implant'.

impact ● **noun** /impakt/ **1** the action of one object coming forcibly into contact with another. **2** a marked effect or influence. ● **verb** /impakt/ **1** N. Amer. come into forcible contact with another object. **2** (often **impact on**) have a strong effect. **3** press firmly.
– DERIVATIVES **impactor** noun.
– ORIGIN from Latin *impingere* 'drive something in or at'.

impacted ● **adjective 1** (of a tooth) wedged between another tooth and the jaw. **2** (of a fractured bone) having the parts crushed together.
– DERIVATIVES **impaction** noun.

impair ● **verb** weaken or damage.
– DERIVATIVES **impairment** noun.
– ORIGIN Old French *empeirier*, from Latin *pejorare* 'make worse'.

impaired ● **adjective** having a disability of a specified kind: *hearing-impaired.*

impala /impaalə/ ● **noun** (pl. same) a graceful antelope of southern and East Africa, with lyre-shaped horns.
– ORIGIN Zulu.

impale ● **verb** transfix or pierce with a sharp instrument.
– DERIVATIVES **impalement** noun **impaler** noun.
– ORIGIN Latin *impalare*, from *palus* 'a stake'.

impalpable ● **adjective 1** unable to be felt by touch. **2** not easily comprehended.

i

Thesaurus

vileness, corruption, dishonesty, dishonourableness; sinfulness, sin, unchastity, depravity, vice, degeneracy, debauchery, dissolution, perversion, lewdness, wantonness, promiscuity; *informal* shadiness; *Brit. informal* crookedness; *formal* turpitude.

immortal ● **adjective 1** *our souls are immortal* UNDYING, deathless, eternal, everlasting, never-ending, endless, lasting, enduring; imperishable, indestructible, inextinguishable, immutable. **2** *an immortal children's classic* TIMELESS, perennial, classic, time-honoured, enduring; famous, famed, renowned, great, eminent, outstanding, acclaimed, celebrated.
● **noun 1** *Greek temples of the immortals* GOD, GODDESS, deity, divine being, supreme being, divinity. **2** *one of the immortals of soccer* GREAT, hero, Olympian.

immortality ● **noun 1** *the immortality of the gods* ETERNAL LIFE, everlasting life, deathlessness; indestructibility, imperishability. **2** *the book has achieved immortality* TIMELESSNESS, legendary status, lasting fame/renown.

immortalize ● **verb** COMMEMORATE, memorialize, eternalize; celebrate, pay tribute to, honour, salute, exalt, glorify; *poetic/literary* eternize.

immovable ● **adjective 1** *lock your bike to something immovable* FIXED, secure, stable, moored, anchored, braced, set firm, set fast; stuck, jammed, stiff, unbudgeable. **2** *he sat immovable* MOTIONLESS, unmoving, stationary, still, stock-still, not moving a muscle, rooted to the spot; transfixed, paralysed, frozen. **3** *she was immovable in her loyalties* STEADFAST, unwavering, unswerving, resolute, determined, firm, unshakeable, unfailing, dogged, tenacious, inflexible, unyielding, unbending, uncompromising, iron-willed; *N. Amer.* rock-ribbed.
– OPPOSITES mobile, moving.

immune ● **adjective** RESISTANT, not subject, not liable, unsusceptible, not vulnerable; protected from, safe from, secure against, not in danger of.
– OPPOSITES susceptible.

immunity ● **noun 1** *an immunity to malaria* RESISTANCE, nonsusceptibility; ability to fight off, protection against, defences against; immunization against, inoculation against. **2** *immunity from prosecution* EXEMPTION, exception, freedom, release, dispensation; *informal* a let-off. **3** *diplomatic immunity* INDEMNITY, privilege, prerogative, right, liberty, licence; legal exemption, impunity, protection.

immunize ● **verb** VACCINATE, inoculate, inject; protect from, safeguard against; *informal* give someone a jab/shot.

immure ● **verb** CONFINE, intern, shut up, lock up, incarcerate, imprison, jail, put behind bars, put under lock and key, hold captive, hold prisoner; detain, hold.

immutable ● **adjective** FIXED, set, rigid, inflexible, permanent, established; unchanging, unchanged, unvarying, unvaried, static, constant, lasting, enduring.
– OPPOSITES variable.

imp ● **noun 1** *imps are thought to sprout from Satan* DEMON, devil, fiend; hobgoblin, goblin, elf, sprite, puck, cacodemon; *archaic* bugbear. **2** *a cheeky young imp* RASCAL, monkey, devil, troublemaker, wretch, urchin, tearaway; *informal* scamp, brat, monster, horror, tyke, whippersnapper; *Brit. informal* perisher; *N. Amer. informal* hellion, varmint; *archaic* scapegrace, rapscallion.

impact ● **noun 1** *the force of the impact* COLLISION, crash, smash, bump, bang, knock. **2** *the job losses will have a major impact* EFFECT, influence; consequences, repercussions, ramifications, reverberations.
● **verb 1** *(N. Amer.) a comet impacted the earth sixty million years ago* CRASH INTO, smash into, collide with, hit, strike, smack into, bang into. **2** *high interest rates have impacted on retail spending* AFFECT, influence, have an effect, make an impression; hit, touch, change, alter, modify, transform, shape.

impair ● **verb** HAVE A NEGATIVE EFFECT ON, harm, damage, diminish, reduce, weaken, lessen, decrease, impede, hinder; undermine, compromise; *formal* vitiate.
– OPPOSITES improve, enhance.

impaired ● **adjective** DISABLED, handicapped, incapacitated; *euphemistic* challenged, differently abled.

impairment ● **noun** DISABILITY, handicap, abnormality, defect, dys-

– DERIVATIVES **impalpably** adverb.

impanel (also **empanel**) ● verb (**impanelled**, **impanelling**; US **impaneled**, **impaneling**) enrol (a jury) or enrol (someone) on to a jury.
– DERIVATIVES **impanelment** noun.
– ORIGIN Old French *empaneller*, from *panel* 'panel'.

impart ● verb **1** communicate (information). **2** give (a quality).
– ORIGIN originally in the sense 'give a share of': from Latin *impartire*, from *pars* 'part'.

impartial ● adjective treating all rivals or disputants equally.
– DERIVATIVES **impartiality** noun **impartially** adverb.

impassable ● adjective impossible to travel along or over.
– DERIVATIVES **impassability** noun.

impasse /ampaas/ ● noun a deadlock.
– ORIGIN French, from *passer* 'to pass'.

impassioned ● adjective filled with or showing great emotion.

impassive ● adjective not feeling or showing emotion.
– DERIVATIVES **impassively** adverb **impassiveness** noun **impassivity** noun.

impasto /impastō/ ● noun Art the process or technique of laying on paint or pigment thickly so that it stands out from a surface.
– ORIGIN Italian, from *pasta* 'a paste'.

impatiens /impatienz/ ● noun a plant of a genus that includes busy Lizzie and its many hybrids.
– ORIGIN from Latin, 'impatient' (because the capsules of the plant readily burst open when touched).

i

impatient ● adjective **1** lacking patience or tolerance. **2** restlessly eager: *impatient for change.*
– DERIVATIVES **impatience** noun **impatiently** adverb.

impeach ● verb **1** call into question the integrity or validity of (a practice). **2** Brit. charge with treason or another crime against the state. **3** chiefly US charge (the holder of a public office) with misconduct.
– DERIVATIVES **impeachable** adjective **impeachment** noun.
– ORIGIN Old French *empecher* 'impede', from Latin *impedicare* 'entangle', from *pes* 'foot'.

impeccable /impekkəb'l/ ● adjective in accordance with the highest standards; faultless.
– DERIVATIVES **impeccability** noun **impeccably** adverb.
– ORIGIN originally in the sense 'not liable to sin': from Latin *impeccabilis*, from *peccare* 'to sin'.

impecunious /impikyōōniəss/ ● adjective having little or no money.
– DERIVATIVES **impecuniosity** noun **impecuniousness** noun.
– ORIGIN from IN-[1] + Latin *pecuniosus* 'wealthy'.

impedance /impeed'nss/ ● noun the effective resistance to an alternating electric current arising from the combined effects of ohmic resistance and reactance.

impede /impeed/ ● verb delay or block the progress or action of.
– ORIGIN Latin *impedire* 'shackle the feet of', from *pes* 'foot'.

impediment /impeddimənt/ ● noun **1** a hindrance or obstruction. **2** (also **speech impediment**) a defect in a person's speech, such as a lisp or stammer.

impedimenta /impeddimentə/ ● plural noun equipment for an activity or expedition, especially when an encumbrance.
– ORIGIN Latin, 'impediments'.

impel /impel/ ● verb (**impelled**, **impelling**) **1** drive, force, or urge to do. **2** drive forward.
– DERIVATIVES **impeller** noun.
– ORIGIN Latin *impellere*, from *in-* 'towards' + *pellere* 'to drive'.

impending /impending/ ● adjective (especially of something bad or momentous) be about to happen.
– ORIGIN from Latin *impendere* 'overhang'.

impenetrable /impennitrəb'l/ ● adjective **1** impossible to get through or into. **2** impossible to understand. **3** impervious to new ideas or influences.
– DERIVATIVES **impenetrability** noun **impenetrably** adverb.

impenitent ● adjective not feeling shame or regret.

Thesaurus

function.

impale ● verb STICK, skewer, spear, spike, transfix; pierce, stab, run through; *poetic/literary* transpierce.

impalpable ● adjective INTANGIBLE, insubstantial, incorporeal; indefinable, elusive, undescribable.

impart ● verb **1** *she had news to impart* COMMUNICATE, pass on, convey, transmit, relay, relate, recount, tell, make known, make public, report, announce, proclaim, spread, disseminate, circulate, promulgate, broadcast; disclose, reveal, divulge; *informal* let on about, blab; *archaic* discover, unbosom. **2** *the brush imparts a good sheen* GIVE, bestow, confer, grant, lend, afford, provide, supply.

impartial ● adjective UNBIASED, unprejudiced, neutral, non-partisan, disinterested, detached, dispassionate, objective, open-minded, equitable, even-handed, fair, just.
– OPPOSITES biased, partisan.

impassable ● adjective UNPASSABLE, unnavigable, untraversable; closed, blocked.

impasse ● noun DEADLOCK, dead end, stalemate, checkmate, standoff; standstill, halt, (full) stop.

impassioned ● adjective EMOTIONAL, heartfelt, wholehearted, earnest, sincere, fervent, ardent, passionate, fervid; *poetic/literary* perfervid; *rare* passional.

impassive ● adjective EXPRESSIONLESS, inexpressive, inscrutable, blank, deadpan, poker-faced, straight-faced; stony, wooden, unresponsive.
– OPPOSITES expressive.

impatience ● noun **1** *he was shifting in his seat with impatience* RESTLESSNESS, restiveness, agitation, nervousness; eagerness, keenness; *informal* jitteriness. **2** *a burst of impatience* IRRITABILITY, testiness, tetchiness, irascibility, querulousness, peevishness, frustration, exasperation, annoyance, pique.

impatient ● adjective **1** *Melissa grew impatient* RESTLESS, restive, agitated, nervous, anxious, ill at ease, edgy, jumpy, keyed up; *Brit.* nervy; *informal* twitchy, jittery, uptight. **2** *they are impatient to get back home* ANXIOUS, eager, keen, yearning, longing, aching; *informal* itching, dying. **3** *an impatient gesture* IRRITATED, annoyed, angry, testy, tetchy, snappy, cross, querulous, peevish, piqued, short-tempered; abrupt, curt, brusque, terse, short; *informal* peeved.
– OPPOSITES calm, reluctant.

impeach ● verb **1** *(N. Amer.) moves to impeach the president* INDICT, charge, accuse, lay charges against, arraign, take to court, put on trial, prosecute. **2** *the headlines impeached their clean image* CHALLENGE, question, call into question, raise doubts about.

impeccable ● adjective FLAWLESS, faultless, unblemished, spotless, stainless, perfect, exemplary; sinless, irreproachable, blameless, guiltless; *informal* squeaky clean.
– OPPOSITES imperfect, sinful.

impecunious ● adjective PENNILESS, poor, impoverished, indigent, insolvent, hard up, poverty-stricken, needy, destitute; in straitened circumstances, unable to make ends meet; *Brit.* on the breadline; *informal* (flat) broke, strapped (for cash), on one's uppers; *Brit. informal* skint, stony broke, in Queer Street; *N. Amer. informal* stone broke; *formal* penurious.
– OPPOSITES wealthy.

impede ● verb HINDER, obstruct, hamper, hold back/up, delay, interfere with, disrupt, retard, slow (down); block, check, stop, thwart, frustrate, baulk, foil, derail; *informal* stymie; *Brit. informal* scupper, throw a spanner in the works; *N. Amer. informal* bork, throw a monkey wrench in the works; *dated* cumber.
– OPPOSITES facilitate.

impediment ● noun **1** *an impediment to economic improvement* HINDRANCE, obstruction, obstacle, barrier, bar, block, check, curb, restriction, limitation; setback, difficulty, snag, hitch, stumbling block; *informal* fly in the ointment, hiccup; *Brit. informal* spanner in the works; *N. Amer. informal* monkey wrench in the works; *archaic* cumber. **2** *a speech impediment* DEFECT; stammer, stutter, lisp.

impedimenta ● plural noun PARAPHERNALIA, trappings, equipment, accoutrements, appurtenances, accessories, bits and pieces, tackle; *informal* stuff, gear; *Brit. informal* clobber, gubbins; *archaic* equipage.

impel ● verb **1** *financial difficulties impelled her to seek work* FORCE, compel, constrain, oblige, require, make, urge, press, pressurize, drive, push, spur, prod, goad, incite, prompt, persuade. **2** *vital energies impel him in unforeseen directions* PROPEL, drive, move, get going, get moving.

impending ● adjective IMMINENT, close (at hand), near, nearing, approaching, coming, forthcoming, upcoming, to come, on the way, about to happen, in store, in the offing, on the horizon, in the air/wind, brewing, looming, threatening, menacing.

impenetrable ● adjective **1** *impenetrable armoured plating* UNBREAKABLE, indestructible, solid, thick, unyielding; impregnable, inviolable, unassailable, unpierceable. **2** *a dark, impenetrable forest* IMPASSABLE, unpassable, inaccessible, unnavigable, untraversable; dense, thick, overgrown. **3** *an impenetrable clique* EX-

– DERIVATIVES **impenitence** noun **impenitently** adverb.

imperative ● adjective **1** of vital importance. **2** giving an authoritative command. **3** Grammar denoting the mood of a verb that expresses a command or exhortation, as in *come here!* ● noun an essential or urgent thing.

– DERIVATIVES **imperatively** adverb **imperativeness** noun.

– ORIGIN Latin *imperativus* 'specially ordered', from *imperare* 'to command'.

imperceptible ● adjective so slight, gradual, or subtle as not to be perceived.

– DERIVATIVES **imperceptibly** adverb.

imperfect ● adjective **1** faulty or incomplete. **2** Grammar (of a tense) denoting a past action in progress but not completed at the time in question.

– DERIVATIVES **imperfection** noun **imperfectly** adverb.

imperial ● adjective **1** relating to an empire or an emperor. **2** characteristic of an emperor; majestic or magnificent. **3** relating to or denoting the system of non-metric weights and measures formerly used for all measures in the UK, and still used for some.

– DERIVATIVES **imperially** adverb.

– ORIGIN Latin *imperialis*, from *imperium* 'command, empire'.

imperialism ● noun a policy of extending a country's power and influence through colonization, use of military force, or other means.

– DERIVATIVES **imperialist** noun & adjective **imperialistic** adjective.

imperil ● verb (**imperilled**, **imperilling**; US **imperiled**, **imperiling**) put into danger.

imperious /impeeriəss/ ● adjective arrogant and domineering.

– DERIVATIVES **imperiously** adverb **imperiousness** noun.

– ORIGIN Latin *imperiosus*, from *imperium* 'command, empire'.

imperishable ● adjective enduring forever.

– DERIVATIVES **imperishably** adverb.

impermanent ● adjective not permanent.

– DERIVATIVES **impermanence** noun **impermanently** adverb.

impermeable /impermiəb'l/ ● adjective not allowing fluid to pass through.

– DERIVATIVES **impermeability** noun.

impersonal ● adjective **1** not influenced by or involving personal feelings. **2** featureless and anonymous. **3** not existing as a person. **4** Grammar (of a verb) used only with a formal subject (in English usually *it*) and expressing an action not attributable to a definite subject (as in *it is snowing*).

– DERIVATIVES **impersonality** noun **impersonally** adverb.

impersonal pronoun ● noun the pronoun *it* when used without definite reference or antecedent, as in *it was snowing*.

impersonate ● verb pretend to be (another person) for entertainment or fraud.

– DERIVATIVES **impersonation** noun **impersonator** noun.

– ORIGIN from IN-² + Latin *persona* 'person'.

impertinent ● adjective **1** not showing proper respect. **2** formal not pertinent; irrelevant.

– DERIVATIVES **impertinence** noun **impertinently** adverb.

imperturbable /impərturbəb'l/ ● adjective unable to be upset or excited.

– DERIVATIVES **imperturbability** noun **imperturbably** adverb.

impervious /imperviəss/ ● adjective **1** not allowing fluid to pass through. **2** (**impervious to**) unable to be affected by.

– DERIVATIVES **imperviously** adverb **imperviousness** noun.

impetigo /impitīgō/ ● noun a contagious bacterial skin infec-

Thesaurus

CLUSIVE, closed, secretive, secret, private; restrictive, restricted, limited. **4** *impenetrable statistics* INCOMPREHENSIBLE, unfathomable, inexplicable, unintelligible, unclear, baffling, bewildering, puzzling, perplexing, confusing, abstruse, opaque; complex, complicated, difficult; archaic wildering.

impenitent ● adjective UNREPENTANT, unrepenting, uncontrite, remorseless, unashamed, unapologetic, unabashed.

imperative ● adjective **1** *it is imperative that you find him* VITALLY IMPORTANT, of vital importance, all-important, vital, crucial, critical, essential, necessary, indispensable, urgent. **2** *the imperative note in her voice* PEREMPTORY, commanding, imperious, authoritative, masterful, dictatorial, assertive, firm, insistent.

– OPPOSITES unimportant, submissive.

imperceptible ● adjective UNNOTICEABLE, undetectable, indistinguishable, indiscernible, invisible, inaudible, impalpable, unobtrusive; slight, small, subtle, faint, fine, negligible; indistinct, unclear, obscure, vague, indefinite, hard to make out.

– OPPOSITES noticeable.

imperfect ● adjective **1** *the good were returned as imperfect* FAULTY, flawed, defective, shoddy, unsound, inferior, second-rate, below standard, substandard; damaged, blemished, broken, cracked, torn, scratched; informal not up to scratch, tenth-rate, crummy; Brit. informal duff. **2** *an imperfect form of the manuscript* INCOMPLETE, unfinished, half-done; unpolished, unrefined, rough. **3** *she spoke imperfect Arabic* BROKEN, faltering, halting, hesitant, rudimentary, limited.

– OPPOSITES flawless.

imperfection ● noun **1** *the glass is free from imperfections* DEFECT, fault, flaw, deformity, discoloration, disfigurement; crack, scratch, chip, dent, blemish, stain, spot, mark. **2** *he was aware of his imperfections* FLAW, fault, failing, deficiency, weakness, weak point, shortcoming, foible, inadequacy, limitation. **3** *the imperfection of the fossil record* INCOMPLETENESS, patchiness, deficiency; roughness, crudeness.

– OPPOSITES strength.

imperial ● adjective **1** *imperial banners* ROYAL, regal, monarchal, monarchial, monarchical, sovereign, kingly, queenly, princely. **2** *her imperial bearing* MAJESTIC, grand, dignified, proud, stately, noble, aristocratic, regal; magnificent, imposing, impressive. **3** *our customers thought we were imperial* IMPERIOUS, high-handed, peremptory, dictatorial, domineering, bossy, arrogant, overweening, overbearing.

imperil ● verb ENDANGER, jeopardize, risk, put in danger, put in jeopardy, expose to danger; threaten, pose a threat to; archaic peril.

imperious ● adjective PEREMPTORY, high-handed, commanding, imperial, overbearing, overweening, domineering, authoritarian, dictatorial, authoritative, lordly, assertive, bossy, arrogant; informal pushy, high and mighty.

imperishable ● adjective ENDURING, everlasting, undying, immortal, perennial, long-lasting; indestructible, inextinguishable, ineradicable, unfading, permanent, never-ending, never dying; poetic/literary sempiternal, perdurable.

impermanent ● adjective TEMPORARY, transient, transitory, passing, fleeting, momentary, ephemeral, fugitive; short-lived, brief, here today and gone tomorrow; poetic/literary evanescent.

impermeable ● adjective WATERTIGHT, waterproof, damp-proof, airtight, (hermetically) sealed.

impersonal ● adjective **1** *the hand of fate is impersonal* NEUTRAL, unbiased, non-partisan, unprejudiced, objective, detached, disinterested, dispassionate, without favouritism. **2** *he remained strangely impersonal* ALOOF, distant, remote, reserved, withdrawn, unemotional, unsentimental, dispassionate, cold, cool, indifferent, unconcerned; formal, stiff, businesslike; informal starchy, standoffish.

– OPPOSITES biased, warm.

impersonate ● verb IMITATE, mimic, do an impression of, ape; parody, caricature, burlesque, travesty, satirize, lampoon; masquerade as, pose as, pass oneself off as; informal take off, send up; N. Amer. informal make like; formal personate; archaic monkey.

impersonation ● noun IMPRESSION, imitation; parody, caricature, burlesque, travesty, lampoon, pastiche; informal take-off, send-up; formal personation.

impertinence ● noun RUDENESS, insolence, impoliteness, bad manners, discourtesy, discourteousness, disrespect, incivility; impudence, cheek, cheekiness, audacity, temerity, effrontery, nerve, gall, boldness, cockiness, brazenness; informal brass (neck); Brit. informal sauce; N. Amer. informal sass, sassiness, chutzpah; archaic assumption.

impertinent ● adjective **1** *she asked a lot of impertinent questions* RUDE, insolent, impolite, ill-mannered, bad-mannered, uncivil, discourteous, disrespectful; impudent, cheeky, audacious, bold, brazen, brash, presumptuous, forward; tactless, undiplomatic; informal brass-necked, saucy; N. Amer. informal sassy; archaic contumelious. **2** (formal) *talk of 'rhetoric' is impertinent to this process* IRRELEVANT, inapplicable, inapposite, inappropriate, immaterial, unrelated, unconnected, not germane; beside the point, out of place.

– OPPOSITES polite, relevant.

imperturbable ● adjective SELF-POSSESSED, composed, {cool, calm, and collected}, cool-headed, self-controlled, serene, relaxed, unexcitable, even-tempered, placid, phlegmatic; unperturbed, unflustered, unruffled; informal unflappable, unfazed, laid-back.

– OPPOSITES excitable.

impervious ● adjective **1** *he seemed impervious to the chill wind* UNAFFECTED, untouched, immune, invulnerable, insusceptible, re-

tion forming pustules and yellow crusty sores.
– ORIGIN Latin, from *impetere* 'to attack'.

impetuous ● adjective **1** acting or done quickly and rashly. **2** moving forcefully or rapidly.
– DERIVATIVES **impetuosity** noun **impetuously** adverb **impetuousness** noun.
– ORIGIN Latin *impetuosus*, from *impetere* 'to attack'.

impetus ● noun **1** the force or energy with which a body moves. **2** a driving force.
– ORIGIN Latin, 'assault, force'.

impi /impi/ ● noun (pl. **impis**) **1** a group of Zulu warriors. **2** an armed band of Zulus involved in urban or rural conflict.
– ORIGIN Zulu.

impiety /impīəti/ ● noun lack of piety or reverence.

impinge ● verb (**impinging**) (usu. **impinge on**) **1** have an effect or impact. **2** come into contact; encroach.
– DERIVATIVES **impingement** noun.
– ORIGIN Latin *impingere* 'drive something in or at'.

impious /impiəss/ ● adjective not showing respect or reverence.
– DERIVATIVES **impiously** adverb.

impish ● adjective mischievous.
– DERIVATIVES **impishly** adverb **impishness** noun.

implacable ● adjective **1** unable to be appeased. **2** relentless; unstoppable.
– DERIVATIVES **implacability** noun **implacably** adverb.

implant ● verb /implaant/ **1** insert or fix (tissue or an artificial object) into the body. **2** establish (an idea) in the mind. ● noun /implaant/ a thing implanted.
– DERIVATIVES **implantation** noun.
– ORIGIN Latin *implantare* 'engraft'.

implausible ● adjective not seeming reasonable or probable.
– DERIVATIVES **implausibility** noun **implausibly** adverb.

implement ● noun /implimənt/ a tool, utensil, or other piece of equipment, used for a particular purpose. ● verb /impliment/ put into effect.
– DERIVATIVES **implementation** noun **implementer** noun.
– ORIGIN from Latin *implere* 'fill up', later 'employ'.

implicate ● verb /implikayt/ **1** show to be involved in a crime. **2** (**be implicated in**) bear some of the responsibility for. **3** convey (a meaning or intention) indirectly; imply.
– DERIVATIVES **implicative** /implikkətiv/ adjective.
– ORIGIN Latin *implicare* 'fold in, involve, imply'.

implication ● noun **1** the implicit conclusion that can be drawn from something. **2** a likely consequence. **3** the action of implicating or the state of being implicated.
– DERIVATIVES **implicational** adjective.

implicit /implissit/ ● adjective **1** implied though not directly expressed. **2** (**implicit in**) always to be found in. **3** with no qualification or question: *implicit faith.*
– DERIVATIVES **implicitly** adverb **implicitness** noun.
– ORIGIN Latin *implicitus*, from *implicare* (see IMPLICATE).

implode /implōd/ ● verb collapse or cause to collapse violently inwards.
– DERIVATIVES **implosion** noun **implosive** adjective.
– ORIGIN from IN-² + Latin *plodere, plaudere* 'to clap', on the pattern of *explode*.

implore ● verb beg earnestly or desperately.
– ORIGIN Latin *implorare* 'invoke with tears'.

imply ● verb (**implies**, **implied**) **1** indicate by suggestion rather than explicit reference. **2** (of a fact or occurrence) suggest as a logical consequence.
– USAGE The words **imply** and **infer** do not mean the same thing. **Imply** is used with a speaker as its subject, as in *he implied that the General had been a traitor*, and indicates that the speaker is

Thesaurus

sistant, indifferent, heedless, oblivious; proof against. **2** *an impervious damp-proof course* IMPERMEABLE, impenetrable, impregnable, waterproof, watertight; (hermetically) sealed.
– OPPOSITES susceptible, permeable.

impetuous ● adjective **1** *an impetuous decision* IMPULSIVE, rash, hasty, overhasty, reckless, heedless, foolhardy, incautious, imprudent, injudicious, ill-considered, unthought-out; spontaneous, impromptu, spur-of-the-moment, precipitate, precipitous, hurried, rushed. **2** *an impetuous flow of water* TORRENTIAL, powerful, forceful, vigorous, violent, raging, relentless, uncontrolled; rapid, fast, fast-flowing.
– OPPOSITES considered, sluggish.

impetus ● noun **1** *the flywheel lost all its impetus* MOMENTUM, propulsion, impulsion, motive force, driving force, drive, thrust; energy, force, power, push, strength. **2** *the sales force were given fresh impetus* MOTIVATION, stimulus, incitement, incentive, inducement, inspiration, encouragement, boost; *informal* a shot in the arm.

impiety ● noun **1** *a world of impiety and immorality* GODLESSNESS, ungodliness, unholiness, irreligion, sinfulness, sin, vice, immorality, unrighteousness; apostasy, atheism, agnosticism, paganism, heathenism, non-belief, unbelief. **2** *one impiety will cost me my eternity in paradise* SIN, transgression, wrongdoing, evil-doing, wrong, misdeed, misdemeanour.
– OPPOSITES faith.

impinge ● verb **1** *these issues impinge on all of us* AFFECT, have an effect, touch, influence, make an impact, leave a mark. **2** *the proposed fencing would impinge on a public bridleway* ENCROACH, intrude, infringe, invade, trespass, obtrude, cut through, interfere with; violate; *archaic* entrench on. **3** *(Physics) electrically charged particles impinge on the lunar surface* STRIKE, hit, collide with.

impious ● adjective GODLESS, ungodly, unholy, irreligious, sinful, immoral, unrighteous, sacrilegious, profane, blasphemous, irreverent; apostate, atheistic, agnostic, pagan, heathen, faithless, non-believing, unbelieving; *rare* nullifidian.

impish ● adjective **1** *he takes an impish delight in shocking the press* MISCHIEVOUS, naughty, wicked, rascally, roguish, playful, sportive; mischief-making, full of mischief. **2** *an impish grin* ELFIN, elflike, pixie-like, puckish; mischievous, roguish.

implacable ● adjective UNAPPEASABLE, unpacifiable, unplacatable, unmollifiable, unforgiving; intransigent, inflexible, unyielding, unbending, uncompromising, unrelenting, ruthless, remorseless, merciless, pitiless, heartless, cruel, hard, harsh, stern, tough.

implant ● verb **1** *the collagen is implanted under the skin* INSERT, embed, bury, lodge, place; graft. **2** *he implanted the idea in my mind* INSTIL, inculcate, insinuate, introduce, inject, plant, sow, root, lodge.
● noun *a silicone implant* TRANSPLANT, graft, implantation, insert.

implausible ● adjective UNLIKELY, improbable, questionable, doubtful, debatable; unconvincing, far-fetched, incredible, unbelievable, unimaginable, inconceivable, fantastic, fanciful, ridiculous, absurd, preposterous; *informal* cock and bull.
– OPPOSITES convincing.

implement ● noun *garden implements* TOOL, utensil, instrument, device, apparatus, gadget, contraption, appliance, machine; *informal* gizmo.
● verb *the cost of implementing the new law* EXECUTE, apply, put into effect/action, put into practice, carry out/through, perform, enact; fulfil, discharge, accomplish, bring about, achieve, realize; *formal* effectuate.

implicate ● verb **1** *he had been implicated in a financial scandal* INCRIMINATE, compromise; involve, connect, embroil, enmesh; *archaic* inculpate. **2** *viruses are implicated in the development of cancer* INVOLVE IN, concern with, associate with, connect with. **3** *when one asks a question one implicates that one desires an answer.* See IMPLY sense 1.

implication ● noun **1** *he was smarting at their implication* SUGGESTION, inference, insinuation, innuendo, hint, intimation, imputation. **2** *important political implications* CONSEQUENCE, result, ramification, repercussion, reverberation, effect. **3** *his implication in the murder case* INCRIMINATION, involvement, connection, entanglement, association; *archaic* inculpation.

implicit ● adjective **1** *implicit assumptions* IMPLIED, inferred, understood, hinted at, suggested, deducible; unspoken, unexpressed, undeclared, unstated, tacit, unacknowledged, taken for granted. **2** *assumptions implicit in the way questions are asked* INHERENT, latent, underlying, inbuilt, incorporated. **3** *an implicit trust in human nature* ABSOLUTE, complete, total, wholehearted, perfect, utter; unqualified, unconditional; unshakeable, unquestioning, firm, steadfast.
– OPPOSITES explicit.

implicitly ● adverb COMPLETELY, absolutely, totally, wholeheartedly, utterly, unconditionally, unreservedly, without reservation.

implied ● adjective IMPLICIT, hinted at, suggested, insinuated, inferred, understood, deducible; unspoken, unexpressed, undeclared, unstated, tacit, unacknowledged, taken for granted.
– OPPOSITES explicit.

implore ● verb **1** *his mother implored him to continue studying* PLEAD WITH, beg, entreat, beseech, appeal to, ask, request, call on; exhort, urge, enjoin, press, push, petition, bid. **2** *(archaic) she im-*

suggesting something though not making an explicit statement. **Infer** is used in sentences such as *we inferred from his words that the General had been a traitor*, and indicates that something in the speaker's words enabled the listeners to deduce that the man was a traitor.
– ORIGIN originally in the sense 'entangle': from Old French *emplier*, from Latin *implicare* 'fold in, involve'.
impolite • adjective not having or showing good manners.
– DERIVATIVES **impolitely** adverb **impoliteness** noun.
impolitic • adjective failing to possess or display prudence.
imponderable • adjective difficult or impossible to assess. • noun an imponderable factor.
import • verb **1** bring (goods or services) into a country from abroad. **2** Computing transfer (data) into a file or document. **3** archaic indicate or signify. • noun **1** an imported article or service. **2** the action or process of importing. **3** the implied meaning of something. **4** importance.
– DERIVATIVES **importable** adjective **importation** noun **importer** noun.
– ORIGIN Latin *importare* 'bring in'.
important • adjective **1** of great significance or value. **2** having high rank or social status.
– DERIVATIVES **importance** noun **importantly** adverb.
importunate /importyoonət/ • adjective persistent or pressing.
– DERIVATIVES **importunately** adverb **importunity** noun (pl. **importunities**).
– ORIGIN Latin *importunus* 'inconvenient', from *Portunus*, the god who protected harbours.
importune /importyo͞on/ • verb **1** harass with persistent requests. **2** (usu. as noun **importuning**) approach to offer one's services as a prostitute.
– ORIGIN Latin *importunari*, from *importunus* (see IMPORTUNATE).
impose • verb **1** force to be accepted, undertaken, or complied with. **2** (often **impose on**) take unfair advantage of someone.
– ORIGIN French *imposer*, from Latin *imponere* 'inflict, deceive'.
imposing • adjective grand and impressive.
– DERIVATIVES **imposingly** adverb.
imposition • noun **1** the action of imposing or process being imposed. **2** something imposed, especially an unfair or resented demand or burden.
impossible • adjective **1** not able to occur, exist, or be done. **2** very difficult to deal with: *an impossible situation*.
– DERIVATIVES **impossibility** noun (pl. **impossibilities**) **impossibly** adverb.
impost /impōst/ • noun **1** a tax or similar compulsory payment. **2** Horse Racing the weight carried by a horse as a handicap.
– ORIGIN from Latin *impostus* 'imposed'.
impostor (also **imposter**) • noun a person who assumes a false identity in order to deceive or defraud.
– ORIGIN Latin, contraction of *impositor*, from *imponere* (see IMPOSE).
imposture • noun an instance of assuming a false identity.
impotent /impətənt/ • adjective **1** helpless or powerless. **2** (of a man) abnormally unable to achieve an erection or orgasm.
– DERIVATIVES **impotence** noun **impotency** noun **impotently** adverb.
impound • verb **1** seize and take legal custody of. **2** shut up (domestic animals) in a pound. **3** (of a dam) hold back or confine

i

Thesaurus

plored pity BEG FOR, plead for, appeal for, call for; ask for, request, sue for.
imply • verb **1** *are you implying he is mad?* INSINUATE, suggest, hint, intimate, say indirectly, indicate, give someone to understand, make out. **2** *the forecasted traffic increase implies more roads* INVOLVE, entail; mean, point to, signify, indicate, signal; necessitate, require.
impolite • adjective RUDE, bad-mannered, ill-mannered, discourteous, uncivil, disrespectful, inconsiderate, boorish, churlish, ill-bred, ungentlemanly, unladylike, ungracious; insolent, impudent, impertinent, cheeky; loutish, rough, crude, indelicate, indecorous; *informal* ignorant, lippy; *archaic* malapert, contumelious.
impolitic • adjective IMPRUDENT, unwise, injudicious, incautious, irresponsible; ill-judged, ill-advised, misguided, rash, reckless, foolhardy, foolish, short-sighted; undiplomatic, tactless.
– OPPOSITES prudent.
import • verb *the UK imports iron ore* BUY FROM ABROAD, bring in, buy in, ship in.
– OPPOSITES export.
• noun **1** *a tax on imports* IMPORTED COMMODITY, foreign commodity. **2** *the import of foreign books* IMPORTATION, importing, bringing in, bringing from abroad, shipping in. **3** *a matter of great import* IMPORTANCE, significance, consequence, momentousness, magnitude, substance, weight, note, gravity, seriousness; *formal* moment. **4** *the full import of her words* MEANING, sense, essence, gist, drift, purport, message, thrust, substance, implication.
– OPPOSITES export, insignificance.
importance • noun **1** *an event of immense importance* SIGNIFICANCE, momentousness, import, consequence, note, noteworthiness, substance; seriousness, gravity, weightiness, urgency. **2** *she had a fine sense of her own importance* POWER, influence, authority, sway, weight, dominance; prominence, eminence, pre-eminence, notability, worth.
– OPPOSITES insignificance.
important • adjective **1** *an important meeting* SIGNIFICANT, consequential, momentous, of great import, major; critical, crucial, vital, pivotal, decisive, urgent, historic; serious, grave, weighty, material; *formal* of great moment. **2** *the important thing is that you do well in your exams* MAIN, chief, principal, key, major, salient, prime, foremost, paramount, overriding, crucial, vital, critical, essential, significant; central, fundamental; *informal* number-one. **3** *the school was important to the community* OF VALUE, valuable, beneficial, necessary, essential, indispensable, vital; of concern, of interest, relevant, pertinent. **4** *he was an important man* POWERFUL, influential, of influence, well-connected, high-ranking; prominent, eminent, pre-eminent, notable, noteworthy, of note; distinguished, esteemed, respected, prestigious, celebrated, famous, great; *informal* major league.
– OPPOSITES trivial, insignificant.
importunate • adjective PERSISTENT, insistent, tenacious, persevering, dogged, unrelenting, tireless, indefatigable; aggressive, high-pressure; *informal* pushy; *formal* exigent, pertinacious.
importune • verb **1** *he importuned her for some spare change* BEG, beseech, entreat, implore, plead with, appeal to, call on; harass, pester, press, badger, bother, nag, harry; *informal* hassle. **2** *they arrested me for importuning* SOLICIT; *informal* proposition; *N. Amer. informal* hustle.
impose • verb **1** *he imposed his ideas on the art director* FOIST, force, inflict, press, urge; *informal* saddle someone with, land someone with. **2** *new taxes will be imposed* LEVY, charge, apply, enforce; set, establish, institute, introduce, bring into effect. **3** *how dare you impose on me like this!* TAKE ADVANTAGE OF, exploit, take liberties with, treat unfairly; bother, trouble, disturb, inconvenience, put out, put to trouble.
– PHRASES **impose oneself** FORCE ONESELF, foist oneself; control, take charge of; *informal* call the shots/tune, be in the driving seat, be in the saddle, run the show.
imposing • adjective IMPRESSIVE, striking, arresting, eye-catching, dramatic, spectacular, stunning, awesome, formidable, splendid, grand, majestic.
– OPPOSITES modest.
imposition • noun **1** *the imposition of an alien culture* IMPOSING, foisting, forcing, inflicting. **2** *the imposition of VAT* LEVYING, charging, application, applying, enforcement, enforcing; setting, establishment, introduction, institution. **3** *it would be no imposition* BURDEN, encumbrance, strain, bother, worry; *informal* hassle. **4** *the levying of special impositions* TAX, levy, duty, charge, tariff, toll, impost; *formal* mulct, exaction.
impossible • adjective **1** *gale force winds made fishing impossible* NOT POSSIBLE, out of the question, unfeasible, impractical, impracticable, non-viable, unworkable; unthinkable, unimaginable, inconceivable. **2** *an impossible dream* UNATTAINABLE, unachievable, unobtainable, hopeless, impractical, implausible, far-fetched, impracticable, unworkable. **3** *food shortages made life impossible* UNBEARABLE, intolerable, unendurable. **4** (*informal*) *an impossible woman* UNREASONABLE, objectionable, difficult, awkward; intolerable, unbearable, unendurable; exasperating, maddening, infuriating.
– OPPOSITES attainable, bearable.
impostor • noun IMPERSONATOR, masquerader, pretender, deceiver, hoaxer, trickster, fraudster; fake, fraud, sham; *informal* phoney.
imposture • noun MISREPRESENTATION, pretence, deceit, deception, trickery, artifice, subterfuge; hoax, trick, ruse, dodge; *informal* con (trick), scam, flimflam; *Brit. informal* wheeze.
impotent • adjective **1** *the legal sanctions are impotent* POWERLESS, ineffective, ineffectual, inadequate, weak, useless, worthless, futile; *poetic/literary* impuissant. **2** *forces which man is impotent to control* UNABLE, incapable, powerless. **3** *an impotent opposition party*

(water).
– DERIVATIVES **impoundment** noun.
impoverish ● verb **1** make poor. **2** exhaust the strength or natural fertility of.
– DERIVATIVES **impoverishment** noun.
– ORIGIN Old French *empoverir*, from *povre* 'poor'.
impracticable ● adjective impossible in practice to do or carry out.
– DERIVATIVES **impracticability** noun **impracticably** adverb.
impractical ● adjective **1** not adapted for use or action; not sensible. **2** chiefly N. Amer. impracticable.
– DERIVATIVES **impracticality** noun **impractically** adverb.
imprecation ● noun formal a spoken curse.
– ORIGIN Latin, from *imprecari* 'invoke (evil)'.
imprecise ● adjective lacking exactness.
– DERIVATIVES **imprecisely** adverb **imprecision** noun.
impregnable ● adjective **1** unable to be captured or broken into. **2** unable to be overcome.
– DERIVATIVES **impregnability** noun **impregnably** adverb.
– ORIGIN Old French *imprenable*, from *in-* 'not' + *prendre* 'take'.
impregnate /impregnayt/ ● verb **1** (usu. **be impregnated with**) soak or saturate with a substance. **2** fill with a feeling or quality. **3** make pregnant.
– DERIVATIVES **impregnation** noun.
– ORIGIN Latin *impregnare* 'make pregnant'.
impresario /imprisaarioō/ ● noun (pl. **impresarios**) a person who organizes and often finances theatrical or musical productions.
– ORIGIN Italian, from *impresa* 'undertaking'.
impress[1] ● verb **1** make (someone) feel admiration and respect. **2** make a mark or design on using a stamp or seal. **3** (**impress on**) emphasize (an idea) in the mind of. ● noun **1** an act of impressing a mark. **2** an impressed mark. **3** a person's characteristic mark or quality.
– ORIGIN Old French *empresser* 'press in'.
impress[2] ● verb historical force to serve in an army or navy.
– DERIVATIVES **impressment** noun.
– ORIGIN from IN-[2] + PRESS[2].
impression ● noun **1** an idea, feeling, or opinion. **2** an effect produced on someone. **3** an imitation of a person or thing, done to entertain. **4** a mark impressed on a surface. **5** the printing of a number of copies of a publication for issue at one time. **6** chiefly Brit. a particular printed version of a book, especially one reprinted with no or only minor alteration.
impressionable ● adjective easily influenced.
– DERIVATIVES **impressionability** noun.
Impressionism ● noun **1** a style or movement in painting concerned with depicting the visual impression of the moment, especially the shifting effects of light. **2** a literary style that seeks to capture a feeling or experience rather than to achieve accurate depiction. **3** Music a style of composition in which clarity of structure and theme is subordinate to harmonic effects.
– DERIVATIVES **Impressionist** noun & adjective.
– ORIGIN from French *impressionniste*, originally applied unfavourably with reference to Monet's painting *Impression: soleil levant* (1872).
impressionist ● noun an entertainer who impersonates famous people.
impressionistic ● adjective **1** based on subjective impressions presented unsystematically. **2** (**Impressionistic**) in the style of Impressionism.
– DERIVATIVES **impressionistically** adverb.
impressive ● adjective evoking admiration through size, quality, or skill.
– DERIVATIVES **impressively** adverb **impressiveness** noun.
imprimatur /imprimaytər/ ● noun **1** an official licence issued

Thesaurus

WEAK, powerless, ineffective, feeble.
– OPPOSITES powerful, effective.
impound ● verb **1** *officials began impounding documents* CONFISCATE, appropriate, take possession of, seize, commandeer, expropriate, requisition, sequester, sequestrate; Law distrain. **2** *the cattle were impounded* PEN IN, shut up/in, fence in, enclose, confine; N. Amer. corral. **3** *unfortunates impounded in prison* LOCK UP, incarcerate, imprison, confine, intern, immure, hold captive, hold prisoner.
impoverish ● verb **1** *the widow had been impoverished* MAKE POOR, make penniless, reduce to penury, bankrupt, ruin, make insolvent, pauperize. **2** *the trees were impoverishing the soil* WEAKEN, sap, exhaust, deplete.
impoverished ● adjective **1** *an impoverished peasant farmer* POOR, poverty-stricken, penniless, destitute, indigent, impecunious, needy, pauperized, down and out, on the breadline; bankrupt, ruined, insolvent; informal (flat) broke, stony broke, on one's uppers, hard up, without a bean, on skid row; Brit. informal skint; N. Amer. informal stone broke; formal penurious. **2** *the soil is impoverished* WEAKENED, exhausted, drained, sapped, depleted, spent; barren, unproductive, unfertile.
– OPPOSITES rich.
impracticable ● adjective UNWORKABLE, non-viable, unfeasible, unachievable, unattainable, unrealizable; impractical.
– OPPOSITES workable, feasible.
impractical ● adjective **1** *an impractical suggestion* UNREALISTIC, unworkable, unfeasible, non-viable, impracticable; ill-thought-out, impossible, absurd, wild; informal cock-eyed, crackpot, crazy. **2** *impractical white ankle boots* UNSUITABLE, not sensible, inappropriate, unserviceable. **3** *an impractical scholar* IDEALISTIC, unrealistic, romantic, dreamy, fanciful, quixotic; informal airy-fairy.
– OPPOSITES practical, sensible.
imprecation ● noun (formal) **1** *the most dreadful imprecations* CURSE, malediction; N. Amer. hex; poetic/literary anathema; archaic execration. **2** *a stream of imprecations* SWEAR WORD, curse, expletive, oath, profanity, four-letter word, obscenity; (**imprecations**) swearing, cursing, foul language, strong language; N. Amer. informal cuss word; archaic execration.
– OPPOSITES blessing.
imprecise ● adjective **1** *a rather imprecise definition* VAGUE, loose, indefinite, inexplicit, indistinct, non-specific, unspecific, broad, general, sweeping; hazy, fuzzy, woolly, nebulous, ambiguous, equivocal, uncertain. **2** *an imprecise estimate* INEXACT, approximate, estimated, rough; N. Amer. informal ballpark.
– OPPOSITES exact.
impregnable ● adjective **1** *an impregnable castle* INVULNERABLE, impenetrable, unassailable, inviolable, secure, strong, well fortified, well defended; invincible, unconquerable, unbeatable, indestructible. **2** *an impregnable parliamentary majority* UNASSAILABLE, unbeatable, undefeatable, unshakeable, invincible, unconquerable, invulnerable.
– OPPOSITES vulnerable.
impregnate ● verb **1** *a pad impregnated with natural oils* INFUSE, soak, steep, saturate, drench. **2** *the woman he had impregnated* MAKE PREGNANT, inseminate, fertilize; informal put in the family way; Brit. informal get up the duff/spout, put in the club; N. Amer. informal knock up; informal, dated get into trouble; archaic get with child.
impresario ● noun ORGANIZER, (stage) manager, producer; promoter, publicist, showman; director, conductor, maestro.
impress ● verb **1** *Hazel had impressed him mightily* MAKE AN IMPRESSION ON, have an impact on, influence, affect, move, stir, rouse, excite, inspire; dazzle, awe, overawe, take someone's breath away, amaze, astonish; informal grab, stick in someone's mind. **2** *goldsmiths impressed his likeness on medallions* IMPRINT, print, stamp, mark, emboss, punch. **3** *you must impress upon her the need to save* EMPHASIZE TO, stress to, bring home to, instil in, inculcate into, drum into, knock into, din into.
– OPPOSITES disappoint.
impression ● noun **1** *he got the impression that she was hiding something* FEELING, feeling in one's bones, sense, fancy, (sneaking) suspicion, inkling, intuition, hunch; notion, idea, funny feeling; informal gut feeling. **2** *a favourable impression* OPINION, view, image, picture, perception, judgement, verdict, estimation. **3** *school made a profound impression on me* IMPACT, effect, influence. **4** *the cap had left a circular impression* INDENTATION, dent, mark, outline, imprint. **5** *he did a good impression of their science teacher* IMPERSONATION, imitation; parody, caricature, burlesque, travesty, lampoon; informal take-off, send-up, spoof; formal personation. **6** *an artist's impression of the gardens* REPRESENTATION, portrayal, depiction, rendition, interpretation, picture, drawing. **7** *a revised impression of the 1981 edition* PRINT RUN, imprint, reprint, issue, edition.
impressionable ● adjective EASILY INFLUENCED, suggestible, susceptible, persuadable, pliable, malleable, pliant, ingenuous, trusting, naive, gullible.
impressive ● adjective **1** *an impressive building* MAGNIFICENT, majestic, imposing, splendid, spectacular, grand, awe-inspiring, stunning, breathtaking; stately, palatial. **2** *they played some impressive football* ADMIRABLE, accomplished, expert, skilled, skilful,

by the Roman Catholic Church to print an ecclesiastical or religious book. **2** authority or approval.
– ORIGIN Latin, 'let it be printed'.

imprint ● verb **1** (usu. **be imprinted**) make (a mark) on an object by pressure. **2** make an impression or mark on. **3** (**imprint on**) (of a young animal) come to recognize (another animal, person, or thing) as a parent. ● noun **1** an impressed mark. **2** a printer's or publisher's name and other details in a publication. **3** a brand name under which books are published, typically the name of a former publishing house now part of a larger group.
– ORIGIN Latin *imprimere* 'impress, imprint'.

imprison ● verb put or keep in prison.
– DERIVATIVES **imprisonment** noun.

improbable ● adjective not likely to be true or to happen.
– DERIVATIVES **improbability** noun (pl. **improbabilities**) **improbably** adverb.

impromptu /impromptyoo/ ● adjective & adverb unplanned or unrehearsed. ● noun (pl. **impromptus**) a short piece of instrumental music, especially a solo, reminiscent of an improvisation.
– ORIGIN from Latin *in promptu* 'in readiness'.

improper ● adjective **1** not conforming with accepted standards of behaviour. **2** unseemly or indecent.
– DERIVATIVES **improperly** adverb.

improper fraction ● noun a fraction in which the numerator is greater than the denominator, such as 5/4.

impropriety /imprəpriəti/ ● noun (pl. **improprieties**) improper behaviour or character.

improve ● verb **1** make or become better. **2** (**improve on/upon**) achieve or produce something better than. **3** (**improving**) giving moral or intellectual benefit.
– DERIVATIVES **improvability** noun **improvable** adjective **improver** noun.
– ORIGIN Old French *emprower*, from *prou* 'profit'.

improvement ● noun **1** an instance of improving or being improved. **2** the action of improving or being improved. **3** a thing that makes something better or is better than something else.

improvident ● adjective lacking care for the future.
– DERIVATIVES **improvidence** noun **improvidently** adverb.

improvise ● verb **1** create and perform (music, drama, or verse) spontaneously or without preparation. **2** make from whatever is available.
– DERIVATIVES **improvisation** noun **improvisational** adjective **improvisatory** adjective **improviser** noun.
– ORIGIN from Latin *improvisus* 'unforeseen'.

imprudent ● adjective not showing care for the consequences of an action; rash.
– DERIVATIVES **imprudence** noun **imprudently** adverb.

impudent /impyoodənt/ ● adjective not showing due respect for another person; impertinent.
– DERIVATIVES **impudence** noun **impudently** adverb.
– ORIGIN originally in the sense 'immodest': from Latin *impudens* 'shameless'.

impugn /impyoon/ ● verb dispute the truth, validity, or honesty of.
– ORIGIN Latin *impugnare* 'assail'.

i

Thesaurus

masterly, consummate; excellent, outstanding, first-class, first-rate, fine; *informal* great, mean, nifty, cracking, ace, wizard; *N. Amer. informal* crackerjack.
– OPPOSITES ordinary, mediocre.

imprint ● verb **1** *patterns can be imprinted in the clay* STAMP, print, impress, mark, emboss. **2** *the image was imprinted on his mind* FIX, establish, stick, lodge, implant, embed.
● noun **1** *her feet left imprints on the floor* IMPRESSION, print, mark, indentation. **2** *colonialism has left its imprint* IMPACT, lasting effect, influence, impression.

imprison ● verb INCARCERATE, send to prison, jail, lock up, put away, intern, detain, hold prisoner, hold captive; *informal* send down, put behind bars, put inside; *Brit. informal* bang up.
– OPPOSITES free, release.

imprisoned ● adjective INCARCERATED, in prison, in jail, jailed, locked up, interned, detained, held prisoner, held captive; *informal* sent down, behind bars, doing time, inside; *Brit. informal* doing porridge, doing bird, banged up.

imprisonment ● noun INCARCERATION, internment, confinement, detention, captivity; *informal* time; *Brit. informal* porridge, bird; *archaic* durance.

improbability ● noun UNLIKELIHOOD, implausibility; doubtfulness, uncertainty, dubiousness.

improbable ● adjective **1** *it seemed improbable that the hot weather should continue* UNLIKELY, doubtful, dubious, debatable, questionable, uncertain; unthinkable, inconceivable, unimaginable, incredible. **2** *an improbable exaggeration* UNCONVINCING, unbelievable, incredible, ridiculous, absurd, preposterous.
– OPPOSITES certain, believable.

impromptu ● adjective *an impromptu lecture* UNREHEARSED, unprepared, unscripted, extempore, extemporized, extemporaneous, improvised, spontaneous, unplanned; *informal* off-the-cuff.
– OPPOSITES prepared, rehearsed.
● adverb *they played the song impromptu* EXTEMPORE, spontaneously, extemporaneously, without preparation, without rehearsal; *informal* off the cuff, off the top of one's head.

improper ● adjective **1** *it is improper for policemen to accept gifts* INAPPROPRIATE, unacceptable, unsuitable, unprofessional, irregular; unethical, corrupt, immoral, dishonest, dishonourable; *informal* not cricket. **2** *it was improper for young ladies to drive a young man home* UNSEEMLY, indecorous, unfitting, unladylike, ungentlemanly, indelicate, impolite; indecent, immodest, immoral. **3** *an extremely improper poem* INDECENT, risqué, off colour, suggestive, naughty, ribald, earthy, smutty, dirty, filthy, vulgar, crude, rude, obscene, lewd; *informal* blue, raunchy, steamy; *Brit. informal* fruity, saucy.
– OPPOSITES acceptable, decent.

impropriety ● noun **1** *a suggestion of impropriety* WRONGDOING, misconduct, dishonesty, corruption, unscrupulousness, unprofessionalism, irregularity; unseemliness, indecorousness, indelicacy, indecency, immorality. **2** *fiscal improprieties* TRANSGRESSION, misdemeanour, offence, misdeed, crime; indiscretion, mistake, peccadillo; *archaic* trespass.

improve ● verb **1** *ways to improve the service* MAKE BETTER, ameliorate, upgrade, refine, enhance, boost, build on, raise; *informal* tweak; *formal* meliorate. **2** *communications improved during the 18th century* GET BETTER, advance, progress, develop; make headway, make progress, pick up, look up. **3** *the dose is not repeated if patient improves* RECOVER, get better, recuperate, gain strength, rally, revive, get back on one's feet, get over something; be on the road to recovery, be on the mend; *informal* turn the corner, take a turn for the better. **4** *resources are needed to improve the offer* INCREASE, make larger, raise, augment, supplement, top up; *informal* up, hike up, bump up.
– OPPOSITES worsen, deteriorate.
– PHRASES **improve on** SURPASS, better, do better than, outdo, exceed, beat, top, cap.

improvement ● noun ADVANCE, development, upgrade, refinement, enhancement, advancement, upgrading, amelioration; boost, augmentation, raising; rally, recovery, upswing.

improvident ● adjective SPENDTHRIFT, thriftless, wasteful, prodigal, profligate, extravagant, free-spending, lavish, immoderate, excessive; imprudent, irresponsible, careless, reckless.
– OPPOSITES thrifty.

improvise ● verb **1** *she was improvising in front of the cameras* EXTEMPORIZE, ad-lib, speak impromptu; *informal* speak off the cuff, speak off the top of one's head, busk it, wing it. **2** *she improvised a sandpit* CONTRIVE, devise, throw together, cobble together, rig up; *Brit. informal* knock up; *informal* whip up, rustle up.

improvised ● adjective **1** *an improvised speech* IMPROMPTU, unrehearsed, unprepared, unscripted, extempore, extemporized, spontaneous, unplanned; *informal* off-the-cuff. **2** *an improvised shelter* MAKESHIFT, thrown together, cobbled together, rough and ready, make-do.
– OPPOSITES prepared, rehearsed.

imprudent ● adjective UNWISE, injudicious, incautious, misguided, ill-advised; thoughtless, unthinking, improvident, irresponsible, short-sighted, foolish.
– OPPOSITES sensible.

impudence ● noun IMPERTINENCE, insolence, effrontery, cheek, cockiness, brazenness; presumption, presumptuousness, disrespect, flippancy, bumptiousness; rudeness, impoliteness, ill manners, discourteousness, gall; *informal* brass neck, chutzpah, nerve; *Brit. informal* sauce; *N. Amer. informal* sassiness.

impudent ● adjective IMPERTINENT, insolent, cheeky, cocky, brazen; presumptuous, forward, disrespectful, insubordinate, flippant, bumptious, brash; rude, impolite, ill-mannered, discourteous, ill-bred; *informal* brass-necked, saucy, lippy; *N. Amer. informal* sassy; *archaic* malapert, contumelious.

impulse ● noun **1** a sudden strong and unreflective urge to act. **2** a driving force; an impetus. **3** a pulse of electrical energy; a brief current. **4** Physics a force acting briefly on a body and producing a change of momentum.
– ORIGIN Latin *impulsus* 'a push', from *impellere* 'impel'.
impulsion ● noun **1** a strong urge to do something. **2** the force or motive behind an action or process.
impulsive ● adjective **1** acting or done without forethought. **2** Physics acting as an impulse.
– DERIVATIVES **impulsively** adverb **impulsiveness** noun **impulsivity** noun.
impunity /impyōōniti/ ● noun (usu. in phrase **with impunity**) exemption from punishment or from the harmful consequences of an action.
– ORIGIN Latin *impunitas*, from *impunis* 'unpunished'.
impure ● adjective **1** mixed with foreign matter; adulterated or tainted. **2** morally wrong, especially in sexual matters. **3** contaminated according to ritual prescriptions.
impurity ● noun (pl. **impurities**) **1** the quality or condition of being impure. **2** a thing which impairs the purity of something.
impute /impyōōt/ ● verb (usu. **impute to**) attribute (something, especially something bad) to someone.
– DERIVATIVES **imputable** adjective **imputation** noun.
– ORIGIN Latin *imputare* 'enter in the account'.
IN ● abbreviation Indiana.
In ● symbol the chemical element indium.
in ● preposition **1** expressing the situation of being enclosed or surrounded. **2** expressing motion that results in being within or surrounded by something. **3** expressing a period of time during which an event takes place or a situation remains the case. **4** expressing the length of time before a future event is expected to take place. **5** expressing a state, condition, or quality. **6** expressing inclusion or involvement. **7** indicating a person's occupation or profession. **8** indicating the language or medium used. **9** expressing a value as a proportion of (a whole). ● adverb **1** expressing movement that results in being enclosed or surrounded. **2** expressing the situation of being enclosed or surrounded. **3** present at one's home or office. **4** expressing arrival at a destination. **5** (of the tide) rising or at its highest level. ● adjective informal fashionable.
– PHRASES **be in for** have good reason to expect (something, typically something unpleasant). **in on** privy to (a secret). **in that** for the reason that. **in with** informal enjoying friendly relations with. **the ins and outs** informal all the details.
– ORIGIN Old English.
in. ● abbreviation inch(es).
in-[1] (also **il-** before *l*; **im-** before *b, m, p*; **ir-** before *r*) ● prefix **1** (added to adjectives) not: *infertile.* **2** (added to nouns) without; a lack of: *inappreciation.*
– ORIGIN Latin.
in-[2] (also **il-** before *l*; **im-** before *b, m, p*; **ir-** before *r*) ● prefix in; into; towards; within: *influx.*
– ORIGIN representing IN or the Latin preposition *in.*
inability ● noun the state of being unable to do something.
in absentia /in absentiə/ ● adverb while not present.
– ORIGIN Latin, 'in absence'.
inaccessible ● adjective **1** unable to be reached or used. **2** difficult to understand or appreciate. **3** not open to advances or influence; unapproachable.
– DERIVATIVES **inaccessibility** noun **inaccessibly** adverb.
inaccurate ● adjective not accurate.
– DERIVATIVES **inaccuracy** noun **inaccurately** adverb.
inaction ● noun lack of action where some is expected or appropriate.
inactivate ● verb make inactive or inoperative.
– DERIVATIVES **inactivation** noun **inactivator** noun.

Thesaurus

– OPPOSITES polite.
impugn ● verb CALL INTO QUESTION, challenge, question, dispute, query, take issue with.
impulse ● noun **1** *she had an impulse to run and hide* URGE, instinct, drive, compulsion, itch; whim, desire, fancy, notion. **2** *a man of impulse* SPONTANEITY, impetuosity, recklessness, rashness. **3** *passions provide the main impulse of poetry* INSPIRATION, stimulation, stimulus, incitement, motivation, encouragement, spur, catalyst. **4** *impulses from the spinal cord to the muscles* PULSE, current, wave, signal.
– PHRASES **on (an) impulse** IMPULSIVELY, spontaneously, on the spur of the moment, without forethought, without premeditation.
impulsive ● adjective **1** *he had an impulsive nature* IMPETUOUS, spontaneous, hasty, passionate, emotional, uninhibited; rash, reckless, foolhardy, madcap, devil-may-care, daredevil. **2** *an impulsive decision* IMPROMPTU, snap, spontaneous, unpremeditated, spur-of-the-moment, extemporaneous; impetuous, precipitate, hasty, rash; sudden, ill-considered, ill-thought-out.
– OPPOSITES cautious, premeditated.
impunity ● noun *the impunity enjoyed by military officers* IMMUNITY, indemnity, exemption (from punishment), non-liability, licence; privilege, special treatment.
– OPPOSITES liability.
– PHRASES **with impunity** WITHOUT PUNISHMENT, scot-free, unpunished.
impure ● adjective **1** *impure gold* ADULTERATED, mixed, combined, blended, alloyed; *technical* admixed. **2** *the water was impure* CONTAMINATED, polluted, tainted, unwholesome, poisoned; dirty, filthy, foul; unhygienic, unsanitary, insanitary; *poetic/literary* befouled. **3** *impure thoughts* IMMORAL, sinful, wrongful, wicked; unchaste, lustful, lecherous, lewd, lascivious, prurient, obscene, indecent, ribald, risqué, improper, crude, coarse; *formal* concupiscent.
– OPPOSITES clean, chaste.
impurity ● noun **1** *the impurity of the cast iron* ADULTERATION, debasement, degradation. **2** *the impurity of the air* CONTAMINATION, pollution; dirtiness, filthiness, uncleanliness, foulness, unwholesomeness. **3** *the impurities in beer* CONTAMINANT, pollutant, foreign body; dross, dirt, filth. **4** *sin and impurity* IMMORALITY, sin, sinfulness, wickedness; unchastity, lustfulness, lechery, lecherousness, lewdness, lasciviousness, prurience, obscenity, dirtiness, indecency, ribaldry, impropriety, crudeness, vulgarity, coarseness; *formal* concupiscence.
impute ● verb ATTRIBUTE, ascribe, assign, credit; connect with, associate with.
in ● preposition **1** *she was hiding in a wardrobe* INSIDE, within, in the middle of; surrounded by, enclosed by. **2** *he was covered in mud* WITH, by. **3** *he put a fruit gum in his mouth* INTO, inside. **4** *they met in 1921* DURING, in the course of, over. **5** *I'll see you in half an hour* AFTER, at the end of, following; within, in less than, in under. **6** *a tax of ten pence in the pound* TO, per, every, each.
– OPPOSITES outside.
● adverb **1** *his mum walked in* INSIDE, indoors, into the room, into the house/building. **2** *the tide's in* HIGH, at its highest level, rising.
– OPPOSITES out.
● adjective **1** *there was no one in* PRESENT, (at) home; inside, indoors, in the house/room. **2** *(informal) beards are in* FASHIONABLE, in fashion, in vogue, popular, (bang) up to date, modern, modish, chic, à la mode, de rigueur; *informal* trendy, all the rage, with it, cool, the in thing, hip. **3** *(informal) I was in with all the right people* IN FAVOUR, popular, friendly, friends; liked, admired, accepted; *informal* in someone's good books.
– OPPOSITES out, unfashionable, unpopular.
– PHRASES **in for** DUE FOR, in line for; expecting, about to receive. **in for it** IN TROUBLE, about to be punished; *informal* for the high jump, in hot/deep water, in (deep) shtook; *Brit. informal* for it. **in on** PRIVY TO, aware of, acquainted with, informed about/of, apprised of; *informal* wise to, in the know about, hip to; *archaic* ware of. **ins and outs** *(informal)* DETAILS, particulars, facts, features, characteristics, nuts and bolts; *informal* nitty gritty.
inability ● noun LACK OF ABILITY, incapability, incapacity, powerlessness, impotence, helplessness; incompetence, ineptitude, unfitness.
inaccessible ● adjective **1** *an inaccessible woodland site* UNREACHABLE, out of reach; cut-off, isolated, remote, in the back of beyond, out of the way, lonely, godforsaken. **2** *the book was elitist and inaccessible* ESOTERIC, obscure, abstruse, recondite, arcane; elitist, exclusive, pretentious.
inaccuracy ● noun **1** *the inaccuracy of recent opinion polls* INCORRECTNESS, inexactness, imprecision, erroneousness, mistakenness, fallaciousness, faultiness. **2** *the article contained a number of inaccuracies* ERROR, mistake, fallacy, slip, oversight, fault, blunder, gaffe; erratum; *Brit.* literal; *informal* howler, boo-boo, typo; *Brit. informal* boob; *N. Amer. informal* blooper, goof.
– OPPOSITES correctness.
inaccurate ● adjective INEXACT, imprecise, incorrect, wrong, erroneous, faulty, imperfect, flawed, defective, unsound, unreliable; fallacious, false, mistaken, untrue; *informal* off beam; *Brit. informal* adrift.
inaction ● noun INACTIVITY, non-intervention; neglect, negligence,

inactive ● adjective not active, working, or energetic.
– DERIVATIVES **inactivity** noun.
inadequate ● adjective **1** insufficient for a purpose. **2** unable to deal with a situation or with life.
– DERIVATIVES **inadequacy** noun (pl. **inadequacies**) **inadequately** adverb.
inadmissible ● adjective **1** (especially of evidence in court) not accepted as valid. **2** not to be allowed.
– DERIVATIVES **inadmissibility** noun.
inadvertent ● adjective not resulting from or achieved through deliberate planning.
– DERIVATIVES **inadvertence** noun **inadvertently** adverb.
– ORIGIN from IN-[1] + Latin *advertere* 'turn the mind to'.
inadvisable ● adjective likely to have unfortunate consequences; unwise.
– DERIVATIVES **inadvisability** noun.
inalienable ● adjective unable to be taken away from or given away by the possessor.
– DERIVATIVES **inalienability** noun **inalienably** adverb.
inamorato /inammərаatō/ ● noun (pl. **inamoratos**; fem. **inamorata**, pl. **inamoratas**) a person's lover.
– ORIGIN Italian, 'enamoured'.
inane ● adjective lacking sense or meaning; silly.
– DERIVATIVES **inanely** adverb **inanity** noun (pl. **inanities**).
– ORIGIN Latin *inanis* 'empty, vain'.
inanimate ● adjective **1** not alive, especially not in the manner of animals and humans. **2** showing no sign of life; lifeless.
inanition /innənish'n/ ● noun exhaustion caused by lack of nourishment.
– ORIGIN Latin, from *inanire* 'make empty'.
inapplicable ● adjective not relevant or appropriate.
– DERIVATIVES **inapplicability** noun.
inapposite /inappəzit/ ● adjective out of place; inappropriate.
inappropriate ● adjective not suitable or appropriate.
– DERIVATIVES **inappropriately** adverb **inappropriateness** noun.
inapt ● adjective not suitable or appropriate.
– DERIVATIVES **inaptly** adverb.
inarguable ● adjective another term for UNARGUABLE.
– DERIVATIVES **inarguably** adverb.
inarticulate /innaartikyoolət/ ● adjective **1** unable to speak distinctly or express oneself clearly. **2** unspoken or not expressed in words. **3** without joints or articulations.
– DERIVATIVES **inarticulacy** noun **inarticulately** adverb **inarticulateness** noun.
inasmuch ● adverb (**inasmuch as**) **1** to the extent that. **2** considering that; since.
inattentive ● adjective not paying attention.
– DERIVATIVES **inattention** noun **inattentively** adverb **inattentiveness** noun.
inaudible ● adjective unable to be heard.
– DERIVATIVES **inaudibility** noun **inaudibly** adverb.
inaugurate /inawgyoorayt/ ● verb **1** begin or introduce (a system, project, etc.). **2** admit formally to office. **3** officially mark the beginning or first public use of (a building, service, etc).
– DERIVATIVES **inaugural** adjective **inauguration** noun **inaugurator** noun.
– ORIGIN from Latin *inauguratus* 'consecrated after interpreting omens', from *augurare* 'to augur'.
inauspicious ● adjective not conducive to success; unpromising.
– DERIVATIVES **inauspiciously** adverb **inauspiciousness** noun.

Thesaurus

apathy, inertia, indolence.
inactivate ● verb DISABLE, deactivate, make inoperative, immobilize.
inactive ● adjective **1** *over the next few days I was horribly inactive* IDLE, indolent, lazy, lifeless, slothful, lethargic, inert, sluggish, unenergetic, listless, torpid. **2** *the device remains inactive while the computer is started up* INOPERATIVE, non-functioning, idle; not working, out of service, unused, not in use.
inactivity ● noun **1** *years of inactivity* IDLENESS, indolence, laziness, lifelessness, slothfulness, lethargy, inertia, sluggishness, listlessness. **2** *government inactivity* INACTION, non-intervention; neglect, negligence, apathy.
– OPPOSITES action.
inadequacy ● noun **1** *the inadequacy of available resources* INSUFFICIENCY, deficiency, scarcity, scarceness, sparseness, dearth, paucity, shortage, want, lack, undersupply; paltriness, meagreness; *formal* exiguity. **2** *her feelings of personal inadequacy* INCOMPETENCE, incapability, unfitness, ineffectiveness, inefficiency, inefficacy, inexpertness, ineptness, uselessness, impotence, powerlessness. **3** *the inadequacies of the present system* SHORTCOMING, defect, fault, failing, weakness, weak point, limitation, flaw, imperfection.
– OPPOSITES abundance, competence.
inadequate ● adjective **1** *inadequate water supplies* INSUFFICIENT, deficient, poor, scant, scanty, scarce, sparse, in short supply; paltry, meagre, niggardly, limited; *informal* measly, pathetic; *formal* exiguous. **2** *inadequate staff* INCOMPETENT, incapable, unsatisfactory, not up to scratch, unfit, ineffective, ineffectual, inefficient, unskilful, inexpert, inept, amateurish, substandard, poor, useless, inferior; *informal* not up to snuff; *Brit. informal* duff, not much cop, no great shakes.
– OPPOSITES sufficient, competent.
inadmissible ● adjective UNALLOWABLE, invalid, unacceptable, impermissible, disallowed, forbidden, prohibited, precluded.
inadvertent ● adjective UNINTENTIONAL, unintended, accidental, unpremeditated, unplanned, innocent, uncalculated, unconscious, unthinking, unwitting, involuntary.
– OPPOSITES deliberate.
inadvertently ● adverb ACCIDENTALLY, by accident, unintentionally, unwittingly.
inadvisable ● adjective UNWISE, ill-advised, imprudent, ill-judged, ill-considered, injudicious, impolitic, foolish, misguided.
– OPPOSITES shrewd.
inalienable ● adjective INVIOLABLE, absolute, sacrosanct; untransferable, non-transferable, non-negotiable; *Law* indefeasible.
inane ● adjective SILLY, foolish, stupid, fatuous, idiotic, ridiculous, ludicrous, asinine, frivolous, vapid; childish, puerile; *informal* dumb, gormless, moronic; *Brit. informal* daft.
– OPPOSITES sensible.
inanimate ● adjective LIFELESS, insentient, without life; dead, defunct.
– OPPOSITES living.
inapplicable ● adjective IRRELEVANT, immaterial, not germane, not pertinent, unrelated, unconnected, extraneous, beside the point; *formal* impertinent.
– OPPOSITES relevant.
inapposite ● adjective INAPPROPRIATE, unsuitable, inapt, out of place, infelicitous, misplaced, ill-judged, ill-advised.
– OPPOSITES appropriate.
inappreciable ● adjective IMPERCEPTIBLE, minute, tiny, slight, small; insignificant, inconsequential, unimportant, negligible, trivial, minor; *informal* piddling, piffling; *formal* exiguous.
– OPPOSITES considerable.
inappropriate ● adjective UNSUITABLE, unfitting, unseemly, unbecoming, unbefitting, improper; incongruous, out of place/keeping, inapposite, inapt; *informal* out of order; *formal* malapropos.
– OPPOSITES suitable.
inapt ● adjective. See INAPPROPRIATE.
inarticulate ● adjective **1** *an inarticulate young man* TONGUE-TIED, lost for words, unable to express oneself; *archaic* mumchance. **2** *an inarticulate reply* UNINTELLIGIBLE, incomprehensible, incoherent, unclear, indistinct, mumbled, muffled. **3** *inarticulate rage* UNSPOKEN, silent, unexpressed, wordless, unvoiced.
– OPPOSITES silver-tongued, fluent.
inattention ● noun **1** *a moment of inattention* DISTRACTION, inattentiveness, preoccupation, absent-mindedness, daydreaming, abstraction. **2** *his inattention to duty* NEGLIGENCE, neglect, disregard; forgetfulness, carelessness, thoughtlessness, heedlessness.
– OPPOSITES concentration.
inattentive ● adjective **1** *an inattentive pupil* DISTRACTED, lacking concentration, preoccupied, absent-minded, daydreaming, dreamy, abstracted, distrait; *informal* miles away. **2** *inattentive service* NEGLIGENT, neglectful, remiss, slack, sloppy, slapdash, lax; forgetful, careless, thoughtless, heedless.
– OPPOSITES alert.
inaudible ● adjective UNHEARD, out of earshot; indistinct, faint, muted, soft, low, muffled, whispered, muttered, murmured, mumbled.
inaugural ● adjective FIRST, opening, initial, introductory, initiatory.
– OPPOSITES final.
inaugurate ● verb **1** *he inaugurated a new policy* INITIATE, begin, start, institute, launch, start off, get going, get under way, establish, lay the foundations of; bring in, usher in; *informal* kick off. **2** *the new President will be inaugurated in January* ADMIT TO OF-

inauthentic ● noun not authentic, genuine, or sincere.
– DERIVATIVES **inauthenticity** noun.
inboard ● adverb & adjective within or towards the centre of a ship, aircraft, or vehicle.
inborn ● adjective existing from birth.
inbound ● adjective & adverb travelling towards a place, especially when returning to the original point of departure.
inbred ● adjective **1** produced by inbreeding. **2** existing from birth; congenital.
inbreed ● verb (past and past part. **inbred**) (often as noun **inbreeding**) breed from closely related people or animals, especially over many generations.
inbuilt ● adjective existing as an original or essential part.
Inc. ● abbreviation N. Amer. Incorporated.
Inca ● noun **1** a member of a South American Indian people living in the central Andes before the Spanish conquest in the early 1530s. **2** the supreme ruler of this people.
– DERIVATIVES **Incan** adjective.
– ORIGIN Quechua, 'lord, royal person'.
incalculable ● adjective **1** too great to be calculated or estimated. **2** not able to be calculated, estimated, or predicted.
– DERIVATIVES **incalculability** noun **incalculably** adverb.
in camera ● adverb see CAMERA.
incandescent ● adjective **1** glowing as a result of being heated. **2** (of an electric light) containing a filament which glows white-hot when heated by a current passed through it. **3** informal extremely angry.
– DERIVATIVES **incandescence** noun **incandescently** adverb.
– ORIGIN from Latin *incandescere* 'glow'.
incant /inkant/ ● verb chant or intone.
incantation ● noun words said as a magic spell or charm.
– DERIVATIVES **incantatory** adjective.
– ORIGIN Latin, from *incantare* 'chant, bewitch'.
incapable ● adjective **1** (**incapable of**) lacking the ability or required quality to do. **2** unable to behave rationally.
– DERIVATIVES **incapability** noun.
incapacitate /inkəpassitayt/ ● verb prevent from functioning in a normal way.
– DERIVATIVES **incapacitant** noun **incapacitation** noun.
incapacity ● noun (pl. **incapacities**) **1** inability to do something or to manage one's affairs. **2** legal disqualification.
incarcerate /inkaarsərayt/ ● verb imprison or confine.
– DERIVATIVES **incarceration** noun.
– ORIGIN Latin *incarcerare*, from *carcer* 'prison'.
incarnate ● adjective /inkaarnət/ (often after a noun) **1** (of a deity or spirit) embodied in flesh; in human form. **2** represented in the ultimate or most typical form: *capitalism incarnate.* ● verb /inkaarnayt/ **1** embody or represent (a deity or spirit) in human form. **2** be the living embodiment of (a quality).
– ORIGIN from Latin *incarnare* 'make flesh', from *caro* 'flesh'.
incarnation ● noun **1** a living embodiment of a deity, spirit, or abstract quality. **2** (**the Incarnation**) (in Christian theology) the embodiment of God the Son in human flesh as Jesus Christ. **3** (with reference to reincarnation) each of a series of earthly lifetimes or forms.
incase ● verb variant spelling of ENCASE.
incautious ● adjective heedless of potential problems or risks.
– DERIVATIVES **incaution** noun **incautiously** adverb.
incendiary /insendiəri/ ● adjective **1** (of a bomb or other device) designed to cause fires. **2** tending to stir up conflict or controversy. ● noun (pl. **incendiaries**) an incendiary device.
– DERIVATIVES **incendiarism** noun.
– ORIGIN Latin *incendiarius*, from *incendium* 'conflagration'.
incense[1] /insenss/ ● noun a gum, spice, or other substance that is burned for the sweet smell it produces. ● verb perfume with incense or a similar fragrance.
– ORIGIN Latin *incensum* 'something burnt, incense'.
incense[2] /insenss/ ● verb make very angry.
– ORIGIN Latin *incendere* 'set fire to'.
incentive ● noun a thing that motivates or encourages someone

i

Thesaurus

FICE, install, instate, swear in; invest, ordain, crown. **3** *the museum was inaugurated in September* OPEN, declare open, unveil; dedicate, consecrate; *N. Amer.* hansel.
inauspicious ● adjective UNPROMISING, unpropitious, unfavourable, unfortunate, infelicitous, ominous; discouraging, disheartening, bleak.
– OPPOSITES promising.
inborn ● adjective INNATE, congenital, connate, connatural; inherent, natural, inbred, inherited, hereditary, in one's genes.
inbred ● adjective. See INBORN.
inbuilt ● adjective **1** *an inbuilt CD-ROM drive* BUILT-IN, integral, incorporated. **2** *our inbuilt survival instinct* INHERENT, intrinsic, innate, congenital, natural, connatural, connate.
incalculable ● adjective INESTIMABLE, indeterminable, untold, immeasurable, incomputable; infinite, endless, limitless, measureless, boundless; enormous, immense, huge, vast, innumerable.
incandescent ● adjective **1** *incandescent fragments of lava* WHITE-HOT, red-hot, burning, fiery, blazing, ablaze, aflame; glowing, aglow, radiant, bright, brilliant, luminous; *poetic/literary* fervid, rutilant, lucent. **2** *the minister was incandescent* FURIOUS, enraged, raging, very angry, incensed, seething, infuriated, fuming, irate, in a temper, beside oneself; *informal* livid, foaming at the mouth, (hopping) mad, wild, apoplectic, steamed up, in a lather, in a paddy; *poetic/literary* wrathful; *archaic* wroth.
incantation ● noun **1** *he muttered some weird incantations* CHANT, invocation, conjuration, magic spell/formula, rune; *N. Amer.* hex, mojo; *NZ* makutu. **2** *ritual incantation* CHANTING, intonation, recitation.
incapable ● adjective **1** *an incapable government* INCOMPETENT, inept, inadequate, not good enough, leaving much to be desired, inexpert, unskilful, ineffective, ineffectual, inefficacious, feeble, unfit, unqualified, unequal to the task; *informal* out of one's depth, not up to it, not up to snuff, useless, hopeless, pathetic, a dead loss. **2** *he was mentally incapable* INCAPACITATED, helpless, powerless, impotent.
– OPPOSITES competent.
incapacitated ● adjective DISABLED, debilitated, indisposed, unfit; immobilized, out of action, out of commission, hors de combat; *informal* laid up.
– OPPOSITES fit.
incapacity ● noun **1** *mental incapacity* DISABILITY, incapability, inability, debility, impairment, indisposition; powerlessness, impotence, helplessness; incompetence, inadequacy, ineffectiveness. **2** *legal incapacity* DISQUALIFICATION, lack of entitlement.
– OPPOSITES capability.
incarcerate ● verb IMPRISON, put in prison, send to prison, jail, lock up, put under lock and key, put away, intern, confine, detain, hold, immure, put in chains, clap in irons, hold prisoner, hold captive; *Brit.* detain at Her Majesty's pleasure; *informal* send down, put behind bars, put inside; *Brit. informal* bang someone up.
– OPPOSITES release.
incarceration ● noun IMPRISONMENT, internment, confinement, detention, custody, captivity, restraint; *informal* time; *Brit. informal* porridge; *archaic* durance, duress.
incarnate ● adjective IN HUMAN FORM, in the flesh, in physical form, in bodily form, made flesh; corporeal, physical, fleshly, embodied.
incarnation ● noun **1** *the incarnation of artistic genius* EMBODIMENT, personification, exemplification, type, epitome; manifestation, bodily form, avatar. **2** *a previous incarnation* LIFETIME, life, existence.
incautious ● adjective RASH, unwise, careless, heedless, thoughtless, reckless, unthinking, imprudent, misguided, ill-advised, ill-judged, injudicious, impolitic, unguarded, foolhardy, foolish; unwary, off-guard, inattentive; *informal* asleep on the job, asleep at the wheel.
– OPPOSITES circumspect.
incendiary ● adjective **1** *an incendiary bomb* COMBUSTIBLE, flammable, inflammable. **2** *an incendiary speech* INFLAMMATORY, rabble-rousing, provocative, seditious, subversive; contentious, controversial.
● noun **1** *an aircraft loaded with incendiaries* EXPLOSIVE, bomb, incendiary device. **2** *incendiaries set the village on fire* ARSONIST, fire-bomber, fire-setter; pyromaniac; *Brit.* fire-raiser; *informal* firebug, pyro; *N. Amer. informal* torch. **3** *a political incendiary* AGITATOR, demagogue, rabble-rouser, firebrand, troublemaker, agent provocateur, revolutionary, insurgent, subversive.
incense[1] ● verb *his taunts used to incense me* ENRAGE, infuriate, anger, madden, outrage, inflame, exasperate, antagonize, provoke; *informal* make someone see red, make someone's blood boil, make someone's hackles rise, drive mad/crazy; *N. Amer. informal* burn up.
– OPPOSITES placate, please.
incense[2] ● noun *a whiff of incense* PERFUME, fragrance, scent.
incensed ● adjective ENRAGED, very angry, furious, infuriated,

to action or increased effort.
– DERIVATIVES **incentivize** (also **incentivise**) verb.
– ORIGIN Latin *incentivum* 'something that sets the tune or incites', from *incantare* 'to chant or bewitch'.
inception • noun the establishment or starting point of an institution or activity.
– ORIGIN Latin, from *incipere* 'begin'.
incertitude • noun a state of uncertainty or hesitation.
incessant • adjective continuing without pause or interruption.
– DERIVATIVES **incessantly** adverb.
– ORIGIN Latin, from *in-* 'not' + *cessare* 'cease'.
incest • noun sexual relations between people classed as being too closely related to marry each other.
– ORIGIN from Latin *in-* 'not' + *castus* 'chaste'.
incestuous /insestyooəss/ • adjective **1** involving or guilty of incest. **2** (of a relationship or community) excessively close and resistant to outside influence.
– DERIVATIVES **incestuously** adverb.
inch • noun **1** a unit of linear measure equal to one twelfth of a foot (2.54 cm). **2** a quantity of rainfall that would cover a horizontal surface to a depth of one inch. **3** a very small amount or distance: *don't yield an inch.* • verb move along slowly and carefully.
– PHRASES **every inch 1** the whole area or distance. **2** entirely; very much so. **give someone an inch and they will take a mile** proverb once concessions have been made to someone they will demand a great deal. **(to) within an inch of one's life** almost to the point of death.
– ORIGIN Latin *uncia* 'twelfth part': compare with OUNCE[1].
inchoate • adjective /inkōayt/ **1** not fully formed or developed; rudimentary. **2** confused or incoherent.
– DERIVATIVES **inchoately** adverb.
– ORIGIN from Latin *inchoare*, variant of *incohare* 'begin'.
incidence • noun **1** the occurrence, rate, or frequency of a disease, crime, or other undesirable thing. **2** Physics the intersection of a line or ray with a surface.
incident • noun **1** an event or occurrence. **2** a violent event, such as an attack. **3** the occurrence of dangerous or exciting events: *the plane landed without incident.* • adjective **1 (incident to)** resulting from. **2** (of light or other radiation) falling on or striking something. **3** Physics relating to incidence.
– ORIGIN from Latin *incidere* 'fall upon, happen to'.
incidental • adjective **1** occurring as a minor accompaniment or by chance in connection with something else. **2 (incidental to)** liable to happen as a consequence of. • noun an incidental detail, expense, etc.
incidentally • adverb **1** by the way. **2** in an incidental manner.
incidental music • noun music used in a film or play as a background.
incinerate /insinnərayt/ • verb destroy by burning.
– DERIVATIVES **incineration** noun.
– ORIGIN Latin *incinerare* 'burn to ashes'.
incinerator • noun an apparatus for incinerating waste material.
incipient /insippiənt/ • adjective beginning to happen or develop.
– DERIVATIVES **incipiently** adverb.
– ORIGIN from Latin *incipere* 'undertake, begin'.
incircle • noun Geometry a circle drawn inside a triangle or other figure so as to touch (but not cross) each side.
incise • verb **1** make a cut or cuts in (a surface). **2** cut (a mark or decoration) into a surface.
– ORIGIN Latin *incidere* 'cut into'.
incision • noun **1** a surgical cut in skin or flesh. **2** the action or process of incising.
incisive • adjective **1** intelligently analytical and concise. **2** (of an action) quick and direct.
– DERIVATIVES **incisively** adverb **incisiveness** noun.
incisor • noun a narrow-edged tooth at the front of the mouth, adapted for cutting.
incite • verb **1** encourage or stir up (violent or unlawful behaviour). **2** urge or persuade to act in a violent or unlawful way.
– DERIVATIVES **incitement** noun **inciter** noun.
– ORIGIN Latin *incitare*, from *citare* 'rouse'.
incivility • noun (pl. **incivilities**) rude or unsociable speech or behaviour.

i

Thesaurus

irate, in a temper, raging, incandescent, fuming, seething, beside oneself, outraged; *informal* mad, hopping mad, wild, livid, apoplectic, hot under the collar, foaming at the mouth, steamed up, in a paddy, fit to be tied; *poetic/literary* wrathful; *archaic* wroth.
incentive • noun INDUCEMENT, motivation, motive, reason, stimulus, stimulant, spur, impetus, encouragement, impulse; incitement, goad, provocation; attraction, lure, bait; *informal* carrot, sweetener, come-on.
– OPPOSITES deterrent.
inception • noun ESTABLISHMENT, institution, foundation, founding, formation, initiation, setting up, origination, constitution, inauguration, opening, day one; beginning, commencement, start, birth, dawn, genesis, origin; *informal* kick-off.
– OPPOSITES end.
incessant • adjective CEASELESS, unceasing, constant, continual, unabating, interminable, endless, unending, never-ending, everlasting, eternal, perpetual, continuous, non-stop, uninterrupted, unbroken, unremitting, persistent, relentless, unrelenting, unrelieved, sustained.
– OPPOSITES intermittent.
incessantly • adverb CONSTANTLY, continually, all the time, non-stop, without stopping, without a break, round the clock, {morning, noon, and night}, interminably, unremittingly, ceaselessly, endlessly; *informal* 24-7.
– OPPOSITES occasionally.
incidence • noun OCCURRENCE, prevalence; rate, frequency; amount, degree, extent.
incident • noun **1** *incidents in his youth* EVENT, occurrence, episode, experience, happening, occasion, proceeding, eventuality, affair, business; adventure, exploit, escapade; matter, circumstance, fact, development. **2** *police are investigating the incident* DISTURBANCE, fracas, melee, commotion, rumpus, scene; fight, skirmish, clash, brawl, free-for-all, encounter, conflict, ruckus, confrontation, altercation, contretemps; *informal* ruction; *Law, dated* affray. **3** *the journey was not without incident* EXCITEMENT, adventure, drama; danger, peril.
incidental • adjective **1** *incidental details* LESS IMPORTANT, secondary, subsidiary; minor, peripheral, background, by-the-way, by-the-by, non-essential, inessential, unimportant, insignificant, inconsequential, tangential, extrinsic, extraneous. **2** *an incidental discovery* CHANCE, accidental, random; fluky, fortuitous, serendipitous, adventitious, coincidental, unlooked-for. **3** *the risks incidental to the job* CONNECTED WITH, related to, associated with, accompanying, attending, attendant on, concomitant with.
– OPPOSITES essential, deliberate.
incidentally • adverb **1** *incidentally, I haven't had a reply yet* BY THE WAY, by the by(e), in passing, en passant, speaking of which; parenthetically; *informal* btw, as it happens. **2** *the infection was discovered incidentally* BY CHANCE, by accident, accidentally, fortuitously, by a fluke, by happenstance; coincidentally, by coincidence.
incinerate • verb BURN, reduce to ashes, consume by fire, carbonize; cremate.
incipient • adjective DEVELOPING, growing, emerging, emergent, dawning, just beginning, inceptive, initial; nascent, embryonic, fledgling, in its infancy, germinal.
– OPPOSITES full-blown.
incise • verb **1** *the wound was incised* CUT (OPEN), make an incision in, slit (open), lance. **2** *an inscription incised in Roman letters* ENGRAVE, etch, carve, cut, chisel, inscribe, score, chase.
incision • noun **1** *a surgical incision* CUT, opening, slit. **2** *incisions on the marble* NOTCH, nick, snick, scratch, scarification.
incisive • adjective PENETRATING, acute, sharp, sharp-witted, razor-sharp, keen, astute, shrewd, trenchant, piercing, perceptive, insightful, percipient, perspicacious, discerning, analytical, clever, smart, quick; concise, succinct, pithy, to the point, crisp, clear; *informal* punchy.
– OPPOSITES rambling, vague.
incite • verb **1** *he was arrested for inciting racial hatred* STIR UP, whip up, encourage, fan the flames of, stoke up, fuel, kindle, ignite, inflame, stimulate, instigate, provoke, excite, arouse, awaken, inspire, trigger, spark off, ferment, foment; *poetic/literary* enkindle, waken. **2** *she incited him to commit murder* EGG ON, encourage, urge, goad, provoke, spur on, drive, stimulate, push, prod, prompt, induce, impel; arouse, rouse, excite, inflame, sting, prick; *informal* put up to.
– OPPOSITES discourage, deter.
incivility • noun RUDENESS, discourtesy, discourteousness, impol-

inclement /inklemmənt/ • adjective (of the weather) unpleasantly cold or wet.
– DERIVATIVES **inclemency** noun.

inclination • noun **1** a natural tendency to act or feel in a particular way. **2** (**inclination for/to/towards**) an interest in or liking for. **3** a slope or slant. **4** the angle at which a straight line or plane is inclined to another.

incline • verb /inklīn/ **1** (usu. **be inclined to/towards/to do**) be favourably disposed towards or willing to do. **2** (usu. **be inclined to/to do**) have a specified tendency or talent. **3** lean or turn away from a given plane or direction, especially the vertical or horizontal. **4** bend (one's head) forwards and downwards. • noun /inklīn/ an inclined surface, slope, or plane.
– ORIGIN Latin *inclinare* 'to bend towards'.

inclined plane • noun a plane inclined at an angle to the horizontal, especially as a means of reducing the force needed to raise a load.

inclose • verb variant spelling of ENCLOSE.

inclosure • noun variant spelling of ENCLOSURE.

include • verb **1** comprise or contain as part of a whole. **2** make or treat as part of a whole or set.
– ORIGIN Latin *includere* 'shut in'.

including • preposition containing as part of the whole being considered.

inclusion • noun **1** the action of including or the state of being included. **2** a person or thing that is included.

inclusive • adjective **1** including all the expected or required services or items. **2** (**inclusive of**) containing (a specified element) as part of a whole. **3** (after a noun) between the limits stated: *the ages of 55 to 59 inclusive.* **4** not excluding any section of society or any party.
– DERIVATIVES **inclusively** adverb **inclusiveness** noun.

incognito /inkogneetō/ • adjective & adverb having one's true identity concealed. • noun (pl. **incognitos**) an assumed or false identity.
– ORIGIN Italian, 'unknown'.

incoherent • adjective **1** incomprehensible or confusing in speech or writing. **2** internally inconsistent; illogical. **3** Physics (of light or other waves) having no fixed phase relationship.
– DERIVATIVES **incoherence** noun **incoherency** noun **incoherently** adverb.

incombustible • adjective (especially of a building material) not inflammable.

income • noun money received, especially on a regular basis, for work or through investments.

incomer • noun chiefly Brit. a person who has come to live in an area in which they have not grown up.

income support • noun (in the UK and Canada) payment made by the state to people on a low income.

income tax • noun tax levied directly on personal income.

incoming • adjective **1** coming in. **2** (of an official or administration) having just been elected or appointed to succeed another. • noun (**incomings**) revenue; income.

incommensurable /inkəmenshərəb'l/ • adjective **1** not able to be judged or measured by the same standards. **2** Mathematics (of numbers) in a ratio that cannot be expressed by means of integers.
– DERIVATIVES **incommensurability** noun.

incommensurate /inkəmenshərət/ • adjective **1** (**incommensurate with**) out of keeping or proportion with. **2** another term for INCOMMENSURABLE (in sense 1).
– DERIVATIVES **incommensurateness** noun.

incommode • verb formal cause inconvenience to.
– ORIGIN Latin *incommodare*, from *in-* 'not' + *commodus* 'convenient'.

incommodious • adjective formal or dated causing inconvenience or discomfort.

incommunicable • adjective not able to be communicated to others.

incommunicado /inkəmyōōnikaadō/ • adjective & adverb not able to communicate with other people.
– ORIGIN Spanish *incomunicado*, from *incomunicar* 'deprive of communication'.

incomparable /inkompərəb'l/ • adjective **1** without an equal in quality or extent. **2** unable to be compared; totally different.
– DERIVATIVES **incomparably** adverb.

Thesaurus

iteness, bad manners, disrespect, boorishness, ungraciousness; insolence, impertinence, impudence.
– OPPOSITES politeness.

inclement • adjective COLD, chilly, bleak, wintry, freezing, snowy, icy; wet, rainy, drizzly, damp; stormy, blustery, wild, rough, squally, windy; unpleasant, bad, foul, nasty, filthy, severe, extreme, harsh.
– OPPOSITES fine.

inclination • noun **1** *his political inclinations* TENDENCY, propensity, proclivity, leaning, predisposition, disposition, predilection, desire, wish, impulse, bent; liking, penchant, partiality, preference, appetite, fancy, interest, affinity; stomach, taste; *informal* yen; *formal* velleity; *archaic* list, humour. **2** *an inclination of his head* BOWING, bow, bending, nod, nodding, lowering. **3** *an inclination of ninety degrees.* See INCLINE noun.
– OPPOSITES aversion.

incline • verb **1** *his prejudice inclines him to overlook obvious facts* PREDISPOSE, lead, make, make of a mind to, dispose, prejudice; prompt, induce, influence, sway; persuade, convince. **2** *I incline to the opposite view* PREFER, favour, go for; tend, lean, swing, veer, gravitate, be drawn. **3** *he inclined his head* BEND, bow, nod, bob, lower, dip. **4** *the columns incline away from the vertical* LEAN, tilt, angle, tip, slope, slant, bend, curve, bank, cant, bevel; list, heel. • noun *a steep incline* SLOPE, gradient, pitch, ramp, bank, ascent, rise, acclivity, upslope, dip, descent, declivity, downslope; hill; *N. Amer.* grade, downgrade, upgrade.

inclined • adjective **1** *I'm inclined to believe her* DISPOSED, minded, of a mind, willing, ready, prepared; predisposed. **2** *she's inclined to gossip* PRONE, given, in the habit of, liable, likely, apt, wont.

include • verb **1** *activities include sports, drama, music, and chess* INCORPORATE, comprise, encompass, cover, embrace, involve, take in, number, contain; consist of, be made up of, be composed of; *formal* comprehend. **2** *don't forget to include the cost of repairs* ALLOW FOR, count, take into account, take into consideration.
– OPPOSITES exclude.

including • preposition INCLUSIVE OF, counting; as well as, plus, together with.

inclusive • adjective **1** *an inclusive price | an inclusive definition* ALL-IN, all-inclusive, comprehensive, in toto, overall, full, all-round, umbrella, catch-all, all-encompassing. **2** *prices are inclusive of VAT* INCLUDING, incorporating, taking in, counting; comprising, covering.

incognito • adverb & adjective UNDER AN ASSUMED NAME, under a false name, in disguise, disguised, under cover, in plain clothes, camouflaged; secretly, anonymously.

incoherent • adjective **1** *a long, incoherent speech* UNCLEAR, confused, muddled, unintelligible, incomprehensible, hard to follow, disjointed, disconnected, disordered, mixed up, garbled, jumbled, scrambled; rambling, wandering, discursive, disorganized, illogical; inarticulate, mumbling, slurred. **2** *she was incoherent and shivering* DELIRIOUS, raving, babbling, hysterical, irrational.
– OPPOSITES lucid.

incombustible • adjective NON-FLAMMABLE, non-combustible; fireproof, flameproof, fire/flame resistant, fire/flame retardant; heatproof, ovenproof.
– OPPOSITES flammable, inflammable.

income • noun EARNINGS, salary, pay, remuneration, wages, stipend; revenue, receipts, takings, profits, gains, proceeds, turnover, yield, dividend, incomings; means; *N. Amer.* take; *formal* emolument.
– OPPOSITES expenditure, outgoings.

incoming • adjective **1** *the incoming train* ARRIVING, entering; approaching, coming (in). **2** *the incoming president* NEWLY ELECTED, newly appointed, succeeding, new, next, future; elect, to-be, designate.
– OPPOSITES outgoing.

incommensurate • adjective OUT OF PROPORTION, not in proportion, disproportionate, inappropriate, out of keeping; insufficient, inadequate; excessive, inordinate, unreasonable, uncalled for, undue, unfair.
– OPPOSITES proportional.

incommunicable • adjective INDESCRIBABLE, inexpressible, unutterable, unspeakable, undefinable, ineffable, beyond words, beyond description; overwhelming, intense, profound.

incomparable • adjective WITHOUT EQUAL, beyond compare, unparalleled, matchless, peerless, unmatched, without parallel, beyond comparison, second to none, in a class of its own, unequalled, unrivalled, inimitable, nonpareil, par excellence; transcendent, su-

incompatible ● adjective **1** (of two things) not able to exist or be used together. **2** (of two people) unable to have a harmonious relationship.
– DERIVATIVES **incompatibility** noun.
incompetent ● adjective **1** not sufficiently skilful to do something successfully. **2** Law not qualified to act in a particular capacity. ● noun an incompetent person.
– DERIVATIVES **incompetence** noun **incompetency** noun **incompetently** adverb.
incomplete ● adjective not complete.
– DERIVATIVES **incompletely** adverb **incompleteness** noun **incompletion** noun.
incomprehensible ● adjective not able to be understood.
– DERIVATIVES **incomprehensibility** noun **incomprehensibly** adverb **incomprehension** noun.
inconceivable ● adjective not capable of being imagined or grasped mentally.
– DERIVATIVES **inconceivably** adverb.
inconclusive ● adjective not conclusive.
– DERIVATIVES **inconclusively** adverb **inconclusiveness** noun.
incongruent /inkonggrooənt/ ● adjective **1** incongruous. **2** Chemistry affecting the components of an alloy or other substance differently.
– DERIVATIVES **incongruence** noun **incongruently** adverb.
incongruous /inkonggrooəss/ ● adjective out of place.
– DERIVATIVES **incongruity** noun (pl. **incongruities**) **incongruously** adverb.
inconsequent ● adjective **1** not connected or following logically. **2** inconsequential.
– DERIVATIVES **inconsequence** noun **inconsequently** adverb.
inconsequential ● adjective not important or significant.
– DERIVATIVES **inconsequentiality** noun **inconsequentially** adverb.
inconsiderable ● adjective small in size, amount, extent, etc.: *a not inconsiderable number.*
inconsiderate ● adjective thoughtlessly causing hurt or inconvenience to others.
– DERIVATIVES **inconsiderately** adverb **inconsiderateness** noun.
inconsistent ● adjective not consistent.
– DERIVATIVES **inconsistency** noun **inconsistently** adverb.
inconsolable ● adjective not able to be comforted or consoled.
– DERIVATIVES **inconsolably** adverb.
inconspicuous ● adjective not clearly visible or attracting attention.
– DERIVATIVES **inconspicuously** adverb **inconspicuousness** noun.
inconstant ● adjective frequently changing; variable or irregular.
– DERIVATIVES **inconstancy** noun.
incontestable ● adjective not able to be disputed.
– DERIVATIVES **incontestably** adverb.
incontinent ● adjective **1** lacking voluntary control over urination or defecation. **2** lacking self-restraint; uncontrolled.
– DERIVATIVES **incontinence** noun **incontinently** adverb.

Thesaurus

perlative, surpassing, unsurpassed, unsurpassable, supreme, top, outstanding, consummate, unique, singular, rare, perfect; *informal* one-in-a-million; *formal* unexampled.
incomparably ● adverb FAR AND AWAY, by far, infinitely, immeasurably, easily; inimitably, supremely, superlatively, transcendently, uniquely.
incompatible ● adjective **1** *she and McBride are totally incompatible* UNSUITED, mismatched, ill-matched, poles apart, worlds apart, like day and night; *Brit.* like chalk and cheese. **2** *incompatible economic objectives* IRRECONCILABLE, conflicting, opposed, opposite, contradictory, antagonistic, antipathetic; clashing, inharmonious, discordant; mutually exclusive. **3** *a theory incompatible with that of his predecessor* INCONSISTENT WITH, at odds with, out of keeping with, at variance with, inconsonant with, different to, divergent from, contrary to, in conflict with, in opposition to, (diametrically) opposed to, counter to, irreconcilable with.
– OPPOSITES well matched, harmonious, consistent.
incompetent ● adjective INEPT, unskilful, unskilled, inexpert, amateurish, unprofessional, bungling, blundering, clumsy, inadequate, substandard, inferior, ineffective, deficient, inefficient, ineffectual, wanting, lacking, leaving much to be desired; incapable, unfit, unqualified; *informal* useless, pathetic, cack-handed, ham-fisted, not up to it, not up to scratch; *Brit. informal* not much cop.
incomplete ● adjective **1** *the project is still incomplete* UNFINISHED, uncompleted, half-finished, half-done, half-completed, partial. **2** *inaccurate or incomplete information* DEFICIENT, insufficient, imperfect, defective, partial, patchy, sketchy, fragmentary, fragmented, scrappy, bitty; abridged, shortened; expurgated, bowdlerized.
incomprehensible ● adjective UNINTELLIGIBLE, impossible to understand, impenetrable, unclear, indecipherable, beyond one's comprehension, beyond one, beyond one's grasp, complicated, complex, involved, baffling, bewildering, mystifying, puzzling, confusing, perplexing; abstruse, esoteric, recondite, arcane, mysterious, Delphic; *informal* over one's head, all Greek to someone; *Brit. informal* double Dutch.
– OPPOSITES intelligible, clear.
inconceivable ● adjective UNBELIEVABLE, beyond belief, incredible, unthinkable, unimaginable, extremely unlikely; impossible, beyond the bounds of possibility, out of the question, preposterous, ridiculous, ludicrous, absurd, incomprehensible; *informal* hard to swallow.
– OPPOSITES likely.
inconclusive ● adjective INDECISIVE, proving nothing; indefinite, indeterminate, unresolved, unproved, unsettled, still open to question/doubt, debatable, unconfirmed; moot; vague, ambiguous; *informal* up in the air, left hanging.
incongruous ● adjective **1** *the women looked incongruous in their smart hats and fur coats* OUT OF PLACE, out of keeping, inappropriate, unsuitable, unsuited; wrong, strange, odd, absurd, bizarre, off-key, extraneous. **2** *an incongruous collection of objects* ILL-MATCHED, ill-assorted, mismatched, unharmonious, discordant, dissonant, conflicting, clashing, jarring, incompatible, different, dissimilar, contrasting, disparate.
– OPPOSITES appropriate, harmonious.
inconsequential ● adjective INSIGNIFICANT, unimportant, of little no/consequence, neither here nor there, incidental, inessential, non-essential, immaterial, irrelevant; negligible, inappreciable, inconsiderable, slight, minor, trivial, trifling, petty; *informal* piddling, piffling.
– OPPOSITES important.
inconsiderable ● adjective INSIGNIFICANT, negligible, trifling, small, tiny, little, minuscule, nominal, token, petty, slight, minor, inappreciable, insubstantial, inconsequential; *informal* piffling; *formal* exiguous.
inconsiderate ● adjective THOUGHTLESS, unthinking, insensitive, selfish, self-centred, unsympathetic, uncaring, heedless, unmindful, unkind, uncharitable, ungracious, impolite, discourteous, rude, disrespectful; tactless, undiplomatic, indiscreet, indelicate; *informal* ignorant.
– OPPOSITES thoughtful.
inconsistent ● adjective **1** *his inconsistent behaviour* ERRATIC, changeable, unpredictable, variable, varying, changing, changeful, inconstant, unstable, irregular, fluctuating, unsteady, unsettled, uneven; self-contradictory, contradictory, paradoxical; capricious, fickle, flighty, whimsical, unreliable, mercurial, volatile, blowing hot and cold, ever-changing, chameleon-like; *informal* up and down; *technical* labile. **2** *he had done nothing inconsistent with his morality* INCOMPATIBLE WITH, conflicting with, in conflict with, at odds with, at variance with, differing from, contrary to, in opposition to, (diametrically) opposed to, irreconcilable with, out of keeping with, out of step with; antithetical to.
inconsolable ● adjective HEARTBROKEN, broken-hearted, grief-stricken, beside oneself with grief, devastated, wretched, sick at heart, desolate, despairing, distraught, comfortless; miserable, unhappy, sad; *poetic/literary* heartsick.
inconspicuous ● adjective UNOBTRUSIVE, unnoticeable, unremarkable, unspectacular, unostentatious, undistinguished, unexceptional, modest, unassuming, discreet, hidden, concealed; unseen, in the background, low-profile.
– OPPOSITES noticeable.
inconstant ● adjective FICKLE, faithless, unfaithful, false, false-hearted; wayward, unreliable, untrustworthy, capricious, volatile, flighty, unpredictable, erratic, blowing hot and cold; *informal* cheating, two-timing.
– OPPOSITES faithful.
incontestable ● adjective INCONTROVERTIBLE, indisputable, undeniable, irrefutable, unassailable, beyond dispute, unquestionable, beyond question, indubitable, beyond doubt; airtight, watertight, unarguable, undebatable, emphatic, categorical, certain, definite, definitive, proven, demonstrable, decisive, conclusive.

incontrovertible ● adjective not able to be denied or disputed.
– DERIVATIVES **incontrovertibly** adverb.
inconvenience ● noun the state or fact of being slightly troublesome or difficult. ● verb cause inconvenience to.
– DERIVATIVES **inconvenient** adjective **inconveniently** adverb.
incorporate ● verb **1** take in or include as part of a whole. **2** constitute (a company, city, or other organization) as a legal corporation. ● adjective constituted as a legal corporation; incorporated.
– DERIVATIVES **incorporation** noun **incorporative** adjective **incorporator** noun.
– ORIGIN Latin *incorporare* 'embody', from *corpus* 'body'.
incorporeal /inkorporiəl/ ● adjective not composed of matter; having no material existence.
incorrect ● adjective not in accordance with fact or standards; wrong.
– DERIVATIVES **incorrectly** adverb **incorrectness** noun.
incorrigible ● adjective not able to be corrected or reformed.
– DERIVATIVES **incorrigibility** noun **incorrigibly** adverb.
– ORIGIN Latin *incorrigibilis*, from *in-* 'not' + *corrigibilis* 'correctable'.
incorruptible ● adjective **1** not susceptible to corruption, especially by bribery. **2** not subject to death or decay.
– DERIVATIVES **incorruptibility** noun.
increase ● verb make or become greater in size, amount, or degree. ● noun an instance or the action of increasing.
– DERIVATIVES **increasing** adjective **increasingly** adverb.
– ORIGIN Latin *increscere*, from *crescere* 'grow'.
incredible ● adjective **1** impossible or hard to believe. **2** informal extraordinarily good.
– DERIVATIVES **incredibility** noun **incredibly** adverb.
incredulous ● adjective unwilling or unable to believe.
– DERIVATIVES **incredulity** noun **incredulously** adverb.
increment /ingkrimənt/ ● noun an increase or addition, especially one of a series on a fixed scale.
– DERIVATIVES **incremental** adjective **incrementally** adverb.
– ORIGIN Latin *incrementum*, from *increscere* 'increase'.
incrementalism ● noun belief in or advocacy of change by degrees.
– DERIVATIVES **incrementalist** noun & adjective.
incriminate /inkrimminayt/ ● verb make (someone) appear guilty of a crime or wrongdoing.
– DERIVATIVES **incrimination** noun **incriminatory** adjective.
– ORIGIN Latin *incriminare* 'accuse', from *crimen* 'crime'.
in-crowd ● noun (**the in-crowd**) informal a small group of people that are particularly fashionable or popular.
incrust ● verb variant spelling of ENCRUST.
incubate /ingkyoobayt/ ● verb **1** (of a bird) sit on (eggs) to keep them warm and bring them to hatching. **2** keep (bacteria, cells, etc.) at a suitable temperature so that they develop. **3** (with reference to an infectious disease) develop slowly without outward or perceptible signs.
– DERIVATIVES **incubation** noun.
– ORIGIN Latin *incubare* 'lie on'.
incubator ● noun **1** an apparatus used to hatch eggs or grow micro-organisms under controlled conditions. **2** an enclosed apparatus providing a controlled and protective environment for the care of premature babies.
incubus /ingkyoobəss/ ● noun (pl. **incubi** /ingkyoobī/) **1** a male demon believed to have sexual intercourse with sleeping women. **2** archaic a nightmare.
– ORIGIN Latin *incubo* 'nightmare', from *incubare* 'lie on'.
inculcate /inkulkayt/ ● verb instil (an idea or habit) by persistent instruction.

Thesaurus

– OPPOSITES questionable.
incontinent ● adjective UNRESTRAINED, uncontrolled, lacking self-restraint, unbridled, unchecked; uncontrollable, ungovernable.
incontrovertible ● adjective INDISPUTABLE, incontestable, undeniable, irrefutable, unassailable, beyond dispute, unquestionable, beyond question, indubitable, beyond doubt, unarguable, undebatable; certain, sure, definite, definitive, proven, decisive, conclusive, demonstrable, emphatic, categorical, airtight, watertight.
– OPPOSITES questionable.
inconvenience ● noun **1** *we apologize for any inconvenience caused* TROUBLE, bother, problems, disruption, difficulty, disturbance; vexation, irritation, annoyance; *informal* aggravation, hassle. **2** *his early arrival was clearly an inconvenience* NUISANCE, trouble, bother, problem, vexation, worry, trial, bind, bore, irritant, thorn in someone's flesh; *informal* headache, pain, pain in the neck, pain in the backside, drag, aggravation, hassle; *N. Amer. informal* pain in the butt.
● verb *I don't want to inconvenience you* TROUBLE, bother, put out, put to any trouble, disturb, impose on, burden; vex, annoy, irritate; *informal* hassle; *formal* discommode.
inconvenient ● adjective AWKWARD, difficult, inopportune, untimely, ill-timed, unsuitable, inappropriate, unfortunate; tiresome, irritating, annoying, vexing, bothersome; *informal* aggravating.
incorporate ● verb **1** *the region was incorporated into Moldavian territory* ABSORB, include, subsume, assimilate, integrate, take in, swallow up. **2** *the model incorporates some advanced features* INCLUDE, contain, comprise, embody, embrace, build in, encompass. **3** *a small amount of salt is incorporated with the butter* BLEND, mix, mingle, meld, combine; fold in, stir in.
incorporeal ● adjective INTANGIBLE, impalpable, non-physical; bodiless, disembodied, discarnate; spiritual, ethereal, unsubstantial, insubstantial, transcendental; ghostly, spectral, supernatural.
– OPPOSITES tangible.
incorrect ● adjective **1** *an incorrect answer* WRONG, erroneous, in error, mistaken, inaccurate, wide of the mark, off target; untrue, false, fallacious; *informal* off beam, out, way out, full of holes. **2** *incorrect behaviour* INAPPROPRIATE, wrong, unsuitable, inapt, inapposite; ill-advised, ill-considered, ill-judged, injudicious, unacceptable, unfitting, out of keeping, improper, unseemly, unbecoming, indecorous; *informal* out of order.
incorrigible ● adjective INVETERATE, habitual, confirmed, hardened, incurable, irredeemable, hopeless, beyond hope/redemption; impenitent, uncontrite, unrepentant, unapologetic, unashamed.
incorruptible ● adjective **1** *an incorruptible man* HONEST, honourable, trustworthy, principled, high-principled, unbribable, moral, ethical, good, virtuous. **2** *an incorruptible substance* IMPERISHABLE, indestructible, indissoluble, enduring, everlasting.
– OPPOSITES venal.
increase ● verb **1** *demand is likely to increase* GROW, get bigger, get larger, enlarge, expand, swell; rise, climb, escalate, soar, surge, rocket, shoot up, spiral; intensify, strengthen, heighten, extend, stretch, spread, widen; multiply, snowball, mushroom, proliferate, balloon, build up, mount up, pile up, accrue, accumulate; *poetic/literary* wax. **2** *higher expectations will increase user demand* ADD TO, make larger, make bigger, augment, supplement, top up, build up, extend, raise, swell, inflate; magnify, intensify, strengthen, amplify, heighten; *informal* up, jack up, hike up, bump up, crank up.
– OPPOSITES decrease, reduce.
● noun *the increase in size | an increase in demand* GROWTH, rise, enlargement, expansion, extension, multiplication, elevation, inflation; increment, addition, augmentation; magnification, intensification, amplification, step up, climb, escalation, surge, upsurge, upswing, spiral, spurt; *informal* hike.
increasingly ● adverb MORE AND MORE, progressively, to an increasing extent, ever more.
incredible ● adjective **1** *I find his story incredible* UNBELIEVABLE, beyond belief, hard to believe, unconvincing, far-fetched, implausible, improbable, highly unlikely, dubious, doubtful; inconceivable, unthinkable, unimaginable, impossible; feeble, weak, thin, lame; *informal* hard to swallow/take, cock-and-bull. **2** *an incredible feat of engineering* MAGNIFICENT, wonderful, marvellous, spectacular, remarkable, phenomenal, prodigious, breathtaking, extraordinary, unbelievable, amazing, stunning, astounding, astonishing, awe-inspiring, staggering, formidable, impressive, supreme, great, awesome, superhuman; *informal* fantastic, terrific, tremendous, stupendous, mind-boggling, mind-blowing, out of this world; *poetic/literary* wondrous.
incredulity ● noun DISBELIEF, incredulousness, scepticism, distrust, mistrust, suspicion, doubt, doubtfulness, dubiousness, lack of conviction; cynicism.
incredulous ● adjective DISBELIEVING, unbelieving, sceptical, distrustful, mistrustful, suspicious, doubtful, dubious, unconvinced; cynical.
increment ● noun INCREASE, addition, supplement, gain, augmentation, boost; *informal* hike.
– OPPOSITES reduction.
incriminate ● verb IMPLICATE, involve; blame, accuse, denounce, inform against, point the finger at; entrap; *informal* frame, set up,

– DERIVATIVES **inculcation** noun.
– ORIGIN Latin *inculcare* 'press in'.

incumbency ● noun (pl. **incumbencies**) the period during which an office is held.

incumbent /inkumb'nt/ ● adjective **1** (**incumbent on/upon**) necessary for (someone) as a duty. **2** currently holding office. ● noun the holder of an office or post.
– ORIGIN Latin *incumbens*, from *incumbere* 'lie or lean on'.

incunabulum /inkyoonabyooləm/ ● noun (pl. **incunabula**) an early printed book, especially one printed before 1501.
– ORIGIN from Latin *incunabula* 'swaddling clothes, cradle'.

incur ● verb (**incurred**, **incurring**) become subject to (something unpleasant) as a result of one's actions.
– ORIGIN Latin *incurrere* 'run into or towards'.

incurable ● adjective not able to be cured. ● noun an incurable person.
– DERIVATIVES **incurability** noun **incurably** adverb.

incurious ● adjective not eager to know something; lacking curiosity.
– DERIVATIVES **incuriosity** noun **incuriously** adverb.

incursion ● noun an invasion or attack, especially a sudden or brief one.
– ORIGIN Latin, from *incurrere* 'run into or towards'.

indebted ● adjective owing money or gratitude.
– DERIVATIVES **indebtedness** noun.
– ORIGIN from Old French *endetter* 'involve in debt'.

indecent ● adjective **1** not conforming with accepted standards of behaviour or morality. **2** not appropriate; unseemly: *indecent haste.*
– DERIVATIVES **indecency** noun **indecently** adverb.

indecent assault ● noun sexual assault that does not involve rape.

indecent exposure ● noun the crime of intentionally showing one's genitals in public.

indecipherable /indisifərəb'l/ ● adjective not able to be read or understood.

indecisive ● adjective **1** not able to make decisions quickly and effectively. **2** not settling an issue: *indecisive results.*
– DERIVATIVES **indecision** noun **indecisively** adverb **indecisiveness** noun.

indecorous ● adjective not in keeping with good taste and propriety; improper.
– DERIVATIVES **indecorously** adverb.

indeed ● adverb **1** used to emphasize a statement, description, or response. **2** used to introduce a further and stronger or more surprising point. **3** used in a response to express interest, incredulity, or contempt.
– ORIGIN originally as *in deed*.

indefatigable /indifattigəb'l/ ● adjective never tiring or stopping.
– DERIVATIVES **indefatigably** adverb.
– ORIGIN Latin *indefatigabilis*, from *fatigare* 'wear out'.

indefensible ● adjective not justifiable by argument.
– DERIVATIVES **indefensibly** adverb.

indefinable ● adjective not able to be defined or described exactly.
– DERIVATIVES **indefinably** adverb.

indefinite ● adjective **1** not clearly expressed or defined; vague. **2** lasting for an unknown or unstated length of time. **3** Grammar (of a word, inflection, or phrase) not determining the person or thing referred to.
– DERIVATIVES **indefinitely** adverb **indefiniteness** noun.

indefinite article ● noun Grammar a determiner (*a* and *an* in English) that introduces a noun phrase and implies that the

i

Thesaurus

stick/pin the blame on, rat on; *Brit. informal* fit up, grass on; *archaic* inculpate.

inculcate ● verb **1** *the beliefs inculcated in him by his father* INSTIL, implant, fix, impress, imprint; hammer into, drum into, drive into, drill into, din into. **2** *they will try to inculcate you with a respect for culture* IMBUE, infuse, inspire, teach.

inculpate ● verb (*archaic*). See INCRIMINATE.

incumbent ● adjective **1** *it is incumbent on the government to give a clear lead* NECESSARY, essential, required, imperative; compulsory, binding, obligatory, mandatory. **2** *the incumbent president* CURRENT, present, in office, in power; reigning.
● noun *the first incumbent of the post* HOLDER, bearer, occupant.

incur ● verb BRING UPON ONESELF, expose oneself to, lay oneself open to; run up; attract, invite, earn, arouse, cause, give rise to, be liable/subject to, meet with, sustain, experience.

incurable ● adjective **1** *an incurable illness* UNTREATABLE, inoperable, irremediable; terminal, fatal, mortal; chronic. **2** *an incurable romantic* INVETERATE, dyed-in-the-wool, confirmed, established, long-established, long-standing, complete, absolute, utter, thorough, thoroughgoing, out-and-out, through and through; unashamed, unapologetic, unrepentant, incorrigible, hopeless.

incursion ● noun ATTACK, assault, raid, invasion, storming, foray, blitz, sortie, sally, advance, push, thrust.
– OPPOSITES retreat.

indebted ● adjective BEHOLDEN, under an obligation, obliged, obligated, grateful, thankful, in someone's debt, owing a debt of gratitude.

indecent ● adjective **1** *indecent photographs* OBSCENE, dirty, filthy, rude, coarse, naughty, vulgar, gross, crude, lewd, salacious, improper, smutty, off colour; pornographic, offensive, prurient, sordid, scatological; ribald, risqué, racy; *informal* blue, nudge-nudge, porn, porno, X-rated, raunchy, skin; *Brit. informal* saucy; *euphemistic* adult. **2** *indecent clothes* REVEALING, short, brief, skimpy, scanty, low-cut, flimsy, thin, see-through; erotic, arousing, sexy, suggestive, titillating. **3** *indecent haste* UNSEEMLY, improper, indecorous, unceremonious, indelicate, unbecoming, ungentlemanly, unladylike, unfitting, unbefitting; untoward, unsuitable, inappropriate; in bad taste, tasteless, unacceptable, offensive, crass.

indecipherable ● adjective ILLEGIBLE, unreadable, hard to read, unintelligible, unclear; scribbled, scrawled, hieroglyphic, squiggly, cramped, crabbed.

indecision ● noun INDECISIVENESS, irresolution, hesitancy, hesitation, tentativeness; ambivalence, doubt, doubtfulness, uncertainty, incertitude; vacillation, equivocation, second thoughts; shilly-shallying, dithering, temporizing; *Brit.* humming and hawing; *Scottish* swithering; *informal* dilly-dallying, sitting on the fence; *formal* dubiety.

indecisive ● adjective **1** *an indecisive result* INCONCLUSIVE, proving nothing, settling nothing, open, indeterminate, undecided, unsettled, borderline, indefinite, unclear, ambiguous; *informal* up in the air. **2** *an indecisive leader* IRRESOLUTE, hesitant, tentative, weak; vacillating, equivocating, dithering, wavering, faltering, shilly-shallying; ambivalent, divided, blowing hot and cold, in two minds, in a dilemma, in a quandary, torn; doubtful, unsure, uncertain; undecided, uncommitted; *informal* iffy, sitting on the fence.

indecorous ● adjective IMPROPER, unseemly, unbecoming, undignified, immodest, indecent, indelicate, unladylike, ungentlemanly; inappropriate, incorrect, unsuitable, undesirable, unfitting, in bad taste, ill-bred.

indecorum ● noun IMPROPRIETY, unseemliness, immodesty, indecency, indelicacy; inappropriateness, unsuitability, undesirability, unacceptability, bad taste.

indeed ● adverb **1** *there was, indeed, quite a furore* AS EXPECTED, to be sure; in fact, in point of fact, as a matter of fact, in truth, actually, as it happens/happened, if truth be told; *archaic* in sooth. **2** *'May I join you?' 'Indeed you may.'* YES, certainly, assuredly, of course, naturally, without (a) doubt, without question, by all means; *informal* you bet, I'll say. **3** *Ian's future with us looked rosy indeed* VERY, extremely, exceedingly, tremendously, immensely, singularly, decidedly, particularly, remarkably, really.

indefatigable ● adjective TIRELESS, untiring, unwearied, unwearying, unflagging; tenacious, determined, dogged, single-minded, assiduous, industrious, unswerving, unfaltering, unshakeable, indomitable; persistent, relentless, unremitting.

indefensible ● adjective **1** *indefensible cruelty* INEXCUSABLE, unjustifiable, unjustified, unpardonable, unforgivable; uncalled for, unprovoked, gratuitous, unreasonable, unnecessary. **2** *an indefensible system of dual justice* UNTENABLE, unsustainable, insupportable, unwarrantable, unwarranted, unjustifiable, unjustified, flawed, unacceptable. **3** *an indefensible island* DEFENCELESS, vulnerable, exposed, open to attack, pregnable, undefended, unfortified, unguarded, unprotected, unarmed.

indefinable ● adjective HARD TO DEFINE, hard to describe, indescribable, inexpressible, nameless; vague, obscure, impalpable, elusive.

indefinite ● adjective **1** *an indefinite period* INDETERMINATE, unspecified, unlimited, unrestricted, undecided, undetermined, undefined, unfixed, unsettled, unknown, uncertain; limitless, infinite, endless, immeasurable. **2** *an indefinite meaning* VAGUE, ill-defined, unclear, loose, general, imprecise, inexact, nebulous,

thing referred to is non-specific.

indefinite pronoun • noun Grammar a pronoun that does not refer to any person or thing in particular, e.g. *anything, everyone*.

indelible /indellib'l/ • adjective **1** (of ink or a mark) unable to be removed. **2** unable to be forgotten.
– DERIVATIVES **indelibly** adverb.
– ORIGIN Latin *indelebilis*, from *in-* 'not' + *delere* 'delete'.

indelicate • adjective **1** lacking sensitive understanding or tact. **2** slightly indecent.
– DERIVATIVES **indelicacy** noun **indelicately** adverb.

indemnify /indemnifi/ • verb (**indemnifies, indemnified**) **1** compensate (someone) for harm or loss. **2** secure (someone) against legal responsibility for their actions.
– DERIVATIVES **indemnification** noun **indemnifier** noun.

indemnity /indemniti/ • noun (pl. **indemnities**) **1** security or protection against a loss or other financial burden. **2** security against or exemption from legal responsibility for one's actions. **3** a sum of money paid as compensation, especially by a country defeated in war.
– ORIGIN Latin *indemnitas*, from *indemnis* 'unhurt, free from loss'.

indent[1] • verb /indent/ **1** form deep recesses or notches in. **2** position or begin (a line or block of text) further from the margin than the main part of the text. **3** make a requisition or written order for something. • noun /indent/ **1** Brit. an official order or requisition for goods or stores. **2** a space left by indenting text. **3** an indentation.
– DERIVATIVES **indenter** noun **indentor** noun.
– ORIGIN Latin *indentare*, from *dens* 'tooth'.

indent[2] /indent/ • verb make a dent or depression in.

indentation • noun **1** the action of indenting or the state of being indented. **2** a deep recess or notch.

indenture /indenchər/ • noun **1** a formal agreement, contract, or list, formerly one of which copies with indented edges were made for the contracting parties. **2** an agreement binding an apprentice to a master. **3** historical a contract by which a person agreed to work for a set period for a colonial landowner in exchange for passage to the colony. • verb chiefly historical bind by an indenture.
– DERIVATIVES **indentureship** noun.

independence • noun the fact or state of being independent.

independent • adjective **1** free from outside control or influence. **2** (of a country) self governing. **3** not depending on another for livelihood or subsistence. **4** not connected with another; separate. **5** (of broadcasting, a school, etc.) not supported by public funds. • noun an independent person or body.
– DERIVATIVES **independency** noun **independently** adverb.

in-depth • adjective comprehensive and thorough.

indescribable • adjective too unusual, extreme, or indefinite to be adequately described.
– DERIVATIVES **indescribably** adverb.

indestructible • adjective not able to be destroyed.
– DERIVATIVES **indestructibility** noun **indestructibly** adverb.

indeterminable • adjective not able to be determined.

indeterminate /inditerminət/ • adjective **1** not exactly known, established, or defined. **2** Mathematics (of a quantity) having no definite or definable value.
– DERIVATIVES **indeterminacy** noun **indeterminately** adverb.

index /indeks/ • noun (pl. **indexes** or especially in technical use **indices** /indiseez/) **1** an alphabetical list of names, subjects, etc., with references to the places in a book where they occur. **2** an alphabetical list or catalogue of books or documents. **3** an indicator, sign, or measure of something. **4** a number representing the relative value or magnitude of something in terms of a standard: *a price index*. **5** Mathematics an exponent or other superscript or subscript number appended to a quantity. • verb **1** record in or provide with an index. **2** link the value of (prices, wages, etc.) automatically to the value of a price index.
– DERIVATIVES **indexable** adjective **indexation** noun **indexer** noun.
– ORIGIN Latin, 'forefinger, informer, sign'.

index finger • noun the forefinger.

index-linked • adjective Brit. adjusted according to the value of a retail price index.

India ink • noun North American term for INDIAN INK.

Indiaman • noun historical a ship engaged in trade with India or the East or West Indies.

Thesaurus

blurred, fuzzy, hazy, obscure, ambiguous, equivocal.
– OPPOSITES fixed, clear.

indefinitely • adverb FOR AN UNSPECIFIED PERIOD, for an unlimited period, without limit, sine die.

indelible • adjective INERADICABLE, permanent, lasting, persisting, enduring, unfading, unforgettable, haunting, never to be forgotten.

indelicate • adjective **1** *an indelicate question* INSENSITIVE, tactless, undiplomatic, impolitic, indiscreet. **2** *an indelicate sense of humour* VULGAR, rude, crude, bawdy, racy, risqué, ribald, earthy, indecent, improper, naughty, indecorous, off colour, dirty, smutty, salacious; *informal* blue, nudge-nudge, raunchy; *Brit. informal* saucy.

indemnify • verb **1** *he should be indemnified for his losses* REIMBURSE, compensate, recompense, repay, pay back, remunerate, recoup. **2** *they are indemnified against breach of contract* INSURE, guarantee, protect, secure, underwrite.

indemnity • noun **1** *no indemnity will be given for loss of cash* INSURANCE, assurance, protection, security, indemnification, surety, guarantee, warranty, safeguard. **2** *indemnity from prosecution* IMMUNITY, exemption, dispensation, freedom; special treatment, privilege. **3** *the company was paid $100,000 in indemnity* COMPENSATION, reimbursement, recompense, repayment, restitution, payment, redress, reparation(s), damages.

indent • verb **1** *a coastline indented by many fjords* NOTCH, make an indentation in, scallop, groove, furrow. **2** *you'll have to indent for a new uniform* ORDER, put in an order for, requisition, apply for, put in for, request, ask for, claim, put in a request/claim for, call for.
• noun *(Brit.) an indent for silk scarves* ORDER, requisition, purchase order, request, call, application; claim.

indentation • noun HOLLOW, depression, dent, dint, cavity, concavity, dip, pit, trough; dimple, cleft; snick, nick, notch; recess, bay, inlet, cove.

indenture • noun CONTRACT, agreement, covenant, compact, bond, warrant; certificate, deed, document, instrument.

independence • noun **1** *the struggle for American independence* SELF-GOVERNMENT, self-rule, home rule, self-determination, sovereignty, autonomy, non-alignment, freedom, liberty. **2** *he valued his independence* SELF-SUFFICIENCY, self-reliance. **3** *the adviser's independence* IMPARTIALITY, neutrality, disinterest, disinterestedness, detachment, objectivity. **4** *independence of spirit* FREEDOM, individualism, unconventionality, unorthodoxy.

independent • adjective **1** *an independent country* SELF-GOVERNING, self-ruling, self-determining, sovereign, autonomous, autarchic, free, non-aligned. **2** *two independent groups of biologists verified the results* SEPARATE, different, unconnected, unrelated, dissociated, discrete. **3** *an independent school* PRIVATE, non-state-run, private-sector, fee-paying; privatized, denationalized. **4** *her grown-up, independent children* SELF-SUFFICIENT, self-supporting, self-reliant, standing on one's own two feet. **5** *independent advice* IMPARTIAL, unbiased, unprejudiced, neutral, disinterested, uninvolved, uncommitted, detached, dispassionate, objective, non-partisan, non-discriminatory, with no axe to grind, without fear or favour. **6** *an independent spirit* FREETHINKING, free, individualistic, unconventional, maverick, bold, unconstrained, unfettered, untrammelled.
– OPPOSITES subservient, related, public, biased.

independently • adverb ALONE, on one's own, separately, unaccompanied, solo; unaided, unassisted, without help, by one's own efforts, under one's own steam, single-handed(ly), off one's own bat, on one's own initiative.

indescribable • adjective INEXPRESSIBLE, indefinable, beyond words/description, incommunicable, ineffable; unutterable, unspeakable; intense, extreme, acute, strong, powerful, profound; incredible, extraordinary, remarkable, prodigious.

indestructible • adjective UNBREAKABLE, shatterproof, durable; lasting, enduring, everlasting, perennial, deathless, undying, immortal, inextinguishable, imperishable; *poetic/literary* adamantine.
– OPPOSITES fragile.

indeterminate • adjective **1** *an indeterminate period of time* UNDETERMINED, uncertain, unknown, unspecified, unstipulated, indefinite, unfixed. **2** *indeterminate background noise* VAGUE, indefinite, unspecific, unclear, nebulous, indistinct; amorphous, shapeless, formless; hazy, faint, shadowy, dim.

index • noun **1** *the library's subject index* LIST, listing, inventory, catalogue, register, directory. **2** *literature is an index to the condition of civilization* GUIDE, sign, indication, indicator, measure, signal, mark, evidence, symptom, token; clue, hint. **3** *the index*

Indian • noun **1** a person from India. **2** an American Indian. • adjective **1** relating to India. **2** relating to American Indians.
– DERIVATIVES **Indianism** noun **Indianize** (also **Indianise**) verb **Indianness** noun.
– USAGE American native peoples were called **Indian** as a result of Christopher Columbus and others believing that, when they reached the east coast of America, they had reached part of India by a new route. The terms **Indian** and **Red Indian** are today regarded as old-fashioned, recalling, as they do, the stereotypical portraits of the Wild West. The term **American Indian**, however, is well established.
Indian club • noun each of a pair of bottle-shaped clubs swung to exercise the arms in gymnastics.
Indian corn • noun maize.
Indian file • noun single file.
Indian ink • noun deep black ink used especially in drawing and technical graphics.
– ORIGIN originally applied to Chinese and Japanese pigments imported to Europe via India.
Indian summer • noun a period of dry, warm weather occurring in late autumn.
India rubber • noun natural rubber.
indicate • verb **1** point out; show. **2** be a sign or symptom of. **3** state briefly or indirectly. **4** suggest as a desirable or necessary course of action. **5** chiefly Brit. (of a driver) use an indicator to signal an intention to change lanes or turn.
– DERIVATIVES **indication** noun.
– ORIGIN Latin *indicare*, from *dicare* 'make known'.
indicative /indikkətiv/ • adjective **1** serving as a sign or indication. **2** Grammar (of a form of a verb) expressing a simple statement of fact, rather than something imagined, wished, or commanded. • noun Grammar an indicative verb.
– DERIVATIVES **indicatively** adverb.
indicator • noun **1** a thing that indicates a state or level. **2** a gauge or meter of a specified kind. **3** a flashing light on a vehicle to show that it is about to change lanes or turn. **4** Brit. an information board or screen in a railway station, airport, etc. **5** Chemistry a compound which changes colour at a specific pH value or in the presence of a particular substance, and can be used to monitor a chemical change.
indices plural of INDEX.
indict /indīt/ • verb formally accuse or charge with a serious crime.
– DERIVATIVES **indictee** noun **indicter** noun.
– ORIGIN Latin *indicere* 'proclaim, appoint'.
indictable • adjective (of an offence) chargeable as a serious crime and warranting a trial by jury.
indictment • noun **1** Law a formal charge or accusation of a serious crime. **2** an indication that a system or situation is bad and deserves to be condemned.
indie informal • adjective (of a pop group or record label) not belonging or affiliated to a major record company.
indifferent • adjective **1** having no particular interest or sympathy; unconcerned. **2** not particularly good; mediocre.
– DERIVATIVES **indifference** noun **indifferently** adverb.
– ORIGIN Latin, 'making no difference'.
indigenize /indijinīz/ (also **indigenise**) • verb bring under the control of native people.
– DERIVATIVES **indigenization** noun.
indigenous • adjective originating or occurring naturally in a particular place; native.
– DERIVATIVES **indigenously** adverb **indigenousness** noun.
– ORIGIN from Latin *indigena* 'a native'.
indigent /indijənt/ • adjective poor; needy. • noun a needy person.
– DERIVATIVES **indigence** noun.
– ORIGIN Latin, from *indigere* 'to lack'.
indigestible • adjective **1** difficult or impossible to digest. **2** difficult to read or understand.
– DERIVATIVES **indigestibility** noun **indigestibly** adverb.
indigestion • noun pain or discomfort in the stomach caused by difficulty in digesting food.
– DERIVATIVES **indigestive** adjective.
indignation • noun annoyance provoked by what is perceived as unfair treatment.
– DERIVATIVES **indignant** adjective **indignantly** adverb.
– ORIGIN Latin, from *indignari* 'regard as unworthy'.
indignity • noun (pl. **indignities**) treatment or circumstances that cause one to feel shame or to lose one's dignity.
indigo /indigō/ • noun (pl. **indigos** or **indigoes**) **1** a dark blue

i

Thesaurus

jumped rapidly up the dial POINTER, indicator, needle, hand, finger, marker.
indicate • verb **1** *sales indicate a growing market for such art* POINT TO, be a sign of, be evidence of, evidence, demonstrate, show, testify to, bespeak, be a symptom of, be symptomatic of, denote, connote, mark, signal, signify, suggest, imply; manifest, reveal, betray, display, reflect, represent; *formal* evince; *poetic/literary* betoken. **2** *the president indicated his willingness to use force* STATE, declare, make known, announce, communicate, mention, reveal, divulge, disclose; put it on record; admit. **3** *please indicate your choice of prize on the form* SPECIFY, designate, stipulate; show. **4** *he indicated the room with a sweep of his arm* POINT TO, point out, gesture towards.
indicated • adjective *in such cases surgery is indicated* ADVISABLE, recommended, suggested, desirable, preferable, best, sensible, wise, commonsensical, prudent, in someone's (best) interests; necessary, needed, required, called for.
indication • noun SIGN, signal, indicator, symptom, mark, manifestation, demonstration, show, evidence; pointer, guide, hint, clue, intimation, omen, augury, portent, warning, forewarning.
indicative • adjective SYMPTOMATIC, expressive, suggestive, representative, symbolic, emblematic; typical, characteristic; *rare* indicatory.
indicator • noun **1** *these tests are a reliable indicator of performance* MEASURE, gauge, barometer, guide, index, mark, sign, signal; standard, touchstone, yardstick, benchmark, criterion, point of reference, guideline, test, litmus test. **2** *the depth indicator* METER, measuring device, measure, gauge, dial. **3** *a position indicator* POINTER, needle, hand, arrow, marker.
indict • verb CHARGE, accuse, arraign, take to court, put on trial, prosecute; summons, cite, prefer charges against; *N. Amer.* impeach.
– OPPOSITES acquit.
indictment • noun CHARGE, accusation, arraignment; citation, summons; *Brit.* plaint; *N. Amer.* impeachment.
indifference • noun **1** *his apparent indifference infuriated her* LACK OF CONCERN, unconcern, disinterest, lack of interest, lack of enthusiasm, apathy, nonchalance; boredom, unresponsiveness, impassivity, dispassion, detachment, coolness. **2** *the indifference of the midfield players* MEDIOCRITY, lack of distinction, amateurism, amateurishness, lack of inspiration.
indifferent • adjective **1** *an indifferent shrug* UNCONCERNED, uninterested, uncaring, casual, nonchalant, offhand, uninvolved, unenthusiastic, apathetic, lukewarm, phlegmatic; unimpressed, bored, unmoved, unresponsive, impassive, dispassionate, detached, cool. **2** *an indifferent performance* MEDIOCRE, ordinary, average, middling, middle-of-the-road, uninspired, undistinguished, unexceptional, unexciting, unremarkable, run-of-the-mill, pedestrian, prosaic, lacklustre, forgettable, amateur, amateurish; *informal* OK, so-so, fair-to-middling, no great shakes, not up to much; *Brit. informal* not much cop; *N. Amer. informal* bush-league; *NZ informal* half-pie.
– OPPOSITES enthusiastic, brilliant.
indigenous • adjective NATIVE, original, autochthonous, aboriginal; earliest, first.
indigent • adjective POOR, impecunious, destitute, penniless, impoverished, poverty-stricken; needy, in need, hard up, on the breadline, deprived, disadvantaged, badly off; *informal* on one's uppers, broke, flat broke, strapped (for cash), without a brass farthing, without a bean/sou, as poor as a church mouse, on one's beam-ends; *Brit. informal* stony broke, skint, boracic; *N. Amer. informal* on skid row; *formal* penurious.
– OPPOSITES rich.
indigestion • noun DYSPEPSIA, heartburn, pyrosis, acidity, stomach ache; (an) upset stomach, (a) stomach upset; *informal* bellyache, tummy ache, collywobbles.
indignant • adjective AGGRIEVED, resentful, affronted, disgruntled, displeased, angry, annoyed, cross, offended, exasperated, irritated, piqued, nettled, in high dudgeon, chagrined; *informal* peeved, vexed, irked, put out, miffed, aggravated, riled, in a huff; *Brit. informal* narked; *N. Amer. informal* sore.
indignation • noun RESENTMENT, umbrage, affront, disgruntlement, displeasure, anger, annoyance, irritation, exasperation, vexation, offence, pique; *informal* aggravation; *poetic/literary* ire.

dye obtained from a tropical plant. **2** a colour between blue and violet in the spectrum.
– ORIGIN Portuguese, from Greek *indikos* 'Indian (dye)'.
indirect • adjective **1** not direct. **2** (of costs) deriving from overhead charges or subsidiary work. **3** (of taxation) levied on goods and services rather than income or profits.
– DERIVATIVES **indirection** noun **indirectly** adverb **indirectness** noun.
indirect object • noun Grammar a noun phrase referring to a person or thing that is affected by the action of a transitive verb but is not the primary object (e.g. *him* in *give him the book*).
indirect question • noun Grammar a question in reported speech (e.g. *they asked who I was*).
indirect speech • noun another term for REPORTED SPEECH.
indiscernible /indisernib'l/ • adjective impossible to see or clearly distinguish.
– DERIVATIVES **indiscernibility** noun **indiscernibly** adverb.
indiscipline • noun lack of discipline.
indiscreet • adjective too ready to reveal things that should remain secret or private.
– DERIVATIVES **indiscreetly** adverb.
indiscretion • noun **1** indiscreet behaviour. **2** an indiscreet act or remark.
indiscriminate /indiskrimminət/ • adjective done or acting at random or without careful judgement.
– DERIVATIVES **indiscriminately** adverb **indiscriminateness** noun.
indispensable • adjective absolutely necessary.
– DERIVATIVES **indispensability** noun **indispensableness** noun **indispensably** adverb.
indisposed • adjective **1** slightly unwell. **2** unwilling.
indisposition • noun **1** a slight illness. **2** unwillingness.
indisputable • adjective unable to be challenged or denied.
– DERIVATIVES **indisputability** noun **indisputably** adverb.
indissoluble /indisolyoob'l/ • adjective unable to be destroyed; lasting.
– DERIVATIVES **indissolubility** noun **indissolubly** adverb.
indistinct • adjective not clear or sharply defined.
– DERIVATIVES **indistinctly** adverb **indistinctness** noun.
indistinguishable • adjective not able to be identified as different or distinct.
– DERIVATIVES **indistinguishably** adverb.
indium /indiəm/ • noun a soft, silvery-white metallic chemical element resembling zinc, used in some alloys and semiconductor devices.
– ORIGIN from INDIGO (because there are two characteristic indigo lines in its spectrum).
individual • adjective **1** single; separate. **2** of or for one particular person. **3** striking or unusual; original. • noun **1** a single human being or item as distinct from a group. **2** a distinctive or original person.
– DERIVATIVES **individualize** (also **individualise**) verb **individually** adverb.
– ORIGIN originally in the sense 'indivisible': from Latin *in-* 'not' + *dividere* 'to divide'.
individualism • noun **1** independence and self-reliance. **2** a social theory favouring freedom of action for individuals.
– DERIVATIVES **individualist** noun & adjective **individualistic** adjective.

i

Thesaurus

indignity • noun SHAME, humiliation, loss of self-respect, loss of pride, loss of face, embarrassment, mortification; disgrace, dishonour, stigma, discredit; affront, insult, abuse, mistreatment, injury, offence, injustice, slight, snub, discourtesy, disrespect; *informal* slap in the face, kick in the teeth.
indirect • adjective **1** *an indirect effect* INCIDENTAL, accidental, unintended, secondary, subordinate, ancillary, collateral, concomitant, contingent. **2** *the indirect route* ROUNDABOUT, circuitous, wandering, meandering, serpentine, winding, tortuous, zigzag. **3** *an indirect attack* OBLIQUE, inexplicit, implicit, implied, allusive.
indirectly • adverb **1** *I heard of the damage indirectly* SECOND-HAND, at second hand, from others; *informal* on the grapevine, on the bush/jungle telegraph. **2** *he referred to the subject indirectly* OBLIQUELY, by implication, allusively.
indiscernible • adjective **1** *an almost indiscernible change* UNNOTICEABLE, imperceptible, invisible, undetectable, indistinguishable, inappreciable, hidden; tiny, minute, minuscule, microscopic, infinitesimal, negligible, inconsequential. **2** *an indiscernible shape* INDISTINCT, nebulous, unclear, fuzzy, obscure, vague, indefinite, amorphous, shadowy, dim, hard to make out.
– OPPOSITES distinct.
indiscreet • adjective **1** *an indiscreet remark* IMPRUDENT, unwise, impolitic, injudicious, incautious, irresponsible, ill-judged, ill-advised, misguided, ill-considered, careless, rash, unwary, hasty, reckless, precipitate, impulsive, foolhardy, foolish, short-sighted; undiplomatic, indelicate, tactless, insensitive; inexpedient, untimely, infelicitous. **2** *her indiscreet behaviour* IMMODEST, indecorous, unseemly, improper, indecent, indelicate.
indiscretion • noun **1** *he was prone to indiscretion* IMPRUDENCE, injudiciousness, incaution, irresponsibility; carelessness, rashness, recklessness, precipitateness, impulsiveness, foolhardiness, foolishness, folly; tactlessness, insensitivity. **2** *his past indiscretions* BLUNDER, lapse, gaffe, mistake, faux pas, error, slip, miscalculation, impropriety; misdemeanour, transgression, peccadillo, misdeed; *informal* slip-up.
indiscriminate • adjective NON-SELECTIVE, unselective, undiscriminating, uncritical, aimless, hit-or-miss, haphazard, random, arbitrary, unsystematic, undirected; wholesale, general, sweeping, blanket; thoughtless, unthinking, unconsidered, casual, careless.
– OPPOSITES selective.
indispensable • adjective ESSENTIAL, necessary, all-important, of the utmost importance, of the essence, vital, crucial, key, needed, required, requisite; invaluable.
– OPPOSITES superfluous.
indisposed • adjective **1** *my wife is indisposed* ILL, unwell, sick, on the sick list, poorly, ailing, not (very) well, out of sorts, under/below par; out of action, hors de combat; *Brit.* off colour; *informal* under the weather. **2** *she was indisposed to help him* RELUCTANT, unwilling, disinclined, loath, unprepared, not disposed, not minded, averse.
– OPPOSITES well, willing.
indisposition • noun **1** *a mild indisposition* ILLNESS, malady, ailment, disorder, sickness, disease, infection; condition, complaint, problem; *informal* bug, virus; *Brit. informal* lurgy. **2** *his indisposition to leave the house* RELUCTANCE, unwillingness, disinclination, aversion.
indisputable • adjective INCONTROVERTIBLE, incontestable, undeniable, irrefutable, unassailable, beyond dispute, unquestionable, beyond question, indubitable, not in doubt, beyond doubt, beyond a shadow of a doubt, unarguable, undebatable, airtight, watertight; unequivocal, unmistakable, certain, sure, definite, definitive, proven, decisive, conclusive, demonstrable, self-evident, clear, clear-cut, plain, obvious, manifest, patent, palpable.
– OPPOSITES questionable.
indistinct • adjective **1** *the distant shoreline was indistinct* BLURRED, out of focus, fuzzy, hazy, misty, foggy, cloudy, shadowy, dim, nebulous; unclear, obscure, vague, faint, indistinguishable, barely perceptible, hard to see, hard to make out. **2** *the last two digits are indistinct* INDECIPHERABLE, illegible, unreadable, hard to read. **3** *indistinct sounds* MUFFLED, muted, low, quiet, soft, faint, inaudible, hard to hear; muttered, mumbled.
– OPPOSITES clear.
indistinguishable • adjective **1** *the two girls were indistinguishable* IDENTICAL, difficult to tell apart, like (two) peas in a pod, like Tweedledum and Tweedledee, very similar, two of a kind. **2** *his words were indistinguishable* UNINTELLIGIBLE, incomprehensible, hard to make out, indistinct, unclear; inaudible.
– OPPOSITES unalike, clear.
individual • adjective **1** *exhibitions devoted to individual artists* SINGLE, separate, discrete, independent; sole, lone, solitary, isolated. **2** *he had his own individual style of music* CHARACTERISTIC, distinctive, distinct, typical, particular, peculiar, personal, personalized, special. **3** *a chic and highly individual apartment* ORIGINAL, unique, exclusive, singular, idiosyncratic, different, unusual, novel, unorthodox, atypical, out of the ordinary.
• noun **1** *Peter was a rather stuffy individual* PERSON, human being, mortal, soul, creature; man, boy, woman, girl; character, personage; *informal* type, sort, beggar, cookie, customer, guy, geezer, devil, bastard; *Brit. informal* bod, gent, punter; *informal, dated* body, cove; *archaic* wight. **2** *she was a real individual* INDIVIDUALIST, free spirit, nonconformist, original, eccentric, character, maverick, rare bird; *Brit. informal* one-off.
individualism • noun INDEPENDENCE, freethinking, freedom of thought, originality; unconventionality, eccentricity.
individualist • noun FREE SPIRIT, individual, nonconformist, ori-

individuality ● noun **1** distinctive quality or character. **2** separate existence.

individuate ● verb distinguish from others of the same kind; single out.

– DERIVATIVES **individuation** noun.

indivisible ● adjective **1** unable to be divided or separated. **2** (of a number) unable to be divided by another number exactly without leaving a remainder.

– DERIVATIVES **indivisibility** noun **indivisibly** adverb.

Indo-Chinese ● adjective relating to the peninsula of Indo-China, which contains Burma (Myanmar), Thailand, Malaya, Laos, Cambodia, and Vietnam.

indoctrinate /indoktrinayt/ ● verb cause to accept a set of beliefs uncritically through repeated instruction.

– DERIVATIVES **indoctrination** noun **indoctrinator** noun.

– ORIGIN originally in the sense 'teach or instruct': from French *endoctriner*, from *doctrine* 'doctrine'.

Indo-European ● noun **1** the family of languages spoken over the greater part of Europe and Asia as far as northern India. **3** a speaker of an Indo-European language. ● adjective relating to Indo-European languages.

indolent /indələnt/ ● adjective wanting to avoid activity or exertion; lazy.

– DERIVATIVES **indolence** noun **indolently** adverb.

– ORIGIN Latin, from *in-* 'not' + *dolere* 'suffer or give pain'.

indomitable /indommitəb'l/ ● adjective impossible to subdue or defeat.

– DERIVATIVES **indomitability** noun **indomitableness** noun **indomitably** adverb.

– ORIGIN Latin *indomitabilis*, from *in-* 'not' + *domitare* 'to tame'.

Indonesian ● noun **1** a person from Indonesia. **2** the group of languages spoken in Indonesia. ● adjective relating to Indonesia.

indoor ● adjective situated, conducted, or used within a building or under cover.

indoors ● adverb into or within a building. ● noun the area or space inside a building.

indorse ● verb US & Law variant spelling of ENDORSE.

indorsement ● noun US & Law variant spelling of ENDORSEMENT.

indrawn ● adjective **1** (of breath) taken in. **2** (of a person) shy and introspective.

indubitable /indyoobitəb'l/ ● adjective impossible to doubt; unquestionable.

– DERIVATIVES **indubitably** adverb.

– ORIGIN Latin *indubitabilis*, from *in-* 'not' + *dubitare* 'to doubt'.

induce /indyooss/ ● verb **1** succeed in persuading or leading (someone) to do something. **2** bring about or give rise to. **3** produce (an electric charge or current or a magnetic state) by induction. **4** Medicine bring on (childbirth or abortion) artificially.

– DERIVATIVES **inducer** noun **inducible** adjective.

– ORIGIN Latin *inducere* 'lead in'.

inducement ● noun **1** a thing that persuades or leads someone to do something. **2** a bribe.

induct ● verb **1** admit formally to a post or organization. **2** US enlist (someone) for military service.

– DERIVATIVES **inductee** noun.

– ORIGIN Latin *inducere* 'lead in'.

inductance ● noun Physics the property of an electric conductor or circuit that causes an electromotive force to be generated by a change in the current flowing.

induction ● noun **1** the action or process of inducting someone to a post, organization, etc. **2** the action or process of inducing something. **3** Logic the inference of a general law from particular instances. **4** the production of an electric or magnetic state by the proximity (without contact) of an electrified or magnetized body. **5** the drawing of the fuel mixture into the cylinders of an internal-combustion engine.

induction coil ● noun a coil for generating intermittent high voltage from a direct current.

induction loop ● noun a sound system in which a loop of wire around an area in a building produces an electromagnetic signal received directly by hearing aids.

inductive ● adjective **1** Logic characterized by the inference of general laws from particular instances. **2** relating to electric or magnetic induction. **3** Physics possessing inductance.

– DERIVATIVES **inductively** adverb **inductiveness** noun **inductivism** noun **inductivist** noun & adjective.

inductor ● noun a circuit component which possesses inductance.

indue ● verb variant spelling of ENDUE.

indulge ● verb **1** (**indulge in**) allow oneself to enjoy the pleasure of. **2** satisfy or yield freely to (a desire or interest). **3** allow (someone) to do or have something.

– DERIVATIVES **indulger** noun.

– ORIGIN Latin *indulgere* 'give free rein to'.

indulgence ● noun **1** the action or fact of indulging. **2** a thing that is indulged in; a luxury. **3** the state or attitude of being in-

i

Thesaurus

ginal, eccentric, maverick, rare bird; *Brit. informal* one-off.

– OPPOSITES conformist.

individualistic ● adjective UNCONVENTIONAL, unorthodox, atypical, singular, unique, original, nonconformist, independent, freethinking; eccentric, maverick, strange, odd, peculiar, idiosyncratic.

individuality ● noun DISTINCTIVENESS, distinction, uniqueness, originality, singularity, particularity, peculiarity, differentness, separateness; personality, character, identity, self.

individually ● adverb ONE AT A TIME, one by one, singly, separately, severally, independently, apart.

– OPPOSITES together.

indoctrinate ● verb BRAINWASH, propagandize, proselytize, inculcate, re-educate, persuade, convince, condition, discipline, mould; instruct, teach, school, drill.

indolence ● noun LAZINESS, idleness, slothfulness, sloth, shiftlessness, inactivity, inaction, inertia, sluggishness, lethargy, languor, languidness, torpor; *poetic/literary* hebetude.

indolent ● adjective LAZY, idle, slothful, loafing, work-shy, do-nothing, sluggardly, shiftless, lackadaisical, languid, inactive, inert, sluggish, lethargic, torpid; slack, lax, remiss, negligent, good-for-nothing, feckless; *informal* bone idle.

– OPPOSITES industrious, energetic.

indomitable ● adjective INVINCIBLE, unconquerable, unbeatable, unassailable, invulnerable, unshakeable; indefatigable, unyielding, unbending, stalwart, stout-hearted, lionhearted, strong-willed, strong-minded, staunch, resolute, firm, steadfast, determined, intransigent, inflexible, adamant; unflinching, courageous, brave, valiant, heroic, intrepid, fearless, plucky, mettlesome, gritty, steely.

– OPPOSITES submissive.

indubitable ● adjective UNQUESTIONABLE, undoubtable, indisputable, unarguable, undebatable, incontestable, undeniable, irrefutable, incontrovertible, unmistakable, unequivocal, certain, sure, positive, definite, absolute, conclusive, watertight; beyond doubt, beyond the shadow of a doubt, beyond dispute, beyond question, not in question, not in doubt.

– OPPOSITES doubtful.

induce ● verb **1** *the pickets induced many workers to stay away* PERSUADE, convince, prevail upon, get, make, prompt, move, inspire, influence, encourage, motivate; coax into, wheedle into, cajole into, talk into, prod into; *informal* twist someone's arm. **2** *these activities induce a feeling of togetherness* BRING ABOUT, cause, produce, effect, create, give rise to, generate, instigate, engender, occasion, set in motion, lead to, result in, trigger off, spark off, whip up, stir up, kindle, arouse, rouse, foster, promote, encourage; *poetic/literary* beget, enkindle.

– OPPOSITES dissuade, prevent.

inducement ● noun INCENTIVE, encouragement, attraction, temptation, stimulus, bait, lure, pull, draw, spur, goad, impetus, motive, motivation, provocation; bribe, reward; *informal* carrot, come-on, sweetener.

– OPPOSITES deterrent.

induct ● verb **1** *the new ministers were inducted into the government* ADMIT TO, allow into, introduce to, initiate into, install in, instate in, swear into; appoint to. **2** *he inducted me into the skills of magic* INTRODUCE TO, acquaint with, familiarize with, make conversant with; ground in, instruct in, teach in, educate in, school in.

indulge ● verb **1** *Sally indulged her passion for long walks* SATISFY, gratify, fulfil, feed, accommodate; yield to, give in to, give way to. **2** *she indulged in a fit of sulks* WALLOW IN, give oneself up to, give way to, yield to, abandon oneself to, give free rein to; luxuriate in, revel in, lose oneself in. **3** *she did not like her children to be indulged* PAMPER, spoil, overindulge, coddle, mollycoddle, cosset, baby, pet, spoon-feed, feather-bed, wrap in cotton wool; pander to, wait on hand and foot, cater to someone's every whim, kill with kindness; *archaic* cocker.

– OPPOSITES frustrate.

dulgent or tolerant. **4** an extension of the time in which a bill or debt has to be paid. **5** chiefly historical (in the Roman Catholic Church) the setting aside or cancellation by the Pope of the punishment still due for sins after absolution.

indulgent • adjective **1** readily indulging someone or overlooking their faults; tolerant or lenient. **2** self-indulgent.
– DERIVATIVES **indulgently** adverb.

industrial • adjective of, used in, or characterized by industry.
– DERIVATIVES **industrially** adverb.

industrial action • noun Brit. action taken by employees of a company as a protest, especially striking or working to rule.

industrial archaeology • noun the study of equipment and buildings formerly used in industry.

industrial estate (N. Amer. **industrial park**) • noun chiefly Brit. an area of land developed as a site for factories and other industrial use.

industrialism • noun a social or economic system in which manufacturing industries are prevalent.

industrialist • noun a person involved in the ownership and management of industry.

industrialize (also **industrialise**) • verb (often as adj. **industrialized**) develop industries in (a country or region) on a wide scale.
– DERIVATIVES **industrialization** noun.

industrial relations • plural noun the relations between management and workers in industry.

industrial-strength • adjective very strong or powerful.

industrious • adjective diligent and hard-working.
– DERIVATIVES **industriously** adverb **industriousness** noun.

industry • noun (pl. **industries**) **1** economic activity concerned with the processing of raw materials and manufacture of goods in factories. **2** a particular branch of economic or commercial activity. **3** hard work.
– ORIGIN Latin *industria* 'diligence'.

-ine[1] • suffix (forming adjectives) belonging to; resembling: *canine*.
– ORIGIN from French *-in, -ine* or Latin *-inus*.

-ine[2] • suffix forming adjectives from the names of minerals, plants, etc.: *crystalline*.
– ORIGIN Greek *-inos*.

-ine[3] • suffix forming feminine nouns such as *heroine*.
– ORIGIN from Greek *-inē* or German *-in*.

-ine[4] • suffix **1** forming chiefly abstract nouns and diminutives such as *doctrine, medicine*. **2** Chemistry forming names of alkaloids, halogens, amino acids, and other substances: *cocaine*.
– ORIGIN Latin *-ina*.

inebriate • verb /ineebriayt/ make drunk; intoxicate. • adjective /ineebriət/ drunk; intoxicated.
– DERIVATIVES **inebriation** noun **inebriety** noun.
– ORIGIN Latin *inebriare* 'intoxicate'.

inedible • adjective not fit for eating.

ineducable /inedyookəb'l/ • adjective considered incapable of being educated.

ineffable /ineffəb'l/ • adjective **1** too great or extreme to be expressed in words. **2** too sacred to be uttered.
– DERIVATIVES **ineffability** noun **ineffably** adverb
– ORIGIN Latin *ineffabilis*, from *in-* 'not' + *effari* 'utter'

ineffective • adjective not producing any or the desired effect.
– DERIVATIVES **ineffectively** adverb **ineffectiveness** noun.

ineffectual • adjective **1** not producing any or the desired effect. **2** lacking adequate forcefulness in a role or situation.
– DERIVATIVES **ineffectuality** noun **ineffectually** adverb **ineffectualness** noun.

inefficient • adjective not achieving maximum productivity; failing to make the best use of time or resources.
– DERIVATIVES **inefficiency** noun **inefficiently** adverb.

inelastic • adjective (of a material) not elastic.
– DERIVATIVES **inelastically** adverb **inelasticity** noun.

inelegant • adjective lacking elegance or refinement.
– DERIVATIVES **inelegance** noun **inelegantly** adverb.

ineligible • adjective not eligible.
– DERIVATIVES **ineligibility** noun **ineligibly** adverb.

ineluctable /iniluktəb'l/ • adjective unable to be resisted or avoided; inescapable.
– DERIVATIVES **ineluctability** noun **ineluctably** adverb.
– ORIGIN Latin *ineluctabilis*, from *in-* 'not' + *eluctari* 'struggle out'.

inept • adjective incompetent; awkward or clumsy.
– DERIVATIVES **ineptitude** noun **ineptly** adverb **ineptness** noun.

Thesaurus

– PHRASES **indulge oneself** TREAT ONESELF, give oneself a treat; have a spree, splash out; *informal* go to town, splurge.

indulgence • noun **1** *the indulgence of all his desires* SATISFACTION, gratification, fulfilment. **2** *excess indulgence contributed to his ill-health* SELF-GRATIFICATION, self-indulgence, overindulgence, intemperance, immoderation, excess, excessiveness, lack of restraint, extravagance, decadence, pleasure-seeking, sybaritism. **3** *they viewed holidays as an indulgence* EXTRAVAGANCE, luxury, treat, non-essential, extra, frill. **4** *her indulgence left him spoilt* PAMPERING, coddling, mollycoddling, cosseting, babying. **5** *his parents view his lapses with indulgence* TOLERANCE, forbearance, understanding, kindess, compassion, sympathy, forgiveness, leniency.

indulgent • adjective GENEROUS, permissive, easy-going, liberal, tolerant, forgiving, forbearing, lenient, kind, kindly, soft-hearted, compassionate, understanding, sympathetic; fond, doting, soft; compliant, obliging, accommodating.
– OPPOSITES strict.

industrial • adjective **1** *industrial areas of the city* MANUFACTURING, factory; commercial, business, trade. **2** *(Brit.) industrial action* STRIKE, protest.

industrialist • noun MANUFACTURER, producer, factory owner; captain of industry, big businessman, magnate, tycoon, capitalist, financier; *informal, derogatory* fat cat.

industrious • adjective HARD-WORKING, diligent, assiduous, conscientious, steady, painstaking, sedulous, persevering, unflagging, untiring, tireless, indefatigable, studious; busy, as busy as a bee, active, bustling, energetic, on the go, vigorous, determined, dynamic, zealous, productive; with one's shoulder to the wheel, with one's nose to the grindstone.
– OPPOSITES indolent.

industry • noun **1** *British industry* MANUFACTURING, production; construction. **2** *the publishing industry* BUSINESS, trade, field, line (of business); *informal* racket. **3** *the kitchen was a hive of industry* ACTIVITY, busyness, energy, vigour, productiveness; hard work, industriousness, diligence, application, dedication.

inebriated • adjective DRUNK, intoxicated, drunken, incapable, tipsy, the worse for drink, under the influence; *informal* tight, merry, in one's cups, three sheets to the wind, pie-eyed, plastered, smashed, wrecked, wasted, sloshed, soused, sozzled, blotto, stewed, pickled, tanked (up), off one's face, out of one's head, ratted; *Brit. informal* legless, bevvied, paralytic, Brahms and Liszt, half cut, out of it, bladdered, trolleyed, squiffy, tiddly; *N. Amer. informal* loaded, trashed, juiced, sauced, out of one's gourd, in the bag, zoned; *euphemistic* tired and emotional; *informal, dated* lit up.
– OPPOSITES sober.

inedible • adjective UNEATABLE, indigestible, unsavoury, unpalatable, unwholesome; stale, rotten, off, bad.

ineffable • adjective **1** *the ineffable beauty of the Everglades* INDESCRIBABLE, inexpressible, beyond words; undefinable, unutterable, untold, unimaginable; overwhelming, breathtaking, staggering, amazing, awesome. **2** *the ineffable name of God* UNUTTERABLE, unmentionable; taboo, forbidden, off limits; *informal* no go.

ineffective • adjective **1** *an ineffective scheme* UNSUCCESSFUL, unproductive, fruitless, unprofitable, abortive, futile, purposeless, worthless, useless, ineffectual, inefficient, inefficacious, inadequate; feeble, inept, lame; *archaic* bootless. **2** *an ineffective president* INEFFECTUAL, inefficient, inefficacious, unsuccessful, powerless, impotent, inadequate, incompetent, incapable, unfit, inept, weak, poor; *informal* useless, hopeless.

ineffectual • adjective. See INEFFECTIVE senses 1, 2.

inefficacious • adjective. See INEFFECTIVE sense 1.

inefficient • adjective **1** *an inefficient worker* INEFFECTIVE, ineffectual, incompetent, inept, incapable, unfit, unskilful, inexpert, amateurish; disorganized, unprepared; negligent, lax, sloppy, slack, careless; *informal* lousy, useless. **2** *inefficient processes* UNECONOMICAL, wasteful, unproductive, time-wasting, slow; deficient, disorganized, unsystematic.

inelegant • adjective **1** *an inelegant bellow of laughter* UNREFINED, uncouth, unsophisticated, unpolished, uncultivated; ill-bred, coarse, vulgar, rude, impolite, unmannerly. **2** *inelegant dancing* GRACELESS, ungraceful, ungainly, uncoordinated, awkward, clumsy, lumbering; inept, unskilful, inexpert; *informal* having two left feet.
– OPPOSITES refined, graceful.

ineligible • adjective **1** *we are ineligible for a grant* UNQUALIFIED, ruled out, disqualified, disentitled; *Law* incompetent. **2** *(dated) she*

inferiority complex ● noun a feeling of general inadequacy caused by actual or supposed inferiority, marked by aggressive behaviour or withdrawal.

infernal ● adjective **1** relating to hell or the underworld. **2** informal terrible; awful.
– DERIVATIVES **infernally** adverb.
– ORIGIN Latin *infernus* 'below, underground'.

inferno ● noun (pl. **infernos**) **1** a large uncontrollable fire. **2** (**Inferno**) hell.
– ORIGIN Italian, from Latin *infernus* 'below, underground'; sense 2 is with reference to *The Divine Comedy* (*c.*1309–20) by the Italian poet Dante.

infertile ● adjective **1** unable to reproduce. **2** (of land) unable to sustain crops or vegetation.
– DERIVATIVES **infertility** noun.

infest ● verb (of insects or organisms) be present in large numbers, typically so as to cause damage or disease.
– DERIVATIVES **infestation** noun.
– ORIGIN originally in the sense 'torment, harass': from Latin *infestare* 'assail'.

infibulation ● noun the practice in some societies of removing the clitoris and labia of a girl or woman and stitching together the edges of the vulva to prevent sexual intercourse.
– DERIVATIVES **infibulate** verb.
– ORIGIN from Latin *infibulare* 'fasten with a clasp'.

infidel /infid'l/ ● noun chiefly archaic a person who has no religion or whose religion is not that of the majority.
– ORIGIN Latin *infidelis*, from *in-* 'not' + *fidelis* 'faithful'.

infidelity ● noun (pl. **infidelities**) **1** the action or state of being sexually unfaithful. **2** lack of religious faith.

infield ● noun Cricket the part of the field closer to the wicket. ● adverb into or towards the infield.
– DERIVATIVES **infielder** noun.

infighting ● noun conflict within a group or organization.
– DERIVATIVES **infighter** noun.

infill ● noun (also **infilling**) material or buildings used to fill a space or hole. ● verb fill or block up (a space or hole).

infiltrate /infiltrayt/ ● verb **1** surreptitiously and gradually enter or gain access to (an organization or place). **2** permeate or cause to permeate by filtration.
– DERIVATIVES **infiltration** noun **infiltrator** noun.

infinite /infinit/ ● adjective **1** limitless in space, extent, or size. **2** very great in amount or degree.
– DERIVATIVES **infinitely** adverb **infiniteness** noun **infinitude** noun.
– ORIGIN Latin *infinitus*.

infinitesimal /infinitessim'l/ ● adjective extremely small.
– DERIVATIVES **infinitesimally** adverb.
– ORIGIN Latin *infinitesimus*, from *infinitus* 'infinite'.

infinitesimal calculus ● noun see CALCULUS.

infinitive /infinnitiv/ ● noun the basic form of a verb, without an inflection binding it to a particular subject or tense (normally occurring in English with the word *to*, as in *to see, to ask*).
– ORIGIN from Latin *infinitus*, from *in-* 'not' + *finitus* 'finished, finite'.

infinity ● noun (pl. **infinities**) **1** the state or quality of being infinite. **2** a very great number or amount. **3** Mathematics a number greater than any assignable quantity or countable number (symbol ∞). **4** a point in space or time that is or seems infinitely distant.

infirm ● adjective physically weak.
– ORIGIN Latin *infirmus*, from *in-* 'not' + *firmus* 'firm'.

infirmary ● noun (pl. **infirmaries**) a hospital or place set aside for the care of the sick or injured.

infirmity ● noun (pl. **infirmities**) physical or mental weakness.

in flagrante delicto /in fləgrantay diliktō/ ● adverb in the very act of wrongdoing, especially in an act of sexual misconduct.
– ORIGIN Latin, 'in the heat of the crime'.

inflame ● verb **1** intensify or aggravate. **2** provoke (someone) to strong feelings. **3** cause inflammation in.

inflammable ● adjective easily set on fire. ● noun a substance which is easily set on fire.
– DERIVATIVES **inflammability** noun **inflammableness** noun **inflammably** adverb.
– USAGE The words **inflammable** and **flammable** both mean 'easily set on fire'. It is, however, safer to use **flammable** if one wishes to avoid ambiguity, as the *in-* prefix of **inflammable** can give the impression that the word means 'non-flammable'.

i

Thesaurus

lower-ranking, subordinate, second-fiddle, junior, minor, lowly, humble, menial, beneath one. **2** *inferior accommodation* SECOND-RATE, substandard, low-quality, low-grade, unsatisfactory, shoddy, deficient; poor, bad, awful, dreadful, wretched; *Brit.* downmarket; *informal* crummy, dire, rotten, lousy, third-rate; *Brit. informal* duff, rubbish, ropy, dodgy.
– OPPOSITES superior, luxury.
● noun *how dare she treat him as an inferior?* SUBORDINATE, junior, underling, minion.

infernal ● adjective **1** *the infernal regions* HELLISH, lower, nether, subterranean, underworld, chthonic; Hadean, Tartarean. **2** *(informal) an infernal nuisance* DAMNABLE, wretched; annoying, irritating, infuriating, exasperating; *informal* damned, damn, flaming, blasted, blessed, pesky, aggravating; *Brit. informal* blinking, blooming, flipping; *Brit. informal, dated* bally, ruddy.

infertile ● adjective **1** *infertile soil* BARREN, unfruitful, unproductive, uncultivatable; sterile, impoverished, arid. **2** *she was infertile* STERILE, barren; childless; *Medicine* infecund.

infest ● verb OVERRUN, spread through, invade, infiltrate, pervade, permeate, inundate, overwhelm; beset, plague.

infested ● adjective OVERRUN, swarming, teeming, crawling, alive, ridden; plagued, beset.

infidel ● noun UNBELIEVER, disbeliever, non-believer, agnostic, atheist; heathen, pagan, idolater, idolatress, heretic, freethinker, dissenter, nonconformist; *archaic* paynim; *rare* nullifidian.

infidelity ● noun UNFAITHFULNESS, adultery, unchastity; faithlessness, disloyalty, treachery, double-dealing, duplicity, deceit; affair; *informal* playing around, fooling around, cheating, two-timing; *formal* fornication; *dated* cuckoldry.

infiltrate ● verb **1** *he infiltrated the smuggling operation* INSINUATE ONESELF INTO, worm one's way into, sneak into, invade, intrude on, butt into; *informal* gatecrash, muscle in on. **2** *mineral solutions infiltrate the rocks* PERMEATE, penetrate, pervade, soak into, seep into/through, get into, enter.

infiltrator ● noun SPY, (secret) agent, plant, intruder, interloper, subversive, informant, informer, mole, entrist, entryist; *N. Amer. informal* spook.

infinite ● adjective **1** *the universe is infinite* BOUNDLESS, unbounded, unlimited, limitless, never-ending, interminable; immeasurable, fathomless; extensive, vast. **2** *an infinite number of birds* COUNTLESS, uncountable, inestimable, innumerable, numberless, immeasurable, incalculable, untold; great, huge, enormous. **3** *she bathed him with infinite care* GREAT, immense, supreme, absolute, real; *informal* no end of.
– OPPOSITES limited, small.

infinitesimal ● adjective MINUTE, tiny, minuscule, very small; microscopic, imperceptible, indiscernible; *Scottish* wee; *informal* teeny, teeny-weeny, itsy-bitsy, tiddly; *Brit. informal* titchy; *N. Amer. informal* little-bitty.
– OPPOSITES huge.

infinity ● noun **1** *the infinity of space* ENDLESSNESS, infinitude, infiniteness, boundlessness, limitlessness; vastness, immensity. **2** *an infinity of different molecules* INFINITE NUMBER; abundance, profusion, host, multitude, mass, wealth; *informal* heap, stack.

infirm ● adjective **1** *she cares for infirm people* FRAIL, weak, feeble, debilitated, decrepit, disabled; ill, unwell, sick, sickly, poorly, indisposed, ailing. **2** *(archaic) he was infirm of purpose* WEAK, uncertain, indefinite, indecisive, irresolute, unresolved, undecided; wavering, vacillating.
– OPPOSITES healthy, strong.

infirmity ● noun **1** *they were excused due to infirmity* FRAILTY, weakness, feebleness, delicacy, debility, decrepitude; disability, impairment; illness, sickness, indisposition, poor health. **2** *the infirmities of old age* AILMENT, malady, illness, disease, disorder, sickness, affliction, complaint, indisposition.

inflame ● verb **1** *the play inflames anti-semitism* INCITE, arouse, rouse, provoke, stir up, whip up, kindle, ignite, touch off, foment, inspire, stimulate, agitate. **2** *he inflamed a sensitive situation* AGGRAVATE, exacerbate, intensify, worsen, compound. **3** *his opinions inflamed his rival* ENRAGE, incense, anger, madden, infuriate, exasperate, provoke, antagonize, rile; *informal* make someone see red, make someone's blood boil.
– OPPOSITES calm, soothe, placate.

inflamed ● adjective SWOLLEN, puffed up; red, hot, burning, itchy; raw, sore, painful, tender; infected, septic.

inflammable ● adjective FLAMMABLE, combustible, incendiary, ig-

inflammation ● noun a condition in which an area of the skin or body becomes reddened, swollen, hot, and often painful, especially as a reaction to injury or infection.

inflammatory ● adjective **1** relating to or causing inflammation. **2** arousing or intended to arouse angry or violent feelings.

inflatable ● adjective capable of being inflated. ● noun a plastic or rubber object that is inflated before use.

inflate ● verb **1** expand by filling with air or gas. **2** increase by a large or excessive amount. **3** exaggerate. **4** bring about inflation of (a currency) or in (an economy).
– ORIGIN Latin *inflare* 'blow into'.

inflation ● noun **1** the action of inflating or the condition of being inflated. **2** a general increase in prices and fall in the purchasing value of money.
– DERIVATIVES **inflationary** adjective **inflationism** noun **inflationist** noun & adjective.

inflect ● verb **1** Grammar change or be changed by inflection. **2** vary the intonation or pitch of (the voice). **3** technical bend or deflect inwards.
– DERIVATIVES **inflective** adjective.
– ORIGIN Latin *inflectere*, from *in-* 'into' + *flectere* 'to bend'.

inflection (chiefly Brit. also **inflexion**) ● noun **1** Grammar a change in the form of a word (typically the ending) to express a grammatical function or attribute such as tense, mood, person, number, case, and gender. **2** a variation in intonation or pitch of the voice. **3** chiefly Mathematics a change of curvature from convex to concave.
– DERIVATIVES **inflectional** adjective **inflectionally** adverb **inflectionless** adjective.

i

inflexible ● adjective **1** not able to be altered or adapted. **2** unwilling to change or compromise. **3** not able to be bent; stiff.
– DERIVATIVES **inflexibility** noun **inflexibly** adverb.

inflict ● verb (**inflict on**) **1** cause (something unpleasant or painful) to be suffered by. **2** impose (something unwelcome) on.
– DERIVATIVES **infliction** noun.
– ORIGIN Latin *infligere* 'strike against'.

in-flight ● adjective occurring or provided during an aircraft flight.

inflorescence /inflәressn'ss/ ● noun Botany **1** the complete flower head of a plant, including stems, stalks, bracts, and flowers. **2** the process of flowering.
– ORIGIN from Latin *inflorescere* 'come into flower'.

inflow ● noun **1** the action of flowing or moving in; influx. **2** something, such as water or money, that flows or moves in.

influence ● noun **1** the power or ability to affect someone's beliefs or actions. **2** a person or thing with such ability or power. **3** the power arising out of status, contacts, or wealth. **4** the power to produce a physical change. ● verb have an influence on.
– PHRASES **under the influence** informal affected by alcoholic drink.
– DERIVATIVES **influencer** noun.
– ORIGIN originally in the sense 'influx': from Latin *influere* 'flow in'.

influential ● adjective having great influence.
– DERIVATIVES **influentially** adverb.

influenza ● noun a highly contagious infection of the respiratory passages, spread by a virus and causing fever, severe aching, and catarrh.
– DERIVATIVES **influenzal** adjective.
– ORIGIN Italian, 'influence, outbreak of an epidemic', from Latin *influere* 'flow in'; the Italian word was applied to an influenza epidemic which began in Italy in 1743, later adopted in England as the name of the disease.

influx ● noun **1** the arrival or entry of large numbers of people or things. **2** an inflow of water into a river, lake, or the sea.
– ORIGIN Latin *influxus*, from *influere* 'flow in'.

infomercial ● noun chiefly N. Amer. an advertising film which promotes a product in an informative and supposedly objective style.
– ORIGIN blend of INFORMATION and COMMERCIAL.

inform ● verb **1** give facts or information to. **2** (**inform on**) give incriminating information about (someone) to the police or other authority. **3** give an essential or formative principle or quality to.
– ORIGIN Latin *informare* 'shape, describe'.

informal ● adjective **1** relaxed, friendly, or unofficial. **2** (of clothes) suitable for everyday wear; casual. **3** referring to the

Thesaurus

nitable; unstable, volatile.
– OPPOSITES fireproof.

inflammation ● noun SWELLING, puffiness; redness, heat, burning; rawness, soreness, tenderness; infection, festering, septicity.

inflammatory ● adjective **1** *an inflammatory lung condition* causing inflammation; *Medicine* erythrogenic. **2** *inflammatory language* PROVOCATIVE, incendiary, stirring, rousing, rabble-rousing, seditious, mutinous; like a red rag to a bull; fiery, passionate; controversial, contentious.

inflate ● verb **1** *the mattress inflated* BLOW UP, fill up, fill with air, aerate, puff up/out, pump up; dilate, distend, swell. **2** *the demand inflated prices* INCREASE, raise, boost, escalate, put up; *informal* hike up, jack up, bump up. **3** *the figures were inflated by the press* EXAGGERATE, magnify, overplay, overstate, enhance, embellish, touch up; increase, amplify, augment.
– OPPOSITES decrease, understate.

inflated ● adjective **1** *an inflated balloon* BLOWN UP, aerated, filled, puffed up/out, pumped up; distended, expanded, engorged, swollen. **2** *inflated prices* HIGH, sky-high, excessive, unreasonable, prohibitive, outrageous, exorbitant, extortionate; *Brit.* over the odds; *informal* steep. **3** *an inflated opinion of himself* EXAGGERATED, magnified, aggrandized, immoderate, overblown, overstated. **4** *inflated language* HIGH-FLOWN, extravagant, exaggerated, elaborate, flowery, ornate, overblown, overwrought, grandiloquent, magniloquent, grandiose, lofty; affected, pretentious; *informal* windy, highfalutin.

inflection ● noun **1** *(Grammar) verbal inflections* CONJUGATION, declension; form, ending, case. **2** *his voice was without inflection* STRESS, cadence, rhythm, accentuation, intonation, emphasis, modulation, lilt.

inflexible ● adjective **1** *his inflexible attitude* STUBBORN, obstinate, obdurate, intractable, intransigent, unbending, immovable, unaccommodating; hidebound, single-minded, pig-headed, mulish, uncompromising, adamant, firm, resolute, diehard, dyed-in-the-wool; *formal* refractory. **2** *inflexible rules* UNALTERABLE, unchangeable, immutable, unvarying, entrenched; firm, fixed, set, established, hard and fast; stringent, strict. **3** *an inflexible structure* RIGID, stiff, unyielding, unbending, unbendable; hard, firm, inelastic.
– OPPOSITES accommodating, pliable.

inflict ● verb **1** *he inflicted an injury on Frank* IMPOSE, exact, wreak; administer to, deal out to, mete out to, cause to, give to. **2** *I won't inflict my pain on my children* IMPOSE, force, thrust, foist; saddle someone with, burden someone with.

infliction ● noun **1** *the infliction of pain* ADMINISTRATION, delivery, application; imposition, perpetration; *formal* exaction. **2** *(informal, dated) they bore the infliction with heroism* AFFLICTION, trial, problem, nuisance, trouble, annoyance, bother, irritant; suffering, torment, tribulation.

influence ● noun **1** *the influence of parents on their children* EFFECT, impact; control, sway, hold, power, authority, mastery, domination, supremacy; guidance, direction; pressure. **2** *a bad influence on young girls* EXAMPLE TO, (role) model for, guide for, inspiration to. **3** *political influence* POWER, authority, sway, leverage, weight, pull, standing, prestige, stature, rank; *informal* clout, muscle, teeth; *N. Amer. informal* drag.
● verb **1** *bosses can influence our careers* AFFECT, have an impact on, determine, guide, control, shape, govern, decide; change, alter, transform. **2** *an attempt to influence the jury* SWAY, bias, prejudice, suborn; pressurize, coerce; dragoon, intimidate, browbeat, brainwash; *informal* twist someone's arm, lean on; *Brit. informal* nobble.

influential ● adjective **1** *an influential leader* POWERFUL, dominant, controlling, strong, authoritative; important, prominent, distinguished. **2** *he was influential in shaping her career* INSTRUMENTAL, significant, important, crucial, pivotal.

influx ● noun **1** *an influx of tourists* INUNDATION, rush, stream, flood, incursion; invasion, intrusion. **2** *influxes of river water* INFLOW, inrush, flood, inundation.

inform ● verb **1** *she informed him that she was ill* TELL, notify, apprise, advise, impart to, communicate to, let someone know; brief, prime, enlighten, send word to; *informal* fill in, clue in/up. **2** *he informed on two villains* DENOUNCE, give away, betray, incriminate, inculpate, report; sell out, stab in the back; *informal* rat, squeal, split, tell, blow the whistle, sell down the river, snitch, peach, stitch up; *Brit. informal* grass, shop, sneak; *Scottish informal*

language of everyday speech and writing, rather than that used in official and formal contexts.
– DERIVATIVES **informality** noun **informally** adverb.
informal vote ● noun Austral./NZ an invalid vote or voting paper.
informant ● noun **1** a person who gives information to another. **2** another term for INFORMER.
informatics /infərmattiks/ ● plural noun (treated as sing.) Computing the science of processing data for storage and retrieval.
information ● noun **1** facts or knowledge provided or learned. **2** what is conveyed or represented by a particular sequence of symbols, impulses, etc.
– DERIVATIVES **informational** adjective.
information superhighway ● noun an extensive electronic network such as the Internet, used for the rapid transfer of information in digital form.
information technology ● noun the study or use of systems such as computers and telecommunications for storing, retrieving, and sending information.
informative ● adjective providing useful information.
– DERIVATIVES **informatively** adverb **informativeness** noun.
informed ● adjective **1** having or showing knowledge. **2** (of a judgement) based on a sound understanding of the facts.
informer ● noun a person who informs on another person to the police or other authority.
infotainment ● noun broadcast material which is intended both to entertain and to inform.
– ORIGIN blend of INFORMATION and ENTERTAINMENT.
infotech ● noun short for INFORMATION TECHNOLOGY.
infra- ● prefix below: *infrasonic.*
– ORIGIN Latin *infra* 'below'.
infraction ● noun chiefly Law a violation or infringement of a law or agreement.
– DERIVATIVES **infractor** noun.
– ORIGIN Latin, from *infringere* 'infringe'.
infra dig /infrə dig/ ● adjective informal beneath one's dignity; demeaning.
– ORIGIN Latin *infra dignitatem* 'beneath dignity'.
infrared ● noun electromagnetic radiation having a wavelength just greater than that of red light but less than that of microwaves, emitted particularly by heated objects. ● adjective of or relating to such radiation.
infrasonic ● adjective relating to or denoting sound waves with a frequency below the lower limit of human audibility.
infrasound ● noun infrasonic sound waves.
infrastructure ● noun the basic physical and organizational structures (e.g. buildings, roads, power supplies) needed for the operation of a society or enterprise.
– DERIVATIVES **infrastructural** adjective.
infrequent ● adjective not occurring often; rare.
– DERIVATIVES **infrequency** noun **infrequently** adverb.
infringe ● verb **1** violate (a law, agreement, etc.). **2** encroach on (a right or privilege).
– DERIVATIVES **infringement** noun **infringer** noun.
– ORIGIN Latin *infringere*, from *in-* 'into' + *frangere* 'to break'.
infuriate ● verb /infyooriayt/ make irritated or angry.
– DERIVATIVES **infuriating** adjective.
– ORIGIN Latin *infuriare.*
infuse ● verb **1** pervade; fill. **2** instil (a quality) in someone or something. **3** soak (tea, herbs, etc.) to extract the flavour or healing properties. **4** Medicine allow (a liquid) to flow into the bloodstream or a part of the body.
– DERIVATIVES **infuser** noun.
– ORIGIN Latin *infundere* 'pour in'.
infusible ● adjective not able to be melted or fused.
– DERIVATIVES **infusibility** noun.
infusion ● noun **1** a drink, remedy, or extract prepared by infusing. **2** the action or process of infusing.
-ing¹ ● suffix **1** denoting a verbal action, activity, or result: *building.* **2** denoting material used for or associated with a process: *piping.* **3** forming the gerund of verbs (such as *painting* as in *I love painting*).
– ORIGIN Old English.
-ing² ● suffix **1** forming the present participle of verbs: *calling.* **2** forming adjectives from nouns: *hulking.*
– ORIGIN from Latin *-ent.*
ingenious /injeeniəss/ ● adjective clever, original, and inventive.
– DERIVATIVES **ingeniously** adverb **ingeniousness** noun.
– ORIGIN Latin *ingeniosus*, from *ingenium* 'mind, intellect'; related to ENGINE.
ingénue /anzhaynyōō/ ● noun an innocent or unsophisticated young woman.
– ORIGIN French, from *ingénu* 'ingenuous'.
ingenuity /injinyōōiti/ ● noun the quality of being ingenious.
– ORIGIN Latin *ingenuitas* 'ingenuousness', from *ingenuus* 'inborn'; the current meaning arose by confusion of *ingenuous* with *ingenious.*
ingenuous /injenyooəss/ ● adjective innocent and unsuspecting.
– DERIVATIVES **ingenuously** adverb **ingenuousness** noun.
– ORIGIN originally in the sense 'noble, generous': from Latin

Thesaurus

clype; N. Amer. informal rat out, finger; Austral./NZ informal dob. **3** *the articles were informed by feminism* SUFFUSE, pervade, permeate, infuse, imbue; characterize, typify.
informal ● adjective **1** *an informal discussion* UNOFFICIAL, casual, relaxed, easy-going, unceremonious; open, friendly, intimate; simple, unpretentious, easy, homely, cosy; informal unstuffy, laid-back, chummy, pally, matey. **2** *an informal speech style* COLLOQUIAL, vernacular, idiomatic, demotic, popular; familiar, everyday, unofficial; simple, natural, unpretentious; informal slangy, chatty, folksy. **3** *informal clothes* CASUAL, relaxed, comfortable, everyday, sloppy, leisure; informal comfy.
– OPPOSITES formal, official, literary, smart.
informality ● noun LACK OF CEREMONY, casualness, unceremoniousness, unpretentiousness; homeliness, cosiness; ease, naturalness, approachability.
information ● noun DETAILS, particulars, facts, figures, statistics, data; knowledge, intelligence; instruction, advice, guidance, direction, counsel, enlightenment; news; informal info, gen, the low-down, the dope, the inside story.
informative ● adjective INSTRUCTIVE, instructional, illuminating, enlightening, revealing, explanatory; factual, educational, educative, edifying, didactic; informal newsy.
informed ● adjective KNOWLEDGEABLE, enlightened, literate, educated; sophisticated, cultured; briefed, up to date, up to speed, in the picture, in the know, au courant, au fait; informal clued up, genned up; Brit. informal switched-on, sussed.
– OPPOSITES ignorant.
informer ● noun INFORMANT, betrayer, traitor, Judas, collaborator, stool pigeon, fifth columnist, spy, double agent, infiltrator, plant; telltale, taleteller; N. Amer. tattletale; informal rat, squealer, whistle-blower, snake in the grass, snitch; Brit. informal grass, supergrass, nark, snout; Scottish informal clype; N. Amer. informal fink, stoolie.
infraction ● noun INFRINGEMENT, contravention, breach, violation, transgression; neglect, dereliction, non-compliance; Law delict, contumacy.
infrequent ● adjective RARE, uncommon, unusual, exceptional, few (and far between), like gold dust, as scarce as hens' teeth; unaccustomed, unwonted; isolated, scarce, scattered; sporadic, irregular, intermittent; informal once in a blue moon; dated seldom.
– OPPOSITES common.
infringe ● verb **1** *the bid infringed EU rules* CONTRAVENE, violate, transgress, break, breach; disobey, defy, flout, fly in the face of; disregard, ignore, neglect; go beyond, overstep, exceed; Law infract. **2** *surveillance could infringe personal liberties* UNDERMINE, erode, diminish, weaken, impair, damage, compromise; limit, curb, check, encroach on.
– OPPOSITES obey, preserve.
infuriate ● verb ENRAGE, incense, anger, madden, inflame; exasperate, antagonize, provoke, rile, annoy, irritate, nettle, gall, irk, vex, pique, get on someone's nerves, try someone's patience; N. Amer. rankle; informal aggravate, make someone see red, get someone's back up, make someone's blood boil, get up someone's nose, needle, hack off, brown off; Brit. informal wind up, get to, nark, cheese off; N. Amer. informal bug, tick off.
– OPPOSITES please.
infuriating ● adjective EXASPERATING, maddening, annoying, irritating, irksome, vexatious, trying, tiresome; informal aggravating, pesky.
infuse ● verb **1** *she was infused with a sense of hope* FILL, suffuse, imbue, inspire, charge, pervade, permeate. **2** *he infused new life into the group* INSTIL, breathe, inject, impart, inculcate, introduce, add. **3** *infuse the dried leaves* STEEP, brew, stew, soak, immerse, souse; Brit. informal mash.
ingenious ● adjective INVENTIVE, creative, imaginative, original, in-

ingenuus 'native, inborn'.

ingest ● verb take (food or drink) into the body by swallowing or absorbing it.
– DERIVATIVES **ingestion** noun **ingestive** adjective.
– ORIGIN Latin *ingerere* 'bring in'.

inglenook ● noun a space on either side of a large fireplace.
– ORIGIN from dialect *ingle* 'fire, fireplace', perhaps from Irish *aingeal* 'live ember' + NOOK.

inglorious ● adjective **1** not worthy of honour. **2** not famous or renowned.
– DERIVATIVES **ingloriously** adverb **ingloriousness** noun.

ingoing ● adjective going towards or into.

ingot /inggət/ ● noun a rectangular block of steel, gold, or other metal.
– ORIGIN originally denoting a mould: perhaps from an Old English word meaning 'pour, cast'.

ingraft ● verb variant spelling of ENGRAFT.

ingrain (also **engrain**) ● verb firmly fix or establish (a habit, belief, or attitude) in a person.
– ORIGIN originally in the sense 'dye with cochineal', from the old use of *grain* meaning 'kermes, cochineal'.

ingrained (also **engrained**) ● adjective **1** (of a habit or attitude) firmly established. **2** (of dirt) deeply embedded.

ingrate /ingrayt/ formal or literary ● noun an ungrateful person. ● adjective ungrateful.
– ORIGIN Latin *ingratus*, from *in-* 'not' + *gratus* 'grateful'.

i

ingratiate /ingrayshiayt/ ● verb (**ingratiate oneself**) bring oneself into favour with someone by flattering or trying to please them.
– DERIVATIVES **ingratiating** adjective **ingratiation** noun.
– ORIGIN from Latin *in gratiam* 'into favour'.

ingratitude ● noun a discreditable lack of gratitude.

ingredient ● noun **1** any of the substances that are combined to make a particular dish. **2** a component part or element.
– ORIGIN from Latin *ingredi* 'enter'.

ingress /ingress/ ● noun **1** the action or fact of entering or coming in. **2** a place or means of access.
– DERIVATIVES **ingression** noun.
– ORIGIN Latin *ingressus*, from *ingredi* 'enter'.

in-group ● noun an exclusive group of people with a shared interest or identity.

ingrown ● adjective **1** growing or having grown within; innate. **2** (of a toenail) having grown into the flesh.
– DERIVATIVES **ingrowing** adjective **ingrowth** noun.

inguinal /inggwinəl/ ● adjective Anatomy of the groin.
– ORIGIN Latin *inguinalis*, from *inguen* 'groin'.

inhabit ● verb (**inhabited**, **inhabiting**) live in or occupy.
– DERIVATIVES **inhabitable** adjective **inhabitation** noun.
– ORIGIN Latin *inhabitare*, from *habitare* 'dwell'.

inhabitant ● noun a person or animal that lives in or occupies a place.

inhalant ● noun **1** a medicinal preparation for inhaling. **2** a solvent or other material producing vapour that is inhaled by drug abusers.

inhale /inhayl/ ● verb breathe in (air, gas, smoke, etc.).
– DERIVATIVES **inhalation** noun.
– ORIGIN Latin *inhalare*.

inhaler ● noun a portable device for administering a drug which is to be inhaled.

inhere /inheer/ ● verb (**inhere in/within**) formal **1** exist essentially or permanently in. **2** Law (of rights, powers, etc.) be vested in a person or group or attached to the ownership of a property.
– ORIGIN Latin *inhaerere* 'stick to'.

inherent /inherrənt, -heer-/ ● adjective existing in something as a permanent or essential attribute.
– DERIVATIVES **inherently** adverb.

inherit ● verb (**inherited**, **inheriting**) **1** receive (money, property, or a title) as an heir at the death of the previous holder. **2** derive (a quality or characteristic) from one's parents or ancestors. **3** receive or be left with (a situation, object, etc.) from a predecessor or former owner.
– DERIVATIVES **inheritable** adjective **inheritor** noun.
– ORIGIN Latin *inhereditare* 'appoint as heir'.

inheritance ● noun **1** a thing that is inherited. **2** the action of inheriting.

inheritance tax ● noun (in the UK) tax levied on property and money acquired by gift or inheritance.

inhibit ● verb (**inhibited**, **inhibiting**) **1** hinder or restrain (an action or process). **2** make (someone) unable to act in a relaxed and natural way.
– DERIVATIVES **inhibited** adjective **inhibitive** adjective.
– ORIGIN Latin *inhibere*.

Thesaurus

novative, pioneering, resourceful, enterprising, inspired; clever, intelligent, smart, brilliant, masterly, talented, gifted, skilful; astute, sharp-witted, quick-witted, shrewd; elaborate, sophisticated.

ingenuous ● adjective NAIVE, innocent, simple, childlike, trusting, trustful, over-trusting, unwary; unsuspicious, unworldly, wide-eyed, inexperienced, green; open, sincere, honest, frank, candid, forthright, artless, guileless, genuine.
– OPPOSITES artful.

inglorious ● adjective SHAMEFUL, dishonourable, ignominious, discreditable, disgraceful, scandalous; humiliating, mortifying, demeaning, ignoble, undignified, wretched.

ingrained, engrained ● adjective **1** *ingrained attitudes* ENTRENCHED, established, deep-rooted, deep-seated, fixed, firm, unshakeable, ineradicable; inveterate, dyed-in-the-wool, abiding, enduring, stubborn. **2** *ingrained dirt* GROUND-IN, fixed, implanted, embedded; permanent, indelible, ineradicable, inexpungible.
– OPPOSITES transient, superficial.

ingratiate ● verb
– PHRASES **ingratiate oneself** CURRY FAVOUR WITH, cultivate, win over, get in someone's good books; toady to, crawl to, grovel to, fawn over, kowtow to, play up to, pander to, flatter, court; *informal* suck up to, rub up the right way, lick someone's boots.

ingratiating ● adjective SYCOPHANTIC, toadying, fawning, unctuous, obsequious; flattering, insincere; smooth-tongued, silver-tongued, slick; greasy, oily, saccharine; *informal* smarmy, slimy, creepy, sucky.

ingratitude ● noun UNGRATEFULNESS, thanklessness, unthankfulness, non-recognition.

ingredient ● adjective CONSTITUENT, component, element; part, piece, bit, strand, portion, unit, feature, aspect, attribute; (**ingredients**) contents, makings.

ingress ● noun **1** *the doors gave ingress to the station* ENTRY, entrance, access, admittance, admission; way in, approach. **2** *the ingress of water* SEEPAGE, leakage, inundation, inrush, intrusion, incursion, entry, entrance.
– OPPOSITES exit.

inhabit ● verb LIVE IN, occupy; settle (in), people, populate, colonize; dwell in, reside in, tenant, lodge in, have one's home in; *formal* be domiciled in, abide in.

inhabitable ● adjective HABITABLE, fit to live in, usable; *informal* liveable-in; *formal* tenantable.

inhabitant ● noun RESIDENT, occupant, occupier, dweller, settler; local, native; (**inhabitants**) population, populace, people, public, community, citizenry, townsfolk, townspeople; *formal* denizen; *archaic* burgher, habitant.

inhale ● verb BREATHE IN, inspire, draw in, suck in, sniff in, drink in; *poetic/literary* inbreathe.

inharmonious ● adjective **1** *inharmonious sounds* UNMELODIOUS, unharmonious, unmusical, tuneless, discordant, dissonant, off-key; harsh, grating, jarring, cacophonous; *archaic* absonant. **2** *an inharmonious modern building* OUT OF PLACE, unsuitable, inappropriate, clashing, conflicting, incompatible, mismatched; jarring, discordant. **3** *his relationships are inharmonious* ANTAGONISTIC, quarrelsome, argumentative, disputatious, cantankerous, confrontational, belligerent.
– OPPOSITES musical, fitting, congenial.

inherent ● adjective INTRINSIC, innate, connate, connatural, immanent, built-in, inborn, ingrained, deep-rooted; essential, fundamental, basic, structural, organic; natural, instinctive, instinctual, congenital, native.
– OPPOSITES acquired.

inherit ● verb **1** *she inherited his farm* BECOME HEIR TO, come into/by, be bequeathed, be left, be willed; *Law* be devised. **2** *Richard inherited the title* SUCCEED TO, assume, take over, come into; *formal* accede to.

inheritance ● noun **1** *a comfortable inheritance* LEGACY, bequest, endowment, bestowal, bequeathal, provision; birthright, heritage, patrimony; *Law* devise. **2** *his inheritance of the title* SUCCESSION TO, accession to, assumption of, elevation to.

inheritor ● noun HEIR, heiress, legatee; successor, next in line; *Law* devisee, grantee, cestui que trust; *Scottish Law* heritor.

inhibit ● verb **1** *the obstacles which inhibit change* IMPEDE, hinder,

inhibition ● noun **1** the action of inhibiting or process of being inhibited. **2** a feeling that makes one unable to act in a relaxed and natural way.

inhibitor ● noun a substance which slows down or prevents a particular chemical reaction or other process.
– DERIVATIVES **inhibitory** adjective.

inhospitable ● adjective **1** (of an environment) harsh and difficult to live in. **2** unwelcoming.
– DERIVATIVES **inhospitableness** noun **inhospitably** adverb **inhospitality** noun.

in-house ● adjective & adverb within an organization.

inhuman ● adjective **1** lacking positive human qualities; cruel and barbaric. **2** not human in nature or character.
– DERIVATIVES **inhumanly** adverb.

inhumane ● adjective without compassion for misery or suffering; cruel.
– DERIVATIVES **inhumanely** adverb.

inhumanity ● noun (pl. **inhumanities**) cruel and brutal behaviour.

inhumation /inhyōōmaysh'n/ ● noun chiefly Archaeology **1** the action or practice of burying the dead. **2** a burial or buried corpse.
– ORIGIN from Latin *inhumare* 'bury', from *humus* 'ground'.

inimical /inimmik'l/ ● adjective tending to obstruct or harm; hostile.
– DERIVATIVES **inimically** adverb.
– ORIGIN Latin *inimicalis*, from *inimicus* 'enemy'.

inimitable /inimmitəb'l/ ● adjective impossible to imitate; unique.
– DERIVATIVES **inimitability** noun **inimitably** adverb.

iniquity /inikwiti/ ● noun (pl. **iniquities**) injustice or immoral behaviour.
– DERIVATIVES **iniquitous** adjective **iniquitously** adverb **iniquitousness** noun.
– ORIGIN Latin *iniquitas*, from *iniquus* 'not equal or just'.

initial ● adjective existing or occurring at the beginning. ● noun the first letter of a name or word. ● verb (**initialled**, **initialling**; N. Amer. **initialed**, **initialing**) mark with one's initials as a sign of approval or endorsement.
– DERIVATIVES **initially** adverb.
– ORIGIN Latin *initialis*, from *initium* 'beginning'.

initialism ● noun an abbreviation consisting of initial letters pronounced separately (e.g. *BBC*).

initiate ● verb /inishiayt/ **1** cause (a process or action) to begin. **2** admit with formal ceremony or ritual into a society or group. **3** (**initiate into**) introduce to (a new activity or skill). ● noun /inishiət/ a person who has been initiated.
– DERIVATIVES **initiation** noun **initiatory** adjective.
– ORIGIN Latin *initiare* 'begin'.

initiative ● noun **1** the ability to act independently and with a fresh approach. **2** the power or opportunity to act before others do. **3** a new development or fresh approach to a problem.
– PHRASES **on one's own initiative** without being prompted by others.

initiator ● noun **1** a person or thing that initiates. **2** Chemistry a substance which starts a chain reaction. **3** an explosive or device used to detonate a main charge.

inject ● verb **1** introduce into the body with a syringe. **2** administer a drug or medicine to (a person or animal) with a syringe. **3** introduce or feed under pressure into another substance. **4** introduce (a new or different element).
– DERIVATIVES **injectable** adjective & noun **injector** noun.
– ORIGIN Latin *inicere* 'throw in'.

injection ● noun **1** an act or the action of injecting or being in-

i

Thesaurus

hamper, hold back, discourage, interfere with, obstruct, slow down, retard; curb, check, suppress, restrict, fetter, cramp, frustrate, stifle, prevent, block, thwart, foil, stop, halt. **2** *she feels inhibited from taking part* PREVENT, disallow, exclude, forbid, prohibit, preclude, ban, bar, interdict.
– OPPOSITES assist, encourage, allow.

inhibited ● adjective SHY, reticent, reserved, self-conscious, diffident, bashful, coy; wary, reluctant, hesitant, insecure, unconfident, unassertive, timid; withdrawn, repressed, undemonstrative; *informal* uptight.

inhibition ● noun **1** *they overcame their inhibitions* SHYNESS, reticence, self-consciousness, reserve, diffidence; wariness, hesitance, hesitancy, insecurity; unassertiveness, timidity; repression, reservation; psychological block; *informal* hang-up. **2** *the inhibition of publishing* HINDRANCE, hampering, discouragement, obstruction, impediment, retardation; suppression, repression, restriction, restraint, constraint, cramping, stifling, prevention; curb, check, bar, barrier.

inhospitable ● adjective **1** *the inhospitable landscape* UNINVITING, unwelcoming; bleak, forbidding, cheerless, hostile, harsh, inimical; uninhabitable, barren, bare, desolate, stark. **2** *forgive me if I seem inhospitable* UNWELCOMING, unfriendly, unsociable, unsocial, antisocial, unneighbourly, uncongenial; cool, cold, frosty, aloof, distant, remote, indifferent, offhand; uncivil, discourteous, ungracious; ungenerous, unkind, unsympathetic; *informal* stand-offish.
– OPPOSITES welcoming.

inhuman ● adjective **1** *inhuman treatment* CRUEL, harsh, inhumane, brutal, callous, sadistic, severe, savage, vicious, barbaric; monstrous, heinous, egregious; merciless, ruthless, pitiless, remorseless, cold-blooded, heartless, hard-hearted; unkind, inconsiderate, unfeeling, uncaring; *Brit. informal* beastly; *dated* dastardly. **2** *hellish and inhuman shapes* NON-HUMAN, non-mortal, monstrous, devilish, ghostly; subhuman, animal; strange, odd, unearthly.
– OPPOSITES humane.

inhumane ● adjective. See INHUMAN sense 1.

inhume ● verb *(poetic/literary)* BURY, inter, lay to rest, entomb; *informal* plant; *poetic/literary* sepulchre.

inimical ● adjective **1** *this is inimical to genuine democracy* HARMFUL, injurious, detrimental, deleterious, prejudicial, damaging, hurtful, destructive, ruinous; antagonistic, contrary, antipathetic, unfavourable, adverse, opposed, hostile; *poetic/literary* malefic. **2** *he fixed her with an inimical gaze* HOSTILE, unfriendly, antagonistic, unkind, unsympathetic, malevolent; unwelcoming, cold, frosty.
– OPPOSITES advantageous, friendly.

inimitable ● adjective UNIQUE, exclusive, distinctive, individual, special, idiosyncratic; incomparable, unparalleled, unrivalled, matchless, peerless, unequalled, unsurpassable, superlative, supreme, beyond compare, second to none, in a class of one's own; *formal* unexampled.

iniquity ● noun **1** *the iniquity of his conduct* WICKEDNESS, sinfulness, immorality, impropriety; vice, evil, sin; villainy, criminality; odiousness, atrocity, egregiousness; outrage, monstrosity, obscenity, reprehensibility. **2** *I will forgive their iniquity* SIN, crime, transgression, wrongdoing, wrong, violation, offence, vice; atrocity, outrage.
– OPPOSITES goodness, virtue.

initial ● adjective *the initial stages* BEGINNING, opening, commencing, starting, inceptive, embryonic, fledgling; first, early, primary, preliminary, elementary, foundational, preparatory; introductory, inaugural.
– OPPOSITES final.
● noun *what do the initials stand for?* INITIAL LETTER; (**initials**) acronym, abbreviation, initialism.
● verb **1** *he initialled the warrant* PUT ONE'S INITIALS ON, sign, countersign, autograph, endorse, inscribe, witness. **2** *they initialled a new agreement* RATIFY, accept, approve, authorize, validate, recognize.

initially ● adverb AT FIRST, at the start, at the outset, in/at the beginning, to begin with, to start with, originally.

initiate ● verb **1** *the government initiated the scheme* BEGIN, start (off), commence; institute, inaugurate, launch, instigate, establish, set up, sow the seeds of, start the ball rolling; originate, pioneer; *informal* kick off. **2** *he was initiated into a cult* INTRODUCE, admit, induct, install, incorporate, enlist, enrol, recruit, sign up, swear in; ordain, invest. **3** *they were initiated into the world of maths* TEACH ABOUT, instruct in, tutor in, school in, prime in, ground in; familiarize with, acquaint with; indoctrinate, inculcate; *informal* show someone the ropes.
– OPPOSITES finish, expel.
● noun *an initiate on the team* NOVICE, starter, beginner, newcomer; learner, student, pupil, trainee, apprentice; new boy, new girl, recruit, tyro, neophyte; postulant, novitiate; *informal* rookie, new kid (on the block), newie, newbie, greenhorn.

initiative ● noun **1** *employers are looking for initiative* ENTERPRISE, resourcefulness, inventiveness, imagination, ingenuity, originality, creativity; drive, dynamism, ambition, motivation, spirit, energy, vision; *informal* get-up-and-go, pep, punch. **2** *he has lost the initiative* ADVANTAGE, upper hand, edge, lead, whip hand, trump card. **3** *a recent initiative on recycling* PLAN, scheme, strategy, stratagem, measure, proposal, step, action, approach.

jected. **2** a substance that is injected. **3** short for FUEL INJECTION.

injection moulding ● noun the shaping of rubber or plastic articles by injecting heated material into a mould.

in-joke ● noun a joke that is shared exclusively by a small group.

injudicious ● adjective showing poor judgement; unwise.
– DERIVATIVES **injudiciously** adverb **injudiciousness** noun.

injunction ● noun **1** Law a judicial order restraining a person from an action, or compelling a person to carry out a certain act. **2** an authoritative warning.
– DERIVATIVES **injunctive** adjective.
– ORIGIN Latin, from *injungere* 'join, attach, impose'.

injure ● verb **1** do physical harm to; wound. **2** offend or hurt.

injured ● adjective **1** harmed or wounded. **2** offended; wronged.

injurious /injooriəss/ ● adjective **1** causing or likely to cause injury. **2** (of language) maliciously insulting; libellous.
– DERIVATIVES **injuriously** adverb **injuriousness** noun.

injury ● noun (pl. **injuries**) **1** an instance of being injured. **2** the fact of being injured; harm or damage.
– ORIGIN Latin *injuria* 'a wrong'.

injury time ● noun Brit. (in soccer and other sports) extra playing time allowed to compensate for time lost as a result of injuries.

injustice ● noun **1** lack of justice. **2** an unjust act or occurrence.

ink ● noun **1** a coloured fluid used for writing, drawing, or printing. **2** Zoology a black liquid ejected by a cuttlefish, octopus, or squid to confuse a predator. ● verb **1** write or mark with ink. **2** cover (type or a stamp) with ink before printing.
– ORIGIN Old French *enque*, from Greek *enkauston*, denoting the purple ink used by Roman emperors for signatures; related to ENCAUSTIC.

ink cap ● noun a mushroom with a tall, narrow cap and slender white stem, that turns into a black liquid after the spores are shed.

ink-jet printer ● noun a printer in which the characters are formed by minute jets of ink.

inkling ● noun a slight suspicion; a hint.
– ORIGIN from archaic *inkle* 'say in an undertone'.

inkstand ● noun a stand for ink bottles, pens, and other stationery items.

inkwell ● noun a container for ink, normally housed in a hole in a desk.

inky ● adjective (**inkier**, **inkiest**) **1** as dark as ink. **2** stained with ink.
– DERIVATIVES **inkiness** noun.

INLA ● abbreviation Irish National Liberation Army.

inlaid past and past participle of INLAY.

inland ● adjective & adverb **1** in or into the interior of a country. **2** (as adjective) chiefly Brit. carried on within the limits of a country; domestic. ● noun the interior of a country or region.
– DERIVATIVES **inlander** noun.

inland revenue ● noun Brit. public revenue consisting of income tax and some other direct taxes.

in-law ● noun a relative by marriage. ● combining form related by marriage: *father-in-law*.

inlay ● verb (past and past part. **inlaid**) ornament by embedding pieces of a different material in a surface. ● noun **1** inlaid decoration. **2** a material or substance used for inlaying. **3** a filling shaped to fit a tooth cavity.
– DERIVATIVES **inlayer** noun.

inlet ● noun **1** a small arm of the sea, a lake, or a river. **2** a place or means of entry. **3** (in tailoring and dressmaking) an inserted piece of material.

in-line ● adjective **1** having parts arranged in a line. **2** constituting an integral part of a continuous sequence of operations or machines.

in-line skate ● noun a type of roller skate in which the wheels are fixed in a single line along the sole.

in loco parentis /in lōkō pərentiss/ ● adverb & adjective in the place of a parent.
– ORIGIN Latin.

inlying /inli-ing/ ● adjective within or near a centre.

inmate ● noun a person living in an institution such as a prison or hospital.
– ORIGIN originally denoting a lodger or subtenant; probably from INN + MATE[1].

in medias res /in meediass rayz/ ● adverb into the middle of things; without preamble.
– ORIGIN Latin.

in memoriam /in mimoriam/ ● preposition in memory of (a dead person).
– ORIGIN Latin.

inmost ● adjective innermost.

inn ● noun a public house, traditionally an establishment also providing food and lodging.
– ORIGIN Old English, related to IN.

innards ● plural noun informal **1** internal organs; entrails. **2** the internal workings of a device or machine.
– ORIGIN representing a dialect pronunciation of INWARDS.

innate /inayt/ ● adjective inborn; natural.

Thesaurus

inject ● verb **1** *he injected a dose of codeine* ADMINISTER, introduce; inoculate, vaccinate; informal shoot (up), mainline, fix (up). **2** *a pump injects air into the valve* INSERT, introduce, feed, push, force, shoot. **3** *he injected new life into the team* INTRODUCE, instil, infuse, imbue, breathe.

injection ● noun INOCULATION, vaccination, vaccine, immunization, booster; dose; informal jab, shot, hype.

injudicious ● adjective IMPRUDENT, unwise, inadvisable, ill-advised, misguided; ill-considered, ill-judged, incautious, hasty, rash, foolish, foolhardy, hare-brained; inappropriate, impolitic, inexpedient; informal dumb.
– OPPOSITES prudent.

injunction ● noun ORDER, ruling, direction, directive, command, instruction; decree, edict, dictum, dictate, fiat, mandate.

injure ● verb **1** *he injured his foot* HURT, wound, damage, harm; cripple, lame, disable; maim, mutilate, deform, mangle, break; Brit. informal knacker; archaic scathe. **2** *a libel injured her reputation* DAMAGE, mar, spoil, ruin, blight, blemish, tarnish, blacken. **3** (archaic) *I have injured no one by my folly* WRONG, do an injustice to, offend against, maltreat, mistreat, ill-use; informal do the dirty on.

injured ● adjective **1** *his injured arm* HURT, wounded, damaged, sore, bruised; crippled, lame, game, disabled; maimed, mutilated, deformed, mangled, broken, fractured; Brit. informal gammy. **2** *the injured party* WRONGED, offended, maltreated, mistreated, ill-used, harmed; defamed, maligned, insulted, dishonoured. **3** *an injured tone* UPSET, hurt, wounded, offended, reproachful, pained, aggrieved, unhappy, put out.
– OPPOSITES healthy, offending.

injurious ● adjective HARMFUL, damaging, deleterious, detrimental, hurtful; disadvantageous, unfavourable, undesirable, adverse, inimical, unhealthy, pernicious; poetic/literary malefic.

injury ● noun **1** *minor injuries* WOUND, bruise, cut, gash, scratch, graze, abrasion, contusion, lesion; Medicine trauma. **2** *they escaped without injury* HARM, hurt, damage, pain, suffering, impairment, affliction, incapacity. **3** *the injury to her feelings* OFFENCE, abuse; affront, insult, slight, snub; wrong, wrongdoing, injustice.

injustice ● noun **1** *the injustice of the world* UNFAIRNESS, unjustness, inequity; cruelty, tyranny, repression, exploitation, corruption; bias, prejudice, discrimination, intolerance. **2** *his sacking was an injustice* WRONG, offence, crime, sin, misdeed, outrage, atrocity, scandal, disgrace, affront.

inkling ● noun IDEA, notion, sense, impression, suggestion, indication, whisper, glimmer, (sneaking) suspicion, fancy, hunch; hint, clue, intimation, sign; informal the foggiest (idea), the faintest (idea).

inky ● adjective **1** *the inky darkness* BLACK, jet-black, pitch-black; sable, ebony, dark; poetic/literary Stygian. **2** *inky fingers* INK-STAINED, stained, blotchy.

inlaid ● adjective INSET, set, studded, lined, panelled; ornamented, decorated; mosaic, intarsia, marquetry.

inland ● adjective **1** *inland areas* INTERIOR, inshore, central, internal, upcountry. **2** *inland trade* DOMESTIC, internal, home, local.
– OPPOSITES coastal, international.
● adverb *the goods were carried inland* UPCOUNTRY, inshore, to the interior.

inlet ● noun **1** COVE, bay, bight, creek, estuary, fjord, sound; Scottish firth. **2** *a fresh air inlet* VENT, flue, shaft, duct, channel, pipe, pipeline.

inmate ● noun **1** *the inmates of the hospital* PATIENT, inpatient; convalescent; resident, inhabitant, occupant. **2** *the prison's inmates* PRISONER, convict, captive, detainee, internee; informal jailbird, con; Brit. informal lag; N. Amer. informal yardbird.

inmost ● adjective. See INNERMOST.

inn ● noun TAVERN, bar, hostelry, taproom; hotel, guest house; Brit.

– DERIVATIVES **innately** adverb **innateness** noun.
– ORIGIN Latin *innatus*, from *innasci* 'be born into'.
inner ● adjective **1** situated inside; close to the centre. **2** mental or spiritual: *inner strength.* **3** private; not expressed. ● noun an inner part.
inner bar ● noun (in the UK) Queen's or King's Counsel collectively.
inner city ● noun an area in or near the centre of a city, especially when associated with social and economic problems.
inner ear ● noun the part of the ear embedded in the temporal bone, consisting of the semicircular canals and cochlea.
innermost ● adjective **1** furthest in; closest to the centre. **2** (of thoughts) most private and deeply felt.
inner tube ● noun a separate inflatable tube inside a pneumatic tyre casing.
inning ● noun Baseball each division of a game during which both sides have a turn at batting.
– ORIGIN Old English, 'a putting or getting in'.
innings ● noun (pl. same) (treated as sing.) Cricket each of the divisions of a game during which one side has a turn at batting.
– PHRASES **a good innings** Brit. informal a long and fulfilling life or career.
innkeeper ● noun chiefly archaic a person who runs an inn.
innocent ● adjective **1** not guilty of a crime or offence. **2** free from moral wrong; not corrupted. **3** not intended to cause offence; harmless. **4** (**innocent of**) without experience or knowledge of. ● noun an innocent person.
– DERIVATIVES **innocence** noun **innocently** adverb.
– ORIGIN Latin, 'not harming', from *in-* 'not' + *nocere* 'to hurt'.
innocuous /inokyooəss/ ● adjective not harmful or offensive.
– DERIVATIVES **innocuously** adverb **innocuousness** noun.
– ORIGIN Latin *innocuus*, from *in-* 'not' + *nocere* 'to hurt'.
Inn of Court ● noun (in the UK) each of the four legal societies having the exclusive right of admitting people to the English bar.
innovate /innəvayt/ ● verb introduce new methods, ideas, or products.
– DERIVATIVES **innovator** noun **innovatory** adjective.
– ORIGIN Latin *innovare* 'renew, alter', from *novus* 'new'.
innovation ● noun **1** the action or process of innovating. **2** a new method, idea, product, etc.
innovative /innəvətiv/ ● adjective **1** featuring new methods; advanced and original: *innovative designs.* **2** (of a person) original and creative in thinking.
innuendo /inyooendō/ ● noun (pl. **innuendoes** or **innuendos**) an allusive or oblique remark, typically a suggestive or disparaging one.
– ORIGIN originally used in legal documents, meaning 'that is to say': from Latin, 'by nodding at, by pointing to', from *in-* 'towards' + *nuere* 'to nod'.
innumerable ● adjective too many to be counted.
– DERIVATIVES **innumerability** noun **innumerably** adverb.
innumerate ● adjective without a basic knowledge of mathematics and arithmetic. ● noun an innumerate person.
– DERIVATIVES **innumeracy** noun.
inoculate /inokyoolayt/ ● verb **1** another term for VACCINATE. **2** introduce (cells or organisms) into a culture medium.
– DERIVATIVES **inoculable** adjective **inoculation** noun **inoculator** noun.
– ORIGIN originally in the sense 'graft a bud or shoot': from Latin *inoculare* 'engraft', from *oculus* 'eye, bud'.
inoffensive ● adjective not objectionable or harmful.
– DERIVATIVES **inoffensively** adverb **inoffensiveness** noun.
inoperable ● adjective **1** Medicine not able to be operated on to beneficial effect. **2** not able to be used or operated. **3** impractical; unworkable.
– DERIVATIVES **inoperability** noun **inoperably** adverb.
inoperative ● adjective not working or taking effect.

i

Thesaurus

pub, public house; *Canadian* beer parlour; *informal* watering hole; *dated* alehouse.
innards ● plural noun *(informal)* ENTRAILS, internal organs, viscera, intestines, bowels, guts; *informal* insides.
innate ● adjective INBORN, inbred, congenital, inherent, natural, intrinsic, instinctive, intuitive, unlearned; hereditary, inherited, in the blood, in the family; inbuilt, deep-rooted, deep-seated, connate, connatural.
– OPPOSITES acquired.
inner ● adjective **1** *inner London* CENTRAL, innermost, mid, middle. **2** *the inner gates* INTERNAL, interior, inside, inmost, innermost, intramural. **3** *the Queen's inner circle* PRIVILEGED, restricted, exclusive, private, confidential, intimate. **4** *the inner meaning* HIDDEN, secret, deep, underlying, unapparent; veiled, esoteric, unrevealed. **5** *one's inner life* MENTAL, intellectual, psychological, spiritual, emotional.
– OPPOSITES external, apparent.
innermost ● adjective **1** *the innermost shrine* CENTRAL, middle, internal, interior. **2** *her innermost feelings* DEEPEST, deep-seated, inward, underlying, intimate, private, personal, secret, hidden, concealed, unexpressed, unrevealed, unapparent; true, real, honest.
innkeeper ● noun LANDLORD, landlady, hotelier, hotel owner, proprietor, manager, manageress; licensee, barman, barmaid; *Brit.* publican.
innocence ● noun **1** *he protested his innocence* GUILTLESSNESS, blamelessness, irreproachability. **2** *the innocence of his bride* VIRGINITY, chastity, chasteness, purity; integrity, morality, decency; *dated* honour; *archaic* virtue. **3** *she took advantage of his innocence* NAIVETY, ingenuousness, credulity, inexperience, gullibility, simplicity, unworldliness, guilelessness, greenness.
innocent ● adjective **1** *he was entirely innocent* GUILTLESS, blameless, in the clear, unimpeachable, irreproachable, above suspicion, faultless; honourable, honest, upright, law-abiding; *informal* squeaky clean. **2** *innocent fun* HARMLESS, innocuous, safe, inoffensive. **3** *nice innocent girls* VIRTUOUS, pure, moral, decent, righteous, upright, wholesome; demure, modest, chaste, virginal; impeccable, spotless, sinless, unsullied, incorrupt, undefiled; *informal* squeaky clean, whiter than white. **4** *she is innocent of guile* FREE FROM, without, lacking (in), clear of, ignorant of, unaware of, untouched by; *poetic/literary* nescient of. **5** *innocent foreigners* NAIVE, ingenuous, trusting, credulous, unsuspicious, unwary, unguarded; impressionable, gullible, easily led; inexperienced, unworldly, unsophisticated, green; simple, artless, guileless; *informal* wet behind the ears, born yesterday.
– OPPOSITES guilty, sinful, worldly, malignant.
● noun *an innocent in a strange land* INGÉNUE, unworldly person; child; novice; *N. Amer. informal* greenhorn; *poetic/literary* babe in arms.
innocuous ● adjective **1** *an innocuous fungus* HARMLESS, safe, nontoxic, innocent; edible, eatable. **2** *an innocuous comment* INOFFENSIVE, unobjectionable, unexceptionable, harmless, mild, tame; anodyne, unremarkable, commonplace, run-of-the-mill.
– OPPOSITES harmful, offensive.
innovation ● noun CHANGE, alteration, revolution, upheaval, transformation, metamorphosis; reorganization, restructuring, rearrangement, remodelling; new measures, new methods, modernization, modernism; novelty, newness; *informal* a shake up, a shakedown.
innovative ● adjective ORIGINAL, innovatory, innovational, new, novel, fresh, unusual, unprecedented, avant-garde, experimental, inventive, ingenious; advanced, modern, state-of-the-art, pioneering, ground-breaking, revolutionary, radical, newfangled.
innovator ● noun PIONEER, trailblazer, ground-breaker, pathfinder; developer, modernizer, reformer, reformist, progressive; experimenter, inventor, creator.
innuendo ● noun INSINUATION, suggestion, intimation, implication, hint, overtone, undertone, allusion, reference; aspersion, slur.
innumerable ● adjective COUNTLESS, numerous, untold, legion, without number, numberless, unnumbered, multitudinous, incalculable, limitless; *informal* umpteen, a slew of, no end of, loads of, stacks of, heaps of, masses of, oodles of, zillions of; *N. Amer. informal* gazillions of; *poetic/literary* myriad.
– OPPOSITES few.
inoculate ● verb IMMUNIZE, vaccinate, inject; protect from, safeguard against; *informal* give someone a jab/shot.
inoculation ● noun IMMUNIZATION, vaccination, vaccine; injection, booster; *informal* jab, shot.
inoffensive ● adjective HARMLESS, innocuous, unobjectionable, unexceptionable; non-aggressive, non-violent, mild, peaceful, peaceable, gentle; tame, innocent.
inoperable ● adjective **1** *an inoperable tumour* UNTREATABLE, incurable, irremediable; malignant; terminal, fatal, deadly, lethal; *archaic* immedicable. **2** *the airfield was left inoperable* UNUSABLE, out of action, out of service, non-active. **3** *the agreement is now inoperable* IMPRACTICAL, unworkable, unfeasible, unrealistic, nonviable, impracticable, unsuitable.
– OPPOSITES curable, workable.

inopportune ● adjective occurring at an inconvenient time.
– DERIVATIVES **inopportunely** adverb **inopportuneness** noun.

inordinate /inordinət/ ● adjective unusually large; excessive.
– DERIVATIVES **inordinately** adverb.
– ORIGIN originally in the sense 'disorderly': from Latin *inordinatus*, from *in-* 'not' + *ordinatus* 'set in order'.

inorganic ● adjective **1** not arising from natural growth. **2** Chemistry relating to or denoting compounds which are not organic (broadly, compounds not containing carbon).
– DERIVATIVES **inorganically** adverb.

inpatient ● noun a patient who is staying day and night in a hospital while receiving treatment.

in propria persona /in prōpriə persōnə/ ● adverb in his or her own person.
– ORIGIN Latin.

input ● noun **1** what is put or taken in or operated on by any process or system. **2** the action or process of putting or feeding something in. **3** a person's contribution. **4** energy supplied to a device or system; an electrical signal. **5** Electronics a place or device from which energy or information enters a system. ● verb (**inputting**; past and past part. **input** or **inputted**) put (data) into a computer.
– DERIVATIVES **inputter** noun.

inquest ● noun **1** a judicial inquiry to ascertain the facts relating to an incident. **2** Brit. an inquiry by a coroner's court into the cause of a death.
– ORIGIN Old French *enqueste*, from Latin *inquirere*, from *quaerere* 'speak'.

inquire ● verb another term for ENQUIRE.
– DERIVATIVES **inquirer** noun.

inquiry ● noun (pl. **inquiries**) another term for ENQUIRY.

inquisition ● noun **1** a period of prolonged and intensive questioning or investigation. **2** the verdict of a coroner's jury.
– DERIVATIVES **inquisitional** adjective.
– ORIGIN Latin, 'examination', from *inquirere* (see INQUEST).

inquisitive ● adjective **1** eagerly seeking knowledge. **2** prying.
– DERIVATIVES **inquisitively** adverb **inquisitiveness** noun.

inquisitor /inkwizzitər/ ● noun a person making an inquiry or conducting an inquisition, especially when regarded as harsh or very searching.
– DERIVATIVES **inquisitorial** adjective.

inquorate /inkworayt/ ● adjective Brit. (of an assembly) not having a quorum.

in re /in ree, ray/ ● preposition in the legal case of; with regard to.
– ORIGIN Latin, 'in the matter of'.

inroad ● noun **1** an instance of something being encroached or intruded upon. **2** a hostile attack.

inrush ● noun a sudden inward rush or flow.
– DERIVATIVES **inrushing** adjective & noun.

INS ● abbreviation (in the US) Immigration and Naturalization Service.

insalubrious /insəlo͞obriəss/ ● adjective seedy; unwholesome.

insane ● adjective **1** in or relating to an unsound state of mind; seriously mentally ill. **2** extremely foolish; irrational.
– DERIVATIVES **insanely** adverb **insanity** noun.
– ORIGIN Latin *insanus*, from *in-* 'not' + *sanus* 'healthy'.

insanitary ● adjective so dirty or germ-ridden as to be a danger to health.

insatiable /insayshəb'l/ ● adjective impossible to satisfy.
– DERIVATIVES **insatiability** noun **insatiably** adverb.

inscribe ● verb **1** write or carve (words or symbols) on a surface. **2** write a dedication to someone in (a book). **3** Geometry draw (a figure) within another so that their boundaries touch but do not intersect.
– DERIVATIVES **inscribable** adjective **inscriber** noun.
– ORIGIN Latin *inscribere*, from *in-* 'into' + *scribere* 'write'.

inscription ● noun **1** words or symbols inscribed on a monument, in a book, etc. **2** the action of inscribing.
– DERIVATIVES **inscriptional** adjective **inscriptive** adjective.

inscrutable /inskro͞otəb'l/ ● adjective impossible to understand or interpret.
– DERIVATIVES **inscrutability** noun **inscrutably** adverb.
– ORIGIN Latin *inscrutabilis*, from *in-* 'not' + *scrutari* 'to search'.

insect ● noun a small invertebrate animal with a head, thorax, and abdomen, six legs, two antennae, and usually one or two

Thesaurus

inoperative ● adjective **1** *the fan is inoperative* OUT OF ORDER, out of service, broken, out of commission, unserviceable, faulty, defective; down; *informal* bust, kaput, on the blink, acting up, shot; *Brit. informal* knackered. **2** *the contract is inoperative* VOID, null and void, invalid, ineffective, non-viable; cancelled, revoked, terminated; worthless, valueless, unproductive, abortive.
– OPPOSITES working, valid.

inopportune ● adjective INCONVENIENT, unsuitable, inappropriate, unfavourable, unfortunate, infelicitous, inexpedient; untimely, ill-timed, unseasonable; awkward, difficult.
– OPPOSITES convenient.

inordinate ● adjective EXCESSIVE, undue, unreasonable, unjustifiable, unwarrantable, disproportionate, unwarranted, unnecessary, needless, uncalled for, exorbitant, extreme; immoderate, extravagant; *informal* over the top, OTT.
– OPPOSITES moderate.

inorganic ● adjective INANIMATE, inert; lifeless, dead, defunct, extinct; mineral.

input ● noun *the errors resulted from invalid input* DATA, details, information, material; facts, figures, statistics, particulars, specifics; *informal* info.
● verb *she input data into the file* FEED IN, put in, load, insert; key in, type in; code, store.

inquest ● noun INQUIRY, investigation, inquisition, probe, examination, review, analysis; hearing.

inquire ● verb. See ENQUIRE.

inquiring ● adjective. See ENQUIRING.

inquiry ● noun. See ENQUIRY.

inquisition ● noun INTERROGATION, questioning, quizzing, cross-examination; investigation, inquiry, inquest; *informal* grilling; *Law* examination.

inquisitive ● adjective CURIOUS, interested, intrigued, agog; prying, spying, eavesdropping, intrusive, busybody, meddlesome; inquiring, questioning, probing; *informal* nosy, nosy-parker, snoopy.
– OPPOSITES uninterested.

insalubrious ● adjective SEEDY, unsavoury, sordid, seamy, sleazy, unpleasant, dismal, wretched; slummy, squalid, shabby, ramshackle, tumbledown, dilapidated, neglected, crumbling, decaying; *informal* scruffy, scuzzy, crummy; *Brit. informal* grotty; *N. Amer. informal* shacky.
– OPPOSITES smart.

insane ● adjective **1** *she was declared insane* MENTALLY ILL, mentally disordered, of unsound mind, certifiable; psychotic, schizophrenic; mad, deranged, demented, out of one's mind, non compos mentis, sick in the head, unhinged, unbalanced, unstable, disturbed, crazed; *informal* crazy, (stark) raving mad, not all there, bonkers, cracked, batty, cuckoo, loony, loopy, nuts, screwy, bananas, wacko, off one's rocker, off one's head, round the bend; *Brit. informal* crackers, barmy, barking (mad), off one's trolley, round the twist, not the full shilling; *N. Amer. informal* buggy, nutso, out of one's tree; *Austral./NZ informal* bushed. **2** *an insane suggestion* FOOLISH, idiotic, stupid, silly, senseless, nonsensical, absurd, ridiculous, ludicrous, preposterous, fatuous, inane, asinine, hare-brained, half-baked; impracticable, implausible, irrational, illogical; *informal* crazy, mad, cock-eyed; *Brit. informal* daft, barmy.
– OPPOSITES sensible, calm.

insanitary ● adjective UNHYGIENIC, unsanitary, unhealthy, insalubrious, dirty, filthy, unclean, impure, contaminated, polluted, foul; infected, infested, germ-ridden; *informal* germy.
– OPPOSITES hygienic.

insanity ● noun **1** *insanity runs in her family* MENTAL ILLNESS, madness, dementia; lunacy, instability; mania, psychosis; *informal* craziness. **2** *it would be insanity to take this loan* FOLLY, foolishness, madness, idiocy, stupidity, lunacy, silliness; *informal* craziness.

insatiable ● adjective UNQUENCHABLE, unappeasable, uncontrollable; voracious, gluttonous, greedy, hungry, ravenous, wolfish; avid, eager, keen; *informal* piggy; *poetic/literary* insatiate.

inscribe ● verb **1** *his name was inscribed above the door* CARVE, write, engrave, etch, cut; imprint, stamp, impress, mark. **2** *a book inscribed to him by the author* DEDICATE, address, name, sign.

inscription ● noun **1** *the inscription on the sarcophagus* ENGRAVING, etching; wording, writing, lettering, legend, epitaph, epigraph. **2** *the book had an inscription* DEDICATION, message; signature, autograph.

inscrutable ● adjective **1** *her inscrutable face* ENIGMATIC, unreadable, mysterious; unexpressive, inexpressive, emotionless, unemotional, expressionless, impassive, blank, vacant, deadpan, dispassionate; *informal* poker-faced. **2** *God's ways are inscrutable* MYS-

pairs of wings.
– ORIGIN from Latin *animal insectum* 'segmented animal', from *insecare* 'cut up or into'.

insectarium /insektairiəm/ (also **insectary** /insektəri/) ● noun (pl. **insectariums** or **insectaries**) a place where insects are kept, exhibited, and studied.

insecticide ● noun a substance used for killing insects.
– DERIVATIVES **insecticidal** adjective.

insectile ● adjective resembling an insect.

insectivore /insektivor/ ● noun **1** an animal that feeds on insects and other invertebrates. **2** Zoology a mammal of an order (Insectivora) that includes the shrews, moles, and hedgehogs.
– DERIVATIVES **insectivorous** adjective.

insecure ● adjective **1** not confident or assured. **2** not firm or firmly fixed. **3** (of a place) easily broken into; not protected.
– DERIVATIVES **insecurely** adverb **insecurity** noun.

inselberg /ins'lberg/ ● noun Geology an isolated hill rising abruptly from a plain.
– ORIGIN German, from *Insel* 'island' + *Berg* 'mountain'.

inseminate /insemminayt/ ● verb introduce semen into (a woman or a female animal).
– DERIVATIVES **insemination** noun **inseminator** noun.
– ORIGIN Latin *inseminare* 'sow'.

insensate ● adjective **1** lacking physical sensation. **2** lacking sympathy; unfeeling. **3** completely lacking sense or reason.
– DERIVATIVES **insensately** adverb.

insensible ● adjective **1** without one's mental faculties; unconscious. **2** numb; without feeling. **3** (**insensible of/to**) unaware of; indifferent to. **4** too small or gradual to be perceived.
– DERIVATIVES **insensibly** adverb **insensibility** noun.

insensitive ● adjective **1** showing or feeling no concern for the feelings of others. **2** not sensitive to physical sensation. **3** not appreciative of or able to respond to something.
– DERIVATIVES **insensitively** adverb **insensitiveness** noun **insensitivity** noun.

insentient ● adjective incapable of feeling; inanimate.
– DERIVATIVES **insentience** noun.

inseparable ● adjective unable to be separated or treated separately.
– DERIVATIVES **inseparability** noun **inseparably** adverb.

insert ● verb /insert/ place, fit, or incorporate into. ● noun /insert/ **1** a loose page or section in a magazine. **2** an ornamental section of cloth inserted into a garment. **3** a shot inserted in a film or video.
– DERIVATIVES **insertable** adjective **inserter** noun.
– ORIGIN Latin *inserere* 'put in'.

insertion ● noun **1** the action of inserting. **2** an amendment or addition inserted in a text. **3** each appearance of an advertisement in a newspaper or periodical. **4** an insert in a garment.

in-service ● adjective (of training) intended to take place during the course of employment.

inset ● noun /inset/ **1** a thing inserted; an insert. **2** a small picture or map inserted within the border of a larger one. ● verb /inset/ (**insetting**; past and past part. **inset** or **insetted**) **1** put in as an inset. **2** decorate with an inset.
– DERIVATIVES **insetter** noun.

inshore ● adjective **1** at sea but close to the shore. **2** operating at sea but near the coast. ● adverb towards or closer to the shore.

inside ● noun **1** the inner side or surface of a thing. **2** the inner part; the interior. **3** (**insides**) informal the stomach and bowels. **4** (**the inside**) informal a position affording private information. **5** the part of a road furthest from the centre. **6** the side of a bend where the edge is shorter. ● adjective **1** situated on or in, or derived from, the inside. **2** (in some sports) denoting positions nearer to the centre of the field. ● preposition & adverb **1** situated or moving within. **2** within (the body or mind of a person). **3** informal in prison. **4** (in some sports) closer to the centre of the field than. **5** in less than (the period of time specified).

inside job ● noun informal a crime committed by or with the assistance of a person associated with the premises where it occurred.

inside leg ● noun the length of a person's leg or trouser leg from crotch to ankle.

inside out ● adverb with the inner surface turned outwards.
– PHRASES **know inside out** know very thoroughly.

insider ● noun a person within an organization, especially someone privy to information unavailable to others.

insider dealing (also **insider trading**) ● noun the illegal practice of trading on the stock exchange to one's own advantage through having access to confidential information.

insidious /insiddiəss/ ● adjective proceeding in a gradual, subtle way, with harmful effect.
– DERIVATIVES **insidiously** adverb **insidiousness** noun.
– ORIGIN Latin *insidiosus* 'cunning'.

insight ● noun **1** the capacity to gain an accurate and intuitive

i

Thesaurus

TERIOUS, inexplicable, unexplainable, incomprehensible, impenetrable, unfathomable, opaque, abstruse, arcane, obscure, cryptic.
– OPPOSITES expressive, transparent.

insecure ● adjective **1** *an insecure young man* UNCONFIDENT, uncertain, unsure, doubtful, hesitant, self-conscious, unassertive, diffident, unforthcoming, shy, timid, retiring, timorous, inhibited, introverted; anxious, fearful, worried; *informal* mousy. **2** *insecure windows* UNGUARDED, unprotected, vulnerable, defenceless, unshielded, exposed, assailable, pregnable; unlocked, unsecured. **3** *an insecure footbridge* UNSTABLE, rickety, rocky, wobbly, shaky, unsteady, precarious; weak, flimsy, unsound, unsafe; *informal* jerry-built; *Brit. informal* dicky, dodgy.
– OPPOSITES confident, stable.

insecurity ● noun **1** *he hid his insecurity* LACK OF CONFIDENCE, self-doubt, diffidence, unassertiveness, timidity, uncertainty, nervousness, inhibition; anxiety, worry, unease. **2** *the insecurity of our situation* VULNERABILITY, defencelessness, peril, danger; instability, fragility, frailty, shakiness, unreliability.

insensate ● adjective. See INSENSIBLE sense 1.

insensible ● adjective **1** *she was insensible on the floor* UNCONSCIOUS, insensate, senseless, insentient, inert, comatose, knocked out, passed out, blacked out; stunned, numb, numbed; *informal* out (cold), out for the count, out of it, zonked (out), dead to the world; *Brit. informal* spark out. **2** *he was insensible to the risks* UNAWARE OF, ignorant of, unconscious of, unmindful of, oblivious to; indifferent to, impervious to, deaf to, blind to, unaffected by; *informal* in the dark about. **3** *he scared even the most insensible person* INSENSITIVE, dispassionate, cool, emotionless, unfeeling, unconcerned, detached, indifferent, hardened, tough; *informal* hard-boiled.
– OPPOSITES conscious, aware, sensitive.

insensitive ● adjective **1** *an insensitive bully* HEARTLESS, unfeeling, inconsiderate, thoughtless, thick-skinned; hard-hearted, cold-blooded, uncaring, unconcerned, unsympathetic, unkind, callous, cruel, merciless, pitiless. **2** *he was insensitive to her feelings* IMPERVIOUS TO, oblivious to, unaware of, unresponsive to, indifferent to, unaffected by, unmoved by, untouched by; *informal* in the dark about.
– OPPOSITES compassionate.

insentient ● adjective INANIMATE, lifeless, inorganic, inert; insensate, unconscious, comatose, anaesthetized, desensitized, numb; *informal* dead to the world, out (cold).

inseparable ● adjective **1** *inseparable friends* DEVOTED, bosom, close, fast, firm, good, best, intimate, boon, faithful; *informal* as thick as thieves. **2** *the laws are inseparable* INDIVISIBLE, indissoluble, inextricable, entangled; (one and) the same.

insert ● verb **1** *he inserted a tape in the machine* PUT, place, push, thrust, slide, slip, load, fit, slot, lodge, install; *informal* pop, stick, bung. **2** *she inserted a clause* ENTER, introduce, incorporate, interpolate, interpose, interject.
– OPPOSITES extract, remove.
● noun *the newspaper carried an insert* ENCLOSURE, insertion, inlay, supplement; circular, advertisement, pamphlet, leaflet; *informal* ad.

inside ● noun **1** *the inside of a volcano* INTERIOR, inner part; centre, core, middle, heart. **2** *(informal) my insides are out of order* STOMACH, gut, bowels, intestines; *informal* belly, tummy, guts.
– OPPOSITES exterior.
● adjective **1** *his inside pocket* INNER, interior, internal, innermost. **2** *inside information* CONFIDENTIAL, classified, restricted, privileged, private, secret, exclusive; *informal* hush-hush.
– OPPOSITES outer, public.
● adverb **1** *she ushered me inside* INDOORS, within, in. **2** *how do you feel inside?* INWARDLY, within, secretly, privately, deep down, at heart, emotionally, intuitively, instinctively. **3** *(informal) if I burgle again I'll be back inside* IN PRISON, in jail, in custody; locked up, imprisoned, incarcerated; *informal* behind bars, doing time; *Brit. informal* banged up.

insider ● noun MEMBER, worker, employee, representative; person in the know.

understanding of something. **2** understanding of this kind.
– DERIVATIVES **insightful** adjective

insignia /insigniə/ ● noun (pl. same) **1** a badge or distinguishing mark of authority, office, or membership. **2** literary a token of something.
– ORIGIN Latin, 'signs, badges', from *insignis* 'distinguished'.

insignificant ● adjective having little or no importance or value.
– DERIVATIVES **insignificance** noun **insignificancy** noun **insignificantly** adverb.

insincere ● adjective not expressing genuine feelings.
– DERIVATIVES **insincerely** adverb **insincerity** noun (pl. **insincerities**).

insinuate /insinyooayt/ ● verb **1** suggest or hint (something bad) in an indirect and unpleasant way. **2** (**insinuate oneself into**) manoeuvre oneself gradually into (a favourable position).
– DERIVATIVES **insinuating** adjective **insinuator** noun.
– ORIGIN originally in the sense 'enter (a document) on the official register': from Latin *insinuare* 'introduce tortuously', from *sinuare* 'to curve'.

insinuation ● noun an unpleasant hint or suggestion.

insipid /insippid/ ● adjective **1** lacking flavour. **2** lacking vigour or interest.
– DERIVATIVES **insipidity** noun **insipidly** adverb **insipidness** noun.
– ORIGIN Latin *insipidus*, from *in-* 'not' + *sapidus* 'tasty, savoury'.

insist ● verb **1** demand or state forcefully, without accepting refusal or contradiction. **2** (**insist on**) persist in (doing).
– ORIGIN Latin *insistere* 'persist', from *sistere* 'stand'.

insistent ● adjective **1** insisting or very demanding. **2** repeated and demanding attention.
– DERIVATIVES **insistence** noun **insistency** noun **insistently** adverb.

in situ /in sityoo/ ● adverb & adjective in the original or appropriate position.
– ORIGIN Latin.

insobriety ● noun drunkenness.

insofar ● adverb variant spelling of **in so far** (see FAR).

insolation /insəlaysh'n/ ● noun technical exposure to the sun's rays.
– ORIGIN Latin, from *insolare*, from *sol* 'sun'.

insole ● noun **1** a removable sole worn inside a shoe for warmth or to improve the fit. **2** the fixed inner sole of a boot or shoe.

insolent ● adjective rude and disrespectful.
– DERIVATIVES **insolence** noun **insolently** adverb.
– ORIGIN Latin, 'immoderate, arrogant'.

insoluble ● adjective **1** impossible to solve. **2** (of a substance) incapable of being dissolved.
– DERIVATIVES **insolubility** noun **insolubly** adverb.

insolvent ● adjective **1** having insufficient money to pay debts owed. **2** relating to bankruptcy. ● noun an insolvent person.
– DERIVATIVES **insolvency** noun.

insomnia ● noun habitual sleeplessness.
– DERIVATIVES **insomniac** noun & adjective.
– ORIGIN Latin, from *insomnis* 'sleepless'.

insomuch ● adverb (**insomuch that/as**) to the extent that.

insouciant /insoosiənt/ ● adjective casually unconcerned.
– DERIVATIVES **insouciance** noun **insouciantly** adverb.
– ORIGIN French, from *in-* 'not' + *souciant* 'worrying'.

inspect ● verb **1** look at closely. **2** examine officially.
– DERIVATIVES **inspection** noun.
– ORIGIN Latin *inspicere* 'look into, examine'.

inspector ● noun **1** an official who ensures that regulations are obeyed. **2** a police officer ranking below a chief inspector.
– DERIVATIVES **inspectorate** noun **inspectorial** adjective **inspectorship** noun.

Thesaurus

insidious ● adjective STEALTHY, subtle, surreptitious, cunning, crafty, artful, sly, wily, underhand, backhanded, indirect; informal sneaky.

insight ● noun **1** *your insight has been invaluable* INTUITION, discernment, perception, awareness, understanding, comprehension, apprehension, appreciation, penetration, acumen, perspicacity, judgement, acuity; vision, prescience, imagination; informal nous, savvy. **2** *an insight into the government* UNDERSTANDING OF, appreciation of, revelation about; introduction to; informal eye-opener.

insignia ● noun BADGE, crest, emblem, symbol, sign, device, mark, seal, colours.

insignificant ● adjective UNIMPORTANT, trivial, trifling, negligible, inconsequential, of no account, inconsiderable; nugatory, paltry, petty, insubstantial, frivolous, pointless, worthless, irrelevant, immaterial, peripheral; informal piddling.

insincere ● adjective FALSE, fake, hollow, artificial, feigned, pretended, put-on; disingenuous, hypocritical, cynical, deceitful, deceptive, duplicitous, double-dealing, two-faced, lying, untruthful, mendacious; informal phoney, pretend, pseud.

insinuate ● verb **1** *he insinuated that she lied* IMPLY, suggest, hint, intimate, indicate, let it be known, give someone to understand; informal make out, tip someone the wink. **2** *he insinuated his hand under hers* SLIDE, slip, manoeuvre, insert, edge.
– PHRASES **insinuate oneself into** WORM ONE'S WAY INTO, ingratiate oneself with, curry favour with; foist oneself on, introduce oneself into; infiltrate, invade, sneak into, intrude on, impinge on; informal muscle in on.

insinuation ● noun IMPLICATION, inference, suggestion, hint, intimation, innuendo, reference, allusion, indication, undertone, overtone; aspersion, slur, allegation.

insipid ● adjective **1** *insipid coffee* TASTELESS, flavourless, savourless, bland, weak, wishy-washy; unappetizing, unpalatable. **2** *insipid pictures* UNIMAGINATIVE, uninspired, uninspiring, characterless, flat, uninteresting, lacklustre, dull, boring, dry (as dust), jejune, humdrum, run-of-the-mill, commonplace, pedestrian, trite, tired, hackneyed, stale, lame, tame, poor, inadequate, sterile, anaemic.
– OPPOSITES tasty, interesting.

insist ● verb **1** *be prepared to insist* STAND FIRM, stand one's ground, be resolute, be determined, hold out, be emphatic, not take no for an answer; persevere, persist; informal stick to one's guns. **2** *she insisted that they pay up* DEMAND, command, require, dictate; urge, exhort. **3** *he insisted that he knew nothing* MAINTAIN, assert, hold, contend, argue, protest, claim, vow, swear, declare, stress, repeat, reiterate; formal aver.

insistence ● noun **1** *she sat down at Anne's insistence* DEMAND, bidding, command, dictate, instruction, requirement, request, entreaty, exhortation; informal say-so; poetic/literary behest. **2** *his insistence that he loved her* ASSERTION, declaration, contention, claim, pronouncement, assurance, affirmation, avowal, profession.

insistent ● adjective **1** *Tony's insistent questioning* PERSISTENT, determined, adamant, importunate, tenacious, unyielding, dogged, unrelenting, inexorable; demanding, pushy, urgent; emphatic, firm, assertive. **2** *an insistent buzzing* INCESSANT, constant, unremitting, repetitive; obtrusive, intrusive.

insobriety ● noun DRUNKENNESS, intoxication, inebriation, tipsiness; informal tightness; poetic/literary crapulence.

insolent ● adjective IMPERTINENT, impudent, cheeky, ill-mannered, bad mannered, unmannerly, rude, impolite, uncivil, discourteous, disrespectful, insubordinate, contemptuous; audacious, bold, cocky, brazen; insulting, abusive; informal fresh, flip, lippy, saucy; N. Amer. informal sassy; archaic contumelious, malapert.
– OPPOSITES polite.

insoluble ● adjective **1** *some problems are insoluble* UNSOLVABLE, unanswerable, unresolvable; unfathomable, impenetrable, unexplainable, inscrutable, inexplicable. **2** *these minerals are insoluble* INDISSOLUBLE.

insolvency ● noun BANKRUPTCY, liquidation, failure, collapse, (financial) ruin; pennilessness, penury; Brit. receivership.

insolvent ● adjective BANKRUPT, ruined, liquidated, wiped out; penniless, impoverished, impecunious; Brit. in receivership, without a penny (to one's name); informal bust, (flat) broke, belly-up, gone to the wall, on the rocks, in the red, hard up, strapped for cash; Brit. informal skint, in Queer Street, stony broke, cleaned out; formal penurious.

insomnia ● noun SLEEPLESSNESS, wakefulness, restlessness; archaic watchfulness.

insouciance ● noun NONCHALANCE, unconcern, indifference, heedlessness, calm, equanimity, composure, ease, airiness; informal cool.
– OPPOSITES anxiety.

insouciant ● adjective NONCHALANT, untroubled, unworried, unruffled, unconcerned, indifferent, blasé, heedless; relaxed, calm, equable, equanimous, serene, composed, easy, carefree, free and easy, happy-go-lucky, light-hearted; informal cool, laid back.
– OPPOSITES anxious.

inspect ● verb EXAMINE, check, scrutinize, investigate, vet, test, monitor, survey, study, look over, scan, explore, probe; assess, appraise, review; informal check out, give something a/the once-over.

inspiration ● noun **1** the process or quality of being inspired. **2** a person or thing that inspires. **3** a sudden clever or timely idea. **4** the process of inhalation.
– DERIVATIVES **inspirational** adjective.
inspiratory /inspīrətəri/ ● adjective Physiology relating to inhalation.
inspire ● verb **1** fill with the urge or ability to do or feel something. **2** create (a feeling) in a person. **3** give rise to. **4** inhale.
– DERIVATIVES **inspirer** noun **inspiring** adjective.
– ORIGIN Latin *inspirare* 'breathe or blow into'.
inspired ● adjective **1** showing or characterized by inspiration. **2** (of air or another substance) having been inhaled.
inspirit ● verb (**inspirited**, **inspiriting**) (usu. as adj. **inspiriting**) encourage and enliven.
– DERIVATIVES **inspiritingly** adverb.
inspissate /inspissayt/ ● verb thicken or congeal.
– ORIGIN Latin *inspissare*.
instability ● noun (pl. **instabilities**) lack of stability.
install (also **instal**) ● verb (**installed**, **installing**) **1** place or fix (equipment) in position ready for use. **2** establish in a new place, condition, or role.
– DERIVATIVES **installer** noun.
– ORIGIN Latin *installare*, from *stallum* 'place, stall'.
installation ● noun **1** the action or process of installing or being installed. **2** a large piece of equipment installed for use. **3** a military or industrial establishment. **4** an art exhibit constructed within a gallery.
instalment (US also **installment**) ● noun **1** a sum of money due as one of several payments made over a period of time. **2** one of several parts of something published or broadcast at intervals.
– ORIGIN Old French *estalement*, from *estaler* 'to fix'.
instance ● noun **1** an example or single occurrence of something. **2** a particular case. ● verb cite as an example.
– PHRASES **for instance** as an example. **in the first** (or **second** etc.) **instance** in the first (or second etc.) place or stage of a proceeding.
– ORIGIN originally in the sense 'urgent entreaty', later 'example to the contrary': from Latin *instantia* 'presence, urgency', from *instare* (see INSTANT).
instant ● adjective **1** immediate. **2** urgent; pressing. **3** (of food) processed to allow quick preparation. ● noun **1** a precise moment of time. **2** a very short time.
– DERIVATIVES **instantly** adverb.
– ORIGIN Latin, from *instare* 'be present, press upon'.
instantaneous /instəntayniəss/ ● adjective **1** occurring or done instantly. **2** Physics existing or measured at a particular instant.
– DERIVATIVES **instantaneity** noun **instantaneously** adverb **instantaneousness** noun.
instantiate /instanshiayt/ ● verb represent as or by a particular instance or example.
– DERIVATIVES **instantiation** noun.
instate ● verb install or establish.
instead ● adverb **1** as an alternative or substitute. **2** (**instead of**) in place of.
instep ● noun the part of a person's foot between the ball and the ankle.
– ORIGIN of unknown origin.
instigate /instigayt/ ● verb **1** bring about or initiate. **2** (**instigate to/to do**) incite (someone) to do.
– DERIVATIVES **instigation** noun **instigator** noun.

i

Thesaurus

inspection ● noun EXAMINATION, check-up, survey, scrutiny, probe, exploration, observation, investigation; assessment, appraisal, review, evaluation; *informal* once-over, going-over, look-see, overhaul.
inspector ● noun EXAMINER, checker, scrutinizer, scrutineer, investigator, surveyor, assessor, appraiser, reviewer, analyst; observer, overseer, supervisor, monitor, watchdog, ombudsman; auditor.
inspiration ● noun **1** *she's a real inspiration to others* STIMULUS, stimulation, motivation, fillip, encouragement, influence, muse, spur, lift, boost, incentive, impulse, catalyst; example, model. **2** *his work lacks inspiration* CREATIVITY, inventiveness, innovation, ingenuity, imagination, originality; artistry, creativity, insight, vision; finesse, flair. **3** *she had a sudden inspiration* BRIGHT IDEA, revelation; *informal* brainwave; *N. Amer. informal* brainstorm. **4** *inspiration pains her* INHALATION, breathing in; respiration.
inspire ● verb **1** *the landscape inspired him to write* STIMULATE, motivate, encourage, influence, rouse, move, stir, energize, galvanize, incite; animate, fire, inspirit, incentivize. **2** *the film inspired a musical* GIVE RISE TO, lead to, bring about, cause, prompt, spawn, engender; *poetic/literary* beget. **3** *Charles inspired awe in her* AROUSE, awaken, prompt, induce, ignite, trigger, kindle, produce, bring out; *poetic/literary* enkindle.
inspired ● adjective OUTSTANDING, wonderful, marvellous, excellent, magnificent, fine, exceptional, first-class, first-rate, virtuoso, supreme, superlative; innovative, innovatory, innovational, ingenious, original; *informal* tremendous, superb, super, ace, wicked, awesome, out of this world; *Brit. informal* brilliant, brill.
– OPPOSITES poor.
inspiring ● adjective INSPIRATIONAL, encouraging, heartening, uplifting, stirring, rousing, stimulating, electrifying; moving, affecting, influential.
instability ● noun **1** *the instability of political life* UNRELIABILITY, uncertainty, unpredictability, insecurity, perilousness, riskiness; impermanence, inconstancy, changeability, variability, fluctuation, mutability. **2** *emotional instability* VOLATILITY, unpredictability, variability, capriciousness, vacillation; frailty, infirmity, weakness, irregularity. **3** *the instability of the foundations* UNSTEADINESS, unsoundness, shakiness, frailty, fragility.
install ● verb **1** *a photocopier was installed in the office* PUT, position, place, locate, situate, station, site, lodge; insert. **2** *they installed a new president* SWEAR IN, induct, instate, inaugurate, invest; appoint, take on; ordain, consecrate, anoint; enthrone, crown. **3** *she installed herself behind the table* ENSCONCE, establish, position, settle, seat, lodge, plant; sit (down); *informal* plonk, park; *Brit. informal* take a pew.
– OPPOSITES remove.
installation ● noun **1** *the installation of radiators* INSTALLING, fitting, putting in; insertion. **2** *the installation of the chancellor* SWEARING IN, induction, instatement, inauguration, investiture; ordination, consecration; enthronement, coronation. **3** *a new computer installation* UNIT, appliance, fixture; equipment, machinery. **4** *an army installation* BASE, camp, post, depot, centre, facility; premises.
instalment ● noun **1** *I pay by monthly instalments* PART PAYMENT; deferred payment; *Brit.* hire purchase, HP; *Brit. informal* the never-never. **2** *a story published in instalments* PART, portion, section, segment, bit; chapter, episode, volume, issue.
instance ● noun **1** *an instance of racism* EXAMPLE, exemplar, occasion, occurrence, case; illustration. **2** *(formal) proceedings began at the instance of the director* INSTIGATION, prompting, suggestion; request, entreaty, demand, insistence; wish, desire.
● verb *as an example I would instance Jones's work* CITE, quote, refer to, mention, allude to, give; specify, name, identify, draw attention to, put forward, offer, advance.
– PHRASES **in the first instance** INITIALLY, at first, at the start, at the outset, in/at the beginning, to begin with, to start with, originally.
instant ● adjective **1** *instant access to your money* IMMEDIATE, instantaneous, on-the-spot, prompt, swift, speedy, rapid, quick, express, lightning; sudden, precipitate, abrupt; *informal* snappy, p.d.q. (pretty damn quick). **2** *instant meals* PRE-PREPARED, pre-cooked, ready mixed, fast; microwaveable, convenience, TV.
– OPPOSITES delayed.
● noun **1** *come here this instant!* MOMENT, time, minute, second; juncture, point. **2** *it all happened in an instant* TRICE, moment, minute, (split) second, twinkling of an eye, flash, no time (at all); *informal* sec, jiffy, the blink of an eye; *Brit. informal* mo; *N. Amer. informal* snap.
instantaneous ● adjective IMMEDIATE, instant, on-the-spot, prompt, swift, speedy, rapid, quick, express, lightning; sudden, hurried, precipitate; *informal* snappy, p.d.q. (pretty damn quick).
– OPPOSITES delayed.
instantly ● adverb IMMEDIATELY, at once, straight away, right away, instantaneously; suddenly, abruptly, all of a sudden; forthwith, there and then, here and now, this/that minute, this/that instant; quickly, rapidly, speedily, promptly; in an instant, in a moment, in a (split) second, in a trice, in/like a flash, like a shot, in the twinkling of an eye, in no time (at all), before you know it; *informal* in a jiffy, pronto, before you can say Jack Robinson, double quick, like (greased) lightning; *archaic* instanter.
instead ● adverb *travel by train instead* AS AN ALTERNATIVE, in lieu, alternatively; rather, by contrast, for preference, by/from choice; on second thoughts, all things being equal, ideally; *N. Amer.* alternately.

– ORIGIN Latin *instigare* 'urge, incite'.

instil /instil/ (also **instill**) ● verb (**instilled, instilling**) **1** gradually but firmly establish (an idea or attitude) in someone's mind. **2** put (a liquid) into something in drops.
– DERIVATIVES **instillation** noun.
– ORIGIN Latin *instillare* 'put in by drops'.

instinct ● noun **1** an inborn tendency or impulse to behave in a certain way. **2** a natural ability or skill. ● adjective (**instinct with**) formal imbued or filled with (a quality).
– DERIVATIVES **instinctual** adjective.
– ORIGIN Latin *instinctus* 'impulse'.

instinctive ● adjective relating to or prompted by instinct; apparently natural or automatic.
– DERIVATIVES **instinctively** adverb.

institute ● noun an organization for the promotion of science, education, etc. ● verb **1** begin or establish. **2** appoint to a position, especially as a cleric.
– ORIGIN from Latin *instituere* 'establish'.

institution ● noun **1** an important organization or public body, such as a university, bank, hospital, or Church. **2** an organization providing residential care for people with special needs. **3** an established law or custom. **4** informal a well-established and familiar person or thing. **5** the action of instituting.

institutional ● adjective **1** of, in, or like an institution. **2** typical of an institution, especially in being regimented or unimaginative.
– DERIVATIVES **institutionally** adverb.

i

institutionalize (also **institutionalise**) ● verb **1** establish as a norm in an organization or culture: *claims that racism is institutionalized in education.* **2** place in a residential institution. **3** (**be/become institutionalized**) suffer the adverse effects of long-term residence in a residential institution.
– DERIVATIVES **institutionalization** noun.

instruct ● verb **1** direct or command. **2** teach. **3** inform of a fact or situation. **4** chiefly Brit. authorize (a solicitor or barrister) to act on one's behalf.
– ORIGIN Latin *instruere* 'construct, equip, teach'.

instruction ● noun **1** a direction or order. **2** teaching or education. **3** a code in a computer program which defines and carries out an operation.
– DERIVATIVES **instructional** adjective.

instructive ● adjective useful and informative.
– DERIVATIVES **instructively** adverb.

instructor (or **instructress**) ● noun **1** a teacher. **2** N. Amer. a university teacher ranking below assistant professor.
– DERIVATIVES **instructorship** noun.

instrument ● noun **1** a tool or implement, especially for precision work. **2** a measuring device, especially in a vehicle or aircraft. **3** (also **musical instrument**) a device for producing musical sounds. **4** a means of pursuing an aim. **5** a person who is made use of. **6** a formal or legal document.
– ORIGIN Latin *instrumentum* 'equipment, implement'.

instrumental ● adjective **1** serving as a means of pursuing an aim. **2** (of music) performed on instruments. **3** relating to an implement or measuring device. ● noun a piece of music performed by instruments, with no vocals.
– DERIVATIVES **instrumentality** noun **instrumentally** adverb.

instrumentalist ● noun a player of a musical instrument.

Thesaurus

– PHRASES **instead of** AS AN ALTERNATIVE TO, as a substitute for, as a replacement for, in place of, in lieu of, in preference to; rather than, as opposed to, as against, as contrasted with, before.

instigate ● verb **1** *they instigated formal proceedings* SET IN MOTION, get under way, get off the ground, start, commence, begin, initiate, launch, institute, set up, inaugurate, establish, organize; actuate, generate, bring about; start the ball rolling; informal kick off. **2** *he instigated men to refuse allegiance* INCITE, encourage, urge, goad, provoke, spur on, push, press, prompt, induce, prevail upon, motivate, influence, persuade, sway; informal put up to.
– OPPOSITES halt, dissuade.

instigation ● noun **1** *they became involved at his instigation* PROMPTING, suggestion; request, entreaty, demand, insistence; wish, desire, persuasion; formal instance. **2** *foreign instigation of the disorder* INITIATION, incitement, provocation, fomentation, encouragement, inducement, inception.

instigator ● noun INITIATOR, prime mover, motivator, architect, designer, planner, inventor, mastermind, originator, author, creator, agent; founder, pioneer, founding father; agitator, fomenter, troublemaker, ringleader.

instil ● verb **1** *we instil vigilance in our children* INCULCATE, implant, ingrain, impress, imprint, introduce; engender, produce, generate, induce, inspire, promote, foster; drum into. **2** *he instilled Monet with a love of nature* IMBUE, inspire, infuse, inculcate; indoctrinate; teach. **3** *she instilled the eye drops* ADMINISTER, introduce, infuse, inject.

instinct ● noun **1** *some instinct told me to be careful* NATURAL TENDENCY, inherent tendency, inclination, urge, drive, compulsion, need; intuition, feeling, sixth sense, insight; nose. **2** *a good instinct for acting* TALENT, gift, ability, aptitude, skill, flair, feel, genius, knack, bent.

instinctive ● adjective INTUITIVE, natural, instinctual, innate, inborn, inherent; unconscious, subconscious, intuitional; automatic, reflex, knee-jerk, mechanical, spontaneous, involuntary, impulsive; informal gut.
– OPPOSITES learned, voluntary.

institute ● noun *a research institute* ORGANIZATION, establishment, institution, foundation, centre; academy, school, college, university; society, association, federation, body, guild.
● verb **1** *we instituted a search* INITIATE, set in motion, get under way, get off the ground, start, commence, begin, launch; set up, inaugurate, found, establish, organize, generate, bring about; start the ball rolling; informal kick off. **2** *he will be instituted as vicar* INSTALL, instate, induct, invest, inaugurate, swear in, initiate; ordain, consecrate, anoint; appoint, create.
– OPPOSITES end, dismiss.

institution ● noun **1** *an academic institution* ESTABLISHMENT, organization, institute, foundation, centre; academy, school, college, university; society, association, body, guild, consortium. **2** *they spent their lives in institutions* (RESIDENTIAL) HOME, hospital, asylum. **3** *the institution of the rector* INSTALLATION, instatement, induction, investiture, inauguration; ordination, consecration, anointing, appointment, creation. **4** *the institution of adoption* PRACTICE, custom, convention, tradition; phenomenon, fact; procedure, usage, method, system, policy; idea, notion, concept. **5** *the institution of legal proceedings* INITIATION, instigation, launch, start, commencement, beginning, inauguration, generation, origination.

institutional ● adjective **1** *an institutional framework for discussions* ORGANIZED, established, bureaucratic, conventional, procedural, prescribed, set, routine, formal, systematic, systematized, methodical, businesslike, orderly, coherent, structured, regulated. **2** *the rooms are rather institutional* IMPERSONAL, formal, regimented, uniform, unvaried, monotonous; insipid, bland, uninteresting, dull; unappealing, uninviting, unattractive, unwelcoming, dreary, drab, colourless; stark, spartan, bare, clinical, sterile.

instruct ● verb **1** *the union instructed them to strike* ORDER, direct, command, tell, enjoin, require, call on, mandate, charge; poetic/literary bid. **2** *nobody instructed him in how to operate it* TEACH, school, coach, train, enlighten, inform, educate, tutor, guide, prepare, prime. **3** *she instructed a solicitor of her own choice* EMPLOY, authorize, brief. **4** *the bank was instructed that money would be withdrawn* INFORM, tell, notify, apprise, advise, brief, prime; informal put in the picture, fill in.

instruction ● noun **1** *do not disobey my instructions* ORDER, command, directive, direction, decree, edict, injunction, mandate, dictate, commandment, bidding; requirement, stipulation; informal say-so; poetic/literary behest. **2** *read the instructions* DIRECTIONS, key, specification; handbook, manual, guide. **3** *he gave instruction in demolition work* TUITION, teaching, coaching, schooling, tutelage; lessons, classes, lectures; training, drill, preparation, grounding, guidance.

instructive ● adjective INFORMATIVE, instructional, informational, illuminating, enlightening, explanatory; educational, educative, edifying, didactic, pedagogic, heuristic; improving, moralistic, homiletic; useful, helpful.

instructor ● noun TRAINER, coach, teacher, tutor; adviser, counsellor, guide; educator; formal pedagogue.

instrument ● noun **1** *a wound made with a sharp instrument* IMPLEMENT, tool, utensil; device, apparatus, contrivance, gadget. **2** *check all the cockpit instruments* MEASURING DEVICE, gauge, meter; indicator, dial, display. **3** *they tuned their instruments* MUSICAL INSTRUMENT. **4** *an instrument of learning* AGENT, agency, cause, channel, medium, means, mechanism, vehicle, organ. **5** *a mere instrument acting under coercion* PAWN, puppet, creature, dupe, cog; tool, cat's paw; informal stooge.

instrumental ● adjective INVOLVED, active, influential, contribu-

instrumentation ● noun **1** the instruments used in a piece of music. **2** the arrangement of a piece of music for particular instruments. **3** measuring instruments collectively.

insubordinate ● adjective disobedient.
– DERIVATIVES **insubordination** noun.

insubstantial ● adjective **1** lacking strength and solidity. **2** imaginary.
– DERIVATIVES **insubstantiality** noun **insubstantially** adverb.

insufferable ● adjective **1** too extreme to bear; intolerable. **2** unbearably arrogant or conceited.
– DERIVATIVES **insufferableness** noun **insufferably** adverb.
– ORIGIN from Latin *sufferre* 'suffer'.

insufficient ● adjective not enough.
– DERIVATIVES **insufficiency** noun **insufficiently** adverb.

insulant ● noun an insulating material.

insular ● adjective **1** isolated from outside influences, and often narrow-minded as a result. **2** relating to or from an island.
– DERIVATIVES **insularity** noun.
– ORIGIN Latin *insularis*, from *insula* 'island'.

insulate ● verb **1** protect by interposing material to prevent loss of heat or intrusion of sound. **2** cover with non-conducting material to prevent the passage of electricity. **3** protect from something unpleasant.
– DERIVATIVES **insulator** noun.
– ORIGIN from Latin *insula* 'island'.

insulating tape ● noun adhesive tape used to cover exposed electric wires.

insulation ● noun **1** the action of insulating or state of being insulated. **2** material used to insulate something.

insulin ● noun a hormone produced in the pancreas, which regulates glucose levels in the blood, and the lack of which causes diabetes.
– ORIGIN from Latin *insula* 'island' (with reference to the islets of Langerhans in the pancreas).

insult ● verb /insult/ speak to or treat with disrespect or abuse. ● noun /insult/ **1** an insulting remark or action. **2** a thing so worthless or contemptible as to be offensive: *the pay offer is an absolute insult.*
– ORIGIN Latin *insultare* 'jump or trample on'.

insuperable /insōōpərəb'l/ ● adjective impossible to overcome.
– DERIVATIVES **insuperably** adverb.
– ORIGIN Latin *insuperabilis*, from *superare* 'overcome'.

insupportable ● adjective **1** unable to be supported or justified. **2** intolerable.
– DERIVATIVES **insupportably** adverb.

insurance ● noun **1** the action of insuring. **2** the business of providing insurance. **3** money paid for insurance, or as compensation under an insurance policy. **4** a thing providing protection against a possible eventuality.

insure ● verb **1** arrange for compensation in the event of damage to or loss of (property, life, or a person), in exchange for regular payments to a company. **2** secure the payment of (a sum) in this way. **3** (**insure against**) protect (someone) against (a possible eventuality). **4** another term for ENSURE.
– DERIVATIVES **insurable** adjective **insurer** noun.
– ORIGIN alteration of ENSURE.

insurgent /insurjənt/ ● adjective rising in active revolt. ● noun a rebel or revolutionary.
– DERIVATIVES **insurgence** noun **insurgency** noun (pl. **insurgencies**).
– ORIGIN from Latin *insurgere* 'rise up'.

insurmountable /insəmowntəb'l/ ● adjective too great to be overcome.
– DERIVATIVES **insurmountably** adverb.

i

Thesaurus

tory; helpful, useful, of service; significant, important; (**be instrumental in**) play a part in, contribute to, be a factor in, have a hand in; add to, help, promote, advance, further; be conducive to, make for, lead to, cause.

insubordinate ● adjective DISOBEDIENT, unruly, wayward, errant, badly behaved, disorderly, undisciplined, delinquent, troublesome, rebellious, defiant, recalcitrant, uncooperative, wilful, intractable, unmanageable, uncontrollable; awkward, difficult, perverse, contrary; *Brit. informal* bolshie.
– OPPOSITES obedient.

insubordination ● noun DISOBEDIENCE, unruliness, indiscipline, bad behaviour, misbehaviour, misconduct, delinquency; rebellion, defiance, mutiny, revolt; recalcitrance, wilfulness, awkwardness, perversity; *informal* acting-up; *Law* contumacy.

insubstantial ● adjective **1** *an insubstantial structure* FLIMSY, slight, fragile, breakable, weak, frail, unstable, shaky, wobbly, rickety, ramshackle, jerry-built. **2** *insubstantial evidence* WEAK, flimsy, feeble, poor, inadequate, insufficient, tenuous, insignificant, inconsequential, unsubstantial, unconvincing, implausible, unsatisfactory, paltry. **3** *the light made her seem insubstantial* INTANGIBLE, impalpable, untouchable, discarnate, unsubstantial, incorporeal; imaginary, unreal, illusory, spectral, ghostlike, vaporous; *Philosophy* immaterial.
– OPPOSITES sturdy, sound, tangible.

insufferable ● adjective **1** *the heat was insufferable* INTOLERABLE, unbearable, unendurable, insupportable, unacceptable, oppressive, overwhelming, overpowering; more than flesh and blood can stand; *informal* too much. **2** *his win made him insufferable* CONCEITED, arrogant, boastful, cocky, cocksure, full of oneself, self-important, swaggering; vain, self-satisfied, self-congratulatory, smug; *informal* swollen-headed, big-headed, too big for one's boots; *poetic/literary* vainglorious.
– OPPOSITES bearable, modest.

insufficient ● adjective INADEQUATE, deficient, poor, scant, scanty; not enough, too little, too few, too small; scarce, sparse, in short supply, lacking, wanting; paltry, meagre, niggardly; incomplete, restricted, limited; *informal* measly, pathetic, piddling.

insular ● adjective **1** *insular people* NARROW-MINDED, small-minded, blinkered, inward-looking, parochial, provincial, small-town, short-sighted, hidebound, set in one's ways, inflexible, rigid, entrenched; illiberal, intolerant, prejudiced, bigoted, biased, partisan, xenophobic; *Brit.* blimpish. **2** *an insular existence* ISOLATED, inaccessible, cut off, segregated, detached, solitary, lonely.
– OPPOSITES broad-minded, cosmopolitan.

insulate ● verb **1** *pipes must be insulated* WRAP, sheathe, cover, encase, enclose, envelop; lag, heatproof, soundproof; pad, cushion. **2** *they were insulated from the impact of the war* PROTECT, save, shield, shelter, screen, cushion, cocoon; isolate, segregate, sequester, detach, cut off.

insulation ● noun **1** *a layer of insulation* LAGGING; blanket, jacket, wrap. **2** *insulation from the rigours of city life* PROTECTION, defence, shelter, screen, shield; isolation, segregation, separation, sequestration, detachment.

insult ● verb *he insulted my wife* ABUSE, be rude to, call someone names, slight, disparage, discredit, libel, slander, malign, defame, denigrate, cast aspersions on; offend, affront, hurt, humiliate, wound; *informal* bad-mouth; *Brit. informal* slag off; *formal* derogate, calumniate; *rare* asperse.
– OPPOSITES compliment.
● noun *he hurled insults at us* ABUSIVE REMARK, jibe, affront, slight, barb, slur, indignity; injury, libel, slander, defamation; abuse, disparagement, aspersions; *informal* dig, put-down, slap in the face, kick in the teeth.

insulting ● adjective ABUSIVE, rude, offensive, disparaging, belittling, derogatory, deprecatory, disrespectful, denigratory, uncomplimentary, pejorative; disdainful, derisive, scornful, contemptuous; defamatory, slanderous, libellous, scurrilous, blasphemous; *informal* bitchy, catty.

insuperable ● adjective INSURMOUNTABLE, invincible, unassailable; overwhelming, hopeless, impossible.

insupportable ● adjective **1** *this view is insupportable* UNJUSTIFIABLE, indefensible, inexcusable, unwarrantable, unreasonable; groundless, unfounded, baseless, unsupported, unsubstantiated, unconfirmed, uncorroborated, invalid, untenable, implausible, weak, flawed, specious, defective. **2** *the heat was insupportable* INTOLERABLE, insufferable, unbearable, unendurable; oppressive, overwhelming, overpowering, more than flesh and blood can stand; *informal* too much.
– OPPOSITES justified, bearable.

insurance ● noun **1** *insurance for his new car* INDEMNITY, indemnification, assurance, (financial) protection, security, cover. **2** *insurance against a third World War* PROTECTION, defence, safeguard, security, precaution, provision; immunity; guarantee, warranty; *informal* backstop.

insure ● verb PROVIDE INSURANCE FOR, indemnify, cover, assure, protect, underwrite; guarantee, warrant.

insurgent ● adjective *insurgent forces* REBELLIOUS, rebel, revolutionary, mutinous, insurrectionist; renegade, seditious, subversive.
– OPPOSITES loyal.
● noun *the troops are fighting insurgents* REBEL, revolutionary,

insurrection /insəreksh'n/ ● noun a violent uprising against authority.
– DERIVATIVES **insurrectionary** adjective **insurrectionist** noun & adjective.
– ORIGIN Latin, from *insurgere* 'rise up'.
insusceptible ● adjective not susceptible.
– DERIVATIVES **insusceptibility** noun.
intact ● adjective not damaged or impaired.
– DERIVATIVES **intactness** noun.
– ORIGIN Latin *intactus* 'untouched'.
intaglio /intaaliō/ ● noun (pl. **intaglios**) **1** an incised or engraved design. **2** a gem with an incised design.
– ORIGIN Italian, from *intagliare* 'engrave'.
intake ● noun **1** an amount or quantity taken in. **2** an act of taking in. **3** a location or structure through which something is taken in.
intangible ● adjective **1** unable to be touched; not solid or real. **2** vague and abstract. ● noun an intangible thing.
– DERIVATIVES **intangibility** noun **intangibly** adverb.
intarsia /intaarsiə/ ● noun **1** a method of knitting in which a separate length or ball of yarn is used for each area of colour. **2** elaborate marquetry or inlaid work.
– ORIGIN Italian *intarsio*; superseding earlier *tarsia* 'marquetry'.
integer /intijər/ ● noun a whole number.
– ORIGIN from Latin, 'intact, whole', from *tangere* 'to touch'; compare with ENTIRE.
integral ● adjective /intigrəl, integ-/ **1** necessary to make a whole complete; fundamental. **2** included as part of a whole. **3** forming a whole; complete. **4** Mathematics of or denoted by an integer or integers. ● noun /intigrəl/ Mathematics a function of which a given function is the derivative, and which may express the area under the curve of a graph of the function.
– DERIVATIVES **integrally** adverb.
– USAGE There are two possible pronunciations for the adjective **integral**: one with the stress on the **in-** and the other with the stress on the **-teg-**. In British English, the second pronunciation is sometimes frowned on, but both are broadly accepted as standard.
integral calculus ● noun Mathematics the part of calculus concerned with the integrals of functions.
integrate ● verb /intigrayt/ **1** combine or be combined to form a whole. **2** bring or come into equal participation in an institution or body. **3** Mathematics find the integral of.
– DERIVATIVES **integrable** /intigrəb'l/ adjective **integrative** /intigrətiv/ adjective **integrator** noun.
– ORIGIN Latin *integrare* 'make whole', from *integer* 'whole, intact'.
integrated circuit ● noun an electronic circuit on a small piece of semiconducting material, performing the same function as a larger circuit of discrete components.
integrated services digital network ● noun a telecommunications network through which sound, images, and data can be transmitted as digitized signals.
integration ● noun **1** the action or process of integrating. **2** the intermixing of peoples or groups previously segregated.
– DERIVATIVES **integrationist** noun.
integrity /integriti/ ● noun **1** the quality of being honest and morally upright. **2** the state of being whole or unified. **3** soundness of construction.
– ORIGIN Latin *integritas*, from *integer* 'intact, whole'.
integument /integyoomənt/ ● noun a tough outer protective layer, especially of an animal or plant.
– ORIGIN Latin *integumentum*, from *integere* 'to cover'.
intellect ● noun **1** the faculty of reasoning and understanding objectively. **2** a person's mental powers. **3** a clever person.
– ORIGIN Latin *intellectus* 'understanding'.
intellectual /intəlektyooəl/ ● adjective **1** relating or appealing to the intellect. **2** having a highly developed intellect. ● noun a person with a highly developed intellect.
– DERIVATIVES **intellectuality** noun **intellectually** adverb.
intellectualism ● noun the exercise of the intellect at the expense of the emotions.
– DERIVATIVES **intellectualist** noun.
intellectualize (also **intellectualise**) ● verb **1** give an intellectual character to. **2** talk or write intellectually.
intellectual property ● noun Law intangible property that is the result of creativity, e.g. patents or copyrights.
intelligence ● noun **1** the ability to acquire and apply knowledge and skills. **2** a person with this ability. **3** the gathering of information of military or political value. **4** information gathered in this way.
– ORIGIN Latin *intelligentia*, from *intelligere* 'understand'.
intelligence quotient ● noun a number representing a person's reasoning ability, compared to the statistical norm, 100 being average.
intelligent ● adjective **1** having intelligence, especially of a high

Thesaurus

revolutionist, mutineer, insurrectionist, agitator, subversive, renegade; guerrilla, freedom fighter, anarchist, terrorist.
– OPPOSITES loyalist.
insurmountable ● adjective INSUPERABLE, unconquerable, invincible, unassailable; overwhelming, hopeless, impossible.
insurrection ● noun REBELLION, revolt, uprising, mutiny, revolution, insurgence, riot, sedition; civil disorder, unrest, anarchy; coup (d'état).
intact ● adjective WHOLE, entire, complete, unbroken, undamaged, unimpaired, faultless, flawless, unscathed, untouched, unspoiled, unblemished, unmarked, perfect, pristine, inviolate, undefiled, unsullied, in one piece; sound, solid.
– OPPOSITES damaged.
intangible ● adjective **1** *the moonlight made things seem intangible* IMPALPABLE, untouchable, incorporeal, discarnate, abstract; ethereal, insubstantial, airy; ghostly, spectral, unearthly, supernatural; Philosophy immaterial. **2** *an intangible atmosphere* INDEFINABLE, indescribable, inexpressible, nameless; vague, obscure, unclear, indefinite, subtle, elusive, fugitive.
integral ● adjective **1** *an integral part of human behaviour* ESSENTIAL, fundamental, basic, intrinsic, inherent, constitutive, innate, structural; vital, necessary, requisite. **2** *the dryer has integral cord storage* BUILT-IN, inbuilt, integrated, incorporated, fitted. **3** *an integral approach to learning* UNIFIED, integrated, comprehensive, composite, combined, aggregate; complete, whole.
– OPPOSITES peripheral, fragmented.
integrate ● verb COMBINE, amalgamate, merge, unite, fuse, blend, mingle, coalesce, consolidate, meld, intermingle, mix; incorporate, unify, assimilate, homogenize; desegregate.
– OPPOSITES separate.
integrated ● adjective **1** *an integrated package of services* UNIFIED, united, consolidated, amalgamated, combined, merged, fused, homogeneous, assimilated, cohesive. **2** *an integrated school* DESEGREGATED, non-segregated, unsegregated, mixed.
integrity ● noun **1** *I never doubted his integrity* HONESTY, probity, rectitude, honour, good character, principle(s), ethics, morals, righteousness, morality, virtue, decency, fairness, scrupulousness, sincerity, truthfulness, trustworthiness. **2** *the integrity of the federation* UNITY, unification, coherence, cohesion, togetherness, solidarity. **3** *the structural integrity of the aircraft* SOUNDNESS, strength, sturdiness, solidity, durability, stability, stoutness, toughness.
– OPPOSITES dishonesty, division, fragility.
intellect ● noun **1** *a film that appeals to the intellect* MIND, brain(s), intelligence, reason, understanding, thought, brainpower, sense, judgement, wisdom, wits; informal nous, grey matter, brain cells, upper storey; Brit. informal loaf; N. Amer. informal smarts. **2** *one of the finest intellects* THINKER, intellectual, sage; mind, brain.
intellectual ● adjective **1** *his intellectual capacity* MENTAL, cerebral, cognitive, psychological; rational, abstract, conceptual, theoretical, analytical, logical; academic. **2** *an intellectual man* INTELLIGENT, clever, academic, educated, well read, erudite, cerebral, learned, knowledgeable, literary, bookish, donnish, highbrow, scholarly, studious, enlightened, sophisticated; informal brainy.
– OPPOSITES physical, stupid.
● noun *intellectuals are appalled by television* HIGHBROW, intelligent person, learned person, academic, bookworm, man/woman of letters, bluestocking; thinker, brain, scholar, sage; genius, Einstein, polymath, mastermind; informal egghead, brains; Brit. informal brainbox, clever clogs, boffin; N. Amer. informal brainiac, rocket scientist.
– OPPOSITES dunce.
intelligence ● noun **1** *a man of great intelligence* INTELLECTUAL CAPACITY, mental capacity, intellect, mind, brain(s), brainpower, judgement, reasoning, understanding, comprehension; acumen, wit, sense, insight, perception, penetration, discernment, quick-wittedness, smartness, canniness, astuteness, intuition, acuity, cleverness, brilliance, ability, talent; informal braininess. **2** *intelligence from our agents* INFORMATION, facts, details, particulars, data,

level. **2** (of a device) able to vary its state or action in response to varying situations and past experience. **3** (of a computer terminal) having its own processing capability.
– DERIVATIVES **intelligently** adverb.
intelligentsia /intellijentsiə/ ● noun (treated as sing. or pl.) intellectuals or highly educated people, regarded as possessing culture and political influence.
intelligible /intellijib'l/ ● adjective able to be understood.
– DERIVATIVES **intelligibility** noun **intelligibly** adverb.
– ORIGIN Latin *intelligibilis*, from *intelligere* 'understand'.
intemperate ● adjective **1** lacking self-control. **2** characterized by excessive indulgence, especially in alcohol.
– DERIVATIVES **intemperance** noun **intemperately** adverb.
intend ● verb **1** have as one's aim or plan. **2** plan that (something) should be, do, or mean something: *the book was intended as a satire*. **3** (**intend for/to do**) design or destine for a particular purpose. **4** (**be intended for**) be meant for the use of.
– DERIVATIVES **intender** noun.
– ORIGIN Latin *intendere* 'intend, extend, direct'.
intended ● adjective planned or meant. ● noun (**one's intended**) informal one's fiancé(e).
intense ● adjective (**intenser, intensest**) **1** of extreme force, degree, or strength. **2** extremely earnest or serious.
– DERIVATIVES **intensely** adverb **intenseness** noun.
– ORIGIN Latin *intensus* 'stretched tightly, strained', from *intendere* 'intend'.
intensifier ● noun **1** a thing that intensifies. **2** Grammar an adverb or prefix used to give force or emphasis.
intensify ● verb (**intensifies, intensified**) make or become more intense.
– DERIVATIVES **intensification** noun.
intensity ● noun (pl. **intensities**) **1** the quality of being intense. **2** chiefly Physics the measurable amount of a property, such as force or brightness.
intensive ● adjective **1** very thorough or vigorous. **2** (of agriculture) aiming to achieve maximum production within a limited area. **3** (in combination) concentrating on or making much use of something: *labour-intensive methods*.
– DERIVATIVES **intensively** adverb **intensiveness** noun.
intensive care ● noun special medical treatment of a dangerously ill patient.
intent ● noun intention or purpose. ● adjective **1** (**intent on/upon**) determined to do. **2** (**intent on/upon**) attentively occupied with. **3** showing earnest and eager attention.
– PHRASES **to all intents and purposes** in all important respects. **with intent** Law with the intention of committing a crime.
– DERIVATIVES **intently** adverb **intentness** noun.
– ORIGIN Old French *entent, entente*, from Latin *intendere* 'intend'.
intention ● noun **1** an aim or plan. **2** the action or fact of intending. **3** (**one's intentions**) a man's plans in respect to marriage.
– DERIVATIVES **intentioned** adjective.
intentional ● adjective deliberate.
– DERIVATIVES **intentionality** noun **intentionally** adverb.
inter /inter/ ● verb (**interred, interring**) place (a corpse) in a grave or tomb.
– ORIGIN Old French *enterrer*, from Latin *in-* 'into' + *terra* 'earth'.
inter- ● prefix **1** between; among: *interbreed*. **2** mutually; reciprocally: *interaction*.
– ORIGIN Latin *inter* 'between, among'.
interact ● verb act so as to have a reciprocal effect.
– DERIVATIVES **interactant** adjective & noun **interaction** noun.
interactive ● adjective **1** influencing each other. **2** (of a computer or other electronic device) allowing a two-way flow of in-

i

Thesaurus

knowledge, reports; *informal* info, gen, dope. **3** *military intelligence* INFORMATION GATHERING, surveillance, observation, reconnaissance, spying, espionage, infiltration, ELINT, Humint; *informal* recon.
intelligent ● adjective **1** *an intelligent writer* CLEVER, bright, brilliant, quick-witted, quick on the uptake, smart, canny, astute, intuitive, insightful, perceptive, perspicacious, discerning; knowledgeable; able, gifted, talented; *informal* brainy. **2** *an intelligent being* RATIONAL, higher-order, capable of thought. **3** *intelligent machines* SELF-REGULATING, capable of learning, smart.
intelligentsia ● plural noun INTELLECTUALS, intelligent people, academics, scholars, literati, cognoscenti, illuminati, highbrows, thinkers, brains; the intelligent; *informal* eggheads; *Brit. informal* boffins.
intelligible ● adjective COMPREHENSIBLE, understandable; accessible, digestible, user-friendly, penetrable, fathomable; lucid, clear, coherent, plain, explicit, precise, unambiguous, self-explanatory.
intemperance ● noun **1** *they were criticized for intemperance* OVERINDULGENCE, immoderation, excess, extravagance, prodigality, profligacy, lavishness; self-indulgence, self-gratification; debauchery, decadence, dissipation, dissolution. **2** *he said intemperance was a disease* DRINKING, alcoholism, alcohol abuse, dipsomania; drunkenness, intoxication, inebriation, insobriety, tipsiness; *formal* inebriety; *poetic/literary* crapulence.
intemperate ● adjective IMMODERATE, excessive, undue, inordinate, extreme, unrestrained, uncontrolled; self-indulgent, overindulgent, extravagant, lavish, prodigal, profligate; imprudent, reckless, wild; dissolute, debauched, wanton, dissipated.
– OPPOSITES moderate.
intend ● verb PLAN, mean, have in mind, have the intention, aim, propose; aspire, hope, expect, be resolved, be determined; want, wish; contemplate, think of, envisage; design, earmark, set aside; *formal* purpose.
intended ● adjective *the foul was not intended* DELIBERATE, intentional, calculated, conscious, planned, studied, knowing, wilful, wanton, purposeful, done on purpose, premeditated, pre-planned, preconceived; *Law* aforethought; *Law, dated* prepense.
– OPPOSITES accidental.
● noun (*informal*) *do you share everything with your intended?* FIANCÉ(E), betrothed, bride-to-be, wife-to-be, husband-to-be, future wife, future husband, prospective spouse.
intense ● adjective **1** *intense heat* EXTREME, great, acute, fierce, severe, high; exceptional, extraordinary; harsh, strong, powerful, potent, vigorous; *informal* serious. **2** *a very intense young man* PASSIONATE, impassioned, ardent, fervent, zealous, vehement, fiery, emotional; earnest, eager, animated, spirited, vigorous, energetic, fanatical, committed.
– OPPOSITES mild, apathetic.
intensify ● verb ESCALATE, increase, step up, boost, raise, strengthen, augment, reinforce; pick up, build up, heighten, deepen, extend, expand, amplify, magnify; aggravate, exacerbate, worsen, inflame, compound.
– OPPOSITES abate.
intensity ● noun **1** *the intensity of the sun* STRENGTH, power, potency, force; severity, ferocity, vehemence, fierceness, harshness; magnitude, greatness, acuteness, extremity. **2** *his eyes had a glowing intensity* PASSION, ardour, fervour, zeal, vehemence, fire, heat, emotion; eagerness, animation, spirit, vigour, strength, energy; fanaticism.
intensive ● adjective THOROUGH, thoroughgoing, in-depth, rigorous, exhaustive, all-out; all-embracing, all-inclusive, comprehensive, complete, full; vigorous, strenuous, detailed, minute, close, meticulous, scrupulous, painstaking, methodical, careful; extensive, widespread, sweeping; determined, resolute, persistent.
– OPPOSITES cursory.
intent ● noun *he tried to divine his father's intent* AIM, intention, purpose, objective, object, goal, target; design, plan, scheme; wish, desire, ambition, idea, aspiration.
● adjective **1** *he was intent on proving his point* BENT, set, determined, insistent, resolved, hell-bent, keen; committed to, obsessive about, fanatical about; determined to, anxious to, impatient to. **2** *an intent expression* ATTENTIVE, absorbed, engrossed, fascinated, enthralled, rapt; focused, earnest, concentrating, intense, studious, preoccupied; alert, watchful.
– PHRASES **to all intents and purposes** IN EFFECT, effectively, in essence, essentially, virtually, practically; more or less, just about, all but, as good as, in all but name, as near as dammit; almost, nearly; *informal* pretty much, pretty well; *poetic/literary* nigh on.
intention ● noun **1** *it is his intention to be leader* AIM, purpose, intent, objective, object, goal, target; design, plan, scheme; resolve, resolution, determination; wish, desire, ambition, idea, dream, aspiration. **2** *he managed, without intention, to upset me* INTENT, intentionality, deliberateness, design, calculation; premeditation, forethought, pre-planning; *Law* malice aforethought.
intentional ● adjective DELIBERATE, calculated, conscious, intended, planned, meant, studied, knowing, wilful, wanton, purposeful, purposive, done on purpose, premeditated, pre-planned, preconceived; *Law* aforethought; *Law, dated* prepense.
intently ● adverb ATTENTIVELY, closely, keenly, earnestly, hard, carefully, fixedly, steadily.
inter ● verb BURY, lay to rest, entomb, inurn; *informal* put six feet

formation between it and a user, responding to the user's input.
– DERIVATIVES **interactively** adverb **interactivity** noun.

inter alia /intər aylia, allia/ ● adverb among other things.
– ORIGIN Latin.

interbreed ● verb (past and past part. **interbred**) breed or cause to breed with an animal of a different race or species.

intercalary /interkələri, -kalləri/ ● adjective (of a day or month) inserted in the calendar to harmonize it with the solar year, e.g. 29 February.
– ORIGIN Latin *intercalarius*, from *intercalare* 'proclaim as inserted in the calendar'.

intercede /intərseed/ ● verb intervene on behalf of another.
– ORIGIN Latin *intercedere*, from *cedere* 'to go'.

intercellular ● adjective located or occurring between cells.

intercept ● verb /intərsept/ obstruct and prevent from continuing to a destination. ● noun /intərsept/ **1** an act of intercepting. **2** Mathematics the point at which a line cuts the axis of a graph.
– DERIVATIVES **interception** noun **interceptor** noun.
– ORIGIN Latin *intercipere* 'catch between'.

intercession /intərsesh'n/ ● noun **1** the action of interceding. **2** the saying a prayer on behalf of another person.
– DERIVATIVES **intercessor** noun **intercessory** adjective.
– ORIGIN Latin, from *intercedere* 'intervene'.

interchange ● verb /intərchaynj/ **1** exchange (things) with each other. **2** put each of (two things) in the other's place. ● noun /intərchaynj/ **1** the action of interchanging. **2** an exchange of words. **3** a road junction on several levels so that traffic streams do not intersect.
– DERIVATIVES **interchangeability** noun **interchangeable** adjective **interchangeably** adverb.

intercity ● adjective existing or travelling between cities.

intercom ● noun an electrical device allowing one-way or two-way communication.
– ORIGIN abbreviation of *intercommunication*.

intercommunicate ● verb **1** engage in two-way communication. **2** (of rooms) have a common connecting door.
– DERIVATIVES **intercommunication** noun.

interconnect ● verb connect with each other.
– DERIVATIVES **interconnection** noun.

intercontinental ● adjective relating to or travelling between continents.

intercooler ● noun an apparatus for cooling gas between successive compressions, especially in a supercharged engine.
– DERIVATIVES **intercool** verb.

intercostal /intərkost'l/ Anatomy ● adjective situated between the ribs. ● noun an intercostal muscle.

intercourse ● noun **1** communication or dealings between people. **2** sexual intercourse.
– ORIGIN Latin *intercursus*, from *intercurrere* 'intervene'.

intercrop ● verb (**intercropped**, **intercropping**) (often as noun **intercropping**) grow (a crop) among plants of a different kind.

intercut ● verb (**intercutting**; past and past part. **intercut**) alternate (scenes) with contrasting scenes in a film.

interdenominational ● adjective relating to more than one religious denomination.

interdepartmental ● adjective relating to more than one department.

interdependent ● adjective dependent on each other.
– DERIVATIVES **interdependence** noun **interdependency** noun.

interdict ● noun /intərdikt/ **1** an authoritative prohibition. **2** (in the Roman Catholic Church) a sentence debarring a person or place from ecclesiastical functions and privileges. ● verb /intərdikt/ chiefly N. Amer. prohibit or forbid.
– DERIVATIVES **interdiction** noun.
– ORIGIN Latin *interdictum*, from *interdicere* 'interpose, forbid by decree'.

interdisciplinary ● adjective relating to more than one branch of knowledge.

interest ● noun **1** the state of wanting to know about something or someone. **2** the quality of exciting curiosity or holding the attention. **3** a subject about which one is concerned or enthusiastic. **4** money paid for the use of money lent. **5** a person's advantage or benefit. **6** a share, right, or stake in property or a financial undertaking. **7** a group having a common concern, especially in politics or business. ● verb **1** excite the curiosity or attention of. **2** (**interest in**) persuade (someone) to undertake or acquire. **3** (**interested**) not impartial: *interested parties*.
– PHRASES **at interest** (of money borrowed) on the condition that interest is payable.
– DERIVATIVES **interestedly** adverb.
– ORIGIN Latin *interesse* 'differ, be important'.

interesting ● adjective arousing curiosity or interest.
– DERIVATIVES **interestingly** adverb **interestingness** noun.

Thesaurus

under, plant; *poetic/literary* sepulchre, inhume.
– OPPOSITES exhume.

intercede ● verb MEDIATE, intermediate, arbitrate, conciliate, negotiate, moderate; intervene, interpose, step in, act; plead, petition.

intercept ● verb STOP, head off, cut off; catch, seize, grab, snatch; obstruct, impede, interrupt, block, check, detain; ambush, challenge, waylay.

intercession ● noun MEDIATION, intermediation, arbitration, conciliation, negotiation; intervention, involvement; pleading, petition, entreaty, agency; diplomacy.

interchange ● verb **1** *they interchange ideas* EXCHANGE, trade, swap, barter, bandy, reciprocate; *archaic* truck. **2** *the terms are often interchanged* SUBSTITUTE, transpose, exchange, switch, swap (round), change (round), reverse, invert, replace.
● noun **1** *the interchange of ideas* EXCHANGE, trade, swap, barter, give and take, traffic, reciprocation, reciprocity; *archaic* truck. **2** *a motorway interchange* JUNCTION, intersection, crossing; *N. Amer.* cloverleaf.

interchangeable ● adjective **1** *the gun has interchangeable barrels* EXCHANGEABLE, transposable, replaceable. **2** *two more or less interchangeable roads* SIMILAR, identical, indistinguishable, alike, the same, uniform, twin, undifferentiated; corresponding, commensurate, equivalent, comparable, equal; *informal* much of a muchness.

intercourse ● noun **1** *social intercourse* DEALINGS, relations, relationships, association, connections, contact; interchange, communication, communion, correspondence; negotiations, bargaining, transactions; trade, traffic; *informal* truck, doings. **2** *she did not consent to intercourse* SEXUAL INTERCOURSE, sex, lovemaking, sexual relations, intimacy, coupling, mating, copulation; *informal* nooky; *Brit. informal* bonking, rumpy pumpy, how's your father; *technical* coitus, coition; *formal* fornication; *dated* carnal knowledge.

interdict ● noun *they breached an interdict* PROHIBITION, ban, bar, veto, proscription, interdiction, embargo, moratorium, injunction.
– OPPOSITES permission.
● verb **1** *they interdicted foreign commerce* PROHIBIT, forbid, ban, bar, veto, proscribe, embargo, disallow, debar, outlaw; stop, suppress; *Law* enjoin, estop. **2** *efforts to interdict asylum seekers* INTERCEPT, stop, head off, cut off; obstruct, impede, block; detain.
– OPPOSITES permit.

interest ● noun **1** *we listened with interest* ATTENTIVENESS, attention, absorption; heed, regard, notice; curiosity, inquisitiveness; enjoyment, delight. **2** *places of interest* ATTRACTION, appeal, fascination, charm, beauty, allure. **3** *this will be of interest to those involved* CONCERN, consequence, importance, import, significance, note, relevance, value, weight; *formal* moment. **4** *her interests include reading* HOBBY, pastime, leisure pursuit, recreation, diversion, amusement, relaxation; passion, enthusiasm; *informal* thing, bag, cup of tea. **5** *a financial interest in the firm* STAKE, share, claim, investment, stock, equity; involvement, concern. **6** *what is your interest in the case?* INVOLVEMENT, partiality, partisanship, preference, loyalty; bias, prejudice. **7** *his attorney guarded his interests* CONCERN, business, affair. **8** *her savings earned interest* DIVIDENDS, profits, returns; a percentage.
– OPPOSITES boredom.
● verb **1** *a topic that interests you* APPEAL TO, be of interest to, attract, intrigue, fascinate; absorb, engross, rivet, grip, captivate; amuse, divert, entertain; arouse one's curiosity, whet one's appetite; *informal* float someone's boat, tickle someone's fancy. **2** *can I interest you in a drink?* persuade to have; sell.
– OPPOSITES bore.
– PHRASES **in someone's interests** OF BENEFIT TO, to the advantage of; for the sake of, for the benefit of.

interested ● adjective **1** *an interested crowd* ATTENTIVE, intent, absorbed, engrossed, fascinated, riveted, gripped, captivated, rapt, agog; intrigued, inquisitive, curious; keen, eager; *informal* all ears, nosy, snoopy. **2** *the government consulted with interested bodies* CONCERNED, involved, affected, connected, related. **3** *no interested*

interface ● noun **1** a point where two things meet and interact. **2** chiefly Physics a surface forming a boundary between two portions of matter or space. **3** a device or program enabling a user to communicate with a computer, or for connecting two items of hardware or software. ● verb **(interface with) 1** interact with. **2** Computing connect with (something) by an interface.

interfacing ● noun an extra layer of material or an adhesive stiffener, applied to the facing of a garment to add support.

interfaith ● adjective relating to or between different religions.

interfere ● verb **1 (interfere with)** prevent from continuing or being carried out properly. **2 (interfere with)** handle or adjust without permission. **3** intervene without invitation or necessity. **4 (interfere with)** Brit. euphemistic sexually molest. **5** Physics interact to produce interference.
– DERIVATIVES **interferer** noun **interfering** adjective.
– ORIGIN Old French *s'entreferir* 'strike each other'.

interference ● noun **1** the action of interfering or process of being interfered with. **2** disturbance to radio signals caused by unwanted signals from other sources. **3** Physics the combination of two or more waveforms to form a resultant in which the wave motions are either reinforced or cancelled (e.g. the combination of beams of light to form a pattern of light and dark bands).
– DERIVATIVES **interferential** adjective.

interferon /intərfeeron/ ● noun a protein released by animal cells which inhibits virus replication.

interfuse ● verb literary join or mix together.
– DERIVATIVES **interfusion** noun.

intergalactic ● adjective relating to or situated between galaxies.

interglacial Geology ● adjective relating to or denoting a period of milder climate between two glacial periods. ● noun an interglacial period.

intergovernmental ● adjective relating to or conducted between governments.

interim /intərim/ ● noun **(the interim)** the intervening time. ● adjective in or for the intervening time; provisional.
– ORIGIN from Latin, 'meanwhile'.

interior ● adjective **1** situated within or inside; inner. **2** remote from the coast or frontier; inland. **3** relating to a country's internal affairs. **4** existing or occurring in the mind or soul. ● noun **1** the interior part. **2** the internal affairs of a country.
– DERIVATIVES **interiorize** (also **interiorise**) verb **interiorly** adverb.
– ORIGIN Latin, 'inner'.

interior angle ● noun the angle between adjacent sides of a straight-sided figure.

interior decoration ● noun the decoration of the interior of a building or room, especially with regard for colour combination and artistic effect.

interior design ● noun the design or decoration of the interior of a room or building.

interiority ● noun the quality of being interior or inward.

interior monologue ● noun a piece of writing expressing a character's thoughts.

interject /intər**jekt**/ ● verb say abruptly, especially as an interruption.
– ORIGIN Latin *interjicere* 'interpose'.

interjection ● noun an exclamation, especially as a part of speech (e.g. *ah!, dear me!*).

interlace ● verb **1** interweave. **2 (interlace with)** mingle or intersperse with.

interlard ● verb **(interlard with)** intersperse (speech or writing) with (contrasting words and phrases).

interleave ● verb **1** insert blank leaves between the pages of (a book). **2** place something between the layers of.

interline ● verb put an extra lining in (a garment, curtain, etc.).

interlinear ● adjective written between the lines of a text.

interlining ● noun material used to interline a garment, curtain, etc.

interlink ● verb join or connect together.
– DERIVATIVES **interlinkage** noun.

interlock ● verb engage with each other by overlapping or fitting together. ● noun **1** a device or mechanism for connecting or coordinating the function of components. **2** (also **interlock fabric**) a fabric with closely interlocking stitches allowing it to stretch.

interlocutor /intər**lok**yootər/ ● noun formal a person who takes part in a conversation.
– DERIVATIVES **interlocution** noun.
– ORIGIN from Latin *interloqui* 'interrupt (with speech)'.

interlocutory /intər**lok**yootəri/ ● adjective **1** Law (of a decree or judgement) given provisionally during the course of a legal action. **2** relating to dialogue.

interloper /intərlōpər/ ● noun a person who interferes in another's affairs; an intruder.
– DERIVATIVES **interlope** verb.
– ORIGIN from INTER- + *-loper* as in archaic *landloper* 'vagabond', from Dutch *landlooper*.

interlude ● noun **1** an intervening period of time or activity that contrasts with what goes before or after: *a romantic interlude.* **2** a pause between the acts of a play. **3** a piece of music played between other pieces or between the verses of a hymn.
– ORIGIN Latin *interludium*, from *inter-* 'between' + *ludus* 'play'.

intermarriage ● noun **1** marriage between people of different races, castes, or religions. **2** marriage between close relations.
– DERIVATIVES **intermarry** verb.

intermediary /intər**mee**diəri/ ● noun (pl. **intermediaries**) a mediator. ● adjective intermediate.

Thesaurus

party can judge the contest PARTISAN, partial, biased, prejudiced, one-sided, preferential.

interesting ● adjective ABSORBING, engrossing, fascinating, riveting, gripping, compelling, compulsive, captivating, engaging, enthralling; appealing, attractive; amusing, entertaining, stimulating, thought-provoking, diverting, intriguing; *informal* unputdownable.

interfere ● verb **1** *don't let emotion interfere with duty* IMPEDE, obstruct, stand in the way of, hinder, inhibit, restrict, constrain, hamper, handicap, cramp, check, block; disturb, disrupt, influence, affect, confuse. **2** *she tried not to interfere in his life* BUTT INTO, barge into, pry into, nose into, intrude into, intervene in, get involved in, encroach on, impinge on; meddle in, tamper with; *informal* poke one's nose into, horn in on, muscle in on, stick one's oar in. **3** *(Brit. euphemistic) he interfered with local children* (SEXUALLY) ABUSE, sexually assault, indecently assault, molest, grope; *informal* feel up, touch up.

interference ● noun **1** *they resent state interference* INTRUSION, intervention, intercession, involvement, trespass, obtrusion; meddling, prying. **2** *radio interference* DISRUPTION, disturbance, static.

interfering ● adjective MEDDLESOME, meddling, intrusive, prying, inquisitive, over-curious, busybody; *informal* nosy, nosy-parker, snoopy.

interim ● noun *in the interim they did more research* MEANTIME, meanwhile, intervening time.
● adjective *an interim advisory body* PROVISIONAL, temporary, pro tem, stopgap, short-term, fill-in, caretaker, acting, intervening, transitional, makeshift, improvised, impromptu.
– OPPOSITES permanent.

interior ● adjective **1** *the house has interior panelling* INSIDE, inner, internal, intramural. **2** *the interior deserts of the US* INLAND, inshore, upcountry, inner, innermost, central. **3** *the country's interior affairs* INTERNAL, home, domestic, national, state, civil, local. **4** *an interior monologue* INNER, mental, spiritual, psychological; private, personal, intimate, secret.
– OPPOSITES exterior, outer, foreign.
● noun **1** *the interior of the yacht* INSIDE, inner part, depths, recesses, bowels, belly; centre, core, heart. **2** *the country's interior* CENTRE, heartland, hinterland.
– OPPOSITES exterior, outside.

interject ● verb **1** *she interjected a comment* INTERPOSE, introduce, throw in, interpolate, add. **2** *he interjected before there was a fight* INTERRUPT, intervene, cut in, break in, butt in, chime in; put one's oar in; *Brit. informal* chip in; *N. Amer. informal* put in one's two cents.

interjection ● noun **1** *an astonished interjection* EXCLAMATION, cry, shout, vociferation, utterance; *dated* ejaculation. **2** *the interjection of a question* INTERPOSITION, interpolation, insertion, addition, introduction.

interlock ● verb INTERCONNECT, interlink, engage, mesh, intermesh, join, unite, connect, couple.

interloper ● noun INTRUDER, encroacher, trespasser, invader, infiltrator; uninvited guest; outsider, stranger, alien; *informal* gatecrasher.

interlude ● noun INTERVAL, intermission, break, recess, pause, respite, rest, breathing space, halt, gap, stop, stoppage, hiatus, lull; *informal* breather, let-up, time out, down time.

intermediate /intərmeediət/ ● adjective **1** coming between two things in time, place, character, etc. **2** having more than basic knowledge or skills but not yet advanced. ● noun an intermediate person or thing. ● verb /intərmeediayt/ mediate.
– DERIVATIVES **intermediacy** noun **intermediation** noun.
– ORIGIN from Latin *inter-* 'between' + *medius* 'middle'.
interment /intermənt/ ● noun the burial of a corpse in a grave or tomb.
intermezzo /intərmetsō/ ● noun (pl. **intermezzi** /intərmetsee/ or **intermezzos**) **1** a short connecting instrumental movement in an opera or other musical work. **2** a short piece for a solo instrument. **3** a light dramatic or other performance between the acts of a play.
– ORIGIN Italian, from Latin *intermedium* 'interval'.
interminable ● adjective endless.
– DERIVATIVES **interminably** adverb.
– ORIGIN Latin *interminabilis*, from *in-* 'not' + *terminare* 'to end'.
intermingle ● verb mix or mingle together.
intermission ● noun **1** a pause or break. **2** an interval between parts of a play or film.
– ORIGIN Latin, from *intermittere* 'discontinue, stop'.
intermittent ● adjective occurring at irregular intervals.
– DERIVATIVES **intermittency** noun **intermittently** adverb.
– ORIGIN Latin, 'ceasing', from *intermittere* (see INTERMISSION).
intermix ● verb mix together.
– DERIVATIVES **intermixable** adjective **intermixture** noun.
intermodal ● adjective involving two or more different modes of transport.
intermolecular ● adjective existing or occurring between molecules.
intern ● noun /intern/ (also **interne**) chiefly N. Amer. **1** a recent medical graduate receiving supervised training in a hospital and acting as an assistant physician or surgeon. **2** a student or trainee who does a job to gain work experience or for a qualification. ● verb **1** /intern/ confine as a prisoner. **2** /intern/ chiefly N. Amer. serve as an intern.
– DERIVATIVES **internment** noun **internship** noun.
– ORIGIN from Latin *internus* 'inward, internal'.
internal ● adjective **1** of or situated on the inside. **2** inside the body. **3** relating to affairs and activities within a country. **4** existing or used within an organization. **5** in or of one's mind or soul. ● noun (**internals**) inner parts or features.
– DERIVATIVES **internality** noun **internally** adverb.
– ORIGIN Latin *internalis*, from *internus* 'inward, internal'.
internal-combustion engine ● noun an engine in which power is generated by the expansion of hot gases from the burning of fuel with air inside the engine.
internal exile ● noun penal banishment from a part of one's own country.
internalize (also **internalise**) ● verb make (attitudes or behaviour) part of one's nature by learning or unconscious assimilation.
– DERIVATIVES **internalization** noun.
internal market ● noun **1** another term for SINGLE MARKET. **2** (in the UK) a system in the National Health Service whereby hospital departments purchase each other's services contractually.
international ● adjective **1** existing or occurring between nations. **2** agreed on or used by all or many nations. ● noun **1** Brit. a game or contest between teams representing different countries. **2** a player who has taken part in such a contest. **3** (**International**) any of four associations founded (1864–1936) to promote socialist or communist action.
– DERIVATIVES **internationality** noun **internationally** adverb.
International Date Line ● noun an imaginary North–South line through the Pacific Ocean, chiefly along the meridian furthest from Greenwich, to the east of which the date is a day earlier than it is to the west.
Internationale /intərnashyənaal/ ● noun **1** (**the Internationale**) a revolutionary song composed in France and adopted by socialists. **2** variant spelling of INTERNATIONAL (in sense 3).
– ORIGIN French, 'international'.
internationalism ● noun **1** the advocacy of cooperation and understanding between nations. **2** the state or process of being international.
– DERIVATIVES **internationalist** noun.
internationalize (also **internationalise**) ● verb make international.
– DERIVATIVES **internationalization** noun.
international law ● noun a body of rules established by custom or treaty and recognized by nations as binding in their relations with one another.
interne ● noun variant spelling of INTERN.
internecine /intərneesīn/ ● adjective **1** destructive to both sides in a conflict. **2** relating to conflict within a group: *internecine rivalries.*
– ORIGIN Latin *internecinus*, from *inter-* 'among' + *necare* 'to kill'.
internee ● noun a prisoner.
Internet ● noun an international information network linking computers, accessible to the public via modem links.
internist ● noun N. Amer. a specialist in internal diseases.
interoperable ● adjective (of computer systems or software) able to operate in conjunction.
– DERIVATIVES **interoperability** noun.
interpenetrate ● verb mix or merge together.
– DERIVATIVES **interpenetration** noun **interpenetrative** adjective.
interpersonal ● adjective relating to relationships or communication between people.
– DERIVATIVES **interpersonally** adverb.
interplanetary ● adjective situated or travelling between planets.
interplant ● verb plant (a crop or plant) together with another.
interplay ● noun the way in which things interact.
Interpol /intərpol/ ● noun an international organization that coordinates investigations made by the police forces of member countries into international crimes.
– ORIGIN from *Inter(national) pol(ice).*
interpolate /interpəlayt/ ● verb **1** insert or introduce (something different or additional). **2** interject (a remark) in a conversation. **3** insert (words) in a book, especially to give a false impression as to its date. **4** Mathematics insert (an intermediate term) into a series by estimating or calculating it from surrounding known values.
– DERIVATIVES **interpolation** noun **interpolator** noun.
– ORIGIN Latin *interpolare* 'refurbish, alter'.
interpose ● verb **1** insert between one thing and another. **2** intervene between parties. **3** say as an interruption. **4** exer-

Thesaurus

intermediary ● noun MEDIATOR, go-between, negotiator, intervenor, interceder, intercessor, arbitrator, arbiter, conciliator, peacemaker; middleman, broker, linkman.
intermediate ● adjective HALFWAY, in-between, middle, mid, midway, median, medial, intermediary, intervening, transitional.
interment ● noun BURIAL, burying, committal, entombment, inhumation; funeral; *archaic* sepulture.
interminable ● adjective (SEEMINGLY) ENDLESS, never-ending, unending, non-stop, everlasting, ceaseless, unceasing, incessant, constant, continual, uninterrupted, sustained; monotonous, long-winded, overlong, rambling.
intermingle ● verb MIX, intermix, mingle, blend, fuse, merge, combine, amalgamate; unite, affiliate, associate, fraternize; *poetic/literary* commingle.
intermission ● noun INTERVAL, interlude, entr'acte, break, recess, pause, rest, respite, breathing space, lull, gap, stop, stoppage, halt; cessation, suspension; *informal* let-up, breather, time out, down time.
intermittent ● adjective SPORADIC, irregular, fitful, spasmodic, broken, fragmentary, discontinuous, isolated, random, patchy, scattered; occasional, periodic.
– OPPOSITES continuous.
intern ● verb *they were interned without trial* IMPRISON, incarcerate, impound, jail, put behind bars, detain, hold (captive), lock up, confine; *informal* put away, put inside, send down; *Brit. informal* bang up.
● noun *an intern at a local firm* TRAINEE, apprentice, probationer, student, novice, beginner.
internal ● adjective **1** *an internal courtyard* INNER, interior, inside, intramural; central. **2** *the state's internal affairs* DOMESTIC, home, interior, civil, local; national, state. **3** *an internal battle with herself* MENTAL, psychological, emotional; personal, private, secret, hidden.
– OPPOSITES external, foreign.
international ● adjective GLOBAL, worldwide, intercontinental, universal; cosmopolitan, multiracial, multinational.
– OPPOSITES national, local.
interplay ● noun INTERACTION, interchange; teamwork, cooperation,

cise or advance (a veto or objection).
– DERIVATIVES **interposition** noun.
– ORIGIN French *interposer*, from Latin *interponere* 'put in'.
interpret • verb (**interpreted**, **interpreting**) **1** explain the meaning of. **2** translate orally the words of a person speaking a different language. **3** understand as having a particular meaning or significance. **4** perform (a creative work) in a way that conveys one's understanding of the creator's ideas.
– DERIVATIVES **interpretable** adjective **interpretative** adjective **interpretive** adjective.
– ORIGIN Latin *interpretari* 'explain, translate'.
interpretation • noun **1** the action of explaining the meaning of something. **2** an explanation or way of explaining. **3** a performer's representation of a creative work.
– DERIVATIVES **interpretational** adjective.
interpreter • noun a person who interprets foreign speech orally.
interracial • adjective existing between or involving different races.
– DERIVATIVES **interracially** adverb.
interregnum /intəregnəm/ • noun (pl. **interregnums** or **interregna** /intəregnə/) a period when normal government is suspended, especially between successive reigns or regimes.
– ORIGIN Latin, from *inter-* 'between' + *regnum* 'reign'.
interrelate • verb relate or connect to one other.
– DERIVATIVES **interrelatedness** noun **interrelation** noun **interrelationship** noun.
interrogate • verb **1** ask questions of (someone) closely, aggressively, or formally. **2** obtain data or information automatically from (a device, database, etc.).
– DERIVATIVES **interrogation** noun **interrogator** noun.
– ORIGIN Latin *interrogare* 'question'.
interrogative /intəroggətiv/ • adjective **1** having the force of a question. **2** Grammar used in questions. • noun a word used in questions, e.g. *how* or *what*.
– DERIVATIVES **interrogatively** adverb.
interrogatory /intəroggətri/ • adjective questioning.
interrupt • verb **1** stop the continuous progress of. **2** stop (a person who is speaking) by saying or doing something. **3** break the continuity of (a line, surface, or view).
– DERIVATIVES **interrupter** (also **interruptor**) noun **interruptible** adjective **interruption** noun **interruptive** adjective.
– ORIGIN Latin *interrumpere* 'break, interrupt'.
intersect • verb **1** divide (something) by passing or lying across it. **2** (of lines, roads, etc.) cross or cut each other.
– ORIGIN Latin *intersecare* 'cut, intersect'.
intersection • noun **1** a point or line common to lines or surfaces that intersect. **2** a point at which two roads intersect.
– DERIVATIVES **intersectional** adjective.
intersex • noun **1** hermaphroditism. **2** a hermaphrodite.
intersexual • adjective **1** existing or occurring between the sexes. **2** hermaphroditic.
– DERIVATIVES **intersexuality** noun.
interspace • noun a space between objects. • verb (usu. **be interspaced**) put or occupy a space between.
intersperse • verb (usu. **be interspersed**) **1** scatter among or between other things. **2** diversify with other things at intervals.
– DERIVATIVES **interspersion** noun.
– ORIGIN Latin *interspergere* 'scatter between'.
interstadial /intərstaydiəl/ Geology • adjective referring to a minor period of less cold climate during a glacial period. • noun an interstadial period.
– ORIGIN from INTER- + Latin *stadium* 'stage'.
interstate • adjective existing or carried on between states, especially of the US. • noun one of a system of motorways running between US states. • adverb Austral. from one state to another.
interstellar /intərstellər/ • adjective occurring or situated between stars.
interstice /interstiss/ • noun a small intervening space.
– ORIGIN Latin *interstitium*, from *intersistere* 'stand between'.
interstitial /intərstish'l/ • adjective of, forming, or occupying interstices.
– DERIVATIVES **interstitially** adverb.
intertextuality • noun the relationship between texts.
– DERIVATIVES **intertextual** adjective.
intertribal • adjective existing or occurring between different tribes.
intertwine • verb twist or twine together.
interval • noun **1** an intervening time or space. **2** a pause or break. **3** Brit. a pause between parts of a theatrical or musical performance or a sports match. **4** the difference in pitch between two sounds.
– DERIVATIVES **intervallic** adjective.
– ORIGIN Latin *intervallum* 'space between ramparts, interval'.
intervene • verb **1** come between so as to prevent or alter the result or course of events. **2** (usu. as adj. **intervening**) occur or be between or among.
– DERIVATIVES **intervener** (also **intervenor**) noun.
– ORIGIN Latin *intervenire* 'come between'.
intervention • noun **1** the action or process of intervening.

i

Thesaurus

reciprocation, reciprocity, give and take.
interpolate • verb INSERT, interpose, enter, add, incorporate, inset, put, introduce.
interpose • verb **1** *he interposed himself between the girls* INSINUATE, place, put. **2** *I must interpose a note of caution* INTRODUCE, insert, interject, add. **3** *they interposed to suppress the custom* INTERVENE, intercede, step in, involve oneself; interfere, intrude, butt in, cut in; *informal* barge in, horn in, muscle in.
interpret • verb **1** *the rabbis interpreted the Jewish laws* EXPLAIN, elucidate, expound, explicate, clarify, illuminate, shed light on. **2** *the remark was interpreted as an invitation* UNDERSTAND, construe, take (to mean), see, regard. **3** *the symbols are difficult to interpret* DECIPHER, decode, make intelligible; understand, comprehend, make sense of; *informal* crack.
interpretation • noun **1** *the interpretation of the Bible's teachings* EXPLANATION, elucidation, expounding, exposition, explication, exegesis, clarification. **2** *she did not care what interpretation he put on her haste* MEANING, understanding, construal, connotation, explanation, inference. **3** *the interpretation of experimental findings* ANALYSIS, evaluation, review, study, examination. **4** *his interpretation of the sonata* RENDITION, rendering, execution, presentation, performance, reading, playing, singing.
interpreter • noun **1** *a Japanese interpreter* TRANSLATOR, dragoman. **2** *a vocal interpreter of his music* PERFORMER, presenter, exponent; singer, player. **3** *interpreters of Soviet history* ANALYST, evaluator, reviewer, commentator.
interrogate • verb QUESTION, cross-question, cross-examine, quiz; interview, examine, debrief, give someone the third degree; *informal* pump, grill.
interrogative • adjective QUESTIONING, inquiring, inquisitive, probing, searching, quizzing, quizzical, curious.
interrupt • verb **1** *she opened her mouth to interrupt* CUT IN (ON), break in (on), barge in (on), intervene (in), put one's oar in; *Brit.* put one's pennyworth in; *N. Amer.* put one's two cents in; *informal* butt in (on), chime in (on); *Brit. informal* chip in (on). **2** *the band had to interrupt their tour* SUSPEND, adjourn, discontinue, break off; stop, halt, cease, end, bring to an end/close; *informal* put on ice, put on a back burner. **3** *the coastal plain is interrupted by large lagoons* BREAK (UP), punctuate; pepper, strew, dot, scatter. **4** *their view was interrupted by houses* OBSTRUCT, impede, block, restrict.
interruption • noun **1** *he was not pleased at her interruption* CUTTING IN, barging in, intervention, intrusion; *informal* butting in. **2** *an interruption of the power supply* DISCONTINUATION, breaking off, suspension, stopping, halting, cessation. **3** *an interruption in her career* INTERVAL, interlude, break, pause, gap.
intersect • verb **1** *the lines intersect at right angles* CROSS, crisscross; *technical* decussate. **2** *the cornfield is intersected by a track* BISECT, divide, cut in two/half, cut across/through; cross, traverse.
intersection • noun **1** *the intersection of the two curves* CROSSING, criss-crossing. **2** *the driver stopped at an intersection* (ROAD) JUNCTION, T-junction, interchange, crossroads; *Brit.* roundabout.
intersperse • verb **1** *giant lobelia were interspersed among the rocks* SCATTER, disperse, spread, strew, dot, sprinkle, pepper; *poetic/literary* bestrew. **2** *the beech trees are interspersed with conifers* INTERMIX, mix, mingle, punctuate.
interstice • noun SPACE, gap, aperture, opening, hole, crevice, chink, slit, slot, crack.
intertwine • verb ENTWINE, interweave, interlace, interwind, twist, coil.
interval • noun **1** *a 15-minute interval* INTERMISSION, interlude, entr'acte, break, recess; half-time. **2** *Baldwin made two speeches in the interval* INTERIM, interlude, intervening time/period, mean-

2 interference by a state in another's affairs. **3** action taken to improve a medical disorder.
– DERIVATIVES **interventional** adjective.
interventionist ● adjective favouring intervention, especially by a government in its domestic economy or by one state in the affairs of another. ● noun an interventionist person.
– DERIVATIVES **interventionism** noun.
interview ● noun **1** an occasion on which a journalist or broadcaster puts a series of questions to a person of public interest. **2** an oral examination of an applicant for a job or college place. **3** a session of formal questioning of a person by the police. ● verb hold an interview with.
– DERIVATIVES **interviewee** noun **interviewer** noun.
– ORIGIN French *entrevue*, from *s'entrevoir* 'see each other'.
inter vivos /intər veevōs/ ● adverb & adjective (especially of a gift as opposed to a legacy) between living people.
– ORIGIN Latin.
interwar ● adjective existing in the period between two wars, especially the two world wars.
interweave ● verb (past **interwove**; past part. **interwoven**) weave or become woven together.
intestate /intestayt/ ● adjective not having made a will before one dies. ● noun a person who has died intestate.
– DERIVATIVES **intestacy** /intestəsi/ noun.
intestine (also **intestines**) ● noun the lower part of the alimentary canal from the end of the stomach to the anus.
– DERIVATIVES **intestinal** adjective.
– ORIGIN Latin *intestinum*, from *intus* 'within'.
intifada /intifaadə/ ● noun the Palestinian uprising against Israeli occupation of the West Bank and Gaza Strip, beginning in 1987.
– ORIGIN Arabic.
intimacy ● noun (pl. **intimacies**) **1** close familiarity or friendship. **2** an intimate act or remark.
intimate[1] /intimət/ ● adjective **1** closely acquainted; familiar. **2** private and personal. **3** euphemistic having a sexual relationship. **4** involving very close connection: *an intimate involvement.* **5** (of knowledge) detailed. **6** having an informal friendly atmosphere. ● noun a very close friend.
– DERIVATIVES **intimately** adverb.
– ORIGIN from Latin *intimare* 'impress, make familiar', from *intimus* 'inmost'.
intimate[2] /intimayt/ ● verb **1** state or make known. **2** imply or hint.
– DERIVATIVES **intimation** noun.
– ORIGIN Latin *intimare* (see INTIMATE[1]).
intimidate ● verb frighten or overawe, especially so as to coerce into doing something.
– DERIVATIVES **intimidation** noun **intimidator** noun **intimidatory** adjective.
– ORIGIN Latin *intimidare* 'make timid'.
into ● preposition **1** expressing motion or direction to a point on or within. **2** expressing a change of state or the result of an action. **3** indicating the direction towards which someone or something is turned. **4** indicating an object of interest. **5** expressing division. **6** informal taking a lively and active interest in.
intolerable ● adjective unable to be endured.
– DERIVATIVES **intolerably** adverb.
intolerant ● adjective not tolerant.
– DERIVATIVES **intolerance** noun **intolerantly** adverb.
intonation ● noun **1** the rise and fall of the voice in speaking. **2** the action of intoning. **3** accuracy of musical pitch.
– DERIVATIVES **intonational** adjective.
intone /intōn/ ● verb say or recite with little rise and fall of the pitch of the voice.
– ORIGIN Latin *intonare*, from *tonus* 'tone'.
in toto /in tōtō/ ● adverb as a whole.
– ORIGIN Latin.
intoxicant ● noun an intoxicating substance.
intoxicate ● verb **1** (of alcoholic drink or a drug) cause (someone) to lose control of their faculties. **2** poison. **3** excite or exhilarate.
– DERIVATIVES **intoxication** noun.
– ORIGIN Latin *intoxicare*, from *toxicum* 'poison'.
intra- /intrə/ ● prefix (added to adjectives) on the inside; within:

Thesaurus

time, meanwhile. **3** *short intervals of still water* STRETCH, distance, span, area.
intervene ● verb **1** *had the war not intervened, they might have married* OCCUR, happen, take place, arise, crop up, come about; result, ensue, follow; poetic/literary come to pass, befall, betide. **2** *she intervened in the row* INTERCEDE, involve oneself, get involved, interpose oneself, step in; interfere, intrude.
intervention ● noun INVOLVEMENT, intercession, interceding, interposing; interference, intrusion.
interview ● noun *all applicants will be called for an interview* MEETING, discussion, conference, examination, interrogation; audience, talk, dialogue, exchange; talks.
● verb *we interviewed seventy subjects for the survey* TALK TO, have a discussion/dialogue with; question, interrogate, cross-examine; poll, canvass, survey, sound out; informal grill, pump; Law examine.
interviewer ● noun QUESTIONER, interrogator, examiner, assessor, appraiser; journalist, reporter.
interweave ● verb **1** *the threads are interwoven* INTERTWINE, entwine, interlace, splice, braid, plait; twist together, weave together, wind together; Nautical marry. **2** *their fates were interwoven* INTERLINK, link, connect; intermix, mix, merge, blend, interlock, knit/bind together.
intestinal ● adjective ENTERIC, gastro-enteric, duodenal, coeliac, gastric, ventral, stomach, abdominal.
intestines ● plural noun GUT, guts, entrails, viscera; small intestine, large intestine; informal insides, innards.
– RELATED TERMS enteric.
intimacy ● noun **1** *the sisters re-established their old intimacy* CLOSENESS, togetherness, affinity, rapport, attachment, familiarity, friendliness, amity, affection, warmth; informal chumminess, palliness; Brit. informal mateyness. **2** *the memory of their intimacy* SEXUAL RELATIONS, (sexual) intercourse, sex, lovemaking, copulation; technical coitus.
intimate[1] ● adjective **1** *an intimate friend* CLOSE, bosom, boon, dear, cherished, faithful, fast, firm; informal chummy, pally. **2** *an intimate atmosphere* FRIENDLY, warm, welcoming, hospitable, relaxed, informal; cosy, comfortable, snug; informal comfy. **3** *intimate thoughts* PERSONAL, private, confidential, secret; innermost, inner, inward, unspoken, undisclosed. **4** *an intimate knowledge of the industry* DETAILED, thorough, exhaustive, deep, in-depth, profound. **5** *intimate relations* SEXUAL, carnal, amorous, amatory.
– OPPOSITES distant, formal.
● noun *his circle of intimates* CLOSE FRIEND, best friend, bosom friend, confidant, confidante; informal chum, pal, crony; Brit. informal mate; N. Amer. informal buddy.
intimate[2] ● verb **1** *he intimated his decision* ANNOUNCE, state, proclaim, make known, make public, disclose, reveal, divulge. **2** *her feelings were subtly intimated* IMPLY, suggest, hint at, insinuate, indicate, signal, allude to, refer to, convey.
intimation ● noun **1** *the early intimation of session dates* ANNOUNCEMENT, statement, communication, notification, notice, reporting, publishing; disclosure, revelation, divulging. **2** *the first intimation of discord* SUGGESTION, hint, indication, sign, signal, inkling, suspicion, impression; clue to, undertone of, whisper of.
intimidate ● verb FRIGHTEN, menace, terrify, scare, terrorize, cow, subdue; threaten, browbeat, bully, pressure, pressurize, harass, harry, hound; informal lean on, bulldoze, steamroller, railroad, use strong-arm tactics on.
intolerable ● adjective UNBEARABLE, insufferable, unsupportable, insupportable, unendurable, beyond endurance, more than flesh and blood can stand, too much to bear.
– OPPOSITES bearable.
intolerant ● adjective **1** *intolerant in religious matters* BIGOTED, narrow-minded, small-minded, parochial, provincial, illiberal, uncompromising; prejudiced, biased, partial, partisan, discriminatory. **2** *foods to which you are intolerant* ALLERGIC, sensitive, hypersensitive.
intonation ● noun **1** *she read the sentence with the wrong intonation* INFLECTION, pitch, tone, timbre, cadence, cadency, lilt, modulation, speech pattern. **2** *the intonation of hymns* CHANTING, incantation, recitation, singing; rare cantillation.
intone ● verb CHANT, sing, recite; rare cantillate.
intoxicate ● verb **1** *one glass of wine intoxicated him* INEBRIATE, make drunk, make intoxicated, befuddle, go to someone's head; informal make legless, make woozy. **2** *he was intoxicated by cinema* EXHILARATE, thrill, elate, delight, captivate, enthral, entrance, enrapture, excite, stir, rouse, inspire, fire with enthusiasm; informal give someone a buzz, give someone a kick; N. Amer. informal give

intramural.
– ORIGIN Latin, 'inside'.
intractable /intraktəb'l/ ● **adjective 1** hard to solve or deal with. **2** stubborn.
– DERIVATIVES **intractability** noun **intractably** adverb.
intramural /intrəmyoorəl/ ● **adjective 1** situated or done within a building. **2** forming part of normal university or college studies.
– ORIGIN from INTRA- + Latin *murus* 'wall'.
Intranet /intrənet/ ● **noun** Computing a private communications network created with Internet technology, accessible only to members of a particular organization.
intransigent /intransijənt/ ● **adjective** refusing to change one's views. ● **noun** an intransigent person.
– DERIVATIVES **intransigence** noun **intransigency** noun **intransigently** adverb.
– ORIGIN from Spanish *los intransigentes* (a name adopted by extreme republicans); ultimately from Latin *transigere* 'come to an understanding'.
intransitive /intransitiv/ ● **adjective** (of a verb) not taking a direct object, e.g. *look* in *look at the sky*. The opposite of TRANSITIVE.
– DERIVATIVES **intransitively** adverb **intransitivity** noun.
intrauterine /intrəyōōtərīn/ ● **adjective** within the uterus.
intrauterine device ● **noun** a contraceptive device fitted inside the uterus and physically preventing the implantation of fertilized ova.
intravenous /intrəveenəss/ ● **adjective** within or into a vein or veins.
– DERIVATIVES **intravenously** adverb.
in tray ● **noun** chiefly Brit. a tray on a desk for incoming letters and documents.
intrepid ● **adjective** fearless; adventurous.
– DERIVATIVES **intrepidity** noun **intrepidly** adverb.
– ORIGIN Latin *intrepidus* 'not alarmed'.
intricacy /intrikəsi/ ● **noun** (pl. **intricacies**) **1** the quality of being intricate. **2** (**intricacies**) details.
intricate ● **adjective** very complicated or detailed.
– DERIVATIVES **intricately** adverb.
– ORIGIN from Latin *intricare* 'entangle', from *tricae* 'tricks'.
intrigue ● **verb** /intreeg/ (**intrigues**, **intrigued**, **intriguing**) **1** arouse the curiosity or interest of. **2** plot something illicit or harmful. ● **noun** /intreeg, intreeg/ **1** the plotting of something illicit or harmful. **2** a secret love affair.
– DERIVATIVES **intriguer** noun **intriguing** adjective.
– ORIGIN French *intriguer* 'tangle, plot', from Latin *intricare* 'entangle'.
intrinsic /intrinsik/ ● **adjective** belonging to the basic nature of someone or something; essential.
– DERIVATIVES **intrinsically** adverb.
– ORIGIN originally in the sense 'interior, inner': from Latin *intrinsecus* 'inwardly, inwards'.
intro- ● **prefix** into; inwards: *introvert.*
– ORIGIN Latin *intro* 'to the inside'.
introduce ● **verb 1** bring into use or operation for the first time. **2** present (someone) by name to another. **3** (**introduce to**) bring (a subject) to the attention of (someone) for the first time. **4** insert or bring into. **5** occur at the start of. **6** provide an opening announcement for. **7** present (new legislation) for debate in a legislative assembly.
– DERIVATIVES **introducer** noun.
– ORIGIN Latin *introducere*, from *ducere* 'to lead'.
introduction ● **noun 1** the action of introducing or being introduced. **2** an act of introducing one person to another. **3** a preliminary thing, such as an explanatory section at the beginning of a book. **4** a thing newly brought in. **5** a book or course of study intended to introduce a subject to a person. **6** a person's first experience of a subject or activity.
introductory ● **adjective** serving as an introduction; basic or preliminary.
introit /introyt/ ● **noun** a psalm or antiphon sung or said while

i

Thesaurus

someone a charge.
intoxicated ● **adjective** DRUNK, inebriated, inebriate, drunken, tipsy, under the influence; *informal* tight, merry, the worse for wear, pie-eyed, in one's cups, three sheets to the wind, plastered, smashed, sloshed, sozzled, well oiled, wrecked, blotto, stewed, pickled, tanked up, soaked, off one's face, out of one's head/skull; *Brit. informal* paralytic, legless, Brahms and Liszt, half cut, bladdered, trolleyed, tiddly; *N. Amer. informal* loaded, trashed, out of one's gourd; *euphemistic* tired and emotional; *formal* bibulous; *poetic/literary* crapulent.
– OPPOSITES sober.
intoxicating ● **adjective 1** *intoxicating drink* ALCOHOLIC, strong, hard, potent, stiff, intoxicant; *formal* spiritous. **2** *an intoxicating sense of freedom* HEADY, exhilarating, thrilling, exciting, rousing, stirring, stimulating, invigorating, electrifying; strong, powerful, potent; *informal* mind-blowing.
– OPPOSITES non-alcoholic.
intoxication ● **noun** DRUNKENNESS, inebriation, insobriety, tipsiness; *informal* tightness; *poetic/literary* crapulence.
intractable ● **adjective 1** *intractable problems* UNMANAGEABLE, uncontrollable, difficult, awkward, troublesome, demanding, burdensome. **2** *an intractable man* STUBBORN, obstinate, obdurate, inflexible, unadaptable, unbending, unyielding, uncompromising, unaccommodating, uncooperative, difficult, awkward, perverse, contrary, pig-headed; *N. Amer.* rock-ribbed; *informal* stiff-necked.
– OPPOSITES manageable, compliant.
intransigent ● **adjective** UNCOMPROMISING, inflexible, unbending, unyielding, unshakeable, unwavering, resolute, rigid, unaccommodating, uncooperative, stubborn, obstinate, obdurate, pig-headed, single-minded, iron-willed; *informal* stiff-necked.
– OPPOSITES compliant.
intrench ● **verb.** See ENTRENCH.
intrenched ● **adjective.** See ENTRENCHED.
intrepid ● **adjective** FEARLESS, unafraid, undaunted, unflinching, unshrinking, bold, daring, audacious, adventurous, heroic, dynamic, spirited, indomitable; brave, courageous, valiant, valorous, stout-hearted, stalwart, plucky; *informal* gutsy, spunky; *archaic* doughty.
– OPPOSITES fearful.
intricate ● **adjective** COMPLEX, complicated, convoluted, tangled, entangled, twisted; elaborate, ornate, detailed, involuted; *Brit. informal* fiddly.
intrigue ● **verb 1** *her answer intrigued him* INTEREST, be of interest to, fascinate, arouse someone's curiosity, attract. **2** *the ministers were intriguing* PLOT, conspire, make secret plans, scheme, manoeuvre, connive, collude, machinate.
● **noun 1** *the intrigue that accompanied the selection of a new leader* PLOTTING, conspiracy, collusion, conniving, scheming, machination, trickery, sharp practice, double-dealing, underhandedness, subterfuge; *informal* dirty tricks. **2** *the king's intrigues with his nobles' wives* (LOVE) AFFAIR, affair of the heart, liaison, amour, fling, flirtation, dalliance; adultery, infidelity, unfaithfulness; *informal* fooling around, playing around, hanky-panky; *Brit. informal* carryings-on.
intriguer ● **noun** CONSPIRATOR, co-conspirator, plotter, schemer, colluder, conniver, machinator, Machiavelli.
intriguing ● **adjective** INTERESTING, fascinating, absorbing, compelling, gripping, riveting, captivating, engaging, enthralling.
intrinsic ● **adjective** INHERENT, innate, inborn, inbred, congenital, connate, connatural, natural; deep-rooted, indelible, ineradicable; integral, basic, fundamental, essential.
introduce ● **verb 1** *he has introduced a new system* INSTITUTE, initiate, launch, inaugurate, establish, found; bring in, set in motion, start, begin, commence, get going, get under way, originate, pioneer; *informal* kick off. **2** *you can introduce new ideas* PROPOSE, put forward, suggest, table; raise, broach, bring up, mention, air, float. **3** *she introduced Lindsey to the young man* PRESENT (FORMALLY), make known, acquaint with. **4** *introducing nitrogen into canned beer* INSERT, inject, put, force, shoot, feed. **5** *she introduced a note of severity into her voice* INSTIL, infuse, inject, add. **6** *the same presenter introduces the programme each week* ANNOUNCE, present, give an introduction to; start off, begin, open.
introduction ● **noun 1** *the introduction of democratic reforms* INSTITUTION, establishment, initiation, launch, inauguration, foundation; start, commencement, inception, origination, pioneering. **2** *an introduction to the king* (FORMAL) PRESENTATION; meeting, audience. **3** *an introduction to the catalogue* FOREWORD, preface, preamble, prologue, prelude; opening (statement), beginning; *informal* intro; *formal* proem, prolegomenon. **4** *an introduction to the history of the period* BASIC EXPLANATION/ACCOUNT OF; the basics, the rudiments, the fundamentals. **5** *a gentle introduction to the life of the school* INITIATION, induction, inauguration.
– OPPOSITES afterword.
introductory ● **adjective 1** *the introductory chapter* OPENING, ini-

the priest approaches the altar for the Eucharist.
– ORIGIN Latin *introitus*, from *introire* 'enter'.
intromission • noun technical the inserting of the penis into the vagina in sexual intercourse.
intron /intron/ • noun Biochemistry a segment of a DNA or RNA molecule which does not code for proteins and interrupts the sequence of genes. Compare with EXON.
– ORIGIN from INTRA-.
introspection • noun the examination of one's own thoughts or feelings.
– DERIVATIVES **introspective** adjective **introspectively** adverb.
– ORIGIN from Latin *introspicere* 'look into', or from *introspectare* 'keep looking into'.
introvert • noun **1** a shy, reticent person. **2** Psychology a person predominantly concerned with their own thoughts and feelings. • adjective (also **introverted**) of or characteristic of an introvert.
– DERIVATIVES **introversion** noun.
– ORIGIN from Latin *intro-* 'to the inside' + *vertere* 'to turn'.
intrude • verb **1** come into a place or situation where one is unwelcome or uninvited. **2** introduce into or enter with adverse effect. **3** Geology (of igneous rock) be forced or thrust into (a pre-existing formation).
– ORIGIN Latin *intrudere*, from *trudere* 'to thrust'.
intruder • noun a person who intrudes, especially into a building with criminal intent.
intrusion • noun **1** the action of intruding. **2** a thing that intrudes.

i

intrusive • adjective **1** intruding or tending to intrude. **2** (of igneous rock) that has been forced when molten into cracks in neighbouring strata.
– DERIVATIVES **intrusively** adverb **intrusiveness** noun.
intuit /intyo͞oit/ • verb understand or work out by intuition.
– ORIGIN Latin *intueri* 'contemplate'.
intuition • noun the ability to understand or know something immediately, without conscious reasoning.
intuitive • adjective **1** instinctive. **2** (chiefly of computer software) easy to use and understand.
– DERIVATIVES **intuitively** adverb **intuitiveness** noun.
Inuit /inyooit/ • noun **1** (pl. same or **Inuits**) a member of an indigenous people of northern Canada and parts of Greenland and Alaska. **2** the language of this people.
– USAGE The term **Inuit** has official status in Canada, and is also used elsewhere as a synonym for **Eskimo** in general. However, the use of **Inuit** to include people from Siberia who are not Inupiaq-speakers, is, strictly speaking, not accurate; **Eskimo** is the only word that covers both groups, and is still widely used.
– ORIGIN Inuit, 'people'.
inundate /inundayt/ • verb (usu. **be inundated**) **1** flood. **2** overwhelm with things to be dealt with.
– DERIVATIVES **inundation** noun.
– ORIGIN Latin *inundare* 'flood', from *unda* 'a wave'.
Inupiaq /ino͞opiak/ (also **Inupiat** /ino͞opiat/, **Inupik** /ino͞opik/) • noun (pl. same) **1** a member of a group of Inuit people inhabiting northern Alaska. **2** the Inuit language.
– ORIGIN Inuit, 'genuine person'.
inure /inyoor/ • verb (usu. **be inured to**) accustom to something, especially something unpleasant.
– ORIGIN from an Old French phrase meaning 'in use or practice'.
in utero /in yo͞otərō/ • adverb & adjective in a woman's uterus; before birth.
– ORIGIN Latin.
in vacuo /in vakyoo-ō/ • adverb in a vacuum.
– ORIGIN Latin.
invade • verb **1** enter (a country) as or with an army so as to subjugate or occupy it. **2** enter in large numbers, especially intrusively. **3** (of a parasite or disease) attack and spread into (an organism or bodily part). **4** encroach on: *his privacy was being invaded.*
– DERIVATIVES **invader** noun.
– ORIGIN Latin *invadere*, from *vadere* 'go'.
invagination • noun chiefly Anatomy & Biology **1** the action or process of being turned inside out or folded back on itself to form a cavity or pouch. **2** a cavity or pouch so formed.
– DERIVATIVES **invaginate** verb.
– ORIGIN Latin, from *vagina* 'sheath'.
invalid[1] /invəlid/ • noun a person made weak or disabled by illness or injury. • verb (**invalided**, **invaliding**) (usu. **be invalided**) remove from active service in the armed forces because of injury or illness.
– DERIVATIVES **invalidism** noun.
– ORIGIN a special sense of INVALID[2], with a change of pronunciation.
invalid[2] /invalid/ • adjective **1** not legally recognized because contravening a regulation or law. **2** not true because based on incorrect information or unsound reasoning.
– DERIVATIVES **invalidate** verb **invalidation** noun **invalidly** adverb.
– ORIGIN Latin *invalidus* 'not strong'.
invalidity • noun **1** Brit. the condition of being an invalid. **2** the

Thesaurus

tial, starting, initiatory, first; prefatory, preliminary. **2** *an introductory course* ELEMENTARY, basic, rudimentary; initiatory, preparatory.
– OPPOSITES final, advanced.
introspection • noun SELF-ANALYSIS, soul-searching, introversion; contemplation, thoughtfulness, pensiveness, meditation, reflection; *informal* navel-gazing; *formal* cogitation.
introspective • adjective INWARD-LOOKING, self-analysing, introverted, introvert; contemplative, thoughtful, pensive, meditative, reflective; *informal* navel-gazing.
introverted • adjective SHY, reserved, withdrawn, reticent, diffident, retiring, quiet; introspective, introvert, inward-looking, indrawn, self-absorbed; contemplative, thoughtful, pensive, meditative, reflective.
– OPPOSITES extroverted.
intrude • verb **1** *intruding on people's privacy* ENCROACH, impinge, trespass, infringe, obtrude, invade, violate, disturb, disrupt; *informal* horn in, muscle in. **2** *he intruded his own personality into his work* FORCE, push, obtrude, impose, thrust.
intruder • noun TRESPASSER, interloper, invader, infiltrator; burglar, housebreaker, thief.
intrusion • noun ENCROACHMENT, obtrusion; invasion, incursion, intervention, disturbance, disruption, infringement, impingement.
intrusive • adjective **1** *an intrusive journalist* INTRUDING, invasive, obtrusive, unwelcome; inquisitive, prying; *informal* nosy. **2** *opinion polls play an intrusive role in elections* INVASIVE, high-profile, prominent; *informal* in one's face. **3** *intrusive questions* PERSONAL, prying, forward, impertinent; *informal* nosy.
intuition • noun **1** *he works according to intuition* INSTINCT, intuitiveness; sixth sense, clairvoyance, second sight. **2** *this confirms an intuition I had* HUNCH, feeling (in one's bones), inkling, (sneaking) suspicion; premonition, presentiment; *informal* gut feeling.
intuitive • adjective INSTINCTIVE, intuitional, instinctual; innate, inborn, inherent, natural, congenital; unconscious, subconscious, involuntary; *informal* gut.
intumescence • noun (*rare*) SWELLING, bulging, bloating, distension, dilatation, turgidity.
inundate • verb **1** *many buildings were inundated* FLOOD, deluge, overrun, swamp, submerge, engulf. **2** *we have been inundated by complaints* OVERWHELM, overrun, overload, swamp, bog down, besiege, snow under.
inundation • noun FLOOD, deluge, torrent, flash flood, freshet; *Brit.* spate.
inure • verb HARDEN, toughen, season, temper, condition; accustom, habituate, familiarize, acclimatize, adjust, adapt.
– OPPOSITES sensitize.
invade • verb **1** *the island was invaded* OCCUPY, conquer, capture, seize, take (over), annex, win, gain, secure; march into, overrun, overwhelm, storm. **2** *someone had invaded our privacy* INTRUDE ON, violate, encroach on, infringe on, trespass on, obtrude on, disturb, disrupt; *informal* horn in on, muscle in on. **3** *the feeling of betrayal invaded my being* PERMEATE, pervade, spread through/over, diffuse through, imbue.
– OPPOSITES withdraw.
invader • noun ATTACKER, raider, marauder; occupier, conqueror; intruder.
invalid[1] • noun *my mother is an invalid* ILL PERSON, sick person, valetudinarian; patient, convalescent.
• adjective *her invalid husband* ILL, sick, ailing, unwell, infirm, valetudinarian, in poor health; incapacitated, bedridden, frail, feeble, weak, debilitated, sickly, poorly.
– OPPOSITES healthy.
• verb *an officer invalided by a chest wound* DISABLE, incapacitate, indispose, hospitalize, put out action, lay up; injure, wound, hurt.
invalid[2] • adjective **1** *the law was invalid* (LEGALLY) VOID, null and

fact of being invalid.

invaluable ● adjective extremely useful.
– DERIVATIVES **invaluably** adverb.

invariable ● adjective **1** never changing. **2** Mathematics (of a quantity) constant.
– DERIVATIVES **invariability** noun.

invariably ● adverb always.

invariant ● adjective never changing. ● noun Mathematics a function which remains unchanged when a specified transformation is applied.
– DERIVATIVES **invariance** noun.

invasion ● noun **1** an instance of invading. **2** the action or process of being invaded.

invasive ● adjective **1** tending to invade or intrude: *invasive grasses.* **2** (of medical procedures) involving the introduction of instruments or other objects into the body.

invective ● noun strongly abusive or critical language.
– ORIGIN Latin *invectivus* 'attacking', from *invehere* (see INVEIGH).

inveigh /invay/ ● verb (**inveigh against**) speak or write about with great hostility.
– ORIGIN originally in the sense 'introduce': from Latin *invehere* 'carry in', *invehi* 'be carried into, attack'.

inveigle /invayg'l/ ● verb (usu. **inveigle someone into**) persuade by deception or flattery.
– DERIVATIVES **inveiglement** noun.
– ORIGIN Old French *aveugler* 'to blind'.

invent ● verb **1** create or design (a new device, process, etc.). **2** make up (a false story, name, etc.).
– DERIVATIVES **inventor** noun.
– ORIGIN Latin *invenire* 'contrive, discover'.

invention ● noun **1** the action of inventing. **2** something invented. **3** a false story. **4** creative ability.

inventive ● adjective having or showing creativity or original thought.
– DERIVATIVES **inventively** adverb **inventiveness** noun.

inventory /invəntri/ ● noun (pl. **inventories**) **1** a complete list of items such as goods in stock or the contents of a building. **2** a quantity of goods in stock. ● verb (**inventories, inventoried**) make an inventory of.
– ORIGIN Latin *inventarium* 'a list of what is found', from *invenire* 'discover'.

inverse /inverss, inverss/ ● adjective opposite in position, direction, order, or effect. ● noun **1** a thing that is the opposite or reverse of another. **2** Mathematics a reciprocal quantity.
– DERIVATIVES **inversely** adverb.
– ORIGIN Latin *inversus*, from *invertere* 'turn inside out'.

inverse proportion (also **inverse ratio**) ● noun a relation between two quantities such that one increases in proportion as the other decreases.

inverse square law ● noun Physics a law stating that the intensity of an effect changes in inverse proportion to the square of the distance from the source.

inversion ● noun **1** the action of inverting or the state of being inverted. **2** (also **temperature** or **thermal inversion**) a reversal of the normal decrease of air temperature with altitude, or of water temperature with depth.
– DERIVATIVES **inversive** adjective.

invert /invert/ ● verb put upside down or in the opposite position, order, or arrangement.
– DERIVATIVES **inverter** noun **invertible** adjective.
– ORIGIN Latin *invertere* 'turn inside out'.

invertebrate /invertibrət/ ● noun an animal having no backbone, such as an arthropod, mollusc, etc. ● adjective relating to such animals.

inverted comma ● noun chiefly Brit. a quotation mark.

inverted snobbery ● noun derogatory the attitude of disdaining anything associated with wealth or high social status, while elevating those things associated with lack of wealth and social position.

invert sugar ● noun a mixture of glucose and fructose obtained by the hydrolysis of sucrose.

invest ● verb **1** put money into financial schemes, shares, or property with the expectation of achieving a profit. **2** devote (time or energy) to an undertaking with the expectation of a worthwhile result. **3** (**invest in**) informal buy (something) whose usefulness will repay the cost. **4** (**invest with**) endow (someone or something) with (a quality or attribute). **5** confer (a rank or office) on.
– DERIVATIVES **investable** (also **investible**) adjective **investor** noun.
– ORIGIN originally in the sense 'clothe': from Latin *investire*,

i

Thesaurus

void, unenforceable, not binding, illegitimate, inapplicable. **2** *the whole theory is invalid* FALSE, untrue, inaccurate, faulty, fallacious, spurious, unconvincing, unsound, weak, wrong, wide of the mark, off target; untenable, baseless, ill-founded, groundless; *informal* off beam, full of holes.
– OPPOSITES binding, true.

invalidate ● verb **1** *a low turnout invalidated the ballot* RENDER INVALID, void, nullify, annul, negate, cancel, overturn, overrule. **2** *this case invalidates the general argument* DISPROVE, refute, explode, contradict, rebut, negate, belie, discredit, debunk; weaken, undermine, compromise; *informal* shoot full of holes; *formal* confute.

invaluable ● adjective INDISPENSABLE, crucial, critical, key, vital, irreplaceable, all-important.
– OPPOSITES dispensable.

invariable ● adjective UNVARYING, unchanging, unvaried; constant, stable, set, steady, predictable, regular, consistent; unchangeable, unalterable, immutable, fixed.
– OPPOSITES varied.

invariably ● adverb ALWAYS, on every occasion, at all times, without fail, without exception; everywhere, in all places, in all cases/instances; regularly, consistently, repeatedly, habitually, unfailingly.
– OPPOSITES sometimes, never.

invasion ● noun **1** *the invasion of the islands* OCCUPATION, conquering, capture, seizure, annexation, annexing, takeover; overrunning, overwhelming, storming. **2** *an invasion of cars* INFLUX, inundation, inrush, flood, torrent, deluge, avalanche. **3** *an invasion of my privacy* VIOLATION, infringement, interruption, intrusion, encroachment, obtrusion, disturbance, disruption, breach.
– OPPOSITES withdrawal.

invective ● noun ABUSE, insults, vituperation, expletives, swear words, swearing, curses, bad/foul language, obloquy; *archaic* contumely.
– OPPOSITES praise.

inveigh ● verb FULMINATE, declaim, protest, rail, rage, remonstrate; denounce, censure, condemn, decry, criticize; disparage, denigrate, run down, abuse, vilify, impugn; *informal* kick up a fuss/stink about, bellyache about, sound off about.
– OPPOSITES support.

inveigle ● verb CAJOLE, wheedle, coax, persuade, talk; tempt, lure, entice, seduce, beguile; *informal* sweet-talk, soft-soap, con; *N. Amer. informal* sucker; *archaic* blandish.

invent ● verb **1** *Louis Braille invented an alphabet to help blind people* ORIGINATE, create, innovate, design, devise, contrive, develop; conceive, think up, dream up, come up with, pioneer. **2** *they invented the story for a laugh* MAKE UP, fabricate, concoct, hatch, dream up; *informal* cook up.

invention ● noun **1** *the invention of the telescope* ORIGINATION, creation, innovation, devising, contriving, development, design. **2** *medieval inventions* INNOVATION, creation, design, contraption, contrivance, construction, device, gadget; *informal* brainchild. **3** *his invention was flagging* INVENTIVENESS, originality, creativity, creativeness, imagination, imaginativeness, inspiration. **4** *a journalistic invention* FABRICATION, concoction, (piece of) fiction, story, tale; lie, untruth, falsehood, fib; myth, fantasy; *informal* tall story, cock-and-bull story.

inventive ● adjective **1** *the most inventive composer of his time* CREATIVE, original, innovational, innovative, imaginative, ingenious, resourceful. **2** *a fresh, inventive comedy* ORIGINAL, innovative, unusual, fresh, novel, new; experimental, avant-garde, groundbreaking, unorthodox, unconventional.
– OPPOSITES unimaginative, hackneyed.

inventor ● noun ORIGINATOR, creator, innovator; designer, deviser, developer, maker, producer; author, architect; pioneer, mastermind, father.

inventory ● noun *a complete inventory of all their belongings* LIST, listing, catalogue, record, register, checklist, log, archive.
● verb *I inventoried his collection* LIST, catalogue, record, register, log.

inverse ● adjective *inverse snobbery* REVERSE, reversed, inverted, opposite, converse, contrary, counter, antithetical.
● noun *alkalinity is the inverse of acidity* OPPOSITE, converse, obverse, antithesis; *informal* flip side.

inversion ● noun REVERSAL, transposition, turning upside down;

from *vestire* 'clothe'; sense 1 is influenced by Italian *investire*.

investigate • verb **1** carry out a systematic or formal inquiry into (an incident or allegation) so as to establish the truth. **2** carry out research into (a subject). **3** make a search or systematic inquiry.
– DERIVATIVES **investigable** adjective **investigation** noun **investigator** noun **investigatory** adjective.
– ORIGIN Latin *investigare* 'trace out'.

investigative /investigətiv/ • adjective **1** of or concerned with investigating. **2** (of journalism or a journalist) investigating and seeking to expose malpractice or the miscarriage of justice.

investiture /investityoor/ • noun **1** the action of formally investing a person with honours or rank. **2** a ceremony at which this takes place.

investment • noun **1** the action or process of investing. **2** a thing worth buying because it may be profitable or useful in the future.

investment trust • noun a limited company which buys and sells shares in selected companies to make a profit for its members.

inveterate /invettərət/ • adjective **1** having a long-standing and firmly established habit or activity: *an inveterate gambler*. **2** (of a feeling or habit) firmly established.
– DERIVATIVES **inveteracy** noun **inveterately** adverb.
– ORIGIN Latin *inveteratus* 'made old'.

invidious /inviddiəss/ • adjective unacceptable, unfair, and likely to arouse resentment or anger in others.
– DERIVATIVES **invidiously** adverb **invidiousness** noun.
– ORIGIN Latin *invidiosus*, from *invidia* 'hostility'.

invigilate /invijilayt/ • verb Brit. supervise candidates during an examination.
– DERIVATIVES **invigilation** noun **invigilator** noun.
– ORIGIN Latin *invigilare* 'watch over'.

invigorate /inviggərayt/ • verb give strength or energy to.
– DERIVATIVES **invigorating** adjective **invigoration** noun.
– ORIGIN Latin *invigorare* 'make strong'.

invincible /invinsib'l/ • adjective too powerful to be defeated or overcome.
– DERIVATIVES **invincibility** noun **invincibly** adverb.
– ORIGIN from Latin *in-* 'not' + *vincibilis* 'able to be overcome'.

in vino veritas /in veenō verritaas/ • exclamation under the influence of alcohol, a person tells the truth.
– ORIGIN Latin, 'truth in wine'.

inviolable /invīələb'l/ • adjective never to be infringed or dishonoured.
– DERIVATIVES **inviolability** noun **inviolably** adverb.

inviolate /invīələt/ • adjective free from injury or violation.
– ORIGIN from Latin *in-* 'not' + *violare* 'violate'.

invisible • adjective **1** unable to be seen, either by nature or because concealed. **2** treated as if unable to be seen; ignored. **3** relating to or denoting earnings which a country makes from the sale of services rather than tangible commodities.
– DERIVATIVES **invisibility** noun **invisibly** adverb.

invitation • noun **1** a written or verbal request inviting someone to go somewhere or to do something. **2** the action of inviting. **3** a situation or action inviting a particular outcome or response: *his tactics were an invitation to disaster*.

invite • verb **1** ask in a friendly or formal way to go somewhere or to do something. **2** request (something) formally or politely. **3** tend to provoke (a particular outcome or response). • noun informal an invitation.
– DERIVATIVES **invitee** noun **inviter** noun.
– ORIGIN Latin *invitare*.

inviting • adjective tempting or attractive.
– DERIVATIVES **invitingly** adverb.

in vitro /in veetrō/ • adjective & adverb (of biological processes) taking place in a test tube, culture dish, or elsewhere outside a living organism.
– ORIGIN Latin, 'in glass'.

in vivo /in veevō/ • adverb & adjective (of biological processes) taking place in a living organism.
– ORIGIN Latin, 'in a living thing'.

invocation /invəkaysh'n/ • noun **1** the action of invoking. **2** an appeal to a deity or the supernatural.
– DERIVATIVES **invocatory** /invokkətri/ adjective.

invoice • noun a list of goods or services provided, with a state-

Thesaurus

reverse, contrary, antithesis, converse.

invert • verb TURN UPSIDE DOWN, upturn, upend, turn around/about, turn inside out, turn back to front, reverse, flip (over).

invest • verb **1** *he invested in a cotton mill* PUT/PLOUGH MONEY INTO, provide capital for, fund, back, finance, underwrite; buy into, buy shares in. **2** *they invested £18 million* SPEND, expend, put in, plough in; venture, speculate, risk; *informal* lay out. **3** *their words were invested with sarcasm* IMBUE, infuse, charge, steep, suffuse, pervade, endow. **4** *the powers invested in the bishop* VEST IN, confer on, bestow on, grant to, entrust to, put in someone's hands. **5** *bishops whom the king had invested* ADMIT TO OFFICE, instate, install, induct, swear in; ordain, crown. **6** (*archaic*) *invested in the full canonicals of his calling* CLOTHE, attire, dress, garb, robe, deck out, accoutre; *archaic* apparel. **7** (*archaic*) *he invested the fort of Arcot* BESIEGE, lay siege to, beleaguer, surround.

investigate • verb ENQUIRE INTO, look into, go into, probe, explore, scrutinize, conduct an investigation into, make inquiries about; inspect, analyse, study, examine, consider, research; *informal* check out, suss out; *N. Amer. informal* scope out.

investigation • noun EXAMINATION, inquiry, study, inspection, exploration, consideration, analysis, appraisal; research, scrutiny, scrutinization, perusal; probe, review, survey.

investigator • noun INSPECTOR, examiner, inquirer, explorer, analyser; researcher, scrutineer, scrutinizer, factfinder, prober, searcher; detective.

investiture • noun INAUGURATION, appointment, installation, instatement, initiation, swearing in; ordination, consecration, crowning, enthronement.

investment • noun **1** *you can lose money by bad investment* INVESTING, speculation; funding, backing, financing, underwriting; buying shares. **2** *it's a good investment* VENTURE, speculation, risk, gamble; asset, acquisition, holding, possession. **3** *an investment of £305,000* STAKE, share, money/capital invested. **4** *a substantial investment of time* SACRIFICE, surrender, loss, forfeiture.

inveterate • adjective **1** *an inveterate gambler* CONFIRMED, hardened, incorrigible, addicted, compulsive, obsessive; *informal* pathological. **2** *an inveterate Democrat* STAUNCH, steadfast, committed, devoted, dedicated, dyed-in-the-wool, out and out, diehard. **3** *mankind's inveterate stupidity* INGRAINED, deep-seated, deep-rooted, entrenched, ineradicable, incurable.

invidious • adjective **1** *that put her in an invidious position* UNPLEASANT, awkward, difficult; undesirable, unenviable. **2** *an invidious comparison* UNFAIR, unjust, iniquitous, unwarranted; deleterious, detrimental.
– OPPOSITES pleasant, fair.

invigorate • verb REVITALIZE, energize, refresh, revive, vivify, brace, rejuvenate, enliven, liven up, perk up, wake up, animate, galvanize, fortify, stimulate, rouse, exhilarate; *informal* buck up, pep up.
– OPPOSITES tire.

invincible • adjective INVULNERABLE, indestructible, unconquerable, unbeatable, indomitable, unassailable; impregnable, inviolable.
– OPPOSITES vulnerable.

inviolable • adjective INALIENABLE, absolute, unalterable, unchallengeable; sacrosanct, sacred, holy.

inviolate • adjective UNTOUCHED, undamaged, unhurt, unharmed, unscathed; unspoiled, unflawed, unsullied, unstained, undefiled, unprofaned, perfect, pristine, pure; intact, unbroken, whole, entire, complete.

invisible • adjective UNABLE TO BE SEEN, not visible; undetectable, indiscernible, inconspicuous, imperceptible; unseen, unnoticed, unobserved, hidden, obscured, out of sight.

invitation • noun **1** *an invitation to dinner* request to attend, call, summons; *informal* invite. **2** *an open door is an invitation to a thief* ENCOURAGEMENT, provocation, temptation, lure, magnet, bait, enticement, attraction, allure; *informal* come-on.

invite • verb **1** *they invited us to Sunday lunch* ASK, summon, have someone over/round, request (the pleasure of) someone's company at. **2** *applications are invited for the posts* ASK FOR, request, call for, appeal for, solicit, seek, summon. **3** *airing such views invites trouble* CAUSE, induce, provoke, create, generate, engender, foster, encourage, lead to; incite, elicit, bring on oneself, arouse.
• noun (*informal*) *an invite to a party*. See INVITATION sense 1.

inviting • adjective TEMPTING, enticing, alluring, beguiling; attractive, appealing, pleasant, agreeable, delightful; appetizing, mouthwatering; fascinating, enchanting, entrancing, captivating, intriguing, irresistible, seductive.
– OPPOSITES repellent.

ment of the sum due. ● verb **1** send an invoice to. **2** send an invoice for (goods or services).
– ORIGIN originally the plural of obsolete *invoy*, from French *envoyer* 'send'.

invoke /invōk/ ● verb **1** appeal to as an authority or in support of an argument. **2** call on (a deity or spirit) in prayer or as a witness. **3** call earnestly for. **4** summon (a spirit) by charms or incantation. **5** give rise to; evoke.
– DERIVATIVES **invoker** noun.
– ORIGIN Latin *invocare*, from *vocare* 'to call'.

involuntary ● adjective **1** done without conscious control. **2** (especially of muscles or nerves) concerned in bodily processes that are not under the control of the will. **3** done against someone's will.
– DERIVATIVES **involuntarily** adverb **involuntariness** noun.

involute /invəlōōt/ ● adjective **1** (also **involuted**) formal complicated. **2** technical curled spirally.
– ORIGIN Latin *involutus* 'wrapped up'.

involution ● noun **1** Physiology the shrinkage of an organ in old age or when inactive. **2** formal the process of complicating or the state of being complicated.
– DERIVATIVES **involutional** adjective.

involve ● verb **1** (of a situation or event) include as a necessary part or result. **2** cause to experience or participate in an activity or situation.
– DERIVATIVES **involvement** noun.
– ORIGIN originally in the senses 'enfold' and 'entangle': from Latin *involvere*, from *volvere* 'to roll'.

involved ● adjective **1** connected, typically on an emotional or personal level. **2** difficult to comprehend; complicated.

invulnerable ● adjective impossible to harm or damage.
– DERIVATIVES **invulnerability** noun **invulnerably** adverb.

-in-waiting ● combining form **1** denoting a position as attendant to a royal personage: *lady-in-waiting.* **2** awaiting a turn or about to happen: *a political administration-in-waiting.*

inward ● adjective **1** directed or proceeding towards the inside. **2** mental or spiritual. ● adverb variant of INWARDS.
– DERIVATIVES **inwardly** adverb **inwardness** noun.

inward investment ● noun investment made within a country from outside.

inward-looking ● adjective self-absorbed or insular.

inwards (also **inward**) ● adverb **1** towards the inside. **2** into or towards the mind, spirit, or soul.

in-your-face ● adjective informal blatantly aggressive or provocative.
– ORIGIN from *in your face*, used as an insult.

I/O ● abbreviation Electronics input-output.

iodide /īədīd/ ● noun a compound of iodine with another element or group.

iodine /īədeen/ ● noun **1** a black, crystalline, non-metallic chemical element of the halogen group. **2** an antiseptic solution of iodine in alcohol.
– ORIGIN from Greek *iōdēs* 'violet-coloured'.

IOM ● abbreviation Isle of Man.

ion /īən/ ● noun an atom or molecule with a net electric charge through loss or gain of electrons, either positive (a **cation**) or negative (an **anion**).
– ORIGIN Greek, 'going'.

-ion ● suffix **1** forming nouns denoting verbal action or an instance of this: *communion.* **2** denoting a resulting state or product: *oblivion.*
– ORIGIN Latin.

ion exchange ● noun the exchange of ions of the same charge between an insoluble solid and a solution in contact with it, used in purification and separation processes.

Ionian /īōniən/ ● noun **1** a member of an ancient people inhabiting Attica, parts of western Asia Minor, and the Aegean islands in pre-classical times. **2** a person from the Ionian Islands, a chain of islands off the western coast of mainland Greece. ● adjective relating to the Ionians, Ionia, or the Ionian Islands.

Ionic /īonnik/ ● adjective relating to a classical order of architecture characterized by a column with scroll shapes on either side of the capital.
– ORIGIN Greek *Iōnikos*, from *Iōnia* 'Ionia' (the ancient Greek name for part of the west coast of Asia Minor).

ionic /īonnik/ ● adjective **1** relating to ions. **2** (of a chemical bond) formed by the electrostatic attraction of oppositely charged ions. Often contrasted with COVALENT.
– DERIVATIVES **ionically** adverb.

ionize /īənīz/ (also **ionise**) ● verb convert (an atom, molecule, or substance) into an ion or ions, typically by removing one or more electrons.
– DERIVATIVES **ionizable** adjective **ionization** noun.

ionizer ● noun a device which produces ions, especially one used to improve the quality of the air in a room.

ionizing radiation ● noun radiation consisting of particles, X-rays, or gamma rays which produce ions in the medium through which it passes.

ionosphere /īonnəsfeer/ ● noun the layer of the atmosphere above the mesosphere, which contains a high concentration of ions and electrons and is able to reflect radio waves.
– DERIVATIVES **ionospheric** adjective.

iota /īōtə/ ● noun **1** the ninth letter of the Greek alphabet (**Ι, ι**), transliterated as 'i'. **2** an extremely small amount: *it won't make an iota of difference.*
– ORIGIN Greek; sense 2 derives from *iota* being the smallest letter of the Greek alphabet (compare with JOT).

IOU ● noun a signed document acknowledging a debt.
– ORIGIN representing the pronunciation of *I owe you.*

IOW ● abbreviation Isle of Wight.

i

Thesaurus

invocation ● noun **1** *her invocation of new methodologies* CITATION, mention, acknowledgement, reference to, allusion to. **2** *the invocation of rain by tribal people* SUMMONING, calling up, conjuring up. **3** *an invocation to the Holy Ghost* PRAYER, intercession, supplication, entreaty, petition, appeal; archaic orison.

invoice ● noun *an invoice for the goods* BILL, account, statement (of charges); N. Amer. check; informal tab; archaic reckoning.
● verb *we'll invoice you for the damage* BILL, charge, send an invoice/bill to.

invoke ● verb **1** *he invoked his statutory rights* CITE, refer to, adduce, instance; resort to, have recourse to, turn to. **2** *I invoked the Madonna* PRAY TO, call on, appeal to, supplicate, entreat, solicit, beg, implore; poetic/literary beseech. **3** *invoking the spirits* SUMMON, call (up), conjure (up). **4** *middle-class moralities invoke peculiar anxieties* BRING FORTH, bring out, elicit, induce, cause, kindle.

involuntary ● adjective **1** *an involuntary shudder* REFLEX, automatic; spontaneous, instinctive, unconscious, unintentional, uncontrollable. **2** *involuntary repatriation* COMPULSORY, obligatory, mandatory, forced, coerced, compelled, imposed, required, prescribed; unwilling, unconsenting, against one's will.
– OPPOSITES deliberate, optional.

involve ● verb **1** *the inspection involved a lot of work* REQUIRE, necessitate, demand, call for; entail, mean, imply, presuppose. **2** *I try to involve everyone in key decisions* INCLUDE, count in, bring in, take into account, take note of; cover, incorporate, encompass, touch on, embrace, comprehend. **3** *many drug addicts involve themselves in crime* IMPLICATE, incriminate, inculpate; associate, connect, concern; embroil, entangle, enmesh; informal mix up.
– OPPOSITES preclude, exclude.

involved ● adjective **1** *social workers involved in the case* ASSOCIATED, connected, concerned. **2** *he had been involved in burglaries* IMPLICATED, incriminated, inculpated, embroiled, entangled, caught up, mixed up. **3** *a long and involved story* COMPLICATED, intricate, complex, elaborate; convoluted, impenetrable, unfathomable. **4** *they were totally involved in their work* ENGROSSED, absorbed, immersed, caught up, preoccupied, busy, engaged, intent.
– OPPOSITES unconnected, straightforward.

involvement ● noun **1** *his involvement in a plot to overthrow the government* PARTICIPATION, action, hand; collaboration, collusion, complicity, implication, incrimination, inculpation; association, connection, attachment, entanglement. **2** *emotional involvement* ATTACHMENT, friendship, intimacy; relationship, relations, bond.

invulnerable ● adjective IMPERVIOUS, insusceptible, immune; indestructible, impenetrable, impregnable, unassailable, inviolable, invincible, secure; proof against.

inward ● adjective **1** *a small inward indentation* TOWARDS THE INSIDE, going in, ingoing; concave. **2** *an inward smile* INTERNAL, inner, interior, innermost; private, personal, hidden, secret, veiled, masked, concealed, unexpressed; archaic privy.
– OPPOSITES outward.
● adverb *the door opened inward.* See INWARDS.

inwardly ● adverb INSIDE, internally, within, deep down (inside), in one's heart (of hearts); privately, secretly, confidentially.

inwards ● adverb INSIDE, into the interior, inward, within.

IP ● abbreviation Computing Internet Protocol.

IPA ● abbreviation International Phonetic Alphabet.

ipecacuanha /ippikakyooaanə/ ● noun the dried root of a South American shrub, used as an emetic and expectorant drug.
– ORIGIN Tupi-Guarani, 'emetic creeper'.

IPO ● abbreviation initial public offering, the first issue of a company's shares to the public, used as a means of raising start-up or expansion capital.

ipsilateral /ipsilattərəl/ ● adjective belonging to or occurring on the same side of the body.
– ORIGIN formed irregularly from Latin *ipse* 'self' + LATERAL.

ipso facto /ipsō faktō/ ● adverb by that very fact or act.
– ORIGIN Latin.

IQ ● abbreviation intelligence quotient.

Ir ● symbol the chemical element iridium.

IRA ● abbreviation Irish Republican Army.

Iranian ● noun a person from Iran. ● adjective relating to Iran.

Iraqi ● noun (pl. **Iraqis**) **1** a person from Iraq. **2** the form of Arabic spoken in Iraq. ● adjective relating to Iraq.

irascible /irassib'l/ ● adjective hot-tempered; irritable.
– DERIVATIVES **irascibility** noun **irascibly** adverb.
– ORIGIN Latin *irascibilis*, from *ira* 'anger'.

irate /īrayt/ ● adjective extremely angry.
– DERIVATIVES **irately** adverb.
– ORIGIN Latin *iratus*, from *ira* 'anger'.

IRC ● abbreviation Computing Internet Relay Chat.

ire /īr/ ● noun chiefly literary anger.
– ORIGIN Latin *ira*.

iridaceous /irridayshəss/ ● adjective Botany relating to or denoting plants of the iris family (Iridaceae).

iridescent /irridess'nt/ ● adjective showing luminous colours that seem to change when seen from different angles.
– DERIVATIVES **iridescence** noun **iridescently** adverb.
– ORIGIN from Latin *iris* 'rainbow'.

iridium /iriddiəm/ ● noun a hard, dense silvery-white metallic element.
– ORIGIN from Latin *iris* 'rainbow' (so named because it forms compounds of various colours).

iridology /irridolləji/ ● noun (in alternative medicine) diagnosis by examination of the iris of the eye.
– DERIVATIVES **iridologist** noun.

iris ● noun **1** a flat, coloured, ring-shaped membrane behind the cornea of the eye, with an adjustable circular opening (pupil) in the centre. **2** a plant with sword-shaped leaves and purple or yellow flowers.
– ORIGIN Greek, 'rainbow, iris'.

Irish ● noun (also **Irish Gaelic**) the Celtic language of Ireland. ● adjective **1** relating to Ireland or Irish. **2** offensive illogical or apparently so.
– DERIVATIVES **Irishman** noun **Irishness** noun **Irishwoman** noun.
– ORIGIN Old English.

Irish coffee ● noun coffee mixed with a dash of Irish whisky and served with cream on top.

Irish moss ● noun another term for CARRAGEEN.

Irish setter ● noun a breed of setter with a long, silky dark red coat and a long feathered tail.

Irish stew ● noun a stew made with mutton, potatoes, and onions.

Irish wolfhound ● noun a large, greyish hound of a rough-coated breed.

irk /urk/ ● verb irritate; annoy.
– DERIVATIVES **irksome** adjective **irksomely** adverb.
– ORIGIN perhaps from Old Norse, 'to work'.

iron ● noun **1** a strong, hard magnetic silvery-grey metal, used in construction and manufacturing. **2** a tool or implement made of iron. **3** a hand-held implement with a flat heated steel base, used to smooth clothes and linen. **4** a golf club used for lofting the ball. **5** (**irons**) fetters or handcuffs. ● verb **1** smooth (clothes) with an iron. **2** (**iron out**) settle (a difficulty or problem).
– PHRASES **have many** (or **other**) **irons in the fire** have a range of options or interests. **an iron hand** (or **fist**) **in a velvet glove** firmness or ruthlessness cloaked in outward gentleness.
– ORIGIN Old English.

Iron Age ● noun a period that followed the Bronze Age, when weapons and tools came to be made of iron.

ironclad ● adjective **1** covered or protected with iron. **2** impossible to weaken or change.

Iron Curtain ● noun (**the Iron Curtain**) a notional barrier separating the former Soviet bloc and the West prior to the decline of communism in eastern Europe in 1989.

ironic /īronnik/ ● adjective **1** using or characterized by irony. **2** happening in the opposite way to what is expected.
– DERIVATIVES **ironical** adjective **ironically** adverb.

ironing ● noun clothes and linen that need to be or have just been ironed.

ironing board ● noun a long, narrow board with folding legs, on which clothes are ironed.

ironist ● noun a person who uses irony.
– DERIVATIVES **ironize** (also **ironise**) verb.

iron lung ● noun a rigid case fitted over a patient's body, used for administering prolonged artificial respiration by means of mechanical pumps.

iron maiden ● noun a former instrument of torture consisting of a coffin-shaped box lined with iron spikes.

iron man ● noun **1** an exceptionally strong or robust man. **2** a

Thesaurus

iota ● noun (LITTLE) BIT, mite, speck, scrap, shred, ounce, scintilla, atom, jot (or tittle); *informal* smidgen; *archaic* scruple.

irascible ● adjective IRRITABLE, quick-tempered, short-tempered, snappish, tetchy, testy, touchy, edgy, crabby, waspish, dyspeptic; crusty, grouchy, cantankerous, curmudgeonly, ill-natured, peevish, querulous, fractious; *informal* prickly, ratty, snappy.

irate ● adjective ANGRY, furious, infuriated, incensed, enraged, incandescent, fuming, seething, cross, mad; raging, ranting, raving, in a frenzy, beside oneself, outraged, up in arms; indignant, annoyed, irritated, irked, piqued; *informal* foaming at the mouth, hot under the collar; *poetic/literary* wrathful; *archaic* wroth.

ire ● noun (*poetic/literary*) ANGER, rage, fury, wrath, outrage, temper, crossness, spleen; annoyance, exasperation, irritation, displeasure, indignation; *poetic/literary* choler.

Ireland ● noun Eire, the Republic of Ireland, the Irish Republic; Hibernia, the Emerald Isle; *poetic/literary* Erin.

iridescent ● adjective SHIMMERING, glittering, sparkling, dazzling, shining, gleaming, glowing, lustrous, scintillating, opalescent; *poetic/literary* glistering, coruscating, effulgent.

irk ● verb IRRITATE, annoy, gall, pique, nettle, exasperate, try someone's patience; anger, infuriate, madden, incense, get on someone's nerves; antagonize, provoke, ruffle someone's feathers, make someone's hackles rise; *Brit.* rub up the wrong way; *informal* get someone's goat, get/put someone's back up, make someone's blood boil, peeve, miff, rile, aggravate, needle, get (to), bug, hack off, brown off, get up someone's nose, give someone the hump, drive mad/crazy, drive up the wall, make someone see red; *Brit. informal* wind up, cheese off, nark, get on someone's wick; *N. Amer. informal* tee off, tick off, rankle, ride, gravel.
– OPPOSITES please.

irksome ● adjective IRRITATING, annoying, vexing, vexatious, galling, exasperating, disagreeable; tiresome, wearisome, tedious, trying, troublesome, bothersome, awkward, difficult, boring, uninteresting; infuriating, maddening; *informal* infernal.

iron ● noun **1** *a ship built of iron* metal, pig iron, cast iron, wrought iron. **2** *she needed some iron in her soul* STRENGTH, toughness, resilience, firmness, robustness, steel, grit; *informal* guts, spunk. **3** *a soldering iron* TOOL, implement, utensil, device. **4** *a hot iron* FLAT IRON, electric iron, steam iron, smoothing iron. **5** *they were clapped in irons* MANACLES, shackles, fetters, chains, handcuffs; *informal* cuffs, bracelets.
● adjective **1** *an iron key* MADE OF IRON, ferric, ferrous. **2** *an iron law of politics* INFLEXIBLE, unbreakable, absolute, unconditional, categorical, incontrovertible, infallible. **3** *an iron will* UNCOMPROMISING, unrelenting, unyielding, unbending, resolute, resolved, determined, firm, rigid, steadfast, unwavering.
– OPPOSITES flexible.
● verb *she irons his shirts* PRESS.
– PHRASES **iron something out 1** *John had ironed out all the minor snags* RESOLVE, straighten out, sort out, clear up, settle, put right, solve, remedy, rectify; *informal* fix, mend. **2** *ironing out differences in national systems* ELIMINATE, eradicate, erase, get rid of; harmonize, reconcile.

ironic ● adjective **1** *Edward's tone was ironic* SARCASTIC, sardonic, dry, caustic, sharp, stinging, scathing, acerbic, acid, bitter, trenchant, mordant, cynical; mocking, satirical, scoffing, derisory, derisive, scornful; *Brit. informal* sarky. **2** *it's ironic that I've ended up writing* PARADOXICAL, incongruous, odd, strange, peculiar, unex-

multi-event sporting contest demanding stamina.

ironmonger ● noun Brit. a retailer of tools and other hardware.
– DERIVATIVES **ironmongery** noun.

iron rations ● plural noun a small emergency supply of food.

ironstone ● noun **1** sedimentary rock containing iron compounds. **2** a kind of dense, opaque stoneware.

ironworks ● noun a place where iron is smelted or iron goods are made.

irony /īrəni/ ● noun (pl. **ironies**) **1** the expression of meaning through the use of language which normally signifies the opposite, typically for humorous effect. **2** a state of affairs that appears perversely contrary to what one expects.
– ORIGIN Greek *eirōneia* 'simulated ignorance'.

Iroquois /irrəkwoy/ ● noun (pl. same) a member of a former confederacy of six American Indian peoples (Mohawk, Oneida, Seneca, Onondaga, Cayuga, and Tuscarora) who lived mainly in southern Ontario and Quebec and northern New York State.
– ORIGIN French, from an Algonquian language.

irradiant ● adjective literary shining brightly.
– DERIVATIVES **irradiance** noun.

irradiate ● verb **1** (often **be irradiated**) expose to radiation. **2** shine light on.
– DERIVATIVES **irradiation** noun.
– ORIGIN Latin *irradiare* 'shine upon', from *radius* 'ray'.

irrational ● adjective not logical or reasonable.
– DERIVATIVES **irrationality** noun **irrationally** adverb.

irrationalism ● noun a system of belief or action that disregards rational principles.
– DERIVATIVES **irrationalist** noun & adjective.

irreconcilable ● adjective **1** incompatible: *the two points of view were irreconcilable.* **2** mutually and implacably hostile.
– DERIVATIVES **irreconcilably** adverb.

irrecoverable ● adjective not able to be recovered or remedied.
– DERIVATIVES **irrecoverably** adverb.

irredeemable ● adjective not able to be saved, improved, or corrected.
– DERIVATIVES **irredeemably** adverb.

irredentist /irridentist/ ● noun **1** a person advocating the restoration to their country of any territory formerly belonging to it. **2** historical (in 19th-century Italian politics) an advocate of the return to Italy of all Italian-speaking districts subject to other countries.
– DERIVATIVES **irredentism** noun.
– ORIGIN Italian *irredentista*, from *irredenta* 'unredeemed'.

irreducible ● adjective not able to be reduced or simplified.
– DERIVATIVES **irreducibly** adverb.

irrefutable /irrifyoōtəb'l/ ● adjective impossible to deny or disprove.
– DERIVATIVES **irrefutably** adverb.

irregardless ● adjective & adverb informal regardless.
– ORIGIN probably a blend of IRRESPECTIVE and REGARDLESS.

irregular ● adjective **1** not regular in shape, arrangement, or occurrence. **2** contrary to a rule, standard, or convention. **3** not belonging to regular army units. **4** Grammar (of a word) having inflections that do not conform to the usual rules. ● noun a member of an irregular military force.
– DERIVATIVES **irregularity** noun (pl. **irregularities**) **irregularly** adverb.

irrelevant ● adjective not relevant.
– DERIVATIVES **irrelevance** noun **irrelevancy** noun (pl. **irrelevancies**) **irrelevantly** adverb.

irreligious ● adjective indifferent or hostile to religion.
– DERIVATIVES **irreligion** noun.

irremediable /irrimeediəb'l/ ● adjective impossible to remedy.
– DERIVATIVES **irremediably** adverb.

irremovable ● adjective incapable of being removed.

irreparable /ireppərəb'l/ ● adjective impossible to rectify or repair.
– DERIVATIVES **irreparably** adverb.

irreplaceable ● adjective impossible to replace if lost or damaged.
– DERIVATIVES **irreplaceably** adverb.

irrepressible ● adjective not able to be restrained.
– DERIVATIVES **irrepressibly** adverb.

i

Thesaurus

pected.
– OPPOSITES sincere.

irony ● noun **1** *that note of irony in her voice* SARCASM, sardonicism, dryness, causticity, sharpness, acerbity, bitterness, trenchancy, mordancy, cynicism; mockery, satire, ridicule, derision, scorn; Brit. informal sarkiness. **2** *the irony of the situation* PARADOX, incongruity, incongruousness, peculiarity.
– OPPOSITES sincerity.

irradiate ● verb ILLUMINATE, light (up), brighten, cast light upon, shine on; poetic/literary illumine.

irrational ● adjective UNREASONABLE, illogical, groundless, baseless, unfounded, unjustifiable; absurd, ridiculous, ludicrous, silly, foolish, senseless.
– OPPOSITES logical.

irreconcilable ● adjective **1** *irreconcilable views* INCOMPATIBLE, at odds, at variance, conflicting, clashing, antagonistic, mutually exclusive, diametrically opposed; disparate, variant, dissimilar, poles apart; rare oppugnant. **2** *irreconcilable enemies* IMPLACABLE, unappeasable, uncompromising, inflexible; mortal, bitter, deadly, sworn, out-and-out.
– OPPOSITES compatible.

irrecoverable ● adjective UNRECOVERABLE, unreclaimable, irretrievable, irredeemable, unsalvageable, gone for ever; written off.

irrefutable ● adjective INDISPUTABLE, undeniable, unquestionable, incontrovertible, incontestable, beyond question, beyond doubt, indisputable; conclusive, definite, definitive, decisive, certain, positive.

irregular ● adjective **1** *irregular features | an irregular coastline* ASYMMETRICAL, non-uniform, uneven, crooked, misshapen, lopsided, twisted; jagged, ragged, serrated, indented. **2** *irregular surfaces* ROUGH, bumpy, uneven, pitted, rutted; lumpy, knobbly, gnarled. **3** *an irregular heartbeat* INCONSISTENT, unsteady, uneven, fitful, patchy, variable, varying, changeable, changing, inconstant, erratic, unstable, unsettled, spasmodic, intermittent, fluctuating. **4** *irregular financial dealings* AGAINST THE RULES, out of order, improper, illegitimate, unscrupulous, unethical, unprofessional, unacceptable, beyond the pale; informal shady; Brit. informal not cricket; Austral./NZ informal over the fence. **5** *an irregular army* GUERRILLA, underground; paramilitary; partisan, mercenary.
– OPPOSITES straight, smooth.

● noun *gun-toting irregulars* GUERRILLA, underground fighter; paramilitary; resistance fighter, partisan, mercenary.

irregularity ● noun **1** *the irregularity of the coastline* ASYMMETRY, non-uniformity, unevenness, crookedness, lopsidedness; jaggedness, raggedness, indentation. **2** *the irregularity of the surface* ROUGHNESS, bumpiness, unevenness; lumpiness, knobbliness. **3** *irregularities in the concrete* BUMP, lump, bulge, hump, protuberance, kink; hole, hollow, pit, crater, depression, dip, indentation, dent; crack, chink, fissure, cranny. **4** *the irregularity of the bus service* INCONSISTENCY, unsteadiness, unevenness, fitfulness, patchiness, inconstancy, instability, variability, changeableness, fluctuation, unpredictability, unreliability. **5** *financial irregularities* IMPROPRIETY, wrongdoing, misconduct, dishonesty, corruption, immorality; informal shadiness, crookedness. **6** *staff noted any irregularity in operation* ABNORMALITY, unusualness, strangeness, oddness, singularity, atypicality, anomaly, deviation, aberration, peculiarity, idiosyncrasy.

irregularly ● adverb **1** *irregularly hexagonal* ASYMMETRICALLY, unevenly. **2** *his heart was beating irregularly* ERRATICALLY, intermittently, in/by fits and starts, fitfully, patchily, haphazardly, unsystematically, unmethodically, inconsistently, unsteadily, unevenly, variably, spasmodically, discontinuously, inconstantly.

irrelevance ● noun INAPPLICABILITY, unrelatedness, inappropriateness, inappositeness; unimportance, inconsequentiality, insignificance; formal impertinence.

irrelevant ● adjective BESIDE THE POINT, immaterial, not pertinent, not germane, off the subject, unconnected, unrelated, peripheral, extraneous, inapposite; unimportant, inconsequential, insignificant, trivial; formal impertinent.

irreligious ● adjective ATHEISTIC, unbelieving, non-believing, agnostic, heretical, faithless, godless, ungodly, impious, profane, infidel, barbarian, heathen, pagan; rare nullifidian.
– OPPOSITES pious.

irreparable ● adjective IRREVERSIBLE, unrectifiable, irrevocable, unrestorable, irrecoverable, unrepairable, beyond repair.
– OPPOSITES repairable.

irreplaceable ● adjective UNIQUE, unrepeatable, incomparable, unparalleled; treasured, prized, cherished.

irrepressible ● adjective **1** *the desire for freedom is irrepressible* INEXTINGUISHABLE, unquenchable, uncontainable, uncontrollable, in-

irreproachable ● adjective beyond criticism.
– DERIVATIVES **irreproachably** adverb.
irresistible ● adjective too tempting or powerful to be resisted.
– DERIVATIVES **irresistibly** adverb.
irresolute ● adjective uncertain.
– DERIVATIVES **irresolutely** adverb **irresolution** noun.
irresolvable ● adjective impossible to solve.
irrespective ● adjective (**irrespective of**) regardless of.
– DERIVATIVES **irrespectively** adverb.
irresponsible ● adjective not showing a proper sense of responsibility.
– DERIVATIVES **irresponsibility** noun **irresponsibly** adverb.
irretrievable ● adjective not able to be retrieved.
– DERIVATIVES **irretrievably** adverb.
irreverent ● adjective disrespectful.
– DERIVATIVES **irreverence** noun **irreverently** adverb.
irreversible ● adjective impossible to be reversed or altered.
– DERIVATIVES **irreversibility** noun **irreversibly** adverb.
irrevocable /irevvəkəb'l/ ● adjective not able to be changed, reversed, or recovered.
– DERIVATIVES **irrevocability** noun **irrevocably** adverb.
– ORIGIN Latin *irrevocabilis*, from *revocare* 'revoke'.
irrigate /irrigayt/ ● verb **1** supply water to (land or crops) by means of channels. **2** Medicine apply a flow of water or medication to (an organ or wound).
– DERIVATIVES **irrigable** adjective **irrigation** noun **irrigator** noun.
– ORIGIN Latin *irrigare* 'moisten'.
irritable ● adjective **1** easily annoyed or angered. **2** Medicine abnormally sensitive.
– DERIVATIVES **irritability** noun **irritableness** noun **irritably** adverb.
irritable bowel syndrome ● noun a condition involving recurrent abdominal pain and diarrhoea or constipation.
irritant ● noun **1** a substance that irritates part of the body. **2** a source of continual annoyance. ● adjective causing irritation to the body.
irritate ● verb **1** make annoyed or angry. **2** cause inflammation in (a part of the body).
– DERIVATIVES **irritating** adjective **irritation** noun.
– ORIGIN Latin *irritare*.
irrupt /irupt/ ● verb enter forcibly or suddenly.
– DERIVATIVES **irruption** noun **irruptive** adjective.
– ORIGIN Latin *irrumpere* 'break into'.
IRS ● abbreviation Internal Revenue Service.
is third person singular present of BE.
ISA ● abbreviation **1** individual savings account. **2** Computing industry standard architecture.
ISBN ● abbreviation international standard book number.
ischaemia /iskeemiə/ (US **ischemia**) ● noun Medicine an inadequate blood supply to a part of the body, especially the heart muscles.
– DERIVATIVES **ischaemic** adjective.
– ORIGIN from Greek *iskhaimos* 'stopping blood'.

i

Thesaurus

destructible, undying, everlasting. **2** *his irrepressible personality* EBULLIENT, exuberant, buoyant, sunny, breezy, jaunty, light-hearted, high-spirited, vivacious, animated, full of life, lively; *informal* bubbly, bouncy, peppy, chipper, chirpy, full of beans.
irreproachable ● adjective IMPECCABLE, exemplary, model, immaculate, outstanding, exceptional, admirable, perfect; above/beyond reproach, blameless, faultless, flawless, unblemished, untarnished, spotless; *informal* squeaky clean, whiter than white.
– OPPOSITES reprehensible.
irresistible ● adjective **1** *her irresistible smile* TEMPTING, enticing, alluring, inviting, seductive; attractive, desirable, fetching, appealing, captivating, beguiling, enchanting. **2** *an irresistible impulse* UNCONTROLLABLE, overwhelming, overpowering, compelling, compulsive, irrepressible, ungovernable, driving, forceful.
irresolute ● adjective INDECISIVE, hesitant, vacillating, equivocating, dithering, wavering, shilly-shallying; ambivalent, blowing hot and cold, in two minds, in a dilemma, in a quandary, torn; doubtful, in doubt, unsure, uncertain, undecided; *informal* sitting on the fence.
– OPPOSITES decisive.
irresolution ● noun INDECISIVENESS, indecision, irresoluteness, hesitancy, hesitation; doubt, doubtfulness, unsureness, uncertainty; vacillation, equivocation, wavering, shilly-shallying, blowing hot and cold, dithering, temporizing, temporization; *Brit.* havering, humming and hawing; *informal* dilly-dallying, sitting on the fence.
irrespective ● adjective REGARDLESS OF, without regard to/for, notwithstanding, whatever, no matter what, without consideration of; *informal* irregardless of.
irresponsible ● adjective **1** *irresponsible behaviour* RECKLESS, rash, careless, thoughtless, incautious, unwise, imprudent, ill-advised, injudicious, misguided, unheeding, hasty, overhasty, precipitate, precipitous, foolhardy, impetuous, impulsive, devil-may-care, hot-headed, delinquent; *N. Amer.* derelict. **2** *an irresponsible teenager* IMMATURE, naive, foolish, hare-brained; unreliable, undependable, untrustworthy, flighty, giddy, scatterbrained, harum-scarum.
– OPPOSITES sensible.
irretrievable ● adjective IRREVERSIBLE, unrectifiable, irremediable, irrecoverable, irreparable, unrepairable, beyond repair.
– OPPOSITES reversible.
irreverent ● adjective DISRESPECTFUL, disdainful, scornful, contemptuous, derisive, disparaging; impertinent, cheeky, flippant, rude, discourteous.
– OPPOSITES respectful.
irreversible ● adjective IRREPARABLE, unrepairable, beyond repair, unrectifiable, irremediable, irrevocable, permanent; unalterable, unchangeable, immutable; *Law* peremptory.
irrevocable ● adjective IRREVERSIBLE, unalterable, unchangeable, immutable, final, binding, permanent; *Law* peremptory.
irrigate ● verb WATER, bring water to, soak, flood, inundate.
irritability ● noun IRASCIBILITY, tetchiness, testiness, touchiness, grumpiness, moodiness, grouchiness, a (bad) mood, cantankerousness, curmudgeonliness, bad temper, short temper, ill humour, peevishness, crossness, fractiousness, pettishness, crabbiness, waspishness, prickliness; *Brit. informal* shirtiness, stroppiness, rattiness; *N. Amer. informal* crankiness, orneriness; *Austral./NZ informal* snakiness; *poetic/literary* choler.
irritable ● adjective BAD-TEMPERED, short-tempered, irascible, tetchy, testy, touchy, grumpy, grouchy, moody, crotchety, in a (bad) mood, cantankerous, curmudgeonly, ill-tempered, ill-humoured, peevish, cross, fractious, pettish, crabby, waspish, prickly, splenetic, dyspeptic, choleric; *informal* on a short fuse; *Brit. informal* shirty, stroppy, ratty; *N. Amer. informal* cranky, ornery, peckish; *Austral./NZ informal* snaky.
– OPPOSITES good-humoured.
irritant ● noun ANNOYANCE, (source of) irritation, thorn in someone's side/flesh, pest, bother, trial, torment, plague, inconvenience, nuisance; *informal* aggravation, peeve, pain (in the neck), headache; *N. Amer. informal* nudnik, burr in/under someone's saddle; *Austral./NZ informal* nark.
irritate ● verb **1** *the smallest things may irritate you* ANNOY, vex, make angry, make cross, anger, exasperate, irk, gall, pique, nettle, put out, antagonize, get on someone's nerves, try someone's patience, ruffle someone's feathers, make someone's hackles rise; infuriate, madden, provoke; *Brit.* rub up the wrong way; *informal* aggravate, miff, rile, needle, get to, bug, hack off, get under someone's skin, get/put someone's back up, get up someone's nose, give someone the hump, drive mad/crazy, drive round the bend/twist, drive up the wall; *Brit. informal* wind up, get on someone's wick; *N. Amer. informal* tee off, tick off, rankle, ride, gravel. **2** *some sand irritated my eyes* INFLAME, aggravate, hurt, chafe, abrade, scratch, scrape, graze.
– OPPOSITES pacify, soothe.
irritated ● adjective ANNOYED, cross, angry, vexed, exasperated, irked, piqued, nettled, put out, fed up, disgruntled, in a bad mood, in a temper, testy, huffy, in a huff, aggrieved; irate, infuriated, incensed; *informal* aggravated, peeved, miffed, mad, riled, hacked off, browned off, hot under the collar; *Brit. informal* cheesed off, brassed off, ratty, shirty; *N. Amer. informal* teed off, ticked off, sore; *Austral./NZ informal* snaky, crook; *archaic* snuffy, wroth.
– OPPOSITES good-humoured.
irritating ● adjective ANNOYING, infuriating, exasperating, maddening, trying, tiresome, vexing, vexatious, irksome, galling; *informal* aggravating.
irritation ● noun **1** *she tried not to show her irritation* ANNOYANCE, exasperation, vexation, indignation, impatience, crossness, displeasure, chagrin, pique; anger, rage, fury, wrath; *informal* aggravation; *poetic/literary* ire. **2** *I realize my presence is an irritation for you* IRRITANT, annoyance, thorn in someone's side/flesh, bother, trial, torment, plague, inconvenience, nuisance; *informal* aggravation,

ISDN ● abbreviation integrated services digital network.
-ise ● suffix variant spelling of -IZE.
– USAGE For the use of **-ise** or **-ize**, see the note at -IZE.
-ish ● suffix forming adjectives: **1** (from nouns) having the qualities or characteristics of: *girlish*. **2** of the nationality of: *Swedish*. **3** (from adjectives) somewhat: *yellowish*. **4** informal denoting an approximate age or time of day: *sixish*.
– ORIGIN Old English.
Ishmaelite /ishməlīt/ ● noun a descendant of Ishmael, a son of Abraham and Hagar, and in Islamic belief the traditional ancestor of Muhammad and of the Arab peoples.
isinglass /īzingglaass/ ● noun **1** a kind of gelatin obtained from fish. **2** chiefly US mica or a similar material in thin transparent sheets.
– ORIGIN alteration, by association with GLASS, of obsolete Dutch *huysenblas* 'sturgeon's bladder'.
Islam /izlaam/ ● noun **1** the monotheistic religion of the Muslims, regarded by them to have been revealed through Muhammad as the Prophet of Allah. **2** the Muslim world.
– DERIVATIVES **Islamist** noun **Islamize** (also **Islamise**) verb.
– ORIGIN Arabic, 'submission'.
Islamic /izlammik/ ● adjective relating to Islam.
– DERIVATIVES **Islamicize** (also **Islamicise**) verb.
island ● noun **1** a piece of land surrounded by water. **2** a thing that is isolated, detached, or surrounded.
– DERIVATIVES **islander** noun.
– ORIGIN Old English.
isle ● noun literary (except in place names) an island.
– ORIGIN Old French *ile*, from Latin *insula*.
islet /īlit/ ● noun a small island.
islets of Langerhans /langərhanz/ ● plural noun groups of cells in the pancreas that secrete the hormones insulin and glucagon.
– ORIGIN named after the German anatomist Paul *Langerhans* (1847–88).
ism /izz'm/ ● noun informal, chiefly derogatory an unspecified system, philosophy, or ideological movement.
-ism ● suffix forming nouns: **1** denoting an action or its result: *baptism*. **2** denoting a state or quality: *barbarism*. **3** denoting a system, principle, or ideological movement: *Anglicanism*. **4** denoting a basis for prejudice or discrimination: *racism*. **5** denoting a peculiarity in language: *colloquialism*. **6** denoting a pathological condition: *alcoholism*.
– ORIGIN Greek *-ismos*.
Ismaili /izmieeli/ ● noun (pl. **Ismailis**) a member of a Shiite Muslim sect believing that Ismail, the son of the sixth Shiite imam, should have become the seventh imam.
isn't ● contraction is not.
ISO ● abbreviation International Organization for Standardization.
– ORIGIN from Greek *isos* 'equal'; the term is technically not an abbreviation.
isobar /īsəbaar/ ● noun Meteorology a line on a map connecting points having the same atmospheric pressure.
– DERIVATIVES **isobaric** adjective.
– ORIGIN from Greek *isobaros* 'of equal weight'.
isochronous /īsokrənəss/ ● adjective **1** occurring at the same time. **2** occupying equal time.
– ORIGIN Greek *isokhronos*, from *isos* 'equal' + *khronos* 'time'.
isohyet /īsəhīit/ ● noun Meteorology a line on a map connecting points having the same amount of rainfall.
– ORIGIN from Greek *isos* 'equal' + *huetos* 'rain'.
isolate ● verb **1** place apart or alone; cut off. **2** Chemistry & Biology obtain or extract (a compound, micro-organism, etc.) in a pure form. **3** cut off the electrical or other connection to (something). ● noun a person or thing that has become isolated.
– DERIVATIVES **isolator** noun.
– ORIGIN from ISOLATED.
isolated ● adjective **1** remote; lonely. **2** single; exceptional.
– ORIGIN French *isolé*, from Latin *insulatus* 'made into an island', from *insula* 'island'.
isolation ● noun the process or fact of isolating or being isolated.
– PHRASES **in isolation** without relation to others; separately.
isolationism ● noun a policy of remaining apart from the political affairs of other countries.
– DERIVATIVES **isolationist** noun.
isoleucine /īsəlōōseen/ ● noun Biochemistry an amino acid that is a constituent of most proteins and is an essential nutrient in the diet.
– ORIGIN from Greek *isos* 'equal' + LEUCINE.
isomer /īsəmər/ ● noun **1** Chemistry each of two or more compounds with the same formula but a different arrangement of atoms and different properties. **2** Physics each of two or more atomic nuclei with the same atomic number and mass number but different energy states.
– DERIVATIVES **isomeric** adjective **isomerism** noun **isomerize** (also **isomerise**) verb.
– ORIGIN from Greek *isomerēs* 'sharing equally'.
isometric ● adjective **1** having equal dimensions. **2** Physiology involving an increase in muscle tension without contraction. **3** (of perspective drawing) in which the three principal dimensions are represented by axes 120° apart.
– DERIVATIVES **isometrically** adverb.
– ORIGIN from Greek *isometria* 'equality of measure'.
isometrics ● plural noun a system of physical exercises in which muscles are caused to act against each other or against a fixed object.
isomorphic /īsəmorfik/ ● adjective corresponding in form and relations.
– DERIVATIVES **isomorphism** noun **isomorphous** adjective.
isosceles /īsossəleez/ ● adjective (of a triangle) having two sides of equal length.
– ORIGIN Greek *isoskelēs*, from *isos* 'equal' + *skelos* 'leg'.
isotherm /īsətherm/ ● noun a line on a map or diagram connecting points having the same temperature.
– DERIVATIVES **isothermal** adjective & noun.
– ORIGIN from Greek *isos* 'equal' + *thermē* 'heat'.
isotonic /īsətonnik/ ● adjective **1** Physiology (of a muscle action) taking place with normal contraction. **2** containing essential salts and minerals in the same concentration as in the body.
– ORIGIN Greek *isotonos*, from *isos* 'equal' + *tonos* 'tone'.
isotope /īsətōp/ ● noun Chemistry each of two or more forms of the same element that contain equal numbers of protons but different numbers of neutrons in their nuclei.
– DERIVATIVES **isotopic** adjective.
– ORIGIN from Greek *isos* 'equal' + *topos* 'place', because the isotopes occupy the same place in the periodic table.
isotropic /īsətroppik/ ● adjective Physics having the same magnitude or properties when measured in different directions.
– ORIGIN from Greek *isos* 'equal' + *tropos* 'a turn'.
ISP ● abbreviation Internet service provider.
Israeli /izrayli/ ● noun (pl. **Israelis**) a person from Israel. ● adjective relating to the modern country of Israel.
Israelite /izrəlīt/ ● noun a member of the ancient Hebrew nation. ● adjective relating to the Israelites.
ISSN ● abbreviation international standard serial number.
issue ● noun **1** an important topic for debate or resolution. **2** the action of issuing. **3** each of a regular series of publications.

i

Thesaurus

pain (in the neck), headache; *N. Amer. informal* nudnik, burr in/under someone's saddle; *Austral./NZ informal* nark.
– OPPOSITES delight.
island ● noun ISLE, islet; atoll; *Brit.* holm; (**islands**) archipelago.
– RELATED TERMS insular.
isolate ● verb **1** *she isolated herself from her family | the contaminated area was isolated* SEPARATE, set/keep apart, segregate, detach, cut off, shut away, divorce, alienate, distance; keep in solitude, cloister, seclude; cordon off, seal off, close off, fence off. **2** *the laser beam can isolate the offending vehicles* IDENTIFY, single out, pick out, point out, spot, recognize, distinguish, pinpoint, locate.
– OPPOSITES integrate.
isolated ● adjective **1** *isolated communities* REMOTE, out of the way, outlying, off the beaten track, secluded, lonely, in the back of beyond, godforsaken, inaccessible, cut-off; *N. Amer.* in the backwoods, lonesome; *Austral./NZ* in the backblocks, in the booay; *informal* in the middle of nowhere, in the sticks; *N. Amer. informal* jerkwater, in the tall timbers; *Austral./NZ informal* Barcoo, beyond the black stump; *archaic* unapproachable. **2** *he lived a very isolated existence* SOLITARY, lonely, companionless, friendless; secluded, cloistered, segregated, unsociable, reclusive, hermitic; *N. Amer.* lonesome. **3** *an isolated incident* UNIQUE, lone, solitary; unusual, uncommon, exceptional, anomalous, abnormal, untypical, freak; *informal* one-off.
– OPPOSITES accessible, sociable, common.
isolation ● noun **1** *patients who need isolation* SEPARATION, segregation, seclusion, keeping apart. **2** *their feeling of isolation* SOLITARI-

4 formal or Law children of one's own. ● verb (**issues, issued, issuing**) 1 supply or distribute. 2 formally send out or make known: *issue a statement.* 3 (**issue from**) come, go, or flow out from.
– PHRASES **at issue** under discussion. **make an issue of** treat too seriously or as a problem. **take issue with** challenge.
– DERIVATIVES **issuer** noun.
– ORIGIN Old French, from Latin *exire* 'go out'.

-ist ● suffix forming personal nouns and some related adjectives: 1 denoting a person who subscribes to a system of beliefs, prejudice or type of discrimination, expressed by nouns ending in *-ism*: *sexist.* 2 denoting a member of a profession or business activity: *dentist.* 3 denoting a person who uses something: *flautist.* 4 denoting a person who does something expressed by a verb ending in *-ize*: *plagiarist.*
– ORIGIN from Greek *-istēs*.

isthmus /issməss/ ● noun (pl. **isthmuses**) a narrow strip of land with sea on either side, linking two larger areas of land.
– DERIVATIVES **isthmian** adjective.
– ORIGIN Greek *isthmos*.

IT ● abbreviation information technology.

it ● pronoun (third person sing.) 1 used to refer to a thing previously mentioned or easily identified. 2 referring to an animal or child of unspecified sex. 3 used to identify a person: *it's me.* 4 used in the normal subject position in statements about time, distance, or weather: *it is raining.* 5 used to refer to something specified later in the sentence: *it is impossible to get there today.* 6 used to emphasize a following part of a sentence: *it is the child who is the victim.* 7 the situation or circumstances. 8 exactly what is needed or desired.
– ORIGIN Old English, neuter of HE.

i

Italian ● noun 1 a person from Italy. 2 the language of Italy, descended from Latin. ● adjective relating to Italy or Italian.
– DERIVATIVES **Italianize** (also **Italianise**) verb.

Italianate ● adjective Italian in character or appearance.

italic /italik/ ● adjective Printing 1 denoting the sloping typeface used especially for emphasis and in foreign words. 2 denoting a style of handwriting, sloping and with pointed letters, resembling 16th-century Italian handwriting. ● noun (also **italics**) an italic typeface or letter.
– DERIVATIVES **italicize** (also **italicise**) verb.
– ORIGIN Greek *Italikos* (in the general sense 'Italian'), from *Italia* 'Italy'.

ITC ● abbreviation Independent Television Commission.

itch ● noun 1 an uncomfortable sensation that causes a desire to scratch the skin. 2 informal an impatient desire. ● verb 1 be the site of or experience an itch. 2 informal feel an impatient desire to do something.
– ORIGIN Old English.

itchy ● adjective (**itchier, itchiest**) having or causing an itch.
– PHRASES **have itchy feet** informal have a strong urge to travel.
– DERIVATIVES **itchiness** noun.

it'd ● contraction 1 it had. 2 it would.

-ite ● suffix 1 forming names denoting people from a country: *Israelite.* 2 often derogatory denoting followers of a movement: *Luddite.* 3 forming names of minerals, rocks, or fossil organisms: *ammonite.* 4 forming names of anatomical or other structures: *dendrite.* 5 forming names of explosives and other commercial products: *dynamite.* 6 Chemistry forming names of salts or esters of acids ending in *-ous*: *sulphite.*
– ORIGIN from Greek *ītes*.

item ● noun an individual article or unit. ● adverb archaic (used to introduce each item in a list) also.
– PHRASES **be an item** informal (of a couple) be in a romantic or sexual relationship.
– ORIGIN Latin, 'in like manner, also'.

itemize (also **itemise**) ● verb present as a list of individual items or parts.

iterate /ittərayt/ ● verb 1 perform or utter repeatedly. 2 make repeated use of a mathematical or computational procedure, applying it each time to the result of the previous application.
– DERIVATIVES **iteration** noun **iterative** adjective.
– ORIGIN Latin *iterare* 'repeat'.

-itic ● suffix forming adjectives and nouns: 1 corresponding to nouns ending in *-ite*: *Semitic.* 2 corresponding to nouns ending in *-itis*: *arthritic.* 3 from other bases: *syphilitic.*
– ORIGIN Greek *-itikos*.

itinerant /ītinnərənt/ ● adjective travelling from place to place. ● noun an itinerant person.
– ORIGIN from Latin *itinerari* 'travel', from *iter* 'journey, road'.

itinerary /ītinnərəri/ ● noun (pl. **itineraries**) a planned route or journey.

-itis ● suffix forming names of inflammatory diseases: *cystitis.*
– ORIGIN from Greek *-itēs*.

it'll ● contraction 1 it shall. 2 it will.

its ● possessive determiner 1 belonging to or associated with a thing previously mentioned or easily identified. 2 belonging to or associated with a child or animal of unspecified sex.
– USAGE A common error in writing is to confuse the possessive **its** (as in *turn the camera on its side*) with the contraction **it's** (short for either **it is** or **it has**, as in *it's my fault; it's been a hot day*).

it's ● contraction 1 it is. 2 it has.

itself ● pronoun (third person sing.) 1 (reflexive) used to refer to something previously mentioned as the subject of the clause: *his horse hurt itself.* 2 (emphatic) used to emphasize a particular thing or animal mentioned.
– PHRASES **in itself** viewed in its essential qualities.

Thesaurus

NESS, loneliness, friendlessness. 3 *the isolation of some mental hospitals* REMOTENESS, seclusion, inaccessibility.

issue ● noun 1 *the committee discussed the issue* MATTER (IN QUESTION), question, point (at issue), affair, case, subject, topic; problem, bone of contention. 2 *the issue of a special stamp* ISSUING, publication, publishing; circulation, distribution, supplying, appearance. 3 *the latest issue of our magazine* EDITION, number, instalment, copy. 4 *(Law) she died without issue* OFFSPRING, descendants, heirs, successors, children, progeny, family; *informal* kids; *archaic* seed, fruit (of one's loins). 5 *an issue of blood* DISCHARGE, emission, release, outflow, outflowing, outflux; secretion, emanation, exudation, effluence; *technical* efflux. 6 *(dated) a favourable issue* (END) RESULT, outcome, consequence, upshot, conclusion, end.
● verb 1 *the minister issued a statement* SEND OUT, put out, release, deliver, publish, announce, broadcast, communicate, circulate, distribute, disseminate. 2 *the captain issued the crew with guns* SUPPLY, provide, furnish, arm, equip, fit out, rig out, kit out; *informal* fix up. 3 *savoury smells issued from the kitchen* EMANATE, emerge, exude, flow (out/forth), pour (out/forth); be emitted. 4 *large profits might issue from the deal* RESULT, follow, ensue, stem, spring, arise, proceed; be the result of, be brought on/about by, be produced by.
– PHRASES **at issue** IN QUESTION, in dispute, under discussion, under consideration, for debate. **take issue** DISAGREE, be in dispute, be in contention, be at variance, be at odds, argue, quarrel; challenge, dispute, (call into) question; *archaic* disaccord.

itch ● noun 1 *I have an itch on my back* tingling, irritation, itchiness. 2 *(informal) the itch to travel* LONGING, yearning, craving, ache, hunger, thirst, urge, hankering; wish, fancy, desire; *informal* yen.
● verb 1 *my chilblains really itch* tingle, be irritated, be itchy. 2 *(informal) he itched to do something to help* LONG, yearn, ache, burn, crave, hanker for/after, hunger, thirst, be eager, be desperate; want, wish, desire, fancy, set one's sights on; *informal* have a yen, be dying, be gagging.

item ● noun 1 *an item of farm equipment | the main item in a badger's diet* THING, article, object, artefact, piece, product; element, constituent, component, ingredient. 2 *the meeting discussed the item* ISSUE, matter, affair, case, situation, subject, topic, question, point. 3 *a news item* REPORT, story, account, article, piece, write-up, bulletin, feature. 4 *items in the profit and loss account* ENTRY, record, statement, listing.

itemize ● verb 1 *Steinburg itemized thirty-two design faults* LIST, catalogue, inventory, record, document, register, detail, specify, identify; enumerate, number. 2 *an itemized bill* ANALYSE, break down, split up.

iterate ● verb REPEAT, recapitulate, go through/over again; say again, restate, reiterate; *informal* recap; *archaic* ingeminate.

itinerant ● adjective *itinerant traders* TRAVELLING, peripatetic, wandering, roving, roaming, touring, nomadic, gypsy, migrant, vagrant, vagabond, of no fixed address/abode.
● noun *an itinerants' lodging house* TRAVELLER, wanderer, roamer, rover, nomad, gypsy, migrant, transient, drifter, vagabond, vagrant, tramp; *dated* bird of passage.

itinerary ● noun (PLANNED) ROUTE, journey, way, road; travel plan, schedule, timetable, programme, tour.

itsy-bitsy (also **itty-bitty**) ● adjective informal very small.
– ORIGIN from a child's form of LITTLE + *bitsy*, from BIT[1].
ITV ● abbreviation Independent Television.
-ity ● suffix forming nouns denoting quality or condition: *humility*.
– ORIGIN Latin *-itas*.
IUD ● abbreviation intrauterine device.
IV ● abbreviation intravenous or intravenously.
I've ● contraction I have.
-ive ● suffix (forming adjectives and nouns derived from them) tending to; having the nature of: *palliative*.
– ORIGIN Latin *-ivus*.
IVF ● abbreviation in vitro fertilization.
ivied ● adjective covered in ivy.
Ivorian /ivoriən/ ● noun a person from the Ivory Coast, a country in West Africa. ● adjective relating to the Ivory Coast.
ivory ● noun (pl. **ivories**) **1** a hard creamy-white substance composing the main part of the tusks of an elephant, walrus, or narwhal. **2** the creamy-white colour of ivory. **3** (**the ivories**) informal the keys of a piano. **4** (**ivories**) informal a person's teeth.
– ORIGIN Old French *ivurie*, from Latin *ebur*.
ivory tower ● noun a state of privileged seclusion or separation from the harsh realities of life.
ivy ● noun a woody evergreen climbing plant, typically with shiny five-pointed leaves.
– ORIGIN Old English.
Ivy League ● noun a group of long-established and prestigious universities in the eastern US.
– ORIGIN with reference to the ivy traditionally growing over their walls.
iwi /eewee/ ● noun (pl. same) NZ a community or people.
– ORIGIN Maori.
-ize (also **-ise**) ● suffix forming verbs meaning: **1** make or become: *privatize*. **2** cause to resemble: *Americanize*. **3** treat in a specified way: *pasteurize*. **4** treat or cause to combine with a specified substance: *carbonize*. **5** perform or subject (someone) to a specified practice: *hospitalize*.
– USAGE The forms **-ize** and **-ise** are, in many cases, straightforward spelling variants. However, the **-ise** spelling is obligatory in certain cases: first, where it forms part of a larger word element, such as *-mise* in **compromise**; and second, in verbs corresponding to nouns with **-s-** in the stem, such as **advertise** and **televise**.
– ORIGIN Greek *-izein*.

Jj

J[1] (also **j**) ● noun (pl. **Js** or **J's**) **1** the tenth letter of the alphabet. **2** denoting the next after I in a set.

J[2] ● abbreviation **1** (in card games) jack. **2** Physics joule(s).

jab ● verb (**jabbed, jabbing**) poke roughly or quickly with something sharp or pointed. ● noun **1** a quick, sharp poke or blow. **2** Brit. informal a hypodermic injection, especially a vaccination.
– ORIGIN apparently symbolic.

jabber ● verb talk rapidly and excitedly but with little sense. ● noun rapid and nonsensical talk.
– ORIGIN imitative.

jabiru /jabbiroo/ ● noun a large black-necked stork with an upturned bill.
– ORIGIN Tupi-Guarani.

jabot /zhabbō/ ● noun an ornamental ruffle on the front of a shirt or blouse.
– ORIGIN French, originally in the sense 'crop of a bird'.

jacaranda /jakkərandə/ ● noun a tropical American tree which has blue trumpet-shaped flowers, fern-like leaves, and fragrant wood.
– ORIGIN Tupi-Guarani.

jacinth /jassinth, jay-/ ● noun a reddish-orange gem variety of zircon.
– ORIGIN Old French *iacinte*, from Latin *hyacinthus* (see HYACINTH).

jack ● noun **1** a device for lifting heavy objects. **2** a playing card bearing a representation of a soldier, page, or knave, normally ranking next below a queen. **3** (also **jack socket**) a socket designed to receive a jack plug. **4** the small white ball at which bowls players aim. **5** a small playing-piece used in tossing and catching games. **6** (**jacks**) a game played by tossing and catching jacks. **7** a small national flag flown at the bow of a vessel in harbour. **8** the male of various animals, e.g. the donkey. **9** used in names of animals and plants that are smaller than similar kinds, e.g. **jack pine**. **10** a perch-like marine fish, typically with a row of large spiky scales along each side. ● verb **1** (**jack up**) raise with a jack. **2** (**jack up**) informal increase by a considerable amount. **3** (**jack in/into**) log into or connect up (a computer or electronic device). **4** (**jack in**) Brit. informal give up. **5** (**jack up**) Austral. give up or refuse to participate.
– PHRASES **every man jack** informal every single person. **jack of all trades (and master of none)** a person who can do many different types of work (but has special skill in none).
– ORIGIN from *Jack*, familiar form of the given name *John*, used originally to denote an ordinary man.

jackal /jakk'l/ ● noun a slender, long-legged wild dog that often hunts or scavenges in packs, found in Africa and southern Asia.
– ORIGIN Turkish *çakal*.

jackanapes /jakkənayps/ ● noun **1** dated an impertinent person. **2** archaic a tame monkey.
– ORIGIN originally as *Jack Napes*, perhaps from a playful name for a tame ape.

jackaroo /jakkəroo/ Austral. informal ● noun a young, inexperienced worker on a sheep or cattle station. ● verb work as a jackaroo.
– ORIGIN alteration of an Aboriginal term meaning 'wandering white man'.

jackass ● noun **1** a stupid person. **2** a male ass or donkey.

jackboot ● noun a large leather military boot reaching to the knee.
– DERIVATIVES **jackbooted** adjective.

jackdaw ● noun a small grey-headed crow, noted for its inquisitiveness.
– ORIGIN from JACK + earlier *daw* (of Germanic origin).

jackeen /jakeen/ ● noun Irish, chiefly derogatory a city-dweller, especially a Dubliner.
– ORIGIN diminutive of the familiar name *Jack*.

jacket ● noun **1** an outer garment extending to the waist or hips, with sleeves. **2** an outer covering placed around something for protection or insulation. **3** the skin of a potato. ● verb (**jacketed, jacketing**) cover with a jacket.
– ORIGIN Old French *jaquet*.

jacket potato ● noun Brit. a baked potato served with the skin on.

Jack Frost ● noun a personification of frost.

jackfruit ● noun the very large edible fruit of an Asian tree, resembling a breadfruit.
– ORIGIN from Portuguese *jaca* + FRUIT.

jackhammer chiefly N. Amer. ● noun a portable pneumatic hammer or drill. ● verb beat or hammer heavily or loudly and repeatedly.

jack-in-the-box ● noun a toy consisting of a box containing a figure on a spring which pops up when the lid is opened.

jackknife ● noun (pl. **jackknives**) **1** a large knife with a folding blade. **2** a dive in which the body is bent at the waist and then straightened. ● verb (**jackknifed, jackknifing**) **1** move (one's body) into a bent or doubled-up position. **2** (of an articulated vehicle) bend into a V-shape in an uncontrolled skidding movement. **3** (of a diver) perform a jackknife.

jack-o'-lantern ● noun **1** a lantern made from a hollowed-out pumpkin or turnip in which holes are cut to represent facial features. **2** archaic a will-o'-the wisp.

jack pine ● noun a small, hardy North American pine with short needles.

jack plug ● noun a plug consisting of a single shaft used to make a connection which transmits a signal, typically used in sound equipment.

jackpot ● noun a large cash prize in a game or lottery.
– PHRASES **hit the jackpot** informal **1** win a jackpot. **2** have great or unexpected success.
– ORIGIN originally used in a form of poker, where the pot accumulated until a player could open the bidding with two jacks or better.

jackrabbit ● noun a North American prairie hare.
– ORIGIN abbreviation of *jackass-rabbit*, because of its long ears.

Jack Russell (also **Jack Russell terrier**) ● noun a terrier of a small working breed with short legs.
– ORIGIN named after the English clergyman Revd John (*Jack*) *Russell* (1795–1883), a breeder of such terriers.

jacksie (also **jacksy**) ● noun Brit. informal a person's bottom.
– ORIGIN diminutive of JACK.

Jack tar ● noun Brit. informal, dated a sailor.

Jack the Lad ● noun informal a brash, cocky young man.

Thesaurus

jab ● verb *he jabbed the Englishman with his finger* POKE, prod, dig, nudge, butt, ram; thrust, stab, push.
● noun *a jab in the ribs* POKE, prod, dig, nudge, butt; thrust, stab, push.

jabber ● verb *they jabbered away non-stop* PRATTLE, babble, chatter, twitter, prate, gabble, rattle on/away, blather; *informal* yak, yap, yabber, yatter, blab, blabber; *Brit. informal* witter, rabbit, natter; *archaic* twaddle, clack.
● noun *stop your jabber!* PRATTLE, babble, chatter, chattering, twitter, twittering, gabble, blather; *informal* yabbering, yatter, blabber; *Brit. informal* wittering, rabbiting, nattering; *archaic* clack.

jack ● verb
– PHRASES **jack something up 1** *they jacked up the car* RAISE, hoist, lift (up), winch up, lever up, hitch up, elevate. **2** *(informal) he may need to jack up interest rates* INCREASE, raise, put up, up, mark up; *informal* hike (up), bump up.

jacket ● noun WRAPPING, wrapper, wrap, sleeve, sheath, sheathing, cover, covering.

jackpot ● noun *this week's lottery jackpot* TOP PRIZE, first prize; pool, bonanza.

– ORIGIN nickname of *Jack* Sheppard, 18th-century thief.
Jacobean /jakkəbeeən/ ● **adjective** relating to or characteristic of the reign of James I of England (1603–1625). ● **noun** a person who lived in the Jacobean period.
– ORIGIN from Latin *Jacobus* 'James'.
Jacobin /jakkəbin/ ● **noun 1** historical a member of a radical democratic club established in Paris in 1789, in the wake of the French Revolution. **2** an extreme political radical. **3** chiefly historical a Dominican friar.
– DERIVATIVES **Jacobinism** noun.
– ORIGIN originally denoting the Dominican friars: from Latin *Jacobus* 'James', after the church of St Jacques in Paris, near which the friars built their first convent; the latter became the headquarters of the French revolutionary group.
Jacobite /jakkəbīt/ ● **noun** a supporter of the deposed James II and his descendants in their claim to the British throne after the Revolution of 1688.
– DERIVATIVES **Jacobitism** noun.
Jacob's ladder ● **noun** a herbaceous plant with blue or white flowers and slender pointed leaves formed in ladder-like rows.
– ORIGIN with biblical allusion to Jacob's dream of a ladder reaching to heaven (Book of Genesis. chapter 28).
jacquard /jakkaard/ ● **noun 1** an apparatus consisting of perforated cards, fitted to a loom for the weaving of figured and brocaded fabrics. **2** a fabric made on a jacquard loom.
– ORIGIN named after the French weaver Joseph M. *Jacquard* (1787–1834).
jacquerie /jaykəri/ ● **noun** a communal uprising or revolt.
– ORIGIN Old French, 'villeins', from *Jacques*, a given name used in the sense 'peasant'.
jacuzzi /jəko͞ozi/ ● **noun** (pl. **jacuzzis**) trademark a large bath incorporating jets of water to massage the body.
– ORIGIN named after the Italian-born American inventor Candido *Jacuzzi* (c.1903–86).
jade[1] ● **noun 1** a hard stone used for ornaments and jewellery. **2** the light bluish green colour of jade.
– ORIGIN from French *le jade*, from Spanish *piedra de ijada* 'stone of the flank' (i.e. stone for colic, which it was believed to cure).
jade[2] ● **noun** archaic **1** a bad-tempered or disreputable woman. **2** an inferior or worn-out horse.
– ORIGIN of unknown origin.
jaded ● **adjective** tired out or lacking enthusiasm after having had too much of something.
– ORIGIN originally in the sense 'disreputable': from JADE[2].
jadeite /jaydīt/ ● **noun** a green, blue, or white form of jade.
jaeger /jaygər/ ● **noun** N. Amer. a skua.
– ORIGIN German *Jäger* 'hunter'.
Jaffa /jaffə/ ● **noun** Brit. a large thick-skinned variety of orange.
– ORIGIN from the city of *Jaffa* in Israel.
jag[1] ● **verb** (**jagged, jagging**) stab, pierce, or prick. ● **noun 1** a sharp projection. **2** chiefly Scottish a prick or injection.
– ORIGIN perhaps symbolic of sudden movement or unevenness.
jag[2] ● **noun** informal, chiefly N. Amer. a bout of unrestrained activity or emotion: *a crying jag*.
– ORIGIN originally in the sense 'a load of hay or wood', later 'as much alcohol as one can hold': of unknown origin.
jagged /jaggid/ ● **adjective** with rough, sharp points protruding.
– DERIVATIVES **jaggedly** adverb **jaggedness** noun.
jaggery /jaggəri/ ● **noun** a coarse brown sugar made in India from the sap of palm trees.
– ORIGIN Portuguese *xagara, jag(a)ra* 'sugar', from Sanskrit.
jaggy ● **adjective** (**jaggier, jaggiest**) **1** jagged. **2** (also **jaggie**) Scottish prickly.
jaguar /jagyooər/ ● **noun** a large, heavily built cat that has a yellowish-brown coat with black spots, found mainly in Central and South America.
– ORIGIN Tupi-Guarani.
Jah /jaa/ ● **noun** the Rastafarian name for God.
– ORIGIN representing a Hebrew abbreviation of YAHWEH.
jail (Brit. also **gaol**) ● **noun** a place for the confinement of people accused or convicted of a crime. ● **verb** put in jail.
– DERIVATIVES **jailer** (also **gaoler**) noun.
– ORIGIN the word came into England from two Old French words, *jaiole* and *gayole* (the latter surviving in the spelling *gaol*): both are from Latin *cavea* 'cage'.
jailbait ● **noun** (treated as sing. or pl.) informal a young woman, or young women collectively, considered in sexual terms but under the age of consent.
jailbird ● **noun** informal a person who is or has repeatedly been in prison.
jailbreak ● **noun** an escape from jail.
jailhouse ● **noun** chiefly N. Amer. a prison.
Jain /jayn/ ● **noun** an adherent of Jainism. ● **adjective** relating to Jainism.
– ORIGIN Sanskrit, relating to a *jina* or great teacher.
Jainism ● **noun** an Indian religion founded in the 6th century BC, characterized by non-violence and asceticism.
– DERIVATIVES **Jainist** noun.
jake ● **adjective** N. Amer. & Austral./NZ informal all right; satisfactory.
– ORIGIN of unknown origin.
jalapeño /haləpaynyō/ ● **noun** (pl. **jalapeños**) a very hot green chilli pepper.
– ORIGIN Spanish, from the Mexican city of *Jalapa*.
jalfrezi /jalfrayzi/ ● **noun** a medium-hot Indian dish consisting of chicken or lamb with fresh chillies, tomatoes, and onions.
– ORIGIN Bengali.
jalopy /jəloppi/ ● **noun** (pl. **jalopies**) informal an old car in a dilapidated condition.
– ORIGIN of unknown origin.
jalousie /zhaloozee/ ● **noun** a blind or shutter made of a row of angled slats.
– ORIGIN French, 'jealousy', from Italian *geloso* 'jealous', also (by extension) 'screen', associated with the screening of women from view in the Middle East.
jam[1] ● **verb** (**jammed, jamming**) **1** squeeze or pack tightly into a space. **2** push roughly and forcibly into a position. **3** block (something such as a road) through crowding. **4** become or make unable to function due to a part becoming stuck. **5** (**jam on**) apply forcibly: *he jammed on the brakes.* **6** make a radio transmission unintelligible by causing interference. **7** informal improvise with other musicians. ● **noun 1** an instance of jamming. **2** informal an awkward situation or predicament. **3** informal an improvised performance by a group of musicians.
– ORIGIN probably symbolic.
jam[2] ● **noun** chiefly Brit. a conserve and spread made from fruit and sugar.
– ORIGIN perhaps from JAM[1].
Jamaican /jəmaykən/ ● **noun** a person from Jamaica. ● **adjective**

j

Thesaurus

– PHRASES **hit the jackpot** (informal) WIN A LARGE PRIZE, win a lot of money, strike it lucky/rich; *informal* clean up, hit the big time.
jaded ● **adjective 1** *a jaded palate* SATIATED, sated, surfeited, glutted; dulled, blunted, deadened. **2** *she felt really jaded* TIRED (OUT), weary, wearied, worn out, exhausted, fatigued, overtired, sapped, drained; *informal* all in, done (in), dead (beat), dead on one's feet, bushed; *Brit. informal* knackered, whacked; *N. Amer. informal* tuckered out.
– OPPOSITES fresh.
jag ● **noun** SHARP PROJECTION, point, barb, thorn.
jagged ● **adjective** SPIKY, barbed, ragged, rough, uneven, irregular, broken; serrated, sawtooth, indented.
– OPPOSITES smooth.
jail ● **noun** *he was thrown into jail* PRISON, penal institution, lock-up, detention centre; *N. Amer.* penitentiary, jailhouse, stockade; *informal* the clink, the slammer, inside, the jug, the brig; *Brit. informal* the nick; *N. Amer. informal* the can, the pen, the cooler, the slam; *Brit. historical* approved school, borstal, bridewell; *N. Amer. historical* reformatory.
● **verb** *she was jailed for killing her husband* IMPRISON, put in prison, send to prison, incarcerate, lock up, put away, intern, detain, hold (prisoner/captive), put into detention; *informal* send down, put behind bars, put inside; *Brit. informal* bang up.
– OPPOSITES acquit, release.
jailer ● **noun** PRISON OFFICER, warder, wardress, warden, guard, captor; *informal* screw; *archaic* turnkey.
jam[1] ● **verb 1** *he jammed a finger in each ear* STUFF, shove, force, ram, thrust, press, push, stick, squeeze, cram. **2** *hundreds of people jammed into the hall* CROWD, pack, pile, press, squeeze, cram; throng, mob, occupy, fill, overcrowd, obstruct, block, clog, congest. **3** *the rudder had jammed* STICK, become stuck, catch, seize (up), become trapped. **4** *dust can jam the mechanism* IMMOBILIZE, paralyse, disable, cripple, put out of action, bring to a standstill.
● **noun 1** *a traffic jam* TAILBACK, hold-up, congestion, bottleneck; *N. Amer.* gridlock; *informal* snarl-up. **2** (informal) *we are in a real jam* PRE-

relating to Jamaica.
jamb /jam/ ● noun a side post of a doorway, window, or fireplace.
– ORIGIN Old French *jambe* 'leg, vertical support', from Greek *kampē* 'joint'.
jambalaya /jambəlīə/ ● noun a Cajun dish of rice with shrimps, chicken, and vegetables.
– ORIGIN Provençal *jambalaia*.
jamboree /jambəree/ ● noun **1** a lavish or boisterous celebration or party. **2** a large rally of Scouts or Guides.
– ORIGIN of unknown origin.
jammy ● adjective (**jammier**, **jammiest**) **1** covered, filled with, or resembling jam. **2** Brit. informal lucky.
jam-packed ● adjective informal extremely crowded or full to capacity.
Jan. ● abbreviation January.
jangle ● verb **1** make or cause to make a ringing metallic sound. **2** (of one's nerves) be set on edge. ● noun an instance of jangling.
– DERIVATIVES **jangly** adjective.
– ORIGIN Old French *jangler*.
janissary /jannisəri/ (also **janizary** /jannizəri/) ● noun (pl. **janissaries**) historical a Turkish infantryman in the Sultan's guard.
– ORIGIN French *janissaire*, from Turkish *yeniçeri*, from *yeni* 'new' + *çeri* 'troops'.
janitor /jannitər/ ● noun chiefly N. Amer. a caretaker of a building.
– DERIVATIVES **janitorial** adjective.
– ORIGIN Latin, from *janua* 'door'.
jankers /jangkərz/ ● noun Brit. military slang punishment for committing a military offence.
– ORIGIN of unknown origin.
Jansenism ● noun a rigorous Christian movement of the 17th and 18th centuries, based on the writings of the Catholic theologian Cornelius Jansen (1585–1638).
– DERIVATIVES **Jansenist** noun.
January ● noun (pl. **Januaries**) the first month of the year.
– ORIGIN from Latin *Januarius mensis* 'month of *Janus*' (the Roman god who presided over doors and beginnings).
Jap ● noun & adjective informal, offensive short for JAPANESE.
japan ● noun a black glossy varnish of a type originating in Japan. ● verb (**japanned**, **japanning**) cover with japan.
Japanese ● noun (pl. same) **1** a person from Japan. **2** the language of Japan. ● adjective relating to Japan.
jape ● noun a practical joke. ● verb say or do something in jest or mockery.
– ORIGIN apparently combining the form of Old French *japer* 'to yelp, yap' with the sense of Old French *gaber* 'to mock'.
japonica /jəponnikə/ ● noun an Asian shrub of the rose family, with bright red flowers followed by edible fruits.
– ORIGIN from Latin, 'Japanese'.
jar[1] ● noun **1** a wide-mouthed cylindrical container made of glass or pottery. **2** Brit. informal a glass of beer.
– ORIGIN French *jarre*, from Arabic.
jar[2] ● verb (**jarred**, **jarring**) **1** send a painful or uncomfortable shock through (a part of the body). **2** strike against something with an unpleasant vibration or jolt. **3** have an unpleasant or incongruous effect. ● noun an instance of jarring.
– DERIVATIVES **jarring** adjective.
– ORIGIN originally denoting a disagreement or dispute: probably imitative.
jardinière /zhaardinyair/ ● noun **1** an ornamental pot or stand for displaying plants. **2** a garnish of mixed vegetables.
– ORIGIN French, 'female gardener'.
jargon ● noun words or expressions used by a particular group that are difficult for others to understand.
– DERIVATIVES **jargonistic** adjective **jargonize** (also **jargonise**) verb.
– ORIGIN originally in the sense 'twittering, chattering': from Old French *jargoun*.
jarrah /jarrə/ ● noun a eucalyptus tree native to western Australia.
– ORIGIN from Nyungar (an extinct Aboriginal language).
jasmine (also **jessamine**) ● noun a shrub or climbing plant with fragrant, often yellow, flowers.
– ORIGIN French *jasmin*, from Persian.
jasper ● noun an opaque reddish-brown variety of chalcedony.
– ORIGIN Old French *jasp(r)e*, from Latin *iaspis*.
jaundice /jawndiss/ ● noun **1** Medicine yellowing of the skin due to a bile disorder. **2** bitterness or resentment.
– DERIVATIVES **jaundiced** adjective.
– ORIGIN Old French *jaunice* 'yellowness'.
jaunt ● noun a short excursion for pleasure. ● verb go on a jaunt.
– ORIGIN of unknown origin.
jaunty ● adjective (**jauntier**, **jauntiest**) having a lively and self-confident manner.
– DERIVATIVES **jauntily** adverb **jauntiness** noun.
– ORIGIN originally in the sense 'well-bred, genteel': from French *gentil* 'well-born'.
Java /jaavə/ ● noun trademark a computer programming language designed to work across different computer systems.
Javan ● noun a person from the Indonesian island of Java. ● adjective relating to Java.
Javanese ● noun (pl. same) **1** a person from Java. **2** the language of central Java. ● adjective relating to Java.
javelin /javvəlin/ ● noun a long, light spear thrown in a competitive sport or as a weapon.
– ORIGIN Old French *javeline*, of Celtic origin.
javelina /havvəleenə/ ● noun North American term for PECCARY.
– ORIGIN Spanish *jabalina* 'wild boar'.
jaw ● noun **1** each of the upper and lower bony structures in vertebrates forming the framework of the mouth and containing the teeth. **2** (**jaws**) the grasping, biting, or crushing mouthparts of an invertebrate. **3** (**jaws**) the gripping parts of a wrench, vice, etc. **4** (**jaws**) the grasping or destructive power of something: *the jaws of death*. ● verb informal talk or gossip at length.
– DERIVATIVES **jawed** adjective.
– ORIGIN Old French *joe* 'cheek, jaw'.

Thesaurus

DICAMENT, plight, tricky situation, difficulty, problem, quandary, dilemma, muddle, mess, imbroglio, mare's nest, dire straits; *informal* pickle, stew, fix, hole, scrape, bind, (tight) spot, (tight) corner, hot/deep water; *Brit. informal* spot of bother.
jam[2] ● noun *raspberry jam* PRESERVE, conserve, jelly, marmalade.
jamb ● noun POST, doorpost, upright, frame.
jamboree ● noun RALLY, gathering, convention, conference; festival, fête, fiesta, gala, carnival, celebration; *informal* bash, shindig, shindy, junket.
jammy ● adjective *(Brit. informal)*. See LUCKY sense 1.
jangle ● verb **1** *keys jangled at his waist* CLANK, clink, jingle, tinkle. **2** *the noise jangled her nerves* GRATE ON, jar on, irritate, disturb, fray, put/set on edge; *informal* get on.
● noun *the jangle of his chains* CLANK, clanking, clink, clinking, jangling, jingle, jingling, tintinnabulation.
janitor ● noun CARETAKER, custodian, porter, concierge, doorkeeper, doorman, warden; cleaner, maintenance man; *N. Amer.* superintendent.
jar[1] ● noun *a jar of honey* (GLASS) CONTAINER, pot, crock, receptacle.
jar[2] ● verb **1** *each step jarred my whole body* JOLT, jerk, shake, vibrate. **2** *her shrill voice jarred on him* GRATE, set someone's teeth on edge, irritate, annoy, irk, exasperate, nettle, disturb, discompose; *informal* rile, aggravate, get on someone's nerves. **3** *the play's symbolism jarred with the realism of its setting* CLASH, conflict, contrast, be incompatible, be at variance, be at odds, be inconsistent, be discordant; *informal* scream at.
jargon ● noun SPECIALIZED LANGUAGE, slang, cant, idiom, argot, patter, gobbledegook; *informal* -speak, -ese.
jarring ● adjective CLASHING, conflicting, contrasting, incompatible, incongruous; discordant, dissonant, inharmonious, harsh, grating, strident, shrill, cacophonous.
– OPPOSITES harmonious.
jaundiced ● adjective BITTER, resentful, cynical, soured, disenchanted, disillusioned, disappointed, pessimistic, sceptical, distrustful, suspicious, misanthropic.
jaunt ● noun (PLEASURE) TRIP, outing, excursion, day trip, day out, mini holiday, short break; tour, drive, ride, run; *informal* spin, tootle.
jaunty ● adjective CHEERFUL, cheery, happy, merry, jolly, joyful; lively, perky, bright, buoyant, bubbly, bouncy, breezy, full of the joys of spring, in good spirits, exuberant, ebullient; carefree, blithe, airy, light-hearted, nonchalant, insouciant, happy-go-lucky; *informal* bright-eyed and bushy-tailed, full of beans, chirpy; *poetic/literary* blithesome.
– OPPOSITES depressed, serious.
javelin ● noun SPEAR, harpoon, dart, gig, shaft, assegai.
jaw ● noun **1** *a broken jaw* JAWBONE, lower/upper jaw; *Anatomy* mandible, maxilla. **2** *the whale seized a seal pup in its jaws* MOUTH,

jawbone ● noun a bone of the jaw, especially that of the lower jaw (the mandible).
jaw-dropping ● adjective informal amazing.
jawline ● noun the contour of the lower edge of a person's jaw.
jay ● noun a noisy bird of the crow family with boldly patterned plumage.
– ORIGIN Latin *gaius*, *gaia*, perhaps from the given name *Gaius*.
jaywalk ● verb chiefly N. Amer. walk in or across a road without regard for approaching traffic.
– DERIVATIVES **jaywalker** noun.
– ORIGIN from JAY in the obsolete sense 'silly person'.
jazz ● noun a type of music of black American origin characterized by improvisation, syncopation, and a regular rhythm. ● verb (**jazz up**) informal make more lively.
– PHRASES **and all that jazz** informal and such similar things.
– ORIGIN of unknown origin.
jazz age ● noun the 1920s in the US, characterized as a period of hedonism, freedom, and exuberance.
jazzy ● adjective (**jazzier**, **jazziest**) **1** of or in the style of jazz. **2** bright, colourful, and showy.
JCB ● noun Brit. trademark a type of mechanical excavator with a shovel at the front and a digging arm at the rear.
– ORIGIN the initials of *J. C. B*amford, the makers.
J-cloth ● noun trademark (in the UK) a type of cloth used for household cleaning.
– ORIGIN *J* from *J*ohnson and Johnson, the original makers.
JCR ● abbreviation Brit. Junior Common (or Combination) Room.
jealous ● adjective **1** envious of someone else's achievements or advantages. **2** resentful of someone regarded as a sexual rival. **3** fiercely protective of one's rights or possessions: *they kept a jealous eye over their interests*. **4** (of God) demanding faithfulness and exclusive worship.
– DERIVATIVES **jealously** adverb **jealousy** noun.
– ORIGIN Old French *gelos*, from Latin *zelosus* 'zealous'.
jean ● noun **1** heavy twilled cotton cloth, especially denim. **2** (**jeans**) hard-wearing trousers made of denim or other cotton fabric.
– ORIGIN Old French *Janne* (now *Gênes*), from Latin *Janua* 'Genoa', the place of original production.
jebel /jebb'l/ ● noun (in the Middle East and North Africa) a mountain or hill, or a range of hills.
– ORIGIN Arabic.
jeep ● noun trademark a small, sturdy motor vehicle with four-wheel drive.
– ORIGIN from the initials *GP*, standing for *general purpose*, influenced by 'Eugene the Jeep', a creature in the *Popeye* comic strip.
jeepers (also **jeepers creepers**) ● exclamation informal, chiefly N. Amer. expressing surprise or alarm.
– ORIGIN alteration of JESUS.
jeer ● verb make rude and mocking remarks at someone. ● noun a rude and mocking remark.
– ORIGIN of unknown origin.
Jeez (also **Jeeze** or **Geez**) ● exclamation informal expressing surprise or annoyance.
– ORIGIN abbreviation of JESUS.
jehad ● noun variant spelling of JIHAD.
Jehovah /jihōvə/ ● noun a form of the Hebrew name of God used in some translations of the Bible.
– ORIGIN Latin *Iehouah*, *Iehoua*, from Hebrew.
Jehovah's Witness ● noun a member of a fundamentalist Christian sect that denies many traditional Christian doctrines and preaches the Second Coming.
jejune /jijo͞on/ ● adjective **1** naive and simplistic. **2** (of ideas or writings) dull.
– ORIGIN Latin *jejunus* 'fasting, barren'.
jejunum /jijo͞onəm/ ● noun Anatomy the part of the small intestine between the duodenum and ileum.
– ORIGIN Latin, 'fasting' (because it is usually found to be empty after death).
Jekyll /jekk'l/ ● noun (in phrase **a Jekyll and Hyde**) a person displaying alternately good and evil personalities.
– ORIGIN after the central character in Robert Louis Stevenson's story *The Strange Case of Dr Jekyll and Mr Hyde* (1886).
jell (also **gel**) ● verb (**jelled**, **jelling**) **1** (of jelly or a similar substance) set or become firmer. **2** take definite form or begin to work well.
jellaba ● noun variant spelling of DJELLABA.
jello (also trademark **Jell-O**) ● noun N. Amer. a fruit-flavoured gelatin dessert made up from a powder.
jelly ● noun (pl. **jellies**) **1** chiefly Brit. a dessert consisting of a sweet, fruit-flavoured liquid set with gelatin to form a semi-solid mass. **2** a small sweet made with gelatin. **3** a similar preparation or a substance of a similar semi-solid consistency. **4** Brit. informal term for GELIGNITE. ● verb (**jellies**, **jellied**) (**jellied**) (of food) set in a jelly.
– ORIGIN Old French *gelee* 'frost, jelly', from Latin *gelare* 'freeze'.
jelly baby ● noun Brit. a jelly sweet in the stylized shape of a baby.
jelly bean ● noun a jelly sweet in the shape of a bean.
jellyfish ● noun a free-swimming marine animal with a soft bell- or saucer-shaped body that has stinging tentacles around the edge.
jelly shoe (also **jelly sandal**) ● noun a sandal made from translucent moulded plastic.
jemmy (N. Amer. **jimmy**) ● noun (pl. **jemmies**) a short crowbar. ● verb (**jemmies**, **jemmied**) informal force open (a window or door) with a jemmy.
– ORIGIN familiar form of the given name *James*.
je ne sais quoi /zhə nə say **kwaa**/ ● noun a quality that cannot be easily identified.
– ORIGIN French, 'I do not know what'.
jenny ● noun (pl. **jennies**) a female donkey or ass.
– ORIGIN familiar form of the given name *Janet*.
jeon /jun/ ● noun (pl. same) a monetary unit of South Korea, equal to one hundredth of a won.
– ORIGIN Korean.
jeopardize /jeppərdīz/ (also **jeopardise**) ● verb put into a situation in which there is a danger of loss, harm, or failure.
jeopardy /jeppərdi/ ● noun danger of loss, harm, or failure.

j

Thesaurus

maw, muzzle; *informal* chops. **3** *(informal) we ought to have a jaw*. See CHAT noun.
– RELATED TERMS mandibular, maxillary.
● verb *(informal) Tom was the type to jaw*. See CHAT verb.
jazz ● verb
– PHRASES **jazz something up** *(informal)* ENLIVEN, liven up, brighten up, make more interesting/exciting, add (some) colour to, ginger up, spice up; *informal* perk up, pep up.
jazzy ● adjective BRIGHT, colourful, brightly coloured, striking, eye-catching, vivid, lively, vibrant, bold, flamboyant, showy, gaudy; *informal* flashy.
– OPPOSITES dull.
jealous ● adjective **1** *he was jealous of his brother's popularity* ENVIOUS, covetous, desirous; resentful, grudging, begrudging, green (with envy). **2** *a jealous lover* SUSPICIOUS, distrustful, mistrustful, doubting, insecure, anxious; possessive, proprietorial, overprotective. **3** *they are very jealous of their rights* PROTECTIVE, vigilant, watchful, heedful, mindful, careful, solicitous.
– OPPOSITES proud, trusting.
jealousy ● noun **1** *he was consumed with jealousy* ENVY, covetousness; resentment, resentfulness, bitterness, spite; *informal* the green-eyed monster. **2** *the jealousy of his long-suffering wife* SUSPICION, suspiciousness, distrust, mistrust, insecurity, anxiety; possessiveness, overprotectiveness. **3** *an intense jealousy of status* PROTECTIVENESS, vigilance, watchfulness, heedfulness, mindfulness, care, solicitousness.
jeans ● plural noun DENIMS, blue jeans; *trademark* Levi's, Wranglers.
jeer ● verb *the demonstrators jeered the police* TAUNT, mock, scoff at, ridicule, sneer at, deride, insult, abuse, jibe (at), scorn, shout disapproval (at); heckle, catcall (at), boo (at), hoot at, whistle at, hiss (at); *archaic* flout at.
– OPPOSITES cheer.
● noun *the jeers of the crowd* TAUNT, sneer, insult, shout, jibe, boo, hiss, catcall; derision, teasing, scoffing, abuse, scorn, heckling, catcalling; *Brit. & Austral./NZ* barracking.
– OPPOSITES applause.
jejune ● adjective **1** *their jejune opinions* NAIVE, innocent, artless, guileless, unworldly, childlike, ingenuous, unsophisticated; credulous, gullible; childish, immature, juvenile, puerile, infantile. **2** *the following poem is rather jejune* BORING, dull, tedious, dreary; uninteresting, unexciting, uninspiring, unimaginative; humdrum, run-of-the-mill, mundane, commonplace; lacklustre, dry, sterile, lifeless, vapid, flat, bland, banal, trite, prosaic; *Brit. informal* samey; *N. Amer. informal* ornery.

– ORIGIN from Old French *ieu parti* '(evenly) divided game', originally used in chess to denote a position in which the chances of winning or losing were evenly balanced.

jerboa /jerbōə/ ● noun a desert-dwelling rodent with very long hind legs found from North Africa to central Asia.
– ORIGIN Latin, from Arabic.

jeremiad /jerrimīad/ ● noun a long, mournful complaint or lamentation; a list of woes.
– ORIGIN French *jérémiade*, with reference to the Lamentations of Jeremiah in the Old Testament.

Jeremiah /jerrimīə/ ● noun a person who complains continually or foretells disaster.

jerk[1] ● noun **1** a quick, sharp, sudden movement. **2** Weightlifting the raising of a barbell above the head from shoulder level by an abrupt straightening of the arms and legs. **3** informal, chiefly N. Amer. a contemptibly foolish person. ● verb **1** move or raise with a jerk. **2** (**jerk around**) N. Amer. informal deal with dishonestly or unfairly. **3** (**jerk off**) vulgar slang, chiefly N. Amer. masturbate.
– DERIVATIVES **jerker** noun.
– ORIGIN probably imitative.

jerk[2] ● verb prepare (pork or chicken) by marinating it in spices and barbecuing it over a wood fire. ● noun jerked meat.
– ORIGIN Spanish *charquear*, from Quechua, 'dried flesh'.

jerkin ● noun a sleeveless jacket.
– ORIGIN of unknown origin.

jerky[1] ● adjective (**jerkier**, **jerkiest**) characterized by abrupt stops and starts.
– DERIVATIVES **jerkily** adverb **jerkiness** noun.

jerky[2] ● noun strips of jerked meat.

j

jeroboam /jerrəbōəm/ ● noun a wine bottle with a capacity four times larger than that of an ordinary bottle.
– ORIGIN named after *Jeroboam*, a king of Israel (Book of Kings 1, chapters 11 and 14).

Jerry ● noun (pl. **Jerries**) Brit. informal, dated a German or Germans collectively.
– ORIGIN probably an alteration of GERMAN.

jerry-built ● adjective badly or hastily built.
– DERIVATIVES **jerry-builder** noun.
– ORIGIN sometimes said to be from the name of a firm of builders in Liverpool, or to allude to the walls of Jericho, which fell down at the sound of Joshua's trumpets (Book of Joshua, chapter 6).

jerrycan (also **jerrican**) ● noun a large flat-sided metal container for storing or transporting liquids.
– ORIGIN from JERRY + CAN[2], because such containers were first used in Germany.

jersey ● noun (pl. **jerseys**) **1** a knitted garment with long sleeves. **2** a distinctive shirt worn by a participant in certain sports. **3** a soft knitted fabric. **4** (**Jersey**) an animal of a breed of light brown dairy cattle from Jersey in the Channel Islands.
– ORIGIN from *Jersey* in the Channel Islands, where the fabric was made.

Jerusalem artichoke ● noun a knobbly tuber with white flesh, eaten as a vegetable.
– ORIGIN alteration of Italian *girasole* 'sunflower'.

jess Falconry ● noun a short leather strap that is fastened round each leg of a hawk, to which a leash may be attached.
– ORIGIN Old French *ges*, from Latin *jactus* 'a throw'.

jessamine /jessəmin/ ● noun variant spelling of JASMINE.

jessie (also **jessy**) ● noun (pl. **jessies**) Brit. informal, derogatory an effeminate, weak, or over-sensitive man.
– ORIGIN from the female given name *Jessie*.

jest ● noun a joke. ● verb speak or act in a joking manner.
– ORIGIN originally in the sense 'exploit, heroic deed': from Old French *geste*, from Latin *gesta* 'actions, exploits'.

jester ● noun historical a professional joker or 'fool' at a medieval court.

Jesuit /jezyooit/ ● noun a member of the society of Jesus, a Roman Catholic order of priests founded by St Ignatius Loyola and others in 1534.

Jesuitical ● adjective **1** of or concerning the Jesuits. **2** secretive or equivocating, in a manner once associated with Jesuits.

Jesus (also **Jesus Christ**) ● noun the central figure of the Christian religion, considered by Christians to be the Christ or Messiah and the Son of God. ● exclamation informal expressing irritation, dismay, or surprise.

jet[1] ● noun **1** a rapid stream of liquid or gas forced out of a small opening. **2** an aircraft powered by jet engines. ● verb (**jetted**, **jetting**) **1** spurt out in a jet. **2** travel by jet aircraft.
– ORIGIN from French *jeter* 'to throw', from Latin *jacere*.

jet[2] ● noun **1** a hard black semi-precious variety of lignite. **2** (also **jet black**) a glossy black colour.
– ORIGIN Old French *jaiet*, from Greek *gagatēs* 'from *Gagai*', a town in Asia Minor.

jeté /zhetay/ ● noun Ballet a spring from one foot to the other, with the following leg extended backwards while in the air.
– ORIGIN French, from *jeter* 'to throw'.

jet engine ● noun an aircraft engine which provides thrust by ejecting a high-speed jet of gas obtained by burning fuel in air.

jet lag ● noun extreme tiredness and other effects felt by a person after a long flight across different time zones.
– DERIVATIVES **jet-lagged** adjective.

jetliner ● noun a large jet aircraft carrying passengers.

jetsam /jetsəm/ ● noun unwanted material or goods that have been thrown overboard from a ship and washed ashore. Compare with FLOTSAM.
– ORIGIN originally as *jetson*; contraction of JETTISON.

jet set ● noun (**the jet set**) informal wealthy people who travel widely and frequently for pleasure.
– DERIVATIVES **jet-setter** noun **jet-setting** adjective.

jet ski ● noun trademark a small jet-propelled vehicle which skims across the surface of water and is ridden in a similar way to a motorcycle. ● verb (**jet-ski**) ride on a jet ski.
– DERIVATIVES **jet-skier** noun **jet-skiing** noun.

jet stream ● noun any of several narrow variable bands of very strong predominantly westerly air currents encircling the globe several miles above the earth.

jettison /jettis'n/ ● verb **1** throw or drop from an aircraft or ship. **2** abandon or discard.
– ORIGIN Old French *getaison*, from Latin *jacere* 'to throw'.

Thesaurus

– OPPOSITES sophisticated, fascinating.

jell ● verb. See GEL.

jeopardize ● verb THREATEN, endanger, imperil, risk, put at risk, put in danger/jeopardy; leave vulnerable; compromise, prejudice, be prejudicial to; be a danger to, pose a threat to; *archaic* peril.
– OPPOSITES safeguard.

jeopardy ● noun DANGER, peril; at risk.

jerk ● noun **1** *she gave the reins a jerk* YANK, tug, pull, wrench, tweak, twitch. **2** *he let the clutch in with a jerk* JOLT, lurch, bump, start, jar, jog, bang, bounce, shake, shock. **3** *(informal) I felt a complete jerk.* See FOOL noun sense 1.
● verb **1** *she jerked her arm free* YANK, tug, pull, wrench, wrest, drag, pluck, snatch, seize, rip, tear. **2** *the car jerked along* JOLT, lurch, bump, rattle, bounce, shake, jounce.

jerky ● adjective **1** *jerky movements* CONVULSIVE, spasmodic, fitful, twitchy, shaky. **2** *the coach drew to a jerky halt* JOLTING, lurching, bumpy, bouncy, jarring.
– OPPOSITES smooth.

jerry-built ● adjective SHODDY, badly built, gimcrack, flimsy, insubstantial, rickety, ramshackle, crude, makeshift; inferior, poor-quality, second-rate, third-rate, low-grade.
– OPPOSITES sturdy.

jersey ● noun PULLOVER, sweater; *Brit.* jumper; *informal* woolly.

jest ● noun *jests were bandied about freely* JOKE, witticism, funny remark, gag, quip, sally, pun; *informal* crack, wisecrack, one-liner.
● verb **1** *surely you are jesting* JOKE, quip, gag, pun; tell jokes, crack jokes; *informal* wisecrack. **2** *she feared that they had not been jesting* FOOL (ABOUT/AROUND), play a practical joke, tease; *informal* kid, have someone on, pull someone's leg; *N. Amer. informal* pull someone's chain, fun; *Brit. informal* wind someone up.
– PHRASES **in jest** IN FUN, as a joke, tongue in cheek, playfully, jokingly, light-heartedly, facetiously, flippantly, frivolously, for a laugh.

jester ● noun **1** *(historical) a court jester* (COURT) FOOL, court jester, clown; *archaic* merry andrew. **2** *the class jester* JOKER, comedian, comic, humorist, wag, wit, prankster, jokester, clown, buffoon; *informal* card, case, caution, hoot, scream, laugh, wisecracker, barrel of laughs; *Austral./NZ informal* hard case.

jet[1] ● noun **1** *a jet of water* STREAM, spurt, squirt, spray, spout; gush, rush, surge, burst. **2** *carburettor jets* NOZZLE, head, spout. **3** *an executive jet* JET PLANE, jetliner; aircraft, plane; *Brit.* aeroplane.
● verb **1** *they jetted out of Heathrow* FLY, travel/go by jet, travel/go by plane. **2** *puffs of gas jetted out* SQUIRT, spurt, shoot, spray; gush, pour, stream, rush, pump, surge, spew, burst.

jetty ● noun (pl. **jetties**) **1** a landing stage or small pier. **2** a construction built out into the water to protect a harbour, riverbank, etc.
– ORIGIN Old French *jetee*, from *jeter* 'to throw'.
jeu d'esprit /zhö despree/ ● noun (pl. **jeux d'esprit** pronunc. same) a light-hearted display of wit.
– ORIGIN French, 'game of the mind'.
jeunesse dorée /zhöness doray/ ● noun young people of wealth, fashion, and flair.
– ORIGIN French, 'gilded youth'.
Jew ● noun a member of the people whose traditional religion is Judaism and who trace their origins to the ancient Hebrew people of Israel.
– ORIGIN from the Hebrew form of the name 'Judah'.
jewel ● noun **1** a precious stone, especially a single crystal or a cut and polished piece of a lustrous or translucent mineral. **2** (**jewels**) pieces of jewellery. **3** a hard precious stone used as a bearing in a watch, compass, etc. **4** a highly valued person or thing.
– DERIVATIVES **jewelled** (US **jeweled**) adjective.
– PHRASES **the jewel in the crown** the most valuable or successful part of something.
– ORIGIN Old French *joel*, from *jeu* 'game, play', from Latin *jocus* 'jest'.
jeweller (US **jeweler**) ● noun a person who makes or sells jewellery.
jeweller's rouge ● noun finely ground ferric oxide, used as a polish for metal and optical glass.
jewellery (US also **jewelry**) ● noun personal ornaments, such as necklaces, rings, or bracelets, that are made from or contain jewels and precious metal.
Jewess ● noun a Jewish woman or girl.
Jewish ● adjective relating to, associated with, or denoting Jews or Judaism.
– DERIVATIVES **Jewishness** noun.
Jewish New Year ● noun another term for ROSH HASHANA.
Jewry /joori/ ● noun (pl. **Jewries**) **1** Jews collectively. **2** historical a Jewish quarter in a town or city.
Jew's harp ● noun a small lyre-shaped musical instrument held between the teeth and struck with a finger.
Jezebel /jezzəbel/ ● noun a shameless or immoral woman.
– ORIGIN the name of the wife of King Ahab in the Bible.
jiao /jow/ ● noun (pl. same) a monetary unit of China, equal to one tenth of a yuan.
– ORIGIN Chinese.
jib[1] ● noun **1** Sailing a triangular staysail set forward of the mast. **2** the projecting arm of a crane.
– ORIGIN of unknown origin.
jib[2] ● verb (**jibbed**, **jibbing**) (usu. **jib at**) **1** be unwilling to do or accept something. **2** (of a horse) stop and refuse to go on.
– DERIVATIVES **jibber** noun.
– ORIGIN perhaps related to French *regimber* 'buck, rear': related to JIBE[1].
jibba /jibbə/ (also **djibba**) ● noun a long coat worn by Muslim men.
– ORIGIN Egyptian.
jibe[1] (also **gibe**) ● noun an insulting or mocking remark. ● verb make jibes.
– ORIGIN perhaps from Old French *giber* 'handle roughly': related to JIB[2].
jibe[2] ● verb & noun US variant of GYBE.
jibe[3] ● verb N. Amer. informal be in accordance; agree.
– ORIGIN of unknown origin.
jiffy (also **jiff**) ● noun informal a moment.
– ORIGIN of unknown origin.
jig ● noun **1** a lively dance with leaping movements and music in compound time. **2** a device that guides tools and holds materials or parts securely. ● verb (**jigged**, **jigging**) **1** dance a jig. **2** move up and down with a quick jerky motion.
– ORIGIN of unknown origin.
jigger[1] ● noun **1** a machine or vehicle with a part that rocks or moves to and fro. **2** a person who dances a jig. **3** a small sail set at the stern of a ship. **4** a small tackle consisting of a double and single block with a rope. **5** a measure of spirits or wine. ● verb Brit. informal **1** rearrange or tamper with. **2** (**jiggered**) damaged, broken, or exhausted.
– PHRASES **I'll be jiggered** Brit. informal, dated expressing astonishment.
jigger[2] ● noun variant spelling of CHIGGER.
jiggery-pokery ● noun informal, chiefly Brit. deceitful or dishonest behaviour.
– ORIGIN probably a variant of Scots *joukery-pawkery*, from *jouk* 'dodge, skulk'.
jiggle ● verb move lightly and quickly from side to side or up and down. ● noun an instance of jiggling.
– DERIVATIVES **jiggly** adjective.
– ORIGIN partly an alteration of JOGGLE, reinforced by JIG.
jigsaw ● noun **1** a puzzle consisting of a picture printed on cardboard or wood and cut into numerous interlocking shapes that have to be fitted together. **2** a machine saw with a fine blade enabling it to cut curved lines in a sheet of wood, metal, etc.
jihad /jihad/ (also **jehad**) ● noun a holy war undertaken by Muslims against unbelievers.
– ORIGIN Arabic, 'effort'.
jilt ● verb abruptly break off a relationship with (a lover).
– ORIGIN originally in the sense 'deceive, trick': of unknown origin.
Jim Crow ● noun US **1** the former practice of segregating black people in the US. **2** offensive a black person.
– DERIVATIVES **Jim Crowism** noun.
– ORIGIN the name of a black character in a plantation song.
jim-jams ● plural noun informal **1** (**the jim-jams**) a fit of depression or nervousness. **2** Brit. pyjamas.
– ORIGIN fanciful reduplication.
jimmy ● noun & verb US spelling of JEMMY.
jingle ● noun **1** a light, loose ringing sound such as that made by metal objects being shaken together. **2** a short easily remembered slogan, verse, or tune. ● verb make or cause to make a jingle.
– DERIVATIVES **jingler** noun **jingly** adjective.

j

Thesaurus

jet[2] ● adjective *her glossy jet hair* BLACK, jet-black, pitch-black, ink-black, ebony, raven, sable, sooty.
jettison ● verb **1** *six aircraft jettisoned their loads* DUMP, drop, ditch, discharge, throw out, tip out, unload, throw overboard. **2** *he jettisoned his unwanted papers | the scheme was jettisoned* DISCARD, dispose of, throw away/out, get rid of; reject, scrap, axe, abandon, drop; *informal* chuck (away/out), dump, ditch, bin, junk, get shut of; *Brit. informal* get shot of; *N. Amer. informal* trash.
– OPPOSITES retain.
jetty ● noun PIER, landing (stage), quay, wharf, dock; breakwater, mole, groyne, dyke; *N. Amer.* dockominium, levee.
jewel ● noun **1** *priceless jewels* GEM, gemstone, (precious) stone, brilliant; baguette; *informal* sparkler, rock; *archaic* bijou. **2** *the jewel of his collection* FINEST EXAMPLE/SPECIMEN, showpiece, pride (and joy), cream, crème de la crème, jewel in the crown, nonpareil, glory, prize, boast, pick, ne plus ultra. **3** *the girl is a jewel* TREASURE, angel, paragon, marvel, find, godsend; *informal* one in a million, a star, the tops; *archaic* nonsuch.
jewellery ● noun JEWELS, gems, gemstones, precious stones, bijouterie, costume jewellery, diamanté; *archaic* bijoux.
Jezebel ● noun IMMORAL WOMAN; seductress, temptress, femme fatale; *informal* tart, vamp, maneater; *N. Amer. informal* tramp; *Brit. informal* scrubber, slapper, slag; *dated* loose woman, trollop, hussy; *archaic* harlot, strumpet.
jib ● verb **1** *the horse jibbed at the final fence* STOP (SHORT) AT, baulk at, shy at; refuse. **2** *some farmers jib at paying large veterinary bills* BAULK AT, fight shy of, recoil from, shrink from; be unwilling, be reluctant, be loath, demur at; *informal* boggle at.
– OPPOSITES clear.
jibe ● noun *cruel jibes* SNIDE REMARK, cutting remark, taunt, sneer, jeer, insult, barb; *informal* dig, put-down.
● verb *Simon jibed in a sarcastic way* JEER, taunt, mock, scoff, sneer.
jiffy ● noun
– PHRASES **in a jiffy** (*informal*) (VERY) SOON, in a second, in a minute, in a moment, in a trice, in a flash, shortly, any second, any minute (now), in no time (at all); *N. Amer.* momentarily; *informal* in a sec, in a jiff, in two shakes (of a lamb's tail), before you can say Jack Robinson; *Brit. informal* in a tick, in two ticks, in a mo; *N. Amer. informal* in a snap, in jig time; *dated* directly.
jig ● verb BOB, jump, spring, skip, hop, prance, bounce, jounce.
jiggle ● verb **1** *Barrett jiggled his foot* SHAKE, joggle, waggle, wiggle. **2** *Thomas jiggled excitedly* FIDGET, wriggle, squirm.
jilt ● verb LEAVE, walk out on, throw over, finish with, break up

– ORIGIN imitative.

jingo /jinggō/ • **noun** (pl. **jingoes**) dated, chiefly derogatory a vociferous supporter of a patriotic war policy.

– PHRASES **by jingo!** an exclamation of surprise.

– ORIGIN originally a conjuror's word; *by jingo* and the noun are from a popular song adopted by those supporting the sending of a British fleet into Turkish waters to resist Russia in 1878.

jingoism • **noun** chiefly derogatory extreme patriotism, especially in the form of aggressive foreign policy.

– DERIVATIVES **jingoist** noun **jingoistic** adjective.

jink • **verb** change direction suddenly and nimbly. • **noun** a sudden quick change of direction.

– ORIGIN originally Scottish as *high jinks*, denoting antics at drinking parties.

jinn /jin/ (also **djinn**) • **noun** (pl. same or **jinns**) (in Arabian and Muslim mythology) an intelligent spirit able to appear in human or animal form.

– ORIGIN Arabic.

jinx • **noun** a person or thing that brings bad luck. • **verb** bring bad luck to.

– ORIGIN probably a variant of Latin *jynx* 'wryneck' (because the bird was used in witchcraft).

jitney /jitni/ • **noun** (pl. **jitneys**) N. Amer. informal a bus or other vehicle carrying passengers for a low fare (originally five cents).

– ORIGIN originally denoting a five-cent piece: of unknown origin.

jitter informal • **noun 1** (**the jitters**) a feeling of extreme nervousness. **2** slight, irregular variation in an electrical signal. • **verb 1** act nervously. **2** suffer from jitter.

– DERIVATIVES **jitteriness** noun **jittery** adjective.

– ORIGIN of unknown origin.

jitterbug • **noun** a fast dance performed to swing music, popular in the 1940s. • **verb** (**jitterbugged**, **jitterbugging**) dance the jitterbug.

jiu-jitsu • **noun** variant spelling of JU-JITSU.

jive • **noun 1** a style of lively dance popular in the 1940s and 1950s, performed to swing music or rock and roll. **2** N. Amer. informal exaggerated or misleading talk. • **verb 1** dance the jive. **2** N. Amer. informal talk in an exaggerated or misleading way.

– DERIVATIVES **jiver** noun.

– ORIGIN originally US, denoting meaningless or misleading speech, later the slang speech associated with black American jazz musicians: of unknown origin.

joanna • **noun** Brit. rhyming slang a piano.

job • **noun 1** a paid position of regular employment. **2** a task or piece of work. **3** informal a crime, especially a robbery. **4** informal a procedure to improve the appearance of something: *a nose job.* • **verb** (**jobbed**, **jobbing**) **1** (usu. as adj. **jobbing**) do casual or occasional work. **2** buy and sell (stocks) on a small scale as a broker-dealer. **3** N. Amer. informal cheat; betray.

– PHRASES **a good job** informal, chiefly Brit. a fortunate fact or circumstance. **jobs for the boys** Brit. the practice of giving paid employment to one's friends, supporters, or relations. **just the job** Brit. informal exactly what is needed. **on the job 1** while working; at work. **2** Brit. informal engaged in sexual intercourse.

– ORIGIN of unknown origin.

jobber • **noun 1** (in the UK) a principal or wholesaler dealing only on the Stock Exchange with brokers, not directly with the public (term officially replaced by **broker-dealer** in 1986). **2** N. Amer. a wholesaler. **3** a person who does casual or occasional work.

jobbery • **noun** the practice of using a public office or position of trust for one's own gain or advantage.

jobcentre • **noun** (in the UK) a government office in a local area, giving information about available jobs and administering benefits to unemployed people.

jobless • **adjective** without a paid job; unemployed.

– DERIVATIVES **joblessness** noun.

job lot • **noun** a batch of articles sold or bought at one time, especially at a discount.

Job's comforter /jōbz/ • **noun** a person who aggravates someone's distress while appearing to offer them comfort.

– ORIGIN alluding to the biblical story of the patriarch *Job.*

job-share • **verb** (of two part-time employees) share a single full-time job. • **noun** an arrangement of such a kind.

– DERIVATIVES **job-sharer** noun.

jobsworth • **noun** Brit. informal an official who mindlessly upholds petty rules.

– ORIGIN from 'it's more than my *job's worth* (not) to...'.

Jock • **noun** informal, often offensive a Scotsman.

– ORIGIN Scottish form of the given name *Jack.*

jock[1] • **noun** informal **1** a disc jockey. **2** N. Amer. an enthusiast or participant in a specified activity: *a computer jock.*

jock[2] • **noun** N. Amer. informal **1** a jockstrap. **2** an enthusiastic male athlete or sports fan.

– DERIVATIVES **jockish** adjective.

jockey • **noun** (pl. **jockeys**) a professional rider in horse races. • **verb** (**jockeys**, **jockeyed**) **1** struggle to gain or achieve something. **2** handle or manipulate in a skilful manner.

– ORIGIN from JOCK, originally denoting an ordinary man, later 'mounted courier' and 'horse dealer'.

jockey cap • **noun** a strengthened cap with a long peak of a kind worn by jockeys.

jockstrap • **noun** a support or protection for the male genitals, worn especially by sportsmen.

– ORIGIN from slang *jock* 'genitals'.

jocose /jəkōss/ • **adjective** formal playful or humorous.

– DERIVATIVES **jocosely** adverb **jocoseness** noun **jocosity** /jəkossiti/ noun (pl. **jocosities**).

– ORIGIN Latin *jocosus*, from *jocus* 'jest, joke'.

jocular /jokyoolər/ • **adjective** fond of or characterized by jok-

Thesaurus

with; *informal* chuck, ditch, dump, drop, run out on, give someone the push/elbow, give someone the old heave-ho, give someone the big E; *poetic/literary* forsake.

jingle • **noun 1** *the jingle of money in the till* CLINK, chink, tinkle, jangle. **2** *the jingle of the bell* TINKLE, ring, ding, ping, ting-a-ling, chime, tintinnabulation. **3** *advertising jingles* SLOGAN, catchphrase; ditty, song, rhyme, tune; *N. Amer. informal* tag line.

• **verb 1** *her bracelets jingled noisily* CLINK, chink, tinkle, jangle. **2** *the bell jingled* TINKLE, ring, ding, ping, chime.

jingoism • **noun** EXTREME PATRIOTISM, chauvinism, extreme nationalism, xenophobia; hawkishness, militarism, belligerence, bellicosity.

jinx • **noun** *the jinx struck six days later* CURSE, spell, hoodoo, malediction; the evil eye, black magic, voodoo, bad luck; *N. Amer.* hex; *archaic* malison.

• **verb** *the family is jinxed* CURSE, cast a spell on, put the evil eye on, hoodoo; *Austral.* point the bone at; *N. Amer.* hex; *Austral. informal* mozz, put the mozz on.

jitters • **plural noun** *(informal)* NERVOUSNESS, nerves, edginess, uneasiness, anxiety, anxiousness, tension, agitation, restlessness; stage fright; *informal* butterflies (in one's stomach), the willies, collywobbles, the heebie-jeebies, jitteriness, the jim-jams.

jittery • **adjective** *(informal)* NERVOUS, on edge, edgy, tense, anxious, ill at ease, uneasy, keyed up, overwrought, jumpy, on tenterhooks, worried, apprehensive; *Brit.* nervy; *informal* with butterflies in one's stomach, like a cat on a hot tin roof, twitchy, uptight, het up, in a tizz/tizzy; *Brit. informal* strung up, like a cat on hot bricks; *N. Amer. informal* spooky, squirrelly, antsy; *Austral./NZ informal* toey; *dated* overstrung.

– OPPOSITES calm.

job • **noun 1** *my job involves a lot of travelling* POSITION (OF EMPLOYMENT), post, situation, appointment; occupation, profession, trade, career, (line of) work, métier, craft; vocation, calling; vacancy, opening; *Austral. informal* grip; *archaic* employ. **2** *this job will take three months* TASK, piece of work, assignment, project; chore, errand; undertaking, venture, operation, enterprise, business. **3** *it's your job to protect her* RESPONSIBILITY, duty, charge, task; role, function, mission; *informal* department, pigeon. **4** *(informal) it was a job to get here on time* DIFFICULT TASK, problem, trouble, struggle, strain, trial, bother; *informal* headache, hassle, pain. **5** *(informal) a bank job* CRIME, felony; raid, robbery, hold-up, burglary, break-in; *informal* stick-up; *N. Amer. informal* heist.

– RELATED TERMS vocational.

– PHRASES **just the job** *(Brit. informal)* THE VERY THING, just the thing, exactly what's needed; *informal* just what the doctor ordered, just the ticket.

jobless • **adjective** UNEMPLOYED, out of work, out of a job, unwaged, between jobs, redundant, laid off; *Brit. informal* signing on, on the dole, 'resting'; *Austral./NZ informal* on the wallaby track.

– OPPOSITES employed.

jockey • **noun** RIDER, horseman, horsewoman, equestrian; *Austral. informal* hoop.

• **verb 1** *he jockeyed himself into the team* MANOEUVRE, ease, edge, work, steer; inveigle, insinuate, ingratiate; *informal* finagle. **2** *min-*

j

ing; humorous.
– DERIVATIVES **jocularity** noun **jocularly** adverb.
– ORIGIN Latin *jocularis*, from *jocus* 'jest, joke'.
jocund /jokkənd/ ● adjective formal cheerful and light-hearted.
– DERIVATIVES **jocundity** noun (pl. **jocundities**) **jocundly** adverb.
– ORIGIN Latin *jocundus*, from *jucundus* 'pleasant, agreeable'.
jodhpurs /jodpərz/ ● plural noun trousers worn for horse riding that are close-fitting below the knee and have reinforced patches on the inside of the leg.
– ORIGIN named after the Indian city of *Jodhpur*.
joe ● noun informal **1** an ordinary man. **2** N. Amer. coffee.
– ORIGIN sense 1 is a familiar form of the given name *Joseph*; sense 2 is of unknown origin.
joey ● noun (pl. **joeys**) Austral. **1** a young kangaroo, wallaby, or possum. **2** informal a baby or young child.
– ORIGIN Aboriginal.
jog ● verb (**jogged**, **jogging**) **1** run at a steady, gentle pace, especially as a form of exercise. **2** (of a horse) move at a slow trot. **3** (**jog along/on**) continue in a steady, uneventful way. **4** nudge or knock slightly. **5** trigger; stimulate. ● noun **1** a spell of jogging. **2** a gentle running pace. **3** a slight push or nudge.
– ORIGIN originally in the sense 'stab, pierce': from JAG[1].
jogger ● noun **1** a person who jogs. **2** (**joggers**) tracksuit trousers worn for jogging.
joggle ● verb move with repeated small bobs or jerks. ● noun a joggling movement.
– ORIGIN from JOG.
jogtrot ● noun a slow trot.
john ● noun informal **1** chiefly N. Amer. a toilet. **2** a prostitute's client.
– ORIGIN from the given name *John*.
John Bull ● noun a personification of England or the typical Englishman.
– ORIGIN from a character in John Arbuthnot's satire *Law is a Bottomless Pit; or, the History of John Bull* (1712).
John Doe ● noun **1** Law, chiefly N. Amer. an anonymous party in a legal action. **2** N. Amer. informal a name used to represent a person in a hypothetical situation.
– ORIGIN originally in legal use as a name of a fictitious plaintiff, corresponding to *Richard Roe*, a fictitious defendant.
John Dory ● noun (pl. **Dories**) an edible dory (fish) of the eastern Atlantic and Mediterranean, with a black oval mark on each side.
johnny ● noun (pl. **johnnies**) Brit. informal **1** a man. **2** a condom.
– ORIGIN familiar form of the given name *John*.
johnny-come-lately ● noun informal a newcomer or late starter.
joie de vivre /zhwaa də veevrə/ ● noun exuberant enjoyment of life.
– ORIGIN French.
join ● verb **1** link or become linked or connected to. **2** unite to form a whole. **3** become a member or employee of. **4** (**join up**) become a member of the armed forces. **5** take part in (an activity). **6** come into the company of. ● noun a place where two or more things are joined.
– PHRASES **join battle** formal begin fighting. **join forces** combine efforts.
– DERIVATIVES **joinable** adjective.
– ORIGIN Old French *joindre*, from Latin *jungere* 'to join'.
joiner ● noun **1** a person who constructs the wooden components of a building. **2** informal a person who readily joins groups.
joinery ● noun **1** the wooden components of a building collectively. **2** the work of a joiner.
joint ● noun **1** a point at which parts are joined. **2** a structure in a body by which two bones are fitted together. **3** the part of a plant stem from which a leaf or branch grows. **4** Brit. a large piece of meat. **5** informal an establishment of a specified kind: *a burger joint*. **6** informal a cannabis cigarette. ● adjective **1** shared, held, or made by two or more people. **2** sharing in an achievement or activity. ● verb **1** provide or fasten with joints. **2** prepare (a board) to be joined to another by planing its edge. **3** point (masonry or brickwork). **4** cut (the body of an animal) into joints.
– PHRASES **out of joint 1** (of a joint of the body) dislocated. **2** in a state of disorder.
– DERIVATIVES **jointless** adjective **jointly** adverb.
– ORIGIN from Old French *joindre* 'to join'.
joint and several ● adjective (of a legal obligation) undertaken by two or more people, each having liability for the whole.
jointer ● noun **1** a plane for preparing a wooden edge for joining to another. **2** a tool for pointing masonry and brickwork. **3** a person who joints pipes or wires.
jointure /joynchər/ ● noun Law an estate settled on a wife for the period during which she survives her husband.
– ORIGIN originally denoting the joint holding of property: from Old French, from Latin *junctura* 'juncture'.
joist /joyst/ ● noun a length of timber or steel supporting part of the structure of a building.
– DERIVATIVES **joisted** adjective.
– ORIGIN Old French *giste* 'beam supporting a bridge', from Latin *jacere* 'lie down'.
jojoba /həhōbə/ ● noun an oil extracted from the seeds of a North American shrub, widely used in cosmetics.
– ORIGIN Mexican Spanish.
joke ● noun **1** a statement made or short story told in order to cause amusement. **2** a trick played for fun. **3** informal a ridiculously inadequate or inappropriate thing. ● verb make jokes.
– DERIVATIVES **jokey** (also **joky**) adjective.
– ORIGIN perhaps from Latin *jocus* 'jest, wordplay'.
joker ● noun **1** a person who is fond of joking. **2** informal a foolish or inept person. **3** a playing card with the figure of a jester, used as a wild card. **4** US a clause in a bill or document affecting its operation in a way not immediately apparent.
– PHRASES **the joker in the pack** an unpredictable person or factor.
jolie laide /zhollee led/ ● noun (pl. **jolies laides** pronunc. same) a woman who is attractive despite having ugly features.
– ORIGIN French, from *jolie* 'pretty' and *laide* 'ugly'.

j

Thesaurus

isters began jockeying for position COMPETE, contend, vie; struggle, fight, scramble, jostle.
jocular ● adjective HUMOROUS, funny, witty, comic, comical, amusing, droll, jokey, hilarious, facetious, tongue-in-cheek, teasing, playful; light-hearted, jovial, cheerful, cheery, merry; *formal* jocose, ludic.
– OPPOSITES solemn.
jocund ● adjective *(formal)*. See CHEERFUL sense 1.
jog ● verb **1** *he jogged along the road* RUN SLOWLY, jogtrot, dogtrot, trot, lope. **2** *things are jogging along quite nicely* CONTINUE, proceed, go on, carry on. **3** *a hand jogged his elbow* NUDGE, prod, poke, push, bump, jar. **4** *something jogged her memory* STIMULATE, prompt, stir, activate, refresh. **5** *she jogged her foot up and down* JOGGLE, jiggle, bob, bounce, jolt, jerk.
● noun *he set off along at a jog* RUN, jogtrot, dogtrot, trot, lope.
joie de vivre ● noun GAIETY, cheerfulness, cheeriness, light-heartedness, happiness, joy, joyfulness, high spirits, jollity, joviality, exuberance, ebullience, liveliness, vivacity, verve, effervescence, buoyancy, zest, zestfulness; *informal* pep, zing; *poetic/literary* blitheness.
– OPPOSITES sobriety.
joint ● noun **1** *a leaky joint in the guttering* JOIN, junction, juncture, intersection, link, linkage, connection; weld, seam; *Anatomy* commissure. **2** *the hip joint* ball-and-socket joint, hinge joint, articulation. **3** *(informal) a classy joint* ESTABLISHMENT, restaurant, bar, club, nightclub. **4** *(informal) he rolled a joint* CANNABIS CIGARETTE, marijuana cigarette; *informal* spliff, reefer, bomb, bomber, stick.
● adjective *matters of joint interest | a joint effort* COMMON, shared, communal, collective; mutual, cooperative, collaborative, concerted, combined, united.
– OPPOSITES separate.
● verb *she jointed the carcass* CUT UP, chop up, butcher, carve.
jointly ● adverb TOGETHER, in partnership, in cooperation, cooperatively, in conjunction, in combination, mutually.
joke ● noun **1** *they were telling jokes* FUNNY STORY, jest, witticism, quip; pun, play on words; *informal* gag, wisecrack, crack, funny, one-liner, killer, rib-tickler, knee-slapper, thigh-slapper; *N. Amer. informal* boffola; *rare* blague. **2** *playing stupid jokes* TRICK, practical joke, prank, stunt, hoax, jape; *informal* leg-pull, spoof. **3** *(informal) he soon became a joke to us* LAUGHING STOCK, figure of fun, object of ridicule; *Brit.* Aunt Sally. **4** *(informal) the present system is a joke* FARCE, travesty, waste of time; *N. Amer. informal* shuck.
● verb **1** *she joked with the guests* TELL JOKES, jest, banter, quip; *informal* wisecrack, josh. **2** *I'm only joking* FOOL (ABOUT/AROUND), play a trick, play a (practical) joke, tease, hoax, pull someone's leg, mess about/around; *informal* kid; *Brit. informal* have someone on, wind someone up; *N. Amer. informal* fun, shuck, pull someone's chain.
joker ● noun HUMORIST, comedian, comedienne, comic, wit, jester;

jollification ● noun merrymaking.
jollity ● noun **1** lively and cheerful activity. **2** the quality of being jolly.
jolly[1] ● adjective (**jollier, jolliest**) **1** happy and cheerful. **2** lively and entertaining. ● verb (**jollies, jollied**) informal encourage in a friendly way: *he jollied her along*. ● adverb Brit. informal very. ● noun (pl. **jollies**) Brit. informal a party or celebration.
– DERIVATIVES **jollily** adverb **jolliness** noun.
– ORIGIN Old French *jolif* 'pretty', perhaps from an Old Norse word meaning 'Yule'.
jolly[2] (also **jolly boat**) ● noun (pl. **jollies**) a clinker-built ship's boat that is smaller than a cutter.
– ORIGIN perhaps related to YAWL.
Jolly Roger ● noun a pirate's flag with a white skull and crossbones on a black background.
– ORIGIN of unknown origin.
jolt ● verb **1** push or shake abruptly and roughly. **2** shock (someone) into taking action. ● noun **1** an act of jolting. **2** a surprise or shock.
– ORIGIN of unknown origin.
jonquil /jongkwil/ ● noun a narcissus with small fragrant yellow flowers and cylindrical leaves.
– ORIGIN Spanish *junquillo*, from Latin *juncus* 'rush, reed'.
Jordanian ● noun a person from Jordan. ● adjective relating to Jordan.
josh informal ● verb tease playfully; banter. ● noun N. Amer. good-natured banter.
– DERIVATIVES **josher** noun.
– ORIGIN of unknown origin.
Joshua tree ● noun a tall branching yucca of SW North America, with clusters of spiky leaves.
– ORIGIN apparently from *Joshua* in the Bible, the plant being likened to a man with a spear.
joss stick ● noun a thin stick of a fragrant substance, burnt as incense.
– ORIGIN from *joss*, denoting a Chinese religious statue or idol: from a Javanese word derived from Latin *deus* 'god'.
jostle ● verb **1** push or bump against roughly. **2** (**jostle for**) struggle or compete forcefully for. ● noun the action of jostling.
– ORIGIN from JOUST.
jot ● verb (**jotted, jotting**) write quickly. ● noun a very small amount: *it made not a jot of difference*.
– ORIGIN from Greek *iōta*, the smallest letter of the Greek alphabet (see IOTA).
jotter ● noun Brit. a small notebook.
jotting ● noun a brief note.

joule /jo͞ol/ ● noun the unit of work or energy in the SI system, equal to the work done by a force of one newton when its point of application moves one metre in the direction of action of the force.
– ORIGIN named after the English physicist James P. *Joule* (1818–89).
jounce /jownss/ ● verb jolt or bounce.
– ORIGIN probably symbolic.
journal ● noun **1** a newspaper or magazine dealing with a particular subject. **2** a diary or daily record. **3** the part of a shaft or axle that rests on bearings.
– ORIGIN Old French *jurnal*, from Latin *diurnus* 'daily'.
journalese ● noun informal a hackneyed writing style supposedly characteristic of journalists.
journalism ● noun the activity or profession of being a journalist.
journalist ● noun a person who writes for newspapers or magazines or prepares news or features to be broadcast on radio or television.
– DERIVATIVES **journalistic** adjective.
journey ● noun (pl. **journeys**) an act of travelling from one place to another. ● verb (**journeys, journeyed**) travel.
– DERIVATIVES **journeyer** noun.
– ORIGIN Old French *jornee* 'day, a day's travel, a day's work', from Latin *diurnus* 'daily'.
journeyman ● noun **1** a skilled worker who is employed by another. **2** a worker who is reliable but not outstanding.
– ORIGIN from JOURNEY in the obsolete sense 'day's work' (because the journeyman was paid by the day).
journo ● noun (pl. **journos**) informal a journalist.
joust /jowst/ ● verb **1** (of a medieval knight) engage in a contest in which two opponents on horseback fight with lances. **2** compete for superiority. ● noun a jousting contest.
– DERIVATIVES **jouster** noun.
– ORIGIN Old French *jouster* 'bring together', from Latin *juxta* 'near'.
Jove /jōv/ ● noun (in phrase **by Jove**) dated used for emphasis or to indicate surprise.
– ORIGIN another name for the Roman god Jupiter.
jovial /jōviəl/ ● adjective cheerful and friendly.
– DERIVATIVES **joviality** noun **jovially** adverb.
– ORIGIN Latin *jovialis* 'of Jupiter', with reference to the supposed influence of the planet Jupiter on those born under it.
Jovian /jōviən/ ● adjective **1** (in Roman mythology) of or like the god Jove (Jupiter). **2** relating to the planet Jupiter.
jowl ● noun **1** the lower part of a cheek, especially when fleshy

Thesaurus

prankster, practical joker, hoaxer, trickster, clown; *informal* card, wisecracker, wag.
jolly ● adjective CHEERFUL, happy, cheery, good-humoured, jovial, merry, sunny, joyful, joyous, light-hearted, in high spirits, bubbly, exuberant, ebullient, cock-a-hoop, gleeful, mirthful, genial, fun-loving; *informal* chipper, chirpy, perky, bright-eyed and bushy-tailed; *formal* jocund, jocose; *dated* gay; *poetic/literary* gladsome, blithe, blithesome.
– OPPOSITES miserable.
● verb (*informal*) *he tried to jolly her along* ENCOURAGE, urge, coax, cajole, persuade.
● adverb (*Brit. informal*) *a jolly good idea*. See VERY adverb.
jolt ● verb **1** *the train jolted the passengers to one side* PUSH, thrust, jar, bump, knock, bang; shake, joggle, jog. **2** *the car jolted along* BUMP, bounce, jerk, rattle, lurch, shudder, judder, jounce. **3** *she was jolted out of her reverie* STARTLE, surprise, shock, stun, shake, take aback; astonish, astound, amaze, stagger, stop someone in their tracks; *informal* rock, floor, knock sideways; *Brit. informal* knock for six.
● noun **1** *a series of sickening jolts* BUMP, bounce, shake, jerk, lurch. **2** *he woke up with a jolt* START, jerk, jump. **3** *the sight of the dagger gave him a jolt* FRIGHT, the fright of one's life, shock, scare, surprise; *informal* turn.
jostle ● verb **1** *she was jostled by noisy students* BUMP INTO/AGAINST, knock into/against, bang into, cannon into, plough into, jolt; push, shove, elbow; mob. **2** *I jostled my way to the exit* PUSH, thrust, barge, shove, force, elbow, shoulder, bulldoze. **3** *people jostled for the best position* STRUGGLE, vie, jockey, scramble.
jot ● verb *I've jotted down a few details* WRITE, note, make a note of, take down, put on paper; scribble, scrawl.
● noun *not a jot of evidence* IOTA, scrap, shred, whit, grain, crumb, ounce, (little) bit, jot or tittle, speck, atom, particle, scintilla, trace, hint; *informal* smidgen, tad; *Austral./NZ informal* skerrick; *archaic* scruple.
journal ● noun **1** *a medical journal* PERIODICAL, magazine, gazette, digest, review, newsletter, news-sheet, bulletin; newspaper, paper; daily, weekly, monthly, quarterly. **2** *he keeps a journal* DIARY, daily record, log, logbook, chronicle; *N. Amer.* daybook.
journalism ● noun **1** *a career in journalism* THE NEWSPAPER BUSINESS, the press, the fourth estate; *Brit.* Fleet Street. **2** *his incisive style of journalism* REPORTING, writing, reportage, feature writing, news coverage; articles, reports, features, pieces, stories.
journalist ● noun REPORTER, correspondent, newspaperman, newspaperwoman, newsman, newswoman, columnist, writer, commentator, reviewer; investigative journalist; *Brit.* pressman; *N. Amer.* legman, wireman; *Austral.* roundsman; *informal* news hound, hack, hackette, stringer, journo; *N. Amer. informal* newsy.
journey ● noun *his journey round the world* TRIP, expedition, tour, trek, voyage, cruise, ride, drive; crossing, passage, flight; travels, wandering, globetrotting; odyssey, pilgrimage; *archaic* peregrination.
● verb *they journeyed south* TRAVEL, go, voyage, sail, cruise, fly, hike, trek, ride, drive, make one's way; go on a trip/expedition, tour; *archaic* peregrinate.
joust (*historical*) ● verb *knights jousted with lances* TOURNEY; fight, spar, clash; *historical* tilt.
● noun *a medieval joust* TOURNAMENT, tourney; combat, contest, fight; *historical* tilt.
jovial ● adjective CHEERFUL, jolly, happy, cheery, good-humoured, convivial, genial, good-natured, friendly, amiable, affable, sociable, outgoing; smiling, merry, sunny, joyful, joyous, high-spirited, exuberant; *informal* chipper, chirpy, perky, bright-eyed

or drooping. **2** N. Amer. the cheek of a pig as meat. **3** the dewlap of cattle or wattle of birds.
– DERIVATIVES **jowled** adjective **jowly** adjective.
– ORIGIN Old English, related to JAW.

joy • noun **1** a feeling of great pleasure and happiness. **2** a cause of joy. **3** Brit. informal success or satisfaction: *you'll get no joy out of her.*
– DERIVATIVES **joyless** adjective.
– ORIGIN Old French *joie*, from Latin *gaudere* 'rejoice'.

joyful • adjective feeling or causing joy.
– DERIVATIVES **joyfully** adverb **joyfulness** noun.

joyous • adjective chiefly literary full of happiness and joy.
– DERIVATIVES **joyously** adverb **joyousness** noun.

joypad • noun a device for a computer games console which uses buttons to control an image on the screen.

joyride • noun informal **1** a fast ride in a stolen vehicle. **2** a ride for enjoyment.
– DERIVATIVES **joyrider** noun **joyriding** noun.

joystick • noun informal **1** the control column of an aircraft. **2** a lever for controlling the movement of an image on a computer screen.

JP • abbreviation Justice of the Peace.

jubilant • adjective happy and triumphant.
– DERIVATIVES **jubilance** noun **jubilantly** adverb.

jubilation /jo͞obilaysh'n/ • noun a feeling of great happiness and triumph.
– ORIGIN from Latin *jubilare* 'shout for joy'.

jubilee • noun **1** a special anniversary, especially one celebrating twenty-five or fifty years of something. **2** Jewish History a year of emancipation and restoration, kept every fifty years.
– ORIGIN from Latin *jubilaeus annus* 'year of jubilee', from a Hebrew word meaning 'ram's-horn trumpet', with which the jubilee year was proclaimed.

Judaean /jo͞odeeən/ • noun a person from Judaea, the southern part of ancient Palestine. • adjective relating to Judaea.

Judaeo- /jo͞odeeō/ (US **Judeo-**) • combining form **1** Jewish; Jewish and ...: *Judaeo-Christian.* **2** relating to Judaea.
– ORIGIN from Latin *Judaeus* 'Jewish'.

Judaic /jo͞odayik/ • adjective relating to Judaism or the ancient Jews.

Judaism /jo͞odayiz'm/ • noun **1** the monotheistic religion of the Jews, based on the Old Testament and the Talmud. **2** Jews collectively.
– DERIVATIVES **Judaist** noun.
– ORIGIN Greek *Ioudaïsmos*, from the Hebrew form of the name 'Judah'.

Judaize /jo͞oday-īz/ (also **Judaise**) • verb **1** make Jewish. **2** follow Jewish customs or religious rites.
– DERIVATIVES **Judaization** noun.

Judas /jo͞odəss/ • noun a person who betrays a friend.
– ORIGIN from *Judas* Iscariot, the disciple who betrayed Christ.

judas (also **judas hole**) • noun a peephole in a door.
– ORIGIN from *Judas* Iscariot (see JUDAS), because of his association with betrayal.

Judas tree • noun a Mediterranean tree with purple flowers that appear before the rounded leaves.
– ORIGIN from a popular notion that Judas Iscariot hanged himself from a tree of this kind.

judder • verb chiefly Brit. shake and vibrate rapidly and forcefully. • noun an instance of juddering.
– DERIVATIVES **juddery** adjective.
– ORIGIN imitative.

Judeo- • combining form US spelling of JUDAEO-.

judge • noun **1** a public officer appointed to decide cases in a law court. **2** a person who decides the results of a competition. **3** a person able or qualified to give an opinion. • verb **1** form an opinion about. **2** give a verdict on in a law court. **3** decide the results of (a competition).
– ORIGIN Old French *juge*, from Latin *judex*, from *jus* 'law' + *dicere* 'to say'.

judgement (also **judgment**) • noun **1** the ability to make considered decisions or form sensible opinions. **2** an opinion or conclusion. **3** a decision of a law court or judge.
– PHRASES **against one's better judgement** contrary to what one feels to be wise.

judgemental (also **judgmental**) • adjective **1** of or concerning the use of judgement. **2** having an excessively critical point of view.
– DERIVATIVES **judgementally** adverb.

Judgement Day • noun the time of the Last Judgement.

judicature /jo͞odikkəchər, jo͞o**dikk**əchər/ • noun **1** the administration of justice. **2** (**the judicature**) judges collectively.

j

Thesaurus

and bushy-tailed; *formal* jocund, jocose; *dated* gay; *poetic/literary* gladsome, blithe, blithesome.
– OPPOSITES miserable.

joy • noun **1** *whoops of joy* DELIGHT, great pleasure, joyfulness, jubilation, triumph, exultation, rejoicing, happiness, gladness, glee, exhilaration, exuberance, elation, euphoria, bliss, ecstasy, rapture; enjoyment, felicity, joie de vivre; *formal* jocundity, jouissance. **2** *it was a joy to be with her* (SOURCE OF) PLEASURE, delight, treat, thrill; *informal* buzz, kick. **3** *(Brit. informal) we still had no joy* SUCCESS, satisfaction, luck, successful result.
– OPPOSITES misery, trial.

joyful • adjective **1** *his joyful mood* CHEERFUL, happy, jolly, merry, sunny, joyous, light-hearted, in good spirits, bubbly, exuberant, ebullient, cock-a-hoop, cheery, smiling, mirthful, radiant; jubilant, overjoyed, thrilled, ecstatic, euphoric, blissful, on cloud nine/seven, elated, delighted, gleeful; jovial, genial, good-humoured, full of the joys of spring; *informal* chipper, chirpy, peppy, over the moon, on top of the world; *Austral./NZ informal* wrapped; *dated* gay; *formal* jocund; *poetic/literary* gladsome, blithe, blithesome. **2** *joyful news* PLEASING, happy, good, cheering, gladdening, welcome, heart-warming; *poetic/literary* gladsome. **3** *a joyful occasion* HAPPY, cheerful, merry, jolly, festive, joyous.
– OPPOSITES sad, distressing.

joyless • adjective **1** *a joyless man* GLOOMY, melancholy, morose, lugubrious, glum, sombre, saturnine, sullen, dour, humourless. **2** *a joyless room* DEPRESSING, cheerless, gloomy, dreary, bleak, dispiriting, drab, dismal, desolate, austere, sombre; unwelcoming, uninviting, inhospitable; *poetic/literary* drear.
– OPPOSITES cheerful, welcoming.

joyous • adjective. See JOYFUL senses 1, 3.

jubilant • adjective OVERJOYED, exultant, triumphant, joyful, rejoicing, cock-a-hoop, exuberant, elated, thrilled, gleeful, euphoric, ecstatic, enraptured, in raptures, walking on air, in seventh heaven, on cloud nine; *informal* over the moon, on top of the world, on a high; *N. Amer. informal* wigged out; *Austral. informal* wrapped.
– OPPOSITES despondent.

jubilation • noun EXULTATION, joy, joyousness, elation, euphoria, ecstasy, rapture, glee, gleefulness, exuberance.

jubilee • noun ANNIVERSARY, commemoration; celebration, festival, jamboree; festivities, revelry.

Judas • noun TRAITOR, betrayer, back-stabber, double-crosser; turncoat, quisling, renegade.

judge • noun **1** *the judge sentenced him to five years* JUSTICE, magistrate, recorder, sheriff; *N. Amer.* jurist; *Brit. informal* beak. **2** *a panel of judges will select the winner* ADJUDICATOR, arbiter, assessor, evaluator, appraiser, examiner, moderator, mediator.
• verb **1** *I judged that she was simply exhausted* FORM THE OPINION, conclude, decide; consider, believe, think, deem, view; deduce, gather, infer, gauge, estimate, guess, surmise, conjecture; regard as, look on as, take to be, rate as, class as; *informal* reckon, figure. **2** *the case was judged by a tribunal* TRY, hear; adjudicate, decide, give a ruling/verdict on. **3** *she was judged innocent of murder* ADJUDGE, pronounce, decree, rule, find. **4** *the competition will be judged by Alan Amey* ADJUDICATE, arbitrate, mediate, moderate. **5** *entries were judged by a panel of experts* ASSESS, appraise, evaluate; examine, review.

judgement • noun **1** *his temper could affect his judgement* DISCERNMENT, acumen, shrewdness, astuteness, (common) sense, perception, perspicacity, percipience, acuity, discrimination, wisdom, wit, judiciousness, prudence, canniness, sharpness, sharp-wittedness, powers of reasoning, reason, logic; *informal* nous, savvy, horse sense, gumption; *Brit. informal* common; *N. Amer. informal* smarts. **2** *a court judgement* VERDICT, decision, adjudication, ruling, pronouncement, decree, finding; sentence. **3** *critical judgement* ASSESSMENT, evaluation, appraisal; review, analysis, criticism, critique. **4** *a judgement on them for their wickedness* PUNISHMENT, retribution, penalty.
– PHRASES **against one's better judgement** RELUCTANTLY, unwillingly, grudgingly. **in my judgement** IN MY OPINION, to my mind, to my way of thinking, I believe, I think, as I see it, in my estimation.

judgemental • adjective CRITICAL, censorious, condemnatory, dis-

– DERIVATIVES **judicatory** adjective.
– ORIGIN from Latin *judicare* 'to judge'.
judicial /joodish'l/ ● **adjective** of, by, or appropriate to a law court or judge.
– DERIVATIVES **judicially** adverb
– ORIGIN from Latin *judicium* 'judgement'.
judicial review ● **noun 1** (in the UK) a procedure by which a court can pronounce on an administrative action by a public body. **2** (in the US) review by the Supreme Court of the constitutional validity of a legislative act.
judiciary /joodishəri/ ● **noun** (pl. **judiciaries**) (usu. **the judiciary**) the judicial authorities of a country.
judicious /joodishəss/ ● **adjective** having or done with good judgement.
– DERIVATIVES **judiciously** adverb **judiciousness** noun.
judo ● **noun** a sport of unarmed combat derived from ju-jitsu, using holds and leverage to unbalance the opponent.
– ORIGIN Japanese, 'gentle way'.
jug ● **noun 1** Brit. a cylindrical container with a handle and a lip, for holding and pouring liquids. **2** N. Amer. a large container for liquids, with a narrow mouth. **3** (**the jug**) informal prison. **4** (**jugs**) vulgar slang a woman's breasts. ● **verb** (**jugged, jugging**) (usu. as adj. **jugged**) stew or boil (a hare or rabbit) in a covered container.
– ORIGIN perhaps from *Jug*, familiar form of the given names *Joan*, *Joanna*, and *Jenny*.
jug band ● **noun** a group of jazz, blues, or folk musicians using simple or improvised instruments such as jugs and washboards.
juggernaut /juggərnawt/ ● **noun** Brit. a large heavy vehicle, especially an articulated truck.
– ORIGIN from a Sanskrit word meaning 'Lord of the world', in reference to an image of the Hindu god Krishna carried in procession on a heavy chariot.
juggle ● **verb 1** continuously toss into the air and catch a number of objects so as to keep at least one in the air at any time. **2** cope with by adroitly balancing (several activities). **3** misrepresent (facts). ● **noun** an act of juggling.
– DERIVATIVES **juggler** noun **jugglery** noun.
– ORIGIN Old French *jogler*, from Latin *joculari* 'to jest'.
Jugoslav ● **noun & adjective** old-fashioned spelling of YUGOSLAV.
jugular /jugyoolər/ ● **adjective** of the neck or throat. ● **noun** a jugular vein.
– ORIGIN from Latin *jugulum* 'collarbone, throat', from *jugum* 'yoke'.
jugular vein ● **noun** any of several large veins in the neck, carrying blood from the head.
juice ● **noun 1** the liquid present in fruit or vegetables. **2** a drink made from this liquid. **3** (**juices**) fluid secreted by the stomach. **4** (**juices**) liquid coming from meat or other food in cooking. **5** informal electrical energy. **6** informal petrol. **7** (**juices**) informal one's vitality or creative faculties. **8** N. Amer. informal alcoholic drink. ● **verb 1** extract the juice from. **2** (**juice up**) informal, chiefly N. Amer. enliven. **3** (**juiced**) N. Amer. informal drunk.
– ORIGIN Latin *jus* 'broth, vegetable juice'.
juicer ● **noun** an appliance for extracting juice from fruit and vegetables.
juicy ● **adjective** (**juicier, juiciest**) **1** full of juice. **2** informal interestingly scandalous. **3** informal profitable.
– DERIVATIVES **juicily** adverb **juiciness** noun.
ju-jitsu /joojitsoo/ (also **jiu-jitsu** or **ju-jutsu** /joojutsoo/) ● **noun** a Japanese system of unarmed combat and physical training.
– ORIGIN Japanese, 'gentle skill'.
juju[1] /joojoo/ ● **noun** a style of Nigerian music characterized by the use of guitars and variable-pitch drums.
– ORIGIN perhaps from a Yoruba word meaning 'dance'.
juju[2] /joojoo/ ● **noun 1** a charm or fetish, especially as used by some West African peoples. **2** supernatural power attributed to such a charm or fetish.
– ORIGIN West African, perhaps from French *joujou* 'toy'.
jujube /joojoob/ ● **noun 1** an edible berry-like fruit of a shrub, formerly taken as a cough cure. **2** chiefly N. Amer. a jujube-flavoured lozenge or sweet.
– ORIGIN Latin *jujuba*, from Greek *zizuphos*.
juke N. Amer. informal ● **noun** (also **juke joint**) a roadhouse, nightclub, or bar providing food, drinks, and music for dancing. ● **verb 1** dance. **2** (in sport) make a sham move to confuse or mislead an opponent. **3** move in a zigzag fashion.
– ORIGIN from Gullah, 'disorderly'.
jukebox ● **noun** a machine that plays a selected musical recording when a coin is inserted.
Jul. ● **abbreviation** July.
julep /joolep/ ● **noun** a sweet drink made from sugar syrup.
– ORIGIN Latin *julapium*, from Persian, 'rose water'.
Julian calendar ● **noun** a calendar introduced by the Roman general Julius Caesar (100–44 BC), in which the year consisted of 365 days, every fourth year having 366 (replaced by the Gregorian calendar).
julienne /joolien/ ● **noun** a portion of food cut into short, thin strips.
– ORIGIN French, from the male given names *Jules* or *Julien*.
July ● **noun** (pl. **Julys**) the seventh month of the year.
– ORIGIN from Latin *Julius mensis* 'month of July', named after the Roman general Julius Caesar.
jumble ● **noun 1** an untidy collection of things. **2** Brit. articles collected for a jumble sale. ● **verb** mix up in a confused way.
– ORIGIN probably symbolic.
jumble sale ● **noun** Brit. a sale of miscellaneous second-hand goods, typically for charity.
jumbo informal ● **noun** (pl. **jumbos**) **1** a very large person or thing. **2** a jumbo jet. ● **adjective** very large.
– ORIGIN probably the second element of MUMBO-JUMBO.
jumbo jet ● **noun** a very large airliner carrying several hundred passengers.
jumbuck /jumbuk/ ● **noun** Austral. informal a sheep.
– ORIGIN perhaps Australian pidgin for *jump up*.
jump ● **verb 1** push oneself off the ground using the muscles in one's legs and feet. **2** move over, onto, or down from by jumping. **3** move suddenly and quickly. **4** make a sudden involuntary movement in surprise. **5** (**jump at/on**) accept eagerly. **6** (often **jump on**) informal attack or criticize suddenly. **7** pass abruptly from one subject or state to another. **8** rise or increase suddenly. **9** (**be jumping**) informal (of a place) be very lively. **10** vulgar slang, chiefly N. Amer. have sexual intercourse with. ● **noun 1** an act of jumping. **2** a large or sudden change or increase. **3** an obstacle to be jumped by a horse.
– PHRASES **get** (or **have**) **the jump on** informal, chiefly N. Amer. get (or have) an advantage over (someone) due to prompt action. **jump down someone's throat** informal respond in a sudden and angry way. **jump out of one's skin** informal be startled. **jump the queue** (or N. Amer. **jump in line**) **1** move ahead of one's proper place in a queue of people. **2** take unfair precedence over others. **jump ship** (of a sailor) leave a ship without permission. **jump through hoops** be made to go through a complicated procedure. **one jump ahead** one stage ahead of a rival.
– DERIVATIVES **jumpable** adjective.
– ORIGIN probably imitative of the sound of feet landing on the ground.

Thesaurus

approving, disparaging, deprecating, negative, overcritical, hypercritical.
judicial ● **adjective** LEGAL, juridical, judicatory; official.
judicious ● **adjective** WISE, sensible, prudent, politic, shrewd, astute, canny, sagacious, commonsensical, sound, well advised, well judged, discerning, percipient, intelligent, smart; *N. Amer. informal* heads-up.
– OPPOSITES ill-advised.
jug ● **noun** PITCHER, ewer, crock, jar, urn; carafe, flask, flagon, decanter; *N. Amer.* creamer; *historical* amphora, jorum.
juggle ● **verb** MISREPRESENT, tamper with, falsify, distort, alter, manipulate, rig, massage, fudge; *informal* fix, doctor; *Brit. informal* fiddle.
juice ● **noun 1** *the juice from two lemons* LIQUID, fluid, sap; extract. **2** *cooking juices* LIQUID, liquor. **3** *(informal) he ran out of juice.* See PETROL.
juicy ● **adjective 1** *a juicy peach* SUCCULENT, tender, moist; ripe; *archaic* mellow. **2** *(informal) juicy gossip* VERY INTERESTING, fascinating, sensational, lurid; scandalous, racy, risqué, spicy; *informal* hot. **3** *(informal) juicy profits* LARGE, substantial, sizeable, generous; lucrative, profitable; *informal* fat, tidy.
– OPPOSITES dry, dull.
jumble ● **noun 1** *the books were in a jumble* UNTIDY HEAP, clutter, muddle, mess, confusion, disarray, disarrangement, tangle; hotchpotch, mishmash, miscellany, motley collection, mixed bag, medley, farrago; *N. Amer.* hodgepodge. **2** *(Brit.) bags of jumble* JUNK, bric-a-brac; *Brit.* lumber.

jumped-up • adjective informal considering oneself to be more important than one really is.

jumper[1] • noun **1** Brit. a pullover or sweater. **2** N. Amer. a pinafore dress.
– ORIGIN probably from dialect *jump* 'short coat', perhaps from Old French *jupe* 'loose jacket or tunic', ultimately from Arabic.

jumper[2] • noun a person or animal that jumps.

jumper cable • noun North American term for JUMP LEAD.

jump jet • noun a jet aircraft that can take off and land vertically.

jump lead • noun Brit. each of a pair of cables for recharging a battery in a motor vehicle by connecting it to the battery in another.

jump-off • noun a deciding round in a showjumping competition.

jump rope • noun N. Amer. a skipping rope.

jump-start • verb start (a car with a flat battery) with jump leads or by a sudden release of the clutch while it is being pushed. • noun an act of jump-starting a car.

jumpstation • noun another term for PORTAL (in sense 2).

jumpsuit • noun a garment incorporating trousers and a sleeved top in one piece.
– ORIGIN originally denoting a garment worn when parachuting.

jumpy • adjective (**jumpier**, **jumpiest**) informal **1** anxious and uneasy. **2** stopping and starting abruptly.
– DERIVATIVES **jumpily** adverb **jumpiness** noun.

Jun. • abbreviation June.

jun /jun/ • noun (pl. same) a monetary unit of North Korea, equal to one hundredth of a won.
– ORIGIN Korean.

junction • noun **1** a point where two or more things meet or are joined. **2** a place where two or more roads or railway lines meet. **3** Electronics a region of transition in a semiconductor between a part where conduction is mainly by electrons and a part where it is mainly by holes. **4** the action of joining or state of being joined.
– ORIGIN Latin, from *jungere* 'to join'.

junction box • noun a box containing a junction of electric wires or cables.

juncture /junkchər/ • noun **1** a particular point in time. **2** a place where things join.
– ORIGIN Latin *junctura* 'joint', from *jungere* 'to join'.

June • noun the sixth month of the year.
– ORIGIN from Latin *Junius mensis* 'month of June', from *Junonius* 'sacred to the goddess Juno'.

June bug • noun chiefly N. Amer. a chafer or similar beetle which often flies in June.

Jungian /yoongiən/ • adjective relating to the Swiss psychologist Carl Jung (1875–1961) or his work. • noun a follower of Jung or his work.

jungle • noun **1** an area of land with dense forest and tangled vegetation, typically in the tropics. **2** a very bewildering or competitive place. **3** a style of dance music with very fast electronic drum tracks and slower synthesized bass lines.
– PHRASES **the law of the jungle** the principle that those who are strongest and most selfish will be most successful.
– DERIVATIVES **junglist** noun & adjective **jungly** adjective.
– ORIGIN Sanskrit, 'rough and arid terrain'.

jungle fever • noun a severe form of malaria.

junglefowl • noun (pl. same) a southern Asian game bird related to the domestic fowl.

junior • adjective **1** of or relating to young or younger people. **2** Brit. of, for, or denoting schoolchildren aged 7–11. **3** N. Amer. of or for students in the third year of a four-year course at college or high school. **4** (after a name) denoting the younger of two with the same name in a family. **5** low or lower in rank or status. • noun **1** a person who is a specified number of years younger than someone else: *he's five years her junior.* **2** Brit. a child at a junior school. **3** N. Amer. a student in the third year at college or high school. **4** (in sport) a young competitor, typically under 16 or 18. **5** N. Amer. informal a nickname for one's son. **6** a person with low rank or status.
– DERIVATIVES **juniority** noun.
– ORIGIN Latin, from *juvenis* 'young'.

junior college • noun (in the US) a college offering courses for two years beyond high school.

junior common room • noun Brit. a room used for social purposes by the undergraduates of a college.

junior high school • noun (in the US and Canada) a school intermediate between an elementary school and a high school.

junior school • noun a school for young children, especially (in England and Wales) for those aged 7–11.

junior technician • noun a rank in the RAF, above senior aircraftman or aircraftwoman and below corporal.

juniper /joonipər/ • noun an evergreen shrub or small tree bearing aromatic berry-like cones.
– ORIGIN Latin *juniperus*.

junk[1] • noun informal **1** useless or worthless articles; rubbish. **2** heroin. • verb informal discard unceremoniously.
– ORIGIN originally denoting an old or inferior rope: of unknown origin.

junk[2] • noun a flat-bottomed sailing boat with a prominent stem, used in China and the East Indies.
– ORIGIN Malay.

junk bond • noun a high-yielding high-risk security, typically issued to finance a takeover.

junket /jungkit/ • noun **1** a dish of sweetened curds of milk. **2** informal an extravagant trip or party. • verb (**junketed**, **junketing**) informal take part in an extravagant trip or party.
– ORIGIN originally denoting a cream cheese made in a rush basket: from Old French *jonquette* 'rush basket', from Latin *juncus* 'rush'.

junk food • noun food with little nutritional value.

junkie (also **junky**) • noun informal a drug addict.

j

Thesaurus

• verb *the photographs are all jumbled up* MIX UP, muddle up, disarrange, disorganize, disorder, put in disarray.

jumbo • adjective (*informal*). See HUGE.

jump • verb **1** *the cat jumped off his lap | Flora began to jump about* LEAP, spring, bound, hop; skip, caper, dance, prance, frolic, cavort. **2** *he jumped the fence* VAULT (OVER), leap over, clear, sail over, hop over, hurdle. **3** *pre-tax profits jumped* RISE, go up, shoot up, soar, surge, climb, increase; *informal* skyrocket. **4** *the noise made her jump* START, jerk, jolt, flinch, recoil; *informal* jump out of one's skin. **5** *Polly jumped at the chance* ACCEPT EAGERLY, leap at, welcome with open arms, seize on, snap up, grab, pounce on. **6** (*informal*) *he jumped the red light* IGNORE, disregard, drive through, overshoot; *informal* run.
• noun **1** *the short jump across the gully* LEAP, spring, vault, bound, hop. **2** *the horse cleared the last jump* OBSTACLE, barrier; fence, hurdle. **3** *a jump in profits* RISE, leap, increase, upsurge, upswing; *informal* hike. **4** *I woke up with a jump* START, jerk, involuntary movement, spasm.
– PHRASES **jump the gun** (*informal*) ACT PREMATURELY, act too soon, be over-hasty, be precipitate; *informal* be ahead of oneself. **jump to it** (*informal*) HURRY UP, get a move on, be quick; *informal* get cracking, shake a leg, look lively, look sharp, pull one's finger out; *Brit. informal* get one's skates on, stir one's stumps; *N. Amer. informal* get a wiggle on; *Austral./NZ informal* get a wriggle on; *dated* make haste.

jumper • noun (*Brit.*) SWEATER, pullover, jersey; *informal* woolly.

jumpy • adjective **1** (*informal*) *he was tired and jumpy* NERVOUS, on edge, edgy, tense, anxious, ill at ease, uneasy, restless, fidgety, keyed up, overwrought, on tenterhooks; *Brit.* nervy; *informal* a bundle of nerves, jittery, like a cat on a hot tin roof, uptight, het up, in a tizz/tizzy; *Brit. informal* strung up, like a cat on hot bricks; *N. Amer. informal* spooky, squirrelly, antsy; *Austral./NZ informal* toey. **2** *jumpy black-and-white footage* JERKY, jolting, lurching, bumpy, jarring; fitful, convulsive.
– OPPOSITES calm.

junction • noun **1** *the junction between the roof and the wall* JOIN, joint, intersection, bond, seam, connection, juncture; *Anatomy* commissure. **2** *the junction of the two rivers* CONFLUENCE, convergence, meeting point, conflux, juncture. **3** *turn right at the next junction* CROSSROADS, intersection, interchange, T-junction; turn, turn-off, exit; *Brit.* roundabout; *N. Amer.* turnout, cloverleaf.

juncture • noun **1** *at this juncture, I am unable to tell you* POINT (IN TIME), time, moment (in time); period, phase. **2** *the juncture of the pipes.* See JUNCTION sense 1. **3** *the juncture of the rivers.* See JUNCTION sense 2.

jungle • noun **1** *the Amazon jungle* TROPICAL FOREST, (tropical) rainforest. **2** *a jungle of bureaucracy* COMPLEXITY, confusion, complication, chaos; labyrinth, maze, tangle, web.

junior • adjective **1** *the junior members of the family* YOUNGER, youngest. **2** *a junior minister* LOW-RANKING, lower-ranking, subordinate, lesser, lower, minor, secondary. **3** *John White Junior* THE

– ORIGIN from JUNK[1].

junk mail ● noun informal unsolicited advertising material sent by post.

junk shop ● noun informal a shop selling second-hand goods or inexpensive antiques.

junky informal ● adjective regarded as junk. ● noun (pl. **junkies**) variant spelling of JUNKIE.

junkyard ● noun N. Amer. a scrapyard.

Junoesque /jo͞onōesk/ ● adjective (of a woman) tall and shapely.

– ORIGIN named after the Roman goddess *Juno*.

junta /juntə/ ● noun a military or political group ruling a country after taking power by force.

– ORIGIN Spanish and Portuguese, 'deliberative or administrative council', from Latin *jungere* 'to join'.

Jurassic /joorassik/ ● adjective Geology relating to the second period of the Mesozoic era (between the Triassic and Cretaceous periods, about 208 to 146 million years ago), a time when large reptiles were dominant and the first birds appeared.

– ORIGIN French *jurassique*, from the *Jura* Mountains on the border of France and Switzerland.

juridical /jooriddik'l/ ● adjective Law relating to judicial proceedings and the law.

– DERIVATIVES **juridically** adverb.

– ORIGIN Latin *juridicus*, from *jus* 'law' + *dicere* 'say'.

jurisdiction /joorisdiksh'n/ ● noun **1** the official power to make legal decisions and judgements. **2** the territory or sphere over which the legal authority of a court or other institution extends. **3** a system of law courts.

– DERIVATIVES **jurisdictional** adjective.

– ORIGIN Latin, from *jus* 'law' + *dicere* 'say'.

jurisprudence /joorispro͞od'nss/ ● noun **1** the theory or philosophy of law. **2** a legal system.

– DERIVATIVES **jurisprudent** adjective & noun **jurisprudential** adjective.

– ORIGIN Latin *jurisprudentia*, from *jus* 'law' + *prudentia* 'knowledge'.

jurist /joorist/ ● noun **1** an expert in law. **2** N. Amer. a lawyer or a judge.

– DERIVATIVES **juristic** adjective.

– ORIGIN Latin *jurista*, from *jus* 'law'.

juror ● noun **1** a member of a jury. **2** historical a person taking an oath.

jury[1] ● noun (pl. **juries**) **1** a body of people (typically twelve) sworn to give a verdict in a legal case on the basis of evidence submitted in court. **2** a body of people judging a competition. ● verb (**juries**, **juried**) chiefly N. Amer. judge (an art or craft exhibit).

– PHRASES **the jury is out** a decision has not yet been reached.

– ORIGIN Old French *juree* 'oath, inquiry', from Latin *jurare* 'swear', from *jus* 'law'.

jury[2] ● adjective Nautical denoting improvised or temporary fittings.

– ORIGIN perhaps from Old French *ajurie* 'aid'.

jury-rigged ● adjective **1** (of a ship) having makeshift rigging. **2** chiefly N. Amer. makeshift; improvised.

jus /zho͞o/ ● noun (especially in French cuisine) a sauce.

– ORIGIN French, 'juice'.

just ● adjective **1** morally right and fair. **2** appropriate or deserved. **3** (of an opinion or appraisal) well founded. ● adverb **1** exactly. **2** exactly or nearly at this or that moment. **3** very recently. **4** barely; by a little. **5** simply; only.

– PHRASES **just in case** as a precaution. **just so 1** arranged or done very carefully. **2** formal expressing agreement.

– DERIVATIVES **justly** adverb **justness** noun.

– ORIGIN Latin *justus*, from *jus* 'law, right'.

justice ● noun **1** just behaviour or treatment. **2** the quality of being just. **3** the administration of law or some other authority according to the principles of just behaviour and treatment. **4** a judge or magistrate.

– PHRASES **bring someone to justice** arrest and try someone in court for a crime. **do oneself justice** perform as well as one is able. **do someone/thing justice** treat or represent someone or something with due fairness.

– ORIGIN Old French *justise* 'administration of the law', from Latin *jus* 'law, right'.

Justice of the Peace ● noun (in the UK) a lay magistrate appointed to hear minor cases, grant licences, etc., in a town or county.

justiciable /justishəb'l/ ● adjective Law subject to trial in a court of law.

justifiable ● adjective able to be justified.

– DERIVATIVES **justifiability** noun **justifiableness** noun **justifiably** adverb.

justify ● verb (**justifies**, **justified**) **1** prove to be right or reasonable. **2** be a good reason for. **3** Printing adjust (text) so that the lines of type fill a given width exactly, forming a straight right edge.

– DERIVATIVES **justification** noun **justificatory** adjective **justifier** noun.

– ORIGIN Latin *justificare* 'do justice to'.

jut ● verb (**jutted**, **jutting**) extend out, over, or beyond the main body or line of something. ● noun a point that sticks out.

Thesaurus

YOUNGER; *Brit.* minor; *N. Amer.* II.

– OPPOSITES senior, older.

junk *(informal)* ● noun *an attic full of junk* RUBBISH, clutter, odds and ends, bits and pieces, bric-a-brac; refuse, litter, scrap, waste, debris, detritus, dross; *Brit.* lumber; *N. Amer.* garbage, trash; *Austral./NZ* mullock; *Brit. informal* odds and sods.

● verb *junk all the rubbish* THROW AWAY/OUT, discard, get rid of, dispose of, scrap, toss out, jettison; *informal* chuck (away/out), dump, ditch, bin, get shut of; *Brit. informal* get shot of.

junket ● noun *(informal)* CELEBRATION, party, jamboree, feast, festivity; spree, excursion, outing, trip, jaunt; *informal* bash, shindy, shindig; *Brit. informal* beanfeast, jolly, bunfight, beano; *Austral. informal* jollo.

junta ● noun FACTION, cabal, clique, party, set, ring, gang, league, confederacy; *historical* junto.

jurisdiction ● noun **1** *an area under French jurisdiction* AUTHORITY, control, power, dominion, rule, administration, command, sway, leadership, sovereignty, hegemony. **2** *foreign jurisdictions* TERRITORY, region, province, district, area, domain, realm.

just ● adjective **1** *a just and democratic society* FAIR, fair-minded, equitable, even-handed, impartial, unbiased, objective, neutral, disinterested, unprejudiced, open-minded, non-partisan; honourable, upright, decent, honest, righteous, moral, virtuous, principled. **2** *a just reward* (WELL) DESERVED, (well) earned, merited; rightful, due, fitting, appropriate, suitable; *formal* condign; *archaic* meet. **3** *just criticism* VALID, sound, well founded, justified, justifiable, warranted, legitimate.

– OPPOSITES unfair, undeserved, unfair.

● adverb **1** *I just saw him* A MOMENT/SECOND AGO, a short time ago, very recently, not long ago. **2** *she's just right for him* EXACTLY, precisely, absolutely, completely, totally, entirely, perfectly, utterly, wholly, thoroughly, in all respects; *informal* down to the ground, to a T, dead. **3** *we just made it* NARROWLY, only just, by a hair's breadth; barely, scarcely, hardly; *informal* by the skin of one's teeth, by a whisker. **4** *she's just a child* ONLY, merely, simply, (nothing) but, no more than. **5** *the colour's just fantastic* REALLY, absolutely, completely, entirely, totally, quite; indeed, truly.

– PHRASES **just about** *(informal)* NEARLY, almost, practically, all but, virtually, as good as, more or less, to all intents and purposes; *informal* pretty much; *poetic/literary* well-nigh, nigh on.

justice ● noun **1** *I appealed to his sense of justice* FAIRNESS, justness, fair play, fair-mindedness, equity, equitableness, even-handedness, impartiality, objectivity, neutrality, disinterestedness, honesty, righteousness, morals, morality. **2** *the justice of his case* VALIDITY, justification, soundness, well-foundedness, legitimacy. **3** *an order made by the justices* JUDGE, magistrate, recorder, sheriff; *N. Amer.* jurist; *Brit. informal* beak.

justifiable ● adjective VALID, legitimate, warranted, well founded, justified, just, reasonable; defensible, tenable, supportable, acceptable.

– OPPOSITES indefensible.

justification ● noun GROUNDS, reason, basis, rationale, premise, rationalization, vindication, explanation; defence, argument, apologia, apology, case.

justify ● verb **1** *directors must justify the expenditure* GIVE GROUNDS FOR, give reasons for, give a justification for, explain, give an explanation for, account for; defend, answer for, vindicate. **2** *the situation justified further investigation* WARRANT, be good reason for, be a justification for.

justly ● adverb **1** *he is justly proud of his achievement* JUSTIFIABLY, with (good) reason, legitimately, rightly, rightfully, deservedly. **2** *they were treated justly* FAIRLY, with fairness, equitably, even-handedly, impartially, without bias, objectively, without preju-

– ORIGIN from JET[1].

Jute ● noun a member of a Germanic people that settled in southern Britain in the 5th century.

– DERIVATIVES **Jutish** adjective.

– ORIGIN Old English.

jute /jo͞ot/ ● noun rough fibre made from the stems of a tropical plant, used for making rope or woven into sacking.

– ORIGIN Bengali.

juvenile /jo͞ovənīl/ ● adjective **1** relating to young people, birds, or animals. **2** childish. ● noun **1** a young person, bird, or animal. **2** Law a person below the age at which ordinary criminal prosecution is possible (18 in most countries).

– DERIVATIVES **juvenility** noun.

– ORIGIN Latin *juvenilis*, from *juvenis* 'young, a young person'.

juvenile court ● noun a court for the trial or legal supervision of juveniles.

juvenile delinquency ● noun the habitual committing of criminal acts by a juvenile.

– DERIVATIVES **juvenile deliquent** noun.

juvenilia /jo͞ovənilliə/ ● plural noun works produced by an author or artist when young.

– ORIGIN Latin, plural of *juvenilis* 'juvenile'.

juxtapose /jukstəpōz/ ● verb place close together.

– DERIVATIVES **juxtaposition** noun.

– ORIGIN French *juxtaposer*, from Latin *juxta* 'next' + French *poser* 'to place'.

Thesaurus

dice; *informal* fairly and squarely.

– OPPOSITES unjustifiably.

jut ● verb STICK OUT, project, protrude, bulge out, overhang, obtrude; *archaic* be imminent.

juvenile ● adjective **1** *juvenile offenders* YOUNG, teenage, adolescent, junior, pubescent, pre-pubescent. **2** *juvenile behaviour* CHILDISH, immature, puerile, infantile, babyish; jejune, inexperienced, callow, green, unsophisticated, naive, foolish, silly.

– OPPOSITES adult, mature.

● noun *many victims are juveniles* YOUNG PERSON, youngster, child, teenager, adolescent, minor, junior; *informal* kid.

– OPPOSITES adult.

juxtapose ● verb PLACE SIDE BY SIDE, set side by side, mix; compare, contrast.

Kk

K[1] (also **k**) ● noun (pl. **Ks** or **K's**) **1** the eleventh letter of the alphabet. **2** denoting the next item after J in a set.

K[2] ● abbreviation **1** kelvin(s). **2** Computing kilobyte(s). **3** kilometre(s). **4** (in card games and chess) king. **5** Köchel (catalogue of Mozart's works). **6** informal thousand. [ORIGIN from KILO-.] ● symbol the chemical element potassium. [ORIGIN from Latin *kalium*.]

k ● abbreviation kilo-. ● symbol used to represent a constant in a formula or equation.

Kabbalah /kəbaalə, kabbələ/ (also **Kabbala**, **Cabbala**, **Cabala**, or **Qabalah**) ● noun the ancient Jewish tradition of mystical interpretation of the Bible.
– DERIVATIVES **Kabbalism** noun **Kabbalist** noun **Kabbalistic** adjective.
– ORIGIN Hebrew, 'tradition'.

kabob ● noun US spelling of KEBAB.

kabuki /kəbōōki/ ● noun a form of traditional Japanese drama performed by men, with highly stylized song, mime, and dance.
– ORIGIN Japanese, interpreted originally as a verb meaning 'act dissolutely', later as if from the words for 'song', 'dance', and 'art'.

Kaddish /kaddish/ ● noun **1** an ancient Jewish prayer sequence recited in the synagogue service. **2** a form of this recited for the dead.
– ORIGIN from Aramaic, 'holy'.

Kaffir /kaffər/ ● noun offensive, chiefly S. African a black African.
– USAGE The word **Kaffir** was originally simply a descriptive term for a particular ethnic group. Now it is a racially abusive and offensive term, and in South Africa its use is actionable.
– ORIGIN Arabic, 'infidel'.

Kaffir lily ● noun a South African plant with strap-like leaves and star-shaped flowers.

kaffiyeh ● noun variant spelling of KEFFIYEH.

kafir /kafeer/ ● noun (among Muslims) a person who is not a Muslim.
– ORIGIN Arabic, 'infidel'; related to KAFFIR.

Kafkaesque /kafkəesk/ ● adjective relating to the Czech novelist Franz Kafka (1883–1924) or his nightmarish fictional world.

kaftan /kaftan/ (also **caftan**) ● noun **1** a man's long belted tunic, worn in the Near East. **2** a woman's long loose dress. **3** a loose shirt or top.
– ORIGIN Persian, partly influenced by French *cafetan*.

kagoul ● noun variant spelling of CAGOULE.

kahuna /kəhōōnə/ ● noun **1** (in Hawaii) a wise man or shaman. **2** N. Amer. informal an important person.
– ORIGIN Hawaiian.

kai /kī/ ● noun NZ informal food.
– ORIGIN Maori.

kaiser /kīzər/ ● noun historical the German Emperor, the Emperor of Austria, or the head of the Holy Roman Empire.
– ORIGIN German, from Latin *Caesar*.

kaka /kaakaa/ ● noun a large New Zealand olive-brown and green parrot with reddish underparts.
– ORIGIN Maori.

kakapo /kaakəpō/ ● noun (pl. **kakapos**) a flightless New Zealand parrot with greenish plumage.
– ORIGIN Maori.

kalanchoe /kallənkōi/ ● noun a tropical succulent plant with clusters of tubular flowers.
– ORIGIN French, from Chinese.

Kalashnikov /kəlashnikof/ ● noun a type of rifle or sub-machine gun made in Russia.
– ORIGIN named after the Russian designer Mikhail T. *Kalashnikov* (born 1919).

kale /kayl/ ● noun a variety of hardy cabbage producing erect stems with large leaves and no compact head.
– ORIGIN northern English form of COLE.

kaleidoscope /kəlīdəskōp/ ● noun **1** a toy consisting of a tube containing mirrors and pieces of coloured glass or paper, whose reflections produce changing patterns when the tube is rotated. **2** a constantly changing pattern or sequence.
– DERIVATIVES **kaleidoscopic** adjective.
– ORIGIN from Greek *kalos* 'beautiful' + *eidos* 'form' + -SCOPE.

kalends ● plural noun variant spelling of CALENDS.

Kama Sutra /kaamə sōōtrə/ ● noun an ancient Sanskrit text on the art of love and sexual technique.
– ORIGIN Sanskrit, 'love thread'.

kameez /kəmeez/ ● noun (pl. same or **kameezes**) a long tunic worn by people from the Indian subcontinent.
– ORIGIN Arabic, perhaps from Latin *camisia* 'chemise, shirt'.

kamikaze /kammikaazi/ ● noun (in the Second World War) a Japanese aircraft loaded with explosives and making a deliberate suicidal crash on an enemy target. ● adjective reckless or potentially self-destructive.
– ORIGIN from the Japanese words for 'divinity' and 'wind', originally referring to the gale that, in Japanese tradition, destroyed the fleet of invading Mongols in 1281.

kampong /kampong/ ● noun a Malaysian enclosure or village.
– ORIGIN Malay; related to COMPOUND[2].

Kampuchean /kampoocheeən/ ● noun & adjective another term for CAMBODIAN.

kana /kaanə/ ● noun the system of syllabic writing used for Japanese.
– ORIGIN Japanese.

kangaroo ● noun a large Australian marsupial with a long powerful tail and strongly developed hindlimbs that enable it to travel by leaping.
– ORIGIN from an Aboriginal language.

kangaroo court ● noun an unofficial court formed by a group of people to try someone regarded as guilty of an offence.

kangaroo paw ● noun an Australian plant with strap-like leaves and tubular flowers with woolly outer surfaces.

kangaroo rat ● noun a hopping rodent with large cheek pouches and long hind legs, found from Canada to Mexico.

kanji /kanji/ ● noun a system of Japanese writing using Chinese characters.
– ORIGIN Japanese, 'Chinese character'.

Kantian /kantiən/ ● adjective relating to the German philosopher Immanuel Kant (1724–1804) or his philosophy. ● noun an adherent of Kant's philosophy.
– DERIVATIVES **Kantianism** noun.

kaolin /kayəlin/ ● noun a fine soft white clay, used for making china and in medicine as an absorbent substance.
– DERIVATIVES **kaolinize** (also **kaolinise**) verb.
– ORIGIN French, from a Chinese word meaning 'high hill', this being the name of a mountain in Jiangxi province where the clay is found.

kapellmeister /kəpelmīstər/ ● noun (in German-speaking countries) the leader or conductor of an orchestra or choir.
– ORIGIN German, from *Kapelle* 'court orchestra' + *Meister* 'master'.

kapok /kaypok/ ● noun a fine fibrous substance which grows around the seeds of a tropical tree, used as stuffing for cushions, soft toys, etc.
– ORIGIN Malay.

Kaposi's sarcoma /kəpōsiz/ ● noun Medicine a form of cancer

Thesaurus

kaleidoscopic ● adjective **1** *kaleidoscopic shapes* MULTICOLOURED, many-coloured, multicolour, many-hued, variegated, particoloured, varicoloured, psychedelic, rainbow, polychromatic. **2** *the kaleidoscopic political landscape* EVER-CHANGING, changeable, shifting, fluid, protean, variable, inconstant, fluctuating, unpredictable, impermanent. **3** *the kaleidoscopic world we are living in*

involving multiple tumours of the lymph nodes or skin, occurring chiefly as a result of Aids.
– ORIGIN named after the Hungarian dermatologist Moritz K. *Kaposi* (1837–1902).
kappa /kappə/ ● noun the tenth letter of the Greek alphabet (Κ, κ), transliterated as 'k'.
– ORIGIN Greek.
kaput /kəpŏŏt/ ● adjective informal broken and useless.
– ORIGIN German *kaputt*, from French *être capot* 'be without tricks in a card game'.
karabiner /karrəbeenər/ (also **carabiner**) ● noun a coupling link with a safety closure, used by rock climbers.
– ORIGIN from German *Karabiner-haken* 'spring hook'.
karakul /karrəkōōl/ (also **caracul**) ● noun **1** a breed of Asian sheep having a dark curled fleece when young. **2** cloth or fur made from or resembling this fleece.
– ORIGIN Russian.
karaoke /karriōki/ ● noun a form of entertainment in which people sing popular songs over pre-recorded backing tracks.
– ORIGIN Japanese, 'empty orchestra'.
karat ● noun US spelling of CARAT (in sense 2).
karate /kəraati/ ● noun an oriental system of unarmed combat using the hands and feet to deliver and block blows.
– ORIGIN Japanese, 'empty hand'.
Karen /kəren/ ● noun (pl. same or **Karens**) **1** a member of a people of eastern Burma (Myanmar) and western Thailand. **2** the language of this people.
– ORIGIN Burmese, 'wild unclean man'.
karma /kaarmə/ ● noun (in Hinduism and Buddhism) the sum of a person's actions in this and previous states of existence, viewed as affecting their future fate.
– DERIVATIVES **karmic** adjective.
– ORIGIN Sanskrit, 'action, effect, fate'.
karri /karri/ ● noun (pl. **karris**) a tall Australian eucalyptus with hard red wood.
– ORIGIN from an Aboriginal word.
karst /kaarst/ ● noun Geology landscape underlain by limestone which has been eroded by dissolution, producing towers, fissures, sinkholes, etc.
– DERIVATIVES **karstic** adjective.
– ORIGIN from German *der Karst*, a limestone region in Slovenia.
kart ● noun a small unsprung motor-racing vehicle with a tubular frame and a rear-mounted engine.
– DERIVATIVES **karting** noun.
– ORIGIN shortening of GO-KART.
kasbah /kazbaa/ (also **casbah**) ● noun **1** a North African citadel. **2** the area of old, narrow streets surrounding such a citadel.
– ORIGIN Arabic.
kasha /kashə/ ● noun (in Russia and Poland) porridge made from cooked buckwheat or similar grain.
– ORIGIN Russian.
Kashmiri /kashmeeri/ ● noun **1** a person from Kashmir, a region on the border of India and Pakistan. **2** the language of Kashmir. ● adjective relating to Kashmir.
katharevousa /kathərevōōsə/ ● noun a form of modern Greek used in traditional literary writing. Compare with DEMOTIC.
– ORIGIN modern Greek, 'purified'.
katydid /kaytidid/ ● noun a large bush cricket native to North America, the male of which makes a characteristic sound which resembles the name.
kauri /kowri/ ● noun (pl. **kauris**) (also **kauri pine**) a tall coniferous forest tree native to New Zealand, which produces valuable wood and resin.
– ORIGIN Maori.
kava /kaavə/ ● noun a narcotic drink made in Polynesia from the crushed roots of a plant of the pepper family.
– ORIGIN Tongan.
kayak /kīak/ ● noun a canoe of a type used originally by the Inuit, made of a light frame with a watertight covering. ● verb (**kayaked**, **kayaking**) travel in a kayak.
– ORIGIN Inuit.
kayo /kayō/ informal ● noun (pl. **kayos**) a knockout. ● verb (**kayoes**, **kayoed**) knock (someone) out.
– ORIGIN representing the pronunciation of *KO*.
Kazakh /kəzak/ ● noun a member of a traditionally nomadic people living chiefly in the central Asian republic of Kazakhstan.
– ORIGIN Turkic, related to COSSACK.
kazillion /kəzilyən/ ● cardinal number another term for GAZILLION.
kazoo /kəzōō/ ● noun a simple musical instrument consisting of a pipe with a hole in it, over which is a membrane that vibrates and produces a buzzing sound when the player hums into it.
– ORIGIN apparently imitative of the sound produced.
KB (also **Kb**) ● abbreviation kilobyte(s).
KBE ● abbreviation (in the UK) Knight Commander of the Order of the British Empire.
KC ● abbreviation King's Counsel.
kcal ● abbreviation kilocalorie(s).
KCB ● abbreviation (in the UK) Knight Commander of the Order of the Bath.
KCMG ● abbreviation (in the UK) Knight Commander of the Order of St Michael and St George.
KCVO ● abbreviation (in the UK) Knight Commander of the Royal Victorian Order.
kea /keeə/ ● noun a New Zealand mountain parrot with a long, narrow bill and mainly olive-green plumage.
– ORIGIN Maori.
kebab /kibab/ (N. Amer. also **kabob**) ● noun a dish of pieces of meat, fish, or vegetables roasted or grilled on a skewer or spit.
– ORIGIN Arabic.
kecks ● plural noun Brit. informal trousers.
– ORIGIN phonetic respelling of obsolete *kicks*.
ked ● noun a wingless bloodsucking insect that is a parasite of sheep.
– ORIGIN of unknown origin.
kedge /kej/ ● verb move (a boat) by hauling in a hawser attached at a distance to an anchor. ● noun a small anchor used for such a purpose.
– ORIGIN perhaps a specific use of dialect *cadge* 'bind, tie'.
kedgeree /kejəree/ ● noun **1** an Indian dish consisting chiefly of rice, split pulses, onions, and eggs. **2** a European dish consisting chiefly of smoked fish, rice, and hard-boiled eggs.
– ORIGIN Sanskrit.
keel ● noun a lengthwise structure along the base of a ship, in some vessels extended downwards as a ridge to increase stability. ● verb (**keel over**) **1** (of a boat or ship) turn over on its side; capsize. **2** fall over; collapse.
– ORIGIN Old Norse.
keelboat ● noun **1** a yacht built with a permanent keel rather than a centreboard. **2** a large, flat freight boat used on American rivers.
keelhaul ● verb **1** historical punish (someone) by dragging them through the water from one side of a boat to the other, under the keel. **2** humorous punish or reprimand severely.
keelson /keels'n/ (also **kelson**) ● noun a structure running the length of a ship, that fastens the timbers or plates of the floor to the keel.
– ORIGIN from Low German *kiel* 'keel of a ship' + *swīn* 'swine' (used as the name of a timber).
keen[1] ● adjective **1** eager; enthusiastic. **2** (**keen on**) interested in or attracted by. **3** (of a blade) sharp. **4** mentally acute or quick. **5** Brit. (of prices) very low; competitive.
– DERIVATIVES **keenly** adverb **keenness** noun.
– ORIGIN Old English, 'wise, clever', also 'brave, daring'.
keen[2] ● verb **1** wail in grief for a dead person. **2** make an eerie wailing sound. ● noun an Irish funeral song accompanied with wailing in lamentation for the dead.
– ORIGIN from Irish *caoinim* 'I wail'.

Thesaurus

MULTIFACETED, varied; complex, intricate, complicated.
– OPPOSITES monochrome, constant.
kaput (*informal*) ● adjective *the TV's kaput* BROKEN, malfunctioning, broken-down, inoperative; *informal* conked out.
– PHRASES **go kaput** BREAK DOWN, go wrong, stop working; *informal* conk out.
keel ● noun *the upturned keel of the boat* BASE, bottom (side), underside.
– PHRASES **keel over 1** *the boat keeled over* CAPSIZE, turn turtle, turn upside down, founder; overturn, turn over, tip over. **2** *the slightest activity made him keel over* COLLAPSE, faint, pass out, black out, lose consciousness, swoon.
keen[1] ● adjective **1** *his publishers were keen to capitalize on his success* EAGER, anxious, intent, impatient, determined, ambitious; *in-*

keep ● verb (past and past part. **kept**) **1** have or retain possession of. **2** retain or reserve for use in the future. **3** put or store in a regular place. **4** (of a perishable commodity) remain in good condition. **5** continue in a specified condition, position, or activity: *she kept quiet about it.* **6** honour, fulfil, or observe (a commitment or undertaking). **7** record or regularly maintain (a note or diary). **8** cause to be late. **9** provide accommodation and food for; support. **10** (**kept**) supported financially in return for sexual favours. ● noun **1** food, clothes, and other essentials for living. **2** the strongest or central tower of a castle. **3** archaic charge; control.
– PHRASES **for keeps** informal permanently; indefinitely. **keep from 1** cause (something) to stay out of. **2** cause (something) to remain a secret from. **3** avoid doing. **4** guard or protect (someone) from. **keep on 1** continue to do. **2** continue to use or employ. **keep to 1** avoid leaving (a path, road, or place). **2** adhere to (a schedule). **3** observe (a promise). **4** confine or restrict oneself to. **keep up 1** move or progress at the same rate as someone or something else. **2** continue (a course of action). **keep up with 1** learn about or be aware of (current events or developments). **2** continue to be in contact with (someone). **keep up with the Joneses** strive not to be outdone by one's neighbours or peers.
– ORIGIN Old English.

keeper ● noun **1** a person who manages or looks after something or someone. **2** a goalkeeper or wicketkeeper. **3** an object which protects or secures another. **4** a bar of soft iron placed across the poles of a horseshoe magnet to maintain its strength.

keep-fit ● noun chiefly Brit. regular exercises to improve personal fitness and health.

keeping ● noun the action of keeping something.
– PHRASES **in** (or **out of**) **keeping with** in (or out of) harmony or conformity with.

keepnet ● noun a fishing net secured in the water and used to keep alive fish that have been caught.

keepsake ● noun a small item kept in memory of the person who gave it or originally owned it.

kef /kef/ ● noun & adjective variant spelling of KIF.

keffiyeh /kefeeyə/ (also **kaffiyeh**) ● noun a Bedouin Arab's headdress.
– ORIGIN Arabic.

keg ● noun **1** a small barrel, especially one of less than 10 gallons or (in the US) 30 gallons. **2** (before another noun) Brit. (of beer)

Thesaurus

k

formal raring, itching, dying. **2** *a keen birdwatcher* ENTHUSIASTIC, avid, eager, ardent, passionate, fervent, fervid, impassioned; conscientious, committed, dedicated, zealous. **3** *they are keen on horses | a girl he was keen on* ENTHUSIASTIC, interested, passionate; attracted to, fond of, taken with, smitten with, enamoured of, infatuated with; *informal* struck on, gone on, mad about, crazy about, nuts about. **4** *a keen cutting edge* SHARP, sharpened, honed, razor-sharp. **5** *keen eyesight* ACUTE, sharp, discerning, sensitive, perceptive, clear. **6** *a keen mind* ACUTE, penetrating, astute, incisive, sharp, perceptive, piercing, razor-sharp, perspicacious, shrewd, discerning, clever, intelligent, brilliant, bright, smart, wise, canny, percipient, insightful. **7** *a keen wind* COLD, icy, freezing, harsh, raw, bitter; penetrating, piercing, biting. **8** *a keen sense of duty* INTENSE, acute, fierce, passionate, burning, fervent, ardent, strong, powerful.
– OPPOSITES reluctant, unenthusiastic.

keen² ● verb *the bereaved gathered to keen* LAMENT, mourn, weep, cry, sorrow, grieve; wail, ululate; *archaic* plain.

keenness ● noun **1** *the company's keenness to sign a deal* EAGERNESS, willingness, readiness, impatience; enthusiasm, fervour, wholeheartedness, zest, zeal, ardour, passion, avidity. **2** *the keenness of the blade* SHARPNESS, razor-sharpness. **3** *keenness of hearing* ACUTENESS, sharpness, sensitivity, perceptiveness, clarity. **4** *the keenness of his mind* ACUITY, sharpness, incisiveness, astuteness, perspicacity, perceptiveness, shrewdness, insight, cleverness, discernment, intelligence, brightness, brilliance, canniness. **5** *the keenness of his sense of loss* INTENSITY, acuteness, strength, power, ferocity.

keep¹ ● verb **1** *you should keep all the old forms* RETAIN (POSSESSION OF), hold on to, keep hold of, not part with; save, store, put by/aside, set aside; *N. Amer.* set by; *informal* hang on to, stash away. **2** *I tried to keep calm* REMAIN, continue to be, stay, carry on being, persist in being. **3** *he keeps going on about the murder* PERSIST IN, keep on, carry on, continue, do something constantly. **4** *I shan't keep you long* DETAIN, keep waiting, delay, hold up, retard, slow down. **5** *most people kept the rules | he had to keep his promise* COMPLY WITH, obey, observe, conform to, abide by, adhere to, stick to, heed, follow; fulfil, carry out, act on, make good, honour, keep to, stand by. **6** *keeping the old traditions* PRESERVE, keep alive/up, keep going, carry on, perpetuate, maintain, uphold, sustain. **7** *the stand where her umbrella was kept* STORE, house, stow, put (away), place, deposit. **8** *the shop keeps a good stock of parchment* (HAVE IN) STOCK, carry, have (for sale), hold. **9** *he stole to keep his family* PROVIDE (FOOD) FOR, support, feed, keep alive, maintain, sustain; take care of, look after. **10** *she keeps rabbits* BREED, rear, raise, farm; own, have as a pet. **11** *his parents kept a shop* MANAGE, run, own, be the proprietor of. **12** *God keep you* LOOK AFTER, care for, take care of, mind, watch over; protect, keep safe, preserve, defend, guard. **13** *today people do not keep the Sabbath* OBSERVE, respect, honour, hold sacred; celebrate, mark, commemorate.
– OPPOSITES throw away, break, abandon.
● noun *money to pay for his keep* MAINTENANCE, upkeep, sustenance, board (and lodging), food, livelihood.
– PHRASES **for keeps** (*informal*) FOREVER, for ever and ever, for evermore, for always, for good (and all), permanently, in perpetuity; *informal* until kingdom come, until doomsday; *archaic* for aye. **keep at** PERSEVERE WITH, persist with, keep going with, carry on with, press on with, work away at, continue with; *informal* stick at, peg away at, plug away at, hammer away at. **keep something back 1** *she kept back some of the money* (KEEP IN) RESERVE, put by/aside, set aside; retain, hold back, keep, hold on to, not part with; *N. Amer.* set by; *informal* stash away. **2** *she kept back the details* CONCEAL, keep secret, keep hidden, withhold, suppress, keep quiet about. **3** *she could hardly keep back her tears* SUPPRESS, stifle, choke back, fight back, hold back/in, repress, keep in check, contain, smother, swallow, bite back. **keep from** REFRAIN FROM, stop oneself, restrain oneself from, prevent oneself from, forbear from, avoid. **keep someone from something 1** *he could hardly keep himself from laughing* PREVENT, stop, restrain, hold back. **2** *keep them from harm* PRESERVE, protect, keep safe, guard, shield, shelter, safeguard, defend. **keep something from someone** KEEP SECRET, keep hidden, hide, conceal, withhold; *informal* keep dark. **keep off 1** *keep off private land* STAY OFF, not enter, keep/stay away from, not trespass on. **2** *Maud tried to keep off political subjects* AVOID, steer clear of, stay away from, evade, sidestep; *informal* duck. **3** *you should keep off alcohol* ABSTAIN FROM, do without, refrain from, give up, forgo, not touch; *informal* swear off; *formal* forswear. **4** *I hope the rain keeps off* STAY AWAY, hold off, not start, not begin. **keep on 1** *they kept on working* CONTINUE, go on, carry on, persist in, persevere in; soldier on, struggle on, keep going. **2** *the commander kept on about vigilance* TALK CONSTANTLY, talk endlessly, keep talking, go on (and on), rant on; *informal* harp on, witter on, rabbit on. **keep someone on** CONTINUE TO EMPLOY, retain in one's service, not dismiss, not sack. **keep on at** NAG, go on at, harp on at, badger, chivvy, harass, hound, pester; *informal* hassle. **keep to 1** *I've got to keep to the rules* OBEY, abide by, observe, follow, comply with, adhere to, respect, keep, stick to, be bound by. **2** *keep to the path* FOLLOW, stick to, stay on. **3** *please keep to the point* STICK TO, restrict oneself to, confine oneself to. **keep someone under** KEEP IN SUBJECTION, hold down, keep down, subdue, suppress, repress, oppress; *informal* squash, trample on. **keep something up** CONTINUE (WITH), keep on with, keep going, carry on with, persist with, persevere with. **keep up with 1** *she walked fast to keep up with him* KEEP PACE WITH, keep abreast of; match, equal. **2** *he kept up with events at home* KEEP INFORMED ABOUT, keep up to date with, keep abreast of; *informal* keep tabs on. **3** *they kept up with him by Christmas cards* REMAIN IN CONTACT WITH, stay in touch with, maintain contact with, keep up one's friendship with.

keep² ● noun *the enemy stormed the keep* FORTRESS, fort, stronghold, tower, donjon, castle, citadel, bastion.

keeper ● noun **1** *keeper of the archives* CURATOR, custodian, guardian, administrator, overseer, steward, caretaker. **2** *the keeper of an inn* PROPRIETOR, owner, master/mistress, landlord/landlady. **3** *you're not her keeper* GUARDIAN, protector, guard, minder, chaperon/chaperone; carer, nursemaid, nurse.

keeping ● noun *the document is in the keeping of the county archivist* SAFE KEEPING, care, custody, charge, possession, trust, protection.
– PHRASES **in keeping with** CONSISTENT WITH, in harmony with, in accord with, in agreement with, in line with, in character with,

supplied in a keg, to which carbon dioxide has been added.
– ORIGIN Old Norse.

keister /keestər/ ● noun N. Amer. informal **1** a person's bottom. **2** dated a suitcase, bag, or box for carrying possessions or merchandise.
– ORIGIN of unknown origin.

kelim ● noun variant spelling of KILIM.

keloid /keeloyd/ ● noun Medicine an area of irregular fibrous tissue formed at the site of a scar or injury.
– ORIGIN from Greek *khēlē* 'crab's claw'.

kelp ● noun **1** a very large brown seaweed having broad fronds divided into strips. **2** the ashes of seaweed used as a source of various salts.
– ORIGIN of unknown origin.

kelpie /kelpi/ ● noun **1** a water spirit of Scottish folklore, typically taking the form of a horse. **2** an Australian breed of sheepdog originally bred from a Scottish collie.
– ORIGIN perhaps from Scottish Gaelic *cailpeach, colpach* 'bullock, colt'.

kelson /kels'n/ ● noun variant spelling of KEELSON.

kelt ● noun a salmon or sea trout after spawning and before returning to the sea.
– ORIGIN of unknown origin.

kelvin ● noun the SI base unit of thermodynamic temperature, equal in magnitude to the degree Celsius.
– ORIGIN named after the British physicist William T. *Kelvin* (1824–1907).

Kelvin scale ● noun the scale of temperature with absolute zero as zero and the freezing point of water as 273.15 kelvins.

kempt ● adjective in a neat and clean condition.
– ORIGIN Old English, 'combed'.

ken ● noun (**one's ken**) one's range of knowledge or sight. ● verb (**kenning**; past and past part. **kenned** or **kent**) Scottish & N. English **1** know. **2** recognize; identify.
– ORIGIN from Old English, 'tell, make known'.

Kendal mint cake ● noun a hard peppermint-flavoured sweet produced in flat rectangular blocks.
– ORIGIN named after the town of *Kendal* in Cumbria.

kendo /kendō/ ● noun a Japanese form of fencing with two-handed bamboo swords.
– ORIGIN Japanese, 'sword way'.

kennel ● noun **1** a small shelter for a dog. **2** (**kennels**) (treated as sing. or pl.) a boarding or breeding establishment for dogs. ● verb (**kennelled, kennelling**; US **kenneled, kenneling**) put or keep (a dog) in a kennel or kennels.
– ORIGIN Old French *chenil*, from Latin *canis* 'dog'.

kenning ● noun a compound expression in Old English and Old Norse poetry with metaphorical meaning, e.g. *oar-steed* = ship.
– ORIGIN from Old Norse, 'know, perceive'; related to KEN.

kent past and past participle of KEN.

Kenyan /kenyən, keen-/ ● noun a person from Kenya. ● adjective relating to Kenya.

kepi /keppi/ ● noun (pl. **kepis**) a French military cap with a horizontal peak.
– ORIGIN French, from Swiss German *Käppi* 'little cap'.

kept past and past participle of KEEP.

keratin /kerrətin/ ● noun a fibrous protein forming the main constituent of hair, feathers, hoofs, claws, and horns.
– ORIGIN from Greek *keras* 'horn'.

keratitis /kerrətītiss/ ● noun Medicine inflammation of the cornea of the eye.

keratotomy /kerrətottəmi/ ● noun a surgical operation involving cutting into the cornea of the eye, especially (**radial keratotomy**) performed to correct myopia.

kerb (US **curb**) ● noun a stone edging to a pavement or raised path.
– ORIGIN variant of CURB.

kerb-crawling ● noun Brit. the action of driving slowly along the edge of the road in search of a prostitute or to harass female pedestrians.
– DERIVATIVES **kerb-crawler** noun.

kerb drill ● noun Brit. a set of precautions taken before crossing the road, as taught to children.

kerbing ● noun **1** the stones forming a kerb. **2** the action of hitting a kerb with a car tyre.

kerbstone ● noun a long, narrow stone or concrete block, laid end to end with others to form a kerb.

kerb weight ● noun the weight of a motor car without occupants or baggage.

kerchief /kercheef/ ● noun **1** a piece of fabric used to cover the head. **2** a handkerchief.
– ORIGIN Old French *cuevrechief*, from *couvrir* 'to cover' + *chief* 'head'.

kerf /kerf/ ● noun **1** a slit made by cutting with a saw. **2** the cut end of a felled tree.
– ORIGIN Old English, related to CARVE.

kerfuffle /kəfuff'l/ ● noun informal, chiefly Brit. a commotion or fuss.
– ORIGIN perhaps from Scots *curfuffle* (from *fuffle* 'to disorder'), or related to Irish *cior thual* 'confusion, disorder'.

kermes /kermeez/ ● noun a red dye obtained from the dried bodies of an insect which makes berry-like galls on the kermes oak.
– ORIGIN Arabic, related to CRIMSON.

kermes oak ● noun a very small evergreen Mediterranean oak with prickly, holly-like leaves.

kern[1] Printing ● noun a part of a metal type projecting beyond the body or shank, or a part of a printed character that overlaps its neighbours. ● verb **1** provide (metal type or a printed character) with a kern. **2** adjust the spacing between (characters).
– ORIGIN perhaps from French *carne* 'corner'.

kern[2] ● noun **1** historical a light-armed Irish foot soldier. **2** archaic a peasant; a rustic.
– ORIGIN from Old Irish *ceithern* 'band of foot soldiers'.

kernel /kern'l/ ● noun **1** a softer part of a nut, seed, or fruit stone contained within its hard shell. **2** the seed and hard husk of a cereal, especially wheat. **3** the central or most important part of something.
– ORIGIN Old English, 'small corn'.

kerosene /kerrəseen/ (also **kerosine**) ● noun a light fuel oil obtained by distilling petroleum, used especially in jet engines and domestic heating boilers; paraffin oil.
– ORIGIN from Greek *kēros* 'wax'.

kerria /kerriə/ ● noun an Asian shrub cultivated for its yellow flowers.
– ORIGIN named after the English botanical collector William *Ker(r)* (died 1814).

kersey /kerzi/ ● noun a kind of coarse, ribbed woollen cloth with a short nap.
– ORIGIN probably from *Kersey*, a town in Suffolk where woollen cloth was made.

kestrel ● noun a small falcon that hunts by hovering with rapidly beating wings.
– ORIGIN perhaps from Old French *crecerelle*.

ketamine /keetəmeen/ ● noun a synthetic compound used as an anaesthetic and pain-killing drug and also illicitly as a hallucinogen.
– ORIGIN blend of KETONE and AMINE.

ketch ● noun a two-masted sailing boat with a mizzenmast stepped forward of the rudder and smaller than its foremast.
– ORIGIN probably from CATCH.

ketchup (US also **catsup**) ● noun a spicy sauce made chiefly from tomatoes and vinegar.
– ORIGIN perhaps from Chinese, 'tomato juice'.

ketone /keetōn/ ● noun Chemistry an organic compound containing the group =C=O bonded to two alkyl groups, e.g. acetone.
– ORIGIN from German *Aketon* 'acetone'.

kettle ● noun a metal or plastic container with a lid, spout, and handle, used for boiling water.
– PHRASES **a different kettle of fish** informal something altogether different from the one just mentioned. **the pot calling the kettle black** used to convey that the criticisms a person is aiming at someone could equally well apply to themselves. **a pretty** (or **fine**) **kettle of fish** informal an awkward state of affairs.
– ORIGIN Latin *catillus* 'little pot'.

kettledrum ● noun a large drum shaped like a bowl, with adjustable pitch.

k

Thesaurus

compatible with; appropriate to, befitting, suitable for.

keepsake ● noun MEMENTO, souvenir, reminder, remembrance, token.

keg ● noun BARREL, cask, vat, butt, tun, hogshead; *historical* firkin.

ken ● noun KNOWLEDGE, awareness, perception, understanding, grasp, comprehension, realization, appreciation, consciousness.

kernel ● noun **1** *the kernel of a nut* seed, grain, core; nut. **2** *the kernel of the argument* ESSENCE, core, heart, essentials, quintes-

Kevlar /kevlaar/ • noun trademark a synthetic fibre of high tensile strength used to make bullet-proof clothing and as a reinforcing agent in tyres and other rubber products.
– ORIGIN an arbitrary formation.

kewpie /kyoopi/ • noun (trademark in the US) a type of doll with a large head, big eyes, chubby cheeks, and a curl or topknot on top of its head.
– ORIGIN from *Cupid*, the Roman god of love (represented as a naked winged boy).

key[1] • noun (pl. **keys**) **1** a small piece of shaped metal which is inserted into a lock and rotated to open or close it. **2** an instrument for grasping and turning a screw, peg, or nut. **3** a lever depressed by the finger in playing an instrument such as the organ, piano, or flute. **4** each of several buttons on a panel for operating a typewriter or computer terminal. **5** a lever operating a mechanical device for making or breaking an electric circuit. **6** a thing providing access or understanding: *a key to success.* **7** an explanatory list of symbols used in a map or table. **8** a word or system for solving a cipher or code. **9** Music a group of notes based on a particular note and comprising a scale. **10** roughness on a surface, provided to assist adhesion of plaster or other material. **11** the dry winged fruit of an ash, maple, or sycamore. • adjective of crucial importance: *a key figure.* • verb (**keys, keyed**) **1** enter or operate on (data) by means of a computer keyboard. **2** (**be keyed up**) be nervous, tense, or excited. **3** (**key into/in with**) be connected or in harmony with.
– DERIVATIVES **keyed** adjective.
– ORIGIN Old English.

key[2] • noun a low-lying island or reef, especially in the Caribbean.
– ORIGIN Spanish *cayo* 'reef'.

k

keyboard • noun **1** a panel of keys for use with a computer or typewriter. **2** a set of keys on a piano or similar musical instrument. **3** an electronic musical instrument with keys arranged as on a piano. • verb enter (data) by means of a keyboard.
– DERIVATIVES **keyboarder** noun.

key grip • noun the person in a film crew who is in charge of the camera equipment.

keyhole • noun a hole in a lock into which the key is inserted.

keyhole surgery • noun minimally invasive surgery carried out through a very small incision.

key money • noun a payment required from a new tenant in exchange for the provision of a key to the premises.

Keynesian /kaynziən/ • adjective relating to the theories of the English economist John Maynard Keynes (1883–1946), who advocated government spending on public works to stimulate the economy and provide employment.
– DERIVATIVES **Keynesianism** noun.

keynote • noun **1** a prevailing tone or central theme. **2** (before another noun) (of a speech) setting out the central theme of a conference. **3** Music the note on which a key is based.

keypad • noun a miniature keyboard or set of buttons for operating a portable electronic device or telephone.

keypunch • noun a device for transferring data by means of punched holes or notches on a series of cards or paper tape.

key ring • noun a metal ring for holding keys together in a bunch.

key signature • noun Music a combination of sharps or flats after the clef at the beginning of each stave, indicating the key of a composition.

keystone • noun **1** a central stone at the summit of an arch, locking the whole together. **2** the central principle or part of a policy or system.

keystroke • noun a single depression of a key on a keyboard.

keyword • noun **1** a word which acts as the key to a cipher or code. **2** a word or concept of great significance. **3** a significant word mentioned in an index. **4** a word used in an information retrieval system to indicate the content of a document.

KG • abbreviation (in the UK) Knight of the Order of the Garter.

kg • abbreviation kilogram(s).

khaki /kaaki/ • noun (pl. **khakis**) **1** a cotton or wool fabric of a dull brownish-yellow colour, used especially in military clothing. **2** a dull brownish-yellow colour.
– ORIGIN from Urdu, 'dust-coloured'.

Khalsa /kulsə/ • noun the company of fully initiated Sikhs to which devout orthodox Sikhs are ritually admitted at puberty.
– ORIGIN from Arabic, 'pure, belonging to'.

khamsin /kamsin/ • noun an oppressive, hot southerly or south-easterly wind blowing in Egypt in spring.
– ORIGIN Arabic, 'fifty' (being the approximate duration in days).

khan /kaan/ • noun a title given to rulers and officials in central Asia, Afghanistan, and certain other Muslim countries.
– DERIVATIVES **khanate** noun.
– ORIGIN originally denoting any of the successors of Genghis Khan: from Turkic, 'lord, prince'.

khat /kaat/ • noun the leaves of an Arabian shrub, which are chewed (or drunk as an infusion) as a stimulant.
– ORIGIN Arabic.

khazi /kaazi/ • noun (pl. **khazies**) Brit. informal a toilet.
– ORIGIN Italian *casa* 'house'.

Khmer /kmair/ • noun **1** a native of the ancient kingdom of Khmer in SE Asia. **2** a person from Cambodia. **3** the language of the Khmers, the official language of Cambodia.
– ORIGIN the name in Khmer.

Khoikhoi /koykoy/ (also **Khoi**) • noun (pl. same) a member of a group of indigenous peoples of South Africa and Namibia.
– USAGE The names **Khoikhoi** or, specifically, **Nama** are now used instead of **Hottentot**, which is regarded as offensive, with reference to people.
– ORIGIN Nama (a Khoikhoi language), 'men of men'.

khoum /koom/ • noun a monetary unit of Mauritania, equal to one fifth of an ouguiya.
– ORIGIN Arabic, 'one fifth'.

kHz • abbreviation kilohertz.

kia ora /kiə orə/ • exclamation (in New Zealand) a greeting wishing good health.
– ORIGIN Maori.

kibble /kibb'l/ • verb grind or chop (beans, grain, etc.) coarsely. • noun N. Amer. ground meal shaped into pellets, especially for pet food.
– ORIGIN of unknown origin.

kibbutz /kiboots/ • noun (pl. **kibbutzim** /kibootsim/) a communal farming settlement in Israel.
– ORIGIN modern Hebrew, 'gathering'.

kibbutznik /kibootsnik/ • noun a member of a kibbutz.

kibitz /kibbits/ • verb N. Amer. informal **1** look on and offer unwelcome advice, especially at a card game. **2** speak informally; chat.
– DERIVATIVES **kibitzer** noun.
– ORIGIN Yiddish.

kibosh /kībosh/ (also **kybosh**) • noun (in phrase **put the kibosh on**) informal put a decisive end to.
– ORIGIN of unknown origin.

kick • verb **1** strike or propel forcibly with the foot. **2** strike out with the foot or feet. **3** informal succeed in giving up (a habit or addiction). **4** (of a gun) recoil when fired. • noun **1** an instance of kicking. **2** informal a sharp stimulant effect. **3** informal a thrill of pleasurable excitement.
– PHRASES **kick against** express disagreement or frustration with. **kick around** (or **about**) informal **1** lie unwanted or unexploited. **2** treat (someone) roughly or without respect. **3** discuss (an idea) casually or experimentally. **kick the bucket** informal

Thesaurus

sence, fundamentals, basics, nub, gist, substance; *informal* nitty-gritty. **3** *a kernel of truth* NUCLEUS, germ, grain, nugget.

key • noun **1** *I put my key in the lock* door key, latchkey, pass key, master key. **2** *the key to the mystery | the key to success* ANSWER, clue, solution, explanation; basis, foundation, requisite, precondition, means, way, route, path, passport, secret, formula. **3** *(Music) a minor key* TONE, pitch, timbre, tone colour. **4** *an austerely intellectual key* STYLE, character, mood, vein, spirit, feel, feeling, flavour, quality, atmosphere.
• adjective *a key figure* CRUCIAL, central, essential, indispensable, pivotal, critical, dominant, vital, principal, prime, chief, major, leading, main, important, significant.
– OPPOSITES peripheral.

keynote • noun THEME, salient point, gist, substance, burden, tenor, pith, marrow, essence, heart, core, basis, essential feature/element.

keystone • noun **1** *the keystone of the door* CORNERSTONE, central stone, quoin. **2** *the keystone of the government's policy* FOUNDATION, basis, linchpin, cornerstone, base, (guiding) principle, core, heart, centre, crux, fundament.

kibosh • noun
– PHRASES **put the kibosh on** *(informal)* PUT A STOP TO, stop, halt, put

die. **kick in** become activated; come into effect. **a kick in the teeth** informal a grave setback or disappointment. **kick off** (of a football match) be started or resumed by a player kicking the ball from the centre spot. **kick oneself** be annoyed with oneself. **kick out** informal expel or dismiss. **kick upstairs** informal remove (someone) from an influential position by giving them an ostensible promotion.
– DERIVATIVES **kicker** noun.
– ORIGIN of unknown origin.

kick-ass ● adjective N. Amer. informal forceful, vigorous, and aggressive.

kickback ● noun **1** a sudden forceful recoil. **2** informal an illicit payment made to someone who has facilitated a transaction or appointment.

kick-boxing ● noun a form of martial art which combines boxing with elements of karate, in particular kicking with bare feet.

kick-down ● noun Brit. a device for changing gear in a motor vehicle with automatic transmission by full depression of the accelerator.

kick drum ● noun informal a bass drum played using a pedal.

kicking ● adjective informal (especially of music) lively and exciting.

kick-off ● noun the start or resumption of a football match, in which a player kicks the ball from the centre spot.

kick-pleat ● noun an inverted pleat in a narrow skirt to allow freedom of movement.

kickshaw ● noun **1** archaic a fancy but insubstantial cooked dish. **2** chiefly N. Amer. an elegant but insubstantial trinket.
– ORIGIN from French *quelque chose* 'something'.

kickstand ● noun a metal rod attached to a bicycle or motorcycle that may be kicked into a vertical position to support the vehicle when it is stationary.

kick-start ● verb **1** start (an engine on a motorcycle) with a downward thrust of a pedal. **2** provide an impetus to start or restart (a process). ● noun **1** an act of kick-starting. **2** a device to kick-start an engine.

kid¹ ● noun **1** informal a child or young person. **2** a young goat. ● verb (**kidded**, **kidding**) (of a goat) give birth.
– PHRASES **handle** (or **treat**) **with kid gloves** deal with very carefully. **kids' stuff** informal something that is easy or simple to do.
– ORIGIN Old Norse.

kid² ● verb (**kidded**, **kidding**) informal **1** deceive playfully; tease. **2** fool into believing something.
– ORIGIN perhaps from KID¹, expressing the notion 'make a child or goat of'.

kid brother (or **kid sister**) ● noun informal a younger brother or sister.

kiddie (also **kiddy**) ● noun (pl. **kiddies**) informal a young child.

kiddiewink ● noun Brit. humorous a small child.

kidnap ● verb (**kidnapped**, **kidnapping**; US also **kidnaped**, **kidnaping**) abduct and hold (someone) captive, typically to obtain a ransom. ● noun an instance of kidnapping.
– DERIVATIVES **kidnapper** noun.
– ORIGIN from KID¹ + slang *nap* 'nab, seize'.

kidney ● noun (pl. **kidneys**) **1** each of a pair of organs in the abdominal cavity, with one concave and one convex side, that excrete urine. **2** the kidney of a sheep, ox, or pig as food. **3** archaic nature or temperament.
– ORIGIN of obscure origin.

kidney bean ● noun a kidney-shaped bean, especially a dark red one from a dwarf French bean plant.

kidney dish ● noun a kidney-shaped receptacle used in medicine.

kidney machine ● noun an artificial kidney or dialysis machine.

kidney stone ● noun a hard mass formed in the kidneys, typically consisting of insoluble calcium compounds.

kidology /kidolləji/ ● noun Brit. informal deliberate deception or teasing.

kieselguhr /keez'lgoor/ ● noun a soft, crumbly sedimentary material consisting of the fossil remains of diatoms, used as a filter, filler, and insulator.
– ORIGIN German, from *Kiesel* 'gravel' + *Guhr* 'yeast'.

kif /kif/ (also **kef**) ● noun a substance, especially cannabis, smoked to produce a drowsy state.
– ORIGIN Arabic, 'enjoyment, well-being'.

Kikuyu /kikōōyōō/ ● noun (pl. same or **Kikuyus**) a member of a people forming the largest ethnic group in Kenya.
– ORIGIN the name in Kikuyu.

kikuyu grass ● noun a creeping perennial grass which is native to Kenya and cultivated elsewhere as a lawn and fodder grass.

kilim /kileem/ (also **kelim**) ● noun a carpet or rug woven without a pile, made in Turkey, Kurdistan, and neighbouring areas.
– ORIGIN Persian.

kill ● verb **1** cause the death of. **2** put an end to. **3** informal overwhelm with an emotion. **4** informal cause pain or anguish to. **5** pass (time). **6** stop (a computing process). **7** (in sport) make (the ball) stop. ● noun **1** an act of killing, especially of one animal by another. **2** an animal or animals killed by a hunter or another animal. **3** informal an act of destroying an enemy aircraft or vessel.
– PHRASES **be in at the kill** be present at or benefit from the successful conclusion of an enterprise. **kill two birds with one stone** proverb achieve two aims at once. **kill with kindness** spoil (someone) with overindulgence.
– ORIGIN probably Germanic and related to QUELL.

Thesaurus

an end to, quash, block, cancel, scotch, thwart, prevent, suppress; *informal* put paid to, stymie; *Brit. informal* scupper.

kick ● verb **1** *her attacker kicked her* BOOT, strike with the foot; *Brit. informal* put the boot into. **2** *(informal) he was struggling to kick his drug habit* GIVE UP, break, abandon, end, stop, cease, desist from, renounce; *informal* shake, pack in, leave off, quit. **3** *the gun kicked hard* RECOIL, spring back.
● noun **1** *a kick on the knee* BLOW WITH THE FOOT; *informal* boot. **2** *(informal) I get a kick out of driving a racing car* THRILL, excitement, stimulation, tingle; fun, enjoyment, amusement, pleasure, gratification; *informal* buzz, high; *N. Amer. informal* charge. **3** *(informal) a drink with a powerful kick* POTENCY, stimulant effect, strength, power; tang, zest, bite, piquancy, edge, pungency; *informal* punch. **4** *(informal) a health kick* CRAZE, enthusiasm, obsession, mania, passion; fashion, vogue, trend; *informal* fad.
– PHRASES **kick against** RESIST, rebel against, oppose, struggle/fight against; defy, disobey, reject, spurn. **kick someone/something around** *(informal)* **1** *we are undervalued and get kicked around* ABUSE, mistreat, maltreat, push around/about, trample on, take for granted; *informal* boss about/around, walk all over. **2** *they began to kick ideas around* DISCUSS, talk over, debate, thrash out, consider, toy with, play with. **kick back** *(N. Amer. informal)* RELAX, unwind, take it easy, rest, slow down, let up, ease up/off, sit back; *N. Amer. informal* chill out, hang loose. **kick off** *(informal)* START, commence, begin, get going, get off the ground, get under way; open, start off, set in motion, launch, initiate, introduce, inaugurate, usher in. **kick someone out** *(informal)* EXPEL, eject, throw out, oust, evict, get rid of, axe; dismiss, discharge; *informal* chuck out, send packing, boot out, give someone their marching orders, sack, fire; *Brit. informal* turf out; *N. Amer. informal* give someone the bum's rush.

kickback ● noun **1** *the kickback from the gun* RECOIL, kick, rebound. **2** *(informal) they paid kickbacks to politicians* BRIBE, payment, inducement; *N. Amer.* payola; *informal* pay-off, sweetener, backhander.

kick-off ● noun *(informal)* BEGINNING, start, commencement, outset, opening.

kid¹ ● noun *(informal) she has three kids* CHILD, youngster, little one, baby, toddler, tot, infant, boy/girl, young person, minor, juvenile, adolescent, teenager, youth, stripling; offspring, son/daughter; *Scottish* bairn; *informal* kiddie, nipper, kiddiewink, shaver, young 'un; *Brit. informal* sprog; *N. Amer. informal* rug rat; *Austral./NZ* ankle-biter; *derogatory* brat; *poetic/literary* babe.

kid² ● verb *(informal)* **1** *I'm not kidding* JOKE, tease, jest, chaff, be facetious, fool about/around; *informal* pull someone's leg, have on, rib; *Brit. informal* wind up; *N. Amer. informal* pull someone's chain, fun, shuck. **2** *why did I kid myself that I'd succeed?* DELUDE, deceive, fool, trick, hoodwink, hoax, beguile, dupe, gull; *informal* con, pull the wool over someone's eyes; *poetic/literary* cozen.

kidnap ● verb ABDUCT, carry off, capture, seize, snatch, take as hostage; *Brit. informal* nobble.

kill ● verb **1** *gangs killed twenty-seven people* MURDER, take/end the life of, make away with, assassinate, eliminate, terminate, dispatch, finish off, put to death, execute; slaughter, butcher, massacre, wipe out, annihilate, exterminate, liquidate, mow down, shoot down, cut down, cut to pieces; *informal* bump off, polish off, do away with, do in, knock off, top, take out, croak, stiff, blow

killdeer /kildeer/ ● noun an American plover with a plaintive call that resembles its name.
killer ● noun **1** a person or thing that kills. **2** informal a formidable person or thing. **3** informal a hilarious joke.
killer bee ● noun informal, chiefly US an Africanized honeybee.
killer cell ● noun a white blood cell which destroys infected or cancerous cells.
killer instinct ● noun a ruthless determination to succeed or win.
killer whale ● noun a large toothed whale with distinctive black-and-white markings and a prominent dorsal fin.
killifish ● noun a small, brightly coloured fish of fresh or brackish water.
– ORIGIN apparently from KILL and FISH[1].
killing ● noun an act of causing death. ● adjective informal overwhelming or unbearable.
– PHRASES **make a killing** have a great financial success.
killing bottle ● noun a bottle containing poisonous vapour to kill insects collected as specimens.
killing field ● noun a place where many people have been killed.
killjoy ● noun a person who spoils the enjoyment of others through resentful or overly sober behaviour.
kiln ● noun a furnace or oven for burning, baking, or drying, especially one for firing pottery.
– ORIGIN Latin *culina* 'kitchen, cooking stove'.
Kilner jar /kilnər/ ● noun trademark a glass jar with a lid which forms an airtight seal, used to bottle fruit and vegetables.
– ORIGIN from the name of the manufacturing company.
kilo ● noun (pl. **kilos**) a kilogram.
kilo- /keelō, killō/ ● combining form denoting a factor of one thousand (10^3): *kilolitre*.
– ORIGIN from Greek *khilioi* 'thousand'.
kilobyte ● noun Computing a unit of memory or data equal to 1,024 bytes.
kilocalorie ● noun a unit of energy of one thousand calories (equal to one large calorie).
kilogram (also **kilogramme**) ● noun the SI unit of mass, equal to 1,000 grams (approximately 2.205 lb).
kilohertz ● noun a measure of frequency equivalent to 1,000 cycles per second.
kilojoule ● noun 1,000 joules, especially as a measure of the energy value of foods.
kilolitre (US **kiloliter**) ● noun 1,000 litres (equivalent to 220 imperial gallons).
kilometre /killəmeetər, kilommitər/ (US **kilometer**) ● noun a metric unit of measurement equal to 1,000 metres (approximately 0.62 miles).
– DERIVATIVES **kilometric** adjective.
– USAGE The first pronunciation of **kilometre**, with the stress on the **kil-** is considered the correct one, especially in British English.
kiloton (also **kilotonne**) ● noun a unit of explosive power equivalent to 1,000 tons of TNT.
kilovolt ● noun 1,000 volts.
kilowatt ● noun 1,000 watts.
kilowatt-hour ● noun a measure of electrical energy equivalent to a power consumption of one thousand watts for one hour.
kilt ● noun a knee-length skirt of pleated tartan cloth, traditionally worn by men as part of Scottish Highland dress. ● verb **1** arrange (a garment or material) in vertical pleats. **2** (**kilt up**) hoist or tuck up (one's skirt or coat).
– DERIVATIVES **kilted** adjective.
– ORIGIN Scandinavian, originally in the sense 'tuck up around the body'.
kilter ● noun (in phrase **out of kilter**) out of harmony or balance.
– ORIGIN of unknown origin.
kimberlite /kimbərlīt/ ● noun a rare, blue-tinged igneous rock sometimes containing diamonds, found in South Africa and Siberia.
– ORIGIN from *Kimberley*, a South African city and diamond-mining centre.
kimchi /kimchi/ ● noun spicy pickled cabbage, the national dish of Korea.
– ORIGIN Korean.
kimono /kimōnō/ ● noun (pl. **kimonos**) a long, loose Japanese robe having wide sleeves and tied with a sash.
– ORIGIN Japanese, 'wearing thing'.
kin ● noun (treated as pl.) one's family and relations. ● adjective (of a person) related.
– ORIGIN Old English.
-kin ● suffix forming diminutive nouns such as *catkin*.
– ORIGIN from Dutch *-kijn*, *-ken*, Low German *-kīn*.
kina[1] /keenə/ ● noun (pl. same) the basic monetary unit of Papua New Guinea, equal to 100 toea.
– ORIGIN from Papuan.
kina[2] /keenə/ ● noun (pl. same) an edible sea urchin occurring on New Zealand coasts.
– ORIGIN Maori.
kinaesthesia /kinnəsstheeziə/ (US **kinesthesia**) ● noun awareness of the position and movement of the parts of the body by means of sensory receptors in the muscles and joints.
– DERIVATIVES **kinaesthetic** adjective.
– ORIGIN from Greek *kinein* 'to move' + *aisthēsis* 'sensation'.
kind[1] ● noun **1** a class or type of people or things having similar

k

Thesaurus

away, dispose of; *N. Amer. informal* ice, rub out, waste, whack, scrag, smoke; *poetic/literary* slay. **2** *this would kill all hopes of progress* DESTROY, put an end to, end, extinguish, dash, quash, ruin, wreck, shatter, smash, crush, scotch, thwart; *informal* put paid to, put the kibosh on, stymie; *Brit. informal* scupper. **3** *we had to kill several hours at the airport* WHILE AWAY, fill (up), occupy, beguile, pass, spend, waste. **4** *(informal) you must rest or you'll kill yourself* EXHAUST, wear out, tire out, overtax, overtire, fatigue, weary, sap, drain, enervate, prostrate; *informal* knock out, shatter; *Brit. informal* knacker. **5** *(informal) my feet were killing me* HURT, cause pain to, torture, torment, cause discomfort to; be painful, be sore, be uncomfortable. **6** *(informal) the music kills me every time I hear it* OVERWHELM, take someone's breath away, move, stir, stun, amaze, stagger; *informal* bowl over, blow away, knock sideways, blow someone's mind. **7** *the engines were at a low rev to kill the noise* MUFFLE, deaden, stifle, dampen, damp down, smother, reduce, diminish, decrease, suppress, tone down, moderate. **8** *a shot to kill the pain* ALLEVIATE, assuage, soothe, allay, dull, blunt, deaden, stifle, suppress, subdue. **9** *(informal) the message has been killed* DELETE, wipe out, erase, remove, destroy, cut (out), cancel; *informal* zap. **10** *(informal) Congress killed the bill* VETO, defeat, vote down, rule against, reject, throw out, overrule, overturn, put a stop to, quash, squash. **11** *(informal) Noel killed the engine* TURN OFF, switch off, stop, shut off/down, cut (out).
– RELATED TERMS -cide.
● noun **1** *the hunter's kill* PREY, quarry, victim, bag. **2** *the wolf was moving in for the kill* DEATH BLOW, killing, dispatch, finish, end, coup de grâce.
killer ● noun **1** *police are searching for the killer* MURDERER, assassin, slaughterer, butcher, serial killer, gunman; exterminator, terminator, executioner; *informal* hit man; *poetic/literary* slayer; *dated* homicide. **2** *a major killer* CAUSE OF DEATH, fatal/deadly illness, threat to life.
killing ● noun *a brutal killing* MURDER, assassination, homicide, manslaughter, elimination, putting/doing to death, execution; slaughter, massacre, butchery, carnage, bloodshed, extermination, annihilation; *poetic/literary* slaying.
● adjective **1** *a killing blow* DEADLY, lethal, fatal, mortal, death-dealing; murderous, homicidal; *poetic/literary* deathly. **2** *(informal) a killing schedule* EXHAUSTING, gruelling, punishing, taxing, draining, wearing, prostrating, crushing, tiring, fatiguing, debilitating, enervating, arduous, tough, demanding, onerous, strenuous, rigorous; *informal* murderous; *Brit. informal* knackering. **3** *(informal) the suspense is killing* UNBEARABLE, intolerable, unendurable, insupportable. **4** *(informal, dated) that's absolutely killing* HILARIOUS, hysterically funny, uproarious, riotous, comical, amusing; *informal* priceless, side-splitting.
– PHRASES **make a killing** *(informal)* MAKE A LARGE PROFIT, make a/one's fortune; *informal* clean up, make a packet, make a pretty penny; *Brit. informal* make a bomb; *N. Amer. informal* make big bucks.
killjoy ● noun SPOILSPORT, prophet of doom; *informal* wet blanket, party-pooper, misery; *Austral./NZ informal* wowser.
kilter
– PHRASES **out of kilter** AWRY, off balance, unbalanced, out of order, disordered, confused, muddled, out of tune, out of step.
kin ● noun *their own kin* RELATIVES, relations, family (members), kindred, kith and kin; kinsfolk, kinsmen/kinswomen, people; *informal* folks.

characteristics. 2 character; nature. 3 each of the elements (bread and wine) of the Eucharist.
– PHRASES **in kind 1** in the same way. 2 (of payment) in goods or services as opposed to money. **kind of** informal rather. **of a kind** hardly or only partly deserving the name. **one of a kind** unique. **two** (or **three, four**, etc.) **of a kind 1** the same or very similar. 2 (of cards) having the same face value but of a different suit.
– USAGE When using **kind** to refer to a plural noun, avoid the ungrammatical construction *these kind*: say *these kinds of questions are not relevant* rather than *these kind of questions are not relevant*.
– ORIGIN Old English, related to KIN.
kind² ● adjective 1 considerate and generous. 2 archaic affectionate; loving.
– ORIGIN Old English, 'natural, native'; in the Middle Ages it meant 'well-born or well-bred', and so 'courteous, gentle, benevolent'.
kindergarten /kindərgaart'n/ ● noun a nursery school.
– ORIGIN German, 'children's garden'.
kindle¹ /kind'l/ ● verb 1 light (a flame); set on fire. 2 arouse (an emotion).
– ORIGIN from Old Norse, 'candle, torch'.
kindle² /kind'l/ ● verb (of a hare or rabbit) give birth.
– ORIGIN probably from KIND¹.
kindling ● noun small sticks or twigs used for lighting fires.
kindly ● adverb 1 in a kind manner. 2 please (used in a polite request). ● adjective (**kindlier, kindliest**) kind; warm-hearted.
– PHRASES **not take kindly to** not welcome or be pleased by. **take kindly** like or be pleased by.
– DERIVATIVES **kindliness** noun.
kindness ● noun 1 the quality of being kind. 2 a kind act.
kindred /kindrid/ ● noun 1 (treated as pl.) one's family and relations. 2 relationship by blood. ● adjective similar in kind; related.
– ORIGIN Old English, from KIN.
kindred spirit ● noun a person whose interests or attitudes are similar to one's own.
kine /kīn/ ● plural noun archaic cows collectively.
kinematics /kinnimattiks, kīni-/ ● plural noun (treated as sing.) the branch of mechanics concerned with the motion of objects without reference to the forces which cause the motion.
– DERIVATIVES **kinematic** adjective.
– ORIGIN from Greek *kinēma* 'motion'.
kinesiology /kineesiolləji/ ● noun the study of the mechanics of body movements.
kinesis /kineesiss/ ● noun (pl. **kineses**) technical movement; motion.
– ORIGIN Greek.
kinesthesia ● noun US spelling of KINAESTHESIA.
kinetic /kinettiks, kī-/ ● adjective 1 relating to or resulting from motion. 2 (of a work of art) depending on movement for its effect.
– DERIVATIVES **kinetically** adverb.
– ORIGIN Greek *kinētikos*, from *kinein* 'to move'.
kinetic energy ● noun Physics energy which a body possesses by virtue of being in motion. Compare with POTENTIAL ENERGY.
kinetics /kinettiks, kī-/ ● plural noun (treated as sing.) 1 the branch of chemistry concerned with the rates of chemical reactions. 2 Physics another term for DYNAMICS (in sense 1).
kinetic theory ● noun the theory which explains the physical properties of matter in terms of the motions of atoms and molecules.
kinetoscope /kineetəskōp, kī-/ ● noun an early motion-picture device in which the images were viewed through a peephole.
kinfolk ● plural noun another term for KINSFOLK.
king ● noun 1 the male ruler of an independent state, especially one who inherits the position by birth. 2 the best or most important person or thing in a sphere or group. 3 a playing card bearing a representation of a king, ranking next below an ace. 4 the most important chess piece, which the opponent has to checkmate in order to win. 5 a piece in draughts with extra capacity for moving, made by crowning an ordinary piece that has reached the opponent's baseline.
– DERIVATIVES **kingly** adjective **kingship** noun.
– ORIGIN Old English, related to KIN.
kingbolt ● noun a kingpin.
King Charles spaniel ● noun a small breed of spaniel with a white, black, and tan coat.
– ORIGIN named after King Charles II of England, Scotland, and

k

Thesaurus

● adjective *my uncle was kin to the brothers* RELATED, akin, allied, connected with, consanguineous; formal cognate.
kind¹ ● noun 1 *all kinds of gifts | the kinds of bird that could be seen* SORT, type, variety, style, form, class, category, genre; genus, species, race, breed. 2 *they were different in kind | the first of its kind* CHARACTER, nature, essence, quality, disposition, make-up; type, style, stamp, manner, description, mould, cast, temperament, ilk; N. Amer. stripe.
– PHRASES **kind of** (informal) RATHER, quite, fairly, somewhat, a little, slightly, a shade; informal sort of, a bit, kinda, pretty, a touch, a tad.
kind² ● adjective *she is such a kind and caring person* KINDLY, good-natured, kind-hearted, warm-hearted, caring, affectionate, loving, warm; considerate, helpful, thoughtful, obliging, unselfish, selfless, altruistic, good, attentive; compassionate, sympathetic, understanding, big-hearted, benevolent, benign, friendly, neighbourly, hospitable, well meaning, public-spirited; generous, liberal, open-handed, bountiful, beneficent, munificent, benignant; Brit. informal decent.
– OPPOSITES inconsiderate, mean.
kind-hearted ● adjective KIND, caring, warm-hearted, kindly, benevolent, good-natured, tender, warm, compassionate, sympathetic, understanding; indulgent, altruistic, benign, beneficent, benignant.
kindle ● verb 1 *he kindled a fire* LIGHT, ignite, set alight, set light to, set fire to, put a match to. 2 *Elvis kindled my interest in music* ROUSE, arouse, wake, awaken; stimulate, inspire, stir (up), excite, evoke, provoke, fire, inflame, trigger, activate, spark off; poetic/literary waken, enkindle.
– OPPOSITES extinguish.
kindliness ● noun KINDNESS, benevolence, warmth, gentleness, tenderness, care, humanity, sympathy, compassion, understanding; generosity, charity, kind-heartedness, warm-heartedness, thoughtfulness, solicitousness.
kindly ● adjective *a kindly old lady* BENEVOLENT, kind, kind-hearted, warm-hearted, generous, good-natured; gentle, warm, compassionate, caring, loving, benign, well meaning; helpful, thoughtful, considerate, good-hearted, nice, friendly, neighbourly; Brit. informal decent.
– OPPOSITES unkind, cruel.
● adverb 1 *she spoke kindly* BENEVOLENTLY, good-naturedly, warmly, affectionately, tenderly, lovingly, compassionately; considerately, thoughtfully, helpfully, obligingly, generously, selflessly, unselfishly, sympathetically. 2 *kindly explain what you mean* PLEASE, if you please, if you wouldn't mind, have the goodness to; archaic prithee, pray.
– OPPOSITES unkindly, harshly.
– PHRASES **not take kindly to** RESENT, object to, take umbrage at, take exception to, take offence at, be annoyed by, be irritated by, feel aggrieved about, be upset by.
kindness ● noun 1 *he thanked her for her kindness* KINDLINESS, kind-heartedness, warm-heartedness, affection, warmth, gentleness, concern, care; consideration, considerateness, helpfulness, thoughtfulness, unselfishness, selflessness, altruism, compassion, sympathy, understanding, big-heartedness, benevolence, benignity, friendliness, neighbourliness, public-spiritedness; hospitality, generosity, magnanimity, charitableness; Brit. informal decency. 2 *she has done us many a kindness* KIND ACT, good deed, good turn, favour, service.
kindred ● noun 1 *his mother's kindred* FAMILY, relatives, relations, kin, kith and kin, one's own flesh and blood; kinsfolk, kinsmen/kinswomen, people; informal folks. 2 *ties of kindred* KINSHIP, family ties, being related, (blood) relationship, consanguinity, common ancestry.
● adjective 1 *industrial relations and kindred subjects* RELATED, allied, connected, comparable, similar, like, parallel, associated, analogous; formal cognate. 2 *a kindred spirit* LIKE-MINDED, in sympathy, in harmony, in tune, of one mind, akin, similar, like, compatible; informal on the same wavelength.
– OPPOSITES unrelated, alien.
king ● noun 1 *the king of France* RULER, sovereign, monarch, crowned head, Crown, emperor, prince, potentate, lord. 2 *the king of world football* STAR, leading light, luminary, superstar, giant, master; informal supremo, megastar.

Ireland.

king cobra ● noun a brownish cobra native to the Indian subcontinent, the largest of all venomous snakes.

kingcup ● noun British term for MARSH MARIGOLD.

kingdom ● noun **1** a country, state, or territory ruled by a king or queen. **2** a realm associated with a particular person or thing. **3** the spiritual reign or authority of God. **4** each of the three divisions (animal, vegetable, and mineral) in which natural objects are classified.

– PHRASES **till** (or **until**) **kingdom come** informal forever. **to kingdom come** informal into the next world.

King Edward ● noun a variety of potato having a white skin mottled with red.

– ORIGIN named after King Edward VII.

kingfisher ● noun a colourful bird with a large head and long sharp beak which dives to catch fish in streams, ponds, etc.

King James Bible (also **King James Version**) ● noun another name for AUTHORIZED VERSION.

kinglet ● noun **1** chiefly derogatory a minor king. **2** chiefly N. Amer. a very small warbler of a group that includes the goldcrest.

kingmaker ● noun a person who brings leaders to power through the exercise of political influence.

– ORIGIN used originally with reference to the Earl of Warwick (1428–71), known as Warwick the *Kingmaker*.

King of Arms ● noun Heraldry (in the UK) a chief herald.

king of beasts ● noun the lion.

king of birds ● noun the eagle.

King of Kings ● noun (in the Christian Church) God.

kingpin ● noun **1** a main or large bolt in a central position. **2** a vertical bolt used as a pivot. **3** a person or thing that is essential to the success of an organization or operation.

king post ● noun an upright post extending from the tie beam to the apex of a roof truss.

k

king prawn ● noun a large edible prawn.

King's Bench ● noun in the reign of a king, the term for QUEEN'S BENCH.

King's Counsel ● noun in the reign of a king, the term for QUEEN'S COUNSEL.

King's evidence ● noun in the reign of a king, the term for QUEEN'S EVIDENCE.

king's evil ● noun historical scrofula, formerly believed to be curable by the royal touch.

king-sized (also **king-size**) ● adjective of a larger size than the standard; very large.

King's speech ● noun in the reign of a king, the term for QUEEN'S SPEECH.

kink ● noun **1** a sharp twist or curve in something long and narrow. **2** a flaw or obstacle in a plan or operation. **3** a quirk of character or behaviour. ● verb form a kink.

– ORIGIN Low German *kinke*, probably from Dutch *kinken* 'to kink'.

kinkajou /kingkəjoo/ ● noun a fruit-eating mammal with a prehensile tail, found in the tropical forests of Central and South America.

– ORIGIN Algonquian.

kinky ● adjective (**kinkier**, **kinkiest**) **1** having kinks or twists. **2** informal involving or given to unusual sexual behaviour.

– DERIVATIVES **kinkily** adverb **kinkiness** noun.

-kins ● suffix equivalent to -KIN, typically expressing endearment.

kinsfolk (also **kinfolk**) ● plural noun (in anthropological or formal use) a person's blood relations, regarded collectively.

kinship ● noun **1** blood relationship. **2** a sharing of characteristics or origins.

kinsman (also **kinswoman**) ● noun (in anthropological or formal use) one of a person's blood relations.

kiosk /keeosk/ ● noun **1** a small open-fronted hut or cubicle from which newspapers, refreshments, tickets, etc. are sold. **2** Brit. a public telephone booth.

– ORIGIN Turkish *köşk* 'pavilion'.

kip[1] informal ● noun **1** Brit. a sleep; a nap. **2** a bed or cheap lodging house. **3** Irish a dirty or sordid place. ● verb (**kipped**, **kipping**) Brit. sleep.

– ORIGIN originally in the sense 'brothel': perhaps related to Danish *kippe* 'hovel, tavern'.

kip[2] ● noun (in Australia) a small piece of wood from which coins are spun in the game of two-up.

– ORIGIN perhaps related to Irish *cipin* 'small stick'.

kip[3] ● noun (pl. same or **kips**) the basic monetary unit of Laos, equal to 100 ats.

– ORIGIN Thai.

kipper ● noun a herring that has been split open, salted, and dried or smoked. ● verb cure (a herring) in such a way.

– ORIGIN Old English, denoting a male salmon in the spawning season.

kipper tie ● noun a brightly coloured and very wide tie.

Kir /keer/ ● noun trademark a drink made from dry white wine and crème de cassis.

– ORIGIN named after Canon Félix *Kir* (1876–1968), a mayor of Dijon, said to have invented the recipe.

kirby grip (also trademark **Kirbigrip**) ● noun Brit. a hairgrip consisting of a thin folded and sprung metal strip.

– ORIGIN named after *Kirby*, Beard, & Co. Ltd, the original manufacturers.

Kirghiz ● noun variant spelling of KYRGYZ.

kirk ● noun Scottish & N. English **1** a church. **2** (**the Kirk** or **the Kirk of Scotland**) the Church of Scotland.

– ORIGIN from the same Old English root as CHURCH.

Kirk session ● noun the lowest court in the Church of Scotland.

kirsch /keersh/ ● noun brandy distilled from the fermented juice of cherries.

– ORIGIN German, from *Kirschenwasser* 'cherry water'.

kirtle /kurt'l/ ● noun archaic **1** a woman's gown or outer petticoat. **2** a man's tunic or coat.

– ORIGIN Old English, probably from Latin *curtus* 'short'.

kismet /kizmet/ ● noun destiny; fate.

– ORIGIN Arabic, 'division, portion, lot'.

kiss ● verb **1** touch or caress with the lips as a sign of love, affection, or greeting. **2** Billiards & Snooker (of a ball) lightly touch (another ball). ● noun **1** a touch or caress with the lips. **2** Billiards & Snooker a slight touch of a ball against another ball. **3** N. Amer. a small cake, biscuit, or sweet.

– PHRASES **kiss someone's arse** (or N. Amer. **ass**) vulgar slang behave obsequiously towards someone. **kiss of death** an action that ensures the failure of an enterprise. **kiss off** N. Amer. informal dismiss rudely or abruptly. **kiss of life** **1** mouth-to-mouth resuscitation. **2** something that revives a failing enterprise. **kiss of peace** a ceremonial kiss signifying unity, especially during

Thesaurus

– PHRASES **a king's ransom** A HUGE AMOUNT, a vast sum; *informal* a (small) fortune, a mint, a packet, a pretty penny, big money; *Brit. informal* a bomb; *N. Amer. informal* big bucks; *Austral. informal* big bickies.

kingdom ● noun **1** *his kingdom stretched to the sea* REALM, domain, dominion, country, empire, land, nation, (sovereign) state, province, territory. **2** *Henry's little kingdom* DOMAIN, province, realm, sphere, dominion, territory, arena, zone. **3** *the plant kingdom* DIVISION, category, classification, grouping, group.

kingly ● adjective **1** *kingly power* ROYAL, regal, monarchical, sovereign, imperial, princely. **2** *kingly robes* REGAL, majestic, stately, noble, lordly, dignified, distinguished, courtly; splendid, magnificent, grand, glorious, rich, gorgeous, resplendent, princely, superb, sumptuous; *informal* splendiferous.

kink ● noun **1** *your fishing line should have no kinks in it* CURL, twist, twirl, loop, crinkle; knot, tangle, entanglement. **2** *a kink in the road* BEND, corner, dog-leg, twist, turn, curve; *Brit.* hairpin bend. **3** *there are still some kinks to iron out* FLAW, defect, imperfection, problem, complication, hitch, snag, shortcoming, weakness; *informal* hiccup, glitch. **4** *their sartorial kinks* PECULIARITY, quirk, idiosyncrasy, eccentricity, oddity, foible, whim, caprice.

kinky ● adjective **1** (*informal*) *a kinky relationship* PERVERTED, abnormal, deviant, unnatural, depraved, degenerate, perverse; *informal* pervy. **2** (*informal*) *kinky underwear* PROVOCATIVE, sexy, sexually arousing, erotic, titillating, naughty, indecent, immodest; *Brit. informal* saucy. **3** *Catriona's long kinky hair* CURLY, crimped, curled, curling, frizzy, frizzed, wavy.

kinsfolk ● noun RELATIVES, relations, kin, kindred, family, kith and kin, kinsmen/kinswomen, people; *informal* folks.

kinship ● noun **1** *ties of kinship* RELATIONSHIP, being related, family ties, blood ties, common ancestry, kindred, consanguinity. **2** *she felt kinship with the others* AFFINITY, sympathy, rapport, harmony, understanding, empathy, closeness, fellow feeling, bond, compatibility; similarity, likeness, correspondence, concordance.

kinsman, kinswoman ● noun RELATIVE, relation, family member; cousin, uncle, nephew, aunt, niece.

kiosk ● noun BOOTH, stand, stall, counter, news-stand.

the Christian Eucharist.
– DERIVATIVES **kissable** adjective.
– ORIGIN Old English.
kiss curl • noun a small curl of hair on the forehead, at the nape of the neck, or in front of the ear.
kisser • noun **1** a person who kisses someone. **2** informal a person's mouth.
kissing cousin • noun a relative known well enough to greet with a kiss.
kissing gate • noun Brit. a small gate hung in a U- or V-shaped enclosure, letting one person through at a time.
kiss-off • noun N. Amer. informal a rude or abrupt dismissal.
kissogram • noun a novelty greeting delivered by a man or woman who accompanies it with a kiss.
kist • noun Scottish & S. African a storage chest.
– ORIGIN variant of CHEST.
Kiswahili /keeswaaheeli/ • noun another term for SWAHILI (the language).
kit[1] • noun **1** a set of articles or equipment for a specific purpose. **2** Brit. the clothing and other items needed for an activity. **3** a set of all the parts needed to assemble something. **4** Brit. a large basket or box, especially for fish. • verb (**kit out**) provide with appropriate clothing or equipment.
– PHRASES **get one's kit off** Brit. informal take off one's clothes.
– ORIGIN Dutch *kitte* 'wooden container'.
kit[2] • noun the young of certain animals, e.g. the beaver, ferret, and mink.
kit[3] • noun historical a small violin, especially one used by a dancing master.
– ORIGIN perhaps from Latin *cithara*, denoting a kind of harp.
kitbag • noun a long, cylindrical canvas bag for carrying a soldier's possessions.
kit-cat • noun a canvas of a standard size (typically 36 × 28 in., 91.5 × 71 cm), especially as used for a portrait showing the sitter's head, shoulders, and hands.
– ORIGIN named after portraits of members of the 18th-century *Kit-Cat* Club, an association of Whigs and literary figures.
kitchen • noun **1** a room where food is prepared and cooked. **2** a set of fitments and units installed in a kitchen.
– ORIGIN Old English, ultimately from Latin *coquere* 'to cook'.
kitchen cabinet • noun informal a group of unofficial advisers considered to be unduly influential.
kitchenette • noun a small kitchen or part of a room equipped as a kitchen.
kitchen garden • noun a garden where vegetables and fruit are grown for domestic use.
kitchen midden • noun a prehistoric refuse heap marking an ancient settlement.
kitchen paper • noun absorbent paper used for drying and cleaning in a kitchen.
kitchen-sink • adjective (of drama) realistic in the depiction of drab or sordid subjects.
kitchen tea • noun Austral./NZ a party before a wedding to which female guests bring kitchen equipment for the bride-to-be.
kitchenware • noun kitchen utensils.
kite • noun **1** a toy consisting of a light frame with thin material stretched over it, flown in the wind at the end of a long string. **2** Brit. informal, dated an aircraft. **3** a long-winged bird of prey with a forked tail and a soaring flight. **4** Geometry a quadrilateral figure having two pairs of equal adjacent sides, symmetrical only about one diagonal. **5** informal a fraudulent cheque, bill, or receipt. • verb **1** fly a kite. **2** informal, chiefly N. Amer. write or use (a fraudulent cheque, bill, or receipt).
– PHRASES **(as) high as a kite** informal intoxicated with drugs or alcohol. **fly a kite** informal try something out to test public opinion.
– ORIGIN Old English.
Kitemark • noun trademark (in the UK) an official kite-shaped mark on goods approved by the British Standards Institution.
kith /kith/ • noun (in phrase **kith and kin**) one's relations.
– ORIGIN Old English, originally in the senses 'knowledge', 'one's native land', and 'friends and neighbours'.
kitsch /kich/ • noun art, objects, or design considered to be excessively garish or sentimental, but appreciated in an ironic or knowing way.
– DERIVATIVES **kitschiness** noun **kitschy** adjective.
– ORIGIN German.
kitten • noun **1** a young cat. **2** the young of certain other animals, such as the rabbit and beaver. • verb give birth to kittens.
– PHRASES **have kittens** Brit. informal be extremely nervous or upset.
– ORIGIN Old French *chitoun*, from *chat* 'cat'.
kitten heel • noun a type of low stiletto heel.
kittenish • adjective playful, lively, or flirtatious.
– DERIVATIVES **kittenishly** adverb **kittenishness** noun.
kittiwake /kittiwayk/ • noun a small gull that nests in colonies on sea cliffs and has a loud call that resembles its name.
kitty[1] • noun (pl. **kitties**) **1** a fund of money for communal use. **2** a pool of money in some card games. **3** (in bowls) the jack.
– ORIGIN originally denoting a jail: of unknown origin.
kitty[2] • noun (pl. **kitties**) a pet name for a cat.
kitty-corner • adjective & adverb another term for CATER-CORNERED.
kiwi • noun (pl. **kiwis**) **1** a flightless, tailless New Zealand bird with hair-like feathers and a long downcurved bill. **2** (**Kiwi**) informal a New Zealander.
– ORIGIN Maori.
kiwi fruit • noun (pl. same) the fruit of an Asian climbing plant, with a thin hairy skin, green flesh, and black seeds.
kJ • abbreviation kilojoule(s).
KKK • abbreviation Ku Klux Klan.
kl • abbreviation kilolitre(s).
Klansman (or **Klanswoman**) • noun a member of the Ku Klux Klan, an extremist right-wing secret society in the US.
klaxon /klaks'n/ • noun trademark a vehicle horn or warning hooter.
– ORIGIN the name of the manufacturers.
Kleenex • noun (pl. same or **Kleenexes**) trademark a paper tissue.
kleptomania /kleptəmayniə/ • noun a recurrent urge to steal.
– DERIVATIVES **kleptomaniac** noun & adjective.
– ORIGIN from Greek *kleptēs* 'thief'.
klieg light /kleeg/ • noun a powerful electric lamp used in filming.
– ORIGIN named after the American brothers, Anton T. *Kliegl* (1872–1927) and John H. *Kliegl* (1869–1959), who invented it.
Klondike /klondik/ • noun a source of valuable material.
– ORIGIN from *Klondike* in Yukon, Canada, where gold was found in 1896.
kludge /kluj/ • noun informal something hastily or badly put together.
– ORIGIN invented word, perhaps influenced by BODGE and FUDGE.
klutz /kluts/ • noun informal, chiefly N. Amer. a clumsy, awkward, or foolish person.
– DERIVATIVES **klutzy** adjective.
– ORIGIN Yiddish, 'wooden block'.
km • abbreviation kilometre(s).
knack • noun **1** an acquired or natural skill at performing a

k

Thesaurus

kismet • noun FATE, destiny, fortune, providence, God's will, one's lot (in life), karma, predestination, preordination, predetermination; luck, chance; *poetic/literary* one's dole.
kiss • verb **1** *he kissed her on the lips* give a kiss to, brush one's lips against, blow a kiss to, air-kiss; *informal* peck, give a smacker to, smooch, canoodle, neck, pet; *Brit. informal* snog; *N. Amer. informal* buss; *informal, dated* spoon; *formal* osculate. **2** *allow your foot just to kiss the floor* BRUSH (AGAINST), caress, touch (gently), stroke, skim over.
• noun **1** *a kiss on the cheek* air kiss, French kiss; X; *informal* peck, smack, smacker, smooch; *Brit. informal* snog; *N. Amer. informal* buss; *formal* osculation. **2** *the kiss of the flowers against her cheeks* GENTLE TOUCH, caress, brush, stroke.
kit • noun **1** *his tool kit* EQUIPMENT, tools, implements, instruments, gadgets, utensils, appliances, tools of the trade, gear, tackle, hardware, paraphernalia; *informal* things, stuff, the necessary; *Military* accoutrements. **2** *(Brit.) their football kit* CLOTHES, clothing, rig, outfit, dress, costume, garments, attire, garb, gear, get-up, rig-out; *formal* apparel. **3** *a model aircraft kit* SET (OF PARTS), DIY kit, do-it-yourself kit, self-assembly set, flat-pack. **4** *(informal) we packed up all our kit* BELONGINGS, luggage, baggage, paraphernalia, effects, impedimenta; *informal* things, stuff, gear; *Brit. informal* clobber.
– PHRASES **kit someone/something out** EQUIP, fit (out/up), furnish, supply, provide, issue; dress, clothe, array, attire, rig out, deck out; *informal* fix up.
kitchen • noun kitchenette, kitchen-diner, cooking area, galley, cookhouse; *N. Amer.* cookery.
kittenish • adjective PLAYFUL, light-hearted, skittish, lively; coquet-

task. **2** a tendency to do something.
– ORIGIN probably related to obsolete *knack* 'sharp blow or sound'.

knacker Brit. ● noun **1** a person who disposes of dead or unwanted animals. **2** (**knackers**) vulgar slang testicles. ● verb informal exhaust; wear out.
– DERIVATIVES **knackered** adjective.
– ORIGIN originally denoting a harness-maker: possibly from obsolete *knack* 'trinket'; sense 2 may be from dialect *knacker* 'castanet'.

knacker's yard ● noun Brit. a place where old or injured animals are slaughtered.

knackwurst /nakwurst/ ● noun a type of short, fat, highly seasoned German sausage.
– ORIGIN German, from *knacken* 'make a cracking noise' + *Wurst* 'sausage'.

knap[1] /nap/ ● noun archaic the crest of a hill.
– ORIGIN Old English.

knap[2] /nap/ ● verb (**knapped**, **knapping**) shape (a stone) by striking it, so as to make a tool or a flat stone for building walls.
– ORIGIN imitative.

knapsack ● noun a soldier's or hiker's bag with shoulder straps, carried on the back.
– ORIGIN Dutch *knapzack*, probably from German *knappen* 'to bite' + *zak* 'sack'.

knapweed ● noun a tough-stemmed plant with purple thistle-like flower heads.
– ORIGIN from *knop* 'knob' (because of its rounded flower heads), from Low German and Dutch *knoppe*.

knave ● noun **1** archaic a dishonest or unscrupulous man. **2** (in cards) a jack.
– DERIVATIVES **knavery** noun **knavish** adjective.
– ORIGIN Old English, 'boy, servant'.

k

knead ● verb **1** work (dough or clay) with the hands. **2** massage as if kneading.
– ORIGIN Old English.

knee ● noun **1** the joint between the thigh and the lower leg. **2** the upper surface of a person's thigh when sitting. **3** something resembling a knee in shape or position, e.g. an angled piece of wood or metal. ● verb (**knees**, **kneed**, **kneeing**) hit with the knee.
– PHRASES **at one's mother's knee** at an early age. **bend** (or **bow**) **one's knee** submit. **bring someone to their knees** reduce someone to a state of weakness or submission.
– ORIGIN Old English.

knee breeches ● plural noun archaic short trousers fastened at or just below the knee.

kneecap ● noun the convex bone in front of the knee joint; the patella. ● verb shoot in the knee or leg as a punishment.

knee-high ● adjective & adverb so high as to reach the knees.
– PHRASES **knee-high to a grasshopper** informal very small or young.

knee-jerk ● noun an involuntary reflex kick caused by a blow on the tendon just below the knee. ● adjective automatic and unthinking: *a kneejerk reaction.*

kneel ● verb (past and past part. **knelt** or chiefly N. Amer. also **kneeled**) fall or rest on a knee or the knees.
– ORIGIN Old English.

kneeler ● noun **1** a person who kneels. **2** a cushion or bench for kneeling on.

knees-up ● noun Brit. informal a lively party.

knee-trembler ● noun informal an act of sexual intercourse between people in a standing position.

knell /nel/ literary ● noun the sound of a bell, especially when rung solemnly for a death or funeral. ● verb (of a bell) ring solemnly.
– ORIGIN Old English.

knelt past and past participle of KNEEL.

Knesset /knessit/ ● noun the parliament of modern Israel.
– ORIGIN Hebrew, 'gathering'.

knew past of KNOW.

knickerbocker ● noun **1** (**knickerbockers**) loose-fitting breeches gathered at the knee or calf. **2** (**Knickerbocker**) informal a New Yorker.
– ORIGIN sense 2 derives from Diedrich *Knickerbocker*, the pretended author of Washington Irving's *History of New York* (1809); sense 1 is said to be from the knee breeches worn by Dutch settlers in Irving's book.

Knickerbocker Glory ● noun Brit. a dessert consisting of ice cream, fruit, and cream in a tall glass.

knickers ● plural noun Brit. **1** a woman's or girl's undergarment covering the body from the waist or hips to the top of the thighs and having two holes for the legs. **2** N. Amer. knickerbockers.
– PHRASES **get one's knickers in a twist** Brit. informal become upset or angry.
– ORIGIN abbreviation of *knickerbockers*.

knick-knack (also **nick-nack**) ● noun a small worthless object, especially an ornament.
– ORIGIN originally in the sense 'a petty trick': reduplication of KNACK.

knife ● noun (pl. **knives**) **1** a cutting instrument consisting of a blade fixed into a handle. **2** a cutting blade on a machine. ● verb **1** stab with a knife. **2** cut like a knife.
– PHRASES **at knifepoint** under threat of injury from a knife. **before you can say knife** informal very quickly. **that one could cut with a knife** (of an accent or atmosphere) very obvious. **stick the knife into** informal treat in a hostile or aggressive manner.
– ORIGIN Old Norse.

knife-edge ● noun **1** the cutting edge of a knife. **2** a very tense or dangerous situation. **3** (before another noun) (of creases or pleats) very fine. **4** a steel wedge on which a pendulum or other device oscillates or is balanced. **5** a narrow, sharp mountain ridge.

knife pleat ● noun a sharp, narrow pleat on a skirt.

knight ● noun **1** (in the Middle Ages) a man raised to honourable military rank after service as a page and squire. **2** (in the UK) a man awarded a non-hereditary title by the sovereign and entitled to use 'Sir' in front of his name. **3** a chess piece, typically shaped like a horse's head, that moves by jumping to the opposite corner of a rectangle two squares by three. **4** (also **knight of the shire**) historical a gentleman representing a shire or county in Parliament. ● verb give (a man) the title of knight.
– PHRASES **knight in shining armour** an idealized chivalrous man.
– DERIVATIVES **knighthood** noun **knightly** adjective.
– ORIGIN Old English, 'boy, youth, servant'.

knight bachelor ● noun (pl. **knights bachelor**) a knight not

Thesaurus

tish, flirtatious, frivolous, flippant, superficial, trivial, shallow, silly; *informal* flirty, dizzy; *poetic/literary* frolicsome.
– OPPOSITES serious.

knack ● noun **1** *a knack for making money | it takes practice to acquire the knack* GIFT, talent, flair, genius, instinct, faculty, ability, capability, capacity, aptitude, aptness, bent, forte, facility; TECHNIQUE, method, trick, skill, art, expertise; *informal* the hang of something. **2** *he has a knack of getting injured at the wrong time* TENDENCY, propensity, habit, proneness, liability, predisposition.

knackered ● adjective *(Brit. informal)* **1** *you look absolutely knackered.* See EXHAUSTED sense 1. **2** *the computer was knackered.* See BROKEN sense 3.

knapsack ● noun RUCKSACK, backpack, haversack, pack, kitbag.

knave ● noun *(archaic).* See SCOUNDREL.

knavery ● noun *(archaic).* See VILLAINY.

knavish ● adjective *(archaic).* See ROGUISH sense 1.

knead ● verb **1** *kneading the dough* PUMMEL, work, pound, squeeze, shape, mould. **2** *she kneaded the base of his neck* MASSAGE, press, manipulate, rub.

kneel ● verb FALL TO ONE'S KNEES, get down on one's knees, genuflect; *historical* kowtow.

knell ● noun *(poetic/literary)* **1** *the knell of the ship's bell* TOLL, tolling, dong, resounding, reverberation; death knell; *archaic* tocsin. **2** *this sounded the knell for the project* (BEGINNING OF THE) END, death knell, death warrant.

knickers ● plural noun *(Brit.)* UNDERPANTS, briefs, French knickers, camiknickers; underwear, lingerie, underclothes, undergarments; *Brit.* pants; *informal* panties, undies; *Brit. informal* knicks, smalls; *dated* drawers; *historical* bloomers, pantalettes.

knick-knack ● noun ORNAMENT, novelty, gewgaw, bibelot, trinket, trifle, bauble, gimcrack, curio; memento, souvenir; *N. Amer.* kickshaw; *N. Amer. informal* tchotchke; *archaic* gaud, whim-wham, bijou.

knife ● noun *a sharp knife* CUTTING TOOL, blade, cutter, carver.
● verb *the victims had been knifed* STAB, hack, gash, run through,

belonging to any particular order.

knight commander • noun a very high class in some orders of knighthood.

knight errant • noun a medieval knight wandering in search of chivalrous adventures.

knight marshal • noun historical an officer of the royal household with judicial functions.

kniphofia /nifōfiə/ • noun a plant of a genus comprising the red-hot pokers.
– ORIGIN named after the German botanist Johann H. *Kniphof* (1704–63).

knit • verb (**knitting**; past and past part. **knitted** or (especially in sense 3) **knit**) **1** make by interlocking loops of yarn with knitting needles or on a machine. **2** make (a plain stitch) in knitting. **3** unite or join together. **4** tighten (one's eyebrows) in a frown. • noun (**knits**) knitted garments.
– DERIVATIVES **knitter** noun **knitting** noun.
– ORIGIN Old English, related to KNOT[1].

knitting needle • noun a long, thin, pointed rod used as part of a pair for hand knitting.

knitwear • noun knitted garments.

knives plural of KNIFE.

knob • noun **1** a rounded lump or ball at the end or on the surface of something. **2** a ball-shaped handle on a door or drawer. **3** a round button on a machine. **4** a small lump of something. **5** chiefly N. Amer. a prominent round hill. **6** vulgar slang a man's penis.
– DERIVATIVES **knobbed** adjective **knobby** adjective.
– ORIGIN Low German *knobbe* 'knot, knob, bud'.

knobble • noun Brit. a small lump on something.
– DERIVATIVES **knobbly** adjective (**knobblier**, **knobbliest**).
– ORIGIN diminutive of KNOB.

knobkerrie /nobkerri/ • noun a short stick with a knobbed head, used as a weapon by the indigenous peoples of South Africa.
– ORIGIN from KNOB + a Nama word meaning 'knobkerrie'.

knock • verb **1** strike a surface noisily to attract attention. **2** collide forcefully with. **3** force to move or fall with a collision or blow. **4** make (a hole, dent, etc.) in something by striking it. **5** informal criticize. **6** (of a motor) make a thumping or rattling noise. • noun **1** a sudden short sound caused by a blow. **2** a blow or collision. **3** a setback.
– PHRASES **knock about** (or **around**) informal **1** travel or spend time without a specific purpose. **2** happen to be present. **knock back** informal consume (a drink) quickly. **knock down 1** (at an auction) confirm (a sale) by a knock with a hammer. **2** informal reduce the price of (an article). **knock it off** informal stop doing something. **knock off** informal **1** stop work. **2** produce (a piece of work) quickly and easily. **3** Brit. informal steal. **4** kill. **be knocking on** informal be growing old. **knock on the head 1** euphemistic kill. **2** Brit. informal put an end to (an idea, plan, etc.). **knock out 1** make unconscious. **2** informal astonish or greatly impress. **3** eliminate from a knockout competition. **4** informal produce (work) at a steady fast rate. **knock spots off** Brit. informal easily outdo. **knock together** assemble (something) roughly and hastily. **knock up** informal **1** chiefly N. Amer. make (a woman) pregnant. **2** Brit. make (something) hurriedly. **the school of hard knocks** painful or difficult but useful life experiences.
– ORIGIN Old English.

knockabout • adjective (of comedy) rough and slapstick. • noun **1** US & Austral. a tramp. **2** Austral./NZ a farm or station handyman.

knock-back • noun informal a refusal or setback.

knock-down • adjective **1** informal (of a price) very low. **2** (of furniture) easily dismantled. • noun Austral./NZ informal an introduction.

knocker • noun **1** an object hinged to a door and rapped by visitors to attract attention. **2** informal a person who buys or sells from door to door. **3** informal a person who continually finds

k

Thesaurus

slash, lacerate, cut, pierce, spike, impale, transfix, bayonet, spear.

knight • noun *knights in armour* CAVALIER, cavalryman, horseman; lord, noble, nobleman; *historical* chevalier, paladin, banneret.
– PHRASES **knight in shining armour** KNIGHT ON A WHITE CHARGER, rescuer, saviour, champion, hero, defender, protector, guardian (angel).

knightly • adjective **1** *tales of knightly deeds* GALLANT, noble, valiant, heroic, courageous, brave, bold, valorous; chivalrous, courteous, honourable. **2** *the knightly classes* UPPER-CLASS, well born, noble, aristocratic; *archaic* gentle.
– OPPOSITES ignoble, low-born.

knit • verb **1** *disparate regions began to knit together* UNITE, unify, come together, draw together, become closer, bond, fuse, coalesce, merge, meld, blend. **2** *we expect broken bones to knit* HEAL, mend, join, fuse. **3** *Marcus knitted his brows* FURROW, tighten, contract, gather, wrinkle.
• noun *silky knits in pretty shades* KNITTED GARMENT, woollen; sweater, pullover, jersey, cardigan; *Brit.* jumper; *informal* woolly; *Brit. informal* cardy.

knob • noun **1** *a black bill with a knob at the base* LUMP, bump, protuberance, protrusion, bulge, swelling, knot, node, nodule, ball; *informal* boss. **2** *the knobs on the radio* DIAL, button. **3** *she turned the knob on the door* DOORKNOB, (door) handle. **4** *a few knobs of butter* NUGGET, lump, pat, ball, dollop, piece; *N. Amer. informal* gob.

knock • verb **1** *he knocked on the door* BANG, tap, rap, thump, pound, hammer; strike, hit, beat. **2** *she knocked her knee on the table* BUMP, bang, hit, strike, crack; injure, hurt, bruise; *informal* bash, thwack. **3** *he knocked into an elderly man* COLLIDE WITH, bump into, bang into, be in collision with, run into, crash into, smash into, plough into; *N. Amer.* impact; *informal* bash into. **4** *(informal) I'm not knocking the company.* See CRITICIZE.
• noun **1** *a sharp knock at the door* TAP, rap, rat-tat, knocking, bang, banging, pounding, hammering, drumming, thump, thud. **2** *the casing is tough enough to withstand knocks* BUMP, blow, bang, jolt, jar, shock; collision, crash, smash, impact. **3** *a knock on the ear* BLOW, bang, hit, slap, smack, crack, punch, cuff, thump, box; *informal* clip, clout, wallop, thwack, belt, bash. **4** *(informal) this isn't a knock on Dave.* See CRITICISM sense 1. **5** *life's hard knocks* SETBACK, reversal, defeat, failure, difficulty, misfortune, bad luck, mishap, (body) blow, disaster, calamity, disappointment, sorrow, trouble, hardship; *informal* kick in the teeth.
– PHRASES **knock about/around** *(informal)* **1** *knocking around the Mediterranean* WANDER AROUND, roam around, rove around, range over, travel around, journey around, voyage around, drift around, gallivant around, potter around; *informal* gad about. **2** *she knocks around with artists* ASSOCIATE, consort, keep company, go around, mix, socialize, be friends, be friendly; *informal* hobnob, hang out, run around, pal around. **knock someone/something about/around** BEAT (UP), batter, hit, punch, thump, thrash, slap; maltreat, mistreat, abuse, ill-treat, assault, attack; *N. Amer.* beat up on; *informal* rough up, do over, lay into, give someone a hiding, clobber, clout, bash, belt, whack, wallop. **knock something back** *(informal)* SWALLOW, gulp down, drink up, quaff, guzzle, slug; *informal* down, swig, swill (down), toss off; *N. Amer. informal* scarf (down/up), snarf (down/up). **knock someone down** FELL, floor, flatten, bring down, knock to the ground; knock over, run over/down. **knock something down 1** *the building was knocked down* DEMOLISH, pull down, tear down, destroy; raze (to the ground), level, flatten, bulldoze. **2** *(informal) the firm has knocked down its prices* REDUCE, lower, cut, decrease, drop, put down, mark down; *informal* slash. **knock off** *(informal)* STOP WORK, finish (working), clock off, leave work. **knock someone off** *(informal).* See KILL verb sense 1. **knock something off 1** *(Brit. informal) someone knocked off the video.* See STEAL verb sense 1. **2** *(informal) we expect you to knock off three stories a day* PRODUCE, make, turn out, create, construct, assemble, put together; complete, finish. **3** *(informal) knock off 10% from the bill* DEDUCT, take off/away, subtract, dock. **knock it off!** *(informal)* STOP IT; *informal* cut it out, give it a rest, leave off, pack it in, lay off; *Brit. informal* give over. **knock someone out 1** *I hit him and knocked him out* KNOCK UNCONSCIOUS, knock senseless; floor, prostrate; *informal* lay out, put out cold, KO, kayo. **2** *England was knocked out* ELIMINATE, beat, defeat, vanquish, overwhelm, trounce. **3** *(informal) walking that far knocked her out* EXHAUST, wear out, tire (out), overtire, fatigue, weary, drain; *informal* do in, take it out of, fag out; *Brit. informal* knacker; *N. Amer. informal* poop. **4** *(informal) the view knocked me out* OVERWHELM, stun, stupefy, amaze, astound, astonish, stagger, take someone's breath away; impress, dazzle, enchant, entrance; *informal* bowl over, flabbergast, knock sideways, blow away; *Brit. informal* knock for six. **knock up** *(Brit. informal)* WARM UP, practise, hit a ball around. **knock someone up 1** *(Brit. informal) we were knocked up at five in the morning* WAKE (UP), awaken, call, rouse, arouse, get out of bed, get up; *poetic/literary* waken. **2** *(informal) he knocked her up* MAKE PREGNANT, impregnate; *informal* put in the family way; *Brit. informal* get in the club; *archaic* get with child. **knock something up** *(Brit. informal)* MAKE QUICKLY, prepare hastily,

fault. **4** (**knockers**) informal a woman's breasts.
– PHRASES **on the knocker** informal **1** Brit. going from door to door. **2** Austral./NZ (of payment) immediately.

knocking shop ● noun Brit. informal a brothel.

knock-kneed ● adjective having legs that curve inwards at the knee.

knock-off ● noun informal a copy or imitation.

knock-on effect ● noun chiefly Brit. a secondary, indirect, or cumulative effect.

knockout ● noun **1** an act of knocking someone out. **2** Brit. a tournament in which the loser in each round is eliminated. **3** informal an extremely attractive or impressive person or thing.

knockout drops ● plural noun a liquid drug added to a drink to cause unconsciousness.

knock-up ● noun Brit. (in racket sports) a period of practice play before a game.

knoll /nōl/ ● noun a small hill or mound.
– ORIGIN Old English.

knot[1] ● noun **1** a fastening made by looping a piece of string, rope, etc. on itself and tightening it. **2** a tangled mass in hair, wool, etc. **3** a protuberance in a stem, branch, or root. **4** a hard mass in wood at the intersection of a trunk with a branch. **5** a hard lump of bodily tissue. **6** a small group of people. **7** a unit of speed equivalent to one nautical mile per hour, used of ships, aircraft, or winds. ● verb (**knotted**, **knotting**) **1** fasten with a knot. **2** tangle. **3** cause (a muscle) to become tense and hard. **4** (of the stomach) tighten as a result of tension.
– PHRASES **at a rate of knots** Brit. informal very fast. **get knotted** Brit. informal go away. **tie (up) in knots** informal confuse completely. **tie the knot** informal get married.
– ORIGIN Old English; sense 7 derives from the former practice of measuring a ship's speed by using a float attached to a long knotted line.

k

knot[2] ● noun (pl. same or **knots**) a short-billed northern sandpiper.
– ORIGIN of unknown origin.

knot garden ● noun an intricately designed formal garden.

knotgrass ● noun a common plant with jointed creeping stems and small pink flowers.

knothole ● noun a hole in a piece of wood where a knot has fallen out.

knotty ● adjective (**knottier**, **knottiest**) **1** full of knots. **2** extremely difficult or intricate.

knotweed ● noun knotgrass or a related plant.

knout /nowt/ ● noun (in imperial Russia) a whip used for punishment.
– ORIGIN Russian *knut*, from Old Norse; related to KNOT[1].

know ● verb (past **knew**; past part. **known**) **1** have knowledge of through observation, inquiry, or information. **2** be absolutely sure of something. **3** be familiar or friendly with. **4** have a good command of (a subject or language). **5** have personal experience of. **6** (usu. **be known as**) regard as having a specified characteristic or title: *the boss was universally known as 'Sir'.* **7** archaic have sexual intercourse with.
– PHRASES **be in the know** be aware of something known only to a few people. **God** (or **goodness** or **heaven**) **knows** I have no idea. **know better than** be wise enough to avoid doing something. **know no bounds** have no limits. **know one's own mind** be decisive and certain. **know the ropes** have experience of the appropriate procedures. **know what's what** informal be experienced and competent in a particular area. **you know** informal implying something generally known or known by the listener.
– DERIVATIVES **knowable** adjective.
– ORIGIN Old English, 'recognize, identify'.

know-all (also **know-it-all**) ● noun informal a person who behaves as if they know everything.

know-how ● noun expertise.

knowing ● adjective **1** suggesting that one has secret knowledge. **2** chiefly derogatory experienced or shrewd, especially excessively or prematurely so. ● noun the state of being aware or informed.
– PHRASES **there is no knowing** no one can tell.
– DERIVATIVES **knowingly** adverb **knowingness** noun.

knowledge ● noun **1** information and skills acquired through experience or education. **2** the sum of what is known. **3** awareness or familiarity gained by experience of a fact or situation: *he denied all knowledge of the incident.*
– PHRASES **come to one's knowledge** become known to one. **to (the best of) my knowledge 1** so far as I know. **2** as I know for certain.

knowledgeable (also **knowledgable**) ● adjective intelligent and well informed.
– DERIVATIVES **knowledgeably** adverb.

Thesaurus

build rapidly, whip up, rig up, throw together, cobble together, improvise, contrive; *informal* rustle up.

knockout ● noun **1** *the match was won by a knockout* STUNNING BLOW, finishing blow, coup de grâce; *informal* KO, kayo. **2** *(informal) she's a knockout!* BEAUTY, vision, picture, sensation, dream; *informal* stunner, dish, looker, good-looker, peach, cracker; *Brit. informal* smasher. **3** *(informal) a technical knockout* MASTERPIECE, sensation, marvel, wonder, triumph, success, feat, coup, master stroke, tour de force.

knoll ● noun *she walked up the grassy knoll* HILLOCK, mound, rise, hummock, hill, hump, tor, bank, ridge, elevation; *Scottish* brae; *formal* eminence.

knot ● noun **1** *tie a small knot* TIE, twist, loop, join, fastening, bond; tangle, entanglement. **2** *a knot in the wood* NODULE, gnarl, node; lump, knob, swelling, gall, protuberance, bump; *archaic* knar. **3** *a small knot of people* CLUSTER, group, band, huddle, bunch, circle, ring, gathering, company, crowd, throng.
● verb *their scarves were knotted round their throats* TIE (UP), fasten, secure, bind, do up.

knotted ● adjective TANGLED, tangly, knotty, entangled, matted, snarled, unkempt, uncombed, tousled; *informal* mussed up.

knotty ● adjective **1** *a knotty legal problem* COMPLEX, complicated, involved, intricate, convoluted, involuted; difficult, hard, thorny, taxing, awkward, tricky, problematic, troublesome. **2** *knotty roots* GNARLED, knotted, knurled, nodular, knobbly, lumpy, bumpy. **3** *a knotty piece of thread* KNOTTED, tangled, tangly, twisted, entangled, snarled, matted.
– OPPOSITES straightforward.

know ● verb **1** *she doesn't know I'm here* BE AWARE, realize, be conscious, be informed; notice, perceive, see, sense, recognize; *informal* savvy, latch on. **2** *I don't know his address* HAVE KNOWLEDGE OF, be informed of, be apprised of; *formal* be cognizant of. **3** *do you know the rules* BE FAMILIAR WITH, be conversant with, be acquainted with, have knowledge of, be versed in, have mastered, have a grasp of, understand, comprehend; have learned, have memorized; *informal* be clued up on. **4** *I don't know many people here* BE ACQUAINTED WITH, have met, be familiar with; be friends with, be friendly with, be on good terms with, be close to, be intimate with; *Scottish* ken; *informal* be thick with. **5** *he had known better times* EXPERIENCE, go through, live through, undergo, taste. **6** *my brothers don't know a saucepan from a frying pan* DISTINGUISH, tell (apart), differentiate, discriminate; recognize, pick out, identify.

know-all ● noun *(informal)* WISEACRE; *informal* smart alec, wise guy, smarty, smarty-pants; *Brit. informal* clever clogs, clever Dick; *N. Amer. informal* know-it-all.

know-how ● noun KNOWLEDGE, expertise, skill, skilfulness, expertness, proficiency, understanding, mastery, technique; ability, capability, competence, capacity, adeptness, dexterity, deftness, aptitude, adroitness, ingenuity, faculty; *informal* savvy.

knowing ● adjective **1** *a knowing smile* SIGNIFICANT, meaningful, eloquent, expressive, suggestive; ARCH, sly, mischievous, impish, teasing, playful. **2** *she's a very knowing child* SOPHISTICATED, worldly, worldly-wise, urbane, experienced; knowledgeable, well informed, enlightened; shrewd, astute, canny, sharp, wily, perceptive. **3** *a knowing infringement of the rules* DELIBERATE, intentional, conscious, calculated, wilful, done on purpose, premeditated, preconceived, planned.

knowingly ● adverb DELIBERATELY, intentionally, consciously, wittingly, on purpose, by design, premeditatedly, wilfully.

knowledge ● noun **1** *his knowledge of history | technical knowledge* UNDERSTANDING, comprehension, grasp, command, mastery; expertise, skill, know-how, proficiency, expertness, accomplishment, adeptness, capacity, capability. **2** *people anxious to display their knowledge* LEARNING, erudition, education, scholarship, schooling, wisdom. **3** *he slipped away without my knowledge* AWARENESS, consciousness, realization, cognition, apprehension, perception, appreciation; *formal* cognizance. **4** *an intimate knowledge of the countryside* FAMILIARITY, acquaintance, conversance, intimacy. **5** *inform the police of your knowledge* INFORMATION, facts, intelligence, news, reports; *informal* info, gen.
– OPPOSITES ignorance.

knowledgeable ● adjective **1** *a knowledgeable old man* WELL IN-

knowledge worker ● noun a person whose job involves handling or using information.

known past participle of KNOW. ● adjective **1** recognized, familiar, or within the scope of knowledge. **2** publicly acknowledged to be: *a known criminal.* **3** Mathematics (of a quantity or variable) having a value that can be stated.

know-nothing ● noun an ignorant person.

knuckle ● noun **1** a part of a finger at a joint where the bone is near the surface. **2** a projection of the carpal or tarsal joint of a quadruped. **3** this projection as a joint of meat. ● verb rub or press with the knuckles.
– PHRASES **knuckle down 1** apply oneself seriously to a task. **2** (also **knuckle under**) submit. **near the knuckle** Brit. informal verging on being indecent or offensive. **rap on** (or **over**) **the knuckles** rebuke or criticize.
– ORIGIN Low German or Dutch *knökel* 'little bone'; the verb *knuckle down* expressed setting the knuckles down to start a game of marbles.

knuckleduster ● noun a metal guard worn over the knuckles in fighting to increase the effect of blows.

knucklehead ● noun informal a stupid person.

knuckle sandwich ● noun informal a punch in the mouth.

knurl /nurl/ ● noun a small projecting knob or ridge.
– DERIVATIVES **knurled** adjective.
– ORIGIN apparently from High German *knorre* 'knobbed protuberance'.

KO[1] ● abbreviation kick-off.

KO[2] ● noun a knockout in a boxing match. ● verb (**KO's**, **KO'd**, **KO'ing**) knock out in a boxing match.

koala /kōaalə/ ● noun a bear-like tree-dwelling Australian marsupial that has thick grey fur and feeds on eucalyptus leaves.
– ORIGIN Dharuk (an Aboriginal language).

koan /kōaan/ ● noun a paradoxical anecdote or riddle, used in Zen Buddhism to show the inadequacy of logical reasoning and provoke enlightenment.
– ORIGIN Japanese, 'matter for public thought'.

kobo /kōbō/ ● noun (pl. same) a monetary unit of Nigeria, equal to one hundredth of a naira.
– ORIGIN corruption of COPPER[1].

kofta /koftə/ ● noun (pl. same or **koftas**) (in Middle Eastern and Indian cookery) a savoury ball of minced meat or vegetables.
– ORIGIN Urdu and Persian, 'pounded meat'.

kohanga reo /kəhəngə rayō/ ● noun NZ a kindergarten where lessons are conducted in Maori.
– ORIGIN Maori, 'language nest'.

kohl /kōl/ ● noun a black powder used as eye make-up.
– ORIGIN Arabic.

kohlrabi /kōlraabi/ ● noun (pl. **kohlrabies**) a variety of cabbage with an edible turnip-like swollen stem.
– ORIGIN German, from Latin *caulis* 'cabbage' + *rapum* 'turnip'.

koi /koy/ ● noun (pl. same) a large common Japanese carp.
– ORIGIN Japanese.

kola ● noun variant spelling of COLA (in sense 2).

kolkhoz /kolkoz/ ● noun (pl. same or **kolkhozes** or **kolkhozy**) a collective farm in the former USSR.
– ORIGIN Russian, from *kollektivnoe khozyaĭstvo* 'collective farm'.

Komodo dragon ● noun a very large lizard native to Komodo and neighbouring Indonesian islands.

Komsomol /komsəmol/ ● noun an organization for communist youth in the former Soviet Union.
– ORIGIN Russian, from *Kommunisticheskiĭ Soyuz Molodëzhi* 'Communist League of Youth'.

kook ● noun N. Amer. informal a mad or eccentric person.
– DERIVATIVES **kooky** adjective.
– ORIGIN probably from CUCKOO.

kookaburra /kŏŏkəburrə/ ● noun a very large, noisy, Australasian kingfisher that feeds on reptiles and birds.
– ORIGIN Wiradhuri (an Aboriginal language).

kop ● noun Brit. a high bank of terracing at a soccer ground.
– ORIGIN Afrikaans, from Dutch, 'head'; the term entered England from *Spion Kop* in South Africa, site of a Boer War battle.

kopek /kōpek/ (also **copeck** or **kopeck**) ● noun a monetary unit of Russia and some other countries of the former USSR, equal to one hundredth of a rouble.
– ORIGIN Russian *kopeĭka* 'small lance' (from the figure on the coin (1535) of Tsar Ivan IV, bearing a lance).

kora /korə/ ● noun a West African musical instrument shaped like a lute and played like a harp.
– ORIGIN a local word.

Koran /koraan/ (also **Quran** or **Qur'an** /kŏŏraan/) ● noun the Islamic sacred book, believed to be the word of God as dictated to Muhammad and written down in Arabic.
– DERIVATIVES **Koranic** /korannik/ adjective.
– ORIGIN Arabic, 'recitation'.

Korean ● noun **1** a person from Korea. **2** the language of Korea. ● adjective relating to Korea.

korma /kormə/ ● noun a mild Indian curry of meat or fish marinaded in yogurt or curds.
– ORIGIN Urdu, from Turkish *kavurma.*

koruna ● noun the basic monetary unit of Bohemia, Moravia, and Slovakia, equal to 100 haleru.
– ORIGIN Czech, 'crown'.

kosher /kōshər/ ● adjective **1** satisfying the requirements of Jewish law with regards to the preparation of food. **2** informal genuine and legitimate. ● verb prepare (food) according to Jewish law.
– ORIGIN Hebrew, 'proper'.

Kosovar /kossəvaar/ ● noun a person from Kosovo, a province of Serbia whose population is largely of Albanian descent.
– DERIVATIVES **Kosovan** noun & adjective.

koto /kōtō/ ● noun (pl. **kotos**) a large Japanese zither, with thirteen strings.
– ORIGIN Japanese.

koumiss /kŏŏmiss/ ● noun a fermented liquor prepared from mare's milk, used as a drink and medicine by Asian nomads.
– ORIGIN Tartar.

kowhai /kōwī/ ● noun a tree native to New Zealand and Chile, with hanging clusters of yellow flowers.
– ORIGIN Maori.

kowtow /kowtow/ ● verb **1** historical kneel and touch the ground with the forehead in submission as part of Chinese custom. **2** be excessively subservient towards someone.
– ORIGIN Chinese.

kph ● abbreviation kilometres per hour.

Kr ● symbol the chemical element krypton.

kraal /kraal/ S. African ● noun **1** a traditional African village of huts. **2** an enclosure for sheep and cattle. ● verb drive (animals) into a kraal.
– ORIGIN Dutch, from Portuguese *curral* 'corral'.

kraft /kraaft/ (also **kraft paper**) ● noun a kind of strong, smooth brown wrapping paper.
– ORIGIN Swedish, 'strength'.

kraken /kraakən/ ● noun a mythical sea monster said to appear off the coast of Norway.
– ORIGIN Norwegian.

Kraut /krowt/ ● noun informal, offensive a German.
– ORIGIN shortening of SAUERKRAUT.

Krebs cycle /krebz/ ● noun Biochemistry the sequence of reactions by which living cells generate energy during aerobic respiration.
– ORIGIN named after the German-born British biochemist Sir Hans *Krebs* (1900–81).

kremlin /kremlin/ ● noun **1** a citadel within a Russian town. **2** (**the Kremlin**) the citadel in Moscow, housing the Russian government.
– ORIGIN Russian *kreml'.*

Thesaurus

FORMED, learned, well read, (well) educated, erudite, scholarly, cultured, cultivated, enlightened. **2** *he is knowledgeable about modern art* ACQUAINTED, familiar, conversant, au courant, au fait; having a knowledge of, up on, up to date with, abreast of; *informal* clued up, genned up; *Brit. informal* switched on.
– OPPOSITES ill-informed.

known ● adjective **1** *a known criminal* RECOGNIZED, well known, widely known, noted, celebrated, notable, notorious; acknowledged, self-confessed, declared, overt. **2** *the known world* FAMILIAR, known about, well known; studied, investigated.

knuckle ● verb
– PHRASES **knuckle under** SURRENDER, submit, capitulate, give in/up, yield, give way, succumb, climb down, back down, admit defeat, lay down one's arms, throw in the towel/sponge.

kowtow ● verb **1** *they kowtowed to the Emperor* PROSTRATE ONESELF, bow (down before), genuflect, do/make obeisance, fall on one's knees before, kneel before. **2** *she didn't have to kowtow to a boss* GROVEL, be obsequious, be servile, be sycophantic, fawn on, bow

krill ● plural noun small shrimp-like planktonic crustaceans which are the principal food of baleen whales.
– ORIGIN Norwegian *kril* 'small fish fry'.
kris /kreess/ ● noun a Malay or Indonesian dagger with a wavy-edged blade.
– ORIGIN Malay.
krona /krōnə/ ● noun **1** (pl. **kronor** pronunc. same) the basic monetary unit of Sweden. **2** (pl. **kronur** pronunc. same) the basic monetary unit of Iceland.
– ORIGIN Swedish and Icelandic, 'crown'.
krone /krōnə/ ● noun (pl. **kroner** pronunc. same) the basic monetary unit of Denmark and Norway.
– ORIGIN Danish and Norwegian, 'crown'.
kroon ● noun (pl. **kroons** or **krooni**) the basic monetary unit of Estonia, equal to 100 sents.
– ORIGIN Estonian, 'crown'.
krugerrand /kroōgərand/ (also **Kruger**) ● noun a South African gold coin with a portrait of President Kruger on the obverse.
– ORIGIN named after Paul *Kruger*, President of Transvaal 1883–99.
krummhorn /krumhorn/ (also **crumhorn**) ● noun a medieval wind instrument with an enclosed double reed and an upward-curving end.
– ORIGIN German, 'crooked horn'.
krypton /kripton/ ● noun an inert gaseous chemical element, present in trace amounts in the air and used in some kinds of electric light.
– ORIGIN from Greek *krupton* 'hidden'.
KS ● abbreviation **1** Kansas. **2** Kaposi's sarcoma.
Kshatriya /kshatriə/ ● noun a member of the second-highest Hindu caste, that of the military.
– ORIGIN Sanskrit, 'rule, authority'.
KStJ ● abbreviation Knight of the Order of St John.
KT ● abbreviation (in the UK) Knight of the Order of the Thistle.
kt ● abbreviation knot(s).
kudos /kyoōdos/ ● noun praise and honour.
– USAGE Despite appearances, **kudos** is not a plural form: there is no singular form **kudo**, and use as a plural, as in *he received many kudos for his work*, is incorrect.
– ORIGIN Greek.
kudu /koōdoō/ ● noun (pl. same or **kudus**) a striped African antelope, the male of which has long spirally curved horns.
– ORIGIN Afrikaans.
Ku Klux Klan /koō kluks klan/ ● noun an extreme white supremacist secret society in the US.
– ORIGIN perhaps from Greek *kuklos* 'circle' and CLAN.
kukri /kookri/ ● noun (pl. **kukris**) a curved knife broadening towards the point, used by Gurkhas.
– ORIGIN Nepalese.
kulak /koolak/ ● noun historical a peasant in Russia wealthy enough to own a farm and hire labour.
– ORIGIN Russian, 'fist, tight-fisted person'.
kumara /koomərə/ ● noun (pl. same) NZ a sweet potato.
– ORIGIN Maori.
kumkum /koomkoom/ ● noun a red pigment used by Hindu women to make a mark on the forehead.
– ORIGIN Sanskrit, 'saffron'.
kümmel /koomm'l/ ● noun a sweet liqueur flavoured with caraway and cumin seeds.
– ORIGIN German, from High German *kumil*, variant of *kumin* 'cumin'.
kumquat /koomkwot/ (also **cumquat**) ● noun an East Asian citrus-like fruit with an edible sweet rind and acid pulp.
– ORIGIN Chinese, 'little orange'.
kuna /koonə/ ● noun (pl. **kune**) the basic monetary unit of Croatia, equal to 100 lipa.
– ORIGIN Serbo-Croat, 'marten' (the fur of the marten was formerly a medium of exchange).
kundalini /koondəleeni/ ● noun (in yoga) latent female energy believed to lie coiled at the base of the spine.
– ORIGIN Sanskrit, 'snake'.
kung fu /kung foō/ ● noun a Chinese martial art resembling karate.
– ORIGIN Chinese, from words meaning 'merit' and 'master'.
Kurd /kurd/ ● noun a member of a mainly pastoral Islamic people living in Kurdistan, a region in the Middle East south of the Caucasus.
– ORIGIN the name in Kurdish.
kurdaitcha /kədīchə/ ● noun Austral. the use among Aboriginals of a bone in spells intended to cause sickness or death.
– ORIGIN from an Aboriginal word.
Kurdish /kurdish/ ● noun the Iranian language of the Kurds. ● adjective relating to the Kurds.
kurgan /koorgaan/ ● noun **1** a prehistoric burial mound of a type found in southern Russia and the Ukraine. **2** (**Kurgan**) a member of the ancient people who built such mounds.
– ORIGIN Russian, from Turkic.
kurrajong /kurrəjong/ ● noun an Australian plant which produces useful tough fibre.
– ORIGIN Dharuk (an Aboriginal language), 'fibre fishing line'.
kurta /kurtə/ ● noun a loose collarless shirt worn by people from the Indian subcontinent.
– ORIGIN Urdu and Persian.
kuru /koōroō/ ● noun Medicine a fatal brain disease occurring in New Guinea, spread by cannibalism.
– ORIGIN a local word.
kurus /kəroōsh/ ● noun (pl. same) a monetary unit of Turkey, equal to one hundredth of a lira.
– ORIGIN Turkish.
Kuwaiti /koowayti/ ● noun a person from Kuwait. ● adjective relating to Kuwait.
kV ● abbreviation kilovolt(s).
kvell /kvel/ ● verb N. Amer. informal feel happy and proud.
– ORIGIN Yiddish, from High German *kveln* 'well up'.
kvetch /kvech/ N. Amer. informal ● noun **1** a person who complains a great deal. **2** a complaint. ● verb complain.
– ORIGIN Yiddish, from High German *quetschen* 'crush'.
kW ● abbreviation kilowatt(s).
kwacha /kwaachə/ ● noun the basic monetary unit of Zambia and Malawi, equal to 100 ngwee in Zambia and 100 tambala in Malawi.
– ORIGIN Bantu, 'dawn', used as a Zambian nationalist slogan calling for a new 'dawn' of freedom.
kwanza ● noun (pl. same or **kwanzas**) the basic monetary unit of Angola, equal to 100 lwei.
– ORIGIN perhaps from a Kiswahili word meaning 'first'.
Kwanzaa /kwanzaa/ ● noun N. Amer. a festival observed by many African Americans from 26 December to 1 January as a celebration of their cultural heritage.
– ORIGIN from Kishwahili, 'first fruits'.
kwashiorkor /kwoshiorkor/ ● noun malnutrition caused by protein deficiency, affecting young children in the tropics.
– ORIGIN a local word in Ghana.
kwela /kwaylə/ ● noun a style of rhythmical popular African music resembling jazz.
– ORIGIN Afrikaans, perhaps from a Zulu word meaning 'mount'.
kWh ● abbreviation kilowatt-hour(s).
KY ● abbreviation Kentucky.
kyat /keeaat/ ● noun (pl. same or **kyats**) the basic monetary unit of Burma (Myanmar), equal to 100 pyas.
– ORIGIN Burmese.
kybosh ● noun variant spelling of KIBOSH.
kyle /kīl/ ● noun Scottish a narrow sea channel.
– ORIGIN Scottish Gaelic *caol* 'strait'.
kylie /kīli/ ● noun Austral. a boomerang.
– ORIGIN from an Aboriginal language.
kyphosis /kīfōsiss/ ● noun Medicine excessive forward curvature of the spine, causing a hunched back. Compare with LORDOSIS.
– ORIGIN Greek *kuphōsis*, from *kuphos* 'bent, hunchbacked'.
Kyrgyz /kergiz/ (also **Kirghiz**) ● noun (pl. same) **1** a member of a people of central Asia, living chiefly in Kyrgyzstan. **2** the language of this people.
– ORIGIN the name in Kyrgyz.
Kyrie /kirriay/ (also **Kyrie eleison** /kirriay ilayizon/) ● noun a short repeated invocation used in many Christian liturgies.
– ORIGIN from Greek *Kuriē eleēson* 'Lord, have mercy'.

Thesaurus

and scrape, toady, truckle, abase oneself, humble oneself; curry favour with, dance attendance on, make up to, ingratiate oneself with; *informal* crawl, creep, suck up, lick someone's boots.

kudos ● noun PRESTIGE, cachet, glory, honour, status, standing, distinction, prestigiousness, fame, celebrity; admiration, respect, esteem, acclaim, praise, credit.

Ll

L[1] (also **l**) ● noun (pl. **Ls** or **L's**) **1** the twelfth letter of the alphabet. **2** denoting the next after K in a set. **3** the Roman numeral for 50. [ORIGIN originally a symbol identified with the letter *L*, because of similarity of form.]
L[2] ● abbreviation **1** (**L.**) Lake, Loch, or Lough. **2** large (as a clothes size). **3** Brit. learner driver. **4** lire. **5** (in tables of sports results) lost.
l ● abbreviation **1** left. **2** (in horse racing) length(s). **3** (**l.**) line. **4** litre(s). **5** (**l.**) archaic pound(s). ● symbol (in mathematical formulae) length.
£ ● abbreviation pound(s).
– ORIGIN the initial letter of Latin *libra* 'pound, balance'.
LA ● abbreviation **1** Los Angeles. **2** Louisiana.
La ● symbol the chemical element lanthanum.
la ● noun Music variant spelling of LAH.
laager /laagər/ S. African ● noun **1** historical an encampment formed by a circle of wagons. **2** an entrenched position or viewpoint. ● verb historical form or enclose with a laager.
– ORIGIN South African Dutch, from Dutch *lager* 'camp'.
lab ● noun informal a laboratory.
label ● noun **1** a small piece of paper, fabric, etc. attached to an object and giving information about it. **2** the name or trademark of a fashion company. **3** a company that produces recorded music. **4** a classifying name applied to a person or thing. **5** Biology & Chemistry a radioactive isotope, fluorescent dye, or enzyme used to make something identifiable. ● verb (**labelled**, **labelling**; US **labeled**, **labeling**) **1** attach a label to. **2** assign to a category. **3** Biology & Chemistry make (a substance, cell, etc.) identifiable using a label.
– ORIGIN Old French, 'ribbon'.
labia plural of LABIUM.
labial ● adjective chiefly Anatomy & Biology relating to the lips or a labium.
labiate ● adjective Botany relating to plants of the mint family (Labiatae), having distinctive two-lobed flowers.
– ORIGIN Latin *labiatus*, from *labium* 'lip'.
labile /laybīl/ ● adjective **1** technical liable to change; easily altered. **2** Chemistry easily broken down or displaced.
– ORIGIN Latin *labilis*, from *labi* 'to fall'.
labium /laybiəm/ ● noun (pl. **labia** /laybiə/) **1** (**labia**) Anatomy the inner and outer folds of the vulva. **2** a fused mouthpart forming the floor of the mouth of an insect.
– ORIGIN Latin, 'lip'.
laboratory /ləborrətri/ ● noun (pl. **laboratories**) a room or building for scientific experiments, research, or teaching, or for the manufacture of drugs or chemicals.
– ORIGIN Latin *laboratorium*, from *laborare* 'to labour'.
labor etc. ● noun US and Australian spelling of LABOUR etc.
laborious /ləboriəss/ ● adjective **1** requiring considerable time and effort. **2** showing obvious signs of effort.
– DERIVATIVES **laboriously** adverb.
labour (US & Austral. **labor**) ● noun **1** work, especially hard physical work. **2** workers collectively. **3** (**Labour**) the Labour Party. **4** the process of childbirth. ● verb **1** work hard. **2** work at an unskilled manual job. **3** have difficulty despite working hard. **4** move with difficulty. **5** (**labour under**) be misled by (a mistaken belief).
– PHRASES **a labour of love** a task done for pleasure, not reward. **labour the point** elaborate something at excessive length.
– ORIGIN Latin *labor* 'toil, trouble'.
labour camp ● noun a prison camp with a regime of hard labour.
Labour Day ● noun a public holiday held in honour of working people in some countries on 1 May, or (in the US and Canada) on the first Monday in September.
laboured (US **labored**) ● adjective **1** done with great difficulty. **2** not spontaneous or fluent.
labourer (US **laborer**) ● noun a person doing unskilled manual work.
labour exchange ● noun former term for JOBCENTRE.
labour force ● noun the members of a population who are able to work.
labour-intensive ● adjective needing a large workforce or a large amount of work in relation to output.
Labourite (US **Laborite**) ● noun a member or supporter of a Labour Party.
Labour Party ● noun a British left-of-centre political party formed to represent the interests of ordinary working people.
labour-saving ● adjective designed to reduce or eliminate work.
labour union ● noun chiefly N. Amer. a trade union.
labra plural of LABRUM.
Labrador /labrədor/ (also **Labrador retriever**) ● noun a breed

Thesaurus

label ● noun **1** *the price is clearly stated on the label* TAG, ticket, tab, sticker, marker, docket, chit, chitty. **2** *a designer label* BRAND (NAME), trade name, trademark, make, logo. **3** *the label the media came up with for me* DESIGNATION, description, tag; name, epithet, nickname, title, sobriquet, pet name, cognomen; formal denomination, appellation.
● verb **1** *label each jar with the date* TAG, put labels on, tab, ticket, mark, docket. **2** *tests labelled him an underachiever* CATEGORIZE, classify, class, describe, designate, identify; mark, stamp, brand, condemn, pigeonhole, stereotype, typecast; call, name, term, dub, nickname.
laborious ● adjective **1** *a laborious job* ARDUOUS, hard, heavy, difficult, strenuous, gruelling, punishing, exacting, tough, onerous, burdensome, back-breaking, trying, challenging; tiring, fatiguing, exhausting, wearying, wearing, taxing, demanding, wearisome; tedious, boring; archaic toilsome. **2** *Doug's slow laborious style* LABOURED, strained, forced, contrived, affected, stiff, stilted, unnatural, artificial, overwrought, heavy, ponderous, convoluted.
– OPPOSITES easy, effortless.
labour ● noun **1** *manual labour* (HARD) WORK, toil, exertion, industry, drudgery, effort, donkey work, menial work; informal slog, grind, sweat, elbow grease; Brit. informal graft; poetic/literary travail, moil. **2** *the conflict between capital and labour* WORKERS, employees, workmen, workforce, staff, working people, blue-collar workers, labourers, labour force, proletariat. **3** *the labours of Hercules* TASK, job, chore, mission, assignment. **4** *a difficult labour* CHILDBIRTH, birth, delivery, nativity; contractions, labour pains; formal parturition; poetic/literary travail; dated confinement; archaic accouchement, lying-in, childbed.
– OPPOSITES rest, management.
● verb **1** *a project on which he had laboured for many years* WORK (HARD), toil, slave (away), grind away, struggle, strive, exert oneself, work one's fingers to the bone, work like a Trojan/slave; informal slog away, plug away, peg away; Brit. informal graft; poetic/literary travail; archaic moil. **2** *Newcastle laboured to break down their defence* STRIVE, struggle, endeavour, work, try hard, make every effort, do one's best, do one's utmost, do all one can, give one's all, go all out, fight, put oneself out, apply oneself, exert oneself; informal bend/lean over backwards, pull out all the stops. **3** *there is no need to labour the point* OVEREMPHASIZE, belabour, overstress, overdo, strain, overplay, make too much of, exaggerate, dwell on, harp on (about). **4** *Rex was labouring under a misapprehension* SUFFER FROM, be a victim of, be deceived by, be misled by.
laboured ● adjective **1** *laboured breathing* STRAINED, difficult, forced, laborious. **2** *a rather laboured joke* CONTRIVED, strained, stilted, forced, unnatural, artificial, overdone, ponderous, overelaborate, laborious, overwrought, unconvincing.
labourer ● noun WORKMAN, worker, working man, labouring man, manual worker, unskilled worker, blue-collar worker, (hired)

of retriever with a black or yellow coat, used as a gun dog or guide dog.
– ORIGIN named after the *Labrador* Peninsula of eastern Canada, where the breed was developed.
labradorite /labrədorit/ ● noun a form of feldspar found in many igneous rocks.
Labrador tea ● noun a northern shrub with fragrant evergreen leaves, sometimes used in Canada to make tea.
labrum /laybrəm/ ● noun (pl. **labra** /laybrə/) Zoology a structure corresponding to a lip, especially the upper border of the mouthparts of a crustacean or insect.
– ORIGIN Latin, 'lip'.
laburnum /ləburnəm/ ● noun a small hardwood tree with hanging clusters of yellow flowers followed by pods of poisonous seeds.
– ORIGIN Latin.
labyrinth /labbərinth/ ● noun **1** a complicated irregular network of passages or paths. **2** an intricate and confusing arrangement. **3** a complex fluid-filled bony structure in the inner ear which contains the organs of hearing and balance.
– DERIVATIVES **labyrinthine** adjective.
– ORIGIN Greek *laburinthos*, referring to the maze constructed by Daedalus in Greek mythology to house the Minotaur.
labyrinthitis /labbərinthītiss/ ● noun Medicine inflammation of the labyrinth or inner ear.
lac[1] ● noun a resinous substance secreted by an Asian insect (the **lac insect**), used to make varnish, shellac, etc.
– ORIGIN Hindi or Persian.
lac[2] ● noun variant spelling of LAKH.
laccolith /lakkəlith/ ● noun Geology a lens-shaped mass of igneous rock intruded between rock strata.
– ORIGIN from Greek *lakkos* 'reservoir' + *lithos* 'stone'.
lace ● noun **1** a fine open fabric of cotton or silk made by looping, twisting, or knitting thread in patterns. **2** a cord or leather strip used to fasten a shoe or garment. ● verb **1** fasten with a lace or laces. **2** entwine. **3** (often **be laced with**) add an ingredient, especially alcohol, to (a drink or dish) to enhance its flavour or strength.
– ORIGIN Old French *laz*, from Latin *laqueus* 'noose'.
lacerate /lassərayt/ ● verb tear or deeply cut (the flesh or skin).
– DERIVATIVES **laceration** noun.
– ORIGIN Latin *lacerare*, from *lacer* 'torn'.
lacewing ● noun a slender delicate insect with large clear membranous wings.
lachrymal /lakrim'l/ (also **lacrimal** or **lacrymal**) ● adjective **1** formal or literary connected with weeping or tears. **2** Physiology & Anatomy concerned with the secretion of tears.
– ORIGIN Latin *lachrymalis*, from *lacrima* 'tear'.
lachrymatory /lakrimətəri/ (also **lacrimatory**) ● adjective technical or literary relating to, causing, or containing tears.
lachrymose /lakrimōss/ ● adjective formal or literary **1** tearful. **2** inducing tears; sad.
lacing ● noun **1** a laced fastening of a shoe or garment. **2** a dash of spirits added to a drink.
lack ● noun the state of being without or not having enough of something. ● verb (also **lack for**) be without or deficient in.
– ORIGIN perhaps partly from Low German *lak* 'deficiency', Dutch *laken* 'lack'.
lackadaisical /lakkədayzik'l/ ● adjective lacking enthusiasm and thoroughness.
– DERIVATIVES **lackadaisically** adverb.
– ORIGIN from the archaic interjection *lackaday, lackadaisy*.
lackey ● noun (pl. **lackeys**) **1** a servant. **2** a servile or obsequious person.
– ORIGIN French *laquais*.
lacking ● adjective absent or deficient.
lacklustre (US **lackluster**) ● adjective **1** lacking in vitality, force, or conviction. **2** not shining; dull.
laconic /ləkonnik/ ● adjective using very few words; terse.
– DERIVATIVES **laconically** adverb.
– ORIGIN Greek *Lakōnikos*, from *Lakōn* 'Laconia, Sparta', the Spartans being known for their terse speech.
lacquer /lakkər/ ● noun **1** a varnish made of shellac or of synthetic substances. **2** the sap of an East Asian tree (the **lacquer tree**) used as a varnish. **3** decorative wooden ware coated with lacquer. **4** Brit. a chemical substance sprayed on hair to keep it in place. ● verb coat with lacquer.

Thesaurus

hand, roustabout, drudge, menial, coolie; Austral./NZ rouseabout; Brit. dated navvy.
labyrinth ● noun **1** *a labyrinth of little streets* MAZE, warren, network, complex, web, entanglement. **2** *the labyrinth of conflicting regulations* TANGLE, web, morass, jungle, confusion, entanglement, convolution; jumble, mishmash; archaic perplexity.
labyrinthine ● adjective **1** *labyrinthine corridors* MAZE-LIKE, winding, twisting, serpentine, meandering, wandering, rambling. **2** *a labyrinthine system* COMPLICATED, intricate, complex, involved, tortuous, convoluted, involuted, tangled, elaborate; confusing, puzzling, mystifying, bewildering, baffling.
lace ● noun **1** *a dress trimmed with white lace* openwork, lacework, tatting; passementerie, bobbinet, needlepoint (lace), filet, bobbin lace, pillow lace, duchesse lace, guipure, rosaline. **2** *brown shoes with laces* SHOELACE, bootlace, shoestring, lacing, thong, tie; archaic latchet.
● verb **1** *he laced up his running shoes* FASTEN, do up, tie up, secure, knot. **2** *he laced his fingers into mine* ENTWINE, intertwine, twine, entangle, interweave, link; braid, plait. **3** *tea laced with rum* FLAVOUR, mix (in), blend, fortify, strengthen, stiffen, season, spice (up), enrich, liven up; doctor, adulterate; informal spike. **4** *her brown hair was laced with grey* STREAK, stripe, striate, line.
– OPPOSITES untie.
– PHRASES **lace into** (informal) **1** *Danny laced into him.* See SET ON at SET[1]. **2** *the newspaper laced into the prime minister.* See CRITICIZE.
lacerate ● verb CUT (OPEN), gash, slash, tear, rip, rend, shred, score, scratch, scrape, graze; wound, injure, hurt.
laceration ● noun **1** *the laceration of her hand* CUTTING (OPEN), gashing, slashing, tearing, ripping, scratching, scraping, grazing, wounding, injury. **2** *a bleeding laceration* GASH, cut, wound, injury, tear, slash, scratch, scrape, abrasion, graze.
lachrymose ● adjective (formal) **1** *she gets quite lachrymose at the mention of his name* TEARFUL, weeping, crying, with tears in one's eyes, close to tears, on the verge of tears, sobbing, snivelling, whimpering; emotional, sad, doleful, maudlin, miserable, forlorn; informal weepy; poetic/literary dolorous. **2** *a lachrymose novel* TRAGIC, sad, poignant, moving, heart-rending, tear-jerking; mawkish, sentimental; Brit. informal soppy.
– OPPOSITES cheerful, comic.
lack ● noun *a lack of cash* ABSENCE, want, need, deficiency, dearth, insufficiency, shortage, shortfall, scarcity, paucity, unavailability, scarceness, deficit; formal exiguity.
– OPPOSITES abundance.
● verb *she's immature and lacks judgement* BE WITHOUT, be in need of, need, be lacking, require, want, be short of, be deficient in, be bereft of, be low on, be pressed for, have insufficient; informal be strapped for.
– OPPOSITES have, possess.
lackadaisical ● adjective CARELESS, lazy, lax, unenthusiastic, half-hearted, lukewarm, indifferent, unconcerned, casual, offhand, blasé, insouciant, relaxed; apathetic, lethargic, listless, sluggish, spiritless, passionless; informal laid back, couldn't-care-less, easy going.
– OPPOSITES enthusiastic.
lackey ● noun **1** *lackeys helped them from their carriage* SERVANT, flunkey, footman, manservant, valet, steward, butler, equerry, retainer, attendant, houseboy, domestic; Brit. informal skivvy; archaic scullion. **2** *a rich man's lackey* TOADY, flunkey, sycophant, flatterer, minion, doormat, stooge, hanger-on, lickspittle; tool, puppet, instrument, pawn, subordinate, underling; informal yes-man, bootlicker.
lacking ● adjective **1** *proof was lacking* ABSENT, missing, non-existent, unavailable. **2** *the advocate general found the government lacking* DEFICIENT, defective, inadequate, wanting, flawed, faulty, insufficient, unacceptable, imperfect, inferior. **3** *the game was lacking in atmosphere* WITHOUT, devoid of, bereft of; deficient in, low on, short on, in need of.
– OPPOSITES present, plentiful.
lacklustre ● adjective UNINSPIRED, uninspiring, unimaginative, dull, humdrum, colourless, characterless, bland, insipid, vapid, flat, dry, lifeless, tame, prosaic, spiritless, lustreless; boring, monotonous, dreary, tedious.
– OPPOSITES inspired.
laconic ● adjective **1** *his laconic comment* BRIEF, concise, terse, succinct, short, pithy; epigrammatic, aphoristic, gnomic. **2** *their laconic press officer* TACITURN, uncommunicative, reticent, quiet, re-

– ORIGIN from obsolete French *lacre* 'sealing wax', from Hindi or Persian (see LAC[1]).
lacrimal ● adjective variant spelling of LACHRYMAL.
lacrimatory ● adjective variant spelling of LACHRYMATORY.
lacrosse /ləkross/ ● noun a team game in which a ball is thrown, carried, and caught with a long-handled stick bearing a net at one end.
– ORIGIN from French *(le jeu de) la crosse* '(the game of) the hooked stick'.
lacrymal ● adjective variant spelling of LACHRYMAL.
lactate[1] /laktayt/ ● verb (of a female mammal) secrete milk.
– ORIGIN Latin *lactare* 'suckle'.
lactate[2] /laktayt/ ● noun Chemistry a salt or ester of lactic acid.
lactation ● noun **1** the secretion of milk by the mammary glands. **2** the suckling of young.
lacteal /laktiəl/ ● adjective conveying milk or milky fluid. ● noun **(lacteals)** Anatomy the lymphatic vessels of the small intestine which absorb digested fats.
– ORIGIN Latin *lacteus*, from *lac* 'milk'.
lactic /laktik/ ● adjective relating to or obtained from milk.
lactic acid ● noun Biochemistry an organic acid present in sour milk, and produced in the muscles during strenuous exercise.
lactose /laktōz/ ● noun Chemistry a compound sugar present in milk.
lacto-vegetarian ● noun a person who eats only dairy products and vegetables.
lacuna /ləkyo͞onə/ ● noun (pl. **lacunae** /ləkyo͞onee/ or **lacunas**) **1** a gap or missing portion. **2** Anatomy a cavity or depression, especially in bone.
– DERIVATIVES **lacunar** adjective.
– ORIGIN Latin, 'pool'.
lacustrine /ləkustrin/ ● adjective technical or literary relating to lakes.
– ORIGIN from Latin *lacus* 'lake'.
lacy ● adjective **(lacier, laciest)** made of, resembling, or trimmed with lace.
lad ● noun informal **1** a boy or young man. **2 (lads)** chiefly Brit. a group of men sharing recreational or working interests. **3** Brit. a boisterously macho or high-spirited man.
– DERIVATIVES **laddish** adjective.
– ORIGIN of unknown origin.
ladder ● noun **1** a structure consisting of a series of bars or steps between two uprights, used for climbing up or down. **2** a hierarchical structure. **3** Brit. a vertical strip of unravelled fabric in tights or stockings. ● verb Brit. develop or cause to develop a ladder in tights or stockings.
– ORIGIN Old English.
ladder-back ● noun an upright chair with a back resembling a ladder.
ladder stitch ● noun a stitch in embroidery consisting of transverse bars.
laddie ● noun informal, chiefly Scottish a boy or young man.
lade /layd/ ● verb (past part. **laden**) archaic put cargo on board (a ship).
– ORIGIN Old English, related to LADLE.
laden ● adjective heavily loaded or weighed down.
la-di-da (also **lah-di-dah**) ● adjective informal pretentious or snobbish.
– ORIGIN imitative of an affected manner of speech.
ladies plural of LADY.
ladies' fingers ● plural noun Brit. another term for OKRA.
ladies' man (also **lady's man**) ● noun informal a man who enjoys spending time and flirting with women.
ladies' night ● noun a function at a men's institution or club to which women are invited.
ladies' room ● noun chiefly N. Amer. a women's toilet in a public or institutional building.
Ladino /ladeenō/ ● noun (pl. **Ladinos**) **1** the language of some Sephardic Jews, based on medieval Spanish with some Hebrew, Greek, and Turkish words. **2** a mestizo or Spanish-speaking white person in Central America.
– ORIGIN Spanish, from Latin *Latinus* (see LATIN).
ladle ● noun a large long-handled spoon with a cup-shaped bowl. ● verb **1** serve or transfer with a ladle. **2 (ladle out)** distribute in large amounts.
– DERIVATIVES **ladleful** noun.
– ORIGIN Old English, related to LADE.
lady ● noun (pl. **ladies**) **1** (in polite or formal use) a woman. **2** a woman of superior social position. **3 (Lady)** a title used by peeresses, female relatives of peers, the wives and widows of knights, etc. **4** a courteous or genteel woman. **5 (the Ladies)** Brit. a women's public toilet.
– PHRASES **it isn't over till the fat lady sings** there is still time for a situation to change. [ORIGIN by association with the final aria in tragic opera.] **My Lady** a polite form of address to female judges and certain noblewomen.
– ORIGIN Old English, from words meaning 'loaf' and 'knead'; compare with LORD.
ladybird ● noun a small beetle with a domed back, typically red or yellow with black spots.
ladybug ● noun North American term for LADYBIRD.
Lady chapel ● noun a chapel dedicated to the Virgin Mary in a church or cathedral.
Lady Day ● noun the feast of the Annunciation, 25 March.
lady-in-waiting ● noun (pl. **ladies-in-waiting**) a woman who attends a queen or princess.
ladykiller ● noun informal a charming man who habitually seduces women.
ladylike ● adjective appropriate for or typical of a well-mannered woman or girl.
lady of the night ● noun euphemistic a prostitute.
lady's bedstraw ● noun a yellow-flowered bedstraw which smells of hay when dried and was formerly used to make mattresses.
lady's finger ● noun Brit. a finger-shaped sponge cake with a sugar topping.
ladyship ● noun **(Her/Your Ladyship)** a respectful form of reference or address to a Lady.
lady's maid ● noun chiefly historical a maid who attended to the personal needs of her mistress.
lady's man ● noun variant spelling of LADIES' MAN.
lady's mantle ● noun a plant with inconspicuous greenish flowers, formerly valued in herbal medicine.
lady's slipper ● noun an orchid whose flower has a pouch- or slipper-shaped lip.
laevulose /leevyo͞olōz/ (US **levulose**) ● noun Chemistry a naturally occurring form of the sugar fructose.
– ORIGIN from Latin *laevus* 'left', because solutions of laevulose rotate the plane of polarised light to the left (i.e. anticlockwise).
lag[1] ● verb **(lagged, lagging)** fall behind; follow after a delay. ● noun (also **time lag**) a period of time between two events; a delay.
– ORIGIN originally in the sense 'hindmost person': related to the dialect adjective *lag* (perhaps from a distortion of LAST[1], or Scandinavian).
lag[2] ● verb **(lagged, lagging)** enclose or cover (a boiler, pipes, etc.) with insulating material.
– ORIGIN from earlier *lag* 'piece of insulating cover'.

I

Thesaurus

served, silent, unforthcoming, brusque.
– OPPOSITES verbose, loquacious.
lad ● noun *(informal)* **1** *a young lad of eight* BOY, schoolboy, youth, youngster, juvenile, stripling; *informal* kid, nipper, whippersnapper; *Scottish informal* laddie; *derogatory* brat. **2** *a hard-working lad* (YOUNG) MAN; *informal* guy, fellow, geezer; *Brit. informal* chap, bloke; *N. Amer. informal* dude, hombre; *Austral./NZ informal* digger.
ladder ● noun **1** *she climbed down the ladder* steps, set of steps. **2** *the academic ladder* HIERARCHY, scale, grading, ranking, pecking order.
laden ● adjective LOADED, burdened, weighed down, overloaded, piled high, fully charged; full, filled, packed, stuffed, crammed; *informal* chock-full, chock-a-block.
la-di-da ● adjective *(informal)* SNOBBISH, pretentious, affected, mannered, pompous, conceited, haughty; *informal* snooty, stuck-up, high and mighty, hoity-toity, uppity, snotty; *Brit. informal* posh, toffee-nosed.
– OPPOSITES common.
ladle ● verb SPOON OUT, dish up/out, serve.
lady ● noun **1** *several ladies were present* WOMAN, female; *Scottish & N. English* lass, lassie; *Brit. informal* bird, bint; *N. Amer. informal* dame, broad, jane; *Austral./NZ informal* sheila; *poetic/literary* maid, damsel; *archaic* wench. **2** *lords and ladies* NOBLEWOMAN, duchess, countess, peeress, viscountess, baroness; *archaic* gentlewoman.
ladylike ● adjective GENTEEL, polite, refined, well bred, cultivated, polished, decorous, proper, respectable, seemly, well mannered,

lag³ ● noun Brit. informal a habitual convict.
– ORIGIN of unknown origin.
lager ● noun a light effervescent beer.
– ORIGIN from German *Lagerbier* 'beer brewed for keeping', from *Lager* 'storehouse'.
lager lout ● noun Brit. informal a young man who behaves offensively as a result of excessive drinking.
laggard /laggərd/ ● noun a person who falls behind others. ● adjective slower than desired or expected.
– DERIVATIVES **laggardly** adjective & adverb.
– ORIGIN from LAG¹.
lagging ● noun material providing heat insulation for a boiler, pipes, etc.
lagniappe /lanyap/ ● noun N. Amer. something given as a bonus or gratuity.
– ORIGIN Louisiana French, from Spanish *la ñapa*.
lagoon ● noun **1** a stretch of salt water separated from the sea by a low sandbank or coral reef. **2** N. Amer. & Austral./NZ a small freshwater lake near a larger lake or river.
– ORIGIN Italian and Spanish *laguna*, from Latin *lacuna* 'pool'.
lah (also **la**) ● noun Music the sixth note of a major scale, coming after 'soh' and before 'te'.
– ORIGIN representing (as an arbitrary name for the note) the first syllable of *labii*, taken from a Latin hymn.
lah-di-dah ● noun variant spelling of LA-DI-DA.
laicize /layisiz/ (also **laicise**) ● verb formal withdraw clerical character, control, or status from.
– DERIVATIVES **laicism** noun **laicization** noun.
– ORIGIN from Latin *laicus* (see LAY²)
laid past and past participle of LAY¹.
laid-back ● adjective informal relaxed and easy-going.
lain past participle of LIE¹.
lair¹ ● noun **1** a wild animal's resting place. **2** a person's hiding place or den.
– ORIGIN Old English, related to LIE¹.
lair² Austral./NZ informal ● noun a flashily dressed man who enjoys showing off. ● verb dress or behave in a flashy manner.
– DERIVATIVES **lairy** adjective.
– ORIGIN from *lairy* (earlier as Cockney slang in the sense 'knowing, conceited'); alteration of LEERY.
laird /laird/ ● noun (in Scotland) a person who owns a large estate.
– DERIVATIVES **lairdship** noun.
– ORIGIN Scots form of LORD.
laissez-faire /lessay fair/ ● noun a policy of non-interference, especially abstention by governments from interfering in the workings of the free market.
– ORIGIN French, 'allow to do'.
laity /layiti/ ● noun (**the laity**) lay people.
lake¹ ● noun **1** a large area of water surrounded by land. **2** (**the Lakes**) another name for the LAKE DISTRICT.
– DERIVATIVES **lakelet** noun.
– ORIGIN Latin *lacus* 'pool, lake'.
lake² ● noun **1** an insoluble pigment made by combining an organic dye and a mordant. **2** a purplish-red pigment of this kind, originally made with lac.
– ORIGIN variant of LAC¹.
Lake District ● noun a region of lakes and mountains in Cumbria.
lakh /lak/ (also **lac**) ● noun Indian a hundred thousand.
– ORIGIN Sanskrit.
la-la land ● noun N. Amer. informal **1** Los Angeles or Hollywood, especially with regard to the film and television industry. **2** a dreamworld.
– ORIGIN reduplication of *LA* (i.e. Los Angeles).
lalapalooza ● noun variant spelling of LOLLAPALOOZA.
laldy /laldi/ ● noun Scottish informal a beating.
– PHRASES **give it laldy** do something vigorously or enthusiastically.
– ORIGIN perhaps imitative, or from an Old English word meaning 'whip, weal'.
Lallans /lalənz/ ● noun a distinctive Scottish literary form of English, based on standard older Scots.
– ORIGIN Scots variant of *Lowlands*.
lallygag /laligag/ ● verb variant spelling of LOLLYGAG.
lam¹ ● verb (**lammed, lamming**) (often **lam into**) informal hit hard or repeatedly.
– ORIGIN perhaps Scandinavian.
lam² N. Amer. informal ● noun (in phrase **on the lam**) in flight, especially from the police. ● verb (**lammed, lamming**) flee.
– ORIGIN from LAM¹.
lama /laamə/ ● noun **1** an honorific title applied to a spiritual leader in Tibetan Buddhism. **2** a Tibetan or Mongolian Buddhist monk.
– ORIGIN Tibetan, 'superior one'.
Lamarckism /lamaarkiz'm/ ● noun the theory of evolution based on the supposed inheritance of acquired characteristics, devised by the French naturalist Jean Baptiste de Lamarck (1744–1829).
– DERIVATIVES **Lamarckian** noun & adjective.
lamasery /laaməsəri/ ● noun (pl. **lamaseries**) a monastery of lamas.
lamb ● noun **1** a young sheep. **2** a mild-mannered, gentle, or innocent person. ● verb **1** (of a ewe) give birth to lambs. **2** tend (ewes) at lambing time.
– DERIVATIVES **lambing** noun.
– ORIGIN Old English.
lambada /lambaadə/ ● noun a fast Brazilian dance which couples perform in close physical contact.
– ORIGIN Portuguese, 'a beating'.
lambaste /lambayst/ (also **lambast** /lambast/) ● verb criticize harshly.
– DERIVATIVES **lambasting** noun.
– ORIGIN originally in the sense 'beat': from LAM¹ + dated *baste*, also meaning 'beat'.
lambda /lamdə/ ● noun the eleventh letter of the Greek alphabet (Λ, λ), transliterated as 'l'.
– ORIGIN Greek.
lambent /lambənt/ ● adjective literary glowing or flickering with a soft radiance.
– ORIGIN from Latin *lambere* 'to lick'.
Lamb of God ● noun a title of Jesus Christ.
Lambrusco /lambrooskō/ ● noun **1** a variety of wine grape grown in the Emilia-Romagna region of North Italy. **2** a sparkling red or white wine made from this grape.
– ORIGIN Italian, 'grape of the wild vine'.
lamb's fry ● noun Brit. lamb's testicles or other offal as food.
lamb's lettuce ● noun a small blue-flowered herbaceous plant, used in salad.
lamb's-tails ● plural noun Brit. catkins from the hazel tree.

Thesaurus

cultured, sophisticated, elegant; *Brit. informal* posh.
– OPPOSITES coarse.
lag ● verb FALL BEHIND, straggle, fall back, trail (behind), hang back, not keep pace, bring up the rear.
– OPPOSITES keep up.
laggard ● noun STRAGGLER, loiterer, lingerer, dawdler, sluggard, snail, idler, loafer; *informal* lazybones, slacker, slowcoach; *N. Amer. informal* slowpoke.
lagoon ● noun inland sea, bay, lake, bight, pool; *Scottish* loch; *Anglo-Irish* lough; *N. Amer.* bayou.
laid-back ● adjective *(informal)* RELAXED, easy-going, equable, free and easy, casual, nonchalant, insouciant, unexcitable, imperturbable, unruffled, blasé, cool, calm, {cool, calm, and collected}, unperturbed, unflustered, unworried, unconcerned; leisurely, unhurried; stoical, phlegmatic, tolerant; *informal* unflappable.
– OPPOSITES uptight.
laid up ● adjective *(informal)* BEDRIDDEN, confined to bed, on the sick list, housebound, incapacitated, injured, disabled; ill, sick, unwell, poorly, ailing, indisposed.
lair ● noun **1** *the lair of a large python* DEN, burrow, hole, tunnel, cave. **2** *a villain's lair* HIDEAWAY, hiding place, hideout, refuge, sanctuary, haven, shelter, retreat; *informal* hidey-hole.
laissez-faire ● noun *laissez-faire is based on self-interest* FREE ENTERPRISE, free trade, non-intervention, free-market capitalism, market forces.
lake ● noun POND, pool, tarn, reservoir, lagoon, waterhole, inland sea; *Scottish* loch, lochan; *Anglo-Irish* lough; *N. Amer.* bayou, pothole (lake); *poetic/literary* mere.
– RELATED TERMS lacustrine.
lam ● verb *(informal).* See HIT verb sense 1.
lambaste ● verb CRITICIZE, chastise, censure, take to task, harangue, rail at, rant at, fulminate against; upbraid, scold, reprimand, rebuke, chide, reprove, admonish, berate; *informal* lay into, pitch into, tear into, give someone a dressing-down, carpet, tell

lame ● adjective **1** walking with difficulty as the result of an injury or illness affecting the leg or foot. **2** (of an explanation or excuse) unconvincingly feeble. **3** dull and uninspiring. ● verb make lame.
– DERIVATIVES **lamely** adverb **lameness** noun.
– ORIGIN Old English.

lamé /laamay/ ● noun fabric with interwoven gold or silver threads.
– ORIGIN French, from Latin *lamina* 'thin plate'.

lamebrained ● adjective informal stupid; dull-witted.

lame duck ● noun **1** an ineffectual or unsuccessful person or thing. **2** N. Amer. a President or administration in the final period of office, after the election of a successor.

lamella /ləmellə/ ● noun (pl. **lamellae** /ləmellee/) **1** a thin layer, membrane, or plate of tissue, especially in bone. **2** Botany a membranous fold in a chloroplast.
– DERIVATIVES **lamellar** adjective **lamellate** adjective.
– ORIGIN Latin, 'small, thin plate'.

lamellibranch /ləmellibrangk/ ● noun another term for BIVALVE.
– ORIGIN from Latin *lamella* + Greek *brankhia* 'gills'.

lament ● noun **1** a passionate expression of grief. **2** a song, piece of music, or poem expressing grief or regret. ● verb **1** mourn (a person's death). **2** (**lamented** or **late lamented**) a conventional way of referring to a dead person. **3** express regret or disappointment about.
– DERIVATIVES **lamentation** noun.
– ORIGIN from Latin *lamenta* (plural) 'weeping'.

lamentable /lammәntәb'l/ ● adjective deplorable or regrettable.
– DERIVATIVES **lamentably** adverb.

lamina /lamminə/ ● noun (pl. **laminae** /lamminee/) technical a thin layer, plate, or scale of sedimentary rock, organic tissue, or other material.
– ORIGIN Latin.

laminar /lamminə/ ● adjective **1** consisting of laminae. **2** Physics (of fluid flow) taking place along unchanging lines, without turbulence.

laminate ● verb /lamminayt/ **1** overlay (a flat surface) with a layer of protective material. **2** manufacture by placing layer on layer. **3** split into layers or leaves. **4** beat or roll (metal) into thin plates. ● noun /lamminət/ a laminated structure or material. ● adjective in the form of a lamina or laminae.
– DERIVATIVES **lamination** noun **laminator** noun.

lamington /lammingtən/ ● noun Austral./NZ a square of sponge cake dipped in melted chocolate and grated coconut.
– ORIGIN apparently from the name of Lord *Lamington*, Governor of Queensland (1895–1901).

Lammas /lamməss/ (also **Lammas Day**) ● noun the first day of August, formerly observed as harvest festival.
– ORIGIN Old English, 'loaf mass'.

lammergeier /lammərgīər/ (also **lammergeyer**) ● noun a long-winged, long-tailed vulture, noted for dropping bones to break them and get at the marrow.
– ORIGIN German, from *Lämmer* 'lambs' + *Geier* 'vulture'.

lamp ● noun **1** an electric, oil, or gas device for giving light. **2** an electrical device producing ultraviolet or other radiation, especially for therapeutic purposes.
– ORIGIN Greek *lampas* 'torch'.

lampblack ● noun a black pigment made from soot.

lampoon /lampoon/ ● verb publicly satirize or ridicule. ● noun a satirical attack.
– ORIGIN French *lampon*, said to be from *lampons* 'let us drink'.

lamprey /lampri/ ● noun (pl. **lampreys**) an eel-like jawless fish that has a sucker mouth with horny teeth and a rasping tongue.
– ORIGIN Latin *lampreda*, probably from *lambere* 'to lick' + *petra* 'stone' (because the lamprey attaches itself to stones by its mouth).

LAN ● abbreviation local area network.

Lancashire hotpot ● noun a stew of meat and vegetables, covered with a layer of sliced potato.

Lancastrian /langkastriən/ ● noun **1** a person from Lancashire or Lancaster. **2** a follower of the House of Lancaster in the Wars of the Roses. ● adjective relating to Lancashire or Lancaster, or the House of Lancaster.

lance ● noun **1** a long weapon with a wooden shaft and a pointed steel head, formerly used by a horseman in charging. **2** a metal pipe supplying a jet of oxygen to a furnace or to make a very hot flame for cutting. ● verb **1** Medicine prick or cut open with a lancet or other sharp instrument. **2** pierce with or as if with a lance.
– ORIGIN Latin *lancea*.

lance corporal ● noun a rank of non-commissioned officer in the British army, above private and below corporal.
– ORIGIN on the analogy of obsolete *lancepesade*, the lowest grade of non-commissioned officer, from Italian *lancia spezzata* 'broken lance'.

lancelet /laanslit/ ● noun a jawless fish-like marine animal that possesses a notochord and typically burrows in sand.

lanceolate /laansiələt/ ● adjective technical of a narrow oval shape tapering to a point at each end.
– ORIGIN Latin *lanceolatus*, from *lanceola* 'a small lance'.

lancer ● noun **1** a soldier of a cavalry regiment armed or formerly armed with lances. **2** (**lancers**) (treated as sing.) a quadrille for eight or sixteen pairs.

lancet /laansit/ ● noun a small, broad two-edged surgical knife with a sharp point.
– ORIGIN Old French *lancette* 'small lance'.

lancet window ● noun a narrow window with an acutely pointed head.

Lancs. ● abbreviation Lancashire.

Land /land/ ● noun (pl. **Länder** /lendər/) a province of Germany or Austria.
– ORIGIN German, 'land'.

land ● noun **1** the part of the earth's surface that is not covered by water. **2** an area of ground in terms of its ownership or use. **3** (**the land**) ground or soil as a basis for agriculture. **4** a country or state. ● verb **1** put or go ashore. **2** come or bring down to the ground. **3** bring (a fish) to land with a net or rod. **4** informal succeed in obtaining or achieving (something desirable). **5** (**land up**) reach a place or destination. **6** (**land up with**) end up with (an unwelcome situation). **7** (**land in**) informal put in (a difficult situation). **8** (**land with**) informal inflict (something unwelcome) on. **9** informal inflict (a blow) on someone.
– PHRASES **how the land lies** what the state of affairs is. **in the land of the living** humorous alive or awake. **the land of Nod** humorous a state of sleep. [ORIGIN punningly, with biblical allusion to the place name *Nod* (Book of Genesis, chapter 4).]
– DERIVATIVES **landless** adjective.
– ORIGIN Old English.

land agent ● noun Brit. **1** a person employed to manage an es-

l

Thesaurus

off, bawl out; *Brit. informal* tick off, have a go at; *N. Amer. informal* chew out; *formal* castigate, excoriate.

lame ● adjective **1** *the mare was lame* LIMPING, hobbling; crippled, disabled, incapacitated; *informal* gammy; *dated* game; *archaic* halt. **2** *a lame excuse* FEEBLE, weak, thin, flimsy, poor; unconvincing, implausible, unlikely.
– OPPOSITES convincing.

lament ● noun **1** *the widow's laments* WAIL, wailing, lamentation, moan, moaning, weeping, crying, sob, sobbing, keening. **2** *a lament for the dead* DIRGE, requiem, elegy, threnody, monody; *Irish* keen; *Scottish & Irish* coronach; *formal* epicedium.
● verb **1** *the mourners lamented* MOURN, grieve, sorrow, wail, weep, cry, sob, keen, beat one's breast; *archaic* plain. **2** *he lamented the modernization of the buildings* BEMOAN, bewail, complain about, deplore; protest against, object to, oppose, fulminate against, inveigh against, denounce.
– OPPOSITES celebrate.

lamentable ● adjective DEPLORABLE, regrettable, terrible, awful, wretched, woeful, dire, disastrous, desperate, grave, appalling, dreadful, egregious; intolerable, pitiful, shameful.

lamentation ● noun WEEPING, wailing, crying, sobbing, moaning, lament, keening, grieving, mourning.

lamp ● noun LIGHT, lantern.

lampoon ● verb *he was mercilessly lampooned* SATIRIZE, mock, ridicule, make fun of, caricature, burlesque, parody, take off, guy, rag, tease; *informal* send up.
● noun *a lampoon of student life* SATIRE, burlesque, parody, skit, caricature, impersonation, travesty, mockery, squib, pasquinade; *informal* send-up, take-off, spoof.

lance ● noun *a knight with a lance* SPEAR, pike, javelin; harpoon.
● verb *the boil was lanced* CUT (OPEN), slit, incise, puncture, prick, pierce.

land ● noun **1** *Lyme Park has 1323 acres of land | publicly owned land* GROUNDS, fields, open space; property, acres, acreage, estate,

tate on behalf of its owners. **2** a person who deals with the sale of land.

landau /landaw/ ● noun a four-wheeled enclosed horse-drawn carriage with adjustable covers.
– ORIGIN named after *Landau* in Germany, where it was first made.

land bank ● noun **1** a large body of land held in trust for future development or disposal. **2** a bank providing loans for land purchase.

land bridge ● noun an area of land formerly connecting two land masses which are now separate.

land crab ● noun a crab that lives in burrows on land and migrates to the sea to breed.

landed ● adjective **1** owning much land, especially through inheritance. **2** consisting of or relating to such land.

lander ● noun a spacecraft designed to land on the surface of a planet or moon.

landfall ● noun **1** an arrival at land on a sea or air journey. **2** a collapse of a mass of land.

landfill ● noun **1** the disposal of waste material by burying it. **2** waste material used in this way.

landform ● noun a natural feature of the earth's surface.

land girl ● noun (in the UK) a woman doing farm work during the Second World War.

landgrave /landgrayv/ ● noun historical the title of certain German princes.
– ORIGIN Low German, from *land* 'land' + *grave* 'count'.

landholder ● noun a landowner.

landing ● noun **1** the action or an instance of coming to or bringing something to land. **2** a place where people and goods can be landed from a boat. **3** a level area at the top of a staircase or between flights of stairs.

landing craft ● noun a boat specially designed for putting troops and military equipment ashore on a beach.

landing gear ● noun the undercarriage of an aircraft.

landing stage ● noun a platform on to which passengers or cargo can be landed from a boat.

landlady ● noun **1** a woman who leases land or property. **2** a woman who keeps lodgings, a boarding house, or (Brit.) a public house.

landline ● noun a conventional telecommunications connection by cable laid across land.

landlocked ● adjective almost or entirely surrounded by land.

landlord ● noun **1** a man (in legal use also a woman) who leases land or property. **2** a man who keeps lodgings, a boarding house, or (Brit.) a public house.

landlordism ● noun the system whereby land or property is owned by landlords to whom tenants pay a fixed rent.

landlubber ● noun informal a person unfamiliar with the sea or sailing.

landmark ● noun **1** an object or feature of a landscape or town that is easily seen and recognized from a distance. **2** an event, discovery, or change marking an important stage or turning point.

land mass ● noun a continent or other large body of land.

landmine ● noun an explosive mine laid on or just under the surface of the ground.

landowner ● noun a person who owns land.
– DERIVATIVES **landownership** noun **landowning** adjective & noun.

landrace ● noun a pig of a large white breed, originally developed in Denmark.
– ORIGIN Danish.

landrail ● noun another term for CORNCRAKE.

landscape ● noun **1** all the visible features of an area of land. **2** a picture representing an area of countryside. **3** the distinctive features of a sphere of intellectual activity: *the political landscape*. **4** (before another noun) (of a format of printed matter) wider than it is high. Compare with PORTRAIT. ● verb improve the appearance of (a piece of land) by changing its contours, planting trees and shrubs, etc.
– DERIVATIVES **landscaper** noun **landscapist** noun.
– ORIGIN Dutch *lantscap*, from *land* 'land' + *scap* (equivalent of -SHIP).

landscape architecture ● noun the art and practice of designing the outdoor environment, especially designing parks or gardens to harmonize with buildings or roads.

landscape gardening ● noun the art and practice of laying out grounds in a way which is ornamental or which imitates natural scenery.

landslide ● noun **1** (chiefly Brit. also **landslip**) the sliding down of a mass of earth or rock from a mountain or cliff. **2** an overwhelming majority of votes for one party in an election.

landsman ● noun a person unfamiliar with the sea or sailing.

landward ● adverb (also **landwards**) towards land. ● adjective facing towards land as opposed to sea.

lane ● noun **1** a narrow road, especially in a rural area. **2** a division of a road intended to separate single lines of traffic according to speed or direction. **3** each of a number of parallel strips of track or water for competitors in a race. **4** a path or course prescribed for or regularly followed by ships or aircraft.
– PHRASES **it's a long lane that has no turning** proverb change is inevitable.
– ORIGIN Old English.

langlauf /langlowf/ ● noun cross-country skiing.
– ORIGIN German, 'long run'.

langouste /longgoost/ ● noun a spiny lobster, especially when prepared and cooked.
– ORIGIN French, from Latin *locusta* 'locust, crustacean'.

langoustine /longgoosteen/ ● noun a Norway lobster.
– ORIGIN French.

language ● noun **1** the method of human communication, either spoken or written, consisting of the use of words in a structured and conventional way. **2** the system of communication used by a particular community or country. **3** the phraseology and vocabulary of a particular group: *legal language*. **4** the manner or style of a piece of writing or speech. **5** Computing a system of symbols and rules for writing programs or algorithms.
– PHRASES **speak the same language** understand one another as a result of shared opinions or values.
– ORIGIN Old French *langage*, from Latin *lingua* 'tongue'.

language engineering ● noun the use of computers to pro-

Thesaurus

lands, real estate; countryside, rural area, green belt; *historical* demesne. **2** *fertile land* SOIL, earth, loam, topsoil, humus. **3** *many people are leaving the land* THE COUNTRYSIDE, the country, rural areas. **4** *Tunisia is a land of variety* COUNTRY, nation, (nation) state, realm, kingdom, province; region, area, domain. **5** *the lookout sighted land* TERRA FIRMA, dry land; coast, coastline, shore.
– RELATED TERMS terrestrial.
● verb **1** *Allied troops landed in France* DISEMBARK, go ashore, debark, alight, get off. **2** *the ship landed at Le Havre* BERTH, dock, moor, (drop) anchor, tie up, put in. **3** *their plane landed at Chicago* TOUCH DOWN, make a landing, come in to land, come down. **4** *a bird landed on the branch* PERCH, settle, come to rest, alight. **5** *(informal) Nick landed the job of editor* OBTAIN, get, acquire, secure, be appointed to, gain, net, win, achieve, attain, bag, carry off; *informal* swing; *Brit. informal* blag. **6** *(informal) that habit landed her in trouble* BRING, lead, cause to be in. **7** *(informal) they landed her with the bill* BURDEN, saddle, encumber; *informal* dump something on someone; *Brit. informal* lumber. **8** *(informal) John landed a punch on Brian's chin* INFLICT, deal, deliver, administer; *informal* fetch.
– OPPOSITES sail, take off.
– PHRASES **land up** FINISH UP, find oneself, end up; *informal* wind up, fetch up.

landing ● noun **1** *a forced landing* ALIGHTING, touchdown; *informal* greaser. **2** *the ferry landing* HARBOUR, berth, dock, jetty, landing stage, pier, quay, wharf, slipway.
– OPPOSITES take-off.

landlady, landlord ● noun **1** *the landlord of the pub* PUBLICAN, licensee, innkeeper, pub-owner, bar-keeper; hotel-keeper, hotelier, restaurateur. **2** *the landlady had objected to the noise* PROPERTY OWNER, proprietor, proprietress, lessor, householder, landowner.
– OPPOSITES tenant.

landmark ● noun **1** *the spire is a landmark for ships* MARKER, mark, indicator, beacon. **2** *one of London's most famous landmarks* MONUMENT, distinctive/prominent feature. **3** *(historical) the landmarks which separated the two states* BOUNDARY MARKER, boundary line, boundary fence. **4** *the ruling was hailed as a landmark* TURNING POINT, milestone, watershed, critical point.

landscape ● noun SCENERY, countryside, topography, country, terrain; outlook, view, prospect, aspect, vista, panorama.

landslide ● noun **1** *floods and landslides* LANDSLIP, mudslide; avalanche. **2** *the Labour landslide* DECISIVE VICTORY, overwhelming majority, triumph.

cess language for purposes such as speech recognition, speech synthesis, and machine translation.

language laboratory ● **noun** a room equipped with audio and visual equipment for learning a foreign language.

language of flowers ● **noun** a set of symbolic meanings attached to different flowers.

langue de chat /lon də **shaa**/ ● **noun** a very thin finger-shaped crisp biscuit or piece of chocolate.
– ORIGIN French, 'cat's tongue'.

langue d'oc /long **dok**/ ● **noun** the form of medieval French spoken south of the Loire, characterized by the use of *oc* to mean 'yes' and forming the basis of modern Provençal.
– ORIGIN Old French, 'language of oc'.

langue d'oïl /long **doyl**/ ● **noun** the form of medieval French spoken north of the Loire, characterized by the use of *oïl* to mean 'yes' and forming the basis of modern French.
– ORIGIN Old French, 'language of oïl'.

languid ● **adjective 1** disinclined to exert oneself physically. **2** weak or faint from illness or fatigue.
– DERIVATIVES **languidly** adverb.

languish ● **verb 1** grow weak or feeble. **2** be kept in an unpleasant place or situation: *he was languishing in jail.* **3** archaic pine with love or grief.
– ORIGIN Old French *languir*, from Latin *languere*.

languor /**lang**gə/ ● **noun 1** tiredness or inactivity, especially when pleasurable. **2** an oppressive stillness of the air.
– DERIVATIVES **languorous** adjective **languorously** adverb.

langur /lang**gə**/ ● **noun** a long-tailed Asian monkey with a characteristic loud call.
– ORIGIN Sanskrit.

laniard ● **noun** variant spelling of LANYARD.

lank ● **adjective 1** (of hair) long, limp, and straight. **2** lanky.
– ORIGIN Old English, 'thin'.

lanky ● **adjective** (**lankier**, **lankiest**) awkwardly thin and tall.
– DERIVATIVES **lankily** adverb **lankiness** noun.

lanolin ● **noun** a fatty substance found naturally on sheep's wool and used as a base for ointments.
– ORIGIN from Latin *lana* 'wool' + *oleum* 'oil'.

lantern ● **noun 1** a lamp with a transparent case protecting the flame or electric bulb. **2** the light chamber at the top of a lighthouse. **3** a square, curved, or polygonal structure on the top of a dome or a room, with glazed or open sides.
– ORIGIN Latin *lanterna*, from Greek *lamptēr* 'lamp'.

lanternfish ● **noun** a deep-sea fish with light-emitting organs on its body.

lantern jawed ● **adjective** having long, thin jaws, giving a drawn look to the face.

lantern slide ● **noun** historical a mounted photographic transparency for projection by a magic lantern.

lanthanide /**lan**thənid/ ● **noun** any of the series of fifteen rare-earth elements from lanthanum to lutetium in the periodic table.

lanthanum /**lan**thənəm/ ● **noun** a silvery-white rare-earth metallic chemical element.
– ORIGIN from Greek *lanthanein* 'escape notice' (because it was long undetected in cerium oxide).

lanyard /**lan**yərd/ (also **laniard**) ● **noun 1** a rope used to secure or raise and lower something such as a ship's sails. **2** a cord passed round the neck, shoulder, or wrist for holding a whistle or similar object.
– ORIGIN Old French *laniere*, altered by association with YARD[1].

Laodicean /layōdi**see**ən/ ● **adjective** archaic half-hearted or indifferent, especially with respect to religion or politics.
– ORIGIN from *Laodicea* in Asia Minor, with reference to the early Christians there (Book of Revelation, chapter 3).

Laotian /**low**sh'n/ ● **noun** a person from the country of Laos in SE Asia. ● **adjective** relating to Laos.

lap[1] ● **noun** the flat area between the waist and knees of a seated person.
– PHRASES **fall** (or **drop**) **into someone's lap** be acquired by or happen to someone without any effort. **in someone's lap** as someone's responsibility. **in the lap of the gods** open to chance. **in the lap of luxury** in conditions of great comfort and wealth.
– DERIVATIVES **lapful** noun.
– ORIGIN Old English, 'fold, flap', later denoting the front of a skirt when held up to carry something.

lap[2] ● **noun 1** one circuit of a track or racetrack. **2** a part of a journey or other endeavour: *the last lap.* **3** an overlapping or projecting part. **4** a single turn of rope, thread, or cable round a drum or reel. ● **verb** (**lapped**, **lapping**) **1** overtake (a competitor in a race) to become one or more laps ahead. **2** (**lap in**) literary enfold (someone or something) protectively in. **3** project beyond or overlap something.
– ORIGIN originally in the sense 'to fold or wrap': from LAP[1].

lap[3] ● **verb** (**lapped**, **lapping**) **1** (of an animal) take up (liquid) with the tongue. **2** (**lap up**) accept with obvious pleasure. **3** (of water) wash against with a gentle rippling sound. ● **noun** the action of water lapping.
– ORIGIN Old English.

laparoscopy /lappə**ros**kəpi/ ● **noun** (pl. **laparoscopies**) a surgical procedure in which a fibre-optic instrument is inserted through the abdominal wall to view the organs in the abdomen or permit small-scale surgery.
– DERIVATIVES **laparoscope** noun **laparoscopic** adjective.
– ORIGIN from Greek *lapara* 'flank'.

laparotomy /lappə**rott**əmi/ ● **noun** (pl. **laparotomies**) a surgical incision into the abdominal cavity, for diagnosis or in preparation for major surgery.

lap dancing ● **noun** erotic dancing in which the dancer performs a striptease near to or on the lap of a paying customer.

lapdog ● **noun 1** a small pampered pet dog. **2** a person who is

Thesaurus

lane ● **noun 1** *country lanes* BYROAD, byway, track, road, street; alley, alleyway. **2** *cycle lanes* | *a three-lane highway* TRACK, way, course; road division.

language ● **noun 1** *the structure of language* SPEECH, writing, communication, conversation, speaking, talking, talk, discourse; words, vocabulary; *archaic* converse. **2** *the English language* TONGUE, mother tongue, native tongue; *informal* lingo. **3** *simple, everyday language* WORDING, phrasing, phraseology, style, vocabulary, terminology, expressions, turns of phrase, parlance, form/mode of expression, usages, locutions, idiolect, choice of words; speech, dialect, patois, slang, idioms, jargon, argot, cant; *informal* lingo.
– RELATED TERMS linguistic.

languid ● **adjective 1** *a languid wave of the hand* RELAXED, unhurried, languorous, slow; listless, lethargic, sluggish, lazy, idle, indolent, apathetic; *informal* laid back; *archaic* otiose. **2** *languid days in the sun* LEISURELY, languorous, relaxed, restful, lazy. **3** *she was pale and languid* SICKLY, weak, faint, feeble, frail, delicate; tired, weary, fatigued.
– OPPOSITES energetic.

languish ● **verb 1** *the plants languished and died* WEAKEN, deteriorate, decline; wither, droop, wilt, fade, waste away; *informal* go downhill. **2** *the general is now languishing in prison* WASTE AWAY, rot, be abandoned, be neglected, be forgotten, suffer, experience hardship. **3** (*archaic*) *she still languished after Richard* PINE FOR, yearn for, ache for, long for, sigh for; grieve for, mourn.
– OPPOSITES thrive.

languor ● **noun 1** *the sultry languor that was stealing over her* LASSITUDE, lethargy, listlessness, torpor, fatigue, weariness, sleepiness, drowsiness; laziness, idleness, indolence, inertia, sluggishness, apathy. **2** *the languor of a hot day* STILLNESS, tranquillity, calm, calmness; oppressiveness, heaviness.
– OPPOSITES vigour.

lank ● **adjective 1** *lank, greasy hair* LIMP, lifeless, lustreless, dull; straggling, straight, long. **2** *his lank figure.* See LANKY.

lanky ● **adjective** TALL, THIN, slender, slim, lean, lank, skinny, spindly, spare, gangling, gangly, gawky, rangy.
– OPPOSITES stocky.

lap[1] ● **noun** *Henry sat on his gran's lap* KNEE, knees, thighs.
– PHRASES **in the lap of the gods** OUT OF ONE'S HANDS, beyond one's control, in the hands of fate. **live in the lap of luxury** BE VERY RICH, want for nothing; *informal* live the life of Riley; *N. Amer. informal* live high on the hog.

lap[2] ● **noun** *a race of eight laps* CIRCUIT, leg, circle, revolution, round.
● **verb 1** *she lapped the other runners* OVERTAKE, outstrip, leave behind, pass, go past; catch up with. **2** (*poetic/literary*) *he was lapped in blankets* WRAP, swathe, envelop, enfold, swaddle.

lap[3] ● **verb 1** *waves lapped against the sea wall* SPLASH, wash, swish, slosh, break, beat, strike, dash, roll; *poetic/literary* plash. **2** *the dog lapped water out of a puddle* DRINK, lick up, sup, swallow, slurp, gulp.

completely under the influence of another.

lapel • noun the part on each side of a coat or jacket immediately below the collar which is folded back against the front opening.
– ORIGIN diminutive of LAP[1].

lapidary /lappidəri/ • adjective **1** relating to the engraving, cutting, or polishing of stones and gems. **2** (of language) elegant and concise. • noun (pl. **lapidaries**) a person who cuts, polishes, or engraves stones and gems.
– ORIGIN Latin *lapidarius*, from *lapis* 'stone'.

lapis lazuli /lappiss lazyooli/ (also **lapis**) • noun **1** a bright blue metamorphic rock used in jewellery. **2** ultramarine, originally made by crushing this rock.
– ORIGIN Latin, 'stone of lapis lazuli', from Persian; related to AZURE.

lap joint • noun a joint made by halving the thickness of each member at the joint and fitting them together.

Laplander /laplandər/ • noun a person from Lapland, a region in northern Europe.

lap of honour • noun Brit. a celebratory circuit of a sports field, track, etc. by the victorious person or team.

Lapp • noun **1** a member of an indigenous people of the extreme north of Scandinavia. **2** the language of this people.
– USAGE Although the term **Lapp** is still widely used and is the most familiar term to many people, the people themselves prefer to be called **Sami**.
– ORIGIN Swedish, perhaps originally a term of contempt and related to High German *lappe* 'simpleton'.

lappet /lappit/ • noun **1** a fold or hanging piece of flesh in some animals. **2** a loose or overlapping part of a garment.
– ORIGIN diminutive of LAP[1].

Lappish • noun the Lapp language. • adjective relating to the Lapps (Sami) or their language.

lapse • noun **1** a brief failure of concentration, memory, or judgement. **2** a decline from previously high standards. **3** an interval of time. **4** Law the termination of a right or privilege through disuse or failure to follow appropriate procedures. • verb **1** (of a right, privilege, or agreement) become invalid because it is not used, claimed, or renewed. **2** cease to follow the rules and practices of a religion or doctrine. **3** (**lapse into**) pass gradually into (a different, often worse, state or condition).
– ORIGIN Latin *lapsus*, from *labi* 'to slip or fall'.

laptop • noun a portable microcomputer suitable for use while travelling.

lapwing • noun a large crested plover with a dark green back, black-and-white head and underparts, and a loud call.
– ORIGIN Old English, from words meaning 'to leap' and 'move from side to side' (because of the way it flies).

larboard /laabord, -bərd/ • noun Nautical archaic term for PORT[3].
– ORIGIN originally as *ladebord* (see LADE, BOARD), referring to the side on which cargo was loaded; the change to *lar-* was due to association with STARBOARD.

larceny /laarsəni/ • noun (pl. **larcenies**) theft of personal property (in English law replaced as a statutory crime by theft in 1968).
– DERIVATIVES **larcenist** noun **larcenous** adjective.
– ORIGIN Old French *larcin*, from Latin *latro* 'robber'.

larch • noun a northern coniferous tree with bunches of deciduous bright green needles and tough wood.
– ORIGIN High German *larche*, from Latin *larix*.

lard • noun fat from the abdomen of a pig, rendered and clarified for use in cooking. • verb **1** insert strips of fat or bacon in (meat) before cooking. **2** (usu. **be larded with**) embellish (talk or writing) excessively with esoteric or technical expressions.
– DERIVATIVES **lardy** adjective.
– ORIGIN Latin *lardum*.

larder • noun a room or large cupboard for storing food.
– ORIGIN originally denoting a store of meat: from Latin *lardarium*, from *lardum* 'lard'.

lardon /laard'n/ (also **lardoon** /laardoon/) • noun a chunk or strip of bacon used to lard meat.
– ORIGIN French.

lardy cake • noun Brit. a cake made with bread dough, lard, and currants.

large • adjective **1** of considerable or relatively great size, extent, or capacity. **2** pursuing an occupation or activity on a significant scale. **3** of wide range or scope. • verb (**large it**) Brit. informal go out and have a good time.
– PHRASES **at large 1** escaped or not yet captured. **2** as a whole.
– DERIVATIVES **largeness** noun **largish** adjective.
– ORIGIN Latin *larga* 'copious'.

large-hearted • adjective sympathetic and generous.

large intestine • noun Anatomy the caecum, colon, and rectum collectively.

largely • adverb on the whole; mostly.

large-scale • adjective extensive.

largesse /laarzhess/ (also **largess**) • noun **1** generosity. **2** money or gifts given generously.
– ORIGIN Old French, from Latin *largus* 'copious'.

largo /laargō/ • adverb & adjective Music in a slow tempo and

Thesaurus

– PHRASES **lap something up** RELISH, revel in, savour, delight in, wallow in, glory in, enjoy.

lapse • noun **1** *a lapse of concentration* FAILURE, failing, slip, error, mistake, blunder, fault, omission; *informal* slip-up. **2** *his lapse into petty crime* DECLINE, fall, falling, slipping, drop, deterioration, degeneration, backsliding, regression, retrogression, descent, sinking, slide. **3** *a lapse of time* INTERVAL, gap, pause, interlude, lull, hiatus, break; passage, course, passing.
• verb **1** *the planning permission has lapsed* EXPIRE, become void, become invalid, run out. **2** *do not let friendships lapse* (COME TO AN) END, cease, stop, terminate, pass, fade, wither, die. **3** *morality has lapsed* DETERIORATE, decline, fall (off), drop, worsen, degenerate, backslide, regress, retrogress, get worse, sink, wane, slump; *informal* go downhill, go to pot, go to the dogs. **4** *she lapsed into silence* REVERT, relapse; drift, slide, slip, sink.

lapsed • adjective **1** *a lapsed Catholic* NON-PRACTISING, backsliding, apostate; *formal* quondam. **2** *a lapsed season ticket* EXPIRED, void, invalid, out of date.
– OPPOSITES practising, valid.

larceny • noun THEFT, stealing, robbery, pilfering, thieving; burglary, housebreaking, breaking and entering; *informal* filching, swiping; *Brit. informal* nicking, pinching; *formal* peculation.

larder • noun PANTRY, (food) store, (food) cupboard; cooler, scullery; *Brit.* buttery; *archaic* spence.

large • adjective **1** *a large house | large numbers of people* BIG, great, huge, sizeable, substantial, immense, enormous, colossal, massive, mammoth, vast, prodigious, tremendous, gigantic, giant, monumental, stupendous, gargantuan, elephantine, titanic, mountainous, monstrous; towering, tall, high; mighty, voluminous, king-size, giant-size; *informal* jumbo, whopping (great), thumping (great), mega, humongous, monster, astronomical; *Brit. informal* whacking (great), ginormous. **2** *a large red-faced man* BIG, burly, heavy, tall, bulky, thickset, chunky, strapping, hulking, hefty, muscular, brawny, solid, powerful, sturdy, strong, rugged; fat, plump, overweight, chubby, stout, meaty, fleshy, portly, rotund, flabby, paunchy, obese, corpulent; *informal* hunky, beefy, tubby, pudgy; *Brit. informal* podgy, fubsy; *N. Amer. informal* zaftig, corn-fed. **3** *a large supply of wool* ABUNDANT, copious, plentiful, ample, liberal, generous, lavish, bountiful, bumper, boundless, good, considerable, superabundant; *poetic/literary* plenteous. **4** *the measure has large economic implications* WIDE-REACHING, far-reaching, wide, sweeping, large-scale, broad, extensive, comprehensive, exhaustive.
– RELATED TERMS macro-, mega-.
– OPPOSITES small, meagre.
– PHRASES **at large 1** *fourteen criminals are still at large* AT LIBERTY, free, (on the) loose, on the run, fugitive; *N. Amer. informal* on the lam. **2** *society at large* AS A WHOLE, generally, in general. **3** *(dated) he spoke at large* IN DETAIL, exhaustively, at length, extensively. **by and large** ON THE WHOLE, generally, in general, all things considered, all in all, for the most part, in the main, as a rule, overall, almost always, mainly, mostly; on average, on balance.

largely • adverb MOSTLY, mainly, to a large/great extent, chiefly, predominantly, primarily, principally, for the most part, in the main; usually, typically, commonly.

large-scale • adjective **1** *a large-scale programme* EXTENSIVE, wide-ranging, far-reaching, comprehensive, exhaustive; mass, nationwide, global. **2** *a large-scale map* ENLARGED, blown-up, magnified.

largesse • noun **1** *Tupper took advantage of his friend's largesse* GENEROSITY, liberality, munificence, bounty, bountifulness, beneficence, altruism, charity, philanthropy, magnanimity, benevolence, charitableness, open-handedness, kindness, big-heartedness; *formal* benefaction. **2** *distributing largesse to the locals* GIFTS, presents, handouts, grants, aid; patronage, sponsorship,

dignified in style.
– ORIGIN Italian, from Latin *largus* 'copious'.

lari /laari/ ● noun (pl. same or **laris**) a monetary unit of the Maldives, equal to one hundredth of a rufiyaa.
– ORIGIN Persian.

lariat /larriət/ ● noun a rope used as a lasso or for tethering.
– ORIGIN from Spanish *la reata*, from *la* 'the' and *reatar* 'tie again'.

lark[1] ● noun a songbird with brown streaky plumage and a song that is delivered on the wing.
– PHRASES **be up with the lark** get out of bed very early in the morning.
– ORIGIN Old English.

lark[2] informal ● noun **1** an amusing adventure or escapade. **2** Brit. an activity regarded as foolish or a waste of time: *he's serious about this music lark.* ● verb behave in a playful and mischievous way.
– DERIVATIVES **larky** adjective.
– ORIGIN perhaps from dialect *lake* 'play', but compare with SKYLARK in the same sense, which is recorded earlier.

larkspur ● noun a Mediterranean plant resembling a delphinium, with spikes of spurred flowers.

larrikin /larrikin/ ● noun Austral./NZ **1** archaic a hooligan. **2** a person who disregards convention.
– ORIGIN English dialect, perhaps from the name *Larry* + -KIN, or from a pronunciation of *larking*.

larva /laarvə/ ● noun (pl. **larvae** /laarvee/) an active immature form of an insect or other animal that undergoes metamorphosis, e.g. a caterpillar or tadpole.
– DERIVATIVES **larval** adjective.
– ORIGIN originally denoting a disembodied spirit: from Latin, 'ghost, mask'.

laryngeal /lərinjiəl/ ● adjective relating to the larynx.

laryngitis /larrinjītiss/ ● noun inflammation of the larynx.

larynx /larrinks/ ● noun (pl. **larynges** /lərinjeez/) the hollow muscular organ forming an air passage to the lungs and containing the vocal cords.
– ORIGIN Greek *larunx*.

lasagne /ləzanjə/ ● noun **1** pasta in the form of sheets or wide strips. **2** an Italian dish consisting of this baked with meat or vegetables and a cheese sauce.
– ORIGIN Italian, from Latin *lasanum* 'chamber pot'.

Lascar /laskər/ ● noun dated a sailor from India or SE Asia.
– ORIGIN Urdu and Persian, 'soldier'.

lascivious /ləsivviəss/ ● adjective feeling or showing an overt or offensive sexual desire.
– DERIVATIVES **lasciviously** adverb **lasciviousness** noun.
– ORIGIN from Latin *lascivia* 'lustfulness'.

laser ● noun a device that generates an intense narrow beam of light by stimulating the emission of photons from excited atoms or molecules.
– ORIGIN acronym from *light amplification by stimulated emission of radiation.*

laserdisc ● noun a disc resembling a large compact disc, used for high-quality video and for interactive multimedia.

laser printer ● noun a computer printer in which a laser is used to form a pattern of electrically charged dots on a light-sensitive drum, which attracts toner.

lash ● verb **1** beat with a whip or stick. **2** beat forcefully against. **3** (**lash out**) launch a verbal or physical attack. **4** (of an animal) move (a part of the body, especially the tail) quickly and violently. **5** fasten securely with a cord or rope. **6** (**lash out**) informal spend money extravagantly. ● noun **1** a sharp blow or stroke with a whip or stick. **2** the flexible leather part of a whip. **3** an eyelash.
– DERIVATIVES **lasher** noun **lashless** adjective.
– ORIGIN probably imitative.

lashing ● noun **1** a whipping or beating. **2** a cord used to fasten something securely.

lashings ● plural noun Brit. informal a copious amount of something, especially food or drink.

lash-up ● noun informal, chiefly Brit. a makeshift, improvised structure or arrangement.

lass (also **lassie**) ● noun chiefly Scottish & N. English a girl or young woman.
– ORIGIN from Old Norse, 'unmarried'.

Lassa fever /lassə/ ● noun an acute and often fatal disease transmitted by a virus and occurring chiefly in West Africa.
– ORIGIN named after the village of *Lassa* in Nigeria, where it was first reported.

lassi /lassi/ ● noun a sweet or savoury Indian drink made from a yogurt or buttermilk base with water.
– ORIGIN Hindi.

lassitude /lassityood/ ● noun physical or mental weariness; lack of energy.
– ORIGIN Latin *lassitudo*, from *lassus* 'tired'.

lasso /lasoo/ ● noun (pl. **lassos** or **lassoes**) a rope with a noose at one end, used especially in North America for catching cattle. ● verb (**lassoes, lassoed**) catch with a lasso.
– DERIVATIVES **lassoer** noun.
– ORIGIN Spanish *lazo*, from Latin *laqueus* 'noose'.

last[1] ● adjective **1** coming after all others in time or order. **2** most recent in time. **3** immediately preceding in order. **4** lowest in importance or rank. **5** (**the last**) the least likely or suitable. **6** only remaining. ● adverb **1** on the last occasion before the present. **2** (in combination) after all others in order: *the last-named film.* **3** (in enumerating points) lastly. ● noun (pl. same) **1** the last person or thing. **2** (**the last of**) the only remaining part of. **3** (**the last**) the end or last moment, especially death.
– PHRASES **at last** (or **at long last**) in the end; after much delay. **last thing** late in the evening, especially just before going to bed.
– ORIGIN Old English, related to LATE.

last[2] ● verb **1** continue for a specified period of time. **2** remain operating or usable for a considerable or specified length of time. **3** (of provisions or resources) be sufficient for (someone) for a specified length of time. **4** (often **last out**) manage to survive or endure.
– ORIGIN Old English, related to LAST[3].

last[3] ● noun a shoemaker's model for shaping or repairing a shoe or boot.
– ORIGIN Old English, from a base meaning 'follow'.

l

Thesaurus

backing, help; *historical* alms.
– OPPOSITES meanness.

lark (*informal*) ● noun **1** *we were just having a bit of a lark* FUN, amusement, laugh, giggle, joke; escapade, prank, trick, jape, practical joke; *informal* leg-pull; (**larks**) antics, high jinks, horseplay, mischief, tomfoolery; *informal* shenanigans, monkey business; *Brit. informal* monkey tricks; *dated* sport. **2** *I've got this snowboarding lark sussed* ACTIVITY; hobby, pastime, task; *informal* business, caper.
● verb *he's always larking about* FOOL ABOUT/AROUND, play tricks, make mischief, monkey about/around, clown about/around, have fun, skylark; *informal* mess about/around; *Brit. informal* muck about/around.

lascivious ● adjective LECHEROUS, lewd, lustful, licentious, libidinous, salacious, lubricious, prurient, dirty, smutty, naughty, suggestive, indecent, ribald; *informal* horny; *Brit. informal* randy; *formal* concupiscent.

lash ● verb **1** *he lashed her repeatedly* WHIP, flog, beat, thrash, horsewhip, scourge, birch, switch, belt, strap, cane; strike, hit; *informal* wallop, whack, lam, larrup, give someone a (good) hiding; *N. Amer. informal* whale. **2** *rain lashed the window panes* BEAT AGAINST, dash against, pound, batter, strike, hit, knock. **3** *the tiger began to lash his tail* SWISH, flick, twitch, whip. **4** *fear lashed them into a frenzy* PROVOKE, incite, arouse, excite, agitate, stir up, whip up, work up. **5** *two boats were lashed together* FASTEN, bind, tie (up), tether, hitch, knot, rope, make fast.
● noun **1** *he brought the lash down upon the prisoner's back* WHIP, horsewhip, switch, scourge, thong, flail, strap, birch, cane; *historical* knout, cat-o'-nine-tails, cat. **2** *twenty lashes* STROKE, blow, hit, strike, welt, thwack, thump; *informal* wallop, whack; *archaic* stripe.
– PHRASES **lash out 1** *the president lashed out at the opposition* CRITICIZE, chastise, censure, attack, condemn, denounce, lambaste, harangue, pillory; berate, upbraid, rebuke, reproach; *informal* lay into; *formal* castigate. **2** *Norman lashed out at Terry with a knife* HIT OUT, strike, let fly, take a swing; set upon/about, turn on, round on, attack; *informal* lay into, tear into, pitch into. **3** (*informal*) *they lashed out on a taxi* SPEND LAVISHLY, be extravagant; *informal* splash out, splurge, shell out, squander money, waste money, fritter money away.

lass ● noun (*Scottish & N. English*) GIRL, young woman, young lady; *Scottish* lassie; *Irish* colleen; *informal* chick, girlie; *Brit. informal* bird, bint; *N. Amer. informal* dame, babe, doll, gal, broad; *Austral./NZ informal* sheila; *poetic/literary* maid, maiden, damsel; *archaic* wench.

last-ditch ● adjective denoting a final desperate attempt to achieve something.
last-gasp ● adjective informal at the last possible moment.
lasting ● adjective enduring or able to endure for a long time.
– DERIVATIVES **lastingly** adverb **lastingness** noun.
Last Judgement ● noun the judgement of humankind expected in some religious traditions to take place at the end of the world.
lastly ● adverb in the last place; last.
last minute (also **last moment**) ● noun the latest possible time before an event.
last name ● noun one's surname.
last post ● noun (in the British armed forces) the second of two bugle calls giving notice of the hour of retiring at night, played also at military funerals and acts of remembrance.
last rites ● plural noun (in the Christian Church) rites administered to a person who is about to die.
Last Supper ● noun the supper eaten by Jesus and his disciples on the night before the Crucifixion.
last trump ● noun the trumpet blast that in some religious beliefs is thought will wake the dead on Judgement Day.
last word ● noun **1** a final or definitive pronouncement. **2** the most modern or advanced example of something: *the last word in luxury.*
lat /lat/ ● noun (pl. **lati** /latti/ or **lats**) the basic monetary unit of Latvia, equal to 100 santims.
– ORIGIN from the first syllable of *Latvija* 'Latvia'.
lat. ● abbreviation latitude.
latch ● noun **1** a bar with a catch and lever used for fastening a door or gate. **2** a spring lock for an outer door, which catches when the door is closed and can only be opened from the outside with a key. ● verb **1** fasten with a latch. **2** (**latch on**) understand. **3** (**latch on to**) associate oneself enthusiastically with.
– PHRASES **on the latch** (of a door or gate) closed but not locked.
– ORIGIN from Old English, 'take hold of, grasp'.
latchkey ● noun (pl. **latchkeys**) a key of an outer door of a house.
latchkey child ● noun a child who is alone at home after school until a parent returns from work.
late ● adjective **1** acting, arriving, or happening after the proper or usual time. **2** belonging or taking place far on in a particular time or period. **3** far on in the day or night. **4** (**the/one's late**) (of a person) no longer alive. **5** (**the/one's late**) no longer having the specified status; former. **6** (**latest**) of most recent date or origin. ● adverb **1** after the proper or usual time. **2** towards the end of a period. **3** far on in the day or night. **4** (**later**) at a time in the near future; afterwards. **5** (**late of**) formerly but not now living or working in (a place). ● noun (**the latest**) the most recent news or fashion.
– PHRASES **at the latest** no later than the time specified. **of late** recently.
– DERIVATIVES **lateness** noun.
– ORIGIN Old English.
latecomer ● noun a person who arrives late.
lateen sail /lateen/ ● noun a triangular sail on a long yard at an angle of 45° to the mast.
– ORIGIN from French *voile Latine* 'Latin sail', so named because it was common in the Mediterranean.
lately ● adverb recently; not long ago.
latent ● adjective existing but not yet developed, manifest, or active.
– DERIVATIVES **latency** noun **latently** adverb.
– ORIGIN from Latin *latere* 'be hidden'.
latent heat ● noun the heat required to convert a solid into a liquid or vapour, or a liquid into a vapour, without change of temperature.
latent image ● noun an image on exposed photographic film that has not yet been made visible by developing.
latent period ● noun Medicine the period between infection and the onset of symptoms.
lateral ● adjective of, at, towards, or from the side or sides. ● noun a lateral part, especially a shoot or branch growing out from the side of a stem.
– DERIVATIVES **laterally** adverb.
– ORIGIN Latin *lateralis*, from *latus* 'side'.
lateral thinking ● noun chiefly Brit. the solving of problems by an indirect and creative approach.
laterite /lattərīt/ ● noun a reddish clayey topsoil, hard when dry, found in tropical regions and sometimes used to make roads.
– ORIGIN from Latin *later* 'brick'.

Thesaurus

lassitude ● noun LETHARGY, listlessness, weariness, languor, sluggishness, tiredness, fatigue, torpor, lifelessness, apathy.
– OPPOSITES vigour.
last[1] ● adjective **1** *the last woman in the queue* REARMOST, hindmost, endmost, at the end, at the back, furthest (back), final, ultimate. **2** *Rembrandt spent his last years in Amsterdam* CLOSING, concluding, final, ending, end, terminal; later, latter. **3** *I'd be the last person to say anything against him* LEAST LIKELY, most unlikely, most improbable; least suitable, most unsuitable, most inappropriate, least appropriate. **4** *we met last year* PREVIOUS, preceding; prior, former. **5** *this was his last chance* FINAL, only remaining.
– OPPOSITES first, early, next.
● adverb *the candidate coming last is eliminated* AT THE END, at/in the rear.
● noun *the most important business was left to the last* END, ending, finish, close, conclusion, finale, termination.
– OPPOSITES beginning.
– PHRASES **at last** FINALLY, in the end, eventually, ultimately, at long last, after a long time, in (the fullness of) time. **the last word** **1** *that's my last word* FINAL DECISION, definitive statement, conclusive comment. **2** *she was determined to have the last word* CONCLUDING REMARK, final say, closing statement. **3** *the last word in luxury and efficiency* THE BEST, the peak, the acme, the epitome, the latest; the pinnacle, the apex, the apogee, the ultimate, the height, the zenith, the nonpareil, the crème de la crème; archaic the nonsuch.
last[2] ● verb **1** *the hearing lasted for six days* CONTINUE, go on, carry on, keep on/going, proceed, take; stay, remain, persist. **2** *how long will he last as manager?* SURVIVE, endure, hold on/out, keep going, persevere; informal stick it out, hang on, hack it. **3** *the car is built to last* ENDURE, wear well, stand up, bear up; informal go the distance.
last-ditch ● adjective LAST-MINUTE, last-chance, eleventh-hour, last-resort, desperate, final; informal last-gasp.
lasting ● adjective ENDURING, long-lasting, long-lived, abiding, continuing, long-term, surviving, persisting, permanent; durable, constant, stable, established, secure, long-standing; unchanging, irreversible, immutable, eternal, undying, everlasting, unending, never-ending; unfading, changeless, indestructible, unceasing, unwavering, unfaltering.
– OPPOSITES ephemeral.
lastly ● adverb FINALLY, in conclusion, to conclude, to sum up, to end, last, ultimately.
– OPPOSITES firstly.
latch ● noun *he lifted the latch* FASTENING, catch, fastener, clasp.
● verb *Jess latched the back door* FASTEN, secure, make fast.
late ● adjective **1** *the train was late* BEHIND TIME, behind schedule, behindhand; tardy, running late, overdue, delayed. **2** *her late husband* DEAD, departed, lamented, passed on/away; formal deceased. **3** *the late government* PREVIOUS, preceding, former, past, prior, earlier, sometime, one-time, ex-, erstwhile; formal quondam.
– OPPOSITES punctual, early.
● adverb **1** *she had arrived late* BEHIND SCHEDULE, behind time, behindhand, belatedly, tardily, at the last minute. **2** *I was working late* AFTER (OFFICE) HOURS, overtime. **3** *I won't have you staying out late* LATE AT NIGHT; informal till all hours.
– PHRASES **of late** RECENTLY, lately, latterly.
lately ● adverb RECENTLY, of late, latterly, in recent times.
lateness ● noun UNPUNCTUALITY, tardiness, delay.
latent ● adjective DORMANT, untapped, unused, undiscovered, hidden, concealed, invisible, unseen, undeveloped, unrealized, unfulfilled, potential.
later ● adjective *a later chapter* SUBSEQUENT, following, succeeding, future, upcoming, to come, ensuing, next; formal posterior; archaic after.
– OPPOSITES earlier.
● adverb **1** *later, the film rights were sold* SUBSEQUENTLY, eventually, then, next, later on, after this/that, afterwards, at a later date, in the future, in due course, by and by, in a while, in time. **2** *two days later a letter arrived* AFTERWARDS, later on, after (that), subsequently, following; formal thereafter.
lateral ● adjective **1** *lateral movements* SIDEWAYS, sidewise, side-

latex /layteks/ ● noun (pl. **latexes** or **latices** /laytiseez/) **1** a milky fluid found in many plants, notably the rubber tree, which coagulates on exposure to the air. **2** a synthetic product resembling this, used to make paints, coatings, etc.
– ORIGIN originally denoting various bodily fluids: from Latin, 'liquid, fluid'.

lath /laath/ ● noun (pl. **laths** /laaths/) a thin, flat strip of wood, especially one of a series forming a foundation for the plaster of a wall.
– ORIGIN Old English, related to LATTICE.

lathe /layth/ ● noun a machine for shaping wood or metal by means of a rotating drive which turns the piece being worked on against changeable cutting tools.
– ORIGIN probably from Old Danish *lad* 'structure, frame'.

lather /laathər/ ● noun **1** a frothy white mass of bubbles produced by soap when mixed with water. **2** heavy sweat visible on a horse's coat as a white foam. **3** (**a lather**) informal a state of agitation or nervous excitement. ● verb **1** form or cause to form a lather. **2** rub with soap until a lather is produced. **3** cover or spread liberally with (a substance). **4** informal thrash.
– ORIGIN Old English.

lathi /laatee/ ● noun (pl. **lathis**) (in the Indian subcontinent) a long metal-bound bamboo stick used as a weapon, especially by police.
– ORIGIN Hindi.

latices plural of LATEX.

Latin ● noun **1** the language of ancient Rome and its empire. **2** a person from a country whose language developed from Latin, e.g. a Latin American. ● adjective **1** relating to the Latin language. **2** relating to countries using languages that developed from Latin, especially Latin America. **3** relating to the Western or Roman Catholic Church.
– DERIVATIVES **Latinism** noun **Latinist** noun **Latinity** noun.
– ORIGIN from Latin *Latinus* 'of Latium' (an ancient region in central Italy).

Latina /lateenə/ ● noun fem. of LATINO.

Latin American ● adjective relating to the parts of the American continent where Spanish or Portuguese is the main national language. ● noun a person from this region.

Latinate /lattinayt/ ● adjective (of language) having the character of Latin.

Latin Church ● noun the Roman Catholic Church as distinguished from Orthodox and Uniate Churches.

Latin cross ● noun a plain cross in which the vertical part below the horizontal is longer than the other three parts.

Latinize (also **Latinise**) ● verb **1** give a Latin or Latinate form to (a word). **2** cause to conform to the ideas and customs of the ancient Romans, the Latin Church, or Latin peoples.
– DERIVATIVES **Latinization** noun.

Latino /lateenō/ ● noun (pl. **Latinos**; fem. **Latina**, pl. **Latinas**) N. Amer. a Latin American inhabitant of the United States.
– ORIGIN Latin American Spanish.

latitude /lattityood/ ● noun **1** the angular distance of a place north or south of the equator. **2** (**latitudes**) regions with reference to their temperature and distance from the equator: *northern latitudes.* **3** scope for freedom of action or thought.
– DERIVATIVES **latitudinal** adjective **latitudinally** adverb.
– ORIGIN Latin *latitudo* 'breadth'.

latitudinarian /lattityoodinairiən/ ● adjective liberal, especially in religious views. ● noun a latitudinarian person.
– DERIVATIVES **latitudinarianism** noun.

latke /lutkə/ ● noun (in Jewish cookery) a pancake, especially one made with grated potato.
– ORIGIN Yiddish.

latrine /lətreen/ ● noun a toilet, especially a communal one in a camp or barracks.
– ORIGIN Latin *latrina*, from *lavare* 'to wash'.

latte /laatay/ ● noun a drink of frothy steamed milk to which a shot of espresso coffee is added.
– ORIGIN Italian, short for *caffè latte* 'milk coffee'.

latter ● adjective **1** nearer to the end than to the beginning. **2** recent: *in latter years.* **3** (**the latter**) denoting the second or second-mentioned of two people or things.
– ORIGIN Old English, 'slower'; related to LATE.

latter-day ● adjective modern or contemporary, especially when resembling some person or thing of the past: *a latter-day Noah.*

Latter-Day Saints ● plural noun the Mormons' name for themselves.

latterly ● adverb **1** recently. **2** in the later stages of a period of time.

lattice ● noun **1** a structure or pattern consisting of strips crossing each other with square or diamond-shaped spaces left between. **2** a regular repeated three-dimensional arrangement of atoms, ions, or molecules in a metal or other crystalline solid.
– DERIVATIVES **latticed** adjective **latticework** noun.
– ORIGIN Old French *lattis*, from *latte* 'lath'.

lattice window ● noun a window with small panes set in diagonally crossing strips of lead.

Latvian ● noun **1** a person from Latvia. **2** the language of Latvia. ● adjective relating to Latvia.

laud /lawd/ ● verb formal praise highly.
– DERIVATIVES **laudation** noun.
– ORIGIN Latin *laudare*, from *laus* 'praise'.

laudable ● adjective deserving praise and commendation.
– DERIVATIVES **laudably** adverb.

laudanum /lawdənəm/ ● noun a solution prepared from opium and formerly used as a narcotic painkiller.
– ORIGIN Latin, perhaps a variant of *ladanum* 'ladanum' (a gum resin obtained from a rock rose).

laudatory /lawdətri/ ● adjective expressing praise and commendation.

lauds /lawdz/ ● noun a service of morning prayer in the Divine Office of the Western Christian Church, traditionally said or chanted at daybreak.
– ORIGIN from the use, in Psalms 148–150, of Latin *laudate!* 'praise ye!'.

laugh ● verb **1** make the sounds and movements that express lively amusement and sometimes also derision. **2** (**laugh at**) make fun of; ridicule. **3** (**laugh off**) dismiss by (something) treating it light-heartedly. **4** (**be laughing**) informal be in a fortunate or successful position. ● noun **1** an act of laughing. **2** (**a laugh**) informal a cause of laughter.
– PHRASES **have the last laugh** be finally vindicated. **he who laughs last laughs longest** proverb don't rejoice too soon, in

Thesaurus

ward, edgewise, edgeways, oblique. **2** *lateral thinking* UNORTHODOX, inventive, creative, imaginative, original, innovative.

latest ● adjective MOST RECENT, newest, just out, just released, fresh, (bang) up to date, up to the minute, state-of-the-art, current, modern, contemporary, fashionable, in fashion, in vogue; *informal* in, with it, trendy, hip, hot, happening, cool.
– OPPOSITES old.

lather ● noun **1** *a rich, soapy lather* FOAM, froth, suds, soapsuds, bubbles; *poetic/literary* spume. **2** *the mare was covered with lather* SWEAT, perspiration. **3** *(informal) Dad was in a right lather* PANIC, fluster, fret, fuss, fever; *informal* flap, sweat, tizzy, dither, twitter, state, stew; *N. Amer. informal* twit; *poetic/literary* pother.

latitude ● noun **1** *Toronto shares the same latitude as Nice* parallel. **2** *he gave them a lot of latitude* FREEDOM, scope, leeway, (breathing) space, flexibility, liberty, independence, free rein, licence, room to manoeuvre, freedom of action.
– OPPOSITES longitude, restriction.

latter ● adjective **1** *the latter half of the season* LATER, closing, end, concluding, final; latest, most recent. **2** *Russia chose the latter option* LAST-MENTIONED, second, last, later.
– OPPOSITES former.

latter-day ● adjective MODERN, present-day, current, contemporary.

latterly ● adverb **1** *latterly, she had been in more pain* RECENTLY, lately, of late, in recent times. **2** *latterly he worked as a political editor* ULTIMATELY, finally, towards the end.

lattice ● noun GRID, latticework, fretwork, open framework, openwork, trellis, trelliswork, network, mesh.

laud ● verb *(formal)* PRAISE, extol, hail, applaud, acclaim, commend, sing the praises of, speak highly of, lionize, eulogize, rhapsodize over/about; *informal* rave about; *archaic* magnify, panegyrize.
– OPPOSITES criticize.

laudable ● adjective PRAISEWORTHY, commendable, admirable, meritorious, worthy, deserving, creditable, estimable, exemplary.
– OPPOSITES shameful.

laudation ● noun *(formal)* PRAISE, honour, applause, acclaim, acclamation, commendation, admiration, homage, distinction, approval, credit, kudos, glory, esteem, approbation, tribute, congratulations, plaudits; *formal* encomium.

laudatory ● adjective COMPLIMENTARY, congratulatory, praising, extolling, adulatory, commendatory, approbatory, flattering, cele-

case your delight at your own good fortune is premature. **laugh on the other side of one's face** be discomfited after feeling confident or triumphant. **laugh out of court** dismiss with contempt as being obviously ridiculous. **laugh up one's sleeve** be secretly or inwardly amused.

– DERIVATIVES **laugher** noun.

– ORIGIN Old English.

laughable • adjective so ludicrous as to be amusing.

– DERIVATIVES **laughably** adverb.

laughing gas • noun non-technical term for NITROUS OXIDE.

laughing hyena • noun a southern African hyena with a loud laughing call.

laughing jackass • noun Austral. the kookaburra.

laughing stock • noun a person subjected to general ridicule.

laughter • noun the action or sound of laughing.

launch[1] • verb **1** move (a boat or ship) from land into the water. **2** send out or hurl (a rocket or other missile). **3** begin (an enterprise) or introduce (a new product). **4** (**launch into**) begin energetically and enthusiastically. • noun an act or instance of launching.

– ORIGIN Old French *launcher*, variant of *lancier* 'to lance'.

launch[2] • noun **1** a large motor boat. **2** historical the largest boat carried on a man-of-war.

– ORIGIN Spanish *lancha* 'pinnace', perhaps from a Malay word meaning 'swift'.

launcher • noun a structure that holds a rocket or missile during launching.

launder • verb **1** wash and iron (clothes or linen). **2** informal pass (illegally obtained money) through legitimate businesses or foreign banks to conceal its origins.

– DERIVATIVES **launderer** noun.

– ORIGIN originally denoting a person who washes linen: from Latin *lavanda* 'things to be washed', from *lavare* 'to wash'.

launderette (also **laundrette**) • noun an establishment with coin-operated washing machines and dryers for public use.

laundress • noun a woman employed to launder clothes and linen.

laundromat • noun chiefly N. Amer. (trademark in the US) a launderette.

laundry • noun (pl. **laundries**) **1** clothes and linen that need to be washed or that have been newly washed. **2** a room or building where clothes and linen are washed and ironed.

laureate /lorriət/ • noun **1** a person given an award for outstanding creative or intellectual achievement. **2** a poet laureate. • adjective literary wreathed with laurel as a mark of honour.

– DERIVATIVES **laureateship** noun.

– ORIGIN from Latin *laurea* 'laurel wreath'.

laurel • noun **1** an aromatic evergreen shrub or small tree with dark green glossy leaves. **2** historical a bay tree. **3** (**laurels**) a crown woven from bay leaves and awarded as an emblem of victory or mark of honour in classical times. **4** (**laurels**) honour or praise.

– PHRASES **look to one's laurels** be careful not to lose one's superior position to a rival. **rest on one's laurels** be so satisfied with what one has already achieved that one makes no further effort.

– ORIGIN Latin *laurus*.

lava • noun hot molten or semi-fluid rock erupted from a volcano or fissure, or solid rock resulting from cooling of this.

– ORIGIN Italian (originally denoting a stream caused by sudden rain), from Latin *lavare* 'to wash'.

lavage /lavvij/ • noun Medicine washing out of a body cavity, such as the colon or stomach, with water or a medicated solution.

– ORIGIN French, from *laver* 'to wash'.

lava lamp • noun a transparent electric lamp containing a viscous liquid in which a suspended waxy substance rises and falls in constantly changing shapes.

lavatorial • adjective **1** relating to or resembling lavatories. **2** (of conversation or humour) characterized by undue reference to lavatories and excretion.

lavatory • noun (pl. **lavatories**) a toilet.

– ORIGIN Latin *lavatorium* 'place for washing', from *lavare* 'to wash'.

lave /layv/ • verb literary wash or wash over.

– ORIGIN Latin *lavare* 'to wash'.

lavender • noun **1** a small aromatic evergreen shrub of the mint family, with narrow leaves and bluish-purple flowers. **2** a pale blue colour with a trace of mauve.

– ORIGIN Latin *lavandula*.

lavender water • noun a perfume made from distilled lavender.

laver /laavər/ (also **purple laver**) • noun an edible seaweed with thin reddish-purple and green sheet-like fronds.

– ORIGIN Latin.

lavish • adjective **1** sumptuously rich, elaborate, or luxurious. **2** giving or given in profusion. • verb (usu. **lavish on**) give or spend in abundant or extravagant quantities.

– DERIVATIVES **lavishly** adverb **lavishness** noun.

– ORIGIN originally in the sense 'profusion': from Old French *lavasse* 'deluge of rain', from Latin *lavare* 'to wash'.

law • noun **1** a rule or system of rules recognized by a country

Thesaurus

bratory, eulogizing, panegyrical; *informal* glowing; *formal* encomiastic.

– OPPOSITES disparaging.

laugh • verb **1** *he started to laugh excitedly* CHUCKLE, chortle, guffaw, giggle, titter, snigger, snicker, tee-hee, burst out laughing, roar/hoot with laughter, dissolve into laughter, split one's sides, be doubled up; *informal* be in stitches, be rolling in the aisles, crease up, fall about, crack up. **2** *people laughed at his theories* RIDICULE, mock, deride, scoff at, jeer at, sneer at, jibe at, make fun of, poke fun at, scorn; lampoon, satirize, parody; *informal* send up, take the mickey out of, pooh-pooh; *Austral./NZ informal* poke mullock at.

• noun **1** *he gave a short laugh* CHUCKLE, chortle, guffaw, giggle, titter, tee-hee, snigger, snicker, roar/hoot of laughter, shriek of laughter, belly laugh. **2** *(informal) he was a right laugh* JOKER, wag, wit, clown, jester, prankster, character; *informal* card, case, caution, hoot, scream, riot, barrel of laughs; *Austral./NZ informal* hard case. **3** *(informal) I entered the contest for a laugh* JOKE, prank, piece of fun, jest, escapade, caper, practical joke; *informal* lark.

– PHRASES **laugh something off** DISMISS, make a joke of, make light of, shrug off, brush aside, scoff at; *informal* pooh-pooh.

laughable • adjective **1** *the idea that nuclear power is safe is laughable* RIDICULOUS, ludicrous, absurd, risible, preposterous; foolish, silly, idiotic, stupid, nonsensical, crazy, insane, outrageous; *informal* cock-eyed; *Brit. informal* daft. **2** *if it wasn't so tragic, it'd be laughable* AMUSING, funny, humorous, hilarious, uproarious, comical, comic, farcical.

laughing stock • noun FIGURE OF FUN, dupe, butt, stooge, Aunt Sally; *informal* fall guy.

laughter • noun **1** *the sound of laughter* LAUGHING, chuckling, chortling, guffawing, giggling, tittering, sniggering; *informal* hysterics. **2** *a source of laughter* AMUSEMENT, entertainment, humour, mirth, merriment, gaiety, hilarity, jollity, jocularity, fun.

launch • verb **1** *he launched the boat* SET AFLOAT, put to sea, put into the water. **2** *they've launched the shuttle* SEND INTO ORBIT, blast off, take off, lift off. **3** *a chair was launched at him* THROW, hurl, fling, pitch, lob, let fly; fire, shoot; *informal* chuck, heave, sling. **4** *the government launched a new campaign* SET IN MOTION, get going, get under way, start, commence, begin, embark on, initiate, inaugurate, set up, organize, introduce, bring into being; *informal* kick off. **5** *he launched into a tirade* START, commence, burst into.

launder • verb WASH (AND IRON), clean; dry-clean.

laundry • noun **1** *a big pile of laundry* (DIRTY) WASHING, dirty clothes. **2** *the facilities include a laundry* WASHROOM, laundry room, launderette; *N. Amer. trademark* laundromat.

laurels • plural noun HONOURS, tributes, praise, plaudits, accolades, kudos, acclaim, acclamation, credit, glory, honour, distinction, fame, renown, prestige, recognition; *informal* brownie points; *formal* laudation.

lavatory • noun TOILET, WC, water closet, (public) convenience, cloakroom, powder room, urinal, privy, latrine, jakes; *N. Amer.* washroom, bathroom, rest room, men's/ladies' room, commode, comfort station; *Nautical* head; *informal* little girls'/boys' room, smallest room; *Brit. informal* loo, bog, the Ladies, the Gents, khazi, lav; *N. Amer. informal* can, john; *Austral./NZ informal* dunny; *archaic* closet, garderobe.

lavish • adjective **1** *lavish parties* SUMPTUOUS, luxurious, gorgeous, costly, expensive, opulent, grand, splendid, rich, fancy; *informal* posh. **2** *he was lavish with his hospitality* GENEROUS, liberal, bountiful, open-handed, unstinting, unsparing, free, munificent, extravagant, prodigal. **3** *lavish amounts of champagne* ABUNDANT, co-

or community as regulating the actions of its members and enforced by the imposition of penalties. **2** such rules as a subject of study or as the basis of the legal profession. **3** statute law and the common law. **4** a statement of fact to the effect that a particular natural or scientific phenomenon always occurs if certain conditions are present. **5** a rule defining correct procedure or behaviour in a sport. **6** something having binding force or effect: *his word was law.* **7** (**the law**) informal the police.
– PHRASES **be a law unto oneself** behave in an unconventional or unpredictable manner. **lay down the law** issue instructions in an authoritative or dogmatic way. **take the law into one's own hands** illegally or violently punish someone according to one's own ideas of justice.
– ORIGIN Old Norse, 'something laid down or fixed'; related to LAY[1].

law-abiding ● adjective obedient to the laws of society.

law agent ● noun (in Scotland) a solicitor.

lawbreaker ● noun a person who breaks the law.

law centre ● noun (in the UK) an independent publicly funded advisory service on legal matters.

law clerk N. Amer. ● noun **1** a judge's research assistant. **2** an articled clerk.

law court ● noun a court of law.

lawful ● adjective conforming to, permitted by, or recognized by law or rules.
– DERIVATIVES **lawfully** adverb **lawfulness** noun.

lawgiver ● noun a person who draws up and enacts laws.

lawless ● adjective not governed by or obedient to laws.
– DERIVATIVES **lawlessly** adverb **lawlessness** noun.

law lord ● noun (in the UK) a member of the House of Lords qualified to perform its legal work.

lawmaker ● noun a legislator.

lawman ● noun (in the US) a law-enforcement officer, especially a sheriff.

lawn[1] ● noun an area of mown grass in a garden or park.
– DERIVATIVES **lawned** adjective.
– ORIGIN Old French *launde* 'wooded district, heath'.

lawn[2] ● noun a fine linen or cotton fabric.
– ORIGIN probably from *Laon*, a French city important for linen manufacture.

lawnmower ● noun a machine for cutting the grass on a lawn.

lawn tennis ● noun dated or formal tennis.

law of averages ● noun the supposed principle that future events are likely to turn out so that they balance any past deviation from a presumed average.

Law Officer (in full **Law Officer of the Crown**) ● noun (in England and Wales) the Attorney General or the Solicitor General, or (in Scotland) the Lord Advocate or the Solicitor General for Scotland.

law of nature ● noun **1** another term for NATURAL LAW. **2** informal a regularly occurring phenomenon observable in society.

lawrencium /lərensiəm/ ● noun a very unstable chemical element made by high-energy collisions.
– ORIGIN named after the American physicist Ernest O. *Lawrence* (1901–58).

lawsuit ● noun a claim or dispute brought to a law court for adjudication.

lawyer ● noun a person who practises or studies law, especially (in the UK) a solicitor or a barrister or (in the US) an attorney.
– DERIVATIVES **lawyering** noun **lawyerly** adjective.

lax ● adjective **1** not sufficiently strict, severe, or careful. **2** (of limbs or muscles) relaxed.
– DERIVATIVES **laxity** noun **laxly** adverb **laxness** noun.
– ORIGIN Latin *laxus* 'loose, lax'.

laxative ● adjective tending to stimulate or facilitate evacuation of the bowels. ● noun a laxative drug or medicine.
– ORIGIN from Latin *laxare* 'loosen'.

lay[1] ● verb (past and past part. **laid**) **1** put down, especially gently or carefully. **2** put down and set in position for use. **3** assign or place: *lay the blame.* **4** (**lay before**) present (material) for consideration and action to. **5** (of a female bird, reptile, etc.) produce (an egg) from inside the body. **6** stake (an amount of money) in a wager. **7** cause (a ghost) to stop appearing; exorcize. **8** vulgar slang have sexual intercourse with. ● noun **1** the general appearance of an area of land. **2** the position or direction in which something lies. **3** vulgar slang a sexual partner or act of sexual intercourse.
– PHRASES **lay about one** strike out wildly. **lay claim to** assert one's right to or possession of. **lay down 1** formulate and enact (a rule or principle). **2** build up a deposit of (a substance). **3** store (wine) in a cellar. **4** pay or wager (money). **lay in/up** build up (a stock) in case of need. **lay into** informal attack violently. **lay off 1** discharge (a worker) temporarily or permanently because of a shortage of work. **2** informal give up. **lay on** chiefly Brit. provide (a service or amenity). **lay something on thick** (or **with a trowel**) informal grossly exaggerate or overemphasize something. **lay open to** expose (someone) to the risk of. **lay out 1** construct or arrange (buildings or gardens) according to a plan. **2** arrange and present (material) for printing and publication. **3** prepare (someone) for burial after death. **4** informal spend (a sum of money). **lay to rest 1** bury (a body) in a grave. **2** soothe and dispel (fear, anxiety, etc.). **lay up 1** put out of action through illness or injury. **2** see **lay in. 3** take (a ship or other vehicle) out of service.
– USAGE The words **lay** and **lie** are often used incorrectly. You *lay* something, as in *they are going to lay the carpet*, but you *lie* down on a bed or other flat surface. The past tense and past participle of **lay** is **laid**, as in *they laid the groundwork* or *she had laid careful plans*; the past tense of **lie** is **lay** (*he lay on the floor*) and the past participle is **lain** (*she had lain on the bed for hours*).
– ORIGIN Old English, related to LIE[1].

lay[2] ● adjective **1** not ordained into or belonging to the clergy. **2** not having professional qualifications or expert knowledge.
– ORIGIN Latin *laicus*, from Greek *laos* 'people'.

lay[3] ● noun **1** a short lyric or narrative poem intended to be

Thesaurus

pious, plentiful, liberal, prolific, generous; *poetic/literary* plenteous.
– OPPOSITES meagre, frugal.
● verb *she lavished money on her children* GIVE FREELY, spend generously, heap, shower.

law ● noun **1** *the law of the land* RULES AND REGULATIONS, body of laws, constitution, statute, legislation, legal code. **2** *a new law was passed* REGULATION, statute, enactment, act, bill, decree, edict, rule, ruling, resolution, dictum, command, order, directive, pronouncement, proclamation, dictate, diktat, fiat, by-law; *N. Amer. formal* ordinance. **3** *a career in the law* THE LEGAL PROFESSION, the bar. **4** *I'll take you to law!* LITIGATION, legal action, lawsuit, justice. **5** *(informal) on the run from the law.* See POLICE noun. **6** *the laws of the game* RULE, regulation, principle, convention, instruction, guideline. **7** *a moral law* PRINCIPLE, rule, precept, directive, injunction, commandment, belief, creed, credo, maxim, tenet, doctrine, canon.
– RELATED TERMS legal.

law-abiding ● adjective HONEST, lawful, righteous, honourable, upright, upstanding, good, decent, virtuous, moral, dutiful, obedient, compliant, disciplined.
– OPPOSITES criminal.

lawbreaker ● noun CRIMINAL, felon, wrongdoer, malefactor, evildoer, offender, transgressor, miscreant; villain, rogue, ruffian; *Law* malfeasant, infractor; *informal* crook, con, jailbird.

law court ● noun COURT, court of law/justice, tribunal.
– RELATED TERMS judicial, juridical.

lawful ● adjective **1** *a verdict of lawful killing* LEGITIMATE, legal, licit, just, permissible, permitted, allowable, allowed, rightful, sanctioned, authorized, warranted, within the law; *informal* legit. **2** *a lawful political organization* LAW-ABIDING, righteous, good, decent, virtuous, moral, orderly, well behaved, peaceful, dutiful, obedient, compliant, disciplined.
– OPPOSITES illegal, criminal.

lawless ● adjective **1** *a lawless rabble* ANARCHIC, disorderly, ungovernable, unruly, disruptive, rebellious, insubordinate, riotous, mutinous. **2** *lawless activities* ILLEGAL, unlawful, lawbreaking, illicit, illegitimate, criminal, felonious, villainous, miscreant; *informal* crooked, shady, bent.
– OPPOSITES orderly, legal.

lawlessness ● noun ANARCHY, disorder, chaos, unruliness, criminality, crime.

lawsuit ● noun (LEGAL) ACTION, suit (at law), case, (legal/judicial) proceedings, litigation, trial.

lawyer ● noun SOLICITOR, legal practitioner, legal adviser, member of the bar, barrister, advocate, counsel, Queen's Counsel, QC; *N. Amer.* attorney, counselor(-at-law); *informal* brief.

lax ● adjective SLACK, slipshod, negligent, remiss, careless, heedless, unmindful, slapdash, offhand, casual; easy-going, lenient, permissive, liberal, indulgent, overindulgent; *informal* sloppy.

l

sung. **2** literary a song.
– ORIGIN Old French *lai*.
lay[4] past of LIE[1].
layabout ● noun derogatory a person who habitually does little or no work.
lay brother (or **lay sister**) ● noun a person who has taken the vows of a religious order but is not ordained and is employed in ancillary or manual work.
lay-by ● noun (pl. **lay-bys**) **1** Brit. an area at the side of a road where vehicles may pull off the road and stop. **2** Austral./NZ & S. African a system of paying a deposit to secure an article for later purchase.
layer ● noun **1** a sheet or thickness of material, typically one of several, covering a surface. **2** (in combination) a person or thing that lays something: *a cable-layer*. **3** a shoot fastened down to take root while attached to the parent plant. ● verb (often as adj. **layered**) **1** arrange or cut in a layer or layers. **2** propagate (a plant) as a layer.
– ORIGIN originally denoting a mason: from LAY[1].
layette ● noun a set of clothing and bedclothes for a newborn child.
– ORIGIN French, originally in the sense 'little drawer'.
layman (or **layperson**) ● noun **1** a non-ordained member of a Church. **2** a person without professional or specialized knowledge.
lay-off ● noun **1** a temporary or permanent discharge of a worker or workers. **2** a temporary break from an activity.
layout ● noun **1** the way in which something, especially a page, is laid out. **2** a thing set out in a particular way.
layover ● noun chiefly N. Amer. a period of rest or waiting before a further stage in a journey.
lay reader ● noun (in the Anglican Church) a layperson licensed to preach and to conduct some services but not to celebrate the Eucharist.
laywoman ● noun a non-ordained female member of a Church.
laze ● verb spend time relaxing or doing very little. ● noun a spell of lazing.
lazy ● adjective (**lazier**, **laziest**) **1** unwilling to work or use energy. **2** showing or characterized by a lack of effort or care.
– DERIVATIVES **lazily** adverb **laziness** noun.
– ORIGIN perhaps related to Low German *lasich* 'languid, idle'.
lazybones ● noun (pl. same) informal a lazy person.
lazy eye ● noun an eye with poor vision due to underuse, especially the unused eye in a squint.
lb ● abbreviation pound(s) (in weight).
– ORIGIN from Latin *libra*.
lbw ● abbreviation Cricket leg before wicket.
l.c. ● abbreviation **1** in the passage cited. [ORIGIN from Latin *loco citato*.] **2** lower case.
LCD ● abbreviation **1** Electronics & Computing liquid crystal display. **2** Mathematics lowest (or least) common denominator.
LCM ● abbreviation Mathematics lowest (or least) common multiple.
L-driver ● noun Brit. a learner driver.
LEA ● abbreviation (in the UK) Local Education Authority.
lea ● noun literary an open area of grassy or arable land.
– ORIGIN Old English.
leach ● verb remove (a soluble substance) from soil or other material by the action of rainwater or another liquid passing

Thesaurus

l

– OPPOSITES strict.
laxative ● noun PURGATIVE, evacuant; *Medicine* aperient, cathartic.
lay[1] ● verb **1** *Curtis laid the newspaper on the table* PUT (DOWN), place, set (down), deposit, rest, situate, locate, position, stow, shove; *informal* stick, dump, park, plonk; *Brit. informal* bung. **2** *the act laid the foundation for the new system* SET IN PLACE, set out/up, establish. **3** *I'll lay money that Michelle will be there* BET, wager, gamble, stake, risk, venture; give odds, speculate; *informal* punt. **4** *they are going to lay charges* BRING (FORWARD), press, prefer, lodge, register, place, file. **5** *he laid the blame at the Prime Minister's door* ASSIGN, attribute, ascribe, allot, attach; hold someone responsible/accountable, find guilty, pin the blame on. **6** *we laid plans for the next voyage* DEVISE, arrange, make (ready), prepare, work out, hatch, design, plan, scheme, plot, conceive, put together, draw up, produce, develop, formulate; *informal* cook up. **7** *this will lay a new responsibility on the court* IMPOSE, apply, entrust, vest, place, put; inflict, encumber, saddle, charge, burden. **8** *the eagles laid two eggs* PRODUCE; *Zoology* oviposit.
– PHRASES **lay something aside** **1** *farmers laying aside areas for conservation* PUT ASIDE, put to one side, keep, save. **2** *producers must lay aside their conservatism* ABANDON, cast aside, reject, renounce, repudiate, disregard, forget, discard; *poetic/literary* forsake. **3** *protesters led the government to lay the plans aside* DEFER, shelve, suspend, put on ice, mothball, set aside, put off/aside; *informal* put on the back burner. **lay something bare** REVEAL, disclose, divulge, show, expose, exhibit, uncover, unveil, unmask, make a clean breast of, make known, make public. **lay something down** **1** *he laid down his glass* PUT DOWN, set down, place down, deposit, rest; *informal* dump, plonk down; *Brit. informal* bung down. **2** *they were forced to lay down their weapons* RELINQUISH, surrender, give up, yield, cede; disarm, give in, submit, capitulate. **3** *the ground rules have been laid down* FORMULATE, stipulate, set down, draw up, frame; prescribe, ordain, dictate, decree; enact, pass, decide, determine, impose, codify. **4** *laying down wine* STORE, put into store, keep. **lay down the law** ORDER SOMEONE ABOUT/AROUND, tell someone what to do, ride roughshod over someone; *informal* boss someone about/around, throw one's weight about/around, push someone about/around. **lay eyes on** *(informal)* SEE, spot, observe, regard, view, catch sight of; *informal* clap/set eyes on; *poetic/literary* behold, espy, descry. **lay hands on** **1** *wait till I lay my hands on you!* CATCH, lay/get hold of, get one's hands on, seize, grab, grasp, capture. **2** *it's not easy to lay your hands on decent champagne* OBTAIN, acquire, get, come by, find, locate, discover, unearth, uncover, pick up, procure, get one's hands on, get possession of, buy, purchase. **3** *the pastor laid hands on the children* BLESS, consecrate; confirm; ordain. **lay something in** STOCK UP WITH/ON, stockpile, store (up), amass, hoard, stow (away), put aside/away/by, garner, collect, squirrel away; *informal* salt away, stash (away). **lay into** *(informal)* **1** *a policeman laying into a protestor*. See ASSAULT verb sense 1. **2** *he laid into her with a string of insults*. See CRITICIZE. **lay it on thick** *(informal)* EXAGGERATE, overdo it, embellish the truth; flatter, praise, soft-soap; *informal* pile it on, sweet-talk. **lay off** *(informal)* GIVE UP, stop, refrain from, abstain from, desist from, cut out; *informal* pack in, leave off, quit. **lay someone off** MAKE REDUNDANT, dismiss, let go, discharge, give notice to; *informal* sack, fire, give someone their cards, give someone their marching orders, give someone the boot/push, give someone the (old) heave-ho. **lay something on** PROVIDE, supply, furnish, line up, organize, prepare, produce, make available; *informal* fix up. **lay someone out** *(informal)* KNOCK OUT/DOWN, knock unconscious, fell, floor, flatten; *informal* KO, kayo; *Brit. informal* knock for six. **lay something out** **1** *Robyn laid the plans out on the desk* SPREAD OUT, set out, display, exhibit. **2** *a paper laying out our priorities* OUTLINE, sketch out, rough out, detail, draw up, formulate, work out, frame, draft. **3** *(informal) he had to lay out £70*. See PAY verb sense 2. **lay waste** DEVASTATE, wipe out, destroy, demolish, annihilate, raze, ruin, wreck, level, flatten, ravage, pillage, sack, despoil.
lay[2] ● adjective **1** *a lay preacher* NON-CLERICAL, non-ordained, secular, temporal; *formal* laic. **2** *a lay audience* NON-PROFESSIONAL, amateur, non-specialist, non-technical, untrained, unqualified.
layabout ● noun IDLER, good-for-nothing, loafer, lounger, shirker, sluggard, laggard, slugabed, malingerer; *informal* skiver, waster, slacker, lazybones; *Austral./NZ informal* bludger; *poetic/literary* wastrel.
layer ● noun COATING, sheet, coat, film, covering, blanket, skin, thickness.
layman ● noun. See LAYPERSON senses 1, 2.
lay-off ● noun REDUNDANCY, dismissal, discharge; *informal* sacking, firing, the sack, the boot, the axe, the elbow.
– OPPOSITES recruitment.
layout ● noun **1** *the layout of the house* ARRANGEMENT, geography, design, organization; plan, map. **2** *the magazine's layout* DESIGN, arrangement, presentation, style, format; structure, organization, composition, configuration.
layperson ● noun **1** *a prayer book for laypeople* UNORDAINED PERSON, member of the congregation, layman, laywoman. **2** *engineering sounds highly specialized to the layperson* NON-EXPERT, layman, non-professional, amateur, non-specialist.
laze ● verb RELAX, unwind, idle, do nothing, loaf (around/about), lounge (around/about), loll (around/about), lie (around/about), take it easy; *informal* hang around/round, veg (out); *N. Amer. informal* bum (around).
lazy ● adjective (BONE) IDLE, indolent, slothful, work-shy, shiftless, inactive, sluggish, lethargic; remiss, negligent, slack, lax, lackadaisical; *archaic* otiose.
– OPPOSITES industrious.
lazybones ● noun *(informal)* IDLER, loafer, layabout, lounger, good-

through it.

– ORIGIN Old English, 'to water'.

lead[1] /leed/ ● verb (past and past part. **led** /led/) **1** cause (a person or animal) to go with one, especially by drawing them along or by preceding them to a destination. **2** be a route or means of access: *the street led into the square.* **3** (**lead to**) result in. **4** influence to do or believe something: *that may lead them to reconsider.* **5** be in charge of. **6** have the advantage in a race or game. **7** be superior to (a competitor). **8** have or experience (a particular way of life). **9** (often **lead (off) with**) begin with a particular action or item. **10** (**lead up to**) precede or result in. **11** (**lead on**) deceive (someone) into believing that one is attracted to them. **12** (in card games) play (the first card) in a trick or round of play. ● noun **1** the initiative in an action: *others followed our lead.* **2** (**the lead**) a position of advantage in a contest; first place. **3** an amount by which a competitor is ahead of the others: *a one-goal lead.* **4** the chief part in a play or film. **5** (before another noun) playing the chief part in a musical group: *the lead singer.* **6** (before another noun) denoting the principal item in a report or text: *the lead article.* **7** a clue to be followed in the resolution of a problem. **8** Brit. a strap or cord for restraining and guiding a dog. **9** a wire conveying electric current from a source to an appliance, or connecting two points of a circuit together. **10** (in card games) an act or the right of playing first in a trick or round of play.

– PHRASES **lead astray** cause to act or think foolishly or wrongly. **lead up the garden path** informal give misleading clues or signals to. **lead with one's chin** informal **1** (of a boxer) leave one's chin unprotected. **2** behave or speak incautiously.

– ORIGIN Old English, related to LOAD and LODE.

lead[2] /led/ ● noun **1** a heavy bluish-grey soft ductile metallic element. **2** graphite used as the part of a pencil that makes a mark. **3** Printing a blank space between lines of print (originally created by a metal strip). **4** Nautical a lump of lead suspended on a line to determine the depth of water. **5** (**leads**) Brit. sheets or strips of lead covering a roof. **6** (**leads**) lead frames holding the glass of a lattice or stained-glass window.

– PHRASES **go down like a lead balloon** (of a speech, proposal, or joke) be poorly received.

– ORIGIN Old English.

lead crystal (also **lead glass**) ● noun glass containing a substantial proportion of lead oxide, making it more refractive.

leaded ● adjective **1** framed, covered, or weighted with lead. **2** (of petrol) containing tetraethyl lead.

leaden ● adjective **1** dull, heavy, or slow. **2** of the dull grey colour of lead. **3** archaic made of lead.

– DERIVATIVES **leadenly** adverb.

leader ● noun **1** a person or thing that leads. **2** a person or thing that is the most successful or advanced in a particular area. **3** the principal player in a music group. **4** Brit. a leading article in a newspaper. **5** (also **Leader of the House**) Brit. a member of the government officially responsible for initiating business in Parliament. **6** a short strip of non-functioning material at each end of a reel of film or recording tape for connection to the spool.

– DERIVATIVES **leaderless** adjective **leadership** noun.

leader board ● noun a scoreboard showing the names and current scores of the leading competitors, especially in a golf match.

lead-in ● noun an introduction or preamble.

leading /leeding/ ● adjective most important or in first place.

leading aircraftman (or **leading aircraftwoman**) ● noun a rank in the RAF immediately above aircraftman (or aircraftwoman).

leading article ● noun Brit. a newspaper article giving the editorial opinion.

leading edge ● noun **1** the foremost edge of an aerofoil, especially a wing or propeller blade. **2** the forefront or vanguard, especially of technological development.

leading light ● noun a person who is prominent or influential in a particular field or organization.

leading man (or **leading lady**) ● noun the actor playing the

l

Thesaurus

for-nothing, do-nothing, shirker, sluggard, laggard, slugabed; *informal* skiver, waster, slacker; *Austral./NZ informal* bludger; *poetic/literary* wastrel.

leach ● verb DRAIN, filter, percolate, filtrate, strain.

lead ● verb **1** *Michelle led them into the house* GUIDE, conduct, show (the way), lead the way, usher, escort, steer, pilot, shepherd; accompany, see, take. **2** *he led us to believe they were lying* CAUSE, induce, prompt, move, persuade, influence, drive, condition, make; incline, dispose, predispose. **3** *this might lead to job losses* RESULT IN, cause, bring on/about, give rise to, be the cause of, make happen, create, produce, occasion, effect, generate, contribute to, promote; provoke, stir up, spark off, arouse, foment, instigate; involve, necessitate, entail; *formal* effectuate. **4** *he led a march to the city centre* BE AT THE HEAD/FRONT OF, head, spearhead. **5** *she led a coalition of radicals* BE THE LEADER OF, be the head of, preside over, head, command, govern, rule, be in charge of, be in command of, be in control of, run, control, be at the helm of; administer, organize, manage; reign over, be in power over; *informal* head up. **6** *Rangers were leading at half-time* BE AHEAD, be winning, be (out) in front, be in the lead, be first. **7** *the champion was leading the field* BE AT THE FRONT OF, be first in, be ahead of, head; outrun, outstrip, outpace, leave behind, draw away from; outdo, outclass, beat; *informal* leave standing. **8** *I just want to lead a normal life* EXPERIENCE, have, live, spend.

– OPPOSITES follow.

● noun **1** *I was in the lead early on* LEADING POSITION, first place, van, vanguard; ahead, in front, winning. **2** *they took the lead in the personal computer market* FIRST POSITION, forefront, primacy, dominance, superiority, ascendancy; pre-eminence, supremacy, advantage, upper hand, whip hand. **3** *sixth-formers should give a lead to younger pupils* EXAMPLE, (role) model, exemplar, paradigm. **4** *playing the lead* LEADING ROLE, star/starring role, title role, principal part; principal character, male lead, female lead, leading man, leading lady. **5** *a labrador on a lead* LEASH, tether, cord, rope, chain. **6** *detectives were following up a new lead* CLUE, pointer, hint, tip, tip-off, suggestion, indication, sign; (**leads**) evidence, information.

● adjective *the lead position* LEADING, first, top, foremost, front, head; chief, principal, premier.

– OPPOSITES last.

– PHRASES **lead something off** BEGIN, start (off), commence, open; *informal* kick off. **lead someone on** DECEIVE, mislead, delude, hoodwink, dupe, trick, fool, pull the wool over someone's eyes; tease, flirt with; *informal* string along, lead up the garden path, take for a ride. **lead the way 1** *he led the way to the kitchen* GUIDE, conduct, show the way. **2** *Britain is leading the way in aerospace technology* TAKE THE INITIATIVE, break (new) ground, blaze a trail, prepare the way. **lead up to** PREPARE THE WAY FOR, pave the way for, lay the groundwork for, set the scene for, work round/up to, approach the subject of.

leaden ● adjective **1** *his eyes were leaden with sleep* DULL, heavy, weighty; listless, lifeless. **2** *he moved on leaden feet* SLUGGISH, heavy, lumbering, slow. **3** *leaden prose* BORING, dull, unimaginative, uninspired, monotonous, heavy, laboured, wooden. **4** *a leaden sky* GREY, greyish, black, dark; cloudy, gloomy, overcast, dull, murky, sunless, louring, oppressive, threatening; *poetic/literary* tenebrous.

– OPPOSITES light, lively.

leader ● noun **1** *the leader of the Democratic Party* CHIEF, head, principal; commander, captain; controller, superior, headman; chairman, chairwoman, chairperson, chair; (managing) director, MD, manager, superintendent, supervisor, overseer, administrator, employer, master, mistress; president, premier, governor; ruler, monarch, king, queen, sovereign, emperor; *informal* boss, skipper, gaffer, guv'nor, number one, numero uno, honcho; *N. Amer. informal* sachem, padrone. **2** *a world leader in the use of video conferencing* PIONEER, front runner, innovator, trailblazer, groundbreaker, trendsetter, torch-bearer; originator, initiator, founder, architect.

– OPPOSITES follower, supporter.

leadership ● noun **1** *the leadership of the Conservative Party* HEADSHIP, directorship, premiership, governorship, governance, administration, captaincy, control, ascendancy, rule, command, power, dominion. **2** *firm leadership* GUIDANCE, direction, control, management, superintendence, supervision; organization, government.

leading ● adjective **1** *he played the leading role in his team's victory* MAIN, chief, major, prime, most significant, principal, foremost, key, central, focal, paramount, dominant, essential. **2** *the leading industrialized countries* MOST POWERFUL, most important, greatest, chief, pre-eminent, principal, dominant. **3** *last season's leading scorer* TOP, highest, best, first; front, lead; unparalleled, matchless,

principal part in a play, film, or television show.
leading question ● noun a question that prompts or encourages the answer wanted.
leading seaman ● noun a rank in the Royal Navy immediately above able seaman.
lead time ● noun the time between the initiation and completion of a production process.
lead-up ● noun an event or sequence that leads up to something else.
leaf ● noun (pl. **leaves**) **1** a flattened, typically green, structure of a plant, that is attached to a stem and is the chief site of photosynthesis and transpiration. **2** the state of having leaves: *the trees were in leaf.* **3** a single thickness of paper, especially in a book. **4** gold, silver, or other metal in the form of very thin foil. **5** a hinged or detachable part, especially of a table. ● verb **1** (of a plant) put out new leaves. **2** (**leaf through**) turn over (pages or papers), reading them quickly or casually.
– PHRASES **turn over a new leaf** start to act or behave in a better way.
– DERIVATIVES **leafage** noun **leafed** (also **leaved**) adjective **leafless** adjective.
– ORIGIN Old English.
leaflet ● noun **1** a printed sheet of paper containing information or advertising and usually distributed free. **2** a small leaf, especially a component of a compound leaf. ● verb (**leafleted**, **leafleting**) distribute leaflets to.
leaf mould ● noun soil consisting chiefly of decayed leaves.
leaf spring ● noun a spring made of a number of strips of metal curved slightly upwards and clamped together one above the other.
leafy ● adjective (**leafier**, **leafiest**) **1** having many leaves. **2** full of trees and shrubs: *a leafy avenue.*
– DERIVATIVES **leafiness** noun.
league[1] ● noun **1** a collection of people, countries, or groups that combine for mutual protection or cooperation. **2** a group of sports clubs which play each other over a period for a championship. **3** a class of quality or excellence: *the two men were not in the same league.* ● verb (**leagues**, **leagued**, **leaguing**) join in a league or alliance.
– PHRASES **in league** conspiring with another or others.
– ORIGIN Italian *lega*, from Latin *ligare* 'to bind'.
league[2] ● noun a former measure of distance by land, usually about three miles.
– ORIGIN Latin *leuga, leuca*.
leaguer ● noun chiefly N. Amer. a member of a particular league, especially a sports player.
league table ● noun Brit. **1** a list of the competitors in a league ranked according to performance. **2** a list in order of merit or achievement.
leak ● verb **1** accidentally allow contents to escape or enter through a hole or crack. **2** (of liquid, gas, etc.) escape or enter accidentally through a hole or crack. **3** intentionally disclose (secret information). **4** (of secret information) become known. ● noun **1** a hole or crack through which contents leak. **2** an instance of leaking.
– PHRASES **have** (or **take**) **a leak** informal urinate.
– DERIVATIVES **leakage** noun **leaker** noun **leaky** adjective.
– ORIGIN probably from Low German or Dutch and related to LACK.
lean[1] ● verb (past and past part. **leaned** or chiefly Brit. **leant**) **1** be in or move into a sloping position. **2** (**lean against/on**) incline from the perpendicular and rest against. **3** (**lean on**) rely on for support. **4** (**lean to/towards**) incline or be partial to (a view or position). **5** (**lean on**) informal intimidate into doing something. ● noun a deviation from the perpendicular; an inclination.
– ORIGIN Old English.
lean[2] ● adjective **1** (of a person) having no superfluous fat; thin. **2** (of meat) containing little fat. **3** offering little reward, substance, or nourishment: *the lean years.* **4** informal (of an industry or company) efficient and with no wastage. **5** (of a vaporized fuel mixture) having a high proportion of air. ● noun the lean part of meat.
– DERIVATIVES **leanly** adverb **leanness** noun.
– ORIGIN Old English.
lean-burn ● adjective (of an internal-combustion engine) designed to run on a lean mixture to reduce pollution.
leaning ● noun a tendency or preference: *communist leanings.*
lean-to ● noun (pl. **lean-tos**) a building sharing a wall with a larger building and having a roof that leans against that wall.
leap ● verb (past or past part. **leaped** or **leapt**) **1** jump or spring a long way. **2** jump across. **3** move quickly and suddenly. **4** (**leap at**) accept eagerly. **5** increase dramatically. ● noun **1** an instance of leaping. **2** a sudden abrupt change or increase.
– PHRASES **a leap in the dark** a daring step or enterprise with unpredictable consequences. **by** (or **in**) **leaps and bounds** with startlingly rapid progress. **leap to the eye** (or **leap out**) be immediately apparent.
– DERIVATIVES **leaper** noun.
– ORIGIN Old English, related to LOPE.
leapfrog ● noun a game in which players in turn vault with

Thesaurus

star.
– OPPOSITES subordinate, minor.
leaf ● noun **1** *sycamore leaves* FROND, leaflet, flag; *Botany* cotyledon, blade, bract. **2** *a sheaf of loose leaves* PAGE, sheet, folio.
– RELATED TERMS foliaceous.
● verb *he leafed through the documents* FLICK, flip, thumb, skim, browse, glance, riffle; scan, run one's eye over, peruse.
– PHRASES **turn over a new leaf** REFORM, improve, mend one's ways, make a fresh start, change for the better; *informal* go straight.
leaflet ● noun PAMPHLET, booklet, brochure, handbill, circular, flyer, handout, bulletin; *N. Amer.* folder, dodger.
league ● noun **1** *a league of nations* ALLIANCE, confederation, confederacy, federation, union, association, coalition, consortium, affiliation, guild, cooperative, partnership, fellowship, syndicate, consociation. **2** *we won the league last year* CHAMPIONSHIP, competition, contest. **3** *the store is not in the same league* CLASS, group, category, level.
● verb *they leagued together with other companies* ALLY, join forces, join together, unite, band together, affiliate, combine, amalgamate, confederate, team up, join up.
– PHRASES **in league with** COLLABORATING WITH, cooperating with, in alliance with, allied with, conspiring with, hand in glove with; *informal* in cahoots with.
leak ● verb **1** *oil leaking from the tanker* SEEP (OUT), escape, ooze (out), emanate, issue, drip, dribble, drain, bleed. **2** *the tanks are leaking gasoline* DISCHARGE, exude, emit, release, drip, dribble, ooze, secrete. **3** *civil servants leaking information* DISCLOSE, divulge, reveal, make public, tell, impart, pass on, relate, communicate, expose, broadcast, publish, release, let slip, bring into the open; *informal* blab, let the cat out of the bag, spill the beans, blow the gaff.
● noun **1** *check that there are no leaks in the bag* HOLE, opening, puncture, perforation, gash, slit, nick, rent, break, crack, fissure, rupture. **2** *a gas leak* DISCHARGE, leakage, leaking, oozing, seeping, seepage, drip, escape. **3** *leaks to the media* DISCLOSURE, revelation, exposé.
leaky ● adjective LEAKING, dripping; cracked, split, punctured, perforated.
– OPPOSITES watertight.
lean[1] ● verb **1** *Polly leaned against the door* REST, recline, be supported. **2** *trees leaning in the wind* SLANT, incline, bend, tilt, be at an angle, slope, tip, list. **3** *he leans towards existentialist philosophy* TEND, incline, gravitate; have a preference for, have a penchant for, be partial to, have a liking for, have an affinity with. **4** *a strong shoulder to lean on* DEPEND, be dependent, rely, count, bank, have faith in, trust. **5** (*informal*) *I got leaned on by villains* INTIMIDATE, coerce, browbeat, bully, pressurize, threaten, put pressure on; *informal* twist someone's arm, put the frighteners on, put the screws on.
lean[2] ● adjective **1** *a tall, lean man* SLIM, thin, slender, spare, wiry, lanky. **2** *a lean harvest* MEAGRE, sparse, poor, mean, inadequate, insufficient, paltry, deficient, insubstantial. **3** *lean times* UNPRODUCTIVE, unfruitful, arid, barren; hard, bad, difficult, tough, impoverished, poverty-stricken.
– OPPOSITES fat, abundant, prosperous.
leaning ● noun INCLINATION, tendency, bent, proclivity, propensity, penchant, predisposition, predilection, partiality, preference, bias, attraction, liking, fondness, taste.
leap ● verb **1** *he leapt over the gate* JUMP (OVER), vault (over), spring over, bound over, hop (over), hurdle, clear. **2** *Claudia leapt to her feet* SPRING, jump (up), bound, dart. **3** *we leapt to the rescue* RUSH, hurry, hasten. **4** *she leapt at the chance* ACCEPT EAGERLY, grasp (with both hands), grab, take advantage of, seize (on), jump at.

parted legs over others who are bending down. ● verb (**leapfrogged, leapfrogging**) **1** perform such a vault. **2** progress by overtaking others to move into a leading position.

leap year ● noun a year, occurring once every four years, which has 366 days including 29 February as an intercalary day.

– ORIGIN probably from the fact that feast days after February in a leap year fell two days later than in the previous year, rather than one day later as in other years, and could be said to have 'leaped' a day.

learn ● verb (past and past part. **learned** or chiefly Brit. **learnt**) **1** acquire knowledge of or skill in (something) through study or experience or by being taught. **2** become aware of by information or from observation. **3** memorize. **4** archaic or informal teach.

– DERIVATIVES **learnable** adjective **learner** noun.

– ORIGIN Old English, related to LORE[1].

learned /lernid/ ● adjective having or characterized by much knowledge acquired by study.

– DERIVATIVES **learnedly** adverb **learnedness** noun.

learning ● noun knowledge or skills acquired through study or by being taught.

learning curve ● noun the rate of a person's progress in gaining experience or new skills.

learning difficulties ● plural noun difficulties in acquiring knowledge and skills to the normal level expected of those of the same age, especially because of mental handicap or cognitive disorder.

learning disability ● noun a condition giving rise to learning difficulties, especially when not associated with physical handicap.

lease ● noun a contract by which one party conveys land, property, services, etc. to another for a specified time, in return for payment. ● verb let or rent on lease.

– PHRASES **a new lease of life** a substantially improved prospect of life or use after recovery or repair.

– DERIVATIVES **leasable** adjective.

– ORIGIN from Old French *lesser*, *laissier* 'let, leave', from Latin *laxus* 'loose, lax'.

leaseback ● noun the leasing of a property back to the vendor.

leasehold ● noun **1** the holding of property by lease. **2** a piece of land or property held by lease.

– DERIVATIVES **leaseholder** noun.

leash ● noun a dog's lead. ● verb put a leash on (a dog).

– ORIGIN from Old French *laissier* in the specific sense 'let run on a slack lead' (see LEASE).

least ● determiner & pronoun (usu. **the least**) smallest in amount, extent, or significance. ● adjective used in names of very small animals and plants: *least shrew*. ● adverb to the smallest extent or degree.

– PHRASES **at least 1** not less than. **2** if nothing else. **3** anyway. **at the least** (or **very least**) **1** not less than. **2** taking the most pessimistic or unfavourable view. **least said, soonest mended** proverb a difficult situation will be resolved more quickly if there is no more discussion of it. **not in the least** not at all. **not least** in particular. **to say the least** to put it mildly.

– ORIGIN Old English, related to LESS.

least significant bit ● noun Computing the bit in a binary number which is of the lowest numerical value.

leastways (also **leastwise**) ● adverb dialect or informal at least.

leat /leet/ ● noun Brit. an open watercourse conducting water to a mill.

– ORIGIN Old English.

leather ● noun **1** a material made from the skin of an animal by tanning or a similar process. **2** a piece of leather as a polishing cloth. **3** (**leathers**) leather clothes worn by a motorcyclist. ● verb **1** (**leathered**) cover with leather. **2** informal beat or thrash.

– ORIGIN Old English.

leatherback turtle ● noun a very large black turtle with a thick leathery shell, living chiefly in tropical seas.

leatherette ● noun imitation leather.

leatherjacket ● noun Brit. the tough-skinned larva of a large crane fly.

leathern ● adjective archaic made of leather.

leathery ● adjective having a tough, hard texture like leather.

– DERIVATIVES **leatheriness** noun.

leave[1] ● verb (past and past part. **left**) **1** go away from. **2** cease living at, attending, or working for: *he left home at 16*. **3** allow or cause to remain; go away without taking. **4** (**be left**) remain to be used or dealt with: *drink left over from the wedding*. **5** cause to be in a particular state or position: *leave the door open*. **6** let (someone) do something without assistance or interference. **7** (**leave to**) entrust (a decision, choice, or action) to. **8** deposit (something) to be collected or attended to. **9** have as (a surviving relative) after one's death. **10** bequeath.

– PHRASES **leave be** informal refrain from disturbing or interfering with (someone). **leave go** informal remove one's hold or grip. **leave hold of** cease holding. **leave much** (or **a lot**) **to be desired** be highly unsatisfactory. **leave off 1** discontinue or stop. **2** cease to wear. **leave out** fail to include.

– DERIVATIVES **leaver** noun.

– ORIGIN Old English.

leave[2] ● noun **1** (also **leave of absence**) time when one has permission to be absent from work or duty. **2** formal permission: *seeking leave to appeal*.

– PHRASES **take one's leave** formal say goodbye. **take leave to do** formal venture or presume to do.

– ORIGIN Old English, related to LIEF and LOVE.

leaven /levv'n/ ● noun **1** a substance, typically yeast, added to

Thesaurus

5 *don't leap to conclusions* FORM HASTILY, reach hurriedly; hurry, hasten, jump, rush. **6** *profits leapt by 55%* INCREASE RAPIDLY, soar, rocket, skyrocket, shoot up, escalate.

● noun **1** *an easy leap* JUMP, vault, spring, bound, hop, skip. **2** *a leap of 33%* SUDDEN RISE, surge, upsurge, upswing, upturn.

– PHRASES **in/by leaps and bounds** RAPIDLY, swiftly, quickly, speedily.

learn ● verb **1** *learning a foreign language* ACQUIRE A KNOWLEDGE OF, acquire skill in, become competent in, become proficient in, grasp, master, take in, absorb, assimilate, digest, familiarize oneself with; study, read up on, be taught, have lessons in; informal get the hang of, get clued up about. **2** *she learnt the poem by heart* MEMORIZE, learn by heart, commit to memory, learn parrot-fashion, get off/down pat; archaic con. **3** *he learned that the school would shortly be closing* DISCOVER, find out, become aware, be informed, hear (tell); gather, understand, ascertain, establish; informal get wind of the fact; Brit. informal suss out.

learned ● adjective SCHOLARLY, erudite, well educated, knowledgeable, widely read, well informed, lettered, cultured, intellectual, academic, literary, bookish, highbrow, studious; informal brainy; formal sapient.

– OPPOSITES ignorant.

learner ● noun BEGINNER, trainee, apprentice, pupil, student, novice, newcomer, starter, probationer, tyro, fledgling, neophyte; N. Amer. tenderfoot; N. Amer. informal greenhorn.

– OPPOSITES veteran.

learning ● noun **1** *a centre of learning* STUDY, studying, education, schooling, tuition, teaching, academic work; research, investigation. **2** *the astonishing range of his learning* SCHOLARSHIP, knowledge, education, erudition, intellect, enlightenment, illumination, edification, book learning, information, understanding, wisdom.

– OPPOSITES ignorance.

lease ● noun *a 15-year lease* LEASEHOLD, rental/hire agreement, charter; rental, tenancy, tenure, period of occupancy.

– RELATED TERMS lessor, lessee.

– OPPOSITES freehold.

● verb **1** *the film crew leased a large hangar* RENT, hire, charter. **2** *they leased the mill to a reputable family* RENT (OUT), let (out), hire (out), sublet, sublease.

leash ● noun **1** *keep your dog on a leash* LEAD, tether, rope, chain, strap, restraint. **2** *he found himself off the parental leash* CONTROL, restraint, check, curb, rein, discipline.

● verb **1** *she leashed the dog* PUT THE LEASH ON, put the lead on, tether, tie up, secure, restrain. **2** *the ire in her face was barely leashed* CURB, control, keep under control, check, restrain, hold back, suppress.

– PHRASES **straining at the leash** EAGER, impatient, anxious, enthusiastic; informal itching, dying.

least ● determiner *I have not the least idea what this means* SLIGHTEST, smallest, minutest, tiniest, littlest.

– PHRASES **at least** AT THE MINIMUM, no/not less than, more than.

leather ● noun *a leather jacket* SKIN, hide.

● verb (informal) *he caught me and leathered me* BEAT, strap, belt, thrash, flog, whip, horsewhip, birch, cane, hit; informal wallop, whack, tan someone's hide, give someone a (good) hiding.

dough to make it ferment and rise. **2** an influence or quality that modifies or improves something: *John's humour was the leaven of his charm.* ● verb **1** (usu. as adj. **leavened**) cause (dough or bread) to ferment and rise by adding leaven. **2** modify or improve.
– ORIGIN Latin *levamen* 'relief', from *levare* 'to lift'.
leaves plural of LEAF.
leave-taking ● noun an act of saying goodbye.
leavings ● plural noun things that have been left as worthless.
Lebanese /lebbəneez/ ● noun (pl. same) a person from Lebanon. ● adjective relating to Lebanon.
Lebensraum /laybənzrowm/ ● noun territory which a state or nation believes is needed for its natural development.
– ORIGIN German, 'living space'.
lech /lech/ informal, derogatory ● noun **1** a lecher. **2** a lecherous urge or desire. ● verb act in a lecherous manner.
lecher ● noun a lecherous man.
– DERIVATIVES **lechery** noun.
lecherous ● adjective having or showing excessive or offensive sexual desire.
– DERIVATIVES **lecherously** adverb **lecherousness** noun.
– ORIGIN Old French *lecheros*, from *lechier* 'live in debauchery or gluttony'; related to LICK.
lecithin /lessithin/ ● noun a substance found in egg yolk and other animal and plant tissues, often used as an emulsifier in food processing.
– ORIGIN from Greek *lekithos* 'egg yolk'.
lectern /lektərn/ ● noun a tall stand with a sloping top from which a speaker can read while standing up.
– ORIGIN Latin *lectrum*, from *legere* 'to read'.
lecture ● noun **1** an educational talk to an audience, especially one of students in a university. **2** a lengthy reprimand or warning. ● verb **1** deliver an educational lecture or lectures. **2** talk seriously or reprovingly to.
– ORIGIN Latin *lectura*, from *legere* 'read, choose'.
lecturer ● noun a person who gives lectures, especially as a teacher in higher education.
lectureship ● noun a post as a lecturer.
LED ● abbreviation light-emitting diode, a semiconductor diode which glows when a voltage is applied.
led past and past participle of LEAD[1].
lederhosen /laydərhōz'n/ ● plural noun leather shorts with braces, traditionally worn by men in Alpine regions.
– ORIGIN German, from *Leder* 'leather' + *Hosen* 'trousers'.
ledge ● noun **1** a narrow horizontal surface projecting from a wall, cliff, etc. **2** an underwater ridge, especially one of rocks near the seashore.
– ORIGIN originally denoting a strip of wood or other material fixed across a door or gate: perhaps from an early form of LAY[1].
ledger ● noun a book or other collection of financial accounts.
– ORIGIN originally denoting a large bible or breviary: probably from variants of LAY[1] and LIE[1], influenced by Dutch *legger* and *ligger*.
ledger line (also **leger line**) ● noun Music a short line added for notes above or below the range of a stave.
lee ● noun **1** shelter from wind or weather given by an object. **2** (also **lee side**) the sheltered side; the side away from the wind. Contrasted with WEATHER.
– ORIGIN Old English, 'shelter'.
leech[1] ● noun **1** a parasitic or predatory worm with suckers at both ends, formerly used in medicine for bloodletting. **2** a person who extorts profit from or lives off others. ● verb (**leech on/off**) habitually exploit or rely on.
– ORIGIN Old English.
leech[2] ● noun archaic a doctor or healer.
– ORIGIN Old English.
leek ● noun a plant related to the onion, with flat overlapping leaves forming an elongated cylindrical bulb which together with the leaf bases is eaten as a vegetable.
– ORIGIN Old English.
leer ● verb look or gaze in a lustful or unpleasant way. ● noun a lustful or unpleasant look.
– ORIGIN originally meaning 'look sideways or askance': perhaps from an Old English word meaning 'cheek'.

L

Thesaurus

leathery ● adjective **1** *leathery skin* ROUGH, rugged, wrinkled, wrinkly, furrowed, lined, wizened, weather-beaten, callous, gnarled. **2** *leathery sides of beef* TOUGH, hard, gristly, chewy, stringy.
leave[1] ● verb **1** *I left the hotel* DEPART FROM, go (away) from, withdraw from, retire from, take oneself off from, exit from, take one's leave of, pull out of, quit, be gone from, decamp from, disappear from, vacate, absent oneself from; say one's farewells/goodbyes, make oneself scarce; *informal* push off, shove off, clear out/off, cut and run, split, vamoose, scoot, make tracks, up sticks; *Brit. informal* sling one's hook. **2** *the next morning we left for Leicester* SET OFF, head, make; set sail. **3** *he's left his wife* ABANDON, desert, cast aside/off, jilt, leave in the lurch, leave high and dry, throw over; *informal* dump, ditch, chuck, drop, walk/run out on; *poetic/literary* forsake. **4** *he left his job in November* RESIGN FROM, retire from, step down from, withdraw from, pull out of, give up; *informal* quit. **5** *she left her handbag on a bus* LEAVE BEHIND, forget, lose, mislay. **6** *I thought I'd leave it to the experts* ENTRUST, hand over, pass on, refer; delegate. **7** *he left her £100,000* BEQUEATH, will, endow, hand down, make over; *Law* demise, devise. **8** *the speech left some feelings of disappointment* CAUSE, produce, generate, give rise to.
– OPPOSITES arrive.
– PHRASES **leave someone in the lurch** LEAVE IN TROUBLE, let down, leave stranded, leave high and dry, abandon, desert. **leave off** (*informal*) STOP, cease, finish, desist from, keep from, break off, lay off, give up, discontinue, refrain from, eschew; *informal* quit, knock off, jack in, swear off; *formal* forswear. **leave someone/something out 1** *Adam left out the address* MISS OUT, omit, fail to include, overlook, forget; skip, miss, jump. **2** *he was left out of the England squad* EXCLUDE, omit, drop, pass over.
leave[2] ● noun **1** *the judge granted leave to appeal* PERMISSION, consent, authorization, sanction, warrant, dispensation, approval, clearance, blessing, agreement, backing, assent, acceptance, licence, acquiescence; *informal* the go-ahead, the green light, the OK, the rubber stamp. **2** *he was on leave* HOLIDAY, vacation, break, time off, furlough, sabbatical, leave of absence; *informal* hols, vac. **3** *I will now take my leave of you* DEPARTURE, leaving, leave-taking, parting, withdrawal, exit, farewell, goodbye.
leaven ● noun *leaven is added to the dough* LEAVENING, fermentation agent, raising agent. ● verb **1** *yeast leavens the bread* RAISE, make rise, puff up, expand. **2** *formal proceedings leavened by humour* PERMEATE, infuse, pervade, imbue, suffuse; enliven, liven up, invigorate, energize, electrify, ginger up, perk up, brighten up, season, spice; *informal* buck up, pep up.
leavings ● plural noun RESIDUE, remainder, remains, remnants, leftovers, scrapings, scraps, oddments, odds and ends, rejects, dregs, refuse, rubbish.
lecher ● noun LECHEROUS MAN, libertine, womanizer, debauchee, rake, roué, profligate, wanton, loose-liver, Don Juan, Casanova, Lothario, Romeo; *informal* lech, dirty old man, goat, wolf; *formal* fornicator.
lecherous ● adjective LUSTFUL, licentious, lascivious, libidinous, prurient, lewd, salacious, lubricious, debauched, dissolute, wanton, dissipated, degenerate, depraved, dirty, filthy; *informal* randy, horny, goatish; *formal* concupiscent.
– OPPOSITES chaste.
lecture ● noun **1** *a lecture on children's literature* SPEECH, talk, address, discourse, disquisition, presentation, oration, lesson. **2** *Dave got a severe lecture* SCOLDING, chiding, reprimand, rebuke, reproof, reproach, upbraiding, admonishment; *informal* dressing-down, telling-off, talking-to, tongue-lashing; *formal* castigation. ● verb **1** *lecturing on the dangers of drugs* GIVE A LECTURE/TALK, talk, make a speech, speak, give an address, discourse, hold forth, declaim, expatiate; *informal* spout, sound off. **2** *she lectures at Dublin University* TEACH, tutor, give instruction, give lessons. **3** *he was lectured by the headmaster* SCOLD, chide, reprimand, rebuke, reprove, reproach, upbraid, berate, chastise, admonish, lambaste, haul over the coals, take to task; *informal* give someone a dressing-down, give someone a talking-to, tell off; *Brit. informal* tick off, carpet; *N. Amer. informal* bawl out; *formal* castigate.
lecturer ● noun **1** *the lecturer is a journalist* (PUBLIC) SPEAKER, speech-maker, orator. **2** *a lecturer in economics* UNIVERSITY/COLLEGE TEACHER, tutor, reader, scholar, don, professor, fellow; academic, academician, preceptor; *formal* pedagogue.
ledge ● noun SHELF, sill, mantel, mantelpiece, shelving; projection, protrusion, overhang, ridge, prominence.
ledger ● noun (ACCOUNT) BOOK, record book, register, log; records, books; balance sheet, financial statement.
lee ● noun SHELTER, protection, cover, refuge, safety, security.

leery • adjective (**leerier**, **leeriest**) cautious or wary.
– DERIVATIVES **leeriness** noun.
– ORIGIN from obsolete *leer* 'looking askance', from LEER.

lees • plural noun the sediment of wine in the barrel; dregs.
– ORIGIN Latin *liae.*

lee shore • noun a shore lying on the leeward side of a ship (and on to which the ship could be blown).

leeward /leeward, lōōərd/ • adjective & adverb on or towards the side sheltered from the wind or towards which the wind is blowing. Contrasted with WINDWARD. • noun the leeward side.

leeway • noun **1** the amount of freedom to move or act that is available: *we have a lot of leeway in how we do our jobs.* **2** the sideways drift of a ship to leeward of the desired course.
– PHRASES **make up (the) leeway** Brit. struggle out of a bad position by recovering lost time.

left[1] • adjective **1** on, towards, or relating to the side of a human body or of a thing which is to the west when the person or thing is facing north. **2** relating to a left-wing person or group. • adverb on or to the left side. • noun **1** (**the left**) the left-hand part, side, or direction. **2** a left turn. **3** a person's left fist, or a blow given with it. **4** (often **the Left**) (treated as sing. or pl.) a group or party favouring radical, reforming, or socialist views.
– PHRASES **have two left feet** be clumsy or awkward. **left, right, and centre** on all sides.
– DERIVATIVES **leftish** adjective **leftmost** adjective **leftward** adjective & adverb **leftwards** adverb.
– ORIGIN Old English, 'weak'.

left[2] past and past participle of LEAVE[1].

left back • noun a defender in soccer or field hockey who plays primarily on the left of the field.

left bank • noun the bank of a river on the left as one faces downstream.

left-field • adjective unconventional or experimental.

left hand • noun **1** the hand of a person's left side. **2** the region or direction on the left side. • adjective **1** on or towards the left side. **2** done with or using the left hand.

left-hand drive • noun a motor-vehicle steering system with the steering wheel and other controls fitted on the left side, for use in countries where vehicles drive on the right.

left-handed • adjective **1** using or done with the left hand. **2** turning to the left; towards the left. **3** (of a screw) advanced by turning anticlockwise. **4** ambiguous.

left-hander • noun **1** a left-handed person. **2** a blow struck with a person's left hand.

leftie • noun variant spelling of LEFTY.

leftism • noun the political views or policies of the left.
– DERIVATIVES **leftist** noun & adjective.

left luggage • noun Brit. travellers' luggage left in temporary storage at a railway station, bus station, or airport.

leftover • noun something, especially food, remaining after the rest has been used. • adjective remaining; surplus.

left wing • noun **1** the radical, reforming, or socialist section of a political party or system. [ORIGIN with reference to the National Assembly in France (1789–91), where the nobles sat to the president's right and the commons to the left.] **2** the left side of a sports team on the field or of an army.
– DERIVATIVES **left-winger** noun.

lefty (also **leftie**) • noun (pl. **lefties**) informal **1** a left-wing person. **2** a left-handed person.

leg • noun **1** each of the limbs on which a person or animal moves and stands. **2** a long, thin support or prop, especially of a chair or table. **3** a section of a journey, process, or race. **4** (in sport) each of two or more games or stages constituting a round or match. **5** (**legs**) informal sustained momentum or success: *some books have legs, others don't.* **6** (also **leg side**) Cricket the half of the field away from which the batsman's feet are pointed when standing to receive the ball. The opposite of OFF.
– PHRASES **get one's leg over** vulgar slang (of a man) have sexual intercourse. **have the legs of** Brit. be able to go faster or further than (a rival). **leg before wicket** Cricket (of a batsman) adjudged to be out through obstructing the ball with the leg (or other part of the body) when the ball would otherwise have hit the wicket. **leg it** informal **1** travel by foot; walk. **2** run away. **not have a leg to stand on** have no sound justification for one's arguments or actions. **on one's last legs** near the end of life, usefulness, or existence.
– DERIVATIVES **legged** adjective **legger** noun.
– ORIGIN Old Norse.

legacy • noun (pl. **legacies**) **1** an amount of money or property left to someone in a will. **2** something handed down by a predecessor. • adjective (of computer hardware or software) that has been superseded but is difficult to replace because of its wide use.
– ORIGIN originally also denoting the function or office of a legate: from Old French *legacie*, from Latin *legatus* 'person delegated'.

legal • adjective **1** of, based on, or required by the law. **2** permitted by law.
– DERIVATIVES **legally** adverb.
– ORIGIN Latin *legalis*, from *lex* 'law'.

legal aid • noun payment from public funds allowed, in cases of need, to help pay for legal advice or proceedings.

legal eagle (also **legal beagle**) • noun informal a lawyer.

Thesaurus

leech • noun PARASITE, bloodsucker, passenger; *informal* scrounger, sponger, freeloader.

leer • verb *Henry leered at her* OGLE, look lasciviously, look suggestively, eye; *informal* give someone a/the once-over, lech after/over.
• noun *a sly leer* LECHEROUS LOOK, lascivious look, ogle; *informal* the once-over.

leery • adjective WARY, cautious, careful, guarded, chary, suspicious, distrustful; worried, anxious, apprehensive.

lees • plural noun SEDIMENT, dregs, deposit, grounds, residue, remains, silt, sludge; *technical* residuum; *poetic/literary* draff; *archaic* grouts.

leeway • noun FREEDOM, scope, latitude, space, room, liberty, flexibility, licence, free hand, free rein.

left • adjective LEFT-HAND, sinistral; *Nautical* port; *Nautical, archaic* larboard; *Heraldry* sinister.
– RELATED TERMS laevo-, sinistro-.
– OPPOSITES right, starboard.

left-handed • adjective **1** *a left-handed golfer* sinistral; *informal* southpaw. **2** *a left-handed compliment* BACKHANDED, ambiguous, equivocal, double-edged; dubious, indirect, cryptic, ironic, sardonic, insincere, hypocritical.
– OPPOSITES right-handed.

leftover • noun **1** *a leftover from the 60s* RESIDUE, survivor, vestige, legacy. **2** *put the leftovers in the fridge* LEAVINGS, uneaten food, remainder, scraps, remnants, remains; excess, surplus.
• adjective *leftover food* REMAINING, left, uneaten, unconsumed; excess, surplus, superfluous, unused, unwanted, spare.

left-wing • adjective SOCIALIST, communist, leftist, Labour, Marxist–Leninist, Bolshevik, Trotskyite, Maoist; *informal* commie, lefty, red, pink.
– OPPOSITES right-wing, conservative.

leg • noun **1** *Lee broke his leg* (LOWER) LIMB, shank; *informal* peg, pin; *archaic* member. **2** *a table leg* UPRIGHT, support, prop. **3** *the first leg of a European tour* PART, stage, portion, segment, section, phase, stretch, lap.
– PHRASES **give someone a leg up** HELP/ASSIST SOMEONE, give someone assistance, lend someone a helping hand, give someone a boost, give someone a flying start. **leg it** (*informal*) **1** *if the dog starts growling, leg it!* RUN (AWAY), flee, make off, make a break for it, escape, hurry; *informal* hightail it, hotfoot it, make a run for it, cut and run, skedaddle, vamoose, show a clean pair of heels, split, scoot, scram; *Brit. informal* scarper. **2** *legging it around London* WALK, march, tramp, trek, trudge, plod, wander, go on foot, go on Shanks's pony. **on its last legs 1** *my car is on its last legs* DILAPIDATED, worn out, rickety, about to fall apart. **2** *a foundry business on its last legs* FAILING, about to go bankrupt, near to ruin, going to the wall; *informal* going bust. **pull someone's leg** TEASE, rag, make fun of, chaff, jest, joke with, play a (practical) joke on, play a trick on, make a monkey out of; hoax, fool, deceive, lead on, hoodwink, dupe, beguile, gull; *informal* kid, have on, rib, take for a ride, take the mickey out of; *Brit. informal* wind up; *N. Amer. informal* put on. **stretch one's legs** GO FOR A WALK, take a stroll, walk, stroll, move about, get some exercise.

legacy • noun **1** *a legacy from a great aunt* BEQUEST, inheritance, heritage, bequeathal, bestowal, endowment, gift, patrimony, settlement, birthright; *Law, dated* hereditament; *formal* benefaction. **2** *the rancorous legacy of the war* CONSEQUENCE, effect, upshot, spin-off, repercussion, aftermath, by-product, result.

legal • adjective **1** *all their actions were legal* LAWFUL, legitimate, licit, within the law, legalized, valid; permissible, permitted, allowable, allowed, above board, admissible, acceptable; author-

lengthways.

lengthy ● adjective (**lengthier**, **lengthiest**) of considerable or unusual duration.
– DERIVATIVES **lengthily** adverb.

lenient /leeniənt/ ● adjective merciful or tolerant.
– DERIVATIVES **lenience** noun **leniency** noun **leniently** adverb.
– ORIGIN from Latin *lenire* 'soothe', from *lenis* 'mild, gentle'.

Leninism ● noun Marxism as interpreted and applied by the Soviet premier Vladimir Ilich Lenin (1870–1924).
– DERIVATIVES **Leninist** noun & adjective.

lens ● noun **1** a piece of transparent material with one or both sides curved for concentrating or dispersing light rays. **2** the light-gathering device of a camera, containing a group of compound lenses. **3** Anatomy the transparent elastic structure behind the iris by which light is focused on to the retina of the eye.
– DERIVATIVES **lensed** adjective.
– ORIGIN Latin, 'lentil' (because of the similarity in shape).

lensman ● noun a professional photographer or cameraman.

Lent ● noun (in the Christian Church) the period preceding Easter, which is devoted to fasting, abstinence, and penitence in commemoration of Christ's fasting in the wilderness.
– ORIGIN abbreviation of LENTEN.

lent past and past participle of LEND.

Lenten ● adjective relating to or appropriate to Lent.
– ORIGIN Old English, 'spring, Lent', related to LONG[1] (perhaps with reference to the lengthening of the day in spring).

lenticular /lentikyoolər/ ● adjective **1** shaped like a lentil; biconvex. **2** relating to the lens of the eye.

lentil ● noun a high-protein pulse which is dried and then soaked and cooked prior to eating.
– ORIGIN Latin *lenticula*, from *lens* 'lentil'.

lento ● adverb & adjective Music slow or slowly.
– ORIGIN Italian.

Leo ● noun **1** Astronomy a large constellation (the Lion), said to represent the lion slain by Hercules. **2** Astrology the fifth sign of the zodiac, which the sun enters about 23 July.
– DERIVATIVES **Leonian** noun & adjective.
– ORIGIN Latin.

leone /liōn/ ● noun the basic monetary unit of Sierra Leone, equal to 100 cents.

leonine /leeənīn/ ● adjective of or resembling a lion or lions.
– ORIGIN Latin *leoninus*, from *leo* 'lion'.

leopard ● noun **1** (fem. **leopardess**) a large solitary cat that has a fawn or brown coat with black spots, found in the forests of Africa and southern Asia. **2** (before another noun) spotted like a leopard.
– PHRASES **a leopard can't change his spots** proverb people can't change their basic nature.
– ORIGIN Greek *leopardos*, from *leōn* 'lion' + *pardos* 'panther'.

leotard ● noun a close-fitting, stretchy one-piece garment covering the body to the top of the thighs, worn for dance, gymnastics, and exercise.
– ORIGIN named after the French trapeze artist Jules *Léotard* (1839–70).

leper ● noun **1** a person suffering from leprosy. **2** a person who is shunned by others.
– ORIGIN Old French *lepre*, from Greek *lepros* 'scaly'.

Lepidoptera /leppidoptərə/ ● plural noun an order of insects comprising the butterflies and moths.
– DERIVATIVES **lepidopteran** adjective & noun **lepidopterist** noun **lepidopterous** adjective.
– ORIGIN from Greek *lepis* 'scale' + *pteron* 'wing'.

leprechaun /leprəkawn/ ● noun (in Irish folklore) a small, mischievous sprite.
– ORIGIN Old Irish *luchorpán*, from *lu* 'small' + *corp* 'body'.

leprosy ● noun a contagious bacterial disease that affects the skin, mucous membranes, and nerves, causing discoloration and lumps on the skin and, in severe cases, disfigurement and deformities.

leprous ● adjective referring to or suffering from leprosy.

leptin ● noun Biochemistry a protein produced by fatty tissue which is believed to regulate fat storage in the body.
– ORIGIN from Greek *leptos* 'fine, thin'.

lepton ● noun Physics a subatomic particle that does not take part in the strong interaction, such as an electron or neutrino.
– ORIGIN from Greek *leptos* 'small'.

lesbian ● noun a homosexual woman. ● adjective referring to lesbians or lesbianism.
– DERIVATIVES **lesbianism** noun.
– ORIGIN from *Lesbos*, the Greek island which was the home of the poet Sappho (early 7th century BC), who expressed affection for women in her poetry.

lese-majesty /leez majisti/ (also **lèse-majesté**) /layz/ ● noun the insulting of a sovereign; treason.
– ORIGIN from Latin *laesa majestas* 'injured sovereignty'.

lesion /leezh'n/ ● noun chiefly Medicine a region in an organ or tissue which has suffered damage through injury or disease.
– ORIGIN from Latin *laedere* 'injure'.

less ● determiner & pronoun **1** a smaller amount of; not as much. **2** fewer in number. ● adverb to a smaller extent; not so much. ● preposition minus.
– USAGE On the difference in use between **less** and **fewer**, see the note at FEW.
– ORIGIN Old English.

-less ● suffix forming adjectives and adverbs: **1** (from nouns) without; free from: *flavourless*. **2** (from verbs) not affected by or not carrying out the action of the verb: *tireless*.
– ORIGIN Old English, 'devoid of'.

lessee ● noun a person who holds the lease of a property.
– ORIGIN Old French *lesse*, from *lesser* 'to let, leave'.

lessen ● verb make or become less.

lesser ● adjective not so great, large, or important as the other or the rest.

lesson ● noun **1** a period of learning or teaching. **2** a thing learned. **3** a thing that serves as a warning or encouragement. **4** a passage from the Bible read aloud during a church service.

Thesaurus

stretch out.
– OPPOSITES shorten.

lengthy ● adjective **1** *a lengthy civil war* (VERY) LONG, long-lasting, prolonged, extended. **2** *lengthy discussions* PROTRACTED, overlong, long-drawn-out; verbose, wordy, prolix, long-winded; tedious, boring, interminable.
– OPPOSITES short.

leniency ● noun MERCIFULNESS, mercy, clemency, forgiveness; tolerance, forbearance, humanity, charity, indulgence, mildness; pity, sympathy, compassion, understanding.

lenient ● adjective MERCIFUL, clement, forgiving, forbearing, tolerant, charitable, humane, indulgent, easy-going, magnanimous, sympathetic, compassionate.
– OPPOSITES severe.

leper ● noun (SOCIAL) OUTCAST, pariah, undesirable, persona non grata.

leprechaun ● noun PIXIE, goblin, elf, sprite, fairy, gnome, imp, brownie.

lesbian ● noun HOMOSEXUAL WOMAN, gay woman; *informal* les, lesbo, lezzy, butch, dyke.
– OPPOSITES heterosexual.
● adjective HOMOSEXUAL, gay; *informal* les, lesbo, lezzy, butch, dykey, queer, bent.
– OPPOSITES straight.

lesion ● noun WOUND, injury, bruise, abrasion, contusion; ulcer, ulceration, (running) sore, abscess; *Medicine* trauma.

less ● pronoun *the fare is less than £1* A SMALLER AMOUNT, not so/as much as, under, below.
– OPPOSITES more.
● determiner *there was less noise now* NOT SO MUCH, smaller, slighter, shorter, reduced; fewer.
● adverb *we must use the car less* TO A LESSER DEGREE, to a smaller extent, not so/as much.
● preposition *list price less 10 per cent* MINUS, subtracting, excepting, without.
– OPPOSITES plus.

lessen ● verb **1** *exercise lessens the risk of heart disease* REDUCE, make less/smaller, minimize, decrease; allay, assuage, alleviate, attenuate, palliate, ease, dull, deaden, blunt, moderate, mitigate, dampen, soften, tone down, dilute, weaken. **2** *the pain began to lessen* GROW LESS, grow smaller, decrease, diminish, decline, subside, abate; fade, die down/off, let up, ease off, tail off, drop (off/away), fall, dwindle, ebb, wane, recede. **3** *his behaviour lessened him in their eyes* DIMINISH, degrade, discredit, devalue, belittle.
– OPPOSITES increase.

lesser ● adjective **1** *a lesser offence* LESS IMPORTANT, minor, secondary, subsidiary, marginal, ancillary, auxiliary, supplementary, peripheral; inferior, insignificant, unimportant, petty. **2** *you look*

l

– ORIGIN Old French *leçon*, from Latin *legere* 'read'.
lessor ● noun a person who leases or lets a property to another.
– ORIGIN Old French, from *lesser* 'let, leave'.
lest ● conjunction formal **1** with the intention of preventing; to avoid the risk of. **2** because of the possibility of.
– USAGE The word **lest** takes the *subjunctive* mood, meaning that the correct construction is *she was worrying lest he be attacked* (not ... *lest he was attacked*).
– ORIGIN Old English, 'whereby less that'.
let[1] ● verb (**letting**; past and past part. **let**) **1** not prevent or forbid; allow. **2** used in the imperative to express an intention, proposal, or instruction: *let's have a drink.* **3** used to express an assumption upon which a theory or calculation is to be based. **4** allow someone to have the use of (a room or property) in return for payment. ● noun Brit. a period during which a room or property is rented.
– PHRASES **let alone** not to mention. **let down** fail to support or help. **let fly** attack physically or verbally. **let go 1** allow to go free. **2** dismiss (an employee). **3** relinquish one's grip on. **let into** set (something) back into (a surface). **let oneself go 1** act in an uninhibited way. **2** become careless or untidy in one's habits or appearance. **let off 1** cause (a gun, firework, or bomb) to fire or explode. **2** refrain from punishing. **3** excuse (someone) from a task or obligation. **let on** informal divulge information. **let out 1** utter (a sound or cry). **2** make (a garment) looser or larger. **let up** informal become less intense. **to let** available for rent.
– DERIVATIVES **letting** noun.
– ORIGIN Old English, 'leave behind, leave out'; related to LATE.
let[2] ● noun (in racket sports) a circumstance under which a service is nullified and has to be retaken, especially (in tennis) when the ball clips the top of the net and falls within bounds.
– PHRASES **let or hindrance** formal obstruction or impediment. **play a let** (in racket sports) play a point again because the ball or one of the players has been obstructed.
– ORIGIN Old English, 'hinder'; related to LATE.
-let ● suffix **1** (forming nouns) denoting a smaller or lesser kind: *booklet.* **2** denoting articles of ornament or dress: *anklet.*
– ORIGIN originally corresponding to French *-ette.*
let-down ● noun a disappointment.
lethal ● adjective **1** sufficient to cause death. **2** very harmful or destructive.
– DERIVATIVES **lethality** noun **lethally** adverb.
– ORIGIN Latin *lethalis*, from *letum* 'death'.
lethargy /lethərji/ ● noun **1** a lack of energy and enthusiasm. **2** Medicine a pathological state of sleepiness or deep unresponsiveness.
– DERIVATIVES **lethargic** adjective **lethargically** adverb.
– ORIGIN from Greek *lēthargos* 'forgetful'.
let-off ● noun informal an instance of unexpectedly escaping or avoiding something.
let's ● contraction let us.
letter ● noun **1** a character representing one or more of the sounds used in speech; any of the symbols of an alphabet. **2** a written, typed, or printed communication, sent by post or messenger. **3** the precise terms of a statement or requirement. **4** (**letters**) literature. ● verb inscribe or provide with letters.
– PHRASES **to the letter** with adherence to every detail.
– DERIVATIVES **lettering** noun.
– ORIGIN Latin *litera* 'letter of the alphabet', (plural) 'epistle, literature, culture'.
letter bomb ● noun an explosive device hidden in a small package and detonated when the package is opened.
letter box ● noun **1** chiefly Brit. a slot in a door through which mail is delivered. **2** (**letterbox**) a format for presenting widescreen films on a standard television screen, in which the image fills the width but not the height of the screen.
letterhead ● noun a printed heading on stationery, stating the

down at us lesser mortals SUBORDINATE, minor, inferior, second-class, subservient, lowly, humble.
– OPPOSITES greater, superior.
lesson ● noun **1** *a maths lesson* CLASS, session, seminar, tutorial, lecture, period (of instruction/teaching). **2** *they should be industrious at their lessons* EXERCISES, assignments, schoolwork, homework. **3** *reading the lesson in assembly* BIBLE READING, scripture, text, reading. **4** *Stuart's accident should be a lesson to all parents* WARNING, deterrent, caution; example, exemplar, message, moral.
lest ● conjunction (JUST) IN CASE, for fear that, in order to avoid.
let ● verb **1** *let him sleep for now* ALLOW, permit, give permission to, give leave to, authorize, sanction, grant the right to, license, empower, enable, entitle; assent to, consent to, agree to, acquiesce in, tolerate, countenance, give one's blessing to, give assent to, give someone/something the nod; informal give the green light to, give the go-ahead to, give the thumbs up to, OK; formal accede to; archaic suffer. **2** *Wilcox opened the door to let her through* ALLOW TO GO, permit to pass; make way for. **3** *they've let their flat* RENT (OUT), let out, lease, hire (out), sublet, sublease.
– OPPOSITES prevent, prohibit.
– PHRASES **let someone down** FAIL (TO SUPPORT), fall short of expectation, disappoint, disillusion; abandon, desert, leave stranded, leave in the lurch. **let something down** LENGTHEN, make longer. **let fly 1** *he let fly with a brick* HURL, fling, throw, propel, pitch, lob, toss, launch; shoot, fire, blast; informal chuck, sling, heave. **2** *she let fly at Geoffrey* LOSE ONE'S TEMPER WITH, lash out at, scold, chastise, chide, rant at, inveigh against, rail against; explode, burst out, let someone have it; informal carpet, give someone a rocket, tear someone off a strip; formal excoriate. **let go** RELEASE (ONE'S HOLD ON), loose/loosen one's hold on, relinquish; archaic unhand. **let someone go** MAKE REDUNDANT, dismiss, discharge, lay off, give notice to, axe; informal sack, fire, give someone their cards, give someone their marching orders, send packing, give someone the boot/push, give someone the (old) heave-ho. **let someone in** ALLOW TO ENTER, allow in, admit, open the door to; receive, welcome, greet. **let someone in on something** INCLUDE, count in, admit, allow to share in, let participate in, inform about, tell about. **let something off** DETONATE, discharge, explode, set off, fire off. **let someone off 1** *I'll let you off this time* PARDON, forgive, grant an amnesty to; deal leniently with, be merciful to, have mercy on; acquit, absolve, exonerate, clear, vindicate; informal let someone off the hook; formal exculpate. **2** *he let me off work* EXCUSE FROM, exempt from, spare from. **let on** (informal) **1** *I never let on that I felt anxious* REVEAL, make known, tell, disclose, mention, divulge, let slip, give away, make public; blab; informal let the cat out of the bag, give the game away. **2** *they all let on they didn't hear me* PRETEND, feign, affect, make out, make believe, simulate. **let something out 1** *I let out a cry of triumph* UTTER, emit, give (vent to), produce, issue, express, voice, release. **2** *she let out that he'd given her a lift home* REVEAL, make known, tell, disclose, mention, divulge, let slip, give away, let it be known, blurt out. **let someone out** RELEASE, liberate, (set) free, let go, discharge; set/turn loose, allow to leave. **let up** (informal) **1** *the rain has let up* ABATE, lessen, decrease, diminish, subside, relent, slacken, die down/off, ease (off), tail off; ebb, wane, dwindle, fade; stop, cease, finish. **2** *you never let up, do you?* RELAX, ease up/off, slow down; pause, break (off), take a break, rest, stop; informal take a breather. **3** *I promise I'll let up on him* TREAT LESS SEVERELY, be more lenient with, be kinder to; informal go easy on.
let-down ● noun DISAPPOINTMENT, anticlimax, comedown, non-event, fiasco, setback, blow; informal washout, damp squib.
lethal ● adjective FATAL, deadly, mortal, death-dealing, life-threatening, murderous, killing; poisonous, toxic, noxious, venomous; dangerous, destructive, harmful, pernicious; poetic/literary deathly, nocuous; archaic baneful.
– OPPOSITES harmless, safe.
lethargic ● adjective SLUGGISH, inert, inactive, slow, torpid, lifeless; languid, listless, lazy, idle, indolent, shiftless, slothful, apathetic, weary, tired, fatigued.
lethargy ● noun SLUGGISHNESS, inertia, inactivity, inaction, slowness, torpor, torpidity, lifelessness, listlessness, languor, languidness, laziness, idleness, indolence, shiftlessness, sloth, apathy, passivity, weariness, tiredness, lassitude, fatigue; poetic/literary hebetude.
– OPPOSITES vigour, energy.
letter ● noun **1** *capital letters* (ALPHABETICAL) CHARACTER, sign, symbol, mark, figure, rune; Linguistics grapheme. **2** *she received a letter* (WRITTEN) MESSAGE, (written) communication, note, line, missive, dispatch; correspondence, news, information, intelligence, word; post, mail; formal epistle. **3** *a man of letters* (BOOK) LEARNING, scholarship, erudition, education, knowledge; intellect, intelligence, enlightenment, wisdom, sagacity, culture.
– RELATED TERMS epistolary.
– PHRASES **to the letter** STRICTLY, precisely, exactly, accurately, closely, faithfully, religiously, punctiliously, literally, verbatim, in every detail.

sender's name and address.

letter of credit ● noun a letter issued by one bank to another to serve as a guarantee for payments made to a specified person.

letterpress ● noun printing from a hard, raised image under pressure, using viscous ink.

letters of administration ● plural noun Law authority to administer the estate of someone who has died without making a will.

letters patent ● plural noun an open document issued by a monarch or government conferring a patent or other right.
– ORIGIN from Latin *litterae patentes*, 'letters lying open'.

lettuce ● noun **1** a cultivated plant with edible leaves that are eaten in salads. **2** used in names of other plants with edible green leaves, e.g. **lamb's lettuce**.
– ORIGIN Old French *letues*, from Latin *lactuca*, from *lac* 'milk' (because of its milky juice).

let-up ● noun informal a pause or reduction in the intensity of something dangerous, difficult, or tiring.

leu /layoo/ ● noun (pl. **lei** /lay/) the basic monetary unit of Romania, equal to 100 bani.
– ORIGIN Romanian, 'lion'.

leucine /looseen/ ● noun Biochemistry a hydrophobic amino acid which is an essential nutrient in the diet of vertebrates.
– ORIGIN from Greek *leukos* 'white'.

leucocyte /lookəsīt/ (also **leukocyte**) ● noun Physiology a colourless cell which circulates in the blood and body fluids and is involved in counteracting foreign substances and disease; a white (blood) cell.
– ORIGIN from Greek *leukos* 'white' + *kutos* 'vessel'.

leucotomy /lookottəmi/ ● noun (pl. **leucotomies**) the surgical cutting of white nerve fibres within the brain, especially in the frontal lobes, formerly used to treat mental illness.

leukaemia /lookeemiə/ (US **leukemia**) ● noun a malignant progressive disease in which the bone marrow and other blood-forming organs produce increased numbers of immature or abnormal white cells, suppressing the production of normal blood cells.
– DERIVATIVES **leukaemic** adjective.
– ORIGIN from Greek *leukos* 'white' + *haima* 'blood'.

lev /lev/ (also **leva** /levvə/) ● noun (pl. **leva** or **levas** or **levs**) the basic monetary unit of Bulgaria, equal to 100 stotinki.
– ORIGIN Bulgarian, 'lion'.

Levant /livant/ ● noun (**the Levant**) historical the eastern part of the Mediterranean.
– DERIVATIVES **Levantine** noun & adjective.
– ORIGIN from French, 'rising' (used to mean 'point of sunrise, east'), from *lever* 'to lift'.

levanter /livantər/ ● noun a strong easterly wind in the Mediterranean region.

levee[1] /levvi, levvay/ ● noun a formal reception of visitors or guests.
– ORIGIN French, from *lever* 'to rise' (such receptions were formerly held by a monarch after rising from bed).

levee[2] /levvi/ ● noun **1** an embankment built to prevent the overflow of a river. **2** a ridge of sediment deposited naturally alongside a river. **3** chiefly N. Amer. a landing place; a quay.
– ORIGIN French, from *lever* 'to lift or rise'.

level ● noun **1** a horizontal plane or line with respect to the distance above or below a given point. **2** a height or distance from the ground or another base. **3** a position or stage on a scale of quantity, extent, rank, or quality. **4** a floor within a multistorey building. **5** a flat area of land. **6** an instrument giving a line parallel to the plane of the horizon for testing whether things are horizontal. ● adjective **1** having a flat, horizontal surface. **2** at the same height as someone or something else. **3** having the same relative position; not in front or behind. **4** calm and steady. ● verb (**levelled**, **levelling**; US **leveled**, **leveling**) **1** make or become level. **2** aim or direct (a weapon, criticism, or accusation). **3** (**level with**) informal be frank or honest with.
– PHRASES **be level pegging** Brit. be equal in score or achievement during a contest. **a level playing field** a situation in which everyone has an equal chance of succeeding. **on the level** informal honest; truthful.
– DERIVATIVES **levelly** adverb **levelness** noun.
– ORIGIN Old French *livel*, from Latin *libra* 'scales, balance'.

level crossing ● noun Brit. a place where a railway and a road cross at the same level.

level-headed ● adjective calm and sensible.
– DERIVATIVES **level-headedly** adverb **level-headedness** noun.

leveller (US **leveler**) ● noun **1** a person or thing that levels something. **2** (**Leveller**) a member of a group of radical dissenters in the English Civil War.

lever ● noun **1** a rigid bar resting on a pivot, used to move a load with one end when pressure is applied to the other. **2** a projecting arm or handle that is moved to operate a mechanism. ● verb **1** lift or move with a lever. **2** move with a concerted physical effort.
– ORIGIN Old French *levier*, from *lever* 'to lift'.

leverage ● noun **1** the exertion of force by means of a lever. **2** the power to influence: *political leverage*.

leveraged buyout ● noun the purchase of a controlling share in a company by its management using outside capital.

leveret /levvərit/ ● noun a young hare in its first year.
– ORIGIN Old French, from Latin *lepus* 'hare'.

leviathan /liviəthən/ ● noun **1** (in biblical use) a sea monster. **2** a very large or powerful thing.
– ORIGIN Hebrew.

levitate ● verb rise or cause to rise and hover in the air.
– DERIVATIVES **levitation** noun.

Thesaurus

lettered ● adjective LEARNED, erudite, academic, (well) educated, well read, widely read, knowledgeable, intellectual, well schooled, enlightened, cultured, cultivated, scholarly, bookish, highbrow, studious.
– OPPOSITES ill-educated.

let-up ● noun *(informal)* ABATEMENT, lessening, decrease, diminishing, diminution, decline, relenting, remission, slackening, weakening, relaxation, dying down, easing off, tailing off, dropping away/off; respite, break, interval, hiatus, suspension, cessation, stop, pause.

level ● adjective **1** *a smooth and level surface* FLAT, smooth, even, uniform, plane, flush, plumb. **2** *he kept his voice level* UNCHANGING, steady, unvarying, even, uniform, regular, constant, invariable, unaltering; calm, unemotional, composed, equable, unruffled, serene, tranquil. **3** *the scores were level* EQUAL, even, drawn, tied, all square, neck and neck, level pegging, on a par, evenly matched; informal even-steven(s). **4** *his eyes were level with hers* ALIGNED, on the same level as, on a level, at the same height as, in line.
– OPPOSITES uneven, unsteady, unequal.
● noun **1** *the post is at research-officer level* RANK, standing, status, position; echelon, degree, grade, gradation, stage, standard, rung; class, stratum, group, grouping, set, classification. **2** *a high level of employment* QUANTITY, amount, extent, measure, degree, volume, size, magnitude, intensity, proportion. **3** *the level of water is rising* HEIGHT, highness, altitude, elevation. **4** *the sixth level* FLOOR, storey, deck.
● verb **1** *tilt the tin to level the mixture* MAKE LEVEL, level out/off, make even, even off/out, make flat, flatten, smooth (out), make uniform. **2** *bulldozers levelled the building* RAZE (TO THE GROUND), demolish, flatten, topple, destroy; tear down, knock down, pull down, bulldoze. **3** *he levelled his opponent with a single blow* KNOCK DOWN/OUT, knock to the ground, lay out, prostrate, flatten, floor, fell; informal KO, kayo. **4** *Carl levelled the score* EQUALIZE, make equal, equal, even (up), make level. **5** *he levelled his pistol at me* AIM, point, direct, train, focus, turn. **6** *(informal) I knew you'd level with me* BE FRANK, be open, be honest, be above board, tell the truth, tell all, hide nothing, be straightforward; informal be upfront.
– PHRASES **on the level** *(informal)* GENUINE, straight, honest, above board, fair, true, sincere, straightforward; informal upfront; N. Amer. informal on the up and up.

level-headed ● adjective SENSIBLE, practical, realistic, prudent, pragmatic, wise, reasonable, rational, mature, judicious, sound, sober, businesslike, no-nonsense, composed, calm, {cool, calm, and collected}, confident, well balanced, equable, cool-headed, self-possessed, having one's feet on the ground; informal unflappable, together.
– OPPOSITES excitable.

lever ● noun **1** *you can insert a lever and prise the rail off* CROWBAR, bar, jemmy. **2** *he pulled the lever* HANDLE, grip, pull, switch.
● verb *he levered the door open* PRISE, force, wrench, pull, wrest, heave; N. Amer. pry; informal jemmy.

leverage ● noun **1** *the long handles provide increased leverage* GRIP, purchase, hold; support, anchorage, force, strength. **2** *they have significant leverage in negotiations* INFLUENCE, power, author-

– ORIGIN from Latin *levis* 'light'.
levity ● noun the treatment of a serious matter with humour or lack of respect.
– ORIGIN Latin *levitas*, from *levis* 'light'.
levy ● noun (pl. **levies**) **1** the imposition of a tax, fee, fine, or subscription. **2** a sum of money raised by a levy. **3** archaic a body of enlisted troops. ● verb (**levies**, **levied**) **1** impose or seize as a levy. **2** archaic enlist for military service. **3** archaic begin to wage (war).
– ORIGIN from Old French *lever* 'raise', from Latin *levis* 'light'.
lewd ● adjective crude and offensive in a sexual way.
– DERIVATIVES **lewdly** adverb **lewdness** noun.
– ORIGIN originally in the sense 'belonging to the laity', later 'belonging to the common people, vulgar': from Old English.
lexical ● adjective **1** relating to the words or vocabulary of a language. **2** relating to a lexicon or dictionary.
– DERIVATIVES **lexically** adverb.
– ORIGIN from Greek *lexikos* 'of words'.
lexicography /leksikogrəfi/ ● noun the practice of compiling dictionaries.
– DERIVATIVES **lexicographer** noun **lexicographic** adjective.
lexicon ● noun **1** the vocabulary of a person, language, or branch of knowledge. **2** a dictionary.
– ORIGIN from Greek *lexikon biblion* 'book of words', from *lexis* 'word'.
lexis ● noun the total stock of words in a language.
– ORIGIN Greek, 'word'.
ley[1] ● noun a piece of land temporarily put down to grass, clover, etc.
– ORIGIN Old English, 'fallow'; related to LAY[1] and LIE[1].
ley[2] (also **ley line**) ● noun a supposed straight line connecting three or more ancient sites, associated by some with lines of energy and other paranormal phenomena.
– ORIGIN variant of LEA.
Leyden jar /līd'n/ ● noun an early form of capacitor consisting of a glass jar with layers of metal foil on the outside and inside.
– ORIGIN named after the city of *Leyden* (or *Leiden*) in the Netherlands, where it was invented in 1745.
leylandii /laylandi-ī/ ● noun (pl. same) a fast-growing conifer, widely grown as a screening plant or for shelter.
– ORIGIN named after the British horticulturalist Christopher J. *Leyland* (1849–1926).

LF ● abbreviation low frequency.
LGV ● abbreviation Brit. large goods vehicle.
Li ● symbol the chemical element lithium.
liability ● noun (pl. **liabilities**) **1** the state of being liable. **2** a thing for which someone is liable, especially a financial obligation. **3** a person or thing likely to cause one embarrassment or put one at a disadvantage.
liable ● adjective **1** responsible by law; legally answerable. **2** (**liable to**) subject by law to. **3** (**liable to do**) likely to do. **4** (**liable to**) likely to experience (something undesirable).
– ORIGIN perhaps from French *lier* 'to bind', from Latin *ligare*.
liaise ● verb **1** cooperate on a matter of mutual concern. **2** (**liaise between**) act as a link to assist communication between.
– ORIGIN from LIAISON.
liaison ● noun **1** communication or cooperation between people or organizations. **2** a sexual relationship, especially one that is secret. **3** the binding or thickening agent of a sauce, often based on egg yolks.
– ORIGIN French, from *lier* 'to bind'.
liana /liaanə/ (also **liane** /liaan/) ● noun a woody climbing plant that hangs from trees, especially in tropical rainforests.
– ORIGIN French *liane* 'clematis, liana'.
liar ● noun a person who tells lies.
lias /līəss/ ● noun Geology (also **blue lias**) a blue-grey clayey limestone deposited in the Jurassic period, found chiefly in SW England.
– ORIGIN Old French *liais* 'hard limestone'.
lib ● noun informal (in the names of political movements) the liberation of a specified group: *women's lib*.
– DERIVATIVES **libber** noun.
libation /lībaysh'n/ ● noun **1** the pouring out of a drink as an offering to a deity. **2** a drink poured out as such an offering. **3** humorous an alcoholic drink.
– ORIGIN Latin, from *libare* 'pour as an offering'.
Lib Dem ● noun informal (in the UK) Liberal Democrat.
libel ● noun **1** Law the publication of a false statement that is damaging to a person's reputation. Compare with SLANDER. **2** a written defamation. ● verb (**libelled**, **libelling**; US **libeled**, **libeling**) Law defame by publishing a libel.
– DERIVATIVES **libellous** (US also **libelous**) adjective.
– ORIGIN originally denoting a document: from Latin *libellus* 'little book'.

Thesaurus

ity, weight, sway, pull, control, say, dominance, advantage, pressure; informal clout, muscle, teeth.
levitate ● noun FLOAT, rise (into the air), hover, be suspended, glide, hang, fly, soar up.
levity ● noun LIGHT-HEARTEDNESS, high spirits, vivacity, liveliness, cheerfulness, cheeriness, humour, gaiety, fun, jocularity, hilarity, frivolity, frivolousness, amusement, mirth, laughter, merriment, glee, comedy, wit, wittiness, jollity, joviality.
– OPPOSITES seriousness.
levy ● verb **1** *a proposal to levy VAT on fuel* IMPOSE, charge, exact, raise, collect; tax. **2** (archaic) *levying troops* CONSCRIPT, call up, enlist, mobilize, rally, muster, marshal, recruit, raise; US draft.
● noun **1** *the levy of taxation* IMPOSITION, raising, collection; formal exaction. **2** *the levy on spirits* TAX, tariff, toll, excise, duty, imposition, impost; formal mulct. **3** (archaic) *not shire levies, but professional soldiers* CONSCRIPTS, troops, (armed) forces, army, militia.
lewd ● adjective **1** *a lewd old man* LECHEROUS, lustful, licentious, lascivious, dirty, prurient, salacious, lubricious, libidinous, lickerish; debauched, depraved, degenerate, decadent, dissipated, dissolute, perverted; informal horny; Brit. informal randy; formal concupiscent. **2** *a lewd song* VULGAR, crude, smutty, dirty, filthy, obscene, pornographic, coarse, off colour, unseemly, indecent, salacious; rude, racy, risqué, naughty, earthy, spicy, bawdy, ribald; informal blue, raunchy, X-rated, nudge-nudge, porno; N. Amer. informal raw; euphemistic adult.
– OPPOSITES chaste, clean.
lexicon ● noun DICTIONARY, wordbook, vocabulary list, glossary, word-finder, thesaurus.
liability ● noun **1** *journalists' liability for defamation* ACCOUNTABILITY, (legal) responsibility, answerability; blame, blameworthiness, culpability, guilt, fault. **2** *they have big liabilities* FINANCIAL OBLIGATIONS, debts, arrears, dues. **3** *an electoral liability* HINDRANCE, encumbrance, burden, handicap, nuisance, inconvenience; obstacle, impediment, disadvantage, weakness, shortcoming; millstone round one's neck, albatross, Achilles heel; archaic cumber. **4** *their liability to the disease* SUSCEPTIBILITY, vulnerability, proneness, tendency, predisposition, propensity.
– OPPOSITES immunity, asset.
liable ● adjective **1** *they are liable for negligence* (LEGALLY) RESPONSIBLE, accountable, answerable, chargeable, blameworthy, at fault, culpable, guilty. **2** *my income is liable to fluctuate wildly* LIKELY, inclined, tending, disposed, apt, predisposed, prone, given. **3** *areas liable to flooding* EXPOSED, prone, subject, susceptible, vulnerable, in danger of, at risk of.
liaise ● verb COOPERATE, work together, collaborate; communicate, network, interface, link up.
liaison ● noun **1** *the branches work in close liaison* COOPERATION, contact, association, connection, collaboration, communication, alliance, partnership. **2** *Dave was my White House liaison* INTERMEDIARY, mediator, middleman, contact, link, linkman, linkwoman, linkperson, go-between, representative, agent. **3** *a secret liaison* (LOVE) AFFAIR, relationship, romance, attachment, fling, amour, affair of the heart, (romantic) entanglement; informal hanky-panky.
liar ● noun FIBBER, deceiver, perjurer, false witness, fabricator; romancer, fabulist; informal storyteller.
libation ● noun **1** *they pour libations into the holy well* (LIQUID) OFFERING, tribute, oblation. **2** (humorous) *would you like a small libation?* (ALCOHOLIC) DRINK, beverage, liquid refreshment; dram, draught, nip, tot; informal tipple; archaic potation.
libel ● noun *she sued two newspapers for libel* DEFAMATION (OF CHARACTER), character assassination, calumny, misrepresentation, scandalmongering; aspersions, denigration, vilification, disparagement, derogation, insult, slander, malicious gossip, traducement; lie, slur, smear, untruth, false report; informal mud-slinging, bad-mouthing.
● verb *she alleged the magazine had libelled her* DEFAME, malign, slander, blacken someone's name, sully someone's reputation, speak ill/evil of, traduce, smear, cast aspersions on, drag someone's name through the mud/mire, besmirch, tarnish, taint,

liberal ● adjective **1** willing to respect and accept behaviour or opinions different from one's own. **2** (of a society, law, etc.) favourable to individual rights and freedoms. **3** (in a political context) favouring individual liberty, free trade, and moderate reform. **4** (**Liberal**) (in the UK) relating to the Liberal Democrat party. **5** (especially of an interpretation of a law) not strictly literal. **6** given, used, or giving in generous amounts. **7** (of education) concerned with broadening general knowledge and experience. ● noun **1** a person of liberal views. **2** (**Liberal**) (in the UK) a Liberal Democrat.
– DERIVATIVES **liberalism** noun **liberality** noun **liberally** adverb.
– ORIGIN originally meaning 'suitable for a free man': from Latin *liberalis*, from *liber* 'free man'.
liberal arts ● plural noun chiefly N. Amer. arts subjects such as literature and history, as distinct from science and technology.
Liberal Democrat ● noun (in the UK) a member of a party formed from the Liberal Party and members of the Social Democratic Party.
liberalize (also **liberalise**) ● verb remove or loosen restrictions on (something, typically an economic or political system).
– DERIVATIVES **liberalization** noun.
liberate ● verb **1** set free, especially from imprisonment or oppression. **2** (**liberated**) free from social conventions, especially with regard to sexual roles.
– DERIVATIVES **liberation** noun **liberationist** noun **liberator** noun.
– ORIGIN Latin *liberare*, from *liber* 'free'.
liberation theology ● noun a movement in Christian theology which attempts to address the problems of poverty and social injustice.
Liberian /lībeeriən/ ● noun a person from Liberia, a country in West Africa. ● adjective relating to Liberia.
libertarian ● noun **1** an adherent of libertarianism. **2** a person who advocates civil liberty.
libertarianism ● noun an extreme laissez-faire political philosophy advocating only minimal state intervention in the lives of citizens.
libertine /libbərteen/ ● noun a man who behaves without moral principles, especially in sexual matters.
– DERIVATIVES **libertinism** noun.
– ORIGIN Latin *libertinus* 'freedman', from *liber* 'free'.
liberty ● noun (pl. **liberties**) **1** the state of being free from oppression or imprisonment. **2** a right or privilege. **3** the power or scope to act as one pleases. **4** informal a presumptuous remark or action.
– PHRASES **take liberties 1** behave in an unduly familiar manner towards a person. **2** treat something freely, without strict faithfulness to the facts or to an original. **take the liberty** do something without first asking permission.
– ORIGIN Latin *libertas*, from *liber* 'free'.
Liberty Hall ● noun a place where one may do as one likes.
libidinous /libiddinəss/ ● adjective having or showing excessive sexual drive.
– ORIGIN Latin *libidinosus*, from *libido* 'desire, lust'.
libido /libeedō/ ● noun (pl. **libidos**) sexual desire.
– DERIVATIVES **libidinal** adjective.
– ORIGIN Latin, 'desire, lust'.
Libra /leebrə/ ● noun **1** Astronomy a small constellation (the Scales or Balance), said to represent a pair of scales symbolizing justice. **2** Astrology the seventh sign of the zodiac, which the sun enters at the northern autumnal equinox (about 23 September).
– DERIVATIVES **Libran** noun & adjective.
– ORIGIN Latin.
librarian ● noun a person in charge of or assisting in a library.
– DERIVATIVES **librarianship** noun.
library ● noun (pl. **libraries**) **1** a building or room containing a collection of books and periodicals for use by the public or the members of an institution. **2** a private collection of books. **3** a collection of films, recorded music, etc., organized systematically and kept for research or borrowing: *a record library*. **4** (also **software library**) Computing a collection of programs and software packages made generally available.
– ORIGIN Latin *libraria* 'bookshop', from *liber* 'book'.
libretto /librettō/ ● noun (pl. **libretti** /libretti/ or **librettos**) the text of an opera or other long vocal work.
– DERIVATIVES **librettist** noun.
– ORIGIN Italian, 'small book'.
Libyan ● noun a person from Libya. ● adjective relating to Libya.
lice plural of LOUSE.
licence (US **license**) ● noun **1** a permit from an authority to own or use something, do a particular thing, or carry on a trade. **2** a writer's or artist's conventional freedom to deviate from facts or accepted rules. **3** freedom to behave without restraint.
– ORIGIN Latin *licentia* 'freedom, licentiousness', from *licere* 'be lawful or permitted'.
license (also **licence**) ● verb **1** grant a licence to. **2** authorize.

Thesaurus

tell lies about, stain, vilify, denigrate, disparage, run down, stigmatize, discredit; *N. Amer.* slur; *formal* derogate, calumniate.
libellous ● adjective DEFAMATORY, denigratory, vilifying, disparaging, derogatory, calumnious, slanderous, false, untrue, traducing, maligning, insulting, scurrilous.
liberal ● adjective **1** *the values of a liberal society* TOLERANT, unprejudiced, unbigoted, broad-minded, open-minded, enlightened; permissive, free (and easy), easy-going, libertarian, indulgent, lenient. **2** *a liberal social agenda* PROGRESSIVE, advanced, modern, forward-looking, forward-thinking, progressivist, enlightened, reformist, radical; *informal* go-ahead. **3** *a liberal education* WIDE-RANGING, broad-based, general. **4** *a liberal interpretation of divorce laws* FLEXIBLE, broad, loose, rough, free, general, non-literal, non-specific, imprecise, vague, indefinite. **5** *liberal coatings of paint* ABUNDANT, copious, ample, plentiful, generous, lavish, luxuriant, profuse, considerable, prolific, rich; *poetic/literary* plenteous. **6** *they were liberal with their cash* GENEROUS, open-handed, unsparing, unstinting, ungrudging, lavish, free, munificent, bountiful, beneficent, benevolent, big-hearted, philanthropic, charitable, altruistic, unselfish; *poetic/literary* bounteous.
– OPPOSITES reactionary, strict, miserly.
liberate ● verb (SET) FREE, release, let out/go, set/let loose, save, rescue; emancipate, enfranchise; *historical* manumit.
– OPPOSITES imprison, enslave.
liberation ● noun **1** *the liberation of prisoners* FREEING, release, rescue, setting free; freedom, liberty; emancipation; *historical* manumission. **2** *women's liberation* FREEDOM, equality, equal rights, emancipation, enfranchisement.
– OPPOSITES confinement, oppression.
liberator ● noun RESCUER, saviour, deliverer, emancipator; *historical* manumitter.
libertine ● noun *an unrepentant libertine* PHILANDERER, playboy, rake, roué, Don Juan, Lothario, Casanova, Romeo; lecher, seducer, womanizer, adulterer, debauchee, profligate, wanton; *informal* skirt-chaser, ladykiller, lech, wolf; *formal* fornicator.
● adjective *libertine sexual intercourse* LICENTIOUS, lustful, libidinous, lecherous, lascivious, lubricious, dissolute, dissipated, debauched, wanton, degenerate, depraved, promiscuous, lewd, prurient, salacious, intemperate, lickerish; *informal* loose, fast, goatish; *formal* concupiscent.
liberty ● noun **1** *personal liberty* FREEDOM, independence, free rein, license, self-determination, free will, latitude. **2** *the essence of British liberty* INDEPENDENCE, freedom, autonomy, sovereignty, self government, self rule, self determination; civil liberties, human rights. **3** *the liberty to go where one pleases* RIGHT, birthright, prerogative, entitlement, privilege, permission, sanction, authorization, authority, licence.
– OPPOSITES constraint, slavery.
– PHRASES **at liberty 1** *he was at liberty for three months* FREE, (on the) loose, at large, unconfined; escaped, out. **2** *she was at liberty to divide her estate how she chose* FREE, permitted, allowed, authorized, able, entitled, eligible. **take liberties** ACT WITH FAMILIARITY, show disrespect, act with impropriety, act indecorously, be impudent; take advantage, exploit.
libidinous ● adjective LUSTFUL, lecherous, lascivious, lewd, carnal, salacious, prurient, licentious, libertine, lubricious, dissolute, debauched, depraved, degenerate, decadent, dissipated, wanton, promiscuous, lickerish; *informal* horny, goatish, wolfish; *Brit. informal* randy; *formal* concupiscent.
libido ● noun SEX DRIVE, sexual appetite; (sexual) desire, passion, sexiness, sensuality, sexuality, lust, lustfulness; *informal* horniness; *Brit. informal* randiness; *formal* concupiscence.
licence ● noun **1** *a driving licence* PERMIT, certificate, document, documentation, authorization, warrant; certification, credentials; pass, papers. **2** *teachers had licence to administer beatings* PERMISSION, authority, right, a free hand, leave, authorization, entitlement, privilege, prerogative; liberty, freedom, power. **3** *they manufacture footwear under licence* FRANCHISE, permission, con-

– DERIVATIVES **licensable** adjective **licenser** (also **licensor**) noun.
– ORIGIN from LICENCE; the spelling *-se* arose by analogy with pairs such as *practice, practise*.
licensee ● noun the holder of a licence, especially to sell alcoholic drinks.
license plate ● noun North American term for NUMBER PLATE.
licentiate /līsenshiət/ ● noun **1** the holder of a certificate of competence to practise a particular profession. **2** (in some foreign universities) a degree between that of bachelor and master or doctor.
– DERIVATIVES **licentiateship** noun.
– ORIGIN from Latin *licentiatus* 'having freedom', from *licentia* 'freedom'.
licentious /līsenshəss/ ● adjective promiscuous and unprincipled in sexual matters.
– DERIVATIVES **licentiously** adverb **licentiousness** noun.
– ORIGIN Latin *licentiosus*, from *licentia* 'freedom'.
lichen /līkən, lichən/ ● noun a simple plant consisting of a fungus living in close association with an alga, typically growing as a crust or covering on rocks, walls, and trees.
– DERIVATIVES **lichened** adjective **lichenous** adjective.
– ORIGIN Greek *leikhēn*.
licit /lissit/ ● adjective not forbidden; lawful.
– ORIGIN Latin *licitus* 'allowed'.
lick ● verb **1** pass the tongue over (something), typically in order to taste, moisten, or clean it. **2** move lightly and quickly like a tongue. **3** informal defeat comprehensively. ● noun **1** an act of licking. **2** informal a small amount or quick application of something: *a lick of paint*. **3** informal a short phrase or solo in jazz or popular music.
– PHRASES **at a lick** informal at a fast pace. **a lick and a promise** informal a hasty wash. **lick someone's boots** (or vulgar slang **arse**) be excessively obsequious towards someone.
– ORIGIN Old English.
lickerish ● adjective lecherous.
– DERIVATIVES **lickerishly** adverb.
– ORIGIN Old French *lecheros* 'lecherous'.
lickety-split ● adverb N. Amer. informal at full speed.
– ORIGIN originally in the phrase *as fast as lickety* 'at full speed': from LICK + SPLIT.
lickspittle ● noun a person who behaves obsequiously to those in power.
licorice ● noun US spelling of LIQUORICE.
lid ● noun **1** a removable or hinged cover for the top of a container. **2** an eyelid.
– DERIVATIVES **lidded** adjective **lidless** adjective.
– ORIGIN Old English.
lido /leedō/ ● noun (pl. **lidos**) a public open-air swimming pool or bathing beach.
– ORIGIN Italian, 'shore' (also the name of a bathing beach near Venice).
lie[1] ● verb (**lying**; past **lay**; past part. **lain**) **1** be in or assume a horizontal or resting position on a supporting surface. **2** be or remain in a specified state. **3** reside or be found. **4** be situated in a specified position or direction. ● noun **1** the way, direction, or position in which something lies or comes to rest. **2** the place of cover of an animal or a bird.
– PHRASES **let lie** take no action regarding (a sensitive matter). **lie in state** (of the corpse of a person of national importance) be laid in a public place of honour before burial. **lie low** keep out of sight; avoid attention. **the lie** (N. Amer. **lay**) **of the land** **1** the features or characteristics of an area. **2** the current situation or state of affairs. **lie with** archaic have sexual intercourse with. **take lying down** accept (an insult, setback, or rebuke) without protest.
– USAGE For the correct use of **lay** and **lie**, see the note at LAY[1].
– ORIGIN Old English.
lie[2] ● noun **1** an intentionally false statement. **2** a situation involving deception or founded on a mistaken impression. ● verb (**lies, lied, lying**) **1** tell a lie or lies. **2** (of a thing) present a false impression.
– PHRASES **give the lie to** serve to show that (something assumed to be true) is not true.
– ORIGIN Old English.
Liebfraumilch /leebfrowmilsh/ ● noun a light white wine from the Rhine region.
– ORIGIN from German *lieb* 'dear' + *Frau* 'lady' (referring to the Virgin Mary, patroness of the convent where it was first made) + *Milch* 'milk'.
Liechtensteiner /liktənstīnər/ ● noun a person from Liechtenstein, a small independent principality in the Alps.
lied /leed/ ● noun (pl. **lieder** /leedər/) a type of German song, typically for solo voice with piano accompaniment.
– ORIGIN German.
lie detector ● noun an instrument for determining whether a person is telling the truth by testing for physiological changes considered to be associated with lying.
lie-down ● noun chiefly Brit. a short rest on a bed or sofa.
lief /leef/ ● adverb (**as lief**) archaic as happily; as gladly.
– ORIGIN Old English, 'dear, pleasant': related to LEAVE[2] and LOVE.

Thesaurus

sent, sanction, warrant, warranty, charter. **4** *the army have too much licence* FREEDOM, liberty, free rein, latitude, independence, scope, impunity, carte blanche. **5** *poetic licence* DISREGARD FOR THE FACTS, inventiveness, invention, creativity, imagination, fancy, freedom, looseness. **6** *the licence of the age* LICENTIOUSNESS, dissoluteness, dissipation, debauchery, immorality, impropriety, decadence, intemperateness, excess, excessiveness, lack of restraint.
license ● verb PERMIT, allow, authorize, grant/give authority to, grant/give permission to; certify, empower, entitle, enable, give approval to, let, qualify, sanction.
– OPPOSITES ban.
licentious ● adjective DISSOLUTE, dissipated, debauched, degenerate, immoral, naughty, wanton, decadent, depraved, sinful, corrupt; lustful, lecherous, lascivious, libidinous, prurient, lubricious, lewd, promiscuous, lickerish; *formal* concupiscent.
– OPPOSITES moral.
licit ● adjective LEGITIMATE, permissible, admissible, allowable; permitted, allowed, sanctioned, authorized, warranted; lawful, legal, statutory, legalized, licensed; *informal* legit.
– OPPOSITES forbidden.
lick ● verb **1** *the spaniel licked his face* pass one's tongue over, touch with one's tongue, tongue; lap, slurp. **2** *flames licking round the coal* FLICKER, play, flit, dance. **3** *(informal) they licked the home side 3-0.* See DEFEAT verb sense 1. **4** *(informal) the government have inflation licked* OVERCOME, get the better of, find an answer/solution to, conquer, beat, control, master, curb, check.
● noun *(informal)* **1** *a lick of paint* DAB, bit, drop, dash, spot, touch, splash; *informal* smidgen. **2** *they ran up at a fair lick* SPEED, rate, pace, tempo; *informal* clip.
licking ● noun *(informal)* **1** *Arsenal took a licking* DEFEAT, beating, trouncing, thrashing; *informal* hiding, pasting, hammering, drubbing; *N. Amer. informal* shellacking. **2** *Ray got the worst licking of his life* THRASHING, beating, flogging, whipping; *informal* walloping, hiding, pasting, lathering; *N. Amer. informal* whaling.
lid ● noun *the lid of a saucepan* COVER, top, cap, covering.
– PHRASES **put a/the lid on** *(informal)* STOP, control, end, put an end/stop to, put paid to. **lift the lid off/on** *(informal)* EXPOSE, reveal, make known, make public, bring into the open, disclose, divulge; *informal* spill the beans, blow the gaff, blab.
lie[1] ● noun *loyalty had made him tell lies* UNTRUTH, falsehood, fib, fabrication, deception, invention, (piece of) fiction, falsification; (little) white lie, half-truth, exaggeration; *informal* tall story, whopper; *Brit. informal* porky (pie).
– RELATED TERMS mendacious.
– OPPOSITES truth.
● verb *he had lied to the police* TELL AN UNTRUTH/LIE, fib, dissemble, dissimulate, tell a white lie, perjure oneself, commit perjury; *informal* lie through one's teeth; *formal* forswear oneself.
– PHRASES **give the lie to** DISPROVE, contradict, negate, deny, refute, rebut, controvert, belie, invalidate, discredit, debunk; challenge, call into question; *informal* shoot full of holes, shoot down (in flames); *formal* confute, gainsay.
lie[2] ● verb **1** *he was lying on a bed* RECLINE, lie down/back, be recumbent, be prostrate, be supine, be prone, be stretched out, sprawl, rest, repose, lounge, loll. **2** *her handbag lay on a chair* BE PLACED, be situated, be positioned, rest. **3** *lying on the border of Switzerland and Austria* BE SITUATED, be located, be placed, be found, be sited. **4** *his body lies in a crypt* BE BURIED, be interred, be laid to rest, rest, be entombed. **5** *the difficulty lies in building real quality into the products* CONSIST, be inherent, be present, be contained, exist, reside.
– OPPOSITES stand.
– PHRASES **lie heavy on** TROUBLE, worry, bother, torment, oppress, nag, prey on one's mind, plague, niggle at, gnaw at, haunt; *informal*

liege /leej/ historical • **adjective** referring to the relationship between a feudal superior and a vassal. • **noun 1** (also **liege lord**) a feudal superior or sovereign. **2** a vassal or subject.
– ORIGIN Old French, from Latin *laeticus*.
lie-in • **noun** chiefly Brit. a prolonged stay in bed in the morning.
lien /leeən/ • **noun** Law a right to keep the property of another person until a debt owed by that person is discharged.
– ORIGIN Old French *loien*, from Latin *ligamen* 'bond'.
lierne /leeern/ • **noun** Architecture a short rib connecting the bosses and intersections of the principal ribs of a vault.
– ORIGIN French, perhaps from dialect *lierne* 'clematis'.
lieu /lyo͞o/ • **noun** (in phrase **in lieu** or **in lieu of**) instead (of).
– ORIGIN French, from Latin *locus* 'place'.
lieutenant /leftennənt/ • **noun 1** a deputy or substitute acting for a superior. **2** a rank of officer in the British army, above second lieutenant and below captain. **3** a rank of officer in the navy, above sub lieutenant and below lieutenant commander.
– DERIVATIVES **lieutenancy** noun (pl. **lieutenancies**).
– ORIGIN Old French, 'place-holding' (see LIEU, TENANT).
lieutenant colonel • **noun** a rank of officer in the army and the US air force, above major and below colonel.
lieutenant commander • **noun** a rank of officer in the navy, above lieutenant and below commander.
lieutenant general • **noun** a high rank of officer in the army, above major general and below general.
life • **noun** (pl. **lives**) **1** the condition that distinguishes animals and plants from inorganic matter, including the capacity for growth and functional activity. **2** the existence of an individual human being or animal. **3** a particular type or aspect of people's existence: *school life*. **4** living things and their activity. **5** a biography. **6** vitality, vigour, or energy. **7** informal a sentence of imprisonment for life. **8** (in various games) each of a specified number of chances each player has before being put out. **9** (before a noun) (in art) based on a living rather than an imagined form: *a life drawing*.
– PHRASES **for the life of me** informal however hard I try. **as large as** (or **larger than**) **life** informal conspicuously present. **not on your life** informal emphatically not. **take one's life in one's hands** risk being killed.
– ORIGIN Old English, related to LIVE[1].
life assurance • **noun** chiefly Brit. another term for LIFE INSURANCE.
lifebelt • **noun** chiefly Brit. a ring of buoyant or inflatable material used to help a person who has fallen into water to stay afloat.
lifeblood • **noun 1** literary blood, as being necessary to life. **2** an indispensable factor or force giving something its vitality.
lifeboat • **noun 1** a specially constructed boat launched from land to rescue people in distress at sea. **2** a small boat kept on a ship for use in an emergency.
lifebuoy • **noun** chiefly Brit. a buoyant support such as a lifebelt for keeping a person afloat in water.
life cycle • **noun** the series of changes in the life of an organism including reproduction.
life expectancy • **noun** the period that a person may expect to live.
life force • **noun** the force that gives something its life, vitality, or strength.
life form • **noun** any living thing.
lifeguard • **noun** a person employed to rescue bathers who get into difficulty at a beach or swimming pool.
Life Guards • **plural noun** (in the UK) a regiment of the Household Cavalry.
life imprisonment • **noun** a long term of imprisonment (rarely the whole of a person's life), which (in the UK) is now the only sentence for murder and the maximum for any crime.
life insurance • **noun** insurance that pays out a sum of money either on the death of the insured person or after a set period.
life jacket • **noun** a sleeveless buoyant or inflatable jacket for keeping a person afloat in water.
lifeless • **adjective 1** dead or apparently dead. **2** devoid of living things. **3** lacking vigour, vitality, or excitement.
– DERIVATIVES **lifelessly** adverb **lifelessness** noun.
lifelike • **adjective** accurate in its representation of a living person or thing.
lifeline • **noun 1** a rope or line thrown to rescue someone in difficulties in water or used by sailors to secure themselves to a boat. **2** a thing which is essential for the continued existence of someone or something or which provides a means of escape. **3** (in palmistry) a line on the palm of a person's hand, regarded as indicating how long they will live.
lifelong • **adjective** lasting or remaining in a particular state throughout a person's life.
life peer (or **peeress**) • **noun** (in the UK) a peer (or peeress) whose title cannot be inherited.
life preserver • **noun** a life jacket or lifebelt.
lifer • **noun** informal a person serving a life sentence.
life raft • **noun** an inflatable raft for use in an emergency at sea.
lifesaver • **noun 1** informal a thing that saves one from serious difficulty. **2** Austral./NZ a lifeguard on a beach.
life sciences • **plural noun** the sciences concerned with the study of living organisms, including biology, botany, and zoology.
life sentence • **noun** a punishment of life imprisonment.
lifespan • **noun** the length of time for which a person or animal lives or a thing functions.
lifestyle • **noun** the way in which one lives.
life support • **noun** Medicine maintenance of vital functions fol-

Thesaurus

bug. **lie low** HIDE (OUT), go into hiding, conceal oneself, keep out of sight, go to earth/ground; *informal* hole up; *Brit. informal, dated* lie doggo.
liege • **noun** (LIEGE) LORD, feudal lord, overlord, master, chief, superior, baron, monarch, sovereign; *historical* suzerain, seigneur.
lieutenant • **noun** DEPUTY, second in command, right-hand man/woman, number two, assistant, aide; *informal* sidekick.
life • **noun 1** *the joy of giving life to a child* EXISTENCE, being, living, animation; sentience, creation, viability. **2** *threats to life on the planet* LIVING BEINGS/CREATURES, the living; human/animal/plant life, fauna, flora, ecosystems; human beings, humanity, humankind, mankind, man. **3** *an easy life* WAY OF LIFE/LIVING, lifestyle, situation, fate, lot. **4** *the last nine months of his life* LIFETIME, life span, days, time on earth, existence. **5** *the life of a Parliament* DURATION, lifetime, existence. **6** *he is full of life* VIVACITY, animation, liveliness, vitality, verve, high spirits, exuberance, zest, buoyancy, enthusiasm, energy, vigour, dynamism, elan, gusto, brio, bounce, spirit, fire; (hustle and) bustle, movement; *informal* oomph, pizzazz, pep, zing, zip, vim. **7** *the life of the party* MOVING SPIRIT, (vital) spirit, life force, lifeblood, heart, soul. **8** *more than 1,500 lives were lost in the accident* PERSON, human being, individual, soul. **9** *a life of Chopin* BIOGRAPHY, autobiography, life story/history, profile, chronicle, account, portrait; *informal* biog, bio. **10** *I'll miss you, but that's life* THE WAY OF THE WORLD, the way things go, the human condition; fate, destiny, providence, kismet, karma, fortune, luck, chance; *informal* the way the cookie crumbles.
– RELATED TERMS animate, bio-.
– OPPOSITES death.
– PHRASES **come to life 1** *the sounds of a barracks coming to life* BECOME ACTIVE, come alive, wake up, awaken, arouse, rouse, stir; *poetic/literary* waken. **2** *the carved angel suddenly came to life* BECOME ANIMATE, come alive. **for dear life** DESPERATELY, with all one's might, with might and main, for all one is worth, as fast/hard as possible, like the devil. **give one's life 1** *he would give his life for her* DIE (TO SAVE), lay down one's life, sacrifice oneself, offer one's life. **2** *he gave his life to the company* DEDICATE ONESELF, devote oneself, give oneself, surrender oneself.
life-and-death • **adjective** VITAL, of vital importance, crucial, critical, urgent, pivotal, momentous, important, key, serious, grave, significant; *informal* earth-shattering; *formal* of great moment.
– OPPOSITES trivial.
lifeblood • **noun** LIFE (FORCE), essential constituent, driving force, vital spark, inspiration, stimulus, essence, crux, heart, soul, core.
life-giving • **adjective** VITALIZING, animating, energizing, invigorating, stimulating; life-preserving, life-sustaining.
lifeless • **adjective 1** *a lifeless body* DEAD, departed, perished, gone, no more, passed on/away, stiff, cold, (as) dead as a doornail; *formal* deceased. **2** *a lifeless rag doll* INANIMATE, without life, inert, insentient. **3** *a lifeless landscape* BARREN, sterile, bare, desolate, stark, arid, infertile, uncultivated, uninhabited; bleak, colourless, characterless, soulless. **4** *a lifeless performance* LACKLUSTRE, spiritless, apathetic, torpid, lethargic; dull, monotonous, boring, tedious, dreary, unexciting, expressionless, emotionless, colourless, characterless. **5** *lifeless hair* LANK, lustreless.
– OPPOSITES alive, animate, lively.
lifelike • **adjective** REALISTIC, true to life, representational, faithful, exact, precise, detailed, vivid, graphic, natural, naturalistic.
– OPPOSITES unrealistic.

lowing disablement or in an adverse environment.

life-threatening ● adjective potentially fatal.

lifetime ● noun **1** the duration of a person's life. **2** the duration of a thing or its usefulness.

lift ● verb **1** raise or be raised to a higher position or level. **2** pick up and move to a different position. **3** formally remove or end (a legal restriction, decision, etc.). **4** (**lift off**) (of an aircraft, spacecraft, etc.) take off, especially vertically. **5** carry off or win (a prize or event). **6** informal steal. ● noun **1** Brit. a platform or compartment housed in a shaft for raising and lowering people or things. **2** an act or instance of lifting. **3** a free ride in another person's vehicle. **4** a device for carrying people up or down a mountain. **5** a feeling of increased cheerfulness. **6** upward force exerted by the air on an aerofoil or other structure.
– PHRASES **lift a finger** (or **hand**) make the slightest effort: *he wouldn't lift a finger to help.*
– DERIVATIVES **liftable** adjective **lifter** noun.
– ORIGIN Old Norse, related to LOFT.

lift-off ● noun the vertical take-off of a spacecraft, rocket, etc.

lig Brit. informal ● verb (**ligged**, **ligging**) take advantage of free parties, shows, or travel offered by companies for publicity purposes. ● noun a free party or show of this type.
– DERIVATIVES **ligger** noun.
– ORIGIN from a dialect variant of LIE[1] meaning 'lie about, loaf'.

ligament ● noun Anatomy **1** a short band of tough, flexible, fibrous tissue which connects two bones or cartilages or holds together a joint. **2** a membranous fold that supports an organ and keeps it in position.
– DERIVATIVES **ligamentous** adjective.
– ORIGIN Latin *ligamentum* 'bond', from *ligare* 'to bind'.

ligand /liggənd/ ● noun Chemistry an ion or molecule that forms a bond to a particular atom or substance.
– ORIGIN from Latin *ligandus* 'that can be tied'.

ligate /ligayt/ ● verb Surgery tie up (an artery or vessel).
– ORIGIN Latin *ligare* 'to tie'.

ligature ● noun **1** a thing used for tying something tightly. **2** a cord used in surgery, especially to tie up a bleeding artery. **3** Music a slur or tie. **4** Printing a character consisting of two or more joined letters, e.g. *æ*. ● verb bind or connect with a ligature.
– ORIGIN Latin *ligatura*, from *ligare* 'to tie'.

light[1] ● noun **1** the natural agent that stimulates sight and makes things visible; electromagnetic radiation from about 390 to 740 nm in wavelength. **2** a source of illumination. **3** a device producing a flame or spark. **4** (**lights**) traffic lights. **5** an expression in someone's eyes. **6** an area that is brighter or paler than its surroundings. **7** enlightenment. **8** (**lights**) a person's opinions, standards, and abilities. **9** a window or opening to let light in. ● verb (past **lit**; past part. **lit** or **lighted**) **1** provide with light. **2** ignite or be ignited. ● adjective **1** having a considerable or sufficient amount of light. **2** (of a colour or object) reflecting a lot of light; pale.
– PHRASES **bring** (or **come**) **to light** make (or become) widely known or evident. **in a —— light** in the way specified. **in (the) light of** taking (something) into consideration. **light at the end of the tunnel** an indication that a period of difficulty is ending. **the light of day** general public attention. **the light of someone's life** a much loved person. **light up 1** become illuminated. **2** ignite a cigarette, pipe, or cigar before smoking it. **3** make or become animated or happy. **see the light 1** understand or realize something. **2** undergo religious conversion. **throw** (or **cast** or **shed**) **light on** help to explain by providing further information.
– DERIVATIVES **lightless** adjective **lightness** noun.
– ORIGIN Old English.

light[2] ● adjective **1** of little weight. **2** deficient in weight. **3** not strongly or heavily built. **4** relatively low in density, amount, or intensity. **5** carrying or suitable for small loads. **6** gentle or delicate. **7** not profound or serious. **8** (of sleep or a sleeper) easily disturbed. **9** easily borne or done. **10** free from worry.
– PHRASES **make light of** treat as unimportant. **make light work of** accomplish quickly and easily. **travel light** travel with a minimum load or little luggage.
– DERIVATIVES **lightish** adjective **lightly** adverb **lightness** noun.
– ORIGIN Old English.

light[3] ● verb (past and past part. **lit** or **lighted**) **1** (**light on/upon**) come upon or discover by chance. **2** (**light into**) N. Amer informal criticize severely; attack.
– ORIGIN Old English, 'descend, alight'.

light box ● noun a box with a translucent top and containing an

Thesaurus

lifelong ● adjective LASTING, long-lasting, long-term, constant, stable, established, steady, enduring, permanent.
– OPPOSITES ephemeral.

lifestyle ● noun WAY OF LIFE/LIVING, life, situation, fate, lot; conduct, behaviour, customs, habits, ways, mores.

lifetime ● noun **1** *he made an exceptional contribution during his lifetime* LIFESPAN, life, days, duration of life, one's time (on earth), existence, one's career. **2** *the lifetime of workstations* DURATION, (active) life, life expectancy, functioning period, period of effectiveness/usefulness. **3** *it would take a lifetime* ALL ONE'S LIFE, a very long time, an eternity, years (on end), aeons; *informal* ages (and ages), an age.

lift ● verb **1** *lift the pack on to your back* RAISE, hoist, heave, haul up, uplift, heft, raise up/aloft, upraise, elevate, hold high; pick up, grab, take up, scoop up, snatch up; winch up, jack up, lever up; *informal* hump; *poetic/literary* upheave. **2** *the news lifted his spirits* BOOST, raise, buoy up, elevate, cheer up, perk up, uplift, brighten up, ginger up, gladden, encourage, stimulate, revive; *informal* buck up. **3** *they lift their game on big occasions* IMPROVE, boost, enhance, revitalize, upgrade, ameliorate. **4** *the fog had lifted* CLEAR, rise, disperse, dissipate, disappear, vanish, dissolve. **5** *the ban has been lifted* CANCEL, remove, withdraw, revoke, rescind, annul, void, discontinue, end, stop, terminate. **6** *lifting carrots* DIG UP, pick, pull up, root out, unearth. **7** *the RAF lifted them to safety* AIRLIFT, transport by air, fly. **8** *he lifted his voice* AMPLIFY, raise, make louder, increase. **9** *(informal) he lifted sections from a 1986 article* PLAGIARIZE, pirate, copy, reproduce, poach; *informal* crib, rip off. **10** *(informal) she lifted a wallet.* See STEAL verb sense 1.
– OPPOSITES drop, put down.
● noun **1** *Alice went up in the lift* ELEVATOR, paternoster (lift); dumb waiter. **2** *give me a lift up* PUSH, hoist, heave, thrust, shove. **3** *he gave me a lift to the airport* (CAR) RIDE, run, drive. **4** *that goal will give his confidence a real lift* BOOST, fillip, stimulus, impetus, encouragement, spur, push; improvement, enhancement; *informal* shot in the arm.
– PHRASES **lift off** TAKE OFF, become airborne, take to the air, take wing; be launched, blast off.

light[1] ● noun **1** *the light of candles* ILLUMINATION, brightness, luminescence, luminosity, shining, gleaming, gleam, brilliance, radiance, lustre, glowing, glow, blaze, glare, dazzle; sunlight, moonlight, starlight, lamplight, firelight; ray of light, beam of light; *poetic/literary* effulgence, refulgence, lambency. **2** *there was a light on in the hall* LAMP, wall light; headlight, headlamp, sidelight; street light, floodlight; lantern; torch, flashlight. **3** *have you got a light?* MATCH, (cigarette) lighter. **4** *we'll be driving in the light* DAYLIGHT (HOURS), daytime, day; natural light, sunlight. **5** *he saw the problem in a different light* ASPECT, angle, slant, approach, interpretation, viewpoint, standpoint, context, hue, complexion. **6** *light dawned on Loretta* UNDERSTANDING, enlightenment, illumination, comprehension, insight, awareness, knowledge. **7** *an eminent legal light* EXPERT, authority, master, leader, guru, leading light, luminary. **8** *he served his party loyally according to his lights* TALENT, skill, ability; intelligence, intellect, knowledge, understanding.
– RELATED TERMS photo-, lumin-.
– OPPOSITES darkness.
● verb *Alan lit a fire* SET ALIGHT, set light to, set burning, set on fire, set fire to, put/set a match to, ignite, kindle, spark (off); *archaic* enkindle.
– OPPOSITES extinguish.
● adjective **1** *a light breakfast room* BRIGHT, full of light, well lit, well illuminated, sunny. **2** *light pastel shades* LIGHT-COLOURED, light-toned, pale, pale-coloured, pastel. **3** *light hair* FAIR, light-coloured, blond(e), golden, flaxen.
– OPPOSITES dark, gloomy.
– PHRASES **bring something to light** REVEAL, disclose, expose, uncover, show up, unearth, dig up/out, bring to notice, identify, hunt out, nose out. **come to light** BE DISCOVERED, be uncovered, be unearthed, come out, become known, become apparent, appear, materialize, transpire, emerge. **in the light of** TAKING INTO CONSIDERATION/ACCOUNT, considering, bearing in mind, taking note of, in view of. **light up** *the dashboard lit up* BECOME BRIGHT, brighten, lighten, shine, gleam, flare, blaze, glint, sparkle, shimmer, glisten, scintillate. **light something up 1** *a flare lit up the night*

electric light, providing an evenly lighted flat surface for viewing transparencies.

light bulb ● noun a glass bulb containing inert gas, fitted into a lamp or ceiling socket, which provides light when an electric current is passed through it.

light-emitting diode ● noun see LED.

lighten[1] ● verb **1** make or become lighter in weight. **2** make or become less serious.

lighten[2] ● verb make or become brighter.

lighter[1] ● noun a device producing a small flame, used to light cigarettes.

lighter[2] ● noun a flat-bottomed barge used to transfer goods to and from ships in harbour.
– ORIGIN from LIGHT[2] (in the sense 'unload'), or from Low German *luchter*.

lightfast ● adjective (of a pigment) not prone to discolour when exposed to light.
– DERIVATIVES **lightfastness** noun.

light-fingered ● adjective prone to steal.

light flyweight ● noun the lowest weight in amateur boxing.

light-footed ● adjective fast, nimble, or stealthy on one's feet.

light-headed ● adjective dizzy and slightly faint.

light-hearted ● adjective amusing and entertaining.
– DERIVATIVES **light-heartedly** adverb.

light heavyweight ● noun a weight in boxing and other sports intermediate between middleweight and heavyweight.

lighthouse ● noun a tower or other structure containing a beacon light to warn ships at sea.

light industry ● noun the manufacture of small or light articles.

lighting ● noun **1** equipment for producing light. **2** the arrangement or effect of lights.

lighting-up time ● noun Brit. the time at which motorists are required by law to switch their vehicles' lights on.

light meter ● noun an instrument measuring the intensity of light, used when taking photographs.

light middleweight ● noun a weight in amateur boxing intermediate between welterweight and middleweight.

lightning ● noun **1** the occurrence of a high-voltage electrical discharge between a cloud and the ground or within a cloud, accompanied by a bright flash. **2** (before another noun) very quick: *lightning speed.*
– ORIGIN from LIGHTEN[2].

lightning conductor (also chiefly N. Amer. **lightning rod**) ● noun Brit. a metal rod or wire fixed in a high and exposed place to divert lightning into the ground.

light pen ● noun **1** Computing a hand-held pen-like photosensitive device used for passing information to a computer. **2** a hand-held device for reading bar codes.

light pollution ● noun excessive brightening of the night sky by street lights and other man-made sources.

lights ● plural noun the lungs of sheep, pigs, or bullocks as food for pets.
– ORIGIN from LIGHT[2] (so named because of their lightness).

lightship ● noun an anchored boat with a beacon light to warn ships at sea.

lightweight ● noun **1** a weight in boxing and other sports intermediate between featherweight and welterweight. **2** informal a person of little importance. ● adjective **1** of thin material or build. **2** informal having little importance.

light welterweight ● noun a weight in amateur boxing intermediate between lightweight and welterweight.

light year ● noun Astronomy a unit of distance equivalent to the distance that light travels in one year, 9.4607×10^{12} km (nearly 6 million million miles).

ligneous /ligniəss/ ● adjective consisting of or resembling wood.
– ORIGIN Latin *ligneus* 'relating to wood'.

lignin ● noun Botany a complex organic polymer deposited in the cell walls of many plants, making them rigid and woody.
– ORIGIN from Latin *lignum* 'wood'.

lignite ● noun soft brownish coal, intermediate between bituminous coal and peat.
– ORIGIN from Latin *lignum* 'wood'.

lignocaine /lignōkayn/ ● noun Medicine a synthetic compound used as a local anaesthetic and in treating abnormal heart rhythms.
– ORIGIN from Latin *lignum* 'wood' + *-caine* (from COCAINE).

likable ● adjective variant spelling of LIKEABLE.

like[1] ● preposition **1** similar to. **2** in the manner of. **3** in a way appropriate to. **4** in this manner. **5** such as. **6** used to ask about someone's or something's characteristics. ● conjunction informal **1** in the same way that. **2** as though. ● noun **1** a similar person or thing. **2** (**the like**) things of the same kind. ● adjective having similar characteristics to another. ● adverb informal used in

Thesaurus

sky MAKE BRIGHT, brighten, illuminate, lighten, throw/cast light on, shine on, irradiate; poetic/literary illumine. **2** *her enthusiasm lit up her face* ANIMATE, irradiate, brighten, cheer up, make cheerful, enliven. **throw/cast/shed light on** EXPLAIN, elucidate, clarify, clear up, interpret.

light[2] ● adjective **1** *it's light and portable* EASY TO LIFT, not heavy, lightweight; easy to carry, portable. **2** *a light cotton robe* FLIMSY, lightweight, insubstantial, thin; delicate, floaty, gauzy, gossamer, diaphanous. **3** *she is light on her feet* NIMBLE, agile, lithe, limber, lissom, graceful; light-footed, fleet-footed, quick, quick-moving, spry, sprightly; informal twinkle-toed; poetic/literary fleet, lightsome. **4** *a light soil* FRIABLE, sandy, easily dug, workable, crumbly, loose. **5** *a light dinner* SMALL, modest, simple, easily digested. **6** *light duties* EASY, simple, undemanding, untaxing; informal cushy. **7** *his eyes gleamed with light mockery* GENTLE, mild, moderate, slight; playful, light-hearted. **8** *light reading* ENTERTAINING, lightweight, diverting, undemanding, middle-of-the-road; frivolous, superficial, trivial. **9** *a light heart* CAREFREE, light-hearted, cheerful, cheery, happy, merry, jolly, blithe, bright, sunny; buoyant, bubbly, jaunty, bouncy, breezy, optimistic, positive, upbeat, ebullient; dated gay. **10** *this is no light matter* UNIMPORTANT, insignificant, trivial, trifling, petty, inconsequential, superficial. **11** *light footsteps* GENTLE, delicate, soft, dainty; faint, indistinct. **12** *her head felt light* DIZZY, giddy, light-headed, faint, vertiginous; informal woozy. **13** (archaic) *light women* PROMISCUOUS, loose, wanton.
– OPPOSITES heavy.

light[3] ● verb
– PHRASES **light into** (N. Amer. informal) **1** *we started lighting into our attackers.* See SET ON at SET[1]. **2** *my father lit into me for being late.* See SCOLD verb. **light on/upon** COME ACROSS, chance on, hit on, happen on, stumble on/across, blunder on, find, discover, uncover, come up with.

lighten[1] ● verb **1** *the sky was beginning to lighten* BECOME/GROW LIGHTER, brighten. **2** *the first touch of dawn lightened the sky* MAKE LIGHTER, make brighter, brighten, light up, illuminate, throw/cast light on, shine on, irradiate; poetic/literary illumine. **3** *he used lemon juice to lighten his hair* WHITEN, make whiter, bleach, blanch, make paler; fade, wash out, decolorize.
– OPPOSITES darken.

lighten[2] ● verb **1** *lightening the burden of taxation* MAKE LIGHTER, lessen, reduce, decrease, diminish, ease; alleviate, mitigate, allay, relieve, palliate, assuage. **2** *an attempt to lighten her spirits* CHEER (UP), brighten, gladden, hearten, perk up, lift, ginger up, enliven, boost, buoy (up), uplift, revive, restore, revitalize.
– OPPOSITES increase, depress.

light-fingered ● adjective THIEVING, stealing, pilfering, shoplifting, dishonest; informal crooked, sticky-fingered.
– OPPOSITES honest.

light-footed ● adjective NIMBLE, light on one's feet, agile, graceful, lithe, spry, sprightly, limber, lissom; swift, fast, quick, quick-moving, fleet-footed; informal twinkle-toed; poetic/literary fleet.
– OPPOSITES clumsy.

light-headed ● adjective DIZZY, giddy, faint, light in the head, muzzy, vertiginous; informal woozy.

light-hearted ● adjective CAREFREE, cheerful, cheery, happy, merry, glad, playful, jolly, jovial, joyful, gleeful, ebullient, high-spirited, lively, blithe, bright, sunny, buoyant, vivacious, bubbly, jaunty, bouncy, breezy; entertaining, amusing, diverting; informal chirpy, upbeat; dated gay.
– OPPOSITES miserable.

lightly ● adverb **1** *Maisie kissed him lightly on the cheek* SOFTLY, gently, faintly, delicately. **2** *season very lightly* SPARINGLY, slightly, sparsely, moderately, delicately. **3** *he has got off lightly* WITHOUT SEVERE PUNISHMENT, easily, leniently, mildly. **4** *her views are not to be dismissed lightly* CARELESSLY, airily, heedlessly, without consideration, uncaringly, indifferently, unthinkingly, thoughtlessly, flippantly, breezily, frivolously.
– OPPOSITES hard, heavily.

lightweight ● adjective **1** *a lightweight jacket* THIN, light, flimsy, insubstantial; summery. **2** *lightweight entertainment* TRIVIAL, in-

speech as a meaningless filler.
– PHRASES **and the like** et cetera. **(as) like as not** probably. **like so** informal in this manner.
– USAGE When writing formal English it is unacceptable to use **like** to mean 'as if', as in *he's behaving like he owns the place*, and it is better to use **as if** or **as though** instead.
– ORIGIN Old Norse; related to ALIKE.
like[2] ● verb **1** find agreeable or satisfactory. **2** wish for; want. ● noun **(likes)** the things one likes.
– ORIGIN Old English, 'be pleasing'.
-like ● combining form (added to nouns) similar to; characteristic of: *crust-like*.
likeable (also **likable**) ● adjective pleasant; easy to like.
– DERIVATIVES **likeably** adverb.
likelihood ● noun the state or fact of being likely.
likely ● adjective **(likelier, likeliest) 1** such as well might be the case; probable. **2** promising. ● adverb probably.
– PHRASES **a likely story!** used to express disbelief. **as likely as not** probably. **not likely!** informal certainly not.
– DERIVATIVES **likeliness** noun.
like-minded ● adjective having similar tastes or opinions.
liken ● verb **(liken to)** point out the resemblance of (someone or something) to.
likeness ● noun **1** resemblance. **2** outward appearance: *humans are made in God's likeness.* **3** a portrait or representation.
likewise ● adverb **1** also; moreover. **2** similarly.
– ORIGIN from the phrase *in like wise*.
liking ● noun **1** a regard or fondness for something. **2** one's taste.
likuta /likoōtə/ ● noun (pl. **makuta** /məkoōtə/) a monetary unit of Zaire (Democratic Republic of Congo), equal to one hundredth of a zaire.
– ORIGIN from a Bantu language.
lilac ● noun **1** a shrub or small tree with fragrant violet, pink, or white blossom. **2** a pale pinkish-violet colour.
– ORIGIN from Persian, 'bluish'.
lilangeni /leelanggayni/ ● noun (pl. **emalangeni** /imalanggayni/) the basic monetary unit of Swaziland, equal to 100 cents.
– ORIGIN from a Bantu prefix used to denote a singular + 'member of a royal family'.
Lilliputian /lillipyoōsh'n/ ● adjective trivial or very small. ● noun a Lilliputian person or thing.
– ORIGIN from the imaginary country of *Lilliput* in Jonathan Swift's *Gulliver's Travels* (1726), inhabited by 6-inch high people.
lilo (also trademark **Li-lo**) ● noun (pl. **lilos**) an inflatable mattress used as a bed or for floating on water.
– ORIGIN alteration of *lie low*.
lilt ● noun **1** a characteristic rising and falling of the voice when speaking. **2** a gentle rhythm in a tune. ● verb speak, sing, or sound with a lilt.
– ORIGIN from obsolete *lulte* 'sound (an alarm)' or 'lift up (the voice)'; of unknown origin.
lily ● noun a bulbous plant with large trumpet-shaped flowers on a tall, slender stem.
– ORIGIN Greek *leirion*.
lily-livered ● adjective cowardly.
lily of the valley ● noun a plant of the lily family, with broad leaves and small white bell-shaped flowers.
lily pad ● noun a leaf of a water lily.
lily-white ● adjective **1** pure white. **2** totally innocent or pure.
lima bean /leemə/ ● noun an edible flat whitish bean.
– ORIGIN from *Lima*, the capital of Peru.
limb[1] ● noun **1** an arm, leg, or wing. **2** a large branch of a tree. **3** a projecting part of a structure, object, or natural feature.
– PHRASES **life and limb** life and bodily faculties. **out on a limb** isolated.
– DERIVATIVES **limbed** adjective **limbless** adjective.
– ORIGIN Old English.
limb[2] ● noun Astronomy a specified edge of the disc of the sun, moon, or other celestial object.
– ORIGIN Latin *limbus* 'hem, border'.
limber[1] ● adjective supple; flexible. ● verb **(limber up)** warm up in preparation for exercise or activity.
– ORIGIN perhaps from LIMBER[2] in the dialect sense 'cart shaft', with allusion to the to-and-fro motion.
limber[2] ● noun the detachable front part of a gun carriage. ● verb attach a limber to (a gun).

l

Thesaurus

substantial, superficial, shallow, unintellectual, undemanding, frivolous; of little merit/value.
– OPPOSITES heavy.
like[1] ● verb **1** *I rather like Colonel Maitland* BE FOND OF, be attached to, have a soft spot for, have a liking for, have regard for, think well of, admire, respect, esteem; be attracted to, fancy, find attractive, be keen on, be taken with; *informal* take a shine to, rate. **2** *Maisie likes veal | she likes gardening* ENJOY, have a taste for, have a preference for, have a liking for, be partial to, find/take pleasure in, be keen on, find agreeable, have a penchant/passion for, find enjoyable; appreciate, love, adore, relish; *informal* have a thing about, be into, be mad about/for, be hooked on, go a bundle on. **3** *feel free to say what you like* CHOOSE, please, wish, want, see/think fit, care to, will. **4** *how would she like it if someone did that to her?* FEEL ABOUT, regard, think about, consider.
– OPPOSITES hate.
like[2] ● preposition **1** *you're just like a teacher* SIMILAR TO, the same as, identical to. **2** *the figure landed like a cat* IN THE SAME WAY/MANNER AS, in the manner of, in a similar way to. **3** *cities like Birmingham* SUCH AS, for example, for instance; in particular, namely, viz. **4** *Richard sounded mean, which isn't like him* CHARACTERISTIC OF, typical of, in character with.
– RELATED TERMS -esque, -ish.
● noun *we shan't see his like again* EQUAL, match, equivalent, counterpart, twin, parallel; *formal* compeer.
● adjective *a like situation* SIMILAR, much the same, comparable, corresponding, resembling, alike, analogous, parallel, equivalent, cognate, related, kindred; identical, same, matching.
– OPPOSITES dissimilar.
likeable ● adjective PLEASANT, nice, friendly, agreeable, affable, amiable, genial, personable, charming, popular, good-natured, engaging, appealing, endearing, convivial, congenial, winning, delightful, enchanting, lovable, adorable, sweet; *informal* darling, lovely.
– OPPOSITES unpleasant.
likelihood ● noun PROBABILITY, chance, prospect, possibility, likeliness, odds, feasibility; risk, threat, danger; hope, promise.
likely ● adjective **1** *it seemed likely that a scandal would break* PROBABLE, (distinctly) possible, to be expected, odds-on, plausible, imaginable; expected, anticipated, predictable, predicted, foreseeable; *informal* on the cards. **2** *a likely explanation* PLAUSIBLE, reasonable, feasible, acceptable, believable, credible, tenable, conceivable. **3** *a likely story!* UNLIKELY, implausible, unbelievable, incredible, untenable, unacceptable, inconceivable. **4** *a likely-looking place* SUITABLE, appropriate, apposite, fit, fitting, acceptable, right; promising, hopeful. **5** *a likely lad* PROMISING, talented, gifted; *informal* up-and-coming.
– OPPOSITES improbable, unbelievable.
● adverb *he was most likely dead* PROBABLY, in all probability, presumably, no doubt, doubtlessly; *informal* (as) like as not.
liken ● verb COMPARE, equate, draw an analogy between, draw a parallel between; link, associate, bracket together.
– OPPOSITES contrast.
likeness ● noun **1** *her likeness to Anne is quite uncanny* RESEMBLANCE, similarity, correspondence, analogy, uniformity, conformity. **2** *the likeness of a naked woman* SEMBLANCE, guise, appearance, (outward) form, shape, image. **3** *a likeness of the last president* REPRESENTATION, image, depiction, portrayal; picture, drawing, sketch, painting, portrait, photograph, study; statue, sculpture.
– OPPOSITES dissimilarity.
likewise ● adverb **1** *an ambush was out of the question, likewise poison* ALSO, in addition, too, as well, to boot; besides, moreover, furthermore. **2** *encourage your family and friends to do likewise* THE SAME, similarly, correspondingly, in the same way, in similar fashion.
liking ● noun FONDNESS, love, affection, penchant, attachment; enjoyment, appreciation, taste, passion; preference, partiality, predilection; desire, fancy, inclination.
lilt ● noun CADENCE, rise and fall, inflection, intonation, rhythm, swing, beat, pulse, tempo.
limb ● noun **1** *his sore limbs* ARM, LEG, appendage; *archaic* member. **2** *the limbs of the tree* BRANCH, bough. **3** *local job centres act as limbs of the Ministry* SECTION, branch, offshoot, arm, wing, subdivision, department, division.
– PHRASES **out on a limb 1** *the portrayal of Scotland as being out on a limb* ISOLATED, segregated, set apart, separate, cut off, solitary.

– ORIGIN apparently related to Latin *limonarius*, from *limo* 'shaft'.

limbic system ● noun a complex system of nerves and networks in the brain, controlling the basic emotions and drives.
– ORIGIN from Latin *limbus* 'edge, border'.

limbo[1] ● noun 1 (in some Christian beliefs) the supposed abode of the souls of unbaptized infants, and of the just who died before Christ. 2 an uncertain period of awaiting a decision or resolution.
– ORIGIN from Latin *limbus* 'hem, border, limbo'.

limbo[2] ● noun (pl. **limbos**) a West Indian dance in which the dancer bends backwards to pass under a horizontal bar which is progressively lowered toward the ground. ● verb dance the limbo.
– ORIGIN from LIMBER[1].

lime[1] ● noun 1 quicklime, slaked lime, or any salt or alkali containing calcium. 2 archaic birdlime. ● verb treat with lime.
– DERIVATIVES **limy** adjective.
– ORIGIN Old English, related to LOAM.

lime[2] ● noun 1 a rounded green citrus fruit similar to a lemon. 2 a bright light green colour. 3 a drink made from lime juice.
– ORIGIN French, from Arabic.

lime[3] (also **lime tree**) ● noun a deciduous tree with heart-shaped leaves and yellowish blossom.
– ORIGIN Old English.

limeade ● noun a drink made from lime juice sweetened with sugar.

limekiln ● noun a kiln in which quicklime is produced.

limelight ● noun 1 (**the limelight**) the focus of public attention. 2 an intense white light produced by heating lime in an oxyhydrogen flame, formerly used in theatres.

limerick ● noun a humorous five-line poem with a rhyme scheme *aabba*.
– ORIGIN said to be from the chorus 'will you come up to Limerick?', sung between improvised verses at a gathering.

limestone ● noun a hard sedimentary rock composed mainly of calcium carbonate.

limewash ● noun a mixture of lime and water for coating walls.

Limey ● noun (pl. **Limeys**) N. Amer. & Austral. informal, chiefly derogatory a British person.
– ORIGIN from the former enforced consumption of lime juice in the British navy.

liminal /limmin'l/ ● adjective technical 1 relating to a transitional or initial stage. 2 at a boundary or threshold.
– DERIVATIVES **liminality** noun.
– ORIGIN from Latin *limen* 'threshold'.

limit ● noun 1 a point beyond which something does not or may not pass. 2 a restriction on the size or amount of something. 3 the furthest extent of one's endurance. ● verb (**limited, limiting**) set or serve as a limit to.
– PHRASES **be the limit** informal be intolerable. **off limits** out of bounds. **within limits** up to a point.
– DERIVATIVES **limiter** noun **limitless** adjective.
– ORIGIN Latin *limes* 'boundary, frontier'.

limitation ● noun 1 a restriction. 2 a defect or failing. 3 (also **limitation period**) Law a legally specified period beyond which an action may be defeated or a property right is not to continue.

limited ● adjective 1 restricted in size, amount, or extent. 2 not great in ability. 3 (of a monarchy or government) exercised under limitations of power prescribed by a constitution. 4 (**Limited**) Brit. denoting a limited company.

limited company ● noun Brit. a private company whose owners are legally responsible for its debts only to the extent of the amount of capital they invested.

limited liability ● noun Brit. the condition of being legally responsible for the debts of a company only to the extent of the nominal value of one's shares.

limn /lim/ ● verb literary depict or describe in painting or words.
– DERIVATIVES **limner** noun.
– ORIGIN originally in the sense 'illuminate a manuscript': from Latin *luminare* 'make light'.

limo ● noun (pl. **limos**) informal a limousine.

limonene ● noun Chemistry a colourless liquid hydrocarbon with a lemon-like scent, present in lemon oil, orange oil, etc.
– ORIGIN from German *Limone* 'lemon'.

Limousin /limoozan/ ● noun a French breed of beef cattle.
– ORIGIN named after *Limousin*, a region of central France.

limousine ● noun a large, luxurious car.
– ORIGIN French, originally denoting a caped cloak worn in the region of *Limousin*; the car originally had an outside driving seat and an enclosed passenger compartment that was likened to the cloak.

limp[1] ● verb 1 walk with difficulty because of an injured leg or foot. 2 (of a damaged ship or aircraft) proceed with difficulty. ● noun a limping gait.
– ORIGIN related to obsolete *limphalt* 'lame'.

limp[2] ● adjective 1 not stiff or firm. 2 without energy or will.
– DERIVATIVES **limply** adverb **limpness** noun.
– ORIGIN perhaps related to LIMP[1].

limpet ● noun a marine mollusc with a shallow conical shell and a muscular foot for clinging tightly to rocks.
– ORIGIN Latin *lampreda* 'limpet, lamprey'.

limpet mine ● noun a mine that attaches magnetically to a ship's hull and explodes after a certain time.

limpid ● adjective 1 (of a liquid or the eyes) clear. 2 (especially of writing or music) clear or melodious.
– DERIVATIVES **limpidity** noun **limpidly** adverb.
– ORIGIN Latin *limpidus*.

Thesaurus

2 *the government would not go out on a limb* IN A PRECARIOUS POSITION, vulnerable; *informal* sticking one's neck out.

limber ● adjective *I have to practise to keep myself limber* LITHE, supple, nimble, lissom, flexible, fit, agile, acrobatic, loose-jointed, loose-limbed.
– OPPOSITES stiff.
– PHRASES **limber up** WARM UP, loosen up, get into condition, get into shape, practise, train, stretch.

limbo ● noun *unbaptized infants are thought to live in limbo* non-existence, void, oblivion.
– PHRASES **in limbo** IN ABEYANCE, unattended to, unfinished; suspended, deferred, postponed, put off, pending, on ice, in cold storage; unresolved, undetermined, up in the air; *informal* on the back burner, on hold.

limelight ● noun THE FOCUS OF ATTENTION, public attention/interest, media attention, the public eye, the glare of publicity, prominence, the spotlight.
– OPPOSITES obscurity.

limit ● noun 1 *the city limits* BOUNDARY (LINE), border, bound, partition line, frontier, edge, demarcation line; perimeter, outside, outline, confine, periphery, margin, rim. 2 *a limit of 4,500 supporters* MAXIMUM, ceiling, limitation, upper limit; restriction, check, control, restraint. 3 *resources are stretched to the limit* UTMOST, breaking point, greatest extent. 4 *(informal) that really is the limit!* THE LAST STRAW, (more than) enough; *informal* the end, it.
● verb *the pressure to limit costs* RESTRICT, curb, cap, (hold in) check, restrain, put a brake on, freeze, peg; regulate, control, govern, delimit.

limitation ● noun 1 *a limitation on the number of newcomers* RESTRICTION, curb, restraint, control, check; impediment, obstacle, obstruction, bar, barrier, block, deterrent. 2 *he is aware of his own limitations* IMPERFECTION, flaw, defect, failing, shortcoming, weak point, deficiency, failure, frailty, weakness, foible.
– OPPOSITES increase, strength.

limited ● adjective 1 *limited resources* RESTRICTED, finite, little, tight, slight, in short supply, short; meagre, scanty, sparse, insubstantial, deficient, inadequate, insufficient, paltry, poor, minimal. 2 *the limited powers of the council* RESTRICTED, curbed, checked, controlled, restrained, delimited, qualified.
– OPPOSITES ample, boundless.

limitless ● adjective BOUNDLESS, unbounded, unlimited, illimitable; infinite, endless, never-ending, unending, everlasting, untold, immeasurable, bottomless, fathomless; unceasing, interminable, inexhaustible, constant, perpetual.

limp[1] ● verb *she limped out of the house* HOBBLE, walk with a limp, walk lamely/unevenly, walk haltingly, falter.
● noun *walking with a limp* LAMENESS, hobble, uneven gait; *Medicine* claudication.

limp[2] ● adjective 1 *a limp handshake* SOFT, flaccid, loose, slack, lax; floppy, drooping, droopy, sagging. 2 *we were all limp with exhaustion* TIRED, fatigued, weary, exhausted, worn out; lethargic, listless, spiritless, weak. 3 *a limp and lacklustre speech* UNINSPIRED, uninspiring, insipid, flat, lifeless, vapid.
– OPPOSITES firm, energetic.

limpid ● adjective 1 *a limpid pool* CLEAR, transparent, glassy, crystal clear, crystalline, translucent, pellucid, unclouded. 2 *his lim-*

limp-wristed ● adjective informal effeminate.
linage ● noun the number of lines in printed or written matter.
linchpin (also **lynchpin**) ● noun **1** a pin through the end of an axle keeping a wheel in position. **2** an indispensable person or thing.
– ORIGIN Old English.
Lincs. ● abbreviation Lincolnshire.
linctus ● noun Brit. thick liquid medicine, especially cough mixture.
– ORIGIN Latin, from *lingere* 'to lick'.
lindane ● noun a synthetic insecticide, now restricted in use owing to its persistence in the environment.
– ORIGIN named after the 20th-century Dutch chemist Teunis van der *Linden*.
linden ● noun a lime tree.
– ORIGIN originally in the sense 'made of wood from the lime tree': from Old English.
line[1] ● noun **1** a long, narrow mark or band. **2** a length of cord, wire, etc. serving a purpose. **3** a row or connected series of people or things. **4** a row of written or printed words. **5** a direction, course, or channel. **6** a telephone connection. **7** a railway track or route. **8** a notional limit or boundary. **9** a connected series of military defences facing an enemy force. **10** an arrangement of soldiers or ships in a column or line formation. **11** a wrinkle in the skin. **12** a contour or outline considered as a feature of design or composition. **13** a range of commercial goods. **14** a sphere of activity. **15** (**lines**) a way of doing something: *thinking along the same lines.* **16** (**lines**) the words of an actor's part. **17** (**lines**) a number of repetitions of a sentence written out as a school punishment. ● verb **1** stand or be positioned at intervals along. **2** (**line up**) arrange in a row. **3** (**line up**) have (someone or something) prepared. **4** (**lined**) marked or covered with lines.
– PHRASES **come** (or **bring**) **into line** conform (or cause to conform). **the end of the line** the point at which one can go no further. **hold the line** not yield to pressure. **in line** under control. **in line for** likely to receive. **in** (or **out of**) **line with** in (or not in) alignment or accordance with. **lay** (or **put**) **it on the line** speak frankly. **line of fire** the expected path of gunfire or a missile. **on the line** at serious risk. **out of line** informal behaving inappropriately or incorrectly.
– ORIGIN Old English, from Latin *linum* 'flax'; later influenced by Old French *ligne*, from Latin *linea*.
line[2] ● verb cover the inner surface of (something) with a layer of different material.
– PHRASES **line one's pocket** informal make money, especially by dishonest means.
– ORIGIN from obsolete *line* 'flax', with reference to the use of linen for linings.
lineage /linni-ij/ ● noun **1** ancestry or pedigree. **2** Biology a sequence of species each of which is considered to have evolved from its predecessor.
lineal /linniəl/ ● adjective **1** in a direct line of descent or ancestry. **2** linear.
– DERIVATIVES **lineally** adverb.
lineament /linniəmənt/ ● noun **1** literary a distinctive feature, especially of the face. **2** Geology a linear feature on the earth's surface.
– ORIGIN Latin *lineamentum*, from *linea* 'a line'.
linear /linniər/ ● adjective **1** arranged in or extending along a straight line. **2** consisting of lines or outlines. **3** involving one dimension only. **4** sequential. **5** Mathematics able to be represented by a straight line on a graph.
– DERIVATIVES **linearity** noun **linearize** (also **linearise**) verb **linearly** adverb.
linear equation ● noun an equation between two variables that gives a straight line when plotted on a graph.
lineation /linniayshən/ ● noun **1** a line or linear marking. **2** the action of drawing lines or marking with lines.
line dancing ● noun a type of country and western dancing in which a line of dancers follow a choreographed pattern of steps.
– DERIVATIVES **line-dance** verb **line dancer** noun.
line drawing ● noun a drawing based on the use of line rather than shading.
lineman ● noun **1** a person who lays and maintains railway tracks. **2** North American term for LINESMAN (in sense 2).
line manager ● noun chiefly Brit. a manager to whom an employee is directly responsible.
– DERIVATIVES **line management** noun.
linen ● noun **1** cloth woven from flax. **2** articles such as sheets or clothes made, or originally made, of linen.

Thesaurus

pid writing LUCID, clear, plain, understandable, intelligible, comprehensible, coherent, explicit, unambiguous, simple, vivid, sharp, crystal clear; *formal* perspicuous.
– OPPOSITES opaque.
line[1] ● noun **1** *he drew a line through the name* dash, rule, bar, score; underline, underscore, stroke, slash, solidus; stripe, strip, band, belt; *technical* stria, striation; *Brit.* oblique. **2** *there were lines round her eyes* WRINKLE, furrow, crease, crinkle, crow's foot. **3** *the classic lines of the exterior* CONTOUR, outline, configuration, shape, figure, delineation, profile. **4** *he headed the ball over the line* | *the county line* BOUNDARY (LINE), limit, border, borderline, bounding line, frontier, demarcation line, dividing line, edge, margin, perimeter. **5** *behind enemy lines* POSITION, formation, front (line); trenches. **6** *he put the washing on the line* CORD, rope, string, cable, wire, thread, twine, strand. **7** *a line of soldiers* FILE, rank, column, string, train, procession; row, queue; *Brit. informal* crocodile. **8** *a line of figures* COLUMN, row. **9** *a long line of crass decisions* SERIES, sequence, succession, chain, string, set, cycle. **10** *the line of flight of some bees* COURSE, route, track, path, way, run. **11** *they took a very tough line with the industry* | *the party line* COURSE (OF ACTION), procedure, technique, tactic, tack; policy, practice, approach, plan, programme, position, stance, philosophy. **12** *her own line of thought* COURSE, direction, drift, tack, tendency, trend. **13** *(informal) don't give me that line!* PATTER, story, piece of fiction, fabrication; *informal* spiel. **14** *he couldn't remember his lines* WORDS, part, script, speech. **15** *their line of work* (LINE OF) BUSINESS, (line of) work, field, trade, occupation, employment, profession, job, career, walk of life; specialty, forte, province, department, sphere, area (of expertise). **16** *a new line of cologne* BRAND, kind, sort, type, variety, make. **17** *a noble line* ANCESTRY, family, parentage, birth, descent, lineage, extraction, genealogy, roots, origin, background; stock, bloodline, pedigree. **18** *the opening line of the poem* SENTENCE, phrase, clause, utterance; passage, extract, quotation, quote, citation. **19** *I should drop Ralph a line* NOTE, letter, card, postcard, message, communication, missive, memorandum; correspondence, word; *informal* memo; *formal* epistle.
– RELATED TERMS linear.
● verb **1** *her face was lined with age* FURROW, wrinkle, crease, mark with lines. **2** *the driveway was lined by poplars* BORDER, edge, fringe, bound, rim.
– PHRASES **draw the line at** STOP SHORT OF, refuse to accept, baulk at; object to, take issue with, take exception to. **in line 1** *the poor stood in line for food* IN A QUEUE, in a row, in a file. **2** *the adverts are in line with the editorial style* IN AGREEMENT, in accord, in accordance, in harmony, in step, in compliance. **3** *in line with the bullseye* IN ALIGNMENT, aligned, level, at the same height; abreast, side by side. **4** *the referee kept him in line* UNDER CONTROL, in order, in check. **in line for** A CANDIDATE FOR, in the running for, on the shortlist for, being considered for. **lay it on the line** SPEAK FRANKLY/HONESTLY, pull no punches, be blunt, not mince one's words, call a spade a spade; *informal* give it to someone straight. **line up** FORM A QUEUE/LINE, get into rows/columns, queue up, fall in; *Military* dress; *Brit. informal* form a crocodile. **line someone/something up 1** *they lined them up and shot them* ARRANGE IN LINES, put in rows, arrange in columns, align, range; *Military* dress. **2** *we've lined up an all-star cast* ASSEMBLE, get together, organize, prepare, arrange, pre-arrange, fix up, lay on; book, schedule, timetable. **on the line** AT RISK, in danger, endangered, imperilled. **toe the line** CONFORM, obey/observe the rules, comply with the rules, abide by the rules.
line[2] ● verb *a cardboard box lined with a blanket* COVER, put a lining in, interline, face, back, pad.
– PHRASES **line one's pockets** *(informal)* MAKE MONEY, accept bribes, embezzle money; *informal* feather one's nest, graft, be on the make.
lineage ● noun ANCESTRY, family, parentage, birth, descent, line, extraction, derivation, genealogy, roots, origin, background; stock, bloodline, breeding, pedigree.
lineaments ● plural noun *(poetic/literary)* (DISTINCTIVE) FEATURES, distinguishing characteristics, hallmarks, properties, traits; form, outline, configuration, physiognomy.
lined[1] ● adjective **1** *lined paper* RULED, feint, striped, banded. **2** *his lined face* WRINKLED, wrinkly, furrowed, wizened.

– ORIGIN originally in the sense 'made of flax': from Old English.
linen basket ● noun chiefly Brit. a basket for soiled clothing.
line-out ● noun Rugby Union a formation of parallel lines of opposing forwards at right angles to the touchline when the ball is thrown in.
liner[1] ● noun **1** a large passenger ship. [ORIGIN because such a ship belonged to a line, or company, providing passenger ships on particular routes.] **2** a fine paintbrush. **3** a cosmetic for outlining or accentuating a facial feature.
liner[2] ● noun a lining of a garment, container, etc.
linesman ● noun **1** (in games played on a field or court) an official who assists the referee or umpire in deciding whether the ball is out of play. **2** Brit. a person who repairs and maintains telephone or electricity power lines.
line-up ● noun **1** a group of people or things assembled for a particular purpose. **2** an identity parade.
ling[1] ● noun a long-bodied edible marine fish of the cod family.
– ORIGIN probably from Dutch; related to LONG[1].
ling[2] ● noun the common heather.
– ORIGIN Old Norse.
-ling ● suffix **1** forming nouns from nouns (e.g. *hireling*, *sapling*). **2** forming nouns from adjectives and adverbs (e.g. *darling*, *underling*). **3** forming diminutive nouns (e.g. *gosling*).
– ORIGIN Old English; sense 3 from Old Norse.
lingam /linggam/ (also **linga** /linggə/) ● noun Hinduism a phallus or phallic object as a symbol of Shiva, the god of reproduction.
– ORIGIN Sanskrit, 'mark, sexual characteristic'.
lingcod /lingkod/ ● noun (pl. same) a large slender greenish-brown fish with golden spots, of the Pacific coast of North America.
linger ● verb **1** be slow or reluctant to leave. **2** (**linger over**) spend a long time over. **3** be slow to fade, disappear, or die.
– DERIVATIVES **lingerer** noun **lingering** adjective.
– ORIGIN from obsolete *leng* 'prolong', of Germanic origin and related to LONG[1].
lingerie /lanzhəri/ ● noun women's underwear and nightclothes.
– ORIGIN French, from *linge* 'linen'.
lingo ● noun (pl. **lingos** or **lingoes**) informal, often humorous **1** a foreign language. **2** the jargon of a particular subject or group.
– ORIGIN probably from Latin *lingua* 'tongue'.
lingua franca /linggwə frangkə/ ● noun (pl. **lingua francas**) a language used as a common language between speakers whose native languages are different.
– ORIGIN Italian, 'Frankish tongue', in reference to a language formerly used in the eastern Mediterranean, consisting of Italian mixed with French, Greek, Arabic, and Spanish.
lingual /linggwəl/ ● adjective technical **1** relating to the tongue. **2** relating to speech or language.
– DERIVATIVES **lingually** adverb.
– ORIGIN Latin *lingualis*, from *lingua* 'tongue, language'.
linguine /linggweenay, -ni/ ● plural noun small ribbons of pasta.
– ORIGIN Italian, 'little tongues'.
linguist ● noun **1** a person skilled in foreign languages. **2** a person who studies linguistics.
– ORIGIN from Latin *lingua* 'language'.
linguistic ● adjective relating to language or linguistics.
– DERIVATIVES **linguistically** adverb.
linguistics ● plural noun (treated as sing.) the scientific study of language and its structure.
– DERIVATIVES **linguistician** noun.

liniment ● noun an ointment rubbed on the body to relieve pain or bruising.
– ORIGIN Latin *linimentum*, from *linire* 'to smear'.
lining ● noun a layer of different material covering or attached to the inside of something.
link ● noun **1** a relationship or connection between people or things. **2** something that facilitates communication between people. **3** a means of contact or transport between two places. **4** a loop in a chain. ● verb make, form, or suggest a link with or between.
– DERIVATIVES **linker** noun.
– ORIGIN Old Norse.
linkage ● noun **1** the action of linking or the state of being linked. **2** a system of links.
linkman ● noun Brit. **1** a person serving as a connection between others. **2** a person providing continuity between items on radio or television.
links ● plural noun **1** (also **golf links**) (treated as sing. or pl.) a golf course, especially on grassland near the sea. **2** sandy ground near the sea, covered by coarse grass.
– ORIGIN Old English, 'rising ground'.
link-up ● noun **1** an instance of two or more people or things linking. **2** a connection enabling people or machines to communicate with each other.
Linnaean /lineeən/ (also **Linnean**) ● adjective relating to the Swedish botanist Linnaeus (Latinized name of Carl von Linné) (1707–78) or his use of names in the classification of animals and plants. ● noun a follower of Linnaeus.
linnet ● noun a mainly brown and grey finch with a reddish breast and forehead.
– ORIGIN Old French *linette*, from *lin* 'flax' (because the bird feeds on flaxseeds).
lino ● noun (pl. **linos**) informal, chiefly Brit. linoleum.
linocut ● noun a design carved in relief on a block of linoleum, used for printing.
linoleic acid /linnəlayik/ ● noun Chemistry a polyunsaturated fatty acid present in linseed oil and other oils and essential in the human diet.
– DERIVATIVES **linoleate** noun.
– ORIGIN from Latin *linum* 'flax'.
linoleum /linōliəm/ ● noun a material consisting of a canvas backing thickly coated with a preparation of linseed oil and powdered cork, used as a floor covering.
– ORIGIN from Latin *linum* 'flax' + *oleum* 'oil'.
linseed ● noun the seeds of the flax plant.
– ORIGIN Old English.
linseed cake ● noun pressed linseed used as cattle food.
linseed oil ● noun oil extracted from linseed, used especially in paint and varnish.
linsey-woolsey /linziwoolzi/ ● noun a strong, coarse fabric with a linen or cotton warp and a woollen weft.
– ORIGIN from *linsey*, originally denoting a coarse linen fabric (probably from *Lindsey*, a village in Suffolk) + WOOL + *-sey* as a rhyming suffix.
lint ● noun **1** short, fine fibres which separate from cloth or yarn during processing. **2** Brit. a fabric with a raised nap on one side, used for dressing wounds. **3** the fibrous material of a cotton boll.
– DERIVATIVES **linty** adjective.
– ORIGIN originally as *lynnet* 'flax prepared for spinning', perhaps

Thesaurus

– OPPOSITES plain, smooth.
lined[2] ● adjective *lined curtains* COVERED, backed, interlined; faced, padded.
liner ● noun **1** *a luxury liner* SHIP, ocean liner, passenger vessel, boat. **2** *her eyes were ringed with liner* EYELINER, eye pencil, kohl (pencil); lipliner.
line-up ● noun **1** *a star-studded line-up* LIST OF PERFORMERS, cast, bill, programme. **2** *United's line-up* LIST OF PLAYERS, team, squad, side. **3** *a long line-up of customers* QUEUE, line, row, column.
linger ● verb **1** *the crowd lingered for a long time* WAIT (AROUND), stay (put), remain; loiter, dawdle, dally, take one's time; informal stick around, hang around/round, hang on; archaic tarry. **2** *the infection can linger for many years* PERSIST, continue, remain, stay, endure, carry on, last, keep on/up.
– OPPOSITES vanish.
lingerie ● noun WOMEN'S UNDERWEAR, underclothes, underclothing, undergarments; nightwear, nightclothes; informal undies, frillies, underthings, unmentionables; Brit. informal smalls.
lingering ● adjective **1** *lingering doubts* REMAINING, surviving, persisting, abiding, nagging, niggling. **2** *a slow, lingering death* PROTRACTED, prolonged, long-drawn-out, long-lasting.
lingo ● noun (informal) **1** *I can't speak the lingo* LANGUAGE, tongue, dialect. **2** *computer lingo* JARGON, terminology, slang, argot, cant, patter, mumbo-jumbo; informal -ese, -speak, gobbledegook.
linguistic ● adjective SEMANTIC, lingual, rhetorical, verbal.
lining ● noun BACKING, interlining, facing, padding, liner.
link ● noun **1** *a chain of steel links* LOOP, ring, connection, connector, coupling, joint. **2** *the links between transport and the environment* CONNECTION, relationship, association, linkage, tie-up. **3** *their links with the labour movement* BOND, tie, attachment, connection, relationship, association, affiliation. **4** *one of the links in the organization* COMPONENT, constituent, element, part, piece.
● verb **1** *four boxes were linked together* JOIN, connect, fasten, attach, bind, unite, combine, amalgamate; clamp, secure, fix, tie,

from Old French *linette* 'linseed', from *lin* 'flax'.

lintel ● noun a horizontal support across the top of a door or window.
– DERIVATIVES **lintelled** (US **linteled**) adjective.
– ORIGIN Old French, from Latin *limen* 'threshold'.

lion ● noun (fem. **lioness**) **1** a large tawny-coloured cat of Africa and NW India, the male of which has a shaggy mane. **2** a brave, strong, or fierce person. **3** a celebrity.
– PHRASES **the lion's den** an intimidating or unpleasant place. **the lion's share** the largest part of something.
– ORIGIN Old French *liun*, from Greek *leōn*.

lion-hearted ● adjective brave and determined.

lionize (also **lionise**) ● verb treat as a celebrity.
– DERIVATIVES **lionization** noun.

lip ● noun **1** either of the two fleshy parts forming the edges of the mouth opening. **2** the edge of a hollow container or an opening. **3** informal impudent talk. **4** another term for LABIUM. ● verb (of water) lap against.
– PHRASES **bite one's lip** stifle laughter or a retort. **curl one's lip** sneer. **pass one's lips** be eaten, drunk, or spoken. **pay lip service to** express superficial or insincere respect or support for.
– DERIVATIVES **lipless** adjective **lipped** adjective.
– ORIGIN Old English.

lipa /leepə/ ● noun (pl. same or **lipas**) a monetary unit of Croatia, equal to one hundredth of a kuna.
– ORIGIN Serbo-Croat, 'lime tree'.

lipase /lippayz, lī-/ ● noun Biochemistry an enzyme secreted by the pancreas that promotes the breakdown of fats.
– ORIGIN from Greek *lipos* 'fat'.

lip gloss ● noun a glossy cosmetic applied to the lips.

lipid ● noun Chemistry any of a class of fats that are insoluble in water and include many natural oils, waxes, and steroids.
– ORIGIN from Greek *lipos* 'fat'.

lipoprotein ● noun Biochemistry a soluble protein that combines with and transports lipids in the blood.

liposome /lippəsōm, lī-/ ● noun a tiny artificial sac of insoluble fat enclosing a water droplet, used to carry drugs into the tissues.
– ORIGIN from Greek *lipos* 'fat' + *sōma* 'body'.

liposuction /lippəsuksh'n, lī-/ ● noun a technique in cosmetic surgery for removing excess fat from under the skin by suction.

lippy informal ● adjective (**lippier**, **lippiest**) impertinent. ● noun (also **lippie**) lipstick.

lip-read ● verb understand speech from observing a speaker's lip movements.
– DERIVATIVES **lip-reader** noun.

lip salve ● noun Brit. a preparation to prevent or relieve sore or chapped lips.

lipstick ● noun coloured cosmetic applied to the lips from a small solid stick.

lip-sync (also **lip-synch**) ● noun the movement of a performer's lips in synchronization with a pre-recorded soundtrack. ● verb perform (a song or speech) in this way.
– DERIVATIVES **lip-syncer** noun.

liquefy /likwifī/ (also **liquify**) ● verb (**liquifies**, **liquified**) make or become liquid.
– DERIVATIVES **liquefaction** noun **liquefactive** adjective **liquefiable** adjective **liquefier** noun.
– ORIGIN Latin *liquefacere*.

liquescent /likwess'nt/ ● adjective becoming or apt to become liquid.

liqueur /likyoor/ ● noun a strong, sweet flavoured alcoholic spirit.
– ORIGIN French.

liquid ● noun a substance with a consistency like that of water or oil, i.e. flowing freely but of constant volume. ● adjective **1** relating to or being a liquid. **2** clear, like water. **3** (of a sound) pure and flowing. **4** not fixed or stable. **5** (of assets) held in or easily converted into cash.
– DERIVATIVES **liquidly** adverb **liquidness** noun.
– ORIGIN Latin *liquidus*, from *liquere* 'be liquid'.

liquidate ● verb **1** wind up the affairs of (a company) by ascertaining liabilities and apportioning assets. **2** convert (assets) into cash. **3** pay off (a debt). **4** informal eliminate; kill.
– DERIVATIVES **liquidation** noun **liquidator** noun.
– ORIGIN originally in the sense 'set out (accounts) clearly': from Latin *liquidare* 'make clear'.

liquid crystal ● noun a liquid with some degree of ordering in the arrangement of its molecules.

liquid crystal display ● noun an electronic visual display in which the application of an electric current to a liquid crystal layer makes it opaque.

liquidity /likwidditi/ ● noun Finance **1** the availability of liquid assets to a market or company. **2** liquid assets.

liquidize (also **liquidise**) ● verb Brit. convert (solid food) into a liquid or purée.

liquidizer (also **liquidiser**) ● noun Brit. a machine for liquidizing.

liquid measure ● noun a unit for measuring the volume of liquids.

liquid paraffin ● noun chiefly Brit. a colourless, odourless oily liquid obtained from petroleum, used as a laxative.

liquify ● verb variant spelling of LIQUEFY.

liquor /likkər/ ● noun **1** alcoholic drink, especially spirits. **2** water used in brewing. **3** liquid that has been produced in or used for cooking. **4** the liquid from which a substance has been crystallized or extracted.
– ORIGIN Latin, related to *liquere* 'be fluid'.

liquorice /likkəriss, -rish/ (US **licorice**) ● noun a sweet, chewy, aromatic black substance made from the juice of a root and used as a sweet and in medicine.
– ORIGIN Old French *licoresse*, from Greek *glukurrhiza* 'sweet root'.

lira /leerə/ ● noun (pl. **lire** /leerə, leeray/) **1** the basic monetary unit of Italy, notionally equal to 100 centesimos. **2** the basic monetary unit of Turkey, equal to 100 kurus.

Thesaurus

couple, yoke. **2** *the evidence linking him with the body* ASSOCIATE, connect, relate, join, bracket.

lion ● noun **1** *a lion ready to attack* big cat, king of the beasts; lioness. **2** *a lion amongst men* HERO, man of courage, brave man; conqueror, champion, conquering hero. **3** *the lions of the symphony hall* CELEBRITY, dignitary, VIP, luminary, star, superstar, big name, leading light; *informal* big shot/noise, celeb, megastar.
– RELATED TERMS leonine.
– PHRASES **beard the lion in his den** DEFY DANGER, face up to danger, confront/brave danger.**the lion's share** MOST, the majority, the larger part/number, the greater part/number, more than half, the bulk.

lionhearted ● adjective BRAVE, courageous, valiant, gallant, intrepid, valorous, fearless, bold, daring; stout-hearted, stalwart, heroic, doughty, plucky; *informal* gutsy, spunky.
– OPPOSITES cowardly.

lionize ● verb CELEBRATE, fête, glorify, honour, exalt, acclaim, admire, praise, extol, applaud, hail, venerate, eulogize; *formal* laud; *archaic* panegyrize.
– OPPOSITES vilify.

lip ● noun **1** *the lip of the crater* EDGE, rim, brim, border, verge, brink. **2** *(informal) I'll have no more of your lip!* INSOLENCE, impertinence, impudence, cheek, rudeness, audacity, effrontery, disrespect, presumptuousness; *informal* mouth; *Brit. informal* sauce, backchat.
– RELATED TERMS labial, labio-.
– PHRASES **keep a stiff upper lip** KEEP CONTROL OF ONESELF, not show emotion, appear unaffected; *informal* keep one's cool.

liquefy ● verb MAKE/BECOME LIQUID, condense, liquidize, melt; deliquesce.

liquid ● adjective **1** *liquid fuels* FLUID, liquefied; melted, molten, thawed, dissolved; *Chemistry* hydrous. **2** *her liquid eyes* CLEAR, limpid, crystal clear, crystalline, pellucid, unclouded. **3** *a liquid voice* PURE, clear, mellifluous, dulcet, mellow, sweet, sweet-sounding, soft, melodious, harmonious; *rare* mellifluent. **4** *liquid assets* CONVERTIBLE, disposable, usable, spendable.
– OPPOSITES solid.
● noun *a vat of liquid* FLUID, moisture, wet, wetness; liquor, solution, juice.

liquidate ● verb **1** *the company was liquidated* CLOSE DOWN, wind up, put into liquidation, dissolve, disband. **2** *he liquidated his share portfolio* CONVERT (TO CASH), cash in, sell off/up. **3** *liquidating the public debt* PAY (OFF), pay in full, settle, clear, discharge, square, honour. **4** *(informal) they were liquidated in bloody purges.* See KILL verb sense 1.

liquidize ● verb PURÉE, cream, liquefy, blend.

liquor ● noun **1** *alcoholic liquor* ALCOHOL, spirits, (alcoholic) drink, intoxicating liquor, intoxicant; *informal* booze, hard stuff, grog,

– ORIGIN Italian, from Latin *libra* 'pound'.

lisle /līl/ • noun a fine, smooth cotton thread formerly used for stockings, gloves, etc.

– ORIGIN from *Lisle*, former spelling of *Lille*, a city in northern France where lisle was made.

lisp • noun a speech defect in which *s* is pronounced like *th* in *thick* and *z* is pronounced like *th* in *this*. • verb speak with a lisp.

– DERIVATIVES **lisper** noun.

– ORIGIN Old English.

lissom (also **lissome**) • adjective slim, supple, and graceful.

– DERIVATIVES **lissomness** noun.

– ORIGIN a contraction formed from LITHE + -SOME[1].

list[1] • noun **1** a number of connected items or names written consecutively. **2** (**lists**) historical palisades enclosing an area for a tournament. **3** a selvedge of a piece of fabric. • verb **1** make a list of. **2** include in a list. **3** archaic enlist for military service.

– PHRASES **enter the lists** issue or accept a challenge.

– ORIGIN the origin of the noun is complex: sense 1 entered English from French *liste*, and developed from an obsolete use of sense 3 denoting a strip of paper; sense 3 itself derives from an Old English word meaning 'a border or edging'; sense 2 is from Old French *lisse*.

list[2] • verb (of a ship) lean over to one side. • noun an instance of listing.

– ORIGIN of unknown origin.

list[3] archaic • verb want; like. • noun desire; inclination.

– ORIGIN Old English.

listed • adjective **1** (of a building in the UK) officially designated as being of historical importance and so protected. **2** denoting companies whose shares are quoted on the main market of the London Stock Exchange.

listen • verb **1** give one's attention to a sound. **2** make an effort to hear something. **3** (**listen in**) listen to a private conversation. **4** (**listen in**) listen to a radio broadcast. **5** respond to advice or a request. • noun an act of listening.

– DERIVATIVES **listener** noun.

– ORIGIN Old English, 'pay attention to'.

listenable • adjective easy or pleasant to listen to.

– DERIVATIVES **listenability** noun.

listening post • noun a station for intercepting electronic communications.

listeria /listeeriə/ • noun a type of bacterium which infects humans and other animals through contaminated food.

– ORIGIN named after the English surgeon Joseph *Lister* (1827–1912).

listeriosis /listeeriōsiss/ • noun disease caused by infection with listeria, which can resemble influenza or meningitis and may cause miscarriage.

listing • noun **1** a list or catalogue. **2** an entry in a list.

listless • adjective lacking energy or enthusiasm.

– DERIVATIVES **listlessly** adverb **listlessness** noun.

– ORIGIN from LIST[3].

list price • noun the price of an article as listed by the manufacturer.

lit past and past participle of LIGHT[1], LIGHT[3].

litany /littəni/ • noun (pl. **litanies**) **1** a series of petitions used in church services, usually recited by the clergy and responded to by the people. **2** a tedious recital.

– ORIGIN Greek *litaneia* 'prayer', from *litē* 'supplication'.

litas /leetass/ • noun (pl. same) the basic monetary unit of Lithuania, equal to 100 centas.

– ORIGIN Lithuanian.

litchi • noun variant spelling of LYCHEE.

-lite • suffix forming names of rocks, minerals, and fossils: *halite*.

– ORIGIN from Greek *lithos* 'stone'.

liter • noun US spelling of LITRE.

literacy • noun the ability to read and write.

literal • adjective **1** using or interpreting words in their usual or most basic sense without metaphor or allegory. **2** (of a translation) representing the exact words of the original text. **3** free from distortion. **4** informal absolute (used for emphasis). **5** relating to a letter or letters of the alphabet. • noun Brit. Printing a misprint of a letter.

– DERIVATIVES **literality** noun **literalize** (also **literalise**) verb **literalness** noun.

– ORIGIN from Latin *litera* 'letter of the alphabet'.

literalism • noun the literal interpretation of words.

– DERIVATIVES **literalist** noun **literalistic** adjective.

literally • adverb **1** in a literal manner or sense. **2** informal used for emphasis (rather than to suggest literal truth).

literary • adjective **1** concerning the writing, study, or content of literature, especially of the kind valued for quality of form. **2** associated with literary works or formal writing.

– DERIVATIVES **literarily** adverb **literariness** noun.

– ORIGIN originally in the sense 'relating to the letters of the alphabet': from Latin *litera* 'letter of the alphabet'.

literary criticism • noun the art or practice of judging the qualities and character of literary works.

literary executor • noun a person entrusted with a dead writer's papers and works.

literary history • noun the history of the treatment of a subject in literature.

literate • adjective **1** able to read and write. **2** knowledgeable in a particular field: *computer literate*. • noun a literate person.

– DERIVATIVES **literately** adverb.

literati /littəraati/ • plural noun educated people who are interested in literature.

– ORIGIN Latin, plural of *literatus* 'acquainted with letters'.

literature • noun **1** written works, especially those regarded as having artistic merit. **2** books and writings on a particular subject. **3** leaflets and other material used to give information or advice.

lithe • adjective slim, supple, and graceful.

Thesaurus

hooch. . **2** *strain the liquor into the sauce* STOCK, broth, bouillon, juice, liquid.

lissom • adjective SUPPLE, lithe, limber, graceful, flexible, loose-limbed, agile, nimble; slim, slender, thin, willowy, sleek, trim.

list[1] • noun *a list of the world's wealthiest people* CATALOGUE, inventory, record, register, roll, file, index, directory, listing, checklist, enumeration.

• verb *the accounts are listed alphabetically* RECORD, register, make a list of, enter; itemize, enumerate, catalogue, file, log, minute, categorize, inventory; classify, group, sort, rank, alphabetize, index.

list[2] • verb *the boat listed to one side* LEAN (OVER), tilt, tip, heel (over), careen, cant, pitch, incline, slant, slope, bank.

listen • verb **1** *are you listening carefully?* HEAR, pay attention, be attentive, attend, concentrate; keep one's ears open, prick up one's ears; informal be all ears, pin back one's ears; poetic/literary hark; archaic hearken. **2** *policy-makers should listen to popular opinion* PAY ATTENTION, take heed, heed, take notice, take note, mind, mark, bear in mind, take into consideration/account.

– PHRASES **listen in** EAVESDROP, spy, overhear, tap, wiretap, bug, monitor.

listless • adjective LETHARGIC, enervated, spiritless, lifeless, vigourless; languid, languorous, inactive, inert, sluggish, torpid.

– OPPOSITES energetic.

litany • noun **1** *repeating the litany* PRAYER, invocation, supplication, devotion; archaic orison. **2** *a litany of complaints* RECITAL, recitation, repetition, enumeration; list, listing, catalogue, inventory.

literacy • noun ABILITY TO READ AND WRITE, reading/writing proficiency; (book) learning, education, scholarship, schooling.

literal • adjective **1** *the literal sense of the word 'dreadful'* STRICT, factual, plain, simple, exact, straightforward; unembellished, undistorted; objective, correct, true, truthful, accurate, genuine, authentic. **2** *a literal translation* WORD-FOR-WORD, verbatim, letter-for-letter; exact, precise, faithful, close, strict, accurate; formal literatim. **3** *his literal, unrhetorical manner* LITERAL-MINDED, down-to-earth, matter-of-fact, no-nonsense, unsentimental; prosaic, unimaginative, pedestrian, uninspired, uninspiring.

– OPPOSITES figurative, loose.

• noun (Brit.) *William corrected two literals* MISPRINT, error, mistake, (slip) of the pen, typographical/typing error/mistake, corrigendum, erratum; informal typo, howler.

literally • adverb VERBATIM, word for word, letter for letter; exactly, precisely, faithfully, closely, strictly, accurately; formal literatim.

literary • adjective **1** *literary works* WRITTEN, poetic, artistic, dramatic. **2** *her literary friends* SCHOLARLY, learned, intellectual, cultured, erudite, bookish, highbrow, lettered, academic, cultivated; well read, widely read, (well) educated. **3** *literary language* FORMAL, written, poetic, dramatic; elaborate, ornate, flowery.

literate • adjective (WELL) EDUCATED, well read, widely read, scholarly, learned, knowledgeable, lettered, cultured, cultivated, sophisti-

– DERIVATIVES **lithely** adverb **litheness** noun.
– ORIGIN Old English, 'gentle, meek, mellow'.
lithium /lithiəm/ ● noun **1** a light, soft, silver-white reactive metallic chemical element. **2** a lithium salt used as a mood-stabilizing drug.
– ORIGIN from Greek *lithos* 'stone'.
lithograph /lithəgraaf/ ● noun a print made by lithography. ● verb print by lithography.
– DERIVATIVES **lithographic** adjective.
lithography /lithogrəfi/ ● noun the process of printing from a flat metal, formerly stone, surface treated so as to repel the ink except where it is required for printing.
– DERIVATIVES **lithographer** noun.
– ORIGIN from Greek *lithos* 'stone'.
lithology /litholləji/ ● noun the study of the physical characteristics of rocks.
– DERIVATIVES **lithological** adjective.
lithosphere /lithəsfeer/ ● noun Geology the rigid outer part of the earth, consisting of the crust and upper mantle.
– DERIVATIVES **lithospheric** adjective.
lithotomy /lithottəmi/ ● noun surgical removal of a calculus (stone) from the bladder, kidney, or urinary tract.
– DERIVATIVES **lithotomist** noun.
– ORIGIN from Greek *lithos* 'stone' + -TOMY.
Lithuanian ● noun **1** a person from Lithuania. **2** the language of Lithuania. ● adjective relating to Lithuania.
litigant ● noun a person involved in litigation.
litigate /littigayt/ ● verb **1** go to law; be a party to a lawsuit. **2** take (a dispute) to a law court.
– DERIVATIVES **litigation** noun **litigator** noun.
– ORIGIN Latin *litigare*, from *lis* 'lawsuit'.
litigious /litijəss/ ● adjective **1** concerned with lawsuits or litigation. **2** having a tendency to go to law to settle disputes.
– DERIVATIVES **litigiously** adverb **litigiousness** noun.
litmus /litməss/ ● noun a dye obtained from certain lichens that is red under acid conditions and blue under alkaline conditions.
– ORIGIN from Old Norse words meaning 'dye' and 'moss'.
litmus paper ● noun paper stained with litmus, used as a test for acids or alkalis.
litmus test ● noun **1** a test using litmus. **2** a decisively indicative test.
litotes /lītōteez/ ● noun ironical understatement in which an affirmative is expressed by the negative of its contrary (e.g. *I shan't be sorry* for *I shall be glad*).
– ORIGIN Greek, from *litos* 'plain, meagre'.
litre (US **liter**) ● noun a metric unit of capacity, formerly the volume of one kilogram of water under standard conditions, now equal to 1,000 cubic centimetres (about 1.75 pints).
– DERIVATIVES **litreage** noun.
– ORIGIN French, from Greek *litra*, a Sicilian monetary unit.
LittD ● abbreviation Doctor of Letters.
– ORIGIN from Latin *Litterarum Doctor*.
litter ● noun **1** rubbish left in an open or public place. **2** an untidy collection of things. **3** a number of young born to an animal at one time. **4** (also **cat litter**) granular absorbent material lining a tray for a cat to urinate and defecate in indoors. **5** straw or other plant matter used as animal bedding. **6** (also **leaf litter**) decomposing leaves and other matter forming a layer on top of soil. **7** historical a vehicle containing a bed or seat enclosed by curtains and carried by men or animals. **8** a framework with a couch for transporting the sick. ● verb make untidy with discarded articles.
– ORIGIN Old French *litiere*, from Latin *lectus* 'bed'.
litterbug (Brit. also **litter lout**) ● noun informal a person who carelessly drops rubbish on the ground.
little ● adjective **1** small in size, amount, or degree. **2** (of a person) young or younger. **3** of short distance or duration. **4** trivial, unimportant, or humble. ● determiner & pronoun **1** (**a little**) a small amount of. **2** (**a little**) a short time or distance. **3** not much. ● adverb (**less**, **least**) **1** (**a little**) to a small extent. **2** hardly or not at all.
– PHRASES **little by little** gradually. **little or nothing** hardly anything.
– DERIVATIVES **littleness** noun.
– ORIGIN Old English.
little end ● noun (in a piston engine) the smaller end of a connecting rod, attached to the piston.
Little Englander ● noun informal a person opposed to an international role or policy for Britain.
little finger ● noun the smallest finger, at the outer side of the hand.
– PHRASES **twist** (or **wind** or **wrap**) **someone around one's little finger** be able to make someone do whatever one wants.
little people ● plural noun **1** the ordinary people of a country or organization. **2** fairies or leprechauns.
littoral /littərəl/ ● adjective relating to the shore of the sea or a lake. ● noun a littoral region.
– ORIGIN Latin *littoralis*, from *litus* 'shore'.
liturgical /liturjik'l/ ● adjective relating to liturgy or public worship.
– DERIVATIVES **liturgically** adverb **liturgist** /littərjist/ noun.
liturgy /littərji/ ● noun (pl. **liturgies**) a prescribed form of public worship used in the Christian Church.
– ORIGIN Greek *leitourgia* 'public service, worship of the gods'.
livable ● adjective variant spelling of LIVEABLE.

l

Thesaurus

cated, well informed.
– OPPOSITES ignorant.
literature ● noun **1** *English literature* WRITTEN WORKS, writings, (creative) writing, literary texts, compositions. **2** *the literature on prototype theory* PUBLICATIONS, published writings, texts, reports, studies. **3** *election literature* PRINTED MATTER, brochures, leaflets, pamphlets, circulars, flyers, handouts, handbills, mailshots, bulletins, documentation, publicity, blurb, notices; informal bumf.
lithe ● adjective AGILE, graceful, supple, limber, lithesome, loose-limbed, nimble, deft, flexible, lissom.
– OPPOSITES clumsy.
litigant ● noun LITIGATOR, opponent (in law), contender, disputant, plaintiff, claimant, complainant, petitioner, appellant, respondent.
litigation ● noun (LEGAL/JUDICIAL) PROCEEDINGS, (legal) action, lawsuit, legal dispute, (legal) case, suit (at law), prosecution, indictment.
litter ● noun **1** *never drop litter* RUBBISH, refuse, junk, waste, debris, scraps, leavings, fragments, detritus; N. Amer. trash, garbage. **2** *the litter of glasses around her* CLUTTER, jumble, muddle, mess, heap, disorder, untidiness, confusion, disarray; informal shambles. **3** *a litter of kittens* BROOD, family; young, offspring, progeny; Law issue. **4** *straw for use as litter* (ANIMAL) BEDDING, straw. **5** *a horse-drawn litter* SEDAN CHAIR, palanquin; stretcher.
● verb *clothes littered the floor* MAKE UNTIDY, mess up, make a mess of, clutter up, be strewn about, be scattered about; informal make a shambles of; poetic/literary bestrew.
little ● adjective **1** *a little writing desk* SMALL, small-scale, compact; mini, miniature, tiny, minute, minuscule; toy, baby, pocket, undersized, dwarf, midget; Scottish wee; informal teeny-weeny, teensy-weensy, itsy-bitsy, tiddly, half-pint; Brit. informal titchy, dinky; N. Amer. informal vest-pocket. **2** *a little man* SHORT, small, slight, petite, diminutive, tiny; elfin, dwarfish, midget, pygmy, Lilliputian; Scottish wee; informal teeny-weeny, pint-sized. **3** *my little sister* YOUNG, younger, junior, small, baby, infant. **4** *I was a bodyguard for a little while* BRIEF, short, short-lived; fleeting, momentary, transitory, transient; fast, quick, hasty, cursory. **5** *a few little problems* MINOR, unimportant, insignificant, trivial, trifling, petty, paltry, inconsequential, nugatory.
– OPPOSITES big, large, elder, important.
● determiner *they have little political influence* HARDLY ANY, not much, slight, scant, limited, restricted, modest, little or no, minimal, negligible.
– OPPOSITES considerable.
● adverb **1** *he is little known as a teacher* HARDLY, barely, scarcely, not much, (only) slightly. **2** *this disease is little seen nowadays* RARELY, seldom, infrequently, hardly (ever), scarcely (ever), not much.
– OPPOSITES well, often.
– PHRASES **a little 1** *add a little water* SOME, a small amount of, a bit of, a touch of, a soupçon of, a dash of, a taste of, a spot of; a shade of, a suggestion of, a trace of, a hint of, a suspicion of; a dribble of, a splash of, a pinch of, a sprinkling of, a speck of; informal a smidgen of, a tad of. **2** *after a little, Oliver came in* A SHORT TIME, a little while, a bit, an interval, a short period; a minute, a moment, a second, an instant; informal a sec, a mo, a jiffy. **3** *this reminds me a little of the Adriatic* SLIGHTLY, faintly, remotely, vaguely; somewhat, a little bit, quite, to some degree. **little by little**

live[1] /liv/ ● verb **1** remain alive. **2** be alive at a specified time. **3** spend one's life in a particular way or under particular circumstances: *they are living in fear.* **4** make one's home in a particular place or with a particular person. **5** (**live in/out**) reside at (or away from) the place where one works or studies. **6** supply oneself with the means of subsistence: *they live by hunting and fishing.* **7** (**live for**) regard as the most important aspect of one's life. **8** survive in someone's mind.
– PHRASES **live and breathe** be devoted to (a subject or activity). **live and let live** proverb you should tolerate the opinions and behaviour of others so that they will similarly tolerate your own. **live down** succeed in making others forget (something regrettable or embarrassing). **live in the past** have outdated ideas and attitudes. **live it up** informal lead a life of extravagance and exciting social activity. **live off** (or **on**) **1** depend on or have available as a source of income or support. **2** eat as a major part of one's diet. **live rough** live outdoors as a result of being homeless. **live together** (of a couple not married to each other) share a home and have a sexual relationship. **live up to** fulfil. **live with 1** share a home and have a sexual relationship with (someone to whom one is not married). **2** accept or tolerate (something unpleasant).
– ORIGIN Old English, related to LIFE and LEAVE[1].

live[2] /līv/ ● adjective **1** living. **2** (of a musical performance) given in concert; not recorded. **3** (of a broadcast) transmitted at the time of occurrence; not recorded. **4** of current or continuing interest and importance. **5** (of a wire or device) connected to a source of electric current. **6** of, containing, or using undetonated explosive. **7** (of coals) burning. **8** (of yogurt) containing the living micro-organisms by which it is formed. ● adverb as or at an actual event or performance.
– PHRASES **go live** Computing (of a system) become operational.
– ORIGIN shortening of ALIVE.

liveable (US also **livable**) ● adjective **1** worth living. **2** fit to live in. **3** (**liveable with**) informal easy to live with.
– DERIVATIVES **liveability** noun.

live action ● noun action in films involving real people or animals, as contrasted with animation or computer-generated effects.

live bait ● noun small living fish or worms used as bait.

live-bearing ● adjective bearing live young rather than laying eggs.
– DERIVATIVES **livebearer** noun.

lived-in ● adjective **1** (of a room or building) showing comforting signs of wear and habitation. **2** informal (of a person's face) marked by experience.

live-in ● adjective **1** (of a domestic employee) resident in an employer's house. **2** living with another in a sexual relationship: *his live-in girlfriend.* **3** (of a course of study, treatment, etc.) residential.

livelihood ● noun a means of securing the necessities of life.
– ORIGIN Old English, 'way of life'.

livelong /livlong/ ● adjective literary (of a period of time) entire: *all this livelong day.*

lively ● adjective (**liveier, liveliest**) **1** full of life and energy. **2** (of a place) full of activity. **3** intellectually stimulating or perceptive.
– PHRASES **look lively** informal move more quickly and energetically.
– DERIVATIVES **livelily** adverb **liveliness** noun.

liven ● verb (**liven up**) make or become more lively or interesting.

liver[1] ● noun **1** a large organ in the abdomen that secretes bile and neutralizes toxins. **2** the flesh of an animal's liver as food.
– ORIGIN Old English.

liver[2] ● noun a person who lives in a specified way: *a clean liver.*

liver fluke ● noun a fluke of which the adult lives in the liver of a vertebrate and the larva in a secondary host such as a snail or fish.

liverish ● adjective **1** slightly ill, as though having a disordered liver. **2** unhappy and bad-tempered.
– DERIVATIVES **liverishly** adverb **liverishness** noun.

Liverpudlian /livvərpudliən/ ● noun **1** a person from the city of Liverpool in NW England. **2** the dialect or accent of people from Liverpool. ● adjective relating to Liverpool.
– ORIGIN humorous formation from *Liverpool* + PUDDLE.

liver sausage ● noun chiefly Brit. a savoury meat paste in the form of a sausage containing cooked liver, or a mixture of liver and pork.

liver spot ● noun a small brown spot on the skin.

liverwort /livvərwurt/ ● noun a small flowerless green plant with leaf-like stems or lobed leaves, lacking true roots and reproducing by spores.

livery ● noun (pl. **liveries**) **1** a special uniform worn by a servant, an official, or a member of a City Company. **2** a distinctive design and colour scheme used on the vehicles or products of a company. **3** the members of a livery company collectively.
– PHRASES **at livery** (of a horse) kept for the owner and fed and cared for at a fixed charge.
– DERIVATIVES **liveried** adjective.
– ORIGIN originally in the sense 'the dispensing of food, provisions, or clothing to servants': from Old French *livree* 'delivered', from Latin *liberare* 'liberate'.

livery company ● noun (in the UK) any of a number of Com-

Thesaurus

GRADUALLY, slowly, by degrees, by stages, step by step, bit by bit, progressively; subtly, imperceptibly.

liturgical ● adjective CEREMONIAL, ritual, solemn; church.

liturgy ● noun RITUAL, worship, service, ceremony, rite, observance, celebration, sacrament; tradition, custom, practice, rubric; formal ordinance.

live[1] ● verb **1** *the greatest mathematician who ever lived* EXIST, be alive, be, have life; breathe, draw breath, walk the earth. **2** *I live in London* RESIDE, have one's home, have one's residence, be settled; be housed, lodge; inhabit, occupy, populate; Scottish stay; formal dwell, be domiciled. **3** *they lived quietly* PASS/SPEND ONE'S LIFE, have a lifestyle; behave, conduct oneself; formal comport oneself. **4** *she had lived a difficult life* EXPERIENCE, spend, pass, lead, have, go through, undergo. **5** *Freddy lived by his wits* SURVIVE, make a living, earn one's living, eke out a living; subsist, support oneself, sustain oneself, make ends meet, keep body and soul together. **6** *you should live a little* ENJOY ONESELF, enjoy life, have fun, live life to the full.
– OPPOSITES die, be dead.
– PHRASES **live it up** (informal) LIVE EXTRAVAGANTLY, live in the lap of luxury, live in clover; carouse, revel, enjoy oneself, have a good time, go on a spree, roister; informal party, push the boat out, paint the town red, have a ball, make whoopee; N. Amer. informal live high on/off the hog; archaic wassail. **live off/on** SUBSIST ON, feed on/off, eat, consume.

live[2] ● adjective **1** *live bait* LIVING, alive, having life, breathing, animate, sentient. **2** *a live performance* IN THE FLESH, personal, in person, not recorded. **3** *a live rail* ELECTRIFIED, charged, powered, active; informal hot. **4** *live coals* (RED) HOT, glowing, aglow; burning, alight, flaming, aflame, blazing, ignited, on fire; poetic/literary afire. **5** *a live grenade* UNEXPLODED, explosive, active; unstable, volatile. **6** *live issue* TOPICAL, current, of current interest, controversial; burning, pressing, important.
– OPPOSITES dead, inanimate, recorded.
– PHRASES **live wire** (informal) ENERGETIC PERSON; informal fireball, human dynamo, powerhouse, life and soul of the party.

livelihood ● noun (SOURCE OF) INCOME, means of support, living, subsistence, keep, maintenance, sustenance, nourishment, daily bread, bread and butter; job, work, employment, occupation.

livelong ● adjective (poetic/literary) ENTIRE, whole, total, complete, full, continuous.

lively ● adjective **1** *a lively young woman* ENERGETIC, active, animated, dynamic, full of life, outgoing, spirited, high-spirited, vivacious, enthusiastic, vibrant, buoyant, exuberant, effervescent, cheerful; bouncy, bubbly, perky, sparkling, zestful; informal full of beans, chirpy, chipper, peppy. **2** *a lively bar* BUSY, crowded, bustling, buzzing; vibrant, boisterous, jolly, festive; informal hopping. **3** *a lively debate* HEATED, vigorous, animated, spirited, enthusiastic, forceful; exciting, interesting, memorable. **4** *a lively portrait of the local community* VIVID, colourful, striking, graphic, bold, strong. **5** *he bowled at a lively pace* BRISK, quick, fast, rapid, swift, speedy, smart; informal nippy, snappy. **6** *the press is making things lively for the Government* AWKWARD, tricky, difficult, challenging, eventful, exciting, busy; informal hairy.
– OPPOSITES quiet, dull.

liven ● verb
– PHRASES **liven up** BRIGHTEN UP, cheer up, perk up, revive, rally, pick up, bounce back; informal buck up. **liven someone/something up** BRIGHTEN UP, cheer up, enliven, animate, raise someone's spirits, perk up, spice up, ginger up, make lively, wake

panies of the City of London descended from the medieval trade guilds.

liveryman ● noun (in the UK) a member of a livery company.

livery stable (also **livery yard**) ● noun a stable where horses are kept at livery or let out for hire.

lives plural of LIFE.

livestock ● noun farm animals regarded as an asset.

live wire ● noun informal an energetic and lively person.

livid ● adjective **1** informal furiously angry. **2** having a dark inflamed appearance.
– DERIVATIVES **lividity** noun **lividly** adverb **lividness** noun.
– ORIGIN Latin *lividus*, from *livere* 'be bluish'.

living ● noun **1** the action of leading one's life; being alive. **2** an income sufficient to live on, or the means of earning it. ● adjective **1** alive. **2** (of a language) still spoken and used. **3** for or related to daily life: *living quarters*.
– PHRASES **in** (or **within**) **living memory** within or during a time that is remembered by people still alive. **the living image of** an exact copy or likeness of.

living room ● noun a room in a house for general everyday use.

living wage ● noun a wage which is high enough to maintain a normal standard of living.

living will ● noun a written statement detailing a person's desires regarding their medical treatment in circumstances in which they are no longer able to express informed consent.

lizard ● noun a four-legged reptile with a long body and tail, movable eyelids, and a rough, scaly, or spiny skin.
– ORIGIN Old French *lesard*, from Latin *lacertus* 'lizard, sea fish, also 'muscle'.

LJ ● abbreviation (pl. **L JJ**) (in the UK) Lord Justice.

ll. ● abbreviation (in textual references) lines.

'll ● contraction shall; will.

llama /laamə/ ● noun a domesticated animal of the camel family found in the Andes, used for carrying loads and valued for its soft woolly fleece.
– ORIGIN Spanish, probably from Quechua.

llano /larnō, lyarnō/ ● noun (pl. **llanos**) (in South America) a treeless grassy plain.
– ORIGIN Spanish, from Latin *planum* 'plain'.

LLB ● abbreviation Bachelor of Laws.
– ORIGIN from Latin *legum baccalaureus*.

LLD ● abbreviation Doctor of Laws.
– ORIGIN from Latin *legum doctor*.

LLM ● abbreviation Master of Laws.
– ORIGIN from Latin *legum magister*.

Lloyd's ● noun **1** an incorporated society of insurance underwriters in London, made up of private syndicates. **2** short for LLOYD'S REGISTER.
– ORIGIN named after the coffee house of Edward *Lloyd* (*fl.* 1688–1726), in which underwriters and merchants congregated.

Lloyd's Register (in full **Lloyd's Register of Shipping**) ● noun a classified list of merchant ships over a certain tonnage, published annually in London.

lm ● abbreviation lumen or lumens.

LMS ● abbreviation (in the UK) local management of schools.

ln ● abbreviation Mathematics natural logarithm.
– ORIGIN from Latin *logarithmus naturalis*.

LNB ● abbreviation low noise blocker, a circuit on a satellite dish which selects the required signal from the transmission.

LNG ● abbreviation liquefied natural gas.

lo ● exclamation archaic used to draw attention to an interesting event.
– PHRASES **lo and behold** used to present a new scene or situation.
– ORIGIN natural exclamation: first recorded in Old English.

loach /lōch/ ● noun a small, elongated freshwater fish with several barbels near the mouth.
– ORIGIN Old French *loche*.

load ● noun **1** a heavy or bulky thing being or about to be carried. **2** a weight or source of pressure. **3** the total number or amount carried in a vehicle or container. **4** (**a load/loads of**) informal a lot of. **5** the amount of work to be done by a person or machine. **6** the amount of power supplied by a source. **7** a burden of responsibility, worry, or grief. ● verb **1** put a load on or in. **2** place (a load or large quantity) on or in a vehicle, container, etc. **3** insert (something) into a device so that it will operate. **4** charge (a firearm) with ammunition. **5** bias towards a particular outcome.
– PHRASES **get a load of** informal take a look at (used to draw attention to someone or something). **load the dice against** (or **in favour of**) put at a disadvantage (or advantage).
– DERIVATIVES **loader** noun.
– ORIGIN Old English, 'journey, conveyance'; related to LEAD[1] and LODE.

loaded ● adjective **1** carrying or bearing a load. **2** weighted or biased towards a particular outcome. **3** charged with an underlying meaning: *a loaded question*. **4** informal wealthy. **5** N. Amer. informal drunk.

load factor ● noun the ratio of the average or actual amount of some quantity and the maximum possible or permissible.

loading ● noun **1** the application of a load to something. **2** the amount of load applied. **3** an increase in an insurance premium due to a factor increasing the risk involved. **4** Austral. an increment added to a basic wage for special skills or qualifications.

load line ● noun another term for PLIMSOLL LINE.

loadmaster ● noun the member of an aircraft's crew responsible for the cargo.

loadstone ● noun variant spelling of LODESTONE.

loaf[1] ● noun (pl. **loaves**) a quantity of bread that is shaped and baked in one piece.
– PHRASES **half a loaf is better than no bread** proverb it is better to accept less than one wants or expects than to have nothing at all. **use one's loaf** Brit. informal use one's common sense. [ORIGIN probably from *loaf of bread*, rhyming slang for 'head'.]
– ORIGIN Old English.

loaf[2] ● verb idle one's time away.
– ORIGIN probably from LOAFER.

l

Thesaurus

up, invigorate, revive, refresh, vivify, galvanize, stimulate, stir up, get going; *informal* buck up, pep up.

livery ● noun UNIFORM, regalia, costume, dress, attire, garb, clothes, clothing, outfit, suit, garments, ensemble; *informal* get-up, gear, kit; *formal* apparel; *archaic* raiment, vestments.

livid ● adjective **1** *(informal) Mum was absolutely livid.* See FURIOUS sense 1. **2** *a livid bruise* PURPLISH, bluish, dark, discoloured, purple, greyish-blue; bruised; angry.

living ● noun **1** *she cleaned floors for a living* LIVELIHOOD, (source of) income, means of support, subsistence, keep, maintenance, sustenance, nourishment, daily bread, bread and butter; job, work, employment, occupation. **2** *the benefits of country living* WAY OF LIFE, lifestyle, way of living, life; conduct, behaviour, activities, habits.
● adjective **1** *living organisms* ALIVE, live, having life, animate, sentient; breathing, existing, existent; *informal* alive and kicking. **2** *a living language* CURRENT, contemporary, present; in use, active, surviving, extant, persisting, remaining, existing, in existence. **3** *a living image of the man* EXACT, faithful, true to life, authentic.
– OPPOSITES dead, extinct.

living room ● noun SITTING ROOM, lounge, front room, reception room, family room.

load ● noun **1** *MacDowell's got a load to deliver* CARGO, freight, consignment, delivery, shipment, goods, merchandise; pack, bundle, parcel; lorryload, truckload, shipload, boatload, vanload; *archaic* lading. **2** *(informal) I bought a load of clothes* A LOT, a great deal, a large amount/quantity, an abundance, a wealth, a mountain; many, plenty; *informal* a heap, a mass, a pile, a stack, a ton, lots, heaps, masses, piles, stacks, tons. **3** *a heavy teaching load* COMMITMENT, responsibility, duty, obligation, charge, burden; trouble, worry, strain, pressure.
● verb **1** *we quickly loaded the van* FILL (UP), pack, lade, charge, stock, stack. **2** *Larry loaded boxes into the jeep* PACK, stow, store, stack, bundle; place, deposit, put away. **3** *loading the committee with responsibilities* BURDEN, weigh down, saddle, charge; overburden, overwhelm, encumber, tax, strain, trouble, worry. **4** *Richard loaded Marshal with honours* REWARD, ply, regale, shower. **5** *he loaded a gun* PRIME, charge, prepare to fire/use. **6** *load the cassette into the camcorder* INSERT, put, place, slot. **7** *the dice are loaded against him* BIAS, rig, fix; weight.
– OPPOSITES unload, remove.

loaded ● adjective **1** *a loaded freight train* FULL, filled, laden, packed, stuffed, crammed, brimming, stacked; *informal* chock-full, chock-a-block. **2** *a loaded gun* PRIMED, charged, ready to fire. **3** *(informal) they are all loaded.*See RICH sense 1. **4** *loaded dice* BIASED, rigged, fixed; weighted. **5** *a politically loaded word* CHARGED, emo-

loafer ● noun **1** a person who idles their time away. **2** trademark a leather shoe shaped like a moccasin, with a flat heel.
– ORIGIN perhaps from German *Landläufer* 'tramp'.
loam ● noun **1** a fertile soil of clay and sand containing humus. **2** a paste of clay and water with sand and chopped straw, used in making bricks and plastering walls.
– DERIVATIVES **loaminess** noun **loamy** adjective.
– ORIGIN Old English, 'clay': related to LIME[1].
loan ● noun **1** a thing that is borrowed, especially a sum of money that is expected to be paid back with interest. **2** the action of lending. ● verb give as a loan.
– PHRASES **on loan** being borrowed.
– DERIVATIVES **loanable** adjective **loanee** noun **loaner** noun.
– ORIGIN Old Norse, related to LEND.
loan shark ● noun informal a moneylender who charges exorbitant rates of interest.
loanword ● noun a word adopted from a foreign language with little or no modification.
loath /lōth/ (also **loth**) ● adjective reluctant; unwilling: *I was loath to leave.*
– ORIGIN Old English, 'hostile'.
loathe /lō<u>th</u>/ ● verb feel hatred or disgust for.
– DERIVATIVES **loather** noun.
– ORIGIN Old English, related to LOATH.
loathsome ● adjective causing hatred or disgust.
– DERIVATIVES **loathsomely** adverb **loathsomeness** noun.
loaves plural of LOAF[1].
lob ● verb (**lobbed**, **lobbing**) throw or hit in a high arc. ● noun **1** (in soccer or tennis) a ball lobbed over an opponent or a stroke producing this result. **2** (in cricket) a ball bowled with a slow underarm action.
– ORIGIN originally in the senses 'cause or allow to hang heavily' and 'behave like a lout': from obsolete *lob* 'lout', 'pendulous object', probably from Low German or Dutch.
lobar /lōbər/ ● adjective chiefly Anatomy & Medicine relating to a lobe, especially a lobe of a lung.
lobate /lōbayt/ ● adjective Biology having a lobe or lobes.
lobby ● noun (pl. **lobbies**) **1** a room out of which one or more other rooms or corridors lead, typically forming a small entrance hall. **2** (in the UK) any of several large halls in the Houses of Parliament in which MPs meet members of the public. **3** (also **division lobby**) each of two corridors in the Houses of Parliament to which MPs retire to vote. **4** a group of people seeking to influence legislators on a particular issue. **5** an organized attempt by members of the public to influence legislators. ● verb (**lobbies**, **lobbied**) seek to influence (a legislator).
– DERIVATIVES **lobbyist** noun.
– ORIGIN originally in the sense 'monastic cloister': from Latin *lobia* 'covered walk'.
lobe ● noun **1** a roundish and flattish projecting or hanging part of something. **2** each of the parts of the cerebrum of the brain.
– DERIVATIVES **lobed** adjective.
– ORIGIN Greek *lobos* 'lobe, pod'.
lobelia /ləbeeliə/ ● noun a plant of the bellflower family, with blue or scarlet flowers.
– ORIGIN named after the Flemish botanist Matthias de *Lobel* (1538–1616).
lobotomize (also **lobotomise**) ● verb Surgery perform a lobotomy on.
– DERIVATIVES **lobotomization** noun.
lobotomy /ləbottəmi/ ● noun (pl. **lobotomies**) a surgical operation involving incision into the prefrontal lobe of the brain, formerly used to treat mental illness.
lobster ● noun **1** a large marine crustacean with stalked eyes and large pincers. **2** the flesh of this animal as food. ● verb catch lobsters.
– ORIGIN Old English, from Latin *locusta* 'crustacean, locust'.
lobster pot ● noun a basket-like trap in which lobsters are caught.
lobster thermidor ● noun a dish of lobster cooked in a cream sauce, returned to its shell, sprinkled with cheese, and browned under the grill.
– ORIGIN *thermidor* from *Thermidor*, the eleventh month of the French Republican calendar.
lobworm ● noun a large earthworm used as fishing bait.
– ORIGIN from LOB in the obsolete sense 'pendulous object'.
local ● adjective **1** relating to a particular area. **2** relating or belonging to one's neighbourhood. **3** (in technical use) relating to a particular region or part: *a local infection.* **4** Computing (of a device) that can be accessed without the use of a network. ● noun **1** a local person or thing. **2** Brit. informal a pub convenient to a person's home.
– DERIVATIVES **locally** adverb **localness** noun.
– ORIGIN Latin *localis*, from *locus* 'place'.
local anaesthetic ● noun an anaesthetic that affects a restricted area of the body.
local area network ● noun a computer network that links devices within a building or group of adjacent buildings.
local authority ● noun Brit. an administrative body in local government.
local derby ● noun see DERBY.
locale /lōkaal/ ● noun a place associated with particular events.
– ORIGIN French *local* 'locality', respelled to indicate stress on the final syllable.
local government ● noun the administration of a particular county or district, with representatives elected by those who live there.
locality ● noun (pl. **localities**) **1** an area or neighbourhood. **2** the position or site of something.
localize (also **localise**) ● verb **1** (often as adj. **localized**) restrict

Thesaurus

tive, sensitive, delicate.
loaf[1] ● noun *(Brit. informal) use your loaf.* See HEAD noun sense 2.
loaf[2] ● verb *he was just loafing around* LAZE, lounge, loll, idle, waste time; *informal* hang around/round; *Brit. informal* hang about, mooch about/around; *N. Amer. informal* bum around.
loafer ● noun IDLER, layabout, good-for-nothing, lounger, shirker, sluggard, laggard, slugabed; *informal* skiver, slacker, slob, lazybones.
loan ● noun *a loan of £7,000* CREDIT, advance; mortgage, overdraft; lending, moneylending; *Brit. informal* sub.
● verb *he loaned me his flat* LEND, advance, give credit; give on loan, lease, charter, hire; *Brit. informal* sub.
– OPPOSITES borrow.
loath ● adjective RELUCTANT, unwilling, disinclined, ill-disposed; against, averse, opposed, resistant.
– OPPOSITES willing.
loathe ● verb HATE, detest, abhor, execrate, have a strong aversion to, feel repugnance towards, not be able to bear/stand, be repelled by; *formal* abominate.
– OPPOSITES love.
loathing ● noun HATRED, hate, detestation, abhorrence, abomination, execration, odium; antipathy, dislike, hostility, animosity, ill feeling, bad feeling, malice, animus, enmity, aversion; repugnance.
– OPPOSITES love.
loathsome ● adjective HATEFUL, detestable, abhorrent, repulsive, odious, repugnant, repellent, disgusting, revolting, sickening, abominable, despicable, contemptible, reprehensible, execrable, damnable; vile, horrible, nasty, obnoxious, gross, foul; *informal* horrid, yucky; *poetic/literary* noisome.
lob ● verb THROW, toss, fling, pitch, hurl, pelt, sling, launch, propel; *informal* chuck, bung, heave.
lobby ● noun **1** *the hotel lobby* ENTRANCE (HALL), hallway, hall, vestibule, foyer, reception area. **2** *the anti-hunt lobby* PRESSURE GROUP, interest group, movement, campaign, crusade, lobbyists, supporters; faction, camp; *Brit.* ginger group.
● verb **1** *readers are urged to lobby their MPs* SEEK TO INFLUENCE, try to persuade, bring pressure to bear on, importune, sway; petition, solicit, appeal to, pressurize. **2** *a group lobbying for better rail services* CAMPAIGN, crusade, press, push, ask, call, demand; promote, advocate, champion.
local ● adjective **1** *the local council* COMMUNITY, district, neighbourhood, regional, city, town, municipal, provincial, village, parish. **2** *a local restaurant* NEIGHBOURHOOD, nearby, near, at hand, close by; accessible, handy, convenient. **3** *a local infection* CONFINED, restricted, contained, localized.
– OPPOSITES national.
● noun **1** *complaints from the locals* LOCAL PERSON, native, inhabitant, resident, parishioner. **2** *(Brit. informal) a pint in the local.* See PUB.
– OPPOSITES outsider.
locale ● noun PLACE, site, spot, area; position, location, setting, scene, venue, background, backdrop, environment; neighbourhood, district, region, locality.

or assign to a particular place. **2** make local in character.
– DERIVATIVES **localizable** adjective **localization** noun.

local time ● noun time as reckoned in a particular region or time zone.

locate ● verb **1** discover the exact place or position of. **2** (**be located**) be situated in a particular place. **3** N. Amer. establish oneself or one's business in a specified place.
– DERIVATIVES **locatable** adjective **locator** noun.
– ORIGIN originally as a legal term meaning 'let out on hire': from Latin *locare* 'to place'.

location ● noun **1** the action or process of locating. **2** a particular place or position. **3** an actual place in which a film or broadcast is made, as distinct from a simulation in a studio.
– DERIVATIVES **locational** adjective.

locative /lokkətiv/ ● adjective Grammar relating to or denoting a case in some languages of nouns, pronouns, and adjectives, expressing location.

loc. cit. ● abbreviation in the passage already cited.
– ORIGIN Latin *loco citato*.

loch /lok, lokh/ ● noun Scottish **1** a lake. **2** a long, narrow arm of the sea.
– ORIGIN Scottish Gaelic.

loci plural of LOCUS.

loci classici plural of LOCUS CLASSICUS.

lock[1] ● noun **1** a mechanism for keeping a door or container fastened, typically operated by a key. **2** a similar device used to prevent the operation of a vehicle or other machine. **3** a short section of a canal or river with gates and sluices at each end which can be opened or closed to change the water level, used for raising and lowering boats. **4** the turning of the front wheels of a vehicle to change its direction of motion. **5** (in wrestling and martial arts) a hold that prevents an opponent from moving a limb. **6** (also **lock forward**) Rugby a player in the second row of a scrum. **7** archaic a mechanism for exploding the charge of a gun. ● verb **1** fasten or be fastened with a lock. **2** enclose or secure by locking a door. **3** (**lock up/away**) imprison. **4** make or become rigidly fixed or immovable. **5** (**lock in**) engage or entangle in: *they were locked in a legal battle.* **6** (**lock on to**) locate and then track (a target) by radar or similar means.
– PHRASES **lock horns** engage in conflict. **lock, stock, and barrel** including everything. [ORIGIN referring to the complete mechanism of a firearm.]
– DERIVATIVES **lockable** adjective.
– ORIGIN Old English.

lock[2] ● noun **1** a section of a person's hair that coils or hangs in a piece. **2** (**locks**) chiefly literary a person's hair. **3** a tuft of wool or cotton.
– DERIVATIVES **locked** adjective.
– ORIGIN Old English.

lockdown ● noun N. Amer. the confining of prisoners to their cells.

locker ● noun a small lockable cupboard or compartment, typically one in a row of several.

locker room ● noun **1** a sports changing room containing rows of lockers. **2** (before another noun) (**locker-room**) characteristic of a men's locker room, especially in being coarse or ribald: *locker-room humour.*

locket ● noun a small ornamental case worn round a person's neck on a chain, ribbon, etc., used to hold an item of sentimental value such as a tiny photograph or a lock of hair.
– ORIGIN Old French *locquet* 'small latch or lock'; related to LOCK[1].

lock forward ● noun another term for LOCK[1] (in sense 6).

lock-in ● noun **1** an arrangement which obliges a person or company to negotiate or trade only with a specific company. **2** a period during which some customers remain in a bar or pub after the doors are locked at closing time, in order to continue drinking privately.

lockjaw ● noun spasm of the jaw muscles, causing the mouth to remain tightly closed, typically as a symptom of tetanus.

locknut ● noun **1** a nut screwed down on another to keep it tight. **2** a nut designed so that, once tightened, it cannot be accidentally loosened.

lockout ● noun the exclusion of employees by their employer from their place of work until certain terms are agreed to.

locksmith ● noun a person who makes and repairs locks.

lock-up ● noun **1** a makeshift jail. **2** Brit. non-residential premises, such as a garage, that can be locked up. **3** an investment in assets which cannot readily be realized or sold on in the short term.

loco[1] ● noun (pl. **locos**) informal a locomotive.

loco[2] ● adjective informal crazy.
– ORIGIN Spanish, 'insane'.

locomotion ● noun movement or the ability to move from one place to another.
– DERIVATIVES **locomotory** adjective.
– ORIGIN from Latin *loco* 'from a place' + *motio* 'motion'.

locomotive ● noun a powered railway vehicle used for pulling trains. ● adjective relating to locomotion.

locomotor (also **locomotory**) ● adjective chiefly Biology relating to locomotion.

locum /lōkəm/ (also **locum tenens**) ● noun a doctor or cleric standing in for another who is temporarily away.
– ORIGIN from Latin *locum tenens* 'one holding a place'.

locus /lōkəss/ ● noun (pl. **loci** /lōsī/) **1** technical a particular position, point, or place. **2** Mathematics a curve or other figure formed by all the points satisfying a particular condition.
– ORIGIN Latin, 'place'.

locus classicus /lōkəss klassikəss/ ● noun (pl. **loci classici** /lōsī klassisī/) the best known or most authoritative passage on a subject.
– ORIGIN Latin, 'classical place'.

locus standi /lōkəss standī/ ● noun (pl. **loci standi** /lōsī standī/) Law the right or capacity to bring an action or to appear in a court.
– ORIGIN Latin, 'place of standing'.

locust ● noun **1** a large tropical grasshopper which migrates in vast swarms and is very destructive to vegetation. **2** (also **locust tree**) a carob tree, false acacia, or similar pod-bearing tree.
– ORIGIN Latin *locusta* 'locust, crustacean'.

locution /ləkyoosh'n/ ● noun **1** a word or phrase. **2** a person's particular style of speech.
– DERIVATIVES **locutionary** adjective.
– ORIGIN Latin, from *loqui* 'speak'.

lode /lōd/ ● noun a vein of metal ore in the earth.

Thesaurus

locality ● noun **1** *the locality of the property* POSITION, location, whereabouts, place, situation, spot, point, site, scene, setting. **2** *other schools in the locality* VICINITY, neighbourhood, area, district, region; *informal* neck of the woods.

localize ● verb LIMIT, restrict, confine, contain, circumscribe, concentrate, delimit.
– OPPOSITES generalize, globalize.

locate ● verb **1** *spotter planes locate the shoals* FIND, discover, pinpoint, detect, track down, run to earth, unearth, sniff out, smoke out, search out, ferret out, uncover. **2** *a company located near Pittsburgh* SITUATE, site, position, place, base; put, build, establish, found, station, install, settle.

location ● noun POSITION, place, situation, site, locality, locale, spot, whereabouts, point; scene, setting, area, environment; bearings, orientation; venue, address; *technical* locus.

lock[1] ● noun *the lock on the door* BOLT, catch, fastener, clasp, bar, hasp, latch.
● verb **1** *he locked the door* BOLT, fasten, bar, secure, seal; padlock, latch, chain. **2** *she locked her wrists together* JOIN, interlock, link, mesh, engage, unite, connect, yoke, mate; couple. **3** *the wheels locked* BECOME STUCK, stick, jam, become/make immovable, become/make rigid. **4** *he locked her in an embrace* CLASP, clench, grasp, embrace, hug, squeeze.
– OPPOSITES unlock, open, separate, divide.
– PHRASES **lock someone out** KEEP OUT, shut out, refuse entrance to, deny admittance to; exclude, bar, debar, ban. **lock someone up** IMPRISON, jail, incarcerate, intern, send to prison, put behind bars, put under lock and key, put in chains, clap in irons, cage, pen, coop up; *informal* send down, put away, put inside.

lock[2] ● noun *a lock of hair* TRESS, tuft, curl, ringlet, hank, strand, wisp, snippet.

locker ● noun CUPBOARD, cabinet, chest, safe, box, case, coffer; compartment, storeroom.

lock-up ● noun **1** *drunks were put in the lock-up overnight* JAIL, prison, cell, detention centre; *N. Amer.* jailhouse; *informal* cooler, slammer, jug, can, nick, stir, clink, quod, chokey. **2** *(Brit.) they stored spare furniture in a lock-up* STOREROOM, store, warehouse, depository; garage.

– ORIGIN Old English, 'way, course'; related to LOAD.

loden /lōd'n/ ● noun **1** a thick waterproof woollen cloth. **2** the dark green colour in which such cloth is often made.
– ORIGIN German.

lodestar ● noun a star that is used to guide the course of a ship, especially the pole star.

lodestone (also **loadstone**) ● noun a piece of magnetite or other naturally magnetized mineral, able to be used as a magnet.

lodge ● noun **1** a small house at the gates of a large house with grounds, occupied by a gatekeeper or other employee. **2** a small country house occupied in season for sports such as hunting and shooting. **3** a porter's quarters at the entrance of a college or other large building. **4** an American Indian tent or other dwelling. **5** a beaver's den. **6** a branch or meeting place of an organization such as the Freemasons. ● verb **1** formally present (a complaint, appeal, etc.). **2** make or become firmly fixed in a place. **3** rent accommodation in another person's house. **4** provide with rented accommodation. **5** (**lodge in/with**) leave (money or a valuable item) for safekeeping in or with.
– ORIGIN Old French *loge* 'arbour, hut', from Latin *lobia* 'covered walk'; related to LOBBY.

lodgement ● noun **1** chiefly literary a place in which a person or thing is lodged. **2** the depositing of money in a particular bank or account.

lodger ● noun a person who pays rent to live in a property with the owner.

lodging ● noun **1** a temporary place of residence. **2** (**lodgings**) a rented room or rooms, usually in the same residence as the owner.

lodging house ● noun a private house providing rented accommodation.

loess /lōiss/ ● noun Geology a loosely compacted yellowish-grey deposit of wind-blown sediment.
– ORIGIN from Swiss German *lösch* 'loose'.

lo-fi (also **low-fi**) ● adjective of or employing sound reproduction of a lower quality than hi-fi.
– ORIGIN from an alteration of LOW¹ + *-fi* on the pattern of *hi-fi*.

loft ● noun **1** a room or storage space directly under the roof of a house or other building. **2** a large, open area in a warehouse or other large building, that has been converted into living space. **3** a gallery in a church or hall. **4** a shelter with nest holes for pigeons. **5** Golf upward inclination given to the ball in a stroke. **6** the thickness of an insulating material such as that in a sleeping bag. ● verb kick, hit, or throw (a ball or missile) high up.
– ORIGIN Old Norse, 'air, upper room'.

lofty ● adjective (**loftier**, **loftiest**) **1** of imposing height. **2** noble; elevated. **3** haughty and aloof. **4** (of wool and other textiles) thick and resilient.
– DERIVATIVES **loftily** adverb **loftiness** noun.

log¹ ● noun **1** a part of the trunk or a large branch of a tree that has fallen or been cut off. **2** (also **logbook**) an official record of events during the voyage of a ship or aircraft. **3** an apparatus for determining the speed of a ship, originally one consisting of a float attached to a knotted line. ● verb (**logged**, **logging**) **1** enter in a log. **2** achieve (a certain distance, speed, or time). **3** (**log in/on** or **out/off**) go through the procedures to begin (or conclude) use of a computer system. **4** cut down (an area of forest) to exploit the wood commercially.
– DERIVATIVES **logger** noun **logging** noun.
– ORIGIN of unknown origin.

log² ● noun short for LOGARITHM.

loganberry ● noun an edible soft fruit, considered to be a hybrid of a raspberry and an American dewberry.
– ORIGIN from the name of the American horticulturalist John H. *Logan* (1841–1928).

logarithm /loggərithəm/ ● noun a quantity representing the power to which a fixed number (the base) must be raised to produce a given number.
– ORIGIN from Greek *logos* 'reckoning, ratio' + *arithmos* 'number'.

logarithmic ● adjective **1** relating to or expressed in terms of logarithms. **2** (of a scale) constructed so that successive points along an axis, or graduations which are an equal distance apart, represent values which are in an equal ratio.
– DERIVATIVES **logarithmically** adverb.

logbook ● noun a book containing an official or systematic record of events.

loge /lōzh/ ● noun a private box or enclosure in a theatre.
– ORIGIN French.

loggerhead ● noun **1** (also **loggerhead turtle**) a large-headed reddish-brown turtle of warm seas. **2** archaic a foolish person.
– PHRASES **at loggerheads** in irreconcilable dispute or disagreement. [ORIGIN perhaps from a use of *loggerhead* in an obsolete sense 'long-handled iron instrument for heating liquids' (when wielded as a weapon).]
– ORIGIN from dialect *logger* 'block of wood for hobbling a horse' + HEAD.

loggia /lōjə/ ● noun a gallery or room with one or more open sides, especially one having one side open to a garden.
– ORIGIN Italian, 'lodge'.

logic ● noun **1** reasoning conducted or assessed according to strict principles of validity. **2** the ability to reason correctly. **3** (**the logic of**) the course of action following as a necessary consequence of. **4** a system or set of principles underlying the arrangements of elements in a computer or electronic device so as to perform a specified task.
– DERIVATIVES **logician** noun.
– ORIGIN from Greek *logikē tekhnē* 'art of reason'.

-logic ● combining form equivalent to -LOGICAL (as in *pharmacologic*).

logical ● adjective **1** of or according to the rules of logic. **2** capable of or showing rational thought. **3** expected or reasonable under the circumstances.
– DERIVATIVES **logicality** noun **logically** adverb.

-logical ● combining form in adjectives corresponding chiefly to

Thesaurus

locomotion ● noun MOVEMENT, motion, moving; travel, travelling; mobility, motility; walking, ambulation, running; progress, progression, passage; formal perambulation.

lodge ● noun **1** *the porter's lodge* GATEHOUSE, cottage. **2** *a hunting lodge* HOUSE, cottage, cabin, chalet; Brit. shooting box. **3** *a beaver's lodge* DEN, lair, hole, sett; retreat, haunt, shelter. **4** *a Masonic lodge* SECTION, branch, wing; hall, clubhouse, meeting room; N. Amer. chapter.
● verb **1** *William lodged at our house* RESIDE, board, stay, live, have lodgings, have rooms, put up, be quartered, stop; N. Amer. room; informal have digs; formal dwell, be domiciled, sojourn; archaic abide. **2** *they were lodged at an inn* ACCOMMODATE, put up, take in, house, board, billet, quarter, shelter. **3** *the government lodged a protest* SUBMIT, register, enter, put forward, advance, lay, present, tender, proffer, put on record, record, table, file. **4** *the money was lodged in a bank* DEPOSIT, put, bank; stash, store, stow, put away, squirrel away. **5** *the bullet lodged in his back* BECOME FIXED, embed itself, become embedded, become implanted, get/become stuck, stick, catch, become caught, wedge.

lodger ● noun BOARDER, paying guest, PG, tenant; N. Amer. roomer.

lodging ● noun ACCOMMODATION, rooms, chambers, living quarters, place to stay, a roof over one's head, housing, shelter; informal digs, pad; formal abode, residence, dwelling, dwelling place, habitation.

lofty ● adjective **1** *a lofty tower* TALL, high, giant, towering, soaring, sky-scraping. **2** *lofty ideals* NOBLE, exalted, high, high-minded, worthy, grand, fine, elevated. **3** *a lofty post in the department* EMINENT, prominent, leading, distinguished, illustrious, celebrated, elevated, esteemed, respected. **4** *lofty disdain* HAUGHTY, arrogant, disdainful, supercilious, condescending, patronizing, scornful, contemptuous, self-important, conceited, snobbish; informal stuck-up, snooty, snotty; Brit. informal toffee-nosed.
– OPPOSITES low, short, base, lowly, modest.

log ● noun **1** *a fallen log* BRANCH, trunk; piece of wood; (**logs**) timber, firewood. **2** *a log of phone calls* RECORD, register, logbook, journal, diary, minutes, chronicle, daybook, record book, ledger, account, tally.
● verb **1** *all complaints are logged* REGISTER, record, make a note of, note down, write down, jot down, put in writing, enter, file, minute. **2** *the pilot had logged 95 hours* ATTAIN, achieve, chalk up, make, do, go, cover.

loggerheads ● plural noun
– PHRASES **at loggerheads** IN DISAGREEMENT, at odds, at variance, wrangling, quarrelling, locking horns, at daggers drawn, in conflict, fighting, at war; informal at each other's throats.

logic ● noun **1** *this case appears to defy all logic* REASON, judgement, logical thought, rationality, wisdom, sense, good sense, common sense, sanity; informal horse sense. **2** *the logic of their argument* REASONING, line of reasoning, rationale, argument, argumentation.

nouns ending in *-logy* (such as *pharmacological* corresponding to *pharmacology*).

logical positivism (also **logical empiricism**) ● noun a form of positivism which considers that the only meaningful philosophical problems are those which can be solved by logical analysis.

logic bomb ● noun Computing a set of instructions secretly incorporated into a program so that if a particular condition is satisfied they will be carried out, usually with harmful effects.

-logist ● combining form indicating a person skilled or involved in a branch of study denoted by a noun ending in *-logy* (such as *biologist* corresponding to *biology*).

logistic ● adjective relating to logistics.
– DERIVATIVES **logistical** adjective.

logistics /ləjistiks/ ● plural noun (treated as sing. or pl.) the detailed coordination of a large and complex operation.
– ORIGIN originally in the sense 'movement and supply of troops and equipment': from French *logistique*, from *loger* 'to lodge'.

logjam ● noun **1** a crowded mass of logs blocking a river. **2** a deadlock. **3** a backlog.

logo /lōgō/ ● noun (pl. **logos**) an emblematic design adopted by an organization to identify its products.
– ORIGIN abbreviation of LOGOGRAM or LOGOTYPE.

logocentric ● adjective regarding words and language as a fundamental expression of an external reality.
– DERIVATIVES **logocentrism** noun.

logogram ● noun a sign or character representing a word or phrase, as used in shorthand and some ancient writing systems.
– ORIGIN from Greek *logos* 'word'.

logorrhoea /loggəreeə/ (US **logorrhea**) ● noun a tendency to be extremely talkative.
– ORIGIN from Greek *logos* 'word' + *rhoia* 'flow'.

logotype ● noun Printing a single piece of type that prints a word, a group of separate letters, or a logo.
– ORIGIN from Greek *logos* 'word'.

logrolling ● noun N. Amer. informal the exchange of favours between politicians by reciprocal voting for each other's proposed legislation.
– ORIGIN from the phrase *you roll my log and I'll roll yours.*

-logy ● combining form **1** (usu. as **-ology**) denoting a subject of study or interest: *psychology.* **2** denoting a characteristic of speech or language: *eulogy.* **3** denoting a type of discourse: *trilogy.*
– ORIGIN from Greek *logos* 'word'.

loin ● noun **1** the part of the body on both sides of the spine between the lowest ribs and the hip bones. **2** (**loins**) literary the region of the sexual organs, regarded as the source of erotic or procreative power. **3** a joint of meat that includes the vertebrae of the loins.
– ORIGIN Old French *loigne*, from Latin *lumbus*.

loincloth ● noun a piece of cloth wrapped round the hips, typically worn by men in some hot countries as their only garment.

loiter ● verb stand around or move without apparent purpose.
– PHRASES **loiter with intent** English Law, dated stand around with the intention of committing an offence.
– DERIVATIVES **loiterer** noun.
– ORIGIN perhaps from Dutch *loteren* 'wag about'.

Lolita /lōleetə/ ● noun (**a Lolita**) a sexually precocious young girl.
– ORIGIN a character in the novel *Lolita* (1958) by Vladimir Nabokov.

loll ● verb **1** sit, lie, or stand in a lazy, relaxed way. **2** hang loosely; droop.
– ORIGIN probably symbolic of dangling.

lollapalooza /lolləpəlōōzə/ (also **lalapalooza**) ● noun N. Amer. informal a particularly impressive or attractive person or thing.
– ORIGIN of fanciful formation.

Lollard /lollərd/ ● noun a follower of the English religious reformer John Wyclif (*c.*1330–84).
– ORIGIN originally a derogatory term, derived from a Dutch word meaning 'mumbler'.

lollipop ● noun **1** a large, flat, rounded boiled sweet on the end of a stick. **2** British term for ICE LOLLY.
– ORIGIN perhaps from dialect *lolly* 'tongue' + POP[1].

lollipop lady (or **lollipop man**) ● noun Brit. informal a person employed to help children cross the road safely near a school by holding up a circular sign on a pole to stop the traffic.

lollop ● verb (**lolloped**, **lolloping**) move in an ungainly way in a series of clumsy bounds.
– ORIGIN probably from LOLL, associated with TROLLOP.

lollo rosso /lollō rossō/ ● noun a variety of lettuce with deeply divided red-edged leaves.
– ORIGIN Italian, from *lolla* 'husk, chaff' + *rosso* 'red'.

lolly ● noun (pl. **lollies**) informal **1** chiefly Brit. a lollipop. **2** Austral./NZ a boiled sweet. **3** Brit. money.

lollygag (also **lallygag**) ● verb (**lollygagged**, **lollygagging**) N. Amer. informal spend time or move aimlessly.
– ORIGIN of unknown origin.

Lombard /lombaard/ ● noun **1** a member of a Germanic people who invaded Italy in the 6th century. **2** a person from Lombardy in northern Italy. **3** the Italian dialect of Lombardy.
– DERIVATIVES **Lombardic** adjective.
– ORIGIN Italian *lombardo*, from Latin *Langobardus*, from LONG[1] + the ethnic name *Bardi*.

Lombardy poplar ● noun a variety of poplar from Italy with a distinctive tall, slender columnar form.

Londoner ● noun a person from London.

London pride ● noun a saxifrage with rosettes of fleshy leaves and stems of pink starlike flowers.

lone ● adjective **1** having no companions; solitary. **2** lacking the support of others: *a lone voice.* **3** literary unfrequented and remote.
– ORIGIN shortening of ALONE.

lonely ● adjective (**lonelier**, **loneliest**) **1** sad because one has no friends or company. **2** solitary. **3** unfrequented and remote.
– DERIVATIVES **loneliness** noun.

lonely hearts ● plural noun people looking for a lover or friend through the personal columns of a newspaper.

loner ● noun a person who prefers not to associate with others.

l

Thesaurus

3 *the study of logic* SCIENCE OF REASONING, science of deduction, science of thought, dialectics, argumentation; *formal* ratiocination.

logical ● adjective **1** *information displayed in a logical fashion* REASONED, well reasoned, rational, sound, cogent, well thought out, valid; coherent, clear, well organized, systematic, orderly, methodical, analytical, consistent, objective; *informal* joined-up. **2** *the logical outcome* NATURAL, reasonable, sensible, understandable; predictable, unsurprising, only to be expected, most likely, likeliest, obvious.
– OPPOSITES illogical, irrational, unlikely, surprising.

logistics ● plural noun ORGANIZATION, planning, plans, management, arrangement, administration, orchestration, coordination, execution, handling, running.

logo ● noun EMBLEM, trademark, device, symbol, design, sign, mark; insignia, crest, seal, coat of arms, shield, badge, motif, monogram, colophon.

loiter ● verb **1** *he loitered at bus stops* LINGER, wait, skulk; loaf, lounge, idle, laze, waste time; *informal* hang around/round; *Brit. informal* hang about, mooch about/around; *archaic* tarry. **2** *they loitered along the river bank* DAWDLE, dally, stroll, amble, saunter, meander, drift, potter, take one's time; *informal* dilly-dally, mosey, tootle; *Brit. informal* mooch.

loll ● verb **1** *he lolled in an armchair* LOUNGE, sprawl, drape oneself, stretch oneself; slouch, slump; laze, luxuriate, put one's feet up, lean back, recline, relax, take it easy. **2** *her head lolled to one side* HANG (LOOSELY), droop, dangle, sag, drop, flop.

lone ● adjective **1** *a lone police officer* SOLITARY, single, solo, unaccompanied, unescorted, alone, by oneself/itself, sole, companionless; detached, isolated, unique; lonely. **2** *a lone parent* SINGLE, unmarried, unattached, partnerless, husbandless, wifeless; separated, divorced, widowed.

loneliness ● noun **1** *his loneliness was unbearable* ISOLATION, friendlessness, abandonment, rejection, unpopularity; *N. Amer.* lonesomeness. **2** *the enforced loneliness of a prison cell* SOLITARINESS, solitude, lack of company, aloneness, separation. **3** *the loneliness of the village* ISOLATION, remoteness, seclusion.

lonely ● adjective **1** *I felt very lonely* ISOLATED, alone, friendless, with no one to turn to, forsaken, abandoned, rejected, unloved, unwanted; *N. Amer.* lonesome. **2** *the lonely life of a writer* SOLITARY, unaccompanied, lone, by oneself/itself, companionless. **3** *a lonely road* DESERTED, uninhabited, unfrequented, unpopulated, desolate, isolated, remote, out of the way, off the beaten track, in the back of beyond, godforsaken; *informal* in the middle of nowhere.
– OPPOSITES popular, sociable, crowded.

lonesome ● adjective chiefly N. Amer. lonely.
– PHRASES **by** (or Brit. **on**) **one's lonesome** informal all alone.
– DERIVATIVES **lonesomeness** noun.
lone wolf ● noun a person who prefers to act alone.
long[1] ● adjective (**longer**, **longest**) **1** of a great distance or duration. **2** relatively great in extent. **3** having a specified length, distance, or duration. **4** (of a ball in sport) travelling a great distance, or further than expected. **5** Phonetics (of a vowel) categorized as long with regard to quality and length (e.g. in standard British English the vowel /o͞o/ in *food*). **6** (of odds or a chance) reflecting or representing a low level of probability. **7** (of a drink) large and refreshing, and in which alcohol, if present, is not concentrated. **8** (**long on**) informal well supplied with. ● noun a long time. ● adverb (**longer**, **longest**) **1** for a long time. **2** at a distant time: *long ago*. **3** throughout a specified period of time: *all day long*. **4** (with reference to the ball in sport) at, to, or over a great distance.
– PHRASES **as** (or **so**) **long as 1** during the whole time that. **2** provided that. **be long** take a long time. **in the long run** (or **term**) eventually. **the long and the short of it** all that can or need be said. **long in the tooth** rather old. [ORIGIN originally said of horses, from the recession of the gums with age.]
– DERIVATIVES **longish** adjective.
– ORIGIN Old English.
long[2] ● verb (**long for/to do**) have a strong wish for or to do.
– ORIGIN Old English, 'grow long', also 'yearn'.
long. ● abbreviation longitude.
longboat ● noun **1** historical a sizeable boat which could be launched from a large sailing ship. **2** another term for LONGSHIP.
longbow ● noun a large bow drawn by hand and shooting a long feathered arrow.
long-distance ● adjective **1** travelling or operating between distant places. **2** Athletics denoting a race distance of 6 miles or 10,000 metres (6 miles 376 yds), or longer. ● adverb between distant places.
long division ● noun division of numbers with details of intermediate calculations written down.
long-drawn (also **long-drawn-out**) ● adjective prolonged, especially unduly.
longe ● noun variant of LUNGE[2].
longevity /lonjevviti/ ● noun long life.
– ORIGIN Latin *longaevitas*, from *longus* 'long' + *aevum* 'age'.
long face ● noun an unhappy or disappointed expression.
longhand ● noun ordinary handwriting (as opposed to shorthand, typing, or printing).
long haul ● noun **1** a long distance (with reference to the transport of goods or passengers). **2** a lengthy and difficult task.
long-headed ● adjective dated having or showing foresight and good judgement.
long hop ● noun Cricket a short-pitched, easily hit ball.
longhorn ● noun a breed of cattle with long horns.
longhouse ● noun a large communal house in parts of Malaysia and Indonesia or among some North American Indians.
longing ● noun a yearning desire. ● adjective having or showing a yearning desire.
– DERIVATIVES **longingly** adverb.
longitude /longgityo͞od/ ● noun the angular distance of a place east or west of a standard meridian, especially the Greenwich meridian.
– ORIGIN Latin *longitudo*, from *longus* 'long'.
longitudinal /longgityo͞odin'l/ ● adjective **1** running lengthwise. **2** relating to longitude.
– DERIVATIVES **longitudinally** adverb.
long johns ● plural noun informal underpants with closely fitted legs extending to the wearer's ankles.
long jump ● noun (**the long jump**) an athletic event in which competitors jump as far as possible along the ground in one leap.
– DERIVATIVES **long jumper** noun.
long leg ● noun Cricket a fielding position far behind the batsman on the leg side.
long-life ● adjective (of perishable goods) treated so as to stay fresh for longer than usual.
longline ● noun a deep-sea fishing line with a large number of hooks attached to it.
long-lived ● adjective living or lasting a long time.
long off ● noun Cricket a fielding position far behind the bowler and towards the off side.
long on ● noun Cricket a fielding position far behind the bowler and towards the on side.
long pig ● noun a translation of a term formerly used in some Pacific Islands for human flesh as food.
long-playing ● adjective (of a record) 12 inches (about 30 cm) in diameter and designed to rotate at 33⅓ revolutions per minute.
long-range ● adjective **1** able to be used or be effective over long distances. **2** relating to a period of time far into the future.
longship ● noun a long, narrow warship with oars and a sail, used by the Vikings.
longshore ● adjective relating to or moving along the seashore.
– ORIGIN from *along shore*.
longshore drift ● noun the movement of material along a coast by waves which approach at an angle to the shore but recede directly away from it.
longshoreman ● noun N. Amer. a docker.
long shot ● noun a venture or guess that has only the slightest chance of succeeding or being accurate.
– PHRASES (**not**) **by a long shot** informal (not) by far or at all.
long-sighted ● adjective unable to see things clearly if they are relatively close to the eyes.
long-standing ● adjective having existed for a long time.
longstop ● noun Cricket a fielding position directly behind the wicketkeeper.
long-suffering ● adjective bearing problems or provocation with patience.
long suit ● noun **1** (in bridge or whist) a holding of several cards of one suit in a hand. **2** an outstanding personal quality or achievement: *tact was not his long suit*.
longueur /lonɢgör/ ● noun a tedious passage or period.
– ORIGIN French, 'length'.
long vacation ● noun Brit. the summer break of three months taken by universities and (formerly) law courts.
long-waisted ● noun (of a dress or a person's body) having a low waist.
long wave ● noun **1** a radio wave of a wavelength above one kilometre (and a frequency below 300 kilohertz). **2** broadcasting using radio waves of 1 to 10 kilometre wavelength.
longways (also **longwise**) ● adverb lengthways.
long-winded ● adjective **1** tediously lengthy. **2** archaic capable of doing something for a long time without becoming breathless.
lonicera /lonissərə/ ● noun a plant of a genus which comprises

Thesaurus

loner ● noun RECLUSE, introvert, lone wolf, hermit, solitary, misanthrope, outsider; *historical* anchorite.
long[1] ● adjective *a long silence* LENGTHY, extended, prolonged, extensive, protracted, long-lasting, long-drawn(-out), spun out, dragged out, seemingly endless, lingering, interminable.
– OPPOSITES short, brief.
– PHRASES **before long** SOON, shortly, presently, in the near future, in a little while, by and by, in a minute, in a moment, in a second; *informal* anon, in a jiffy; *Brit. informal* in a tick, in two ticks, in a mo; *dated* directly; *poetic/literary* ere long.
long[2] ● verb *I longed for the holidays* YEARN, pine, ache, hanker for/after, hunger, thirst, itch, be eager, be desperate; crave, dream of, set one's heart on; *informal* have a yen, be dying.
longing ● noun *a longing for the countryside* YEARNING, pining, craving, ache, burning, hunger, thirst, hankering; *informal* yen, itch.
● adjective *a longing look* YEARNING, pining, craving, hungry, thirsty, hankering, wistful, covetous.
long-lasting ● adjective ENDURING, lasting, abiding, long-lived, long-running, long-established, long-standing, lifelong, deep-rooted, time-honoured, traditional, permanent.
– OPPOSITES short-lived, ephemeral.
long-lived ● adjective. See LONG-LASTING.
long-standing ● adjective WELL ESTABLISHED, long-established; time-honoured, traditional, age-old; abiding, enduring, long-lived, surviving, persistent, prevailing, perennial, deep-rooted, long-term, confirmed.
– OPPOSITES new, recent.
long-suffering ● adjective PATIENT, forbearing, tolerant, uncomplaining, stoical, resigned; easy-going, indulgent, charitable, accommodating, forgiving.
– OPPOSITES impatient, complaining.
long-winded ● adjective VERBOSE, wordy, lengthy, long, overlong, prolix, prolonged, protracted, long-drawn-out, interminable; dis-

the honeysuckles.
– ORIGIN named after the German botanist Adam *Lonitzer* (1528–86).

Lonsdale belt • noun an ornate belt awarded to a professional boxer winning a British title fight.
– ORIGIN named after the fifth Earl of *Lonsdale*, Hugh Cecil Lowther (1857–1944), who presented the first one.

loo[1] • noun Brit. informal a toilet.
– ORIGIN origin uncertain: one theory suggests the source is *Waterloo*, a trade name for iron cisterns in the early 20th century.

loo[2] • noun a gambling card game, popular from the 17th to the 19th centuries, in which a player who fails to win a trick must pay a sum to a pool.
– ORIGIN abbreviation of *lanterloo*, a meaningless refrain in old songs.

loofah /lo͞ofə/ • noun a fibrous cylindrical object used like a bath sponge, consisting of the dried inner parts of a marrow-like tropical fruit.
– ORIGIN Egyptian Arabic.

look • verb **1** direct one's gaze in a specified direction. **2** have an outlook in a specified direction. **3** have the appearance or give the impression of being. • noun **1** an act of looking. **2** an expression of a feeling or thought by looking at someone. **3** the appearance of someone or something. **4** (**looks**) a person's facial appearance considered aesthetically. **5** a style or fashion. • exclamation (also **look here!**) used to call attention to what one is going to say.
– PHRASES **look after** take care of. **look at 1** regard in a specified way. **2** examine (a matter) and consider what action to take. **look before you leap** proverb one shouldn't act without first considering the possible consequences or dangers. **look down on** (also **look down one's nose at**) regard with a feeling of superiority. **look for** attempt to find. **look in** make a short visit or call. **look into** investigate. **look like** informal show a likelihood of. **look lively** (or **sharp**) informal be quick; get moving. **look on** watch without getting involved. **look out 1** be vigilant and take notice. **2** Brit. search for and produce (something). **look over** inspect (something) to establish its merits. **look to 1** rely on (someone) to do something. **2** hope or expect to do. **3** archaic make sure. **look up 1** improve. **2** search for and find (a piece of information) in a reference work. **3** informal make social contact with. **look up to** have a great deal of respect for.
– ORIGIN Old English.

lookalike • noun a person or thing that closely resembles another.

looker • noun **1** a person with a specified appearance: *she's not a bad looker*. **2** informal a very attractive person.

look-in • noun informal a chance of participation or success.

looking glass • noun a mirror.

lookism • noun prejudice or discrimination on the grounds of appearance.
– DERIVATIVES **lookist** noun & adjective.

lookout • noun **1** a place from which to keep watch or view landscape. **2** a person stationed to keep watch. **3** informal, chiefly Brit. a good or bad prospect or outcome. **4** (**one's lookout**) Brit. informal one's own concern.
– PHRASES **be on the lookout** (or **keep a lookout**) **for 1** be alert to. **2** keep searching for.

look-see • noun informal a brief look or inspection.

loom[1] • noun an apparatus for making fabric by weaving yarn or thread.
– ORIGIN Old English, 'tool'.

loom[2] • verb **1** appear as a vague form, especially one that is threatening. **2** (of an event regarded as threatening) seem about to happen.
– ORIGIN probably from Low German or Dutch.

loon[1] • noun informal a silly or foolish person. • verb Brit. informal act in a foolish or desultory way.
– ORIGIN from LOON[2] (referring to the bird's actions when escaping from danger), perhaps influenced by LOONY.

loon[2] • noun North American term for DIVER (in sense 2).
– ORIGIN probably from Shetland dialect *loom*.

loons (also **loon pants**) • plural noun Brit. dated close-fitting casual trousers widely flared from the knees downwards.
– ORIGIN of unknown origin.

loony informal • noun (pl. **loonies**) a mad or silly person. • adjective (**loonier, looniest**) mad or silly.
– DERIVATIVES **looniness** noun.
– ORIGIN abbreviation of LUNATIC.

loony bin • noun informal, derogatory an institution for people with mental illnesses.

Thesaurus

cursive, diffuse, rambling, tortuous, meandering, repetitious; *informal* windy; *Brit. informal* waffly.
– OPPOSITES concise, succinct, laconic.

look • verb **1** *Mrs Wright looked at him* GLANCE, gaze, stare, gape, peer; peep, peek, take a look; watch, observe, view, regard, examine, inspect, eye, scan, scrutinize, survey, study, contemplate, consider, take in, ogle; *informal* take a gander, rubberneck, give someone/something a/the once-over, get a load of; *Brit. informal* take a dekko, take a butcher's, take a shufti, clock, gawp; *N. Amer. informal* eyeball; *poetic/literary* behold. **2** *her room looked out on Broadway* COMMAND A VIEW, face, overlook, front. **3** *they looked shocked* SEEM (TO BE), appear (to be), have the appearance/air of being, give the impression of being, give every appearance/indication of being, strike someone as being.
– OPPOSITES ignore.
• noun **1** *have a look at this report* GLANCE, view, examination, study, inspection, observation, scan, survey, peep, peek, glimpse, gaze, stare; *informal* eyeful, gander, look-see, once-over, squint, recce; *Brit. informal* shufti, dekko, butcher's, gawp. **2** *the look on her face* EXPRESSION, mien. **3** *that rustic look* APPEARANCE, air, aspect, bearing, cast, manner, mien, demeanour, facade, impression, effect. **4** *this season's look* FASHION, style, vogue, mode.
– PHRASES **look after** TAKE CARE OF, care for, attend to, minister to, tend, mind, keep an eye on, keep safe, be responsible for, protect; nurse, babysit, childmind. **look back on** REFLECT ON, think back to, remember, recall, reminisce about. **look down on** DISDAIN, scorn, regard with contempt, look down one's nose at, sneer at, despise. **look for** SEARCH FOR, hunt for, try to find, seek, cast about/around/round for, try to track down, forage for, scout out, quest for/after. **look forward to** AWAIT WITH PLEASURE, eagerly anticipate, lick one's lips over, be unable to wait for, count the days until. **look into** INVESTIGATE, enquire into, ask questions about, go into, probe, explore, follow up, research, study, examine; *informal* check out, give something a/the once-over; *N. Amer. informal* scope out. **look like** RESEMBLE, bear a resemblance to, look similar to, take after, have the look of, have the appearance of, remind one of, make one think of; *informal* be the spitting image of, be a dead ringer for. **look on/upon** REGARD, consider, think of, deem, judge, see, view, count, reckon. **look out** BEWARE, watch out, mind out, be on (one's) guard, be alert, be wary, be vigilant, be careful, take care, be cautious, pay attention, take heed, keep one's eyes open/peeled, keep an eye out, watch your step. **look something over** INSPECT, examine, scan, cast an eye over, take stock of, vet, view, look through, peruse, run through, read through; *informal* take a dekko at, give something a/the once-over; *N. Amer.* check out; *N. Amer. informal* eyeball. **look to 1** *we must look to the future* CONSIDER, think about, turn one's thoughts to, focus on, take heed of, pay attention to, attend to, address, mind, heed. **2** *they look to the government for help* TURN TO, resort to, have recourse to, fall back on, rely on. **look up** IMPROVE, get better, pick up, come along/on, progress, make progress, make headway, perk up, rally, take a turn for the better. **look someone up** *(informal)* VISIT, pay a visit to, call on, go to see, look in on; *N. Amer.* visit with, go see; *informal* drop in on. **look up to** ADMIRE, have a high opinion of, think highly of, hold in high regard, regard highly, rate highly, respect, esteem, value.

lookalike • noun DOUBLE, twin, clone, duplicate, exact likeness, replica, copy, facsimile, Doppelgänger; *informal* spitting image, dead ringer, dead spit.

lookout • noun **1** *he saw the smoke from the lookout* OBSERVATION POST, lookout point, lookout station, lookout tower, watchtower. **2** *the lookout sighted sails* WATCHMAN, watch, guard, sentry, sentinel, picket; *historical* vedette. **3** *(informal) it would be a poor lookout for her* OUTLOOK, prospect, chance of success, future. **4** *(Brit. informal) that's your lookout* PROBLEM, concern, business, affair, responsibility, worry; *informal* pigeon.
– PHRASES **be on the lookout/keep a lookout** KEEP WATCH, keep an eye out, keep one's eyes peeled, keep a vigil, be alert, be on the qui vive.

loom • verb **1** *ghostly shapes loomed out of the fog* EMERGE, appear, come into view, take shape, materialize, reveal itself. **2** *the church loomed above him* SOAR, tower, rise, rear up; overhang,

loop ● noun **1** a shape produced by a curve that bends round and crosses itself. **2** (also **loop-the-loop**) a manoeuvre in which an aircraft describes a vertical circle in the air. **3** an endless strip of tape or film allowing continuous repetition. **4** a complete circuit for an electric current. **5** Computing a programmed sequence of instructions that is repeated until or while a particular condition is satisfied. **6** (also **loop line**) a length of railway track which is connected at either end to the main line. ● verb **1** form into a loop or loops; encircle. **2** follow a course that forms a loop or loops. **3** put into or execute a loop of tape, film, or computing instructions. **4** (also **loop the loop**) circle an aircraft vertically in the air.
– PHRASES **in** (or **out of**) **the loop** informal, chiefly N. Amer. aware (or unaware) of information known to only a privileged few.
– ORIGIN of unknown origin.

looper ● noun a kind of moth caterpillar which moves forward by arching itself into loops.

loophole ● noun **1** an ambiguity or inadequacy in the law or a set of rules. **2** an arrow slit in a wall.
– ORIGIN from obsolete *loop* 'embrasure' + HOLE.

loopy ● adjective (**loopier, loopiest**) informal mad or silly.
– DERIVATIVES **loopiness** noun.

loose /lo͞oss/ ● adjective **1** not firmly or tightly fixed in place. **2** not held, tied, or packaged together. **3** not bound or tethered. **4** not fitting tightly or closely. **5** not dense or compact. **6** relaxed: *her loose, easy stride.* **7** careless and indiscreet: *loose talk.* **8** not strict; inexact. **9** dated promiscuous or immoral. **10** (of the ball in a game) in play but not in any player's possession. ● verb **1** unfasten or set free. **2** relax (one's grip). **3** (usu. **loose off**) discharge; fire.
– PHRASES **hang** (or **stay**) **loose** informal, chiefly N. Amer. be relaxed. **on the loose** having escaped from confinement.
– DERIVATIVES **loosely** adverb **looseness** noun.
– USAGE The word **loose** is sometimes confused with **lose**; as a verb **loose** means 'unfasten or set free', while **lose** means 'cease to have' or 'become unable to find'. It is therefore incorrect to say *this would cause them to loose 20 percent*, the correct version being ... *to lose 20 per cent.*
– ORIGIN Old Norse.

loose box ● noun Brit. a stable or stall in which a horse is kept without a tether.

loose cannon ● noun an unpredictable person who is liable to cause unintentional damage.

loose cover ● noun Brit. a removable fitted cloth cover for a chair or sofa.

loose end ● noun a detail that is not yet settled or explained.
– PHRASES **be at a loose end** (or N. Amer. **at loose ends**) have nothing specific to do.

loose forward ● noun Rugby a forward who plays at the back of the scrum.

loose-leaf ● adjective (of a notebook or folder) having each sheet of paper separate and removable.

loosen ● verb **1** make or become loose. **2** (**loosen up**) warm up in preparation for an activity.
– PHRASES **loosen someone's tongue** make someone talk freely.
– DERIVATIVES **loosener** noun.

loose scrum ● noun Rugby a scrum formed by the players round the ball during play, not ordered by the referee.

loosestrife /lo͞osstrīf/ ● noun a waterside plant with a tall upright spike of purple or yellow flowers.
– ORIGIN from the plant's Greek name *lusimakheion*, actually from *Lusimakhos*, the name of its discoverer, but imagined as being from *luein* 'undo, loose' + *makhē* 'battle'.

loot ● noun **1** private property taken from an enemy in war or stolen by thieves. **2** informal money. ● verb steal goods from somewhere, especially during a war or riot.
– DERIVATIVES **looter** noun.
– ORIGIN Sanskrit, 'rob'.

lop ● verb (**lopped, lopping**) **1** cut off (a branch or limb) from a tree or body. **2** informal remove (something unnecessary or burdensome). ● noun (also **lop and top**) branches and twigs lopped off trees.
– DERIVATIVES **lopper** noun.
– ORIGIN of unknown origin.

lope ● verb run with a long bounding stride. ● noun a long bounding stride.
– ORIGIN Old Norse, 'leap'.

lop-eared ● adjective (of an animal) having drooping ears.
– DERIVATIVES **lop ears** plural noun.
– ORIGIN from archaic *lop* 'hang loosely or limply'.

lopsided ● adjective with one side lower or smaller than the other.
– DERIVATIVES **lopsidedly** adverb **lopsidedness** noun.

loquacious /lokwayshəss/ ● adjective talkative.
– DERIVATIVES **loquaciously** adverb **loquaciousness** noun **loquacity** noun.
– ORIGIN Latin *loquax*, from *loqui* 'to talk'.

loquat /lōkwot/ ● noun a small egg-shaped yellow fruit from an East Asian tree.
– ORIGIN Chinese dialect, 'rush orange'.

Thesaurus

overshadow, dominate. **3** *without reforms, disaster looms* BE IMMINENT, be on the horizon, impend, threaten, brew, be just around the corner.

loop ● noun *a loop of rope* COIL, hoop, ring, circle, noose, oval, spiral, curl, bend, curve, arc, twirl, whorl, twist, hook, zigzag, helix, convolution, incurvation.
● verb **1** *Dave looped rope around their hands* COIL, wind, twist, snake, wreathe, spiral, curve, bend, turn. **2** *he looped the cables together* FASTEN, tie, join, connect, knot, bind.

loophole ● noun MEANS OF EVASION, means of avoidance; ambiguity, omission, flaw, inconsistency, discrepancy.

loose ● adjective **1** *a loose floorboard* NOT FIXED IN PLACE, not secure, unsecured, unattached; detached, unfastened; wobbly, unsteady, movable. **2** *she wore her hair loose* UNTIED, unpinned, unbound, hanging free, down, flowing. **3** *there's a wolf loose* FREE, at large, at liberty, on the loose, escaped; unconfined, untied, unchained, untethered. **4** *a loose interpretation* VAGUE, indefinite, inexact, imprecise, approximate; broad, general, rough; liberal. **5** *a loose jacket* BAGGY, generously cut, slack, roomy; oversized, shapeless, bagging, sagging, sloppy. **6** (dated) *a loose woman* PROMISCUOUS, of easy virtue, fast, wanton, unchaste, immoral; licentious, dissolute; N. Amer. informal roundheeled; dated fallen; derogatory whorish, sluttish.
– OPPOSITES secure, literal, narrow, tight, chaste.
● verb **1** *the hounds have been loosed* FREE, set free, unloose, turn loose, set loose, let loose, let go, release; untie, unchain, unfasten, unleash. **2** *the fingers loosed their hold* RELAX, slacken, loosen; weaken, lessen, reduce, diminish, moderate. **3** *Brian loosed off a shot* FIRE, discharge, shoot, let go, let fly with.
– OPPOSITES confine, tighten.
– PHRASES **at a loose end** WITH NOTHING TO DO, unoccupied, unemployed, at leisure, idle, adrift, with time to kill; bored, twiddling one's thumbs, kicking one's heels. **break loose** ESCAPE, make one's escape, get away, get free, break free, free oneself. **let loose.** See LOOSE verb sense 1. **on the loose** FREE, at liberty, at large, escaped; on the run, fugitive; N. Amer. informal on the lam.

loose-limbed ● adjective SUPPLE, limber, lithe, lissom, willowy; agile, nimble.

loosen ● verb **1** *you simply loosen two screws* MAKE SLACK, slacken, unstick; unfasten, detach, release, disconnect, undo, unclasp, unlatch, unbolt. **2** *her fingers loosened* BECOME SLACK, slacken, become loose, let go, ease; work loose, work free. **3** *Philip loosened his grip* WEAKEN, relax, slacken, loose, lessen, reduce, moderate, diminish. **4** *you need to loosen up* RELAX, unwind, ease up/off; informal let up, hang loose, lighten up, go easy.
– OPPOSITES tighten.

loot ● noun *a bag full of loot* BOOTY, spoils, plunder, stolen goods, contraband, pillage; informal swag, hot goods, ill-gotten gains, boodle.
● verb *troops looted the cathedral* PLUNDER, pillage, despoil, ransack, sack, raid, rifle, rob, burgle; strip, clear out.

lop ● verb CUT, chop, hack, saw, hew, slash, axe; prune, sever, clip, trim, snip, dock, crop.

lope ● verb STRIDE, run, bound; lollop.

lopsided ● adjective CROOKED, askew, awry, off-centre, uneven, out of true, out of line, asymmetrical, tilted, at an angle, aslant, slanting, squint; Scottish agley; informal cock-eyed; Brit. informal skew-whiff, wonky.
– OPPOSITES even, level, balanced.

loquacious ● adjective TALKATIVE, voluble, communicative, expansive, unreserved, chatty, gossipy, gossiping, garrulous; informal having the gift of the gab, gabby, gassy; Brit. informal able to talk the hind legs off a donkey.
– OPPOSITES reticent, taciturn.

loquitur /lokwitər/ ● verb he or she speaks (as a stage direction).
– ORIGIN Latin, from *loqui* 'talk, speak'.

lord ● noun **1** a man of noble rank or high office. **2** (**Lord**) a title given formally to a baron, less formally to a marquess, earl, or viscount, and as a courtesy title to a younger son of a duke or marquess. **3** (**the Lords**) the House of Lords, or its members collectively. **4** a master or ruler. **5** (**Lord**) a name for God or Christ. ● exclamation (**Lord**) used in exclamations expressing surprise or worry, or for emphasis. ● verb (**lord it over**) act in a superior and domineering manner towards.
– PHRASES **the Lord's Day** Sunday. **the Lord's Prayer** the prayer taught by Christ to his disciples, beginning 'Our Father.'
– ORIGIN Old English, 'bread-keeper'; compare with LADY.

Lord Advocate ● noun the principal Law Officer of the Crown in Scotland.

Lord Chamberlain (also **Lord Chamberlain of the Household**) ● noun (in the UK) the official in charge of the royal household, formerly the licenser of plays.

Lord Chancellor ● noun (in the UK) the highest officer of the Crown, presiding in the House of Lords, the Chancery Division, or the Court of Appeal.

Lord Chief Justice ● noun (in the UK) the officer presiding over the Queen's Bench Division and the Court of Appeal.

Lord Justice ● noun (pl. **Lords Justices**) (in the UK) a judge in the Court of Appeal.

Lord Lieutenant ● noun (in the UK) the chief executive authority and head of magistrates in each county.

lordly ● adjective (**lordlier**, **lordliest**) of, characteristic of, or suitable for a lord.
– DERIVATIVES **lordliness** noun.

Lord Mayor ● noun the title of the mayor in London and some other large cities.

Lord of Appeal (in full **Lord of Appeal in Ordinary**) ● noun formal term for LAW LORD.

lordosis /lordōsiss/ ● noun Medicine excessive backward curvature of the spine, causing concavity of the back. Compare with KYPHOSIS.
– ORIGIN Greek, from *lordos* 'bent backwards'.

Lord President of the Council ● noun (in the UK) the cabinet minister presiding at the Privy Council.

Lord Privy Seal ● noun (in the UK) a senior cabinet minister without specified official duties.

Lord Provost ● noun the head of a municipal corporation or borough in certain Scottish cities.

lords and ladies ● noun another term for CUCKOO PINT.

lordship ● noun **1** supreme power or rule. **2** (**His/Your** etc. **Lordship**) a form of address to a judge, bishop, or titled man. **3** archaic the authority or state of being a lord.

Lords spiritual ● plural noun the bishops in the House of Lords.

Lords temporal ● plural noun the members of the House of Lords other than the bishops.

Lord Treasurer ● noun see TREASURER.

lore[1] ● noun a body of traditions and knowledge on a subject: *farming lore.*
– ORIGIN Old English, 'instruction'; related to LEARN.

lore[2] ● noun Zoology the surface on each side of a bird's head between the eye and the upper base of the beak, or between the eye and nostril in snakes.
– ORIGIN Latin *lorum* 'strap'.

lorgnette /lornyet/ (also **lorgnettes**) ● noun a pair of glasses or opera glasses held by a long handle at one side.
– ORIGIN French, from *lorgner* 'to squint'.

lorikeet /lorrikeet/ ● noun a small bird of the lory family, found chiefly in New Guinea.
– ORIGIN from LORY, on the pattern of *parakeet.*

loris /loriss/ ● noun (pl. **lorises**) a small, slow-moving nocturnal primate living in dense vegetation in South Asia.
– ORIGIN French, perhaps from obsolete Dutch *loeris* 'clown'.

lorry ● noun (pl. **lorries**) Brit. a large, heavy motor vehicle for transporting goods or troops.
– PHRASES **fall off of the back a lorry** informal (of goods) be acquired in dubious circumstances.
– ORIGIN perhaps from the given name *Laurie.*

lory /lori/ ● noun (pl. **lories**) a small Australasian or SE Asian parrot.
– ORIGIN Malay.

lose /lo͞oz/ ● verb (past and past part. **lost**) **1** be deprived of or cease to have or retain. **2** become unable to find. **3** fail to win. **4** earn less (money) than one is spending. **5** waste or fail to take advantage of. **6** (**be lost**) be destroyed or killed. **7** evade or shake off (a pursuer). **8** (**lose oneself in/be lost in**) be or become deeply absorbed in. **9** (of a watch or clock) become slow by (a specified amount of time).
– PHRASES **lose face** lose one's credibility. **lose heart** become discouraged. **lose it** informal lose control of one's temper or emotions. **lose one's mind** (or **marbles**) informal go insane. **lose out** be disadvantaged. **lose one's** (or **the**) **way** become lost.
– USAGE On the confusion of **lose** and **loose**, see the note at LOOSE.
– ORIGIN Old English, 'perish, destroy', also 'become unable to find'.

loser ● noun **1** a person or thing that loses or has lost. **2** informal a person who fails frequently.

losing battle ● noun a struggle in which failure seems certain.

loss ● noun **1** the fact or process of losing something or someone. **2** the feeling of grief after losing a valued person or thing. **3** a person or thing that is badly missed when lost. **4** a defeat in sport.

Thesaurus

loquacity ● noun TALKATIVENESS, volubility, expansiveness, garrulousness, garrulity, chattiness; *informal* the gift of the gab.
– OPPOSITES reticence, taciturnity.

lord ● noun **1** *lords and ladies* NOBLE, nobleman, peer, aristocrat, patrician, grandee, seigneur. **2** *it is my duty to obey my lord's wishes* MASTER, ruler, leader, chief, superior, monarch, sovereign, king, emperor, prince, governor, commander, suzerain, liege, liege lord. **3** *let us pray to our Lord* GOD, the Father, the Almighty, Jehovah, the Creator; JESUS CHRIST, the Messiah, the Saviour, the Son of God, the Redeemer, the Lamb of God, the Prince of Peace, the King of Kings. **4** *a press lord* MAGNATE, tycoon, mogul, captain, baron, king; industrialist, proprietor; *informal* big shot, honcho; *derogatory* fat cat.
– OPPOSITES commoner, servant, inferior.
– PHRASES **lord it over someone** ORDER ABOUT/AROUND, dictate to, ride roughshod over, pull rank on, tyrannize, have under one's thumb; be overbearing, put on airs, swagger; *informal* boss about/around, walk all over, push around, throw one's weight about/around.

lordly ● adjective **1** *lordly titles* NOBLE, aristocratic, princely, kingly, regal, royal, imperial, courtly, stately; magnificent, majestic, grand, august. **2** *in lordly tones* IMPERIOUS, arrogant, haughty, self-important, swaggering; supercilious, disdainful, scornful, contemptuous, condescending, patronizing, superior; dictatorial, authoritarian, peremptory, autocratic; *informal* bossy, high and mighty, snooty, uppity, hoity-toity; *Brit. informal* toffee-nosed.
– OPPOSITES lowly, humble.

lore ● noun **1** *Arthurian legend and lore* MYTHOLOGY, myths, legends, stories, traditions, folklore, oral tradition, mythos, mythus. **2** *cricket lore* KNOWLEDGE, learning, wisdom; *informal* know-how, how-tos.

lorry ● noun TRUCK, wagon, van, juggernaut, trailer; articulated lorry, heavy-goods vehicle, HGV; *dated* pantechnicon.

lose ● verb **1** *I've lost my watch* MISLAY, misplace, be unable to find, lose track of, leave (behind), fail to keep/retain, fail to keep sight of. **2** *he's lost a lot of blood* BE DEPRIVED OF, suffer the loss of; no longer have. **3** *he lost his pursuers* ESCAPE FROM, evade, elude, dodge, avoid, give someone the slip, shake off, throw off, throw off the scent; leave behind, outdistance, outstrip, outrun. **4** *their lost their way* STRAY FROM, wander from, depart from, go astray from, fail to keep to. **5** *you've lost your opportunity* NEGLECT, waste, squander, fail to grasp, fail to take advantage of, let pass, miss, forfeit; *informal* pass up, lose out on. **6** *they always lose at football* BE DEFEATED, be beaten, suffer defeat, be the loser, be conquered, be vanquished, be trounced, be worsted; *informal* come a cropper, go down, take a licking, be bested.
– OPPOSITES find, regain, seize, win.
– PHRASES **lose out** BE DEPRIVED OF AN OPPORTUNITY, fail to benefit, be disadvantaged, be the loser. **lose out on** BE UNABLE TO TAKE ADVANTAGE OF, fail to benefit from; *informal* miss out on. **lose out to** BE DEFEATED BY, be beaten by, suffer defeat at the hands of, lose to, be conquered by, be vanquished by, be trounced by, be worsted by, be beaten into second place by; *informal* go down to, be bested by.

loser ● noun **1** *the loser still gets the silver medal* DEFEATED PERSON, also-ran, runner-up. **2** (*informal*) *he's a complete loser* FAILURE, non-achiever, underachiever, ne'er-do-well, dead loss; write-off, has-

– PHRASES **at a loss 1** uncertain or puzzled. **2** making less money than is spent in operation or production.
– ORIGIN Old English, 'destruction'.
loss adjuster ● noun an insurance agent who assesses the amount of compensation that should be paid to a claimant.
loss-leader ● noun a product sold at a loss to attract customers.
lost past and past participle of LOSE.
– PHRASES **be lost for words** be so surprised or upset that one cannot think what to say. **be lost on** fail to be noticed or appreciated by. **get lost!** informal go away!
lost cause ● noun a person or thing that can no longer hope to succeed or be changed for the better.
lost generation ● noun **1** a generation with many of its men killed in war, especially the First World War. **2** an unfulfilled generation maturing during a period of instability.
lot ● pronoun informal **1** (**a lot** or **lots**) a large number or amount; a great deal. **2** (**the lot**) chiefly Brit. the whole number or quantity. ● adverb (**a lot** or **lots**) informal a great deal. ● noun **1** (treated as sing. or pl.) informal a particular group or set of people or things. **2** an item or set of items for sale at an auction. **3** a method of deciding something by random selection, especially of one from a number of pieces of paper. **4** a person's destiny, luck, or condition in life. **5** chiefly N. Amer. a plot of land. **6** (also **parking lot**) N. Amer. a car park. ● verb (**lotted**, **lotting**) divide into lots for sale at an auction.
– PHRASES **draw** (or **cast**) **lots** decide by lot. **fall to someone's lot** become someone's task or responsibility. **throw in one's lot with** decide to share the fate of.
– ORIGIN Old English.
loth ● adjective variant spelling of LOATH.
Lothario /ləthaariō/ ● noun (pl. **Lotharios**) a womanizer.
– ORIGIN from a character in Nicholas Rowe's tragedy *The Fair Penitent* (1703).
loti /lōti, lo͞oti/ ● noun (pl. **maloti** /məlōti, məlo͞oti/) the basic monetary unit of Lesotho.
– ORIGIN Sesotho (a Bantu language).
lotion ● noun a thick liquid preparation applied to the skin as a medicine or cosmetic.
– ORIGIN Latin, from *lavare* 'to wash'.
lottery ● noun (pl. **lotteries**) **1** a means of raising money by selling numbered tickets and giving prizes to the holders of numbers drawn at random. **2** something whose success is governed by chance.
– ORIGIN probably from Dutch *loterij*, from *lot* 'lot'.
lotto ● noun **1** a children's game similar to bingo, using illustrated counters or cards. **2** chiefly N. Amer. a lottery.
– ORIGIN Italian.
lotus ● noun **1** a large water lily. **2** (in Greek mythology) a legendary plant whose fruit induces a dreamy forgetfulness and an unwillingness to leave.
– ORIGIN Greek *lōtos*, from Semitic.
lotus-eater ● noun a person given to indulgence in pleasure and luxury.
lotus position ● noun a cross-legged position for meditation, with the feet resting on the thighs.
louche /lo͞osh/ ● adjective disreputable or dubious in a rakish or appealing way.
– ORIGIN French, 'squinting'.
loud ● adjective **1** producing or capable of producing much noise. **2** strong in expression: *loud protests.* **3** obtrusive or gaudy. ● adverb with a great deal of volume.
– PHRASES **out loud** audibly.
– DERIVATIVES **louden** verb **loudly** adverb **loudness** noun.
– ORIGIN Old English.
loudhailer ● noun chiefly Brit. a megaphone.
loudmouth ● noun informal a person who talks too much, especially tactlessly.
loudspeaker ● noun an apparatus that converts electrical impulses into sound.
lough /lok, lokh/ ● noun Anglo-Irish spelling of LOCH.
lounge ● verb recline or stand in a relaxed or lazy way. ● noun **1** Brit. a sitting room. **2** a public sitting room in a hotel or theatre. **3** a seating area in an airport for waiting passengers.
– ORIGIN of unknown origin.

Thesaurus

been; *informal* flop, non-starter, no-hoper, washout, lemon.
– OPPOSITES winner, success.
loss ● noun **1** *the loss of the documents* MISLAYING, misplacement, forgetting. **2** *loss of earnings* DEPRIVATION, disappearance, privation, forfeiture, diminution, erosion, reduction, depletion. **3** *the loss of her husband* DEATH, dying, demise, passing (away/on), end, quietus; bereavement; *formal* decease; *archaic* expiry. **4** *British losses in the war* CASUALTY, fatality, victim; dead; missing; death toll, number killed/dead/wounded. **5** *a loss of £15,000* DEFICIT, debit, debt, indebtedness, deficiency.
– OPPOSITES recovery, profit.
– PHRASES **at a loss** BAFFLED, nonplussed, mystified, puzzled, perplexed, bewildered, bemused, at sixes and sevens, confused, dumbfounded, stumped, stuck, blank; *informal* clueless, flummoxed, bamboozled, fazed, floored, beaten; *N. Amer. informal* discombobulated.
lost ● adjective **1** *her lost keys* MISSING, mislaid, misplaced, vanished, disappeared, gone missing/astray, forgotten, nowhere to be found; absent, not present, strayed. **2** *I think we're lost* OFF COURSE, off track, disorientated, having lost one's bearings, going round in circles, adrift, at sea, stray, astray. **3** *a lost opportunity* MISSED, forfeited, neglected, wasted, squandered, gone by the board; *informal* down the drain. **4** *lost traditional values* BYGONE, past, former, one-time, previous, old, olden, departed, vanished, forgotten, consigned to oblivion, extinct, dead, gone. **5** *lost species and habitats* EXTINCT, died out, defunct, vanished, gone; destroyed, wiped out, ruined, wrecked, exterminated, eradicated. **6** *a lost cause* HOPELESS, beyond hope, futile, forlorn, failed, beyond remedy, beyond recovery. **7** *lost souls* DAMNED, fallen, irredeemable, irreclaimable, irretrievable, past hope, past praying for, condemned, cursed, doomed, excommunicated; *poetic/literary* accursed. **8** *lost in thought* ENGROSSED, absorbed, rapt, immersed, deep, intent, engaged, wrapped up.
– OPPOSITES current, saved.
lot ● pronoun *a lot of money | lots of friends* A LARGE AMOUNT, a fair amount, a good/great deal, a great quantity, quantities, an abundance, a wealth, a profusion, plenty; many, a great many, a large number, a considerable number, numerous, scores; *informal* hundreds, hundreds, thousands, millions, billions, loads, masses, heaps, a pile, piles, oodles, stacks, scads, reams, wads, pots, oceans, a mountain, mountains, miles, tons, zillions, more than one can shake a stick at; *Brit. informal* a shedload, lashings; *N. Amer. informal* gobs, a bunch, gazillions.
– OPPOSITES a little, not much, a few, not many.
● adverb *I work in pastels a lot* A GREAT DEAL, a good deal, to a great extent, much; often, frequently, regularly.
– OPPOSITES a little, not much.
● noun **1** *(informal) what do your lot think?* GROUP, set, crowd, circle, band, crew; *informal* bunch, gang, mob; *Brit. informal* shower. **2** *the books were auctioned as a number of lots* ITEM, article; batch, set, collection, group, bundle, quantity, assortment, parcel. **3** *his lot in life* FATE, destiny, fortune, doom; situation, circumstances, state, condition, position, plight, predicament. **4** *(N. Amer.) some youngsters playing ball in a vacant lot* PATCH OF GROUND, piece of ground, plot, area, tract, parcel; *N. Amer.* plat.
– PHRASES **draw/cast lots** DECIDE RANDOMLY, spin/toss a coin, throw dice, draw straws. **throw in one's lot with** JOIN FORCES WITH, join up with, form an alliance with, ally with, align oneself with, link up with, make common cause with.
lotion ● noun OINTMENT, cream, salve, balm, rub, emollient, moisturizer, lubricant, unguent, liniment, embrocation.
lottery ● noun **1** *a national lottery* RAFFLE, (prize) draw, sweepstake, sweep, tombola, pools. **2** *the race is something of a lottery* GAMBLE, speculation, game of chance, matter of luck.
loud ● adjective **1** *loud music* NOISY, blaring, booming, deafening, roaring, thunderous, thundering, ear-splitting, ear-piercing, piercing; carrying, clearly audible; lusty, powerful, forceful, stentorian; *Music* forte, fortissimo. **2** *loud complaints* VOCIFEROUS, clamorous, insistent, vehement, emphatic, urgent. **3** *a loud T-shirt* GARISH, gaudy, flamboyant, lurid, glaring, showy, ostentatious; vulgar, tasteless; *informal* flash, flashy, naff, kitsch, tacky.
– OPPOSITES quiet, soft, gentle, sober, tasteful.
loudly ● adverb AT HIGH VOLUME, at the top of one's voice; noisily, deafeningly, thunderously, piercingly; stridently, lustily, powerfully, forcefully; *Music* forte, fortissimo; *informal* as if to wake the dead.
– OPPOSITES quietly, softly.
loudmouth ● noun *(informal)* BRAGGART, boaster, blusterer, swaggerer; *informal* blabbermouth, big mouth; *N. Amer. informal* blowhard.
loudspeaker ● noun SPEAKER, monitor, woofer, tweeter;

lounge bar ● noun Brit. a bar in a pub or hotel that is more comfortable or smarter than the public bar.

lounge lizard ● noun informal an idle, pleasure-seeking man who spends his time in fashionable society.

lounger ● noun **1** a comfortable chair, especially an outdoor chair that reclines. **2** a person spending their time lazily or in a relaxed way.

lounge suit ● noun Brit. a man's suit for ordinary day wear.

lour /lowr/ (also **lower**) ● verb **1** scowl. **2** (of the sky) look dark and threatening. ● noun **1** a scowl. **2** a louring appearance of the sky.
– ORIGIN of unknown origin.

louse ● noun **1** (pl. **lice**) a small wingless parasitic insect which infests human skin and hair. **2** (pl. **lice**) a related insect which lives on the skin of mammals or birds. **3** (pl. **louses**) informal a contemptible person. ● verb (**louse up**) informal spoil (something).
– ORIGIN Old English.

lousy ● adjective (**lousier**, **lousiest**) **1** informal very poor or bad. **2** infested with lice. **3** (**lousy with**) informal teeming with (something undesirable).
– DERIVATIVES **lousily** adverb **lousiness** noun.

lout ● noun an uncouth or aggressive man or boy.
– DERIVATIVES **loutish** adjective.
– ORIGIN perhaps from archaic *lout* 'to bow down'.

louvre /lo͞ovər/ (US also **louver**) ● noun **1** each of a set of angled slats fixed at regular intervals in a door, shutter, or cover to allow air or light through. **2** a domed structure on a roof, with side openings for ventilation.
– DERIVATIVES **louvred** adjective.
– ORIGIN Old French *lover*, *lovier* 'skylight'.

lovable (also **loveable**) ● adjective inspiring love or affection.
– DERIVATIVES **lovableness** noun **lovably** adverb.

lovage /luvvij/ ● noun a large edible white-flowered plant of the parsley family.
– ORIGIN Old French *luvesche*, from Latin *ligusticus* 'of or from Liguria (in NW Italy)'.

lovat /luvvət/ ● noun a muted green used especially in tweed and woollen garments.
– ORIGIN from *Lovat*, a place in Highland Scotland.

love ● noun **1** an intense feeling of deep affection. **2** a deep romantic or sexual attachment to someone. **3** a great interest and pleasure in something. **4** a person or thing that one loves. **5** (in tennis, squash, etc.) a score of zero. [ORIGIN apparently from the phrase *play for love* (i.e. the love of the game, not for money).] ● verb **1** feel love for. **2** like very much. **3** (**loving**) showing love or great care.
– PHRASES **love me, love my dog** proverb if you love someone, you must accept everything about them, even their faults or weaknesses. **make love 1** have sexual intercourse. **2** (**make love to**) dated pay amorous attention to. **there's no love lost between** there is mutual dislike between.
– DERIVATIVES **loveless** adjective **lovingly** adverb.
– ORIGIN Old English, related to LEAVE[2] and LIEF.

loveable ● adjective variant spelling of LOVABLE.

love affair ● noun **1** a romantic or sexual relationship, especially outside marriage. **2** an intense enthusiasm for something.

love apple ● noun archaic a tomato.

lovebird ● noun **1** a very small African or Madagascan parrot, noted for the affectionate behaviour of mated birds. **2** (**lovebirds**) informal an affectionate couple.

love bite ● noun a temporary red mark on the skin caused by biting or sucking during sexual play.

love child ● noun a child born to parents who are not married to each other.

love handles ● plural noun informal deposits of excess fat at the waistline.

love-in ● noun informal (especially among hippies in the 1960s) a gathering at which people are encouraged to express friendship and physical attraction.

love-in-a-mist ● noun a plant whose blue flowers are surrounded by thread-like green bracts, giving them a hazy appearance.

love interest ● noun an actor whose main role in a story or film is that of a lover of the central character.

love-lies-bleeding ● noun a South American plant with long drooping tassels of crimson flowers.

love life ● noun the part of one's life concerning relationships with lovers.

lovelorn ● adjective unhappy because of unrequited love.

Thesaurus

loudhailer, megaphone; public address system, PA (system); *informal* squawk box.

lounge ● verb *he just lounges in his room* LAZE, lie, loll, lie back, lean back, recline, stretch oneself, drape oneself, relax, rest, repose, take it easy, put one's feet up, unwind, luxuriate; sprawl, slump, slouch, flop; loaf, idle, do nothing.
● noun *she sat in the lounge* LIVING ROOM, sitting room, front room, drawing room, morning room, reception room, salon, family room; *dated* parlour.

lour, lower ● verb SCOWL, frown, look sullen, glower, glare, give someone black looks, look daggers, look angry; *informal* give someone dirty looks.
– OPPOSITES smile.

louring, lowering ● adjective OVERCAST, dark, leaden, grey, cloudy, clouded, gloomy, threatening, menacing, promising rain.
– OPPOSITES sunny, bright.

lousy (*informal*) ● adjective **1** *a lousy film.* See AWFUL sense 2. **2** *the lousy, double-crossing snake!* See DESPICABLE. **3** *I felt lousy.* See ILL adjective sense 1.
– PHRASES **be lousy with.** See CRAWL sense 3.

lout ● noun RUFFIAN, hooligan, thug, boor, oaf, hoodlum, rowdy; *informal* tough, roughneck, bruiser, yahoo, lug; *Brit. informal* yob, yobbo.
– OPPOSITES smoothie, gentleman.

loutish ● adjective UNCOUTH, rude, impolite, unmannerly, ill-mannered, ill-bred, coarse; thuggish, boorish, oafish, uncivilized, wild, rough; *informal* slobbish; *Brit. informal* yobbish.
– OPPOSITES polite, well behaved.

lovable ● adjective ADORABLE, dear, sweet, cute, charming, darling, lovely, likeable, delightful, captivating, enchanting, engaging, bewitching, pleasing, appealing, winsome, winning, fetching, endearing.
– OPPOSITES hateful, loathsome.

love ● noun **1** *his friendship with Helen grew into love* DEEP AFFECTION, fondness, tenderness, warmth, intimacy, attachment, endearment; devotion, adoration, doting, idolization, worship; passion, ardour, desire, lust, yearning, infatuation, besottedness. **2** *her love of fashion* LIKING, enjoyment, appreciation, taste, delight, relish, passion, zeal, appetite, zest, enthusiasm, keenness, fondness, soft spot, weakness, bent, leaning, proclivity, inclination, disposition, partiality, predilection, penchant. **3** *their love for their fellow human beings* COMPASSION, care, caring, regard, solicitude, concern, friendliness, friendship, kindness, charity, goodwill, sympathy, kindliness, altruism, unselfishness, philanthropy, benevolence, fellow feeling, humanity. **4** *he was her one true love* BELOVED, loved one, love of one's life, dear, dearest, dear one, darling, sweetheart, sweet, angel, honey; lover, inamorato, inamorata, amour; *archaic* paramour. **5** *their love will survive* RELATIONSHIP, love affair, romance, liaison, affair of the heart, amour. **6** *my mother sends her love* BEST WISHES, regards, good wishes, greetings, kind/kindest regards.
– RELATED TERMS amatory, phil-.
– OPPOSITES hatred.
● verb **1** *she loves him dearly* CARE VERY MUCH FOR, feel deep affection for, hold very dear, adore, think the world of, be devoted to, dote on, idolize, worship; be in love with, be infatuated with, be smitten with, be besotted with; *informal* be mad/crazy/nuts/wild/potty about, have a pash on, carry a torch for. **2** *Laura loved painting* LIKE VERY MUCH, delight in, enjoy greatly, have a passion for, take great pleasure in, derive great pleasure from, relish, savour; have a weakness for, be partial to, have a soft spot for, have a taste for, be taken with; *informal* get a kick out of, have a thing about, be mad/crazy/nuts/wild/potty about, be hooked on, go a bundle on, get off on, get a buzz out of.
– OPPOSITES hate.
– PHRASES **fall in love with** BECOME INFATUATED WITH, give/lose one's heart to; *informal* fall for, be bowled over by, be swept off one's feet by, develop a crush on. **in love with** INFATUATED WITH, besotted with, enamoured of, smitten with, consumed with desire for; captivated by, bewitched by, enthralled by, entranced by; devoted to, doting on; *informal* mad/crazy/nuts/wild/potty about.

love affair ● noun **1** *he had a love affair with a teacher* RELATIONSHIP, affair, romance, liaison, affair of the heart, affaire de cœur, intrigue, fling, amour, involvement, romantic entanglement; flirtation, dalliance; *Brit. informal* carry-on. **2** *a love affair with the motor car* ENTHUSIASM, mania, devotion, passion.

loveless ● adjective PASSIONLESS, unloving, unfeeling, heartless,

– ORIGIN from LOVE + past participle of obsolete *lese* 'lose'.

lovely ● adjective (**lovelier**, **loveliest**) **1** exquisitely beautiful. **2** informal very pleasant. ● noun (pl. **lovelies**) informal a beautiful woman or girl.

– DERIVATIVES **loveliness** noun.

love nest ● noun informal a secluded place where two lovers spend time together.

lover ● noun **1** a person having a sexual or romantic relationship with another. **2** a person who enjoys a specified thing: *a music lover*.

love seat ● noun a sofa designed in an S-shape so that two people can face each other.

lovesick ● adjective pining or feeling weak due to being in love.

– DERIVATIVES **lovesickness** noun.

lovey-dovey ● adjective informal very affectionate or romantic.

loving cup ● noun a two-handled cup passed round at banquets.

loving kindness ● noun tenderness and consideration.

low[1] ● adjective **1** of less than average height. **2** situated not far above the ground, horizon, etc. **3** below average in amount, extent, or intensity. **4** lacking importance, prestige, or quality; inferior. **5** (of a sound) deep. **6** (of a sound) not loud. **7** unfavourable: *a low opinion*. **8** depressed or lacking energy. **9** unscrupulous or dishonest. ● noun **1** a low point, level or figure. **2** an area of low barometric pressure. ● adverb **1** in or into a low position or state. **2** quietly or at a low pitch.

– DERIVATIVES **lowish** adjective **lowness** noun.

– ORIGIN Old Norse, related to LIE[1].

low[2] ● verb (of a cow) moo. ● noun a moo.

– ORIGIN Old English.

lowboy ● noun N. Amer. a low chest or table with drawers.

lowbrow ● adjective informal, chiefly derogatory not highly intellectual or cultured.

Low Church ● noun a tradition within the Anglican Church giving relatively little emphasis to ritual and sacraments.

low comedy ● noun comedy bordering on farce.

low-down informal ● adjective mean and unfair. ● noun (**the low-down**) the relevant information.

lower[1] ● adjective comparative of LOW[1]. **1** less high. **2** Geology & Archaeology older (and hence forming more deeply buried strata): *the Lower Cretaceous*. **3** (in place names) situated to the south.

– DERIVATIVES **lowermost** adjective.

lower[2] ● verb **1** cause to move downward or be less high. **2** make or become less in amount, extent, or value. **3** (**lower oneself**) demean oneself.

lower[3] ● verb & noun variant spelling of LOUR.

lower animals ● plural noun invertebrate animals, regarded as having relatively primitive characteristics.

lower case ● noun small or non-capital letters.

lower class ● noun the working class.

lower court ● noun Law a court whose decisions may be overruled by another on appeal.

lower house (also **lower chamber**) ● noun **1** the larger, typically elected, body of a parliament with two chambers. **2** (**the Lower House**) (in the UK) the House of Commons.

lower plants ● plural noun plants without vascular systems, e.g. algae, mosses, and liverworts.

lower regions ● plural noun archaic hell.

lowest common denominator ● noun **1** Mathematics the lowest common multiple of the denominators of several vulgar fractions. **2** the least desirable common feature of members of a group.

lowest common multiple ● noun Mathematics the lowest quantity that is a multiple of two or more given quantities.

low-fi ● adjective variant spelling of LO-FI.

Thesaurus

cold, icy, frigid.

– OPPOSITES loving, passionate.

lovelorn ● adjective LOVESICK, unrequited in love, crossed in love; spurned, jilted, rejected; pining, moping.

lovely ● adjective **1** *a lovely young woman* BEAUTIFUL, pretty, attractive, good-looking, appealing, handsome, adorable, exquisite, sweet, personable, charming; enchanting, engaging, winsome, seductive, gorgeous, alluring, ravishing, glamorous; *Scottish & N. English* bonny; *informal* tasty, knockout, stunning, drop-dead gorgeous; *Brit. informal* smashing, fit; *N. Amer. informal* cute, foxy; *formal* beauteous; *archaic* comely, fair. **2** *a lovely view* SCENIC, picturesque, pleasing, easy on the eye; magnificent, stunning, splendid. **3** *(informal) we had a lovely day* DELIGHTFUL, very pleasant, very nice, very agreeable, marvellous, wonderful, sublime, superb, fine, magical; *informal* terrific, fabulous, heavenly, divine, amazing, glorious.

– OPPOSITES ugly, horrible.

lover ● noun **1** *she had a secret lover* BOYFRIEND, GIRLFRIEND, ladylove, beloved, love, darling, sweetheart, inamorata, inamorato; mistress; partner, significant other; *informal* bit on the side, bit of fluff, toy boy, fancy man, fancy woman; *dated* beau; *archaic* swain, concubine, paramour. **2** *a dog lover* DEVOTEE, admirer, fan, enthusiast, aficionado; *informal* buff, freak, nut.

– RELATED TERMS -phile.

lovesick ● adjective LOVELORN, pining, languishing, longing, yearning, infatuated; frustrated.

loving ● adjective AFFECTIONATE, fond, devoted, adoring, doting, solicitous, demonstrative; caring, tender, warm, warm-hearted, close; amorous, ardent, passionate, amatory.

– OPPOSITES cold, cruel.

low[1] ● adjective **1** *a low fence* SHORT, small, little; squat, stubby, stunted, dwarf; shallow. **2** *she was wearing a low dress* LOW-CUT, skimpy, revealing, plunging. **3** *low prices* CHEAP, economical, moderate, reasonable, modest, bargain, bargain-basement, rock-bottom. **4** *supplies were low* SCARCE, scanty, scant, skimpy, meagre, sparse, few, little, paltry; reduced, depleted, diminished. **5** *low quality* INFERIOR, substandard, poor, bad, low-grade, below par, second-rate, unsatisfactory, deficient, defective. **6** *of low birth* HUMBLE, lowly, low-ranking, plebeian, proletarian, peasant, poor; common, ordinary. **7** *low expectations* UNAMBITIOUS, unaspiring, modest. **8** *a low opinion* UNFAVOURABLE, poor, bad, adverse, negative. **9** *a rather low thing to have done* DESPICABLE, contemptible, reprehensible, lamentable, disgusting, shameful, mean, abject, unworthy, shabby, uncharitable, base, dishonourable, unprincipled, ignoble, sordid; nasty, cruel, foul, bad; *informal* rotten, low-down; *Brit. informal* beastly; *dated* dastardly; *archaic* scurvy. **10** *low comedy* UNCOUTH, uncultured, unsophisticated, rough, rough-hewn, unrefined, tasteless, crass, common, vulgar, coarse, crude. **11** *a low voice* QUIET, soft, faint, gentle, muted, subdued, muffled, hushed, quietened, whispered, stifled, murmured. **12** *a low note* BASS, low-pitched, deep, rumbling, booming, sonorous. **13** *she was feeling low* DEPRESSED, dejected, despondent, downhearted, downcast, low-spirited, down, fed up, morose, miserable, dismal, heavy-hearted, mournful, forlorn, woebegone, crestfallen, dispirited; without energy, enervated, flat, sapped, weary; *informal* down in the mouth, down in the dumps, blue.

– OPPOSITES high, expensive, plentiful, superior, noble, favourable, admirable, decent, exalted, loud, cheerful, lively.

● noun *the dollar fell to an all-time low* NADIR, low point, lowest point, lowest level, depth, rock bottom.

– OPPOSITES high.

low[2] ● verb *cattle were lowing* MOO, bellow.

lowbrow ● adjective *(informal)* MASS-MARKET, tabloid, popular, intellectually undemanding, lightweight, accessible, unpretentious; uncultured, unsophisticated, trashy, philistine, simplistic; *Brit.* downmarket; *informal* dumbed-down, rubbishy.

– OPPOSITES highbrow, intellectual.

low-down *(informal)* ● adjective *a low-down trick* UNFAIR, mean, despicable, reprehensible, contemptible, lamentable, disgusting, shameful, low, unworthy, shabby, base, dishonourable, unprincipled, sordid, underhand; *informal* rotten, dirty; *Brit. informal* beastly; *dated* dastardly; *archaic* scurvy.

– OPPOSITES kind, honourable.

● noun *he gave us the low-down* FACTS, information, story, data, facts and figures, intelligence, news; *informal* info, rundown, the score, the gen, the latest, the word, the dope.

lower[1] ● adjective **1** *the lower house of parliament* SUBORDINATE, inferior, lesser, junior, minor, secondary, lower-level, subsidiary, subservient. **2** *her lower lip* BOTTOM, bottommost, nether, under; underneath, further down, beneath. **3** *a lower price* CHEAPER, reduced, cut, slashed.

– OPPOSITES upper, higher, increased.

lower[2] ● verb **1** *she lowered the mask* MOVE DOWN, let down, take down, haul down, drop, let fall. **2** *lower your voice* SOFTEN, modulate, quieten, hush, tone down, muffle, turn down, mute. **3** *they are lowering their prices* REDUCE, decrease, lessen, bring down, mark down, cut, slash, axe, diminish, curtail, prune, pare (down). **4** *the water level lowered* SUBSIDE, fall (off), recede, ebb, wane; abate, die down, let up, moderate, diminish, lessen. **5** *don't lower yourself to their level* DEGRADE, debase, demean, abase, humiliate, downgrade, discredit, shame, dishonour, disgrace; belittle, cheap-

low frequency ● noun (in radio) 30–300 kilohertz.
low gear ● noun a gear that causes a wheeled vehicle to move slowly.
Low German ● noun a German dialect spoken in much of northern Germany.
low-impact ● adjective **1** (of exercises) putting little stress on the body. **2** affecting or altering the environment as little as possible.
low-key ● adjective modest or restrained.
lowland /lōlənd/ ● noun **1** (also **lowlands**) low-lying country. **2** (**the Lowlands**) the part of Scotland lying south and east of the Highlands.
– DERIVATIVES **lowlander** noun.
low-level ● adjective **1** of relatively little importance. **2** Computing denoting a programming language that is close to machine code in form.
low life ● noun **1** disreputable or criminal people or activities. **2** (**lowlife**) informal a disreputable or criminal person.
lowlight ● noun **1** (**lowlights**) darker dyed streaks in the hair. **2** informal a disappointing or dull event or feature.
low-loader ● noun Brit. a truck with a low floor and no sides, for heavy loads.
lowly ● adjective (**lowlier**, **lowliest**) **1** low in status or importance. **2** (of an organism) primitive or simple. ● adverb to a low degree.
– DERIVATIVES **lowliness** noun.
low-lying ● adjective at low altitude above sea level.
low-minded ● adjective vulgar or sordid.
low relief ● noun see RELIEF (sense 8).
low-rider ● noun US a customized vehicle with a chassis that can be lowered nearly to the road.
low-rise ● adjective (of a building) having few storeys.
low season ● noun Brit. the least popular time of year for a holiday, when prices are lowest.
low spirits ● plural noun sadness and despondency.
Low Sunday ● noun the Sunday after Easter.
– ORIGIN perhaps in contrast to the high days of Holy Week and Easter.
low technology ● noun less advanced technological development or equipment.
low tide ● noun the state of the tide when at its lowest level.
low water ● noun low tide.
low-water mark ● noun **1** the level reached by the sea at low tide. **2** a minimum recorded level or value.
lox /loks/ ● noun N. Amer. smoked salmon.
– ORIGIN Yiddish.
loyal ● adjective showing firm and constant support or allegiance to a person or institution.
– DERIVATIVES **loyally** adverb.
– ORIGIN French, from Latin *legalis* 'legal'.
loyalist ● noun **1** a person who remains loyal to the established ruler or government. **2** (**Loyalist**) a supporter of union between Great Britain and Northern Ireland.
– DERIVATIVES **loyalism** noun.
loyal toast ● noun a toast to one's sovereign.
loyalty ● noun (pl. **loyalties**) **1** the state of being loyal. **2** a strong feeling of support or allegiance.
loyalty card ● noun Brit. a card issued by a retailer to its customers, on which credits are accumulated for future discounts every time a transaction is recorded.
lozenge /lozinj/ ● noun **1** a rhombus or diamond shape. **2** a small medicinal tablet, originally of this shape, sucked to soothe a sore throat.
– ORIGIN Old French *losenge*, probably from Latin *lausiae lapides* 'stone slabs'.
LP ● abbreviation long-playing (gramophone record).
LPG ● abbreviation liquefied petroleum gas.
L-plate ● noun Brit. a sign bearing the letter L, attached to a vehicle to indicate that the driver is a learner.
Lr ● symbol the chemical element lawrencium.
LSD ● noun a synthetic crystalline compound, lysergic acid diethylamide, which is a powerful hallucinogenic drug.
LSE ● abbreviation London School of Economics.
LSO ● abbreviation London Symphony Orchestra.
Lt ● abbreviation Lieutenant.
Ltd ● abbreviation Brit. (after a company name) Limited.
Lu ● symbol the chemical element lutetium.
lubber ● noun archaic or dialect a big, clumsy person.
– DERIVATIVES **lubberly** adjective & adverb.
– ORIGIN perhaps from Old French *lobeor* 'swindler, parasite' from *lober* 'deceive'.
lubber line ● noun a line on a compass, showing the direction straight ahead.
lube /lo͞ob/ informal, chiefly N. Amer. & Austral./NZ ● noun a lubricant. ● verb lubricate.
lubricant ● noun a substance, e.g. oil or grease, for lubricating an engine or component. ● adjective lubricating.
lubricate /lo͞obrikayt/ ● verb apply oil or grease to (an engine or component) to minimize friction.
– DERIVATIVES **lubrication** noun **lubricator** noun.
– ORIGIN Latin *lubricare* 'make slippery', from *lubricus* 'slippery'.
lubricious /loobrishəss/ (also **lubricous** /lo͞obrikəss/) ● adjective **1** lewd. **2** smooth and slippery with oil or grease.
– DERIVATIVES **lubriciously** adverb **lubricity** noun.
luce /lo͞oss/ ● noun (pl. same) a pike (fish), especially when full-grown.
– ORIGIN Old French *lus, luis*, from Latin *lucius*.
lucent /lo͞oss'nt/ ● adjective literary shining.
– DERIVATIVES **lucency** noun.
– ORIGIN from Latin *lucere* 'shine'.
lucerne /loosern/ ● noun another term for ALFALFA.
– ORIGIN modern Provençal *luzerno* 'glow-worm' (with reference to its shiny seeds).
lucid /lo͞ossid/ ● adjective **1** clear; easy to understand. **2** showing an ability to think clearly. **3** literary bright or luminous.
– DERIVATIVES **lucidity** noun **lucidly** adverb.
– ORIGIN Latin *lucidus*, from *lux* 'light'.
Lucifer /lo͞osifər/ ● noun **1** the Devil. **2** literary the planet Venus in the morning. **3** (**lucifer**) archaic a match.
– ORIGIN Latin, 'light-bringing, morning star'.
luck ● noun **1** success or failure apparently brought by chance. **2** chance considered as a force causing success or failure. **3** good fortune. ● verb informal **1** (**luck into/upon**) chance to find or acquire. **2** (**luck out**) N. Amer. succeed due to good luck.

Thesaurus

en, devalue; (**lower oneself**) stoop, sink, descend.
– OPPOSITES raise, increase.
lower³ ● verb *he lowered at her*. See LOUR.
low-grade ● adjective POOR-QUALITY, inferior, substandard, second-rate; shoddy, cheap, reject, trashy, gimcrack; *Brit. informal* duff, ropy, twopenny-halfpenny, rubbishy; *N. Amer. informal* two-bit, bum, cheapjack.
– OPPOSITES top-quality, first-class.
low-key ● adjective RESTRAINED, modest, understated, muted, subtle, quiet, low-profile, inconspicuous, unostentatious, unobtrusive, discreet, toned-down.
– OPPOSITES ostentatious, obtrusive.
lowly ● adjective HUMBLE, low, low-born, low-bred, low-ranking, plebeian, proletarian; common, ordinary, plain, average, modest, simple; inferior, ignoble, subordinate, obscure.
– OPPOSITES aristocratic, exalted.
loyal ● adjective FAITHFUL, true, devoted; constant, steadfast, staunch, dependable, reliable, trusted, trustworthy, trusty, dutiful, dedicated, unchanging, unwavering, unswerving; patriotic.
– OPPOSITES treacherous.
loyalty ● noun ALLEGIANCE, faithfulness, obedience, adherence, homage, devotion; steadfastness, staunchness, dependability, reliability, trustiness, trustworthiness, duty, dedication, commitment; patriotism; *historical* fealty.
– OPPOSITES treachery.
lozenge ● noun **1** *the pattern consists of overlapping lozenges* DIAMOND, rhombus. **2** *a throat lozenge* PASTILLE, drop; cough sweet, jujube; *dated* cachou.
lubricant ● noun GREASE, oil, lubrication, lubricator, emollient, lotion, unguent; *informal* lube.
lubricate ● verb **1** *lubricate the washer with silicone grease* OIL, GREASE, wax, polish. **2** *oil money lubricates an elaborate system of patronage* FACILITATE, ease, smooth the way for, oil the wheels of.
– OPPOSITES impede.
lucid ● adjective **1** *a lucid description* INTELLIGIBLE, comprehensible, understandable, cogent, coherent, articulate; clear, transparent; plain, simple, vivid, sharp, straightforward, unambiguous, graphic; *formal* perspicuous. **2** *he was not lucid enough to explain* RATIONAL, sane, in one's right mind, in possession of one's faculties, compos mentis, able to think clearly, balanced, sensible, clear-

– PHRASES **one's luck is in** one is fortunate. **no such luck** informal unfortunately not. **try one's luck** attempt something risky. **worse luck** informal unfortunately.
– ORIGIN Low German *lucke*.
luckily ● adverb it is fortunate that.
luckless ● adjective unfortunate.
lucky ● adjective (**luckier**, **luckiest**) having, bringing, or resulting from good luck.
lucky bag ● noun Brit. another term for GRAB BAG.
lucky dip ● noun Brit. a game in which small prizes are concealed in a container and chosen at random by participants.
lucrative /lo͞okrətiv/ ● adjective profitable.
– DERIVATIVES **lucratively** adverb.
– ORIGIN Latin *lucrativus*, from *lucrari* 'to gain'.
lucre /lo͞okər/ ● noun literary money, especially when gained dishonourably.
– ORIGIN Latin *lucrum*.
lucubrate /lo͞okjoobrayt/ ● verb archaic discourse learnedly in writing.
– ORIGIN Latin *lucubrare* 'work by lamplight'.
lucubration ● noun formal **1** study; meditation. **2** a piece of writing, especially a pedantic or over-elaborate one.
Lucullan /lookullən/ ● adjective (especially of a meal) luxurious.
– ORIGIN from the name of Licinius *Lucullus*, an ancient Roman general famous for his lavish banquets.
lud ● noun (**m'lud** or **my lud**) Brit. used to address a judge in court.
– ORIGIN alteration of LORD.
Luddite /luddīt/ ● noun **1** a member of any of the bands of English workers who opposed mechanization and destroyed machinery in the early 19th century. **2** a person opposed to industrialization or new technology.
– DERIVATIVES **Luddism** noun **Ludditism** noun.
– ORIGIN perhaps named after Ned *Lud*, a participant in the destruction of machinery.
ludic /lo͞odik/ ● adjective formal spontaneous; playful.
– ORIGIN French *ludique*, from Latin *ludere* 'to play'.
ludicrous ● adjective absurd; ridiculous.
– DERIVATIVES **ludicrously** adverb **ludicrousness** noun.
– ORIGIN Latin *ludicrus*, probably from *ludicrum* 'stage play'.
ludo ● noun Brit. a board game in which players move counters according to throws of a dice.
– ORIGIN Latin, 'I play'.
luff ● noun Sailing the edge of a fore-and-aft sail next to the mast or stay. ● verb **1** steer (a yacht) nearer the wind. **2** raise or lower (the jib of a crane).
– ORIGIN Old French *lof*.
Luftwaffe /lo͝oftvaffə/ ● noun the German air force until the end of the Second World War.
– ORIGIN German, from *Luft* 'air' + *Waffe* 'weapon'.
lug[1] ● verb (**lugged**, **lugging**) carry or drag with great effort. ● noun a box for transporting fruit.
– ORIGIN probably Scandinavian.
lug[2] ● noun **1** Scottish & N. English or informal an ear. **2** a projection on an object by which it may be carried or fixed in place. **3** informal, chiefly N. Amer. a lout.
– ORIGIN probably Scandinavian.
luge /lo͞ozh/ ● noun a light toboggan ridden in a sitting or lying position. ● verb ride on a luge.
– ORIGIN Swiss French.
Luger /lo͞ogər/ ● noun (trademark in the US) a type of German automatic pistol.
– ORIGIN named after the German firearms expert George *Luger* (1849–1923).
luggage ● noun suitcases or other bags for a traveller's belongings.
– ORIGIN from LUG[1].
lugger ● noun a small ship with two or three masts and a lugsail on each.
lughole ● noun Brit. informal an ear.
lugsail /lugsayl, -s'l/ ● noun an asymmetrical four-sided sail, bent on and hoisted from a steeply inclined yard.
– ORIGIN probably from LUG[2].
lugubrious /loogo͞obriəss/ ● adjective mournful; sad and dismal.
– DERIVATIVES **lugubriously** adverb **lugubriousness** noun.
– ORIGIN Latin *lugubris*, from *lugere* 'mourn'.
lugworm ● noun a bristle worm living in muddy sand and leaving characteristic worm casts, used as fishing bait.
– ORIGIN from earlier *lug* 'lugworm', of unknown origin.
lukewarm ● adjective **1** only moderately warm. **2** unenthusiastic.
– ORIGIN from dialect *luke*, related to LEE.
lull ● verb **1** calm or send to sleep with soothing sounds or movements. **2** cause to feel deceptively secure. **3** allay (doubts, fears, etc.), typically by deception. **4** (of noise or a storm) abate. ● noun a temporary period of quiet or inactivity.
– ORIGIN imitative of sounds used to quieten a child.
lullaby ● noun (pl. **lullabies**) a soothing song sung to send a

l

Thesaurus

headed, sober; *informal* all there.
– OPPOSITES confusing, confused.
luck ● noun **1** *with luck you'll make it* GOOD FORTUNE, good luck; fluke, stroke of luck; *informal* lucky break. **2** *I wish you luck* SUCCESS, prosperity, good fortune, good luck. **3** *it is a matter of luck whether it hits or misses* FORTUNE, fate, destiny, lot, stars, karma, kismet; fortuity, serendipity; chance, accident, a twist of fate; *Austral./NZ informal* mozzle.
– OPPOSITES bad luck, misfortune.
– PHRASES **in luck** FORTUNATE, lucky, blessed with good luck, born under a lucky star; successful, having a charmed life; *Brit. informal* jammy. **out of luck** UNFORTUNATE, unlucky, luckless, hapless, unsuccessful, cursed, jinxed, ill-fated; *informal* down on one's luck; *poetic/literary* star-crossed.
luckily ● adverb FORTUNATELY, happily, providentially, opportunely, by good fortune, as luck would have it, propitiously; mercifully, thankfully.
– OPPOSITES unfortunately.
luckless ● adjective UNLUCKY, unfortunate, unsuccessful, hapless, out of luck, cursed, jinxed, doomed, ill-fated; *informal* down on one's luck; *poetic/literary* star-crossed.
– OPPOSITES lucky.
lucky ● adjective **1** *the lucky winner* FORTUNATE, in luck, blessed, blessed with good luck, favoured, born under a lucky star, charmed; successful, prosperous; born with a silver spoon in one's mouth; *Brit. informal* jammy. **2** *a lucky escape* PROVIDENTIAL, fortunate, advantageous, timely, opportune, serendipitous, expedient, heaven-sent, auspicious; chance, fortuitous, fluky, accidental.
– OPPOSITES unfortunate.
lucrative ● adjective PROFITABLE, profit-making, gainful, remunerative, moneymaking, paying, high-income, well paid, bankable; rewarding, worthwhile; thriving, flourishing, successful, booming.
– OPPOSITES unprofitable.
lucre ● noun MONEY, cash, funds, capital, finances, riches, wealth, spoils, ill-gotten gains, Mammon; *informal* dough, bread, loot, the ready, readies, moolah; *Brit. informal* dosh, brass, lolly, spondulicks, wonga, ackers; *archaic* pelf.
ludicrous ● adjective ABSURD, ridiculous, farcical, laughable, risible, preposterous, foolish, mad, insane, idiotic, stupid, inane, silly, asinine, nonsensical; *informal* crazy; *rare* derisible.
– OPPOSITES sensible.
lug ● verb CARRY, lift, bear, tote, heave, hoist, shoulder, manhandle; haul, drag, tug, tow, transport, move, convey, shift; *informal* hump, schlep; *Scottish informal* humph.
luggage ● noun BAGGAGE; bags, suitcases, cases, trunks. See also BAG noun sense 2.
lugubrious ● adjective MOURNFUL, gloomy, sad, unhappy, doleful, glum, melancholy, woeful, miserable, woebegone, forlorn, long-faced, sombre, solemn, serious, sorrowful, morose, dour, cheerless, joyless, dismal; funereal, sepulchral; *informal* down in the mouth; *poetic/literary* dolorous.
– OPPOSITES cheerful.
lukewarm ● adjective **1** *lukewarm coffee* TEPID, slightly warm, warmish, blood-warm, at skin temperature, at room temperature, chambré. **2** *a lukewarm response* INDIFFERENT, cool, half-hearted, apathetic, unenthusiastic, tepid, offhand, lackadaisical, perfunctory, non-committal; *informal* laid-back, unenthused, couldn't-careless; *rare* Laodicean.
– OPPOSITES hot, cold, enthusiastic.
lull ● verb **1** *the sound of the bells lulled us to sleep* SOOTHE, calm, hush; rock to sleep. **2** *his suspicions were soon lulled* ASSUAGE, allay, ease, alleviate, soothe, quiet, quieten; reduce, diminish; quell, banish, dispel. **3** *the noise had lulled* ABATE, die down, subside, let up, moderate, slacken, lessen, dwindle, decrease, diminish.
– OPPOSITES waken, agitate, arouse, intensify.

child to sleep.
– ORIGIN from LULL + *bye-bye*, a sound used as a refrain in lullabies.
lulu ● noun informal an outstanding example of a person or thing.
– ORIGIN perhaps from *Lulu*, familiar form of the given name *Louise*.
lum /lum/ ● noun Scottish & N. English a chimney.
– ORIGIN perhaps from Old French *lum* 'light'.
luma /lo͞omə/ ● noun (pl. same or **lumas**) a monetary unit of Armenia, equal to one hundredth of a dram.
– ORIGIN Armenian.
lumbago /lumbaygō/ ● noun pain in the lower back.
– ORIGIN Latin, from *lumbus* 'loin'.
lumbar /lumbər/ ● adjective relating to the lower back.
– ORIGIN Latin *lumbaris*, from *lumbus* 'loin'.
lumbar puncture ● noun Medicine the withdrawal of spinal fluid from the lower back through a hollow needle, usually for diagnosis.
lumber[1] ● verb move in a slow, heavy, awkward way.
– ORIGIN perhaps symbolic of clumsy movement.
lumber[2] ● noun **1** chiefly Brit. disused articles of furniture that inconveniently take up space. **2** chiefly N. Amer. partly prepared timber. ● verb **1** (usu. **be lumbered with**) Brit. informal burden with an unwanted responsibility. **2** chiefly N. Amer. cut and prepare forest timber for transport and sale.
– ORIGIN perhaps from LUMBER[1]; later associated with obsolete *lumber* 'pawnbroker's shop'.
lumberjack (also **lumberman**) ● noun a person who fells trees, cuts them into logs, or transports them.
lumberjacket ● noun a thick jacket, typically with a bright check pattern, of the kind worn by lumberjacks.
lumber room ● noun Brit. a room for storing disused or bulky things.
lumen /lo͞omen/ ● noun Physics the SI unit of luminous flux, equal to the amount of light emitted per second in a unit solid angle of one steradian from a uniform source of one candela.
– ORIGIN Latin, 'light'.
luminaire /lo͞ominair/ ● noun a complete electric light unit.
– ORIGIN French.
luminance /lo͞ominənss/ ● noun **1** Physics the intensity of light emitted from a surface per unit area in a given direction. **2** the component of a television signal which carries information on the brightness of the image.
luminary /lo͞ominəri/ ● noun (pl. **luminaries**) **1** a person who inspires or influences others. **2** literary a natural light-giving body, especially the sun or moon.
luminesce /lo͞ominess/ ● verb emit light by luminescence.
luminescence /lo͞ominess'nss/ ● noun the emission of light by a substance that has not been heated, as in fluorescence and phosphorescence.
– DERIVATIVES **luminescent** adjective.
luminosity ● noun luminous quality.
luminous /lo͞ominəss/ ● adjective **1** bright or shining, especially in the dark. **2** Physics relating to visible light.
– DERIVATIVES **luminously** adverb.
– ORIGIN Latin *luminosus*, from *lumen* 'light'.
lumme /lummi/ ● exclamation Brit. informal, dated an expression of surprise.
– ORIGIN from *Lord love me*.
lummox /lumməks/ ● noun informal, chiefly N. Amer. a clumsy, stupid person.
– ORIGIN of unknown origin.
lump[1] ● noun **1** a compact mass, especially one without a definite or regular shape. **2** a swelling under the skin. **3** informal a heavy, ungainly, or slow-witted person. **4** (**the lump**) Brit. informal casual employment in the building trade. ● verb **1** (often **lump together**) treat as alike, regardless of particulars. **2** Brit. carry (a heavy load) somewhere with difficulty.
– PHRASES **a lump in the throat** a feeling of tightness in the throat caused by strong emotion.
– ORIGIN perhaps Germanic.
lump[2] ● verb (**lump it**) informal accept or tolerate something whether one likes it or not.
– ORIGIN originally in the sense 'look sulky': symbolic.
lumpectomy ● noun (pl. **lumpectomies**) a surgical operation in which a lump, typically a tumour, is removed from the breast.
lumpen ● adjective **1** lumpy and misshapen. **2** boorish and stupid. **3** (in Marxist contexts) uninterested in revolutionary advancement.
– ORIGIN abbreviation of LUMPENPROLETARIAT.
lumpenproletariat /lumpənprōlitairiət/ ● noun (in Marxist terminology) the apolitical lower orders of society uninterested in revolutionary advancement.
– ORIGIN from German *Lumpen* 'rag, rogue' + PROLETARIAT.
lumpfish ● noun a North Atlantic lumpsucker with edible roe.
– ORIGIN from Low German *lumpen*, Dutch *lompe*, possibly related to LUMP[1].
lumpish ● adjective **1** roughly or clumsily formed. **2** stupid and lethargic.
– DERIVATIVES **lumpishly** adverb **lumpishness** noun.
lumpsucker ● noun a round-bodied northern coastal fish with an abdominal sucker and spiny fins.
lump sum ● noun a single payment made at one time, as opposed to many instalments.
lumpy ● adjective (**lumpier**, **lumpiest**) **1** full of or covered with lumps. **2** (of water) formed by the wind into small waves.
– DERIVATIVES **lumpily** adverb **lumpiness** noun.
lunacy ● noun (pl. **lunacies**) **1** insanity (not in technical use). **2** extreme folly.
– ORIGIN from LUNATIC.

l

Thesaurus

● noun **1** *a lull in the fighting* PAUSE, respite, interval, break, hiatus, suspension, interlude, intermission, breathing space; *informal* let-up, breather. **2** *the lull before the storm* CALM, stillness, quiet, tranquillity, peace, silence, hush.
– OPPOSITES agitation, activity.
lullaby ● noun CRADLE SONG, berceuse.
lumber[1] ● verb *elephants lumbered past* LURCH, stumble, trundle, shamble, shuffle, waddle; trudge, clump, stump, plod, tramp; *informal* galumph.
lumber[2] ● noun **1** *a spare room packed with lumber* JUMBLE, clutter, odds and ends, bits and pieces, flotsam and jetsam, cast-offs; refuse, rubbish, litter; *N. Amer.* trash; *informal* junk, odds and sods, gubbins, clobber. **2** *the lumber trade* TIMBER, wood.
● verb *(Brit. informal) she was lumbered with a husband and child* BURDEN, saddle, encumber, hamper; load, oppress, trouble, tax; *informal* land, dump something on someone.
– OPPOSITES free.
lumbering ● adjective CLUMSY, awkward, heavy-footed, slow, blundering, bumbling, inept, maladroit, uncoordinated, ungainly, ungraceful, gauche, lumpish, hulking, ponderous; *informal* clodhopping.
– OPPOSITES nimble, agile.
luminary ● noun LEADING LIGHT, guiding light, inspiration, role model, hero, heroine, leader, expert, master, panjandrum; lion, legend, great, giant.
– OPPOSITES nobody.
luminous ● adjective SHINING, bright, brilliant, radiant, dazzling, glowing, gleaming, scintillating, lustrous; luminescent, phosphorescent, fluorescent, incandescent.
– OPPOSITES dark.
lump[1] ● noun **1** *a lump of coal* CHUNK, hunk, piece, mass, block, wedge, slab, cake, nugget, ball, brick, cube, pat, knob, clod, gobbet, dollop, wad; *informal* glob; *N. Amer. informal* gob. **2** *a lump on his head* SWELLING, bump, bulge, protuberance, protrusion, growth, outgrowth, hump.
● verb *it is convenient to lump them together* COMBINE, put, group, bunch, aggregate, unite, pool, merge, collect, throw, consider together.
lump[2] ● verb *(informal) I'm afraid you'll have to lump it* PUT UP WITH, bear, endure, take, tolerate, accept.
lumpish ● adjective **1** *lumpish furniture* CUMBERSOME, unwieldy, heavy, hulking, chunky, bulky, ponderous. **2** *a lumpish young girl* STUPID, obtuse, dense, dim-witted, dull-witted, slow-witted, slow; lethargic, bovine, sluggish, listless; *informal* thick, dumb, dopey, slow on the uptake, moronic; *Brit. informal* dozy.
– OPPOSITES elegant, quick-witted, sharp.
lumpy ● adjective **1** *a lumpy mattress* BUMPY, knobbly, bulging, uneven, rough, gnarled. **2** *lumpy custard* CLOTTED, curdled, congealed, coagulated.
lunacy ● noun **1** *originality demands a degree of lunacy* INSANITY, madness, mental illness, dementia, mania, psychosis; *informal* craziness. **2** *the lunacy of gambling* FOLLY, foolishness, foolhardiness, stupidity, silliness, idiocy, madness, rashness, recklessness, imprudence, irresponsibility, injudiciousness; *informal* craziness; *Brit.*

lunar /lōōnər/ ● **adjective** of, determined by, or resembling the moon.
– ORIGIN from Latin *luna* 'moon'.
lunar day ● **noun** the interval between two successive crossings of the meridian by the moon (roughly 24 hours and 50 minutes).
lunar eclipse ● **noun** an eclipse in which the moon passes into the earth's shadow.
lunar month ● **noun 1** a month measured between successive new moons (roughly 29½ days). **2** (in general use) a period of four weeks.
lunar year ● **noun** a period of twelve lunar months (approximately 354 days).
lunate /lōōnayt/ ● **adjective** crescent-shaped.
– ORIGIN from Latin *luna* 'moon'.
lunatic ● **noun 1** a person who is mentally ill (not in technical use). **2** an extremely foolish person.
– ORIGIN Latin *lunaticus*, from *luna* 'moon' (from the belief that changes of the moon caused intermittent insanity).
lunatic fringe ● **noun** an extreme or eccentric minority.
lunation /lōōnaysh'n/ ● **noun** Astronomy a lunar month.
lunch ● **noun** a meal eaten in the middle of the day. ● **verb** eat lunch.
– PHRASES **out to lunch** informal unbalanced or stupid. **there's no such thing as a free lunch** proverb it isn't possible to get something for nothing.
– DERIVATIVES **luncher** noun.
– ORIGIN abbreviation of LUNCHEON.
luncheon ● **noun** formal lunch.
– ORIGIN originally in the sense 'thick piece, hunk': possibly from Spanish *lonja* 'slice'.
luncheonette ● **noun** N. Amer. a small restaurant serving light lunches.
luncheon meat ● **noun** finely minced cooked pork mixed with cereal, sold in a tin.
luncheon voucher ● **noun** Brit. a voucher given to employees as part of their pay and exchangeable for food at certain restaurants and shops.
lunette /loonet/ ● **noun 1** an arched aperture or window in a domed ceiling. **2** a crescent-shaped or semicircular alcove containing a painting or statue. **3** a fortification with two faces forming a projecting angle. **4** Christian Church a holder for the consecrated host in a monstrance. **5** a ring on a vehicle, by which it can be towed.
– ORIGIN French, 'little moon'.
lung ● **noun** each of the pair of organs within the ribcage into which air is drawn in breathing, so that oxygen can pass into the blood and carbon dioxide be removed.
– DERIVATIVES **lunged** adjective **lungful** noun.
– ORIGIN Old English, related to LIGHT² and LIGHTS.
lunge¹ ● **noun 1** a sudden forward movement of the body. **2** a thrust in fencing, in which the leading leg is bent while the back leg remains straightened. ● **verb** (**lunging** or **lungeing**) make a lunge.
– ORIGIN from French *allonger* 'lengthen'.
lunge² (also **longe**) ● **noun** a long rein on which a horse is made to move in a circle round its trainer.
– ORIGIN French *longe*, from *allonge* 'lengthening out'.
lungfish ● **noun** an elongated freshwater fish with one or two sacs which function as lungs, enabling it to breath air and live dormant in mud to survive drought.
lungi /lōōnggee/ ● **noun** (pl. **lungis**) a length of cotton cloth worn as a loincloth in India or as a skirt in Burma (Myanmar).
– ORIGIN Urdu.
lungwort ● **noun 1** a bristly pink-flowered plant with white-spotted leaves said to resemble a diseased lung. **2** a large lichen which grows on trees, formerly used to treat lung disease.
lunk (also **lunkhead**) ● **noun** informal a slow-witted person.
– ORIGIN probably from an alteration of LUMP¹.
lupin /lōōpin/ (also **lupine** pronunc. same) ● **noun** a plant with deeply divided leaves and tall colourful tapering spikes of flowers.
– ORIGIN Latin *lupinus*.
lupine /lōōpīn/ ● **adjective** of or like a wolf or wolves.
– ORIGIN Latin *lupinus*, from *lupus* 'wolf'.
lupus /lōōpəss/ ● **noun** an ulcerous skin condition, especially one due to direct infection with tuberculosis.
– ORIGIN Latin, 'wolf'.
lupus erythematosus /erritheemətōsəss/ ● **noun** an inflammatory disease causing scaly red patches on the skin.
– ORIGIN Latin, from Greek *eruthēma* 'reddening'.
lurch¹ ● **noun** a sudden unsteady movement. ● **verb** make such a movement; stagger.
– ORIGIN of unknown origin.
lurch² ● **noun** (in phrase **leave in the lurch**) leave (someone) in a difficult situation without assistance or support.
– ORIGIN French *lourche*, a game resembling backgammon, used in the phrase *demeurer lourche* 'be discomfited'.
lurcher ● **noun** Brit. a cross-bred dog, typically a retriever, collie, or sheepdog crossed with a greyhound, originally used for hunting and by poachers.
– ORIGIN from obsolete *lurch*, variant of LURK.
lure /loor/ ● **verb** tempt to do something or to go somewhere. ● **noun 1** a thing that lures a person or animal to do something. **2** the attractive qualities of a person or thing. **3** a type of bait used in fishing or hunting. **4** Falconry a bunch of feathers with a piece of meat attached to a long string, swung around the head of a falconer to recall a hawk.
– ORIGIN Old French *luere*.
lurex /looreks/ ● **noun** trademark yarn or fabric incorporating a glittering metallic thread.
– ORIGIN of unknown origin.
lurgy /lurgi/ ● **noun** (pl. **lurgies**) Brit. informal, humorous an unspecified illness.
– ORIGIN of unknown origin.
lurid /lyoorid/ ● **adjective 1** unpleasantly vivid in colour. **2** (of a description) shocking or sensational.
– DERIVATIVES **luridly** adverb **luridness** noun.
– ORIGIN originally in the sense 'pale and dismal': from Latin *luridus*, related to *luror* 'wan or yellow colour'.
lurk ● **verb 1** be or remain hidden so as to wait in ambush. **2** be present in a latent or barely discernible state. ● **noun** Austral./NZ informal a dodge or scheme.
– DERIVATIVES **lurker** noun.
– ORIGIN perhaps from LOUR.
luscious ● **adjective 1** having a pleasingly rich, sweet taste. **2** richly verdant or opulent. **3** (of a woman) sexually attractive.
– DERIVATIVES **lusciously** adverb **lusciousness** noun.
– ORIGIN perhaps an alteration of obsolete *licious*, shortened form of DELICIOUS.

Thesaurus

informal daftness.
– OPPOSITES sanity, sense, prudence.
lunatic ● **noun** *he drives like a lunatic* MANIAC, madman, madwoman, imbecile, psychopath, psychotic; fool, idiot; eccentric; *informal* loony, nut, nutcase, head case, psycho, moron; *Brit. informal* nutter; *N. Amer. informal* screwball.
● **adjective 1** *a lunatic prisoner.* See MAD sense 1. **2** *a lunatic idea.* See MAD sense 3.
lunch ● **noun** MIDDAY MEAL, luncheon; *Brit.* dinner.
lunge ● **noun** *Darren made a lunge at his attacker* THRUST, dive, rush, charge, grab.
● **verb** *he lunged at Finn with a knife* THRUST, dive, spring, launch oneself, rush, make a grab.
lurch ● **verb 1** *he lurched into the kitchen* STAGGER, stumble, wobble, sway, reel, roll, weave, pitch, totter, blunder. **2** *the ship lurched* SWAY, reel, list, heel, rock, roll, pitch, toss, jerk, shake, judder, flounder, swerve.
lure ● **verb** *consumers are frequently lured into debt* TEMPT, entice, attract, induce, coax, persuade, inveigle, allure, seduce, win over, cajole, beguile, bewitch, ensnare.
– OPPOSITES deter, put off.
● **noun** *the lure of the stage* TEMPTATION, enticement, attraction, pull, draw, appeal; inducement, allurement, fascination, interest; *informal* come-on.
lurid ● **adjective 1** *lurid food colourings* BRIGHT, brilliant, vivid, glaring, shocking, fluorescent, flaming, dazzling, intense, gaudy, loud. **2** *the lurid details* SENSATIONAL, sensationalist, exaggerated, overdramatized, extravagant, colourful; salacious, graphic, explicit, unrestrained, prurient, shocking; gruesome, gory, grisly; *informal* tacky, shock-horror, juicy, full-frontal.
– OPPOSITES muted, restrained.
lurk ● **verb** SKULK, loiter, lie in wait, lie low, hide, conceal oneself, take cover, keep out of sight.
luscious ● **adjective 1** *luscious fruit* DELICIOUS, succulent, lush,

lush[1] ● adjective **1** (of vegetation) luxuriant. **2** rich or luxurious. **3** informal sexually attractive.
– DERIVATIVES **lushly** adverb **lushness** noun.
– ORIGIN perhaps from Old French *lasche* 'lax', by association with LUSCIOUS.

lush[2] ● noun informal, chiefly N. Amer. a drunkard.
– ORIGIN perhaps a humorous use of LUSH[1].

lusophone /lo͞osəfōn/ ● adjective Portuguese-speaking.
– ORIGIN from *luso-* (representing *Lusitania*, an ancient Roman province corresponding to modern Portugal) + -PHONE.

lust ● noun **1** strong sexual desire. **2** a passionate desire for something. **3** Theology a sensuous appetite regarded as sinful. ● verb (usu. **lust for/after**) feel lust for someone or something.
– ORIGIN Old English.

lustful ● adjective filled with lust; lecherous.
– DERIVATIVES **lustfully** adverb **lustfulness** noun.

lustra plural of LUSTRUM.

lustral /lustrəl/ ● adjective relating to or used in ceremonial purification.
– ORIGIN Latin *lustralis*, from *lustrum* (see LUSTRUM).

lustre (US **luster**) ● noun **1** a gentle sheen or soft glow. **2** glory or distinction. **3** a thin metallic coating giving an iridescent glaze to ceramics. **4** (also **lustreware**) ceramics with an iridescent metallic glaze. **5** a fabric or yarn with a sheen.
– DERIVATIVES **lustred** adjective **lustreless** adjective.
– ORIGIN French, from Latin *lustrare* 'illuminate'.

lustrous ● adjective having lustre; shining.
– DERIVATIVES **lustrously** adverb **lustrousness** noun.

lustrum /lustrəm/ ● noun (pl. **lustra** /lustrə/ or **lustrums**) chiefly literary or historical a period of five years.
– ORIGIN Latin, originally denoting a purificatory sacrifice after a five-yearly census.

lusty ● adjective (**lustier**, **lustiest**) healthy and strong; vigorous.
– DERIVATIVES **lustily** adverb **lustiness** noun.

lute[1] ● noun a stringed instrument with a long neck and a rounded body with a flat front, played by plucking.
– ORIGIN Old French *lut*, *leut*, probably from Arabic.

lute[2] ● noun **1** liquid clay or cement used to seal a joint, protect a graft, etc. **2** a rubber seal for a jar. ● verb seal, join, or coat with lute.
– ORIGIN Latin *lutum* 'potter's clay'.

lutenist /lo͞otənist/ (also **lutanist**) ● noun a lute player.

lutetium /lo͞oteeshəm/ ● noun a rare silvery-white metallic chemical element of the lanthanide series.
– ORIGIN from Latin *Lutetia*, the ancient name of Paris, where its discoverer Georges Urbain (1872–1938) lived.

Lutheran ● noun **1** a follower of the German protestant theologian Martin Luther (1483–1546). **2** a member of the Lutheran Church. ● adjective **1** of or characterized by the theology of Martin Luther. **2** relating to the Lutheran Church.
– DERIVATIVES **Lutheranism** noun.

Lutheran Church ● noun the Protestant Church founded on the doctrines of Martin Luther, with justification by faith alone as a cardinal doctrine.

luthier /lo͞otiər/ ● noun a maker of stringed instruments.
– ORIGIN French, from *luth* 'lute'.

lutist ● noun **1** a lute player. **2** a lute maker.

lutz /lo͝ots/ ● noun a jump in skating from the backward outside edge of one skate to the backward outside edge of the other, with a full turn in the air.
– ORIGIN probably from the name of Gustave *Lussi* (born 1898), who invented it.

luvvy (also **luvvie**) ● noun (pl. **luvvies**) Brit. informal an effusive or affected actor or actress.

lux /luks/ ● noun (pl. same) the SI unit of illuminance, equal to one lumen per square metre.
– ORIGIN Latin, 'light'.

luxe /luks, lo͝oks/ ● noun luxury.
– ORIGIN French.

Luxembourger /luksəmbergər/ ● noun a person from Luxembourg.

Luxemburgish /luksəmburgish/ ● noun a form of German spoken in Luxembourg.

luxuriant /lugzyooriənt/ ● adjective **1** (of vegetation) rich and profuse in growth. **2** (of hair) thick and healthy.
– DERIVATIVES **luxuriance** noun **luxuriantly** adverb.
– ORIGIN from Latin *luxuriare* 'grow rankly', from *luxuria* 'luxury, rankness'.

luxuriate /lugzyooriayt/ ● verb (**luxuriate in/over**) enjoy as a luxury.

luxurious ● adjective **1** characterized by luxury. **2** giving self-indulgent pleasure.
– DERIVATIVES **luxuriously** adverb **luxuriousness** noun.

luxury ● noun (pl. **luxuries**) **1** the state of great comfort and ex-

L

Thesaurus

juicy, mouth-watering, sweet, tasty, appetizing; *informal* scrumptious, scrummy, yummy, moreish; *N. Amer. informal* nummy; *poetic/literary* ambrosial. **2** *a luscious Swedish beauty* SEXY, sexually attractive, nubile, ravishing, gorgeous, seductive, alluring, sultry, beautiful, stunning; *informal* fanciable, tasty, drop-dead gorgeous, curvy; *Brit. informal* fit; *N. Amer. informal* foxy, cute; *Austral./NZ informal* spunky.
– OPPOSITES unappetizing, plain, scrawny.

lush ● adjective **1** *lush vegetation* LUXURIANT, rich, abundant, profuse, exuberant, riotous, prolific, vigorous; dense, thick, rank, rampant; *informal* jungly. **2** *a lush, ripe peach* SUCCULENT, luscious, juicy, soft, tender, ripe. **3** *a lush apartment* LUXURIOUS, de luxe, sumptuous, palatial, opulent, lavish, elaborate, extravagant, fancy; *informal* plush, ritzy, posh, swanky; *Brit. informal* swish; *N. Amer. informal* swank.
– OPPOSITES barren, sparse, shrivelled, austere.

lust ● noun **1** *his lust for her* SEXUAL DESIRE, sexual appetite, sexual longing, ardour, desire, passion; libido, sex drive, sexuality, biological urge; lechery, lecherousness, lasciviousness; *informal* horniness, the hots; *Brit. informal* randiness. **2** *a lust for power* GREED, desire, craving, covetousness, eagerness, avidity, cupidity, longing, yearning, hunger, thirst, appetite, hankering.
– OPPOSITES dread, aversion.
● verb **1** *he lusted after his employer's wife* DESIRE, be consumed with desire for, find sexually attractive, crave, covet, ache for, burn for, pant for; *informal* have the hots for, lech after/over, fancy, have a thing about/for, drool over, have the horn for. **2** *she lusted after adventure* CRAVE, desire, covet, want, wish for, long for, yearn for, dream of, hanker for, hanker after, hunger for, thirst for, ache for.
– OPPOSITES dread, avoid.

lustful ● adjective LECHEROUS, lascivious, libidinous, licentious, salacious, goatish; wanton, unchaste, impure, naughty, immodest, indecent, dirty, prurient; passionate, sensual, sexy, erotic; *informal* horny, randy, raunchy; *formal* concupiscent.
– OPPOSITES chaste, pure.

lustily ● adverb HEARTILY, vigorously, loudly, at the top of one's voice, powerfully, forcefully, strongly; *informal* like mad, like crazy.
– OPPOSITES feebly, quietly.

lustre ● noun **1** *her hair lost its lustre* SHEEN, gloss, shine, glow, gleam, shimmer, burnish, polish, patina. **2** *the lustre of the Milky Way* BRILLIANCE, brightness, radiance, sparkle, dazzle, flash, glitter, glint, gleam, luminosity, luminescence.
– OPPOSITES dullness, dark.

lustreless ● adjective DULL, lacklustre, matt, unpolished, tarnished, dingy, dim, dark.
– OPPOSITES lustrous, bright.

lustrous ● adjective SHINY, shining, satiny, glossy, gleaming, shimmering, burnished, polished; radiant, bright, brilliant, luminous; dazzling, sparkling, glistening, twinkling.
– OPPOSITES dull, dark.

lusty ● adjective **1** *lusty young men* HEALTHY, strong, fit, vigorous, robust, hale and hearty, energetic; rugged, sturdy, muscular, muscly, strapping, hefty, husky, burly, powerful; *informal* beefy; *dated* stalwart. **2** *lusty singing* LOUD, vigorous, hearty, strong, powerful, forceful.
– OPPOSITES feeble, quiet.

luxuriant ● adjective LUSH, rich, abundant, profuse, exuberant, riotous, prolific, vigorous; dense, thick, rank, rampant; *informal* jungly.
– OPPOSITES barren, sparse.

luxuriate ● verb REVEL, bask, delight, take pleasure, wallow; (**luxuriate in**) enjoy, relish, savour, appreciate; *informal* get a kick out of, get a thrill out of.
– OPPOSITES dislike.

luxurious ● adjective **1** *a luxurious hotel* OPULENT, sumptuous, de luxe, grand, palatial, splendid, magnificent, well appointed, extravagant, fancy; *Brit.* upmarket; *informal* plush, posh, classy, ritzy, swanky; *Brit. informal* swish; *N. Amer. informal* swank. **2** *a luxurious lifestyle* SELF-INDULGENT, sensual, pleasure-loving, pleasure-seeking,

travagant living. **2** an inessential but desirable item. ● adjective of the nature of a luxury.
– ORIGIN originally meaning 'lechery': from Latin *luxuria*, from *luxus* 'excess'.

LVO ● abbreviation Lieutenant of the Royal Victorian Order.

lwei /ləway/ ● noun (pl. same) a monetary unit of Angola, equal to one hundredth of a kwanza.
– ORIGIN a local word.

lx ● abbreviation Physics lux.

-ly[1] ● suffix forming adjectives meaning: **1** having the qualities of: *brotherly*. **2** recurring at intervals of: *hourly*.
– ORIGIN Old English, related to LIKE[1].

-ly[2] ● suffix forming adverbs from adjectives: *greatly*.
– ORIGIN Old English.

lycanthrope /līkənthrōp/ ● noun a werewolf.

lycanthropy /līkanthrəpi/ ● noun the mythical transformation of a person into a wolf.
– DERIVATIVES **lycanthropic** adjective.
– ORIGIN Greek *lukanthrōpia*, from *lukos* 'wolf' + *anthrōpos* 'man'.

lycée /leesay/ ● noun (pl. pronounced same) a French secondary school funded by the state.
– ORIGIN French, from Latin *lyceum* (see LYCEUM).

Lyceum /līseeəm/ ● noun **1** the garden in ancient Athens in which Aristotle taught philosophy. **2** (**lyceum**) US archaic a literary institution, lecture hall, or teaching place.
– ORIGIN Latin, from Greek *Lukeios*, a name for the god Apollo (from whose neighbouring temple the Lyceum in Athens was named).

lychee /līchee/ (also **litchi**) ● noun a small rounded fruit with sweet white scented flesh, a large stone, and thin rough skin.
– ORIGIN Chinese.

lychgate /lichgayt/ ● noun a roofed gateway to a churchyard, formerly used at burials for sheltering a coffin until the clergyman's arrival.
– ORIGIN from Old English *līc* 'body'.

Lycra /līkrə/ ● noun trademark an elastic polyurethane fibre or fabric used especially for close-fitting sports clothing.
– ORIGIN of unknown origin.

Lydian ● noun a person from the ancient region of Lydia in western Asia Minor. ● adjective relating to Lydia.

lye ● noun a strongly alkaline solution, especially of potassium hydroxide, used for washing or cleansing.
– ORIGIN Old English, related to LATHER.

lying[1] present participle of LIE[1].

lying[2] present participle of LIE[2].

lyke wake /līk/ ● noun Brit. a night spent watching over a dead body.
– ORIGIN from Old English *līc* 'body'; related to LYCHGATE.

Lyme disease /līm/ ● noun a form of arthritis caused by bacteria that are transmitted by ticks.
– ORIGIN named after *Lyme*, a town in Connecticut, US, where an outbreak occurred.

lymph /limf/ ● noun **1** a colourless fluid containing white blood cells, which bathes the tissues and drains through the lymphatic system into the bloodstream. **2** fluid exuding from a sore or inflamed tissue.
– ORIGIN Latin *lympha, limpa* 'water'.

lymphatic ● adjective **1** relating to lymph or its secretion. **2** archaic (of a person) pale, flabby, or sluggish. ● noun a vein-like vessel conveying lymph in the body.
– ORIGIN originally in the sense 'frenzied, mad': from Greek *numpholēptos* 'seized by nymphs'; now associated with LYMPH.

lymphatic system ● noun the network of vessels through which lymph drains from the tissues into the blood.

lymph node (also **lymph gland**) ● noun each of a number of small swellings in the lymphatic system where lymph is filtered and lymphocytes are formed.

lymphocyte /limfəsīt/ ● noun a form of small leucocyte (white blood cell) with a single round nucleus, occurring especially in the lymphatic system.

lymphoid /limfoyd/ ● adjective relating to tissue responsible for producing lymphocytes and antibodies.

lymphoma /limfōmə/ ● noun (pl. **lymphomas** or **lymphomata** /limfōmətə/) cancer of the lymph nodes.

lynch ● verb (of a group) kill (someone) for an alleged offence without a legal trial, especially by hanging.
– DERIVATIVES **lyncher** noun.
– ORIGIN from *Lynch's law*, named after Captain William *Lynch*, head of a self-constituted judicial tribunal in Virginia *c.*1780.

lynchet /linchit/ ● noun a ridge or ledge formed along the downhill side of a plot by ploughing in ancient times.
– ORIGIN probably from dialect *linch* 'rising ground'; related to LINKS.

lynchpin ● noun variant spelling of LINCHPIN.

lynx ● noun a wild cat with a short tail and tufted ears.
– ORIGIN Greek *lunx*.

lynx-eyed ● adjective keen-sighted.

lyonnaise /liənayz/ ● adjective (of sliced potatoes) cooked with onions or with a white wine and onion sauce.
– ORIGIN French, 'characteristic of the city of Lyons'.

lyrate /līrayt/ ● adjective Biology lyre-shaped.

lyre ● noun a stringed instrument like a small U-shaped harp with strings fixed to a crossbar, used especially in ancient Greece.
– ORIGIN Greek *lura*.

lyrebird ● noun a large Australian songbird, the male of which has a long lyre-shaped tail.

lyric ● noun **1** (also **lyrics**) the words of a song. **2** a lyric poem or verse. ● adjective **1** (of poetry) expressing the writer's emotions, usually briefly and in stanzas or recognized forms. **2** (of a singing voice) using a light register.
– ORIGIN Greek *lurikos*, from *lura* 'lyre'.

lyrical ● adjective **1** (of literature, art, or music) expressing the writer's emotions in an imaginative and beautiful way. **2** (of poetry) lyric. **3** relating to the words of a popular song.
– PHRASES **wax lyrical** talk in a highly enthusiastic and effusive way.
– DERIVATIVES **lyrically** adverb.

lyricism ● noun an artist's expression of emotion in an imaginative and beautiful way.

lyricist ● noun a person who writes the words to popular songs.

lyrist ● noun **1** /lirist/ a person who plays the lyre. **2** /lirrist/ a lyric poet.

lysergic acid /līserjik/ ● noun a crystalline compound prepared from natural ergot alkaloids or synthetically, from which the drug LSD (**lysergic acid diethylamide**) can be made.
– ORIGIN from *hydrolysis* + *ergot*.

lysin /līsin/ ● noun Biology an antibody or other substance able to cause lysis of cells (especially bacteria).

lysine /līseen/ ● noun Biochemistry an amino acid which is a constituent of most proteins and is an essential nutrient in the diet of vertebrates.
– ORIGIN German *Lysin*, from LYSIS.

lysis /līsiss/ ● noun Biology the disintegration of a cell by rupture of the cell wall or membrane.
– ORIGIN Greek *lusis* 'loosening'

lytic /littik/ ● adjective Biology relating to or causing lysis.

Thesaurus

epicurean, hedonistic, sybaritic, lotus-eating.
– OPPOSITES plain, basic, abstemious.

luxury ● noun **1** *we'll live in luxury* OPULENCE, luxuriousness, sumptuousness, grandeur, splendour, magnificence, lavishness, the lap of luxury, a bed of roses, milk and honey; *informal* the life of Riley. **2** *a TV is his only luxury* INDULGENCE, extravagance, self-indulgence, treat, extra, non-essential, frill.
– OPPOSITES simplicity, necessity.

lying ● noun *she was no good at lying* UNTRUTHFULNESS, fabrication, fibbing, perjury, white lies; falseness, falsity, dishonesty, mendacity, telling stories, invention, misrepresentation, deceit, duplicity; *poetic/literary* perfidy.
● adjective *he was a lying womanizer* UNTRUTHFUL, false, dishonest, mendacious, deceitful, deceiving, duplicitous, double-dealing, two-faced; *poetic/literary* perfidious.
– OPPOSITES truthful.

lynch ● verb EXECUTE ILLEGALLY, hang; *informal* string up.

lyric ● adjective **1** *a lyric poem* EXPRESSIVE, emotional, deeply felt, personal, subjective, passionate. **2** *a lyric soprano* LIGHT, silvery, clear, sweet.

lyrical ● adjective **1** *lyrical love poetry* EXPRESSIVE, emotional, deeply felt, personal, subjective, passionate. **2** *she was lyrical about her success* ENTHUSIASTIC, rhapsodic, effusive, rapturous, ecstatic, euphoric, carried away.
– OPPOSITES unenthusiastic.

lyrics ● plural noun WORDS, libretto, book, text, lines.

l

Mm

M[1] (also **m**) ● noun (pl. **Ms** or **M's**) **1** the thirteenth letter of the alphabet. **2** the Roman numeral for 1,000. [ORIGIN from Latin *mille.*]

M[2] ● abbreviation **1** male. **2** medium. **3** mega-. **4** Monsieur. **5** motorway.

m ● abbreviation **1** married. **2** masculine. **3** Physics mass. **4** Chemistry meta-. **5** metre(s). **6** mile(s). **7** milli-. **8** million(s). **9** minute(s).

MA ● abbreviation **1** Massachusetts. **2** Master of Arts.

ma ● noun informal one's mother.

ma'am ● noun madam.

mac ● noun Brit. informal a mackintosh.

macabre /məkaabrə, -bər/ ● adjective disturbing and horrifying because concerned with death and injury.
– ORIGIN French, from *Danse Macabre* 'dance of death', perhaps from *Macabé* 'a Maccabee' (a member of a 2nd-century BC Jewish sect led by Judas Maccabaeus), with reference to a miracle play depicting the slaughter of the Maccabees.

macadam ● noun broken stone used with tar or bitumen for surfacing roads and paths.
– ORIGIN named after the British surveyor John L. *McAdam* (1756–1836).

macadamia /makədaymiə/ ● noun the round edible nut of an Australian tree.
– ORIGIN named after the Australian chemist John *Macadam* (1827–65).

macaque /məkaak/ ● noun a medium-sized monkey with a long face and cheek pouches for holding food.
– ORIGIN from Bantu *makaku* 'some monkeys'.

macaroni ● noun **1** pasta in the form of narrow tubes. **2** (pl. **macaronies**) an 18th-century British dandy affecting Continental fashions.
– ORIGIN Italian *maccaroni*, from Greek *makaria* 'food made from barley'.

macaronic /makəronnik/ ● adjective (of language, especially verse) containing a mixture of words from two or more languages.
– ORIGIN originally in the sense 'a jumble or medley'; from obsolete Italian *macaronico*, a humorous formation from MACARONI.

macaroon ● noun a light biscuit made with egg white and ground almonds or coconut.
– ORIGIN French *macaron*, from Italian *maccarone* 'macaroni'.

macaw /məkaw/ ● noun a large long-tailed parrot with brightly coloured plumage, native to Central and South America.
– ORIGIN Portuguese *macau.*

mace[1] ● noun **1** historical a heavy club with a spiked metal head. **2** a staff of office, especially the symbol of the Speaker's authority in the House of Commons. **3** (**Mace**) trademark an irritant chemical used in an aerosol to disable attackers.
– ORIGIN Old French *masse* 'large hammer'.

mace[2] ● noun the reddish outer covering of the nutmeg, dried as a spice.
– ORIGIN Latin *macir.*

macédoine /massidwaan/ ● noun a mixture of vegetables or fruit cut into small pieces.
– ORIGIN French, 'Macedonia', with reference to the mixture of peoples in the Macedonian Empire of Alexander the Great.

Macedonian ● noun a person from the republic of Macedonia (formerly part of Yugoslavia), ancient Macedonia, or the modern Greek region of Macedonia. ● adjective relating to Macedonia.

macerate /massərayt/ ● verb soften or break up (food) by soaking in a liquid.
– DERIVATIVES **maceration** noun.
– ORIGIN Latin *macerare.*

Mach /maak/ ● noun used with a numeral (as **Mach 1**, **Mach 2**, etc.) to indicate the speed of sound, twice the speed of sound, etc.
– ORIGIN named after the Austrian physicist Ernst *Mach* (1838–1916).

machair /makə/ ● noun (in Scotland) low-lying coastal land formed from sand and shell fragments deposited by the wind.
– ORIGIN Scottish Gaelic.

machete /məsheti/ ● noun a broad, heavy knife used as an implement or weapon.
– ORIGIN Spanish, from *macho* 'hammer'.

Machiavellian /makiəvelliən/ ● adjective cunning, scheming, and unscrupulous.
– ORIGIN from the name of the Italian statesman and writer Niccolò *Machiavelli* (1469–1527), whose work *The Prince* (1532) advises that the acquisition and use of power may necessitate unethical methods.

machicolation ● noun (in medieval fortifications) an opening between the supports of a projecting structure, through which stones or burning objects could be dropped on attackers.
– DERIVATIVES **machicolated** adjective.
– ORIGIN from Provençal *machacol*, from *macar* 'to crush' + *col* 'neck'.

machinations /mashinayshənz/ ● plural noun plots and intrigues; scheming.
– ORIGIN Latin, from *machinari* 'contrive'.

machine ● noun **1** an apparatus using mechanical power and having several parts, for performing a particular task. **2** an efficient and well-organized group of powerful people. ● verb make or operate on with a machine.
– ORIGIN Greek *mēkhanē*, from *mēkhos* 'contrivance'.

machine code (also **machine language**) ● noun a computer programming language consisting of instructions which a computer can respond to directly.

machine gun ● noun an automatic gun that fires bullets in rapid succession for as long as the trigger is pressed.

machine-readable ● adjective in a form that a computer can process.

machinery ● noun **1** machines collectively, or the components of a machine. **2** the organization or structure of something.

machine tool ● noun a fixed powered tool for cutting or shaping metal, wood, etc.

machine translation ● noun translation carried out by a computer.

machinist ● noun a person who operates a machine or who makes machinery.

Thesaurus

macabre ● adjective **1** *a macabre ritual* GRUESOME, grisly, grim, gory, morbid, ghastly, unearthly, grotesque, hideous, horrific, shocking, dreadful, loathsome, repugnant, repulsive, sickening. **2** *a macabre joke* BLACK, weird, unhealthy; *informal* sick.

mace ● noun CLUB, cudgel, stick, staff, shillelagh, bludgeon, truncheon; *Brit.* life preserver; *N. Amer.* nightstick, billy, billy club, blackjack; *Brit. informal* cosh.

macerate ● verb PULP, mash, squash, soften, liquefy, soak.

Machiavellian ● adjective DEVIOUS, cunning, crafty, artful, wily, sly, scheming, treacherous, two-faced, tricky, double-dealing, unscrupulous, deceitful, dishonest; *poetic/literary* perfidious; *informal* foxy.
– OPPOSITES straightforward, ingenuous.

machinations ● plural noun SCHEMING, plotting, intrigues, conspiracies, ruses, tricks, wiles, stratagems, tactics, manoeuvring.

machine ● noun **1** *it is quicker done by machine* APPARATUS, appliance, device, contraption, contrivance, mechanism, engine, gadget, tool. **2** *an efficient publicity machine* ORGANIZATION, system, structure, arrangement, machinery; *informal* set-up.
– RELATED TERMS mechanical.

machinery ● noun **1** *road-making machinery* EQUIPMENT, apparatus, plant, hardware, gear, tackle; mechanism; instruments,

machismo /məchizmō/ ● **noun** strong or aggressive masculine pride.
– ORIGIN Mexican Spanish, from *macho* 'male'.
macho /machō/ ● **adjective** aggressively masculine.
– ORIGIN Mexican Spanish.
mackerel ● **noun** a fast-swimming sea fish with a greenish-blue back, important as a food fish.
– ORIGIN Old French *maquerel*.
mackerel sky ● **noun** a sky dappled with rows of small white fleecy clouds, like the pattern on a mackerel's back.
mackintosh (also **macintosh**) ● **noun** Brit. a full-length waterproof coat.
– ORIGIN named after the Scottish inventor Charles *Macintosh* (1766–1843).
macramé /məkraami/ ● **noun** the craft of knotting cord or string in patterns to make decorative articles.
– ORIGIN French, from Turkish, 'tablecloth or towel'.
macro ● **noun** (pl. **macros**) Computing a single instruction that expands automatically into a set of instructions to perform a particular task. ● **adjective** large-scale; overall.
macro- ● **combining form 1** long; over a long period: *macroevolution*. **2** large or large-scale: *macrocosm*.
– ORIGIN from Greek *makros* 'long, large'.
macrobiotic ● **adjective** (of diet) consisting of pure wholefoods, based on Buddhist principles of the balance of yin and yang.
– ORIGIN from Greek *makros* 'long' + *bios* 'life'.
macrocarpa ● **noun** a Californian cypress tree with a large spreading crown of horizontal branches.
– ORIGIN from Greek *makros* 'long' + *karpos* 'fruit'.
macrocosm ● **noun 1** the whole of a complex structure. **2** the universe; the cosmos.
– DERIVATIVES **macrocosmic** adjective.
– ORIGIN from Greek *makros kosmos* 'big world'.
macroeconomics ● **plural noun** (treated as sing.) the branch of economics concerned with large-scale or general economic factors, such as interest rates.
macro lens ● **noun** a camera lens suitable for taking photographs unusually close to the subject.
macromolecule ● **noun** Chemistry a molecule containing a very large number of atoms, such as a protein, nucleic acid, or synthetic polymer.
– DERIVATIVES **macromolecular** adjective.
macron ● **noun** a written or printed mark (¯) used to indicate a long vowel in some languages, or a stressed vowel in verse.
macroscopic ● **adjective 1** visible to the naked eye; not microscopic. **2** relating to large-scale or general analysis.
macula /makyoolə/ ● **noun** (pl. **maculae** /makyoolee/) **1** (also **macule**) a dark permanent spot on the skin. **2** an oval yellowish area near the centre of the retina in the eye, which is the region of keenest vision.
– ORIGIN Latin; related to IMMACULATE.
macumba /məkumbə/ ● **noun** a religious cult practised by black people in Brazil, using sorcery, ritual dance, and fetishes.
– ORIGIN Portuguese.
mad ● **adjective** (**madder**, **maddest**) **1** mentally ill. **2** extremely foolish or ill-advised. **3** showing impulsiveness, confusion, or frenzy. **4** informal very enthusiastic about something. **5** informal very angry. **6** (of a dog) rabid.
– DERIVATIVES **madly** adverb **madness** noun.
– ORIGIN Old English.
Madagascan /maddəgaskən/ ● **noun** a person from Madagascar. ● **adjective** relating to Madagascar.
madam ● **noun 1** a polite form of address for a woman. **2** Brit. informal a conceited or precocious girl. **3** a female brothel-keeper.
– ORIGIN French *ma dame* 'my lady'.
Madame /mədaam/ ● **noun** (pl. **Mesdames**) /maydaam/ a title or form of address for a French-speaking woman.
madcap ● **adjective** impulsive or reckless.
mad cow disease ● **noun** informal term for BSE.
madden ● **verb 1** drive insane. **2** irritate or annoy greatly.
madder ● **noun** a red dye or pigment obtained from the roots of a plant.
– ORIGIN Old English.
madding ● **adjective** literary **1** acting madly; frenzied. **2** maddening.
made past and past participle of MAKE.
Madeira ● **noun** a fortified white wine from the island of Madeira.
Madeira cake ● **noun** Brit. a close-textured, rich kind of sponge cake.
Madeiran /mədeerən/ ● **noun** a person from Madeira, an island in the Atlantic Ocean off NW Africa. ● **adjective** relating to Ma-

m

Thesaurus

tools; gadgetry, technology. **2** *the machinery of local government* WORKINGS, organization, system, structure, administration, institution; *informal* set-up.
machinist ● **noun** OPERATOR, operative, machine-minder.
machismo ● **noun** (AGGRESSIVE) MASCULINITY, toughness, male chauvinism, sexism, laddishness; virility, manliness.
macho ● **adjective** *a macho, non-caring image* (AGGRESSIVELY) MALE, (unpleasantly) masculine; manly, virile, red-blooded; *informal* butch, laddish.
– OPPOSITES wimpish.
● **noun 1** *he was a macho at heart* RED-BLOODED MALE, macho man, muscleman; *informal* he-man, tough guy. **2** *macho is out.* See MACHISMO.
– OPPOSITES wimp.
mackintosh ● **noun** *(Brit.)* RAINCOAT, gabardine, trench coat, waterproof; *Brit.* pakamac; *N. Amer.* slicker; *Brit. informal* mac; *trademark* Burberry, Drizabone.
macrocosm ● **noun 1** *the law of the macrocosm* UNIVERSE, cosmos, creation, outer space. **2** *the individual is a microcosm of the social macrocosm* SYSTEM, structure, totality, entirety, complex.
– OPPOSITES microcosm.
mad ● **adjective 1** *he was killed by his mad brother* INSANE, mentally ill, certifiable, deranged, demented, of unsound mind, out of one's mind, not in one's right mind, sick in the head, crazy, crazed, lunatic, non compos mentis, unhinged, disturbed, raving, psychotic, psychopathic, mad as a hatter, mad as a March hare, away with the fairies; *informal* mental, off one's head, off one's nut, nuts, nutty, off one's rocker, not right in the head, round the bend, stark staring/raving mad, bats, batty, bonkers, dotty, cuckoo, cracked, loopy, loony, doolally, bananas, loco, dippy, screwy, schizoid, touched, gaga, up the pole, not all there, not right upstairs; *Brit. informal* barmy, crackers, barking, barking mad, round the twist, off one's trolley, not the full shilling; *N. Amer. informal* nutso, out of one's tree, meshuga, wacko, gonzo; *Austral./NZ informal* bushed; *NZ informal* porangi; (**be mad**) *informal* have a screw loose, have bats in the/one's belfry; *Austral. informal* have kangaroos in the/one's top paddock; (**go mad**) lose one's reason, lose one's mind, take leave of one's senses; *informal* lose one's marbles, crack up. **2** *(informal) I'm still mad at him* ANGRY, furious, infuriated, irate, raging, enraged, fuming, incensed, seeing red, beside oneself; *informal* livid, spare; *informal, dated* in a wax; *Brit. informal* aerated; *N. Amer. informal* sore; *poetic/literary* wrathful; (**go mad**) lose one's temper, get in a rage, rant and rave; *informal* explode, go off the deep end, go ape, flip, flip one's lid; *Brit. informal* do one's nut; *N. Amer. informal* flip one's wig. **3** *some mad scheme* FOOLISH, insane, stupid, lunatic, foolhardy, idiotic, senseless, absurd, impractical, silly, inane, asinine, wild, unwise, imprudent; *informal* crazy, crackpot, crackbrained; *Brit. informal* daft. **4** *(informal) he's mad about jazz* ENTHUSIASTIC, passionate; ardent, fervent, avid, fanatical; devoted to, infatuated with, in love with, hot for; *informal* crazy, dotty, nuts, wild, hooked on, gone on; *Brit. informal* potty; *N. Amer. informal* nutso. **5** *it was a mad dash to get ready* FRENZIED, frantic, frenetic, feverish, hysterical. wild, hectic, manic.
– OPPOSITES sane, pleased, sensible, indifferent, calm.
– PHRASES **like mad** *(informal)* **1** *I ran like mad* FAST, quickly, rapidly, speedily, hastily, hurriedly. **2** *he had to fight like mad* ENERGETICALLY, enthusiastically, madly, furiously, with a will, for all one is worth, passionately, intensely, ardently, fervently; *informal* like crazy, hammer and tongs; *Brit. informal* like billy-o.
madcap ● **adjective 1** *a madcap scheme* RECKLESS, rash, foolhardy, foolish, hare-brained, wild, hasty, imprudent, ill-advised; *informal* crazy, crackpot, crackbrained. **2** *a madcap comedy* ZANY, eccentric, unconventional.
● **noun** *she was a boisterous madcap* ECCENTRIC, crank, maniac, madman/madwoman, lunatic; oddity, character, maniac, individual; *informal* crackpot, oddball, weirdo, loony, nut; *Brit. informal* nutter; *N. Amer. informal* screwball.
madden ● **verb 1** *what maddens people most is his vagueness* INFURIATE, exasperate, irritate; incense, anger, enrage, provoke, upset, agitate, vex, irk, make someone's hackles rise, make someone see red; *informal* aggravate, make someone's blood boil, make livid, get up someone's nose, get someone's goat, get someone's

deira.

madeleine ● noun a small rich sponge cake, often decorated with coconut and jam.
– ORIGIN probably named after *Madeleine* Paulmier, 19th-century French pastry cook.

Mademoiselle /maddəmwəzel/ ● noun (pl. **Mesdemoiselles**) /maydamwəzel/ a title or form of address for an unmarried French-speaking woman.
– ORIGIN French, from *ma* 'my' + *demoiselle* 'damsel'.

made-up ● adjective **1** wearing make-up. **2** invented; untrue.

madhouse ● noun **1** dated a mental institution. **2** informal a scene of extreme confusion or uproar.

madman ● noun **1** a man who is mentally ill. **2** a foolish or reckless person.

Madonna ● noun (**the Madonna**) the Virgin Mary.
– ORIGIN Italian, from *ma* 'my' + *donna* 'lady'.

madras ● noun **1** a strong cotton fabric, typically patterned with colourful stripes or checks. **2** a hot spiced curry dish.
– ORIGIN named after the Indian city of *Madras*.

madrigal ● noun a 16th- or 17th-century part song for several voices, typically unaccompanied.
– ORIGIN Italian *madrigale*, from Latin *carmen matricale* 'simple song'.

maelstrom /maylstrəm/ ● noun **1** a powerful whirlpool. **2** a scene of confused movement or upheaval.
– ORIGIN Dutch, from *maalen* 'grind, whirl' + *stroom* 'stream'.

maenad /meenad/ ● noun (in ancient Greece) a female follower of the god Bacchus, traditionally associated with frenzied rites.
– ORIGIN Greek *Mainas*, from *mainesthai* 'to rave'.

maestro /mīstrō/ ● noun (pl. **maestri** /mīstri/ or **maestros**) **1** a distinguished male conductor or performer of classical music. **2** a distinguished man in any sphere.
– ORIGIN Italian, 'master'.

Mae West ● noun informal, dated an inflatable life jacket.
– ORIGIN named (by RAF personnel during the Second World War) after the American film actress *Mae West* (1892–1980), noted for her large bust.

MAFF ● abbreviation (in the UK) Ministry of Agriculture, Fisheries, and Food.

Mafia ● noun **1** (**the Mafia**) an international criminal organization originating in Sicily. **2** (**mafia**) a group exerting a hidden sinister influence.
– ORIGIN Italian, originally meaning 'bragging'.

mafic /maffik/ ● adjective referring or relating to a group of dark-coloured minerals that contain large amounts of iron and magnesium. Often contrasted with FELSIC.
– ORIGIN blend of MAGNESIUM and FERRIC.

Mafioso /maffiōsō/ ● noun (pl. **Mafiosi** /maffiōsi/) a member of the Mafia.

magazine ● noun **1** a periodical publication containing articles and illustrations. **2** a regular television or radio programme comprising a variety of items. **3** a chamber holding a supply of cartridges to be fed automatically to the breech of a gun. **4** a store for arms, ammunition, and explosives.
– ORIGIN French *magasin*, from an Arabic word meaning 'storehouse'.

magdalen /magdəlin/ ● noun archaic a reformed prostitute.
– ORIGIN from the name of St Mary *Magdalene* (to whom Jesus appeared after his resurrection), commonly identified with the sinner mentioned in the Gospel of Luke, chapter 7.

magenta /məjentə/ ● noun **1** a light mauvish crimson. **2** the dye fuchsin.
– ORIGIN named after *Magenta* in Italy, site of a battle (1859) fought shortly before the dye was discovered.

maggot ● noun a soft-bodied legless larva, especially one of a fly or other insect and found in decaying matter.
– ORIGIN perhaps an alteration of dialect *maddock*, from Old Norse.

magi plural of MAGUS.

magic ● noun **1** the power of apparently influencing events by using mysterious or supernatural forces. **2** conjuring tricks performed to entertain. **3** mysterious and enchanting quality. **4** informal exceptional skill or talent. ● adjective **1** having or apparently having supernatural powers. **2** informal very exciting or good. ● verb (**magicked**, **magicking**) move, change, or create by or as if by magic.
– DERIVATIVES **magical** adjective **magically** adverb.
– ORIGIN from Greek *magikē tekhnē* 'art of a magus': magi were regarded as magicians.

magic carpet ● noun a mythical carpet that is able to transport people through the air.

magician ● noun **1** a person with magical powers. **2** a conjuror.

m

Thesaurus

back up; *Brit. informal* nark; *N. Amer. informal* tee off, tick off. **2** *they were maddened with pain* DRIVE MAD, drive insane, derange, unhinge, unbalance; *informal* drive round the bend.

made-up ● adjective INVENTED, fabricated, trumped up, concocted, fictitious, fictional, false, untrue, specious, spurious, bogus, apocryphal, imaginary, mythical.

madhouse ● noun **1** *(dated) his father is shut up in a madhouse* MENTAL HOSPITAL, mental institution, psychiatric hospital, asylum; *informal* nuthouse, funny farm, loony bin; *dated* lunatic asylum. **2** *(informal) the place was a total madhouse* BEDLAM, mayhem, chaos, pandemonium, uproar, turmoil, disorder, madness, all hell broken loose; *N. Amer.* three-ring circus.

madly ● adverb **1** *she was smiling madly* INSANELY, deliriously, wildly, like a lunatic; *informal* crazily, barmily. **2** *it was fun, hurtling madly downhill* FAST, furiously, hurriedly, quickly, speedily, hastily, energetically; *informal* like mad, like crazy. **3** *(informal) he loved her madly* INTENSELY, fervently, wildly, unrestrainedly, to distraction. **4** *(informal) his job isn't madly glamorous* VERY, extremely, really, exceedingly, exceptionally, remarkably, extraordinarily, immensely, tremendously, wildly, all that, hugely; *informal* awfully, terribly, terrifically, fantastically.
– OPPOSITES sanely, slowly, slightly.

madman, madwoman ● noun LUNATIC, maniac, psychotic, psychopath; *informal* loony, nut, nutcase, head case, psycho; *Brit. informal* nutter; *N. Amer. informal* screwball.

madness ● noun **1** *today madness is called mental illness* INSANITY, mental illness, dementia, derangement; lunacy, instability; mania, psychosis; *informal* craziness. **2** *it would be madness to do otherwise* FOLLY, foolishness, idiocy, stupidity, insanity, lunacy, silliness; *informal* craziness. **3** *it's absolute madness in here* BEDLAM, mayhem, chaos, pandemonium, uproar, turmoil, disorder, all hell broken loose; *N. Amer.* three-ring circus.
– OPPOSITES sanity, common sense, good sense, calm.

maelstrom ● noun **1** *a maelstrom in the sea* WHIRLPOOL, vortex, eddy, swirl; *poetic/literary* Charybdis. **2** *the maelstrom of war* TURBULENCE, tumult, turmoil, disorder, disarray, chaos, confusion, upheaval, pandemonium, bedlam, whirlwind.

maestro ● noun VIRTUOSO, master, expert, genius, wizard, prodigy; *informal* ace, whizz, pro, hotshot.
– OPPOSITES tyro, beginner.

magazine ● noun JOURNAL, periodical, supplement, colour supplement; *informal* glossy, mag, 'zine.

magenta ● adjective REDDISH-PURPLE, purplish-red, crimson, plum, carmine red, fuchsia.

maggot ● noun GRUB, larva.

magic ● noun **1** *do you believe in magic?* SORCERY, witchcraft, wizardry, necromancy, enchantment, the supernatural, occultism, the occult, black magic, the black arts, voodoo, shamanism; charm, hex, spell, jinx; *N. Amer.* mojo. **2** *he does magic at children's parties* CONJURING TRICKS, sleight of hand, legerdemain, illusion, prestidigitation. **3** *the magic of the stage* ALLURE, attraction, excitement, fascination, charm, glamour. **4** *a taste of soccer magic* SKILL, brilliance, ability, accomplishment, adeptness, adroitness, deftness, dexterity, aptitude, expertise, art, finesse, talent.
● adjective **1** *a magic spell* SUPERNATURAL, enchanted, occult. **2** *a magic place* FASCINATING, captivating, charming, glamorous, magical, enchanting, entrancing, spellbinding, magnetic, irresistible, hypnotic. **3** *(informal) we had a magic time* MARVELLOUS, wonderful, excellent, admirable; *informal* terrific, fabulous, fab, brilliant, brill.

magical ● adjective **1** *magical incantations* SUPERNATURAL, magic, occult, shamanistic, mystical, paranormal, preternatural, otherworldly. **2** *the news had a magical effect* EXTRAORDINARY, remarkable, exceptional, outstanding, incredible, phenomenal, unbelievable, amazing, astonishing, astounding, stunning, staggering, marvellous, magnificent, wonderful, sensational, breathtaking, miraculous; *informal* fantastic, fabulous, stupendous, out of this world, terrific, tremendous, brilliant, mind-boggling, mind-blowing, awesome; *poetic/literary* wondrous. **3** *this magical small land* ENCHANTING, entrancing, spellbinding, bewitching, beguiling, fascinating, captivating, alluring, enthralling, charming, attractive, lovely, delightful, beautiful; *informal* dreamy, heavenly, divine, gorgeous.

magic lantern ● noun a simple form of projector formerly used for showing photographic slides.
magic mushroom ● noun informal a toadstool with hallucinogenic properties if eaten.
magisterial /majisteeriəl/ ● adjective **1** very authoritative. **2** domineering; dictatorial. **3** relating to a magistrate.
– DERIVATIVES **magisterially** adverb.
– ORIGIN from Latin *magister* 'master'.
magistracy ● noun (pl. **magistracies**) **1** the office or authority of a magistrate. **2** magistrates collectively.
magistrate ● noun a civil officer who administers the law, especially one who conducts a court concerned with minor offences and holds preliminary hearings for more serious ones.
– ORIGIN Latin *magistratus* 'administrator', from *magister* 'master'.
maglev ● noun a transport system in which trains glide above a track, supported by magnetic repulsion and propelled by a linear motor.
– ORIGIN short for *magnetic levitation*.
magma ● noun hot fluid or semi-fluid material within the earth's crust from which lava and other igneous rock is formed by cooling.
– ORIGIN Greek, from *massein* 'knead'.
Magna Carta ● noun a charter of liberty and political rights signed by King John of England in 1215.
– ORIGIN Latin, 'great charter'.
magna cum laude /magnə kum **law**day/ ● adverb & adjective chiefly N. Amer. with great distinction.
– ORIGIN Latin, 'with great praise'.
magnanimous /mag**nann**iməss/ ● adjective generous or forgiving, especially towards a rival or less powerful person.
– DERIVATIVES **magnanimity** noun **magnanimously** adverb.
– ORIGIN from Latin *magnus* 'great' + *animus* 'soul'.
magnate ● noun a wealthy and influential person, especially in business.
– ORIGIN Latin *magnas* 'great man'.
magnesia ● noun **1** magnesium oxide. **2** hydrated magnesium carbonate used as an antacid and laxative.
– ORIGIN Greek, denoting a mineral from Magnesia in Asia Minor.
magnesium ● noun a silvery-white metallic element which burns with a brilliant white flame.
magnet ● noun **1** a piece of iron or other material that has the property of attracting similar objects or aligning itself in an external magnetic field. **2** a person or thing that has a powerful attraction.
– ORIGIN from Greek *magnēs lithos* 'lodestone'.
magnetic ● adjective **1** having the property of magnetism. **2** very attractive or alluring.
– DERIVATIVES **magnetically** adverb.
magnetic equator ● noun the irregular imaginary line, passing round the earth near the equator, on which a magnetic needle has no dip.
magnetic field ● noun a region around a magnet within which the force of magnetism acts.
magnetic induction ● noun **1** the strength of a magnetic field. **2** the process by which an object or material is magnetized by a magnetic field around it.
magnetic north ● noun the direction in which the north end of a compass needle will point in response to the earth's magnetic field.
magnetic pole ● noun **1** each of the points near the extremities of the axis of rotation of the earth where a magnetic needle dips vertically. **2** each of the two points of a magnet to and from which the lines of magnetic force are directed.
magnetic resonance imaging ● noun a technique for producing images of bodily organs by measuring the properties of atomic nuclei in a strong magnetic field.
magnetic storm ● noun a disturbance of the magnetic field of the earth.
magnetic tape ● noun tape used in recording sound, pictures, or computer data.
magnetism ● noun **1** the property displayed by magnets and produced by the motion of electric charges, which results in attraction or repulsion between objects. **2** the ability to attract and charm people.
magnetite ● noun a grey-black magnetic mineral which is an important form of iron ore.
magnetize (also **magnetise**) ● verb make magnetic.
magneto ● noun (pl. **magnetos**) a small electric generator containing a permanent magnet and used to provided high-voltage pulses, especially (formerly) in the ignition systems of internal-combustion engines.
magnetohydrodynamics ● plural noun (treated as sing.) the branch of physics concerned with the behaviour of an electrically conducting fluid in a magnetic field.
magnetometer /maggni**tomm**itər/ ● noun an instrument used for measuring magnetic forces, especially the earth's magnetism.
magnetosphere ● noun the region surrounding the earth or another body in which its magnetic field is predominant.
magnetron ● noun an electron tube for amplifying or generating microwaves, with the flow of electrons controlled by an external magnetic field.
Magnificat /mag**niff**ikat/ ● noun the hymn of the Virgin Mary (Gospel of Luke, chapter 1) used as a canticle, especially at vespers and evensong.
– ORIGIN Latin, 'magnifies', from the opening words, which translate as 'my soul magnifies the Lord'.
magnificence ● noun **1** the quality of being magnificent. **2** (**His/Your** etc. **Magnificence**) a title or form of address for a monarch or other distinguished person.
magnificent ● adjective **1** impressively beautiful, elaborate, or extravagant. **2** very good; excellent.
– DERIVATIVES **magnificently** adverb.
– ORIGIN Latin *magnificus*, from *magnus* 'great'.

Thesaurus

– OPPOSITES predictable, boring.
magician ● noun **1** SORCERER, sorceress, witch, wizard, warlock, enchanter, enchantress, necromancer, shaman. **2** CONJUROR, illusionist, prestidigitator.
magisterial ● adjective **1** *a magisterial pronouncement* AUTHORITATIVE, masterful, assured, lordly, commanding, assertive. **2** *his magisterial style of questioning* DOMINEERING, dictatorial, autocratic, imperious, overbearing, peremptory, high-handed, arrogant, supercilious, patronizing; informal bossy.
– OPPOSITES untrustworthy, humble, hesitant, tentative.
magnanimity ● noun GENEROSITY, charity, benevolence, beneficence, big-heartedness, altruism, philanthropy, humanity, chivalry, nobility; clemency, mercy, leniency, forgiveness, indulgence.
– OPPOSITES meanness, selfishness.
magnanimous ● adjective GENEROUS, charitable, benevolent, beneficent, big-hearted, handsome, princely, altruistic, philanthropic, chivalrous, noble; forgiving, merciful, lenient, indulgent, clement.
– OPPOSITES mean-spirited, selfish.
magnate ● noun TYCOON, mogul, captain of industry, baron, lord, king; industrialist, proprietor; informal big shot, honcho; derogatory fat cat.
magnet ● noun **1** *you can tell steel by using a magnet* LODESTONE; electromagnet, solenoid. **2** *a magnet for tourists* ATTRACTION, focus, draw, lure.
magnetic ● adjective **1** *a magnetic personality* ALLURING, attractive, fascinating, captivating, enchanting, enthralling, appealing, charming, prepossessing, engaging, entrancing, seductive, inviting, irresistible, charismatic.
magnetism ● noun *his sheer magnetism* ALLURE, attraction, fascination, appeal, draw, drawing power, pull, charm, enchantment, seductiveness, magic, spell, charisma.
magnification ● noun **1** *optical magnification* ENLARGEMENT, enhancement, increase, augmentation, extension, expansion, amplification, intensification. **2** *the magnification of marginal details* EXAGGERATION, overstatement, overemphasis, overplaying, dramatization, colouring, embroidery, embellishment, inflation, hyperbole, aggrandizement; informal blowing up (out of all proportion), making a big thing out of something.
– OPPOSITES reduction, understatement.
magnificence ● noun SPLENDOUR, resplendence, grandeur, impressiveness, glory, majesty, nobility, pomp, stateliness, elegance, sumptuousness, opulence, luxury, lavishness, richness, brilliance, dazzle, skill, virtuosity.
– OPPOSITES modesty, tawdriness, weakness.
magnificent ● adjective **1** *a magnificent view of the mountains* SPLENDID, spectacular, impressive, striking, glorious, superb, ma-

m

magnifico /magniffikō/ ● noun (pl. **magnificoes**) informal an important, powerful, or well-known person.
– ORIGIN from Italian, 'high-minded, excellent', originally used as a title of a Venetian nobleman.
magnify ● verb (**magnifies, magnified**) **1** make (something) appear larger than it is, especially with a lens or microscope. **2** intensify or exaggerate. **3** archaic extol; glorify.
– DERIVATIVES **magnification** noun **magnifier** noun.
– ORIGIN Latin *magnificare*, from *magnus* 'great'.
magnifying glass ● noun a lens that produces an enlarged image, used to examine small or finely detailed things.
magniloquent /magnilləkwənt/ ● adjective formal using high-flown language.
magnitude ● noun **1** great size, extent, or importance. **2** size. **3** Astronomy the brightness of a star, as represented by a number on a logarithmic scale.
– ORIGIN Latin *magnitudo*, from *magnus* 'great'.
magnolia ● noun **1** a tree or shrub with large waxy flowers. **2** a pale creamy-white colour like that of magnolia blossom.
– ORIGIN named after the French botanist Pierre *Magnol* (1638–1715).
magnox ● noun a magnesium-based alloy used to enclose uranium fuel elements in some nuclear reactors.
magnum ● noun (pl. **magnums**) **1** a wine bottle of twice the standard size, normally 1½ litres. **2** (trademark in the US) a gun designed to fire cartridges that are more powerful than its calibre would suggest.
– ORIGIN Latin, 'great thing'.
magnum opus /magnəm ōpəss/ ● noun (pl. **magnum opuses** or **magna opera**) a large and important work of art, music, or literature, especially a person's most important work.
– ORIGIN Latin, 'great work'.
magpie ● noun **1** a long-tailed bird of the crow family with pied plumage and a raucous voice. **2** a black-and-white Australian butcher bird with musical calls. **3** a person who obsessively collects things or who chatters idly.
– ORIGIN probably a shortening of dialect *maggot the pie*, *maggoty-pie*, from *Magot*, a former familiar form of the name *Marguerite*, + Latin *pica* 'magpie'.
maguey /magway/ ● noun an agave plant, especially one yielding pulque.
– ORIGIN from Taino (an extinct Caribbean language).
magus /maygəss/ ● noun (pl. **magi** /mayji/) **1** a member of a priestly class of ancient Persia. **2** a sorcerer. **3** (**the Magi**) the three wise men from the East who brought gifts to the infant Jesus.
– ORIGIN Latin, from Old Persian.
Magyar /magyaar/ ● noun **1** a member of a people predominating in Hungary. **2** the Hungarian language.
– ORIGIN the name in Hungarian.
maharaja /maahəraajə/ (also **maharajah**) ● noun historical an Indian prince.
– ORIGIN Hindi, from Sanskrit, 'great raja'.
maharani /maahəraani/ ● noun a maharaja's wife or widow.
– ORIGIN Hindi, from Sanskrit, 'great queen'.
Maharishi /maahərishi/ ● noun a great Hindu sage or spiritual leader.
– ORIGIN Sanskrit, 'great sage or saint'.
mahatma /məhatmə/ ● noun (in the Indian subcontinent) a holy person or sage.
– ORIGIN Sanskrit, 'great soul'.
Mahayana /maahəyaanə/ ● noun one of the two major traditions of Buddhism (the other being Theravada), practised especially in China, Tibet, Japan, and Korea.
– ORIGIN Sanskrit, 'great vehicle'.
Mahdi /maadi/ ● noun (pl. **Mahdis**) (in popular Muslim belief) a leader who will rule before the end of the world and restore religion and justice.
– ORIGIN Arabic, 'he who is guided in the right way'.
Mahican /mahikən/ (also **Mohican**) ● noun a member of an American Indian people formerly inhabiting the Upper Hudson Valley. ● adjective relating to the Mahicans.
– ORIGIN the name in the extinct Mahican language, said to mean 'wolf'.
mah-jong /maajong/ (also **mah-jongg**) ● noun a Chinese game played with 136 or 144 rectangular tiles.
– ORIGIN Chinese dialect, 'sparrows'.
mahogany ● noun **1** hard reddish-brown wood from a tropical tree, used for furniture. **2** a rich reddish-brown colour.
– ORIGIN of unknown origin.
mahonia /məhōniə/ ● noun an evergreen shrub with clusters of small fragrant yellow flowers.
– ORIGIN named after the American botanist Bernard Mc*Mahon* (*c*.1775–1816).
mahout /məhowt/ ● noun (in the Indian subcontinent and SE Asia) a person who works with and rides an elephant.
– ORIGIN Hindi.
maid ● noun **1** a female domestic servant. **2** archaic or literary a girl or young woman. **3** archaic or literary a virgin.
maiden ● noun **1** archaic or literary a girl or young woman. **2** archaic or literary a virgin. **3** (also **maiden over**) Cricket an over in which no runs are scored. ● adjective **1** (of an older woman) unmarried. **2** first of its kind: *a maiden voyage.*
– ORIGIN Old English.
maidenhair fern ● noun a fern with slender-stalked fronds.
maidenhead ● noun archaic **1** a girl's or woman's virginity. **2** the hymen.
maiden name ● noun the surname of a married woman before her marriage.
maid of honour ● noun **1** an unmarried noblewoman attending a queen or princess. **2** N. Amer. a principal bridesmaid.
maidservant ● noun dated a female domestic servant.
mail[1] ● noun **1** letters and parcels sent by post. **2** the postal system. **3** email. ● verb **1** send by post. **2** send post or email to.
– ORIGIN originally in the sense 'travelling bag': from Old French *male* 'wallet'.
mail[2] ● noun historical flexible armour made of metal rings or plates.
– ORIGIN Old French *maille*, from Latin *macula* 'spot or mesh'; related to IMMACULATE.

m

Thesaurus

jestic, awesome, awe-inspiring, breathtaking. **2** *a magnificent apartment overlooking the lake* SUMPTUOUS, resplendent, grand, impressive, imposing, monumental, palatial, stately, opulent, luxurious, lavish, rich, dazzling, beautiful, elegant; *informal* splendiferous, ritzy, posh. **3** *a magnificent performance* MASTERLY, skilful, virtuoso, brilliant.
– OPPOSITES uninspiring, modest, tawdry, poor, weak.
magnify ● verb **1** *the lens magnifies the image* ENLARGE, boost, enhance, maximize, increase, augment, extend, expand, amplify, intensify; *informal* blow up. **2** *the problem gets magnified* EXAGGERATE, overstate, overemphasize, overplay, dramatize, colour, embroider, embellish, inflate, make a mountain out of (a molehill); *informal* blow up (out of all proportion), make a big thing out of.
– OPPOSITES reduce, minimize, understate.
magnitude ● noun **1** *the magnitude of the task* IMMENSITY, vastness, hugeness, enormity; size, extent, expanse, greatness, largeness, bigness. **2** *events of tragic magnitude* IMPORTANCE, import, significance, weight, consequence, mark, notability, note; *formal* moment. **3** *a change in magnitude on the Richter scale* VALUE, figure, number, measure, order, quantity, vector, index, indicator. **4** *a star of magnitude 4.2* BRIGHTNESS, brilliance, radiance, luminosity.
– OPPOSITES smallness, triviality.
– PHRASES **of the first magnitude** OF THE UTMOST IMPORTANCE, of the greatest significance, very important, of great consequence; *formal* of great moment.
maid ● noun **1** *the maid cleared the table* FEMALE SERVANT, maidservant, housemaid, parlourmaid, lady's maid, chambermaid, maid-of-all-work, domestic; help, cleaner, cleaning woman/lady; *Brit. informal* daily, skivvy, Mrs Mop; *Brit. dated* charwoman, charlady, char, tweeny. **2** *(poetic/literary) a village maid and her swain* GIRL, young woman, young lady, lass, miss; *Scottish* (wee) lassie; *poetic/literary* maiden, damsel, nymph; *archaic* wench. **3** *(poetic/literary) she was no longer a maid* VIRGIN, chaste woman, unmarried girl, celibate; *formal* virgo intacta; *poetic/literary* maiden.
maiden ● noun *(poetic/literary)*. See MAID senses 2, 3.
● adjective **1** *a maiden aunt* UNMARRIED, spinster, unwed, unwedded, single, husbandless, celibate. **2** *a maiden voyage* FIRST, initial, inaugural, introductory, initiatory.
maidenly ● adjective VIRGINAL, immaculate, intact, chaste, pure, virtuous; demure, reserved, retiring, decorous, seemly.
– OPPOSITES fast, slatternly.
mail ● noun *the mail arrived* POST, letters, correspondence; postal system, postal service, post office; delivery, collection; e-mail; *in-*

mailbag ● noun a large sack or bag for carrying mail.
mailbox ● noun chiefly N. Amer. **1** a box on a post at the entrance to a person's property, into which mail is delivered. **2** a post box.
mailer ● noun **1** chiefly N. Amer. the sender of a letter or package by post. **2** Computing a program that sends email messages.
mailing ● noun something sent by mail, especially a piece of mass advertising.
mailing list ● noun a list of the names and addresses of people to whom advertising matter or information may be mailed regularly.
maillot /mīyō/ ● noun (pl. pronounced same) **1** a pair of tights worn for dancing or gymnastics. **2** a jersey or top worn in cycling. **3** chiefly N. Amer. a woman's one-piece swimsuit.
– ORIGIN French.
mailman ● noun N. Amer. a postman.
mail order ● noun the ordering of goods by post.
mailshot ● noun Brit. a piece of advertising material sent to a large number of addresses.
maim ● verb wound or injure (someone) so that part of the body is permanently damaged.
– ORIGIN Old French *mahaignier*.
main ● adjective chief in size or importance. ● noun **1** a principal water or gas pipe or electricity cable. **2** (**the mains**) Brit. public water, gas, or electricity supply through pipes or cables. **3** (**the main**) archaic or literary the open ocean.
– PHRASES **by main force** through sheer strength. **in the main** on the whole.
– ORIGIN from Old English, 'physical force'.
main brace ● noun the rope attached to the main yard of a sailing ship.
main drag ● noun informal, chiefly N. Amer. the main street of a town.
mainframe ● noun **1** a large high-speed computer, especially one supporting numerous workstations. **2** the central processing unit and primary memory of a computer.
mainland ● noun a large continuous extent of land as opposed to offshore islands and detached territories.
mainline ● verb informal inject (a drug) intravenously.
main line ● noun **1** a chief railway line. **2** informal a principal vein as a site for a drug injection.
mainly ● adverb more than anything else; for the most part.
main man ● noun N. Amer. informal a close and trusted friend.
mainmast ● noun the principal mast of a ship.
mainspring ● noun **1** the principal spring in a watch, clock, etc. **2** a prime source of motivation or support.
mainstay ● noun **1** a stay which extends from the maintop to the foot of the foremast of a sailing ship. **2** the chief support or main part.
mainstream ● noun normal or conventional ideas, attitudes, or activities. ● adjective belonging to or characteristic of the mainstream.
maintain ● verb **1** cause or enable (a condition or state of affairs) to continue. **2** keep (a building, machine, etc.) in good condition by checking or repairing it regularly. **3** provide with necessities for life or existence. **4** assert to be the case.
– ORIGIN Old French *maintenir*, from Latin *manu tenere* 'hold in the hand'.
maintained school ● noun Brit. a school financed with public money.
maintenance ● noun **1** the process of maintaining or being maintained. **2** provision for one's former husband or wife after divorce.
maintop ● noun a platform around the head of the lower section of a sailing ship's mainmast.
maiolica /məyollikə/ ● noun fine Italian earthenware with coloured decoration on an opaque white glaze.
– ORIGIN Italian, from *Maiolica* 'Majorca' (from or via where such earthenware was shipped).
maisonette ● noun a set of rooms for living in, typically on two storeys of a larger building.
– ORIGIN French *maisonnette* 'small house'.
maize ● noun chiefly Brit. a cereal plant yielding large grains (corn or sweetcorn) set in rows on a cob.
– ORIGIN Spanish *maíz*, from Taino (an extinct Caribbean language).
majestic ● adjective impressively beautiful or dignified.
– DERIVATIVES **majestically** adverb.
majesty ● noun (pl. **majesties**) **1** impressive dignity or beauty. **2** royal power. **3** (**His**, **Your**, etc. **Majesty**) a title given to a sovereign or a sovereign's wife or widow.
– ORIGIN Latin *majestas*, from *major* 'major'.
majolica /məjollikə/ ● noun a kind of earthenware made in imitation of Italian maiolica, especially in England during the 19th century.
major ● adjective **1** important, serious, or significant. **2** greater or more important; main. **3** Music based on intervals of a semitone between the third and fourth, and seventh and eighth degrees. Contrasted with MINOR. ● noun **1** a rank of officer in the army and the US air force, above captain and below lieutenant colonel. **2** an officer in charge of a section of band instruments. **3** Music a major key, interval, or scale. **4** N. Amer. a student's principal subject or course. **5** N. Amer. a student specializing in a specified subject. ● verb (**major in**) N. Amer. & Austral./NZ specialize in (a particular subject) at college or university.
– ORIGIN Latin, comparative of *magnus* 'great'.

m

Thesaurus

formal snail mail; *N. Amer.* the mails.
● verb *we mailed the parcels* SEND, post, dispatch, direct, forward, redirect, ship; e-mail.
maim ● verb INJURE, wound, cripple, disable, incapacitate, impair, mar, mutilate, lacerate, disfigure, deform, mangle.
main ● adjective *the main item* PRINCIPAL, chief, head, leading, foremost, most important, major, ruling, dominant, central, focal, key, prime, master, premier, primary, first, fundamental, supreme, predominant, (most) prominent, pre-eminent, paramount, overriding, cardinal, crucial, critical, pivotal, salient, elemental, essential, staple.
– OPPOSITES subsidiary, minor.
● noun *(poetic/literary) the Spanish Main* SEA, ocean, deep; *informal, dated* the drink; *Brit. informal, dated* the briny.
– PHRASES **in the main.** See MAINLY.
mainly ● adverb MOSTLY, for the most part, in the main, on the whole, largely, by and large, to a large extent, predominantly, chiefly, principally, primarily; generally, usually, typically, commonly, on average, as a rule, almost always.
mainspring ● noun MOTIVE, motivation, impetus, driving force, incentive, impulse, prime mover, reason, fountain, fount, root, generator.
mainstay ● noun CENTRAL COMPONENT, central figure, centrepiece, prop, linchpin, cornerstone, pillar, bulwark, buttress, chief support, backbone, anchor, foundation, base, staple.
mainstream ● adjective NORMAL, conventional, ordinary, orthodox, conformist, accepted, established, recognized, common, usual, prevailing, popular.
– OPPOSITES fringe.
maintain ● verb **1** *they wanted to maintain peace* PRESERVE, conserve, keep, retain, keep going, keep alive, keep up, prolong, perpetuate, sustain, carry on, continue. **2** *the council maintains the roads* KEEP IN GOOD CONDITION, keep in (good) repair, keep up, service, care for, take good care of, look after. **3** *the costs of maintaining a family* SUPPORT, provide for, keep, sustain; nurture, feed, nourish. **4** *he always maintained his innocence | he maintains that he is innocent* INSIST (ON), declare, assert, protest, affirm, avow, profess, claim, allege, contend, argue, swear (to), hold to; *formal* aver; *rare* asseverate.
– OPPOSITES break, discontinue, neglect, deny.
maintenance ● noun **1** *the maintenance of peace* PRESERVATION, conservation, keeping, prolongation, perpetuation, carrying on, continuation, continuance. **2** *car maintenance* UPKEEP, service, servicing, repair(s), care, aftercare. **3** *the maintenance of his children* SUPPORT, keeping, upkeep, sustenance; nurture, feeding, nourishment. **4** *absent fathers are forced to pay maintenance* FINANCIAL SUPPORT, child support, alimony, provision; keep, subsistence, living expenses.
– OPPOSITES breakdown, discontinuation, neglect.
majestic ● adjective STATELY, dignified, distinguished, solemn, magnificent, grand, splendid, resplendent, glorious, sumptuous, impressive, august, noble, awe-inspiring, monumental, palatial; statuesque, Olympian, imposing, marvellous, sonorous, resounding, heroic.
– OPPOSITES modest, wretched.
majesty ● noun **1** *the majesty of the procession* STATELINESS, dignity, distinction, solemnity, magnificence, pomp, grandeur, grandness, splendour, resplendence, glory, impressiveness, au-

Majorcan /məyorkən/ ● noun a person from Majorca. ● adjective relating to Majorca.

major-domo ● noun (pl. **major-domos**) the chief steward of a large household.

– ORIGIN Spanish and Italian, from Latin *major domus* 'highest official of the household'.

major general ● noun a rank of officer in the army and the US air force, above brigadier or brigadier general and below lieutenant general.

majoritarian ● adjective governed by or believing in decision by a majority.

majority ● noun (pl. **majorities**) **1** the greater number. **2** Brit. the number by which the votes cast for one party or candidate exceed those for the next. **3** the age when a person is legally considered a full adult, usually 18 or 21.

– USAGE Strictly speaking, **majority** should be used with plural nouns to mean 'the greater number', as in *the majority of cases*. Use with nouns that do not take a plural to mean 'the greatest part', as in *she ate the majority of the meal*, is not considered good English.

majority rule ● noun the principle that the greater number should exercise greater power.

majority verdict ● noun English Law a verdict agreed by all but one or two of the members of a jury.

major league ● noun N. Amer. the highest-ranking league in a particular professional sport, especially baseball.

major planet ● noun any of the nine principal planets of the solar system, as distinct from an asteroid or moon.

major prophet ● noun any of the prophets after whom the longer prophetic books of the Bible are named: Isaiah, Jeremiah, and Ezekiel.

majuscule /majəskyool/ ● noun a large letter, either capital or uncial.

– ORIGIN from Latin *majuscula littera* 'somewhat greater letter'.

make ● verb (past and past part. **made**) **1** form by putting parts together or combining substances. **2** cause to be or come about. **3** force to do something. **4** (**make into**) alter (something) so that it forms (something else). **5** constitute, amount to, or serve as. **6** estimate as or decide on. **7** gain or earn (money or profit). **8** arrive at or achieve. **9** (**make it**) become successful. **10** prepare to go in a particular direction or do a particular thing: *he made towards the car.* **11** arrange bedclothes tidily on (a bed) ready for use. ● noun the manufacturer or trade name of a product.

– PHRASES **have (got) it made** informal be in a position where success is certain. **make after** pursue. **make away with 1** another way of saying **make off with**. **2** kill furtively and illicitly. **make do** manage with the limited means available. **make for 1** move towards. **2** tend to result in or be received as. **3** (**be made for**) be eminently suited for. **make it up to** compensate for unfair treatment. **make of 1** ascribe (attention or importance) to. **2** understand or derive (advantage) from. **make off** leave hurriedly. **make off with** carry away illicitly. **make or break** be the factor which decides whether (something) will succeed or fail. **make out 1** manage with difficulty to see, hear, or understand. **2** represent as or pretend. **3** draw up (a list or document). **4** informal make progress; fare. **make over 1** transfer the possession of. **2** give (someone) a new image with cosmetics, hairstyling, and clothes. **make sail** spread a sail or sails, especially to begin a voyage. **make time** find an occasion when time is available to do something. **make up 1** put together or prepare from parts or ingredients. **2** concoct or invent (a story). **3** (also **make up for**) compensate for. **4** be reconciled after a quarrel. **5** apply cosmetics to. **make up one's mind** make a decision. **make way** allow room for someone or something else. **on the make** informal **1** intent on gain. **2** looking for a sexual partner.

– ORIGIN Old English, related to MATCH[1].

Thesaurus

gustness, nobility. **2** *the majesty invested in the monarch* SOVEREIGNTY, authority, power, dominion, supremacy.

– OPPOSITES modesty, wretchedness.

major ● adjective **1** *the major English poets* GREATEST, best, finest, most important, chief, main, prime, principal, capital, cardinal, leading, star, foremost, outstanding, first-rate, pre-eminent, arch-. **2** *an issue of major importance* CRUCIAL, vital, great, considerable, paramount, utmost, prime. **3** *a major factor* IMPORTANT, big, significant, weighty, crucial, key, sweeping, substantial. **4** *major surgery* SERIOUS, radical, complicated, difficult.

– OPPOSITES minor, little, trivial.

majority ● noun **1** *the majority of cases* LARGER PART/NUMBER, greater part/number, best/better part, most, more than half; bulk, mass, weight, (main) body, preponderance, predominance, generality, lion's share. **2** *a majority in the election* (WINNING) MARGIN, superiority of numbers/votes; landslide. **3** *my son has reached his majority* COMING OF AGE, legal age, adulthood, maturity, manhood/womanhood; age of consent.

– OPPOSITES minority.

make ● verb **1** *he makes models* CONSTRUCT, build, assemble, put together, manufacture, produce, fabricate, create, form, fashion, model. **2** *she made me drink it* FORCE, compel, coerce, press, drive, pressure, pressurize, oblige, require; have someone do something, prevail on, dragoon, bludgeon, strong-arm, impel, constrain; informal railroad. **3** *don't make such a noise* CAUSE, create, give rise to, produce, bring about, generate, engender, occasion, effect, set up, establish, institute, found, develop, originate; poetic/literary beget. **4** *she made a little bow* PERFORM, execute, give, do, accomplish, achieve, bring off, carry out, effect. **5** *they made him chairman* APPOINT, designate, name, nominate, select, elect, vote in, install; induct, institute, invest, ordain. **6** *he had made a will* FORMULATE, frame, draw up, devise, make out, prepare, compile, compose, put together; draft, write, pen. **7** *I've made a mistake* PERPETRATE, commit, be responsible for, be guilty of, be to blame for. **8** *he's made a lot of money* ACQUIRE, obtain, gain, get, realize, secure, win, earn; gross, net, clear; bring in, take (in). **9** *he made tea* PREPARE, get ready, put together, concoct, cook, dish up, throw together, whip up, brew; informal fix; Brit. informal mash. **10** *we've got to make a decision* REACH, come to, settle on, determine on, conclude. **11** *she made a short announcement* UTTER, give, deliver, give voice to, enunciate, recite, pronounce. **12** *the sofa makes a good bed* BE, act as, serve as, function as, constitute, do duty for. **13** *he'll make the first eleven* GAIN A PLACE IN, get into, gain access to, enter; achieve, attain. **14** *he just made his train* CATCH, get, arrive/be in time for, arrive at, reach; get to.

– OPPOSITES destroy, lose, miss.

● noun **1** *what make is the car?* BRAND, marque, label. **2** *a man of a different make from his brother* CHARACTER, nature, temperament, temper, disposition, kidney, mould, stamp.

– PHRASES **make as if/though** FEIGN, pretend, make a show/pretence of, affect, feint, make out; informal put it on. **make away with 1** *she decided to make away with him* KILL, murder, dispatch, eliminate; informal bump off, do away with, do in, do for, knock off, top, croak, stiff, blow away; N. Amer. informal ice, rub out, smoke, waste; poetic/literary slay. **2** *they made away with the evidence* DISPOSE OF, get rid of, destroy, throw away, jettison, ditch, dump; informal do away with. **make believe** PRETEND, fantasize, daydream, build castles in the air, build castles in Spain, dream, imagine, play-act, play. **make do** SCRAPE BY/ALONG, get by/along, manage, cope, survive, muddle through/along, improvise, make ends meet, keep the wolf from the door, keep one's head above water; informal make out; (**make do with**) make the best of, get by on, put up with. **make for 1** *she made for the door* GO FOR/TOWARDS, head for/towards, aim for, make one's way towards, move towards, direct one's steps towards, steer a course towards, be bound for, make a beeline for. **2** *constant arguing doesn't make for a happy marriage* CONTRIBUTE TO, be conducive to, produce, promote, facilitate, foster; formal conduce to. **make it 1** *he never made it as a singer* SUCCEED, be a success, distinguish oneself, get ahead, make good; informal make the grade, arrive, crack it. **2** *she's very ill—is she going to make it?* SURVIVE, come through, pull through, get better, recover. **make love.** See HAVE SEX at SEX. **make off** RUN AWAY/OFF, take to one's heels, beat a hasty retreat, flee, make one's getaway, make a quick exit, run for it, make a run for it, take off, take flight, bolt, make oneself scarce, decamp, do a disappearing act; informal clear off/out, beat it, leg it, cut and run, skedaddle, vamoose, hightail it, hotfoot it, show a clean pair of heels, fly the coop, split, scoot, scram; Brit. informal scarper, do a runner; N. Amer. informal take a powder. **make off with** TAKE, steal, purloin, pilfer, abscond with, run away/off with, carry off, snatch; kidnap, abduct; informal walk away/off with, swipe, filch, snaffle, nab, lift, 'liberate', 'borrow', snitch; Brit. informal pinch, half-inch, nick, whip, knock off; N. Amer. informal heist, glom. **make out** (informal) *how did you make out?* GET ON/ALONG, fare, do, proceed, go, progress, manage, survive, cope, get by. **make something out 1** *I could just make out a figure in the distance* SEE, discern, distinguish, per-

make-believe • noun a state of fantasy or pretence. • adjective imitating something real; pretend.

makeover • noun a complete transformation of a person's appearance with cosmetics, hairstyling, and clothes.

maker • noun **1** a person or thing that makes something. **2** (**our, the**, etc. **Maker**) God.

– PHRASES **meet one's Maker** chiefly humorous die.

makeshift • adjective interim and temporary. • noun a temporary substitute or device.

make-up • noun **1** cosmetics applied to the face. **2** composition or constitution. **3** Printing the arrangement of type, illustrations, etc. on a printed page.

makeweight • noun **1** something put on a scale to make up the required weight. **2** an extra person or thing needed to complete something.

making • noun **1** the process of making something. **2** (**makings**) the necessary qualities.

– PHRASES **be the making of** bring about the success or favourable development of.

mako /maakō/ • noun (pl. **makos**) a large shark with a deep blue back and white underparts.

– ORIGIN Maori.

makuta plural of LIKUTA.

makutu /məkōotōo/ • noun NZ a magic spell.

– ORIGIN Maori.

mal- • combining form **1** in an unpleasant degree: *malodorous*. **2** in a faulty or improper manner: *malfunction*. **3** not: *maladroit*.

– ORIGIN from Latin *male* 'badly'.

malacca /məlakkə/ • noun a walking stick made of cane obtained from a Malaysian palm.

– ORIGIN from the name *Malacca* (or Melaka), a state of Malaysia.

malachite /maləkīt/ • noun a bright green copper-containing mineral.

– ORIGIN Old French *melochite*, from Greek *malakhē* 'mallow'.

maladjusted • adjective failing to cope with the demands of a normal social environment.

maladminister • verb formal manage or administer badly or dishonestly.

– DERIVATIVES **maladministration** noun.

maladroit /malədroyt/ • adjective inefficient or ineffective; clumsy.

malady • noun (pl. **maladies**) a disease or ailment.

– ORIGIN from Old French *malade* 'ill'.

Malagasy /maləgassi/ • noun (pl. same or **Malagasies**) **1** a person from Madagascar. **2** the language of Madagascar.

malaise • noun a general feeling of unease, ill health, or low spirits.

– ORIGIN French.

malapert /maləpert/ • adjective archaic presumptuous and impudent.

– ORIGIN from MAL- + archaic *apert* 'insolent'.

malapropism /maləproppiz'm/ (US also **malaprop**) • noun the mistaken use of a word in place of a similar-sounding one (e.g. 'dance a *flamingo*' instead of *flamenco*).

– ORIGIN from the name of the character Mrs *Malaprop* in Richard Sheridan's play *The Rivals* (1775).

malaria • noun a disease characterized by recurrent attacks of fever, caused by a blood parasite transmitted by mosquitoes in tropical and subtropical regions.

– DERIVATIVES **malarial** adjective.

– ORIGIN from Italian *mala aria* 'bad air' (the disease was formerly attributed to unhealthy vapours given off by marshes).

malarkey /məlaarki/ • noun informal nonsense.

– ORIGIN of unknown origin.

malathion /maləthīən/ • noun a synthetic insecticide containing phosphorus, relatively harmless to plants and other ani-

Thesaurus

m

ceive, pick out, detect, observe, recognize; *poetic/literary* descry, espy. **2** *he couldn't make out what she was saying* UNDERSTAND, comprehend, follow, grasp, fathom, work out, make sense of, interpret, decipher, make head or tail of, get, get the drift of, catch. **3** *she made out that he was violent* ALLEGE, claim, assert, declare, maintain, affirm, suggest, imply, hint, insinuate, indicate, intimate, impute; *formal* aver. **4** *he made out a receipt for $20* WRITE OUT, fill out, fill in, complete, draw up. **make something over to someone** TRANSFER, sign over, turn over, hand over/on/down, give, leave, bequeath, bestow, pass on, assign, consign, entrust; *Law* devolve, convey. **make up** *let's kiss and make up* BE FRIENDS AGAIN, bury the hatchet, declare a truce, make peace, forgive and forget, shake hands, become reconciled, settle one's differences, mend fences, call it quits. **make something up 1** *exports make up 42% of earnings* COMPRISE, form, compose, constitute, account for. **2** *Gina brought a friend to make up a foursome* COMPLETE, round off, finish. **3** *the pharmacist made up the prescription* PREPARE, mix, concoct, put together. **4** *he made up an excuse* INVENT, fabricate, concoct, dream up, think up, hatch, trump up; devise, manufacture, formulate, coin; *informal* cook up. **5** *she made up her face* APPLY MAKE-UP/COSMETICS TO, powder, rouge; (**make oneself up**) *informal* put on one's face, do/paint one's face, apply one's warpaint, doll oneself up. **make up for 1** *she tried to make up for what she'd said* ATONE FOR, make amends for, compensate for, make recompense for, make reparation for, make redress for, make restitution for, expiate. **2** *job satisfaction can make up for low pay* OFFSET, counterbalance, counteract, compensate for; balance, neutralize, cancel out, even up, redeem. **make up one's mind** DECIDE, come to a decision, make/reach a decision; settle on a plan of action, come to a conclusion, reach a conclusion; determine, resolve. **make up to** *(informal)* CURRY FAVOUR WITH, cultivate, try to win over, court, ingratiate oneself with; *informal* suck up to, butter up; *N. Amer. informal* shine up to; *archaic* blandish. **make way** MOVE ASIDE, clear the way, make a space, make room, stand back.

make-believe • noun *that was sheer make-believe* FANTASY, pretence, daydreaming, imagination, invention, fancy, dream, fabrication, play-acting, charade, masquerade.

– OPPOSITES reality.

• adjective *make-believe adventures* IMAGINARY, imagined, made-up, fantasy, dreamed-up, fanciful, fictitious, fictive, feigned, fake, mock, sham, simulated; *informal* pretend, phoney.

– OPPOSITES real, actual.

maker • noun CREATOR, manufacturer, builder, constructor, producer, fabricator.

makeshift • adjective TEMPORARY, provisional, stopgap, standby, rough and ready, improvised, ad hoc, extempore, thrown together, cobbled together.

– OPPOSITES permanent.

make-up • noun **1** *she used excessive make-up* COSMETICS, maquillage; greasepaint, face paint; *informal* warpaint, slap. **2** *the cellular make-up of plants and trees* COMPOSITION, constitution, structure, configuration, arrangement, organization, formation. **3** *jealousy isn't part of his make-up* CHARACTER, nature, temperament, personality, disposition, mentality, persona, psyche; *informal* what makes someone tick.

making • noun **1** *the making of cars* MANUFACTURE, mass-production, building, construction, assembly, production, creation, putting together, fabrication, forming, moulding, forging. **2** *she has the makings of a champion* QUALITIES, characteristics, ingredients; potential, promise, capacity, capability; essentials, essence, beginnings, rudiments, basics, stuff.

– OPPOSITES destruction.

– PHRASES **in the making** *a hero in the making* BUDDING, up and coming, emergent, developing, nascent, potential, promising, incipient.

maladjusted • adjective DISTURBED, unstable, neurotic, unbalanced, unhinged, dysfunctional; *informal* mixed up, screwed up, hung up, messed up.

– OPPOSITES normal, stable.

maladministration • noun *(formal)* MISMANAGEMENT, mishandling, misgovernment, misrule, incompetence, inefficiency, bungling; malpractice, misconduct; *Law* malfeasance; *formal* malversation.

– OPPOSITES probity, efficiency.

maladroit • adjective BUNGLING, awkward, inept, clumsy, bumbling, incompetent, unskilful, heavy-handed, gauche, tactless, inconsiderate, undiplomatic, impolitic; *informal* ham-fisted, cack-handed.

– OPPOSITES adroit, skilful.

malady • noun ILLNESS, sickness, disease, infection, ailment, disorder, complaint, indisposition, affliction, infirmity; *informal* bug, virus; *Brit. informal* lurgy; *Austral. informal* wog.

malaise • noun UNHAPPINESS, uneasiness, unease, discomfort, melancholy, depression, despondency, dejection, angst, Weltschmerz, ennui; lassitude, listlessness, languor, weariness; indisposition, ailment, infirmity, illness, sickness, disease.

– OPPOSITES comfort, well-being.

malapropism • noun WRONG WORD, solecism, misuse, misapplication, infelicity, slip of the tongue.

mals.
– ORIGIN from elements of its chemical name.
Malawian /məlaawiən/ ● noun a person from Malawi in south central Africa. ● adjective relating to Malawi.
Malay ● noun **1** a member of a people inhabiting Malaysia and Indonesia. **2** the Austronesian language of the Malays.
Malayan ● noun another term for MALAY. ● adjective relating to Malays or Malaya (now part of Malaysia).
Malaysian ● noun a person from Malaysia. ● adjective relating to Malaysia.
malcontent ● noun a discontented person.
mal de mer /mal də **mair**/ ● noun seasickness.
– ORIGIN French.
Maldivian /mawl**div**viən/ ● noun a person from the Maldives, a country consisting of a chain of islands in the Indian Ocean. ● adjective relating to the Maldives.
male ● adjective **1** relating to the sex that can fertilize or inseminate the female to give rise to offspring. **2** relating to or characteristic of men. **3** (of a plant or flower) bearing stamens but lacking functional pistils. **4** (of a fitting) manufactured to fit inside a corresponding female part. ● noun a male person, animal, or plant.
– DERIVATIVES **maleness** noun.
– ORIGIN Old French *masle*, from Latin *masculus*, from *mas* 'a male'.
malediction /mali**diksh**'n/ ● noun a curse.
– ORIGIN from Latin *maledicere* 'speak evil of'.
malefactor /**mal**ifaktər/ ● noun a person who commits a crime or some other wrong.
– ORIGIN from Latin *malefacere* 'do wrong'.
malefic /mə**lef**fik/ ● adjective literary causing harm.
– DERIVATIVES **maleficent** adjective.
– ORIGIN from Latin *male* 'ill' + *-ficus* 'doing'.
malevolent /mə**lev**vələnt/ ● adjective wishing evil to others.
– DERIVATIVES **malevolence** noun **malevolently** adverb.
– ORIGIN Latin, from *male* 'ill' + *velle* 'to wish'.
malfeasance /mal**feez**'nss/ ● noun Law wrongdoing, especially (US) by a public official.
– ORIGIN Old French *malfaisance*.
malformation ● noun abnormality of shape or form in a part of the body.
– DERIVATIVES **malformed** adjective.
malfunction ● verb (of a piece of equipment or machinery) fail to function normally. ● noun a failure of this type.
Malian /**maa**liən/ ● noun a person from Mali, a country in West Africa. ● adjective relating to Mali.
malice ● noun the desire to do harm to someone; ill will.
– ORIGIN Old French, from Latin *malus* 'bad'.
malice aforethought ● noun Law the intention to kill or harm, held to distinguish murder from unlawful killing.
malicious ● adjective characterized by malice; intending or intended to do harm.
– DERIVATIVES **maliciously** adverb **maliciousness** noun.
malign /mə**līn**/ ● adjective harmful or evil. ● verb speak ill of.
– DERIVATIVES **malignity** /mə**lig**niti/ noun **malignly** adverb.
– ORIGIN Latin *malignus* 'tending to evil'.
malignancy ● noun (pl. **malignancies**) **1** the presence of a malignant tumour; cancer. **2** a cancerous growth. **3** the quality of being malign or malevolent.
malignant ● adjective **1** harmful; malevolent. **2** (of a tumour) tending to invade normal tissue or to recur after removal; cancerous. Contrasted with BENIGN.
– ORIGIN originally in the sense 'likely to rebel against God or authority': from Latin *malignare* 'contrive maliciously'.
malinger ● verb exaggerate or feign illness in order to escape duty or work.
– DERIVATIVES **malingerer** noun.
– ORIGIN from French *malingre* 'weak, sickly'.
mall /mal, mawl/ ● noun **1** a large enclosed shopping area from which traffic is excluded. **2** a sheltered walk or promenade.
– ORIGIN probably a shortening of PALL-MALL: from *The Mall* in St James's Park, London, former site of a pall-mall alley.
mallard ● noun a common duck, the male of which has a dark green head and white collar.
– ORIGIN Old French, 'wild drake', from *masle* 'male'.
malleable ● adjective **1** able to be hammered or pressed into shape without breaking or cracking. **2** easily influenced.
– DERIVATIVES **malleability** noun.

m

Thesaurus

malapropos ● adjective *(formal)* INAPPROPRIATE, unsuitable, inappposite, infelicitous, unfitting, inapt, unseemly, inopportune, ill-timed, untimely.
malcontent ● noun *a group of malcontents* TROUBLEMAKER, mischief-maker, agitator, dissident, rebel; discontent, complainer, grumbler, moaner; *informal* stirrer, whinger, grouch, bellyacher; *N. Amer. informal* kvetch.
● adjective *a malcontent employee* DISAFFECTED, discontented, dissatisfied, disgruntled, fed up, unhappy, annoyed, irritated, displeased, resentful; rebellious, dissentient, troublemaking, grumbling, complaining; *informal* browned off, hacked off, peeved, bellyaching; *Brit. informal* cheesed off, brassed off; *N. Amer. informal* teed off, ticked off.
– OPPOSITES happy.
male ● adjective *male sexual jealousy* MASCULINE, he-; virile, manly, macho, red-blooded.
– OPPOSITES female.
● noun *two males walked past.* See MAN noun sense 1.
– RELATED TERMS andro-.
– OPPOSITES female.
malediction ● noun CURSE, damnation, oath; spell; *N. Amer.* hex; *formal* imprecation; *poetic/literary* anathema; *archaic* execration.
– OPPOSITES blessing.
malefactor ● noun WRONGDOER, miscreant, offender, criminal, culprit, villain, lawbreaker, felon, evil-doer, delinquent, sinner, transgressor; *informal* crook, baddy; *Austral. informal* crim; *Law* malfeasant; *archaic* trespasser.
malevolence ● noun MALICE, hostility, hatred, hate, ill will, enmity, ill feeling, balefulness, venom, rancour, malignity, vindictiveness, viciousness, vengefulness; *poetic/literary* maleficence.
– OPPOSITES benevolence.
malevolent ● adjective MALICIOUS, hostile, evil-minded, baleful, evil-intentioned, venomous, evil, malign, malignant, rancorous, vicious, vindictive, vengeful; *poetic/literary* malefic, maleficent.
– OPPOSITES benevolent.
malformation ● noun DEFORMITY, distortion, crookedness, misshapenness, disfigurement, abnormality, warp.
malformed ● adjective DEFORMED, misshapen, misproportioned, ill-proportioned, disfigured, distorted, crooked, contorted, twisted, warped, wry; abnormal, grotesque, monstrous; *Scottish* thrawn.
malfunction ● verb *the computer has malfunctioned* CRASH, go wrong, break down, fail, stop working; *informal* conk out, go kaput, fall over, act up; *Brit. informal* play up, pack up.
● noun *a computer malfunction* CRASH, breakdown, fault, failure, bug; *informal* glitch.
malice ● noun SPITE, malevolence, ill will, vindictiveness, vengefulness, revenge, malignity, evil intentions, animus, enmity; *informal* bitchiness, cattiness; *poetic/literary* maleficence.
– OPPOSITES benevolence.
malicious ● adjective SPITEFUL, malevolent, evil-intentioned, vindictive, vengeful, malign, mean, nasty, hurtful, mischievous, wounding, cruel, unkind; *informal* bitchy, catty; *poetic/literary* malefic, maleficent.
– OPPOSITES benevolent.
malign ● adjective *a malign influence* HARMFUL, evil, bad, baleful, hostile, inimical, destructive, malignant, injurious; *poetic/literary* malefic, maleficent.
– OPPOSITES beneficial.
● verb *he maligned an innocent man* DEFAME, slander, libel, blacken someone's name/character, smear, vilify, speak ill of, cast aspersions on, run down, traduce, denigrate, disparage, slur, abuse, revile; *informal* bad-mouth, knock; *Brit. informal* rubbish, slag off; *formal* derogate, calumniate; *rare* asperse.
– OPPOSITES praise.
malignant ● noun **1** *a malignant disease* VIRULENT, very infectious, invasive, uncontrollable, dangerous, deadly, life-threatening, fatal. **2** *a malignant growth* CANCEROUS; *technical* metastatic. **3** *a malignant thought* SPITEFUL, malicious, malevolent, evil-intentioned, vindictive, vengeful, malign, mean, nasty, hurtful, mischievous, wounding, cruel, unkind; *informal* bitchy, catty; *poetic/literary* malefic, maleficent.
– OPPOSITES benign, benevolent.
malinger ● verb PRETEND TO BE ILL, feign/fake illness, sham; shirk; *informal* put it on; *Brit. informal* skive, swing the lead; *N. Amer. informal* gold-brick.
malingerer ● noun SHIRKER, idler, layabout; *informal* slacker; *Brit. in-*

– ORIGIN from Latin *malleus* 'a hammer'.
mallee /mali/ ● noun a low-growing bushy Australian eucalyptus.
– ORIGIN from an Aboriginal language.
mallet ● noun **1** a hammer with a large wooden head. **2** a long-handled wooden stick with a head like a hammer, for hitting a croquet or polo ball.
– ORIGIN Old French *maillet*, from Latin *malleus* 'hammer'.
mallow ● noun a herbaceous plant with pink or purple flowers.
– ORIGIN Latin *malva*; related to MAUVE.
malmsey /maamzi/ ● noun a sweet fortified Madeira wine.
– ORIGIN from *Monemvasia*, a port in Greece; malmsey was formerly a strong, sweet white wine imported from Greece.
malnourished ● adjective suffering from malnutrition.
– DERIVATIVES **malnourishment** noun.
malnutrition ● noun lack of proper nutrition.
malocclusion ● noun Dentistry imperfect positioning of the teeth when the jaws are closed.
malodorous ● adjective smelling very unpleasant.
malpractice ● noun improper, illegal, or negligent professional activity or treatment.
malt ● noun barley or other grain that has been steeped, germinated, and dried, used for brewing or distilling. ● verb **1** convert (grain) into malt. **2** (**malted**) mixed with malt or a malt extract.
– ORIGIN Old English, related to MELT.
maltase /mawltayz/ ● noun an enzyme, present in saliva and pancreatic juice, which catalyses the breakdown of maltose and similar sugars to form glucose.
Maltese ● noun (pl. same) a person from Malta. ● adjective relating to Malta.
Maltese cross ● noun a cross with arms of equal length which broaden from the centre and have their ends indented in a shallow V-shape.
– ORIGIN so named because the cross was formerly worn by the Knights of Malta, a religious order.
Malthusian /malthyoōziən/ ● adjective relating to the theory of the English economist Thomas Malthus (1766–1834) that, if unchecked, the population tends to increase at a greater rate than its means of subsistence. ● noun an adherent of Malthus.
malt liquor ● noun alcoholic liquor made from malt by fermentation rather than distillation, for example beer.
maltose /mawltōz/ ● noun a sugar produced by the breakdown of starch, e.g. by enzymes found in malt and saliva.
maltreat ● verb treat badly or brutally.
– DERIVATIVES **maltreatment** noun.
maltster ● noun a person who makes malt.
malt whisky ● noun whisky made only from malted barley and not blended with grain whisky.
malversation /malvərsaysh'n/ ● noun formal corrupt behaviour by a person in public office or a position of trust.
– ORIGIN French, from Latin *male* 'badly' + *versari* 'behave'.
mama (also **mamma**) ● noun dated or N. Amer. one's mother.
– ORIGIN imitative of a child's first syllables *ma, ma*.
mamba ● noun a large, agile, highly venomous African snake.
– ORIGIN Zulu.
mambo ● noun (pl. **mambos**) a Latin American dance similar to the rumba.
– ORIGIN American Spanish.
mammal ● noun a warm-blooded vertebrate animal that has hair or fur, secretes milk, and (typically) bears live young.
– DERIVATIVES **mammalian** adjective.
– ORIGIN from Latin *mamma* 'breast'.
mammary ● adjective relating to the human female breasts or the milk-secreting organs of other mammals. ● noun (pl. **mammaries**) informal a breast.
– ORIGIN from Latin *mamma* 'breast'.
mammogram /maməgram/ ● noun an image obtained by mammography.
mammography /mamogrəfi/ ● noun a technique using X-rays to diagnose and locate tumours of the breasts.
Mammon ● noun wealth regarded as an evil influence or false object of worship.
– ORIGIN New Testament Greek *mamōnas*, from an Aramaic word meaning 'riches'; see Gospel of Matthew, chapter 6 and Gospel of Luke, chapter 16.
mammoth ● noun a large extinct form of elephant with a hairy coat and long curved tusks. ● adjective huge; enormous.
– ORIGIN Russian.
mammy ● noun (pl. **mammies**) informal **1** a child's name for their mother. **2** offensive (formerly in the US) a black nursemaid or nanny in charge of white children.
man ● noun (pl. **men**) **1** an adult human male. **2** a male member of a workforce, team, etc. **3** a husband or lover. **4** a person. **5** human beings in general. **6** a figure or token used in a board game. ● verb (**manned**, **manning**) provide (a place or machine) with the personnel to run, operate, or defend it. ● exclamation informal, chiefly N. Amer. used for emphasis or to express surprise, admiration, or delight.
– PHRASES **every man for himself and the devil take the hindmost** proverb everyone should (or does) look after their own interests rather than considering those of others. **man about town** a fashionable and sociable man. **man and boy** from childhood. **the man in the street** the average man. **man of the cloth** a clergyman. **man of God** a clergyman. **man of letters** a male scholar or author. **man of straw** (also **straw man**) **1** a person who is a sham. **2** a person undertaking a financial commitment without adequate means. **to a man** without exception.
– USAGE Traditionally the word **man** has been used to refer not only to adult males but also to human beings in general. There is a historical explanation for this: in Old English the principal sense of **man** was 'a human being', and the words **wer** and **wif** were used to refer specifically to 'a male person' and 'a female person' respectively. Subsequently, **man** replaced **wer** as the normal term for 'a male person', but at the same time the older sense 'a human being' remained in use. The generic use of **man** to refer to 'human beings in general' is now widely regarded as old-fashioned or sexist. Acceptable alternatives include the **the human race** or **humankind**.
– ORIGIN Old English.
-man ● combining form **1** in nouns denoting a man of a specified nationality or origin (*Frenchman*). **2** in nouns denoting a person belonging to a specified group or having a specified occupation or role (*chairman*). **3** a ship of a specified kind (*merchantman*).
– USAGE Traditionally, the form **-man** was combined with other words to create a term denoting an occupation or role, as in **fireman** and **chairman**. As the role of women in society has changed, many of these terms ending in **-man** have come to be regarded as sexist and outdated. As a result, there has been a gradual shift away from **-man** compounds except where referring to a specific male person. Alternative neutral terms which are now well-established include **firefighter**, **police officer**, and **chair/chairperson**.

Thesaurus

formal skiver, lead-swinger; *N. Amer. informal* gold brick.
mall ● noun SHOPPING PRECINCT, shopping centre, shopping complex, arcade, galleria; *N. Amer.* plaza.
malleable ● adjective **1** *a malleable substance* PLIABLE, ductile, plastic, pliant, soft, workable. **2** *a malleable young woman* EASILY INFLUENCED, suggestible, susceptible, impressionable, amenable, compliant, pliable, tractable; biddable, complaisant, manipulable, persuadable, like putty in someone's hands.
– OPPOSITES hard, intractable.
malnutrition ● noun UNDERNOURISHMENT, malnourishment, poor diet, inadequate diet, unhealthy diet, lack of food.
malodorous ● adjective FOUL-SMELLING, evil-smelling, fetid, smelly, stinking, reeking, rank, high, putrid, noxious; *informal* stinky; *Brit. informal* niffy, pongy, whiffy, humming; *N. Amer. informal* funky; *poetic/literary* noisome, mephitic.
– OPPOSITES fragrant.
malpractice ● noun WRONGDOING, professional misconduct, breach of ethics, unprofessionalism, unethical behaviour; negligence, carelessness, incompetence.
maltreat ● verb ILL-TREAT, mistreat, abuse, ill-use, misuse, mishandle; knock about/around, hit, beat, strike, manhandle, harm, hurt, persecute, molest; *informal* beat up, rough up, do over.
maltreatment ● noun ILL-TREATMENT, mistreatment, abuse, ill use, ill usage, misuse, mishandling; violence, harm, persecution, molestation.
mammoth ● adjective HUGE, enormous, gigantic, giant, colossal, massive, vast, immense, mighty, stupendous, monumental, Herculean, epic, prodigious, mountainous, monstrous, titanic, towering, elephantine, king-size(d), gargantuan, Brobdingnagian; *informal* mega, monster, whopping, humongous, jumbo, bumper, astro-

m

mana /maanə/ ● noun (in Polynesian, Melanesian, and Maori belief) pervasive supernatural or magical power.
– ORIGIN Maori.

manacle ● noun a metal band or chain fastened around a person's hands or ankles to restrict their movement. ● verb fetter with a manacle or manacles.
– ORIGIN Old French *manicle* 'handcuff', from Latin *manus* 'hand'.

manage ● verb **1** be in charge of; run. **2** supervise (staff). **3** administer and regulate (resources). **4** succeed in doing or dealing with. **5** succeed despite difficulties; cope. **6** be free to attend (an appointment).
– DERIVATIVES **manageable** adjective **managing** adjective.
– ORIGIN originally in the sense 'put (a horse) through the paces of the manège': from Italian *maneggiare*, from Latin *manus* 'hand'.

management ● noun **1** the process of managing. **2** the managers of an organization.

manager ● noun **1** a person who manages an organization, group of staff, or sports team. **2** a person in charge of the business affairs of a sports player, actor, or performer.
– DERIVATIVES **managerial** adjective **managership** noun.

manageress ● noun a female manager.

mañana /manyaanə/ ● adverb tomorrow, or at some time in the future.
– ORIGIN Spanish.

manat /mannat/ ● noun (pl. same) the basic monetary unit of Azerbaijan and Turkmenistan.

man-at-arms ● noun archaic a soldier.

manatee /mannətee/ ● noun a sea cow of tropical Atlantic coasts, with a rounded tail flipper.
– ORIGIN Carib.

Manchester ● noun Austral./NZ cotton textiles; household linen.
– ORIGIN from the city of *Manchester*, historically a centre of cotton manufacture.

manciple ● noun chiefly archaic a person responsible for the supply of provisions in a monastery, college, or Inn of Court.
– ORIGIN Latin *manceps* 'buyer'.

Mancunian ● noun a person from Manchester. ● adjective relating to Manchester.
– ORIGIN from *Mancunium*, the Latin name for Manchester.

mandala /mandələ/ ● noun an intricate circular motif symbolizing the universe in Hinduism and Buddhism.
– ORIGIN Sanskrit, 'disc, circle'.

mandamus /mandaymæss/ ● noun Law a judicial writ issued as a command to a lower court or ordering a person to perform a public or legal duty.
– ORIGIN Latin, 'we command'.

mandarin ● noun **1** (**Mandarin**) the standard literary and official form of Chinese. **2** a high-ranking official in the former imperial Chinese civil service. **3** a powerful official or senior bureaucrat. **4** (also **mandarine**) a small citrus fruit with a loose yellow-orange skin.
– ORIGIN Hindi *mantrī* 'counsellor'; sense 4 perhaps derives from the colour of the fruit being likened to the official's yellow robes.

mandarin collar ● noun a close-fitting upright collar.

mandarin duck ● noun a small tree-nesting East Asian duck, the male of which has an orange ruff and sail-like feathers on each side of the body.

mandate ● noun /mandayt/ **1** an official order or authorization. **2** the authority to carry out a policy, regarded as given by the electorate to a party or candidate that wins an election. **3** historical a commission from the League of Nations to a member state to administer a territory. ● verb /mandayt/ **1** give (someone) authority to act in a certain way. **2** make compulsory.
– ORIGIN Latin *mandatum* 'something commanded'.

mandatory /mandətəri/ ● adjective required by law or mandate; compulsory.
– DERIVATIVES **mandatorily** adverb.

Mandelbrot set ● noun Mathematics a particular set of complex numbers which has a highly convoluted fractal boundary when plotted.
– ORIGIN named after the Polish-born mathematician Benoit B. *Mandelbrot* (born 1924).

mandible ● noun **1** the lower jawbone. **2** either of the upper and lower parts of a bird's beak. **3** either half of the crushing organ in an insect's mouthparts.
– ORIGIN from Latin *mandere* 'to chew'.

mandolin ● noun **1** a musical instrument resembling a lute, having paired metal strings plucked with a plectrum. **2** (also **mandoline**) a kitchen utensil consisting of a frame with adjustable blades, for slicing vegetables.

Thesaurus

nomical; *Brit. informal* whacking, whacking great, ginormous.
– OPPOSITES tiny.

man ● noun **1** *a handsome man* MALE, adult male, gentleman; youth; *informal* guy, fellow, geezer, gent; *Brit. informal* bloke, chap, lad, cove; *Scottish & Irish informal* bodach; *N. Amer. informal* dude, hombre; *Austral./NZ informal* digger. **2** *all men are mortal* HUMAN BEING, human, person, mortal, individual, personage, soul. **3** *the evolution of man* THE HUMAN RACE, the human species, Homo sapiens, humankind, humanity, human beings, humans, people, mankind. **4** *the men voted to go on strike* WORKER, workman, labourer, hand, blue-collar worker. See also STAFF noun sense 1. **5** *have you met her new man?* BOYFRIEND, partner, husband, spouse, lover, admirer, fiancé; common-law husband, live-in lover, significant other, cohabitee; *informal* fancy man, toy boy, sugar daddy, intended; *N. Amer. informal* squeeze; *dated* beau, steady, young man; *archaic* leman. **6** *his man brought him a cocktail* MANSERVANT, valet, gentleman's gentleman, Jeeves, attendant, retainer; page, footman, flunkey; *Military, dated* batman; *N. Amer.* houseman.
– RELATED TERMS male, masculine, virile.
– OPPOSITES woman.
● verb **1** *the office is manned from 9 a.m. to 5 p.m.* STAFF, crew, occupy, people. **2** *firemen manned the pumps* OPERATE, work, use, utilize.
– PHRASES **man to man** FRANKLY, openly, honestly, directly, candidly, plainly, forthrightly, without beating about the bush; woman to woman. **to a man** WITHOUT EXCEPTION, with no exceptions, bar none, one and all, everyone, each and every one, unanimously, as one.

manacle ● verb SHACKLE, fetter, chain, put/clap in irons, handcuff, restrain; secure; *informal* cuff.

manacles ● plural noun HANDCUFFS, shackles, chains, irons, fetters, restraints, bonds; *informal* cuffs, bracelets; *Brit. archaic* darbies.

manage ● verb **1** *she manages a staff of 80 people* BE IN CHARGE OF, run, be head of, head, direct, control, preside over, lead, govern, rule, command, superintend, supervise, oversee, administer, organize, conduct, handle, guide, be at the helm of; *informal* head up. **2** *how much work can you manage this week?* ACCOMPLISH, achieve, do, carry out, perform, undertake, bring about/off, effect, finish; succeed in, contrive, engineer. **3** *will you be able to manage without him?* COPE, get along/on, make do, be/fare/do all right, carry on, survive, get by, muddle through/along, fend for oneself, shift for oneself, make ends meet, weather the storm; *informal* make out, hack it. **4** *she can't manage that horse* CONTROL, handle, master; cope with, deal with.

manageable ● adjective **1** *a manageable amount of work* ACHIEVABLE, doable, practicable, possible, feasible, reasonable, attainable, viable. **2** *a manageable child* COMPLIANT, tractable, pliant, pliable, malleable, biddable, docile, amenable, governable, controllable, accommodating, acquiescent, complaisant, yielding. **3** *a manageable tool* USER-FRIENDLY, easy to use, handy.
– OPPOSITES difficult, impossible.

management ● noun **1** *he's responsible for the management of the firm* ADMINISTRATION, running, managing, organization; charge, care, direction, leadership, control, governing, governance, ruling, command, superintendence, supervision, overseeing, conduct, handling, guidance, operation. **2** *workers are in dispute with the management* MANAGERS, employers, directors, board of directors, board, directorate, executives, administrators, administration; owners, proprietors; *informal* bosses, top brass.
– OPPOSITES workers.

manager ● noun **1** *the works manager* EXECUTIVE, head of department, line manager, supervisor, principal, administrator, head, director, managing director, employer, superintendent, foreman, forewoman, overseer; proprietor; *informal* boss, chief, head honcho, governor; *Brit. informal* gaffer, guv'nor. **2** *the band's manager* ORGANIZER, controller, comptroller; impresario.

mandate ● noun **1** *he called an election to seek a mandate for his policies* AUTHORITY, approval, acceptance, ratification, endorsement, sanction, authorization. **2** *a mandate from the UN* INSTRUCTION, directive, decree, command, order, injunction, edict, charge, commission, bidding, ruling, fiat; *formal* ordinance.

mandatory ● adjective OBLIGATORY, compulsory, binding, required,

– DERIVATIVES **mandolinist** noun.
– ORIGIN Italian *mandolino* 'little mandola' (a *mandola* being an early form of mandolin).
mandragora /mandraggərə/ ● noun literary the mandrake, especially when used as a narcotic.
– ORIGIN Latin.
mandrake ● noun a plant with a forked fleshy root supposedly resembling the human form, used in herbal medicine and magic.
– ORIGIN Latin *mandragora*; the form *mandrake* developed by association with *man*, because of the forked shape of the root (formerly believed to shriek when pulled from the earth), and with *drake* in its Old English sense 'dragon'.
mandrel ● noun **1** a shaft or spindle in a lathe to which work is fixed while being turned. **2** a cylindrical rod round which metal or other material is forged or shaped.
– ORIGIN of unknown origin.
mandrill ● noun a large West African baboon with a red and blue face, the male having a blue rump.
– ORIGIN probably from MAN + DRILL³.
mane ● noun **1** a growth of long hair on the neck of a horse, lion, or other mammal. **2** a person's long flowing hair.
– ORIGIN Old English.
manège /manezh/ ● noun **1** a riding school. **2** the movements in which a horse is trained in a riding school.
– ORIGIN French, from Italian (see MANAGE).
manes /maanayz/ ● plural noun (in Roman mythology) the souls of dead ancestors, worshipped as gods.
– ORIGIN Latin.
maneuver ● noun & verb US spelling of MANOEUVRE.
man Friday ● noun a male helper or follower.
– ORIGIN a character in Daniel Defoe's novel *Robinson Crusoe* (1719).
manful ● adjective brave and resolute.
– DERIVATIVES **manfully** adverb.
manga ● noun Japanese cartoons, comic books, and animated films with a science-fiction or fantasy theme.
– ORIGIN Japanese, from *man* 'indiscriminate' + *ga* 'picture'.
mangabey /manggəbay/ ● noun a long-tailed monkey from West and central Africa.
– ORIGIN by erroneous association with *Mangabey*, a region of Madagascar.
manganese ● noun a hard grey metallic element used in special steels and magnetic alloys.
– ORIGIN Italian, alteration of *magnesia*.
mange ● noun a skin disease in some animals (occasionally communicable to humans) caused by mites, characterized by severe itching and hair loss.
– ORIGIN from Old French *mangier* 'eat'.
mangel /mangg'l/ (also **mangel-wurzel**) ● noun another term for MANGOLD.
manger ● noun a long trough from which horses or cattle feed.
– ORIGIN Old French *mangeure*, from Latin *manducare* 'chew'.
mangetout /monzhtoo/ ● noun (pl. same or **mangetouts** pronunc. same) chiefly Brit. a variety of pea with an edible pod.
– ORIGIN French, 'eat all'.
mangey ● adjective variant spelling of MANGY.
mangle¹ ● noun chiefly Brit. a machine having two or more cylinders turned by a handle, between which wet laundry is squeezed to remove excess moisture.
– ORIGIN from Greek *manganon* 'axis, engine'.
mangle² ● verb destroy or severely damage by tearing or crushing.
– ORIGIN Old French *mahaignier* 'maim'.
mango ● noun (pl. **mangoes** or **mangos**) a fleshy oval yellowish-red tropical fruit.
– ORIGIN Portuguese *manga*.
mangold ● noun a variety of beet with a large root, grown as feed for farm animals.
– ORIGIN German *Mangoldwurzel*.
mangonel /manggən'l/ ● noun historical a military device for throwing stones.
– ORIGIN from Greek *manganon* 'axis of a pulley'.
mangosteen ● noun a tropical fruit with juicy white segments of flesh inside a thick reddish-brown rind.
– ORIGIN Malay.
mangrove ● noun a tree or shrub which grows in tropical coastal swamps and has tangled roots that grow above ground and form dense thickets.
– ORIGIN probably from Taino (an extinct Caribbean language); also associated with GROVE.
mangy (also **mangey**) ● adjective (**mangier**, **mangiest**) **1** having mange. **2** in poor condition; shabby.
manhandle ● verb **1** move (a heavy object) with effort. **2** handle roughly by dragging or pushing.
manhole ● noun a covered opening allowing access to a sewer or other underground structure.
manhood ● noun **1** the state or period of being a man rather than a child. **2** the men of a country or society. **3** the qualities traditionally associated with men, such as strength and sexual potency.
mania ● noun **1** mental illness marked by periods of excitement, delusions, and overactivity. **2** an obsession.
– ORIGIN Greek, 'madness'.
-mania ● combining form **1** referring to a specified type of mental abnormality or obsession: *kleptomania*. **2** denoting extreme enthusiasm or admiration: *bibliomania*.
– DERIVATIVES **-maniac** combining form.
maniac ● noun **1** a person exhibiting extremely wild or violent behaviour. **2** informal an obsessive enthusiast.
– DERIVATIVES **maniacal** /mənīək'l/ adjective **maniacally** adverb.
manic ● adjective **1** relating to or affected by mania. **2** showing wild excitement and energy.
– DERIVATIVES **manically** adverb.
manic depression ● noun a mental disorder marked by alternating periods of elation and depression.

Thesaurus

requisite, necessary, essential, imperative.
– OPPOSITES optional.
manful ● adjective BRAVE, courageous, bold, plucky, gallant, manly, heroic, intrepid, fearless, stout-hearted, valiant, valorous, dauntless, doughty; resolute, with gritted teeth, determined; informal gutsy, spunky.
– OPPOSITES cowardly.
manfully ● adverb BRAVELY, courageously, boldly, gallantly, pluckily, heroically, intrepidly, fearlessly, valiantly, dauntlessly; resolutely, determinedly, hard, strongly, vigorously, with might and main, like a Trojan; with all one's strength, to the best of one's abilities, as best one can, desperately.
mange ● noun SCABIES, scab, rash, eruption, skin infection.
manger ● noun TROUGH, feeding trough, fodder rack, feeder, crib.
mangle ● verb **1** *the bodies were mangled beyond recognition* MUTILATE, maim, disfigure, damage, injure, crush; hack, cut up, lacerate, tear apart, butcher, maul. **2** *he's mangling the English language* SPOIL, ruin, mar, mutilate, make a mess of, wreck; informal murder, make a hash of, butcher.
mangy ● adjective **1** *a mangy cat* SCABBY, scaly, scabious, diseased. **2** *a mangy old armchair* SCRUFFY, moth-eaten, shabby, worn; dirty, squalid, sleazy, seedy; informal tatty, the worse for wear, scuzzy; Brit. informal grotty.
manhandle ● verb **1** *he was manhandled by a gang of youths* PUSH, shove, jostle, hustle; maltreat, ill-treat, mistreat, maul, molest; informal paw, rough up; N. Amer. informal roust. **2** *we manhandled the piano down the stairs* HEAVE, haul, push, shove; pull, tug, drag, lug, carry, lift, manoeuvre; informal hump.
manhood ● noun **1** *the transition from boyhood to manhood* MATURITY, sexual maturity, adulthood. **2** *an insult to his manhood* VIRILITY, manliness, machismo, masculinity, maleness; mettle, spirit, strength, fortitude, determination, bravery, courage, intrepidity, valour, heroism, boldness.
mania ● noun **1** *fits of mania* MADNESS, derangement, dementia, insanity, lunacy, psychosis, mental illness; delirium, frenzy, hysteria, raving, wildness. **2** *his mania for gadgets* OBSESSION, compulsion, fixation, fetish, fascination, preoccupation, passion, enthusiasm, desire, urge, craving; craze, fad, rage; informal thing, yen.
maniac ● noun **1** *a homicidal maniac* LUNATIC, madman, madwoman, psychopath; informal loony, fruitcake, nutcase, nut, psycho, head case, headbanger, sicko; Brit. informal nutter; N. Amer. informal screwball, crazy, meshuggener. **2** (informal) *a football maniac* ENTHUSIAST, fan, devotee, aficionado; informal freak, fiend, fanatic, nut, buff, addict.
manic ● adjective **1** *a manic grin* MAD, insane, deranged, demented, maniacal, lunatic, crazed, wild, demonic, hysterical, raving, unhinged, unbalanced; informal crazy. **2** *manic activity* FRENZIED, fever-

– DERIVATIVES **manic-depressive** adjective & noun.

Manichaean /mannikeeən/ (also **Manichean**) ● adjective 1 chiefly historical of or relating to Manichaeism. 2 of or characterized by dualistic contrast or conflict between opposites. ● noun an adherent of Manichaeism.
– DERIVATIVES **Manichaeanism** noun.

Manichaeism /mannikeeiz'm/ (also **Manicheism**) ● noun a religious system with Christian, Gnostic, and pagan elements, founded in Persia in the 3rd century by Manes (c.216–c.276) and based on a belief in an ancient conflict between light and darkness.
– ORIGIN from Latin *Manichaeus*, 'of Manes'.

manicure ● noun a cosmetic treatment of the hands and nails. ● verb 1 give a manicure to. 2 (**manicured**) (of a lawn or garden) neatly trimmed and maintained.
– DERIVATIVES **manicurist** noun.
– ORIGIN from Latin *manus* 'hand' + *cura* 'care'.

manifest[1] ● adjective clear and obvious. ● verb 1 show or demonstrate. 2 become apparent. 3 (of a ghost) appear.
– DERIVATIVES **manifestly** adverb.
– ORIGIN Latin *manifestus* 'caught in the act, flagrant'.

manifest[2] ● noun 1 a document listing a ship's contents, cargo, crew, and passengers. 2 a list of passengers or cargo in an aircraft. 3 a list of the wagons forming a freight train. ● verb record in a manifest.
– ORIGIN Italian *manifesto* 'manifesto'.

manifestation ● noun 1 a sign or embodiment of something. 2 the materialization of a god or spirit.

manifesto ● noun (pl. **manifestos**) a public declaration of policy and aims.
– ORIGIN Italian, from Latin *manifestus* 'caught in the act, flagrant'.

manifold ● adjective 1 many and various. 2 having many different forms. ● noun 1 a pipe or chamber branching into several openings. 2 (in an internal-combustion engine) the part conveying air and fuel from the carburettor to the cylinders or leading from the cylinders to the exhaust pipe.
– ORIGIN Old English.

manikin (also **mannikin**) ● noun 1 a very small person. 2 a jointed model of the human body.
– ORIGIN Dutch *manneken* 'little man'.

Manila (also **Manilla**) ● noun 1 (also **Manila hemp**) a plant fibre used for rope, matting, paper, etc. 2 strong brown paper, originally made from Manila hemp. 3 a cigar or cheroot made in Manila.
– ORIGIN from *Manila*, the capital of the Philippines; the plant yielding the fibre is native to the Philippines.

manioc /manniok/ ● noun another term for CASSAVA.
– ORIGIN Tupi.

maniple /mannip'l/ ● noun a subdivision of a Roman legion, consisting of either 120 or 60 men.
– ORIGIN Latin *manipulus* 'handful, troop'.

manipulate ● verb 1 handle or control with dexterity. 2 examine or treat (a part of the body) by feeling or moving it with the hand. 3 control or influence cleverly or unscrupulously. 4 alter or present (data) so as to mislead.
– DERIVATIVES **manipulable** adjective **manipulation** noun **manipulator** noun.
– ORIGIN from Latin *manipulus* 'handful'.

manipulative ● adjective 1 tending to manipulate others cleverly or unscrupulously. 2 relating to manipulation of an object or part of the body.
– DERIVATIVES **manipulatively** adverb **manipulativeness** noun.

manitou /mannitoo/ ● noun (among certain North American Indians) a good or evil spirit.
– ORIGIN Algonquian.

mankind ● noun human beings collectively; the human race.

manky ● adjective (**mankier**, **mankiest**) Brit. informal 1 inferior; worthless. 2 grimy; dirty.
– ORIGIN probably from obsolete *mank* 'mutilated, defective'.

manly ● adjective (**manlier**, **manliest**) 1 possessing qualities traditionally associated with men, such as courage and strength. 2 befitting a man.
– DERIVATIVES **manliness** noun.

man-made ● adjective made or caused by human beings.

manna ● noun 1 (in the Bible) the substance miraculously supplied as food to the Israelites in the wilderness (Exod. 16). 2 an unexpected and freely given benefit. 3 a sweet edible laxative gum obtained from a tree.
– ORIGIN Hebrew and Arabic, referring to a sweet substance exuded from the tamarisk tree.

manned ● adjective having a human crew.

mannequin ● noun a dummy used to display clothes in a shop window.
– ORIGIN French, from Dutch *manneken* 'little man'; related to MANIKIN.

manner ● noun 1 a way in which something is done or happens. 2 a person's outward bearing or way of behaving towards others. 3 (**manners**) polite social behaviour. 4 a style in literature or art. 5 literary a kind or sort.
– PHRASES **all manner of** many different kinds of. **in a manner of speaking** in some sense. **to the manner born** naturally at ease in a specified job or situation. [ORIGIN with allusion to Shakespeare's *Hamlet* I. iv. 17.]
– ORIGIN from Latin *manuarius* 'of the hand', from *manus* 'hand'.

mannered ● adjective 1 behaving in a specified way: *well-*

m

Thesaurus

ish, frenetic, hectic, intense; informal hyper, mad.
– OPPOSITES sane, calm.

manifest ● verb 1 *she manifested signs of depression* DISPLAY, show, exhibit, demonstrate, betray, present, reveal; formal evince. 2 *strikes manifest bad industrial relations* BE EVIDENCE OF, be a sign of, indicate, show, attest, reflect, bespeak, prove, establish, evidence, substantiate, corroborate, confirm; poetic/literary betoken.
– OPPOSITES hide, mask.
● adjective *his manifest lack of interest* OBVIOUS, clear, plain, apparent, evident, patent, palpable, distinct, definite, blatant, overt, glaring, barefaced, explicit, transparent, conspicuous, undisguised, unmistakable, noticeable, perceptible, visible, recognizable.
– OPPOSITES secret.

manifestation ● noun 1 *the manifestation of anxiety* DISPLAY, demonstration, show, exhibition, presentation. 2 *manifestations of global warming* SIGN, indication, evidence, token, symptom, testimony, proof, substantiation, mark, reflection, example, instance. 3 *a supernatural manifestation* APPARITION, appearance, materialization, visitation.

manifesto ● noun POLICY STATEMENT, mission statement, platform, programme, declaration, proclamation, pronouncement, announcement.

manifold ● adjective MANY, numerous, multiple, multifarious, legion, diverse, various, several, varied, different, miscellaneous, assorted, sundry; poetic/literary myriad, divers.

manikin ● noun MIDGET, dwarf, homunculus, pygmy, Tom Thumb.

manipulate ● verb 1 *he manipulated some knobs and levers* OPERATE, work; turn, pull. 2 *she manipulated the muscles of his back* MASSAGE, rub, knead, feel, palpate. 3 *the government tried to manipulate the situation* CONTROL, influence, use/turn to one's advantage, exploit, manoeuvre, engineer, steer, direct; twist someone round one's little finger. 4 *they accused him of manipulating the data* FALSIFY, rig, distort, alter, change, doctor, massage, juggle, tamper with, tinker with, interfere with, misrepresent; informal cook, fiddle.

manipulative ● adjective SCHEMING, calculating, cunning, crafty, wily, shrewd, devious, designing, conniving, Machiavellian, artful, guileful, slippery, slick, sly, unscrupulous, disingenuous; informal foxy.

manipulator ● noun EXPLOITER, user, manoeuvrer, conniver, puppet master, wheeler-dealer; informal operator, thimblerigger.

mankind ● noun THE HUMAN RACE, man, humanity, human beings, humans, Homo sapiens, humankind, people, men and women.

manly ● adjective 1 *his manly physique* VIRILE, masculine, strong, all-male, muscular, muscly, strapping, well built, sturdy, robust, rugged, tough, powerful, brawny, red-blooded, vigorous; informal hunky. 2 *their manly deeds* BRAVE, courageous, bold, valiant, valorous, fearless, plucky, macho, manful, intrepid, daring, lionhearted, heroic, gallant, chivalrous, swashbuckling, adventurous, stout-hearted, dauntless, doughty, resolute, determined, stalwart; informal gutsy, spunky.
– OPPOSITES effeminate, cowardly.

man-made ● adjective ARTIFICIAL, synthetic, manufactured; imitation, ersatz, simulated, mock, fake, plastic.
– OPPOSITES natural, real.

mannequin ● noun 1 *mannequins in a shop window* DUMMY, model, figure. 2 *mannequins on the catwalk* MODEL, fashion model,

mannered. **2** (of an artistic style) marked by highly distinctive or exaggerated features.

mannerism ● noun **1** a habitual gesture or way of speaking or behaving. **2** the use of a highly distinctive style in art, literature, or music. **3** (**Mannerism**) a style of 16th-century Italian art characterized by distortions in scale and perspective.
– DERIVATIVES **mannerist** noun & adjective.

mannerly ● adjective well-mannered; polite.

mannikin ● noun variant spelling of MANIKIN.

mannish ● adjective (of a woman) having an appearance and characteristics that are associated with men.

mannitol /mannitol/ ● noun a sweet-tasting form of alcohol found in many plants and used in foods and medical products.
– ORIGIN from MANNA.

manoeuvrable (US **maneuverable**) ● adjective (of a craft or vessel) able to be manoeuvred easily while in motion.
– DERIVATIVES **manoeuvrability** noun.

manoeuvre (US **maneuver**) ● noun **1** a physical movement or series of moves requiring skill and care. **2** a carefully planned scheme or action. **3** (**manoeuvres**) a large-scale military exercise. ● verb (**manoeuvred**, **manoeuvring**) **1** perform a physical manoeuvre. **2** carefully manipulate in order to achieve an end.
– ORIGIN French *manœuvrer*, from Latin *manus* 'hand' + *operari* 'to work'.

man-of-war (also **man-o'-war**) ● noun historical an armed sailing ship.

manometer /mənommitər/ ● noun an instrument for measuring the pressure acting on a column of fluid.
– ORIGIN from Greek *manos* 'thin, rare, rarefied'.

manor ● noun **1** a large country house with lands. **2** chiefly historical a unit of land consisting of a lord's demesne and lands rented to tenants.
– DERIVATIVES **manorial** adjective.
– ORIGIN Old French *maner* 'dwelling', from Latin *manere* 'remain'.

manpower ● noun the number of people working or available for work or service.

manqué /mongkay/ ● adjective that might have been; unfulfilled: *an actor manqué.*
– ORIGIN French, from *manquer* 'to lack'.

m

mansard ● noun **1** a roof having four sides, in each of which the lower part of the slope is steeper than the upper part. **2** Brit. another term for GAMBREL.
– ORIGIN named after the 17th-century French architect François *Mansart*.

manse ● noun a house provided for the minister in the Presbyterian and some other churches.
– ORIGIN Latin *mansus* 'house, dwelling'.

manservant ● noun a male servant.

mansion ● noun a large, impressive house.
– ORIGIN Latin, 'place where someone stays', from *manere* 'remain'.

mansion block ● noun Brit. a large block of flats.

manslaughter ● noun the crime of killing a person without intention to do so.

manta ● noun a very large ray of tropical seas.
– ORIGIN Latin American Spanish, 'large blanket'.

mantel (also **mantle**) ● noun a mantelpiece or mantelshelf.
– ORIGIN specialized use of MANTLE.

mantelpiece ● noun **1** a structure surrounding a fireplace. **2** a mantelshelf.

mantelshelf ● noun a shelf forming the top of a mantelpiece.

manticore /mantikor/ ● noun a mythical beast having the body of a lion, the face of a man, and the sting of a scorpion.
– ORIGIN from Greek *mantikhōras*, from an Old Persian word meaning 'a man-eating creature'.

mantilla /mantillə/ ● noun (in Spain) a lace or silk scarf worn by women over the hair and shoulders.
– ORIGIN Spanish, 'little mantle or shawl'.

mantis (also **praying mantis**) ● noun (pl. same or **mantises**) a slender predatory insect with a triangular head, typically waiting motionless for prey with its forelegs folded like hands in prayer.
– ORIGIN Greek, 'prophet'.

mantle ● noun **1** a woman's loose sleeveless cloak or shawl. **2** a close covering, such as that of snow. **3** (also **gas mantle**) a mesh cover fixed round a gas jet to give an incandescent light when heated. **4** an important role or responsibility that passes from one person to another. [ORIGIN with allusion to the passing of Elijah's cloak (his mantle) to Elisha (2 Kings 2:13).] **5** Geology the region of the earth's interior between the crust and the core, consisting of hot, dense silicate rocks. ● verb literary cloak, envelop, or suffuse.
– ORIGIN Latin *mantellum* 'cloak'.

mantra ● noun **1** (originally in Hinduism and Buddhism) a word or sound repeated to aid concentration in meditation. **2** a Vedic hymn.
– ORIGIN Sanskrit, 'instrument of thought'.

mantrap ● noun a trap for catching people.

manual ● adjective **1** made or worked with the hands. **2** using or working with the hands: *a manual worker.* ● noun **1** a book giving instructions or information. **2** an organ keyboard played with the hands not the feet.
– DERIVATIVES **manually** adverb.
– ORIGIN Latin *manualis*, from *manus* 'hand'.

manufactory ● noun (pl. **manufactories**) archaic a factory.

manufacture ● verb **1** make (something), especially on a large scale using machinery. **2** (**manufactured**) made or produced in

Thesaurus

supermodel; *informal* clothes horse.

manner ● noun **1** *it was dealt with in a very efficient manner* WAY, fashion, mode, means, method, system, style, approach, technique, procedure, process, methodology, modus operandi, form. **2** *(poetic/literary) what manner of person is he?* KIND, sort, type, variety, nature, breed, stamp, class, category, genre, order. **3** *her unfriendly manner* DEMEANOUR, air, aspect, attitude, bearing, cast, behaviour, conduct; mien; *formal* comportment. **4** *the life and manners of Victorian society* CUSTOMS, habits, ways, practices, conventions, usages. **5** *it's bad manners to stare* BEHAVIOUR, conduct, way of behaving; form. **6** *you ought to teach him some manners* CORRECT BEHAVIOUR, etiquette, social graces, good form, protocol, politeness, decorum, propriety, gentility, civility, Ps and Qs, breeding; *informal* the done thing; *archaic* convenances.

mannered ● adjective AFFECTED, pretentious, unnatural, artificial, contrived, stilted, stiff, forced, put-on, theatrical, precious, stagy, camp; *informal* pseudo.
– OPPOSITES natural.

mannerism ● noun IDIOSYNCRASY, quirk, oddity, foible, trait, peculiarity, habit, characteristic.

mannerly ● adjective. See POLITE sense 1.

mannish ● adjective UNFEMININE, unwomanly, masculine, unladylike, Amazonian; *informal* butch.
– OPPOSITES feminine, girlish.

manoeuvre ● verb **1** *I manoeuvred the car into the space* STEER, guide, drive, negotiate, navigate, pilot, direct, manipulate, move, work, jockey. **2** *he manoeuvred things to suit himself* MANIPULATE, contrive, manage, engineer, devise, plan, fix, organize, arrange, set up, orchestrate, choreograph, stage-manage; *informal* wangle. **3** *he began manoeuvring for the party leadership* INTRIGUE, plot, scheme, plan, lay plans, conspire, pull strings.
● noun **1** *a tricky parking manoeuvre* OPERATION, exercise, activity, move, movement, action. **2** *diplomatic manoeuvres* STRATAGEM, tactic, gambit, ploy, trick, dodge, ruse, plan, scheme, operation, device, plot, machination, artifice, subterfuge, intrigue. **3** *military manoeuvres* TRAINING EXERCISES, exercises, war games, operations.

manse ● noun MINISTER'S HOUSE, vicarage, parsonage, rectory, deanery.

manservant ● noun VALET, attendant, retainer, equerry, gentleman's gentleman, man, Jeeves; steward, butler, footman, flunkey, page, houseboy, lackey; *N. Amer.* houseman; *Military, dated* batman.

mansion ● noun STATELY HOME, hall, seat, manor, manor house, country house; *informal* palace, pile; *formal* residence.
– OPPOSITES hovel.

mantle ● noun **1** *a dark green velvet mantle* CLOAK, cape, shawl, wrap, stole; *historical* pelisse. **2** *a thick mantle of snow* COVERING, layer, blanket, sheet, veil, curtain, canopy, cover, cloak, pall, shroud. **3** *the mantle of leadership* ROLE, burden, onus, duty, responsibility.
● verb *(poetic/literary) heavy mists mantled the forest* COVER, envelop, veil, cloak, curtain, shroud, swathe, wrap, blanket, conceal, hide, obscure, surround, clothe; *poetic/literary* enshroud.

manual ● adjective **1** *manual work* DONE WITH ONE'S HANDS, labouring, physical, blue-collar. **2** *a manual typewriter* HAND-OPERATED, hand, non-automatic.

a merely mechanical way. **3** invent or fabricate (evidence or a story). ● noun the process of manufacturing.
– DERIVATIVES **manufacturable** adjective **manufacturer** noun.
– ORIGIN French, from Italian *manifattura*, influenced by Latin *manu factum* 'made by hand'.

manuka /maanōōkə, manōōkə/ ● noun a small tree with aromatic leaves, native to New Zealand and Tasmania.
– ORIGIN Maori.

manumit ● verb (**manumitted**, **manumitting**) historical release from slavery; set free.
– DERIVATIVES **manumission** noun.
– ORIGIN Latin *manumittere* 'send forth from the hand'.

manure ● noun animal dung used for fertilizing land. ● verb apply manure to.
– ORIGIN originally in the sense 'cultivate (land)': from Old French *manouvrer* (see MANOEUVRE).

manuscript ● noun **1** a handwritten book, document, or piece of music. **2** a text submitted for printing and publication.
– ORIGIN from Latin *manu* 'by hand' + *scriptus* 'written'.

Manx ● noun the Celtic language formerly spoken in the Isle of Man, still used for some ceremonial purposes. ● adjective relating to the Isle of Man.
– ORIGIN from Old Irish *Manu* 'Isle of Man' + *-skr* (equivalent of -ISH).

Manx cat ● noun a breed of cat that has no tail.

many ● determiner, pronoun, & adjective (**more**, **most**) a large number of. ● noun (**the many**) the majority of people.
– PHRASES **a good** (or **great**) **many** a large number.
– ORIGIN Old English.

manzanilla /manzənillə/ ● noun a pale, very dry Spanish sherry.
– ORIGIN Spanish, 'chamomile' (because the flavour is considered reminiscent of that of chamomile).

Maoism /mowiz'm/ ● noun the communist doctrines of Mao Zedong (1893–1976), Chinese head of state 1949–59, as formerly practised in China.
– DERIVATIVES **Maoist** noun & adjective.

Maori /mowri/ ● noun (pl. same or **Maoris**) **1** a member of the aboriginal people of New Zealand. **2** the Polynesian language of this people.
– ORIGIN Maori.

map ● noun **1** a flat diagram of an area of land or sea showing physical features, cities, roads, etc. **2** a diagram or collection of data showing the arrangement, distribution, or sequence of something. ● verb (**mapped**, **mapping**) **1** represent or record on a map. **2** (**map out**) plan in detail.
– PHRASES **off the map** very distant or remote. **put on the map** bring to prominence. **wipe off the map** obliterate totally.
– ORIGIN Latin *mappa* 'sheet, napkin'.

maple ● noun a tree or shrub with lobed leaves, winged fruits, and syrupy sap.
– ORIGIN Old English.

maple leaf ● noun the leaf of the maple, used as the Canadian national emblem.

maple syrup ● noun sugary syrup produced from the sap of a maple tree.

maquette /maket/ ● noun a sculptor's small preliminary model or sketch.
– ORIGIN French, from Italian *machietta* 'little spot'.

maquis /makee/ ● noun (pl. same) **1** (**the Maquis**) the French resistance movement during the German occupation of France in the Second World War. **2** dense evergreen scrub characteristic of coastal regions in the Mediterranean.
– ORIGIN French, 'brushwood'.

Mar. ● abbreviation March.

mar ● verb (**marred**, **marring**) harm the appearance or quality of.
– ORIGIN Old English.

marabou /marrəbōō/ ● noun **1** an African stork with a massive bill and large neck pouch. **2** down feathers from marabou used as trimming for hats or clothing.
– ORIGIN French, from Arabic, 'holy man'.

maraca /mərakkə/ ● noun a hollow gourd or gourd-shaped container filled with small beans, stones, etc., shaken as a percussion instrument.
– ORIGIN Portuguese, from Tupi.

marae /mərī/ ● noun (pl. same) the courtyard of a Maori meeting house, especially as a social or ceremonial forum.
– ORIGIN Polynesian, denoting a sacrificial altar or sacred enclosure.

maraschino /marrəsheenō/ ● noun (pl. **maraschinos**) a strong, sweet liqueur made from small black Dalmatian cherries.
– ORIGIN Italian, from *marasca* (the name of the cherry), from *amaro* 'bitter'.

maraschino cherry ● noun a cherry preserved in maraschino.

marathon ● noun **1** a long-distance running race, strictly one of 26 miles 385 yards (42.195 km). **2** a long-lasting and difficult task.
– ORIGIN from *Marathōn* in Greece, the scene of a victory over the Persians in 490 BC; the modern race is based on the tradition that a messenger ran from Marathon to Athens (22 miles) with the news.

maraud /mərawd/ ● verb make a plundering raid.
– DERIVATIVES **marauder** noun.
– ORIGIN from French *maraud* 'rogue'.

marble ● noun **1** a hard form of limestone, typically variegated or mottled, which may be polished and is used in sculpture and building. **2** a small ball of coloured glass used as a toy. **3** (**marbles**) (treated as sing.) a game in which marbles are rolled along the ground. **4** (**one's marbles**) informal one's mental faculties.

Thesaurus

● noun *a training manual* HANDBOOK, instruction book, instructions, guide, companion, ABC, guidebook; informal bible.

manufacture ● verb **1** *the company manufactures laser printers* MAKE, produce, mass-produce, build, construct, assemble, put together, create, fabricate, prefabricate, turn out, process, engineer. **2** *a story manufactured by the press* MAKE UP, invent, fabricate, concoct, hatch, dream up, think up, trump up, devise, formulate, frame, contrive; informal cook up.
● noun *the manufacture of aircraft engines* PRODUCTION, making, manufacturing, mass-production, construction, building, assembly, creation, fabrication, prefabrication, processing.

manufacturer ● noun MAKER, producer, builder, constructor, creator; factory owner, industrialist, captain of industry, baron of industry.

manure ● noun DUNG, muck, excrement, droppings, ordure, guano, cowpats; fertilizer; N. Amer. informal cow chips, horse apples.

manuscript ● noun DOCUMENT, text, script, paper, typescript; codex, palimpsest, scroll; autograph, holograph.

many ● determiner & adjective **1** *many animals were killed* NUMEROUS, a great/good deal of, a lot of, plenty of, countless, innumerable, scores of, crowds of, droves of, an army of, a horde of, a multitude of, a multiplicity of, multitudinous, multiple, untold; several, various, sundry, diverse, assorted, multifarious; copious, abundant, profuse, an abundance of, a profusion of; frequent; informal lots of, umpteen, loads of, masses of, stacks of, scads of, heaps of, piles of, bags of, tons of, oodles of, dozens of, hundreds of, thousands of, millions of, billions of, zillions of, a slew of, more —— than one can shake a stick at; Brit. informal a shedload of; N. Amer. informal gazillions of; Austral./NZ informal a swag of; poetic/literary myriad, divers. **2** *sacrificing the individual for the sake of the many* THE PEOPLE, the common people, the masses, the multitude, the populace, the public, the rank and file; derogatory the hoi polloi, the common herd, the mob, the proletariat, the riff-raff, the great unwashed, the proles.
– RELATED TERMS multi-, poly-.
– OPPOSITES few.

map ● noun PLAN, chart, cartogram; road map, A to Z, street plan, guide; atlas, globe; sketch map, relief map, contour map; Mercator projection, Peters projection; N. Amer. plat, plot.
– RELATED TERMS cartography.
● verb *the region was mapped from the air* CHART, plot, delineate, draw, depict, portray.
– PHRASES **map something out** OUTLINE, set out, lay out, sketch out, trace out, rough out, block out, delineate, detail, draw up, formulate, work out, frame, draft, plan, plot out, arrange, design, programme.

mar ● verb **1** *an ugly scar marred his features* SPOIL, impair, disfigure, detract from, blemish, scar; mutilate, deface, deform. **2** *the celebrations were marred by violence* SPOIL, ruin, impair, damage, wreck; harm, hurt, blight, taint, tarnish, sully, stain, pollute; informal foul up; formal vitiate.
– OPPOSITES enhance.

marauder ● noun RAIDER, plunderer, pillager, looter, robber, pirate, freebooter, bandit, highwayman, rustler; poetic/literary brigand;

● verb give (something) the appearance of marble.
– DERIVATIVES **marbled** adjective.
– ORIGIN Greek *marmaros* 'shining stone'.
marbling ● noun **1** colouring or marking that resembles marble. **2** streaks of fat in lean meat.
marc ● noun **1** the skins and other remains from grapes that have been pressed for winemaking. **2** an alcoholic spirit distilled from this.
– ORIGIN French, from *marcher* in the early sense 'to tread or trample'.
marcasite /maarkəsīt, -zeet/ ● noun **1** a semi-precious stone consisting of iron pyrites. **2** a piece of polished metal cut as a gem.
– ORIGIN Latin *marcasita*, from Arabic.
March ● noun the third month of the year.
– ORIGIN from Latin *Martius mensis* 'month of Mars'.
march[1] ● verb **1** walk in a military manner with a regular measured tread. **2** proceed quickly and with determination. **3** force (someone) to walk somewhere quickly. **4** take part in an organized procession to make a protest. ● noun **1** an act of marching. **2** a procession organized as a protest. **3** a piece of music written to accompany marching.
– PHRASES **on the march 1** engaged in marching. **2** making progress.
– DERIVATIVES **marcher** noun.
– ORIGIN French *marcher* 'to walk'.
march[2] ● noun (**Marches**) an area of land on the border between two countries or territories. ● verb (**march with**) have a common frontier with.
– ORIGIN Old French *marche*, related to MARK[1].
March hare ● noun informal a brown hare in the breeding season, noted for its leaping, boxing, and chasing in circles.
marching orders ● noun **1** instructions for troops to depart. **2** informal a dismissal.
marchioness /maarshəness/ ● noun **1** the wife or widow of a marquess. **2** a woman holding the rank of marquess in her own right.
– ORIGIN Latin *marchionissa*, 'female ruler of a border territory'.
marchpane ● noun archaic marzipan.
Mardi Gras /maardi **graa**/ ● noun a carnival held in some countries on Shrove Tuesday.
– ORIGIN French, 'fat Tuesday', alluding to the last day of feasting before the fast and penitence of Lent.
mare[1] /mair/ ● noun the female of a horse or other equine animal.
– ORIGIN Old English.
mare[2] /maaray/ ● noun (pl. **maria** /maariə/) Astronomy a large basalt plain on the surface of the moon.
– ORIGIN Latin *mare* 'sea'; these areas were once thought to be seas, as they appear dark by contrast with surrounding highland areas.
mare's nest ● noun **1** a muddle. **2** an illusory discovery.
mare's tail ● noun **1** a water plant with whorls of narrow leaves around a tall stout stem. **2** (**mare's tails**) long straight streaks of cirrus cloud.
margarine ● noun a butter substitute made from vegetable oils or animal fats.
– ORIGIN French, from Greek *margaron* 'pearl' (because of the lustre of the crystals of esters from which it was first made).
margarita ● noun a cocktail made with tequila and citrus fruit juice.
– ORIGIN Spanish equivalent of the given name *Margaret*.
marge ● noun Brit. informal short for MARGARINE.
margin ● noun **1** an edge or border. **2** the blank border on each side of the print on a page. **3** the furthest reach or limit. **4** an amount above or below a given level.
– PHRASES **margin of error** a small amount allowed for in case of miscalculation or change of circumstances.
– ORIGIN Latin *margo* 'edge'.
marginal ● adjective **1** relating to or situated at or in a margin. **2** of minor importance. **3** (of a decision or distinction) very narrow. **4** chiefly Brit. (of a parliamentary seat) having a small majority. ● noun chiefly Brit. a marginal parliamentary seat.
– DERIVATIVES **marginality** noun.
marginalia /maarjinayliə/ ● plural noun notes written or printed in the margin of a book or manuscript.
marginalize (also **marginalise**) ● verb treat as marginal or peripheral.
– DERIVATIVES **marginalization** noun.
marginally ● adverb to only a limited extent; slightly.
margin call ● noun Stock Exchange a demand by a broker that an investor deposit further cash or securities to cover possible losses.
margrave ● noun historical the hereditary title of some princes of the Holy Roman Empire.
– ORIGIN Dutch, from *marke* 'boundary' + *grave* 'count'.
marguerite /maargəreet/ ● noun another term for OX-EYE DAISY.
– ORIGIN French equivalent of the given name *Margaret*.
maria plural of MARE[2].
mariachi /mariaachi/ ● noun (pl. **mariachis**) (in Mexico) a musician performing traditional folk music.
– ORIGIN Mexican Spanish, 'street singer'.
mariculture /marikulchər/ ● noun the cultivation of fish or other marine life for food.
– ORIGIN from Latin *mare* 'sea'.
Marie Rose ● noun a cold sauce made from mayonnaise and tomato purée and served with seafood.
– ORIGIN of unknown origin.
marigold ● noun a plant of the daisy family with yellow or orange flowers.
– ORIGIN from the given name *Mary* + dialect *gold*, referring to the corn or garden marigold in Old English.
marijuana /marrihwaanə/ ● noun cannabis.
– ORIGIN Latin American Spanish.
marimba ● noun a deep-toned xylophone of African origin.
– ORIGIN from Kimbundu (a Bantu language of western Angola).
marina ● noun a purpose-built harbour with moorings for yachts and small boats.
– ORIGIN Italian or Spanish, from Latin *mare* 'sea'.
marinade ● noun /marin**ayd**/ a mixture of ingredients such as oil, vinegar, and herbs, in which food is soaked before cooking in order to flavour or soften it. ● verb /marinayd/ another term for MARINATE.
– ORIGIN French, from Spanish *marinar* 'pickle in brine', ultimately from Latin *mare* 'sea'.
marinara /maarinaarə/ ● noun (in Italian cooking) a sauce made from tomatoes, onions, and herbs.
– ORIGIN from Italian *alla marinara* 'sailor-style'.
marinate ● verb soak in a marinade.
– DERIVATIVES **marination** noun.
marine ● adjective **1** relating to the sea. **2** relating to shipping or naval matters. ● noun a member of a body of troops trained to serve on land or sea, in particular (in the UK) a member of the Royal Marines or (in the US) a member of the Marine Corps.
– PHRASES **tell that to the marines** a scornful expression of disbelief. [ORIGIN referring to the *horse marines*, an imaginary corps of cavalrymen employed to serve as marines (thus out of their element).]

Thesaurus

archaic buccaneer, corsair, reaver, cateran, mosstrooper.
marauding ● adjective PREDATORY, rapacious, thieving, plundering, pillaging, looting, freebooting, piratical.
march ● verb **1** *the men marched past* STRIDE, walk, troop, step, pace, tread; footslog, slog, tramp, hike, trudge; parade, file, process; *Brit. informal* yomp. **2** *she marched in without even knocking* STALK, stride, strut, flounce, storm, stomp, sweep. **3** *time marches on* ADVANCE, progress, move on, roll on.
● noun **1** *a 20-mile march* HIKE, trek, tramp, slog, footslog, walk; route march, forced march; *Brit. informal* yomp. **2** *police sought to ban the march* PARADE, procession, march past, cortège; demonstration; *informal* demo. **3** *the march of technology* PROGRESS, advance, progression, development, evolution; passage.
marches ● plural noun *the Welsh marches* BORDERS, boundaries, borderlands, frontiers; *historical* marcher lands.
margin ● noun **1** *the margin of the lake* EDGE, side, verge, border, perimeter, brink, brim, rim, fringe, boundary, limits, periphery, bound, extremity; *poetic/literary* marge, bourn, skirt. **2** *there's no margin for error* LEEWAY, latitude, scope, room, room for manoeuvre, space, allowance, extra, surplus. **3** *they won by a narrow margin* GAP, majority, amount, difference.
marginal ● adjective **1** *the difference is marginal* SLIGHT, small, tiny, minute, insignificant, minimal, negligible. **2** *a very marginal case* BORDERLINE, disputable, questionable, doubtful.
marijuana ● noun CANNABIS, hashish, bhang, hemp, kif, ganja, sinsemilla, skunkweed; *informal* dope, hash, grass, pot, blow, draw,

– ORIGIN Latin *marinus*, from *mare* 'sea'.

mariner • noun formal or literary a sailor.

Mariolatry /mairiɒlətri/ • noun idolatrous worship of the Virgin Mary.

marionette • noun a puppet worked by strings.
– ORIGIN French, from the given name *Marion*.

marital • adjective relating to marriage or the relations between husband and wife.
– DERIVATIVES **maritally** adverb.
– USAGE Do not confuse **marital**, which means 'relating to marriage' with **martial** 'of war'.
– ORIGIN from Latin *maritus* 'husband'.

maritime • adjective **1** relating to shipping or other activity taking place at sea. **2** living or found in or near the sea. **3** (of a climate) moist and temperate owing to the influence of the sea.
– ORIGIN Latin *maritimus*, from *mare* 'sea'.

marjoram • noun **1** (also **sweet marjoram**) an aromatic plant of the mint family, used as a herb in cooking. **2** (also **wild marjoram**) another term for OREGANO.
– ORIGIN Latin *majorana*.

mark[1] • noun **1** a small area on a surface having a different colour from its surroundings. **2** something that indicates position or acts as a pointer. **3** a line, figure, or symbol made to identify or record something. **4** a sign or indication of a quality or feeling. **5** a characteristic feature or property of something. **6** a level or stage. **7** a point awarded for a correct answer or for proficiency in an examination. **8** a particular model or type of a vehicle or machine. • verb **1** make a mark on. **2** write a word or symbol on (an object) in order to identify it. **3** indicate the position of. **4** (**mark out**) distinguish or delineate. **5** indicate or acknowledge (a significant event). **6** (**mark up** or **down**) increase or reduce the indicated price of (an item). **7** assess and give a mark to (written work). **8** notice or pay careful attention to. **9** Brit. (in team games) stay close to (an opponent) in order to prevent them getting or passing the ball.
– PHRASES **be quick off the mark** be fast in responding. **make a mark** have a lasting or significant effect. **mark time 1** (of troops) march on the spot without moving forward. **2** engage temporarily in routine activities. **near** (or **close**) **to the mark** almost accurate. **off** (or **wide of**) **the mark** incorrect or inaccurate. **on the mark** correct; accurate. **on your marks** be ready to start (used to instruct competitors in a race). **up to the mark** up to the required standard or normal level.
– ORIGIN Old English.

mark[2] • noun the basic monetary unit of Germany, equal to 100 pfennig.
– ORIGIN Old Norse, probably related to MARK[1].

marked • adjective **1** having a visible mark or other identifying feature. **2** clearly noticeable. **3** singled out as a target for attack: *a marked man*.
– DERIVATIVES **markedly** adverb **markedness** noun.

marker • noun **1** an object used to indicate a position, place, or route. **2** a felt-tip pen with a broad tip. **3** (in team games) a player who marks an opponent. **4** a person who marks a test or examination.

market • noun **1** a regular gathering for the purchase and sale of food, livestock, or other commodities. **2** an outdoor space or large hall where vendors sell their goods. **3** a particular area of commercial or competitive activity. **4** demand for a particular commodity or service. • verb (**marketed**, **marketing**) advertise or promote.
– PHRASES **on the market** available for sale.
– DERIVATIVES **marketable** adjective **marketer** noun.
– ORIGIN Latin *mercatus*, from *mercari* 'buy'.

marketeer • noun a person who sells goods or services in a market.

market garden • noun a place where vegetables and fruit are grown for sale.

marketing • noun the promotion and selling of products or services.

market-maker • noun Stock Exchange a dealer in securities or other assets who undertakes to buy or sell at specified prices at all times.

marketplace • noun **1** an open space where a market is held. **2** a competitive or commercial arena.

market research • noun the activity of gathering information about consumers' needs and preferences.

market town • noun a town of moderate size where a regular

m

Thesaurus

the weed, skunk; *Brit. informal* wacky baccy; *N. Amer. informal* locoweed.

marinate • verb SOUSE, soak, steep, immerse, marinade.

marine • adjective **1** *marine plants* SEAWATER, sea, saltwater, oceanic; aquatic; *technical* pelagic, thalassic. **2** *a marine insurance company* MARITIME, nautical, naval; seafaring, seagoing, ocean-going.

mariner • noun (*poetic/literary*) SAILOR, seaman, seafarer; *informal* Jack tar, tar, sea dog, salt, bluejacket, matelot; *N. Amer. informal* shellback.

marital • adjective MATRIMONIAL, married, wedded, conjugal, nuptial, marriage; *Law* spousal; *poetic/literary* connubial.

maritime • adjective **1** *maritime law* NAVAL, marine, nautical; seafaring, seagoing, sea, ocean-going. **2** *maritime regions* COASTAL, seaside, littoral.

mark • noun **1** *a dirty mark* BLEMISH, streak, spot, fleck, dot, blot, stain, smear, speck, speckle, blotch, smudge, smut, fingermark, fingerprint; bruise, discoloration; birthmark; *informal* splotch, splodge; *technical* stigma; *poetic/literary* smirch. **2** *a punctuation mark* SYMBOL, sign, character; diacritic. **3** *books bearing the mark of a well-known bookseller* LOGO, seal, stamp, imprint, symbol, emblem, device, insignia, badge, brand, trademark, monogram, hallmark, logotype, watermark. **4** *unemployment passed the three million mark* POINT, level, stage, degree. **5** *a mark of respect* SIGN, token, symbol, indication, badge, emblem; symptom, evidence, proof. **6** *the war left its mark on him* IMPRESSION, imprint, traces; effect, impact, influence. **7** *the mark of a civilized society* CHARACTERISTIC, feature, trait, attribute, quality, hallmark, badge, stamp, property, indicator. **8** *he got good marks for maths* GRADE, grading, rating, score, percentage. **9** *the bullet missed its mark* TARGET, goal, aim, bullseye; objective, object, end.
• verb **1** *be careful not to mark the paintwork* DISCOLOUR, stain, smear, smudge, streak, blotch, blemish; dirty, pockmark, bruise; *informal* splotch, splodge; *poetic/literary* smirch. **2** *her possessions were clearly marked* PUT ONE'S NAME ON, name, initial, label; hallmark, watermark, brand. **3** *I've marked the relevant passages* INDICATE, label, flag, tick; show, identify, designate, delineate, denote. **4** *a festival to mark the town's 200th anniversary* CELEBRATE, observe, recognize, acknowledge, keep, honour, solemnize, pay tribute to, salute, commemorate, remember, memorialize. **5** *the incidents marked a new phase in their campaign* REPRESENT, signify, be a sign of, indicate, herald. **6** *his style is marked by simplicity and concision* CHARACTERIZE, distinguish, identify, typify, brand, signalize, stamp. **7** *I have a pile of essays to mark* ASSESS, evaluate, appraise, correct; *N. Amer.* grade. **8** *it'll cause trouble, you mark my words!* TAKE HEED OF, pay heed to, heed, listen to, take note of, pay attention to, attend to, note, mind, bear in mind, take into consideration.
– PHRASES **make one's mark** BE SUCCESSFUL, distinguish oneself, succeed, be a success, prosper, get ahead/on, make good; *informal* make it, make the grade, find a place in the sun. **mark something down** REDUCE, decrease, lower, cut, put down, discount; *informal* slash. **mark someone out 1** *his honesty marked him out from the rest* SET APART, separate, single out, differentiate, distinguish. **2** *she is marked out for fame* DESTINE, ordain, predestine, preordain. **mark something up** INCREASE, raise, up, put up, hike (up), escalate; *informal* jack up. **of mark** (*dated*) IMPORTANT, distinguished, eminent, pre-eminent, prominent, notable, famous, great, prestigious; of importance, of consequence, of note, of high standing, of distinction. **quick off the mark** ALERT, quick, quick-witted, bright, clever, perceptive, sharp, sharp-witted, observant, wide awake, on one's toes; *informal* on the ball, quick on the uptake. **wide of the mark** INACCURATE, incorrect, wrong, erroneous, off target, off beam, out, mistaken, misguided, misinformed.

marked • adjective NOTICEABLE, pronounced, decided, distinct, striking, clear, glaring, blatant, unmistakable, obvious, plain, manifest, patent, palpable, prominent, signal, significant, conspicuous, notable, recognizable, identifiable, distinguishable, discernible, apparent, evident; written all over one.
– OPPOSITES imperceptible.

market • noun **1** SHOPPING CENTRE, marketplace, mart, flea market, bazaar, souk, fair; *archaic* emporium. **2** *there's no market for such goods* DEMAND, call, want, desire, need, requirement. **3** *the market is sluggish* TRADE, trading, business, commerce, buying and selling, dealing.
• verb *the product was marketed worldwide* SELL, retail, vend, merchandise, trade, peddle, hawk; advertise, promote.

market is held.
market value ● noun the amount for which something can be sold in an open market.
marking ● noun **1** an identification mark. **2** (also **markings**) a pattern of marks on an animal's fur, feathers, or skin.
markka /maarkə/ ● noun the basic monetary unit of Finland, equal to 100 penniä.
– ORIGIN Finnish.
marksman ● noun a person skilled in shooting.
– DERIVATIVES **marksmanship** noun.
mark-up ● noun **1** the amount added to the cost price of goods to cover overheads and profit. **2** Computing a set of codes assigned to different elements of a text.
marl[1] ● noun an unconsolidated sedimentary rock or soil consisting of clay and lime, formerly used as fertilizer.
– ORIGIN Old French *marle*, from Latin *marga*, of Celtic origin.
marl[2] ● noun a mottled yarn or fabric.
– ORIGIN shortening of *marbled*.
marlin ● noun a large, edible, fast-swimming fish of warm seas, with a pointed snout.
– ORIGIN from MARLINSPIKE (with reference to its pointed snout).
marlinspike (also **marlinespike**) ● noun a pointed metal tool used by sailors to separate strands of rope or wire.
– ORIGIN from *marl* 'fasten with marline' (rope made of two strands), from Dutch *marlen* 'keep binding'.
marmalade ● noun a preserve made from citrus fruit, especially bitter oranges.
– ORIGIN Portuguese *marmelada* 'quince jam', from *marmelo* 'quince'.
Marmite ● noun trademark a dark savoury spread made from yeast extract and vegetable extract.
marmite ● noun a cooking pot.
– ORIGIN from Old French *marmite* 'hypocritical' (with reference to the hidden contents of the lidded pot), from *marmotter* 'to mutter' + *mite* 'cat'.
marmoreal /maamoriəl/ ● adjective literary made of or resembling marble.
– ORIGIN Latin *marmoreus*, from *marmor* 'marble'.
marmoset /maarməzet/ ● noun a small tropical American monkey with a silky coat and a long tail.
– ORIGIN Old French *marmouset* 'grotesque image'.
marmot ● noun a heavily built burrowing rodent.
– ORIGIN French *marmotte*, from Latin *mus montanus* 'mountain mouse'.
Maronite /marənīt/ ● noun a member of a Christian sect living chiefly in Lebanon and in communion with the Roman Catholic Church.
– ORIGIN from the name of John *Maro*, a 7th-century Syrian religious leader.
maroon[1] ● noun **1** a dark brownish-red colour. **2** chiefly Brit. a firework that makes a loud bang, used as a signal or warning.
– ORIGIN from French *marron* 'chestnut'; sense 2 is so named because the firework makes the noise of a chestnut bursting in the fire.
maroon[2] ● verb (**be marooned**) be abandoned alone in an inaccessible place.
– ORIGIN from *Maroon*, a member of a group of black people descended from runaway slaves and living in parts of Suriname and the West Indies, from Spanish *cimarrón* 'runaway slave'.
marque ● noun a make of car, as distinct from a specific model.
– ORIGIN French, from *marquer* 'to brand'.
marquee ● noun **1** chiefly Brit. a large tent used for social or commercial functions. **2** N. Amer. a roof-like projection over the entrance to a theatre, hotel, or other building. **3** (before another noun) N. Amer. leading; pre-eminent: *a marquee player*.
– ORIGIN from MARQUISE (formerly a synonym for *marquee*), taken as a plural; sense 3 is with allusion to the practice of billing the name of an entertainer over the entrance to a theatre.
marquess ● noun a British nobleman ranking above an earl and below a duke. Compare with MARQUIS.
– ORIGIN variant of MARQUIS.
marquetry /maarkitri/ ● noun inlaid work made from small pieces of variously coloured wood, used for the decoration of furniture.
– ORIGIN from French *marqueter* 'become variegated'.
marquis /maarkwiss/ ● noun **1** (in some European countries) a nobleman ranking above a count and below a duke. Compare with MARQUESS. **2** variant spelling of MARQUESS.
– ORIGIN Old French *marchis*, from the base of MARCH[2].
marquise /maarkeez/ ● noun **1** the wife or widow of a marquis, or a woman holding the rank of marquis in her own right. **2** a ring set with a pointed oval gem or cluster of gems.
– ORIGIN French, feminine of MARQUIS.
marram grass ● noun a coarse grass of coastal sand dunes.
– ORIGIN Old Norse.
marriage ● noun **1** the formal union of a man and a woman, by which they become husband and wife. **2** a combination of two or more elements.
– PHRASES **marriage of convenience** a marriage concluded primarily to achieve a practical purpose.
– ORIGIN Old French *mariage*, from *marier* 'marry'.
marriageable ● adjective fit or suitable for marriage.
married ● adjective united by marriage. ● noun (**marrieds**) married people.
marron /marən/ ● noun (pl. same or **marrons**) a large Australian freshwater crayfish.
– ORIGIN from an Aboriginal language.
marron glacé /marron glassay/ ● noun (pl. **marrons glacés** pronunc. same) a chestnut preserved in and coated with sugar.
– ORIGIN French, 'iced chestnut'.
marrow ● noun **1** Brit. a long gourd with a thin green skin and white flesh, eaten as a vegetable. **2** (also **bone marrow**) a soft fatty substance in the cavities of bones, in which blood cells are produced.
– PHRASES **to the marrow** to one's innermost being.
– ORIGIN Old English.
marrowbone ● noun a bone containing edible marrow.
marrowfat pea ● noun a pea of a large variety which is processed and sold in cans.
marry[1] ● verb (**marries, married**) **1** take as one's wife or husband in marriage. **2** join (two people) in marriage. **3** (**marry into**) become a member of (a family) by marriage. **4** join together; combine harmoniously.
– PHRASES **marry in haste, repent at leisure** proverb those who rush impetuously into marriage may spend a long time regretting doing so.
– ORIGIN Old French *marier*, from Latin *maritus*, 'married, husband'.
marry[2] ● exclamation archaic expressing surprise, indignation, or emphatic assertion.
– ORIGIN variant of *Mary* (mother of Jesus).
Marsala /maarsaalə/ ● noun a dark, sweet fortified dessert wine produced in Sicily.
– ORIGIN named after *Marsala*, a town in Sicily.
marsh ● noun an area of low-lying land which is flooded in wet seasons or at high tide and typically remains waterlogged.
– DERIVATIVES **marshy** adjective.
– ORIGIN Old English.

Thesaurus

– PHRASES **on the market** ON SALE, (up) for sale, on offer, available, obtainable; *N. Amer.* on the block.
marksman, markswoman ● noun SNIPER, sharpshooter, good shot; *informal* crack shot; *N. Amer. informal* deadeye, shootist.
maroon ● verb STRAND, cast away, cast ashore; abandon, leave behind, leave, leave in the lurch, desert; *informal* leave high and dry.
marriage ● noun **1** *a proposal of marriage* (HOLY) MATRIMONY, wedlock. **2** *the marriage took place at St Margaret's* WEDDING, wedding ceremony, marriage ceremony, nuptials, union; *archaic* espousal. **3** *a marriage of jazz, pop, and gospel* UNION, alliance, fusion, mixture, mix, blend, amalgamation, combination, merger.
– RELATED TERMS conjugal, marital, matrimonial.
– OPPOSITES divorce, separation.
married ● adjective **1** *a married couple* WEDDED, wed; *informal* spliced, hitched. **2** *married bliss* MARITAL, matrimonial, conjugal, nuptial; *Law* spousal; *poetic/literary* connubial.
– OPPOSITES single.
marrow ● noun *the marrow of his statement* ESSENCE, core, nucleus, pith, kernel, heart, quintessence, gist, substance, sum and substance, meat, nub; *informal* nitty-gritty.
marry ● verb **1** *the couple married last year* GET/BE MARRIED, wed, be wed, become man and wife, plight/pledge one's troth; *informal* tie the knot, walk down the aisle, take the plunge, get spliced, get hitched, say 'I do'. **2** *John wanted to marry her* WED, take to wife/husband; *informal* make an honest woman of; *archaic* espouse. **3** *the show marries poetry with art* JOIN, unite, combine, fuse, mix,

m

marshal ● noun **1** an officer of the highest rank in the armed forces of some countries. **2** chiefly historical a high-ranking officer of state. **3** (in the US) a federal or municipal law officer. **4** an official responsible for supervising public events. **5** (in the UK) an official accompanying a judge on circuit. ● verb (**marshalled**, **marshalling**; US **marshaled**, **marshaling**) **1** assemble (a group of people, especially soldiers) in order. **2** bring together (facts, information, etc.) in an organized way. **3** direct the movement of (an aircraft) on the ground at an airport.
– ORIGIN Old French *mareschal* 'farrier, commander', from Latin *mariscalcus*.

marshalling yard ● noun a large railway yard in which freight wagons are organized into trains.

Marshal of the Royal Air Force ● noun the highest rank of officer in the RAF.

Marsh Arab ● noun a member of a semi-nomadic Arab people inhabiting marshland in southern Iraq.

marsh gas ● noun methane generated by decaying matter in marshes.

marshmallow ● noun a spongy sweet made from a mixture of sugar, albumen, and gelatin.

marsh mallow ● noun a tall pink-flowered plant growing in marshes, whose roots were formerly used to make marshmallow.

marsh marigold ● noun a plant with large yellow flowers which grows in damp ground and shallow water.

marsupial /maarsoōpiəl/ ● noun a mammal, such as a kangaroo or a wombat, whose young are born incompletely developed and are carried and suckled in a pouch on the mother's belly.
– ORIGIN from Greek *marsupion* 'little purse'.

mart ● noun a trade centre or market.
– ORIGIN Dutch, variant of *marct* 'market'.

Martello tower ● noun any of a number of small circular defensive forts erected along the coasts of Britain during the Napoleonic Wars.
– ORIGIN alteration of Cape *Mortella* in Corsica, where such a tower proved difficult for the English to capture in 1794.

marten ● noun a weasel-like forest mammal that is hunted for fur in some countries.
– ORIGIN from Old French *peau martrine* 'marten fur', from Germanic.

martial ● adjective of or appropriate to war; warlike.
– DERIVATIVES **martially** adverb.
– USAGE On the confusion of **martial** and **marital**, see the note at MARITAL.
– ORIGIN from Latin *martialis*, from *Mars*, the name of the Roman god of war.

martial arts ● plural noun various sports or skills, mainly of Japanese origin, which originated as forms of self-defence or attack, such as judo, karate, and kung fu.

martial law ● noun military government, involving the suspension of ordinary law.

Martian ● adjective relating to the planet Mars. ● noun a supposed inhabitant of Mars.

martin ● noun used in names of small short-tailed swallows, e.g. **house martin**.
– ORIGIN probably from the name of St *Martin* of Tours.

martinet ● noun a strict disciplinarian.
– ORIGIN named after Jean *Martinet*, 17th-century French drill master.

martingale ● noun **1** a strap or set of straps running from the noseband or reins to the girth of a horse, used to prevent the horse from raising its head too high. **2** a gambling system that involves a continual doubling of the stakes.
– ORIGIN French, from an Arabic word meaning 'the fastening'.

Martiniquan /maartineek'n/ (also **Martinican**) ● noun a person from Martinique, a French island in the Lesser Antilles. ● adjective relating to Martinique.

martyr ● noun **1** a person who is killed because of their religious or other beliefs. **2** a person who exaggerates their difficulties in order to obtain sympathy or admiration. ● verb make a martyr of.
– DERIVATIVES **martyrdom** noun.
– ORIGIN Greek *martur* 'witness'.

martyrology ● noun (pl. **martyrologies**) **1** the study of the lives of martyrs. **2** a list of martyrs.

marvel ● verb (**marvelled**, **marvelling**; US **marveled**, **marveling**) be filled with wonder. ● noun a person or thing that causes a feeling of wonder.
– ORIGIN Old French *merveille*, from Latin *mirabilis* 'wonderful', from *mirari* 'wonder at'.

marvellous (US **marvelous**) ● adjective **1** causing great wonder; extraordinary. **2** extremely good or pleasing.
– DERIVATIVES **marvellously** adverb.

Marxism ● noun the political and economic theories of Karl Marx (1818–83) and Friedrich Engels (1820–95), later developed by their followers to form the basis for the theory and practice of communism.
– DERIVATIVES **Marxist** noun & adjective.

Marxism–Leninism ● noun the doctrines of Marx as interpreted and put into effect by Lenin in the Soviet Union.

marzipan ● noun a sweet paste of ground almonds, sugar, and egg whites, used to coat cakes or to make confectionery.
– ORIGIN from Italian *marzapane*, perhaps from Arabic.

Masai /maasī/ (also **Maasai**) ● noun (pl. same or **Masais**) a member of a pastoral people living in Tanzania and Kenya.
– ORIGIN Masai.

masala /məsaalə/ ● noun a mixture of spices ground into a paste or powder and used in Indian cookery.
– ORIGIN Urdu, from Arabic, 'ingredients, materials'.

mascara ● noun a cosmetic for darkening and thickening the eyelashes.
– ORIGIN Italian, 'mask'.

mascarpone /maskəpōnay/ ● noun a soft, mild Italian cream cheese.
– ORIGIN Italian.

mascot ● noun a person, animal, or object that is identified with a person, group, team, etc. and supposed to bring good luck.
– ORIGIN French *mascotte*, from Provençal *masco* 'witch'.

masculine ● adjective **1** relating to men; male. **2** having the qualities or appearance traditionally associated with men.

m

Thesaurus

blend, merge, amalgamate, link, connect, couple, knit, yoke.
– OPPOSITES divorce, separate.

marsh ● noun SWAMP, marshland, bog, peat bog, swampland, morass, mire, quagmire, slough, fen, fenland, wetland; *N. Amer.* bayou; *Scottish & N. English* moss; *archaic* quag.

marshal ● verb **1** *the king marshalled an army* ASSEMBLE, gather together, collect, muster, call together, draw up, line up, align, array, organize, group, arrange, deploy, position, order, dispose; mobilize, rally, round up. **2** *guests were marshalled to their seats* USHER, guide, escort, conduct, lead, shepherd, steer, take.

marshy ● adjective BOGGY, swampy, muddy, squelchy, soggy, waterlogged, miry, fenny; *Scottish & N. English* mossy; *Ecology* paludal.
– OPPOSITES dry, firm.

martial ● adjective MILITARY, soldierly, soldier-like, army, naval; warlike, fighting, combative, militaristic; *informal* gung-ho.

martinet ● noun DISCIPLINARIAN, slave-driver, stickler for discipline, (hard) taskmaster, authoritarian, tyrant.

martyr ● verb PUT TO DEATH, kill, martyrize; burn, burn at the stake, immolate, stone to death, throw to the lions, crucify.

martyrdom ● noun DEATH, suffering, torture, torment, agony, ordeal; killing, sacrifice, crucifixion, immolation, burning, auto-da-fé; *Christianity* Passion.

marvel ● verb *she marvelled at their courage* BE AMAZED, be astonished, be surprised, be awed, stand in awe, wonder; stare, gape, goggle, not believe one's eyes/ears, be dumbfounded; *informal* be flabbergasted.
● noun *the marvels of technology* WONDER, miracle, sensation, spectacle, phenomenon; *informal* something else, something to shout about, eye-opener.

marvellous ● adjective **1** *his solo climb was marvellous* AMAZING, astounding, astonishing, awesome, breathtaking, sensational, remarkable, spectacular, stupendous, staggering, stunning; phenomenal, prodigious, miraculous, extraordinary, incredible, unbelievable; *poetic/literary* wondrous. **2** *marvellous weather* EXCELLENT, splendid, wonderful, magnificent, superb, glorious, sublime, lovely, delightful, too good to be true; *informal* super, great, amazing, fantastic, terrific, tremendous, sensational, heavenly, divine, gorgeous, grand, fabulous, fab, awesome, to die for, magic, ace, wicked, mind-blowing, far out, out of this world; *Brit. informal* smashing, brilliant, brill; *N. Amer. informal* boss; *Austral./NZ informal* beaut, bonzer; *Brit. informal, dated* champion, wizard, corking, rip-

3 Grammar referring to a gender of nouns and adjectives conventionally regarded as male.
– DERIVATIVES **masculinity** noun.
– ORIGIN from Latin *masculus* 'male'.
maser /mayzə/ ● noun a form of laser generating a beam of microwaves.
– ORIGIN acronym from *microwave amplification by the stimulated emission of radiation*.
mash ● noun **1** a soft mass made by crushing a substance into a pulp. **2** bran mixed with hot water, given as a warm food to horses. **3** Brit. informal boiled and mashed potatoes. **4** (in brewing) a mixture of powdered malt and hot water, which is left standing until the sugars dissolve to form the wort. ● verb **1** reduce or beat to a mash. **2** (in brewing) mix (powdered malt) with hot water to form wort. **3** Brit. informal (with reference to tea) brew or infuse.
– ORIGIN Old English.
mask ● noun **1** a covering for all or part of the face, worn as a disguise, for protection or hygiene, or for theatrical effect. **2** a respirator used to filter inhaled air or to supply gas for inhalation. **3** a likeness of a person's face moulded or sculpted in clay or wax. **4** a face pack. ● verb **1** cover with a mask. **2** conceal or disguise. **3** cover so as to protect during a process such as painting.
– DERIVATIVES **masked** adjective.
– ORIGIN French *masque*, from Italian *maschera* or *mascara*, probably from Latin *masca* 'witch, spectre', but influenced by an Arabic word meaning 'buffoon'.
masked ball ● noun a ball at which participants wear masks to conceal their faces.
masking tape ● noun adhesive tape used in painting to cover areas on which paint is not wanted.
masochism /massəkiz'm/ ● noun the tendency to derive pleasure from one's own pain or humiliation.
– DERIVATIVES **masochist** noun **masochistic** adjective.
– ORIGIN named after Leopold von Sacher-*Masoch* (1835–95), the Austrian novelist who described it.
mason ● noun **1** a builder and worker in stone. **2** (**Mason**) a Freemason.
– ORIGIN Old French *masson*.
Masonic ● adjective relating to Freemasons.
masonry ● noun **1** stonework. **2** (**Masonry**) Freemasonry.
masque /maask/ ● noun a form of dramatic entertainment popular in the 16th and 17th centuries, consisting of dancing and acting performed by masked players.
– ORIGIN probably from *masker* 'person wearing a mask', influenced by French *masque* 'mask'.
masquerade ● noun **1** a false show or pretence. **2** a masked ball. ● verb **1** pretend to be someone that one is not. **2** be disguised or passed off as something else.
– ORIGIN French *mascarade*, from Italian *maschera* 'mask'.
Mass ● noun **1** the Christian Eucharist or Holy Communion, especially in the Roman Catholic Church. **2** a musical setting of parts of the liturgy used in the Mass.
– ORIGIN Latin *missa*, from *mittere* 'dismiss', perhaps from the last words of the service, *Ite, missa est* 'Go, it is the dismissal'.
mass ● noun **1** a body of matter with no definite shape. **2** a large number of people or objects gathered together. **3** (before another noun) done by or affecting large numbers: *a mass exodus*. **4** (**the masses**) the ordinary people. **5** (**the mass of**) the majority of. **6** (**a mass of**) a large amount of. **7** Physics the quantity of matter which a body contains, as measured by its acceleration under a given force or by the force exerted on it by a gravitational field. ● verb assemble into a single body or mass.
– ORIGIN Latin *massa*, from Greek *maza* 'barley cake'.
massacre ● noun **1** a brutal slaughter of a large number of people. **2** informal a very heavy defeat. ● verb **1** brutally kill (a large number of people). **2** informal inflict a heavy defeat on.
– ORIGIN French.
massage ● noun the rubbing and kneading of parts of the body with the hands to relieve tension or pain. ● verb **1** give a massage to. **2** manipulate (figures) to give a more acceptable result. **3** gently flatter (someone's ego).
– ORIGIN French, probably from Portuguese *amassar* 'knead', from *massa* 'dough'.
massage parlour ● noun **1** an establishment in which massage is provided for payment. **2** euphemistic a brothel.
masseur ● noun (fem. **masseuse**) a person who provides massage professionally.
– ORIGIN French, from *masser* 'to massage'.
massif /masseef/ ● noun a compact group of mountains.
– ORIGIN from French, 'massive'.
massive ● adjective **1** large and heavy or solid. **2** exceptionally large, intense, or severe. **3** forming a solid or continuous mass.
– DERIVATIVES **massively** adverb **massiveness** noun.
– ORIGIN French *massif*, from Latin *massa* 'mass'.

m

Thesaurus

ping, spiffing, top-hole; *N. Amer. informal, dated* swell.
– OPPOSITES commonplace, awful.
masculine ● adjective **1** *a masculine trait* MALE, man's, men's; male-oriented. **2** *a powerfully masculine man* VIRILE, macho, manly, all-male, muscular, muscly, strong, strapping, well built, rugged, robust, brawny, powerful, red-blooded, vigorous; *informal* hunky. **3** *a rather masculine woman* MANNISH, unfeminine, unwomanly, unladylike, Amazonian; *informal* butch.
– OPPOSITES feminine, effeminate.
masculinity ● noun VIRILITY, manliness, maleness, machismo, vigour, strength, muscularity, ruggedness, robustness.
mash ● verb *mash the potatoes* PULP, crush, purée, cream, smash, squash, pound, beat.
● noun *first pound the garlic to a mash* PULP, purée, mush, paste.
mask ● noun **1** *she wore a mask to conceal her face* DISGUISE, false face; *historical* domino, visor; *archaic* vizard. **2** *he dropped his mask of good humour* PRETENCE, semblance, veil, screen, front, false front, facade, veneer, blind, false colours, disguise, guise, concealment, cover, cover-up, cloak, camouflage.
● verb *poplar trees masked the factory* HIDE, conceal, disguise, cover up, obscure, screen, cloak, camouflage, veil.
masquerade ● noun **1** *a grand masquerade* MASKED BALL, masque, fancy-dress party. **2** *he couldn't keep up the masquerade much longer* PRETENCE, deception, pose, act, front, facade, disguise, dissimulation, cover-up, bluff, play-acting, make-believe; *informal* put-on.
● verb *a woman masquerading as a man* PRETEND TO BE, pose as, pass oneself off as, impersonate, disguise oneself as; *formal* personate.
Mass ● noun EUCHARIST, Holy Communion, Communion, the Lord's Supper.
mass ● noun **1** *a soggy mass of fallen leaves* PILE, heap; accumulation, aggregation, accretion, concretion, build-up. **2** *a mass of cyclists* CROWD, horde, large group, throng, host, troop, army, herd, flock, drove, swarm, mob, pack, press, crush, flood, multitude. **3** *the mass of the population* MAJORITY, greater part/number, best/better part, major part, most, bulk, main body, lion's share. **4** THE COMMON PEOPLE, the populace, the public, the people, the rank and file, the crowd, the third estate; *derogatory* the hoi polloi, the mob, the proletariat, the common herd, the great unwashed. **5** *(informal) masses of food.* See LOT pronoun.
● adjective *mass hysteria* WIDESPREAD, general, wholesale, universal, large-scale, extensive, pandemic.
● verb *they began massing troops in the region* ASSEMBLE, marshal, gather together, muster, round up, mobilize, rally.
massacre ● noun **1** *a cold-blooded massacre of innocent civilians* SLAUGHTER, wholesale/mass slaughter, indiscriminate killing, mass murder, mass execution, annihilation, liquidation, decimation, extermination; carnage, butchery, bloodbath, bloodletting, pogrom, genocide, ethnic cleansing, holocaust, Shoah, night of the long knives; *poetic/literary* slaying. **2** *(informal) the match was an 8–0 massacre.* See ROUT noun sense 2.
● verb **1** *thousands were brutally massacred* SLAUGHTER, butcher, murder, kill, annihilate, exterminate, execute, liquidate, eliminate, decimate, wipe out, mow down, cut down, put to the sword, put to death; *poetic/literary* slay. **2** *(informal) they were massacred in the final.* See TROUNCE.
massage ● noun RUB, rub-down, rubbing, kneading, palpation, manipulation, pummelling; shiatsu, reflexology, acupressure, hydromassage, Swedish massage, osteopathy; effleurage, tapotement, Rolfing.
● verb **1** *he massaged her tired muscles* RUB, knead, palpate, manipulate, pummel, work. **2** *the statistics have been massaged* ALTER, tamper with, manipulate, doctor, falsify, juggle, fiddle with, tinker with, distort, change, rig, interfere with, misrepresent; *informal* fix, cook, fiddle.
massive ● adjective HUGE, enormous, vast, immense, large, big, mighty, great, colossal, tremendous, prodigious, gigantic, gargan-

mass market ● noun an unrestricted arena of commercial activity in which goods are produced in large quantities for the broad population.
mass noun ● noun a noun denoting something which cannot be counted, in English usually a noun which has no plural form and is not used with *a* or *an*, e.g. *luggage, happiness*. Contrasted with COUNT NOUN.
mass number ● noun Physics the total number of protons and neutrons in a nucleus.
mass-produced ● adjective produced in large quantities by an automated mechanical process.
mast[1] ● noun **1** a tall upright post or spar on a boat, generally carrying a sail or sails. **2** any tall upright post, especially a flagpole or a television or radio transmitter.
– PHRASES **before the mast** historical serving as an ordinary seaman (quartered in the forecastle). **nail one's colours to the mast** declare openly and firmly what one believes.
– ORIGIN Old English.
mast[2] ● noun the fruit of beech and other forest trees, especially as food for pigs.
– ORIGIN Old English.
mastectomy ● noun (pl. **mastectomies**) a surgical operation to remove a breast.
– ORIGIN from Greek *mastos* 'breast'.
master ● noun **1** a man in a position of authority, control, or ownership. **2** a skilled practitioner of a particular art or activity. **3** the head of a college or school. **4** chiefly Brit. a male schoolteacher. **5** a person who holds a second or further degree. **6** an original film, recording, or document from which copies can be made. **7** a title prefixed to the name of a boy. ● adjective **1** (of an artist) having great skill or proficiency: *a master painter*. **2** skilled in a particular trade and able to teach others: *a master builder*. **3** main; principal. ● verb **1** acquire complete knowledge or skill in. **2** gain control of; overcome. **3** make a master copy of (a film or record).
– ORIGIN Latin *magister*.
master-at-arms ● noun a warrant officer responsible for police duties on board a ship.
masterclass ● noun a class given to students by a musician regarded as a master.
masterful ● adjective **1** powerful and able to control others. **2** performed or performing very skilfully.
– DERIVATIVES **masterfully** adverb.
– USAGE Strictly, there is a distinction between **masterful** and **masterly**: both mean 'very skilful', but only **masterful** means 'powerful and able to control others'.
master key ● noun a key that opens several locks, each of which also has its own key.
masterly ● adjective performed or performing very skilfully.
mastermind ● noun **1** a person with outstanding intellect. **2** a person who plans and directs a complex scheme or enterprise. ● verb be the mastermind of.
master of ceremonies ● noun a person in charge of procedure at a state occasion, formal event, or entertainment, who introduces the speakers or performers.
Master of the Rolls ● noun (in England and Wales) the judge who presides over the Court of Appeal.
masterpiece ● noun a work of outstanding skill.
– ORIGIN originally referring to a piece of work by a craftsman accepted as qualification for membership of a guild as an acknowledged master.
mastery ● noun **1** comprehensive knowledge or command of a subject or skill. **2** control or superiority.
masthead ● noun **1** the highest part of a ship's mast. **2** the name of a newspaper or magazine printed at the top of the first or editorial page.
mastic ● noun **1** an aromatic gum from the bark of a Mediterranean tree, used in making varnish and chewing gum and as a flavouring. **2** a putty-like waterproof filler and sealant used in building.
– ORIGIN Greek *mastikhē*, from *mastikhan* 'grind the teeth'.
masticate ● verb chew (food).
– DERIVATIVES **mastication** noun.
– ORIGIN Latin *masticare*, from Greek *mastikhan* 'grind the teeth'.
mastiff ● noun a dog of a large, strong breed with drooping ears and pendulous lips.
– ORIGIN Old French *mastin*, from Latin *mansuetus* 'tame'.
mastitis ● noun inflammation of the mammary gland in the breast or udder.
– ORIGIN from Greek *mastos* 'breast'.
mastodon /mastədon/ ● noun a large extinct elephant-like mammal of the Miocene to Pleistocene epochs.
– ORIGIN from Greek *mastos* 'breast' + *odous* 'tooth' (with reference to nipple-shaped tubercles on the crowns of its molar teeth).
mastoid ● noun **1** (also **mastoid process**) Anatomy a conical projection of the temporal bone behind the ear, to which neck muscles are attached, and which has air spaces linked to the middle ear. **2** (**mastoids**) (treated as sing.) informal mastoiditis.
mastoiditis ● noun Medicine inflammation of the mastoid.
masturbate ● verb stimulate one's genitals with one's hand for sexual pleasure.
– DERIVATIVES **masturbation** noun **masturbator** noun **masturbatory** adjective.

m

Thesaurus

tuan, mammoth, monstrous, monumental, giant, towering, elephantine, mountainous, titanic; epic, Herculean, Brobdingnagian; *informal* jumbo, mega, monster, whopping, humongous, hulking, bumper, astronomical; *Brit. informal* whacking, ginormous.
– OPPOSITES tiny.
mast ● noun **1** *a ship's mast* spar, boom, yard, gaff, foremast, mainmast, topmast, mizzenmast, mizzen, royal mast. **2** *the mast on top of the building* FLAGPOLE, flagstaff, pole, post, rod, upright; aerial, transmitter, pylon.
master ● noun **1** *(historical) he acceded to his master's wishes* LORD, overlord, lord and master, ruler, sovereign, monarch, liege (lord), suzerain. **2** *the dog's master* OWNER, keeper. **3** *a chess master* EXPERT, adept, genius, past master, maestro, virtuoso, professional, doyen, authority; *informal* ace, pro, wizard, whizz, hotshot; *Brit. informal* dab hand; *N. Amer. informal* maven, crackerjack. **4** *the master of the ship* CAPTAIN, commander; *informal* skipper. **5** *the geography master* TEACHER, schoolteacher, schoolmaster, tutor, instructor, preceptor; *formal* pedagogue. **6** *their spiritual master* GURU, teacher, leader, guide, mentor; swami, Maharishi; Roshi.
– OPPOSITES servant, amateur, pupil.
● verb **1** *I managed to master my fears* OVERCOME, conquer, beat, quell, quash, suppress, control, overpower, triumph over, subdue, vanquish, subjugate, prevail over, govern, curb, check, bridle, tame, defeat, get the better of, get a grip on, get over; *informal* lick. **2** *it took ages to master the technique* LEARN, become proficient in, know inside out, know backwards; pick up, grasp, understand; *informal* get the hang of.
● adjective **1** *a master craftsman* EXPERT, adept, proficient, skilled, skilful, deft, dexterous, adroit, practised, experienced, masterly, accomplished, complete, demon, brilliant; *informal* crack, ace, mean, wizard; *N. Amer. informal* crackerjack. **2** *the master bedroom* PRINCIPAL, main, chief; biggest.
masterful ● adjective **1** *a masterful man* COMMANDING, powerful, imposing, magisterial, lordly, authoritative; dominating, domineering, overbearing, overweening, imperious. **2** *their masterful handling of the situation* EXPERT, adept, clever, masterly, skilful, skilled, adroit, proficient, deft, dexterous, accomplished, polished, consummate; *informal* crack, ace.
– OPPOSITES weak, inept.
masterly ● adjective. See MASTERFUL sense 2.
mastermind ● verb *he masterminded the whole campaign* PLAN, control, direct, be in charge of, run, conduct, organize, arrange, preside over, orchestrate, stage-manage, engineer, manage, coordinate; conceive, devise, originate, initiate, think up, frame, hatch, come up with; *informal* be the brains behind.
● noun *the mastermind behind the project* GENIUS, mind, intellect, author, architect, organizer, originator, prime mover, initiator, inventor; *informal* brain, brains, bright spark.
masterpiece ● noun CHEF-D'ŒUVRE, pièce de résistance, masterwork, magnum opus, finest/best work, tour de force.
master stroke ● noun STROKE OF GENIUS, coup, triumph, coup de maître, tour de force.
mastery ● noun **1** *her mastery of the language* PROFICIENCY, ability, capability; knowledge, understanding, comprehension, familiarity, command, grasp, grip. **2** *they played with tactical mastery* SKILL, skilfulness, expertise, dexterity, finesse, adroitness, virtuosity, prowess, deftness, proficiency; *informal* know-how. **3** *man's mastery over nature* CONTROL, domination, command, ascendancy, supremacy, pre-eminence, superiority; triumph, victory, the upper hand, the whip hand, rule, government, power, sway, au-

– ORIGIN Latin *masturbari.*
mat ● noun **1** a thick piece of material placed on the floor and used as protection from dirt or as a decorative rug. **2** a piece of resilient material for landing on in gymnastics or similar sports. **3** a small piece of material placed on a surface to protect it from the heat or moisture of an object placed on it. **4** a thick, untidy layer of hairy or woolly material.
– PHRASES **on the mat** informal being reprimanded by someone in authority.
– ORIGIN Old English.
Matabele /mattəbeeli/ ● noun the Ndebele people collectively, particularly those of Zimbabwe.
– ORIGIN Sotho (a Bantu language).
matador ● noun a bullfighter whose task is to kill the bull.
– ORIGIN Spanish, 'killer'.
match[1] ● noun **1** a contest in which people or teams compete against each other. **2** an equal contender. **3** an exact equivalent. **4** a corresponding pair. **5** a potential husband or wife. **6** a marriage. ● verb **1** correspond or cause to correspond; make or be harmonious. **2** be equal to. **3** place in competition with another.
– ORIGIN Old English, 'mate, companion'.
match[2] ● noun **1** a short, thin stick tipped with a mixture that ignites when rubbed against a rough surface, used to light a fire. **2** historical a piece of wick or cord which burned uniformly, used for lighting gunpowder.
– ORIGIN Old French *meche.*
matchboard ● noun interlocking boards joined together by tongue and groove.
matchbox ● noun a small box in which matches are sold.
matchless ● adjective unequalled; incomparable.
matchlock ● noun historical a type of gun with a lock containing a piece of match.
matchmaker ● noun a person who tries to bring about marriages or relationships between other people.
match play ● noun golf in which the score is reckoned by holes won.
match point ● noun (in tennis) a point which if won by one of the players will also win them the match.
matchstick ● noun **1** the stem of a match. **2** (before another noun) drawn using thin straight lines: *matchstick men.*
matchwood ● noun very small pieces or splinters of wood.
mate[1] ● noun **1** Brit. informal a friend or companion. **2** (in combination) a fellow member or occupant: *his teammates.* **3** the sexual partner of an animal. **4** an assistant. **5** an officer on a merchant ship subordinate to the master. ● verb **1** (of animals or birds) come together for breeding. **2** join or connect mechanically.
– ORIGIN Low German, 'comrade'.
mate[2] ● noun & verb Chess short for CHECKMATE.
maté /matay/ (also **yerba maté**) ● noun a bitter tea-like infusion made in South America from the leaves of a shrub.
– ORIGIN Quechua.
matelassé /matəlassay/ ● noun a fabric having a raised design like quilting.
– ORIGIN French, from *matelas* 'mattress'.
matelot /matlō/ ● noun Brit. informal a sailor.
– ORIGIN French, from Dutch *mattenoot* 'bed companion' (because sailors had to share hammocks).
mater /maytə/ ● noun Brit. informal, dated mother.
– ORIGIN Latin.
materfamilias /maytəfəmilliəss/ ● noun (pl. **matresfamilias**) the female head of a family or household.
– ORIGIN Latin.
material ● noun **1** the matter from which something is or can be made. **2** items needed for doing or creating something. **3** cloth or fabric. ● adjective **1** consisting of or referring to physical objects rather than ideas or spirit. **2** important; essential; relevant.
– DERIVATIVES **materiality** noun **materially** adverb.
– ORIGIN Latin *materia* 'matter', from *mater* 'mother'.
materialism ● noun **1** a tendency to consider material possessions and physical comfort as more important than spiritual values. **2** Philosophy the doctrine that nothing exists except matter and its movements and modifications.
– DERIVATIVES **materialist** noun & adjective **materialistic** adjective.
materialize (also **materialise**) ● verb **1** become actual fact; happen. **2** appear in bodily form.
– DERIVATIVES **materialization** noun.

m

Thesaurus

thority, jurisdiction, dominion, sovereignty.
masticate ● verb CHEW, munch, champ, chomp, crunch, eat; ruminate, chew the cud; *formal* manducate.
mat ● noun **1** *the hall mat* RUG, runner, carpet, drugget; doormat, welcome mat, hearthrug; dhurrie, numdah; kilim, flokati; *N. Amer.* floorcloth. **2** *he placed his glass on the mat* COASTER, beer mat, doily; table mat, place mat; *Brit.* drip mat. **3** *a thick mat of hair* MASS, tangle, knot, mop, thatch, shock, mane.
● verb *his hair was matted with blood* TANGLE, entangle, knot, ravel, snarl up.
match ● noun **1** *a football match | a boxing match* CONTEST, competition, game, tournament, tie, cup tie, event, fixture, trial, test, meet, bout, fight; friendly, (local) derby; play-off, replay, rematch; *archaic* tourney. **2** *he was no match for the champion* EQUAL, rival, equivalent, peer, counterpart; *formal* compeer. **3** *the vase was an exact match of the one she already owned* LOOKALIKE, double, twin, duplicate, mate, fellow, companion, counterpart, pair; replica, copy; *informal* spitting image, spit and image, dead spit, dead ringer. **4** *a love match* MARRIAGE, betrothal, relationship, partnership, union.
● verb **1** *the curtains matched the duvet cover* GO WITH, coordinate with, complement, suit; be the same as, be similar to. **2** *did their statements match?* CORRESPOND, be in agreement, tally, agree, match up, coincide, accord, conform, square. **3** *no one can match him at chess* EQUAL, be a match for, measure up to, compare with, parallel, be in the same league as, be on a par with, touch, keep pace with, keep up with, emulate, rival, vie with, compete with, contend with; *informal* hold a candle to.
– PHRASES **match up to** MEASURE UP TO, come up to, meet with, be equal to, be as good as, satisfy, fulfil, answer to.
matching ● adjective CORRESPONDING, equivalent, parallel, analogous; coordinating, complementary, toning; paired, twin, identical, like, like (two) peas in a pod, alike.
– OPPOSITES different, clashing.
matchless ● adjective INCOMPARABLE, unrivalled, inimitable, beyond compare/comparison, unparalleled, unequalled, without equal, peerless, second to none, unsurpassed, unsurpassable, nonpareil, unique, consummate, perfect, rare, transcendent, surpassing; *formal* unexampled.
matchmaker ● noun MARRIAGE BROKER, shadchan; marriage bureau, dating agency; go-between.
mate ● noun **1** *(Brit. informal) he's gone out with his mates* FRIEND, companion, boon companion, intimate, familiar, confidant; playmate, playfellow, schoolmate, classmate, workmate; *informal* pal, chum; *Brit. informal* china, mucker; *N. English informal* marra; *N. Amer. informal* buddy, amigo, compadre, homeboy; *archaic* compeer. **2** *she's finally found her ideal mate* PARTNER, husband, wife, spouse, lover, live-in lover, significant other, companion, helpmate, helpmeet, consort; *informal* better half, hubby, missus, missis; *Brit. informal* other half, dutch, trouble and strife. **3** *I can't find the mate to this sock* MATCH, fellow, twin, companion, pair, other half, equivalent. **4** *a plumber's mate* ASSISTANT, helper, apprentice.
● verb *pandas rarely mate in captivity* BREED, couple, copulate.
material ● noun **1** *the decomposition of organic material* MATTER, substance, stuff, medium. **2** *the materials for a new building* CONSTITUENT, raw material, element, component. **3** *cleaning materials* THINGS, items, articles, stuff, necessaries; *Brit. informal* gubbins. **4** *curtain material* FABRIC, cloth, textiles. **5** *material for a magazine article* INFORMATION, data, facts, facts and figures, statistics, evidence, details, particulars, background, notes; *informal* info, gen, dope, low-down.
● adjective **1** *the material world* PHYSICAL, corporeal, tangible, non-spiritual, mundane, worldly, earthly, secular, temporal, concrete, real, solid, substantial. **2** *she was too fond of material pleasures* SENSUAL, physical, carnal, corporal, fleshly, bodily. **3** *information that could be material to the inquiry* RELEVANT, pertinent, applicable, germane; apropos, to the point; vital, essential, key. **4** *the storms caused material damage* SIGNIFICANT, major, important.
– OPPOSITES spiritual, aesthetic, irrelevant.
materialistic ● adjective CONSUMERIST, money-oriented, acquisitive, greedy; worldly, capitalistic, bourgeois.
materialize ● verb **1** *the forecast investment boom did not materialize* HAPPEN, occur, come about, take place, come into being, transpire; *informal* come off; *formal* eventuate; *poetic/literary* come to pass. **2** *Harry materialized at the door* APPEAR, turn up, arrive, make/put in an appearance, present oneself/itself, emerge, sur-

materiel /məteeriel/ ● noun military materials and equipment.
– ORIGIN French *matériel*.
maternal ● adjective **1** relating to or characteristic of a mother. **2** related through the mother's side of the family.
– DERIVATIVES **maternally** adverb.
– ORIGIN French *maternel*, from Latin *mater* 'mother'.
maternity ● noun **1** motherhood. **2** (before another noun) relating to the period during pregnancy and shortly after childbirth: *maternity clothes*.
mateship ● noun Austral./NZ informal companionship or friendship.
matey ● adjective (**matier**, **matiest**) Brit. informal familiar and friendly.
– DERIVATIVES **mateyness** (also **matiness**) noun **matily** adverb.
mathematics ● plural noun (usu. treated as sing.) the branch of science concerned with number, quantity, and space, either as abstract ideas (**pure mathematics**) or as applied to physics, engineering, and other subjects (**applied mathematics**).
– DERIVATIVES **mathematical** adjective **mathematically** adverb **mathematician** noun.
– ORIGIN from Greek *mathēma* 'science', from *manthanein* 'learn'.
maths (N. Amer. **math**) ● noun short for MATHEMATICS.
Matilda ● noun Austral./NZ informal, archaic a bushman's bundle of rolled-up bedding and clothes.
– ORIGIN from the given name *Matilda*.
matinee /mattinay/ ● noun an afternoon performance in a theatre or cinema.
– ORIGIN originally referring to performances in the morning, later extended to any performance earlier than the evening: from French *matin* 'morning'.
matinee coat ● noun Brit. a baby's short coat.
matinee idol ● noun informal, dated a handsome actor admired chiefly by women.
matins ● noun a service of morning prayer, especially in the Anglican Church.
– ORIGIN Old French *matines* 'mornings', from Latin *Matuta*, goddess of the dawn.
maître d'hôtel /maytrə dōtel/ ● noun (pl. **maîtres d'hôtel** pronunc. same) **1** the head waiter of a restaurant. **2** the manager of a hotel.
– ORIGIN French, 'master of the house'.
matriarch /maytriaark/ ● noun **1** a woman who is the head of a family or tribe. **2** a powerful older woman.
– DERIVATIVES **matriarchal** adjective **matriarchy** noun.
– ORIGIN from Latin *mater* 'mother', on the false analogy of *patriarch*.
matrices plural of MATRIX.
matricide /matrissīd/ ● noun **1** the killing of one's mother. **2** a person who kills their mother.
– DERIVATIVES **matricidal** adjective.
– ORIGIN from Latin *mater* 'mother' + *-cidium* 'killing'.
matriculate ● verb enrol or be enrolled at a college or university.
– DERIVATIVES **matriculation** noun.
– ORIGIN Latin *matriculare*, from *matricula* 'register', diminutive of *matrix*.
matrilineal ● adjective based on kinship with the mother or the female line.
– DERIVATIVES **matrilineally** adverb.
matrimony ● noun the state or ceremony of being married.
– DERIVATIVES **matrimonial** adjective.
– ORIGIN Latin *matrimonium*, from *mater* 'mother'.
matrix /maytriks/ ● noun (pl. **matrices** /maytriseez/ or **matrixes**) **1** an environment or material in which something develops. **2** a mould in which something is cast or shaped. **3** Mathematics a rectangular array of quantities in rows and columns that is manipulated according to particular rules. **4** a grid-like array of elements; a lattice. **5** a mass of fine-grained rock in which gems, crystals, or fossils are embedded.
– ORIGIN Latin, 'womb', from *mater* 'mother'.
matron ● noun **1** a woman in charge of domestic and medical arrangements at a boarding school. **2** a dignified or staid married woman. **3** Brit., dated a woman in charge of nursing in a hospital. **4** chiefly US a female prison officer.
– DERIVATIVES **matronly** adjective.
– USAGE In sense 3, the official term is now **senior nursing officer**.
– ORIGIN Latin *matrona*, from *mater* 'mother'.
matron of honour ● noun a married woman attending the bride at a wedding.
matt (also **matte**) ● adjective not shiny; dull and flat. ● noun **1** a matt colour, paint, or finish. **2** a sheet of cardboard placed on the back of a picture, as a mount or to form a border.
– ORIGIN French *mat*.
matte ● noun **1** a mask used to obscure part of an image in a film and allow another image to be substituted. **2** an impure product of the smelting of sulphide ores.
matted ● adjective (of hair or fur) tangled into a thick mass.
matter ● noun **1** physical substance or material in general, as distinct from mind and spirit; (in physics) that which occupies space and possesses mass. **2** an affair or situation under consideration; a topic. **3** (**the matter**) the reason for a problem. **4** written or printed material. **5** Logic the particular content of a proposition, as distinct from its form. **6** Law something to be tried or proved in court; a case. ● verb be important or significant.
– PHRASES **as a matter of fact** in reality; in fact. **for that matter** and indeed also. **in the matter of** as regards. **a matter of 1** no more than (a specified period). **2** a question of. **a matter of course** the natural or expected thing. **no matter 1** regardless of. **2** it is of no importance.
– ORIGIN Latin *materia*, from *mater* 'mother'.
matter-of-fact ● adjective **1** concerned only with factual content. **2** unemotional and practical.
matting ● noun material used for mats, especially coarse fabric woven from a natural fibre.
mattock ● noun an agricultural tool similar to a pickaxe, but with one arm of the head curved like an adze and the other like a chisel edge.
– ORIGIN Old English.
mattress ● noun a fabric case filled with soft, firm, or springy material used for sleeping on.
– ORIGIN Arabic, 'carpet or cushion'.
maturation ● noun **1** the action or process of maturing. **2** the formation of pus in a boil, abscess, etc.
mature ● adjective **1** fully grown or physically developed; adult.

Thesaurus

face, reveal oneself/itself, show one's face, pop up; *informal* show up, fetch up, pitch up.
materially ● adverb SIGNIFICANTLY, greatly, much, very much, to a great extent, considerably, substantially, a great deal, appreciably, markedly, fundamentally, seriously, gravely.
maternal ● adjective **1** *her maternal instincts* MOTHERLY, protective, caring, nurturing, loving, devoted, affectionate, fond, warm, tender, gentle, kind, kindly, comforting. **2** *his maternal grandparents* ON ONE'S MOTHER'S SIDE, on the distaff side.
mathematical ● adjective **1** *mathematical symbols* ARITHMETICAL, numerical; statistical, algebraic, geometric, trigonometric. **2** *mathematical precision* RIGOROUS, meticulous, scrupulous, punctilious, scientific, strict, precise, exact, accurate, pinpoint, correct, careful, unerring.
matrimonial ● adjective MARITAL, conjugal, married, wedded; nuptial; *Law* spousal; *poetic/literary* connubial.
matrimony ● noun MARRIAGE, wedlock, union; nuptials.
– OPPOSITES divorce.
matted ● adjective TANGLED, tangly, knotted, knotty, tousled, dishevelled, uncombed, unkempt, ratty; *black English* natty.
matter ● noun **1** *decaying vegetable matter* MATERIAL, substance, stuff. **2** *the heart of the matter* AFFAIR, business, proceeding, situation, circumstance, event, happening, occurrence, incident, episode, experience; subject, topic, issue, question, point, point at issue, case, concern. **3** *it is of little matter now* IMPORTANCE, consequence, significance, note, import, weight; *formal* moment. **4** *what's the matter?* PROBLEM, trouble, difficulty, complication; upset, worry. **5** *the matter of the sermon* CONTENT, subject matter, text, argument, substance. **6** *an infected wound full of matter* PUS, suppuration, purulence, discharge.
● verb *it doesn't matter what you wear* BE IMPORTANT, make any/a difference, be of importance, be of consequence, signify, be relevant, count; *informal* cut any ice.
– PHRASES **as a matter of fact** ACTUALLY, in (actual) fact, in point of fact, as it happens, really, believe it or not, in reality, in truth, to tell the truth. **no matter** IT DOESN'T MATTER, it makes no difference/odds, it's not important, never mind, don't worry about it.
matter-of-fact ● adjective UNEMOTIONAL, practical, down-to-earth, sensible, realistic, rational, sober, unsentimental, pragmatic,

2 like an adult in mental or emotional development. **3** (of thought or planning) careful and thorough. **4** (of certain foodstuffs or drinks) ready for consumption; full-flavoured. **5** (of a bill) due for payment. ● **verb 1** become mature. **2** (of an insurance policy, security, etc.) reach the end of its term and hence become payable.
– DERIVATIVES **maturely** adverb.
– ORIGIN Latin *maturus* 'timely, ripe'.
maturity ● **noun 1** the state, fact, or period of being mature. **2** the time when an insurance policy, security, etc. matures.
matutinal /matyootīnəl/ ● **adjective** formal of or occurring in the morning.
– ORIGIN Latin *matutinus* 'early'.
matzo /matsō/ (also **matzoh**) ● **noun** (pl. **matzos** or **matzoth** /matsōt/) a crisp biscuit of unleavened bread, traditionally eaten by Jews during Passover.
– ORIGIN Yiddish, from Hebrew.
maudlin ● **adjective** self-pityingly or tearfully sentimental.
– ORIGIN from the name of Mary *Magdalen* in the Bible, typically depicted weeping.
maul ● **verb 1** wound by scratching and tearing. **2** handle or treat savagely or roughly. ● **noun 1** Rugby Union a loose scrum formed around a player with the ball off the ground. **2** another term for BEETLE[2] (in sense 1).
– ORIGIN from Latin *malleus* 'hammer'.
maulstick ● **noun** a light stick with a padded leather ball at one end, held by a painter to support and steady the brush hand.
– ORIGIN Dutch *maalstok* 'paint stick'.
maunder ● **verb** move, talk, or act in a rambling or aimless manner.
– ORIGIN perhaps from obsolete *maunder* 'to beg'.
Maundy ● **noun** a public ceremony on the Thursday before Easter (**Maundy Thursday**) at which the British monarch distributes specially minted coins (**Maundy money**) to a group of people.
– ORIGIN Old French *mande*, from Latin *mandatum novum* 'new commandment' (referring to Christ's words in the Gospel of John, chapter 13).
Mauritanian /moritayniən/ ● **noun** a person from Mauritania, a country in West Africa. ● **adjective** relating to Mauritania.
Mauritian /mərish'n/ ● **noun** a person from the island of Mauritius in the Indian Ocean. ● **adjective** relating to Mauritius.
mausoleum /mawsəleeəm/ ● **noun** (pl. **mausolea** /mawsəleeə/ or **mausoleums**) a building housing a tomb or tombs.
– ORIGIN Greek *Mausōleion*, from *Mausōlos*, the name of a king of the 4th century BC to whose tomb the name was originally applied.
mauve ● **noun** a pale purple colour.
– ORIGIN French, 'mallow', from Latin *malva*.
maven /mayv'n/ ● **noun** N. Amer. informal an expert or connoisseur.
– ORIGIN Yiddish.
maverick ● **noun 1** an unorthodox or independent-minded person. **2** N. Amer. an unbranded calf or yearling.
– ORIGIN from Samuel A. *Maverick*, a 19th-century Texas rancher who did not brand his cattle.
maw ● **noun** the jaws or throat, especially of a voracious animal.
– ORIGIN Old English.
mawkish ● **adjective 1** sentimental in a feeble or sickly way. **2** archaic or dialect having a faint sickly flavour.
– ORIGIN from obsolete *mawk* 'maggot'.
max ● **abbreviation** maximum.
maxi ● **noun** (pl. **maxis**) a skirt or coat reaching to the ankle.
maxilla /maksillə/ ● **noun** (pl. **maxillae** /maksillee/) **1** Anatomy the bone of the upper jaw. **2** Zoology (in arthropods) each of a pair of chewing mouthparts.
– DERIVATIVES **maxillary** adjective.
– ORIGIN Latin, 'jaw'.
maxim ● **noun** a short statement expressing a general truth or rule of conduct.
– ORIGIN from Latin *propositio maxima* 'most important proposition'.
maximize (also **maximise**) ● **verb 1** make as great or large as possible. **2** make the best use of.
– DERIVATIVES **maximization** noun **maximizer** noun.
maximum ● **noun** (pl. **maxima** or **maximums**) the greatest amount, size, or intensity possible or attained. ● **adjective** greatest in amount, size, or intensity.
– DERIVATIVES **maximal** adjective.
– ORIGIN Latin, 'greatest thing'.
maxwell ● **noun** Physics a unit used in measuring the strength of a magnetic field.
– ORIGIN named after the Scottish physicist J. C. *Maxwell* (1831–79).
May ● **noun 1** the fifth month of the year. **2** (**may**) the hawthorn or its blossom.
– ORIGIN from Latin *Maius mensis* 'month of the goddess *Maia*'.
may ● **modal verb** (3rd sing. present **may**; past **might**) **1** expressing possibility. **2** expressing permission. **3** expressing a wish or hope.
– PHRASES **be that as it may** nevertheless.
– USAGE When expressing or asking permission, *may* is regarded as more correct (and more polite) than *can*, so that it is better to say *May we leave now?* rather than *Can we leave now?* The verb *can* should be used to express ability or capability (*can he move?* = is he physically able to move?; *may he move?* = is he allowed to move?).
– ORIGIN Old English.
Maya /mīyə/ ● **noun** (pl. same or **Mayas**) a member of a Central American people whose civilization died out *c.*900 AD.
– DERIVATIVES **Mayan** adjective & noun.

Thesaurus

businesslike, commonsensical, level-headed, hard-headed, no-nonsense, factual, literal, straightforward, plain, unembellished, unvarnished, unadorned.
mature ● **adjective 1** *a mature woman* ADULT, grown-up, grown, fully grown, full-grown, of age, fully developed, in one's prime. **2** *he's very mature for his age* SENSIBLE, responsible, adult, level-headed, reliable, dependable; wise, discriminating, shrewd, sophisticated. **3** *mature cheese* RIPE, ripened, mellow; ready to eat/drink. **4** *on mature reflection, he decided not to go* CAREFUL, thorough, deep, considered.
– OPPOSITES adolescent, childish.
● **verb 1** *kittens mature when they are about a year old* BE FULLY GROWN, be full-grown; come of age, reach adulthood, reach maturity. **2** *he's matured since he left home* GROW UP, become more sensible/adult; blossom. **3** *leave the cheese to mature* RIPEN, mellow; age. **4** *their friendship didn't have time to mature* DEVELOP, grow, evolve, bloom, blossom, flourish, thrive.
maturity ● **noun 1** *her progress from childhood to maturity* ADULTHOOD, majority, coming-of-age, manhood/womanhood. **2** *he displayed a maturity beyond his years* RESPONSIBILITY, sense, level-headedness; wisdom, discrimination, shrewdness, sophistication.
maudlin ● **adjective 1** *maudlin self-pity* SENTIMENTAL, over-sentimental, emotional, over-emotional, tearful, lachrymose; informal weepy. **2** *a maudlin ballad* MAWKISH, sentimental, over-sentimental; Brit. twee; informal mushy, slushy, sloppy, schmaltzy, cheesy, corny, toe-curling; Brit. informal soppy; N. Amer. informal cornball, three-hankie.
maul ● **verb 1** *he had been mauled by a lion* SAVAGE, attack, tear to pieces, lacerate, claw, scratch. **2** *she hated being mauled by men* MOLEST, feel, fondle, manhandle; informal grope, paw, touch up. **3** *his book was mauled by the critics.* See CRITICIZE.
maunder ● **verb 1** *he maundered on about his problems* RAMBLE, prattle, blather, blether, rattle, chatter, jabber, babble; informal yak, yatter; Brit. informal rabbit, witter, waffle, natter, chunter. **2** *she maundered across the road* WANDER, drift, meander, amble, potter; Brit. informal mooch.
mausoleum ● **noun** TOMB, sepulchre, crypt, vault, charnel house, burial chamber, catacomb, undercroft.
maverick ● **noun** INDIVIDUALIST, nonconformist, free spirit, unorthodox person, original, eccentric; rebel, dissenter, dissident.
– OPPOSITES conformist.
maw ● **noun** MOUTH, jaws, muzzle; throat, gullet; informal trap, chops, kisser; Brit. informal gob.
mawkish ● **adjective** SENTIMENTAL, over-sentimental, maudlin, cloying, sickly, saccharine, sugary, syrupy, nauseating; Brit. twee; informal mushy, slushy, sloppy, schmaltzy, weepy, cutesy, lovey-dovey, cheesy, corny, sick-making, toe-curling; Brit. informal soppy; N. Amer. informal cornball, hokey, three-hankie.
maxim ● **noun** SAYING, adage, aphorism, proverb, motto, saw, axiom, apophthegm, dictum, precept, epigram; truism, cliché.
maximum ● **adjective** *the maximum amount* GREATEST, highest, biggest, largest, top, topmost, most, utmost, maximal.
– OPPOSITES minimum.
● **noun** *production levels are near their maximum* UPPER LIMIT, limit,

– ORIGIN the name in Maya.
maybe ● adverb perhaps; possibly.
May Day ● noun 1 May, celebrated as a springtime festival or as a day honouring workers.
Mayday ● noun an international radio distress signal used by ships and aircraft.
– ORIGIN from the pronunciation of French *m'aidez* 'help me'.
mayflower ● noun a North American plant of the heather family with clusters of pink or white flowers.
mayfly ● noun a slender insect with transparent wings which lives as an adult for only a very short time.
mayhem ● noun violent disorder; chaos.
– ORIGIN originally meaning 'the crime of maliciously injuring someone': from Old French, related to MAIM.
mayn't ● contraction may not.
mayonnaise /mayənayz/ ● noun a thick creamy dressing made from egg yolks, oil, and vinegar.
– ORIGIN French, meaning 'from Port *Mahon*' (the capital of Minorca).
mayor ● noun the elected head of a city or borough council.
– DERIVATIVES **mayoral** adjective **mayorship** noun.
– ORIGIN from Latin *major* 'greater'.
mayoralty ● noun (pl. **mayoralties**) the period or term of office of a mayor.
mayoress ● noun **1** the wife of a mayor. **2** a woman elected as mayor.
maypole ● noun a decorated pole with long ribbons attached to the top, traditionally used for dancing round on May Day.
mayweed ● noun a wild chamomile found as a weed of waste ground.
– ORIGIN from *maythen*, an earlier name for this plant.
maze ● noun **1** a puzzle consisting of a network of paths and walls or hedges through which one has to find a way. **2** a confusing mass of information.
– ORIGIN originally denoting delusion: related to AMAZE.
mazel tov /mazəl tov/ ● exclamation (among Jews) congratulations; good luck.
– ORIGIN modern Hebrew, 'good star'.
mazurka ● noun a lively Polish dance in triple time.
– ORIGIN Polish, referring to a woman from the province of Mazovia.
MB ● abbreviation **1** Bachelor of Medicine. [ORIGIN Latin *Medicinae Baccalaureus*.] **2** Manitoba. **3** (also **Mb**) Computing megabyte(s).
MBA ● abbreviation Master of Business Administration.
MBE ● abbreviation Member of the Order of the British Empire.
MBO ● abbreviation management buyout.
MC ● abbreviation **1** Master of Ceremonies. **2** (in the US) Member of Congress. **3** Military Cross.
MCC ● abbreviation Marylebone Cricket Club.
McCarthyism ● noun a campaign against alleged communists in the US government and other institutions carried out under Senator Joseph McCarthy from 1950–4.
– DERIVATIVES **McCarthyite** adjective & noun.
McCoy ● noun (in phrase **the real McCoy**) informal the real thing; the genuine article.
– ORIGIN origin uncertain: perhaps from *the real Mackay*, an advertising slogan used by the whisky distillers G. Mackay and Co.; the form *McCoy* may come from the name of the American inventor Elijah *McCoy*.
McGuffin ● noun an object or device in a film or a book which serves merely as a trigger for the plot.
– ORIGIN a Scottish surname, said to have been borrowed by the English film director Alfred Hitchcock from a humorous story involving such a pivotal factor.
m-commerce ● noun commercial transactions conducted electronically by mobile phone.
MD ● abbreviation **1** Doctor of Medicine. [ORIGIN Latin *Medicinae Doctor*.] **2** Brit. Managing Director. **3** Maryland.
Md ● symbol the chemical element mendelevium.
MDF ● abbreviation medium density fibreboard.
MDMA ● abbreviation methylenedioxymethamphetamine, the drug Ecstasy.
ME ● abbreviation **1** Maine. **2** myalgic encephalomyelitis.
me¹ ● pronoun (first person sing.) **1** used as the object of a verb or preposition or after 'than', 'as', or the verb 'to be', to refer to the speaker himself or herself. **2** N. Amer. informal to or for myself.
– USAGE The pronoun *me* should be used as the object of a verb or preposition, as in *John hates me* or *Come with me!* It is wrong to use *me* as the subject of a verb, as in *John and me went to the shops*; in this case *I* should be used instead.
– ORIGIN Old English.
me² (also **mi**) ● noun Music the third note of a major scale, coming after 'ray' and before 'fah'.
– ORIGIN *mi*, an arbitrary name for the note, taken from the first syllable of *mira*, in a Latin hymn.
mea culpa /mayə kulpə/ ● noun an acknowledgement that one is at fault.
– ORIGIN Latin, 'by my fault'.
mead¹ ● noun an alcoholic drink of fermented honey and water.
– ORIGIN Old English.
mead² ● noun literary a meadow.
meadow ● noun **1** an area of grassland, especially one used for hay. **2** a piece of low ground near a river.
– ORIGIN Old English, related to MOW.
meadowlark ● noun an American songbird, typically brown with yellow and black underparts.
meadow saffron ● noun a poisonous lilac-flowered autumn crocus.
meadowsweet ● noun a tall meadow plant with heads of creamy-white fragrant flowers.
meagre (US **meager**) ● adjective **1** lacking in quantity or quality. **2** lean; thin.
– DERIVATIVES **meagreness** noun.
– ORIGIN Old French *maigre*, from Latin *macer*.
meal¹ ● noun **1** any of the regular daily occasions when food is eaten. **2** the food eaten on such an occasion.
– PHRASES **make a meal of** Brit. informal carry out (a task) with unnecessary effort.
– ORIGIN Old English.
meal² ● noun **1** the edible part of any grain or pulse ground to powder; flour. **2** any powdery substance made by grinding.
– ORIGIN Old English.
meal beetle ● noun a dark brown beetle which is a pest of stored grain and cereal products.
mealie ● noun chiefly S. African a maize plant or cob.
– ORIGIN Afrikaans *mielie*, from Portuguese *milho* 'maize, millet'.
meal ticket ● noun a person or thing that is exploited as a source of income.
mealworm ● noun the larva of the meal beetle.
mealy ● adjective (**mealier**, **mealiest**) **1** of, like, or containing meal. **2** pale in colour.
mealy bug ● noun a small sap-sucking scale insect which is coated with a white powdery wax resembling meal and which can be a serious pest.
mealy-mouthed ● adjective reluctant to speak frankly.
– ORIGIN perhaps from German *Mehl im Maule behalten* 'carry meal in the mouth' (i.e. be unstraightforward in speech), or related to Latin *mel* 'honey'.
mean¹ ● verb (past and past part. **meant**) **1** intend to express or refer to. **2** (of a word) have as its explanation in the same lan-

Thesaurus

utmost, uttermost, greatest, most, extremity, peak, height, ceiling, top.
– OPPOSITES minimum.
maybe ● adverb PERHAPS, possibly, conceivably, it could be, it is possible, for all one knows; *N. English* happen; *poetic/literary* peradventure, perchance.
mayhem ● noun CHAOS, disorder, havoc, bedlam, pandemonium, tumult, uproar, turmoil, commotion, all hell broken loose, maelstrom, trouble, disturbance, confusion, riot, anarchy, violence; *informal* madhouse.
maze ● noun LABYRINTH, complex network, warren; web, tangle, jungle, snarl.
meadow ● noun FIELD, paddock; pasture, pastureland; *poetic/literary* lea, mead.
meagre ● adjective **1** *their meagre earnings* INADEQUATE, scanty, scant, paltry, limited, restricted, modest, insufficient, sparse, deficient, negligible, skimpy, slender, poor, miserable, pitiful, puny, miserly, niggardly, beggarly; *informal* measly, stingy, pathetic, piddling; *formal* exiguous. **2** *a tall, meagre man* THIN, lean, skinny, spare, scrawny, scraggy, gangling, gangly, spindly, stringy, bony, raw-boned, gaunt, underweight, underfed, undernourished, emaciated, skeletal, cadaverous.
– OPPOSITES abundant, fat.
meal ● noun snack; feast, banquet; *informal* bite (to eat), spread,

guage or its equivalent in another language. **3** intend to occur or be the case. **4** have as a consequence. **5** intend or design for a particular purpose. **6** be of specified importance.
– PHRASES **mean business** be in earnest. **mean well** have good intentions, but not always carry them out.
– ORIGIN Old English.

mean² ● adjective **1** unwilling to give or share; not generous. **2** unkind or unfair. **3** vicious or aggressive. **4** poor in quality and appearance; inferior. **5** dated of low birth or social class. **6** informal excellent.
– DERIVATIVES **meanly** adverb **meanness** noun.
– ORIGIN originally in the sense 'common to two or more persons': from Old English.

mean³ ● noun **1** the average or central value of a set of quantities. **2** something in the middle of two extremes. ● adjective **1** calculated as a mean. **2** equally far from two extremes.
– ORIGIN Latin *medianus* 'middle'.

meander /miandər/ ● verb **1** follow a winding course. **2** wander in a leisurely or aimless way. ● noun a winding bend of a river or road.
– ORIGIN Greek, from the name of the winding river *Maeander* in SW Turkey.

meaning ● noun **1** what is meant by a word, idea, or action. **2** worthwhile quality; purpose. ● adjective expressive.

meaningful ● adjective **1** having meaning. **2** worthwhile. **3** expressive.
– DERIVATIVES **meaningfully** adverb **meaningfulness** noun.

meaningless ● adjective having no meaning or significance.
– DERIVATIVES **meaninglessly** adverb **meaninglessness** noun.

means ● plural noun (also treated as sing.) **1** an agent or method for achieving a result. **2** financial resources; income. **3** substantial resources; wealth.
– PHRASES **by all means** of course. **by means of** by using. **by no means** certainly not. **a means to an end** a thing that is not valued in itself but is useful in achieving an aim.
– ORIGIN plural of MEAN³, the early sense being 'intermediary'.

means-test ● verb subject to or base on a means test. ● noun (**means test**) an official investigation of a person's finances to determine whether the person qualifies for state assistance.

meant past and past participle of MEAN¹.

meantime ● adverb (also **in the meantime**) meanwhile.

meanwhile ● adverb **1** (also **in the meanwhile**) in the intervening period of time. **2** at the same time.

measles ● plural noun (treated as sing.) an infectious disease spread by a virus, causing fever and a red rash.
– ORIGIN probably from Dutch *masel* 'spot'.

measly ● adjective (**measlier**, **measliest**) informal ridiculously small or few.

measure ● verb **1** determine the size, amount, or degree of (something) by comparison with a standard unit. **2** be of (a specified size). **3** (**measure out**) take an exact quantity of. **4** (**measure up**) reach the required or expected standard. ● noun **1** a means of achieving a purpose. **2** a legislative bill. **3** a standard unit used to express size, amount, or degree. **4** a measuring device marked with such units. **5** (**a measure of**) a certain amount or degree of. **6** (**a measure of**) an indication of the extent or quality of. **7** (**measures**) a group of rock strata. **8** a metrical unit or group in poetry.

Thesaurus

m

blowout, feed; *Brit. informal* nosh-up; *formal* repast, collation; *poetic/literary* refection.
– RELATED TERMS prandial.

mean¹ ● verb **1** *flashing lights mean the road is blocked* SIGNIFY, convey, denote, designate, indicate, connote, show, express, spell out; stand for, represent, symbolize; imply, suggest, intimate, hint at, insinuate, drive at, refer to, allude to; *poetic/literary* betoken. **2** *she didn't mean to break it* INTEND, aim, plan, design, have in mind, contemplate, purpose, propose, set out, aspire, desire, want, wish, expect. **3** *he was hit by a bullet meant for a soldier* INTEND, design; destine, predestine. **4** *the closures will mean a rise in unemployment* ENTAIL, involve, necessitate, lead to, result in, give rise to, bring about, cause, engender, produce. **5** *this means a lot to me* MATTER, be important, be significant. **6** *a red sky in the morning usually means rain* PRESAGE, portend, foretell, augur, promise, foreshadow, herald, signal, bode; *poetic/literary* betoken, foretoken.

mean² ● adjective **1** *he's too mean to leave a tip* MISERLY, niggardly, close-fisted, parsimonious, penny-pinching, cheese-paring, Scrooge-like; *informal* tight-fisted, stingy, tight, mingy, money-grubbing; *N. Amer. informal* cheap; *formal* penurious; *archaic* near, niggard. **2** *a mean trick* UNKIND, nasty, unpleasant, spiteful, malicious, unfair, cruel, shabby, foul, despicable, contemptible, obnoxious, vile, odious, loathsome, base, low; *informal* horrible, horrid, hateful, rotten, low-down; *Brit. informal* beastly. **3** *the truth was obvious to even the meanest intelligence* INFERIOR, poor, limited, restricted. **4** *her flat was mean and cold* SQUALID, shabby, dilapidated, sordid, seedy, slummy, sleazy, insalubrious, wretched, dismal, dingy, miserable, run down, down at heel; *informal* scruffy, scuzzy, crummy, grungy; *Brit. informal* grotty. **5** *a man of mean birth* LOWLY, humble, ordinary, low, low-born, modest, common, base, proletarian, plebeian, obscure, undistinguished, ignoble; *archaic* baseborn. **6** *(informal) he's a mean cook.* See EXCELLENT.
– OPPOSITES generous, kind, luxurious, noble.

mean³ ● noun *a mean between saving and splashing out* MIDDLE COURSE, middle way, midpoint, happy medium, golden mean, compromise, balance; median, norm, average.
● adjective *the mean temperature* AVERAGE, median, middle, medial, medium, normal, standard.

meander ● verb **1** *the river meandered gently through the meadow* ZIGZAG, wind, twist, turn, curve, curl, bend, snake. **2** *we meandered along the path* STROLL, saunter, amble, wander, ramble, drift, maunder; *Scottish* stravaig; *informal* mosey, tootle.

meandering ● adjective **1** *a meandering stream* WINDING, windy, zigzag, twisting, turning, curving, serpentine, sinuous, twisty. **2** *meandering reminiscences* RAMBLING, maundering, circuitous, roundabout, digressive, discursive, indirect, tortuous, convoluted.
– OPPOSITES straight, succinct.

meaning ● noun **1** *the meaning of his remark* SIGNIFICANCE, sense, signification, import, thrust, drift, gist, implication, tenor, message, essence, substance, purport, intention. **2** *the word has several different meanings* DEFINITION, sense, explanation, denotation, connotation, interpretation. **3** *my life has no meaning* VALUE, validity, worth, consequence, account, use, usefulness, significance, point. **4** *his smile was full of meaning* EXPRESSIVENESS, significance, eloquence, implications, insinuations.
– RELATED TERMS semantic.
● adjective *a meaning look.* See MEANINGFUL sense 3.

meaningful ● adjective **1** *a meaningful remark* SIGNIFICANT, relevant, important, consequential, telling, material, valid, worthwhile. **2** *a meaningful relationship* SINCERE, deep, serious, in earnest, significant, important. **3** *a meaningful glance* EXPRESSIVE, eloquent, pointed, significant, meaning; pregnant, speaking, telltale, revealing, suggestive.
– OPPOSITES inconsequential.

meaningless ● adjective **1** *a jumble of meaningless words* UNINTELLIGIBLE, incomprehensible, incoherent. **2** *she felt her life was meaningless* FUTILE, pointless, aimless, empty, hollow, vain, purposeless, valueless, useless, of no use, worthless, senseless, trivial, trifling, unimportant, insignificant, inconsequential.
– OPPOSITES worthwhile.

means ● plural noun **1** *the best means to achieve your goal* METHOD, way, manner, mode, measure, technique, expedient, agency, medium, instrument, channel, vehicle, avenue, course, process, procedure. **2** *she doesn't have the means to support herself* MONEY, resources, capital, income, finance, funds, cash, the wherewithal, assets; *informal* dough, bread; *Brit. informal* dosh, brass, lolly, spondulicks, ackers. **3** *a man of means* WEALTH, riches, affluence, substance, fortune, property, money, capital.
– PHRASES **by all means** OF COURSE, certainly, definitely, surely, absolutely, with pleasure; *N. Amer. informal* sure thing. **by means of** USING, utilizing, employing, through, with the help of; as a result of, by dint of, by way of, by virtue of. **by no means** NOT AT ALL, in no way, not in the least, not in the slightest, not the least bit, not by a long shot, certainly not, absolutely not, definitely not, on no account, under no circumstances; *Brit.* not by a long chalk; *informal* no way.

meantime ● adverb. See MEANWHILE.

meanwhile ● adverb **1** *meanwhile, I'll stay here* FOR NOW, for the moment, for the present, for the time being, meantime, in the meantime, in the interim, in the interval. **2** *cook for a further half hour; meanwhile, make the stuffing* AT THE SAME TIME, simultaneously, concurrently, the while.

measurable ● adjective **1** *a measurable amount* QUANTIFIABLE, assessable, gaugeable, computable. **2** *a measurable improvement* AP-

– PHRASES **for good measure** as an amount or item beyond that which is strictly required. **have the measure of** understand the character or abilities of.
– DERIVATIVES **measurable** adjective **measurably** adverb.
– ORIGIN Latin *mensura*, from *metiri* 'to measure'.
measured ● adjective **1** slow and regular in rhythm. **2** carefully considered and restrained.
measureless ● adjective literary having no limits.
measurement ● noun **1** the action of measuring. **2** an amount, size, or extent found by measuring. **3** a standard unit used in measuring.
meat ● noun **1** the flesh of an animal as food. **2** the main substance or chief part: *let's get to the meat of the matter.*
– PHRASES **easy meat** informal a person who is easily overcome or outwitted. **one man's meat is another man's poison** proverb things liked or enjoyed by one person may be distasteful to another.
– ORIGIN Old English, 'food', 'article of food'.
meatball ● noun a ball of minced or chopped meat.
meat loaf ● noun minced or chopped meat baked in the shape of a loaf.
meatspace ● noun Computing the physical world as opposed to cyberspace or another virtual environment.
meatus /miaytuss/ ● noun (pl. same or **meatuses**) Anatomy a passage or opening leading into the body.
– ORIGIN Latin, 'passage'.
meaty ● adjective (**meatier**, **meatiest**) **1** resembling or full of meat. **2** fleshy or muscular. **3** substantial.
– DERIVATIVES **meatiness** noun.
Mecca ● noun a place which attracts many people of a particular group or with a particular interest.
– ORIGIN from the city of *Mecca* in Saudi Arabia, the holiest city for Muslims.
mechanic ● noun a skilled worker who repairs and maintains machinery.
– ORIGIN Greek, from *mēkhanē* 'machine'.
mechanical ● adjective **1** relating to or operated by a machine or machinery. **2** lacking thought or spontaneity. **3** relating to physical forces or motion.
– DERIVATIVES **mechanically** adverb.
mechanical advantage ● noun the ratio of the force produced by a machine to the force applied to it.
mechanical drawing ● noun a scale drawing done with precision instruments.
mechanical engineering ● noun the branch of engineering concerned with the design, construction, and use of machines.
mechanics ● plural noun **1** (treated as sing.) the branch of study concerned with motion and forces producing motion. **2** machinery or working parts. **3** the physical or practical aspects of something.
mechanism ● noun **1** a piece of machinery. **2** the way in which something works or is brought about.
mechanistic ● adjective Philosophy relating to the idea that all natural processes can be explained in purely physical or deterministic terms.
mechanize (also **mechanise**) ● verb equip with or make reliant on machines or automatic devices.
– DERIVATIVES **mechanization** noun.
meconium /mikōniəm/ ● noun Medicine the dark green substance forming the first faeces of a newborn infant.
– ORIGIN Latin, 'poppy juice'.
med. ● abbreviation **1** medium. **2** informal medical.
medal ● noun a metal disc with an inscription or design, awarded for achievement or to commemorate an event.
– ORIGIN Latin *medalia* 'half a denarius'.
medallion ● noun **1** a piece of jewellery in the shape of a medal, worn as a pendant. **2** a decorative oval or circular painting, panel, or design.
medallist (US **medalist**) ● noun a person awarded a medal.
meddle ● verb interfere in something that is not one's concern.
– DERIVATIVES **meddler** noun **meddlesome** adjective.
– ORIGIN Old French, from Latin *miscere* 'to mix'.
Mede /meed/ ● noun a member of a people who inhabited ancient Media (present-day Azerbaijan, NW Iran, and NE Iraq).

Thesaurus

m

PRECIABLE, noticeable, significant, visible, perceptible, definite, obvious.
measure ● verb **1** *they measured the length of the room* CALCULATE, compute, count, meter, quantify, weigh, size, evaluate, assess, gauge, plumb, determine. **2** *I had better measure my words* CHOOSE CAREFULLY, consider, plan. **3** *she did not need to measure herself against some ideal* COMPARE WITH, pit against, set against, test against, judge by.
● noun **1** *cost-cutting measures* ACTION, act, course (of action), deed, proceeding, procedure, step, means, expedient; manoeuvre, initiative, programme, operation. **2** *the Senate passed the measure* STATUTE, act, bill, law, legislation. **3** *the original dimensions were in imperial measure* SYSTEM, standard, units, scale. **4** *use a measure to check the size* RULER, tape measure, rule, gauge, meter, scale, level, yardstick. **5** *a measure of egg white* QUANTITY, amount, portion. **6** *the states retain a measure of independence* CERTAIN AMOUNT, degree; some. **7** *sales are the measure of the company's success* YARDSTICK, test, standard, barometer, touchstone, litmus test, criterion, benchmark. **8** *poetic measure* METRE, cadence, rhythm; foot.
– PHRASES **beyond measure** IMMENSELY, extremely, vastly, greatly, excessively, immeasurably, incalculably, infinitely. **for good measure** AS A BONUS, as an extra, into the bargain, to boot, in addition, besides, as well. **get/have the measure of** EVALUATE, assess, gauge, judge, weigh up; understand, fathom, read, be wise to, see through; informal have someone's number. **measure something off** MARK OFF, measure out, demarcate, delimit, delineate, outline, describe, define, stake out. **measure up** PASS MUSTER, match up, come up to standard, fit/fill the bill, be acceptable; informal come up to scratch, make the grade, cut the mustard, be up to snuff. **measure someone up** EVALUATE, rate, assess, appraise, judge, weigh up; informal size up. **measure up to** MEET, come up to, equal, match, bear comparison with, be on a level with; achieve, satisfy, fulfil.
measured ● adjective **1** *his measured tread* REGULAR, steady, even, rhythmic, rhythmical, unfaltering; slow, dignified, stately, sedate, leisurely, unhurried. **2** *his measured tones* THOUGHTFUL, careful, carefully chosen, studied, calculated, planned, considered, deliberate, restrained.
measureless ● adjective BOUNDLESS, limitless, unlimited, unbounded, untold, immense, vast, endless, inexhaustible, infinite, illimitable, immeasurable, incalculable.
measurement ● noun **1** *measurement of the effect is difficult* QUANTIFICATION, computation, calculation, mensuration; evaluation, assessment, gauging. **2** *all measurements are given in metric form* SIZE, dimension, proportions, magnitude, amplitude; mass, bulk, volume, capacity, extent; value, amount, quantity, area, length, height, depth, weight, width, range.
meat ● noun **1** FLESH, animal flesh. **2** (archaic) *meat and drink* FOOD, nourishment, sustenance, provisions, rations, fare, foodstuff(s), provender, daily bread; informal grub, eats, chow, nosh; Brit. informal scoff; formal comestibles; dated victuals; poetic/literary viands; archaic commons. **3** *the meat of the matter* SUBSTANCE, pith, marrow, heart, kernel, core, nucleus, nub, essence, essentials, gist, fundamentals, basics; informal nitty-gritty.
meaty ● adjective **1** *a tall, meaty young man* BEEFY, brawny, burly, muscular, muscly, powerful, sturdy, strapping, well built, solidly built, thickset; fleshy, stout. **2** *a good, meaty story* INTERESTING, thought-provoking, three-dimensional, stimulating; substantial, satisfying, meaningful, deep, profound.
mechanical ● adjective **1** *a mechanical device* MECHANIZED, machine-driven, automated, automatic, power-driven, robotic. **2** *a mechanical response* AUTOMATIC, unthinking, robotic, involuntary, reflex, knee-jerk, habitual, routine, unemotional, unfeeling, lifeless; perfunctory, cursory, careless, casual.
– OPPOSITES manual, conscious.
mechanism ● noun **1** *an electrical mechanism* MACHINE, piece of machinery, appliance, apparatus, device, instrument, contraption, gadget; informal gizmo. **2** *the train's safety mechanism* MACHINERY, workings, works, movement, action, gears, components. **3** *a formal mechanism for citizens to lodge complaints* PROCEDURE, process, system, operation, method, technique, means, medium, agency, channel.
mechanize ● verb AUTOMATE, industrialize, motorize, computerize.
medal ● noun DECORATION, ribbon, star, badge, laurel, palm, award; honour; Military slang fruit salad; Brit. informal gong.
meddle ● verb **1** *don't meddle in my affairs* INTERFERE, butt in, intrude, intervene, pry; informal poke one's nose in, horn in on, muscle in on, snoop, put/stick one's oar in; N. Amer. informal kibitz. **2** *someone had been meddling with her things* FIDDLE, interfere, tamper, tinker, finger; Brit. informal muck about/around.

media ● noun **1** the means of mass communication, especially television, radio, and newspapers collectively. **2** plural of MEDIUM.
– USAGE The word **media** comes from the Latin plural of **medium**. In the normal sense 'television, radio, and the press collectively', it often behaves as a collective noun (for example like **staff**), and can be used with either a singular or a plural verb. Although some people regard the singular use as incorrect, it is now generally accepted in standard English.
mediaeval ● adjective variant spelling of MEDIEVAL.
medial ● adjective situated in the middle.
– DERIVATIVES **medially** adverb.
– ORIGIN originally in the sense 'relating to the average': from Latin *medialis*, from *medius* 'middle'.
median ● adjective **1** technical situated in the middle. **2** referring to the middle term (or mean of the middle two terms) of a series of values arranged in order of magnitude. ● noun **1** a median value. **2** Geometry a straight line drawn from one of the angles of a triangle to the middle of the opposite side.
– ORIGIN Latin *medianus*, from *medius* 'middle'.
mediate ● verb **1** try to settle a dispute between two other parties. **2** technical be a medium for (a process or effect).
– DERIVATIVES **mediation** noun **mediator** noun.
– ORIGIN Latin *mediare* 'place in the middle'.
medic ● noun informal a medical practitioner or student.
medical ● adjective relating to the science or practice of medicine. ● noun an examination to assess a person's physical health.
– DERIVATIVES **medically** adverb.
– ORIGIN from Latin *medicus* 'physician'.
medical officer ● noun a doctor in charge of the health services of a local authority or other organization.
medicament /midikkəmənt/ ● noun a medicine.
medicate ● verb **1** administer medicine or a drug to. **2** (**medicated**) containing a medicinal substance.
– ORIGIN Latin *medicari* 'administer remedies to'.
medication ● noun **1** a medicine or drug. **2** treatment with medicines.
Medicean /meddicheeən, medeechiən/ ● adjective relating to the Medici, a powerful Italian family who effectively ruled Florence in the 15th century.
medicinal ● adjective **1** having healing properties. **2** relating to medicines.
– DERIVATIVES **medicinally** adverb.
medicine ● noun **1** the science or practice of the treatment and prevention of disease. **2** a drug or other preparation taken by mouth in order to treat or prevent disease.
– PHRASES **give someone a dose of their own medicine** treat someone in the same unpleasant way that they treated others.
– ORIGIN from Latin *medicus* 'physician'.
medicine ball ● noun a large, heavy solid ball thrown and caught for exercise.
medicine man ● noun (among North American Indians) a shaman.
– ORIGIN from *medicine* in the sense 'spell or charm believed to have healing or magical power'.
medico ● noun (pl. **medicos**) another term for MEDIC.
medieval (also **mediaeval**) ● adjective **1** relating to the Middle Ages. **2** informal very old-fashioned or outdated.
– DERIVATIVES **medievalize** (also **medievalise**) verb **medievally** adverb.
– ORIGIN from Latin *medium aevum* 'middle age'.
medievalist (also **medievalist**) ● noun a scholar of medieval history or literature.
medina /medeenə/ ● noun the old quarter of a North African town.
– ORIGIN Arabic, 'town'.
mediocracy ● noun (pl. **mediocracies**) a dominant class consisting of mediocre people.
mediocre /meediōkər/ ● adjective of only average or fairly low quality.
– ORIGIN Latin *mediocris* 'of middle height or degree' (literally 'somewhat rugged or mountainous'), from *medius* 'middle' + *ocris* 'rugged mountain'.
mediocrity ● noun (pl. **mediocrities**) **1** the quality or state of being mediocre. **2** a person of mediocre ability.
meditate ● verb **1** focus one's mind for a time for spiritual purposes or for relaxation. **2** (**meditate on/about**) think carefully about.
– ORIGIN Latin *meditari* 'contemplate', related to METE[1].
meditation ● noun **1** the action or practice of meditating. **2** a discourse expressing considered thoughts on a subject.
meditative ● adjective involving or absorbed in meditation.
– DERIVATIVES **meditatively** adverb.
Mediterranean ● adjective relating to the Mediterranean Sea or the countries around it.
– ORIGIN Latin *mediterraneus* 'inland', from *medius* 'middle' + *terra* 'land'.
Mediterranean climate ● noun a climate that has warm, wet winters and calm, hot, dry summers.
medium ● noun (pl. **media** or **mediums**) **1** a means by which something is expressed, communicated, or achieved. **2** a substance through which a force or other influence is transmitted. **3** a form of storage for computer software, such as magnetic tape or disks. **4** a liquid with which pigments are mixed to make paint. **5** (pl. **mediums**) a person claiming to be able to communicate between the dead and the living. **6** the middle state between two extremes. ● adjective between two extremes; average.
– ORIGIN Latin, 'middle'.

m

Thesaurus

meddlesome ● adjective INTERFERING, meddling, intrusive, prying, busybody; *informal* nosy, nosy-parker.
mediate ● verb **1** *Austria tried to mediate between the belligerents* ARBITRATE, conciliate, moderate, act as peacemaker, make peace; intervene, step in, intercede, act as an intermediary, liaise. **2** *a tribunal was set up to mediate disputes* RESOLVE, settle, arbitrate in, umpire, reconcile, referee; mend, clear up; *informal* patch up. **3** *he attempted to mediate a solution to the conflict* NEGOTIATE, bring about, effect; *formal* effectuate.
mediation ● noun ARBITRATION, conciliation, reconciliation, intervention, intercession, good offices; negotiation, shuttle diplomacy.
mediator ● noun ARBITRATOR, arbiter, negotiator, conciliator, peacemaker, go-between, middleman, intermediary, moderator, intervenor, intercessor, broker, honest broker, liaison officer; umpire, referee, adjudicator, judge.
medicinal ● adjective CURATIVE, healing, remedial, therapeutic, restorative, corrective, health-giving; medical; *archaic* sanative.
medicine ● noun MEDICATION, medicament, drug, prescription, dose, treatment, remedy, cure; nostrum, panacea, cure-all; *archaic* physic.
– RELATED TERMS pharmaceutical.
medieval ● adjective **1** *medieval times* OF THE MIDDLE AGES, of the Dark Ages, Dark-Age; Gothic. **2** *(informal) the plumbing's a bit medieval* PRIMITIVE, antiquated, archaic, antique, antediluvian, old-fashioned, out of date, outdated, outmoded, anachronistic, passé, obsolete; *informal* out of the ark; *N. Amer. informal* horse-and-buggy, clunky.
– OPPOSITES modern.
mediocre ● adjective ORDINARY, average, middling, middle-of-the-road, uninspired, undistinguished, indifferent, unexceptional, unexciting, unremarkable, run-of-the-mill, pedestrian, prosaic, lacklustre, forgettable, amateur, amateurish; *informal* OK, so-so, (plain) vanilla, fair-to-middling, no great shakes, not up to much; *Brit. informal* not much cop; *N. Amer. informal* bush-league; *NZ informal* half-pie.
– OPPOSITES excellent.
meditate ● verb CONTEMPLATE, think, consider, ponder, muse, reflect, deliberate, ruminate, chew the cud, brood, mull over; be in a brown study, be deep/lost in thought, debate with oneself; pray; *informal* put on one's thinking cap; *formal* cogitate.
meditation ● noun CONTEMPLATION, thought, thinking, musing, pondering, consideration, reflection, deliberation, rumination, brooding, reverie, brown study, concentration; prayer; *formal* cogitation.
meditative ● adjective PENSIVE, thoughtful, contemplative, reflective, musing, ruminative, introspective, brooding, deep/lost in thought, in a brown study; prayerful; *formal* cogitative.
medium ● noun **1** *using technology as a medium for job creation* MEANS, method, way, form, agency, avenue, channel, vehicle, organ, instrument, mechanism. **2** *organisms growing in their natural medium* HABITAT, element, environment, surroundings, milieu, setting, conditions. **3** *she consulted a medium* SPIRITUALIST, spiritist, necromancer. **4** *a happy medium* MIDDLE WAY, middle course, middle ground, middle, mean, median, midpoint; com-

medium frequency • noun (in radio) a frequency between 300 kilohertz and 3 megahertz.

medium wave • noun chiefly Brit. a radio wave of a frequency between 300 kilohertz and 3 megahertz.

medlar • noun a small brown apple-like fruit.
– ORIGIN Old French *medler*, from Greek *mespilē*.

medley • noun (pl. **medleys**) **1** a varied mixture. **2** a collection of songs or other musical items performed as a continuous piece.
– ORIGIN originally denoting hand-to-hand combat, also cloth made of variegated wool: from Old French *medlee* 'melee', from Latin *misculare* 'to mix'.

Medoc /maydok/ • noun a red wine produced in the Médoc area of SW France.

medulla /medullə/ • noun **1** Anatomy a distinct inner region of an organ or tissue. **2** Botany the soft internal tissue of a plant.
– ORIGIN Latin, 'pith or marrow'.

medulla oblongata /oblonggaatə/ • noun the part of the spinal cord extending into the brain.

medusa /midyōōzə/ • noun (pl. **medusae** /midyōōzee/ or **medusas**) Zoology the free-swimming stage in the life cycle of a jellyfish or related organism.
– ORIGIN from *Medusa*, a gorgon in Greek mythology with snakes in her hair.

meed • noun archaic a deserved share or reward.
– ORIGIN Old English.

meek • adjective quiet, gentle, and submissive.
– DERIVATIVES **meekly** adverb **meekness** noun.
– ORIGIN Old Norse, 'soft, gentle'.

meerkat • noun a small southern African mongoose.
– ORIGIN Dutch, 'sea cat': the name originally applied to a kind of monkey, perhaps with the notion 'from overseas'.

meerschaum /meershəm/ • noun **1** a soft white clay-like material. **2** a tobacco pipe with a bowl made from meerschaum.
– ORIGIN German, 'sea foam'.

meet[1] • verb (past and past part. **met**) **1** come together with at the same place and time. **2** see or be introduced to for the first time. **3** come into contact with; touch or join. **4** encounter (a situation). **5** (**meet with**) receive (a reaction). **6** fulfil or satisfy (a requirement). • noun a gathering or meeting, especially for races or foxhunting.
– ORIGIN Old English.

meet[2] • adjective archaic suitable or proper.
– ORIGIN originally in the sense 'made to fit'; related to METE.

meeting • noun **1** an organized gathering of people for a discussion or other purpose. **2** a coming together of two or more people.

mega • adjective informal **1** very large. **2** excellent.

mega- • combining form **1** large. **2** denoting a factor of one million (10^6).
– ORIGIN Greek *megas* 'great'.

megabucks • plural noun informal a huge sum of money.

megabyte • noun Computing a unit of information equal to one million or (strictly) 1,048,576 bytes.

megaflop • noun Computing a unit of computing speed equal to one million or (strictly) 1,048,576 floating-point operations per second.

megahertz • noun (pl. same) a unit of frequency equal to one million hertz.

megalith • noun a large stone that forms a prehistoric monument or part of one.
– DERIVATIVES **megalithic** adjective.

megalomania • noun **1** obsession with the exercise of power. **2** the delusion that one has great power or importance.
– DERIVATIVES **megalomaniac** noun & adjective.

megaphone • noun a large cone-shaped device for amplifying and directing the voice.

megapode /megəpōd/ • noun a large ground-dwelling Australasian or SE Asian bird that builds a large mound of plant debris to incubate its eggs.
– ORIGIN from Greek *pous* 'foot'.

megastar • noun informal a very famous entertainer or sports player.

megaton • noun a unit of explosive power equivalent to one million tons of TNT.

megawatt • noun a unit of electrical or other power equal to one million watts.

meiosis /mīōsiss/ • noun (pl. **meioses** /mīōseez/) **1** Biology a type of cell division that results in daughter cells each with half the number of chromosomes of the parent cell. Compare with MITOSIS. **2** another term for LITOTES.
– DERIVATIVES **meiotic** adjective.
– ORIGIN Greek *meiōsis* 'lessening'.

Meistersinger /mīstəsingər/ • noun (pl. same) a member of one of the guilds of German lyric poets and musicians which flourished from the 12th to 17th century.
– ORIGIN German, 'master singer'.

meitnerium /mītneeriəm/ • noun a very unstable chemical element made by high-energy atomic collisions.
– ORIGIN named after the Swedish physicist Lise *Meitner* (1878–1968).

melaleuca /meləlōōkə/ • noun an Australian shrub or tree which bears spikes of bottlebrush-like flowers.
– ORIGIN from Greek *melas* 'black' + *leukos* 'white' (because of the fire-blackened white bark of some species).

melamine /melləmeen/ • noun a hard plastic used chiefly for laminated coatings.
– ORIGIN from German *melam* (an arbitrary formation denoting an organic chemical compound), + AMINE.

melancholia /mellənkōliə/ • noun severe depression.

melancholy • noun deep and long-lasting sadness. • adjective sad or depressed.
– DERIVATIVES **melancholic** adjective.
– ORIGIN Greek *melankholia*, from *melas* 'black' + *kholē* 'bile', an excess of which was formerly believed to cause depression.

Melanesian • adjective relating to Melanesia in the western

m

Thesaurus

promise, golden mean.
• adjective *medium height* AVERAGE, middling, medium-sized, middle-sized, moderate, normal, standard.

medley • noun ASSORTMENT, miscellany, mixture, melange, variety, mixed bag, mix, collection, selection, pot-pourri, patchwork; motley collection, ragbag, gallimaufry, mishmash, hotchpotch, jumble; *N. Amer.* hodgepodge.

meek • adjective SUBMISSIVE, yielding, obedient, compliant, tame, biddable, tractable, acquiescent, deferential, timid, unprotesting, unresisting, like a lamb to the slaughter; quiet, mild, gentle, docile, lamblike, shy, diffident, unassuming, self-effacing.
– OPPOSITES assertive.

meet • verb **1** *I met an old friend on the train* ENCOUNTER, meet up with, come face to face with, run into/across, come across/upon, chance on, happen on, light on, stumble across/on; *informal* bump into. **2** *she first met Paul at a party* GET TO KNOW, be introduced to, make the acquaintance of. **3** *the committee met on Saturday* ASSEMBLE, gather, come together, get together, congregate, convene; *formal* foregather. **4** *the place where three roads meet* CONVERGE, connect, touch, link up, intersect, cross, join. **5** *he met death bravely* FACE, encounter, undergo, experience, go through, suffer, endure, bear; cope with, handle. **6** *the announcement was met with widespread hostility* GREET, receive, answer, treat. **7** *he does not meet the job's requirements* FULFIL, satisfy, fill, measure up to, match (up to), conform to, come up to, comply with, answer. **8** *shipowners would meet the cost of oil spills* PAY, settle, clear, honour, discharge, pay off, square.
• noun *an athletics meet.* See MEETING sense 5.
– PHRASES **meet someone halfway.** See HALFWAY.

meeting • noun **1** *he stood up to address the meeting* GATHERING, assembly, conference, congregation, convention, summit, forum, convocation, conclave, council of war, rally; *N. Amer.* caucus; *informal* get-together. **2** *she demanded a meeting with the minister* CONSULTATION, audience, interview. **3** *he intrigued her on their first meeting* ENCOUNTER, contact; appointment, assignation, rendezvous; *poetic/literary* tryst. **4** *the meeting of land and sea* CONVERGENCE, coming together, confluence, conjunction, union, junction, abutment; intersection, T-junction, crossing. **5** *an athletics meeting* EVENT, tournament, meet, rally, competition, match, game, contest.

megalomania • noun DELUSIONS OF GRANDEUR, folie de grandeur, thirst for power; self-importance, egotism, conceit, conceitedness.

melancholy • adjective *a melancholy expression* SAD, sorrowful, unhappy, desolate, mournful, lugubrious, gloomy, despondent, dejected, depressed, downhearted, downcast, disconsolate, glum, miserable, wretched, dismal, morose, woeful, woebegone, doleful, joyless, heavy-hearted; *informal* down in the dumps, down in the mouth, blue.

Pacific. ● noun a person from Melanesia.
melange /mayl**o**NZH/ ● noun a varied mixture.
– ORIGIN French *mélange*, from *mêler* 'to mix'.
melanin ● noun a dark pigment in the hair and skin, responsible for tanning of skin exposed to sunlight.
– ORIGIN from Greek *melas* 'black'.
melanoma /melənōmə/ ● noun a form of skin cancer which develops in melanin-forming cells.
Melba sauce ● noun a sauce made from puréed raspberries thickened with icing sugar.
– ORIGIN named after the Australian opera singer Dame Nellie *Melba* (1861–1931).
Melba toast ● noun very thin crisp toast.
meld ● verb blend; combine.
– ORIGIN perhaps a blend of MELT and WELD.
melee /mellay/ ● noun **1** a confused fight. **2** a disorderly mass.
– ORIGIN French *mêlée*; related to MEDLEY.
mellifluous /məliflooəss/ ● adjective pleasingly smooth and musical to hear.
– DERIVATIVES **mellifluously** adverb **mellifluousness** noun.
– ORIGIN from Latin *mel* 'honey' + *fluere* 'to flow'.
mellotron ● noun an electronic keyboard instrument in which each key controls the playback of a single pre-recorded musical sound.
– ORIGIN from MELLOW + *-tron*, element of ELECTRONIC.
mellow ● adjective **1** pleasantly smooth or soft in sound, taste, or colour. **2** relaxed and good-humoured. ● verb make or become mellow.
– ORIGIN perhaps related to MEAL².
melodeon ● noun **1** a small accordion. **2** a small organ similar to the harmonium.
melodic ● adjective **1** relating to melody. **2** pleasant-sounding.
– DERIVATIVES **melodically** adverb.
melodious ● adjective pleasant-sounding; tuneful.
melodrama ● noun **1** a sensational play with exaggerated characters and exciting events. **2** behaviour or events resembling melodrama.
– ORIGIN originally denoting a play, especially of a romantic or sensational nature, interspersed with songs and music: from Greek *melos* 'music' + French *drame* 'drama'.
melodramatic ● adjective like a melodrama; overdramatic or sensationalized.
– DERIVATIVES **melodramatically** adverb.
melody ● noun (pl. **melodies**) **1** a sequence of notes that is musically satisfying; a tune. **2** the main part in harmonized music.
– ORIGIN from Greek *melos* 'song'.
melon ● noun a large round fruit with sweet pulpy flesh and many seeds.
– ORIGIN Greek, from *mēlon* 'apple' + *pepōn* 'gourd'.
melt ● verb **1** make or become liquid by heating. **2** gradually disappear or disperse. **3** become or make more tender or loving.
– ORIGIN Old English, related to MALT.
meltdown ● noun **1** an accident in a nuclear reactor in which the fuel overheats and melts the reactor core. **2** a disastrous collapse or breakdown.
melting point ● noun the temperature at which a solid will melt.
melting pot ● noun **1** a place where different peoples, styles, etc., are mixed together and influence each other. **2** a changing and uncertain situation.
member ● noun **1** a person or organization belonging to a group or society. **2** a part of a complex structure. **3** archaic a part of the body, especially a limb.
– DERIVATIVES **membership** noun.
– ORIGIN Latin *membrum* 'limb'.
membrane ● noun **1** a skin-like covering or sheet in an organism or cell. **2** a thin skin-like sheet of material.
– DERIVATIVES **membraneous** adjective **membranous** adjective.
– ORIGIN Latin, from *membrum* 'limb'.
meme /meem/ ● noun Biology an element of behaviour or culture passed on by imitation or other non-genetic means.
– DERIVATIVES **memetic** adjective.
– ORIGIN Greek *mimēma* 'that which is imitated', on the pattern of *gene*.
memento ● noun (pl. **mementos** or **mementoes**) an object kept as a reminder.
– ORIGIN Latin, 'remember!'
memento mori /mimentō mori/ ● noun (pl. same) an object kept as a reminder that death is inevitable.
– ORIGIN Latin, 'remember (that you have) to die'.
memo ● noun (pl. **memos**) informal a memorandum.
memoir ● noun **1** a historical account or biography written from personal knowledge. **2** (**memoirs**) an account written by a public figure of their life and experiences.
– ORIGIN French *mémoire* 'memory'.
memorabilia ● plural noun objects kept or collected because of their associations with memorable people or events.
memorable ● adjective worth remembering or easily remembered.
– DERIVATIVES **memorably** adverb.
memorandum ● noun (pl. **memoranda** or **memorandums**) **1** a written message in business or diplomacy. **2** a note recording something.
– ORIGIN Latin, 'something to be brought to mind'.
memorial ● noun an object or structure established in memory of a person or event. ● adjective in memory of someone.

Thesaurus

– OPPOSITES cheerful.
● noun *a feeling of melancholy* SADNESS, sorrow, unhappiness, woe, desolation, melancholia, dejection, depression, despondency, gloom, gloominess, misery; *informal* the dumps, the blues.
melange ● noun MIXTURE, medley, assortment, blend, variety, mixed bag, mix, miscellany, selection, pot-pourri, patchwork; motley collection, ragbag, gallimaufry, mishmash, hotchpotch, jumble; *N. Amer.* hodgepodge.
melee, mêlée ● noun FRACAS, disturbance, rumpus, tumult, commotion, disorder, fray; brawl, fight, scuffle, struggle, skirmish, free-for-all, tussle; *informal* scrap, set-to, ruction; *N. Amer. informal* rough house.
mellifluous ● adjective SWEET-SOUNDING, dulcet, honeyed, mellow, soft, liquid, silvery, soothing, rich, smooth, euphonious, harmonious, tuneful, musical.
– OPPOSITES cacophonous.
mellow ● adjective **1** *the mellow tone of his voice* DULCET, sweet-sounding, tuneful, melodious, mellifluous; soft, smooth, warm, full, rich. **2** *a mellow wine* FULL-BODIED, mature, well matured, full-flavoured, rich, smooth. **3** *a mellow mood* GENIAL, affable, amiable, good-humoured, good-natured, amicable, pleasant, relaxed, easy-going; jovial, jolly, cheerful, happy, merry.
melodious ● adjective TUNEFUL, melodic, musical, mellifluous, dulcet, sweet-sounding, silvery, silvery-toned, harmonious, euphonious, lyrical; *informal* easy on the ear.
– OPPOSITES discordant.
melodramatic ● adjective EXAGGERATED, histrionic, extravagant, over-dramatic, overdone, over-sensational, sensationalized, over-emotional, sentimental; theatrical, stagy, actressy; *informal* hammy.
melody ● noun **1** *familiar melodies* TUNE, air, strain, theme, song, refrain, piece of music. **2** *his unique gift for melody* MELODIOUSNESS, tunefulness, lyricism, musicality, euphony.
melt ● verb **1** *the snow was beginning to melt* LIQUEFY, thaw, defrost, soften, dissolve, deliquesce. **2** *his smile melted her heart* SOFTEN, disarm, touch, affect, move. **3** *his anger melted away* VANISH, disappear, fade away, dissolve, evaporate; *poetic/literary* evanesce.
member ● noun **1** *a member of the club* SUBSCRIBER, associate, fellow, life member, founder member, card-carrying member. **2** *a member of a mathematical set* CONSTITUENT, element, component, part, portion, piece, unit. **3** *(archaic) many victims had injured members* LIMB, organ; arm, leg, appendage.
membrane ● noun LAYER, sheet, skin, film, tissue, integument, overlay; *technical* pellicle.
memento ● noun SOUVENIR, keepsake, reminder, remembrance, token, memorial; trophy, relic.
memoir ● noun **1** *a touching memoir of her childhood* ACCOUNT, history, record, chronicle, narrative, story, portrayal, depiction, sketch, portrait, profile, biography, monograph. **2** *he published his memoirs in 1955* AUTOBIOGRAPHY, life story, life, memories, recollections, reminiscences; journal, diary.
memorable ● adjective UNFORGETTABLE, catchy, haunting, indelible; momentous, significant, historic, notable, noteworthy, important, consequential, remarkable, special, signal, outstanding, extraordinary, striking, vivid, arresting, impressive, distinctive, distinguished, famous, celebrated, renowned, illustrious, glorious.
memorandum ● noun **1** *a memorandum from the managing director* MESSAGE, communication, note, e-mail, letter, missive; *informal*

– DERIVATIVES **memorialist** noun **memorialize** (also **memorialise**) verb.

memorize (also **memorise**) ● verb learn by heart.

memory ● noun (pl. **memories**) **1** the faculty by which the mind stores and remembers information. **2** a person or thing remembered. **3** the length of time over which people's memory extends. **4** a computer's equipment or capacity for storing data or program instructions for retrieval.
– PHRASES **in memory of** so as to commemorate.
– ORIGIN Old French *memorie*, from Latin *memoria*.

memsahib /memsaab/ ● noun Indian, dated a respectful form of address for a married white woman.
– ORIGIN from an Indian pronunciation of *ma'am* + SAHIB.

men plural of MAN.

menace ● noun **1** a dangerous or troublesome person or thing. **2** a threatening quality. ● verb put at risk; threaten.
– DERIVATIVES **menacing** adjective.
– ORIGIN from Latin *minax* 'threatening'.

ménage à trois /maynaa<u>zh</u> aa **trwaa**/ ● noun an arrangement in which a married couple and the lover of one of them live together.
– ORIGIN French, 'household of three'.

menagerie /mənajəri/ ● noun a collection of wild animals kept in captivity for showing to the public.
– ORIGIN French, from *ménage* 'household'.

menaquinone /mennə**kwinn**ōn/ ● noun Biochemistry vitamin K, a compound produced by intestinal bacteria and essential for the blood-clotting process.
– ORIGIN from its chemical name.

menarche /menaarki/ ● noun the first occurrence of menstruation.
– ORIGIN from Greek *mēn* 'month' + *arkhē* 'beginning'.

mend ● verb **1** restore to the correct or working condition. **2** improve. ● noun a repair in a material.
– PHRASES **mend (one's) fences** make peace with a person. **on the mend** improving in health or condition.
– DERIVATIVES **mendable** adjective **mender** noun.
– ORIGIN shortening of AMEND.

mendacious ● adjective untruthful.
– DERIVATIVES **mendaciously** adverb **mendacity** noun.
– ORIGIN Latin *mendax* 'lying'.

mendelevium /mendəleeviəm/ ● noun a very unstable chemical element made by high-energy collisions.
– ORIGIN named after the Russian chemist Dimitri *Mendeleev* (1834–1907).

Mendelism /mendəliz'm/ ● noun the theory of heredity based on characteristics transmitted as genes, as developed by the Austrian botanist G. J. Mendel (1822–84).
– DERIVATIVES **Mendelian** adjective.

mendicant /mendikənt/ ● adjective **1** habitually engaged in begging. **2** (of a religious order) originally dependent on alms. ● noun **1** a beggar. **2** a member of a mendicant order.
– ORIGIN from Latin *mendicus* 'beggar'.

menfolk ● plural noun the men of a family or community considered collectively.

menhir /menheer/ ● noun a tall upright prehistoric stone erected as a monument.
– ORIGIN from Breton *men* 'stone' + *hir* 'long'.

menial ● adjective (of work) requiring little skill and lacking prestige. ● noun a person with a menial job.
– ORIGIN Old French, from *mesnee* 'household'.

meninges /mininjeez/ ● plural noun (sing. **meninx**) the three membranes that enclose the brain and spinal cord.
– ORIGIN from Greek *mēninx* 'membrane'.

meningitis /menninjītiss/ ● noun a disease in which the meninges become inflamed owing to infection with a bacterium or virus.

meniscus /miniskəss/ ● noun (pl. **menisci** /minissī/) **1** Physics the curved upper surface of a liquid in a tube. **2** a thin lens convex on one side and concave on the other.
– ORIGIN Greek *mēniskos* 'crescent'.

menopause ● noun the ceasing of menstruation or the period in a woman's life (typically between 45 and 50) when this occurs.
– DERIVATIVES **menopausal** adjective.
– ORIGIN from Greek *mēn* 'month' + PAUSE.

menorah /minōrə/ ● noun a candelabrum used in Jewish worship, typically with eight branches.
– ORIGIN Hebrew.

menses /menseez/ ● plural noun blood discharged from the uterus at menstruation.
– ORIGIN Latin, plural of *mensis* 'month'.

menstrual ● adjective of or relating to menstruation.
– ORIGIN Latin *menstrualis*, from *mensis* 'month'.

menstruate ● verb (of a non-pregnant woman) discharge blood from the lining of the womb at intervals of about one lunar month.
– DERIVATIVES **menstruation** noun.

mensuration ● noun **1** measurement. **2** the part of geometry concerned with ascertaining lengths, areas, and volumes.
– ORIGIN Latin, from *mensurare* 'to measure'.

-ment ● suffix **1** forming nouns expressing the means or result of an action: *treatment*. **2** forming nouns from adjectives: *merriment*.

m

Thesaurus

memo. **2** *hasty memoranda and jottings-down* RECORD, minute, note, aide-memoire, reminder.

memorial ● noun **1** *the war memorial* MONUMENT, cenotaph, mausoleum; statue, plaque, cairn; tombstone, gravestone, headstone; shrine. **2** *the Festschrift is a memorial to his life's work* TRIBUTE, testimonial; remembrance, memento.
● adjective *a memorial service* COMMEMORATIVE, remembrance, commemorating; monumental.

memorize ● verb COMMIT TO MEMORY, remember, learn by heart, get off by heart, learn, learn by rote, become word-perfect in, get off pat; archaic con.

memory ● noun **1** *she is losing her memory* ABILITY TO REMEMBER, powers of recall. **2** *happy memories of her young days* RECOLLECTION, remembrance, reminiscence; impression. **3** *the town built a statue in memory of him* COMMEMORATION, remembrance; honour, tribute, recognition, respect. **4** *a computer's memory* MEMORY BANK, store, cache, disk, RAM, ROM.
– RELATED TERMS mnemonic.

menace ● noun **1** *an atmosphere full of menace* THREAT, ominousness, intimidation, warning, ill omen. **2** *a menace to British society* DANGER, peril, risk, hazard, threat; jeopardy. **3** *that child is a menace* NUISANCE, pest, annoyance, plague, torment, troublemaker, mischief-maker, thorn in someone's side/flesh.
● verb **1** *the elephants are still menaced by poaching* THREATEN, be a danger to, put at risk, jeopardize, imperil. **2** *a gang of skinheads menaced local residents* INTIMIDATE, threaten, terrorize, frighten, scare, terrify.

menacing ● adjective THREATENING, ominous, intimidating, frightening, terrifying, alarming, forbidding, black, thunderous, glowering, unfriendly, hostile, sinister, baleful, warning; formal minatory.
– OPPOSITES friendly.

mend ● verb **1** *workmen were mending faulty cabling* REPAIR, fix, put back together, piece together, restore; sew (up), stitch, darn, patch, cobble; rehabilitate, renew, renovate; informal patch up. **2** *'How's Walter?' 'He'll mend.'* GET BETTER, get well, recover, recuperate, improve; be well, be cured, heal. **3** *quarrels could be mended by talking* PUT/SET RIGHT, set straight, straighten out, sort out, rectify, remedy, cure, right, resolve, square, settle, put to rights, correct, retrieve, improve, make better. **4** *he mended the fire* STOKE (UP), make up, add fuel to.
– OPPOSITES break, worsen.

mendacious ● adjective LYING, untruthful, dishonest, deceitful, false, dissembling, insincere, disingenuous, hypocritical, fraudulent, double-dealing, two-faced, two-timing, duplicitous, perjured; untrue, fictitious, falsified, fabricated, fallacious, invented, made up; euphemistic economical with the truth; poetic/literary perfidious.
– OPPOSITES truthful.

mendicant ● noun BEGGAR, tramp, vagrant, vagabond; N. Amer. hobo; informal scrounger, sponger; N. Amer. informal bum, mooch, moocher, schnorrer.

menial ● adjective *a menial job* UNSKILLED, lowly, humble, low-grade, low-status, inferior, degrading; routine, humdrum, boring, dull.
● noun *they were treated like menials* SERVANT, drudge, minion, factotum, lackey; informal wage slave, gofer; Brit. informal dogsbody, skivvy; N. Amer. informal peon; archaic scullion.

menstruation ● noun PERIODS, menses, menorrhoea, menstrual cycle; menarche; informal the curse, monthlies, one's/the time of the month.

– ORIGIN from French or Latin.
mental ● adjective **1** of, done by, or occurring in the mind. **2** relating to disorders or illnesses of the mind. **3** informal mad.
– DERIVATIVES **mentally** adverb.
– USAGE The use of **mental** in sense 2 (e.g. as in **mental hospital**) is now regarded as old-fashioned, even offensive, and has been largely replaced by **psychiatric** in both general and official use. The terms **mental handicap** and **mentally handicapped** have now fallen out of favour and have been replaced in official contexts by terms such as **learning difficulties**.
– ORIGIN from Latin *mens* 'mind'.
mental age ● noun a person's mental ability expressed as the age at which an average person reaches the same ability.
mental block ● noun an inability to recall something or to perform a mental action.
mental handicap ● noun intellectual capacity that is underdeveloped to an extent which prevents normal function in society.
mentality ● noun (pl. **mentalities**) **1** a characteristic way of thinking. **2** the capacity for intelligent thought.
menthol ● noun a mint-tasting substance found chiefly in peppermint oil, used as a flavouring and in decongestants.
– DERIVATIVES **mentholated** adjective.
– ORIGIN Latin *mentha* 'mint'.
mention ● verb **1** refer to briefly. **2** refer to by name as being noteworthy. ● noun **1** a reference to someone or something. **2** a formal acknowledgement of something noteworthy.
– PHRASES **be mentioned in dispatches** Brit. be commended for one's actions by name in an official military report. **mention someone in one's will** leave a legacy to someone.
– ORIGIN Latin, related to MIND.
mentor ● noun **1** an experienced and trusted adviser. **2** an experienced person in an organization or institution who trains and counsels new employees or students.
– ORIGIN from the name of *Mentor*, the adviser of the young Telemachus in Homer's *Odyssey*.
menu ● noun **1** a list of dishes available in a restaurant. **2** the food available or to be served in a restaurant or at a meal. **3** Computing a list of commands or facilities displayed on screen.
– ORIGIN French, 'detailed list'.
meow ● noun & verb variant spelling of MIAOW.
MEP ● abbreviation Member of the European Parliament.
Mephistophelian /meffistofeeliən/ (also **Mephistophelean**) ● adjective wicked or evil.
– ORIGIN from *Mephistopheles*, an evil spirit to whom Faust, in the German legend, sold his soul.
mephitic /mifitik/ ● adjective literary foul-smelling; noxious.
– ORIGIN from Latin *mephitis* 'noxious exhalation'.
mercantile ● adjective relating to trade or commerce.
– ORIGIN from Italian *mercante* 'merchant'.
mercantilism /merkəntiliz'm/ ● noun chiefly historical the economic theory that trade generates wealth and is stimulated by the accumulation of bullion, which a government should encourage by means of protectionism.
– DERIVATIVES **mercantilist** noun & adjective.
Mercator projection ● noun a world map projection made on to a cylinder in such a way that all parallels of latitude have the same length as the equator.
– ORIGIN from *Mercator*, Latinized name of the Flemish geographer G. Kremer (1512–94).
mercenary ● adjective motivated chiefly by the desire for gain. ● noun (pl. **mercenaries**) a professional soldier hired to serve in a foreign army.
– ORIGIN from Latin *mercenarius* 'hireling', from *merces* 'reward'.
mercer ● noun chiefly historical a dealer in textile fabrics, especially silk and other fine materials.
– ORIGIN Old French *mercier*, from Latin *merx* 'goods'.
mercerized (also **mercerised**) ● adjective (of cotton) treated with caustic alkali to give strength and lustre.
– ORIGIN named after J. *Mercer* (1791–1866), said to have invented the process.
merchandise ● noun /merchəndiss/ goods for sale. ● verb /merchəndīz/ (also **merchandize**) promote the sale of.
– DERIVATIVES **merchandiser** noun.
– ORIGIN from Old French *marchand* 'merchant'.
merchant ● noun **1** a wholesale trader. **2** N. Amer. & Scottish a retail trader. **3** informal, chiefly derogatory a person fond of a particular activity: *a speed merchant.* ● adjective (of ships, sailors, or shipping activity) involved with commerce.
– ORIGIN Old French *marchant*, from Latin *mercari* 'to trade', from *merx* 'merchandise'.
merchantable ● adjective saleable.
merchant bank ● noun chiefly Brit. a bank dealing in commercial loans and investment.
merchantman ● noun a ship conveying merchandise.
merchant navy (US **merchant marine**) ● noun a country's commercial shipping.
merchant prince ● noun a merchant with sufficient wealth to wield political influence.
merciful ● adjective **1** showing mercy. **2** giving relief from suffering.
mercifully ● adverb **1** in a merciful manner. **2** to one's great relief.
merciless ● adjective showing no mercy.
– DERIVATIVES **mercilessly** adverb **mercilessness** noun.
mercurial /merkyooriəl/ ● adjective **1** subject to sudden changes

Thesaurus

mensuration ● noun MEASUREMENT, measuring, calculation, computation, quantification.
mental ● adjective **1** *mental faculties* INTELLECTUAL, cerebral, brain, rational, cognitive. **2** *a mental disorder* PSYCHIATRIC, psychological, psychogenic. **3** (informal) *he's completely mental.* See MAD sense 1.
– OPPOSITES physical.
mentality ● noun **1** *I can't understand the mentality of these people* WAY OF THINKING, mind set, cast of mind, frame of mind, turn of mind, mind, psychology, mental attitude, outlook, disposition, make-up. **2** *a person of limited mentality* INTELLECT, intellectual capabilities, intelligence, IQ, (powers of) reasoning, rationality.
mentally ● adverb IN ONE'S MIND, in one's head, inwardly, intellectually, cognitively.
mention ● verb **1** *don't mention the war* ALLUDE TO, refer to, touch on/upon; bring up, raise, broach, introduce, moot. **2** *Jim mentioned that he'd met them before* STATE, say, indicate, let someone know, disclose, divulge, reveal. **3** *I'll gladly mention your work to my friends* RECOMMEND, commend, put in a good word for, speak well of.
● noun **1** *he made no mention of your request* REFERENCE, allusion, remark, statement, announcement, indication. **2** *a mention in dispatches* TRIBUTE, citation, acknowledgement, recognition. **3** *my book got a mention on the show* RECOMMENDATION, commendation, a good word.
– PHRASES **don't mention it** DON'T APOLOGIZE, it doesn't matter, it makes no difference/odds, it's not important, never mind, don't worry. **not to mention** IN ADDITION TO, as well as; not counting, not including, to say nothing of, aside from, besides.
mentor ● noun **1** *his political mentors* ADVISER, guide, guru, counsellor, consultant; confidant(e). **2** *regular meetings between mentor and trainee* TRAINER, teacher, tutor, instructor.
menu ● noun BILL OF FARE, carte du jour, set menu, table d'hôte.
mephitic ● adjective (poetic/literary). See MALODOROUS.
mercantile ● adjective COMMERCIAL, trade, trading, business, merchant, sales.
mercenary ● adjective **1** *mercenary self-interest* MONEY-ORIENTED, grasping, greedy, acquisitive, avaricious, covetous, bribable, venal, materialistic; informal money-grubbing. **2** *mercenary soldiers* HIRED, paid, bought, professional.
● noun *a group of mercenaries* SOLDIER OF FORTUNE, professional soldier, hired soldier; informal hired gun; historical freelance, condottiere.
merchandise ● noun *a wide range of merchandise* GOODS, wares, stock, commodities, lines, produce, products.
● verb *a new product that can be easily merchandised* PROMOTE, market, sell, retail; advertise, publicize, push; informal hype (up), plug.
merchant ● noun TRADER, dealer, wholesaler, broker, agent, seller, buyer, buyer and seller, vendor, distributor.
merciful ● adjective **1** *God is merciful* FORGIVING, compassionate, clement, pitying, forbearing, lenient, humane, mild, soft-hearted, tender-hearted, gracious, kind, sympathetic, humanitarian, liberal, tolerant, indulgent, generous, magnanimous, benign, benevolent. **2** *a merciful silence fell* WELCOME, blessed.
– OPPOSITES cruel.
– PHRASES **be merciful to** HAVE MERCY ON, have pity on, show mercy to, spare, pardon, forgive, be lenient on/to; informal go/be easy on, let off.

of mood. **2** of or containing the element mercury.
– ORIGIN Latin *mercurialis* 'relating to the god Mercury', from *Mercurius* 'Mercury'.
Mercurian ● adjective relating to the planet Mercury.
mercury ● noun a heavy silvery-white liquid metallic element used in some thermometers and barometers.
– DERIVATIVES **mercuric** adjective **mercurous** adjective.
– ORIGIN from *Mercury*, the Roman messenger of the gods.
mercy ● noun (pl. **mercies**) **1** compassion or forgiveness shown towards an enemy or offender in one's power. **2** something to be grateful for. **3** (before another noun) motivated by compassion: *a mercy killing*. ● exclamation archaic used to express surprise or fear.
– PHRASES **at the mercy of** in the power of; defenceless against.
– ORIGIN Latin *merces* 'reward, pity'.
mere[1] ● adjective **1** that is nothing more than what is specified. **2** (**the merest**) the smallest or slightest.
– ORIGIN Latin *merus* 'pure, undiluted'.
mere[2] ● noun chiefly literary a lake or pond.
– ORIGIN Old English.
merely ● adverb just; only.
meretricious /meritrishəss/ ● adjective showily but falsely attractive.
– ORIGIN from Latin *meretrix* 'prostitute', from *mereri* 'be hired'.
merganser /merganzər/ ● noun a fish-eating diving duck with a long, thin serrated and hooked bill.
– ORIGIN from Latin *mergus* 'diver' + *anser* 'goose'.
merge ● verb **1** combine or be combined into a whole. **2** blend gradually into something else.
– ORIGIN originally in the sense 'immerse oneself in an activity': from Latin *mergere* 'to dip, plunge'.
merger ● noun a merging of two things, especially companies, into one.
meridian ● noun **1** a circle of constant longitude passing through a given place on the earth's surface and the poles. **2** Astronomy a circle passing through the celestial poles and the zenith of a given place on the earth's surface. **3** any of twelve pathways in the body, believed by practitioners of Chinese medicine to be a channel for vital energy.
– ORIGIN from Latin *meridianum* 'noon' (because the sun crosses a meridian at noon).
meridional /məriddiən'l/ ● adjective **1** of or relating to the south, especially southern Europe. **2** of or relating to a meridian.
meringue /mərang/ ● noun **1** beaten egg whites and sugar baked until crisp. **2** a small cake made of meringue.
– ORIGIN French.
merino /məreenō/ ● noun (pl. **merinos**) **1** a breed of sheep with long, fine wool. **2** a soft woollen or wool-and-cotton material, originally of merino wool.
– ORIGIN Spanish.
meristem /merristem/ ● noun a region of plant tissue consisting of actively dividing cells.
– ORIGIN from Greek *meristos* 'divisible'.
merit ● noun **1** superior quality; excellence. **2** a good point or quality. ● verb (**merited**, **meriting**) deserve.
– ORIGIN Latin *meritum* 'due reward', from *mereri* 'earn, deserve'.
meritocracy ● noun (pl. **meritocracies**) **1** government or leadership by people of great merit. **2** a society governed by meritocracy.
– DERIVATIVES **meritocratic** adjective.
meritorious ● adjective deserving reward or praise.
merlin ● noun a small dark falcon.
– ORIGIN Old French *merilun*.
Merlot /merlō/ ● noun a variety of black wine grape originally from the Bordeaux region of France.
– ORIGIN French.
mermaid ● noun a mythical sea creature with a woman's head and trunk and a fish's tail.
– ORIGIN from MERE[2] (in the obsolete sense 'sea') + MAID.
mermaid's purse ● noun the horny egg case of a skate, ray, or small shark.
merman ● noun the male equivalent of a mermaid.
merriment ● noun gaiety and fun.
merry ● adjective (**merrier**, **merriest**) **1** cheerful and lively. **2** Brit. informal slightly drunk.
– PHRASES **make merry** indulge in merriment.
– DERIVATIVES **merrily** adjective **merriness** noun.
– ORIGIN Old English, 'pleasing, delightful'.
merry-go-round ● noun **1** a revolving machine with model horses or cars on which people ride for amusement. **2** a continuous cycle of activities or events.

Thesaurus

mercifully ● adverb LUCKILY, fortunately, happily, thank goodness/God/heavens.
merciless ● adjective RUTHLESS, remorseless, pitiless, unforgiving, unsparing, implacable, inexorable, relentless, inflexible, inhumane, inhuman, unsympathetic, unfeeling, intolerant, rigid, severe, cold-blooded, hard-hearted, stony-hearted, heartless, harsh, callous, cruel, brutal, barbarous, cut-throat.
– OPPOSITES compassionate.
mercurial ● adjective VOLATILE, capricious, temperamental, excitable, fickle, changeable, unpredictable, variable, protean, mutable, erratic, quicksilver, inconstant, inconsistent, unstable, unsteady, fluctuating, ever-changing, moody, flighty, wayward, whimsical, impulsive; *technical* labile.
– OPPOSITES stable.
mercy ● noun **1** *he showed no mercy to the others* LENIENCY, clemency, compassion, grace, pity, charity, forgiveness, forbearance, quarter, humanity; soft-heartedness, tender-heartedness, kindness, sympathy, liberality, indulgence, tolerance, generosity, magnanimity, beneficence. **2** *we must be thankful for small mercies* BLESSING, godsend, boon, favour, piece/stroke of luck.
– OPPOSITES ruthlessness, cruelty.
– PHRASES **at the mercy of 1** *they found themselves at the mercy of the tyrant* IN THE POWER OF, under/in the control of, in the clutches of, under the heel of, subject to. **2** *he was at the mercy of the elements* DEFENCELESS AGAINST, vulnerable to, exposed to, susceptible to, prey to, (wide) open to.
mere ● adjective NO MORE THAN, just, only, merely; no better than.
merely ● adverb ONLY, purely, solely, simply, just, but.
meretricious ● adjective WORTHLESS, valueless, cheap, tawdry, trashy, Brummagem, tasteless, kitsch; false, artificial, fake, imitation; *informal* tacky.
merge ● verb **1** *the company merged with a European firm* JOIN (TOGETHER), join forces, amalgamate, unite, affiliate, team up, link (up). **2** *the two organizations were merged* AMALGAMATE, bring together, join, consolidate, conflate, unite, unify, combine, incorporate, integrate, link (up), knit, yoke. **3** *the two colours merged* MINGLE, blend, fuse, mix, intermix, intermingle, coalesce; *poetic/literary* commingle.
– OPPOSITES separate.
merger ● noun AMALGAMATION, combination, union, fusion, coalition, affiliation, unification, incorporation, consolidation, link-up, alliance.
– OPPOSITES split.
merit ● noun **1** *composers of outstanding merit* EXCELLENCE, quality, calibre, worth, worthiness, credit, value, distinction, eminence. **2** *the merits of the scheme* GOOD POINT, strong point, advantage, benefit, value, asset, plus.
– OPPOSITES inferiority, fault, disadvantage.
● verb *the accusation did not merit a response* DESERVE, earn, be deserving of, warrant, rate, justify, be worthy of, be worth, be entitled to, have a right to, have a claim to/on.
meritorious ● adjective PRAISEWORTHY, laudable, commendable, admirable, estimable, creditable, worthy, deserving, excellent, exemplary, good.
– OPPOSITES discreditable.
merriment ● noun HIGH SPIRITS, high-spiritedness, exuberance, cheerfulness, gaiety, fun, effervescence, verve, buoyancy, levity, zest, liveliness, cheer, joy, joyfulness, joyousness, jolliness, jollity, happiness, gladness, jocularity, conviviality, festivity, merrymaking, revelry, mirth, glee, gleefulness, laughter, hilarity, light-heartedness, amusement, pleasure.
– OPPOSITES misery.
merry ● adjective **1** *merry throngs of students* CHEERFUL, cheery, in high spirits, high-spirited, bright, sunny, smiling, light-hearted, buoyant, lively, carefree, without a care in the world, joyful, joyous, jolly, convivial, festive, mirthful, gleeful, happy, glad, laughing; *informal* chirpy; *formal* jocund; *dated* gay; *poetic/literary* blithe, blithesome. **2** (*Brit. informal*) *after three beers he began to feel quite merry* TIPSY, mellow, slightly drunk; *Brit. informal* tiddly, squiffy.
– OPPOSITES miserable.
– PHRASES **make merry** HAVE FUN, have a good time, enjoy oneself, have a party, celebrate, carouse, feast, {eat, drink, and be

merrymaking ● noun fun; festivity.
mesa /maysə/ ● noun an isolated flat-topped hill with steep sides.
– ORIGIN Spanish, 'table'.
mésalliance /mezalliənss/ ● noun a marriage to a person of a lower social class.
– ORIGIN French, 'misalliance'.
mescal ● noun **1** alcoholic liquor distilled from a type of agave. **2** a peyote cactus.
– ORIGIN Nahuatl.
mescaline /meskəlin/ (also **mescalin**) ● noun a hallucinogenic drug made from the peyote cactus.
Mesdames /maydaam/ plural of MADAME.
Mesdemoiselles /maydamwəzel/ plural of MADEMOISELLE.
mesembryanthemum /mizembrianthimum/ ● noun a succulent plant with brightly coloured daisy-like flowers.
– ORIGIN from Greek *mesēmbria* 'noon' + *anthemon* 'flower'.
mesh ● noun **1** material made of a network of wire or thread. **2** the spacing of the strands of a net. **3** a complex or constricting situation. ● verb **1** (**mesh with**) be in harmony with. **2** become entangled or entwined. **3** (of a gearwheel) lock together with another.
– ORIGIN probably from Old English.
mesmeric ● adjective causing one to become transfixed and unaware of one's surroundings; hypnotic.
– DERIVATIVES **mesmerically** adverb.
mesmerism ● noun **1** historical a therapeutic technique involving hypnotism. **2** hypnotism.
– DERIVATIVES **mesmerist** noun.
– ORIGIN named after the Austrian physician Franz A. *Mesmer* (1734–1815).
mesmerize (also **mesmerise**) ● verb capture the whole attention of; fascinate.
meso- /messō/ ● combining form middle; intermediate: *mesomorph*.
– ORIGIN from Greek *mesos* 'middle'.
mesoderm ● noun the middle layer of cells or tissues of an embryo, or the parts that come from the mesoderm, such as cartilage, muscles, and bone.
– DERIVATIVES **mesodermal** adjective.
– ORIGIN from Greek *mesos* 'middle' + *derma* 'skin'.
Mesolithic ● adjective relating to the middle part of the Stone Age, between the end of the glacial period and the beginnings of agriculture.
– ORIGIN from Greek *mesos* 'middle' + *lithos* 'stone'.
mesomorph ● noun a person with a compact and muscular body. Compare with ECTOMORPH, ENDOMORPH.
– DERIVATIVES **mesomorphic** adjective.
– ORIGIN from *mesodermal* (the mesoderm being the layer of the embryo giving rise to these physical characteristics).
meson /meezon/ ● noun Physics a subatomic particle, intermediate in mass between an electron and a proton, that transmits the strong interaction binding nucleons together.
– ORIGIN from Greek *mesos* 'middle'.
Mesopotamian /messəpətaymiən/ ● adjective relating to Mesopotamia, an ancient region of what is now Iraq. ● noun a person from Mesopotamia.
mesosphere ● noun the region of the earth's atmosphere above the stratosphere and below the thermosphere.
Mesozoic /mesōzōic/ ● adjective Geology relating to the era between the Palaeozoic and Cenozoic eras, about 245 to 65 million years ago, with evidence of the first mammals, birds, and flowering plants.
– ORIGIN from Greek *mesos* 'middle' + *zōion* 'animal'.
mesquite /messkeet/ ● noun a spiny tree of the south-western US and Mexico, yielding wood, medicinal products, and edible pods.
– ORIGIN Mexican Spanish *mezquite*.
mess ● noun **1** a dirty or untidy state. **2** a state of confusion or difficulty. **3** a portion of semi-solid food. **4** euphemistic a domestic animal's excrement. **5** a place providing meals and recreational facilities for members of the armed forces. ● verb **1** make untidy or dirty. **2** (**mess about/around**) behave in a silly or playful way. **3** (**mess with**) informal meddle with. **4** eat communally in an armed forces' mess. **5** (of a domestic animal) defecate.
– ORIGIN Old French *mes* 'portion of food', from Latin *missum* 'something put on the table'.
message ● noun **1** a verbal or written communication. **2** a significant point or central theme. ● verb send a message to, especially by email.
– PHRASES **get the message** informal understand what is meant. **on** (or **off**) **message** (of a politician) stating (or deviating from) the official party line.
– ORIGIN Old French, from Latin *mittere* 'send'.
Messeigneurs plural of MONSEIGNEUR.
messenger ● noun a person who carries a message.
messenger RNA ● noun the form of RNA in which genetic information transcribed from DNA is transferred to a ribosome.
messiah ● noun **1** (**the Messiah**) the promised liberator of the Jewish nation prophesied in the Hebrew Bible. **2** (**the Messiah**) Jesus regarded by Christians as the Messiah of these prophecies. **3** a leader or saviour.
– ORIGIN Hebrew, 'anointed'.
messianic /messiannik/ ● adjective **1** relating to the Messiah. **2** inspired by belief in a messiah.
– DERIVATIVES **messianism** noun.
Messieurs plural of MONSIEUR.
Messrs plural of MR.
– ORIGIN abbreviation of MESSIEURS.
mess tin ● noun Brit. a rectangular metal food dish forming part of a soldier's kit.
messy ● adjective (**messier, messiest**) **1** untidy or dirty. **2** confused and difficult to deal with.
– DERIVATIVES **messily** adverb **messiness** noun.
mestizo /mesteezō/ ● noun (pl. **mestizos**; fem. **mestiza**, pl. **mestizas**) a Latin American of mixed race, especially the offspring

m

Thesaurus

merry}, revel, roister; *informal* party, have a ball.
merry-go-round ● noun CAROUSEL; *Brit.* roundabout.
mesh ● noun **1** *wire mesh* NETTING, net, network; web, webbing, lattice, latticework. **2** *a mesh of political intrigue* ENTANGLEMENT, net, tangle, web.
● verb **1** *one gear meshes with the input gear* ENGAGE, connect, lock, interlock. **2** *don't get meshed in the weeds* ENTANGLE, enmesh, snare, trap, catch. **3** *our ideas just do not mesh* HARMONIZE, fit together, match, dovetail.
mesmerize ● verb ENTHRAL, spellbind, entrance, dazzle, bewitch, charm, captivate, enchant, fascinate, transfix, grip, hypnotize.
mess ● noun **1** *please clear up the mess* UNTIDINESS, disorder, disarray, clutter, shambles, jumble, muddle, chaos; *Brit. informal* tip. **2** *cat mess* EXCREMENT, muck, faeces, excreta. **3** *I've got to get out of this mess* PLIGHT, predicament, tight spot/corner, difficulty, trouble, quandary, dilemma, problem, muddle, mix-up, imbroglio; *informal* jam, fix, pickle, stew, hole, scrape. **4** *he made a mess of the project* MUDDLE, bungle; *informal* botch, hash, foul-up; *Brit. informal* cock-up; *N. Amer. informal* snafu.
– PHRASES **make a mess of** MISMANAGE, mishandle, bungle, fluff, spoil, ruin, wreck; *informal* mess up, botch, make a hash of, muck up, foul up; *Brit. informal* make a pig's ear of, make a Horlicks of, cock up. **mess about/around** POTTER ABOUT, pass the time, fiddle about/around, footle about/around, play about/around, fool about/around; fidget, toy, trifle, tamper, tinker, interfere, meddle, monkey (about/around); *informal* piddle about/around; *Brit. informal* muck about/around, lark (about/around). **mess something up** **1** *he messed up my kitchen* DIRTY; clutter up, disarrange, jumble, dishevel, rumple; *N. Amer. informal* muss up; *poetic/literary* befoul. **2** *(informal) Eddie messed things up.* See MAKE A MESS OF.
message ● noun **1** *are there any messages for me?* COMMUNICATION, piece of information, news, note, memorandum, memo, e-mail, letter, missive, report, bulletin, communiqué, dispatch. **2** *the message of his teaching* MEANING, sense, import, idea; point, thrust, gist, essence, content, subject (matter), substance, implication, drift, lesson.
– PHRASES **get the message** *(informal)* UNDERSTAND, get the point, comprehend; *informal* catch on, latch on, get the picture.
messenger ● noun MESSAGE-BEARER, postman, courier, runner, dispatch rider, envoy, emissary, agent, go-between; *historical* herald; *archaic* legate.
messy ● adjective **1** *messy oil spills | messy hair* DIRTY, filthy, grubby, soiled, grimy; mucky, muddy, slimy, sticky, sullied, spotted, stained, smeared, smudged; dishevelled, scruffy, rumpled, matted, unkempt, tousled, bedraggled, tangled; *informal* yucky; *Brit. informal* gungy. **2** *a messy kitchen* DISORDERLY, disordered, in a muddle, chaotic, confused, disorganized, in disarray, disarranged; untidy, cluttered, in a jumble; *informal* like a bomb's hit it; *Brit. informal*

of a Spaniard and an American Indian.
– ORIGIN Spanish, 'mixed'.

Met ● abbreviation informal meteorological.

met past and past participle of MEET[1].

meta- (also **met-** before a vowel or h) ● combining form forming words referring to: **1** a change of position or condition: *metamorphosis*. **2** position behind, after, or beyond: *metacarpus*. **3** something of a higher or second-order kind: *metalanguage*.
– ORIGIN from Greek *meta* 'with, across, or after'.

metabolism /mitabbəliz'm/ ● noun the chemical processes in a living organism by which food is used for tissue growth or energy production.
– DERIVATIVES **metabolic** adjective.
– ORIGIN from Greek *metabolē* 'change'.

metabolite /mitabbəlīt/ ● noun a substance formed in or necessary for metabolism.

metabolize (also **metabolise**) ● verb process or be processed by metabolism.

metacarpus ● noun (pl. **metacarpi**) the group of five bones of the hand between the wrist and the fingers.
– DERIVATIVES **metacarpal** adjective & noun.
– ORIGIN Greek *metakarpion*.

metal ● noun **1** a solid material which is typically hard, shiny, malleable, fusible, and ductile, with good electrical and thermal conductivity, e.g. iron, copper, and gold. **2** (also **road metal**) broken stone used in road-making.
– ORIGIN Greek *metallon* 'mine, quarry, or metal'.

metalanguage ● noun a form of language used to describe or analyse another language.

metal detector ● noun an electronic device that gives an audible signal when it is close to metal.

metalled ● adjective **1** made from or coated with metal. **2** surfaced with road metal.

metallic ● adjective **1** of or resembling metal. **2** (of sound) sharp and ringing.
– DERIVATIVES **metallically** adverb.

metalliferous ● adjective containing or producing metal.

metallize (also **metallise**, US also **metalize**) ● verb **1** coat with metal. **2** make metallic.

metallography /mettəlogrəfi/ ● noun the descriptive science of the structure and properties of metals.
– DERIVATIVES **metallographic** adjective.

metallurgy /mitalərji/ ● noun the science concerned with the properties, production, and purification of metals.
– DERIVATIVES **metallurgical** adjective **metallurgist** noun.

metalwork ● noun **1** the art of making things from metal. **2** metal objects collectively.

metamorphic ● adjective (of rock) having undergone transformation by heat, pressure, or other natural agencies.
– DERIVATIVES **metamorphism** noun.

metamorphose /mettəmorfōz/ ● verb **1** change completely in form or nature. **2** (of an insect or amphibian) undergo metamorphosis. **3** subject (rock) to metamorphism.

metamorphosis /mettəmorfəsiss/ ● noun (pl. **metamorphoses** /mettəmorfəseez/) **1** the transformation of an insect or amphibian from an immature form or larva to an adult form in distinct stages. **2** a change in form or nature.
– ORIGIN Greek, from *metamorphoun* 'transform, change shape'.

metaphor ● noun **1** a figure of speech in which a word or phrase is applied to something to which it is not literally applicable (e.g. *food for thought*). **2** a thing symbolic of something else.
– ORIGIN from Greek, from *metapherein* 'to transfer'.

metaphorical (also **metaphoric**) ● adjective of the nature of or relating to metaphor.
– DERIVATIVES **metaphorically** adverb.

metaphysic ● noun a system of metaphysics.

metaphysical ● adjective **1** relating to metaphysics. **2** transcending physical matter. **3** referring to a group of 17th century English poets (in particular John Donne, George Herbert, Andrew Marvell, and Henry Vaughan) known for their subtlety of thought and complex imagery.
– DERIVATIVES **metaphysically** adverb.

metaphysics ● plural noun (usu. treated as sing.) **1** philosophy concerned with abstract concepts such as the nature of existence or of truth and knowledge. **2** informal abstract talk; mere theory.
– DERIVATIVES **metaphysician** noun.
– ORIGIN from Greek *ta meta ta phusika* 'the things after the Physics', referring to the sequence of Aristotle's works.

metastable /mettəstayb'l/ ● adjective Physics **1** (of a state of equilibrium) stable provided it is only subjected to small forces. **2** theoretically unstable but so long-lived as to be stable for practical purposes.

metastasis /mitastəsiss/ ● noun (pl. **metastases** /mitastəseez/) Medicine the development of secondary tumours at a distance from a primary site of cancer.
– ORIGIN Greek, 'removal or change'.

metatarsus ● noun (pl. **metatarsi**) the bones of the foot, between the ankle and the toes.
– DERIVATIVES **metatarsal** adjective & noun.

metathesis /mitathisiss/ ● noun (pl. **metatheses** /mitathiseez/) Grammar the transposition of sounds or letters in a word.
– DERIVATIVES **metathetic** adjective.
– ORIGIN Greek, 'transposition'.

metazoan /metəzōən/ ● noun an animal other than a protozoan or sponge.
– ORIGIN from META- + Greek *zōion* 'animal'.

mete ● verb (**mete out**) deal out or allot (justice, punishment, etc.).
– ORIGIN Old English, 'measure'; related to MEET[2].

metempsychosis /mettempsikōsiss/ ● noun (pl. **metempsychoses** /mettempsikōseez/) the supposed transmigration at death of the soul into a new body.
– ORIGIN Greek *metempsukhōsis*, from *psukhē* 'soul'.

meteor ● noun a small body of matter from outer space that becomes incandescent as a result of friction with the earth's atmosphere and appears as a shooting star.
– ORIGIN from Greek, from *meteōros* 'lofty'.

meteoric ● adjective **1** relating to meteors or meteorites. **2** (of progress or development) very rapid.

meteorite ● noun a piece of rock or metal that has fallen to the earth from space.

meteoroid ● noun a small body that would become a meteor if it entered the earth's atmosphere.

meteorology /meetiərolәji/ ● noun the study of atmospheric processes and phenomena, especially for weather forecasting.
– DERIVATIVES **meteorological** adjective **meteorologist** noun.

meter[1] ● noun a device that measures and records the quantity, degree, or rate of something. ● verb measure with a meter.
– ORIGIN originally in the sense 'person who measures': from METE.

meter[2] ● noun US spelling of METRE[1], METRE[2].

-meter ● combining form **1** in names of measuring instruments: *thermometer*. **2** in nouns referring to lines of poetry with a

m

Thesaurus

shambolic. **3** *a messy legal battle* COMPLEX, intricate, tangled, confused, convoluted; unpleasant, nasty, bitter, acrimonious.
– OPPOSITES clean, tidy.

metallic ● adjective **1** *a metallic sound* TINNY, jangling, jingling; grating, harsh, jarring, dissonant. **2** *metallic paint* METALLIZED, burnished; shiny, glossy, lustrous.

metamorphose ● verb TRANSFORM, change, mutate, transmute, transfigure, convert, alter, modify, remodel, recast, reconstruct; humorous transmogrify; formal transubstantiate.

metamorphosis ● noun TRANSFORMATION, mutation, transmutation, change, alteration, conversion, modification, remodelling, reconstruction; humorous transmogrification; formal transubstantiation.

metaphor ● noun FIGURE OF SPEECH, image, trope, analogy, comparison, symbol, word painting/picture.

metaphorical ● adjective FIGURATIVE, allegorical, symbolic; imaginative, extended.
– OPPOSITES literal.

metaphysical ● adjective **1** *metaphysical questions* ABSTRACT, theoretical, conceptual, notional, philosophical, speculative, intellectual, academic. **2** *Good and Evil are inextricably linked in a metaphysical battle* TRANSCENDENTAL, spiritual, supernatural, paranormal.

mete ● verb
– PHRASES **mete something out** DISPENSE, hand out, allocate, allot, apportion, issue, deal out, dole out, dish out, assign, administer.

meteor ● noun FALLING STAR, shooting star, meteorite, meteoroid, bolide.

meteoric ● adjective RAPID, lightning, swift, fast, quick, speedy, accelerated, instant, sudden, spectacular.

specified number of measures: *hexameter*.
– ORIGIN from Greek *metron* 'measure'.
methadone ● noun a powerful synthetic painkiller, used as a substitute for morphine and heroin in the treatment of addiction.
– ORIGIN from its chemical name.
methamphetamine /methamfettəmeen/ ● noun a synthetic drug related to amphetamine, used illegally as a stimulant.
methane /meethayn/ ● noun a colourless, odourless flammable gas which is the main constituent of natural gas.
– ORIGIN from METHYL.
methanol ● noun a poisonous flammable alcohol, used to make methylated spirit.
methedrine /methədrin/ ● noun (trademark in the UK) another term for METHAMPHETAMINE.
methinks ● verb (past **methought**) archaic or humorous it seems to me.
– ORIGIN Old English.
methionine /mithīəneen/ ● noun Biochemistry a sulphur-containing amino acid which is a constituent of most proteins and is essential in the diet.
– ORIGIN from METHYL + Greek *theion* 'sulphur'.
method ● noun **1** a way of doing something. **2** orderliness of thought or behaviour.
– ORIGIN Greek *methodos* 'pursuit of knowledge'.
method acting ● noun an acting technique in which an actor tries to identify completely with a character's emotions.
methodical (also **methodic**) ● adjective characterized by method or order.
– DERIVATIVES **methodically** adverb.
Methodist ● noun a member of a Christian Protestant denomination originating in the 18th-century evangelistic movement of Charles and John Wesley. ● adjective relating to Methodists or Methodism.
– DERIVATIVES **Methodism** noun.
– ORIGIN probably from the notion of following a specified 'method' of Bible study.
methodology ● noun (pl. **methodologies**) a system of methods used in a particular field.
– DERIVATIVES **methodological** adjective **methodologist** noun.
methought past of METHINKS.
meths ● noun Brit. informal methylated spirit.
Methuselah ● noun **1** humorous a very old person. **2** (**methuselah**) a wine bottle of eight times the standard size.
– ORIGIN named after the biblical patriarch *Methuselah*, said to have lived for 969 years (Book of Genesis, chapter 5).
methyl /meethīl/ ● noun Chemistry the radical $-CH_3$, derived from methane.
– ORIGIN from Greek *methu* 'wine' + *hulē* 'wood'.
methyl alcohol ● noun methanol.
methylate ● verb **1** mix with methanol or methylated spirit. **2** Chemistry introduce a methyl radical into (a molecule).
– DERIVATIVES **methylation** noun.
methylated spirit (also **methylated spirits**) ● noun alcohol for use as a solvent or fuel, made unfit for drinking by the addition of methanol and a violet dye.
metical /mettikal/ ● noun (pl. **meticais** /mettikīsh/) the basic monetary unit of Mozambique, equal to 100 centavos.
– ORIGIN Portuguese, from Arabic, 'to weigh'.
meticulous ● adjective very careful and precise.
– DERIVATIVES **meticulously** adverb **meticulousness** noun.
– ORIGIN originally in the sense 'fearful', later 'overcareful about detail': from Latin *meticulosus* 'fearful'.
métier /metyay/ ● noun **1** a trade, profession, or occupation. **2** a person's strength or special ability.
– ORIGIN French, from Latin *ministerium* 'service'.
metonym /mettənim/ ● noun a word or expression used as a substitute for something with which it is closely associated, e.g. *Washington* for the US government.
– DERIVATIVES **metonymic** adjective **metonymy** noun.
– ORIGIN from Greek *metōnumia* 'change of name'.
metope /metəpi/ ● noun Architecture a square space between triglyphs in a Doric frieze.
– ORIGIN Greek, from *meta* 'between' + *opē* 'hole for a beam end'.
metre[1] (US **meter**) ● noun the fundamental unit of length in the metric system, equal to 100 centimetres (approx. 39.37 inches).
– ORIGIN French, from Greek *metron* 'measure'.
metre[2] (US **meter**) ● noun **1** the rhythm of a piece of poetry, determined by the number and length of feet in a line. **2** the basic rhythmic pattern of a piece of music.
– ORIGIN Greek *metron* 'measure'.
metric ● adjective relating to or using the metric system.
metrical ● adjective **1** of or composed in poetic metre. **2** of or involving measurement.
– DERIVATIVES **metrically** adverb.
metricate ● verb convert to a metric system of measurement.
– DERIVATIVES **metrication** noun.
metric system ● noun the decimal measuring system based on the metre, litre, and gram as units of length, capacity, and weight or mass.
metric ton (also **metric tonne**) ● noun a unit of weight equal to 1,000 kilograms (2,205 lb).
metro ● noun (pl. **metros**) an underground railway system in a city, especially Paris.
– ORIGIN French, abbreviation of *métropolitain*, from *Chemin de Fer Métropolitain* 'Metropolitan Railway'.
metronome ● noun a musicians' device that marks time at a selected rate by giving a regular tick.
– DERIVATIVES **metronomic** adjective.
– ORIGIN from Greek *metron* 'measure' + *nomos* 'law'.
metropolis /mitroppəliss/ ● noun the principal city of a country or region.
– ORIGIN Greek, from *mētēr* 'mother' + *polis* 'city'.
metropolitan ● adjective **1** relating to a metropolis. **2** relating to the parent state of a colony. **3** Christian Church relating to a metropolitan or his see. ● noun **1** Christian Church a bishop having authority over the bishops of a province. **2** an inhabitant of a metropolis.
metropolitan county ● noun (in England) each of six units of local government centred on a large urban area (established in 1974, although their councils were abolished in 1986).
mettle ● noun spirit and resilience in the face of difficulty.
– PHRASES **be on one's mettle** be ready to show one's ability or courage.
– ORIGIN variant spelling of METAL.
meunière /mönyair/ ● adjective (after noun) cooked or served in lightly browned butter with lemon juice and parsley.
– ORIGIN from French *à la meunière* 'in the manner of a miller's wife'.
mew[1] ● verb (of a cat or gull) make a characteristic high-pitched crying noise. ● noun a mewing noise.
– ORIGIN imitative.
mew[2] Falconry ● noun a cage or building for trained hawks, especially while they are moulting. ● verb **1** (of a trained hawk)

m

Thesaurus

– OPPOSITES gradual.
meteorologist ● noun WEATHER FORECASTER, met officer, weatherman, weatherwoman.
method ● noun **1** *they use very old-fashioned methods* PROCEDURE, technique, system, practice, routine, modus operandi, process; strategy, tactic, plan. **2** *there's method in his madness* ORDER, orderliness, organization, structure, form, system, logic, planning, design.
– OPPOSITES disorder.
methodical ● adjective ORDERLY, well ordered, well organized, (well) planned, efficient, businesslike, systematic, structured, logical, analytic, disciplined; meticulous, punctilious.
meticulous ● adjective CAREFUL, conscientious, diligent, scrupulous, punctilious, painstaking, accurate; thorough, studious, rigorous, detailed, perfectionist, fastidious, methodical, particular.
– OPPOSITES careless.
métier ● noun **1** *he had another métier besides the priesthood* OCCUPATION, job, work, profession, business, employment, career, vocation, trade, craft, line (of work); *N. Amer.* specialty. **2** *television is more my métier* FORTE, strong point, strength, speciality, talent, bent; *informal* thing, cup of tea.
metropolis ● noun CAPITAL (CITY), chief town, county town; big city, conurbation, megalopolis; *informal* big smoke; *archaic* wen.
mettle ● noun **1** *a man of mettle* SPIRIT, fortitude, strength of character, moral fibre, steel, determination, resolve, resolution, backbone, grit, courage, courageousness, bravery, valour, fearlessness, daring; *informal* guts, spunk; *Brit. informal* bottle. **2** *Frazer was of a very different mettle* CALIBRE, character, disposition, nature, temperament, personality, make-up, stamp.
mettlesome ● adjective SPIRITED, game, gritty, intrepid, fearless,

moult. **2** confine (a moulting trained hawk) to a mew. **3** (**mew up**) confine in a restricting place or situation.
– ORIGIN from Old French *muer* 'to moult'.
mewl • verb **1** cry feebly or querulously. **2** mew.
– ORIGIN imitative.
mews • noun (pl. same) Brit. a row of houses or flats converted from stables in a small street or square.
– ORIGIN from MEW²: first referring to the royal stables on the site of the hawk mews at Charing Cross, London.
Mexican • noun a person from Mexico. • adjective relating to Mexico.
Mexican wave • noun an effect resembling a moving wave produced by successive sections of a stadium crowd standing, raising their arms, lowering them, and sitting down again.
– ORIGIN because first observed at the 1986 soccer World Cup in Mexico City.
meze /mayzay/ (also **mezze**) • noun (pl. same or **mezes**) (in Turkish, Greek, and Middle Eastern cookery) a selection of hot and cold hors d'oeuvres.
– ORIGIN Turkish, 'appetizer'.
mezzanine /mezəneen/ • noun **1** a low storey between two others, typically between the ground and first floors. **2** N. Amer. the lowest balcony of a theatre or the front rows of the balcony.
– ORIGIN from Italian *mezzano* 'middle'.
mezzo /metsō/ (also **mezzo-soprano**) • noun (pl. **mezzos**) a female singer with a voice pitched between soprano and contralto.
– ORIGIN Italian, from Latin *medius* 'middle'.
mezzotint /metsōtint/ • noun a print made from an engraved metal plate, the surface of which has been scraped and polished to give areas of shade and light respectively.
– ORIGIN from Italian *mezzo* 'half' + *tinto* 'tint'.
MF • abbreviation medium frequency.
Mg • symbol the chemical element magnesium.
mg • abbreviation milligram(s).
Mgr • abbreviation **1** (**mgr**) manager. **2** Monseigneur. **3** Monsignor.
MHR • abbreviation (in the US and Australia) Member of the House of Representatives.
MHz • abbreviation megahertz.
MI • abbreviation Michigan.
mi • noun variant spelling of ME².
mi. • abbreviation mile(s).
MI5 • abbreviation Military Intelligence section 5, the former name for the UK governmental agency responsible for internal security and counter-intelligence on British territory (now officially named the Security Service).
MI6 • abbreviation Military Intelligence section 6, the former name for the UK governmental agency responsible for counter-intelligence overseas (now officially named the Secret Intelligence Service).
MIA • abbreviation chiefly US missing in action.
mia-mia /mīəmīə/ • noun Austral. an Aboriginal hut or shelter.
– ORIGIN an Aboriginal word.
miaow (also **meow**) • noun the characteristic cry of a cat. • verb make a miaow.
– ORIGIN imitative.
miasma /miazmə/ • noun literary **1** an unpleasant or unhealthy vapour. **2** an oppressive or unpleasant atmosphere.
– ORIGIN Greek, 'defilement'.
mic • noun informal a microphone.
mica /mīkə/ • noun a silicate mineral found as minute shiny scales in granite and other rocks.
– ORIGIN Latin, 'crumb'.
mice plural of MOUSE.
Michaelmas /mikəlməss/ • noun the day of the Christian festival of St Michael, 29 September.
– ORIGIN Old English, 'Saint Michael's Mass', referring to the Archangel Michael.
Michaelmas daisy • noun an aster with numerous pinkish-lilac daisy-like flowers which bloom around Michaelmas.
Michaelmas term • noun Brit. (in some universities) the autumn term.
mickery (also **mickerie**) • noun (pl. **mickeries**) Austral. a waterhole or excavated well, especially in a dry river bed.
– ORIGIN from an Aboriginal language.
mickey • noun (**take the mickey**) informal, chiefly Brit. tease or ridicule someone.
– DERIVATIVES **mickey-taking** noun.
– ORIGIN of unknown origin.
Mickey Finn • noun informal a surreptitiously drugged or doctored drink.
– ORIGIN perhaps the name of a notorious Chicago saloon-keeper (*c.*1896–1906).
Mickey Mouse • adjective informal ineffective or insignificant.
– ORIGIN from the name of the character created by the American cartoonist Walt Disney (1901–66).
mickle (also **muckle**) archaic or Scottish & N. English • noun a large amount. • adjective very large.
– PHRASES **many a little makes a mickle** (also **many a mickle makes a muckle**) many small amounts accumulate to make a large amount.
– ORIGIN Old English.
– USAGE The forms **mickle** and **muckle** are merely variants of the same (now dialect) word meaning 'a large amount'. However, the alternative form of the proverb (originally a misquotation) has led to a misunderstanding that **mickle** means 'a small amount'.
Micmac /mikmak/ • noun (pl. same or **Micmacs**) a member of an American Indian people inhabiting the Maritime Provinces of Canada.
– ORIGIN the Micmacs' name for themselves.
micro • noun (pl. **micros**) a microcomputer or microprocessor. • adjective extremely small or small-scale.
micro- • combining form **1** very small or of reduced size: *microchip*. **2** denoting a factor of one millionth (10^{-6}): *microfarad*.
– ORIGIN from Greek *mikros* 'small'.
microanalysis • noun the analysis of chemical compounds using a sample of a few milligrams.
microbe /mikrōb/ • noun a micro-organism, especially a bacterium causing disease or fermentation.
– DERIVATIVES **microbial** adjective.
– ORIGIN from Greek *mikros* 'small' + *bios* 'life'.
microbiology • noun the scientific study of micro-organisms.
microbrewery • noun chiefly N. Amer. a brewery producing limited quantities of beer.
microchip • noun a tiny wafer of semiconducting material used to make an integrated circuit.
microcircuit • noun a minute electric circuit, especially an integrated circuit.
microclimate • noun the climate of a very small or restricted area.
microcode • noun Computing a very low-level instruction set controlling the operation of a computer.
microcomputer • noun a small computer with a microprocessor as its central processor.
microcosm /mīkrōkoz'm/ • noun **1** a thing regarded as encapsulating in miniature the characteristics of something much larger. **2** humankind regarded as the epitome of the universe.
– DERIVATIVES **microcosmic** adjective.
– ORIGIN from Greek *mikros kosmos* 'little world'.
microdot • noun **1** a photograph, especially of a printed document, reduced to a very small size. **2** a tiny tablet of LSD.
microeconomics • plural noun (treated as sing.) the part of economics concerned with single factors and the effects of individual decisions.
microelectronics • plural noun (usu. treated as sing.) the design, manufacture, and use of microchips and microcircuits.
microfibre • noun a very fine synthetic yarn.
microfiche /mīkrōfeesh/ • noun a flat piece of film containing greatly reduced photographs of the pages of a newspaper, book, etc.
– ORIGIN from Greek *mikros* 'small' + French *fiche* 'slip of paper, index card'.

m

Thesaurus

courageous, brave, plucky, daring; tenacious, determined, resolved, resolute, indomitable.
mew • verb **1** *the cat mewed plaintively* MIAOW, mewl, cry. **2** *above them, seagulls mewed* CRY, screech.
mewl • verb WHIMPER, cry, whine; *informal* grizzle; *poetic/literary* pule.
miasma • noun (*poetic/literary*) STINK, reek, stench, smell, odour, malodour; *Brit. informal* pong, niff, whiff.
miasmic, miasmal • adjective (*poetic/literary*) FOUL-SMELLING, fetid, smelly, stinking (to high heaven), reeking, rank, noxious, malodorous; *Brit. informal* niffy, pongy, whiffy; *poetic/literary* noisome,

microfilm • noun a length of film containing greatly reduced photographs of a newspaper, book, etc.
microgram • noun one millionth of a gram.
micrograph • noun a photograph taken using a microscope.
microgravity • noun very weak gravity, as in an orbiting spacecraft.
microinstruction • noun Computing a single instruction in microcode.
microlight • noun chiefly Brit. a very small, light, one- or two-seater aircraft.
microlitre (US also **microliter**) • noun one millionth of a litre.
micromesh • noun a material consisting of a very fine mesh.
micrometer /mīkrommitər/ • noun a gauge which measures small distances or thicknesses.
micrometre (US **micrometer**) • noun one millionth of a metre.
micron • noun one millionth of a metre.
Micronesian • noun a person from Micronesia, an island group in the western Pacific. • adjective relating to Micronesia.
micronutrient • noun a chemical element or substance required in trace amounts by living organisms.
micro-organism • noun a microscopic organism, especially a bacterium, virus, or fungus.
microphone • noun an instrument for converting sound waves into electrical energy which may then be amplified, transmitted, or recorded.
microphotograph • noun a photograph reduced to a very small size.
microprocessor • noun an integrated circuit containing all the functions of a central processing unit of a computer.
microprogram • noun a microinstruction program.
micro scooter • noun a two-wheeled foldable aluminium scooter for both children and adults.
microscope • noun an optical instrument for magnifying very small objects.
– ORIGIN from Greek *mikros* 'small' + *skopein* 'look at'.
microscopic • adjective **1** so small as to be visible only with a microscope. **2** informal very small. **3** relating to a microscope.
– DERIVATIVES **microscopically** adverb.
microscopy /mīkroskəpi/ • noun the use of a microscope.
microsecond • noun one millionth of a second.
microstructure • noun the fine structure in a material which can be made visible and examined with a microscope.
microsurgery • noun intricate surgery performed using miniaturized instruments and a microscope.
microwave • noun **1** an electromagnetic wave with a wavelength in the range 0.001–0.3 m, shorter than that of a normal radio wave but longer than those of infrared radiation. **2** (also **microwave oven**) an oven that uses microwaves to cook or heat food. • verb cook (food) in a microwave oven.
micturate /miktyoorayt/ • verb formal urinate.
– DERIVATIVES **micturition** noun.
– ORIGIN Latin *micturire*.
mid • adjective of or in the middle part or position of a range. • preposition literary in the middle of; amid.
mid- • combining form **1** referring to the middle of: *midsection*. **2** in the middle; medium; half: *midway*.
– ORIGIN Old English.
Midas touch • noun the ability to make a lot of money out of anything one undertakes.
– ORIGIN from *Midas*, king of Phrygia, who in Greek mythology was given by Dionysus the power to turn everything he touched into gold.
midbrain • noun Anatomy a small central part of the brainstem, developing from the middle of the primitive or embryonic brain.
midday • noun the middle of the day; noon.
midden • noun a dunghill or refuse heap.
– ORIGIN Scandinavian.
middle • adjective **1** at an equal distance from the extremities of something; central. **2** intermediate in rank, quality, or ability. • noun **1** a middle point or position. **2** informal a person's waist and stomach.
middle age • noun the period between youth and old age, about 45 to 60.
middle-aged • adjective of middle age.
Middle Ages • plural noun the period of European history from the fall of the Roman Empire in the West (5th century) to the fall of Constantinople (1453), or, more narrowly, from *c.*1000 to 1453.
Middle America • noun the conservative middle classes of the United States, characterized as inhabiting the Midwest.
middlebrow • adjective informal, chiefly derogatory demanding or involving only a moderate degree of intellectual application.
middle C • noun Music the C near the middle of the piano keyboard, written on the first ledger line below the treble stave or the first ledger line above the bass stave.
middle class • noun the social group between the upper and working classes; professional and business people.
middle distance • noun **1** the part of a real or painted landscape between the foreground and the background. **2** Athletics a race distance between 800 and 5,000 metres.
middle ear • noun the air-filled central cavity of the ear, behind the eardrum.
Middle East • noun an area of SW Asia and northern Africa, stretching from the Mediterranean to Pakistan, in particular Iran, Iraq, Israel, Jordan, Lebanon, and Syria.
– DERIVATIVES **Middle Eastern** adjective.
Middle England • noun the conservative middle classes in England.
Middle English • noun the English language from *c.*1150 to *c.*1470.
middle ground • noun an area of compromise or possible agreement between two extreme positions.
middleman • noun **1** a person who buys goods from producers and sells them to retailers or consumers. **2** a person who arranges business or political deals between other people.
middle name • noun a person's name placed after the first name and before the surname.
middle of the road • adjective **1** moderate. **2** conventional and unadventurous.
middle school • noun (in the UK) a school for children from about 9 to 13 years old.
middleweight • noun a weight in boxing and other sports intermediate between welterweight and light heavyweight.
middling • adjective moderate or average. • adverb informal fairly or moderately.
Middx • abbreviation Middlesex.
midfield • noun **1** (chiefly in soccer) the central part of the field. **2** the players who play in a central position between attack and defence.
– DERIVATIVES **midfielder** noun.
midge • noun **1** a small two-winged fly that forms swarms near water, of which many kinds feed on blood. **2** informal a small person.
– ORIGIN Old English.
midget • noun **1** an extremely small person. **2** (before another noun) extremely small: *a midget submarine*.
MIDI • noun a standard for interconnecting electronic musical

Thesaurus

mephitic.
microbe • noun MICRO-ORGANISM, bacillus, bacterium, virus, germ; *informal* bug.
microscopic • adjective TINY, very small, minute, infinitesimal, minuscule; little, micro, diminutive; *Scottish* wee; *informal* teeny-weeny, teensy-weensy, itsy-bitsy, eensy-weensy; *Brit. informal* titchy, tiddly.
– OPPOSITES huge.
midday • noun NOON, twelve noon, high noon, noontide, noonday.
– OPPOSITES midnight.
middle • noun **1** *a shallow dish with a spike in the middle* CENTRE, midpoint, halfway point, dead centre, focus, hub; eye, heart, core, kernel. **2** *he had a towel round his middle* MIDRIFF, waist, belly, stomach; *informal* tummy, tum.
– OPPOSITES outside.
• adjective **1** *the middle point* CENTRAL, mid, mean, medium, medial, median, midway, halfway. **2** *the middle level* INTERMEDIATE, intermediary.
– RELATED TERMS meso-.
middleman • noun INTERMEDIARY, go-between; dealer, broker, agent, factor, wholesaler, distributor.
middling • adjective AVERAGE, standard, normal, middle-of-the-road; moderate, ordinary, commonplace, everyday, workaday, tolerable, passable; run-of-the-mill, fair, mediocre, undistinguished, unexceptional, unremarkable; *informal* OK, so-so, bog-standard, fair-to-middling, (plain) vanilla; *NZ informal* half-pie.

instruments and computers.
– ORIGIN from *musical instrument digital interface*.
midi • noun (pl. **midis**) a woman's calf-length skirt, dress, or coat.
midi- • combining form of medium-size or length.
midi system • noun Brit. a set of compact stacking hi-fi equipment components.
midland • noun **1** the middle part of a country. **2** (**the Midlands**) the inland counties of central England. • adjective (also **midlands**) of or in a midland or the Midlands.
– DERIVATIVES **midlander** noun.
midlife • noun the central period of a person's life, between around 45 and 60 years old.
midnight • noun twelve o'clock at night; the middle of the night.
midnight blue • noun a very dark blue.
midnight sun • noun the sun when seen at midnight during the summer within either the Arctic or Antarctic Circle.
mid-off • noun Cricket a fielding position on the off side near the bowler.
mid-on • noun Cricket a fielding position on the on side near the bowler.
midrib • noun a large strengthened vein along the midline of a leaf.
midriff • noun the front of the body between the chest and the waist.
– ORIGIN Old English.
midship • noun the middle part of a ship or boat.
midshipman • noun **1** a rank of officer in the Royal Navy, above naval cadet and below sub lieutenant. **2** a naval cadet in the US navy.
midships • adverb & adjective another term for AMIDSHIPS.
midst archaic or literary • preposition in the middle of. • noun the middle point or part.
– PHRASES **in our** (or **your**, **their**, etc.) **midst** among us (or you or them).
midstream • noun the middle of a stream or river.
– PHRASES **in midstream** part-way through an activity, speech, etc.
midsummer • noun **1** the middle part of summer. **2** the summer solstice.
Midsummer Day (also **Midsummer's Day**) • noun 24 June.
midterm • noun the middle of a period of office, an academic term, or a pregnancy.
midway • adverb & adjective in or towards the middle.
midweek • noun the middle of the week. • adjective & adverb in the middle of the week.
Midwest • noun the region of northern states of the US from Ohio west to the Rocky Mountains.
– DERIVATIVES **Midwestern** adjective.
midwicket • noun Cricket a fielding position on the leg side, level with the middle of the pitch.
midwife • noun a nurse who is trained to assist women in childbirth.
– DERIVATIVES **midwifery** /midwifəri/ noun.
– ORIGIN probably from obsolete *mid* 'with' + WIFE (in the sense 'woman').
midwinter • noun **1** the middle part of winter. **2** the winter solstice.
mien /meen/ • noun a person's look or manner.
– ORIGIN probably from French *mine* 'expression'.
miffed • adjective informal offended or irritated.
– ORIGIN perhaps imitative.
might[1] • modal verb (3rd sing. present **might**) past of MAY[1]. **1** used to express possibility or make a suggestion. **2** used politely or tentatively in questions and requests.
might[2] • noun great power or strength.
– PHRASES **with might and main** with all one's strength or power.
– ORIGIN Old English, related to MAY.
mightn't • contraction might not.
mighty • adjective (**mightier**, **mightiest**) **1** possessing great power or strength. **2** informal very large. • adverb informal, chiefly N. Amer. extremely.
– DERIVATIVES **mightily** adverb **mightiness** noun.
mignonette /minyənet/ • noun a plant with spikes of small fragrant greenish flowers.
– ORIGIN French, from *mignon* 'small and sweet'.
migraine /meegrayn, mīgrayn/ • noun a recurrent throbbing headache, typically affecting one side of the head and often accompanied by nausea and disturbed vision.
– USAGE The standard pronunciation of **migraine** in British English is /**mee**grayn/, which is closer to the pronunciation of the original word in French. However, many people in Britain say /**mī**grayn/, and this pronunciation is standard in the US.
– ORIGIN French, from Greek *hēmikrania*, from *hēmi-* 'half' + *kranion* 'skull'.
migrant • noun **1** an animal that migrates. **2** a worker who moves from one place to another to find work. • adjective tending to migrate or having migrated.
migrate • verb **1** (of an animal) move from one habitat to another according to the seasons. **2** move to settle in a new area in order to find work. **3** Computing transfer from one system to another.
– DERIVATIVES **migration** noun **migratory** adjective.
– ORIGIN Latin *migrare* 'move, shift', the root also of EMIGRATE and IMMIGRATE.
mihrab /meeraab/ • noun a niche in the wall of a mosque, at the point nearest to Mecca, towards which the congregation faces to pray.
– ORIGIN Arabic, 'place for prayer'.

m

Thesaurus

midget • noun *the inhabitants must have been midgets* SMALL PERSON, dwarf, homunculus, Lilliputian, manikin, gnome, pygmy; *informal* shrimp.
• adjective **1** *a story about midget matadors* DIMINUTIVE, dwarfish, petite, very small, pygmy; *informal* pint-sized; *N. Amer. informal* sawn-off. **2** *a midget camera* MINIATURE, pocket, dwarf, baby.
– OPPOSITES giant.
midnight • noun TWELVE MIDNIGHT, the middle of the night, the witching hour.
– OPPOSITES midday.
midst *(poetic/literary)* • noun MIDDLE, centre, heart, core, midpoint, kernel, nub; depth(s), thick; (**in the midst of**) in the course of, halfway through, at the heart/core of.
– PHRASES **in our midst** AMONG US, amid us, in our group, with us.
midway • adverb HALFWAY, in the middle, at the midpoint, in the centre; part-way, at some point.
mien • noun APPEARANCE, look, expression, countenance, aura, demeanour, attitude, air, manner, bearing; *formal* comportment.
miffed • adjective *(informal)*. See ANNOYED.
might • noun STRENGTH, force, power, vigour, energy, brawn, powerfulness, forcefulness.
– PHRASES **with might and main** WITH ALL ONE'S STRENGTH, as hard as one can, as hard as possible, (with) full force, forcefully, powerfully, strongly, vigorously.
mightily • adverb **1** *he is mightily impressive* EXTREMELY, exceedingly, enormously, immensely, tremendously, hugely, dreadfully, very (much); *informal* awfully, majorly, mega; *N. Amer. informal* mighty, plumb; *informal, dated* devilish. **2** *Ann and I laboured mightily* STRENUOUSLY, energetically, powerfully, hard, with all one's might, with might and main, all out, heartily, vigorously, diligently, assiduously, persistently, indefatigably; *informal* like mad, like crazy; *Brit. informal* like billy-o.
mighty • adjective **1** *a mighty blow* POWERFUL, forceful, violent, vigorous, hefty, thunderous. **2** *a mighty warrior* FEARSOME, ferocious; big, tough, robust, muscular, strapping. **3** *mighty industrial countries* DOMINANT, influential, strong, powerful, important, predominant. **4** *mighty oak trees* HUGE, enormous, massive, gigantic, big, large, giant, colossal, mammoth, immense; *informal* monster, whopping (great), thumping (great), humongous, jumbo(-sized); *Brit. informal* whacking (great), ginormous.
– OPPOSITES feeble, puny, tiny.
• adverb *(N. Amer. informal) I'm mighty pleased to see you* EXTREMELY, exceedingly, enormously, immensely, tremendously, hugely, mightily, very (much); *informal* awfully, dreadfully, majorly, mega; *Brit. informal* well, jolly; *N. Amer. informal* plumb; *informal, dated* devilish, frightfully.
migrant • noun *economic migrants* IMMIGRANT, EMIGRANT; nomad, itinerant, traveller, vagrant, transient, rover, wanderer, drifter.
• adjective *migrant workers* TRAVELLING, wandering, drifting, nomadic, roving, roaming, itinerant, vagrant, transient.
migrate • verb **1** *rural populations migrated to urban areas* RELOCATE, resettle, move (house); emigrate, go abroad, go overseas; *N. Amer.* pull up stakes; *Brit. informal* up sticks; *dated* remove. **2** *wildebeest migrate across the Serengeti* ROAM, wander, drift, rove, travel

mikado /mikaadō/ ● noun historical a title given to the emperor of Japan.
– ORIGIN Japanese, from *mi* 'august' + *kado* 'gate'.
mike informal ● noun a microphone.
mil[1] ● abbreviation informal millions.
mil[2] ● noun one thousandth of an inch.
– ORIGIN from Latin *millesimum* 'thousandth'.
milady ● noun historical or humorous used to address or refer to an English noblewoman.
milch ● adjective (of a domestic mammal) giving or kept for milk.
– ORIGIN from Old English *-milce* in *thrimilce* 'May' (when cows could be milked three times a day).
milch cow ● noun a source of easy profit.
mild ● adjective **1** gentle and not easily provoked. **2** of moderate severity, intensity, or effect. **3** not sharp or strong in flavour. **4** (of weather) moderately warm; less cold than expected. ● noun Brit. a kind of dark beer not strongly flavoured with hops.
– DERIVATIVES **mildish** adjective **mildly** adverb **mildness** noun.
– ORIGIN Old English.
mildew ● noun a coating of minute fungi on plants or damp organic material such as paper or leather. ● verb affect with mildew.
– ORIGIN Old English.
mild steel ● noun steel containing a small percentage of carbon, that is strong and tough but not readily tempered.
mile ● noun **1** (also **statute mile**) a unit of linear measure equal to 1,760 yards (approximately 1.609 kilometres). **2** (**miles**) informal a very long way. ● adverb (**miles**) informal by a great amount or a long way.
– PHRASES **be miles away** informal be lost in thought. **go the extra mile** try particularly hard to achieve something. **run a mile** informal run rapidly away; flee. **stand** (or **stick**) **out a mile** informal be very obvious or incongruous.
– ORIGIN from Latin *milia*, plural of *mille* 'thousand'; a Roman 'mile' consisted of 1,000 paces (approximately 1,620 yards).
mileage (also **milage**) ● noun **1** a number of miles travelled or covered. **2** informal actual or potential benefit or advantage.
mileometer ● noun variant spelling of MILOMETER.
milepost ● noun chiefly N. Amer. & Austral. **1** a milestone. **2** a post one mile from the finishing post of a race.
miler ● noun informal a person or horse trained to run over races of a mile.
milestone ● noun **1** a stone set up beside a road to mark the distance in miles to a particular place. **2** an event marking a significant new development or stage.
milfoil ● noun **1** the common yarrow. **2** (also **water milfoil**) an aquatic plant with whorls of fine submerged leaves.
– ORIGIN from Latin *mille* 'thousand' + *folium* 'leaf'.
miliary /milliəri/ ● adjective Medicine (of a disease) accompanied by a rash with small round lesions resembling millet seed.
– ORIGIN from Latin *milium* 'millet'.
milieu /meelyö/ ● noun (pl. **milieux** or **milieus**) a person's social environment.
– ORIGIN French, from *mi* 'mid' + *lieu* 'place'.
militant ● adjective favouring confrontational methods in support of a cause. ● noun a militant person.
– DERIVATIVES **militancy** noun **militantly** adverb.
militaria ● plural noun military articles of historical interest.
militarism ● noun the belief that a country should maintain and readily use strong armed forces.
– DERIVATIVES **militarist** noun & adjective.
militaristic ● adjective characterized by militarism.
militarize (also **militarise**) ● verb **1** equip with military resources. **2** give a military character to.
military ● adjective relating to or characteristic of soldiers or armed forces. ● noun (**the military**) the armed forces of a country.
– DERIVATIVES **militarily** adverb.
– ORIGIN Latin *militaris*, from *miles* 'soldier'.
military attaché ● noun an army officer serving with an embassy or attached as an observer to a foreign army.
Military Cross ● noun (in the UK and Commonwealth) a decoration awarded for distinguished active service on land (originally for officers).
military honours ● plural noun ceremonies performed by troops as a mark of respect at the burial of a member of the armed forces.
military-industrial complex ● noun a country's military establishment and arms industries regarded as a powerful vested interest.
Military Medal ● noun (in the UK and Commonwealth) a decoration awarded for distinguished active service on land (originally for enlisted men).
military police ● noun a body responsible for disciplinary duties in the armed forces.
militate ● verb (**militate against**) be a powerful or conclusive factor in preventing.
– USAGE On the confusion between **militate** and **mitigate**, see the note at MITIGATE.
– ORIGIN Latin *militare* 'wage war', from *miles* 'soldier'.
militia /milishə/ ● noun **1** a military force raised from the civilian population to supplement a regular army in an emergency. **2** a rebel force opposing a regular army.
– ORIGIN Latin, 'military service'.
militiaman ● noun a member of a militia.
milk ● noun **1** an opaque white fluid produced by female mammals for the nourishment of their young. **2** the milk of cows as a food and drink for humans. **3** the milk-like juice of certain plants, such as the coconut. ● verb **1** draw milk from (a cow or other animal). **2** exploit or defraud over a period of time. **3** take full advantage of (a situation).
– PHRASES **it's no use crying over spilt milk** proverb there is no point in regretting something which has already happened. **milk and honey** prosperity and abundance. **milk of human kindness** care and compassion for others. [ORIGIN from Shakespeare's *Macbeth*.]
– ORIGIN Old English.
milk-and-water ● adjective feeble; ineffective.
milk bar ● noun Brit. a snack bar selling milk drinks.
milk chocolate ● noun solid chocolate made with the addition of milk.
milk fever ● noun an acute illness in cows or other female animals that have just produced young.
milk float ● noun Brit. an open-sided electrically powered van used for delivering milk to houses.
milkmaid ● noun chiefly archaic a girl or woman who works in a dairy.
milkman ● noun a man who delivers milk to houses.
milk pudding ● noun Brit. a baked pudding made of milk and a grain such as rice, sago, or tapioca.
milk round ● noun Brit. **1** a regular milk delivery along a fixed route. **2** a series of visits to universities and colleges by re-

m

Thesaurus

(around).
migratory ● adjective MIGRANT, migrating, moving, travelling.
mild ● adjective **1** *a mild tone of voice* GENTLE, tender, soft-hearted, tender-hearted, sensitive, sympathetic, warm, placid, calm, tranquil, serene, peaceable, good-natured, amiable, affable, genial, easy-going. **2** *a mild punishment* LENIENT, light; compassionate, merciful, humane. **3** *he was eyeing her with mild interest* SLIGHT, faint, vague, minimal, nominal, token, feeble. **4** *mild weather* WARM, balmy, temperate, clement. **5** *a mild curry* BLAND, insipid.
– OPPOSITES harsh, strong, severe.
mildewy ● adjective MOULDY, mildewed, rotten, decaying.
milieu ● noun ENVIRONMENT, sphere, background, backdrop, setting, context, atmosphere; location, conditions, surroundings, environs.
militant ● adjective *militant supporters* AGGRESSIVE, violent, belligerent, bellicose, vigorous, forceful, active, fierce, combative, pugnacious; radical, extremist, extreme, zealous, fanatical.
● noun *the demands of the militants* ACTIVIST, extremist, radical, young turk, zealot.
militaristic ● adjective WARMONGERING, warlike, martial, hawkish, pugnacious, combative, aggressive, belligerent, bellicose; informal gung-ho.
– OPPOSITES peaceable.
military ● adjective *military activity* FIGHTING, service, army, armed, defence, martial.
– OPPOSITES civilian.
● noun *the military took power* (ARMED) FORCES, services, militia; army, navy, air force, marines.
militate ● verb TEND TO PREVENT, work against, hinder, discourage, prejudice, be detrimental to.
milk ● verb **1** *Pam was milking the cows* DRAW MILK FROM, express milk from. **2** *milk a little of the liquid* DRAW OFF, siphon (off), pump

cruiting staff from large companies.
milk run • noun a routine, uneventful journey, especially by aircraft.
– ORIGIN RAF slang in the Second World War for a sortie that was as simple as a milkman's round.
milkshake • noun a cold drink made from milk whisked with ice cream.
milksop • noun a timid and indecisive person.
milk stout • noun a kind of sweet stout made with lactose.
milk tooth • noun a temporary tooth in a child or young mammal.
milky • adjective **1** containing milk. **2** of a soft white colour or clouded appearance.
– DERIVATIVES **milkily** adverb **milkiness** noun.
Milky Way • noun the galaxy of which our solar system is a part, visible at night as a faint band of light crossing the sky.
mill[1] • noun **1** a building equipped with machinery for grinding grain into flour. **2** a device or piece of machinery for grinding grain or other solid substances. **3** a building fitted with machinery for a manufacturing process. • verb **1** grind in a mill. **2** cut or shape (metal) with a rotating tool. **3** produce regular ribbed markings on the edge of (a coin). **4** (**mill about/around**) move around in a confused mass.
– PHRASES **go** (or **put**) **through the mill** undergo (or cause to undergo) an unpleasant experience.
– ORIGIN Latin *mola* 'grindstone, mill'.
mill[2] • noun N. Amer. a monetary unit used only in calculations, worth one thousandth of a dollar.
– ORIGIN from Latin *millesimum* 'thousandth part'.
millboard • noun stiff grey pasteboard, used for the covers of books.
millefeuille /meelfö-i/ • noun a cake consisting of thin layers of puff pastry filled with jam and cream.
– ORIGIN French, 'thousand-leaf'.
millenarian /millinairiən/ • adjective **1** relating to or believing in Christian millenarianism. **2** seeking rapid and radical change. • noun a person who believes in millenarianism.
– USAGE Note that **millenarian**, **millenarianism**, and **millenary** are spelt with only one **n**; see the note at MILLENNIUM.
– ORIGIN Latin *millenarius* 'having a thousand'.
millenarianism • noun the belief in a future thousand-year age of blessedness, beginning with or culminating in the Second Coming of Christ.
– DERIVATIVES **millenarianist** noun & adjective.
millenary /milennəri/ • noun (pl. **millenaries**) **1** a period of a thousand years. **2** a thousandth anniversary. • adjective consisting of a thousand.
millennial • adjective relating to a millennium.
millennialism • noun another term for MILLENARIANISM.
– DERIVATIVES **millennialist** noun & adjective.
millennium /milleniəm/ • noun (pl. **millennia** or **millenniums**) **1** a period of a thousand years, especially when calculated from the traditional date of the birth of Christ. **2** (**the millennium**) the point at which one period of a thousand years ends and another begins. **3** (**the millennium**) Christian Theology the prophesied thousand-year reign of Christ at the end of the age. **4** an anniversary of a thousand years.
– USAGE The correct spelling is **millennium**, with two **n**s. The spelling with one **n** is a common error, formed by confusion with other words such as **millenarian**, correctly spelled with only one **n**. The differences in spelling are explained by different origins. **Millennium** was formed by analogy with words like **biennium**, while **millenarian** was formed on the Latin *milleni* 'a thousand each'.
– ORIGIN from Latin *mille* 'thousand' + *annus* 'year'.
millennium bug • noun an inability in older computing software to deal correctly with dates of 1 January 2000 or later.
miller • noun a person who owns or works in a grain mill.
miller's thumb • noun a small freshwater fish with a broad flattened head.
millesimal /milessim'l/ • adjective relating to division into thousandths; thousandth.
– ORIGIN Latin *millesimus*, from *mille* 'thousand'.
millet • noun a cereal which bears a large crop of small seeds, used to make flour or alcoholic drinks.
– ORIGIN French, from Latin *milium*.
milli- • combining form a thousand, especially a factor of one thousandth (10^{-3}): *milligram*.
– ORIGIN from Latin *mille* 'thousand'.
milliard • noun Brit., dated one thousand million; a billion.
millibar • noun one thousandth of a bar, a unit of atmospheric pressure equivalent to 100 pascals.
millieme /milyem/ • noun a monetary unit of Egypt, equal to one thousandth of a pound.
– ORIGIN from French, 'thousandth'.
milligram (also **milligramme**) • noun one thousandth of a gram.
millilitre (US **milliliter**) • noun one thousandth of a litre.
millimetre (US **millimeter**) • noun one thousandth of a metre.
milliner • noun a person who makes or sells women's hats.
– DERIVATIVES **millinery** noun.
– ORIGIN from the name of the Italian city *Milan*, originally meaning 'native of Milan', later 'a vendor of fancy goods from Milan'.
million • cardinal number (pl. **millions** or (with numeral or quantifying word) same) **1** the number equivalent to the product of a thousand and a thousand; 1,000,000 or 10^6. **2** (also **millions**) informal a very large number or amount.
– DERIVATIVES **millionth** ordinal number.
millionaire • noun (fem. **millionairess**) a person whose assets are worth one million pounds or dollars or more.
millipede • noun a small invertebrate animal (an arthropod) with an elongated body composed of many segments, most of which bear two pairs of legs.
– ORIGIN from Latin *mille* 'thousand' + *pes* 'foot'.
millisecond • noun one thousandth of a second.
millpond • noun **1** the pool created by a mill dam, providing the head of water that powers a watermill. **2** a very still and calm stretch of water.
mill race • noun the channel carrying the swift current of water that drives a mill wheel.
millstone • noun **1** each of a pair of circular stones used for grinding grain. **2** a burden of responsibility.
millstone grit • noun a coarse sandstone occurring in Britain immediately below the coal measures.
millstream • noun the flowing water that drives a mill wheel.
mill wheel • noun a wheel used to drive a watermill.
milo • noun a drought-resistant variety of sorghum, an important cereal in the central US.
– ORIGIN Sesotho (an African language).
milometer /milommitər/ (also **mileometer**) • noun Brit. an instrument on a vehicle for recording the number of miles travelled.
milord • noun historical or humorous used to address or refer to an English nobleman.
Milquetoast /milktōst/ • noun chiefly N. Amer. a timid or submissive person.
– ORIGIN from the name of an American cartoon character, Caspar *Milquetoast*, created by H. T. Webster in 1924.
milt • noun **1** the semen of a male fish. **2** the reproductive gland of a male fish.
– ORIGIN Old English, perhaps related to MELT.
Miltonian (also **Miltonic**) • adjective relating to the English poet John Milton (1608–74).
mime • noun **1** the expression of action, character, or emotion by gesture alone, especially as a form of theatrical performance. **2** (in ancient Greece and Rome) a simple farcical drama including mimicry. **3** a performer of mime. • verb **1** use mime to act out. **2** pretend to sing or play an instrument as a record-

m

Thesaurus

off, tap, drain, extract. **3** *milking rich clients* EXPLOIT, take advantage of, cash in on, suck dry; *informal* bleed, squeeze, fleece.
– RELATED TERMS dairy, lactic.
milksop • noun NAMBY-PAMBY, coward, weakling; *informal* drip, mummy's boy, sissy, jellyfish, wimp; *Brit. informal* wet, big girl's blouse; *N. Amer. informal* pantywaist, pussy; *archaic* poltroon.
milky • adjective PALE, white, milk-white, whitish, off-white, cream, creamy, chalky, pearly, nacreous, ivory, alabaster.
– OPPOSITES swarthy.
mill • noun **1** *a steel mill* FACTORY, (processing) plant, works, workshop, shop, foundry, industrial unit. **2** *a pepper mill* GRINDER, quern, crusher.
• verb *the wheat is milled into flour* GRIND, pulverize, powder, granulate, pound, crush, press; *technical* comminute, triturate; *archaic* bray, levigate.
– PHRASES **mill around/about** THRONG, swarm, seethe, crowd.

ing is being played.
– ORIGIN Greek *mimos*.
mimeograph ● noun a duplicating machine which produces copies from a stencil, now superseded by the photocopier.
– ORIGIN from Greek *mimeomai* 'I imitate'.
mimesis /mimeessiss/ ● noun **1** imitative representation of the real world in art and literature. **2** Biology mimicry of another animal or plant.
– ORIGIN Greek, from *mimeisthai* 'to imitate'.
mimetic /mimettik/ ● adjective relating to or practising mimesis or mimicry.
mimic ● verb (**mimicked**, **mimicking**) **1** imitate in order to entertain or ridicule. **2** (of an animal or plant) take on the appearance of (another) to deter predators or for camouflage. **3** replicate the effects of. ● noun **1** a person skilled in mimicking. **2** an animal or plant that mimics.
mimicry ● noun **1** imitation of someone or something to entertain or ridicule. **2** Biology the close external resemblance of an animal or plant to another.
mimosa /mimōzə/ ● noun **1** an acacia tree with delicate fernlike leaves and yellow flowers. **2** a plant of a genus that includes the sensitive plant (*Mimosa pudica*).
– ORIGIN probably from Latin *mimus* 'mime' (because the plant seemingly mimics an animal's sensitivity to touch).
mimsy ● adjective rather feeble and prim.
– ORIGIN a nonsense word coined by Lewis Carroll from MISERABLE and FLIMSY.
min. ● abbreviation **1** minimum. **2** minute(s).
minaret ● noun a slender tower of a mosque, with a balcony from which Muslims are called to prayer.
– ORIGIN Arabic.
minatory /minnətəri/ ● adjective formal threatening.
– ORIGIN from Latin *minari* 'threaten'.
mince ● verb **1** cut up or shred (meat) into very small pieces. **2** walk in an affected manner with short, quick steps and swinging hips. ● noun chiefly Brit. minced meat.
– PHRASES **mince (one's) words** voice one's disapproval delicately or gently.
– DERIVATIVES **mincer** noun **mincing** adjective.
– ORIGIN Old French *mincier*, from Latin *minutia* 'smallness'.
mincemeat ● noun a mixture of currants, raisins, apples, candied peel, sugar, spices, and suet.
– PHRASES **make mincemeat of** informal defeat decisively.
mince pie ● noun chiefly Brit. a pie containing mincemeat, typically eaten at Christmas.
mind ● noun **1** the faculty of consciousness and thought. **2** a person's intellect or memory. **3** a person identified with their intellectual faculties. **4** a person's attention or will. ● verb **1** be distressed or annoyed by; object to. **2** remember or take care to do. **3** give attention to; watch out for. **4** take care of temporarily. **5** (**be minded**) be inclined to do. **6** (also **mind you**) introducing a qualification to a previous statement.
– PHRASES **be in** (or **of**) **two minds** be unable to decide between alternatives. **be of one mind** share the same opinion. **give someone a piece of one's mind** rebuke someone. **have a** (or **a good** or **half a**) **mind to do** be inclined to do. **have in mind 1** be thinking of. **2** intend to do. **in one's mind's eye** in one's imagination. **mind one's Ps & Qs** be careful to be polite and avoid giving offence. [ORIGIN perhaps referring to the care a young pupil must pay in differentiating the tailed letters *p* and *q*.] **never mind 1** do not be concerned or distressed. **2** let alone. **out of one's mind** having lost control of one's mental faculties. **put one in mind of** remind one of. **to my mind** in my opinion.
– ORIGIN Old English.
mind-bending ● adjective informal altering one's state of mind.
mind-blowing ● adjective informal overwhelmingly impressive.
mind-boggling ● adjective informal overwhelming.
minded ● adjective inclined to think in a particular way: *liberal-minded*.
minder ● noun **1** a person employed to look after someone or something. **2** informal a bodyguard.
mindful ● adjective **1** (**mindful of/that**) aware of or recognizing that. **2** formal inclined or intending to do something.
mind game ● noun a series of actions planned for its psychological effect on another.
mindless ● adjective **1** acting or done without justification and with no concern for the consequences. **2** (**mindless of**) not thinking of or concerned about. **3** (of an activity) simple and repetitive.
– DERIVATIVES **mindlessly** adverb **mindlessness** noun.

m

Thesaurus

millstone ● noun BURDEN, encumbrance, dead weight, cross to bear, albatross; duty, obligation, liability, misfortune; *archaic* cumber.
mime ● noun *a mime of someone fencing* DUMB SHOW, pantomime.
● verb *she mimed picking up a phone* ACT OUT, pantomime, gesture, simulate, represent, indicate by dumb show.
mimic ● verb **1** *she mimicked his accent* IMITATE, copy, impersonate, do an impression of, ape, caricature, parody, lampoon, burlesque; *informal* send up, take off, spoof; *archaic* monkey. **2** *most hoverflies mimic wasps* RESEMBLE, look like, have the appearance of, simulate; *N. Amer. informal* make like.
● noun *he was a superb mimic* IMPERSONATOR, impressionist, imitator, mimicker; parodist, caricaturist, lampooner, lampoonist; *informal* copycat; *historical* zany; *archaic* ape.
● adjective *they were waging mimic war* SIMULATED, mock, imitation, make-believe, sham; *informal* pretend, copycat.
mimicry ● noun IMITATION, imitating, impersonation, copying, aping; *archaic* apery.
minatory ● adjective (*formal*) MENACING, threatening, baleful, intimidating, admonitory, warning, cautionary; *rare* minacious, comminatory.
mince ● verb **1** *mince the meat and onions* GRIND, chop up, cut up, dice; *N. Amer.* hash. **2** *she minced out of the room* WALK AFFECTEDLY; *N. Amer. informal* sashay.
– PHRASES **not mince (one's) words** TALK STRAIGHT, not beat about the bush, call a spade a spade, speak straight from the shoulder, pull no punches; *informal* tell it like it is; *N. Amer. informal* talk turkey.
mincing ● adjective AFFECTED, dainty, effeminate, niminy-piminy; pretentious; *informal* camp, sissy; *Brit. informal* poncey.
mind ● noun **1** *a good teacher must stretch pupils' minds* BRAIN, intelligence, intellect, intellectual capabilities, brains, brainpower, wits, understanding, reasoning, judgement, sense, head; *informal* grey matter, brainbox, brain cells; *Brit. informal* loaf; *N. Amer. informal* smarts. **2** *he kept his mind on the job* ATTENTION, thoughts, concentration, attentiveness. **3** *the tragedy affected her mind* SANITY, mental faculties, senses, wits, reason, reasoning, judgement; *informal* marbles. **4** *his words stuck in her mind* MEMORY, recollection. **5** *a great mind* INTELLECT, thinker, brain, scholar, academic. **6** *I've a mind to complain* INCLINATION, desire, wish, urge, notion, fancy, intention, will. **7** *of the same mind* OPINION, way of thinking, outlook, attitude, view, viewpoint, point of view.
– RELATED TERMS mental.
– OPPOSITES body.
● verb **1** *do you mind if I smoke?* CARE, object, be bothered, be annoyed, be upset, take offence, disapprove, dislike it, look askance; *informal* give/care a damn, give/care a toss, give/care a hoot, give/care a rap. **2** *mind the step!* BE CAREFUL OF, watch out for, look out for, beware of, be on one's guard for, be wary of. **3** *mind you wipe your feet* BE/MAKE SURE (THAT), see (that); remember to, don't forget to. **4** *her husband was minding the baby* LOOK AFTER, take care of, keep an eye on, attend to, care for, tend. **5** *mind what your mother says* PAY ATTENTION TO, heed, pay heed to, attend to, take note/notice of, note, mark, listen to, be mindful of; obey, follow, comply with; *archaic* regard.
– PHRASES **be in two minds** BE UNDECIDED, be uncertain, be unsure, hesitate, waver, vacillate, dither; *Brit.* haver, hum and haw; *informal* dilly-dally, shilly-shally. **bear/keep in mind** REMEMBER, note, be mindful of, take note of; *formal* take cognizance of. **cross one's mind** OCCUR TO ONE, enter one's mind/head, strike one, hit one, dawn on one. **give someone a piece of one's mind.** See REPRIMAND verb. **have something in mind** THINK OF, contemplate; intend, plan, propose, desire, want, wish. **mind out** TAKE CARE, be careful, watch out, look out, beware, be on one's guard, be wary. **never mind 1** *never mind the cost* DON'T BOTHER ABOUT, don't worry about, disregard, forget. **2** *never mind, it's all right now* DON'T APOLOGIZE, forget it, don't worry about it, it doesn't matter. **out of one's mind 1** *you must be out of your mind!* See MAD sense 1. **2** *I've been out of my mind with worry* FRANTIC, beside oneself, distraught, in a frenzy. **put someone in mind of** REMIND OF, recall, conjure up, suggest; RESEMBLE, look like. **to my mind** IN MY OPINION, in my view, as I see it, personally, in my estimation, in my book, if you ask me.
mindful ● adjective AWARE, conscious, sensible, alive, alert, acquainted, heedful, wary, chary; *informal* wise, hip; *formal* cognizant,

mind-numbing ● adjective so extreme or intense as to prevent normal thought.
mindset ● noun a habitual way of thinking.
mindshare ● noun consumer awareness of a product or brand, as opposed to market share.
mine[1] ● possessive pronoun referring to a thing or things belonging to or associated with the speaker. ● possessive determiner archaic (used before a vowel) my.
– ORIGIN Old English, related to ME[1].
mine[2] ● noun **1** an excavation in the earth for extracting coal or other minerals. **2** an abundant source. **3** a type of bomb placed on or in the ground or water, which detonates on contact. **4** historical a passage tunnelled under the wall of a besieged fortress, in which explosives were placed. ● verb **1** obtain from a mine. **2** excavate for coal or other minerals. **3** lay a mine or mines on or in.
– ORIGIN Old French.
minefield ● noun **1** an area planted with explosive mines. **2** a subject or situation presenting unseen hazards.
miner ● noun a person who works in a mine.
mineral ● noun **1** a solid inorganic substance of natural occurrence, such as copper and silicon. **2** an inorganic substance needed by the human body for good health, such as calcium and iron. **3** a substance obtained by mining. **4** (**minerals**) Brit. fizzy soft drinks.
– ORIGIN Latin *minera* 'ore'.
mineralize (also **mineralise**) ● verb convert into or impregnate with a mineral substance.
– DERIVATIVES **mineralization** noun.
mineralogy ● noun the scientific study of minerals.
– DERIVATIVES **mineralogical** adjective **mineralogist** noun.
mineral oil ● noun petroleum, or a distillation product of petroleum.
mineral water ● noun water having some dissolved salts naturally present.
mineshaft ● noun a deep, narrow shaft that gives access to a mine.
minestrone /minnistrōni/ ● noun an Italian soup containing vegetables and pasta.
– ORIGIN from Italian *minestrare* 'serve at table'.
minesweeper ● noun a warship equipped for detecting and removing or destroying tethered explosive mines.
Ming ● adjective (of Chinese porcelain) made during the Ming dynasty (1368–1644), characterized by elaborate designs and vivid colours.
– ORIGIN Chinese, 'clear or bright'.
mingle ● verb **1** mix together. **2** move around and chat at a social function.
– ORIGIN from obsolete *meng* 'mix or blend'.
mingy ● adjective informal mean; ungenerous.
– ORIGIN perhaps a blend of MEAN[2] and STINGY.
mini ● adjective miniaturized; very small of its kind. ● noun (pl. **minis**) a very short skirt or dress.
mini- ● combining form very small or minor of its kind; miniature: *minibus*.
– ORIGIN from MINIATURE, reinforced by MINIMUM.
miniature ● adjective of a much smaller size than normal. ● noun **1** a thing that is much smaller than normal. **2** a very small and minutely detailed portrait. **3** a picture or decorated letter in an illuminated manuscript.
– DERIVATIVES **miniaturize** (also **miniaturise**) verb.
– ORIGIN from Latin *minium* 'red lead, vermilion' (which was used to mark particular words in manuscripts).
miniaturist ● noun an artist who paints miniatures.
minibar ● noun a refrigerator in a hotel room containing a selection of drinks.
minibus ● noun a small bus for about ten to fifteen passengers.
minicab ● noun Brit. a car that is available for hire as a taxi but can only be ordered in advance.
minicam ● noun a hand-held video camera.
minicomputer ● noun a computer of medium power, more than a microcomputer but less than a mainframe.
minidisc ● noun a disc similar to a small CD but able to record sound or data as well as play it back.
minidress ● noun a very short dress.
minigolf ● noun an informal version of golf played on a series of short obstacle courses.
minikin ● adjective chiefly archaic small; insignificant.
– ORIGIN from Dutch *minne* 'love, friendship' + -KIN.
minim ● noun **1** Music, chiefly Brit. a note having the time value of two crotchets or half a semibreve, represented by a ring with a stem. **2** one sixtieth of a fluid drachm, about one drop of liquid.
– ORIGIN from Latin *minimus* 'smallest'.
minima plural of MINIMUM.
minimal ● adjective **1** of a minimum amount, quantity, or degree. **2** Art characterized by the use of simple forms or structures. **3** Music characterized by the repetition and gradual alteration of short phrases.
– DERIVATIVES **minimally** adverb.
minimalist ● noun **1** an advocate or practitioner of minimal art or music. **2** an advocate of moderate political reform. ● adjective **1** relating to minimal art or music. **2** advocating moderate political reform.
– DERIVATIVES **minimalism** noun.
minimize (also **minimise**) ● verb **1** reduce to the smallest possible amount or degree. **2** represent or estimate at less than the true value.
– DERIVATIVES **minimization** noun **minimizer** noun.
minimum ● noun (pl. **minima** or **minimums**) the least or smallest amount, extent, or intensity possible or recorded. ● adjective smallest or lowest in amount, extent, or intensity.
– ORIGIN Latin.

m

Thesaurus

regardful.
– OPPOSITES heedless.
mindless ● adjective **1** *a mindless idiot* STUPID, idiotic, brainless, imbecilic, imbecile, asinine, witless, foolish, empty-headed, slow-witted, obtuse, feather-brained, doltish; *informal* dumb, pig-ignorant, brain-dead, cretinous, moronic, thick, birdbrained, peabrained, dopey, dim, half-witted, dippy, fat-headed, boneheaded; *N. Amer. informal* chowderheaded. **2** *mindless acts of vandalism* UNTHINKING, thoughtless, senseless, gratuitous, wanton, indiscriminate, unreasoning. **3** *a mindless task* MECHANICAL, automatic, routine; tedious, boring, monotonous, brainless, mind-numbing.
– PHRASES **mindless of** INDIFFERENT TO, heedless of, unaware of, unmindful of, careless of, blind to.
mine ● noun **1** *a coal mine* PIT, excavation, quarry, workings, diggings; strip mine; *Brit.* opencast mine; *N. Amer.* open-pit mine. **2** *a mine of information* RICH SOURCE, repository, store, storehouse, reservoir, gold mine, treasure house, treasury, reserve, fund, wealth, stock. **3** *he was killed by a mine* EXPLOSIVE, landmine, limpet mine, magnetic mine, depth charge.
● verb **1** *the iron ore was mined from shallow pits* QUARRY, excavate, dig (up), extract, remove; strip-mine. **2** *medical data was mined for relevant statistics* SEARCH, delve into, scour, scan, read through, survey. **3** *the entrance to the harbour had been mined* DEFEND WITH MINES, lay with mines.
miner ● noun PITMAN, digger, collier, faceworker, haulier; tinner; *dated* hewer.
mingle ● verb **1** *fact and fiction are skilfully mingled in his novels* MIX, blend, intermingle, intermix, interweave, interlace, combine, merge, fuse, unite, join, amalgamate, meld, mesh; *poetic/literary* commingle; *archaic* commix. **2** *wedding guests mingled in the marquee* SOCIALIZE, circulate, fraternize, get together, associate with others; *informal* hobnob.
– OPPOSITES separate.
miniature ● adjective *a miniature railway* SMALL-SCALE, mini; tiny, little, small, minute, baby, toy, pocket, dwarf, pygmy, minuscule, diminutive; *Scottish* wee; *N. Amer.* vest-pocket; *informal* teeny, teeny-weeny, teensy, teensy-weensy, itsy-bitsy, eensy, eensy-weensy; *Brit. informal* titchy, tiddly.
– OPPOSITES giant.
minimal ● adjective VERY LITTLE, minimum, the least (possible); nominal, token, negligible.
– OPPOSITES maximum.
minimize ● verb **1** *the aim is to minimize costs* KEEP DOWN, keep at/to a minimum, reduce, decrease, cut down, lessen, curtail, diminish, prune; *informal* slash. **2** *we should not minimize his contribution* BELITTLE, make light of, play down, underestimate, underrate, downplay, undervalue, understate; *informal* pooh-pooh; *archaic* hold cheap; *rare* misprize.
– OPPOSITES maximize, exaggerate.
minimum ● noun *costs will be kept to the minimum* LOWEST LEVEL, lower limit, bottom level, rock bottom; least, lowest, slightest.
– OPPOSITES maximum.

minimum wage ● noun the lowest wage permitted by law or by agreement.
minion ● noun a servile or unimportant follower of a powerful person.
– ORIGIN from French *mignon* 'pretty, dainty, sweet'; the term was originally used in a derogatory way to refer to a homoerotic relationship between a male minion and his patron.
mini-pill ● noun a contraceptive pill containing a progestogen and not oestrogen.
miniseries ● noun a television drama shown in a small number of episodes.
miniskirt ● noun a very short skirt.
minister ● noun **1** a head of a government department. **2** a diplomatic agent, usually ranking below an ambassador, representing a state or sovereign in a foreign country. **3** a member of the clergy, especially in the Presbyterian and Nonconformist Churches. **4** archaic a person or thing used to achieve or convey something: *ministers of death*. ● verb **1** (**minister to**) attend to the needs of. **2** archaic provide.
– ORIGIN Latin, 'servant', from *minus* 'less'.
ministerial ● adjective relating to a minister or ministers.
– DERIVATIVES **ministerially** adverb.
Minister of State ● noun (in the UK) a government minister ranking below a Secretary of State.
Minister of the Crown ● noun (in the UK and Canada) a member of the cabinet.
Minister without Portfolio ● noun a government minister with cabinet status but not in charge of a specific department of state.
ministration ● noun **1** (**ministrations**) the provision of assistance or care. **2** the services of a minister of religion or of a religious institution. **3** the action of administering the sacrament.
– DERIVATIVES **ministrant** noun.
ministry ● noun (pl. **ministries**) **1** a government department headed by a minister. **2** a period of government under one Prime Minister. **3** the work or office of a minister of religion.
minivan ● noun a small van fitted with seats for passengers.
miniver ● noun white fur used for lining or trimming clothes.
– ORIGIN from Old French *menu vair* 'little vair' (vair being the fur of a red squirrel, used in medieval times as a trimming or lining for garments).
mink ● noun a semiaquatic stoat-like carnivore widely farmed for its fur.
– ORIGIN Swedish.
minke /mingkə/ ● noun a small rorqual whale with a dark grey back and white underparts.
– ORIGIN probably from *Meincke*, a 19th-century Norwegian whaler who mistook it for a different whale.
min-min (also **min-min light**) ● noun Austral. a will-o'-the-wisp.
– ORIGIN probably from an Aboriginal language.
minneola ● noun a thin-skinned deep reddish fruit that is a hybrid of the tangerine and grapefruit.
– ORIGIN named after a town in Florida, US.
Minnesinger /minnəsingər/ ● noun a German lyric poet and singer of the 12th–14th centuries, who performed songs of courtly love.
– ORIGIN German, 'love singer'.
minnow ● noun **1** a small freshwater fish of the carp family. **2** a small or unimportant person.
– ORIGIN probably from Old English, influenced by Old French *menu* 'small, minnow'.
Minoan /minōən/ ● adjective relating to a Bronze Age civilization centred on Crete (*c.*3000–1050 BC).
– ORIGIN named after the legendary Cretan king *Minos*, to whom a palace excavated at Knossos was attributed.
minor ● adjective **1** having little importance, seriousness, or significance. **2** Music having or based on intervals of a semitone between the second and third degrees, and (usually) the fifth and sixth, and the seventh and eighth. Contrasted with MAJOR. **3** Brit. dated (added to a surname in public schools) indicating the younger of two brothers. ● noun **1** a person under the age of full legal responsibility. **2** Music a minor key, interval, or scale. **3** N. Amer. a student's subsidiary subject or course. ● verb (**minor in**) N. Amer. study or qualify in as a subsidiary subject.
– ORIGIN Latin, 'smaller, less'.
Minorcan /minorkən/ ● noun a person from Minorca. ● adjective relating to Minorca.
minor canon ● noun a member of the Christian clergy who assists in the daily services of a cathedral but is not a member of the chapter.
minority ● noun (pl. **minorities**) **1** the smaller number or part; a number or part representing less than half of the whole. **2** a relatively small group of people differing from the majority in race, religion, language, etc. **3** the state or period of being a minor.
minor league ● noun N. Amer. a league below the level of the major league in baseball or American football.
minor planet ● noun an asteroid.
minor prophet ● noun any of the twelve prophets after whom the shorter prophetic books of the Bible, from Hosea to Malachi, are named.
Minotaur /minətawr/ ● noun Greek Mythology a creature who was half-man and half-bull, kept in a labyrinth on Crete by King Minos and killed by Theseus.
– ORIGIN Greek *Minōtauros*, 'bull of Minos'.
minster ● noun a large or important church, typically one of cathedral status in the north of England that was built as part of a monastery.
– ORIGIN from Greek *monastērion* 'monastery'.
minstrel ● noun a medieval singer or musician.
– ORIGIN Old French *menestral* 'entertainer, servant', from Latin *ministerialis* 'officer'.
minstrelsy ● noun the practice of performing as a minstrel.
mint[1] ● noun **1** an aromatic plant, several kinds of which are used as culinary herbs. **2** the flavour of mint, especially peppermint. **3** a peppermint sweet.
– DERIVATIVES **minty** adjective.
– ORIGIN Greek *minthē*.
mint[2] ● noun **1** a place where money is coined. **2** (**a mint**) informal a large sum of money. ● adjective in pristine condition; as new. ● verb **1** make (a coin) by stamping metal. **2** produce for the first time.
– ORIGIN from Latin *moneta* 'money'.

Thesaurus

● adjective *the minimum amount of effort* MINIMAL, least, smallest, least possible, slightest, lowest, minutest.
minion ● noun UNDERLING, henchman, flunkey, lackey, hanger-on, follower, servant, hireling, vassal, stooge; *informal* yes-man, bootlicker; *Brit. informal* poodle; *N. Amer. informal* suck-up.
minister ● noun **1** *a government minister* MEMBER OF THE GOVERNMENT, cabinet minister, secretary of state, undersecretary. **2** *a minister of religion* CLERGYMAN, clergywoman, cleric, ecclesiastic, pastor, vicar, rector, priest, parson, father, man/woman of the cloth, man/woman of God, churchman, churchwoman; curate, chaplain; *informal* reverend, padre, Holy Joe, sky pilot; *Austral. informal* josser. **3** *the British minister in Egypt* AMBASSADOR, chargé d'affaires, plenipotentiary, envoy, emissary, diplomat, consul, representative; *archaic* legate.
● verb *doctors were ministering to the injured* TEND, care for, take care of, look after, nurse, treat, attend to, see to, administer to, help, assist.
ministrations ● plural noun ATTENTION, treatment, help, assistance, aid, care, services.
ministry ● noun **1** *the ministry for foreign affairs* (GOVERNMENT) DEPARTMENT, bureau, agency, office. **2** *he's training for the ministry* HOLY ORDERS, the priesthood, the cloth, the church. **3** *the ministry of Jesus* TEACHING, preaching, evangelism. **4** *Gladstone's first ministry* PERIOD OF OFFICE, term (of office), administration.
minor ● adjective **1** *a minor problem* SLIGHT, small; unimportant, insignificant, inconsequential, inconsiderable, subsidiary, negligible, trivial, trifling, paltry, petty; *N. Amer.* nickel-and-dime; *informal* piffling, piddling. **2** *a minor poet* LITTLE KNOWN, unknown, lesser, unimportant, insignificant, obscure; *N. Amer.* minor-league; *informal* small-time; *N. Amer. informal* two-bit. **3** *(Brit. dated) Smith minor* JUNIOR, younger.
– OPPOSITES major, important.
● noun *the heir to the throne was a minor* CHILD, infant, youth, adolescent, teenager, boy, girl; *informal* kid, kiddie.
– OPPOSITES adult.
minstrel ● noun *(historical)* MUSICIAN, singer, balladeer; *historical* troubadour, jongleur; *poetic/literary* bard.
mint ● noun **1** COINAGE FACTORY, money factory. **2** *(informal) the bank made a mint out of the deal* A VAST SUM OF MONEY, a king's ransom, millions, billions; *informal* a (small) fortune, a tidy sum, a bundle, a

mint julep • noun a long drink consisting of bourbon, crushed ice, sugar, and fresh mint.

mint sauce • noun chopped spearmint in vinegar and sugar, traditionally eaten with lamb.

minuet • noun a stately ballroom dance in triple time, popular in the 18th century. • verb (**minueted**, **minueting**) dance a minuet.
– ORIGIN from French *menuet* 'fine, delicate'.

minus • preposition **1** with the subtraction of. **2** (of temperature) falling below zero by: *minus 40° centigrade.* **3** informal lacking: *he was minus a finger.* • adjective **1** (before a number) below zero; negative. **2** (after a grade) rather worse than: *C minus.* **3** having a negative electric charge. • noun **1** (also **minus sign**) the symbol -, indicating subtraction or a negative value. **2** informal a disadvantage.
– ORIGIN Latin, neuter of *minor* 'less'.

minuscule • adjective **1** extremely tiny. **2** in lower-case letters, as distinct from capitals or uncials.
– USAGE The correct spelling is **minuscule** rather than **miniscule**.
– ORIGIN from Latin *minuscula littera* 'somewhat smaller letter'.

minute[1] /minit/ • noun **1** a period of time equal to sixty seconds or a sixtieth of an hour. **2** (**a minute**) informal a very short time. **3** (also **arc minute** or **minute of arc**) a sixtieth of a degree of angular measurement.
– PHRASES **up to the minute** up to date.
– ORIGIN from Latin *pars minuta prima* 'first very small part'.

minute[2] /mīnyoot/ • adjective (**minutest**) **1** extremely small. **2** precise and meticulous.
– DERIVATIVES **minutely** adverb **minuteness** noun.
– ORIGIN Latin *minutus* 'lessened, made small'.

minute[3] /minit/ • noun **1** (**minutes**) a summarized record of the points discussed at a meeting. **2** an official memorandum. • verb **1** record or note (the points discussed at a meeting). **2** send a minute to.
– ORIGIN French *minute*, from the notion of a rough copy in 'small writing'.

minute steak • noun a thin slice of steak cooked very quickly.

minutiae /minyooshi-ee/ (also **minutia** /minyooshiə/) • plural noun small or precise details.
– ORIGIN Latin, from *minutia* 'smallness'.

minx • noun humorous or derogatory an impudent, cunning, or boldly flirtatious girl or young woman.
– ORIGIN of unknown origin.

Miocene /mīoseen/ • adjective Geology relating to the fourth epoch of the Tertiary period (23.3 to 5.2 million years ago), a time when the first apes appeared.
– ORIGIN from Greek *meiōn* 'less' + *kainos* 'new'.

mirabelle • noun **1** a sweet yellow plum-like fruit. **2** a liqueur distilled from mirabelles.
– ORIGIN French.

mirabile dictu /miraabilay **dik**too/ • adverb wonderful to relate.
– ORIGIN Latin.

miracle • noun **1** an extraordinary and welcome event attributed to a divine agency. **2** a remarkable and very welcome occurrence. **3** an outstanding example, specimen, or achievement.
– ORIGIN Latin *miraculum* 'object of wonder'.

miracle play • noun a mystery play.

miraculous • adjective **1** having the character of a miracle. **2** very surprising and welcome.
– DERIVATIVES **miraculously** adverb.

mirage /mirraazh/ • noun **1** an optical illusion caused by atmospheric conditions, especially the appearance of a sheet of water in a desert or on a hot road caused by the refraction of light by heated air. **2** something illusory.
– ORIGIN French, from Latin *mirare* 'look at'; cf. MIRROR.

MIRAS /mīrass/ • abbreviation (in the UK) mortgage interest relief at source.

mire • noun **1** a stretch of swampy or boggy ground. **2** a difficult situation from which it is hard to escape. • verb (**be mired**) **1** become stuck in or covered with mud. **2** be in difficulties.
– ORIGIN Old Norse; related to MOSS.

mirepoix /meerpwaa/ • noun a mixture of chopped sautéed vegetables used in various sauces.
– ORIGIN named after the 18th-century French general Duc de *Mirepoix*.

miro /meerō/ • noun (pl. **miros**) an evergreen coniferous New Zealand tree which yields useful wood.
– ORIGIN Maori.

mirror • noun **1** a surface, typically of glass coated with a metal amalgam, which reflects a clear image. **2** something accurately representing something else. • verb **1** show a reflection of. **2** correspond to.
– ORIGIN Old French *mirour*, from Latin *mirare* 'look at'; compare with MIRAGE.

mirrorball • noun a revolving ball covered with small mirrored

m

Thesaurus

packet, a pile; *Brit. informal* a bomb, big money; *N. Amer. informal* big bucks; *Austral. informal* big bickies, motser.
• adjective *in mint condition* BRAND NEW, pristine, perfect, immaculate, unblemished, undamaged, unmarked, unused, first-class, excellent.
• verb **1** *the shilling was minted in 1742* COIN, stamp, strike, cast, forge, manufacture. **2** *the slogan had been freshly minted* CREATE, invent, make up, think up, dream up.

minuscule • adjective TINY, minute, microscopic, very small, little, micro, diminutive, miniature, baby, dwarf; *Scottish* wee; *informal* teeny, teeny-weeny, teensy, teensy-weensy, itsy-bitsy, eensy, eensy-weensy, tiddly; *Brit. informal* titchy.
– OPPOSITES huge.

minute[1] • noun **1** *it'll only take a minute* MOMENT, short time, little while, second, bit, instant; *informal* sec, jiffy; *Brit. informal* tick, mo, two ticks. **2** *at that minute, Tony and Catherine walked in* POINT (IN TIME), moment, instant, juncture. **3** *their objection was noted in the minutes* RECORD(S), proceedings, log, notes; transcript, summary, résumé.
– PHRASES **at the minute** *(Brit. informal)* AT PRESENT, at the moment, now, currently. **in a minute** VERY SOON, any minute (now), in a moment/second/instant, in a trice, shortly, in a short time, in (less than) no time, before long; *N. Amer.* momentarily; *informal* anon, in a jiffy, in two shakes, before you can say Jack Robinson; *Brit. informal* in a tick, in a mo, in two ticks; *N. Amer. informal* in a snap; *poetic/literary* ere long. **this minute** AT ONCE, immediately, directly, this second, instantly, straight away, right away/now, forthwith; *informal* pronto, straight off, right off, toot sweet; *archaic* straight. **up to the minute** LATEST, newest, up to date, modern, fashionable, smart, chic, stylish, all the rage, in vogue; *informal* trendy, with it, in. **wait a minute** BE PATIENT, wait a moment/second, just a moment/minute/second, hold on; *informal* hang on, hold your horses; *Brit. informal* hang about.

minute[2] • adjective **1** *minute particles* TINY, minuscule, microscopic, very small, little, micro, diminutive, miniature, baby, toy, dwarf, pygmy, Lilliputian; *Scottish* wee; *informal* teeny, teeny-weeny, teensy, teensy-weensy, itsy-bitsy, eensy, eensy-weensy; *Brit. informal* titchy, tiddly. **2** *a minute chance of success* NEGLIGIBLE, slight, infinitesimal, minimal, insignificant, inappreciable. **3** *minute detail* EXHAUSTIVE, painstaking, meticulous, rigorous, scrupulous, punctilious, detailed.
– OPPOSITES huge.

minutely • adverb EXHAUSTIVELY, painstakingly, meticulously, rigorously, scrupulously, punctiliously, in detail.

minutiae • plural noun DETAILS, niceties, finer points, particulars, trivia, trivialities.

minx • noun *(humorous)* TEASE, seductress, coquette, Lolita; *informal* floozie, vamp; *dated* hussy; *archaic* strumpet, trollop.

miracle • noun **1** *Christ's first miracle* SUPERNATURAL PHENOMENON, mystery, prodigy. **2** *Germany's economic miracle* WONDER, marvel, sensation, phenomenon.

miraculous • adjective **1** *the miraculous help of St Blaise* SUPERNATURAL, preternatural, inexplicable, unaccountable, magical. **2** *a miraculous escape* AMAZING, astounding, remarkable, extraordinary, incredible, unbelievable, sensational; *informal* mind-boggling, mind-blowing.

mirage • noun OPTICAL ILLUSION, hallucination, phantasmagoria, apparition, fantasy, chimera, vision, figment of the imagination; *poetic/literary* phantasm.

mire • noun **1** *it's a mire out there* SWAMP, bog, morass, quagmire, slough; swampland, marshland, wetland. **2** *her horse was spattered with mire* MUD, slime, dirt, filth, muck. **3** *struggling to pull Russia out of the mire* MESS, difficulty, plight, predicament, tight spot, trouble, quandary, muddle; *informal* jam, fix, pickle, hot water.
• verb **1** *Frank's horse got mired in a bog* BOG DOWN, sink (down). **2** *the children were mired* DIRTY, soil, muddy; *poetic/literary* begrime. **3** *he has become mired in lawsuits* ENTANGLE, tangle up, embroil,

facets, used to provide lighting effects at discos.
mirror image • noun an image which is identical in form to another but has the structure reversed, as if seen in a mirror.
mirror site • noun Computing an Internet site which stores contents copied from another site.
mirth • noun amusement, especially as expressed in laughter.
– DERIVATIVES **mirthful** adjective.
– ORIGIN Old English, related to MERRY.
MIRV • abbreviation multiple independently targeted re-entry vehicle, an intercontinental nuclear missile with several independent warheads.
miry • adjective very muddy or boggy.
MIS • abbreviation Computing management information systems.
mis- • prefix **1** (added to verbs and their derivatives) wrongly, badly, or unsuitably: *mismanage.* **2** occurring in some nouns expressing a sense with negative force: *misadventure.*
– ORIGIN Old English.
misadventure • noun **1** (also **death by misadventure**) Law death caused accidentally during the performance of a legal act without negligence or intent to harm. **2** a mishap.
misalliance • noun an unsuitable or unhappy alliance or marriage.
misandry • noun hatred of men.
– ORIGIN from Greek *miso-* 'hating' + *aner* 'man'.
misanthrope /mizzənthrōp/ (also **misanthropist**) • noun a person who dislikes and avoids other people.
– DERIVATIVES **misanthropic** adjective **misanthropy** noun.
– ORIGIN from Greek *misein* 'to hate' + *anthrōpos* 'man'.
misapprehension • noun a mistaken belief.
misappropriate • verb dishonestly or unfairly take for one's own use.
– DERIVATIVES **misappropriation** noun.
misbegotten • adjective **1** badly conceived, designed, or planned. **2** contemptible. **3** archaic (of a child) illegitimate.
misbehave • verb behave badly.
– DERIVATIVES **misbehaviour** noun.
misbelief • noun a wrong or false belief or opinion.
miscalculate • verb calculate or assess wrongly.
– DERIVATIVES **miscalculation** noun.
miscarriage • noun **1** the spontaneous expulsion of a fetus from the womb before it is able to survive independently. **2** an unsuccessful outcome; a failure.
miscarriage of justice • noun a failure of a court or judicial system to fulfil the objective of justice.
miscarry • verb (**miscarries, miscarried**) **1** have a miscarriage. **2** (of a plan) fail.
miscast • verb (past and past part. **miscast**) (**be miscast**) (of an actor) be given an unsuitable role.
miscegenation /missijinaysh'n/ • noun the interbreeding of people of different races.
– ORIGIN from Latin *miscere* 'to mix' + *genus* 'race'.
miscellanea /missəlayniə/ • plural noun miscellaneous items collected together.
miscellaneous • adjective **1** of various types. **2** composed of things of different kinds.
– DERIVATIVES **miscellaneously** adverb.
– ORIGIN Latin *miscellus* 'mixed', from *miscere* 'to mix'.
miscellany /misellәni/ • noun (pl. **miscellanies**) a collection of different things; a mixture.
mischance • noun bad luck.
mischief • noun **1** playful misbehaviour. **2** harm or injury caused by someone or something.
– PHRASES **do someone a mischief** informal injure someone.
– ORIGIN Old French *meschief,* from *meschever* 'come to an unfortunate end'.
mischievous /mischivәss/ • adjective **1** causing or disposed to

Thesaurus

m

catch up, mix up, involve.
mirror • noun **1** *a quick look in the mirror* LOOKING GLASS, reflecting surface; full-length mirror, hand mirror, wing mirror, rear-view mirror; *Brit.* glass. **2** *the Frenchman's life was a mirror of his own* REFLECTION, twin, replica, copy, match, parallel.
– RELATED TERMS catoptric, specular.
• verb *pop music mirrored the mood of desperation* REFLECT, match, reproduce, imitate, simulate, copy, mimic, echo, parallel, correspond to.
mirth • noun MERRIMENT, high spirits, mirthfulness, cheerfulness, cheeriness, hilarity, glee, laughter, gaiety, buoyancy, blitheness, euphoria, exhilaration, light-heartedness, joviality, joy, joyfulness, joyousness.
– OPPOSITES misery.
mirthful • adjective MERRY, high-spirited, cheerful, cheery, gleeful, jocular, buoyant, euphoric, exhilarated, elated, light-hearted, jovial, joyous, jolly, festive.
– OPPOSITES miserable.
mirthless • adjective HUMOURLESS, unamused, grim, sour, surly, dour, sullen, sulky, gloomy, mournful, melancholy, doleful, miserable, grumpy.
– OPPOSITES cheerful.
miry • adjective MUDDY, slushy, slimy, swampy, marshy, boggy, squelchy, waterlogged.
misadventure • noun ACCIDENT, problem, difficulty, misfortune, mishap; setback, reversal (of fortune), stroke of bad luck, blow; failure, disaster, tragedy, calamity, woe, trial, tribulation, catastrophe.
misanthrope • noun HATER OF MANKIND, cynic; recluse, hermit; *informal* grouch, grump; *historical* anchorite.
misanthropic • adjective ANTISOCIAL, unsociable, unfriendly, reclusive, uncongenial, cynical, jaundiced.
misapply • verb MISUSE, mishandle, misemploy, abuse; distort, garble, warp, misinterpret, misconstrue, misrepresent.
misapprehend • verb MISUNDERSTAND, misinterpret, misconstrue, misconceive, mistake, misread, get the wrong idea about, take something the wrong way.
misapprehension • noun MISUNDERSTANDING, misinterpretation, misreading, misjudgement, misconception, misbelief, the wrong idea, false impression, delusion.
misappropriate • verb EMBEZZLE, expropriate, steal, thieve, pilfer, pocket, help oneself to, make off with; *informal* swipe, filch, rip off, snitch; *Brit. informal* pinch, nick, whip, knock off; *formal* peculate.
misappropriation • noun EMBEZZLEMENT, expropriation, stealing, theft, thieving, pilfering; *formal* peculation.
misbegotten • adjective **1** *a misbegotten scheme* ILL-CONCEIVED, ill-advised, badly planned, badly thought-out, hare-brained. **2** *you misbegotten hound!* CONTEMPTIBLE, despicable, wretched, miserable, confounded; *informal* infernal, damned, flaming; *dated* cursed, accursed. **3** *(archaic) misbegotten children.* See ILLEGITIMATE sense 2.
misbehave • verb BEHAVE BADLY, be misbehaved, be naughty, be disobedient, get up to mischief, get up to no good; be bad-mannered, be rude; *informal* carry on, act up.
misbehaviour • noun BAD BEHAVIOUR, misconduct, naughtiness, disobedience, mischief, mischievousness; bad/poor manners, rudeness; *informal* acting-up.
misbelief • noun FALSE BELIEF, delusion, illusion, fallacy, error, mistake, misconception, misapprehension.
miscalculate • verb MISJUDGE, make a mistake (about), calculate wrongly, estimate wrongly, overestimate, underestimate, overvalue, undervalue; go wrong, err, be wide of the mark.
miscalculation • noun ERROR OF JUDGEMENT, misjudgement, mistake, overestimate, underestimate.
miscarriage • noun **1** *she's had a miscarriage* (SPONTANEOUS) ABORTION, stillbirth. **2** *the miscarriage of the project* FAILURE, foundering, ruin, ruination, collapse, breakdown, thwarting, frustration, undoing, non-fulfilment, mismanagement.
miscarry • verb **1** *the shock caused her to miscarry* LOSE ONE'S BABY, have a miscarriage, abort, have a (spontaneous) abortion. **2** *our plan miscarried* GO WRONG, go awry, go amiss, be unsuccessful, be ruined, fail, misfire, abort, founder, come to nothing, fall through, fall flat; *informal* flop, go up in smoke.
– OPPOSITES succeed.
miscellaneous • adjective VARIOUS, varied, different, assorted, mixed, sundry, diverse, disparate; diversified, motley, multifarious, heterogeneous; *poetic/literary* divers.
miscellany • noun ASSORTMENT, mixture, melange, blend, variety, mixed bag, mix, medley, diversity, collection, selection, assemblage, pot-pourri, mishmash, hotchpotch, ragbag, salmagundi, gallimaufry, omnium gatherum; *N. Amer.* hodgepodge.
mischance • noun ACCIDENT, misfortune, mishap, misadventure, setback, disaster, tragedy, calamity, catastrophe, reversal, upset, blow; bad luck, ill fortune.
mischief • noun **1** *the boys are always getting up to mischief* NAUGHTINESS, bad behaviour, misbehaviour, mischievousness, misconduct, disobedience; pranks, tricks, larks, capers, nonsense, devilry, funny business; *informal* monkey business, shenanigans, hanky-panky; *Brit. informal* monkey tricks, carryings-on, jiggery-

mischief. **2** intended to cause trouble.
– DERIVATIVES **mischievously** adverb **mischievousness** noun.
miscible /missib'l/ ● adjective (of liquids) capable of being mixed together.
– ORIGIN from Latin *miscere* 'to mix'.
misconceive ● verb **1** fail to understand correctly. **2** (**be misconceived**) be badly judged or planned.
misconception ● noun a false or mistaken idea or belief.
misconduct ● noun /misskondukt/ unacceptable or improper behaviour. ● verb /misskəndukt/ (**misconduct oneself**) behave in an improper manner.
misconstruction ● noun the action of misconstruing something.
misconstrue ● verb (**misconstrues**, **misconstrued**, **misconstruing**) interpret wrongly.
miscreant /misskriənt/ ● noun **1** a person who behaves badly or unlawfully. **2** archaic a heretic. ● adjective behaving badly or unlawfully.
– ORIGIN Old French *mescreant*, from *mescreire* 'disbelieve'.
miscue ● verb (**miscues**, **miscued**, **miscueing** or **miscuing**) (in billiards and snooker) fail to cue the ball properly. ● noun an act of miscueing the ball.
misdeed ● noun a wrongful act.
misdemeanour (US **misdemeanor**) ● noun **1** a minor wrongdoing. **2** Law a non-indictable offence, regarded in the US (and formerly the UK) as less serious than a felony.
misdiagnose ● verb diagnose incorrectly.
– DERIVATIVES **misdiagnosis** noun.
misdial ● verb (**misdialled**, **misdialling**; US **misdialed**, **misdialing**) dial a telephone number incorrectly.
misdirect ● verb direct or instruct wrongly.
– DERIVATIVES **misdirection** noun.
misdoing ● noun a misdeed.
mise en scène /meez ON sen/ ● noun **1** the arrangement of scenery and stage properties in a play. **2** the setting of an event.
– ORIGIN French, 'putting on stage'.
miser ● noun a person who hoards wealth and spends as little as possible.
– ORIGIN from Latin, 'wretched'.
miserable ● adjective **1** wretchedly unhappy or depressed. **2** causing unhappiness or discomfort. **3** habitually morose and humourless. **4** pitiably small or inadequate. **5** Austral./NZ & Scottish miserly.
– DERIVATIVES **miserableness** noun **miserably** adverb.
miserere /mizzərairi/ ● noun a psalm, prayer, or cry for mercy.
– ORIGIN Latin, 'have mercy!', from *miser* 'wretched'.
misericord /mizerrikord/ ● noun a ledge projecting from the underside of a hinged seat in a choir stall, giving support to someone standing when the seat is folded up.
– ORIGIN from Latin *misericors* 'compassionate', from *misereri* 'to pity' + *cor* 'heart'.
miserly ● adjective **1** having the characteristics of a miser. **2** (of a quantity) pitiably small.
– DERIVATIVES **miserliness** noun.
misery ● noun (pl. **miseries**) **1** wretched unhappiness. **2** a cause of this. **3** Brit. informal a person who is constantly miserable.
misfire ● verb **1** (of a gun) fail to fire properly. **2** (of an internal-combustion engine) fail to ignite the fuel correctly. **3** fail to produce the intended result.
misfit ● noun **1** a person whose behaviour or attitude sets them apart from others. **2** something that does not fit or fits badly.
misfortune ● noun **1** bad luck. **2** an unfortunate event.
misgivings ● plural noun feelings of doubt or apprehension.

Thesaurus

pokery. **2** *the mischief in her eyes* IMPISHNESS, roguishness, devilment. **3** (informal) *you'll do yourself a mischief* HARM, hurt, injury, damage.
mischievous ● adjective **1** *a mischievous child* NAUGHTY, badly behaved, misbehaving, disobedient, troublesome, full of mischief; rascally, roguish. **2** *a mischievous smile* PLAYFUL, teasing, wicked, impish, roguish, arch. **3** *a mischievous allegation* MALICIOUS, malevolent, spiteful, venomous, poisonous, evil-intentioned, evil, baleful, vindictive, vengeful, vitriolic, rancorous, malign, malignant, pernicious, mean, nasty, harmful, hurtful, cruel, unkind; informal bitchy, catty; poetic/literary malefic, maleficent.
– OPPOSITES well behaved.
misconceive ● verb MISUNDERSTAND, misinterpret, misconstrue, misapprehend, mistake, misread; miscalculate, err, be mistaken, get the wrong idea.
misconception ● noun MISAPPREHENSION, misunderstanding, mistake, error, misinterpretation, misconstruction, misreading, misjudgement, misbelief, miscalculation, false impression, illusion, fallacy, delusion.
misconduct ● noun **1** *allegations of misconduct* WRONGDOING, unlawfulness, lawlessness, crime, felony, criminality, sin, sinfulness; unprofessionalism, unethical behaviour, malpractice, negligence, impropriety; formal maladministration, malversation. **2** *misconduct in the classroom* MISBEHAVIOUR, bad behaviour, misdeeds, misdemeanours, disorderly conduct, mischief, naughtiness, rudeness.
misconstruction ● noun MISUNDERSTANDING, misinterpretation, misapprehension, misconception, misreading, misjudgement, misbelief, miscalculation, false impression.
misconstrue ● verb MISUNDERSTAND, misinterpret, misconceive, misapprehend, mistake, misread; be mistaken about, get the wrong idea about, get it/someone wrong.
miscreant ● noun CRIMINAL, culprit, wrongdoer, malefactor, offender, villain, lawbreaker, evil-doer, delinquent, reprobate; Law malfeasant.
misdeed ● noun WRONGDOING, wrong, evil deed, crime, felony, misdemeanour, misconduct, offence, error, transgression, sin; archaic trespass.
misdemeanour ● noun WRONGDOING, evil deed, crime, felony; misdeed, misconduct, offence, error, peccadillo, transgression, sin; archaic trespass.
miser ● noun PENNY-PINCHER, pinchpenny, niggard, cheese-parer, Scrooge; informal skinflint, meanie, money-grubber, cheapskate; N. Amer. informal tightwad.
– OPPOSITES spendthrift.
miserable ● adjective **1** *I'm too miserable to eat* UNHAPPY, sad, sorrowful, dejected, depressed, downcast, downhearted, down, despondent, disconsolate, wretched, glum, gloomy, dismal, melancholy, woebegone, doleful, forlorn, heartbroken; informal blue, down in the mouth/dumps. **2** *their miserable surroundings* DREARY, dismal, gloomy, drab, wretched, depressing, grim, cheerless, bleak, desolate; poor, shabby, squalid, seedy, dilapidated. **3** *miserable weather* UNPLEASANT, disagreeable, depressing; wet, rainy, stormy; informal rotten. **4** *a miserable old grouch* GRUMPY, sullen, gloomy, bad-tempered, ill-tempered, dour, surly, sour, glum, moody, unsociable, saturnine, lugubrious, irritable, churlish, cantankerous, crotchety, cross, crabby, grouchy, testy, peevish, crusty, waspish. **5** *miserable wages* INADEQUATE, meagre, scanty, paltry, small, poor, pitiful, niggardly; informal measly, stingy, pathetic; formal exiguous. **6** *all that fuss about a few miserable pounds* WRETCHED, confounded; informal blithering, flaming, blessed, damned, blasted; dated accursed.
– OPPOSITES cheerful, lovely.
miserliness ● noun MEANNESS, niggardliness, close-fistedness, closeness, parsimony, parsimoniousness; informal stinginess, tight-fistedness; N. Amer. cheapness; archaic nearness.
miserly ● adjective **1** *his miserly great-uncle* MEAN, niggardly, parsimonious, close, close-fisted, penny-pinching, cheese-paring, Scrooge-like; informal stingy, tight, tight-fisted; N. Amer. informal cheap; archaic near. **2** *the prize is a miserly £300* MEAGRE, inadequate, paltry, negligible, miserable, pitiful, niggardly, beggarly; informal measly, stingy, pathetic; formal exiguous.
– OPPOSITES generous.
misery ● noun **1** *periods of intense misery* UNHAPPINESS, distress, wretchedness, suffering, anguish, anxiety, angst, torment, pain, grief, heartache, heartbreak, despair, despondency, dejection, depression, desolation, gloom, melancholy, melancholia, woe, sadness, sorrow; informal the dumps, the blues; poetic/literary dolour. **2** *the miseries of war* AFFLICTION, misfortune, difficulty, problem, ordeal, trouble, hardship, deprivation; pain, sorrow, trial, tribulation, woe. **3** (Brit. informal) *he's a real old misery* KILLJOY, dog in the manger, spoilsport; informal sourpuss, grouch, grump, party-pooper.
– OPPOSITES contentment, pleasure.
misfire ● verb GO WRONG, go awry, be unsuccessful, fail, founder, fall through/flat; backfire; informal flop, go up in smoke.
misfit ● noun NONCONFORMIST, eccentric, maverick, individualist, square peg in a round hole; informal oddball, weirdo, freak; N. Amer. informal screwball.
misfortune ● noun PROBLEM, difficulty, trouble, setback, adver-

misgovern ● verb govern unfairly or poorly.
misguided ● adjective showing faulty judgement or reasoning.
mishandle ● verb handle unwisely or wrongly.
mishap ● noun an unlucky accident.
mishear ● verb (past and past part. **misheard**) hear incorrectly.
mishit ● verb (**mishitting**; past and past part. **mishit**) hit or kick (a ball) badly.
mishmash ● noun a confused mixture.
– ORIGIN reduplication of MASH.
misidentify ● verb (**misidentifies**, **misidentified**) identify incorrectly.
– DERIVATIVES **misidentification** noun.
misinform ● verb give false or inaccurate information to.
– DERIVATIVES **misinformation** noun.
misinterpret ● verb (**misinterpreted**, **misinterpreting**) interpret wrongly.
– DERIVATIVES **misinterpretation** noun.
misjudge ● verb **1** form an incorrect opinion of. **2** judge wrongly: *the horse misjudged the fence.*
– DERIVATIVES **misjudgement** (also **misjudgment**) noun.
mislay ● verb (past and past part. **mislaid**) lose (an object) by temporarily forgetting where one has left it.
mislead ● verb (past and past part. **misled**) give the wrong impression to.
– DERIVATIVES **misleading** adjective.
mismanage ● verb manage badly or wrongly.
– DERIVATIVES **mismanagement** noun.
mismatch ● noun **1** a failure to correspond or match. **2** an unequal sporting contest. ● verb match unsuitably or incorrectly.
misnomer ● noun **1** an inaccurate or misleading name. **2** the wrong use of a name or term.
– ORIGIN from Old French *mesnommer* 'misname', from Latin *nomen* 'name'.
miso /meesō/ ● noun paste made from fermented soya beans and barley or rice malt, used in Japanese cookery.
– ORIGIN Japanese.
misogynist /misojənist/ ● noun a man who hates women.
– DERIVATIVES **misogynistic** adjective.
misogyny /misojəni/ ● noun hatred of women.
– ORIGIN from Greek *misos* 'hatred' + *gunē* 'woman'.
misplace ● verb put in the wrong place.
misplaced ● adjective **1** incorrectly placed. **2** unwise or inappropriate.
misprint ● noun an error in printed text. ● verb print incorrectly.
mispronounce ● verb pronounce wrongly.
– DERIVATIVES **mispronunciation** noun.
misquote ● verb quote inaccurately.
– DERIVATIVES **misquotation** noun.
misread ● verb (past and past part. **misread**) read or interpret wrongly.
misrepresent ● verb give a false or misleading account of.
– DERIVATIVES **misrepresentation** noun.
misrule ● noun **1** unfair or inefficient government. **2** disruption of peace; disorder. ● verb govern badly.
miss[1] ● verb **1** fail to hit, reach, or come into contact with. **2** be too late for. **3** fail to notice, hear, or understand. **4** fail to be present. **5** avoid. **6** (**miss out**) omit. **7** notice or feel the loss or absence of. ● noun **1** a failure to hit, catch, or reach something. **2** an unsuccessful record or film.
– PHRASES **give something a miss** Brit. informal decide not to do or have something. **a miss is as good as a mile** proverb the fact of failure or escape is not affected by the narrowness of the margin. **miss the boat** informal be too slow to take advantage of something.
– ORIGIN Old English.
miss[2] ● noun **1** (**Miss**) a title prefixed to the name of an unmarried woman or girl. **2** (**Miss**) used as a form of address to a teacher. **3** derogatory or humorous a girl or young woman.
– ORIGIN abbreviation of *mistress*.

Thesaurus

m

sity, stroke of bad luck, reversal (of fortune), misadventure, mishap, blow, failure, accident, disaster; sorrow, misery, woe, trial, tribulation.
misgiving ● noun QUALM, doubt, reservation; suspicion, distrust, mistrust, lack of confidence, second thoughts; trepidation, scepticism, unease, uneasiness, anxiety, apprehension, disquiet.
misguided ● adjective **1** *the policy is misguided* ERRONEOUS, fallacious, unsound, misplaced, misconceived, ill-advised, ill-considered, ill-judged, inappropriate, unwise, injudicious, imprudent. **2** *you are quite misguided* MISINFORMED, misled, labouring under a misapprehension, wrong, mistaken, deluded.
mishandle ● verb **1** *the officer mishandled the situation* BUNGLE, fluff, make a mess of, mismanage, spoil, ruin, wreck; *informal* botch, make a hash of, mess up, muck up; *Brit. informal* make a pig's ear of, make a Horlicks of. **2** *he mishandled his wife* BULLY, persecute, ill-treat, mistreat, maltreat, abuse, knock about/around, hit, beat; *informal* beat up. **3** *the equipment could be dangerous if mishandled* MISUSE, abuse, handle/treat roughly.
mishap ● noun ACCIDENT, trouble, problem, difficulty, setback, adversity, reversal (of fortune), misfortune, blow; failure, disaster, tragedy, catastrophe, calamity.
mishmash ● noun JUMBLE, confusion, hotchpotch, ragbag, patchwork, farrago, assortment, medley, miscellany, mixture, melange, blend, mix, pot-pourri, conglomeration, gallimaufry, omnium gatherum, salmagundi; *N. Amer.* hodgepodge.
misinform ● verb MISLEAD, misguide, give wrong information, delude, take in, deceive, lie to, hoodwink; *informal* lead up the garden path, take for a ride; *N. Amer. informal* give someone a bum steer.
misinformation ● noun DISINFORMATION, false/misleading information; lie, fib; *N. Amer. informal* bum steer.
misinterpret ● verb MISUNDERSTAND, misconceive, misconstrue, misapprehend, mistake, misread; confuse, take amiss, be mistaken, get the wrong idea.
misjudge ● verb GET THE WRONG IDEA ABOUT, get wrong, judge incorrectly, estimate wrongly; overestimate, underestimate, overvalue, undervalue, underrate, be wrong about, miscalculate, misread.
mislay ● verb LOSE, misplace, put in the wrong place, be unable to find, forget the whereabouts of.
– OPPOSITES find.
mislead ● verb DECEIVE, delude, take in, lie to, fool, hoodwink, throw off the scent, pull the wool over someone's eyes, misguide, misinform, give wrong information to; *informal* lead up the garden path, take for a ride; *N. Amer. informal* give someone a bum steer.
misleading ● adjective DECEPTIVE, confusing, deceiving, equivocal, ambiguous, fallacious, specious, spurious, false.
mismanage ● verb BUNGLE, fluff, make a mess of, mishandle, misconduct, spoil, ruin, wreck; *informal* botch, make a hash of, mess up, muck up; *Brit. informal* make a pig's ear of, make a Horlicks of.
mismatch ● noun DISCREPANCY, inconsistency, contradiction, incongruity, incongruousness, conflict, discord, irreconcilability.
mismatched ● adjective ILL-ASSORTED, ill-matched, incongruous, unsuited, incompatible, inconsistent, at odds; out of keeping, clashing, dissimilar, unalike, different, at variance, disparate, unrelated, divergent, contrasting.
– OPPOSITES matching.
misogynist ● noun WOMAN-HATER, anti-feminist, (male) chauvinist, sexist; *informal* male chauvinist pig, MCP.
misplace ● verb LOSE, mislay, put in the wrong place, be unable to find, forget the whereabouts of.
– OPPOSITES find.
misplaced ● adjective **1** *his comments were misplaced* MISGUIDED, unwise, ill-advised, ill-considered, ill-judged, inappropriate. **2** *misplaced keys* LOST, mislaid, missing.
misprint ● noun MISTAKE, error, typographical mistake/error, typing mistake/error, corrigendum, erratum; *Brit.* literal; *informal* typo.
misquote ● verb MISREPORT, misrepresent, misstate, take/quote out of context, distort, twist, slant, bias, put a spin on, falsify.
misrepresent ● verb GIVE A FALSE ACCOUNT/IDEA OF, misstate, misreport, misquote, quote/take out of context, misinterpret, put a spin on, falsify, distort.
misrule ● noun **1** *the misrule of Edward IV* BAD GOVERNMENT, misgovernment, mismanagement, malpractice, incompetence; *formal* maladministration. **2** *the misrule at football games* LAWLESSNESS, anarchy, disorder, chaos, mayhem.
– OPPOSITES order.
miss[1] ● verb **1** *the shot missed her by inches* FAIL TO HIT, be/go wide of, fall short of. **2** *Mandy missed the catch* FAIL TO CATCH, drop, fumble, fluff, mishandle, misfield, mishit. **3** *I've missed my bus* BE TOO LATE FOR, fail to catch/get. **4** *I missed what you said* FAIL TO HEAR, mishear. **5** *you can't miss the station* FAIL TO SEE/NOTICE, overlook. **6** *she never missed a meeting* FAIL TO ATTEND, be absent from, play truant from, cut, skip; *Brit. informal* skive off. **7** *don't miss this exciting opportunity!* LET SLIP, fail to take advantage of, let go/pass, pass up. **8** *I left early to miss the rush-hour traffic* AVOID, beat,

missal ● noun a book of the texts used in the Catholic Mass.
– ORIGIN from Latin *missa* 'Mass'.
misshapen ● adjective not having the normal or natural shape.
missile ● noun **1** an object which is forcibly propelled at a target. **2** a weapon that is self-propelled or directed by remote control, carrying conventional or nuclear explosive.
– ORIGIN Latin, from *mittere* 'send'.
missing ● adjective **1** absent and of unknown whereabouts. **2** not present when expected or supposed to be.
missing link ● noun a hypothetical fossil form intermediate between humans and apes.
mission ● noun **1** an important assignment, typically involving travel abroad. **2** an organization or institution involved in a long-term assignment abroad. **3** a military or scientific expedition. **4** the vocation of a religious organization to spread its faith. **5** a strongly felt aim or calling.
– ORIGIN Latin, from *mittere* 'send'.
missionary ● noun (pl. **missionaries**) a person sent on a religious mission. ● adjective of or characteristic of a missionary or religious mission.
missionary position ● noun a position for sexual intercourse in which a couple lie face to face with the woman underneath the man.
– ORIGIN said to come from the fact that early missionaries advocated the position as 'proper' to primitive peoples.
missioner ● noun a missionary.
mission statement ● noun a summary of the aims and values of an organization.
missis ● noun variant spelling of MISSUS.
missive ● noun formal or humorous a letter.
– ORIGIN Latin *missivus*, from *mittere* 'send'.
misspell ● verb (past and past part. **misspelt** or **misspelled**) spell wrongly.
misspend ● verb (past and past part. **misspent**) spend foolishly or wastefully.
misstate ● verb state wrongly or inaccurately.
– DERIVATIVES **misstatement** noun.
misstep ● noun **1** a badly judged step. **2** a mistake.
missus (also **missis**) ● noun **1** informal or humorous a person's wife. **2** informal a form of address to a woman.
missy ● noun (pl. **missies**) an affectionate or disparaging form of address to a young girl.
mist ● noun **1** a cloud of tiny water droplets in the atmosphere, limiting visibility to a lesser extent than fog. **2** a condensed vapour settling on a surface. ● verb cover or become covered with mist.
– ORIGIN Old English.
mistake ● noun **1** a thing that is incorrect. **2** an error of judgement. ● verb (past **mistook**; past part. **mistaken**) **1** be wrong about. **2** (**mistake for**) confuse (someone or something) with.
– ORIGIN Old Norse, 'take in error'.
mistaken ● adjective **1** wrong in one's opinion or judgement. **2** based on a misunderstanding or faulty judgement.
– DERIVATIVES **mistakenly** adverb.
mister ● noun **1** variant form of MR. **2** informal a form of address to a man.
mistime ● verb choose an inappropriate moment to do or say.
mistle thrush ● noun a large thrush with a spotted breast and harsh rattling call.
– ORIGIN so named because of the bird's fondness for mistletoe berries.
mistletoe ● noun an evergreen parasitic plant which grows on broadleaf trees and bears white berries in winter.
– ORIGIN Old English.
mistook past of MISTAKE.
mistral /misstrəl/ ● noun a strong, cold north-westerly wind that blows through the Rhône valley and southern France.
– ORIGIN French, from Latin *magistralis ventus* 'master wind'.
mistranslate ● verb translate incorrectly.
– DERIVATIVES **mistranslation** noun.
mistreat ● verb treat badly or unfairly.
– DERIVATIVES **mistreatment** noun.
mistress ● noun **1** a woman in a position of authority, control, or ownership. **2** a woman skilled in a particular subject or activity. **3** a woman (other than a wife) having a sexual relationship with a married man. **4** chiefly Brit. a female schoolteacher. **5** (**Mistress**) archaic Mrs.
– ORIGIN Old French *maistresse*, from *maistre* 'master'.
Mistress of the Robes ● noun Brit. a woman of high rank in charge of the Queen's wardrobe.

m

Thesaurus

evade, escape, dodge, sidestep, elude, circumvent, steer clear of, find a way round, bypass. **9** *she missed him when he was away* PINE FOR, yearn for, ache for, long for, long to see.
– OPPOSITES hit, catch.
● noun *one hit and three misses* FAILURE, omission, slip, blunder, error, mistake.
– PHRASES **miss someone/something out** LEAVE OUT, exclude, miss (off), fail to mention, pass over, skip; Brit. informal give something a miss.
miss² ● noun *a headstrong young miss* YOUNG WOMAN, young lady, girl, schoolgirl, missy; Scottish lass, lassie; Irish colleen; informal girlie, chick, bit, doll; Brit. informal bird, bint; N. Amer. informal broad, dame; Austral./NZ informal sheila; poetic/literary maiden, maid, damsel; archaic wench.
misshapen ● adjective DEFORMED, malformed, distorted, crooked, twisted, warped, out of shape, bent, asymmetrical, irregular, misproportioned, ill-proportioned, disfigured, grotesque.
missing ● adjective **1** *his wallet is missing* LOST, mislaid, misplaced, absent, gone (astray), unaccounted for. **2** *passion was missing from her life* ABSENT, not present, lacking, wanting.
– OPPOSITES present.
mission ● noun **1** *a mercy mission to Romania* ASSIGNMENT, commission, expedition, journey, trip, undertaking, operation; task, job, labour, work, duty, charge, trust. **2** *her mission in life* VOCATION, calling, goal, aim, quest, purpose, function. **3** *a trade mission* DELEGATION, deputation, commission, legation, delegacy. **4** *a teacher in a mission* missionary post, missionary station. **5** *a bombing mission* SORTIE, operation, raid.
missionary ● noun EVANGELIST, apostle, proselytizer, preacher, minister, priest.
missive ● noun MESSAGE, communication, letter, word, note, memorandum, line, communiqué, dispatch, news; informal memo; formal epistle; poetic/literary tidings.
misspent ● adjective WASTED, dissipated, squandered, thrown away, frittered away, misused, misapplied.
misstate ● verb MISREPORT, misrepresent, take/quote out of context, distort, twist, put a spin on, falsify.
mist ● noun *the mist was clearing* HAZE, fog, smog, murk, cloud, Scotch mist; poetic/literary brume, fume.
– PHRASES **mist over/up** *her glasses were misting up* STEAM UP, become misty, fog over/up, film over, cloud over.
mistake ● noun **1** *I assumed it had been a mistake* ERROR, fault, inaccuracy, omission, slip, blunder, miscalculation, misunderstanding, oversight, misinterpretation, gaffe, faux pas, solecism; informal slip-up, boo-boo, howler, boner; Brit. informal boob, clanger, bloomer; N. Amer. informal goof. **2** *spelling mistakes* MISPRINT, typographical error/mistake, typing error/mistake, corrigendum, erratum; Brit. literal; informal typo.
● verb **1** *men are apt to mistake their own feelings* MISUNDERSTAND, misinterpret, get wrong, misconstrue, misread. **2** *children often mistake vitamin pills for sweets* CONFUSE WITH, mix up with, take for, misinterpret as.
– PHRASES **be mistaken** BE WRONG, be in error, be under a misapprehension, be misinformed, be misguided; informal be barking up the wrong tree, get the wrong end of the stick. **make a mistake** GO WRONG, err, make an error, blunder, miscalculate; informal slip up, make a boo-boo, make a howler; Brit. informal boob; N. Amer. informal drop the ball, goof (up).
mistaken ● adjective WRONG, erroneous, inaccurate, incorrect, off beam, false, fallacious, unfounded, misguided, misinformed.
– OPPOSITES correct.
mistakenly ● adverb **1** *we often mistakenly imagine that when a problem is diagnosed it is solved* WRONGLY, in error, erroneously, incorrectly, falsely, fallaciously, inaccurately. **2** *Matt mistakenly opened the letter* BY ACCIDENT, accidentally, inadvertently, unintentionally, unwittingly, unconsciously, by mistake.
– OPPOSITES correctly, intentionally.
mistimed ● adjective ILL-TIMED, badly timed, inopportune, inappropriate, untimely, unseasonable.
mistreat ● verb ILL-TREAT, maltreat, abuse, knock about/around, hit, beat, strike, molest, injure, harm, hurt; misuse, mishandle; informal beat up, rough up.
mistreatment ● noun ILL-TREATMENT, maltreatment, abuse, beating, molestation, injury, harm; mishandling, manhandling.

mistrial ● noun a trial made invalid through an error in proceedings.
mistrust ● verb have no trust in. ● noun lack of trust.
– DERIVATIVES **mistrustful** adjective.
misty ● adjective (**mistier**, **mistiest**) **1** full of or covered with mist. **2** indistinct or dim in outline.
– DERIVATIVES **mistily** adverb **mistiness** noun.
misunderstand ● verb (past and past part. **misunderstood**) fail to understand correctly.
misunderstanding ● noun **1** a failure to understand. **2** a disagreement.
misuse ● verb **1** use wrongly. **2** treat badly or unfairly. ● noun the action of misusing something.
mite[1] ● noun a minute arachnid, several kinds of which are parasitic.
– ORIGIN Old English.
mite[2] ● noun **1** a small child or animal. **2** a very small amount. ● adverb (**a mite**) informal slightly.
– ORIGIN Dutch (originally referring to a small Flemish copper coin of low value).
miter ● noun & verb US spelling of MITRE.
mither /mīthər/ ● verb dialect, chiefly N. English **1** make a fuss. **2** pester.
– ORIGIN of unknown origin.
mitigate ● verb **1** make less severe, serious, or painful. **2** (**mitigating**) (of a fact or circumstance) lessening the gravity or culpability of an action.
– DERIVATIVES **mitigation** noun.
– USAGE The words **mitigate** and **militate** are often confused; **mitigate** means 'make (something bad) less severe', while **militate** is used in constructions with **against** to mean 'be a powerful factor in preventing'.
– ORIGIN Latin *mitigare* 'soften, alleviate'.
mitochondrion /mītəkondriən/ ● noun (pl. **mitochondria** /mītəkondriə/) Biology a structure found in large numbers in most cells, in which respiration and energy production occur.
– DERIVATIVES **mitochondrial** adjective.
– ORIGIN from Greek *mitos* 'thread' + *khondrion* 'small granule'.
mitosis /mītōsiss/ ● noun (pl. **mitoses**) Biology a type of cell division in which daughter cells have the same number and kind of chromosomes as the parent nucleus. Compare with MEIOSIS.
– ORIGIN from Greek *mitos* 'thread'.
mitral /mītrəl/ ● adjective Anatomy referring to the valve between the left atrium and the left ventricle of the heart.
– ORIGIN from Latin *mitra* 'belt or turban' (from the valve's shape).
mitre (US **miter**) ● noun **1** a tall cleft headdress that tapers to a point at front and back, worn by bishops and senior abbots. **2** a joint made between two pieces of wood or other material at an angle of 90°, in which the line of the join bisects this angle. ● verb join by means of a mitre.
– ORIGIN Greek *mitra* 'belt or turban'.
mitt ● noun **1** a mitten. **2** a fingerless glove. **3** informal a person's hand.
mitten ● noun a glove having a single section for all four fingers, with a separate section for the thumb.
– ORIGIN Old French *mitaine*, perhaps from *mite*, a pet name for a cat (because mittens were often made of fur).
mix ● verb **1** combine or be combined to form a whole. **2** make by mixing ingredients. **3** combine (signals or soundtracks) into one to produce a recording. **4** (**mix up**) spoil the order or arrangement of. **5** (**mix up**) confuse (a person or thing) with another. **6** associate with others socially. ● noun **1** a mixture. **2** the proportion of different people or things constituting a mixture. **3** a version of a recording mixed in a different way from the original.
– PHRASES **be mixed up in** (or **with**) be involved in or with (dubious actions or people).
– ORIGIN back-formation from MIXED.
mixed ● adjective **1** consisting of different kinds, qualities or elements. **2** of or for members of both sexes.
– ORIGIN Latin *mixtus*, from *miscere* 'to mix'.
mixed bag ● noun a diverse assortment.
mixed economy ● noun an economic system combining private and state enterprise.
mixed farming ● noun farming of both crops and livestock.
mixed grill ● noun a dish of various grilled meats.
mixed marriage ● noun a marriage between people of different races or religions.
mixed metaphor ● noun a combination of incompatible metaphors (e.g. *this tower of strength will forge ahead*).
mixed-up ● adjective informal suffering from psychological or emotional problems.
mixer ● noun **1** a machine or device for mixing things. **2** a per-

m

Thesaurus

mistress ● noun LOVER, girlfriend, kept woman; courtesan, concubine; *informal* fancy woman, bit on the side; *archaic* paramour.
mistrust ● verb **1** *I mistrust his motives* BE SUSPICIOUS OF, be mistrustful of, be distrustful of, be sceptical of, be wary of, be chary of, distrust, have doubts about, have misgivings about, have reservations about, suspect. **2** *don't mistrust your impulses* QUESTION, challenge, doubt, have no confidence/faith in.
● noun **1** *mistrust of Russia was widespread* SUSPICION, distrust, doubt, misgivings, wariness. **2** *their mistrust of David's competence?* QUESTIONING, lack of confidence/faith in, doubt about.
mistrustful ● adjective SUSPICIOUS, chary, wary, distrustful, doubtful, dubious, uneasy, sceptical, leery.
misty ● adjective **1** *misty weather* HAZY, foggy, cloudy; smoggy. **2** *a misty figure* BLURRY, fuzzy, blurred, dim, indistinct, unclear, vague. **3** *misty memories* VAGUE, unclear, indefinite, hazy, nebulous.
– OPPOSITES clear.
misunderstand ● verb MISAPPREHEND, misinterpret, misconstrue, misconceive, mistake, misread; be mistaken, get the wrong idea, receive a false impression; *informal* be barking up the wrong tree, get (hold of) the wrong end of the stick.
misunderstanding ● noun **1** *a fundamental misunderstanding of juvenile crime* MISINTERPRETATION, misconstruction, misreading, misapprehension, misconception, the wrong idea, false impression. **2** *we have had some misunderstandings* DISAGREEMENT, difference (of opinion), dispute, falling-out, quarrel, argument, altercation, squabble, wrangle, row, clash; *informal* spat, scrap, tiff.
misuse ● verb **1** *misusing public funds* PUT TO WRONG USE, misemploy, embezzle, use fraudulently; abuse, squander, waste. **2** *she had been misused by her husband* ILL-TREAT, maltreat, mistreat, abuse, knock about/around, hit, beat, strike, molest, injure, harm, hurt; mishandle, manhandle; *informal* beat up, rough up.
● noun **1** *a misuse of company assets* WRONG USE, embezzlement, fraud; squandering, waste. **2** *the misuse of drugs* ILLEGAL USE, abuse.
mitigate ● verb ALLEVIATE, reduce, diminish, lessen, weaken, lighten, attenuate, take the edge off, allay, ease, assuage, palliate, relieve, tone down.
– OPPOSITES aggravate.
mitigating ● adjective EXTENUATING, exonerative, justificatory, justifying, vindicatory, vindicating, qualifying; *formal* exculpatory.
mitigation ● noun **1** *the mitigation of the problems* ALLEVIATION, reduction, diminution, lessening, easing, weakening, assuagement, palliation, relief. **2** *what did she say in mitigation?* EXTENUATION, explanation, excuse.
mix ● verb **1** *mix all the ingredients together* BLEND, mix up, mingle, combine, put together, jumble; fuse, unite, unify, join, amalgamate, incorporate, meld, marry, coalesce, homogenize, intermingle, intermix; *technical* admix; *poetic/literary* commingle; *archaic* commix. **2** *she mixes with all sorts* ASSOCIATE, socialize, fraternize, keep company, consort; mingle, circulate; *N. Amer.* rub elbows; *informal* hang out/around, knock about/around, hobnob; *Brit. informal* hang about. **3** *we just don't mix* BE COMPATIBLE, get along/on, be in harmony, see eye to eye, agree; *informal* hit it off, click, be on the same wavelength.
– OPPOSITES separate.
● noun *a mix of ancient and modern* MIXTURE, blend, mingling, combination, compound, fusion, alloy, union, amalgamation; medley, melange, collection, selection, assortment, variety, mixed bag, miscellany, pot-pourri, jumble, hotchpotch, ragbag, patchwork, farrago, gallimaufry, omnium gatherum, salmagundi; *N. Amer.* hodgepodge.
– PHRASES **mix something up 1** *mix up the rusk with milk.* See MIX verb sense 1. **2** *I mixed up the dates* CONFUSE, get confused, muddle (up), get muddled up, mistake. **mixed up in** INVOLVED IN, embroiled in, caught up in.
mixed ● adjective **1** *a mixed collection* ASSORTED, varied, variegated, miscellaneous, disparate, diverse, diversified, motley, sundry, jumbled, heterogeneous. **2** *chickens of mixed breeds* HYBRID, half-caste, cross-bred, interbred. **3** *mixed reactions* AMBIVALENT, equivo-

son considered in terms of their ability to mix socially. **3** a soft drink that can be mixed with alcohol. **4** (in recording and cinematography) a device for merging input signals to produce a combined output.

mixer tap ● noun a single tap through which both hot and cold water can be drawn simultaneously.

mixture ● noun **1** a substance made by mixing other substances together. **2** (**a mixture of**) a combination of different things in which the components are individually distinct. **3** the charge of gas or vapour mixed with air admitted to the cylinder of an internal-combustion engine.

mix-up ● noun a confusion or misunderstanding.

mizzen (also **mizen**) ● noun **1** (also **mizzenmast**) the mast aft of a ship's mainmast. **2** (also **mizzensail**) a sail on a mizzenmast.
– ORIGIN from Italian *mezzano* 'middle'.

mizzle chiefly dialect ● noun light rain; drizzle. ● verb (**it mizzles**, **it is mizzling**, etc.) rain lightly.
– ORIGIN probably from MIST.

Mk ● abbreviation **1** the German mark. **2** mark (of a vehicle or machine).

ml ● abbreviation **1** mile or miles. **2** millilitre or millilitres.

MLA ● abbreviation Member of the Legislative Assembly.

MLitt ● abbreviation Master of Letters.
– ORIGIN from Latin *Magister Litterarum*.

Mlle ● abbreviation (pl. **Mlles**) Mademoiselle.

MM ● abbreviation **1** Messieurs. **2** Military Medal.

mm ● abbreviation millimetre or millimetres.

Mme ● abbreviation (pl. **Mmes**) Madame.

MMR ● abbreviation measles, mumps, and rubella (a vaccination given to children).

MN ● abbreviation Minnesota.

Mn ● symbol the chemical element manganese.

mnemonic /nimonnik/ ● noun a pattern of letters or words formulated as an aid to memory. ● adjective **1** aiding or designed to aid the memory. **2** relating to the power of memory.
– ORIGIN from Greek *mnēmōn* 'mindful'.

MO ● abbreviation **1** Medical Officer. **2** Missouri. **3** modus operandi. **4** money order.

Mo ● symbol the chemical element molybdenum.

mo ● noun informal, chiefly Brit. a moment.

moa /mōə/ ● noun a large extinct flightless bird resembling the emu, formerly found in New Zealand.
– ORIGIN Maori.

moan ● noun **1** a low mournful sound, usually expressive of suffering. **2** informal a trivial complaint. ● verb **1** utter or make a moan. **2** informal complain; grumble.
– DERIVATIVES **moaner** noun.
– ORIGIN of unknown origin.

moat ● noun a deep, wide defensive ditch surrounding a castle or town, typically filled with water.
– DERIVATIVES **moated** adjective.
– ORIGIN Old French *mote* 'mound'.

mob ● noun **1** a disorderly crowd of people. **2** Brit. informal a group of people. **3** (**the Mob**) N. Amer. the Mafia. **4** (**the mob**) informal, derogatory the ordinary people. **5** Austral./NZ a flock or herd of animals. ● verb (**mobbed**, **mobbing**) **1** crowd round or into in an unruly way. **2** (of birds or animals) crowd round so as to harass (a predator).
– ORIGIN from Latin *mobile vulgus* 'excitable crowd'.

mob cap ● noun a large, soft indoor hat covering the hair, worn by women in the 18th and early 19th centuries.
– ORIGIN variant of obsolete *mab* 'slut'.

mobe (also **mobey**) ● noun informal a mobile phone.

mobile ● adjective **1** able to move or be moved freely or easily. **2** (of a shop, library, etc.) accommodated in a vehicle so as to travel around. **3** able or willing to move between occupations, places of residence, or social classes. **4** (of the features of the face) readily changing expression. ● noun **1** a decorative structure suspended so as to turn freely in the air. **2** a mobile phone.
– PHRASES **upwardly** (or **downwardly**) **mobile** moving to a higher (or lower) social class.
– ORIGIN Latin *mobilis*, from *movere* 'to move'.

mobile home ● noun a large caravan used as permanent living accommodation.

mobile phone ● noun a portable telephone using a cellular radio system.

mobility ● noun the quality of being mobile.

mobility allowance ● noun Brit. a state travel benefit for people with disabilities.

mobilize (also **mobilise**) ● verb **1** prepare and organize (troops) for active service. **2** organize (people or resources) for a particular task. **3** make mobile.
– DERIVATIVES **mobilization** noun **mobilizer** noun.

Möbius strip /möbiəss/ ● noun a surface with one continuous side formed by joining the ends of a rectangle after twisting one end through 180°.
– ORIGIN named after the German mathematician August F. *Möbius*.

mobster ● noun informal a gangster.

moccasin ● noun **1** a soft leather shoe with the sole turned up and sewn to the upper, originally worn by North American Indians. **2** a venomous American pit viper.
– ORIGIN Virginia Algonquian.

mocha /mokə/ ● noun **1** a fine-quality coffee. **2** a drink or flavouring made with this, typically with chocolate added. **3** a soft leather made from sheepskin.
– ORIGIN named after *Mocha*, a port on the Red Sea, from where the coffee and leather were first shipped.

mock ● verb **1** tease scornfully; ridicule. **2** mimic contemptuous-

Thesaurus

cal, contradictory, conflicting, confused, muddled.
– OPPOSITES homogeneous.

mixed up ● adjective *(informal)* CONFUSED, at sea, befuddled, bemused, bewildered, muddled; maladjusted, disturbed, neurotic, unbalanced; *informal* hung up, messed up.

mixer ● noun **1** *a kitchen mixer* BLENDER, food processor, liquidizer, beater, churn. **2** *she was never really a mixer* SOCIABLE PERSON, socializer, extrovert, socialite.

mixture ● noun **1** *the pudding mixture* BLEND, mix, brew, combination, concoction; composition, compound, alloy, amalgam. **2** *a strange mixture of people* ASSORTMENT, miscellany, medley, melange, blend, variety, mixed bag, mix, diversity, collection, selection, pot-pourri, mishmash, hotchpotch, ragbag, patchwork, farrago, gallimaufry, omnium gatherum, salmagundi; *N. Amer.* hodgepodge. **3** *the animals were a mixture of genetic strands* CROSS, cross-breed, mongrel, hybrid, half-breed, half-caste.

mix-up ● noun CONFUSION, muddle, misunderstanding, mistake, error.

moan ● noun **1** *moans of pain* GROAN, wail, whimper, sob, cry. **2** *the moan of the wind* SOUGH, sigh, murmur. **3** *(informal) there were moans about the delay* COMPLAINT, complaining, grouse, grousing, grumble, grumbling, whine, whining, carping; *informal* gripe, griping, grouch, grouching, bellyache, bitch, whinge, whingeing, beef, beefing.
● verb **1** *he moaned in agony* GROAN, wail, whimper, sob, cry. **2** *the wind moaned in the trees* SOUGH, sigh, murmur. **3** *(informal) you're always moaning about the weather* COMPLAIN, grouse, grumble, whine, carp; *informal* gripe, grouch, bellyache, bitch, beef, whinge; *N. English informal* mither.

mob ● noun **1** *troops dispersed the mob* CROWD, horde, multitude, rabble, mass, throng, group, gang, gathering, assemblage; *archaic* rout. **2** *(informal) the mob were excluded from political life* THE COMMON PEOPLE, the masses, the rank and file, the commonality, the commonalty, the third estate, the plebeians, the proletariat; the hoi polloi, the lower classes, the rabble, the riff-raff, the great unwashed; *informal* the proles, the plebs. **3** *(Brit. informal) he stood out from the rest of the mob* GROUP, set, crowd, lot, circle, coterie, clan, faction, pack, band, ring; *informal* gang, bunch.
● verb **1** *the Chancellor was mobbed when he visited Berlin* SURROUND, swarm around, besiege, jostle. **2** *reporters mobbed her hotel* CROWD (INTO), fill, pack, throng, press into, squeeze into.

mobile ● adjective **1** *both patients are mobile* ABLE TO MOVE (AROUND), moving, walking; *Zoology* motile; *Medicine* ambulant. **2** *her mobile face* EXPRESSIVE, eloquent, revealing, animated. **3** *a mobile library* TRAVELLING, transportable, portable, movable; itinerant, peripatetic. **4** *highly mobile young people* ADAPTABLE, flexible, versatile, adjustable.
– OPPOSITES motionless, static.

mobility ● noun **1** *restricted mobility* ABILITY TO MOVE, movability. **2** *the mobility of Billy's face* EXPRESSIVENESS, eloquence, animation. **3** *mobility in the workforce* ADAPTABILITY, flexibility, versatility, adjustability.

mobilize ● verb **1** *the government mobilized the troops* MARSHAL, deploy, muster, rally, call up, assemble, mass, organize, prepare.

ly. ● adjective **1** not authentic or real. **2** (of an examination, battle, etc.) arranged for training or practice. ● noun (**mocks**) Brit. informal examinations taken in school as training for public examinations.
– DERIVATIVES **mocking** adjective.
– ORIGIN Old French *mocquer* 'deride'.

mocker ● noun a person who mocks.
– PHRASES **put the mockers on** Brit. informal **1** put an end to. **2** bring bad luck to.

mockery ● noun (pl. **mockeries**) **1** ridicule. **2** an absurd representation of something.
– PHRASES **make a mockery of** cause to appear foolish or absurd.

mock-heroic ● adjective consciously grandiose in style in order to satirize a mundane subject.

mockingbird ● noun a long-tailed American songbird, noted for its mimicry of the calls of other birds.

mock orange ● noun a bushy shrub (philadelphus) with white flowers whose perfume resembles that of orange blossom.

mock turtle soup ● noun imitation turtle soup made from a calf's head.

mock-up ● noun a model or replica of a machine or structure for instructional or experimental purposes.

MOD ● abbreviation (in the UK) Ministry of Defence.

mod ● adjective informal modern. ● noun Brit. (especially in the 1960s) a young person of a group characterized by a stylish appearance and the riding of motor scooters.

modal ● adjective **1** relating to mode or form as opposed to substance. **2** Grammar relating to the mood of a verb. **3** Music using melodies or harmonies based on modes other than the ordinary major and minor scales.
– DERIVATIVES **modality** noun **modally** adverb.

modal verb ● noun Grammar an auxiliary verb expressing necessity or possibility, e.g. *must, shall, will.*

mod cons ● plural noun modern conveniences, i.e. the amenities and appliances characteristic of a well-equipped modern house.

mode ● noun **1** a way in which something occurs or is done. **2** a style in clothes, art, etc. **3** Music a set of notes forming a scale and from which melodies and harmonies are constructed. **4** Statistics the value that occurs most frequently in a given data set.
– ORIGIN originally in the musical sense: from Latin *modus* 'measure, manner'.

model ● noun **1** a three-dimensional representation of a person or thing, typically on a smaller scale. **2** (in sculpture) a figure made in clay or wax which is then reproduced in a more durable material. **3** something used as an example. **4** a simplified mathematical description of a system or process, used to assist calculations and predictions. **5** an excellent example of a quality. **6** a person employed to display clothes by wearing them. **7** a person employed to pose for an artist. **8** a particular design or version of a product. ● verb (**modelled, modelling**; US **modeled, modeling**) **1** fashion or shape (a figure) in clay, wax, etc. **2** (in drawing, painting, etc.) cause to appear three-dimensional. **3** devise a mathematical model of. **4** (**model on**) use as an example for something else. **5** display (clothes) by wearing them. **6** work as a model.
– DERIVATIVES **modeller** noun.

modem /mōdem/ ● noun a device for interconverting digital and analogue signals, especially to enable a computer to be connected to a telephone line.
– ORIGIN blend of *modulator* and *demodulator*.

moderate ● adjective **1** average in amount, intensity, or degree. **2** (of a political position) not radical or extreme. ● noun a person with moderate views. ● verb **1** make or become less extreme or intense. **2** review (examination papers or results) to ensure consistency of marking. **3** preside over (a deliberative body or a debate).
– DERIVATIVES **moderately** adverb.
– ORIGIN from Latin *moderare* 'reduce, control'; related to MODEST.

moderation ● noun **1** the avoidance of extremes in one's actions or opinions. **2** the process of moderating.

moderator ● noun **1** an arbitrator or mediator. **2** a chairman of a debate. **3** a person who moderates examination papers.

modern ● adjective **1** relating to the present or to recent times. **2** characterized by or using the most up-to-date techniques or equipment. **3** (in art, architecture, etc.) marked in style or content by a significant departure from traditional values. ● noun a person who advocates a departure from traditional styles or values.
– DERIVATIVES **modernity** noun **modernly** adverb **modernness** noun.
– ORIGIN Latin *modernus*, from *modo* 'just now'.

m

Thesaurus

2 *mobilizing support for the party* GENERATE, arouse, awaken, excite, incite, provoke, foment, prompt, stimulate, stir up, galvanize, encourage, inspire, whip up; poetic/literary waken.

mock ● verb **1** *the local children mocked the old people* RIDICULE, jeer at, sneer at, deride, scorn, make fun of, laugh at, scoff at, tease, taunt; informal take the mickey out of, josh; N. Amer. informal goof on, rag on, pull someone's chain; Austral./NZ informal poke mullock at, sling off at. **2** *they mocked the way he speaks* PARODY, ape, take off, satirize, lampoon, imitate, mimic; informal send up.
● adjective *mock leather* IMITATION, artificial, man-made, simulated, synthetic, ersatz, fake, reproduction, dummy, sham, false, spurious, bogus, counterfeit, pseudo; informal pretend, phoney.
– OPPOSITES genuine.

mockery ● noun **1** *the mockery in his voice* RIDICULE, derision, jeering, sneering, contempt, scorn, scoffing, teasing, taunting, sarcasm. **2** *the trial was a mockery* TRAVESTY, charade, farce, parody.

mocking ● adjective SNEERING, derisive, contemptuous, scornful, sardonic, sarcastic, ironic.

mode ● noun **1** *an informal mode of policing* MANNER, way, fashion, means, method, system, style, approach, technique, procedure, process, practice. **2** *the camera is in manual mode* FUNCTION, position, operation. **3** *the mode for active wear* FASHION, vogue, style, look, trend; craze, rage, fad.

model ● noun **1** *a working model* REPLICA, copy, representation, mock-up, dummy, imitation, duplicate, reproduction, facsimile. **2** *the American model of airline deregulation* PROTOTYPE, stereotype, archetype, type, version; mould, template, framework, pattern, design, blueprint. **3** *she was a model as a teacher* IDEAL, paragon, perfect example/specimen; perfection, acme, epitome, nonpareil, crème de la crème. **4** *a top model* FASHION MODEL, supermodel, mannequin; informal clothes horse. **5** *an artist's model* SITTER, poser, subject. **6** *the latest model of car* VERSION, type, design, variety, kind, sort. **7** *this dress is a model* ORIGINAL (DESIGN), exclusive; informal one-off.
● adjective **1** *model trains* REPLICA, TOY, miniature, dummy, imitation, duplicate, reproduction, facsimile. **2** *model farms* PROTOTYPICAL, prototypal, archetypal. **3** *a model teacher* IDEAL, perfect, exemplary, classic, flawless, faultless.

moderate ● adjective **1** *moderate success* AVERAGE, modest, medium, middling, ordinary, common, commonplace, everyday, workaday; tolerable, passable, adequate, fair; mediocre, indifferent, unexceptional, unremarkable, run-of-the-mill; informal OK, so-so, bog-standard, fair-to-middling, (plain) vanilla, no great shakes, not up to much; NZ informal half-pie. **2** *moderate prices* REASONABLE, acceptable; inexpensive, low, fair, modest. **3** *moderate views* MIDDLE-OF-THE-ROAD, non-extreme, non-radical. **4** *moderate behaviour* RESTRAINED, controlled, sober; tolerant, lenient.
– OPPOSITES great, unreasonable, extreme.
● verb **1** *the wind has moderated* DIE DOWN, abate, let up, calm down, lessen, decrease, diminish; recede, weaken, subside. **2** *you can help to moderate her anger* CURB, control, check, temper, restrain, subdue; repress, tame, lessen, decrease, lower, reduce, diminish, alleviate, allay, appease, assuage, ease, soothe, calm, tone down; archaic remit. **3** *the Speaker moderates the assembly* CHAIR, take the chair of, preside over.
– OPPOSITES increase.

moderately ● adverb SOMEWHAT, quite, rather, fairly, reasonably, comparatively, relatively, to some extent; tolerably, passably, adequately; informal pretty.

moderation ● noun **1** *he urged them to show moderation* SELF-RESTRAINT, restraint, self-control, self-discipline; moderateness, temperance, leniency, fairness. **2** *a moderation of their confrontational style* RELAXATION, easing (off), reduction, abatement, weakening, slackening, tempering, softening, diminution, diminishing, lessening; decline, modulation, modification, mitigation, allaying; informal let-up.
– PHRASES **in moderation** IN MODERATE QUANTITIES/AMOUNTS, within (sensible) limits; moderately.

modern ● adjective **1** *modern times* PRESENT-DAY, contemporary, present, current, twenty-first-century, latter-day, recent. **2** *her clothes are very modern* FASHIONABLE, in fashion, in style, in vogue, up to date, all the rage, trendsetting, stylish, voguish, modish, chic, à la mode; the latest, new, newest, newfangled, modernistic, advanced; informal trendy, cool, in, with it, now, hip, happening; N.

modernism ● noun **1** modern ideas, methods, or styles. **2** a movement in the arts or religion that aims to break with traditional forms or ideas.
– DERIVATIVES **modernist** noun & adjective **modernistic** adjective.
modernize (also **modernise**) ● verb adapt to the requirements of current times; make modern.
– DERIVATIVES **modernization** noun **modernizer** noun.
modest ● adjective **1** unassuming in the estimation of one's abilities or achievements. **2** relatively moderate, limited, or small. **3** decent; decorous.
– DERIVATIVES **modestly** adverb.
– ORIGIN Latin *modestus* 'keeping due measure', related to *modus* 'measure'.
modesty ● noun the quality or state of being modest.
modicum /moddikəm/ ● noun a small quantity of something.
– ORIGIN from Latin *modicus* 'moderate', from *modus* 'measure'.
modification ● noun **1** the action of modifying. **2** a change made.
modifier ● noun **1** a person or thing that modifies. **2** Grammar a word that qualifies the sense of a noun (e.g. *good* and *family* in *a good family house*).
modify ● verb (**modifies**, **modified**) make partial changes to.
– ORIGIN Latin *modificare*, from *modus* 'measure'.
modish /mōdish/ ● adjective fashionable.
– DERIVATIVES **modishly** adverb **modishness** noun.
modiste /modeest/ ● noun dated a fashionable milliner or dressmaker.
– ORIGIN French, from *mode* 'fashion'.
modular ● adjective **1** employing or involving modules. **2** Mathematics of or relating to a modulus.
– DERIVATIVES **modularity** noun.
modulate ● verb **1** exert a controlling influence on; regulate. **2** vary the strength, tone, or pitch of (one's voice). **3** adjust the amplitude or frequency of (an oscillation or signal). **4** Music change from one key to another.
– DERIVATIVES **modulation** noun **modulator** noun.
– ORIGIN Latin *modulari* 'measure'.
module ● noun **1** each of a set of parts or units that can be used to construct a more complex structure. **2** each of a set of independent units of study or training forming part of a course. **3** an independent self-contained unit of a spacecraft.
– ORIGIN Latin *modulus*, from *modus* 'measure'.
modulus /modyooləss/ ● noun (pl. **moduli** /**mod**yoolī/) **1** Mathematics the magnitude of a number irrespective of whether it is positive or negative. **2** a constant factor relating a physical effect to the force producing it.
modus operandi /mōdəss oppərandi/ ● noun (pl. **modi operandi** /mōdi oppərandi/) a way of operating or doing something.
– ORIGIN Latin.
modus vivendi /mōdəss vivendi/ ● noun (pl. **modi vivendi** /mōdi vivendi/) **1** a way of living. **2** an arrangement allowing conflicting parties to coexist peacefully.
– ORIGIN Latin.
moggie (also **moggy**) ● noun (pl. **moggies**) Brit. informal a cat.
– ORIGIN variant of *Maggie*, familiar form of the given name *Margaret*.
Mogul /mōgəl/ (also **Moghul** or **Mughal**) ● noun **1** a member of the Muslim dynasty of Mongol origin which ruled much of India in the 16th–19th centuries. **2** (**mogul**) an important or powerful person.
– ORIGIN Persian, 'Mongol'.
MOH ● abbreviation Ministry of Health.
mohair ● noun a yarn or fabric made from the hair of the angora goat.
– ORIGIN Arabic, 'cloth made of goat's hair' (literally 'choice, select').
Mohawk ● noun (pl. same or **Mohawks**) **1** a member of an American Indian people originally inhabiting parts of what is now upper New York State. **2** chiefly N. Amer. a Mohican haircut.
– ORIGIN from an American Indian language, meaning 'maneaters'.
Mohegan /mōheegən/ ● noun a member of an American Indian people formerly inhabiting western parts of Connecticut and Massachusetts. Compare with MAHICAN. ● adjective relating to the Mohegans.
– ORIGIN Mohegan, 'people of the tidal waters'.
Mohican[1] /mōheekən/ ● noun a hair style in which the sides of the head are shaved and a central strip of hair is made to stand erect.
– ORIGIN erroneously associated with the American Indian people; compare with HURON.
Mohican[2] ● adjective & noun old-fashioned variant of MAHICAN or MOHEGAN.
Moho ● noun Geology the boundary between the earth's crust and the mantle.
– ORIGIN short for *Mohorovičić discontinuity*, named after the Yugoslav seismologist Andrija *Mohorovičić* (1857–1936).
moidore /moydōr/ ● noun a Portuguese gold coin, current in England in the 18th century.
– ORIGIN from Portuguese *moeda d'ouro* 'money of gold'.
moiety /moyəti/ ● noun (pl. **moieties**) **1** formal a half. **2** technical each of two parts into which a thing is or can be divided.
– ORIGIN Old French *moite*, from Latin *medius* 'mid, middle'.
moil archaic, dialect, or N. Amer. ● verb **1** work hard. **2** move around in confusion. ● noun **1** hard work. **2** confusion.
– ORIGIN Old French *moillier* 'paddle in mud, moisten'.
moire /mwaar/ (also **moiré** /**mwaa**ray/) ● noun silk fabric treated to give it an appearance like that of rippled water.
– ORIGIN from French *moire* 'mohair' (the treatment originally being used on mohair fabric).
moist ● adjective slightly wet; damp.
– DERIVATIVES **moisten** verb **moistly** adverb **moistness** noun.
– ORIGIN Old French *moiste*, from Latin *mucidus* 'mouldy'.
moisture ● noun water or other liquid diffused in a small quan-

m

Thesaurus

Amer. informal tony.
– OPPOSITES past, old-fashioned.
modernity ● noun CONTEMPORANEITY, contemporaneousness, modernness, modernism; fashionableness, vogue; *informal* trendiness.
modernize ● verb **1** *they are modernizing their manufacturing facilities* UPDATE, bring up to date, streamline, rationalize, overhaul; renovate, remodel, refashion, revamp. **2** *we must modernize to survive* GET UP TO DATE, move with the times, innovate; *informal* get in the swim, get with it.
modest ● adjective **1** *she was modest about her poetry* SELF-EFFACING, self-deprecating, humble, unpretentious, unassuming, unostentatious; shy, bashful, self-conscious, diffident, reserved, reticent, coy. **2** *modest success* MODERATE, fair, limited, tolerable, passable, adequate, satisfactory, acceptable, unexceptional. **3** *a modest house* SMALL, ordinary, simple, plain, humble, inexpensive, unostentatious, unpretentious. **4** *her modest dress* DECOROUS, decent, seemly, demure, proper.
– OPPOSITES conceited, great, grand.
modesty ● noun **1** *Hannah's modesty cloaks many talents* SELF-EFFACEMENT, humility, unpretentiousness; shyness, bashfulness, self-consciousness, reserve, reticence, timidity. **2** *the modesty of his aspirations* LIMITED SCOPE, moderation. **3** *the modesty of his home* UNPRETENTIOUSNESS, simplicity, plainness. **4** *her maidenly modesty* DECORUM, decorousness, decency, seemliness, demureness.
modicum ● noun SMALL AMOUNT, particle, speck, fragment, scrap, crumb, grain, morsel, shred, dash, drop, pinch, jot, iota, whit, atom, smattering, scintilla, hint, suggestion; *informal* smidgen, tad; *archaic* scantling.
modification ● noun **1** *the design is undergoing modification* ALTERATION, adjustment, change, adaptation, refinement, revision. **2** *some minor modifications were made* REVISION, refinement, improvement, amendment, adaptation, adjustment, change, alteration. **3** *the modification of his views* SOFTENING, moderation, tempering, qualification.
modify ● verb **1** *their economic policy has been modified* ALTER, change, adjust, adapt, amend, revise, reshape, refashion, restyle, revamp, rework, remodel, refine; *informal* tweak. **2** *he modified his more extreme views* MODERATE, revise, temper, soften, tone down, qualify.
modish ● adjective FASHIONABLE, stylish, chic, modern, contemporary, all the rage, in vogue, voguish, up to the minute, à la mode; *informal* trendy, cool, with it, in, now, hip, happening; *N. Amer. informal* kicky, tony.
modulate ● verb **1** *the cells modulate the body's response* REGULATE, adjust, set, modify, moderate. **2** *she modulated her voice* ADJUST, change the tone of.
modus operandi ● noun METHOD (OF WORKING), way, MO, manner, technique, style, procedure, approach, methodology, strategy, plan, formula; *formal* praxis.
mogul ● noun MAGNATE, tycoon, VIP, notable, personage, baron,

tity as vapour, within a solid, or condensed on a surface.

moisturize (also **moisturise**) ● verb make (something, especially skin) less dry.

moisturizer (also **moisturiser**) ● noun a cosmetic preparation for moisturizing the skin.

mojo ● noun (pl. **mojos**) chiefly US **1** a magic charm or spell. **2** supernatural power or luck.
– ORIGIN probably African.

moke ● noun Brit. informal a donkey.
– ORIGIN of unknown origin.

moko /mōkō/ ● noun (pl. **mokos**) NZ a traditional Maori tattoo.
– ORIGIN Maori.

mol /mōl/ ● noun Chemistry short for MOLE⁴.

molar¹ ● noun a grinding tooth at the back of a mammal's mouth.
– ORIGIN from Latin *mola* 'millstone'.

molar² ● adjective acting on or by means of large masses or units.
– ORIGIN from Latin *moles* 'mass'.

molar³ ● adjective Chemistry **1** of or relating to one mole of a substance. **2** (of a solution) containing one mole of solute per litre of solvent.

molasses ● noun **1** a thick, dark brown liquid obtained from raw sugar during the refining process. **2** N. Amer. golden syrup.
– ORIGIN from Latin *mellacium* 'must', from *mel* 'honey'.

mold ● noun & verb US spelling of MOULD¹⁻³.

Moldavian ● noun a person from Moldavia, a former principality of SE Europe. ● adjective relating to Moldavia.

molder ● verb & noun US spelling of MOULDER.

molding ● noun US spelling of MOULDING.

Moldovan /moldōvən/ ● noun a person from Moldova, a country in SE Europe. ● adjective relating to Moldova.

moldy ● adjective US spelling of MOULDY.

mole¹ ● noun **1** a small burrowing insect-eating mammal with dark velvety fur, a long muzzle, and very small eyes. **2** a spy who manages to achieve an important position within the security defences of a country. **3** someone within an organization who anonymously betrays confidential information.
– ORIGIN Germanic.

mole² ● noun a small dark blemish on the skin where there is a high concentration of melanin.
– ORIGIN Old English.

mole³ ● noun **1** a large solid structure serving as a pier, breakwater, or causeway. **2** a harbour formed by a mole.
– ORIGIN Latin *moles* 'mass'.

mole⁴ ● noun Chemistry the SI unit of amount of substance, equal to the quantity containing as many elementary units as there are atoms in 0.012 kg of carbon-12.
– ORIGIN from German *Molekul* 'molecule'.

mole⁵ ● noun Medicine an abnormal mass of tissue in the uterus.
– ORIGIN French, from Latin *mola* in the sense 'false conception'.

mole⁶ /mōlay/ ● noun a highly spiced Mexican savoury sauce containing chilli peppers and chocolate.
– ORIGIN Mexican Spanish, from Nahuatl, 'sauce, stew'.

molecular /məlekyoolər/ ● adjective relating to or consisting of molecules.

molecular biology ● noun the branch of biology concerned with the macromolecules (e.g. proteins and DNA) essential to life.

molecular weight ● noun another term for RELATIVE MOLECULAR MASS.

molecule /mollikyōōl/ ● noun a group of atoms chemically bonded together, representing the smallest fundamental unit of a compound that can take part in a chemical reaction.
– ORIGIN French, from Latin *molecula* 'small mass', from *moles* 'mass'.

molehill ● noun a small mound of earth thrown up by a burrowing mole.
– PHRASES **make a mountain out of a molehill** exaggerate the importance of a minor problem.

moleskin ● noun **1** the skin of a mole used as fur. **2** a thick, strong cotton fabric with a shaved pile surface.

molest ● verb **1** pester or harass in a hostile way. **2** assault or abuse sexually.
– DERIVATIVES **molestation** noun **molester** noun.
– ORIGIN Latin *molestare* 'annoy', from *molestus* 'troublesome'.

moll ● noun informal **1** a gangster's female companion. **2** a prostitute.
– ORIGIN familiar form of the given name *Mary*.

mollify ● verb (**mollifies, mollified**) **1** appease the anger or anxiety of. **2** reduce the severity of.
– DERIVATIVES **mollification** noun.
– ORIGIN from Latin *mollis* 'soft'.

mollusc /molləsk/ (US **mollusk**) ● noun Zoology an invertebrate animal of a large group including snails, slugs, and mussels, with a soft unsegmented body and often an external shell.
– DERIVATIVES **molluscan** adjective.
– ORIGIN from Latin *mollis* 'soft'.

molly (also **mollie**) ● noun a small fish which is bred for aquaria in many colours, especially black.
– ORIGIN from the name of Count *Mollien* (1758–1850), French statesman.

mollycoddle ● verb treat indulgently or overprotectively. ● noun an effeminate man or boy.
– ORIGIN from *molly* 'girl' (see MOLL) + CODDLE.

molly-dooker /molidōōkər/ ● noun Austral. informal a left-handed person.
– ORIGIN from *Molly* (see MOLL) + *-dook* representing a pronunciation of DUKE (in sense 3).

mollymawk ● noun chiefly Austral./NZ an albatross.
– ORIGIN Dutch *mallemok*, from *mal* 'foolish' + *mok* 'gull'.

moloch /mōlok/ ● noun a spiny lizard of grotesque appearance, found in arid inland Australia.
– ORIGIN named after a Caananite idol to whom children were sacrificed.

Molotov cocktail ● noun a crude incendiary device consisting of a bottle of flammable liquid ignited by means of a wick.
– ORIGIN named after the Soviet statesman Vyacheslav *Molotov*, who organized the production of similar grenades in World War II.

molt ● verb & noun US spelling of MOULT.

molten ● adjective (especially of metal and glass) liquefied by heat.
– ORIGIN archaic past participle of MELT.

molto ● adverb Music very.
– ORIGIN Italian.

molybdenum /məlibdənəm/ ● noun a brittle silver-grey metallic element used in some steels and other alloys.
– ORIGIN from Greek *molubdos* 'lead'.

mom ● noun North American term for MUM¹.

moment ● noun **1** a brief period of time. **2** an exact point in time. **3** formal importance. **4** Physics a turning effect produced by

Thesaurus

captain, king, lord, grandee, nabob; *informal* bigwig, big shot, big noise, top dog; *N. Amer. informal* top banana, big enchilada.

moist ● adjective **1** *the air was moist* DAMP, dampish, steamy, humid, muggy, clammy, dank, wet, wettish, soggy, sweaty, sticky. **2** *a moist fruitcake* SUCCULENT, juicy, soft. **3** *her eyes grew moist* TEARFUL, watery, misty.
– OPPOSITES dry.

moisten ● verb DAMPEN, wet, damp, water, humidify; *poetic/literary* bedew.

moisture ● noun WETNESS, wet, water, liquid, condensation, steam, vapour, dampness, damp, humidity, clamminess, mugginess, dankness, wateriness.

moisturizer ● noun LOTION, cream, balm, emollient, salve, unguent, lubricant; *technical* humectant.

mole¹ ● noun *the mole on his left cheek* MARK, freckle, blotch, spot, blemish.

mole² ● noun *a well-placed mole* SPY, (secret) agent, undercover agent, operative, plant, infiltrator; *N. Amer. informal* spook; *archaic* intelligencer.

mole³ ● noun *the mole protecting the harbour* BREAKWATER, groyne, dyke, pier, sea wall, causeway.

molest ● verb **1** *the crowd were molesting the police* HARASS, harry, pester, beset, persecute, torment; *N. Amer. informal* roust. **2** *he molested a ten-year-old boy* (SEXUALLY) ABUSE, (sexually) assault, interfere with, rape, violate; *informal* grope, paw; *poetic/literary* ravish.

mollify ● verb **1** *they mollified the protesters* APPEASE, placate, pacify, conciliate, soothe, calm (down). **2** *mollifying the fears of the public* ALLAY, assuage, alleviate, mitigate, ease, reduce, moderate, temper, tone down.
– OPPOSITES enrage.

mollycoddle ● verb *his parents mollycoddle him* PAMPER, cosset, coddle, spoil, indulge, overindulge, pet, baby, nanny, nursemaid,

a force on an object, expressed as the product of the force and the distance from its line of action to a given point.
– PHRASES **have one's** (or **its**) **moments** be very good at times. **moment of truth** a time of crisis or test. [ORIGIN from a Spanish phrase, referring originally to the final sword-thrust in a bullfight.] **of the moment** currently popular, famous, or important.
– ORIGIN Latin *momentum* (see MOMENTUM).
momentarily • adverb **1** for a very short time. **2** N. Amer. very soon.
momentary • adjective very brief or short-lived.
momentous • adjective of great importance or significance.
– DERIVATIVES **momentously** adverb **momentousness** noun.
momentum • noun (pl. **momenta**) **1** impetus gained by movement or progress. **2** Physics the quantity of motion of a moving body, equal to the product of its mass and velocity.
– ORIGIN Latin *movimentum*, from *movere* 'to move'.
mommy • noun (pl. **mommies**) North American term for MUMMY[1].
Mon. • abbreviation Monday.
monad /monnad/ • noun technical a single unit; the number one.
– ORIGIN Greek *monas* 'unit', from *monos* 'alone'.
monarch • noun **1** a sovereign head of state. **2** a large migratory orange and black butterfly.
– DERIVATIVES **monarchic** adjective **monarchical** adjective.
– ORIGIN from Greek *monos* 'alone' + *arkhein* 'to rule'.
monarchism • noun support for the principle of monarchy.
– DERIVATIVES **monarchist** noun & adjective.
monarchy • noun (pl. **monarchies**) **1** government by a monarch. **2** a state with a monarch.
monastery • noun (pl. **monasteries**) a community of monks living under religious vows.
– ORIGIN Greek *monastērion*, from *monazein* 'live alone'.
monastic • adjective **1** relating to monks or nuns or their communities. **2** resembling monks or their way of life, especially in being austere or reclusive.
– DERIVATIVES **monastically** adverb **monasticism** noun.
monaural /monnawrəl/ • adjective **1** of or involving one ear. **2** another term for MONOPHONIC.
Monday • noun the day of the week before Tuesday and following Sunday.
– ORIGIN Old English, 'day of the moon', from Latin *lunae dies*.
Monégasque /monaygask/ • noun a person from Monaco. • adjective relating to Monaco.
– ORIGIN French.
monetarism • noun the theory that inflation is best controlled by limiting the supply of money circulating in an economy.
– DERIVATIVES **monetarist** noun & adjective.
monetary • adjective relating to money or currency.
– DERIVATIVES **monetarily** adverb.
monetize (also **monetarize**, **monetarise**) • verb **1** convert into or express in the form of currency. **2** (as **monetized**) (of a society) adapted to the use of money.
– DERIVATIVES **monetization** noun.
money • noun **1** a medium of exchange in the form of coins and banknotes. **2** wealth. **3** payment or financial gain. **4** (**moneys** or **monies**) formal sums of money.
– PHRASES **for my money** in my opinion. **money for old rope** (or **money for jam**) Brit. informal money or reward earned for little or no effort. **money talks** proverb wealth gives power and influence to those who possess it. **put one's money where one's mouth is** informal take action to support one's statements.
– ORIGIN Latin *moneta* 'mint, money', originally a title of the goddess Juno, in whose temple in ancient Rome money was minted.
moneybags • noun informal a wealthy person.
moneyed • adjective having much money; affluent.
money-grubbing • adjective informal greedily concerned with making money; grasping.
money market • noun the trade in short-term loans between banks and other financial institutions.
money of account • noun denominations of money used in reckoning but not current as coins.
money order • noun a printed order for payment of a specified sum, issued by a bank or post office.
money spider • noun a very small black spider.
money-spinner • noun chiefly Brit. a thing that brings in a large profit.
money supply • noun the total amount of money in circulation or in existence in a country.
-monger • combining form **1** referring to a dealer or trader in a specified commodity (*fishmonger*). **2** chiefly derogatory referring to a person engaging in a particular activity (*rumour-monger*).
– ORIGIN from Latin *mango* 'dealer'.
mongo • noun (pl. same or **mongos**) a monetary unit of Mongolia, equal to one hundredth of a tugrik.
– ORIGIN Mongolian, 'silver'.
Mongol • noun **1** a person from Mongolia. **2** (**mongol**) offensive a

m

Thesaurus

wait on hand and foot, wrap in cotton wool.
• noun *the boy's a mollycoddle!* See DRIP noun sense 2.
molten • adjective LIQUEFIED, liquid, fluid, melted, flowing.
moment • noun **1** *he thought for a moment* LITTLE WHILE, short time, bit, minute, instant, (split) second; *informal* sec, jiffy; *Brit. informal* tick, mo, two ticks. **2** *the moment they met* POINT (IN TIME), time, hour. **3** *(formal) issues of little moment* IMPORTANCE, import, significance, consequence, note, weight, concern, interest.
– PHRASES **in a moment** VERY SOON, in a minute, in a second, in a trice, shortly, any minute (now), in the twinkling of an eye, in (less than) no time, in no time at all; *N. Amer.* momentarily; *informal* in a jiffy, in two shakes (of a lamb's tail), before you can say Jack Robinson, in the blink of an eye; *Brit. informal* in a tick, in two ticks, in a mo; *N. Amer. informal* in a snap; *poetic/literary* ere long.
momentarily • adverb **1** *he paused momentarily* BRIEFLY, for a moment, for a second, for an instant, fleetingly. **2** *(N. Amer.) my husband will be here momentarily.* See IN A MOMENT at MOMENT.
momentary • adjective BRIEF, short, short-lived, fleeting, passing, transient, ephemeral; *poetic/literary* evanescent.
– OPPOSITES lengthy.
momentous • adjective IMPORTANT, significant, historic, portentous, critical, crucial, life-and-death, decisive, pivotal, consequential, of consequence, far-reaching, earth-shattering; *formal* of moment.
– OPPOSITES insignificant.
momentum • noun IMPETUS, energy, force, power, strength, thrust, speed, velocity.
monarch • noun SOVEREIGN, ruler, Crown, crowned head, potentate; king, queen, emperor, empress, prince, princess.
monarchy • noun **1** *a constitutional monarchy* KINGDOM, sovereign state, principality, empire. **2** *hereditary monarchy* KINGSHIP, sovereignty, autocracy, monocracy, absolutism.
monastery • noun RELIGIOUS COMMUNITY; friary, abbey, priory, cloister.
monastic • adjective **1** *a monastic community* CLOISTERED, cloistral, claustral. **2** *a monastic existence* AUSTERE, ascetic, simple, solitary, monkish, celibate, quiet, cloistered, sequestered, secluded, reclusive, hermit-like, hermitic.
monetary • adjective FINANCIAL, fiscal, pecuniary, money, cash, economic, budgetary.
money • noun **1** *I haven't got enough money* (HARD) CASH, ready money; the means, the wherewithal, funds, capital, finances, (filthy) lucre; banknotes, notes, coins, change, specie, silver, copper, currency; *Brit.* sterling; *N. Amer.* bills; *N. Amer. & Austral.* roll; *informal* dough, bread, loot, readies, shekels, moolah, the necessary; *Brit. informal* dosh, brass, lolly, spondulicks; *N. Amer. informal* dinero, bucks, mazuma; *US informal* greenbacks, simoleons, jack, rocks; *Austral./NZ informal* Oscar; *Brit. dated* l.s.d.; *archaic* pelf. **2** *she married him for his money* WEALTH, riches, fortune, affluence, (liquid) assets, resources, means. **3** *the money here is better* PAY, salary, wages, remuneration; *formal* emolument.
– RELATED TERMS pecuniary, monetary, numismatic.
– PHRASES **for my money** IN MY OPINION, to my mind, in my view, as I see it, personally, in my estimation, in my judgement, if you ask me. **in the money** *(informal)* RICH, wealthy, affluent, well-to-do, well off, prosperous, moneyed, in clover, opulent; *informal* rolling in it, loaded, stinking rich, well heeled, made of money.
moneyed • adjective RICH, wealthy, affluent, well-to-do, well off, prosperous, in clover, opulent, of means, of substance; *informal* in the money, rolling in it, loaded, stinking/filthy rich, well heeled, made of money.
– OPPOSITES poor.
money-grubbing • adjective *(informal)* ACQUISITIVE, avaricious, grasping, money-grabbing, rapacious, mercenary, materialistic; *N. Amer. informal* grabby.
moneymaking • adjective PROFITABLE, profit-making, remunera-

person with Down's syndrome.
– DERIVATIVES **mongolism** noun (offensive).
– USAGE The term **mongol** was adopted in the late 19th century to refer to a person suffering from **Down's syndrome**, owing to the similarity of some of the physical symptoms of the disorder with the normal facial characteristics of East Asian people. In modern English, this use is now unacceptable and considered offensive; it has therefore mostly been replaced by the term **Down's syndrome**.
Mongolian • **noun 1** a person from Mongolia. **2** the language of Mongolia. • **adjective** relating to Mongolia.
Mongoloid • **adjective 1** relating to the broad division of humankind including the indigenous peoples of east Asia, SE Asia, and Arctic North America. **2** (**mongoloid**) offensive affected with Down's syndrome. • **noun** a person of a Mongoloid physical type.
– USAGE The term **Mongoloid** belongs to a set of terms introduced by 19th-century anthropologists attempting to categorize human races. Such terms are associated with outdated notions of racial types, and so are now potentially offensive and best avoided.
mongoose • **noun** (pl. **mongooses**) a small carnivorous mammal with a long body and tail, native to Africa and Asia.
– ORIGIN Marathi (a central Indian language).
mongrel • **noun 1** a dog of no definable breed. **2** offensive a person of mixed descent. **3** something of mixed origin or nature.
– ORIGIN apparently related to MINGLE and AMONG.
monies plural of MONEY, as used in financial contexts.
moniker (also **monicker**) • **noun** informal a name.
– DERIVATIVES **monikered** adjective.
– ORIGIN of unknown origin.
monism /moniz'm/ • **noun** Philosophy a theory or doctrine that denies the existence of a distinction or duality, such as that between matter and mind.
– DERIVATIVES **monist** noun & adjective.
– ORIGIN from Greek *monos* 'single'.
monitor • **noun 1** a person or device that monitors something. **2** a television used to view a picture from a particular camera or a display from a computer. **3** a loudspeaker used by performers to hear what is being played or recorded. **4** a school pupil with disciplinary or other special duties. **5** (also **monitor lizard**) a large tropical lizard. • **verb** keep under observation, especially so as to regulate, record, or control.
– ORIGIN from Latin *monere* 'warn'.
monk • **noun** a man belonging to a religious community typically living under vows of poverty, chastity, and obedience.
– DERIVATIVES **monkish** adjective.
– ORIGIN from Greek *monakhos* 'solitary'.
monkey • **noun** (pl. **monkeys**) **1** a small to medium-sized primate typically having a long tail and living in trees in tropical countries. **2** a mischievous child. **3** Brit. informal a sum of £500. • **verb** (**monkeys, monkeyed**) **1** (**monkey about/around**) behave in a silly or playful way. **2** (**monkey with**) tamper with.
– PHRASES **make a monkey of** (or **out of**) make a fool of. **not give a monkey's** informal not care at all.
– ORIGIN of unknown origin, perhaps from Low German.
monkey business • **noun** informal mischievous or underhand behaviour.
monkey nut • **noun** Brit. a peanut.
monkey puzzle • **noun** a coniferous tree with branches covered in spirals of tough spiny leaves.
monkey suit • **noun** informal a man's evening dress or formal suit.
monkey tricks • **plural noun** Brit. informal mischievous behaviour.
monkey wrench • **noun** a spanner with large adjustable jaws.
monkfish • **noun 1** an anglerfish, especially when used as food. **2** an angel shark.
monk seal • **noun** a seal with a dark back and pale underside, found in warm waters of the northern hemisphere.
monkshood • **noun** an aconite with blue or purple flowers.
mono • **adjective 1** monophonic. **2** monochrome. • **noun 1** monophonic reproduction. **2** monochrome reproduction.
mono- (also **mon-** before a vowel) • **combining form 1** one; alone; single (*monochromatic*). **2** Chemistry (forming names of compounds) containing one atom or group of a specified kind.
– ORIGIN from Greek *monos* 'alone'.
monoamine /monnōaymeen/ (also **monamine**) • **noun** a chemical compound having a single amine group in its molecule, especially one which is a neurotransmitter.
monobasic • **adjective** Chemistry (of an acid) having one replaceable hydrogen atom.
monobloc • **adjective** made as or contained in a single casting.
monochromatic • **adjective 1** containing only one colour. **2** Physics (of light or other radiation) of a single wavelength or frequency.
monochrome • **noun** representation or reproduction in black and white or in varying tones of one colour. • **adjective** consisting of or displaying images in black and white or in varying tones of one colour.
– ORIGIN from Greek *monokhrōmatos* 'of a single colour'.
monocle • **noun** a lens worn to improve sight in one eye.
– ORIGIN from Latin *monoculus* 'one-eyed'.
monoclonal /monnōklōn'l/ • **adjective** Biology relating to a clone or line of clones produced from a single individual or cell.
monocoque /monnəkok/ • **noun** an aircraft or vehicle structure in which the chassis is integral with the body.
– ORIGIN French, from *mono-* 'single' + *coque* 'shell'.
monocotyledon /monōkotileedən/ • **noun** a flowering plant whose seeds have a single cotyledon.
monocular • **adjective** with, for, or using one eye. • **noun** an optical instrument for viewing distant objects with one eye.
– ORIGIN Latin *monoculus* 'having one eye'.
monoculture • **noun** the cultivation of a single crop in a particular area.
monocycle • **noun** a unicycle.
monody /monnədi/ • **noun** (pl. **monodies**) **1** an ode sung by a single actor in a Greek tragedy. **2** music with only one melodic line.
– ORIGIN from Greek *monōdos* 'singing alone'.
monoecious /məneeshəs/ • **adjective** (of a plant or invertebrate animal) having both the male and female reproductive organs in the same individual. Compare with DIOECIOUS.
– ORIGIN from Greek *monos* 'single' + *oikos* 'house'.
monogamy • **noun** the state of having only one husband, wife, or sexual partner at any one time.
– DERIVATIVES **monogamist** noun **monogamous** adjective.
– ORIGIN from Greek *monos* 'single' + *gamos* 'marriage'.
monoglot • **adjective** using or speaking only one language. • **noun** a monoglot person.
– ORIGIN from Greek *monos* 'single' + *glōtta* 'tongue'.

Thesaurus

tive, lucrative, successful, financially rewarding.
– OPPOSITES loss-making.
mongrel • **noun** *a rough-haired mongrel* CROSS-BREED, cross, mixed breed, half-breed; tyke, cur, mutt; *NZ* kuri; *Austral. informal* mong, bitzer.
• **adjective** *a mongrel bitch* CROSS-BRED, of mixed breed, half-breed.
– OPPOSITES pedigree.
monitor • **noun 1** *monitors covered all entrances* DETECTOR, scanner, recorder; security camera, CCTV. **2** *UN monitors* OBSERVER, watchdog, overseer, supervisor. **3** *a computer monitor* SCREEN, visual display unit, VDU. **4** *a school monitor* PREFECT, praepostor; senior boy/girl, senior pupil.
• **verb** *his movements were closely monitored* OBSERVE, watch, track, keep an eye on, keep under observation, keep watch on, keep under surveillance, record, note, oversee; *informal* keep tabs on, keep a beady eye on.
monk • **noun** brother, religious, coenobite, contemplative, mendicant; friar; abbot, prior; novice, oblate, postulant; Benedictine, Black Monk, Cluniac, Carthusian, Cistercian, White Monk.
– RELATED TERMS monastic, monastery.
monkey • **noun 1** SIMIAN, primate, ape. **2** *you little monkey!* See RASCAL.
– PHRASES **make a monkey (out) of** MAKE SOMEONE LOOK FOOLISH, make a fool of, make a laughing stock of, ridicule, make fun of, poke fun at. **monkey about/around** FOOL ABOUT/AROUND, play about/around, clown about/around, footle about/around; *informal* mess about/around, horse about/around, lark (about/around); *Brit. informal* muck about/around. **monkey with** TAMPER WITH, fiddle with, interfere with, meddle with, tinker with, play with; *informal* mess with; *Brit. informal* muck about/around with.
monkey business • **noun** *(informal)* MISCHIEF, misbehaviour, mischievousness, devilry, devilment, tomfoolery; dishonesty, trickery, chicanery, skulduggery; *informal* shenanigans, funny business, hanky-panky; *Brit. informal* monkey tricks, jiggery-pokery; *N. Amer. in-*

monogram ● noun a motif of two or more interwoven letters, typically a person's initials.
– DERIVATIVES **monogrammed** adjective.
monograph ● noun a scholarly written study of a single subject.
– DERIVATIVES **monographic** adjective.
monohull ● noun a boat with only one hull, as opposed to a catamaran or multihull.
monohydrate ● noun a chemical compound containing water and another substance that has one mole of water per mole of the other substance.
monolingual ● adjective speaking or expressed in only one language.
monolith ● noun **1** a large single upright block of stone, especially a pillar or monument. **2** a massive and indivisible organization or institution.
– ORIGIN from Greek *monos* 'single' + *lithos* 'stone'.
monolithic ● adjective **1** formed of a single large block of stone. **2** massive and uniform or indivisible.
monologue ● noun **1** a long speech by one actor in a play or film. **2** a long, tedious speech by one person during a conversation.
– ORIGIN from Greek *monologos* 'speaking alone'.
monomania ● noun obsessive preoccupation with one thing.
– DERIVATIVES **monomaniac** noun.
monomer /monnəmər/ ● noun Chemistry a molecule that can be linked to other identical molecules to form a polymer.
monomial /mənōmiəl/ ● noun an algebraic expression consisting of one term.
– ORIGIN from MONO-, on the pattern of *binomial*.
monophonic ● adjective (of sound reproduction) using only one transmission channel. Compare with STEREOPHONIC.
monoplane ● noun an aircraft with one pair of wings.
monopod ● noun a one-legged support for a camera or fishing rod.
– ORIGIN from Greek *monos* 'single' + *pous* 'foot'.
monopole ● noun **1** Physics a single electric charge or magnetic pole, especially a hypothetical isolated magnetic pole. **2** a radio aerial or pylon consisting of a single pole.
monopolist ● noun a person who has a monopoly.
– DERIVATIVES **monopolistic** adjective.
monopolize (also **monopolise**) ● verb take exclusive control or use of.
– DERIVATIVES **monopolization** noun.
monopoly ● noun (pl. **monopolies**) **1** the exclusive possession or control of the supply of a commodity or service. **2** an organization having a monopoly, or a commodity or service controlled by one. **3** exclusive possession or control of something.
– ORIGIN Greek *monopōlion*, from *monos* 'single' + *pōlein* 'sell'.
monopsony /mənopsəni/ ● noun (pl. **monopsonies**) Economics a market situation in which there is only one buyer.
– ORIGIN from Greek *opsōnein* 'buy provisions'.
monorail ● noun a railway in which the track consists of a single rail.
monosaccharide ● noun a sugar (e.g. glucose) that cannot be broken down to give a simpler sugar.
monoski ● noun a single broad ski attached to both feet.
monosodium glutamate ● noun a compound made by the breakdown of vegetable protein and used as a flavour enhancer in food.
monosyllabic ● adjective **1** consisting of one syllable. **2** using brief words because reluctant to converse.
monosyllable ● noun a word of one syllable.
monotheism /monnətheeiz'm/ ● noun the belief that there is a single god.
– DERIVATIVES **monotheist** noun & adjective **monotheistic** adjective.
monotone ● noun a continuing sound that is unchanging in pitch.
monotonous ● adjective **1** tedious because repetitious. **2** without variation of tone or pitch.
– DERIVATIVES **monotonously** adverb **monotony** noun.
monotreme /monnətreem/ ● noun a mammal which possesses a cloaca and lays eggs, i.e. a platypus or an echidna.
– ORIGIN from Greek *monos* 'single' + *trēma* 'hole'.
monounsaturated ● adjective referring to fats whose molecules are saturated except for one multiple bond, believed to be healthier in the diet than polyunsaturated fats.
monoxide ● noun Chemistry an oxide containing one atom of oxygen.
Monseigneur /monsenyör/ ● noun (pl. **Messeigneurs** /messenyör/) a title or form of address for a French-speaking prince, cardinal, archbishop, or bishop.
– ORIGIN French, 'my lord'.
Monsieur /məsyör/ ● noun (pl. **Messieurs** /mesyör/) a title or form of address for a French-speaking man, corresponding to *Mr* or *sir*.
– ORIGIN French, 'my lord'.
Monsignor /monseenyər/ ● noun (pl. **Monsignori** /monseenyori/) the title of various senior Roman Catholic priests and officials.
– ORIGIN Italian.
monsoon ● noun **1** a seasonal prevailing wind in the region of the Indian subcontinent and SE Asia, bringing rain when blowing from the south-west. **2** the rainy season (typically May to September) accompanying the south-west monsoon.
– DERIVATIVES **monsoonal** adjective.
– ORIGIN Arabic, 'season'.
mons pubis /monz pyōōbiss/ ● noun the rounded mass of fatty tissue lying over the joint of the pubic bones.
– ORIGIN Latin, 'mount of the pubes'.
monster ● noun **1** a large, ugly, and frightening imaginary creature. **2** an inhumanly cruel or wicked person. **3** (before another noun) informal extraordinarily large.
– ORIGIN Latin *monstrum* 'divine portent or warning, monster', from *monere* 'warn'.
monstera /monsteerə/ ● noun a tropical American climbing plant of a genus including the Swiss cheese plant.
– ORIGIN perhaps from Latin *monstrum* 'monster'.
monstrance /monstrənss/ ● noun (in the Roman Catholic Church) a receptacle in which the consecrated Host is displayed for veneration.
– ORIGIN from Latin *monstrare* 'to show'.
monstrosity ● noun (pl. **monstrosities**) **1** something outrageously or offensively wrong. **2** a grossly malformed animal, plant, or bodily part.
monstrous ● adjective **1** very large and ugly or frightening.

m

Thesaurus

formal monkeyshines.
monocle ● noun EYEGLASS, glass.
monolith ● noun STANDING STONE, menhir, sarsen (stone), megalith.
monolithic ● adjective **1** *a monolithic building* MASSIVE, huge, vast, colossal, gigantic, immense, giant, enormous; featureless, characterless. **2** *the old monolithic Communist party* INFLEXIBLE, rigid, unbending, unchanging, fossilized.
monologue ● noun SOLILOQUY, speech, address, lecture, sermon; *formal* oration.
monomania ● noun OBSESSION, fixation, consuming passion, mania, compulsion.
monopolize ● verb **1** *the company has monopolized the market* CORNER, control, take over, gain control/dominance over; *archaic* engross. **2** *he monopolized the conversation* DOMINATE, take over; *informal* hog. **3** *she monopolized the guest of honour* TAKE UP ALL THE ATTENTION OF, keep to oneself; *informal* tie up.
monotonous ● adjective **1** *a monotonous job* TEDIOUS, boring, dull, uninteresting, unexciting, wearisome, tiresome, repetitive, repetitious, unvarying, unchanging, unvaried, humdrum, routine, mechanical, mind-numbing, soul-destroying; colourless, featureless, dreary; *informal* deadly; *Brit. informal* samey; *N. Amer. informal* dullsville. **2** *a monotonous voice* TONELESS, flat, uninflected, soporific.
– OPPOSITES interesting.
monotony ● noun **1** *the monotony of everyday life* TEDIUM, tediousness, lack of variety, dullness, boredom, repetitiveness, repetitiousness, uniformity, routineness, wearisomeness, tiresomeness; lack of excitement, uneventfulness, dreariness, colourlessness, featurelessness; *informal* deadliness. **2** *the monotony of her voice* TONELESSNESS, flatness.
monster ● noun **1** *legendary sea monsters* FABULOUS CREATURE, mythical creature. **2** *her husband is a monster* BRUTE, fiend, beast, devil, demon, barbarian, savage, animal; *informal* swine, pig. **3** *the boy's a little monster* RASCAL, imp, monkey, wretch, devil; *informal* horror, scamp, scallywag, tyke; *Brit. informal* perisher, pickle; *N. Amer. informal* varmint, hellion; *archaic* scapegrace, rapscallion. **4** *he's a monster of a man* GIANT, mammoth, colossus, leviathan, titan; *informal* jumbo.

2 outrageously evil or wrong.
– DERIVATIVES **monstrously** adverb **monstrousness** noun.
mons Veneris /monz vennəriss/ ● noun (in women) the mons pubis.
– ORIGIN Latin, 'mount of Venus'.
montage /montaazh/ ● noun **1** the technique of making a picture or film by putting together pieces from other pictures or films. **2** a picture or film resulting from this.
– ORIGIN French, from *monter* 'to mount'.
montane /montayn/ ● adjective of or inhabiting mountainous country.
– ORIGIN Latin, from *mons* 'mountain'.
montbretia /monbreeshə/ ● noun a plant with small orange trumpet-shaped flowers.
– ORIGIN named after the French botanist A. F. E. Coquebert de *Montbret* (1780–1801).
Montenegrin /montinegrin/ ● noun a person from Montenegro, a republic in the Balkans. ● adjective relating to Montenegro.
Montessori /montisori/ ● noun a system of education that seeks to develop a child's natural interests and activities rather than use formal teaching methods.
– ORIGIN named after the Italian educationist Maria *Montessori* (1870–1952).
month ● noun **1** each of the twelve named periods into which a year is divided. **2** a period of time between the same dates in successive calendar months. **3** a period of 28 days or four weeks.
– PHRASES **a month of Sundays** informal a very long time.
– ORIGIN Old English, related to MOON (since in many early civilizations the calendar month was calculated as beginning with the new moon).
monthly ● adjective done, produced, or occurring once a month. ● adverb once a month. ● noun (pl. **monthlies**) **1** a magazine published once a month. **2** (**monthlies**) informal a menstrual period.
monty ● noun (**the full monty**) Brit. informal the full amount expected, desired, or possible.
– ORIGIN of unknown origin; perhaps from *the full Montague Burton*, apparently meaning 'Sunday-best three-piece suit' (from the name of a tailor), or in reference to 'the full cooked English breakfast' insisted upon by Field Marshal *Montgomery* (1887–1976).
monument ● noun **1** a statue or structure erected to commemorate a person or event. **2** a structure or site of historical importance. **3** an enduring and memorable example or reminder.
– ORIGIN Latin *monumentum*, from *monere* 'remind'.
monumental ● adjective **1** very large or impressive. **2** of or serving as a monument.
– DERIVATIVES **monumentality** noun **monumentally** adverb.
monumental mason ● noun Brit. a person who makes tombstones and similar items.
moo ● verb (**moos**, **mooed**) make the characteristic deep vocal sound of cattle. ● noun (pl. **moos**) such a sound.
– ORIGIN imitative.
mooch ● verb Brit. informal loiter in a bored or listless way.
– ORIGIN originally meaning 'to hoard', later (in English dialect) 'play truant to pick blackberries': probably from Old French *muscher* 'hide, skulk'.
mood ● noun **1** a temporary state of mind. **2** a fit of bad temper or depression. **3** the atmosphere of a work of art. **4** Grammar a form or category of a verb expressing fact, command, question, wish, or conditionality.
– ORIGIN Old English.
moody ● adjective (**moodier**, **moodiest**) **1** given to sudden bouts of gloominess or sullenness. **2** giving a melancholy or mysterious impression.
– DERIVATIVES **moodily** adverb **moodiness** noun.
moolah ● noun informal money.
– ORIGIN of unknown origin.
mooli /mooli/ ● noun a variety of large white slender radish.
– ORIGIN from Sanskrit, 'root'.
moon ● noun **1** (also **Moon**) the natural satellite of the earth, orbiting it every 28 days and shining by reflected light from the sun. **2** a natural satellite of any planet. **3** literary or humorous a month. ● verb **1** (usu. **moon about/around**) behave or move in a listless or dreamy manner. **2** informal expose one's buttocks to someone as an insult or joke.
– PHRASES **over the moon** Brit. informal delighted.
– ORIGIN Old English, related to MONTH.
moon boot ● noun a thickly padded boot with a fabric or plastic outer surface.
mooncalf ● noun a foolish person.
moon daisy ● noun another term for OX-EYE DAISY.
moon-faced ● adjective having a round face.
Moonie ● noun informal, often derogatory a member of the Unification Church.
– ORIGIN named after its founder, the Korean religious leader Sun Myung *Moon* (born 1920).
moonlight ● noun the light of the moon. ● verb (past and past part. **moonlighted**) informal do a second job, especially at night, without declaring it for tax purposes.
– DERIVATIVES **moonlighter** noun **moonlit** adjective.
moonscape ● noun a rocky and barren landscape resembling the moon's surface.
moonshine ● noun informal **1** foolish talk or ideas. **2** chiefly N. Amer. illicitly distilled or smuggled liquor.
moonstone ● noun a pearly white semi-precious form of feldspar.
moonstruck ● adjective slightly deranged, especially because of being in love.
moonwalk ● verb move or dance in a way reminiscent of the weightless movement of walking on the moon.
moony ● adjective (**moonier**, **mooniest**) dreamy, especially through being in love.
Moor ● noun a member of a NW African Muslim people of mixed Berber and Arab descent.
– DERIVATIVES **Moorish** adjective.

m

Thesaurus

● adjective *(informal) a monster carp.* See HUGE.
monstrosity ● noun **1** *a concrete monstrosity* EYESORE, blot on the landscape, carbuncle, excrescence. **2** *a biological monstrosity* MUTANT, mutation, freak (of nature), monster, abortion.
monstrous ● adjective **1** *a monstrous creature* GROTESQUE, hideous, ugly, ghastly, gruesome, horrible, horrific, horrifying, grisly, disgusting, repulsive, repellent, dreadful, frightening, terrifying, malformed, misshapen. **2** *a monstrous tidal wave.* See HUGE. **3** *monstrous acts of violence* APPALLING, heinous, egregious, evil, wicked, abominable, terrible, horrible, dreadful, vile, outrageous, shocking, disgraceful; unspeakable, despicable, vicious, savage, barbaric, barbarous, inhuman; *Brit. informal* beastly.
– OPPOSITES lovely, small.
monument ● noun **1** *a stone monument* MEMORIAL, statue, pillar, column, obelisk, cross; cenotaph, tomb, mausoleum, shrine. **2** *a monument was placed over the grave* GRAVESTONE, headstone, tombstone. **3** *a monument to a past era of aviation* TESTAMENT, record, reminder, remembrance, memorial, commemoration.
monumental ● adjective **1** *a monumental task* HUGE, great, enormous, gigantic, massive, colossal, mammoth, immense, tremendous, mighty, stupendous. **2** *a monumental error of judgement* TERRIBLE, dreadful, awful, colossal, staggering, huge, enormous, unforgivable, egregious. **3** *Beethoven's monumental works* IMPRESSIVE, striking, outstanding, remarkable, magnificent, majestic, stupendous, ambitious, large-scale, grand, awe-inspiring, important, significant, distinguished, memorable, immortal. **4** *a monumental inscription* COMMEMORATIVE, memorial, celebratory, commemorating.
mood ● noun **1** *she's in a good mood* FRAME/STATE OF MIND, humour, temper; disposition, spirit, tenor. **2** *he's obviously in a mood* BAD MOOD, (bad) temper, sulk, pet, fit of pique; low spirits, the doldrums, the blues; *informal* the dumps, grump; *Brit. informal* paddy. **3** *the mood of the film* ATMOSPHERE, feeling, spirit, ambience, aura, character, tenor, flavour, feel, tone.
– PHRASES **in the mood** IN THE RIGHT FRAME OF MIND, feeling like, wanting to, inclined to, disposed to, minded to, eager to, willing to.
moody ● adjective TEMPERAMENTAL, emotional, volatile, capricious, changeable, mercurial; sullen, sulky, morose, glum, depressed, dejected, despondent, doleful, dour, sour, saturnine; *informal* blue, down in the dumps/mouth.
– OPPOSITES cheerful.
moon ● noun SATELLITE.
– RELATED TERMS lunar.
● verb **1** *stop mooning about* WASTE TIME, loaf, idle, mope; *Brit. informal* mooch; *N. Amer. informal* lollygag. **2** *he's mooning over her photograph* MOPE, pine, brood, daydream, fantasize, be in a reverie.
– PHRASES **many moons ago** *(informal)* A LONG TIME AGO, ages ago, years ago; *informal* donkey's years ago; *Brit. informal* yonks ago. **once**

– ORIGIN Greek *Mauros* 'inhabitant of Mauretania' (an ancient region of N. Africa).
moor[1] • noun a stretch of open uncultivated upland.
– ORIGIN Old English.
moor[2] • verb **1** make fast (a boat) by attaching it by cable or rope to the shore or to an anchor. **2** be secured somewhere in this way.
– ORIGIN probably from Germanic.
moorhen • noun an aquatic bird with mainly blackish plumage and a red and yellow bill.
mooring (also **moorings**) • noun **1** a place where a boat is moored. **2** the ropes or cables by which a boat is moored.
moose • noun (pl. same) North American term for ELK.
– ORIGIN from Abnaki (an American Indian language).
moot • adjective subject to debate or uncertainty: *a moot point.* • verb put forward for discussion. • noun **1** (in Anglo-Saxon and medieval England) a legislative or judicial assembly. **2** Law a mock trial set up to examine a hypothetical case as an academic exercise.
– ORIGIN Old English, 'assembly or meeting'; related to MEET[1].
mop • noun **1** a bundle of thick loose strings or a sponge attached to a handle, used for wiping floors. **2** a thick mass of disordered hair. • verb (**mopped**, **mopping**) **1** clean or soak up by wiping. **2** (**mop up**) clear up or put an end to.
– ORIGIN perhaps ultimately related to Latin *mappa* 'napkin'.
mope • verb be listless and in low spirits.
– ORIGIN perhaps Scandinavian.
moped • noun a light motorcycle with an engine capacity below 50 cc.
– ORIGIN from Swedish *trampcykel med motor och pedaler* 'pedal cycle with motor and pedals'.
moppet • noun informal an endearing small child.
– ORIGIN from obsolete *moppe* 'baby or rag doll'.
moquette /moket/ • noun a thick pile fabric used for carpets and upholstery.
– ORIGIN French.
MOR • abbreviation (of music) middle-of-the-road.
moraine /mərayn/ • noun a mass of rocks and sediment carried down and deposited by a glacier.
– ORIGIN from French dialect *morre* 'snout'.
moral • adjective **1** concerned with the principles of right and wrong behaviour and the goodness or badness of human character. **2** conforming to accepted standards of behaviour. **3** psychological rather than physical or practical: *moral support.* • noun **1** a lesson about right or wrong that can be derived from a story or experience. **2** (**morals**) standards of behaviour, or principles of right and wrong.
– DERIVATIVES **morally** adverb.
– ORIGIN Latin *moralis*, from *mos* 'custom'.
morale • noun the level of a person's or group's confidence and spirits.
– ORIGIN French *moral*, respelled to preserve the final stress in pronunciation.
moralist • noun **1** a person who teaches or promotes morality. **2** a person who behaves morally.
– DERIVATIVES **moralistic** adjective.
morality • noun (pl. **moralities**) **1** principles concerning the distinction between right and wrong or good and bad behaviour. **2** moral behaviour. **3** the extent to which an action is right or wrong. **4** a system of values and moral principles.
morality play • noun a play presenting a moral lesson and having personified qualities as the main characters, popular in the 15th and 16th centuries.
moralize (also **moralise**) • verb **1** comment on moral issues, especially disapprovingly. **2** improve the morals of. **3** interpret as giving moral lessons.
– DERIVATIVES **moralization** noun **moralizer** noun.
moral majority • noun **1** the part of society favouring strict moral standards. **2** (**Moral Majority**) a right-wing Christian movement in the US.
moral philosophy • noun the branch of philosophy concerned with ethics.
moral victory • noun a defeat that can be interpreted as a victory in moral terms.
morass /mərass/ • noun **1** an area of muddy or boggy ground. **2** a complicated or confused situation.
– ORIGIN Dutch *moeras*, from Latin *mariscus*.
moratorium • noun (pl. **moratoriums** or **moratoria**) **1** a temporary prohibition of an activity. **2** Law a legal authorization to debtors to postpone payment.
– ORIGIN Latin, from *morari* 'to delay'.
Moravian /mərayviən/ • noun **1** a person from Moravia in the Czech Republic. **2** a member of a Protestant Church founded by emigrants from Moravia. • adjective relating to Moravia or the Moravian Church.
moray (also **moray eel**) • noun an eel-like predatory fish of warm seas.
– ORIGIN Portuguese *moréia* from Greek *muraina*.
morbid • adjective **1** having or showing an unhealthy interest in unpleasant subjects, especially death and disease. **2** Medicine of the nature of or indicative of disease.
– DERIVATIVES **morbidity** noun **morbidly** adverb.
– ORIGIN from Latin *morbus* 'disease'.
mordant • adjective (especially of humour) sharply sarcastic.

m

Thesaurus

in a blue moon *(informal)* HARDLY EVER, scarcely ever, rarely, very seldom. **over the moon** *(Brit. informal)*. See ECSTATIC.
moonshine • noun *(informal)*. See RUBBISH noun sense 2.
moor[1] • verb *a boat was moored to the quay* TIE UP, secure, make fast, fix firmly, anchor, berth, dock.
moor[2] • noun *a walk on the moor* UPLAND, moorland; grouse moor; *Brit.* heath, fell, wold.
moot • adjective *a moot point* DEBATABLE, arguable, questionable, open to discussion/question, at issue, open to doubt, disputable, controversial, contentious, disputed, unresolved, unsettled, up in the air.
• verb *the idea was first mooted in the 1930s* RAISE, bring up, broach, mention, put forward, introduce, advance, propose, suggest.
mop • noun *her tousled mop of hair* SHOCK, mane, tangle, mass.
• verb *a man was mopping the floor* WASH, clean, wipe.
– PHRASES **mop something up 1** *I mopped up the spilt coffee* WIPE UP, clean up, sponge up. **2** *troops mopped up the last pockets of resistance* FINISH OFF, deal with, dispose of, take care of, clear up, eliminate.
mope • verb **1** *it's no use moping* BROOD, sulk, be miserable, be despondent, pine, eat one's heart out, fret, grieve; *informal* be down in the dumps/mouth; *poetic/literary* repine. **2** *she was moping about the house* LANGUISH, moon, idle, loaf; *Brit. informal* mooch; *N. Amer. informal* lollygag.
• noun *she's regarded as a mope* MELANCHOLIC, depressive, pessimist, killjoy; *informal* sourpuss, party-pooper, spoilsport, grouch, grump; *Brit. informal* misery.
moral • adjective **1** *moral issues* ETHICAL, social, having to do with right and wrong. **2** *a very moral man* VIRTUOUS, good, righteous, upright, upstanding, high-minded, principled, honourable, honest, just, noble, incorruptible, scrupulous, respectable, decent, law-abiding, clean-living. **3** *moral support* PSYCHOLOGICAL, emotional, mental.
– OPPOSITES dishonourable.
• noun **1** *the moral of the story* LESSON, message, meaning, significance, signification, import, point, teaching. **2** *he has no morals* MORAL CODE, code of ethics, moral standards/values, principles, standards, (sense of) morality, scruples.
morale • noun CONFIDENCE, self-confidence, self-esteem, spirit(s), team spirit.
moral fibre • noun STRENGTH OF CHARACTER, fibre, fortitude, resolve, backbone, spine, mettle, firmness of purpose.
morality • noun **1** *the morality of nuclear weapons* ETHICS, rights and wrongs, ethicality. **2** *a sharp decline in morality* VIRTUE, goodness, good behaviour, righteousness, rectitude, uprightness; morals, principles, honesty, integrity, propriety, honour, justice, decency. **3** *orthodox Christian morality* MORAL STANDARDS, morals, ethics, standards/principles of behaviour, mores, standards.
moralize • verb PONTIFICATE, sermonize, lecture, preach; *informal* preachify.
morass • noun **1** *the muddy morass* QUAGMIRE, swamp, bog, marsh, mire, marshland, slough; *N. Amer.* moor. **2** *a morass of paperwork* CONFUSION, chaos, muddle, tangle, entanglement, imbroglio, jumble, clutter.
moratorium • noun EMBARGO, ban, prohibition, suspension, postponement, stay, stoppage, halt, freeze, standstill, respite.
morbid • adjective **1** *a morbid fascination with contemporary warfare* GHOULISH, macabre, unhealthy, gruesome, unwholesome; *informal* sick. **2** *I felt decidedly morbid* GLOOMY, glum, melancholy, mor-

● noun 1 a substance that combines with a dye and thereby fixes it in a material. 2 a corrosive liquid used to etch the lines on a printing plate.
– ORIGIN from Latin *mordere* 'to bite'.

more ● determiner & pronoun a greater or additional amount or degree. ● adverb 1 forming the comparative of adjectives and adverbs. 2 to a greater extent. 3 again. 4 (**more than**) extremely.
– PHRASES **more and more** at an increasing rate. **more or less** to a certain extent. **no more 1** nothing further. 2 no further. 3 (**be no more**) no longer exist.
– ORIGIN Old English.

moreish ● adjective Brit. informal so pleasant to eat that one wants more.

morel /mərell/ ● noun an edible fungus having a brown oval or pointed cap with an irregular honeycombed surface.
– ORIGIN French *morille*, from Dutch *morilje*.

morello ● noun (pl. **morellos**) a kind of sour dark cherry used in cooking.
– ORIGIN from Italian, 'blackish'.

moreover ● adverb as a further matter; besides.

mores /morayz/ ● plural noun the customs and conventions of a community.
– ORIGIN Latin, plural of *mos* 'custom'.

morganatic /morgənattik/ ● adjective (of a marriage) between a man of high rank and a woman of low rank who retains her former status, their children having no claim to the father's possessions or title.
– ORIGIN from Latin *matrimonium ad morganaticam* 'marriage with a morning gift' (because a gift given by a husband on the morning after the marriage was the wife's sole entitlement).

morgue ● noun 1 a mortuary. 2 informal a newspaper's files of miscellaneous information kept for reference.
– ORIGIN French, originally the name of a building in Paris where bodies were kept until identified.

moribund ● adjective 1 at the point of death. 2 in terminal decline; lacking vigour.
– ORIGIN Latin *moribundus*, from *mori* 'to die'.

Mormon ● noun a member of the Church of Jesus Christ of Latter-Day Saints, a religion founded in the US in 1830 by Joseph Smith Jr.
– DERIVATIVES **Mormonism** noun.
– ORIGIN the name of a prophet to whom Smith attributed *The Book of Mormon*, a collection of supposed revelations.

morn ● noun literary morning.
– ORIGIN Old English.

mornay ● adjective denoting or served in a cheese-flavoured white sauce.
– ORIGIN named after *Mornay*, the eldest son of the French cook Joseph Voiron, the inventor of the sauce.

morning ● noun 1 the period of time between midnight and noon, especially from sunrise to noon. 2 sunrise. ● adverb (**mornings**) informal every morning.
– ORIGIN from MORN, on the pattern of *evening*.

morning-after pill ● noun a contraceptive pill that is effective within about thirty-six hours after intercourse.

morning coat ● noun a man's tailcoat.

morning dress ● noun a man's formal dress of morning coat and striped trousers.

morning glory ● noun a climbing plant of the convolvulus family with trumpet-shaped flowers.

morning sickness ● noun nausea occurring in the mornings during early pregnancy.

morning star ● noun a planet, especially Venus, when visible in the east before sunrise.

Moroccan ● noun a person from Morocco in North Africa. ● adjective relating to Morocco.

morocco ● noun fine flexible leather made (originally in Morocco) from goatskins tanned with sumac.

moron ● noun informal a stupid person.
– DERIVATIVES **moronic** adjective.
– ORIGIN from Greek *mōros* 'foolish'.

morose ● adjective sullen and ill-tempered.
– DERIVATIVES **morosely** adverb **moroseness** noun.
– ORIGIN Latin *morosus* 'peevish'.

morph ● verb (in computer animation) change smoothly and gradually from one image to another.
– ORIGIN from METAMORPHOSIS.

-morph ● combining form denoting something having a specified form or character (*biomorph*, *ectomorph*).
– ORIGIN from Greek *morphē* 'form'.

morpheme /morfeem/ ● noun Linguistics a meaningful morphological unit of a language that cannot be further divided (e.g. *in*, *come*, *-ing*, forming *incoming*).
– DERIVATIVES **morphemic** adjective.

morphia ● noun dated morphine.

morphic resonance ● noun a supposed paranormal influence by which (according to the theory of the British biologist Rupert Sheldrake) a pattern of events or behaviour makes subsequent occurrences of similar patterns more likely.

morphine ● noun a narcotic drug obtained from opium and used medicinally to relieve pain.
– ORIGIN named after the Roman god of sleep, *Morpheus*.

morphology ● noun 1 the branch of biology concerned with the forms and structures of living organisms. 2 the study of the forms of words.
– DERIVATIVES **morphological** adjective **morphologist** noun.

morris dancing ● noun traditional English folk dancing performed outdoors by groups of dancers wearing costumes with small bells attached and carrying handkerchiefs or sticks.
– ORIGIN from *Moorish* (see MOOR).

morrow ● noun (**the morrow**) archaic or literary the following day.
– ORIGIN Old English, related to MORN.

Morse (also **Morse code**) ● noun a code in which letters are represented by combinations of long and short light or sound signals.
– ORIGIN named after its American inventor Samuel F. B. *Morse* (1791–1872).

morsel ● noun a small piece of food; a mouthful.

Thesaurus

ose, dismal, sombre, doleful, despondent, dejected, sad, depressed, downcast, down, disconsolate, miserable, unhappy, downhearted, dispirited, low; *informal* blue, down in the dumps/mouth.
– OPPOSITES wholesome, cheerful.

mordant ● adjective CAUSTIC, trenchant, biting, cutting, acerbic, sardonic, sarcastic, scathing, acid, sharp, keen; critical, bitter, virulent, vitriolic; *formal* mordacious.

more ● determiner *I could do with some more clothes* ADDITIONAL, further, added, extra, increased, new, other, supplementary.
– OPPOSITES less, fewer.
● adverb 1 *he was able to concentrate more on his writing* TO A GREATER EXTENT, further, some more, better. 2 *he was rich, and more, he was handsome* MOREOVER, furthermore, besides, what's more, in addition, also, as well, too, to boot, on top of that, into the bargain; *archaic* withal, forbye.
● pronoun *we're going to need more* EXTRA, an additional amount/number, an addition, an increase.
– OPPOSITES less, fewer.
– PHRASES **more or less** APPROXIMATELY, roughly, nearly, almost, close to, about, of the order of, in the region of.

moreover ● adverb BESIDES, furthermore, what's more, in addition, also, as well, too, to boot, additionally, on top of that, into the bargain, more; *archaic* withal, forbye.

mores ● plural noun CUSTOMS, conventions, ways, way of life, traditions, practices, habits; *formal* praxis.

morgue ● noun MORTUARY, funeral parlour; *Brit.* chapel of rest.

moribund ● adjective 1 *the patient was moribund* DYING, expiring, on one's deathbed, near death, at death's door, not long for this world. 2 *the moribund shipbuilding industry* DECLINING, in decline, waning, dying, stagnating, stagnant, crumbling, on its last legs.
– OPPOSITES thriving.

morning ● noun 1 *I've got a meeting this morning* BEFORE NOON, before lunch(time), a.m.; *poetic/literary* morn; *Nautical & N. Amer.* forenoon. 2 *morning is on its way* DAWN, daybreak, sunrise, first light, cockcrow; *N. Amer.* sunup; *poetic/literary* dayspring, dawning, aurora.
– RELATED TERMS matutinal.
– PHRASES **morning, noon, and night** ALL THE TIME, without a break, constantly, continually, incessantly, ceaselessly, perpetually, unceasingly; *informal* 24-7.

moron ● noun (*informal*). See FOOL noun sense 1.

moronic ● adjective (*informal*). See STUPID sense 1.

morose ● adjective SULLEN, sulky, gloomy, bad-tempered, ill-tempered, dour, surly, sour, glum, moody, ill-humoured, melancholy, melancholic, doleful, miserable, depressed, dejected, despondent, downcast, unhappy, in low spirits, low, down, fed up, grumpy, irritable, churlish, cantankerous, crotchety, cross,

– ORIGIN Old French, 'little bite'.

mortadella /mɔːtəˈdɛlə/ ● noun a type of smooth-textured Italian sausage containing pieces of fat.

– ORIGIN from Latin *murtatum* 'sausage seasoned with myrtle berries'.

mortal ● adjective **1** subject to death. **2** causing death. **3** (of fear, pain, etc.) intense. **4** (of conflict or an enemy) lasting until death; never to be reconciled. **5** without exception; imaginable: *every mortal thing*. **6** Christian Theology (of a sin) regarded as depriving the soul of divine grace. Often contrasted with VENIAL. ● noun a human being.

– DERIVATIVES **mortally** adverb.

– ORIGIN from Latin *mors* 'death'.

mortality ● noun **1** the state of being mortal. **2** death, especially on a large scale. **3** (also **mortality rate**) the number of deaths in a given area or period, or from a particular cause.

mortar ● noun **1** a mixture of lime with cement, sand, and water, used to bond bricks or stones. **2** a cup-shaped receptacle in which substances are crushed or ground with a pestle. **3** a short cannon for firing bombs at high angles. ● verb **1** fix or bond using mortar. **2** attack with bombs fired from a mortar.

– ORIGIN Latin *mortarium* 'receptacle in which substances are crushed or ground'; sense 1 is probably a transferred use of sense 2, the mortar being mixed in a trough or other receptacle,

mortar board ● noun **1** an academic cap with a stiff, flat square top and a tassel. **2** a small square board held horizontally by a handle on the underside, used for holding mortar.

mortgage ● noun **1** a legal agreement by which a person takes out a loan using as security real property (usually a house which is being purchased). **2** an amount of money borrowed or lent under such an agreement. ● verb transfer the title to (a property) to a creditor as security for the payment of a loan.

– ORIGIN Old French, 'dead pledge'.

mortgagee ● noun the lender in a mortgage.

mortgagor ● noun the borrower in a mortgage.

mortician ● noun chiefly N. Amer. an undertaker.

mortify ● verb (**mortifies**, **mortified**) **1** cause to feel embarrassed or humiliated. **2** subdue (physical urges) by self-denial or discipline. **3** be affected by gangrene or necrosis.

– DERIVATIVES **mortification** noun **mortifying** adjective.

– ORIGIN Old French *mortifier*, from Latin *mors* 'death'.

mortise (also **mortice**) ● noun a hole or recess designed to receive a corresponding projection (a tenon) so that the two are held together. ● verb **1** join by a mortise and tenon. **2** cut a mortise in.

– ORIGIN Old French *mortaise*.

mortise lock ● noun a lock set into the framework of a door in a recess or mortise.

mortuary ● noun (pl. **mortuaries**) a room or building in which dead bodies are kept until burial or cremation. ● adjective relating to burial or tombs.

– ORIGIN originally denoting a gift claimed by a parish priest from a deceased person's estate, later meaning 'a funeral': from Latin *mortuus* 'dead'.

morwong ● noun a brightly coloured marine fish of Australian waters.

– ORIGIN probably from an Aboriginal language.

Mosaic ● adjective of or associated with the biblical Hebrew prophet Moses.

mosaic ● noun a picture or pattern produced by arranging together small variously coloured pieces of stone, tile, or glass.

– DERIVATIVES **mosaicist** noun.

– ORIGIN French *mosaïque*, from Latin *musivum* 'decoration with small square stones'.

mosaic disease ● noun a virus disease that causes mottled leaves in tobacco and other plants.

mosasaur /mōzəsawr/ ● noun a large fossil marine reptile with paddle-like limbs and a long flattened tail.

– ORIGIN from Latin *Mosa*, the river Meuse (near which it was first discovered) + Greek *sauros* 'lizard'.

Moselle /mōzel/ (also **Mosel**) ● noun a light medium-dry white wine from the valley of the River Moselle.

mosey informal ● verb (**moseys**, **moseyed**) walk or move in a leisurely manner. ● noun a leisurely walk.

– ORIGIN of unknown origin.

mosh ● verb informal dance to rock music in a violent manner involving jumping up and down and deliberately colliding with other dancers.

– ORIGIN perhaps from MASH or MUSH[1].

Moslem ● noun & adjective variant spelling of MUSLIM.

mosque ● noun a Muslim place of worship.

– ORIGIN French, from Arabic.

mosquito ● noun (pl. **mosquitoes**) a small slender fly, some kinds of which transmit parasitic diseases through the bite of the bloodsucking female.

– ORIGIN Spanish and Portuguese, 'little fly'.

mosquito net ● noun a fine net hung across a door or window or around a bed to keep mosquitoes away.

moss ● noun **1** a small flowerless green plant which grows in low carpets or rounded cushions in damp habitats and reproduces by means of spores. **2** Scottish & N. English a peat bog.

– DERIVATIVES **mossy** adjective.

– ORIGIN Old English.

moss agate ● noun agate with moss-like markings.

moss stitch ● noun alternate plain and purl stitches in knitting.

most ● determiner & pronoun **1** greatest in amount or degree. **2** the majority of. ● adverb **1** to the greatest extent. **2** forming the superlative of adjectives and adverbs. **3** very. **4** N. Amer. informal almost.

– PHRASES **at (the) most** not more than. **for the most part** in most cases; usually. **make the most of** use or represent to the best advantage.

– ORIGIN Old English.

-most ● suffix forming superlative adjectives and adverbs from prepositions and other words indicating relative position (e.g. *innermost*).

– ORIGIN Old English, related to MOST.

Most Honourable ● noun (in the UK) a title given to marquesses, members of the Privy Council, and holders of the Order of the Bath.

mostly ● adverb **1** on the whole; mainly. **2** usually.

Most Reverend ● noun the title of an Anglican archbishop or

m

Thesaurus

crabby, grouchy, testy, snappish, peevish, crusty; *informal* blue, down in the dumps/mouth.

– OPPOSITES cheerful.

morsel ● noun MOUTHFUL, bite, nibble, bit, soupçon, taste, spoonful, forkful, sliver, drop, dollop, spot, gobbet; titbit, bonne bouche; *informal* smidgen.

mortal ● adjective **1** *mortal remains | all men are mortal* PERISHABLE, physical, bodily, corporeal, fleshly, earthly; human, impermanent, transient, ephemeral. **2** *a mortal blow* DEADLY, fatal, lethal, death-dealing, murderous, terminal. **3** *mortal enemies* IRRECONCILABLE, deadly, sworn, bitter, out-and-out, implacable. **4** *a mortal sin* UNPARDONABLE, unforgivable. **5** *living in mortal fear* EXTREME, (very) great, terrible, awful, dreadful, intense, severe, grave, dire, unbearable. **6** *the punishment is out of all mortal proportion* CONCEIVABLE, imaginable, perceivable, possible, earthly.

– OPPOSITES venial.

● noun *we are mere mortals* HUMAN (BEING), person, man/woman; earthling.

mortality ● noun **1** *a sense of his own mortality* IMPERMANENCE, transience, ephemerality, perishability; humanity; corporeality. **2** *the causes of mortality* DEATH, loss of life, dying.

mortification ● noun **1** *scarlet with mortification* EMBARRASSMENT, humiliation, chagrin, discomfiture, discomposure, shame. **2** *the mortification of the flesh* SUBDUING, suppression, subjugation, control, controlling; disciplining, chastening, punishment.

mortify ● verb **1** *I'd be mortified if my friends found out* EMBARRASS, humiliate, chagrin, shame, discomfit, abash, horrify, appal. **2** *he was mortified at being excluded* HURT, wound, affront, offend, put out, pique, irk, annoy, vex; *informal* rile. **3** *mortifying the flesh* SUBDUE, suppress, subjugate, control; discipline, chasten, punish. **4** *the cut had mortified* BECOME GANGRENOUS, fester, putrefy, gangrene, rot, decay, decompose.

mortuary ● noun MORGUE, funeral parlour; *Brit.* chapel of rest.

most ● pronoun *most of the guests brought flowers* NEARLY ALL, almost all, the greatest part/number, the majority, the bulk, the preponderance.

– OPPOSITES little, few.

– PHRASES **for the most part** MOSTLY, mainly, in the main, on the whole, largely, by and large, to a large extent, predominantly, chiefly, principally, basically, generally, usually, typically, com-

an Irish Roman Catholic bishop.

MOT ● noun (in the UK) a compulsory annual test of motor vehicles of more than a specified age.
– ORIGIN abbreviation of *Ministry of Transport*.

mote ● noun a speck.
– ORIGIN Old English.

motel ● noun a roadside hotel for motorists.
– ORIGIN blend of MOTOR and HOTEL.

motet /mōtet/ ● noun a short piece of sacred choral music.
– ORIGIN Old French, 'little word'.

moth ● noun a chiefly nocturnal insect resembling a butterfly but holding its wings flat when at rest and generally having feathery antennae.
– ORIGIN Old English.

mothball ● noun a small ball of naphthalene or camphor, placed among stored clothes to deter clothes moths. ● verb **1** store (clothes) among or in mothballs. **2** put into storage or on hold indefinitely.
– PHRASES **in mothballs** in storage or on hold.

moth-eaten ● adjective damaged or apparently damaged by clothes moths; shabby or threadbare.

mother ● noun **1** a female parent. **2** (**Mother**) (especially as a title or form of address) the head of a female religious community. **3** informal an extreme or very large example of: *the mother of all traffic jams.* ● verb look after kindly and protectively, sometimes excessively so.
– DERIVATIVES **motherhood** noun **motherless** adjective.
– ORIGIN Old English.

motherboard ● noun a printed circuit board containing the main components of a microcomputer.

mother country ● noun a country in relation to its colonies.

Mothering Sunday ● noun Brit. the fourth Sunday in Lent, traditionally a day for honouring one's mother.

mother-in-law ● noun (pl. **mothers-in-law**) the mother of one's husband or wife.

motherland ● noun one's native country.

mother lode ● noun a principal vein of an ore or mineral.

motherly ● adjective of or characteristic of a mother, especially in being caring, protective, and kind.
– DERIVATIVES **motherliness** noun.

mother-of-pearl ● noun a smooth pearly substance lining the shells of oysters, abalones, and certain other molluscs.

Mother's Day ● noun a day of the year on which children honour their mothers (in Britain Mothering Sunday, and in North America the second Sunday in May).

mother's ruin ● noun Brit. informal gin.

Mother Superior ● noun the head of a female religious community.

mother tongue ● noun a person's native language.

motif /mōteef/ ● noun **1** a single or repeated image forming a design. **2** a dominant or recurrent theme in an artistic, musical, or literary work. **3** a decorative device applied to a garment or textile.
– ORIGIN French.

motile /mōtīl/ ● adjective (of cells, gametes, and single-celled organisms) capable of motion.
– DERIVATIVES **motility** noun.
– ORIGIN from Latin *motus* 'motion', on the pattern of *mobile*.

motion ● noun **1** the action of moving. **2** a movement or gesture. **3** a piece of moving mechanism. **4** a formal proposal put to a legislature or committee. **5** Brit. an emptying of the bowels. **6** Brit. a piece of excrement. ● verb direct (someone) with a gesture.
– PHRASES **go through the motions** do something in a perfunctory way.
– DERIVATIVES **motional** adjective **motionless** adjective.
– ORIGIN from Latin *movere* 'to move'.

motion picture ● noun chiefly N. Amer. a cinema film.

motivate ● verb **1** provide with a motive for doing something. **2** stimulate the interest of.
– DERIVATIVES **motivator** noun.

motivation ● noun **1** the reason or reasons behind one's actions or behaviour. **2** enthusiasm.
– DERIVATIVES **motivational** adjective.

motive ● noun **1** a factor inducing a person to act in a particular way. **2** a motif. ● adjective producing physical or mechanical motion.
– DERIVATIVES **motiveless** adjective.
– ORIGIN Latin *motivus*, from *movere* 'to move'.

motive power ● noun the energy used to drive machinery.

mot juste /mō zhoost/ ● noun (pl. **mots justes** pronunc. same) (**the mot juste**) the most appropriate word or expression.
– ORIGIN French, 'appropriate word'.

motley ● adjective incongruously varied in appearance or character. ● noun a varied mixture.
– ORIGIN of unknown origin.

motocross ● noun cross-country racing on motorcycles.

motor ● noun **1** a machine that supplies motive power for a vehicle or other device. **2** Brit. informal a car. ● adjective **1** giving or producing motion or action. **2** Physiology relating to muscular movement or the nerves activating it. ● verb informal, chiefly Brit.

m

Thesaurus

monly, as a rule, on balance, on average.

mostly ● adverb **1** *the other passengers were mostly businessmen* MAINLY, for the most part, on the whole, in the main, largely, chiefly, predominantly, principally, primarily. **2** *I mostly wear jeans* USUALLY, generally, in general, as a rule, ordinarily, normally, customarily, typically, most of the time, almost always.

mote ● noun SPECK, particle, grain, spot, fleck, atom, scintilla.

moth-eaten ● adjective THREADBARE, worn (out), well worn, old, shabby, scruffy, tattered, ragged; *informal* tatty, the worse for wear; *N. Amer. informal* raggedy.

mother ● noun **1** *I will ask my mother* FEMALE PARENT, materfamilias, matriarch; *informal* ma, mam, mammy, old lady, old woman; *Brit. informal* mum, mummy; *N. Amer. informal* mom, mommy; *Brit. informal, dated* mater. **2** *the foal's mother* DAM. **3** *the wish was mother of the deed* SOURCE, origin, genesis, fountainhead, inspiration, stimulus; *poetic/literary* wellspring.
– RELATED TERMS maternal, matri-.
– OPPOSITES child, father.
● verb **1** *she mothered her husband* LOOK AFTER, care for, take care of, nurse, protect, tend, raise, rear; pamper, coddle, cosset, fuss over. **2** *she mothered an illegitimate daughter* GIVE BIRTH TO, have, bear, produce; *N. Amer.* birth; *archaic* be brought to bed of.
– OPPOSITES neglect.

motherly ● adjective MATERNAL, maternalistic, protective, caring, loving, devoted, affectionate, fond, warm, tender, gentle, kind, kindly, understanding, compassionate.

motif ● noun **1** *a colourful tulip motif* DESIGN, pattern, decoration, figure, shape, device, emblem, ornament. **2** *a recurring motif in Pinter's work* THEME, idea, concept, subject, topic, leitmotif, element.

motion ● noun **1** *the rocking motion of the boat | a planet's motion around the sun* MOVEMENT, moving, locomotion, rise and fall, shifting; progress, passage, passing, transit, course, travel, travelling. **2** *a motion of the hand* GESTURE, movement, signal, sign, indication; wave, nod, gesticulation. **3** *the motion failed to obtain a majority* PROPOSAL, proposition, recommendation, suggestion.
– RELATED TERMS kinetic.
● verb *he motioned her to sit down* GESTURE, signal, direct, indicate; wave, beckon, nod, gesticulate.
– PHRASES **in motion** MOVING, on the move, going, travelling, running, functioning, operational. **set in motion** START, commence, begin, activate, initiate, launch, get under way, get going, get off the ground; trigger off, set off, spark off, generate, cause.

motionless ● adjective UNMOVING, still, stationary, stock-still, immobile, static, not moving a muscle, rooted to the spot, transfixed, paralysed, frozen.
– OPPOSITES moving.

motivate ● verb **1** *she was primarily motivated by the desire for profit* PROMPT, drive, move, inspire, stimulate, influence, activate, impel, push, propel, spur (on). **2** *it's the teacher's job to motivate the child* INSPIRE, stimulate, encourage, spur (on), excite, inspirit, incentivize, fire with enthusiasm.

motivation ● noun **1** *his motivation was financial* MOTIVE, motivating force, incentive, stimulus, stimulation, inspiration, inducement, incitement, spur, reason. **2** *staff motivation* ENTHUSIASM, drive, ambition, initiative, determination, enterprise; *informal* get-up-and-go.

motive ● noun **1** *the motive for the attack* REASON, motivation, motivating force, rationale, grounds, cause, basis, object, purpose, intention; incentive, inducement, incitement, lure, inspiration, stimulus, stimulation, spur. **2** *religious motives in art* MOTIF, theme, idea, concept, subject, topic, leitmotif.
● adjective *motive power* KINETIC, driving, impelling, propelling, propulsive, motor.

travel in a car.
– ORIGIN Latin, 'mover', from *movere* 'to move'.
motorbike ● noun a motorcycle.
motorboat ● noun a boat powered by a motor.
motorcade ● noun a procession of motor vehicles.
– ORIGIN from MOTOR, on the pattern of *cavalcade*.
motor car ● noun chiefly Brit. a car.
motorcycle ● noun a two-wheeled vehicle that is powered by a motor.
– DERIVATIVES **motorcycling** noun **motorcyclist** noun.
motor drive ● noun a battery-driven motor in a camera, used to wind the film rapidly between exposures.
motorist ● noun the driver of a car.
motorman ● noun the driver of a train or tram.
motormouth ● noun informal a person who talks rapidly and incessantly.
motor neuron ● noun a nerve cell forming part of a pathway along which impulses pass from the brain or spinal cord to a muscle or gland.
motor neuron disease ● noun a progressive disease involving degeneration of the motor neurons and wasting of the muscles.
motor racing ● noun the sport of racing in specially developed fast cars.
motor vehicle ● noun a road vehicle powered by an internal-combustion engine.
motorway ● noun Brit. a road designed for fast traffic, typically with three lanes in each direction.
motte /mot/ ● noun historical a mound forming the site of a castle or camp.
– ORIGIN French, 'mound', related to MOAT.
mottle ● noun a mottled marking.
mottled ● adjective marked with patches of a different colour.
– ORIGIN probably from MOTLEY.
motto ● noun (pl. **mottoes** or **mottos**) a short sentence or phrase encapsulating a belief or ideal.
– ORIGIN Italian, 'word'.
moue /moō/ ● noun a pout.
– ORIGIN French.
mouflon /moōflon/ (also **moufflon**) ● noun a small wild sheep with chestnut-brown wool, found in mountainous country.
– ORIGIN French, from Italian *muflone*.
mould[1] (US **mold**) ● noun **1** a hollow container used to give shape to molten or hot liquid material when it cools and hardens. **2** something made in this way, especially a jelly or mousse. **3** a distinctive type, style, or character. ● verb **1** form (an object) out of a malleable substance. **2** give a shape to (a malleable substance). **3** influence the development of.
– PHRASES **break the mould** end a restrictive pattern of events or behaviour by doing things differently.
– ORIGIN probably from Old French *modle*, from Latin *modus* 'measure'.
mould[2] (US **mold**) ● noun a furry growth of minute fungi occurring typically in moist warm conditions on organic matter.
– ORIGIN probably from obsolete *moul* 'grow mouldy'.
mould[3] (US **mold**) ● noun chiefly Brit. soft loose earth, especially when rich in organic matter.
– ORIGIN Old English, related to MEAL[2].
mouldboard ● noun the board or plate in a plough that turns the earth over.
moulder (US **molder**) ● verb slowly decay.
– ORIGIN perhaps from MOULD[3].
moulding (US **molding**) ● noun a moulded strip of wood, stone, or plaster as a decorative architectural feature.
mouldy (US **moldy**) ● adjective (**mouldier**, **mouldiest**) **1** covered with or smelling of mould. **2** informal boring or worthless.
– DERIVATIVES **mouldiness** noun.
moules marinière /moōl marinyair/ (also **moules à la marinière**) ● plural noun mussels served in their shells and cooked in a wine and onion sauce.
– ORIGIN French, 'mussels in the marine style'.
moult (US **molt**) ● verb shed old feathers, hair, or skin, to make way for a new growth. ● noun a period of moulting.
– ORIGIN from Latin *mutare* 'to change': see MUTATE.
mound ● noun **1** a raised mass of earth or other compacted material. **2** a small hill. **3** a heap or pile. ● verb heap up into a mound.
– ORIGIN originally in the sense 'boundary hedge or fence': of obscure origin.
mount[1] ● verb **1** climb up or on to. **2** get up on (an animal or bicycle) to ride it. **3** (**be mounted**) be on horseback; be provided with a horse. **4** increase in size, number, or intensity. **5** organize and initiate. **6** put or fix in place or on a support. **7** set in or attach (a picture) to a backing. ● noun **1** (also **mounting**) something on which an object is mounted for support or display. **2** a horse used for riding.
– PHRASES **mount guard** keep watch.
– DERIVATIVES **mountable** adjective **mounted** adjective.
mount[2] ● noun archaic or in place names a mountain or hill.
mountain ● noun **1** a mass of land rising abruptly and to a large height from the surrounding level. **2** a large pile or quantity. **3** a surplus stock of a commodity.
– PHRASES **if the mountain won't come to Muhammad, Muhammad must go to the mountain** proverb if someone won't do as you wish or a situation can't be arranged to suit you, you must accept it and change your plans accordingly. [ORIGIN with allusion to a well-known story about Muhammad told by Francis Bacon (*Essays* xii).] **move mountains** achieve spectacular and apparently impossible results.
mountain ash ● noun a rowan tree.

m

Thesaurus

motley ● adjective MISCELLANEOUS, disparate, diverse, assorted, varied, diversified, heterogeneous.
– OPPOSITES homogeneous.
mottled ● adjective BLOTCHY, blotched, spotted, spotty, speckled, streaked, streaky, marbled, flecked, freckled, dappled, stippled, piebald, skewbald, brindled, brindle; *N. Amer.* pinto; *informal* splotchy.
motto ● noun MAXIM, saying, proverb, aphorism, adage, saw, axiom, apophthegm, formula, expression, phrase, dictum, precept; slogan, catchphrase; truism, cliché, platitude.
mould[1] ● noun **1** *the molten metal is poured into a mould* CAST, die, form, matrix, shape, template, pattern, frame. **2** *an actress in the traditional Hollywood mould* PATTERN, form, shape, format, model, kind, type, style; archetype, prototype. **3** *he is a figure of heroic mould* CHARACTER, nature, temperament, disposition; calibre, kind, sort, variety, stamp, type.
● verb **1** *a figure moulded from clay* SHAPE, form, fashion, model, work, construct, make, create, manufacture, sculpt, sculpture; forge, cast. **2** *moulding US policy* DETERMINE, direct, control, guide, lead, influence, shape, form, fashion, make.
mould[2] ● noun *walls stained with mould* MILDEW, fungus, must, mouldiness, mustiness.
mould[3] ● noun *leaf mould* EARTH, soil, dirt, loam, humus.
moulder ● verb DECAY, decompose, rot (away), go mouldy, go off, go bad, spoil, putrefy.
mouldy ● adjective MILDEWED, mildewy, musty, mouldering, fusty; decaying, decayed, rotting, rotten, bad, spoiled, spoilt, decomposing.
mound ● noun **1** *a mound of leaves* HEAP, pile, stack, mountain; mass, accumulation, assemblage. **2** *high on the mound* HILLOCK, hill, knoll, rise, hummock, hump, embankment, bank, ridge, elevation, acclivity; *Geology* drumlin; *Scottish* brae. **3** *a burial mound* BARROW, tumulus; motte.
● verb *mound up the rice on a serving plate* PILE (UP), heap (up).
mount ● verb **1** *he mounted the stairs* GO UP, ascend, climb (up), scale. **2** *the committee mounted the platform* CLIMB ON TO, jump on to, clamber on to, get on to. **3** *they mounted their horses* GET ASTRIDE, bestride, get on to, hop on to. **4** *the museum is mounting an exhibition* (PUT ON) DISPLAY, exhibit, present, install; organize, put on, stage. **5** *the company mounted a takeover bid* ORGANIZE, stage, prepare, arrange, set up; launch, set in motion, initiate. **6** *their losses mounted rapidly* INCREASE, grow, rise, escalate, soar, spiral, shoot up, rocket, climb, accumulate, build up, multiply. **7** *cameras were mounted above the door* INSTALL, place, fix, set, put up, put in position.
– OPPOSITES descend.
● noun **1** *he hung on to his mount's bridle* HORSE; *archaic* steed. **2** *a decorated photograph mount* SETTING, backing, support, mounting, frame, stand.
mountain ● noun **1** *a range of mountains* PEAK, height, mount, prominence, summit, pinnacle, alp; (**mountains**) range, massif, sierra; *Scottish* ben, Munro. **2** *a huge mountain of paperwork* GREAT DEAL, lot; profusion, abundance, quantity, backlog; *informal* heap, pile, stack, slew, lots, loads, heaps, piles, tons, masses; *N. Amer.* in-

mountain bike ● noun a sturdy bicycle with broad deep-treaded tyres and multiple gears, originally intended for riding on mountainous terrain.
mountaineering ● noun the sport or activity of climbing mountains.
– DERIVATIVES **mountaineer** noun.
mountain goat ● noun a goat that lives on mountains, proverbial for its agility.
mountain lion ● noun N. Amer. a puma.
mountainous ● adjective **1** having many mountains. **2** huge; enormous.
mountebank /mowntibangk/ ● noun a swindler.
– ORIGIN originally meaning 'a person who sold patent medicines in public places': from Italian *monta in banco!* 'climb on the bench!', with allusion to the raised platform used by mountebanks to attract an audience.
Mountie ● noun informal a member of the Royal Canadian Mounted Police.
mourn ● verb feel deep sorrow following the death or loss of.
– ORIGIN Old English.
mourner ● noun a person who attends a funeral as a relative or friend of the dead person.
mournful ● adjective feeling, showing, or causing sadness or grief.
– DERIVATIVES **mournfully** adverb **mournfulness** noun.
mourning ● noun **1** the experience or expression of deep sorrow for someone who has died. **2** black clothes conventionally worn in a period of mourning.
mouse ● noun (pl. **mice**) **1** a small rodent with a pointed snout, relatively large ears and eyes, and a long thin tail. **2** a timid and quiet person. **3** (pl. also **mouses**) Computing a small handheld device which controls cursor movements on a computer screen, with buttons which are pressed to control functions. ● verb /mowz/ hunt for or catch mice.
– DERIVATIVES **mouser** noun.
– ORIGIN Old English.
mousetrap ● noun **1** a trap for catching mice, traditionally baited with cheese. **2** Brit. informal poor-quality cheese.
moussaka /moosaakə/ ● noun a Greek dish of minced lamb layered with aubergines and tomatoes and topped with a cheese sauce.
– ORIGIN Turkish, 'that which is fed liquid' (i.e. a dish to which liquid is added during cooking).
mousse ● noun **1** a sweet or savoury dish made as a smooth light mass in which the main ingredient is whipped with cream or egg white. **2** an aerated or light preparation for the skin or hair.
– ORIGIN French, 'moss or froth'.
mousseline /mōōsleen/ ● noun **1** a fine, semi-opaque fabric similar to muslin. **2** a soft, light mousse. **3** (also **sauce mousseline**) hollandaise sauce made frothy with whipped cream or beaten egg white.
– ORIGIN French, related to MUSLIN.
moustache (US also **mustache**) ● noun a strip of hair left to grow above a man's upper lip.
– DERIVATIVES **moustached** adjective.
– ORIGIN French, from Greek *mustax*.
mousy (also **mousey**) ● adjective (**mousier**, **mousiest**) **1** of or like a mouse. **2** (of hair) of a dull, light brown colour. **3** timid and ineffectual.
mouth ● noun **1** the opening in the body of most animals through which food is taken and sounds are emitted. **2** an opening or entrance to a structure that is hollow, concave, or almost completely enclosed. **3** the place where a river enters the sea. **4** informal impudent talk. ● verb **1** move the lips as if to form (words). **2** say in an insincere or pompous way. **3** (**mouth off**) informal talk in an opinionated or abusive way. **4** take in or touch with the mouth.
– PHRASES **be all mouth (and no trousers)** informal tend to talk boastfully but not to act on one's words. **keep one's mouth shut** informal say nothing, especially to avoid revealing a secret.
– ORIGIN Old English.
mouthbrooder ● noun a freshwater fish which protects its eggs (and in some cases its young) by carrying them in its mouth.
mouthful ● noun **1** a quantity of food or drink that fills or can be put in the mouth. **2** a long or complicated word or phrase.
– PHRASES **give someone a mouthful** Brit. informal talk to someone in an angry or abusive way.
mouth organ ● noun a harmonica.
mouthpart ● noun any of the appendages surrounding the mouth of an insect or other arthropod and adapted for feeding.
mouthpiece ● noun **1** a part of a musical instrument, telephone, etc. that is designed to be put in or against the mouth. **2** a person or publication expressing the views of another person or an organization.
mouth-to-mouth ● adjective (of artificial respiration) in which a person breathes into someone's lungs through their mouth.
mouthwash ● noun an antiseptic liquid for rinsing the mouth or gargling.
mouth-watering ● adjective **1** smelling or looking delicious. **2** very attractive or tempting.
mouthy ● adjective (**mouthier**, **mouthiest**) informal inclined to talk a lot, especially in an impudent way.
movable (also **moveable**) ● adjective **1** capable of being moved. **2** denoting a religious feast day occurring on a different date each year. **3** Law (of property) of the nature of a chattel, as dis-

Thesaurus

formal gobs. **3** *a butter mountain* SURPLUS, surfeit, glut, oversupply.
– PHRASES **move mountains 1** *faith can move mountains* PERFORM MIRACLES, work/do wonders. **2** *his fans move mountains to attend his performances* MAKE EVERY EFFORT, pull out all the stops, do one's utmost/best; *informal* bend/lean over backwards.
mountainous ● adjective **1** *a mountainous region* HILLY, craggy, rocky, alpine; upland, highland. **2** *mountainous waves* HUGE, enormous, gigantic, massive, giant, colossal, immense, tremendous, mighty; *informal* whopping (great), thumping (great), humongous; *Brit. informal* whacking (great), ginormous.
– OPPOSITES flat, tiny.
mountebank ● noun SWINDLER, charlatan, confidence trickster, fraud, fraudster, impostor, trickster, hoaxer, quack; *informal* con man, flimflammer, sharp; *N. Amer. informal* grifter, bunco artist; *Austral. informal* magsman, illywhacker.
mourn ● verb **1** *Isobel mourned her husband* GRIEVE FOR, sorrow over, lament for, weep for, wail/keen over; *archaic* plain for. **2** *he mourned the loss of the beautiful buildings* DEPLORE, bewail, bemoan, rue, regret.
mournful ● adjective SAD, sorrowful, doleful, melancholy, melancholic, woeful, grief-stricken, miserable, unhappy, heartbroken, broken-hearted, gloomy, dismal, desolate, dejected, despondent, depressed, downcast, disconsolate, woebegone, forlorn, rueful, lugubrious, joyless, cheerless; *poetic/literary* dolorous.
– OPPOSITES cheerful.
mourning ● noun **1** *a period of mourning* GRIEF, grieving, sorrowing, lamentation, lament, keening, wailing, weeping; *poetic/literary* dole. **2** *she was dressed in mourning* BLACK (CLOTHES), (widow's) weeds; *archaic* sables.
moustache ● noun WHISKERS, mustachios, handlebar moustache, walrus moustache, burnsides; *informal* tash; *N. Amer. informal* stash.
mousy ● adjective **1** *mousy hair* LIGHTISH BROWN, brownish, brownish-grey, dun-coloured; dull, lacklustre. **2** *a small, mousy woman* TIMID, quiet, fearful, timorous, shy, self-effacing, diffident, unassertive, unforthcoming, withdrawn, introverted, introvert.
mouth ● noun **1** *open your mouth* lips, jaws; maw, muzzle; *informal* trap, chops, kisser; *Brit. informal* gob, cakehole; *N. Amer. informal* puss, bazoo. **2** *the mouth of the cave* ENTRANCE, opening, entry, way in, access, ingress. **3** *the mouth of the bottle* OPENING, rim, lip. **4** *the mouth of the river* OUTFALL, outlet, debouchment; estuary, firth. **5** *(informal) he's all mouth* BOASTING, bragging, idle talk, bombast, braggadocio; *informal* hot air. **6** *(informal) you've got a lot of mouth* IMPUDENCE, cheek, cheekiness, insolence, impertinence, effrontery, presumption, presumptuousness, rudeness, disrespect; *informal* lip, (brass) neck; *Brit. informal* sauce, backchat; *N. Amer. informal* sass, sassiness, back talk.
● verb *he mouthed platitudes* UTTER, speak, say; pronounce, enunciate, articulate, voice, express; say insincerely, say for form's sake.
– PHRASES **down in the mouth** *(informal)*. See UNHAPPY sense 1. **keep one's mouth shut** *(informal)* SAY NOTHING, keep quiet, not breathe a word, not tell a soul; *informal* keep mum, not let the cat out of the bag. **mouth off** *(informal)* RANT, spout, declaim, sound off.
mouthful ● noun **1** *a mouthful of pizza* BITE, nibble, taste, bit, piece; spoonful, forkful. **2** *a mouthful of beer* DRAUGHT, sip, swallow, drop, gulp, slug; *informal* swig. **3** *'sesquipedalian' is a bit of a mouthful* TONGUE-TWISTER, long word, difficult word.

m

tinct from land or buildings.

move • verb **1** go or cause to go in a specified direction or manner. **2** change or cause to change position. **3** change one's place of residence. **4** change from one state, sphere, or activity to another. **5** take or cause to take action. **6** make progress. **7** provoke compassion, affection, or other feelings in. **8** propose for discussion and resolution at a meeting or legislative assembly. **9** empty (the bowels). • noun **1** an instance of moving. **2** an action taken towards achieving a purpose. **3** a manoeuvre in a sport or game. **4** a player's turn during a board game.
– PHRASES **get a move on** informal hurry up. **make a move 1** take action. **2** Brit. set off; leave somewhere. **make a move on** (or **put the moves on**) informal make a proposition of a sexual nature to. **move in** (or **out**) start (or cease) living or working in a place. **move in/within** be socially active in (a particular sphere) or among (a particular group).
– DERIVATIVES **mover** noun.
– ORIGIN Latin *movere*.

movement • noun **1** an act of moving. **2** the process of moving or the state of being moved. **3** a group of people working to advance a shared cause. **4** a series of organized actions to advance a shared cause. **5** a trend or development. **6** (**movements**) a person's activities during a particular period of time. **7** Music a principal division of a musical work. **8** the moving parts of a mechanism, especially a clock or watch.

movie • noun chiefly N. Amer. a cinema film.

moving • adjective **1** in motion. **2** arousing strong emotion.
– DERIVATIVES **movingly** adverb.

mow • verb (past part. **mowed** or **mown**) **1** cut down or trim (grass or a cereal crop) with a machine or scythe. **2** (**mow down**) kill by gunfire or by knocking down with a motor vehicle.
– DERIVATIVES **mower** noun.
– ORIGIN Old English, related to MEAD².

moxa • noun a downy substance obtained from the dried leaves of an Asian plant, burnt on or near the skin in Eastern medicine as a counterirritant.
– ORIGIN from Japanese *moe kusa* 'burning herb'.

moxibustion • noun (in Eastern medicine) the burning of moxa as a counterirritant.

Mozambican /mōzambeekən/ • noun a person from Mozambique. • adjective relating to Mozambique.

Mozartian /mōtzaartiən/ • adjective relating to the Austrian composer Wolfgang Amadeus Mozart (1756–91).

mozzarella /motsərellə/ • noun a firm white Italian cheese made from buffalo's or cow's milk.
– ORIGIN Italian, from *mozzare* 'cut off'.

mozzie (also **mossie**) • noun (pl. **mozzies**) informal, chiefly Austral./NZ a mosquito.

MP • abbreviation **1** Member of Parliament. **2** military police.

MP3 • noun a means of compressing a sound sequence into a very small file, used as a way of downloading audio files from the Internet.

MPD • abbreviation multiple personality disorder.

mpg • abbreviation miles per gallon.

mph • abbreviation miles per hour.

MPhil • abbreviation Master of Philosophy.

MPV • abbreviation multi-purpose vehicle.

Mr • noun **1** a title used before a man's surname or full name. **2** a title used to address the male holder of an office.
– ORIGIN abbreviation of MASTER.

MRI • abbreviation magnetic resonance imaging.

Mrs • noun a title used before a married woman's surname or full name.
– ORIGIN abbreviation of MISTRESS.

Mrs Grundy • noun a person with very conventional standards of propriety.
– ORIGIN a person repeatedly mentioned in T. Morton's comedy *Speed the Plough* (1798).

MS • abbreviation **1** manuscript. **2** Mississippi. **3** multiple sclerosis.

Ms • noun a title used before the surname or full name of a woman regardless of her marital status (a neutral alternative to **Mrs** or **Miss**).

MSc • abbreviation Master of Science.

MS-DOS • abbreviation Computing, trademark Microsoft disk operating system.

MSG • abbreviation monosodium glutamate.

Msgr • abbreviation **1** Monseigneur. **2** Monsignor.

MSP • abbreviation Member of the Scottish Parliament.

MT • abbreviation Montana.

Mt • abbreviation (in place names) Mount. • symbol the chemical elem-

m

Thesaurus

mouthpiece • noun **1** *the flute's mouthpiece* EMBOUCHURE. **2** *a mouthpiece for the government* SPOKESPERSON, spokesman, spokeswoman, agent, representative, propagandist, voice.

movable • adjective **1** *movable objects* PORTABLE, transportable, transferable; mobile. **2** *movable feasts* VARIABLE, changeable, alterable.
– OPPOSITES fixed.

movables • plural noun POSSESSIONS, belongings, effects, property, goods, chattels, paraphernalia, impedimenta; *informal* gear.
– OPPOSITES fixtures, fittings.

move • verb **1** *she moved to the door* | *don't move!* GO, walk, proceed, progress, advance; budge, stir, shift, change position. **2** *he moved the chair closer to the fire* CARRY, transport, transfer, shift. **3** *things were moving too fast* (MAKE) PROGRESS, make headway, advance, develop. **4** *he urged the council to move quickly* TAKE ACTION, act, take steps, do something, take measures; *informal* get moving. **5** *she's moved to Cambridge* RELOCATE, move house, move away/out, change address/house, leave, go away, decamp; *Brit. informal* up sticks; *N. Amer. informal* pull up stakes. **6** *I was deeply moved by the story* AFFECT, touch, impress, shake, upset, disturb, make an impression on. **7** *she was moved to find out more about it* INSPIRE, prompt, stimulate, motivate, provoke, influence, rouse, induce, incite. **8** *they are not prepared to move on this issue* CHANGE, budge, shift one's ground, change one's tune, change one's mind, have second thoughts; do a U-turn, do an about-face; *Brit.* do an about-turn. **9** *she moves in the art worlds* CIRCULATE, mix, socialize, keep company, associate; *informal* hang out/around; *Brit. informal* hang about. **10** *I move that we adjourn* PROPOSE, submit, suggest, advocate, recommend, urge.
• noun **1** *his eyes followed her every move* MOVEMENT, motion, action; gesture, gesticulation. **2** *his recent move to London* RELOCATION, change of house/address, transfer, posting. **3** *the latest move in the war against drugs* INITIATIVE, step, action, act, measure, manoeuvre, tactic, stratagem. **4** *it's your move* TURN, go; opportunity, chance.
– PHRASES **get a move on** *(informal)* HURRY UP, speed up, move faster; *informal* get cracking, get moving, step on it, shake a leg; *Brit. informal* get one's skates on, stir one's stumps; *N. Amer. informal* get a wiggle on; *dated* make haste. **make a move 1** *waiting for the other side to make a move* DO SOMETHING, take action, act, take the initiative; *informal* get moving. **2** *(Brit.) I'd better be making a move* LEAVE, take one's leave, be on one's way, get going, depart, be off; *informal* push off, shove off, split. **on the move 1** *she's always on the move* TRAVELLING, in transit, moving, journeying, on the road; *informal* on the go. **2** *the economy is on the move* PROGRESSING, making progress, advancing, developing.

movement • noun **1** *Rachel made a sudden movement* | *there was almost no movement* MOTION, move; gesture, gesticulation, sign, signal; action, activity. **2** *the movement of supplies* TRANSPORTATION, shift, shifting, conveyance, moving, transfer. **3** *the labour movement* POLITICAL GROUP, party, faction, wing, lobby, camp. **4** *a movement to declare war on poverty* CAMPAIGN, crusade, drive, push. **5** *there have been movements in the financial markets* DEVELOPMENT, change, fluctuation, variation. **6** *the movement towards equality* TREND, tendency, drift, swing. **7** *some movement will be made by the end of the month* PROGRESS, progression, advance. **8** *a symphony in three movements* PART, section, division. **9** *the clock's movement* MECHANISM, machinery, works, workings; *informal* innards, guts.

movie • noun **1** *a horror movie* FILM, (motion) picture, feature (film); *informal* flick; *dated* moving picture. **2** *let's go to the movies* THE CINEMA, the pictures, the silver screen; *informal* the flicks, the big screen.

moving • adjective **1** *moving parts* | *a moving train* IN MOTION, operating, operational, working, going, on the move, active; movable, mobile. **2** *a moving book* AFFECTING, touching, poignant, heartwarming, heart-rending, emotional, disturbing; inspiring, inspirational, stimulating, stirring. **3** *the party's moving force* DRIVING, motivating, dynamic, stimulating, inspirational.
– OPPOSITES fixed, stationary.

mow • verb *she had mown the grass* CUT (DOWN), trim; crop, clip.
– PHRASES **mow someone/something down** KILL, gun down, shoot

ent meitnerium.

MTB ● abbreviation **1** Brit. motor torpedo boat. **2** mountain bike.

mu /myōō/ ● noun the twelfth letter of the Greek alphabet (M, μ), transliterated as 'm'. ● symbol (μ) 'micro-' in abbreviations for units, e.g. μg for *microgram.*

– ORIGIN Greek.

much ● determiner & pronoun (**more, most**) **1** a large amount. **2** indicating that someone or something is a poor specimen: *I'm not much of a gardener.* ● adverb **1** to a great extent; a great deal. **2** for a large part of one's time; often.

– PHRASES **a bit much** informal somewhat excessive or unreasonable. (**as**) **much as** even though. **so much the better** (or **worse**) that is even better (or worse). **too much** too difficult or exhausting to tolerate.

– ORIGIN Old English, related to MICKLE.

muchness ● noun (in phrase (**much**) **of a muchness**) very similar.

mucilage /myōōssilij/ ● noun **1** a viscous secretion or bodily fluid. **2** a viscous or gelatinous solution extracted from plants, used in medicines and adhesives.

– DERIVATIVES **mucilaginous** /myōōssilajinəss/ adjective.

– ORIGIN Latin *mucilago* 'musty juice'.

muck ● noun **1** dirt or rubbish. **2** manure. ● verb **1** (**muck up**) informal spoil. **2** (**muck about/around**) Brit. informal behave in a silly or aimless way. **3** (**muck about/around with**) Brit. informal interfere with. **4** (**muck in**) Brit. informal share tasks or accommodation. **5** (**muck out**) chiefly Brit. remove manure and other dirt from (a stable).

– PHRASES **Lord** (or **Lady**) **Muck** Brit. informal a socially pretentious man (or woman). **where there's muck there's brass** proverb dirty or unpleasant activities are also lucrative.

– ORIGIN probably Scandinavian.

mucker ● noun Brit. informal a friend or companion.

muckle ● noun & adjective variant form of MICKLE.

muckraking ● noun the action of searching out and publicizing scandal about famous people.

– ORIGIN coined by President Theodore Roosevelt in a speech (1906) alluding to the man with the *muck rake* in Bunyan's *Pilgrim's Progress.*

m

mucky ● adjective (**muckier, muckiest**) **1** covered with or consisting of muck; dirty. **2** sordid or indecent.

mucosa /myookōsə/ ● noun (pl. **mucosae** /myookōsee/) a mucous membrane.

mucous ● adjective relating to or covered with mucus.

mucous membrane ● noun a mucus-secreting tissue lining many body cavities and tubular organs, including the respiratory passages.

mucus ● noun **1** a slimy substance secreted by the mucous membranes and glands of animals for lubrication, protection, etc. **2** mucilage from plants.

– ORIGIN Latin, related to Greek *mussesthai* 'blow the nose', *mukter* 'nose, nostril'.

mud ● noun **1** soft, sticky matter consisting of mixed earth and water. **2** damaging information or allegations.

– PHRASES **drag through the mud** slander or criticize publicly. (**here's**) **mud in your eye!** informal used as a toast. **one's name is mud** informal one is in disgrace or unpopular.

– ORIGIN probably from Low German *mudde.*

mudbank ● noun a bank of mud on the bed of a river or the bottom of the sea.

mudbath ● noun **1** a bath in the mud of mineral springs, taken to relieve rheumatic complaints. **2** a muddy place.

muddle ● verb **1** bring into a disordered or confusing state. **2** confuse or perplex (someone). **3** (**muddle up**) confuse (two or more things) with each other. **4** (**muddle along/through**) cope more or less satisfactorily. ● noun a muddled state.

– DERIVATIVES **muddled** adjective **muddly** adjective.

– ORIGIN originally in the sense 'wallow in mud': perhaps from Dutch *modden* 'dabble in mud'.

muddle-headed ● adjective disorganized or confused.

muddy ● adjective (**muddier, muddiest**) **1** covered in, full of, or reminiscent of mud. **2** clouded; not bright or clear. ● verb (**muddies, muddied**) **1** cause to become muddy. **2** make unclear.

mudflap ● noun a flap hung behind the wheel of a vehicle to protect against mud and stones thrown up from the road.

mudflat ● noun a stretch of muddy land left uncovered at low tide.

mudguard ● noun a curved strip fitted over a wheel of a bicycle or motorcycle to protect against water and dirt thrown up from the road.

mudlark ● noun a person who scavenges in river mud for objects of value.

mud pack ● noun a paste applied to the face to improve the condition of the skin.

mudskipper ● noun a small goby of tropical mangrove swamps which is able to move around out of water.

mud-slinging ● noun informal the casting of insults and accusations.

mudstone ● noun a dark sedimentary rock formed from consolidated mud.

Thesaurus

down, cut down, cut to pieces, butcher, slaughter, massacre, annihilate, wipe out; *informal* blow away.

much ● determiner *did you get much help?* A LOT OF, a great/good deal of, a great/large amount of, plenty of, ample, copious, abundant, plentiful, considerable; *informal* lots of, loads of, heaps of, masses of, tons of.

– OPPOSITES little.

● adverb **1** *it didn't hurt much* GREATLY, to a great extent/degree, a great deal, a lot, considerably, appreciably. **2** *does he come here much?* OFTEN, frequently, many times, repeatedly, regularly, habitually, routinely, usually, normally, commonly; *informal* a lot.

● pronoun *he did so much for our team* A LOT, a great/good deal, plenty; *informal* lots, loads, heaps, masses.

– PHRASES **much of a muchness** *(informal)* VERY SIMILAR, much the same, very alike, practically identical.

muck ● noun **1** *I'll just clean off the muck* DIRT, grime, filth, mud, slime, mess; *informal* crud, gunk, grunge, gloop; *Brit. informal* gunge, grot; *N. Amer. informal* guck, glop. **2** *spreading muck on the fields* DUNG, manure, ordure, excrement, excreta, droppings, faeces, sewage; *N. Amer. informal* cow chips, horse apples.

– PHRASES **muck something up** *(informal)* MAKE A MESS OF, mess up, bungle, spoil, ruin, wreck; *informal* botch, make a hash of, muff, fluff, foul up, louse up; *Brit. informal* make a pig's ear of, make a Horlicks of; *N. Amer. informal* goof up. **muck about/around** *(Brit. informal)* **1** *he was mucking about with his mates* FOOL ABOUT/AROUND, play about/around, clown about/around, footle about/around; *informal* mess about/around, horse about/around, lark (about/around). **2** *someone's been mucking about with the video* INTERFERE, fiddle (about/around), play about/around, tamper, meddle, tinker; *informal* mess (about/around).

mucky ● adjective DIRTY, filthy, grimy, muddy, grubby, messy, soiled, stained, smeared, slimy, sticky, bespattered; *informal* cruddy, grungy, gloopy; *Brit. informal* gungy, grotty; *Austral./NZ informal* scungy; *poetic/literary* besmirched, begrimed, befouled.

– OPPOSITES clean.

mud ● noun MIRE, sludge, ooze, silt, clay, dirt, soil.

muddle ● verb **1** *the papers have got muddled up* CONFUSE, mix up, jumble (up), disarrange, disorganize, disorder, disturb, mess up. **2** *it would only muddle you* BEWILDER, confuse, bemuse, perplex, puzzle, baffle, nonplus, mystify.

● noun **1** *the files are in a muddle* MESS, confusion, jumble, tangle, hotchpotch, mishmash, chaos, disorder, disarray, disorganization; *N. Amer.* hodgepodge. **2** *a bureaucratic muddle* BUNGLE, mix-up, misunderstanding; *informal* foul-up; *N. Amer. informal* snafu.

– PHRASES **muddle along/through** COPE, manage, get by/along, scrape by/along, make do.

muddled ● adjective **1** *a muddled pile of photographs* JUMBLED, in a jumble, in a muddle, in a mess, chaotic, in disorder, in disarray, topsy-turvy, disorganized, disordered, disorderly, mixed up, at sixes and sevens; *informal* higgledy-piggledy. **2** *she felt muddled* CONFUSED, bewildered, bemused, perplexed, disorientated, disoriented, in a muddle, befuddled; *N. Amer. informal* discombobulated. **3** *muddled thinking* INCOHERENT, confused, muddle-headed, woolly.

– OPPOSITES orderly, clear.

muddy ● adjective **1** *muddy ground* WATERLOGGED, boggy, marshy, swampy, squelchy, squishy, mucky, slimy, spongy, wet, soft, heavy; *archaic* quaggy. **2** *muddy boots* MUD-CAKED, muddied, dirty, filthy, mucky, grimy, soiled; *poetic/literary* begrimed. **3** *muddy water* MURKY, cloudy, muddied, turbid; *N. Amer.* riled, roily. **4** *a muddy pink* DINGY, dirty, drab, dull, sludgy.

– OPPOSITES clean, clear.

● verb **1** *don't muddy your boots* MAKE MUDDY, dirty, soil, spatter, bespatter; *poetic/literary* besmirch, begrime. **2** *these results muddy the situation* MAKE UNCLEAR, obscure, confuse, obfuscate, blur,

muesli /myoozli/ • noun (pl. **mueslis**) a mixture of oats and other cereals, dried fruit, and nuts, eaten with milk at breakfast.
– ORIGIN Swiss German.

muezzin /mooezzin/ • noun a man who calls Muslims to prayer from the minaret of a mosque.
– ORIGIN from Arabic, 'proclaim'.

muff[1] • noun 1 a short tube made of fur or other warm material into which the hands are placed for warmth. 2 vulgar slang a woman's genitals.
– ORIGIN Dutch *mof*.

muff[2] informal • verb handle clumsily; bungle. • noun a mistake or failure, especially a failure to catch a ball cleanly.
– ORIGIN of unknown origin.

muffin • noun 1 (N. Amer. **English muffin**) a thick, flattened bread roll made from yeast dough and eaten split, toasted, and buttered. 2 chiefly N. Amer. a small domed cake.
– ORIGIN of unknown origin.

muffle • verb 1 wrap or cover for warmth. 2 make (a sound) quieter or less distinct by covering its source.
– ORIGIN from Old French *moufle* 'thick glove'.

muffler • noun 1 a wrap or scarf worn around the neck and face. 2 a device for deadening the sound of a drum or other instrument. 3 N. Amer. a silencer for a motor vehicle exhaust.

mufti[1] /mufti/ • noun (pl. **muftis**) a Muslim legal expert empowered to give rulings on religious matters.
– ORIGIN from Arabic, 'decide a point of law'.

mufti[2] /mufti/ • noun civilian clothes when worn by military or police staff.
– ORIGIN perhaps from MUFTI[1].

mug[1] • noun 1 a large cylindrical cup with a handle. 2 informal a person's face. 3 Brit. informal a stupid or gullible person. 4 US informal a thug. • verb (**mugged**, **mugging**) 1 attack and rob (someone) in a public place. 2 informal make faces before an audience or a camera.
– PHRASES **a mug's game** informal an activity likely to be unsuccessful or dangerous.
– ORIGIN probably Scandinavian.

mug[2] • verb (**mugged**, **mugging**) (**mug up**) Brit. informal learn or study (a subject) quickly and intensively, especially for an exam.
– ORIGIN of unknown origin.

mugger[1] • noun a person who attacks and robs another in a public place.

mugger[2] • noun a large short-snouted Indian crocodile, venerated by many Hindus.
– ORIGIN Hindi.

muggins • noun (pl. same or **mugginses**) Brit. informal a foolish and gullible person.
– ORIGIN perhaps a use of the surname *Muggins*, with allusion to MUG[1].

muggy • adjective (**muggier**, **muggiest**) (of the weather) unpleasantly warm and humid.
– ORIGIN from dialect *mug* 'mist, drizzle'.

Mughal • noun variant spelling of MOGUL.

mugshot • noun informal a photograph of a person's face made for an official purpose, especially police records.

mugwort • noun a plant with aromatic divided leaves that are dark green above and whitish below.
– ORIGIN Old English, from MIDGE + WORT.

mugwump • noun N. Amer. a person who remains aloof or independent, especially from party politics.
– ORIGIN Algonquian, 'great chief'.

Muhammadan (also **Mohammedan**) • noun & adjective archaic term for MUSLIM (not favoured by Muslims).
– ORIGIN from the name of the Arab prophet and founder of Islam *Muhammad*.

mujahedin /mujaahideen/ (also **mujaheddin**, **mujahideen**) • plural noun Islamic guerrilla fighters.
– ORIGIN Persian and Arabic, 'people who fight a holy war'.

mukluk /mukluk/ • noun N. Amer. a high, soft sealskin boot worn in the American Arctic.
– ORIGIN from Yupik (an Eskimo language), 'bearded seal'.

mulatto /myoolattō/ • noun (pl. **mulattoes** or **mulattos**) a person with one white and one black parent. • adjective relating to such a person.
– ORIGIN Spanish *mulato* 'young mule, mulatto'.

mulberry • noun 1 a dark red or white fruit resembling the loganberry. 2 a dark red or purple colour.
– ORIGIN Latin *morum* 'mulberry'.

mulch • noun a mass of leaves, bark, or compost spread around or over a plant for protection or to enrich the soil. • verb cover with or apply mulch.
– ORIGIN probably from dialect *mulch* 'soft'.

mulct /mulkt/ formal • verb extract money from (someone) by fining or taxing them or by fraudulent means. • noun a fine or compulsory payment.
– ORIGIN from Latin *mulcta* 'a fine'.

mule[1] • noun 1 the offspring of a male donkey and a female horse, typically sterile. 2 a hybrid plant or animal, especially a sterile one. 3 a stupid or obstinate person. 4 informal a courier for illegal drugs. 5 historical a kind of spinning machine producing yarn on spindles.
– ORIGIN Latin *mulus*, *mula*.

mule[2] • noun a slipper or light shoe without a back.
– ORIGIN French, 'slipper'.

mule deer • noun a North American deer with long ears and black markings on the tail.

muleteer /myooliteer/ • noun a person who drives mules.

mulga /mulgə/ • noun 1 a small Australian acacia tree or shrub, which forms dense scrubby growth and is also grown for its wood. 2 (**the mulga**) Austral. informal the outback.
– ORIGIN from an Aboriginal language.

muliebrity /myooliebriti/ • noun formal womanly qualities; womanhood.
– ORIGIN from Latin *mulier* 'woman'.

mulish • adjective stubborn (like a mule).

mull[1] • verb (**mull over**) think about at length.
– ORIGIN origin uncertain.

mull[2] • verb warm (wine or beer) and add sugar and spices to it.
– ORIGIN of unknown origin.

mull[3] • noun (in Scottish place names) a promontory.
– ORIGIN perhaps from Scottish Gaelic or Icelandic.

mull[4] • noun humus formed under non-acid conditions.
– ORIGIN Danish *muld* 'soil'.

mull[5] • noun a thin muslin used in bookbinding for joining the spine of a book to its cover.
– ORIGIN Hindi.

mullah /mullə/ • noun a Muslim learned in Islamic theology and sacred law.
– ORIGIN Arabic.

mullein /mullin/ • noun a plant with woolly leaves and tall

Thesaurus

cloud, befog.
– OPPOSITES clarify.

muff • verb *(informal)* MISHANDLE, mismanage, mess up, make a mess of, bungle; *informal* botch, make a hash of, fluff, foul up, louse up; *Brit. informal* make a pig's ear of, make a Horlicks of; *N. Amer. informal* goof up.

muffle • verb 1 *everyone was muffled up in coats* WRAP (UP), swathe, enfold, envelop, cloak. 2 *the sound of their footsteps was muffled* DEADEN, dull, dampen, damp down, mute, soften, quieten, tone down, mask, stifle, smother.

muffled • adjective INDISTINCT, faint, muted, dull, soft, stifled, smothered.
– OPPOSITES loud.

mug[1] • noun 1 *a china mug* BEAKER, cup; tankard, glass, stein, flagon; *dated* seidel; *archaic* stoup. 2 *(informal) her ugly mug.* See FACE noun sense 1. 3 *(Brit. informal) he's no mug.* See FOOL noun sense 1.
• verb *he was mugged by a gang of youths* ASSAULT, attack, set upon, beat up, rob; *informal* jump, rough up, lay into; *Brit. informal* duff up, do over.

mug[2] • verb
– PHRASES **mug something up** *(Brit. informal) she's mugging up the Highway Code* STUDY, read up, cram; *informal* bone up (on); *Brit. informal* swot; *archaic* con.

muggy • adjective HUMID, close, sultry, sticky, oppressive, airless, stifling, suffocating, stuffy, clammy, damp, heavy, fuggy, like a Turkish bath, like a sauna.
– OPPOSITES fresh.

mulish • adjective OBSTINATE, stubborn, pig-headed, recalcitrant, intransigent, unyielding, inflexible, bull-headed, stiff-necked; *Brit. informal* bloody-minded, bolshie.

mull • verb
– PHRASES **mull something over** PONDER, consider, think over/

spikes of yellow flowers.
– ORIGIN Celtic.
muller /mullər/ • noun a stone used for grinding materials such as artists' pigments.
– ORIGIN perhaps from Old French *moldre* 'to grind'.
mullet • noun any of various chiefly marine fish that are widely caught for food.
– ORIGIN Greek *mullos*.
mulligatawny /mulligətawni/ • noun a spicy meat soup originally made in India.
– ORIGIN Tamil, 'pepper water'.
mullion • noun a vertical bar between the panes of glass in a window.
– DERIVATIVES **mullioned** adjective.
– ORIGIN probably an altered form of obsolete *monial*, from Old French *moinel* 'middle'.
mullock • noun **1** Austral./NZ or dialect rubbish or nonsense. **2** Austral./NZ rock which contains no gold or from which gold has been extracted.
– ORIGIN from obsolete *mul* 'dust, rubbish', from Dutch.
mulloway • noun a large edible predatory fish of Australian coastal waters.
– ORIGIN from an Aboriginal language.
multi- • combining form more than one; many: *multicultural*.
– ORIGIN from Latin *multus* 'much, many'.
multicast • verb (past and past part. **multicast**) send (data) across a computer network to several users at the same time. • noun a set of multicast data.
multicoloured (also **multicolour**; US **-colored**, **-color**) • adjective having many colours.
multicultural • adjective relating to or constituting several cultural or ethnic groups.
– DERIVATIVES **multiculturalism** noun **multiculturalist** noun & adjective.
multidisciplinary • adjective involving several academic disciplines or professional specializations.
multifaceted • adjective having many facets or aspects.
multifarious /multifairiəss/ • adjective having great variety and diversity; many and varied.
– ORIGIN Latin *multifarius*.
multiform • adjective existing in many forms or kinds.
multigym • noun an apparatus on which a number of exercises can be performed.
multihull • noun a boat with two or more, especially three, hulls.
multilateral • adjective involving three or more participants.
– DERIVATIVES **multilateralism** noun **multilaterally** adverb.
multilingual • adjective in or using several languages.
multimedia • adjective using more than one medium of expression or communication. • noun Computing an extension of hypertext allowing the provision of audio and video material.
multimillion • adjective consisting of several million.
multimillionaire • noun a person with assets worth several million pounds or dollars.
multinational • adjective **1** including or involving several countries or nationalities. **2** operating in several countries. • noun a company operating in several countries.
– DERIVATIVES **multinationally** adverb.
multi-occupation • noun the occupation of a building by a number of independent individuals or groups, typically tenants.
multiparty • adjective of or involving several political parties.
multiphase • adjective **1** in or relating to more than one phase. **2** (of an electrical device or circuit) polyphase.
multiple • adjective **1** having or involving several parts or elements. **2** numerous and varied. **3** (of a disease or injury) complex in its nature or effect; affecting several parts of the body. • noun **1** a number that may be divided by another a certain number of times without a remainder. **2** chiefly Brit. a shop with several branches.
– ORIGIN Latin *multiplus*.
multiple-choice • adjective (of a question in an examination) accompanied by several possible answers, from which the candidate must choose the correct one.
multiple sclerosis • noun see SCLEROSIS.
multiple unit • noun a passenger train of two or more carriages powered by integral motors.
multiplex • adjective **1** consisting of many elements in a complex relationship. **2** (of a cinema) having several separate screens within one building. **3** involving simultaneous transmission of several messages along a single channel of communication. • noun **1** a multiplex system or signal. **2** a multiplex cinema.
– ORIGIN Latin.
multiplicand /multiplikand/ • noun a quantity which is to be multiplied by another (the multiplier).
multiplication • noun **1** the process of multiplying. **2** Mathematics the process of combining matrices, vectors, or other quantities under specific rules to obtain their product.
multiplication sign • noun the sign ×, used to indicate that one quantity is to be multiplied by another.
multiplication table • noun a list of multiples of a particular number, typically from 1 to 12.
multiplicative /multiplikativ/ • noun subject to or of the nature of multiplication.
multiplicity • noun (pl. **multiplicities**) a large number or variety.
multiplier • noun **1** a quantity by which a given number (the multiplicand) is to be multiplied. **2** a device for increasing the intensity of an electric current, force, etc. to a measurable level.
multiply¹ /multiplī/ • verb (**multiplies**, **multiplied**) **1** obtain from (a number) another which contains the first number a specified number of times. **2** increase in number or quantity. **3** increase in number by reproducing.
– ORIGIN Latin *multiplicare*.
multiply² /multipli/ • adverb in different ways or respects.
multipolar • adjective **1** having many poles or extremities. **2** polarized in several ways or directions.
– DERIVATIVES **multipolarity** noun.
multiprocessing (also **multiprogramming**) • noun Computing another term for MULTITASKING.
multiprocessor • noun a computer with more than one central processor.
multi-purpose • adjective having several purposes.
multiracial • adjective consisting of or relating to people of many races.
multi-storey • adjective (of a building) having several storeys. • noun Brit. informal a multi-storey car park.
multitasking • noun Computing the execution of more than one program or task simultaneously.
multi-track • adjective relating to or made by the mixing of several separately recorded tracks of sound. • verb record using multi-track recording.
multitude • noun **1** a large number of people or things. **2** (**the multitude**) the mass of ordinary people.
– ORIGIN Latin *multitudo*, from *multus* 'many'.
multitudinous /multityōōdinəss/ • adjective **1** very numerous.

Thesaurus

about, reflect on, contemplate, turn over in one's mind, chew over, cogitate on, give some thought to; *archaic* pore on.
multicoloured • adjective KALEIDOSCOPIC, psychedelic, colourful, multicolour, many-coloured, many-hued, rainbow, jazzy, varicoloured, variegated, harlequin, polychromatic.
– OPPOSITES monochrome.
multifarious • adjective DIVERSE, many, numerous, various, varied, diversified, multiple, multitudinous, multiplex, manifold, multifaceted, different, heterogeneous, miscellaneous, assorted; *poetic/literary* myriad, divers.
– OPPOSITES homogeneous.
multiple • adjective NUMEROUS, many, various, different, diverse, several, manifold, multifarious, multitudinous; *poetic/literary* myriad, divers.
multiplicity • noun ABUNDANCE, scores, mass, host, array, variety; range, diversity, heterogeneity, plurality, profusion; *informal* loads, stacks, heaps, masses, tons; *poetic/literary* myriad.
multiply • verb **1** *their difficulties seem to be multiplying* INCREASE, grow, become more numerous, accumulate, proliferate, mount up, mushroom, snowball. **2** *the rabbits have multiplied* BREED, reproduce, procreate.
– OPPOSITES decrease.
multitude • noun **1** *a multitude of birds* A LOT, a great/large number, a great/large quantity, host, horde, mass, swarm, abundance, profusion; scores, quantities, droves; *informal* slew, lots, loads, masses, stacks, heaps, tons, dozens, hundreds, thousands,

2 consisting of many individuals or elements.

multivalent /multivaylənt/ ● adjective **1** having many applications, interpretations, or values. **2** Chemistry another term for POLYVALENT.

multum in parvo /multəm in paarvō/ ● noun a great deal in a small space.
– ORIGIN Latin, 'much in little'.

mum[1] ● noun Brit. informal one's mother.

mum[2] ● adjective (**keep mum**) informal remain silent so as not to reveal a secret.
– PHRASES **mum's the word** do not reveal a secret.
– ORIGIN imitative of a sound made with closed lips.

mumble ● verb **1** say something indistinctly and quietly. **2** bite or chew with toothless gums. ● noun a quiet and indistinct utterance.
– ORIGIN from MUM[2].

mumbo-jumbo ● noun informal language or ritual causing or intended to cause confusion or bewilderment.
– ORIGIN from *Mumbo Jumbo*, the supposed name of an African idol.

mummer ● noun **1** an actor in a mummers' play. **2** archaic or derogatory an actor in the theatre.
– ORIGIN Old French *momeur*, from *momer* 'act in a mime'.

mummers' play (also **mumming play**) ● noun a traditional English folk play typically featuring Saint George and involving miraculous resurrection.

mummery ● noun (pl. **mummeries**) **1** a performance by mummers. **2** ridiculous ceremony.

mummify ● verb (**mummifies, mummified**) **1** (especially in ancient Egypt) preserve (a body) as a mummy. **2** dry up (a body) and so preserve it.
– DERIVATIVES **mummification** noun.

mummy[1] ● noun (pl. **mummies**) Brit. informal one's mother.
– ORIGIN perhaps an alteration of earlier MAMMY.

mummy[2] ● noun (pl. **mummies**) (especially in ancient Egypt) a body that has been preserved for burial by embalming and wrapping in bandages.
– ORIGIN Arabic, 'embalmed body', perhaps from a Persian word meaning 'wax'.

mumps ● plural noun (treated as sing.) an infectious disease spread by a virus, causing swelling of the salivary glands at the sides of the face.
– ORIGIN from obsolete *mump* 'grimace'.

mumsy Brit. informal ● adjective (of a woman) homely and unfashionable. ● noun chiefly humorous one's mother.

munch ● verb eat steadily and audibly.
– ORIGIN imitative of the sound of eating.

Munchausen's syndrome /munshowz'nz/ ● noun Psychiatry a mental disorder in which a person feigns severe illness so as to obtain medical attention.
– ORIGIN from the name of Baron *Munchausen*, the hero of a book of fantastic tales (1785).

munchies ● plural noun informal **1** snacks or small items of food. **2** (**the munchies**) a sudden strong desire for food.

mundane /mundayn/ ● adjective **1** lacking interest or excitement. **2** of this earthly world rather than a heavenly or spiritual one.
– DERIVATIVES **mundanely** adverb **mundaneness** noun **mundanity** noun.
– ORIGIN from Latin *mundus* 'world'.

mung bean ● noun a small round green bean grown in the tropics, chiefly as a source of bean sprouts.
– ORIGIN Hindi.

municipal ● adjective relating to a municipality.
– DERIVATIVES **municipally** adverb.
– ORIGIN Latin *municipalis*, from *municipium* 'free city' + *capere* 'take'.

municipality ● noun (pl. **municipalities**) a town or district that has local government.

munificent /myooniffis'nt/ ● adjective very generous.
– DERIVATIVES **munificence** noun **munificently** adverb.
– ORIGIN Latin *munificus*, from *munus* 'gift'.

muniments /myoonimənts/ ● plural noun chiefly Law title deeds or other documents proving a person's title to land.
– ORIGIN from Latin *munimentum* 'defence', later 'title deed'.

munitions ● plural noun military weapons, ammunition, equipment, and stores.
– ORIGIN Latin, 'fortification', from *munire* 'fortify'.

Munro ● noun (pl. **-os**) any of the 277 mountains in Scotland that are at least 3,000 feet high (approximately 914 metres).
– ORIGIN named after Sir Hugh Thomas *Munro*, who published a list of all such mountains in 1891.

muntjac /muntjak/ ● noun a small SE Asian deer with a dog-like bark and small tusks.
– ORIGIN Sundanese.

muon /myooon/ ● noun Physics an unstable meson with a mass around 200 times that of the electron.
– ORIGIN contraction of the earlier name *mu-meson*.

mural ● noun a painting executed directly on a wall. ● adjective on, like, or relating to a wall.
– ORIGIN from Latin *murus* 'wall'.

murder ● noun **1** the unlawful premeditated killing of one person by another. **2** informal a very difficult or unpleasant situation or experience. ● verb **1** kill unlawfully and with premeditation. **2** informal spoil by poor performance. **3** informal, chiefly Brit. consume (food or drink) with relish.
– PHRASES **get away with murder** informal succeed in doing whatever one chooses without being punished. **murder will out** murder cannot remain undetected. **scream blue murder** informal protest noisily.
– DERIVATIVES **murderer** noun **murderess** noun.
– ORIGIN Old English.

m

Thesaurus

millions; *N. Amer. informal* gazillions. **2** *Father Peter addressed the multitude* CROWD, gathering, assembly, congregation, flock, throng, horde, mob; *formal* concourse. **3** *political power in the hands of the multitude* THE (COMMON) PEOPLE, the populace, the masses, the rank and file, the commonality, the commonalty, the plebeians; the hoi polloi, the mob, the proletariat, the common herd, the rabble, the proles, the plebs.

multitudinous ● adjective NUMEROUS, many, abundant, profuse, prolific, copious, multifarious, innumerable, countless, infinite, numberless; *poetic/literary* divers, myriad.

mum[1] ● noun *(Brit. informal) my mum looks after me.* See MOTHER noun sense 1.

mum[2] *(informal)* ● adjective *he was keeping mum* SILENT, quiet, mute, dumb, tight-lipped, unforthcoming, reticent; *archaic* mumchance.
– PHRASES **mum's the word** *(informal)* SAY NOTHING, keep quiet, don't breathe a word, don't tell a soul, keep it secret, keep it to yourself, keep it under your hat; *informal* don't let on, keep shtum, don't let the cat out of the bag.

mumble ● verb MUTTER, murmur, speak indistinctly, talk under one's breath.

mumbo-jumbo ● noun NONSENSE, gibberish, claptrap, rubbish, balderdash, blather, hocus-pocus; *informal* gobbledegook, double Dutch, argle-bargle.

munch ● verb CHEW, champ, chomp, masticate, crunch, eat; *formal* manducate.

mundane ● adjective **1** *her mundane life* HUMDRUM, dull, boring, tedious, monotonous, tiresome, wearisome, unexciting, uninteresting, uneventful, unvarying, unremarkable, repetitive, repetitious, routine, ordinary, everyday, day-to-day, run-of-the-mill, commonplace, workaday; *informal* (plain) vanilla. **2** *the mundane world* EARTHLY, worldly, terrestrial, material, temporal, secular; *poetic/literary* sublunary.
– OPPOSITES extraordinary, spiritual.

municipal ● adjective CIVIC, civil, metropolitan, urban, city, town, borough.
– OPPOSITES rural.

municipality ● noun BOROUGH, town, city, district; *N. Amer.* precinct, township; *Scottish* burgh.

munificence ● noun GENEROSITY, bountifulness, open-handedness, magnanimity, lavishness, liberality, philanthropy, charitableness, largesse, big-heartedness, beneficence; *poetic/literary* bounty, bounteousness.

munificent ● adjective GENEROUS, bountiful, open-handed, magnanimous, philanthropic, princely, handsome, lavish, liberal, charitable, big-hearted, beneficent; *poetic/literary* bounteous.
– OPPOSITES mean.

murder ● noun **1** *a brutal murder* KILLING, homicide, assassination, liquidation, extermination, execution, slaughter, butchery, massacre; manslaughter; *poetic/literary* slaying. **2** *(informal) driving there was murder* HELL (ON EARTH), a nightmare, an ordeal, a trial, misery, torture, agony.
● verb **1** *someone tried to murder him* KILL, put/do to death, assas-

murderous • adjective **1** capable of, intending, or involving murder or extreme violence. **2** informal extremely arduous or unpleasant.
– DERIVATIVES **murderously** adverb **murderousness** noun.

murex /myooreks/ • noun (pl. **murices** /myooriseez/ or **murexes**) a predatory tropical marine mollusc with a spiny shell.
– ORIGIN Latin.

murine /myoorīn/ • adjective Zoology relating to mice or related rodents.
– ORIGIN from Latin *mus* 'mouse'.

murk • noun darkness or fog causing poor visibility.
– ORIGIN Old English.

murky • adjective (**murkier**, **murkiest**) **1** dark and gloomy. **2** (of water) dirty or cloudy. **3** deliberately obscure so as to conceal dishonesty or immorality.
– DERIVATIVES **murkily** adverb **murkiness** noun.

murmur • noun **1** a quietly spoken utterance. **2** a low continuous background noise. **3** a subdued complaint. **4** Medicine a recurring sound heard in the heart through a stethoscope and usually indicating disease or damage. • verb **1** say something in a murmur. **2** make a low continuous sound. **3** complain in a subdued way.
– ORIGIN Latin.

Murphy's Law • noun a supposed law of nature, to the effect that anything that can go wrong will go wrong.

murrain /murrin/ • noun **1** an infectious disease affecting cattle, in particular redwater fever. **2** archaic a plague or crop blight.
– ORIGIN Old French *morine*, from Latin *mori* 'to die'.

Muscadet /muskəday/ • noun a dry white wine from the Loire region of France.
– ORIGIN French, from *muscade* 'nutmeg'.

muscat /muskat/ • noun **1** a variety of grape with a musky scent. **2** a sweet or fortified white wine made from these grapes.
– ORIGIN from Provençal *musc* 'musk'.

muscatel /muskətel/ • noun **1** a muscat grape or a raisin made from such a grape. **2** a sweet wine made from muscat grapes.

muscle • noun **1** a band of fibrous tissue in the body that has the ability to contract, producing movement in or maintaining the position of a part of the body. **2** power or strength. • verb (**muscle in/into**) informal interfere forcibly in (another's affairs).
– DERIVATIVES **muscly** adjective.
– ORIGIN Latin *musculus*, diminutive of *mus* 'mouse' (some muscles being thought to be mouse-like in form).

muscle-bound • adjective having over-developed muscles.

muscleman • noun a large, strong man, especially a bodyguard or hired thug.

muscovado /muskəvaadō/ • noun unrefined sugar made from sugar cane.
– ORIGIN from Portuguese *mascabado açúcar* 'sugar of the lowest quality'.

Muscovite • noun **1** a native or citizen of Moscow. **2** (**muscovite**) a silver-grey form of mica. • adjective relating to Moscow.

Muscovy /muskəvi/ • noun archaic Russia.
– ORIGIN Russian *Moskva* 'Moscow'.

Muscovy duck • noun a large tropical American duck with glossy greenish-black plumage.

muscular • adjective **1** of or affecting the muscles. **2** having well-developed muscles.
– DERIVATIVES **muscularity** noun **muscularly** adverb.

muscular dystrophy • noun a hereditary condition marked by progressive weakening and wasting of the muscles.

musculature • noun the muscular system or arrangement of a body or an organ.

musculoskeletal • adjective relating to the musculature and skeleton together.

muse[1] • noun **1** (**Muse**) (in Greek and Roman mythology) each of nine goddesses who preside over the arts and sciences. **2** a woman who is the inspiration for a creative artist.
– ORIGIN Greek *mousa*.

muse[2] • verb **1** be absorbed in thought. **2** say to oneself in a thoughtful manner.
– ORIGIN Old French *muser* 'meditate, waste time'.

museum • noun a building in which objects of interest or significance are stored and exhibited.
– ORIGIN Greek *mouseion* 'seat of the Muses'.

museum piece • noun Brit. an old-fashioned or useless person or object.

mush[1] • noun **1** a soft, wet, pulpy mass. **2** cloying sentimentality. • verb reduce to mush.
– ORIGIN apparently a variant of MASH.

mush[2] • exclamation a command urging on dogs that pull a dog sled.
– ORIGIN probably an alteration of French *marchez!* or *marchons!* 'advance!'.

mush[3] • noun Brit. informal **1** a person's mouth or face. **2** used as a term of address to a man.
– ORIGIN probably from Romany, 'man'.

mushroom • noun **1** a spore-producing body of a fungus, typically having the form of a domed cap at the top of a stalk and often edible. **2** a pale pinkish-brown colour. • verb increase or develop rapidly.
– ORIGIN Old French *mousseron*.

mushroom cloud • noun a mushroom-shaped cloud of dust

m

Thesaurus

sinate, execute, liquidate, eliminate, dispatch, butcher, slaughter, massacre, wipe out; *informal* bump off, do in, do away with, knock off, blow away, blow someone's brains out, take out, dispose of; *N. Amer. informal* ice, rub out, smoke, waste; *poetic/literary* slay. **2** *(informal) Anna was murdering a Mozart sonata.* See MANGLE sense 2. **3** *(informal) he murdered his opponent.* See TROUNCE.

murderer, murderess • noun KILLER, assassin, serial killer, butcher, slaughterer; *informal* hit man, hired gun; *dated* homicide; *poetic/literary* slayer.

murderous • adjective **1** *a murderous attack* HOMICIDAL, brutal, violent, savage, ferocious, fierce, vicious, bloodthirsty, barbarous, barbaric; fatal, lethal, deadly, mortal, death-dealing; *archaic* sanguinary. **2** *(informal) a murderous schedule* ARDUOUS, gruelling, strenuous, punishing, onerous, exhausting, taxing, difficult, rigorous; *informal* killing, hellish.

murky • adjective **1** *a murky winter afternoon* DARK, gloomy, grey, leaden, dull, dim, overcast, cloudy, clouded, sunless, dismal, dreary, bleak; *poetic/literary* tenebrous. **2** *murky water* DIRTY, muddy, cloudy, turbid; *N. Amer.* riled, roily. **3** *her murky past* QUESTIONABLE, suspicious, suspect, dubious, dark, mysterious, secret; *informal* shady.
– OPPOSITES bright, clear.

murmur • noun **1** *his voice was a murmur* WHISPER, undertone, mutter, mumble. **2** *there were murmurs in Tory ranks* COMPLAINT, grumble, grouse; *informal* gripe, moan. **3** *the murmur of bees* HUM, humming, buzz, buzzing, thrum, thrumming, drone; sigh, rustle; *poetic/literary* susurration, murmuration.
• verb **1** *he heard them murmuring in the hall* MUTTER, mumble, whisper, talk under one's breath, speak softly. **2** *no one murmured at the delay* COMPLAIN, mutter, grumble, grouse; *informal* gripe, moan. **3** *the wind was murmuring through the trees* RUSTLE, sigh; burble, purl; *poetic/literary* whisper.

muscle • noun **1** *he had muscle but no brains* STRENGTH, power, muscularity, brawn, burliness; *informal* beef, beefiness; *poetic/literary* thew. **2** *financial muscle* INFLUENCE, power, strength, might, force, forcefulness, weight; *informal* clout.
– PHRASES **muscle in** *(informal)* INTERFERE WITH, force one's way into, impose oneself on, encroach on; *informal* horn in on.

muscular • adjective **1** *muscular tissue* FIBROUS, sinewy. **2** *he's very muscular* STRONG, brawny, muscly, sinewy, powerfully built, well muscled, burly, strapping, sturdy, powerful, athletic; *Physiology* mesomorphic; *informal* hunky, beefy; *poetic/literary* thewy. **3** *a muscular economy* VIGOROUS, robust, strong, powerful, dynamic, potent, active.

muse[1] • noun *the poet's muse* INSPIRATION, creative influence, stimulus; *formal* afflatus.

muse[2] • verb *I mused on Toby's story* PONDER, consider, think over/about, mull over, reflect on, contemplate, turn over in one's mind, chew over, give some thought to, cogitate on; think, be lost in contemplation/thought, daydream; *archaic* pore on.

mush • noun **1** *some sort of greyish mush* PAP, pulp, slop, paste, purée, mash; *informal* gloop, goo, gook; *N. Amer. informal* glop. **2** *romantic mush* SENTIMENTALITY, mawkishness; *informal* schmaltz, corn, slush; *N. Amer. informal* slop.

mushroom • noun FUNGUS, field mushroom, chanterelle, button mushroom, cep, champignon, shiitake, oyster mushroom.
• verb *ecotourism mushroomed in the 1980s* PROLIFERATE, grow/develop rapidly, burgeon, spread, increase, expand, boom,

and debris formed after a nuclear explosion.

mushy ● adjective (**mushier**, **mushiest**) **1** in the form of mush. **2** informal cloyingly sentimental.
– DERIVATIVES **mushiness** noun.

music ● noun **1** the art of combining vocal or instrumental sounds in a pleasing way. **2** the sound so produced. **3** the written or printed signs representing such sound.
– PHRASES **music to one's ears** something very pleasant to hear or learn.
– ORIGIN Old French *musique*, from Greek *mousikē tekhnē* 'art of the Muses'.

musical ● adjective **1** relating to or accompanied by music. **2** fond of or skilled in music. **3** pleasant-sounding. ● noun a play or film in which singing and dancing play an essential part.
– DERIVATIVES **musicality** noun **musically** adverb.

musical box ● noun Brit. a small box which plays a tune when the lid is opened.

musical chairs ● plural noun **1** a party game in which players compete for a decreasing number of chairs when the accompanying music is stopped. **2** a situation in which people frequently exchange jobs or positions.

musical comedy ● noun a musical.

music centre ● noun Brit. a combined radio, cassette player, and record or compact disc player.

music hall ● noun **1** a form of variety entertainment popular in Britain *c.*1850–1918. **2** a theatre where such entertainment took place.

musician ● noun a person who plays a musical instrument or is otherwise musically gifted.
– DERIVATIVES **musicianly** adjective **musicianship** noun.

musicology ● noun the study of music as an academic subject.
– DERIVATIVES **musicological** adjective **musicologist** noun.

musique concrète /myoozeek conkret/ ● noun music constructed by mixing recorded sounds.
– ORIGIN French, 'concrete music'.

musk ● noun **1** a strong-smelling substance secreted by the male musk deer, used as an ingredient in perfumery. **2** (also **musk plant**) a musk-scented plant related to the monkey flower.
– DERIVATIVES **muskiness** noun **musky** adjective (**muskier**, **muskiest**).
– ORIGIN Persian, perhaps from a Sanskrit word meaning 'scrotum' (because of the similarity in shape of a musk deer's musk bag).

musk deer ● noun a small East Asian deer, the male of which produces musk in an abdominal sac.

muskeg ● noun a swamp or bog in northern North America.
– ORIGIN from Cree (an American Indian language of central Canada).

musket ● noun historical a light gun with a long barrel, typically smooth-bored and fired from the shoulder.
– ORIGIN French *mousquet*, from Italian *moschetto* 'crossbow bolt'.

musketeer ● noun historical **1** a soldier armed with a musket. **2** a member of the household troops of the French king in the 17th and 18th centuries.

musketry ● noun **1** musket fire. **2** musketeers collectively. **3** the art or technique of handling a musket.

musk ox ● noun a large heavily built goat-antelope with a thick shaggy coat, native to the tundra of North America and Greenland.

muskrat ● noun a large semiaquatic North American rodent with a musky smell, valued for its fur.

Muslim (also **Moslem**) ● noun a follower of Islam. ● adjective relating to Muslims or Islam.
– ORIGIN Arabic, related to ISLAM.

muslin ● noun lightweight cotton cloth in a plain weave.
– ORIGIN Italian *mussolina*, from *Mussolo* 'Mosul' (the place in Iraq where it was formerly made).

muso ● noun (pl. **musos**) Brit. informal a musician or keen music fan.

musquash /muskwosh/ ● noun **1** Brit. the fur of the muskrat. **2** archaic a muskrat.
– ORIGIN from Abnaki (an American Indian language of Maine and Quebec).

muss informal, chiefly N. Amer. ● verb make untidy or messy. ● noun a mess or muddle.
– ORIGIN apparently a variant of MESS.

mussel ● noun **1** a marine mollusc with a dark brown or purplish-black shell. **2** a freshwater mollusc, some kinds of which produce small pearls.
– ORIGIN Latin *musculus* 'muscle'.

Mussulman /musəlmən/ ● noun (pl. **Mussulmans** or **Mussulmen**) & adjective archaic term for MUSLIM.
– ORIGIN Persian, from *muslim* (see MUSLIM).

must[1] ● modal verb (past **had to** or in reported speech **must**) **1** be obliged to; should. **2** expressing insistence. **3** expressing an opinion about something that is very likely. ● noun informal something that should not be overlooked or missed.
– ORIGIN Old English.

must[2] ● noun grape juice before or during fermentation.
– ORIGIN from Latin *mustus* 'new'.

must[3] ● noun mustiness or mould.
– ORIGIN back-formation from MUSTY.

must[4] (also **musth**) ● noun the frenzied state of a rutting male elephant or camel.
– ORIGIN from Persian, 'intoxicated'.

mustache ● noun US spelling of MOUSTACHE.

mustachios ● plural noun a long or elaborate moustache.
– ORIGIN Italian *mostaccio*.

mustang ● noun a small lightly built feral horse of the southwestern US.
– ORIGIN from a blend of Spanish *mestengo* and *mostrenco*, both meaning 'wild or masterless cattle'.

mustard ● noun **1** a hot-tasting yellow or brown paste made from the crushed seeds of a plant, eaten with meat or used in cooking. **2** a brownish yellow colour.
– ORIGIN Old French *moustarde*, from Latin *mustum* 'must' (because mustard was originally prepared with grape must).

mustard gas ● noun a liquid whose vapour causes severe irritation and blistering, used in chemical weapons.

mustelid /mustilid/ ● noun Zoology a mammal of a family including the weasels, martens, skunks, and otters.
– ORIGIN Latin *Mustelidae* (the weasel family), from *mustela* 'weasel'.

muster ● verb **1** bring (troops) together, especially for inspection or in preparation for battle. **2** (of people) gather together. **3** summon up (a feeling or attitude). **4** Austral./NZ round up (livestock). ● noun **1** an instance of mustering troops. **2** Austral./NZ a rounding up of livestock.
– PHRASES **pass muster** be accepted as satisfactory.
– ORIGIN Old French *moustrer*, from Latin *monstrare* 'to show'.

m

Thesaurus

explode, snowball, rocket, skyrocket; thrive, flourish, prosper.
– OPPOSITES contract.

mushy ● adjective **1** *cook until the fruit is mushy* SOFT, semi-liquid, pulpy, pappy, sloppy, spongy, squashy, squelchy, squishy; *informal* gooey, gloopy; *Brit. informal* squidgy. **2** *(informal) a mushy film* SENTIMENTAL, mawkish, emotional, saccharine; *informal* slushy, schmaltzy, weepy, corny; *Brit. informal* soppy; *N. Amer. informal* cornball, sappy, hokey, three-hankie.
– OPPOSITES firm.

musical ● adjective TUNEFUL, melodic, melodious, harmonious, sweet-sounding, sweet, mellifluous, euphonious, euphonic; *rare* mellifluent.
– OPPOSITES discordant.

musician ● noun PLAYER, performer, instrumentalist, accompanist, soloist, virtuoso, maestro; *historical* minstrel.

musing ● noun MEDITATION, thinking, contemplation, deliberation, pondering, reflection, rumination, introspection, daydreaming, dreaming, reverie, preoccupation, brooding; *formal* cogitation.

muss ● verb *(N. Amer. informal)* RUFFLE, tousle, dishevel, rumple, mess up, make a mess of, disarrange, make untidy.

must[1] ● verb *I must go* OUGHT TO, should, have (got) to, need to, be obliged to, be required to, be compelled to.
● noun *(informal) this video is a must* NOT TO BE MISSED, very good; necessity, essential, requirement, requisite.

must[2] ● noun *a smell of must* MOULD, mustiness, mouldiness, mildew, fustiness.

muster ● verb **1** *they mustered 50,000 troops* ASSEMBLE, mobilize, rally, raise, summon, gather (together), mass, collect, convene, call up, call to arms, recruit, conscript; *US* draft; *archaic* levy. **2** *reporters mustered outside her house* CONGREGATE, assemble, gather together, come together, collect together, convene, mass, rally; *formal* foregather. **3** *she mustered her courage* SUMMON (UP), screw up, call up, rally.
● noun *the colonel called a muster* ROLL-CALL, assembly, rally, meet-

musth • noun variant spelling of MUST[4].
mustn't • contraction must not.
musty • adjective (**mustier**, **mustiest**) **1** having a stale or mouldy smell or taste. **2** unoriginal or outdated.
– DERIVATIVES **mustiness** noun.
– ORIGIN perhaps an alteration of *moisty* 'moist'.
mutable /myōōtəb'l/ • adjective liable to change.
– DERIVATIVES **mutability** noun.
– ORIGIN Latin *mutabilis*, from *mutare* 'to change'.
mutagen /myōōtəjən/ • noun a substance which causes genetic mutation.
mutant • adjective resulting from or showing the effect of mutation. • noun a mutant form.
mutate • verb undergo mutation.
mutation • noun **1** the process or an instance of changing. **2** a change in genetic structure which results in a variant form and may be transmitted to subsequent generations. **3** a distinct form resulting from such a change.
– DERIVATIVES **mutational** adjective.
– ORIGIN Latin, from *mutare* 'to change'.
mutatis mutandis /myōōtaatiss myōōtandiss/ • adverb (used when comparing two or more cases) making necessary alterations while not affecting the main point.
– ORIGIN Latin, 'things being changed that have to be changed'.
mute • adjective **1** refraining from speech or temporarily speechless. **2** dated lacking the power of speech. **3** (of a letter) not pronounced. • noun **1** dated a person without the power of speech. **2** historical a professional attendant or mourner at a funeral. **3** a clamp placed over the bridge of a stringed instrument to deaden the resonance of the strings. **4** a pad or cone placed in the opening of a wind instrument. • verb **1** deaden or muffle the sound of. **2** reduce the strength or intensity of. **3** (**muted**) (of colour or lighting) not bright; subdued.
– DERIVATIVES **mutely** adverb **muteness** noun.
– USAGE To describe a person without the power of speech as **mute** (especially as in **deaf mute**) is today likely to cause offence. Since there are no accepted alternative terms in general use, the solution may be to use a longer construction, such as *she is both deaf and unable to speak*.
– ORIGIN Latin *mutus*.
mute swan • noun the commonest Eurasian swan, having an orange-red bill with a black knob at the base.
mutilate • verb **1** inflict a violent and disfiguring injury on (someone). **2** inflict serious damage on (something).
– DERIVATIVES **mutilation** noun **mutilator** noun.
– ORIGIN Latin *mutilare* 'maim'.
mutineer • noun a person who mutinies.
mutinous • adjective tending to mutiny; rebellious.
– DERIVATIVES **mutinously** adverb.
mutiny • noun (pl. **mutinies**) an open rebellion against authority, especially by soldiers or sailors against their officers. • verb (**mutinies**, **mutinied**) engage in mutiny; rebel.
– ORIGIN from French *mutin* 'mutineer, rebellious'.
mutt • noun informal **1** humorous or derogatory a dog, especially a mongrel. **2** a stupid or incompetent person.
– ORIGIN abbreviation of MUTTONHEAD.
mutter • verb **1** say in a barely audible voice. **2** talk or grumble in secret or in private. • noun a barely audible utterance.
– ORIGIN imitative of the sound of muttering.
mutton • noun the flesh of mature sheep used as food.
– PHRASES **mutton dressed as lamb** Brit. informal, derogatory a middle-aged or old woman dressed in a style suitable for a much younger woman.
– ORIGIN Old French *moton*, from Latin *multo*, probably of Celtic origin.
mutton-chop whiskers • plural noun whiskers on a man's cheek that are narrow at the top and broad and rounded at the bottom.
muttonhead • noun informal, dated a dull or stupid person.
mutual • adjective **1** experienced or done by each of two or more parties towards the other or others. **2** (of two or more parties) having the same specified relationship to each other. **3** held in common by two or more parties. **4** (of a building society or insurance company) owned by its members and dividing its profits between them.
– DERIVATIVES **mutuality** noun **mutually** adverb.
– USAGE Traditionally it has been held that the only correct use of **mutual** is in describing a reciprocal relationship, as in *mutual respect* (sense 1). The use of **mutual** to mean 'held in common' (sense 3), has been thought incorrect, although it has a long and respectable history (e.g. in the title of Dickens's novel *Our Mutual Friend*) and is now generally accepted as standard English.
– ORIGIN Old French *mutuel*, from Latin *mutuus* 'mutual, borrowed'.
mutual fund • noun N. Amer. a fund in which the combined contributions of many people are invested in various securities and bonds, dividends being paid in proportion to the contributors' holdings.
mutual induction • noun the production of an electric current in a circuit by a change in the current in an adjacent circuit linked to the first by a magnetic field.
muumuu /mōōmōō/ • noun a loose, brightly coloured dress as traditionally worn by Hawaiian women.
– ORIGIN Hawaiian, 'cut off'.
muzak • noun trademark recorded light background music played in public places.
– ORIGIN alteration of MUSIC.
muzzle • noun **1** the projecting part of an animal's face, including the nose and mouth. **2** a guard fitted over an animal's muz-

m

Thesaurus

ing, gathering, assemblage, congregation, convention; parade, review.
– PHRASES **pass muster** BE GOOD ENOUGH, come up to standard, come up to scratch, measure up, be acceptable/adequate, fill/fit the bill; *informal* make the grade, come/be up to snuff.
musty • adjective **1** *the room smelled musty* MOULDY, stale, fusty, damp, dank, mildewy, smelly, stuffy, airless, unventilated; *N. Amer. informal* funky. **2** *the play seemed musty* UNORIGINAL, uninspired, unimaginative, hackneyed, stale, flat, tired, banal, trite, clichéd, old-fashioned, outdated; *informal* old hat.
– OPPOSITES fresh.
mutable • adjective *the mutable nature of fashion* CHANGEABLE, variable, varying, fluctuating, shifting, inconsistent, unpredictable, inconstant, uneven, unstable, protean; *poetic/literary* fluctuant.
– OPPOSITES invariable.
mutant • noun FREAK (OF NATURE), deviant, monstrosity, monster, mutation.
mutate • verb CHANGE, metamorphose, evolve; transmute, transform, convert; *humorous* transmogrify.
mutation • noun **1** ALTERATION, change, variation, modification, transformation, metamorphosis, transmutation; *humorous* transmogrification. **2** *a genetic mutation* MUTANT, freak (of nature), deviant, monstrosity, monster.
mute • adjective **1** *Yasmin remained mute* SILENT, speechless, dumb, unspeaking, tight-lipped, taciturn; *informal* mum; *archaic* mumchance. **2** *a mute appeal* WORDLESS, silent, dumb, unspoken, unvoiced, unexpressed. **3** *the church was mute* QUIET, silent, hushed. **4** *he was deaf and mute* DUMB, unable to speak; *Medicine* aphasic.
– OPPOSITES voluble, spoken.
• verb **1** *the noise was muted by the heavy curtains* DEADEN, muffle, dampen, soften, quieten; stifle, smother, suppress. **2** *Bruce muted his criticisms* RESTRAIN, soften, tone down, moderate, temper.
– OPPOSITES intensify.
muted • adjective **1** *the muted hum of traffic* MUFFLED, faint, indistinct, quiet, soft, low. **2** *muted tones* SUBDUED, pastel, delicate, subtle, understated, restrained.
mutilate • verb **1** *the bodies had been mutilated* MANGLE, maim, disfigure, butcher, dismember; cripple. **2** *the carved screen had been mutilated* VANDALIZE, damage, deface, ruin, destroy, wreck, violate, desecrate; *N. Amer. informal* trash.
mutinous • adjective REBELLIOUS, insubordinate, subversive, seditious, insurgent, insurrectionary, rebel, riotous.
mutiny • noun *a mutiny over pay arrears* INSURRECTION, rebellion, revolt, riot, uprising, insurgence, insubordination.
• verb *thousands of soldiers mutinied* RISE UP, rebel, revolt, riot, disobey/defy authority, be insubordinate.
mutt • noun (*informal*) **1** *a long-haired mutt* MONGREL, hound, dog, cur; *Austral. informal* mong, bitzer. **2** *he pitied the poor mutt.* See FOOL noun sense 1.
mutter • verb **1** *a group of men stood muttering* TALK UNDER ONE'S BREATH, murmur, mumble, whisper, speak in an undertone. **2** *back-benchers muttered about the reshuffle* GRUMBLE, complain, grouse, carp, whine; *informal* moan, gripe, beef, whinge; *Brit. informal*

zle to stop it biting or feeding. **3** the open end of the barrel of a firearm. ● verb **1** put a muzzle on (an animal). **2** prevent (someone) expressing their opinions freely.
– ORIGIN Latin *musum*.

muzzy ● adjective (**muzzier**, **muzziest**) **1** dazed or confused. **2** blurred or indistinct.
– DERIVATIVES **muzzily** adverb **muzziness** noun.
– ORIGIN of unknown origin.

MV ● abbreviation motor vessel.

MVO ● abbreviation Member of the Royal Victorian Order.

MVP ● abbreviation chiefly N. Amer. most valuable player.

MW ● abbreviation **1** medium wave. **2** megawatt(s).

MY ● abbreviation motor yacht.

my ● possessive determiner **1** belonging to or associated with the speaker. **2** used in various expressions of surprise.
– PHRASES **My Lady** (or **Lord**) a polite form of address to certain titled people.
– ORIGIN Old English.

myalgia /mīaljə/ ● noun pain in a muscle or group of muscles.
– DERIVATIVES **myalgic** adjective.
– ORIGIN from Greek *mus* 'muscle' + *algos* 'pain'.

myalgic encephalomyelitis ● noun another term for CHRONIC FATIGUE SYNDROME.

myall /mīəl/ ● noun **1** Austral. an Australian Aboriginal living in a traditional way. **2** an Australian acacia tree with hard scented wood.
– ORIGIN sense 1 is from an Aboriginal word, meaning 'person of another tribe'; sense 2 is perhaps a transferred use of sense 1, with reference to trade in wood between the speakers of two different Aboriginal languages.

myasthenia /mīəstheeniə/ ● noun a rare chronic autoimmune disease marked by muscular weakness without atrophy.
– ORIGIN from Greek *mus* 'muscle' + *asthenia* 'weakness'.

mycelium /mīseeliəm/ ● noun (pl. **mycelia**) Botany a network of fine white filaments (hyphae) constituting the vegetative part of a fungus.
– ORIGIN from Greek *mukēs* 'fungus'.

Mycenaean /mīsineeən/ (also **Mycenean**) ● adjective relating to a late Bronze Age civilization in Greece represented by finds at Mycenae and other ancient cities of the Peloponnese. ● noun an inhabitant of Mycenae or member of the Mycenaean people.

mycology /mīkoləji/ ● noun the scientific study of fungi.
– DERIVATIVES **mycological** adjective **mycologist** noun.
– ORIGIN from Greek *mukēs* 'fungus'.

mycoprotein ● noun protein derived from fungi, especially as produced for human consumption.

myelin ● noun a whitish fatty substance forming a sheath around many nerve fibres.
– ORIGIN from Greek *muelos* 'marrow'.

myelitis /mīəlītis/ ● noun Medicine inflammation of the spinal cord.

myeloid /mīəloyd/ ● adjective relating to bone marrow or the spinal cord.
– ORIGIN from Greek *muelos* 'marrow'.

myeloma /mīəlōmə/ ● noun (pl. **myelomas** or **myelomata** /mīəlōmətə/) a malignant tumour of the bone marrow.

mynah (also **mynah bird**) ● noun a southern Asian or Australasian starling with a loud call, some kinds of which can mimic human speech.
– ORIGIN Hindi.

myocardium /mīəkaardiəm/ ● noun Anatomy the muscular tissue of the heart.
– DERIVATIVES **myocardial** adjective.
– ORIGIN from Greek *mus* 'muscle' + *kardia* 'heart'.

myopia /mīōpiə/ ● noun **1** short-sightedness. **2** lack of foresight or intellectual insight.
– DERIVATIVES **myopic** adjective.
– ORIGIN from Greek *muein* 'shut' + *ōps* 'eye'.

myositis /mīəsītiss/ ● noun Medicine inflammation and degeneration of muscle tissue.
– ORIGIN from Greek *mus* 'muscle'.

myosotis /mīəsōtis/ ● noun a plant of a genus which includes the forget-me-nots.
– ORIGIN from Greek *mus* 'mouse' + *ous* 'ear'.

myotonia /mīətōniə/ ● noun inability to relax voluntary muscle after vigorous effort.
– DERIVATIVES **myotonic** adjective.

myriad /miriəd/ literary ● noun **1** (also **myriads**) an indefinitely great number. **2** (in classical times) a unit of ten thousand. ● adjective innumerable.
– ORIGIN Greek *murias*, from *murioi* '10,000'.

myriapod /miriəpod/ ● noun Zoology a centipede, millipede, or other arthropod having an elongated body with numerous leg-bearing segments.
– ORIGIN from Greek *murioi* '10,000' + *pous* 'foot'.

myrmecology /mermikoləji/ ● noun the branch of entomology concerned with ants.
– ORIGIN from Greek *murmēx* 'ant'.

myrmidon /mermidon/ ● noun a hired ruffian or unscrupulous subordinate.
– ORIGIN from Greek *Murmidones*, a warlike people of Thessaly who accompanied Achilles to Troy.

myrrh /mur/ ● noun a fragrant gum resin obtained from certain trees and used in perfumery, medicines, and incense.
– ORIGIN Greek *murra*, of Semitic origin.

myrtle ● noun an evergreen shrub with glossy aromatic foliage and white flowers followed by purple-black oval berries.
– ORIGIN Greek *murtos*.

myself ● pronoun (first person sing.) **1** (reflexive) used by a speaker to refer to himself or herself as the object of a verb or preposition when he or she is the subject of the clause. **2** (emphatic) I or me personally. **3** literary term for **I**[2].
– ORIGIN Old English.

mysterious ● adjective **1** difficult or impossible to understand, explain, or identify. **2** deliberately enigmatic.
– DERIVATIVES **mysteriously** adverb **mysteriousness** noun.

mystery[1] ● noun (pl. **mysteries**) **1** something that is difficult or impossible to understand or explain. **2** secrecy or obscurity. **3** a novel, play, or film dealing with a puzzling crime. **4** (**mysteries**) the secret rites of an ancient or tribal religion. **5** chiefly Christian Theology a religious belief based on divine revelation. **6** an incident in the life of Jesus or of a saint as a focus of devotion in the Roman Catholic Church.
– ORIGIN Greek *mustērion*, related to MYSTIC.

mystery[2] ● noun (pl. **mysteries**) archaic a handicraft or trade.
– ORIGIN from Latin *ministerium* 'ministry'.

mystery play ● noun a popular medieval play based on biblical stories or the lives of the saints.

mystery tour ● noun Brit. a pleasure excursion to an unspecified destination.

mystic ● noun a person who seeks by contemplation and self-surrender to attain unity with the Deity and reach truths be-

m

Thesaurus

chunter; *N. Amer. informal* kvetch.

mutual ● adjective RECIPROCAL, reciprocated, requited, returned; common, joint, shared.

muzzle ● noun *the dog's velvety muzzle* SNOUT, nose, mouth, maw. ● verb *attempts to muzzle the media* GAG, silence, censor, stifle, restrain, check, curb, fetter.

muzzy ● adjective **1** *she felt muzzy* GROGGY, light-headed, faint, dizzy, befuddled, befogged; *informal* dopey, woozy. **2** *a slightly muzzy picture* BLURRED, blurry, fuzzy, unfocused, unclear, ill-defined, foggy, hazy.
– OPPOSITES clear.

myopic ● adjective **1** *a myopic patient* SHORT-SIGHTED, near-sighted. **2** *the government's myopic attitude* UNIMAGINATIVE, uncreative, unadventurous, narrow-minded, small-minded, short-term.
– OPPOSITES long-sighted, far-sighted.

myriad (*poetic/literary*) ● noun *myriads of insects* MULTITUDE, a large/great number/quantity, scores, quantities, mass, host, droves, horde; *informal* lots, loads, masses, stacks, tons, hundreds, thousands, millions; *N. Amer. informal* gazillions.
● adjective *the myriad lights of the city* INNUMERABLE, countless, infinite, numberless, untold, unnumbered, immeasurable, multitudinous, numerous; *poetic/literary* divers.

mysterious ● adjective **1** *he vanished in mysterious circumstances* PUZZLING, strange, peculiar, curious, funny, queer, odd, weird, bizarre, mystifying, inexplicable, baffling, perplexing, incomprehensible, unexplainable, unfathomable. **2** *he was being very mysterious* ENIGMATIC, inscrutable, secretive, reticent, evasive, furtive, surreptitious.
– OPPOSITES straightforward.

mystery ● noun **1** *his death remains a mystery* PUZZLE, enigma, conundrum, riddle, secret, (unsolved) problem. **2** *her past is shrouded in mystery* SECRECY, obscurity, uncertainty, mystique.

yond human understanding. ● adjective mystical.
– ORIGIN Greek *mustēs* 'initiated person', from *muein* 'close the eyes or lips' or 'initiate'.

mystical ● adjective **1** relating to mystics or mysticism. **2** having a spiritual significance that transcends human understanding. **3** inspiring a sense of spiritual mystery and awe.
– DERIVATIVES **mystically** adverb.

mysticism ● noun **1** the beliefs or state of mind characteristic of mystics. **2** vague or ill-defined religious or spiritual belief.

mystify ● verb (**mystifies**, **mystified**) **1** utterly bewilder. **2** make obscure or mysterious.
– DERIVATIVES **mystification** noun **mystifying** adjective
– ORIGIN French *mystifier*, from *mystique* 'mystic' or from *mystère* 'mystery'.

mystique ● noun **1** a fascinating aura of mystery, awe, and power. **2** an air of secrecy surrounding an activity or subject, making it impressive or baffling to the layperson.
– ORIGIN French.

myth ● noun **1** a traditional story concerning the early history of a people or explaining a natural or social phenomenon, typically involving the supernatural. **2** a widely held but false belief. **3** a fictitious person or thing.
– ORIGIN Greek *muthos*.

mythical ● adjective **1** occurring in or characteristic of myths or folk tales. **2** fictitious.
– DERIVATIVES **mythic** adjective **mythically** adverb.

mythological ● adjective **1** relating to or found in mythology; mythical. **2** fictitious.
– DERIVATIVES **mythologically** adverb.

mythologize (also **mythologise**) ● verb convert into myth or mythology; make the subject of a myth.

mythology ● noun (pl. **mythologies**) **1** a collection of myths. **2** a set of widely held but exaggerated or fictitious stories or beliefs. **3** the study of myths.
– DERIVATIVES **mythologist** noun.

mythomania ● noun an abnormal or pathological tendency to exaggerate or tell lies.
– DERIVATIVES **mythomaniac** noun & adjective.

mythopoeia /mithəpeeə/ ● noun the making of a myth or myths.
– DERIVATIVES **mythopoeic** adjective **mythopoetic** adjective.
– ORIGIN Greek.

myxomatosis /miksəmətōsiss/ ● noun a highly infectious and usually fatal disease of rabbits, spread by a virus and causing inflammation and discharge around the eyes.
– ORIGIN from Greek *muxa* 'slime, mucus'.

Thesaurus

3 *a murder mystery* THRILLER, detective story/novel, murder story; *informal* whodunnit.

mystic, mystical ● adjective **1** *a mystic experience* SPIRITUAL, religious, transcendental, paranormal, other-worldly, supernatural, occult, metaphysical. **2** *mystic rites* SYMBOLIC, symbolical, allegorical. **3** *a figure of mystical significance* CRYPTIC, concealed, hidden, abstruse, arcane, esoteric, inscrutable, inexplicable, unfathomable, mysterious, secret, enigmatic.

mystify ● verb BEWILDER, puzzle, perplex, baffle, confuse, confound, bemuse, nonplus, throw; *informal* flummox, stump, bamboozle, faze, fox.

mystique ● noun CHARISMA, glamour, romance, mystery, magic, charm, appeal, allure.

myth ● noun **1** *ancient Greek myths* (FOLK) TALE, (folk) story, legend, fable, saga, mythos, mythus; lore, folklore. **2** *the myths surrounding childbirth* MISCONCEPTION, fallacy, false notion, old wives' tale, fairy story/tale, fiction; *informal* (tall) story, cock and bull story.

mythical ● adjective **1** *mythical beasts* LEGENDARY, mythological, fabled, fabulous, folkloric, fairy-tale, storybook; fantastical, imaginary, imagined, fictitious. **2** *her mythical child* IMAGINARY, fictitious, make-believe, fantasy, invented, made-up, non-existent; *informal* pretend.

mythological ● adjective FABLED, fabulous, folkloric, fairy-tale, legendary, mythical, mythic, traditional; fictitious, imaginary.

mythology ● noun MYTH(S), legend(s), folklore, folk tales/stories, lore, tradition.

Nn

N[1] (also **n**) ● **noun** (pl. **Ns** or **N's**) the fourteenth letter of the alphabet.

N[2] ● **abbreviation** **1** (used in recording moves in chess) knight. [ORIGIN representing the pronunciation of *kn-*.] **2** (chiefly in place names) New. **3** Physics newton(s). **4** North or Northern. ● **symbol** the chemical element nitrogen.

n ● **abbreviation** **1** nano- (10^{-9}). **2** Grammar neuter. **3** Grammar noun. ● **symbol** an unspecified or variable number.

'n (also **'n'**) ● **contraction** informal and (e.g. *rock 'n roll*).

Na ● **symbol** the chemical element sodium.
– ORIGIN from Latin *natrium*.

n/a ● **abbreviation** **1** not applicable. **2** not available.

NAAFI /naffi/ Brit. ● **abbreviation** Navy, Army, and Air Force Institutes. ● **noun** a canteen or shop run by the NAAFI.

naan ● **noun** variant spelling of NAN[2].

nab ● **verb** (**nabbed**, **nabbing**) informal **1** catch (a wrong-doer). **2** take or grab suddenly.
– ORIGIN of unknown origin.

Nabataean /nabbəteeən/ (also **Nabatean**) ● **noun** a member of an ancient Arabian people having a kingdom with its capital at Petra (now in Jordan). ● **adjective** relating to the Nabataeans.

nabob /naybob/ ● **noun** **1** historical a Muslim official or governor under the Mogul empire. **2** a very wealthy or influential person.
– ORIGIN Urdu.

nacelle /nəsel/ ● **noun** the streamlined outer casing of an aircraft engine.
– ORIGIN originally denoting the car of an airship: from French, from Latin *navicella* 'small ship'.

nacho /nachō/ ● **noun** (pl. **nachos**) a small piece of tortilla topped with melted cheese, peppers, etc.
– ORIGIN perhaps from Mexican Spanish *Nacho*, familiar form of *Ignacio*, first name of the chef credited with creating the dish, or from Spanish *nacho* 'flat-nosed'.

nacre /naykər/ ● **noun** mother-of-pearl.
– DERIVATIVES **nacreous** adjective.
– ORIGIN French.

nada /naadə/ ● **pronoun** N. Amer. informal nothing.
– ORIGIN Spanish.

nadir /naydeer, nad-/ ● **noun** **1** Astronomy the point on the celestial sphere directly opposite the zenith and below an observer. **2** the lowest or most unsuccessful point.
– ORIGIN from Arabic, 'opposite to the zenith.'.

naevus /neevəss/ (US **nevus**) ● **noun** (pl. **naevi** /neevī/) a birthmark or a mole on the skin.
– ORIGIN Latin.

naff Brit. informal ● **verb** **1** (**naff off**) go away. **2** (**naffing**) used to emphasize annoyance. ● **adjective** lacking taste or style.
– DERIVATIVES **naffness** noun.
– ORIGIN the verb is a euphemism for FUCK; the origin of the adjective is unknown.

NAFTA (also **Nafta**) ● **abbreviation** North American Free Trade Agreement.

nag[1] ● **verb** (**nagged**, **nagging**) **1** harass (someone) constantly to do something to which they are averse. **2** be persistently worrying or painful to. ● **noun** a persistent feeling of anxiety.
– ORIGIN originally dialect in the sense 'gnaw': perhaps Scandinavian or Low German.

nag[2] ● **noun** informal, often derogatory a horse, especially an old or decrepit one.
– ORIGIN of unknown origin.

Nahuatl /naawaat'l, naawaat'l/ ● **noun** **1** a member of a group of peoples native to southern Mexico and Central America, including the Aztecs. **2** the language of these peoples.
– ORIGIN Nahuatl.

naiad /nīad/ ● **noun** (pl. **naiads** or **naiades** /nīədeez/) (in classical mythology) a water nymph.
– ORIGIN Greek *Naias*, from *naein* 'to flow'.

naif /nīeef/ ● **adjective** naive. ● **noun** a naive person.
– ORIGIN French.

nail ● **noun** **1** a small metal spike with a broadened flat head, hammered in to join things together or to serve as a hook. **2** a horny covering on the upper surface of the tip of the finger and toe in humans and other primates. ● **verb** **1** fasten with a nail or nails. **2** informal detect or catch (someone, especially a suspected criminal). **3** (**nail down**) extract a firm commitment from. **4** (**nail down**) identify precisely.
– PHRASES **a nail in the coffin** an action or event likely to have a detrimental or destructive effect. **on the nail** (of payment) without delay.
– ORIGIN Old English.

nail-biting ● **adjective** causing great anxiety or tension.

nail file ● **noun** a small file or emery board for smoothing and shaping the fingernails and toenails.

nail polish (also **nail varnish**) ● **noun** a glossy coloured substance applied to the fingernails or toenails.

naira /nīrə/ ● **noun** the basic monetary unit of Nigeria, equal to 100 kobo.
– ORIGIN contraction of *Nigeria*.

naive /nīeev/ (also **naïve**) ● **adjective** **1** lacking experience, wisdom, or judgement. **2** (of art or an artist) produced in or adopting a simple, childlike style which deliberately rejects sophisticated techniques.
– DERIVATIVES **naively** adverb.
– ORIGIN French, from Latin *nativus* 'native, natural'.

naivety /nīeevti/ (also **naiveté**) /nīeevtay/ ● **noun** **1** lack of ex-

Thesaurus

nab ● **verb** *(informal)* CATCH, capture, apprehend, arrest, seize; *informal* nail, cop, pull in, pick up; *Brit. informal* nick.

nabob ● **noun** VERY RICH PERSON, tycoon, magnate, millionaire, billionaire, multimillionaire; *informal* fat cat.

nadir ● **noun** THE LOWEST POINT/LEVEL, the all-time low, the bottom, rock-bottom; *informal* the pits.
– OPPOSITES zenith.

nag[1] ● **verb** **1** *she's constantly nagging me* HARASS, keep on at, go on at, badger, give someone a hard time, chivvy, hound, harry, criticize, find fault with, moan at, grumble at; henpeck; *informal* hassle; *N. Amer. informal* ride; *Austral. informal* heavy. **2** *this has been nagging me for weeks* TROUBLE, worry, bother, plague, torment, niggle, prey on one's mind; annoy, irritate; *informal* bug, aggravate.
● **noun** *she's such a nag* SHREW, nagger, harpy, termagant, harridan; *archaic* scold.

nag[2] ● **noun** *(informal) she rode the old nag* WORN-OUT HORSE, old horse, hack; *N. Amer. informal* plug, crowbait; *Austral./NZ informal* moke; *archaic* jade.

nagging ● **adjective** **1** *his nagging wife* SHREWISH, complaining, grumbling, fault-finding, scolding, carping, criticizing. **2** *a nagging pain* PERSISTENT, continuous, niggling, unrelenting, unremitting, unabating.

nail ● **noun** **1** *fastened with nails* TACK, spike, pin, rivet; hobnail. **2** *biting her nails* FINGERNAIL, thumbnail, toenail.
– RELATED TERMS ungual.
● **verb** **1** *a board was nailed to the wall* FASTEN, attach, fix, affix, secure, tack, hammer, pin. **2** *(informal) nailing suspects* CATCH, capture, apprehend, arrest, seize; *informal* collar, nab, cop, pull in, pick up; *Brit. informal* nick. **3** *the pictures had nailed the lie* EXPOSE, reveal, uncover, unmask, bring to light, detect, identify.
– PHRASES **hard as nails** CALLOUS, hard-hearted, heartless, unfeeling, unsympathetic, uncaring, insensitive, unsentimental, hard-bitten, tough, lacking compassion. **on the nail** IMMEDIATELY, at once, without delay, straight away, right away, promptly, directly, now, this minute; *N. Amer.* on the barrelhead.

naive ● **adjective** INNOCENT, unsophisticated, artless, ingenuous, in-

perience, wisdom, or judgement. **2** innocence or unsophistication.

naked ● adjective **1** without clothes. **2** (of an object) without the usual covering or protection. **3** not concealed; undisguised: *naked aggression.* **4** exposed to harm; vulnerable.
– PHRASES **the naked eye** vision unassisted by a telescope, microscope, or other optical instrument. **naked of** devoid of.
– DERIVATIVES **nakedly** adverb **nakedness** noun.
– ORIGIN Old English.

Nama /naamə/ ● noun (pl. same or **Namas**) **1** a member of a people of South Africa and SW Namibia. **2** the language of this people.
– USAGE **Nama** or **Khoikhoi** are the standard accepted terms in this context. The older word **Hottentot** is obsolete, and may now cause offence.
– ORIGIN Nama.

namby-pamby ● adjective lacking courage or vigour; feeble. ● noun (pl. **namby-pambies**) a namby-pamby person.
– ORIGIN fanciful formation from the name of *Ambrose* Philips (1674–1749), an English pastoral poet ridiculed for his insipid verse.

name ● noun **1** a word or words by which someone or something is known, addressed, or referred to. **2** a famous person. **3** a reputation, especially a good one: *he made a name for himself in the theatre.* **4** (in the UK) an insurance underwriter belonging to a Lloyd's syndicate. ● verb **1** give a name to. **2** identify or mention by name. **3** specify (a sum, time, or place). **4** appoint or nominate: *she was named Prime Minister.*
– PHRASES **call names** insult (someone) verbally. **have to one's name** in one's possession. **in all but name** existing in practice but not formally recognized as such. **in someone's name 1** formally registered as belonging to or reserved for someone. **2** on behalf of someone. **in the name of** for the sake of. **name the day** arrange the date for a specific occasion, especially a wedding. **name names** mention specific names, especially in accusation. **the name of the game** informal the main purpose or most important aspect of a situation.
– DERIVATIVES **nameable** adjective.
– ORIGIN Old English.

namecheck ● verb publicly mention the name of, especially in acknowledgement or for publicity purposes.

name day ● noun the feast day of a saint after whom a person is named.

name-dropping ● noun the casual mention of famous people as if one knows them, so as to impress.

nameless ● adjective **1** having no name. **2** not identified by name; anonymous. **3** too horrific or unpleasant to be described.

namely ● adverb that is to say.

nameplate ● noun a plate attached to something and bearing the name of the owner, occupier, or the thing itself.

namesake ● noun a person or thing with the same name as another.
– ORIGIN from the phrase *for the name's sake.*

Namibian /nəmibiən/ ● noun a person from Namibia, a country in southern Africa. ● adjective relating to Namibia.

nan¹ /nan/ ● noun Brit. informal one's grandmother.
– ORIGIN abbreviation of NANNY, or a child's pronunciation of GRAN.

nan² /naan/ (also **naan**) ● noun a type of leavened Indian bread of a flattened teardrop shape.
– ORIGIN Urdu and Persian.

nana¹ /naanə/ ● noun Brit. informal a silly person.
– ORIGIN perhaps a shortening of *banana.*

nana² /nannə/ (Brit. also **nanna**) ● noun informal one's grandmother.
– ORIGIN child's pronunciation of NANNY or GRAN.

nancy (also **nance**, **nancy boy**) ● noun (pl. **nancies**) informal, derogatory an effeminate or homosexual man.
– ORIGIN familiar form of the name *Ann.*

nandrolone /nandrəlōn/ ● noun an anabolic steroid with tissue-building properties, used illegally to enhance performance in sport.
– ORIGIN shortened form of its chemical name.

nankeen /nangkeen/ ● noun a yellowish cotton cloth.
– ORIGIN named after the city of *Nanking* in China, where it was first made.

nanny ● noun (pl. **nannies**) **1** a woman employed to look after a child in its own home. **2** (before another noun) interfering and overprotective: *the nanny state.* **3** (also **nanny goat**) a female goat. ● verb (**nannies**, **nannied**) be overprotective towards.
– ORIGIN familiar form of the name *Ann.*

nano- /nannō/ ● combining form **1** denoting a factor of one thousand millionth (10^{-9}): *nanosecond.* **2** extremely small; submicroscopic: *nanomachine.*
– ORIGIN from Greek *nanos* 'dwarf'.

nanobacterium /nannōbakteeriəm/ ● noun a kind of microorganism about a tenth the size of the smallest normal bacteria, claimed to exist in various environments.

nanobe /nannōb/ ● noun another term for NANOBACTERIUM.

nanometre /nannōmeetər/ (US **nanometer**) ● noun one thousand millionth of a metre.

nanosecond ● noun one thousand millionth of a second.

nanotechnology ● noun technology on an atomic or molecular scale, concerned with dimensions of less than 100 nanometres.

nap¹ ● noun a short sleep, especially during the day. ● verb (**napped**, **napping**) have a nap.
– ORIGIN Old English.

nap² ● noun short raised fibres on the surface of certain fabrics, especially velvet.
– ORIGIN Dutch or Low German *noppe.*

nap³ ● noun **1** a card game resembling whist in which players declare the number of tricks they expect to take, up to five. **2** Brit. a tipster's prediction of the most likely winner. ● verb (**napped**, **napping**) Brit. name (a horse or greyhound) as a likely winner of a race.

Thesaurus

experienced, guileless, unworldly, trusting; gullible, credulous, immature, callow, raw, green; *informal* wet behind the ears.
– OPPOSITES worldly.

naivety ● noun INNOCENCE, ingenuousness, guilelessness, unworldliness, trustfulness; gullibility, credulousness, credulity, immaturity, callowness.

naked ● adjective **1** *a naked woman* NUDE, bare, in the nude, stark naked, having nothing on, stripped, unclothed, undressed, in a state of nature; *informal* without a stitch on, in one's birthday suit, in the raw/buff, in the altogether, in the nuddy, mother naked; *Brit. informal* starkers; *N. Amer. informal* buck naked. **2** *a naked flame* UNPROTECTED, uncovered, exposed, unguarded. **3** *the naked branches of the trees* BARE, barren, denuded, stripped, uncovered. **4** *I felt naked and exposed* VULNERABLE, helpless, weak, powerless, defenceless, exposed, open to attack. **5** *the naked truth | naked hostility* UNDISGUISED, plain, unadorned, unvarnished, unqualified, stark, bald; overt, obvious, open, patent, evident, apparent, manifest, unmistakable, blatant.
– OPPOSITES clothed, covered.

nakedness ● noun **1** *she covered her nakedness* NUDITY, state of undress, bareness. **2** *the nakedness of the landscape* BARENESS, barrenness, starkness.

namby-pamby ● adjective WEAK, feeble, spineless, effeminate, effete, limp-wristed, ineffectual; *informal* wet, weedy, wimpy, sissy.

name ● noun **1** *her name's Gemma* designation, honorific, title, tag, epithet, label; *informal* moniker, handle; *formal* denomination, appellation. **2** *the top names in the fashion industry* CELEBRITY, star, superstar, VIP, leading light, big name, luminary; expert, authority; *informal* celeb, somebody, megastar, big noise, big shot, bigwig, big gun. **3** *the good name of the firm* REPUTATION, character, repute, standing, stature, esteem, prestige, cachet, kudos; renown, popularity, notability, distinction.
– RELATED TERMS nominal, onomastic.
● verb **1** *they named the child Phoebe* CALL, give a name to, dub; label, style, term, title, entitle; baptize, christen; *formal* denominate. **2** *the driver was named as Jason Penter* IDENTIFY, specify. **3** *he has named his successor* CHOOSE, select, pick, decide on, nominate, designate.

named ● adjective **1** *a girl named Anne* CALLED, by the name of, baptized, christened, known as; dubbed, entitled, styled, termed, labelled. **2** *named individuals* SPECIFIED, designated, identified, cited, mentioned, singled out.

nameless ● adjective **1** *pictures taken by a nameless photographer* UNNAMED, unidentified, anonymous, incognito, unspecified, unacknowledged, uncredited; unknown, unsung, uncelebrated. **2** *nameless fears* UNSPEAKABLE, unutterable, inexpressible, indescribable; indefinable, vague, unspecified, unspecifiable.

namely ● adverb THAT IS (TO SAY), to be specific, specifically, viz, to wit.

nanny ● noun *the children's nanny* NURSEMAID, au pair, childmind-

– PHRASES **go nap 1** try to take all five tricks in nap. **2** score or win five times.
– ORIGIN abbreviation of *napoleon*, the original name of the card game.
napalm /naypaam/ • **noun** a highly flammable jelly-like form of petrol, used in incendiary bombs and flame-throwers.
– ORIGIN from *naphthenic* and *palmitic acids* (compounds used in its manufacture).
nape • **noun** the back of a person's neck.
– ORIGIN of unknown origin.
nap hand • **noun** a series of five winning points, victories, etc.
naphtha /nafthə/ • **noun** a flammable oil distilled from coal, shale, or petroleum.
– ORIGIN Greek.
naphthalene /nafthəleen/ • **noun** a white crystalline substance distilled from coal tar, used in mothballs and for chemical manufacture.
napkin • **noun 1** a square piece of cloth or paper used at a meal to wipe the fingers or lips and to protect garments. **2** Brit. dated a baby's nappy.
– ORIGIN from Old French *nappe* 'tablecloth' + -KIN.
Napoleonic /nəpōlionnik/ • **adjective** relating to or characteristic of the French emperor Napoleon I (1769–1821) or his time.
napper • **noun** Brit. informal a person's head.
– ORIGIN of unknown origin.
nappy • **noun** (pl. **nappies**) Brit. a piece of absorbent material wrapped round a baby's bottom and between its legs to absorb and retain urine and faeces.
– ORIGIN abbreviation of NAPKIN.
narcissism /naarsisiz'm/ • **noun** excessive or erotic interest in oneself and one's physical appearance.
– DERIVATIVES **narcissist** noun **narcissistic** adjective.
– ORIGIN from *Narcissus*, a beautiful youth in Greek mythology who fell in love with his reflection in a pool.
narcissus /naarsissəss/ • **noun** (pl. **narcissi** or **narcissuses**) a daffodil with a flower that has white or pale outer petals and a shallow orange or yellow centre.
– ORIGIN Greek *narkissos*, perhaps from *narkē* 'numbness', with reference to its narcotic effects.
narcolepsy /naarkəlepsi/ • **noun** a nervous illness characterized by an extreme tendency to fall asleep whenever in relaxing surroundings.
– DERIVATIVES **narcoleptic** adjective & noun.
– ORIGIN from Greek *narkē* 'numbness'.
narcosis /naarkōsiss/ • **noun** a state of stupor, drowsiness, or unconsciousness produced by drugs.
– ORIGIN Greek *narkōsis*, from *narkoun* 'make numb'.
narcotic • **noun 1** an addictive drug, especially an illegal one, affecting mood or behaviour. **2** Medicine a drug which induces drowsiness, stupor, or insensibility and relieves pain. • **adjective** relating to narcotics.
nark informal • **noun 1** chiefly Brit. a police informer. **2** Austral./NZ an annoying person or thing. • **verb** chiefly Brit. annoy.
– ORIGIN Romany *nāk* 'nose'.
narky • **adjective** Brit. informal irritable.
Narragansett /narrəgansət/ (also **Narraganset**) • **noun** (pl. same or **Narragansetts**) a member of an American Indian people originally of Rhode Island.
– ORIGIN Narragansett, 'people of the promontory'.
narrate • **verb 1** give an account of. **2** provide a commentary for (a film, television programme, etc.).
– DERIVATIVES **narration** noun **narrator** noun.
– ORIGIN Latin *narrare.*
narrative • **noun 1** an account of connected events; a story. **2** the narrated part of a literary work, as distinct from dialogue. • **adjective** in the form of a narrative or concerned with narration.
– DERIVATIVES **narratively** adverb.
narrow • **adjective** (**narrower**, **narrowest**) **1** of small width in comparison to length. **2** limited in extent, amount, or scope. **3** barely achieved: *a narrow escape.* • **verb 1** become or make narrower. **2** (**narrow down**) reduce (the number of possibilities or options). • **noun** (**narrows**) a narrow channel connecting two larger areas of water.
– DERIVATIVES **narrowly** adverb **narrowness** noun.
– ORIGIN Old English.
narrowboat • **noun** Brit. a canal boat less than 7 ft (2.1 metres) wide and steered with a tiller rather than a wheel.
narrowcast • (past and past part. **narrowcast** or **narrowcasted**) transmit a television programme, especially by cable, to a comparatively small or specialist audience.
narrow gauge • **noun** a railway gauge which is narrower than the standard gauge of 4 ft 8½ inches (1.435 m).
narrow-minded • **adjective** unwilling to listen to or tolerate the views of others; prejudiced.
narthex /naartheks/ • **noun** an antechamber or large porch in a church.
– ORIGIN Greek.
narwhal /naarwəl/ • **noun** a small Arctic whale, the male of which has a long spirally twisted tusk.

n

Thesaurus

er, childcarer; governess; *dated* nurse.
• **verb** *stop nannying me* MOLLYCODDLE, cosset, coddle, wrap in cotton wool, baby, feather-bed; spoil, pamper, indulge, overindulge.
nap¹ • **verb** *they were napping on the sofa* DOZE, sleep (lightly), take a nap, catnap, rest, take a siesta; *informal* snooze, snatch forty winks, get some shut-eye; *Brit. informal* have a kip, get some zizz; *N. Amer. informal* catch some Zs, catch a few Zs.
• **noun** *she is taking a nap* (LIGHT) SLEEP, catnap, siesta, doze, lie-down, rest; *informal* snooze, forty winks, shut-eye; *Brit. informal* kip, zizz.
– PHRASES **catch someone napping** CATCH OFF GUARD, catch unawares, (take by) surprise, catch out, find unprepared; *informal* catch someone with their trousers/pants down; *Brit. informal* catch on the hop.
nap² • **noun** *the nap of the velvet* PILE, fibres, threads, weave, surface, grain.
nappy • **noun** *N. Amer.* diaper; *Brit. dated* napkin.
narcissism • **noun** VANITY, self-love, self-admiration, self-absorption, self-obsession, conceit, self-centredness, self-regard, egotism, egoism.
– OPPOSITES modesty.
narcissistic • **adjective** VAIN, self-loving, self-admiring, self-absorbed, self-obsessed, conceited, self-centred, self-regarding, egotistic, egotistical, egoistic.
narcotic • **noun** SOPORIFIC (DRUG), opiate, sleeping pill; painkiller, pain reliever, analgesic, anodyne, palliative, anaesthetic; tranquillizer, sedative; *informal* downer; *Medicine* stupefacient.
• **adjective** SOPORIFIC, sleep-inducing, opiate; painkilling, pain-relieving, analgesic, anodyne, anaesthetic, tranquillizing, sedative; *Medicine* stupefacient.
narked • **adjective** *(Brit. informal).* See ANNOYED.
narrate • **verb** TELL, relate, recount, describe, chronicle, give a report of, report; voice-over.
narration • **noun 1** *a narration of past events* ACCOUNT, narrative, chronicle, description, report, relation, chronicling. **2** *his narration of the story* VOICE-OVER, commentary.
narrative • **noun** ACCOUNT, chronicle, history, description, record, report.
narrator • **noun 1** *the narrator of 'the Arabian Nights'* STORYTELLER, teller of tales, relater, chronicler, romancer; raconteur, anecdotalist; *Austral. informal* magsman. **2** *the film's narrator* VOICE-OVER, commentator.
– OPPOSITES listener, audience.
narrow • **adjective 1** *the path became narrower* SMALL, tapered, tapering, narrowing; *archaic* strait. **2** *her narrow waist* SLENDER, slim, slight, spare, attenuated, thin. **3** *a narrow space* CONFINED, cramped, tight, restricted, limited, constricted. **4** *a narrow range of products* LIMITED, restricted, circumscribed, small, inadequate, insufficient, deficient. **5** *a narrow view of the world.* See NARROW-MINDED. **6** *nationalism in the narrowest sense of the word* STRICT, literal, exact, precise. **7** *a narrow escape* BY A VERY SMALL MARGIN, close, near, by a hair's breadth; *informal* by a whisker.
– OPPOSITES wide, broad.
• **verb** *the path narrowed* | *narrowing the gap between rich and poor* GET/BECOME/MAKE NARROWER, get/become/make smaller, taper, diminish, decrease, reduce, contract, shrink; *archaic* straiten.
narrowly • **adverb 1** *one bullet narrowly missed him* (ONLY) JUST, barely, scarcely, hardly, by a hair's breadth; *informal* by a whisker. **2** *she looked at me narrowly* CLOSELY, carefully, searchingly, attentively.
narrow-minded • **adjective** INTOLERANT, illiberal, reactionary, conservative, parochial, provincial, insular, small-minded, petty, blinkered, inward-looking, narrow, hidebound, prejudiced, bigoted; *Brit.* parish-pump, blimpish; *N. Amer. informal* jerkwater.

– ORIGIN Danish *narhval*, perhaps from an Old Norse word meaning 'corpse', with reference to the whale's skin colour.

nary /nairi/ ● adjective informal or dialect form of NOT.
– ORIGIN from *ne'er a* 'never a'.

NASA /nassə/ ● abbreviation (in the US) National Aeronautics and Space Administration.

nasal ● adjective **1** relating to the nose. **2** (of a speech sound) pronounced by the breath resonating in the nose, e.g. *m, n, ng*, or French *en, un*. **3** (of speech) characterized by resonance in the nose as well as the mouth.
– DERIVATIVES **nasally** adverb.
– ORIGIN from Latin *nasus* 'nose'.

nasalize (also **nasalise**) ● verb say or speak nasally.
– DERIVATIVES **nasalization** noun.

nascent /nassn't, nay-/ ● adjective just coming into existence and beginning to develop.
– ORIGIN from Latin *nasci* 'be born'.

nasturtium ● noun a trailing garden plant with round leaves and bright orange, yellow, or red flowers.
– ORIGIN Latin, apparently from *naris* 'nose' + *torquere* 'to twist' (referring to its pungent scent).

nasty ● adjective (**nastier**, **nastiest**) **1** unpleasant, disgusting, or repugnant. **2** spiteful, violent, or bad-tempered. **3** likely to cause or having caused harm; dangerous or serious: *a nasty bang on the head*. ● noun (pl. **nasties**) informal a nasty person or thing.
– DERIVATIVES **nastily** adverb **nastiness** noun.
– ORIGIN of unknown origin.

Nat. ● abbreviation **1** national. **2** nationalist.

natal /nayt'l/ ● adjective relating to the place or time of one's birth.
– ORIGIN Latin *natalis*, from *nasci* 'be born'.

natch ● adverb informal naturally.

nates /nayteez/ ● plural noun Anatomy the bottom.
– ORIGIN Latin, plural of *natis* 'buttock, rump'.

nation ● noun a large body of people united by common descent, culture, or language, inhabiting a particular state or territory.
– ORIGIN Latin, from *nasci* 'be born'.

national ● adjective **1** relating to or characteristic of a nation. **2** owned, controlled, or financially supported by the state. ● noun a citizen of a particular country.
– DERIVATIVES **nationally** adverb.

national curriculum ● noun a curriculum of study laid down to be taught in state schools.

national debt ● noun the total amount of money which a country's government has borrowed.

national grid ● noun Brit. **1** the network of high-voltage power lines between major power stations. **2** the metric system of geographical coordinates used in maps of the British Isles.

National Guard ● noun (in the US) the primary reserve military force partly maintained by the states but also available for federal use.

National Insurance ● noun (in the UK) a system of compulsory payments by employees and employers to provide state assistance for people who are sick, unemployed, or retired.

nationalism ● noun **1** patriotic feeling, often to an excessive degree. **2** advocacy of political independence for a particular country.
– DERIVATIVES **nationalist** noun & adjective **nationalistic** adjective.

nationality ● noun (pl. **nationalities**) **1** the status of belonging to a particular nation. **2** an ethnic group forming a part of one or more political nations.

nationalize (also **nationalise**) ● verb transfer (an industry or business) from private to state ownership or control.
– DERIVATIVES **nationalization** noun.

national park ● noun an area of environmental importance or natural beauty protected by the state and accessible to the public.

national service ● noun a period of compulsory service in the armed forces during peacetime.

National Socialism ● noun historical the political doctrine of the Nazi Party of Germany.

nation state ● noun a sovereign state of which most of the citizens or subjects are united also by factors which define a nation, such as language or common descent.

nationwide ● adjective & adverb throughout the whole nation.

native ● noun **1** a person born in a specified place. **2** a local inhabitant. **3** an indigenous animal or plant. **4** dated, offensive a non-white original inhabitant of a country as regarded by European colonists or travellers. ● adjective **1** associated with a person's place of birth. **2** (of a plant or animal) of indigenous origin or growth. **3** of the indigenous inhabitants of a place. **4** in a person's character; innate: *native wit*.
– USAGE In contexts such as *a native of Boston* the use of the noun **native** is quite acceptable. But when used as a noun without qualification, as in *this dance is a favourite with the natives*, it has an old-fashioned feel and, because of its associations with a colonial European attitude to non-white people in remote places, it may cause offence.
– ORIGIN Latin *nativus*, from *nasci* 'be born'.

Native American ● noun a member of any of the indigenous peoples of North and South America and the Caribbean Islands. ● adjective relating to these peoples.
– USAGE In the US, **Native American** is now the current accepted

Thesaurus

– OPPOSITES tolerant.

narrows ● plural noun STRAIT(S), sound, channel, waterway, (sea) passage.

nascent ● adjective JUST BEGINNING, budding, developing, growing, embryonic, incipient, young, fledgling, evolving, emergent, dawning, burgeoning.

nastiness ● noun **1** *my mother tried to shut herself off from nastiness* UNPLEASANTNESS, disagreeableness, offensiveness, vileness, foulness. **2** *her uncharacteristic nastiness* UNKINDNESS, unpleasantness, unfriendliness, disagreeableness, rudeness, churlishness, spitefulness, maliciousness, meanness, ill temper, ill nature, viciousness, malevolence; *informal* bitchiness, cattiness. **3** *I abhor such nastiness* OBSCENITY, indecency, offensiveness, crudity, vulgarity, pornography, smuttiness, lewdness, licentiousness.

nasty ● adjective **1** *a nasty smell* UNPLEASANT, disagreeable, disgusting, distasteful, awful, dreadful, horrible, terrible, vile, foul, abominable, frightful, loathsome, revolting, repulsive, odious, sickening, nauseating, repellent, repugnant, horrendous, appalling, atrocious, offensive, objectionable, obnoxious, unsavoury, unappetizing, off-putting; noxious, foul-smelling, smelly, stinking, rank, fetid, malodorous, mephitic; *informal* ghastly, horrid, gruesome, diabolical, yucky, skanky, God-awful, gross; *Brit. informal* beastly, grotty, whiffy, pongy, niffy; *N. Amer. informal* lousy, funky; *Austral. informal* on the nose; *poetic/literary* miasmal, noisome. **2** *the weather turned nasty* UNPLEASANT, disagreeable, foul, filthy, inclement; wet, stormy, cold, blustery. **3** *she can be really nasty* UNKIND, unpleasant, unfriendly, disagreeable, rude, churlish, spiteful, malicious, mean, ill-tempered, ill-natured, vicious, malevolent, obnoxious, hateful, hurtful; *informal* bitchy, catty. **4** *a nasty accident | a nasty cut* SERIOUS, dangerous, bad, awful, dreadful, terrible, severe; painful, ugly. **5** *she had the nasty habit of appearing unannounced* ANNOYING, irritating, infuriating, disagreeable, unpleasant, maddening, exasperating. **6** *they wrote nasty things on the wall* OBSCENE, indecent, offensive, crude, rude, dirty, filthy, vulgar, foul, gross, disgusting, pornographic, smutty, lewd; *informal* sick.
– OPPOSITES nice.

nation ● noun COUNTRY, (sovereign/nation) state, land, realm, kingdom, republic; fatherland, motherland; people, race.

national ● adjective **1** *national politics* STATE, public, federal, governmental; civic, civil, domestic, internal. **2** *a national strike* NATIONWIDE, countrywide, state, general, widespread.
– OPPOSITES local, international.
● noun *a French national* CITIZEN, subject, native; voter.

nationalism ● noun PATRIOTISM, patriotic sentiment, xenophobia, chauvinism, jingoism.

nationalistic ● adjective PATRIOTIC, nationalist, xenophobic, chauvinistic, jingoistic.

nationality ● noun **1** *British nationality* CITIZENSHIP. **2** *all the main nationalities of Ethiopia* ETHNIC GROUP, ethnic minority, tribe, clan, race, nation.

nationwide ● adjective NATIONAL, countrywide, state, general, widespread, extensive.

native ● noun *a native of Sweden* INHABITANT, resident, local; citizen, national; aborigine, autochthon; *formal* dweller.
– OPPOSITES foreigner.
● adjective **1** *the native population* INDIGENOUS, original, first, earliest, aboriginal, autochthonous. **2** *native produce | native plants* DOMESTIC, home-grown, home-made, local; indigenous. **3** *a native instinct for politics* INNATE, inherent, inborn, instinctive, intuitive,

term in many contexts. See also AMERICAN INDIAN.

native speaker ● noun a person who has spoken the language in question from earliest childhood.

nativity ● noun (pl. **nativities**) **1** a person's birth. **2** (**the Nativity**) the birth of Jesus Christ.

NATO (also **Nato**) ● abbreviation North Atlantic Treaty Organization.

natron /naytrən/ ● noun a mineral salt found in dried lake beds, consisting of hydrated sodium carbonate.
– ORIGIN Spanish, from Greek *nitron* 'nitre'.

natter informal ● verb chat casually and at length. ● noun a lengthy chat.
– ORIGIN originally dialect, in the sense 'grumble, fret': imitative.

natterjack toad ● noun a small toad with a bright yellow stripe down its back.
– ORIGIN perhaps from NATTER (because of its loud croak) + JACK.

natty ● adjective (**nattier**, **nattiest**) informal smart and fashionable.
– DERIVATIVES **nattily** adverb **nattiness** noun.
– ORIGIN perhaps related to NEAT.

natural ● adjective **1** existing in or derived from nature; not made, caused by, or processed by humankind. **2** in accordance with nature; normal or to be expected: *a natural death.* **3** born with a particular skill or quality: *a natural leader.* **4** relaxed and unaffected. **5** (of a parent or child) related by blood. **6** archaic illegitimate. **7** Music (of a note) not sharpened or flattened. ● noun **1** a person with an innate gift or talent. **2** an off-white colour. **3** Music a natural note or a sign (♮) denoting one. **4** archaic a person mentally handicapped from birth.
– DERIVATIVES **naturalness** noun.

natural gas ● noun flammable gas, consisting largely of methane, occurring naturally underground and used as fuel.

natural history ● noun the scientific study of animals or plants, especially as concerned with observation rather than experiment.

naturalism ● noun an artistic or literary movement or style based on the highly detailed and unidealized depiction of daily life.

naturalist ● noun **1** an expert in or student of natural history. **2** an exponent or practitioner of naturalism.

naturalistic ● adjective **1** derived from or imitating real life or nature. **2** based on the theory of naturalism.
– DERIVATIVES **naturalistically** adverb.

naturalize (also **naturalise**) ● verb **1** admit (a foreigner) to the citizenship of a country. **2** introduce (a non-native plant or animal) into a region and establish it in the wild. **3** alter (an adopted foreign word) so that it conforms more closely to the adopting language.
– DERIVATIVES **naturalization** noun.

natural law ● noun **1** a body of unchanging moral principles regarded as inherent in all human beings and forming a basis for human conduct. **2** an observable law relating to natural phenomena.

natural logarithm ● noun Mathematics a logarithm to the base *e* (2.71828 ...).

naturally ● adverb **1** in a natural manner. **2** of course.

natural numbers ● plural noun the sequence of whole numbers 1, 2, 3, etc., used for counting.

natural philosophy ● noun archaic natural science, especially physical science.

natural resources ● plural noun naturally occurring materials which can be exploited for economic gain.

natural science ● noun a branch of science which deals with the physical world, e.g. physics, chemistry, geology, biology.

natural selection ● noun the evolutionary process whereby organisms better adapted to their environment tend to survive and produce more offspring.

nature ● noun **1** the physical world, including plants, animals, the landscape, and natural phenomena, as opposed to humans or human creations. **2** the inherent qualities or characteristics of a person or thing. **3** a kind, sort, or class: *topics of a religious nature.* **4** hereditary characteristics as an influence on or determinant of personality. Often contrasted with NURTURE.
– PHRASES **in the nature of things** inevitable or inevitably.
– DERIVATIVES **natured** adjective.
– ORIGIN Latin *natura* 'birth, nature, quality', from *nasci* 'be born'.

nature reserve ● noun an area of land managed so as to preserve its flora, fauna, and physical features.

nature trail ● noun a signposted path through the countryside designed to draw attention to natural features.

naturism ● noun nudism.
– DERIVATIVES **naturist** noun & adjective.

naturopathy /naychəroppəthi/ ● noun a system of alternative medicine involving the treatment or prevention of diseases by diet, exercise, and massage rather than by using drugs.
– DERIVATIVES **naturopath** noun **naturopathic** adjective.

naught ● pronoun archaic nothing. ● noun N. Amer. nought.
– ORIGIN Old English.

naughty ● adjective (**naughtier**, **naughtiest**) **1** (especially of a child) disobedient; badly behaved. **2** informal mildly rude or indecent.
– DERIVATIVES **naughtily** adverb **naughtiness** noun.
– ORIGIN originally in the sense 'possessing nothing': from NAUGHT.

n

Thesaurus

natural; hereditary, inherited, congenital, inbred, connate, connatural. **4** *her native tongue* MOTHER, vernacular.
– OPPOSITES immigrant.

nativity ● noun BIRTH, childbirth, delivery; *formal* parturition.

natter *(informal)* ● verb *they nattered away.* See CHAT verb.
● noun *she rang up for a natter.* See CHAT noun.

natty ● adjective *(informal)* SMART, stylish, fashionable, dapper, debonair, dashing, spruce, well dressed, chic, elegant, trim; *N. Amer.* trig; *informal* snazzy, trendy, snappy, nifty; *N. Amer. informal* sassy, spiffy, fly, kicky.
– OPPOSITES scruffy.

natural ● adjective **1** *a natural occurrence* NORMAL, ordinary, everyday, usual, regular, common, commonplace, typical, routine, standard, established, customary, accustomed, habitual. **2** *natural produce* UNPROCESSED, organic, pure, wholesome, unrefined, pesticide-free, additive-free. **3** *Alex is a natural leader* BORN, naturally gifted, untaught. **4** *his natural instincts* INNATE, inborn, inherent, native, instinctive, intuitive; hereditary, inherited, inbred, congenital, connate, connatural. **5** *she seemed very natural* UNAFFECTED, spontaneous, uninhibited, relaxed, unselfconscious, genuine, open, artless, guileless, ingenuous, unpretentious, without airs. **6** *it was quite natural to think she admired him* REASONABLE, logical, understandable, (only) to be expected, predictable. **7** *(archaic) his natural son* ILLEGITIMATE, born out of wedlock; *dated* born on the wrong side of the blanket; *archaic* bastard, misbegotten, baseborn.
– OPPOSITES abnormal, artificial, affected.

naturalist ● noun NATURAL HISTORIAN, life scientist, wildlife expert; biologist, botanist, zoologist, ornithologist, entomologist, ecologist, conservationist, environmentalist.

naturalistic ● adjective REALISTIC, real-life, true-to-life, lifelike, graphic, representational, photographic.
– OPPOSITES abstract.

naturalize ● verb **1** *he was naturalized in 1950* GRANT CITIZENSHIP TO, make a citizen, give a passport to, enfranchise. **2** *coriander has been naturalized in southern Britain* ESTABLISH, introduce, acclimatize, domesticate; *N. Amer.* acclimate.

naturally ● adverb **1** *he's naturally shy* BY NATURE, by character, inherently, innately, congenitally. **2** *try to act naturally* NORMALLY, in a natural manner/way, unaffectedly, spontaneously, genuinely, unpretentiously; *informal* natural. **3** *naturally, they wanted everything kept quiet* OF COURSE, as might be expected, needless to say; obviously, clearly, it goes without saying.
– OPPOSITES self-consciously.

naturalness ● noun UNSELFCONSCIOUSNESS, spontaneity, spontaneousness, straightforwardness, genuineness, openness, ingenuousness, lack of sophistication, unpretentiousness.

nature ● noun **1** *the beauty of nature* THE NATURAL WORLD, Mother Nature, Mother Earth, the environment; the universe, the cosmos; wildlife, flora and fauna, the countryside. **2** *such crimes are, by their very nature, difficult to hide* ESSENCE, inherent/basic/essential qualities, inherent/basic/essential features, character, complexion. **3** *it was not in Daisy's nature to be bitchy* CHARACTER, personality, disposition, temperament, make-up, psyche, constitution. **4** *experiments of a similar nature* KIND, sort, type, variety, category, ilk, class, species, genre, style, cast, order, kidney, mould, stamp; *N. Amer.* stripe.

naturist ● noun NUDIST.

naught ● noun *(archaic)* NOTHING (AT ALL), nil, zero; *N. English* nowt; *informal* zilch, sweet Fanny Adams, sweet FA; *Brit. informal* damn all, not

nausea /nawziə/ ● noun **1** a feeling of sickness with an inclination to vomit. **2** disgust or revulsion.
– ORIGIN Greek *nausia* 'seasickness', from *naus* 'ship'.
nauseate ● verb cause to feel sick or disgusted.
nauseous ● adjective **1** affected with nausea. **2** causing nausea.
– DERIVATIVES **nauseously** adverb.
nautical ● adjective of or concerning sailors or navigation; maritime.
– DERIVATIVES **nautically** adverb.
– ORIGIN Greek *nautikos*, from *nautēs* 'sailor'.
nautical mile ● noun a unit used in measuring distances at sea, equal to 1,852 metres (approximately 2,025 yards).
nautilus /nawtiləss/ ● noun (pl. **nautiluses** or **nautili** /nawtilī/) a swimming mollusc with a spiral shell and numerous short tentacles around the mouth.
– ORIGIN Greek *nautilos* 'sailor'.
Navajo /navvəhō/ (also **Navaho**) ● noun (pl. same or **Navajos**) **1** a member of an American Indian people of New Mexico and Arizona. **2** the language of this people.
– ORIGIN from an American Indian word meaning 'fields adjoining a dry gully'.
naval ● adjective of or relating to a navy or navies.
– ORIGIN Latin *navalis*, from *navis* 'ship'.
navarin /navvərin/ ● noun a casserole of lamb or mutton with vegetables.
– ORIGIN French.
nave[1] ● noun the central part of a church apart from the side aisles, chancel, and transepts.
– ORIGIN Latin *navis* 'ship'.
nave[2] ● noun the hub of a wheel.
– ORIGIN Old English, related to NAVEL.
navel ● noun the small hollow in the centre of a person's belly caused by the detachment of the umbilical cord.
– ORIGIN Old English.
navel-gazing ● noun absorption in oneself or a single issue.
navel orange ● noun a variety of orange having a navel-like depression at the top containing a small secondary fruit.
navigable ● adjective of sufficient depth or width to be used by boats and ships.
– DERIVATIVES **navigability** noun.
navigate ● verb **1** plan and direct the route or course of a ship, aircraft, or other form of transport. **2** sail or travel over. **3** guide (a vessel or vehicle) over a specified route.
– ORIGIN Latin *navigare* 'to sail'.
navigation ● noun **1** the process or activity of navigating. **2** the passage of ships.
– DERIVATIVES **navigational** adjective.
navigation lights ● plural noun lights shown by a ship or aircraft at night to indicate its position and orientation.
navigator ● noun **1** a person who navigates a ship, aircraft, etc. **2** historical a person who explores by sea. **3** Computing a browser program for accessing data on the World Wide Web or another information system.
navvy ● noun (pl. **navvies**) Brit. dated a labourer employed in the excavation and construction of a road or railway.
– ORIGIN abbreviation of NAVIGATOR in the former sense 'builder of a *navigation*' (a dialect word for a canal).
navy ● noun (pl. **navies**) **1** the branch of a state's armed services which conducts military operations at sea. **2** (also **navy blue**) a dark blue colour.
– ORIGIN Old French *navie* 'ship, fleet', from Latin *navis* 'ship'.
nawab /nəwaab/ ● noun Indian **1** historical a native governor during the time of the Mogul empire. **2** a Muslim nobleman or person of high status.
– ORIGIN Urdu, from Arabic, 'deputy'.
nay ● adverb **1** or rather: *it will take months, nay years.* **2** archaic or dialect no. ● noun a negative answer.
– ORIGIN Old Norse.
Nazarene /nazzəreen/ ● noun **1** a native or inhabitant of the town of Nazareth in Israel. **2** (**the Nazarene**) Jesus Christ. **3** a member of an early sect of Jewish Christians. ● adjective relating to Nazareth or Nazarenes.
Nazi /naatzi/ ● noun (pl. **Nazis**) **1** historical a member of the National Socialist German Workers' Party. **2** derogatory a person with extreme racist or authoritarian views.
– DERIVATIVES **Nazism** noun.
– ORIGIN German, representing the pronunciation of *Nati-* in *Nationalsozialist.*
NB ● abbreviation **1** New Brunswick. **2** nota bene.
Nb ● symbol the chemical element niobium.
nb ● abbreviation Cricket no-ball.
NC ● abbreviation **1** network computer. **2** North Carolina.
NCO ● abbreviation non-commissioned officer.
ND ● abbreviation North Dakota.
Nd ● symbol the chemical element neodymium.
Ndebele /əndəbeeli, -bayli/ ● noun (pl. same or **Ndebeles**) a member of a people of Zimbabwe and NE South Africa.
– ORIGIN Nguni (a Bantu language).
NE ● abbreviation **1** Nebraska. **2** north-east or north-eastern.
Ne ● symbol the chemical element neon.
né /nay/ masc. of NÉE.
Neanderthal /niandərtaal/ ● noun **1** (also **Neanderthal man**) an extinct human living in ice age Europe between *c.*120,000–35,000 years ago. **2** informal an uncivilized or uncouth man.
– ORIGIN from *Neanderthal*, a region in Germany where remains of Neanderthal man were found.
neap /neep/ (also **neap tide**) ● noun a tide just after the first or third quarters of the moon when there is least difference between high and low water.
– ORIGIN Old English.
Neapolitan /neeəpollit'n/ ● noun a person from the Italian city

Thesaurus

a sausage; *N. Amer. informal* zip, nada, diddly-squat; *archaic* nought.
naughty ● adjective **1** *a naughty boy* BADLY BEHAVED, disobedient, bad, misbehaved, misbehaving, wayward, defiant, unruly, insubordinate, wilful, delinquent, undisciplined, uncontrollable, ungovernable, unbiddable, disorderly, disruptive, fractious, recalcitrant, wild, wicked, obstreperous, difficult, troublesome, awkward, contrary, perverse, incorrigible; mischievous, playful, impish, roguish, rascally; *informal* brattish; *formal* refractory. **2** *(informal) naughty jokes* INDECENT, risqué, rude, racy, ribald, bawdy, suggestive, improper, indelicate, indecorous; vulgar, dirty, filthy, smutty, crude, coarse; *informal* raunchy; *Brit. informal* fruity, saucy; *N. Amer. informal* gamy; *euphemistic* adult.
– OPPOSITES well behaved, decent.
nausea ● noun **1** *symptoms include nausea and a headache* SICKNESS, biliousness, queasiness; vomiting, retching, gagging; travel-sickness, seasickness, carsickness, airsickness. **2** *it induces a feeling of nausea* DISGUST, revulsion, repugnance, repulsion, distaste, aversion, loathing, abhorrence.
nauseate ● verb CAUSE TO FEEL SICK, sicken, make sick, turn someone's stomach, make someone's gorge rise; *N. Amer. informal* gross out.
nauseating ● adjective SICKENING, stomach-churning, nauseous, emetic, sickly; disgusting, revolting, offensive, loathsome, obnoxious, foul; *N. Amer.* vomitous; *informal* sick-making, gross, gut-churning.
nauseous ● adjective **1** *the food made her feel nauseous* SICK, nauseated, queasy, bilious, green about/at the gills, ill, unwell; seasick, carsick, airsick, travel-sick; *N. Amer. informal* barfy. **2** *a nauseous stench.* See NAUSEATING.
nautical ● adjective MARITIME, marine, naval, seafaring; boating, sailing.
navel ● noun **1** *informal* belly button, tummy button; *Anatomy* umbilicus. **2** *the navel of Byzantine culture* CENTRE, central point, hub, focal point, focus, nucleus, heart, core; *poetic/literary* omphalos.
– RELATED TERMS umbilical, omphalo-.
navigable ● adjective PASSABLE, negotiable, traversable; clear, open, unobstructed, unblocked.
navigate ● verb **1** *he navigated the yacht across the Atlantic* STEER, pilot, guide, direct, helm, captain; *Nautical* con; *informal* skipper. **2** *the upper reaches are dangerous to navigate* SAIL (ACROSS/OVER), cross, traverse, negotiate. **3** *I'll drive—you can navigate* MAP-READ, give directions.
navigation ● noun **1** *the navigation of the ship* STEERING, piloting, sailing, guiding, directing, guidance. **2** *the skills of navigation* HELMSMANSHIP, steersmanship, seamanship, map-reading, chart-reading.
navigator ● noun HELMSMAN, steersman, pilot, guide; *N. Amer.* wheelman.
navvy ● noun LABOURER, manual worker, workman, worker, hand, coolie, roustabout; *Austral./NZ* rouseabout; *archaic* mechanic.
navy ● noun **1** *a 600-ship navy* FLEET, flotilla, armada. **2** *a navy suit* NAVY BLUE, dark blue, indigo.

of Naples. ● adjective **1** relating to Naples. **2** (of ice cream) made in layers of different colours and flavours.

near ● adverb **1** at or to a short distance in space or time. **2** almost. ● preposition (also **near to**) **1** at or to a short distance in space or time from. **2** close to (a state or in terms of resemblance). ● adjective **1** at a short distance away in space or time. **2** close to being: *a near disaster*. **3** closely related. **4** located on the nearside of a vehicle. ● verb approach.
– DERIVATIVES **nearness** noun.
– ORIGIN Old Norse.

nearby ● adjective & adverb not far away.

Near East ● noun the countries of SW Asia between the Mediterranean and India (including the Middle East).
– DERIVATIVES **Near Eastern** adjective.

nearly ● adverb very close to; almost.
– PHRASES **not nearly** nothing like; far from.

near miss ● noun **1** a narrowly avoided collision. **2** a bomb or shot that just misses its target.

nearside ● noun chiefly Brit. **1** the side of a vehicle nearest the kerb. **2** the left side of a horse.

near-sighted ● adjective short-sighted.

neat ● adjective **1** tidy or carefully arranged. **2** done with or demonstrating skill or efficiency. **3** (of a drink of spirits) not diluted or mixed with anything else. **4** N. Amer. informal excellent.
– DERIVATIVES **neatly** adverb **neatness** noun.
– ORIGIN French *net*, from Latin *nitidus* 'shining'; related to NET².

neaten ● verb make neat.

neath ● preposition literary beneath.

neat's-foot oil ● noun oil obtained by boiling the feet of cattle, used to dress leather.
– ORIGIN from *neat*, an archaic word for a cow or ox.

neb ● noun Scottish & N. English a nose, snout, or bird's beak.
– ORIGIN Old English.

Nebuchadnezzar /nebyookədnezzər/ ● noun a very large wine bottle, equivalent in capacity to about twenty regular bottles.
– ORIGIN from *Nebuchadnezzar* II, king of Babylon in the 6th century BC.

nebula /nebyoolə/ ● noun (pl. **nebulae** /nebyoolee/ or **nebulas**) Astronomy a cloud of gas or dust in outer space, visible in the night sky either as a bright patch or as a dark silhouette against other glowing matter.
– DERIVATIVES **nebular** adjective.
– ORIGIN Latin, 'mist'.

nebulizer /nebyoolīzər/ (also **nebuliser**) ● noun a device for producing a fine spray of liquid, used for example for inhaling a medicinal drug.
– DERIVATIVES **nebulize** (also **nebulise**) verb.

nebulous ● adjective **1** in the form of a cloud or haze; hazy. **2** vague or ill-defined: *nebulous concepts*. **3** Astronomy relating to a nebula or nebulae.
– DERIVATIVES **nebulosity** noun.

necessarily ● adverb as a necessary result; inevitably.

necessary ● adjective **1** required to be done, achieved, or present; needed. **2** that must be; inevitable: *a necessary result*. ● noun **1** (**necessaries**) the basic requirements of life, such as food and warmth. **2** (**the necessary**) informal the action, item, or money required.
– ORIGIN Latin *necessarius*, from *necesse* 'be needful'.

necessitate ● verb **1** make necessary as a result. **2** force or compel to do something.

necessitous ● adjective lacking the necessities of life; poor.

necessity ● noun (pl. **necessities**) **1** the state or fact of being required or indispensable. **2** an indispensable thing. **3** a situation enforcing a particular course: *created more by necessity than design*.
– PHRASES **necessity is the mother of invention** proverb when the need for something becomes imperative, you are forced to find ways of getting or achieving it.

Thesaurus

nay ● adverb OR RATHER, (and) indeed, and even, in fact, actually, in truth.

near ● adverb **1** *her children all live near* CLOSE (BY), nearby, close/near at hand, in the neighbourhood, in the vicinity, at hand, within reach, on the doorstep, a stone's throw away; *informal* within spitting distance; *archaic* nigh. **2** *near perfect conditions* ALMOST, just about, nearly, practically, virtually; *poetic/literary* well-nigh.
● preposition *a hotel near the seafront* CLOSE TO, close by, by, a short distance from, in the vicinity of, in the neighbourhood of, within reach of, a stone's throw away from; *informal* within spitting distance of.
● adjective **1** *the nearest house* CLOSE, nearby, close/near at hand, at hand, a stone's throw away, within reach, accessible, handy, convenient; *informal* within spitting distance. **2** *the final judgement is near* IMMINENT, in the offing, close/near at hand, at hand, (just) round the corner, impending, looming. **3** *a near relation* CLOSELY RELATED, close, related. **4** *a near escape* NARROW, close, by a hair's breadth; *informal* by a whisker.
– OPPOSITES far, distant.
● verb **1** *by dawn we were nearing Moscow* APPROACH, draw near/nearer to, get close/closer to, advance towards, close in on. **2** *the death toll is nearing 3,000* VERGE ON, border on, approach.

nearby ● adjective *one of the nearby villages* NOT FAR AWAY/OFF, close/near at hand, close (by), near, within reach, at hand, neighbouring; accessible, handy, convenient.
– OPPOSITES faraway.
● adverb *her mother lives nearby* CLOSE (BY), close/near at hand, near, a short distance away, in the neighbourhood, in the vicinity, at hand, within reach, on the doorstep, (just) round the corner.

nearly ● adverb ALMOST, (just) about, more or less, practically, virtually, all but, as good as, not far off, to all intents and purposes; not quite; *informal* pretty much, pretty well; *poetic/literary* well-nigh.

near miss ● noun CLOSE THING, near thing, narrow escape; *informal* close shave.

nearness ● noun **1** *the town's nearness to Rome* CLOSENESS, proximity, propinquity; accessibility, handiness; *archaic* vicinity. **2** *the nearness of death* IMMINENCE, closeness, immediacy.

near-sighted ● adjective SHORT-SIGHTED, myopic.

neat ● adjective **1** *the bedroom was neat and clean* TIDY, orderly, well ordered, in (good) order, shipshape (and Bristol fashion), in apple-pie order, spick and span, uncluttered, straight, trim. **2** *he's very neat* SMART, spruce, dapper, trim, well groomed, well turned out; *N. Amer.* trig; *informal* natty. **3** *her neat script* WELL FORMED, regular, precise, elegant, well proportioned. **4** *this neat little gadget* COMPACT, well designed, handy; *Brit. informal* dinky. **5** *his neat footwork* SKILFUL, deft, dexterous, adroit, adept, expert; *informal* nifty. **6** *a neat solution* CLEVER, ingenious, inventive. **7** *neat gin* UNDILUTED, straight, unmixed; *N. Amer. informal* straight up. **8** *(N. Amer. informal) we had a really neat time.* See WONDERFUL.
– OPPOSITES untidy.

neaten ● verb TIDY (UP), make neat/neater, straighten (up), smarten (up), spruce up, put in order; *N. Amer. informal* fix up.

neatly ● adverb **1** *neatly arranged papers* TIDILY, methodically, systematically; smartly, sprucely. **2** *the point was neatly put* CLEVERLY, aptly, elegantly. **3** *a neatly executed header* SKILFULLY, deftly, adroitly, adeptly, expertly.

neatness ● noun **1** *the neatness of the cottage* TIDINESS, orderliness, trimness, spruceness; smartness. **2** *the neatness of her movements* GRACE, gracefulness, nimbleness, deftness, dexterity, agility.

nebulous ● adjective **1** *the figure was nebulous* INDISTINCT, indefinite, unclear, vague, hazy, cloudy, fuzzy, misty, blurred, blurry, foggy; faint, shadowy, obscure, formless, amorphous. **2** *nebulous ideas* VAGUE, ill-defined, unclear, hazy, uncertain, indefinite, indeterminate, imprecise, unformed, muddled, confused, ambiguous.
– OPPOSITES clear.

necessarily ● adverb AS A CONSEQUENCE, as a result, automatically, as a matter of course, certainly, surely, definitely, incontrovertibly, undoubtedly, inevitably, unavoidably, inescapably, ineluctably, of necessity; *formal* perforce.

necessary ● adjective **1** *planning permission is necessary* OBLIGATORY, requisite, required, compulsory, mandatory, imperative, needed, de rigueur; essential, indispensable, vital. **2** *a necessary consequence* INEVITABLE, unavoidable, inescapable, inexorable, ineluctable; predetermined, preordained.
● noun *(informal) could you lend me the necessary?* See MONEY sense 1.

necessitate ● verb MAKE NECESSARY, entail, involve, mean, require, demand, call for, be grounds for, warrant, constrain, force.

necessitous ● adjective NEEDY, poor, short of money, disadvantaged, underprivileged, in straitened circumstances, impoverished, poverty-stricken, penniless, impecunious, destitute, pauperized, indigent; *Brit.* on the breadline, without a penny to one's name; *informal* on one's uppers, hard up, without two pennies to

neck ● noun **1** the part of the body connecting the head to the rest of the body. **2** a narrow connecting or end part, such as the part of a bottle near the mouth. **3** the part of a violin, guitar, or other instrument that bears the fingerboard. **4** the length of a horse's head and neck as a measure of its lead in a race. **5** informal impudence or nerve: *he had the neck to charge me full fare.* ● verb **1** informal kiss and caress amorously. **2** Brit. informal swallow (a drink).
– PHRASES **get** (or **catch**) **it in the neck** informal be severely criticized or punished. **neck and neck** level in a race or competition. **neck of the woods** informal a particular locality. **up to one's neck in** informal heavily or busily involved in.
– DERIVATIVES **neckless** adjective.
– ORIGIN Old English, 'nape of the neck'.

neckband ● noun a strip of material round the neck of a garment.

neckcloth ● noun a cravat.

neckerchief ● noun a square of cloth worn round the neck.

necklace ● noun an ornamental chain or string of beads, jewels, or links worn round the neck. ● verb (in South Africa) kill by placing a tyre soaked with petrol round a victim's neck and setting it alight.

necklet ● noun a close-fitting, typically rigid ornament worn around the neck.

neckline ● noun the edge of a woman's garment at or below the neck.

necktie ● noun N. Amer. or dated a tie worn around the neck.

necromancy /nekrōmansi/ ● noun **1** prediction of the future by allegedly communicating with the dead. **2** witchcraft or black magic.
– DERIVATIVES **necromancer** noun **necromantic** adjective.
– ORIGIN from Greek *nekros* 'corpse'.

necrophilia /nekrəfilliə/ ● noun sexual intercourse with or attraction towards corpses.
– DERIVATIVES **necrophiliac** noun.

necrophobia ● noun extreme or irrational fear of death or dead bodies.

necropolis /nekroppəliss/ ● noun a cemetery, especially a large ancient one.
– ORIGIN from Greek *nekros* 'corpse' + *polis* 'city'.

necropsy /nekropsi/ ● noun (pl. **necropsies**) another term for AUTOPSY.

necrosis /nekrōsiss/ ● noun Medicine the death of most or all of the cells in an organ or tissue due to disease, injury, or failure of the blood supply.
– DERIVATIVES **necrotic** adjective.
– ORIGIN from Greek *nekros* 'corpse'.

necrotizing /nekrətīzing/ (also **necrotising**) ● adjective causing or accompanied by necrosis.

nectar ● noun **1** a sugary fluid produced by flowers to encourage pollination by insects, made into honey by bees. **2** (in Greek and Roman mythology) the drink of the gods. **3** a delicious drink.
– DERIVATIVES **nectarivorous** adjective.
– ORIGIN Greek *nektar*.

nectarine /nektəreen/ ● noun a variety of peach with smooth, brightly coloured skin and rich firm flesh.
– ORIGIN originally in the sense 'nectar-like': from NECTAR.

nectary ● noun (pl. **nectaries**) Botany a nectar-secreting gland in a flower or on a leaf or stem.

née /nay/ ● adjective (masc. **né**) born (used in citing a person's former name, especially a married woman's maiden name): *Mrs. Hargreaves, née Liddell.*
– ORIGIN French.

need ● verb **1** require (something) because it is essential or very important. **2** expressing necessity or obligation: *need I say more?* ● noun **1** circumstances in which a thing or course of action is required. **2** a thing that is wanted or required. **3** a state of poverty, distress, or misfortune.
– PHRASES **needs must when the Devil drives** proverb sometimes you have to do something you would rather not.
– ORIGIN Old English.

needful ● adjective **1** formal necessary; requisite. **2** archaic needy. ● noun (**the needful**) informal what is necessary.

needle ● noun **1** a very thin pointed piece of metal with a hole or eye for thread at the blunter end, used in sewing. **2** a similar, larger instrument without an eye, used in knitting, crochet, etc. **3** the pointed hollow end of a hypodermic syringe. **4** a stylus used to play records. **5** a thin pointer on a dial, compass, etc. **6** the thin, sharp, stiff leaf of a fir or pine tree. **7** Brit. informal hostility or antagonism provoked by rivalry. ● verb **1** prick or pierce with or as with a needle. **2** informal provoke or annoy by continual criticism.
– ORIGIN Old English.

needlecord ● noun Brit. fine-ribbed corduroy fabric.

needlepoint ● noun **1** closely stitched embroidery worked over canvas. **2** (also **needlelace**) lace made by hand using a needle rather than bobbins.

needless ● adjective unnecessary; avoidable.
– PHRASES **needless to say** of course.
– DERIVATIVES **needlessly** adverb.

needlewoman ● noun a woman who has particular sewing

n

Thesaurus

rub together; *Brit. informal* in Queer Street; *formal* penurious.
– OPPOSITES wealthy.

necessity ● noun **1** *the VCR is now regarded as a necessity* ESSENTIAL, indispensable item, requisite, prerequisite, necessary, basic, sine qua non, desideratum. **2** *political necessity forced him to resign* FORCE OF CIRCUMSTANCE, obligation, need, call, exigency; force majeure. **3** *the necessity of growing old* INEVITABILITY, certainty, inescapability, inexorability, ineluctability. **4** *necessity made them steal* POVERTY, need, neediness, want, deprivation, privation, penury, destitution, indigence.
– PHRASES **of necessity** NECESSARILY, inevitably, unavoidably, inescapably, ineluctably; as a matter of course, naturally, automatically, certainly, surely, definitely, incontrovertibly, undoubtedly; *formal* perforce.

neck ● noun *technical* cervix; *archaic, informal* scrag.
– RELATED TERMS cervical, jugular.
● verb *(informal)* KISS, caress, pet; *informal* smooch, canoodle; *Brit. informal* snog; *N. Amer. informal* make out; *informal, dated* spoon.
– PHRASES **neck and neck** LEVEL, equal, tied, side by side; *Brit.* level pegging; *informal* even-steven(s).

necklace ● noun CHAIN, choker, necklet; beads, pearls; pendant, locket; *historical* torc.

necromancer ● noun SORCERER, sorceress, (black) magician, wizard, warlock, witch, enchantress, occultist, diviner; spiritualist, medium.

necromancy ● noun SORCERY, (black) magic, witchcraft, witchery, wizardry, the occult, occultism, voodoo, hoodoo; divination; spiritualism.

necropolis ● noun CEMETERY, graveyard, churchyard, burial ground; *informal* boneyard; *historical* potter's field; *archaic* God's acre.

née ● adjective *Jill Wyatt, née Peters* BORN, formerly, previously; *formal* heretofore.

need ● verb **1** *do you need money?* REQUIRE, be in need of, have need of, want; be crying out for, be desperate for; demand, call for, necessitate, entail, involve; lack, be without, be short of. **2** *you needn't come* HAVE TO, be obliged to, be compelled to. **3** *she needed him so much* YEARN FOR, pine for, long for, desire, miss.
● noun **1** *there's no need to apologize* NECESSITY, obligation, requirement, call, demand. **2** *basic human needs* REQUIREMENT, essential, necessity, want, requisite, prerequisite, demand, desideratum. **3** *their need was particularly pressing* NEEDINESS, want, poverty, deprivation, privation, hardship, destitution, indigence. **4** *my hour of need* DIFFICULTY, trouble, distress; crisis, emergency, urgency, extremity.
– PHRASES **in need** NEEDY, necessitous, deprived, disadvantaged, underprivileged, poor, impoverished, poverty-stricken, destitute, impecunious, indigent; *Brit.* on the breadline; *formal* penurious.

needed ● adjective NECESSARY, required, wanted, desired, lacking; essential, requisite, compulsory, obligatory, mandatory.
– OPPOSITES optional.

needful ● adjective *(formal)* NECESSARY, needed, required, requisite; essential, imperative, vital, indispensable.

needle ● noun **1** *a needle and thread* darner, bodkin. **2** *the virus is transmitted via needles* hypodermic needle; *informal* hype, spike. **3** *the needle on the meter* INDICATOR, pointer, marker, arrow, hand. **4** *put the needle on the record* STYLUS.
● verb *(informal) why had she let Leo needle her?* See ANNOY.

needless ● adjective UNNECESSARY, inessential, non-essential, unneeded, undesired, unwanted, uncalled for; gratuitous, pointless; dispensable, expendable, superfluous, redundant, excessive, supererogatory.
– OPPOSITES necessary.

skills.
needlework • noun sewing or embroidery.
needn't • contraction need not.
needy • adjective (**needier**, **neediest**) **1** lacking the necessities of life; very poor. **2** needing emotional support; insecure.
– DERIVATIVES **neediness** noun.
neem /neem/ • noun a tropical tree which yields wood, oil, medicinal products, and insecticide.
– ORIGIN Sanskrit.
neep • noun Scottish & N. English a turnip.
– ORIGIN Latin *napus*.
ne'er /nair/ • contraction literary or dialect never.
ne'er-do-well • noun a person who is lazy and irresponsible.
nefarious /nifairiəss/ • adjective wicked or criminal.
– ORIGIN from Latin *nefas* 'wrong'.
negate /nigayt/ • verb **1** make ineffective; nullify. **2** deny the existence of. **3** Grammar make (a clause, sentence, etc.) negative in meaning.
– ORIGIN Latin *negare* 'deny'.
negation • noun **1** the contradiction or denial of something. **2** the absence or opposite of something actual or positive: *evil is not merely the negation of goodness.* **3** Mathematics replacement of positive by negative.
negative • adjective **1** characterized by the absence rather than the presence of distinguishing features: *a negative test result.* **2** expressing or implying denial, disagreement, or refusal. **3** pessimistic, undesirable, or unwelcome. **4** (of a quantity) less than zero. **5** of, containing, producing, or denoting the kind of electric charge carried by electrons. **6** (of a photographic image) showing light and shade or colours reversed from those of the original. **7** Grammar stating that something is not the case. • noun **1** a word or statement expressing denial, refusal, or negation. **2** a negative photographic image from which positive prints may be made. • verb **1** reject, veto, or contradict. **2** make ineffective; neutralize.
– DERIVATIVES **negatively** adverb **negativity** noun.
negative equity • noun potential indebtedness arising when the market value of a property falls below the outstanding amount of a mortgage secured on it.
negative pole • noun the south-seeking pole of a magnet.
negative sign • noun a minus sign.
neglect • verb **1** fail to give proper care or attention to. **2** fail to do something. • noun **1** the state of being neglected. **2** the action of neglecting.
– ORIGIN Latin *neglegere* 'disregard'.
neglectful • adjective failing to give proper care or attention.
negligee /neglizhay/ • noun a woman's light, filmy dressing gown.
– ORIGIN French, 'given little thought or attention'.
negligence • noun **1** lack of proper care and attention. **2** Law breach of a duty of care which results in damage.
– DERIVATIVES **negligent** adjective.
negligible /neglijib'l/ • adjective so small or unimportant as to be not worth considering.
– DERIVATIVES **negligibly** adverb.
– ORIGIN obsolete French, from *négliger* 'to neglect'.
negotiable • adjective **1** open to discussion or modification. **2** able to be traversed; passable. **3** (of a document) able to be transferred or assigned to the legal ownership of another person.
– DERIVATIVES **negotiability** noun.
negotiate • verb **1** try to reach an agreement or compromise by discussion. **2** obtain or bring about by negotiating. **3** find a way over or through (an obstacle or difficult path). **4** transfer (a cheque, bill, etc.) to the legal ownership of another.
– DERIVATIVES **negotiation** noun **negotiator** noun.
– ORIGIN Latin *negotiari* 'do in the course of business'.
Negress /neegris/ • noun a woman or girl of black African

Thesaurus

– PHRASES **needless to say** OF COURSE, as one would expect, not unexpectedly, it goes without saying, obviously, naturally; *informal* natch.
needlework • noun SEWING, stitching, embroidery, needlepoint, needlecraft, tapestry, crewel work.
needy • adjective POOR, deprived, disadvantaged, underprivileged, necessitous, in need, needful, hard up, in straitened circumstances, poverty-stricken, indigent, impoverished, pauperized, destitute, impecunious, penniless, moneyless; *Brit.* on the breadline; *informal* on one's uppers, broke, strapped (for cash), without two pennies to rub together; *Brit. informal* skint, stony broke, in Queer Street; *N. Amer. informal* stone broke; *formal* penurious.
– OPPOSITES wealthy.
ne'er-do-well • noun GOOD-FOR-NOTHING, layabout, loafer, idler, shirker, sluggard, slugabed, drone; *informal* waster, lazybones; *Brit. informal* skiver; *N. Amer. informal* bum, gold brick; *archaic* wastrel.
nefarious • adjective WICKED, evil, sinful, iniquitous, egregious, heinous, atrocious, vile, foul, abominable, odious, depraved, monstrous, fiendish, diabolical, unspeakable, despicable; villainous, criminal, corrupt, illegal, unlawful; *dated* dastardly.
– OPPOSITES good.
negate • verb **1** *they negated the court's ruling* INVALIDATE, nullify, neutralize, cancel; undo, reverse, annul, void, revoke, rescind, repeal, retract, countermand, overrule, overturn; *Law* avoid; *formal* abrogate. **2** *he negates the political nature of education* DENY, dispute, contradict, controvert, refute, rebut, reject, repudiate; *formal* gainsay.
– OPPOSITES validate, confirm.
negation • noun **1** *negation of the findings* DENIAL, contradiction, repudiation, refutation, rebuttal; nullification, cancellation, revocation, repeal, retraction; *Law* disaffirmation; *formal* abrogation. **2** *evil is not just the negation of goodness* OPPOSITE, reverse, antithesis, contrary, inverse, converse; absence, want.
negative • adjective **1** *a negative reply* OPPOSING, opposed, contrary, anti-, dissenting, dissentient; saying 'no', in the negative. **2** *stop being so negative* PESSIMISTIC, defeatist, gloomy, cynical, fatalistic, dismissive, antipathetic; unenthusiastic, uninterested, unresponsive. **3** *a negative effect on the economy* HARMFUL, bad, adverse, damaging, detrimental, unfavourable, disadvantageous.
– OPPOSITES positive, optimistic, favourable.
• noun *he murmured a negative* 'NO', refusal, rejection, veto; dissension, contradiction; denial.
• verb **1** *the bill was negatived by the house* REJECT, turn down, refuse, veto, squash; *informal* give the thumbs down to. **2** *his arguments were negatived* DISPROVE, belie, invalidate, refute, rebut, discredit; contradict, deny, negate; *formal* gainsay. **3** *they tried to negative the effect of the tax* NEUTRALIZE, cancel out, counteract, nullify, negate; offset, balance, counterbalance.
– OPPOSITES ratify, prove.
negativity • noun PESSIMISM, defeatism, gloom, cynicism, hopelessness, despair, despondency; apathy, indifference.
neglect • verb **1** *she neglected the children* FAIL TO LOOK AFTER, leave alone, abandon; *poetic/literary* forsake. **2** *he's neglecting his work* PAY NO ATTENTION TO, let slide, not attend to, be remiss about, be lax about, leave undone, shirk. **3** *don't neglect our advice* DISREGARD, ignore, pay no attention to, take no notice of, pay no heed to, overlook; disdain, scorn, spurn. **4** *I neglected to inform her* FAIL, omit, forget.
– OPPOSITES cherish, heed, remember.
• noun **1** *the place had an air of neglect* DISREPAIR, dilapidation, deterioration, shabbiness, disuse, abandonment. **2** *her doctor was guilty of neglect* NEGLIGENCE, dereliction of duty, remissness, carelessness, heedlessness, unconcern, laxity, slackness, irresponsibility; *formal* delinquency. **3** *the relative neglect of women* DISREGARD, ignoring, overlooking; inattention to, indifference to, heedlessness to.
– OPPOSITES care, attention.
neglected • adjective **1** *neglected animals* UNCARED FOR, abandoned; mistreated, maltreated; *poetic/literary* forsaken. **2** *a neglected cottage* DERELICT, dilapidated, tumbledown, ramshackle, untended. **3** *a neglected masterpiece of prose* DISREGARDED, forgotten, overlooked, ignored, unrecognized, unnoticed, unsung, underestimated, undervalued, unappreciated.
neglectful • adjective. See NEGLIGENT.
negligent • adjective NEGLECTFUL, remiss, careless, lax, irresponsible, inattentive, heedless, thoughtless, unmindful, forgetful; slack, sloppy; *N. Amer.* derelict; *formal* delinquent.
– OPPOSITES dutiful.
negligible • adjective TRIVIAL, trifling, insignificant, unimportant, minor, inconsequential; minimal, small, slight, inappreciable, infinitesimal, nugatory, petty; paltry, inadequate, insufficient, meagre, pitiful; *informal* minuscule, piddling, measly, poxy; *formal* exiguous.
– OPPOSITES significant.
negotiable • adjective **1** *the salary will be negotiable* OPEN TO DISCUSSION, discussable, flexible, open to modification; unsettled, un-

n

origin.

– USAGE The term **Negress** is now regarded as old-fashioned or even offensive; **black** is the preferred term.

Negritude /negrityōōd/ ● noun the quality, fact, or awareness of being of black African origin.

Negro ● noun (pl. **Negroes**) a member of a dark-skinned group of peoples originally native to Africa south of the Sahara.

– USAGE The term **Negro** is now regarded as old-fashioned or even offensive; **black** is the preferred term.

– ORIGIN from Latin *niger* 'black'.

Negroid ● adjective relating to the division of humankind represented by the indigenous peoples of central and southern Africa.

– USAGE The term **Negroid** is associated with outdated notions of racial types; it is potentially offensive and best avoided.

Negrophobia ● noun intense or irrational dislike or fear of black people.

– DERIVATIVES **Negrophobe** noun.

neigh ● noun a characteristic high whinnying sound made by a horse. ● verb utter a neigh.

– ORIGIN imitative.

neighbour (US **neighbor**) ● noun **1** a person living next door to or very near to another. **2** a person or place in relation to others next to it. ● verb be situated next to or very near (another).

– DERIVATIVES **neighbourly** adjective.

– ORIGIN from the Old English words for 'near' and 'inhabitant, peasant, farmer'.

neighbourhood (US **neighborhood**) ● noun **1** a district or community within a town or city. **2** the area surrounding a particular place, person, or object.

– PHRASES **in the neighbourhood of** approximately.

neighbourhood watch ● noun a scheme of systematic local vigilance by householders to discourage crime, especially burglary.

neither /nīthər, nee-/ ● determiner & pronoun not the one nor the other of two people or things; not either. ● adverb **1** used before the first of two (or occasionally more) alternatives (the others being introduced by 'nor') to indicate that they are each untrue or each do not happen. **2** used to introduce a further negative statement.

– ORIGIN Old English.

n

nekton /nektən/ ● noun Zoology aquatic animals that are able to swim and move independently of water currents, as distinct from plankton.

– DERIVATIVES **nektonic** adjective.

– ORIGIN Greek, from *nēkhein* 'to swim'.

nelly ● noun (pl. **nellies**) informal **1** a silly person. **2** derogatory an effeminate homosexual man.

– PHRASES **not on your nelly** Brit. certainly not. [ORIGIN originally as *not on your Nelly Duff*, rhyming slang for 'puff' (i.e. breath of life).]

– ORIGIN from the given name *Nelly*.

nelson ● noun a wrestling hold in which one arm is passed under the opponent's arm from behind and the hand is applied to the neck (**half nelson**), or both arms and hands are applied (**full nelson**).

– ORIGIN apparently from the surname *Nelson*.

nematode /nemmətōd/ ● noun Zoology a worm of a group with slender, unsegmented, cylindrical bodies (including the roundworms, threadworms, and eelworms).

– ORIGIN from Greek *nēma* 'thread'.

nem. con. ● adverb with no one dissenting; unanimously.

– ORIGIN abbreviation of Latin *nemine contradicente*.

nemesis /nemmisiss/ ● noun (pl. **nemeses** /nemmiseez/) **1** an inescapable agent of retribution: *inflationary excess brought its nemesis in subsequent deflation.* **2** retribution caused by such an agent.

– ORIGIN Greek, 'retribution', personified as the goddess of divine punishment.

neo- /neeō/ ● combining form **1** new: *neonate.* **2** a new or revived form of: *neoclassicism.*

– ORIGIN from Greek *neos* 'new'.

neoclassical (also **neoclassic**) ● adjective relating to the revival of a classical style in the arts.

– DERIVATIVES **neoclassicism** noun **neoclassicist** noun & adjective.

neocortex ● noun (pl. **neocortices**) Anatomy a part of the cerebral cortex of the brain, concerned with sight and hearing in mammals.

– DERIVATIVES **neocortical** adjective.

neodymium /neeədimmiəm/ ● noun a silvery-white metallic element of the lanthanide series.

– ORIGIN from NEO- + *didymium*, name given to a mixture of the elements praseodymium and neodymium, from Greek *didumos* 'twin'.

neo-Impressionism ● noun a late 19th-century artistic movement which sought to improve on Impressionism through a systematic approach to form and colour, especially by using pointillist technique.

– DERIVATIVES **neo-Impressionist** adjective & noun.

Neolithic /neeəlithik/ ● adjective relating to the later part of the Stone Age, when ground or polished stone weapons and implements prevailed.

– ORIGIN from NEO- + Greek *lithos* 'stone'.

neologism /neeolləjiz'm/ ● noun a newly coined word or expression.

– ORIGIN from NEO- + Greek *logos* 'word'.

neon ● noun **1** an inert gaseous element giving an orange glow when electricity is passed through it, used in fluorescent lighting. **2** (before another noun) very bright or fluorescent in colour: *bold neon colours.*

– ORIGIN Greek, 'something new'.

neonatal /neeənayt'l/ ● adjective relating to newborn children.

– DERIVATIVES **neonatology** noun.

neonate /neeənayt/ ● noun a newborn child or mammal.

– ORIGIN from Greek *neos* 'new' + Latin *nasci* 'be born'.

neon tetra ● noun a small brightly coloured tropical freshwater fish, popular in aquaria.

– ORIGIN *tetra* is an abbreviation of Latin *Tetragonopterus* 'tetragonal-finned', a former genus name.

neophobia ● noun extreme or irrational fear or dislike of anything new or unfamiliar.

– DERIVATIVES **neophobic** adjective.

neophyte /neeəfit/ ● noun **1** a person who is new to a subject,

Thesaurus

decided. **2** *the path was negotiable* PASSABLE, navigable, crossable, traversable; clear, unblocked, unobstructed. **3** *negotiable cheques* transferable; valid.

negotiate ● verb **1** *she refused to negotiate* DISCUSS TERMS, talk, consult, parley, confer, debate; compromise; mediate, intercede, arbitrate, moderate, conciliate; bargain, haggle. **2** *he negotiated a new contract* ARRANGE, broker, work out, thrash out, agree on; settle, clinch, conclude, pull off, bring off, transact; informal sort out, swing. **3** *I negotiated the obstacles* GET ROUND, get past, get over, clear, cross; surmount, overcome, deal with, cope with.

negotiation ● noun **1** *the negotiations resume next week* DISCUSSION(S), talks, deliberations; conference, debate, dialogue, consultation; mediation, arbitration, conciliation. **2** *the negotiation of the deal* ARRANGEMENT, brokering; settlement, conclusion, completion, transaction.

negotiator ● noun MEDIATOR, arbitrator, arbiter, moderator, go-between, middleman, intermediary, intercessor, intervener, conciliator; representative, spokesperson, broker, bargainer.

neigh ● verb WHINNY, bray, nicker, snicker, whicker.

neighbourhood ● noun **1** *a quiet neighbourhood* DISTRICT, area, locality, locale, quarter, community; part, region, zone; informal neck of the woods; Brit. informal manor; N. Amer. informal hood, nabe. **2** *in the neighbourhood of Canterbury* VICINITY, environs, purlieus, precincts, vicinage.

– PHRASES **in the neighbourhood of** APPROXIMATELY, about, around, roughly, in the region of, of the order of, nearly, almost, close to, just about, practically, there or thereabouts, circa; Brit. getting on for.

neighbouring ● adjective ADJACENT, adjoining, bordering, connecting, abutting; proximate, near, close (at hand), next-door, nearby, in the vicinity, vicinal.

– OPPOSITES remote.

neighbourly ● adjective OBLIGING, helpful, friendly, kind, amiable, amicable, affable, genial, agreeable, hospitable, companionable, well disposed, civil, cordial, good-natured, nice, pleasant, generous; considerate, thoughtful, unselfish; Brit. informal decent.

– OPPOSITES unfriendly.

nemesis ● noun **1** *this could be the bank's nemesis* DOWNFALL, undoing, ruin, ruination, destruction, Waterloo. **2** *the nemesis that his crime deserved* RETRIBUTION, vengeance, punishment, just des-

skill, or belief. **2** a novice in a religious order, or a newly ordained priest.
– ORIGIN from Greek *neophutos* 'newly planted'.

neoplasm ● noun a new and abnormal growth of tissue in the body, especially a malignant tumour.
– DERIVATIVES **neoplastic** adjective.
– ORIGIN from NEO- + Greek *plasma* 'formation'.

Neoplatonism /neeōplaytəniz'm/ ● noun a philosophical and religious system dating from the 3rd century, combining Platonic and other Greek thought with oriental mysticism.
– DERIVATIVES **Neoplatonic** adjective **Neoplatonist** noun.

neoprene /neeōpreen/ ● noun a synthetic substance resembling rubber.
– ORIGIN from NEO- + *prene* (perhaps from PROPYL + -ENE).

neoteny /neeottəni/ ● noun Zoology **1** the retention of juvenile features in an adult animal. **2** the sexual maturity of an animal in a larval state, as in the axolotl.
– DERIVATIVES **neotenic** adjective **neotenous** adjective.
– ORIGIN from Greek *neos* 'new' + *teinein* 'extend'.

Nepalese /neppəleez/ ● noun a person from Nepal. ● adjective relating to Nepal.

Nepali /nipawli/ ● noun (pl. same or **Nepalis**) **1** a person from Nepal. **2** the official language of Nepal.

nephew ● noun a son of one's brother or sister, or of one's brother-in-law or sister-in-law.
– ORIGIN Old French *neveu*, from Latin *nepos* 'grandson, nephew'.

nephridium /nifriddiəm/ ● noun (pl. **nephridia**) Zoology (in many invertebrates) a minute tube open to the exterior via which bodily wastes and excess water are expelled.
– ORIGIN Latin, from Greek *nephrion* 'little kidney'.

nephrite /nefrīt/ ● noun a pale green or white form of jade.
– ORIGIN from Greek *nephros* 'kidney' (with reference to its supposed efficacy in treating kidney disease).

nephritis /nifrītiss/ ● noun inflammation of the kidneys.
– ORIGIN from Greek *nephros* 'kidney'.

nephrosis /nifrōsiss/ ● noun kidney disease.
– DERIVATIVES **nephrotic** adjective.

ne plus ultra /nay plōōss ōōltraa/ ● noun (**the ne plus ultra**) the perfect or most extreme example.
– ORIGIN Latin, 'not further beyond', the supposed inscription on the Pillars of Hercules (at the Strait of Gibraltar) prohibiting passage by ships.

nepotism /neppətiz'm/ ● noun favouritism shown to relatives or friends, especially by giving them jobs.
– DERIVATIVES **nepotistic** adjective.
– ORIGIN Italian *nepotismo*, from *nipote* 'nephew' (with reference to privileges bestowed on the 'nephews' of popes, often really their illegitimate sons).

Neptunian ● adjective relating to the planet Neptune.

neptunium ● noun a rare radioactive metallic element produced from uranium by the capture of neutrons.
– ORIGIN from *Neptune*, on the pattern of *uranium* (Neptune being the next planet beyond Uranus).

nerd ● noun informal a person who lacks social skills or is boringly studious.
– DERIVATIVES **nerdish** adjective **nerdy** adjective.
– ORIGIN of unknown origin.

Nereid /neeri-id/ ● noun Greek Mythology any of the sea nymphs, daughters of the old sea god Nereus.

neroli /neerəli/ (also **neroli oil**) ● noun an essential oil distilled from the flowers of the Seville orange.
– ORIGIN Italian, said to be the name of a 17th-century Italian princess who discovered the oil.

nerve ● noun **1** a fibre or bundle of fibres in the body that transmits impulses of sensation between the brain or spinal cord and other parts of the body. **2** (**nerves** or **one's nerve**) steadiness and courage in a demanding situation: *the journey tested her nerves to the full.* **3** (**nerves**) nervousness. **4** informal impudence or audacity. ● verb (**nerve oneself**) brace oneself for a demanding situation.
– PHRASES **get on someone's nerves** informal irritate someone. **touch** (or **hit**) **a** (**raw**) **nerve** refer to a sensitive topic.
– ORIGIN Latin *nervus*; related to Greek *neuron* (see NEURON).

nerve cell ● noun a neuron.

nerve centre ● noun **1** a group of connected nerve cells performing a particular function. **2** the control centre of an organization or operation.

nerve gas ● noun a poisonous vapour which disrupts the transmission of nerve impulses, causing death or disablement.

nerveless ● adjective **1** lacking vigour or feeling. **2** confident. **3** Anatomy & Biology lacking nerves or nervures.

nerve-racking (also **nerve-wracking**) ● adjective stressful; frightening.

nervous ● adjective **1** easily agitated or alarmed. **2** apprehensive or anxious. **3** relating to or affecting the nerves.
– DERIVATIVES **nervously** adverb **nervousness** noun.

nervous breakdown ● noun a period of mental illness resulting from severe depression or stress.

nervous system ● noun the network of nerve cells and fibres which transmits nerve impulses between parts of the body.

n

Thesaurus

erts; fate, destiny.

neologism ● noun NEW WORD, new expression, new term, new phrase, coinage; made-up word, nonce-word.

neophyte ● noun **1** *a neophyte of the monastery* NOVICE, novitiate; postulant, catechumen. **2** *cooking classes are offered to neophytes* BEGINNER, learner, novice, newcomer; initiate, tyro, fledgling; trainee, apprentice, probationer; *N. Amer.* tenderfoot; *informal* rookie, newbie, newie; *N. Amer. informal* greenhorn.

ne plus ultra ● noun THE LAST WORD, the ultimate, the perfect example, the height, the acme, the zenith, the epitome, the quintessence; *archaic* the nonsuch.

nepotism ● noun FAVOURITISM, preferential treatment, the old boy network, looking after one's own, bias, partiality, partisanship; *Brit.* jobs for the boys, the old school tie.
– OPPOSITES impartiality.

nerd ● noun *(informal)* BORE; *informal* dork, dweeb, geek; *Brit. informal* anorak, spod; *N. Amer. informal* Poindexter.

nerve ● noun **1** *the nerves that transmit pain* nerve fibre, neuron, axon; *Physiology* dendrite. **2** *the match will be a test of nerve* CONFIDENCE, assurance, cool-headedness, self-possession; courage, bravery, pluck, boldness, intrepidity, fearlessness, daring; determination, will power, spirit, backbone, fortitude, mettle, grit, stout-heartedness; *informal* guts, spunk; *Brit. informal* bottle; *N. Amer. informal* moxie. **3** *(informal) he had the nerve to chat her up* AUDACITY, cheek, effrontery, gall, temerity, presumption, boldness, brazenness, impudence, impertinence, front, arrogance, cockiness; *informal* face, brass neck, chutzpah; *Brit. informal* sauce. **4** *pre-wedding nerves* ANXIETY, tension, nervousness, stress, worry, cold feet, apprehension; *informal* butterflies (in one's stomach), collywobbles, the jitters, the shakes; *Brit. informal* the (screaming) abdabs.
– RELATED TERMS neural, neuro-.
– PHRASES **get on someone's nerves** *(informal)* IRRITATE, annoy, irk, anger, bother, vex, provoke, displease, exasperate, infuriate, gall, pique, needle, ruffle someone's feathers, try someone's patience; jar on, grate on, rankle; *Brit.* rub up the wrong way; *informal* aggravate, get to, bug, miff, peeve, rile, nettle, get up someone's nose, hack off, get someone's goat; *Brit. informal* nark, get on someone's wick, wind up. **nerve oneself** BRACE ONESELF, steel oneself, summon one's courage, gear oneself up, prepare oneself; fortify oneself; *informal* psych oneself up; *poetic/literary* gird one's loins.

nerveless ● adjective **1** *her nerveless fingers* INERT, lifeless; weak, powerless, feeble. **2** *a nerveless lack of restraint* CONFIDENT, self-confident, self-assured, self-possessed, cool, calm, {cool, calm, and collected}, composed, relaxed.
– OPPOSITES nervous.

nerve-racking ● adjective STRESSFUL, anxious, worrying, fraught, nail-biting, tense, difficult, trying, worrisome, daunting, frightening; *informal* scary, hairy.

nervous ● adjective **1** *a nervous woman* HIGHLY STRUNG, anxious, edgy, tense, excitable, jumpy, skittish, brittle, neurotic; timid, mousy, shy, fearful; *Brit.* nervy. **2** *he was so nervous he couldn't eat* ANXIOUS, worried, apprehensive, on edge, edgy, tense, stressed, agitated, uneasy, restless, worked up, keyed up, overwrought, jumpy; fearful, frightened, scared, shaky, in a cold sweat; *informal* with butterflies in one's stomach, jittery, twitchy, in a state, uptight, wired, in a flap, het up; *Brit. informal* strung up, having kittens; *N. Amer. informal* spooky, squirrelly. **3** *a nervous disorder* NEUROLOGICAL, neural, neuro-.
– OPPOSITES relaxed, calm.

nervous breakdown ● noun (MENTAL) COLLAPSE, breakdown, crisis, trauma; nervous exhaustion, mental illness; *informal* crack-up.

nervousness ● noun ANXIETY, edginess, tension, agitation, stress, worry, apprehension, uneasiness, disquiet, fear, trepidation, perturbation, alarm; *Brit.* nerviness; *informal* butterflies (in one's stom-

nervous wreck ● noun informal a stressed or emotionally exhausted person.

nervure /nervyoor/ ● noun **1** Entomology each of the hollow veins forming the framework of an insect's wing. **2** Botany the principal vein of a leaf.
– ORIGIN French, from *nerf* 'nerve'.

nervy ● adjective (**nervier**, **nerviest**) **1** chiefly Brit. nervous or tense. **2** N. Amer. informal bold or impudent.
– DERIVATIVES **nervily** adverb **nerviness** noun.

nescient /nessiənt/ ● adjective literary ignorant.
– DERIVATIVES **nescience** noun.
– ORIGIN from Latin *nescire* 'to not know'.

ness ● noun a headland or promontory.
– ORIGIN Old English, related to NOSE.

-ness ● suffix **1** forming nouns denoting a state or condition: *liveliness.* **2** forming nouns denoting something in a certain state: *wilderness.*
– ORIGIN Old English.

nest ● noun **1** a structure made by a bird for laying eggs and sheltering its young. **2** a place where an animal or insect breeds or shelters. **3** a place filled with undesirable people or things: *a nest of spies.* **4** a set of similar objects of graduated sizes, fitting together for storage. ● verb **1** use or build a nest. **2** fit (an object or objects) inside a larger one.
– ORIGIN Old English.

nest box (also **nesting box**) ● noun a box provided for a bird to nest in.

nest egg ● noun **1** a sum of money saved for the future. **2** a real or artificial egg left in a nest to induce hens to lay there.

nestle ● verb **1** settle comfortably within or against something. **2** (of a place) lie in a sheltered position.
– ORIGIN Old English, related to NEST.

nestling ● noun a bird that is too young to leave the nest.

net[1] ● noun **1** an open-meshed material of twine or cord. **2** a piece or structure of net for catching fish or insects. **3** a fine fabric with a very open weave. **4** (**the net**) the goal in football. **5** (**nets**) (in cricket) a practice area enclosed by net. **6** a trap. **7** a system for selecting or recruiting someone. **8** a communications or computer network. **9** (**the Net**) the Internet. ● verb (**netted**, **netting**) **1** catch or obtain with or as if with a net. **2** (in sport) score (a goal). **3** cover with a net.
– ORIGIN Old English.

n

net[2] (Brit. also **nett**) ● adjective **1** (of an amount, value, or price) remaining after a deduction of tax or other contributions. Often contrasted with GROSS. **2** (of a price) to be paid in full. **3** (of a weight) excluding that of the packaging. **4** (of an effect or result) overall. ● verb (**netted**, **netting**) acquire (a sum) as clear profit.
– ORIGIN originally in the senses 'clean' and 'smart': from French *net* 'neat'.

netball ● noun a team game in which goals are scored by throwing a ball through a netted hoop.

nether /ne<u>th</u>ər/ ● adjective lower in position.
– DERIVATIVES **nethermost** adjective.
– ORIGIN Old English.

nether regions ● plural noun **1** (also **netherworld**) hell; the underworld. **2** euphemistic a person's genitals and bottom.

net profit ● noun the actual profit after working expenses have been paid.

netsuke /netsŏŏki/ ● noun (pl. same or **netsukes**) a carved Japanese ornament of wood or ivory, formerly worn tucked into the sash of a kimono.
– ORIGIN Japanese.

nett ● adjective & verb Brit. variant spelling of NET².

netting ● noun fabric made of net.

nettle ● noun a plant having jagged leaves covered with stinging hairs. ● verb annoy.
– PHRASES **grasp the nettle** Brit. tackle a difficulty boldly.
– ORIGIN Old English.

nettlerash ● noun another term for URTICARIA.

network ● noun **1** an arrangement of intersecting horizontal and vertical lines. **2** a complex system of railways, roads, etc. **3** a group of broadcasting stations that connect to broadcast a programme simultaneously. **4** a number of interconnected computers, operations, etc. **5** a group of people who interact together. ● verb **1** connect as or operate with a network. **2** Brit. broadcast on a network. **3** interact with others to exchange information and develop contacts.
– DERIVATIVES **networker** noun.

neural ● adjective relating to a nerve or the nervous system.
– DERIVATIVES **neurally** adverb.

neuralgia /nyooraljə/ ● noun intense pain along the course of a nerve, especially in the head or face.
– DERIVATIVES **neuralgic** adjective.

neurasthenia /nyoorəsstheeniə/ ● noun Medicine, dated a condition of tiredness, headache, and irritability, typically ascribed to emotional disturbance.
– DERIVATIVES **neurasthenic** adjective & noun.

neuritis /nyooritiss/ ● noun Medicine inflammation of a peripheral nerve or nerves.

neuro- ● combining form relating to nerves or the nervous system.
– ORIGIN from Greek *neuron* 'nerve, sinew, tendon'.

neurogenic /nyoorōjennik/ ● adjective caused by or arising in the nervous system.

neuroleptic /nyoorōleptik/ Medicine ● adjective tending to reduce nervous tension by depressing nerve functions.
– ORIGIN from NEURO- + Greek *lēpsis* 'seizing'.

neurology ● noun the branch of medicine and biology concerned with the nervous system.
– DERIVATIVES **neurological** adjective **neurologist** noun.

neuron (also **neurone**) ● noun a specialized cell transmitting nerve impulses.
– DERIVATIVES **neuronal** adjective.
– USAGE In scientific sources the standard spelling is **neuron**. The spelling **neurone** is found only in non-technical sources.
– ORIGIN Greek *neuron* 'sinew, tendon, nerve'.

neuropathology ● noun the pathology of the nervous system.
– DERIVATIVES **neuropathological** adjective **neuropathologist** noun.

neuropathy /nyooroppəthi/ ● noun Medicine disease or disorder of the nervous system.
– DERIVATIVES **neuropathic** adjective.

neurophysiology ● noun the physiology of the nervous system.
– DERIVATIVES **neurophysiological** adjective **neurophysiologist**

Thesaurus

ach), collywobbles, the jitters, the willies, the heebie-jeebies, the shakes; *Brit. informal* the (screaming) abdabs.

nervy ● adjective. See NERVOUS senses 1, 2.

nest ● noun **1** *the birds built a nest* ROOST, eyrie. **2** *the animals disperse rapidly from the nest* LAIR, den, burrow, set. **3** *a cosy love nest* HIDEAWAY, hideout, retreat, shelter, refuge, snuggery, den; *informal* hidey-hole. **4** *a nest of intrigue* HOTBED, den, breeding ground, cradle.

nest egg ● noun (LIFE) SAVINGS, cache, funds, reserve.

nestle ● verb SNUGGLE, cuddle, huddle, nuzzle, settle, burrow, snug down.

nestling ● noun CHICK, fledgling, baby bird.

net[1] ● noun **1** *fishermen mending their nets* FISHING NET, dragnet, drift net, trawl net, landing net, gill net, cast net. **2** *a dress of green net* NETTING, meshwork, webbing, tulle, fishnet, openwork, lace, latticework. **3** *he managed to escape the net* TRAP, snare.
● verb *they netted big criminals* CATCH, capture, trap, entrap, snare, ensnare, bag, hook, land; *informal* nab, collar.

net[2] ● adjective **1** *net earnings* AFTER TAX, after deductions, take-home, final; *informal* bottom line. **2** *the net result* FINAL, end, ultimate, closing; overall, actual, effective.
– OPPOSITES gross.
● verb *she netted £50,000* EARN, make, get, gain, obtain, acquire, accumulate, take home, bring in, pocket, realize, be paid; *informal* rake in.

nether ● adjective LOWER, low, bottom, bottommost, under, basal; underground.
– OPPOSITES upper.

netherworld ● noun HELL, the underworld, the infernal regions, the abyss; eternal damnation, perdition; Hades, Acheron, Gehenna, Tophet, Sheol; *poetic/literary* the pit.
– OPPOSITES heaven.

nettle ● verb IRRITATE, annoy, irk, gall, vex, anger, exasperate, infuriate, provoke; upset, displease, offend, affront, pique, get on someone's nerves, try someone's patience, ruffle someone's feathers; *Brit.* rub up the wrong way; *N. Amer.* rankle; *informal* peeve, aggravate, miff, rile, needle, get to, bug, get up someone's nose, hack off, get someone's goat; *Brit. informal* nark, get on someone's wick, wind up; *N. Amer. informal* tick off.

network ● noun **1** *a network of arteries* WEB, lattice, net, matrix,

noun.

neurosis /nyoorōsiss/ ● noun (pl. **neuroses** /nyoorōseez/) a relatively mild mental illness not caused by organic disease and involving symptoms such as depression, anxiety, obsessive behaviour, or hypochondria.

neurosurgery ● noun surgery performed on the nervous system.

– DERIVATIVES **neurosurgeon** noun **neurosurgical** adjective.

neurotic ● adjective **1** having, caused by, or relating to neurosis. **2** abnormally sensitive, anxious, or obsessive. ● noun a neurotic person.

– DERIVATIVES **neurotically** adverb **neuroticism** noun.

neurotoxin /nyoorōtoksin/ ● noun a poison which acts on the nervous system.

neurotransmitter ● noun Physiology a chemical substance released from a nerve fibre and bringing about the transfer of an impulse to another nerve, muscle, etc.

– DERIVATIVES **neurotransmission** noun.

neuter ● adjective **1** Grammar (of a noun) not masculine, feminine, or common. **2** (of an animal) lacking developed sexual organs, or having had them removed. **3** (of a plant or flower) having neither functional pistils nor stamens. ● noun Grammar a neuter word. ● verb **1** castrate or spay. **2** make ineffective.

– ORIGIN Latin, 'neither'.

neutral ● adjective **1** impartial or unbiased. **2** having no strongly marked characteristics. **3** Chemistry neither acid nor alkaline; having a pH of about 7. **4** electrically neither positive nor negative. ● noun **1** an impartial or unbiased state or person. **2** a neutral colour or shade. **3** a disengaged position of gears. **4** an electrically neutral point, terminal, etc.

– DERIVATIVES **neutrality** noun **neutrally** adverb.

– ORIGIN Latin *neutralis* 'of neuter gender'.

neutralism ● noun a policy of political neutrality.

– DERIVATIVES **neutralist** noun.

neutralize (also **neutralise**) ● verb **1** make ineffective by applying an opposite force or effect. **2** make chemically neutral. **3** disarm (a bomb). **4** euphemistic kill or destroy.

– DERIVATIVES **neutralization** noun.

neutrino /nyootreenō/ ● noun (pl. **neutrinos**) a subatomic particle with a mass close to zero and no electric charge.

– ORIGIN Italian, from *neutro* 'neutral'.

neutron ● noun a subatomic particle of about the same mass as a proton but without an electric charge.

– ORIGIN from NEUTRAL.

neutron bomb ● noun a nuclear weapon that produces large numbers of neutrons rather than heat or blast, causing harm to life but not property.

neutron star ● noun Astronomy an extremely dense star composed predominantly of neutrons.

névé /nayvay/ ● noun uncompressed granular snow, especially at the head of a glacier.

– ORIGIN Swiss French, 'glacier'.

never ● adverb **1** not ever. **2** not at all. **3** Brit. informal (expressing surprise) definitely or surely not.

– PHRASES **never a one** not one. **the never-never** Brit. informal hire purchase. **never-never land** an imaginary perfect place. [ORIGIN the name of the ideal country in J. M. Barrie's *Peter Pan* (1904).] **well I never!** informal expressing great surprise.

– ORIGIN Old English.

nevermore ● adverb literary never again.

nevertheless ● adverb in spite of that.

nevus ● noun (pl. **nevi**) US spelling of NAEVUS.

new ● adjective **1** not existing before; made, introduced, or discovered recently or now for the first time. **2** not previously used or owned. **3** (often **new to**) seen, experienced, or acquired recently or now for the first time. **4** (**new to/at**) inexperienced at or unaccustomed to. **5** reinvigorated, restored, or reformed. **6** (in place names) discovered or founded later than and named after. ● adverb newly.

– DERIVATIVES **newness** noun.

– ORIGIN Old English.

New Age ● noun a broad movement characterized by alternative approaches to traditional Western culture, involving spirituality, mysticism, environmentalism, etc.

newborn ● adjective **1** recently born. **2** regenerated. ● noun a newborn child or animal.

newcomer ● noun **1** a person who has recently arrived. **2** a novice.

newel /nyooəl/ ● noun **1** the central supporting pillar of a spiral or winding staircase. **2** (also **newel post**) the top or bottom supporting post of a stair rail.

– ORIGIN Old French *nouel* 'knob', from Latin *nodus* 'knot'.

newfangled ● adjective derogatory newly developed and unfamiliar.

n

Thesaurus

mesh, criss-cross, grid, reticulum, reticulation; *Anatomy* plexus. **2** *a network of lanes* MAZE, labyrinth, warren, tangle. **3** *a network of friends* SYSTEM, complex, nexus, web.

neurosis ● noun MENTAL ILLNESS, mental disorder, psychological disorder; psychoneurosis, psychopathy; obsession, phobia, fixation; *Medicine* neuroticism.

neurotic ● adjective **1** *(Medicine) neurotic patients* MENTALLY ILL, mentally disturbed, unstable, unbalanced, maladjusted; psychopathic, phobic, obsessive-compulsive. **2** *a neurotic, self-obsessed woman* OVER-ANXIOUS, oversensitive, nervous, tense, highly strung, paranoid; obsessive, fixated, hysterical, overwrought, irrational; *Brit.* nervy; *informal* twitchy.

– OPPOSITES stable, calm.

neuter ● adjective ASEXUAL, sexless, unsexed; androgynous, epicene. ● verb *have your pets neutered* STERILIZE, castrate, spay, geld, cut, fix, desex; *N. Amer. & Austral.* alter; *Brit. informal* doctor; *archaic* emasculate.

neutral ● adjective **1** *she's neutral on this issue* IMPARTIAL, unbiased, unprejudiced, objective, open-minded, non-partisan, disinterested, dispassionate, detached, impersonal, unemotional, indifferent, uncommitted. **2** *Switzerland remained neutral* UNALIGNED, non-aligned, unaffiliated, unallied, uninvolved; non-combatant. **3** *a neutral topic of conversation* INOFFENSIVE, bland, unobjectionable, unexceptionable, anodyne, unremarkable, ordinary, commonplace; safe, harmless, innocuous. **4** *a neutral background* PALE, light; beige, cream, taupe, oatmeal, ecru, buff, fawn, grey; colourless, uncoloured, achromatic; indeterminate, insipid, nondescript, dull, drab.

– OPPOSITES biased, partisan, provocative, colourful.

neutralize ● verb COUNTERACT, offset, counterbalance, balance, counterpoise, countervail, compensate for, make up for; cancel out, nullify, negate, negative; equalize.

never ● adverb **1** *his room is never tidy* NOT EVER, at no time, not at any time, not once; *poetic/literary* ne'er. **2** *she will never agree to it* NOT AT ALL, certainly not, not for a moment, under no circumstances, on no account; *informal* no way, not on your life, not in a million years; *Brit. informal* not on your nelly.

– OPPOSITES always, definitely.

never-ending ● adjective **1** *never-ending noise* INCESSANT, continuous, unceasing, ceaseless, constant, continual, perpetual, unfaltering, uninterrupted, unbroken, steady, unremitting, relentless, persistent, interminable, non-stop, endless, unending, everlasting, eternal. **2** *never-ending tasks* ENDLESS, countless, innumerable, numberless, untold, unlimited, limitless, boundless; *poetic/literary* myriad.

nevertheless ● adverb NONETHELESS, even so, however, but, still, yet, though; in spite of that, despite that, be that as it may, for all that, that said, just the same, all the same; notwithstanding, regardless, anyway, anyhow; *informal* still and all.

new ● adjective **1** *new technology* RECENTLY DEVELOPED, up to date, latest, current, state-of-the-art, contemporary, advanced, recent, modern. **2** *new ideas* NOVEL, original, fresh, imaginative, creative, experimental; contemporary, modernist, up to date; newfangled, ultra-modern, avant-garde, futuristic; *informal* way out, far out. **3** *is your boat new?* UNUSED, brand new, pristine, fresh, in mint condition. **4** *new neighbours moved in* DIFFERENT, another, alternative; unfamiliar, unknown, strange; unaccustomed, untried. **5** *they had a new classroom built* ADDITIONAL, extra, supplementary, further, another, fresh. **6** *I came back a completely new woman* REINVIGORATED, restored, revived, improved, refreshed, regenerated, reborn, renewed.

– RELATED TERMS neo-.

– OPPOSITES old, hackneyed, second-hand, present.

newborn ● adjective *newborn babies* JUST BORN, recently born. ● noun *the bacteria are fatal to newborns* YOUNG BABY, tiny baby, infant; *Medicine* neonate.

newcomer ● noun **1** *a newcomer to the village* (NEW) ARRIVAL, immigrant, incomer, settler; stranger, outsider, foreigner, alien; *N. English* offcomer; *informal* johnny-come-lately, new kid on the block; *Austral. informal* blow-in. **2** *photography tips for the newcomer* BEGINNER,

– ORIGIN from dialect *newfangle* 'liking what is new'.
Newfoundland /nyoofowndlənd/ • noun a dog of a very large breed with a thick coarse coat.
– ORIGIN named after *Newfoundland* in Canada.
New Guinean • noun a person from New Guinea. • adjective relating to New Guinea.
newly • adverb **1** recently. **2** again; afresh. **3** in a new or different manner.
newly-wed • noun a recently married person.
new man • noun a man who rejects sexist attitudes and the traditional male role.
new maths (N. Amer. **new math**) • plural noun (usu. treated as sing.) a system of teaching mathematics to children, with emphasis on investigation by them and on set theory.
new moon • noun the phase of the moon when it first appears as a slender crescent.
news • noun **1** newly received or noteworthy information about recent events. **2** (**the news**) a broadcast or published news report. **3** (**news to**) informal information not previously known to.
– PHRASES **no news is good news** proverb without information to the contrary you can assume that all is well.
news agency • noun an organization that collects and distributes news items.
newsagent • noun Brit. a person or shop selling newspapers, magazines, etc.
newsboy • noun a boy who sells or delivers newspapers.
newscast • noun a broadcast news report.
newscaster • noun a newsreader.
news conference • noun a press conference.
newsflash • noun a single item of important news broadcast separately and often interrupting other programmes.
newsgroup • noun a group of Internet users who exchange email on a topic of mutual interest.
newsletter • noun a bulletin issued periodically to those in a particular group.
newsman • noun a male reporter or journalist.
newspaper • noun a daily or weekly publication consisting of folded unstapled sheets and containing news, articles, and advertisements.
newspeak • noun ambiguous euphemistic language used in political propaganda.
– ORIGIN the name of an artificial official language in George Orwell's novel *Nineteen Eighty-Four* (1949).
newsprint • noun cheap, low-quality absorbent printing paper used for newspapers.
newsreader • noun Brit. a person who reads out broadcast news bulletins.
newsreel • noun a short cinema film of news and current affairs.
newsroom • noun the area in a newspaper or broadcasting office where news is processed.
news-stand • noun a stand for the sale of newspapers.
New Stone Age • noun the Neolithic period.
New Style • noun the calculation of dates using the Gregorian calendar.
news wire • noun an Internet news service.
newsworthy • adjective noteworthy as news.
newsy • adjective informal full of news.
newt • noun a small slender-bodied amphibian with a well-developed tail.
– ORIGIN from *an ewt* (from Old English *efeta* 'eft'), interpreted (by wrong division) as *a newt*.
New Testament • noun the second part of the Christian Bible, recording the life and teachings of Christ and his earliest followers.
newton • noun Physics the SI unit of force, equal to the force that would give a mass of one kilogram an acceleration of one metre per second per second.
– ORIGIN named after the English scientist Sir Isaac *Newton* (1642–1727).
Newtonian • adjective Physics relating to or arising from the work of Sir Isaac Newton.
new town • noun a planned urban centre created in an undeveloped or rural area.
new wave • noun **1** another term for NOUVELLE VAGUE. **2** a style of rock music popular in the late 1970s, deriving from punk.
New World • noun North and South America regarded collectively, in contrast to Europe, Asia, and Africa.
new year • noun **1** the calendar year just begun or about to begin. **2** the period immediately before and after 31 December.
New Year's Day • noun 1 January.
New Year's Eve • noun 31 December.
New Yorker • noun a person from the state or city of New York.
New Zealander • noun a person from New Zealand.
next • adjective **1** coming immediately after the present one in time, space, or order. **2** (of a day of the week) nearest (or the nearest but one) after the present. • adverb **1** immediately afterwards. **2** following in the specified order: *the next oldest.* • noun the next person or thing.
– PHRASES **next of kin** a person's closest living relative or relatives. **next to 1** beside. **2** following in order or importance. **3** almost. **4** in comparison with. **the next world** (in some religious beliefs) the place where one goes after death.
– ORIGIN Old English.
next door • adverb & adjective in or to the next house or room.
– PHRASES **next door to 1** in the next house or room to. **2** almost.
nexus /neksəss/ • noun (pl. same or **nexuses**) **1** a connection. **2** a connected group or series. **3** the central and most important point.
– ORIGIN Latin, from *nectere* 'bind'.
Nez Percé /nez perss, persay/ • noun (pl. same or **Nez Percés**) a member of an American Indian people of central Idaho.
– ORIGIN French, 'pierced nose'.
NF • abbreviation **1** National Front. **2** Newfoundland.
NFL • abbreviation (in the US) National Football League.
ngaio /nīō/ • noun (pl. **ngaios**) a small New Zealand tree with edible fruit and light white wood.
– ORIGIN Maori.
NGO • abbreviation non-governmental organization.
ngultrum /ənggoōltrəm/ • noun (pl. same) the basic monetary unit of Bhutan, equal to 100 chetrum.
– ORIGIN from Dzongkha, the official language of Bhutan.
ngwee /əngway/ • noun (pl. same) a monetary unit of Zambia, equal to one hundredth of a kwacha.
– ORIGIN a local word.
NH • abbreviation New Hampshire.
NHS • abbreviation (in the UK) National Health Service.
NI • abbreviation **1** (in the UK) National Insurance. **2** Northern Ireland.
Ni • symbol the chemical element nickel.
niacin /nīəsin/ • noun another term for NICOTINIC ACID.

n

Thesaurus

novice, learner; trainee, apprentice, probationer, tyro, initiate, neophyte; *N. Amer.* tenderfoot; *informal* rookie, newbie; *N. Amer. informal* greenhorn.
newfangled • adjective NEW, the latest, modern, ultra-modern, up to the minute, state-of-the-art, advanced, contemporary; new-fashioned; *informal* trendy, flash.
– OPPOSITES dated.
newly • adverb RECENTLY, (only) just, lately, freshly; not long ago, a short time ago, only now, of late; new-.
news • noun REPORT, announcement, story, account; article, news flash, newscast, headlines, press release, communication, communiqué, bulletin; message, dispatch, statement, intelligence; disclosure, revelation, word, talk, gossip; *informal* scoop; *poetic/literary* tidings.
newspaper • noun PAPER, journal, gazette, news-sheet; tabloid, broadsheet, quality (paper), national (paper), local (paper), daily (paper), weekly (paper); free sheet, scandal sheet; *informal* rag; *N. Amer. informal* tab.
newsworthy • adjective INTERESTING, topical, notable, noteworthy, important, significant, momentous, historic, remarkable, sensational.
– OPPOSITES unremarkable.
next • adjective **1** *the next chapter* FOLLOWING, succeeding, upcoming, to come. **2** *the next house in the street* NEIGHBOURING, adjacent, adjoining, next-door, bordering, connected, attached; closest, nearest.
– OPPOSITES previous.
• adverb *where shall we go next?* THEN, after, afterwards, after this/that, following that/this, later, subsequently; *formal* thereafter, thereupon.
– OPPOSITES before.
– PHRASES **next to** BESIDE, by, alongside, by the side of, next door

nib • noun **1** the pointed end part of a pen, which distributes the ink. **2** (**nibs**) shelled and crushed coffee or cocoa beans.
– ORIGIN originally in the sense 'beak, nose': probably from Dutch *nib* or Low German *nibbe*, related to NEB.
nibble • verb **1** take small bites out of. **2** gently bite at. **3** gradually erode. **4** show cautious interest in a project. • noun **1** an instance of nibbling. **2** a small piece of food bitten off. **3** (**nibbles**) informal small savoury snacks.
– ORIGIN probably Low German or Dutch.
niblet • noun a small piece of food.
niblick /niblik/ • noun Golf, dated an iron with a heavy, lofted head, used for playing out of bunkers.
– ORIGIN of unknown origin.
nibs • noun (**his nibs**) informal a mock title used to refer to a self-important man.
– ORIGIN of unknown origin.
NiCad /nīkad/ (also US trademark **Nicad**) • noun a battery or cell containing nickel, cadmium, and potassium hydroxide.
– ORIGIN blend of NICKEL and CADMIUM.
Nicam /nīkam/ • noun a digital system used in British television to provide video signals with high-quality stereo sound.
– ORIGIN acronym from *near instantaneously companded* (i.e. compressed and expanded) *audio multiplex*.
Nicaraguan /nikkəragyooən/ • noun a person from Nicaragua in Central America. • adjective relating to Nicaragua.
nice • adjective **1** pleasant; agreeable; satisfactory. **2** good-natured; kind. **3** (**nice and ——**) satisfactory in terms of the quality described. **4** fine or subtle: *a nice distinction*. **5** archaic fastidious.
– DERIVATIVES **nicely** adverb **niceness** noun.
– ORIGIN original senses included 'stupid' and 'coy, reserved': from Latin *nescius* 'ignorant'.
nicety • noun (pl. **niceties**) **1** a fine detail or distinction. **2** accuracy. **3** a detail of etiquette.
– PHRASES **to a nicety** precisely.
niche /neesh, nitch/ • noun **1** a shallow recess, especially one in a wall to display an ornament. **2** (**one's niche**) a comfortable or suitable position in life. **3** a specialized but profitable corner of the market. **4** Ecology a role taken by a type of organism within its community.
– ORIGIN French, 'recess', from Latin *nidus* 'nest'.
nick[1] • noun **1** a small cut or notch. **2** (**the nick**) Brit. informal prison or police station. **3** Brit. informal condition: *in good nick*. **4** the junction between the floor and side walls in a squash court. • verb **1** make a nick or nicks in. **2** Brit. informal steal. **3** Brit. informal arrest.
– PHRASES **in the nick of time** only just in time.
– ORIGIN of unknown origin.
nick[2] • verb (often **nick off**) Austral./NZ informal go quickly or furtively.
– ORIGIN probably a figurative use of NICK[1] in the sense 'to steal'.
nickel • noun **1** a silvery-white metallic chemical element resembling iron, used in alloys. **2** N. Amer. informal a five-cent coin. • verb (**nickelled**, **nickelling**; US **nickeled**, **nickeling**) coat with nickel.
– ORIGIN from German *Kupfernickel*, the copper-coloured ore from which nickel was first obtained, from *Kupfer* 'copper' + *Nickel* 'demon' (with reference to the ore's failure to yield copper).
nickel-and-dime • adjective N. Amer. of little importance; petty.
– ORIGIN originally denoting a store selling articles at five or ten cents.
nickel brass • noun an alloy of copper, zinc, and nickel.
nickelodeon /nikkəlōdiən/ • noun N. Amer. **1** informal, dated a jukebox. **2** historical a cinema charging one nickel.
– ORIGIN from NICKEL (the coin) + a shortened form of MELODEON.
nickel silver • noun another term for GERMAN SILVER.
nickel steel • noun stainless steel containing chromium and nickel.
nicker[1] • noun (pl. same) Brit. informal a pound sterling.
– ORIGIN of unknown origin.
nicker[2] • verb (of a horse) give a soft breathy whinny. • noun a nickering sound.
– ORIGIN imitative.
nick-nack • noun variant spelling of KNICK-KNACK.
nickname • noun a familiar or humorous name for a person or thing. • verb give a nickname to.
– ORIGIN from *an eke-name* (*eke* meaning 'addition': see EKE[2]), misinterpreted (by wrong division) as *a neke name*.
Niçois /neeswaa/ (also **Niçoise** /neeswaaz/) • adjective (after a noun) garnished with tomatoes, capers, and anchovies: *salade Niçoise*.
– ORIGIN French, 'relating to the city of Nice'.
nicotiana /nikkotiaanə/ • noun an ornamental plant related to tobacco, with tubular flowers that are particularly fragrant at night.
nicotine • noun a toxic oily liquid which is the chief active constituent of tobacco.
– ORIGIN named after Jaques *Nicot*, a 16th-century diplomat who introduced tobacco to France.
nicotine patch • noun a patch impregnated with nicotine, worn on the skin by a person trying to give up smoking.
nicotinic acid • noun Biochemistry a vitamin of the B complex which occurs in milk, wheat germ, meat, and other foods.
nictation • noun technical blinking.
– ORIGIN Latin, from *nictare* 'to blink'.
nictitating membrane • noun Zoology a whitish membrane forming an inner eyelid in birds, reptiles, and some mammals.
nidification /niddifikaysh'n/ • noun Zoology nest-building.
– ORIGIN Latin, from *nidus* 'nest'.
nidus /nīdəss/ • noun (pl. **nidi** /nīdī/ or **niduses**) **1** a place in which something is formed or deposited. **2** Medicine a place in which bacteria have multiplied or may multiply.
– ORIGIN Latin, 'nest'.
niece • noun a daughter of one's brother or sister, or of one's brother-in-law or sister-in-law.
– ORIGIN Old French, from Latin *neptis* 'granddaughter'.
niello /niellō/ • noun **1** a black compound of sulphur with silver, lead, or copper, used for filling in engraved designs in silver or other metals. **2** objects decorated with niello.
– ORIGIN Italian, from Latin *niger* 'black'.
Nietzschean /neechiən/ • adjective relating to the German philosopher Friedrich Wilhelm Nietzsche (1844–1900).
niff Brit. informal • noun an unpleasant smell. • verb stink.
– DERIVATIVES **niffy** adjective.
– ORIGIN perhaps from SNIFF.
nifty • adjective (**niftier**, **niftiest**) informal particularly good, effective, or stylish.
– DERIVATIVES **niftily** adverb.

n

Thesaurus

to, adjacent to, side by side with; close to, near, neighbouring, adjoining.
nibble • verb **1** *they nibbled at mangoes* TAKE SMALL BITES (FROM), pick, gnaw, peck, snack on; toy with; taste, sample; *informal* graze (on). **2** *the mouse nibbled his finger* PECK, nip, bite.
• noun **1** *the fish enjoyed a nibble on the lettuce* BITE, gnaw, chew; taste. **2** *(informal) nuts and nibbles* MORSEL, mouthful, bite; snack, titbit, canapé, hors d'oeuvre, bonne bouche.
nice • adjective **1** *have a nice time* ENJOYABLE, pleasant, agreeable, good, satisfying, gratifying, delightful, marvellous; entertaining, amusing, diverting; *informal* lovely, great; *N. Amer. informal* neat. **2** *nice people* PLEASANT, likeable, agreeable, personable, congenial, amiable, affable, genial, friendly, charming, delightful, engaging; sympathetic, compassionate, good. **3** *nice manners* POLITE, courteous, civil, refined, polished, genteel, elegant. **4** *that's a rather nice distinction* SUBTLE, fine, delicate, minute, precise, strict, close; careful, meticulous, scrupulous. **5** *it's a nice day* FINE, pleasant, agreeable; dry, sunny, warm, mild.
– OPPOSITES unpleasant, nasty, rough.
nicety • noun **1** *legal niceties* SUBTLETY, fine point, nuance, refinement, detail. **2** *great nicety of control* PRECISION, accuracy, exactness, meticulousness.
niche • noun **1** *a niche in the wall* RECESS, alcove, nook, cranny, hollow, bay, cavity, cubbyhole, pigeonhole. **2** *he found his niche in life* IDEAL POSITION, place, function, vocation, calling, métier, job.
nick • noun **1** *a slight nick in the blade* CUT, scratch, incision, snick, notch, chip, gouge, gash; dent, indentation. **2** *(Brit. informal) she's in the nick.* See PRISON. **3** *(Brit. informal) he's under arrest at the nick* POLICE STATION, station; *N. Amer.* precinct, station house; *informal* cop shop. **4** *(Brit. informal) the car's in good nick* CONDITION, repair, shape, state, order, form, fettle, trim.
• verb **1** *I nicked my toe* CUT, scratch, incise, snick, gouge, gash, score. **2** *(Brit. informal) she nicked his wallet.* See STEAL verb sense 1. **3** *(Brit. informal) Steve's been nicked.* See ARREST verb sense 1.
– PHRASES **in the nick of time** JUST IN TIME, not a moment too soon, at the critical moment; *N. Amer. informal* under the wire.

– ORIGIN of unknown origin.

nigella /nijellə/ ● noun a plant of a genus which includes love-in-a-mist.
– ORIGIN Latin, from *niger* 'black'.

Niger–Congo ● adjective denoting or belonging to a large group of languages in Africa, named after the Rivers Niger and Congo.

Nigerian /nījeeriən/ ● noun a person from Nigeria. ● adjective relating to Nigeria.

niggard /niggərd/ ● noun a miserly person.
– ORIGIN Scandinavian.

niggardly ● adjective ungenerous or meagre.

nigger ● noun offensive a black person.
– PHRASES **a nigger in the woodpile** dated a hidden cause of trouble.
– USAGE The word **nigger** has had strong offensive connotations since the 17th century. Recently, however, it has begun to be used by black people as a mildly disparaging or ironically affectionate way of referring to other black people. Despite this, when used by white people it remains strongly offensive, and should be avoided.
– ORIGIN from Spanish *negro* 'black'.

niggle ● verb **1** cause slight but persistent annoyance, discomfort, or anxiety. **2** find fault with in a petty way. ● noun a trifling worry, dispute, or criticism.
– DERIVATIVES **niggly** adjective.
– ORIGIN apparently Scandinavian.

nigh ● adverb, preposition, & adjective archaic near.
– ORIGIN Old English.

night ● noun **1** the time from sunset to sunrise. **2** the darkness of night. **3** literary nightfall. **4** an evening. ● adverb (**nights**) informal at night.
– ORIGIN Old English.

night blindness ● noun less technical term for NYCTALOPIA.

nightcap ● noun **1** historical a cap worn in bed. **2** a hot or alcoholic drink taken at bedtime.

nightclothes ● plural noun clothes worn in bed.

nightclub ● noun a club that is open at night, usually having a bar and disco.

nightdress ● noun a light, loose garment worn by a woman or girl in bed.

nightfall ● noun dusk.

nightgown ● noun **1** a nightdress. **2** archaic a dressing gown.

nightie ● noun informal a nightdress.

nightingale ● noun a small brownish migratory thrush noted for its rich melodious song, often heard at night.
– ORIGIN Old English, from NIGHT and a base meaning 'sing'.

nightjar ● noun a nocturnal bird with grey-brown camouflaged plumage, large eyes and gape, and a distinctive call.

nightlife ● noun social activities or entertainment available at night.

night light ● noun a lamp or candle providing a dim light during the night.

nightly ● adjective **1** happening or done every night. **2** happening, done, or existing in the night. ● adverb every night.

nightmare ● noun **1** a frightening or unpleasant dream. **2** a very unpleasant experience or prospect.
– DERIVATIVES **nightmarish** adjective.
– ORIGIN originally denoting a female evil spirit thought to lie upon and suffocate sleepers: from Old English *mære* 'incubus'.

night owl (also **night bird**) ● noun informal a person who is habitually active or wakeful at night.

night safe ● noun Brit. a safe with access from the outer wall of a bank, used for deposits when the bank is closed.

night school ● noun an institution providing evening classes.

nightshirt ● noun a long shirt worn in bed.

nightside ● noun Astronomy the side of a planet or moon facing away from the sun and therefore in darkness.

night soil ● noun human excrement collected at night from cesspools and privies.

nightspot ● noun informal a nightclub.

nightstick ● noun N. Amer. a police officer's truncheon.

nightwatchman ● noun **1** a person who guards a building at night. **2** Cricket an inferior batsman sent in to bat near the end of a day's play.

nigrescent /nigress'nt/ ● adjective literary blackish.
– DERIVATIVES **nigrescence** noun.
– ORIGIN from Latin *nigrescere* 'grow black'.

nigritude /nigrityōōd/ ● noun archaic blackness.

nihilism /nīhiliz'm/ ● noun **1** the rejection of all religious and moral principles. **2** Philosophy extreme scepticism, maintaining that nothing has a real existence.
– DERIVATIVES **nihilist** noun **nihilistic** adjective.
– ORIGIN from Latin *nihil* 'nothing'.

nihil obstat /nīhil obstat/ ● noun (in the Roman Catholic Church) a certificate affirming that a book is not open to objection on doctrinal or moral grounds.
– ORIGIN Latin, 'nothing hinders'.

-nik ● suffix (forming nouns) denoting a person associated with a specified thing or quality: *beatnik*.
– ORIGIN from Russian (on the pattern of *sputnik*) and Yiddish.

Nikkei index /nikkay/ (also **Nikkei average**) ● noun a figure indicating the relative price of representative shares on the Tokyo Stock Exchange.
– ORIGIN abbreviation of *Ni(hon) Kei(zai Shimbun)* 'Japanese Economic Journal'.

nil ● noun nothing; zero. ● adjective non-existent.
– ORIGIN Latin, contraction of *nihil* 'nothing'.

nil desperandum /nil despərandəm/ ● exclamation do not despair.
– ORIGIN from Latin *nil desperandum Teucro duce* 'no need to despair with Teucer as your leader', from Horace's *Odes* 1.vii.27.

Nilotic /nīlottik/ ● adjective **1** relating to the River Nile or to the Nile region of Africa. **2** referring or belonging to a family of

Thesaurus

nickname ● noun SOBRIQUET, byname, tag, label, epithet, cognomen; pet name, diminutive, endearment; *informal* moniker; *formal* appellation.

nifty ● adjective (*informal*) **1** *nifty camerawork* SKILFUL, deft, agile, capable. **2** *a nifty little gadget* USEFUL, handy, practical. **3** *a nifty suit* FASHIONABLE, stylish, smart.
– OPPOSITES clumsy.

niggardly ● adjective **1** *a niggardly person* MEAN, miserly, parsimonious, close-fisted, penny-pinching, cheese-paring, grasping, ungenerous, illiberal; *informal* stingy, tight, tight-fisted; *N. Amer. informal* cheap. **2** *niggardly rations* MEAGRE, inadequate, scanty, scant, skimpy, paltry, sparse, insufficient, deficient, short, lean, small, slender, poor, miserable, pitiful, puny; *informal* measly, stingy, pathetic, piddling.
– OPPOSITES generous.

niggle ● verb **1** *his behaviour does niggle me* IRRITATE, annoy, bother, provoke, exasperate, upset, gall, irk, rankle with; *informal* rile, get to, bug. **2** *he niggles on about taxes* COMPLAIN, fuss, carp, cavil, grumble, grouse; *informal* moan, nit-pick.
● noun *niggles about the lack of equipment* QUIBBLE, trivial complaint, criticism, grumble, grouse, cavil; *informal* gripe, moan, beef, grouch.

night ● noun night-time; (hours of) darkness, dark.
– RELATED TERMS nocturnal.
– OPPOSITES day.
– PHRASES **night and day** ALL THE TIME, around the clock, {morning, noon, and night}, {day in, day out}, ceaselessly, endlessly, incessantly, unceasingly, interminably, constantly, perpetually, continually, relentlessly; *informal* 24-7.

nightclub ● noun DISCO, discotheque, night spot, club, bar; *N. Amer.* cafe; *informal* niterie.

nightfall ● noun SUNSET, sundown, dusk, twilight, evening, close of day, dark; *poetic/literary* eventide.
– OPPOSITES dawn.

nightly ● adjective **1** *nightly raids* EVERY NIGHT, each night, night after night. **2** *his nightly wanderings* NOCTURNAL, night-time.
● adverb *a band plays there nightly* EVERY NIGHT, each night, night after night.

nightmare ● noun **1** *she woke from a nightmare* BAD DREAM, night terrors; *archaic* incubus. **2** *the journey was a nightmare* ORDEAL, trial, torment, horror, hell, misery, agony, torture, murder; curse, bane.

nightmarish ● adjective UNEARTHLY, spine-chilling, hair-raising, horrific, macabre, hideous, unspeakable, gruesome, grisly, ghastly, harrowing, disturbing; *informal* scary, creepy.

nihilism ● noun SCEPTICISM, disbelief, unbelief, agnosticism, atheism; negativity, cynicism, pessimism; rejection, denial.

nihilist ● noun SCEPTIC, disbeliever, unbeliever, agnostic, atheist; negativist, cynic, pessimist.

nil ● noun NOTHING, none; nought, zero, 0; *Tennis* love; *Cricket* a duck;

languages spoken in Egypt, Sudan, Kenya, and Tanzania.
– ORIGIN Greek *Neilōtikos*, from *Neilos* 'Nile'.

nimble ● adjective (**nimbler**, **nimblest**) quick and agile in movement, action, or thought.
– DERIVATIVES **nimbly** adverb.
– ORIGIN Old English.

nimbostratus /nimbōstraytəss, -straatəss/ ● noun cloud forming a low thick grey layer, from which rain or snow often falls.

nimbus /nimbəss/ ● noun (pl. **nimbi** /nimbī/ or **nimbuses**) **1** a large grey rain cloud. **2** a luminous cloud or a halo surrounding a supernatural being or saint.
– ORIGIN Latin, 'cloud, aureole'.

Nimby /nimbi/ ● noun (pl. **Nimbys**) informal a person who objects to the siting of unpleasant developments in their neighbourhood.
– ORIGIN acronym from *not in my back yard*.

niminy-piminy ● adjective affectedly prim or refined.
– ORIGIN fanciful coinage.

nimrod /nimrod/ ● noun a skilful hunter.
– ORIGIN from the great-grandson of Noah, known for his skill as a hunter (see Book of Genesis, chapter 10).

nincompoop /ningkəmpoop/ ● noun informal a stupid person.
– ORIGIN perhaps from the given name *Nicholas*, or from the name of the Pharisee *Nicodemus*, known for his naive questioning of Christ.

nine ● cardinal number **1** one less than ten; 9. (Roman numeral: **ix** or **IX**.) **2** (**the Nine**) Greek Mythology the nine Muses.
– PHRASES **dressed (up) to the nines** dressed very smartly or fancily.
– ORIGIN Old English.

ninepins ● plural noun (usu. treated as sing.) the traditional form of the game of skittles, using nine pins.
– PHRASES **go down** (or **drop** or **fall**) **like ninepins** succumb in large numbers.

nineteen ● cardinal number one more than eighteen; 19. (Roman numeral: **xix** or **XIX**.)
– DERIVATIVES **nineteenth** ordinal number.

nineteenth hole ● noun informal, humorous the bar in a golf clubhouse, as reached after a round of eighteen holes.

ninety ● cardinal number (pl. **nineties**) ten less than one hundred; 90. (Roman numeral: **xc** or **XC**.)
– DERIVATIVES **ninetieth** ordinal number.

ninja /ninjə/ ● noun a person skilled in ninjutsu.
– ORIGIN Japanese, 'spy'.

ninjutsu /ninjootsoo/ ● noun the traditional Japanese technique of espionage, characterized by stealth and camouflage.
– ORIGIN Japanese, 'art or science of stealth'.

ninny ● noun (pl. **ninnies**) informal a foolish and weak person.
– ORIGIN perhaps from INNOCENT.

ninth ● ordinal number **1** constituting number nine in a sequence; 9th. **2** (**a ninth/one ninth**) each of nine equal parts into which something is divided. **3** Music an interval spanning nine consecutive notes in a diatonic scale.
– DERIVATIVES **ninthly** adverb.

niobium /nīōbiəm/ ● noun a silver-grey metallic chemical element.
– ORIGIN from *Niobe*, daughter of Tantalus in Greek mythology (because the element was first found in the substance *tantalite*).

Nip ● noun informal, offensive a Japanese person.
– ORIGIN abbreviation of *Nipponese*, from *Nippon* (the Japanese name for Japan).

nip[1] ● verb (**nipped**, **nipping**) **1** pinch, squeeze, or bite sharply. **2** (of cold or frost) cause pain or harm to. **3** Brit. informal go quickly. ● noun **1** an act of nipping. **2** a feeling of biting cold.
– PHRASES **nip in the bud** suppress or destroy at an early stage.
– ORIGIN probably Low German or Dutch.

nip[2] ● noun a small quantity or sip of spirits.
– ORIGIN probably an abbreviation of archaic *nipperkin* 'small measure'.

nip and tuck ● adverb & adjective closely contested; neck and neck. ● noun informal a cosmetic surgical operation.

nipper ● noun **1** informal a child. **2** (**nippers**) pliers, pincers, or a similar tool. **3** the claw of a crab or lobster.

nipple ● noun **1** the small projection in which the mammary ducts of female mammals terminate and from which milk can be secreted. **2** the corresponding vestigial structure in a male. **3** a small projection on a machine from which oil or other fluid is dispensed. **4** a short section of pipe with a screw thread at each end for coupling.
– ORIGIN perhaps a diminutive of NEB.

nipplewort ● noun a yellow-flowered plant found in woods and on wasteland.

nippy ● adjective (**nippier**, **nippiest**) informal **1** quick; nimble. **2** chilly.

nirvana /nərvaanə/ ● noun **1** the ultimate goal of Buddhism, a state in which there is no suffering or desire, and no sense of self. **2** a state of perfect happiness.
– ORIGIN Sanskrit, from a word meaning 'be extinguished'.

Nissen hut /niss'n/ ● noun chiefly Brit. a tunnel-shaped hut of corrugated iron with a cement floor.
– ORIGIN named after the British engineer Peter N. *Nissen* (1871–1930).

nit ● noun informal **1** the egg or young form of a parasitic insect, especially the egg of a human head louse. **2** Brit. a stupid person.
– ORIGIN Old English.

niterie /nītəri/ ● noun (pl. **niteries**) informal a nightclub.

nit-picking ● noun informal fussy or pedantic fault-finding.
– DERIVATIVES **nit-pick** verb **nit-picker** noun.

nitrate /nītrayt/ ● noun a salt or ester of nitric acid. ● verb treat with nitric acid.
– DERIVATIVES **nitration** noun.

nitre /nītər/ (US **niter**) ● noun potassium nitrate; saltpetre.
– ORIGIN Old French, from Greek *nitron*.

nitric acid ● noun a colourless or pale yellow acid with strong corrosive and oxidizing properties.

nitric oxide ● noun a colourless toxic gas that reacts with oxygen to form nitrogen dioxide.

nitride /nītrīd/ ● noun a compound of nitrogen with another element or group.

nitrify /nītrifī/ ● verb (**nitrifies**, **nitrified**) convert (ammonia or another nitrogen compound) into nitrites or nitrates.
– DERIVATIVES **nitrification** noun.

nitrile /nītrīl/ ● noun an organic compound containing a cyanide group.

nitrite /nītrīt/ ● noun a salt or ester of nitrous acid.

nitro ● noun short for NITROGLYCERINE.

nitro- /nītrō/ ● combining form of or containing nitric acid, nitrates, or nitrogen.

nitrobenzene ● noun a yellow oily liquid made by nitrating benzene, used in chemical synthesis.

nitrocellulose ● noun a highly flammable material used to make explosives and celluloid.

n

Thesaurus

N. English nowt; *informal* zilch, nix, not a dicky bird; *Brit. informal* sweet Fanny Adams, sweet FA, not a sausage; *N. Amer. informal* zip, nada, a goose egg; *dated* cipher; *archaic* naught.

nimble ● adjective **1** *he was nimble on his feet* AGILE, sprightly, light, spry, lively, quick, graceful, lithe, limber; skilful, deft, dextrous, adroit; *informal* nippy, twinkle-toed; *poetic/literary* lightsome. **2** *a nimble mind* QUICK-WITTED, quick, alert, lively, wide awake, observant, astute, perceptive, penetrating, discerning, shrewd, sharp; intelligent, bright, smart, clever, brilliant; *informal* brainy, quick on the uptake.
– OPPOSITES clumsy, dull.

nincompoop ● noun *(informal)*. See IDIOT.

nine ● cardinal number NONET.
– RELATED TERMS nona-.

nip ● verb **1** *the child nipped her* BITE, nibble, peck; pinch, tweak, squeeze, grip. **2** *(Brit. informal) I'm just nipping out* RUSH, dash, dart, hurry, scurry, scamper; go; *informal* pop, whip.
● noun *penguins can give a serious nip* BITE, peck, nibble; pinch, tweak.
– PHRASES **nip something in the bud** CUT SHORT, curtail, check, curb, thwart, frustrate, stop, halt, arrest, stifle, obstruct, block, squash, quash, subdue, crack down on, stamp out; *informal* put the kibosh on. **nip something off** CUT, snip, trim, clip, prune, lop, dock, crop; remove, take off.

nipple ● noun TEAT, dug; *Anatomy* mamilla.

nippy ● adjective *(informal)* **1** *he's too big to be nippy* AGILE, light-footed, nimble, light on one's feet, spry, supple, limber; *informal* twinkle-toed; *poetic/literary* lightsome. **2** *a nippy hatchback* FAST, quick, lively; *informal* zippy. **3** *it's a bit nippy in here* COLD, chilly, icy, bitter, raw.
– OPPOSITES lumbering, slow, warm.

nirvana ● noun PARADISE, heaven; bliss, ecstasy, joy, peace, seren-

nitrogen /nītrəjən/ ● **noun** a colourless, odourless, relatively unreactive gaseous chemical element, forming about 78 per cent of the earth's atmosphere.
– DERIVATIVES **nitrogenous** adjective.
nitrogen dioxide ● **noun** a reddish-brown poisonous gas formed when many metals dissolve in nitric acid.
nitrogen narcosis ● **noun** Medicine a drowsy state induced by breathing air under pressure, e.g. in deep-sea diving.
nitroglycerine (also **nitroglycerin**) ● **noun** an explosive yellow liquid made from glycerol, used in dynamite.
nitrous /nītrəs/ ● **adjective** of or containing nitrogen.
nitrous acid ● **noun** an unstable, weak acid made by the action of acids on nitrites.
nitrous oxide ● **noun** a colourless gas with a sweetish odour, used as an anaesthetic.
nitty-gritty ● **noun** informal the most important aspects or practical details of a matter.
– ORIGIN of unknown origin.
nitwit ● **noun** informal a silly or foolish person.
– ORIGIN apparently from NIT + WIT[1].
nix informal ● **pronoun** nothing. ● **exclamation 1** expressing denial or refusal. **2** Brit. dated used as a warning that a person in authority is approaching. ● **verb** put an end to; cancel.
– ORIGIN German, colloquial variant of *nichts* 'nothing'.
nixie ● **noun** a female water sprite.
– ORIGIN German.
Nizari /nizaari/ ● **noun** a member of an Ismaili Muslim sect led by the Aga Khan.
– ORIGIN named after the 12th-century Egyptian imam *Nizar*.
NJ ● **abbreviation** New Jersey.
NM ● **abbreviation** New Mexico.
nm ● **abbreviation 1** nanometre. **2** (also **n.m.**) nautical mile.
NMR ● **abbreviation** Physics nuclear magnetic resonance.
NNE ● **abbreviation** north-north-east.
NNW ● **abbreviation** north-north-west.
No[1] ● **noun** variant spelling of NOH.
No[2] ● **symbol** the chemical element nobelium.
no ● **determiner 1** not any. **2** quite the opposite of. **3** hardly any. ● **exclamation** used to give a negative response. ● **adverb 1** (with comparative) not at all. **2** Scottish not. ● **noun** (pl. **noes**) a negative answer or decision, especially in voting.
– PHRASES **no longer** not now as formerly. **no through road** a street where passage is blocked or prohibited. **not take no for an answer** persist in spite of refusals. **no two ways about it** no possible doubt about something. **no way** informal under no circumstances; not at all. **or no** or not.
– ORIGIN Old English.
no. ● **abbreviation** number.
– ORIGIN from Latin *numero*, from *numerus*.
n.o. ● **abbreviation** Cricket not out.
no-account ● **adjective** informal, chiefly N. Amer. unimportant or worthless.
Noachian /nōaykiən/ ● **adjective** relating to the biblical patriarch Noah or his time.
nob[1] ● **noun** Brit. informal a person of wealth or high social position.
– DERIVATIVES **nobby** adjective.
– ORIGIN of unknown origin.
nob[2] ● **noun** informal a person's head.
– ORIGIN apparently from KNOB.
no-ball ● **noun** Cricket an unlawfully delivered ball, counting as an extra run to the batting side if not scored from.
nobble ● **verb** Brit. informal **1** try to influence or thwart by underhand or unfair methods. **2** tamper with (a racehorse) to prevent it from winning a race. **3** accost or seize. **4** obtain dishonestly or steal.
– ORIGIN probably from dialect *knobble*, *knubble* 'knock, strike with the knuckles'.
Nobelist /nōbellist/ ● **noun** chiefly N. Amer. a winner of a Nobel Prize.
nobelium /nōbeeliəm/ ● **noun** a very unstable chemical element made by high-energy collisions.
– ORIGIN named after Alfred *Nobel* (see NOBEL PRIZE).
Nobel Prize ● **noun** any of six international prizes awarded annually for outstanding work in physics, chemistry, physiology or medicine, literature, economics, and the promotion of peace.
– ORIGIN named after the Swedish chemist and engineer Alfred *Nobel* (1833–96), who endowed the prizes.
nobility ● **noun 1** the quality of being noble. **2** the aristocracy.
noble ● **adjective** (**nobler**, **noblest**) **1** belonging to the aristocracy. **2** having fine personal qualities or high moral principles. **3** imposing; magnificent. ● **noun 1** (especially in former times) a person of noble rank or birth. **2** a former English gold coin.
– PHRASES **the noble art** (or **science**) (**of self-defence**) chiefly archaic boxing.
– DERIVATIVES **nobly** adverb.
– ORIGIN Old French, from Latin *nobilis* 'noted, high-born'.
noble gas ● **noun** Chemistry any of the gaseous elements helium, neon, argon, krypton, xenon, and radon, which form compounds with difficulty or not at all.
nobleman (or **noblewoman**) ● **noun** a man (or woman) who belongs to the aristocracy; a peer (or peeress).
noble metal ● **noun** a metal (e.g. gold, silver, or platinum) that resists attack by acids and other reagents and does not corrode.
noble rot ● **noun** a grey mould cultivated on grapes in order to perfect certain wines.
noble savage ● **noun** a representative of primitive mankind as idealized in Romantic literature.
noblesse /nōbless/ ● **noun** the nobility of a foreign country.
– PHRASES **noblesse oblige** /obleezh/ privilege entails responsibility.
– ORIGIN French, 'nobility'.
nobody ● **pronoun** no person; no one. ● **noun** (pl. **nobodies**) a person of no importance or authority.
nock Archery ● **noun** a notch at either end of a bow or at the end of an arrow, for receiving the bowstring. ● **verb** fit (an arrow) to the bowstring.
– ORIGIN perhaps from Dutch *nocke* 'point, tip'.
no-claims bonus ● **noun** Brit. a reduction in an insurance premium when no claim has been made during an agreed preceding period.
noctambulist /noktambyoolist/ ● **noun** rare a sleepwalker.
– DERIVATIVES **noctambulism** noun.
– ORIGIN from Latin *nox* 'night' + *ambulare* 'walk'.
noctuid /noktyo͝oid/ ● **noun** Entomology a moth of a large family (Noctuidae) whose members typically have pale or colourful hindwings.
– ORIGIN from Latin *noctua* 'night owl'.
noctule /noktyo͞ol/ ● **noun** a large golden-brown bat.
– ORIGIN Italian *nottola* 'bat'.

Thesaurus

ity, tranquillity; enlightenment.
– OPPOSITES hell.
nit-picking ● **adjective** *(informal)*. See PEDANTIC.
nitty-gritty ● **noun** *(informal)* BASICS, essentials, fundamentals, substance, quintessence, heart of the matter; nub, crux, gist, meat, kernel, marrow; *informal* brass tacks, nuts and bolts.
nitwit ● **noun** *(informal)*. See IDIOT.
no ● **adverb** absolutely not, most certainly not, of course not, under no circumstances, by no means, not at all, negative, never, not really; *informal* nope, nah, not on your life, no way; *Brit. informal* no fear, not on your nelly; *archaic* nay.
– OPPOSITES yes.
nobble ● **verb** *(Brit. informal)* **1** *he nobbled the jury* BRIBE, suborn, buy, pay off, corrupt, get at; influence, persuade, win over, sway, control, manipulate; *informal* grease someone's palm, oil someone's palm. **2** *a stable lad nobbled the horse* DRUG, dope; tamper with, interfere with; disable, incapacitate. **3** *I stopped him nobbling her money* STEAL, thieve, embezzle; *informal* rob. **4** *people tried to nobble her at parties* ACCOST, waylay, detain, catch, confront, importune; *informal* buttonhole.
nobility ● **noun 1** *a member of the nobility* ARISTOCRACY, aristocrats, peerage, peers (of the realm), lords, nobles, noblemen, noblewomen, patricians; *informal* aristos; *Brit. informal* nobs. **2** *the nobility of his deed* VIRTUE, goodness, honour, decency, integrity; magnanimity, generosity, selflessness.
noble ● **adjective 1** *a noble family* ARISTOCRATIC, patrician, blue-blooded, high-born, titled; *archaic* gentle. **2** *a noble cause* RIGHTEOUS, virtuous, good, honourable, upright, decent, worthy, moral, ethical, reputable; magnanimous, unselfish, generous. **3** *a noble pine forest* MAGNIFICENT, splendid, grand, stately, imposing, dignified, proud, striking, impressive, majestic, glorious, awesome, monumental, statuesque, regal, imperial.
– OPPOSITES humble, dishonourable, base.
● **noun** *Scottish nobles* ARISTOCRAT, nobleman, noblewoman, lord,

nocturn • noun (in the Roman Catholic Church) a part of matins originally said at night.

nocturnal • adjective done, occurring, or active at night.
– DERIVATIVES **nocturnally** adverb.
– ORIGIN from Latin *nocturnus* 'of the night'.

nocturnal emission • noun an involuntary ejaculation of semen during sleep.

nocturne /noktern/ • noun **1** Music a short composition of a romantic nature. **2** Art a picture of a night scene.
– ORIGIN French.

nod • verb (**nodded**, **nodding**) **1** lower and raise one's head slightly and briefly in greeting, assent, or understanding, or as a signal. **2** let one's head fall forward when drowsy or asleep. **3** (**nod off**) informal fall asleep. **4** make a mistake due to a momentary lack of attention. **5** Soccer head (the ball) without great force. **6** (**nod through**) informal approve (something) by general agreement and without discussion. • noun **1** an act of nodding. **2** a gesture of acknowledgement or concession.
– PHRASES **be on nodding terms** know someone slightly. **give someone/thing the nod 1** select or approve someone or something. **2** give someone a signal. **a nodding acquaintance** a slight acquaintance. **a nod's as good as a wink to a blind horse** said to convey that a hint or suggestion has been understood without the need of further explanation. **on the nod** Brit. informal **1** by general agreement and without discussion. **2** dated on credit.
– ORIGIN perhaps Low German.

noddle • noun informal, dated a person's head.
– ORIGIN of unknown origin.

noddy • noun (pl. **noddies**) **1** dated a silly or foolish person. **2** a tropical tern with mainly dark-coloured plumage.
– ORIGIN sense 2 perhaps refers to the birds' nodding during courtship.

node • noun technical **1** a point in a network at which lines intersect or branch. **2** a computer or other device attached to a network. **3** Botany the part of a plant stem from which one or more leaves emerge. **4** Anatomy a small mass of distinct tissue. **5** Physics & Mathematics a point at which the amplitude of vibration of a wave is zero.
– DERIVATIVES **nodal** adjective.
– ORIGIN Latin *nodus* 'knot'.

nodose /nōdōss/ • adjective technical characterized by hard or tight lumps; knotty.
– DERIVATIVES **nodosity** noun.

nodule • noun **1** a small swelling or aggregation of cells in the body. **2** a swelling on a root of a leguminous plant, containing nitrogen-fixing bacteria. **3** a small rounded lump of matter distinct from its surroundings.
– DERIVATIVES **nodular** adjective.
– ORIGIN Latin *nodulus* 'little knot'.

Noel • noun Christmas.
– ORIGIN French, from Latin *natalis* 'relating to birth'.

noetic /nōettik/ • adjective relating to mental activity or the intellect.
– ORIGIN from Greek *noētos* 'intellectual'.

nog • noun archaic a small block or peg of wood.
– ORIGIN of unknown origin.

noggin • noun informal **1** a person's head. **2** a small quantity of alcoholic drink, typically a quarter of a pint.
– ORIGIN of unknown origin.

nogging • noun **1** brickwork in a timber frame. **2** a horizontal piece of wood fixed to a framework to strengthen it.
– ORIGIN from NOG.

no-go area • noun Brit. an area to which entry is dangerous, impossible, or forbidden.

Noh /nō/ (also **No**) • noun traditional Japanese masked drama with dance and song.
– ORIGIN Japanese.

no-hitter • noun Baseball a game in which a pitcher yields no hits to the opposing team.

no-hoper • noun informal a person who is not expected to be successful.

nohow • adverb informal **1** chiefly US used to emphasize a negative. **2** archaic not well or in good order.

noise • noun **1** a sound, especially one that is loud, unpleasant, or disturbing. **2** continuous or repeated loud, confused sounds. **3** (**noises**) conventional remarks expressing some emotion or purpose. **4** technical irregular fluctuations accompanying and tending to obscure an electrical signal. • verb **1** (usu. **be noised about**) dated talk about or make known publicly. **2** literary make much noise.
– PHRASES **noises off 1** sounds made offstage to be heard by the audience of a play. **2** distracting or intrusive background noise.
– DERIVATIVES **noiseless** adjective.
– ORIGIN Old French, from Latin *nausea* 'nausea, seasickness'.

noisette /nwaazet/ • noun **1** a small round piece of meat. **2** a chocolate made with hazelnuts.
– ORIGIN French, 'little nut'.

noisome /noysəm/ • adjective literary **1** having an extremely offensive smell. **2** disagreeable; unpleasant.
– ORIGIN from obsolete *noy* (shortened form of ANNOY).

noisy • adjective (**noisier**, **noisiest**) full of or making a lot of noise.
– DERIVATIVES **noisily** adverb **noisiness** noun.

nolle prosequi /nolli prossikwī/ • noun Law a formal notice that a plaintiff or prosecutor has abandoned a suit.
– ORIGIN Latin, 'refuse to pursue'.

nomad • noun **1** a member of a people continually moving to find fresh pasture for its animals and having no permanent home. **2** a wanderer.
– DERIVATIVES **nomadism** noun.
– ORIGIN Greek *nomas*, from *nemein* 'to pasture'.

nomadic • adjective having the life of a nomad; wandering.
– DERIVATIVES **nomadically** adverb.

no-man's-land • noun **1** disputed ground between two opposing armies. **2** a piece of unowned land or wasteland.

nom de guerre /nom də gair/ • noun (pl. **noms de guerre** pronunc. same) an assumed name under which a person engages in combat.
– ORIGIN French, 'war name'.

nom de plume /nom də plo͞om/ • noun (pl. **noms de plume** pronunc. same) a pen name.
– ORIGIN French.

nomen /nōmen/ • noun the second personal name of a citizen of ancient Rome, indicating their family, e.g. Marcus *Tullius* Cicero.
– ORIGIN Latin, 'name'.

nomenclature /nōmenkləchər, nōmənklaychər/ • noun **1** the selecting of names for things in a particular field. **2** a body or system of names. **3** formal the term or terms applied to someone or something.
– DERIVATIVES **nomenclatural** /-klachərəl, -kləchoorəl/ adjective.
– ORIGIN Latin *nomenclatura*, from *nomen* 'name' + *clatura* 'calling, summoning'.

nomenklatura /nomenklətyoorə/ • noun (in the former Soviet Union) a list of influential public positions to be filled by Party

n

Thesaurus

lady, peer (of the realm), peeress, patrician; *informal* aristo; *Brit. informal* nob.

nod • verb **1** *she nodded her head* INCLINE, bob, bow, dip, wag. **2** *he nodded to me to start* SIGNAL, gesture, gesticulate, motion, sign, indicate.
• noun **1** *she gave a nod to the manager* SIGNAL, indication, sign, cue; gesture. **2** *a quick nod of his head* INCLINATION, bob, bow, dip.
– PHRASES **give someone the nod 1** *the winger was given the nod* SELECT, choose, pick, go for; *Brit.* cap. **2** *the Lords will give the treaty the nod* APPROVE, agree to, sanction, ratify, endorse, rubber-stamp; *informal* OK, give something the green light, give something the thumbs up. **nod off** *(informal)* FALL ASLEEP, go to sleep, doze off, drop off; *informal* drift off, flake out, go out like a light; *N. Amer. informal* sack out.

node • noun *(technical)* JUNCTION, intersection, interchange, fork, confluence, convergence.

noise • noun SOUND, din, hubbub, clamour, racket, uproar, tumult, commotion, pandemonium, babel; *informal* hullabaloo; *Brit. informal* row.
– OPPOSITES silence.

noisome • adjective *(poetic/literary)*. See ODIOUS.

noisy • adjective **1** *a noisy crowd* ROWDY, clamorous, boisterous, turbulent, rackety; chattering, talkative, vociferous, shouting, screaming. **2** *noisy music* LOUD, fortissimo, blaring, booming, deafening, thunderous, tumultuous, clamorous, ear-splitting, piercing, strident, cacophonous, raucous.
– OPPOSITES quiet, soft.

nomad • noun ITINERANT, traveller, migrant, wanderer, roamer,

appointees.
– ORIGIN Russian, from Latin *nomenclatura*.
nominal • adjective **1** existing in name only. **2** relating to or consisting of names. **3** (of a sum of money) very small; far below the real value or cost. **4** Grammar relating to or functioning as a noun.
– DERIVATIVES **nominally** adverb.
– ORIGIN Latin *nominalis*, from *nomen* 'name'.
nominalism • noun Philosophy the doctrine that universals or general ideas are mere names without any corresponding reality. Often contrasted with REALISM.
– DERIVATIVES **nominalist** noun.
nominalize (also **nominalise**) • verb Grammar form a noun from (a verb or adjective).
– DERIVATIVES **nominalization** noun.
nominal value • noun **1** the face value of a coin, note, etc. **2** the price of a share, bond, or stock when it was issued, rather than its current market value.
nominate • verb **1** put forward as a candidate for election or for an honour or award. **2** appoint to a job or position. **3** specify formally.
– DERIVATIVES **nomination** noun **nominator** noun.
– ORIGIN Latin *nominare* 'to name'.
nominative /**nomm**inətiv/ • adjective **1** Grammar denoting a case of nouns, pronouns, and adjectives expressing the subject of a verb. **2** /**nomm**inaytiv/ of or appointed by nomination as distinct from election. • noun Grammar a word in the nominative case.
nominee • noun **1** a person who is nominated. **2** a person or company in whose name a company, stock, etc. is registered.
-nomy • combining form denoting a specified area of knowledge or its laws: *astronomy*.
– ORIGIN Greek *-nomia*.
non- • prefix expressing negation or absence: *non-recognition*.
– USAGE The prefixes **non-** and **un-** both have the meaning 'not', but tend to be used with a difference of emphasis, **non-** being weaker and more neutral than **un-**. For example, **unnatural** implies that something is not natural in a bad way, whereas **non-natural** is neutral.
– ORIGIN Latin, 'not'.
nona- /**nonn**ə, **nō**nə/ • combining form nine; having nine: *nonagon*.
– ORIGIN from Latin *nonus* 'ninth'.
nonage /**nō**nij, **non**-/ • noun formal the period of immaturity or youth.
– ORIGIN Old French.
nonagenarian /nonəjə**nair**iən, nōn-/ • noun a person between 90 and 99 years old.
– ORIGIN Latin *nonagenarius*, from *nonaginta* 'ninety'.
nonagon /**non**əgən/ • noun a plane figure with nine straight sides and angles.
– DERIVATIVES **nonagonal** adjective.
non-aligned • adjective (chiefly during the cold war) neutral towards the superpowers: *non-aligned countries*.
– DERIVATIVES **non-alignment** noun.
non-allergenic (also **non-allergic**) • adjective not causing an allergic reaction.
non-being • noun the state of not being; non-existence.
non-belligerent • adjective not engaged in a war or conflict. • noun a non-belligerent nation or person.
nonce[1] /nonss/ • adjective (of a word or expression) coined for one occasion.
– PHRASES **for the nonce** for the present; temporarily.
– ORIGIN from obsolete *then anes* 'the one (purpose)' from *then* 'the' + *ane* 'one', altered by wrong division.
nonce[2] /nonss/ • noun Brit. informal a sexual deviant, especially a child molester.
– ORIGIN of unknown origin.
nonchalant /**non**shələnt/ • adjective casually calm and relaxed.
– DERIVATIVES **nonchalance** noun **nonchalantly** adverb.
– ORIGIN French, 'not being concerned'.
non-com • noun Military slang a non-commissioned officer.
non-combatant • noun a person who is not engaged in fighting during a war, especially a civilian, army chaplain, or army doctor.
non-commissioned • adjective (of a military officer) not holding a rank conferred by a commission.
non-committal • adjective not displaying commitment to a definite opinion or policy.
– DERIVATIVES **non-committally** adverb.
non compos mentis /non komposs **men**tiss/ • adjective not in one's right mind.
– ORIGIN Latin, 'not having control of one's mind'.
non-conductor • noun a substance that does not conduct heat or electricity.
– DERIVATIVES **non-conducting** adjective.
nonconformist • noun **1** a person who does not conform to prevailing ideas or established practice. **2** (**Nonconformist**) a member of a Protestant Church which dissents from the established Church of England. • adjective not conforming to prevailing ideas or established practice.
– DERIVATIVES **nonconformism** noun **nonconformity** noun.
non-content • noun a member of the House of Lords who votes against a particular motion.
non-contributory • adjective **1** (of a pension) funded by regular payments by the employer, not the employee. **2** (of a state benefit) paid irrespective of taxes or other contributions made by recipients.
non-cooperation • noun failure to cooperate, especially as a form of protest.
non-delivery • noun chiefly Law failure to provide or deliver goods.
non-denominational • adjective open or acceptable to people of any Christian denomination.
nondescript • adjective lacking distinctive or interesting characteristics.
– ORIGIN originally in the sense 'not previously described scientifically': from NON- + obsolete *descript* 'described, engraved'.
non-destructive • adjective (of methods of testing) not involving damage to the specimen.
none • pronoun **1** not any. **2** no one. • adverb (**none the**) (with com-

Thesaurus

rover; gypsy, Bedouin; transient, drifter, vagabond, vagrant, tramp; *dated* bird of passage.
nominal • adjective **1** *the nominal head of the campaign* IN NAME ONLY, titular, formal, official; theoretical, supposed, ostensible, so-called. **2** *a nominal rent* TOKEN, symbolic; tiny, minute, minimal, small, insignificant, trifling; *Brit.* peppercorn; *informal* minuscule, piddling, piffling; *N. Amer. informal* nickel-and-dime.
– OPPOSITES real, considerable.
nominate • verb **1** *you may nominate a candidate* PROPOSE, recommend, suggest, name, put forward, present, submit. **2** *he nominated his assistant* APPOINT, select, choose, elect, commission, designate, name, delegate.
non-believer • noun UNBELIEVER, disbeliever, sceptic, doubter, doubting Thomas, cynic, nihilist; atheist, agnostic, freethinker; infidel, pagan, heathen.
nonce • adjective *a nonce word* neological; *informal* one-off.
– PHRASES **for the nonce** FOR THE TIME BEING, temporarily, pro tem, for now, for the moment, for the interim, for a while, for the present, in the meantime; provisionally.
nonchalant • adjective CALM, composed, unconcerned, cool, {cool, calm, and collected}, cool as a cucumber; indifferent, blasé, dispassionate, apathetic, casual, insouciant; *informal* laid-back.
– OPPOSITES anxious.
non-combatant • adjective NON-FIGHTING, non-participating, civilian; pacifist, neutral, non-aligned.
non-committal • adjective EVASIVE, equivocal, guarded, circumspect, reserved; discreet, uncommunicative, tactful, diplomatic, vague; *informal* cagey.
– PHRASES **be non-committal** PREVARICATE, give nothing away, dodge the issue, sidestep the issue, hedge, fence, pussyfoot around, beat about the bush, equivocate, temporize, shilly-shally, vacillate, waver; *Brit.* hum and haw; *informal* sit on the fence.
non compos mentis • adjective. See INSANE sense 1.
nonconformist • noun DISSENTER, dissentient, protester, rebel, renegade, schismatic; freethinker, apostate, heretic; individualist, free spirit, maverick, eccentric, original, deviant, misfit, dropout, outsider; *informal* freak, oddball, odd fish, weirdo; *N. Amer. informal* screwball, kook.
nondescript • adjective UNDISTINGUISHED, unremarkable, unexceptional, featureless, characterless, unmemorable; ordinary, commonplace, average, run-of-the-mill, mundane; uninteresting, uninspiring, colourless, bland; *informal* bog-standard; *Brit. informal* com-

parative) by no amount: *none the wiser*.

– USAGE Some traditionalists maintain that **none** can only take a singular verb (as in *none of them is coming tonight* rather than *none of them are coming tonight*). However, **none** is descended from Old English **nān** meaning 'not one', and has been used for around a thousand years with either a singular or a plural verb, depending on the context and the emphasis needed.

– ORIGIN Old English.

nonentity ● noun (pl. **nonentities**) **1** an unimportant person or thing. **2** non-existence.

– ORIGIN Latin *nonentitas* 'non-existence'.

nones /nōnz/ ● plural noun **1** (in the ancient Roman calendar) the ninth day before the ides. **2** a service forming part of the Divine Office of the Western Christian Church, traditionally said at the ninth hour of the day (3 p.m.).

– ORIGIN Latin *nonas*, from *nonus* 'ninth'.

non-essential ● adjective not absolutely necessary. ● noun a non-essential thing.

non est factum /nōn est faktəm/ ● noun Law a plea that a written agreement is invalid because the defendant was mistaken about its character when signing it.

– ORIGIN Latin, 'it was not done'.

nonesuch ● noun variant spelling of NONSUCH.

nonet /nōnet/ ● noun **1** a group of nine. **2** a musical composition for nine voices or instruments.

– ORIGIN Italian *nonetto*.

nonetheless (also **none the less**) ● adverb in spite of that; nevertheless.

non-event ● noun an unexpectedly insignificant or uninteresting occasion.

non-existent ● adjective not existing or not real or present.

– DERIVATIVES **non-existence** noun.

nonfeasance /nonfeez'nss/ ● noun Law failure to perform an act required by law.

– ORIGIN from NON- + *feasance* (see MALFEASANCE).

non-ferrous ● adjective (of metal) other than iron or steel.

non-fiction ● noun prose writing that is informative or factual rather than fictional.

– DERIVATIVES **non-fictional** adjective.

non-flammable ● adjective not catching fire easily.

non-fulfilment ● noun failure to fulfil or carry out something.

non-functional ● adjective **1** having no function. **2** not in working order.

nong /nong/ ● noun Austral./NZ informal a foolish or stupid person.

– ORIGIN of unknown origin.

non-governmental ● adjective not belonging to or associated with any government.

non-inflammable ● adjective not catching fire easily.

non-interference ● noun failure or refusal to interfere.

non-intervention ● noun the policy of not becoming involved in the affairs of others.

– DERIVATIVES **non-interventionist** adjective & noun.

non-invasive ● adjective **1** (of medical procedures) not involving the introduction of instruments into the body. **2** not tending to spread undesirably.

Nonjuror ● noun historical a member of the clergy who refused to take the oath of allegiance to William and Mary in 1689.

non-linear ● adjective **1** not linear. **2** Mathematics (of an equation or function) containing a variable raised to a power less than or greater than 1, and hence not able to be represented by a straight line.

non-member ● noun a person, country, etc. that is not a member of a particular organization.

non-metal ● noun an element or substance that is not a metal.

– DERIVATIVES **non-metallic** adjective.

non-natural ● adjective not produced by or involving natural processes.

non-negotiable ● adjective **1** not open to discussion or modification. **2** not able to be transferred to the legal ownership of another person.

no-no ● noun (pl. **no-nos**) informal a thing that is not possible or acceptable.

no-nonsense ● adjective simple and straightforward; sensible.

non-operational ● adjective **1** not involving active duties. **2** not working or in use.

nonpareil /nonpərayl/ ● adjective unrivalled. ● noun an unrivalled person or thing.

– ORIGIN French, 'not equal'.

non-person ● noun a person regarded as non-existent or insignificant.

nonplussed /nonplusst/ ● adjective **1** surprised and confused. **2** N. Amer. informal unperturbed.

– USAGE In standard English **nonplussed** means 'surprised and confused'. A new meaning, 'not disconcerted; unperturbed', has developed recently in North American English, probably on the assumption that the prefix *non-* must have a negative meaning; this is not yet accepted as standard usage.

– ORIGIN from Latin *non plus* 'not more'.

non-productive ● adjective not producing or able to produce.

– DERIVATIVES **non-productively** adverb.

non-profit ● adjective not making or intended to make a profit.

non-proliferation ● noun the prevention of an increase or spread of something, especially possession of nuclear weapons.

non-resident ● adjective **1** not living in a particular country or a place of work. **2** Computing (of software) not kept permanently in memory. ● noun a person not living in a particular place.

nonsense ● noun **1** words that make no sense. **2** foolish or unacceptable behaviour. **3** an absurd or unthinkable scheme, situation, etc.

– DERIVATIVES **nonsensical** adjective **nonsensically** adverb.

Thesaurus

mon or garden.

– OPPOSITES distinctive.

none ● pronoun **1** *none of the fish are unusual* NOT ONE, not a one. **2** *none of this concerns me* NO PART, not a bit, not any. **3** *none can know better than you* NOT ONE, no one, nobody, not a soul, not a single person, no man.

– OPPOSITES all.

– PHRASES **none the ——** *we were left none the wiser* NOT AT ALL, not a bit, not the slightest bit, in no way, by no means any.

nonentity ● noun NOBODY, unimportant person, cipher, nonperson, nothing, small fry, lightweight, mediocrity; *informal* nohoper, non-starter.

– OPPOSITES celebrity.

non-essential ● adjective UNNECESSARY, inessential, unessential, needless, unneeded, superfluous, uncalled for, redundant, dispensable, expendable, unimportant, extraneous.

nonetheless ● adverb NEVERTHELESS, even so, however, but, still, yet, though; in spite of that, despite that, be that as it may, for all that, that said, just the same, all the same; notwithstanding, regardless, anyway, anyhow; *informal* still and all.

non-existent ● adjective IMAGINARY, imagined, unreal, fictional, fictitious, made up, invented, fanciful; fantastic, mythical; illusory, hallucinatory, chimerical, notional, shadowy, insubstantial; missing, absent; *poetic/literary* illusive.

– OPPOSITES real.

non-intervention ● noun LAISSEZ-FAIRE, non-participation, noninterference, inaction, passivity, neutrality; live and let live.

non-observance ● noun INFRINGEMENT, breach, violation, contravention, transgression, non-compliance, infraction; dereliction, neglect.

nonpareil ● adjective *a nonpareil storyteller* INCOMPARABLE, matchless, unrivalled, unparalleled, unequalled, peerless, beyond compare, second to none, unsurpassed, unbeatable, inimitable; unique, consummate, superlative, supreme; *formal* unexampled.

– OPPOSITES mediocre.

● noun *Britain's nonpareil of the 1980s* BEST, finest, crème de la crème, peak of perfection, elite, jewel in the crown, ne plus ultra, paragon; *archaic* nonsuch.

nonplus ● verb SURPRISE, stun, dumbfound, confound, take aback, disconcert, throw (off balance); puzzle, perplex, baffle, bemuse, bewilder; *informal* faze, flummox, stump, bamboozle, fox; *N. Amer. informal* discombobulate.

nonsense ● noun **1** *he was talking nonsense* RUBBISH, balderdash, gibberish, claptrap, blarney, blather, garbage; *informal* hogwash, rot, guff, baloney, tripe, drivel, gobbledegook, bilge, bosh, bunk, hot air, piffle, poppycock, phooey, twaddle; *Brit. informal* cobblers, codswallop, tosh, double Dutch; *Scottish & N. English informal* havers; *N. Amer. informal* flapdoodle, bushwa, applesauce; *informal, dated* bunkum, tommyrot. **2** *she stands no nonsense* MISCHIEF, naughtiness, bad behaviour, misbehaviour, misconduct, misdemeanour; pranks, tricks, clowning, buffoonery, funny business; *informal* tomfoolery, monkey business, shenanigans, hanky-panky; *Brit. informal* monkey tricks, jiggery-pokery. **3** *they dismissed the concept as a nonsense* ABSURDITY, folly, stupidity, ludicrousness, inanity, fool-

non sequitur /non sekwitər/ • noun a conclusion that does not logically follow from the previous argument or statement.
– ORIGIN Latin, 'it does not follow'.
non-specific • adjective not specific; indefinite.
non-specific urethritis • noun Medicine urethritis which is not associated with gonorrhoea.
non-standard • adjective **1** not average, normal, or usual. **2** (of language) not of the form accepted as standard.
non-starter • noun **1** a person or animal that fails to take part in a race. **2** informal something that has no chance of succeeding.
non-stick • adjective (of a pan or surface) covered with a substance that prevents food sticking to it during cooking.
non-stop • adjective **1** continuing without stopping or pausing. **2** having no intermediate stops on the way to a destination. • adverb without stopping or pausing.
nonsuch (also **nonesuch**) • noun archaic a person or thing regarded as perfect or excellent.
non-U • adjective informal, chiefly Brit. (of language or behaviour) not characteristic of the upper social classes.
non-uniform • adjective not uniform; varying.
non-verbal • adjective not involving or using words or speech.
non-violent • adjective not using violence.
– DERIVATIVES **non-violence** noun.
non-white • adjective (of a person) not white or not of predominantly European origin. • noun a non-white person.
noodle[1] • noun (usu. **noodles**) a very thin, long strip of pasta or a similar flour paste.
– ORIGIN German *Nudel*.
noodle[2] • noun informal **1** a stupid or silly person. **2** a person's head.
– ORIGIN of unknown origin.
noodle[3] • verb Austral. informal search (an old working) for opals.
– ORIGIN of unknown origin.
nook • noun a corner or recess offering seclusion or security.
– PHRASES **every nook and cranny** every part of something.
– ORIGIN of unknown origin.
nooky (also **nookie**) • noun informal sexual activity or intercourse.
– ORIGIN perhaps from NOOK.
noon • noun twelve o'clock in the day; midday.
– ORIGIN from Latin *nona hora* 'ninth hour', originally referring to the ninth hour from sunrise, i.e. approximately 3 p.m.
noonday • noun the middle of the day.
no one • pronoun no person; not a single person.
noontide (also **noontime**) • noun literary noon.
noose • noun a loop with a running knot which tightens as the rope or wire is pulled, used especially to hang offenders or trap animals. • verb catch or hold with a noose.
– PHRASES **put one's head in a noose** bring about one's own downfall.
– ORIGIN probably from Old French *nous*, from Latin *nodus* 'knot'.
nootropic /nōətrōpik, -troppik/ • adjective (of drugs) used to enhance memory or other mental functions.
– ORIGIN from Greek *noos* 'mind' + *tropē* 'turning'.
no place • noun N. Amer. nowhere.
nor • conjunction & adverb **1** and not; and not either. **2** archaic or dialect than.
– ORIGIN Old English.
nor' • abbreviation north: *nor'west*.
noradrenaline /norədrennəlin/ (also **norepinephrine**) • noun Biochemistry an adrenal hormone which functions as a neurotransmitter and is also used as a drug to raise blood pressure.
Nordic • adjective **1** relating to Scandinavia, Finland, and Iceland. **2** referring to a tall, blonde physical type associated with northern Europe. • noun a native of Scandinavia, Finland, or Iceland.
– ORIGIN French *nordique*, from *nord* 'north'.
Nordic skiing • noun cross-country skiing and ski jumping.
Norfolk jacket • noun a loose belted jacket with box pleats, typically made of tweed.
NOR gate • noun Electronics a gate circuit which produces an output only when there are no signals on any of the input connections.
norm • noun **1** (**the norm**) the usual or standard thing. **2** a required or acceptable standard.
– ORIGIN Latin *norma* 'precept, rule, carpenter's square'.
normal • adjective **1** conforming to a standard; usual, typical, or expected. **2** technical intersecting a given line or surface at right angles. • noun **1** the normal state or condition. **2** technical a line at right angles to a given line or surface.
– DERIVATIVES **normalcy** noun (chiefly N. Amer.) **normality** noun **normally** adverb.
normal distribution • noun Statistics a function that represents the distribution of variables as a symmetrical bell-shaped graph.
normalize (also **normalise**) • verb bring to a normal or standard state.
– DERIVATIVES **normalization** noun.
normal school • noun (especially in North America and France) a teacher training college.
Norman • noun **1** a member of a people of mixed Frankish and Scandinavian origin who settled in Normandy in the 10th century and who conquered England in 1066. **2** (also **Norman French**) the northern form of Old French spoken by the Normans. **3** a person from modern Normandy. • adjective **1** relating to the Normans or Normandy. **2** of the style of Romanesque architecture used in Britain under the Normans.
– ORIGIN Old French *Normant*, from an Old Norse word meaning 'Northman'.
normative • adjective formal relating to a standard or norm.
normotensive /normōtensiv/ • adjective Medicine having normal blood pressure.
Norse historical • noun **1** an ancient or medieval form of Norwegian or a related Scandinavian language. **2** (treated as pl.) Norwegians or Scandinavians. • adjective relating to Norway or Scandinavia.
– DERIVATIVES **Norseman** noun.
– ORIGIN Dutch *noordsch*, from *noord* 'north'.

Thesaurus

ishness, idiocy, insanity, madness.
– OPPOSITES sense, wisdom.
nonsensical • adjective **1** *her nonsensical way of talking* MEANINGLESS, senseless, illogical. **2** *a nonsensical generalization* FOOLISH, insane, stupid, idiotic, illogical, irrational, senseless, absurd, silly, inane, hare-brained, ridiculous, ludicrous, preposterous; *informal* crazy, crackpot, nutty; *Brit. informal* daft.
– OPPOSITES logical, sensible.
non-stop • adjective *non-stop entertainment* CONTINUOUS, constant, continual, perpetual, incessant, unceasing, ceaseless, uninterrupted, round-the-clock; unremitting, relentless, persistent.
– OPPOSITES occasional.
• adverb *we worked non-stop* CONTINUOUSLY, continually, incessantly, unceasingly, ceaselessly, all the time, constantly, perpetually, round the clock, steadily, relentlessly, persistently; *informal* 24-7.
– OPPOSITES occasionally.
nook • noun RECESS, corner, alcove, niche, bay, inglenook, cavity, cubbyhole, pigeonhole; opening, gap, aperture; hideaway, hiding place, hideout, shelter; *informal* hidey-hole.
noon • noun MIDDAY, twelve o'clock, twelve hundred hours, twelve noon, high noon, noonday; *poetic/literary* noontime, noontide.
– RELATED TERMS meridian.
no one • pronoun NOBODY, not a soul, not anyone, not a single person, never a one, none.
norm • noun **1** *norms of diplomatic behaviour* CONVENTION, standard; criterion, yardstick, benchmark, touchstone, rule, formula, pattern, guide, guideline, model, exemplar. **2** *such teams are now the norm* STANDARD, usual, the rule; normal, typical, average, unexceptional, par for the course, expected.
normal • adjective **1** *this is the normal procedure in most universities* USUAL, standard, ordinary, customary, conventional, habitual, accustomed, expected, wonted; typical, stock, common, everyday, regular, routine, established, set, fixed, traditional. **2** *a normal couple* ORDINARY, average, typical, run-of-the-mill, middle-of-the-road, common, conventional, mainstream, unremarkable, unexceptional; *N. Amer.* garden-variety; *informal* bog-standard, a dime a dozen; *Brit. informal* common or garden; *N. Amer. informal* ornery. **3** *the man was not normal* SANE, in one's right mind, right in the head, of sound mind, compos mentis, lucid, rational, coherent; *informal* all there.
– OPPOSITES unusual, insane.
normality • noun NORMALCY, business as usual, the daily round; routine, order, regularity.
normally • adverb **1** *she wanted to walk normally* NATURALLY, conventionally, ordinarily; as usual, as normal. **2** *normally we'd keep quiet about this* USUALLY, ordinarily, as a rule, generally, in gen-

north ● noun **1** the direction in which a compass needle normally points, towards the horizon on the left-hand side of a person facing east. **2** the northern part of a country, region, or town. ● adjective **1** lying towards, near, or facing the north. **2** (of a wind) blowing from the north. ● adverb to or towards the north.
– PHRASES **north by east** (or **west**) between north and north-north-east (or north-north-west).
– DERIVATIVES **northbound** adjective & adverb.
– ORIGIN Old English.
North American ● noun a person from North America, especially a citizen of the US or Canada. ● adjective relating to North America.
Northants ● abbreviation Northamptonshire.
north-east ● noun **1** the point of the horizon midway between north and east. **2** the north-eastern part of a country, region, or town. ● adjective **1** lying towards, near, or facing the north-east. **2** (of a wind) from the north-east. ● adverb to or towards the north-east.
– DERIVATIVES **north-eastern** adjective.
north-easterly ● adjective & adverb in a north-eastward position or direction. ● noun a wind blowing from the north-east.
north-eastward ● adverb (also **north-eastwards**) towards the north-east. ● adjective situated in, directed towards, or facing the north-east.
northerly ● adjective & adverb **1** in a northward position or direction. **2** (of a wind) blowing from the north. ● noun a north wind.
northern ● adjective **1** situated in, directed towards, or facing the north. **2** (usu. **Northern**) living in, coming from, or characteristic of the north.
– DERIVATIVES **northernmost** adjective.
northerner ● noun a person from the north of a region or country.
Northern Lights ● plural noun the aurora borealis.
northing ● noun **1** distance travelled or measured northward. **2** a figure or line representing northward distance on a map.
northland (also **northlands**) ● noun literary the northern part of a country or region.
north light ● noun good natural light without direct sun.
north-north-east ● noun the compass point or direction midway between north and north-east.
north-north-west ● noun the compass point or direction midway between north and north-west.
North Star ● noun the Pole Star.
Northumb. ● abbreviation Northumberland.
northward ● adjective in a northerly direction. ● adverb (also **northwards**) towards the north.
north-west ● noun **1** the point of the horizon midway between north and west. **2** the north-western part of a country, region, or town. ● adjective **1** lying towards, near, or facing the north-west. **2** (of a wind) from the north-west. ● adverb to or towards the north-west.
– DERIVATIVES **north-western** adjective.
north-westerly ● adjective & adverb in a north-westward position or direction. ● noun a wind blowing from the north-west.
north-westward ● adverb (also **north-westwards**) towards the north-west. ● adjective situated in, directed towards, or facing the north-west.
Norwegian /norweejən/ ● noun **1** a person from Norway. **2** the Scandinavian language spoken in Norway. ● adjective relating to Norway.
– ORIGIN from Latin *Norvegia* 'Norway'.
nose ● noun **1** the facial part projecting above the mouth, containing the nostrils and used in breathing and smelling. **2** the front end of an aircraft, car, or other vehicle. **3** the sense of smell. **4** an instinctive talent for detecting something. **5** an act of looking around or prying. **6** the aroma of a wine. ● verb **1** (of an animal) thrust its nose against or into something. **2** look around or pry into something. **3** make one's way slowly forward. **4** smell or sniff (something).
– PHRASES **by a nose** (of a victory) by a very narrow margin. **cut off one's nose to spite one's face** disadvantage oneself through a wilful attempt to gain an advantage. **get up someone's nose** informal irritate or annoy someone. **keep one's nose clean** informal stay out of trouble. **keep one's nose out of** refrain from interfering in. **nose to tail** (of vehicles) moving or standing close behind one another. **on the nose 1** informal, chiefly N. Amer. precisely. **2** informal (of betting) on a horse to win (as opposed to being placed). **put someone's nose out of joint** informal offend someone or hurt their pride. **turn one's nose up at** informal show distaste or contempt for. **under someone's nose** informal directly in front of someone.
– ORIGIN Old English.
nosebag ● noun a bag containing fodder, hung from a horse's head and into which it can reach to eat.
noseband ● noun the strap of a bridle that passes over the horse's nose and under its chin.
nosebleed ● noun an instance of bleeding from the nose.
nosedive ● noun **1** a steep downward plunge by an aircraft. **2** a sudden dramatic deterioration. ● verb make a nosedive.
no-see-um ● noun N. Amer. a minute biting insect.
nosegay ● noun a small sweet-scented bunch of flowers.
– ORIGIN from GAY in the obsolete sense 'ornament'.
nose job ● noun informal a cosmetic surgery operation on a person's nose.
nosey ● adjective & verb variant spelling of NOSY.
nosh informal ● noun food. ● verb eat enthusiastically or greedily.
– ORIGIN originally denoting a snack bar: from Yiddish.
no-show ● noun a person who has made a reservation or appointment but neither keeps nor cancels it.
nosh-up ● noun Brit. informal a large meal.
nosocomial /nossəkōmiəl/ ● adjective Medicine (of a disease) originating in a hospital.
– ORIGIN from Greek *nosokomos* 'person who tends the sick'.
nosology /nosolləji/ ● noun the branch of medical science concerned with the classification of diseases.
– ORIGIN from Greek *nosos* 'disease'.
nostalgia ● noun sentimental longing or wistful affection for the past.
– DERIVATIVES **nostalgic** adjective **nostalgically** adverb.
– ORIGIN originally in the sense 'acute homesickness': from Latin, from Greek *nostos* 'return home' + *algos* 'pain'.
nostril ● noun either of two external openings of the nose that

Thesaurus

eral, mostly, for the most part, by and large, mainly, most of the time, on the whole; typically, customarily, traditionally.
north ● adjective NORTHERN, northerly, boreal.
North American Indian ● noun NATIVE AMERICAN, American Indian; *dated* Red Indian.
nose ● noun **1** *a punch on the nose* snout, muzzle, proboscis, trunk; *informal* beak, conk, snoot, schnozzle, hooter, sniffer. **2** *he has a good nose* SENSE OF SMELL. **3** *a nose for scandal* INSTINCT, feeling, sixth sense, intuition, insight, perception. **4** *wine with a fruity nose* SMELL, bouquet, aroma, fragrance, perfume, scent, odour. **5** *the plane's nose dipped* nose-cone, bow, prow, front end; *informal* droop-snoot.
– RELATED TERMS nasal, rhinal.
● verb **1** *the dog nosed the ball* NUZZLE, nudge, push. **2** *she's nosing into my business* PRY, inquire, poke about/around, interfere (in), meddle (in); be a busybody, stick/poke one's nose in; *informal* be nosy (about), snoop; *Austral./NZ informal* stickybeak. **3** *he nosed the car into the traffic* EASE, inch, edge, move, manoeuvre, steer, guide.
– PHRASES **by a nose** (ONLY) JUST, barely, narrowly, by a hair's breadth, by the skin of one's teeth; *informal* by a whisker. **nose around/about/round** INVESTIGATE, explore, ferret (about/around), rummage, search; delve into, peer into; prowl around; *informal* snoop about/around/round. **nose something out** DETECT, find, discover, bring to light, track down, dig up, ferret out, root out, uncover, unearth, sniff out. **on the nose** *(informal)* EXACTLY, precisely, sharp, on the dot, promptly, prompt, dead (on); *informal* bang (on); *Brit. informal* spot on; *N. Amer. informal* on the button.
nosedive ● noun **1** *the plane went into a nosedive* DIVE, descent, drop, plunge, plummet, fall. **2** *sterling took a nosedive* FALL, drop, plunge, plummet, tumble, decline, slump; *informal* crash.
– OPPOSITES climb, rise.
● verb **1** *the device nosedived to earth* DIVE, plunge, pitch, drop, plummet. **2** *a series of strikes caused the economy to nosedive* FALL, take a header, drop, sink, plunge, plummet, tumble, slump, go down, decline; *informal* crash.
– OPPOSITES soar, rise.
nosegay ● noun POSY, bouquet, bunch, spray, sprig, buttonhole, corsage, boutonnière, tussie-mussie.
nosh *(informal)* ● noun *all kinds of nosh.* See FOOD sense 1.
● verb *they noshed smoked salmon.* See EAT sense 1.
nostalgia ● noun REMINISCENCE, remembrance, recollection; wist-

admit air to the lungs and smells to the olfactory nerves.
– ORIGIN Old English, 'nose hole'.
nostrum ● noun **1** a quack medicine. **2** a favourite method for bringing about reform.
– ORIGIN Latin, 'something of our own making'.
nosy (also **nosey**) ● adjective (**nosier**, **nosiest**) informal too inquisitive about other people's affairs.
– DERIVATIVES **nosily** adverb **nosiness** noun.
nosy parker ● noun an overly inquisitive person.
– ORIGIN from a 1907 picture postcard caption, 'The adventures of Nosey Parker', referring to a peeping Tom in Hyde Park.
not ● adverb **1** used to form or express a negative. **2** less than: *not ten feet away.*
– ORIGIN contraction of NOUGHT.
nota bene /nōtə bennay/ ● verb formal take special note.
– ORIGIN Latin, 'note well!'
notability ● noun (pl. **notabilities**) a famous or important person.
notable ● adjective worthy of attention or notice. ● noun a famous or important person.
notably ● adverb **1** in particular. **2** in a notable way.
notarize (also **notarise**) ● verb have (a document) legalized by a notary.
notary (in full **notary public**) ● noun (pl. **notaries**) a person authorized to perform certain legal formalities, especially to draw up or certify contracts, deeds, etc.
– DERIVATIVES **notarial** adjective.
– ORIGIN Latin *notarius* 'secretary'.
notation ● noun **1** a system of written symbols used to represent numbers, amounts, or elements in a field such as music or mathematics. **2** a note or annotation.
– DERIVATIVES **notate** verb **notational** adjective.
notch ● noun **1** an indentation or incision on an edge or surface. **2** a point or degree in a scale. ● verb **1** make notches in. **2** (**notch up**) score or achieve.
– ORIGIN Old French.
note ● noun **1** a brief written record of facts, topics, or thoughts, used as an aid to memory. **2** a short written message or document. **3** Brit. a banknote. **4** a single tone of definite pitch made by a musical instrument or voice, or a symbol representing this. **5** a bird's song or call. **6** a particular quality or tone expressing a mood or attitude. **7** a basic component of a fragrance or flavour. ● verb **1** pay attention to. **2** record in writing.
– PHRASES **hit the right** (or **wrong**) **note** say or do something in the right (or wrong) way. **of note** important. **take note** pay attention.
– ORIGIN from Latin *nota* 'a mark' and *notare* 'to mark'.
notebook ● noun **1** a small book for writing notes in. **2** a portable computer smaller than a laptop.
noted ● adjective well known.
notelet ● noun a small folded sheet of notepaper with a decorative design on the front.
notepad ● noun **1** a pad of paper for writing notes on. **2** a pocket-sized personal computer in which text is input using a stylus.
notepaper ● noun paper for writing letters on.
noteworthy ● adjective interesting or significant.
NOT gate ● noun Electronics a gate circuit which produces an output only when there is no input signal.
nothing ● pronoun **1** not anything. **2** something of no importance or concern. **3** nought. ● adverb not at all.
– PHRASES **for nothing 1** without payment or charge. **2** to no purpose. **nothing but** only. **nothing doing** informal **1** there is no prospect of success or agreement. **2** nothing is happening. **sweet nothings** words of affection exchanged by lovers. **think nothing of it** do not apologize or feel bound to show gratitude.
– ORIGIN Old English.
nothingness ● noun **1** the absence or ending of existence.

Thesaurus

fulness, regret, sentimentality.
nostalgic ● adjective WISTFUL, evocative, romantic, sentimental; regretful, dewy-eyed, maudlin.
nostrum ● noun **1** *they have to prove their nostrums work* MEDICINE, quack remedy, potion, elixir, panacea, cure-all, wonder drug; *informal* magic bullet. **2** *right-wing nostrums* MAGIC FORMULA, recipe for success, remedy, cure, prescription, answer.
nosy ● adjective *(informal)* PRYING, inquisitive, curious, busybody, spying, eavesdropping, intrusive; *informal* snooping, snoopy; *Austral. informal* stickybeak.
notability ● noun *the patronage of local notabilities.* See NOTABLE noun.
notable ● adjective **1** *notable examples of workmanship* NOTEWORTHY, remarkable, outstanding, important, significant, momentous, memorable; marked, striking, impressive; uncommon, unusual, special, exceptional, signal. **2** *a notable author* PROMINENT, important, well known, famous, famed, noted, distinguished, great, eminent, illustrious, respected, esteemed, renowned, celebrated, acclaimed, influential, prestigious, of note.
– OPPOSITES unremarkable, unknown.
● noun *movie stars and other notables* CELEBRITY, public figure, VIP, personage, notability, dignitary, worthy, luminary; star, superstar, (big) name; *informal* celeb, somebody, bigwig, big shot, big cheese, big fish, megastar; *Brit. informal* nob; *N. Amer. informal* kahuna, high muckamuck.
– OPPOSITES nonentity.
notably ● adverb **1** *other countries, notably the USA* IN PARTICULAR, particularly, especially, specially; primarily, principally. **2** *these are notably short-lived birds* REMARKABLY, especially, specially, very, extremely, exceptionally, singularly, particularly, peculiarly, distinctly, significantly, unusually, extraordinarily, uncommonly, incredibly, really, decidedly, surprisingly, conspicuously; *informal* seriously; *Brit. informal* jolly, dead.
notation ● noun **1** *algebraic notation* SYMBOLS, alphabet, syllabary, script; code, cipher, hieroglyphics. **2** *notations in the margin* ANNOTATION, jotting, comment, footnote, entry, memo, gloss, explanation; *historical* scholium.
notch ● noun **1** *a notch in the end of the arrow* NICK, cut, incision, score, scratch, slit, snick, slot, groove, cleft, indentation. **2** *her opinion of Nick dropped a notch* DEGREE, level, rung, point, mark, measure, grade.
● verb *notch the plank* NICK, cut, score, incise, carve, scratch, slit, snick, gouge, groove, furrow.
– PHRASES **notch something up** SCORE, achieve, attain, gain, earn, make; rack up, chalk up; register, record.
note ● noun **1** *a note in her diary* RECORD, entry, item, notation, jotting, memorandum, reminder, aide-memoire; *informal* memo. **2** *he will take notes of the meeting* MINUTES, records, details; report, account, commentary, transcript, proceedings, transactions; synopsis, summary, outline. **3** *notes in the margins* ANNOTATION, footnote, commentary, comment; marginalia, exegesis; *historical* scholium. **4** *he dropped me a note* MESSAGE, communication, letter, line; *formal* epistle, missive. **5** *(Brit.) a £20 note* BANKNOTE; *N. Amer.* bill; *US informal* greenback; (**notes**) paper money. **6** *this is worthy of note* ATTENTION, consideration, notice, heed, observation, regard. **7** *a composer of note* DISTINCTION, importance, eminence, prestige, fame, celebrity, acclaim, renown, repute, stature, standing, consequence, account. **8** *there was a note of hopelessness in her voice* TONE, intonation, inflection, sound; hint, indication, sign, element, suggestion.
● verb **1** *we will note your suggestion* BEAR IN MIND, be mindful of, consider, observe, heed, take notice of, pay attention to, take in. **2** *the letter noted the ministers' concern* MENTION, refer to, touch on, indicate, point out, make known, state. **3** *note the date in your diary* WRITE DOWN, put down, jot down, take down, inscribe, enter, mark, record, register, pencil.
notebook ● noun NOTEPAD, exercise book; register, logbook, log, diary, daybook, journal, record; *Brit.* jotter, pocketbook; *N. Amer.* scratch pad; *informal* memo pad.
noted ● adjective RENOWNED, well known, famous, famed, prominent, celebrated; notable, of note, important, eminent, distinguished, illustrious, acclaimed, esteemed; of distinction, of repute.
– OPPOSITES unknown.
noteworthy ● adjective NOTABLE, interesting, significant, important; remarkable, impressive, striking, outstanding, memorable, unique, special; unusual, extraordinary, singular, rare.
– OPPOSITES unexceptional.
nothing ● noun **1** *there's nothing I can do* NOT A THING, not anything, nil, zero; *N. English* nowt; *informal* zilch, sweet Fanny Adams, sweet FA, nix, not a dicky bird; *Brit. informal* damn all, not a sausage; *N. Amer. informal* zip, nada; *archaic* naught. **2** *forget it—it's nothing* A TRIFLING MATTER, a trifle; neither here nor there; *informal* no big deal. **3** *he treats her as nothing* A NOBODY, an unimportant person, a nonentity, a cipher, a non-person; *Brit.* small beer. **4** *the share value fell to nothing* ZERO, nought, 0; *Tennis* love; *Cricket* a duck.

2 insignificance.
notice ● noun **1** attention; observation. **2** advance notification or warning. **3** a formal declaration of one's intention to end an agreement, typically one concerning employment or tenancy. **4** a displayed sheet or placard giving news or information. **5** a small published announcement or advertisement. **6** a short published review. ● verb **1** become aware of. **2** (**be noticed**) be recognized as noteworthy. **3** archaic remark on.
– PHRASES **at short** (or **a moment's**) **notice** with little warning. **put someone on notice** (or **serve notice**) warn someone of something about or likely to occur. **take** (**no**) **notice** (**of**) pay (no) attention (to).
– ORIGIN Latin *notitia*, from *notus* 'known'.
noticeable ● adjective easily seen; clear or apparent.
– DERIVATIVES **noticeably** adverb.
notifiable ● adjective (of an infectious disease) that must be officially reported.
notify ● verb (**notifies**, **notified**) inform, typically in a formal or official manner.
– DERIVATIVES **notification** noun.
– ORIGIN Latin *notificare* 'make known'.
notion ● noun **1** a concept or belief. **2** an impulse or desire. **3** a vague awareness or understanding. **4** (**notions**) chiefly N. Amer. items used in sewing, such as buttons and pins.
– ORIGIN Latin, 'idea'.
notional ● adjective hypothetical or imaginary.
– DERIVATIVES **notionally** adverb.
notochord /nōtəkord/ ● noun Zoology a skeletal rod of cartilage supporting the body in embryonic and some adult chordate animals.
– ORIGIN from Greek *nōton* 'back' + CHORD².
notorious ● adjective famous for some bad quality or deed.
– DERIVATIVES **notoriety** noun **notoriously** adverb.
– ORIGIN Latin *notorius*, from *notus* 'known'.
Notts. ● abbreviation Nottinghamshire.
notwithstanding ● preposition in spite of. ● adverb nevertheless. ● conjunction although.
nougat /nōogaa, nuggət/ ● noun a sweet made from sugar or honey, nuts, and egg white.
– ORIGIN French, from Provençal *noga* 'nut'.
nougatine /nōogəteen/ ● noun nougat covered with chocolate.
nought ● noun the digit 0. ● pronoun variant spelling of NAUGHT.
– PHRASES **noughts and crosses** a game in which two players seek to complete a row of either three noughts or three crosses drawn alternately in the spaces of a grid of nine squares.
noumenon /nowmənon/ ● noun (pl. **noumena**) (in Kantian philosophy) a thing as it is in itself, as distinct from what is knowable by the senses.
– DERIVATIVES **noumenal** adjective.
– ORIGIN Greek, 'something conceived'.
noun ● noun Grammar a word (other than a pronoun) used to identify any of a class of people, places, or things (**common noun**), or to name a particular one of these (**proper noun**).
– ORIGIN Old French, from Latin *nomen* 'name'.
noun phrase ● noun Grammar a word or group of words that function in a sentence as subject, object, or prepositional object.
nourish ● verb **1** provide with the food or other substances necessary for growth and health. **2** keep (a feeling or belief) in one's mind for a long time.
– ORIGIN Old French *norir*, from Latin *nutrire*.
nourishment ● noun **1** the food or other substances necessary for growth, health, and good condition. **2** the action of nourishing.
nous /nowss/ ● noun **1** Brit. informal practical intelligence. **2** Philosophy the mind or intellect.
– ORIGIN Greek, 'mind, intelligence'.
nouveau riche /nōovō reesh/ ● noun (treated as pl.) people who have recently acquired wealth, typically those perceived as lacking good taste.
– ORIGIN French, 'new rich'.
nouvelle cuisine /nōovel kwizeen/ ● noun a modern style of

Thesaurus

– OPPOSITES something.
– PHRASES **be/have nothing to do with 1** *it has nothing to do with you* BE UNCONNECTED WITH, be unrelated to; be irrelevant to, be inapplicable to, be inapposite to. **2** *I'll have nothing to do with him* AVOID, have no truck with, have no contact with, steer clear of, give a wide berth to. **for nothing 1** *she hosted the show for nothing* FREE (OF CHARGE), gratis, without charge, at no cost, for free, on the house. **2** *all this trouble for nothing* IN VAIN, to no avail, to no purpose, with no result, needlessly, pointlessly. **nothing but** *he's nothing but a nuisance* MERELY, only, just, solely, simply, purely, no more than.
nothingness ● noun **1** *the nothingness of death* OBLIVION, nullity, blankness; void, vacuum; rare nihility. **2** *the nothingness of it all overwhelmed him* UNIMPORTANCE, insignificance, triviality, pointlessness, uselessness, worthlessness.
notice ● noun **1** *nothing escaped his notice* ATTENTION, observation, awareness, consciousness, perception; regard, consideration, scrutiny; watchfulness, vigilance, attentiveness. **2** *a notice on the wall* POSTER, bill, handbill, advertisement, announcement, bulletin; flyer, leaflet, pamphlet; sign, card; informal ad; Brit. informal advert. **3** *times may change without notice* NOTIFICATION, (advance) warning, announcement; information, news, communication, word. **4** *I handed in my notice* RESIGNATION. **5** *the film got bad notices* REVIEW, write-up, critique, criticism; Brit. informal crit.
● verb *I noticed that the door was open* OBSERVE, perceive, note, see, discern, detect, spot, distinguish, mark, remark; Brit. informal clock; poetic/literary behold.
– OPPOSITES overlook.
– PHRASES **take no notice (of)** IGNORE, pay no attention (to), disregard, pay no heed (to), take no account (of), brush aside, shrug off, turn a blind eye (to), pass over, let go, overlook, look the other way.
noticeable ● adjective DISTINCT, evident, obvious, apparent, manifest, patent, plain, clear, marked, conspicuous, unmistakable, undeniable, pronounced, prominent, striking, arresting; perceptible, discernible, detectable, observable, visible, appreciable.
noticeboard ● noun PINBOARD, cork board, bulletin board; hoarding.
notification ● noun **1** *the notification of the victim's wife* INFORMING, telling, alerting. **2** *she received notification that he was on the way* INFORMATION, word, advice, news, intelligence; communication, message; poetic/literary tidings.
notify ● verb **1** *we will notify you as soon as possible* INFORM, tell, advise, apprise, let someone know, put in the picture; alert, warn. **2** *births should be notified to the registrar* REPORT, make known, announce, declare, communicate, disclose.
notion ● noun **1** *he had a notion that something was wrong* IDEA, belief, conviction, opinion, view, thought, impression, perception; hypothesis, theory; (funny) feeling, (sneaking) suspicion, hunch. **2** *Claire had no notion of what he meant* UNDERSTANDING, idea, awareness, knowledge, clue, inkling. **3** *he got a notion to return* IMPULSE, inclination, whim, desire, wish, fancy.
notional ● adjective HYPOTHETICAL, theoretical, speculative, conjectural, suppositional, putative, conceptual; imaginary, fanciful, unreal, illusory.
– OPPOSITES actual.
notoriety ● noun INFAMY, disrepute, ill repute, bad name, dishonour, discredit; dated ill fame.
notorious ● adjective INFAMOUS, scandalous; well known, famous, famed, legendary.
notwithstanding ● preposition *notwithstanding his workload, he is a dedicated father* DESPITE, in spite of, regardless of, for all.
● adverb *she is bright—notwithstanding, she is now jobless* NEVERTHELESS, nonetheless, even so, all the same, in spite of this, despite this, however, still, yet, that said, just the same, anyway, in any event, at any rate.
● conjunction *notwithstanding that there was no space, they played on* ALTHOUGH, even though, though, in spite of the fact that, despite the fact that.
nought ● noun **1** *the batsman was out for nought* NIL, zero, 0; Tennis love; Cricket a duck. **2** (archaic) *my work has all been for nought.* See NAUGHT.
nourish ● verb **1** *patients must be well nourished* FEED, provide for, sustain, maintain. **2** *we nourish the talents of children* ENCOURAGE, promote, foster, nurture, cultivate, stimulate, boost, advance, assist, help, aid, strengthen, enrich. **3** *the hopes Ursula nourished* CHERISH, nurture, foster, harbour, nurse, entertain, maintain, hold, have.
nourishing ● adjective NUTRITIOUS, nutritive, wholesome, good for one, healthy, health-giving, healthful, beneficial, sustaining.
– OPPOSITES unhealthy.
nourishment ● noun FOOD, sustenance, nutriment, nutrition, sub-

cookery that emphasizes fresh, wholesome ingredients and the presentation of the dishes.
– ORIGIN French, 'new cookery'.
nouvelle vague /no͞ovel vaag/ ● noun a grouping of stylistically innovative French film directors in the late 1950s and 1960s.
– ORIGIN French, 'new wave'.
Nov. ● abbreviation November.
nova /nōvə/ ● noun (pl. **novae** /nōvee/ or **novas**) Astronomy a star suddenly increasing in brightness and then slowly returning to normal.
– ORIGIN Latin, from *novus* 'new' (because such stars were thought to be newly formed).
novation /nōvaysh'n/ ● noun Law the substitution of a new contract in place of an old one.
– ORIGIN Latin, from *novare* 'make new'.
novel[1] ● noun a fictitious prose narrative of book length.
– ORIGIN from Italian *novella storia* 'new story'.
novel[2] ● adjective interestingly new or unusual.
– ORIGIN Latin *novellus*, from *novus* 'new'.
novelette ● noun chiefly derogatory a short novel, typically a light romantic one.
novelist ● noun a writer of novels.
– DERIVATIVES **novelistic** adjective.
novelize (also **novelise**) ● verb convert into a novel.
– DERIVATIVES **novelization** noun.
novella /nəvellə/ ● noun a short novel or long short story.
– ORIGIN Italian.
novelty ● noun (pl. **novelties**) **1** the quality of being novel. **2** a new or unfamiliar thing. **3** a small and inexpensive toy or ornament. **4** (before another noun) intended to be amusingly striking or unusual: *a novelty teapot*.
November ● noun the eleventh month of the year.
– ORIGIN Latin, from *novem* 'nine' (being originally the ninth month of the Roman year).
novena /nəveenə/ ● noun (in the Roman Catholic Church) a form of worship consisting of special prayers or services on nine successive days.
– ORIGIN Latin, from *novem* 'nine'.
novice ● noun **1** a person new to and inexperienced in a job or situation. **2** a person who has entered a religious order and is under probation, before taking vows. **3** a racehorse that has not yet won a major prize or reached a qualifying level of performance.
– ORIGIN Latin *novicius*, from *novus* 'new'.
novitiate /nəvishiət/ (also **noviciate**) ● noun **1** the period or state of being a novice. **2** a religious novice. **3** a place housing religious novices.
now ● adverb **1** at the present time. **2** at or from this precise moment. **3** under the present circumstances. ● conjunction as a consequence of the fact.
– PHRASES **now and again** (or **then**) from time to time.
– ORIGIN Old English.
nowadays ● adverb at the present time, in contrast with the past.
nowhere ● adverb not in or to any place. ● pronoun **1** no place. **2** a place that is remote or uninteresting.
– PHRASES **from** (or **out of**) **nowhere** appearing or happening suddenly and unexpectedly. **get** (or **go**) **nowhere** make no progress. **nowhere near** not nearly.
nowise ● adverb archaic not at all.
nowt ● pronoun & adverb N. English nothing.
noxious ● adjective harmful, poisonous, or very unpleasant.
– ORIGIN from Latin *noxa* 'harm'.
nozzle ● noun a spout used to control a jet of liquid or gas.
– ORIGIN from NOSE.
NP ● abbreviation notary public.
Np ● symbol the chemical element neptunium.
NS ● abbreviation **1** (in calculating dates) New Style. **2** Nova Scotia.
ns ● abbreviation nanosecond.
n/s ● abbreviation (in personal advertisements) non-smoker; non-smoking.
NSPCC ● abbreviation (in the UK) National Society for the Prevention of Cruelty to Children.
NSU ● abbreviation Medicine non-specific urethritis.
NSW ● abbreviation New South Wales.
NT ● abbreviation **1** National Trust. **2** New Testament. **3** Northern Territory. **4** Northwest Territories.
-n't ● contraction not, used with auxiliary verbs (e.g. *can't*).
nth /enth/ ● adjective **1** Mathematics denoting an unspecified term in a series. **2** denoting the last or latest item in a long series.
nu /nyo͞o/ ● noun the thirteenth letter of the Greek alphabet (Ν, ν), transliterated as 'n'.
– ORIGIN Greek.
nuance /nyo͞onss/ ● noun a subtle difference in or shade of meaning, expression, colour, etc. ● verb (usu. **be nuanced**) give nuances to.
– ORIGIN French, from Latin *nubes* 'cloud'.
nub ● noun **1** (**the nub**) the crux or central point of a matter. **2** a small lump or protuberance.
– DERIVATIVES **nubby** adjective.
– ORIGIN apparently from dialect *knub* 'protuberance', from Low German.
nubbin ● noun a small lump or residual part.

Thesaurus

sistence, provisions, provender, fare; *informal* grub, nosh, chow, eats; *Brit. informal* scoff; *N. Amer. informal* chuck; *formal* comestibles; *dated* victuals.
nouveau riche ● plural noun THE NEW RICH, parvenus, arrivistes, upstarts, social climbers, vulgarians.
novel[1] ● noun *a writer of historical novels* BOOK, paperback, hardback; STORY, tale, narrative, romance; best-seller; *informal* blockbuster.
novel[2] ● adjective *a novel way of making money* NEW, original, unusual, unfamiliar, unconventional, unorthodox; different, fresh, imaginative, innovative, innovatory, innovational, inventive, modern, neoteric, avant-garde, pioneering, ground-breaking, revolutionary; rare, unique, singular, unprecedented; experimental, untested, untried; strange, exotic, newfangled.
– OPPOSITES traditional.
novelist ● noun WRITER, author, fictionist, man/woman of letters; *informal* penman, scribbler.
novelty ● noun **1** *the novelty of our approach* ORIGINALITY, newness, freshness, unconventionality, unfamiliarity; difference, imaginativeness, creativity, innovation, modernity. **2** *we sell seasonal novelties* KNICK-KNACK, trinket, bauble, toy, trifle, gewgaw, gimcrack, ornament; *N. Amer.* kickshaw.
novice ● noun **1** *a five-day course for novices* BEGINNER, learner, neophyte, newcomer, initiate, tyro, fledgling; apprentice, trainee, probationer, student, pupil; *N. Amer.* tenderfoot; *informal* rookie, newie, newbie; *N. Amer. informal* greenhorn. **2** *a novice who was never ordained* NEOPHYTE, novitiate; postulant, proselyte, catechumen.
– OPPOSITES expert, veteran.
novitiate ● noun **1** *a three-year novitiate* PROBATIONARY PERIOD, probation, trial period, test period, apprenticeship, training period, traineeship, training, initiation. **2** *two young novitiates* NOVICE, neophyte; postulant, proselyte, catechumen.
now ● adverb **1** *I'm extremely busy now* AT THE MOMENT, at present, at the present (time/moment), at this moment in time, currently; *N. Amer.* presently; *Brit. informal* at the minute. **2** *television is now the main source of news* NOWADAYS, today, these days, in this day and age; in the present climate. **3** *you must leave now* AT ONCE, straight away, right away, right now, this minute, this instant, immediately, instantly, directly, without further ado, promptly, without delay, as soon as possible; *informal* pronto, straight off, a.s.a.p.
– PHRASES **as of now** FROM THIS TIME ON, from now on, henceforth, henceforward, from this day forward, in future; *formal* hereafter. **for now** FOR THE TIME BEING, for the moment, for the present, for the meantime; *archaic* for the nonce. **not now** LATER (ON), sometime, one day, some day, one of these days, sooner or later, in due course, by and by, eventually, ultimately. **now and again** OCCASIONALLY, now and then, from time to time, sometimes, every so often, (every) now and again, at times, on occasion(s), (every) once in a while; periodically, once in a blue moon.
nowadays ● adverb THESE DAYS, today, at the present time, in these times, in this day and age, now, currently, at the moment, at present, at this moment in time; in the present climate; *N. Amer.* presently.
noxious ● adjective POISONOUS, toxic, deadly, harmful, dangerous, pernicious, damaging, destructive; unpleasant, nasty, disgusting, awful, dreadful, horrible, terrible; vile, revolting, foul, nauseating, appalling, offensive; malodorous, fetid, putrid; *informal* ghastly, horrid; *poetic/literary* noisome; *archaic* disgustful.
– OPPOSITES innocuous.

Nubian /nyoobiən/ ● adjective relating to Nubia, an ancient region corresponding to southern Egypt and northern Sudan. ● noun **1** a person from Nubia. **2** the language spoken by the Nubians. **3** a short-haired breed of goat with long hanging ears and long legs, originally from Africa.

nubile /nyoobīl/ ● adjective (of a girl or woman) youthful but sexually mature and attractive.
– DERIVATIVES **nubility** noun.
– ORIGIN from Latin *nubilis* 'marriageable'.

nubuck /nyoobuk/ ● noun cowhide leather which has been rubbed on the flesh side to give a suede-like effect.

nuchal /nyook'l/ ● adjective Anatomy relating to the nape of the neck.
– ORIGIN from Latin *nucha* 'medulla oblongata'.

nuciferous /nyoosiffərəss/ ● adjective Botany bearing nuts.
– ORIGIN from Latin *nux* 'nut'.

nuclear ● adjective **1** relating to a nucleus. **2** using energy released in the fission or fusion of atomic nuclei. **3** possessing or involving nuclear weapons.

nuclear family ● noun a couple and their dependent children, regarded as a basic social unit.

nuclear fuel ● noun a substance that will undergo nuclear fission and can be used as a source of nuclear energy.

nuclear magnetic resonance ● noun the absorption of electromagnetic radiation by nuclei of atoms, when surrounded by a magnetic field, used as a means of determining chemical structures and forming images of internal body tissues.

nuclear medicine ● noun the branch of medicine concerned with the use of radioactive substances in research, diagnosis, and treatment.

nuclear physics ● plural noun (treated as sing.) the science of atomic nuclei and their interactions, especially in the generation of nuclear energy.

nuclear power ● noun power generated by a nuclear reactor.

nuclear waste ● noun radioactive waste material, especially from the use or reprocessing of nuclear fuel.

nuclear winter ● noun a period of abnormal cold and darkness predicted to follow a nuclear war, caused by smoke and dust blocking the sun's rays.

nuclease /nyookliayz/ ● noun Biochemistry an enzyme that cuts nucleic acid chains into smaller units.

nucleate ● verb /nyookliayt/ (usu. as adj. **nucleated**) **1** form a nucleus. **2** form around a central area. ● adjective /nyookliət/ chiefly Biology having a nucleus.
– DERIVATIVES **nucleation** noun.

nuclei plural of NUCLEUS.

nucleic acid /nyookleeik, -klayik/ ● noun Biochemistry a complex organic substance, especially DNA or RNA, whose molecules consist of long chains of nucleotides.

nucleon /nyooklion/ ● noun Physics a proton or neutron.

nucleoside ● noun Biochemistry an organic compound consisting of a purine or pyrimidine base linked to a sugar, e.g. adenosine.

nucleotide ● noun Biochemistry a compound consisting of a nucleoside linked to a phosphate group, forming the basic structural unit of nucleic acids.

nucleus /nyookliəss/ ● noun (pl. **nuclei** /nyookli-ī/) **1** the central and most important part of an object or group. **2** Physics the positively charged central core of an atom, containing nearly all its mass. **3** Biology a structure present in most cells, containing the genetic material.
– ORIGIN Latin, 'kernel, inner part', from *nux* 'nut'.

nude ● adjective wearing no clothes. ● noun a naked human figure as a subject in art or photography.
– DERIVATIVES **nudity** noun.
– ORIGIN Latin *nudus* 'plain, explicit'.

nudge ● verb **1** prod with one's elbow to attract attention. **2** touch or push lightly. **3** give gentle encouragement to. ● noun a light touch or push.
– ORIGIN of unknown origin.

nudibranch /nyoodibrangk/ ● noun Zoology a mollusc of an order comprising the sea slugs.
– ORIGIN from Latin *nudus* 'nude' + *branchia* 'gill'.

nudist ● noun a person who goes naked wherever possible.
– DERIVATIVES **nudism** noun.

nugatory /nyoogətəri/ ● adjective **1** worthless. **2** useless or invalid.
– ORIGIN Latin *nugatorius*, from *nugari* 'to trifle'.

nugget ● noun **1** a small lump of gold or other precious metal found ready-formed in the earth. **2** a small but valuable fact.
– ORIGIN apparently from dialect *nug* 'lump', of unknown origin.

nuisance ● noun a person or thing causing inconvenience or annoyance.
– ORIGIN Old French, 'hurt', from Latin *nocere* 'to harm'.

Nuits St George /nwee san zhorzh/ ● noun a red burgundy wine produced in district of Nuits St Georges, in France.

nuke informal ● noun a nuclear weapon. ● verb attack or destroy with nuclear weapons.

null ● adjective **1** (usu. in phrase **null and void**) having no legal force; invalid. **2** having or associated with the value zero. **3** having no positive substance. ● noun **1** a dummy letter in a cipher. **2** Electronics a condition in which no signal is generated. ● verb Electronics cancel out.
– ORIGIN Latin *nullus* 'none'.

nulla-nulla /nullənullə/ (also **nulla**) ● noun a hardwood club used as a weapon by Australian Aboriginals.
– ORIGIN from an Aboriginal language.

null hypothesis ● noun (in a statistical test) the theory that any observed differences between two groups are due to sampling or experimental error.

nullify ● verb (**nullifies, nullified**) **1** make null and void. **2** cancel out.
– DERIVATIVES **nullification** noun.

nullity ● noun (pl. **nullities**) **1** the state of being null. **2** a thing that is null.

numb ● adjective deprived of the power of sensation. ● verb make numb.
– DERIVATIVES **numbly** adverb **numbness** noun.
– ORIGIN from obsolete *nomen* 'taken', from Germanic.

numbat ● noun a small termite-eating Australian marsupial

n

Thesaurus

nuance ● noun FINE DISTINCTION, subtle difference; shade, shading, gradation, variation, degree; subtlety, nicety, overtone.

nub ● noun CRUX, central point, main point, core, heart (of the matter), nucleus, essence, quintessence, kernel, marrow, meat, pith; gist, substance; *informal* nitty-gritty.

nubile ● adjective SEXUALLY MATURE, marriageable; sexually attractive, desirable, sexy, luscious; *informal* beddable.

nucleus ● noun **1** *the nucleus of the banking world* CORE, centre, central part, heart, nub, hub, middle, eye, focus, focal point, pivot, crux. **2** *a nucleus of union men supported him* SMALL GROUP, caucus, cell, coterie, clique, faction.

nude ● adjective (STARK) NAKED, bare, unclothed, undressed, disrobed, stripped, unclad, in a state of nature, au naturel; *informal* without a stitch on, in one's birthday suit, in the raw, in the altogether, in the buff, in the nuddy; *Brit. informal* starkers; *Scottish informal* in the scud; *N. Amer. informal* buck naked.
– OPPOSITES clothed.

nudge ● verb **1** *he nudged Ben* POKE, elbow, dig, prod, jog, jab. **2** *the canoe nudged a bank* TOUCH, bump (against), push (against), run into. **3** *we nudged them into action* PROMPT, encourage, stimulate, prod, galvanize. **4** *unemployment was nudging 3,000,000* APPROACH, near, come close to, be verging on, border on.
● noun **1** *Maggie gave him a nudge* POKE, dig (in the ribs), prod, jog, jab, push. **2** *after a little nudge, she remembered Lilian* REMINDER, prompt, prompting, prod, encouragement.

nugatory ● adjective **1** *a nugatory observation* WORTHLESS, unimportant, inconsequential, valueless, trifling, trivial, insignificant, meaningless. **2** *the shortages will render nugatory our hopes* FUTILE, useless, vain, unavailing, null, invalid.

nugget ● noun LUMP, nub, chunk, piece, hunk, wad, gobbet; *N. Amer. informal* gob.

nuisance ● noun ANNOYANCE, inconvenience, bore, bother, irritation, problem, trouble, trial, burden; pest, plague, thorn in one's side/flesh; *informal* pain (in the neck), hassle, bind, drag, aggravation, headache; *Scottish informal* nyaff, skelf; *N. Amer. informal* nudnik; *Austral./NZ informal* nark.
– OPPOSITES blessing.

null ● adjective **1** *their marriage was declared null* INVALID, null and void, void; annulled, nullified, cancelled, revoked. **2** *his null life* CHARACTERLESS, colourless, empty, insipid, vapid, dull, boring.
– OPPOSITES valid, interesting.

nullify ● verb **1** *they nullified the legislation* ANNUL, render null and void, void, invalidate; repeal, reverse, rescind, revoke, cancel, abolish; countermand, do away with, terminate, quash; *Law* vac-

with a black-and-white striped back.
– ORIGIN from an Aboriginal language.
number ● noun **1** a quantity or value expressed by a word, symbol, or figure. **2** a quantity or amount of something countable. **3** (**a number of**) several. **4** a single issue of a magazine. **5** a song, dance, or other musical item. **6** informal an item of clothing of a particular type, regarded with approval: *a little black number*. **7** a grammatical classification of words that consists typically of singular and plural. ● verb **1** amount to. **2** mark with a number or give a number to. **3** count or estimate. **4** include as a member of a group.
– PHRASES **by numbers** following simple instructions identified or as if identified by numbers. **have someone's number** informal understand a person's real motives or character. **someone's days are numbered** someone will not survive for much longer. **someone's number is up** informal someone is finished or doomed to die. **without number** too many to count.
– DERIVATIVES **numberless** adjective.
– ORIGIN Old French *nombre*, from Latin *numerus*.
number cruncher ● noun informal **1** a computer for performing complicated calculations. **2** often derogatory a statistician or other person dealing with numerical data.
numbered account ● noun a bank account, especially in a Swiss bank, identified only by a number and not bearing the owner's name.
number one ● noun informal **1** oneself. **2** the foremost person or thing. **3** a first lieutenant in the navy.
number plate ● noun Brit. a sign on the front and rear of a vehicle displaying its registration number.
numbers game ● noun **1** often derogatory the manipulation of statistics. **2** N. Amer. a lottery based on the occurrence of unpredictable numbers.
number two ● noun informal a second in command.
numbskull (also **numskull**) ● noun informal a stupid or foolish person.
numen /nyoōmən/ ● noun (pl. **numina** /nyoōminə/) a spirit or deity that presides over a place.
– ORIGIN Latin.
numerable ● adjective able to be counted.
numeral ● noun a figure, word, or group of figures denoting a number. ● adjective of or denoting a number.
numerate /nyoōmərət/ ● adjective having a good basic knowledge of arithmetic.
– DERIVATIVES **numeracy** noun.
– ORIGIN from Latin *numerus* 'a number', on the pattern of *literate*.
numeration ● noun the action or process of numbering or calculating.
numerator ● noun the number above the line in a vulgar fraction showing how many of the parts indicated by the denominator are taken, e.g. 2 in ⅔.
numerical ● adjective of, relating to, or expressed as a number or numbers.
– DERIVATIVES **numerically** adverb.
numerology ● noun the branch of knowledge concerned with the occult significance of numbers.
– DERIVATIVES **numerological** adjective **numerologist** noun.
numerous ● adjective **1** many. **2** consisting of many members.
– DERIVATIVES **numerously** adverb.
Numidian /nyoōmiddiən/ ● noun a person from the ancient region of Numidia in North Africa. ● adjective relating to Numidia.
numina plural of NUMEN.
numinous /nyoōminəss/ ● adjective having a strong religious or spiritual quality.
– ORIGIN from Latin *numen* (see NUMEN).
numismatic ● adjective of or relating to coins or medals.
– DERIVATIVES **numismatically** adverb.
– ORIGIN from Greek *nomisma* 'current coin'.
numismatics ● plural noun (usu. treated as sing.) the study or collection of coins, banknotes, and medals.
– DERIVATIVES **numismatist** noun.
numskull ● noun variant spelling of NUMBSKULL.
nun ● noun **1** a member of a female religious community, typically one living under vows of poverty, chastity, and obedience. **2** a pigeon of a breed with a crest on its neck.
– ORIGIN Latin *nonna*, feminine of *nonnus* 'monk'.
nunatak /nunnətak/ ● noun an isolated peak of rock projecting above a surface of inland ice or snow.
– ORIGIN Eskimo.
Nunc Dimittis /nungk dimittiss/ ● noun the Song of Simeon (Gospel of Luke, chapter 2) used as a canticle in Christian liturgy.
– ORIGIN Latin, the opening words of the canticle, '(Lord), now you let (your servant) depart'.
nuncio ● noun (pl. **nuncios**) (in the Roman Catholic Church) a papal ambassador to a foreign government or court.
– ORIGIN Italian, from Latin *nuntius* 'messenger'.
nunnery ● noun (pl. **nunneries**) a religious house of nuns.
nuptial /nupsh'l/ ● adjective **1** of or relating to marriage or weddings. **2** Zoology relating to breeding. ● noun (**nuptials**) a wedding.
– ORIGIN Latin *nuptialis*, from *nuptiae* 'wedding'.
nurse[1] ● noun **1** a person trained to care for the sick or infirm.

Thesaurus

ate; *formal* abrogate. **2** *the costs would nullify any tax relief* CANCEL OUT, neutralize, negate, negative.
– OPPOSITES ratify.
numb ● adjective *his fingers were numb* WITHOUT SENSATION, without feeling, numbed, benumbed, desensitized, insensible, senseless, unfeeling; anaesthetized; dazed, stunned, stupefied, paralysed, immobilized, frozen.
– OPPOSITES sensitive.
● verb *the cold numbed her senses* DEADEN, benumb, desensitize, dull; anaesthetize; daze, stupefy, paralyse, immobilize, freeze.
– OPPOSITES sensitize.
number ● noun **1** *a whole number* NUMERAL, integer, figure, digit; character, symbol; decimal, unit; cardinal number, ordinal number. **2** *a large number of complaints* AMOUNT, quantity; total, aggregate, tally; quota. **3** *the wedding of one of their number* GROUP, company, crowd, circle, party, band, crew, set; *informal* gang. **4** *the band performed another number* SONG, piece (of music), tune, track; routine, sketch, dance, act.
– RELATED TERMS numerical.
● verb **1** *visitors numbered more than two million* ADD UP TO, amount to, total, come to. **2** *he numbers the fleet at a thousand* CALCULATE, count, total, compute, reckon, tally; assess; *Brit.* tot up; *formal* enumerate. **3** *each paragraph is numbered* assign a number to, mark with a number; itemize, enumerate. **4** *he numbers her among his friends* INCLUDE, count, reckon, deem. **5** *his days are numbered* LIMIT, restrict, fix.
– PHRASES **a number of** SEVERAL, various, quite a few, sundry. **without number** COUNTLESS, innumerable, unlimited, endless, limitless, untold, numberless, uncountable, uncounted; numerous, many, multiple, manifold, legion.
numberless ● adjective INNUMERABLE, countless, unlimited, endless, limitless, untold, uncountable, uncounted; numerous, many, multiple, manifold, legion; *informal* more —— than one can shake a stick at; *poetic/literary* myriad.
numbing ● adjective **1** *menthol has a numbing action* DESENSITIZING, deadening, benumbing, anaesthetic, anaesthetizing; paralysing. **2** *numbing cold* FREEZING, raw, bitter, biting, arctic. **3** *hours of numbing boredom* STUPEFYING, mind-numbing, stultifying, paralysing; soporific.
numbskull ● noun *(informal)*. See IDIOT.
numeral ● noun NUMBER, integer, figure, digit; character, symbol, unit.
numerous ● adjective (VERY) MANY, a lot of, scores of, countless, numberless, innumerable; several, quite a few, various; plenty of, copious, a quantity of, an abundance of, a profusion of, a multitude of; frequent; *informal* umpteen, lots of, loads of, masses of, stacks of, heaps of, bags of, tons of, oodles of, hundreds of, thousands of, millions of, more —— than one can shake a stick at; *Brit. informal* a shedload of; *N. Amer. informal* gazillions of; *Austral./NZ informal* a swag of; *poetic/literary* myriad.
– OPPOSITES few.
numinous ● adjective SPIRITUAL, religious, divine, holy, sacred; mysterious, other-worldly, unearthly, transcendent.
nun ● noun sister, abbess, prioress, Mother Superior, Reverend Mother; novice; bride of Christ, religious, conventual, contemplative, canoness; *poetic/literary* vestal; *historical* anchoress.
nuncio ● noun (PAPAL) AMBASSADOR, legate, envoy, messenger.
nunnery ● noun CONVENT, priory, abbey, cloister, religious community.
nuptial ● adjective MATRIMONIAL, marital, marriage, wedding, conju-

2 dated a person employed or trained to take charge of young children. • **verb 1** give medical and other attention to. **2** feed or be fed at the breast. **3** treat or hold carefully or protectively. **4** harbour (a belief or feeling) for a long time.
– DERIVATIVES **nursing** noun.
– ORIGIN Old French *nourice*, from Latin *nutrire* 'nourish'.
nurse[2] (also **nurse shark**) • **noun** a slow-moving Australian shark of shallow inshore waters.
– ORIGIN probably from HUSS, by wrong division of *an huss*.
nursemaid • **noun** a woman or girl employed to look after a young child or children.
nursery • **noun** (pl. **nurseries**) **1** a room in a house for the special use of young children. **2** (also **day nursery**) a nursery school. **3** a place where young plants and trees are grown for sale or for planting elsewhere.
nurseryman • **noun** a worker in or owner of a plant or tree nursery.
nursery nurse • **noun** Brit. a person trained to look after young children and babies in nurseries, crèches, etc.
nursery rhyme • **noun** a simple traditional song or poem for children.
nursery school • **noun** a school for young children, mainly between the ages of three and five.
nursery slope • **noun** a gentle ski slope suitable for beginners.
nursing home • **noun** a small private institution for the elderly providing residential accommodation with health care.
nursling • **noun** dated a baby that is being breastfed.
nurture • **verb 1** rear and encourage the development of (a child). **2** cherish (a hope, belief, or ambition). • **noun 1** the action or process of nurturing. **2** upbringing, education, and environment as a factor determining personality. Often contrasted with NATURE.
– ORIGIN Old French *noureture* 'nourishment', from Latin *nutrire* 'feed, cherish'.
nut • **noun 1** a fruit consisting of a hard or tough shell around an edible kernel. **2** the hard kernel of such a fruit. **3** a small flat piece of metal or other material, typically square or hexagonal, with a threaded hole through it for screwing on to a bolt. **4** informal a crazy or eccentric person. **5** informal an obsessive enthusiast: *a football nut.* **6** informal a person's head. **7** a small lump of coal or other material. **8** (**nuts**) vulgar slang a man's testicles. • **verb** (**nutted, nutting**) informal butt with one's head.
– PHRASES **do one's nut** Brit. informal be extremely angry or agitated. **nuts and bolts** informal the basic practical details. **a tough** (or **hard**) **nut to crack** informal a problem or an opponent that is hard to solve or overcome.
– DERIVATIVES **nutty** adjective.
– ORIGIN Old English.
nutation /nyōōtaysh'n/ • **noun** a periodic variation in the inclination of an axis of rotation, especially that causing the earth's precession to follow a wavy rather than a circular path.
– ORIGIN Latin, from *nutare* 'to nod'.
nutcase • **noun** informal a mad or foolish person.
nutcracker • **noun 1** (**nutcrackers**) a device for cracking nuts. **2** a bird of the crow family that feeds on the seeds of conifers.
nuthatch • **noun** a small grey-backed songbird which climbs up and down tree trunks.
– ORIGIN from an obsolete word related to HACK[1], from the bird's habit of hacking at nuts with its beak.
nut loaf • **noun** a baked vegetarian dish made from ground or chopped nuts, vegetables, and herbs.
nutmeg • **noun** a spice made from the seed of a tropical tree native to the Moluccas.
– ORIGIN partial translation of Old French *nois muguede* 'musky nut'.
nutria /nyōōtriə/ • **noun** the skin or fur of the coypu.
– ORIGIN Spanish, 'otter'.
nutrient • **noun** a substance that provides nourishment essential for life and growth.
– ORIGIN from Latin *nutrire* 'nourish'.
nutriment /nyōōtrimənt/ • **noun** nourishment; sustenance.
nutrition • **noun 1** the process of taking in and assimilating nutrients. **2** the branch of science concerned with this process.
– DERIVATIVES **nutritional** adjective **nutritionist** noun.
– ORIGIN Latin, from *nutrire* 'nourish'.
nutritious • **adjective** full of nutrients; nourishing.
– DERIVATIVES **nutritiously** adverb.
nutritive • **adjective 1** of or relating to nutrition. **2** nutritious.
nuts • **adjective** informal mad.
nutshell • **noun** the hard woody covering around the kernel of a nut.
– PHRASES **in a nutshell** in the fewest possible words.
nutter • **noun** Brit. informal a mad or eccentric person.
nux vomica /nuks vommikə/ • **noun** a spiny southern Asian tree with berry-like fruit and toxic seeds that contain strychnine.
– ORIGIN Latin, 'nut causing vomiting'.
nuzzle • **verb** rub or push against gently with the nose and mouth.
– ORIGIN from NOSE.
NV • **abbreviation** Nevada.
NVQ • **abbreviation** (in the UK) National Vocational Qualification.
NW • **abbreviation 1** north-west. **2** north-western.
NY • **abbreviation** New York.

Thesaurus

gal, bridal; married, wedded; *poetic/literary* connubial; *Law* spousal.
nuptials • **plural noun** WEDDING (CEREMONY), marriage, union; *archaic* espousal.
nurse • **noun 1** *skilled nurses* CARER, caregiver; *informal* Florence Nightingale, nursey; *N. Amer. informal* candy-striper. **2** *(dated) she had been his nurse in childhood* NANNY, nursemaid, nursery nurse, childminder, governess, au pair, childcarer, babysitter, ayah.
• **verb 1** *they nursed smallpox patients* CARE FOR, take care of, look after, tend, minister to. **2** *I nursed my sore finger* TREAT, medicate, tend; dress, bandage, soothe; *informal* doctor. **3** *Rosa was nursing her baby* BREASTFEED, suckle, feed. **4** *they nursed old grievances* HARBOUR, foster, entertain, bear, have, hold (on to), cherish, cling to, retain. **5** *our unity needs to be nursed* NURTURE, encourage, promote, boost, assist, help, cultivate; protect, safeguard.
nursemaid • **noun.** See NURSE noun sense 2.
nurture • **verb 1** *she nurtured her children into adulthood* BRING UP, care for, take care of, look after, tend, rear, raise, support, foster; parent, mother. **2** *we nurtured these plants* CULTIVATE, grow, keep, tend. **3** *he nurtured my love of art* ENCOURAGE, promote, stimulate, develop, foster, cultivate, boost, contribute to, assist, help, abet, strengthen, fuel.
– OPPOSITES neglect, hinder.
• **noun 1** *we are what nature and nurture have made us* UPBRINGING, rearing, raising, childcare; training, education. **2** *the nurture of ideas* ENCOURAGEMENT, promotion, fostering, development, cultivation.
– OPPOSITES nature.
nut • **noun 1** *nuts in their shells* kernel. **2** *(informal) he smacked her on the nut* HEAD, skull, cranium, crown; *informal* noodle, noggin, dome; *Brit. informal* bonce; *informal, dated* conk, noddle. **3** *(informal) some nut arrived at the office* MANIAC, lunatic, madman, madwoman; eccentric; *informal* loony, nutcase, fruitcake, head case, crank, crackpot, weirdo; *Brit. informal* nutter; *N. Amer. informal* screwball, crazy; *N. Amer. & Austral./NZ informal* dingbat. **4** *(informal) a movie nut* ENTHUSIAST, fan, devotee, aficionado; *informal* freak, fiend, fanatic, addict, buff; *N. Amer. informal* jock.
– PHRASES **do one's nut** *(Brit. informal)* BE VERY ANGRY, be furious, lose one's temper, go into a rage; *informal* go mad, go crazy, go wild, go bananas, have a fit, blow one's top, hit the roof, go off the deep end, go ape, flip, lose one's rag; *Brit. informal* go spare. **off one's nut** *(informal).* See MAD sense 1.
nutriment • **noun** NOURISHMENT, nutrients, sustenance, goodness, nutrition, food.
nutrition • **noun** NOURISHMENT, nutriment, nutrients, sustenance, food; *informal* grub, chow, nosh; *Brit. informal* scoff; *poetic/literary* viands; *dated* victuals; *archaic* aliment.
– RELATED TERMS trophic.
nutritious • **adjective** NOURISHING, good for one, full of nutrients, nutritive, nutrimental; wholesome, healthy, healthful, beneficial, sustaining.
nuts • **adjective** *(informal)* **1** *they thought we were nuts.* See MAD sense 1. **2** *he's nuts about her* INFATUATED WITH, keen on, devoted to, in love with, smitten with, enamoured of, hot for; *informal* mad, crazy, nutty, wild, hooked on, gone on; *Brit. informal* potty.
nuts and bolts • **plural noun** *(informal)* PRACTICAL DETAILS, fundamentals, basics, practicalities, essentials, mechanics; *informal* nitty-gritty, ins and outs, brass tacks.
nutty • **adjective** *(informal)* **1** *they're all nutty.* See MAD sense 1. **2** *she's nutty about Elvis.* See NUTS sense 2.
nuzzle • **verb 1** *the horse nuzzled at her pocket* NUDGE, nose, prod,

nyala /nyaalə/ ● **noun** (pl. same) a southern African antelope with a conspicuous crest on the neck and back and lyre-shaped horns.
– ORIGIN Zulu.

NYC ● **abbreviation** New York City.

nyctalopia /niktəlōpiə/ ● **noun** Medicine abnormal inability to see in very dim light.
– ORIGIN from Greek *nux* 'night' + *alaos* 'blind' + *ōps* 'eye'.

nyctophobia /niktəfōbiə/ ● **noun** extreme or irrational fear of the night or of darkness.
– ORIGIN from Greek *nux* 'night'.

nylon ● **noun** **1** a tough, lightweight, elastic synthetic polymer with a protein-like chemical structure. **2** fabric or yarn made of such polymers. **3** (**nylons**) nylon stockings or tights.
– ORIGIN an invented word.

nymph ● **noun** **1** a mythological spirit of nature imagined as a beautiful maiden. **2** literary a beautiful young woman. **3** an immature form of a dragonfly or other insect that does not undergo complete metamorphosis.
– DERIVATIVES **nymphal** adjective.
– ORIGIN Greek *numphē* 'nymph, bride'.

nymphet ● **noun** an attractive and sexually mature young girl.

nympho ● **noun** (pl. **nymphos**) informal a nymphomaniac.

nympholepsy /nimfəlepsi/ ● **noun** literary frenzy caused by desire for the unattainable.
– DERIVATIVES **nympholeptic** adjective.
– ORIGIN from Greek *numpholēptos* 'caught by nymphs'.

nymphomania ● **noun** uncontrollable or excessive sexual desire in a woman.
– DERIVATIVES **nymphomaniac** noun.

nystagmus /nistagməss/ ● **noun** Medicine rapid involuntary movements of the eyes.
– ORIGIN Greek *nustagmos* 'nodding, drowsiness'.

NZ ● **abbreviation** New Zealand.

Thesaurus

push. **2** *she nuzzled up to her boyfriend* SNUGGLE, cuddle, nestle, burrow, embrace, hug.

nymph ● **noun** **1** *a nymph with winged sandals* SPRITE, sylph, spirit. **2** (*poetic/literary*) *a skinny nymph with brown eyes* GIRL, belle, nymphet, sylph; young woman, young lady; *Scottish & N. English* lass; *Brit. dated* rosebud; *poetic/literary* maid, maiden, damsel.

n

Oo

O¹ (also **o**) ● noun (pl. **Os** or **O's**) **1** the fifteenth letter of the alphabet. **2** (also **oh**) zero, especially when spoken). **3** a human blood type (in the ABO system) lacking both the A and B antigens.

O² ● symbol the chemical element oxygen.

O³ ● exclamation **1** archaic spelling of OH¹. **2** used before a name in the vocative.

oaf ● noun a stupid, boorish, or clumsy man.
– DERIVATIVES **oafish** adjective.
– ORIGIN originally in the sense 'elf's child, changeling', later 'idiot child': from Old Norse, 'elf'.

oak ● noun **1** a large tree which bears acorns and typically has lobed leaves and hard durable wood. **2** a smoky flavour or nose characteristic of wine aged in oak barrels.
– PHRASES **great oaks from little acorns grow** proverb something of small or modest proportions may grow into something very large or impressive.
– DERIVATIVES **oaken** adjective (archaic) **oaky** adjective.
– ORIGIN Old English.

oak apple ● noun a spongy spherical gall which forms on oak trees, caused by wasp larvae.

oakum ● noun chiefly historical loose fibre obtained by untwisting old rope, used especially in caulking wooden ships.
– ORIGIN Old English, 'off-combings'.

OAP ● abbreviation Brit. old-age pensioner.

oar ● noun a pole with a flat blade, used for rowing or steering a boat.
– PHRASES **put one's oar in** informal give an opinion without being asked.
– ORIGIN Old English.

oarlock ● noun N. Amer. a rowlock.

oarsman (or **oarswoman**) ● noun a rower.

OAS ● abbreviation Organization of American States.

oasis ● noun (pl. **oases**) **1** a fertile spot in a desert where water rises to ground level. **2** an area or period of calm in the midst of a difficult or hectic place or situation.
– ORIGIN Greek, from Egyptian.

oast ● noun a kiln for drying hops.
– ORIGIN Old English.

oast house ● noun a building containing an oast, typically conical in shape with a cowl on top.

oat ● noun a cereal plant with a loose branched cluster of florets, cultivated in cool climates.
– PHRASES **feel one's oats** N. Amer. informal feel lively and energetic. **get one's oats** Brit. informal have sexual intercourse. **sow one's wild oats** go through a period of wild or promiscuous behaviour while young.
– DERIVATIVES **oaty** adjective.
– ORIGIN Old English.

oatcake ● noun a savoury oatmeal biscuit.

oater ● noun informal, chiefly US a western film.
– ORIGIN with allusion to oats as feed for horses.

oath ● noun (pl. **oaths**) **1** a solemn promise, especially one that calls on a deity as a witness. **2** an obscene or blasphemous utterance.
– PHRASES **under** (or **on**) **oath** having sworn to tell the truth, especially in a court of law.
– ORIGIN Old English.

oatmeal ● noun meal made from ground oats, used in making porridge and oatcakes.

ob- (also **oc-** before *c*; **of-** before *f*; **op-** before *p*) ● prefix forming words meaning: **1** to, towards: *obverse.* **2** against: *opponent.* **3** finality; completeness: *obsolete.* **4** technical in a direction or manner contrary to the usual.
– ORIGIN Latin *ob* 'towards, against, in the way of'.

obbligato /obligaatō/ (US also **obligato**) ● noun (pl. **obbligatos** or **obbligati**) an instrumental part integral to a piece of music and not to be omitted in performance.
– ORIGIN from Italian, 'obligatory'.

obdurate /obdyoorət/ ● adjective stubbornly refusing to change one's opinion or course of action.
– DERIVATIVES **obduracy** noun **obdurately** adverb **obdurateness** noun.
– ORIGIN Latin *obduratus*, from *durare* 'harden'.

OBE ● abbreviation Officer of the Order of the British Empire.

obeah /ōbiə/ (also **obi**) ● noun a kind of sorcery practised especially in the Caribbean.
– ORIGIN Akan.

obedient ● adjective willing to obey an order or submit to another's authority.
– DERIVATIVES **obedience** noun **obediently** adverb.
– ORIGIN from Latin *oboedire* 'obey'.

obeisance /ōbays'nss/ ● noun **1** deferential respect or homage. **2** a gesture expressing this, such as a bow.
– DERIVATIVES **obeisant** adjective.
– ORIGIN Old French *obeissance*, from *obeir* 'obey'.

obelisk ● noun **1** a tapering stone pillar of square or rectangular cross section, set up as a monument or landmark. **2** another term for OBELUS.
– ORIGIN Greek *obeliskos* 'small pointed pillar'.

obelus /obbələss/ ● noun (pl. **obeli** /obbəlī/) **1** a symbol (†) used in printed matter as a reference mark or to indicate that a person is deceased. **2** a mark (– or ÷) used in ancient manuscripts to mark a word or passage as spurious or doubtful.
– ORIGIN Greek *obelos* 'pointed pillar', also 'critical mark'.

obese ● adjective very fat.
– DERIVATIVES **obesity** noun.
– ORIGIN Latin *obesus*.

Thesaurus

oaf ● noun LOUT, boor, barbarian, Neanderthal, churl, bumpkin, yokel; fool, idiot, imbecile; *informal* cretin, ass, goon, oik, yahoo, ape, lump, clod, meathead, bonehead, lamebrain; *Brit. informal* clot, plonker, berk, pillock, yob, yobbo; *Scottish informal* nyaff, gowk; *N. Amer. informal* bozo, dumbhead, lummox, klutz, goofus, clunk, turkey; *Austral. informal* hoon, dingbat, galah, drongo; *archaic* lubber.

oafish ● adjective STUPID, foolish, idiotic; loutish, awkward, gawkish, clumsy, lumbering, ape-like, cloddish, Neanderthal, uncouth, uncultured, boorish, rough, coarse, brutish, ill-mannered, unrefined; *informal* clodhopping, blockheaded, boneheaded, thickheaded; *Brit. informal* yobbish; *archaic* lubberly.

oasis ● noun **1** *an oasis near Cairo* WATERING HOLE, watering place, water hole, spring. **2** *a cool oasis in a hot summer* REFUGE, haven, retreat, sanctuary, sanctum, harbour, asylum.

oath ● noun **1** *an oath of allegiance* vow, pledge, promise, avowal, affirmation, word (of honour), bond, guarantee; *formal* troth. **2** *he uttered a stream of oaths* SWEAR WORD, profanity, expletive, four-letter word, dirty word, obscenity, vulgarity, curse, malediction; *informal* cuss (word); *formal* imprecation.

obdurate ● adjective STUBBORN, obstinate, intransigent, inflexible, unyielding, unbending, pig-headed, mulish, stiff-necked; headstrong, unshakeable, intractable, unpersuadable, immovable, inexorable, uncompromising, iron-willed, adamant, firm, determined; *Brit. informal* bloody-minded.
– OPPOSITES malleable.

obedient ● adjective COMPLIANT, biddable, acquiescent, tractable, amenable, malleable, pliable, pliant; dutiful, good, law-abiding, deferential, respectful, duteous, well trained, well disciplined, manageable, governable, docile, tame, meek, passive, submissive, unresisting, yielding.
– OPPOSITES rebellious.

obeisance ● noun **1** *a gesture of obeisance* RESPECT, homage, worship, adoration, reverence, veneration, honour, submission, deference. **2** *she made a deep obeisance* BOW, curtsy, bob,

obey ● verb **1** submit to the authority of. **2** carry out (an order). **3** behave in accordance with (a principle or law).
– ORIGIN Old French *obeir*, from Latin *oboedire*, from *audire* 'hear'.
obfuscate /obfuskayt/ ● verb make unclear or unintelligible.
– DERIVATIVES **obfuscation** noun **obfuscatory** adjective.
– ORIGIN Latin *obfuscare* 'darken'.
obi /ōbi/ ● noun (pl. **obis**) a broad sash worn round the waist of a Japanese kimono.
– ORIGIN Japanese, 'belt'.
obit /obbit, ōbit/ ● noun informal an obituary.
obiter dictum /obbitər diktəm/ ● noun (pl. **obiter dicta** /obbitər diktə/) **1** Law a judge's expression of opinion uttered in court or when giving judgement, which is not essential to the decision and is therefore without binding authority. **2** an incidental remark.
– ORIGIN Latin, 'something said in passing'.
obituarist ● noun a writer of obituaries.
obituary /əbityoori/ ● noun (pl. **obituaries**) an announcement that someone has died, especially as published in a newspaper in the form of a brief biography.
– ORIGIN from Latin *obitus* 'death'.
object ● noun /objikt/ **1** a material thing that can be seen and touched. **2** a person or thing to which an action or feeling is directed. **3** a goal or purpose. **4** Grammar a noun or noun phrase governed by a transitive verb or by a preposition. ● verb /əbjekt/ express disapproval or opposition.
– PHRASES **no object** not influencing or restricting choices or decisions: *money is no object.*
– DERIVATIVES **objector** noun.
– ORIGIN Latin *objectum* 'thing presented to the mind'.
objectify ● verb (**objectifies, objectified**) **1** express (something abstract) in a concrete form. **2** degrade to the status of an object.
– DERIVATIVES **objectification** noun.
objection ● noun **1** an expression of disapproval or opposition. **2** the action of challenging or disagreeing: *a letter of objection.*
objectionable ● adjective arousing distaste or opposition.
– DERIVATIVES **objectionableness** noun **objectionably** adverb.
objective ● adjective **1** not influenced by personal feelings or opinions. **2** not dependent on the mind for existence; actual. **3** Grammar relating to a case of nouns and pronouns used for the object of a transitive verb or a preposition. ● noun **1** a goal or aim. **2** the lens in a telescope or microscope nearest to the object observed.
– DERIVATIVES **objectively** adverb **objectivity** noun **objectivize** (also **objectivise**) verb.
objectivism ● noun **1** the tendency to emphasize what is external to or independent of the mind. **2** Philosophy the belief that moral truths exist independently of human knowledge or perception of them.
– DERIVATIVES **objectivist** noun & adjective.
object lesson ● noun a striking practical example of a principle or ideal.
objet d'art /obzhay daar/ ● noun (pl. **objets d'art** pronunc. same) a small decorative or artistic object.
– ORIGIN French, 'object of art'.
objet trouvé /obzhay troovay/ ● noun (pl. **objets trouvés** pronunc. same) an ordinary object found at random and considered as a work of art.
– ORIGIN French, 'found object'.
objurgation /objərgaysh'n/ ● noun rare a severe rebuke.
– DERIVATIVES **objurgate** verb.
– ORIGIN Latin, from *objurgare* 'chide'.
oblate[1] /oblayt/ ● adjective Geometry (of a spheroid) flattened at the poles. Often contrasted with PROLATE.
– ORIGIN Latin *oblatus* 'carried inversely'.
oblate[2] /oblayt/ ● noun a person dedicated to a religious life, but typically not having taken full monastic vows.
– ORIGIN from Latin *oblatus* 'offered'.
oblation ● noun **1** a thing presented or offered to a god. **2** Christian Church the presentation of bread and wine to God in the Eucharist.
– DERIVATIVES **oblational** adjective **oblatory** adjective.
– ORIGIN Latin, from *offerre* 'to offer'.
obligate ● verb **1** compel legally or morally. **2** US commit (assets) as security. ● adjective Biology restricted to a particular function or mode of life.
– ORIGIN Latin *obligare*, from *ligare* 'to bind'.
obligation ● noun **1** an act or course of action to which a person is morally or legally bound. **2** the condition of being morally or legally bound to do something. **3** a debt of gratitude for a service or favour.
obligato ● noun US variant spelling of OBBLIGATO.

Thesaurus

genuflection, salaam; *archaic* reverence; *historical* kowtow.
obelisk ● noun COLUMN, pillar, needle, shaft, monolith, monument.
obese ● adjective FAT, overweight, corpulent, gross, stout, fleshy, outsize, heavy, portly, paunchy, pot-bellied, beer-bellied, well upholstered, well padded, broad in the beam, bulky, bloated, flabby; *informal* porky, roly-poly, blubbery; *Brit. informal* podgy; *archaic* pursy.
– OPPOSITES thin.
obey ● verb **1** *I obeyed him without question* DO WHAT SOMEONE SAYS, carry out someone's orders; submit to, defer to, bow to, yield to. **2** *he refused to obey the order* CARRY OUT, perform, act on, execute, discharge, implement, fulfil. **3** *health and safety regulations have to be obeyed* COMPLY WITH, adhere to, observe, abide by, act in accordance with, conform to, respect, follow, keep to, stick to; play it by the book, toe the line.
– OPPOSITES defy, ignore.
obfuscate ● verb OBSCURE, confuse, blur, muddle, complicate, muddy, cloud, befog; muddy the waters.
– OPPOSITES clarify.
obituary ● noun DEATH NOTICE; *informal* obit; *formal* necrology.
object ● noun **1** *wooden objects* THING, article, item, device, gadget; *informal* doodah, thingamajig, thingamabob, thingummy, whatsit, whatchamacallit, thingy; *Brit. informal* gubbins; *N. Amer. informal* doodad, dingus. **2** *he became the object of criticism* TARGET, butt, focus, recipient, victim. **3** *his object was to resolve the crisis* OBJECTIVE, aim, goal, target, purpose, end (in view), plan, object of the exercise, point; ambition, design, intent, intention, idea.
● verb *teachers objected to the scheme* PROTEST ABOUT, oppose, raise objections to, express disapproval of, take exception to, take issue with, take a stand against, argue against, quarrel with, condemn, draw the line at, demur at, mind, complain about, cavil at, quibble about; beg to differ; *informal* kick up a fuss/stink about.
– OPPOSITES approve, accept.
objection ● noun PROTEST, protestation, demur, demurral, complaint, expostulation, grievance, cavil, quibble; opposition, argument, counter-argument, disagreement, disapproval, dissent; *informal* niggle.
objectionable ● adjective UNPLEASANT, disagreeable, distasteful, displeasing, off-putting, undesirable, obnoxious, offensive, nasty, horrible, horrid, disgusting, awful, terrible, dreadful, frightful, appalling, insufferable, odious, vile, foul, unsavoury, repulsive, repellent, repugnant, revolting, abhorrent, loathsome, hateful, detestable, reprehensible, deplorable; *informal* ghastly; *Brit. informal* beastly; *formal* exceptionable, rebarbative.
– OPPOSITES pleasant.
objective ● adjective **1** *an interviewer must try to be objective* IMPARTIAL, unbiased, unprejudiced, non-partisan, disinterested, neutral, uninvolved, even-handed, equitable, fair, fair-minded, just, open-minded, dispassionate, detached. **2** *the world of objective knowledge* FACTUAL, actual, real, empirical, verifiable.
– OPPOSITES biased, subjective.
● noun *our objective is to build a profitable business* AIM, intention, purpose, target, goal, intent, object, object of the exercise, point, end (in view); idea, design, plan, ambition, aspiration, desire, hope.
objectively ● adverb IMPARTIALLY, without bias, without prejudice, even-handedly, dispassionately, detachedly, equitably, fairly, justly, with an open mind, without fear or favour.
objectivity ● noun IMPARTIALITY, lack of bias/prejudice, fairness, fair-mindedness, neutrality, even-handedness, justice, open-mindedness, disinterest, detachment, dispassion, dispassionateness.
oblation ● noun RELIGIOUS OFFERING, offering, sacrifice, peace offering, burnt offering, first fruits, libation.
obligate ● verb OBLIGE, compel, commit, bind, require, constrain, force, impel, make.
obligation ● noun **1** *his professional obligations* DUTY, commitment, responsibility; function, task, job, assignment, commission, burden, charge, onus, liability, accountability, requirement, debt; *archaic* devoir. **2** *a sense of obligation* DUTY, compulsion, indebted-

obligatory ● adjective **1** required by a legal or other rule; compulsory. **2** (of a ruling) having binding force.
– DERIVATIVES **obligatorily** adverb.

oblige ● verb **1** compel legally or morally. **2** perform a service or favour for. **3** (**be obliged**) be indebted or grateful.
– ORIGIN Latin *obligare*, from *ligare* 'to bind'.

obliging ● adjective willing to do a service or kindness; helpful.
– DERIVATIVES **obligingly** adverb.

oblique /əbleek/ ● adjective **1** neither parallel nor at right angles; slanting. **2** not explicit or direct. **3** Geometry (of a line, plane figure, or surface) inclined at other than a right angle. ● noun Brit. another term for SLASH (in sense 3).
– DERIVATIVES **obliquely** adverb **obliqueness** noun **obliquity** /əblikwiti/ noun.
– ORIGIN Latin *obliquus*.

obliterate /əblittərayt/ ● verb **1** destroy completely. **2** blot out or erase.
– DERIVATIVES **obliteration** noun.
– ORIGIN Latin *obliterare* 'strike out, erase', from *littera* 'letter'.

oblivion ● noun **1** the state of being unaware of what is happening around one. **2** the state of being forgotten. **3** destruction or extinction.
– ORIGIN Latin, from *oblivisci* 'forget'.

oblivious ● adjective not aware of what is happening around one.
– DERIVATIVES **obliviously** adverb **obliviousness** noun.

oblong ● adjective having a rectangular shape. ● noun an oblong object or flat figure.
– ORIGIN Latin *oblongus* 'longish'.

obloquy /obləkwi/ ● noun **1** strong public condemnation. **2** disgrace brought about by public condemnation.
– ORIGIN from Latin *obloqui* 'speak against'.

obnoxious /əbnokshəss/ ● adjective extremely unpleasant.
– DERIVATIVES **obnoxiously** adverb **obnoxiousness** noun.
– ORIGIN originally in the sense 'vulnerable': from Latin *obnoxius* 'exposed to harm'.

oboe /ōbō/ ● noun a woodwind instrument of treble pitch, played with a double reed and having an incisive tone.
– DERIVATIVES **oboist** noun.
– ORIGIN Italian, or from French *hautbois*, from *haut* 'high' + *bois* 'wood'.

obscene ● adjective **1** offending accepted standards of decency; offensive or disgusting. **2** morally repugnant through being excessive: *obscene pay rises*.
– DERIVATIVES **obscenely** adverb.
– ORIGIN Latin *obscaenus* 'ill-omened, abominable'.

obscenity ● noun (pl. **obscenities**) **1** the state or quality of being obscene. **2** an obscene action, image, or expression.

obscurantism /obskyoorantiz'm/ ● noun the practice of preventing the facts or full details of something from becoming known.
– DERIVATIVES **obscurantist** noun & adjective.
– ORIGIN from Latin *obscurare* 'make dark'.

obscure ● adjective (**obscurer**, **obscurest**) **1** not discovered or known about; uncertain. **2** not well known. **3** not clearly expressed or easily understood. **4** hard to make out; indistinct. ● verb conceal or make unclear.
– DERIVATIVES **obscuration** noun **obscurely** adverb **obscurity** noun.
– ORIGIN Latin *obscurus* 'dark'.

obsequies /obsikwiz/ ● plural noun funeral rites.

Thesaurus

ness; duress, necessity, pressure, constraint.
– PHRASES **under an obligation** BEHOLDEN, obliged, in someone's debt, indebted, obligated, owing someone a debt of gratitude, duty-bound, honour-bound.

obligatory ● adjective COMPULSORY, mandatory, prescribed, required, demanded, statutory, enforced, binding, incumbent; requisite, necessary, imperative, unavoidable, inescapable, essential.
– OPPOSITES optional.

oblige ● verb **1** *both parties are obliged to accept the decision* REQUIRE, compel, bind, constrain, obligate, leave someone no option, force. **2** *I'll be happy to oblige you* DO SOMEONE A FAVOUR, accommodate, help, assist, serve; gratify someone's wishes, indulge, humour.

obliged ● adjective THANKFUL, grateful, appreciative, much obliged; beholden, indebted, in someone's debt.

obliging ● adjective HELPFUL, accommodating, willing, cooperative, considerate, complaisant, agreeable, amenable, generous, kind, neighbourly, hospitable, pleasant, good-natured, amiable, gracious, unselfish, civil, courteous, polite; Brit. informal decent.
– OPPOSITES unhelpful.

oblique ● adjective **1** *an oblique line* SLANTING, slanted, sloping, at an angle, angled, diagonal, aslant, slant, slantwise, skew, on the skew, askew, squint; N. Amer. cater-cornered. **2** *an oblique reference* INDIRECT, inexplicit, roundabout, circuitous, circumlocutory, implicit, implied, elliptical, evasive, backhanded. **3** *an oblique glance* SIDELONG, sideways, furtive, covert, sly, surreptitious.
– OPPOSITES straight, direct.
● noun SLASH, solidus, backslash, diagonal, virgule.

obliquely ● adverb **1** *the sun shone obliquely across the tower* DIAGONALLY, at an angle, slantwise, sideways, sidelong, aslant. **2** *he referred obliquely to the war* INDIRECTLY, in a roundabout way, not in so many words, circuitously, evasively.

obliterate ● verb **1** *he tried to obliterate the memory* ERASE, eradicate, expunge, efface, wipe out, blot out, rub out, remove all traces of. **2** *a nuclear explosion that would obliterate a city* DESTROY, wipe out, annihilate, demolish, liquidate, wipe off the face of the earth, wipe off the map; informal zap. **3** *clouds were darkening, obliterating the sun* HIDE, obscure, blot out, block, cover, screen.

oblivion ● noun **1** *they drank themselves into oblivion* UNCONSCIOUSNESS, insensibility, stupor, stupefaction; coma, blackout; poetic/literary the waters of Lethe. **2** *they rescued him from artistic oblivion* OBSCURITY, limbo, anonymity, neglect, disregard.
– OPPOSITES consciousness, fame.

oblivious ● adjective UNAWARE, unconscious, heedless, unmindful, insensible, unheeding, ignorant, blind, deaf, unsuspecting, unobservant; unconcerned, impervious, unaffected.
– OPPOSITES conscious.

obloquy ● noun **1** *he endured years of contempt and obloquy* VILIFICATION, opprobrium, vituperation, condemnation, denunciation, abuse, criticism, censure, defamation, denigration, revilement, calumny, insults, flak; formal castigation, excoriation; archaic contumely. **2** *conduct to which no moral obloquy could reasonably attach* DISGRACE, dishonour, shame, discredit, stigma, humiliation, loss of face, ignominy, odium, opprobrium, disfavour, disrepute, ill repute, infamy, notoriety, scandal.
– OPPOSITES praise, honour.

obnoxious ● adjective UNPLEASANT, disagreeable, nasty, distasteful, offensive, objectionable, unsavoury, unpalatable, awful, terrible, dreadful, frightful, revolting, repulsive, repellent, repugnant, disgusting, odious, vile, foul, abhorrent, loathsome, nauseating, sickening, hateful, insufferable, intolerable; informal horrible, horrid, ghastly, gross, putrid, sick-making, yucky, God-awful; Brit. informal beastly; archaic disgustful, loathly.
– OPPOSITES delightful.

obscene ● adjective **1** *obscene literature* PORNOGRAPHIC, indecent, smutty, dirty, filthy, X-rated, 'adult', explicit, lewd, rude, vulgar, coarse, crude, immoral, improper, off colour; scatological, profane; informal blue, porn, porno, skin. **2** *an obscene crime* SHOCKING, scandalous, vile, foul, atrocious, outrageous, heinous, odious, abhorrent, abominable, disgusting, hideous, repugnant, repulsive, revolting, repellent, loathsome, nauseating, sickening, awful, dreadful, terrible, frightful.

obscenity ● noun **1** *the book was banned on the grounds of obscenity* INDECENCY, immorality, impropriety, smuttiness, smut, lewdness, rudeness, vulgarity, dirt, filth, coarseness, crudity; profanity, profaneness. **2** *the men scowled and muttered obscenities* EXPLETIVE, swear word, oath, profanity, curse, four-letter word, dirty word, blasphemy; informal cuss, cuss word; formal imprecation.

obscure ● adjective **1** *his origins and parentage remain obscure* UNCLEAR, uncertain, unknown, in doubt, doubtful, dubious, mysterious, hazy, vague, indeterminate, concealed, hidden. **2** *obscure references to Proust* MYSTIFYING, puzzling, perplexing, baffling, ambiguous, cryptic, enigmatic, Delphic, oracular, oblique, opaque, elliptical, unintelligible, incomprehensible, impenetrable, unfathomable; abstruse, recondite, arcane, esoteric; informal as clear as mud. **3** *an obscure Peruvian painter* LITTLE KNOWN, unknown, unheard of, undistinguished, unimportant, nameless, minor; unsung, unrecognized, forgotten. **4** *an obscure shape* INDISTINCT, faint, vague, nebulous, ill-defined, unclear, blurred, blurry, misty, hazy.
– OPPOSITES clear, plain, famous, distinct.
● verb **1** *grey clouds obscured the sun* HIDE, conceal, cover, veil, shroud, screen, mask, cloak, cast a shadow over, shadow, block,

– ORIGIN Latin, from *exsequiae* 'funeral rites', influenced by *obsequium* 'dutiful service'.

obsequious /əbseekwiəss/ ● adjective obedient or attentive to an excessive or servile degree.
– DERIVATIVES **obsequiously** adverb **obsequiousness** noun.
– ORIGIN from Latin *obsequium* 'compliance', from *obsequi* 'follow, comply with'.

observance ● noun **1** compliance with the requirements of law, morality, or ritual. **2** (**observances**) acts performed for religious or ceremonial reasons.

observant ● adjective **1** quick to notice things. **2** observing the rules of a religion.

observation ● noun **1** the action or process of closely observing or monitoring. **2** the ability to notice significant details. **3** a comment based on something one has seen, heard, or noticed.
– DERIVATIVES **observational** adjective.

observatory ● noun (pl. **observatories**) a room or building housing an astronomical telescope or other scientific equipment for the study of natural phenomena.

observe ● verb **1** notice; perceive. **2** watch attentively; monitor. **3** make a remark; say. **4** fulfil or comply with.
– DERIVATIVES **observable** adjective **observer** noun.
– ORIGIN Latin *observare* 'to watch'.

obsess ● verb **1** (usu. **be obsessed**) fill the mind of (someone) continually and disturbingly. **2** informal, chiefly N. Amer. be preoccupied in this way.
– ORIGIN originally in the sense 'haunt, possess', referring to an evil spirit: from Latin *obsidere* 'besiege'.

obsession ● noun **1** the state of being obsessed. **2** an idea or thought that intrudes on someone's mind.
– DERIVATIVES **obsessional** adjective.

obsessive ● adjective **1** obsessed with someone or something. **2** affecting the mind continually and disturbingly.
– DERIVATIVES **obsessively** adverb **obsessiveness** noun.

obsessive–compulsive ● adjective Psychiatry relating to a disorder in which a person feels compelled to perform certain actions repeatedly to alleviate persistent fears or intrusive thoughts.

obsidian /əbsiddiən/ ● noun a dark glass-like volcanic rock formed by the rapid solidification of lava without crystallization.
– ORIGIN Latin *obsidianus*, error for *obsianus*, from *Obsius*, the name (in Pliny) of the discoverer of a similar stone.

obsolescent /obsəless'nt/ ● adjective becoming obsolete.
– DERIVATIVES **obsolesce** verb **obsolescence** noun.
– ORIGIN from Latin *obsolescere* 'fall into disuse'.

obsolete ● adjective **1** no longer produced or used; out of date. **2** Biology rudimentary or vestigial.
– ORIGIN Latin *obsoletus* 'grown old, worn out', from *obsolescere* 'fall into disuse'.

obstacle ● noun a thing that blocks one's way or hinders progress.
– ORIGIN Latin *obstaculum*, from *obstare* 'impede'.

obstacle race ● noun a race in which runners have to negotiate fences, pits, and similar obstacles.

obstetrician /obstətrish'n/ ● noun a physician or surgeon qualified to practise in obstetrics.

obstetrics ● plural noun the branch of medicine and surgery concerned with childbirth.
– DERIVATIVES **obstetric** adjective.
– ORIGIN from Latin *obstetrix* 'midwife', from *obstare* 'be present'.

obstinate ● adjective **1** stubbornly refusing to change one's opinion or chosen course of action. **2** hard to deal with or overcome: *an obstinate problem.*

Thesaurus

obliterate, eclipse, darken. **2** *recent events have obscured the issue* CONFUSE, complicate, obfuscate, cloud, blur, muddy; muddy the waters; *poetic/literary* befog.
– OPPOSITES reveal, clarify.

obscurity ● noun **1** *the discovery rescued him from relative obscurity* INSIGNIFICANCE, inconspicuousness, unimportance, anonymity; limbo, twilight, oblivion. **2** *poems of impenetrable obscurity* INCOMPREHENSIBILITY, impenetrability, unintelligibility, opacity. **3** *the obscurities in his poems and plays* ENIGMA, puzzle, mystery, difficulty, problem.
– OPPOSITES fame, clarity.

O

obsequies ● plural noun FUNERAL RITES, funeral service, funeral, burial, interment, entombment, inhumation, last offices; *formal* exequies; *archaic* sepulture.

obsequious ● adjective SERVILE, ingratiating, sycophantic, fawning, unctuous, oily, oleaginous, grovelling, cringing, subservient, submissive, slavish; *informal* slimy, bootlicking, smarmy.

observable ● adjective NOTICEABLE, visible, perceptible, perceivable, detectable, distinguishable, discernible, recognizable, evident, apparent, manifest, obvious, patent, clear, distinct, plain, unmistakable; *archaic* sensible.

observance ● noun **1** *strict observance of the rules* COMPLIANCE, adherence, accordance, respect, observation, fulfilment, obedience; keeping, obeying. **2** *religious observances* RITE, ritual, ceremony, ceremonial, celebration, practice, service, office, festival, tradition, custom, usage, formality, form.

observant ● adjective ALERT, sharp-eyed, sharp, eagle-eyed, hawk-eyed, having eyes like a hawk, keen-eyed, watchful, heedful, aware; on the lookout, on the qui vive, on guard, attentive, vigilant, having one's eyes open/peeled; *informal* beady-eyed, not missing a trick, on the ball.
– OPPOSITES inattentive.

observation ● noun **1** *detailed observation of the animal's behaviour* MONITORING, watching, scrutiny, examination, inspection, survey, surveillance, attention, consideration, study. **2** *his observations were concise and to the point* REMARK, comment, statement, utterance, pronouncement, declaration; opinion, impression, thought, reflection. **3** *the observation of the law* OBSERVANCE, compliance, adherence, respect, obedience; keeping, obeying.

observe ● verb **1** *she observed that all the chairs were occupied* NOTICE, see, note, perceive, discern, spot; *poetic/literary* espy, descry. **2** *she was alarmed to discover he had been observing her* WATCH, look at, eye, contemplate, view, survey, regard, keep an eye on, scrutinize, keep under observation, keep watch on, keep under surveillance, monitor, keep a weather eye on; *informal* keep tabs on, keep a beady eye on; *poetic/literary* behold. **3** *'You look tired,' she observed* REMARK, comment, say, mention, declare, announce, state, pronounce; *formal* opine. **4** *both countries agreed to observe the ceasefire* COMPLY WITH, abide by, keep, obey, adhere to, heed, honour, fulfil, respect, follow, consent to, acquiesce in, accept. **5** *townspeople observed the one-year anniversary of the flood* COMMEMORATE, mark, keep, memorialize, remember, celebrate.

observer ● noun **1** *a casual observer might not have noticed* SPECTATOR, onlooker, watcher, looker-on, fly on the wall, viewer, witness; *informal* rubberneck; *poetic/literary* beholder. **2** *industry observers expect the deal to be finalized today* COMMENTATOR, reporter; monitor.

obsess ● verb PREOCCUPY, be uppermost in someone's mind, prey on someone's mind, prey on, possess, haunt, consume, plague, torment, hound, bedevil, beset, take control of, take over, have a hold on, eat up, grip.

obsessed ● adjective FIXATED, possessed, consumed; infatuated, besotted; *informal* smitten, hung up; *N. Amer. informal* hipped.

obsession ● noun FIXATION, ruling/consuming passion, passion, mania, idée fixe, compulsion, preoccupation, infatuation, addiction, fetish, craze; hobby horse; phobia, complex, neurosis; *informal* bee in one's bonnet, hang-up, thing.

obsessive ● adjective ALL-CONSUMING, consuming, compulsive, controlling, obsessional, fanatical, neurotic, excessive, besetting, tormenting, inescapable; *informal* pathological.

obsolescent ● adjective DYING OUT, on the decline, declining, waning, on the wane, disappearing, past its prime, ageing, moribund, on its last legs, out of date, outdated, old-fashioned, outmoded; *informal* on the way out, past it.

obsolete ● adjective OUT OF DATE, outdated, outmoded, old-fashioned, démodé, passé; no longer in use, disused, fallen into disuse, superannuated, outworn, antiquated, antediluvian, anachronistic, discontinued, old, dated, archaic, ancient, fossilized, extinct, defunct, dead, bygone; *informal* out of the ark, prehistoric; *Brit. informal* past its sell-by date.
– OPPOSITES current, modern.

obstacle ● noun BARRIER, hurdle, stumbling block, obstruction, bar, block, impediment, hindrance, snag, catch, drawback, hitch, handicap, deterrent, complication, difficulty, problem, disadvantage, curb, check; *informal* fly in the ointment; *Brit. informal* spanner in the works; *poetic/literary* trammel.
– OPPOSITES advantage, aid.

obstinacy ● noun STUBBORNNESS, inflexibility, intransigence, intractability, obduracy, mulishness, pig-headedness, wilfulness, contrariness, perversity, recalcitrance, implacability; persistence,

– DERIVATIVES **obstinacy** noun **obstinately** adverb.
– ORIGIN Latin *obstinatus*, from *obstinare* 'persist'.
obstreperous /əbstreppərəss/ ● adjective noisy and difficult to control.
– DERIVATIVES **obstreperously** adverb **obstreperousness** noun.
– ORIGIN from Latin *obstrepere*, from *strepere* 'make a noise'.
obstruct ● verb **1** be in the way of; block. **2** prevent or hinder.
– DERIVATIVES **obstructive** adjective **obstructor** noun.
– ORIGIN Latin *obstruere*, from *struere* 'pile up'.
obstruction ● noun **1** the action of obstructing or the state of being obstructed. **2** a thing that obstructs.
obstructionism ● noun the practice of deliberately blocking or delaying the course of legislative or other procedures.
– DERIVATIVES **obstructionist** noun & adjective.
obtain ● verb **1** come into possession of; get. **2** formal be prevalent, customary, or established.
– DERIVATIVES **obtainable** adjective.
– ORIGIN Latin *obtinere*.
obtrude ● verb **1** become obtrusive. **2** impose or force on someone.
– ORIGIN Latin *obtrudere*, from *trudere* 'to push'.
obtrusive ● adjective noticeable or prominent in an unwelcome or intrusive way.
– DERIVATIVES **obtrusively** adverb **obtrusiveness** noun.
obtuse ● adjective **1** annoyingly insensitive or slow to understand. **2** (of an angle) more than 90° and less than 180°. **3** not sharp-pointed or sharp-edged; blunt.
– DERIVATIVES **obtusely** adverb **obtuseness** noun.
– ORIGIN Latin *obtusus*, from *obtundere* 'beat against'.
obverse ● noun **1** the side of a coin or medal bearing the head or principal design. **2** the opposite or counterpart of a fact or truth. ● adjective **1** denoting the obverse of a coin or medal. **2** corresponding to something as its opposite or counterpart.
– DERIVATIVES **obversely** adverb.
– ORIGIN Latin *obversus*, from *obvertere* 'turn towards'.
obviate /obviayt/ ● verb **1** remove (a need or difficulty). **2** avoid; prevent.
– DERIVATIVES **obviation** noun.
– ORIGIN Latin *obviare*, from *via* 'way'.
obvious ● adjective **1** easily perceived or understood; clear. **2** derogatory predictable and lacking in subtlety.
– DERIVATIVES **obviously** adverb **obviousness** noun.
– ORIGIN originally in the sense 'frequently encountered': from Latin *ob viam* 'in the way'.
OC ● abbreviation Officer Commanding.
ocarina /okkəreenə/ ● noun a small wind instrument with holes for the fingers, typically having the shape of a bird.
– ORIGIN Italian, from *oca* 'goose' (referring to its shape).
Occam's razor (also **Ockham's razor**) ● noun the scientific principle that in explaining a thing no more assumptions should be made than are necessary.
– ORIGIN named after the 13th-century English philosopher William of *Occam*.
occasion ● noun **1** a particular event, or the time at which it takes place. **2** a suitable or opportune time. **3** a special event or celebration. **4** reason or justification: *we have occasion to rejoice.* ● verb cause.
– PHRASES **on occasion** from time to time. **rise to the occasion** perform well in response to a special situation.
– ORIGIN Latin, 'juncture, reason', from *occidere* 'go down, set'.
occasional ● adjective **1** occurring infrequently or irregularly. **2** produced on or intended for particular occasions: *occasional verse.*
– DERIVATIVES **occasionally** adverb.

Thesaurus

tenacity, tenaciousness, doggedness, single-mindedness, determination; Brit. informal bloody-mindedness, bolshiness; formal refractoriness, pertinacity.
obstinate ● adjective STUBBORN, unyielding, inflexible, unbending, intransigent, intractable, obdurate, mulish, stubborn as a mule, pig-headed, self-willed, strong-willed, headstrong, wilful, contrary, perverse, recalcitrant, uncooperative, unmanageable, stiff-necked, uncompromising, implacable, unrelenting, immovable, unshakeable; persistent, tenacious, dogged, single-minded, adamant, determined; Brit. informal bloody-minded, bolshie; N. Amer. informal balky; formal refractory, pertinacious.
– OPPOSITES compliant.
obstreperous ● adjective UNRULY, unmanageable, disorderly, undisciplined, uncontrollable, rowdy, disruptive, truculent, difficult, rebellious, mutinous, riotous, out of control, wild, turbulent, uproarious, boisterous; noisy, loud, clamorous, raucous, vociferous; Brit. informal stroppy, bolshie, rumbustious; N. Amer. informal rambunctious; formal refractory.
– OPPOSITES quiet, restrained.
obstruct ● verb **1** *ensure that air bricks and vents are not obstructed* BLOCK (UP), clog (up), get in the way of, occlude, cut off, shut off, bung up, choke, dam up; barricade, bar; Brit. informal gunge up. **2** *he was charged with obstructing the traffic* HOLD UP, bring to a standstill, stop, halt, block. **3** *fears that the regime would obstruct the distribution of food* IMPEDE, hinder, interfere with, hamper, block, interrupt, hold up, stand in the way of, frustrate, thwart, baulk, inhibit, hamstring, sabotage; slow down, retard, delay, stonewall, stop, halt, restrict, limit, curb, put a brake on, bridle; N. Amer. informal bork.
– OPPOSITES clear, facilitate.
obstruction ● noun OBSTACLE, barrier, stumbling block, hurdle, bar, block, impediment, hindrance, snag, difficulty, catch, drawback, hitch, handicap, deterrent, curb, check, restriction; blockage, stoppage, congestion, bottleneck, hold-up; Medicine occlusion; informal fly in the ointment; Brit. informal spanner in the works.
obstructive ● adjective UNHELPFUL, uncooperative, awkward, difficult, unaccommodating, disobliging, perverse, contrary; Brit. informal bloody-minded, bolshie; N. Amer. informal balky.
– OPPOSITES helpful.
obtain ● verb **1** *the newspaper obtained a copy of the letter* GET, acquire, come by, secure, procure, come into the possession of, pick up, be given; gain, earn, achieve, attain; informal get hold of, get/lay one's hands on, get one's mitts on, land. **2** (formal) *rules obtaining in other jurisdictions* PREVAIL, be in force, apply, exist, be in use, be in effect, stand, hold, be the case.
– OPPOSITES lose.
obtainable ● adjective AVAILABLE, to be had, in circulation, on the market, on offer, in season, at one's disposal, at hand, attainable, procurable, accessible; informal up for grabs, on tap, get-at-able.
obtrusive ● adjective CONSPICUOUS, prominent, noticeable, obvious, unmistakable, intrusive, out of place; informal sticking out a mile, sticking out like a sore thumb.
– OPPOSITES inconspicuous.
obtuse ● adjective STUPID, foolish, slow-witted, slow, dull-witted, unintelligent, ignorant, simple-minded; insensitive, imperceptive, uncomprehending; informal dim, dim-witted, dense, dumb, slow on the uptake, half-witted, brain-dead, moronic, cretinous, thick, dopey, dozy, wooden-headed, boneheaded; Brit. informal divvy; Scottish & N. English informal glaikit; N. Amer. informal dumb-ass, chowder-headed.
– OPPOSITES clever.
obviate ● verb PRECLUDE, prevent, remove, get rid of, do away with, get round, rule out, eliminate, make unnecessary.
obvious ● adjective CLEAR, crystal clear, plain, evident, apparent, manifest, patent, conspicuous, pronounced, transparent, palpable, prominent, marked, decided, distinct, noticeable, perceptible, visible, discernible; unmistakable, indisputable, self-evident, incontrovertible, incontestable, undeniable, as plain as a pikestaff, as clear as day, staring someone in the face; overt, open, undisguised, unconcealed, frank, glaring, blatant, written all over someone; informal as plain as the nose on your face, sticking out like a sore thumb, sticking out a mile.
– OPPOSITES imperceptible.
obviously ● adverb CLEARLY, evidently, plainly, patently, visibly, discernibly, manifestly, noticeably; unmistakably, undeniably, incontrovertibly, demonstrably, unquestionably, undoubtedly, without doubt, doubtless; of course, naturally, needless to say, it goes without saying.
– OPPOSITES perhaps.
occasion ● noun **1** *a previous occasion* TIME, instance, juncture, point; event, occurrence, affair, incident, episode, experience; situation, case, circumstance. **2** *a family occasion* SOCIAL EVENT, event, affair, function, celebration, party, get-together, gathering; informal do, bash. **3** *I doubt if the occasion will arise* OPPORTUNITY, right moment, chance, opening, window. **4** *it's the first time I've had occasion to complain* REASON, cause, call, grounds, justification, need, motive.
● verb *her situation occasioned a good deal of sympathy* CAUSE, give rise to, bring about, result in, lead to, prompt, elicit, call forth, produce, create, arouse, generate, engender, precipitate, provoke,

Occident /oksidənt/ ● noun (**the Occident**) formal or literary the countries of the West.
– ORIGIN from Latin *occidere* 'go down, set', with reference to the setting of the sun.
occidental ● adjective relating to the countries of the West. ● noun (**Occidental**) a person from the West.
occiput /oksiput/ ● noun Anatomy the back of the head.
– DERIVATIVES **occipital** adjective.
– ORIGIN Latin, from *caput* 'head'.
Occitan /oksitən/ ● noun the medieval or modern language of Languedoc (southern France), including Provençal.
– DERIVATIVES **Occitanian** noun & adjective.
– ORIGIN French, from Old French *oc* 'yes' (see LANGUE D'OC).
occlude /əklōōd/ ● verb **1** stop, close up, or obstruct. **2** Chemistry (of a solid) absorb and retain (a gas or impurity). **3** (of a tooth) come into contact with another in the opposite jaw.
– ORIGIN Latin *occludere*.
occluded front ● noun a composite weather front produced when a cold front catches up with a warm front, so that the warm air in between them is forced upwards.
occlusion ● noun technical the process of occluding or blocking up.
– DERIVATIVES **occlusive** adjective.
occult /okult, okkult/ ● noun (**the occult**) supernatural beliefs, practices, or phenomena. ● adjective **1** relating to the occult. **2** beyond ordinary knowledge or experience; esoteric. **3** Medicine (of a disease or process) present but not readily discernible. ● verb /okult/ **1** cut off from view by interposing something. **2** Astronomy (of a celestial body) conceal (another body) from view.
– DERIVATIVES **occultation** noun **occultism** noun **occultist** noun.
– ORIGIN from Latin *occulere* 'conceal'.
occupancy ● noun **1** the action or fact of occupying a place. **2** the proportion of accommodation occupied or used.
occupant ● noun **1** a person who occupies a place at a given time. **2** the holder of a position or office.
occupation ● noun **1** a job or profession. **2** the action, state, or period of occupying or being occupied. **3** a way of spending time.
– DERIVATIVES **occupational** adjective **occupationally** adverb.
occupational hazard ● noun a risk arising as a consequence of a particular occupation.
occupational therapy ● noun the use of particular activities as an aid to recovery from physical or mental illness.
– DERIVATIVES **occupational therapist** noun.
occupy ● verb (**occupies, occupied**) **1** live or have one's place of business in. **2** take control of (a place) by military conquest or settlement. **3** enter and stay in (a building) without authority. **4** fill or take up (a space, time or position). **5** keep busy, active, or preoccupied.
– DERIVATIVES **occupier** noun.
– ORIGIN Latin *occupare* 'seize'.
occur ● verb (**occurred, occurring**) **1** happen; take place. **2** exist or be found to be present. **3** (**occur to**) come into the mind of.
– ORIGIN Latin *occurrere* 'go to meet, present itself'.
occurrence /əkurrənss/ ● noun **1** the fact or frequency of something occurring. **2** a thing that occurs; an incident or event.
ocean ● noun **1** a very large expanse of sea; in particular, each of the Atlantic, Pacific, Indian, Arctic, and Antarctic Oceans. **2** (**the ocean**) chiefly N. Amer. the sea.
– ORIGIN Greek *ōkeanos* 'great stream encircling the earth's disc'.
oceanarium /ōshənairiəm/ ● noun (pl. **oceanariums** or **oceanaria** /ōshənairiə/) a large seawater aquarium.
Oceanian /ōshiaaniən/ ● adjective relating to Oceania, the islands of the Pacific Ocean and adjacent seas. ● noun a person from Oceania; a Polynesian.
oceanic /ōshiannik/ ● adjective **1** relating to the ocean. **2** (**Oceanic**) Oceanian.
oceanography ● noun the branch of science concerned with the physical and biological properties and phenomena of the sea.
– DERIVATIVES **oceanographer** noun **oceanographic** adjective.
oceanology ● noun **1** oceanography. **2** the branch of technology and economics concerned with human use of the sea.
– DERIVATIVES **oceanological** adjective **oceanologist** noun.
ocelot /ossəlot/ ● noun a medium-sized striped and spotted wild cat, native to South and Central America.
– ORIGIN French, from a Nahuatl word meaning 'field tiger'.
och /ok, o<u>kh</u>/ ● exclamation Scottish & Irish expressing surprise, regret, or disbelief.

Thesaurus

O

stir up, inspire, spark off, trigger; poetic/literary beget.
– PHRASES **on occasion.** See OCCASIONALLY.
occasional ● adjective INFREQUENT, intermittent, irregular, periodic, sporadic, odd, random, uncommon, few and far between, isolated, rare; N. Amer. sometime.
– OPPOSITES regular, frequent.
occasionally ● adverb SOMETIMES, from time to time, (every) now and then, (every) now and again, at times, every so often, (every) once in a while, on occasion, periodically, at intervals, irregularly, sporadically, infrequently, intermittently, on and off, off and on.
– OPPOSITES often.
occlude ● verb BLOCK (UP), stop (up), obstruct, clog (up), close, shut, bung up, choke.
occult ● noun *his interest in the occult* THE SUPERNATURAL, supernaturalism, magic, black magic, witchcraft, sorcery, necromancy, wizardry, the black arts, occultism, diabolism, devil worship, devilry, voodoo, hoodoo, white magic, mysticism; NZ makutu. ● adjective **1** *occult powers* SUPERNATURAL, magic, magical, mystical, mystic, psychic, preternatural, transcendental; cabbalistic, hermetic. **2** *the typically occult language of the time* ESOTERIC, arcane, recondite, abstruse, secret; obscure, incomprehensible, impenetrable, puzzling, perplexing, mystifying, mysterious, enigmatic.
occupancy ● noun OCCUPATION, tenancy, tenure, residence, residency, inhabitation, habitation, living, lease, holding, owner-occupancy; formal dwelling.
occupant ● noun **1** *the occupants of the houses* RESIDENT, inhabitant, owner, householder, tenant, renter, leaseholder, lessee; addressee; Brit. occupier, owner-occupier; formal dweller. **2** *the first occupant of the post* INCUMBENT, holder.
occupation ● noun **1** *his father's occupation* JOB, profession, (line) of work, trade, employment, position, post, situation, business, career, métier, vocation, calling, craft; Austral. informal grip; archaic employ. **2** *her leisure occupations* PASTIME, activity, hobby, pursuit, interest, entertainment, recreation, amusement, divertissement. **3** *a property suitable for occupation by older people* RESIDENCE, residency, habitation, inhabitation, occupancy, tenancy, tenure, lease, living in; formal dwelling. **4** *the Roman occupation of Britain* CONQUEST, capture, invasion, seizure, takeover, annexation, overrunning, subjugation, subjection, appropriation; colonization, rule, control, suzerainty.
occupational ● adjective JOB-RELATED, work, professional, vocational, employment, business, career.
occupied ● adjective **1** *tasks which kept her occupied all day* BUSY, engaged, working, at work, active; informal tied up, hard at it, on the go. **2** *all the tables were occupied* IN USE, full, engaged, taken. **3** *only two of the flats are occupied* INHABITED, lived-in, tenanted, settled.
– OPPOSITES free, vacant.
occupy ● verb **1** *Carol occupied the basement flat* LIVE IN, inhabit, be the tenant of, lodge in; move into, take up residence in; people, populate, settle; Scottish stay in; formal reside in, dwell in. **2** *two windows occupied almost the whole of the end wall* TAKE UP, fill, fill up, cover, use up. **3** *he occupies a senior post at the Treasury* HOLD, fill, have; informal hold down. **4** *I need something to occupy my mind* ENGAGE, busy, employ, distract, absorb, engross, preoccupy, hold, interest, involve, entertain, amuse, divert. **5** *the region was occupied by Soviet troops* CAPTURE, seize, take possession of, conquer, invade, overrun, take over, colonize, garrison, annex, subjugate.
occur ● verb **1** *the accident occurred at about 3.30* HAPPEN, take place, come about, transpire, materialize, arise, crop up; N. Amer. informal go down; poetic/literary come to pass, befall, betide; archaic hap; formal eventuate. **2** *the disease occurs chiefly in tropical climates* BE FOUND, be present, exist, appear, prevail, present itself, manifest itself, turn up. **3** *an idea occurred to her* ENTER ONE'S HEAD/MIND, cross one's mind, come to mind, spring to mind, strike one, hit one, dawn on one, suggest itself.
occurrence ● noun **1** *vandalism used to be a rare occurrence* EVENT, incident, happening, phenomenon, affair, matter, circumstance. **2** *the occurrence of cancer increases with age* EXISTENCE, instance, appearance, manifestation, materialization, development; frequency, incidence, rate, prevalence; Statistics distribution.

oche /okki/ (also **hockey**) ● noun Brit. the line behind which darts players stand when throwing.
– ORIGIN perhaps related to Old French *ocher* 'cut a notch in'.

ochlocracy /oklokrəsi/ ● noun formal government by the populace; mob rule.
– ORIGIN from Greek *okhlos* 'mob' + *-kratia* 'power'.

ochre /ōkər/ (US also **ocher**) ● noun an earthy pigment containing ferric oxide, varying from light yellow to brown or red.
– DERIVATIVES **ochreous** /ōkriəss/ adjective **ochrous** adjective.
– ORIGIN Greek *ōkhra*.

ocker ● noun Austral. informal a boorish or uncultivated Australian.
– ORIGIN alteration of *Oscar*, an Australian TV character.

Ockham's razor ● noun variant spelling of OCCAM'S RAZOR.

o'clock ● adverb used to specify the hour when telling the time.
– ORIGIN contraction of *of the clock*.

OCR ● abbreviation optical character recognition.

Oct. ● abbreviation October.

octa- (also **oct-** before a vowel) ● combining form eight; having eight: *octahedron*.
– ORIGIN Greek *oktō* 'eight'.

octad /oktad/ ● noun a group or set of eight.
– ORIGIN from Greek *oktō* 'eight'.

octagon ● noun a plane figure with eight straight sides and eight angles.
– DERIVATIVES **octagonal** adjective.

octahedron /oktəheedrən/ ● noun (pl. **octahedra** /oktəheedrə/ or **octahedrons**) a three-dimensional shape having eight plane faces, in particular eight equal triangular faces.
– DERIVATIVES **octahedral** adjective.

octal /oktəl/ ● adjective relating to a system of numerical notation that has 8 rather than 10 as a base.

octane ● noun Chemistry a liquid hydrocarbon present in petroleum spirit.

octane number (or **octane rating**) ● noun a figure indicating the anti-knock properties of a fuel, based on a comparison with a standard mixture.

octant /oktənt/ ● noun **1** an arc of a circle equal to one eighth of its circumference, or the sector of the circle defined by it. **2** each of eight parts into which a space or solid body is divided by three intersecting planes.
– ORIGIN Latin, from *octo* 'eight'.

octave /oktiv/ ● noun **1** Music a series of eight notes occupying the interval between (and including) two notes, one having twice or half the pitch of the other. **2** Music the interval between two such notes, or the notes themselves sounding together. **3** a group or stanza of eight lines.
– ORIGIN originally referring to a period of eight days following and including a Church festival; from Latin *octava dies* 'eighth day'.

octavo /oktaavō/ ● noun (pl. **octavos**) a size of book page that results from folding each printed sheet into eight leaves (sixteen pages).
– ORIGIN from Latin *in octavo* 'in an eighth'.

octennial ● adjective lasting for or recurring every eight years.
– ORIGIN from Latin *octennium* 'period of eight years'.

octet ● noun **1** a group of eight musicians. **2** a musical composition for eight voices or instruments. **3** a group of eight lines of verse.

octo- (also **oct-** before a vowel) ● combining form eight; having eight: *octosyllabic*.
– ORIGIN Latin *octo* or Greek *oktō* 'eight'.

October ● noun the tenth month of the year.
– ORIGIN from Latin *octo* 'eight', October being originally the eighth month of the Roman year.

octogenarian /oktəjinairiən/ ● noun a person who is between 80 and 89 years old.
– ORIGIN from Latin *octoginta* 'eighty'.

octopus ● noun (pl. **octopuses**) a mollusc with eight sucker-bearing arms, a soft body, beak-like jaws, and no internal shell.
– DERIVATIVES **octopoid** adjective.
– USAGE The standard plural in English of **octopus** is **octopuses**. However, since the word comes from Greek, the Greek plural form **octopodes** is still occasionally used. The plural form **octopi**, formed according to rules for Latin plurals, is incorrect.
– ORIGIN Greek, from *oktō* 'eight' + *pous* 'foot'.

octoroon /oktəroon/ ● noun archaic a person who is one-eighth black by descent.

octuple /oktyoop'l/ ● adjective **1** consisting of eight parts or things. **2** eight times as many or as much. ● verb make or become eight times as many or as large.
– ORIGIN from Latin *octo* 'eight' + *-plus* (as in *duplus* 'double').

octuplet ● noun each of eight children born at one birth.

ocular /okyoolər/ ● adjective of or connected with the eyes or vision. ● noun an eyepiece.
– ORIGIN Latin *ocularis*, from *oculus* 'eye'.

ocularist ● noun a person who makes artificial eyes.

oculist /okyoolist/ ● noun a person who specializes in the medical treatment of diseases or defects of the eye; an ophthalmologist.
– ORIGIN French *oculiste*, from Latin *oculus* 'eye'.

oculus /okyooləss/ ● noun (pl. **oculi** /okyoolee/) Architecture **1** a circular window. **2** the central boss of a volute. **3** an opening at the apex of a dome.
– ORIGIN Latin, 'eye'.

OD informal ● verb (**OD's**, **OD'd**, **OD'ing**) take an overdose of a drug. ● noun an overdose.

odalisque /ōdəlisk/ ● noun historical a female slave or concubine in a harem.
– ORIGIN French, from Turkish *oda* 'chamber' + *lik* 'function'.

odd ● adjective **1** unusual or unexpected; strange. **2** (of whole numbers such as 3 and 5) having one left over as a remainder when divided by two. **3** (in combination) in the region of: *fifty-odd years*. **4** occasional: *we have the odd drink together*. **5** spare; unoccupied: *an odd five minutes*. **6** detached from a pair or set.
– PHRASES **odd one out** a person or thing differing in some way from the other members of a group or set. **odds and ends** miscellaneous articles or remnants.
– DERIVATIVES **oddly** adverb **oddness** noun.
– ORIGIN Old Norse.

oddball ● noun informal a strange or eccentric person.

oddity ● noun (pl. **oddities**) **1** the quality of being strange. **2** a strange person or thing.

odd-job man ● noun a man who does casual or isolated jobs of work of a routine domestic or manual nature.

oddment ● noun an item or remnant from a larger piece or set.

odds ● plural noun **1** the ratio between the amounts staked by the parties to a bet, based on the expected probability either way. **2** (**the odds**) the chances of something happening or being the case. **3** (**the odds**) the balance of advantage; superiority in strength, power, or resources: *she clung to the lead against all the odds*.
– PHRASES **at odds** in conflict or at variance. **it makes no odds** informal, chiefly Brit. it does not matter. **lay** (or **give**) **odds** offer a bet with odds favourable to the other better. **over the odds** Brit.

O

Thesaurus

ocean ● noun **1** *the ocean was calm* THE SEA; *informal* the drink; *Brit. informal* the briny; *poetic/literary* the deep, the waves, the main. **2** *(informal) she had oceans of energy*. See LOT pronoun.

odd ● adjective **1** *an odd man* STRANGE, peculiar, weird, queer, funny, bizarre, eccentric, unusual, unconventional, outlandish, quirky, zany; *informal* wacky, kooky, screwy, oddball, offbeat, off the wall. **2** *quite a few odd things had happened* STRANGE, unusual, peculiar, funny, curious, bizarre, weird, uncanny, queer, outré, unexpected, unfamiliar, abnormal, atypical, anomalous, different, out of the ordinary, out of the way, exceptional, rare, extraordinary, remarkable, puzzling, mystifying, mysterious, perplexing, baffling, unaccountable, uncommon, irregular, singular, deviant, aberrant, freak, freakish. **3** *we have the odd drink together | he does odd jobs for friends* OCCASIONAL, casual, irregular, isolated, random, sporadic, periodic; miscellaneous, various, varied, sundry. **4** *odd shoes* MISMATCHED, unmatched, unpaired; single, lone, solitary, extra, surplus, leftover, remaining.
– OPPOSITES normal, ordinary, regular.
– PHRASES **odd man out** OUTSIDER, exception, oddity, nonconformist, maverick, individualist, misfit, fish out of water, square peg in a round hole.

oddity ● noun **1** *she was regarded as a bit of an oddity* ECCENTRIC, crank, misfit, maverick, nonconformist, rare bird; *informal* character, oddball, weirdo, crackpot, nut, freak; *Brit. informal* nutter; *N. Amer. informal* screwball, kook; *informal, dated* case. **2** *his work remains an oddity in some respects* ANOMALY, aberration, curiosity, rarity. **3** *the oddities of human nature* PECULIARITY, idiosyncrasy, eccentricity, quirk, irregularity, twist.

oddments ● plural noun **1** *oddments of material* SCRAPS, remnants, odds and ends, bits, pieces, bits and pieces, bits and bobs, left-

(especially of a price) above what is generally considered acceptable. **take odds** offer a bet with odds unfavourable to the other better.

odds-on ● adjective **1** (especially of a horse) rated at evens or less to win. **2** very likely to happen or succeed.

ode ● noun a poem expressing noble feelings, often addressed to a person or celebrating an event.
– ORIGIN Greek *ōidē* 'song', from *aeidein* 'sing'.

odiferous /ōdiffərəss/ ● adjective variant spelling of ODORIFEROUS.

odious ● adjective extremely unpleasant; repulsive.
– DERIVATIVES **odiously** adverb **odiousness** noun.
– ORIGIN from Latin *odium* 'hatred'.

odium ● noun general or widespread hatred or disgust.
– ORIGIN Latin.

odometer /ōdommitər/ ● noun chiefly N. Amer. an instrument for measuring the distance travelled by a wheeled vehicle.
– ORIGIN French *odomètre*, from Greek *hodos* 'way'.

odontology /ōdontolləji/ ● noun the scientific study of the structure and diseases of teeth.
– DERIVATIVES **odontologist** noun.
– ORIGIN from Greek *odous* 'tooth'.

odor ● noun US spelling of ODOUR.

odorant ● noun a substance used to give a scent or odour to a product.

odoriferous /ōdəriffərəss/ ● adjective having an odour.
– ORIGIN from Latin *odorifer* 'odour-bearing'.

odour (US **odor**) ● noun **1** a distinctive smell. **2** a lingering quality or impression.
– PHRASES **be in good** (or **bad**) **odour** informal be in or out of favour.
– DERIVATIVES **odorous** adjective **odourless** adjective.
– ORIGIN Latin *odor*.

odyssey /oddisi/ ● noun (pl. **odysseys**) a long eventful journey.
– DERIVATIVES **odyssean** /oddiseeən/ adjective.
– ORIGIN the title of a Greek epic poem attributed to Homer, describing the adventures of Odysseus.

OECD ● abbreviation Organization for Economic Cooperation and Development.

OED ● abbreviation Oxford English Dictionary.

oedema /ideemə/ (US **edema**) ● noun an excess of watery fluid in the cavities or tissues of the body.
– DERIVATIVES **oedematous** adjective.
– ORIGIN Greek *oidēma*, from *oidein* 'to swell'.

Oedipus complex ● noun (in Freudian theory) the complex of emotions aroused in a young child by an unconscious sexual desire for the parent of the opposite sex.
– DERIVATIVES **Oedipal** adjective.
– ORIGIN by association with *Oedipus* in Greek mythology, who unwittingly killed his father and married his mother.

OEM ● abbreviation original equipment manufacturer.

oenology /eenolləji/ (US also **enology**) ● noun the study of wines.
– DERIVATIVES **oenological** adjective **oenologist** noun.
– ORIGIN from Greek *oinos* 'wine'.

oenophile /eenəfīl/ (US also **enophile**) ● noun a connoisseur of wines.
– DERIVATIVES **oenophilist** /eenoffilist/ noun.

o'er ● adverb & preposition archaic or literary form of OVER.

oesophagus /eesoffəgəss/ (US **esophagus**) ● noun (pl. **oesophagi** /eesoffəjī/ or **oesophaguses**) the part of the alimentary canal which connects the throat to the stomach.
– DERIVATIVES **oesophageal** /eesoffəjeeəl/ adjective.
– ORIGIN Greek *oisophagos*.

oestradiol /eestrədīol/ (US **estradiol**) ● noun a major oestrogen produced in the ovaries.

oestrogen /eestrəjən/ (US **estrogen**) ● noun any of a group of steroid hormones which promote the development and maintenance of female characteristics of the body.
– ORIGIN from OESTRUS.

oestrus /eestrəss/ (US **estrus**) ● noun a recurring period of sexual receptivity and fertility in many female mammals.
– DERIVATIVES **oestrous** adjective.
– ORIGIN Greek *oistros* 'gadfly or frenzy'.

oeuvre /övrə/ ● noun the body of work of an artist, composer, author, etc.
– ORIGIN French.

of ● preposition **1** expressing the relationship between a part and a whole. **2** belonging to; coming from. **3** expressing the relationship between a scale or measure and a value. **4** made from. **5** expressing the relationship between a direction and a point of reference. **6** expressing the relationship between a general category and something which belongs to such a category. **7** N. Amer. expressing time in relation to the following hour.
– USAGE It is incorrect to write the word **of** instead of **have** in constructions such as *I could have told you* (not *I could of told you*). This common mistake is made because the pronunciation of **have** in unstressed contexts is the same as that of **of**, so the two words are confused when it comes to writing them down.
– ORIGIN Old English.

off ● adverb **1** away from the place in question. **2** so as to be removed or separated. **3** starting a journey or race. **4** so as to bring to an end or be discontinued. **5** (of an electrical appliance or power supply) not functioning or so as to cease to function. **6** having specified material goods or wealth: *badly off.* ● preposition **1** moving away and often down from. **2** situated or leading in a direction away from. **3** so as to be removed, separated, or absent from. **4** informal having a temporary dislike of. ● adjective **1** unsatisfactory or inadequate: *an off day.* **2** (of food) no longer fresh. **3** located on the side of a vehicle that is normally furthest from the kerb. **4** Brit. informal annoying or unfair. **5** Brit. informal unwell. ● noun **1** (also **off side**) Cricket the half of the field towards which the batsman's feet are pointed when standing to receive the ball. The opposite of LEG. **2** Brit. informal the start of a race or journey. ● verb informal N. Amer. kill; murder.
– PHRASES **off and on** intermittently.
– ORIGIN Old English.

O

Thesaurus

overs, fragments, snippets, offcuts, ends, shreds, tail ends; *Brit. informal* fag ends. **2** *a cellar full of oddments.* See ODDS AND ENDS at ODDS.

odds ● plural noun **1** *the odds are that he is no longer alive* LIKELIHOOD, probability, chances, chance, balance. **2** *the odds are in our favour* ADVANTAGE, edge; superiority, supremacy, ascendancy.
– PHRASES **at odds 1** *he was at odds with his colleagues* IN CONFLICT, in disagreement, on bad terms, at cross purposes, at loggerheads, quarrelling, arguing, at daggers drawn, at each other's throats; *N. Amer.* on the outs. **2** *behaviour at odds with the interests of the company* AT VARIANCE, out of keeping, out of line, in opposition, conflicting, contrary, incompatible, inconsistent, irreconcilable. **odds and ends** BITS AND PIECES, bits and bobs, bits, pieces, stuff, paraphernalia, things, sundries, miscellanea, bric-a-brac, knick-knacks, oddments; *informal* junk; *Brit. informal* odds and sods, clobber, gubbins.

odious ● adjective REVOLTING, repulsive, repellent, repugnant, disgusting, offensive, objectionable, vile, foul, abhorrent, loathsome, nauseating, sickening, hateful, detestable, execrable, abominable, monstrous, appalling, reprehensible, deplorable, insufferable, intolerable, despicable, contemptible, unspeakable, atrocious, awful, terrible, dreadful, frightful, obnoxious, unsavoury, unpalatable, unpleasant, disagreeable, nasty, distasteful; *informal* ghastly, horrible, horrid, gross, God-awful; *Brit. informal* beastly; *archaic* disgustful, loathly.
– OPPOSITES delightful.

odium ● noun DISGUST, abhorrence, repugnance, revulsion, loathing, detestation, hatred, hate, obloquy, dislike, distaste, disfavour, antipathy, animosity, animus, enmity, hostility, contempt; disgrace, shame, opprobrium, discredit, dishonour.
– OPPOSITES approval.

odorous ● adjective SMELLY, malodorous, pungent, acrid, foul-smelling, evil-smelling, stinking, reeking, fetid, rank; *informal* stinky; *Brit. informal* pongy, niffy; *poetic/literary* miasmic, noisome, mephitic.

odour ● noun **1** *an odour of sweat* SMELL, stench, stink, reek; *Brit. informal* pong, whiff, niff, hum; *N. Amer. informal* funk; *poetic/literary* miasma. **2** *an odour of suspicion* ATMOSPHERE, air, aura, quality, flavour, savour, hint, suggestion, impression, whiff.

odyssey ● noun JOURNEY, voyage, trek, travels, quest, crusade, pilgrimage, wandering, journeying; *archaic* peregrination.

off ● adverb & adjective **1** *Kate's off today* AWAY, absent, unavailable, not at work, off duty, on holiday, on leave; free, at leisure; *N. Amer.* on vacation. **2** *the game's off* CANCELLED, postponed, called off. **3** *strawberries are off* UNAVAILABLE, finished, sold out. **4** *the fish was a bit off* ROTTEN, bad, stale, mouldy, high, sour, rancid, turned, spoiled, putrid, putrescent. **5** *(Brit. informal) I felt decidedly off.* See OFF COLOUR sense 1. **6** *(Brit. informal) that remark was a bit off* UNFAIR,

offal ● noun **1** the entrails and internal organs of an animal used as food. **2** decaying or waste matter.
– ORIGIN probably from Dutch *afval*, from *af* 'off' + *vallen* 'to fall'.
offbeat ● adjective **1** Music not coinciding with the beat. **2** informal unconventional; unusual. ● noun Music any of the normally unaccented beats in a bar.
off break ● noun Cricket a ball which spins from the off side towards the leg side after pitching.
off-colour ● adjective **1** Brit. slightly unwell. **2** slightly indecent or obscene.
offcut ● noun a piece of waste material that is left behind after cutting a larger piece.
offence (US **offense**) ● noun **1** an illegal act; a breach of a law or rule. **2** resentment or hurt. **3** the action of making a military attack. **4** N. Amer. the attacking team in a sport.
offend ● verb **1** cause to feel hurt or resentful. **2** be displeasing to. **3** commit an act that is illegal or that goes against an accepted principle.
– DERIVATIVES **offender** noun.
– ORIGIN Latin *offendere* 'strike against'.
offense ● noun US spelling of OFFENCE.
offensive ● adjective **1** causing offence. **2** involved or used in active attack. **3** chiefly N. Amer. relating to the team in possession of the ball or puck in a game. ● noun a military campaign of attack.
– PHRASES **be on the offensive** be ready to act aggressively.
– DERIVATIVES **offensively** adverb **offensiveness** noun.

OFFER ● abbreviation (in the UK) Office of Electricity Regulation.
offer ● verb **1** present for acceptance, refusal, or consideration. **2** express willingness to do something for someone. **3** provide (access or opportunity). **4** present (a prayer or sacrifice) to a deity. **5** (**offer up**) place in the desired position for fixing. ● noun **1** an expression of readiness to do or give something. **2** an amount of money that someone is willing to pay for something. **3** a specially reduced price. **4** a proposal of marriage.
– PHRASES **on offer 1** available. **2** for sale at a reduced price.
– DERIVATIVES **offerer** noun.
– ORIGIN Latin *offerre* 'bestow, present'.
offering ● noun **1** a small gift or donation. **2** a religious sacrifice.
offertory /offərtəri/ ● noun (pl. **offertories**) Christian Church **1** the offering of the bread and wine at the Eucharist. **2** a collection of money made at a religious service.
– ORIGIN Latin *offertorium*.
offhand ● adjective ungraciously nonchalant or cool in manner. ● adverb without previous consideration.
office ● noun **1** a room, set of rooms, or building used as a place for non-manual work. **2** a position of authority or service. **3** tenure of an official position. **4** (**offices**) service done for others: *the good offices of the rector*. **5** (also **Divine Office**) Christian Church the services of prayers and psalms said daily by Catholic priests or other clergy. **6** (**offices**) Brit. dated the parts of a large house given over to household work or to storage.
– ORIGIN Latin *officium* 'performance of a task', from *opus* 'work'

Thesaurus

unjust, uncalled for, below the belt, unjustified, unjustifiable, unreasonable, unwarranted, unnecessary; *informal* a bit much; *Brit. informal* out of order. **7** *(Brit. informal) he was really off with me* UNFRIENDLY, aloof, cool, cold, distant; *informal* stand-offish.
– PHRASES **off and on** PERIODICALLY, at intervals, on and off, (every) once in a while, every so often, (every) now and then/again, from time to time, occasionally, sometimes, intermittently, irregularly.
offbeat ● adjective *(informal)* UNCONVENTIONAL, unorthodox, unusual, eccentric, idiosyncratic, outré, strange, bizarre, weird, peculiar, odd, freakish, outlandish, out of the ordinary, Bohemian, alternative, left-field, zany, quirky; *informal* wacky, freaky, way-out, off the wall, kooky, oddball.
– OPPOSITES conventional.
off colour ● adjective **1** *(Brit.) I'm feeling a bit off colour* UNWELL, ill, poorly, out of sorts, indisposed, not oneself, sick, queasy, nauseous, peaky, liverish, green about the gills, run down, washed out, below par; *informal* under the weather, rough; *Brit. informal* ropy, off; *Scottish informal* wabbit, peely-wally; *Austral./NZ informal* crook. **2** *off-colour jokes* SMUTTY, dirty, rude, crude, suggestive, indecent, indelicate, risqué, racy, bawdy, naughty, blue, vulgar, ribald, broad, salacious, coarse; *informal* raunchy; *Brit. informal* fruity, saucy; *euphemistic* adult.
– OPPOSITES well.
offence ● noun **1** *he denied having committed any offence* CRIME, illegal/unlawful act, misdemeanour, breach of the law, felony, wrongdoing, wrong, misdeed, peccadillo, sin, transgression, infringement; *Law* malfeasance; *archaic* trespass. **2** *an offence to basic justice* AFFRONT, slap in the face, insult, outrage, violation. **3** *I do not want to cause offence* ANNOYANCE, anger, resentment, indignation, irritation, exasperation, wrath, displeasure, hard/bad/ill feelings, disgruntlement, pique, vexation, animosity.
– PHRASES **take offence** BE OFFENDED, take exception, take something personally, feel affronted, feel resentful, take something amiss, take umbrage, get upset, get annoyed, get angry, get into a huff; *Brit. informal* get the hump.
offend ● verb **1** *I'm sorry if I offended him* HURT SOMEONE'S FEELINGS, give offence to, affront, displease, upset, distress, hurt, wound; annoy, anger, exasperate, irritate, vex, pique, gall, irk, nettle, tread on someone's toes; *Brit.* rub up the wrong way; *informal* rile, rattle, peeve, needle, put someone's nose out of joint, put someone's back up. **2** *the smell of cigarette smoke offended him* DISPLEASE, be distasteful to, be disagreeable to, be offensive to, disgust, repel, revolt, sicken, nauseate; *informal* turn off; *N. Amer. informal* gross out. **3** *criminals who offend again and again* BREAK THE LAW, commit a crime, do wrong, sin, transgress; *archaic* trespass.
offended ● adjective AFFRONTED, insulted, aggrieved, displeased, upset, hurt, wounded, disgruntled, put out, annoyed, angry, cross, exasperated, indignant, irritated, vexed, piqued, irked, stung, galled, nettled, resentful, in a huff, huffy, in high dudgeon; *informal* riled, miffed, peeved, aggravated; *Brit. informal* narked; *N. Amer. informal* sore.
– OPPOSITES pleased.
offender ● noun WRONGDOER, criminal, lawbreaker, miscreant, malefactor, felon, delinquent, culprit, guilty party, sinner, transgressor; *Law* malfeasant.
offensive ● adjective **1** *offensive remarks* INSULTING, rude, impertinent, insolent, derogatory, disrespectful, personal, hurtful, wounding, abusive; annoying, exasperating, irritating, galling, provocative, outrageous; discourteous, uncivil, impolite; *formal* exceptionable. **2** *an offensive smell* UNPLEASANT, disagreeable, nasty, distasteful, displeasing, objectionable, off-putting, awful, terrible, dreadful, frightful, obnoxious, abominable, disgusting, repulsive, repellent, repugnant, revolting, abhorrent, loathsome, odious, vile, foul, sickening, nauseating; *informal* ghastly, horrible, horrid, gross, God-awful; *Brit. informal* beastly; *archaic* disgustful. **3** *an offensive air action* HOSTILE, attacking, aggressive, invading, combative, belligerent, on the attack.
– OPPOSITES complimentary, pleasant, defensive.
● noun *a military offensive* ATTACK, assault, onslaught, drive, invasion, push, thrust, charge, sortie, sally, foray, raid, incursion, blitz, campaign.
offer ● verb **1** *Frank offered another suggestion* PUT FORWARD, proffer, give, present, come up with, suggest, recommend, propose, advance, submit, tender, render. **2** *she offered to help* VOLUNTEER, volunteer one's services, be at someone's disposal, be at someone's service, step/come forward, show willing. **3** *the product is offered at a competitive price* PUT UP FOR SALE, put on the market, sell, market, put under the hammer; *Law* vend. **4** *he offered $200* BID, tender, put in a bid of, put in an offer of. **5** *a job offering good career prospects* PROVIDE, afford, supply, give, furnish, present, hold out. **6** *she offered no resistance* ATTEMPT, try, give, show, express; *formal* essay. **7** *birds were offered to the gods* SACRIFICE, offer up, immolate.
– OPPOSITES withdraw, refuse.
● noun **1** *offers of help* PROPOSAL, proposition, suggestion, submission, approach, overture. **2** *the highest offer* BID, tender, bidding price.
– PHRASES **on offer** ON SALE, up for sale, on the market; available, obtainable, to be had; *N. Amer.* on the block.
offering ● noun **1** *you may place offerings in the charity box* CONTRIBUTION, donation, gift, present, handout, widow's mite; charity; *formal* benefaction; *historical* alms. **2** *many offerings were made to the goddess* SACRIFICE, oblation, burnt offering, immolation, libation, first fruits.
offhand ● adjective *an offhand manner* CASUAL, careless, uninterested, unconcerned, indifferent, cool, nonchalant, blasé, insouciant, cavalier, glib, perfunctory, cursory, unceremonious, ungracious, dismissive, discourteous, uncivil, impolite, terse, abrupt, curt; *informal* off, couldn't-care-less, take-it-or-leave-it.
● adverb *I can't think of a better answer offhand* ON THE SPUR OF THE

+ *facere* 'do'.
office boy (or **office girl**) ● noun a young person employed in an office to carry out routine tasks.
officer ● noun **1** a person holding a position of authority, especially a member of the armed forces who holds a commission or a member of the police force. **2** a holder of a public, civil, or ecclesiastical office.
official ● adjective **1** relating to an authority or public body and its activities and responsibilities. **2** having the approval or authorization of such a body. ● noun a person holding public office or having official duties.
– DERIVATIVES **officialdom** noun **officially** adverb.
official birthday ● noun (in the UK) a day in June chosen for the observance of the sovereign's birthday.
officialese ● noun formal and wordy language considered to be characteristic of official documents.
official secret ● noun Brit. a piece of information that is important for national security and is officially classified as confidential.
officiant /əfish'nt/ ● noun a priest or minister who performs a religious service or ceremony.
officiate /əfishiayt/ ● verb **1** act as an official. **2** perform a religious service or ceremony.
– DERIVATIVES **officiation** noun **officiator** noun.
– ORIGIN Latin *officiare* 'perform divine service'.
officinal /offiseen'l, əfissin'l/ ● adjective (of a herb or drug) used in medicine.
– ORIGIN from Latin *officinalis* 'storeroom for medicines'.
officious ● adjective asserting authority or interfering in an overbearing way.
– DERIVATIVES **officiously** adverb **officiousness** noun.
offing ● noun the more distant part of the sea in view.
– PHRASES **in the offing** likely to happen or appear soon.
offish ● adjective informal aloof or distant in manner.
off-key ● adjective & adverb **1** Music not in the correct key or of the correct pitch. **2** inappropriate.
off-licence ● noun Brit. a shop selling alcoholic drink for consumption elsewhere.
off-limits ● adjective out of bounds.
off-line ● adjective not connected to a computer.
offload ● verb **1** unload (a cargo). **2** rid oneself of.
off-peak ● adjective & adverb at a time when demand is less.
off-piste ● adjective & adverb Skiing away from prepared ski runs.
offprint ● noun a printed copy of an article that originally appeared as part of a larger publication.
off-putting ● adjective unpleasant or disconcerting.
off-ramp ● noun N. Amer. an exit road from a motorway.
off-road ● adverb away from the road; on rough terrain.
off season ● noun a time of year when a particular activity is not engaged in or a business is quiet.
offset ● noun **1** a consideration or amount that diminishes or balances the effect of a contrary one. **2** the amount by which something is out of line. **3** a side shoot from a plant serving for propagation. **4** a method of printing in which ink is transferred from a plate or stone to a uniform rubber surface and from that to the paper. ● verb (**offsetting**; past and past part. **offset**) **1** counterbalance; compensate for. **2** place out of line. **3** transfer an impression by means of offset printing.
offshoot ● noun **1** a side shoot on a plant. **2** a thing that develops from something else.
offshore ● adjective & adverb **1** situated at sea some distance from the shore. **2** (of the wind) blowing towards the sea from the land. **3** relating to the business of extracting oil or gas from the seabed. **4** made, situated, or registered abroad. **5** relating to a foreign country.
offside ● adjective & adverb (in games such as football) occupying a position on the field where playing the ball or puck is not allowed. ● noun **1** the fact of being offside. **2** chiefly Brit. the side of a vehicle furthest from the kerb. **3** the right side of a horse.
offspring ● noun (pl. same) a person's child or children, or the young of an animal.
offstage ● adjective & adverb (in a theatre) not on the stage and so not visible to the audience.
off-white ● noun a white colour with a grey or yellowish tinge.
Ofgas ● abbreviation (in the UK) Office of Gas Supply.
Ofsted ● abbreviation (in the UK) Office for Standards in Education.
OFT ● abbreviation (in the UK) Office of Fair Trading.
oft (also **oft-times**) ● adverb archaic or literary often.
– ORIGIN Old English.
Oftel ● abbreviation (in the UK) Office of Telecommunications.
often (also archaic or N. Amer. **oftentimes**) ● adverb (**oftener**, **oftenest**) **1** frequently. **2** in many instances.
– USAGE The comparative and superlative forms **oftener** and **oftenest** are not incorrect, but are rarely used now in British English, the more usual constructions being **more often** and

O

Thesaurus

MOMENT, without consideration, extempore, impromptu, ad lib; extemporaneously, spontaneously; *informal* off the cuff, off the top of one's head, just like that.
office ● noun **1** *her office in Aldersgate Street* PLACE OF WORK, place of business, workplace, workroom. **2** *the newspaper's Paris office* BRANCH, division, section, bureau, department; agency. **3** *he assumed the office of President* POST, position, appointment, job, occupation, role, situation, function, capacity. **4** *he was saved by the good offices of his uncle* ASSISTANCE, help, aid, services, intervention, intercession, mediation, agency. **5** *(dated) the offices of a nurse* DUTY, job, task, chore, obligation, assignment, responsibility, charge, commission.
officer ● noun **1** *an officer in the army* military officer, commissioned officer, non-commissioned officer, NCO, commanding officer, CO. **2** *all officers carry warrant cards.* See POLICE OFFICER. **3** *the officers of the society* OFFICIAL, office-holder, committee member, board member; public servant, administrator, executive, functionary, bureaucrat; *derogatory* apparatchik.
official ● adjective **1** *an official inquiry* AUTHORIZED, approved, validated, authenticated, certified, accredited, endorsed, sanctioned, licensed, recognized, accepted, legitimate, legal, lawful, valid, bona fide, proper, ex cathedra; *informal* kosher. **2** *an official function* CEREMONIAL, formal, solemn, ceremonious; bureaucratic; *informal* stuffed-shirt.
– OPPOSITES unauthorized, informal.
● noun *a union official* OFFICER, office-holder, administrator, executive, appointee, functionary; bureaucrat, mandarin; representative, agent; *Brit.* jack-in-office; *derogatory* apparatchik.
officiate ● verb **1** *he officiated in the first two matches* BE IN CHARGE OF, take charge of, preside over; oversee, superintend, supervise, conduct, run. **2** *Father Buckley officiated at the wedding service* CONDUCT, perform, celebrate, solemnize.
officious ● adjective SELF-IMPORTANT, bumptious, self-assertive, pushy, overbearing, overzealous, domineering, opinionated, interfering, intrusive, meddlesome, meddling; *informal* bossy.
– OPPOSITES self-effacing.
offing ● noun
– PHRASES **in the offing** ON THE WAY, coming, (close) at hand, near, imminent, in prospect, on the horizon, in the wings, just around the corner, in the air, in the wind, brewing, upcoming, forthcoming; *informal* on the cards.
off-key ● adjective **1** *an off-key rendition of 'Amazing Grace'* OUT OF TUNE, flat, tuneless, discordant, unharmonious. **2** *the cinematic effects are distractingly off-key* INCONGRUOUS, inappropriate, unsuitable, out of place, out of keeping, jarring, dissonant, inharmonious.
– OPPOSITES harmonious.
offload ● verb **1** *the cargo was being offloaded* UNLOAD, remove, empty (out), tip (out); *archaic* unlade. **2** *he offloaded 5,000 of the shares* DISPOSE OF, dump, jettison, get rid of, transfer, shift; palm off, foist, fob off.
off-putting ● adjective **1** *an off-putting aroma* UNPLEASANT, unappealing, uninviting, unattractive, disagreeable, offensive, distasteful, unsavoury, unpalatable, unappetizing, objectionable, nasty, disgusting, repellent; *informal* horrid, horrible. **2** *her manner was off-putting* DISCOURAGING, disheartening, demoralizing, dispiriting, daunting, disconcerting, unnerving, unsettling; *formal* rebarbative.
offset ● verb COUNTERBALANCE, balance (out), cancel (out), even out/up, counteract, countervail, neutralize, compensate for, make up for, make good, redeem.
offshoot ● noun **1** *the plant's offshoots* SIDE SHOOT, shoot, sucker, tendril, runner, scion, slip, offset, stolon; twig, branch, bough, limb. **2** *an offshoot of Cromwell's line* DESCENDANT, scion. **3** *an offshoot of the growth of interest in heritage* OUTCOME, result, effect, consequence, upshot, product, by-product, spin-off, development, ramification.
offspring ● noun CHILDREN, sons and daughters, progeny, family,

most often. However **oftener** and **oftenest** do occur more frequently in North American English. The form **oftentimes**, which developed as an extension of **oft-times**, is also archaic in British English although still used in North America.

Ofwat • abbreviation (in the UK) Office of Water Services.

ogee /ōjee/ Architecture • adjective showing in section an S-shaped curve. • noun an S-shaped line or moulding.
– ORIGIN apparently from OGIVE (with which it was originally synonymous).

ogee arch • noun an arch with two ogee curves meeting at the apex.

ogham /oggəm/ (also **ogam**) • noun an ancient British and Irish alphabet, consisting of characters formed by strokes across or on either side of a continuous line.
– ORIGIN Irish *ogam*.

ogive /ōjiv/ • noun Architecture **1** a pointed or Gothic arch. **2** one of the diagonal groins or ribs of a vault.
– DERIVATIVES **ogival** adjective.
– ORIGIN French.

ogle • verb stare at lecherously. • noun a lecherous look.
– DERIVATIVES **ogler** noun.
– ORIGIN probably from Low German or Dutch.

ogre • noun (fem. **ogress**) **1** (in folklore) a man-eating giant. **2** a cruel or terrifying person.
– DERIVATIVES **ogreish** (also **ogrish**) adjective.
– ORIGIN French.

OH • abbreviation Ohio.

oh[1] • exclamation **1** expressing surprise, disappointment, joy, or other emotion. **2** used to acknowledge something that has just been said.

oh[2] • noun variant spelling of O[1] (in sense 2).

ohm • noun the SI unit of electrical resistance, transmitting a current of one ampere when subjected to a potential difference of one volt. (Symbol: Ω)
– ORIGIN named after the German physicist G. S. *Ohm* (1789–1854).

OHMS • abbreviation on Her (or His) Majesty's Service.

Ohm's law • noun Physics a law stating that electric current is proportional to voltage and inversely proportional to resistance.

ohnosecond • noun Computing, informal a moment in which one realizes that one has made an error, typically by pressing the wrong key.

OHP • abbreviation Brit. overhead projector.

-oid • suffix forming adjectives and nouns: **1** Zoology denoting an animal belonging to a higher taxon with a name ending in *-oidea*: *hominoid*. **2** denoting form or resemblance: *asteroid*.
– DERIVATIVES **-oidal** suffix.
– ORIGIN Greek *-oeidēs*; related to *eidos* 'form'.

OIEO • abbreviation Brit. offers in excess of.

oik (also **oick**) • noun informal an uncouth or obnoxious person.
– ORIGIN of unknown origin.

oil • noun **1** a viscous liquid obtained from petroleum, used especially as a fuel or lubricant. **2** any of various viscous liquids which are insoluble in water and are obtained from animals or plants. **3** Chemistry any of a group of natural esters of glycerol and various fatty acids, which are liquid at room temperature. **4** (also **oils**) oil paint. • verb lubricate, coat, or impregnate with oil.
– ORIGIN Old French *oile*, from Latin *oleum* 'oil, olive oil'.

oilcake • noun a mass of compressed linseed or other plant material left after oil has been extracted, used as fodder or fertilizer.

oilcan • noun a can with a long nozzle used for applying oil to machinery.

oilcloth • noun cotton fabric treated with oil to make it waterproof.

oiler • noun **1** an oil tanker. **2** an oilcan. **3** N. Amer. informal an oil well. **4** (**oilers**) N. Amer. informal oilskin garments.

oilfield • noun an area of land or seabed underlain by strata yielding significant quantities of mineral oil.

oil-fired • adjective (especially of a heating system or power station) using oil as fuel.

oil lamp • noun a lamp using oil as fuel.

oil paint • noun a paste made with ground pigment and a drying oil such as linseed oil, used by artists.

oil palm • noun a tropical West African palm which is the chief source of palm oil.

oil platform • noun a structure designed to stand on the seabed to provide a stable base above water for the drilling and regulation of oil wells.

oil rig • noun an oil platform.

oilseed • noun any of a number of seeds from cultivated crops yielding oil, e.g. rape, peanut, or cotton.

oil shale • noun fine-grained sedimentary rock from which oil can be extracted.

oilskin • noun **1** heavy cotton cloth waterproofed with oil. **2** (**oilskins**) a set of garments made of oilskin.

oil slick • noun a film or layer of oil floating on an expanse of water.

oilstone • noun a fine-grained flat stone used with oil for sharpening chisels, planes, or other tools.

oil well • noun an artificially made well or shaft in rock from which mineral oil is drawn.

oily • adjective (**oilier**, **oiliest**) **1** containing, covered with, or soaked in oil. **2** resembling oil. **3** (of a person) unpleasantly smooth and ingratiating.
– DERIVATIVES **oiliness** noun.

oink • noun the characteristic grunting sound of a pig. • verb make such a sound.
– ORIGIN imitative.

ointment • noun a smooth substance that is rubbed on the skin for medicinal purposes.
– ORIGIN Old French *oignement*, from Latin *unguentum*, from *unguere* 'anoint'.

OIRO • abbreviation Brit. offers in the region of.

Ojibwa /əjibway/ • noun (pl. same or **Ojibwas**) a member of an American Indian people of the area around Lake Superior.
– ORIGIN Ojibwa, said to mean 'puckered', with reference to their moccasins.

OK[1] (also **okay**) informal • exclamation **1** expressing agreement or acquiescence. **2** introducing an utterance. • adjective **1** satisfactory, but not especially good. **2** permissible. • adverb in a satisfactory manner or to a satisfactory extent. • noun an authorization or approval. • verb (**OK's**, **OK'd**, **OK'ing**) give approval to.
– ORIGIN probably an abbreviation of *orl korrect*, humorous form of *all correct*, popularized as a slogan during President Van Buren's re-election campaign of 1840 in the US; his nickname *Old Kinderhook* (derived from his birthplace) provided the initials.

OK[2] • abbreviation Oklahoma.

okapi /ōkaapi/ • noun (pl. same or **okapis**) a large mammal of the giraffe family that lives in the rainforests of northern Zaire (Democratic Republic of Congo), having a dark chestnut coat with stripes on the hindquarters and upper legs.
– ORIGIN a local word.

okay • exclamation, adjective, adverb, noun, & verb variant spelling of OK[1].

okey-dokey (also **okey-doke**) • exclamation variant form of OK[1].

Okie • noun (pl. **Okies**) US informal **1** a person from the state of Oklahoma. **2** derogatory a migrant agricultural worker from Oklahoma who was forced to leave their farm during the depression

Thesaurus

youngsters, babies, infants, brood; descendants, heirs, successors; *Law* issue; *informal* kids; *Brit. informal* sprogs, brats; *derogatory* spawn; *archaic* fruit of one's loins.

often • adverb FREQUENTLY, many times, many a time, a lot, on many/numerous occasions, as often as not, repeatedly; regularly, routinely, usually, habitually, commonly, generally, in many cases/instances, ordinarily; *N. Amer.* oftentimes; *poetic/literary* oft, oft-times.
– OPPOSITES seldom.

ogle • verb LEER AT, stare at, eye, make eyes at; *informal* eye up, give someone the glad eye, lech after, undress with one's eyes, give someone the come-on; *Austral./NZ informal* perv on.

ogre • noun **1** *an ogre with two heads* MONSTER, giant, troll. **2** *he is not the ogre he sometimes seems to be* BRUTE, fiend, monster, beast, barbarian, savage, animal, tyrant; *informal* bastard, swine, pig.

ogress • noun **1** *a one-eyed ogress* MONSTER, giantess. **2** *the French teacher was a real ogress* HARRIDAN, tartar, termagant, gorgon, virago; *informal* battleaxe.

oily • adjective **1** *oily substances* GREASY, oleaginous; *technical* sebaceous; *formal* pinguid. **2** *oily food* GREASY, fatty, buttery, swimming in oil/fat. **3** *an oily man* UNCTUOUS, ingratiating, smooth-talking, fulsome, flattering; obsequious, sycophantic, oleaginous; *informal*

of the 1930s.

okra /okrə, ōkrə/ ● noun the long ridged seed pods of a tropical plant of the mallow family, eaten as a vegetable.
– ORIGIN a West African word.

old ● adjective (**older**, **oldest**) **1** having lived for a long time; no longer young. **2** made or built long ago. **3** possessed or used for a long time. **4** dating from far back; long-established or known. **5** former; previous. **6** of a specified age. **7** informal expressing affection, familiarity, or contempt: *good old Mum.*
– PHRASES **of old 1** in or belonging to the past. **2** for a long time. **the old days** a period in the past. **the old country** the native country of a person who has gone to live abroad. **the old school** the traditional form or type: *a gentleman of the old school.* **you can't put an old head on young shoulders** proverb you can't expect a young person to have the wisdom or maturity associated with older people.
– DERIVATIVES **oldish** adjective **oldness** noun.
– ORIGIN Old English.

old age ● noun **1** the later part of normal life. **2** the state of being old.

old-age pensioner ● noun an old person, especially one receiving a retirement pension.

old boy ● noun **1** a former male pupil of a school. **2** informal an elderly man. **3** an affectionate form of address to a man or boy.

old boy network (also **old boys' network**) ● noun an informal system through which men use their positions of influence to help others who went to the same school or university, or who share a similar social background.

olde /ōld, ōldi/ (also **olde worlde**) ● adjective pseudo-archaic old-fashioned in a way that is intended to be attractively quaint.

olden ● adjective of a former age.

Old English ● noun the language of the Anglo-Saxons (up to about 1150), an inflected language with a Germanic vocabulary.

Old English sheepdog ● noun a large sheepdog of a breed with a shaggy blue-grey and white coat.

old-fashioned ● adjective **1** relating to styles or views that are no longer current. **2** disapproving: *he gave her an old-fashioned look.*

Old French ● noun the French language up to *c.*1400.

old girl ● noun **1** a former female pupil of a school. **2** informal an elderly woman. **3** an affectionate term of address to a girl or woman.

Old Glory ● noun US informal the US national flag.

old gold ● noun a dull brownish-gold colour.

old guard ● noun the original or long-standing members of a group, regarded as being unwilling to accept change.

old hand ● noun a person with a lot of experience.

old hat ● adjective informal tediously familiar or out of date.

oldie ● noun informal an old person or thing.

old lady ● noun **1** an elderly woman. **2** (**one's old lady**) informal one's mother, wife, or girlfriend.

old maid ● noun **1** derogatory a single woman regarded as too old for marriage. **2** a prim and fussy person. **3** a card game in which players collect pairs and try not to be left with an odd penalty card, typically a queen.

old man ● noun **1** an elderly man. **2** (**one's old man**) informal one's father, husband, or male partner. **3** Brit. informal an affectionate form of address between men or boys.

old man's beard ● noun **1** a wild clematis with grey fluffy hairs around the seeds. **2** a lichen forming shaggy greyish growths on trees.

old master ● noun a great artist of former times, especially of the 13th–17th century in Europe.

Old Nick ● noun an informal name for the Devil.

Old Norse ● noun the North Germanic language of medieval Norway, Iceland, Denmark, and Sweden, from which the modern Scandinavian languages are derived.

old stager ● noun informal a very experienced or long-serving person.

oldster ● noun informal, chiefly N. Amer. an older person.

Old Stone Age ● noun the Palaeolithic period.

Old Style ● noun the method of calculating dates using the Julian calendar.

old sweat ● noun informal a veteran soldier.

Old Testament ● noun the first part of the Christian Bible, comprising thirty-nine books and corresponding approximately to the Hebrew Bible.

old-time ● adjective pleasingly traditional or old-fashioned.

old-timer ● noun informal a very experienced or long-serving person.

old wives' tale ● noun a widely held traditional belief that is now thought to be unscientific or incorrect.

old woman ● noun **1** an elderly woman. **2** (**one's old woman**) informal one's mother, wife, or female partner. **3** derogatory a fussy or timid person.

Old World ● noun Europe, Asia, and Africa, regarded collectively as the part of the world known before the discovery of the Americas.

O

Thesaurus

smarmy, slimy.

ointment ● noun LOTION, cream, salve, liniment, embrocation, rub, gel, balm, emollient, unguent; *technical* humectant.

OK, okay *(informal)* ● exclamation *OK, I'll go with him* ALL RIGHT, right, right then, right you are, very well, very good, fine; *informal* okey-doke(y); *Brit. informal* righto, righty-ho.
● adjective **1** *the film was OK* SATISFACTORY, all right, acceptable, competent; adequate, tolerable, passable, reasonable, fair, decent, not bad, average, middling, moderate, unremarkable, unexceptional; *informal* so-so, fair-to-middling. **2** *Jo's feeling OK now* FINE, all right, well, in good shape, in good health, fit, healthy, as fit as a fiddle/flea. **3** *it is OK for me to come?* PERMISSIBLE, allowable, acceptable, all right, in order, permitted, fitting, suitable, appropriate.
– OPPOSITES unsatisfactory, ill.
● noun *he's just given me the OK* AUTHORIZATION, approval, seal of approval, agreement, consent, assent, permission, endorsement, ratification, sanction, approbation, confirmation, blessing, leave; *informal* the go-ahead, the green light, the thumbs up, say-so.
– OPPOSITES refusal.
● verb *the move must be okayed by the president* AUTHORIZE, approve, agree to, consent to, sanction, pass, ratify, endorse, allow, give something the nod, rubber-stamp; *informal* give the go-ahead, give the green light, give the thumbs up; *formal* accede to.
– OPPOSITES refuse, veto.

old ● adjective **1** *old people* ELDERLY, aged, older, senior, advanced in years, venerable; in one's dotage, long in the tooth, grey-haired, grizzled, hoary, past one's prime, not as young as one was, ancient, decrepit, doddering, doddery, not long for this world, senescent, senile, superannuated; *informal* getting on, past it, over the hill, no spring chicken. **2** *old farm buildings* DILAPIDATED, broken-down, run down, tumbledown, ramshackle, decaying, crumbling, disintegrating. **3** *old clothes* WORN, worn out, shabby, threadbare, holey, torn, frayed, patched, tattered, moth-eaten, ragged; old-fashioned, out of date, outmoded; cast-off, hand-me-down; *informal* tatty. **4** *old cars* ANTIQUE, veteran, vintage. **5** *she's old for her years* MATURE, wise, sensible, experienced, worldly-wise, knowledgeable. **6** *in the old days* BYGONE, past, former, olden, of old, previous, early, earlier, earliest; medieval, ancient, classical, primeval, primordial, prehistoric. **7** *the same old phrases* HACKNEYED, hack, banal, trite, overused, overworked, tired, worn out, stale, clichéd, platitudinous, unimaginative, stock, conventional; out of date, outdated, old-fashioned, outmoded, hoary; *informal* old hat, corny, played out. **8** *an old girlfriend* FORMER, previous, ex-, one-time, sometime, erstwhile; *formal* quondam.
– OPPOSITES young, new, modern.
– PHRASES **old age** DECLINING YEARS, advanced years, age, oldness, winter/autumn of one's life, senescence, senility, dotage. **old man 1** SENIOR CITIZEN, pensioner, OAP, elder, grandfather; patriarch; *informal* greybeard, codger; *Brit. informal* buffer; *archaic* grandsire, ancient. **2** *(informal) her old man was away.* See HUSBAND noun. **old person** SENIOR CITIZEN, senior, (old-age) pensioner, OAP, elder, geriatric, dotard, Methuselah; *N. Amer.* golden ager; *informal* old stager, old-timer, oldie, wrinkly, crock, crumbly; *N. Amer. informal* oldster, woopie. **old woman 1** SENIOR CITIZEN, pensioner, OAP, crone; *informal* old dear; *archaic* beldam, grandam. **2** *(informal) his old woman threw him out.* See WIFE.

old-fashioned ● adjective OUT OF DATE, outdated, dated, out of fashion, outmoded, unfashionable, passé, démodé, frumpy; outworn, old, old-time, behind the times, archaic, obsolescent, obsolete, ancient, antiquated, superannuated, defunct; medieval, prehistoric, antediluvian, old-fogeyish, conservative, backward-looking, quaint, anachronistic, fusty, moth-eaten, olde worlde; *informal* old hat, square, not with it, out of the ark; *N. Amer. informal* horse-and-buggy, clunky, rinky-dink.
– OPPOSITES modern.

OLE ● abbreviation Computing object linking and embedding.
ole ● adjective US informal old.
olé /ōlay/ ● exclamation bravo!
– ORIGIN Spanish.
oleaginous /ōliajinəss/ ● adjective **1** oily or greasy. **2** exaggeratedly complimentary; obsequious.
– ORIGIN Latin *oleaginus* 'of the olive tree'.
oleander /ōliandər/ ● noun an evergreen shrub grown in warm countries for its clusters of white, pink, or red flowers, that are poisonous if eaten.
– ORIGIN Latin.
olefin /ōlifin/ (also **olefine**) ● noun Chemistry another term for ALKENE.
– ORIGIN from French *oléfiant* 'oil-forming'.
oleic acid /ōleeik/ ● noun Chemistry an unsaturated fatty acid present in many fats and soaps.
– ORIGIN from Latin *oleum* 'oil'.
oleograph ● noun a print textured to resemble an oil painting.
– ORIGIN from Latin *oleum* 'oil'.
O level ● noun historical (in the UK except Scotland) the lower of the two main levels of the GCE examination.
– ORIGIN short for ORDINARY LEVEL.
olfaction /olfakshən/ ● noun the sense of smell.
– DERIVATIVES **olfactive** adjective.
– ORIGIN from Latin *olfactus* 'a smell'.
olfactory /olfaktəri/ ● adjective relating to the sense of smell.
– ORIGIN from Latin *olfacere* 'to smell'.
olibanum /olibbənəm/ ● noun frankincense.
– ORIGIN Greek *libanos*.
oligarch /olligaark/ ● noun a ruler in an oligarchy.
oligarchy ● noun (pl. **oligarchies**) **1** a small group of people having control of a state. **2** a state governed by such a group.
– DERIVATIVES **oligarchic** adjective.
– ORIGIN from Greek *oligoi* 'few' + *arkhein* 'to rule'.
Oligocene /olligəseen/ ● adjective Geology relating to the third epoch of the Tertiary period (35.4 to 23.3 million years ago), a time when the first primates appeared.
– ORIGIN from Greek *oligos* 'few' + *kainos* 'new'.
oligopoly /olligoppəli/ ● noun (pl. **oligopolies**) a state of limited competition, in which a market is shared by a small number of producers or sellers.
– DERIVATIVES **oligopolist** noun **oligopolistic** adjective.
oligopsony /olligopsəni/ ● noun (pl. **oligopsonies**) a state of the market in which only a small number of buyers exists for a product.
– ORIGIN from Greek *oligos* 'small' + *opsōnein* 'buy provisions'.
oligotrophic /olligōtrōfik, -troff-/ ● adjective Ecology (of a body of water) relatively poor in plant nutrients and containing abundant oxygen in the deeper parts.
– DERIVATIVES **oligotrophy** noun.
olivaceous /ollivayshəss/ ● adjective technical olive green.
olive ● noun **1** a small oval fruit with a hard stone and bitter flesh, green when unripe and bluish black when ripe. **2** the small evergreen tree which yields this fruit. **3** (also **olive green**) a greyish-green colour like that of an unripe olive. **4** a slice of beef or veal made into a roll with stuffing inside and stewed. **5** a metal ring or fitting tightened under a threaded nut to form a seal. ● adjective (of a person's complexion) yellowish brown; sallow.
– ORIGIN Latin *oliva*, from Greek *elaion* 'oil'.
olive branch ● noun an offer of reconciliation.
– ORIGIN in allusion to the story of Noah in the Book of Genesis, in which a dove returns with an olive branch after the Flood.
olive drab ● noun a dull olive-green colour, used in some military uniforms.
olive oil ● noun an oil obtained from olives, used in cookery and salad dressings.
olivine /olliveen/ ● noun a green or brown silicate mineral found in many igneous rocks.
Olmec /olmek/ ● noun (pl. same or **Olmecs**) **1** a member of a prehistoric people who lived on the Gulf of Mexico. **2** a native people inhabiting this area during the 15th and 16th centuries.
– ORIGIN Nahuatl, 'inhabitants of the rubber country'.
-ology ● combining form common form of -LOGY.
oloroso /ollərōsō/ ● noun a heavy, dark, medium-sweet sherry.
– ORIGIN from Spanish, 'fragrant'.
Olympiad /əlimpiad/ ● noun **1** a staging of the ancient or modern Olympic Games. **2** a period of four years between Olympic Games, used by the ancient Greeks in dating events.
Olympian ● adjective **1** associated with Mount Olympus in NE Greece, traditional home of the Greek gods. **2** superior and aloof like a god. **3** relating to the Olympic Games. ● noun **1** any of the twelve Greek gods regarded as living on Mount Olympus. **2** a very superior or exalted person. **3** a competitor in the Olympic Games.
Olympic ● adjective relating to ancient Olympia or the Olympic Games. ● noun (**the Olympics**) the Olympic Games.
Olympic Games ● plural noun **1** a sports festival held every four years in different countries, instigated in 1896. **2** an ancient Greek festival with athletic, literary, and musical competitions, held at Olympia every four years.
OM ● abbreviation (in the UK) Order of Merit.
om /ōm/ ● noun Hinduism & Tibetan Buddhism a mystic syllable, considered the most sacred mantra.
– ORIGIN Sanskrit, sometimes regarded as three sounds, *a-u-m*, symbolic of the three major Hindu deities.
-oma ● suffix (forming nouns) denoting tumours and other abnormal growths: *carcinoma*.
– ORIGIN Greek.
Omaha /ōməhaa/ ● noun (pl. same or **Omahas**) a member of an American Indian people of NE Nebraska.
– ORIGIN Omaha, 'upstream people'.
Omani /ōmaani/ ● noun a person from Oman in the Arabian peninsula. ● adjective relating to Oman.
ombre /ombər/ ● noun a card game for three people using a pack of forty cards, popular in the 17th–18th centuries.
– ORIGIN Spanish *hombre* 'man', with reference to one player seeking to win the pool.
ombré /ombray/ ● adjective (of a fabric) graduated from light to dark in colour.
– ORIGIN French, 'shaded'.
ombudsman /omboŏdzmən/ ● noun an official appointed to investigate individuals' complaints against bad or dishonest administration, especially that of public authorities.
– ORIGIN Swedish, 'legal representative'.
omega /ōmigə/ ● noun **1** the last letter of the Greek alphabet (**Ω**, **ω**), transliterated as 'o' or 'ō'. **2** the last of a series; the final development.
– ORIGIN from Greek *ō mega* 'the great O'.
omelette (US also **omelet**) ● noun a dish of beaten eggs cooked in a frying pan and usually served with a savoury topping or filling.
– PHRASES **one can't make an omelette without breaking eggs** proverb one cannot always accomplish something without risking bad effects elsewhere.
– ORIGIN French, from *lemele* 'knife blade'.
omen ● noun **1** an event regarded as a sign of future good fortune or evil. **2** prophetic significance: *a bird of evil omen*.
– ORIGIN Latin.
omertà /ōmairtaa/ ● noun the Mafia code of silence about criminal activity.
– ORIGIN Italian, 'humility'.
omicron /ōmīkron/ ● noun the fifteenth letter of the Greek alphabet (**O**, **o**), transliterated as 'o'.
– ORIGIN from Greek *o mikron* 'small o'.
ominous ● adjective giving the worrying impression that something bad is going to happen.
– DERIVATIVES **ominously** adverb **ominousness** noun.
– ORIGIN Latin *ominosus*, from *omen* 'omen'.
omission ● noun **1** the action of leaving something out. **2** a failure to do something. **3** something that has been left out or not done.

O

Thesaurus

old-time ● adjective FORMER, past, bygone, old-fashioned; traditional, folk, old-world, quaint.
– OPPOSITES modern.
Olympian ● adjective ALOOF, distant, remote, unfriendly, uncommunicative, unforthcoming, cool; *informal* stand-offish.
– OPPOSITES friendly.
omen ● noun PORTENT, sign, signal, token, forewarning, warning, foreshadowing, prediction, forecast, prophesy, harbinger, augury, auspice, presage; writing on the wall, indication, hint; *poetic/literary* foretoken.
ominous ● adjective THREATENING, menacing, baleful, forbidding, sinister, inauspicious, unpropitious, portentous, unfavourable,

omit ● verb (**omitted**, **omitting**) **1** leave out or exclude. **2** fail to do.
– DERIVATIVES **omissible** adjective.
– ORIGIN Latin *omittere* 'let go'.
omni- ● combining form **1** all; of all things: *omnifarious.* **2** in all ways or places: *omnipresent.*
– ORIGIN from Latin *omnis* 'all'.
omnibus ● noun **1** a volume containing several works previously published separately. **2** a single edition of two or more consecutive programmes previously broadcast separately. **3** dated a bus.
– ORIGIN Latin, 'for all'.
omnicompetent ● adjective able to deal with all matters or solve all problems.
– DERIVATIVES **omnicompetence** noun.
omnidirectional ● adjective Telecommunications receiving signals from or transmitting in all directions.
omnifarious /omnifairiəss/ ● adjective formal comprising or relating to all sorts or varieties.
– ORIGIN Latin *omnifarius.*
omnipotent /omnippət'nt/ ● adjective having unlimited or very great power.
– DERIVATIVES **omnipotence** noun.
– ORIGIN Latin *omnipotens.*
omnipresent ● adjective **1** (of God) present everywhere at the same time. **2** widely or constantly encountered.
– DERIVATIVES **omnipresence** noun.
omniscient /omnissiənt/ ● adjective knowing everything.
– DERIVATIVES **omniscience** noun **omnisciently** adverb.
– ORIGIN Latin *omnisciens,* from *scire* 'to know'.
omnisexual ● adjective not restricted in sexual choice with regard to gender or activity.
omnium gatherum /omniəm ga<u>th</u>ərəm/ ● noun a miscellaneous collection.
– ORIGIN mock Latin, from Latin *omnium* 'of all' and GATHER + the Latin suffix *-um.*
omnivore /omnivor/ ● noun an omnivorous animal.
omnivorous /omnivvərəss/ ● adjective **1** feeding on a variety of food of both plant and animal origin. **2** indiscriminate in taking in or using whatever is available.
– DERIVATIVES **omnivorously** adverb.
omophagy /ōmoffəji/ (also **omophagia**) ● noun the eating of raw food, especially raw meat.
– ORIGIN from Greek *ōmos* 'raw' + *-phagia* 'eating'.
omphalos /omfəloss/ ● noun (pl. **omphaloi** /omfəloy/) **1** (in ancient Greece) a conical stone at Delphi representing the navel of the earth. **2** a boss on an ancient Greek shield.
– ORIGIN Greek, 'navel, boss'.

O

ON ● abbreviation Ontario.
on ● preposition **1** in contact with and supported by (a surface). **2** on to. **3** in the possession of. **4** forming a distinctive part of the surface of. **5** about; concerning. **6** as a member of (a committee, jury, etc.). **7** having (the thing mentioned) as a target, aim, or focus. **8** stored in or broadcast by. **9** in the course of or while travelling in. **10** indicating the day or time when something takes place. **11** engaged in. **12** regularly taking (a drug or medicine). **13** paid for by. **14** added to. ● adverb **1** in contact with and supported by a surface. **2** (of clothing) being worn. **3** further forward; with continued movement or action. **4** taking place or being presented. **5** (of an electrical appliance or power supply) functioning. **6** on duty or on stage. ● noun (also **on side**) Cricket the leg side.
– PHRASES **be on about** Brit. informal talk about tediously and at length. **be on at** Brit. informal nag or grumble at. **be on to** informal **1** be close to uncovering an illegal or undesirable activity engaged in by (someone). **2** (**be on to something**) have an idea that is likely to lead to an important discovery. **on and on** continually; at tedious length. **on to** moving to a location on the surface of or aboard.
– ORIGIN Old English.
onager /onnəgər/ ● noun a wild ass of a race native to northern Iran.
– ORIGIN Greek *onagros* 'wild ass'.
onanism /ōnəniz'm/ ● noun formal **1** masturbation. **2** sexual intercourse in which the penis is withdrawn before ejaculation.
– DERIVATIVES **onanist** noun **onanistic** adjective.
– ORIGIN from *Onan* in the Bible, who practised coitus interruptus (Book of Genesis, chapter 38).
once ● adverb **1** on one occasion or for one time only. **2** at all; on even one occasion: *he never once complained.* **3** formerly. **4** multiplied by one. ● conjunction as soon as; when.
– PHRASES **all at once 1** suddenly. **2** all at the same time. **at once 1** immediately. **2** simultaneously. **for once** (or **this once**) on this occasion only. **once again** (or **more**) one more time. **once and for all** (or **once for all**) now and for the last time; finally. **once** (or **every once**) **in a while** occasionally. **once or twice** a few times. **once upon a time** at some time in the past.
once-over ● noun informal a rapid inspection, search, or piece of work.
oncer ● noun Brit. informal (formerly) a one-pound note.
oncogene /ongkəjeen/ ● noun Medicine a gene which in certain circumstances can transform a cell into a tumour cell.
– ORIGIN from Greek *onkos* 'mass'.
oncogenic /ongkəjennik/ ● adjective Medicine causing development of a tumour or tumours.
oncology /ongkolləji/ ● noun the study and treatment of tumours.
– DERIVATIVES **oncological** adjective **oncologist** noun.
oncoming ● adjective approaching from the front; moving towards one.

Thesaurus

unpromising; black, dark, gloomy; *formal* minatory; *poetic/literary* direful.
– OPPOSITES promising.
omission ● noun **1** *the omission of recent publications from his biography* EXCLUSION, leaving out; deletion, cut, excision, elimination. **2** *the damage was not caused by any omission on behalf of the carrier* NEGLIGENCE, neglect, neglectfulness, dereliction, forgetfulness, oversight, default, lapse, failure.
omit ● verb **1** *they omitted his name from the list* LEAVE OUT, exclude, leave off, take out, miss out, miss, drop, cut; delete, eliminate, rub out, cross out, strike out. **2** *I omitted to mention our guest lecturer* FORGET, neglect, fail; leave undone, overlook, skip.
– OPPOSITES add, include, remember.
omnipotence ● noun ALL-POWERFULNESS, supremacy, supreme power, unlimited power; pre-eminence, invincibility.
omnipotent ● adjective ALL-POWERFUL, almighty, supreme, pre-eminent; invincible, unconquerable.
omnipresent ● adjective UBIQUITOUS, all-pervasive, everywhere; rife, pervasive, prevalent.
omniscient ● adjective ALL-KNOWING, all-wise, all-seeing.
omnivorous ● adjective **1** *most duck species are omnivorous* ABLE TO EAT ANYTHING; *rare* pantophagous, omnivorant. **2** *an omnivorous reader* UNDISCRIMINATING, indiscriminate, unselective.
on ● adverb **1** *the computer's on* FUNCTIONING, in operation, working, in use. **2** *she droned on* INTERMINABLY, at length, for a long time, continuously, endlessly, ceaselessly, without a pause/break.
– OPPOSITES off.
– PHRASES **on and off.** See OFF AND ON at OFF. **on and on** FOR A LONG TIME, for ages, for hours, at (great) length, incessantly, ceaselessly, constantly, continuously, continually, endlessly, unendingly, eternally, forever, interminably, unremittingly, relentlessly, indefatigably, without stopping, without let-up, without a pause/break, without cease.
once ● adverb **1** *I only met him once* ON ONE OCCASION, one time, one single time. **2** *he did not once help* EVER, at any time, on any occasion, at all. **3** *they were friends once* FORMERLY, previously, in the past, at one time, at one point, once upon a time, time was when, in days/times gone by, in times past, in the (good) old days, long ago; *archaic* sometime, erstwhile, whilom; *poetic/literary* in days/times of yore.
– OPPOSITES often, now.
● conjunction *he'll be all right once she's gone* AS SOON AS, when, after.
– PHRASES **at once 1** *you must leave at once* IMMEDIATELY, right away, right now, this moment/instant/second/minute, now, straight away, instantly, directly, forthwith, promptly, without delay/hesitation, without further ado; quickly, as fast as possible, as soon as possible, a.s.a.p., speedily; *informal* like a shot, in/like a flash, before you can say Jack Robinson. **2** *all the guests arrived at once* AT THE SAME TIME, at one and the same time, (all) together, simultaneously; as a group, in unison, in concert, in chorus. **once and for all** CONCLUSIVELY, decisively, finally, positively, definitely, definitively, irrevocably; for good, for always, forever, permanently. **once in a while** OCCASIONALLY, from time to time,

oncost ● noun Brit. an overhead expense.

one ● cardinal number **1** the lowest cardinal number; 1. (Roman numeral: **i** or **I.**) **2** single, or a single person or thing. **3** (before a person's name) a certain. **4** informal, chiefly N. Amer. a noteworthy example of. **5** identical; the same. ● pronoun **1** used to refer to a person or thing previously mentioned or easily identified. **2** a person of a specified kind. **3** (third person sing.) used to refer to the speaker, or any person, as representing people in general.
– PHRASES **at one** in agreement or harmony. **one after another** (or **the other**) following one another in quick succession. **one and all** everyone. **one and only** unique; single. **one another** each other. **one by one** separately and in succession. **one day** at a particular but unspecified time in the past or future. **one or another** (or **the other**) a particular but unspecified one out of a set of items. **one or two** informal a few.
– ORIGIN Old English.

one-armed bandit ● noun informal a fruit machine operated by pulling a long handle at the side.

one-dimensional ● adjective lacking depth; superficial.

one-horse race ● noun a contest in which one competitor is clearly superior to all the others.

one-horse town ● noun informal a small town with few and poor facilities.

Oneida /ōnīdə/ ● noun (pl. same or **Oneidas**) a member of an American Indian people formerly inhabiting upper New York State.
– ORIGIN from a local word meaning 'erected stone', the name of successive principal Oneida settlements, near which a large boulder was traditionally erected.

oneiric /ənīrik/ ● adjective formal relating to dreams or dreaming.
– ORIGIN from Greek *oneiros* 'dream'.

one-liner ● noun informal a short joke or witty remark.

one-man band ● noun **1** a street entertainer who plays many instruments at the same time. **2** a person who runs a business alone.

oneness ● noun **1** the state of being unified, whole, or in harmony. **2** the state of being one in number.

one-night stand (also **one-nighter**) ● noun **1** informal a sexual relationship lasting only one night. **2** a single performance of a play or show in a particular place.

one-off informal, chiefly Brit. ● adjective done, made, or happening only once. ● noun **1** something done, made, or happening only once. **2** a unique or remarkable person.

onerous /onnərəss, ōnə-/ ● adjective **1** involving an oppressive amount of effort and difficulty. **2** Law involving heavy obligations.
– ORIGIN Latin *onerosus*, from *onus* 'burden'.

oneself ● pronoun (third person sing.) **1** (reflexive) used as the object of a verb or preposition when this is the same as the subject of the clause and the subject is 'one'. **2** (emphatic) used to emphasize that one does something individually or unaided. **3** in one's normal and individual state of body or mind.

one-sided ● adjective **1** unfairly biased. **2** (of a contest or conflict) grossly unequal. **3** occurring on or having one side only.

one-step ● noun a vigorous kind of foxtrot in duple time.

one-time ● adjective former.

one-track mind ● noun informal a mind preoccupied with one subject, especially sex.

one-trick pony ● noun informal a person or thing with only one special feature, talent, or area of expertise.

one-two ● noun **1** a pair of punches in quick succession with alternate hands. **2** chiefly Soccer a move in which a player plays a short pass to a teammate and moves forward to receive an immediate return pass.

one-upmanship ● noun informal the technique of gaining an advantage or feeling of superiority over someone else.

one-way ● adjective moving or allowing movement in one direction only.

ongoing ● adjective continuing; still in progress.

onion ● noun an edible bulb used as a vegetable, having a pungent taste and smell and composed of several concentric layers.
– PHRASES **know one's onions** informal be very knowledgeable.
– DERIVATIVES **oniony** adjective.
– ORIGIN Old French *oignon*, from Latin *unio*.

onion dome ● noun a dome which bulges in the middle and rises to a point, used in Russian church architecture.

online ● adjective & adverb **1** controlled by or connected to a computer. **2** in or into operation or existence.

onlooker ● noun a non-participating observer; a spectator.
– DERIVATIVES **onlooking** adjective.

only ● adverb **1** and no one or nothing more besides. **2** no longer ago than. **3** not until. **4** with the negative or unfortunate result that. ● adjective **1** alone of its or their kind; single or solitary. **2** alone deserving consideration. ● conjunction informal except that.
– PHRASES **only just 1** by a very small margin. **2** very recently. **only too** —— to an extreme or regrettable extent.
– ORIGIN Old English, related to ONE.

o.n.o. ● abbreviation Brit. or nearest offer.

onomastics ● plural noun (usu. treated as sing.) the study of the history and origin of proper names, especially personal names.
– DERIVATIVES **onomastic** adjective.
– ORIGIN Greek *onomastikos*, from *onoma* 'name'.

onomatopoeia /onnəmattəpeeə/ ● noun **1** the formation of a word from a sound associated with what is named (e.g. *cuckoo*, *sizzle*). **2** the use of such words for rhetorical effect.
– DERIVATIVES **onomatopoeic** adjective **onomatopoeically** adverb.
– ORIGIN Greek *onomatopoiia* 'word-making'.

Onondaga /onnəndaagə/ ● noun (pl. same or **Onondagas**) a member of an Iroquois people formerly inhabiting an area near Syracuse, New York.
– ORIGIN from the name of their main settlement, literally 'on the hill'.

onrush ● noun a surging rush forward.
– DERIVATIVES **onrushing** adjective.

onset ● noun **1** the beginning of something, especially something unpleasant. **2** archaic a military attack.

onshore ● adjective & adverb **1** situated or occurring on land. **2** (of the wind) blowing from the sea towards the land.

onside ● adjective & adverb **1** (in sport) not offside. **2** informal in or

Thesaurus

(every) now and then/again, every so often, on occasion, at times, sometimes, off and on, at intervals, periodically, sporadically, intermittently.

oncoming ● adjective APPROACHING, advancing, nearing, forthcoming, on the way, imminent, impending, looming, gathering, (close) at hand, about to happen, to come.

one ● cardinal number **1** UNIT, item; *technical* monad. **2** *only one person came* A SINGLE, a solitary, a sole, a lone. **3** *her one concern was her daughter* ONLY, single, solitary, sole. **4** *they have now become one* UNITED, a unit, unitary, amalgamated, consolidated, integrated, combined, incorporated, allied, affiliated, linked, joined, unified, in league, in partnership; wedded, married.
– RELATED TERMS mono-, uni-.

onerous ● adjective BURDENSOME, arduous, strenuous, difficult, hard, severe, heavy, back-breaking, oppressive, weighty, uphill, effortful, formidable, laborious, Herculean, exhausting, tiring, taxing, demanding, punishing, gruelling, exacting, wearing, wearisome, fatiguing; *archaic* toilsome.
– OPPOSITES easy.

oneself ● pronoun
– PHRASES **by oneself.** See BY.

one-sided ● adjective **1** *a one-sided account* BIASED, prejudiced, partisan, partial, preferential, discriminatory, slanted, inequitable, unfair, unjust. **2** *a one-sided game* UNEQUAL, uneven, unbalanced.
– OPPOSITES impartial.

one-time ● adjective FORMER, ex-, old, previous, sometime, erstwhile; lapsed; *formal* quondam.

ongoing ● adjective **1** *negotiations are ongoing* IN PROGRESS, under way, going on, continuing, taking place, proceeding, progressing, advancing; unfinished. **2** *an ongoing struggle* CONTINUOUS, continuing, uninterrupted, unbroken, non-stop, constant, ceaseless, unceasing, unending, endless, never-ending, unremitting, relentless, unfaltering.

onlooker ● noun EYEWITNESS, witness, observer, looker-on, fly on the wall, spectator, watcher, viewer, bystander; sightseer; *informal* rubberneck; *poetic/literary* beholder.

only ● adverb **1** *there was only enough for two* AT MOST, at best, (only) just, no/not more than; barely, scarcely, hardly. **2** *he only works on one picture at a time* EXCLUSIVELY, solely, to the exclusion of everything else. **3** *you're only saying that* MERELY, simply, just. ● adjective *their only son* SOLE, single, one (and only), solitary, lone, unique; exclusive.

onomatopoeic ● adjective IMITATIVE, echoic.

onset ● noun START, beginning, commencement, arrival, (first) ap-

into a position of agreement.

onslaught ● noun **1** a fierce or destructive attack. **2** an overwhelmingly large quantity of people or things.
– ORIGIN Dutch *aenslag*, from *aen* 'on' + *slag* 'blow'.

onstage ● adjective & adverb (in a theatre) on the stage and so visible to the audience.

on-stream ● adjective & adverb in or into industrial production or useful operation.

ontic /ontik/ ● adjective Philosophy relating to entities and the facts about them.
– ORIGIN from Greek *ōn* 'being'.

onto ● preposition variant form of **on to** (see ON).
– USAGE The preposition **onto** written as one word (instead of **on to**) is widely used, but is still not wholly accepted as part of standard British English. It is also important to note the distinction between the preposition **onto** or **on to** and the use of the adverb **on** followed by the preposition **to**: *she climbed on to* (or *onto*) *the roof* but *let's go on to* (not *onto*) *the next point*.

ontogeny /ontojəni/ ● noun Biology the development of an individual organism or feature from the earliest stage to maturity. Compare with PHYLOGENY.
– DERIVATIVES **ontogenic** adjective.
– ORIGIN from Greek *ōn* 'being' + *genesis* 'birth'.

ontology /ontolləji/ ● noun Philosophy the branch of metaphysics concerned with the nature of being.
– DERIVATIVES **ontological** adjective **ontologist** noun.

onus /ōnəss/ ● noun a burden, duty, or responsibility.
– ORIGIN Latin, 'load or burden'.

onward ● adverb (also **onwards**) **1** in a continuing forward direction; ahead. **2** so as to make progress or become more successful. ● adjective moving forward.

-onym ● combining form forming nouns: **1** denoting a type of name: *pseudonym*. **2** denoting a word having a specified relationship to another: *antonym*.
– ORIGIN from Greek *onoma* 'name'.

onyx /onniks/ ● noun a semi-precious variety of agate with different colours in layers.
– ORIGIN Greek *onux* 'fingernail, onyx'.

oocyte /ōəsīt/ ● noun Biology a cell in an ovary which may divide to form an ovum.
– ORIGIN from Greek *ōion* 'egg' + *kutos* 'vessel'.

oodles ● plural noun informal a very great number or amount.
– ORIGIN of unknown origin.

oojah /oojaa/ (also **oojamaflip** /oojəməflip/) ● noun informal something that one cannot or does not want to name.
– ORIGIN of unknown origin.

oolite /ōəlīt/ ● noun Geology limestone consisting of a mass of rounded grains (ooliths) made up of concentric layers.
– DERIVATIVES **oolitic** adjective.
– ORIGIN Latin *oolites* 'egg stone'.

oology /ōolləji/ ● noun the study or collecting of birds' eggs.
– DERIVATIVES **oologist** noun.

oolong /oolong/ ● noun a kind of dark-coloured partly fermented China tea.
– ORIGIN Chinese, 'black dragon'.

oompah ● noun informal the rhythmical sound of deep-toned brass instruments in a band.
– ORIGIN imitative.

oomph (also **umph**) ● noun informal the quality of being exciting, energetic, or sexually attractive.
– ORIGIN perhaps imitative.

oops ● exclamation informal used to show recognition of a mistake or minor accident.

ooze ● verb **1** slowly trickle or seep out. **2** give a powerful impression of: *she oozes sex appeal*. ● noun **1** the sluggish flow of a fluid. **2** wet mud or slime, especially that found at the bottom of a river, lake, or sea. **3** an infusion of oak bark or other vegetable matter, used in tanning.
– DERIVATIVES **oozy** adjective.
– ORIGIN Old English, 'juice or sap'.

OP ● abbreviation **1** observation post. **2** (in the Roman Catholic Church) Order of Preachers (Dominican). [ORIGIN Latin *Ordo Praedicatorum*.] **3** organophosphate(s).

Op. (also **op.**) ● abbreviation Music (before a number given to each work of a particular composer) opus.

op ● noun informal **1** a surgical operation. **2** (**ops**) military operations. **3** a radio or telephone operator.

opacify /ōpassifī/ ● verb (**opacifies, opacified**) technical make or become opaque.

opacity /ōpassiti/ ● noun the condition of being opaque.

opah /ōpə/ ● noun a large deep-bodied fish with a dark blue back and crimson fins, living in deep oceanic waters.
– ORIGIN a West African word.

opal ● noun a quartz-like gemstone that is typically semi-transparent and shows many small points of shifting colour against a pale or dark ground.
– ORIGIN Latin *opalus*, probably from a Sanskrit word meaning 'precious stone'.

opalescent ● adjective showing many small points of shifting colour against a pale or dark ground.
– DERIVATIVES **opalescence** noun.

opaline /ōpəleen/ ● adjective opalescent. ● noun translucent or semi-translucent glass.

opaque /ōpayk/ ● adjective (**opaquer, opaquest**) **1** not able to be seen through; not transparent. **2** difficult or impossible to understand. ● noun Photography a substance for producing opaque areas on negatives.
– DERIVATIVES **opaquely** adverb.
– ORIGIN Latin *opacus* 'darkened'.

op art ● noun a form of abstract art that gives the illusion of movement by its use of pattern and colour.
– ORIGIN abbreviation of *optical art* on the pattern of *pop art*.

op. cit. ● adverb in the work already cited.
– ORIGIN from Latin *opere citato*.

OPEC ● abbreviation Organization of the Petroleum Exporting Countries.

open ● adjective **1** allowing access, passage, or view; not closed, fastened, or restricted. **2** exposed to view or attack; not covered or protected. **3** (**open to**) vulnerable or subject to. **4** spread out, expanded, or unfolded. **5** officially admitting customers or visitors; available for business. **6** (of an offer or opportunity) still available. **7** frank and communicative. **8** not finally settled; still admitting of debate. **9** (often **open to**) accessible, receptive, or available. **10** (**open to**) admitting of; making possible. **11** Music (of a string) allowed to vibrate along its whole length. **12** Phonetics (of a vowel) produced with a relatively wide opening of the mouth and the tongue kept low. **13** (of an electric circuit) having a break in the conducting path. ● verb **1** make or become open. **2** spread out; unfold or be unfolded. **3** formally begin or establish. **4** make available or more widely known. **5** (**open on to/into**) give access to. **6** (**open out/up**) become more communicative or confiding. **7** break the conducting path of (an electric circuit). ● noun **1** (**the open**) fresh air or open countryside. **2** (**Open**) a championship or competition with no restrictions on who may compete.
– PHRASES **the open air** a free or unenclosed space outdoors. **in open court** in a court of law, before the judge and the public. **in** (or **into**) **the open** not concealed or secret. **open-and-shut**

Thesaurus

pearance, inception, day one; outbreak.
– OPPOSITES end.

onslaught ● noun ASSAULT, attack, offensive, advance, charge, onrush, rush, storming, sortie, sally, raid, descent, incursion, invasion, foray, push, thrust, drive, blitz, bombardment, barrage, salvo; *historical* broadside.

onus ● noun BURDEN, responsibility, liability, obligation, duty, weight, load, charge, encumbrance; cross to bear, millstone round one's neck, albatross.

ooze ● verb **1** *blood oozed from the wound* SEEP, discharge, flow, exude, trickle, drip, dribble, issue, filter, percolate, escape, leak, drain, empty, bleed, sweat, well; *Medicine* extravasate. **2** *she was positively oozing charm* EXUDE, gush, drip, pour forth, emanate, radiate.
● noun **1** *the ooze of blood* SEEPAGE, seeping, discharge, flow, exudation, trickle, drip, dribble, percolation, escape, leak, leakage, drainage; secretion; *Medicine* extravasation. **2** *the ooze on the ocean floor* MUD, slime, alluvium, silt, mire, sludge, muck, dirt, deposit.

opalescent ● adjective IRIDESCENT, prismatic, rainbow-like, kaleidoscopic, multicoloured, many-hued, lustrous, shimmering, glittering, sparkling, variegated, shot, moire, opaline, milky, pearly, nacreous.

opaque ● adjective **1** *opaque glass* NON-TRANSPARENT, cloudy, filmy, blurred, smeared, smeary, misty, dirty, muddy, muddied, grimy. **2** *the technical jargon was opaque to her* OBSCURE, unclear, mysterious, puzzling, perplexing, baffling, mystifying, confusing, un-

admitting no doubt or dispute; straightforward. **open up** (or **open fire**) begin shooting.
– DERIVATIVES **openable** adjective **openness** noun.
– ORIGIN Old English.

opencast (N. Amer. **open-pit**) ● adjective Brit. (of mining) in which coal or ore is extracted from a level near the earth's surface, rather than from shafts.

open day ● noun Brit. a day when members of the public may visit a place or institution to which they do not usually have access.

open-ended ● adjective having no predetermined limit or boundary.

opener ● noun **1** a device for opening something. **2** a person or thing that opens or begins, for example the first goal in a match or a cricketer who opens the batting.
– PHRASES **for openers** informal to start with; first of all.

open-faced ● adjective **1** having a frank or ingenuous expression. **2** (also **open-face**) chiefly N. Amer. (of a sandwich or pie) without an upper layer of bread or pastry.

open-handed ● adjective **1** (of a blow) delivered with the palm of the hand. **2** generous.

open-hearted ● adjective unrestrainedly warm and kind.

open-hearth process ● noun a steel-making process in which scrap iron or steel, limestone, and pig iron are melted together in a furnace.

open-heart surgery ● noun surgery in which the heart is exposed and the blood made to bypass it.

open house ● noun **1** a place or situation in which all visitors are welcome. **2** N. Amer. an open day.

opening ● noun **1** an aperture or gap. **2** a beginning; an initial part. **3** a ceremony at which a building, show, etc. is declared to be open. **4** an opportunity to achieve something. **5** an available job or position. ● adjective coming at the beginning; initial.

open letter ● noun a letter addressed to a particular person but intended for publication in a newspaper or journal.

openly ● adverb without concealment or deception; frankly or honestly.

open market ● noun an unrestricted market with free access by and competition of buyers and sellers.

open marriage ● noun a marriage in which both partners agree that each may have sexual relations with others.

open mind ● noun a mind willing to consider new ideas.
– DERIVATIVES **open-minded** adjective.

open-necked ● adjective (of a shirt) worn with the collar unbuttoned and without a tie.

open-plan ● adjective having large rooms with few or no internal dividing walls.

open prison ● noun Brit. a prison with the minimum of restrictions on prisoners' movements and activities.

open question ● noun a matter that is not yet decided or cannot be decided.

open range ● noun N. Amer. an area of land without fences or other barriers.

open-reel ● adjective another term for REEL-TO-REEL.

open sandal ● noun a sandal that does not cover the toes.

open sandwich ● noun a sandwich without a top slice of bread.

open season ● noun the annual period when restrictions on the killing of certain types of wildlife are lifted.

open secret ● noun a supposed secret that is in fact known to many people.

open-toed ● adjective (of a shoe) not covering the toes.

open-topped (also **open-top**) ● adjective (of a vehicle) having no roof, or having a folding or detachable roof.

open verdict ● noun Law a verdict of a coroner's jury affirming that a suspicious death has occurred but not specifying the cause.

openwork ● noun ornamental work in cloth, leather, etc. with regular patterns of openings and holes.

opera[1] ● noun **1** a dramatic work set to music for singers and instrumentalists. **2** a building for the performance of opera.
– ORIGIN Italian, from Latin, 'labour, work'.

opera[2] plural of OPUS.

operable ● adjective **1** able to be operated. **2** able to be treated by means of a surgical operation.

opéra bouffe /opperaa boof/ ● noun (pl. **opéras bouffes**) a French comic opera.
– ORIGIN French, from Italian (see OPERA BUFFA).

Thesaurus

fathomable, incomprehensible, unintelligible, impenetrable, hazy, foggy; *informal* as clear as mud.
– OPPOSITES transparent, clear.

open ● adjective **1** *the door's open* NOT SHUT, not closed, unlocked, unbolted, unlatched, off the latch, unfastened, unsecured; ajar, gaping, yawning. **2** *a blue silk shirt, open at the neck* UNFASTENED, not done up, undone, unbuttoned, unzipped, loose. **3** *the main roads are open* CLEAR, passable, navigable, unblocked, unobstructed. **4** *open countryside | open spaces* UNENCLOSED, rolling, sweeping, extensive, wide (open), unfenced, exposed, unsheltered; spacious, airy, uncrowded, uncluttered; undeveloped, unbuilt-up. **5** *a map was open beside him* SPREAD OUT, unfolded, unfurled, unrolled, extended, stretched out. **6** *the bank wasn't open* OPEN FOR BUSINESS, open to the public. **7** *the position is still open* AVAILABLE, vacant, free, unfilled; *informal* up for grabs. **8** *the system is open to abuse* VULNERABLE, subject, susceptible, liable, exposed, an easy target for, at risk of. **9** *she was open about her feelings* FRANK, candid, honest, forthcoming, communicative, forthright, direct, unreserved, plain-spoken, outspoken, free-spoken, not afraid to call a spade a spade; *informal* upfront. **10** *open hostility* OVERT, obvious, patent, manifest, palpable, conspicuous, plain, undisguised, unconcealed, clear, apparent, evident; blatant, flagrant, barefaced, brazen. **11** *the case is still open* UNRESOLVED, undecided, unsettled, up in the air; open to debate, open for discussion, arguable, debatable, moot. **12** *an open mind* IMPARTIAL, unbiased, unprejudiced, objective, disinterested, non-partisan, non-discriminatory, neutral, dispassionate, detached. **13** *I'm open to suggestions* RECEPTIVE, amenable, willing/ready to listen, responsive. **14** *what other options are open to us?* AVAILABLE, accessible, on hand, obtainable, on offer. **15** *an open meeting* PUBLIC, general, unrestricted, non-exclusive, non-restrictive.
– OPPOSITES shut.
● verb **1** *she opened the front door* UNFASTEN, unlatch, unlock, unbolt, unbar; throw wide. **2** *Katherine opened the parcel* UNWRAP, undo, untie, unseal. **3** *shall I open another bottle?* UNCORK, broach, crack (open). **4** *Adam opened the map* SPREAD OUT, unfold, unfurl, unroll, straighten out. **5** *he opened his heart to her* REVEAL, uncover, expose, lay bare, bare, pour out, disclose, divulge. **6** *we're hoping to open next month* START TRADING, open for business, set up shop, put up one's plate; *N. Amer. informal* hang out one's shingle. **7** *Sir Bryan opened the meeting* BEGIN, start, commence, initiate, set in motion, launch, get going, get under way, set the ball rolling, get off the ground; inaugurate; *informal* kick off, get the show on the road. **8** *the lounge opens on to a terrace* GIVE ACCESS, lead, be connected, communicate with.
– OPPOSITES close, shut, end.

open air ● adjective OUTDOOR, out-of-doors, outside, alfresco.
– OPPOSITES indoor.

open-handed ● adjective GENEROUS, magnanimous, charitable, benevolent, beneficent, munificent, bountiful, altruistic, philanthropic; *poetic/literary* bounteous.
– OPPOSITES tight-fisted.

opening ● noun **1** *an opening in the centre of the roof* HOLE, gap, aperture, orifice, vent, crack, slit, chink; spyhole, peephole; *Anatomy* foramen. **2** *the opening in the wall* DOORWAY, gateway, entrance, (means of) entry, way in/out, exit. **3** *United created openings but were unable to score* OPPORTUNITY, chance, window (of opportunity), possibility. **4** *an opening with a stockbroker* VACANCY, position, job. **5** *the opening of the session* BEGINNING, start, commencement, outset; introduction, prefatory remarks, opening statement; *informal* kick-off; *formal* proem. **6** *a gallery opening* OPENING CEREMONY, official opening, launch, inauguration; opening/first night, premiere.

openly ● adverb **1** *drugs were openly on sale* PUBLICLY, blatantly, flagrantly, overtly. **2** *he spoke openly of his problems* FRANKLY, candidly, explicitly, honestly, sincerely, forthrightly, bluntly, without constraint, straight from the shoulder.
– OPPOSITES secretly.

open-minded ● adjective **1** *open-minded attitudes* UNBIASED, unprejudiced, neutral, non-judgemental, non-discriminatory, objective, disinterested; tolerant, liberal, permissive, broad-minded. **2** *musicians need to be open-minded* RECEPTIVE, open (to suggestions), amenable, flexible, willing to change.
– OPPOSITES prejudiced, narrow-minded.

open-mouthed ● adjective ASTOUNDED, amazed, in amazement, surprised, stunned, bowled over, staggered, thunderstruck,

opera buffa /oppərə boofə/ ● noun (pl. **opera buffas** or **opere buffe** /oppəray boofay/) a comic opera, especially in Italian.
– ORIGIN Italian, 'comic opera'.
opera cloak ● noun a cloak of rich material worn over evening clothes, especially by women.
opera glasses ● plural noun small binoculars for use at the opera or theatre.
opera hat ● noun a collapsible top hat.
opera house ● noun a theatre for the performance of opera.
operand /opparand/ ● noun Mathematics the quantity on which an operation is to be done.
– ORIGIN Latin *operandum* 'thing to be operated on'.
operant /oppərənt/ Psychology ● adjective involving the modification of behaviour by the effect of its own consequences. ● noun an item of behaviour that is spontaneous rather than a response to a stimulus.
opera seria /oppərə seeriə/ ● noun an opera, especially one of the 18th century in Italian, on a serious theme.
– ORIGIN Italian, 'serious opera'.
operate ● verb **1** (of a machine, process, etc.) be in action; function. **2** control the functioning of (a machine or process). **3** (with reference to an organization) manage or be managed. **4** (of an armed force) conduct military activities. **5** be in effect. **6** perform a surgical operation.
– ORIGIN Latin *operari*, from *opus* 'work'.
operatic ● adjective **1** relating to or characteristic of opera. **2** extravagantly theatrical.
– DERIVATIVES **operatically** adverb.
operatics ● plural noun (often treated as sing.) the production or performance of operas.
operating profit ● noun a gross profit before deduction of expenses.
operating system ● noun the low-level software that supports a computer's basic functions.
operating table ● noun a table on which a patient is placed during a surgical operation.
operating theatre (N. Amer. **operating room**) ● noun a room in which surgical operations are performed.
operation ● noun **1** the action or process of operating. **2** an act of surgery performed on a patient. **3** a concerted action involving a number of people, especially members of the armed forces or the police. **4** a business organization; a company. **5** Mathematics a process in which a number, quantity, expression, etc., is altered or manipulated according to set formal rules.
operational ● adjective **1** in or ready for use. **2** relating to the operation of an organization.
– DERIVATIVES **operationally** adverb.
operations room ● noun a room from which military or police operations are directed.
operative ● adjective **1** functioning; having effect. **2** (of a word) having the most relevance or significance in a phrase. **3** relating to surgery. ● noun **1** a worker, especially a skilled one. **2** a private detective or secret agent.
– DERIVATIVES **operatively** adverb.
operator ● noun **1** a person who operates equipment or a machine. **2** a person who works at the switchboard of a telephone exchange. **3** a person or company that runs a business or enterprise. **4** informal a person who acts in a specified, especially manipulative, way: *a smooth operator*. **5** Mathematics a symbol or function denoting an operation (e.g. ×, +).
opera window ● noun chiefly US a small window behind the rear side window of a motor car.
operculum /ōperkyooləm/ ● noun (pl. **opercula** /ōperkyoolə/) Zoology **1** a flap of skin protecting a fish's gills, typically stiffened by bony plates. **2** a plate that closes the aperture of a gastropod mollusc's shell.
– ORIGIN Latin, 'lid, covering'.
operetta ● noun a short opera on a light or humorous theme.
– ORIGIN Italian, 'little opera'.
ophicleide /offiklīd/ ● noun an obsolete bass brass instrument with keys.
– ORIGIN French, from Greek *ophis* 'serpent' + *kleis* 'key'.
ophidian /ōfiddiən/ ● noun Zoology an animal of the group which includes the snakes.
– ORIGIN Greek *ophis*.
ophthalmia /ofthalmiə/ ● noun Medicine inflammation of the eye, especially conjunctivitis.
– ORIGIN Greek, from *ophthalmos* 'eye'.
ophthalmic ● adjective relating to the eye and its diseases.
ophthalmic optician ● noun Brit. an optician qualified to prescribe and dispense glasses and contact lenses and to detect eye diseases.
ophthalmology /ofthalmolləji/ ● noun the study and treatment of disorders and diseases of the eye.
– DERIVATIVES **ophthalmological** adjective **ophthalmologist** noun.
ophthalmoscope /ofthalməskōp/ ● noun an instrument for inspecting the retina and other parts of the eye.
– DERIVATIVES **ophthalmoscopic** adjective **ophthalmoscopy** noun.
opiate /ōpiət/ ● adjective relating to, resembling, or containing opium. ● noun **1** a drug derived from or related to opium. **2** something that induces a false and unrealistic sense of contentment.
– DERIVATIVES **opiated** adjective.
opine ● verb formal hold and state as one's opinion.
– ORIGIN Latin *opinari* 'think, believe'.
opinion ● noun **1** a view or judgement not necessarily based on fact or knowledge. **2** the beliefs or views of people in general: *public opinion*. **3** an estimation of quality or worth. **4** a formal statement of advice by an expert or professional.
– PHRASES **a matter of opinion** something not capable of being proven either way.
– ORIGIN Latin, from *opinari* 'think, believe'.

O

Thesaurus

aghast, stupefied, taken aback, shocked, speechless, dumbfounded, dumbstruck; *informal* flabbergasted; *Brit. informal* gobsmacked.
operate ● verb **1** *he can operate the machine* WORK, make go, run, use, utilize, handle, control, manage; drive, steer, manoeuvre. **2** *the machine ceased to operate* FUNCTION, work, go, run, be in working/running order, be operative. **3** *the way the law operates in practice* TAKE EFFECT, act, apply, be applied, function. **4** *Hechstetter operated the mines until 1634* DIRECT, control, manage, run, govern, administer, superintend, head (up), supervise, oversee, be in control/charge of. **5** *doctors decided to operate* do an operation, perform surgery.
operation ● noun **1** *the slide bars ensure smooth operation* FUNCTIONING, working, running, performance, action. **2** *the operation of the factory* MANAGEMENT, running, governing, administration, supervision. **3** *a heart bypass operation* SURGERY, surgical operation. **4** *a military operation* ACTION, activity, exercise, undertaking, enterprise, manoeuvre, campaign. **5** *their mining operations* BUSINESS, enterprise, company, firm; *informal* outfit.
– PHRASES **in operation.** See OPERATIONAL.
operational ● adjective (UP AND) RUNNING, working, functioning, operative, in operation, in use, in action; in working order, workable, serviceable, functional, usable.
operative ● adjective **1** *the act is not operative at the moment* IN FORCE, in operation, in effect, valid. **2** *the steam railway is operative.* See OPERATIONAL. **3** *the operative word* KEY, significant, relevant, applicable, pertinent, apposite, germane, crucial, critical, pivotal.
– OPPOSITES invalid.
● noun **1** *the operatives clean the machines* MACHINIST, (machine) operator, mechanic, engineer, worker, workman, (factory) hand, blue-collar worker. **2** *an operative of the CIA* (SECRET) AGENT, undercover agent, spy, mole, plant, double agent; *N. Amer. informal* spook; *archaic* intelligencer. **3** *a private operative* (PRIVATE) DETECTIVE, (private) investigator, sleuth; *informal* private eye; *N. Amer. informal* gumshoe.
operator ● noun **1** *a machine operator* MACHINIST, mechanic, operative, engineer, worker. **2** *a tour operator* CONTRACTOR, entrepreneur, promoter, arranger, fixer. **3** *(informal) a ruthless operator* MANIPULATOR, manoeuvrer, string-puller, mover and shaker, wheeler-dealer; *N. Amer. informal* wire-puller.
opiate ● noun DRUG, narcotic, sedative, tranquillizer, depressant, soporific, anaesthetic, painkiller, analgesic, anodyne; morphine, opium; *informal* dope; *Medicine* stupefacient.
opine ● verb *(formal)* SUGGEST, say, declare, observe, comment, remark; think, believe, consider, maintain, imagine, reckon, guess, assume, presume, take it, suppose; *N. Amer. informal* allow.
opinion ● noun *she did not share her husband's opinion* BELIEF, judgement, thought(s), (way of) thinking, mind, (point of) view, viewpoint, attitude, stance, position, standpoint.
– PHRASES **a matter of opinion** OPEN TO QUESTION, debatable, open to debate, a moot point. **be of the opinion** BELIEVE, think, consider, maintain, reckon, estimate, feel, be convinced; *N. Amer. informal*

opinionated ● adjective assertively dogmatic in one's views.
opinion poll ● noun an assessment of public opinion by questioning of a representative sample.
opioid /ōpioyd/ ● noun a compound resembling opium in its properties or effects. ● adjective relating to such compounds.
opium ● noun **1** an addictive drug prepared from the juice of a poppy, used as a narcotic and in medicine as a painkiller. **2** something that induces a false and unrealistic sense of contentment.
– ORIGIN Latin, from Greek *opion* 'poppy juice'.
opossum /əpossəm/ ● noun **1** an American marsupial which has a naked prehensile tail and hind feet with an opposable thumb. **2** Austral./NZ a possum.
– ORIGIN Algonquian, 'white dog'.
oppo ● noun (pl. **oppos**) Brit. informal a colleague or friend.
– ORIGIN abbreviation of *opposite number*.
opponent ● noun **1** a person who competes with or fights another in a contest, game, or argument. **2** a person who disagrees with or resists a proposal or practice.
– ORIGIN from Latin *opponere* 'set against'.
opportune /oppərtyoon/ ● adjective done or occurring at an especially convenient or appropriate time.
– DERIVATIVES **opportunely** adverb.
– ORIGIN Latin *opportunus*, from *ob-* 'in the direction of' + *portus* 'harbour', originally describing the wind driving towards the harbour, hence the idea 'seasonable'.
opportunist ● noun a person who takes advantage of opportunities as and when they arise, regardless of planning or principle. ● adjective opportunistic.
– DERIVATIVES **opportunism** noun.
opportunistic ● adjective **1** exploiting immediate opportunities, especially in an unplanned or selfish way. **2** Medicine (of an infection) occurring when the immune system is depressed.
– DERIVATIVES **opportunistically** adverb.
opportunity ● noun (pl. **opportunities**) **1** a favourable time or set of circumstances for doing something. **2** a career opening: *job opportunities.*
opposable ● adjective Zoology (of the thumb of a primate) capable of facing and touching the other digits on the same hand.
oppose ● verb **1** (also **be opposed to**) disapprove of, resist, or be hostile to. **2** compete with or fight. **3** (**opposed**) (of two or more things) contrasting or conflicting. **4** (**opposing**) opposite.
– DERIVATIVES **opposer** noun.
– ORIGIN Old French *opposer*, from Latin *opponere* 'set against'.
opposite ● adjective **1** situated on the other or further side; facing. **2** completely different. **3** being the other of a contrasted pair. **4** (of angles) between opposite sides of the intersection of two lines. ● noun an opposite person or thing. ● adverb in an opposite position. ● preposition **1** in a position opposite to. **2** co-starring beside.
– DERIVATIVES **oppositely** adverb.
– ORIGIN Latin *oppositus*, from *opponere* 'set against'.
opposite number ● noun a person's counterpart in another organization or country.
opposite sex ● noun (**the opposite sex**) women in relation to men or vice versa.
opposition ● noun **1** resistance or dissent. **2** a group of opponents. **3** (**the Opposition**) Brit. the principal parliamentary party opposed to that in office. **4** a contrast or antithesis. **5** Astronomy the apparent position of two celestial objects that are directly opposite each other in the sky.
– DERIVATIVES **oppositional** adjective.
oppress ● verb **1** keep in subjection and hardship. **2** cause to feel distressed or anxious.
– DERIVATIVES **oppression** noun **oppressor** noun.
– ORIGIN Old French *oppresser*, from Latin *opprimere* 'press against'.
oppressive ● adjective **1** harsh and authoritarian. **2** weighing heavily on the mind or spirits. **3** (of weather) close and sultry.
– DERIVATIVES **oppressively** adverb **oppressiveness** noun.
opprobrious /əprōbriəss/ ● adjective highly scornful.
– DERIVATIVES **opprobriously** adverb.
opprobrium /əprōbriəm/ ● noun **1** harsh criticism or scorn. **2** public disgrace arising from shameful conduct.

Thesaurus

allow; formal opine. **in my opinion** IT SEEMS TO ME, as I see it, to my mind, (according) to my way of thinking, personally, in my estimation, if you ask me.
opinionated ● adjective DOGMATIC, of fixed views; inflexible, uncompromising, prejudiced, bigoted.
opponent ● noun **1** *his Republican opponent* RIVAL, adversary, opposer, the opposition, fellow contestant, (fellow) competitor, enemy, antagonist, combatant, contender, challenger; poetic/literary foe. **2** *an opponent of the reforms* OPPOSER, objector, dissenter.
– OPPOSITES ally, supporter.
opportune ● adjective AUSPICIOUS, propitious, favourable, advantageous, golden, felicitous; timely, convenient, suitable, appropriate, apt, fitting.
– OPPOSITES disadvantageous.
opportunism ● noun EXPEDIENCY, pragmatism, Machiavellianism; striking while the iron is hot, making hay while the sun shines.
opportunity ● noun (LUCKY) CHANCE, golden opportunity, favourable time/occasion/moment; time, occasion, moment, opening, option, window (of opportunity), possibility, scope, freedom; informal shot, break, look-in.
oppose ● verb BE AGAINST, object to, be hostile to, be in opposition to, disagree with, dislike, disapprove of; resist, take a stand against, put up a fight against, stand up to, fight, challenge; take issue with, dispute, argue with/against, quarrel with; informal be anti; formal gainsay.
– OPPOSITES support.
opposed ● adjective **1** *the population is opposed to the nuclear power plants* AGAINST, (dead) set against; in opposition, averse, hostile, antagonistic, antipathetic, resistant; informal anti. **2** *their interests were opposed* CONFLICTING, contrasting, incompatible, irreconcilable, antithetical, contradictory, clashing, at variance, at odds, divergent, poles apart.
– OPPOSITES in favour of.
– PHRASES **as opposed to** IN CONTRAST WITH, as against, as contrasted with, rather than, instead of.
opposing ● adjective **1** *the two opposing points of view* CONFLICTING, contrasting, opposite, incompatible, irreconcilable, contradictory, antithetical, clashing, at variance, at odds, divergent, opposed, poles apart. **2** *opposing sides in the war* RIVAL, opposite, enemy. **3** *the opposing page* OPPOSITE, facing.
opposite ● adjective **1** *they sat opposite each other* FACING, face to face with, across from; informal eyeball to eyeball with. **2** *the opposite page* FACING, opposing. **3** *opposite views* CONFLICTING, contrasting, incompatible, irreconcilable, antithetical, contradictory, clashing, at variance, at odds, different, differing, divergent, dissimilar, unalike, disagreeing, opposed, opposing, poles apart. **4** *opposite sides in a war* RIVAL, opposing, enemy.
– OPPOSITES same.
● noun *in fact the opposite was true* REVERSE, converse, antithesis, contrary, inverse, obverse, antipode; the other side of the coin; informal flip side.
opposition ● noun **1** *the proposal met with opposition* RESISTANCE, hostility, antagonism, antipathy, objection, dissent, disapproval; defiance, non-compliance, obstruction. **2** *they beat the opposition* OPPONENTS, opposing side, other side/team, competition, opposers, rivals, adversaries. **3** *the opposition between the public and the private domains* CONFLICT, clash, disparity, antithesis, polarity.
oppress ● verb **1** *the invaders oppressed the people* PERSECUTE, abuse, maltreat, ill-treat, tyrannize, crush, repress, suppress, subjugate, subdue, keep down, grind down, rule with a rod of iron, ride roughshod over. **2** *the gloom oppressed her* DEPRESS, make gloomy/despondent, weigh down, weigh heavily on, cast down, dampen someone's spirits, dispirit, dishearten, discourage, sadden, get down; archaic deject.
oppressed ● adjective PERSECUTED, downtrodden, abused, maltreated, ill-treated, tyrannized, subjugated, repressed, subdued, crushed; disadvantaged, underprivileged.
oppression ● noun PERSECUTION, abuse, maltreatment, ill-treatment, tyranny, repression, suppression, subjection, subjugation; cruelty, brutality, injustice, hardship, misery, suffering.
oppressive ● adjective **1** *an oppressive dictatorship* HARSH, cruel, brutal, repressive, tyrannical, autocratic, dictatorial, despotic, undemocratic; ruthless, merciless, pitiless. **2** *an oppressive sense of despair* OVERWHELMING, overpowering, unbearable, unendurable, intolerable. **3** *it was grey and oppressive* MUGGY, close, heavy, hot, humid, sticky, steamy, airless, stuffy, stifling, sultry.
– OPPOSITES lenient.
oppressor ● noun PERSECUTOR, tyrant, despot, autocrat, dictator, subjugator, tormentor.
opprobrious ● adjective ABUSIVE, vituperative, derogatory, dispara-

– ORIGIN Latin, 'infamy'.
oppugn /əpyoōn/ ● verb archaic dispute the truth or validity of.
– ORIGIN Latin *oppugnare* 'attack, besiege'.
opsimath /opsimath/ ● noun rare a person who begins to learn or study only late in life.
– ORIGIN from Greek *opse* 'late' + the stem *math-* 'learn'.
opt ● verb make a choice.
– PHRASES **opt out 1** choose not to participate. **2** Brit. (of a school or hospital) decide to withdraw from local authority control.
– ORIGIN Latin *optare* 'choose, wish'.
optative /optətiv, optaytiv/ ● adjective Grammar (of a mood of verbs, especially in Greek) expressing a wish, equivalent in meaning to English *let's* or *if only*.
optic ● adjective relating to the eye or vision. ● noun **1** a lens or similar component in an optical instrument. **2** Brit. trademark a device fastened to the neck of an inverted bottle for measuring out spirits.
– ORIGIN Greek *optikos*, from *optos* 'seen'.
optical ● adjective relating to vision, light, or optics.
– DERIVATIVES **optically** adverb.
optical brightener ● noun a fluorescent substance added to detergents to produce a whitening effect on laundry.
optical character recognition ● noun the identification of printed characters using photoelectric devices and computer software.
optical fibre ● noun a thin glass fibre through which light can be transmitted.
optical glass ● noun a very pure kind of glass used for lenses.
optical illusion ● noun a thing that deceives the eye by appearing to be other than it is.
optician ● noun a person qualified to prescribe and dispense glasses and contact lenses, and to detect eye diseases (**ophthalmic optician**), or to make and supply glasses and contact lenses (**dispensing optician**).
optic nerves ● plural noun Anatomy the pair of nerves transmitting impulses from the eyes to the brain.
optics ● plural noun (usu. treated as sing.) the branch of science concerned with vision and the behaviour of light.
optimal ● adjective best or most favourable.
– DERIVATIVES **optimality** noun **optimally** adverb.
optimism ● noun **1** hopefulness and confidence about the future or success of something. **2** Philosophy the doctrine that this world is the best of all possible worlds.
– DERIVATIVES **optimist** noun **optimistic** adjective **optimistically** adverb.
– ORIGIN French *optimisme*, from Latin *optimum* (see OPTIMUM).
optimize (also **optimise**) ● verb make the best or most effective use of (a situation or resource).
– DERIVATIVES **optimization** noun **optimizer** noun.
optimum ● adjective most likely to lead to a favourable outcome. ● noun (pl. **optima** or **optimums**) the most favourable conditions for growth, reproduction, or success.
– ORIGIN from Latin, 'best thing'.
option ● noun **1** a thing that is or may be chosen. **2** the freedom or right to choose. **3** a right to buy or sell something at a specified price within a set time.
– PHRASES **keep** (or **leave**) **one's options open** not commit oneself.
optional ● adjective available to be chosen but not obligatory.
– DERIVATIVES **optionality** noun **optionally** adverb.
optometrist ● noun chiefly N. Amer. a person who practises optometry; an opthalmic optician.
optometry ● noun the occupation of measuring eyesight, prescribing corrective lenses, and detecting eye disease.
opulent ● adjective ostentatiously rich and luxurious.
– DERIVATIVES **opulence** noun **opulently** adverb.
– ORIGIN Latin *opulens* 'wealthy, splendid'.
opuntia /əpunshə/ ● noun a cactus of a genus that comprises the prickly pears.
– ORIGIN Latin, a name given to a plant growing around *Opus*, a city in ancient Greece.
opus /ōpəs, oppəs/ ● noun (pl. **opuses** or **opera** /oppərə/) **1** Music a separate composition or set of compositions. **2** an artistic work, especially one on a large scale.
– ORIGIN Latin, 'work'.
opus Dei /ōpəss dayee, oppəss/ ● noun **1** Christian Church public worship regarded as humankind's primary duty to God. **2** (**Opus Dei**) a Roman Catholic organization aiming to re-establish Christian ideals in society.
– ORIGIN Latin, 'work of God'.
OR ● abbreviation Oregon.
or[1] ● conjunction **1** used to link alternatives. **2** introducing a synonym or explanation of a preceding word or phrase. **3** otherwise. **4** literary either.
– ORIGIN Old English.
or[2] ● noun gold or yellow, as a conventional heraldic colour.
– ORIGIN French, from Latin *aurum* 'gold'.
-or[1] ● suffix (forming nouns) denoting a person or thing performing the action of a verb: *escalator*.
– ORIGIN Latin.
-or[2] ● suffix forming nouns denoting a state or condition: *terror*.
– ORIGIN Latin.
orache /orrəch/ (also **orach**) ● noun a plant with red, yellow, or green leaves sometimes eaten as a vegetable.
– ORIGIN Old French *arasche*, from Greek *atraphaxus*.
oracle ● noun **1** (in ancient Greece or Rome) a priest or priestess who acted as a medium for divine advice or prophecy. **2** an infallible authority.
– ORIGIN Latin *oraculum*, from *orare* 'speak'.
oracular /orakyoolər/ ● adjective **1** relating to an oracle. **2** hard to interpret. **3** holding or claiming the authority of an oracle.
oracy /orrəsi/ ● noun Brit. the ability to express oneself fluently and grammatically in speech.
– ORIGIN from Latin *os* 'mouth', on the pattern of *literacy*.

Thesaurus

ging, denigratory, pejorative, deprecatory, insulting, offensive; scornful, contemptuous, derisive; *informal* bitchy; *archaic* contumelious.
opprobrium ● noun **1** *the government endured months of opprobrium* VILIFICATION, abuse, vituperation, condemnation, criticism, flak, censure, denunciation, defamation, denigration, disparagement, obloquy, derogation, slander, revilement, calumny, calumniation, execration, bad press, invective, mud-slinging, badmouthing; *Brit. informal* stick; *formal* castigation, excoriation; *archaic* contumely. **2** *the opprobrium of being associated with thugs* DISGRACE, shame, dishonour, stigma, humiliation, loss of face, ignominy, disrepute, infamy, notoriety, scandal.
– OPPOSITES praise, honour.
opt ● verb CHOOSE, select, pick (out), decide on, go for, settle on, plump for/on.
optimism ● noun HOPEFULNESS, hope, confidence, buoyancy, sanguineness, positiveness, positive attitude.
optimistic ● adjective **1** *she felt optimistic about the future* POSITIVE, confident, hopeful, sanguine, bullish, buoyant; *informal* upbeat. **2** *the forecast is optimistic* ENCOURAGING, promising, hopeful, reassuring, favourable, auspicious, propitious.
– OPPOSITES pessimistic.
optimum ● adjective BEST, most favourable, most advantageous, ideal, perfect, prime, optimal.
option ● noun CHOICE, alternative, possibility, course of action.
optional ● adjective VOLUNTARY, discretionary, non-compulsory, non-mandatory; *Law* permissive.
– OPPOSITES compulsory.
opulence ● noun **1** *the opulence of the room* LUXURIOUSNESS, sumptuousness, lavishness, richness, luxury, luxuriance, splendour, magnificence, grandeur, splendidness; *informal* plushness. **2** *a display of opulence* WEALTH, affluence, wealthiness, richness, riches, prosperity, prosperousness, money.
– OPPOSITES poverty.
opulent ● adjective **1** *his opulent home* LUXURIOUS, sumptuous, palatial, lavishly appointed, rich, splendid, magnificent, grand, grandiose, fancy; *informal* plush, plushy, swanky; *Brit. informal* swish; *N. Amer. informal* swank. **2** *an opulent family* WEALTHY, rich, affluent, well off, well-to-do, moneyed, prosperous, of substance; *informal* well heeled, rolling in money, loaded, stinking/filthy rich, made of money. **3** *her opulent red hair* COPIOUS, abundant, profuse, prolific, plentiful, luxuriant.
– OPPOSITES spartan, poor.
opus ● noun COMPOSITION, work (of art), oeuvre.
oracle ● noun **1** *the oracle of Apollo* PROPHET, PROPHETESS, sibyl, seer, augur, prognosticator, diviner, soothsayer, fortune teller. **2** *our oracle on Africa* AUTHORITY, expert, specialist, pundit, mentor, adviser.
oracular ● adjective **1** *his every utterance was given oracular significance* PROPHETIC, prophetical, sibylline, predictive, prescient,

oral • adjective **1** spoken rather than written. **2** relating to the mouth. **3** done or taken by the mouth. • noun a spoken examination or test.
– DERIVATIVES **orally** adverb.
– ORIGIN Latin *oralis*, from *os* 'mouth'.
oral history • noun the collection and study of historical information from people's personal memories.
oralism • noun the teaching of deaf people to communicate by the use of speech and lip-reading rather than sign language.
– DERIVATIVES **oralist** adjective & noun.
orality • noun **1** the quality of being verbally communicated. **2** Psychoanalysis the focusing of sexual energy and feeling on the mouth.
oral sex • noun sexual activity in which the genitals of one partner are stimulated by the mouth of the other.
Orange • adjective relating to Orangemen or their Order.
– ORIGIN named after the Protestant king William of *Orange* (William III of Great Britain and Ireland, 1650–1702).
orange • noun **1** a large round citrus fruit with a tough bright reddish-yellow rind. **2** a drink made from or flavoured with orange juice. **3** a bright reddish-yellow colour. • adjective reddish yellow.
– DERIVATIVES **orangey** (also **orangy**) adjective.
– ORIGIN Old French *orenge*, from Arabic.
orangeade • noun Brit. a fizzy soft drink flavoured with orange.
orange flower water • noun a solution of neroli in water, used in perfumery and as a food flavouring.
Orangeman • noun a member of the Orange Order.
Orange Order • noun a Protestant political society in Northern Ireland.
orange pekoe • noun a type of black tea made from young leaves.
orangery • noun (pl. **orangeries**) a building like a large conservatory where orange trees are grown.
orange stick • noun a thin pointed stick for manicuring the fingernails.
orang-utan /ərangootan/ (also **-utang** /-ootang/) • noun a large tree-dwelling ape with long red hair, native to Borneo and Sumatra.
– ORIGIN Malay, 'forest person'.
orate • verb make a long or pompous speech.
oration • noun a formal speech, especially one given on a ceremonial occasion.
– ORIGIN Latin, from *orare* 'speak, pray'.
orator • noun a proficient public speaker.
– DERIVATIVES **oratorial** adjective.
oratorio /orrətoriō/ • noun (pl. **oratorios**) a large-scale musical work on a religious theme for orchestra and voices.
– ORIGIN Italian, from the musical services held in the church of the Oratory of St Philip Neri in Rome.
oratory[1] /orrətri/ • noun (pl. **oratories**) a small chapel for private worship.
oratory[2] /orrətri/ • noun **1** formal public speaking. **2** rhetorical or eloquent language.
– DERIVATIVES **oratorical** /orrətorrik'l/ adjective.
orb • noun **1** a spherical object or shape. **2** a golden globe with a cross on top, forming part of the regalia of a monarch.
– ORIGIN Latin *orbis* 'ring'.
orbicular /orbikyoolər/ • adjective **1** technical having the shape of a flat ring or disc. **2** literary spherical or rounded.
orbit • noun **1** the regularly repeated elliptical course of a celestial object or spacecraft around a star or planet. **2** a field of activity or influence. **3** the path of an electron round an atomic nucleus. **4** Anatomy the eye socket. • verb (**orbited**, **orbiting**) move in orbit round (a star or planet).
– ORIGIN Latin *orbita* 'course, track'.
orbital • adjective **1** relating to an orbit or orbits. **2** Brit. (of a road) passing round the outside of a town.
orbital sander • noun a sander in which the sanding surface has a minute circular motion without rotating relative to the object being worked on.
orbiter • noun a spacecraft designed to go into orbit, especially one that does not subsequently land.
orc • noun a member of an imaginary race of ugly, aggressive human-like creatures.
– ORIGIN perhaps from Latin *orcus* 'hell' or Italian *orco* 'monster'; the word was popularized by the fantasy adventures of of the British writer J. R. R. Tolkien (1892–1973).
orca /orkə/ • noun another term for KILLER WHALE.
– ORIGIN French *orque* or Latin *orca*.
Orcadian /orkaydiən/ • adjective relating to the Orkney Islands. • noun a person from the Orkney Islands.
– ORIGIN from *Orcades*, the Latin name for the Orkney Islands.
orchard • noun a piece of enclosed land planted with fruit trees.
– ORIGIN Old English, from Latin *hortus* 'garden' + the base of YARD[2].
orchestra • noun **1** (treated as sing. or pl.) a large group of musicians with string, woodwind, brass, and percussion sections. **2** (also **orchestra pit**) the part of a theatre where the orchestra plays, typically in front of the stage and on a lower level. **3** N. Amer. the stalls in a theatre. **4** the semicircular space in front of an ancient Greek theatre stage where the chorus danced and sang.
– DERIVATIVES **orchestral** adjective **orchestrally** adverb.
– ORIGIN Greek *orkhēstra*, from *orkheisthai* 'to dance'.
orchestrate • verb **1** arrange or score (music) for orchestral performance. **2** direct (a situation) to produce a desired effect.
– DERIVATIVES **orchestration** noun **orchestrator** noun.
orchid • noun a plant of a large family with complex showy flowers.
– DERIVATIVES **orchidaceous** adjective.
– ORIGIN Greek *orkhis* 'testicle' (because of the shape of the tuber).
orchitis /orkītiss/ • noun Medicine inflammation of one or both of the testicles.
– ORIGIN Latin, from Greek *orkhis* 'testicle'.
ordain • verb **1** make (someone) a priest or minister. **2** order officially. **3** (of God or fate) decide in advance.
– ORIGIN Latin *ordinare*, from *ordo* 'order'.
ordeal • noun **1** a prolonged painful or horrific experience. **2** an ancient test of guilt or innocence in which the accused was subjected to severe pain, survival of which was taken as divine proof of innocence.
– ORIGIN Old English.
order • noun **1** the arrangement of people or things according to a particular sequence or method. **2** a state in which everything

O

Thesaurus

prognostic, divinatory, augural. **2** *oracular responses* ENIGMATIC, cryptic, abstruse, unclear, obscure, confusing, mystifying, puzzling, mysterious, arcane; ambiguous, equivocal.
oral • adjective *an oral agreement* SPOKEN, verbal, unwritten, vocal, uttered, said.
– OPPOSITES written.
• noun *a French oral* ORAL EXAMINATION; *Brit.* viva (voce).
orate • verb DECLAIM, make a speech, hold forth, speak, discourse, pontificate, preach, sermonize, sound off, spout off; *informal* spiel; *formal* perorate.
oration • noun SPEECH, address, lecture, talk, homily, sermon, discourse, declamation; *informal* spiel.
orator • noun (PUBLIC) SPEAKER, speech-maker, lecturer, declaimer, rhetorician; *informal* spieler.
oratorical • adjective RHETORICAL, grandiloquent, magniloquent, high-flown, orotund, bombastic, grandiose, pompous, pretentious, overblown, turgid, flowery, florid.
oratory • noun RHETORIC, eloquence, grandiloquence, magniloquence, public speaking, speech-making, declamation.
orb • noun SPHERE, globe, ball, circle.
orbit • noun **1** *the earth's orbit around the sun* COURSE, path, circuit, track, trajectory, rotation, revolution, circle. **2** *the problem comes outside our orbit* SPHERE (OF INFLUENCE), area of activity, range, scope, ambit, compass, jurisdiction, authority, remit, domain, realm, province, territory; *informal* bailiwick.
• verb *Mercury orbits the sun* REVOLVE ROUND, circle round, go round, travel round.
orchestra • noun ENSEMBLE; *informal* band.
orchestrate • verb **1** *the piece was orchestrated by Mozart* ARRANGE, adapt, score. **2** *orchestrating a campaign of civil disobedience* ORGANIZE, arrange, plan, set up, bring about, mobilize, mount, stage, stage-manage, mastermind, coordinate, direct, engineer.
ordain • verb **1** *the Church of England voted to ordain women* CONFER HOLY ORDERS ON, appoint, anoint, consecrate. **2** *the path ordained by God* PREDETERMINE, predestine, preordain, prescribe, determine, designate. **3** *he ordained that anyone hunting in the forest was to pay a fine* DECREE, rule, order, command, lay down, legislate, prescribe, pronounce.

is in its correct place. **3** a state in which the laws and rules regulating public behaviour are observed. **4** an authoritative command or direction. **5** a request for something to be made, supplied, or served. **6** the prescribed procedure followed in a meeting, law court, or religious service. **7** quality or nature: *poetry of the highest order.* **8** a social class or system. **9** a rank in the Christian ministry. **10** (**orders** or **holy orders**) the rank of an ordained minister of the Church. **11** a society of monks, nuns, or friars (or formerly knights) living under the same rule. **12** an institution founded by a monarch to honour good conduct: *the Order of the Garter.* **13** Biology a principal taxonomic category that ranks below class and above family. **14** any of the five classical styles of architecture (Doric, Ionic, Corinthian, Tuscan, and Composite). ● **verb 1** give an order. **2** request that (something) be made, supplied, or served. **3** arrange methodically.
– PHRASES **in order 1** in the correct condition for operation or use. **2** appropriate in the circumstances. **in order for** (or **that**) so that. **in order to** with the purpose of doing. **of** (or **in** or **on**) **the order of** approximately. **on order** (of goods) requested but not yet received. **the order of the day 1** the prevailing state of affairs. **2** the day's business to be considered in a meeting or parliament. **out of order 1** not working properly or at all. **2** Brit. informal unacceptable or wrong.
– ORIGIN Latin *ordo* 'row, series'.
Order in Council ● **noun** Brit. a sovereign's order on an administrative matter, given on the advice of the Privy Council.
orderly ● **adjective 1** neatly and methodically arranged. **2** well behaved. ● **noun** (pl. **orderlies**) **1** a hospital attendant responsible for cleaning and other non-medical tasks. **2** a soldier who carries orders or performs minor tasks for an officer.
– DERIVATIVES **orderliness** noun.
orderly officer ● **noun** Brit. Military the officer in charge of the security and administration of a unit for a particular day.
orderly room ● **noun** Military the room in a barracks used for regimental or company business.
order of magnitude ● **noun 1** a class in a system of classification determined by size, typically in powers of ten. **2** size or quantity.
Order Paper ● **noun** Brit. a paper on which the day's parliamentary business is entered.
ordinal ● **adjective 1** relating to order in a series. **2** Biology relating to a taxonomic order. ● **noun** Christian Church, chiefly historical a book with the forms of service used at ordinations.
– ORIGIN Latin *ordinalis* 'relating to order'.
ordinal number ● **noun** a number defining a thing's position in a series, such as 'first' or 'second'.
ordinance ● **noun** formal **1** an authoritative order. **2** a religious rite. **3** N. Amer. a by-law.
– ORIGIN Old French *ordenance*, from Latin *ordinare* 'arrange, ordain'.
ordinand /ordinand/ ● **noun** a person who is training to be ordained as a priest or minister.
– ORIGIN Latin *ordinandus.*
ordinary ● **adjective 1** with no distinctive features; normal or usual. **2** (of a judge, archbishop, or bishop) exercising authority by virtue of office and not by delegation. ● **noun** (pl. **ordinaries**) **1** (**Ordinary**) those parts of a Roman Catholic service, especially the Mass, which do not vary from day to day. **2** a rule or book laying down the order of divine service. **3** Heraldry any of the simplest principal charges used in coats of arms.
– PHRASES **out of the ordinary** unusual.
– DERIVATIVES **ordinarily** adverb **ordinariness** noun.
– ORIGIN Latin *ordinarius* 'orderly', from *ordo* 'order'.
ordinary grade ● **noun** (in Scotland) the lower of the two main levels of the Scottish Certificate of Education examination. Compare with HIGHER.
ordinary level ● **noun** fuller form of O LEVEL.
ordinary seaman ● **noun** the lowest rank of sailor in the Royal Navy, below able seaman.

Thesaurus

ordeal ● **noun** UNPLEASANT EXPERIENCE, painful experience, trial, tribulation, nightmare, trauma, hell (on earth), trouble, difficulty, torture, torment, agony.
order ● **noun 1** *a list in alphabetical order* SEQUENCE, arrangement, organization, disposition, system, series, succession; grouping, classification, categorization, codification, systematization. **2** *some semblance of order* TIDINESS, neatness, orderliness, trimness. **3** *the police were needed to keep order* PEACE, control, law (and order), lawfulness, discipline, calm, (peace and) quiet, peacefulness, peaceableness. **4** *his sense of order* ORDERLINESS, organization, method, system; symmetry, uniformity, regularity; routine. **5** *the equipment was in good order* CONDITION, state, repair, shape. **6** *I had to obey his orders* COMMAND, instruction, directive, direction, decree, edict, injunction, mandate, dictate, commandment, rescript; law, rule, regulation, diktat; demand, bidding, requirement, stipulation; *informal* say-so; *formal* ordinance; *poetic/literary* behest. **7** *the company has won the order* COMMISSION, purchase order, request, requisition; booking, reservation. **8** *the lower orders of society* CLASS, level, rank, grade, degree, position, category; *dated* station. **9** *the established social order* (CLASS) SYSTEM, hierarchy, pecking order, grading, ranking, scale. **10** *(Biology) the higher orders of insects* TAXONOMIC GROUP, class, family, species, breed; taxon. **11** *a religious order* COMMUNITY, brotherhood, sisterhood. **12** *the Orange Order* ORGANIZATION, association, society, fellowship, fraternity, confraternity, sodality, lodge, guild, league, union, club; sect. **13** *skills of a very high order* TYPE, kind, sort, nature, variety; quality, calibre, standard.
– OPPOSITES chaos.
● **verb 1** *he ordered me to return* INSTRUCT, command, direct, enjoin, tell, require, charge; *formal* adjure; *poetic/literary* bid. **2** *he ordered that their assets be confiscated* DECREE, ordain, rule, legislate, dictate, prescribe. **3** *you can order your tickets by phone* REQUEST, apply for, place an order for; book, reserve; *formal* bespeak. **4** *the messages are ordered chronologically* ORGANIZE, put in order, arrange, sort out, marshal, dispose, lay out; group, classify, categorize, catalogue, codify, systematize, systemize.
– PHRASES **in order 1** *list the dates in order* IN SEQUENCE, in alphabetical order, in numerical order, in order of priority. **2** *he found everything in order* TIDY, neat, orderly, straight, trim, shipshape (and Bristol fashion), in apple-pie order; in position, in place. **3** *I think it's in order for me to take the credit* APPROPRIATE, fitting, suitable, acceptable, (all) right, permissible, permitted, allowable; *informal* okay. **order someone about/around** TELL SOMEONE WHAT TO DO, give orders to, dictate to; lay down the law; *informal* boss about/around, push about/around. **out of order 1** *the lift's out of order* NOT WORKING, not in working order, not functioning, broken, broken-down, out of service, out of commission, faulty, defective, inoperative; down; *informal* conked out, bust, (gone) kaput; *N. Amer. informal* on the fritz, out of whack. **2** *(Brit. informal) that's really out of order* UNACCEPTABLE, unfair, unjust, unjustified, uncalled for, below the belt, unreasonable, unwarranted, beyond the pale; *informal* not on, a bit much; *Brit. informal* a bit thick, off, not cricket; *Austral./NZ informal* over the fence.
orderly ● **adjective 1** *an orderly room* NEAT, tidy, well ordered, in order, trim, in apple-pie order, spick and span; *Brit. informal, dated* shipshape (and Bristol fashion). **2** *the orderly presentation of information* (WELL) ORGANIZED, efficient, methodical, systematic, meticulous, punctilious; coherent, structured, logical, well planned, well regulated, systematized. **3** *the crowd was orderly* WELL BEHAVED, law-abiding, disciplined, peaceful, peaceable, non-violent.
– OPPOSITES untidy, disorganized.
ordinance ● **noun** *(formal)* **1** *the president issued an ordinance* EDICT, decree, law, injunction, fiat, command, order, rule, ruling, dictum, dictate, directive, mandate. **2** *religious ordinances* RITE, ritual, ceremony, sacrament, observance, service.
ordinarily ● **adverb** USUALLY, normally, as a (general) rule, generally, in general, for the most part, mainly, mostly, most of the time, typically, habitually, commonly, routinely.
ordinary ● **adjective 1** *the ordinary course of events* USUAL, normal, standard, typical, common, customary, habitual, everyday, regular, routine, day-to-day. **2** *my life seemed very ordinary* AVERAGE, normal, run-of-the-mill, standard, typical, middle-of-the-road, conventional, unremarkable, unexceptional, workaday, undistinguished, nondescript, colourless, commonplace, humdrum, mundane, unmemorable, pedestrian, prosaic, quotidian, uninteresting, uneventful, dull, boring, bland, suburban, hackneyed; *N. Amer.* garden-variety; *informal* bog-standard, (plain) vanilla, nothing to write home about, no great shakes; *Brit. informal* common or garden; *N. Amer. informal* ornery.
– OPPOSITES unusual.
– PHRASES **out of the ordinary** UNUSUAL, exceptional, remarkable, extraordinary, unexpected, surprising, unaccustomed, unfamiliar, abnormal, atypical, different, special, exciting, memorable, noteworthy, unique, singular, outstanding; unconventional, un-

O

ordinary share ● noun Brit. a share which entitles the holder to dividends proportionate to the company's profits. Compare with PREFERENCE SHARE.
ordinate /ordinət/ ● noun Mathematics a straight line from a point on a graph drawn parallel to the vertical axis and meeting the other; the *y*-coordinate.
– ORIGIN Latin *linea ordinata applicata* 'line applied parallel'.
ordination ● noun the action of ordaining someone as a priest or minister.
ordnance /ordnənss/ ● noun **1** mounted guns; cannon. **2** US munitions. **3** a government department dealing with military stores and materials.
– ORIGIN variant of ORDINANCE.
ordnance datum ● noun Brit. the mean sea level as defined for Ordnance Survey.
Ordnance Survey ● noun (in the UK) an official survey organization preparing detailed maps of the whole country.
– ORIGIN originally prepared by the government department dealing with military stores and materials.
Ordovician /ordəvishiən/ ● adjective Geology relating to the second period of the Palaeozoic era (between the Cambrian and Silurian periods), about 510 to 439 million years ago, a time when the first vertebrates appeared.
– ORIGIN from *Ordovices*, the Latin name of an ancient British tribe in North Wales.
ordure /ordyoor/ ● noun excrement; dung.
– ORIGIN Old French, from Latin *horridus* 'rough, horrible'.
ore ● noun a naturally occurring material from which a metal or valuable mineral can be extracted.
– ORIGIN Old English, 'unwrought metal'.
øre /örə/ ● noun (pl. same) a monetary unit of Denmark and Norway, equal to one hundredth of a krone.
– ORIGIN Danish and Norwegian.
öre /örə/ ● noun (pl. same) a monetary unit of Sweden, equal to one hundredth of a krona.
– ORIGIN Swedish.
oread /oriad/ ● noun Greek & Roman Mythology a nymph believed to inhabit mountains.
– ORIGIN Greek *Oreias*, from *oros* 'mountain'.
oregano /orrigaanō/ ● noun an aromatic plant with small purple flowers and leaves used as a herb in cookery.
– ORIGIN Spanish, from Greek *origanon*.
orfe /orf/ ● noun a silvery freshwater fish of the carp family.
– ORIGIN German.
organ ● noun **1** a distinct part of an animal or plant adapted for a particular function, for example the heart or kidneys. **2** a large musical keyboard instrument with rows of pipes supplied with air from bellows. **3** a smaller keyboard instrument producing similar sounds electronically. **4** a newspaper or periodical which puts forward the views of a political party or movement. **5** euphemistic a man's penis.
– DERIVATIVES **organist** noun.
– ORIGIN Greek *organon* 'tool, sense organ'.
organdie /orgəndi/ (US also **organdy**) ● noun a fine, translucent, stiff cotton muslin.
– ORIGIN French *organdi*.
organelle /orgənel/ ● noun Biology an organized or specialized structure within a cell.
– ORIGIN Latin *organella* 'little tool'.
organ-grinder ● noun a street musician who plays a barrel organ.
organic ● adjective **1** relating to or derived from living matter. **2** not involving or produced with chemical fertilizers or other artificial chemicals. **3** Chemistry relating to or denoting compounds containing carbon and chiefly or ultimately of biological origin. **4** relating to or affecting a bodily organ or organs. **5** (of the elements of a whole) harmoniously related. **6** characterized by natural development.
– DERIVATIVES **organically** adverb.
organism ● noun **1** an individual animal, plant, or single-celled life form. **2** a whole with interdependent parts.
organization (also **organisation**) ● noun **1** the action of organizing. **2** a systematic arrangement or approach. **3** an organized body of people with a particular purpose, e.g. a business.
– DERIVATIVES **organizational** adjective **organizationally** adverb.
organize (also **organise**) ● verb **1** arrange systematically; order. **2** Brit. make arrangements or preparations for. **3** form (people) into a trade union or other political group.
– DERIVATIVES **organizer** noun.
– ORIGIN Latin *organizare*, from *organum* 'instrument, tool'.
organo- /orgənō/ ● combining form forming names of classes of chemical compounds containing a particular element bonded to organic groups: *organophosphorus compounds*.
organophosphorus /orgənōfosfərəss/ ● adjective referring to synthetic organic compounds containing phosphorus, especially pesticides and nerve gases of this kind.
– DERIVATIVES **organophosphate** noun.
organza /organzə/ ● noun a thin, stiff, transparent dress fabric made of silk or a synthetic yarn.
– ORIGIN probably from *Lorganza*, a US trademark.
orgasm ● noun the climax of sexual excitement, characterized by intensely pleasurable sensations centred in the genitals. ● verb have an orgasm.
– ORIGIN Greek *orgasmos*, from *organ* 'swell or be excited'.
orgasmic ● adjective **1** relating to orgasm. **2** informal very enjoyable.
– DERIVATIVES **orgasmically** adverb.
orgastic ● adjective relating to orgasm.
orgiastic ● adjective relating to or resembling an orgy.
– DERIVATIVES **orgiastically** adverb.
orgulous /orgyooləss/ ● adjective literary haughty.
– ORIGIN Old French *orguillus*, from *orguill* 'pride'.
orgy ● noun (pl. **orgies**) **1** a wild party with excessive drinking and indiscriminate sexual activity. **2** excessive indulgence in a specified activity: *an orgy of killing*.
– ORIGIN from Greek *orgia* 'secret rites or revels'.
oriel /oriəl/ ● noun a large upper-storey bay with a window (an **oriel window**), supported by brackets or on corbels.
– ORIGIN Old French *oriol* 'gallery'.
orient ● noun /oriənt/ (**the Orient**) literary the countries of the

O

Thesaurus

orthodox, strange, peculiar, odd, queer, curious, bizarre, outlandish; *informal* offbeat.
ordnance ● noun GUNS, cannon, artillery, weapons, arms; munitions.
ordure ● noun EXCREMENT, excreta, dung, manure, muck, droppings, faeces, stools, night soil, sewage; *informal* pooh; *Brit. informal* cack, big jobs; *N. Amer. informal* poop.
organ ● noun **1** *the internal organs* BODY PART, biological structure. **2** *the official organ of the Communist Party* NEWSPAPER, paper, journal, periodical, magazine, newsletter, gazette, publication, mouthpiece; *informal* rag.
organic ● adjective **1** *organic matter* LIVING, live, animate, biological, biotic. **2** *organic vegetables* PESTICIDE-FREE, additive-free, natural. **3** *the love scenes were an organic part of the drama* ESSENTIAL, fundamental, integral, intrinsic, vital, indispensable, inherent. **4** *a society is an organic whole* STRUCTURED, organized, coherent, integrated, coordinated, ordered, harmonious.
organism ● noun **1** *fish and other organisms* LIVING THING, being, creature, animal, plant, life form. **2** *a complex political organism* STRUCTURE, system, organization, entity.
organization ● noun **1** *the organization of conferences* PLANNING, arrangement, coordination, administration, organizing, running, management. **2** *the overall organization of the book* STRUCTURE, arrangement, plan, pattern, order, form, format, framework, composition, constitution. **3** *his lack of organization* EFFICIENCY, order, orderliness, planning. **4** *a large international organization* COMPANY, firm, corporation, institution, group, consortium, conglomerate, agency, association, society; *informal* outfit.
organize ● verb **1** *organizing and disseminating information* (PUT IN) ORDER, arrange, sort (out), assemble, marshal, put straight, group, classify, collocate, categorize, catalogue, codify, systematize, systemize; *rare* methodize. **2** *they organized a search party* MAKE ARRANGEMENTS FOR, arrange, coordinate, sort out, put together, fix up, set up, orchestrate, take care of, see to/about, deal with, manage, conduct, administrate, mobilize; schedule, timetable, programme; *formal* concert.
organized ● adjective (WELL) ORDERED, well run, well regulated, structured; orderly, efficient, neat, tidy, methodical; *informal* together.
– OPPOSITES inefficient.
orgiastic ● adjective DEBAUCHED, wild, riotous, wanton, dissolute, depraved.
orgy ● noun **1** *a drunken orgy* WILD PARTY, debauch, carousal, revel, revelry; *informal* binge, booze-up, bender, love-in; *Brit. informal* rave-

East, especially east Asia. • **adjective** /orient/ literary oriental. • **verb** /orient/ **1** align or position relative to the points of a compass or other specified positions. **2** (**orient oneself**) find one's position in relation to unfamiliar surroundings. **3** tailor to specified circumstances.
– ORIGIN from Latin *oriens* 'rising or east', from *oriri* 'to rise'.

oriental • **adjective** of, from, or characteristic of the Far East. • **noun** often offensive a person of Far Eastern descent.
– DERIVATIVES **orientalism** noun **orientalist** noun **orientalize** (also **orientalise**) verb **orientally** adverb.
– USAGE The term **oriental** is now regarded as old-fashioned and potentially offensive as a term denoting people from the Far East. In US English, **Asian** is the standard accepted term in modern use; in British English, where **Asian** tends to denote people from the Indian subcontinent, specific terms such as **Chinese** or **Japanese** are more likely to be used.

orientate • **verb** another term for ORIENT.

orientation • **noun** **1** the action of orienting. **2** a relative position. **3** a person's attitude or inclination, especially as regards political or sexual matters.
– DERIVATIVES **orientational** adjective.

orientation course • **noun** chiefly N. Amer. a course giving information to newcomers to a university or other organization.

orienteering • **noun** a competitive sport in which runners have to find their way across rough country with the aid of a map and compass.
– DERIVATIVES **orienteer** noun & verb.

orifice /orrifiss/ • **noun** an opening, particularly one in the body such as a nostril.
– ORIGIN French, from Latin *os* 'mouth' + *facere* 'make'.

oriflamme /orriflam/ • **noun** literary a scarlet banner or knight's standard.
– ORIGIN Old French, from Latin *aurum* 'gold' + *flamma* 'flame'.

origami /orrigaami/ • **noun** the Japanese art of folding paper into decorative shapes and figures.
– ORIGIN Japanese, from words meaning 'fold' + 'paper'.

origin • **noun** **1** the point where something begins or arises. **2** a person's social background or ancestry. **3** Mathematics a fixed point from which coordinates are measured.
– ORIGIN Latin *origo*, from *oriri* 'to rise'.

original • **adjective** **1** existing from the beginning; first or earliest. **2** produced first-hand; not a copy. **3** inventive or novel. • **noun** the earliest form of something, from which copies can be made.
– DERIVATIVES **originally** adverb.

originality • **noun** **1** the ability to think independently or creatively. **2** the quality of being new or unusual.

original sin • **noun** (in Christian theology) the tendency to evil of all human beings, held to be a consequence of the Fall.

originate • **verb** **1** have a specified beginning. **2** create or initiate.
– DERIVATIVES **origination** noun **originator** noun.

oriole /oriōl/ • **noun** a brightly coloured tree-dwelling bird with a musical call.
– ORIGIN Latin *oriolus*, from *aureus* 'golden'.

orison /orriz'n/ • **noun** literary a prayer.
– ORIGIN Old French *oreison*, from Latin *oration* 'discourse, prayer'.

Orlon /orlon/ • **noun** trademark a synthetic acrylic fibre and fabric used for clothing, knitwear, etc.
– ORIGIN invented word, on the pattern of *nylon*.

ormolu /orməloo/ • **noun** a gold-coloured alloy of copper, zinc, and tin used in decoration.
– ORIGIN from French *or moulu* 'powdered gold'.

ornament • **noun** **1** an object designed to add beauty to something. **2** decorative items collectively; decoration. **3** (**ornaments**) Music embellishments made to a melody.
– DERIVATIVES **ornamentation** noun.
– ORIGIN Latin *ornamentum*, from *ornare* 'adorn'.

ornamental • **adjective** serving or intended as an ornament. • **noun** a plant grown for its attractive appearance.
– DERIVATIVES **ornamentally** adverb.

ornate • **adjective** elaborately or highly decorated.
– DERIVATIVES **ornately** adverb **ornateness** noun.
– ORIGIN from Latin *ornare* 'adorn'.

ornery /ornəri/ • **adjective** N. Amer. informal bad-tempered.
– ORIGIN representing a dialect pronunciation of ORDINARY.

ornithine /ornitheen/ • **noun** Biochemistry an amino acid which is produced by the body and is important in protein metabolism.
– ORIGIN from Greek *ornis* 'bird' (because it was first obtained from a constituent of bird droppings).

ornithischian /ornithiskiən/ • **noun** Palaeontology a herbivorous dinosaur of a group with pelvic bones resembling those of birds. Compare with SAURISCHIAN.
– ORIGIN from Greek *ornis* 'bird' + *iskhion* 'hip joint'.

ornithology /ornithollәji/ • **noun** the scientific study of birds.
– DERIVATIVES **ornithological** adjective **ornithologist** noun.
– ORIGIN from Greek *ornis* 'bird'.

ornithopter • **noun** chiefly historical a flying machine with flapping wings.

O

Thesaurus

up; *N. Amer. informal* toot; *poetic/literary* bacchanal; *archaic* wassail. **2** *an orgy of spending* BOUT, excess, spree; *informal* binge.

oriental • **adjective** EASTERN, Far Eastern, Asian; *poetic/literary* orient.

orientation • **noun** **1** *the orientation of the radar station* POSITIONING, location, position, situation, placement, alignment. **2** *his orientation to his new way of life* ADAPTATION, adjustment, acclimatization. **3** *broadly Marxist in orientation* ATTITUDE, inclination. **4** *orientation courses* INDUCTION, training, initiation, briefing.

orient, orientate • **verb** **1** *there were no street names to enable her to orient herself* GET/FIND ONE'S BEARINGS, establish one's location. **2** *you need to orientate yourself to your new way of life* ADAPT, adjust, familiarize, acclimatize, accustom, attune; *N. Amer.* acclimate. **3** *magazines oriented to the business community* AIM, direct, pitch, design, intend. **4** *the fires are oriented in line with the sunset* ALIGN, place, position, dispose.

orifice • **noun** OPENING, hole, aperture, slot, slit, cleft.

origin • **noun** **1** *the origins of life* BEGINNING, start, commencement, origination, genesis, birth, dawning, dawn, emergence, creation, birthplace, cradle; source, basis, cause, root(s); *formal* radix. **2** *the Latin origin of the word* SOURCE, derivation, root(s), provenance, etymology; *N. Amer.* provenience. **3** *his Scottish origins* DESCENT, ancestry, parentage, pedigree, lineage, line (of descent), heritage, birth, extraction, family, stock, blood, bloodline.

original • **adjective** **1** *the original inhabitants* INDIGENOUS, native, aboriginal, autochthonous; first, earliest, early. **2** *two original Rembrandts* AUTHENTIC, genuine, actual, true, bona fide; *informal* pukka, kosher. **3** *the film is highly original* INNOVATIVE, creative, imaginative, innovatory, inventive; new, novel, fresh, refreshing; unusual, unconventional, unorthodox, ground-breaking, pioneering, avant-garde, unique, distinctive.
• **noun** **1** *a copy of the original* ARCHETYPE, prototype, source, master. **2** *he really is an original* INDIVIDUALIST, individual, eccentric, nonconformist, free spirit, maverick; *informal* character, oddball; *Brit. informal* one-off, odd bod; *N. Amer. informal* screwball, kook.

originality • **noun** INVENTIVENESS, ingenuity, creativeness, creativity, innovation, novelty, freshness, imagination, imaginativeness, individuality, unconventionality, uniqueness, distinctiveness.

originally • **adverb** (AT) FIRST, in/at the beginning, to begin with, initially, in the first place, at the outset.

originate • **verb** **1** *the disease originates from Africa* ARISE, have its origin, begin, start, stem, spring, emerge, emanate. **2** *Bill Levy originated the idea* INVENT, create, initiate, devise, think up, dream up, conceive, formulate, form, develop, generate, engender, produce, mastermind, pioneer; *poetic/literary* beget.

originator • **noun** INVENTOR, creator, architect, author, father, mother, initiator, innovator, founder, pioneer, mastermind; *poetic/literary* begetter.

ornament • **noun** **1** *small tables covered with ornaments* KNICK-KNACK, trinket, bauble, bibelot, gewgaw, gimcrack, furbelow; *informal* whatnot, doodah; *N. Amer. informal* tchotchke; *archaic* whim-wham, kickshaw, bijou. **2** *the dress had no ornament at all* DECORATION, adornment, embellishment, ornamentation, trimming, accessories.
• **verb** *the room was highly ornamented* DECORATE, adorn, embellish, trim, bedeck, deck (out), festoon; *poetic/literary* bedizen, furbelow.

ornamental • **adjective** DECORATIVE, fancy, ornate, ornamented.

ornamentation • **noun** DECORATION, adornment, embellishment, ornament, trimming, accessories.

ornate • **adjective** **1** *an ornate mirror* ELABORATE, decorated, embellished, adorned, ornamented, fancy, fussy, ostentatious, showy; *informal* flash, flashy. **2** *ornate language* ELABORATE, flowery, florid; grandiose, pompous, pretentious, high-flown, orotund, magniloquent, grandiloquent, rhetorical, oratorical, bombastic, over-

– ORIGIN French *ornithoptère*.

orogeny /orojəni/ • **noun** Geology a process in which a section of the earth's crust is folded and deformed by lateral compression to form a mountain range.
– DERIVATIVES **orogenesis** noun **orogenic** adjective.
– ORIGIN from Greek *oros* 'mountain'.

orotund /orrətund/ • **adjective 1** (of the voice) resonant and impressive. **2** (of writing or style) pompous.
– ORIGIN from Latin *ore rotundo* 'with rounded mouth'.

orphan • **noun** a child whose parents are dead. • **verb** (usu. **be orphaned**) make an orphan.
– ORIGIN from Greek *orphanos* 'bereaved'.

orphanage • **noun** a residential institution for the care and education of orphans.

orpiment /orpimənt/ • **noun** a bright yellow mineral formerly used as a dye and artist's pigment.
– ORIGIN Latin *auripigmentum*, from *aurum* 'gold' + *pigmentum* 'pigment'.

orrery /orrəri/ • **noun** (pl. **orreries**) a clockwork model of the solar system.
– ORIGIN named after the fourth Earl of *Orrery* (1676–1731), for whom one was made.

orris (also **orris root**) • **noun** a preparation of the fragrant rootstock of an iris, used in perfumery.
– ORIGIN alteration of IRIS.

ortho- • **combining form 1** straight; rectangular; upright: *orthodontics*. **2** correct: *orthography*.
– ORIGIN from Greek *orthos* 'straight, right'.

orthodontics /orthədontiks/ • **plural noun** (treated as sing.) the treatment of irregularities in the teeth and jaws.
– DERIVATIVES **orthodontic** adjective **orthodontist** noun.
– ORIGIN from Greek *odous* 'tooth'.

orthodox • **adjective 1** conforming with traditional or generally accepted beliefs. **2** conventional; normal. **3** (**Orthodox**) relating to Orthodox Judaism or the Orthodox Church.
– DERIVATIVES **orthodoxly** adverb.
– ORIGIN Greek *orthodoxos*, from *doxa* 'opinion'.

Orthodox Church • **noun** a Christian Church acknowledging the authority of the patriarch of Constantinople.

Orthodox Judaism • **noun** a branch of Judaism which teaches strict adherence to rabbinical interpretation of Jewish law and its traditional observances.

orthodoxy • **noun** (pl. **orthodoxies**) **1** orthodox theory, doctrine, or practice. **2** the state of being orthodox. **3** the whole community of Orthodox Jews or Orthodox Christians.

orthogonal /orthoggən'l/ • **adjective** of or involving right angles; at right angles.

orthographic projection • **noun** a method of projection in which an object is depicted using parallel lines to project its outline on to a plane.

orthography /orthogrəfi/ • **noun** (pl. **orthographies**) the conventional spelling system of a language.
– DERIVATIVES **orthographic** adjective.

orthopaedics /orthəpeediks/ (US **orthopedics**) • **plural noun** (treated as sing.) the branch of medicine concerned with the correction of deformities of bones or muscles.
– DERIVATIVES **orthopaedic** adjective **orthopaedist** noun.
– ORIGIN from Greek *paideia* 'rearing of children'.

orthoptics • **plural noun** (treated as sing.) the study or treatment of irregularities of the eyes, especially those of the eye muscles.
– DERIVATIVES **orthoptic** adjective **orthoptist** noun.

orthotics /orthottiks/ • **plural noun** (treated as sing.) the branch of medicine concerned with the provision and use of artificial supports or braces.
– DERIVATIVES **orthotic** adjective & noun **orthotist** noun.

ortolan /ortələn/ (also **ortolan bunting**) • **noun** a small songbird formerly eaten as a delicacy, the male having an olive-green head and yellow throat.
– ORIGIN Provençal, 'gardener' (because the bird frequents gardens).

Orwellian • **adjective** relating to the work of the British novelist George Orwell (1903–50), especially the totalitarian state depicted in *Nineteen Eighty-four*.

-ory[1] • **suffix** (forming nouns) denoting a place for a particular function: *dormitory*.
– ORIGIN Latin *-oria, -orium*.

-ory[2] • **suffix** forming adjectives relating to or involving a verbal action: *compulsory*.
– ORIGIN Latin *-orius*.

oryx /orriks/ • **noun** a large long-horned antelope of arid regions of Africa and Arabia.
– ORIGIN Greek *orux* 'stonemason's pickaxe' (because of its pointed horns).

orzo /ortsō/ • **noun** small pieces of pasta, shaped like grains of barley or rice.
– ORIGIN Italian, 'barley'.

OS • **abbreviation 1** Computing operating system. **2** Ordinary Seaman. **3** (in the UK) Ordnance Survey. **4** (as a size of clothing) outsize.

Os • **symbol** the chemical element osmium.

Oscar • **noun** (trademark in the US) the nickname for a gold statuette given as an Academy award.
– ORIGIN one speculative explanation claims that the statuette reminded an executive director of the Academy of Motion Picture Arts and Sciences of her uncle Oscar.

oscillate /ossilayt/ • **verb 1** move or swing back and forth at a regular rate. **2** waver between extremes of opinion or emotion.
– DERIVATIVES **oscillation** noun **oscillator** noun **oscillatory** /osillətri, ossilaytri/ adjective.
– ORIGIN Latin *oscillare* 'to swing'.

oscilloscope • **noun** a device for viewing oscillations by a display on the screen of a cathode ray tube.

osculation /oskyoolaysh'n/ • **noun** humorous kissing.
– ORIGIN from Latin *osculari* 'to kiss'.

osculum /oskyooləm/ • **noun** (pl. **oscula** /oskyoolə/) Zoology a large aperture in a sponge through which water is expelled.
– ORIGIN Latin, 'little mouth'.

-ose[1] • **suffix** (forming adjectives) having a specified quality: *bellicose*.
– ORIGIN Latin *-osus*.

-ose[2] • **suffix** Chemistry forming names of sugars and other carbohydrates: *cellulose*.
– ORIGIN from *(gluc)ose*.

osier /ōziər/ • **noun** a small willow with long flexible shoots used in basketwork.
– ORIGIN Old French.

-osis • **suffix** (pl. **-oses**) denoting a process, condition, or pathological state: *metamorphosis*.
– ORIGIN Greek.

-osity • **suffix** forming nouns from adjectives ending in *-ose* (such as *verbosity* from *verbose*) and from adjectives ending in *-ous* (such as *pomposity* from *pompous*).
– ORIGIN French *-osité* or Latin *-ositas*.

osmium /ozmiəm/ • **noun** a hard, dense silvery-white metallic element.
– ORIGIN from Greek *osmē* 'smell' (from the pungent smell of one of its oxides).

osmoregulation • **noun** Biology the maintenance of constant osmotic pressure in the fluids of an organism by the control of water and salt concentrations.
– DERIVATIVES **osmoregulatory** adjective.

osmosis /ozmōsiss/ • **noun 1** Biology & Chemistry a process by

Thesaurus

wrought, overblown; *informal* highfalutin, purple.
– OPPOSITES plain.

orotund • **adjective 1** *Halliwell's orotund voice* DEEP, sonorous, strong, powerful, full, rich, resonant, loud, booming. **2** *the orotund rhetoric of his prose* POMPOUS, pretentious, affected, fulsome, grandiose, ornate, overblown, flowery, florid, high-flown, magniloquent, grandiloquent, rhetorical, oratorical; *informal* highfalutin, purple.

orthodox • **adjective 1** *orthodox views* CONVENTIONAL, mainstream, conformist, (well) established, traditional, traditionalist, prevalent, popular, conservative, unoriginal. **2** *an orthodox Hindu* CONSERVATIVE, traditional, observant, devout, strict.
– OPPOSITES unconventional.

orthodoxy • **noun 1** *a pillar of orthodoxy* CONVENTIONALITY, conventionalism, conformism, conservatism, traditionalism, conformity. **2** *Christian orthodoxies* DOCTRINE, belief, conviction, creed, dogma, credo, theory, tenet, teaching.

oscillate • **verb 1** *the pendulum started to oscillate* SWING (TO AND FRO), swing back and forth, sway; *N. Amer. informal* wigwag. **2** *oscillating between fear and bravery* WAVER, swing, fluctuate, alternate, see-saw, yo-yo, sway, vacillate, hover; *informal* wobble.

oscillation • **noun 1** *the oscillation of the pendulum* SWINGING (TO

which molecules of a solvent pass through a semipermeable membrane from a less concentrated solution into a more concentrated one. **2** the gradual assimilation of ideas.
– DERIVATIVES **osmotic** adjective.
– ORIGIN Greek *ōsmos* 'a push'.
osmotic pressure /ozmottik/ ● noun Chemistry the pressure that would have to be applied to a pure solvent to prevent it from passing into a given solution by osmosis.
osprey ● noun (pl. **ospreys**) a large fish-eating bird of prey with a white underside and crown.
– ORIGIN apparently from Latin *ossifraga*, from *os* 'bone' + *frangere* 'to break'.
osseous /ossiəss/ ● adjective chiefly Zoology & Medicine consisting of or turned into bone.
– ORIGIN Latin *osseus* 'bony'.
ossicle ● noun Anatomy a very small bone, especially one of those which transmit sounds within the middle ear.
– ORIGIN Latin *ossiculum* 'little bone'.
ossify /ossifī/ ● verb (**ossifies**, **ossified**) **1** turn into bone or bony tissue. **2** cease developing; become inflexible.
– DERIVATIVES **ossification** noun.
– ORIGIN from Latin *os* 'bone'.
ossuary /ossyoori/ ● noun (pl. **ossuaries**) a container or room for the bones of the dead.
– ORIGIN Latin *ossuarium*, from *os* 'bone'.
ostensible ● adjective apparently true, but not necessarily so.
– DERIVATIVES **ostensibly** adverb.
– ORIGIN Latin *ostensibilis*, from *ostendere* 'stretch out to view'.
ostentation ● noun flamboyant display which is intended to impress.
– DERIVATIVES **ostentatious** adjective.
– ORIGIN from Latin *ostendere* 'stretch out to view'.
osteo- ● combining form of or relating to the bones: *osteoporosis*.
– ORIGIN from Greek *osteon* 'bone'.
osteoarthritis ● noun Medicine degeneration of joint cartilage, causing pain and stiffness.
osteogenesis imperfecta /ostiōjennisiss impərfektə/ ● noun Medicine an inherited disorder characterized by extreme fragility of the bones.
osteology /ostiolləji/ ● noun the study of the skeleton and bone.
– DERIVATIVES **osteological** adjective **osteologist** noun.
osteomyelitis /ostiōmī-ilītiss/ ● noun Medicine inflammation of bone or bone marrow.
osteopathy /ostioppəthi/ ● noun a system of complementary medicine involving the manipulation of the skeleton and musculature.
– DERIVATIVES **osteopath** noun **osteopathic** adjective.
osteoporosis /ostiōpərōsiss/ ● noun a medical condition in which the bones become brittle and fragile, typically as a result of hormonal changes, or deficiency of calcium or vitamin D.
– DERIVATIVES **osteoporotic** adjective.
– ORIGIN from Greek *poros* 'passage, pore'.
ostinato /ostinaatō/ ● noun (pl. **ostinatos** or **ostinati** /ostinaati/) a continually repeated musical phrase or rhythm.
– ORIGIN from Italian, 'obstinate'.
ostler /oslər/ (also **hostler**) ● noun historical a man employed at an inn to look after customers' horses.
– ORIGIN Old French *hostelier* 'innkeeper', from *hostel* (see HOSTEL).
Ostpolitik /ostpoliteek/ ● noun historical the foreign policy of détente of western European countries with reference to the former communist bloc.
– ORIGIN German, 'east politics'.
ostracize /ostrəsīz/ (also **ostracise**) ● verb exclude from a society or group.
– DERIVATIVES **ostracism** noun.
– ORIGIN Greek *ostrakizein*, from *ostrakon* 'shell or potsherd' (on which names were written in voting to banish unpopular citizens).
ostrich ● noun **1** a large flightless swift-running African bird with a long neck and long legs. **2** a person who refuses to accept unpleasant truths. [ORIGIN from the popular belief that ostriches bury their heads in the sand if pursued.]
– ORIGIN Old French *ostriche*, from Latin *avis* 'bird' + *struthio*, from Greek *strouthos* 'sparrow or ostrich'.
Ostrogoth /ostrəgoth/ ● noun a member of the eastern branch of the Goths, who conquered Italy in the 5th–6th centuries AD.
– ORIGIN Latin *Ostrogothi* 'East Goths'. Compare with VISIGOTH.
OT ● abbreviation **1** occupational therapist; occupational therapy. **2** Old Testament.
OTC ● abbreviation **1** (in the UK) Officers' Training Corps. **2** over the counter.
other ● adjective & pronoun **1** used to refer to a person or thing that is different from one already mentioned or known. **2** additional. **3** alternative of two. **4** those not already mentioned. **5** (usu. **the Other**) Philosophy & Sociology that which is distinct from, different from, or opposite to something or oneself.
– PHRASES **no other** archaic nothing else. **the other day** (or **night**, **week**, etc.) a few days (or nights, weeks, etc.) ago.
– ORIGIN Old English.
other half ● noun Brit. informal one's wife, husband, or partner.
otherness ● noun the quality or fact of being different.
other place ● noun Brit. humorous **1** hell, as opposed to heaven. **2** the House of Lords as regarded by the House of Commons, and vice versa.
other ranks ● plural noun Brit. (in the armed forces) all those who are not commissioned officers.
otherwise ● adverb **1** in different circumstances; or else. **2** in other respects. **3** in a different way. **4** alternatively. ● adjective in a different state or situation.
other woman ● noun the mistress of a married man.
other-worldly ● adjective **1** relating to an imaginary or spiritual world. **2** unworldly.
otic /ōtik/ ● adjective Anatomy relating to the ear.
– ORIGIN Greek *ōtikos*, from *ous* 'ear'.
otiose /ōtiōss, ōshi-/ ● adjective serving no practical purpose; pointless.
– ORIGIN Latin *otiosus*, from *otium* 'leisure'.
otitis /ətītiss/ ● noun Medicine inflammation of part of the ear, especially the middle ear (**otitis media**).
– ORIGIN from Greek *ous* 'ear'.
OTT ● abbreviation Brit. informal over the top.
otter ● noun a semiaquatic fish-eating mammal with an elongated body, dense fur, and webbed feet.
– ORIGIN Old English.
Ottoman ● adjective historical **1** relating to the Turkish dynasty of

Thesaurus

AND FRO), swing, swaying. **2** *his oscillation between commerce and art* WAVERING, swinging, fluctuation, see-sawing, yo-yoing, vacillation.
ossify ● verb **1** *these cartilages may ossify* TURN INTO BONE, become bony, harden, solidify, rigidify, petrify, fossilize. **2** *the political regime ossified* BECOME INFLEXIBLE, become rigid, fossilize, rigidify, stagnate.
ostensible ● adjective APPARENT, outward, superficial, professed, supposed, alleged, purported.
– OPPOSITES genuine.
ostensibly ● adverb APPARENTLY, seemingly, on the face of it, to all intents and purposes, outwardly, superficially, allegedly, supposedly, purportedly.
ostentation ● noun SHOWINESS, show, ostentatiousness, pretentiousness, vulgarity, conspicuousness, display, flamboyance, gaudiness, brashness, extravagance, ornateness, exhibitionism; *informal* flashiness, glitz, glitziness, ritziness.
ostentatious ● adjective SHOWY, pretentious, conspicuous, flamboyant, gaudy, brash, vulgar, loud, extravagant, fancy, ornate, over-elaborate; *informal* flash, flashy, over the top, OTT, glitzy, ritzy; *N. Amer. informal* superfly.
– OPPOSITES restrained.
ostracism ● noun EXCLUSION, rejection, shunning, spurning, the cold shoulder, snubbing, avoidance, banishment; blackballing, blacklisting.
ostracize ● verb EXCLUDE, shun, spurn, cold-shoulder, reject, shut out, avoid, ignore, snub, cut dead, keep at arm's length, leave out in the cold; blackball, blacklist; *Brit.* send to Coventry; *informal* freeze out; *Brit. informal* blank.
– OPPOSITES welcome.
other ● adjective **1** *these homes use other fuels* ALTERNATIVE, different, dissimilar, disparate, distinct, separate, contrasting. **2** *are there any other questions?* MORE, further, additional, extra, added, supplementary.
otherwise ● adverb **1** *hurry up, otherwise we'll be late* OR (ELSE), if not. **2** *she's exhausted, but otherwise she's fine* IN OTHER RESPECTS, apart from that. **3** *he could not have acted otherwise* IN ANY OTHER WAY, differently.

Osman I (Othman I), founded in *c.*1300. **2** relating to the Ottoman Empire ruled by the successors of Osman I. **3** Turkish. ● noun (pl. **Ottomans**) a Turk, especially of the Ottoman period.
– ORIGIN Arabic.

ottoman ● noun (pl. **ottomans**) a low upholstered seat without a back or arms, typically serving also as a box.

OU ● abbreviation (in the UK) Open University.

oubliette /ōōbliet/ ● noun a secret dungeon with access only through a trapdoor in its ceiling.
– ORIGIN French, from *oublier* 'forget'.

ouch ● exclamation used to express pain.
– ORIGIN natural exclamation.

ought ● modal verb (3rd sing. present and past **ought**) **1** used to indicate duty or correctness. **2** used to indicate something that is probable. **3** used to indicate a desirable or expected state. **4** used to give or ask advice.
– USAGE The standard construction for the negative is *he ought not to have gone.* The constructions *he didn't ought to have gone* and *he hadn't ought to have gone* are found in dialect but are not acceptable in standard modern English. The reason for this is that the verb **ought** is a modal verb and therefore behaves differently from ordinary verbs in certain constructions, such as the formation of a negative.
– ORIGIN Old English.

oughtn't ● contraction ought not.

ouguiya /ōōgeeyə/ (also **ougiya**) ● noun the basic monetary unit of Mauritania, equal to five khoums.
– ORIGIN Arabic, from Latin *uncia* 'ounce'.

Ouija board /weejə/ ● noun trademark a board with letters, numbers, and other signs around its edge, to which a pointer moves, supposedly in answer to questions at a seance.
– ORIGIN from French *oui* 'yes' + German *ja* 'yes'.

ounce ● noun **1** a unit of weight of one sixteenth of a pound avoirdupois (approximately 28 grams). **2** a unit of one twelfth of a pound troy or apothecaries' measure, equal to 480 grains (approximately 31 grams). **3** a very small amount.
– ORIGIN Latin *uncia* 'twelfth part (of a pound or foot)'; compare with INCH.

our ● possessive determiner **1** belonging to or associated with the speaker and one or more others. **2** belonging to or associated with people in general. **3** used in formal contexts by a royal person to refer to something belonging to himself or herself. **4** informal, chiefly N. English used with a name to refer to a relative or friend of the speaker.
– ORIGIN Old English.

Our Father ● noun **1** God. **2** the Lord's Prayer.

Our Lady ● noun the Virgin Mary.

Our Lord ● noun God or Jesus.

ours ● possessive pronoun used to refer to something belonging to or associated with the speaker and one or more others.

ourself ● pronoun (first person pl.) used instead of 'ourselves', typically when 'we' refers to people in general.

ourselves ● pronoun (first person pl.) **1** used as the object of a verb or preposition when this is the same as the subject of the clause and the subject is the speaker and one or more other people considered together. **2** (emphatic) we or us personally.

-ous ● suffix forming adjectives: **1** characterized by: *mountainous.* **2** Chemistry denoting an element in a lower valency: *sulphurous.* Compare with -IC.
– ORIGIN Latin *-osus.*

ousel ● noun variant spelling of OUZEL.

oust /owst/ ● verb drive out or expel from a position or place.
– ORIGIN Old French *ouster* 'take away', from Latin *obstare* 'oppose, hinder'.

out ● adverb **1** moving away from a place. **2** away from one's usual base or residence. **3** outdoors. **4** so as to be revealed, heard, or known. **5** at or to an end: *the romance fizzled out.* **6** at a specified distance away from the target. **7** to sea, away from the land. **8** (of the tide) falling or at its lowest level. **9** no longer in prison. ● preposition non-standard contraction of **out of.** ● adjective **1** not at home or one's place of work. **2** in existence, use, or the public domain. **3** open about one's homosexuality. **4** not possible or worth considering. **5** no longer existing. **6** informal no longer fashionable. **7** unconscious. **8** mistaken. **9** (of the ball in tennis, squash, etc.) outside the playing area. **10** Cricket & Baseball no longer batting. ● verb informal reveal the homosexuality of.
– PHRASES **out and about** engaging in normal activity after an illness. **out for** intent on having. **out of 1** from. **2** not having (something). **out of it** informal **1** not included. **2** unaware of what is happening. **out to do** keenly striving to do. **out with it** say what you are thinking.
– USAGE It is better to write **out of** rather than simply **out** in constructions such as *he threw it out of the window.*
– ORIGIN Old English.

out- ● prefix **1** to the point of surpassing or exceeding: *outperform.* **2** external; separate; from outside: *outbuildings.* **3** away from; outward: *outpost.*

outage ● noun a period when a power supply or other service is not available.

out and out ● adjective absolute. ● adverb completely.

outback ● noun (**the outback**) a remote or sparsely populated inland area, especially in Australia.

outbalance ● verb be more valuable or important than.

outbid ● verb (**outbidding**; past and past part. **outbid**) bid more for something than.

outboard ● adjective & adverb **1** on, towards, or near the outside of a ship or aircraft. **2** (of a motor) portable and attachable to the outside of the stern of a boat. ● noun **1** an outboard motor. **2** a boat with such a motor.

outbound ● adjective & adverb outward bound.

outbreak ● noun a sudden or violent occurrence of war, disease, etc.

outbuilding ● noun a smaller detached building in the grounds of a main building.

outburst ● noun a sudden violent occurrence or release of something.

outcast ● noun a person rejected by their society or social group. ● adjective rejected or cast out.

outclass ● verb be far superior to.

outcome ● noun a consequence.

outcrop ● noun a part of a rock formation that is visible on the surface. ● verb (**outcropped**, **outcropping**) appear as an outcrop.

Thesaurus

other-worldly ● adjective ETHEREAL, dreamy, spiritual, mystic, mystical; unearthly, unworldly, supernatural.

ounce ● noun PARTICLE, scrap, bit, speck, iota, whit, jot, trace, atom, shred, crumb, fragment, grain, drop, spot; *informal* smidgen.

oust ● verb DRIVE OUT, expel, force out, throw out, remove (from office/power), eject, get rid of, depose, topple, unseat, overthrow, bring down, overturn, dismiss, dislodge, displace; *informal* boot out, kick out; *Brit. informal* turf out; *dated* out.

out ● adjective & adverb **1** *she's out at the moment* NOT HERE, not at home, not in, (gone) away, elsewhere, absent. **2** *the secret was out* REVEALED, (out) in the open, common/public knowledge, known, disclosed, divulged. **3** *the roses are out* IN FLOWER, flowering, in (full) bloom, blooming, in blossom, blossoming, open. **4** *the book should be out soon* AVAILABLE, obtainable, in the shops, published, in print. **5** *the fire was nearly out* EXTINGUISHED, no longer alight. **6** *(informal) grunge is out* UNFASHIONABLE, out of fashion, dated, outdated, passé; *informal* old hat, not with it, not in. **7** *smoking is out* FORBIDDEN, not permitted, not allowed, proscribed, unacceptable; *informal* not on. **8** *he was slightly out in his calculations* MISTAKEN, inaccurate, incorrect, wrong, in error.
– OPPOSITES in.
● verb *(informal) it was not our intention to out him* EXPOSE, unmask.
– PHRASES **out cold** UNCONSCIOUS, knocked out, out for the count; *informal* KO'd, kayoed.

out-and-out ● adjective UTTER, downright, thoroughgoing, absolute, complete, thorough, total, unmitigated, outright, real, perfect, consummate; *N. Amer.* full-bore; *informal* deep-dyed; *Brit. informal* right; *Austral./NZ informal* fair.

outbreak ● noun **1** *a fresh outbreak of killings* ERUPTION, flare-up, upsurge, outburst, rash, wave, spate, flood, explosion, burst, flurry; *formal* boutade. **2** *on the outbreak of war* START, beginning, commencement, onset, outset.

outburst ● noun ERUPTION, explosion, burst, outbreak, flare-up, access, rush, flood, storm, outpouring, surge, upsurge, outflowing; *formal* boutade.

outcast ● noun PARIAH, persona non grata, reject, outsider.

outclass ● verb SURPASS, be superior to, be better than, outshine, overshadow, eclipse, outdo, outplay, outmanoeuvre, outstrip, get the better of, upstage; top, cap, beat, defeat, exceed; *informal* be a cut above, be head and shoulders above, run rings round; *archaic*

outcry ● noun (pl. **outcries**) a strong expression of public disapproval.
outdated ● adjective obsolete.
outdistance ● verb leave (a competitor or pursuer) far behind.
outdo ● verb (**outdoes**, **outdoing**; past **outdid**; past part. **outdone**) be superior to in action or performance.
outdoor ● adjective **1** done, situated, or used outdoors. **2** liking the outdoors.
outdoors ● adverb in or into the open air. ● noun any area outside buildings or shelter.
outer ● adjective **1** outside; external. **2** further from the centre or the inside. ● noun Brit. the division of a target furthest from the bullseye.
outer bar ● noun (**the outer bar**) (in the UK) barristers who are not Queen's or King's Counsels.
outermost ● adjective furthest from the centre.
outer space ● noun the physical universe beyond the earth's atmosphere.
outface ● verb disconcert or defeat by bold confrontation.
outfall ● noun the place where a river or drain empties into the sea, a river, or a lake.
outfield ● noun the outer part of a cricket or baseball field.
outfit ● noun **1** a set of clothes worn together. **2** informal a group of people undertaking a particular activity together. ● verb (**outfitted**, **outfitting**) (usu. **be outfitted**) provide with an outfit of clothes.
outfitter (also **outfitters**) ● noun Brit. dated a shop selling men's clothing.
outflank ● verb **1** move round the side of (an enemy) so as to outmanoeuvre them. **2** outwit.
outflow ● noun **1** the action of flowing or moving out. **2** something, such as water or money, that flows or moves out.
outfox ● verb informal defeat with superior cunning.
outgas ● verb (**outgases**, **outgassing**, **outgassed**) release or give off as a gas or vapour.
outgoing ● adjective **1** friendly and confident. **2** leaving an office or position. **3** going out or away from a place. ● noun Brit. (**outgoings**) one's regular expenditure.
outgrow ● verb (past **outgrew**; past part. **outgrown**) **1** grow too big for. **2** leave behind as one matures. **3** grow faster or taller than.
outgrowth ● noun **1** something that grows out of something else. **2** a natural development or result.
outgun ● verb (**outgunned**, **outgunning**) have more or better weaponry than.
outhouse ● noun a smaller building built on to or in the grounds of a house.
outing ● noun **1** a short trip taken for pleasure. **2** informal a public appearance in something, especially a sporting fixture. **3** the practice of revealing someone's homosexuality.
outlandish ● adjective bizarre or unfamiliar.
– ORIGIN Old English, 'not native'.
outlast ● verb last longer than.
outlaw ● noun **1** a fugitive from the law. **2** historical a person deprived of the benefit and protection of the law. ● verb **1** make illegal; ban. **2** historical deprive of the benefit and protection of the law.
– DERIVATIVES **outlawry** noun.
outlay ● noun an amount of money spent.
outlet ● noun **1** a pipe or hole through which water or gas may escape. **2** a point from which goods are sold or distributed. **3** an output socket in an electrical device. **4** a means of expressing one's talents, energy, or emotions. **5** the mouth of a river.
outlier /owtlīər/ ● noun **1** a thing detached from a main body or system. **2** Geology a younger rock formation among older rocks.
outline ● noun **1** a line or lines enclosing or indicating the shape of an object in a sketch or diagram. **2** the contours or outer edges of an object. **3** a general plan showing essential features but no detail. ● verb **1** draw or define the outer edge or shape of. **2** give a summary of.

Thesaurus

outrival.
outcome ● noun (END) RESULT, consequence, net result, upshot, after-effect, aftermath, conclusion, issue, end (product).
outcry ● noun **1** *an outcry of passion* SHOUT, exclamation, cry, yell, howl, roar, scream; *informal* holler. **2** *public outcry* PROTEST(S), protestation(s), complaints, objections, furore, fuss, commotion, uproar, outbursts, opposition, dissent; *informal* hullabaloo, ballyhoo, ructions, stink.
outdated ● adjective OLD-FASHIONED, out of date, outmoded, out of fashion, unfashionable, dated, passé, old, behind the times, behindhand, obsolete, antiquated; *informal* out, old hat, square, not with it, out of the ark; *N. Amer. informal* horse-and-buggy, clunky.
– OPPOSITES modern.
outdistance ● verb **1** *the colt outdistanced the train* OUTRUN, outstrip, outpace, leave behind, get (further) ahead of; overtake, pass. **2** *the mill outdistanced all its rivals* SURPASS, outshine, outclass, outdo, exceed, transcend, top, cap, beat, better, leave behind; *informal* leave standing; *archaic* outrival.
outdo ● verb SURPASS, outshine, overshadow, eclipse, outclass, outmanoeuvre, get the better of, put in the shade, upstage; exceed, transcend, top, cap, beat, better, leave behind, get ahead of; *informal* be a cut above, be head and shoulders above, run rings round; *archaic* outrival.
outdoor ● adjective OPEN-AIR, out-of-doors, outside, al fresco, not under cover.
– OPPOSITES indoor.
outer ● adjective **1** *the outer layer* OUTSIDE, outermost, outward, exterior, external, surface. **2** *outer areas of the city* OUTLYING, distant, remote, faraway, furthest, peripheral; suburban.
– OPPOSITES inner.
outface ● verb STAND UP TO, face down, cow, overawe, intimidate.
outfit ● noun **1** *a new outfit* COSTUME, suit, uniform, ensemble, attire, clothes, clothing, dress, garb; *informal* get-up, gear, togs; *Brit. informal* kit, rig-out; *formal* apparel; *archaic* habit, raiment. **2** *a studio lighting outfit* KIT, equipment, tools, implements, tackle, apparatus, paraphernalia, things, stuff. **3** *a local manufacturing outfit* ORGANIZATION, set-up, enterprise, company, firm, business; group, band, body, team.
● verb *enough swords to outfit an army* EQUIP, kit out, fit out/up, rig out, supply, arm; dress, attire, clothe, deck out; *archaic* apparel, invest, habit.
outfitter ● noun CLOTHIER, tailor, couturier, costumier, dressmaker, seamstress; *dated* modiste.
outflow ● noun DISCHARGE, outflowing, outpouring, outrush, rush, flood, deluge, issue, spurt, jet, cascade, stream, torrent, gush, outburst; flow, flux; *technical* efflux.
outgoing ● adjective **1** *outgoing children* EXTROVERT, uninhibited, unreserved, demonstrative, affectionate, warm, friendly, genial, cordial, affable, easy-going, sociable, convivial, lively, gregarious; communicative, responsive, open, forthcoming, frank. **2** *the outgoing president* DEPARTING, retiring, leaving.
– OPPOSITES introverted, incoming.
outgoings ● plural noun EXPENSES, expenditure, spending, outlay, payments, costs, overheads.
outgrowth ● noun PROTUBERANCE, swelling, excrescence, growth, lump, bump, bulge; tumour, cancer, boil, carbuncle, pustule.
outing ● noun **1** *family outings* (PLEASURE) TRIP, excursion, jaunt, expedition, day out, (mystery) tour, drive, ride, run; *informal* junket, spin. **2** *the outing of public figures by the press* EXPOSURE, unmasking, revelation.
outlandish ● adjective WEIRD, queer, far out, quirky, zany, eccentric, idiosyncratic, unconventional, unorthodox, funny, bizarre, unusual, singular, extraordinary, strange, unfamiliar, peculiar, odd, curious; *informal* offbeat, off the wall, way-out, wacky, freaky, kooky, kinky, oddball; *N. Amer. informal* in left field.
– OPPOSITES ordinary.
outlast ● verb OUTLIVE, survive, live/last longer than; ride out, weather, withstand.
outlaw ● noun *bands of outlaws* FUGITIVE, (wanted) criminal, outcast, exile, pariah; bandit, robber; *dated* desperado.
● verb **1** *they voted to outlaw fox-hunting* BAN, bar, prohibit, forbid, veto, make illegal, proscribe, interdict. **2** *she feared she would be outlawed* BANISH, exile, expel.
– OPPOSITES permit.
outlay ● noun EXPENDITURE, expenses, spending, outgoings, cost, price, payment, investment.
outlet ● noun **1** *a central-heating outlet* VENT (HOLE), way out, egress; outfall, opening, channel, conduit, duct. **2** *an outlet for farm produce* MARKET, retail outlet, marketplace, shop, store. **3** *an outlet for their energies* MEANS OF EXPRESSION, (means of) release, vent, avenue, channel.
outline ● noun **1** *the outline of the building* SILHOUETTE, profile, shape, contours, form, line, delineation; diagram, sketch; *poetic/literary* lineaments. **2** *an outline of expenditure for each depart-*

outlive ● verb live or last longer than.
outlook ● noun **1** a person's point of view or attitude to life. **2** a view. **3** the prospect for the future.
outlying ● adjective situated far from a centre.
outmanoeuvre ● verb **1** evade by moving faster or more skilfully. **2** use skill and cunning to gain an advantage.
outmatch ● verb be superior to.
outmoded ● adjective old-fashioned.
outnumber ● verb be more numerous than.
out-of-body experience ● noun a sensation of being outside one's body, typically of observing oneself from a distance.
out-of-court ● adjective Law (of a settlement) made without the intervention of a court.
out of date ● adjective **1** old-fashioned. **2** no longer valid.
outpace ● verb go faster than.
outpatient ● noun a patient attending a hospital for treatment without staying overnight.
outperform ● verb perform better than.
outplacement ● noun the provision of assistance to redundant employees in finding new employment.
outplay ● verb play better than.
outpost ● noun **1** a small military camp at a distance from the main army. **2** a remote part of a country or empire.
outpouring ● noun **1** something that streams out rapidly. **2** an outburst of strong emotion.
output ● noun **1** the amount of something produced. **2** the process of producing something. **3** the power, energy, etc. supplied by a device or system. **4** Electronics a place where power or information leaves a system. ● verb (**outputting**; past and past part. **output** or **outputted**) (of a computer) produce or supply (data).
outrage ● noun **1** an extremely strong reaction of anger or indignation. **2** an extremely cruel, immoral, or shocking act. ● verb **1** arouse outrage in. **2** violate (a standard, law, etc.) flagrantly.
– ORIGIN Old French, from Latin *ultra* 'beyond'.
outrageous ● adjective **1** shockingly bad or excessive. **2** very bold and unusual.
– DERIVATIVES **outrageously** adverb **outrageousness** noun.
outran past of OUTRUN.
outrank ● verb **1** have a higher rank than. **2** be better or more important than.
outré /o͞otray/ ● adjective unusual and typically rather shocking.
– ORIGIN French, 'exceeded'.
outreach ● verb /owtreech/ reach further than. ● noun /owtreech/ **1** the extent or length of reaching out. **2** an organization's involvement with the community.
outrider ● noun a person in a vehicle or on horseback who escorts or guards another vehicle.
outrigger ● noun **1** a spar or framework projecting from or over a boat's side. **2** a stabilizing float fixed parallel to a canoe or small ship. **3** a boat fitted with an outrigger.
outright ● adverb **1** altogether. **2** openly. **3** immediately. ● adjective **1** open and direct. **2** complete.
outrun ● verb (**outrunning**; past **outran**; past part. **outrun**) **1** run or travel faster or further than. **2** exceed.
outsell ● verb (past and past part. **outsold**) be sold in greater quantities than.
outset ● noun the start or beginning.
outshine ● verb (past and past part. **outshone**) **1** shine more brightly than. **2** be much better than.
outside ● noun **1** the external side or surface of something. **2** the external appearance of someone or something. **3** the part of a path nearer to a road. **4** the side of a curve where the edge is longer. ● adjective **1** situated on or near the outside. **2** not of

Thesaurus

ment ROUGH IDEA, thumbnail sketch, (quick) rundown, summary, synopsis, résumé, precis; essence, main points, gist, (bare) bones, draft, sketch.
● verb **1** *the plane was outlined against the sky* SILHOUETTE, define, demarcate; sketch, delineate, trace. **2** *she outlined the plan briefly* ROUGH OUT, sketch out, draft, give a rough idea of, summarize, precis.
outlive ● verb LIVE ON AFTER, live longer than, outlast, survive.
outlook ● noun **1** *the two men were wholly different in outlook* POINT OF VIEW, viewpoint, views, opinion, (way of) thinking, perspective, attitude, standpoint, stance, frame of mind. **2** *a lovely open outlook* VIEW, vista, prospect, panorama, scene, aspect. **3** *the outlook for the economy* PROSPECTS, expectations, hopes, lookout, future.
outlying ● adjective DISTANT, remote, outer, out of the way, faraway, far-flung, inaccessible, off the beaten track.
outmanoeuvre ● verb **1** *the English army were outmanoeuvred* OUTFLANK, circumvent, bypass. **2** *he outmanoeuvred his critics* OUTWIT, outsmart, out-think, outplay, steal a march on, trick, get the better of; *informal* outfox, put one over on.
outmoded ● adjective OUT OF DATE, old-fashioned, out of fashion, outdated, dated, behind the times, antiquated, obsolete, passé; *informal* old hat, out of the ark.
out of date ● adjective **1** *this design is out of date* OLD-FASHIONED, outmoded, out of fashion, unfashionable, frumpish, frumpy, outdated, dated, old, passé, behind the times, behindhand, obsolete, antiquated; *informal* out, old hat, square, not with it, out of the ark; *N. Amer. informal* horse-and-buggy, clunky. **2** *many of the facts are out of date* SUPERSEDED, obsolete, expired, lapsed, invalid, (null and) void.
– OPPOSITES fashionable, current.
out of the way ● adjective **1** *out-of-the-way places* OUTLYING, distant, remote, faraway, far-flung, isolated, lonely, godforsaken, inaccessible, off the beaten track. **2** *I find his methods out of the way* STRANGE, unusual, peculiar, odd, funny, curious, bizarre, weird, queer, unfamiliar, out of the ordinary, extraordinary, remarkable, singular.
– OPPOSITES accessible.
out of work ● adjective UNEMPLOYED, jobless, out of a job; redundant, laid off; *Brit. informal* on the dole; *Austral. informal* on the wallaby track.
outpouring ● noun OUTFLOW, outflowing, outrush, rush, flood, deluge, discharge, issue, spurt, jet, cascade, stream, torrent, gush, outburst, flow, flux; *technical* efflux.
output ● noun PRODUCTION, amount/quantity produced, yield, gross domestic product, out-turn; works, writings.
outrage ● noun **1** *widespread public outrage* INDIGNATION, fury, anger, rage, disapproval, wrath, resentment. **2** *it is an outrage* SCANDAL, offence, insult, injustice, disgrace. **3** *the bomb outrage* ATROCITY, act of violence/wickedness, crime, wrong, barbarism, inhumane act.
● verb *his remarks outraged his parishioners* ENRAGE, infuriate, incense, anger, scandalize, offend, give offence to, affront, shock, horrify, disgust, appal.
outrageous ● adjective **1** *outrageous acts of cruelty* SHOCKING, disgraceful, scandalous, atrocious, appalling, monstrous, heinous; evil, wicked, abominable, terrible, horrendous, dreadful, foul, nauseating, sickening, vile, nasty, odious, loathsome, unspeakable; *Brit. informal* beastly. **2** *the politician's outrageous promises* FAR-FETCHED, (highly) unlikely, doubtful, dubious, questionable, implausible, unconvincing, unbelievable, incredible, preposterous, extravagant, excessive. **3** *outrageous clothes* EYE-CATCHING, flamboyant, showy, gaudy, ostentatious; shameless, brazen, shocking; *informal* saucy, flashy.
outré ● adjective WEIRD, queer, outlandish, far out, freakish, quirky, zany, eccentric, off-centre, unconventional, unorthodox, funny, bizarre, fantastic, unusual, singular, extraordinary, strange, unfamiliar, peculiar, odd, out of the way; *informal* way-out, wacky, freaky, kooky, oddball, off the wall; *N. Amer. informal* offbeat, in left field.
outright ● adverb **1** *he rejected the proposal outright* COMPLETELY, entirely, wholly, fully, totally, categorically, absolutely, utterly, flatly, unreservedly. **2** *I told her outright* EXPLICITLY, directly, forthrightly, openly, frankly, candidly, honestly, sincerely, bluntly, plainly, in plain language, truthfully, to someone's face, straight from the shoulder; *Brit. informal* straight up. **3** *they were killed outright* INSTANTLY, instantaneously, immediately, at once, straight away, then and there, on the spot. **4** *paintings have to be bought outright* ALL AT ONCE, in one go.
● adjective **1** *an outright lie* OUT-AND-OUT, absolute, complete, downright, utter, sheer, categorical, unqualified, unconditional. **2** *the outright winner* DEFINITE, unequivocal, clear, unqualified, incontestable, unmistakable.
outrun ● verb RUN FASTER THAN, outstrip, outdistance, outpace, leave behind, lose; *informal* leave standing.
outset ● noun START, starting point, beginning, commencement, dawn, birth, origin, inception, opening, launch, inauguration; *informal* the word go.
– OPPOSITES end.
outshine ● verb SURPASS, overshadow, eclipse, outclass, put in the

or belonging to a particular group. **3** (in hockey, soccer, etc.) denoting positions nearer to the sides of the field. ● **preposition & adverb** **1** situated or moving beyond the boundaries of. **2** (in hockey, soccer, etc.) closer to the side of the field than. **3** beyond the limits or scope of. **4** not being a member of.
– PHRASES **at the outside** at the most. **an outside chance** a remote possibility. **outside of** informal, chiefly N. Amer. **1** beyond the boundaries of. **2** apart from.
outside broadcast ● **noun** Brit. a radio or television programme recorded or broadcast live on location.
outside interest ● **noun** an interest not connected with one's work or studies.
outsider ● **noun** **1** a person who does not belong to a particular group. **2** a competitor thought to have little chance of success.
outsize ● **adjective** (also **outsized**) exceptionally large.
outskirts ● **plural noun** the outer parts of a town or city.
outsmart ● **verb** defeat with superior intelligence.
outsold past and past participle of OUTSELL.
outsole ● **noun** the outer sole of a boot or shoe.
outsource ● **verb** **1** obtain by contract from an outside supplier. **2** contract (work) out.
outspoken ● **adjective** frank in stating one's opinions.
– DERIVATIVES **outspokenness** noun.
outspread ● **adjective** fully extended or expanded.
outstanding ● **adjective** **1** exceptionally good. **2** clearly noticeable. **3** not yet dealt with or paid.
– DERIVATIVES **outstandingly** adverb.
outstation ● **noun** **1** a branch of an organization situated far from its headquarters. **2** Austral./NZ a part of a farming estate that is separate from the main estate.
outstay ● **verb** stay beyond the limit of (one's expected or permitted time).
outstretch ● **verb** extend or stretch out.
outstrip ● **verb** (**outstripped**, **outstripping**) **1** move faster than and overtake. **2** exceed; surpass.
out-take ● **noun** a sequence of a film or recording rejected in editing.
out tray ● **noun** a tray on a desk for letters and documents that have been dealt with.
out-turn ● **noun** **1** the amount of something produced. **2** a result or consequence.
outvote ● **verb** defeat by gaining more votes.
outward ● **adjective** **1** of, on, or from the outside. **2** going out or away from a place. ● **adverb** outwards.
– DERIVATIVES **outwardly** adverb.
outward bound ● **adjective** going away from home. ● **noun** (**Outward Bound**) trademark an organization providing outdoor activities for young people.
outwards ● **adverb** towards the outside; away from the centre or a place.
outwash ● **noun** material carried away from a glacier by meltwater.
outweigh ● **verb** be heavier, greater, or more significant than.
outwit ● **verb** (**outwitted**, **outwitting**) deceive by greater ingenuity.
outwith ● **preposition** Scottish outside; beyond.
outwork ● **noun** **1** an outer section of a fortification or system of defence. **2** Brit. work done outside the factory or office which provides it.
– DERIVATIVES **outworker** noun.
ouzel /o͞oz'l/ (also **ousel**) ● **noun** used in names of birds resembling the blackbird, e.g. **ring ouzel**.
– ORIGIN Old English, 'blackbird'.
ouzo /o͞ozō/ ● **noun** a Greek aniseed-flavoured spirit.
– ORIGIN modern Greek.
ova plural of OVUM.
oval ● **adjective** having a rounded and slightly elongated outline; egg-shaped. ● **noun** **1** an oval object or design. **2** an oval sports field or track. **3** a ground for Australian Rules football.
– ORIGIN Latin *ovalis*, from *ovum* 'egg'.
Oval Office ● **noun** the office of the US President in the White House.
ovarian ● **adjective** relating to the ovaries.
ovariectomy /ōvəriektəmi/ ● **noun** (pl. **ovariectomies**) surgical removal of one or both ovaries.
ovariotomy /ōvəriottəmi/ ● **noun** another term for OVARIECTOMY.
ovary ● **noun** (pl. **ovaries**) **1** a female reproductive organ in which ova or eggs are produced. **2** Botany the base of the carpel of a flower, containing one or more ovules.
– ORIGIN Latin *ovarium*, from *ovum* 'egg'.
ovate /ōvayt/ ● **adjective** oval; egg-shaped.
– ORIGIN Latin *ovatus*.
ovation ● **noun** an enthusiastic and sustained round of applause, cheering, etc.
– ORIGIN Latin, from *ovare* 'exult'.
oven ● **noun** **1** an enclosed compartment in which food is cooked

Thesaurus

shade, upstage, exceed, transcend, top, cap, beat, better; *informal* be a cut above, be head and shoulders above, run rings round; *archaic* outrival.
outside ● **noun** *the outside of the building* OUTER/EXTERNAL SURFACE, exterior, outer side/layer, case, skin, shell, covering, facade.
– RELATED TERMS ecto-, exo-, extra-.
● **adjective** **1** *outside lights* EXTERIOR, external, outer, outdoor, out-of-doors. **2** *outside contractors* INDEPENDENT, hired, temporary, freelance, casual, external, extramural. **3** *an outside chance* SLIGHT, slender, slim, small, tiny, faint, negligible, remote, vague.
● **adverb** *they went outside | shall we eat outside?* OUTDOORS, out of doors.
– OPPOSITES inside.
outsider ● **noun** STRANGER, visitor, non-member; foreigner, alien, immigrant, emigrant, émigré; incomer, newcomer, parvenu.
outsize ● **adjective** **1** *her outsize handbag* HUGE, oversized, enormous, gigantic, very big/large, great, giant, colossal, massive, mammoth, vast, immense, tremendous, monumental, prodigious, mountainous, king-sized; *informal* mega, monster, whopping (great), thumping (great), humongous, jumbo, bumper; *Brit. informal* whacking (great), ginormous. **2** *an outsize actor* VERY LARGE, big, massive, fat, corpulent, stout, heavy, plump, portly, ample, bulky; *informal* pudgy, tubby; *Brit. informal* podgy; *archaic* pursy.
outskirts ● **plural noun** OUTLYING DISTRICTS, edges, fringes, suburbs, suburbia; purlieus, borders, environs.
outsmart ● **verb** OUTWIT, outmanoeuvre, outplay, steal a march on, trick, get the better of; *informal* outfox, pull a fast one on, put one over on.
outspoken ● **adjective** FORTHRIGHT, direct, candid, frank, straightforward, honest, open, straight from the shoulder, plain-spoken; blunt, abrupt, bluff, brusque; *archaic* free-spoken.
outspread ● **adjective** FULLY EXTENDED, outstretched, spread out, fanned out, unfolded, unfurled, (wide) open, opened out.
outstanding ● **adjective** **1** *an outstanding painter* EXCELLENT, marvellous, magnificent, superb, fine, wonderful, superlative, exceptional, first-class, first-rate; *informal* great, terrific, tremendous, super, amazing, fantastic, sensational, fabulous, ace, crack, A1, mean, awesome, out of this world; *Brit. informal* smashing, brilliant; *N. Amer. informal* neat; *Austral. informal* bonzer. **2** *an outstanding decorative element* REMARKABLE, extraordinary, exceptional, striking, eye-catching, arresting, impressive, distinctive, unforgettable, memorable, special, momentous, significant, notable, noteworthy; *informal* out of this world. **3** *how much work is still outstanding?* TO BE DONE, undone, unattended to, unfinished, incomplete, remaining, pending, ongoing. **4** *outstanding debts* UNPAID, unsettled, owing, owed, to be paid, payable, due, overdue, undischarged; *N. Amer.* delinquent.
– OPPOSITES unexceptional.
outstrip ● **verb** **1** *he outstripped the police cars* GO FASTER THAN, outrun, outdistance, outpace, leave behind, get (further) ahead of, lose; *informal* leave standing. **2** *demand far outstrips supply* SURPASS, exceed, be more than, top, eclipse.
outward ● **adjective** EXTERNAL, outer, outside, exterior; surface, superficial, seeming, apparent, ostensible.
– OPPOSITES inward.
outwardly ● **adverb** EXTERNALLY, on the surface, superficially, on the face of it, to all intents and purposes, apparently, ostensibly, seemingly.
outweigh ● **verb** BE GREATER THAN, exceed, be superior to, prevail over, have the edge on/over, override, supersede, offset, cancel out, (more than) make up for, outbalance, compensate for.
outwit ● **verb** OUTSMART, outmanoeuvre, outplay, steal a march on, trick, gull, get the better of; *informal* outfox, pull a fast one on, put one over on.
outworn ● **adjective** OUT OF DATE, outdated, old-fashioned, out of fashion, outmoded, dated, behind the times, antiquated, obsolete, defunct, passé; *informal* old hat, out of the ark.
– OPPOSITES up to date.

or heated. **2** a small furnace or kiln.
– ORIGIN Old English.
oven glove • noun a padded glove for handling hot dishes from an oven.
ovenproof • adjective suitable for use in an oven.
oven-ready • adjective (of food) sold as a prepared dish, ready for cooking in an oven.
ovenware • noun ovenproof dishes.
over • preposition **1** extending upwards from or above. **2** above so as to cover or protect. **3** expressing movement or a route across. **4** beyond and falling or hanging from. **5** expressing duration. **6** at a higher level, layer, or intensity than. **7** higher or more than. **8** expressing authority or control. **9** on the subject of. • adverb **1** expressing movement or a route across an area. **2** beyond and falling or hanging from a point. **3** in or to the place indicated. **4** expressing action and result. **5** finished. **6** expressing repetition of a process. • noun Cricket a sequence of six balls bowled by a bowler from one end of the pitch.
– PHRASES **be over** be no longer affected by. **over against 1** adjacent to. **2** in contrast with. **over and above** in addition to. **over and out** indicating that a message on a two-way radio has finished.
– ORIGIN Old English.
over- • prefix **1** excessively: *overambitious*. **2** completely: *overjoyed*. **3** upper; outer; extra: *overcoat*. **4** over; above: *overcast*.
overachieve • verb do better than expected.
– DERIVATIVES **overachievement** noun **overachiever** noun.
overact • verb act a role in an exaggerated manner.
overactive • adjective excessively active.
– DERIVATIVES **overactivity** noun.
overall • adjective **1** inclusive of everything; total. **2** taking everything into account. • adverb taken as a whole. • noun (also **overalls**) Brit. a loose-fitting garment worn over ordinary clothes for protection.
overambitious • adjective excessively ambitious.
overanxious • adjective excessively anxious.
– DERIVATIVES **overanxiety** noun.
overarch • verb **1** form an arch over. **2** (**overarching**) all-embracing.
overarm • adjective & adverb (of a throw, stroke with a racket, etc.) made with the hand brought forward and down from above shoulder level.
overate past of OVEREAT.
overawe • verb (usu. **be overawed**) subdue or inhibit with a sense of awe.
overbalance • verb **1** fall or cause to fall due to loss of balance. **2** outweigh.
overbearing • adjective unpleasantly overpowering.
overbite • noun the overlapping of the lower teeth by the upper.
overblown • adjective **1** excessive or exaggerated. **2** (of a flower) past its prime.
overboard • adverb from a ship into the water.
– PHRASES **go overboard 1** be very enthusiastic. **2** go too far.
overbook • verb accept more reservations for (a flight or hotel) than there is room for.
overburden • verb burden excessively.
overcame past of OVERCOME.
overcapacity • noun an excess of productive capacity.
overcast • adjective **1** cloudy; dull. **2** edged with stitching to prevent fraying. • verb (past and past part. **overcast**) stitch over (a raw edge) to prevent fraying.
overcautious • adjective excessively cautious.
– DERIVATIVES **overcaution** noun.
overcharge • verb charge too high a price.
overcheck • noun a check pattern superimposed on a colour or design.
overcloud • verb mar, dim, or obscure.
overcoat • noun **1** a long warm coat. **2** a top, final layer of paint or varnish.
overcome • verb (past **overcame**; past part. **overcome**) **1** succeed in dealing with (a problem). **2** defeat. **3** (usu. **be overcome**) (of an emotion) overwhelm.
overcommit • verb (**overcommits**, **overcommitting**, **overcommitted**) (**overcommit oneself**) undertake to do more than one is capable of.
overcompensate • verb take excessive measures to compensate for something.
– DERIVATIVES **overcompensation** noun **overcompensatory** adjective.
overconfident • adjective excessively confident.
– DERIVATIVES **overconfidence** noun.
overcook • verb cook for too long.
overcrowd • verb fill beyond what is usual or comfortable.

Thesaurus

O

oval • adjective EGG-SHAPED, ovoid, ovate, oviform, elliptical; *Botany* obovate.
ovation • noun (ROUND OF) APPLAUSE, handclapping, clapping, cheering, cheers, bravos, acclaim, acclamation, tribute, standing ovation; *informal* (big) hand.
oven • noun (KITCHEN) STOVE, microwave (oven), (kitchen) range; roaster.
over • preposition **1** *there will be cloud over most of the country* ABOVE, on top of, higher (up) than, atop, covering. **2** *he walked over the grass* ACROSS, around, throughout. **3** *he has three people over him* SUPERIOR TO, above, higher up than, in charge of, responsible for. **4** *over 200,000 people live in the area* MORE THAN, above, in excess of, upwards of. **5** *a discussion over unemployment* ON THE SUBJECT OF, about, concerning, apropos of, with reference to, regarding, relating to, in connection with.
– OPPOSITES under.
• adverb **1** *a flock of geese flew over* OVERHEAD, on high, above, past, by. **2** *the relationship is over* AT AN END, finished, concluded, terminated, ended, no more, a thing of the past. **3** *he had some money over* LEFT (OVER), remaining, unused, surplus, in excess, in addition.
– PHRASES **over and above** IN ADDITION TO, on top of, plus, as well as, besides, along with. **over and over** REPEATEDLY, again and again, over and over again, time and (time) again, many times over, frequently, constantly, continually, persistently, ad nauseam.
overact • verb EXAGGERATE, overdo it, overplay it; *informal* ham it up, camp it up.
overall • adjective *the overall cost* ALL-INCLUSIVE, general, comprehensive, universal, all-embracing, gross, net, final, inclusive; wholesale, complete, across the board, global, worldwide.
• adverb *overall, things have improved* GENERALLY (SPEAKING), in general, altogether, all in all, on balance, on average, for the most part, in the main, on the whole, by and large, to a large extent.
overawe • verb INTIMIDATE, daunt, cow, disconcert, unnerve, subdue, dismay, frighten, alarm, scare, terrify; *informal* psych out; *N. Amer. informal* buffalo.
overbalance • verb FALL OVER, topple over, lose one's balance, tip over, keel over; push over, upend, upset.
overbearing • adjective DOMINEERING, dominating, autocratic, tyrannical, despotic, oppressive, high-handed, bullying; *informal* bossy.
overblown • adjective OVERWRITTEN, florid, grandiose, pompous, over-elaborate, flowery, overwrought, pretentious, high-flown, turgid, grandiloquent, magniloquent, orotund; *informal* highfalutin.
overcast • adjective CLOUDY, clouded (over), sunless, darkened, dark, grey, black, leaden, heavy, dull, murky, dismal, dreary.
– OPPOSITES bright.
overcharge • verb **1** *clients are being overcharged* SWINDLE, charge too much, cheat, defraud, fleece, short-change; *informal* rip off, sting, screw, rob, diddle, do, rook; *N. Amer. informal* gouge. **2** *the decoration is overcharged* OVERSTATE, overdo, exaggerate, over-embroider, over-embellish; overwrite, overdraw.
overcome • verb **1** *we overcame the home team* DEFEAT, beat, conquer, trounce, thrash, rout, vanquish, overwhelm, overpower, get the better of, triumph over, prevail over, win over/against, outdo, outclass, worst, crush; *informal* drub, slaughter, clobber, hammer, lick, best, crucify, demolish, wipe the floor with, make mincemeat of, blow out of the water, take to the cleaners; *Brit. informal* stuff; *N. Amer. informal* shellac, skunk. **2** *they overcame their fear of flying* GET THE BETTER OF, prevail over, control, get/bring under control, master, conquer, defeat, beat; get over, get a grip on, curb, subdue; *informal* lick, best.
• adjective *I was overcome* OVERWHELMED, emotional, moved, affected, speechless.
overconfident • adjective COCKSURE, cocky, smug, conceited, self-assured, brash, blustering, overbearing, presumptuous, riding/heading for a fall; *informal* too big for one's boots.
overcritical • adjective FAULT-FINDING, hypercritical, captious, carping, cavilling, quibbling, hair-splitting, over-particular; fussy, finicky, fastidious, pedantic, over-scrupulous, punctilious; *informal* nit-picking, pernickety; *archaic* overnice.

overdetermine ● verb technical determine, account for, or cause in more than one way or with more conditions than are necessary.
– DERIVATIVES **overdetermination** noun.
overdevelop ● verb (**overdeveloped**, **overdeveloping**) develop to excess.
– DERIVATIVES **overdevelopment** noun.
overdo ● verb (**overdoes**; past **overdid**; past part. **overdone**) **1** do (something) excessively or in an exaggerated manner. **2** (**overdo it/things**) exhaust oneself. **3** use or add too much of. **4** (**overdone**) overcooked.
overdose ● noun an excessive and dangerous dose of a drug. ● verb take an overdose.
– DERIVATIVES **overdosage** noun.
overdraft ● noun a deficit in a bank account caused by drawing more money than the account holds.
overdramatize (also **overdramatise**) ● verb react to or portray in an excessively dramatic way.
– DERIVATIVES **overdramatic** adjective.
overdrawn ● adjective **1** (of a bank account) in a state in which the amount of money withdrawn exceeds the amount held. **2** having an overdrawn bank account.
overdress ● verb dress too elaborately or formally.
overdrive ● noun **1** a gear in a motor vehicle providing a gear ratio higher than that of the usual top gear. **2** a state of high or excessive activity. ● verb drive or work to exhaustion.
– DERIVATIVES **overdriven** adjective.
overdub ● verb (**overdubbed**, **overdubbing**) record (additional sounds) on an existing recording. ● noun an instance of overdubbing.
overdue ● adjective not having arrived, happened, or been done at the expected or required time.
overeager ● adjective excessively eager.
over easy ● adjective N. Amer. (of an egg) fried on both sides, with the yolk remaining slightly liquid.
overeat ● verb (past **overate**; past part. **overeaten**) eat too much.
over-egg ● verb (in phrase **over-egg the pudding**) go too far in doing something; exaggerate.
overemotional ● adjective excessively emotional.
overemphasize (also **overemphasise**) ● verb place excessive emphasis on.
– DERIVATIVES **overemphasis** noun.
overenthusiasm ● noun excessive enthusiasm.
– DERIVATIVES **overenthusiastic** adjective.
overestimate ● verb form too high an estimate of. ● noun an excessively high estimate.
– DERIVATIVES **overestimation** noun.
overexcite ● verb excite excessively.
– DERIVATIVES **overexcitable** adjective **overexcitement** noun.
overexert ● verb (**overexert oneself**) exert oneself excessively.
– DERIVATIVES **overexertion** noun.
overexpose ● verb expose too much.
– DERIVATIVES **overexposure** noun.
overextend ● verb (usu. **be overextended**) **1** make too long. **2** impose excessive work or commitments on.
overfall ● noun **1** a turbulent stretch of open water caused by a strong current or tide over a submarine ridge, or by a meeting of currents. **2** a place where surplus water overflows from a dam, pool, etc.
overfamiliar ● adjective **1** too well known. **2** inappropriately informal.
– DERIVATIVES **overfamiliarity** noun.
overfeed ● verb (past and past part. **overfed**) feed too much.
overfill ● verb fill to excess.
overfish ● verb deplete (a body or water or stock of fish) by too much fishing.
overflow ● verb **1** flow over the brim of a receptacle. **2** be excessively full or crowded. **3** (**overflow with**) be very full of (an emotion). ● noun **1** the overflowing of a liquid. **2** the excess not able to be accommodated by a space. **3** (also **overflow pipe**) an outlet for excess water.
overgarment ● noun a garment worn over others.
overgeneralize (also **overgeneralise**) ● verb express in a way that is too general.
overgenerous ● adjective excessively generous.
overglaze ● noun decoration or a second glaze applied to glazed ceramic. ● adjective (of decoration) applied on a glazed surface.
overground ● adverb & adjective on or above the ground.
overgrown ● adjective **1** covered with plants that have been allowed to grow wild. **2** grown too large.
overgrowth ● noun excessive growth.
overhand ● adjective & adverb **1** overarm. **2** with the palm downward or inward.
overhang ● verb (past and past part. **overhung**) jut out or hang over. ● noun an overhanging part.
overhaul ● verb **1** examine and repair. **2** Brit. overtake. ● noun an act of overhauling.
– ORIGIN originally in nautical use in the sense 'release (rope tackle) by slackening'.
overhead ● adverb above one's head; in the sky. ● adjective **1** situated overhead. **2** (of a driving mechanism) above the object driven. **3** (of an expense) incurred in the upkeep or running of premises or a business. ● noun **1** an overhead cost or expense. **2** a transparency for use with an overhead projector.
overhead projector ● noun a device that projects an enlarged image of a transparency by means of an overhead mirror.
overhear ● verb (past and past part. **overheard**) hear accidentally or secretly.
overheat ● verb **1** make or become too hot. **2** Economics (of an economy) show marked inflation when increased demand re-

O

Thesaurus

overcrowded ● adjective OVERFULL, overflowing, full to overflowing/bursting, crammed full, congested, overpopulated, overpeopled, crowded, swarming, teeming; *informal* bursting at the seams, full to the gunwales, jam-packed.
overdo ● verb **1** *she overdoes the cockney scenes* EXAGGERATE, overstate, overemphasize, overplay, go overboard with, overdramatize; *informal* ham up, camp up. **2** *don't overdo the drink* HAVE/USE/EAT/DRINK TOO MUCH OF, overindulge in, have/use/eat/drink to excess. **3** *they overdid the beef* OVERCOOK, burn.
– OPPOSITES understate.
– PHRASES **overdo it** WORK TOO HARD, overwork, do too much, burn the candle at both ends, overtax oneself, drive/push oneself too hard, work/run oneself into the ground, wear oneself to a shadow, wear oneself out; *informal* kill oneself, knock oneself out.
overdone ● adjective **1** *the flattery was overdone* EXCESSIVE, too much, undue, immoderate, inordinate, disproportionate, inflated, overstated, overworked, exaggerated, overemphasized, overenthusiastic, over-effusive; *informal* a bit much, over the top, OTT. **2** *overdone food* OVERCOOKED, dried out, burnt.
– OPPOSITES understated, underdone.
overdue ● adjective **1** *the ship is overdue* LATE, behind schedule, behind time, delayed, unpunctual. **2** *an a overdue payments* UNPAID, unsettled, owing, owed, payable, due, outstanding, undischarged; *N. Amer.* delinquent.
– OPPOSITES early, punctual.
overeat ● verb EAT TOO MUCH, be greedy, gorge (oneself), overindulge (oneself), feast, gourmandize, gluttonize; *informal* binge, make a pig of oneself, pig out; *N. Amer. informal* scarf out.
overemphasize ● verb PLACE/LAY TOO MUCH EMPHASIS ON, overstress, place/lay too much stress on, exaggerate, make too much of, overplay, overdo, over-dramatize; *informal* make a big thing about/of, blow up out of all proportion.
– OPPOSITES understate, play down.
overflow ● verb *cream overflowed the edges of the shallow dish* SPILL OVER, flow over, brim over, well over, pour forth, stream forth, flood.
● noun **1** *an overflow from the tank* OVERSPILL, spill, spillage, flood. **2** *to accommodate the overflow, five more offices were built* SURPLUS, excess, additional people/things, extra people/things, remainder, overspill.
overflowing ● adjective OVERFULL, full to overflowing/bursting, spilling over, running over, crammed full, overcrowded, overloaded; *informal* bursting/bulging at the seams, jam-packed.
overhang ● verb STICK OUT (OVER), stand out (over), extend (over), project (over), protrude (over), jut out (over), bulge out (over), hang over.
overhaul ● verb **1** *I've been overhauling the gearbox* SERVICE, maintain, repair, mend, fix up, rebuild, renovate, recondition, refit, refurbish; *informal* do up, patch up. **2** *(Brit.) Kenyon overhauled him in the race* OVERTAKE, pass, go past/by, go faster than, get/pull ahead of, outstrip.
overhead ● adverb *a burst of thunder erupted overhead* (UP) ABOVE, high up, (up) in the sky, on high, above/over one's head.
● adjective *overhead lines* AERIAL, elevated, raised, suspended.

sults in rising prices.
overindulge ● verb **1** have too much of something enjoyable. **2** gratify the wishes of (someone) to an excessive extent.
– DERIVATIVES **overindulgence** noun **overindulgent** adjective.
overinflated ● adjective **1** filled with too much air. **2** (of a price or value) excessive. **3** exaggerated.
overissue ● verb (**overissues**, **overissued**, **overissuing**) issue (banknotes, shares, etc.) beyond the authorized amount or the issuer's ability to pay. ● noun the action of overissuing.
overjoyed ● adjective extremely happy.
overkill ● noun **1** the amount by which destruction or the capacity for destruction exceeds what is necessary. **2** excessive treatment or action; too much of something.
overladen ● adjective bearing too large a load.
overlaid past and past participle of OVERLAY[1].
overlain past participle of OVERLIE.
overland ● adjective & adverb by land. ● verb Austral./NZ historical **1** drive (livestock) over a long distance. **2** travel a long distance by land.
overlander ● noun **1** Austral./NZ historical a person who overlands livestock. **2** a person who travels a long distance overland.
overlap ● verb (**overlapped**, **overlapping**) **1** extend over so as to cover partly. **2** partly coincide. ● noun an overlapping part or amount.
overlay[1] ● verb (past and past part. **overlaid**) (often **be overlaid with**) **1** coat the surface of. **2** lie on top of. **3** (of a quality or feeling) become more prominent than (a previous one). ● noun **1** a covering. **2** a transparent sheet over artwork or a map, giving additional detail. **3** Computing replacement of a block of stored instructions or data with another.
overlay[2] past of OVERLIE.
overleaf ● adverb on the other side of the page.
overlie ● verb (**overlying**; past **overlay**; past part. **overlain**) lie on top of.
overload ● verb **1** load excessively. **2** put too great a demand on. ● noun an excessive amount.
overlock ● verb prevent fraying of (an edge of cloth) by oversewing it.
– DERIVATIVES **overlocker** noun.
overlook ● verb **1** fail to notice. **2** ignore or disregard. **3** have a view of from above. ● noun N. Amer. a commanding position or view.
overlord ● noun a ruler, especially a feudal lord.
overly ● adverb excessively.
overlying present participle of OVERLIE.
overman ● verb (**overmanned**, **overmanning**) provide with more people than necessary. ● noun an overseer in a colliery.
overmantel ● noun an ornamental structure over a mantelpiece.
overmaster ● verb literary overcome.
overmatch ● verb chiefly N. Amer. be stronger, better armed, or more skilful than.
overmuch ● adverb, determiner, & pronoun too much.
overnight ● adverb **1** for the duration of a night. **2** during the course of a night. **3** suddenly. ● adjective **1** for use overnight. **2** done or happening overnight. **3** sudden. ● verb **1** stay overnight. **2** N. Amer. convey (goods) overnight.
overnighter ● noun **1** a person who stays overnight. **2** N. Amer. an overnight trip or stay. **3** an overnight bag.
overpaint ● verb cover with paint. ● noun paint added as a covering layer.
overpass ● noun a bridge by which a road or railway line passes over another.
overpay ● verb (past and past part. **overpaid**) pay too much.
overplay ● verb overemphasize.
– PHRASES **overplay one's hand** spoil one's chance of success through excessive confidence.
overpopulate ● verb populate (an area) in excessive numbers.
overpower ● verb **1** defeat with superior strength. **2** be too intense for.
– DERIVATIVES **overpowering** adjective.
overprice ● verb charge too high a price for.
overproduce ● verb **1** produce an excess of. **2** record or produce (a song or film) in an excessively elaborate way.
– DERIVATIVES **overproduction** noun.
overprotective ● adjective excessively protective.
overqualified ● adjective too highly qualified.
overran past of OVERRUN.
overrate ● verb rate more highly than is deserved.
– DERIVATIVES **overrated** adjective.
overreach ● verb (**overreach oneself**) fail through being too ambitious or trying too hard.
overreacher ● noun N. Amer. a fraudster.
overreact ● verb react more emotionally or forcibly than is justified.
– DERIVATIVES **overreaction** noun.
override ● verb (past **overrode**; past part. **overridden**) **1** use one's authority to reject or cancel. **2** interrupt the action of (an automatic function). **3** be more important than. **4** overlap. **5** travel or move over. ● noun **1** the action or process of overriding. **2** a device on a machine for overriding an automatic function. **3** an excess or increase on a budget, salary, or cost.

Thesaurus

overheads ● plural noun (RUNNING) COSTS, operating costs, fixed costs, expenses; *Brit.* oncosts.
overindulge ● verb **1** *we all overindulge at Christmas* DRINK/EAT TOO MUCH, overeat, overdrink, be greedy, be intemperate, overindulge oneself, overdo it, drink/eat to excess, gorge (oneself), feast, gourmandize, gluttonize; *informal* binge, stuff oneself, go overboard, make a pig of oneself, pig oneself; *N. Amer. informal* scarf out. **2** *his mother had overindulged him* SPOIL, give in to, indulge, humour, pander to, pamper, mollycoddle, baby.
overindulgence ● noun INTEMPERANCE, immoderation, excess, overeating, overdrinking, gorging; *informal* binge.
overjoyed ● adjective ECSTATIC, euphoric, thrilled, elated, delighted, on cloud nine/seven, in seventh heaven, jubilant, rapturous, jumping for joy, delirious, blissful, in raptures, as pleased as Punch, cock-a-hoop, as happy as a sandboy, as happy as Larry; *informal* over the moon, on top of the world, tickled pink; *N. Amer. informal* as happy as a clam; *Austral. informal* wrapped.
– OPPOSITES unhappy.
overlay ● verb *the area was overlaid with marble* COVER, face, surface, veneer, inlay, laminate, plaster; coat, varnish, glaze.
● noun *an overlay of glass-fibre insulation* COVERING, cover, layer, face, surface, veneer, lamination; coat, varnish, glaze, wash.
overload ● verb **1** *avoid overloading the ship* OVERBURDEN, put too much in, overcharge, weigh down. **2** *don't overload the wiring* STRAIN, overtax, overwork, overuse, swamp, oversupply, overwhelm.
● noun *there was an overload of demands* EXCESS, overabundance, superabundance, profusion, glut, surfeit, surplus, superfluity; avalanche, deluge, flood.
overlook ● verb **1** *he overlooked the mistake* FAIL TO NOTICE, fail to spot, miss. **2** *his work has been overlooked* DISREGARD, neglect, ignore, pay no attention/heed to, pass over, forget. **3** *she was willing to overlook his faults* DELIBERATELY IGNORE, not take into consideration, disregard, take no notice of, make allowances for, turn a blind eye to, excuse, pardon, forgive. **4** *the breakfast room overlooks the garden* HAVE A VIEW OF, look over/across, look on to, look out on/over, give on to, command a view of.
overly ● adverb UNDULY, excessively, inordinately, too; wildly, absurdly, ridiculously, outrageously, unreasonably, exorbitantly, impossibly.
overpower ● verb **1** *the prisoners might overpower the crew* GAIN CONTROL OVER, overwhelm, prevail over, get the better of, gain mastery over, overthrow, overturn, subdue, suppress, subjugate, repress, bring someone to their knees, conquer, defeat, triumph over, worst, trounce; *informal* thrash, lick, best, clobber, wipe the floor with. **2** *he was overpowered by grief* OVERCOME, overwhelm, stun, shake, devastate, take aback, leave speechless; *informal* bowl over, knock sideways; *Brit. informal* knock/hit for six.
overpowering ● adjective **1** *overpowering grief* OVERWHELMING, oppressive, unbearable, unendurable, intolerable, shattering. **2** *an overpowering smell* STIFLING, suffocating, strong, pungent, powerful; nauseating, offensive, acrid, fetid, mephitic. **3** *overpowering evidence* IRREFUTABLE, undeniable, indisputable, incontestable, incontrovertible, compelling, conclusive.
overrate ● verb OVERESTIMATE, overvalue, think too much of, attach too much importance to. praise too highly.
– OPPOSITES underestimate.
overreach ● verb
– PHRASES **overreach oneself** TRY TO DO TOO MUCH, overestimate one's ability, overdo it, overstretch oneself, wear/burn oneself out, bite off more than one can chew.
overreact ● verb REACT DISPROPORTIONATELY, act irrationally, lose

overriding • adjective **1** more important than any other considerations. **2** extending or moving over.
overripe • adjective too ripe.
overrode past of OVERRIDE.
overrule • verb reject or disallow by exercising one's superior authority.
overrun • verb (**overrunning**; past **overran**; past part. **overrun**) **1** spread over or occupy in large numbers. **2** move or extend over or beyond. **3** exceed (an expected or allowed time or cost).
oversail • verb (of a part of a building) project beyond (a lower part).
– ORIGIN from French *saillir* 'jut out'.
oversaw past of OVERSEE.
overseas • adverb in or to a foreign country. • adjective relating to a foreign country. • noun foreign countries regarded collectively.
oversee • verb (**oversees**; past **oversaw**; past part. **overseen**) supervise.
– DERIVATIVES **overseer** noun.
oversell • verb (past and past part. **oversold**) **1** sell more of (something) than exists or can be delivered. **2** exaggerate the merits of.
oversensitive • adjective excessively sensitive.
– DERIVATIVES **oversensitivity** noun.
oversew • verb (past part. **oversewn** or **oversewed**) **1** sew (the edges of two pieces of fabric) together, having the stitches passing over the join. **2** join the sections of (a book) in such a way.
oversexed • adjective having unusually strong sexual desires.
overshadow • verb **1** tower above and cast a shadow over. **2** cast a feeling of sadness over. **3** appear more prominent, important, or successful than.
overshoe • noun a protective shoe worn over a normal shoe.
overshoot • verb (past and past part. **overshot**) **1** move or travel past unintentionally. **2** exceed (a financial target or limit).
oversight • noun an unintentional failure to notice or do something.
oversimplify • verb (**oversimplifies**, **oversimplified**) simplify (something) so much that a distorted impression of it is given.
– DERIVATIVES **oversimplification** noun.
oversized (also **oversize**) • adjective bigger than the usual size.
overskirt • noun an outer skirt forming a second layer over a skirt or dress.
oversleep • verb (past and past part. **overslept**) sleep longer or later than one has intended.
oversold past and past participle of OVERSELL.
overspend • verb (past and past part. **overspent**) spend too much.
overspill • noun Brit. a surplus population moving from an overcrowded area to live elsewhere.
overstaff • verb provide with more members of staff than are necessary.
overstate • verb exaggerate or state too emphatically.
– DERIVATIVES **overstatement** noun.
overstay • verb stay longer than the duration or limits of.
oversteer • verb (of a vehicle) turn more sharply than is desirable.
overstep • verb (**overstepped**, **overstepping**) go beyond (a set or accepted limit).
– PHRASES **overstep the mark** go beyond what is intended or acceptable.
overstimulate • verb stimulate excessively.
– DERIVATIVES **overstimulation** noun.
overstitch • noun a stitch made over an edge or over another stitch. • verb sew with an overstitch.
overstock • verb stock with more than is necessary or sustainable. • noun chiefly N. Amer. a supply or quantity in excess of demand.
overstrain • verb subject to an excessive demand on strength, resources, or abilities.
overstress • verb **1** subject to too much stress. **2** lay too much emphasis on.
overstretch • verb **1** stretch too much. **2** be too demanding of.
overstrung • adjective (of a piano) with strings in sets crossing each other obliquely.
overstuff • verb cover (furniture) completely with a thick layer of stuffing.
oversubscribed • adjective **1** (of something for sale) applied for in greater quantities than are available. **2** (of a course or institution) having more applications than available places.
overt /ōvert/ • adjective done or shown openly.
– DERIVATIVES **overtly** adverb **overtness** noun.
– ORIGIN Old French, 'opened', from Latin *aperire* 'to open'.
overtake • verb (past **overtook**; past part. **overtaken**) **1** catch up with and pass while travelling in the same direction. **2** become greater or more successful than. **3** come suddenly or unexpectedly upon.
overthrow • verb (past **overthrew**; past part. **overthrown**) **1** remove forcibly from power. **2** put an end to through force. **3** throw (a ball) further than the intended distance. • noun **1** a defeat or removal from power. **2** a throw which sends a ball past its intended recipient or target.

Thesaurus

one's sense of proportion, blow something up out of all proportion; *Brit. informal* go over the top.
override • verb **1** *the court could not override her decision* DISALLOW, overrule, countermand, veto, quash, overturn, overthrow; cancel, reverse, rescind, revoke, repeal, annul, nullify, invalidate, negate, void; *Law* vacate; *formal* abrogate; *archaic* recall. **2** *the government can override all opposition* DISREGARD, pay no heed to, take no account of, turn a deaf ear to, ignore, ride roughshod over. **3** *a positive attitude will override any negative thoughts* OUTWEIGH, supersede, take precedence over, take priority over, offset, cancel out, (more than) make up for, outbalance, compensate for.
overriding • adjective MOST IMPORTANT, of greatest importance, of greatest significance, uppermost, top, first (and foremost), highest, pre-eminent, predominant, principal, primary, paramount, chief, main, major, foremost, central, key, focal, pivotal; *informal* number-one.
overrule • verb COUNTERMAND, cancel, reverse, rescind, repeal, revoke, retract, disallow, override, veto, quash, overturn, overthrow, annul, nullify, invalidate, negate, void; *Law* vacate; *formal* abrogate; *archaic* recall.
overrun • verb **1** *guerrillas overran the barracks* INVADE, storm, occupy, swarm into, surge into, inundate, overwhelm. **2** *the talks overran the deadline* EXCEED, go beyond/over, run over.
oversee • verb SUPERVISE, superintend, be in charge/control of, be responsible for, look after, keep an eye on, inspect, administer, organize, manage, direct, preside over.
overseer • noun SUPERVISOR, foreman, forewoman, team leader, controller, (line) manager, manageress, head (of department), superintendent, captain; *informal* boss, chief, governor; *Brit. informal* gaffer, guv'nor; *N. Amer. informal* straw boss; *Austral. informal* pannikin boss; *Mining* overman.
overshadow • verb **1** *a massive hill overshadows the town* CAST A SHADOW OVER, shade, darken, conceal, obscure, screen; dominate, overlook. **2** *this feeling of tragedy overshadowed his story* CAST GLOOM OVER, blight, take the edge off, mar, spoil, ruin. **3** *he was overshadowed by his brilliant elder brother* OUTSHINE, eclipse, surpass, exceed, be superior to, outclass, outstrip, outdo, upstage; *informal* be head and shoulders above.
oversight • noun **1** *a stupid oversight* MISTAKE, error, omission, lapse, slip, blunder; *informal* slip-up, boo-boo; *Brit. informal* boob; *N. Amer. informal* goof. **2** *the omission was due to oversight* CARELESSNESS, inattention, negligence, forgetfulness, laxity. **3** *school governors have oversight of the curriculum* SUPERVISION, surveillance, superintendence, charge, care, administration, management.
overstate • verb EXAGGERATE, overdo, overemphasize, overplay, dramatize, embroider, embellish; *informal* blow up out of all proportion.
– OPPOSITES understate.
overstatement • noun EXAGGERATION, overemphasis, dramatization, embroidery, embellishment, enhancement, hyperbole.
overt • adjective UNDISGUISED, unconcealed, plain (to see), clear, apparent, conspicuous, obvious, noticeable, manifest, patent, open, blatant.
– OPPOSITES covert.
overtake • verb **1** *a green car overtook the taxi* PASS, go past/by, get/pull ahead of, leave behind, outdistance, outstrip. **2** *tourism overtook coffee as the main earner of foreign currency* OUTSTRIP, surpass, overshadow, eclipse, outshine, outclass; dwarf, put in the shade, exceed, top, cap; *archaic* outrival. **3** *the calamity which overtook us* BEFALL, happen to, come upon, hit, strike, overwhelm, overcome, be visited on; *poetic/literary* betide.
overthrow • verb **1** *the President was overthrown* REMOVE (FROM OFFICE/POWER), bring down, topple, depose, oust, displace, unseat. **2** *an attempt to overthrow the military regime* PUT AN END TO, defeat,

overtime • noun **1** time worked in addition to one's normal working hours. **2** N. Amer. extra time played at the end of a tied game. • adverb in addition to normal working hours.
overtire • verb exhaust.
– DERIVATIVES **overtired** adjective.
overtone • noun **1** a musical tone which is a part of the harmonic series above a fundamental note, and may be heard with it. **2** a subtle or subsidiary quality, implication, or connotation.
overtop • verb (**overtopped**, **overtopping**) **1** exceed in height. **2** (especially of water) rise over the top of. • adverb & preposition chiefly Canadian over.
overtrousers • plural noun protective or waterproof trousers worn over other trousers.
overture • noun **1** an orchestral piece at the beginning of a musical work. **2** an independent orchestral composition in one movement. **3** an introduction to something more substantial. **4** (**overtures**) approaches made with the aim of opening negotiations or establishing a relationship.
– ORIGIN originally in the sense 'aperture': from Old French, from Latin *apertura* 'aperture'.
overturn • verb **1** turn over and come to rest upside down. **2** abolish, invalidate, or reverse (a decision, system, belief, etc.).
overuse • verb use too much. • noun excessive use.
overvalue • verb (**overvalues**, **overvalued**, **overvaluing**) **1** overestimate the importance of. **2** fix the value of (something, especially a currency) at too high a level.
– DERIVATIVES **overvaluation** noun.
overview • noun a general review or summary. • verb give an overview of.
overweening • adjective **1** showing excessive confidence or pride. **2** excessive; immoderate.
– ORIGIN from archaic *ween* 'think or suppose', from Old English.
overweight • adjective above a normal, desirable, or permitted weight.
overwhelm • verb **1** submerge beneath a huge mass. **2** defeat completely; overpower. **3** have a strong emotional effect on.
– DERIVATIVES **overwhelming** adjective.
– ORIGIN from archaic *whelm* 'engulf or submerge', from Old English.
overwind • verb (past and past part. **overwound**) wind (a mechanism) beyond the proper stopping point.
overwinter • verb **1** spend the winter in a specified place. **2** (of an insect, plant, etc.) live or survive through the winter. **3** maintain through the winter.
overwork • verb **1** work or cause to work too hard. **2** use (a word or idea) too much and so make it weaker in effect. • noun excessive work.
overwound past and past participle of OVERWIND.
overwrite • verb (past **overwrote**; past part. **overwritten**) **1** write on top of (other writing). **2** Computing destroy (data) or the data in (a file) by entering new data in its place. **3** write too elaborately or ornately. **4** (in insurance) accept more risk than the premium income limits allow.
overwrought • adjective **1** in a state of nervous excitement or anxiety. **2** (of a piece of writing or a work of art) too elaborate or complicated.
– ORIGIN archaic past participle of OVERWORK.
overzealous • adjective overly enthusiastic or energetic.
oviduct /ōvidukt/ • noun Anatomy & Zoology the tube through which an ovum or egg passes from an ovary.
oviform • adjective egg-shaped.
– ORIGIN from Latin *ovum* 'egg'.
ovine /ōvīn/ • adjective relating to sheep.
– ORIGIN Latin *ovinus*, from *ovis* 'sheep'.
oviparous /ōvippərəss/ • adjective Zoology producing young by means of eggs which are hatched after they have been laid by the parent, as in birds. Compare with VIVIPAROUS and OVOVIVIPAROUS.
ovipositor /ōvipozzitər/ • noun Zoology a tubular organ through which a female insect or fish deposits eggs.
ovoid /ōvoyd/ • adjective **1** (of a solid or a three-dimensional surface) more or less egg-shaped. **2** (of a plane figure) oval. • noun an ovoid body or surface.
– ORIGIN Latin *ovoides*, from *ovum* 'egg'.
ovoviviparous /ōvōvippərəss/ • adjective Zoology producing young by means of eggs which are hatched within the body of the parent, as in some snakes. Compare with OVIPAROUS and VIVIPAROUS.
ovulate /ovyoolayt/ • verb discharge ova or ovules from the ovary.
– DERIVATIVES **ovulation** noun.
ovule • noun Botany the part of the ovary of seed plants that contains the female germ cell and after fertilization becomes the seed.
– DERIVATIVES **ovular** adjective.
– ORIGIN Latin *ovulum* 'little egg'.
ovum • noun (pl. **ova**) a mature female reproductive cell, which

Thesaurus

conquer.
• noun **1** *the overthrow of the Shah* REMOVAL (FROM OFFICE/POWER), downfall, fall, toppling, deposition, ousting, displacement, supplanting, unseating. **2** *the overthrow of capitalism* ENDING, defeat, displacement, fall, collapse, downfall, demise.
overtone • noun CONNOTATION, hidden meaning, implication, association, undercurrent, undertone, echo, vibrations, hint, suggestion, insinuation, intimation, suspicion, feeling, nuance.
overture • noun **1** *the overture to Don Giovanni* PRELUDE, introduction, opening, introductory movement. **2** *the overture to a long debate* PRELIMINARY, prelude, introduction, lead-in, precursor, start, beginning. **3** *peace overtures* (OPENING) MOVE, approach, advances, feeler, signal, proposal, proposition.
overturn • verb **1** *the boat overturned* CAPSIZE, turn turtle, keel over, tip over, topple over, turn over; Nautical pitchpole; archaic overset. **2** *I overturned the stool* UPSET, tip over, topple over, turn over, knock over, upend. **3** *the Senate may overturn this ruling* CANCEL, reverse, rescind, repeal, revoke, retract, countermand, disallow, override, overrule, veto, quash, overthrow, annul, nullify, invalidate, negate, void; Law vacate; formal abrogate; archaic recall.
overused • adjective HACKNEYED, overworked, worn out, time-worn, tired, played out, clichéd, stale, trite, banal, stock, unoriginal.
overweening • adjective OVERCONFIDENT, conceited, cocksure, cocky, smug, haughty, supercilious, lofty, patronizing, arrogant, proud, vain, self-important, imperious, overbearing; informal high and mighty, uppish.
– OPPOSITES unassuming.
overweight • adjective FAT, obese, stout, corpulent, gross, fleshy, plump, portly, chubby, rotund, paunchy, pot-bellied, flabby, well upholstered, well padded, broad in the beam; informal porky, tubby, blubbery; Brit. informal podgy, fubsy; archaic pursy.
– OPPOSITES skinny.
overwhelm • verb **1** *advancing sand dunes could overwhelm the village* SWAMP, submerge, engulf, bury, deluge, flood, inundate. **2** *Spain overwhelmed Russia in the hockey* DEFEAT (UTTERLY/HEAVILY), trounce, rout, beat (hollow), conquer, vanquish, be victorious over, triumph over, worst, overcome, overthrow, crush; informal thrash, lick, best, clobber, wipe the floor with. **3** *she was overwhelmed by a sense of tragedy* OVERCOME, strike, dumbfound, shake, devastate, floor, leave speechless; informal bowl over, knock sideways; Brit. informal knock/hit for six.
overwhelming • adjective **1** *an overwhelming number of players were unavailable* VERY LARGE, enormous, immense, inordinate, massive, huge. **2** *overwhelming desire to laugh* VERY STRONG, forceful, uncontrollable, irrepressible, irresistible, overpowering, compelling.
overwork • verb **1** *we should not overwork* WORK TOO HARD, work/run oneself into the ground, wear oneself to a shadow, work one's fingers to the bone, burn the candle at both ends, overtax oneself, burn oneself out, do too much, overdo it, strain oneself, overload oneself, drive/push oneself too hard; informal kill oneself, knock oneself out. **2** *my colleagues did not overwork me* DRIVE (TOO HARD), exploit, drive into the ground, tax, overtax, overburden, put upon, impose on.
overworked • adjective **1** *overworked staff* STRESSED (OUT), stress-ridden, overtaxed, overburdened, overloaded, exhausted, worn out. **2** *an overworked phrase* HACKNEYED, overused, worn out, tired, played out, clichéd, threadbare, stale, trite, banal, stock, unoriginal.
overwrought • adjective **1** *she was too overwrought to listen* TENSE, agitated, nervous, on edge, edgy, keyed up, worked up, highly strung, neurotic, overexcited, beside oneself, distracted, distraught, frantic, hysterical; informal in a state, in a tizzy, uptight, wound up, het up; Brit. informal strung up. **2** *the painting is overwrought* OVER-ELABORATE, over-ornate, overblown, overdone,

can divide to give rise to an embryo usually only after fertilization by a male cell.
– ORIGIN Latin, 'egg'.
ow ● exclamation expressing sudden pain.
– ORIGIN natural exclamation.
owe ● verb **1** be required to pay (money or goods) to (someone) in return for something received. **2** be morally obliged to show (gratitude, respect, etc.) or to offer (an explanation) to (someone). **3** (**owe something to**) have something because of. **4** be indebted to someone or something for: *I owe my life to you.*
– ORIGIN Old English.
owing ● adjective yet to be paid or supplied.
– PHRASES **owing to** because of or on account of.
owl ● noun a nocturnal bird of prey with large eyes, a hooked beak, and typically a loud hooting call.
– ORIGIN Old English, ultimately imitative of the bird's call.
owlet ● noun a young or small owl.
owlish ● adjective **1** like an owl, especially in being wise or solemn. **2** (of glasses or eyes) resembling the large round eyes of an owl.
– DERIVATIVES **owlishly** adverb.
own ● adjective & pronoun **1** (with a possessive) belonging or relating to the person specified. **2** done or produced by the person specified. **3** particular to the person or thing specified; individual. ● verb **1** possess. **2** formal admit or acknowledge that something is the case. **3** (**own up**) admit to having done something wrong or embarrassing.
– PHRASES **be one's own man** (or **woman**) act independently. **come into its** (or **one's**) **own** become fully effective. **hold one's own** retain a position of strength in a challenging situation.
– ORIGIN Old English, related to OWE.
own brand ● noun Brit. a product manufactured specially for a retailer and bearing the retailer's name.
owner ● noun a person who owns something.
– DERIVATIVES **ownership** noun.
owner-occupier ● noun Brit. a person who owns the house or flat in which they live.
own goal ● noun (in soccer) a goal scored when a player accidentally strikes or deflects the ball into their own team's goal.
owt /owt/ ● pronoun N. English anything.
– ORIGIN variant of AUGHT[1].
ox ● noun (pl. **oxen**) **1** a domesticated bovine animal kept for milk or meat; a cow or bull. **2** a castrated bull, especially as a draught animal.
– ORIGIN Old English.
oxalic acid /oksalik/ ● noun Chemistry a poisonous crystalline organic acid, present in rhubarb leaves, wood sorrel, and other plants.
– DERIVATIVES **oxalate** /oksəlayt/ noun.
– ORIGIN from Greek *oxalis* 'wood sorrel'.
oxalis /oksəliss/ ● noun a plant of a genus which includes the wood sorrel, typically having three-lobed leaves and white, yellow, or pink flowers.
– ORIGIN Greek, from *oxus* 'sour' (because of its sharp-tasting leaves).
oxbow ● noun **1** a loop formed by a horseshoe bend in a river. **2** the U-shaped collar of an ox-yoke.
oxbow lake ● noun a curved lake formed from a horseshoe bend in a river where the main stream has cut across the neck and no longer flows around the loop of the bend.
Oxbridge ● noun Oxford and Cambridge universities regarded together.
oxen plural of ox.
ox-eye daisy ● noun a daisy which has large white flowers with yellow centres.
Oxford ● noun a type of lace-up shoe with a low heel.
– ORIGIN named after the city of *Oxford*.
Oxford bags ● plural noun Brit. wide baggy trousers.
Oxford blue ● noun Brit. **1** a dark blue, adopted as the colour of Oxford University. **2** a person who has represented Oxford University in a particular sport.
oxhide ● noun leather made from the hide of an ox.
oxidant ● noun an oxidizing agent.
oxidation ● noun Chemistry the process of oxidizing or the result of being oxidized.
– DERIVATIVES **oxidative** adjective.
oxide ● noun Chemistry a compound of oxygen with another element or group.
oxidize (also **oxidise**) ● verb **1** cause to combine with oxygen. **2** Chemistry cause to undergo a reaction in which electrons are lost to another substance or molecule. The opposite of REDUCE.
– DERIVATIVES **oxidization** noun **oxidizer** noun.
oxidizing agent ● noun a substance that tends to bring about oxidation by being reduced and gaining electrons.
oxlip ● noun a woodland primula with yellow flowers that hang down one side of the stem.
– ORIGIN Old English, 'ox slime', i.e. ox dung.
Oxon ● abbreviation **1** Oxfordshire. **2** (in degree titles) of Oxford University.
– ORIGIN from *Oxonia*, Latinized form of Oxford from its old form *Oxenford*.
Oxonian /oksōniən/ ● adjective relating to Oxford or Oxford University. ● noun **1** a person from Oxford. **2** a member of Oxford University.
oxtail ● noun the tail of an ox (used in making soup).
oxter /okstər/ ● noun Scottish & N. English a person's armpit.
– ORIGIN Old English.
ox tongue ● noun the tongue of an ox (used as meat).
oxyacetylene ● adjective denoting welding or cutting techniques using a very hot flame produced by mixing acetylene and oxygen.
oxygen ● noun a colourless, odourless, gaseous chemical element, forming about 20 per cent of the earth's atmosphere and essential to life.
– ORIGIN from French *principe oxygène* 'acidifying constituent' (because at first it was held to be the essential component of acids).
oxygenate ● verb supply, treat, or enrich with oxygen.
– DERIVATIVES **oxygenated** adjective **oxygenation** noun.
oxygenator ● noun Medicine **1** an apparatus for oxygenating the blood. **2** an aquatic plant which enriches the surrounding water with oxygen.
oxygen bar ● noun an establishment where people pay to inhale pure oxygen for its reputedly therapeutic effects.
oxyhaemoglobin ● noun Biochemistry a bright red substance formed by the combination of haemoglobin with oxygen, present in oxygenated blood.
oxymoron /oksimoron/ ● noun a figure of speech or expressed

Thesaurus

contrived, overworked, strained.
– OPPOSITES calm, understated.
owe ● verb BE IN DEBT (TO), be indebted (to), be in arrears (to), be under an obligation (to).
owing ● adjective *the rent was owing* UNPAID, to be paid, payable, due, overdue, undischarged, owed, outstanding, in arrears; *N. Amer.* delinquent.
– PHRASES **owing to** BECAUSE OF, as a result of, on account of, due to, as a consequence of, thanks to, in view of; *formal* by reason of.
own ● adjective *he has his own reasons* PERSONAL, individual, particular, private, personalized, unique.
● verb **1** *I own this house* BE THE OWNER OF, possess, be the possessor of, have in one's possession, have (to one's name). **2** *she had to own that she agreed* ADMIT, concede, grant, accept, acknowledge, agree, confess.
– PHRASES **get one's own back** *(informal)* HAVE/GET/TAKE ONE'S REVENGE (ON), be revenged (on), hit back, get (back at), get even (with), settle accounts (with), repay, pay someone back, give someone their just deserts, retaliate (against/on), take reprisals (against), exact retribution (on), give someone a taste of their own medicine. **hold one's own** STAND FIRM, stand one's ground, keep one's end up, keep one's head above water, compete, survive, cope, get on/along. **on one's own 1** *I am all on my own* (ALL) ALONE, (all) by oneself, solitary, unaccompanied, companionless; *informal* by one's lonesome; *Brit. informal* on one's tod, on one's Jack Jones. **2** *she works well on her own* UNAIDED, unassisted, without help, without assistance, (all) by oneself, independently. **own up** CONFESS (TO), admit to, admit guilt, plead guilty, accept blame/responsibility, tell the truth (about), make a clean breast of it, tell all; *informal* come clean (about).
owner ● noun POSSESSOR, holder, proprietor/proprietress, homeowner, freeholder, landlord, landlady.
– RELATED TERMS proprietary.
ox ● noun bull, bullock, steer; *Farming* beef.

idea in which apparently contradictory terms appear in conjunction (e.g. *bittersweet*).
– DERIVATIVES **oxymoronic** adjective.
– ORIGIN from Greek *oxumōros* 'pointedly foolish'.

oxytocin /oksitōsin/ ● **noun** Biochemistry a hormone released by the pituitary gland that causes contraction of the womb during labour and stimulates the flow of milk into the breasts.
– ORIGIN from Greek *oxutokia* 'sudden delivery'.

oyez /ōyez/ (also **oyes**) ● **exclamation** a call given by a public crier or a court officer to command silence and attention before an announcement.
– ORIGIN Old French, 'hear!', from Latin *audire* 'to hear'.

oyster ● **noun 1** a bivalve marine mollusc with a rough, flattened, irregularly oval shell, several kinds of which are farmed for food or pearls. **2** a shade of greyish white. **3** an oval morsel of meat on each side of the backbone in poultry.
– PHRASES **the world is one's oyster** one is able to enjoy a broad range of opportunities. [ORIGIN from Shakespeare's *Merry Wives of Windsor* (II. ii. 5).]
– ORIGIN Old French *oistre*, from Greek *ostreon*.

oystercatcher ● **noun** a wading bird with black or black-and-white plumage and a strong orange-red bill, feeding chiefly on shellfish.

oyster mushroom ● **noun** an edible fungus with a greyish-brown oyster-shaped cap.

oyster sauce ● **noun** a sauce made with oysters and soy sauce, used especially in oriental cookery.

oy vey /oy vay/ (also **oy**) ● **exclamation** indicating dismay or grief (used mainly by Yiddish-speakers).
– ORIGIN Yiddish, 'oh woe'.

Oz ● **noun & adjective** informal Australia or Australian.
– ORIGIN from the abbreviation of *Australia*.

oz ● **abbreviation** ounce(s).
– ORIGIN Italian *onza* 'ounce'.

ozone ● **noun 1** a pungent, toxic form of oxygen with three atoms in its molecule, formed in electrical discharges or by ultraviolet light. **2** informal fresh invigorating air.
– ORIGIN German *Ozon*, from Greek *ozein* 'to smell'.

ozone-friendly ● **adjective** (of manufactured products) not containing chemicals that are destructive to the ozone layer.

ozone hole ● **noun** a region of marked thinning of the ozone layer in high latitudes, chiefly in winter, due to CFCs and other atmospheric pollutants.

ozone layer ● **noun** a layer in the earth's stratosphere at an altitude of about 10 km (6.2 miles) containing a high concentration of ozone, which absorbs most of the ultraviolet radiation reaching the earth from the sun.

Ozzie ● **noun** variant spelling of AUSSIE.

Pp

P[1] (also **p**) ● noun (pl. **Ps** or **P's**) the sixteenth letter of the alphabet.
P[2] ● abbreviation **1** (in tables of sports results) games played. **2** (on road signs and street plans) parking. ● symbol the chemical element phosphorus.
p ● abbreviation **1** page. **2** Brit. penny or pence.
PA ● abbreviation **1** Pennsylvania. **2** Brit. personal assistant. **3** public address.
Pa ● abbreviation pascal(s). ● symbol the chemical element protactinium.
pa ● noun informal father.
– ORIGIN abbreviation of PAPA.
p.a. ● abbreviation per annum.
paan /paan/ (also **pan**) ● noun Indian betel leaves prepared and used as a stimulant.
– ORIGIN Sanskrit, 'feather, leaf'.
pa'anga /paaaanggə/ ● noun (pl. same) the basic monetary unit of Tonga, equal to 100 seniti.
– ORIGIN Tongan.
pabulum /pabyooləm/ (also **pablum**) /pabləm/ ● noun bland intellectual matter or entertainment.
– ORIGIN originally in the sense 'food': from Latin, from *pascere* 'to feed'.
paca /pakkə/ ● noun a large nocturnal South American rodent that has a reddish-brown coat patterned with rows of white spots.
– ORIGIN Tupi.
pacamac ● noun variant spelling of PAKAMAC.
pace[1] /payss/ ● noun **1** a single step taken when walking or running. **2** a gait of a horse, especially one of the recognized trained gaits. **3** speed or rate of motion, development, or change. ● verb **1** walk at a steady speed, especially without a particular destination and as an expression of anxiety. **2** measure (a distance) by walking it and counting the number of steps taken. **3** lead (another runner in a race) in order to establish a competitive speed. **4** (**pace oneself**) do something at a restrained and steady rate or speed. **5** move or develop (something) at a particular rate or speed. **6** (of a trained horse) move with a distinctive lateral gait in which both legs on the same side are lifted together.
– PHRASES **keep pace with** move or progress at the same speed as. **off the pace** behind the leader in a race or contest. **put someone through their paces** make someone demonstrate their abilities. **stand** (or **stay**) **the pace** be able to keep up with others.
– ORIGIN Latin *passus* 'stretch (of the leg)'.
pace[2] /paachay, paysi/ ● preposition with due respect to.
– ORIGIN Latin, 'in peace'.
pacemaker ● noun **1** (also **pacesetter**) a competitor who sets the pace at the beginning of a race or competition. **2** an artificial device for stimulating and regulating the heart muscle.
pacer ● noun **1** a pacemaker. **2** chiefly US a horse bred or trained to pace.
pacey ● adjective variant spelling of PACY.
pacha ● noun variant spelling of PASHA.
pachinko /pəchingkō/ ● noun a Japanese form of pinball.
– ORIGIN Japanese.
pachuco /pəchookō/ ● noun (pl. **pachucos**) chiefly US a member of a gang of young Mexican-Americans.
– ORIGIN from Mexican Spanish, 'flashily dressed'.
pachyderm /pakkiderm/ ● noun a very large mammal with thick skin, especially an elephant, rhinoceros, or hippopotamus.
– ORIGIN Greek *pakhudermos*, from *pakhus* 'thick' + *derma* 'skin'.
pacific ● adjective **1** peaceful in character or intent. **2** (**Pacific**) relating to the Pacific Ocean. ● noun (**the Pacific**) the Pacific Ocean.
– DERIVATIVES **pacifically** adverb.
– ORIGIN Latin *pacificus* 'peacemaking', from *pax* 'peace'.
pacifier ● noun **1** a person or thing that pacifies. **2** N. Amer. a baby's dummy.
pacifism ● noun the belief that disputes should be settled by peaceful means and that war and violence are unjustifiable.
– DERIVATIVES **pacifist** noun & adjective.
pacify ● verb (**pacifies, pacified**) **1** quell the anger or agitation of. **2** bring peace to (a country or warring factions).
– DERIVATIVES **pacification** noun.
– ORIGIN Latin *pacificare*, from *pax* 'peace'.
pack[1] ● noun **1** a cardboard or paper container and the items inside it. **2** Brit. a set of playing cards. **3** a collection of related documents. **4** a group of animals that live and hunt together. **5** chiefly derogatory a group or set of similar things or people. **6** (**the pack**) the main body of competitors following the leader in a race or competition. **7** Rugby a team's forwards considered as a group. **8** (**Pack**) an organized group of Cub Scouts or Brownies. **9** a rucksack. **10** pack ice. **11** a hot or cold pad of absorbent material, used for treating an injury. ● verb **1** fill (a suitcase or bag) with clothes and other items needed for travel. **2** place in a container for transport or storage. **3** be capable of being folded up for transport or storage. **4** cram a large number of things into. **5** (**packed** or Brit. **packed out**) crowded or filled with people. **6** cover, surround, or fill. **7** informal carry (a gun). **8** Rugby (of players) form a scrum.
– PHRASES **pack a punch 1** hit with skill or force. **2** have a powerful effect. **pack in** informal give up (an activity or job). **pack someone off** informal send someone somewhere peremptorily or without much notice. **pack up** Brit. informal (of a machine) break down. **send someone packing** informal dismiss someone peremptorily.
– DERIVATIVES **packable** adjective **packer** noun.
– ORIGIN Low German *pak*.
pack[2] ● verb fill (a jury or committee) with people likely to support a particular verdict or decision.
– ORIGIN probably from obsolete *pact* 'enter into an agreement with'.

Thesaurus

pace ● noun **1** *he stepped back a pace* STEP, stride. **2** *a slow, steady pace* GAIT, stride, walk, march. **3** *he drove home at a furious pace* SPEED, rate, velocity; *informal* clip, lick.
● verb *she paced up and down* WALK, stride, tread, march, pound, patrol.
pacific ● adjective **1** *a pacific community* PEACE-LOVING, peaceable, pacifist, non-violent, non-aggressive, non-belligerent. **2** *their pacific intentions* CONCILIATORY, peacemaking, placatory, propitiatory, appeasing, mollifying, mediatory, dovish; *formal* irenic. **3** *pacific waters* CALM, still, smooth, tranquil, placid, waveless, unruffled, like a millpond.
– OPPOSITES aggressive, stormy.
pacifism ● noun PEACEMAKING, conscientious objection(s), passive resistance, peace-mongering, non-violence.
pacifist ● noun PEACE-LOVER, conscientious objector, passive resister, peacemaker, peace-monger, dove; *Brit. informal* conchie.
– OPPOSITES warmonger.
pacify ● verb PLACATE, appease, calm (down), conciliate, propitiate, assuage, mollify, soothe.
– OPPOSITES enrage.
pack ● noun **1** *a pack of cigarettes* PACKET, container, package, box, carton, parcel. **2** *a 45lb pack* BACKPACK, rucksack, knapsack, kitbag, bag, load. **3** *a pack of wolves* GROUP, herd, troop. **4** *a pack of youngsters* CROWD, mob, group, band, troupe, party, set, clique, gang, rabble, horde, throng, huddle, mass, assembly, gathering, host; *informal* crew, bunch.

package ● noun **1** an object or group of objects wrapped in paper or packed in a box. **2** N. Amer. a packet. **3** (also **package deal**) a set of proposals or terms offered or agreed as a whole. **4** informal a package holiday. **5** Computing a collection of related programs or subroutines. ● verb **1** put into a box or wrapping. **2** present in a favourable way. **3** combine (various products) for sale as one unit. **4** commission and produce (an illustrated book) to sell as a complete product to publishers.
– DERIVATIVES **packaged** adjective **packager** noun.

package holiday (also **package tour**) ● noun a holiday organized by a travel agent, with arrangements for transport and accommodation made at an inclusive price.

packaging ● noun materials used to wrap or protect goods.

pack animal ● noun **1** an animal used to carry loads. **2** an animal that lives and hunts in a pack.

pack drill ● noun a military punishment of marching up and down carrying full equipment.

packed lunch ● noun a cold lunch carried in a bag or box to work or school or on an excursion.

packet ● noun **1** a paper or cardboard container. **2** Computing a block of data transmitted across a network. **3** (**a packet**) informal, chiefly Brit. a large sum of money. ● verb (**packeted**, **packeting**) wrap up in a packet.
– ORIGIN from PACK[1].

packet boat ● noun dated a boat travelling at regular intervals between two ports, originally carrying mail and later taking passengers.

packetize ● verb Computing partition or separate (data) into units for transmission in a packet-switching network.

packet switching ● noun Computing & Telecommunications data transmission in which a message is broken into parts and reassembled at the destination.

packhorse ● noun a horse used to carry loads.

pack ice ● noun (in polar seas) an expanse of large pieces of floating ice driven together into a mass.

packing ● noun **1** material used to protect fragile goods in transit. **2** material used to seal a join or assist in lubricating an axle.

packing case ● noun a large, strong box used for transportation or storage.

packsack ● noun N. Amer. a rucksack.

packsaddle ● noun chiefly N. Amer. a saddle adapted for securing the loads carried by a pack animal.

pact ● noun a formal agreement between individuals or parties.
– ORIGIN Latin *pactum* 'something agreed'.

pacy (also **pacey**) ● adjective (**pacier**, **paciest**) fast-moving.

pad[1] ● noun **1** a thick piece of soft or absorbent material. **2** the fleshy underpart of an animal's foot or of a human finger. **3** a protective guard worn over a part of the body by a sports player. **4** a number of sheets of blank paper fastened together at one edge. **5** a flat-topped structure or area used for helicopter take-off and landing or for rocket-launching. **6** informal a person's home. ● verb (**padded**, **padding**) **1** fill or cover with a pad or padding. **2** (**pad out**) lengthen (a speech or piece of writing) with unnecessary material. **3** chiefly N. Amer. defraud by adding false items to (an expenses claim or bill).
– ORIGIN originally in the sense 'bundle of straw to lie on': the senses may not be of common origin; the meaning 'underpart of an animal's foot' is perhaps related to Low German *pad* 'sole of the foot'.

pad[2] ● verb (**padded**, **padding**) walk with steady steps making a soft, dull sound. ● noun the sound of such steps.
– ORIGIN Low German *padden*.

padding ● noun **1** soft material such as foam or cloth used to pad or stuff something. **2** superfluous material in a book, speech, etc. introduced in order to make it reach a desired length.

paddle[1] ● noun **1** a short pole with a broad blade at one or both ends, used to propel a small boat through the water. **2** a paddle-shaped implement for stirring or mixing. **3** a short-handled bat such as that used in table tennis. **4** each of the boards fitted round the circumference of a paddle wheel or mill wheel. **5** the fin or flipper of an aquatic mammal or bird. ● verb **1** propel (a boat) with a paddle or paddles. **2** (of a bird or other animal) swim with short fast strokes.
– DERIVATIVES **paddler** noun.
– ORIGIN of unknown origin.

paddle[2] ● verb walk with bare feet in shallow water. ● noun a spell of paddling.
– DERIVATIVES **paddler** noun.
– ORIGIN of obscure origin; compare with Low German *paddeln* 'tramp about'.

paddle steamer (also **paddle boat**) ● noun a boat powered by steam and propelled by paddle wheels.

paddle wheel ● noun a large steam-driven wheel with paddles round its circumference, attached to the side or stern of a ship and propelling the ship by its rotation.

paddling pool ● noun a shallow artificial pool for children to paddle in.

paddock ● noun **1** a small field or enclosure for horses. **2** an enclosure adjoining a racecourse or track where horses or cars are gathered and displayed before a race. **3** Austral./NZ a field or plot of land enclosed by fencing or defined by natural boundaries. ● verb keep or enclose (a horse) in a paddock.
– ORIGIN of unknown origin.

Paddy ● noun (pl. **Paddies**) informal, chiefly offensive an Irishman.
– ORIGIN familiar form of the Irish given name *Padraig*.

paddy[1] ● noun (pl. **paddies**) **1** a field where rice is grown. **2** rice still in the husk.
– ORIGIN Malay.

Thesaurus

● verb **1** *she helped pack the hamper* FILL (UP), put things in, load. **2** *they packed their belongings* STOW, put away, store, box up. **3** *the glasses were packed in straw* WRAP (UP), package, parcel, swathe, swaddle, encase, enfold, envelop, bundle. **4** *Christmas shoppers packed the store* THRONG, crowd (into), fill (to overflowing), cram, jam, squash into, squeeze into. **5** *pack the cloth against the wall* COMPRESS, press, squash, squeeze, jam, tamp.
– PHRASES **pack something in** (informal) **1** *she has packed in her job* RESIGN FROM, leave, give up; informal quit, chuck; Brit. informal jack in. **2** *he should pack in smoking* GIVE UP, abstain from, drop, desist from, refrain from, discontinue; informal quit, leave off; formal forswear. **pack someone off** (informal) SEND OFF, dispatch, bundle off. **pack up 1** (Brit. informal) *something is bound to pack up over Christmas* BREAK (DOWN), stop working, fail, develop a fault, malfunction, go wrong; informal act up, conk out, go kaput. **2** (informal) *it's time to pack up* STOP, call it a day, finish, cease; informal knock off, quit, pack/jack it in. **pack something up** PUT AWAY, tidy up/away, clear up/away.

package ● noun **1** *the delivery of a package* PARCEL, packet, container, box. **2** *a complete package of services* COLLECTION, bundle, combination.
● verb *goods packaged in recyclable materials* WRAP (UP), gift-wrap; pack (up), parcel (up), box, encase.

packaging ● noun WRAPPING, wrappers, packing, covering.

packed ● adjective CROWDED, full, filled (to capacity), crammed, jammed, solid, overcrowded, overfull, teeming, seething, swarming; informal jam-packed, chock-full, chock-a-block, full to the gunwales, bursting/bulging at the seams.

packet ● noun **1** *a packet of cigarettes* PACK, carton, (cardboard) box, container, case, package. **2** (informal) *that must have cost a packet* A CONSIDERABLE/LARGE SUM OF MONEY, a king's ransom, millions, billions; informal a (small) fortune, pots/heaps of money, a mint, a bundle, a pile, a tidy sum, a pretty penny, big money; Brit. informal a bomb, loadsamoney; N. Amer. informal big bucks, gazillions; Austral. informal big bickies, motser.

pact ● noun AGREEMENT, treaty, entente, protocol, deal, settlement, concordat; armistice, truce; formal concord.

pad[1] ● noun **1** *a pad over the eye* PIECE OF COTTON WOOL, dressing, pack, padding, wadding, wad. **2** *a seat pad* CUSHION, squab. **3** *making notes on a pad* NOTEBOOK, notepad, writing pad, memo pad, jotter, block, sketch pad, sketchbook; N. Amer. scratch pad.
● verb *a quilted jacket padded with duck feathers* STUFF, fill, pack, wad.
– PHRASES **pad something out** EXPAND UNNECESSARILY, fill out, amplify, increase, flesh out, lengthen, spin out, overdo, elaborate.

pad[2] ● verb *he padded along towards the bedroom* WALK QUIETLY, tread warily, creep, tiptoe, steal, pussyfoot.

padding ● noun **1** *padding around the ankle* WADDING, cushioning, stuffing, packing, filling, lining. **2** *a concise style with no padding* VERBIAGE, verbosity, wordiness, prolixity; Brit. informal waffle.

paddle[1] ● noun *use the paddles to row ashore* OAR, scull, blade.
● verb *we paddled around the bay* ROW GENTLY, pull, scull.

paddle[2] ● verb *children were paddling in the water* SPLASH ABOUT, wade; dabble.

paddy[2] ● **noun** Brit. informal a fit of temper.
– ORIGIN from PADDY; associated with obsolete *paddywhack* 'Irishman given to brawling'.
paddy wagon ● **noun** N. Amer. informal a police van.
– ORIGIN from PADDY, perhaps because formerly many American police officers were of Irish descent.
padlock ● **noun** a detachable lock hanging by a pivoted hook on the object fastened. ● **verb** secure with a padlock.
– ORIGIN *pad-* is of unknown origin.
padre /paadray/ ● **noun** informal a chaplain in the armed services.
– ORIGIN Latin *pater* 'father'.
padrone /padrōnay/ ● **noun** a patron or master, especially a Mafia boss.
– ORIGIN Italian.
padsaw ● **noun** a small saw with a narrow blade, for cutting curves.
paean /peeən/ ● **noun** a song of praise or triumph.
– ORIGIN Greek *paian* 'hymn of thanksgiving to Apollo'; the hymn addressed Apollo by the name *Paian*, originally the Homeric name of the physician of the gods.
paediatrics /peediatriks/ (US **pediatrics**) ● **plural noun** (treated as sing.) the branch of medicine concerned with children and their diseases.
– DERIVATIVES **paediatric** adjective **paediatrician** noun.
– ORIGIN from Greek *pais* 'child' + *iatros* 'physician'.
paedophile (US **pedophile**) ● **noun** a person who is sexually attracted to children.
– DERIVATIVES **paedophilia** noun **paedophiliac** adjective & noun.
– ORIGIN from Greek *pais* 'child'.
paella /pīellə/ ● **noun** a Spanish dish of rice, saffron, chicken, seafood, and vegetables, traditionally cooked in a large shallow pan.
– ORIGIN Catalan, from Latin *patella* 'pan'.
paeony ● **noun** variant spelling of PEONY.
pagan ● **noun** a person holding religious beliefs other than those of the main world religions. ● **adjective** relating to pagans or their beliefs.
– DERIVATIVES **paganism** noun.
– ORIGIN Latin *paganus* 'rustic', later 'civilian' (i.e. a person who was not a 'soldier' in Christ's army).
page[1] ● **noun 1** one side of a leaf of a book, magazine, or newspaper, or the material written or printed on it. **2** both sides of such a leaf considered as a single unit. **3** Computing a section of data displayed on a screen at one time. **4** a particular episode considered as part of a longer history. ● **verb 1** (**page through**) leaf through. **2** Computing move through and display (text) one page at a time.
– ORIGIN Latin *pagina*, from *pangere* 'fasten'.
page[2] ● **noun 1** a boy or young man employed in a hotel or club to run errands, open doors, etc. **2** a young boy attending a bride at a wedding. **3** historical a boy in training for knighthood, ranking next below a squire in the personal service of a knight. **4** historical a man or boy employed as the personal attendant of a person of rank. ● **verb** summon over a public address system or by means of a pager.
– ORIGIN Old French, from Greek *paidion* 'small boy'.
pageant /pajənt/ ● **noun 1** a public entertainment consisting of a procession of people in elaborate costumes, or an outdoor performance of a historical scene. **2** (also **beauty pageant**) N. Amer. a beauty contest. **3** historical a scene erected on a fixed stage or moving vehicle as a public show.
– ORIGIN of unknown origin.
pageantry ● **noun** elaborate display or ceremony.
pageboy ● **noun 1** a page in a hotel or attending a bride at a wedding. **2** a woman's hairstyle consisting of a shoulder-length bob with the ends rolled under.
pager ● **noun** a small radio device which bleeps or vibrates to inform the wearer that someone wishes to contact them or that it has received a short text message.
Page Three ● **noun** Brit. trademark (before another noun) characteristic of a feature which formerly appeared daily on page three of the *Sun* newspaper, comprising a picture of a topless young woman.
paginate /pajinayt/ ● **noun** assign numbers to the pages of a book, journal, etc.
– DERIVATIVES **pagination** noun.
pagoda /pəgōdə/ ● **noun** a Hindu or Buddhist temple or other sacred building, typically having a many-tiered tower.
– ORIGIN Portuguese *pagode*.
paid past and past participle of PAY.
– PHRASES **put paid to** informal stop abruptly; destroy.
paid-up ● **adjective 1** with all subscriptions or charges paid in full. **2** committed to a cause, group, etc.: *a fully paid-up postmodernist.*
pail ● **noun** a bucket.
– ORIGIN origin uncertain.
pain ● **noun 1** a strongly unpleasant bodily sensation such as is caused by illness or injury. **2** mental suffering or distress. **3** (also **pain in the neck** or vulgar slang **pain in the arse**) informal an annoying or tedious person or thing. **4** (**pains**) great care or trouble. ● **verb** cause pain to.
– PHRASES **on** (or **under**) **pain of** on penalty of.
– ORIGIN Old French *peine*, from Latin *poena* 'penalty, pain'.
pained ● **adjective** showing or suffering pain, especially mental pain.
painful ● **adjective 1** affected with or causing pain. **2** informal very bad: *their attempts at reggae are painful.*
– DERIVATIVES **painfully** adverb **painfulness** noun.
painkiller ● **noun** a medicine for relieving pain.
painless ● **adjective 1** not causing pain. **2** involving little effort

p

Thesaurus

paddock ● **noun** FIELD, meadow, pasture; pen, pound; *N. Amer.* corral.
paddy ● **noun** *(Brit. informal)* RAGE, (bad) temper, (bad) mood, pet, fit of pique, tantrum; *informal* grump, stress; *Brit. informal* strop; *N. Amer. informal* blowout, hissy fit.
padlock ● **verb** LOCK (UP), fasten, secure.
padre ● **noun** *(informal)* PRIEST, chaplain, minister (of religion), pastor, father, parson, clergyman, cleric, ecclesiastic, man of the cloth, churchman, vicar, rector, curate, preacher; *informal* reverend, Holy Joe, sky pilot; *Austral. informal* josser.
paean ● **noun** SONG OF PRAISE, hymn, alleluia; plaudit, glorification, eulogy, tribute, panegyric, accolade, acclamation; *formal* encomium.
pagan ● **noun** *pagans worshipped the sun* HEATHEN, infidel, idolater, idolatress; *archaic* paynim.
● **adjective** *the pagan festival* HEATHEN, ungodly, irreligious, infidel, idolatrous; *rare* nullifidian.
page[1] ● **noun 1** *a book of 672 pages* FOLIO, sheet, side, leaf. **2** *a glorious page in his life* PERIOD, time, stage, phase, epoch, era, chapter.
page[2] ● **noun 1** *a page in a hotel* ERRAND BOY, messenger boy; *N. Amer.* bellboy, bellhop. **2** *a page at a wedding* ATTENDANT, pageboy, train-bearer.
● **verb** *could you please page Mr Johnson?* CALL (FOR), summon, send for.
pageant ● **noun** PARADE, procession, cavalcade, tableau (vivant); spectacle, extravaganza, show.
pageantry ● **noun** SPECTACLE, display, ceremony, magnificence, pomp, splendour, grandeur, show; *informal* razzle-dazzle, razzmatazz.
pain ● **noun 1** *she endured great pain* SUFFERING, agony, torture, torment, discomfort. **2** *a pain in the stomach* ACHE, aching, soreness, throb, throbbing, sting, stinging, twinge, shooting pain, stab, pang; discomfort, irritation, tenderness. **3** *the pain of losing a loved one* SORROW, grief, heartache, heartbreak, sadness, unhappiness, distress, desolation, misery, wretchedness, despair; agony, torment, torture. **4** *(informal) that child is a pain.* See NUISANCE. **5** *he took great pains to hide his feelings* CARE, effort, bother, trouble.
● **verb 1** *her foot is still paining her* HURT, cause pain, be painful, be sore, be tender, ache, throb, sting, twinge, cause discomfort; *informal* kill. **2** *the memory pains her* SADDEN, grieve, distress, trouble, perturb, oppress, cause anguish to.
– PHRASES **be at pains** TRY HARD, make a great effort, take (great) pains, put oneself out; strive, endeavour, try, do one's best, do one's utmost, go all out; *informal* bend/fall/lean over backwards.
pained ● **adjective** UPSET, hurt, wounded, injured, insulted, offended, aggrieved, displeased, disgruntled, annoyed, angered, angry, cross, indignant, irritated, resentful; *informal* riled, miffed, aggravated, peeved, hacked off, browned off; *Brit. informal* narked, cheesed off; *N. Amer. informal* teed off, ticked off, sore.
painful ● **adjective 1** *a painful arm* SORE, hurting, tender, aching, throbbing. **2** *a painful experience* DISAGREEABLE, unpleasant, nasty, bitter, distressing, upsetting, traumatic, miserable, sad, heartbreaking, agonizing, harrowing.

or stress.
– DERIVATIVES **painlessly** adverb **painlessness** noun.
painstaking ● adjective very careful and thorough.
– DERIVATIVES **painstakingly** adverb.
paint ● noun **1** a coloured substance which is spread over a surface to give a thin decorative or protective coating. **2** dated cosmetic make up. ● verb **1** apply paint to. **2** apply (a liquid) to a surface with a brush. **3** depict or produce with paint. **4** give a description of.
– PHRASES **paint the town red** informal go out and enjoy oneself flamboyantly.
– ORIGIN from Old French *peindre*, from Latin *pingere* 'to paint'.
paintball ● noun a combat game in which participants shoot capsules of paint at each other with air guns.
paintbox ● noun a box holding a palette of dry paints for painting pictures.
paintbrush ● noun a brush for applying paint.
painted lady ● noun a butterfly with predominantly orange-brown wings and darker markings.
painter[1] ● noun **1** an artist who paints pictures. **2** a person who paints buildings.
painter[2] ● noun a rope attached to the bow of a boat for tying it to a quay.
– ORIGIN origin uncertain.
painterly ● adjective **1** of or appropriate to a painter; artistic. **2** (of a painting) characterized by qualities of colour, stroke, and texture rather than of line.
painting ● noun **1** the action of painting. **2** a painted picture.
paint shop ● noun the part of a factory in which goods are painted.
paintwork ● noun chiefly Brit. painted surfaces in a building or on a vehicle.
pair ● noun **1** a set of two things used together or regarded as a unit. **2** an article consisting of two joined or corresponding parts. **3** two people or animals related in some way or considered together. **4** two opposing members of a parliament who absent themselves from voting by mutual arrangement. ● verb **1** join or connect to form a pair. **2** (**pair off/up**) form a couple.
– ORIGIN Old French *paire*, from Latin *par* 'equal'.
paisa /pīsaa/ ● noun (pl. **paise** /pīsay/) a monetary unit of India, Pakistan, and Nepal, equal to one hundredth of a rupee.
– ORIGIN Hindi.
paisley /payzli/ ● noun a distinctive intricate pattern of curved feather-shaped figures based on an Indian pine cone design.
– ORIGIN named after the town of *Paisley* in Scotland, where a cloth incorporating this design was made.
Paiute /pīoot/ ● noun (pl. same or **Paiutes**) a member of either of two American Indian peoples (the **Southern Paiute** and the **Northern Paiute**) of the western US.
– ORIGIN Spanish *Payuchi, Payuta*.
pajamas ● plural noun US spelling of PYJAMAS.
pakamac /pakkəmak/ (also **pacamac**) ● noun Brit. a lightweight plastic mackintosh that can be folded up into a small pack when not required.
pak choi /pak choy/ (also N. Amer. **bok choy**) ● noun a Chinese cabbage with smooth-edged tapering leaves.
– ORIGIN Chinese, 'white vegetable'.
Pakeha /paakihaa/ ● noun NZ a white New Zealander, as opposed to a Maori.
– ORIGIN Maori.
Paki ● noun (pl. **Pakis**) Brit. informal, offensive a Pakistani.
Pakistani /paakistaani, pakkistanni/ ● noun a person from Pakistan. ● adjective relating to Pakistan.
pakora /pəkorə/ ● noun (in Indian cookery) a piece of battered and deep-fried vegetable or meat.
– ORIGIN Hindi.
PAL ● abbreviation phase alternate line (the television broadcasting system used in most of Europe).
– ORIGIN so named because the colour information in alternate lines is inverted in phase.
pal informal ● noun a friend. ● verb (**palled, palling**) (**pal up**) form a friendship.
– ORIGIN Romany, 'brother, mate', from Sanskrit.
palace ● noun a large, impressive building forming the official residence of a sovereign, president, archbishop, etc.
– ORIGIN Old French *paleis*, from Latin *Palatium*, the name of the Palatine hill in Rome, where the house of the emperor was situated.
palace coup (also **palace revolution**) ● noun the non-violent overthrow of a sovereign or government by senior officials within the ruling group.
paladin /palədin/ ● noun historical **1** any of the twelve peers of Charlemagne's court. **2** a brave, chivalrous knight.
– ORIGIN French, from Latin *palatinus* 'of the palace'.
Palaearctic /paliaarktik, payli-/ (also chiefly US **Palearctic**) ● adjective Zoology relating to a region comprising Eurasia north of the Himalayas, together with North Africa and part of the Arabian peninsula.
palaeo- /paliō, payliō/ (US **paleo-**) ● combining form older or ancient: *Palaeolithic*.
– ORIGIN from Greek *palaios* 'ancient'.
Palaeocene /paliōseen, pay-/ (US **Paleocene**) ● adjective Geology relating to the earliest epoch of the Tertiary period (between the Cretaceous period and the Eocene epoch, about 65 to 56.5 million years ago), a time of rapid development of mammals.
– ORIGIN from Greek *palaios* 'ancient' + *kainos* 'new'.
palaeography /paliografi, pay-/ (US **paleography**) ● noun the study of ancient writing systems and manuscripts.
– DERIVATIVES **palaeographer** noun **palaeographic** adjective.
Palaeolithic /palliəlithik, pay-/ (US **Paleolithic**) ● adjective Archaeology relating to the early phase of the Stone Age, up to the end of the glacial period.
– ORIGIN from Greek *palaios* 'ancient' + *lithos* 'stone'.
palaeontology /paliontolləji, pay-/ (US **paleontology**) ● noun the branch of science concerned with fossil animals and plants.
– DERIVATIVES **palaeontological** adjective **palaeontologist** noun.
– ORIGIN from Greek *palaios* 'ancient' + *onta* 'beings'.
Palaeozoic /paliəzōik, pay-/ (US **Paleozoic**) ● adjective Geology relating to the era between the Precambrian aeon and the Mesozoic era, about 570 to 245 million years ago, which ended with the rise to dominance of the reptiles.
– ORIGIN from Greek *palaios* 'ancient' + *zōē* 'life'.
palaestra /pəleestrə, -līstrə/ (also **palestra**) ● noun (in ancient Greece and Rome) a wrestling school or gymnasium.
– ORIGIN Greek *palaistra*, from *palaiein* 'wrestle'.
palais /palay/ ● noun Brit. a public hall for dancing.

p

Thesaurus

painfully ● adverb DISTRESSINGLY, disturbingly, unendurably, unbearably, uncomfortably, unpleasantly; dreadfully; *informal* terribly, awfully; *informal, dated* frightfully.
painkiller ● noun ANALGESIC, pain reliever, anodyne, anaesthetic, narcotic; palliative.
painless ● adjective **1** *any killing of animals should be painless* WITHOUT PAIN, pain-free. **2** *getting rid of him proved painless* EASY, trouble-free, effortless, simple, plain sailing; *informal* as easy as pie, a piece of cake, child's play, a cinch.
– OPPOSITES painful, difficult.
painstaking ● adjective CAREFUL, meticulous, thorough, assiduous, sedulous, attentive, diligent, industrious, conscientious, punctilious, scrupulous, rigorous, particular; pedantic, fussy.
– OPPOSITES slapdash.
paint ● noun COLOURING, colourant, tint, dye, stain, pigment, colour. ● verb **1** *simply paint the ceiling* COLOUR, apply paint to, decorate, whitewash, emulsion, gloss, spray-paint, airbrush. **2** *painting slogans on a wall* DAUB, smear, spray-paint, airbrush. **3** *Rembrandt painted his mother* PORTRAY, picture, paint a picture of, depict, represent. **4** *you paint a very stark picture of the suffering* TELL, recount, outline, sketch, describe, depict, evoke, conjure up.
– PHRASES **paint the town red** (*informal*) CELEBRATE, carouse, enjoy oneself, have a good/wild time, have a party; *informal* go out on the town, whoop it up, make whoopee, live it up, party, have a ball, push the boat out.
painting ● noun PICTURE, illustration, portrayal, depiction, representation, image, artwork; oil (painting), watercolour, canvas.
pair ● noun **1** *a pair of gloves* SET (OF TWO), matching set, two of a kind. **2** *the pair were arrested* TWO, couple, duo, brace, twosome, duplet; twins; *archaic* twain. **3** *a pair of lines* COUPLET; *Prosody* distich. **4** *the happy pair* COUPLE, man/husband and wife.
● verb *a cardigan paired with a matching skirt* MATCH, put together, couple, twin.
– PHRASES **pair off/up** GET TOGETHER, team up, form a couple, make a twosome.
pal (*informal*) ● noun *my best pal*. See FRIEND sense 1.
– PHRASES **pal up** BECOME FRIENDLY, make friends, form a friendship; *N. Amer. informal* buddy up.

– ORIGIN from French *palais de danse* 'dancing hall'.
palanquin /palənkeen/ (also **palankeen**) ● noun (in India and the East) a covered litter for one passenger.
– ORIGIN Portuguese *palanquim*, from Sanskrit, 'bed, couch'.
palatable /palətəb'l/ ● adjective **1** pleasant to taste. **2** (of an action or proposal) acceptable.
– DERIVATIVES **palatability** noun **palatably** adverb.
palatal /palət'l/ ● adjective **1** relating to the palate. **2** Phonetics (of a speech sound) made by placing the blade of the tongue against or near the hard palate (e.g. *y* in *yes*).
– DERIVATIVES **palatalize** (also **palatalise**) verb.
palate ● noun **1** the roof of the mouth, separating the cavities of the mouth and nose in vertebrates. **2** a person's ability to distinguish between and appreciate different flavours. **3** a person's taste or liking.
– ORIGIN Latin *palatum*.
palatial ● adjective resembling a palace, especially in being spacious or grand.
– DERIVATIVES **palatially** adverb.
palatinate /pəlattinət/ ● noun historical **1** a territory under the jurisdiction of a Count Palatine. **2** (**the Palatinate**) the territory of the German Empire ruled by the Count Palatine of the Rhine.
palatine /palətīn/ ● adjective chiefly historical **1** (of an official or feudal lord) having local authority that elsewhere belongs only to a sovereign. **2** (of a territory) subject to such authority.
– ORIGIN French, from Latin *palatinus* 'of the palace'.
palaver /pəlaavər/ informal ● noun **1** prolonged and tedious fuss or discussion. **2** dated a parley or improvised conference between two sides. ● verb talk unnecessarily at length.
– ORIGIN Portuguese *palavra* 'word', from Latin *parabola* 'comparison'.
palazzo /pəlatsō/ ● noun (pl. **palazzos** or **palazzi** /pəlatsee/) a large, grand building, especially in Italy.
– ORIGIN Italian, 'palace'.
palazzo pants ● plural noun women's loose wide-legged trousers.
pale[1] ● adjective **1** of a light shade or hue; approaching white. **2** (of a person's face) having little colour, through shock, fear, illness, etc. **3** unimpressive or inferior: *a pale imitation.* ● verb **1** become pale in one's face. **2** seem or become less important.
– DERIVATIVES **palely** adverb **paleness** noun.
– ORIGIN Old French, from Latin *pallidus*.
pale[2] ● noun **1** a wooden stake used with others to form a fence. **2** a boundary. **3** archaic or historical an area within set boundaries or subject to a particular jurisdiction. **4** Heraldry a broad vertical stripe down the middle of a shield.
– PHRASES **beyond the pale** outside the boundaries of acceptable behaviour.
– ORIGIN Old French *pal*, from Latin *palus* 'stake'.
Palearctic ● adjective chiefly US variant spelling of PALAEARCTIC.
paleface ● noun a name supposedly used by North American Indians for a white person.
paleo- ● combining form US spelling of PALAEO-.
Palestinian /paləstinniən/ ● adjective relating to Palestine. ● noun a member of the native Arab population of Palestine.
palestra /pəleestrə, -līstrə/ ● noun variant spelling of PALAESTRA.
palette /palit/ ● noun **1** a thin board on which an artist lays and mixes colours. **2** the range of colours used by an artist. **3** the range of tonal colour in a musical piece.
– ORIGIN French, 'little shovel'.
palette knife ● noun **1** a thin steel blade with a handle for mixing colours or applying or removing paint. **2** Brit. a kitchen knife with a long, blunt, flexible, round-ended blade.
palfrey /pawlfri/ ● noun (pl. **palfreys**) archaic a docile horse ridden especially by women.
– ORIGIN Old French *palefrei*, from Greek *para* 'beside, extra' + Latin *veredus* 'light horse'.
palimony /paliməni/ ● noun informal, chiefly N. Amer. compensation made by one member of an unmarried couple to the other after separation.
– ORIGIN from PAL + ALIMONY.
palimpsest /palimpsest/ ● noun **1** a parchment or other surface on which writing has been applied over earlier writing which has been erased. **2** something reused or altered but still bearing visible traces of its earlier form: *the house is a palimpsest of the taste of successive owners.*
– ORIGIN from Greek *palin* 'again' + *psēstos* 'rubbed smooth'.
palindrome /palindrōm/ ● noun a word or sequence that reads the same backwards as forwards, e.g. *madam*.
– DERIVATIVES **palindromic** /pallindrommik/ adjective.
– ORIGIN from Greek *palindromos* 'running back again'.
paling /payling/ ● noun **1** a fence made from stakes. **2** a stake used in such a fence.
palinode /palinōd/ ● noun a poem in which the poet retracts a view or sentiment expressed in a former poem.
– ORIGIN from Greek *palin* 'again' + *ōidē* 'song'.
palisade /palisayd/ ● noun **1** a fence of stakes or iron railings forming an enclosure or defence. **2** (**palisades**) US a line of high cliffs.
– ORIGIN French *palissade*, from Latin *palus* 'stake'
pall[1] /pawl/ ● noun **1** a cloth spread over a coffin, hearse, or tomb. **2** a dark cloud of smoke, dust, etc. **3** an enveloping air of gloom or fear. **4** an ecclesiastical pallium.
– ORIGIN Latin *pallium* 'covering, cloak'.
pall[2] /pawl/ ● verb become less appealing or interesting through familiarity.
– ORIGIN shortening of APPAL.
Palladian /pəlaydiən/ ● adjective in the neoclassical style of the Italian architect Andrea Palladio (1508–80), especially with reference to English architecture of the 18th century.
– DERIVATIVES **Palladianism** noun.
palladium /pəlaydiəm/ ● noun a rare silvery-white metallic element resembling platinum.
– ORIGIN from *Pallas*, an asteroid discovered (1803) just before the element.

Thesaurus

palace ● noun ROYAL/OFFICIAL RESIDENCE, castle, château, schloss, mansion, stately home.
– RELATED TERMS palatial.
palatable ● adjective **1** *palatable meals* TASTY, appetizing, flavourful, flavoursome, delicious, mouth-watering, toothsome, succulent; *informal* scrumptious, yummy, scrummy, moreish; *formal* comestible. **2** *the truth is not always palatable* PLEASANT, acceptable, pleasing, agreeable, to one's liking.
– OPPOSITES disagreeable.
palate ● noun **1** *the tea burned her palate* ROOF OF THE MOUTH, hard/soft palate. **2** *menus to suit the tourist palate* (SENSE OF) TASTE, appetite, stomach. **3** *wine with a peachy palate* FLAVOUR, taste.
palatial ● adjective LUXURIOUS, de luxe, magnificent, sumptuous, splendid, grand, opulent, lavish, stately, regal; fancy; *Brit.* upmarket; *informal* plush, swanky, posh, ritzy, swish.
– OPPOSITES modest.
palaver *(informal)* ● noun **1** *what was all that palaver about?* FUSS (AND BOTHER), bother, commotion, trouble, rigmarole, folderol; *informal* song and dance, performance, to-do, carrying-on, kerfuffle, hoo-ha, hullabaloo, ballyhoo. **2** *(dated) they were having a palaver.* See PARLEY noun.
● verb *don't stand there palavering.* See TALK verb sense 3.
pale[1] ● noun **1** *the pales of a fence* STAKE, post, pole, picket, upright. **2** *outside the pale of decency* BOUNDARY, confines, bounds, limits.
– PHRASES **beyond the pale** UNACCEPTABLE, unseemly, improper, unsuitable, unreasonable, intolerable, disgraceful, deplorable, outrageous, scandalous, shocking; *informal* not on, not the done thing, out of order, out of line; *Austral./NZ informal* over the fence; *formal* exceptionable.
pale[2] ● adjective **1** *she looked pale and drawn* WHITE, pallid, pasty, wan, colourless, anaemic, bloodless, washed out, peaky, ashen, grey, whitish, whey-faced, drained, sickly, sallow, as white as a sheet, deathly pale; milky, creamy, cream, ivory, milk-white, alabaster; *informal* like death warmed up. **2** *pale colours* LIGHT, light-coloured, pastel, muted, subtle, soft; faded, bleached, washed out. **3** *the pale light of morning* DIM, faint, weak, feeble. **4** *a pale imitation* FEEBLE, weak, insipid, bland, poor, inadequate; uninspired, unimaginative, lacklustre, spiritless, lifeless; *informal* pathetic.
– OPPOSITES dark.
● verb **1** *his face paled* GO/TURN WHITE, grow/turn pale, blanch, lose colour. **2** *everything else pales by comparison* DECREASE IN IMPORTANCE, lose significance, pale into insignificance.
palisade ● noun FENCE, paling, barricade, stockade.
pall[1] ● noun **1** *a rich velvet pall* FUNERAL CLOTH, coffin covering. **2** *a pall of black smoke* CLOUD, covering, cloak, veil, shroud, layer, blanket.
– PHRASES **cast a pall over** SPOIL, cast a shadow over, overshadow, cloud, put a damper on.

pall-bearer ● noun a person helping to carry or escorting a coffin at a funeral.

pallet[1] ● noun **1** a straw mattress. **2** a crude or makeshift bed.
– ORIGIN Old French *paillete*, from Latin *palea* 'straw'.

pallet[2] ● noun **1** a portable platform on which goods can be moved, stacked, and stored. **2** a flat wooden blade with a handle, used to shape clay or plaster. **3** an artist's palette.
– DERIVATIVES **palletize** (also **palletise**) verb.
– ORIGIN French, 'little blade', from Latin *pala* 'spade'.

pallia plural of PALLIUM.

palliasse /paliass/ ● noun a straw mattress.
– ORIGIN French *paillasse*, from Latin *palea* 'straw'.

palliate /paliayt/ ● verb **1** make (the symptoms of a disease) less severe without removing the cause. **2** make (something bad) less severe.
– DERIVATIVES **palliation** noun.
– ORIGIN Latin *palliare* 'to cloak'.

palliative /paliətiv/ ● adjective relieving pain or alleviating a problem without dealing with the cause. ● noun a palliative remedy or medicine.

pallid ● adjective **1** pale, especially because of poor health. **2** feeble or insipid.
– ORIGIN Latin *pallidus* 'pale'.

pallium /paliəm/ ● noun (pl. **pallia** /paliə/ or **palliums**) **1** a clerical garment conferred by the Pope on an archbishop, consisting of a narrow circular band placed round the shoulders. **2** a man's large rectangular cloak worn in antiquity.
– ORIGIN Latin, 'covering, cloak'.

pall-mall /palmal/ ● noun a 16th- and 17th-century game in which a ball was driven through an iron ring suspended at the end of a long alley.
– ORIGIN from Italian *palla* 'ball' + *maglio* 'mallet'.

pallor ● noun an unhealthy pale appearance.
– ORIGIN Latin, from *pallere* 'be pale'.

pally ● adjective (**pallier**, **palliest**) informal having a close, friendly relationship.

palm[1] ● noun **1** (also **palm tree**) an evergreen tree with a crown of very long feathered or fan-shaped leaves, growing in warm regions. **2** a leaf of a palm awarded as a prize or viewed as a symbol of victory.
– ORIGIN Latin *palma* 'palm (of a hand)', its leaf being likened to a spread hand.

palm[2] ● noun the inner surface of the hand between the wrist and fingers. ● verb **1** conceal (a small object) in the hand, especially as part of a trick. **2** (**palm off**) sell or dispose of (something) by misrepresentation or fraud. **3** (**palm off**) informal persuade (someone) to accept something by deception. **4** deflect (a ball) with the palm of the hand.
– PHRASES **in the palm of one's hand** under one's control or influence. **read someone's palm** tell someone's fortune by looking at the lines on their palm.
– ORIGIN Latin *palma*.

palmate /palmayt/ ● adjective chiefly Botany & Zoology shaped like an open hand with a number of lobes resembling fingers.

palmer ● noun historical a pilgrim, especially one who had returned from the Holy Land with a palm branch or leaf as a sign of having undertaken the pilgrimage.
– ORIGIN Latin *palmarius* 'pilgrim', from *palma* 'palm'.

palmetto /palmettō/ ● noun (pl. **palmettos**) an American palm with large fan-shaped leaves.
– ORIGIN Spanish *palmito* 'small palm'.

palmier /palmiay/ ● noun (pl. pronounced same) a sweet crisp pastry shaped like a palm leaf.
– ORIGIN French, 'palm tree'.

palmistry ● noun the supposed interpretation of a person's character or prediction of their future by examining the hand.
– DERIVATIVES **palmist** noun.

Palm Sunday ● noun the Sunday before Easter, on which Christ's entry into Jerusalem is celebrated by processions in which branches of palms are carried.

palmtop ● noun a computer small and light enough to be held in one hand.

palm wine ● noun an alcoholic drink made from fermented palm sap.

palmy ● adjective (**palmier**, **palmiest**) comfortable and prosperous: *the palmy days of the 1970s.*

palomino /paləmeenō/ ● noun (pl. **palominos**) a pale golden or tan-coloured horse with a white mane and tail.
– ORIGIN Latin American Spanish, from Spanish, 'young pigeon'.

palp /palp/ ● noun Zoology each of a pair of elongated segmented feelers near the mouth of an arthropod.
– ORIGIN Latin *palpus*, from *palpare* 'to feel'.

palpable /palpəb'l/ ● adjective **1** able to be touched or felt. **2** so intense as to be almost touched or felt: *a palpable sense of loss.*
– DERIVATIVES **palpably** adverb.
– ORIGIN Latin *palpabilis*, from *palpare* 'feel, touch gently'.

palpate /palpayt/ ● verb examine (a part of the body) by touch, especially for medical purposes.
– DERIVATIVES **palpation** noun.

palpitate /palpitayt/ ● verb **1** (of the heart) beat rapidly or irregularly. **2** shake; tremble.
– ORIGIN Latin *palpitare* 'tremble, throb'.

palpitation ● noun **1** throbbing or trembling. **2** (**palpitations**) a noticeably rapid, strong, or irregular heartbeat.

palpus /palpəss/ ● noun (pl. **palpi** /palpī/) another term for PALP.

palsy /pawlzi/ ● noun (pl. **palsies**) dated paralysis, especially when accompanied by involuntary tremors. ● verb (**be palsied**) be affected with palsy.
– ORIGIN Old French *paralisie*, from Latin *paralysis.*

palter /pawltər/ ● verb archaic **1** equivocate or prevaricate. **2** (**palter with**) trifle with.
– ORIGIN of unknown origin.

paltry ● adjective (**paltrier**, **paltriest**) **1** (of an amount) very small or meagre. **2** petty; trivial.
– DERIVATIVES **paltriness** noun.
– ORIGIN probably from dialect *pelt* 'rubbish'.

p

Thesaurus

pall[2] ● verb *the high life was beginning to pall* BECOME/GROW TEDIOUS, become/grow boring, lose its/their interest, lose attraction, wear off; weary, sicken, nauseate; irritate, irk.

palliate ● verb **1** *the treatment works by palliating symptoms* ALLEVIATE, ease, relieve, soothe, take the edge off, assuage, moderate, temper, diminish, decrease, blunt, deaden. **2** *there is no way to palliate his dirty deed* DISGUISE, hide, gloss over, conceal, cover (up), camouflage, mask; excuse, justify, extenuate, mitigate.

palliative ● adjective *palliative medicine* SOOTHING, alleviating, sedative, calmative.
● noun *antibiotics and palliatives* PAINKILLER, analgesic, pain reliever, sedative, tranquillizer, anodyne, calmative, opiate, bromide.

pallid ● adjective **1** *a pallid child* PALE, white, pasty, wan, colourless, anaemic, washed out, peaky, whey-faced, ashen, grey, whitish, drained, sickly, sallow; *informal* like death warmed up. **2** *pallid watercolours* INSIPID, uninspired, colourless, uninteresting, unexciting, unimaginative, lifeless, spiritless, sterile, bland.

pallor ● noun PALENESS, pallidness, lack of colour, wanness, ashen hue, pastiness, peakiness, greyness, sickliness, sallowness.

pally ● adjective *(informal)* FRIENDLY, on good terms, close, intimate; *informal* matey, buddy-buddy.

palm[1] ● noun
– PHRASES **grease someone's palm** *(informal)* BRIBE, buy (off), corrupt, suborn, give an inducement to; *informal* give a backhander to, give a sweetener to. **have someone in the palm of one's hand** HAVE CONTROL OVER, have influence over, have someone eating out of one's hand, have someone on a string; *N. Amer.* have someone in one's hip pocket. **palm something off** FOIST, fob off, get rid of, dispose of, unload.

palm[2] ● noun *the palm of victory* PRIZE, trophy, award, crown, laurel wreath, laurels, bays.

palmistry ● noun FORTUNE TELLING, palm-reading, clairvoyancy, chiromancy.

palmy ● adjective HAPPY, fortunate, glorious, prosperous, halcyon, golden, rosy.

palpable ● adjective **1** *a palpable bump* TANGIBLE, touchable, noticeable, detectable. **2** *his reluctance was palpable* PERCEPTIBLE, perceivable, visible, noticeable, discernible, detectable, observable, tangible, unmistakable, transparent, self-evident; obvious, clear, plain (to see), evident, apparent, manifest, staring one in the face, written all over someone.
– OPPOSITES imperceptible.

palpitate ● verb **1** *her heart began to palpitate* BEAT RAPIDLY, pound, throb, pulsate, pulse, thud, thump, hammer, race. **2** *palpitating with terror* TREMBLE, quiver, quake, shake (like a leaf).

paltry ● adjective **1** *a paltry sum of money* SMALL, meagre, trifling, insignificant, negligible, inadequate, insufficient, derisory, pitiful,

palynology /palinolləji/ • noun the study of pollen grains and other spores, especially as found in archaeological or geological deposits.
– DERIVATIVES **palynological** adjective **palynologist** noun.
– ORIGIN from Greek *palunein* 'sprinkle'.
pampas /pampəss/ • noun (treated as sing. or pl.) large treeless plains in South America.
– ORIGIN Quechua, 'plain'.
pampas grass • noun a tall South American grass with silky flowering plumes.
pamper • verb indulge (someone) with a great deal of attention and comfort; spoil.
– ORIGIN originally meaning 'cram with food': probably from Low German or Dutch.
pamphlet /pamflit/ • noun a small booklet or leaflet containing information or arguments about a single subject. • verb (**pamphleted**, **pamphleting**) distribute pamphlets to.
– ORIGIN from *Pamphilet*, the familiar name of the 12th-century Latin love poem *Pamphilus, seu de Amore*.
pamphleteer • noun a writer of pamphlets, especially controversial political ones.
– DERIVATIVES **pamphleteering** noun.
pan¹ /pan/ • noun **1** a metal container for cooking food in. **2** a bowl fitted at either end of a pair of scales. **3** Brit. the bowl of a toilet. **4** a shallow bowl in which gravel and mud is shaken and washed by people seeking gold. **5** a hollow in the ground in which water collects or in which salt is deposited after evaporation. **6** a part of the lock that held the priming in old types of gun. **7** a steel drum. • verb (**panned**, **panning**) **1** informal criticize severely. **2** (**pan out**) informal end up or conclude. **3** wash gravel in a pan to separate out (gold).
– PHRASES **go down the pan** informal fail or be totally useless.
– ORIGIN Old English, perhaps from Latin *patina* 'dish'.
pan² /pan/ • verb (**panned**, **panning**) swing (a video or film camera) to give a panoramic effect or follow a subject. • noun a panning movement.
– ORIGIN abbreviation of PANORAMA.
pan³ /paan/ • noun variant spelling of PAAN.
pan- • combining form including everything or everyone, especially the whole of a continent, people, etc: *pan-African*.
– ORIGIN Greek, from *pas* 'all'.
panacea /pannəseeə/ • noun a solution or remedy for all difficulties or diseases.
– ORIGIN Greek *panakeia*, from *panakēs* 'all-healing'.
panache /pənash/ • noun flamboyant confidence of style or manner.
– ORIGIN originally denoting a tuft or plume of feathers: from French, from Latin *pinnaculum* 'little feather'.
panama • noun a man's wide-brimmed hat of straw-like material, originally made from the leaves of a tropical palm tree.
– ORIGIN named after the country of *Panama*.
Panamanian /pannəmayniən/ • noun a person from Panama. • adjective relating to Panama.
panatella /pannətellə/ • noun a long thin cigar.
– ORIGIN Latin American Spanish *panatela* 'long thin biscuit'.
pancake • noun **1** a thin, flat cake of batter, fried and turned in a pan. **2** theatrical make-up consisting of a flat solid layer of compressed powder. • verb **1** (of an aircraft) make a pancake landing. **2** informal flatten or become flattened.
– PHRASES (**as**) **flat as a pancake** completely flat.
Pancake Day • noun Shrove Tuesday, when pancakes are traditionally eaten.
pancake landing • noun an emergency landing in which an aircraft levels out close to the ground and drops vertically with its undercarriage still retracted.
pancake race • noun a race in which each competitor must toss a pancake from a pan as they run.
pancetta /panchettə/ • noun Italian cured belly of pork.
– ORIGIN Italian, 'little belly'.
panchromatic • adjective (of black-and-white photographic film) sensitive to all visible colours of the spectrum.
pancreas /pangkriəss/ • noun (pl. **pancreases**) a large gland behind the stomach which secretes digestive enzymes into the duodenum.
– DERIVATIVES **pancreatic** adjective.
– ORIGIN from Greek *pan* 'all' + *kreas* 'flesh'.
pancreatitis /pangkriətitiss/ • noun Medicine inflammation of the pancreas.
panda • noun **1** (also **giant panda**) a large black-and-white bear-like mammal native to bamboo forests in China. **2** (also **red panda**) a raccoon-like Himalayan mammal with thick reddish-brown fur and a bushy tail.
– ORIGIN Nepali.
panda car • noun Brit. informal a small police patrol car (originally black and white or blue and white).
pandanus /pandaynəss, -dann-/ • noun a tropical tree or shrub with a twisted stem, long, narrow spiny leaves that yield fibre, and fibrous edible fruit.
– ORIGIN Malay.
pandemic /pandemmik/ • adjective (of a disease) prevalent over a whole country or large part of the world. • noun an outbreak of such a disease.
– ORIGIN from Greek *pan* 'all' + *dēmos* 'people'.
pandemonium /pandimōniəm/ • noun wild and noisy disorder or confusion; uproar.
– ORIGIN originally meaning 'the place of all demons', in Milton's *Paradise Lost*: from Greek *pan* 'all' + *daimōn* 'demon'.
pander • verb (**pander to**) gratify or indulge (an immoral or distasteful desire or habit). • noun dated a pimp or procurer.
– ORIGIN from *Pandare*, a character in Chaucer's *Troilus and Criseyde* who acts as a lovers' go-between.
pandit (also **pundit**) • noun a Hindu scholar learned in Sanskrit and Hindu philosophy and religion.
– ORIGIN from Sanskrit, 'learned'.
Pandora's box • noun a process that once begun generates many complicated problems.
– ORIGIN from *Pandora* in Greek mythology, who was sent to earth with a jar or box of evils and contrary to instructions opened it, letting the evils escape.
pane • noun **1** a single sheet of glass in a window or door. **2** a sheet or page of stamps.
– ORIGIN Latin *pannus* 'piece of cloth'.
paneer /pəneer/ • noun a type of milk curd cheese used in Indian, Iranian, and Afghan cooking.
– ORIGIN Hindi or Persian, 'cheese'.
panegyric /pannijirrik/ • noun a speech or text in praise of someone or something.
– DERIVATIVES **panegyrical** adjective.

Thesaurus

pathetic, miserable, niggardly, beggarly; *informal* measly, piddling, poxy; *formal* exiguous. **2** *naval glory struck him as paltry* WORTHLESS, petty, trivial, unimportant, insignificant, inconsequential, of little account.
– OPPOSITES considerable.
pamper • verb SPOIL, indulge, overindulge, cosset, mollycoddle, coddle, baby, wait on someone hand and foot.
pamphlet • noun BROCHURE, leaflet, booklet, circular, flyer, handbill; *N. Amer.* mailer, folder, dodger.
pan¹ • noun **1** *a heavy pan* SAUCEPAN, frying pan, wok, skillet. **2** *salt pans* HOLLOW, pit, depression, dip, crater, concavity.
• verb **1** *(informal) the movie was panned by the critics.* See CRITICIZE. **2** *prospectors panned for gold* SIFT FOR, search for, look for.
– OPPOSITES praise.
– PHRASES **pan out 1** *Harold's idea hadn't panned out* SUCCEED, be successful, work (out), turn out well. **2** *the deal panned out badly* TURN OUT, work out, end (up), come out, fall out, evolve; *formal* eventuate.
pan² • verb *the camera panned to the building* SWING (ROUND), sweep, move, turn, circle.
panacea • noun UNIVERSAL CURE, cure-all, cure for all ills, universal remedy, elixir, wonder drug; *informal* magic bullet.
panache • noun FLAMBOYANCE, confidence, self-assurance, style, stylishness, flair, elan, dash, verve, zest, spirit, brio, éclat, vivacity, gusto, liveliness, vitality, energy; *informal* pizzazz, oomph, zip, zing.
pancake • noun CRÊPE, galette; blin, tortilla, tostada, chapatti, dosa, latke, blintze; *N. Amer.* flapjack, slapjack.
pandemic • adjective WIDESPREAD, prevalent, pervasive, rife, rampant.
pandemonium • noun BEDLAM, chaos, mayhem, uproar, turmoil, tumult, commotion, confusion, anarchy, furore, hubbub, rumpus; *informal* hullabaloo.
– OPPOSITES peace.
pander • verb
– PHRASES **pander to** INDULGE, gratify, satisfy, cater to, give in to,

– ORIGIN from Greek *panēgurikos* 'of public assembly'.

panegyrize /pannijirīz/ (also **panegyrise**) ● verb speak or write in praise of.
– DERIVATIVES **panegyrist** noun.

panel ● noun **1** a distinct, usually rectangular section of a door, vehicle, garment, etc. **2** a flat board on which instruments or controls are fixed. **3** a small group of people brought together to investigate or decide on a matter. **4** chiefly N. Amer. a jury, or a list of available jurors.
– DERIVATIVES **panelled** (US **paneled**) adjective.
– ORIGIN originally in the sense 'piece of parchment or cloth', later 'list': from Latin *pannus* 'piece of cloth'.

panel beater ● noun Brit. a person whose job is to beat out the bodywork of motor vehicles.

panel game ● noun Brit. a broadcast quiz played by a team of people.

panelling (US **paneling**) ● noun panels collectively, when used to decorate a wall.

panellist (US **panelist**) ● noun a member of a panel, especially in a broadcast game or discussion.

panel pin ● noun Brit. a light, thin nail with a very small head.

panel saw ● noun Brit. a light saw with small teeth, for cutting thin wood.

panel truck ● noun N. Amer. a small enclosed delivery truck.

panettone /pannitōnay/ ● noun (pl. **panettoni** /pannitōni/) a rich Italian bread with fruit, eaten at Christmas.
– ORIGIN Italian, from *pane* 'bread'.

pan-fry ● verb (**pan-fries**, **pan-frying**, **pan-fried**) fry in a pan in shallow fat.

pang ● noun a sudden sharp pain or painful emotion.
– ORIGIN perhaps an alteration of PRONG.

panga /pangga/ ● noun a bladed African tool like a machete.
– ORIGIN Swahili.

Pangloss /panggloss/ ● noun a person who is optimistic regardless of the circumstances.
– DERIVATIVES **Panglossian** adjective.
– ORIGIN from the name of the tutor and philosopher in Voltaire's *Candide* (1759).

pangolin /panggōlin/ ● noun an insect-eating mammal whose body is covered with horny overlapping scales.
– ORIGIN Malay, 'roller' (from the animal's habit of rolling into a ball).

panhandle N. Amer. ● noun a narrow strip of territory projecting from the main territory of one state into another. ● verb informal beg in the street.
– DERIVATIVES **panhandler** noun.

panic ● noun **1** sudden uncontrollable fear or anxiety. **2** informal frenzied hurry to do something. ● verb (**panicked**, **panicking**) feel or cause to feel panic.
– DERIVATIVES **panicky** adjective.
– ORIGIN from the name of the Greek god *Pan*, noted for causing terror.

panic attack ● noun a sudden overwhelming feeling of acute and disabling anxiety.

panic button ● noun a button for summoning help in an emergency.

panicle /pannik'l/ ● noun Botany a loose branching cluster of flowers, as in oats.
– ORIGIN Latin *panicula*, from *panus* 'ear of millet'.

panic stations ● plural noun (treated as sing.) Brit. informal a state of alarm or emergency.

panino /paneenō/ ● noun (pl. **panini** /paneeni/) a filled sandwich made with a baguette or Italian bread roll.
– ORIGIN Italian, 'bread roll'.

Panjabi ● noun (pl. **Panjabis**) & adjective variant spelling of PUNJABI.

panjandrum /panjandrəm/ ● noun a person who has or claims to have a great deal of authority or influence.
– ORIGIN from *Grand Panjandrum*, an invented phrase in a nonsense verse (1755) by Samuel Foote.

pannage /pannij/ ● noun chiefly historical the right of feeding pigs or other animals in a wood.
– ORIGIN Old French *pasnage*, from Latin *pastio* 'pasturing'.

panne /pan/ ● noun a shining fabric resembling velvet, with a flattened pile.
– ORIGIN French.

pannier ● noun **1** a bag or box fitted on either side of the rear wheel of a bicycle or motorcycle. **2** a basket, especially each of a pair carried by a beast of burden. **3** historical part of a skirt looped up round the hips and supported on a frame.
– ORIGIN Old French *panier*, from Latin *panarium* 'bread basket'.

pannikin ● noun a small metal drinking cup.

panoply /pannəpli/ ● noun a complete or impressive collection or display.
– DERIVATIVES **panoplied** adjective.
– ORIGIN originally in the sense 'complete protection', later 'complete set of arms or suit of armour': from Greek *pan* 'all' + *hopla* 'arms'.

panoptic /panoptik/ ● adjective showing or seeing the whole at one view.
– ORIGIN Greek *panoptos* 'seen by all'.

panopticon /panoptikən/ ● noun historical a circular prison with cells arranged around a central well, from which prisoners could at all times be observed.

panorama ● noun **1** an unbroken view of a surrounding region. **2** a complete survey of a subject or sequence of events.
– DERIVATIVES **panoramic** adjective **panoramically** adverb.
– ORIGIN from Greek *pan* 'all' + *horama* 'view'.

pan pipes ● plural noun a musical instrument made from a row of short pipes fixed together.
– ORIGIN from the name of the Greek rural god *Pan*.

pansexual ● adjective another term for OMNISEXUAL.

panstick ● noun a kind of matt cosmetic foundation in stick form, used in theatrical make-up.
– ORIGIN from PANCAKE + STICK[1].

pansy ● noun **1** a plant of the viola family, with flowers in rich colours. **2** informal, derogatory an effeminate or homosexual man.
– ORIGIN French *pensée* 'thought, pansy'.

pant ● verb **1** breathe with short, quick breaths, typically from exertion or excitement. **2** (usu. **pant for**) long for or to do something. ● noun a short, quick breath.
– ORIGIN Old French *pantaisier* 'be agitated, gasp', from Greek *phantasioun* 'cause to imagine'.

Pantagruelian /pantəgrooelliən/ ● adjective literary enormous.

p

Thesaurus

accommodate, comply with.

pane ● noun SHEET OF GLASS, windowpane.

panegyric ● noun EULOGY, speech of praise, paean, accolade, tribute.

panel ● noun **1** *a control panel* CONSOLE, instrument panel, dashboard; instruments, controls, dials. **2** *a panel of judges* GROUP, team, body, committee, board.

pang ● noun **1** *hunger pangs* (SHARP) PAIN, shooting pain, twinge, stab, spasm. **2** *a pang of remorse* QUALM, twinge, prick.

panic ● noun *a wave of panic* ALARM, anxiety, nervousness, fear, fright, trepidation, dread, terror, agitation, hysteria, consternation, perturbation, dismay, apprehension; *informal* flap, fluster, cold sweat, funk, tizzy; *N. Amer. informal* swivet.
● verb **1** *there's no need to panic* BE ALARMED, be scared, be nervous, be afraid, take fright, be agitated, be hysterical, lose one's nerve, get overwrought, get worked up; *informal* flap, get in a flap, lose one's cool, get into a tizzy, run around like a headless chicken, freak out, get in a stew; *Brit. informal* get the wind up, go into a (flat) spin, have kittens. **2** *talk of love panicked her* FRIGHTEN, alarm, scare, unnerve; *informal* throw into a tizzy, freak out; *Brit. informal* put the wind up.

panic-stricken ● adjective ALARMED, frightened, scared (stiff), terrified, terror-stricken, petrified, horrified, horror-stricken, fearful, afraid, panicky, frantic, in a frenzy, nervous, agitated, hysterical, beside oneself, worked up, overwrought; *informal* in a cold sweat, in a (blue) funk, in a flap, in a fluster, in a tizzy; *Brit. informal* in a flat spin.

panoply ● noun **1** *the full panoply of America's military might* ARRAY, range, collection. **2** *all the panoply of religious liturgy* TRAPPINGS, regalia; splendour, spectacle, ceremony, ritual.

panorama ● noun **1** *he surveyed the panorama* (SCENIC) VIEW, vista, prospect, scene, scenery, landscape, seascape. **2** *a panorama of the art scene* OVERVIEW, survey, review, presentation, appraisal.

panoramic ● adjective **1** *a panoramic view* SWEEPING, wide, extensive, scenic, commanding. **2** *a panoramic look at the 20th century* WIDE-RANGING, extensive, broad, far-reaching, comprehensive, all-embracing.

pant ● verb **1** *he was panting as they reached the top* BREATHE HEAVILY, breathe hard, puff (and blow), huff and puff, gasp, wheeze. **2** *it makes you pant for more* YEARN FOR, long for, crave, hanker

– ORIGIN from *Pantagruel*, the name of a giant in Rabelais' *Gargantua and Pantagruel* (1532).

pantalettes (chiefly N. Amer. also **pantalets**) ● plural noun women's long underpants with a frill at the bottom of each leg, worn in the 19th century.

pantaloons ● plural noun **1** women's baggy trousers gathered at the ankles. **2** historical men's close-fitting breeches fastened below the calf or at the foot.
– ORIGIN from *Pantalone*, a character in Italian commedia dell'arte represented as a foolish old man wearing pantaloons.

pantechnicon /panteknikən/ ● noun Brit. a large van for transporting furniture.
– ORIGIN from Greek *pan* 'all' + *tekhnikon* 'piece of art', originally the name of a London bazaar selling artistic work, later converted into a furniture warehouse.

pantheism /panthi-iz'm/ ● noun **1** the belief that God can be identified with the universe, or that the universe is a manifestation of God. **2** rare worship that admits or tolerates all gods.
– DERIVATIVES **pantheist** noun **pantheistic** adjective.

pantheon /panthiən/ ● noun **1** all the gods of a people or religion collectively. **2** an ancient temple dedicated to all the gods. **3** a collection of particularly famous or important people.
– ORIGIN originally referring especially to a circular temple in Rome: from Greek *pan* 'all' + *theion* 'holy'.

panther ● noun **1** a leopard, especially a black one. **2** N. Amer. a puma or a jaguar.
– ORIGIN Greek *panthēr*.

panties ● plural noun informal legless underpants worn by women and girls; knickers.

pantihose ● plural noun variant spelling of PANTYHOSE.

pantile /pantīl/ ● noun a roof tile curved to form an S-shaped section, fitted to overlap its neighbour.
– ORIGIN from PAN[1] + TILE.

panto ● noun (pl. **pantos**) Brit. informal a pantomime.

panto- ● combining form all; universal: *pantomime*.
– ORIGIN from Greek *pas* 'all'.

pantograph ● noun **1** an instrument for copying a plan or drawing on a different scale by a system of hinged and jointed rods. **2** a jointed framework conveying a current to an electric train or tram from overhead wires.

pantomime ● noun **1** Brit. a theatrical entertainment involving music, topical jokes, and slapstick comedy, usually produced around Christmas. **2** informal a ridiculous or confused action or situation. ● verb express or represent by extravagant and exaggerated mime.
– ORIGIN originally in the sense 'actor using mime', later 'entertainment in which performers mime': from Greek *pantomimos* 'imitator of all'.

p

pantothenic acid /pantəthennik/ ● noun Biochemistry a vitamin of the B complex, found in rice, bran, and other foods, and essential for the oxidation of fats and carbohydrates.
– ORIGIN from Greek *pantothen* 'from every side' (alluding to its widespread occurrence).

pantry ● noun (pl. **pantries**) a small room or cupboard in which food, crockery, and cutlery are kept.
– ORIGIN from Old French *paneter* 'baker', from Latin *panis* 'bread'.

pants ● plural noun **1** Brit. underpants or knickers. **2** chiefly N. Amer. trousers. **3** Brit. informal rubbish; nonsense.
– PHRASES **catch someone with their pants** (or **trousers**) **down** informal catch someone in an embarrassingly unprepared state. **fly** (or **drive**) **by the seat of one's pants** informal rely on instinct rather than logic or knowledge. **scare** (or **bore** etc.) **the pants off** informal make extremely scared, bored, etc.
– ORIGIN abbreviation of PANTALOONS.

pantsuit (also **pants suit**) ● noun chiefly N. Amer. a trouser suit.

panty girdle (also **pantie girdle**) ● noun a woman's control undergarment with a crotch shaped like pants.

pantyhose (also **pantihose**) ● plural noun N. Amer. women's thin nylon tights.

pantywaist ● noun N. Amer. informal a feeble or effeminate person.
– ORIGIN from the literal sense 'child's garment consisting of panties attached to a bodice'.

panzer /panzər/ ● noun a German armoured unit.
– ORIGIN German, 'coat of mail'.

pap[1] ● noun **1** bland soft or semi-liquid food suitable for babies or invalids. **2** (in Africa and the Caribbean) maize porridge. **3** worthless or trivial reading matter or entertainment.
– ORIGIN probably from Latin *pappare* 'eat'.

pap[2] ● noun archaic or dialect a woman's breast or nipple.
– ORIGIN probably Scandinavian.

papa /pəpaa/ ● noun N. Amer. or dated one's father.
– ORIGIN French, from Greek *papas*.

papacy /paypəsi/ ● noun (pl. **papacies**) the pope's office or tenure.
– ORIGIN from Latin *papa* 'pope'.

papain /pəpayin/ ● noun a protein-digesting enzyme obtained from unripe papaya fruit, used to tenderize meat and as a food supplement.

papal /payp'l/ ● adjective relating to the pope or the papacy.
– DERIVATIVES **papally** adverb.

paparazzo /pappəratsō/ ● noun (pl. **paparazzi** /pappəratsi/) a freelance photographer who pursues celebrities to get photographs of them.
– ORIGIN Italian, the name of a character in Fellini's film *La Dolce Vita* (1960).

papaw /pəpaw/ ● noun variant spelling of PAWPAW.

papaya /pəpiə/ ● noun a tropical fruit like an elongated melon, with edible orange flesh and small black seeds.
– ORIGIN Spanish and Portuguese, from Carib.

paper ● noun **1** material manufactured in thin sheets from the pulp of wood or other fibrous substances, used for writing or printing on or as wrapping material. **2** (**papers**) sheets of paper covered with writing or printing; documents. **3** (before another noun) officially documented but having no real existence or use: *a paper profit*. **4** a newspaper. **5** a government report or policy document. **6** an essay or dissertation read at a seminar or published in a journal. **7** a set of examination questions. ● verb **1** cover with wallpaper. **2** (**paper over**) disguise (an awkward problem) instead of resolving it. **3** theatrical slang fill (a theatre) by giving out free tickets.
– PHRASES **on paper 1** in writing. **2** in theory rather than in reality.
– DERIVATIVES **paperless** adjective **papery** noun.
– ORIGIN Old French *papir*, from Latin *papyrus* 'paper-reed' (see PAPYRUS).

paperback ● noun a book bound in stiff paper or flexible card.

paper boy (or **paper girl**) ● noun a boy (or girl) who delivers newspapers to people's homes.

paperchase ● noun Brit. a cross-country race in which the run-

Thesaurus

after/for, ache for, hunger for, thirst for, be hungry for, be thirsty for, wish for, desire, want; *informal* itch for, be dying for; *archaic* be athirst for.
● noun *breathing in shallow pants* GASP, puff, wheeze, breath.

panting ● adjective OUT OF BREATH, breathless, short of breath, puffed out, puffing (and blowing), huffing and puffing, gasping (for breath), wheezing, wheezy.

pantry ● noun LARDER, store, storeroom; *Brit. historical* still room; *archaic* spence.

pants ● plural noun **1** *(Brit.)* UNDERPANTS, briefs, Y-fronts, boxer shorts, boxers, long johns, (French) knickers, bikini briefs; *Brit.* camiknickers; *N. Amer.* shorts, undershorts; *informal* panties; *Brit. informal* kecks, knicks, smalls; *dated* drawers, bloomers, unmentionables; *N. Amer. dated* step-ins. **2** *(N. Amer.)*. See TROUSERS.

pap ● noun **1** *tasteless pap* SOFT FOOD, mush, slop, pulp, purée, mash; *informal* goo, gloop, gook; *N. Amer. informal* glop. **2** *commercial pap* TRIVIA, pulp (fiction), rubbish, nonsense, froth; *Brit.* candyfloss; *informal* dreck, drivel, trash, twaddle.

paper ● noun **1** *a sheet of paper* writing paper, notepaper, foolscap. **2** *the local paper* NEWSPAPER, journal, gazette, periodical; tabloid, broadsheet, quality paper, daily, weekly, evening paper, Sunday paper; *informal* rag; *N. Amer. informal* tab. **3** *the paper was peeling off the walls* WALLPAPER, wallcovering; *Brit.* woodchip; *trademark* Anaglypta. **4** *toffee papers* WRAPPER, wrapping. **5** *a three-hour paper* EXAM, examination, test. **6** *he has just published a paper* ESSAY, article, monograph, thesis, work, dissertation, treatise, study, report, analysis, tract, critique, exegesis, review; *N. Amer.* theme. **7** *personal papers* DOCUMENTS, certificates, letters, files, deeds, records, archives, paperwork, documentation; *Law* muniments. **8** *they asked us for our papers* IDENTIFICATION PAPERS/DOCUMENTS, identity card, ID, credentials.
● verb *we papered the walls* WALLPAPER, hang wallpaper on.
– PHRASES **paper something over** COVER UP, hide, conceal, disguise, camouflage, gloss over. **on paper 1** *he put his thoughts down on*

ners follow a trail marked by torn-up paper.
paper clip • noun a piece of bent wire or plastic used for holding several sheets of paper together.
paperknife • noun a blunt knife used for opening envelopes.
paper money • noun money in the form of banknotes.
paper round (N. Amer. **paper route**) • noun a job of regularly delivering newspapers.
paper-thin • adjective very thin or insubstantial.
paper tiger • noun a person or thing that appears threatening but is ineffectual.
paper trail • noun chiefly N. Amer. the total amount of written evidence of someone's activities.
paperweight • noun a small, heavy object for keeping loose papers in place.
paperwork • noun routine work involving written documents.
papier mâché /papyay mashay/ • noun a malleable mixture of paper and glue that becomes hard when dry.
– ORIGIN French, 'chewed paper'.
papilla /pəpillə/ • noun (pl. **papillae** /pəpillee/) **1** a small rounded protuberance on a part or organ of the body. **2** a small fleshy projection on a plant.
– DERIVATIVES **papillary** adjective.
– ORIGIN Latin, 'nipple'.
papilloma /pappilōmə/ • noun (pl. **papillomas** or **papillomata** /pappilōmətə/) Medicine a small wart-like growth, usually benign.
papillon /pappiyoN/ • noun a dog of a toy breed with ears suggesting the form of a butterfly.
– ORIGIN French, 'butterfly'.
papist /paypist/ chiefly derogatory • noun **1** a Roman Catholic. **2** a supporter of the papacy. • adjective **1** Roman Catholic. **2** supporting the papacy.
– DERIVATIVES **papism** noun **papistry** noun.
papoose /pəpōōss/ • noun chiefly offensive a young North American Indian child.
– ORIGIN Algonquian.
pappardelle /papaardellay/ • plural noun pasta in the form of broad flat ribbons.
– ORIGIN Italian, from *pappare* 'eat hungrily'.
pappus /pappəss/ • noun (pl. **pappi** /pappī/) Botany a tuft of hairs on a seed which helps the seed be carried by the wind.
– ORIGIN Greek *pappos*.
pappy[1] • noun (pl. **pappies**) a child's word for father.
pappy[2] • adjective of the nature of pap.
paprika /paprikə, pəpreekə/ • noun a deep orange-red powdered spice made from certain varieties of sweet pepper.
– ORIGIN Hungarian.
Pap test • noun a smear test carried out to detect cancer of the cervix or womb.
– ORIGIN named after the American scientist George N. *Papanicolaou* (1883–1962).
Papuan • noun **1** a person from Papua or Papua New Guinea. **2** a group of languages spoken in Papua New Guinea and neighbouring islands. • adjective relating to Papua or its languages.
papule /papyōōl/ • noun Medicine a small pimple or swelling on the skin, often forming part of a rash.
– ORIGIN Latin *papula*.
papyrus /pəpīrəss/ • noun (pl. **papyri** /pəpīrī/ or **papyruses**) **1** a material prepared in ancient Egypt from the pithy stem of a water plant, used for writing or painting on. **2** the tall aquatic sedge from which papyrus was obtained.
– ORIGIN Greek *papuros*.

par • noun **1** Golf the number of strokes a first-class player should normally require for a particular hole or course. **2** (usu. in phrases **above** or **below** or **under par**) the usual or expected level or amount. **3** Stock Exchange the face value of a share or other security. • verb (**parred**, **parring**) Golf play (a hole) in par.
– PHRASES **on a par with** equal to. **par for the course** what is normal or expected in any given circumstances.
– ORIGIN Latin, 'equal', also 'equality'.
para[1] /parrə/ • noun informal a paratrooper.
para[2] /parrə/ • noun (pl. same or **paras**) a monetary unit of Bosnia–Herzegovina, Montenegro, and Serbia, equal to one hundredth of a dinar.
– ORIGIN Turkish, from Persian 'piece, portion'.
para- (also **par-**) • prefix **1** beside; adjacent to: *parathyroid*. **2** beyond or distinct from, but comparable to: *paramilitary*.
– ORIGIN from Greek *para* 'beside, beyond'.
parable • noun a simple story used to illustrate a moral or spiritual lesson.
– ORIGIN Latin *parabola* 'comparison, discourse, allegory', from Greek *parabolē* (see PARABOLA).
parabola /pərabbələ/ • noun (pl. **parabolas** or **parabolae** /pərabbəlee/) a symmetrical open plane curve of the kind formed by the intersection of a cone with a plane parallel to its side.
– ORIGIN Latin, from Greek *parabolē* 'placing side by side'.
parabolic /parrəbollik/ • adjective **1** of or like a parabola or part of one. **2** of or expressed in parables.
paraboloid /pərabbəloyd/ • noun a three-dimensional figure generated by rotating a parabola about its axis of symmetry.
paracetamol /parrəseetəmol, -settə-/ • noun (pl. same or **paracetamols**) Brit. a synthetic compound used to relieve pain and reduce fever.
– ORIGIN abbreviation of its chemical name.
parachute • noun a cloth canopy which allows a person or heavy object attached to it to descend slowly when dropped from a high position. • verb drop or cause to drop by parachute.
– DERIVATIVES **parachutist** noun.
– ORIGIN from French *para-* 'protection against' + *chute* 'fall'.
Paraclete /parrəkleet/ • noun (in Christian theology) the Holy Spirit as advocate or counsellor.
– ORIGIN from Greek *paraklētos* 'called in aid'.
paracrine /parrəkrīn/ • adjective Physiology referring or relating to a hormone which has an effect only in the vicinity of the gland secreting it.
– ORIGIN from PARA- + Greek *krinein* 'to separate'.
parade • noun **1** a public procession. **2** a formal march or gathering of troops for inspection or display. **3** a series or succession. **4** a boastful or ostentatious display. **5** Brit. a public square, promenade, or row of shops. • verb **1** walk, march, or display in a parade. **2** display (something) publicly in order to impress or attract attention. **3** (**parade as**) appear falsely as.
– ORIGIN French, 'a showing', from Latin *parare* 'prepare'.
parade ground • noun a place where troops gather for parade.
paradiddle /parrədidd'l/ • noun Music a simple drum roll consisting of four even strokes.
– ORIGIN imitative.
paradigm /parrədīm/ • noun **1** a typical example, pattern, or model of something. **2** a conceptual model underlying the theories and practice of a scientific subject. **3** Grammar a table of all the inflected forms of a word, serving as a model for other words of the same conjugation or declension.
– DERIVATIVES **paradigmatic** /parrədigmattik/ adjective **paradigmatically** adverb.

Thesaurus

paper IN WRITING, in black and white, in print. **2** *the combatants were evenly matched on paper* IN THEORY, theoretically, supposedly.
papery • adjective THIN, paper-thin, flimsy, delicate, insubstantial, light, lightweight.
par • noun
– PHRASES **below par 1** *their performances have been below par* SUBSTANDARD, inferior, not up to scratch, under par, below average, second-rate, mediocre, poor, undistinguished; *informal* not up to snuff; *N. Amer. informal* bush-league. **2** *I'm feeling below par* SLIGHTLY UNWELL, not (very) well, not oneself, out of sorts; ill, unwell, poorly, washed out, run down, peaky; *Brit.* off (colour); *informal* under the weather, not up to snuff, lousy, rough; *Brit. informal* ropy, grotty; *Austral./NZ informal* crook; *dated* queer. **on a par with** AS GOOD AS, comparable with, in the same class/league as, equivalent to, equal to, on a level with, of the same standard as. **par for the course** NORMAL, typical, standard, usual, what one would expect. **up to par** GOOD ENOUGH, up to the mark, satisfactory, acceptable, adequate, up to scratch; *informal* up to snuff.
parable • noun ALLEGORY, moral story/tale, fable, exemplum, apologue.
parade • noun **1** *a St George's Day parade* PROCESSION, march, cavalcade, motorcade, spectacle, display, pageant; review, dress parade, tattoo; *Brit.* march past. **2** *she made a great parade of doing the housework* EXHIBITION, show, display, performance, spectacle, fuss; *informal* hoo-ha, to-do. **3** *she walked along the parade* PROMENADE, walkway, esplanade, mall; *N. Amer.* boardwalk; *Brit. informal* prom.
• verb **1** *the teams paraded through the city* MARCH, process, file,

– ORIGIN Greek *paradeigma*, from *paradeiknunai* 'show side by side'.

paradigm shift ● noun a fundamental change in approach or underlying assumptions.

paradise /parrədīss/ ● noun **1** (in some religions) heaven as the place where the good live after death. **2** the Garden of Eden. **3** an ideal or idyllic place or state.
– DERIVATIVES **paradisal** adjective **paradisiacal** /parrədisīək'l/ (also **paradisical** /parrədissik'l/) adjective.
– ORIGIN Old French *paradis*, from Greek *paradeisos* 'royal park'.

parador /parrədor/ ● noun (pl. **paradors** or **paradores** /parrədorayz/) a hotel in Spain owned and administered by the government.
– ORIGIN Spanish.

paradox ● noun **1** a seemingly absurd or self-contradictory statement or proposition that may in fact be true. **2** a person or thing that combines contradictory features or qualities.
– DERIVATIVES **paradoxical** adjective **paradoxically** adverb.
– ORIGIN originally in the sense 'statement contrary to accepted opinion': from Greek *paradoxon* 'contrary opinion'.

paraffin ● noun **1** (Brit. **paraffin wax**) a flammable waxy solid obtained from petroleum or shale and used for sealing and waterproofing and in candles. **2** (also **paraffin oil** or **liquid paraffin**) Brit. a liquid fuel made similarly, especially kerosene. **3** Chemistry old-fashioned term for ALKANE.
– ORIGIN German, from Latin *parum* 'little' + *affinis* 'related' (from its low reactivity).

paragliding ● noun a sport in which a person glides through the air by means of a wide parachute after jumping from or being hauled to a height.
– DERIVATIVES **paraglide** verb **paraglider** noun.

paragon ● noun **1** a model of excellence or of a particular quality. **2** a perfect diamond of 100 carats or more.
– ORIGIN Italian *paragone* 'touchstone'.

paragraph ● noun a distinct section of a piece of writing, beginning on a new line and often indented.
– ORIGIN French *paragraphe*, from Greek *paragraphos* 'short stroke marking a break in sense'.

paragraph mark ● noun a symbol (usually ¶) used to mark a new paragraph or as a reference mark.

Paraguayan /parrəgwīən/ ● noun a person from Paraguay. ● adjective relating to Paraguay.

parakeet /parrəkeet/ (also **parrakeet**) ● noun a small parrot with predominantly green plumage and a long tail.
– ORIGIN Old French *paroquet*, Italian *parrocchetto*, and Spanish *periquito*; related to PARROT.

paralegal chiefly N. Amer. ● adjective relating to auxiliary aspects of the law. ● noun a person trained in subsidiary legal matters but not fully qualified as a lawyer.

paralipsis /parrəlipsiss/ ● noun Rhetoric the device of giving emphasis by professing to say little or nothing of a subject, as in *not to mention their unpaid debts.*
– ORIGIN Greek *paraleipsis* 'passing over'.

parallax /parrəlaks/ ● noun **1** the apparent difference in the position of an object when viewed from different positions, e.g. through the viewfinder and the lens of a camera. **2** Astronomy the angular difference in the apparent positions of a star observed from opposite sides of the earth's orbit.
– DERIVATIVES **parallactic** adjective.
– ORIGIN Greek *parallaxis* 'a change'.

parallel ● adjective **1** (of lines, planes, or surfaces) side by side and having the same distance continuously between them. **2** occurring or existing at the same time or in a similar way; corresponding: *a parallel universe.* **3** Computing involving the simultaneous performance of operations. ● noun **1** a person or thing that is similar or comparable to another. **2** a similarity or comparison. **3** (also **parallel of latitude**) each of the imaginary parallel circles of constant latitude on the earth's surface. **4** Printing two parallel lines (‖) as a reference mark. ● verb (**paralleled**, **paralleling**) **1** run or lie parallel to. **2** be similar or corresponding to.
– PHRASES **in parallel 1** taking place at the same time and having some connection. **2** (of electrical components or circuits) connected to common points at each end, so that the current is divided between them.
– DERIVATIVES **parallelism** noun.
– ORIGIN Greek *parallēlos*, from *para-* 'alongside' + *allēlos* 'one another'.

parallel bars ● plural noun a pair of parallel rails on posts, used in gymnastics.

parallelepiped /parrəleleppiped, parrəlellipīped/ ● noun Geometry a solid body of which each face is a parallelogram.
– ORIGIN from Greek *parallēlos* 'beside another' + *epipedon* 'plane surface'.

parallel imports ● plural noun goods imported by unlicensed distributors for sale at less than the manufacturer's official retail price.

parallelogram /parrəlelləgram/ ● noun a plane figure with four straight sides and opposite sides parallel.

Paralympics ● plural noun (usu. treated as sing.) an international athletic competition for disabled athletes.
– DERIVATIVES **Paralympic** adjective.
– ORIGIN blend of *paraplegic* and *Olympics*.

paralyse (chiefly US also **paralyze**) ● verb **1** cause (a person or part of the body) to become partly or wholly incapable of movement. **2** bring to a standstill by causing disruption.

paralysis /pəralisiss/ ● noun (pl. **paralyses** /pəraliseez/) **1** the loss of the ability to move part or most of the body. **2** inability to act or function.
– ORIGIN Greek *paralusis*, from *paraluesthai* 'be disabled at the side'.

paralytic ● adjective **1** relating to paralysis. **2** informal, chiefly Brit.

Thesaurus

troop. **2** *she paraded up and down* STRUT, swagger, stride. **3** *he was keen to parade his knowledge* DISPLAY, exhibit, make a show of, flaunt, show (off), demonstrate.

paradigm ● noun MODEL, pattern, example, exemplar, standard, prototype, archetype.

paradisal ● adjective HEAVENLY, idyllic, blissful, divine, sublime, perfect.

paradise ● noun **1** *the souls in paradise* (THE KINGDOM OF) HEAVEN, the heavenly kingdom, Elysium, the Elysian Fields, Valhalla, Avalon. **2** *Adam and Eve's expulsion from Paradise* THE GARDEN OF EDEN, Eden. **3** *a tropical paradise* UTOPIA, Shangri-La, heaven, idyll, nirvana. **4** *this is sheer paradise!* BLISS, heaven, ecstasy, delight, joy, happiness, nirvana, heaven on earth.
– OPPOSITES hell.

paradox ● noun CONTRADICTION (IN TERMS), self-contradiction, inconsistency, incongruity, anomaly, conflict; enigma, puzzle, mystery, conundrum.

paradoxical ● adjective CONTRADICTORY, self-contradictory, inconsistent, incongruous, anomalous; illogical, puzzling, baffling, incomprehensible, inexplicable.

paragon ● noun PERFECT EXAMPLE, shining example, model, epitome, archetype, ideal, exemplar, nonpareil, embodiment, personification, quintessence, apotheosis, acme; jewel, gem, angel, treasure; *informal* one in a million, the tops; *archaic* a nonsuch.

paragraph ● noun **1** *the concluding paragraph* SECTION, subdivision, part, subsection, division, portion, segment, passage. **2** *a paragraph in the newspaper* REPORT, article, item, piece, write-up, mention.

parallel ● adjective **1** *parallel lines* SIDE BY SIDE, aligned, collateral, equidistant. **2** *parallel careers* SIMILAR, analogous, comparable, corresponding, like, of a kind, akin, related, equivalent, matching. **3** *a parallel universe* COEXISTING, coexistent, concurrent; contemporaneous, simultaneous, synchronous.
– OPPOSITES divergent.
● noun **1** *an exact parallel* COUNTERPART, analogue, equivalent, likeness, match, twin, duplicate, mirror. **2** *there is an interesting parallel between these figures* SIMILARITY, likeness, resemblance, analogy, correspondence, equivalence, correlation, relation, symmetry, parity.
● verb **1** *his experiences parallel mine* RESEMBLE, be similar to, be like, bear a resemblance to; correspond to, be analogous to, be comparable/equivalent to, equate with/to, correlate with, imitate, echo, remind one of, duplicate, mirror, follow, match. **2** *her performance has never been paralleled* EQUAL, match, rival, emulate.

paralyse ● verb **1** *both of his legs were paralysed* DISABLE, cripple, immobilize, incapacitate, debilitate; *formal* torpefy. **2** *Maisie was paralysed by the sight of him* IMMOBILIZE, transfix, become rooted to the spot, freeze, stun, render motionless. **3** *the capital was paralysed by a general strike* BRING TO A STANDSTILL, immobilize, bring to a (grinding) halt, freeze, cripple, disable.

paralysed ● adjective DISABLED, crippled, handicapped, incapaci-

extremely drunk.
– DERIVATIVES **paralytically** adverb.

paramagnetic • adjective very weakly attracted by a magnet, but not retaining any permanent magnetism.
– DERIVATIVES **paramagnetism** noun.

paramecium /parrəmeesiəm/ • noun Zoology a single-celled freshwater animal which has a characteristic slipper-like shape.
– ORIGIN Latin, from Greek *paramēkēs* 'oval'.

paramedic • noun a person who is trained to do medical work, especially emergency first aid, but is not a fully qualified doctor.
– DERIVATIVES **paramedical** adjective.

parameter /pərammitər/ • noun **1** a measurable or quantifiable characteristic of a system. **2** Mathematics a quantity which is fixed for the case in question but may vary in other cases. **3** a limit or boundary which defines the scope of a process or activity.
– DERIVATIVES **parametric** adjective **parametrically** adverb.
– ORIGIN from Greek *para-* 'beside' + *metron* 'measure'.

paramilitary • adjective organized on similar lines to a military force. • noun (pl. **paramilitaries**) a member of a paramilitary organization.

paramotor /parrəmōtər/ • noun (trademark in the US) a motorized and steerable parachute, powered by a motor and propeller strapped to the pilot's back.
– DERIVATIVES **paramotoring** noun.

paramount • adjective **1** more important than anything else; supreme. **2** having supreme power.
– DERIVATIVES **paramountcy** noun.
– ORIGIN from Old French *par* 'by' + *amont* 'above'.

paramour • noun archaic or derogatory a lover, especially the illicit partner of a married person.
– ORIGIN from Old French *par amour* 'by love'.

paranoia /parrənoyə/ • noun **1** a mental condition characterized by delusions of persecution, unwarranted jealousy, or exaggerated self-importance. **2** unjustified suspicion and mistrust of others.
– DERIVATIVES **paranoiac** /parrənoyik, -nōik/ (also **paranoic**) adjective & noun **paranoiacally** adverb.
– ORIGIN Latin, from Greek *para* 'irregular' + *noos* 'mind'.

paranoid • adjective of, characterized by, or suffering from paranoia. • noun a person who is paranoid.

paranormal • adjective supposedly beyond the scope of normal scientific understanding.
– DERIVATIVES **paranormally** adverb.

parapente /parrəpont/ • verb (usu. as noun **parapenting**) glide while suspended from a wing-like parachute launched from high ground. • noun a parachute used for this purpose.
– DERIVATIVES **parapenter** noun.
– ORIGIN French, from *para(chute)* + *pente* 'slope'.

parapet /parrəpit/ • noun **1** a low protective wall along the edge of a roof, bridge, or balcony. **2** a protective wall or bank along the top of a military trench.
– ORIGIN French, or from Italian *parapetto*, 'chest-high wall'.

paraphernalia /parrəfərnayliə/ • noun (treated as sing. or pl.) miscellaneous articles, especially the equipment needed for a particular activity.
– ORIGIN originally in the sense 'property owned by a married woman': from Latin, from Greek *parapherna* 'property apart from a dowry'.

paraphilia /parrəfilliə/ • noun Psychiatry a condition characterized by abnormal sexual desires involving extreme or dangerous activities.
– DERIVATIVES **paraphiliac** adjective & noun.

paraphrase • verb express the meaning of (something) using different words. • noun a rewording of a passage.

paraplegia /parrəpleejə/ • noun paralysis of the legs and lower body.
– DERIVATIVES **paraplegic** adjective & noun.
– ORIGIN Greek, from *paraplēssein* 'strike at the side'.

parapsychology • noun the study of mental phenomena which are outside the sphere of orthodox psychology (such as hypnosis or telepathy).
– DERIVATIVES **parapsychological** adjective **parapsychologist** noun.

paraquat /parrəkwot/ • noun a toxic fast-acting herbicide.
– ORIGIN from PARA- + QUATERNARY.

parasailing • noun the sport of gliding through the air wearing an open parachute while being towed by a motor boat.
– DERIVATIVES **parasail** noun & verb.

parascending • noun Brit. paragliding or parasailing.
– DERIVATIVES **parascend** verb **parascender** noun.

parasite • noun **1** an organism which lives in or on another organism and benefits at the other's expense. **2** derogatory a person who lives off or exploits others.
– DERIVATIVES **parasitism** noun **parasitology** noun.
– ORIGIN Greek *parasitos* 'person eating at another's table'.

parasitic /parrəsittik/ • adjective **1** (of an organism) living as a parasite. **2** resulting from infestation by a parasite. **3** derogatory habitually relying on or exploiting others.
– DERIVATIVES **parasitical** adjective **parasitically** adverb.

parasitize /parrəsitīz/ (also **parasitise**) • verb infest or exploit as a parasite.

parasitoid /parrəsitoyd/ • noun an insect (e.g. an ichneumon wasp) whose larvae live as parasites which eventually kill their hosts.

parasol • noun **1** a light umbrella used to give shade from the sun. **2** (also **parasol mushroom**) a tall mushroom with a broad scaly greyish-brown cap.
– ORIGIN Italian *parasole*, from *para-* 'protecting against' + *sole* 'sun'.

parastatal /parrəstayt'l/ • adjective (of an organization or industry) having some political authority and serving the state indirectly.

parasympathetic • adjective Physiology relating to a system of nerves arising from the brain and the lower end of the spinal cord and supplying the internal organs, blood vessels, and glands.

paratha /pəraatə/ • noun (in Indian cookery) a flat, thick piece of unleavened bread fried on a griddle.
– ORIGIN Hindi.

parathion /parrəthiən/ • noun a highly toxic synthetic insecticide containing phosphorus and sulphur.

parathyroid • noun Anatomy a gland next to the thyroid which secretes a hormone that regulates calcium levels in a person's body.

Thesaurus

tated, paralytic, powerless, immobilized, useless; *Medicine* paraplegic, quadriplegic, tetraplegic, monoplegic, hemiplegic, paretic, paraparetic.

paralysis • noun **1** *the disease can cause paralysis* IMMOBILITY, powerlessness, incapacity, debilitation; *Medicine* paraplegia, quadriplegia, tetraplegia, monoplegia, hemiplegia, diplegia, paresis, paraparesis. **2** *complete paralysis of the ports* SHUTDOWN, immobilization, stoppage.

paralytic • adjective **1** *her hands became paralytic* PARALYSED, crippled, disabled, incapacitated, powerless, immobilized, useless. **2** *(Brit. informal) everyone was paralytic.* See DRUNK adjective.

parameter • noun FRAMEWORK, variable, limit, boundary, limitation, restriction, criterion, guideline.

paramount • adjective MOST IMPORTANT, of greatest/prime importance; uppermost, supreme, chief, overriding, predominant, foremost, prime, primary, principal, highest, main, key, central, leading, major, top; *informal* number-one.

paramour • noun *(archaic)* LOVER, significant other; mistress, girlfriend, kept woman, other woman, inamorata; boyfriend, other man, inamorato; *informal* fancy woman/man, toy boy, sugar daddy, bit on the side, bit of fluff; *archaic* concubine, courtesan.

paranoia • noun PERSECUTION COMPLEX, delusions, obsession, psychosis.

paranoid • adjective OVER-SUSPICIOUS, paranoiac, suspicious, mistrustful, fearful, insecure; *Brit. informal* para.

parapet • noun **1** *Marian leaned over the parapet* BALUSTRADE, barrier, wall. **2** *the sandbags making up the parapet* BARRICADE, rampart, bulwark, bank, embankment, fortification, defence, earthwork, bastion.

paraphernalia • plural noun EQUIPMENT, stuff, things, apparatus, kit, implements, tools, utensils, material(s), appliances, accoutrements, appurtenances, odds and ends, bits and pieces; *informal* gear; *Brit. informal* clobber; *archaic* equipage.

paraphrase • verb *paraphrasing literary texts* REWORD, rephrase, put/express in other words, rewrite, gloss.
• noun *this paraphrase of St Paul's words* REWORDING, rephrasing, rewriting, rewrite, rendition, rendering, gloss.

parasite • noun HANGER-ON, cadger, leech, passenger; *informal* blood-

paratroops • plural noun troops equipped to be dropped by parachute from aircraft.
– DERIVATIVES **paratrooper** noun.
paratyphoid • noun a fever resembling typhoid, caused by related bacteria.
par avion /paar avyon/ • adverb by airmail.
– ORIGIN French, 'by aeroplane'.
parboil • verb partly cook by boiling.
– ORIGIN Latin *perbullire* 'boil thoroughly', confused with PART.
parcel • noun **1** an object or collection of objects wrapped in paper in order to be carried or sent by post. **2** a quantity or amount of something, in particular land. • verb (**parcelled**, **parcelling**; US **parceled**, **parceling**) **1** make (something) into a parcel by wrapping it. **2** (**parcel out**) divide (something) into portions and then distribute it.
– ORIGIN Old French *parcelle*, from Latin *particula* 'small part'.
parch • verb **1** make dry through intense heat. **2** (**parched**) informal extremely thirsty. **3** roast (corn, peas, etc.) lightly.
– ORIGIN of unknown origin.
parchment • noun **1** a stiff material made from the skin of a sheep or goat, formerly used for writing on. **2** (also **parchment paper**) stiff translucent paper treated to resemble parchment. **3** informal a diploma or other formal document.
– ORIGIN Old French *parchemin*, from a blend of Latin *pergamina* 'writing material from Pergamum' and *Parthica pellis* 'Parthian skin' (a kind of scarlet leather).
pard • noun archaic or literary a leopard.
– ORIGIN Greek *pardos*.
pardon • noun **1** the action of forgiving or being forgiven for an error or offence. **2** a remission of the legal consequences of an offence or conviction. **3** Christian Church, historical an indulgence. • verb **1** forgive or excuse (a person, error, or offence). **2** give (an offender) a pardon. • exclamation used to ask a speaker to repeat something because one did not hear or understand it.
– DERIVATIVES **pardonable** adjective.
– ORIGIN Latin *perdonare* 'concede, remit'.
pardoner • noun historical a person licensed to sell papal pardons or indulgences.
pare • verb **1** trim by cutting away the outer edges of. **2** (often **pare away/down**) reduce or diminish in a number of small successive stages.
– ORIGIN Old French *parer*, from Latin *parare* 'prepare'.
paregoric /parrigorrik/ • noun a medicine containing opium and camphor, formerly used to treat diarrhoea and coughing in children.
– ORIGIN from Greek *parēgorikos* 'soothing', from *parēgorein* 'speak in the assembly', hence 'soothe, console'.
parenchyma /pərengkimə/ • noun **1** Anatomy the functional tissue of an organ as distinguished from the connective and supporting tissue. **2** Botany soft cellular tissue forming the pulp of fruits, pith of stems, etc.
– ORIGIN Greek *parenkhuma* 'something poured in besides'.
parent • noun **1** a father or mother. **2** an animal or plant from which younger ones are derived. **3** an organization or company which owns or controls a number of subsidiaries. **4** archaic a forefather or ancestor. • verb be or act as a parent to.
– DERIVATIVES **parental** adjective **parentally** adverb **parenthood** noun.
– ORIGIN from Latin *parere* 'bring forth'.
parentage • noun the identity and origins of one's parents; lineage.
parenteral /pərentərəl/ • adjective Medicine relating to nutrition involving a part of the body other than the mouth and alimentary canal.
– ORIGIN from PARA- + Greek *enteron* 'intestine'.
parenthesis /pərenthisiss/ • noun (pl. **parentheses** /pərenthiseez/) **1** a word or phrase inserted as an explanation or afterthought, in writing usually marked off by brackets, dashes, or commas. **2** (**parentheses**) a pair of round brackets () used to include such a word or phrase.
– ORIGIN Greek, from *parentithenai* 'put in beside'.
parenthetic • adjective relating to or inserted as a parenthesis.
– DERIVATIVES **parenthetical** adjective **parenthetically** adverb.
parergon /pərergən/ • noun (pl. **parerga** /pərergə/) formal a supplementary or subsidiary piece of work.
– ORIGIN Greek, from *para-* 'beside, additional' + *ergon* 'work'.
paresis /pəreesiss, parrisiss/ • noun (pl. **pareses** /pəreeseez, parriseez/) Medicine **1** muscular weakness or partial paralysis caused by nerve damage or disease. **2** inflammation of the brain in the later stages of syphilis.
– DERIVATIVES **paretic** adjective.
– ORIGIN Latin, from Greek *parienai* 'let go'.
pareu /paarayoo/ • noun a kind of Polynesian sarong.
– ORIGIN Tahitian.
par excellence /paar eksəlonss/ • adjective (after a noun) better or more than all others of the same kind: *a designer par excellence*.
– ORIGIN French, 'by excellence'.
parfait /paarfay/ • noun **1** a rich cold dessert made with whipped cream, eggs, and fruit. **2** a dessert consisting of layers of ice cream, meringue, and fruit, served in a tall glass.
– ORIGIN from French, 'perfect'.
pargana /pərgunnə/ • noun a group of villages or a subdivision of a district in India.
– ORIGIN Urdu, 'district'.
pargeting /paarjiting/ • noun patterned or decorative plaster or mortar.
– DERIVATIVES **pargeted** adjective.
– ORIGIN from Old French *parjeter*, from *par-* 'all over' + *jeter* 'to throw'.
parhelion /paarheeliən/ • noun (pl. **parhelia** /paarheeliə/) a bright spot in the sky on either side of the sun, formed by refraction of sunlight through ice crystals high in the atmosphere.
– ORIGIN from Greek *para-* 'beside' + *hēlios* 'sun'.
pariah /pərīə/ • noun **1** an outcast. **2** historical a member of a low caste or of no caste in southern India.
– ORIGIN from a Tamil word meaning 'hereditary drummers' (pariahs were drummers because they were not allowed to join in with religious processions).

Thesaurus

sucker, sponger, scrounger, freeloader; *N. Amer. informal* mooch; *Austral./NZ informal* bludger.
parcel • noun **1** *a parcel of clothes* PACKAGE, packet; pack, bundle, box, case, bale. **2** *a parcel of land* PLOT, piece, patch, tract; *Brit.* allotment; *N. Amer.* lot, plat.
• verb **1** *she parcelled up the papers* PACK (UP), package, wrap (up), gift-wrap, tie up, bundle up. **2** *parcelling out commercial farmland* DIVIDE UP, portion out, distribute, share out, allocate, allot, apportion, hand out, dole out, dish out; *informal* divvy up.
parched • adjective **1** *the parched earth* (BONE) DRY, dried up/out, arid, desiccated, dehydrated, baked, burned, scorched; withered, shrivelled. **2** *(informal) I'm parched.* See THIRSTY sense 1.
– OPPOSITES soaking.
pardon • noun **1** *pardon for your sins* FORGIVENESS, absolution, clemency, mercy, lenience, leniency. **2** *he offered them a full pardon* REPRIEVE, free pardon, amnesty, exoneration, release, acquittal, discharge; *formal* exculpation.
• verb **1** *I know she will pardon me* FORGIVE, absolve, have mercy on; excuse, condone, overlook. **2** *they were subsequently pardoned* EXONERATE, acquit, amnesty; reprieve, release, free; *informal* let off; *formal* exculpate.
– OPPOSITES blame, punish.
• exclamation *Pardon?* WHAT (DID YOU SAY), eh, pardon me, I beg your pardon, sorry, excuse me; *informal* come again.
pardonable • adjective EXCUSABLE, forgivable, condonable, understandable, minor, slight, venial.
– OPPOSITES inexcusable.
pare • verb **1** *pare the peel from the lemon* CUT (OFF), trim (off), peel (off), strip (off), skin; *technical* decorticate. **2** *domestic operations have been pared down* REDUCE, diminish, decrease, cut (back/down), trim, slim down, prune, curtail.
parent • noun **1** *her parents have divorced* MOTHER, FATHER, birth/biological parent, progenitor; adoptive parent, foster-parent, step-parent, guardian; *poetic/literary* begetter. **2** *the parent of rock and roll* SOURCE, origin, genesis, root, author, architect; precursor, forerunner, predecessor, antecedent; *formal* radix.
• verb *those who parent young children* BRING UP, look after, take care of, rear, raise.
parentage • noun ORIGINS, extraction, birth, family, ancestry, lineage, heritage, pedigree, descent, blood, stock, roots.
parenthetical • adjective INCIDENTAL, supplementary, in brackets, in parentheses, parenthetic; explanatory, qualifying.
parenthetically • adverb INCIDENTALLY, by the way, by the by(e), in passing, in parenthesis.

p

pariah dog ● noun another term for PYE-DOG.
Parian /pairiən/ ● adjective relating to the Greek island of Paros, famous as a source of marble.
parietal /pərīit'l/ ● adjective Anatomy & Biology relating to the wall of the body or of a body cavity.
– ORIGIN from Latin *paries* 'wall'.
parietal bone ● noun a bone forming the central side and upper back part of each side of the skull.
parietal lobe ● noun either of the paired lobes of the brain at the top of the head.
pari-mutuel /parrimyo͞otyooəl/ ● noun a form of betting in which those backing the first three places divide the losers' stakes.
– ORIGIN French, 'mutual stake'.
parings ● plural noun thin strips pared off from something.
pari passu /parri passo͞o/ ● adverb side by side; equally or equivalently.
– ORIGIN Latin, 'with equal step'.
parish ● noun **1** (in the Christian Church) a small administrative district with its own church and clergy. **2** (also **civil parish**) Brit. the smallest unit of local government in rural areas.
– ORIGIN Old French *paroche*, from Greek *paroikia* 'staying temporarily'.
parish council ● noun the administrative body in a civil parish.
parishioner ● noun a person who lives in a particular Church parish.
parish-pump ● adjective Brit. of local importance only; parochial.
parish register ● noun a book recording christenings, marriages, and burials at a parish church.
Parisian /pərizziən/ ● adjective relating to Paris. ● noun a person from Paris.
Parisienne /pərizzien/ ● noun a Parisian girl or woman.
parity[1] /parriti/ ● noun **1** equality or equivalence. **2** Mathematics the fact of being an even or an odd number.
– ORIGIN Latin *paritas*, from *par* 'equal'.
parity[2] /parriti/ ● noun Medicine the fact or condition of having borne a specified number of children.
– ORIGIN from Latin *parere* 'bring forth, produce'.
park ● noun **1** a large public garden in a town, used for recreation. **2** a large area of woodland and pasture attached to a country house. **3** an area devoted to a specified purpose: *a wildlife park*. **4** an area in which vehicles may be parked. **5** (**the park**) Brit. informal a football pitch. ● verb **1** stop and leave (a vehicle) temporarily. **2** informal leave (something) in a convenient place until required. **3** (**park oneself**) informal sit down.
– ORIGIN Old French *parc*, from Latin *parricus*.
parka ● noun **1** a large windproof hooded jacket. **2** a hooded jacket made of animal skin, worn by Eskimos.
– ORIGIN Russian.
parkin ● noun Brit. soft, dark gingerbread made with oatmeal and treacle or molasses.
– ORIGIN perhaps from the family name *Parkin*.
parking meter ● noun a machine next to a parking space in a street, into which coins are inserted to pay for parking a vehicle.
parking ticket ● noun a notice informing a driver of a fine imposed for parking illegally.
Parkinson's disease ● noun a progressive disease of the brain and nervous system marked by involuntary trembling, muscular rigidity, and slow, imprecise movement.
– DERIVATIVES **Parkinsonism** noun.
– ORIGIN named after the English surgeon James *Parkinson* (1755–1824).
Parkinson's law ● noun the notion that work expands so as to fill the time available for its completion.
– ORIGIN named after the English writer Cyril Northcote *Parkinson* (1909–93).
parkland (also **parklands**) ● noun open land consisting of fields and scattered groups of trees.
parkway ● noun **1** N. Amer. an open landscaped highway. **2** Brit. (in names) a railway station with extensive parking facilities.
parky ● adjective Brit. informal chilly.
– ORIGIN of unknown origin.
parlance /paarlənss/ ● noun a way of using words associated with a particular subject: *medical parlance*.
– ORIGIN Old French, from *parler* 'speak'.
parlay /paarlay/ ● verb (**parlay into**) N. Amer. turn (an initial stake) into (a greater amount) by further gambling.
– ORIGIN French *paroli*, from Latin *par* 'equal'.
parley /paarli/ ● noun (pl. **parleys**) a meeting between opponents or enemies to discuss terms for an armistice. ● verb (**parleys, parleyed**) hold a parley.
– ORIGIN perhaps from Old French *parlee* 'spoken'.
parliament /paarləmənt/ ● noun **1** (**Parliament**) (in the UK) the highest legislature, consisting of the Sovereign, the House of Lords, and the House of Commons. **2** a similar body in other countries.
– ORIGIN Old French *parlement* 'speaking'.
parliamentarian ● noun **1** a member of parliament who is well versed in parliamentary procedures and debates. **2** historical a supporter of Parliament in the English Civil War; a Roundhead. ● adjective relating to parliament or parliamentarians.
parliamentary /paarləmentri/ ● adjective relating to, enacted by, or suitable for a parliament.
parliamentary private secretary ● noun (in the UK) a Member of Parliament assisting a government minister.
parlour (US **parlor**) ● noun **1** dated a sitting room. **2** a room in a public building, monastery, etc. for receiving guests or private conversation. **3** a shop or business providing specified goods or services: *an ice-cream parlour*. **4** a room or building equipped for milking cows.
– ORIGIN Old French *parlur* 'place for speaking', from Latin *parlare* 'speak'.
parlour game ● noun an indoor game, especially a word game.
parlourmaid ● noun historical a maid employed to wait at table.
parlous /paarləss/ ● adjective archaic or humorous dangerously uncertain; precarious.
– ORIGIN contraction of PERILOUS.
Parma ham ● noun a strongly flavoured Italian cured ham, eaten uncooked and thinly sliced.
– ORIGIN named after the Italian city of *Parma*.
Parmesan /paarmizan/ ● noun a hard, dry Italian cheese used chiefly in grated form.

p

Thesaurus

parenthood ● noun CHILDCARE, child-rearing, motherhood, fatherhood, parenting.
pariah ● noun OUTCAST, persona non grata, leper, undesirable, unperson.
parings ● plural noun PEELINGS, clippings, peel, rind, cuttings, trimmings, shavings.
parish ● noun **1** *the parish of Poplar* DISTRICT, community. **2** *the vicar scandalized the parish* PARISHIONERS, churchgoers, congregation, flock, fold, community.
– RELATED TERMS parochial.
parity ● noun EQUALITY, equivalence, uniformity, consistency, correspondence, congruity, levelness, unity, coequality.
park ● noun **1** *we were playing in the park* PUBLIC GARDEN, recreation ground, playground, play area. **2** *fifty acres of park* PARKLAND, grassland, woodland, garden(s), lawns, grounds, estate. **3** *the liveliest player on the park* (PLAYING) FIELD, football field, pitch.
● verb **1** *he parked his car* LEAVE, position; stop, pull up. **2** *(informal) park your bag by the door* PUT (DOWN), place, deposit, leave, stick, shove, dump; *informal* plonk; *Brit. informal* bung.
– PHRASES **park oneself** *(informal)* SIT DOWN, seat oneself, settle (oneself), install oneself; *informal* plonk oneself.
parlance ● noun JARGON, language, phraseology, talk, speech, argot, patois, cant; *informal* lingo, -ese, -speak.
parley ● noun *a peace parley* NEGOTIATION, talk(s), conference, summit, discussion, powwow; *informal* confab; *formal* colloquy, confabulation; *dated* palaver.
● verb *the two parties were willing to parley* DISCUSS TERMS, talk, hold talks, negotiate, deliberate; *informal* powwow.
parliament ● noun **1** *the Queen's speech to Parliament* THE HOUSES OF PARLIAMENT, Westminster, the (House of) Commons, the (House of) Lords. **2** *the Russian parliament* LEGISLATURE, legislative assembly, congress, senate, (upper/lower) house, (upper/lower) chamber, diet, assembly.
parliamentary ● adjective LEGISLATIVE, law-making, governmental, congressional, senatorial, democratic, elected, representative.
parlour ● noun **1** *(dated) tea in the parlour* SITTING ROOM, living room, lounge, front room, drawing room; *Brit.* reception room. **2** *a beauty parlour* SALON, shop, establishment, store.
parlous ● adjective *(archaic)* BAD, dire, dreadful, awful, terrible, grave, serious, desperate, precarious; sorry, poor, lamentable,

– ORIGIN from Italian *Parmigiano* 'of *Parma*'.

parmigiana /paarmijaanə/ ● adjective cooked or served with Parmesan cheese: *veal parmigiana.*
– ORIGIN Italian.

parochial /pərōkiəl/ ● adjective **1** relating to a parish. **2** having a narrow outlook or scope.
– DERIVATIVES **parochialism** noun.
– ORIGIN Latin *parochialis*, from Greek *paroikia* (see PARISH).

parody ● noun (pl. **parodies**) **1** an amusingly exaggerated imitation of the style of a writer, artist, or genre. **2** a feeble imitation. ● verb (**parodies, parodied**) produce a parody of.
– DERIVATIVES **parodic** adjective **parodist** noun.
– ORIGIN Greek *parōidia* 'burlesque poem or song'.

parole ● noun **1** the temporary or permanent release of a prisoner before the expiry of a sentence, on the promise of good behaviour. **2** historical a prisoner of war's word of honour not to escape or, if released, to act as a non-belligerent. ● verb release (a prisoner) on parole.
– DERIVATIVES **parolee** noun.
– ORIGIN Old French, 'word', from Latin *parabola* 'speech'.

paronomasia /parrənəmayziə/ ● noun a pun.
– ORIGIN Greek, from *para-* 'beside' + *onomasia* 'naming'.

parotid /pərottid/ ● adjective relating to a pair of large salivary glands situated just in front of each ear.
– ORIGIN Greek, from *para-* 'beside' + *ous* 'ear'.

parotitis /parrətītiss/ ● noun Medicine inflammation of a parotid gland, especially (**infectious parotitis**) mumps.

paroxysm /parrəksiz'm/ ● noun a sudden attack or outburst: *a paroxysm of weeping.*
– DERIVATIVES **paroxysmal** adjective.
– ORIGIN Greek *paroxusmos*, from *paroxunein* 'exasperate'.

parquet /paarki, -kay/ ● noun flooring composed of wooden blocks arranged in a geometric pattern.
– DERIVATIVES **parquetry** noun.
– ORIGIN French, 'small compartment, wooden flooring'.

parr ● noun (pl. same) a young salmon or trout up to two years old.
– ORIGIN of unknown origin.

parrakeet ● noun variant spelling of PARAKEET.

parricide /parrisīd/ ● noun **1** the killing of a parent or other near relative. **2** a person who commits parricide.
– DERIVATIVES **parricidal** adjective.
– ORIGIN Latin *parricidium*, with unknown first element associated with Latin *pater* 'father' and *parens* 'parent'.

parrot ● noun a mainly tropical bird with brightly coloured plumage and a strong downcurved hooked bill, some kinds of which are able to mimic human speech. ● verb (**parroted, parroting**) repeat mechanically.
– ORIGIN probably from French dialect *perrot*, diminutive of the male name *Pierre* 'Peter'.

parrotbill ● noun a titmouse-like songbird with brown and grey plumage and a short arched bill.

parrot-fashion ● adverb repeated without thought or understanding.

parrotfish ● noun **1** a brightly coloured sea fish with a parrot-like beak. **2** Austral./NZ a brightly coloured wrasse.

parry ● verb (**parries, parried**) **1** ward off (a weapon or attack) with a countermove. **2** avoid answering (a question) directly. ● noun (pl. **parries**) an act of parrying.
– ORIGIN probably from French *parer* 'ward off'.

parse /paarz/ ● verb **1** analyse (a sentence) into its component parts and describe their syntactic roles. **2** Computing analyse (text) into logical syntactic components.
– DERIVATIVES **parser** noun.
– ORIGIN perhaps from Old French *pars* 'parts'.

parsec ● noun a unit of astronomical distance equal to about 3.25 light years, corresponding to the distance at which the radius of the earth's orbit subtends an angle of one second of arc.
– ORIGIN blend of PARALLAX and SECOND².

Parsee /paarsee/ ● noun a descendant of a group of Zoroastrian Persians who fled to India during the 7th–8th centuries.
– ORIGIN from a Persian word meaning 'Persian'.

parsimony /paarsiməni/ ● noun extreme unwillingness to spend money or use resources.
– DERIVATIVES **parsimonious** adjective.
– ORIGIN Latin *parsimonia, parcimonia*, from *parcere* 'be sparing'.

parsley ● noun a herb with crinkly or flat leaves, used for seasoning or garnishing food.
– ORIGIN Greek *petroselinon*, from *petra* 'rock' + *selinon* 'parsley'.

parsnip ● noun the long tapering cream-coloured root of a plant of the parsley family, eaten as a vegetable.
– ORIGIN Old French *pasnaie*, from Latin *pastinaca*; the change in ending was influenced by NEEP.

parson ● noun **1** (in the Church of England) a parish priest. **2** informal any clergyman.
– ORIGIN Latin *persona* 'person', later 'rector'.

parsonage ● noun a church house provided for a parson.

parson's nose ● noun informal the piece of fatty flesh at the rump of a cooked fowl.

part ● noun **1** a piece or segment which is combined with others to make up a whole. **2** some but not all of something. **3** a specified fraction of a whole. **4** a measure allowing comparison between the amounts of different ingredients used in a mixture. **5** a role played by an actor or actress. **6** a person's contribution to an action or situation. **7** (**parts**) informal a region. **8** Music a melody or other constituent of harmony assigned to a particular voice or instrument. **9** (**parts**) abilities: *a man of many parts.* ● verb **1** move apart or divide to leave a central space. **2** leave or cause to leave someone's company. **3** (**part with**) give up possession of; hand over. ● adverb partly: *part jazz, part blues.*
– PHRASES **be part and parcel of** be an essential element of. **for my** (or **his, her**, etc.) **part** as far as I am (or he, she, etc. is) concerned. **in part** to some extent. **on the part of** used to ascribe responsibility for something to someone. **part company** go in different directions. **take part** join in or be involved in an activity. **take the part of** give support and encouragement to.
– ORIGIN Latin *pars*; the verb is from Latin *partire* 'divide, share'.

p

Thesaurus

hopeless; unsafe, perilous, dangerous, risky; *informal* dicey, hairy, chronic, woeful.

parochial ● adjective NARROW-MINDED, small-minded, provincial, narrow, small-town, conservative, illiberal, intolerant; *Brit.* parish-pump; *N. Amer. informal* jerkwater.
– OPPOSITES broad-minded.

parochialism ● noun NARROW-MINDEDNESS, provincialism, small-mindedness.

parody ● noun **1** *a parody of the gothic novel* SATIRE, burlesque, lampoon, pastiche, pasquinade, caricature, imitation, mockery; *informal* spoof, take-off, send-up. **2** *a parody of the truth* DISTORTION, travesty, caricature, misrepresentation, perversion, corruption, debasement.
● verb *parodying schoolgirl fiction* SATIRIZE, burlesque, lampoon, caricature, mimic, imitate, ape, copy, make fun of, travesty, take off; *informal* send up.

paroxysm ● noun SPASM, attack, fit, burst, bout, convulsion, seizure, outburst, eruption, explosion, access; *formal* boutade.

parrot ● noun PSITTACINE.
● verb *they parroted slogans without appreciating their significance* REPEAT (MINDLESSLY), repeat mechanically, echo.

parrot-fashion ● adverb MECHANICALLY, by rote, mindlessly, automatically.

parry ● verb **1** *Sharpe parried the blow* WARD OFF, fend off; deflect, hold off, block, counter, repel, repulse. **2** *I parried her constant questions* EVADE, sidestep, avoid, dodge, answer evasively, field, fend off.

parsimonious ● adjective MEAN, miserly, niggardly, close-fisted, close, penny-pinching, ungenerous, Scrooge-like; *informal* tight-fisted, tight, stingy, mingy; *N. Amer. informal* cheap; *formal* penurious; *archaic* near.
– OPPOSITES generous.

parsimony ● noun MEANNESS, miserliness, parsimoniousness, niggardliness, close-fistedness, closeness, penny-pinching; *informal* stinginess, minginess, tightness, tight-fistedness; *N. Amer.* cheapness; *formal* penuriousness; *archaic* nearness.

parson ● noun VICAR, rector, clergyman, cleric, chaplain, pastor, curate, man of the cloth, ecclesiastic, minister, priest, preacher; *informal* reverend, padre; *Austral. informal* josser.

part ● noun **1** *the last part of the cake | a large part of their life* BIT, slice, chunk, lump, hunk, wedge, fragment, scrap, piece; portion, proportion, percentage, fraction. **2** *car parts* COMPONENT, bit, constituent, element, module. **3** *body parts* PART OF THE BODY, organ, limb, member. **4** *the third part of the book* SECTION, division, volume, chapter, act, scene, instalment. **5** *another part of the country* DISTRICT, neighbourhood, quarter, section, area, region. **6** *the part*

partake ● verb (past **partook**; past part. **partaken**) formal **1** (**partake in**) participate in (an activity). **2** (**partake of**) be characterized by. **3** (**partake of**) eat or drink.
– ORIGIN from earlier *partaker* 'person who takes a part'.

parterre /paartair/ ● noun a group of flower beds laid out in a formal pattern.
– ORIGIN French, from *par terre* 'on the ground'.

part exchange ● noun Brit. a transaction in which an article that one already owns is given as part of the payment for a more expensive one, with the balance in money.

parthenogenesis /paarthinōjennisiss/ ● noun Biology reproduction from an ovum without fertilization, especially in some invertebrates and lower plants.
– DERIVATIVES **parthenogenetic** adjective.
– ORIGIN from Greek *parthenos* 'virgin' + *genesis* 'creation'.

Parthian /paarthiən/ ● noun a person from Parthia, an ancient kingdom which lay SE of the Caspian Sea. ● adjective relating to Parthia.

Parthian shot ● noun another term for PARTING SHOT.
– ORIGIN from the practice among Parthian horsemen of shooting arrows backwards while fleeing.

partial ● adjective **1** existing only in part; incomplete. **2** favouring one side in a dispute above the other; biased. **3** (**partial to**) having a liking for.
– DERIVATIVES **partiality** noun **partially** adverb.

participate ● verb take part.
– DERIVATIVES **participant** noun **participation** noun **participative** adjective **participator** noun **participatory** adjective.
– ORIGIN Latin *participare* 'share in'.

participle /paartissip'l/ ● noun Grammar a word formed from a verb (e.g. *going, gone, being, been*) and used as an adjective or noun (as in *burnt toast, good breeding*) or used to make compound verb forms (*is going, has been*).
– DERIVATIVES **participial** /paartisippiəl/ adjective.
– ORIGIN from Latin *participium* 'sharing'.

particle ● noun **1** a minute portion of matter. **2** Physics a component of the physical world smaller than an atom, e.g. an electron, proton, neutrino, or photon. **3** Grammar a minor function word that has comparatively little meaning and does not inflect, e.g. *in, up, off,* or *over*, used with verbs to make phrasal verbs.
– ORIGIN Latin *particula* 'little part'.

particle board ● noun another term for CHIPBOARD.

particle physics ● plural noun (treated as sing.) the branch of physics concerned with the properties and interactions of subatomic particles.

particoloured (US **particolored**) ● adjective partly of one colour, partly of another or others.

particular ● adjective **1** relating to an individual member of a specified group or class. **2** more than is usual; special: *particular care.* **3** fastidious about something. ● noun a detail.
– PHRASES **in particular** especially.
– ORIGIN Latin *particularis*, from *particula* 'small part'.

particularity ● noun (pl. **particularities**) **1** the quality of being individual. **2** fullness or minuteness of detail. **3** (**particularities**) small details.

particularize (also **particularise**) ● verb formal treat individually or in detail.
– DERIVATIVES **particularization** noun.

particularly ● adverb **1** more than is usual; especially or very. **2** in particular; specifically.

particulate /paartikyoolayt/ ● adjective relating to or in the form of minute particles. ● noun (**particulates**) matter in such a form.

Thesaurus

of Juliet (THEATRICAL) ROLE, character, persona. **7** *he's learning his part* LINES, words, script, speech; libretto, lyrics, score. **8** *he was jailed for his part in the affair* INVOLVEMENT, role, function, hand, work, responsibility, capacity, position, participation, contribution; *informal* bit.
– OPPOSITES whole.
● verb **1** *the curtains parted* SEPARATE, divide (in two), split (in two), move apart. **2** *we parted on bad terms* LEAVE, take one's leave, say goodbye/farewell, say one's goodbyes/farewells, go one's (separate) ways, go away, depart.
– OPPOSITES join, meet.
● adjective *a part payment* INCOMPLETE, partial, half, semi-, limited, inadequate, insufficient, unfinished.
– OPPOSITES complete.
● adverb *it is part finished* TO A CERTAIN EXTENT/DEGREE, to some extent/degree, partly, partially, in part, half, relatively, comparatively, (up) to a point, somewhat; not totally, not entirely, (very) nearly, almost, just about, all but.
– OPPOSITES completely.
– PHRASES **for the most part.** See MOST. **in good part.** See GOOD. **in part** TO A CERTAIN EXTENT/DEGREE, to some extent/degree, partly, partially, slightly, in some measure, (up) to a point. **on the part of** (MADE/DONE) BY, carried out by, caused by, from. **part with** GIVE UP/AWAY, relinquish, forgo, surrender, hand over, deliver up, dispose of. **take part** PARTICIPATE, join in, get involved, enter, play a part/role, be a participant, contribute, have a hand, help, assist, lend a hand; *informal* get in on the act. **take part in** PARTICIPATE IN, engage in, join in, get involved in, share in, play a part/role in, be a participant in, contribute to, be associated with, have a hand in. **take someone's part** SUPPORT, give one's support to, take the side of, side with, stand by, stick up for, be supportive of, back (up), give one's backing to, be loyal to, defend, come to the defence of, champion.

partake ● verb **1** (*formal*) *visitors can partake in golf* PARTICIPATE IN, take part in, engage in, join in, get involved in. **2** *she had partaken of lunch* CONSUME, have, eat, drink, devour; *informal* wolf down, polish off. **3** *Bohemia partakes of both East and West* HAVE THE QUALITIES/ATTRIBUTES OF, suggest, evoke, be characterized by.

partial ● adjective **1** *a partial recovery* INCOMPLETE, limited, qualified, imperfect, fragmentary, unfinished. **2** *a very partial view of the situation* BIASED, prejudiced, partisan, one-sided, slanted, skewed, coloured, unbalanced.
– OPPOSITES complete, unbiased.
– PHRASES **be partial to** LIKE, love, enjoy, have a liking for, be fond of, be keen on, have a soft spot for, have a taste for, have a penchant for; *informal* adore, be mad about/on, have a thing about, be crazy about, be nutty about; *Brit. informal* be potty about; *N. Amer. informal* cotton to; *Austral./NZ informal* be shook on.

partiality ● noun **1** *his partiality towards their cause* BIAS, prejudice, favouritism, favour, partisanship. **2** *her partiality for brandy* LIKING, love, fondness, taste, soft spot, predilection, penchant, passion.

partially ● adverb TO A LIMITED EXTENT/DEGREE, to a certain extent/degree, partly, in part, not totally, not entirely, relatively, moderately, (up) to a point, somewhat, comparatively, slightly.

participant ● noun PARTICIPATOR, contributor, party, member; entrant, competitor, player, contestant, candidate.

participate ● verb TAKE PART, engage, join, get involved, share, play a part/role, be a participant, partake, have a hand in, be associated with; cooperate, help, assist, lend a hand.

participation ● noun INVOLVEMENT, part, contribution, association.

particle ● noun **1** *minute particles of rock* (TINY) BIT, (tiny) piece, speck, spot, fleck; fragment, sliver, splinter. **2** *he never showed a particle of sympathy* IOTA, jot, whit, bit, scrap, shred, crumb, drop, hint, touch, trace, suggestion, whisper, suspicion, scintilla; *informal* smidgen.

particular ● adjective **1** *a particular group of companies* SPECIFIC, certain, distinct, separate, discrete, definite, precise; single, individual. **2** *an issue of particular importance* (EXTRA) SPECIAL, especial, exceptional, unusual, singular, uncommon, notable, noteworthy, remarkable, unique; *formal* peculiar. **3** *he was particular about what he ate* FUSSY, fastidious, finicky, meticulous, punctilious, discriminating, selective, painstaking, exacting, demanding; *informal* pernickety, choosy, picky; *Brit. informal* faddy.
– OPPOSITES general, careless.
● noun *the same in every particular* DETAIL, item, point, specific, element, aspect, respect, regard, particularity, fact, feature.
– PHRASES **in particular 1** *nothing in particular* SPECIFIC, special. **2** *the poor, in particular, were hit by rising prices* PARTICULARLY, specifically, especially, specially.

particularity ● noun **1** *the particularity of each human being* INDIVIDUALITY, distinctiveness, uniqueness, singularity, originality. **2** *a great degree of particularity* DETAIL, precision, accuracy, thoroughness, scrupulousness, meticulousness.

particularize ● verb SPECIFY, detail, itemize, list, enumerate, spell out, cite, stipulate, instance.

particularly ● adverb **1** *the acoustics are particularly good* ESPECIALLY, specially, very, extremely, exceptionally, singularly, peculiarly, unusually, extraordinarily, remarkably, outstandingly, amazingly, incredibly, really; *informal* seriously, majorly, awfully,

– ORIGIN from Latin *particula* 'particle'.

parting ● noun **1** the action or an act of parting. **2** Brit. a line of scalp revealed by combing the hair away in opposite directions on either side.

parting shot ● noun a cutting remark made at the moment of departure.

parti pris /paarti pree/ ● noun (pl. **partis pris** pronunc. same) a preconceived view; a bias. ● adjective prejudiced; biased.
– ORIGIN French, 'side taken'.

partisan /paartizan, paartizan/ ● noun **1** a strong, often uncritical, supporter of a party, cause, or person. **2** a member of an armed group fighting secretly against an occupying force. ● adjective prejudiced.
– DERIVATIVES **partisanship** noun.
– ORIGIN French, from Italian *partigiano*, from *parte* 'part'.

partita /paarteetə/ ● noun (pl. **partitas** or **partite partite** /paarteetay/) Music a suite, typically for a solo instrument or chamber ensemble.
– ORIGIN from Italian, 'divided off'.

partition ● noun **1** a structure dividing a space into parts, especially a light interior wall. **2** division into parts, especially the division of a country into self-governing parts. ● verb **1** divide into parts. **2** divide or separate (a room or part of a room) with a partition.
– DERIVATIVES **partitionist** noun.
– ORIGIN Latin, from *partiri* 'divide into parts'.

partitive /paartitiv/ Grammar ● adjective (of a grammatical construction) indicating that only a part of a whole is referred to (e.g. *a slice of bacon, some of the children*). ● noun a noun or pronoun used as the first term in such a construction.

partly ● adverb to some extent; not completely.

partner ● noun **1** a person who takes part in an undertaking with another or others, especially in a business with shared risks and profits. **2** either of two people doing something as a couple or pair. **3** either member of a married couple or of an established unmarried couple. ● verb be the partner of.
– ORIGIN Old French *parcener*, from Latin *partitio* 'partition'.

partnership ● noun **1** the state of being a partner or partners. **2** an association of two or more people as partners.

part of speech ● noun a category to which a word is assigned in accordance with its syntactic functions, e.g. noun, pronoun, adjective, verb.

partook past of PARTAKE.

partridge ● noun (pl. same or **partridges**) a short-tailed game bird with mainly brown plumage.
– ORIGIN Old French *perdriz*, from Latin *perdix*.

part song ● noun a secular song with three or more voice parts, typically unaccompanied.

part-time ● adjective & adverb for only part of the usual working day or week.

parturient /paartyooriənt/ ● adjective technical about to give birth; in labour.

parturition /paartyoorish'n/ ● noun formal or technical the action of giving birth; childbirth.
– ORIGIN Latin, from *parturire* 'be in labour'.

part-way ● adverb part of the way.

party ● noun (pl. **parties**) **1** a social gathering of invited guests. **2** a formally organized political group that puts forward candidates for local or national office. **3** a group of people taking part in an activity or trip. **4** a person or group forming one side in an agreement or dispute. **5** informal, dated a person: *an old party came in to clean*. ● verb (**parties**, **partied**) informal enjoy oneself at a party or other lively gathering.
– PHRASES **be party** (or **a party**) **to** be involved in.
– ORIGIN Old French *partie*, from Latin *partiri* 'divide into parts'.

party line ● noun **1** a policy or policies officially adopted by a political party. **2** a telephone line shared by two or more subscribers.

party politics ● plural noun (treated as sing. or pl.) politics that relate to political parties rather than to the public good.

party-pooper ● noun informal a person who throws gloom over social enjoyment.

party wall ● noun a wall common to two adjoining buildings or rooms.

parvenu /paarvənoo/ ● noun chiefly derogatory a person from a humble background who has recently acquired wealth, influence, or celebrity.
– ORIGIN from French, 'arrived'.

parvovirus /paarvōvīrəss/ ● noun any of a class of very small viruses causing contagious disease in dogs and other animals.
– ORIGIN from Latin *parvus* 'small'.

pas /paa/ ● noun (pl. same) a step in in classical ballet.
– ORIGIN French.

pascal /pask'l/ ● noun the SI unit of pressure, equal to one newton per square metre.
– ORIGIN named after the French scientist Blaise *Pascal* (1623–62).

Pascal's triangle ● noun Mathematics a triangular array of numbers in which each number is the sum of the two numbers im-

Thesaurus

p

terribly; *Brit. informal* jolly, dead, well; *informal, dated* devilish, frightfully. **2** *he particularly asked that I should help you* SPECIFICALLY, explicitly, expressly, in particular, especially, specially.

parting ● noun **1** *an emotional parting* FAREWELL, leave-taking, goodbye, adieu, departure; valediction. **2** *they kept their parting quiet* SEPARATION, break-up, split, divorce, rift, estrangement; *Brit. informal* bust-up. **3** *the parting of the Red Sea* DIVISION, dividing, separation, separating, splitting, breaking up/apart, partition, partitioning.
● adjective *a parting kiss* FAREWELL, goodbye, last, final, valedictory.

partisan ● noun **1** *Conservative partisans* SUPPORTER, follower, adherent, devotee, champion; fanatic, fan, enthusiast, stalwart, zealot; *N. Amer.* booster. **2** *the partisans opened fire from the woods* GUERRILLA, freedom fighter, resistance fighter, underground fighter, irregular (soldier).
● adjective *partisan attitudes* BIASED, prejudiced, one-sided, discriminatory, coloured, partial, interested, sectarian, factional.
– OPPOSITES unbiased.

partisanship ● noun BIAS, prejudice, one-sidedness, discrimination, favouritism, favour, partiality, sectarianism, factionalism.

partition ● noun **1** *the partition of Palestine* DIVIDING UP, partitioning, separation, division, dividing, subdivision, splitting (up), breaking up, break-up. **2** *room partitions* SCREEN, (room) divider, (dividing) wall, barrier, panel, separator.
● verb **1** *the resolution partitioned Poland* DIVIDE (UP), subdivide, separate, split (up), break up; share (out), parcel out. **2** *the huge hall was partitioned* SUBDIVIDE, divide (up); separate (off), section off, screen off.

partly ● adverb TO A CERTAIN EXTENT/DEGREE, to some extent/degree, in part, partially, a little, somewhat, not totally, not entirely, relatively, moderately, (up) to a point, in some measure, slightly.
– OPPOSITES completely.

partner ● noun **1** *business partners* COLLEAGUE, associate, coworker, fellow worker, collaborator, comrade, teammate; *Brit. informal* oppo; *Austral./NZ informal* offsider; *archaic* compeer. **2** *his partner in crime* ACCOMPLICE, confederate, accessory, collaborator, fellow conspirator, helper; *informal* sidekick. **3** *your relationship with your partner* SPOUSE, husband, wife, consort; lover, girlfriend, boyfriend, fiancé, fiancée, significant other, live-in lover, common-law husband/wife, man, woman, mate; *informal* hubby, missus, old man, old lady/woman, better half, intended, POSSLQ; *Brit. informal* other half.

partnership ● noun **1** *close partnership* COOPERATION, association, collaboration, coalition, alliance, union, affiliation, relationship, connection. **2** *thriving partnerships* COMPANY, firm, business, corporation, organization, association, consortium, syndicate.

parturition ● noun *(formal)* CHILDBIRTH, birth, delivery, labour; *dated* confinement; *poetic/literary* travail; *archaic* childbed, accouchement.

party ● noun **1** *150 people attended the party* (SOCIAL) GATHERING, (social) function, get-together, celebration, reunion, festivity, jamboree, reception, at-home, soirée, social; dance, ball, ceilidh, frolic, carousal, carouse; *N. Amer.* fête, hoedown, shower, bake, cookout, levee; *Austral./NZ* corroboree; *informal* bash, shindig, rave, disco, do, shebang, bop, hop; *Brit. informal* rave-up, knees-up, beanfeast, beano, bunfight; *N. Amer. informal* blast, wingding, kegger; *Austral./NZ informal* shivoo, rage, ding, jollo, rort. **2** *a party of British tourists* GROUP, company, body, gang, band, crowd, pack, contingent; *informal* bunch, crew, load. **3** *the left-wing parties* FACTION, political party, group, grouping, cabal, junta, bloc, camp, caucus. **4** *(informal) don't mention a certain party* PERSON, individual, somebody, someone.
● verb *(informal) let's party!* CELEBRATE, have fun, enjoy oneself, have a party, have a good/wild time, go on a spree, rave it up, carouse, make merry; *informal* go out on the town, paint the town red, whoop it up, let one's hair down, make whoopee, live it up, have a ball.
– PHRASES **be a party to** GET INVOLVED IN/WITH, be associated with, be

mediately above, and 1 is at the apex and at both ends of each row.

paschal /pask'l/ ● adjective **1** relating to Easter. **2** relating to the Jewish Passover.
– ORIGIN from Latin *pascha* 'feast of Passover', from Hebrew.

pas de deux /paa də dö/ ● noun (pl. same) a dance for a couple.
– ORIGIN French, 'step of two'.

pasha /pashə/ (also **pacha**) ● noun historical the title of a Turkish officer of high rank.
– ORIGIN Turkish.

pashmina /pashmeenə/ ● noun **1** fine-quality material made from goat's wool. **2** a shawl made from this material.
– ORIGIN from a Persian word meaning 'wool, down'.

Pashto /pushtō/ ● noun the language of the Pathans, spoken in Afghanistan and northern Pakistan.
– ORIGIN the name in Pashto.

paso doble /passō dōblay/ ● noun (pl. **paso dobles**) a fast-paced ballroom dance based on a Latin American marching style.
– ORIGIN Spanish, 'double step'.

pasque flower /pask/ ● noun a spring-flowering plant with purple flowers and fern-like foliage.
– ORIGIN French *passe-fleur*; later associated with archaic *pasque* 'Easter'.

pass[1] ● verb **1** move or go onward, past, through, or across. **2** change from one state or condition to another. **3** transfer (something) to someone. **4** kick, hit, or throw (the ball) to a teammate. **5** (of time) go by. **6** occupy or spend (time). **7** be done or said: *not another word passed between them.* **8** come to an end. **9** be successful in (an examination, test, or course). **10** declare to be satisfactory. **11** approve or put into effect (a proposal or law) by voting. **12** utter (remarks) or pronounce (a judgement or sentence). **13** forgo one's turn or an opportunity to do or have something. **14** discharge (urine or faeces) from the body. ● noun **1** an act of passing. **2** a success in an examination. **3** an official document authorizing the holder to have access to, use, or do something. **4** informal an amorous or sexual advance. **5** a particular state of affairs. **6** Computing a single scan through a set of data or a program.
– PHRASES **come to a pretty pass** reach a regrettable state of affairs. **pass as/for** be accepted as. **pass away** euphemistic die. **pass one's eye over** read cursorily. **pass off 1** happen or be carried through in a specified (usually satisfactory) way. **2** evade or lightly dismiss (an awkward remark). **pass off as** falsely represent (something) as. **pass out 1** become unconscious. **2** Brit. complete one's initial training in the armed forces. **pass over 1** ignore the claims of (someone) to advancement. **2** avoid mentioning or considering. **pass up** refrain from taking up (an opportunity).
– DERIVATIVES **passer** noun.
– ORIGIN Old French *passer*, from Latin *passus* 'pace'.

pass[2] ● noun a route over or through mountains.
– PHRASES **sell the pass** Brit. betray a cause.
– ORIGIN variant of PACE[1], influenced by PASS[1] and French *pas*.

passable ● adjective **1** acceptable, but not outstanding. **2** able to be travelled along or on.
– DERIVATIVES **passably** adverb.

passage ● noun **1** the action or process of passing. **2** a way through something; a passageway. **3** a journey by sea or air. **4** the right to pass through somewhere: *a permit for safe passage.* **5** a short section from a text, musical composition, etc.
– PHRASES **work one's passage** work in return for a free place on a voyage.

passageway ● noun a corridor or other narrow passage between buildings or rooms.

passata /pəsaatə/ ● noun a thick paste made from sieved tomatoes.
– ORIGIN Italian.

passband ● noun the range of frequencies that is transmitted by an electronic filter without loss of signal strength.

passbook ● noun a book issued by a bank or building society to an account holder, recording transactions.

passé /passay/ ● adjective no longer fashionable; out of date.
– ORIGIN French, 'gone by'.

passel /pass'l/ ● noun US informal a large group.
– ORIGIN representing a pronunciation of PARCEL.

passenger ● noun **1** a person travelling in a vehicle, ship, or aircraft other than the driver, pilot, or crew. **2** a member of a team who does very little effective work.
– ORIGIN from Old French *passager* 'passing, transitory'.

passepartout /paspaartoo/ ● noun a simple picture frame consisting of pieces of glass and card taped together at the edges.
– ORIGIN French, 'passes everywhere'.

passer-by ● noun (pl. **passers-by**) a person who happens to be walking past something or someone.

Thesaurus

a participant in.

parvenu ● noun UPSTART, social climber, arriviste.

pass[1] ● verb **1** *the traffic passing through the village* GO, proceed, move, progress, make one's way, travel. **2** *a car passed him* OVERTAKE, go past/by, pull ahead of, overhaul, leave behind. **3** *time passed* ELAPSE, go by/past, advance, wear on, roll by, tick by. **4** *he passed the time writing letters* OCCUPY, spend, fill, use (up), employ, while away. **5** *pass me the salt* HAND (OVER), let someone have, give, reach. **6** *he passed the ball back* KICK, hit, throw, lob. **7** *her estate passed to her grandson* BE TRANSFERRED, go, be left, be bequeathed, be handed down/on, be passed on; Law devolve. **8** *his death passed almost unnoticed* HAPPEN, occur, take place, come about, transpire; poetic/literary befall. **9** *the storm passed* COME TO AN END, fade (away), blow over, run its course, die out, finish, end, cease. **10** *God's peace passes all human understanding* SURPASS, exceed, transcend. **11** *he passed the exam* BE SUCCESSFUL IN, succeed in, gain a pass in, get through; informal sail through, scrape through. **12** *the Senate passed the bill* APPROVE, vote for, accept, ratify, adopt, agree to, authorize, endorse, legalize, enact; informal OK. **13** *she could not let that comment pass* GO (UNNOTICED), stand, go unremarked, go undisputed. **14** *we should not pass judgement* DECLARE, pronounce, utter, express, deliver, issue. **15** *passing urine* DISCHARGE, excrete, evacuate, expel, emit, release.
– OPPOSITES stop, fail, reject.
● noun **1** *you must show your pass* PERMIT, warrant, authorization, licence. **2** *a cross-field pass* KICK, hit, throw, shot.
– PHRASES **come to pass** (poetic/literary) HAPPEN, come about, occur, transpire, arise; poetic/literary befall. **make a pass at** (informal) MAKE (SEXUAL) ADVANCES TO, proposition; informal come on to, make a play for; N. Amer. informal hit on, put the make on. **pass away/on.** See DIE sense 1. **pass as/for** BE MISTAKEN FOR, be taken for, be accepted as. **pass off 1** *the rally passed off peacefully* TAKE PLACE, go off, happen, occur, be completed, turn out. **2** *when the dizziness passed off he sat up* WEAR OFF, fade (away), pass, die down. **pass someone off** MISREPRESENT, falsely represent; disguise. **pass out** FAINT, lose consciousness, black out. **pass something over** DISREGARD, overlook, ignore, pay no attention to, let pass, gloss over, take no notice of, pay no heed to, turn a blind eye to. **pass something up** TURN DOWN, reject, refuse, decline, give up, forgo, let pass, miss (out on); informal give something a miss.

pass[2] ● noun *a pass through the mountains* ROUTE, way, road, passage, cut, gap; N. Amer. notch.

passable ● adjective **1** *the beer was passable* ADEQUATE, all right, fairly good, acceptable, satisfactory, moderately good, not (too) bad, average, tolerable, fair; mediocre, middling, ordinary, indifferent, unremarkable, unexceptional; informal OK, so-so, nothing to write home about, no great shakes, not up to much; NZ informal half-pie. **2** *the road is still passable* NAVIGABLE, traversable, negotiable, unblocked, unobstructed, open, clear.

passably ● adverb QUITE, rather, somewhat, fairly, reasonably, moderately, comparatively, relatively, tolerably; informal pretty.

passage ● noun **1** *their passage through the country* TRANSIT, progress, passing, movement, motion, travelling. **2** *the passage of time* PASSING, advance, course, march. **3** *a passage from the embassy* SAFE CONDUCT, warrant, visa; admission, access. **4** *the overnight passage* VOYAGE, crossing, trip, journey. **5** *clearing a passage to the front door* WAY (THROUGH), route, path. **6** *a passage to the kitchen.* See PASSAGEWAY sense 1. **7** *a passage between the buildings.* See PASSAGEWAY sense 2. **8** *the nasal passages* DUCT, orifice, opening, channel; inlet, outlet. **9** *the passage to democracy* TRANSITION, development, progress, move, change, shift. **10** *the passage of the bill* ENACTMENT, passing, ratification, approval, adoption, authorization, legalization. **11** *a passage from 'Macbeth'* EXTRACT, excerpt, quotation, quote, citation, reading, piece, selection.

passageway ● noun **1** *secret passageways* CORRIDOR, hall, passage, hallway, walkway, aisle. **2** *a narrow passageway off the main street* ALLEY, alleyway, passage, lane, path, pathway, footpath, track, thoroughfare; N. Amer. areaway.

passé ● adjective. See OLD-FASHIONED.

passenger ● noun **1** *rail passengers* TRAVELLER, commuter, fare

passerine /passəreen/ ● adjective denoting birds of a large group (the order Passeriformes) distinguished by having feet adapted for perching and including all songbirds.
– ORIGIN from Latin *passer* 'sparrow'.

passim /passim/ ● adverb (of references) at various places throughout the text.
– ORIGIN Latin, 'everywhere'.

passing ● adjective **1** done quickly and casually. **2** (of a resemblance or similarity) slight. ● noun **1** the ending of something. **2** euphemistic a person's death.
– PHRASES **in passing** briefly and casually.

passing shot ● noun Tennis a shot aiming the ball beyond and out of reach of one's opponent.

passion ● noun **1** very strong emotion. **2** intense sexual love. **3** an outburst of very strong emotion. **4** an intense enthusiasm for something. **4** (**the Passion**) the suffering and death of Jesus.
– DERIVATIVES **passionless** adjective.
– ORIGIN Latin, from *pati* 'suffer'.

passionate ● adjective showing or caused by passion.
– DERIVATIVES **passionately** adverb.

passion flower ● noun a climbing plant with a flower whose component parts are said to suggest objects associated with Christ's Crucifixion.

passion fruit ● noun the edible purple fruit of some species of passion flower.

passion play ● noun a play about Christ's crucifixion.

passivate /passivayt/ ● verb technical make (a metal or other substance) unreactive by coating or otherwise altering the surface.
– DERIVATIVES **passivation** noun.

passive ● adjective **1** accepting or allowing what happens or what others do, without active response or resistance. **2** Grammar (of verbs) in which the subject undergoes the action of the verb (e.g. *they were killed* as opposed to the active form *he killed them*). **3** (of a circuit or device) containing no source of energy or electromotive force. **4** Chemistry unreactive because of a thin inert surface layer of oxide. ● noun Grammar a passive form of a verb.
– DERIVATIVES **passively** adverb **passiveness** noun **passivity** noun.
– ORIGIN Latin *passivus*, from *pati* 'suffer'.

passive resistance ● noun non-violent opposition to authority, especially a refusal to cooperate with legal requirements.

passive smoking ● noun the involuntary inhaling of smoke from other people's cigarettes, cigars, or pipes.

pass key ● noun **1** a key given only to those who are officially allowed access. **2** a master key.

Passover ● noun the major Jewish spring festival, commemorating the liberation of the Israelites from slavery in Egypt.
– ORIGIN from *pass over*, with reference to the exemption of the Israelites from the death of their firstborn (Book of Exodus, chapter 12).

passport ● noun **1** an official government document certifying the holder's identity and citizenship and entitling them to travel abroad under its protection. **2** a thing that enables someone to do or achieve something: *qualifications are a passport to success.*

password ● noun a secret word or phrase used to gain admission.

past ● adjective **1** gone by in time and no longer existing. **2** (of time) that has gone by. **3** Grammar (of a tense) expressing a past action or state. ● noun **1** a past period or the events in it. **2** a person's or thing's history or earlier life. **3** Grammar a past tense or form of a verb. ● preposition **1** beyond in time or space. **2** in front of or from one side to the other of. **3** beyond the scope, limits, or power of. ● adverb **1** so as to pass from one side to the other. **2** used to indicate the passage of time.
– PHRASES **not put it past** believe to be capable of doing something wrong or rash. **past it** informal too old to be any good at anything.
– ORIGIN variant of *passed*, past participle of PASS[1].

pasta ● noun dough formed into various shapes (e.g. spaghetti, lasagne), cooked as part of a dish or in boiling water and served with a savoury sauce.
– ORIGIN Italian, 'paste'.

paste ● noun **1** a thick, soft, moist substance. **2** an adhesive made from water and starch, used especially for sticking paper. **3** a hard glassy substance used in making imitation gems. **4** a mixture of kaolin and water, used for making porcelain. ● verb **1** coat or stick with paste. **2** Computing insert (a section of text) into a document. **3** informal beat or defeat severely.
– ORIGIN Latin *pasta* 'paste', probably from Greek *pastē* 'barley porridge'.

pasteboard ● noun thin board made by pasting together sheets of paper.

pastel ● noun **1** a crayon made of powdered pigments bound

Thesaurus

p

payer. **2** *we can't afford passengers* HANGER-ON, idler, parasite; *informal* freeloader.

passing ● adjective **1** *of passing interest* FLEETING, transient, transitory, ephemeral, brief, short-lived, temporary, momentary; *poetic/literary* evanescent. **2** *a passing glance* HASTY, rapid, hurried, brief, quick; cursory, superficial, casual, perfunctory.
● noun **1** *the passing of time* PASSAGE, course, progress, advance. **2** *Jack's passing* DEATH, demise, passing away/on, end, loss, quietus; *formal* decease. **3** *the passing of the new bill* ENACTMENT, ratification, approval, adoption, authorization, legalization, endorsement.
– PHRASES **in passing** INCIDENTALLY, by the by/way, en passant.

passion ● noun **1** *the passion of activists* FERVOUR, ardour, enthusiasm, eagerness, zeal, zealousness, vigour, fire, fieriness, energy, fervency, animation, spirit, spiritedness, fanaticism. **2** *he worked himself up into a passion* (BLIND) RAGE, fit of anger/temper, temper, towering rage, tantrum, fury, frenzy; *Brit. informal* paddy. **3** *hot with passion* LOVE, (sexual) desire, lust, ardour, infatuation, lasciviousness, lustfulness. **4** *his passion for football* ENTHUSIASM, love, mania, fascination, obsession, fanaticism, fixation, compulsion, appetite, addiction; *informal* thing. **5** *English literature is a passion with me* OBSESSION, preoccupation, craze, mania, hobby horse. **6** *the Passion of Christ* CRUCIFIXION, suffering, agony, martyrdom.
– OPPOSITES apathy.

passionate ● adjective **1** *a passionate entreaty* INTENSE, impassioned, ardent, fervent, vehement, fiery, heated, emotional, heartfelt, eager, excited, animated, spirited, energetic, fervid, frenzied, wild, consuming, violent; *poetic/literary* perfervid. **2** *McGregor is passionate about sport* VERY KEEN, very enthusiastic, addicted; *informal* mad, crazy, hooked, nuts; *N. Amer. informal* nutso; *Austral./NZ informal* shook. **3** *a passionate kiss* AMOROUS, ardent, hot-blooded, aroused, loving, sexy, sensual, erotic, lustful; *informal* steamy, hot, turned on. **4** *a passionate woman* EXCITABLE, emotional, fiery, volatile, mercurial, quick-tempered, highly strung, impulsive, temperamental.
– OPPOSITES apathetic.

passionless ● adjective UNEMOTIONAL, cold, cold-blooded, emotionless, frigid, cool, unfeeling, unloving, unresponsive, undemonstrative, impassive.

passive ● adjective **1** *a passive role* INACTIVE, non-active, non-participative, uninvolved. **2** *passive victims* SUBMISSIVE, acquiescent, unresisting, unassertive, compliant, pliant, obedient, docile, tractable, malleable, pliable. **3** *the woman's face was passive* EMOTIONLESS, impassive, unemotional, unmoved, dispassionate, passionless, detached, unresponsive, undemonstrative, apathetic, phlegmatic.
– OPPOSITES active.

passport ● noun **1** TRAVEL PERMIT, (travel) papers, visa, laissez-passer. **2** *qualifications are the passport to success* KEY, path, way, route, avenue, door, doorway.

password ● noun WORD OF IDENTIFICATION; *Military, archaic* watchword, countersign.

past ● adjective **1** *memories of times past* GONE (BY), over (and done with), no more, done, bygone, former, (of) old, olden, long-ago; *poetic/literary* of yore. **2** *the past few months* LAST, recent, preceding. **3** *a past chairman* PREVIOUS, former, foregoing, erstwhile, one-time, sometime, ex-; *formal* quondam.
– OPPOSITES present, future.
● noun *details about her past* HISTORY, background, life (story).
● preposition **1** *she walked past the cafe* IN FRONT OF, by. **2** *he's past retirement age* BEYOND, in excess of.
● adverb *they hurried past* ALONG, by, on.
– PHRASES **in the past** FORMERLY, previously, in days/years/times gone by, in former times, in the (good) old days, in days of old, in olden times, once (upon a time); *poetic/literary* in days of yore, in yesteryear.

paste ● noun **1** *blend the ingredients to a paste* PURÉE, pulp, mush, blend. **2** *wallpaper paste* ADHESIVE, glue, gum, fixative; *N. Amer.*

with gum or resin. **2** a picture created using pastels. **3** a pale shade of a colour. ● adjective (of a colour) pale.
– DERIVATIVES **pastellist** (also **pastelist**) noun.
– ORIGIN Italian *pastello*, from *pasta* 'paste'.
pastern /pastərn/ ● noun the part of a horse's or other animal's foot between the fetlock and the hoof.
– ORIGIN Old French *pasturon* from *pasture* 'strap for hobbling a horse'.
paste-up ● noun a document prepared for copying or printing by pasting various sections on a backing.
pasteurize /paastyərīz/ (also **pasteurise**) ● verb make (milk or other food) safe to eat by destroying most of the micro-organisms in it, especially by heating.
– DERIVATIVES **pasteurization** noun.
– ORIGIN named after the French chemist Louis *Pasteur* (1822–95).
pastiche /pasteesh/ ● noun an artistic work in a style that imitates that of another work, artist, or period.
– DERIVATIVES **pasticheur** /pastishör/ noun.
– ORIGIN Italian *pasticcio*, from Latin *pasta* 'paste'.
pastille /pastil/ ● noun **1** a small sweet or lozenge. **2** a small pellet of aromatic paste burnt as a perfume or deodorizer.
– ORIGIN Latin *pastillus* 'little loaf, lozenge'.
pastime ● noun an activity done regularly for enjoyment; a hobby.
– ORIGIN from PASS[1] + TIME.
pastis /pastiss, pasteess/ ● noun (pl. same) an aniseed-flavoured aperitif.
– ORIGIN French.
past master ● noun a person who is experienced or expert in an activity.
pastor /paastər/ ● noun a minister in charge of a Christian church or congregation, especially in some non-episcopal churches.
– ORIGIN Latin, 'shepherd'.
pastoral /paastərəl/ ● adjective **1** relating to the farming or grazing of sheep or cattle. **2** (of a literary, artistic, or musical work) portraying country life, especially in an idealized form. **3** relating to the giving of spiritual guidance by a member of the clergy. **4** relating to a teacher's responsibility for the general well-being of pupils or students. ● noun a pastoral poem, picture, or piece of music.
– DERIVATIVES **pastoralism** noun.
pastoralist ● noun (especially in Australia and New Zealand) a sheep or cattle farmer.
past participle ● noun Grammar the form of a verb, typically ending in *-ed* in English, which is used in forming perfect and passive tenses and sometimes as an adjective, e.g. *looked* in *have you looked?*, *lost* in *lost property*.
pastrami /pastraami/ ● noun highly seasoned smoked beef.
– ORIGIN Yiddish.
pastry ● noun (pl. **pastries**) **1** a dough of flour, fat, and water, used as a base and covering in baked dishes such as pies. **2** a cake consisting of sweet pastry with a cream, jam, or fruit filling.
– ORIGIN from PASTE.
pasturage ● noun **1** land used for pasture. **2** the pasturing of animals.
pasture ● noun **1** land covered with grass, suitable for grazing cattle or sheep. **2** grass growing on such land. ● verb put (animals) to graze in a pasture.
– PHRASES **pastures new** somewhere offering new opportunities. [ORIGIN suggested by 'Tomorrow to fresh woods and pastures new' (Milton's *Lycidas*).] **put out to pasture** force to retire.
– ORIGIN Latin *pastura* 'grazing', from *pascere* 'graze'.
pasty[1] /pasti/ (also **pastie**) ● noun (pl. **pasties**) chiefly Brit. a folded pastry case filled with seasoned meat and vegetables.
– ORIGIN Old French *pastee*, from Latin *pasta* 'paste'.
pasty[2] /paysti/ ● adjective (**pastier**, **pastiest**) **1** of or like paste. **2** (of a person's skin) unhealthily pale.
pat[1] ● verb (**patted**, **patting**) **1** tap quickly and gently with the flat of the hand. **2** mould or position with gentle taps. ● noun **1** an act of patting. **2** a compact mass of a soft substance.
– PHRASES **a pat on the back** an expression of congratulation or encouragement.
– ORIGIN probably imitative.
pat[2] ● adjective prompt but glib or unconvincing: *a pat answer*. ● adverb conveniently or opportunely.
– PHRASES **have off** (or **down**) **pat** have (something) memorized perfectly.
– ORIGIN apparently originally 'as if with a pat'; related to PAT[1].
pataca /pətaakə/ ● noun the basic monetary unit of Macao, equivalent to 100 avos.
– ORIGIN Spanish and Portuguese.
Patagonian /pattəgōniən/ ● noun a person from the South American region of Patagonia. ● adjective relating to Patagonia.
patch ● noun **1** a piece of material used to mend a hole or strengthen a weak point. **2** a small area differing in colour, composition, or texture from its surroundings. **3** a small plot of land: *a cabbage patch*. **4** Brit. informal a brief period of time: *a bad patch*. **5** Brit. informal an area for which someone is responsible or in which they operate. **6** a shield worn over a sightless or injured eye. **7** an adhesive piece of drug-impregnated material worn on the skin so that the drug may be gradually absorbed. **8** a temporary electrical or telephone connection. **9** Computing a small piece of code inserted to correct or enhance a program. ● verb **1** mend, strengthen, or protect by means of a patch. **2** (**patch up**) informal treat (injuries) or repair (something) hastily or temporarily. **3** (**patch up**) informal settle (a quarrel or dispute). **4** (**patch together**) assemble hastily. **5** connect by a temporary electrical, radio, or telephonic connection.
– PHRASES **not a patch on** Brit. informal greatly inferior to.
– DERIVATIVES **patcher** noun.
– ORIGIN perhaps from Old French dialect *pieche* 'piece'.
patchouli /pəchōōli/ ● noun an aromatic oil obtained from a SE

Thesaurus

mucilage. **3** *fish paste* SPREAD, pâté.
● verb *a notice was pasted on the door* GLUE, stick, gum, fix, affix.
pastel ● adjective PALE, soft, light, light-coloured, muted, subtle, subdued, soft-hued.
– OPPOSITES dark, bright.
pastiche ● noun **1** *a pastiche of literary models* MIXTURE, blend, medley, melange, miscellany, mixed bag, pot-pourri, mix, compound, composite, collection, assortment, conglomeration, hotchpotch, jumble, ragbag; *N. Amer.* hodgepodge. **2** *a pastiche of 18th-century style* IMITATION, parody; *informal* take-off.
pastille ● noun LOZENGE, sweet, drop; tablet, pill.
pastime ● noun HOBBY, leisure activity/pursuit, sport, game, recreation, amusement, diversion, entertainment, interest, sideline.
past master ● noun EXPERT, master, wizard, genius, old hand, veteran, maestro, connoisseur, authority, grandmaster; *informal* ace, pro, star, hotshot; *Brit. informal* dab hand; *N. Amer. informal* maven, crackerjack.
pastor ● noun PRIEST, minister (of religion), parson, clergyman, cleric, chaplain, ecclesiastic, man of the cloth, churchman, vicar, rector, curate, preacher; *informal* reverend, padre; *Austral. informal* josser.
pastoral ● adjective **1** *a pastoral scene* RURAL, country, countryside, rustic, agricultural, bucolic; *poetic/literary* sylvan, Arcadian. **2** *his pastoral duties* PRIESTLY, clerical, ecclesiastical, ministerial.
– OPPOSITES urban.
pastry ● noun **1** *pastries for tea* TART, tartlet, pie, pasty, patty. **2** *two layers of pastry* CRUST, piecrust, croute.
pasture ● noun GRAZING (LAND), grassland, grass, pastureland, pasturage, ley; meadow, field; *Austral./NZ* run; *poetic/literary* lea, mead, greensward.
pasty ● adjective PALE, pallid, wan, colourless, anaemic, ashen, white, grey, pasty-faced, washed out, sallow.
pat[1] ● verb *Brian patted her on the shoulder* TAP, slap lightly, clap, touch.
● noun **1** *a pat on the cheek* TAP, light blow, clap, touch. **2** *a pat of butter* PIECE, dab, lump, portion, knob, mass, gobbet, ball, curl.
– PHRASES **pat someone on the back** CONGRATULATE, praise, take one's hat off to; commend, compliment, applaud, acclaim.
pat[2] ● adjective *pat answers* GLIB, simplistic, facile, unconvincing.
● adverb *his reply came rather pat* OPPORTUNELY, conveniently, at just/exactly the right moment, expediently, favourably, appropriately, fittingly, auspiciously, providentially, felicitously, propitiously.
– PHRASES **off pat** WORD-PERFECT, by heart, by rote, by memory, parrot-fashion. **get something off pat** MEMORIZE, commit to memory, remember, learn by heart, learn (by rote).
patch ● noun **1** *a patch over one eye* COVER, eyepatch, covering, pad. **2** *a reddish patch on her wrist* BLOTCH, mark, spot, smudge, speckle, smear, stain, streak, blemish; *informal* splodge, splotch. **3** *a patch of ground* PLOT, area, piece, strip, tract, parcel; bed; *Brit.* al-

Asian shrub, used in perfumery, insecticides, and medicine.
– ORIGIN Tamil.

patch pocket • noun a pocket made of a separate piece of cloth sewn on to the outside of a garment.

patch test • noun an allergy test in which a range of substances are applied to the skin in light scratches or under a plaster.

patchwork • noun **1** needlework in which small pieces of cloth in different designs are sewn edge to edge. **2** a thing composed of many different elements: *a patchwork of educational courses.*

patchy • adjective (**patchier**, **patchiest**) **1** existing or happening in small, isolated areas: *patchy fog.* **2** uneven in quality; inconsistent.
– DERIVATIVES **patchily** adverb **patchiness** noun.

pate /payt/ • noun archaic or humorous a person's head.
– ORIGIN of unknown origin.

pâté /pattay/ • noun a rich savoury paste made from finely minced or mashed meat, fish, or other ingredients.
– ORIGIN French, from Old French *paste* 'pie of seasoned meat'.

pâté de foie gras /pattay də fwaa graa/ • noun a pâté made from fatted goose liver.

patella /pətellə/ • noun (pl. **patellae** /pətelllee/) Anatomy the kneecap.
– DERIVATIVES **patellar** adjective.
– ORIGIN Latin, 'small dish'.

paten /patt'n/ • noun a plate for holding the bread during the Eucharist.
– ORIGIN Greek *patanē* 'a plate'.

patent /patt'nt, payt'nt/ • noun a government licence giving an individual or body the sole right to make, use, or sell an invention for a set period. • adjective /payt'nt/ **1** easily recognizable; obvious. **2** made and marketed under a patent. • verb obtain a patent for.
– DERIVATIVES **patentable** adjective **patently** /paytəntli/ adverb.
– ORIGIN from Latin *patere* 'lie open'; see also LETTERS PATENT.

patentee /paytəntee/ • noun a person or body that obtains or holds a patent.

patent leather • noun glossy varnished leather.

patent medicine • noun a medicine made and marketed under a patent and available without prescription.

pater /paytər/ • noun Brit. informal, dated father.
– ORIGIN Latin.

paterfamilias /paytərfəmilliass/ • noun (pl. **patresfamilias** /paytreez-/) the male head of a family or household.
– ORIGIN Latin, 'father of the family'.

paternal • adjective **1** of, like, or appropriate to a father. **2** related through the father.
– DERIVATIVES **paternally** adverb.

paternalism • noun the policy of restricting the freedom and responsibilities of subordinates or dependents in their supposed best interest.
– DERIVATIVES **paternalist** noun & adjective **paternalistic** adjective.

paternity • noun **1** the state of being a father. **2** descent from a father.

paternity suit • noun chiefly N. Amer. a court case held to establish the identity of a child's father.

paternoster /pattərnostər/ • noun (in the Roman Catholic Church) the Lord's Prayer, especially in Latin.
– ORIGIN from Latin *pater noster* 'our father', the first words of the Lord's Prayer.

path • noun **1** a way or track laid down for walking or made by continual treading. **2** the direction in which a person or thing moves. **3** a course of action or conduct.
– ORIGIN Old English.

-path • combining form **1** denoting a practitioner of curative treatment: *homeopath.* **2** denoting a person who suffers from a disease: *psychopath.*
– ORIGIN from -PATHY or from Greek *-pathēs* '-sufferer'.

Pathan /pətaan/ • noun a member of a Pashto-speaking people inhabiting NW Pakistan and SE Afghanistan.
– ORIGIN Hindi.

path-breaking • adjective pioneering; innovative.

pathetic • adjective **1** arousing pity. **2** informal miserably inadequate. **3** archaic relating to the emotions.
– DERIVATIVES **pathetically** adverb.
– ORIGIN Greek *pathētikos* 'sensitive', from *pathos* 'suffering'.

pathetic fallacy • noun the attribution of human feelings to inanimate things or animals.

pathfinder • noun a person who goes ahead and discovers or shows others a way.

pathname • noun Computing a description of where an item is to be found in a hierarchy of directories.

patho- • combining form relating to disease: *pathology.*
– ORIGIN from Greek *pathos* 'suffering, disease'.

pathogen /pathəjən/ • noun a micro-organism that can cause disease.
– DERIVATIVES **pathogenic** adjective.

pathological (US **pathologic**) • adjective **1** of or caused by a disease. **2** informal compulsive: *a pathological liar.* **3** relating to pathology.
– DERIVATIVES **pathologically** adverb.

pathology • noun **1** the branch of medicine concerned with the causes and effects of diseases. **2** the typical behaviour of a disease.
– DERIVATIVES **pathologist** noun.

pathos /paythoss/ • noun a quality that evokes pity or sadness.
– ORIGIN Greek, 'suffering'.

pathway • noun **1** a path or its course. **2** a sequence of changes or events constituting a progression.

-pathy • combining form **1** denoting feelings: *telepathy.* **2** denoting disorder in a part of the body: *neuropathy.* **3** denoting curative treatment: *hydropathy.*
– ORIGIN from Greek *patheia* 'suffering, feeling'.

patience • noun **1** the capacity to tolerate delay, trouble, or suffering without becoming angry or upset. **2** chiefly Brit. a card game for one player.
– ORIGIN Latin *patientia*, from *pati* 'suffer'.

patient • adjective having or showing patience. • noun a person

Thesaurus

lotment; *N. Amer.* lot. **4** *(Brit. informal) they are going through a difficult patch* PERIOD, time, spell, phase, stretch; *Brit. informal* spot.
• verb *her jeans were neatly patched* MEND, repair, put a patch on, sew (up), stitch (up).
– PHRASES **patch something up** *(informal)* **1** *the houses were being patched up* REPAIR, mend, fix hastily, do a makeshift repair on. **2** *he's trying to patch things up with his wife* RECONCILE, make up, settle, remedy, put to rights, rectify, clear up, set right, make good, resolve, square.

patchwork • noun ASSORTMENT, miscellany, mixture, melange, medley, blend, mixed bag, mix, collection, selection, assemblage, combination, pot-pourri, jumble, mishmash, hotchpotch, ragbag; *N. Amer.* hodgepodge.

patchy • adjective **1** *their teaching has been patchy* UNEVEN, bitty, varying, variable, intermittent, fitful, sporadic, erratic, irregular. **2** *patchy evidence* FRAGMENTARY, inadequate, insufficient, rudimentary, limited, sketchy.
– OPPOSITES uniform, comprehensive.

patent • noun *there is a patent on the chemical* COPYRIGHT, licence, legal protection, registered trademark.
• adjective **1** *patent nonsense* OBVIOUS, clear, plain, evident, manifest, self-evident, transparent, overt, conspicuous, blatant, downright, barefaced, flagrant, undisguised, unconcealed, unmistakable. **2** *patent medicines* PROPRIETARY, patented, licensed, branded.

paternal • adjective **1** *paternal concern* FATHERLY, fatherlike, patriarchal; protective, solicitous, compassionate, sympathetic. **2** *his paternal grandfather* ON ONE'S FATHER'S SIDE, patrilineal.
– OPPOSITES maternal.

paternity • noun FATHERHOOD.

path • noun **1** *a path down to the beach* FOOTPATH, pathway, footway, pavement, track, trail, trackway, bridleway, bridle path, lane, alley, alleyway, passage, passageway; cycle path/track; *N. Amer.* sidewalk, bikeway. **2** *journalists blocked his path* ROUTE, way, course; direction, bearing, line; orbit, trajectory. **3** *the best path towards a settlement* COURSE OF ACTION, route, road, avenue, line, approach, tack, strategy, tactic.

pathetic • adjective **1** *a pathetic groan* PITIFUL, pitiable, piteous, moving, touching, poignant, plaintive, distressing, upsetting, heartbreaking, heart-rending, harrowing, wretched, forlorn. **2** *(informal) a pathetic excuse* FEEBLE, woeful, sorry, poor, pitiful, lamentable, deplorable, contemptible, inadequate, paltry, insufficient, insubstantial, unsatisfactory.

pathfinder • noun PIONEER, trailblazer, ground-breaker, trendsetter, leader, torch-bearer, pacemaker.

pathological • adjective **1** *a pathological condition* MORBID, diseased. **2** *(informal) a pathological liar* COMPULSIVE, obsessive, inveter-

receiving or registered to receive medical treatment.
– DERIVATIVES **patiently** adverb.

patina /pattinə/ ● noun **1** a green or brown film on the surface of old bronze. **2** a sheen on wooden furniture produced by age and polishing. **3** a superficial covering or appearance gained over time: *rugs with a patina of cigarette ash.*
– DERIVATIVES **patinated** adjective **patination** noun.
– ORIGIN Latin, 'shallow dish'.

patio ● noun (pl. **patios**) **1** a paved outdoor area adjoining a house. **2** a roofless inner courtyard in a Spanish or Spanish-American house.
– ORIGIN Spanish.

patio door ● noun a large glass sliding door leading to a patio, garden, or balcony.

patisserie /pətissəri/ ● noun **1** a shop where pastries and cakes are sold. **2** pastries and cakes collectively.
– ORIGIN French, from Latin *pasticium* 'pastry'.

patois /patwaa/ ● noun (pl. same or /patwaaz/) the dialect of a region, differing in various respects from the standard language of the country.
– ORIGIN French, 'rough speech'.

patresfamilias plural of PATERFAMILIAS.

patriarch /paytriaark/ ● noun **1** the male head of a family or tribe. **2** a biblical figure regarded as a father of the human race, especially Abraham, Isaac, and Jacob, and their forefathers, or the sons of Jacob. **3** a powerful or respected older man. **4** a high-ranking bishop in certain Christian churches. **5** the head of an independent Orthodox Church.
– DERIVATIVES **patriarchal** adjective **patriarchate** noun.
– ORIGIN Greek *patriarkhēs*, from *patria* 'family' + *arkhēs* 'ruling'.

patriarchy ● noun (pl. **patriarchies**) **1** a form of social organization in which the father or eldest male is the head of the family and descent is reckoned through the male line. **2** a system of society in which men hold most or all of the power.

patrician /pətrish'n/ ● noun **1** an aristocrat. **2** a member of the nobility in ancient Rome. ● adjective relating to or characteristic of aristocrats; upper-class.
– ORIGIN Latin *patricius* 'having a noble father', from *pater* 'father'.

patricide /patrisid/ ● noun **1** the killing of one's father. **2** a person who kills their father.
– ORIGIN Latin *patricidium*, alteration of *parricidium* 'parricide'.

patrilineal ● adjective relating to or based on relationship to the father or descent through the male line.

patrimony /patriməni/ ● noun (pl. **patrimonies**) **1** property inherited from one's father or male ancestor. **2** heritage.
– ORIGIN Latin *patrimonium*, from *pater* 'father'.

patriot /paytriət, pat-/ ● noun a person who vigorously supports their country and is prepared to defend it.
– DERIVATIVES **patriotic** adjective **patriotically** adverb **patriotism** noun.
– ORIGIN Latin *patriota* 'fellow countryman', from Greek *patris* 'fatherland'.

patristic /pətristik/ ● adjective relating to the early Christian theologians or their writings.
– ORIGIN German *patristisch*, from Latin *pater* 'father'.

patrol ● noun **1** a person or group sent to keep watch over an area, especially a detachment of guards or police. **2** the action of patrolling an area. **3** a military or naval expedition to carry out reconnaissance. **4** a unit of six to eight Scouts or Guides forming part of a troop. ● verb (**patrolled**, **patrolling**) keep watch over (an area) by regularly walking or travelling around it.
– DERIVATIVES **patroller** noun.
– ORIGIN from French *patrouiller* 'paddle in mud'.

patrolman ● noun N. Amer. a patrolling police officer.

patron ● noun **1** a person who gives financial or other support to a person, organization, cause, etc. **2** a regular customer of a restaurant, hotel, etc.
– DERIVATIVES **patroness** noun.
– ORIGIN Latin *patronus* 'defender', from *pater* 'father'.

patronage /patrənij, pay-/ ● noun **1** support given by a patron. **2** the power to control appointments to office or the right to privileges. **3** a patronizing manner. **4** the regular custom attracted by a restaurant, hotel, etc.

patronize (also **patronise**) ● verb **1** treat condescendingly. **2** be a patron of.

patron saint ● noun the protecting or guiding saint of a person or place.

patronymic /patrənimik/ ● noun a name derived from the name of a father or ancestor, e.g. *Johnson, O'Brien, Ivanovich.*
– ORIGIN Greek *patrōnumikos*, from *patēr* 'father' + *onoma* 'name'.

patsy ● noun (pl. **patsies**) informal, chiefly N. Amer. a person who is taken advantage of or tricked.
– ORIGIN of unknown origin.

patten /patt'n/ ● noun historical a shoe or clog with a raised sole or set on an iron ring, worn to raise the feet above wet ground.

Thesaurus

ate, habitual, persistent, chronic, hardened, confirmed.

pathos ● noun POIGNANCY, tragedy, sadness, pitifulness, piteousness, pitiableness.

patience ● noun **1** *she tried everyone's patience* FORBEARANCE, tolerance, restraint, self-restraint, stoicism; calmness, composure, equanimity, serenity, tranquillity, imperturbability, understanding, indulgence. **2** *a task requiring patience* PERSEVERANCE, persistence, endurance, tenacity, assiduity, application, staying power, doggedness, determination, resolve, resolution, resoluteness; *formal* pertinacity.

patient ● adjective **1** *I must ask you to be patient* FORBEARING, uncomplaining, tolerant, resigned, stoical; calm, composed, even-tempered, imperturbable, unexcitable, accommodating, understanding, indulgent; *informal* unflappable, cool. **2** *a good deal of patient work* PERSEVERING, persistent, tenacious, indefatigable, dogged, determined, resolved, resolute, single-minded; *formal* pertinacious.
● noun *a doctor's patient* SICK PERSON, case; invalid, convalescent, outpatient, inpatient.

patio ● noun TERRACE; courtyard, quadrangle, quad; *N. Amer.* sun deck.

patois ● noun VERNACULAR, (local) dialect, regional language; jargon, argot, cant; *informal* (local) lingo.

patriarch ● noun SENIOR FIGURE, father, paterfamilias, leader, elder.

patrician ● noun *the great patricians* ARISTOCRAT, grandee, noble, nobleman, noblewoman, lord, lady, peer, peeress.
● adjective *patrician families* ARISTOCRATIC, noble, titled, blue-blooded, high-born, upper-class, landowning; *informal* upper-crust; *archaic* gentle.

patrimony ● noun HERITAGE, inheritance, birthright; legacy, bequest, endowment, bequeathal; *Law, dated* hereditament.

patriot ● noun NATIONALIST, loyalist; chauvinist, jingoist, flag-waver.

patriotic ● adjective NATIONALIST, nationalistic, loyalist, loyal; chauvinistic, jingoistic, flag-waving.
– OPPOSITES traitorous.

patriotism ● noun NATIONALISM, allegiance/loyalty to one's country, patriotic sentiment; chauvinism, jingoism, flag-waving.
– OPPOSITES treachery.

patrol ● noun **1** *anti-poaching patrols* VIGIL, guard, watch, monitoring, policing, beat-pounding, patrolling; reconnoitre, surveillance; *informal* recce. **2** *the patrol stopped a suspect* PATROLMAN, PATROLWOMAN, sentinel, sentry; scout, scouting party, task force.
● verb *a security guard was patrolling a housing estate* KEEP GUARD (ON), guard, keep watch (on); police, pound the beat (of), make the rounds (of); stand guard (over), keep a vigil (on), defend, safeguard.

patron ● noun **1** *a patron of the arts* SPONSOR, backer, financier, benefactor, benefactress, contributor, subscriber, donor; philanthropist, promoter, friend, supporter; *informal* angel. **2** *club patrons* CUSTOMER, client, frequenter, consumer, user, visitor, guest; *informal* regular.

patronage ● noun **1** *art patronage* SPONSORSHIP, backing, funding, financing, promotion, assistance, support. **2** *political patronage* POWER OF APPOINTMENT, favouritism, nepotism, preferential treatment. **3** *a slight note of patronage* CONDESCENSION, patronizing, patronization, disdain, disrespect, scorn, contempt. **4** *thank you for your patronage* CUSTOM, trade, business.

patronize ● verb **1** *don't patronize me!* TREAT CONDESCENDINGLY, condescend to, look down on, talk down to, put down, treat like a child, treat with disdain. **2** *they patronized local tradesmen* DO BUSINESS WITH, buy from, shop at, be a customer of, be a client of, deal with, trade with, frequent, support. **3** *he patronized a national museum* SPONSOR, back, fund, finance, be a patron of, support, champion.

patronizing ● adjective CONDESCENDING, supercilious, superior, im-

– ORIGIN Old French *patin.*

patter[1] ● verb **1** make a repeated light tapping sound. **2** run with quick light steps. ● noun a repeated light tapping sound.
– ORIGIN from PAT[1].

patter[2] ● noun **1** rapid continuous talk, such as that used by a comedian or salesman. **2** the jargon of a profession or social group. ● verb talk trivially and at length.
– ORIGIN originally in the sense 'recite rapidly': from PATERNOSTER (from the rapid and mechanical way in which the prayer was often said).

pattern ● noun **1** a repeated decorative design. **2** a regular or discernible form or order in which a series of things occur: *working patterns.* **3** a model, design, or set of instructions for making something. **4** an example for others to follow. **5** a model from which a mould is made for a casting. **6** a sample of cloth or wallpaper. ● verb **1** decorate with a pattern. **2** give a regular or discernible form to.
– ORIGIN from PATRON in the former sense 'something serving as a model', from the idea of a patron giving an example to be copied.

patty ● noun (pl. **patties**) **1** N. Amer. a small flat cake of minced food, especially meat. **2** a small pie or pasty.
– ORIGIN alteration of French *pâté.*

paua /powə/ ● noun **1** a large New Zealand abalone or its shell. **2** a Maori fish hook made from an abalone shell.
– ORIGIN Maori.

paucity /pawsiti/ ● noun smallness or insufficiency of supply or quantity.
– ORIGIN from Latin *paucus* 'few'.

Pauline /pawlīn/ ● adjective relating to or characteristic of St Paul.

paunch ● noun a large or protruding abdomen or stomach. ● verb disembowel (an animal).
– DERIVATIVES **paunchy** adjective.
– ORIGIN Old French *paunche,* from Latin *pantex* 'intestines'.

pauper ● noun **1** a very poor person. **2** historical a recipient of public charity.
– DERIVATIVES **pauperism** noun **pauperize** (also **pauperise**) verb.
– ORIGIN from Latin, 'poor'.

pause ● noun **1** a temporary stop in action or speech. **2** Music a mark (𝄐) over a note or rest that is to be lengthened by an unspecified amount. ● verb stop temporarily.
– PHRASES **give pause** (or **give pause for thought**) **to** cause to stop and think before doing something.
– ORIGIN Greek *pausis,* from *pausein* 'to stop'.

pavane /pəvan/ (also **pavan** /pavv'n/) ● noun a stately dance in slow duple time, popular in the 16th and 17th centuries.
– ORIGIN French, perhaps from Italian *pavana* 'Paduan', from the dialect name of the city of *Padua.*

pave ● verb cover (a piece of ground) with flat stones or bricks.
– PHRASES **pave the way for** create the circumstances to enable (something) to happen.
– DERIVATIVES **paver** noun **paving** noun.
– ORIGIN Old French *paver.*

pavement ● noun **1** Brit. a raised paved or asphalted path for pedestrians at the side of a road. **2** N. Amer. the hard surface of a road or street. **3** Geology a horizontal expanse of bare rock with cracks or joints.
– ORIGIN Latin *pavimentum* 'trodden down floor'.

pavilion ● noun **1** Brit. a building at a sports ground used for changing and taking refreshments. **2** a summer house or other decorative shelter in a park or large garden. **3** a marquee with a peak and crenellated decorations, used at a show or fair. **4** a temporary display stand or other structure at a trade exhibition.
– ORIGIN Old French *pavillon,* from Latin *papilio* 'butterfly or tent'.

pavlova ● noun a dessert consisting of a meringue base or shell filled with whipped cream and fruit.
– ORIGIN named after the Russian ballerina Anna *Pavlova* (1881–1931).

Pavlovian /pavlōviən/ ● adjective relating to conditioned reflexes as described by the Russian physiologist Ivan P. Pavlov (1849–1936), famous for training dogs to respond instantly to various stimuli.

paw ● noun **1** an animal's foot having claws and pads. **2** informal a person's hand. ● verb **1** feel or scrape with a paw or hoof. **2** informal touch or handle clumsily or lasciviously.
– ORIGIN Old French *poue.*

pawky ● adjective (**pawkier, pawkiest**) chiefly Scottish & N. English drily humorous; sardonic.
– ORIGIN from Scots and northern English *pawk* 'trick'.

pawl /pawl/ ● noun **1** a pivoted bar or lever whose free end engages with the teeth of a cogwheel or ratchet, allowing it to move or turn in one direction only. **2** each of a set of short stout bars used to prevent a capstan, windlass, or winch from recoiling.
– ORIGIN perhaps from Low German and Dutch *pal.*

pawn[1] ● noun **1** a chess piece of the smallest size and value. **2** a person used by others for their own purposes.
– ORIGIN Old French *poun,* from Latin *pedo* 'foot soldier'.

pawn[2] ● verb deposit (an object) with a pawnbroker as security for money lent. ● noun the state of being pawned: *everything was in pawn.*
– ORIGIN from Old French *pan* 'pledge, security'.

pawnbroker ● noun a person licensed to lend money at interest on the security of an article deposited with him or her.

Pawnee /pawnee/ ● noun (pl. same or **Pawnees**) a member of an American Indian confederacy formerly living in Nebraska, and now mainly in Oklahoma.
– ORIGIN from a North American Indian language.

pawnshop ● noun a pawnbroker's shop.

p

Thesaurus

perious, disdainful, scornful, contemptuous; *informal* uppity, high and mighty.

patter[1] ● verb **1** *raindrops pattered against the window* GO PITTER-PATTER, tap, drum, beat, pound, rat-a-tat, go pit-a-pat, thrum. **2** *she pattered across the floor* SCURRY, scuttle, skip, trip.
● noun *the patter of rain* PITTER-PATTER, tapping, pattering, drumming, beat, beating, pounding, rat-a-tat, pit-a-pat, clack, thrum, thrumming.

patter[2] ● noun **1** *this witty patter* PRATTLE, prating, blather, blither, drivel, chatter, jabber, babble; *informal* yabbering, yatter; *archaic* twaddle. **2** *the salesmen's patter* (SALES) PITCH, sales talk; *informal* line. **3** *the local patter* SPEECH, language, parlance, dialect; *informal* lingo.
● verb *she pattered on incessantly* PRATTLE, prate, blather, blither, drivel, chatter, jabber, babble; *informal* yabber, yatter; *Brit. informal* rabbit, witter.

pattern ● noun **1** *the pattern on the wallpaper* DESIGN, decoration, motif, marking, ornament, ornamentation. **2** *working patterns* SYSTEM, order, arrangement, method, structure, scheme, plan, form, format, framework. **3** *this would set the pattern for a generation* MODEL, example, criterion, standard, basis, point of reference, gauge, norm, yardstick, touchstone, benchmark; blueprint, archetype, prototype. **4** *textile patterns* SAMPLE, specimen, swatch.
● verb *someone else is patterning my life* SHAPE, influence, model, fashion, mould, style, determine, control.

patterned ● adjective DECORATED, ornamented, fancy, adorned, embellished.
– OPPOSITES plain.

paucity ● noun SCARCITY, sparseness, sparsity, dearth, shortage, poverty, insufficiency, deficiency, lack, want; *formal* exiguity.
– OPPOSITES abundance.

paunch ● noun POT BELLY, beer belly; *informal* beer gut, pot; *dated* corporation.

pauper ● noun POOR PERSON, indigent, down-and-out; *informal* have-not.

pause ● noun *a pause in the conversation* STOP, cessation, break, halt, interruption, check, lull, respite, breathing space, discontinuation, hiatus, gap, interlude; adjournment, suspension, rest, wait, hesitation; *informal* let-up, breather.
● verb *Hannah paused for a moment* STOP, cease, halt, discontinue, break off, take a break; adjourn, rest, wait, hesitate, falter, waver; *informal* take a breather.

pave ● verb *the yard was paved* TILE, surface, flag.
– PHRASES **pave the way for** PREPARE (THE WAY) FOR, make preparations for, get ready for, lay the foundations for, herald, precede.

pavement ● noun FOOTPATH, walkway, footway; *N. Amer.* sidewalk.

paw ● noun FOOT, forepaw, hind paw.
● verb (*informal*) **1** *their offspring were pawing each other* HANDLE ROUGHLY, maul, manhandle. **2** *some Casanova tried to paw her* FONDLE, feel, maul, molest; *informal* grope, feel up, touch up.

pawn[1] ● verb *he pawned his watch* PLEDGE, put in pawn, give as security, use as collateral; *informal* hock, put in hock.

pawpaw /pawpaw/ (also **papaw**) /pəpaw/ ● noun **1** a papaya. **2** US the sweet oblong yellow fruit of a North American tree.
– ORIGIN Spanish and Portuguese *papaya*, from Carib.
pax ● noun (in the Christian Church) the kiss of peace.
– ORIGIN Latin, 'peace'.
pay ● verb (past and past part. **paid**) **1** give (someone) money due for work, goods, or an outstanding debt. **2** give (a sum of money) thus owed. **3** be profitable or advantageous: *crime doesn't pay.* **4** suffer a loss or misfortune as a consequence of an action: *someone's got to pay for all that grief.* **5** give (attention, respect, or a compliment) to. **6** give what is due or deserved to. **7** make (a visit or a call) to. ● noun money paid for work.
– PHRASES **he who pays the piper calls the tune** proverb the person providing the money for something has the right to determine how it's spent. **hit** (or **strike**) **pay dirt** N. Amer. informal find or reach a source of profit. [ORIGIN from *pay dirt* in the sense 'ground containing a profitable amount of ore'.] **pay back** take revenge on. **pay dearly** suffer for a misdemeanour or failure. **pay one's last respects** show respect towards a dead person by attending their funeral. **pay off 1** dismiss with a final payment. **2** informal yield good results. **pay out** let out (a rope) by slackening it. **pay through the nose** informal pay much more than a fair price.
– DERIVATIVES **payer** noun.
– ORIGIN originally in the sense 'pacify', the notion of 'payment' deriving from the sense of 'pacifying' a creditor: from Old French *payer* 'appease', from Latin *pax* 'peace'.
payable ● adjective **1** that must be paid. **2** able to be paid.
payback ● noun **1** profit from an investment equal to the initial outlay. **2** informal an act of revenge.
pay bed ● noun (in the UK) a hospital bed for private patients in a National Health Service hospital.
pay channel ● noun a television channel for which viewers pay a subscription fee additional to that already paid for a cable or satellite service.
PAYE ● abbreviation (in the UK) pay as you earn, a system whereby an employer deducts income tax from an employee's wages.
payee ● noun a person to whom money is paid or to be paid.
paying guest ● noun a lodger.
payload ● noun **1** the part of a vehicle's load which earns revenue; passengers and cargo. **2** an explosive warhead carried by an aircraft or missile. **3** the load carried by a spacecraft.
paymaster ● noun **1** a person who pays another and therefore controls them. **2** an official who pays troops or workers.
payment ● noun **1** the action of paying or the process of being paid. **2** an amount paid or payable.
pay-off ● noun informal **1** a payment, especially a bribe. **2** the return on investment or on a bet. **3** a final outcome.
payola /payōlə/ ● noun chiefly N. Amer. bribery in return for the unofficial promotion of a product in the media.
– ORIGIN from PAY + *-ola* as in *Victrola*, a make of gramophone; the term originally referred to the bribery of a disc jockey to promote a record.
payphone ● noun a public telephone operated by coins or by a credit or prepaid card.
payroll ● noun a list of a company's employees and the amount of money they are to be paid.
Pb ● symbol the chemical element lead.
– ORIGIN from Latin *plumbum*.
pb ● abbreviation paperback.
PC ● abbreviation **1** personal computer. **2** police constable. **3** (also **pc**) politically correct; political correctness.
p.c. ● abbreviation per cent.
PCB ● abbreviation **1** Electronics printed circuit board. **2** Chemistry polychlorinated biphenyl.
PCP ● abbreviation phencyclidine.
PCV ● abbreviation Brit. passenger-carrying vehicle.
Pd ● symbol the chemical element palladium.
PDQ ● abbreviation informal pretty damn quick.
PDSA ● abbreviation (in the UK) People's Dispensary for Sick Animals.
PDT ● abbreviation Pacific Daylight Time.
PE ● abbreviation **1** physical education. **2** Prince Edward Island.
pea ● noun **1** a spherical green seed eaten as a vegetable. **2** the climbing leguminous plant which has pods containing peas.
– ORIGIN from PEASE, which was interpreted as being plural but in fact meant 'pea' in Old English; from Greek *pison*.
peace ● noun **1** freedom from disturbance; tranquillity. **2** freedom from or the ending of war. **3** (**the peace**) Christian Church an action such as a handshake, signifying unity, performed during the Eucharist.
– PHRASES **at peace 1** free from anxiety or distress. **2** euphemistic dead. **hold one's peace** remain silent. **keep the peace** refrain or prevent others from disturbing civil order. **make** (**one's**) **peace** become reconciled.
– ORIGIN Old French *pais*, from Latin *pax*.
peaceable ● adjective **1** inclined to avoid war. **2** free from conflict; peaceful.
– DERIVATIVES **peaceably** adverb.
peace dividend ● noun a sum of public money available for other purposes when spending on defence is reduced.
peaceful ● adjective **1** free from disturbance; calm. **2** not involving war or violence. **3** inclined to avoid conflict.
– DERIVATIVES **peacefully** adverb **peacefulness** noun.
peacekeeping ● noun the active maintenance of a truce, espe-

Thesaurus

pawn² ● noun *a pawn in the battle for the throne* PUPPET, dupe, hostage, tool, cat's paw, instrument.
pay ● verb **1** *I must pay him for his work* REWARD, reimburse, recompense, give payment to, remunerate. **2** *you must pay a few more pounds* SPEND, expend, pay out, dish out, disburse; *informal* lay out, shell out, fork out, cough up; *N. Amer. informal* ante up, pony up. **3** *he paid his debts* DISCHARGE, settle, pay off, clear, liquidate. **4** *hard work will pay dividends* YIELD, return, produce. **5** *he made the buses pay* BE PROFITABLE, make money, make a profit. **6** *it may pay you to be early* BE ADVANTAGEOUS TO, benefit, be of advantage to, be beneficial to. **7** *paying compliments* BESTOW, grant, give, offer. **8** *he will pay for his mistakes* SUFFER (THE CONSEQUENCES), be punished, atone, pay the penalty/price.
● noun *equal pay for women* SALARY, wages, payment; earnings, remuneration, reimbursement, income, revenue; *formal* emolument(s).
– PHRASES **pay someone back/out** GET ONE'S REVENGE ON, be revenged on, avenge oneself on, get back at, get even with, settle accounts with, pay someone out, exact retribution on. **pay something back** REPAY, pay off, give back, return, reimburse, refund. **pay for** DEFRAY THE COST OF, settle up for, finance, fund; treat someone to; *informal* foot the bill for, shell out for, fork out for, cough up for; *N. Amer. informal* ante up for, pony up for. **pay someone off 1** *Tim paid off the driver* PAY WHAT ONE OWES, discharge. **2** *paying off the police* BRIBE, suborn, buy (off); *informal* grease someone's palm. **pay something off** PAY (IN FULL), settle, discharge, clear, liquidate. **pay off** *(informal)* MEET WITH SUCCESS, be successful, be effective, get results. **pay something out** SPEND, expend, pay, dish out, put up, part with, hand over; *informal* shell out, fork out/up, lay out, cough up. **pay up** MAKE PAYMENT, settle up, pay (in full); *informal* cough up.
payable ● adjective DUE, owed, owing, outstanding, unpaid, overdue, in arrears; *N. Amer.* delinquent.
payment ● noun **1** *discounts for early payment* REMITTANCE, settlement, discharge, clearance, liquidation. **2** *monthly payments* INSTALMENT, premium. **3** *extra payment for good performance* SALARY, wages, pay, earnings, fee(s), remuneration, reimbursement, income; *formal* emolument(s).
pay-off ● noun *(informal)* **1** *the lure of enormous pay-offs* PAYMENT, payout, reward; bribe, inducement, 'incentive'; *N. Amer.* payola; *informal* kickback, sweetener, backhander; *Austral. informal* sling. **2** *a pay-off of £160,000* RETURN (ON INVESTMENT), yield, payback, profit, gain, dividend. **3** *a dramatic pay-off* OUTCOME, denouement, culmination, conclusion, development, result.
peace ● noun **1** *can't a man get any peace around here?* TRANQUILLITY, calm, restfulness, peace and quiet, peacefulness, quiet, quietness; privacy, solitude. **2** *peace of mind* SERENITY, peacefulness, tranquillity, equanimity, calm, calmness, composure, ease, contentment, contentedness. **3** *we pray for peace* LAW AND ORDER, lawfulness, order, peacefulness, peaceableness, harmony, nonviolence; *formal* concord. **4** *a lasting peace* TREATY, truce, ceasefire, armistice, cessation/suspension of hostilities.
– OPPOSITES noise, war.
peaceable ● adjective **1** *a peaceable man* PEACE-LOVING, nonviolent, non-aggressive, easy-going, placid, gentle, inoffensive, good-natured, even-tempered, amiable, amicable, friendly, affable, genial, pacific, dovelike, dovish; *formal* irenic. **2** *a peaceable society* PEACEFUL, strife-free, harmonious; law-abiding, disciplined, order-

cially by an international military force.
– DERIVATIVES **peacekeeper** noun.
peacenik ● noun informal, often derogatory a member of a pacifist movement.
peace offering ● noun a conciliatory gift.
peace sign ● noun a sign of peace made by holding up the hand with palm out-turned and the first two fingers extended in a V-shape.
peacetime ● noun a period when a country is not at war.
peach[1] ● noun **1** the round stone fruit of a tree native to China, with juicy yellow flesh and downy yellow skin flushed with red. **2** a pinkish-orange colour. **3** informal an exceptionally good or attractive person or thing.
– DERIVATIVES **peachy** adjective.
– ORIGIN Old French *pesche*, from Latin *persicum malum* 'Persian apple'.
peach[2] ● verb (**peach on**) informal inform on.
– ORIGIN related to IMPEACH.
peach Melba ● noun ice cream and peaches with Melba sauce.
peacock ● noun a large crested pheasant of which the male has very long tail feathers with eye-like markings that can be fanned out in display.
– ORIGIN Old English, from Latin *pavo* 'peacock' + COCK.
peacock blue ● noun a greenish-blue colour like that of a peacock's neck.
peacock butterfly ● noun a brightly coloured butterfly with conspicuous eye-like markings.
peafowl ● noun a peacock or peahen.
pea green ● noun a bright green colour.
peahen ● noun a female peafowl, which has drabber colours and a shorter tail than the male.
pea jacket (also **pea coat**) ● noun a short double-breasted overcoat of coarse woollen cloth, formerly worn by sailors.
– ORIGIN Dutch *pijjakker*, from *pij* 'coat of coarse cloth' + *jekker* 'jacket'.
peak ● noun **1** the pointed top of a mountain. **2** a mountain with a pointed top. **3** a stiff brim at the front of a cap. **4** the point of highest activity, achievement, intensity, etc. ● verb reach a highest point or maximum. ● adjective maximum; characterized by maximum activity or demand.
– ORIGIN probably from *peaked*, a variant of *picked*, a dialect word meaning 'pointed'.
peaked[1] ● adjective (of a cap) having a peak.
peaked[2] ● adjective pale from illness or fatigue.
– ORIGIN from archaic *peak* 'to decline in health and spirits'.
peaky ● adjective (**peakier**, **peakiest**) pale from illness or fatigue.
peal ● noun **1** a loud or prolonged ringing of a bell or bells. **2** a loud repeated or reverberating sound of thunder or laughter. **3** a set of bells. ● verb ring or resound in a peal.
– ORIGIN shortening of APPEAL.
peanut ● noun **1** the oval edible seed of a plant native to South America, whose seeds develop in underground pods. **2** (**peanuts**) informal a paltry sum of money.
peanut butter ● noun a spread made from ground roasted peanuts.
pear ● noun a yellowish-green or brownish-green edible fruit, narrow at the stalk and wider towards the tip.
– PHRASES **go pear-shaped** Brit. informal go wrong. [ORIGIN RAF slang.]
– ORIGIN Old English, from Latin *pirum*.
pear drop ● noun a boiled sweet in the shape of a pear, with a pungently sweet flavour.
pearl[1] ● noun **1** a hard, shiny spherical mass, typically white or bluish-grey, formed within the shell of an oyster or other mollusc and highly prized as a gem. **2** a thing of great worth. **3** a very pale bluish grey or white colour. ● verb **1** literary form pearl-like drops. **2** (**pearling**) diving or fishing for pearl oysters.
– PHRASES **cast pearls before swine** offer valuable things to people who do not appreciate them.
– ORIGIN Old French *perle*.
pearl[2] ● noun Brit. another term for PICOT.
– ORIGIN variant of PURL[1].
pearl barley ● noun barley reduced to small round grains by grinding.
pearled ● adjective literary decorated with pearls.
pearlescent ● adjective having a lustre resembling that of mother-of-pearl.
pearl onion ● noun a very small onion used for pickling.
pearly ● adjective (**pearlier**, **pearliest**) like a pearl in lustre or colour. ● noun (**pearlies**) Brit. **1** a pearly king's or queen's clothes or pearl buttons. **2** informal a person's teeth.
Pearly Gates ● plural noun informal the gates of heaven.
– ORIGIN from a reference in the Book of Revelation to twelve gates, each fashioned from a single pearl.
pearly king (or **pearly queen**) ● noun a London costermonger (or his wife) wearing traditional ceremonial clothes covered with pearl buttons.
Pearmain /pairmayn, pərmayn/ ● noun a pear-shaped variety of dessert apple with firm white flesh.
– ORIGIN Old French *parmain*, probably named after the Italian city of *Parma*.
peasant ● noun **1** a poor smallholder or agricultural labourer of low social status. **2** informal an ignorant, rude, or unsophisticated person.
– DERIVATIVES **peasantry** noun.
– ORIGIN Old French *paisent*, from *pais* 'country'.
pease ● plural noun archaic peas.
pease pudding ● noun chiefly Brit. a dish of split peas boiled with onion and carrot and mashed to a pulp.
pea-shooter ● noun a toy weapon consisting of a small tube out of which dried peas are blown.
pea-souper ● noun Brit. a very thick yellowish fog.
peat ● noun partly decomposed vegetable matter forming a deposit on acidic, boggy ground, dried for use in gardening and as fuel.
– DERIVATIVES **peaty** adjective.
– ORIGIN Anglo-Latin *peta*.
peat moss ● noun **1** a large absorbent moss which grows in dense masses on boggy ground. **2** a peat bog.
peau-de-soie /pōdəswaa/ ● noun a smooth, finely ribbed satin fabric of silk or rayon.
– ORIGIN French, 'skin of silk'.
pebble ● noun **1** a small stone made smooth and round by the action of water or sand. **2** (before another noun) informal with very thick lenses: *pebble glasses*.
– DERIVATIVES **pebbly** adjective.
– ORIGIN Old English.
pebble-dash ● noun mortar with pebbles in it, used as a coating for external walls.
pec ● noun informal a pectoral muscle.

Thesaurus

ly, civilized.
– OPPOSITES aggressive.
peaceful ● adjective **1** *everything was quiet and peaceful* TRANQUIL, calm, restful, quiet, still, relaxing, soothing, undisturbed, untroubled, private, secluded. **2** *his peaceful mood* SERENE, calm, tranquil, composed, placid, at ease, untroubled, unworried, content. **3** *peaceful relations* HARMONIOUS, at peace, peaceable, on good terms, amicable, friendly, cordial, non-violent.
– OPPOSITES noisy, agitated, hostile.
peacemaker ● noun ARBITRATOR, arbiter, mediator, negotiator, conciliator, go-between, intermediary, pacifier, appeaser, peacemonger, pacifist, peace-lover, dove; *informal* peacenik.
peak ● noun **1** *the peaks of the mountains* SUMMIT, top, crest, pinnacle, apex, crown, cap. **2** *the highest peak* MOUNTAIN, hill, height, mount, alp; *Scottish* ben, Munro. **3** *the peak of a cap* BRIM, visor. **4** *the peak of his career* HEIGHT, high point/spot, pinnacle, summit, top, climax, culmination, apex, zenith, crowning point, acme, apogee, prime, heyday.
● verb *Labour support has peaked* REACH ITS HEIGHT, climax, reach a climax, come to a head.
● adjective *peak loads* MAXIMUM, top, greatest, highest; ultimate, best, optimum.
peaky ● adjective PALE, pasty, wan, drained, washed out, drawn, pallid, anaemic, ashen, grey, pinched, sickly, sallow; ill, unwell, poorly, indisposed, run down; *Brit.* off (colour); *informal* under the weather, rough, lousy, seedy; *Brit. informal* grotty, ropy.
peal ● noun **1** *a peal of bells* CHIME, carillon, ring, ringing, tintinnabulation. **2** *peals of laughter* SHRIEK, shout, scream, howl, gale, fit, roar, hoot. **3** *a peal of thunder* RUMBLE, roar, boom, crash, clap, crack.
● verb **1** *the bell pealed* RING (OUT), chime (out), clang, sound, ding, jingle. **2** *the thunder pealed* RUMBLE, roar, boom, crash, resound.

pecan /peekən/ ● noun a smooth pinkish-brown nut like a walnut, obtained from a hickory tree of the southern US.
– ORIGIN from an American Indian.

peccadillo /pekkədillō/ ● noun (pl. **peccadilloes** or **peccadillos**) a minor sin or fault.
– ORIGIN Spanish, from Latin *peccare* 'to sin'.

peccant /pekkənt/ ● adjective archaic **1** at fault. **2** diseased.
– ORIGIN Latin, 'sinning'.

peccary /pekkəri/ ● noun (pl. **peccaries**) a gregarious piglike mammal found from the south-western US to Paraguay.
– ORIGIN Carib.

peccavi /pekaavi/ ● exclamation archaic used to express one's guilt.
– ORIGIN Latin, 'I have sinned'.

peck[1] ● verb **1** (of a bird) strike or bite with its beak. **2** kiss lightly or perfunctorily. **3** (**peck at**) informal eat (food) listlessly or daintily. **4** type slowly and laboriously. ● noun **1** an act of pecking. **2** a light or perfunctory kiss.
– ORIGIN of unknown origin.

peck[2] ● noun a measure of capacity for dry goods, equal to a quarter of a bushel (2 imperial gallons = 9.092 l, or 8 US quarts = 8.81 l).
– ORIGIN Old French *pek*.

pecker ● noun N. Amer. vulgar slang a man's penis.
– PHRASES **keep your pecker up** Brit. informal remain cheerful. [ORIGIN *pecker* probably in the sense 'beak'.]

pecking order ● noun a hierarchy of status among members of a group, originally as observed among hens.

peckish ● adjective informal hungry.

Pecksniffian /peksniffiən/ ● adjective affecting high moral principles; hypocritical.
– ORIGIN from Mr *Pecksniff*, a character in Dickens's *Martin Chuzzlewit* (1844).

pecorino /pekkəreenō/ ● noun an Italian cheese made from ewes' milk.
– ORIGIN from Italian, 'of ewes'.

pecten /pekten/ ● noun (pl. **pectens** or **pectines** /pektineez/) Zoology **1** a comb-like structure. **2** a scallop.
– ORIGIN Latin, 'a comb'.

pectin ● noun a soluble jelly-like substance present in ripe fruits, used as a setting agent in jams and jellies.
– ORIGIN from Greek *pektos* 'congealed'.

pectoral /pektərəl/ ● adjective of, on, or relating to the breast or chest. ● noun **1** a pectoral muscle. **2** an ornamental breastplate.
– ORIGIN Latin *pectoralis*, from *pectus* 'breast, chest'.

pectoral muscle ● noun each of four large paired muscles which cover the front of the ribcage.

peculation /pekyoolaysh'n/ ● noun formal embezzlement of public funds.
– ORIGIN from Latin *peculari* 'embezzle'.

peculiar ● adjective **1** strange or odd. **2** (**peculiar to**) belonging exclusively to. **3** formal particular. ● noun a parish or church exempt from the jurisdiction of the diocese in which it lies, and subject to the direct jurisdiction of the monarch or an archbishop.
– DERIVATIVES **peculiarly** adverb.
– ORIGIN Latin *peculiaris* 'of private property', from *peculium* 'property'.

peculiarity ● noun (pl. **pecularities**) **1** an unusual or distinctive feature or habit. **2** the state of being peculiar.

pecuniary ● adjective formal of or relating to money.
– ORIGIN Latin *pecuniarius*, from *pecunia* 'money'.

pedagogue /peddəgog/ ● noun formal or humorous a teacher, especially a strict or pedantic one.
– ORIGIN Greek *paidagōgos*, denoting a slave who accompanied a child to school, from *pais* 'boy' + *agōgos* 'guide'.

pedagogy /peddəgogi, -goji/ ● noun the profession, science, or theory of teaching.
– DERIVATIVES **pedagogic** (also **pedagogical**) adjective.

pedal[1] /pedd'l/ ● noun **1** each of a pair of foot-operated levers for powering a bicycle or other vehicle. **2** a foot-operated throttle, brake, or clutch control. **3** a foot-operated lever on a piano, organ, etc. for sustaining or softening the tone. **4** Music a pedal note. ● verb (**pedalled**, **pedalling**; US **pedaled**, **pedaling**) **1** move (a bicycle, pedalo, etc.) by working the pedals. **2** use the pedals of a piano, organ, etc.
– DERIVATIVES **pedaller** (US **pedaler**) noun.
– USAGE Confusion can arise between the words **pedal** and **peddle**. **Pedal** is a noun denoting a foot-operated lever; as a verb it means 'move (a bicycle or similar) by means of pedals'. **Peddle** is a verb meaning 'sell (goods)'. The associated noun from pedal is **pedaller** (US **pedaler**), and the noun from **peddle** is **pedlar** or **peddler**.
– ORIGIN French *pédale*, from Latin *pedalis* 'a foot in length'.

pedal[2] /pedd'l, peed'l/ ● adjective chiefly Medicine & Zoology relating to the foot or feet.
– ORIGIN Latin *pedalis*, from *pes* 'foot'.

pedal note ● noun Music **1** the lowest or fundamental note of a harmonic series in some brass and wind instruments. **2** (also **pedal point**) a note sustained in one part (usually the bass) through successive harmonies.

pedalo /peddəlō/ ● noun (pl. **pedalos** or **pedaloes**) Brit. a small pedal-operated pleasure boat.

pedal pusher ● noun **1** (**pedal pushers**) women's calf-length trousers. **2** informal a cyclist.

pedant /pedd'nt/ ● noun a person excessively concerned with minor detail or with displaying technical knowledge.
– DERIVATIVES **pedantic** adjective **pedantically** adverb **pedantry** noun.
– ORIGIN French *pédant*, probably related to PEDAGOGUE.

peddle ● verb **1** sell (goods) by going from place to place. **2** sell (an illegal drug or stolen item). **3** derogatory promote (an idea)

p

Thesaurus

peasant ● noun **1** *peasants working the land* AGRICULTURAL WORKER, small farmer, rustic, swain, villein, serf. **2** *(informal) you peasants!* See BOOR.

peccadillo ● noun MISDEMEANOUR, petty offence, indiscretion, lapse, misdeed.

peck ● verb **1** *the cockerel pecked my heel* BITE, nip, strike, hit, tap, rap, jab. **2** *he pecked her on the cheek* KISS, give someone a peck. **3** *(informal) the old lady pecked at her food* NIBBLE, pick at, take very small bites from, toy with, play with.

peculiar ● adjective **1** *something peculiar began to happen* STRANGE, unusual, odd, funny, curious, bizarre, weird, queer, unexpected, unfamiliar, abnormal, atypical, anomalous, out of the ordinary; exceptional, extraordinary, remarkable; puzzling, mystifying, mysterious, perplexing, baffling; suspicious, eerie, unnatural; *informal* fishy, creepy, spooky. **2** *peculiar behaviour* BIZARRE, eccentric, strange, odd, weird, queer, funny, unusual, abnormal, idiosyncratic, unconventional, outlandish, quirky; *informal* wacky, freaky, oddball, offbeat, off the wall; *N. Amer. informal* wacko. **3** *(informal) I feel a bit peculiar.* See UNWELL. **4** *mannerisms peculiar to the islanders* CHARACTERISTIC OF, typical of, representative of, indicative of, suggestive of, exclusive to. **5** *(formal) their own peculiar contribution* DISTINCTIVE, characteristic, distinct, individual, special, unique, personal.
– OPPOSITES ordinary.

peculiarity ● noun **1** *a legal peculiarity* ODDITY, anomaly, abnormality. **2** *a physical peculiarity* IDIOSYNCRASY, mannerism, quirk, foible. **3** *one of the peculiarities of the city* CHARACTERISTIC, feature, (essential) quality, property, trait, attribute, hallmark, trademark. **4** *the peculiarity of this notion* STRANGENESS, oddness, bizarreness, weirdness, queerness, unexpectedness, unfamiliarity, anomalousness, incongruity. **5** *there is a certain peculiarity about her appearance* OUTLANDISHNESS, bizarreness, unconventionality, idiosyncrasy, weirdness, oddness, eccentricity, unusualness, abnormality, queerness, strangeness, quirkiness; *informal* wackiness, freakiness.

pecuniary ● adjective *(formal)* FINANCIAL, monetary, money, fiscal, economic.

pedagogic ● adjective EDUCATIONAL, educative, pedagogical, teaching, instructional, instructive, didactic; academic, scholastic.

pedagogue *(formal)* ● noun TEACHER, schoolteacher, schoolmaster, schoolmistress, master, mistress, tutor; lecturer, academic, don, professor, instructor, educator, educationalist, educationist; *Austral./NZ informal* chalkie.

pedant ● noun DOGMATIST, purist, literalist, formalist, doctrinaire, perfectionist; quibbler, hair-splitter, casuist, sophist; *informal* nitpicker.

pedantic ● adjective OVER-SCRUPULOUS, scrupulous, precise, exact, perfectionist, punctilious, meticulous, fussy, fastidious, finical, finicky; dogmatic, purist, literalist, literalistic, formalist; casuistic, casuistical, sophistic, sophistical; captious, hair-splitting, quibbling; *informal* nit-picking, pernickety; *archaic* overnice.

pedantry ● noun DOGMATISM, purism, literalism, formalism; over-

persistently or widely.
– USAGE On the confusion between **pedal** and **peddle**, see the note at PEDAL[1].
– ORIGIN from PEDLAR.
peddler ● noun variant spelling of PEDLAR.
pederasty ● noun sexual intercourse between a man and a boy.
– DERIVATIVES **pederast** noun **pederastic** adjective.
– ORIGIN Greek *paiderastia*, from *pais* 'boy' + *erastēs* 'lover'.
pedestal ● noun **1** the base or support on which a statue, obelisk, or column is mounted. **2** each of the two supports of a kneehole desk or table. **3** the supporting column of a washbasin or toilet pan.
– ORIGIN Italian *piedestallo*, from *piè* 'foot' + *di* 'of' + *stallo* 'stall'.
pedestrian ● noun a person walking rather than travelling in a vehicle. ● adjective dull; uninspired.
– DERIVATIVES **pedestrianly** adverb.
– ORIGIN from Latin *pedester* 'going on foot'.
pedestrianize (also **pedestrianise**) ● verb make (a street or area) accessible only to pedestrians.
– DERIVATIVES **pedestrianization** noun.
pediatrics ● plural noun US spelling of PAEDIATRICS.
pedicel /peddis'l/ ● noun **1** Botany a small stalk bearing an individual flower in a cluster. **2** Anatomy & Zoology another term for PEDICLE.
– ORIGIN Latin *pedicellus* 'small foot'.
pedicle /peddik'l/ ● noun **1** Anatomy & Zoology a small stalk-like connecting structure. **2** Medicine part of a skin graft left temporarily attached to its original site.
– ORIGIN Latin *pediculus* 'small foot'.
pedicure ● noun a cosmetic treatment of the feet and toenails.
– ORIGIN French, from Latin *pes* 'foot' + *curare* 'attend to'.
pedigree ● noun **1** the record of descent of an animal, showing it to be pure-bred. **2** a person's lineage or ancestry. **3** the history or provenance of a person or thing.
– ORIGIN from Old French *pé de grue* 'crane's foot', a mark used to denote succession in pedigrees.
pediment ● noun Architecture the triangular upper part of the front of a classical building, typically set over a portico.
– ORIGIN perhaps an alteration of PYRAMID.
pedlar (also **peddler**) ● noun **1** a travelling trader who sells small goods. **2** a person who sells illegal drugs or stolen goods. **3** a person who promotes an idea or view.
– ORIGIN perhaps from dialect *ped* 'pannier'.
pedometer /pidommitər/ ● noun an instrument for estimating the distance travelled on foot by recording the number of steps taken.
– ORIGIN from Latin *pes* 'foot'.
peduncle /pidungk'l/ ● noun **1** Botany the stalk carrying a flower or fruit. **2** Zoology a stalk-like connecting structure.
– DERIVATIVES **pedunculate** adjective.
– ORIGIN Latin *pedunculus*, from *pes* 'foot'.
pee informal ● verb (**pees**, **peed**, **peeing**) urinate. ● noun **1** an act of urinating. **2** urine.
– ORIGIN euphemistic use of the initial letter of PISS.
peek ● verb **1** look quickly or furtively. **2** stick out slightly so as to be just visible. ● noun a quick or furtive look.
– ORIGIN of unknown origin.
peekaboo ● noun a game played with a young child, which involves hiding and suddenly reappearing, saying 'peekaboo'. ● adjective **1** (of a garment) made of transparent fabric or having a pattern of small holes. **2** (of a hairstyle) concealing one eye with a fringe or wave.
peel[1] ● verb **1** remove the outer covering or skin from (a fruit, vegetable, etc.). **2** (of a surface or object) lose parts of its outer layer or covering in small strips or pieces. ● noun the outer covering or rind of a fruit or vegetable.
– DERIVATIVES **peelings** plural noun.
– PHRASES **peel off 1** (also **peel away**) remove (a thin outer covering). **2** remove (an article of clothing). **3** leave a formation or group by veering away.
– ORIGIN originally in the sense 'plunder': from Latin *pilare* 'to strip hair from', from *pilus* 'hair'.
peel[2] (also **pele**) ● noun a late medieval square defensive tower typical of the border counties of England and Scotland.
– ORIGIN Old French *pel* 'stake, palisade', from Latin *palus* 'stake'.
peeler[1] ● noun a utensil for peeling fruit and vegetables.
peeler[2] ● noun Brit. informal, archaic a police officer.
– ORIGIN from the name of the British Prime Minister Sir Robert *Peel* (1788–1850) who established the Metropolitan Police.
peen (also **pein**) ● noun the rounded or wedge-shaped end of a hammer head opposite the face. ● verb strike with a peen.
– ORIGIN probably Scandinavian.
peep[1] ● verb **1** look quickly and furtively. **2** (**peep out**) come slowly or partially into view. ● noun **1** a quick or furtive look. **2** a momentary or partial view of something.
– ORIGIN symbolic.
peep[2] ● noun a weak or brief high-pitched sound. ● verb make a peep.
– PHRASES **not a peep** not the slightest utterance or complaint.
– ORIGIN imitative.

Thesaurus

p

scrupulousness, scrupulousness, perfectionism, fastidiousness, punctiliousness, meticulousness; captiousness, quibbling, hair-splitting, casuistry, sophistry; *informal* nit-picking.
peddle ● verb **1** *they are peddling water filters* SELL (FROM DOOR TO DOOR), hawk, tout, vend; trade (in), deal in, traffic in. **2** *peddling unorthodox views* ADVOCATE, champion, preach, put forward, proclaim, propound, promote.
pedestal ● noun *a bust on a pedestal* PLINTH, base, support, mounting, stand, foundation, pillar, column, pier; *Architecture* socle.
– PHRASES **put someone on a pedestal** IDEALIZE, lionize, look up to, respect, hold in high regard, think highly of, admire, esteem, revere, worship.
pedestrian ● noun *accidents involving pedestrians* WALKER, person on foot.
– OPPOSITES driver.
● adjective *pedestrian lives* DULL, boring, tedious, monotonous, uneventful, unremarkable, tiresome, wearisome, uninspired, unimaginative, unexciting, uninteresting; unvarying, unvaried, repetitive, routine, commonplace, workaday; ordinary, everyday, run-of-the-mill, mundane, humdrum; *informal* bog-standard, (plain) vanilla; *Brit. informal* common or garden.
– OPPOSITES exciting.
pedigree ● noun *a long pedigree* ANCESTRY, descent, lineage, line (of descent), genealogy, family tree, extraction, derivation, origin(s), heritage, parentage, bloodline, background, roots.
● adjective *a pedigree cat* PURE-BRED, thoroughbred, pure-blooded.
pedlar ● noun **1** *pedlars of watches* TRAVELLING SALESMAN, door-to-door salesman, huckster; street trader, hawker; *Brit. informal* fly-pitcher; *archaic* chapman, packman. **2** *a drug pedlar* TRAFFICKER, dealer; *informal* pusher.
peek ● verb **1** *they peeked from behind the curtains* (HAVE A) PEEP, have a peek, spy, take a sly/stealthy look, sneak a look; *informal* take a gander, have a squint; *Brit. informal* have a dekko, have/take a butcher's, take a shufti. **2** *the deer's antlers peeked out from the trees* APPEAR (SLOWLY/PARTLY), show, come into view/sight, become visible, emerge, peep (out).
● noun *a peek at the map* SECRET LOOK, sly look, stealthy look, sneaky look, peep, glance, glimpse, hurried/quick look; *informal* gander, squint; *Brit. informal* dekko, butcher's, shufti.
peel ● verb **1** *peel and core the fruit* PARE, skin, take the skin/rind off; hull, shell, husk, shuck; *technical* decorticate. **2** *use a long knife to peel the veneer* TRIM (OFF), peel off, pare, strip (off), shave (off), remove. **3** *the wallpaper was peeling* FLAKE (OFF), peel off, come off in layers/strips.
● noun *orange peel* RIND, skin, covering, zest; hull, pod, integument, shuck.
– PHRASES **keep one's eyes peeled** KEEP A (SHARP) LOOKOUT, look out, keep one's eyes open, keep watch, be watchful, be alert, be on the alert, be on the qui vive, be on guard; *Brit.* keep one's eyes skinned. **peel something off** TAKE OFF, strip off, remove, pull off, slip out of.
peep[1] ● verb **1** *I peeped through the keyhole* LOOK QUICKLY, cast a brief look, take a secret look, sneak a look, (have a) peek, glance; *informal* take a gander, have a squint; *Brit. informal* have a dekko, have/take a butcher's, take a shufti. **2** *the moon peeped through the clouds* APPEAR (SLOWLY/PARTLY), show, come into view/sight, become visible, emerge, peek, peer out.
● noun *I'll just take a peep at it* QUICK LOOK, brief look, sneaky look, peek, glance; *informal* gander, squint; *Brit. informal* dekko, butcher's, shufti.
peep[2] ● noun **1** *I heard a quiet peep* CHEEP, chirp, chirrup, tweet, twitter, chirr, warble. **2** *there's been not a peep out of the children* SOUND, noise, cry, word. **3** *the painting was sold without a peep* COMPLAINT, grumble, mutter, murmur, grouse, objection, protest,

peeper ● noun **1** a person who peeps. **2** (**peepers**) informal a person's eyes.
peephole ● noun a small hole in a door through which callers may be identified.
peeping Tom ● noun a person who gains sexual pleasure from secretly watching people undress or engage in sexual activity.
– ORIGIN the name of the tailor said to have watched Lady Godiva ride naked through Coventry.
peep show ● noun a form of entertainment in which pictures are viewed through a lens or hole set into a box.
peepul /peep'l/ (also **pipal**) ● noun another term for BO TREE.
– ORIGIN Sanskrit.
peer[1] ● verb **1** look with difficulty or concentration. **2** be just visible.
– ORIGIN perhaps a variant of dialect *pire* or perhaps partly from a shortening of APPEAR.
peer[2] ● noun **1** a member of the nobility in Britain or Ireland, comprising the ranks of duke, marquess, earl, viscount, and baron. **2** a person of the same age, status, or ability as another specified person.
– PHRASES **without peer** unrivalled.
– ORIGIN Old French, from Latin *par* 'equal'.
peerage ● noun **1** the title and rank of peer or peeress. **2** (**the peerage**) peers collectively.
peeress ● noun **1** a woman holding the rank of a peer in her own right. **2** the wife or widow of a peer.
peer group ● noun a group of people of approximately the same age, status, and interests.
peerless ● adjective unequalled or unrivalled.
peer of the realm ● noun a hereditary peer who has the right to sit in the House of Lords.
peeve informal ● verb annoy; irritate. ● noun a cause of annoyance.
– ORIGIN from PEEVISH.
peevish ● adjective irritable.
– DERIVATIVES **peevishly** adverb **peevishness** noun.
– ORIGIN originally in the sense 'foolish, mad, spiteful': of unknown origin.
peewit ● noun Brit. the lapwing.
– ORIGIN imitative of the bird's call.
peg ● noun **1** a short projecting pin or bolt used for hanging things on, securing something in place, or marking a position. **2** a clip for holding things together or hanging up clothes. **3** chiefly Indian a measure of spirits. **4** a point or limit on a scale. **5** informal a person's leg. ● verb (**pegged**, **pegging**) **1** fix, attach, or mark with a peg or pegs. **2** fix (a price, rate, etc.) at a particular level. **3** (**peg out**) informal die. **4** (**peg away**) informal work hard over a long period.
– PHRASES **off the peg** chiefly Brit. (of clothes) ready-made. **a square peg in a round hole** a person in a situation unsuited to their abilities or character. **take someone down a peg or two** make someone less arrogant.
– ORIGIN probably Low German.
pegboard ● noun a board with a regular pattern of small holes for pegs.
peg leg ● noun informal a wooden leg.
pegmatite /pegmətīt/ ● noun Geology a coarse-grained granite or other igneous rock with large crystals.
– ORIGIN from Greek *pēgma* 'thing joined together'.
Peigan /peegən/ (also **Piegan**) ● noun (pl. same or **Peigans**) a member of a North American Indian people of the Blackfoot confederacy.
– ORIGIN Blackfoot.
peignoir /paynwaar/ ● noun a woman's light dressing gown or negligee.
– ORIGIN French, from *peigner* 'to comb' (because the garment was originally worn while combing the hair).
pein ● noun & verb variant spelling of PEEN.
pejorative /pijorrətiv/ ● adjective expressing contempt or disapproval.
– DERIVATIVES **pejoratively** adverb.
– ORIGIN French *péjoratif*, from Latin *pejorare* 'make worse'.
Pekinese (also **Pekingese**) ● noun (pl. same) a lapdog of a short-legged breed with long hair and a snub nose. ● adjective relating to Beijing (Peking).
Peking duck ● noun a Chinese dish consisting of strips of roast duck served with shredded vegetables and a sweet sauce.
pekoe /peekō/ ● noun a high-quality black tea made from young leaves.
– ORIGIN Chinese dialect, 'white down' (the leaves being picked young when covered with down).
pelage /pellij/ ● noun the fur, hair, or wool of a mammal.
– ORIGIN French, from Old French *pel* 'hair'.
pelagic /pilajik/ ● adjective **1** relating to the open sea. **2** (chiefly of fish) inhabiting the upper layers of the open sea.
– ORIGIN Greek *pelagikos*, from *pelagios* 'of the sea'.
pelargonium /pellərgōniəm/ ● noun a shrubby plant cultivated for its red, pink, or white flowers.
– ORIGIN Latin, from Greek *pelargos* 'stork', apparently on the pattern of *geranium*.
pele ● noun variant spelling of PEEL[2].
pelf ● noun archaic money, especially when gained dishonestly.
– ORIGIN from a variant of Old French *pelfre* 'spoils'; related to PILFER.
pelican ● noun a large waterbird with a long bill and an extensible throat pouch for scooping up fish.
– ORIGIN Greek *pelekan*, probably from *pelekus* 'axe' (with reference to its bill).
pelican crossing ● noun (in the UK) a pedestrian crossing with traffic lights operated by pedestrians.
pelisse /pəleess/ ● noun historical **1** a woman's ankle-length cloak with armholes or sleeves. **2** a fur-lined cloak, especially as part

Thesaurus

protestation; *informal* moan, gripe, grouch.
● verb *the fax peeped* CHEEP, chirp, chirrup, tweet, twitter, chirr.
peephole ● noun OPENING, gap, cleft, spyhole, slit, crack, chink, keyhole, squint, judas (hole).
peer[1] ● verb *he peered at the manuscript* LOOK CLOSELY, try to see, narrow one's eyes, screw up one's eyes, squint.
peer[2] ● noun **1** *hereditary peers* ARISTOCRAT, lord, lady, peer of the realm, peeress, noble, nobleman, noblewoman, titled man/woman, patrician. **2** *his academic peers* EQUAL, coequal, fellow, confrère; contemporary; *formal* compeer.
peerage ● noun ARISTOCRACY, nobility, peers and peeresses, lords and ladies, patriciate; the House of Lords, the Lords.
peerless ● adjective INCOMPARABLE, matchless, unrivalled, inimitable, beyond compare/comparison, unparalleled, unequalled, without equal, second to none, unsurpassed, unsurpassable, nonpareil; unique, consummate, perfect, rare, transcendent, surpassing; *formal* unexampled.
peeve ● verb *(informal)* IRRITATE, annoy, vex, anger, exasperate, irk, gall, pique, nettle, put out, get on someone's nerves, try someone's patience, ruffle someone's feathers; *Brit.* rub up the wrong way; *informal* aggravate, rile, needle, get to, bug, hack off, get someone's goat, get/put someone's back up, get up someone's nose, give someone the hump; *Brit. informal* wind up, get on someone's wick; *N. Amer. informal* tee off, tick off.
peeved ● adjective *(informal)* IRRITATED, annoyed, cross, angry, vexed, displeased, disgruntled, indignant, exasperated, galled, irked, put out, aggrieved, offended, affronted, piqued, nettled, in high dudgeon; *informal* aggravated, miffed, riled, hacked off, browned off; *Brit. informal* narked, cheesed off, brassed off; *N. Amer. informal* teed off, ticked off, sore.
peevish ● adjective IRRITABLE, fractious, fretful, cross, petulant, querulous, pettish, crabby, crotchety, cantankerous, curmudgeonly, grumpy, bad-tempered, short-tempered, touchy, testy, tetchy, snappish, irascible, waspish, prickly, crusty, dyspeptic, splenetic, choleric; *N. English* mardy; *Brit. informal* ratty, like a bear with a sore head; *N. Amer. informal* cranky, ornery.
– OPPOSITES good-humoured.
peg ● noun PIN, nail, dowel, skewer, spike, rivet, brad, screw, bolt, hook, spigot; *Mountaineering* piton; *Golf* tee.
● verb **1** *the flysheet is pegged to the ground* FIX, pin, attach, fasten, secure, make fast. **2** *we decided to peg our prices* HOLD DOWN, keep down, fix, set, hold, freeze.
– PHRASES **peg away** *(informal)* WORK HARD, slog away, plod away, hammer away, grind away, slave away, exert oneself; persevere, persist, keep at it; *informal* beaver away, plug away, stick at it, soldier on; *Brit. informal* graft away. **take someone down a peg or two** HUMBLE, humiliate, mortify, bring down, shame, embarrass, abash, put someone in their place, chasten, subdue, squash, deflate, make someone eat humble pie; *informal* show up, settle someone's hash, cut down to size; *N. Amer. informal* make someone eat crow.
pejorative ● adjective DISPARAGING, derogatory, denigratory, depre-

of a hussar's uniform.
– ORIGIN French, from Latin *pellicia vestis* 'garment of fur'.
pellagra /pilagrə/ ● noun a disease characterized by dermatitis, diarrhoea, and mental disturbance, caused by a dietary deficiency.
– ORIGIN Italian, from *pelle* 'skin'.
pellet ● noun **1** a small, rounded, compressed mass of a substance. **2** a piece of small shot or other lightweight bullet. **3** a small mass of bones and feathers regurgitated by a bird of prey. ● verb (**pelleted, pelleting**) **1** form into pellets. **2** hit with or as if with pellets.
– DERIVATIVES **pelletize** (also **pelletise**) verb.
– ORIGIN Old French *pelote* 'metal ball', from Latin *pila* 'ball'.
pellicle /pellik'l/ ● noun technical a thin skin, cuticle, or membrane.
– ORIGIN Latin *pellicula*, from *pellis* 'skin'.
pell-mell ● adjective & adverb in a confused, rushed, or disorderly way.
– ORIGIN French *pêle-mêle*, from *mesler* 'to mix'.
pellucid /piloōsid/ ● adjective **1** translucently clear. **2** easily understood.
– ORIGIN Latin *pellucidus*, from *perlucere* 'shine through'.
Pelmanism /pelməniz'm/ ● noun **1** a system of memory training originally devised by the Pelman Institute for the Scientific Development of Mind, Memory, and Personality. **2** a card game involving finding matching pairs.
pelmet ● noun a narrow border fitted across the top of a door or window to conceal the curtain fittings.
– ORIGIN probably from French *palmette* 'small palm leaf'.
pelota /pilōtə/ ● noun a Basque or Spanish ball game played in a walled court with basket-like rackets.
– ORIGIN Spanish, 'ball'.
peloton /pellәton/ ● noun the main group of cyclists in a race.
– ORIGIN French, 'small ball'.
pelt[1] ● verb **1** hurl missiles at. **2** (**pelt down**) (chiefly of rain) fall very heavily. **3** informal run very quickly.
– PHRASES (**at**) **full pelt** as fast as possible.
– ORIGIN of unknown origin.
pelt[2] ● noun **1** the skin of an animal with the fur, wool, or hair still on it. **2** the raw skin of a sheep or goat, stripped and ready for tanning.
– ORIGIN either from Latin *pellis* 'skin', or from PELTRY.
peltate /peltayt/ ● adjective Botany shield-shaped.
– ORIGIN from Greek *peltē* 'shield'.
peltry ● noun animal pelts collectively.
– ORIGIN Old French *pelterie*, from Latin *pellis* 'skin'.
pelvic floor ● noun the muscular base of the abdomen, attached to the pelvis.
pelvic girdle ● noun (in vertebrates) the enclosing structure formed by the pelvis.
pelvic inflammatory disease ● noun inflammation of the female reproductive organs, accompanied by fever and pain.
pelvis /pelviss/ ● noun (pl. **pelvises** or **pelves** /pelveez/) **1** the large bony frame at the base of the spine to which the lower limbs are attached. **2** (**renal pelvis**) the broadened top part of the ureter into which the kidney tubules drain.
– DERIVATIVES **pelvic** adjective.
– ORIGIN Latin, 'basin'.
pelycosaur /pellikəsawr/ ● noun a fossil reptile with a spiny sail-like crest on the back.
– ORIGIN from Greek *pelux* 'bowl' + *sauros* 'lizard'.
Pembs. ● abbreviation Pembrokeshire.
pemmican /pemmikən/ ● noun a cake made from a paste of pounded dried meat, melted fat, and other ingredients,
– ORIGIN Cree: pemmican was originally made by North American Indians and later adapted by Arctic explorers.
pemphigus /pemfigəss/ ● noun Medicine a skin disease in which watery blisters form on the skin.
– ORIGIN Latin, from Greek *pemphix* 'bubble'.
pen[1] ● noun **1** an instrument for writing or drawing with ink. **2** an electronic device used with a writing surface to enter commands into a computer. **3** the tapering internal shell of a squid. ● verb (**penned, penning**) write or compose.
– PHRASES **the pen is mightier than the sword** proverb writing is more effective than military power or violence.
– ORIGIN Latin *penna* 'feather' (pens were originally made from a quill feather).
pen[2] ● noun **1** a small enclosure for farm animals. **2** a covered dock for a submarine or other warship. ● verb (**penned, penning**) **1** put or keep in a pen. **2** (**pen up/in**) confine (someone) in a restricted space.
– ORIGIN Old English.
pen[3] ● noun a female swan.
– ORIGIN of unknown origin.
penal ● adjective **1** relating to the punishment of offenders under the legal system. **2** extremely severe: *penal rates of interest*.
– ORIGIN Old French, from Latin *poena* 'pain, penalty'.
penalize (also **penalise**) ● verb **1** subject to a penalty or punishment. **2** Law make (an action) legally punishable. **3** put in an unfavourable position.
– DERIVATIVES **penalization** noun.
penal servitude ● noun imprisonment with hard labour.
penalty ● noun (pl. **penalties**) **1** a punishment imposed for breaking a law, rule, or contract. **2** something unpleasant suffered as a result of an action or circumstance: *feeling cold is one of the penalties of old age*. **3** a penalty kick or shot.
– PHRASES **under** (or **on**) **penalty of** under the threat of.
penalty area (also **penalty box**) ● noun Soccer the rectangular area marked out in front of each goal, within which a foul by a defender involves the award of a penalty kick.
penalty kick ● noun **1** Soccer a free shot at the goal awarded to the attacking team after a foul within an area around the goal. **2** Rugby a place kick awarded to a team after an offence by an opponent.

Thesaurus

catory, defamatory, slanderous, libellous, abusive, insulting, slighting; *informal* bitchy.
– OPPOSITES complimentary.
pellet ● noun **1** *a pellet of mud* LITTLE BALL, little piece. **2** *pellet wounds* BULLET, shot, lead shot, buckshot. **3** *rabbit pellets* EXCREMENT, excreta, droppings, faeces, dung.
pell-mell ● adverb **1** *men streamed pell-mell from the building* HELTER-SKELTER, headlong, (at) full tilt, hotfoot, post-haste, hurriedly, hastily, recklessly, precipitately; *archaic* hurry-scurry. **2** *the sacks' contents were thrown pell-mell to the ground* UNTIDILY, anyhow, in disarray, in a mess, in a muddle; *informal* all over the place, every which way, any old how; *Brit. informal* all over the shop; *N. Amer. informal* all over the map, all over the lot.
pellucid ● adjective **1** *the pellucid waters* TRANSLUCENT, transparent, clear, crystal clear, crystalline, glassy, limpid, unclouded. **2** *pellucid prose* LUCID, limpid, clear, crystal clear, articulate; coherent, comprehensible, understandable, intelligible, straightforward, simple, well constructed; *formal* perspicuous.
pelt[1] ● verb **1** *they pelted him with snowballs* BOMBARD, shower, attack, assail, pepper. **2** *rain was pelting down* POUR DOWN, teem down, stream down, tip down, rain cats and dogs, rain hard; *Brit. informal* bucket down, come down in stair rods. **3** *(informal) they pelted into the factory* DASH, run, race, rush, sprint, bolt, dart, career, charge, shoot, hurtle, hare, fly, speed, zoom, streak; hasten, hurry; *informal* tear, belt, hotfoot it, scoot, leg it, go like a bat out of hell; *Brit. informal* bomb; *N. Amer. informal* hightail it.
pelt[2] ● noun *an animal's pelt* SKIN, hide, fleece, coat, fur; *archaic* fell.
pen[1] ● noun *you'll need a pen and paper* fountain pen, ballpoint (pen), rollerball; fibre tip (pen), felt tip (pen), highlighter, marker pen; *Brit. trademark* biro.
● verb *he penned a number of articles* WRITE, compose, draft, dash off; write down, jot down, set down, take down, scribble.
pen[2] ● noun *a sheep pen* ENCLOSURE, fold, sheepfold, pound, compound, stockade; sty, coop; *N. Amer.* corral.
● verb *the hostages had been penned up in a basement* CONFINE, coop (up), cage, shut in, box up/in, lock up/in, trap, imprison, incarcerate, immure.
penal ● adjective **1** *a penal institution* DISCIPLINARY, punitive, corrective, correctional. **2** *penal rates of interest* EXORBITANT, extortionate, excessive, outrageous, preposterous, unreasonable, inflated, sky-high.
penalize ● verb **1** *if you break the rules you will be penalized* PUNISH, discipline, inflict a penalty on. **2** *people with certain medical positions would be penalized* HANDICAP, disadvantage, put at a disadvantage, cause to suffer.
– OPPOSITES reward.
penalty ● noun **1** *increased penalties for dumping oil at sea* PUNISHMENT, sanction, punitive action, retribution; fine, forfeit, sentence; penance; *formal* mulct. **2** *the penalties of old age* DISADVANTAGE, difficulty, drawback, handicap, downside, minus; trial, tribula-

penance ● noun **1** voluntary self-punishment expressing repentance for wrongdoing. **2** a sacrament in which a member of the Church confesses sins to a priest and is given absolution. **3** a religious duty imposed as part of this sacrament.
– ORIGIN Old French, from Latin *paenitentia* 'repentance'.

pence plural of PENNY (used for sums of money).

penchant /poNshoN/ ● noun a strong liking or inclination: *a penchant for champagne*.
– ORIGIN French, 'leaning, inclining'.

pencil ● noun an instrument for writing or drawing, typically consisting of a thin stick of graphite enclosed in wood or a cylindrical case. ● verb (**pencilled**, **pencilling**; US **penciled**, **penciling**) **1** write, draw, or colour with a pencil. **2** (**pencil in**) arrange or note down provisionally.
– ORIGIN originally denoting a fine paintbrush: from Old French *pincel*, from Latin *penis* 'tail'.

pencil skirt ● noun a very narrow straight skirt.

pendant ● noun **1** a piece of jewellery that hangs from a necklace chain. **2** a light designed to hang from the ceiling. ● adjective hanging downwards.
– ORIGIN from Old French, 'hanging'.

pendent ● adjective **1** hanging down. **2** pending.
– DERIVATIVES **pendency** noun.

pending ● adjective **1** awaiting decision or settlement. **2** about to happen. ● preposition until.
– ORIGIN anglicized spelling of PENDANT.

pendulous ● adjective hanging down; drooping.

pendulum ● noun a weight hung from a fixed point so that it can swing freely, especially one regulating the mechanism of a clock.
– DERIVATIVES **pendular** adjective.
– ORIGIN Latin, 'thing hanging down'.

peneplain /peeniplayn/ ● noun Geology a level land surface produced by erosion over a long period.
– ORIGIN from Latin *paene* 'almost'.

penetralia /pennitrayliə/ ● plural noun the innermost parts of a building.
– ORIGIN Latin, 'innermost things'.

penetrant ● noun a substance which can penetrate cracks, pores, etc.

penetrate ● verb **1** force a way into or through. **2** infiltrate (an enemy organization or a competitor's market). **3** understand or gain insight into. **4** (**penetrating**) (of a sound) clearly heard through or above other sounds. **5** (of a man) insert the penis into the vagina or anus of (a sexual partner).
– DERIVATIVES **penetrable** adjective **penetration** noun **penetrative** adjective **penetrator** noun.
– ORIGIN Latin *penetrare* 'go into'.

penetrometer /pennitrommitər/ ● noun an instrument for determining the hardness of a substance by measuring the penetration of a rod driven into it by a known force.

penfriend ● noun a person with whom one becomes friendly by exchanging letters.

penguin ● noun a flightless black and white seabird of the southern hemisphere, with wings used as flippers.
– ORIGIN originally denoting the great auk: of unknown origin.

penicillin ● noun an antibiotic produced naturally by certain blue moulds and now usually prepared synthetically.
– ORIGIN from Latin *penicillum* 'paintbrush'.

peninsula ● noun a long, narrow piece of land projecting out into a sea or lake.
– DERIVATIVES **peninsular** adjective.
– ORIGIN Latin, from *paene* 'almost' + *insula* 'island'.

penis /peeniss/ ● noun (pl. **penises** or **penes** /peeneez/) the male organ of copulation and urination.
– DERIVATIVES **penile** adjective.
– ORIGIN Latin, 'tail'.

penitent ● adjective feeling sorrow and regret for having done wrong. ● noun a person who repents or submits to penance.
– DERIVATIVES **penitence** noun **penitential** adjective **penitently** adverb.
– ORIGIN from Latin *paenitere* 'repent'.

penitentiary /pennitenshəri/ ● noun (pl. **penitentiaries**) **1** (in North America) a prison for people convicted of serious crimes. **2** (in the Roman Catholic Church) a priest appointed to administer penance.

penknife ● noun a small knife with a blade which folds into the handle.

penlight ● noun a small electric torch shaped like a pen.

penman ● noun **1** historical a clerk. **2** dated a person with a specified ability in handwriting. **3** archaic an author.

pen name ● noun a literary pseudonym.

pennant ● noun **1** a tapering flag flown at the masthead of a ship in commission. **2** a long triangular or swallow-tailed flag.

Thesaurus

tion, bane, affliction, burden, trouble.
– OPPOSITES reward.

penance ● noun ATONEMENT, expiation, self-punishment, self-mortification, self-abasement, amends; punishment, penalty.

penchant ● noun LIKING, fondness, preference, taste, relish, appetite, partiality, soft spot, love, passion, desire, fancy, whim, weakness, inclination, bent, bias, proclivity, predilection, predisposition.

pencil ● noun **1** *a sharpened pencil* lead pencil, propelling pencil. **2** *a pencil of light* BEAM, ray, shaft, finger, gleam.
● verb **1** *he pencilled his name inside the cover* WRITE, write down, jot down, scribble, note, take down. **2** *pencil a line along the top of the moulding* DRAW, trace, sketch.

pendant ● noun NECKLACE, locket, medallion.

pendent ● adjective HANGING, suspended, dangling, pendulous, pensile, pendant, drooping, droopy, trailing.

pending ● adjective **1** *nine cases were still pending* UNRESOLVED, undecided, unsettled, awaiting decision/action, undetermined, open, hanging fire, (up) in the air, ongoing, outstanding, not done, unfinished, incomplete; *informal* on the back burner. **2** *with a general election pending* IMMINENT, impending, about to happen, forthcoming, upcoming, on the way, coming, approaching, looming, gathering, near, nearing, close, close at hand, in the offing, to come.
● preposition *they were released on bail pending an appeal* AWAITING, until, till, until there is/are.

pendulous ● adjective DROOPING, dangling, trailing, droopy, sagging, saggy, floppy; hanging, pendent, pensile.

penetrable ● adjective **1** *a penetrable subsoil* PERMEABLE, pervious, porous. **2** *books which are barely penetrable to anyone under 50* UNDERSTANDABLE, fathomable, comprehensible, intelligible.

penetrate ● verb **1** *the knife penetrated his lungs* PIERCE, puncture, make a hole in, perforate, stab, prick, gore, spike. **2** *they penetrated the enemy territory* INFILTRATE, slip into, sneak into, insinuate oneself into. **3** *fear penetrated her bones* PERMEATE, pervade, fill, spread throughout, suffuse, seep through. **4** *he seemed to have penetrated the mysteries of nature* UNDERSTAND, comprehend, apprehend, fathom, grasp, perceive, discern, get to the bottom of, solve, resolve, make sense of, interpret, puzzle out, work out, unravel, decipher, make head or tail of; *informal* crack, get, figure out; *Brit. informal* suss out. **5** *his words finally penetrated* REGISTER, sink in, be understood, be comprehended, become clear, fall into place; *informal* click.

penetrating ● adjective **1** *a penetrating wind* PIERCING, cutting, biting, stinging, keen, sharp, harsh, raw, freezing, chill, wintry, cold. **2** *a penetrating voice* SHRILL, strident, piercing, carrying, loud, high, high-pitched, piping, ear-splitting, screechy, intrusive. **3** *a penetrating smell* PUNGENT, pervasive, strong, powerful, sharp, acrid; heady, aromatic. **4** *her penetrating gaze* OBSERVANT, searching, intent, alert, shrewd, perceptive, probing, piercing, sharp, keen. **5** *a penetrating analysis* PERCEPTIVE, insightful, keen, sharp, sharp-witted, intelligent, clever, smart, incisive, piercing, razor-edged, trenchant, astute, shrewd, clear, acute, percipient, perspicacious, discerning, sensitive, thoughtful, deep, profound.
– OPPOSITES mild, soft.

penetration ● noun **1** *skin penetration by infective larvae* PERFORATION, piercing, puncturing, puncture, stabbing, pricking. **2** *remarks of great penetration* INSIGHT, discernment, perception, perceptiveness, intelligence, sharp-wittedness, cleverness, incisiveness, keenness, sharpness, trenchancy, astuteness, shrewdness, acuteness, clarity, acuity, percipience, perspicacity, discrimination, sensitivity, thoughtfulness, profundity; *formal* perspicuity.

peninsula ● noun CAPE, promontory, point, head, headland, foreland, ness, horn, bill, bluff, mull.

penitence ● noun REPENTANCE, contrition, regret, remorse, remorsefulness, ruefulness, sorrow, sorrowfulness, pangs of conscience, self-reproach, shame, guilt, compunction; *archaic* rue.

penitent ● adjective REPENTANT, contrite, remorseful, sorry, apologetic, regretful, conscience-stricken, rueful, ashamed, shamefaced, abject, in sackcloth and ashes.

3 N. Amer. a flag identifying a sports team, club, etc.
– ORIGIN blend of PENDANT and PENNON.

penne /pennay/ ● plural noun pasta in the form of short wide tubes.
– ORIGIN Italian, 'quills'.

penni /penni/ ● noun (pl. **penniä** /pennyaa/) a monetary unit of Finland, equal to one hundredth of a markka.
– ORIGIN Finnish.

penniless ● adjective without money; destitute.

pennon ● noun less common term for PENNANT.
– ORIGIN Old French, from Latin *penna* 'feather'.

penny ● noun (pl. **pennies** (for separate coins); **pence** (for a sum of money)) **1** a British bronze coin worth one hundredth of a pound. **2** a former British coin worth one twelfth of a shilling and 240th of a pound. **3** N. Amer. informal a one-cent coin.
– PHRASES **a bad penny always turns up** proverb someone or something unwelcome will always reappear. **in for a penny, in for a pound** willing to see an undertaking through, however much this entails. **look after the pennies and the pounds will look after themselves** proverb if you concentrate on saving small amounts of money, you'll soon amass a large amount. **not a penny** no money at all. **pennies from heaven** unexpected benefits. **the penny dropped** informal someone has finally realized something. **penny wise and pound foolish** economical in small matters but extravagant in large ones. **two** (or **ten**) **a penny** informal plentiful and thus of little value.
– ORIGIN Old English.

penny dreadful ● noun historical or humorous a cheap, sensational comic or storybook.

penny-farthing ● noun Brit. an early type of bicycle with a very large front wheel and a small rear wheel.

penny-pinching ● adjective unwilling to spend money; miserly. ● noun miserliness.
– DERIVATIVES **penny-pincher** noun.

penny plain ● adjective plain and simple.
– ORIGIN with reference to prints of characters sold for toy theatres, costing one penny for black-and-white ones, and two pennies for coloured ones.

pennyroyal ● noun a small-leaved plant of the mint family, used in herbal medicine.
– ORIGIN from Old French *puliol real* 'royal thyme'.

pennyweight ● noun a unit of weight, 24 grains or one twentieth of an ounce troy.

penny whistle ● noun another term for TIN WHISTLE.

pennywort ● noun a plant with small rounded leaves, growing in crevices or marshy places.

pennyworth ● noun **1** an amount of something worth a penny. **2** (**one's pennyworth**) Brit. one's contribution to a discussion.

p

penology /peenolləji/ ● noun the study of the punishment of crime and of prison management.
– DERIVATIVES **penological** adjective **penologist** noun.
– ORIGIN from Latin *poena* 'penalty'.

pen pal ● noun informal a penfriend.

pen-pusher ● noun informal a clerical worker.

pensée /poNsay/ ● noun a thought written down in a concise or witty form.
– ORIGIN French.

pension¹ ● noun **1** a regular payment made to retired people and to some widows and disabled people, either by the state or from an investment fund. **2** chiefly historical a regular payment made to a royal favourite or to an artist or scholar. ● verb (**pension off**) dismiss (someone) from employment and pay them a pension.
– DERIVATIVES **pensionable** adjective **pensioner** noun.
– ORIGIN Latin, 'payment', from *pendere* 'to pay'.

pension² /poNsyon/ ● noun a small hotel or boarding house in France and other European countries.
– ORIGIN French.

pensione /pensiōnay/ ● noun (pl. **pensioni** /pensiōni/) a small hotel or boarding house in Italy.
– ORIGIN Italian.

pensive ● adjective engaged in deep thought.
– DERIVATIVES **pensively** adverb **pensiveness** noun.
– ORIGIN Old French *pensif*, from Latin *pensare* 'ponder'.

penstemon /penstimən, pensteemən/ (also **pentstemon**) ● noun a North American plant with snapdragon-like flowers.
– ORIGIN Latin, from PENTA- + Greek *stēmōn* 'warp', used to mean 'stamen'.

penstock ● noun **1** a sluice for controlling the flow of water. **2** a channel for conveying water to a hydroelectric station.
– ORIGIN from PEN² (meaning 'mill dam') + STOCK.

penta- ● combining form five; having five: *pentagon*.
– ORIGIN Greek *pente* 'five'.

pentacle /pentək'l/ ● noun a pentagram.
– ORIGIN Latin *pentaculum*.

pentad ● noun a group or set of five.

pentagon ● noun **1** a plane figure with five straight sides and five angles. **2** (**the Pentagon**) the headquarters of the US Department of Defense, near Washington DC.
– DERIVATIVES **pentagonal** adjective.

pentagram ● noun a five-pointed star drawn using a continuous line, often used as a mystic and magical symbol.

pentahedron /pentəheedrən/ ● noun (pl. **pentahedra** /pentəheedrə/ or **pentahedrons**) a solid figure with five plane faces.
– DERIVATIVES **pentahedral** adjective.

pentameter /pentammitər/ ● noun a line of verse consisting of five metrical feet, or (in Greek and Latin verse) of two halves each of two feet and a long syllable.

pentane /pentayn/ ● noun Chemistry a volatile liquid hydrocarbon present in petroleum spirit.
– ORIGIN from Greek *pente* 'five' (denoting five carbon atoms).

pentaprism ● noun a five-sided prism that deviates light from any direction.

Pentateuch /pentətyook/ ● noun the first five books of the Old Testament and Hebrew Scriptures (Genesis, Exodus, Leviticus, Numbers, and Deuteronomy).
– ORIGIN Greek, from *penta-* 'five' + *teukhos* 'implement, book'.

pentathlon ● noun an athletic event comprising five different events for each competitor, in particular (**modern pentathlon**) a men's event involving fencing, shooting, swimming, riding, and cross-country running.
– DERIVATIVES **pentathlete** noun.
– ORIGIN Greek, from *pente* 'five' + *athlon* 'contest'.

pentatonic /pentətonnik/ ● adjective Music of or referring to a scale of five notes.

Pentecost ● noun **1** the Christian festival celebrating the descent of the Holy Spirit on the disciples of Jesus after his Ascension, held on Whit Sunday. **2** the Jewish festival of Shavuoth.
– ORIGIN from Greek *pentēkostē hēmera* 'fiftieth day' (because the

Thesaurus

– OPPOSITES unrepentant.

pen name ● noun PSEUDONYM, nom de plume, assumed name, alias, professional name.

pennant ● noun FLAG, standard, ensign, colour(s), banner, banderole, guidon; *Brit.* pendant; *Nautical* burgee.

penniless ● adjective DESTITUTE, poverty-stricken, impoverished, poor, indigent, impecunious, in penury, moneyless, without a sou, necessitous, needy, on one's beam-ends; bankrupt, insolvent; *Brit.* on the breadline, without a penny (to one's name); *informal* (flat) broke, cleaned out, strapped for cash, on one's uppers, without a brass farthing, bust; *Brit. informal* stony broke, skint; *N. Amer. informal* stone broke; *formal* penurious.
– OPPOSITES wealthy.

penny ● noun
– PHRASES **a pretty penny** *(informal)* A LOT OF MONEY, millions, billions, a king's ransom; *informal* a (small) fortune, lots/pots/heaps of money, a mint, a killing, a bundle, a packet, a tidy sum, big money, telephone numbers, an arm and a leg; *Brit. informal* a bomb, loadsamoney; *N. Amer. informal* big bucks; *Austral. informal* big bickies, motser, motza. **two/ten a penny** *(informal)* NUMEROUS, abundant, thick on the ground, plentiful; in large numbers, by the yard; very common, ubiquitous; *N. Amer. informal* a dime a dozen.

penny-pincher ● noun MISER, Scrooge, niggard; *informal* skinflint, meanie, money-grubber, cheapskate; *N. Amer. informal* tightwad.
– OPPOSITES spendthrift.

penny-pinching ● adjective MEAN, miserly, niggardly, parsimonious, close-fisted, cheese-paring, grasping, Scrooge-like; *informal* stingy, mingy, tight, tight-fisted, money-grubbing; *formal* penurious; *archaic* near.
– OPPOSITES generous.

pension ● noun OLD-AGE PENSION, retirement pension, regular payment, superannuation; allowance, benefit, support, welfare.

pensioner ● noun RETIRED PERSON, old-age pensioner, OAP, senior citizen; *N. Amer.* senior, retiree.

Jewish festival is held on the fiftieth day after the second day of Passover).

Pentecostal ● adjective **1** relating to Pentecost. **2** (in Christian use) emphasizing baptism in the Holy Spirit, evidenced by 'speaking in tongues', prophecy, healing, and exorcism.

– DERIVATIVES **Pentecostalism** noun **Pentecostalist** adjective & noun.

penthouse ● noun **1** a flat on the top floor of a tall building. **2** archaic an outhouse built on the side of a building.

– ORIGIN Old French *apentis*, from Latin *appendicium* 'appendage', changed by association with *house*.

pentimento /pentimentō/ ● noun (pl. **pentimenti** /pentimenti/) a visible trace of earlier painting beneath the paint on a canvas.

– ORIGIN Italian, 'repentance'.

pentose /pentōz/ ● noun Chemistry any simple sugar whose molecules contain five carbon atoms (e.g. ribose).

Pentothal /pentəthal/ ● noun trademark an anaesthetic and sedative drug reputedly used as a truth drug.

pentstemon ● noun variant spelling of PENSTEMON.

penultimate ● adjective last but one.

– ORIGIN from Latin *paene* 'almost' + *ultimus* 'last'.

penumbra /pinumbrə/ ● noun (pl. **penumbrae** /pinumbree/ or **penumbras**) the partially shaded outer region of the shadow cast by an object.

– DERIVATIVES **penumbral** adjective.

– ORIGIN from Latin *paene* 'almost' + *umbra* 'shadow'.

penurious /pinyooriəss/ ● adjective formal **1** extremely poor. **2** parsimonious.

– DERIVATIVES **penuriously** adverb.

penury /penyoori/ ● noun extreme poverty.

– ORIGIN Latin *penuria*.

peon /peeən/ ● noun **1** /also payon/ an unskilled Spanish-American worker. **2** /also pyoon/ (in the Indian subcontinent and SE Asia) a person of low rank.

– ORIGIN from Portuguese *peão* and Spanish *peón*, from Latin *pedo* 'walker, foot soldier'.

peony /peeəni/ (also **paeony**) ● noun a herbaceous or shrubby plant cultivated for its showy flowers.

– ORIGIN Greek *paiōnia*, from *Paiōn*, the physician of the gods.

people ● plural noun **1** human beings in general or considered collectively. **2** (**the people**) the mass of citizens; the populace. **3** (**one's people**) one's relatives, or one's employees or supporters. **4** (pl. **peoples**) (treated as sing. or pl.) the members of a particular nation, community, or ethnic group. ● verb **1** (usu. **be peopled**) inhabit. **2** fill with a particular group of inhabitants.

– ORIGIN Old French *poeple*, from Latin *populus* 'populace'.

people carrier ● noun a motor vehicle with three rows of seats.

PEP ● abbreviation Brit. personal equity plan.

pep informal ● noun liveliness. ● verb (**pepped**, **pepping**) (**pep up**) make more lively.

– DERIVATIVES **peppy** adjective.

– ORIGIN abbreviation of PEPPER.

peplum /pepləm/ ● noun a short flared, gathered, or pleated strip of fabric attached at the waist of a woman's jacket, dress, or blouse.

– ORIGIN originally denoting a woman's loose outer tunic or shawl, worn in ancient Greece: from Greek *peplos*.

pepper ● noun **1** a pungent, hot-tasting powder made from peppercorns, used to flavour food. **2** a capsicum. ● verb **1** sprinkle or season with pepper. **2** (usu. **be peppered with**) scatter liberally over or through. **3** hit repeatedly with small missiles or gunshot.

– DERIVATIVES **peppery** adjective.

– ORIGIN Greek *peperi*, from Sanskrit.

peppercorn ● noun the dried berry of a climbing vine, used whole as a spice or crushed or ground to make pepper.

peppercorn rent ● noun Brit. a very low or nominal rent.

– ORIGIN from the former practice of stipulating the payment of a peppercorn as a nominal rent.

peppermint ● noun **1** a plant of the mint family which produces aromatic leaves and oil, used as a flavouring in food. **2** a sweet flavoured with peppermint oil.

pepperoni /peppərōni/ ● noun beef and pork sausage seasoned with pepper.

– ORIGIN Italian *peperone* 'chilli'.

pepper pot ● noun Brit. a container with a perforated top for sprinkling pepper.

pepper spray ● noun an aerosol spray containing irritant oils derived from cayenne pepper, used as a disabling weapon.

pep pill ● noun informal a pill containing a stimulant drug.

pepsin ● noun the chief digestive enzyme in the stomach, which breaks down proteins into polypeptides.

– ORIGIN from Greek *pepsis* 'digestion'.

pep talk ● noun informal a talk intended to make someone feel more courageous or enthusiastic.

peptic ● adjective relating to digestion.

– ORIGIN Greek *peptikos* 'able to digest'.

peptic ulcer ● noun an ulcer in the lining of the stomach or duodenum.

peptide ● noun Biochemistry a compound consisting of two or more linked amino acids.

– ORIGIN German *Peptid*, from *Polypeptid* 'polypeptide'.

per ● preposition **1** for each. **2** by means of. **3** (**as per**) in accord-

Thesaurus

pensive ● adjective THOUGHTFUL, reflective, contemplative, musing, meditative, introspective, ruminative, absorbed, preoccupied, deep/lost in thought, in a brown study, brooding; *formal* cogitative.

pent-up ● adjective REPRESSED, suppressed, stifled, smothered, restrained, confined, bottled up, held in/back, kept in check, curbed, bridled.

penurious ● adjective (*formal*) **1** *a penurious student* POOR, as poor as a church mouse, poverty-stricken, destitute, necessitous, impecunious, impoverished, indigent, needy, in need/want, badly off, in reduced/straitened circumstances, hard up, on one's beam-ends, unable to make ends meet, penniless, without a sou; *Brit.* on the breadline, without a penny (to one's name); *informal* (flat) broke, strapped for cash, on one's uppers; *Brit. informal* stony broke, skint, without a brass farthing, in Queer Street; *N. Amer. informal* stone broke. **2** *a penurious old skinflint* MEAN, miserly, niggardly, parsimonious, penny-pinching, close-fisted, cheese-paring, Scrooge-like; *informal* stingy, mingy, tight, tight-fisted, money-grubbing; *archaic* near.

– OPPOSITES wealthy, generous.

penury ● noun EXTREME POVERTY, destitution, pennilessness, impecuniousness, impoverishment, indigence, pauperism, privation, beggary.

people ● noun **1** *crowds of people* HUMAN BEINGS, persons, individuals, humans, mortals, (living) souls, personages, {men, women, and children}; *informal* folk, peeps. **2** *the British people* CITIZENS, subjects, electors, voters, taxpayers, residents, inhabitants, (general) public, citizenry, nation, population, populace. **3** *a man of the people* THE COMMON PEOPLE, the proletariat, the masses, the populace, the rank and file, the commonality, the commonalty, the third estate, the plebeians; *derogatory* the hoi polloi, the common herd, the great unwashed, the proles, the plebs. **4** *her people don't live far away* FAMILY, parents, relatives, relations, folk, kinsmen, kin, kith and kin, kinsfolk, flesh and blood, nearest and dearest; *informal* folks. **5** *the peoples of Africa* RACE, (ethnic) group, tribe, clan.

● verb *the Indians who once peopled Newfoundland* POPULATE, settle (in), colonize, inhabit, live in, occupy; *formal* reside in, be domiciled in, dwell in.

pep (*informal*) ● noun *a performance full of pep* DYNAMISM, life, energy, spirit, liveliness, animation, bounce, sparkle, effervescence, verve, spiritedness, ebullience, high spirits, enthusiasm, vitality, vivacity, fire, dash, panache, elan, zest, exuberance, vigour, gusto, brio; *informal* feistiness, get-up-and-go, oomph, pizzazz, vim.

– PHRASES **pep something up** ENLIVEN, animate, liven up, put some/new life into, invigorate, vitalize, revitalize, vivify, ginger up, energize, galvanize, put some spark into, stimulate, get something going, perk up; brighten up, cheer up; *informal* buck up.

pepper ● verb **1** *salt and pepper the potatoes* ADD PEPPER TO, season, flavour. **2** *stars peppered the desert skies* SPRINKLE, fleck, dot, spot, stipple; cover, fill. **3** *another burst of bullets peppered the tank* BOMBARD, pelt, shower, rain down on, attack, assail, batter, strafe, rake, blitz, hit.

peppery ● adjective **1** *a peppery sauce* SPICY, spiced, peppered, hot, highly seasoned, piquant, pungent, sharp. **2** *a peppery old man* IRRITABLE, cantankerous, irascible, bad-tempered, ill-tempered, grumpy, grouchy, crotchety, short-tempered, tetchy, testy, crusty, crabby, curmudgeonly, peevish, cross, fractious, pettish, prickly, waspish; *informal* snappish, snappy, chippy; *N. Amer. informal* cranky,

ance with. **4** Heraldry divided by a line in the direction of.
– PHRASES **as per usual** as usual.
– ORIGIN Latin, 'through, by means of'.

per- ● prefix **1** through; all over: *pervade.* **2** completely; very: *perfect.* **3** Chemistry having the maximum proportion of some element in combination: *peroxide.*

peradventure archaic or humorous ● adverb perhaps. ● noun uncertainty or doubt.
– ORIGIN from Old French *per* (or *par) auenture* 'by chance'.

perambulate /pərambyoolayt/ ● verb **1** formal walk or travel from place to place. **2** Brit. historical walk round (a parish, forest, etc.) in order to officially assert and record its boundaries.
– DERIVATIVES **perambulation** noun **perambulatory** adjective.
– ORIGIN Latin *perambulare* 'walk about'.

perambulator ● noun formal term for PRAM.

per annum ● adverb for each year.
– ORIGIN Latin.

perborate /pəborayt/ ● noun Chemistry a salt which is an oxidized borate containing a peroxide linkage, especially a sodium salt of this kind used as a bleach.

percale /pərkayl/ ● noun a closely woven fine cotton fabric.
– ORIGIN French.

per capita /pər kappitə/ (also **per caput** /kappoot/) ● adverb & adjective for each person; in relation to people taken individually.
– ORIGIN Latin, 'by heads'.

perceive ● verb **1** become aware or conscious of through the senses. **2** regard as.
– DERIVATIVES **perceivable** adjective **perceiver** noun.
– ORIGIN Old French *perçoivre*, from Latin *percipere* 'seize, understand'.

per cent ● adverb by a specified amount in or for every hundred. ● noun one part in every hundred.

percentage ● noun **1** a rate, number, or amount in each hundred. **2** a proportion of a larger sum of money granted as an allowance or commission. **3** any proportion or share in relation to a whole.

percentile /pərsentīl/ ● noun Statistics **1** each of 100 equal groups into which a population can be divided according to the distribution of values of a particular variable. **2** each of the 99 intermediate values of a particular variable which divide a frequency distribution into 100 such groups.

percept /persept/ ● noun Philosophy **1** something that is perceived. **2** a mental concept that results from perceiving.

perceptible ● adjective able to be perceived.
– DERIVATIVES **perceptibly** adverb.

perception ● noun **1** the ability to see, hear, or become aware of something through the senses. **2** the process of perceiving. **3** a way of understanding or interpreting something. **4** intuitive understanding and insight.
– ORIGIN Latin, from *percipere* 'seize, understand'.

perceptive ● adjective having or showing acute insight.
– DERIVATIVES **perceptively** adverb **perceptiveness** noun.

perceptual ● adjective relating to the ability to perceive.
– DERIVATIVES **perceptually** adverb.

perch[1] ● noun **1** a branch, bar, etc. on which a bird rests or roosts. **2** a high or narrow seat or resting place. ● verb **1** sit, rest, or place somewhere. **2** (**be perched**) (of a building) be situated above or on the edge of something.
– ORIGIN from PERCH[3].

perch[2] ● noun (pl. same or **perches**) a freshwater fish with a high spiny dorsal fin and dark vertical bars.
– ORIGIN Old French *perche*, from Greek *perkē*.

perch[3] ● noun historical **1** a measure of length equal to a quarter of a chain or 5½ yards (approximately 5.029 m). **2** (also **square perch**) a measure of area equal to 160th of an acre or 30¼ square yards (approximately 25.29 sq. metres).
– ORIGIN Old French *perche*, from Latin *pertica* 'measuring rod, pole'.

perchance ● adverb archaic or literary by some chance; perhaps.
– ORIGIN from Old French *par cheance* 'by chance'.

percheron /pershəron/ ● noun a powerful draught horse of a grey or black breed, originally from France.
– ORIGIN French (the animal was originally bred in le *Perche*, a district of northern France).

percipient /pərsippiənt/ ● adjective having a perceptive understanding. ● noun (especially in philosophy or with reference to psychic phenomena) a person who is able to perceive things.
– DERIVATIVES **percipience** noun **percipiently** adverb.

percolate ● verb **1** filter through a porous surface or substance. **2** (of information or ideas) spread gradually through a group of people. **3** prepare (coffee) in a percolator.
– DERIVATIVES **percolation** noun.
– ORIGIN Latin *percolare* 'strain through'.

percolator ● noun a machine for making coffee, consisting of a pot in which boiling water is circulated through a small chamber that holds the ground beans.

percuss /pərkuss/ ● verb Medicine gently tap (a part of the body) as part of a diagnosis.

percussion ● noun **1** (before another noun) (of a musical instrument) played by being struck or shaken. **2** percussion instruments forming a band or section of an orchestra. **3** the striking of one solid object with or against another.
– DERIVATIVES **percussionist** noun **percussive** adjective.
– ORIGIN Latin, from *percutere* 'strike forcibly'.

percussion cap ● noun a small amount of explosive powder contained in metal or paper and exploded by striking.

percutaneous /perkyootayniəss/ ● adjective Medicine made or done through the skin.
– DERIVATIVES **percutaneously** adverb.
– ORIGIN from Latin *per cutem* 'through the skin'.

per diem /pər deeem/ ● adverb & adjective for each day.
– ORIGIN Latin.

perdition /pərdish'n/ ● noun (in Christian theology) a state of eternal damnation into which a sinful person who has not repented passes after death.
– ORIGIN Latin, from *perdere* 'destroy'.

perdurable /pərdyoorəb'l/ ● adjective formal enduring continuously; permanent.

père /pair/ ● noun used after a surname to distinguish a father

Thesaurus

ornery.
– OPPOSITES mild, bland, affable.

perceive ● verb **1** *I immediately perceived the flaws in her story* DISCERN, recognize, become aware of, see, distinguish, realize, grasp, understand, take in, make out, find, identify, hit on, comprehend, apprehend, appreciate, sense, divine; informal figure out; Brit. informal twig; formal become cognizant of. **2** *he perceived a flush creeping up her neck* SEE, discern, detect, catch sight of, spot, observe, notice. **3** *he was perceived as too negative* REGARD, look on, view, consider, think of, judge, deem, adjudge.

perceptible ● adjective NOTICEABLE, perceivable, detectable, discernible, visible, observable, recognizable, appreciable; obvious, apparent, evident, manifest, patent, clear, distinct, plain, conspicuous.

perception ● noun **1** *our perception of our own limitations* RECOGNITION, awareness, consciousness, appreciation, realization, knowledge, grasp, understanding, comprehension, apprehension; formal cognizance. **2** *popular perceptions of old age* IMPRESSION, idea, conception, notion, thought, belief, judgement, estimation. **3** *he talks with great perception* INSIGHT, perceptiveness, percipience, perspicacity, understanding, sharpness, sharp-wittedness, intelligence, intuition, cleverness, incisiveness, trenchancy, astuteness, shrewdness, acuteness, acuity, discernment, sensitivity, penetration, thoughtfulness, profundity; formal perspicuity.

perceptive ● adjective INSIGHTFUL, discerning, sensitive, intuitive, observant; piercing, penetrating, percipient, perspicacious, penetrative, clear-sighted, far-sighted, intelligent, clever, canny, keen, sharp, sharp-witted, astute, shrewd, quick, smart, acute, discriminating; informal on the ball; N. Amer. informal heads-up.
– OPPOSITES obtuse.

perch ● noun *the budgerigar's perch* POLE, rod, branch, roost, rest, resting place.
● verb **1** *three swallows perched on the telegraph wire* ROOST, sit, rest; alight, settle, land, come to rest. **2** *she perched her glasses on her nose* PUT, place, set, rest, balance. **3** *the church is perched on a hill* BE LOCATED, be situated, be positioned, be sited, stand.

perchance ● adverb (poetic/literary) MAYBE, perhaps, possibly, for all one knows, it could be, it's possible, conceivably; N. English happen; poetic/literary peradventure.

percipient ● adjective. See PERCEPTIVE.

percolate ● verb **1** *water percolated through the soil* FILTER, drain, drip, ooze, seep, trickle, dribble, leak, leach. **2** *these views began to percolate through society as a whole* SPREAD, be disseminated, filter, pass; permeate, pervade. **3** *he put some coffee on to percolate*

from a son of the same name.
– ORIGIN French, 'father'.
peregrinations /perrigrinaysh'nz/ ● **plural noun** archaic or humorous travel or wandering from place to place.
– DERIVATIVES **peregrinate** /perrigrinayt/ verb.
– ORIGIN from Latin *peregrinari* 'travel abroad'.
peregrine /perrigrin/ ● **noun** a powerful falcon with a bluish-grey back and wings and pale underparts, that breeds chiefly on mountains and coastal cliffs.
– ORIGIN Latin, 'pilgrim falcon', because falconers' birds were caught full-grown on migration, not taken from the nest.
peremptory /pərempṭəri, perrimp-/ ● **adjective 1** insisting on immediate attention or obedience; brusque and imperious. **2** Law not open to appeal or challenge; final.
– DERIVATIVES **peremptorily** adverb **peremptoriness** noun.
– ORIGIN Latin *peremptorius* 'deadly, decisive'.
perennial ● **adjective 1** lasting through a year or several years. **2** (of a plant) living for several years. Compare with ANNUAL, BIENNIAL. **3** lasting or doing something for a long time or for ever. ● **noun** a perennial plant.
– DERIVATIVES **perennially** adverb.
– ORIGIN from Latin *perennis* 'lasting the year through'.
perestroika /perristroykə/ ● **noun** the economic and political reforms practised in the former Soviet Union during the 1980s under Mikhail Gorbachev.
– ORIGIN Russian, 'restructuring'.
perfect ● **adjective** /perfikt/ **1** having all the required elements, qualities, or characteristics. **2** free from any flaw; faultless. **3** complete; absolute: *it made perfect sense.* **4** Grammar (of a tense) denoting a completed action or a state or habitual action which began in the past, formed in English with *have* or *has* and the past participle, as in *they have eaten.* **5** Mathematics (of a number) equal to the sum of its positive divisors, e.g. the number 6, whose divisors (1, 2, 3) also add up to 6. ● **verb** /pərfekt/ **1** make perfect. **2** bring to completion.
– DERIVATIVES **perfecter** noun **perfectible** adjective.
– ORIGIN Latin *perfectus* 'completed'.
perfection ● **noun 1** the process of perfecting or the state of being perfect. **2** a perfect person or thing.
perfectionism ● **noun 1** refusal to accept any standard short of perfection. **2** Philosophy the doctrine that religious, moral, social, or political perfection is attainable.
– DERIVATIVES **perfectionist** noun & adjective.
perfectly ● **adverb 1** in a perfect way. **2** absolutely; completely.
perfect pitch ● **noun** the ability to recognize the pitch of a note or produce any given note.
perfervid /pərfervid/ ● **adjective** literary intense and impassioned.
– ORIGIN from Latin *per-* 'utterly' + *fervidus* 'glowing hot, fiery'.
perfidious ● **adjective** literary deceitful and untrustworthy: *a perfidious lover.*
– DERIVATIVES **perfidiously** adverb **perfidiousness** noun.
perfidy /perfidi/ ● **noun** literary deceitfulness; untrustworthiness.
– ORIGIN Latin *perfidia*, from *perfidus* 'treacherous'.
perforate /perfərayt/ ● **verb** pierce and make a hole or holes in.
– DERIVATIVES **perforation** noun **perforator** noun.
– ORIGIN Latin *perforare* 'pierce through'.
perforce ● **adverb** formal necessarily; inevitably.
– ORIGIN from Old French *par force* 'by force'.
perform ● **verb 1** carry out, accomplish, or fulfil (an action, task, or function). **2** work, function, or do something to a specified standard. **3** present entertainment to an audience. **4** (of an investment) yield a profitable return.
– DERIVATIVES **performable** adjective **performer** noun.
– ORIGIN Old French *parfournir*.
performance ● **noun 1** the action or process of performing. **2** an act of performing a play, concert, song, etc. **3** informal a display of exaggerated behaviour; a fuss. **4** the capabilities of a machine or product.

Thesaurus

BREW; *informal* perk.
perdition ● **noun** DAMNATION, eternal punishment; hell, hellfire, doom.
peregrinations ● **plural noun** *(archaic)* TRAVELS, wanderings, journeys, globetrotting, voyages, expeditions, odysseys, trips, treks, excursions; *formal* perambulations.
peremptory ● **adjective 1** *a peremptory reply* BRUSQUE, imperious, high-handed, brisk, abrupt, summary, commanding, dictatorial, autocratic, overbearing, dogmatic, arrogant, overweening, lordly, magisterial, authoritarian; emphatic, firm, insistent; *informal* bossy. **2** *a peremptory order of the court* IRREVERSIBLE, binding, absolute, final, conclusive, decisive, definitive, categorical, irrefutable, incontrovertible; *Law* unappealable.
perennial ● **adjective** ABIDING, enduring, lasting, everlasting, perpetual, eternal, continuing, unending, never-ending, endless, undying, ceaseless, persisting, permanent, constant, continual, unfailing, unchanging, never-changing.
perfect ● **adjective 1** *she strove to be the perfect wife* IDEAL, model, without fault, faultless, flawless, consummate, quintessential, exemplary, best, ultimate, copybook; unrivalled, unequalled, matchless, unparalleled, beyond compare, without equal, second to none, too good to be true, Utopian, incomparable, nonpareil, peerless, inimitable, unexcelled, unsurpassed, unsurpassable. **2** *an E-type Jaguar in perfect condition* FLAWLESS, mint, as good as new, pristine, impeccable, immaculate, superb, superlative, optimum, prime, optimal, peak, excellent, faultless, as sound as a bell, unspoiled, unblemished, undamaged, spotless, unmarred; *informal* tip-top, A1. **3** *a perfect copy* EXACT, precise, accurate, faithful, correct, unerring, right, true, strict; *Brit. informal* spot on; *N. Amer. informal* on the money. **4** *the perfect Christmas present for golfers everywhere* IDEAL, just right, right, appropriate, fitting, fit, suitable, apt, made to order, tailor-made; very; *Brit. informal* spot on, just the job. **5** *she felt a perfect idiot* ABSOLUTE, complete, total, real, out-and-out, thorough, thoroughgoing, downright, utter, sheer, arrant, unmitigated, unqualified, veritable, in every respect, unalloyed; *Brit. informal* right; *Austral./NZ informal* fair.
● **verb** *he's busy perfecting his bowling technique* IMPROVE, better, polish (up), hone, refine, put the finishing/final touches to, brush up, fine-tune.
perfection ● **noun 1** *the perfection of his technique* IMPROVEMENT, betterment, refinement, refining, honing. **2** *for her, he was still perfection* THE IDEAL, a paragon, the ne plus ultra, the beau idéal, a nonpareil, the crème de la crème, the last word, the ultimate; *informal* one in a million, the tops, the best/greatest thing since sliced bread, the bee's knees; *archaic* a nonsuch.
perfectionist ● **noun** PURIST, stickler for perfection, idealist; pedant; *archaic* precisian.
perfectly ● **adverb 1** *a perfectly cooked meal* SUPERBLY, superlatively, excellently, flawlessly, faultlessly, to perfection, without fault, ideally, inimitably, incomparably, impeccably, immaculately, exquisitely, consummately; *N. Amer.* to a fare-thee-well; *informal* like a dream, to a T. **2** *I think we understand each other perfectly* ABSOLUTELY, utterly, completely, altogether, entirely, wholly, totally, thoroughly, fully, in every respect. **3** *you know perfectly well that is not what I meant* VERY, quite, full; *N. English* right; *informal* damn, damned; *Brit. informal* jolly, bloody; *N. Amer. informal* darned.
perfidious ● **adjective** *(poetic/literary)* TREACHEROUS, duplicitous, deceitful, disloyal, faithless, unfaithful, traitorous, treasonous, false, false-hearted, double-dealing, two-faced, untrustworthy.
– OPPOSITES faithful.
perfidy ● **noun** *(poetic/literary)* TREACHERY, duplicity, deceit, deceitfulness, disloyalty, infidelity, faithlessness, unfaithfulness, betrayal, treason, double-dealing, untrustworthiness, breach of trust; *poetic/literary* perfidiousness.
perforate ● **verb** PIERCE, penetrate, enter, puncture, prick, bore through, riddle.
perforce ● **adverb** *(formal)* NECESSARILY, of necessity, inevitably, unavoidably, by force of circumstances, needs must; *informal* like it or not; *formal* nolens volens.
perform ● **verb 1** *I have my duties to perform* CARRY OUT, do, execute, discharge, bring about, bring off, accomplish, achieve, fulfil, complete, conduct, effect, dispatch, work, implement; *informal* pull off; *formal* effectuate; *archaic* acquit oneself of. **2** *a car which performs well at low speeds* FUNCTION, work, operate, run, go, respond, behave, act, acquit oneself/itself. **3** *the play has been performed in Britain* STAGE, put on, present, mount, enact, act, produce. **4** *the band performed live in Hyde Park* APPEAR, play, be on stage.
– OPPOSITES neglect.
performance ● **noun 1** *the evening performance* SHOW, production, showing, presentation, staging; concert, recital; *Brit.* house; *informal* gig. **2** *their performance of Mozart's concerto in E flat* RENDITION, rendering, interpretation, playing, acting, representation. **3** *the continual performance of a single task* CARRYING OUT, execution, discharge, accomplishment, completion, fulfilment, dispatch, implementation; *formal* effectuation. **4** *the performance of the processor* FUNCTIONING, working, operation, running, behaviour, cap-

p

performance art ● noun an art form that combines visual art with dramatic performance.

performing arts ● plural noun forms of creative activity that are performed in front of an audience, such as drama, music, and dance.

perfume /perfyo͞om/ ● noun **1** a fragrant liquid used to give a pleasant smell to one's body. **2** a pleasant smell. ● verb /pərfyo͞om/ **1** give a pleasant smell to. **2** impregnate with perfume or a sweet-smelling ingredient.
– DERIVATIVES **perfumed** adjective.
– ORIGIN originally denoting pleasant-smelling smoke used in fumigation: from French *parfum*, from obsolete Italian *parfumare* 'to smoke through'.

perfumery ● noun (pl. **perfumeries**) **1** the process of producing and selling perfumes. **2** a shop that sells perfumes.
– DERIVATIVES **perfumer** noun.

perfunctory /pərfungktəri/ ● adjective carried out with a minimum of effort or reflection.
– DERIVATIVES **perfunctorily** adverb.
– ORIGIN Latin *perfunctorius* 'careless'.

perfuse ● verb permeate or suffuse with a liquid, colour, quality, etc.
– DERIVATIVES **perfusion** noun.
– ORIGIN Latin *perfundere* 'pour through'.

pergola /pergələ/ ● noun an arched structure forming a framework for climbing or trailing plants.
– ORIGIN Latin *pergula* 'projecting roof'.

perhaps ● adverb **1** expressing uncertainty or possibility. **2** used when making a polite request or suggestion.
– ORIGIN from PER + HAP.

peri- ● prefix **1** round; about: *pericardium*. **2** Astronomy denoting the point nearest to a specified celestial body: *perihelion*.
– ORIGIN Greek *peri* 'about, around'.

perianth /perrianth/ ● noun Botany the outer part of a flower, consisting of the calyx (sepals) and corolla (petals).
– ORIGIN from Greek *peri* 'around' + *anthos* 'flower'.

pericardium /perrikaardiəm/ ● noun (pl. **pericardia** /perrikaardiə/) Anatomy the membrane enclosing the heart.
– DERIVATIVES **pericardial** adjective.
– ORIGIN Latin, from Greek *peri* 'around' + *kardia* 'heart'.

pericarp ● noun Botany the part of a fruit formed from the wall of the ripened ovary.
– ORIGIN from Greek *peri-* 'around' + *karpos* 'fruit'.

peridot /perridot/ ● noun a green semi-precious stone.
– ORIGIN French.

peridotite /perridotīt/ ● noun Geology a dense, coarse-grained rock that is rich in magnesium and iron, thought to be the main constituent of the earth's mantle.

p

perigee /perrijee/ ● noun Astronomy the point in the orbit of the moon or a satellite at which it is nearest to the earth. The opposite of APOGEE.
– ORIGIN from Greek *peri-* 'around' + *gē* 'earth'.

perihelion /perriheeliən/ ● noun (pl. **perihelia** /perriheeliə/) Astronomy the point in the orbit of a planet, asteroid, or comet at which it is closest to the sun. The opposite of APHELION.
– ORIGIN from Greek *peri-* 'around' + *hēlios* 'sun'.

peril ● noun a situation of serious and immediate danger.
– PHRASES **at one's peril** at one's own risk. **in** (or **at**) **peril of** **1** very likely to suffer from. **2** at risk of losing or injuring.
– ORIGIN Old French, from Latin *periculum* 'danger'.

perilous ● adjective full of danger or risk.
– DERIVATIVES **perilously** adverb **perilousness** noun.

perimeter ● noun **1** the continuous line forming the boundary of a closed figure. **2** the outermost parts or boundary of an area or object. **3** an instrument for measuring a person's field of vision.
– DERIVATIVES **perimetric** adjective.
– ORIGIN from Greek *peri-* 'around' + *metron* 'measure'.

perinatal ● adjective relating to the time immediately before and after a birth.
– DERIVATIVES **perinatally** adverb.

perineum /perrineeəm/ ● noun (pl. **perinea**) Anatomy the area between the anus and the scrotum or vulva.
– DERIVATIVES **perineal** adjective.
– ORIGIN Greek *perinaion*.

period ● noun **1** a length or portion of time. **2** a distinct portion of time with particular characteristics. **3** a major division of geological time, forming part of an era. **4** a lesson in a school. **5** (also **menstrual period**) a monthly flow of blood and other material from the lining of the uterus, occurring in women of child-bearing age when not pregnant. **6** chiefly N. Amer. a full stop. **7** Physics the interval of time between recurrences of a phenomenon. ● adjective belonging to or characteristic of a past historical time: *period furniture*.
– ORIGIN originally denoting the time during which something runs its course: from Greek *periodos* 'orbit, recurrence, course'.

periodic /peerioddik/ ● adjective appearing or occurring at intervals.
– DERIVATIVES **periodicity** noun.

periodical ● adjective **1** occurring or appearing at intervals. **2** (of a magazine or newspaper) published at regular intervals. ● noun a periodical magazine or newspaper.
– DERIVATIVES **periodically** adverb.

periodic table ● noun a table of the chemical elements arranged in order of atomic number, usually in rows, with elements having similar atomic structure appearing in vertical columns.

period piece ● noun an object or work that is set in or reminiscent of an earlier historical period.

perioperative ● adjective Medicine (of a process or treatment) occurring or performed at or around the time of an operation.

peripatetic /perripətettik/ ● adjective **1** travelling from place to place. **2** working or based in a succession of places.
– DERIVATIVES **peripatetically** adverb.
– ORIGIN Greek *peripatētikos* 'walking up and down'.

peripheral ● adjective **1** relating to or situated on the periphery. **2** of secondary importance; marginal. **3** (of a device) able to be attached to and used with a computer, though not an integral

Thesaurus

abilities, capability, capacity, power, potential. **5** *(informal) he made a great performance of telling her about it* FUSS, production, palaver, scene; *NZ* bobsy-die; *informal* song and dance, to-do, hoo-ha, business, pantomime.

performer ● noun ACTOR, ACTRESS, thespian, artiste, artist, entertainer, trouper, player, musician, singer, dancer, comic, comedian, comedienne.

perfume ● noun **1** *a bottle of perfume* SCENT, fragrance, eau de toilette, toilet water, eau de cologne, cologne, aftershave. **2** *the heady perfume of lilacs* SMELL, scent, fragrance, aroma, bouquet, redolence.

perfumed ● adjective SWEET-SMELLING, scented, fragrant, fragranced, perfumy, aromatic.

perfunctory ● adjective CURSORY, desultory, quick, brief, hasty, hurried, rapid, token, casual, superficial, careless, half-hearted, sketchy, mechanical, automatic, routine, offhand, inattentive.
– OPPOSITES careful, thorough.

perhaps ● adverb MAYBE, for all one knows, it could be, it may be, it's possible, possibly, conceivably; *N. English* happen; *poetic/literary* peradventure, perchance.

peril ● noun DANGER, jeopardy, risk, hazard, insecurity, uncertainty, menace, threat, perilousness; pitfall, problem.

perilous ● adjective DANGEROUS, fraught with danger, hazardous, risky, unsafe, treacherous; precarious, vulnerable, uncertain, insecure, exposed, at risk, in jeopardy, in danger, touch-and-go; *informal* dicey.
– OPPOSITES safe.

perimeter ● noun **1** *the perimeter of a circle* CIRCUMFERENCE, outside, outer edge. **2** *the perimeter of the vast estate* BOUNDARY, border, limits, bounds, confines, edge, margin, fringe(s), periphery, borderline, verge; *poetic/literary* bourn, marge.

period ● noun **1** *a six-week period* TIME, spell, interval, stretch, term, span, phase, bout, run, duration, chapter, stage; while; *Brit. informal* patch. **2** *the post-war period* ERA, age, epoch, time, days, years; *Geology* aeon. **3** *a double Maths period* LESSON, class, session. **4** *women who suffer from painful periods* MENSTRUATION, menstrual flow; *informal* the curse, monthlies, time of the month; *technical* menses. **5** *(N. Amer.) a comma instead of a period* FULL STOP, full point, point, stop.

periodic ● adjective REGULAR, periodical, at fixed intervals, recurrent, recurring, repeated, cyclical, cyclic, seasonal; occasional, infrequent, intermittent, sporadic, spasmodic, odd.

periodical ● noun *articles in specialist periodicals* JOURNAL, publication, magazine, newspaper, paper, review, digest, gazette, newsletter, organ, quarterly; *informal* mag, book, glossy.
● adjective *the island has periodical earthquakes.* See PERIODIC.

part of it. **4** Anatomy near the surface of the body. ● **noun** Computing a peripheral device.
– DERIVATIVES **peripherality** noun **peripherally** adverb.
peripheral nervous system ● **noun** Anatomy the nervous system outside the brain and spinal cord.
periphery /pəriffəri/ ● **noun** (pl. **peripheries**) **1** the outer limits or edge of an area or object. **2** a marginal or secondary position, part, or aspect.
– ORIGIN Greek *periphereia* 'circumference'.
periphrasis /pərifrəsiss/ ● **noun** (pl. **periphrases** /pərifrəseez/) the use of indirect and roundabout language; circumlocution.
– DERIVATIVES **periphrastic** adjective.
– ORIGIN from Greek *peri-* 'around' + *phrazein* 'declare'.
periscope ● **noun** a tube attached to a set of mirrors or prisms, by which an observer in a submerged submarine or behind an obstacle can see things that are otherwise out of sight.
– DERIVATIVES **periscopic** adjective.
perish ● **verb** **1** die. **2** suffer complete ruin or destruction. **3** rot or decay. **4** (**be perished**) Brit. be suffering from extreme cold.
– PHRASES **perish the thought** informal may the thought or idea prove unfounded.
– ORIGIN Latin *perire* 'pass away'.
perishable ● **adjective** (of food) likely to rot quickly. ● **noun** (**perishables**) perishable foodstuffs.
perisher ● **noun** Brit. informal a mischievous or awkward person, especially a child.
perishing ● **adjective** Brit. informal **1** extremely cold. **2** dated used for emphasis or to express annoyance.
– DERIVATIVES **perishingly** adverb.
peristalsis /perristalsiss/ ● **noun** the contraction and relaxation of the muscles of the intestines, creating wave-like movements which push the contents of the intestines forward.
– DERIVATIVES **peristaltic** adjective.
– ORIGIN from Greek *peristallein* 'wrap around'.
peristyle ● **noun** a row of columns surrounding a courtyard or internal garden or edging a veranda or porch.
– ORIGIN from Greek *peri-* 'around' + *stulos* 'pillar'.
peritoneum /perritəneeəm/ ● **noun** (pl. **peritoneums** or **peritonea** /perritəneeə/) the membrane lining the cavity of the abdomen and covering the abdominal organs.
– DERIVATIVES **peritoneal** adjective.
– ORIGIN Latin, from *peritonos* 'stretched round'.
peritonitis /perritənītiss/ ● **noun** inflammation of the peritoneum.
periwig ● **noun** a wig of a kind worn in the 17th and 18th centuries, retained by judges and barristers as part of their professional dress.
– ORIGIN alteration of PERUKE.
periwinkle[1] ● **noun** a plant with flat five-petalled flowers and glossy leaves.
– ORIGIN Latin *pervinca*.
periwinkle[2] ● **noun** another term for WINKLE.
– ORIGIN of unknown origin.
perjure ● **verb** (**perjure oneself**) Law commit perjury.
– DERIVATIVES **perjurer** noun.
– ORIGIN Latin *perjurare* 'swear falsely'.
perjured ● **adjective** Law **1** (of evidence) involving deliberate untruth. **2** guilty of perjury.
perjury /perjəri/ ● **noun** Law the offence of deliberately telling an untruth in court when under oath.
perk[1] ● **verb** (**perk up**) make or become more cheerful or lively.
– ORIGIN originally in the senses 'perch' and 'be lively'): perhaps from Old French *percher* 'to perch'.
perk[2] ● **noun** a benefit or privilege to which an employee is entitled.
– ORIGIN abbreviation of PERQUISITE.
perk[3] ● **verb** informal (with reference to coffee) percolate.
perky ● **adjective** (**perkier**, **perkiest**) **1** cheerful and lively. **2** cheeky.
– DERIVATIVES **perkily** adverb **perkiness** noun.
perlite /perlit/ ● **noun** a form of obsidian consisting of glassy globules, used as insulation or in plant growth media.
– ORIGIN French, from *perle* 'pearl'.
perm[1] ● **noun** (also **permanent wave**) a method of setting the hair in waves or curls and treating it with chemicals so that the style lasts for several months. ● **verb** treat (the hair) in such a way.
perm[2] Brit. informal ● **noun** a permutation, especially a selection of a specified number of matches in a football pool. ● **verb** make a selection of (so many) from a larger number.
permaculture ● **noun** the development of agricultural ecosystems intended to be sustainable and self-sufficient.
– ORIGIN blend of PERMANENT and AGRICULTURE.
permafrost ● **noun** a thick subsurface layer of soil that remains below freezing point throughout the year.
permanent ● **adjective** lasting or intending to last indefinitely; not temporary.
– DERIVATIVES **permanence** noun **permanency** noun **permanently** adverb.
– ORIGIN from Latin *permanere* 'remain to the end'.

Thesaurus

p

peripatetic ● **adjective** NOMADIC, itinerant, travelling, wandering, roving, roaming, migrant, migratory, unsettled.
peripheral ● **adjective** **1** *the city's peripheral housing estates* OUTLYING, outer, on the edge/outskirts, surrounding. **2** *peripheral issues* SECONDARY, subsidiary, incidental, tangential, marginal, minor, unimportant, lesser, inessential, non-essential, immaterial, ancillary.
– OPPOSITES central.
periphery ● **noun** EDGE, outer edge, margin, fringe, boundary, border, perimeter, rim, verge, borderline; outskirts, outer limits/reaches, bounds; *poetic/literary* bourn, marge.
– OPPOSITES centre.
periphrastic ● **adjective** CIRCUMLOCUTORY, circuitous, roundabout, indirect, tautological, pleonastic, prolix, verbose, wordy, long-winded, rambling, wandering, tortuous, diffuse.
perish ● **verb** **1** *millions of soldiers perished* DIE, lose one's life, be killed, fall, expire, meet one's death, be lost, lay down one's life, breathe one's last, pass away, go the way of all flesh, give up the ghost, go to glory, meet one's maker, go to one's last resting place, cross the great divide; *informal* kick the bucket, turn up one's toes, shuffle off this mortal coil, buy it, croak; *Brit. informal* snuff it, pop one's clogs; *N. Amer. informal* bite the big one, buy the farm; *archaic* decease, depart this life. **2** *must these hopes perish so soon?* COME TO AN END, die (away), disappear, vanish, fade, dissolve, evaporate, melt away, wither. **3** *the wood had perished* GO BAD, go off, spoil, rot, go mouldy, moulder, putrefy, decay, decompose.
– OPPOSITES live, survive.
perjure ● **verb**
– PHRASES **perjure oneself** LIE UNDER OATH, lie, commit perjury, give false evidence/testimony; *formal* forswear oneself, be forsworn.
perjury ● **noun** LYING UNDER OATH, giving false evidence/testimony, making false statements, wilful falsehood.
perk[1] ● **verb**
– PHRASES **perk up 1** *you seem to have perked up* CHEER UP, brighten up, liven up, take heart; *informal* buck up. **2** *the economy is finally starting to perk up* RECOVER, rally, improve, revive, take a turn for the better, look up, pick up, bounce back. **perk someone/something up** *you could do with something to perk you up* CHEER UP, liven up, brighten up, raise someone's spirits, give someone a boost/lift, revitalize, invigorate, energize, enliven, ginger up, put new life/heart into, put some spark into, rejuvenate, refresh, vitalize; *informal* buck up, pep up.
perk[2] ● **noun** *a job with a lot of perks* FRINGE BENEFIT, additional benefit, benefit, advantage, bonus, extra, plus; *informal* freebie; *Brit. informal* golden hello; *formal* perquisite.
perky ● **adjective** CHEERFUL, lively, vivacious, animated, bubbly, effervescent, bouncy, spirited, high-spirited, in high spirits, cheery, merry, buoyant, ebullient, exuberant, jaunty, frisky, sprightly, spry, bright, sunny, jolly, full of the joys of spring, sparkly, pert; *informal* full of beans, bright-eyed and bushy-tailed, chirpy, chipper; *N. Amer. informal* peppy; *dated* gay.
permanence ● **noun** STABILITY, durability, permanency, fixity, fixedness, changelessness, immutability, constancy, continuity, immortality, indestructibility, perpetuity, endlessness.
permanent ● **adjective** **1** *permanent brain damage* LASTING, enduring, indefinite, continuing, perpetual, everlasting, eternal, abiding, constant, irreparable, irreversible, lifelong, indissoluble, indelible, standing, perennial, unending, endless, never-ending, immutable, undying, imperishable, indestructible, ineradicable; *poetic/literary* sempiternal, perdurable. **2** *a permanent job* LONG-TERM, stable, secure, durable.
– OPPOSITES temporary.
permanently ● **adverb** **1** *the attack left her permanently disabled* FOR ALL TIME, forever, for good, for always, for ever and ever, (for)

permanent magnet ● noun a magnet that retains its magnetic properties in the absence of an inducing field or current.

Permanent Undersecretary (also **Permanent Secretary**) ● noun (in the UK) a senior civil servant who is a permanent adviser to a Secretary of State.

permanent wave ● noun see PERM[1].

permanent way ● noun Brit. the finished foundation of a railway together with the track.

permanganate /pərmanggənayt/ ● noun Chemistry a salt containing the anion MnO_4^-, typically deep purplish-red and with strong oxidizing properties.

permeable ● adjective allowing liquids or gases to pass through; capable of being permeated.
– DERIVATIVES **permeability** noun.

permeate ● verb spread throughout; pervade.
– DERIVATIVES **permeation** noun **permeator** noun.
– ORIGIN Latin *permeare* 'pass through'.

Permian /permiən/ ● adjective Geology of or relating to the last period of the Palaeozoic era (between the Carboniferous and Triassic periods), about 290 to 245 million years ago, a time when reptiles proliferated and many marine animals became extinct.
– ORIGIN from *Perm*, a Russian province with extensive deposits from this period.

permissible ● adjective allowable; permitted.
– DERIVATIVES **permissibility** noun.

permission ● noun authorization; consent.

permissive ● adjective **1** allowing or characterized by freedom of behaviour, especially in sexual matters. **2** Law allowed but not obligatory; optional.
– DERIVATIVES **permissively** adverb **permissiveness** noun.

permit ● verb /pərmit/ (**permitted**, **permitting**) **1** give permission to (someone) or for (something). **2** make possible. **3** (**permit of**) formal allow for; admit of. ● noun /permit/ an official document giving permission to do something.
– ORIGIN Latin *permittere*, from *mittere* 'send, let go'.

permittivity /permitivviti/ ● noun Physics the ability of a substance to store electrical energy in an electric field.

permutation ● noun **1** each of several possible ways in which a set or number of things can be ordered or arranged. **2** Mathematics the action of changing the arrangement of a set of items. **3** Brit. a selection of a specified number of matches in a football pool.
– DERIVATIVES **permutational** adjective.
– ORIGIN Latin, from *permutare* 'change completely'

permute (also **permutate**) ● verb alter the sequence of; rearrange.

pernicious /pərnishəss/ ● adjective having a harmful effect, especially in a gradual or subtle way.
– DERIVATIVES **perniciously** adverb **perniciousness** noun.
– ORIGIN Latin *perniciosus* 'destructive'.

pernicious anaemia ● noun a deficiency in the production of red blood cells through a lack of vitamin B_{12}.

pernickety ● adjective informal, chiefly Brit. **1** fussy; over-fastidious. **2** requiring a precise or careful approach.
– ORIGIN of unknown origin.

Pernod /pernō/ ● noun trademark an aniseed-flavoured aperitif.
– ORIGIN named after the manufacturing firm *Pernod* Fils.

perorate /perrərayt/ ● verb formal **1** speak at length. **2** sum up and conclude a speech.
– ORIGIN Latin *perorare* 'speak at length'.

peroration ● noun the concluding part of a speech; the summing up.

peroxide ● noun **1** Chemistry a compound containing two oxygen atoms bonded together. **2** hydrogen peroxide, especially as used as a bleach for the hair. ● verb bleach (hair) with peroxide.

perpendicular /perpəndikyoolər/ ● adjective **1** at an angle of 90° to a given line, plane, or surface. **2** at an angle of 90° to the ground; vertical. **3** (**Perpendicular**) of the latest stage of English Gothic church architecture (late 14th to mid 16th centuries), characterized by broad arches and elaborate fan vaulting. ● noun a perpendicular line.
– DERIVATIVES **perpendicularity** noun **perpendicularly** adverb.
– ORIGIN Latin *perpendicularis*, from *perpendiculum* 'plumb line'.

perpetrate /perpitrayt/ ● verb carry out or commit (a bad or illegal action).
– DERIVATIVES **perpetration** noun **perpetrator** noun.
– ORIGIN Latin *perpetrare* 'perform'.

perpetual /pərpetyooəl/ ● adjective **1** never ending or changing. **2** occurring repeatedly; seemingly continual.
– DERIVATIVES **perpetually** adverb.
– ORIGIN Latin *perpetualis*, from *perpetuus* 'continuing throughout'.

perpetual motion ● noun the motion of a hypothetical ma-

Thesaurus

p

evermore, until hell freezes over, in perpetuity, indelibly, immutably, until the end of time; *N. Amer.* forevermore; *informal* for keeps, until the cows come home, until doomsday, until kingdom come; *archaic* for aye. **2** *I was permanently hungry* CONTINUALLY, constantly, perpetually, always.

permeable ● adjective POROUS, pervious, penetrable, absorbent, absorptive.

permeate ● verb **1** *the delicious smell permeated the entire flat* PERVADE, spread through, fill, filter through, diffuse through, imbue, penetrate, pass through, percolate through, perfuse, charge, suffuse, steep, impregnate, inform. **2** *these resins are able to permeate the timber* SOAK THROUGH, penetrate, seep through, saturate, percolate through, leach through.

permissible ● adjective PERMITTED, allowable, allowed, acceptable, legal, lawful, legitimate, admissible, licit, authorized, sanctioned, tolerated; *informal* legit, OK.
– OPPOSITES forbidden.

permission ● noun AUTHORIZATION, consent, leave, authority, sanction, licence, dispensation, assent, acquiescence, agreement, approval, seal of approval, approbation, endorsement, blessing, imprimatur, clearance, allowance, tolerance, sufferance, empowerment; *informal* the go-ahead, the thumbs up, the OK, the green light, say-so.

permissive ● adjective LIBERAL, broad-minded, open-minded, free, free and easy, easy-going, live-and-let-live, latitudinarian, laissez-faire, libertarian, unprescriptive, tolerant, forbearing, indulgent, lenient; overindulgent, lax, soft.
– OPPOSITES intolerant, strict.

permit ● verb *I cannot permit you to leave* ALLOW, let, authorize, give someone permission, sanction, grant, give someone the right, license, empower, enable, entitle, qualify; consent to, assent to, give one's blessing to, give the nod to, acquiesce in, agree to, tolerate, countenance, admit of; legalize, legitimize, legitimate; *informal* give the go-ahead to, give the thumbs up to, OK, give the OK to, give the green light to, say the word; *formal* accede to; *archaic* suffer.
– OPPOSITES ban, forbid.
● noun *I need to see your permit* AUTHORIZATION, licence, pass, ticket, warrant, document, certification; passport, visa.

permutation ● noun VARIATION, alteration, modification, change, shift, transformation, transmutation, mutation; *humorous* transmogrification.

pernicious ● adjective HARMFUL, damaging, destructive, injurious, hurtful, detrimental, deleterious, dangerous, adverse, inimical, unhealthy, unfavourable, bad, evil, baleful, wicked, malign, malevolent, malignant, noxious, poisonous, corrupting; *poetic/literary* maleficent.
– OPPOSITES beneficial.

pernickety ● adjective (*informal*) FUSSY, difficult to please, difficult, finicky, over-fastidious, fastidious, over-particular, particular, faddish, punctilious, hair-splitting, critical, overcritical; *informal* nit-picking, choosy, picky; *Brit. informal* faddy; *N. Amer. informal* persnickety.
– OPPOSITES easy-going.

peroration ● noun **1** *the peroration of his speech* CONCLUSION, ending, close, closing remarks; summation, summing-up. **2** *an hour-long peroration* SPEECH, lecture, talk, address, oration, sermon, disquisition, discourse, declamation, harangue, diatribe; *informal* spiel.

perpendicular ● adjective **1** *the perpendicular stones* UPRIGHT, vertical, erect, plumb, straight (up and down), on end, standing, upended. **2** *lines perpendicular to each other* AT RIGHT ANGLES, at 90 degrees. **3** *the perpendicular hillside* STEEP, sheer, precipitous, abrupt, bluff, vertiginous.
– OPPOSITES horizontal.

perpetrate ● verb COMMIT, carry out, perform, execute, do, effect, bring about, accomplish; be guilty of, be to blame for, be responsible for, inflict, wreak; *informal* pull off; *formal* effectuate.

perpetual ● adjective **1** *deep caves in perpetual darkness* EVERLASTING, never-ending, eternal, permanent, unending, endless, without

chine which, once activated, would run forever unless subject to an external force or to wear.

perpetuate ● verb cause to continue indefinitely.
– DERIVATIVES **perpetuation** noun **perpetuator** noun.
– ORIGIN Latin *perpetuare* 'make permanent'.

perpetuity ● noun (pl. **perpetuities**) **1** the state or quality of lasting forever. **2** a bond or other security with no fixed maturity date.
– PHRASES **in** (or **for**) **perpetuity** for ever.

perplex ● verb cause to feel baffled; puzzle greatly.
– DERIVATIVES **perplexity** noun (pl. **perplexities**).
– ORIGIN from Latin *perplexus* 'entangled'.

perquisite /perkwizit/ ● noun **1** formal a special right or privilege enjoyed as a result of one's position. **2** historical a thing which has served its primary use and to which a subordinate or employee has a customary right.
– ORIGIN Latin *perquisitum* 'acquisition'.

perry ● noun (pl. **perries**) an alcoholic drink made from the fermented juice of pears.
– ORIGIN Old French *pere*, from Latin *pirum* 'pear'.

per se /per say/ ● adverb by or in itself or themselves.
– ORIGIN Latin.

persecute ● verb **1** subject to prolonged hostility and ill-treatment. **2** persistently harass or annoy.
– DERIVATIVES **persecution** noun **persecutor** noun.
– ORIGIN Old French *persecuter*, from Latin *persequi* 'follow with hostility'.

persecution complex ● noun an irrational and obsessive feeling that others are scheming against one.

persevere ● verb continue in a course of action in spite of difficulty or lack of success.
– DERIVATIVES **perseverance** noun.
– ORIGIN Latin *perseverare* 'abide by strictly'.

Persian ● noun **1** a person from Persia (now Iran). **2** the language of ancient Persia or modern Iran. **3** a long-haired breed of domestic cat with a broad round head and stocky body. ● adjective relating to Persia or Iran.

Persian carpet ● noun a carpet or rug with a traditional Persian design incorporating stylized symbolic imagery.

Persian lamb ● noun the silky, tightly curled fleece of the karakul, used to make clothing.

persiflage /persiflaazh/ ● noun formal light mockery or banter.
– ORIGIN from French *persifler* 'to banter'.

persimmon /pərsimmən/ ● noun an edible fruit resembling a large tomato, with very sweet flesh.
– ORIGIN Algonquian.

persist ● verb **1** continue doing something in spite of difficulty or opposition. **2** continue to exist.
– ORIGIN Latin *persistere* 'continue steadfastly'.

persistent ● adjective **1** persisting or having a tendency to persist. **2** continuing or recurring; prolonged. **3** Botany & Zoology (of a horn, leaf, etc.) remaining attached instead of falling off in the normal manner.
– DERIVATIVES **persistence** noun **persistently** adverb.

persistent vegetative state ● noun a condition in which a patient is kept alive by medical intervention but displays no sign of higher brain function.

persnickety ● adjective North American term for PERNICKETY.

person ● noun (pl. **people** or **persons**) **1** a human being regarded as an individual. **2** an individual's body: *concealed on his person.* **3** Grammar a category used in the classification of pronouns, verb forms, etc. according to whether they indicate the speaker (**first person**), the person spoken to (**second person**), or a third party (**third person**). **4** Christian Theology each of the three modes of being of God, namely the Father, the Son, and the Holy Ghost.
– PHRASES **in person** physically present.
– USAGE The words **people** and **persons** can both be used as the plural of **person** but they are not used in exactly the same way. **People** is by far the commoner of the two words and is used in most ordinary contexts. **Persons**, on the other hand, tends to be restricted to official or formal contexts, as in *this vehicle is authorized to carry twenty persons.*
– ORIGIN Latin *persona* 'actor's mask, character in a play', later 'human being'.

-person ● combining form used as a neutral alternative to *-man* in

Thesaurus

end, lasting, long-lasting, constant, abiding, enduring, perennial, timeless, ageless, deathless, undying, immortal; unfailing, unchanging, never-changing, changeless, unfading; poetic/literary sempiternal, perdurable. **2** *a perpetual state of fear* CONSTANT, permanent, uninterrupted, continuous, unremitting, unending, unceasing, persistent, unbroken. **3** *her mother's perpetual nagging* INTERMINABLE, incessant, ceaseless, endless, without respite, relentless, unrelenting, persistent, continual, continuous, non-stop, never-ending, recurrent, repeated, unremitting, sustained, round-the-clock, unabating; informal eternal.
– OPPOSITES temporary, intermittent.

perpetuate ● verb KEEP ALIVE, keep going, preserve, conserve, sustain, maintain, continue, extend, carry on, keep up, prolong; immortalize, commemorate, memorialize, eternalize.

perpetuity ● noun
– PHRASES **in perpetuity** FOREVER, permanently, for always, for good, for good and all, perpetually, (for) evermore, for ever and ever, for all time, until the end of time, until hell freezes over, eternally, for eternity, everlastingly; N. Amer. forevermore; informal for keeps, until doomsday; archaic for aye.

perplex ● verb PUZZLE, baffle, mystify, bemuse, bewilder, confound, confuse, nonplus, disconcert, dumbfound, throw, throw/catch off balance, exercise, worry; informal flummox, be all Greek to, stump, bamboozle, floor, beat, faze, fox; N. Amer. informal discombobulate; archaic wilder, maze.

perplexing ● adjective PUZZLING, baffling, mystifying, mysterious, bewildering, confusing, disconcerting, worrying, unaccountable, difficult to understand, beyond one, paradoxical, peculiar, funny, strange, weird, odd.

perplexity ● noun **1** *he scratched his head in perplexity* CONFUSION, bewilderment, puzzlement, bafflement, incomprehension, mystification, bemusement; informal bamboozlement; N. Amer. informal discombobulation. **2** *the perplexities of international relations* COMPLEXITY, complication, intricacy, problem, difficulty, mystery, puzzle, enigma, paradox.

perquisite ● noun (formal). See PERK[2].

per se ● adverb IN ITSELF, of itself, by itself, as such, intrinsically; by its very nature, in essence, by definition, essentially.

persecute ● verb **1** *they were persecuted for their religious beliefs* OPPRESS, abuse, victimize, ill-treat, mistreat, maltreat, tyrannize, torment, torture; martyr. **2** *she was persecuted by the press* HARASS, hound, plague, badger, harry, intimidate, pick on, pester, bother, bedevil, bully, victimize, terrorize; N. Amer. devil; informal hassle, give someone a hard time, get on someone's back; Austral. informal heavy.

persecution ● noun **1** *victims of religious persecution* OPPRESSION, victimization, maltreatment, ill-treatment, mistreatment, abuse, ill-usage, discrimination, tyranny; informal witch hunt. **2** *the persecution I endured at school* HARASSMENT, hounding, intimidation, bullying.

perseverance ● noun PERSISTENCE, tenacity, determination, staying power, indefatigability, steadfastness, purposefulness; patience, endurance, application, diligence, dedication, commitment, doggedness, assiduity, tirelessness, stamina; intransigence, obstinacy; informal stickability; N. Amer. informal stick-to-it-iveness; formal pertinacity.

persevere ● verb PERSIST, continue, carry on, go on, keep on, keep going, struggle on, hammer away, be persistent, be determined, see/follow something through, keep at it, press on/ahead, not take no for an answer, be tenacious, stand one's ground, stand fast/firm, hold on, go the distance, stay the course, plod on, plough on, stop at nothing, leave no stone unturned; informal soldier on, hang on, plug away, peg away, stick to one's guns, stick it out, hang in there.
– OPPOSITES give up.

persist ● verb **1** *Corbett persisted with his questioning.* See PERSEVERE. **2** *if dry weather persists, water the lawn thoroughly* CONTINUE, hold, carry on, last, keep on, keep up, remain, linger, stay, endure.

persistence ● noun. See PERSEVERANCE.

persistent ● adjective **1** *a very persistent man* TENACIOUS, persevering, determined, resolute, purposeful, dogged, single-minded, tireless, indefatigable, patient, unflagging, untiring, insistent, importunate, relentless, unrelenting; stubborn, intransigent, obstinate, obdurate; formal pertinacious. **2** *persistent rain* CONSTANT, continuous, continuing, continual, non-stop, never-ending, steady, uninterrupted, unbroken, interminable, incessant, unceasing, endless, unending, perpetual, unremitting, unrelenting, relentless,

nouns denoting status, authority, etc.: *salesperson.*

persona /persōnə/ ● noun (pl. **personas** or **personae** /persōnee/) **1** Psychoanalysis the aspect of a person's character that is presented to or perceived by others. Compare with ANIMA. **2** a role or character adopted by an author or actor.
– ORIGIN Latin, 'mask, character played by an actor'.

personable ● adjective having a pleasant appearance and manner.
– DERIVATIVES **personably** adverb.

personage ● noun a person (used to express their importance or elevated status).
– ORIGIN Old French, reinforced by Latin *personagium* 'effigy'.

personal ● adjective **1** of, affecting, or belonging to a particular person. **2** involving the presence or action of a particular individual. **3** concerning a person's private rather than professional life. **4** making inappropriate or offensive reference to a person's character or appearance. **5** relating to a person's body. **6** Grammar of one of the three persons. **7** existing as a self-aware entity, not as an abstraction or an impersonal force: *a personal God.* ● noun (**personals**) chiefly N. Amer. advertisements or messages in the personal column of a newspaper.

personal assistant ● noun a secretary or administrative assistant working for one particular person.

personal column ● noun a section of a newspaper devoted to private advertisements or messages.

personal computer ● noun a microcomputer designed for use by one person at a time.

personal equity plan ● noun (in the UK) a scheme whereby individuals may invest a limited sum each year in British companies without liability for tax on dividends or capital gains.

personal identification number ● noun a number allocated to an individual and used to validate electronic transactions.

personality ● noun (pl. **personalities**) **1** the characteristics or qualities that form an individual's character. **2** qualities that make someone interesting or popular. **3** a celebrity.

personality disorder ● noun Psychiatry a deeply ingrained pattern of inappropriate or inadequate behaviour.

personalize (also **personalise**) ● verb **1** design or produce (something) to meet someone's individual requirements. **2** make (something) identifiable as belonging to a particular person. **3** cause (an issue or argument) to become concerned with personalities or feelings. **4** personify.
– DERIVATIVES **personalization** noun.

personally ● adverb **1** in person. **2** from one's own viewpoint; subjectively.
– PHRASES **take personally** interpret (a remark or action) as directed against oneself and be upset or offended by it.

personal organizer ● noun a loose-leaf notebook with a diary and address book.

personal pension ● noun a pension scheme that is independent of the contributor's employer.

personal pronoun ● noun each of the pronouns in English (*I, you, he, she, it, we, they, me, him, her, us,* and *them*) that show contrasts of person, gender, number, and case.
– USAGE **I**, **we**, **they**, **he**, and **she** are **subjective** personal pronouns, which means they are used as the subject of the sentence, often coming before the verb (*she lives in Paris*). **Me**, **us**, **them**, **him**, and **her**, on the other hand, are **objective** personal pronouns, which means that they are used as the object of a verb or preposition (*John hates me*). This explains why it is incorrect to say *John and me went to the shops*: the personal pronoun is in subject position, so it must be **I**. Where a personal pronoun is used alone, however, the traditional analysis starts to break down. It is sometimes claimed that statements such as *she's younger than me* and *I've not been here as long as her* are incorrect and that the correct forms are *she's younger than I* and *I've not been here as long as she.* This is based on the assumption that **than** and **as** are conjunctions and so the personal pronoun is still subjective even though there is no verb (in full form it would be *she's younger than I am*). Yet for most native speakers the supposed 'correct' form sounds stilted and is almost never used. It would perhaps be more accurate to say that objective personal pronouns are now used in all cases where the pronoun is not explicitly subjective, and it is therefore acceptable to say *she's taller than him* and *I didn't do as well as her.*

personal property ● noun Law all of someone's property except land and buildings. Compare with REAL PROPERTY.

personal stereo ● noun a small portable cassette or compact disc player, used with headphones.

personalty /persənəlti/ ● noun Law a person's personal property. Compare with REALTY.

persona non grata ● noun (pl. **personae non gratae**) an unacceptable or unwelcome person.
– ORIGIN Latin.

personate ● verb formal play the part of or pretend to be.
– DERIVATIVES **personation** noun.

personify ● verb (**personifies, personified**) **1** represent (a quality or concept) by a figure in human form. **2** attribute a personal nature or human characteristics to (something non-human). **3** represent or embody (a quality or concept) in a physical form.
– DERIVATIVES **personification** noun.

personnel ● plural noun people employed in an organization or engaged in an undertaking.
– ORIGIN from French, 'personal'.

personnel carrier ● noun an armoured vehicle for transporting troops.

perspective ● noun **1** the art of representing three-dimensional objects on a two-dimensional surface so as to convey the impression of height, width, depth, and relative distance. **2** a view

p

Thesaurus

unrelieved, sustained. **3** *a persistent cough* CHRONIC, permanent, nagging, frequent; repeated, habitual.
– OPPOSITES irresolute, intermittent.

person ● noun HUMAN BEING, individual, man/woman, human, being, (living) soul, mortal, creature; personage, character, customer; informal type, sort, beggar, cookie; Brit. informal bod; informal, dated body, dog, cove; archaic wight.
– PHRASES **in person** PHYSICALLY, in the flesh, in propria persona, personally; oneself; informal as large as life.

persona ● noun IMAGE, face, public face, character, personality, identity, self; front, facade, guise, exterior, role, part.

personable ● adjective PLEASANT, agreeable, likeable, nice, amiable, affable, charming, congenial, genial, engaging, pleasing; attractive, presentable, good-looking, nice-looking, pretty, appealing; Scottish couthy; Scottish & N. English bonny, canny; dated taking.
– OPPOSITES disagreeable, unattractive.

personage ● noun IMPORTANT PERSON, VIP, luminary, celebrity, personality, name, famous name, household name, public figure, star, leading light, dignitary, notable, notability, worthy, panjandrum; person; informal celeb, somebody, big shot, big noise; Brit. informal nob; N. Amer. informal big wheel, big kahuna.

personal ● adjective **1** *a highly personal style* DISTINCTIVE, characteristic, unique, individual, one's own, particular, peculiar, idiosyncratic, individualized, personalized. **2** *a personal appearance* IN PERSON, in the flesh, actual, live, physical. **3** *his personal life* PRIVATE, intimate; confidential, secret. **4** *a personal friend* INTIMATE, close, dear, great, bosom. **5** *I have personal knowledge of the family* DIRECT, empirical, first-hand, immediate, experiential. **6** *personal remarks* DEROGATORY, disparaging, belittling, insulting, critical, rude, slighting, disrespectful, offensive, pejorative.
– OPPOSITES public, general.

personality ● noun **1** *her cheerful personality* CHARACTER, nature, disposition, temperament, make-up, persona, psyche. **2** *she had loads of personality* CHARISMA, magnetism, strength/force of personality, character, charm, presence. **3** *a famous TV personality* CELEBRITY, VIP, star, superstar, name, famous name, household name, big name, somebody, leading light, luminary, notable, personage, notability; informal celeb.

personalize ● verb **1** *products which can be personalized to your requirements* CUSTOMIZE, individualize. **2** *attempts to personalize God* PERSONIFY, humanize, anthropomorphize.

personally ● adverb **1** *I'd like to thank him personally* IN PERSON, oneself. **2** *personally, I think it's a good idea* FOR MY PART, for myself, to my way of thinking, to my mind, in my estimation, as far as I am concerned, in my view/opinion, from my point of view, from where I stand, as I see it, if you ask me, for my money, in my book; privately.
– PHRASES **take something personally** TAKE OFFENCE, take something amiss, be offended, be upset, be affronted, take umbrage, take exception, feel insulted, feel hurt.

personification ● noun EMBODIMENT, incarnation, epitome, quintessence, essence, type, symbol, soul, model, exemplification, exemplar, image, representation.

personify ● verb EPITOMIZE, embody, be the incarnation of, typify,

or prospect. **3** a particular way of regarding something. **4** understanding of the relative importance of things.
– DERIVATIVES **perspectival** adjective.
– ORIGIN originally in the sense 'optics': from Latin *perspectiva ars* 'science of optics'.

perspex • noun trademark a tough transparent plastic used as a substitute for glass.
– ORIGIN from Latin *perspicere* 'look through'.

perspicacious /perspikayshəss/ • adjective having a ready insight into and understanding of things.
– DERIVATIVES **perspicaciously** adverb **perspicacity** noun.
– ORIGIN from Latin *perspicax* 'seeing clearly'.

perspicuous /pərspikyooəss/ • adjective **1** clearly expressed and easily understood; lucid. **2** expressing things clearly.
– DERIVATIVES **perspicuity** noun **perspicuously** adverb.
– ORIGIN Latin *perspicuus* 'transparent, clear'.

perspiration • noun **1** sweat. **2** the process of perspiring.

perspire • verb give out sweat through the pores of the skin.
– ORIGIN Latin *perspirare*, from *spirare* 'breathe'.

persuade • verb **1** induce (someone) to do something through reasoning or argument. **2** cause (someone) to believe something.
– DERIVATIVES **persuadable** adjective **persuader** noun.
– ORIGIN Latin *persuadere*, from *suadere* 'advise'.

persuasion • noun **1** the process of persuading or of being persuaded. **2** a belief or set of beliefs. **3** a group or sect holding a particular belief.

persuasive • adjective **1** good at persuading someone to do or believe something. **2** providing sound reasoning or argument: *a persuasive speech*.
– DERIVATIVES **persuasively** adverb **persuasiveness** noun.

pert • adjective **1** attractively lively or cheeky. **2** (of a bodily feature or garment) neat and suggestive of jauntiness.
– DERIVATIVES **pertly** adverb **pertness** noun.
– ORIGIN originally in the sense 'manifest': from Latin *apertus* 'opened'.

pertain • verb **1** be appropriate, related, or applicable. **2** chiefly Law belong as a part, appendage, or accessory. **3** be in effect or existence at a particular place or time.
– ORIGIN Latin *pertinere* 'extend to, have reference to'.

pertinacious /pertinayshəss/ • adjective formal stubborn; persistent.
– DERIVATIVES **pertinaciously** adverb **pertinacity** noun.
– ORIGIN from Latin *pertinax* 'holding fast'.

pertinent • adjective relevant; appropriate.
– DERIVATIVES **pertinence** noun **pertinently** adverb.
– ORIGIN from Latin *pertinere* 'extend to, have reference to'.

perturb • verb **1** make anxious or unsettled. **2** alter the normal or regular state or path of.
– ORIGIN Latin *perturbare*, from *turbare* 'disturb'.

perturbation • noun **1** anxiety; uneasiness. **2** the action of perturbing a system, moving object, or process.

pertussis /pərtussiss/ • noun medical term for WHOOPING COUGH.
– ORIGIN Latin, from *tussis* 'a cough'.

peruke /pərook/ • noun archaic a wig or periwig.
– ORIGIN French *perruque*.

peruse /pərooz/ • verb read or examine thoroughly or carefully.
– DERIVATIVES **perusal** noun **peruser** noun.
– ORIGIN originally in the sense 'use up, wear out': perhaps from PER- + USE.

Peruvian /pəroovian/ • noun a person from Peru. • adjective relating to Peru.

perv (also **perve**) informal • noun **1** a sexual pervert. **2** Austral./NZ a lecherous look. • verb Austral./NZ gaze lecherously.
– DERIVATIVES **pervy** adjective.

pervade • verb spread or be present throughout; suffuse.
– DERIVATIVES **pervasion** noun.
– ORIGIN Latin *pervadere* 'go or come through'.

pervasive • adjective spreading widely through something; widespread.
– DERIVATIVES **pervasively** adverb **pervasiveness** noun.

perverse • adjective **1** showing a deliberate and obstinate desire

Thesaurus

exemplify, represent, symbolize, stand for, body forth.

personnel • noun STAFF, employees, workforce, workers, labour force, manpower, human resources; *informal* liveware.

perspective • noun **1** *her perspective on things had changed* OUTLOOK, view, viewpoint, point of view, standpoint, position, stand, stance, angle, slant, attitude, frame of mind, frame of reference, approach, way of looking, interpretation. **2** *a perspective of the whole valley* VIEW, vista, panorama, prospect, bird's-eye view, outlook, aspect.

perspicacious • adjective DISCERNING, shrewd, perceptive, astute, penetrating, observant, percipient, sharp-witted, sharp, smart, alert, clear-sighted, far-sighted, acute, clever, canny, intelligent, insightful, wise, sage, sensitive, intuitive, understanding, aware, discriminating; *informal* on the ball; *N. Amer. informal* heads-up.
– OPPOSITES stupid.

perspicuous • adjective *(formal)*. See CLEAR adjective sense 1.

perspiration • noun SWEAT, moisture; a lather; *informal* a muck sweat; *Medicine* diaphoresis, hidrosis.

perspire • verb SWEAT, be dripping/pouring with sweat, glow; *informal* be in a muck sweat.

persuadable • adjective MALLEABLE, tractable, pliable, compliant, amenable, adaptable, accommodating, cooperative, flexible, acquiescent, yielding, biddable, complaisant, like putty in one's hands, suggestible.

persuade • verb **1** *he tried to persuade her to come with him* PREVAIL ON, talk into, coax, convince, make, get, induce, win over, bring round, coerce, influence, sway, inveigle, entice, tempt, lure, cajole, wheedle; *Law* procure; *informal* sweet-talk, twist someone's arm. **2** *shortage of money persuaded them to abandon the scheme* CAUSE, lead, move, dispose, incline.
– OPPOSITES dissuade, deter.

persuasion • noun **1** *Monica needed plenty of persuasion* COAXING, persuading, coercion, inducement, convincing, blandishment, encouragement, urging, inveiglement, cajolery, enticement, wheedling; *informal* sweet-talking, arm-twisting; *formal* suasion. **2** *various political and religious persuasions* GROUP, grouping, sect, denomination, party, camp, side, faction, affiliation, school of thought, belief, creed, credo, faith, philosophy.

persuasive • adjective CONVINCING, cogent, compelling, potent, forceful, powerful, eloquent, impressive, influential, sound, valid, strong, effective, winning, telling; plausible, credible.
– OPPOSITES unconvincing.

pert • adjective **1** *a pert little hat* JAUNTY, neat, trim, stylish, smart, perky, rakish; *informal* natty; *N. Amer. informal* saucy. **2** *a young girl with a pert manner* IMPUDENT, impertinent, cheeky, irreverent, forward, insolent, disrespectful, flippant, familiar, presumptuous, bold, as bold as brass, brazen; *informal* fresh, lippy, saucy; *N. Amer. informal* sassy; *archaic* malapert.

pertain • verb **1** *developments pertaining to the economy* CONCERN, relate to, be related to, be connected with, be relevant to, apply to, be pertinent to, refer to, have a bearing on, appertain to, bear on, affect, involve, touch; *archaic* regard. **2** *the stock and assets pertaining to the business* BELONG TO, be a part of, be included in. **3** *the economic situation which pertained in Britain at that time* EXIST, be the order of the day, be the case, prevail; *formal* obtain.

pertinacious • adjective *(formal)* DETERMINED, tenacious, persistent, persevering, purposeful, resolute, dogged, indefatigable, insistent, single-minded, unrelenting, relentless, tireless, unshakeable; stubborn, obstinate, inflexible, unbending.
– OPPOSITES irresolute, tentative.

pertinent • adjective RELEVANT, to the point, apposite, appropriate, suitable, fitting, fit, apt, applicable, material, germane, to the purpose, apropos; *formal* ad rem.
– OPPOSITES irrelevant.

perturb • verb WORRY, upset, unsettle, disturb, concern, trouble, disquiet; disconcert, discomfit, unnerve, alarm, bother, distress, dismay, gnaw at, agitate, fluster, ruffle, discountenance, exercise; *informal* rattle.
– OPPOSITES reassure.

perturbed • adjective UPSET, worried, unsettled, disturbed, concerned, troubled, anxious, ill at ease, uneasy, fretful, disquieted; disconcerted, discomposed, unnerved, alarmed, bothered, distressed, dismayed, agitated, flustered, ruffled, shaken, discountenanced; *informal* twitchy, rattled, fazed; *N. Amer. informal* discombobulated.
– OPPOSITES calm.

peruse • verb READ, study, scrutinize, inspect, examine, wade through, look through; browse through, leaf through, scan, run one's eye over, glance through, flick through, skim through, thumb through, dip into; *archaic* con.

pervade • verb PERMEATE, spread through, fill, suffuse, be diffused through, imbue, penetrate, filter through, percolate through, in-

to behave unacceptably. **2** contrary to that which is accepted or expected. **3** sexually perverted.
– DERIVATIVES **perversely** adverb **perverseness** noun **perversity** noun (pl. **perversities**).

perversion ● noun **1** the action of perverting. **2** abnormal or unacceptable sexual behaviour.

pervert ● verb **1** alter from an original meaning or state to a corruption of what was first intended. **2** lead away from what is right, natural, or acceptable. ● noun a person with abnormal or unacceptable sexual behaviour.
– ORIGIN Latin *pervertere* 'turn about'.

perverted ● adjective sexually abnormal and unacceptable.
– DERIVATIVES **pervertedly** adverb.

pervious /perviəss/ ● adjective allowing water to pass through; permeable.
– ORIGIN Latin *pervius* 'having a passage through'.

peseta /pəsaytə/ ● noun the basic monetary unit of Spain, equal to 100 centimos.
– ORIGIN Spanish, 'little weight'.

pesewa /peseewə/ ● noun a monetary unit of Ghana, equal to one hundredth of a cedi.
– ORIGIN Akan, 'penny'.

pesky ● adjective (**peskier**, **peskiest**) informal annoying.
– ORIGIN perhaps related to PEST.

peso /paysō/ ● noun (pl. **pesos**) the basic monetary unit of several Latin American countries and of the Philippines.
– ORIGIN Spanish, 'weight'.

pessary /pessəri/ ● noun (pl. **pessaries**) **1** a small soluble medicinal or contraceptive block inserted into the vagina. **2** a device inserted into the vagina to support the uterus.
– ORIGIN Latin *pessarium*, from Greek *pessos* 'oval stone'.

pessimism ● noun **1** lack of hope or confidence in the future. **2** Philosophy a belief that this world is as bad as it could be or that evil will ultimately prevail over good.
– DERIVATIVES **pessimist** noun **pessimistic** adjective **pessimistically** adverb.
– ORIGIN from Latin *pessimus* 'worst'.

pest ● noun **1** a destructive animal that attacks crops, food, or livestock. **2** informal an annoying person or thing.
– ORIGIN French *peste* or Latin *pestis* 'plague'.

pester ● verb trouble or annoy with persistent requests or interruptions.
– ORIGIN originally in the sense 'overcrowd or impede', later 'infest': from French *empestrer* 'encumber'.

pesticide ● noun a substance for destroying insects or other pests.

pestiferous ● adjective **1** literary harbouring infection and disease. **2** humorous annoying.
– ORIGIN from Latin *pestifer* 'bringing pestilence'.

pestilence ● noun archaic a fatal epidemic disease, especially bubonic plague.
– ORIGIN Latin *pestilentia*, from *pestis* 'a plague'.

pestilent ● adjective **1** deadly. **2** informal, dated annoying. **3** archaic harmful to morals or public order.

pestilential ● adjective **1** relating to or tending to cause infectious diseases. **2** of the nature of a pest. **3** informal annoying.

pestle /pess'l/ ● noun a heavy tool with a rounded end, used for crushing and grinding substances in a mortar.
– ORIGIN Latin *pistillum*, from *pinsere* 'to pound'.

pesto /pestō/ ● noun a sauce of crushed basil leaves, pine nuts, garlic, Parmesan cheese, and olive oil, served with pasta.
– ORIGIN Italian, from *pestare* 'pound, crush'.

pet[1] ● noun **1** a domestic or tamed animal or bird kept for companionship or pleasure. **2** a person treated with special favour. **3** used as an affectionate form of address. ● adjective **1** relating to or kept as a pet. **2** favourite or particular: *my pet hate.* ● verb (**petted**, **petting**) **1** stroke or pat (an animal). **2** caress sexually.
– ORIGIN of unknown origin.

pet[2] ● noun a fit of sulking or bad temper.
– ORIGIN of unknown origin.

peta- /pettə/ ● combining form denoting a factor of one thousand million million (10^{15}).
– ORIGIN alteration of PENTA- based on the supposed analogy of *tera-* and *tetra-*.

petal ● noun each of the segments of the corolla of a flower.

Thesaurus

fuse, perfuse, flow through; charge, steep, saturate, impregnate, inform.

pervasive ● adjective PREVALENT, pervading, permeating, extensive, ubiquitous, omnipresent, universal, rife, widespread, general.

perverse ● adjective **1** *he is being deliberately perverse* AWKWARD, contrary, difficult, unreasonable, uncooperative, unhelpful, obstructive, disobliging, recalcitrant, stubborn, obstinate, obdurate, mulish, pig-headed, bull-headed; *informal* cussed; *Brit. informal* bloody-minded, bolshie; *N. Amer. informal* balky; *formal* refractory; *archaic* froward, contumacious. **2** *a verdict that is manifestly perverse* ILLOGICAL, irrational, unreasonable, wrong, wrong-headed. **3** *an evil life dedicated to perverse pleasure* PERVERTED, depraved, unnatural, abnormal, deviant, degenerate, immoral, warped, twisted, corrupt; wicked, base, evil; *informal* kinky, sick, pervy.
– OPPOSITES accommodating, reasonable.

p

perversion ● noun **1** *a twisted perversion of the truth* DISTORTION, misrepresentation, falsification, travesty, misinterpretation, misconstruction, twisting, corruption, subversion, misuse, misapplication, debasement. **2** *sexual perversion* DEVIANCE, abnormality; depravity, degeneracy, debauchery, corruption, vice, wickedness, immorality.

perversity ● noun **1** *out of sheer perversity, he refused* CONTRARINESS, awkwardness, recalcitrance, stubbornness, obstinacy, obduracy, mulishness, pig-headedness; *informal* cussedness; *Brit. informal* bloody-mindedness; *formal* refractoriness. **2** *the perversity of the decision* UNREASONABLENESS, irrationality, illogicality, wrong-headedness.

pervert ● verb **1** *people who attempt to pervert the rules* DISTORT, corrupt, subvert, twist, bend, abuse, misapply, misuse, misrepresent, misinterpret, falsify. **2** *men can be perverted by power* CORRUPT, lead astray, debase, warp, pollute, poison, deprave, debauch.
● noun *a sexual pervert* DEVIANT, degenerate; *informal* perv, dirty old man, sicko.

perverted ● adjective UNNATURAL, deviant, warped, corrupt, twisted, abnormal, unhealthy, depraved, perverse, aberrant, immoral, debauched, debased, degenerate, evil, wicked, vile, amoral, wrong, bad; *informal* sick, sicko, kinky, pervy.

pessimism ● noun DEFEATISM, negativity, doom and gloom, gloominess, cynicism, fatalism; hopelessness, depression, despair, despondency, angst; *informal* looking on the black side.

pessimist ● noun DEFEATIST, fatalist, prophet of doom, cynic, doomsayer, doomster, Cassandra; sceptic, doubter, doubting Thomas; misery, killjoy, Job's comforter; *informal* doom (and gloom) merchant, wet blanket; *N. Amer. informal* gloomy Gus.
– OPPOSITES optimist.

pessimistic ● adjective GLOOMY, negative, defeatist, downbeat, cynical, bleak, fatalistic, dark, black, despairing, despondent, depressed, hopeless; suspicious, distrustful, doubting.
– OPPOSITES optimistic.

pest ● noun *(informal)* NUISANCE, annoyance, irritation, irritant, thorn in one's flesh/side, vexation, trial, the bane of one's life, menace, problem, trouble, worry, bother; *informal* pain (in the neck), aggravation, headache; *Scottish informal* skelf; *N. Amer. informal* nudnik; *Austral./NZ informal* nark.

pester ● verb BADGER, hound, harass, plague, annoy, bother, trouble, keep after, persecute, torment, bedevil, harry, worry, beleaguer, chivvy, nag; *informal* hassle, bug, get on someone's back; *N. English informal* mither; *N. Amer. informal* devil.

pestilence ● noun *(archaic)*. See PLAGUE noun sense 1.

pestilential ● adjective **1** *pestilential fever* PLAGUE-LIKE, infectious, contagious, communicable, epidemic, virulent; *informal* catching; *poetic/literary* pestiferous. **2** *(informal) a pestilential man!* ANNOYING, irritating, infuriating, exasperating, maddening, tiresome, irksome, vexing, vexatious; *informal* aggravating, pesky, infernal.

pet[1] ● noun *the teacher's pet* FAVOURITE, darling, the apple of one's eye; *Brit. informal* blue-eyed boy/girl; *N. Amer. informal* fair-haired boy/girl.
● adjective **1** *a pet lamb* TAME, domesticated, domestic; *Brit.* house-trained; *N. Amer.* housebroken. **2** *his pet theory* FAVOURITE, favoured, cherished, dear to one's heart; particular, special, personal.
● verb **1** *the cats came to be petted* STROKE, caress, fondle, pat. **2** *she had always been petted by her parents* PAMPER, spoil, mollycoddle, coddle, cosset, baby, indulge, overindulge, wrap in cotton wool. **3** *couples were petting in their cars* KISS AND CUDDLE, kiss, cuddle, embrace, caress; *informal* canoodle, neck, smooch; *Brit. informal* snog; *N. Amer. informal* make out, get it on; *informal, dated* spoon.
– PHRASES **pet name** AFFECTIONATE NAME, term of endearment, en-

– ORIGIN Greek *petalon* 'leaf'.
pétanque /pətangk/ ● noun a game similar to boule, played chiefly in Provence.
– ORIGIN French, from Provençal *pèd tanco* 'foot fixed (to the ground)', describing the start position.
petard /pitaard/ ● noun historical a small bomb made of a metal or wooden box filled with powder.
– PHRASES **be hoist with** (or **by**) **one's own petard** have one's schemes against others backfiring on one. [ORIGIN from Shakespeare's *Hamlet* (III. iv. 207); *hoist* is in the sense 'lifted and removed'.]
– ORIGIN French, from *péter* 'break wind'.
peter ● verb (usu. **peter out**) diminish or come to an end gradually.
– ORIGIN of unknown origin.
peterman ● noun archaic a safe-breaker.
Peter Pan ● noun a person who retains youthful features, or who is immature.
– ORIGIN the hero of J. M. Barrie's play of the same name (1904).
Peter Principle ● noun the principle that members of a hierarchy are promoted until they reach the level at which they are no longer competent.
– ORIGIN named after the American educationalist Laurence J. *Peter* (1919–90).
petersham ● noun a corded tape used for stiffening in making dresses and hats.
– ORIGIN named after the English army officer Lord *Petersham* (1790–1851).
Peters projection ● noun a world map projection in which areas are shown in correct proportion but with distorted shape.
– ORIGIN named after the German historian Arno *Peters* (born 1916).
pethidine /pethideen/ ● noun a painkiller used especially for women in labour.
pétillant /pettiyon/ ● adjective (of wine) slightly sparkling.
– ORIGIN French.
petiole /pettiōl/ ● noun Botany the stalk that joins a leaf to a stem.
– ORIGIN Latin *petiolus* 'little foot, stalk'.
petit bourgeois ● adjective of or characteristic of the lower middle class, especially in being conventional and conservative. ● noun (pl. **petits bourgeois** pronunc. same) a petit bourgeois person.
– ORIGIN French, 'little citizen'.
petite ● adjective (of a woman) attractively small and dainty.
– ORIGIN French, feminine of *petit* 'small'.
petite bourgeoisie (also **petit bourgeoisie**) ● noun the lower middle class.
– ORIGIN French, 'little townsfolk'.
petit four /petti for/ ● noun (pl. **petits fours** /petti forz/) a very small fancy cake, biscuit, or sweet.
– ORIGIN French, 'little oven'.
petition ● noun **1** a formal written request, typically one signed by many people, appealing to authority concerning a cause. **2** an appeal or request. **3** Law an application to a court for a writ, judicial action, etc. ● verb make or present a petition to.
– DERIVATIVES **petitioner** noun.
– ORIGIN Latin, from *petere* 'aim at, seek, lay claim to'.
petit mal /petti mal/ ● noun a mild form of epilepsy with only momentary spells of unconsciousness. Compare with GRAND MAL.
– ORIGIN French, 'little sickness'.
petit point /petti poynt/ ● noun embroidery on canvas, using small diagonal stitches.
– ORIGIN French, 'little stitch'.
petits pois /petti pwaa/ ● plural noun small, fine peas.
– ORIGIN French, 'small peas'.
pet name ● noun a name used to express fondness or familiarity.
petrel /petrəl/ ● noun a seabird of a kind that typically flies far from land.
– ORIGIN from the name of St *Peter*, because of the bird's habit of flying low with legs dangling, and so appearing to walk on the water (as did St Peter in the Gospel of Matthew).
Petri dish /petri, peetri/ ● noun a shallow transparent dish with a flat lid, used for the culture of micro-organisms.
– ORIGIN named after the German bacteriologist Julius R. *Petri* (1852–1922).
petrify ● verb (**petrifies, petrified**) **1** change (organic matter) into stone by encrusting or replacing its original substance with a mineral deposit. **2** paralyse with fear. **3** deprive of vitality.
– DERIVATIVES **petrifaction** noun **petrification** noun.
– ORIGIN Latin *petrificare*, from *petra* 'rock'.
petrochemical ● adjective **1** relating to the chemical properties and processing of petroleum and natural gas. **2** relating to the chemistry of rocks. ● noun a chemical obtained from petroleum and natural gas.
– ORIGIN sense 1 from PETROLEUM; sense 2 from Greek *petros* 'stone', *petra* 'rock'.
petrodollar ● noun a notional unit of currency earned from the export of petroleum.
petroglyph /petrəglif/ ● noun a rock carving.
– ORIGIN from Greek *petros* 'rock' + *glyphē* 'carving'.
petrography /petrografi/ ● noun the study of the composition and properties of rocks.
– DERIVATIVES **petrographer** noun **petrographic** adjective.
petrol ● noun Brit. **1** refined petroleum used as fuel in motor vehicles. **2** (also **petrol blue**) a shade of intense greenish or greyish blue.
petrolatum /petrəlaytəm/ ● noun another term for PETROLEUM JELLY.
– ORIGIN Latin, from PETROL.
petrol bomb ● noun Brit. a crude bomb consisting of a bottle containing petrol and a cloth wick.
petroleum ● noun a hydrocarbon oil found in rock strata and extracted and refined to produce fuels including petrol, paraffin, and diesel oil; oil.
– ORIGIN Latin, from *petra* 'rock' + *oleum* 'oil'.
petroleum jelly ● noun a translucent solid mixture of hydrocarbons, used as a lubricant or ointment.
petrology /pitrolləji/ ● noun the study of the origin, structure, and composition of rocks.
– DERIVATIVES **petrological** adjective **petrologist** noun.
petticoat ● noun **1** a woman's light, loose undergarment in the form of a skirt or dress. **2** (before another noun) informal, often derogatory associated with women: *petticoat government*.
– ORIGIN from obsolete *petty coat* 'small coat'.
pettifog ● verb (**pettifogged, pettifogging**) archaic **1** quibble about petty points. **2** practise legal deception or trickery.
– DERIVATIVES **pettifoggery** noun.
pettifogger ● noun archaic an inferior legal practitioner.
– ORIGIN from PETTY + obsolete *fogger* 'underhand dealer', probably from *Fugger*, a family of merchants in Augsburg in the 15th and 16th centuries.
pettifogging ● adjective petty; trivial.
pettish ● adjective petulant.
– DERIVATIVES **pettishly** adverb **pettishness** noun.
petty ● adjective (**pettier, pettiest**) **1** trivial. **2** mean; small-

p

Thesaurus

dearment, nickname, diminutive, hypocoristic.
pet² ● noun *Mum's in a pet* BAD MOOD, mood, bad temper, temper, sulk, fit of pique, huff; *Brit. informal* paddy, strop.
peter ● verb
– PHRASES **peter out** FIZZLE OUT, fade (away), die away/out, dwindle, diminish, taper off, tail off, trail away/off, wane, ebb, melt away, evaporate, disappear, come to an end, subside.
petite ● adjective SMALL, dainty, diminutive, slight, little, tiny, elfin, delicate, small-boned; *Scottish* wee; *informal* pint-sized.
petition ● noun **1** *over 1,000 people signed the petition* APPEAL, round robin. **2** *petitions to Allah* ENTREATY, supplication, plea, prayer, appeal, request, invocation, suit; *archaic* orison.
● verb *they petitioned the king to revoke the decision* APPEAL TO, request, ask, call on, entreat, beg, implore, plead with, apply to, press, urge; *formal* adjure; *poetic/literary* beseech.
petrified ● adjective **1** *she looked petrified* TERRIFIED, terror-stricken, horrified, scared/frightened out of one's wits, scared/frightened to death. **2** *petrified remains of prehistoric animals* OSSIFIED, fossilized, calcified.
petrify ● verb TERRIFY, horrify, frighten, scare, scare/frighten to death, scare/frighten the living daylights out of, scare/frighten the life out of, strike terror into, put the fear of God into; paralyse, transfix; *informal* scare the pants off; *Irish informal* scare the bejesus out of.
petrol ● noun FUEL, unleaded, superunleaded, diesel; *N. Amer.* gasoline, gas; *informal* juice.

minded. **3** minor. **4** Law (of a crime) of lesser importance. Compare with GRAND.
– DERIVATIVES **pettily** adverb **pettiness** noun.
– ORIGIN from the pronunciation of French *petit* 'small'.
petty bourgeois ● noun variant of PETIT BOURGEOIS.
petty bourgeoisie ● noun variant of PETITE BOURGEOISIE.
petty cash ● noun an accessible store of money for expenditure on small items.
petty officer ● noun a rank of non-commissioned officer in the navy, above leading seaman or seaman and below chief petty officer.
petty treason ● noun see TREASON.
petulant /petyoolənt/ ● adjective childishly sulky or bad-tempered.
– DERIVATIVES **petulance** noun **petulantly** adverb.
– ORIGIN Latin *petulans* 'impudent'.
petunia ● noun a South American plant with white, purple, or red funnel-shaped flowers.
– ORIGIN Guarani, 'tobacco' (to which these plants are related).
pew ● noun **1** (in a church) a long bench with a back. **2** Brit. informal a seat.
– ORIGIN originally denoting a raised, enclosed place for particular worshippers: from Old French *puye* 'balcony', from Latin *podium* 'elevated place'.
pewter ● noun a grey alloy of tin with copper and antimony (formerly, tin and lead).
– ORIGIN Old French *peutre*.
peyote /payōti/ ● noun **1** a small spineless cactus native to Mexico and the southern US. **2** a hallucinogenic drug prepared from this, containing mescaline.
– ORIGIN Nahuatl.
Pf. ● abbreviation pfennig.
pfennig /fennig/ ● noun a monetary unit of Germany, equal to one hundredth of a mark.
– ORIGIN German, related to PENNY.
PFI ● abbreviation (in the UK) Private Finance Initiative, a scheme whereby public services such as the National Health Service raise funds for capital projects from commercial organizations.
PG ● abbreviation (in film classification) parental guidance, indicating that some scenes may be considered unsuitable for children.
pH ● noun Chemistry a figure expressing acidity or alkalinity (7 is neutral, lower values are more acid and higher values more alkaline).
– ORIGIN from *p* representing German *Potenz* 'power' + *H*, the symbol for hydrogen.
phaeton /fayt'n/ ● noun **1** historical a light, open four-wheeled horse-drawn carriage. **2** US a vintage touring car.
– ORIGIN from *Phaethōn*, son of the sun god Helios in Greek mythology, who was allowed to drive the solar chariot for a day with fatal results.
phage /fayj/ ● noun Biology a kind of virus which acts as a parasite of bacteria, infecting them and reproducing inside them.
– ORIGIN short for *bacteriophage*, from BACTERIUM + Greek *phagein* 'eat'.
phagocyte /faggəsit/ ● noun a type of body cell which engulfs and absorbs bacteria and other small particles.
– DERIVATIVES **phagocytic** adjective.
– ORIGIN from Greek *phago-* 'eating' + *kutos* 'vessel'.
phalange /falanj/ ● noun **1** Anatomy another term for PHALANX (in sense 3). **2** (**Phalange**) a right-wing Maronite party in Lebanon. [ORIGIN abbreviation of French *Phalanges Libanaises* 'Lebanese phalanxes'.]
– DERIVATIVES **Phalangist** noun & adjective.
phalangeal ● adjective Anatomy relating to a phalanx or the phalanges.
phalanger /fəlanjər/ ● noun a tree-dwelling marsupial native to Australia and New Guinea.
– ORIGIN Greek *phalangion* 'spider's web' (because of the animal's webbed toes).
phalanx /falangks/ ● noun (pl. **phalanxes**) **1** a group of similar people or things. **2** a body of troops or police officers in close formation. **3** (pl. **phalanges** /fəlanjeez/) Anatomy a bone of the finger or toe.
– ORIGIN Greek.
phalarope /falərōp/ ● noun a small wading or swimming bird with lobed feet.
– ORIGIN French, from Greek *phalaris* 'coot' + *pous* 'foot'.
phallic ● adjective relating to or resembling a phallus or erect penis.
– DERIVATIVES **phallically** adverb.
phallocentric /falōsentrik/ ● adjective focused on the phallus as a symbol of male dominance.
– DERIVATIVES **phallocentrism** noun.
phallus /faləss/ ● noun (pl. **phalli** /falī/ or **phalluses**) **1** a penis, especially when erect. **2** a representation of an erect penis symbolizing fertility or potency.
– DERIVATIVES **phallicism** noun.
– ORIGIN Greek *phallos*.
phantasm /fantaz'm/ ● noun literary an illusion or apparition.
– DERIVATIVES **phantasmal** adjective.
– ORIGIN Greek *phantasma*, from *phantazein* 'make visible'.
phantasmagoria /fantazməgoriə/ ● noun a sequence of real or imaginary images like that seen in a dream.
– DERIVATIVES **phantasmagoric** adjective **phantasmagorical** adjective.
– ORIGIN originally the name of a London exhibition (1802) of optical illusions: probably from French *fantasmagorie*, from *fantasme* 'phantasm'.
phantom ● noun **1** a ghost. **2** a figment of the imagination. **3** (before another noun) not really existing; illusory.
– ORIGIN Greek *phantasma* (see PHANTASM).
phantom limb ● noun a sensation experienced by a person who has had a limb amputated that the limb is still there.
phantom pregnancy ● noun a condition in which signs of pregnancy are present in a woman who is not pregnant.
pharaoh /fairō/ ● noun a ruler in ancient Egypt.
– DERIVATIVES **pharaonic** /fairayonnik/ adjective.
– ORIGIN Greek *Pharaō*, from an Egyptian word meaning 'great house'.
Pharisee /farrisee/ ● noun **1** a member of an ancient Jewish sect noted for their strict observance of the traditional and written law. **2** a self-righteous or hypocritical person.
– DERIVATIVES **Pharisaic** /farrisayik/ adjective **Pharisaical** adjective.
– ORIGIN Greek *Pharisaios*, from an Aramaic word meaning 'separated ones'.
pharmaceutical /faarməsyōōtik'l/ ● adjective relating to medicinal drugs. ● noun a compound manufactured for use as a medicinal drug.
– DERIVATIVES **pharmaceutically** adverb.
– ORIGIN Greek *pharmakeutikos*, from *pharmakon* 'drug'.
pharmacist ● noun a person qualified to prepare and dispense medicinal drugs.
pharmacology ● noun the branch of medicine concerned with the uses, effects, and action of drugs.
– DERIVATIVES **pharmacologic** adjective **pharmacological** adjective **pharmacologist** noun.
pharmacopoeia /faarməkəpeeə/ (US also **pharmacopeia**) ● noun **1** a book containing a list of medicinal drugs with their effects and directions for use. **2** a stock of medicinal drugs.
– ORIGIN Greek *pharmakopoiia* 'art of preparing drugs'.
pharmacy ● noun (pl. **pharmacies**) **1** a place where medicinal drugs are prepared or sold. **2** the science or practice of preparing and dispensing medicinal drugs.

Thesaurus

petticoat ● noun SLIP, underskirt, half-slip, underslip, undergarment; *archaic* kirtle; *historical* crinoline.
petty ● adjective **1** *petty regulations* TRIVIAL, trifling, minor, small, unimportant, insignificant, inconsequential, inconsiderable, negligible, paltry, footling, pettifogging; *informal* piffling, piddling, fiddling. **2** *a petty form of revenge* SMALL-MINDED, mean, ungenerous, shabby, spiteful.
– OPPOSITES important, magnanimous.
petulant ● adjective PEEVISH, bad-tempered, querulous, pettish, fretful, cross, irritable, sulky, snappish, crotchety, touchy, tetchy, testy, fractious, grumpy, disgruntled, crabbed, crabby; *informal* grouchy; *Brit. informal* ratty; *N. English informal* mardy; *N. Amer. informal* cranky.
– OPPOSITES good-humoured.
phantasmagorical ● adjective DREAMLIKE, psychedelic, kaleidoscopic, surreal, unreal, hallucinatory, fantastic, fantastical, chimerical.
phantom ● noun **1** *a phantom who haunts lonely roads* GHOST, apparition, spirit, spectre, wraith; *informal* spook; *poetic/literary* phantasm, shade. **2** *the phantoms of an overactive imagination* DELU-

pharyngeal /farrinjeeəl/ ● adjective relating to the pharynx.

pharyngitis /farrinjītiss/ ● noun inflammation of the pharynx.

pharynx /farringks/ ● noun (pl. **pharynges** /farinjeez/) the membrane-lined cavity behind the nose and mouth, connecting them to the oesophagus.
– ORIGIN Greek *pharunx.*

phase ● noun **1** a distinct period or stage in a process of change or development. **2** each of the aspects of the moon or a planet, according to the amount of its illumination. **3** Physics the relationship between the cycles of an oscillating system and a fixed reference point or another system. **4** Chemistry a distinct and homogeneous form of matter separated by its surface from other forms. ● verb **1** carry out in gradual stages. **2** (**phase in/out**) gradually introduce or withdraw (something).
– PHRASES **in** (or **out of**) **phase** in (or out of) synchrony.
– ORIGIN French, from Greek *phasis* 'appearance'.

phasic /fayzik/ ● adjective relating to a phase or phases.

phat ● adjective black slang excellent.
– ORIGIN originally used to describe a woman, in the sense 'sexy, attractive': of uncertain origin.

phatic /fattik/ ● adjective (of language) used for general social interaction rather than to convey specific meaning, e.g. *nice morning, isn't it?*
– ORIGIN from Greek *phatos* 'spoken' or *phatikos* 'affirming'.

PhD ● abbreviation Doctor of Philosophy.
– ORIGIN from Latin *philosophiae doctor.*

pheasant ● noun a large long-tailed game bird, the male of which typically has showy plumage.
– ORIGIN Greek *phasianos* 'bird of Phasis', a river in the Caucasus from which the bird is said to have spread westwards.

phencyclidine /fensīklideen/ ● noun a drug used as a veterinary anaesthetic and in hallucinogenic drugs such as angel dust.

phenobarbitone /feenōbaarbitōn/ (US **phenobarbital**) /feenōbaarbit'l/ ● noun a narcotic and sedative barbiturate drug used to treat epilepsy.

phenol /feenol/ ● noun Chemistry **1** a toxic white crystalline solid obtained from coal tar. Also called CARBOLIC ACID. **2** any compound with a hydroxyl group linked directly to a benzene ring.
– DERIVATIVES **phenolic** adjective.
– ORIGIN from French *phène* 'benzene'.

phenology /finolləji/ ● noun the study of cyclic and seasonal natural phenomena, especially in relation to climate and plant and animal life.
– DERIVATIVES **phenological** adjective.
– ORIGIN from PHENOMENON.

phenolphthalein /feenolthayleen/ ● noun Chemistry a crystalline solid used as an acid–base indicator and medicinally as a laxative.
– ORIGIN from the chemical name.

phenom ● noun N. Amer. informal an unusually gifted person.
– ORIGIN abbreviation of PHENOMENON.

phenomena plural of PHENOMENON.

phenomenal ● adjective **1** extraordinary. **2** perceptible by the senses or through immediate experience.
– DERIVATIVES **phenomenally** adverb.

phenomenology /finomminolləji/ ● noun Philosophy **1** the science of phenomena as distinct from that of the nature of being. **2** an approach that concentrates on the study of consciousness and the objects of direct experience.
– DERIVATIVES **phenomenological** adjective **phenomenologist** noun.

phenomenon ● noun (pl. **phenomena**) **1** a fact or situation that is observed to exist or happen, especially one whose cause is in question. **2** Philosophy the object of a person's perception. **3** a remarkable person or thing.
– USAGE The word **phenomenon** comes from Greek, and its plural form is **phenomena**. In standard English it is a mistake to treat **phenomena** as if it were a singular form.
– ORIGIN Greek *phainomenon* 'thing appearing to view'.

phenotype /feenōtīp/ ● noun Biology the observable characteristics of an individual resulting from the interaction of its genotype with the environment.
– ORIGIN from Greek *phainein* 'to show'.

phenyl /feenīl, fennil/ ● noun Chemistry the radical $-C_6H_5$, derived from benzene.
– ORIGIN French *phényle*, from Greek *phaino-* 'shining' (because first used in names of by-products of the manufacture of gas for illumination).

phenylalanine /feenīlaləneen, fenil-/ ● noun Biochemistry an amino acid which is widely distributed in plant proteins and is an essential nutrient in the diet.

pheromone /ferrəmōn/ ● noun a chemical substance released by an animal and causing a response in others of its species.
– ORIGIN from Greek *pherein* 'convey' + HORMONE.

phi /fī/ ● noun the twenty-first letter of the Greek alphabet (Φ, φ), transliterated as 'ph' or (in modern Greek) 'f'.
– ORIGIN Greek.

phial /fīəl/ ● noun a small cylindrical glass bottle, typically for medicines.
– ORIGIN Greek *phialē*, denoting a broad flat container.

phil- ● combining form variant spelling of PHILO- before a vowel or *h.*

philadelphus /filladelfəss/ ● noun a mock orange.
– ORIGIN from Greek *philadelphos* 'loving one's brother'.

philander /filandər/ ● verb (of a man) enter into casual sexual relationships with women.
– DERIVATIVES **philanderer** noun.
– ORIGIN earlier as in the sense 'man, husband', often used in literature as the given name of a lover: from Greek *philandros* 'fond of men'.

philanthrope /fillənthrōp/ ● noun archaic a philanthropist.

philanthropist ● noun a person who seeks to help others, especially by donating money to good causes.

philanthropy ● noun the desire to help others, especially through donation of money to good causes.
– DERIVATIVES **philanthropic** adjective **philanthropically** adverb.
– ORIGIN Greek *philanthrōpia*, from *philanthrōpos* 'man-loving'.

philately /filattəli/ ● noun the collection and study of postage stamps.
– DERIVATIVES **philatelic** adjective **philatelist** noun.
– ORIGIN from Greek *philo-* 'loving' + *ateleia* 'exemption from payment', used to mean a franking mark or postage stamp exempting the recipient from payment.

-phile ● combining form denoting a person or thing having a fondness for or tendency towards a specified thing: *bibliophile.*

Thesaurus

SION, figment of the imagination, hallucination, illusion, chimera, vision, mirage.

phase ● noun **1** *the final phase of the campaign* STAGE, period, chapter, episode, part, step, point, time, juncture. **2** *he's going through a difficult phase* PERIOD, stage, time, spell; *Brit. informal* patch. **3** *the phases of the moon* ASPECT, shape, form, appearance, state, condition.
– PHRASES **phase something in** INTRODUCE GRADUALLY, begin to use, ease in. **phase something out** WITHDRAW GRADUALLY, discontinue, stop using, run down, wind down.

phenomenal ● adjective REMARKABLE, exceptional, extraordinary, amazing, astonishing, astounding, sensational, stunning, incredible, unbelievable; marvellous, magnificent, wonderful, outstanding, singular, out of the ordinary, unusual, unprecedented; *informal* fantastic, terrific, tremendous, stupendous, awesome, out of this world; *poetic/literary* wondrous.
– OPPOSITES ordinary.

phenomenon ● noun **1** *a rare phenomenon* OCCURRENCE, event, happening, fact, situation, circumstance, experience, case, incident, episode. **2** *the band was a pop phenomenon* MARVEL, sensation, wonder, prodigy, miracle, rarity, nonpareil.

philander ● verb WOMANIZE, have affairs, flirt; *informal* play around, carry on, play the field, play away, sleep around; *N. Amer. informal* fool around.

philanderer ● noun WOMANIZER, Casanova, Don Juan, Lothario, flirt, ladies' man, playboy, rake, roué; *informal* stud, skirt-chaser, ladykiller, wolf; *informal, dated* gay dog.

philanthropic ● adjective CHARITABLE, generous, benevolent, humanitarian, public-spirited, altruistic, magnanimous, munificent, open-handed, bountiful, liberal, generous to a fault, beneficent, caring, compassionate, unselfish, kind, kind-hearted, big-hearted; *formal* eleemosynary.
– OPPOSITES selfish, mean.

philanthropist ● noun BENEFACTOR, benefactress, patron, patroness, donor, contributor, sponsor, backer, helper, good Samaritan; do-gooder, Lady Bountiful; *historical* almsgiver.

philanthropy ● noun BENEVOLENCE, generosity, humanitarianism, public-spiritedness, altruism, social conscience, charity, charitableness, brotherly love, fellow feeling, magnanimity, munificence, liberality, largesse, open-handedness, bountifulness,

– ORIGIN from Greek *philos* 'loving'.
philharmonic ● adjective (in the names of orchestras) devoted to music.
philhellene /filheleen/ ● noun **1** a lover of Greece and Greek culture. **2** historical a supporter of Greek independence.
– DERIVATIVES **philhellenic** adjective **philhellenism** noun.
-philia ● combining form denoting fondness, especially an abnormal love for or inclination towards something: *paedophilia*.
– DERIVATIVES **-philiac** combining form **-philic** combining form **-philous** combining form.
– ORIGIN from Greek *philia* 'fondness'.
philippic /filippik/ ● noun poetic/literary a bitter verbal attack or denunciation.
– ORIGIN from Greek *philippikos*, the name given to Demosthenes' speeches against Philip II of Macedon, and Cicero's against Mark Antony.
Philippine /fillipeen/ ● adjective relating to the Philippines.
Philistine /fillistīn/ ● noun **1** a member of a people of ancient Palestine who came into conflict with the Israelites. **2** (**philistine**) a person who is hostile or indifferent to culture and the arts.
– DERIVATIVES **philistinism** /fillistiniz'm/ noun.
– ORIGIN Greek *Philistinos*, from Hebrew.
Phillips ● adjective trademark referring to a screw with a cross-shaped slot for turning, or a corresponding screwdriver.
– ORIGIN the name of the American manufacturer Henry F. *Phillips* (died 1958).
phillumenist /filoōmənist/ ● noun a collector of matchbox or matchbook labels.
– DERIVATIVES **phillumeny** noun.
– ORIGIN from PHIL- + Latin *lumen* 'light'.
philo- (also **phil-** before a vowel or *h*) ● combining form denoting a liking for a specified thing: *philology*.
– ORIGIN from Greek *philein* 'to love' or *philos* 'loving'.
philodendron /filladendrən/ ● noun (pl. **philodendrons** or **philodendra** /filladendrə/) a tropical American climbing plant grown as a greenhouse or indoor plant.
– ORIGIN from PHILO- + Greek *dendron* 'tree'.
philology ● noun **1** the study of the structure, historical development, and relationships of a language or languages. **2** chiefly N. Amer. literary or classical scholarship.
– DERIVATIVES **philological** adjective **philologist** noun.
– ORIGIN originally in the sense 'love of learning': from Greek *philologia*.
philoprogenitive /fillōprəjennitiv/ ● adjective formal **1** having many offspring. **2** loving one's offspring.
– DERIVATIVES **philoprogenitiveness** noun.
philosopher ● noun a person engaged or learned in philosophy.
philosopher's stone ● noun a mythical substance supposed to change any metal into gold or silver.
philosophical ● adjective **1** relating to the study of philosophy. **2** calm in difficult circumstances.
– DERIVATIVES **philosophic** adjective **philosophically** adverb.
philosophize (also **philosophise**) ● verb theorize about fundamental or serious issues.
philosophy ● noun (pl. **philosophies**) **1** the study of the fundamental nature of knowledge, reality, and existence. **2** the theories of a particular philosopher. **3** a theory or attitude that guides one's behaviour. **4** the study of the theoretical basis of a branch of knowledge or experience.
– ORIGIN Greek *philosophia* 'love of wisdom'.
philtre /filtər/ (US **philter**) ● noun a love potion.
– ORIGIN Greek *philtron*, from *philein* 'to love'.
phiz /fiz/ (also **phizog**, **fizzog** /fizog/) ● noun Brit. informal one's face or expression.
– ORIGIN abbreviation of PHYSIOGNOMY.
phlebitis /flibītiss/ ● noun Medicine inflammation of the walls of a vein.
– ORIGIN from Greek *phleps* 'vein'.
phlebotomy /flibottəmi/ ● noun (pl. **phlebotomies**) the surgical opening or puncture of a vein to withdraw blood or introduce a fluid.
– DERIVATIVES **phlebotomist** noun.
phlegm /flem/ ● noun **1** the thick viscous substance secreted by the mucous membranes of the respiratory passages. **2** (in medieval science and medicine) one of the four bodily humours, believed to be associated with a calm or apathetic temperament. **3** calmness of temperament.
– DERIVATIVES **phlegmy** adjective.
– ORIGIN Greek *phlegma* 'inflammation', from *phlegein* 'to burn'.
phlegmatic /flegmattik/ ● adjective unemotional and stolidly calm.
– DERIVATIVES **phlegmatically** adverb.
phloem /flōəm/ ● noun Botany the tissue in plants which conducts food materials downwards from the leaves.
– ORIGIN from Greek *phloos* 'bark'.
phlox /floks/ ● noun a plant with dense clusters of colourful scented flowers.
– ORIGIN Greek, 'flame'.
-phobe ● combining form denoting a person having a fear or dislike of a specified thing: *homophobe*.
– ORIGIN from Greek *phobos* 'fear'.
phobia ● noun an extreme or irrational fear of something.
– DERIVATIVES **phobic** adjective & noun.
-phobia ● combining form extreme or irrational fear or dislike of a specified thing: *arachnophobia*.
– DERIVATIVES **-phobic** combining form.
Phoenician /fəneesh'n/ ● noun a member of an ancient people inhabiting Phoenicia in the eastern Mediterranean. ● adjective relating to Phoenicia.
phoenix /feeniks/ ● noun (in classical mythology) a unique bird that periodically burned itself on a funeral pyre and was born again from the ashes.
– ORIGIN Greek *phoinix* 'Phoenician, reddish purple, or phoenix'.
phone ● noun **1** a telephone. **2** (**phones**) informal headphones or earphones. ● verb telephone.
-phone ● combining form **1** denoting an instrument using or connected with sound: *megaphone*. **2** denoting a person who uses a specified language: *francophone*.
– ORIGIN from Greek *phōnē* 'sound, voice'.

Thesaurus

beneficence, unselfishness, humanity, kindness, kind-heartedness, compassion; *historical* almsgiving.
philippic ● noun *(poetic/literary)* TIRADE, diatribe, harangue, lecture, attack, onslaught, denunciation, rant, polemic, broadside, fulmination, condemnation, criticism, censure; *informal* blast.
philistine ● adjective UNCULTURED, lowbrow, anti-intellectual, uncultivated, uncivilized, uneducated, unenlightened, commercial, materialist, bourgeois; ignorant, crass, boorish, barbarian.
philosopher ● noun THINKER, theorist, theorizer, theoretician, metaphysicist, metaphysician; scholar, intellectual, sage, wise man.
philosophical ● adjective **1** *a philosophical question* THEORETICAL, metaphysical. **2** *a philosophical mood* THOUGHTFUL, reflective, pensive, meditative, contemplative, introspective, ruminative; *formal* cogitative. **3** *he was philosphical about losing the contract* CALM, composed, cool, collected, {cool, calm, and collected}, self-possessed, serene, tranquil, stoical, impassive, dispassionate, phlegmatic, unperturbed, imperturbable, unruffled, patient, forbearing, long-suffering, resigned, rational, realistic.
philosophize ● verb THEORIZE, speculate; pontificate, preach, sermonize, moralize.
philosophy ● noun **1** *the philosophy of Aristotle* THINKING, thought, reasoning. **2** *her political philosophy* BELIEFS, credo, convictions, ideology, ideas, thinking, notions, theories, doctrine, tenets, principles, views, school of thought.
phlegm ● noun **1** MUCUS, catarrh. **2** *British phlegm and perseverance* CALMNESS, coolness, composure, equanimity, tranquillity, placidity, placidness, impassivity, stolidity, imperturbability, impassiveness, dispassionateness; *informal* cool, unflappability.
phlegmatic ● adjective CALM, cool, composed, {cool, calm, and collected}, controlled, serene, tranquil, placid, impassive, stolid, imperturbable, unruffled, dispassionate, philosophical; *informal* unflappable.
– OPPOSITES excitable.
phobia ● noun ABNORMAL FEAR, irrational fear, obsessive fear, dread, horror, terror, hatred, loathing, detestation, aversion, antipathy, revulsion; complex, neurosis; *informal* thing, hang-up.
phone ● noun **1** *she spent hours on the phone* TELEPHONE, mobile (phone), cellphone, car phone, cordless phone, speakerphone; extension; *Brit. informal* blower; *Brit. rhyming slang* dog and bone. **2** *give me a phone sometime* CALL, telephone call, phone call; *Brit.* ring; *informal* buzz; *Brit. informal* tinkle, bell.
● verb *I'll phone you later* TELEPHONE, call, give someone a call; *Brit.* ring, ring up, give someone a ring; *informal* call up, give someone a

phone book ● noun a telephone directory.

phonecard ● noun a prepaid card allowing the user to make calls on a public telephone.

phone-in ● noun a radio or television programme during which listeners or viewers telephone the studio and participate.

phoneme /fōneem/ ● noun Phonetics any of the distinct units of sound that distinguish one word from another, e.g. *p*, *b*, *d*, and *t* in *pad*, *pat*, *bad*, and *bat*.
– ORIGIN Greek *phōnēma* 'sound, speech', from *phōnein* 'speak'.

phonetic ● adjective Phonetics **1** of or relating to speech sounds. **2** (of a system of writing) having a direct correspondence between symbols and sounds.
– DERIVATIVES **phonetically** adverb.
– ORIGIN Greek *phōnētikos*, from *phōnein* 'speak'.

phonetics ● plural noun (treated as sing.) the study and classification of speech sounds.

phoney (also **phony**) informal ● adjective (**phonier**, **phoniest**) not genuine. ● noun (pl. **phoneys** or **phonies**) a fraudulent person or thing.
– DERIVATIVES **phonily** adverb.
– ORIGIN of unknown origin.

phonic /fonnik/ ● adjective relating to speech sounds.

phonics ● plural noun (treated as sing.) a method of teaching people to read by correlating sounds with alphabetic symbols.

phono ● adjective denoting a type of plug used with audio and video equipment, in which one conductor is cylindrical and the other is a central prong that extends beyond it.
– ORIGIN abbreviation of PHONOGRAPH.

phono- ● combining form relating to sound: *phonograph*.
– ORIGIN from Greek *phōnē* 'sound, voice'.

phonograph ● noun **1** Brit. an early form of gramophone. **2** N. Amer. a record player.
– DERIVATIVES **phonographic** adjective.

phonology /fənolləji/ ● noun the system of contrastive relationships among the fundamental speech sounds of a language.
– DERIVATIVES **phonological** adjective.

phony ● adjective & noun variant spelling of PHONEY.

phooey informal ● exclamation used to express disdain or disbelief. ● noun nonsense.
– ORIGIN imitative.

phormium /formiəm/ ● noun the flax-lily of New Zealand.
– ORIGIN Latin, from Greek *phormion* 'small basket' (with reference to the use made of the fibres).

phosgene /fozjeen/ ● noun Chemistry a poisonous gas formerly used in warfare.
– ORIGIN from Greek *phōs* 'light' (the gas was originally made by the action of sunlight on chlorine and carbon monoxide).

phosphate /fosfayt/ ● noun Chemistry a salt or ester of phosphoric acid.

phosphine /fosfeen/ ● noun Chemistry a foul-smelling gas formed from phosphorus and hydrogen.

phospholipid /fosfəlippid/ ● noun Biochemistry a lipid containing a phosphate group in its molecule.

phosphor /fosfər/ ● noun **1** a synthetic fluorescent or phosphorescent substance. **2** old-fashioned term for PHOSPHORUS.

phosphorescence ● noun **1** light emitted by a substance without combustion or perceptible heat. **2** Physics the emission of radiation in a similar manner to fluorescence but continuing after excitation ceases.
– DERIVATIVES **phosphoresce** verb **phosphorescent** adjective.

phosphoric /fosforrik/ ● adjective relating to or containing phosphorus.

phosphoric acid ● noun Chemistry a crystalline acid obtained by treating phosphates with sulphuric acid.

phosphorus /fosfərəss/ ● noun a poisonous non-metallic chemical element existing as a yellowish waxy solid which ignites spontaneously in air and glows in the dark, and as a less reactive form used in making matches.
– DERIVATIVES **phosphorous** adjective.
– USAGE The correct spelling for the noun referring to the chemical element is **phosphorus**, while the correct spelling for the adjective is **phosphorous**.
– ORIGIN Greek *phōsphoros*, from *phōs* 'light' + *-phoros* '-bringing'.

photic ● adjective **1** technical relating to light. **2** Ecology referring to the layers of the ocean reached by sufficient sunlight to allow plant growth.

photo ● noun (pl. **photos**) a photograph.

photo- ● combining form **1** relating to light. **2** relating to photography.
– ORIGIN sense 1 from Greek *phōs* 'light'.

photocall ● noun Brit. an occasion on which famous people pose for photographers by arrangement.

photocell ● noun short for PHOTOELECTRIC CELL.

photochemistry ● noun the branch of chemistry concerned with the chemical effects of light.
– DERIVATIVES **photochemical** adjective.

photochromic ● adjective (of glass, lenses, etc.) undergoing a reversible change in colour when exposed to bright light.

photocopier ● noun a machine for making photocopies.

photocopy ● noun (pl. **photocopies**) a photographic copy of something produced by a process involving the action of light on a specially prepared surface. ● verb (**photocopies**, **photocopied**) make a photocopy of.
– DERIVATIVES **photocopiable** adjective.

photoelectric ● adjective characterized by or involving the emission of electrons from a surface by the action of light.

photoelectric cell ● noun a device using a photoelectric effect to generate current.

photo finish ● noun a close finish of a race in which the winner is identifiable only from a photograph of competitors crossing the line.

photofit ● noun Brit. a picture of a person made from composite photographs of facial features.

photogenic /fōtəjennik/ ● adjective **1** looking attractive in photographs. **2** Biology producing or emitting light.

photograph ● noun a picture made with a camera, in which an image is focused on to film and then made visible and permanent by chemical treatment. ● verb take a photograph of.
– DERIVATIVES **photographer** noun **photographic** adjective.

photographic memory ● noun an ability to remember information or visual images in great detail.

photography ● noun the taking and processing of photographs.

photogravure /fōtōgrəvyoor/ ● noun an image produced from a photographic negative transferred to a metal plate and etched in.
– ORIGIN French, 'photo-engraving'.

photojournalism ● noun the communicating of news by photographs.
– DERIVATIVES **photojournalist** noun.

photolysis /fōtollisiss/ ● noun Chemistry the decomposition or separation of molecules by the action of light.

photometer /fōtommitər/ ● noun an instrument measuring the intensity of light.
– DERIVATIVES **photometric** adjective **photometry** noun.

photomicrograph ● noun another term for MICROGRAPH.

photomontage /fōtōmontaazh/ ● noun a picture consisting of numerous photographs placed together or overlapping.

photon /fōton/ ● noun Physics a particle representing a quantum of light or other electromagnetic radiation.
– DERIVATIVES **photonic** adjective.

photo opportunity ● noun a photocall.

photophobia ● noun extreme sensitivity to light.
– DERIVATIVES **photophobic** adjective.

photorealism ● noun a style of art and sculpture characterized

Thesaurus

buzz; *Brit. informal* give someone a bell/tinkle, get on the blower to; *N. Amer. informal* get someone on the horn.

phoney *(informal)* ● adjective *a phoney address* BOGUS, false, fake, fraudulent, spurious; counterfeit, forged, feigned; pseudo, imitation, sham, man-made, mock, ersatz, synthetic, artificial; simulated, pretended, contrived, affected, insincere; *informal* pretend, put-on; *Brit. informal* cod.
– OPPOSITES authentic.
● noun **1** *he's nothing but a phoney* IMPOSTOR, sham, fake, fraud, charlatan; *informal* con artist. **2** *the diamond's a phoney* FAKE, imitation, counterfeit, forgery.

photocopy ● noun COPY, facsimile, duplicate; *trademark* Xerox, photostat, Ozalid.

photograph ● noun *a photograph of her father* PICTURE, photo, snap, snapshot, shot, likeness, print, slide, transparency, still, enlargement; *Brit.* enprint; *informal* tranny.
● verb *she was photographed leaving the castle* TAKE SOMEONE'S PICTURE/PHOTO, snap, shoot, film.

photographer ● noun LENSMAN, paparazzo; cameraman; *informal* snapper; *N. Amer. informal* shutterbug.

by the highly detailed depiction of ordinary life with the impersonality of a photograph.
– DERIVATIVES **photorealist** noun & adjective **photorealistic** adjective.
photoreceptor ● noun a structure in an organism that responds to light.
photosensitive ● adjective responding to light.
– DERIVATIVES **photosensitivity** noun.
photostat ● noun trademark **1** a type of machine for making photocopies on special paper. **2** a copy made by a photstat. ● verb (**photostatted**, **photostatting**) copy with a photostat.
photosynthesis ● noun the process by which green plants use sunlight to synthesize nutrients from carbon dioxide and water.
– DERIVATIVES **photosynthesize** (also **photosynthesise**) verb **photosynthetic** adjective.
phototropism /fōtōtrōpiz'm/ ● noun Biology the orientation of a plant or other organism either towards or away from a source of light.
– DERIVATIVES **phototropic** adjective.
photovoltaic /fōtōvoltayik/ ● adjective relating to the production of electric current at the junction of two substances exposed to light.
phrasal verb ● noun Grammar an idiomatic phrase consisting of a verb and an adverb or preposition, as in *break down* or *see to*.
phrase ● noun **1** a small group of words standing together as a conceptual unit. **2** Music a group of notes forming a distinct unit within a longer passage. **3** an idiomatic or pithy expression. ● verb put into a particular form of words.
– DERIVATIVES **phrasal** adjective.
– ORIGIN Greek *phrasis*, from *phrazein* 'declare, tell'.
phrase book ● noun a book listing useful expressions in a foreign language and their translations.
phraseology /frayziolləji/ ● noun (pl. **phraseologies**) a particular or characteristic mode of expression.
phrasing ● noun division of music into phrases.
phreaking ● noun informal, chiefly N. Amer. the action of hacking into telecommunications systems, especially to obtain free calls.
– DERIVATIVES **phreak** noun **phreaker** noun.
– ORIGIN alteration of *freaking* by association with *phone*.
phrenology /frinolləji/ ● noun chiefly historical the study of the shape and size of the cranium as a supposed indication of character.
– DERIVATIVES **phrenologist** noun.
– ORIGIN from Greek *phrēn* 'mind'.
Phrygian /frijiən/ ● noun a person from Phrygia, an ancient region of west central Asia Minor. ● adjective relating to Phrygia.
phthisis /fthīsiss/ ● noun archaic pulmonary tuberculosis or a similar progressive wasting disease.
– ORIGIN Greek, from *phthinein* 'to decay'.
phut ● exclamation used to represent a dull abrupt sound as of a slight impact or explosion.
– ORIGIN perhaps from a Hindi word meaning 'to burst'.
phyla plural of PHYLUM.
phylactery /filaktəri/ ● noun (pl. **phylacteries**) a small leather box containing Hebrew texts, worn by Jewish men at morning prayer.
– ORIGIN Greek *phulaktērion* 'amulet', from *phulassein* 'to guard'.
phyllo ● noun variant spelling of FILO.
phylloquinone /fillōkwinnōn/ ● noun vitamin K_1, a compound found in cabbage, spinach, and other leafy green vegetables, and essential for the blood-clotting process.
– ORIGIN from Greek *phullon* 'leaf' + QUINONE.
phylloxera /filoksərə, fillokseerə/ ● noun a plant louse that is a pest of vines.
– ORIGIN from Greek *phullon* 'leaf' + *xēros* 'dry'.
phylogeny /fīlojəni/ ● noun Biology the evolutionary development and diversification of species. Compare with ONTOGENY.
phylum /fīləm/ ● noun (pl. **phyla** /fīlə/) Zoology a principal taxonomic category that ranks above class and below kingdom.
– ORIGIN Greek *phulon* 'race'.
physalis /fisayliss/ ● noun a plant of a genus that includes the Cape gooseberry and Chinese lantern.
– ORIGIN Greek *phusallis* 'bladder'.
physic archaic ● noun medicinal drugs or medical treatment.
– ORIGIN Latin *physica*, from Greek *phusikē epistēmē* 'knowledge of nature'.
physical ● adjective **1** relating to the body as opposed to the mind. **2** relating to things perceived through the senses as opposed to the mind. **3** involving bodily contact or activity. **4** relating to physics or the operation of natural forces. ● noun a medical examination to determine a person's bodily fitness.
– DERIVATIVES **physicality** noun **physically** adverb.
physical chemistry ● noun the branch of chemistry concerned with the application of the techniques and theories of physics to the study of chemical systems.
physical education ● noun instruction in physical exercise and games, especially in schools.
physical geography ● noun the branch of geography concerned with natural features.
physical sciences ● plural noun the sciences concerned with the study of inanimate natural objects, including physics, chemistry, and astronomy.
physical therapy ● noun US term for PHYSIOTHERAPY.
– DERIVATIVES **physical therapist** noun.
physician ● noun a person qualified to practise medicine.
– PHRASES **physician, heal thyself** proverb before attempting to correct others, make sure that you aren't guilty of the same faults yourself. [ORIGIN with biblical allusion to the Gospel of Luke, chapter 4.]
physics ● plural noun (treated as sing.) **1** the branch of science concerned with the nature and properties of matter and energy. **2** the physical properties and phenomena of something.
– DERIVATIVES **physicist** noun.
– ORIGIN Latin *physica* 'natural things'.
physio ● noun (pl. **physios**) informal physiotherapy or a physiotherapist.
physiognomy /fizzionnəmi/ ● noun (pl. **physiognomies**) a person's facial features or expression, especially when regarded as indicative of character.
– ORIGIN Greek *phusiognōmonia*, from *phusis* 'nature' + *gnōmōn* 'judge or interpreter'.
physiology ● noun **1** the branch of biology concerned with the normal functions of living organisms and their parts. **2** the way in which a living organism or bodily part functions.
– DERIVATIVES **physiological** adjective **physiologist** noun.
physiotherapy (US **physical therapy**) ● noun the treatment of disease, injury, or deformity by physical methods such as massage and exercise.
– DERIVATIVES **physiotherapist** noun.
physique ● noun the form, size, and development of a person's body.
– ORIGIN French, 'physical' (used as a noun).
phytoplankton /fītōplangktən/ ● noun Biology plankton consisting of microscopic plants.
– ORIGIN from Greek *phuton* 'a plant'.
pi /pī/ ● noun **1** the sixteenth letter of the Greek alphabet (Π, π), transliterated as 'p'. **2** the numerical value of the ratio of the circumference of a circle to its diameter (approximately 3.14159).
– ORIGIN Greek: sense 2 from the initial letter of *periphereia* 'circumference'.

Thesaurus

photographic ● adjective **1** *a photographic record* PICTORIAL, in photographs; cinematic, filmic. **2** *a photographic memory* DETAILED, graphic, exact, precise, accurate, vivid.
phrase ● noun *familiar words and phrases* EXPRESSION, group of words, construction, locution, term, turn of phrase; idiom, idiomatic expression; saying, tag.
● verb *how could I phrase the question?* EXPRESS, put into words, put, word, style, formulate, couch, frame, articulate, verbalize.
phraseology ● noun WORDING, choice of words, phrasing, way of speaking/writing, usage, idiom, diction, parlance, words, language, vocabulary, terminology; jargon; *informal* lingo, -speak, -ese.
physical ● adjective **1** *physical pleasure* BODILY, corporeal, corporal, somatic; carnal, fleshly, non-spiritual. **2** *hard physical work* MANUAL, labouring, blue-collar. **3** *the physical universe* MATERIAL, concrete, tangible, palpable, solid, substantial, real, actual, visible.
– OPPOSITES mental, spiritual.
physician ● noun DOCTOR, doctor of medicine, MD, medical practitioner, general practitioner, GP, clinician; specialist, consultant; *informal* doc, medic, medico; *Brit. informal* quack; *informal, dated* sawbones.
physiognomy ● noun FACE, features, countenance, expression, look, mien; *informal* mug; *Brit. informal* phizog, phiz; *Brit. rhyming slang*

p

pia /pīə/ (in full **pia mater**) • **noun** Anatomy the delicate innermost membrane enveloping the brain and spinal cord.
– ORIGIN Latin, (in full) 'tender mother', translating an Arabic phrase.

pianism • **noun** skill or artistry in playing the piano or composing piano music.
– DERIVATIVES **pianistic** adjective.

pianissimo /peeənissimō/ • **adverb & adjective** Music very soft or softly.
– ORIGIN Italian, 'softest'.

piano¹ /piannō/ • **noun** (pl. **pianos**) a large keyboard musical instrument with metal strings, which are struck by hammers when the keys are depressed.
– DERIVATIVES **pianist** noun.
– ORIGIN Italian, abbreviation of PIANOFORTE.

piano² /pyaanō/ • **adverb & adjective** Music soft or softly.
– ORIGIN Italian, 'soft'.

piano accordion • **noun** an accordion with the melody played on a small vertical keyboard like that of a piano.

pianoforte /piannōfortay/ • **noun** formal term for PIANO¹.
– ORIGIN from Italian *piano e forte* 'soft and loud', expressing the gradation in tone.

pianola /peeənōlə/ • **noun** trademark a piano equipped to be played automatically with a roll of perforated paper which controls the movement of the keys to produce a particular tune.

piano nobile /pyaanō nōbilay/ • **noun** Architecture the main storey of a large house, usually the first floor.
– ORIGIN Italian, 'noble floor'.

piastre /piastər/ (US also **piaster**) • **noun** a monetary unit of several Middle Eastern countries, equal to one hundredth of a pound.
– ORIGIN from Italian *piastra d'argento* 'plate of silver'.

piazza /piatsə/ • **noun** a public square or marketplace.
– ORIGIN Italian.

pibroch /peebrok, -brokh/ • **noun** a form of music for the Scottish bagpipes involving elaborate variations on a theme.
– ORIGIN Scottish Gaelic *piobaireachd* 'art of piping'.

pic • **noun** informal a picture, photograph, or film.

pica /pīkə/ • **noun** Printing **1** a unit of type size and line length equal to 12 points (about ⅙ inch or 4.2 mm). **2** a size of letter in typewriting, with 10 characters to the inch (about 3.9 to the centimetre).
– ORIGIN Latin, literally 'magpie', commonly identified with a 15th-century book of rules about Church feasts, although there is no known copy of this book printed in 'pica' type.

picador /pikkədor/ • **noun** (in bullfighting) a person on horseback who goads the bull with a lance.
– ORIGIN Spanish, from *picar* 'to prick'.

picaresque /pikkəresk/ • **adjective** relating to fiction dealing with the adventures of a dishonest but appealing hero.
– ORIGIN Spanish *picaresco*, from *pícaro* 'rogue'.

picayune /pikkəyo͞on/ N. Amer. • **adjective** informal petty; worthless. • **noun 1** informal an insignificant person or thing. **2** dated a coin of little value.
– ORIGIN French *picaillon*, denoting a Piedmontese copper coin, also used to mean 'cash'.

piccalilli /pikkəlilli/ • **noun** (pl. **piccalillies** or **piccalillis**) a pickle of chopped vegetables, mustard, and hot spices.
– ORIGIN probably from a blend of PICKLE and CHILLI.

piccaninny /pikkəninni/ (US **pickaninny**) • **noun** (pl. **piccaninnies**) offensive a small black child.
– ORIGIN from Spanish *pequeño* or Portuguese *pequeno* 'little'.

piccolo • **noun** (pl. **piccolos**) a small flute sounding an octave higher than the ordinary one.
– ORIGIN Italian, 'small flute'.

pick¹ • **verb 1** (often **pick up**) take hold of and move. **2** remove (a flower or fruit) from where it is growing. **3** choose from a number of alternatives. **4** remove unwanted matter from (one's nose or teeth) with a finger or a pointed instrument. • **noun 1** an act of selecting something. **2** (**the pick of**) informal the best person or thing in a particular group.
– PHRASES **pick and choose** select only the best from among a number of alternatives. **pick at 1** repeatedly pull at (something) with one's fingers. **2** eat in small amounts. **pick someone's brains** informal obtain information by questioning someone with expertise. **pick a fight** provoke an argument or fight. **pick holes in** find fault with. **pick a lock** open a lock with an instrument other than the proper key. **pick off** shoot (one of a group) from a distance. **pick on** single out for unfair treatment. **pick out 1** distinguish from among a group. **2** play (a tune) slowly or with difficulty on a guitar or similar instrument. **pick over** (or **pick through**) sort through (a number of items) carefully. **pick someone's pockets** steal something from a person's pocket. **pick up 1** go to collect. **2** improve or increase. **3** informal casually strike up a relationship with (someone) as a sexual overture. **4** return to (an earlier point or topic). **5** obtain, acquire, or learn. **6** become aware of or sensitive to. **7** detect or receive (a signal or sound). **pick one's way** walk slowly and carefully.
– DERIVATIVES **picker** noun.
– ORIGIN of unknown origin.

pick² (also **pickaxe**) • **noun 1** a tool consisting of a curved iron bar with one or both ends pointed, mounted at right angles to its handle, used for breaking up hard ground or rock. **2** a plectrum.
– ORIGIN variant of PIKE².

picket • **noun 1** a person or group of people standing outside a workplace trying to persuade others not to enter during a strike. **2** (also **picquet**) a soldier or small body of troops sent out to watch for the enemy. **3** a pointed wooden stake driven into the ground. • **verb** (**picketed, picketing**) act as a picket outside (a workplace).
– ORIGIN originally denoting a pointed stake, on which a soldier was required to stand on one foot as a military punishment: from French *piquet* 'pointed stake'.

pickings • **plural noun 1** profits or gains, especially those made effortlessly or dishonestly. **2** scraps or leftovers.

pickle • **noun 1** a relish consisting of vegetables or fruit preserved in vinegar, brine, or mustard. **2** liquid used to preserve food or other perishable items. **3** (**a pickle**) informal a difficult

p

Thesaurus

boat race; *N. Amer. informal* puss; *poetic/literary* visage, lineaments.

physique • **noun** BODY, build, figure, frame, anatomy, shape, form, proportions; muscles, musculature; *informal* vital statistics, bod.

pick • **verb 1** *I got a job picking apples* HARVEST, gather (in), collect, pluck; *poetic/literary* cull. **2** *pick the time that suits you best* CHOOSE, select, pick out, single out, take, opt for, plump for, elect, decide on, settle on, fix on, sift out, sort out; name, nominate. **3** *Beth picked at her food* NIBBLE, toy with, play with, eat like a bird. **4** *people were singing and picking guitars* STRUM, twang, thrum, pluck. **5** *he tried to pick a fight* PROVOKE, start, cause, incite, stir up, whip up, instigate, prompt, bring about.
• **noun 1** *take your pick* CHOICE, selection, option, decision; preference, favourite. **2** *(informal) the pick of the crop* BEST, finest, top, choice, choicest, prime, cream, flower, prize, pearl, gem, jewel, jewel in the crown, crème de la crème, elite.
– PHRASES **pick on** BULLY, victimize, tyrannize, torment, persecute, criticize, harass, hound, taunt, tease; *informal* get at, have it in for, have a down on, be down on, needle. **pick something out 1** *one painting was picked out for special mention* CHOOSE, select, pick, single out, opt for, plump for, decide on, elect, settle on, fix on, sift out, sort out; name, nominate. **2** *she picked out Jessica in the crowd* SEE, make out, distinguish, discern, spot, perceive, detect, notice, recognize, identify, catch sight of, glimpse; *poetic/literary* espy, behold, descry. **pick up** IMPROVE, recover, be on the road to recovery, rally, make a comeback, bounce back, perk up, look up, take a turn for the better, turn the/a corner, be on the mend, make headway, make progress. **pick someone/something up** LIFT, take up, raise, hoist, scoop up, gather up, snatch up. **pick someone up 1** *I'll pick you up after lunch* FETCH, collect, call for. **2** *(informal) he was picked up by the police* ARREST, apprehend, detain, take into custody, seize; *informal* nab, run in, bust; *Brit. informal* nick. **3** *(informal) he picked her up in a club* TAKE UP WITH; *informal* get off with, pull, cop off with. **pick something up 1** *we picked it up at a flea market* FIND, discover, come across, stumble across, happen on, chance on; acquire, obtain, come by, get, procure; purchase, buy; *informal* get hold of, get/lay one's hands on, get one's mitts on, bag, land. **2** *he picked up the story in the 1950s* RESUME, take up, start again, recommence, continue, carry on with, go on with. **3** *she picked up a virus* CATCH, contract, get, go/come down with. **4** *he told us the bits of gossip he'd picked up* HEAR, hear tell, get wind of, be told, learn; glean, garner. **5** *we're picking up a distress signal* RECEIVE, detect, get, hear.

picket • **noun 1** *forty pickets were arrested* STRIKER, demonstrator, protester, objector, picketer; flying picket. **2** *fences made of cedar*

situation. ● verb **1** preserve (food) in pickle. **2** (**pickled**) informal drunk.
– ORIGIN Dutch or Low German *pekel*.
pick-me-up ● noun (*informal*) informal a thing that makes one feel more energetic or cheerful.
pickpocket ● noun a person who steals from people's pockets.
pickup ● noun **1** (also **pickup truck**) a small van or truck with low sides. **2** an act of picking up or collecting a person or goods. **3** an improvement. **4** a device on an electric guitar which converts sound vibrations into electrical signals for amplification. **5** the cartridge of a record player, carrying the stylus.
picky ● adjective (**pickier**, **pickiest**) informal fastidious, especially excessively so.
picnic ● noun a packed meal eaten outdoors, or an occasion when such a meal is eaten. ● verb (**picnicked**, **picnicking**) have or take part in a picnic.
– PHRASES **be no picnic** informal be difficult or unpleasant.
– DERIVATIVES **picnicker** noun.
– ORIGIN French *pique-nique*.
pico- ● combining form denoting a factor of one million millionth (10^{-12}): *picosecond*.
– ORIGIN from Spanish *pico*, 'beak, peak, little bit'.
picot /peekō/ ● noun a small decorative loop or series of loops in lace or embroidery, typically used to decorate a border.
– ORIGIN French, 'small peak or point'.
picric acid /pikrik/ ● noun Chemistry a bitter yellow compound obtained by nitrating phenol, used in making explosives.
– ORIGIN from Greek *pikros* 'bitter'.
Pict ● noun a member of an ancient people inhabiting northern Scotland in Roman times.
– ORIGIN Latin *Picti*, perhaps from *pingere* 'to paint or tattoo'.
pictograph (also **pictogram**) ● noun **1** a pictorial symbol for a word or phrase. **2** a pictorial representation of statistics on a chart, graph, or computer screen.
– DERIVATIVES **pictographic** adjective.
– ORIGIN from Latin *pingere* 'to paint'.
pictorial ● adjective of or expressed in pictures; illustrated. ● noun a newspaper or periodical with pictures as a main feature.
– DERIVATIVES **pictorially** adverb.
– ORIGIN Latin *pictorius*, from *pictor* 'painter'.
picture ● noun **1** a painting, drawing, or photograph. **2** an image on a television screen. **3** a cinema film. **4** (**the pictures**) the cinema. **5** an impression formed from an account or description. **6** informal a state of being fully informed: *in the picture*. ● verb **1** represent in a picture. **2** form a mental image of.
– PHRASES **be** (or **look**) **a picture 1** be beautiful. **2** look amusingly startled. (**as**) **pretty as a picture** very pretty.
– ORIGIN Latin *pictura*, from *pingere* 'to paint'.
picture postcard ● noun **1** a postcard with a picture on one side. **2** (before another noun) (of a view) prettily picturesque.
picturesque ● adjective visually attractive in a quaint or charming manner.
– DERIVATIVES **picturesquely** adverb **picturesqueness** noun.
picture window ● noun a large window consisting of one pane of glass.
piddle ● verb informal **1** urinate. **2** (**piddle about/around**) spend time in trifling activities. **3** (**piddling**) pathetically trivial.
– ORIGIN probably from a blend of PISS and PUDDLE.
pidgin ● noun a grammatically simplified form of a language with elements taken from local languages, used for communication between people not sharing a common language.
– ORIGIN Chinese alteration of English *business*.
pi-dog ● noun variant spelling of PYE-DOG.
pie[1] ● noun a baked dish of savoury or sweet ingredients encased in or topped with pastry.
– PHRASES **pie in the sky** informal a pleasant prospect that is very unlikely to be realized.
– ORIGIN probably the same word as obsolete *pie* 'magpie', the various combinations of ingredients being compared to objects randomly collected by a magpie.
pie[2] ● noun a former monetary unit of the Indian subcontinent, equal to one twelfth of an anna.
– ORIGIN Sanskrit, 'quarter'.
piebald ● adjective (of a horse) having irregular patches of two colours, typically black and white. ● noun a piebald horse.
– ORIGIN from *pie* in *magpie* + *bald* in the obsolete sense 'streaked with white'.
piece ● noun **1** a portion separated from or regarded distinctly from the whole. **2** an item used in constructing something or forming part of a set. **3** a musical or written work. **4** a figure or token used to make moves in a board game. **5** a coin of specified value. **6** informal, chiefly N. Amer. a firearm. ● verb (**piece together**) assemble from individual parts.
– PHRASES **go to pieces** become so nervous or upset that one is unable to function normally. **in one piece** unharmed or undamaged. (**all**) **of a piece** entirely consistent. **piece by piece** in slow and small stages. **piece of work** informal a person of a specified kind, especially an unpleasant one. **say one's piece**

Thesaurus

p

pickets STAKE, post, paling; upright, stanchion, pier, piling.
● verb *over 200 people picketed the factory* DEMONSTRATE AT, form a picket at, man the picket line at; blockade, shut off.
pickle ● noun **1** *a jar of pickle* RELISH, chutney, piccalilli. **2** *steep the vegetables in pickle* MARINADE, brine, vinegar. **3** *(informal) they got into an awful pickle* PLIGHT, predicament, mess, difficulty, trouble, dire/desperate straits, problem; *informal* tight corner, tight spot, jam, fix, scrape, bind, hole, hot water, fine kettle of fish; *Brit. informal* spot of bother.
● verb *fish pickled in brine* PRESERVE, souse, marinate, conserve; bottle, can, tin.
pick-me-up ● noun *(informal)* **1** *a drink that's a very good pick-me-up* TONIC, restorative, energizer, stimulant, refresher, reviver; *informal* bracer; *Medicine* analeptic. **2** *his winning goal was a perfect pick-me-up* BOOST, boost to the spirits, fillip, stimulant, stimulus; *informal* shot in the arm.
pickpocket ● noun THIEF, petty thief, sneak thief; *archaic* cutpurse.
pickup ● noun IMPROVEMENT, recovery, revival, upturn, upswing, rally, comeback, resurgence, renewal, turn for the better.
– OPPOSITES slump.
picnic ● noun **1** *a picnic on the beach* OUTDOOR MEAL, alfresco meal; *N. Amer.* cookout. **2** *(informal) working for him was no picnic* EASY TASK/JOB, child's play, five-finger exercise, gift, walkover; *informal* doddle, piece of cake, money for old rope, money for jam, cinch, breeze, kids' stuff, cakewalk, pushover; *N. Amer. informal* duck soup; *Austral./NZ informal* bludge.
pictorial ● adjective ILLUSTRATED, in pictures, in picture form, in photographs, photographic, graphic.
picture ● noun **1** *pictures in an art gallery* PAINTING, DRAWING, sketch, oil painting, watercolour, print, canvas, portrait, portrayal, illustration, artwork, depiction, likeness, representation, image, icon, miniature; fresco, mural, wall painting; *informal* oil. **2** *we were told not to take pictures* PHOTOGRAPH, photo, snap, snapshot, shot, print, slide, transparency, exposure, still, enlargement; *Brit.* enprint. **3** *a picture of the sort of person the child should be* CONCEPT, idea, impression, view, (mental) image, vision, visualization, notion. **4** *the picture of health* PERSONIFICATION, embodiment, epitome, essence, quintessence, perfect example, soul, model. **5** *a picture starring Robert de Niro* FILM, movie, feature film, motion picture; *informal* flick; *dated* moving picture. **6** *we went to the pictures* THE CINEMA, the movies, the silver screen, the big screen; *informal* the flicks.
● verb **1** *he was pictured with his guests* PHOTOGRAPH, take a photograph/photo of, snap, shoot, film. **2** *in the drawing they were pictured against a snowy background* PAINT, DRAW, sketch, depict, delineate, portray, show, illustrate. **3** *Anne still pictured Richard as he had been* VISUALIZE, see in one's mind's eye, conjure up a picture/image of, imagine, see, evoke.
– PHRASES **put someone in the picture** INFORM, fill in, explain the situation/circumstances to, bring up to date, update, brief, keep posted; *informal* clue in, bring up to speed.
picturesque ● adjective **1** *a picturesque village* ATTRACTIVE, pretty, beautiful, lovely, scenic, charming, quaint, pleasing, delightful. **2** *a picturesque description* VIVID, graphic, colourful, impressive, striking.
– OPPOSITES ugly, dull.
piddling ● adjective *(informal)* TRIVIAL, trifling, petty, footling, slight, small, insignificant, unimportant, inconsequential, inconsiderable, negligible; meagre, inadequate, insufficient, paltry, scant, scanty, derisory, pitiful, miserable, puny, niggardly, beggarly, mere; *informal* measly, pathetic, piffling, mingy, poxy; *N. Amer. informal* nickel-and-dime.
pie ● noun PASTRY, tart, tartlet, quiche, pasty, patty, turnover, strudel.

give one's opinion or make a prepared statement. **tear** (or **pull**) **to pieces** criticize harshly.
– ORIGIN Old French.
pièce de résistance /pyess de rayzistonss/ ● noun the most important or remarkable feature of a creative work.
– ORIGIN French, 'piece (i.e. means) of resistance'.
piecemeal ● adjective & adverb done piece by piece over a period of time.
– ORIGIN from PIECE + an Old English word meaning 'measure, quantity taken at one time'.
piecework ● noun work paid for according to the amount produced.
pie chart ● noun a diagram in which a circle is divided into sectors that each represent a proportion of the whole.
pied /pīd/ ● adjective having two or more different colours.
– ORIGIN originally in the sense 'black and white like a magpie'.
pied-à-terre /pyaydaatair/ ● noun (pl. **pieds-à-terre** pronunc. same) a small flat, house, or room kept for occasional use, one's permanent residence being elsewhere.
– ORIGIN French, 'foot to earth'.
Pied Piper ● noun a person who entices others to follow them, especially to their doom.
– ORIGIN from the piper in German legend who rid the town of Hamelin of rats by enticing them away with his music, and when refused the promised payment lured away the town's children.
pie-eyed ● adjective informal very drunk.
Piegan ● noun (pl. same or **Piegans**) & adjective variant spelling of PEIGAN.
pier ● noun **1** a structure leading out to sea and used as a landing stage for boats or as a place of entertainment. **2** Brit. a long narrow structure projecting from an airport terminal and giving access to an aircraft. **3** the pillar of an arch or supporting a bridge. **4** a wall between windows or other adjacent openings.
– ORIGIN Latin *pera*.
pierce ● verb **1** make a hole in or through with a sharp object. **2** force or cut a way through. **3** (**piercing**) very sharp, cold, or high-pitched.
– DERIVATIVES **piercer** noun.
– ORIGIN Old French *percer*, from Latin *pertundere* 'bore through'.
Pierrot /pīərō/ ● noun a male character in French pantomime, with a sad white-painted face, a loose white costume, and a pointed hat.
– ORIGIN French, familiar form of the male given name *Pierre* 'Peter'.
pietà /pyaytaa/ ● noun a picture or sculpture of the Virgin Mary holding the dead body of Christ.
– ORIGIN Italian, from Latin *pietas* 'dutifulness'.
piety /pīəti/ ● noun (pl. **pieties**) **1** the quality of being pious or reverent. **2** a conventional belief accepted unthinkingly.
– ORIGIN Latin *pietas*, from *pius* 'dutiful'.
piezo /pīeezō/ ● adjective piezoelectric.
piezoelectricity /pī-eezōillektrissiti/ ● noun electric polarization produced in certain crystals by the application of mechanical stress.
– DERIVATIVES **piezoelectric** adjective.
– ORIGIN from Greek *piezein* 'press, squeeze'.
piffle ● noun informal nonsense.
– ORIGIN imitative.
piffling ● adjective informal trivial; unimportant.
pig ● noun **1** a domesticated mammal with sparse bristly hair and a flat snout, kept for its meat. **2** a wild animal related to the domestic pig. **3** informal a greedy, dirty, or unpleasant person. **4** informal, derogatory a police officer. **5** an oblong mass of iron or lead from a smelting furnace. ● verb (**pigged**, **pigging**) informal gorge oneself with food.
– PHRASES **make a pig of oneself** informal overeat. **make a pig's ear of** Brit. informal handle ineptly. **a pig in a poke** something that is bought or accepted without first being seen or assessed.
– DERIVATIVES **piglet** noun.
– ORIGIN probably from the first part of an Old English word meaning 'acorn' or 'pig bread' (i.e. food for pigs).
pigeon ● noun a stout bird with a small head, short legs, and a cooing voice.
– ORIGIN Old French *pijon* 'young bird', from Latin *pipio*, 'young cheeping bird'.
pigeon-chested (also **pigeon-breasted**) ● adjective having a narrow, projecting chest.
pigeonhole ● noun **1** a small recess for a domestic pigeon to nest in. **2** each of a set of small compartments where letters or messages may be left for individuals. **3** a category to which someone or something is assigned. ● verb assign to a particular category, especially a restrictive one.
pigeon-toed ● adjective having the toes or feet turned inwards.

Thesaurus

– PHRASES **pie in the sky** *(informal)* FALSE HOPE, illusion, delusion, fantasy, pipe dream, daydream, castle in the air, castle in Spain.
piebald ● adjective. See PIED.
piece ● noun **1** *a piece of cheese | a piece of wood* BIT, slice, chunk, segment, section, lump, hunk, wedge, slab, block, cake, bar, cube, stick, length; offcut, sample, fragment, sliver, splinter, wafer, chip, crumb, scrap, remnant, shred, shard, snippet; mouthful, morsel; *Brit. informal* wodge. **2** *the pieces of a clock* COMPONENT, part, bit, section, segment, constituent, element; unit, module. **3** *a piece of furniture* ITEM, article, specimen. **4** *a piece of the profit* SHARE, portion, slice, quota, part, bit, percentage, amount, quantity, ration, fraction, division; *informal* cut, rake-off; *Brit. informal* whack. **5** *pieces from his private collection* WORK (OF ART), creation, production; composition, opus. **6** *the reporter who wrote the piece* ARTICLE, item, story, report, essay, study, review, composition, column. **7** *the pieces on a chess board* TOKEN, counter, man, disc, chip, marker.
– PHRASES **in one piece 1** *the camera was still in one piece* UNBROKEN, entire, whole, intact, undamaged, unharmed. **2** *I'll bring her back in one piece* UNHURT, uninjured, unscathed, safe, safe and sound. **in pieces** BROKEN, in bits, shattered, smashed, in smithereens; *informal* bust. **go/fall to pieces** HAVE A BREAKDOWN, break down, go out of one's mind, lose control, lose one's head, fall apart; *informal* crack up, lose it, come/fall apart at the seams, freak, freak out.
pièce de résistance ● noun MASTERPIECE, magnum opus, chef-d'œuvre, masterwork, tour de force, showpiece, prize, jewel in the crown.
piecemeal ● adverb A LITTLE AT A TIME, piece by piece, bit by bit, gradually, slowly, in stages, in steps, step by step, little by little, by degrees, in/by fits and starts.
pied ● adjective PARTICOLOURED, multicoloured, variegated, black and white, brown and white, piebald, skewbald, dappled, brindle, spotted, mottled, speckled, flecked; *N. Amer.* pinto.
pier ● noun **1** *a boat was tied to the pier* JETTY, quay, wharf, dock, landing, landing stage. **2** *the piers of the bridge* SUPPORT, cutwater, pile, piling, abutment, buttress, stanchion, prop, stay, upright, pillar, post, column.
pierce ● verb **1** *the metal pierced his flesh* PENETRATE, puncture, perforate, prick, lance; stab, spike, stick, impale, transfix, bore through, drill through. **2** *his anguish pierced her to the quick* HURT, wound, pain, sting, sear, grieve, distress, upset, trouble, harrow, afflict; affect, move.
piercing ● adjective **1** *a piercing shriek* SHRILL, ear-splitting, high-pitched, penetrating, strident, loud. **2** *the piercing wind* BITTER, biting, cutting, penetrating, sharp, keen, stinging, raw; freezing, frigid, glacial, arctic, chill. **3** *a piercing pain* INTENSE, excruciating, agonizing, sharp, stabbing, shooting, stinging, severe, extreme, fierce, searing, racking. **4** *his piercing gaze* SEARCHING, probing, penetrating, penetrative, shrewd, sharp, keen. **5** *his piercing intelligence* PERCEPTIVE, percipient, perspicacious, penetrating, discerning, discriminating, intelligent, quick-witted, sharp, sharp-witted, shrewd, insightful, keen, acute, astute, clever, smart, incisive, razor-edged, trenchant.
piety ● noun DEVOUTNESS, devotion, piousness, religion, holiness, godliness, saintliness; veneration, reverence, faith, religious duty, spirituality, religious zeal, fervour; pietism, religiosity.
piffle ● noun *(informal)*. See NONSENSE sense 1.
piffling ● adjective *(informal)* INADEQUATE, insufficient, tiny, small, minimal, trifling, paltry, pitiful, negligible; miserly, miserable; *informal* measly, stingy, lousy, pathetic, piddling, mingy, poxy.
pig ● noun **1** *a herd of pigs* HOG, boar, sow, porker, swine, piglet; *children's word* piggy. **2** *(informal) he's eaten the lot, the pig* GLUTTON, guzzler; *informal* hog, greedy guts; *Brit. informal* gannet. **3** *(informal) he's been an absolute pig lately informal* BASTARD, beast, louse, swine; *Brit. informal* toerag; *informal, dated* rotter, heel, stinker.
– RELATED TERMS porcine.
pigeonhole ● noun *journalistic pigeonholes* CATEGORY, categorization, class, classification, group, grouping, designation, slot.
● verb **1** *they were pigeonholed as an indie guitar band* CATEGORIZE,

piggery ● noun (pl. **piggeries**) **1** a farm or enclosure where pigs are kept. **2** behaviour regarded as characteristic of pigs, especially greed or unpleasantness.

piggish ● adjective resembling a pig, especially in being unpleasant.

piggy ● noun (pl. **piggies**) a child's word for a pig or piglet. ● adjective resembling a pig, especially in features or appetite.
– PHRASES **piggy in the middle** chiefly Brit. **1** a game in which two people attempt to throw a ball to each other without a third person in the middle catching it. **2** a person who is placed in an awkward situation between two others.

piggyback ● noun a ride on someone's back and shoulders. ● adverb on the back and shoulders of another person. ● verb carry by or as if by means of a piggyback.

piggy bank ● noun a money box, especially one shaped like a pig.

pig-headed ● adjective stupidly obstinate.

pig iron ● noun crude iron as first obtained from a smelting furnace.

pigment ● noun **1** the natural colouring matter of animal or plant tissue. **2** a substance used for colouring or painting. ● verb colour with or as if with pigment.
– DERIVATIVES **pigmentary** adjective **pigmentation** noun.
– ORIGIN Latin *pigmentum*, from *pingere* 'to paint'.

pigmy ● noun variant spelling of PYGMY.

pigskin ● noun leather made from the hide of a domestic pig.

pigsty ● noun (pl. **pigsties**) **1** a pen or enclosure for a pig or pigs. **2** a very dirty or untidy house or room.

pigswill ● noun kitchen refuse and scraps fed to pigs.

pigtail ● noun a plaited lock of hair worn singly at the back or on each side of the head.
– DERIVATIVES **pigtailed** adjective.

pika /pīkə/ ● noun a small mammal related to the rabbits, found mainly in mountains and deserts.
– ORIGIN from a Siberian language.

pike[1] ● noun (pl. same) a long-bodied predatory freshwater fish with long teeth.
– ORIGIN from PIKE[2] (because of the fish's pointed jaw).

pike[2] ● noun historical a weapon with a pointed metal head on a long wooden shaft.
– ORIGIN French *pique*, from *piquer* 'pierce', from *pic* 'pick, pike'.

pike[3] ● noun a jackknife position in diving or gymnastics.
– ORIGIN of unknown origin.

pikelet ● noun a thin kind of crumpet.
– ORIGIN from Welsh *bara pyglyd* 'pitchy bread'.

piker ● noun N. Amer. & Austral./NZ informal **1** a gambler who makes only small bets. **2** a mean or cautious person.

pikestaff ● noun historical the wooden shaft of a pike.
– PHRASES **(as) plain as a pikestaff** very obvious. [ORIGIN the phrase is an altered version of *as plain as a packstaff*, the staff being that of a pedlar, on which he rested his pack of wares.]

pilaf /pilaf/ (also **pilaff**, **pilau** /pilow/, **pulao** /pəlow/) ● noun a Middle Eastern or Indian dish of spiced rice or wheat and often meat and vegetables.
– ORIGIN Turkish.

pilaster /pilastər/ ● noun a rectangular column, especially one projecting from a wall.
– ORIGIN Latin *pilastrum*, from *pila* 'pillar'.

Pilates /pilaateez/ ● noun a system of exercises using special apparatus, designed to improve physical strength, flexibility, and posture.
– ORIGIN named after the German physical fitness specialist Joseph *Pilates* (1880–1967).

pilchard ● noun a small marine food fish of the herring family.
– ORIGIN of unknown origin.

pile[1] ● noun **1** a heap of things laid or lying one on top of another. **2** informal a large amount. **3** a large imposing building. ● verb **1** place (things) one on top of the other. **2** (**pile up**) form a pile or very large quantity. **3** (**pile on**) informal intensify or exaggerate for effect. **4** (**pile into/out of**) get into or out of (a vehicle) in a disorganized manner.
– PHRASES **make a pile** informal make a lot of money.
– ORIGIN Latin *pila* 'pillar, pier'.

pile[2] ● noun a heavy stake or post driven into the ground to support foundations.
– ORIGIN Old English, 'dart, arrow', also 'pointed stake'.

pile[3] ● noun the soft projecting surface of a carpet or a fabric, consisting of many small threads.
– ORIGIN Latin *pilus* 'hair'.

piledriver ● noun **1** a machine for driving piles into the ground. **2** Brit. informal a forceful act, blow, or shot.

piles ● plural noun haemorrhoids.
– ORIGIN probably from Latin *pila* 'ball' (because of the globular form of external haemorrhoids).

pile-up ● noun *(informal)* informal **1** a crash involving several vehicles. **2** an accumulation of a specified thing.

pilfer ● verb steal (things of little value).
– DERIVATIVES **pilferage** noun.
– ORIGIN Old French *pelfrer* 'to pillage'.

pilgrim ● noun a person who journeys to a sacred place for religious reasons.
– ORIGIN Provençal *pelegrin*, from Latin *peregrinus* 'foreign'; related to PEREGRINE.

pilgrimage ● noun a pilgrim's journey.

pill ● noun **1** a small round mass of solid medicine for swallowing whole. **2** (**the Pill**) a contraceptive pill. ● verb (of knitted fabric) form small balls of fluff on its surface.
– PHRASES **a bitter pill** an unpleasant or painful necessity. **sugar** (or **sweeten**) **the pill** make an unpleasant or painful necessity more palatable.
– ORIGIN Latin *pilula* 'little ball'.

pillage ● verb rob or steal with violence, especially in wartime. ● noun the action of pillaging.
– DERIVATIVES **pillager** noun.
– ORIGIN Old French, from *piller* 'to plunder'.

pillar ● noun **1** a tall vertical structure used as a support for a

p

Thesaurus

compartmentalize, classify, characterize, label, brand, tag, designate. **2** *the plan was pigeonholed last year* POSTPONE, put off, put back, defer, shelve, hold over, put to one side, put on ice, mothball, put in cold storage; *N. Amer.* table; *informal* put on the back burner.

pig-headed ● adjective OBSTINATE, stubborn (as a mule), mulish, bull-headed, obdurate, headstrong, self-willed, wilful, perverse, contrary, recalcitrant, stiff-necked; uncooperative, inflexible, uncompromising, intractable, intransigent, unyielding; *Brit. informal* bloody-minded, bolshie; *formal* refractory.

pigment ● noun COLOURING MATTER, colouring, colourant, colour, tint, dye, dyestuff.

pile[1] ● noun **1** *a pile of stones* HEAP, stack, mound, pyramid, mass, quantity; collection, accumulation, assemblage, store, stockpile, hoard. **2** *(informal) I've a pile of work to do* GREAT DEAL, lot, large quantity/amount, quantities, reams, mountain; abundance, cornucopia, plethora; *informal* load, heap, mass, slew, ocean, stack, ton; *Brit. informal* shedload; *Austral./NZ informal* swag. **3** *(informal) he'd made his pile in the fur trade* FORTUNE, millions, billions; *informal* small fortune, bomb, packet, bundle, wad; *Brit. informal* loadsamoney. **4** *a huge Victorian pile* MANSION, stately home, manor, manor house, country house; edifice.
● verb **1** *he piled up the plates* HEAP (UP), stack (up), put on top of each other. **2** *he piled his plate with fried eggs* LOAD, heap, fill (up), lade, stack, charge, stock. **3** *his debts were piling up* INCREASE, grow, mount up, escalate, soar, spiral, leap up, shoot up, rocket, climb, accumulate, accrue, build up, multiply. **4** *we piled into the car* CROWD, climb, pack, squeeze, push, shove.
– PHRASES **pile it on** *(informal)* EXAGGERATE, overstate the case, make a mountain out of a molehill, overdo it, overplay it, over-dramatize; *informal* lay it on thick, lay it on with a trowel.

pile[2] ● noun *a wall supported by timber piles* POST, stake, pillar, column, support, foundation, piling, abutment, pier, cutwater, buttress, stanchion, upright.

pile[3] ● noun *a carpet with a short pile* NAP, fibres, threads.

pile-up ● noun *(informal)* CRASH, multiple crash, collision, multiple collision, smash, accident, road accident; *Brit.* RTA (road traffic accident); *N. Amer.* wreck; *informal* smash-up; *Brit. informal* shunt.

pilfer ● verb STEAL, thieve, take, snatch, purloin, loot; *informal* swipe, rob, nab, rip off, lift, 'liberate', 'borrow', filch, snaffle; *Brit. informal* pinch, half-inch, nick, whip, knock off, nobble; *N. Amer. informal* heist.

pilgrim ● noun worshipper, devotee, believer; traveller, crusader, haji; *poetic/literary* wayfarer; *historical* palmer.

pilgrimage ● noun RELIGIOUS JOURNEY, religious expedition, hajj, crusade, mission.

pill ● noun TABLET, capsule, caplet, pellet, lozenge, pastille; *Veterinary Medicine* bolus.

building or as an ornament. **2** a person or thing providing reliable support.
– PHRASES **from pillar to post** from one place to another in an unsatisfactory manner.
– DERIVATIVES **pillared** adjective.
– ORIGIN Latin *pila* 'pillar'.
pillar box ● noun (in the UK) a large red cylindrical public postbox.
pillbox ● noun **1** a small box for holding pills. **2** a hat of a similar shape. **3** a small, partly underground, concrete fort used as an outpost.
pillion ● noun a seat for a passenger behind a motorcyclist.
– ORIGIN originally denoting a woman's light saddle, or a cushion attached to a saddle for an additional passenger: from Irish *pillín* 'small cushion'.
pillock ● noun Brit. informal a stupid person.
– ORIGIN from obsolete *pillicock* 'penis'.
pillory ● noun (pl. **pillories**) a wooden framework with holes for the head and hands, in which offenders were formerly imprisoned and exposed to public abuse. ● verb (**pillories, pilloried**) **1** put in a pillory. **2** attack or ridicule publicly.
– ORIGIN Old French *pilori*, perhaps related to a Catalan word meaning 'peephole'.
pillow ● noun a rectangular cloth bag stuffed with feathers or other soft materials, used to support the head when lying or sleeping. ● verb support (one's head) as if on a pillow.
– DERIVATIVES **pillowy** adjective.
– ORIGIN Latin *pulvinus* 'cushion'.
pillowcase ● noun a removable cloth cover for a pillow.
pillow fight ● noun a mock fight using pillows.
pillow talk ● noun intimate conversation in bed.
pilot ● noun **1** a person who operates the flying controls of an aircraft. **2** a person with local knowledge qualified to take charge of a ship entering or leaving a harbour. **3** something done or produced as an experiment or test before wider introduction. ● verb (**piloted, piloting**) **1** act as a pilot of (an aircraft or ship). **2** test (a scheme, project, etc.) before introducing it more widely.
– DERIVATIVES **pilotage** noun.
– ORIGIN Latin *pilotus*, from Greek *pēdon* 'oar'.
pilot chute ● noun a small parachute used to bring the main one into operation.
pilotfish ● noun a fish of warm seas that often swims close to large fish such as sharks.
pilot light ● noun **1** a small gas burner kept alight permanently to light a larger burner when needed. **2** an electric indicator light or control light.
pilot officer ● noun the lowest rank of officer in the RAF.
pilot whale ● noun a black toothed whale with a square bulbous head.
Pilsner /pilznər/ (also **Pilsener**) ● noun a lager beer with a strong hop flavour, originally brewed at Pilsen (Plzeň) in the Czech Republic.
PIM ● abbreviation personal information manager.
pimento /pimentō/ ● noun (pl. **pimentos**) variant spelling of PIMIENTO.
pimiento /pimmientō/ (also **pimento**) ● noun (pl. **pimientos**) a red sweet pepper.
– ORIGIN Spanish, from Latin *pigmentum* 'pigment', later 'spice'.
pimp ● noun **1** a man who controls prostitutes and arranges clients for them, taking a percentage of their earnings in return. **2** Austral. informal a telltale or informer. ● verb **1** act as a pimp. **2** (**pimp on**) Austral. informal inform on.
– ORIGIN of unknown origin.
pimpernel ● noun a low-growing plant with bright five-petalled flowers.
– ORIGIN Old French *pimpernelle*, from Latin *piper* 'pepper'.
pimple ● noun a small, hard inflamed spot on the skin.
– DERIVATIVES **pimpled** adjective **pimply** adjective.
– ORIGIN related to an Old English word meaning 'break out in pustules'.
PIN (also **PIN number**) ● abbreviation personal identification number.
pin ● noun **1** a thin piece of metal with a sharp point at one end and a round head at the other, used for fastening pieces of cloth, paper, etc. **2** a metal projection from a plug or an integrated circuit. **3** a small brooch or badge. **4** Medicine a steel rod used to join the ends of fractured bones while they heal. **5** Golf a stick with a flag placed in a hole to mark its position. **6** a metal peg in a hand grenade that prevents its explosion. **7** a skittle in bowling. **8** (**pins**) informal legs. ● verb (**pinned, pinning**) **1** attach or fasten with a pin or pins. **2** hold someone firmly so they are unable to move. **3** (**pin down**) force (someone) to be specific about their intentions. **4** (**pin down**) restrict the actions of (an enemy) by firing at them. **5** (**pin on**) fix (blame or responsibility) on.
– PHRASES **pin one's ears back** listen carefully. **pin one's hopes** (or **faith**) **on** rely heavily on.
– ORIGIN Latin *pinna* 'point, tip, edge'.
pina colada /peenə kəlaadə/ ● noun a cocktail made with rum, pineapple juice, and coconut.
– ORIGIN Spanish, 'strained pineapple'.
pinafore ● noun **1** (also **pinafore dress**) a collarless, sleeveless dress worn over a blouse or jumper. **2** Brit. a woman's loose sleeveless garment worn over clothes to keep them clean.
– ORIGIN from PIN + AFORE (because the term originally denoted an apron with a bib pinned on the front of a dress).
pinball ● noun a game in which small metal balls are shot across a sloping board and score points by striking targets.
pince-nez /pansnay/ ● noun (treated as sing. or pl.) a pair of eye-

p

Thesaurus

pillage ● verb **1** *the abbey was pillaged* RANSACK, rob, plunder, despoil, raid, loot; sack, devastate, lay waste, ravage, rape. **2** *columns pillaged from an ancient town* STEAL, pilfer, thieve, take, snatch, purloin, loot; *informal* swipe, rob, nab, rip off, lift, 'liberate', 'borrow', filch, snaffle; *Brit. informal* pinch, half-inch, nick, whip, knock off, nobble; *N. Amer. informal* heist.
● noun *the rebels were intent on pillage* ROBBERY, robbing, raiding, plunder, looting, sacking, rape, marauding; *poetic/literary* rapine.
pillar ● noun **1** *stone pillars* COLUMN, post, support, upright, baluster, pier, pile, pilaster, stanchion, prop, newel; obelisk, monolith. **2** *a pillar of the community* STALWART, mainstay, bastion, rock; leading light, worthy, backbone, support, upholder, champion.
pillory ● noun *offenders were put in the pillory* STOCKS.
● verb **1** *he was pilloried by the press* ATTACK, criticize, censure, condemn, denigrate, lambaste, savage, stigmatize, denounce; *informal* knock, slam, pan, bash, crucify, hammer; *Brit. informal* slate, rubbish, slag off; *N. Amer. informal* pummel; *Austral./NZ informal* bag, monster; *formal* excoriate. **2** *they were pilloried at school* RIDICULE, jeer at, sneer at, deride, mock, scorn, make fun of, poke fun at, laugh at, scoff at, tease, taunt, rag; *informal* kid, rib, josh, take the mickey out of; *N. Amer. informal* razz, pull someone's chain.
pillow ● noun *his head rested on the pillow* CUSHION, bolster, pad; headrest.
● verb *she pillowed her head on folded arms* CUSHION, cradle, rest, lay, support.
pilot ● noun **1** *a fighter pilot* AIRMAN/AIRWOMAN, flyer; captain, commander, co-pilot, wingman; *informal* skipper; *N. Amer. informal* jock; *dated* aviator, aeronaut. **2** *a harbour pilot* NAVIGATOR, helmsman, steersman, coxswain. **3** *a pilot for a TV series* TRIAL EPISODE; sample, experiment.
● adjective *a pilot project* EXPERIMENTAL, exploratory, trial, test, sample, speculative; preliminary.
● verb **1** *he piloted the jet to safety* NAVIGATE, guide, manoeuvre, steer, control, direct, captain, shepherd; fly, aviate; drive; sail; *informal* skipper. **2** *the questionnaire has been piloted* TEST, trial, try out; assess, investigate, examine, appraise, evaluate.
pimp ● noun PROCURER, procuress; brothel-keeper, madam; *Brit. informal* ponce; *archaic* bawd.
pimple ● noun SPOT, pustule, bleb, boil, swelling, eruption, blackhead, carbuncle, blister; (**pimples**) acne; *informal* whitehead, zit; *Scottish informal* plook; *technical* comedo, papule.
pin ● noun **1** *fasten the hem with a pin* TACK, safety pin, nail, staple, fastener. **2** *a broken pin in the machine* BOLT, peg, rivet, dowel, screw. **3** *they wore name pins* BADGE, brooch.
● verb **1** *she pinned the brooch to her dress* ATTACH, fasten, affix, fix, tack, clip; join, secure. **2** *they pinned him to the ground* HOLD, press, hold fast, hold down; restrain, pinion, immobilize. **3** *they pinned the crime on him* BLAME FOR, hold responsible for, attribute to, impute to, ascribe to; lay something at someone's door; *informal* stick on.
– PHRASES **pin someone/something down 1** *our troops can pin down the enemy* CONFINE, TRAP, hem in, corner, close in, shut in, hedge in, pen in, restrain, entangle, enmesh, immobilize. **2** *she tried to pin him down to a plan* CONSTRAIN, make someone commit

glasses with a nose clip instead of earpieces.
– ORIGIN French, 'that pinches the nose'.
pincer ● noun **1** (**pincers**) a tool made of two pieces of metal with blunt concave jaws arranged like the blades of scissors, used for gripping and pulling things. **2** a front claw of a lobster or similar crustacean.
– ORIGIN from Old French *pincier* 'to pinch'.
pincer movement ● noun a movement by two separate bodies of troops converging on the enemy.
pinch ● verb **1** grip (the flesh) tightly between finger and thumb. **2** (of a shoe) hurt (a foot) by being too tight. **3** tighten (the lips or a part of the face). **4** informal, chiefly Brit. steal. **5** informal arrest. **6** live in a frugal way. ● noun **1** an act of pinching. **2** an amount of an ingredient that can be held between fingers and thumb.
– PHRASES **at** (or N. Amer. **in**) **a pinch** if absolutely necessary. **feel the pinch** experience financial hardship.
– ORIGIN Old French *pincier* 'to pinch'.
pinchbeck ● noun an alloy of copper and zinc resembling gold, used in cheap jewellery. ● adjective appearing valuable, but actually cheap or tawdry.
– ORIGIN named after the English watchmaker Christopher *Pinchbeck* (died 1732).
pinch-hit ● verb Baseball & Cricket bat instead of another, typically at a critical point in the game.
– DERIVATIVES **pinch-hitter** noun.
pincushion ● noun **1** a small pad for holding pins. **2** optical distortion in which straight lines along the edge of a screen or lens bulge towards the centre.
pine[1] ● noun (also **pine tree**) an evergreen coniferous tree having clusters of long needle-shaped leaves.
– ORIGIN Latin *pinus*.
pine[2] ● verb **1** suffer a mental and physical decline, especially because of a broken heart. **2** (**pine for**) miss and long for the return of.
– ORIGIN Old English, from Latin *poena* 'punishment'.
pineal gland /pīniəl/ (also **pineal body**) ● noun a small gland situated at the back of the skull within the brain, secreting a hormone-like substance in some mammals.
– ORIGIN from Latin *pinea* 'pine cone' (with reference to its shape).
pineapple ● noun a large juicy tropical fruit consisting of edible yellow flesh surrounded by a tough segmented skin and topped with a tuft of leaves.
– ORIGIN originally denoting a pine cone: from PINE[1] + APPLE.
pine cone ● noun the conical or rounded woody fruit of a pine tree.
pine marten ● noun a tree-dwelling weasel-like mammal with a dark brown coat.
pine nut ● noun the edible seed of various pine trees.
ping ● noun an abrupt high-pitched ringing sound. ● verb make or cause to make such a sound.
– ORIGIN imitative.
ping-pong ● noun informal table tennis.
– ORIGIN imitative of the sound of a bat striking a ball.
pinguid /pinggwid/ ● adjective formal fatty, greasy, or oily.
– ORIGIN from Latin *pinguis* 'fat'.
pinhead ● noun **1** the flattened head of a pin. **2** informal a stupid person.
pinhole ● noun a very small hole.
pinhole camera ● noun a camera with a pinhole aperture and no lens.
pinion[1] /pinyən/ ● noun the outer part of a bird's wing including the flight feathers. ● verb **1** tie or hold the arms or legs of. **2** cut off the pinion of (a bird) to prevent flight.
– ORIGIN Old French *pignon*, from Latin *pinna*, *penna* 'feather'.
pinion[2] /pinyən/ ● noun a small cogwheel or spindle engaging with a large cogwheel.
– ORIGIN French *pignon* (earlier *pignol*), from Latin *pinea* 'pine cone'.
pink[1] ● adjective **1** of a colour intermediate between red and white, as of coral or salmon. **2** informal, often derogatory left-wing. **3** relating to or associated with homosexuals: *the pink economy*. ● noun **1** pink colour, pigment, or material. **2** (**the pink**) informal the best condition or degree. **3** informal, often derogatory a left-wing person.
– DERIVATIVES **pinkish** adjective **pinky** adjective.
– ORIGIN from PINK[2].
pink[2] ● noun a plant with sweet-smelling pink or white flowers and slender grey-green leaves.
– ORIGIN perhaps short for *pink eye*, 'small or half-shut eye'.
pink[3] ● verb cut a scalloped or zigzag edge on.
– ORIGIN originally in the sense 'pierce or nick slightly': compare with Low German *pinken* 'strike, peck'.
pink[4] ● verb Brit. (of a vehicle engine) make rattling sounds as a result of over-rapid combustion in the cylinders.
– ORIGIN imitative.
pink gin ● noun Brit. gin flavoured with angostura bitters.
pinkie ● noun informal the little finger.
– ORIGIN partly from Dutch *pink*.
pinking shears ● plural noun shears with a serrated blade, used to cut a zigzag edge in fabric.
pinko ● noun (pl. **pinkos** or **pinkoes**) informal, derogatory, chiefly N. Amer. a person with left-wing or liberal views.
pin money ● noun a small sum of money for spending on inessentials.
– ORIGIN originally denoting an allowance to a woman from her husband for dress and other personal expenses.
pinna /pinnə/ ● noun (pl. **pinnae** /pinnee/) Anatomy the external part of the ear; the auricle.
– ORIGIN Latin, from *penna* 'feather, wing, fin'.
pinnace /pinniss/ ● noun chiefly historical a small boat forming part of the equipment of a larger vessel.
– ORIGIN French *pinace*, probably from Latin *pinus* 'pine tree'.
pinnacle ● noun **1** a high pointed piece of rock. **2** a small pointed turret built as an ornament on a roof. **3** the most successful point.
– ORIGIN Latin *pinnaculum*, from *pinna* 'wing, point'.
pinnate ● adjective Botany & Zoology having leaflets or other parts

Thesaurus

themselves, pressure, pressurize, tie down, nail down. **3** *it evoked a memory but he couldn't pin it down* DEFINE, put one's finger on, put into words, express, name, specify, identify, pinpoint, place.
pinch ● verb **1** *he pinched my arm* NIP, tweak, squeeze, grasp. **2** *my new shoes pinch my toes* HURT, pain; squeeze, crush, cramp; be uncomfortable. **3** *I scraped and pinched to afford it* ECONOMIZE, scrimp (and save), be sparing, be frugal, cut back, tighten one's belt, retrench, cut one's coat according to one's cloth; *informal* be stingy, be tight. **4** *(informal) he was pinched for drink-driving* ARREST, apprehend, take into custody, detain, seize, catch, take in, haul in; *informal* collar, nab, pick up, run in, nick, bust, nail, do. **5** *(Brit. informal) you pinched his biscuits* STEAL, thieve, take, snatch, pilfer, purloin, loot; *informal* swipe, rob, nab, lift, 'liberate', 'borrow', filch; *Brit. informal* nick, half-inch, whip, knock off, nobble; *N. Amer. informal* heist.
● noun **1** *he gave her arm a pinch* NIP, tweak, squeeze. **2** *a pinch of salt* BIT, touch, dash, spot, trace, soupçon, speck, taste; *informal* smidgen, tad.
– PHRASES **at a pinch** IF NECESSARY, if need be, in an emergency, just possibly, with difficulty; *N. Amer.* in a pinch; *Brit. informal* at a push. **feel the pinch** SUFFER HARDSHIP, be short of money, be poor, be impoverished.
pinched ● adjective *their pinched faces* STRAINED, stressed, fraught, tense, taut; tired, worn, drained, sapped; wan, peaky, pale, grey, blanched; thin, drawn, haggard, gaunt.
– OPPOSITES healthy.
pine ● verb **1** *I am pining away from love* LANGUISH, decline, weaken, waste away, wilt, wither, fade, sicken, droop; brood, mope, moon. **2** *he was pining for his son* YEARN, long, ache, sigh, hunger, languish; miss, mourn, lament, grieve over, shed tears for, bemoan, rue, eat one's heart out over; *informal* itch.
pinion ● verb HOLD DOWN, pin down, restrain, hold fast, immobilize; tie, bind, truss (up), shackle, fetter, hobble, manacle, handcuff; *informal* cuff.
pink ● adjective ROSE, rosy, rosé, pale red, salmon, coral; flushed, blushing.
● noun *(informal) she's in the pink of condition* PRIME, perfection, best, finest, height; utmost, greatest, apex, zenith, acme, bloom.
– PHRASES **in the pink** *(informal)* IN GOOD HEALTH, very healthy, in rude health, very well, hale and hearty; blooming, flourishing, thriving, vigorous, strong, lusty, robust, in fine fettle, (as) fit as a fiddle, in excellent shape.
pinnacle ● noun **1** *pinnacles of rock* PEAK, needle, aiguille, hoodoo, crag, tor; summit, crest, apex, tip; *Geology* inselberg. **2** *the pinnacles of the clock tower* TURRET, minaret, spire, finial, shikara, mirador. **3** *the pinnacle of the sport* HIGHEST LEVEL, peak, height, high

arranged on either side of a stem or axis like the vanes of a feather.
– ORIGIN Latin *pinnatus* 'feathered'.

PIN number • noun see PIN.

pinny • noun (pl. **pinnies**) informal a pinafore.

Pinot /peenō/ • noun any of several varieties of black or white wine grape.
– ORIGIN French, from *pin* 'pine' (because of the shape of the grape cluster).

pinpoint • noun a tiny dot or point. • adjective absolutely precise. • verb find or locate exactly.

pinprick • noun **1** a prick caused by a pin. **2** a very small dot or amount.

pins and needles • plural noun (treated as sing.) a tingling sensation in a limb recovering from numbness.

pinstripe • noun a very narrow stripe in cloth, used especially for formal suits.
– DERIVATIVES **pinstriped** adjective.

pint • noun **1** a unit of liquid or dry capacity equal to one eighth of a gallon, in Britain equal to 0.568 litre and in the US equal to 0.473 litre (for liquid measure) or 0.551 litre (for dry measure). **2** Brit. informal a pint of beer.
– ORIGIN Old French *pinte*, of unknown origin.

pintail • noun a duck with a long pointed tail.

pintle • noun a pin or bolt on which a rudder turns.
– ORIGIN Old English, 'penis'.

pinto /pintō/ • noun (pl. **pintos**) N. Amer. a piebald horse.
– ORIGIN from Spanish, 'mottled'.

pinto bean • noun a medium-sized speckled variety of kidney bean.

pint-sized • adjective informal very small.

pin-tuck • noun a very narrow ornamental tuck in a garment.

pin-up • noun a poster featuring a sexually attractive person.

pinwheel • noun **1** a small cogwheel in which the teeth are formed by pins set into the rim. **2** a small Catherine wheel.

Pinyin /pinyin/ • noun the standard system of romanized spelling for transliterating Chinese.
– ORIGIN Chinese, 'spell-sound'.

pion /pīon/ • noun Physics a meson with a mass around 270 times that of the electron.
– ORIGIN contraction of the earlier name *pi-meson*.

pioneer • noun **1** a person who explores or settles in a new region. **2** a developer of new ideas or techniques. **3** a member of an infantry group preparing roads or terrain for the main body of troops. • verb be a pioneer of.
– ORIGIN French *pionnier* 'foot soldier'.

pious • adjective **1** devoutly religious. **2** making a hypocritical display of virtue. **3** (of a hope) sincere but unlikely to be fulfilled.
– DERIVATIVES **piously** adverb **piousness** noun.
– ORIGIN Latin *pius* 'dutiful'.

pip[1] • noun a small hard seed in a fruit.
– ORIGIN abbreviation of PIPPIN.

pip[2] • noun **(the pips)** Brit. a series of short high-pitched sounds used as a signal on the radio or within the telephone system.
– ORIGIN imitative.

pip[3] • noun **1** Brit. a star indicating rank on the shoulder of an army officer's uniform. **2** any of the spots on a playing card, dice, or domino. **3** an image of an object on a radar screen.
– ORIGIN of unknown origin.

pip[4] • noun a disease of poultry or other birds causing thick mucus in the throat and white scale on the tongue.
– PHRASES **give someone the pip** informal, dated make someone angry or depressed.
– ORIGIN Dutch *pippe*, probably from Latin *pituita* 'slime'.

pip[5] • verb **(pipped, pipping)** Brit. informal **1 (be pipped)** be defeated by a small margin or at the last moment. **2** dated hit or wound with a gun.
– PHRASES **pip at the post** defeat at the last moment.
– ORIGIN from PIP[1] or PIP[3].

pip[6] • verb **(pipped, pipping)** (of a young bird) crack (the shell of the egg) when hatching.
– ORIGIN perhaps imitative.

pipal /peep'l/ • noun variant spelling of PEEPUL.

pipe • noun **1** a tube used to convey water, gas, oil, etc. **2** a device for smoking tobacco, consisting of a narrow tube that opens into a small bowl in which the tobacco is burned, the smoke being drawn through the tube to the mouth. **3** a wind instrument consisting of a single tube with holes along its length that are covered by the fingers to produce different notes. **4** one of the cylindrical tubes by which notes are produced in an organ. **5 (pipes)** bagpipes. **6** a high-pitched cry or song, especially that of a bird. • verb **1** convey through a pipe. **2** transmit (music, a programme, a signal, etc.) by wire or cable. **3** play (a tune) on a pipe. **4** sing or say in a high, shrill voice. **5** decorate with piping.
– PHRASES **pipe down** informal stop talking; be less noisy. **pipe up** say something suddenly. **put that in one's pipe and smoke it** informal one will have to accept a particular fact, even if it is unwelcome.
– ORIGIN from Latin *pipare* 'to peep, chirp'.

pipeclay • noun a fine white clay, used especially for making tobacco pipes or for whitening leather.

pipe cleaner • noun a piece of wire covered with fibre, used to clean a tobacco pipe.

piped music • noun pre-recorded background music played through loudspeakers.

pipe dream • noun an unattainable or fanciful hope or scheme.
– ORIGIN referring to a dream experienced when smoking an opium pipe.

pipeline • noun **1** a long pipe for conveying oil, gas, etc. over a distance. **2** (in surfing) the hollow formed by the breaking of a large wave. **3** Computing a linear sequence of specialized modules used for pipelining. • verb **1** convey by a pipeline. **2** Computing execute using the technique of pipelining.
– PHRASES **in the pipeline** in the process of being developed.

pipelining • noun **1** the laying or use of pipelines. **2** Computing a form of computer organization in which successive steps of an instruction sequence are executed in turn, so that another instruction can be begun before the previous one is finished.

Thesaurus

point, top, apex, zenith, apogee, acme.
– OPPOSITES nadir.

pinpoint • noun *a pinpoint of light* POINT, spot, speck, dot, speckle.
• adjective *pinpoint accuracy* PRECISE, strict, exact, meticulous, scrupulous, punctilious, accurate, careful.
• verb *pinpoint the cause of the trouble* IDENTIFY, determine, distinguish, discover, find, locate, detect, track down, spot, diagnose, recognize, pin down, home in on, put one's finger on.

pioneer • noun **1** *the pioneers of the Wild West* SETTLER, colonist, colonizer, frontiersman/woman, explorer, trailblazer. **2** *a pioneer of motoring* DEVELOPER, innovator, trailblazer, ground-breaker, spearhead; founder, founding father, architect, creator.
• verb *he pioneered the sale of insurance* INTRODUCE, develop, evolve, launch, instigate, initiate, spearhead, institute, establish, found, be the father/mother of, originate, set in motion, create; lay the groundwork, prepare the way, blaze a trail, break new ground.

pious • adjective **1** *a pious family* RELIGIOUS, devout, God-fearing, churchgoing, spiritual, prayerful, holy, godly, saintly, dedicated, reverent, dutiful, righteous. **2** *a pious platitude* SANCTIMONIOUS, hypocritical, insincere, self-righteous, holier-than-thou, pietistic, churchy; *informal* goody-goody; *Brit. informal* pi. **3** *a pious hope* FORLORN, vain, doomed, hopeless, desperate; unlikely, unrealistic.
– OPPOSITES irreligious, sincere.

pip • noun SEED, stone, pit.

pipe • noun **1** *a central-heating pipe* TUBE, conduit, hose, main, duct, line, channel, pipeline, drain; tubing, piping, siphon. **2** *he smokes a pipe* briar (pipe), meerschaum, chibouk; hookah, narghile, hubble-bubble, bong; *Brit.* churchwarden; *Scottish & N. English* cutty. **3** *she was playing a pipe* WHISTLE, penny whistle, flute, recorder, fife; chanter. **4** *regimental pipes and drums* BAGPIPES, uillean pipes; pan pipes.
• verb **1** *the beer is piped into barrels* SIPHON, feed, channel, run, convey. **2** *programmes piped in from London* TRANSMIT, feed, patch. **3** *he heard a tune being piped* PLAY ON A PIPE, tootle, whistle; *poetic/literary* flute. **4** *a curlew piped* CHIRP, cheep, chirrup, twitter, warble, trill, peep, sing, shrill.
– PHRASES **pipe down** *(informal)* BE QUIET, be silent, hush, stop talking, hold one's tongue; *informal* shut up, shut one's mouth, button it, button one's lip, belt up, put a sock in it.

pipe dream • noun FANTASY, false hope, illusion, delusion, daydream, chimera; castle in the air, castle in Spain; *informal* pie in the sky.

pipeline • noun *a gas pipeline* PIPE, conduit, main, line, duct, tube.

pipe organ ● noun an organ using pipes instead of or as well as reeds.

piper ● noun a person who plays a pipe or bagpipes.

pipette /pipet/ ● noun a slender tube used in a laboratory for handling small quantities of liquid, the liquid being drawn into the tube by suction. ● verb pour or draw off using a pipette.
– ORIGIN French, 'little pipe'.

piping ● noun **1** lengths of pipe. **2** lines of icing or cream, used to decorate cakes and desserts. **3** thin cord covered in fabric and inserted along the length of a seam or hem for decoration.
– PHRASES **piping hot** (of food or water) very hot. [ORIGIN with reference to the whistling sound made by very hot liquid or food.]

pipistrelle /pippistrel/ ● noun a small insect-eating bat.
– ORIGIN French, from Latin *vespertilio* 'bat', from *vesper* 'evening'.

pipit /pippit/ ● noun a ground-dwelling songbird of open country, typically having brown streaky plumage.
– ORIGIN probably imitative.

pipkin ● noun a small earthenware pot.
– ORIGIN of unknown origin.

pippin ● noun a red and yellow dessert apple.
– ORIGIN originally denoting a seed of a fruit: from Old French *pepin*.

pipsqueak ● noun informal an insignificant or contemptible person.

piquant /peekont/ ● adjective **1** having a pleasantly sharp taste or appetizing flavour. **2** pleasantly stimulating or exciting.
– DERIVATIVES **piquancy** noun **piquantly** adverb.
– ORIGIN French, 'stinging, pricking'.

pique /peek/ ● noun irritation or resentment arising from hurt pride. ● verb (**piques, piqued, piquing**) **1** stimulate (interest or curiosity). **2** (**be piqued**) feel hurt and irritated or resentful.
– ORIGIN French *piquer* 'prick, irritate'.

piqué /peekay/ ● noun firm fabric woven in a ribbed or raised pattern.
– ORIGIN French, 'backstitched'.

piquet[1] /piket/ ● noun a trick-taking card game for two players.
– ORIGIN French.

piquet[2] ● noun variant spelling of PICKET (in sense 2).

piracy ● noun **1** the practice of attacking and robbing ships at sea. **2** the unauthorized use or reproduction of another's work.

piranha /piraanə/ ● noun a freshwater fish with very sharp teeth that it uses to tear flesh from prey.
– ORIGIN Portuguese, from two Tupi words meaning 'fish' and 'tooth'.

pirate ● noun **1** a person who attacks and robs ships at sea. **2** (before another noun) denoting a text, film, recording, etc. that has been reproduced and used for profit without permission: *pirate videos*. **3** (before another noun) denoting an organization that is broadcasting without official authorization: *a pirate radio station*. ● verb **1** dated rob or plunder (a ship). **2** reproduce (a film, recording, etc.) for profit without permission.
– DERIVATIVES **piratic** adjective.
– ORIGIN Greek *peiratēs*, from *peirein* 'to attempt, attack'.

piripiri /pirripirri/ ● noun (pl. **piripiris**) a New Zealand plant of the rose family, with prickly burrs.
– ORIGIN Maori.

pirogue /pirrōg/ ● noun (in Central America and the Caribbean) a long narrow canoe made from a single tree trunk.
– ORIGIN French, probably from Carib.

pirouette /pirrooet/ ● noun (in ballet) an act of spinning on one foot. ● verb perform a pirouette.
– ORIGIN French, 'spinning top'.

piscatorial /piskətoriəl/ (also **piscatory**) ● adjective formal relating to fishing.
– ORIGIN from Latin *piscator* 'fisherman', from *piscis* 'fish'.

Pisces /pīseez/ ● noun **1** Astronomy a large constellation (the Fish or Fishes), said to represent a pair of fishes tied together by their tails. **2** Astrology the twelfth sign of the zodiac, which the sun enters about 20 February.
– DERIVATIVES **Piscean** /pīseeən/ noun & adjective.
– ORIGIN Latin, plural of *piscis* 'fish'.

pisciculture /pissikulchər/ ● noun the controlled breeding and rearing of fish.
– ORIGIN from Latin *piscis* 'fish'.

piscina /piseenə/ ● noun (pl. **piscinas** or **piscinae** /piseenee/) **1** a stone basin near the altar in some churches, for draining water used in the Mass. **2** (in ancient Roman architecture) a bathing pool.
– ORIGIN Latin, 'fish pond'.

piscine /pissīn/ ● adjective relating to fish.

piscivorous /pisivvərəss/ ● adjective Zoology feeding on fish.
– DERIVATIVES **piscivore** noun.

piss vulgar slang ● verb urinate. ● noun **1** urine. **2** an act of urinating.
– PHRASES **be on the piss** Brit. be engaged in a heavy drinking session. **piss about/around** Brit. mess around. **piss off** go away. **piss someone off** annoy someone. **take the piss** Brit. tease or mock.
– DERIVATIVES **pisser** noun.
– ORIGIN Old French *pisser*.

piss artist ● noun Brit. vulgar slang **1** a drunkard. **2** an incompetent person.

pissed ● adjective vulgar slang **1** Brit. drunk. **2** (**pissed off** or N. Amer. **pissed**) very annoyed.

pissoir /piswaar/ ● noun a public urinal.
– ORIGIN French.

piss-up ● noun Brit. vulgar slang a heavy drinking session.

pissy ● adjective vulgar slang **1** relating to urine. **2** contemptible or inferior.

pistachio /pistaashiō/ ● noun (pl. **pistachios**) a small nut with an edible pale green kernel, the seed of an Asian tree.
– ORIGIN Greek *pistakion*, from Old Persian.

piste /peest/ ● noun a course or run for skiing.
– ORIGIN French, 'racetrack'.

pistil /pistil/ ● noun Botany the female organs of a flower, comprising the stigma, style, and ovary.
– ORIGIN Latin *pistillum* 'pestle'.

pistol ● noun a small firearm designed to be held in one hand.
– ORIGIN French *pistole*, from Czech *pišt'ala*, originally in the sense 'whistle', hence 'a firearm' by the resemblance in shape.

pistol-whip ● verb (**pistol-whips, pistol-whipping, pistol-whipped**) hit or beat with the butt of a pistol.

piston ● noun **1** a disc or short cylinder fitting closely inside a tube in which it moves up and down against a liquid or gas, used to derive or impart motion in an internal-combustion engine or pump. **2** a valve in a brass instrument, depressed to

Thesaurus

– PHRASES **in the pipeline** ON THE WAY, coming, forthcoming, upcoming, imminent, about to happen, near, close, brewing, in the offing, in the wind.

pipsqueak ● noun (*informal*) NOBODY, nonentity, insignificant person, non-person, cipher, small fry; upstart, stripling; *informal* squirt, whippersnapper; *N. Amer. informal* picayune; *archaic, informal* dandiprat.

piquant ● adjective **1** *a piquant sauce* SPICY, tangy, peppery, hot; tasty, flavoursome, flavourful, appetizing, savoury; pungent, sharp, tart, zesty, strong, salty. **2** *a piquant story* INTRIGUING, stimulating, interesting, fascinating, colourful, exciting, lively; spicy, provocative, racy; *informal* juicy.
– OPPOSITES bland, dull.

pique ● noun *a fit of pique* IRRITATION, annoyance, resentment, anger, displeasure, indignation, petulance, ill humour, vexation, exasperation, disgruntlement, discontent; offence, umbrage.
● verb **1** *his curiosity was piqued* STIMULATE, arouse, rouse, provoke, whet, awaken, excite, kindle, stir, galvanize. **2** *she was piqued by his neglect* IRRITATE, annoy, bother, vex, displease, upset, offend, affront, anger, exasperate, infuriate, gall, irk, nettle; *informal* peeve, aggravate, miff, rile, bug, needle, get someone's back up, hack off, get someone's goat; *Brit. informal* nark, give someone the hump; *N. Amer. informal* tick off, tee off.

piracy ● noun **1** *piracy on the high seas* ROBBERY AT SEA, freebooting; *archaic* buccaneering. **2** *software piracy* ILLEGAL COPYING, plagiarism, copyright infringement, bootlegging.

pirate ● noun **1** *pirates boarded the ship* FREEBOOTER, marauder, raider; *historical* privateer; *archaic* buccaneer, corsair. **2** *software pirates* COPYRIGHT INFRINGER, plagiarist, plagiarizer.
● verb *designers may pirate good ideas* REPRODUCE ILLEGALLY, copy illegally, plagiarize, poach, steal, appropriate, bootleg; *informal* crib, lift, rip off; *Brit. informal* nick, pinch.

pirouette ● noun *she did a little pirouette* SPIN, twirl, whirl, turn.
● verb *she pirouetted before the mirror* SPIN ROUND, twirl, whirl, turn round, revolve, pivot.

pistol ● noun REVOLVER, gun, handgun, side arm; automatic, six-

alter the pitch of a note.
– ORIGIN Italian *pistone*, variant of *pestone* 'large pestle'.

pistou /peestōō/ ● noun a paste made from crushed basil, garlic, and cheese, used in Provençal dishes.
– ORIGIN Provençal, related to PESTO.

pit¹ ● noun **1** a large hole in the ground. **2** a mine or excavation for coal, chalk, etc. **3** a hollow or indentation in a surface. **4** a sunken area in a workshop floor allowing access to a car's underside. **5** an area at the side of a track where racing cars are serviced and refuelled. **6** an orchestra pit. **7** a part of the floor of an exchange in which a particular stock or commodity is traded. **8** chiefly historical an enclosure in which animals are made to fight. **9** (**the pit**) literary hell. **10** (**the pits**) informal a very bad place or situation. **11** Brit. informal a person's bed. ● verb (**pitted, pitting**) **1** (**pit against**) set in conflict or competition with. **2** make a hollow or indentation in the surface of.
– PHRASES **the pit of the stomach** the region of the lower abdomen.
– DERIVATIVES **pitted** adjective.
– ORIGIN Old English, from Latin *puteus* 'well, shaft'.

pit² chiefly N. Amer. ● noun the stone of a fruit. ● verb (**pitted, pitting**) remove the pit from (fruit).
– ORIGIN apparently from Dutch; related to PITH.

pita ● noun chiefly N. Amer. variant spelling of PITTA.

pit-a-pat (also **pitapat**) ● adverb with a sound like quick light taps. ● noun a sound of this kind.
– ORIGIN imitative.

pit bull terrier ● noun an American variety of bull terrier, noted for its ferocity.

pitch¹ ● noun **1** the degree of highness or lowness in a sound or tone, as governed by the rate of vibrations producing it. **2** the steepness of a roof. **3** a particular level of intensity. **4** Brit. an area of ground marked out or used for play in an outdoor team game. **5** a form of words used to persuade or influence: *a sales pitch*. **6** Brit. a place where a street vendor or performer stations themselves. **7** a swaying or oscillation of a ship, aircraft, or vehicle around a horizontal axis perpendicular to the direction of motion. ● verb **1** set at a particular musical pitch. **2** throw or fall heavily or roughly. **3** set or aim at a particular level, target, or audience. **4** set up and fix in position. **5** (**pitch in**) informal join in enthusiastically with a task or activity. **6** (**pitch up**) informal arrive. **7** (of a moving ship, aircraft, or vehicle) rock or oscillate around a lateral axis, so that the front moves up and down. **8** (often as adj. **pitched**) (with reference to a roof) slope or cause to slope downwards.
– PHRASES **make a pitch** make an attempt at or bid for something.
– ORIGIN perhaps related to an Old English word meaning 'stigmata'.

pitch² ● noun a sticky resinous black or dark brown substance which hardens on cooling, obtained by distilling tar or turpentine and used for waterproofing.
– ORIGIN Old English.

pitch-black (also **pitch-dark**) ● adjective completely dark.

pitchblende /pichblend/ ● noun a form of the mineral uraninite occurring in brown or black pitch-like masses and containing radium.
– ORIGIN German *Pechblende*, from *Pech* 'pitch' + *Blende*, denoting a zinc ore.

pitched battle ● noun a battle in which the time and place are determined beforehand, rather than a casual or chance skirmish.

pitcher¹ ● noun a large jug.
– ORIGIN Old French *pichier* 'pot', from Latin *picarium*.

pitcher² ● noun Baseball the player who pitches the ball.

pitcher plant ● noun a plant with a deep pitcher-shaped fluid-filled pouch in which insects are trapped and absorbed.

pitchfork ● noun a farm tool with a long handle and two sharp metal prongs, used for lifting hay. ● verb **1** lift with a pitchfork. **2** thrust suddenly into an unexpected and difficult situation.
– ORIGIN from obsolete *pickfork*, influenced by PITCH¹ in the sense 'throw'.

pitch pine ● noun a pine tree with hard, heavy, resinous wood.

pitchy ● adjective (**pitchier, pitchiest**) as dark as pitch.

piteous ● adjective deserving or arousing pity.
– DERIVATIVES **piteously** adverb **piteousness** noun.
– ORIGIN Old French *piteus*, from Latin *pietas* 'dutifulness'.

pitfall ● noun **1** a hidden or unsuspected danger or difficulty. **2** a covered pit for use as a trap.

pith ● noun **1** spongy white tissue lining the rind of citrus fruits. **2** spongy tissue in the stems and branches of many plants. **3** the true nature or essence of something. **4** vigorous and concise expression.
– ORIGIN Old English.

pithead ● noun the top of a mineshaft and the area around it.

pith helmet ● noun a head covering made from the dried pith of the sola or a similar plant, used for protection from the sun.

pithos /pithoss/ ● noun (pl. **pithoi** /pithoy/) Archaeology a large earthenware storage jar.
– ORIGIN Greek.

pithy ● adjective (**pithier, pithiest**) **1** (of a fruit or plant) containing much pith. **2** (of language or style) terse and vigorously expressive.
– DERIVATIVES **pithily** adverb **pithiness** noun.

pitiable ● adjective **1** deserving or arousing pity. **2** contemptibly poor or small.
– DERIVATIVES **pitiably** adverb.

pitiful ● adjective **1** deserving or arousing pity. **2** very small or

Thesaurus

shooter, thirty-eight, derringer; *informal* gat; *N. Amer. informal* piece, shooting iron; *trademark* Colt, Luger.

pit¹ ● noun **1** *a pit in the ground* HOLE, ditch, trench, trough, hollow, excavation, cavity, crater, pothole; shaft, mineshaft. **2** *pit closures* COAL MINE, colliery, quarry. **3** *the pits in her skin* POCKMARK, pock, hollow, indentation, depression, dent, dint, dimple.
● verb **1** *his skin had been pitted by acne* MARK, pockmark, scar, blemish, disfigure. **2** *raindrops pitted the bare earth* MAKE HOLES IN, make hollows in, dent, indent, dint.
– PHRASES **pit someone/something against** SET AGAINST, match against, put in opposition to, put in competition with; compete with, contend with, vie with, wrestle with. **the pits** (*informal*) THE WORST, the lowest of the low; rock-bottom, extremely bad, awful, terrible, dreadful, deplorable; *informal* appalling, lousy, abysmal, dire; *Brit. informal* chronic.

pit² ● noun *cherry pits* STONE, pip, seed.

pitch¹ ● noun **1** *the pitch was unfit for cricket* PLAYING FIELD, field, ground, sports field; stadium, arena; *Brit.* park. **2** *her voice rose in pitch* TONE, timbre, key, modulation, frequency. **3** *the pitch of the roof* GRADIENT, slope, slant, angle, steepness, tilt, incline, inclination. **4** *her anger reached such a pitch that she screamed* LEVEL, intensity, point, degree, height, extent. **5** *a pitch of the ball* THROW, fling, hurl, toss, lob; delivery; *informal* chuck, heave. **6** *his sales pitch* PATTER, talk; *informal* spiel, line. **7** *street traders reserved their pitches* SITE, place, spot, station; *Scottish* stance; *Brit. informal* patch.
● verb **1** *he pitched the note into the fire* THROW, toss, fling, hurl, cast, lob, flip, propel, bowl; *informal* chuck, sling, heave, bung; *N. Amer. informal* peg; *Austral. informal* hoy; *NZ informal* biff; *dated* shy. **2** *he pitched overboard* FALL, tumble, topple, plunge, plummet. **3** *they pitched their tents* PUT UP, set up, erect, raise. **4** *the boat pitched* LURCH, toss (about), plunge, roll, reel, sway, rock, keel, list, wallow, labour.
– PHRASES **make a pitch for** TRY TO OBTAIN, try to acquire, try to get, bid for, make a bid for. **pitch in** HELP (OUT), assist, lend a hand, join in, participate, contribute, do one's bit, chip in, cooperate, collaborate; *Brit. informal* muck in. **pitch into** ATTACK, turn on, lash out at, set upon, assault, fly at, tear into, weigh into, belabour; *informal* lay into, let someone have it, take a pop at; *N. Amer. informal* light into.

pitch² ● noun *cement coated with pitch* bitumen, asphalt, tar.

pitch-black ● adjective BLACK, dark, pitch-dark, inky, jet-black, coal-black, jet, ebony; starless, moonless; *poetic/literary* Stygian.

pitcher ● noun JUG, ewer, jar; *N. Amer.* creamer; *historical* jorum.

piteous ● adjective SAD, pitiful, pitiable, pathetic, heart-rending, heartbreaking, moving, touching; plaintive, poignant, forlorn; poor, wretched, miserable.

pitfall ● noun HAZARD, danger, risk, peril, difficulty, catch, snag, stumbling block, drawback.

pith ● noun **1** *the pith of the argument* ESSENCE, main point, fundamentals, heart, substance, nub, core, quintessence, crux, gist, meat, kernel, marrow, burden; *informal* nitty-gritty. **2** *he writes with pith and exactitude* SUCCINCTNESS, conciseness, concision, pithiness, brevity; cogency, weight, depth, force.

pithy ● adjective SUCCINCT, terse, concise, compact, short (and sweet), brief, condensed, to the point, epigrammatic, crisp, thumbnail; significant, meaningful, expressive, telling; *formal* com-

poor; inadequate.
– DERIVATIVES **pitifully** adverb **pitifulness** noun.

pitiless ● adjective showing no pity; harsh or cruel.
– DERIVATIVES **pitilessly** adverb **pitilessness** noun.

piton /peeton/ ● noun a peg or spike driven into a crack to support a climber or a rope.
– ORIGIN French, 'eye bolt'.

pitot /peetō/ (also **pitot tube**) ● noun a device for measuring the speed of flow of a fluid, consisting of an open-ended right-angled tube pointing in opposition to the flow.
– ORIGIN named after the French physicist Henri *Pitot* (1695–1771).

pit pony ● noun Brit. historical a pony used to haul loads in a coal mine.

pit stop ● noun a brief stop at a pit for servicing and refuelling cars during a motor race.

pitta /pittə/ (also chiefly N. Amer. **pita**) ● noun flat hollow unleavened bread which can be split open to hold a filling.
– ORIGIN Modern Greek, 'cake or pie'.

pittance ● noun a very small or inadequate amount of money.
– ORIGIN originally denoting a small bequest to a religious establishment to provide extra food and wine for a festival: from Old French *pitance*, from Latin *pietas* 'pity'.

pitter-patter ● noun a sound as of quick light steps or taps. ● adverb with this sound.

pituitary gland /pityōōitəri/ (also **pituitary body**) ● noun a pea-sized gland attached to the base of the brain, important in controlling growth and development.
– ORIGIN Latin *pituitarius* 'secreting phlegm'.

pity ● noun (pl. **pities**) **1** a feeling of sorrow and compassion caused by the sufferings of others. **2** a cause for regret or disappointment. ● verb (**pities**, **pitied**) feel pity for.
– PHRASES **for pity's sake** informal used to express impatience or make an urgent appeal. **more's the pity** informal used to express regret.
– ORIGIN Old French *pite* 'compassion', from Latin *pietas* 'piety'.

pivot ● noun **1** the central point, pin, or shaft on which a mechanism turns or oscillates. **2** a person or thing playing a central part in an activity or organization. ● verb (**pivoted**, **pivoting**) **1** turn on or as if on a pivot. **2** (**pivot on**) depend on.
– DERIVATIVES **pivotable** adjective.
– ORIGIN French.

pivotal ● adjective **1** fixed on or as if on a pivot. **2** of crucial or central importance.

pix ● noun variant spelling of PYX.

pixel ● noun Electronics a minute area of illumination on a display screen, one of many from which an image is composed.
– ORIGIN abbreviation of *picture element*.

pixelate /piksəlayt/ (also **pixellate** or **pixilate**) ● verb **1** divide (an image) into pixels, for display or for storage in a digital format. **2** display (a person's image) as a small number of large pixels in order to disguise their identity.
– DERIVATIVES **pixelation** noun.

pixie (also **pixy**) ● noun (pl. **pixies**) a supernatural being in folklore, typically portrayed as a tiny man with pointed ears and a pointed hat.
– DERIVATIVES **pixieish** adjective.
– ORIGIN of unknown origin.

pixilate ● verb variant spelling of PIXELATE.

pixilated (also **pixillated**) ● adjective **1** crazy; confused. **2** informal drunk.
– DERIVATIVES **pixilation** noun.
– ORIGIN from *pixie-led*, 'led astray by pixies'.

pizza ● noun a dish of Italian origin, consisting of a flat, round base of dough baked with a topping of tomatoes, cheese, and other ingredients.
– ORIGIN Italian, 'pie'.

pizzazz (also **pizazz** or **pzazz**) ● noun informal a combination of vitality and style.
– ORIGIN said to have been invented by Diana Vreeland, fashion editor of *Harper's Bazaar* in the 1930s.

pizzeria /peetsəreeə/ ● noun a place where pizzas are sold.
– ORIGIN Italian.

pizzicato /pitsikaatō/ Music ● adverb & adjective plucking the strings of a violin or other stringed instrument with one's finger. ● noun (pl. **pizzicatos** or **pizzicati** /pitsikaati/) this technique of playing.
– ORIGIN Italian, 'pinched'.

pizzle ● noun dialect or archaic the penis of an animal, especially a bull.
– ORIGIN Low German *pēsel* or Flemish *pezel*.

pl. ● abbreviation **1** (also **Pl.**) place. **2** plural.

placable /plakkəb'l/ ● adjective archaic easily calmed or placated.
– ORIGIN Latin *placabilis*, from *placare* 'appease'.

placard /plakkaard/ ● noun a sign for public display, either posted on a wall or carried during a demonstration. ● verb /also plakaard/ cover with placards.
– ORIGIN Old French *placquart*, from *plaquier* 'to plaster, lay flat'.

placate /pləkayt/ ● verb make less angry or hostile: calm or appease.
– DERIVATIVES **placatory** adjective.
– ORIGIN Latin *placare*.

place ● noun **1** a particular position or location. **2** a portion of space occupied by or set aside for someone or something. **3** a vacancy or available position. **4** a position in a sequence or hierarchy. **5** the position of a figure in a series indicated in decimal notation. **6** (in place names) a square or short street. **7** informal a person's home. ● verb **1** put in a particular position or situation. **2** find an appropriate place or role for. **3** allocate or award a specified position in a sequence or hierarchy. **4** (**be placed**) Brit. achieve a specified position in a race. **5** remember the relevant background or circumstances of. **6** arrange for the implementation of (an order, bet, etc.). **7** Rugby & American Football score (a goal) by a place kick.
– PHRASES **go places** informal **1** travel. **2** be increasingly success-

Thesaurus

pendious.
– OPPOSITES verbose.

pitiful ● adjective **1** *a child in a pitiful state* DISTRESSING, sad, piteous, pitiable, pathetic, heart-rending, heartbreaking, moving, touching, tear-jerking; plaintive, poignant, forlorn; poor, sorry, wretched, abject, miserable. **2** *a pitiful £50 a month* PALTRY, miserable, meagre, insufficient, trifling, negligible, pitiable, derisory; *informal* pathetic, measly, piddling, mingy; *Brit. informal* poxy. **3** *his performance was pitiful* DREADFUL, awful, terrible, lamentable, hopeless, poor, bad, feeble, pitiable, woeful, inadequate, below par, deplorable, laughable; *informal* pathetic, useless, appalling, lousy, abysmal, dire.

pitiless ● adjective MERCILESS, unmerciful, unpitying, ruthless, cruel, heartless, remorseless, hard-hearted, cold-hearted, harsh, callous, severe, unsparing, unforgiving, unfeeling, uncaring, unsympathetic, uncharitable, brutal, inhuman, inhumane, barbaric, sadistic.
– OPPOSITES merciful.

pittance ● noun A TINY AMOUNT, next to nothing, very little; *informal* peanuts, chicken feed, slave wages; *N. Amer. informal* chump change.

pitted ● adjective **1** *his skin was pitted* POCKMARKED, pocked, scarred, marked, blemished. **2** *the pitted lane* POTHOLED, rutted, rutty, holey, bumpy, rough, uneven.
– OPPOSITES smooth.

pity ● noun **1** *a voice full of pity* COMPASSION, commiseration, condolence, sympathy, fellow feeling, understanding; sorrow, regret, sadness. **2** *it's a pity he never had children* SHAME, sad thing, bad luck, misfortune; *informal* crime, bummer, sin.
– OPPOSITES indifference, cruelty.
● verb *they pitied me* FEEL SORRY FOR, feel for, sympathize with, empathize with, commiserate with, take pity on, be moved by, condole with, grieve for.
– PHRASES **take pity on** FEEL SORRY FOR, relent, be compassionate towards, be sympathetic towards, have mercy on, help (out), put someone out of their misery.

pivot ● noun **1** *the machine turns on a pivot* FULCRUM, axis, axle, swivel; pin, shaft, hub, spindle, hinge, kingpin, gudgeon. **2** *the pivot of government policy* CENTRE, focus, hub, heart, nucleus, crux, keystone, cornerstone, linchpin, kingpin.
● verb **1** *the panel pivots inwards* ROTATE, turn, swivel, revolve, spin. **2** *it all pivoted on his response* DEPEND, hinge, turn, centre, hang, rely, rest; revolve around.

pivotal ● adjective CENTRAL, crucial, vital, critical, focal, essential, key, decisive.

pixie ● noun ELF, fairy, sprite, imp, brownie, puck, leprechaun; *poetic/literary* faerie, fay.

placard ● noun NOTICE, poster, sign, bill, advertisement; banner; *informal* ad; *Brit. informal* advert.

placate ● verb PACIFY, calm, appease, mollify, soothe, win over, conciliate, propitiate, make peace with, humour; *Austral./NZ* square

ful. **in one's place** in one's appropriate (but inferior) position or status. **in place 1** working or ready to work. **2** N. Amer. on the spot; not travelling any distance. **in place of** instead of. **out of place 1** not in the proper position. **2** in a setting where one is or feels incongruous. **put someone in his** (or **her**) **place** deflate or humiliate someone regarded as being arrogant. **take place** occur. **take one's place** take up one's usual or recognized position. **take the place of** replace.
– ORIGIN Old French, from Greek *plateia hodos* 'broad way'.

placebo /pləseebō/ ● noun (pl. **placebos**) **1** a medicine prescribed for the psychological benefit to the patient rather than for any physiological effect. **2** a substance that has no therapeutic effect, used as a control in testing new drugs.
– ORIGIN Latin, 'I shall be acceptable or pleasing'.

place kick American Football, Rugby, & Soccer ● noun a kick made after the ball is first placed on the ground. ● verb (**place-kick**) take a place kick.
– DERIVATIVES **place-kicker** noun.

placeman ● noun Brit. derogatory a person appointed to a position chiefly for personal profit and as a reward for political support.

placement ● noun **1** the action of placing or the fact of being placed. **2** a temporary posting of someone in a workplace, especially to gain work experience.

place name ● noun the name of a geographical location, such as a town, lake, or mountain.

placenta /pləsentə/ ● noun (pl. **placentae** /pləsentee/ or **placentas**) a flattened circular organ in the uterus of a pregnant mammal, nourishing and maintaining the fetus through the umbilical cord.
– DERIVATIVES **placental** adjective.
– ORIGIN Latin, from Greek *plakous* 'flat cake'.

placenta praevia (US **placenta previa**) ● noun Medicine a condition in which the placenta partially or wholly blocks the neck of the uterus, so interfering with normal delivery of a baby.
– ORIGIN from Latin *praevia* 'going before'.

placer ● noun a deposit of sand or gravel in the bed of a river or lake, containing particles of valuable minerals.
– ORIGIN Latin American Spanish, 'deposit, shoal'.

placid ● adjective not easily upset or excited; calm.
– DERIVATIVES **placidity** noun **placidly** adverb.
– ORIGIN Latin *placidus*, from *placere* 'to please'.

placing ● noun **1** the action of placing or the fact of being placed. **2** a ranking given to a competitor.

placket ● noun **1** an opening in a garment, covering fastenings or for access to a pocket. **2** a flap of material used to strengthen such an opening.
– ORIGIN from PLACARD in an obsolete sense 'garment worn under an open coat'.

plagiarize /playjərīz/ (also **plagiarise**) ● verb take (the work or idea of someone else) and pass it off as one's own.
– DERIVATIVES **plagiarism** noun **plagiarist** noun **plagiarizer** noun.
– ORIGIN from Latin *plagiarius* 'kidnapper', from Greek *plagion* 'a kidnapping'.

plague ● noun **1** a contagious disease spread by bacteria and characterized by fever and delirium. **2** an unusually and unpleasantly large quantity of insects or animals. ● verb (**plagues**, **plagued**, **plaguing**) **1** cause continual trouble or distress to. **2** pester or harass continually.
– ORIGIN Latin *plaga* 'stroke, wound'.

plaice ● noun (pl. same) a brown flatfish with orange spots, commercially important as a food fish.
– ORIGIN Old French *plaiz*, from Greek *platus* 'broad'.

plaid /plad/ ● noun fabric woven in a chequered or tartan design.
– ORIGIN Scottish Gaelic *plaide* 'blanket'.

plain ● adjective **1** not decorated or elaborate; simple or ordinary. **2** without a pattern; in only one colour. **3** unmarked; without identification. **4** easy to perceive or understand; clear. **5** (of language) clearly expressed; direct. **6** (of a woman or girl) not beautiful or attractive. **7** sheer; simple: *plain stupidity.* **8** (of a knitting stitch) made by putting the needle through the front of the stitch from left to right. Compare with PURL[1]. ● adverb informal **1** simply: *that's plain stupid.* **2** clearly; unequivocally. ● noun a large area of flat land with few trees.
– DERIVATIVES **plainly** adverb **plainness** noun.
– ORIGIN Latin *planus* 'flat, plain'.

plain chocolate ● noun Brit. dark, slightly bitter, chocolate

Thesaurus

someone off.
– OPPOSITES provoke.

place ● noun **1** *an ideal place for dinner* LOCATION, site, spot, setting, position, situation, area, region, locale; venue; *technical* locus. **2** *foreign places* COUNTRY, state, area, region, town, city; locality, district; *poetic/literary* clime. **3** *a place of her own* HOME, house, flat, apartment; accommodation, property, pied-à-terre; rooms, quarters; *informal* pad, digs; *Brit. informal* gaff; *formal* residence, abode, dwelling (place), domicile, habitation. **4** *if I were in your place, I'd agree* SITUATION, position, circumstances; *informal* shoes. **5** *a place was reserved for her* SEAT, chair, space. **6** *I offered him a place in the company* JOB, position, post, appointment, situation, office; employment. **7** *I know my place* STATUS, position, standing, rank, niche; *dated* estate, station. **8** *it was not her place to sort it out* RESPONSIBILITY, duty, job, task, role, function, concern, affair, charge; right, privilege, prerogative.
● verb **1** *books were placed on the table* PUT (DOWN), set (down), lay, deposit, position, plant, rest, stand, station, situate, leave; *informal* stick, dump, bung, park, plonk, pop; *N. Amer. informal* plunk. **2** *the trust you placed in me* PUT, lay, set, invest. **3** *a survey placed the company sixth* RANK, order, grade, class, classify, categorize; put, set, assign. **4** *Joe couldn't quite place her* IDENTIFY, recognize, remember, put a name to, pin down; locate, pinpoint. **5** *we were placed with foster parents* ACCOMMODATE, house; allocate, assign, appoint.
– PHRASES **in place 1** *the veil was held in place by pearls* IN POSITION, in situ. **2** *the plans are in place* READY, set up, all set, established, arranged, in order. **in place of** INSTEAD OF, rather than, as a substitute for, as a replacement for, in exchange for, in lieu of; in someone's stead. **out of place 1** *she never had a hair out of place* OUT OF POSITION, out of order, in disarray, disarranged, in a mess, messy, topsy-turvy, muddled. **2** *he said something out of place* INAPPROPRIATE, unsuitable, unseemly, improper, untoward, out of keeping, unbecoming, wrong. **3** *she seemed out of place in a launderette* INCONGRUOUS, out of one's element, like a fish out of water; uncomfortable, uneasy. **put someone in their place** HUMILIATE, take down a peg or two, deflate, crush, squash, humble; *informal* cut down to size, settle someone's hash; *N. Amer. informal* make someone eat crow. **take place** HAPPEN, occur, come about, transpire, crop up, materialize, arise; *N. Amer. informal* go down; *poetic/literary* come to pass, befall, betide. **take the place of** REPLACE, stand in for, substitute for, act for, fill in for, cover for, relieve.

placement ● noun **1** *the placement of the chairs* POSITIONING, placing, arrangement, position, deployment, location, disposition. **2** *teaching placements* JOB, post, assignment, posting, position, appointment, engagement.

placid ● adjective **1** *she's normally very placid* EVEN-TEMPERED, calm, tranquil, equable, equanimous, unexcitable, serene, mild, {cool, calm, and collected}, composed, self-possessed, poised, easy-going, level-headed, steady, unruffled, unperturbed, phlegmatic; *informal* unflappable. **2** *a placid village* QUIET, calm, tranquil, still, peaceful, undisturbed, restful, sleepy.
– OPPOSITES excitable, bustling.

plagiarism ● noun COPYING, infringement of copyright, piracy, theft, stealing; *informal* cribbing.

plagiarize ● verb COPY, infringe the copyright of, pirate, steal, poach, appropriate; *informal* rip off, crib, 'borrow'; *Brit. informal* pinch, nick.

plague ● noun **1** *they died of the plague* BUBONIC PLAGUE, pneumonic plague, the Black Death; disease, sickness, epidemic; *dated* contagion; *archaic* pestilence. **2** *a plague of cat fleas* INFESTATION, epidemic, invasion, swarm, multitude, host. **3** *theft is the plague of restaurants* BANE, curse, scourge, affliction, blight.
● verb **1** *he was plagued by poor health* AFFLICT, bedevil, torment, trouble, beset, dog, curse. **2** *he plagued her with questions* PESTER, harass, badger, bother, torment, persecute, bedevil, harry, hound, trouble, irritate, nag, annoy, vex, molest; *informal* hassle, bug, aggravate; *N. English informal* mither; *N. Amer. informal* devil.

plain ● adjective **1** *it was plain that something was wrong* OBVIOUS, (crystal) clear, evident, apparent, manifest, patent; discernible, perceptible, noticeable, recognizable, unmistakable, transparent; pronounced, marked, striking, conspicuous, self-evident, indisputable; as plain as a pikestaff, writ large; *informal* standing/sticking out like a sore thumb, standing/sticking out a mile. **2** *plain English* INTELLIGIBLE, comprehensible, understandable,

without added milk.

plain clothes ● plural noun ordinary clothes rather than uniform, especially when worn by police officers.

plain flour ● noun Brit. flour that does not contain a raising agent.

plain sailing ● noun smooth and easy progress.
– ORIGIN probably from *plane sailing*, denoting the practice of determining a ship's position on the theory that it is moving on a plane.

plainsong (also **plainchant**) ● noun unaccompanied medieval church music sung in free rhythm corresponding to the accentuation of the words.

plaint ● noun **1** Law, Brit. an accusation; a charge. **2** chiefly literary a complaint or lamentation.
– ORIGIN Old French *plainte*, from *plaindre* 'complain'.

plaintiff ● noun Law a person who brings a case against another in a court of law. Compare with DEFENDANT.
– ORIGIN Old French *plaintif* 'plaintive'.

plaintive ● adjective sounding sad and mournful.
– DERIVATIVES **plaintively** adverb **plaintiveness** noun.
– ORIGIN Old French, from *plaindre* 'complain'.

plain weave ● noun a style of weave in which the weft alternates over and under the warp.

plait ● noun Brit. a single length of hair, rope, or other material made up of three or more interlaced strands. ● verb form into a plait or plaits.
– ORIGIN Old French *pleit* 'a fold', from Latin *plicare* 'to fold'.

plan ● noun **1** a detailed proposal for doing or achieving something. **2** an intention or decision about what one is going to do. **3** a scheme for the regular payment of contributions towards a pension, insurance policy, etc. **4** a map or diagram. **5** a scale drawing of a horizontal section of a building. ● verb (**planned, planning**) **1** decide on and arrange in advance. **2** (**plan for**) make preparations for. **3** make a plan of (something to be made or built).
– DERIVATIVES **planner** noun.
– ORIGIN French, from earlier *plant* 'ground plan, plane surface'.

planar /playnər/ ● adjective Mathematics relating to or in the form of a plane.

planchette /plaanshet/ ● noun a small board supported on castors and fitted with a vertical pencil, used for automatic writing and in seances.
– ORIGIN French, 'small plank'.

plane[1] ● noun **1** a flat surface on which a straight line joining any two points would wholly lie. **2** a level of existence or thought. ● adjective **1** completely level or flat. **2** relating to two-dimensional surfaces or magnitudes. ● verb **1** soar without moving the wings; glide. **2** (of a boat, surfboard, etc.) skim over the surface of water.
– ORIGIN Latin *planum* 'flat surface', from *planus* 'plain'.

plane[2] ● noun an aeroplane.

plane[3] (also **planer**) ● noun a tool consisting of a block with a projecting steel blade, used to smooth a wooden surface by paring shavings from it. ● verb smooth with a plane.
– ORIGIN Latin *plana*, from *planare* 'make level'.

plane[4] (also **plane tree**) ● noun a tall spreading tree with maple-like leaves and a peeling bark.
– ORIGIN Old French, from Greek *platanos*, from *platus* 'broad'.

planet ● noun **1** a celestial body moving in an elliptical orbit round a star. **2** (**the planet**) the earth. **3** chiefly Astrology & historical a celestial body distinguished from the fixed stars by having an apparent motion of its own (including the moon and sun).
– DERIVATIVES **planetary** adjective **planetology** noun.
– ORIGIN Greek *planētēs* 'wanderer, planet', from *planan* 'wander'.

planetarium /plannitairiəm/ ● noun (pl. **planetariums** or **planetaria** /plannitairiə/) a building in which images of stars, planets, and constellations are projected onto a domed ceiling.
– ORIGIN Latin, from *planetarius* 'relating to the planets'.

planetary nebula ● noun Astronomy a ring-shaped nebula formed by an expanding shell of gas round an ageing star.

planetesimal /plannitessim'l/ Astronomy ● noun a minute planet; a body which could come together with many others under gravitation to form a planet. ● adjective relating to such bodies.
– ORIGIN from PLANET, on the pattern of *infinitesimal*.

planetoid ● noun another term for ASTEROID.

plangent /planjənt/ ● adjective chiefly literary (of a sound) loud and resonant, with a mournful tone.
– DERIVATIVES **plangency** noun **plangently** adverb.
– ORIGIN from Latin *plangere* 'to lament'.

planimeter /plənimmitər/ ● noun an instrument for measuring the area of a plane figure.
– DERIVATIVES **planimetric** adjective **planimetry** noun.

planisphere /plannisfeer/ ● noun a map formed by the projection of a sphere, especially a star map that can be adjusted to show the constellations at a specific time and place.
– DERIVATIVES **planispheric** adjective.
– ORIGIN from Latin *planus* 'level' + *sphaera* 'sphere'.

plank ● noun **1** a long, flat piece of timber, used in flooring. **2** a fundamental part of a political or other programme.
– PHRASES **walk the plank** (formerly) be forced by pirates to walk blindfold along a plank over the side of a ship to one's death in the sea.
– DERIVATIVES **planked** adjective.
– ORIGIN Latin *planca* 'board', from *plancus* 'flat-footed'.

planking ● noun planks collectively, especially when used for flooring or as part of a boat.

plankton ● noun small and microscopic organisms living in the sea or fresh water, consisting chiefly of diatoms, protozoans, and small crustaceans.
– DERIVATIVES **planktic** adjective **planktonic** adjective.
– ORIGIN from Greek *planktos* 'wandering', from *plazein* 'wander'.

planned economy ● noun an economy in which production, investment, prices, and incomes are determined centrally by the government.

p

Thesaurus

clear, coherent, uncomplicated, lucid, unambiguous, simple, straightforward, user-friendly; *formal* perspicuous. **3** *plain speaking* CANDID, frank, outspoken, forthright, direct, honest, truthful, blunt, bald, explicit, unequivocal; *informal* upfront. **4** *a plain dress* SIMPLE, ordinary, unadorned, unembellished, unornamented, unostentatious, unfussy, homely, basic, modest, unsophisticated, without frills; restrained, muted; everyday, workaday. **5** *a plain girl* UNATTRACTIVE, unprepossessing, ugly, ill-favoured, unlovely, ordinary; *N. Amer.* homely; *informal* not much to look at; *Brit. informal* no oil painting. **6** *it was plain bad luck* SHEER, pure, downright, out-and-out, unmitigated.
– OPPOSITES obscure, fancy, attractive, pretentious.
● adverb *(informal) this is just plain stupid* DOWNRIGHT, utterly, absolutely, completely, totally, really, thoroughly, positively, simply, unquestionably, undeniably; *informal* plumb.
● noun *the plains of North America* GRASSLAND, flatland, lowland, pasture, meadowland, prairie, savannah, steppe; tableland, tundra, pampas, veld.

plain-spoken ● adjective CANDID, frank, outspoken, forthright, direct, honest, truthful, open, blunt, straightforward, explicit, unequivocal, unambiguous, not afraid to call a spade a spade; *informal* upfront.
– OPPOSITES evasive.

plaintive ● adjective MOURNFUL, sad, wistful, doleful, pathetic, pitiful, piteous, melancholy, sorrowful, unhappy, wretched, woeful, forlorn, woebegone; *poetic/literary* dolorous.

plan ● noun **1** *a plan for raising money* SCHEME, idea, proposal, proposition, suggestion; project, programme, system, method, procedure, strategy, stratagem, formula, recipe; way, means, measure, tactic. **2** *her plan was to win a medal* INTENTION, aim, idea, intent, objective, object, goal, target, ambition. **3** *plans for the clubhouse* BLUEPRINT, drawing, diagram, sketch, layout; illustration, representation; *N. Amer.* plat.
● verb **1** *plan your route in advance* ORGANIZE, arrange, work out, design, outline, map out, prepare, schedule, formulate, frame, develop, devise, concoct; plot, scheme, hatch, brew; *N. Amer.* slate. **2** *he plans to buy a house* INTEND, aim, propose, mean, hope, want, wish, desire, envisage; *formal* purpose. **3** *I'm planning a new garden* DESIGN, draw up, sketch out, map out; *N. Amer.* plat.

plane[1] ● noun **1** *a horizontal plane* FLAT SURFACE, level surface; the flat, horizontal. **2** *a higher plane of achievement* LEVEL, degree, standard, stratum; position, rung, echelon.
● adjective *a plane surface* FLAT, level, horizontal, even; smooth, regular, uniform; *technical* planar.
● verb **1** *seagulls planed overhead* SOAR, glide, float, drift, wheel. **2** *boats planed across the water* SKIM, glide.

plane[2] ● noun *the plane took off* AIRCRAFT, airliner, (jumbo) jet, jetliner; flying machine; *Brit.* aeroplane; *N. Amer.* airplane, ship.

planet ● noun CELESTIAL BODY, heavenly body, satellite, moon, earth, asteroid, planetoid; *poetic/literary* orb.

planning • noun **1** the process of making plans for something. **2** the control of urban development by a local government authority.

planning permission • noun Brit. formal permission from a local authority for the erection or alteration of buildings.

plant • noun **1** a living organism (such as a tree, grass, or fern) that absorbs water and inorganic substances through its roots and makes nutrients in its leaves by photosynthesis. **2** a place where an industrial or manufacturing process takes place. **3** machinery used in an industrial or manufacturing process. **4** a person placed in a group as a spy or informer. **5** a thing put among someone's belongings to incriminate or discredit them. • verb **1** place (a seed, bulb, or plant) in the ground so that it can grow. **2** (**plant out**) transfer (a seedling or young plant) from a protected container to the open ground. **3** place or fix in a specified position. **4** secretly place (a bomb). **5** put or hide (something) among someone's belongings as a plant. **6** send (someone) to join a group to act as a spy or informer. **7** establish (an idea) in someone's mind.
– DERIVATIVES **plantlet** noun.
– ORIGIN from Latin *planta* 'sprout, cutting' and *plantare* 'plant, fix in place'.

Plantagenet /plantajinit/ • noun a member of the English royal dynasty which ruled from 1154 until 1485.
– ORIGIN from Latin *planta genista* 'sprig of broom', said to be worn as a crest by and given as a nickname to Geoffrey, count of Anjou, the father of Henry II.

plantain[1] /plantin/ • noun a low-growing plant, typically with a rosette of leaves and a slender green flower spike.
– ORIGIN Old French, from Latin *planta* 'sole of the foot' (because of its broad leaves that grow along the ground).

plantain[2] /plantin/ • noun a type of banana containing high levels of starch and little sugar, which is harvested green and widely used as a cooked vegetable in the tropics.
– ORIGIN probably by assimilation of a South American word to the Spanish *plá(n)tano* 'plane tree'.

plantar /plantər/ • adjective Anatomy relating to the sole of the foot.
– ORIGIN from Latin *planta* 'sole'.

plantation • noun **1** a large estate on which crops such as coffee, sugar, and tobacco are grown. **2** an area in which trees have been planted.

planter • noun **1** a manager or owner of a plantation. **2** a decorative container in which plants are grown.

plantigrade /plantigrayd/ • adjective walking on the soles of the feet, like a human or a bear. Compare with DIGITIGRADE.
– ORIGIN Latin *plantigradus*, from *planta* 'sole' + *-gradus* '-walking'.

plaque /plak, plaak/ • noun **1** an ornamental tablet fixed to a wall in commemoration of a person or event. **2** a sticky deposit on teeth in which bacteria proliferate. **3** Medicine a small raised patch on or within the body, caused by local damage or deposition of material. **4** a flat counter used in gambling.
– ORIGIN French, from Dutch *plakken* 'to stick'.

plash • noun **1** a splashing sound. **2** a pool or puddle. • verb make or hit with a splash.
– DERIVATIVES **plashy** adjective.
– ORIGIN probably imitative.

plasma /plazmə/ • noun **1** the colourless fluid part of blood, lymph, or milk, in which corpuscles or fat globules are suspended. **2** Physics a gas of positive ions and free electrons with little or no overall electric charge. **3** a bright green translucent ornamental variety of quartz. **4** (also **plasm** /plazz'm/) cytoplasm or protoplasm.
– DERIVATIVES **plasmatic** adjective **plasmic** adjective.
– ORIGIN Greek, from *plassein* 'to shape'.

plaster • noun **1** a soft mixture of lime with sand or cement and water for spreading on walls and ceilings to form a smooth hard surface when dried. **2** (also **plaster of Paris**) a hard white substance made by adding water to powdered gypsum, used for setting broken bones and making sculptures and casts. **3** (also **sticking plaster**) an adhesive strip of material for covering cuts and wounds. • verb **1** cover with plaster; apply plaster to. **2** coat thickly; daub. **3** make (hair) lie flat by applying liquid to it.
– DERIVATIVES **plasterer** noun.
– ORIGIN Latin *plastrum*, from Greek *emplastron* 'daub, salve'; sense 2 of the noun derives from the fact that the gypsum originally came from Paris.

plasterboard • noun board made of plaster set between two sheets of paper, used to line interior walls and ceilings.

plastered • adjective informal very drunk.

plasterwork • noun plaster as part of the interior of a building, especially when formed into decorative shapes.

plastic • noun **1** a synthetic material made from organic polymers, that can be moulded into shape while soft and then set into a rigid or slightly elastic form. **2** informal credit cards or other plastic cards that can be used as money. • adjective **1** made of plastic. **2** easily shaped or moulded. **3** relating to moulding or modelling in three dimensions. **4** artificial; unnatural.
– DERIVATIVES **plastically** adverb **plasticity** noun.
– ORIGIN Greek *plastikos*, from *plassein* 'to mould'.

plastic bullet • noun a bullet made of PVC or another plastic, used for riot control.

plastic explosive • noun a putty-like explosive capable of being moulded by hand.

plasticine (also **Plasticine**) • noun trademark a soft modelling material.

plasticize • verb **1** make plastic or mouldable. **2** treat or coat with plastic.
– DERIVATIVES **plasticization** noun.

plasticizer • noun a solvent added to a synthetic resin to promote plasticity and to reduce brittleness.

plasticky • adjective **1** resembling plastic. **2** artificial or of inferior quality.

plastic surgery • noun the reconstruction or repair of parts of the body by the transfer of tissue, either in the treatment of injury or for cosmetic reasons.

plastique /plasteek/ • noun plastic explosive.
– ORIGIN French, 'plastic'.

plastron /plastrən/ • noun **1** a large pad worn by a fencer to protect the chest. **2** an ornamental front part of a woman's bodice, fashionable in the late 19th century. **3** a man's starched shirt front. **4** the part of a tortoise's or turtle's shell forming the underside.
– ORIGIN French, from Italian *piastra* 'breastplate', from Latin *emplastrum* 'a plaster'.

plat du jour /pla doo zhoor/ • noun (pl. **plats du jour** pronunc. same) a dish specially prepared by a restaurant on a particular day, in addition to the usual menu.
– ORIGIN French, 'dish of the day'.

p

Thesaurus

plangent • adjective (poetic/literary) MELANCHOLY, mournful, plaintive; sonorous, resonant, loud.

plank • noun BOARD, floorboard, timber, stave.

planning • noun PREPARATION(S), organization, arrangement, design; forethought, groundwork.

plant • noun **1** *garden plants* flower, vegetable, herb, shrub, weed; (**plants**) vegetation, greenery, flora, herbage, verdure. **2** *a CIA plant* SPY, informant, informer, (secret) agent, mole, infiltrator, operative; N. Amer. informal spook. **3** *the plant commenced production* FACTORY, works, foundry, mill, workshop, yard; archaic manufactory.
– RELATED TERMS phyto-, -phyte.
• verb **1** *plant the seeds this autumn* sow, scatter, seed; bed out, transplant. **2** *he planted his feet on the ground* PLACE, put, set, position, situate, settle; informal plonk. **3** *she planted the idea in his mind* INSTIL, implant, impress, imprint, put, place, introduce, fix, establish, lodge. **4** *letters were planted to embarrass them* HIDE, conceal, secrete.

plaque • noun PLATE, tablet, panel, sign, plaquette, cartouche; Brit. brass.

plaster • noun **1** *the plaster covering the bricks* PLASTERWORK, stucco, pargeting; trademark Artex. **2** *a statuette made of plaster* PLASTER OF PARIS, gypsum. **3** *waterproof plasters* STICKING PLASTER, (adhesive) dressing, bandage; trademark Elastoplast, Band-Aid.
• verb **1** *bread plastered with butter* COVER THICKLY, smother, spread, smear, cake, coat. **2** *his hair was plastered down with sweat* FLATTEN (DOWN), smooth down, slick down.

plastic • adjective **1** *at high temperatures the rocks become plastic* MALLEABLE, mouldable, pliable, pliant, ductile, flexible, soft, workable, bendable; informal bendy. **2** *the plastic minds of children* IMPRESSIONABLE, malleable, receptive, pliable, pliant, flexible; compliant, tractable, biddable, persuadable, susceptible, manipulable.

plate ● noun **1** a flat dish from which food is eaten or served. **2** bowls, cups, and other utensils made of gold or silver. **3** a thin, flat piece of metal used to join or strengthen or forming part of a machine. **4** a small, flat piece of metal bearing a name or inscription and fixed to a wall or door. **5** a sheet of metal or other material bearing an image of type or illustrations, from which multiple copies are printed. **6** a printed photograph or illustration in a book. **7** Botany & Zoology a thin, flat organic structure or formation. **8** Geology each of the several rigid pieces of the earth's lithosphere which together make up the earth's surface. **9** a horizontal timber laid along the top of a wall to support the ends of joists or rafters. ● verb cover (a metal object) with a thin coating of a different metal.
– PHRASES **be handed something on a plate** informal acquire something with little or no effort. **on one's plate** chiefly Brit. occupying one's time or energy.
– DERIVATIVES **plater** noun.
– ORIGIN from Old French *plat* 'platter' or *plate* 'sheet of metal', from Greek *platus* 'flat'.

plate armour ● noun protective armour of metal plates, as worn by knights in the Middle Ages.

plateau /plattō/ ● noun (pl. **plateaux** /plattōz/ or **plateaus**) **1** an area of fairly level high ground. **2** a state or period of little or no change following a period of activity or progress. ● verb (**plateaus, plateaued, plateauing**) reach a plateau.
– ORIGIN French, from *plat* 'level'.

plate glass ● noun thick fine-quality glass used for shop windows and doors, originally cast in plates.

platelet ● noun Physiology a small colourless disc-shaped cell fragment without a nucleus, found in large numbers in blood and involved in clotting.

platen /platt'n/ ● noun **1** a plate in a small letterpress printing press which presses the paper against the type. **2** a cylindrical roller in a typewriter against which the paper is held.
– ORIGIN French *platine* 'flat piece', from *plat* 'flat'.

plate tectonics ● plural noun (treated as sing.) a theory explaining the structure of the earth's crust as resulting from the movement of lithospheric plates.

platform ● noun **1** a raised level surface on which people or things can stand. **2** a raised structure along the side of a railway track where passengers get on and off trains. **3** a raised structure standing in the sea from which oil or gas wells can be drilled. **4** the declared policy of a political party or group. **5** an opportunity for the expression or exchange of views. **6** a very thick sole on a shoe. **7** Computing a standard for the hardware of a computer system, which determines the kinds of software it can run.
– ORIGIN French *plateforme* 'ground plan', literally 'flat shape'.

platinize (also **platinise**) ● verb coat with platinum.
– DERIVATIVES **platinization** noun.

platinoid ● noun an alloy of copper with zinc, nickel, and sometimes tungsten, used for its high electrical resistance.

platinum /plattinəm/ ● noun **1** a precious silvery-white metallic chemical element used in jewellery and in some electrical and laboratory apparatus. **2** (before another noun) greyish-white or silvery like platinum.
– ORIGIN Spanish *platina*, from *plata* 'silver'.

platinum blonde ● adjective (of hair) silvery-blonde.

platinum disc ● noun a framed platinum disc awarded to a recording artist for sales of a record exceeding a specified high figure.

platitude ● noun a remark or statement that has been used too often to be interesting or thoughtful.
– DERIVATIVES **platitudinize** (also **platitudinise**) verb **platitudinous** adjective.
– ORIGIN French, from *plat* 'flat'.

Platonic /plətonnik/ ● adjective **1** of or associated with the Greek philosopher Plato (*c*.429–*c*.347 BC) or his ideas. **2** (**platonic**) (of love or friendship) intimate and affectionate but not sexual.
– DERIVATIVES **platonically** adverb.

Platonism /playtəniz'm/ ● noun the philosophy of Plato, especially his theories on the relationship between abstract ideas or entities and their corresponding objects or forms in the material world.
– DERIVATIVES **Platonist** noun & adjective.

platoon ● noun a subdivision of a company of soldiers, usually commanded by a subaltern or lieutenant and divided into three sections.
– ORIGIN French *peloton* 'platoon', literally 'small ball'.

platter ● noun **1** a large flat serving dish. **2** the rotating metal disc forming the turntable of a record player. **3** Computing a rigid rotating disk on which data is stored in a disk drive; a hard disk.
– PHRASES **be handed something on a (silver) platter** informal acquire something with little or no effort.
– ORIGIN Old French *plater*, from *plat*; related to PLATE.

platypus /plattipəss/ (also **duck-billed platypus**) ● noun (pl. **platypuses**) a semiaquatic egg-laying Australian mammal with a sensitive pliable bill like that of a duck and webbed feet with venomous spurs.
– ORIGIN from Greek *platupous* 'flat-footed'.

plaudits ● plural noun praise; enthusiastic approval.
– ORIGIN from Latin *plaudite* 'applaud!' (said by ancient Roman actors at the end of a play).

plausible ● adjective **1** seeming reasonable or probable. **2** skilled at producing persuasive or deceptive arguments: *a plausible liar*.
– DERIVATIVES **plausibility** noun **plausibly** adverb.
– ORIGIN originally in the sense 'deserving applause': from Latin *plaudere* 'applaud'.

play ● verb **1** engage in games or other activities for enjoyment rather than for a serious or practical purpose. **2** take part in (a sport or contest). **3** compete against. **4** take a specified position in a sports team. **5** represent (a character) in a play or film. **6** perform on or have the skill to perform on (a musical instrument). **7** produce (notes) from a musical instrument; perform (a piece of music). **8** move (a piece) or display (a playing card) in one's turn in a game. **9** make (a record player, radio, etc.) produce sounds. **10** be cooperative: *he needs financial backing, but the banks won't play*. **11** move lightly and quickly; flicker. ● noun **1** games and other activities engaged in for enjoyment. **2** the progress of a sporting match. **3** a move or manoeuvre in a sport or game. **4** the state of being active, operative, or effective: *luck came into play*. **5** a dramatic work for the stage or to be broadcast. **6** the ability or freedom of movement in a mechanism. **7** light and constantly changing movement.
– PHRASES **be played out** drained of strength or life. **make great**

Thesaurus

3 *a plastic smile* ARTIFICIAL, false, fake, superficial, pseudo, bogus, unnatural, insincere; *informal* phoney, pretend.
– OPPOSITES rigid, intractable, genuine.

plate ● noun **1** *a dinner plate* DISH, platter, salver, paten; *historical* trencher; *archaic* charger. **2** *a plate of spaghetti* PLATEFUL, helping, portion, serving. **3** *steel plates* PANEL, sheet, layer, pane, slab. **4** *a brass plate on the door* PLAQUE, sign, tablet, plaquette, cartouche; *Brit.* brass. **5** *the book has colour plates* PICTURE, print, illustration, photograph, photo.
● verb *the roof was plated with steel* COVER, coat, overlay, laminate, veneer; electroplate, galvanize, gild.

plateau ● noun **1** *a windswept plateau* UPLAND, tableland, plain, mesa, highland. **2** *prices reached a plateau* quiescent period; letup, respite, lull.

platform ● noun **1** *he made a speech from the platform* STAGE, dais, rostrum, podium, soapbox. **2** *the Democratic Party's platform* POLICY, programme, party line, manifesto, plan, principles, objectives, aims.

platitude ● noun CLICHÉ, truism, commonplace, banality, old chestnut, bromide.

platitudinous ● adjective HACKNEYED, overworked, overused, clichéd, banal, trite, commonplace, well worn, stale, tired, unoriginal; *informal* corny, old hat.
– OPPOSITES original.

platonic ● adjective NON-SEXUAL, non-physical, chaste; intellectual, friendly.
– OPPOSITES sexual.

platoon ● noun UNIT, patrol, troop, squad, squadron, team, company, corps, outfit, detachment, contingent.

platter ● noun PLATE, dish, salver, paten, tray; *historical* trencher; *archaic* charger.

plaudits ● plural noun PRAISE, acclaim, commendation, congratulations, accolades, compliments, cheers, applause, tributes, bouquets; a pat on the back; *informal* a (big) hand.
– OPPOSITES criticism.

plausible ● adjective CREDIBLE, reasonable, believable, likely, feas-

play of ostentatiously draw attention to. **make a play for** informal attempt to attract or attain. **play both ends against the middle** keep one's options open by supporting opposing sides. **play about** (or **around**) **1** behave in a casual or irresponsible way. **2** informal (of a married person) have an affair. **play-act** engage in pretence in an attention-seeking manner. **play along 1** perform a piece of music at the same time as it is playing on a tape or record. **2** pretend to cooperate. **play by ear 1** perform (music) without having to read from a score. **2** (**play it by ear**) proceed instinctively according to circumstances rather than according to rules or a plan. **play down** disguise the importance or significance of. **play fast and loose** behave irresponsibly or immorally. **play for time** use excuses or unnecessary manoeuvres to gain time. **play into someone's hands** act in such a way as unintentionally to give someone an advantage. **play off** bring (two or more people or parties) into conflict for one's own advantage. **play on** exploit (someone's weak or vulnerable point). **a play on words** a pun. **play** (or **play it**) **safe** avoid taking risks. **play up 1** emphasize the extent or importance of. **2** (**play up to**) humour or flatter. **3** Brit. informal fail to function properly; cause problems. **play with 1** treat inconsiderately for one's own amusement. **2** tamper with. **play with fire** take foolish risks.

– DERIVATIVES **playable** adjective.

– ORIGIN Old English, 'to exercise'.

playback • noun the replaying of previously recorded sound or moving images.

playboy • noun a wealthy man who spends his time seeking pleasure.

player • noun **1** a person taking part in a sport or game. **2** a person who is involved and influential in an activity. **3** a person who plays a musical instrument. **4** a device for playing compact discs, cassettes, etc. **5** an actor.

player-manager • noun a person who both plays in a sports team and manages it.

playful • adjective **1** fond of games and amusement. **2** intended for amusement; light-hearted.

– DERIVATIVES **playfully** adverb **playfulness** noun.

playground • noun an outdoor area provided for children to play on.

playgroup (also **playschool**) • noun Brit. a regular play session for pre-school children, organized by parents.

playhouse • noun **1** a theatre. **2** a toy house for children to play in.

playing card • noun each of a set of rectangular pieces of card with numbers and symbols on one side (usually 52 cards divided into four suits), used to play various games.

playing field • noun a field used for outdoor team games.

playlist • noun a list of recorded songs or pieces of music chosen to be broadcast on a radio station.

playmaker • noun a player in a team game who leads attacks or brings teammates into attacking positions.

playmate • noun a friend with whom a child plays.

play-off • noun an additional match played to decide the outcome of a contest.

playpen • noun a small portable enclosure in which a baby or small child can play safely.

playscheme • noun a local project providing recreational facilities and activities for children.

playsuit • noun an all-in-one stretchy garment for a baby or toddler, covering the body, arms, and legs.

plaything • noun **1** a toy. **2** a person who is treated as amusing but unimportant.

playwright • noun a person who writes plays.

plaza • noun **1** a public square or similar open space in a built-up area. **2** N. Amer. a shopping centre.

– ORIGIN Spanish, 'place'.

plc (also **PLC**) • abbreviation Brit. public limited company.

plea • noun **1** a request made in an urgent and emotional manner. **2** Law a formal statement by or on behalf of a defendant, stating guilt or innocence in response to a charge, offering an allegation of fact, or claiming that a point of law should apply. **3** Lawan excuse or claim of mitigating circumstances.

– ORIGIN Old French *plait*, *plaid* 'agreement, discussion', from Latin *placere* 'to please'.

plea-bargaining • noun Law an arrangement between prosecutor and defendant whereby the defendant pleads guilty to a lesser charge in the expectation of leniency.

Thesaurus

ible, tenable, possible, conceivable, imaginable; convincing, persuasive, cogent, sound, rational, logical, thinkable.

– OPPOSITES unlikely.

play • verb **1** *the children played with toys* AMUSE ONESELF, entertain oneself, enjoy oneself, have fun; relax, occupy oneself, divert oneself; frolic, frisk, romp, caper; *informal* mess about/around, lark (about/around); *dated* sport. **2** *I used to play football* TAKE PART IN, participate in, be involved in, compete in, do. **3** *Liverpool play Oxford on Sunday* COMPETE AGAINST, take on, challenge, vie with. **4** *he was to play Macbeth* ACT (THE PART OF), take the role of, appear as, portray, depict, impersonate, represent, render, perform; *formal* personate. **5** *he learned to play the flute* PERFORM ON, make music on; blow, sound. **6** *the sunlight played on the water* DANCE, flit, ripple, touch; sparkle, glint.

• noun **1** *a balance between work and play* AMUSEMENT, entertainment, relaxation, recreation, diversion, distraction, leisure; enjoyment, pleasure, fun, games, fun and games; horseplay, merrymaking, revelry; *informal* living it up; *dated* sport. **2** *a Shakespeare play* DRAMA, theatrical work; teleplay, screenplay, comedy, tragedy; production, performance, show, sketch. **3** *she knew the play of the real world* ACTION, activity, operation, working, function; interaction, interplay. **4** *there was a little play in the rope* MOVEMENT, slack, give; room to manoeuvre, scope, latitude.

– PHRASES **play around** *(informal)* WOMANIZE, philander, have affairs, flirt; *informal* carry on, mess about/around, play the field, sleep around; *Brit. informal* play away; *N. Amer. informal* fool around. **play at** PRETEND TO BE, pass oneself off as, masquerade as, profess to be, pose as, impersonate; fake, feign, simulate, affect; *N. Amer. informal* make like. **play ball** *(informal)* COOPERATE, collaborate, play the game, show willing, help, lend a hand, assist, contribute; *informal* pitch in. **play something down** MAKE LIGHT OF, make little of, gloss over, de-emphasize, downplay, understate; soft-pedal, tone down, diminish, trivialize, underrate, underestimate, undervalue; disparage, belittle, scoff at, sneer at, shrug off; *informal* pooh-pooh. **play for time** STALL, temporize, delay, hold back, hang fire, procrastinate, drag one's feet. **play it by ear** IMPROVISE, extemporize, ad lib; *informal* busk it, wing it. **play on** *they play on our fears* EXPLOIT, take advantage of, use, turn to (one's) account, profit by, capitalize on, trade on, milk, abuse. **play the fool** CLOWN ABOUT/AROUND, fool about/around, mess about/around, lark about/around, monkey about/around, joke; *informal* horse about/around, act the goat; *Brit. informal* muck about/around. **play the game** PLAY FAIR, be fair, play by the rules, conform, be a good sport, toe the line. **play up** *(Brit. informal)* **1** *the boys really did play up* MISBEHAVE, be bad, be naughty, get up to mischief, be disobedient, cause trouble. **2** *the boiler's playing up* MALFUNCTION, not work, be defective, be faulty; *informal* go on the blink, act up. **3** *his leg was playing up* BE PAINFUL, hurt, ache, be sore, cause discomfort; *informal* kill someone, give someone gyp. **play something up** EMPHASIZE, accentuate, call attention to, point up, underline, highlight, spotlight, foreground, feature, stress, accent. **play up to** INGRATIATE ONESELF WITH, curry favour with, court, fawn over, make up to, keep someone sweet, toady to, crawl to, pander to, flatter; *informal* soft-soap, suck up to, butter up, lick someone's boots.

playboy • noun SOCIALITE, pleasure-seeker, sybarite; ladies' man, womanizer, philanderer, rake, roué; *informal* ladykiller.

player • noun **1** *a tournament for young players* PARTICIPANT, contestant, competitor, contender; sportsman/woman, athlete. **2** *the players in the orchestra* MUSICIAN, performer, instrumentalist, soloist, virtuoso. **3** *the players of the Royal Shakespeare Company* ACTOR, actress, performer, thespian, entertainer, artist(e), trouper.

playful • adjective **1** *a playful mood* FRISKY, jolly, lively, full of fun, frolicsome, sportive, high-spirited, exuberant, perky; mischievous, impish, rascally, tricksy; *informal* full of beans; *dated* gay; *formal* ludic. **2** *a playful remark* LIGHT-HEARTED, in jest, joking, jokey, teasing, humorous, jocular, good-natured, tongue-in-cheek, facetious, frivolous, flippant, arch; *informal* waggish.

– OPPOSITES serious.

playground • noun PLAY AREA, park, playing field, recreation ground; *Brit. informal* rec.

playmate • noun FRIEND, playfellow, companion; *informal* chum, pal; *Brit. informal* mate; *N. Amer. informal* buddy.

plaything • noun TOY, game.

playwright • noun DRAMATIST, dramaturge, scriptwriter, screenwriter, writer, scenarist; tragedian.

plea • noun **1** *a plea for aid* APPEAL, entreaty, supplication, peti-

pleach /pleech/ • verb entwine (tree branches) to form a hedge or provide cover for an outdoor walkway.
– ORIGIN Old French *plaissier*, from Latin *plectere* 'plait'.

plead • verb (past and past part. **pleaded** or N. Amer., Scottish, or dialect **pled**) **1** make an emotional appeal. **2** present and argue for (a position), especially in court or in another public context. **3** Law state formally in court whether one is guilty or not guilty of the offence with which one is charged. **4** Law invoke (a reason or a point of law) as an accusation or defence. **5** offer or present as an excuse for doing or not doing something.
– DERIVATIVES **pleader** noun.
– ORIGIN Old French *plaidier* 'go to law', from *plaid* 'agreement, discussion' (see PLEA).

pleadable • adjective Law able to be offered as a formal plea in court.

pleading • noun **1** the action of making an emotional or earnest appeal. **2** Law a formal statement of the cause of an action or defence. • adjective earnestly appealing.
– DERIVATIVES **pleadingly** adverb.

pleasance • noun literary a secluded enclosure or part of a garden.
– ORIGIN Old French *plaisance*, from *plaisir* 'please'.

pleasant • adjective **1** giving a sense of happy satisfaction or enjoyment. **2** friendly and likeable.
– DERIVATIVES **pleasantly** adverb **pleasantness** noun.
– ORIGIN Old French *plaisant*, from *plaisir* 'please'.

pleasantry • noun (pl. **pleasantries**) **1** an inconsequential remark made as part of a polite conversation. **2** a mildly amusing joke.

please • verb **1** cause to feel happy and satisfied. **2** wish or desire: *do as you please*. **3** (**please oneself**) take only one's own wishes into consideration. **4** (**if you please**) used in polite requests or to express indignation. • adverb used in polite requests or questions, or to accept an offer.
– DERIVATIVES **pleasing** adjective.
– ORIGIN Old French *plaisir*, from Latin *placere*.

pleased • adjective **1** feeling or showing pleasure and satisfaction. **2** (**pleased to do**) willing or glad to do.

pleasurable • adjective pleasing; enjoyable.
– DERIVATIVES **pleasurably** adverb.

pleasure • noun **1** a feeling of happy satisfaction and enjoyment. **2** an event or activity from which one derives enjoyment. **3** (before another noun) intended for entertainment rather than business: *pleasure boats*. **4** sensual gratification. • verb give pleasure (especially of a sexual nature) to.
– PHRASES **at one's pleasure** formal as and when someone wishes.
– ORIGIN from Old French *plaisir* 'to please'.

pleat • noun a fold in a garment or other item made of cloth, held by stitching the top or side. • verb fold or form into pleats.
– ORIGIN variant of PLAIT.

pleb • noun informal, derogatory a member of the lower social classes.
– DERIVATIVES **plebby** adjective.
– ORIGIN abbreviation of PLEBEIAN.

plebeian /plibeeən/ • noun **1** (in ancient Rome) a commoner. **2** a member of the lower social classes. • adjective **1** relating to the plebeians of ancient Rome. **2** lower-class or lacking in refinement.
– ORIGIN from Latin *plebs* 'the common people'.

plebiscite /plebbisīt/ • noun **1** the direct vote of all the members of an electorate on an important public question. **2** (in ancient Rome) a law enacted by the plebeians' assembly.
– DERIVATIVES **plebiscitary** /plebissitəri/ adjective.
– ORIGIN French *plébiscite*, from Latin *plebs* 'the common people' + *scitum* 'decree'.

plectrum • noun (pl. **plectrums** or **plectra**) a thin flat piece of plastic or tortoiseshell used to pluck the strings of a guitar or similar musical instrument.
– ORIGIN Greek *plēktron* 'something with which to strike', from *plēssein* 'to strike'.

pled North American, Scottish, or dialect past participle of PLEAD.

pledge • noun **1** a solemn promise or undertaking. **2** Law a thing that is given as security for the fulfilment of a contract or the payment of a debt and is liable to forfeiture in the event of failure. **3** (**the pledge**) a solemn undertaking to abstain from alcohol. **4** a thing given as a token of love, favour, or loyalty. **5** archaic the drinking of a person's health; a toast. • verb **1** solemnly undertake to do or give something. **2** Law give as security on a loan. **3** archaic drink to the health of.
– ORIGIN originally denoting a person acting as surety for another: from Old French *plege*, from Latin *plebium*.

Thesaurus

p

tion, request, call, suit, solicitation. **2** *her plea of a headache was unconvincing* CLAIM, explanation, defence, justification; excuse, pretext.

plead • verb **1** *he pleaded with her to stay* BEG, implore, entreat, appeal to, supplicate, petition, request, ask, call on; poetic/literary beseech. **2** *she pleaded ignorance* CLAIM, use as an excuse, assert, allege, argue, state.

pleasant • adjective **1** *a pleasant evening* ENJOYABLE, pleasurable, nice, agreeable, pleasing, satisfying, gratifying, good; entertaining, amusing, delightful, charming; fine, balmy; informal lovely, great. **2** *the staff are pleasant* FRIENDLY, agreeable, amiable, nice, genial, cordial, likeable, amicable, good-humoured, good-natured, personable; hospitable, approachable, gracious, courteous, polite, obliging, helpful, considerate; charming, lovely, delightful, sweet, sympathetic; N. English & Scottish canny; Scottish couthy.
– OPPOSITES disagreeable.

pleasantry • noun **1** *we exchanged pleasantries* BANTER, badinage; polite remark, casual remark; N. Amer. informal josh. **2** *he laughed at his own pleasantry* JOKE, witticism, quip, jest, gag, bon mot; informal wisecrack, crack.

please • verb **1** *he'd do anything to please her* MAKE HAPPY, give pleasure to, make someone feel good; delight, charm, amuse, entertain; satisfy, gratify, humour, oblige, content, suit; informal tickle someone pink. **2** *do as you please* LIKE, want, wish, desire, see fit, think fit, choose, will, prefer.
– OPPOSITES annoy.
• adverb *please sit down* IF YOU PLEASE, if you wouldn't mind, if you would be so good; kindly, pray; archaic prithee.

pleased • adjective HAPPY, glad, delighted, gratified, grateful, thankful, content, contented, satisfied; thrilled, elated, overjoyed, cock-a-hoop; informal over the moon, tickled pink, on cloud nine; Brit. informal chuffed; N. English informal made up; Austral. informal wrapped; humorous gruntled.
– OPPOSITES unhappy.

pleasing • adjective **1** *a pleasing day* NICE, agreeable, pleasant, pleasurable, satisfying, gratifying, good, enjoyable, entertaining, amusing, delightful; informal lovely, great. **2** *her pleasing manner* FRIENDLY, amiable, pleasant, agreeable, affable, nice, genial, likeable, good-humoured, charming, engaging, delightful, winning; informal lovely.

pleasurable • adjective PLEASANT, enjoyable, delightful, nice, pleasing, agreeable, gratifying; fun, entertaining, amusing, diverting; informal lovely, great.

pleasure • noun **1** *she smiled with pleasure* HAPPINESS, delight, joy, gladness, glee, satisfaction, gratification, contentment, enjoyment, amusement. **2** *his greatest pleasures in life* JOY, amusement, diversion, recreation, pastime; treat, thrill. **3** *don't mix business and pleasure* ENJOYMENT, fun, entertainment; recreation, leisure, relaxation; informal jollies. **4** *a life of pleasure* HEDONISM, indulgence, self-indulgence, self-gratification, lotus-eating. **5** *what's your pleasure?* WISH, desire, preference, will, inclination, choice.
– PHRASES **take pleasure in** ENJOY, delight in, love, like, adore, appreciate, relish, savour, revel in, glory in; informal get a kick out of, get a thrill out of. **with pleasure** GLADLY, willingly, happily, readily; by all means, of course; archaic fain.

pleat • noun *a curtain pleat* FOLD, crease, gather, tuck, crimp; pucker.
• verb *the dress is pleated at the front* FOLD, crease, gather, tuck, crimp; pucker.

plebeian • noun *plebeians and gentry lived together* PROLETARIAN, commoner, working-class person, worker; peasant; informal pleb, prole.
– OPPOSITES aristocrat.
• adjective **1** *people of plebeian descent* LOWER-CLASS, working-class, proletarian, common, peasant; mean, humble, lowly. **2** *plebeian tastes* UNCULTURED, uncultivated, unrefined, lowbrow, philistine, uneducated; coarse, uncouth, common, vulgar; informal plebby; Brit. informal non-U.
– OPPOSITES noble, refined.

plebiscite • noun VOTE, referendum, ballot, poll.

pledge • noun **1** *his election pledge* PROMISE, undertaking, vow, word (of honour), commitment, assurance, oath, guarantee. **2** *he*

Pleistocene /plīstəseen/ ● **adjective** Geology relating to the first epoch of the Quaternary period (between the Pliocene and Holocene epochs, from 1.64 million to about 10,000 years ago), a time which included the ice ages and the appearance of humans.
– ORIGIN from Greek *pleistos* 'most' + *kainos* 'new'.

plenary /pleenəri/ ● **adjective** **1** unqualified; absolute. **2** (of a meeting at a conference or assembly) to be attended by all participants. ● **noun** a plenary meeting.
– ORIGIN Latin *plenus* 'full'.

plenipotentiary /plennipətenshəri/ ● **noun** (pl. **plenipotentiaries**) a person appointed by a government to act on its behalf with full and independent power. ● **adjective** **1** having full power to take independent action. **2** (of power) absolute.
– ORIGIN from Latin *plenus* 'full' + *potentia* 'power'.

plenitude ● **noun** formal **1** an abundance. **2** the condition of being full or complete.
– ORIGIN Old French, from Latin *plenus* 'full'.

plenteous ● **adjective** literary plentiful.

plentiful ● **adjective** existing in or yielding great quantities; abundant.
– DERIVATIVES **plentifully** adverb.

plentitude ● **noun** another term for PLENITUDE.

plenty ● **pronoun** a large or sufficient amount or quantity. ● **noun** a situation in which food and other necessities are available in sufficiently large quantities. ● **adverb** informal fully; sufficiently.
– ORIGIN Old French *plente*, from Latin *plenus* 'full'.

plenum /pleenəm/ ● **noun** **1** an assembly of all the members of a group or committee. **2** Physics a space completely filled with matter, or the whole of space so regarded.
– ORIGIN Latin, 'full space'.

pleonasm /pleeōnaz'm/ ● **noun** the use of more words than are necessary to convey meaning (e.g. *see with one's eyes*).
– DERIVATIVES **pleonastic** adjective.
– ORIGIN Greek *pleonasmos*, from *pleonazein* 'be superfluous'.

plesiosaur /pleesiəsawr/ ● **noun** a large fossil marine reptile of the Mesozoic era, with large paddle-like limbs and a long flexible neck.
– ORIGIN from Greek *plēsios* 'near' (because closely related to the lizards) + *sauros* 'lizard'.

plessor ● **noun** variant spelling of PLEXOR.

plethora /plethərə/ ● **noun** an excessive amount of: *a plethora of complaints.*
– ORIGIN Latin, from Greek *plēthein* 'be full'.

pleura /ploorə/ ● **noun** (pl. **pleurae** /plooree/) Anatomy each of a pair of membranes lining the thorax and enveloping the lungs.
– DERIVATIVES **pleural** adjective.
– ORIGIN Greek, 'side of the body, rib'.

pleurisy /poorisi/ ● **noun** inflammation of the pleurae, causing pain during breathing.
– DERIVATIVES **pleuritic** adjective.

plexiglas /pleksiglaass/ ● **noun** trademark, chiefly N. Amer. a tough transparent plastic made of an acrylic resin, used as a substitute for glass.
– ORIGIN from Greek *plēxis* 'percussion'.

plexor (also **plessor**) ● **noun** a small hammer with a rubber head, used to test reflexes.
– ORIGIN from Greek *plēxis* 'percussion'.

plexus ● **noun** (pl. same or **plexuses**) **1** Anatomy a network of nerves or vessels in the body. **2** an intricate network or weblike formation.
– DERIVATIVES **plexiform** adjective.
– ORIGIN Latin, 'plaited formation', from *plectere* 'to plait'.

pliable ● **adjective** **1** easily bent; flexible. **2** easily influenced or swayed.
– DERIVATIVES **pliability** noun.
– ORIGIN French, from Latin *plicare* 'to bend or fold'.

pliant ● **adjective** pliable.
– DERIVATIVES **pliancy** noun **pliantly** adverb.

plié /pleeay/ Ballet ● **noun** a movement in which a dancer bends the knees and straightens them again, having the feet turned right out and heels firmly on the ground.
– ORIGIN French, 'bent'.

pliers ● **plural noun** pincers with parallel flat jaws, used for gripping small objects or bending wire.
– ORIGIN from French *plier* 'to bend'.

plight[1] ● **noun** a dangerous or difficult situation.
– ORIGIN Old French *plit* 'fold'.

plight[2] ● **verb** archaic **1** solemnly pledge or promise (faith or loyalty). **2** (**be plighted to**) be engaged to be married to.
– ORIGIN Old English.

plimsoll (also **plimsole**) ● **noun** Brit. a light rubber-soled canvas sports shoe.
– ORIGIN probably from the resemblance of the side of the sole to a PLIMSOLL LINE.

Plimsoll line ● **noun** a marking on a ship's side showing the limit of legal submersion when loaded with cargo.
– ORIGIN named after the English politician Samuel *Plimsoll*, responsible for the Merchant Shipping Act of 1876.

plink ● **verb** **1** emit a short, sharp, metallic ringing sound. **2** chiefly N. Amer. shoot at (a target) casually. ● **noun** a plinking sound.
– DERIVATIVES **plinky** adjective.
– ORIGIN imitative.

plinth ● **noun** **1** a heavy base supporting a statue or vase. **2** Architecture the lower square slab at the base of a column.
– ORIGIN Greek *plinthos* 'tile, brick, squared stone'.

Pliocene /plīəseen/ ● **adjective** Geology relating to the last epoch of the Tertiary period (between the Miocene and Pleistocene epochs, 5.2 to 1.64 million years ago), a time when the first hominids appeared.
– ORIGIN from Greek *pleiōn* 'more' + *kainos* 'new'.

pliosaur /plīəsawr/ ● **noun** a plesiosaur with a short neck, large head, and massive toothed jaws.
– ORIGIN from Greek *pleiōn* 'more' + *sauros* 'lizard' (because of its greater similarity to a lizard than the ichthyosaur).

PLO ● **abbreviation** Palestine Liberation Organization.

plod ● **verb** (**plodded**, **plodding**) **1** walk doggedly and slowly with heavy steps. **2** work slowly and perseveringly at a dull task. ● **noun** **1** a slow, heavy walk. **2** (also **PC Plod**) Brit. informal a police officer.
– DERIVATIVES **plodder** noun.

Thesaurus

gave it as a pledge to a creditor SURETY, bond, security, collateral, guarantee, deposit. **3** *a pledge of my sincerity* TOKEN, symbol, sign, earnest, mark, testimony, proof, evidence.
● **verb** **1** *he pledged to root out corruption* PROMISE, vow, swear, undertake, engage, commit oneself, declare, affirm, avow. **2** *they pledged £100 million* PROMISE (TO GIVE), donate, contribute, give, put up; Brit. covenant. **3** *his home is pledged as security against the loan* MORTGAGE, put up as collateral, guarantee, pawn.

plenary ● **adjective** **1** *the council has plenary powers* UNCONDITIONAL, unlimited, unrestricted, unqualified, absolute, sweeping, comprehensive; plenipotentiary. **2** *a plenary session of the parliament* FULL, complete, entire.

plenipotentiary ● **noun** *a plenipotentiary in Paris* DIPLOMAT, dignitary, ambassador, minister, emissary, chargé d'affaires, envoy.
● **adjective** *plenipotentiary powers.* See PLENARY sense 1.

plenitude ● **noun** *(formal)* ABUNDANCE, lot, wealth, profusion, cornucopia, plethora, superabundance; informal load, slew, heap, ton; Brit. informal shedload.

plenteous ● **adjective** *(poetic/literary).* See PLENTIFUL.

plentiful ● **adjective** ABUNDANT, copious, ample, profuse, rich, lavish, generous, bountiful, large, great, bumper, superabundant, inexhaustible, prolific; informal a gogo, galore; poetic/literary plenteous.
– OPPOSITES scarce.

plenty ● **noun** *times of plenty* PROSPERITY, affluence, wealth, opulence, comfort, luxury; plentifulness, abundance; poetic/literary plenteousness.
● **pronoun** *there are plenty of books* A LOT OF, many, a great deal of, a plethora of, enough (and to spare), no lack of, sufficient, a wealth of; informal loads of, lots of, heaps of, stacks of, masses of, tons of, oodles of, scads of, a slew of.

plethora ● **noun** EXCESS, abundance, superabundance, surplus, glut, superfluity, surfeit, profusion, too many, too much, enough and to spare; informal more —— than one can shake a stick at.
– OPPOSITES dearth.

pliable ● **adjective** **1** *leather is pliable* FLEXIBLE, pliant, bendable, elastic, supple, malleable, workable, plastic, springy, ductile; informal bendy. **2** *pliable teenage minds* MALLEABLE, impressionable, flexible, adaptable, pliant, compliant, biddable, tractable, yielding, amenable, susceptible, suggestible, persuadable, manipulable, receptive.
– OPPOSITES rigid, obdurate.

pliant ● **adjective.** See PLIABLE senses 1, 2.

– ORIGIN probably symbolic of a heavy gait.

plonk[1] informal • verb **1** set down heavily or carelessly. **2** play unskilfully on a musical instrument. • noun a sound as of something being set down heavily.

– ORIGIN imitative.

plonk[2] • noun Brit. informal cheap wine.

– ORIGIN originally Australian: probably an alteration of *blanc* in French *vin blanc* 'white wine'.

plonker • noun Brit. informal a foolish or inept person.

– ORIGIN originally a dialect word meaning 'something large of its kind': from PLONK[1].

plop • noun a sound as of a small, solid object dropping into water without a splash. • verb (**plopped**, **plopping**) fall or drop with such a sound.

– ORIGIN imitative.

plosive • adjective Phonetics referring to a consonant (e.g. *d* and *t*) that is produced by stopping the airflow using the lips, teeth, or palate, followed by a sudden release of air.

– ORIGIN shortening of EXPLOSIVE.

plot • noun **1** a secret plan to do something illegal or harmful. **2** the main sequence of events in a play, novel, or film. **3** a small piece of ground marked out for building, gardening, etc. **4** a graph showing the relation between two variables. **5** chiefly US a diagram, chart, or map. • verb (**plotted**, **plotting**) **1** secretly make plans to carry out (something illegal or harmful). **2** devise the plot of (a play, novel, or film). **3** mark (a route or position) on a chart or graph.

– DERIVATIVES **plotless** adjective **plotter** noun.

– ORIGIN Old English, 'small piece of ground'; sense 1 is associated with Old French *complot* 'dense crowd, secret project'.

plough (US **plow**) • noun **1** a large farming implement with one or more blades fixed in a frame, drawn over soil to turn it over and cut furrows. **2** (**the Plough**) a prominent formation of seven stars in the constellation Ursa Major (the Great Bear). • verb **1** turn up (earth) with a plough. **2** (**plough through/into**) (of a vehicle) move in a fast or uncontrolled manner through or into. **3** advance or progress laboriously or forcibly. **4** (of a ship or boat) travel through (an area of water). **5** (**plough in**) invest (money) in a business.

– DERIVATIVES **ploughable** adjective.

– ORIGIN Old English.

ploughman's lunch • noun Brit. a meal of bread and cheese with pickle and salad.

ploughshare • noun the main cutting blade of a plough.

plover /pluvvər/ • noun a short-billed wading bird, typically found by water but sometimes frequenting grassland.

– ORIGIN Old French, from Latin *pluvia* 'rain'.

plow • noun & verb US spelling of PLOUGH.

ploy • noun a cunning manoeuvre to gain an advantage.

– ORIGIN originally Scots and northern English in the sense 'pastime': of unknown origin.

pluck • verb **1** take hold of (something) and quickly remove it from its place. **2** pull out (a hair, feather, etc.) **3** pull the feathers from (a bird's carcass) to prepare it for cooking. **4** pull at or twitch. **5** sound (a stringed musical instrument) with one's finger or a plectrum. **6** (**pluck up**) summon up (courage) in order to do something frightening. • noun **1** spirited and determined courage. **2** the heart, liver, and lungs of an animal as food.

– ORIGIN Old English.

plucky • adjective (**pluckier**, **pluckiest**) determined and courageous in the face of difficulties.

– DERIVATIVES **pluckily** adverb **pluckiness** noun.

plug • noun **1** a piece of solid material fitting tightly into a hole and blocking it up. **2** a device consisting of an insulated casing with metal pins that fit into holes in a socket to make an electrical connection. **3** informal an electrical socket. **4** informal a piece of publicity promoting a product or event. **5** a piece of tobacco cut from a larger cake for chewing. **6** Fishing a lure with one or more hooks attached. • verb (**plugged**, **plugging**) **1** block or fill in (a hole or cavity). **2** (**plug in**) connect (an electrical appliance) to the mains by means of a socket. **3** (**plug into**) have or gain access to (an information system or area of activity). **4** informal promote (a product or event) by mentioning it publicly. **5** informal shoot or hit. **6** (**plug away**) informal proceed steadily and laboriously with a task.

– DERIVATIVES **plugger** noun.

– ORIGIN Dutch and Low German *plugge*.

plughole • noun Brit. a hole at the lowest point of a bath or sink, through which the water drains away.

plug-in • noun Computing a module or piece of software which can be added to an existing system to give extra features.

plug-ugly informal, chiefly N. Amer. • noun (pl. **plug-uglies**) a thug or villain. • adjective very ugly.

– ORIGIN by association with PLUG in the sense 'hit with the fist'.

plum • noun **1** an oval fleshy fruit which is purple, reddish, or yellow when ripe, containing a flattish pointed stone. **2** a reddish-purple colour. **3** (before another noun) informal highly desirable: *a plum job.*

– PHRASES **have a plum in one's mouth** Brit. have an upper-class accent.

– ORIGIN Latin *prunum*.

plumage /plōōmij/ • noun a bird's feathers.

– ORIGIN Old French, from *plume* 'feather'.

plumb[1] • verb **1** measure (the depth of water). **2** explore or experience fully or to extremes. **3** test (an upright surface) to determine the vertical. • noun a lead ball or other heavy object attached to a line for finding the depth of water or determining

p

Thesaurus

plight • noun PREDICAMENT, difficult situation, dire straits, trouble, difficulty, extremity, bind; *informal* dilemma, tight corner, tight spot, hole, pickle, jam, fix.

plod • verb **1** *Mum plodded wearily upstairs* TRUDGE, walk heavily, clump, stomp, tramp, lumber, slog; *Brit. informal* trog. **2** *I have to plod through the whole book* WADE, plough, trawl, toil, labour; *informal* slog.

plot • noun **1** *a plot to overthrow him* CONSPIRACY, intrigue, secret plan; machinations. **2** *the plot of her novel* STORYLINE, story, scenario, action, thread; *formal* diegesis. **3** *a three-acre plot* PIECE OF GROUND, patch, area, tract, acreage; *Brit.* allotment; *N. Amer.* lot, plat; *N. Amer. & Austral./NZ* homesite.

• verb **1** *he plotted their downfall* PLAN, scheme, arrange, organize, hatch, concoct, devise, dream up; *informal* cook up. **2** *his brother was plotting against him* CONSPIRE, scheme, intrigue, collude, connive, machinate. **3** *the fifty-three sites were plotted* MARK, chart, map, represent, graph.

plotter • noun CONSPIRATOR, schemer, intriguer, machinator; planner.

plough • verb **1** *the fields were ploughed* TILL, furrow, harrow, cultivate, work, break up. **2** *the car ploughed into a lamp post* CRASH, smash, career, plunge, bulldoze, hurtle, cannon, run, drive; *N. Amer. informal* barrel. **3** *they ploughed through deep snow* TRUDGE, plod, toil, wade; *informal* slog; *Brit. informal* trog.

ploy • noun RUSE, tactic, move, device, stratagem, scheme, trick, gambit, plan, manoeuvre, dodge, subterfuge, wile; *Brit. informal* wheeze.

pluck • verb **1** *he plucked a thread from his lapel* REMOVE, pick (off), pull (off/out), extract, take (off). **2** *she plucked at his T-shirt* PULL (AT), tug (at), clutch (at), snatch (at), grab, catch (at), tweak, jerk; *informal* yank. **3** *the turkeys are plucked* DEPLUME, remove the feathers from. **4** *she plucked the guitar strings* STRUM, pick, thrum, twang; play pizzicato.

• noun *the task took a lot of pluck* COURAGE, bravery, nerve, backbone, spine, daring, spirit, intrepidity, fearlessness, mettle, grit, determination, fortitude, resolve, stout-heartedness, dauntlessness, valour, heroism, audacity; *informal* guts, spunk, gumption; *Brit. informal* bottle; *N. Amer. informal* moxie.

plucky • adjective BRAVE, courageous, bold, daring, fearless, intrepid, spirited, game, valiant, valorous, stout-hearted, dauntless, resolute, determined, undaunted, unflinching, audacious, unafraid, doughty, mettlesome; *informal* gutsy, spunky.

– OPPOSITES timid.

plug • noun **1** *she pulled out the plug* STOPPER, bung, cork, seal, spigot, spile; *N. Amer.* stopple. **2** *a plug of tobacco* WAD, quid, twist, chew. **3** *(informal) a plug for his new book* ADVERTISEMENT, promotion, commercial, recommendation, mention, good word; *informal* hype, push, puff, ad, boost, ballyhoo; *Brit. informal* advert.

• verb **1** *plug the holes* STOP (UP), seal (up/off), close (up/off), cork, stopper, bung, block (up/off), fill (up); *N. Amer.* stopple. **2** *(informal) she plugged her new film* PUBLICIZE, promote, advertise, mention, bang the drum for, draw attention to; *informal* hype (up), push, puff. **3** *(informal) don't move or I'll plug you* SHOOT, gun down; *informal* blast, pump full of lead.

– PHRASES **plug away** *(informal)* TOIL, labour, slave away, soldier on, persevere, persist, keep on, plough on; *informal* slog away, beaver

the vertical on an upright surface. ● adverb informal **1** exactly: *plumb in the centre.* **2** N. Amer. extremely or completely. ● adjective vertical.
– ORIGIN Latin *plumbum* 'lead'.
plumb² ● verb (**plumb in**) install (a bath, washing machine, etc.) and connect it to water and drainage pipes.
– ORIGIN from PLUMBER.
plumbago /plumbaygō/ ● noun (pl. **plumbagos**) **1** an evergreen shrub or climber with grey or blue flowers. **2** old-fashioned term for GRAPHITE.
– ORIGIN from Latin *plumbum* 'lead'.
plumb bob ● noun a ball of lead or other heavy material forming the weight of a plumb line.
plumber ● noun a person who fits and repairs the pipes and fittings of water supply, sanitation, or heating systems.
– ORIGIN originally denoting a person dealing in and working with lead: from Old French *plommier*, from Latin *plumbum* 'lead'.
plumbing ● noun **1** the system of pipes, tanks, and fittings required for the water supply, heating, and sanitation in a building. **2** the work of installing and maintaining such a system.
plumbism /plumbiz'm/ ● noun technical poisoning due to the absorption of lead into the body.
plumb line ● noun a line with a plumb attached to it.
plum duff ● noun dated a plum pudding.
plume ● noun **1** a long, soft feather or arrangement of feathers. **2** a long spreading cloud of smoke or vapour. **3** Geology a column of magma rising by convection in the earth's mantle. ● verb **1** (**plumed**) decorated with feathers. **2** (of smoke or vapour) spread out in a plume.
– ORIGIN Latin *pluma* 'down'.
plummet ● verb (**plummeted**, **plummeting**) **1** fall or drop straight down at high speed. **2** decrease rapidly in value or amount. ● noun **1** a steep and rapid fall or drop. **2** a plumb bob or plumb line.
– ORIGIN from Old French *plommet* 'small sounding lead', from *plomb* 'lead'.
plummy ● adjective (**plummier**, **plummiest**) **1** resembling a plum. **2** Brit. informal (of a person's voice) typical of the English upper classes. **3** Brit. informal choice; highly desirable.
plump¹ ● adjective **1** full and rounded in shape. **2** rather fat. ● verb (**plump up**) make or become full and round.
– DERIVATIVES **plumpish** adjective **plumpness** noun.
– ORIGIN originally in the sense 'blunt, forthright': related to Dutch *plomp*, Low German *plump* 'blunt, obtuse'.
plump² ● verb **1** set or sit down heavily or unceremoniously. **2** (**plump for**) decide in favour of (one of two or more possibilities). ● adverb informal with a sudden or heavy fall.
– ORIGIN probably imitative.
plum pudding ● noun a rich suet pudding containing raisins, currants, and spices.
plum tomato ● noun a plum-shaped variety of tomato.
plumule /plo͝omyo͞ol/ ● noun **1** the rudimentary shoot or stem of an embryo plant. **2** a bird's down feather.
– ORIGIN Latin *plumula* 'small feather'.
plumy ● adjective resembling or decorated with feathers.
plunder ● verb enter forcibly and steal goods from, especially during war or civil disorder. ● noun **1** the action of plundering. **2** goods obtained by plundering.
– DERIVATIVES **plunderer** noun.
– ORIGIN German *plündern*, 'rob of household goods', from High German *plunder* 'household effects'.
plunge ● verb **1** fall or move suddenly and uncontrollably. **2** jump or dive quickly and energetically. **3** (**plunge in**) embark impetuously on (a course of action). **4** (**be plunged into**) suddenly bring into a specified condition or state: *the area was was plunged into darkness.* **5** push or thrust quickly. ● noun an act or instance of plunging.
– PHRASES **take the plunge** informal commit oneself to a bold course of action after consideration.
– ORIGIN Old French *plungier* 'thrust down', from Latin *plumbum* 'lead, plummet'.
plunge pool ● noun **1** a deep basin at the foot of a waterfall formed by the action of the falling water. **2** a small, deep swimming pool.
plunger ● noun **1** a part of a device or mechanism that works with a plunging or thrusting movement. **2** a device consisting of a rubber cup on a long handle, used to clear blocked pipes by means of suction.
plunk informal ● verb **1** play a keyboard or pluck a stringed instrument in an inexpressive way. **2** US hit (someone) abruptly. **3** chiefly N. Amer. set down heavily or abruptly. ● noun **1** a plunking sound. **2** US a heavy blow. **3** N. Amer. an act of setting something down heavily.
– ORIGIN probably imitative.
pluperfect ● adjective Grammar (of a tense) denoting an action completed prior to some past point of time, formed in English by *had* and the past participle (as in *he had gone by then*).
– ORIGIN from Latin *plus quam perfectum* 'more than perfect' (referring to the perfect tense).
plural ● adjective **1** more than one in number. **2** Grammar (of a word or form) denoting more than one. ● noun Grammar a plural word or form.
– DERIVATIVES **plurally** adverb.

Thesaurus

p

away, peg away.
plum ● adjective *(informal) a plum job* EXCELLENT, very good, wonderful, marvellous, choice, first-class; *informal* great, terrific, cushy.
plumb¹ ● verb *an attempt to plumb her psyche* EXPLORE, probe, delve into, search, examine, investigate, fathom, penetrate, understand.
● adverb **1** *(informal) it went plumb through the screen* RIGHT, exactly, precisely, directly, dead, straight; *informal* (slap) bang. **2** *(N. Amer. informal) he's plumb crazy* UTTERLY, absolutely, completely, downright, totally, quite, thoroughly. **3** *(archaic) the bell hangs plumb* VERTICALLY, perpendicularly, straight down.
● adjective *a plumb drop* VERTICAL, perpendicular, straight.
– PHRASES **plumb the depths** FIND, experience the extremes, reach the lowest point; reach rock bottom.
plumb² ● verb *he plumbed in the washing machine* INSTALL, put in, fit.
plume ● noun *ostrich plumes* FEATHER, quill; *Ornithology* plumule, covert.
– PHRASES **plume oneself** CONGRATULATE ONESELF, preen oneself, pat oneself on the back, pride oneself, boast about.
plummet ● verb **1** *the plane plummeted to the ground* PLUNGE, nosedive, dive, drop, fall, descend, hurtle. **2** *share prices plummeted* FALL STEEPLY, plunge, tumble, drop rapidly, go down, slump; *informal* crash, nosedive.
plummy ● adjective *(Brit. informal) a plummy voice* UPPER-CLASS, refined, aristocratic, grand; *Brit.* Home Counties; *Scottish* Kelvinside, Morningside; *Brit. informal* posh, Sloaney.
plump¹ ● adjective *a plump child* CHUBBY, fat, stout, rotund, well padded, ample, round, chunky, portly, overweight, fleshy, paunchy, bulky, corpulent; *informal* tubby, roly-poly, pudgy, beefy, porky, blubbery; *Brit. informal* podgy, fubsy; *N. Amer. informal* zaftig, corn-fed.
– OPPOSITES thin.
plump² ● verb **1** *Jack plumped down on to a chair* FLOP, COLLAPSE, sink, fall, drop, slump; *informal* plonk oneself; *N. Amer. informal* plank oneself. **2** *she plumped her bag on the table* PUT (DOWN), set (down), place, deposit, dump, stick; *informal* plonk; *Brit. informal* bung; *N. Amer. informal* plunk. **3** *I plumped for a cream cake* CHOOSE, decide on, go for, opt for, pick, settle on, select, take, elect.
plunder ● verb **1** *they plundered the countryside* PILLAGE, loot, rob, raid, ransack, despoil, strip, ravage, lay waste, devastate, sack, rape. **2** *money plundered from pension funds* STEAL, purloin, thieve, seize, pillage; embezzle.
● noun **1** *the plunder of the villages* LOOTING, pillaging, plundering, raiding, ransacking, devastation, sacking; *poetic/literary* rapine. **2** *the army took huge quantities of plunder* BOOTY, loot, stolen goods, spoils, ill-gotten gains; *informal* swag.
plunge ● verb **1** *Joy plunged into the sea* DIVE, jump, throw oneself, launch oneself. **2** *the aircraft plunged to the ground* PLUMMET, nosedive, drop, fall, pitch, tumble, descend. **3** *the car plunged down an alley* CHARGE, hurtle, career, plough, cannon, tear; *N. Amer. informal* barrel. **4** *oil prices plunged* FALL SHARPLY, plummet, drop, go down, tumble, slump; *informal* crash, nosedive. **5** *he plunged the dagger into her back* THRUST, jab, stab, sink, stick, ram, drive, push, shove, force. **6** *plunge the pears into water* IMMERSE, submerge, dip, dunk. **7** *the room was plunged into darkness* THROW, cast, pitch.
● noun **1** *a plunge into the deep end* DIVE, jump, nosedive, fall, pitch, drop, plummet, descent. **2** *a plunge in profits* FALL, drop, slump; *informal* nosedive, crash.
– PHRASES **take the plunge** COMMIT ONESELF, go for it, throw caution

– ORIGIN Latin *pluralis*, from *plus* 'more'.
pluralism ● noun **1** a political system of power-sharing among a number of political parties. **2** the existence or toleration of a diversity of ethnic groups or differing cultures and views within a society. **3** Philosophy a theory or system that recognizes more than one ultimate principle. **4** the holding of more than one ecclesiastical office or position at the same time by one person.
– DERIVATIVES **pluralist** noun & adjective **pluralistic** adjective.
plurality ● noun (pl. **pluralities**) **1** the fact or state of being plural. **2** a large number of people or things. **3** US the number of votes cast for a candidate who receives more than any other but does not receive an absolute majority.
pluralize (also **pluralise**) ● verb **1** make more numerous. **2** give a plural form to (a word).
– DERIVATIVES **pluralization** noun.
plural society ● noun a society composed of different ethnic groups or cultural traditions.
plus ● preposition **1** with the addition of. **2** informal together with. ● adjective **1** (after a number or amount) at least: *$500,000 plus.* **2** (after a grade) rather better than: *B plus.* **3** (before a number) above zero; positive: *plus 60 degrees centigrade.* **4** having a positive electric charge. ● noun **1** a plus sign. **2** informal an advantage. ● conjunction informal furthermore; also.
– ORIGIN Latin, 'more'.
plus ça change /plōō sa **shonj**/ ● exclamation used to express the observation that certain things remain fundamentally unchanged.
– ORIGIN French, from *plus ça change, plus c'est la même chose* 'the more it changes, the more it stays the same'.
plus fours ● plural noun men's baggy knickerbockers reaching below the knee, formerly worn for hunting and golf.
– ORIGIN so named because the overhang at the knee required an extra four inches of material.
plush ● noun a rich fabric of silk, cotton, or wool, with a long, soft nap. ● adjective informal expensively luxurious.
– DERIVATIVES **plushy** adjective.
– ORIGIN obsolete French *pluche*, from Latin *pilus* 'hair'.
plus sign ● noun the symbol +, indicating addition or a positive value.
plutocracy /plōō**tok**rəsi/ ● noun (pl. **plutocracies**) **1** government by the wealthy. **2** a society governed by the wealthy. **3** an elite or ruling class whose power derives from their wealth.
– DERIVATIVES **plutocratic** adjective.
– ORIGIN from Greek *ploutos* 'wealth' + *kratos* 'strength, authority'.
plutocrat ● noun often derogatory a person whose power derives from their wealth.
Plutonian ● adjective relating to the planet Pluto.
plutonic ● adjective **1** Geology (of igneous rock) formed by solidification at considerable depth beneath the earth's surface. **2** (**Plutonic**) relating to the underworld or the Greek god Pluto.
plutonium ● noun a radioactive metallic element formed by the radioactive decay of uranium and used as a fuel in nuclear reactors and as an explosive in atomic weapons.
– ORIGIN from the planet *Pluto*, on the pattern of *neptunium* (Pluto being the next planet beyond Neptune).
pluvial ● adjective relating to or characterized by rainfall.
– ORIGIN Latin *pluvialis*, from *pluvia* 'rain'.
ply[1] ● noun (pl. **plies**) **1** a thickness or layer of a folded or laminated material. **2** each of a number of multiple layers or strands of which something is made.
– ORIGIN French *pli* 'fold', from Latin *plicare* 'to fold'.
ply[2] ● verb (**plies, plied**) **1** work steadily with (a tool) or at (one's job). **2** (of a vessel or vehicle) travel regularly over a route, typically for commercial purposes. **3** (**ply with**) provide (someone) with (food or drink) in a continuous or insistent way. **4** (**ply with**) direct (numerous questions) at (someone).
– ORIGIN shortening of APPLY.
plywood ● noun thin strong board consisting of two or more layers of wood glued together.
PM ● abbreviation **1** post-mortem. **2** Prime Minister.
Pm ● symbol the chemical element promethium.
p.m. ● abbreviation after noon.
– ORIGIN from Latin *post meridiem.*
PMS ● abbreviation premenstrual syndrome.
PMT ● abbreviation chiefly Brit. premenstrual tension.
pneumatic ● adjective containing or operated by air or gas under pressure.
– DERIVATIVES **pneumatically** adverb.
– ORIGIN Greek *pneumatikos*, from *pneuma* 'wind'.
pneumatic drill ● noun a large, heavy drill driven by compressed air, used for breaking up a hard surface.
pneumatics ● plural noun (treated as sing.) the science of the mechanical properties of gases.
pneumococcus /nyōōmə**kok**kəss/ ● noun (pl. **pneumococci** /nyōōmə**kok**k(s)ī/) a bacterium associated with pneumonia and some forms of meningitis.
– DERIVATIVES **pneumococcal** adjective.
pneumonia /nyōō**mō**niə/ ● noun a lung infection in which the air sacs fill with pus.
– DERIVATIVES **pneumonic** adjective.
– ORIGIN from Greek *pneumōn* 'lung'.
PNG ● abbreviation Papua New Guinea.
P. & O. ● abbreviation Peninsular and Oriental Shipping Company (or Line).
PO ● abbreviation **1** postal order. **2** Post Office.
Po ● symbol the chemical element polonium.
poach[1] ● verb cook by simmering in a small amount of liquid.
– ORIGIN Old French *pochier* (earlier in the sense 'enclose in a bag'), from *poche* 'bag, pocket'.
poach[2] ● verb **1** illegally take (game or fish) from private or protected areas. **2** take or acquire in an unfair or clandestine way.
– ORIGIN apparently related to POKE[1]; perhaps also partly from Old French *pochier* (see POACH[1]).
poacher[1] ● noun a pan for poaching eggs or other food.
poacher[2] ● noun a person who poaches game or fish.
PO box ● noun short for POST OFFICE BOX.
pochard /**pō**chərd/ ● noun a diving duck, the male of which typically has a reddish-brown head.
– ORIGIN of unknown origin.
pock ● noun a pockmark.
– DERIVATIVES **pocked** adjective.
– ORIGIN Old English.
pocket ● noun **1** a small bag sewn into or on clothing, used for carrying small articles. **2** a small, isolated patch, group, or area. **3** (**one's pocket**) informal one's financial resources. **4** a pouch-like storage compartment in a suitcase, car door, etc. **5** an opening at the corner or on the side of a billiard table into which balls are struck. ● adjective of a suitable size for carrying in a pocket. ● verb (**pocketed, pocketing**) **1** put into one's pocket. **2** take for oneself, especially dishonestly. **3** Billiards & Snooker drive (a ball) into a pocket.
– PHRASES **in** (or **out of**) **pocket** having gained (or lost) money in a transaction. **in someone's pocket** dependent on someone, especially financially, and therefore under their influence. **line one's pocket** make money, especially dishonestly. **put one's**

p

Thesaurus

to the wind(s), risk it; *informal* jump in at the deep end, go for broke.
plurality ● noun *a plurality of theories* WIDE VARIETY, diversity, range, lot, multitude, multiplicity, galaxy, wealth, profusion, abundance, plethora, host; *informal* load, stack, heap, mass.
plus ● preposition **1** *three plus three makes six* AND, added to. **2** *(informal) he wrote four novels plus various poems* AS WELL AS, together with, along with, in addition to, and, not to mention, besides.
– OPPOSITES minus.
● noun *(informal) one of the pluses of the job* ADVANTAGE, good point, asset, pro, (fringe) benefit, bonus, extra, attraction; *informal* perk; *formal* perquisite.
– OPPOSITES disadvantage.
plush ● adjective *(informal)* LUXURIOUS, luxury, de luxe, sumptuous, palatial, lavish, opulent, magnificent, lush, rich, expensive, fancy, grand; *Brit.* upmarket; *informal* posh, ritzy, swanky, classy; *Brit. informal* swish; *N. Amer. informal* swank.
– OPPOSITES austere.
plutocrat ● noun RICH PERSON, magnate, millionaire, billionaire, multimillionaire; nouveau riche; *informal* fat cat, moneybags.
ply[1] ● verb **1** *the gondolier plied his oar* USE, wield, work, manipulate, handle, operate, utilize, employ. **2** *he plied a profitable trade* ENGAGE IN, carry on, pursue, conduct, practise; *archaic* prosecute. **3** *ferries ply between all lake resorts* GO REGULARLY, travel, shuttle, go back and forth. **4** *she plied me with scones* PROVIDE, supply, lavish, shower, regale. **5** *he plied her with questions* BOMBARD, assail, beset, pester, plague, harass, importune; *informal* hassle.
ply[2] ● noun *a three-ply tissue* LAYER, thickness, strand, sheet, leaf.

hand in one's pocket spend or provide one's own money.
– DERIVATIVES **pocketable** adjective.
– ORIGIN Old French *pokete* 'little bag', from *poke* 'pouch'.

pocketbook • noun **1** Brit. a notebook. **2** US a wallet, purse, or handbag.

pocket borough • noun (before the 1832 Reform Act) a borough in which the election of political representatives was controlled by one person or family.

pocket knife • noun a penknife.

pocket money • noun Brit. **1** a small regular allowance given to a child by their parents. **2** a small amount of money for minor expenses.

pocket watch • noun a watch on a chain, intended to be carried in a jacket or waistcoat pocket.

pockmark • noun **1** a pitted scar or mark on the skin left by a pustule or spot. **2** a mark or pitted area disfiguring a surface. • verb cover or disfigure with pockmarks.

pod[1] • noun **1** a long seed-case of a leguminous plant such as the pea. **2** a self-contained or detachable unit on an aircraft or spacecraft. • verb (**podded**, **podding**) **1** remove (peas or beans) from their pods prior to cooking. **2** (of a plant) bear or form pods.
– ORIGIN from dialect *podware*, *podder* 'field crops', of unknown origin.

pod[2] • noun a small herd or school of marine animals, especially whales.
– ORIGIN of unknown origin.

podge • noun Brit. informal **1** a short, fat person. **2** excess weight; fat.
– ORIGIN of unknown origin.

podgy • adjective (**podgier**, **podgiest**) Brit. informal rather fat; chubby.

podiatry /pədīətri/ • noun another term for CHIROPODY.
– DERIVATIVES **podiatrist** noun.
– ORIGIN from Greek *pous* 'foot' + *iatros* 'physician'.

podium /pōdiəm/ • noun (pl. **podiums** or **podia** /pōdiə/) **1** a small platform on which a person may stand to be seen by an audience. **2** N. Amer. a lectern.
– ORIGIN Greek *podion* 'little foot'.

podzol /podzol/ (also **podsol** /podsol/) • noun an infertile acidic soil with a grey subsurface layer, typical of coniferous woodland.
– ORIGIN from Russian *pod* 'under' + *zola* 'ashes'.

poem • noun a literary composition in verse, typically concerned with the expression of feelings or imaginative description.
– ORIGIN Grek *poēma*, variant of *poiēma* 'fiction, poem', from *poiein* 'create'.

poesy /pōizi/ • noun archaic or literary poetry.
– ORIGIN Greek *poēsis*, *poiēsis* 'making, poetry'.

poet • noun **1** a person who writes poems. **2** a person possessing special powers of imagination or expression.
– DERIVATIVES **poetess** noun.

poetaster /pōitastər/ • noun a person who writes inferior poetry.

poetic (also **poetical**) • adjective relating to or of the nature of poetry.
– DERIVATIVES **poetically** adverb.

poeticize (also **poeticise**) • verb **1** make poetic in character. **2** write or speak poetically.
– DERIVATIVES **poeticism** noun.

poetic justice • noun fitting or deserved punishment or reward.

poetic licence • noun departure from convention or factual accuracy for artistic effect.

poetics • plural noun (treated as sing.) the study of linguistic techniques in poetry and literature.

poetize (also **poetise**) • verb represent in poetic form.

Poet Laureate • noun (pl. **Poets Laureate**) a poet appointed by the British sovereign to write poems for royal and official occasions.

poetry • noun **1** poems collectively or as a literary genre. **2** a quality of beauty and emotional intensity regarded as characteristic of poetry.

po-faced • adjective Brit. humourless and disapproving.
– ORIGIN perhaps from *po* 'chamber pot', influenced by *poker-faced*.

pogo • verb (**pogoes**, **pogoed**) informal jump up and down as if on a pogo stick as a form of dancing to rock music.

pogo stick • noun a toy for bouncing around on, consisting of a spring-loaded pole with a handle at the top and rests for the feet near the bottom.

pogrom /pogrəm/ • noun an organized massacre of an ethnic group, originally that of Jews in Russia or eastern Europe.
– ORIGIN Russian, 'devastation'.

poignant /poynyənt/ • adjective evoking a keen sense of sadness or regret.
– DERIVATIVES **poignancy** noun **poignantly** adverb.
– ORIGIN from Old French *poindre* 'to prick', from Latin *pungere*.

poikilotherm /poykilləthermˌ/ • noun Zoology an organism that cannot regulate its body temperature except by behavioural means such as basking or burrowing. Often contrasted with HOMEOTHERM.
– DERIVATIVES **poikilothermic** adjective.
– ORIGIN from Greek *poikilos* 'varied'.

poinciana /poynsiaanə/ • noun a tropical tree with showy red or red and yellow flowers.
– ORIGIN named after M. de *Poinci*, a 17th-century governor of the Antilles.

poinsettia /poynsettiə/ • noun a small shrub with large showy scarlet bracts surrounding the small yellow flowers.
– ORIGIN named after the American diplomat and botanist Joel R. *Poinsett* (1779–1851).

point • noun **1** the tapered, sharp end of a tool, weapon, or other object. **2** a particular spot, place, or moment. **3** an item, detail, or idea in a discussion, text, etc. **4** (**the point**) the most significant or relevant factor or element. **5** advantage or purpose: *what's the point of it all?* **6** a positive feature or characteristic. **7** a unit of scoring or of measuring value, achievement, or extent. **8** a full stop or a decimal point. **9** a very small dot or mark on a surface. **10** (in geometry) something having position but not spatial extent, magnitude, dimension, or direction. **11** each of thirty-two directions marked at equal distances round a compass. **12** a narrow piece of land jutting out into the sea. **13** (**points**) Brit. a junction of two railway lines, with a pair of linked tapering rails that can be moved sideways to allow a

p

Thesaurus

poach • verb **1** *he's been poaching salmon* HUNT ILLEGALLY, catch illegally; steal. **2** *workers were poached by other firms* STEAL, appropriate, purloin, take; *informal* nab, swipe; *Brit. informal* nick, pinch.

pocket • noun **1** *a bag with two pockets* POUCH, compartment. **2** *the jewellery was beyond her pocket* MEANS, budget, resources, finances, funds, money, wherewithal; *N. Amer.* pocketbook. **3** *pockets of disaffection* (ISOLATED) AREA, patch, region, island, cluster, centre.
• adjective *a pocket dictionary* SMALL, little, miniature, mini, compact, concise, abridged, potted, portable; *N. Amer.* vest-pocket.
• verb *he pocketed $900,000 of their money* STEAL, take, appropriate, thieve, purloin, misappropriate, embezzle; *informal* filch, swipe, snaffle; *Brit. informal* pinch, nick, whip.

pockmark • noun SCAR, pit, pock, mark, blemish.

pod • noun SHELL, husk, hull, case; *N. Amer.* shuck; *Botany* pericarp, capsule.

podgy • adjective *(Brit. informal)* CHUBBY, plump, fat, stout, rotund, well padded, ample, round, chunky, portly, overweight, fleshy, paunchy, bulky, corpulent; *informal* tubby, roly-poly, pudgy, beefy, porky, blubbery; *N. Amer. informal* zaftig, corn-fed.
– OPPOSITES thin.

podium • noun PLATFORM, stage, dais, rostrum, stand, soapbox.

poem • noun VERSE, rhyme, piece of poetry, song, verselet.

poet • noun WRITER OF POETRY, versifier, rhymester, rhymer, sonneteer, lyricist, lyrist; laureate; *poetic/literary* bard; *derogatory* poetaster; *historical* troubadour, balladeer; *archaic* rhymist.

poetic • adjective **1** *poetic compositions* POETICAL, verse, metrical, lyrical, lyric, elegiac. **2** *poetic language* EXPRESSIVE, figurative, symbolic, flowery, artistic, elegant, fine, beautiful; sensitive, imaginative, creative.

poetry • noun POEMS, verse, versification, metrical composition, rhymes, balladry; *archaic* poesy.

pogrom • noun MASSACRE, slaughter, mass murder, annihilation, extermination, decimation, carnage, bloodbath, bloodletting, butchery, genocide, holocaust, ethnic cleansing.

poignancy • noun PATHOS, pitifulness, piteousness, sadness, sorrow, mournfulness, wretchedness, misery, tragedy.

poignant • adjective TOUCHING, moving, sad, affecting, pitiful, pit-

train to pass from one line to the other. **14** Printing a unit of measurement for type sizes and spacing (in the UK and US 0.351 mm, in Europe 0.376 mm). **15** Brit. a socket in a wall for connecting a device to an electrical supply or communications network. **16** each of a set of electrical contacts in the distributor of a motor vehicle. **17** Cricket a fielding position on the off side near the batsman. **18** Ballet another term for POINTE. ● **verb** **1** direct someone's attention in a particular direction by extending one's finger. **2** direct or aim (something). **3** face in or indicate a particular direction. **4** (**point out**) make someone aware of (a fact or circumstance). **5** (often **point to**) cite or function as evidence. **6** (**point up**) reveal the true nature or importance of. **7** give a sharp, tapered point to. **8** fill in or repair the joints of (brickwork or tiling) with smoothly finished mortar or cement.

– PHRASES **a case in point** an example that illustrates what is being discussed. **make a point of** make a special effort to do something. **on the point of** on the verge or brink of. **score points** deliberately make oneself appear superior by making clever remarks. **take someone's point** chiefly Brit. accept the validity of someone's idea or argument. **up to a point** to some extent.

– ORIGIN partly from Old French *pointe*, from Latin *puncta* 'pricking'; partly from Old French *point*, from Latin *punctum* 'something that is pricked'.

point-blank ● **adjective** **1** (of a shot or missile) fired from very close to its target. **2** without explanation or qualification.

point duty ● **noun** Brit. the duties of a police officer stationed at a junction to control traffic.

pointe /pwant/ ● **noun** (pl. pronounced same) Ballet the tips of the toes.

– ORIGIN French, 'tip'.

pointed ● **adjective** **1** having a sharpened or tapered tip or end. **2** (of a remark or look) clearly directed and unambiguous in intent.

– DERIVATIVES **pointedly** adverb.

pointer ● **noun** **1** a long, thin piece of metal on a scale or dial which moves to give a reading. **2** a rod used for pointing to features on a map or chart. **3** a hint or tip. **4** a breed of dog that on scenting game stands rigid looking towards it. **5** Computing a cursor or a link.

pointillism /pwantiliz'm/ ● **noun** a technique of neo-Impressionist painting using tiny dots of various pure colours, which become blended in the viewer's eye.

– DERIVATIVES **pointillist** noun & adjective.

– ORIGIN from French *pointiller* 'mark with dots'.

pointing ● **noun** mortar or cement used to fill the joints of brickwork or tiling.

pointless ● **adjective** having little or no sense or purpose.

– DERIVATIVES **pointlessly** adverb **pointlessness** noun.

point of order ● **noun** (pl. **points of order**) a query in a formal debate or meeting as to whether correct procedure is being followed.

point of view ● **noun** (pl. **points of view**) **1** a particular attitude or way of considering a matter. **2** the position from which something or someone is observed.

point-to-point ● **noun** (pl. **point-to-points**) an amateur cross-country steeplechase for horses used in hunting.

pointy ● **adjective** (**pointier**, **pointiest**) informal having a pointed tip or end.

poise[1] ● **noun** **1** graceful and elegant bearing. **2** composure and dignity of manner. ● **verb** **1** be or cause to be balanced or suspended. **2** (**poised**) composed and elegant or self-assured. **3** (**be poised to do**) be ready and prepared to do.

– ORIGIN Old French *pois*, from Latin *pensum* 'weight'.

poise[2] ● **noun** Physics a unit used to express the viscosity of a liquid, equal to 0.1 newton seconds per square metre.

– ORIGIN named after the French physician Jean L. M. *Poiseuille* (1799–1869).

poisha /poyshə/ ● **noun** (pl. same) a monetary unit of Bangladesh, equal to one hundredth of a taka.

– ORIGIN Bengali, alteration of PAISA.

poison ● **noun** **1** a substance that causes death or injury when introduced into or absorbed by a living organism. **2** a destructive or corrupting influence. ● **verb** **1** administer poison to. **2** contaminate with poison. **3** corrupt or prove harmful to.

– DERIVATIVES **poisoner** noun.

– ORIGIN Old French, 'magic potion', from Latin *potio* 'potion'.

Thesaurus

eous, pathetic, sorrowful, mournful, wretched, miserable, distressing, heart-rending, tear-jerking, plaintive, tragic.

p

point[1] ● **noun** **1** *the point of a needle* TIP, (sharp) end, extremity; prong, spike, tine, nib, barb. **2** *points of light* PINPOINT, dot, spot, speck, fleck. **3** *a meeting point* PLACE, position, location, site, spot, area. **4** *this point in her life* TIME, stage, juncture, period, phase. **5** *the tension had reached such a high point* LEVEL, degree, stage, pitch, extent. **6** *an important point* DETAIL, item, fact, thing, argument, consideration, factor, element; subject, issue, topic, question, matter. **7** *get to the point* HEART OF THE MATTER, most important part, essence, nub, keynote, core, pith, crux; meaning, significance, gist, substance, thrust, burden, relevance; *informal* brass tacks, nitty-gritty. **8** *what's the point of this?* PURPOSE, aim, object, objective, goal, intention; use, sense, value, advantage. **9** *he had his good points* ATTRIBUTE, characteristic, feature, trait, quality, property, aspect, side.

● **verb** **1** *she pointed the gun at him* AIM, direct, level, train. **2** *the evidence pointed to his guilt* INDICATE, suggest, evidence, signal, signify, denote, bespeak, reveal, manifest.

– PHRASES **beside the point** IRRELEVANT, immaterial, unimportant, neither here nor there, inconsequential, incidental, out of place, unconnected, peripheral, tangential, extraneous. **in point of fact** IN FACT, as a matter of fact, actually, in actual fact, really, in reality, as it happens, in truth. **make a point of** MAKE AN EFFORT TO, go out of one's way to, put emphasis on. **on the point of** (JUST) ABOUT TO, on the verge of, on the brink of, going to, all set to. **point of view** OPINION, view, belief, attitude, feeling, sentiment, thoughts; position, perspective, viewpoint, standpoint, outlook. **point something out** IDENTIFY, show, designate, draw attention to, indicate, specify, detail, mention. **point something up** EMPHASIZE, highlight, draw attention to, accentuate, underline, spotlight, foreground, put emphasis on, stress, play up, accent, bring to the fore. **to the point** RELEVANT, pertinent, apposite, germane, applicable, apropos, appropriate, apt, fitting, suitable, material; *formal* ad rem. **up to a point** PARTLY, to some extent, to a certain degree, in part, somewhat, partially.

point[2] ● **noun** *the ship rounded the point* PROMONTORY, headland, foreland, cape, peninsula, bluff, ness, horn.

point-blank ● **adverb** **1** *he fired the pistol point-blank* AT CLOSE RANGE, close up, close to. **2** *she couldn't say it point-blank* BLUNTLY, directly, straight, frankly, candidly, openly, explicitly, unequivocally, unambiguously, plainly, flatly, categorically, outright.

● **adjective** *a point-blank refusal* BLUNT, direct, straight, straightforward, frank, candid, forthright, explicit, unequivocal, plain, clear, flat, decisive, unqualified, categorical, outright.

pointed ● **adjective** **1** *a pointed stick* SHARP, tapering, tapered, conical, jagged, spiky, spiked, barbed; *informal* pointy. **2** *a pointed remark* CUTTING, trenchant, biting, incisive, acerbic, caustic, scathing, venomous, sarcastic; *informal* sarky; *N. Amer. informal* snarky.

pointer ● **noun** **1** *the pointer moved to 100rpm* INDICATOR, needle, arrow, hand. **2** *he used a pointer on the chart* STICK, rod, cane; cursor. **3** *a pointer to the outcome of the election* INDICATION, indicator, clue, hint, sign, signal, evidence, intimation, inkling, suggestion. **4** *I can give you a few pointers* TIP, hint, suggestion, guideline, recommendation.

pointless ● **adjective** SENSELESS, futile, hopeless, fruitless, useless, needless, in vain, unavailing, aimless, idle, worthless, valueless; absurd, insane, stupid, silly, foolish.

– OPPOSITES valuable.

poise ● **noun** **1** *poise and good deportment* GRACE, gracefulness, elegance, balance, control. **2** *despite the setback she retained her poise* COMPOSURE, equanimity, self-possession, aplomb, presence of mind, self-assurance, self-control, nerve, calm, sangfroid, dignity; *informal* cool, unflappability.

● **verb** **1** *she was poised on one foot* BALANCE, hold (oneself) steady, be suspended, remain motionless, hang, hover. **2** *he was poised for action* PREPARE ONESELF, ready oneself, brace oneself, gear oneself up, stand by.

poison ● **noun** **1** *a deadly poison* TOXIN, toxicant, venom; *archaic* bane. **2** *Marianne would spread her poison* MALICE, ill will, hate, malevolence, bitterness, spite, spitefulness, venom, acrimony, rancour; bad influence, cancer, corruption, pollution.

– RELATED TERMS toxic.

● **verb** **1** *her mother poisoned her* GIVE POISON TO; murder. **2** *a blackmailer poisoning baby foods* CONTAMINATE, put poison in, adulterate, spike, lace, doctor. **3** *the Amazon is being poisoned* POLLUTE,

poisoned chalice ● noun something offered which is apparently appealing or beneficial but which is likely to prove a source of problems to the recipient.

poison ivy ● noun a North American climbing plant which secretes an irritant oil from its leaves.

poisonous ● adjective **1** producing or of the nature of poison. **2** extremely unpleasant or malicious.
– DERIVATIVES **poisonously** adverb.

poison pen letter ● noun an anonymous letter that is libellous or abusive.

poison pill ● noun Finance a tactic used by a company threatened with an unwelcome takeover bid to make itself unattractive to the bidder.

poke[1] ● verb **1** jab or prod with a finger or a sharp object. **2** make (a hole) by jabbing or prodding. **3** (**poke about/around**) look or search around a place. **3** (often **poke out**) thrust out or protrude in a particular direction. ● noun an act of poking.
– PHRASES **poke fun at** tease or make fun of. **poke one's nose into** *(informal)* informal take an intrusive interest in. **take a poke at** informal hit, punch, or criticize.
– ORIGIN origin uncertain.

poke[2] ● noun chiefly Scottish a bag or small sack.
– ORIGIN variant of Old French *poche* 'pocket'; related to POUCH.

poke bonnet ● noun a woman's bonnet with a projecting brim, popular in the early 19th century.

poker[1] ● noun a metal rod with a handle, used for prodding and stirring an open fire.

poker[2] ● noun a card game in which the players bet on the value of the hands dealt to them, sometimes using bluff.
– ORIGIN perhaps related to German *pochen* 'to brag', *Pochspiel* 'bragging game'.

poker face ● noun an impassive expression that hides one's true feelings.

pokerwork ● noun British term for PYROGRAPHY.

pokey ● noun informal, chiefly N. Amer. prison.
– ORIGIN variant of *pogey* (Canadian informal term meaning 'hostel for the needy', later 'unemployment benefit'), perhaps influenced by POKY.

poky (also **pokey**) ● adjective (**pokier**, **pokiest**) **1** (of a room or building) uncomfortably small and cramped. **2** N. Amer. annoyingly slow.
– ORIGIN from POKE[1] (in the sense 'confine'.

Polack /pōlak/ ● noun derogatory, chiefly N. Amer. a person from Poland or of Polish descent.
– ORIGIN Polish.

polar ● adjective **1** relating to the North or South Poles of the earth or their adjacent area. **2** having an electrical or magnetic field. **3** directly opposite in character or tendency.

polar bear ● noun a large white arctic bear which lives mainly on the pack ice.

polarity ● noun (pl. **polarities**) **1** the state of having poles or opposites. **2** the direction of a magnetic or electric field.

polarize (also **polarise**) ● verb **1** divide into two sharply contrasting groups or sets of beliefs. **2** Physics restrict the vibrations of (a transverse wave, especially light) to one direction. **3** give magnetic or electric polarity to.
– DERIVATIVES **polarization** noun.

Polaroid ● noun trademark **1** a composite material with the property of polarizing light, produced in thin plastic sheets. **2** (**Polaroids**) sunglasses with lenses of polaroid. **3** a type of camera that produces a finished print rapidly after each exposure. **4** a photograph taken with such a camera.

polder /pōldər/ ● noun a piece of land reclaimed from the sea or a river, especially in the Netherlands.
– ORIGIN Dutch.

Pole ● noun a person from Poland.

pole[1] ● noun **1** a long, slender rounded piece of wood or metal, typically used as a support. **2** a wooden shaft at the front of a cart or carriage drawn by animals and attached to their yokes or collars. **3** Brit. historical another term for PERCH[3] (in sense 1). **4** (also **square pole**) Brit. historical another term for PERCH[3] (in sense 2). ● verb propel (a boat) with a pole.
– PHRASES **up the pole** Brit. informal mad.
– ORIGIN Old English, related to Latin *palus* 'stake'.

pole[2] ● noun **1** either of the two locations (**North Pole** or **South Pole**) on the earth which are the ends of the axis of rotation. **2** Geometry each of the two points at which the axis of a circle cuts the surface of a sphere. **3** each of the two opposite points of a magnet at which magnetic forces are strongest. **4** the positive or negative terminal of an electric cell or battery. **5** each of two opposed principles or ideas.
– PHRASES **be poles apart** have nothing in common.
– ORIGIN Greek *polos* 'pivot, axis, sky'.

poleaxe (US also **poleax**) ● noun **1** a battleaxe. **2** a butcher's axe used to slaughter animals. ● verb **1** kill or knock down with or as if with a poleaxe. **2** shock greatly.
– ORIGIN from POLL + AXE.

polecat ● noun **1** a weasel-like mammal with dark brown fur and an unpleasant smell. **2** N. Amer. a skunk.
– ORIGIN perhaps from Old French *pole* 'chicken' + CAT.

polemic /pəlemmik/ ● noun **1** a strong verbal or written attack. **2** (also **polemics**) the practice of engaging in controversial debate. ● adjective (also **polemical**) of or involving disputatious or controversial debate.
– DERIVATIVES **polemicist** noun **polemicize** (also **polemicise**) verb.
– ORIGIN Greek *polemikos*, from *polemos* 'war'.

polenta /pəlentə/ ● noun (in Italian cookery) maize flour or a dough made from this, which is boiled and then fried or baked.
– ORIGIN Latin, 'pearl barley'.

pole position ● noun the most favourable position at the start of a motor race.
– ORIGIN from the use of *pole* in horse racing to mean the starting position next to the inside boundary fence.

Pole Star ● noun a fairly bright star located within one degree of the celestial north pole, in the constellation Ursa Minor.

pole vault ● noun an athletic event in which competitors attempt to vault over a high bar with the aid of an extremely

Thesaurus

contaminate, taint, blight, spoil; *poetic/literary* befoul. **4** *they poisoned his mind* PREJUDICE, bias, jaundice, embitter, sour, envenom, warp, corrupt, subvert.

poisonous ● adjective **1** *a poisonous snake* VENOMOUS, deadly. **2** *a poisonous chemical* TOXIC, noxious, deadly, fatal, lethal, mortal, death-dealing. **3** *a poisonous glance* MALICIOUS, malevolent, hostile, vicious, spiteful, bitter, venomous, vindictive, vitriolic, rancorous, malign, pernicious, mean, nasty; *informal* bitchy, catty.
– OPPOSITES harmless, non-toxic, benevolent.

poke ● verb **1** *she poked him in the ribs* PROD, jab, dig, nudge, butt, shove, jolt, stab, stick. **2** *leave the cable poking out* STICK OUT, jut out, protrude, project, extend.
● noun **1** *Carrie gave him a poke* PROD, jab, dig, elbow, nudge. **2** *a poke in the arm* JAB, dig, nudge, shove, stab.
– PHRASES **poke about/around** SEARCH, hunt, rummage (around), forage, grub, root about/around, scavenge, nose around, ferret (about/around); sift through, rifle through, scour, comb, probe; *Brit. informal* rootle (around). **poke fun at** MOCK, make fun of, ridicule, laugh at, jeer at, sneer at, deride, scorn, scoff at, pillory, lampoon, tease, taunt, rag, chaff, jibe at; *informal* send up, take the mickey out of, kid, rib; *Brit. informal* wind up; *N. Amer. informal* goof on, rag on; *Austral./NZ informal* poke mullock at. **poke one's nose into** *(informal)* PRY INTO, interfere in, intrude on, butt into, meddle with; *informal* snoop into.

poky ● adjective SMALL, little, tiny, cramped, confined, restricted, boxy; *euphemistic* compact, bijou.
– OPPOSITES spacious.

polar ● adjective **1** *polar weather* ARCTIC, cold, freezing, icy, glacial, chilly, gelid. **2** *two polar types of interview* OPPOSITE, opposed, dichotomous, extreme, contrary, contradictory, antithetical.

polarity ● noun DIFFERENCE, dichotomy, separation, opposition, contradiction, antithesis, antagonism.

pole[1] ● noun POST, pillar, stanchion, paling, stake, stick, support, prop, batten, bar, rail, rod, beam; staff, stave, cane, baton.

pole[2] ● noun *points of view at opposite poles* EXTREMITY, extreme, limit, antipode.
– PHRASES **poles apart** COMPLETELY DIFFERENT, directly opposed, antithetical, incompatible, irreconcilable, worlds apart, at opposite extremes; *Brit.* like chalk and cheese.

polemic ● noun **1** *a polemic against injustice* DIATRIBE, invective, rant, tirade, broadside, attack, harangue, condemnation, criticism, stricture, admonition, rebuke; abuse; *informal* blast; *formal* castigation; *poetic/literary* philippic. **2** *he is skilled in polemics* ARGUMENTATION, argument, debate, contention, disputation, discussion, altercation; *formal* contestation.
● adjective *his famous polemic book*. See POLEMICAL.

long flexible pole.

police ● noun (treated as pl.) **1** a civil force responsible for the prevention and detection of crime and the maintenance of public order. **2** members of such a force. ● verb **1** maintain law and order in (an area), with or as with a police force. **2** regulate, administer, or control.
– ORIGIN originally in the sense 'public order': from Latin *politia* 'policy, government'.

policeman (or **policewoman**) ● noun a member of a police force.

police officer ● noun a policeman or policewoman.

police state ● noun a totalitarian state in which political police secretly supervise and control citizens' activities.

police station ● noun the office of a local police force.

policy[1] ● noun (pl. **policies**) **1** a course or principle of action adopted or proposed by an organization or individual. **2** archaic prudent or expedient conduct or action.
– ORIGIN Greek *politeia* 'citizenship', from *polis* 'city'.

policy[2] ● noun (pl. **policies**) a contract of insurance.
– ORIGIN French *police* 'bill of lading, contract of insurance'.

polio ● noun short for POLIOMYELITIS.

poliomyelitis /pōliōmīəlītiss/ ● noun an infectious disease, caused by a virus, that affects the central nervous system and can cause temporary or permanent paralysis.
– ORIGIN from Greek *polios* 'grey' + *muelos* 'marrow'.

Polish /pōlish/ ● noun the language of Poland. ● adjective relating to Poland.

polish /pollish/ ● verb **1** make smooth and shiny by rubbing. **2** improve or refine. **3** (**polish off**) informal finish or consume quickly. ● noun **1** a substance used to make something smooth and shiny when rubbed in. **2** an act of polishing. **3** smoothness or glossiness produced by polishing. **4** refinement or elegance.
– DERIVATIVES **polisher** noun.
– ORIGIN Latin *polire.*

politburo /pollitbyoorō/ ● noun (pl. **politburos**) the principal policy-making committee of a communist party, especially that of the former USSR.
– ORIGIN from Russian *politicheskoe byuro* 'political bureau'.

polite ● adjective (**politer**, **politest**) **1** courteous and well-mannered. **2** cultured and refined: *polite society.*
– DERIVATIVES **politely** adverb **politeness** noun.
– ORIGIN Latin *politus* 'polished, made smooth', from *polire* 'to polish'.

politesse /pollitess/ ● noun formal politeness or etiquette.
– ORIGIN French.

politic ● adjective **1** (of an action) sensible and wise in the circumstances. **2** (also **politick**) archaic prudent and shrewd. ● verb (**politicked**, **politicking**) often derogatory engage in political activity.
– ORIGIN Greek *politikos*, from *politēs* 'citizen'.

political ● adjective **1** relating to the government or public affairs of a country. **2** related to or interested in politics. **3** chiefly derogatory acting in the interests of status within an organization rather than on principle.
– DERIVATIVES **politically** adverb.

political correctness ● noun the avoidance of terms or behaviour considered to be discriminatory or offensive to certain groups of people.

politically correct (or **incorrect**) ● adjective exhibiting (or failing to exhibit) political correctness.

political prisoner ● noun a person imprisoned for their political beliefs or actions.

political science ● noun the study of political activity and behaviour.

politician ● noun **1** a person who is professionally involved in politics, especially as a holder of an elected office. **2** chiefly US a person who acts in a manipulative and devious way, typically to gain advancement.

politicize (also **politicise**) ● verb **1** make politically aware or politically active. **2** engage in or talk about politics.
– DERIVATIVES **politicization** noun.

politick ● adjective archaic spelling of POLITIC.

politico ● noun (pl. **politicos**) informal, chiefly derogatory a politician or person with strong political views.

politics ● plural noun (usu. treated as sing.) **1** the activities associated with governing a country or area, and with the political relations between states. **2** a particular set of political beliefs or principles. **3** activities aimed at gaining power within an organization: *office politics.* **4** the principles relating to or inherent in a sphere or activity, especially when concerned with power and status: *the politics of gender.*

polity ● noun (pl. **polities**) **1** a form or process of civil govern-

Thesaurus

p

polemical ● adjective CRITICAL, hostile, bitter, polemic, virulent, vitriolic, venomous, caustic, trenchant, cutting, acerbic, sardonic, sarcastic, scathing, sharp, incisive, devastating.

police ● noun the police force, police officers, policemen, policewomen, officers of the law, the forces of law and order; *Brit.* constabulary; *informal* the cops, the fuzz, (the long arm of) the law, the boys in blue; *Brit. informal* the (Old) Bill, coppers, bobbies, busies, the force; *N. Amer. informal* the heat; *informal, derogatory* pigs, the filth.
● verb **1** *we must police the area* GUARD, watch over, protect, defend, patrol; control, regulate. **2** *the regulations will be policed by the ministry* ENFORCE, regulate, oversee, supervise, monitor, observe, check.

police officer ● noun POLICEMAN, POLICEWOMAN, officer (of the law); *Brit.* constable; *N. Amer.* patrolman, trooper, roundsman; *informal* cop; *Brit. informal* copper, bobby, rozzer, busy, (PC) plod; *N. Amer. informal* uniform; *informal, derogatory* pig; *archaic* peeler.

policy ● noun **1** *government policy* PLANS, strategy, stratagem, approach, code, system, guidelines, theory; line, position, stance, attitude. **2** *(archaic) it's good policy to listen* PRACTICE, custom, procedure, conduct, convention.

polish ● verb **1** *I polished his shoes* SHINE, wax, buff, rub up/down; gloss, burnish; varnish, oil, glaze, lacquer, japan, shellac. **2** *polish up your essay* PERFECT, refine, improve, hone, enhance; brush up, revise, edit, correct, rewrite, go over, touch up; *informal* clean up.
● noun **1** *furniture polish* WAX, glaze, varnish; lacquer, japan, shellac. **2** *a good surface polish* SHINE, gloss, lustre, sheen, sparkle, patina, finish. **3** *his polish made him stand out* SOPHISTICATION, refinement, urbanity, suaveness, elegance, style, grace, finesse, cultivation, civility, gentility, breeding, courtesy, (good) manners; *informal* class.
– PHRASES **polish something off** *(informal)* **1** *he polished off an apple pie* EAT, finish, consume, devour, guzzle, wolf down, down, bolt; drink up, drain, quaff, gulp (down); *informal* binge on, stuff oneself with, get outside of, murder, put away, scoff, shovel down, pig out on, sink, swill, knock back; *Brit. informal* shift, gollop; *N. Amer. informal* scarf (down/up), snarf (down/up). **2** *the enemy tried to polish him off* DESTROY, finish off, despatch, do away with, eliminate, kill, liquidate; *informal* bump off, knock off, do in, take out, dispose of; *N. Amer. informal* rub out. **3** *I'll polish off the last few pages* COMPLETE, finish, deal with, accomplish, discharge, do; end, conclude, close, finalize, round off, wind up; *informal* wrap up, sew up.

polished ● adjective **1** *a polished table* SHINY, glossy, gleaming, lustrous, glassy; waxed, buffed, burnished; varnished, glazed, lacquered, japanned, shellacked. **2** *a polished performance* EXPERT, accomplished, masterly, masterful, skilful, adept, adroit, dexterous; impeccable, flawless, perfect, consummate, exquisite, outstanding, excellent, superb, superlative, first-rate, fine; *informal* ace. **3** *polished manners* REFINED, cultivated, civilized, well bred, polite, courteous, genteel, decorous, respectable, urbane, suave, sophisticated.
– OPPOSITES dull, inexpert, gauche.

polite ● adjective **1** *a very polite girl* WELL MANNERED, civil, courteous, mannerly, respectful, deferential, well behaved, well bred, gentlemanly, ladylike, genteel, gracious, urbane; tactful, diplomatic. **2** *polite society* CIVILIZED, refined, cultured, sophisticated, genteel, courtly.
– OPPOSITES rude, uncivilized.

politic ● adjective WISE, prudent, sensible, judicious, canny, sagacious, shrewd, astute; recommended, advantageous, beneficial, profitable, desirable, advisable; appropriate, suitable, fitting, apt.
– OPPOSITES unwise.

political ● adjective **1** *the political affairs of the nation* GOVERNMENTAL, government, constitutional, ministerial, parliamentary, diplomatic, legislative, administrative, bureaucratic; public, civic, state. **2** *he's a political man* POLITICALLY ACTIVE, party (political); militant, factional, partisan.

politician ● noun LEGISLATOR, elected official, Member of Parliament, MP, minister, statesman, stateswoman, public servant; senator, congressman/woman; *informal* politico, pol.

politics ● noun **1** *a career in politics* GOVERNMENT, affairs of state, public affairs; diplomacy. **2** *he studies politics* POLITICAL SCIENCE, civics, statecraft. **3** *what are his politics?* POLITICAL VIEWS, political

ment or constitution. **2** a state as a political entity.
– ORIGIN Greek *politeia* 'citizenship, government'.

polka /polkə/ ● noun a lively dance of Bohemian origin in duple time.
– ORIGIN Czech *půlka* 'half-step'.

polka dot ● noun each of a number of round dots repeated to form a regular pattern.

poll /pōl/ ● noun **1** the process of voting in an election. **2** a record of the number of votes cast. **3** dialect a person's head. ● verb **1** record the opinion or vote of. **2** (of an electoral candidate) receive a specified number of votes. **3** Telecommunications & Computing check the status of (a device), especially as part of a repeated cycle. **4** cut the horns off (an animal, especially a young cow).
– ORIGIN perhaps from Low German.

pollack /pollək/ (also **pollock**) ● noun an edible greenish-brown fish of the cod family.
– ORIGIN perhaps from Celtic.

pollard /pollərd/ ● verb cut off the top and branches of (a tree) to encourage new growth. ● noun a tree that has been pollarded.
– ORIGIN from POLL.

pollen ● noun a powdery substance discharged from the male part of a flower, containing the fertilizing agent.
– ORIGIN Latin, 'fine powder'.

pollen count ● noun an index of the amount of pollen in the air.

pollinate ● verb deposit pollen in and fertilize (a flower or plant).
– DERIVATIVES **pollination** noun **pollinator** noun.

pollock ● noun variant spelling of POLLACK.

pollster /pōlstər/ ● noun a person who conducts or analyses opinion polls.

poll tax ● noun a tax levied on every adult, without reference to their income or resources.

pollute ● verb **1** contaminate with harmful or poisonous substances. **2** corrupt.
– DERIVATIVES **pollutant** adjective & noun **polluter** noun **pollution** noun.
– ORIGIN Latin *polluere* 'pollute, defile'.

polly (also **pollie**) ● noun (pl. **pollies**) Austral./NZ informal a politician.

Pollyanna ● noun an excessively cheerful or optimistic person.
– ORIGIN the name of the optimistic heroine created by the American author Eleanor H. Porter (1868–1920).

polo ● noun a game similar to hockey, played on horseback with a long-handled mallet.
– ORIGIN Balti, 'ball'.

polonaise /pollənayz/ ● noun a slow stately dance of Polish origin in triple time. ● adjective (of a dish, especially a vegetable dish) garnished with chopped hard-boiled egg yolk, breadcrumbs, and parsley.
– ORIGIN from French, 'Polish'.

polo neck ● noun Brit. a high, close-fitting, turned-over collar on a sweater.

polonium /pəlōniəm/ ● noun a rare radioactive metallic element.
– ORIGIN from Latin *Polonia* 'Poland' (the native country of Marie Curie, the element's co-discoverer).

polony /pəlōni/ ● noun (pl. **polonies**) Brit. another term for BOLOGNA.
– ORIGIN apparently an alteration of *Bologna*.

polo shirt ● noun a casual short-sleeved shirt with a collar and two or three buttons at the neck.

poltergeist /poltərgīst/ ● noun a supernatural being supposedly responsible for physical disturbances such as throwing objects about.
– ORIGIN German, from *poltern* 'create a disturbance' + *Geist* 'ghost'.

poltroon /poltrōōn/ ● noun archaic or literary an utter coward.
– ORIGIN Italian *poltrone*, perhaps from *poltro* 'lazy'.

poly ● noun (pl. **polys**) informal **1** polythene. **2** Brit. a polytechnic.

poly- ● combining form **1** many; much: *polychrome*. **2** Chemistry forming names of polymers: *polyester*.
– ORIGIN from Greek *polus* 'much', *polloi* 'many'.

polyamide /polliaymīd, polliammīd/ ● noun a polymer, e.g. nylon, made by linking an amino group of one molecule and a carboxylic acid group of another.

polyandry /polliandri/ ● noun polygamy in which a woman has more than one husband.
– DERIVATIVES **polyandrous** adjective.
– ORIGIN from Greek *anēr* 'male'.

polyanthus /pollianthəss/ ● noun (pl. same) a cultivated hybrid of the wild primrose and primulas.
– ORIGIN from Greek *anthos* 'flower'.

polycarbonate ● noun a synthetic resin in which the polymer units are linked through carbonate groups.

polychlorinated biphenyl ● noun any of a class of toxic chlorinated organic compounds, formed as waste in some industrial processes.

polychromatic ● adjective multicoloured.

polychrome ● adjective painted, printed, or decorated in several colours. ● noun varied colouring.
– DERIVATIVES **polychromy** noun.
– ORIGIN from Greek *khrōma* 'colour'.

polyester ● noun a synthetic resin in which the polymer units are linked by ester groups, used chiefly to make textile fibres.

polyethylene /polliethileen/ ● noun another term for POLYTHENE.

polygamy ● noun the practice or custom of having more than one wife or husband at the same time.
– DERIVATIVES **polygamist** noun **polygamous** adjective.
– ORIGIN from Greek *polugamos* 'often marrying'.

polyglot /polliglot/ ● adjective knowing, using, or written in several languages. ● noun a person who knows or uses several languages.
– ORIGIN Greek *poluglōttos* 'many-tongued'.

polygon /polligən/ ● noun Geometry a plane figure with at least three straight sides and angles, and typically five or more.
– DERIVATIVES **polygonal** adjective.

polygraph ● noun a machine for recording changes in a person's physiological characteristics, such as pulse and breathing rates, used especially as a lie detector.

polygyny /pəlijini/ ● noun polygamy in which a man has more than one wife.
– DERIVATIVES **polygynous** /pəlijinəss/ adjective.
– ORIGIN from Greek *gunē* 'woman'.

polyhedron /polliheedrən/ ● noun (pl. **polyhedra** /polliheedrə/ or **polyhedrons**) Geometry a solid figure with many plane faces, typically more than six.
– DERIVATIVES **polyhedral** adjective.

polymath /pollimath/ ● noun a person of wide-ranging knowledge or learning.
– DERIVATIVES **polymathic** adjective.
– ORIGIN from Greek *polumathēs* 'having learned much'.

polymer /pollimər/ ● noun Chemistry a substance with a molecular structure formed from many identical small molecules bonded together.
– DERIVATIVES **polymeric** adjective **polymerize** (also **polymerise**) verb.
– ORIGIN from Greek *polumeros* 'having many parts'.

polymerase /pollimərayz, pəlimmərayz/ ● noun Biochemistry an enzyme which brings about the formation of a particular polymer, especially DNA or RNA.

polymorphism ● noun the occurrence of something in several different forms.
– DERIVATIVES **polymorphic** adjective **polymorphous** adjective.

Polynesian ● noun **1** a person from Polynesia, a large group of Pacific islands including New Zealand, Hawaii, and Samoa. **2** a group of languages spoken in Polynesia. ● adjective relating to Polynesia.

p

Thesaurus

leanings, party politics. **4** *office politics* POWER STRUGGLE, machinations, manoeuvring, opportunism, realpolitik.

poll ● noun **1** *a second-round poll* VOTE, ballot, show of hands, referendum, plebiscite; election. **2** *the poll was unduly low* VOTING FIGURES, vote, returns, count, tally. **3** *a poll to investigate holiday choices* SURVEY, opinion poll, straw poll, canvass, market research, census.
● verb **1** *most of those polled supported him* CANVASS, survey, ask, question, interview, ballot. **2** *she polled 119 votes* GET, gain, register, record, return.

pollute ● verb **1** *fish farms will pollute the lake* CONTAMINATE, adulterate, taint, poison, foul, dirty, soil, infect; poetic/literary befoul. **2** *propaganda polluted this nation* CORRUPT, poison, warp, pervert, deprave, defile, blight, sully; poetic/literary besmirch.
– OPPOSITES purify.

pollution ● noun **1** *pollution in the rivers* CONTAMINATION, adulter-

polynomial /pollinōmiəl/ ● **noun** Mathematics an expression consisting of several terms, especially terms containing different powers of the same variable.
– ORIGIN from POLY-, on the pattern of *binomial*.

polyp /pollip/ ● **noun 1** Zoology the sedentary form of an organism such as a sea anemone or coral, in some cases forming a distinct stage in the animal's life-cycle. **2** Medicine a small growth protruding from a mucous membrane.
– DERIVATIVES **polypoid** adjective & noun.
– ORIGIN Greek *polupous* 'cuttlefish, polyp', from *polu-* 'many' + *pous* 'foot'.

polypeptide ● **noun** Biochemistry a peptide consisting of many amino-acids bonded together in a chain, e.g. in a protein.

polyphonic ● **adjective 1** having many sounds or voices. **2** Music (especially of vocal music) in two or more parts each having a melody of its own; contrapuntal.
– DERIVATIVES **polyphony** noun (pl. **polyphonies**).
– ORIGIN from Greek *polu-* 'many' + *phōnē* 'voice, sound'.

polyploid /polliployd/ ● **adjective** Genetics (of a cell or nucleus) containing more than two matching sets of chromosomes.
– DERIVATIVES **polyploidy** noun.

polypropylene /polliprōpileen/ ● **noun** a synthetic resin which is a polymer of propylene.

polyptych /polliptik/ ● **noun** a painting, especially an altarpiece, consisting of more than three panels joined by hinges or folds.
– ORIGIN from Greek *poluptukhos* 'having many folds'.

polyrhythm ● **noun** Music the use of two or more different rhythms simultaneously.
– DERIVATIVES **polyrhythmic** adjective.

polysaccharide ● **noun** a carbohydrate (e.g. starch or cellulose) whose molecules consist of chains of sugar molecules.

polysemy /polliseemi/ ● **noun** the coexistence of many possible meanings for a word or phrase.
– DERIVATIVES **polysemous** adjective.
– ORIGIN from Greek *sēma* 'sign'.

polystyrene /pollistīreen/ ● **noun** a synthetic resin which is a polymer of styrene.

polysyllabic ● **adjective** having more than one syllable.
– DERIVATIVES **polysyllable** noun.

polytechnic ● **noun** an institution of higher education offering courses at degree level or below (little used after 1992, when British polytechnics became able to call themselves 'universities').

polytheism /pollithee-iz'm/ ● **noun** the belief in or worship of more than one god.
– DERIVATIVES **polytheist** noun **polytheistic** adjective.
– ORIGIN from Greek *polutheos* 'of many gods'.

polythene ● **noun** chiefly Brit. a tough, light, flexible plastic made by polymerizing ethylene, chiefly used for packaging.
– ORIGIN contraction of *polyethylene*.

polytunnel ● **noun** an elongated polythene-covered frame under which plants are grown outdoors.

polyunsaturated ● **adjective** referring to fats whose molecules contain several double or triple bonds, believed to be less healthy in the diet than monounsaturated fats.
– DERIVATIVES **polyunsaturates** plural noun.

polyurethane /polliyoorəthayn/ ● **noun** a synthetic resin in which the polymer units are linked by urethane groups.

polyvalent /pollivaylənt/ ● **adjective** having many different functions, forms, or aspects.

polyvinyl acetate ● **noun** a synthetic resin made by polymerizing vinyl acetate, used chiefly in paints and adhesives.

polyvinyl chloride ● **noun** a tough chemically resistant synthetic resin made by polymerizing vinyl chloride.

Pom ● **noun** short for POMMY.

pomade /pəmayd/ ● **noun** a scented preparation for dressing the hair. ● **verb** (**pomaded**) dressed with pomade.
– ORIGIN French *pommade*, from Latin *pomum* 'apple' (from which it was formerly made).

pomander /pəmandər/ ● **noun** a ball or perforated container of mixed aromatic substances used to perfume a room or cupboard or (formerly) carried as protection against infection.
– ORIGIN from Latin *pomum de ambra* 'apple of ambergris'.

pome /pōm/ ● **noun** Botany a fruit consisting of a fleshy enlarged receptacle and a tough central core containing the seeds, e.g. an apple.
– ORIGIN Latin *pomum* 'apple'.

pomegranate /pommigrannit/ ● **noun** a round tropical fruit with a tough golden-orange outer skin and sweet red flesh containing many seeds.
– ORIGIN from Latin *pomum granatum* 'apple having many seeds'.

pomelo /pumməlō/ (also **pummelo**) ● **noun** (pl. **pomelos**) a large citrus fruit similar to a grapefruit, with a thick yellow skin and bitter pulp.
– ORIGIN of unknown origin.

Pomeranian ● **noun** a small dog of a breed with long silky hair, a pointed muzzle, and pricked ears.
– ORIGIN from *Pomerania*, a region of central Europe.

pomfret /pomfrit/ ● **noun** an edible deep-bodied sea fish.
– ORIGIN apparently from Portuguese *pampo*.

pomiculture /pōmikulchər/ ● **noun** fruit-growing.
– ORIGIN from Latin *pomum* 'fruit'.

pommel /pumm'l/ ● **noun 1** the upward curving or projecting front part of a saddle. **2** a rounded knob on the end of the handle of a sword, dagger, or old-fashioned gun. ● **verb** (**pommelled, pommelling**; US **pommeled, pommeling**) pummel.
– ORIGIN Old French *pomel*, from Latin *pomum* 'fruit, apple'.

pommel horse ● **noun** a vaulting horse fitted with a pair of curved handgrips.

Pommy (also **Pommie**) ● **noun** (pl. **Pommies**) Austral./NZ informal, derogatory a British person.
– ORIGIN said by some to be short for *pomegranate*, as a near rhyme to *immigrant*.

pomp ● **noun 1** ceremony and splendid display. **2** (**pomps**) archaic vain and boastful display.
– ORIGIN Greek *pompē* 'procession, pomp', from *pempein* 'send'.

pompadour /pompədoor/ ● **noun 1** a woman's hairstyle in which the hair is turned back off the forehead in a roll. **2** N. Amer. a men's hairstyle in which the hair is combed back from the forehead without a parting.
– ORIGIN named after Madame de *Pompadour* (1721–64), the mistress of Louis XV of France.

pompano /pompənō/ ● **noun** (pl. **pompanos**) **1** an edible fish of the west coast of North America. **2** another term for JACK (in sense 10).
– ORIGIN Spanish *pámpano*, perhaps from *pámpana* 'vine leaf', because of its shape.

pompom (also **pompon**) ● **noun 1** a small woollen ball attached to a garment for decoration. **2** a dahlia, chrysanthemum, or aster with small tightly clustered petals.
– ORIGIN French *pompon* 'tuft, topknot'.

pom-pom ● **noun** Brit. an automatic quick-firing two-pounder cannon of the Second World War period.
– ORIGIN imitative of the sound of the discharge.

pompous ● **adjective** affectedly grand, solemn, or self-important.
– DERIVATIVES **pomposity** noun **pompously** adverb.

ponce Brit. informal ● **noun 1** a man who lives off a prostitute's earnings. **2** derogatory an effeminate man. ● **verb 1** (**ponce about/around**) behave in an affected or ineffectual way. **2** (**ponce off**) ask for or obtain (something to which one is not entitled) from (someone).
– DERIVATIVES **poncey** (also **poncy**) adjective.
– ORIGIN perhaps from POUNCE[1].

poncho ● **noun** (pl. **ponchos**) a garment made of a thick piece of woollen cloth with a slit in the middle for the head.
– ORIGIN Latin American Spanish.

pond ● **noun 1** a fairly small body of still water. **2** (**the pond**) humorous the Atlantic ocean.
– ORIGIN alteration of POUND[3].

ponder ● **verb** consider carefully.
– ORIGIN Latin *ponderare* 'weigh', from *pondus* 'weight'.

Thesaurus

ation, impurity; dirt, filth, infection. **2** *the pollution of young minds* CORRUPTION, defilement, poisoning, warping, depravation, sullying, violation.

pomp ● **noun** CEREMONY, ceremonial, solemnity, ritual, display, spectacle, pageantry; show, showiness, ostentation, splendour, grandeur, magnificence, majesty, stateliness, glory, opulence, brilliance, drama, resplendence, splendidness; *informal* razzmatazz.

pompous ● **adjective** SELF-IMPORTANT, imperious, overbearing, domineering, magisterial, pontifical, sententious, grandiose, affected, pretentious, puffed up, arrogant, vain, haughty, proud, conceited, egotistic, supercilious, condescending, patronizing; *informal* snooty, uppity, uppish.

ponderable ● adjective literary worthy of consideration; thought-provoking.

ponderosa /pondərōzə/ (also **ponderosa pine**) ● noun a tall North American pine tree, planted for wood and as an ornamental.
– ORIGIN feminine of Latin *ponderosus* 'massive'.

ponderous ● adjective **1** slow and clumsy because of great weight. **2** dull or laborious.
– DERIVATIVES **ponderously** adverb.
– ORIGIN Latin *ponderosus*, from *pondus* 'weight'.

pondweed ● noun a submerged aquatic plant of still or running water.

pong Brit. informal ● noun a strong, unpleasant smell. ● verb smell strongly and unpleasantly.
– DERIVATIVES **pongy** adjective.
– ORIGIN of unknown origin.

ponga /pungə/ ● noun a tree fern found in forests throughout New Zealand.
– ORIGIN Maori.

pongee /ponjee/ ● noun a soft, unbleached type of Chinese fabric, originally made from uneven threads of raw silk and now also other fibres such as cotton.
– ORIGIN Chinese, either from a word meaning 'own loom' or from a word meaning 'home-woven'.

poniard /ponyərd/ ● noun historical a small, slim dagger.
– ORIGIN French *poignard*, from Latin *pugnus* 'fist'.

pons /ponz/ ● noun (pl. **pontes** /**ponteez**/) Anatomy the part of the brainstem that links the medulla oblongata and the thalamus.
– ORIGIN Latin, 'bridge'.

Pontefract cake /pontifrakt/ ● noun Brit. a flat, round liquorice sweet.
– ORIGIN named after *Pontefract* (earlier *Pomfret*), a town in Yorkshire where the sweets were first made.

pontiff ● noun the Pope.
– ORIGIN Latin *pontifex* 'high priest', from *pons* 'bridge' + *-fex*, from *facere* 'to make'.

pontifical /pontiffik'l/ ● adjective **1** papal. **2** characterized by a pompous air of infallibility.
– DERIVATIVES **pontifically** adverb.

pontificate ● verb /pontiffikayt/ **1** express one's opinions in a pompous and dogmatic way. **2** (in the Roman Catholic Church) officiate as bishop, especially at Mass. ● noun /pontiffikət/ (also **Pontificate**) (in the Roman Catholic Church) the office or term of office of pope or bishop.
– DERIVATIVES **pontificator** noun.

pontoon[1] /pontōōn/ ● noun Brit. a card game in which players try to acquire cards with a value totalling twenty-one.
– ORIGIN probably an alteration of French *vingt-et-un* 'twenty-one'.

pontoon[2] /pontōōn/ ● noun **1** a flat-bottomed boat or hollow metal cylinder used with others to support a temporary bridge or floating landing stage. **2** a bridge or landing stage supported by pontoons. **3** a large flat-bottomed barge or lighter equipped for careening ships and salvage work.
– ORIGIN French *ponton*, from Latin *pons* 'bridge'.

pony ● noun (pl. **ponies**) **1** a horse of a small breed, especially one below 15 hands. **2** Brit. informal twenty-five pounds sterling.
– ORIGIN probably from French *poulenet* 'small foal'.

ponytail ● noun a hairstyle in which the hair is drawn back and tied at the back of the head.

pony-trekking ● noun Brit. the leisure activity of riding across country on a pony or horse.

poo ● exclamation, noun, & verb variant spelling of POOH.

pooch ● noun informal a dog.
– ORIGIN of unknown origin.

poodle ● noun **1** a breed of dog with a curly coat that is usually clipped. **2** Brit. a servile or obsequious person.
– ORIGIN German *Pudelhund*, from *puddeln* 'splash in water' (the poodle being a water-dog).

poof[1] /pŏŏf, pōōf/ (also **pouf**, **poofter**) ● noun Brit. informal, derogatory an effeminate or homosexual man.
– DERIVATIVES **poofy** adjective.
– ORIGIN perhaps an alteration of *puff* in the obsolete sense 'braggart'.

poof[2] /pŏŏf/ (also **pouf**) ● exclamation describing a sudden disappearance or expressing contemptuous dismissal.
– ORIGIN symbolic.

pooh (also **poo**) informal ● exclamation **1** expressing disgust at an unpleasant smell. **2** expressing impatience or contempt. ● noun **1** excrement. **2** an act of defecating. ● verb defecate.
– ORIGIN natural exclamation.

pooh-bah /pōōbaa/ ● noun a pompous person having much influence or holding many offices simultaneously.
– ORIGIN named after a character in W. S. Gilbert's *The Mikado* (1885).

pooh-pooh ● verb informal dismiss as being foolish or impractical.

pool[1] ● noun **1** a small area of still water. **2** (also **swimming pool**) an artificial pool for swimming in. **3** a small, shallow patch of liquid lying on a surface. **4** a deep place in a river.
– ORIGIN Old English.

pool[2] ● noun **1** a shared supply of vehicles, people, commodities, or funds to be drawn on when needed. **2** the total amount of players' stakes in gambling or sweepstakes. **3** (**the pools** or **football pools**) a form of gambling on the results of football matches, the winners receiving large sums accumulated from entry money. **4** a game played on a billiard table using 16 balls. **5** an arrangement between competing commercial ventures to fix prices and share business so as to eliminate competition. ● verb **1** put (money or other assets) into a common fund. **2** share for the benefit of all.
– ORIGIN French *poule* 'stake, kitty', associated with POOL[1].

poop[1] (also **poop deck**) ● noun a raised deck at the stern of a ship, especially a sailing ship.
– ORIGIN Latin *puppis* 'stern'.

poop[2] N. Amer. informal ● noun excrement. ● verb defecate.
– ORIGIN imitative.

pooped ● adjective N. Amer. informal exhausted.
– ORIGIN of unknown origin.

pooper scooper ● noun an implement for clearing up dog excrement.

poor ● adjective **1** lacking sufficient money to live at a comfortable or normal standard. **2** of a low or inferior standard or quality. **3** (**poor in**) lacking in. **4** deserving pity or sympathy.
– PHRASES **the poor man's ——** an inferior or cheaper substitute for the thing specified. **poor relation** a person or thing that is considered inferior to others of the same type. **take a poor view of** regard with disapproval.
– ORIGIN Old French *poure*, from Latin *pauper*.

poorhouse ● noun Brit. another term for WORKHOUSE.

p

Thesaurus

– OPPOSITES modest.

pond ● noun POOL, waterhole, lake, tarn, reservoir, swim; *Brit.* stew; *Scottish* lochan; *N. Amer.* pothole; *Austral./NZ* tank.

ponder ● verb THINK ABOUT, contemplate, consider, review, reflect on, mull over, meditate on, muse on, deliberate about, cogitate on, dwell on, brood on, ruminate on, chew over, puzzle over, turn over in one's mind.

ponderous ● adjective **1** *a ponderous dance* CLUMSY, heavy, awkward, lumbering, slow, cumbersome, ungainly, graceless, uncoordinated, blundering; *informal* clodhopping, clunky. **2** *his ponderous sentences* LABOURED, laborious, awkward, clumsy, forced, stilted, unnatural, artificial; stodgy, lifeless, plodding, pedestrian, boring, dull, tedious, monotonous; over-elaborate, convoluted, windy.
– OPPOSITES light, lively.

pontifical ● adjective POMPOUS, cocksure, self-important, arrogant, superior; opinionated, dogmatic, doctrinaire, authoritarian, domineering; adamant, obstinate, stubborn, single-minded, inflexible.

– OPPOSITES humble.

pontificate ● verb HOLD FORTH, expound, declaim, preach, lay down the law, sound off, dogmatize, sermonize, moralize, lecture; *informal* preachify, mouth off.

pooh-pooh ● verb *(informal)* DISMISS, reject, spurn, rebuff, wave aside, disregard, discount; play down, make light of, belittle, deride, mock, scorn, scoff at, sneer at; *Austral./NZ informal* wipe.

pool[1] ● noun **1** *pools of water* PUDDLE, pond; *poetic/literary* plash. **2** *the hotel has a pool* SWIMMING POOL, baths, lido; *Brit.* swimming bath(s); *N. Amer.* natatorium.

pool[2] ● noun **1** *a pool of skilled labour* SUPPLY, reserve(s), reservoir, fund; store, stock, accumulation, cache. **2** *a pool of money for emergencies* FUND, reserve, kitty, pot, bank, purse.
● verb *they pooled their skills* COMBINE, amalgamate, group, join, unite, merge; fuse, conglomerate, integrate; share.

poor ● adjective **1** *a poor family* POVERTY-STRICKEN, penniless, moneyless, impoverished, necessitous, impecunious, indigent, needy,

poorly • adverb in a poor manner. • adjective chiefly Brit. unwell.
poor white • noun derogatory a member of an impoverished white underclass, especially one living in the southern US.
pootle • verb Brit. informal move or travel in a leisurely manner.
– ORIGIN blend of TOOTLE and *poodle* in the same sense.
pop[1] • verb (**popped, popping**) **1** make or cause to make a sudden short explosive sound. **2** go or come quickly or unexpectedly. **3** put or place quickly. **4** (of a person's eyes) open wide and appear to bulge. **5** informal take or inject (a drug). • noun **1** a sudden short explosive sound. **2** informal, dated or N. Amer. fizzy soft drink.
– PHRASES **have** (or **take**) **a pop at** informal attack. **pop off** (or Brit. **pop one's clogs**) informal die. **pop the question** informal propose marriage.
– ORIGIN imitative.
pop[2] • noun (also **pop music**) popular modern commercial music, typically with a strong melody and beat. • adjective **1** relating to pop music. **2** often derogatory (especially of a scientific or academic subject) made accessible to the general public.
pop[3] • noun chiefly US informal term for FATHER.
– ORIGIN abbreviation of POPPA.
popadom • noun variant spelling of POPPADOM.
pop art • noun art based on modern popular culture and the mass media.
popcorn • noun maize kernels which swell up and burst open when heated and are then eaten as a snack.
pop culture • noun commercial culture based on popular taste.
pope • noun (**the Pope**) the Bishop of Rome as head of the Roman Catholic Church.
– PHRASES **is the Pope (a) Catholic?** informal used to indicate that something is blatantly obvious.
– ORIGIN Greek *papas* 'bishop, patriarch', variant of *pappas* 'father'.
popery • noun derogatory, chiefly archaic Roman Catholicism.
pop-eyed • adjective informal having bulging or staring eyes.
popgun • noun a child's toy gun which shoots a harmless pellet or cork.
popinjay /poppinjay/ • noun dated a vain or foppish person.
– ORIGIN Old French *papingay* 'parrot', from Arabic.
popish • adjective derogatory Roman Catholic.
poplar • noun a tall, slender tree, often grown in shelter belts or for wood and pulp.
– ORIGIN Latin *populus*.
poplin • noun a plain-woven fabric, typically a lightweight cotton, with a corded surface.
– ORIGIN obsolete French *papeline*, perhaps from Italian *papalina* 'papal', because first made in the town of Avignon (residence of popes in exile, 1309–77).
popliteal /poplittiəl/ • adjective Anatomy relating to or situated in the hollow at the back of the knee.
– ORIGIN Latin *popliteus*, from *poples* 'ham, hock'.
poppa • noun N. Amer. informal term for FATHER.
– ORIGIN alteration of PAPA.
poppadom /poppədəm/ (also **poppadum** or **popadom**) • noun (in Indian cookery) a large disc of unleavened spiced bread made from ground lentils fried in oil.
– ORIGIN Tamil.
popper • noun **1** Brit. informal a press stud. **2** informal a small vial of amyl nitrite used for inhalation, which makes a popping sound when opened.
poppet • noun Brit. informal an endearingly sweet or pretty child.
– ORIGIN Latin *puppa* 'girl, doll'; related to PUPPET.
popping crease • noun Cricket a line across the pitch in front of the stumps, behind which the batsman must keep the bat or one foot grounded to avoid the risk of being stumped or run out.
– ORIGIN from POP[1], perhaps in the obsolete sense 'strike'.
poppy[1] • noun a plant with showy flowers (typically red, pink, or yellow) and large seed capsules, and including species which produce drugs such as opium and codeine.
– ORIGIN Old English, from Latin *papaver*.
poppy[2] • adjective (of popular music) tuneful and immediately appealing.
poppycock • noun informal nonsense.
– ORIGIN Dutch dialect *pappekak*, from *pap* 'soft' + *kak* 'dung'.
Poppy Day • noun Brit. another name for REMEMBRANCE SUNDAY.
popster • noun informal a pop musician.
popsy (also **popsie**) • noun (pl. **popsies**) informal, chiefly Brit. an attractive young woman.
– ORIGIN alteration of POPPET.
populace /popyooləss/ • noun (treated as sing. or pl.) the general public.
– ORIGIN Italian *popolaccio* 'common people'.
popular • adjective **1** liked or admired by many or by a particular group. **2** intended for or suited to the taste or means of the general public: *the popular press.* **3** (of a belief or attitude) widely held among the general public. **4** (of political activity) carried on by the people as a whole.
– DERIVATIVES **popularity** noun **popularly** adverb.
– ORIGIN Latin *popularis*, from *populus* 'people'.

Thesaurus

destitute, pauperized, on one's beam-ends, unable to make ends meet, without a sou; insolvent, in debt; *Brit.* on the breadline, without a penny (to one's name); *informal* (flat) broke, hard up, cleaned out, strapped, on one's uppers, without two pennies to rub together; *Brit. informal* skint, in Queer Street; *formal* penurious. **2** *poor workmanship* SUBSTANDARD, below par, bad, deficient, defective, faulty, imperfect, inferior; appalling, abysmal, atrocious, awful, terrible, dreadful, unsatisfactory, second-rate, third-rate, shoddy, crude, lamentable, deplorable, inadequate, unacceptable; *informal* crummy, rubbishy, dire, dismal, bum, rotten, tenth-rate; *Brit. informal* ropy, duff, rubbish, dodgy. **3** *a poor crop* MEAGRE, scanty, scant, paltry, disappointing, limited, reduced, modest, insufficient, inadequate, sparse, spare, deficient, insubstantial, skimpy, short, small, lean, slender; *informal* measly, stingy, pathetic, piddling; *formal* exiguous. **4** *poor soil* UNPRODUCTIVE, barren, unyielding, unfruitful, uncultivatable; arid, sterile. **5** *the waters are poor in nutrients* DEFICIENT, lacking, wanting; short of, low on. **6** *you poor thing!* UNFORTUNATE, unlucky, luckless, unhappy, hapless, ill-fated, ill-starred, pitiable, pitiful, wretched.
– OPPOSITES rich, superior, good, fertile, lucky.
poorly • adverb *the text is poorly written* BADLY, deficiently, defectively, imperfectly, incompetently; appallingly, abysmally, atrociously, awfully, dreadfully; crudely, shoddily, inadequately.
• adjective *she felt poorly* ILL, unwell, not (very) well, ailing, indisposed, out of sorts, under/below par, peaky; sick, queasy, nauseous; *Brit.* off colour; *informal* under the weather, funny, peculiar, lousy, rough; *Brit. informal* ropy, grotty; *Scottish informal* wabbit; *Austral./NZ informal* crook; *Brit. informal, dated* queer; *dated* seedy.
pop • verb **1** *champagne corks popped* GO BANG, go off; crack, snap, burst, explode. **2** *I'm just popping home* GO; drop in, stop by, visit; *informal* tootle, whip; *Brit. informal* nip. **3** *pop a bag over the pot* PUT, place, slip, slide, stick, set, lay, install, position, arrange.
• noun **1** *the balloons burst with a pop* BANG, crack, snap; explosion, report. **2** *(informal) a bottle of pop* FIZZY DRINK, soft drink, carbonated drink; *N. Amer.* soda; *Scottish informal* scoosh.
– PHRASES **pop up** APPEAR (SUDDENLY), occur (suddenly), arrive, materialize, come along, happen, emerge, arise, crop up, turn up, present itself, come to light; *informal* show up.
pope • noun PONTIFF, Bishop of Rome, Holy Father, Vicar of Christ, His Holiness.
– RELATED TERMS papal, pontifical.
pop music • noun POP, popular music, chart music.
poppycock • noun *(informal)* NONSENSE, rubbish, claptrap, balderdash, blather, moonshine, garbage; *informal* rot, tripe, hogwash, baloney, drivel, bilge, bosh, bunk, eyewash, piffle, phooey, twaddle; *Brit. informal* cobblers, codswallop, tosh; *N. Amer. informal* applesauce, bushwa; *informal, dated* bunkum, tommyrot.
populace • noun POPULATION, inhabitants, residents, natives; community, country, (general) public, people, nation; common people, man/woman in the street, masses, multitude, rank and file, commonality, commonalty, third estate, plebeians, proletariat; *informal* proles, plebs; *Brit. informal* Joe Public; *formal* denizens; *derogatory* the hoi polloi, common herd, rabble, riff-raff.
popular • adjective **1** *the restaurant is very popular* WELL LIKED, favoured, sought-after, in demand, desired, wanted; commercial, marketable, fashionable, in vogue, all the rage, hot; *informal* in, cool, big; *Brit. informal, dated* all the go. **2** *popular science* NON-SPECIALIST, non-technical, amateur, lay person's, general, middle-of-the-road; accessible, simplified, plain, simple, easy, straightforward, understandable; mass-market, middlebrow, lowbrow, pop. **3** *popular opinion* WIDESPREAD, general, common, current, prevalent, prevailing, standard, stock; ordinary, usual, accepted, established, acknowledged, conventional, orthodox. **4** *a popular movement for independence* MASS, general, communal, collective, social,

popular front ● noun a political party or coalition representing left-wing elements.

popularize (also **popularise**) ● verb **1** make popular. **2** make (something scientific or academic) accessible or interesting to the general public.
– DERIVATIVES **popularization** noun **popularizer** noun.

populate ● verb **1** form the population of. **2** cause people to settle in.
– ORIGIN Latin *populare* 'supply with people'.

population ● noun **1** all the inhabitants of a place. **2** a particular group within this. **3** the action of populating an area. **4** Biology a community of interbreeding organisms.

populist ● noun a member or supporter of a political party who seeks to appeal to or represent the interests and views of ordinary people. ● adjective relating to populists.
– DERIVATIVES **populism** noun.

populous ● adjective having a large population.

pop-up ● noun **1** (of a book or greetings card) containing folded pictures that rise up to form a three-dimensional scene or figure when opened. **2** (of an electric toaster) operating so as to push up a piece of toast when it is ready. **3** Computing (of a menu or other utility) able to be superimposed on the screen being worked on and suppressed rapidly.

porbeagle /porbeeg'l/ ● noun a large shark found chiefly in the open seas of the North Atlantic and in the Mediterranean.
– ORIGIN Cornish dialect, perhaps from Cornish *porth* 'harbour' + *bugel* 'shepherd'.

porcelain /porsəlin/ ● noun **1** a white vitrified translucent ceramic. **2** articles made of this.
– ORIGIN Italian *porcellana* 'cowrie shell', hence 'chinaware' (from its resemblance to the polished surface of cowrie shells).

porch ● noun **1** a covered shelter projecting over the entrance of a building. **2** N. Amer. a veranda.
– ORIGIN Old French *porche*, from Latin *porticus* 'colonnade'.

porcine /porsīn/ ● adjective relating to or resembling a pig or pigs.
– ORIGIN Latin *porcinus*, from *porcus* 'pig'.

porcini /porcheeni/ ● plural noun ceps (wild mushrooms), especially when used as food.
– ORIGIN Italian, 'little pigs'.

porcupine ● noun a large rodent with defensive spines or quills on the body and tail.
– ORIGIN from Latin *porcus* 'pig' + *spina* 'thorn'.

pore[1] ● noun a minute opening in the skin or other surface through which gases, liquids, or microscopic particles may pass.
– ORIGIN Greek *poros* 'passage, pore'.

pore[2] ● verb **1** (**pore over/through**) be absorbed in the reading or study of. **2** (**pore on/over**) archaic ponder.
– ORIGIN perhaps related to PEER[1].

pork ● noun the flesh of a pig used as food, especially when uncured.
– ORIGIN Latin *porcus* 'pig'.

pork barrel ● noun N. Amer. informal the use of government funds for projects designed to win votes.
– ORIGIN from the farmers' practice of keeping a reserve supply of meat in a barrel, later meaning 'a supply of money'.

porker ● noun **1** a young pig raised and fattened for food. **2** informal, derogatory a fat person.

pork pie ● noun a raised pie made with minced, cooked pork, eaten cold.

pork-pie hat ● noun a hat with a flat crown and a brim turned up all round.

porky ● adjective (**porkier**, **porkiest**) **1** informal fleshy or fat. **2** of or resembling pork. ● noun (pl. **porkies**) (also **porky-pie**) Brit. rhyming slang a lie.

porn (also **porno**) informal ● noun pornography. ● adjective pornographic.

pornography ● noun printed or visual material intended to stimulate sexual excitement.
– DERIVATIVES **pornographer** noun **pornographic** adjective.
– ORIGIN Greek *pornographos* 'writing about prostitutes'.

porous ● adjective (of a rock or other material) having minute spaces through which liquid or air may pass.
– DERIVATIVES **porosity** noun.
– ORIGIN from Latin *porus* 'pore'.

porphyria /porfirriə/ ● noun Medicine a rare hereditary disease in which the body fails to break down haemoglobin properly, causing mental disturbance, extreme sensitivity to light, and excretion of dark pigments in the urine.
– ORIGIN from *porphyrin* (a pigment made by breakdown of haemoglobin), from Greek *porphura* 'purple'.

porphyritic /porfirittik/ ● adjective Geology referring or relating to a rock texture containing distinct crystals embedded in a compact groundmass.

porphyry /porfiri/ ● noun (pl. **porphyries**) a hard, typically reddish igneous rock containing crystals of feldspar.
– ORIGIN Greek *porphuritēs*, from *porphura* 'purple'.

porpoise /porpəss, -poyz/ ● noun a small toothed whale with a blunt rounded snout.
– ORIGIN Old French *porpois*, from Latin *porcus* 'pig' + *piscis* 'fish'.

porridge ● noun **1** a dish consisting of oatmeal boiled with water or milk. **2** Brit. informal time spent in prison.
– ORIGIN alteration of POTTAGE.

porringer /porrinjər/ ● noun historical a small bowl, often with a handle, used for soup or similar dishes.
– ORIGIN Old French *potager*, from *potage* 'contents of a pot'.

port[1] ● noun **1** a town or city with a harbour. **2** a harbour.
– PHRASES **any port in a storm** proverb in difficult circumstances one welcomes any source of relief or escape. **port of call** a place where a ship or person stops on a journey.
– ORIGIN Latin *portus* 'harbour'.

port[2] (also **port wine**) ● noun a sweet dark red fortified wine from Portugal.
– ORIGIN shortened form of *Oporto*, a port in Portugal from which the wine is shipped.

port[3] ● noun the side of a ship or aircraft that is on the left when one is facing forward. The opposite of STARBOARD. ● verb turn (a ship or its helm) to port.
– ORIGIN probably originally the side turned towards the port.

port[4] ● noun **1** an opening in the side of a ship for boarding or loading. **2** a porthole. **3** an opening for the passage of steam, liquid, or gas. **4** an opening in the body of an aircraft or in a

Thesaurus

collaborative, group, civil, public.
– OPPOSITES highbrow.

popularize ● verb **1** *tobacco was popularized by Sir Walter Raleigh* MAKE POPULAR, make fashionable; market, publicize; *informal* hype. **2** *he popularized the subject* SIMPLIFY, make accessible, give mass-market appeal to. **3** *the report popularized the unfounded notion* GIVE CURRENCY TO, spread, propagate, give credence to.

popularly ● adverb **1** *old age is popularly associated with illness* WIDELY, generally, universally, commonly, usually, customarily, habitually, conventionally, traditionally, as a rule. **2** *the rock was popularly known as 'Arthur's Seat'* INFORMALLY, unofficially; by lay people. **3** *the President is popularly elected* DEMOCRATICALLY, by the people.

populate ● verb **1** *the state is populated by 40,000 people* INHABIT, occupy, people; live in, reside in. **2** *an attempt to populate the island* SETTLE, colonize, people, occupy, move into, make one's home in.

population ● noun INHABITANTS, residents, people, citizens, citizenry, public, community, populace, society, natives, occupants; *formal* denizens.
– RELATED TERMS demo-.

populous ● adjective DENSELY POPULATED, crowded, congested, packed, jammed, crammed, teeming, swarming, seething, crawling; *informal* jam-packed.
– OPPOSITES deserted.

porch ● noun VESTIBULE, foyer, entrance (hall), entry, portico, lobby; *N. Amer.* ramada, stoop; *Architecture* lanai, tambour, narthex.

pore[1] ● noun *pores in the skin* OPENING, orifice, aperture, hole, outlet, inlet, vent; *Biology* stoma, foramen.

pore[2] ● verb *they pored over the map* STUDY, read intently, peruse, scrutinize, scan, examine, go over.

pornographic ● adjective OBSCENE, indecent, crude, lewd, dirty, vulgar, smutty, filthy; erotic, titillating, arousing, suggestive, sexy, risqué; off colour, adult, X-rated, hard-core, soft-core; *informal* porn, porno, blue, skin.
– OPPOSITES wholesome.

pornography ● noun EROTICA, pornographic material, dirty books; smut, filth, vice; *informal* (hard/soft) porn, porno, girlie magazines, skin flicks.

porous ● adjective PERMEABLE, penetrable, pervious, cellular, holey;

wall or armoured vehicle through which a gun may be fired. **5** Electronics a socket in a computer network into which a device can be plugged.
– ORIGIN Latin *porta* 'gate'.
port[5] ● verb **1** Computing transfer (software) from one system or machine to another. **2** Military carry (a weapon) diagonally across and close to the body with the barrel or blade near the left shoulder. ● noun **1** Military the position required by an order to port a weapon. **2** Computing an instance of porting software.
– ORIGIN from French *porter* 'carry' or Old French *port* 'bearing, gait', both from Latin *portare* 'carry'.
port[6] ● noun Austral. informal a suitcase or travelling bag.
– ORIGIN abbreviation of PORTMANTEAU.
portable ● adjective **1** able to be easily carried or moved. **2** (of a loan or pension) capable of being transferred or adapted. **3** Computing (of software) able to be ported. ● noun a portable object.
– DERIVATIVES **portability** noun.
portage /portij/ ● noun **1** the carrying of a boat or its cargo between two navigable waters. **2** a place at which this is necessary. ● verb carry (a boat or its cargo) between navigable waters.
– ORIGIN French, from *porter* 'carry'.
Portakabin ● noun Brit. trademark a portable building used as a temporary office, classroom, etc.
portal ● noun **1** a doorway, gate, or gateway, especially a large and imposing one. **2** Computing an Internet site providing a directory of links to other sites.
– ORIGIN from Latin *porta* 'door, gate'.
portal vein ● noun a vein conveying blood to the liver from the spleen, stomach, pancreas, and intestines.
portamento /portəmentō/ ● noun (pl. **portamentos** or **portamenti** /portəmenti/) Music a slide from one note to another, especially in singing or playing the violin.
– ORIGIN Italian, 'carrying'.
portcullis ● noun a strong, heavy grating that can be lowered to block a gateway.
– ORIGIN from Old French *porte coleice* 'sliding door'.
portend ● verb be a sign or warning that (something momentous or disastrous) is likely to happen.
– ORIGIN Latin *portendere* 'foretell, presage'.
portent /portent/ ● noun **1** a sign or warning that something momentous or disastrous is likely to happen. **2** archaic an exceptional or wonderful person or thing.
– ORIGIN Latin *portentum* 'omen, token'.
portentous ● adjective **1** of or like a portent; ominous. **2** excessively solemn.
– DERIVATIVES **portentously** adverb **portentousness** noun.
porter[1] ● noun **1** a person employed to carry luggage and other loads. **2** a hospital employee who moves equipment or patients. **3** dark brown bitter beer brewed from charred or browned malt. [ORIGIN so called because it was originally made for porters.] **4** N. Amer. a sleeping-car attendant.
– DERIVATIVES **porterage** noun.
– ORIGIN Old French *porteour*, from Latin *portare* 'carry'.
porter[2] ● noun Brit. an employee in charge of the entrance of a large building.
– ORIGIN Old French *portier*, from Latin *porta* 'gate, door'.
porterhouse ● noun historical, chiefly N. Amer. an establishment at which porter and sometimes steaks were served.
porterhouse steak ● noun a thick steak cut from the thick end of a sirloin.
portfolio ● noun (pl. **portfolios**) **1** a thin, flat case for carrying drawings, maps, etc. **2** a set of pieces of creative work intended to demonstrate a person's ability. **3** a range of investments held. **4** the position and duties of a Minister or Secretary of State.
– ORIGIN Italian *portafogli*, from *portare* 'carry' + *foglio* 'leaf'.
porthole ● noun **1** a small window on the outside of a ship or aircraft. **2** historical an opening for firing a cannon through.
portico /portikō/ ● noun (pl. **porticoes** or **porticos**) a roof supported by columns at regular intervals, typically attached as a porch to a building.
– ORIGIN Italian, from Latin *porticus* 'porch'.
portière /portiair/ ● noun a curtain hung over a door or doorway.
– ORIGIN French, from *porte* 'door'.
portion ● noun **1** a part or a share. **2** an amount of food suitable for or served to one person. **3** archaic a person's destiny or lot. **4** archaic a dowry. ● verb **1** divide into portions and share out. **2** archaic give a dowry to.
– ORIGIN Latin, from *pro portione* 'in proportion'.
Portland cement ● noun cement which resembles Portland stone when hard.
Portland stone ● noun limestone from the Isle of Portland in Dorset, valued as a building material.
portly ● adjective (**portlier**, **portliest**) (especially of a man) rather fat.
– DERIVATIVES **portliness** noun.
– ORIGIN originally in the sense 'stately or dignified': from PORT[5] in the archaic sense 'bearing'.
portmanteau /portmantō/ ● noun (pl. **portmanteaus** or **portmanteaux** /portmantōz/) **1** a large travelling bag made of stiff leather and opening into two equal parts. **2** (before another noun) consisting of two or more aspects or qualities: *a portmanteau movie.*
– ORIGIN French *portemanteau*, from *porter* 'carry' + *manteau* 'mantle'.
portmanteau word ● noun a word blending the sounds and combining the meanings of two others, e.g. *brunch* from *breakfast* and *lunch.*
portrait ● noun **1** an artistic representation of a person, especially one depicting only the face or head and shoulders. **2** a written or filmed description. **3** a format of printed matter which is higher than it is wide. Compare with LANDSCAPE.
– DERIVATIVES **portraitist** noun **portraiture** noun.
– ORIGIN French, from Old French *portraire* 'portray'.

Thesaurus

absorbent, absorptive, spongy.
– OPPOSITES impermeable.
port[1] ● noun **1** *the German port of Kiel* SEAPORT, entrepôt. **2** *shells exploded down by the port* HARBOUR, dock(s), haven, marina; anchorage, moorage, harbourage, roads.
port[2] ● noun *push the supply pipes into the ports* APERTURE, opening, outlet, inlet, socket, vent.
portable ● adjective TRANSPORTABLE, movable, mobile, travel; lightweight, compact, handy, convenient.
portal ● noun DOORWAY, gateway, entrance, exit, opening; door, gate; *N. Amer.* entryway; *formal* egress.
portend ● verb PRESAGE, augur, foreshadow, foretell, prophesy; be a sign, warn, be an omen, indicate, herald, signal, bode, promise, threaten, signify, spell, denote; *poetic/literary* betoken, foretoken, forebode.
portent ● noun **1** *a portent of things to come* OMEN, sign, signal, token, forewarning, warning, foreshadowing, prediction, forecast, prophesy, harbinger, augury, auspice, presage; writing on the wall, indication, hint; *poetic/literary* foretoken. **2** *the word carries terrifying portent* SIGNIFICANCE, importance, import, consequence, meaning, weight; *formal* moment.
portentous ● adjective **1** *portentous signs* OMINOUS, warning, premonitory, prognosticatory; threatening, menacing, foreboding, ill-omened, inauspicious, unfavourable. **2** *portentous dialogue* POMPOUS, bombastic, self-important, pontifical, solemn, sonorous, grandiloquent.
porter[1] ● noun *a porter helped with the bags* CARRIER, bearer; *N. Amer.* redcap, skycap.
porter[2] ● noun *(Brit.) the college porter* DOORMAN, doorkeeper, commissionaire, gatekeeper.
portion ● noun **1** *the upper portion of the chimney* PART, piece, bit, section, segment. **2** *her portion of the allowance* SHARE, slice, quota, quantum, part, percentage, amount, quantity, ration, fraction, division, allocation, measure; *informal* cut, rake-off; *Brit. informal* whack. **3** *a portion of cake* HELPING, serving, amount, quantity; plateful, bowlful; slice, piece, chunk, wedge, slab, hunk; *Brit. informal* wodge. **4** *(archaic) poverty was certain to be his portion.* See DESTINY sense 1.
● verb *she portioned out the food* SHARE OUT, allocate, allot, apportion; distribute, hand out, deal out, dole out, give out, dispense, mete out; *informal* divvy up.
portly ● adjective STOUT, plump, fat, overweight, heavy, corpulent, fleshy, paunchy, pot-bellied, well padded, rotund, stocky, bulky; *informal* tubby, roly-poly, beefy, porky, pudgy; *Brit. informal* podgy; *N. Amer. informal* corn-fed.
– OPPOSITES slim.
portrait ● noun **1** *a portrait of the King* PAINTING, picture, drawing, sketch, likeness, image, study, miniature; *informal* oil; *formal* por-

portray ● verb **1** depict in a work of art or literature. **2** describe in a particular way. **3** (of an actor) play the part of.
– DERIVATIVES **portrayal** noun **portrayer** noun.
– ORIGIN Old French *portraire*, from *traire* 'to draw'.
Portuguese /portyoogeez/ ● noun (pl. same) **1** a person from Portugal. **2** the Romance language of Portugal and Brazil. ● adjective relating to Portugal.
Portuguese man-of-war ● noun a floating jellyfish-like marine animal with a conspicuous, often blue float and long stinging tentacles.
pose ● verb **1** present or constitute (a problem, danger, question, etc.). **2** assume a particular position in order to be photographed, painted, or drawn. **3** (**pose as**) pretend to be. **4** behave affectedly in order to impress. ● noun **1** a position assumed in order to be painted, drawn, or photographed. **2** a way of behaving adopted in order to impress or give a false impression.
– ORIGIN Old French *poser*, from Latin *pausare* 'to pause'.
poser ● noun **1** a person who poses; a poseur. **2** a puzzling question or problem.
poseur /pōzör/ ● noun (fem. **poseuse** /pōzöz/) a person who behaves affectedly in order to impress.
– ORIGIN French.
posey (also **posy**) ● adjective informal pretentious.
posh informal ● adjective **1** elegant or stylishly luxurious. **2** chiefly Brit. upper-class. ● adverb Brit. in an upper-class way. ● verb (**posh up**) Brit. smarten (something) up.
– DERIVATIVES **poshly** adverb **poshness** noun.
– ORIGIN perhaps from obsolete slang *posh* 'a dandy'; there is no evidence for the well-known theory that *posh* is formed from the initials of *port out starboard home* (referring to the more comfortable accommodation, out of the heat of the sun, on ships between England and India).
posit /pozzit/ ● verb (**posited**, **positing**) **1** put forward as fact or as a basis for argument. **2** put in position; place.
– ORIGIN Latin, 'placed', from *ponere*.
position ● noun **1** a place where someone or something is located or has been put. **2** the correct place. **3** a way in which someone or something is placed or arranged. **4** a situation or set of circumstances. **5** high rank or social standing. **6** a job. **7** a point of view or attitude. **8** a place where part of a military force is posted. ● verb put or arrange in a particular position.
– DERIVATIVES **positional** adjective **positionally** adverb.
– ORIGIN Latin, from *ponere* 'to place'.
positive ● adjective **1** characterized by the presence rather than the absence of distinguishing features. **2** expressing or implying affirmation, agreement, or permission. **3** constructive, optimistic, or confident. **4** with no possibility of doubt; certain. **5** (of a quantity) greater than zero. **6** of, containing, or producing the kind of electric charge opposite to that carried by electrons. **7** (of a photographic image) showing light and shade or colours true to the original. **8** Grammar (of an adjective or adverb) expressing a quality in its basic, primary degree. Contrasted with COMPARATIVE and SUPERLATIVE. ● noun a positive quality, attribute, or image.
– DERIVATIVES **positively** adverb **positiveness** noun **positivity** noun.
– ORIGIN originally referring to laws as being formally 'laid down': from Old French *positif*, from Latin *ponere* 'to place'.
positive discrimination ● noun Brit. the favouring of individuals belonging to groups which suffer discrimination.
positive pole ● noun the north-seeking pole of a magnet.
positive sign ● noun a plus sign.
positive vetting ● noun Brit. the investigation of the background and character of a candidate for a Civil Service post that involves access to secret material.
positivism ● noun Philosophy **1** a system recognizing only that which can be scientifically verified or logically proved, and therefore rejecting metaphysics and theism. **2** another term for LOGICAL POSITIVISM.
– DERIVATIVES **positivist** noun & adjective **positivistic** adjective.
positron /pozzitron/ ● noun Physics a subatomic particle with the same mass as an electron and a numerically equal but positive charge.
posse /possi/ ● noun **1** N. Amer. historical a body of men summoned

Thesaurus

traiture. **2** *a vivid portrait of Italy* DESCRIPTION, portrayal, representation, depiction, impression, account; sketch, vignette, profile.
portray ● verb **1** *he portrays Windermere in sunny weather* PAINT, draw, sketch, picture, depict, represent, illustrate, render. **2** *the dons portrayed by Waugh* DESCRIBE, depict, characterize, represent, delineate, evoke. **3** *he portrays her as a doormat* REPRESENT, depict, characterize, describe, present. **4** *the actor portrays a spy* PLAY, act the part of, take the role of, represent, appear as; *formal* personate.
portrayal ● noun **1** *a portrayal of a parrot* PAINTING, picture, portrait, drawing, sketch, representation, depiction, study. **2** *her portrayal of adolescence* DESCRIPTION, representation, characterization, depiction, evocation. **3** *Brando's portrayal of Corleone* PERFORMANCE AS, representation, interpretation, rendering; *formal* personation.
pose ● verb **1** *pollution poses a threat to health* CONSTITUTE, present, create, cause, produce, be. **2** *the question posed earlier* RAISE, ask, put, set, submit, advance, propose, suggest, moot. **3** *she posed for the artist* BE A MODEL, model, sit. **4** *he posed her on the sofa* POSITION, place, put, arrange, dispose, locate, situate. **5** *fashion victims were posing at the bar* BEHAVE AFFECTEDLY, strike a pose, posture, attitudinize, put on airs; *informal* show off.
● noun **1** *a sexy pose* POSTURE, position, stance, attitude, bearing. **2** *her pose of aggrieved innocence* PRETENCE, act, affectation, facade, show, front, display, masquerade, posture.
– PHRASES **pose as** PRETEND TO BE, impersonate, pass oneself off as, masquerade as, profess to be, represent oneself as; *formal* personate.
poser[1] ● noun *this situation's a bit of a poser* DIFFICULT QUESTION, vexed question, awkward problem, tough one, puzzle, mystery, conundrum, puzzler, enigma, riddle; *informal* dilemma, facer, toughie, stumper.
poser[2] ● noun *he's such a poser* EXHIBITIONIST, poseur, poseuse, posturer; *informal* show-off, pseud.
poseur ● noun. See POSER[2].
posh ● adjective **1** *(informal) a posh hotel* SMART, stylish, fancy, high-class, fashionable, chic, luxurious, luxury, de luxe, exclusive, opulent, lavish, grand, showy; *Brit.* upmarket; *informal* classy, swanky, snazzy, plush, ritzy, flash, la-di-da; *Brit. informal* swish; *N. Amer. informal* swank, tony. **2** *(Brit. informal) a posh accent* UPPER-CLASS, aristocratic; *Brit.* upmarket, Home Counties; *informal* upper-crust, top-drawer; *Brit. informal* plummy, Sloaney, U.
posit ● verb POSTULATE, put forward, advance, propound, submit, hypothesize, propose, assert.
position ● noun **1** *the aircraft's position* LOCATION, place, situation, spot, site, locality, setting, area; whereabouts, bearings, orientation; *technical* locus. **2** *a standing position* POSTURE, stance, attitude, pose. **3** *our financial position* SITUATION, state, condition, circumstances; predicament, plight, strait(s). **4** *the two parties jockeyed for position* ADVANTAGE, the upper hand, the edge, the whip hand, primacy; *Austral./NZ* the box seat; *N. Amer. informal* the catbird seat. **5** *their position in society* STATUS, place, level, rank, standing; stature, prestige, influence, reputation, importance, consequence, class; *dated* station. **6** *a secretarial position* JOB, post, situation, appointment, role, occupation, employment; office, capacity, duty, function; opening, vacancy, placement. **7** *the government's position on the matter* VIEWPOINT, opinion, outlook, attitude, stand, standpoint, stance, perspective, approach, slant, thinking, policy, feelings.
● verb *he positioned a chair between them* PUT, place, locate, situate, set, site, stand, station; plant, stick, install; arrange, dispose; *informal* plonk, park.
positive ● adjective **1** *a positive response* AFFIRMATIVE, favourable, good, approving, enthusiastic, supportive, encouraging. **2** *do something positive* CONSTRUCTIVE, practical, useful, productive, helpful, worthwhile, beneficial, effective. **3** *she seems a lot more positive* OPTIMISTIC, hopeful, confident, cheerful, sanguine, buoyant; *informal* upbeat. **4** *positive economic signs* FAVOURABLE, good, promising, encouraging, heartening, propitious, auspicious. **5** *positive proof* DEFINITE, conclusive, certain, categorical, unequivocal, incontrovertible, indisputable, undeniable, unmistakable, irrefutable, reliable, concrete, tangible, clear-cut, explicit, firm, decisive, real, actual. **6** *I'm positive he's coming back* CERTAIN, sure, convinced, confident, satisfied, assured; as sure as eggs is eggs.
– OPPOSITES negative, pessimistic, doubtful, unsure.
positively ● adverb **1** *I could not positively identify the voice* CONFIDENTLY, definitely, emphatically, categorically, with certainty, conclusively, unquestionably, undoubtedly, indisputably, unmistakably, assuredly. **2** *he was positively livid* ABSOLUTELY, really, down-

p

by a sheriff to enforce the law. **2** (also **posse comitatus** /possi kommitaytəss/) Brit. historical the men of a county forming a body whom the sheriff could summon to repress a riot or for other purposes. [ORIGIN Latin *comitatus* 'of the county'.] **3** informal a group of people with a common characteristic, interest, or purpose.
– ORIGIN from Latin, 'be able', later 'power'.

possess ● verb **1** have as property; own. **2** (also **be possessed of**) have as an ability, quality, or characteristic. **3** (of a demon or spirit) have complete power over. **4** (of an emotion, idea, etc.) dominate the mind of.
– PHRASES **what possessed you?** used to express surprise at an extremely unwise action.
– DERIVATIVES **possessor** noun **possessory** adjective.
– ORIGIN Old French *possesser*, from Latin *possidere* 'occupy, hold'.

possession ● noun **1** the state of possessing something. **2** a thing owned or possessed. **3** the state of being possessed by a demon, emotion, etc. **4** (in sport) temporary control of the ball by a player or team.

possessive ● adjective **1** demanding someone's total attention and love. **2** unwilling to share one's possessions. **3** Grammar expressing possession.
– DERIVATIVES **possessively** adverb **possessiveness** noun.

possessive determiner ● noun Grammar a determiner indicating possession, for example *my*.

possessive pronoun ● noun Grammar a pronoun indicating possession, for example *mine*.

posset /possit/ ● noun a drink made of hot milk curdled with ale or wine and flavoured with spices, formerly drunk as a delicacy or as a remedy for colds.
– ORIGIN of unknown origin.

possibility ● noun (pl. **possibilities**) **1** a thing that is possible. **2** the state or fact of being possible. **3** (**possibilities**) unspecified qualities of a promising nature.

possible ● adjective **1** capable of existing, happening, or being achieved. **2** that may be so, but that is not certain or probable. ● noun **1** a possible candidate for a job or member of a team. **2** (**the possible**) that which is likely or achievable.
– ORIGIN Latin *possibilis*, from *posse* 'be able'.

possibly ● adverb **1** perhaps. **2** in accordance with what is possible.

possum ● noun **1** a tree-dwelling Australasian marsupial. **2** N. Amer. informal an opossum.
– PHRASES **play possum 1** pretend to be unconscious or dead (as an opossum does when threatened). **2** feign ignorance.
– ORIGIN shortening of OPOSSUM.

post[1] ● noun **1** a long, sturdy, upright piece of timber or metal used as a support or a marker. **2** (**the post**) a starting post or winning post. ● verb **1** display (a notice) in a public place. **2** announce or publish. **3** achieve or record (a particular score or result).
– ORIGIN Latin *postis* 'doorpost'.

post[2] ● noun chiefly Brit. **1** the official service or system that delivers letters and parcels. **2** letters and parcels delivered. **3** a single collection or delivery of post. ● verb **1** chiefly Brit. send via the postal system. **2** (in bookkeeping) enter (an item) in a ledger.
– PHRASES **keep posted** keep (someone) informed of the latest developments or news.
– ORIGIN originally denoting one of a series of couriers who carried mail on horseback between stages: from French *poste*, from Latin *ponere* 'to place'.

post[3] ● noun **1** a place where someone is on duty or where an activity is carried out. **2** a job. ● verb **1** station in a particular place. **2** send to a place to take up an appointment.
– ORIGIN Italian *posto*, from Latin *ponere* 'to place'.

post- ● prefix after in time or order: *post-date*.
– ORIGIN Latin *post* 'after, behind'.

postage ● noun **1** the sending of letters and parcels by post. **2** the amount required to send something by post.

postage stamp ● noun an adhesive stamp applied to a letter or parcel to indicate the amount of postage paid.

postal ● adjective relating to or carried out by post.
– PHRASES **go postal** US informal go mad, especially from stress. [ORIGIN with reference to cases in which postal employees have run amok and shot colleagues.]
– DERIVATIVES **postally** adverb.

postal card ● noun US term for POSTCARD.

postal code ● noun another term for POSTCODE.

postal order ● noun Brit. an order for payment of a specified sum to a named person, issued by the Post Office.

postbag ● noun British term for MAILBAG.

postbellum ● adjective occurring or existing after a war, in particular the American Civil War.
– ORIGIN from Latin *post* 'after' + *bellum* 'war'.

Thesaurus

p

right, thoroughly, completely, utterly, totally, extremely, fairly; *informal* plain.

possess ● verb **1** *the only hat she possessed* OWN, have (to one's name), hold. **2** *he did not possess a sense of humour* HAVE, be blessed with, be endowed with; enjoy, boast. **3** *a supernatural force possessed him* TAKE CONTROL OF, take over, control, dominate, influence; bewitch, enchant, enthral. **4** *she was possessed by a need to talk to him* OBSESS, haunt, preoccupy, consume; eat someone up, prey on one's mind.
– PHRASES **possess oneself of** ACQUIRE, obtain, get (hold of), procure, get one's hands on; take, seize; *informal* get one's mitts on.

possessed ● adjective MAD, demented, insane, crazed, berserk, out of one's mind; bewitched, enchanted, haunted, under a spell.

possession ● noun **1** *the estate came into their possession* OWNERSHIP, control, hands, keeping, care, custody, charge, hold, title, guardianship. **2** *her possession of the premises* OCCUPANCY, occupation, tenure, holding, tenancy. **3** *she packed her possessions* BELONGINGS, things, property, (worldly) goods, (personal) effects, assets, chattels, movables, valuables; stuff, bits and pieces; luggage, baggage; *informal* gear, junk; *Brit. informal* clobber. **4** *colonial possessions* COLONY, dependency, territory, holding, protectorate.
– PHRASES **take possession of** SEIZE, appropriate, impound, expropriate, sequestrate, sequester, confiscate; take, get, acquire, obtain, procure, possess oneself of, get hold of, get one's hands on; capture, commandeer, requisition; *Law* distrain; *Scottish Law* poind; *informal* get one's mitts on.

possessive ● adjective **1** *he was very possessive* PROPRIETORIAL, overprotective, controlling, dominating, jealous, clingy. **2** *kids are possessive of their own property* COVETOUS, selfish, unwilling to share; grasping, greedy, acquisitive; *N. Amer. informal* grabby.

possibility ● noun **1** *there is a possibility that he might be alive* CHANCE, likelihood, probability, hope; risk, hazard, danger, fear. **2** *they discussed the possibility of launching a new project* FEASIBILITY, practicability, chances, odds, achievability, probability. **3** *buying a smaller house is one possibility* OPTION, alternative, choice, course of action, solution. **4** *the idea has distinct possibilities* POTENTIAL, promise, prospects.

possible ● adjective **1** *it's not possible to check the figures* FEASIBLE, practicable, viable, within the bounds/realms of possibility, attainable, achievable, workable; *informal* on, doable. **2** *a possible reason for his disappearance* CONCEIVABLE, plausible, imaginable, believable, likely, potential, probable, credible. **3** *a possible future leader* POTENTIAL, prospective, likely, probable.
– OPPOSITES unlikely.

possibly ● adverb **1** *possibly he took the boy with him* PERHAPS, maybe, it is possible, for all one knows, very likely; *poetic/literary* peradventure, perchance, mayhap. **2** *you can't possibly refuse* CONCEIVABLY, under any circumstances, by any means. **3** *could you possibly help me?* PLEASE, kindly, be so good as to.

post[1] ● noun *wooden posts* POLE, stake, upright, shaft, prop, support, picket, strut, pillar, pale, paling, stanchion, puncheon.
● verb **1** *the notice posted on the wall* AFFIX, attach, fasten, display, pin (up), put up, stick (up), tack (up). **2** *the group posted a net profit* ANNOUNCE, report, make known, publish.

post[2] ● noun *(Brit.)* **1** *the winners will be notified by post* MAIL, the postal service; airmail, surface mail, registered mail; *informal* snail mail. **2** *did we get any post?* LETTERS, correspondence, mail.
● verb **1** *(Brit.) post the order form today* SEND (OFF), mail, put in the post/mail, get off. **2** *post the transaction in the second column* RECORD, write in, enter, register.
– PHRASES **keep someone posted** KEEP INFORMED, keep up to date, keep in the picture, keep briefed, update, fill in; *informal* keep up to speed.

post[3] ● noun **1** *there were seventy candidates for the post* JOB, position, appointment, situation, place; vacancy, opening; *Austral. informal* grip. **2** *Back to your posts!* (ASSIGNED) POSITION, station, observation post.
● verb **1** *he'd been posted to Berlin* SEND, assign to a post, dispatch.

postbox ● noun a large public box into which letters are posted for collection by the post office.
postcard ● noun a card for sending a message by post without an envelope.
post-chaise /pōstshayz/ ● noun (pl. **post-chaises** pronunc. same) historical a horse-drawn carriage for transporting passengers or mail.
postcode ● noun Brit. a group of letters and numbers added to a postal address to assist the sorting of mail.
post-coital ● adjective occurring or done after sexual intercourse.
– DERIVATIVES **post-coitally** adverb.
post-date ● verb **1** assign a date later than the actual one to (a document or event). **2** occur or come at a later date than.
postdoctoral ● adjective (of research) undertaken after the completion of a doctorate.
poster ● noun a large printed picture or notice used for decoration or advertisement.
poste restante /pōst restənt, restont/ ● noun Brit. a department in a post office that keeps letters until they are collected by the person they are addressed to.
– ORIGIN French, 'mail remaining'.
posterior ● adjective **1** chiefly Anatomy further back in position; of or nearer the rear or hind end. The opposite of ANTERIOR. **2** formal coming after in time or order; later. ● noun humorous a person's buttocks.
– ORIGIN Latin, from *posterus* 'following'.
posterity ● noun all future generations of people.
– ORIGIN Old French *posterite*, from Latin *posterus* 'following'.
postern /postərn/ ● noun a back or side entrance.
– ORIGIN Old French *posterne*, from Latin *posterus* 'following'.
poster paint ● noun an opaque paint with a water-soluble binder.
post-feminist ● adjective moving beyond or rejecting some of the earlier ideas of feminism as out of date. ● noun a person holding post-feminist views.
postgraduate ● adjective relating to study undertaken after completing a first degree. ● noun a person engaged in postgraduate study.
post-haste ● adverb with great speed.
– ORIGIN from the direction 'haste, post, haste', formerly given on letters.
post horn ● noun historical a valveless horn used to signal the arrival or departure of a mounted courier or mail coach.
posthumous /postyooməss/ ● adjective occurring, awarded, or appearing after the death of the originator.
– DERIVATIVES **posthumously** adverb.
– ORIGIN Latin *postumus* 'last', later associated with *humus* 'ground'.
postilion /postilyən/ (also **postillion**) ● noun the rider of the leading nearside horse of a team or pair drawing a coach, when there is no coachman.
– ORIGIN French *postillon*, from Italian *postiglione* 'post boy'.
post-Impressionism ● noun a late 19th-century and early 20th-century style of art in which colour, line, and form were used to express the emotional response of the artist.
– DERIVATIVES **post-Impressionist** noun & adjective.
post-industrial ● adjective (of an economy or society) no longer relying on heavy industry.
posting ● noun chiefly Brit. an appointment to a job, especially one abroad or in the armed forces.
postlude ● noun Music a concluding piece of music.
– ORIGIN from POST-, on the pattern of *prelude*.
postman (or **postwoman**) ● noun Brit. a person who is employed to deliver or collect post.
postman's knock ● noun Brit. a children's game in which imaginary letters are delivered in exchange for kisses.
postmark ● noun an official mark stamped on a letter or parcel, giving the date of posting and cancelling the postage stamp. ● verb stamp with a postmark.
postmaster (or **postmistress**) ● noun a person in charge of a post office.
postmaster general ● noun the head of a country's postal service.
postmillennialism ● noun (among fundamentalist Christians) the doctrine that the Second Coming of Christ will be the culmination of the prophesied millennium of blessedness.
– DERIVATIVES **postmillennialist** noun.
postmodernism ● noun a style and concept in the arts characterized by distrust of theories and ideologies and by the drawing of attention to conventions.
– DERIVATIVES **postmodern** adjective **postmodernist** noun & adjective **postmodernity** noun.
post-mortem ● noun **1** an examination of a dead body to determine the cause of death. **2** an analysis of an event made after it has occurred. ● adjective happening after death.
– ORIGIN Latin, 'after death'.
post-natal ● adjective occurring in or relating to the period after childbirth.
– DERIVATIVES **post-natally** adverb.
post office ● noun **1** the public department or corporation responsible for postal services and (in some countries) telecommunications. **2** a building where postal business is transacted.
post office box ● noun a numbered box in a post office where letters for a person or organization are kept until called for.
post-operative ● adjective relating to the period following a surgical operation.
post-partum /pōstpaartəm/ ● adjective relating to the period following childbirth or the birth of young.
– ORIGIN from Latin *post partum* 'after childbirth'.
postpone ● verb arrange for (something) to take place at a time later than that first scheduled.
– DERIVATIVES **postponement** noun.
– ORIGIN Latin *postponere*, from *post* 'after' + *ponere* 'to place'.
postpositive ● adjective (of a word) placed after or as a suffix on the word that it relates to.
postprandial ● adjective **1** formal or humorous during or relating to the period after a meal. **2** Medicine occurring after a meal.
– ORIGIN from Latin *prandium* 'a meal'.
postscript ● noun an additional remark at the end of a letter, following the signature.
– ORIGIN Latin *postscriptum*, from *postscribere* 'write under, add'.
post-structuralism ● noun an extension and critique of structuralism, especially as used in critical textual analysis, which emphasizes plurality of meaning and rejects the binary oppositions of structuralism.
– DERIVATIVES **post-structural** adjective **post-structuralist** noun & adjective.
post-traumatic stress disorder ● noun a condition of persistent stress occurring as a result of injury or severe psychological shock.
postulant /postyoolənt/ ● noun a candidate seeking admission into a religious order.
postulate ● verb /postyoolayt/ **1** suggest or assume the exist-

p

Thesaurus

2 *armed guards were posted beside the exit* PUT ON DUTY, station, position, situate, locate.
poster ● noun NOTICE, placard, bill, sign, advertisement, affiche, playbill; *Brit.* fly-poster.
posterior ● adjective **1** *the posterior part of the skull* REAR, hind, back, hinder; *technical* dorsal, caudal. **2** *(formal) a date posterior to the Reform Bill* LATER THAN, subsequent to, following, after.
– OPPOSITES anterior, previous.
● noun *(humorous) her plump posterior*. See BOTTOM noun sense 6.
posterity ● noun **1** *their names are recorded for posterity* FUTURE GENERATIONS, the future. **2** *(archaic) the posterity of Abraham* DESCENDANTS, heirs, successors, offspring, children, progeny; *Law* issue; *archaic* seed.
post-haste ● adverb AS QUICKLY AS POSSIBLE, without delay, (very) quickly, speedily, without further/more ado, with all speed, promptly, immediately, at once, straight away, right away; *informal* pronto, straight off.
postman, postwoman ● noun POSTAL WORKER; *N. Amer.* mailman; *Brit. informal* postie.
post-mortem ● noun **1** *the hospital carried out a post-mortem* AUTOPSY, post-mortem examination, PM, necropsy. **2** *a post-mortem of her failed relationship* ANALYSIS, evaluation, assessment, appraisal, examination, review.
postpone ● verb PUT OFF/BACK, delay, defer, reschedule, adjourn, shelve; *N. Amer.* put over, take a rain check on; *informal* put on ice, put on the back burner; *rare* remit, respite.
– OPPOSITES bring forward.
postponement ● noun DEFERRAL, deferment, delay, putting off/back, rescheduling, adjournment, shelving.
postscript ● noun **1** *a handwritten postscript* AFTERTHOUGHT, PS,

ence, fact, or truth of (something) as a basis for reasoning or belief. **2** nominate or elect to an ecclesiastical office subject to the sanction of a higher authority. ● noun /postyoolət/ a thing postulated.
– DERIVATIVES **postulation** noun.
– ORIGIN Latin *postulare* 'ask'.
posture ● noun **1** a particular position of the body. **2** the way in which a person holds their body. **3** an approach or attitude towards something. ● verb behave in a way that is intended to impress or mislead others.
– DERIVATIVES **postural** adjective.
– ORIGIN Latin *positura* 'position'.
postviral syndrome (also **postviral fatigue syndrome**) ● noun myalgic encephalomyelitis following infection by a virus.
posy[1] ● noun (pl. **posies**) a small bunch of flowers.
– ORIGIN originally in the sense 'motto or line of verse inscribed inside a ring': contraction of POESY.
posy[2] ● adjective variant spelling of POSEY.
pot[1] ● noun **1** a rounded or cylindrical container, especially one of ceramic, used for storage or cooking. **2** a flowerpot. **3** (**the pot**) the total sum of the bets made on a round in poker, brag, etc. **4** Billiards & Snooker a shot in which a player strikes a ball into a pocket. **5** (chiefly in rugby) an attempt to score a goal with a kick. ● verb (**potted**, **potting**) **1** plant in a pot. **2** preserve (food) in a sealed pot or jar. **3** make pottery. **4** Billiards & Snooker strike (a ball) into a pocket. **5** score (a goal). **6** informal hit or kill by shooting.
– PHRASES **go to pot** informal deteriorate through neglect. **a watched pot never boils** proverb time seems to drag endlessly when you're waiting anxiously for something to happen.
– ORIGIN Old English.
pot[2] ● noun informal cannabis.
– ORIGIN probably from Mexican Spanish *potiguaya* 'cannabis leaves'.
potable /pōtəb'l/ ● adjective formal drinkable.
– DERIVATIVES **potability** noun.
– ORIGIN French, from Latin *potare* 'to drink'.
potage /potaazh/ ● noun thick soup.
– ORIGIN French; compare with POTTAGE.
potager /pottəjər/ ● noun a kitchen garden.
– ORIGIN from French *jardin potager* 'garden providing vegetables for the pot'.
potash ● noun an alkaline potassium compound, especially potassium carbonate or hydroxide.
– ORIGIN from *pot-ashes*, because originally obtained by leaching vegetable ashes and evaporating the solution in iron pots.
potassium /pətassiəm/ ● noun a soft silvery-white reactive metallic element of the alkali-metal group.
– ORIGIN from POTASH.
potassium hydroxide ● noun a strongly alkaline white compound used in many industrial processes, e.g. soap manufacture.
potation /pōtaysh'n/ ● noun archaic or humorous **1** the action of drinking alcohol. **2** an alcoholic drink.
– ORIGIN Latin, from *potare* 'to drink'.
potato ● noun a starchy plant tuber which is cooked and eaten as a vegetable.
– ORIGIN Spanish *patata* 'sweet potato', from Taino (an extinct Caribbean language).
pot-au-feu /potōfö/ ● noun a French soup of meat and vegetables cooked in a large pot.
– ORIGIN French, 'pot on the fire'.
pot belly ● noun a protruding stomach.
potboiler ● noun informal a book, film, etc. produced purely to make the writer or artist a living by catering to popular taste.
pot-bound ● adjective (of a plant) having roots which fill the pot, leaving no room for them to expand.
poteen /poteen/ ● noun chiefly Irish illicitly made whisky.
– ORIGIN from Irish *fuisce poitín* 'little pot of whisky'.
potent ● adjective **1** having great power, influence, or effect. **2** (of a male) able to achieve an erection or to reach an orgasm.
– DERIVATIVES **potency** noun **potently** adverb.
– ORIGIN from Latin *posse* 'be powerful, be able'.
potentate ● noun a monarch or ruler.
– ORIGIN Latin *potentatus* 'dominion'.
potential ● adjective having the capacity to develop into something in the future. ● noun **1** qualities or abilities that may be developed and lead to future success or usefulness. **2** (often **potential for/to do**) the possibility of something happening or of someone doing something in the future. **3** Physics the quantity determining the energy of mass in a gravitational field or of charge in an electric field.
– DERIVATIVES **potentiality** noun **potentially** adverb.
– ORIGIN Latin *potentialis*, from *potentia* 'power'.
potential difference ● noun Physics the difference of electrical potential between two points.
potential energy ● noun Physics energy possessed by a body by virtue of its position or state. Compare with KINETIC ENERGY.
potentiate /pətenshiayt/ ● verb increase the power or effect of (a drug, physiological reaction, etc.).
potentilla /pōtəntillə/ ● noun a small shrub with yellow or red flowers.
– ORIGIN from Latin *potent-* 'being powerful' (with reference to its herbal qualities).
potentiometer /pətenshiommitər/ ● noun an instrument for measuring or adjusting an electromotive force.
pother /pothər/ ● noun a commotion or fuss.
– ORIGIN of unknown origin.
pothole ● noun **1** a deep natural underground cave formed by the eroding action of water. **2** a hole in a road surface. ● verb Brit. explore underground potholes as a pastime.
– DERIVATIVES **potholed** adjective **potholer** noun **potholing** noun.
– ORIGIN from dialect *pot* 'pit'.
potion ● noun a liquid with healing, magical, or poisonous properties.
– ORIGIN Latin, 'drink, poisonous draught', related to *potare* 'to drink'.
potlatch ● noun (among some North American Indian peoples) a ceremonial feast at which possessions are given away or destroyed to display wealth.
– ORIGIN from an American Indian language of Vancouver Island.
pot luck ● noun the chance that whatever is available will prove to be good or acceptable.
potoroo /pottərōō/ ● noun a small long-nosed marsupial with

Thesaurus

additional remark. **2** *he added postscripts of his own* ADDENDUM, supplement, appendix, codicil, afterword, addition.
postulate ● verb PUT FORWARD, suggest, advance, posit, hypothesize, propose; assume, presuppose, presume, take for granted.
posture ● noun **1** *a kneeling posture* POSITION, pose, attitude, stance. **2** *good posture* BEARING, carriage, stance, comportment; Brit. deportment. **3** *trade unions adopted a militant posture* ATTITUDE, stance, standpoint, point of view, opinion, position, frame of mind.
● verb *Keith postured, flexing his biceps* POSE, strike an attitude, strut.
posy ● noun BOUQUET, bunch (of flowers), spray, nosegay, corsage; buttonhole, boutonnière.
pot ● noun **1** *pots and pans* COOKING UTENSIL, pan, saucepan, casserole, stewpot, stockpot. **2** *earthenware pots* FLOWERPOT, planter, jardinière. **3** *Jim raked in half the pot* BANK, kitty, pool, purse, jackpot.
– PHRASES **go to pot** *(informal)* DETERIORATE, decline, degenerate, go to (rack and) ruin, go downhill, go to seed, become run down; informal go to the dogs, go down the tubes; Austral./NZ informal go to the pack.
pot-bellied ● adjective PAUNCHY, beer-bellied, portly, rotund; informal tubby, roly-poly.
pot belly ● noun PAUNCH, (beer) belly; informal beer gut, pot, tummy.
potency ● noun **1** *the potency of his words* FORCEFULNESS, force, effectiveness, persuasiveness, cogency, influence, strength, authoritativeness, authority, power, powerfulness; poetic/literary puissance. **2** *the potency of the drugs* STRENGTH, powerfulness, power, effectiveness; formal efficacy; efficaciousness.
potent ● adjective **1** *a potent political force* POWERFUL, strong, mighty, formidable, influential, dominant, forceful; poetic/literary puissant. **2** *a potent argument* FORCEFUL, convincing, cogent, compelling, persuasive, powerful, strong. **3** *a potent drug* STRONG, powerful, effective; formal efficacious.
– OPPOSITES weak.
potentate ● noun RULER, monarch, sovereign, king, queen, emperor, empress.
potential ● adjective *a potential source of conflict* POSSIBLE, likely, prospective, future, probable; latent, inherent, undeveloped.
● noun *economic potential* POSSIBILITIES, potentiality, prospects; promise, capability, capacity.

long hindlimbs, native to Australia and Tasmania.
– ORIGIN probably from an Aboriginal language.
pot-pourri /pōpooree/ • noun (pl. **pot-pourris**) **1** a mixture of dried petals and spices placed in a bowl to perfume a room. **2** a mixture of things; a medley.
– ORIGIN originally denoting a stew made of different kinds of meat: from French, 'rotten pot'.
pot roast • noun a piece of meat cooked slowly in a covered pot.
potsherd /potsherd/ • noun a piece of broken pottery.
potshot • noun a shot aimed unexpectedly or at random.
– ORIGIN originally a *shot* at an animal intended for the *pot*, i.e. for food, rather than for display (which would require skilled shooting).
pottage • noun archaic soup or stew.
– ORIGIN Old French *potage* 'that which is put into a pot'; compare with POTAGE and PORRIDGE.
potted • adjective **1** grown or preserved in a pot. **2** (of an account) put into a short, accessible form.
potter[1] • verb **1** occupy oneself in a leisurely but pleasant manner. **2** move or go in a casual, unhurried way. • noun a spell of pottering.
– ORIGIN originally in the sense 'poke repeatedly': from dialect *pote* 'to push, kick, or poke'.
potter[2] • noun a person who makes ceramic ware.
potter's field • noun historical a burial place for paupers and strangers.
– ORIGIN with biblical allusion to the Gospel of Matthew, chapter 27.
potter's wheel • noun a horizontal revolving disc on which wet clay is shaped into pots, bowls, etc.
pottery • noun (pl. **potteries**) **1** articles made of fired clay. **2** the craft or profession of making such ware. **3** a factory or workshop where such ware is made.
potting shed • noun a shed used for potting plants and storing garden tools and supplies.
potty[1] • adjective (**pottier**, **pottiest**) informal, chiefly Brit. **1** foolish; crazy. **2** extremely enthusiastic about someone or something.
– DERIVATIVES **pottiness** noun.
– ORIGIN of unknown origin.
potty[2] • noun (pl. **potties**) informal a receptacle for a child to urinate or defecate into.
pouch • noun **1** a small flexible bag, typically carried in a pocket or attached to a belt. **2** a pocket-like receptacle in an animal's body, especially that in which marsupials carry their young. • verb put, make, or form into a pouch.
– DERIVATIVES **pouched** adjective **pouchy** adjective.
– ORIGIN Old French *poche* 'bag'.
pouf[1] • noun variant spelling of POOF[1] or POUFFE. • exclamation variant spelling of POOF[2].
pouf[2] /pōōf/ • noun **1** a part of a dress in which a large mass of material has been gathered so that it stands away from the body. **2** a bouffant hairstyle.
– ORIGIN French.
pouffe /pōōf/ (also **pouf**) • noun a cushioned footstool or low seat with no back.
– ORIGIN French.
poult /pōlt/ • noun a young domestic fowl being raised for food.
– ORIGIN contraction of PULLET.
poulterer • noun Brit. a dealer in poultry.
poultice /pōltiss/ • noun a soft moist mass of flour, plant material, etc., applied to the skin to relieve inflammation. • verb apply a poultice to.
– ORIGIN from Latin *puls* 'pottage, pap'.
poultry /pōltri/ • noun chickens, turkeys, ducks, and geese; domestic fowl.
– ORIGIN Old French *pouletrie*, from *poulet* 'pullet'.
pounce[1] • verb **1** spring or swoop suddenly so as to seize or attack. **2** take swift advantage of a mistake or sign of weakness. • noun an act of pouncing.
– ORIGIN originally denoting a tool for punching, later a claw or talon: origin uncertain.
pounce[2] • noun **1** a fine powder formerly used to prevent ink from spreading on paper or to prepare parchment to receive writing. **2** a fine powder dusted over a perforated pattern to transfer the design to the surface beneath.
– ORIGIN French *poncer*, from Latin *pumex* 'pumice'.
pound[1] • noun **1** a unit of weight equal to 16 oz avoirdupois (0.4536 kg), or 12 oz troy (0.3732 kg). **2** (also **pound sterling**) (pl. **pounds sterling**) the basic monetary unit of the UK, equal to 100 pence. **3** another term for PUNT[4]. **4** the basic monetary unit of several Middle Eastern countries, equal to 100 piastres. **5** the basic monetary unit of Cyprus, equal to 100 cents. **6** a monetary unit of the Sudan, equal to one tenth of a dinar.
– PHRASES **one's pound of flesh** something to which one is strictly entitled, but which it is ruthless to demand. [ORIGIN with allusion to Shakespeare's *Merchant of Venice*.]
– DERIVATIVES **pounder** noun.
– ORIGIN Old English, from Latin *libra pondo*, denoting a Roman 'pound weight' of 12 ounces.
pound[2] • verb **1** strike or hit heavily and repeatedly. **2** walk or run with heavy steps. **3** beat of throb with a strong regular rhythm. **4** (**pound out**) produce (a document or piece of music) with heavy strokes on a keyboard or instrument. **5** crush or grind into a powder or paste. **6** informal defeat resoundingly.
– ORIGIN Old English.
pound[3] • noun **1** a place where stray dogs or illegally parked vehicles may officially be taken and kept until claimed. **2** archaic a trap or prison.
– ORIGIN uncertain.
poundage • noun Brit. **1** a commission of a particular amount of the sum involved in a transaction. **2** a percentage of the total earnings of a business, paid as wages. **3** weight.
pound cake • noun a rich cake originally made with a pound of each chief ingredient.
pour • verb **1** flow or cause to flow in a steady stream. **2** (of rain) fall heavily. **3** prepare and serve (a drink). **4** come or go in a steady stream. **5** (**pour out**) express (one's feelings) in an unrestrained way.
– PHRASES **it never rains but it pours** proverb misfortunes or difficult situations tend to arrive all at the same time. **pour oil on troubled waters** try to calm a dispute with placatory words.
– DERIVATIVES **pourer** noun.
– ORIGIN of unknown origin.
poussin /pōōsan/ • noun a chicken killed young for eating.

p

Thesaurus

potion • noun CONCOCTION, mixture, brew, elixir, philtre, drink, decoction; medicine, tonic; *poetic/literary* draught.
pot-pourri • noun MIXTURE, assortment, collection, selection, assemblage, medley, miscellany, mix, variety, mixed bag; ragbag, hotchpotch, mishmash, jumble; *N. Amer.* hodgepodge.
potter • verb *we pottered down to the library* AMBLE, wander, meander, stroll, saunter, maunder; *informal* mosey, tootle, toddle; *N. Amer. informal* putter.
– PHRASES **potter about/around** DO NOTHING MUCH, fiddle about/around, footle about/around; *informal* mess about/around; *Brit. informal* muck about/around; *N. Amer. informal* putter about/around, lollygag.
pottery • noun CHINA, crockery, ceramics, earthenware, stoneware.
potty • adjective (*Brit. informal*) **1** *I'm going potty.* See CRAZY sense 1. **2** *she's potty about you.* See CRAZY sense 3.
pouch • noun **1** *a leather pouch* BAG, purse, sack, sac, pocket; *Scottish* sporran. **2** *a kangaroo's pouch Zoology* marsupium.
pounce • verb *two men pounced on him* JUMP ON, spring, leap, dive, lunge, fall on, set on, attack suddenly; *informal* jump, mug.
• noun *a sudden pounce* LEAP, spring, jump, dive, lunge, bound.
pound[1] • verb **1** *the two men pounded him with their fists* BEAT, strike, hit, batter, thump, pummel, punch, rain blows on, belabour, hammer, thrash, set on, tear into; *informal* bash, clobber, wallop, beat the living daylights out of, whack, thwack, lay into, pitch into; *Brit. informal* slosh; *N. Amer. informal* light into, whale. **2** *waves pounded the seafront* BEAT AGAINST, crash against, batter, dash against, lash, buffet. **3** *gunships pounded the capital* BOMBARD, bomb, shell, fire on; *archaic* cannonade. **4** *pound the cloves with salt* CRUSH, grind, pulverize, mill, mash, pulp; *technical* triturate; *archaic* levigate. **5** *I heard him pounding along the gangway* WALK/RUN HEAVILY, stomp, lumber, clomp, clump, tramp, trudge. **6** *her heart was pounding* THROB, thump, thud, hammer, pulse, race, go pit-a-pat; *poetic/literary* pant, thrill.
pound[2] • noun **1** *a pound of apples* pound weight, lb. **2** *ten pounds* pound sterling, £; *Brit. informal* quid, smacker, nicker.
pound[3] • noun *a dog pound* ENCLOSURE, compound, pen, yard.
pour • verb **1** *blood was pouring from his nose* STREAM, flow, run, gush, course, jet, spurt, surge, spill. **2** *Amy poured wine into his*

– ORIGIN French.
pout ● verb push one's lips forward as an expression of petulant annoyance or in order to make oneself look sexually attractive. ● noun a pouting expression.
– DERIVATIVES **pouty** adjective.
– ORIGIN perhaps related to Swedish dialect *puta* 'be inflated'.
pouter ● noun a kind of pigeon that is able to inflate its crop to a considerable extent.
poverty ● noun **1** the state of being extremely poor. **2** the state of being insufficient in amount.
– ORIGIN Old French *poverte*, from Latin *pauper* 'poor'.
poverty trap ● noun Brit. a situation in which an increase in someone's income is offset by a consequent loss of state benefits.
POW ● abbreviation prisoner of war.
powder ● noun **1** fine dry particles produced by the grinding, crushing, or disintegration of a solid substance. **2** a cosmetic in this form applied to a person's face. **3** dated a medicine in this form. **4** loose, dry, newly fallen snow. **5** gunpowder. ● verb **1** sprinkle or cover with powder. **2** make into a powder.
– PHRASES **keep one's powder dry** remain cautious and alert. **take a powder** N. Amer. informal depart quickly.
– DERIVATIVES **powdery** adjective.
– ORIGIN Old French *poudre*, from Latin *pulvis* 'dust'.
powder blue ● noun a soft, pale blue.
powder keg ● noun **1** a barrel of gunpowder. **2** a potentially explosive situation.
powder monkey ● noun **1** historical a boy employed on a sailing warship to carry powder to the guns. **2** N. Amer. a person who works with explosives.
powder puff ● noun a soft pad for applying powder to the face.
powder room ● noun euphemistic a women's toilet in a public building.
power ● noun **1** the ability to do something or act in a particular way. **2** the capacity to influence other people or the course of events. **3** a right or authority given or delegated to a person or body. **4** political authority or control. **5** physical strength or force. **6** a country viewed in terms of its international influence and military strength: *a world power.* **7** capacity or performance of an engine or other device. **8** energy that is produced by mechanical, electrical, or other means. **9** Physics the rate of doing work, measured in watts or horse power. **10** Mathematics the product obtained when a number is multiplied by itself a certain number of times. ● verb **1** supply with power. **2** (**power up/down**) switch (a device) on or off. **3** move or cause to move with speed or force.
– PHRASES **do someone a power of good** informal be very beneficial to someone. **the powers that be** the authorities. [ORIGIN with biblical allusion to Epistle to the Romans, chapter 13.]
– DERIVATIVES **powered** adjective.
– ORIGIN Old French *poeir*, from Latin *posse* 'be able'.
powerboat ● noun a fast motor boat.
power broker ● noun a person who exerts influence to affect the distribution of political or economic power.
power cut ● noun a temporary withdrawal or failure of an electrical power supply.
powerful ● adjective having power. ● adverb chiefly dialect very.
– DERIVATIVES **powerfully** adverb.
powerhouse ● noun a person or thing having great energy or power.
powerless ● adjective without ability, influence, or power.
– DERIVATIVES **powerlessly** adverb **powerlessness** noun.
power of attorney ● noun Law the authority to act for another person in specified legal or financial matters.
power pack ● noun **1** a unit which stores and supplies electrical power. **2** a transformer for converting an alternating current (from the mains) to a direct current.
power plant ● noun **1** a power station. **2** an apparatus which provides power for a machine, building, etc.
power play ● noun **1** tactics exhibiting or intended to increase a person's power. **2** offensive tactics in a team sport involving the concentration of players in a particular area.
power station ● noun an installation where electrical power is generated.
power steering ● noun steering aided by power from the vehicle's engine.
power train ● noun the mechanism that transmits the drive from the engine of a vehicle to its axle.
Powhatan /powətan/ ● noun (pl. same or **Powhatans**) a member of an American Indian people of eastern Virginia.
– ORIGIN Virginia Algonquian.
powwow ● noun **1** a North American Indian ceremony involving feasting and dancing. **2** informal a meeting for discussion among friends or colleagues. ● verb informal hold a powwow.
– ORIGIN Narragansett, 'magician'.
pox ● noun **1** any disease caused by a virus and producing a rash of pimples that become pus-filled and leave pockmarks on

Thesaurus

glass TIP, let flow, splash, spill, decant; *informal* slosh, slop. **3** *it was pouring with rain* RAIN HEAVILY/HARD, teem down, pelt down, tip down, come down in torrents/sheets, rain cats and dogs; *informal* be chucking it down; *Brit. informal* bucket down, come down in stair rods; *N. Amer. informal* rain pitchforks. **4** *people poured off the train* THRONG, crowd, swarm, stream, flood.
pout ● verb *Crystal pouted sullenly* LOOK PETULANT, pull a face, look sulky.
● noun *a childish pout* PETULANT EXPRESSION, sulky expression, moue.
poverty ● noun **1** *abject poverty* PENURY, destitution, pauperism, pauperdom, indigence, pennilessness, impoverishment, neediness, need, hardship, impecuniousness. **2** *the poverty of choice* SCARCITY, deficiency, dearth, shortage, paucity, insufficiency, absence, lack. **3** *the poverty of her imagination* INFERIORITY, mediocrity, poorness, sterility.
– OPPOSITES wealth, abundance.
poverty-stricken ● adjective EXTREMELY POOR, impoverished, destitute, penniless, on one's beam-ends, as poor as a church mouse, in penury, impecunious, indigent, needy, in need/want; *Brit.* on the breadline, without a penny (to one's name); *informal* on one's uppers, without two pennies/farthings to rub together; *Brit. informal* in Queer Street; *formal* penurious.
powder ● noun DUST, fine particles; talcum powder, talc; *historical* pounce.
● verb **1** *she powdered her face* DUST, sprinkle/cover with powder. **2** *the grains are powdered* CRUSH, grind, pulverize, pound, mill; *technical* comminute; *archaic* levigate. **3** *powdered milk* dry, freeze-dry; *technical* lyophilize.
powdered ● adjective dried, freeze-dried; *technical* lyophilized.
powdery ● adjective FINE, dry, fine-grained, powder-like, dusty, chalky, floury, sandy, crumbly, friable.
power ● noun **1** *the power of speech* ABILITY, capacity, capability, potential, faculty, competence. **2** *the unions wield enormous power* CONTROL, authority, influence, dominance, mastery, domination, dominion, sway, weight, leverage; *informal* clout, teeth; *N. Amer. informal* drag; *poetic/literary* puissance. **3** *police have the power to stop and search* AUTHORITY, right, authorization, warrant, licence. **4** *a major European power* STATE, country, nation. **5** *he hit the ball with as much power as he could* STRENGTH, powerfulness, might, force, forcefulness, vigour, energy; brawn, muscle; *informal* punch; *Brit. informal* welly; *poetic/literary* thew. **6** *the power of his arguments* FORCEFULNESS, powerfulness, potency, strength, force, cogency, persuasiveness. **7** *the new engine has more power* DRIVING FORCE, horsepower, hp, acceleration; *informal* oomph, grunt. **8** *generating power from waste* ENERGY, electrical power. **9** *(informal) the holiday did him a power of good* A GREAT DEAL OF, a lot of, much; *informal* lots of, loads of.
– OPPOSITES inability, weakness.
– PHRASES **have someone in/under one's power** HAVE CONTROL OVER, have influence over, have under one's thumb, have at one's mercy, have in one's clutches, have in the palm of one's hand; *N. Amer.* have in one's hip pocket; *informal* have over a barrel. **the powers that be** THE AUTHORITIES, the people in charge, the government.
powerful ● adjective **1** *powerful shoulders* STRONG, muscular, muscly, sturdy, strapping, robust, brawny, burly, athletic, manly, well built, solid; *informal* beefy, hunky; *dated* stalwart; *poetic/literary* stark, thewy. **2** *a powerful drink* INTOXICATING, hard, strong, stiff; *formal* spirituous. **3** *a powerful blow* VIOLENT, forceful, hard, mighty. **4** *he felt a powerful desire to kiss her* INTENSE, keen, fierce, passionate, ardent, burning, strong, irresistible, overpowering, overwhelming. **5** *a powerful nation* INFLUENTIAL, strong, important, dominant, commanding, potent, forceful, formidable; *poetic/literary* puissant. **6** *a powerful critique* COGENT, compelling, convincing, persuasive, forceful; dramatic, graphic, vivid, moving.

healing. **2** (**the pox**) historical smallpox. **3** (**the pox**) informal syphilis.
– PHRASES **a pox on ——** archaic expressing anger with someone.
– ORIGIN alteration of *pocks*, plural of POCK.

poxy • adjective (**poxier**, **poxiest**) informal, chiefly Brit. of poor quality; worthless.

p. & p. • abbreviation Brit. postage and packing.

pp • abbreviation **1** (**pp.**) pages. **2** (also **p.p.**) per procurationem (used when signing a letter on someone else's behalf). [ORIGIN from Latin, 'through the agency of'.] **3** Music pianissimo.

PPE • abbreviation philosophy, politics, and economics.

ppm • abbreviation **1** part(s) per million. **2** Computing page(s) per minute.

PPS • abbreviation **1** post (additional) postscript. **2** Brit. Parliamentary Private Secretary.

PPV • abbreviation pay-per-view.

PR • abbreviation **1** proportional representation. **2** public relations.

Pr • symbol the chemical element praseodymium.

practicable • adjective able to be done or put into practice successfully.
– DERIVATIVES **practicability** noun **practicably** adverb.
– USAGE Although they are related, **practicable** and **practical** do not mean exactly the same thing: **practicable** means 'able to be done successfully', whereas the closest senses of **practical** are 'likely to be effective, feasible' and 'suitable for a particular purpose'.

practical • adjective **1** of or concerned with practice rather than theory. **2** likely to be effective in real circumstances; feasible. **3** suitable for a particular purpose. **4** realistic in approach. **5** skilled at manual tasks. **6** so nearly the case that it can be regarded as so; virtual. • noun Brit. an examination or lesson involving the practical application of theories and procedures.
– ORIGIN from Greek *praktikos* 'concerned with action'.

practicality • noun (pl. **practicalities**) **1** the quality or state of being practical. **2** (**practicalities**) the aspects of a situation that involve action or experience rather than theories or ideas.

practical joke • noun a trick played on someone in order to make them look foolish and to amuse others.

practically • adverb **1** in a practical way. **2** virtually; almost.

practice • noun **1** the actual application of a plan or method, as opposed to the theories relating to it. **2** the customary way of doing something. **3** the practising of a profession. **4** the business or premises of a doctor or lawyer. **5** the action or process of practising something so as to become proficient in it. • verb US spelling of PRACTISE.
– USAGE It should be noted that **practice** is the spelling for the noun, and in America for the verb as well; **practise** is the British spelling of the verb.
– ORIGIN from PRACTISE, on the pattern of pairs such as *advise, advice*.

practise (US **practice**) • verb **1** perform (an activity) or exercise (a skill) repeatedly in order to improve or maintain proficiency in it. **2** carry out or perform (an activity or custom) habitually or regularly. **3** be engaged in (a particular profession). **4** observe the teaching and rules of (a religion). **5** archaic scheme or plot for an evil purpose.
– ORIGIN Old French *practiser*, from Latin *practicare* 'perform, carry out'.

practised (US **practiced**) • adjective expert as the result of much experience.

practitioner • noun a person engaged in an art, discipline, or profession, especially medicine.

praenomen /preenōmen/ • noun the first or personal name given to a citizen of ancient Rome.
– ORIGIN Latin, from *prae* 'before' + *nomen* 'name'.

praepostor /pripostər/ • noun Brit. (at some public schools) a prefect or monitor.
– ORIGIN from Latin *praepositus* 'head, chief'; compare with PROVOST.

praesidium • noun variant spelling of PRESIDIUM.

praetor /preetər, -tor/ (US also **pretor**) • noun each of two ancient Roman magistrates ranking below consul.
– DERIVATIVES **praetorian** adjective & noun.
– ORIGIN Latin, perhaps from *prae* 'before' + *ire* 'go'.

praetorian guard • noun (in ancient Rome) the bodyguard of the emperor.

pragmatic • adjective **1** dealing with things in a practical rather than theoretical way. **2** relating to philosophical or political pragmatism.
– DERIVATIVES **pragmatically** adverb.
– ORIGIN Greek *pragmatikos* 'relating to fact'.

pragmatism • noun **1** a pragmatic attitude or policy. **2** Philosophy an approach that evaluates theories or beliefs in terms of the success of their practical application.
– DERIVATIVES **pragmatist** noun.

prairie • noun (in North America) a large open area of grassland.
– ORIGIN French, from Latin *pratum* 'meadow'.

prairie chicken • noun a large North American grouse found on the prairies.

prairie dog • noun a gregarious ground squirrel that lives in burrows in the grasslands of North America.

prairie oyster • noun **1** a drink made with a raw egg and seasoning, drunk as a cure for a hangover. **2** (**prairie oysters**) chiefly N. Amer. the testicles of a calf as food.

praise • verb **1** express warm approval of or admiration for. **2** express respect and gratitude towards (a deity). • noun **1** the expression of approval or admiration. **2** the expression of respect and gratitude as an act of worship.
– PHRASES **praise be** expressing relief, joy, or gratitude.
– ORIGIN Old French *preisier* 'to prize, praise', from Latin *pretium* 'price'.

praiseworthy • adjective deserving of praise.

Thesaurus

– OPPOSITES weak, gentle.

powerless • adjective IMPOTENT, helpless, ineffectual, ineffective, useless, defenceless, vulnerable; *poetic/literary* impuissant.

practicable • adjective REALISTIC, feasible, possible, within the bounds/realms of possibility, viable, reasonable, sensible, workable, achievable; *informal* doable.

practical • adjective **1** *practical experience* EMPIRICAL, hands-on, actual, active, applied, heuristic, experiential. **2** *there are no practical alternatives* FEASIBLE, practicable, realistic, viable, workable, possible, reasonable, sensible; *informal* doable. **3** *practical clothes* FUNCTIONAL, sensible, utilitarian, workaday. **4** *try to be more practical* REALISTIC, sensible, down-to-earth, businesslike, commonsensical, hard-headed, no-nonsense; *informal* hard-nosed. **5** *a practical certainty* VIRTUAL, effective, near.
– OPPOSITES theoretical.

practicality • noun **1** *the practicality of the proposal* FEASIBILITY, practicability, viability, workability. **2** *practicality of design* FUNCTIONALISM, functionality, serviceability, utility. **3** *his calm practicality* (COMMON) SENSE, realism, pragmatism. **4** *the practicalities of army life* PRACTICAL DETAILS; *informal* nitty gritty, nuts and bolts.

practical joke • noun TRICK, joke, prank, jape, hoax; *informal* leg-pull.

practically • adverb **1** *the cinema was practically empty* ALMOST, (very) nearly, virtually, just about, all but, more or less, as good as, to all intents and purposes, verging on, bordering on; *informal* pretty nearly, pretty well; *poetic/literary* well-nigh. **2** *'You can't afford it,' he pointed out practically* REALISTICALLY, sensibly, reasonably.

practice • noun **1** *the practice of radiotherapy* APPLICATION, exercise, use, operation, implementation, execution. **2** *common practice* CUSTOM, procedure, policy, convention, tradition; *formal* praxis. **3** *it takes lots of practice | the team's final practice* TRAINING, rehearsal, repetition, preparation; practice session, dummy run, run-through; *informal* dry run. **4** *the practice of medicine* PROFESSION, career, business, work. **5** *a small legal practice* BUSINESS, firm, office, company; *informal* outfit.
– PHRASES **in practice** IN REALITY, realistically, practically. **out of practice** RUSTY, unpractised. **put something into practice** USE, make use of, put to use, utilize, apply.

practise • verb **1** *he practised the songs every day* REHEARSE, run through, go over/through, work on/at; polish, perfect. **2** *the performers were practising* TRAIN, rehearse, prepare, go through one's paces. **3** *we still practise these rituals today* CARRY OUT, perform, observe. **4** *she practises medicine* WORK AT, pursue a career in.

practised • adjective EXPERT, experienced, seasoned, skilled, skilful, accomplished, proficient, talented, able, adept, consummate, master, masterly; *informal* crack, ace, mean; *N. Amer. informal* crackerjack.

pragmatic • adjective PRACTICAL, matter of fact, sensible, down-to-earth, commonsensical, businesslike, having both/one's feet on

– DERIVATIVES **praiseworthily** adverb **praiseworthiness** noun.

praline /praaleen/ ● noun a smooth sweet substance made from nuts boiled in sugar, used as a filling for chocolates.
– ORIGIN named after Marshal de Plessis-*Praslin* (1598–1675), the French soldier whose cook invented it.

pram ● noun Brit. a four-wheeled carriage for a baby, pushed by a person on foot.
– ORIGIN contraction of PERAMBULATOR.

prance ● verb **1** (of a horse) move with high springy steps. **2** walk with ostentatious, exaggerated movements. ● noun an act of prancing.
– ORIGIN of unknown origin.

prandial /prandiəl/ ● adjective during or relating to a meal.
– ORIGIN from Latin *prandium* 'meal'.

prang Brit. informal ● verb crash (a motor vehicle or aircraft). ● noun a collision or crash.
– ORIGIN imitative.

prank ● noun a practical joke or mischievous act.
– DERIVATIVES **prankish** adjective.
– ORIGIN of unknown origin.

prankster ● noun a person fond of playing pranks.

prase /prayz/ ● noun a translucent greenish variety of quartz.
– ORIGIN Greek *prasios* 'leek green', from *prason* 'leek'.

praseodymium /prayziədimmiəm/ ● noun a silvery-white metallic element of the lanthanide series.
– ORIGIN from Greek *prasios* 'leek green' (because of its green salts) + *didymium* (see NEODYMIUM).

prat ● noun informal **1** Brit. a stupid person. **2** a person's bottom.
– ORIGIN of unknown origin.

prate ● verb talk foolishly or at tedious length.
– ORIGIN from Dutch or Low German *praten*, probably imitative.

pratfall ● noun informal a fall on to one's bottom.

prattle ● verb talk at length in a foolish or inconsequential way. ● noun foolish or inconsequential talk.
– ORIGIN Low German *pratelen*, related to PRATE.

prawn ● noun a marine crustacean which resembles a large shrimp.
– ORIGIN of unknown origin.

prawn cracker ● noun (in Chinese cooking) a light prawn-flavoured crisp which puffs up when deep-fried.

praxis /praksiss/ ● noun **1** practice, as distinguished from theory. **2** custom.
– ORIGIN Greek, 'doing'.

pray ● verb **1** address a prayer to God or another deity. **2** wish or hope earnestly for a particular outcome. ● adverb formal or archaic used in polite requests or questions: *pray continue.*
– ORIGIN Old French *preier*, from Latin *precari* 'entreat'.

prayer ● noun **1** a request for help or expression of thanks addressed to God or another deity. **2** (**prayers**) a religious service at which people gather to pray together. **3** an earnest hope or wish.
– PHRASES **not have a prayer** informal have no chance.

prayerful ● adjective **1** characterized by the use of prayer. **2** given to praying; devout.
– DERIVATIVES **prayerfully** adverb.

prayer wheel ● noun a small revolving cylinder inscribed with or containing prayers, used by Tibetan Buddhists.

praying mantis ● noun see MANTIS.

pre- ● prefix before (in time, place, order, degree, or importance): *pre-adolescent.*
– ORIGIN from Latin *prae-*.

preach ● verb **1** deliver a religious address to an assembled group of people. **2** earnestly advocate (a principle). **3** (**preach at**) give moral advice to (someone) in a self-righteous way.
– DERIVATIVES **preacher** noun.
– ORIGIN Old French *prechier*, from Latin *praedicare* 'proclaim'.

preachify ● verb (**preachifies, preachified**) informal preach or moralize tediously.

preachy ● adjective informal giving moral advice in a self-righteous way.

preamble /preeamb'l/ ● noun a preliminary statement; an introduction.
– ORIGIN Old French *preambule*, from Latin *praeambulus* 'going before'.

preamplifier ● noun an electronic device that amplifies a very weak signal and transmits it to a main amplifier.

pre-arrange ● verb arrange or agree in advance.

prebend /prebb'nd/ ● noun historical **1** the allowance granted to a canon or member of a chapter. **2** the property from which such an allowance was derived. **3** another term for PREBENDARY.
– DERIVATIVES **prebendal** adjective.
– ORIGIN from Latin *praebenda* 'things to be supplied, pension'.

prebendary /prebbəndəri/ ● noun (pl. **prebendaries**) **1** an honorary canon. **2** historical a canon whose income came from a prebend.

prebuttal /pributt'l/ ● noun (in politics) a response formulated in anticipation of a criticism; a pre-emptive rebuttal.

Precambrian /preekambriən/ ● adjective Geology relating to the earliest aeon of the earth's history, preceding the Cambrian period and ending about 570 million years ago, a time when living organisms first appeared.

precancerous ● adjective Medicine (of a cell or medical condition) likely to develop into cancer if untreated.

precarious ● adjective **1** not securely held or in position; likely to fall. **2** dependent on chance; uncertain.
– DERIVATIVES **precariously** adverb **precariousness** noun.

Thesaurus

the ground, hard-headed, no-nonsense; *informal* hard-nosed.
– OPPOSITES impractical.

praise ● verb **1** *the police praised Pauline for her courage* COMMEND, express admiration for, applaud, pay tribute to, speak highly of, eulogize, compliment, congratulate, sing the praises of, rave about, go into raptures about, heap praise on, wax lyrical about, make much of, pat on the back, take one's hat off to, lionize, admire, hail; *N. Amer. informal* ballyhoo; *formal* laud. **2** *we praise God* WORSHIP, glorify, honour, exalt, adore, pay tribute to, give thanks to, venerate, reverence; *formal* laud; *archaic* magnify.
– RELATED TERMS laudatory.
– OPPOSITES criticize.
● noun **1** *James was full of praise for the medical teams* APPROVAL, acclaim, admiration, approbation, acclamation, plaudits, congratulations, commendation; tribute, accolade, compliment, a pat on the back, eulogy, panegyric; *formal* laudation, encomium. **2** *give praise to God* HONOUR, thanks, glory, worship, devotion, adoration, reverence.

praiseworthy ● adjective COMMENDABLE, laudable, admirable, worthy (of admiration), meritorious, estimable, exemplary.

pram ● noun *(Brit.)* pushchair; *N. Amer.* baby carriage, stroller; *formal* perambulator.

prance ● verb CAVORT, dance, jig, trip, caper, jump, leap, spring, bound, skip, hop, frisk, romp, frolic.

prank ● noun (PRACTICAL) JOKE, trick, piece of mischief, escapade, stunt, caper, jape, game, hoax, antic; *informal* lark, leg-pull.

prattle ● verb *he prattled on for ages.* See CHAT verb.
● noun *childish prattle.* See CHATTER noun.

pray ● verb **1** *let us pray* SAY ONE'S PRAYERS, make one's devotions, offer a prayer/prayers. **2** *she prayed God to forgive her* INVOKE, call on, implore, appeal to, entreat, beg, petition, supplicate; *poetic/literary* beseech.

prayer ● noun **1** *the priest's murmured prayers* INVOCATION intercession, devotion; *archaic* orison. **2** *a quick prayer that she wouldn't bump into him* APPEAL, plea, entreaty, petition, supplication, invocation; *rare* obsecration.
– PHRASES **not have a prayer** *(informal)* HAVE NO HOPE, have/stand no chance, not have/stand (the ghost of) a chance; *informal* not have a hope in hell, not have/stand an earthly; *Austral./NZ informal* not have Buckley's (chance).

preach ● verb **1** *he preached to a large congregation* GIVE A SERMON, sermonize, address, speak. **2** *preaching the good news of Jesus* PROCLAIM, teach, spread, propagate, expound. **3** *they preach toleration* ADVOCATE, recommend, advise, urge, teach, counsel. **4** *who are you to preach at me?* MORALIZE, sermonize, pontificate, lecture, harangue; *informal* preachify.
– RELATED TERMS homiletic.

preacher ● noun MINISTER (OF RELIGION), parson, clergyman, clergywoman, member of the clergy, priest, man/woman of the cloth, man/woman of God, cleric, churchman, churchwoman, evangelist; *informal* reverend, padre, Holy Joe, sky pilot; *N. Amer. informal* preacher man; *Austral. informal* josser.

preaching ● noun RELIGIOUS TEACHING, message, sermons.

preachy ● adjective *(informal)* MORALISTIC, moralizing, sanctimonious, self-righteous, holier-than-thou, sententious.

preamble ● noun INTRODUCTION, preface, prologue; foreword, prelude, front matter; *informal* intro, prelims; *formal* exordium, proem, prolegomenon.

– ORIGIN from Latin *precarius* 'obtained by entreaty', from *prex* 'prayer'.

precast ● adjective (especially of concrete) cast in its final shape before positioning.

precaution ● noun **1** a measure taken in advance to prevent something undesirable from happening. **2** (**precautions**) informal contraception.
– DERIVATIVES **precautionary** adjective.
– ORIGIN Latin, from *praecavere* 'beware of in advance'.

precede ● verb **1** come or go before in time, order, or position. **2** (**precede with**) preface or introduce (something) with.
– DERIVATIVES **preceding** adjective.
– ORIGIN Latin *praecedere* 'go before'.

precedence /pressid'nss/ ● noun **1** the condition of preceding others in importance, order, or rank. **2** an acknowledged or legally determined right to such precedence.

precedent ● noun /pressid'nt/ **1** an earlier event or action serving as an example or guide. **2** Law a previous case or legal decision that may or must be followed in subsequent similar cases. ● adjective /priseed'nt, pressi-/ preceding in time, order, or importance.

precentor /prisentər/ ● noun **1** a person who leads a congregation in its singing or (in a synagogue) prayers. **2** a minor canon who administers the musical life of a cathedral.
– ORIGIN Latin *praecentor*, from *praecinere* 'sing before'.

precept /preesept/ ● noun **1** a general rule regulating behaviour or thought. **2** a writ or warrant. **3** Brit. an order issued by one local authority to another specifying the rate of tax to be charged on its behalf.
– ORIGIN Latin *praeceptum* 'something advised'.

preceptor /priseptər/ ● noun a teacher or instructor.

precession ● noun **1** the slow movement of the axis of a spinning body around another axis. **2** Astronomy the slow retrograde motion of the equinoctial points along the ecliptic, resulting in the earlier occurrence of equinoxes each year.
– DERIVATIVES **precess** verb **precessional** adjective.
– ORIGIN from Latin *praecedere* 'go before'.

precinct /preesingkt/ ● noun **1** the area within the walls or boundaries of a place. **2** an enclosed or defined area of ground around a cathedral, church, or college. **3** Brit. a specially designated area in a town, especially one closed to traffic. **4** N. Amer. a district of a city or town as defined for policing or electoral purposes.
– ORIGIN Latin *praecinctum*, from *praecingere* 'encircle'.

preciosity /preshiossiti/ ● noun over-refinement in language or art.

precious ● adjective **1** having great value. **2** greatly loved or treasured. **3** ironic considerable: *a precious lot you know!* **4** derogatory affectedly concerned with elegant or refined language or manners.
– PHRASES **precious little** (or **few**) informal extremely little (or few).
– DERIVATIVES **preciously** adverb **preciousness** noun.
– ORIGIN Latin *pretiosus*, from *pretium* 'price'.

precious metal ● noun a valuable metal such as gold, silver, or platinum.

precious stone ● noun a highly attractive and valuable piece of mineral, used in jewellery.

precipice ● noun a tall and very steep rock face or cliff.
– ORIGIN originally in the sense 'headlong fall': from Latin *praecipitium*, from *praeceps* 'steep, headlong'.

precipitancy ● noun rashness or suddenness of action.

precipitant ● noun **1** a cause of an action or event. **2** Chemistry a substance that causes precipitation.

precipitate ● verb /prisippitayt/ **1** cause (something bad) to happen unexpectedly or prematurely. **2** cause to move suddenly and with force. **3** Chemistry cause (a substance) to be deposited in solid form from a solution. **4** cause (moisture or dust) to be deposited from the atmosphere or from a vapour or suspension. ● adjective /prisippitət/ done, acting, or occurring suddenly or without careful consideration. ● noun /prisippitayt, -tət/ Chemistry a substance precipitated from a solution.
– DERIVATIVES **precipitately** adverb **precipitator** noun.
– ORIGIN Latin *praecipitare* 'throw headlong'.

precipitation ● noun **1** rain, snow, sleet, or hail that falls to or condenses on the ground. **2** Chemistry the action or process of precipitating. **3** archaic sudden and unthinking action.

precipitous /prisippitəss/ ● adjective **1** dangerously high or steep. **2** (of a change in a condition or situation) sudden and dramatic. **3** hasty; precipitate.
– DERIVATIVES **precipitously** adverb.

precis /praysi/ ● noun (pl. same or /prayseez/) a summary of a text or speech. ● verb (**precises** /prayseez/, **precised** /prayseed/, **precising** /prayseeing/) make a precis of.
– ORIGIN from French, 'precise'.

precise ● adjective **1** marked by exactness of expression or detail. **2** very attentive to detail. **3** exact; particular: *at that precise moment.*
– DERIVATIVES **precisely** adverb **preciseness** noun.
– USAGE Strictly speaking, **precise** does not mean the same as **accurate**. **Accurate** means 'correct in all details', while **precise** contains a notion of trying to specify details exactly: if you say 'It's 4.04 and 12 seconds' you are being *precise*, but not necessarily *accurate* (your watch might be slow).
– ORIGIN Old French *prescis*, from Latin *praecidere* 'cut short'.

precision ● noun **1** the quality or condition of being precise.

p

Thesaurus

pre-arranged ● adjective ARRANGED BEFOREHAND, agreed in advance, predetermined, pre-established, pre-planned.

precarious ● adjective UNCERTAIN, insecure, unpredictable, risky, hazardous, dangerous, unsafe; unsettled, unstable, unsteady, shaky; *informal* dicey, chancy, iffy; *Brit. informal* dodgy; *archaic* parlous.
– OPPOSITES safe.

precaution ● noun SAFEGUARD, preventative/preventive measure, safety measure, insurance; *informal* backstop.

precautionary ● adjective PREVENTATIVE, preventive, safety.

precede ● verb **1** *adverts preceded the film* GO/COME BEFORE, lead (up) to, pave/prepare the way for, herald, introduce, usher in; *archaic* forgo. **2** *Catherine preceded him into the studio* GO AHEAD OF, go in front of, go before, go first, lead the way. **3** *he preceded the book with a poem* PREFACE, introduce, begin, open.
– OPPOSITES follow.

precedence ● noun *quarrels over precedence* PRIORITY, rank, seniority, superiority, primacy, pre-eminence, eminence.
– PHRASES **take precedence over** TAKE PRIORITY OVER, outweigh, prevail over, come before.

precedent ● noun MODEL, exemplar, example, pattern, previous case, prior instance/example; paradigm, criterion, yardstick, standard.

preceding ● adjective FOREGOING, previous, prior, former, precedent, earlier, above, aforementioned, antecedent; *formal* anterior, prevenient.

precept ● noun **1** *the precepts of Orthodox Judaism* PRINCIPLE, rule, tenet, canon, doctrine, command, order, decree, dictate, dictum, injunction, commandment; *Judaism* mitzvah; *formal* prescript. **2** *precepts that her grandmother used to quote* MAXIM, saying, adage, axiom, aphorism, apophthegm.

precinct ● noun **1** *a pedestrian precinct* AREA, zone, sector. **2** *within the precincts of the City* BOUNDS, boundaries, limits, confines. **3** *the cathedral precinct* ENCLOSURE, close, court.

precious ● adjective **1** *precious works of art* VALUABLE, costly, expensive; invaluable, priceless, beyond price. **2** *her most precious possession* VALUED, cherished, treasured, prized, favourite, dear, dearest, beloved, darling, adored, loved, special. **3** *his precious manners* AFFECTED, over-refined, pretentious; *informal* la-di-da; *Brit. informal* poncey.

precipice ● noun CLIFF (FACE), steep cliff, rock face, sheer drop, crag, bluff, escarpment, scarp; *poetic/literary* steep.

precipitate ● verb **1** *the incident precipitated a crisis* BRING ABOUT/ON, cause, lead to, give rise to, instigate, trigger, spark, touch off, provoke, hasten, accelerate, expedite. **2** *they were precipitated down the mountain* HURL, catapult, throw, plunge, launch, fling, propel.
● adjective **1** *their actions were precipitate* HASTY, overhasty, rash, hurried, rushed; impetuous, impulsive, spur-of-the-moment, precipitous, incautious, imprudent, injudicious, ill-advised, reckless, harum-scarum; *informal* previous; *poetic/literary* temerarious. **2** *a precipitate decline.* See PRECIPITOUS sense 2.

precipitous ● adjective **1** *a precipitous drop* STEEP, sheer, perpendicular, abrupt, sharp, vertical. **2** *his fall from power was precipitous* SUDDEN, rapid, swift, abrupt, headlong, speedy, quick, fast. **3** *he was too precipitous.* See PRECIPITATE adjective sense 1.

precis ● noun *a precis of the report* SUMMARY, synopsis, résumé, abstract, outline, summarization, summation; abridgement, digest, overview, epitome; *N. Amer.* wrap-up; *rare* conspectus.

2 (before another noun) very accurate: *a precision instrument.*
preclude ● verb prevent (something) from happening or (someone) from doing something.
– DERIVATIVES **preclusion** noun.
– ORIGIN Latin *praecludere* 'shut off, impede'.
precocious ● adjective having developed certain abilities or inclinations at an earlier age than usual.
– DERIVATIVES **precociously** adverb **precociousness** noun **precocity** noun.
– ORIGIN from Latin *praecox*, from *praecoquere* 'ripen fully'.
precognition /preekognish'n/ ● noun foreknowledge of an event, especially through supposed paranormal means.
– DERIVATIVES **precognitive** adjective.
precoital ● adjective occurring before sexual intercourse.
– DERIVATIVES **precoitally** adverb.
pre-Columbian ● adjective relating to the Americas before the arrival of Christopher Columbus in 1492.
preconceived ● adjective (of an idea or opinion) formed before having evidence for its truth or usefulness.
preconception ● noun a preconceived idea or prejudice.
precondition ● noun a condition that must be fulfilled before other things can happen or be done. ● verb bring into a desired or necessary state beforehand.
precursor ● noun a person or thing that comes before another of the same kind.
– DERIVATIVES **precursory** adjective.
– ORIGIN Latin *praecursor*, from *praecurrere* 'precede'.
predacious /pridayshəss/ (also **predaceous**) ● adjective (of an animal) predatory.
pre-date ● verb exist or occur at a date earlier than.
predation /pridaysh'n/ ● noun Zoology the preying of one animal on others.
– ORIGIN Latin, from *praeda* 'plunder'; compare with PREY.
predator ● noun **1** an animal that preys on others. **2** a person who exploits others.
predatory ● adjective **1** (of an animal) naturally preying on others. **2** seeking to exploit others.
predecease ● verb formal die before (another person).
predecessor ● noun **1** a person who held a job or office before the current holder. **2** a thing that has been followed or replaced by another.
– ORIGIN Latin *praedecessor*, from *prae* 'beforehand' + *decessor* 'retiring officer'.
predestinarian /pridestinairiən/ ● noun a person who believes in the doctrine of predestination. ● adjective upholding or relating to the doctrine of predestination.
predestination ● noun (in Christian theology) the doctrine, associated particularly with Calvinism, that God has ordained all that will happen.
predestine ● verb **1** (of God) destine (someone) for a particular fate or purpose. **2** determine (an outcome) in advance by divine will or fate.
– DERIVATIVES **predestined** adjective.
predetermine ● verb **1** establish or decide in advance. **2** predestine.
– DERIVATIVES **predetermination** noun.
predeterminer ● noun Grammar a word or phrase that occurs before a determiner, for example *both* or *a lot of.*
predicable /preddikəb'l/ ● adjective that may be predicated or affirmed.
predicament ● noun **1** a difficult situation. **2** Philosophy each of the ten categories in Aristotelian logic.
– ORIGIN originally in the sense 'category', later 'state of being': from Latin *praedicamentum* 'something predicated'.
predicate ● noun /preddikət/ **1** Grammar the part of a sentence or clause containing a verb and stating something about the subject (e.g. *went home* in *John went home*). **2** Logic something which is affirmed or denied concerning an argument of a proposition. ● verb /preddikayt/ **1** Grammar & Logic assert (something) about the subject of a sentence or an argument of proposition. **2** (**predicate on/upon**) found or base (something) on.
– DERIVATIVES **predication** noun.
– ORIGIN Latin *praedicatum*, from *praedicare* 'make known beforehand, declare'.
predicative /pridikkətiv/ ● adjective **1** Grammar (of an adjective or noun) forming or contained in the predicate, as *old* in *the dog is old* (but not in *the old dog*). Contrasted with ATTRIBUTIVE. **2** Logic acting as a predicate.
– DERIVATIVES **predicatively** adverb.
predict ● verb state that (a specified event) will happen in the future.
– DERIVATIVES **predictive** adjective **predictor** noun.
– ORIGIN Latin *praedicere* 'make known beforehand, declare'.
predictable ● adjective **1** able to be predicted. **2** derogatory always behaving or occurring in the way expected.
– DERIVATIVES **predictability** noun **predictably** adverb.
prediction ● noun **1** a thing predicted; a forecast. **2** the action of predicting.
predigest ● verb **1** (of an animal) treat (food) by a process similar to digestion to make it more easily digestible when subsequently eaten. **2** simplify (information) so that it is easier to absorb.
predilection /preedileksh'n/ ● noun a preference or special liking for something.

p

Thesaurus

● verb *precising a passage* SUMMARIZE, sum up, give a summary/precis of, give the main points of; abridge, condense, shorten, synopsize, abstract, outline, abbreviate; *archaic* epitomize.
precise ● adjective **1** *precise measurements* EXACT, accurate, correct, specific, detailed, explicit, unambiguous, definite. **2** *at that precise moment the car stopped* EXACT, particular, very, specific. **3** *the attention to detail is very precise* METICULOUS, careful, exact, scrupulous, punctilious, conscientious, particular, methodical, strict, rigorous.
– OPPOSITES inaccurate.
precisely ● adverb **1** *at 2 o'clock precisely* EXACTLY, sharp, on the dot; promptly, prompt, dead (on), on the stroke of ——, on the dot of ——; *informal* bang (on); *Brit. informal* spot on; *N. Amer. informal* on the button/nose. **2** *precisely the kind of man I am looking for* EXACTLY, absolutely, just, in all respects; *informal* to a T. **3** *fertilization can be timed precisely* ACCURATELY, exactly; clearly, distinctly, strictly. **4** *'You mean he's gone?' 'Precisely.'* YES, exactly, absolutely, (that's) right, quite so, indubitably, definitely; *informal* you bet, I'll say.
precision ● noun EXACTNESS, exactitude, accuracy, correctness, preciseness; care, carefulness, meticulousness, scrupulousness, punctiliousness, methodicalness, rigour, rigorousness.
preclude ● verb PREVENT, make it impossible for, rule out, stop, prohibit, debar, bar, hinder, impede, inhibit, exclude.
precocious ● adjective ADVANCED FOR ONE'S AGE, forward, mature, gifted, talented, clever, intelligent, quick; *informal* smart.
– OPPOSITES backward.
preconceived ● adjective PREDETERMINED, prejudged; prejudiced, biased.
preconception ● noun PRECONCEIVED IDEA/NOTION, presupposition, assumption, presumption, prejudgement; prejudice.
precondition ● noun PREREQUISITE, (necessary/essential) condition, requirement, necessity, essential, imperative, sine qua non; *informal* must.
precursor ● noun **1** *a three-stringed precursor of the guitar* FORERUNNER, predecessor, forefather, father, antecedent, ancestor, forebear. **2** *a precursor of disasters to come* HARBINGER, herald, sign, indication, portent, omen.
precursory ● adjective PRELIMINARY, prior, previous, introductory, preparatory, prefatory; *formal* anterior, prevenient.
predatory ● adjective **1** *predatory birds* PREDACIOUS, carnivorous, hunting, raptorial; of prey. **2** *a predatory gleam in his eyes* EXPLOITATIVE, wolfish, rapacious, vulturine, vulturous.
predecessor ● noun **1** *the Prime Minister's predecessor* FORERUNNER, precursor, antecedent. **2** *our Victorian predecessors* ANCESTOR, forefather, forebear, antecedent.
– OPPOSITES successor, descendant.
predestined ● adjective PREORDAINED, ordained, predetermined, destined, fated.
predetermined ● adjective **1** *a predetermined budget* PREARRANGED, established in advance, preset, set, fixed, agreed. **2** *our predetermined fate* PREDESTINED, preordained.
predicament ● noun DIFFICULT SITUATION, mess, difficulty, plight, quandary, muddle, mare's nest; *informal* hole, fix, jam, pickle, scrape, bind, tight spot/corner, dilemma.
predicate ● verb BASE, be dependent, found, establish, rest, ground, premise.
predict ● verb FORECAST, foretell, foresee, prophesy, anticipate, tell in advance, envision, envisage; *poetic/literary* previse; *archaic* augur, presage.
predictable ● adjective FORESEEABLE, (only) to be expected, antici-

– ORIGIN French, from Latin *praediligere* 'prefer'.

predispose • verb make liable or inclined to a specified attitude, action, or condition.

– DERIVATIVES **predisposition** noun.

predominant • adjective **1** present as the strongest or main element. **2** having the greatest control or power.

– DERIVATIVES **predominance** noun **predominantly** adverb.

predominate • verb **1** be the strongest or main element. **2** have or exert control or power.

predominately • adverb mainly; for the most part.

pre-echo • noun **1** a faint copy heard just before an actual sound in a recording, caused by the accidental transfer of signals. **2** a foreshadowing.

pre-eclampsia • noun a condition in pregnancy characterized especially by high blood pressure.

– DERIVATIVES **pre-eclamptic** adjective & noun.

pre-embryo • noun a fertilized ovum in the first fourteen days after fertilization, before implantation in the womb.

pre-eminent • adjective surpassing all others.

– DERIVATIVES **pre-eminence** noun **pre-eminently** adverb.

pre-empt • verb **1** take action in order to prevent (something) happening or (someone) from doing something. **2** obtain or take in advance.

– DERIVATIVES **pre-emptive** adjective **pre-emptor** noun.

pre-emption • noun **1** the action of pre-empting or forestalling. **2** the purchase of goods or shares before the opportunity is offered to others.

– ORIGIN Latin, from *praeemere* 'buy in advance'.

preen • verb **1** (of a bird) tidy and clean its feathers with its beak. **2** devote effort to making oneself look attractive. **3** (**preen oneself**) congratulate or pride oneself.

– ORIGIN probably related to obsolete *prune*, from Latin *ungere* 'anoint'.

pre-exist • verb exist before or from an earlier time.

– DERIVATIVES **pre-existence** noun **pre-existent** adjective **pre-existing** adjective.

prefab • noun informal a prefabricated building.

prefabricate • verb manufacture sections of (a building) to enable easy assembly on site.

– DERIVATIVES **prefabricated** adjective **prefabrication** noun.

preface /preffəss/ • noun **1** an introduction to a book, stating its subject, scope, or aims. **2** the preliminary part of a speech. • verb **1** provide with a preface. **2** (**preface with/by**) begin (a speech or event) with or by doing something.

– DERIVATIVES **prefatory** /preffətəri/ adjective.

– ORIGIN Old French, from Latin *praefari* 'speak before'.

prefect • noun **1** chiefly Brit. a senior pupil authorized to enforce discipline in a school. **2** a chief officer, magistrate, or regional governor in certain countries.

– DERIVATIVES **prefectoral** adjective **prefectorial** adjective.

– ORIGIN Latin *praefectus*, from *praeficere* 'set in authority over'.

prefecture • noun **1** a district under the government of a prefect. **2** a prefect's office, tenure, or residence.

– DERIVATIVES **prefectural** adjective.

prefer • verb (**preferred**, **preferring**) **1** like (someone or something) better than another or others; tend to choose. **2** formal submit (a charge or information) for consideration. **3** archaic promote to a prestigious position.

– ORIGIN Latin *praeferre* 'bear or carry before'.

preferable • adjective more desirable or suitable.

– DERIVATIVES **preferability** noun.

preferably • adverb ideally; if possible.

preference • noun **1** a greater liking for one alternative over another or others. **2** a thing preferred. **3** favour shown to one person over another or others.

preference share (N. Amer. **preferred share**) • noun a share which entitles the holder to a fixed dividend whose payment takes priority over that of ordinary share dividends.

preferential • adjective **1** of or involving preference or partiality. **2** (of a creditor) having a claim for repayment which will be met before those of other creditors.

– DERIVATIVES **preferentially** adverb.

Thesaurus

pated, foreseen, unsurprising; *informal* inevitable.

prediction • noun FORECAST, prophecy, prognosis, prognostication, augury; projection, conjecture, guess.

predilection • noun LIKING, fondness, preference, partiality, taste, penchant, weakness, soft spot, fancy, inclination, leaning, bias, propensity, bent, proclivity, predisposition, appetite.

– OPPOSITES dislike.

predispose • verb **1** *lack of exercise may predispose an individual to high blood pressure* MAKE SUSCEPTIBLE, make liable, make prone, make vulnerable, put at risk of. **2** *attitudes which predispose people to behave badly* LEAD, influence, sway, induce, prompt, dispose; bias, prejudice.

predisposed • adjective INCLINED, prepared, ready, of a mind, disposed, minded, willing.

predisposition • noun **1** *a predisposition to heart disease* SUSCEPTIBILITY, proneness, tendency, liability, inclination, disposition, vulnerability. **2** *their political predispositions* PREFERENCE, predilection, inclination, leaning.

predominance • noun **1** *the predominance of women carers* PREVALENCE, dominance, preponderance. **2** *Soviet military predominance* SUPREMACY, mastery, control, power, ascendancy, dominance, pre-eminence, superiority.

predominant • adjective **1** *our predominant objectives* MAIN, chief, principal, most important, primary, prime, central, leading, foremost, key, paramount; *informal* number-one. **2** *the predominant political forces* CONTROLLING, dominant, predominating, more/most powerful, pre-eminent, ascendant, superior, in the ascendancy.

– OPPOSITES subsidiary.

predominantly • adverb MAINLY, mostly, for the most part, chiefly, principally, primarily, predominately, in the main, on the whole, largely, by and large, typically, generally, usually.

predominate • verb **1** *small-scale producers predominate* BE IN THE MAJORITY, preponderate, be predominant, prevail, be most prominent. **2** *private interest predominates over the public good* PREVAIL, dominate, be dominant, carry most weight; override, outweigh.

pre-eminence • noun SUPERIORITY, supremacy, greatness, excellence, distinction, prominence, predominance, eminence, importance, prestige, stature, fame, renown, celebrity.

pre-eminent • adjective GREATEST, leading, foremost, best, finest, chief, outstanding, excellent, distinguished, prominent, eminent, important, top, famous, renowned, celebrated, illustrious, supreme; *N. Amer.* marquee.

– OPPOSITES undistinguished.

pre-eminently • adverb PRIMARILY, principally, above all, chiefly, mostly, mainly, in particular.

pre-empt • verb **1** *his action may have pre-empted war* FORESTALL, prevent. **2** *many tables were already pre-empted by family parties* COMMANDEER, occupy, seize, arrogate, appropriate, take over, secure, reserve.

preen • verb **1** *the robin preened its feathers* CLEAN, tidy, groom, smooth, arrange; *archaic* plume. **2** *she preened before the mirror* ADMIRE ONESELF, primp oneself, prink oneself, groom oneself, spruce oneself up; *informal* titivate oneself, doll oneself up; *Brit. informal* tart oneself up; *N. Amer. informal* gussy oneself up.

– PHRASES **preen oneself** CONGRATULATE ONESELF, be pleased with oneself, be proud of oneself, pat oneself on the back, feel self-satisfied.

preface • noun *the preface to the novel* INTRODUCTION, foreword, preamble, prologue, prelude; front matter; *informal* prelims, intro; *formal* exordium, proem, prolegomenon.
• verb *the chapter is prefaced by a poem* PRECEDE, introduce, begin, open, start.

prefatory • adjective INTRODUCTORY, preliminary, opening, initial, preparatory, initiatory, precursory.

– OPPOSITES closing.

prefect • noun *(Brit.)* MONITOR; *Brit.* praepostor.

prefer • verb **1** *I prefer white wine to red* LIKE BETTER, would rather (have), would sooner (have), favour, be more partial to; choose, select, pick, opt for, go for, plump for. **2** *(formal) do you want to prefer charges?* BRING, press, file, lodge, lay. **3** *(archaic) he was preferred to the post* PROMOTE, upgrade, raise, elevate.

preferable • adjective BETTER, best, more desirable, more suitable, advantageous, superior, preferred, recommended.

preferably • adverb IDEALLY, if possible, for preference, from choice.

preference • noun **1** *her preference for boys' games* LIKING, partiality, predilection, proclivity, fondness, taste, inclination, leaning, bias, bent, penchant, predisposition. **2** *my preference is rock* FAVOURITE, (first) choice, selection; *informal* cup of tea, thing; *N. Amer. informal* druthers. **3** *preference will be given to applicants speaking Japanese* PRIORITY, favour, precedence, preferential treatment.

– PHRASES **in preference to** RATHER THAN, instead of, in place of,

preferment ● noun promotion or appointment to a position or office.

prefigure ● verb **1** be an early indication or version of. **2** archaic imagine beforehand.
– DERIVATIVES **prefiguration** noun **prefigurative** adjective **prefigurement** noun.

prefix ● noun **1** a word, letter, or number placed before another. **2** an element placed at the beginning of a word to alter its meaning (e.g. *non-*, *re-*) or (in some languages) as an inflection. **3** a title placed before a name (e.g. *Mr*). ● verb **1** add as a prefix. **2** add a prefix to.

preggers ● adjective informal pregnant.

pregnancy ● noun (pl. **pregnancies**) the condition or period of being pregnant.

pregnant ● adjective **1** (of a woman or female animal) having a child or young developing in the uterus. **2** full of meaning or significance.
– ORIGIN Latin *praegnans*, probably from *prae* 'before' + the base of *gnasci* 'be born'.

preheat ● verb heat beforehand.

prehensile /prihensīl/ ● adjective (chiefly of an animal's limb or tail) capable of grasping.
– ORIGIN from Latin *prehendere* 'to grasp'.

prehistoric ● adjective relating to prehistory.

prehistory ● noun **1** the period of time before written records. **2** the events or conditions leading up to a particular phenomenon.
– DERIVATIVES **prehistorian** noun.

pre-ignition ● noun premature combustion of the fuel–air mixture in an internal-combustion engine.

pre-industrial ● adjective before industrialization.

prejudge ● verb form a judgement on (an issue or person) prematurely and without having adequate information.

prejudice ● noun **1** preconceived opinion that is not based on reason or experience. **2** unjust behaviour formed on such a basis. **3** chiefly Law harm that may result from some action or judgement. ● verb **1** give rise to prejudice in (someone); make biased. **2** chiefly Law cause harm to (a state of affairs).
– PHRASES **without prejudice** Law without detriment to any existing right or claim.
– ORIGIN Latin *praejudicium*, from *prae* 'in advance' + *judicium* 'judgement'.

prejudicial ● adjective harmful to someone or something.

prelapsarian /preelapsairiən/ ● adjective Theology or literary before the Fall of Man; innocent and unspoilt.
– ORIGIN from PRE- + Latin *lapsus* 'a fall'.

prelate /prellət/ ● noun formal or historical a bishop or other high ecclesiastical dignitary.
– ORIGIN Latin *praelatus* 'civil dignitary'.

preliminary ● adjective preceding or done in preparation for something fuller or more important. ● noun (pl. **preliminaries**) **1** a preliminary action or event. **2** a preliminary round in a sporting competition.
– ORIGIN Latin *praeliminaris*, from *prae* 'before' + *limen* 'threshold'.

preliterate ● adjective relating to a society or culture that has not developed the use of writing.

pre-loved ● adjective informal second-hand.

prelude ● noun **1** an action or event serving as an introduction to something more important. **2** a piece of music serving as an introduction to a longer piece. **3** the introductory part of a poem or other literary work. ● verb serve as a prelude or introduction to.
– ORIGIN Latin *praeludium*, from *praeludere* 'play beforehand'.

premarital ● adjective occurring or existing before marriage.

premature ● adjective **1** occurring or done before the proper time. **2** (of a baby) born before the end of the full term of gestation.
– DERIVATIVES **prematurely** adverb **prematurity** noun.
– ORIGIN Latin *praematurus* 'very early'.

pre-med ● noun **1** chiefly N. Amer. a premedical student or course of study. **2** short for PREMEDICATION.

premedication ● noun medication given in preparation for an operation or other treatment.

premeditated ● adjective (of an action, especially a crime) planned in advance.
– DERIVATIVES **premeditation** noun.

premenopausal ● adjective closely preceding the menopause.

premenstrual ● adjective of, occurring, or experienced before menstruation.

Thesaurus

sooner than.

preferential ● adjective SPECIAL, better, privileged, superior, favourable; partial, discriminatory, partisan, biased.

p

preferment ● noun PROMOTION, advancement, elevation, being upgraded, a step up (the ladder); *informal* a kick upstairs.
– OPPOSITES demotion.

prefigure ● verb FORESHADOW, presage, be a harbinger of, herald; *poetic/literary* foretoken.

pregnancy ● noun gestation.
– RELATED TERMS antenatal, maternity.

pregnant ● adjective **1** *she is heavily pregnant* EXPECTING A BABY, expectant, carrying a child; *informal* expecting, in the family way, preggers, with a bun in the oven; *Brit. informal* up the duff, in the (pudding) club, up the spout; *N. Amer. informal* knocked up, having swallowed a watermelon seed; *Austral. informal* with a joey in the pouch; *informal, dated* in trouble; *archaic* with child, in a delicate condition, in an interesting condition; *technical* gravid, parturient. **2** *a rite pregnant with religious significance* FILLED, charged, heavy; full of. **3** *a pregnant pause* MEANINGFUL, significant, suggestive, expressive, charged.

prehistoric ● adjective **1** *prehistoric times* PRIMITIVE, primeval, primordial, primal, ancient, early, antediluvian. **2** *the special effects look prehistoric* OUT OF DATE, outdated, outmoded, old-fashioned, passé, antiquated, archaic, behind the times, primitive, antediluvian; *informal* out of the ark; *N. Amer. informal* horse and buggy, clunky.
– RELATED TERMS archaeo-.
– OPPOSITES modern.

prejudice ● noun **1** *male prejudices about women* PRECONCEIVED IDEA, preconception, prejudgement. **2** *they are motivated by prejudice* BIGOTRY, bias, partisanship, partiality, intolerance, discrimination, unfairness, inequality. **3** *without prejudice to the interests of others* DETRIMENT, harm, damage, injury, hurt, loss.
● verb **1** *the article could prejudice the jury* BIAS, influence, sway, predispose, make biased, make partial, colour. **2** *this could prejudice his chances of victory* DAMAGE, be detrimental to, be prejudicial to, injure, harm, hurt, spoil, impair, undermine, hinder, compromise.

prejudiced ● adjective BIASED, bigoted, discriminatory, partisan, intolerant, narrow-minded, unfair, unjust, inequitable, coloured.
– OPPOSITES impartial.

prejudicial ● adjective DETRIMENTAL, damaging, injurious, harmful, disadvantageous, hurtful, deleterious.
– OPPOSITES beneficial.

preliminary ● adjective *the discussions are still at a preliminary stage* PREPARATORY, introductory, initial, opening, prefatory, precursory; early, exploratory.
– OPPOSITES final.
● noun **1** *he began without any preliminaries* INTRODUCTION, preamble, opening/prefatory remarks, formalities. **2** *a preliminary to the resumption of war* PRELUDE, preparation, preparatory measure, preliminary action.
– PHRASES **preliminary to** IN PREPARATION FOR, before, in advance of, prior to, preparatory to.

prelims ● plural noun *(informal)* FRONT MATTER, preliminary material, introduction, foreword, preface, preamble; *informal* intro; *formal* exordium, proem, prolegomenon.

prelude ● noun **1** *a ceasefire was a prelude to peace negotiations* PRELIMINARY, overture, opening, preparation, introduction, start, commencement, beginning, lead-in, precursor. **2** *an orchestral prelude* OVERTURE, introductory movement, introduction, opening. **3** *the passage forms a prelude to Part III* INTRODUCTION, preface, prologue, foreword, preamble; *informal* intro; *formal* exordium, proem, prolegomenon.

premature ● adjective **1** *his premature death* UNTIMELY, (too) early, unseasonable, before time. **2** *a premature baby* PRETERM; *informal* prem. **3** *such a step would be premature* RASH, overhasty, hasty, precipitate, precipitous, impulsive, impetuous; *informal* previous.
– OPPOSITES overdue.

prematurely ● adverb **1** *Sam was born prematurely* TOO SOON, too early, ahead of time; preterm. **2** *don't act prematurely* RASHLY, over-hastily, hastily, precipitately, precipitously.

premeditated ● adjective PLANNED, intentional, deliberate, preplanned, calculated, cold-blooded, conscious, pre-arranged.

premenstrual syndrome • noun a complex of symptoms (including emotional tension and fluid retention) experienced by some women prior to menstruation.

premier • adjective first in importance, order, or position. • noun a Prime Minister or other head of government.
– DERIVATIVES **premiership** noun.
– ORIGIN Old French, from Latin *primarius* 'principal'.

premiere • noun the first performance of a musical or theatrical work or the first showing of a film. • verb give the premiere of.
– ORIGIN French, feminine of *premier* (see PREMIER).

premise • noun /premmiss/ (Brit. also **premiss**) **1** Logic a previous statement from which another is inferred. **2** an underlying assumption. • verb /primīz/ (**premise on/upon**) base (an argument, theory, etc.) on.
– ORIGIN Old French *premisse*, from Latin. *praemissa propositio* 'proposition set in front'.

premises • plural noun a house or building, together with its land and outbuildings, occupied by a business or considered in an official context.

premium • noun (pl. **premiums**) **1** an amount paid for a contract of insurance. **2** a sum added to an ordinary price or other payment. **3** (before another noun) (of a commodity) superior and more expensive.
– PHRASES **at a premium 1** scarce and in demand. **2** above the usual price. **put** (or **place**) **a premium on** regard as particularly valuable.
– ORIGIN Latin *praemium* 'booty, reward', from *prae* 'before' + *emere* 'buy, take'.

Premium Bond (also **Premium Savings Bond**) • noun (in the UK) a government security offering no interest or capital gain but entered in regular draws for cash prizes.

premolar (also **premolar tooth**) • noun a tooth situated between the canines and molar teeth.

premonition /premmənish'n/ • noun a strong feeling that something is about to happen.
– DERIVATIVES **premonitory** adjective.
– ORIGIN Latin, from *praemonere* 'forewarn'.

prenatal • adjective before birth.
– DERIVATIVES **prenatally** adverb.

prenuptial • adjective before marriage.

prenuptial agreement • noun an agreement made by a couple before they marry concerning ownership of assets in the event of a divorce.

preoccupation • noun **1** the state of being preoccupied. **2** a matter that preoccupies someone.

preoccupy • verb (**preoccupies**, **preoccupied**) dominate the mind of (someone) to the exclusion of other thoughts.

preordain • verb decide or determine beforehand.

prep[1] • noun informal **1** Brit. (especially in a private school) school work done outside lessons. **2** a period set aside for this.
– ORIGIN abbreviation of PREPARATION.

prep[2] informal, chiefly N. Amer. • verb (**prepped**, **prepping**) prepare; make ready. • noun preparation.

pre-packed (also **pre-packaged**) • adjective (of goods) packed or wrapped on the site of production or before sale.

prepaid past and past participle of PREPAY.

preparation • noun **1** the action of preparing or the state of being prepared. **2** something done to prepare for an event or undertaking. **3** a specially made up substance, especially a medicine or food.

preparative • adjective preparatory.

preparatory • adjective **1** serving as or carrying out preparation. **2** Brit. relating to education in a preparatory school.

preparatory school • noun **1** Brit. a private school for pupils between the ages of seven and thirteen. **2** N. Amer. a private school that prepares pupils for college or university.

prepare • verb **1** make ready for use or consideration. **2** make or get ready to do or deal with something. **3** (**be prepared to do**) be willing to do. **4** make (a substance) by chemical reaction.
– DERIVATIVES **preparer** noun.
– ORIGIN Latin *praeparare*, from *prae* 'before' + *parare* 'make ready'.

preparedness • noun a state of readiness, especially for war.

prepay • verb (past and past part. **prepaid**) pay for in advance.
– DERIVATIVES **prepayment** noun.

pre-plan • verb plan in advance.

Thesaurus

– OPPOSITES spontaneous.

premeditation • noun (ADVANCE) PLANNING, forethought, preplanning, (criminal) intent; *Law* malice aforethought.

premier • adjective *a premier chef* LEADING, foremost, chief, principal, head, top-ranking, top, prime, primary, first, highest, preeminent, senior, outstanding, master; *N. Amer.* ranking; *informal* top-notch.
• noun *the Italian premier* HEAD OF GOVERNMENT, prime minister, PM, president, chancellor.

premiere • noun FIRST PERFORMANCE, first night, opening night.

premise • noun *the premise that human life consists of a series of choices* PROPOSITION, assumption, hypothesis, thesis, presupposition, postulation, postulate, supposition, presumption, surmise, conjecture, speculation, assertion, belief.
• verb *they premised that the cosmos is indestructible* POSTULATE, hypothesize, conjecture, posit, theorize, suppose, presuppose, surmise, assume.

premises • plural noun BUILDING(S), property, site, office.

premium • noun **1** *monthly premiums of £30* (REGULAR) PAYMENT, instalment. **2** *you must pay a premium for organic fruit* SURCHARGE, additional payment, extra amount. **3** *a foreign service premium* BONUS, extra; incentive, inducement; *informal* perk; *formal* perquisite.
– PHRASES **at a premium** SCARCE, in great demand, hard to come by, in short supply, thin on the ground. **put/place a premium on 1** *I place a high premium on our relationship* VALUE GREATLY, attach great/special importance to, set great store by, put a high value on. **2** *the high price of oil put a premium on the coal industry* MAKE VALUABLE, make invaluable, make important.

premonition • noun FOREBODING, presentiment, intuition, (funny) feeling, hunch, suspicion, feeling in one's bones; misgiving, apprehension, fear; *archaic* presage.

preoccupation • noun **1** *an air of preoccupation* PENSIVENESS, concentration, engrossment, absorption, self-absorption, musing, thinking, deep thought, brown study, brooding; abstraction, absent-mindedness, distraction, forgetfulness, inattentiveness, wool-gathering, daydreaming. **2** *their main preoccupation was feeding their family* OBSESSION, concern; passion, enthusiasm, hobby horse.

preoccupied • adjective **1** *officials preoccupied with their careers* OBSESSED, concerned, absorbed, engrossed, intent, involved, wrapped up. **2** *she looked preoccupied* LOST/DEEP IN THOUGHT, in a brown study, pensive, absent-minded, distracted, abstracted.

preoccupy • verb ENGROSS, concern, absorb, take up someone's attention, distract, obsess, occupy, prey on someone's mind.

preordain • verb PREDESTINE, destine, foreordain, ordain, fate, predetermine, determine.

preparation • noun **1** *the preparation of contingency plans* DEVISING, putting together, drawing up, construction, composition, production, getting ready, development. **2** *preparations for the party* ARRANGEMENTS, planning, plans, preparatory measures. **3** *preparation for exams* INSTRUCTION, teaching, coaching, training, tutoring, drilling, priming. **4** *a preparation to kill off mites* MIXTURE, compound, concoction, solution, tincture, medicine, potion, cream, ointment, lotion.

preparatory • adjective *preparatory work* PRELIMINARY, initial, introductory, prefatory, opening, preparative, precursory.
– PHRASES **preparatory to** IN PREPARATION FOR, before, prior to, preliminary to.

prepare • verb **1** *I want you to prepare a report* MAKE/GET READY, put together, draw up, produce, arrange, assemble, construct, compose, formulate. **2** *the meal was easy to prepare* COOK, make, get, put together, concoct; *informal* fix, rustle up; *Brit. informal* knock up. **3** *preparing for war* GET READY, make preparations, arrange things, make provision, get everything set. **4** *athletes preparing for the Olympics* TRAIN, get into shape, practise, get ready. **5** *I must prepare for my exams* STUDY, revise; *Brit. informal* swot. **6** *this course prepares students for their exams* INSTRUCT, coach, train, tutor, drill, prime. **7** *prepare yourself for a shock* BRACE, make ready, tense, steel, steady.

prepared • adjective **1** *he needs to be well prepared* READY, (all) set, equipped, primed; waiting, on hand, poised, in position. **2** *I'm not prepared to cut the price* WILLING, ready, disposed, predisposed, (favourably) inclined, of a mind, minded.

preponderance • noun **1** *the preponderance of women among older people* PREVALENCE, predominance, dominance. **2** *the preponderance of evidence* BULK, majority, greater quantity, larger part,

p

preponderant ● adjective predominant in influence, number, or importance.
– DERIVATIVES **preponderance** noun **preponderantly** adverb.
preponderate ● verb be preponderant.
– ORIGIN Latin *praeponderare* 'weigh more'.
preposition /preppəzish'n/ ● noun Grammar a word governing a noun or pronoun and expressing a relation to another word or element, as in 'she arrived *after* dinner' and 'what did you do it *for*?'.
– DERIVATIVES **prepositional** adjective.
prepossessing ● adjective attractive or appealing in appearance.
preposterous ● adjective utterly absurd or ridiculous.
– DERIVATIVES **preposterously** adverb **preposterousness** noun.
– ORIGIN Latin *praeposterus* 'reversed, absurd'.
preppy (also **preppie**) N. Amer. informal ● noun (pl. **preppies**) a pupil of an expensive preparatory school. ● adjective (**preppier**, **preppiest**) typical of such a person, especially with reference to their neat style of dress.
preprandial ● adjective formal or humorous done or taken before dinner.
– ORIGIN from Latin *prandium* 'a meal'.
pre-production ● noun work done on a film, broadcast programme, etc. before full-scale production begins.
pre-program ● verb Computing program in advance for ease of use.
prep school ● noun short for PREPARATORY SCHOOL.
pre-pubescent ● adjective relating to or in the period preceding puberty.
prepuce /preepyooss/ ● noun Anatomy **1** technical term for FORESKIN. **2** the fold of skin surrounding the clitoris.
– ORIGIN French, from Latin *praeputium*.
prequel ● noun a story or film containing events which precede those of an existing work.
– ORIGIN from PRE- + SEQUEL.
Pre-Raphaelite /preeraffəlīt/ ● noun a member of a group of English 19th-century artists who sought to emulate the style of Italian artists from before the time of Raphael. ● adjective **1** relating to the Pre-Raphaelites. **2** (of women) suggesting Pre-Raphaelite painting in appearance, typically with long auburn hair and pale skin.
– DERIVATIVES **Pre-Raphaelitism** noun.
pre-record ● verb (often as adj. **pre-recorded**) record (sound or film) in advance.
prerequisite /preerekwizit/ ● adjective required as a prior condition. ● noun a prerequisite thing.
prerogative /priroggətiv/ ● noun **1** a right or privilege exclusive to a particular individual or class. **2** (in UK law) the right of the sovereign, theoretically unrestricted but usually delegated to government or the judiciary.
– ORIGIN Latin *praerogativa* 'the verdict of the political division which was chosen to vote first in the assembly'.
presage /pressij/ ● verb /also prisayj/ be a sign or warning of (an imminent event). ● noun an omen or portent.
– ORIGIN Latin *praesagire* 'forebode'.
presbyter /prezbitər/ ● noun historical **1** an elder or minister of the Christian Church. **2** formal (in presbyterian Churches) an elder.
– DERIVATIVES **presbyteral** /prezbittərəl/ adjective **presbyterial** adjective.
– ORIGIN Greek *presbuteros* 'elder'.
Presbyterian /prezbiteeriən/ ● adjective relating to a Protestant Church or denomination governed by elders all of equal rank. ● noun a member of a Presbyterian Church.
– DERIVATIVES **Presbyterianism** noun.
presbytery /prezbitəri/ ● noun (pl. **presbyteries**) **1** (treated as sing. or pl.) a body of Church elders. **2** the house of a Roman Catholic parish priest. **3** chiefly Architecture the eastern part of a church chancel.
pre-school ● adjective relating to the time before a child is old enough to go to school.
prescient /pressiənt/ ● adjective having knowledge of events before they take place.
– DERIVATIVES **prescience** noun **presciently** adverb.
– ORIGIN from Latin *praescire* 'know beforehand'.
prescribe ● verb **1** recommend and authorize the use of (a medicine or treatment). **2** state authoritatively that (an action or procedure) should be carried out.
– USAGE On the confusion between **prescribe** and **proscribe**, see the note at PROSCRIBE.
– ORIGIN Latin *praescribere* 'direct in writing'.
prescription ● noun **1** an instruction written by a medical practitioner authorizing a patient to be issued with a medicine or treatment. **2** the action of prescribing. **3** an authoritative recommendation or ruling. **4** (also **positive prescription**) Law the establishment of a claim founded on the basis of long usage or custom.
prescriptive ● adjective **1** relating to the imposition of a rule or method. **2** (of a right, title, etc.) legally established by long usage.
– DERIVATIVES **prescriptivism** noun **prescriptivist** noun & adjective.
– ORIGIN Latin *praescriptivus* 'relating to a legal exception', from *praescribere* 'direct in writing'.
preseason ● adjective before the start of the season for a particular sport.
presence ● noun **1** the state or fact of being present. **2** the impressive manner or appearance of a person. **3** a person or thing that is present but not seen. **4** a group of soldiers or police stationed in a particular place: *the USA would maintain a presence in the region.*
– PHRASES **make one's presence felt** have a strong influence on a situation. **presence of mind** the ability to remain calm and take quick, sensible action in the face of sudden difficulty.
– ORIGIN Latin *praesentia* 'being at hand'.

Thesaurus

best/better part, most; almost all. **3** *the preponderance of the trade unions* PREDOMINANCE, dominance, ascendancy, supremacy, power.
preponderant ● adjective DOMINANT, predominant, pre-eminent, in control, more/most powerful, superior, supreme, ascendant, in the ascendancy.
preponderate ● verb BE IN THE MAJORITY, predominate, be predominant; be more/most important, prevail, dominate.
prepossessing ● adjective ATTRACTIVE, beautiful, pretty, handsome, good-looking, fetching, charming, delightful, enchanting, captivating; archaic fair.
– OPPOSITES ugly.
preposterous ● adjective ABSURD, ridiculous, foolish, stupid, ludicrous, farcical, laughable, comical, risible, nonsensical, senseless, insane; outrageous, monstrous; informal crazy.
– OPPOSITES sensible.
prerequisite ● noun *a prerequisite for the course* (NECESSARY) CONDITION, precondition, essential, requirement, requisite, necessity, sine qua non; informal must.
● adjective *the prerequisite qualifications* NECESSARY, required, called for, essential, requisite, obligatory, compulsory.
– OPPOSITES unnecessary.
prerogative ● noun ENTITLEMENT, right, privilege, advantage, due, birthright.
presage ● verb *the owl's hooting presages death* PORTEND, augur, foreshadow, foretell, prophesy, be an omen of, herald, be a sign of, be the harbinger of, warn of, be a presage of, signal, bode, promise, threaten; poetic/literary betoken, foretoken, forebode.
● noun *a sombre presage of his final illness* OMEN, sign, indication, portent, warning, forewarning, harbinger, augury, prophecy, foretoken.
prescience ● noun FAR-SIGHTEDNESS, foresight, foreknowledge; psychic powers, clairvoyance; prediction, prognostication, divination, prophesy, augury; insight, intuition, perception, percipience.
prescient ● adjective PROPHETIC, predictive, visionary; psychic, clairvoyant; far-sighted, prognostic, divinatory; insightful, intuitive, perceptive, percipient.
prescribe ● verb **1** *the doctor prescribed antibiotics* WRITE A PRESCRIPTION FOR, authorize. **2** *traditional values prescribe a life of domesticity* ADVISE, recommend, advocate, suggest, endorse, champion, promote. **3** *rules prescribing your duty* STIPULATE, lay down, dictate, specify, determine, establish, fix.
prescription ● noun **1** *the doctor wrote a prescription* INSTRUCTION, authorization; informal script; archaic recipe. **2** *he fetched the prescription from the chemist* MEDICINE, drug, medication. **3** *a painless prescription for improvement* METHOD, measure; recommendation, suggestion, recipe, formula.
prescriptive ● adjective DICTATORIAL, narrow, rigid, authoritarian, arbitrary, repressive, dogmatic.
presence ● noun **1** *presence of a train was indicated electrically*

present[1] /prezz'nt/ ● adjective **1** being or occurring in a particular place. **2** existing or occurring now. **3** Grammar (of a tense or participle) expressing an action now going on or habitually performed, or a condition now existing. ● noun **1** (**the present**) the period of time now occurring. **2** Grammar a present tense or form of a verb.
– PHRASES **at present** now. **for the present** for now; temporarily. **these presents** Law, formal this document.
– ORIGIN Latin *praesens* 'being at hand', from *praeesse* 'be before'.

present[2] /prizent/ ● verb **1** give formally or ceremonially. **2** offer for acceptance or consideration. **3** formally introduce (someone) to someone else. **4** put (a show or exhibition) before the public. **5** introduce and appear in (a television or radio show). **6** be the cause of (a problem). **7** exhibit (a particular appearance) to others. **8** (**present oneself**) appear formally before others. **9** (**present with**) Medicine (of a patient) come forward for medical examination for (a particular condition or symptom).
– PHRASES **present arms** hold a rifle vertically in front of the body as a salute.
– ORIGIN Latin *praesentare* 'place before'.

present[3] /prezz'nt/ ● noun a thing given to someone as a gift.
– ORIGIN Old French, originally in the phrase *mettre une chose en present à quelqu'un* 'put a thing into the presence of a person'.

presentable ● adjective clean, smart, or decent enough to be seen in public.

presentation ● noun **1** the action or an instance of presenting or being presented. **2** the manner or style in which something is presented.
– DERIVATIVES **presentational** adjective **presentationally** adverb.

presenteeism ● noun the practice of being present at work for longer than required.

presenter ● noun a person who introduces and appears in a television or radio programme.

presentiment /prizentimənt/ ● noun an intuitive feeling or foreboding about the future.
– ORIGIN obsolete French *présentiment*, from Latin *praesentientire* 'perceive beforehand'.

presentism ● noun the tendency to interpret past events in terms of modern values and concepts.
– DERIVATIVES **presentist** adjective.

presently ● adverb **1** after a short time; soon. **2** at the present time; now.

present participle ● noun Grammar the form of a verb, ending in *-ing* in English, which is used in forming continuous tenses (e.g. *I'm thinking*), as a noun (e.g. *good thinking*), and as an adjective (e.g. *running water*).

preservation ● noun **1** the action of preserving. **2** the state of being preserved, especially to a specified degree.

preservationist ● noun a supporter of the preservation of something, especially of historic buildings or artefacts.

preservative ● noun a substance used to preserve foodstuffs or other materials against decay. ● adjective acting to preserve something.

preserve ● verb **1** maintain in its original or existing state. **2** keep safe from harm or injury. **3** keep alive (a memory or quality). **4** treat (food) to prevent its decomposition. **5** prepare (fruit) for long-term storage by boiling it with sugar. ● noun **1** a foodstuff made with fruit preserved in sugar. **2** something regarded as reserved for a particular person or group. **3** a place where game is protected and kept for private hunting.
– DERIVATIVES **preservable** adjective **preserver** noun.
– ORIGIN Latin *praeservare*, from *prae-* 'before' + *servare* 'to keep'.

preset ● verb (**presetting**; past and past part. **preset**) set (a value that controls the operation of a device) in advance of its use.

pre-shrunk ● adjective (of a fabric or garment) shrunk during manufacture to prevent further shrinking in use.
– DERIVATIVES **pre-shrink** verb.

Thesaurus

EXISTENCE, being there. **2** *I requested the presence of an adjudicator* ATTENDANCE, appearance; company, companionship. **3** *a woman of presence* AURA, charisma, (strength/force of) personality; poise, self-assurance, self-confidence. **4** *she felt a presence in the castle* GHOST, spirit, spectre, phantom, apparition, supernatural being; informal spook; poetic/literary shade.
– OPPOSITES absence.
– PHRASES **presence of mind** COMPOSURE, equanimity, self-possession, level-headedness, self-assurance, calmness, sangfroid, imperturbability; alertness, quick-wittedness; informal cool, unflappability.

present[1] ● adjective **1** *a doctor must be present at the ringside* IN ATTENDANCE, here, there, near, nearby, (close/near) at hand, available. **2** *organic compounds are present in the waste* IN EXISTENCE, existing, existent. **3** *the present economic climate* CURRENT, present-day, existing; archaic instant.
– OPPOSITES absent.
● noun *forget the past and think about the present* NOW, today, the present time/moment, the here and now.
– OPPOSITES past, future.
– PHRASES **at present** AT THE MOMENT, just now, right now, at the present time, currently, at this moment in time. **for the present** FOR THE TIME BEING, for now, for the moment, for a while, temporarily, pro tem. **the present day** MODERN TIMES, nowadays.

present[2] ● verb **1** *Eddy presented a cheque to the winner* HAND OVER/OUT, give (out), confer, bestow, award, grant, accord. **2** *the committee presented its report* SUBMIT, set forth, put forward, proffer, offer, tender, table. **3** *may I present my wife?* INTRODUCE, make known, acquaint someone with. **4** *I called to present my warmest compliments* OFFER, give, express. **5** *they presented their new product last month* DEMONSTRATE, show, put on show/display, exhibit, display, launch, unveil. **6** *presenting good quality opera* STAGE, put on, produce, perform. **7** *she presents a TV show* HOST, introduce, compère, be the presenter of; N. Amer. informal emcee. **8** *the authorities present him as a common criminal* REPRESENT, describe, portray, depict.
– PHRASES **present oneself 1** *he presented himself at ten* BE PRESENT, make an appearance, appear, turn up, arrive. **2** *an opportunity that presented itself* OCCUR, arise, happen, come about/up, appear, crop up, turn up.

present[3] ● noun *a birthday present* GIFT, donation, offering, contribution; informal prezzie, freebie; formal benefaction.

presentable ● adjective **1** *I'm making the place look presentable* TIDY, neat, straight, clean, spick and span, in good order, shipshape (and Bristol fashion). **2** *make yourself presentable* SMARTLY DRESSED, tidily dressed, tidy, well groomed, trim, spruce; informal natty. **3** *presentable videos* FAIRLY GOOD, passable, all right, satisfactory, moderately good, not (too) bad, average, fair; informal OK.

presentation ● noun **1** *the presentation of his certificate* AWARDING, presenting, giving, handing over/out, bestowal, granting, award. **2** *the presentation of food* APPEARANCE, arrangement, packaging, disposition, display, layout. **3** *her presentation to the Queen* INTRODUCTION, making known. **4** *the presentation of new proposals* SUBMISSION, proffering, offering, tendering, advancing, proposal, suggestion, mooting, tabling. **5** *a sales presentation* DEMONSTRATION, talk, lecture, address, speech, show, exhibition, display, introduction, launch, launching, unveiling. **6** *a presentation of his latest play* STAGING, production, performance, mounting, showing.

present-day ● adjective CURRENT, present, contemporary, latter-day, present-time, twenty-first-century, modern; up to date, up to the minute, fashionable, trendsetting, the latest, new, newest, newfangled; informal trendy, now.

presentiment ● noun PREMONITION, foreboding, intuition, (funny) feeling, hunch, feeling in one's bones, sixth sense; archaic presage.

presently ● adverb **1** *I shall see you presently* SOON, shortly, directly, quite soon, in a short time, in a little while, at any moment/minute/second, in next to no time, before long; N. Amer. momentarily; informal pretty soon, any moment now, in a jiffy, before you can say Jack Robinson, in two shakes of a lamb's tail; Brit. informal in a mo; poetic/literary ere long. **2** *he is presently abroad* AT PRESENT, currently, at the/this moment, at the present moment/time, now, nowadays, these days; Brit. informal at the minute.

preservation ● noun **1** *wood preservation* CONSERVATION, protection, care. **2** *the preservation of the status quo* CONTINUATION, conservation, maintenance, upholding, sustaining, perpetuation. **3** *the preservation of food* CONSERVING, bottling, canning, freezing, drying; curing, smoking, pickling.

preserve ● verb **1** *oil helps preserve wood* CONSERVE, protect, maintain, care for, look after. **2** *they wish to preserve the status quo* CONTINUE (WITH), conserve, keep going, maintain, uphold, sustain, perpetuate. **3** *preserving him from harassment* GUARD, protect, keep, defend, safeguard, shelter, shield. **4** *spices enable us to preserve food* CONSERVE, bottle, can, freeze, dry; cure, smoke, pickle.
● noun **1** *strawberry preserve* JAM, jelly, marmalade, conserve. **2** *the preserve of an educated middle-class* DOMAIN, area, field,

p

preside ● verb **1** be in a position of authority in a meeting, court, etc. **2** (**preside over**) be in charge of (a situation).
– ORIGIN Latin *praesidere*, from *prae* 'before' + *sedere* 'sit'.
presidency ● noun (pl. **presidencies**) **1** the office or status of president. **2** the period of this.
president ● noun **1** the elected head of a republican state. **2** the head of a society, council, or other organization. **3** Christian Church the celebrant at a Eucharist.
– DERIVATIVES **presidential** adjective.
– ORIGIN from Latin *praesidere* 'preside'.
presidium /prisiddiəm, priziddiəm/ (also **praesidium**) ● noun a standing executive committee in a communist country.
– ORIGIN Russian *prezidium*, from Latin *praesidere* 'preside'.
press[1] ● verb **1** move into a position of contact with something by exerting continuous physical force. **2** exert continuous physical force on (something), especially to operate a device. **3** apply pressure to (something) to flatten or shape it. **4** move in a specified direction by pushing. **5** (**press on/ahead**) continue in one's action. **6** forcefully put forward (an opinion or claim). **7** make strong efforts to persuade or force to do something. **8** extract (juice or oil) by crushing or squeezing fruit, vegetables, etc. **9** (of time) be short. **10** (**be pressed to do**) have difficulty doing. **11** Weightlifting raise (a weight) by gradually pushing it upwards from the shoulders. ● noun **1** a device for applying pressure in order to flatten or shape something or to extract juice or oil. **2** a printing press. **3** (**the press**) (treated as sing. or pl.) newspapers or journalists collectively. **4** coverage in newspapers and magazines. **5** a printing or publishing business. **6** a closely packed mass of people or things.
– PHRASES **go to press** go to be printed. **press (the) flesh** informal, chiefly N. Amer. greet people by shaking hands.
– ORIGIN Latin *pressare* 'keep pressing'.
press[2] ● verb **1** (**press into**) put to a specified use, especially as a makeshift measure. **2** historical force to enlist in the army or navy.
– ORIGIN alteration of obsolete *prest* 'pay given on enlistment' (by association with PRESS[1]), from Latin *praestare* 'provide'.
press conference ● noun a meeting held with journalists in order to make an announcement or answer questions.
press gang ● noun historical a body of men employed to enlist men forcibly into service in the army or navy. ● verb (**press-gang**) force into service.
pressie ● noun variant spelling of PREZZIE.
pressing ● adjective **1** requiring quick or immediate action or attention. **2** expressing something strongly or persistently. ● noun an object made by moulding under pressure.
pressman ● noun chiefly Brit. a journalist.
press release ● noun an official statement issued to journalists.
press stud ● noun Brit. a small fastener engaged by pressing its two halves together.
press-up ● noun Brit. an exercise in which a person lies facing the floor and raises their body by pressing down on their hands.
pressure ● noun **1** the continuous physical force exerted on or against an object by something in contact with it. **2** the use of persuasion or intimidation to make someone do something. **3** a feeling of stressful urgency. **4** the force per unit area exerted by a fluid against a surface. ● verb attempt to persuade or coerce into doing something.
– ORIGIN Latin *pressura*, from *pressare* 'to press'.
pressure cooker ● noun an airtight pot in which food can be cooked quickly under steam pressure.
pressure group ● noun a group that tries to influence public policy in the interest of a particular cause.
pressure point ● noun **1** a point on the surface of the body sensitive to pressure. **2** a point where an artery can be pressed against a bone to inhibit bleeding.
pressurize (also **pressurise**) ● verb **1** produce or maintain raised pressure artificially in. **2** attempt to persuade or coerce into doing something.
– DERIVATIVES **pressurization** noun.
prestidigitation /prestidijitaysh'n/ ● noun formal sleight of hand performed as entertainment.
– DERIVATIVES **prestidigitator** noun.
– ORIGIN French, from *preste* 'nimble' + Latin *digitus* 'finger'.
prestige ● noun respect and admiration attracted through a perception of high achievements or quality.
– DERIVATIVES **prestigious** adjective.
– ORIGIN French, 'illusion, glamour'.
presto ● adverb & adjective Music in a quick tempo. ● exclamation (Brit. also **hey presto**) announcing the successful completion of a conjuring trick or other surprising achievement.
– ORIGIN Italian, 'quick, quickly'.
prestressed ● adjective strengthened by the application of stress during manufacture, especially (of concrete) by means of

Thesaurus

p

sphere, orbit, realm, province, territory; *informal* turf, bailiwick. **3** *a game preserve* SANCTUARY, (game) reserve, reservation.
preside ● verb *the chairman presides at the meeting* CHAIR, be chairman/chairwoman/chairperson, officiate (at), conduct, lead.
– PHRASES **preside over** BE IN CHARGE OF, be responsible for, be at the head/helm of, head, be head of, manage, administer, be in control of, control, direct, lead, govern, rule, command, supervise, oversee; *informal* head up, be boss of, be in the saddle, be in the driving/driver's seat.
president ● noun **1** *terrorists assassinated the president* HEAD OF STATE. **2** *the president of the society* HEAD, chief, director, leader, governor, principal, master; *N. Amer. informal* prexy. **3** *the president of the company* CHAIRMAN, chairwoman; managing director, MD, chief executive (officer), CEO.
press ● verb **1** *press the paper down firmly* PUSH (DOWN), press down, depress, hold down, force, thrust, squeeze, compress. **2** *his shirt was pressed* SMOOTH (OUT), iron, remove creases from. **3** *we pressed the grapes* CRUSH, squeeze, squash, mash, pulp, pound, pulverize, macerate. **4** *she pressed the child to her bosom* CLASP, hold close, hug, cuddle, squeeze, clutch, grasp, embrace. **5** *Winnie pressed his hand* SQUEEZE, grip, clutch. **6** *the crowd pressed round* CLUSTER, gather, converge, congregate, flock, swarm, throng, crowd. **7** *the government pressed its claim* PLEAD, urge, advance insistently, present, submit, put forward. **8** *they pressed him to agree* URGE, put pressure on, pressurize, force, push, coerce, dragoon, steamroller, browbeat; *informal* lean on, put the screws on, twist someone's arm, railroad, bulldoze. **9** *they pressed for a ban on the ivory trade* CALL, ask, clamour, push, campaign, demand.
● noun **1** *a private press* PUBLISHING HOUSE, printing company; printing press. **2** *the freedom of the press* THE MEDIA, the newspapers, the papers, the news media, the fourth estate; journalists, newspapermen, newsmen, newspaper women, reporters, pressmen, presswomen; *informal* journos, news hounds; *N. Amer. informal* newsies; *Brit. dated* Fleet Street. **3** *the company had some bad press* (PRESS) REPORTS, press coverage, press articles, press reviews.
– PHRASES **be pressed for** HAVE TOO LITTLE, be short of, have insufficient, lack, be lacking (in), be deficient in, need, be/stand in need of; *informal* be strapped for. **press on** PROCEED, keep going, continue, carry on, make progress, make headway, press ahead, forge on/ahead, push on, keep on, struggle on, persevere, keep at it, stay with it, plod on, plough on; *informal* soldier on, plug away, peg away, stick at it.
pressing ● adjective **1** *a pressing problem* URGENT, critical, crucial, acute, desperate, serious, grave, life-and-death. **2** *a pressing engagement* IMPORTANT, high-priority, critical, crucial, compelling, inescapable.
pressure ● noun **1** *a confined gas exerts a constant pressure* PHYSICAL FORCE, load, stress, thrust; compression, weight. **2** *they put pressure on us to borrow money* COERCION, force, compulsion, constraint, duress; pestering, harassment, nagging, badgering, intimidation, arm-twisting, pressurization, persuasion. **3** *she had a lot of pressure from work* STRAIN, stress, tension, trouble, difficulty; *informal* hassle.
● verb *they pressured him into resigning*. See PRESSURIZE.
pressurize ● verb *he tried to pressurize Buffy into selling* COERCE, pressure, put pressure on, press, push, persuade, force, bulldoze, hound, harass, nag, harry, badger, goad, pester, browbeat, bully, bludgeon, intimidate, dragoon, twist someone's arm; *informal* railroad, lean on; *N. Amer. informal* hustle.
prestige ● noun STATUS, standing, stature, prestigiousness, reputation, repute, regard, fame, note, renown, honour, esteem, celebrity, importance, prominence, influence, eminence; kudos, cachet; *informal* clout.
prestigious ● adjective **1** *prestigious journals* REPUTABLE, distinguished, respected, esteemed, eminent, august, highly regarded, well thought of, acclaimed, authoritative, celebrated, illustrious, leading, renowned. **2** *a prestigious job* IMPRESSIVE, important, prominent, high-ranking, influential, powerful, glamorous; well

tensioned rods or wires inserted before setting.

presumably ● adverb as may reasonably be presumed.

presume ● verb **1** suppose that something is probably the case. **2** take for granted. **3** be arrogant enough to do something. **4** (**presume on/upon**) unjustifiably regard (something) as entitling one to privileges.
– DERIVATIVES **presumable** adjective.
– ORIGIN Latin *praesumere* 'anticipate'.

presumption ● noun **1** an act or instance of presuming something to be the case. **2** an idea that is presumed to be true. **3** arrogant or disrespectful behaviour. **4** chiefly Law an attitude adopted towards something in the absence of contrary factors.

presumptive ● adjective **1** presumed in the absence of further information. **2** presumptuous.
– DERIVATIVES **presumptively** adverb.

presumptuous ● adjective failing to observe the limits of what is permitted or appropriate.
– DERIVATIVES **presumptuously** adverb **presumptuousness** noun.

presuppose ● verb **1** require as a precondition of possibility or coherence. **2** tacitly assume to be the case.
– DERIVATIVES **presupposition** noun.

prêt-à-porter /prettəportay/ ● noun designer clothing sold ready-to-wear.
– ORIGIN French, 'ready to wear'.

pretence (US **pretense**) ● noun **1** an act or the action of pretending. **2** affected and ostentatious behaviour. **3** (**pretence to**) a claim, especially a false or ambitious one.

pretend ● verb **1** make it appear that something is the case when in fact it is not. **2** engage in an imaginative game. **3** simulate (an emotion or quality). **4** (**pretend to**) lay claim to (a quality or title). ● adjective informal imaginary; make-believe.
– ORIGIN Latin *praetendere* 'stretch forth, claim'.

pretender ● noun a person who claims or aspires to a title or position.

pretense ● noun US spelling of PRETENCE.

pretension ● noun **1** (**pretension to**) a claim or assertion of a claim to. **2** (**pretensions**) aspirations or claims to a specified status or quality: *literary pretensions.* **3** pretentiousness.

pretentious ● adjective attempting to impress by affecting greater importance or merit than is actually possessed.
– DERIVATIVES **pretentiously** adverb **pretentiousness** noun.

preterite /prettərit/ (US also **preterit**) Grammar ● adjective expressing a past action or state. ● noun a simple past tense or form.
– ORIGIN Latin *praeteritus*, from *praeterire* 'pass, go by'.

preterm ● adjective & adverb Medicine born or occurring after a pregnancy significantly shorter than normal.

preternatural /preetənachərəl/ ● adjective beyond what is normal or natural.
– DERIVATIVES **preternaturally** adverb.
– ORIGIN from Latin *praeter* 'past, beyond'.

pretext ● noun an ostensible or false reason used to justify an action.
– ORIGIN Latin *praetextus* 'outward display', from *praetexere* 'to disguise'.

pretreat ● verb treat with a chemical before use.
– DERIVATIVES **pretreatment** noun.

prettify ● verb (**prettifies**, **prettified**) make superficially pretty.
– DERIVATIVES **prettification** noun.

pretty ● adjective (**prettier**, **prettiest**) **1** attractive in a delicate way without being truly beautiful. **2** informal used ironically to express displeasure: *he led me a pretty dance.* ● adverb informal to a moderately high degree; fairly. ● noun (pl. **pretties**) informal a pretty thing; a trinket.
– PHRASES **be sitting pretty** informal be in an advantageous position. **a pretty penny** informal a large sum of money.
– DERIVATIVES **prettily** adverb **prettiness** noun.
– ORIGIN Old English, 'cunning, crafty', later 'clever, skilful, pleasing'.

pretty boy ● noun informal, often derogatory a foppish or effeminate

Thesaurus

paid, expensive; *Brit.* upmarket.
– OPPOSITES obscure, minor.

presumably ● adverb I PRESUME, I expect, I assume, I take it, I suppose, I imagine, I dare say, I guess, in all probability, probably, in all likelihood, as likely as not, doubtless, undoubtedly, no doubt.

presume ● verb **1** *I presumed that it had once been an attic* ASSUME, suppose, dare say, imagine, take it, expect, believe, think, surmise, guess, judge, conjecture, speculate, postulate, presuppose. **2** *let me presume to give you some advice* VENTURE, dare, have the audacity/effrontery, be so bold as, take the liberty of.
– PHRASES **presume on** TAKE (UNFAIR) ADVANTAGE OF, exploit, take liberties with; count on, bank on, place reliance on.

presumption ● noun **1** *this presumption may be easily rebutted* ASSUMPTION, supposition, presupposition, belief, guess, judgement, surmise, conjecture, speculation, hypothesis, postulation, inference, deduction, conclusion. **2** *he apologized for his presumption* BRAZENNESS, audacity, boldness, audaciousness, temerity, arrogance, presumptuousness, forwardness; cockiness, insolence, impudence, bumptiousness, impertinence, effrontery, cheek, cheekiness; rudeness, impoliteness, disrespect, familiarity; *informal* nerve, brass neck, chutzpah; *N. Amer. informal* sass, sassiness; *archaic* assumption.

presumptive ● adjective **1** *a presumptive diagnosis* CONJECTURAL, speculative, tentative; theoretical, unproven, unconfirmed. **2** *the heir presumptive* PROBABLE, likely, prospective, assumed, supposed, expected.

presumptuous ● adjective BRAZEN, overconfident, arrogant, bold, audacious, forward, familiar, impertinent, insolent, impudent, cocky; cheeky, rude, impolite, uncivil, bumptious; *N. Amer. informal* sassy; *archaic* assumptive.

presuppose ● verb **1** *this presupposes the existence of a policy-making group* REQUIRE, necessitate, imply, entail, mean, involve, assume. **2** *I had presupposed that theme parks make people happy* PRESUME, assume, take it for granted, take it as read, suppose, surmise, think, accept, consider.

presupposition ● noun PRESUMPTION, assumption, preconception, supposition, hypothesis, surmise, thesis, theory, premise, belief, postulation.

pretence ● noun **1** *cease this pretence* MAKE-BELIEVE, putting on an act, acting, dissembling, shamming, faking, feigning, simulation, dissimulation, play-acting, posturing; deception, deceit, deceitfulness, fraud, fraudulence, duplicity, subterfuge, trickery, dishonesty, hypocrisy, falsity, lying, mendacity. **2** *he made a pretence of being unconcerned* (FALSE) SHOW, semblance, affectation, (false) appearance, outward appearance, impression, (false) front, guise, facade, display. **3** *she had dropped any pretence to faith* CLAIM, profession. **4** *he was absolutely without pretence* PRETENTIOUSNESS, display, ostentation, affectation, showiness, posturing, humbug.
– OPPOSITES honesty.

pretend ● verb **1** *they just pretend to listen* MAKE AS IF, profess, affect; dissimulate, dissemble, put it on, put on a false front, go through the motions, sham, fake it. **2** *I'll pretend to be the dragon* PUT ON AN ACT, make believe, play at, act, play-act, impersonate. **3** *it was useless to pretend innocence* FEIGN, sham, fake, simulate, put on, counterfeit, affect. **4** *he cannot pretend to sophistication* CLAIM, lay claim to, purport to have, profess to have.
● adjective *(informal) a pretend conversation* IMAGINARY, imagined, pretended, make-believe, made-up, fantasy, fantasized, dreamed-up, unreal, invented, fictitious, mythical, feigned, fake, mock, sham, simulated, artificial, ersatz, false, pseudo; *informal* phoney.

pretended ● adjective FAKE, faked, affected, assumed, professed, spurious, mock, imitation, simulated, make-believe, pseudo, sham, false, bogus; *informal* pretend, phoney.

pretender ● noun CLAIMANT, aspirant.

pretension ● noun **1** *the author has no pretension to exhaustive coverage* ASPIRATION, claim, assertion, pretence, profession. **2** *she spoke without pretension* PRETENTIOUSNESS, affectation, affectedness, ostentation, ostentatiousness, artificiality, airs, posing, posturing, show, flashiness; pomposity, pompousness, grandiosity, grandiloquence, magniloquence.

pretentious ● adjective AFFECTED, ostentatious, showy; overambitious, pompous, artificial, inflated, overblown, high-sounding, flowery, grandiose, elaborate, extravagant, flamboyant, ornate, grandiloquent, magniloquent; *N. Amer.* sophomoric; *informal* flashy, highfalutin, la-di-da, pseudo; *Brit. informal* poncey.

preternatural ● adjective EXTRAORDINARY, exceptional, unusual, uncommon, singular, unprecedented, remarkable, phenomenal, abnormal, inexplicable, unaccountable; strange, mysterious, fantastic.

pretext ● noun (FALSE) EXCUSE, ostensible reason, alleged reason; guise, ploy, pretence, ruse.

prettify ● verb BEAUTIFY, make attractive, make pretty, titivate, adorn, ornament, decorate, smarten (up); *informal* doll up, do up,

man.

pretzel /pretz'l/ ● noun chiefly N. Amer. a crisp biscuit baked in the shape of a knot or stick and flavoured with salt.
– ORIGIN German.

prevail ● verb **1** prove more powerful; be victorious. **2** (**prevail on/upon**) persuade to do something. **3** be widespread or current.
– DERIVATIVES **prevailing** adjective.
– ORIGIN Latin *praevalere* 'have greater power'.

prevailing wind ● noun a wind from the predominant or most usual direction.

prevalent ● adjective widespread in a particular area at a particular time.
– DERIVATIVES **prevalence** noun.
– ORIGIN from Latin *praevalere* (see PREVAIL).

prevaricate /privarrikayt/ ● verb avoid giving a direct answer when asked a question.
– DERIVATIVES **prevarication** noun **prevaricator** noun.
– ORIGIN originally in the sense 'transgress': from Latin *praevaricari* 'walk crookedly, deviate'.

prevent ● verb **1** keep from happening or arising. **2** stop (someone) from doing something.
– PHRASES **prevention is better than cure** proverb it's easier to stop something happening in the first place than to repair the damage after it has happened.
– DERIVATIVES **preventable** adjective **prevention** noun.
– ORIGIN Latin *praevenire* 'precede, hinder'.

preventative ● adjective & noun another term for PREVENTIVE.
– DERIVATIVES **preventatively** adverb.

preventer ● noun **1** a person or thing that prevents something. **2** Sailing an extra line rigged to support a piece of rigging or to prevent the boom from gybing.

preventive ● adjective designed to prevent something from occurring. ● noun a preventive medicine or other treatment.

preview ● noun **1** a viewing or display of something before it is acquired or becomes generally available. **2** a publicity article or trailer of a forthcoming film, book, etc. ● verb provide or have a preview of (a product, film, etc.).

previous ● adjective **1** existing or occurring before in time or order. **2** informal over-hasty.
– PHRASES **previous to** before.
– DERIVATIVES **previously** adverb.
– ORIGIN Latin *praevius* 'going before'.

prey ● noun **1** an animal hunted and killed by another for food. **2** a person who is easily exploited or harmed. **3** a person vulnerable to distressing emotions. ● verb (**prey on/upon**) **1** hunt and kill for food. **2** take advantage of; exploit. **3** cause constant distress to.
– ORIGIN Old French *preie*, from Latin *praeda* 'booty'.

prezzie (also **pressie**) ● noun Brit. informal a present.

priapic /priappik/ ● adjective **1** phallic. **2** Medicine having a persistently erect penis.
– DERIVATIVES **priapism** noun.
– ORIGIN from Greek *Priapos*, a god of fertility.

price ● noun **1** the amount of money expected, required, or given in payment for something. **2** something endured in order to achieve an objective. **3** the odds in betting. ● verb decide the price of.
– PHRASES **at any price** no matter what is involved. **at a price** requiring great expense or involving unwelcome consequences. **a price on someone's head** a reward offered for someone's capture or death. **what price ——?** **1** what has or would become of ——? **2** what is the chance of ——?
– ORIGIN Old French *pris*, from Latin *pretium* 'value, reward'.

priceless ● adjective **1** so precious that its value cannot be determined. **2** informal very amusing or absurd.

price tag ● noun the cost of something.

pricey ● adjective (**pricier**, **priciest**) informal expensive.

Thesaurus

give something a facelift; *Brit. informal* tart up.

pretty ● adjective *a pretty child* ATTRACTIVE, lovely, good-looking, nice-looking, personable, fetching, prepossessing, appealing, charming, delightful, cute, as pretty as a picture; *Scottish & N. English* bonny; *informal* easy on the eye; *poetic/literary* beauteous; *archaic* fair, comely.
– OPPOSITES plain, ugly.
● adverb *(informal) a pretty large sum* QUITE, rather, somewhat, fairly, reasonably, comparatively, relatively.
● verb *she's prettying herself* BEAUTIFY, make attractive, make pretty, prettify, titivate, adorn, ornament, smarten; *informal* do oneself up; *Brit. informal* tart oneself up.

prevail ● verb **1** *common sense will prevail* WIN (OUT/THROUGH), triumph, be victorious, carry the day, come out on top, succeed, prove superior, conquer, overcome; rule, reign. **2** *the conditions that prevailed in the 1950s* EXIST, be in existence, be present, be the case, occur, be prevalent, be current, be the order of the day, be customary, be common, be widespread; *formal* obtain.
– PHRASES **prevail on/upon** PERSUADE, induce, talk someone into, coax, convince, make, get, press someone into, argue someone into, urge, pressure someone into, pressurize someone into, coerce; *informal* sweet-talk, soft-soap.

prevailing ● adjective CURRENT, existing, prevalent, usual, common, general, widespread.

prevalence ● noun COMMONNESS, currency, widespread presence, generality, popularity, pervasiveness, universality, extensiveness; rampancy, rifeness.

prevalent ● adjective WIDESPREAD, prevailing, frequent, usual, common, current, popular, general, universal; endemic, rampant, rife.
– OPPOSITES rare.

prevaricate ● verb BE EVASIVE, beat about the bush, hedge, fence, shilly-shally, dodge (the issue), sidestep (the issue), equivocate; temporize, stall (for time); *Brit.* hum and haw; *archaic* palter; *rare* tergiversate.

prevent ● verb STOP, put a stop to, avert, nip in the bud, fend off, stave off, ward off; hinder, impede, hamper, obstruct, baulk, foil, thwart, forestall, counteract, inhibit, curb, restrain, preclude, pre-empt, save, help; disallow, prohibit, forbid, proscribe, exclude, debar, bar; *poetic/literary* stay.
– OPPOSITES allow.

preventive ● adjective **1** *preventive maintenance* PRE-EMPTIVE, deterrent, precautionary, protective. **2** *preventive medicine* PROPHYLACTIC, disease-preventing.
● noun **1** *a preventive against crime* PRECAUTIONARY MEASURE, deterrent, safeguard, security, protection, defence. **2** *disease preventives* PROPHYLACTIC (DEVICE), prophylactic medicine, preventive drug.

previous ● adjective **1** *the previous five years | her previous boyfriend* FOREGOING, preceding, antecedent; old, earlier, prior, former, ex-, past, last, sometime, one-time, erstwhile; *formal* quondam, anterior; *archaic* whilom. **2** *(informal) I was a bit previous* OVERHASTY, hasty, premature, precipitate, impetuous; *informal* ahead of oneself.
– OPPOSITES next.
– PHRASES **previous to** BEFORE, prior to, until, (leading) up to, earlier than, preceding; *formal* anterior to.

previously ● adverb FORMERLY, earlier (on), before, hitherto, once, at one time, in the past, in days/times gone by, in bygone days, in times past, in former times; in advance, already, beforehand; *formal* heretofore.

prey ● noun **1** *the lions killed their prey* QUARRY, kill. **2** *she was easy prey* VICTIM, target, dupe, gull; *informal* sucker, soft touch, pushover; *N. Amer. informal* patsy, sap, schlemiel; *Austral./NZ informal* dill.
– OPPOSITES predator.
– PHRASES **prey on 1** *hoverfly larvae prey on aphids* HUNT, catch; eat, feed on, live on/off. **2** *they prey on the elderly* EXPLOIT, victimize, pick on, take advantage of; trick, swindle, cheat, hoodwink, fleece; *informal* con. **3** *the problem preyed on his mind* OPPRESS, weigh (heavily) on, lie heavy on, gnaw at; trouble, worry, beset, disturb, distress, haunt, nag, torment, plague, obsess.

price ● noun **1** *the purchase price* COST, asking price, charge, fee, fare, levy, amount, sum; outlay, expense, expenditure; valuation, quotation, estimate; *informal, humorous* damage. **2** *spinsterhood was the price of her career* CONSEQUENCE, result, cost, penalty, sacrifice; downside, snag, drawback, disadvantage, minus. **3** *he had a price on his head* REWARD, bounty, premium.
● verb *a ticket is priced at £5.00* FIX/SET THE PRICE OF, cost, value, rate; estimate.
– PHRASES **at a price** AT A HIGH PRICE/COST, at considerable cost, for a great deal of money. **at any price** WHATEVER THE PRICE, at whatever cost, no matter (what) the cost. **beyond price.** See PRICELESS sense 1.

priceless ● adjective **1** *priceless works of art* OF INCALCULABLE VALUE/WORTH, of immeasurable value/worth, invaluable, beyond price; irreplaceable, incomparable, unparalleled. **2** *(informal) that's priceless!* See HILARIOUS sense 1.

prick ● verb **1** press briefly or puncture with a sharp point. **2** feel a sensation as though a sharp point were sticking into one. **3** (often **prick up**) (chiefly of a horse or dog) make (the ears) stand erect when alert. **4** (**prick out**) plant (seedlings) in small holes made in the earth. ● noun **1** an act of pricking something. **2** a sharp pain caused by being pierced with a fine point. **3** a small hole or mark made by pricking. **4** vulgar slang a man's penis. **5** vulgar slang a man regarded as stupid, unpleasant, or contemptible.
– PHRASES **kick against the pricks** hurt oneself by persisting in useless resistance. [ORIGIN with biblical allusion to Acts of the Apostles, chapter 9.]
– DERIVATIVES **pricker** noun.
– ORIGIN Old English.
prickle ● noun **1** a short spine or pointed outgrowth on the surface of a plant or on the skin of an animal. **2** a tingling or mildly painful sensation on the skin. ● verb experience or produce a prickle.
– ORIGIN Old English, related to PRICK.
prickly ● adjective (**pricklier**, **prickliest**) **1** covered in or resembling prickles. **2** having or causing a prickling sensation. **3** ready to take offence.
prickly heat ● noun an itchy skin rash experienced in hot moist weather.
prickly pear ● noun a cactus with flattened, jointed stems which produces prickly, pear-shaped fruits.
pride ● noun **1** a feeling of deep pleasure or satisfaction derived from achievements, qualities, or possessions. **2** a cause or source of such a feeling. **3** consciousness of one's own dignity. **4** the quality of having an excessively high opinion of oneself. **5** a group of lions forming a social unit. ● verb (**pride oneself on/upon**) be especially proud of (a quality or skill).
– PHRASES **pride goes** (or **comes**) **before a fall** proverb if you're too self-important, something will happen to make you look foolish. **pride of place** the most prominent or important position.
– DERIVATIVES **prideful** adjective.
– ORIGIN Old English, related to PROUD.
prie-dieu /preedjö/ ● noun (pl. **prie-dieux** pronunc. same) a narrow desk on which to kneel for prayer.
– ORIGIN French, 'pray God'.
priest ● noun **1** an ordained minister of the Catholic, Orthodox, or Anglican Church, authorized to perform certain ceremonies. **2** a person who performs ceremonies in a non-Christian religion.
– DERIVATIVES **priesthood** noun **priestly** adjective.
– ORIGIN Old English, related to PRESBYTER.
priestess ● noun a female priest of a non-Christian religion.
prig ● noun a self-righteously moralistic person.
– DERIVATIVES **priggish** adjective.
– ORIGIN originally in the sense 'tinker, petty thief', later 'disliked person': of unknown origin.
prim ● adjective (**primmer**, **primmest**) feeling or showing disapproval of anything improper; stiffly correct.
– DERIVATIVES **primly** adverb **primness** noun.
– ORIGIN probably from Old French *prin*, 'excellent, delicate', from Latin *primus* 'first'.
prima ballerina /preemə/ ● noun the chief female dancer in a ballet or ballet company.
– ORIGIN Italian.
primacy /prīməsi/ ● noun the fact of being primary or preeminent.
– ORIGIN Latin *primatia*, from *primas* 'of the first rank'.
prima donna ● noun **1** the chief female singer in an opera or opera company. **2** a very temperamental and self-important person.
– ORIGIN Italian, 'first lady'.
primaeval ● adjective variant spelling of PRIMEVAL.
prima facie /prīmə fayshee/ ● adjective & adverb Law at first sight; accepted as so until proved otherwise.
– ORIGIN Latin, from *primus* 'first' + *facies* 'face'.
primal ● adjective **1** basic; primitive; primeval. **2** Psychology relating to feelings or behaviour postulated to form the origins of emotional life: *primal fears*.
– ORIGIN Latin *primalis*, from *primus* 'first'.
primarily ● adverb for the most part; mainly.
primary ● adjective **1** of chief importance; principal. **2** earliest in time or order. **3** relating to education for children between the ages of about five and eleven. ● noun (pl. **primaries**) (in the US) a preliminary election to appoint delegates to a party confer-

Thesaurus

– OPPOSITES worthless, cheap.
pricey ● adjective (*informal*). See EXPENSIVE.
prick ● verb **1** *prick the potatoes with a fork* PIERCE, puncture, make/put a hole in, stab, perforate, nick, jab. **2** *his eyes began to prick* STING, smart, burn, prickle. **3** *his conscience pricked him* TROUBLE, worry, distress, perturb, disturb, cause someone anguish, afflict, torment, plague, prey on, gnaw at. **4** *ambition pricked him on to greater effort* GOAD, prod, incite, provoke, urge, spur, stimulate, encourage, inspire, motivate, push, propel, impel. **5** *the horse pricked up its ears* RAISE, erect.
● noun **1** *a prick in the leg* JAB, sting, pinprick, stab. **2** *the prick of tears behind her eyelids* STING, stinging, smart, smarting, burning. **3** *the prick of conscience* PANG, twinge, stab.
– PHRASES **prick up one's ears** LISTEN CAREFULLY, pay attention, become attentive, begin to take notice, attend; *informal* be all ears; *poetic/literary* hark.
prickle ● noun **1** *the cactus is covered with prickles* THORN, needle, barb, spike, point, spine; *technical* spicule. **2** *Willie felt a cold prickle of fear* TINGLE, tingling (sensation), prickling sensation, chill, thrill; *Medicine* paraesthesia.
● verb *its tiny spikes prickled his skin* STING, prick.
prickly ● adjective **1** *a prickly hedgehog* SPIKY, spiked, thorny, barbed, spiny; briary, brambly; rough, scratchy; *technical* spiculate, spicular, aculeate, spinose. **2** *my skin feels prickly* TINGLY, tingling, prickling. **3** *a prickly character.* See IRRITABLE. **4** *the prickly question of the refugees* PROBLEMATIC, awkward, ticklish, tricky, delicate, sensitive, difficult, knotty, thorny, tough, troublesome, bothersome, irksome, vexatious.
pride ● noun **1** *their triumphs were a source of pride* SELF-ESTEEM, dignity, honour, self-respect, self-worth, self-regard, pride in oneself. **2** *take pride in a good job well done* PLEASURE, joy, delight, gratification, fulfilment, satisfaction, sense of achievement. **3** *he refused her offer out of pride* ARROGANCE, vanity, self-importance, hubris, conceit, conceitedness, self-love, self-adulation, self-admiration, narcissism, egotism, superciliousness, haughtiness, snobbery, snobbishness; *informal* big-headedness; *poetic/literary* vainglory. **4** *the bull is the pride of the herd* BEST, finest, top, cream, pick, choice, prize, glory, the jewel in the crown. **5** *the vegetable garden was the pride of the gardener* SOURCE OF SATISFACTION, pride and joy, treasured possession, joy, delight.
– OPPOSITES shame, humility.
– PHRASES **pride oneself on** BE PROUD OF, be proud of oneself for, take pride in, take satisfaction in, congratulate oneself on, pat oneself on the back for; *archaic* pique oneself on/in.
priest ● noun CLERGYMAN, CLERGYWOMAN, minister (of religion), cleric, ecclesiastic, pastor, vicar, rector, parson, churchman, churchwoman, man/woman of the cloth, man/woman of God, father, curate, chaplain, curé, evangelist, preacher; *Scottish* kirkman; *N. Amer.* dominie; *informal* reverend, padre, Holy Joe, sky pilot; *Austral. informal* josser; *dated* divine.
priestly ● adjective CLERICAL, pastoral, priestlike, ecclesiastical, sacerdotal, hieratic, rectorial; *archaic* vicarial.
prig ● noun PRUDE, puritan, killjoy, Mrs Grundy; *informal* goody-goody, holy Joe; *N. Amer. informal* bluenose.
priggish ● adjective SELF-RIGHTEOUS, holier-than-thou, sanctimonious, moralistic, prudish, puritanical, prim, strait-laced, stuffy, prissy, narrow-minded; *informal* goody-goody, starchy.
– OPPOSITES broad-minded.
prim ● adjective DEMURE, (prim and) proper, formal, stuffy, strait-laced, prudish; prissy, mimsy, priggish, puritanical; *Brit.* po-faced; *informal* starchy.
primacy ● noun GREATER IMPORTANCE, priority, precedence, preeminence, superiority, supremacy, ascendancy, dominance, dominion, leadership.
prima donna ● noun LEADING SOPRANO, leading lady, diva, (opera) star, principal singer.
primal ● adjective **1** *primal masculine instincts* BASIC, fundamental, essential, elemental, vital, central, intrinsic, inherent. **2** *the primal source of living things* ORIGINAL, initial, earliest, first, primitive, primeval.
primarily ● adverb **1** *the bishop was primarily a leader of the local community* FIRST (AND FOREMOST), firstly, essentially, in essence, fundamentally, principally, predominantly, basically. **2** *such work is undertaken primarily for large institutions* MOSTLY, for the most

ence or to select candidates for an election.
– ORIGIN Latin *primarius*, from *primus* 'first'.
primary care ● noun health care provided in the community by medical practitioners and specialist clinics.
primary colour ● noun any of a group of colours from which all others can be obtained by mixing.
primary industry ● noun Economics an industry concerned with obtaining or providing raw materials, such as mining or agriculture.
primate ● noun **1** a mammal of an order including monkeys, apes, and humans. **2** Christian Church the chief bishop or archbishop of a province.
– ORIGIN from Latin *primas* 'of the first rank', from *primus* 'first'.
primatology ● noun the branch of zoology concerned with primates.
– DERIVATIVES **primatologist** noun.
primavera /preeməverrə/ ● adjective (of a pasta dish) made with lightly sautéed spring vegetables.
– ORIGIN from Spanish or Italian, denoting the season of spring.
prime[1] ● adjective **1** of first importance; main. **2** of the best possible quality; excellent. **3** (of a number) divisible only by itself and one (e.g. 2, 3, 5, 7). ● noun **1** a time of greatest vigour or success in a person's life. **2** a prime number. **3** Printing a symbol (′) written as a distinguishing mark or to denote minutes or feet. **4** Christian Church a service traditionally said at the first hour of the day (i.e. 6 a.m.), but now little used.
– ORIGIN from Latin *prima hora* 'first hour' from *primus* 'first'.
prime[2] ● verb **1** make (something, especially a firearm or bomb) ready for use or action. **2** introduce liquid into (a pump) to facilitate its working. **3** prepare (someone) for a situation by giving them relevant information. **4** cover (a surface) with primer.
– PHRASES **prime the pump** stimulate growth or success by supplying money.
– ORIGIN originally in the sense 'fill, load': probably from Latin *primus* 'first'.
prime minister ● noun the head of an elected government; the principal minister of a sovereign or state.
prime mover ● noun **1** the originator of a plan or project. **2** an initial source of motive power.
primer[1] ● noun a substance painted on a surface as a preparatory coat.
primer[2] ● noun a book providing a basic introduction to a subject or used for teaching reading.
– ORIGIN from Latin *primarius liber* 'primary book' and *primarium manuale* 'primary manual'.
prime time ● noun the time at which a radio or television audience is expected to be greatest.
primeval /prīmeev'l/ (also **primaeval**) ● adjective **1** of the earliest time in history. **2** (of behaviour or emotion) instinctive and unreasoning.
– ORIGIN Latin *primaevus*, from *primus* 'first' + *aevum* 'age'.
primitive ● adjective **1** relating to the earliest times in history or stages in development. **2** denoting a preliterate, non-industrial society of simple organization. **3** offering an extremely basic level of comfort or convenience. **4** (of behaviour or emotion) instinctive and unreasoning. ● noun **1** a person belonging to a primitive society. **2** a painter employing a simple, naive style that deliberately rejects subtlety or conventional techniques.
– DERIVATIVES **primitively** adverb **primitiveness** noun.
– ORIGIN Latin *primitivus* 'first of its kind', from *primus* 'first'.
primitivism ● noun **1** adoption of a primitive lifestyle or technique. **2** instinctive and unreasoning behaviour.
– DERIVATIVES **primitivist** noun & adjective.
primogeniture /preemōjennichər/ ● noun **1** the state of being the firstborn child. **2** a rule of inheritance by the firstborn child.
– ORIGIN Latin *primogenitura*, from *primo* 'first' + *genitura* 'birth, begetting'.
primordial /prīmordiəl/ ● adjective existing at or from the beginning of time; primitive.
– ORIGIN Latin *primordialis* 'first of all'.
primordial soup ● noun a solution rich in organic compounds in which life on earth is supposed to have originated.
primp ● verb make minor adjustments to (one's hair, clothes, or make-up).
– ORIGIN related to PRIM.
primrose ● noun **1** a woodland and hedgerow plant which produces pale yellow flowers. **2** a pale yellow colour.
– PHRASES **primrose path** the pursuit of pleasure, especially when bringing disastrous consequences. [ORIGIN with allusion to Shakespeare's *Hamlet* I. iii. 50.]
– ORIGIN probably related to Latin *prima rosa* 'first rose'.
primula /primyoolə/ ● noun a plant of a genus that includes primroses, cowslips, and polyanthuses.
– ORIGIN Latin, from *primulus* 'little first flower'.
Primus /prīməss/ ● noun trademark a portable cooking stove that burns vaporized oil.
primus inter pares /preeməss intər paareez/ ● noun the senior or representative member of a group.
– ORIGIN Latin, 'first among equals'.
prince ● noun **1** a son or other close male relative of a monarch. **2** a male monarch of a small state. **3** (in some European countries) a nobleman.
– DERIVATIVES **princedom** noun.
– ORIGIN from Latin *princeps* 'first, chief, sovereign'.
Prince Charming ● noun a handsome and honourable young male lover.
– ORIGIN from French *Roi Charmant*, 'King Charming', the title of an eighteenth-century fairy tale.
prince consort ● noun the husband of a reigning female sovereign who is himself a prince.
princeling ● noun **1** chiefly derogatory the ruler of a small principality or domain. **2** a young prince.
princely ● adjective **1** relating to or suitable for a prince. **2** (of a sum of money) generous.
Prince of Darkness ● noun the Devil.
prince royal (or **princess royal**) ● noun the eldest son (or daughter) of a reigning monarch.

p

Thesaurus

part, chiefly, mainly, in the main, on the whole, largely, to a large extent, especially, generally, usually, typically, commonly, as a rule.
primary ● adjective **1** *our primary role* MAIN, chief, key, prime, central, principal, foremost, first, most important, predominant, paramount; *informal* number-one. **2** *the primary cause* ORIGINAL, earliest, initial, first; essential, fundamental, basic.
– OPPOSITES secondary.
prime[1] ● adjective **1** *his prime reason for leaving* MAIN, chief, key, primary, central, principal, foremost, first, most important, paramount, major; *informal* number-one. **2** *the prime cause of flooding* FUNDAMENTAL, basic, essential, primary, central. **3** *prime agricultural land* TOP-QUALITY, top, best, first-class, first-rate, grade A, superior, supreme, choice, select, finest; excellent, superb, fine; *informal* tip-top, A1, top-notch. **4** *a prime example* ARCHETYPAL, prototypical, typical, classic, excellent, characteristic, quintessential.
– OPPOSITES secondary, inferior.
● noun *he is in his prime* HEYDAY, best days/years, prime of one's life; youth, salad days; peak, pinnacle, high point/spot, zenith.
prime[2] ● verb **1** *he primed the gun* PREPARE, load, get ready. **2** *Lucy had primed him carefully* BRIEF, fill in, prepare, put in the picture, inform, advise, instruct, coach, drill; *informal* clue in, give someone the low-down.
prime minister ● noun PREMIER, first minister, head of the government.
primeval ● adjective **1** *primeval forest* ANCIENT, earliest, first, prehistoric, antediluvian, primordial; pristine, original, virgin. **2** *primeval fears* INSTINCTIVE, primitive, basic, primal, primordial, intuitive, inborn, innate, inherent.
primitive ● adjective **1** *primitive times* ANCIENT, earliest, first, prehistoric, antediluvian, primordial, primeval, primal. **2** *primitive peoples* UNCIVILIZED, barbarian, barbaric, barbarous, savage, ignorant, uncultivated. **3** *primitive tools* CRUDE, simple, rough (and ready), basic, rudimentary, unrefined, unsophisticated, rude, makeshift. **4** *primitive art* SIMPLE, natural, unsophisticated, unaffected, undeveloped, unpretentious.
– OPPOSITES sophisticated, civilized.
primordial ● adjective **1** *the primordial oceans* ANCIENT, earliest, first, prehistoric, antediluvian, primeval. **2** *their primordial desires* INSTINCTIVE, primitive, basic, primal, primeval, intuitive, inborn, innate, inherent.
primp ● verb GROOM, tidy, arrange, brush, comb; smarten (up), spruce up; *informal* titivate, doll up; *Brit. informal* tart up; *N. Amer. informal* gussy up.
prince ● noun RULER, sovereign, monarch, king, princeling; crown prince; emir, sheikh, sultan, maharaja, raja.

princess ● noun **1** a daughter or other close female relative of a monarch. **2** the wife or widow of a prince. **3** a female monarch of a small state.

principal ● adjective **1** first in order of importance; main. **2** denoting an original sum of money invested or lent. ● noun **1** the most important person in an organization or group. **2** the head of a school or college. **3** a sum of money lent or invested, on which interest is paid. **4** a person for whom another acts as a representative. **5** Law a person directly responsible for a crime.
– DERIVATIVES **principalship** noun.
– USAGE The words **principal** and **principle** are pronounced in the same way but they do not have the same meaning. **Principal** is normally an adjective meaning 'main or most important', whereas **principle** is normally used as a noun meaning 'a basis of a system of thought or belief'.
– ORIGIN Latin *principalis* 'first, original', from *princeps* 'first, chief'.

principal boy ● noun Brit. a woman who takes the leading male role in a pantomime.

principality ● noun (pl. **principalities**) **1** a state ruled by a prince. **2** (**the Principality**) Brit. Wales.

principally ● adverb for the most part; chiefly.

principle ● noun **1** a fundamental truth or proposition serving as the foundation for belief or action. **2** a rule or belief governing one's personal behaviour. **3** morally correct behaviour and attitudes. **4** a general scientific theorem or natural law. **5** a fundamental source or basis of something. **6** Chemistry an active or characteristic constituent of a substance.
– PHRASES **in principle** in theory. **on principle** because of one's adherence to a particular belief.
– ORIGIN Latin *principium* 'source', from *princeps* 'first, chief'.

principled ● adjective acting in accordance with morality.

prink ● verb (**prink oneself**) make minor adjustments to one's appearance.
– ORIGIN probably related to archaic *prank* 'dress or adorn in a showy manner'.

print ● verb **1** produce (books, newspapers, etc.) by a process involving the transfer of text or designs to paper. **2** produce (text or a picture) in such a way. **3** produce a paper copy of (information stored on a computer). **4** produce (a photographic print) from a negative. **5** write clearly without joining the letters. **6** mark with a coloured design. ● noun **1** the text appearing in a book, newspaper, etc. **2** an indentation or mark left on a surface by pressure. **3** a printed picture or design. **4** a photograph printed on paper from a negative or transparency. **5** a copy of a motion picture on film. **6** a piece of fabric or clothing with a coloured pattern or design.
– PHRASES **in print 1** (of a book) available from the publisher. **2** in published form. **out of print** (of a book) no longer available from the publisher.
– DERIVATIVES **printable** adjective.
– ORIGIN Old French *preinte* 'pressed', from Latin *premere* 'to press'.

printed circuit ● noun an electronic circuit based on thin strips of a conductor on an insulating board.

printer ● noun **1** a person whose job is commercial printing. **2** a machine for printing text or pictures.

printing ● noun **1** the production of books, newspapers, etc. **2** a single impression of a book. **3** handwriting in which the letters are written separately.

printing press ● noun a machine for printing from type or plates.

printmaker ● noun a person who prints pictures or designs from plates or blocks.
– DERIVATIVES **printmaking** noun.

printout ● noun Computing a page of printed material from a computer's printer.

print run ● noun the number of copies of a book, magazine, etc. printed at one time.

prion /preeon/ ● noun Microbiology a submicroscopic protein particle believed to be the cause of certain brain diseases such as BSE.
– ORIGIN by rearrangement of elements from *pro(teinaceous) in(fectious particle)*.

prior[1] ● adjective existing or coming before in time, order, or importance.
– PHRASES **prior to** before.
– ORIGIN Latin, 'former, elder'.

prior[2] ● noun (fem. **prioress**) **1** (in an abbey) the person next in rank below an abbot (or abbess). **2** the head of a house of friars (or nuns).
– ORIGIN Latin *prior* (see PRIOR[1]).

prioritize (also **prioritise**) ● verb **1** designate or treat as most important. **2** determine the relative importance of (items or tasks).
– DERIVATIVES **prioritization** noun.

priority ● noun (pl. **priorities**) **1** the condition of being regarded as more important. **2** a thing regarded as more important than others. **3** the right to proceed before other traffic.

priory ● noun (pl. **priories**) a monastery or nunnery governed by a prior or prioress.

prise (US **prize**) ● verb **1** use force in order to open or move apart. **2** (**prise out of/from**) obtain (something) from (someone) with effort or difficulty.

Thesaurus

princely ● adjective **1** *princely buildings.* See SPLENDID sense 1. **2** *a princely sum.* See HANDSOME sense 3.

principal ● adjective *the principal cause of poor air quality* MAIN, chief, primary, leading, foremost, first, most important, predominant, dominant, (most) prominent; key, crucial, vital, essential, basic, prime, central, focal; premier, paramount, major, overriding, cardinal, pre-eminent, uppermost, highest, top, topmost; *informal* number-one.
– OPPOSITES minor.
● noun **1** *the principal of the firm* CHIEF, chief executive (officer), CEO, chairman, chairwoman, managing director, MD, president, director, manager, head; *informal* boss; *Brit. informal* gaffer, governor. **2** *the school's principal* HEAD (TEACHER), headmaster, headmistress; dean, rector, chancellor, vice-chancellor, president, provost; *N. Amer. informal* prexy. **3** *the film's principals* LEADING ACTOR/ACTRESS, leading player/performer, leading role, lead, star. **4** *repayment of the principal* CAPITAL (SUM), debt, loan.

principally ● adverb MAINLY, mostly, chiefly, for the most part, in the main, on the whole, largely, to a large extent, predominantly, basically, primarily.

principle ● noun **1** *elementary principles* TRUTH, proposition, concept, idea, theory, assumption, fundamental, essential. **2** *the principle of laissez-faire* DOCTRINE, belief, creed, credo, (golden) rule, criterion, tenet, code, ethic, dictum, dogma, canon, law. **3** *a woman of principle | sticking to one's principles* MORALS, morality, (code of) ethics, beliefs, ideals, standards; integrity, uprightness, righteousness, virtue, probity, (sense of) honour, decency, conscience, scruples.
– PHRASES **in principle 1** *there is no reason, in principle, why we couldn't work together* IN THEORY, theoretically, on paper. **2** *he has accepted the idea in principle* IN GENERAL, in essence, on the whole, in the main.

principled ● adjective MORAL, ethical, virtuous, righteous, upright, upstanding, high-minded, honourable, honest, incorruptible.

prink ● verb GROOM, tidy, arrange, smarten (up), spruce up, preen, primp; *informal* titivate, doll up; *Brit. informal* tart up; *N. Amer. informal* gussy up.

print ● verb **1** *four newspapers are printed in the town* SET IN PRINT, send to press, run off, reprint. **2** *patterns were printed on the cloth* IMPRINT, impress, stamp, mark. **3** *they printed 30,000 copies* PUBLISH, issue, release, circulate. **4** *the incident is printed on her memory* REGISTER, record, impress, imprint, engrave, etch, stamp, mark.
● noun **1** *small print* TYPE, printing, letters, lettering, characters, type size, typeface, font. **2** *prints of his left hand* IMPRESSION, fingerprint, footprint. **3** *sporting prints* PICTURE, design, engraving, etching, lithograph, linocut, woodcut. **4** *prints and negatives* PHOTOGRAPH, photo, snap, snapshot, picture, still; *Brit.* enprint. **5** *soft floral prints* PRINTED CLOTH/FABRIC, patterned cloth/fabric, chintz.
– PHRASES **in print** PUBLISHED, printed, available in bookshops. **out of print** NO LONGER AVAILABLE, unavailable, unobtainable.

prior ● adjective *by prior arrangement* EARLIER, previous, preceding, foregoing, antecedent, advance; *formal* anterior.
– OPPOSITES subsequent.
– PHRASES **prior to** BEFORE, until, till, up to, previous to, earlier than, preceding, leading up to; *formal* anterior to.

priority ● noun **1** *safety is our priority* PRIME CONCERN, most important consideration, primary issue. **2** *giving priority to primary education* PRECEDENCE, greater importance, preference, pre-eminence, predominance, primacy. **3** *traffic on the roundabout*

– ORIGIN from Old French *prise* 'a grasp, taking hold'.
prism ● noun **1** a piece of glass or other transparent material of regular shape, used to separate white light into a spectrum of colours. **2** Geometry a solid geometric figure whose two ends are similar, equal, and parallel rectilinear figures, and whose sides are parallelograms.
– ORIGIN Greek *prisma* 'thing sawn', from *prizein* 'to saw'.
prismatic ● adjective **1** relating to or having the form of a prism. **2** (of colours) formed, separated, or distributed by or as by a prism.
prison ● noun a building for the confinement of criminals or those awaiting trial.
– ORIGIN Old French *prisun*, from Latin *prehendere* 'lay hold of'.
prison camp ● noun a camp where prisoners of war or political prisoners are kept.
prisoner ● noun **1** a person legally committed to prison. **2** a person captured and kept confined. **3** a person trapped by circumstances.
– PHRASES **take no prisoners** be ruthlessly aggressive in the pursuit of one's objectives.
prisoner of conscience ● noun a person imprisoned for their political or religious views.
prisoner of war ● noun a person captured and imprisoned by the enemy in war.
prissy ● adjective (**prissier**, **prissiest**) fussily respectable; prim.
– DERIVATIVES **prissily** adverb **prissiness** noun.
– ORIGIN perhaps a blend of PRIM and SISSY.
pristine /pristeen/ ● adjective **1** in its original condition. **2** clean and fresh as if new.
– ORIGIN Latin *pristinus* 'former'.
prithee /prithee/ ● exclamation archaic please.
– ORIGIN abbreviation of *I pray thee*.
privacy /privvəsi, pri-/ ● noun a state in which one is not observed or disturbed by others.
private ● adjective **1** for or belonging to one particular person or group only. **2** (of a service or industry) provided by an individual or commercial company rather than the state. **3** (of thoughts, feelings, etc.) not to be shared or revealed. **4** (of a person) not choosing to share their thoughts and feelings. **5** (of a person) having no official or public position. **6** not connected with one's work or official position: *the president visited the country in a private capacity*. **7** (of a place) secluded. ● noun **1** the lowest rank in the army, below lance corporal. **2** (**privates**) informal short for PRIVATE PARTS.
– PHRASES **in private** with no one else present.
– DERIVATIVES **privately** adverb.
– ORIGIN Latin *privatus* 'withdrawn from public life' from *privus* 'single, individual'.
private company ● noun Brit. a company whose shares may not be offered to the public for sale.
private detective (also **private investigator**) ● noun a freelance detective carrying out investigations for private clients.
private enterprise ● noun business or industry managed by independent companies rather than the state.
privateer /prīvəteer/ ● noun chiefly historical an armed ship owned by private individuals, holding a government commission and authorized for use in war.
private eye ● noun informal a private detective.
private life ● noun one's personal relationships, interests, etc., as distinct from one's professional or public life.
private means ● plural noun Brit. income derived from investments, property, etc., rather than from employment.
private member ● noun (in the UK, Canada, Australia, and New Zealand) a member of a parliament who is not a minister or does not hold government office.
private parts ● plural noun euphemistic a person's genitals.
private practice ● noun **1** the work of a doctor, lawyer, etc. who is self-employed. **2** Brit. medical practice that is not part of the National Health Service.
private school ● noun **1** Brit. an independent school supported mainly by the payment of fees. **2** N. Amer. a school supported mainly by private individuals.
private secretary ● noun **1** a secretary who deals with the personal concerns of their employer. **2** a civil servant acting as an aide to a senior government official.
private sector ● noun the part of the national economy not under direct state control.
private soldier ● noun a soldier of the lowest rank (in the US, one who is also not a recruit).
private view ● noun a chance for invited guests to see an art exhibition before it opens to the public.
privation /prīvaysh'n/ ● noun a state in which essentials such as food and warmth are lacking.
– ORIGIN Latin, from *privare* 'bereave, deprive'.
privatize (also **privatise**) ● verb transfer (a business or industry) from public to private ownership.
– DERIVATIVES **privatization** noun.
privet /privvit/ ● noun a shrub with small white flowers and poisonous black berries.
– ORIGIN of unknown origin.
privilege ● noun **1** a special right, advantage, or immunity for a particular person or group. **2** an opportunity to do something

Thesaurus

has priority RIGHT OF WAY.
priory ● noun RELIGIOUS HOUSE, abbey, cloister; monastery, friary; convent, nunnery.
prise ● verb **1** *I prised the lid off* LEVER, jemmy; wrench, wrest, twist; *N. Amer.* pry, jimmy. **2** *he had to prise information from them* WRING, wrest, worm out, winkle out, screw, squeeze, extract.
prison ● noun JAIL, lock-up, penal institution, detention centre; *Brit.* young offender institution; *N. Amer.* jailhouse, penitentiary, correctional facility; *informal* clink, slammer, stir, jug, brig; *Brit. informal* nick; *N. Amer. informal* can, pen, cooler, pokey, slam; *Brit. informal, dated* chokey, quod; *Brit. historical* approved school, borstal, bridewell; *Brit. Military* glasshouse; (**be in prison**) *informal* be inside, be behind bars, do time; *Brit. informal* do bird, do porridge.
– RELATED TERMS custodial.
prisoner ● noun **1** *a prisoner serving a life sentence* CONVICT, detainee, inmate; *informal* jailbird, con; *Brit. informal* (old) lag; *N. Amer. informal* yardbird. **2** *the army took many prisoners* PRISONER OF WAR, POW, internee, captive.
prissy ● adjective PRUDISH, priggish, prim, prim and proper, strait-laced, Victorian, old-maidish, schoolmistressy, schoolmarmish; *Brit.* po-faced; *informal* starchy.
– OPPOSITES broad-minded.
pristine ● adjective IMMACULATE, perfect, in mint condition, as new, unspoilt, spotless, flawless, clean, fresh, new, virgin, pure, unused.
– OPPOSITES dirty, spoilt.
privacy ● noun SECLUSION, solitude, isolation, freedom from disturbance, freedom from interference.
private ● adjective **1** *his private plane* PERSONAL, own, individual, special, exclusive, privately owned. **2** *private talks* CONFIDENTIAL, secret, classified, unofficial, off the record, closet, in camera; backstage, privileged, one-on-one, tête-à-tête. **3** *private thoughts* INTIMATE, personal, secret; innermost, undisclosed, unspoken, unvoiced. **4** *a very private man* RESERVED, introvert, introverted, self-contained, reticent, discreet, uncommunicative, unforthcoming, retiring, unsociable, withdrawn, solitary, reclusive, hermitic. **5** *they found a private place in which to talk* SECLUDED, solitary, undisturbed, concealed, hidden, remote, isolated, out of the way, sequestered. **6** *we can be private here* UNDISTURBED, uninterrupted; alone, by ourselves. **7** *the Queen attended in a private capacity* UNOFFICIAL, personal. **8** *private industry* INDEPENDENT, non-state; privatized, denationalized; commercial, private-enterprise.
– OPPOSITES public, open, extrovert, busy, crowded, official, state, nationalized.
● noun *a private in the army* PRIVATE SOLDIER, common soldier; trooper; *Brit.* sapper, gunner, ranker; *US* GI; *Brit. informal* Tommy, squaddie.
– PHRASES **in private** IN SECRET, secretly, privately, behind closed doors, in camera, à huis clos; in confidence, confidentially, between ourselves, entre nous, off the record; *formal* sub rosa.
private detective ● noun PRIVATE INVESTIGATOR; *Brit.* enquiry agent; *informal* private eye, PI, sleuth, snoop; *N. Amer. informal* shamus, gumshoe; *informal, dated* private dick.
privately ● adverb **1** *we must talk privately* IN SECRET, secretly, in private, behind closed doors, in camera, à huis clos; in confidence, confidentially, between ourselves, entre nous, off the record; *formal* sub rosa. **2** *privately, I am glad* SECRETLY, inwardly, deep down, personally, unofficially. **3** *he lived very privately* OUT OF THE PUBLIC EYE, out of public view, in seclusion, in solitude, alone.
– OPPOSITES publicly.
privation ● noun DEPRIVATION, hardship, destitution, impoverish-

regarded as a special honour: *she had the privilege of giving the opening lecture.* **3** the right to say or write something without the risk of punishment, especially in parliament.
– DERIVATIVES **privileged** adjective.
– ORIGIN Latin *privilegium* 'bill or law affecting an individual', from *privus* 'private' + *lex* 'law'.
privy ● adjective (**privy to**) sharing in the knowledge of (something secret). ● noun (pl. **privies**) a toilet in a small shed outside a house.
– DERIVATIVES **privily** adverb.
– ORIGIN Old French *prive* 'private', also 'private place', from Latin *privatus* 'withdrawn from public life'.
Privy Council ● noun a body of advisers appointed by a sovereign or a Governor General.
– DERIVATIVES **privy counsellor** (also **privy councillor**) noun.
privy purse ● noun (in the UK) an allowance from the public revenue for the monarch's private expenses.
privy seal ● noun (in the UK) a seal affixed to state documents.
prix fixe /pree fiks/ ● noun a meal of several courses costing a fixed price.
– ORIGIN French, 'fixed price'.
prize¹ ● noun **1** a thing given as a reward to a winner or in recognition of an outstanding achievement. **2** something of great value that is worth struggling to achieve. ● adjective **1** having been or likely to be awarded a prize. **2** outstanding of its kind. ● verb value highly.
– ORIGIN Old French *preisier* 'praise'.
prize² ● verb US spelling of PRISE.
prizefight ● noun a boxing match for prize money.
– DERIVATIVES **prizefighter** noun.
PRO ● abbreviation Public Record Office.
pro¹ ● noun (pl. **pros**) informal **1** a professional. **2** a prostitute. ● adjective professional.
pro² ● noun (pl. **pros**) (usu. in phrase **pros and cons**) an advantage or argument in favour of something. ● preposition & adverb in favour of.
– ORIGIN Latin, 'for, on behalf of'.
pro-¹ ● prefix **1** favouring; supporting: *pro-choice.* **2** acting as a substitute for: *proconsul.* **3** denoting motion forwards, out, or away: *propel.*
– ORIGIN Latin *pro* 'in front of, on behalf of, instead of, on account of'.
pro-² ● prefix before in time, place, or order: *proactive.*
– ORIGIN Greek *pro* 'before'.
proactive ● adjective creating or controlling a situation rather than just responding to it.
– DERIVATIVES **proactively** adverb.
pro-am ● adjective involving professionals and amateurs. ● noun a pro-am event.
probabilistic ● adjective based on or adapted to a theory of probability; involving chance variation.
probability ● noun (pl. **probabilities**) **1** the extent to which something is probable. **2** a probable or most probable event.
– PHRASES **in all probability** most probably.
probable ● adjective likely to happen or be the case. ● noun a person likely to become or do something.
– ORIGIN Latin *probabilis*, from *probare* 'to test, demonstrate'.
probable cause ● noun Law, chiefly N. Amer. reasonable grounds (for making a search, preferring a charge, etc.).
probably ● adverb almost certainly; as far as one knows or can tell.
probate ● noun **1** the official proving of a will. **2** a verified copy of a will with a certificate as handed to the executors.
– ORIGIN Latin *probatum* 'something proved'.
probation ● noun **1** Law the release of an offender from detention, subject to a period of good behaviour under supervision. **2** the process of testing the character or abilities of a person in a certain role.
– DERIVATIVES **probationary** adjective.
probationer ● noun **1** a person serving a probationary period in a job or position. **2** an offender on probation.
probation officer ● noun a person who supervises offenders on probation.
probe ● noun **1** a blunt-ended surgical instrument for exploring a wound or part of the body. **2** a small measuring or testing device, especially an electrode. **3** an investigation. **4** (also **space probe**) an unmanned exploratory spacecraft. ● verb **1** physically explore or examine. **2** enquire into closely.
– DERIVATIVES **prober** noun **probing** adjective.
– ORIGIN Latin *proba* 'proof', later 'examination', from *probare* 'to prove'.
probity /prōbiti/ ● noun honesty and decency.
– ORIGIN Latin *probitas*, from *probus* 'good'.
problem ● noun **1** an unwelcome or harmful matter needing to be dealt with. **2** a thing that is difficult to achieve. **3** Physics & Mathematics an inquiry starting from given conditions to investigate or demonstrate something.
– ORIGIN Greek *problēma*, from *proballein* 'put forth'.

Thesaurus

ment, want, need, neediness, austerity.
– OPPOSITES plenty, luxury.
privilege ● noun **1** *senior pupils have certain privileges* ADVANTAGE, benefit; prerogative, entitlement, right; concession, freedom, liberty. **2** *it was a privilege to meet her* HONOUR, pleasure. **3** *parliamentary privilege* IMMUNITY, exemption, dispensation.
privileged ● adjective **1** *a privileged background* WEALTHY, rich, affluent, prosperous; LUCKY, fortunate, elite, favoured; (socially) advantaged. **2** *privileged information* CONFIDENTIAL, private, secret, restricted, classified, not for publication, off the record, inside; *informal* hush-hush. **3** *MPs are privileged* IMMUNE (FROM PROSECUTION), protected, exempt, excepted.
– OPPOSITES underprivileged, disadvantaged, public, liable.
privy ● adjective *he was not privy to the discussions* IN THE KNOW ABOUT, acquainted with, in on, informed of, advised of, apprised of; *informal* genned up on, clued up on, wise to; *formal* cognizant of.
● noun *he went out to the privy.* See TOILET sense 1.
prize ● noun **1** *an art prize* AWARD, reward, premium, purse; trophy, medal; honour, accolade, crown, laurels, palm. **2** *the prizes of war* SPOILS, booty, plunder, loot, pickings.
● adjective **1** *a prize bull* CHAMPION, award-winning, prize-winning, winning, top, best. **2** *a prize example* OUTSTANDING, excellent, superlative, superb, supreme, very good, prime, fine, magnificent, marvellous, wonderful; *informal* great, terrific, tremendous, fantastic. **3** *a prize idiot* UTTER, complete, total, absolute, real, perfect, positive, veritable; *Brit. informal* right, bloody; *Austral./NZ informal* fair.
– OPPOSITES second-rate.
● verb *many collectors prize his work* VALUE, set great store by, rate highly, attach great importance to, esteem, hold in high regard, think highly of, treasure, cherish.
prized ● adjective TREASURED, precious, cherished, much loved, beloved, valued, esteemed, highly regarded.
prizewinner ● noun CHAMPION, winner, gold medallist, victor; *informal* champ, number one.
probability ● noun **1** *the probability of winning* LIKELIHOOD, prospect, expectation, chance, chances, odds. **2** *relegation is a distinct probability* PROBABLE EVENT, good/fair/reasonable bet, prospect, possibility.
probable ● adjective LIKELY, most likely, odds-on, expected, anticipated, predictable, foreseeable, ten to one; *informal* on the cards, a good/fair/reasonable bet.
– OPPOSITES unlikely.
probably ● adverb IN ALL LIKELIHOOD, in all probability, as like(ly) as not, (very/most) likely, ten to one, the chances are, doubtless, no doubt; *archaic* like enough.
probation ● noun TRIAL PERIOD, test period, experimental period, trial.
probe ● noun *a probe into an air crash* INVESTIGATION, enquiry, examination, inquest, exploration, study, analysis.
● verb **1** *hands probed his body* EXAMINE, feel, feel around, explore, prod, poke, check. **2** *police probed the tragedy* INVESTIGATE, enquire into, look into, study, examine, scrutinize, go into, carry out an inquest into.
probity ● noun INTEGRITY, honesty, uprightness, decency, morality, rectitude, goodness, virtue, right-mindedness, trustworthiness, truthfulness, honour.
– OPPOSITES untrustworthiness.
problem ● noun **1** *they ran into a problem* DIFFICULTY, trouble, worry, complication, difficult situation; snag, hitch, drawback, stumbling block, obstacle, hurdle, hiccup, setback, catch; predicament, plight; misfortune, mishap, misadventure; *informal* dilemma, headache, prob, facer. **2** *I don't want to be a problem* NUISANCE, bother, pest, irritant, thorn in one's side/flesh, vexation; *informal* drag, pain, pain in the neck. **3** *arithmetical problems* PUZZLE, question, poser, enigma, riddle, conundrum; *informal* teaser, brainteaser.

problematic • adjective presenting a problem.
– DERIVATIVES **problematical** adjective **problematically** adverb.
problematize (also **problematise**) • verb make into or regard as a problem.
pro bono publico /prō bonnō po͝oblikō/ • adverb & adjective 1 for the public good. 2 (usu. **pro bono**) chiefly N. Amer. denoting legal work undertaken without charge.
– ORIGIN Latin.
proboscis /prəbossis/ • noun (pl. **proboscses** /prəbosseez/, **proboscides** /prəbossideez/, or **proboscises**) 1 the nose of a mammal, especially when long and mobile like an elephant's trunk. 2 an elongated sucking organ or mouthpart of an insect or worm.
– ORIGIN Greek *proboskis* 'means of obtaining food'.
proboscis monkey • noun a monkey native to the forests of Borneo, the male of which has a large dangling nose.
procedure • noun 1 an established or official way of doing something. 2 a series of actions conducted in a certain manner.
– DERIVATIVES **procedural** adjective **procedurally** adverb.
– ORIGIN French *procédure*, from Latin *procedere* (see PROCEED).
proceed • verb 1 begin a course of action. 2 go on to do something. 3 (of an action) carry on or continue. 4 move forward. 5 Law start a lawsuit against someone.
– ORIGIN Latin *procedere*, from *pro-* 'forward' + *cedere* 'go'.
proceedings • plural noun 1 an event or a series of activities with a set procedure. 2 Law action taken in a court to settle a dispute. 3 a report of a set of meetings or a conference.
proceeds • plural noun money obtained from an event or activity.
process[1] /prōsess/ • noun 1 a series of actions or steps towards achieving a particular end. 2 a natural series of changes: *the ageing process.* 3 Law a summons to appear in court. 4 Biology & Anatomy a natural appendage or outgrowth on or in an organism. 5 (before another noun) Printing relating to printing using ink in three colours (cyan, magenta, and yellow) and black. • verb 1 perform a series of operations to change or preserve. 2 Computing operate on (data) by means of a program. 3 deal with, using an established procedure.
– ORIGIN Latin *processus* 'progression, course', from *procedere* (see PROCEED).
process[2] /prəsess/ • verb walk in procession.
– ORIGIN from PROCESSION.
procession • noun 1 a number of people or vehicles moving forward in an orderly fashion. 2 the action of moving in such a way. 3 a relentless succession of people or things.
processional • adjective of or used in a religious or ceremonial procession. • noun a book of litanies and hymns used in religious processions.
processor • noun 1 a machine that processes something. 2 Computing a central processing unit.
pro-choice • adjective advocating the right of a woman to choose to have an abortion.
proclaim • verb 1 announce officially or publicly. 2 declare (someone) officially or publicly to be. 3 indicate clearly.
– DERIVATIVES **proclamation** noun.
– ORIGIN Latin *proclamare* 'cry out'.
proclivity /prəklivviti/ • noun (pl. **proclivities**) a tendency to do or choose something regularly; an inclination or predisposition.
– ORIGIN Latin *proclivitas*, from *proclivis* 'inclined'.
proconsul /prōkons'l/ • noun 1 a governor of a province in ancient Rome. 2 a governor or deputy consul of a modern colony.
procrastinate /prəkrastinayt/ • verb delay or postpone action.
– DERIVATIVES **procrastination** noun **procrastinator** noun.
– ORIGIN Latin *procrastinare* 'defer till the morning'.
procreate • verb produce young.
– DERIVATIVES **procreation** noun **procreative** adjective.
– ORIGIN Latin *procreare* 'generate, bring forth'.
Procrustean /prōkrustiən/ • adjective enforcing conformity without regard to natural variation or individuality.
– ORIGIN from *Procrustes*, a robber in Greek mythology who fitted victims to a bed by stretching or cutting off parts of them.
proctology /proktolləji/ • noun the branch of medicine concerned with the anus and rectum.
– DERIVATIVES **proctological** adjective **proctologist** noun.
– ORIGIN from Greek *prōktos* 'anus'.
proctor • noun Brit. a disciplinary officer at certain universities.
– ORIGIN contraction of PROCURATOR.
procumbent /prəkumbənt/ • adjective Botany growing loosely along the ground.
– ORIGIN from Latin *procumbere* 'fall forwards'.
procuracy /prəkyoorəsi/ • noun (pl. **procuracies**) the position or office of a procurator.
procurator /prokyooraytər/ • noun Law 1 an agent representing others in a court in countries retaining Roman civil law. 2 (in Scotland) a lawyer practising before the lower courts.
– ORIGIN Latin *procurator* 'administrator, finance agent'.
procurator fiscal • noun (pl. **procurators fiscal** or **procurator fiscals**) (in Scotland) a local coroner and public prosecutor.
procure • verb 1 obtain. 2 Law persuade or cause to do something.
– DERIVATIVES **procurable** adjective **procurement** noun.
– ORIGIN Latin *procurare* 'take care of, manage'.
procurer • noun (fem. **procuress**) 1 a person who obtains a

Thesaurus

• adjective *a problem child* TROUBLESOME, difficult, unmanageable, unruly, disobedient, uncontrollable, recalcitrant, delinquent.
– OPPOSITES well behaved, manageable.
problematic • adjective DIFFICULT, hard, taxing, troublesome, tricky, awkward, controversial, ticklish, complicated, complex, knotty, thorny, prickly, vexed; *informal* sticky; *Brit. informal* dodgy.
– OPPOSITES easy, simple, straightforward.
procedure • noun COURSE OF ACTION, line of action, policy, series of steps, method, system, strategy, way, approach, formula, mechanism, methodology, MO (modus operandi), technique; routine, drill, practice.
proceed • verb 1 *she was uncertain how to proceed* BEGIN, make a start, get going, move, set something in motion; TAKE ACTION, act, go on, go ahead, make progress, make headway. 2 *he proceeded down the road* GO, make one's way, advance, move, progress, carry on, press on, push on. 3 *we should proceed with the talks* GO AHEAD, carry on, go on, continue, keep on, get on, get ahead; pursue, prosecute. 4 *there is not enough evidence to proceed against him* TAKE SOMEONE TO COURT, start/take proceedings against, start an action against, sue. 5 *all power proceeds from God* ORIGINATE, spring, stem, come, derive, arise, issue, flow, emanate.
– OPPOSITES stop.
proceedings • plural noun 1 *the evening's proceedings* EVENTS, activities, happenings, goings-on, doings. 2 *the proceedings of the meeting* REPORT, transactions, minutes, account, record(s); annals, archives. 3 *legal proceedings* LEGAL ACTION, court/judicial proceedings, litigation; lawsuit, case, prosecution.
proceeds • plural noun PROFITS, earnings, receipts, returns, takings, income, revenue; *Sport* gate (money/receipts); *N. Amer.* take.
process • noun 1 *investigation is a long process* PROCEDURE, operation, action, activity, exercise, affair, business, job, task, undertaking. 2 *a new canning process* METHOD, system, technique, means, practice, way, approach, methodology.
• verb *applications are processed rapidly* DEAL WITH, attend to, see to, sort out, handle, take care of, action.
– PHRASES **in the process of** IN THE MIDDLE OF, in the course of, in the midst of, in the throes of, busy with, occupied in/with, taken up with/by, involved in.
procession • noun 1 *a procession through the town* PARADE, march, march past, cavalcade, motorcade, cortège; column, file, train. 2 *a procession of dance routines* SERIES, succession, stream, string, sequence, run.
proclaim • verb 1 *messengers proclaimed the good news* DECLARE, announce, pronounce, state, make known, give out, advertise, publish, broadcast, promulgate, trumpet, blazon. 2 *the men proclaimed their innocence* ASSERT, declare, profess, maintain, protest. 3 *he proclaimed himself president* DECLARE, pronounce, announce. 4 *cheap paint soon proclaims its cheapness* DEMONSTRATE, indicate, show, reveal, manifest, betray, testify to, signify.
proclamation • noun DECLARATION, announcement, pronouncement, statement, notification, publication, broadcast, promulgation, blazoning; assertion, profession, protestation; DECREE, order, edict, ruling.
proclivity • noun INCLINATION, tendency, leaning, disposition, proneness, propensity, bent, bias, penchant, predisposition; predilection, partiality, liking, preference, taste, fondness, weakness.
procrastinate • verb DELAY, put off doing something, postpone action, defer action, be dilatory, use delaying tactics, stall, temporize, drag one's feet/heels, take one's time, play for time, play a waiting game.

woman as a prostitute for another person. **2** Law a person who causes someone to do something or something to happen.

Prod (also **Proddie**, **Proddy**) ● **noun** informal, offensive (especially in Ireland) a Protestant.
– ORIGIN abbreviation representing a pronunciation.

prod ● **verb** (**prodded**, **prodding**) **1** poke with a finger or pointed object. **2** stimulate or persuade to do something. ● **noun** **1** a poke. **2** a stimulus or reminder. **3** a pointed implement, typically used as a goad.
– ORIGIN perhaps symbolic, or a blend of POKE[1] and dialect *brod* 'to goad, prod'.

prodigal ● **adjective** **1** wastefully extravagant. **2** lavish. ● **noun** **1** a prodigal person. **2** (also **prodigal son**) a person who leaves home to lead a prodigal life but returns repentant. [ORIGIN with allusion to the parable in the Gospel of Luke, chapter 15.]
– DERIVATIVES **prodigality** noun **prodigally** adverb.
– ORIGIN Latin *prodigalis*, from *prodigus* 'lavish'.

prodigious /prədijəss/ ● **adjective** impressively large.
– DERIVATIVES **prodigiously** adverb.
– ORIGIN Latin *prodigiosus*, from *prodigium* 'portent'.

prodigy ● **noun** (pl. **prodigies**) **1** a person, especially a young one, with exceptional abilities. **2** an outstanding example of a quality. **3** an amazing or unusual thing: *omens and prodigies*.
– ORIGIN Latin *prodigium* 'portent'.

produce ● **verb** /prədyōōss/ **1** make, manufacture, or create. **2** cause to happen or exist. **3** show or provide for inspection or use. **4** administer the financial and managerial aspects of (a film or broadcast) or the staging of (a play). **5** supervise the making of (a musical recording). ● **noun** /prodyōōss/ things that have been produced or grown: *dairy produce*.
– DERIVATIVES **producer** noun **producible** adjective.
– ORIGIN Latin *producere* 'bring forth, extend, produce'.

product ● **noun** **1** an article or substance manufactured for sale. **2** a result of an action or process. **3** a substance produced during a natural, chemical, or manufacturing process. **4** Mathematics a quantity obtained by multiplying quantities together.
– ORIGIN Latin *productum* 'something produced'.

production ● **noun** **1** the action of producing or the process of being produced. **2** the amount of something produced. **3** a film, record, or play, viewed in terms of its making or staging.

production line ● **noun** an assembly line.

productive ● **adjective** **1** producing or able to produce large amounts of goods or crops. **2** achieving or producing a significant amount or result.
– DERIVATIVES **productively** adverb **productiveness** noun.

productivity ● **noun** **1** the state or quality of being productive. **2** the effectiveness of productive effort.

product placement ● **noun** a practice in which companies pay for their products to be featured in films and television programmes.

profane ● **adjective** **1** secular rather than religious. **2** not respectful of religious practice. **3** (of language) blasphemous or obscene. ● **verb** treat with irreverence.
– DERIVATIVES **profanation** noun.
– ORIGIN Latin *profanus* 'outside the temple, not sacred'.

profanity ● **noun** (pl. **profanities**) **1** profane language or behaviour. **2** an oath or swear word.

profess ● **verb** **1** claim that one has (a quality or feeling). **2** affirm one's faith in or allegiance to (a religion).
– ORIGIN Latin *profiteri* 'declare publicly'.

Thesaurus

procreate ● **verb** PRODUCE OFFSPRING, reproduce, multiply, propagate, breed.

procure ● **verb** **1** *he managed to procure a coat* OBTAIN, acquire, get, find, come by, secure, pick up; buy, purchase; *informal* get hold of, get one's hands on. **2** *the police found that he was procuring* PIMP; *Brit. informal* ponce.

prod ● **verb** **1** *Cassie prodded him in the chest* POKE, jab, dig, elbow, butt, stab. **2** *they hoped to prod the government into action* SPUR, stimulate, stir, rouse, prompt, drive, galvanize; persuade, urge, chivvy; incite, goad, egg on, provoke.
● **noun** **1** *a prod in the ribs* POKE, jab, dig, elbow, butt, thrust. **2** *they need a prod to get them to do act* STIMULUS, push, prompt, reminder, spur; incitement, goad.

prodigal ● **adjective** **1** *prodigal habits die hard* WASTEFUL, extravagant, spendthrift, profligate, improvident, imprudent. **2** *a composer who is prodigal with his talents* GENEROUS, lavish, liberal, unstinting, unsparing; *poetic/literary* bounteous. **3** *a dessert prodigal with whipped cream* ABOUNDING IN, abundant in, rich in, covered in, awash with.
– OPPOSITES thrifty, mean, deficient.

prodigious ● **adjective** ENORMOUS, huge, colossal, immense, vast, great, massive, gigantic, mammoth, tremendous, inordinate, monumental; amazing, astonishing, astounding, staggering, stunning, remarkable, phenomenal, terrific, miraculous, impressive, striking, startling, sensational, spectacular, extraordinary, exceptional, breathtaking, incredible; *informal* humongous, stupendous, fantastic, fabulous, mega, awesome; *Brit. informal* ginormous; *poetic/literary* wondrous.
– OPPOSITES small, unexceptional.

prodigy ● **noun** **1** *a seven-year-old prodigy* GENIUS, mastermind, virtuoso, wunderkind, wonder child; *informal* whizz-kid, whizz, wizard. **2** *Germany seemed a prodigy of industrial discipline* MODEL, classic example, paragon, paradigm, epitome, exemplar, archetype.

produce ● **verb** **1** *the company produces furniture* MANUFACTURE, make, construct, build, fabricate, put together, assemble, turn out, create; mass-produce; *informal* churn out. **2** *the vineyards produce excellent wines* YIELD, grow, give, supply, provide, furnish, bear, bring forth. **3** *she produced ten puppies* GIVE BIRTH TO, bear, deliver, bring forth, bring into the world. **4** *he produced five novels* CREATE, originate, fashion, turn out; compose, write, pen; paint. **5** *she produced an ID card* PULL OUT, extract, fish out; present, offer, proffer, show. **6** *no evidence was produced* PRESENT, offer, provide, furnish, advance, put forward, bring forward, come up with. **7** *that will produce a reaction* GIVE RISE TO, bring about, cause, occasion, generate, engender, lead to, result in, effect, induce, set off; provoke, precipitate, breed, spark off, trigger; *poetic/literary* beget. **8** *James produced the play* STAGE, put on, mount, present.
– RELATED TERMS -facient, -genic.
● **noun** *fresh produce* FOOD, foodstuff(s), products; harvest, crops, fruit, vegetables, greens; *Brit.* greengrocery.

producer ● **noun** **1** *a car producer* MANUFACTURER, maker, builder, constructor, fabricator. **2** *coffee producers* GROWER, farmer. **3** *the producer of the show* IMPRESARIO, manager, administrator, promoter, regisseur.

product ● **noun** **1** *a household product* ARTEFACT, commodity, manufactured article; creation, invention; (**products**) goods, wares, merchandise, produce. **2** *his skill is a product of experience* RESULT, consequence, outcome, effect, upshot, fruit, by-product, spin-off.

production ● **noun** **1** *the production of cars* MANUFACTURE, making, construction, building, fabrication, assembly, creation; mass-production. **2** *the production of literary works* CREATION, origination, fashioning; composition, writing. **3** *literary productions* WORK, opus, creation; publication, composition, piece; work of art, painting, picture. **4** *agricultural production* OUTPUT, yield; productivity. **5** *admission only on production of a ticket* PRESENTATION, proffering, showing. **6** *a theatre production* PERFORMANCE, staging, presentation, show, piece, play.

productive ● **adjective** **1** *a productive artist* PROLIFIC, inventive, creative; energetic. **2** *productive talks* USEFUL, constructive, profitable, fruitful, gainful, valuable, effective, worthwhile, helpful. **3** *productive land* FERTILE, fruitful, rich, fecund.
– OPPOSITES sterile, barren.

productivity ● **noun** **1** *workers have boosted productivity* EFFICIENCY, work rate; output, yield, production. **2** *the productivity of the soil* FRUITFULNESS, fertility, richness, fecundity.
– OPPOSITES sterility, barrenness.

profane ● **adjective** **1** *subjects both sacred and profane* SECULAR, lay, non-religious, temporal; *formal* laic. **2** *a profane man* IRREVERENT, irreligious, ungodly, godless, unbelieving, impious, disrespectful, sacrilegious. **3** *profane language* OBSCENE, blasphemous, indecent, foul, vulgar, crude, filthy, dirty, smutty, coarse, rude, offensive, indecorous.
– OPPOSITES religious, sacred, reverent, decorous.
● **verb** *invaders profaned our temples* DESECRATE, violate, defile, treat sacrilegiously.

profanity ● **noun** **1** *he hissed a profanity | an outburst of profanity* OATH, swear word, expletive, curse, obscenity, four-letter word, dirty word; blasphemy, swearing, foul language, bad language, cursing; *informal* cuss, cuss word; *formal* imprecation; *archaic* execration. **2** *some traditional festivals were tainted with profanity* SACRILEGE, blasphemy, irreligion, ungodliness, impiety, irreverence,

p

professed ● adjective **1** (of a quality or feeling) claimed openly but often falsely. **2** self-acknowledged.
– DERIVATIVES **professedly** adverb.

profession ● noun **1** a paid occupation, especially one involving training and a formal qualification. **2** (treated as sing. or pl.) a body of people engaged in a profession. **3** an open but typically false claim. **4** a declaration of belief in a religion.
– PHRASES **the oldest profession** humorous prostitution.

professional ● adjective **1** relating to or belonging to a profession. **2** engaged in an activity as a paid occupation rather than as an amateur. **3** worthy of or appropriate to a professional person; competent. ● noun **1** a professional person. **2** a person having impressive competence in a particular activity.
– DERIVATIVES **professionalize** (also **professionalise**) verb **professionally** adverb.

professional foul ● noun (especially in soccer) a deliberate foul to deprive an opponent of an advantage.

professionalism ● noun the competence or skill expected of a professional.

professor ● noun **1** a university academic of the highest rank. **2** N. Amer. a university teacher. **3** a person who affirms a faith in or allegiance to something.
– DERIVATIVES **professorial** adjective **professorship** noun.
– ORIGIN Latin.

proffer ● verb offer for acceptance.
– ORIGIN Old French *proffrir*, from Latin *pro-* 'before' + *offerre* 'to offer'.

proficient ● adjective competent; skilled.
– DERIVATIVES **proficiency** noun **proficiently** adverb.
– ORIGIN from Latin *proficere* 'to advance'.

profile ● noun **1** an outline of something, especially a face, as seen from one side. **2** a short descriptive article about someone. **3** the extent to which a person or organization attracts public notice: *her high profile as an opera star.* ● verb **1** describe in a short article. **2** (**be profiled**) appear in outline.
– PHRASES **in profile** as seen from one side. **keep a low profile** remain inconspicuous.
– DERIVATIVES **profiler** noun.
– ORIGIN obsolete Italian *profilo* 'a drawing or border', from *profilare*, from Latin *filum* 'thread'.

profiling ● noun the analysis of a person's psychological and behavioural characteristics.

profit ● noun **1** a financial gain, especially the difference between an initial outlay and the subsequent amount earned. **2** advantage; benefit. ● verb (**profited**, **profiting**) benefit, especially financially.
– DERIVATIVES **profitless** adjective.
– ORIGIN Latin *profectus* 'progress, profit', from *proficere* 'to advance'.

profitable ● adjective **1** (of a business or activity) yielding profit or financial gain. **2** beneficial; useful: *he'd had a profitable day.*
– DERIVATIVES **profitability** noun **profitably** adverb.

profit and loss account ● noun an account to which incomes and gains are credited and expenses and losses debited, so as to show the net profit or loss.

profiteer ● verb (often as noun **profiteering**) make an excessive or unfair profit. ● noun a person who profiteers.

profiterole ● noun a small ball of choux pastry filled with cream and covered with chocolate sauce.
– ORIGIN French, 'small profit'.

profit margin ● noun the amount by which revenue from sales exceeds costs in a business.

profit-sharing ● noun a system in which the people who work for a company receive a direct share of its profits.

profligate /profligət/ ● adjective **1** recklessly extravagant or wasteful. **2** licentious; dissolute. ● noun a profligate person.
– DERIVATIVES **profligacy** noun.
– ORIGIN Latin *profligatus* 'dissolute', from *profligare* 'overthrow, ruin'.

pro forma /prō formə/ ● adverb as a matter of form or polite-

Thesaurus

disrespect.

profess ● verb **1** *he professed his love* DECLARE, announce, proclaim, assert, state, affirm, avow, maintain, protest; *formal* aver. **2** *she professed to loathe publicity* CLAIM, pretend, purport, affect; make out; *informal* let on. **3** *the Emperor professed Christianity* AFFIRM ONE'S FAITH IN, affirm one's allegiance to, avow, confess.

professed ● adjective **1** *his professed ambition* CLAIMED, supposed, ostensible, self-styled, apparent, pretended, purported. **2** *a professed Christian* DECLARED, self-acknowledged, self-confessed, confessed, sworn, avowed, confirmed.

profession ● noun **1** *his chosen profession of teaching* CAREER, occupation, calling, vocation, métier, line (of work), walk of life, job, business, trade, craft; *informal* racket. **2** *a profession of allegiance* DECLARATION, affirmation, statement, announcement, proclamation, assertion, avowal, vow, claim, protestation; *formal* averment.

professional ● adjective **1** *people in professional occupations* WHITE-COLLAR, non-manual. **2** *a professional cricketer* PAID, salaried. **3** *a thoroughly professional performance* EXPERT, accomplished, skilful, masterly, masterful, fine, polished, skilled, proficient, competent, able, experienced, practised, trained, seasoned, businesslike, deft; *informal* ace, crack, top-notch. **4** *not a professional way to behave* APPROPRIATE, fitting, proper, honourable, ethical, correct, comme il faut.
– OPPOSITES manual, amateur, amateurish, inappropriate, unethical.
● noun **1** *affluent young professionals* WHITE-COLLAR WORKER, office worker. **2** *his first season as a professional* PROFESSIONAL PLAYER, paid player, salaried player; *informal* pro. **3** *she was a real professional on stage* EXPERT, virtuoso, old hand, master, maestro, past master; *informal* pro, ace, wizard, whizz, hotshot; *Brit. informal* dab hand; *N. Amer. informal* maven, crackerjack.
– OPPOSITES manual worker, amateur.

professor ● noun holder of a chair, head of faculty, head of department; *N. Amer.* full professor; *informal* prof.

proffer ● verb OFFER, tender, submit, extend, volunteer, suggest, propose, put forward; hold out.
– OPPOSITES refuse, withdraw.

proficiency ● noun SKILL, expertise, experience, accomplishment, competence, mastery, prowess, professionalism, deftness, adroitness, dexterity, finesse, ability, facility; *informal* know-how.
– OPPOSITES incompetence.

proficient ● adjective SKILLED, skilful, expert, experienced, accomplished, competent, masterly, adept, adroit, deft, dexterous, able, professional, consummate, complete, master; *informal* crack, ace, mean.
– OPPOSITES incompetent.

profile ● noun **1** *his handsome profile* SIDE VIEW, outline, silhouette, contour, shape, form, figure, lines. **2** *she wrote a profile of the organization* DESCRIPTION, account, study, portrait, portrayal, depiction, rundown, sketch, outline.
● verb *he was profiled in the Irish Times* DESCRIBE, write about, give an account of, portray, depict, sketch, outline.
– PHRASES **keep a low profile** LIE LOW, keep quiet, keep out of the public eye, avoid publicity, keep out of sight.

profit ● noun **1** *the firm made a profit* (FINANCIAL) GAIN, return(s), yield, proceeds, earnings, winnings, surplus, excess; *informal* pay dirt, bottom line. **2** *there was little profit in going on* ADVANTAGE, benefit, value, use, good, avail; *informal* mileage.
– OPPOSITES loss, disadvantage.
● verb **1** *the company will not profit from the disposal* MAKE MONEY, make a profit; *informal* rake it in, clean up, make a packet, make a killing, make a bundle; *N. Amer. informal* make big bucks, make a fast/quick buck. **2** *how will that profit us?* BENEFIT, be beneficial to, be of benefit to, be advantageous to, be of advantage to, be of use to, be of value to, do someone good, help, be of service to, serve, assist, aid.
– OPPOSITES lose, disadvantage.
– PHRASES **profit by/from** BENEFIT FROM, take advantage of, derive benefit from, capitalize on, make the most of, turn to one's advantage, put to good use, do well out of, exploit, gain from; *informal* cash in on.

profitable ● adjective **1** *a profitable company* MONEYMAKING, profit-making, commercial, successful, money-spinning, solvent, in the black, gainful, remunerative, financially rewarding, paying, lucrative, bankable. **2** *profitable study* BENEFICIAL, useful, advantageous, valuable, productive, worthwhile; rewarding, fruitful, illuminating, informative, well spent.
– OPPOSITES loss-making, fruitless, useless.

profiteer ● verb *a shopkeeper was charged with profiteering* OVERCHARGE, racketeer; cheat someone, fleece someone; *informal* rip someone off, rob someone.
● noun *he was a war profiteer* RACKETEER, exploiter, black marketeer; *informal* bloodsucker.

p

ness. ● **adjective** done or produced as a matter of form. ● **noun** a standard document or form.
– ORIGIN Latin.
profound ● **adjective** (**profounder**, **profoundest**) **1** very great or intense. **2** showing great knowledge or insight. **3** demanding deep study or thought. **4** archaic very deep.
– DERIVATIVES **profoundly** adverb **profoundness** noun **profundity** noun.
– ORIGIN Latin *profundus* 'deep'.
profuse ● **adjective 1** plentiful; abundant. **2** archaic extravagant.
– DERIVATIVES **profusely** adverb **profuseness** noun **profusion** noun.
– ORIGIN Latin *profusus* 'lavish, spread out'.
progenitive ● **adjective** formal able to produce offspring.
progenitor /prōjennitər/ ● **noun 1** an ancestor or parent. **2** the originator of an artistic, political, or intellectual movement.
– DERIVATIVES **progenitorial** adjective.
– ORIGIN Latin, from *progignere* 'beget'.
progeniture /prōjennichər/ ● **noun** formal **1** the production of offspring. **2** offspring.
progeny /projini/ ● **noun** (treated as sing. or pl.) offspring.
– ORIGIN Old French *progenie*, from Latin *progignere* 'beget'.
progeria /prōjeeriə/ ● **noun** Medicine a rare syndrome in children characterized by physical symptoms suggestive of premature old age.
– ORIGIN from Greek *progērōs* 'prematurely old'.
progesterone /prəjestərōn/ ● **noun** Biochemistry a steroid hormone released by the corpus luteum that stimulates the uterus to prepare for pregnancy.
progestogen /prəjestəjən/ ● **noun** Biochemistry a steroid hormone that maintains pregnancy and prevents further ovulation.
prognathous /prognaythoss/ ● **adjective** (of a jaw or chin) projecting.
– ORIGIN from PRO-² + Greek *gnathos* 'jaw'.
prognosis /prognōsiss/ ● **noun** (pl. **prognoses** /prognōseez/) a forecast, especially of the likely course of a disease or ailment.
– ORIGIN Greek, from *pro-* 'before' + *gignōskein* 'know'.
prognostic /prognostik/ ● **adjective** predicting the likely course of a disease or ailment.
– DERIVATIVES **prognostically** adverb.
prognosticate ● **verb** foretell; prophesy.
– DERIVATIVES **prognostication** noun **prognosticator** noun.
prograde /prōgrayd/ ● **adjective** chiefly Astronomy proceeding in the normal direction; not retrograde.
– ORIGIN from PRO-¹ + RETROGRADE.
programmatic ● **adjective** of the nature of or according to a programme, schedule, or method.
– DERIVATIVES **programmatically** adverb.
programme (US **program**) ● **noun 1** a planned series of events. **2** a radio or television broadcast. **3** a set of related measures or activities with a long-term aim. **4** a sheet or booklet detailing items or performers at an event. **5** (**program**) a series of coded software instructions to control the operation of a computer or other machine. ● **verb** (**programmed**, **programming**; US **programed**, **programing**) **1** (**program**) provide (a computer) with a program. **2** cause to behave in a predetermined way. **3** arrange according to a plan or schedule.
– DERIVATIVES **programmable** adjective **programmer** noun.
– ORIGIN Greek *programma*, from *prographein* 'write publicly'.
programme music ● **noun** music intended to evoke images or tell a story.
progress ● **noun 1** forward movement towards a destination. **2** development towards a better, more complete, or more modern condition. **3** Brit. archaic a state journey or official tour. ● **verb** move or develop towards a destination or a more advanced condition.
– ORIGIN Latin *progressus* 'an advance', from *progredi* 'move forward'.
progression ● **noun 1** a gradual movement or development towards a destination or a more advanced state. **2** a succession. **3** a sequence of numbers following a mathematical rule.
– DERIVATIVES **progressional** adjective.
progressive ● **adjective 1** proceeding gradually or in stages. **2** favouring innovation or social reform. **3** (of tax) increasing as a proportion of the sum taxed as that sum increases. **4** (of a card game or dance) involving successive changes of partner. **5** archaic engaging in or constituting forward motion. ● **noun** a person advocating social reform.
– DERIVATIVES **progressively** adverb **progressiveness** noun.

Thesaurus

profligate ● **adjective 1** *profligate local authorities* WASTEFUL, extravagant, spendthrift, improvident, prodigal. **2** *a profligate lifestyle* DISSOLUTE, degenerate, dissipated, debauched, corrupt, depraved; PROMISCUOUS, loose, wanton, licentious, libertine, decadent, abandoned, fast; SYBARITIC, voluptuary.
– OPPOSITES thrifty, frugal, moral, upright.
● **noun** *he was an out-and-out profligate* LIBERTINE, debauchee, degenerate, dissolute, roué, rake, loose-liver; sybarite, voluptuary; *dated* rip.
profound ● **adjective 1** *profound relief* HEARTFELT, intense, keen, great, extreme, acute, severe, sincere, earnest, deep, deep-seated, overpowering, overwhelming, fervent, ardent. **2** *profound silence* COMPLETE, utter, total, absolute. **3** *a profound change* FAR-REACHING, radical, extensive, sweeping, exhaustive, thoroughgoing. **4** *a profound analysis* WISE, learned, clever, intelligent, scholarly, sage, erudite, discerning, penetrating, perceptive, astute, thoughtful, insightful, percipient, perspicacious; *rare* sapient. **5** *profound truths* COMPLEX, abstract, deep, weighty, difficult, abstruse, recondite, esoteric.
– OPPOSITES superficial, mild, slight, simple.
profuse ● **adjective 1** *profuse apologies* COPIOUS, prolific, abundant, liberal, unstinting, fulsome, effusive, extravagant, lavish, gushing; *informal* over the top, gushy. **2** *profuse blooms* LUXURIANT, plentiful, copious, abundant, lush, rich, exuberant, riotous, teeming, rank, rampant; *informal* jungly.
– OPPOSITES meagre, sparse.
profusion ● **noun** ABUNDANCE, mass, host, cornucopia, riot, plethora, superabundance; *informal* sea, wealth; *formal* plenitude.
progenitor ● **noun 1** *the progenitor of an illustrious family* ANCESTOR, forefather, forebear, parent, primogenitor; *Law* stirps; *archaic* begetter. **2** *the progenitor of modern jazz* ORIGINATOR, creator, founder, architect, inventor, pioneer.
progeny ● **noun** OFFSPRING, young, babies, children, sons and daughters, family, brood; DESCENDANTS, heirs, scions; *Law* issue; *archaic* seed, fruit of one's loins.
prognosis ● **noun** FORECAST, prediction, prognostication, prophecy, divination, augury.
prognosticate ● **verb** FORECAST, predict, prophesy, foretell, foresee, forewarn of.
prognostication ● **noun** PREDICTION, forecast, prophecy, prognosis, divination, augury.
programme ● **noun 1** *our programme for the day* SCHEDULE, agenda, calendar, timetable; order of events, line-up. **2** *the government's reform programme* SCHEME, plan of action, series of measures, strategy. **3** *a television programme* BROADCAST, production, show, presentation, transmission, performance, telecast; *informal* prog. **4** *a programme of study* COURSE, syllabus, curriculum. **5** *a theatre programme* GUIDE, list of performers; *N. Amer.* playbill.
● **verb** *they programmed the day well* ARRANGE, organize, schedule, plan, map out, timetable, line up; *N. Amer.* slate.
progress ● **noun 1** *boulders made progress difficult* FORWARD MOVEMENT, advance, going, progression, headway, passage. **2** *scientific progress* DEVELOPMENT, advance, advancement, headway, step(s) forward; improvement, betterment, growth.
– OPPOSITES relapse.
● **verb 1** *they progressed slowly down the road* GO, make one's way, move, move forward, go forward, proceed, advance, go on, continue, make headway, work one's way. **2** *the school has progressed rapidly* DEVELOP, make progress, advance, make headway, take steps forward, move on, get on, gain ground; improve, get better, come on, come along, make strides; thrive, prosper, blossom, flourish; *informal* be getting there.
– OPPOSITES relapse.
– PHRASES **in progress** UNDER WAY, going on, ongoing, happening, occurring, taking place, proceeding, continuing; unfinished, on the stocks; *N. Amer.* in the works.
progression ● **noun 1** *progression to the next stage* PROGRESS, advancement, movement, passage, march; development, evolution, growth. **2** *a progression of peaks on the graph* SUCCESSION, series, sequence, string, stream, chain, concatenation, train, row, cycle.
progressive ● **adjective 1** *progressive deterioration* CONTINUING, continuous, increasing, growing, developing, ongoing, accelerating, escalating; gradual, step-by-step, cumulative. **2** *progressive views* MODERN, liberal, advanced, forward-thinking, enlightened, enterprising, innovative, pioneering, dynamic, bold, avant-garde, reforming, reformist, radical; *informal* go-ahead.

prohibit ● verb (**prohibited**, **prohibiting**) **1** formally forbid by law, rule, etc. **2** make impossible; prevent.
– DERIVATIVES **prohibitory** adjective.
– ORIGIN Latin *prohibere* 'keep in check'.

prohibition /prōhibish'n, prō-i-/ ● noun **1** the action of prohibiting. **2** an order that forbids. **3** (**Prohibition**) the prevention by law of the manufacture and sale of alcohol in the US from 1920 to 1933.
– DERIVATIVES **Prohibitionist** noun.

prohibitive ● adjective **1** serving to forbid, restrict, or prevent. **2** (of a price or charge) excessively high.
– DERIVATIVES **prohibitively** adverb.

project ● noun **1** an enterprise carefully planned to achieve a particular aim. **2** a piece of research work by a school or college student. **3** N. Amer. a government-subsidized estate or block of homes. ● verb **1** estimate or forecast on the basis of present trends. **2** plan. **3** extend outwards beyond something else; protrude. **4** throw or cause to move forward or outward. **5** cause (light, shadow, or an image) to fall on a surface. **6** present, promote, or display (a view or image). **7** (**project on to**) attribute (an emotion) to (another person), especially unconsciously. **8** Geometry draw straight lines through (a figure) to produce a corresponding figure on a surface or line. **9** represent (the earth's surface, the heavens, etc.) on a plane surface.
– ORIGIN Latin *projectum* 'something prominent', from *proicere* 'throw forth'.

projectile ● noun a missile fired or thrown at a target. ● adjective **1** relating to a projectile. **2** propelled with great force.

projection ● noun **1** an estimate or forecast based on present trends. **2** the projecting of an image, sound, etc. **3** a mental image viewed as reality. **4** the unconscious transfer of one's own desires or emotions to another person. **5** a protruding thing. **6** a map or diagram made by projecting a given figure, area, etc.
– DERIVATIVES **projective** adjective **projectionist** noun.

projector ● noun an apparatus for projecting slides or film on to a screen.

prokaryote /prōkarriət/ ● noun Biology a single-celled organism with neither a distinct nucleus with a membrane nor other specialized structures (i.e. the bacteria and archaea). Compare with EUKARYOTE.
– DERIVATIVES **prokaryotic** adjective.
– ORIGIN from PRO-² + Greek *karuon* 'nut, kernel'.

prolactin /prōlaktin/ ● noun Biochemistry a hormone from the pituitary gland stimulating milk production after childbirth.

prolapse ● noun /prōlaps/ **1** a slipping forward or down of a part or organ of the body. **2** a prolapsed part or organ. ● verb /prōlaps/ undergo prolapse.
– ORIGIN from Latin *prolabi* 'slip forward'.

prolate /prōlayt/ ● adjective Geometry (of a spheroid) lengthened in the direction of a polar diameter. Often contrasted with OBLATE¹.
– ORIGIN Latin *prolatus* 'carried forward'.

prole informal, derogatory ● noun a member of the working class. ● adjective working class.
– ORIGIN abbreviation of PROLETARIAT.

prolegomenon /prōligomminən/ ● noun (pl. **prolegomena**) a critical or discursive introduction to a book.
– ORIGIN Greek, from *prolegein* 'say beforehand'.

prolepsis /prōlepsiss/ ● noun (pl. **prolepses** /prōlepseez/) **1** Rhetoric the anticipation and answering of possible objections. **2** the representation of something as happening before it actually does, as in *he was a dead man when he entered*.
– ORIGIN Greek, from *prolambanein* 'anticipate'.

proletarian /prōlitairiən/ ● adjective relating to the proletariat. ● noun a member of the proletariat.
– ORIGIN Latin *proletarius* (from *proles* 'offspring'), denoting a person without wealth, who served the state only by producing offspring.

proletariat ● noun (treated as sing. or pl.) **1** workers or working-class people. **2** the lowest class of citizens in ancient Rome.

pro-life ● adjective seeking to ban abortion and euthanasia.
– DERIVATIVES **pro-lifer** noun.

proliferate /prəliffərayt/ ● verb reproduce rapidly; increase rapidly in number.
– DERIVATIVES **proliferation** noun **proliferative** adjective.
– ORIGIN from Latin *prolificus* (see PROLIFIC).

prolific ● adjective **1** producing much fruit or foliage or many offspring. **2** (of an artist, author, etc.) producing many works. **3** plentiful.
– DERIVATIVES **prolifically** adverb.
– ORIGIN Latin *prolificus*, from *proles* 'offspring'.

proline /prōleen/ ● noun Biochemistry an amino acid which is a constituent of most proteins, especially collagen.
– ORIGIN contraction of the chemical name *pyrrolidine*-2-carboxylic acid.

prolix /prōliks/ ● adjective (of speech or writing) tediously lengthy.
– DERIVATIVES **prolixity** noun **prolixly** adverb.
– ORIGIN Latin *prolixus* 'poured forth, extended'.

prologue (US **prolog**) ● noun **1** an introductory section or scene in a literary, dramatic, or musical work. **2** an event or action

Thesaurus

– OPPOSITES conservative, reactionary.
● noun *he is very much a progressive* INNOVATOR, reformer, reformist, liberal, libertarian.

prohibit ● verb **1** *state law prohibits gambling* FORBID, ban, bar, interdict, proscribe, make illegal, embargo, outlaw, disallow, veto; Law enjoin. **2** *a cash shortage prohibited the visit* PREVENT, stop, rule out, preclude, make impossible.
– OPPOSITES allow.

prohibited ● adjective ILLEGAL, illicit, against the law, verboten; Islam haram; informal not on, out, no go; formal non licet.
– OPPOSITES permitted.

prohibition ● noun **1** *the prohibition of cannabis* BANNING, forbidding, prohibiting, barring, debarment, vetoing, proscription, interdiction, outlawing. **2** *a prohibition was imposed* BAN, bar, interdict, veto, embargo, injunction, moratorium.

prohibitive ● adjective **1** *prohibitive costs* EXCESSIVELY HIGH, sky-high, over-inflated; out of the question, beyond one's means; extortionate, unreasonable, exorbitant; informal steep, criminal. **2** *prohibitive regulations* PROSCRIPTIVE, prohibitory, restrictive, repressive.

project ● noun **1** *an engineering project* SCHEME, plan, programme, enterprise, undertaking, venture; proposal, idea, concept. **2** *a history project* ASSIGNMENT, piece of work, piece of research, task.
● verb **1** *profits are projected to rise* FORECAST, predict, expect, estimate, calculate, reckon. **2** *his projected book* INTEND, plan, propose, devise, design, outline. **3** *balconies projected over the lake* STICK OUT, jut (out), protrude, extend, stand out, bulge out, poke out, thrust out, cantilever. **4** *seeds are projected from the tree* PROPEL, discharge, launch, throw, cast, fling, hurl, shoot. **5** *the sun projected his shadow on the wall* CAST, throw, send, shed, shine. **6** *she tried to project a calm image* CONVEY, put across, put over, communicate, present, promote.

projectile ● noun MISSILE, brickbat; rocket, bomb.

projecting ● adjective STICKING OUT, protuberant, protruding, prominent, jutting, overhanging, proud, bulging; informal sticky-out.
– OPPOSITES sunken, flush.

projection ● noun **1** *a sales projection* FORECAST, prediction, prognosis, expectation, estimate. **2** *tiny projections on the cliff face* PROTUBERANCE, protrusion, sticking-out bit, prominence, eminence, outcrop, outgrowth, jut, jag, snag; overhang, ledge, shelf; informal sticky-out bit.

proletarian ● adjective *a proletarian background* WORKING-CLASS, plebeian, cloth-cap, common.
– OPPOSITES aristocratic.
● noun *disaffected proletarians* WORKING-CLASS PERSON, worker, plebeian, commoner, man/woman/person in the street; derogatory prole.
– OPPOSITES aristocrat.

proletariat ● noun THE WORKERS, working-class people, wage-earners, the labouring classes, the common people, the lower classes, the masses, the commonalty, the rank and file, the third estate, the plebeians; derogatory the hoi polloi, the plebs, the proles, the great unwashed, the mob, the rabble.
– OPPOSITES aristocracy.

proliferate ● verb INCREASE RAPIDLY, grow rapidly, multiply, rocket, mushroom, snowball, burgeon, run riot.
– OPPOSITES decrease, dwindle.

prolific ● adjective **1** *a prolific crop of tomatoes* PLENTIFUL, abundant, bountiful, profuse, copious, luxuriant, rich, lush; fruitful, fecund; poetic/literary plenteous, bounteous. **2** *a prolific composer* PRODUCTIVE, creative, inventive, fertile.

prolix ● adjective LONG-WINDED, verbose, wordy, pleonastic, discur-

leading to another.
– ORIGIN Greek *prologos*, from *pro-* 'before' + *logos* 'saying'.
prolong ● verb **1** extend the duration of. **2** technical extend in spatial length.
– DERIVATIVES **prolongation** noun.
– ORIGIN Latin *prolongare*.
prolonged ● adjective continuing for a long time; lengthy.
prom ● noun informal **1** Brit. short for PROMENADE (in sense 1). **2** Brit. a promenade concert. **3** N. Amer. a formal dance, especially one at a high school or college.
promenade /prommənaad/ ● noun **1** a paved public walk, especially one along a seafront. **2** a leisurely walk, ride, or drive in a public place. **3** N. Amer. old-fashioned term for PROM (in sense 3). ● verb take a promenade.
– ORIGIN French, from *se promener* 'to walk'.
promenade concert ● noun Brit. a concert of classical music at which part of the audience stands in an area without seating.
promenade deck ● noun an upper, open-air deck on a passenger ship.
promenader ● noun **1** a person who takes a promenade. **2** Brit. a person standing at a promenade concert.
Promethean /prəmeethiən/ ● adjective daring or skilful like Prometheus, a demigod in Greek mythology who stole fire from the gods and gave it to the human race.
promethium /prəmeethiəm/ ● noun an unstable radioactive metallic chemical element of the lanthanide series, made by high-energy collisions.
– ORIGIN named after *Prometheus* (see PROMETHEAN).
prominence ● noun **1** the state of being prominent. **2** a thing that projects or protrudes.
prominent ● adjective **1** important; famous. **2** protuberant. **3** particularly noticeable.
– DERIVATIVES **prominently** adverb.
– ORIGIN from Latin *prominere* 'jut out'.
promiscuous /prəmiskyooəss/ ● adjective **1** having or characterized by many transient sexual relationships. **2** indiscriminate or casual: *a promiscuous mixing of styles*.
– DERIVATIVES **promiscuity** noun **promiscuously** adverb.
– ORIGIN Latin *promiscuus* 'indiscriminate'.
promise ● noun **1** an assurance that one will do something or that something will happen. **2** potential excellence. ● verb **1** make a promise. **2** give good grounds for expecting. **3** (**promise oneself**) firmly intend.
– ORIGIN Latin *promissum*, from *promittere* 'put forth, promise'.
promised land ● noun **1** (**the Promised Land**) (in the Bible) the land of Canaan, promised to Abraham and his descendants (Book of Genesis, chapter 12). **2** a place or situation where great happiness is expected.
promisee ● noun Law a person to whom a promise is made.
promising ● adjective showing great potential.
– DERIVATIVES **promisingly** adverb.
promisor ● noun Law a person who makes a promise.
promissory /prommisəri/ ● adjective chiefly Law conveying or implying a promise.
promissory note ● noun a signed document containing a written promise to pay a stated sum.
promo /prōmō/ ● noun (pl. **promos**) informal a promotional film, video, etc.
promontory /prommənteri/ ● noun (pl. **promontories**) **1** a point of high land jutting out into the sea or a lake. **2** Anatomy a protuberance on an organ or other bodily structure.
– ORIGIN Latin *promontorium*, influenced by *mons* 'mountain'.
promote ● verb **1** further the progress of (a cause, venture, or aim); support. **2** publicize (a product or celebrity). **3** raise to a higher position or rank. **4** transfer (a sports team) to a higher division.
– ORIGIN Latin *promovere* 'move forward'.
promoter ● noun **1** the organizer of a sporting event or theatrical production. **2** a supporter of a cause or aim.
promotion ● noun **1** activity that supports or encourages. **2** the publicizing of a product or celebrity. **3** (**promotions**) the activity or business of organizing such publicity. **4** elevation to a higher position or rank. **5** the transfer of a sports team to a higher division.
– DERIVATIVES **promotional** adjective.
prompt ● verb **1** cause or bring about. **2** (**prompt to/to do**) cause (someone) to take a course of action. **3** assist or encour-

Thesaurus

sive, rambling, long-drawn-out, overlong, lengthy, protracted, interminable; *informal* windy; *Brit. informal* waffly.
prologue ● noun INTRODUCTION, foreword, preface, preamble, prelude; *informal* intro; *formal* exordium, proem, prolegomenon.
– OPPOSITES epilogue.
prolong ● verb LENGTHEN, extend, draw out, drag out, protract, spin out, stretch out, string out, elongate; carry on, continue, keep up, perpetuate.
– OPPOSITES shorten.
promenade ● noun **1** *the tree-lined promenade* ESPLANADE, front, seafront, parade, walk, boulevard, avenue; *N. Amer.* boardwalk; *Brit. informal* prom. **2** *our nightly promenade* WALK, stroll, turn, amble, airing; *dated* constitutional.
● verb *we promenaded in the park* WALK, stroll, saunter, wander, amble, stretch one's legs, take a turn.
prominence ● noun **1** *his rise to prominence* FAME, celebrity, eminence, pre-eminence, importance, distinction, greatness, note, notability, prestige, stature, standing, position, rank. **2** *the press gave prominence to the reports* GOOD COVERAGE, importance, precedence, weight, a high profile, top billing. **3** *a rocky prominence* HILLOCK, hill, hummock, mound; outcrop, crag, spur, rise; ridge, arête; peak, pinnacle; promontory, cliff, headland.
prominent ● adjective **1** *a prominent surgeon* IMPORTANT, well known, leading, eminent, distinguished, notable, noteworthy, noted, illustrious, celebrated, famous, renowned, acclaimed, famed, influential; *N. Amer.* major-league. **2** *prominent cheekbones* PROTUBERANT, protruding, projecting, jutting (out), standing out, sticking out, proud, bulging, bulbous. **3** *a prominent feature of the landscape* CONSPICUOUS, noticeable, easily seen, obvious, unmistakable, eye-catching, pronounced, salient, striking, dominant; obtrusive.
– OPPOSITES unimportant, unknown, inconspicuous.
promiscuity ● noun LICENTIOUSNESS, wantonness, immorality; *informal* sleeping around, sluttishness, whorishness; *dated* looseness.
– OPPOSITES chastity, virtue.
promiscuous ● adjective **1** *a promiscuous woman* LICENTIOUS, sexually indiscriminate, wanton, immoral, of easy virtue, fast; *informal* easy, swinging, sluttish, whorish; *N. Amer. informal* roundheeled; *Brit. informal* slaggy; *dated* loose, fallen; *archaic* light. **2** *promiscuous reading* INDISCRIMINATE, undiscriminating, unselective, random, haphazard, irresponsible, unthinking, unconsidered.
– OPPOSITES chaste, virtuous, selective.
promise ● noun **1** *you broke your promise* WORD (OF HONOUR), assurance, pledge, vow, guarantee, oath, bond, undertaking, agreement, commitment, contract, convenant. **2** *he shows promise* POTENTIAL, ability, aptitude, capability, capacity. **3** *a promise of fine weather* INDICATION, hint, suggestion, sign.
● verb **1** *she promised to go* GIVE ONE'S WORD, swear, pledge, vow, undertake, guarantee, contract, engage, give an assurance, commit oneself, bind oneself, swear/take an oath, covenant; *archaic* plight. **2** *the skies promised sunshine* INDICATE, lead one to expect, point to, denote, signify, be a sign of, be evidence of, give hope of, bespeak, presage, augur, herald, bode, portend; *poetic/literary* betoken, foretoken, forebode.
promising ● adjective **1** *a promising start* GOOD, encouraging, favourable, hopeful, full of promise, auspicious, propitious, bright, rosy, heartening, reassuring. **2** *a promising actor* WITH POTENTIAL, budding, up-and-coming, rising, coming, in the making.
– OPPOSITES unfavourable, hopeless.
promontory ● noun HEADLAND, point, cape, head, foreland, horn, bill, ness, naze, peninsula; *Scottish* mull.
promote ● verb **1** *she's been promoted at work* UPGRADE, give promotion to, elevate, advance, move up; *archaic* prefer. **2** *an organization promoting justlce* ENCOURAGE, further, advance, assist, aid, help, contribute to, foster, nurture, develop, boost, stimulate, forward, work for. **3** *she is promoting her new film* ADVERTISE, publicize, give publicity to, beat/bang the drum for, market, merchandise; *informal* push, plug, hype, puff, boost; *N. Amer. informal* ballyhoo, flack.
– OPPOSITES demote, obstruct, play down.
promoter ● noun ADVOCATE, champion, supporter, backer, proponent, protagonist, campaigner; *N. Amer.* booster.
promotion ● noun **1** *her promotion at work* UPGRADING, preferment, elevation, advancement, step up (the ladder). **2** *the promotion of justice* ENCOURAGEMENT, furtherance, furthering, advancement, assistance, aid, help, contribution to, fostering, boosting,

age (a hesitating speaker). **4** supply a forgotten word or line to (an actor). ● **noun 1** an act of prompting. **2** a word or phrase used in prompting an actor. **3** a prompter. **4** Computing a word or symbol on a VDU screen to show that input is required. ● **adjective** done or acting without delay. ● **adverb** Brit. exactly or punctually: *12 o'clock prompt.*
– DERIVATIVES **promptly** adverb **promptness** noun.
– ORIGIN Latin *promptus* 'brought to light', also 'prepared, ready', from *promere* 'to produce'.
prompt book ● **noun** a copy of a play used by a prompter.
prompter ● **noun** a person who prompts the actors during the performance of a play.
prompt note ● **noun** a note sent as a reminder of payment due.
promulgate /prommәlgayt/ ● **verb 1** promote or make widely known. **2** put (a law or decree) into effect by official proclamation.
– DERIVATIVES **promulgation** noun **promulgator** noun.
– ORIGIN Latin *promulgare* 'expose to public view', from *mulgere* 'cause to come forth' (literally 'to milk').
pronate /prōnayt/ ● **verb** technical put or hold (a hand, foot, or limb) with the palm or sole turned downwards. Compare with SUPINATE.
– DERIVATIVES **pronation** noun.
– ORIGIN from Latin *pronus* 'leaning forward'.
pronator ● **noun** Anatomy a muscle involved in pronation.
prone ● **adjective 1** (**prone to**/**to do**) likely or liable to suffer from, do, or experience (something unfortunate). **2** lying flat, especially face downwards. **3** archaic with a downward slope or direction.
– DERIVATIVES **proneness** noun.
– ORIGIN Latin *pronus* 'leaning forward'.
prong ● **noun 1** each of two or more projecting pointed parts on a fork or other article. **2** each of the separate parts of an attack or operation. ● **verb** pierce or stab with a fork.
– DERIVATIVES **pronged** adjective.
– ORIGIN perhaps related to Low German *prange* 'pinching instrument'.
pronghorn ● **noun** a deer-like North American mammal with black horns.
pronominal /prōnommin'l/ ● **adjective** relating to or serving as a pronoun.
– DERIVATIVES **pronominally** adverb.
pronoun ● **noun** a word used instead of a noun to indicate someone or something already mentioned or known, e.g. *I, she, this.*
pronounce /prәnownss/ ● **verb 1** make the sound of (a word or part of a word). **2** declare or announce. **3** (**pronounce on**) pass judgement or make a decision on.
– DERIVATIVES **pronounceable** adjective **pronouncement** noun **pronouncer** noun.
– ORIGIN Latin *pronuntiare*, from *nuntiare* 'announce'.
pronounced ● **adjective** very noticeable.
– DERIVATIVES **pronouncedly** adverb.
pronto ● **adverb** informal promptly.
– ORIGIN Spanish.
pronunciation /prәnunsiaysh'n/ ● **noun** the way in which a word is pronounced.
– USAGE The word **pronunciation** is often pronounced incorrectly with the second syllable rhyming with **bounce**, whereas it should be pronounced with the second syllable rhyming with **dunce**.
pro-nuncio /prōnunsiō/ ● **noun** (pl. **pro-nuncios**) a papal ambassador to a country that does not give the Pope's ambassador automatic precedence.
proof ● **noun 1** evidence establishing a fact or the truth of a statement. **2** the proving of the truth of a statement. **3** a series of stages in the resolution of a mathematical or philosophical problem. **4** archaic a test or trial. **5** Printing a trial impression of a page used for making corrections before final printing. **6** a trial photographic print. **7** a specially struck specimen coin. **8** the strength of distilled alcoholic liquor, relative to proof spirit taken as a standard of 100. ● **adjective** (in combination) resistant: *bulletproof.* ● **verb 1** make waterproof. **2** make a proof of (a printed work). **3** proofread (a text).
– PHRASES **the proof of the pudding is in the eating** proverb the real value of something can be judged only from practical experience or results.
– ORIGIN Old French *proeve*, from Latin *probare* 'to test, prove'.
proof positive ● **noun** final or absolute proof of something.
proofread ● **verb** read (printer's proofs or other material) and mark any errors.
– DERIVATIVES **proofreader** noun.
proof spirit ● **noun** a mixture of alcohol and water used as a standard of strength of distilled alcoholic liquor.
prop[1] ● **noun 1** a pole or beam used as a temporary support. **2** a source of support or assistance. **3** (also **prop forward**) Rugby a forward at either end of the front row of a scrum. ● **verb** (**propped, propping**) **1** support with a prop. **2** lean (something) against something else. **3** (**prop up**) support or assist (someone) to stop them failing or declining.
– ORIGIN probably from Dutch *proppe* 'support (for vines)'.
prop[2] ● **noun** a portable object used on the set of a play or film.
– ORIGIN abbreviation of PROPERTY.
prop[3] ● **noun** informal an aircraft propeller.
propaganda ● **noun** information, especially of a biased or mis-

Thesaurus

stimulation; N. Amer. boosterism. **3** *the promotion of her new film* ADVERTISING, publicizing, marketing; publicity, campaign, propaganda; *informal* hard sell, plug, hype, puff; N. Amer. *informal* ballyhoo.
prompt ● **verb 1** *curiosity prompted him to look* INDUCE, make, move, motivate, lead, dispose, persuade, incline, encourage, stimulate, prod, impel, spur on, inspire. **2** *the statement prompted a hostile reaction* GIVE RISE TO, bring about, cause, occasion, result in, lead to, elicit, produce, bring on, engender, induce, precipitate, trigger, spark off, provoke. **3** *the actors needed prompting* REMIND, cue, feed, help out; jog someone's memory.
– OPPOSITES deter.
● **adjective** *a prompt reply* QUICK, swift, rapid, speedy, fast, direct, immediate, instant, expeditious, early, punctual, in good time, on time, timely.
– OPPOSITES slow, late.
● **adverb** *at 3.30 prompt* EXACTLY, precisely, sharp, on the dot, dead, punctually, on the nail; *informal* bang on; N. Amer. *informal* on the button, on the nose.
● **noun** *he stopped, and Julia supplied a prompt* REMINDER, cue, feed.
promptly ● **adverb 1** *William arrived promptly at 7.30* PUNCTUALLY, on time; *informal* on the dot, bang on; Brit. *informal* spot on; N. Amer. *informal* on the button, on the nose. **2** *I expect the matter to be dealt with promptly* WITHOUT DELAY, straight away, right away, at once, immediately, now, as soon as possible; QUICKLY, swiftly, rapidly, speedily, fast, expeditiously; N. Amer. momentarily; *informal* pronto, a.s.a.p., p.d.q. (pretty damn quick).
– OPPOSITES late, slowly.
promulgate ● **verb 1** *they promulgated their own views* MAKE KNOWN, make public, publicize, spread, communicate, propagate, disseminate, broadcast, promote, preach; *poetic/literary* bruit abroad. **2** *the law was promulgated in 1942* PUT INTO EFFECT, enact, implement, enforce.
prone ● **adjective 1** *softwood is prone to rotting | prone to rot* SUSCEPTIBLE, vulnerable, subject, open, liable, given, predisposed, likely, disposed, inclined, apt; at risk of. **2** *his prone body* (LYING) FACE DOWN, face downwards, on one's stomach/front; LYING FLAT, horizontal, prostrate.
– OPPOSITES resistant, immune, upright.
prong ● **noun** TINE, spike, point, tip, projection.
pronounce ● **verb 1** *his name is difficult to pronounce* SAY, enunciate, articulate, utter, voice, sound, vocalize, get one's tongue round. **2** *the doctor pronounced that I had a virus* ANNOUNCE, proclaim, declare, affirm, assert; judge, rule, decree; *rare* asseverate.
pronounced ● **adjective** NOTICEABLE, marked, strong, conspicuous, striking, distinct, prominent, unmistakable, obvious, recognizable, identifiable.
– OPPOSITES slight.
pronouncement ● **noun** ANNOUNCEMENT, proclamation, declaration, assertion; judgement, ruling, decree; *formal* ordinance; *rare* asseveration.
pronunciation ● **noun** ACCENT, manner of speaking, speech, diction, delivery, elocution, intonation; articulation, enunciation, voicing, vocalization, sounding; *rare* orthoepy.
proof ● **noun 1** *proof of ownership* EVIDENCE, verification, corroboration, authentication, confirmation, certification, documentation, validation, attestation, substantiation. **2** *the proofs of a book* PAGE PROOF, galley proof, galley, pull, slip; revise.
● **adjective** *no system is proof against theft* RESISTANT, immune, unaffected, invulnerable, impenetrable, impervious, repellent.
prop ● **noun 1** *the roof is held up by props* POLE, post, support, up-

leading nature, used to promote a political cause or point of view.
– ORIGIN originally denoting a committee of Roman Catholic cardinals responsible for foreign missions: from Latin *congregatio de propaganda fide* 'congregation for propagation of the faith'.
propagandist chiefly derogatory ● noun a person who spreads propaganda. ● adjective consisting of or spreading propaganda.
– DERIVATIVES **propagandize** (also **propagandise**) verb.
propagate ● verb **1** breed by natural processes from the parent stock. **2** promote (an idea, knowledge, etc.) widely. **3** transmit in a particular direction.
– DERIVATIVES **propagation** noun.
– ORIGIN Latin *propagare* 'multiply from layers or shoots'.
propagator ● noun **1** a covered, heated container of earth or compost, used for germinating seedlings. **2** a person who propagates an idea, knowledge, etc.
propane /prōpayn/ ● noun a flammable hydrocarbon gas present in natural gas and used as bottled fuel.
propel ● verb (**propelled**, **propelling**) drive or push forwards.
– ORIGIN Latin *propellere* 'to drive forward'.
propellant ● noun **1** a compressed fluid in which the active contents of an aerosol are dispersed. **2** an explosive that fires bullets from a firearm. **3** a substance used to provide thrust in a rocket engine. ● adjective (also **propellent**) capable of propelling.
propeller ● noun a revolving shaft with two or more angled blades, for propelling a ship or aircraft.
propeller shaft ● noun a shaft transmitting power from an engine to a propeller or to the wheels of a vehicle.
propelling pencil ● noun a pencil with a thin lead that may be extended as the point is worn away.
propensity ● noun (pl. **propensities**) an inclination or tendency.
– ORIGIN from Latin *propensus* 'inclined'.
proper ● adjective **1** truly what something is said or regarded to be; genuine. **2** (after a noun) strictly so called: *the World Cup proper.* **3** suitable or appropriate; correct. **4** respectable, especially excessively so. **5** (**proper to**) belonging or relating exclusively to. **6** Heraldry in the natural colours. ● adverb Brit. informal or dialect thoroughly.
– ORIGIN Old French *propre*, from Latin *proprius* 'one's own, special'.
proper fraction ● noun a fraction that is less than one, with the numerator less than the denominator.
properly ● adverb **1** in a proper manner. **2** in the strict sense. **3** informal, chiefly Brit. completely.
proper noun (also **proper name**) ● noun a name for an individual person, place, or organization, having an initial capital letter.
propertied ● adjective owning property and land.
property ● noun (pl. **properties**) **1** a thing or things belonging to someone. **2** a building and the land belonging to it. **3** Law the right to the possession, use, or disposal of something; ownership. **4** a characteristic: *a perfumed oil with calming properties.* **5** old-fashioned term for PROP².
– ORIGIN Latin *proprietas*, from *proprius* 'one's own, special'.
prophecy /proffisi/ ● noun (pl. **prophecies**) **1** a prediction. **2** the faculty or practice of prophesying.
– ORIGIN Greek *prophēteia*, from *prophētēs* 'spokesman'.
prophesy /proffisī/ ● verb (**prophesies**, **prophesied**) **1** predict. **2** speak or write by divine inspiration.
prophet ● noun (fem. **prophetess**) **1** an inspired teacher or proclaimer of the will of God. **2** a person who predicts the future. **3** a person who advocates a new belief or theory.
– PHRASES **a prophet is not without honour save in his own country** proverb a person's gifts and talents are rarely appreciated by those close to him. [ORIGIN with biblical allusion to the Gospel of Matthew, chapter 13.]
– ORIGIN Greek *prophētēs* 'spokesman'.
prophetic /prəfettik/ ● adjective **1** accurately predicting the future. **2** relating to or characteristic of a prophet or prophecy.
– DERIVATIVES **prophetical** adjective **prophetically** adverb.
prophylactic /proffilaktik/ ● adjective intended to prevent disease. ● noun **1** a preventative medicine or course of action. **2** chiefly N. Amer. a condom.
– ORIGIN Greek *prophulaktikos*, from *phulassein* 'to guard'.
prophylaxis /proffilaksiss/ ● noun action taken to prevent disease.
– ORIGIN Latin, from Greek *phulaxis* 'act of guarding'.
propinquity /prəpingkwiti/ ● noun **1** nearness in time or space. **2** technical close kinship.
– ORIGIN Latin *propinquitas*, from *propinquus* 'near'.
propitiate /prəpishiayt/ ● verb win or regain the favour of; appease.
– DERIVATIVES **propitiatory** adjective.
– ORIGIN Latin *propitiare* 'make favourable', from *propitius* 'favourable, gracious'.

Thesaurus

p

right, brace, buttress, stay, strut, stanchion, shore, pier, pillar, pile, piling, bolster, truss, column. **2** *a prop for the economy* MAINSTAY, pillar, anchor, backbone, support, foundation, cornerstone. ● verb **1** *he propped his bike against the wall* LEAN, rest, stand, balance, steady. **2** *this post is propping the wall up* HOLD UP, shore up, bolster up, buttress, support, brace, underpin. **3** *they prop up loss-making industries* SUBSIDIZE, underwrite, fund, finance; support, bolster, shore up.
propaganda ● noun INFORMATION, promotion, advertising, publicity; agitprop, disinformation, counter-information, the big lie; *informal* info, hype, plugging.
propagandist ● noun PROMOTER, champion, supporter, proponent, advocate, campaigner, crusader, publicist, evangelist, apostle; *informal* plugger.
propagate ● verb **1** *an easy plant to propagate* BREED, grow, cultivate. **2** *these shrubs propagate easily* REPRODUCE, multiply, proliferate, increase, spread, self-seed, self-sow. **3** *they propagated socialist ideas* SPREAD, disseminate, communicate, make known, promulgate, circulate, broadcast, publicize, proclaim, preach, promote; *poetic/literary* bruit abroad.
propel ● verb **1** *a boat propelled by oars* MOVE, power, push, drive. **2** *he propelled the ball into the air* THROW, thrust, toss, fling, hurl, launch, pitch, project, send, shoot. **3** *confusion propelled her into action* SPUR, drive, prompt, precipitate, catapult, motivate, force, impel.
propeller ● noun ROTOR, screw, airscrew; *informal* prop.
propensity ● noun TENDENCY, inclination, predisposition, proneness, proclivity, readiness, liability, disposition, leaning, weakness.
proper ● adjective **1** *he's not a proper scientist* REAL, genuine, actual, true, bona fide; *informal* kosher. **2** *the proper channels* RIGHT, correct, accepted, orthodox, conventional, established, official, formal, regular, acceptable, appropriate; *archaic* meet. **3** *they were terribly proper* RESPECTABLE, decorous, seemly, decent, refined, ladylike, gentlemanly, genteel; formal, conventional, correct, comme il faut, done, orthodox, polite, punctilious. **4** *(Brit. informal) a proper mess* COMPLETE, absolute, real, perfect, total, thorough, utter, out-and-out, positive, unmitigated, consummate; *Brit. informal* right; *Austral./NZ informal* fair.
– OPPOSITES fake, inappropriate, wrong, unconventional.
property ● noun **1** *lost property* POSSESSIONS, belongings, things, effects, stuff, chattels, movables; resources, assets, valuables, fortune, capital, riches, wealth; *Law* personalty, goods and chattels; *informal* gear. **2** *private property* BUILDING(S), premises, house(s), land, estates; *Law* real property, realty; *N. Amer.* real estate. **3** *healing properties* QUALITY, attribute, characteristic, feature, power, trait, mark, hallmark.
prophecy ● noun **1** *her prophecy is coming true* PREDICTION, forecast, prognostication, prognosis, divination, augury. **2** *the gift of prophecy* FORETELLING THE FUTURE, fortune telling, crystal-gazing, prediction, second sight, prognostication, divination, augury, soothsaying.
prophesy ● verb PREDICT, foretell, forecast, foresee, forewarn of, prognosticate.
prophet, prophetess ● noun SEER, soothsayer, fortune teller, clairvoyant, diviner; oracle, augur, sibyl.
– PHRASES **prophet of doom** PESSIMIST, doom-monger, doomsayer, doomster, Cassandra, Jeremiah; *informal* doom (and gloom) merchant.
prophetic ● adjective PRESCIENT, predictive, far-seeing, prognostic, divinatory, sibylline, apocalyptic; *rare* vatic, mantic.
prophylactic ● adjective *prophylactic measures* PREVENTIVE, preventative, precautionary, protective, inhibitory. ● noun *a prophylactic against malaria* PREVENTIVE MEASURE, precaution, safeguard, safety measure; preventive medicine.
prophylaxis ● noun PREVENTIVE TREATMENT, prevention, protection, precaution.
propitiate ● verb APPEASE, placate, mollify, pacify, make peace

propitiation ● noun **1** appeasement. **2** atonement, especially that of Christ.
propitious /prəpishəss/ ● adjective **1** favourable. **2** archaic favourably disposed towards someone.
– DERIVATIVES **propitiously** adverb **propitiousness** noun.
prop jet ● noun a turboprop aircraft or engine.
propolis /proppəliss/ ● noun a resinous substance collected by honeybees from tree buds for constructing and varnishing honeycombs.
– ORIGIN Greek, 'suburb', also 'bee glue', from *polis* 'city'.
proponent /prəpōnənt/ ● noun a person who advocates a theory, proposal, or project.
– ORIGIN from Latin *proponere* 'put forward'.
proportion ● noun **1** a part, share, or number considered in relation to a whole. **2** the ratio of one thing to another. **3** the correct or pleasing relation of things or between the parts of a whole. **4** (**proportions**) dimensions; size. ● verb formal adjust so as to have a particular or suitable relationship to something else.
– PHRASES **in** (or **out of**) **proportion 1** according (or not according) to a particular relationship in size, amount, or degree. **2** regarded without (or with) exaggeration. **sense of proportion** the ability to judge the relative importance of things.
– DERIVATIVES **proportioned** adjective.
– ORIGIN Latin, from *pro portione* 'in respect of a share'.
proportional ● adjective corresponding in size or amount to something else.
– DERIVATIVES **proportionality** noun **proportionally** adverb.
proportional representation ● noun an electoral system in which parties gain seats in proportion to the number of votes cast for them.
proportionate ● adjective another term for PROPORTIONAL.
– DERIVATIVES **proportionately** adverb.
proposal ● noun **1** a plan or suggestion. **2** the action of proposing something. **3** an offer of marriage.
propose ● verb **1** put forward (an idea or plan) for consideration by others. **2** nominate for an office or position. **3** put forward (a motion) to a legislature or committee. **4** plan or intend. **5** make an offer of marriage to someone.
– DERIVATIVES **proposer** noun.
– ORIGIN Latin *proponere* 'put forward'.
proposition ● noun **1** a statement expressing a judgement or opinion. **2** a proposed scheme or plan. **3** informal an offer of sexual intercourse. **4** a matter or person to be dealt with: *it's a tough proposition.* **5** Mathematics a formal statement of a theorem or problem. ● verb informal make an offer, especially of sexual intercourse, to.
– DERIVATIVES **propositional** adjective.
propound /prəpownd/ ● verb put forward (an idea, theory, etc.) for consideration.
– DERIVATIVES **propounder** noun.
– ORIGIN Latin *proponere* 'put forward'.
proprietary ● adjective **1** relating to or characteristic of an owner or ownership. **2** (of a product) marketed under a registered trade name.
– ORIGIN from Latin *proprietarius* 'proprietor', from *proprietas* 'property'.
proprietary name (also **proprietary term**) ● noun a name of a product or service registered as a trademark.
proprietor ● noun (fem. **proprietress**) **1** the owner of a business. **2** a holder of property.
proprietorial /prəpriətoriəl/ ● adjective **1** relating to an owner. **2** possessive.
– DERIVATIVES **proprietorially** adverb.
propriety ● noun (pl. **proprieties**) **1** correctness of behaviour or morals. **2** appropriateness; rightness. **3** (**proprieties**) the details or rules of conventionally accepted behaviour.
– ORIGIN originally in the sense 'peculiarity, essential quality': from Latin *proprietas* 'property'.
propulsion ● noun the action of propelling or driving forward.
– DERIVATIVES **propulsive** adjective.
propyl /prōpīl/ ● noun Chemistry the radical $-C_3H_7$, derived from propane.
propylene /prōpileen/ ● noun Chemistry a gaseous hydrocarbon of the alkene series.
pro rata /prō raatə/ ● adjective proportional. ● adverb proportionally.
– ORIGIN Latin, 'according to the rate'.
prorogue /prərōg/ ● verb (**prorogues, prorogued, proroguing**) discontinue a session of (a legislative assembly) without dissolving it.
– DERIVATIVES **prorogation** /prōrəgaysh'n/ noun.
– ORIGIN Latin *prorogare* 'prolong, extend'.
prosaic /prōzayik/ ● adjective **1** having the style of prose. **2** commonplace; unromantic.
– DERIVATIVES **prosaically** adverb.
proscenium /prəseeniəm/ ● noun (pl. **prosceniums** or **proscenia** /prəseeniə/) **1** the part of a stage in front of the curtain. **2** (also **proscenium arch**) an arch framing the opening between the stage and the auditorium.

Thesaurus

p

with, conciliate, make amends to, soothe, calm.
– OPPOSITES provoke.
propitious ● adjective FAVOURABLE, auspicious, promising, providential, advantageous, optimistic, bright, rosy, heaven-sent, hopeful; opportune, timely.
– OPPOSITES inauspicious, unfortunate.
proponent ● noun ADVOCATE, champion, supporter, backer, promoter, protagonist, campaigner; *N. Amer.* booster.
proportion ● noun **1** *a small proportion of the land* PART, portion, amount, quantity, bit, piece, percentage, fraction, section, segment, share. **2** *the proportion of water to alcohol* RATIO, distribution, relative amount/number; relationship. **3** *the drawing is out of proportion* BALANCE, symmetry, harmony, correspondence, correlation, agreement. **4** *men of huge proportions* SIZE, dimensions, magnitude, measurements; mass, volume, bulk; expanse, extent, width, breadth.
proportional ● adjective CORRESPONDING, proportionate, comparable, in proportion, pro rata, commensurate, equivalent, consistent, relative, analogous.
– OPPOSITES disproportionate.
proposal ● noun **1** *the proposal was rejected* SCHEME, plan, idea, project, programme, manifesto, motion, proposition, suggestion, submission. **2** *the proposal of a new constitution* PUTTING FORWARD, proposing, suggesting, submitting.
– OPPOSITES withdrawal.
propose ● verb **1** *he proposed a solution* PUT FORWARD, suggest, submit, advance, offer, present, move, come up with, lodge, table, nominate. **2** *do you propose to go?* INTEND, mean, plan, have in mind/view, resolve, aim, purpose, think of, aspire, want. **3** *you've proposed to her!* ASK SOMEONE TO MARRY YOU, make an offer of marriage, offer marriage; *informal* pop the question; *dated* ask for someone's hand in marriage.
– OPPOSITES withdraw.
proposition ● noun **1** *the analysis derives from one proposition* THEORY, hypothesis, thesis, argument, premiss, theorem, concept, idea, statement. **2** *a business proposition* PROPOSAL, scheme, plan, project, idea, programme, bid. **3** *doing it for real is a very different proposition* TASK, job, undertaking, venture, activity, affair, problem.
● verb *he never dared proposition her* PROPOSE SEX WITH, make sexual advances to, make an indecent proposal to, make an improper suggestion to; *informal* give someone the come-on.
propound ● verb PUT FORWARD, advance, offer, proffer, present, set forth, submit, tender, suggest, introduce, postulate, propose, pose, posit; advocate, promote, peddle, spread.
proprietor, proprietress ● noun OWNER, possessor, holder, master/mistress; landowner, landlord/landlady; innkeeper, hotelkeeper, hotelier, shopkeeper; *Brit.* publican.
propriety ● noun **1** *he behaves with the utmost propriety* DECORUM, respectability, decency, correctness, protocol, appropriateness, suitability, good manners, courtesy, politeness, rectitude, morality, civility, modesty, demureness; sobriety, refinement, discretion. **2** *he was careful to preserve the proprieties in public* ETIQUETTE, convention(s), social grace(s), niceties, one's Ps and Qs, protocol, standards, civilities, formalities, accepted behaviour, good form, the done thing, the thing to do, punctilio.
– OPPOSITES indecorum.
propulsion ● noun THRUST, motive force, impetus, impulse, drive, driving force, actuation, push, pressure, power.
prosaic ● adjective ORDINARY, everyday, commonplace, conventional, straightforward, routine, run-of-the-mill, workaday; UNIMAGINATIVE, uninspired, uninspiring, matter-of-fact, dull, dry, dreary, tedious, boring, humdrum, mundane, pedestrian, tame, plodding; bland, insipid, banal, trite, literal, factual, unpoetic, unemotional,

– ORIGIN Greek *proskēnion*, from *pro* 'before' + *skēnē* 'stage'.
prosciutto /prəshoōtō/ ● noun raw cured Italian ham.
– ORIGIN Italian.
proscribe ● verb **1** forbid, especially by law. **2** denounce or condemn. **3** historical outlaw (someone).
– DERIVATIVES **proscription** noun **proscriptive** adjective.
– USAGE The words **proscribe** and **prescribe** are often confused. **Proscribe** is a rather formal word meaning 'condemn or forbid', whereas **prescribe** is a much commoner word that means either 'issue a medical prescription' or 'recommend with authority'.
– ORIGIN originally in the sense 'post up the name of (an outlaw etc.)': from Latin *proscribere* 'publish by writing'.
prose ● noun ordinary written or spoken language, without metrical structure. ● verb talk tediously.
– ORIGIN from Latin *prosa oratio* 'straightforward discourse'.
prosecute ● verb **1** institute legal proceedings against (someone) or with reference to (a crime). **2** continue (a course of action) with a view to completion. **3** archaic carry on (a trade or pursuit).
– DERIVATIVES **prosecutable** adjective.
– ORIGIN Latin *prosequi* 'pursue, accompany'.
prosecution ● noun **1** the prosecuting of someone in respect of a criminal charge. **2** (**the prosecution**) (treated as sing. or pl.) the party prosecuting someone in a lawsuit. **3** the continuation of a course of action.
prosecutor ● noun **1** a person, especially a public official, who prosecutes someone. **2** a lawyer who conducts the case against a defendant.
– DERIVATIVES **prosecutorial** adjective.
proselyte /prossilit/ ● noun **1** a convert from one opinion, religion, or party to another. **2** a Gentile who has converted to Judaism.
– DERIVATIVES **proselytism** /prossilitiz'm/ noun.
– ORIGIN Greek *prosēluthos* 'stranger, convert'.
proselytize /prossilitiz/ (also **proselytise**) ● verb convert from one religion, belief, or opinion to another.
– DERIVATIVES **proselytizer** noun.
prosody /prossədi/ ● noun **1** the patterns of rhythm and sound used in poetry. **2** the theory or study of these patterns, or the rules governing them. **3** the patterns of stress and intonation in a language.
– DERIVATIVES **prosodic** adjective **prosodist** noun.
– ORIGIN Greek *prosōidia* 'song sung to music, tone of a syllable', from *ōidē* 'song'.
prospect ● noun **1** the possibility or likelihood of some future event occurring. **2** a mental picture of a future or anticipated event. **3** (**prospects**) chances or opportunities for success. **4** a potential customer or person likely to be successful. **5** an extensive view of landscape. ● verb search for mineral deposits, especially by means of drilling and excavation.
– DERIVATIVES **prospector** noun.
– ORIGIN Latin *prospectus* 'view', from *prospicere* 'look forward'.
prospective ● adjective expected or likely to happen or be in the future.
– DERIVATIVES **prospectively** adverb.
prospectus ● noun (pl. **prospectuses**) a printed booklet advertising a school or university or giving details of a share offer.
– ORIGIN Latin, 'view, prospect'.
prosper ● verb succeed or flourish, especially financially.
– ORIGIN Latin *prosperare*, from *prosperus* 'doing well'.
prosperous ● adjective successful or flourishing, especially financially.
– DERIVATIVES **prosperity** noun **prosperously** adverb.
prostaglandin /prostəglandin/ ● noun Biochemistry any of a group of compounds which have hormone-like effects such as causing uterine contractions.
prostate ● noun a gland surrounding the neck of the bladder in male mammals and releasing a fluid component of semen.
– DERIVATIVES **prostatic** adjective.
– ORIGIN Greek *prostatēs* 'one that stands before'.
prosthesis /prosstheesiss/ ● noun (pl. **prostheses** /prosstheeseez/) an artificial body part.
– DERIVATIVES **prosthetic** /prossthettik/ adjective.
– ORIGIN Greek, from *prostithenai* 'add'.
prosthetics /prossthettiks/ ● plural noun **1** artificial body parts; prostheses. **2** pieces of flexible material applied to actors' faces to transform their appearance. **3** (treated as sing.) the branch of surgery concerned with the making and fitting of artificial body parts.
– DERIVATIVES **prosthetist** /prosthitist/ noun.
prostitute ● noun a person, typically a woman, who engages in sexual activity for payment. ● verb (often **prostitute oneself**) **1** offer (someone) as a prostitute. **2** put to an unworthy or corrupt use for the sake of gain.
– DERIVATIVES **prostitution** noun.
– ORIGIN Latin *prostituere* 'expose publicly, offer for sale'.

Thesaurus

unsentimental.
– OPPOSITES interesting, imaginative, inspired.
proscribe ● verb **1** *gambling was proscribed* FORBID, prohibit, ban, bar, interdict, make illegal, embargo, outlaw, disallow, veto; *Law* enjoin. **2** *the book was proscribed by the Church* CONDEMN, denounce, attack, criticize, censure, damn, reject.
– OPPOSITES allow, authorize, accept.
proscription ● noun **1** *the proscription of alcohol* BANNING, forbidding, prohibition, prohibiting, barring, debarment, vetoing, interdiction, outlawing. **2** *a proscription was imposed* BAN, prohibition, bar, interdict, veto, embargo, moratorium. **3** *the proscription of his recordings* CONDEMNATION, denunciation, attacking, criticism, censuring, damning, rejection.
– OPPOSITES allowing, authorization, acceptance.
prosecute ● verb **1** *they prosecute offenders* TAKE TO COURT, bring/institute legal proceedings against, bring an action against, take legal action against, sue, try, bring to trial, put on trial, put in the dock, bring a suit against, indict, arraign; *N. Amer.* impeach; *informal* have the law on. **2** *they helped him prosecute the war* PURSUE, fight, wage, carry on, conduct, direct, engage in, proceed with, continue (with), keep on with.
– OPPOSITES defend, let off, give up.
proselyte ● noun CONVERT, new believer, catechumen.
proselytize ● verb **1** *I'm not here to proselytize* EVANGELIZE, convert, save, redeem, win over, preach (to), recruit, act as a missionary. **2** *he wanted to proselytize his ideas* PROMOTE, advocate, champion, advance, further, spread, proclaim, peddle, preach, endorse, urge, recommend, boost.
prospect ● noun **1** *there is little prospect of success* LIKELIHOOD, hope, expectation, anticipation, (good/poor) chance, odds, probability, possibility, promise, lookout; fear, danger. **2** *her job prospects* POSSIBILITIES, potential, promise, expectations, outlook. **3** *a daunting prospect* VISION, thought, idea; task, undertaking. **4** *Jimmy is an exciting prospect* CANDIDATE, possibility; *informal* catch. **5** *there is a pleasant prospect from the lounge* VIEW, vista, outlook, perspective, panorama, aspect, scene; picture, spectacle, sight.
● verb *they are prospecting for oil* SEARCH, look, explore, survey, scout, hunt, reconnoitre, examine, inspect.
– PHRASES **in prospect** EXPECTED, likely, coming soon, on the way, to come, at hand, near, imminent, in the offing, in store, on the horizon, just around the corner, in the air, in the wind, brewing, looming; *informal* on the cards.
prospective ● adjective POTENTIAL, possible, probable, likely, future, eventual, -to-be, soon-to-be, in the making; intending, aspiring, would-be; forthcoming, approaching, coming, imminent.
prospectus ● noun BROCHURE, pamphlet, description, particulars, announcement, advertisement; syllabus, curriculum, catalogue, programme, list, scheme, schedule.
prosper ● verb FLOURISH, thrive, do well, bloom, blossom, burgeon, progress, do all right for oneself, get ahead, get on (in the world), be successful; *informal* go places.
– OPPOSITES fail, flounder.
prosperity ● noun SUCCESS, profitability, affluence, wealth, opulence, luxury, the good life, milk and honey, (good) fortune, ease, plenty, comfort, security, well-being.
– OPPOSITES hardship, failure.
prosperous ● adjective THRIVING, flourishing, successful, strong, vigorous, profitable, lucrative, expanding, booming, burgeoning; AFFLUENT, wealthy, rich, moneyed, well off, well-to-do, opulent, substantial, in clover; *informal* on a roll, on the up and up, in the money.
– OPPOSITES ailing, poor.
prostitute ● noun WHORE, sex worker, call girl; rent boy; *informal* tart, pro, moll, working girl, member of the oldest profession; *Brit. informal* tom, woman on the game, renter; *N. Amer. informal* hooker, hustler, chippy; *black English* ho; *dated* streetwalker, woman of the streets, lady/woman of the night, scarlet woman, cocotte; *archaic*

prostrate ● adjective /prostrayt/ **1** lying stretched out on the ground with one's face downwards. **2** completely overcome with distress or exhaustion. **3** Botany growing along the ground. ● verb /prostrayt/ **1** (**prostrate oneself**) throw oneself flat on the ground in reverence or submission. **2** (**be prostrated**) be completely overcome with stress or exhaustion.
– DERIVATIVES **prostration** noun.
– ORIGIN Latin *prosternere* 'throw down'.

prosy /prōzi/ ● adjective (**prosier**, **prosiest**) (of speech or writing) dull and unimaginative.

protactinium /prōtaktinniəm/ ● noun a rare radioactive metallic chemical element formed as a product of the natural decay of uranium.

protagonist ● noun **1** the leading character in a drama, film, or novel. **2** a prominent figure in a real situation. **3** an advocate or champion of a cause or idea.
– ORIGIN Greek *prōtagōnistēs*, from *prōtos* 'first in importance' + *agōnistēs* 'actor'.

protea /prōtiə/ ● noun a chiefly South African evergreen shrub with large cone-like flower heads surrounded by brightly coloured bracts.
– ORIGIN from *Proteus* (see PROTEAN), with reference to the many species of the genus.

protean /prōteeən/ ● adjective tending or able to change or adapt; variable or versatile.
– ORIGIN from the Greek sea god *Proteus*, who was able to change shape at will.

protect ● verb **1** keep safe from harm or injury. **2** Economics shield (a domestic industry) from competition by imposing import duties on foreign goods. **3** (**protected**) (of a threatened plant or animal species) safeguarded through legislation against collecting or hunting.
– ORIGIN Latin *protegere* 'cover in front'.

protection ● noun **1** the action of protecting or the state of being protected. **2** a person or thing that protects. **3** the payment of money to criminals to prevent them from attacking oneself or one's property.

protectionism ● noun Economics the theory or practice of shielding a country's domestic industries from foreign competition by taxing imports.
– DERIVATIVES **protectionist** noun & adjective.

protective ● adjective serving, intended, or wishing to protect. ● noun Brit. **1** a thing that protects. **2** dated a condom.
– DERIVATIVES **protectively** adverb **protectiveness** noun.

protective custody ● noun the detention of a person for their own protection.

protector ● noun **1** a person or thing that protects. **2** (**Protector**) historical a regent in charge of a kingdom during the minority, absence, or incapacity of the sovereign.
– DERIVATIVES **protectress** noun.

protectorate ● noun **1** a state that is controlled and protected by another. **2** (**Protectorate**) historical the position or period of office of a Protector, in particular that of Oliver Cromwell and his son Richard as heads of state in England 1653–9.

protégé /prottizhay, prō-/ ● noun (fem. **protégée**) a person who is guided and supported by an older and more experienced person.
– ORIGIN French, 'protected'.

protein ● noun any of a class of organic compounds forming structural components of body tissues and constituting an important part of the diet.
– ORIGIN from Greek *prōteios* 'primary'.

pro tem /prō tem/ ● adverb & adjective for the time being.
– ORIGIN abbreviation of Latin *pro tempore*.

Proterozoic /prōtərəzōik/ ● adjective Geology relating to the later part of the Precambrian aeon (between the Archaean aeon and the Cambrian period, about 2,500 to 570 million years ago), in which the earliest forms of life evolved.
– ORIGIN from Greek *proteros* 'former' + *zōē* 'life'.

protest ● noun **1** a statement or action expressing disapproval or objection. **2** an organized public demonstration objecting to an official policy or course of action. ● verb **1** express an objection to what someone has said or done. **2** take part in a public protest. **3** state emphatically in response to an accusation or criticism: *she protested her innocence.*
– DERIVATIVES **protester** (also **protestor**) noun.
– ORIGIN Latin *protestari* 'assert formally', from *testis* 'a witness'.

Protestant /prottistənt/ ● noun a member or follower of any of

Thesaurus

courtesan, strumpet, harlot, trollop, woman of ill repute, lady of pleasure, wench.
● verb *they prostituted their art* BETRAY, sacrifice, sell, sell out, debase, degrade, demean, devalue, cheapen, lower, shame, misuse, pervert; abandon one's principles, be untrue to oneself.

p

prostitution ● noun WHORING, the sex industry, streetwalking, Mrs Warren's profession, sex tourism; *informal* the oldest profession, the trade; rough trade; *Brit. informal* the game; *N. Amer. informal* hooking, hustling; *dated* whoredom; *archaic* harlotry.

prostrate ● adjective **1** *the prostrate figure on the ground* PRONE, lying flat, lying down, stretched out, spreadeagled, sprawling, horizontal, recumbent; *rare* procumbent. **2** *his wife was prostrate with shock* OVERWHELMED, overcome, overpowered, brought to one's knees, stunned, dazed; speechless, helpless; *informal* knocked/hit for six. **3** *the fever left me prostrate* WORN OUT, exhausted, fatigued, tired out, sapped, dog-tired, spent, drained, debilitated, enervated, laid low; *informal* all in, done in, dead, dead beat, dead on one's feet, ready to drop, fagged out, bushed, frazzled, worn to a frazzle; *Brit. informal* whacked, knackered; *N. Amer. informal* pooped.
– OPPOSITES upright, fresh.
● verb *she was prostrated by the tragedy* OVERWHELM, overcome, overpower, bring to one's knees, devastate, debilitate, weaken, enfeeble, enervate, lay low, wear out, exhaust, tire out, drain, sap, wash out, take it out of; *informal* knacker, frazzle, do in; *N. Amer. informal* poop.
– PHRASES **prostrate oneself** THROW ONESELF FLAT/DOWN, lie down, stretch oneself out, throw oneself at someone's feet; *dated* measure one's length.

prostration ● noun COLLAPSE, weakness, debility, lassitude, exhaustion, fatigue, tiredness, enervation, emotional exhaustion.

protagonist ● noun **1** *the protagonist of his second novel* MAIN/LEADING CHARACTER, hero/heroine, leading man/lady, title role, lead. **2** *a protagonist of deregulation* CHAMPION, advocate, upholder, supporter, backer, promoter, proponent, exponent, campaigner, fighter, crusader; apostle, apologist; *N. Amer.* booster.
– OPPOSITES opponent.

protean ● adjective **1** *the protean nature of mental disorders* EVER-CHANGING, variable, changeable, mutable, kaleidoscopic, inconstant, inconsistent, unstable, shifting, unsettled, fluctuating, fluid, wavering, vacillating, mercurial, volatile; *technical* labile. **2** *a remarkably protean composer* VERSATILE, adaptable, flexible, all-round, multifaceted, multitalented, many-sided.
– OPPOSITES constant, consistent, limited.

protect ● verb KEEP SAFE, keep from harm, save, safeguard, preserve, defend, shield, cushion, insulate, hedge, shelter, screen, secure, fortify, guard, watch over, look after, take care of, keep; inoculate.
– OPPOSITES expose, neglect, attack, harm.

protection ● noun **1** *protection against biological and nuclear attack* DEFENCE, security, shielding, preservation, conservation, safe keeping, safeguarding, safety, sanctuary, shelter, refuge, lee, immunity, insurance, indemnity. **2** *under the protection of the Church* SAFE KEEPING, care, charge, keeping, protectorship, guidance, aegis, auspices, umbrella, guardianship, support, patronage, championship, providence. **3** *protection against noise* BARRIER, buffer, shield, screen, hedge, cushion, preventative, armour, refuge, bulwark.

protective ● adjective **1** *protective clothing should be worn at all times* PRESERVATIVE, protecting, safeguarding, shielding, defensive, safety, precautionary, preventive, preventative. **2** *he felt protective towards the girl* SOLICITOUS, caring, warm, paternal/maternal, fatherly/motherly, gallant, chivalrous; overprotective, possessive, jealous.

protector ● noun **1** *a protector of the environment* DEFENDER, preserver, guardian, guard, champion, watchdog, ombudsman, knight in shining armour, guardian angel, patron, chaperon, escort, keeper, custodian, bodyguard, minder; *informal* hired gun. **2** *ear protectors* GUARD, shield, buffer, cushion, pad, screen.

protégé, *fem.* **protégée** ● noun PUPIL, student, trainee, apprentice; disciple, follower; discovery, find, ward.

protest ● noun **1** *he resigned as a protest* OBJECTION, complaint, exception, disapproval, challenge, dissent, demurral, remonstration, fuss, outcry. **2** *women staged a protest* DEMONSTRATION, (protest) march, rally; sit-in, occupation; work-to-rule, industrial action, stoppage, strike, walkout, mutiny, picket, boycott; *informal* demo.
– OPPOSITES support, approval.

the Western Christian Churches that are separate from the Roman Catholic Church in accordance with the principles of the Reformation. ● adjective relating to or belonging to any of the Protestant Churches.
– DERIVATIVES **Protestantism** noun.
– ORIGIN Protestants are so called after the declaration (Latin *protestatio*) of Martin Luther and his supporters dissenting from the decision of the Diet of Spires (1529), which reaffirmed the edict of the Diet of Worms against the Reformation.

Protestant ethic (also **Protestant work ethic**) ● noun the view that a person's duty and responsibility is to achieve success through hard work and thrift.

protestation /prottistaysh'n/ ● noun **1** an emphatic declaration that something is or is not the case. **2** an objection or protest.

prothalamium /prōthəlaymiəm/ ● noun (pl. **prothalamia** /prōthəlaymiə/) literary a song or poem celebrating a forthcoming wedding.
– ORIGIN from *Prothalamion*, the title of a poem (1597) by Spenser, on the pattern of *epithalamium*.

protist /prōtist/ ● noun Biology a primitive organism of a kind including the protozoans, slime moulds, and simple algae and fungi.
– ORIGIN Greek *prōtista*, from *prōtistos* 'very first'.

protium /prōtiəm/ ● noun Chemistry the common, stable isotope of hydrogen, as distinct from deuterium and tritium.
– ORIGIN Latin, from Greek *prōtos* 'first'.

proto- ● combining form **1** original; primitive: *prototype*. **2** first; relating to a precursor: *protozoon*.
– ORIGIN from Greek *prōtos* 'first'.

protocol ● noun **1** the official procedure or system of rules governing affairs of state or diplomatic occasions. **2** the accepted code of behaviour in a particular situation. **3** the original draft of a diplomatic document, especially of the terms of a treaty. **4** a formal record of scientific experimental observations. **5** Computing a set of rules governing the exchange or transmission of data between devices.
– ORIGIN originally in the sense 'original note of an agreement': from Greek *prōtokollon* 'first page, flyleaf'.

proton /prōton/ ● noun Physics a stable subatomic particle occurring in all atomic nuclei, with a positive electric charge equal in magnitude to that of an electron.
– ORIGIN Greek, 'first thing'.

protoplasm /prōtəplaz'm/ ● noun Biology the material comprising the living part of a cell, including the cytoplasm, nucleus, and other organelles.
– DERIVATIVES **protoplasmic** adjective.
– ORIGIN Greek *prōtoplasma*, from *protos* 'first' + *plasma* (see PLASMA).

prototype ● noun **1** a first or preliminary form from which other forms are developed or copied. **2** a typical example of something.
– DERIVATIVES **prototypical** adjective **prototypically** adverb.

protozoan /prōtəzōən/ ● noun a single-celled microscopic animal such as an amoeba. ● adjective relating to protozoans.
– ORIGIN from Greek *protos* 'first' + *zōion* 'animal'.

protract ● verb prolong; draw out.
– DERIVATIVES **protracted** adjective.
– ORIGIN Latin *protrahere* 'prolong'.

protraction ● noun **1** the action of prolonging or the state of being prolonged. **2** the action of extending a part of the body.

protractor ● noun an instrument for measuring angles, typically in the form of a flat semicircle marked with degrees along the curved edge.

protrude ● verb extend beyond or above a surface.
– DERIVATIVES **protrusion** noun.
– ORIGIN Latin *protrudere* 'to thrust forward'.

protuberance /prətyoōbərənss/ ● noun **1** a thing that protrudes. **2** the state of protruding.

protuberant ● adjective protruding; bulging.
– ORIGIN from Latin *protuberare* 'swell out'.

proud ● adjective **1** (often **proud of**) feeling pride or satisfaction in one's own or another's achievements. **2** having or showing a high opinion of oneself. **3** conscious of one's own dignity. **4** (often **proud of**) slightly projecting from a surface. **5** literary imposing; splendid.
– PHRASES **do proud** informal **1** cause to feel pleased or satisfied. **2** treat or entertain very well.
– DERIVATIVES **proudly** adverb.
– ORIGIN Old French *prud* 'valiant', from Latin *prodesse* 'be of value'.

prove /proōv/ ● verb (past part. **proved** or **proven** /proōv'n or

Thesaurus

● verb **1** *residents protested at the plans* EXPRESS OPPOSITION, object, dissent, take issue, make/take a stand, put up a fight, kick, take exception, complain, express disapproval, disagree, demur, remonstrate, make a fuss; cry out, speak out, rail, inveigh, fulminate; informal kick up a fuss/stink. **2** *people protested outside the cathedral* DEMONSTRATE, march, hold a rally, sit in, occupy somewhere; work to rule, take industrial action, stop work, down tools, strike, go on strike, walk out, mutiny, picket somewhere; boycott something. **3** *he protested his innocence* INSIST ON, maintain, assert, affirm, announce, proclaim, declare, profess, contend, argue, claim, vow, swear (to), stress; formal aver, asseverate.
– OPPOSITES acquiesce, support, deny.

protestation ● noun **1** *his protestations of innocence* DECLARATION, announcement, profession, assertion, insistence, claim, affirmation, assurance, oath, vow; rare aver, asseveration. **2** *we helped him despite his protestations* OBJECTION, protest, exception, complaint, disapproval, opposition, challenge, dissent, demurral, remonstration, fuss, outcry; informal stink.
– OPPOSITES denial, acquiescence, support.

protester ● noun **1** *the council lost protesters' letters* OBJECTOR, opposer, opponent, complainant, complainer, dissenter, dissident, nonconformist. **2** *the protesters were moved on* DEMONSTRATOR, protest marcher; striker, mutineer, picket.

protocol ● noun **1** *a stickler for protocol* ETIQUETTE, conventions, formalities, customs, rules of conduct, procedure, ritual, accepted behaviour, propriety, proprieties, one's Ps and Qs, decorum, good form, the done thing, the thing to do, punctilio. **2** *the two countries signed a protocol* AGREEMENT, treaty, entente, concordat, convention, deal, pact, contract, compact; formal concord.

prototype ● noun **1** *a protoype of the weapon* ORIGINAL, first example/model, master, mould, template, framework, mock-up, pattern, sample; DESIGN, guide, blueprint. **2** *the prototype of an ideal wife* TYPICAL EXAMPLE, paradigm, archetype, exemplar.

protract ● verb PROLONG, lengthen, extend, draw out, drag out, spin out, stretch out, string out, elongate; carry on, continue, keep up, perpetuate.
– OPPOSITES curtail, shorten.

protracted ● adjective PROLONGED, long-lasting, extended, long-drawn-out, spun out, dragged out, strung out, lengthy, long.
– OPPOSITES short.

protrude ● verb STICK OUT, jut (out), project, extend, stand out, bulge out, poke out, thrust out, cantilever.

protruding ● adjective STICKING OUT, protuberant, projecting, prominent, jutting, overhanging, proud, bulging; informal sticky-out.
– OPPOSITES sunken, flush.

protrusion ● noun **1** *the neck vertebrae have short vertical protrusions* BUMP, lump, knob, protuberance, projection, sticking-out bit, prominence, swelling, eminence, outcrop, outgrowth, jut, jag, snag; ledge, shelf, ridge; informal sticky-out bit. **2** *protrusion of the lips* STICKING OUT, jutting, projection, obtrusion, prominence; swelling, bulging.

protuberance ● noun **1** *a protuberance can cause drag* BUMP, lump, knob, projection, protrusion, sticking-out bit, prominence, swelling, eminence, outcrop, outgrowth, jut, jag, snag; ledge, shelf, ridge; informal sticky-out bit. **2** *the protuberance of the incisors* STICKING OUT, jutting, projection, obtrusion, prominence; swelling, bulging.

protuberant ● adjective STICKING OUT, protruding, projecting, prominent, jutting, overhanging, proud, bulging; informal sticky-out.
– OPPOSITES sunken, flush.

proud ● adjective **1** *the proud parents beamed* PLEASED, glad, happy, delighted, joyful, overjoyed, thrilled, satisfied, gratified, content. **2** *a proud day* PLEASING, gratifying, satisfying, cheering, heartwarming; happy, good, glorious, memorable, notable, red-letter. **3** *they were poor but proud* SELF-RESPECTING, dignified, noble, worthy; independent. **4** *I'm not too proud to admit I'm wrong* ARROGANT, conceited, vain, self-important, full of oneself, puffed up, jumped-up, smug, complacent, disdainful, condescending, scornful, supercilious, snobbish, imperious, pompous, overbearing, bumptious, haughty; informal big-headed, swollen-headed, too big for one's boots, high and mighty, stuck-up, uppity, snooty, highfalutin; Brit. informal toffee-nosed; poetic/literary vainglorious; rare hubris-

prōv'n/) **1** demonstrate by evidence or argument the truth or existence of. **2** show or be seen to be: *the scheme has proved a great success.* **3** (**prove oneself**) demonstrate one's abilities or courage. **4** Law establish the genuineness and validity of (a will). **5** subject (a gun) to a testing process. **6** (of bread dough) rise through the action of yeast.
– DERIVATIVES **provable** adjective.
– USAGE **Prove** has two past participles, **proved** and **proven**, which can be used more or less interchangeably. However, **proven** is always used when the word is an adjective coming before the noun: *a proven talent*, not *a proved talent.*
– ORIGIN Old French *prover*, from Latin *probare* 'test, approve, demonstrate'.

provenance /provvənənss/ ● noun **1** the origin or earliest known history of something. **2** a record of ownership of a work of art or an antique.
– ORIGIN French, from Latin *provenire* 'come from'.

Provençal /provvonsaal/ ● noun **1** a person from Provence. **2** the language of Provence. ● adjective relating to Provence.

provençale /provvonsaal/ ● adjective (after a noun) cooked in a sauce made with tomatoes, garlic, and olive oil, as characteristic of Provençal cuisine.
– ORIGIN from French *à la provençale* 'in the Provençal style'.

provender /provvindər/ ● noun **1** animal fodder. **2** archaic or humorous food.
– ORIGIN Old French *provendre*, from Latin *praebenda* 'things to be supplied'.

proverb ● noun a short saying stating a general truth or piece of advice.
– ORIGIN Latin *proverbium*, from *verbum* 'word'.

proverbial ● adjective **1** referred to in a proverb or idiom. **2** well known, especially so as to be stereotypical.
– DERIVATIVES **proverbially** adverb.

provide ● verb **1** make available for use; supply. **2** (**provide with**) equip or supply (someone) with. **3** (**provide for**) make adequate preparation or arrangements for. **4** stipulate in a will or other legal document.
– DERIVATIVES **provider** noun.
– ORIGIN Latin *providere* 'foresee, attend to'.

provided ● conjunction on the condition or understanding that.

providence ● noun **1** the protective care of God or of nature as a spiritual power. **2** timely preparation for future eventualities.

provident ● adjective making or indicating timely preparation for the future.
– DERIVATIVES **providently** adverb.

providential ● adjective **1** occurring at a favourable time; opportune. **2** involving divine foresight or interference.
– DERIVATIVES **providentially** adverb.

providing ● conjunction on the condition or understanding that.

province ● noun **1** a principal administrative division of a country or empire. **2** (**the provinces**) the whole of a country outside the capital, especially when regarded as lacking in sophistication or culture. **3** (**one's province**) an area in which one has special knowledge, interest, or responsibility.
– ORIGIN Latin *provincia* 'charge, province'.

provincial ● adjective **1** relating to a province or the provinces. **2** unsophisticated or narrow-minded. ● noun **1** an inhabitant of a province. **2** an inhabitant of the regions outside the capital city of a country.
– DERIVATIVES **provincialism** noun **provinciality** noun **provincially** adverb.

proving ground ● noun an area or situation in which a person or thing is tested or proved.

provision ● noun **1** the action of providing or supplying. **2** something supplied or provided. **3** (**provision for/against**) arrangements for future eventualities or requirements. **4** (**provisions**) supplies of food, drink, or equipment, especially for a journey. **5** a condition or requirement in a legal document.

Thesaurus

tic. **5** *the proud ships* MAGNIFICENT, splendid, resplendent, grand, noble, stately, imposing, dignified, striking, impressive, majestic, glorious, awe-inspiring, awesome, monumental. **6** *the switch is proud of the wall* PROJECTING, sticking out/up, jutting (out), protruding, prominent, raised, convex, elevated.
– OPPOSITES ashamed, shameful, humble, modest, unimpressive, concave, flush.

p

prove ● verb **1** *that proves I'm right* SHOW (TO BE TRUE), demonstrate (the truth of), show beyond doubt, manifest; witness to, give substance to, determine, substantiate, corroborate, verify, ratify, validate, authenticate, document, bear out, confirm; *formal* evince. **2** *the rumour eventually proved to be correct* TURN OUT, be found, happen.
– OPPOSITES disprove.
– PHRASES **prove oneself** DEMONSTRATE ONE'S ABILITIES/QUALITIES, show one's (true) mettle, show what one is made of.

provenance ● noun ORIGIN, source, place of origin; birthplace, fount, roots, pedigree, derivation, root, etymology; *N. Amer.* provenience; *formal* radix.

proverb ● noun SAYING, adage, saw, maxim, axiom, motto, bon mot, aphorism, apophthegm, epigram, gnome, dictum, precept; words of wisdom.

proverbial ● adjective WELL KNOWN, famous, famed, renowned, traditional, time-honoured, legendary; notorious, infamous.

provide ● verb **1** *the Foundation will provide funds* SUPPLY, give, issue, furnish, come up with, dispense, bestow, impart, produce, yield, bring forth, bear, deliver, donate, contribute, pledge, advance, spare, part with, allocate, distribute, allot, put up; *informal* fork out, lay out; *N. Amer. informal* ante up, pony up. **2** *he was provided with enough tools* EQUIP, furnish, issue, supply, outfit; fit out, rig out, kit out, arm, provision; *informal* fix up. **3** *he had to provide for his family* FEED, nurture, nourish; SUPPORT, maintain, keep, sustain, provide sustenance for, fend for, finance, endow. **4** *the test may provide the answer* MAKE AVAILABLE, present, offer, afford, give, add, bring, yield, impart. **5** *we have provided for further restructuring* PREPARE, allow, make provision, be prepared, arrange, get ready, plan, cater. **6** *the banks have to provide against bad debts* TAKE PRECAUTIONS, take steps/measures, guard, forearm oneself; make provision for. **7** *the Act provides that factories must be kept clean* STIPULATE, lay down, make it a condition, require, order, ordain, demand, prescribe, state, specify.
– OPPOSITES refuse, withhold, deprive, neglect.

provided ● conjunction ON CONDITION THAT, if, providing (that), provided that, presuming (that), assuming (that), on the assumption that, as long as, given (that), with the provision/proviso that, with/on the understanding that, contingent on.

providence ● noun **1** *a life mapped out by providence* FATE, destiny, nemesis, kismet, God's will, divine intervention, predestination, predetermination, the stars; one's lot (in life); *archaic* one's portion. **2** *he had a streak of providence* PRUDENCE, foresight, forethought, far-sightedness, judiciousness, shrewdness, circumspection, wisdom, sagacity, common sense; careful budgeting, thrift, economy.

provident ● adjective PRUDENT, far-sighted, judicious, shrewd, circumspect, forearmed, wise, sagacious, sensible; economical, thrifty.
– OPPOSITES improvident.

providential ● adjective OPPORTUNE, advantageous, favourable, auspicious, propitious, heaven-sent, welcome, golden, lucky, happy, fortunate, felicitous, timely, well timed, seasonable, convenient, expedient.
– OPPOSITES inopportune.

provider ● noun SUPPLIER, donor, giver, contributor, source.

providing ● conjunction. See PROVIDED.

province ● noun **1** *a province of the Ottoman Empire* TERRITORY, region, state, department, canton, area, district, sector, zone, division. **2** *people in the provinces* NON-METROPOLITAN AREAS/COUNTIES, the rest of the country, middle England/America, rural areas/districts, the countryside, the backwoods, the wilds; *informal* the sticks, the middle of nowhere; *N. Amer. informal* the boondocks. **3** *that's outside my province* RESPONSIBILITY, area of activity, area of interest, knowledge, department, sphere, world, realm, field, domain, territory, orbit, preserve, line of country; business, affair, concern; speciality, forte; jurisdiction, authority; *informal* pigeon, bailiwick, turf.

provincial ● adjective **1** *the provincial government* REGIONAL, state, territorial, district, local; sectoral, zonal, cantonal, county. **2** *provincial areas* NON-METROPOLITAN, small-town, non-urban, outlying, rural, country, rustic, backwoods, backwater; *informal* one-horse; *N. Amer. informal* hick, freshwater. **3** *they're so dull and provincial* UNSOPHISTICATED, narrow-minded, parochial, small-town, suburban, insular, parish-pump, inward-looking, conservative; small-minded, blinkered, bigoted, prejudiced; *N. Amer. informal* jerkwater, corn-fed.
– OPPOSITES national, metropolitan, cosmopolitan, sophisticated, broad-minded.
● noun *they were dismissed as provincials* (COUNTRY) BUMPKIN, coun-

● verb supply with provisions.

provisional ● adjective **1** arranged or existing for the present, possibly to be changed later. **2** (**Provisional**) relating to the unofficial wings of the IRA and Sinn Fein. ● noun (**Provisional**) a member of the Provisional wing of the IRA or Sinn Fein.
– DERIVATIVES **provisionality** noun **provisionally** adverb.

proviso /prəvīzō/ ● noun (pl. **provisos**) a condition attached to an agreement.
– ORIGIN from Latin *proviso quod* 'it being provided that'.

provisory ● adjective **1** subject to a proviso; conditional. **2** provisional.

provitamin ● noun Biochemistry a substance which is converted into a vitamin within an organism.

Provo /prōvō/ ● noun (pl. **Provos**) informal a member of the Provisional IRA or Sinn Fein.

provocation ● noun **1** the action of provoking. **2** action or speech that provokes.

provocative ● adjective **1** deliberately causing annoyance or anger. **2** deliberately arousing sexual desire or interest.
– DERIVATIVES **provocatively** adverb **provocativeness** noun.

provoke ● verb **1** stimulate or cause (a strong or unwelcome reaction or emotion) in someone. **2** deliberately annoy or anger. **3** incite to do or feel something, especially by arousing anger.
– ORIGIN Latin *provocare* 'to challenge'.

provolone /provvəlōnay, provvəlōni/ ● noun an Italian soft smoked cheese made from cow's milk.
– ORIGIN Italian, from *provola* 'buffalo's milk cheese'.

provost /provvəst/ ● noun **1** Brit. the position of head in certain university colleges and public schools. **2** N. Amer. a senior administrative officer in certain universities. **3** Scottish a mayor. **4** the head of a chapter in a cathedral. **5** short for PROVOST MARSHAL. **6** historical the chief magistrate of a European town.
– ORIGIN Old English, from Latin *propositus*, *praepositus* 'head, chief'.

provost marshal ● noun **1** the head of military police in camp or on active service. **2** the master-at-arms of a ship in which a court martial is held.

prow /prow/ ● noun the pointed front part of a ship; the bow.
– ORIGIN Old French *proue*, from Greek *prōira*.

prowess ● noun **1** skill or expertise in a particular activity or field. **2** bravery in battle.
– ORIGIN Old French *proesce*, from *prou* 'valiant'.

prowl ● verb move about stealthily or restlessly as if in search of prey. ● noun an act of prowling.
– DERIVATIVES **prowler** noun.
– ORIGIN of unknown origin.

proximal ● adjective chiefly Anatomy situated nearer to the centre of the body or an area or the point of attachment. The opposite of DISTAL.
– DERIVATIVES **proximally** adverb.

proximate ● adjective **1** closest in space, time, or relationship. **2** nearly accurate; approximate.
– DERIVATIVES **proximately** adverb.
– ORIGIN Latin *proximatus* 'drawn near', from *proximus* 'nearest'.

proximity ● noun nearness in space, time, or relationship.

proxy ● noun (pl. **proxies**) **1** the authority to represent someone else, especially in voting. **2** a person authorized to act on behalf of another. **3** a figure used to represent the value of something in a calculation.
– ORIGIN contraction of PROCURACY.

Prozac /prōzak/ ● noun trademark fluoxetine, a drug which reduces the uptake of serotonin in the brain and is taken to treat depression.
– ORIGIN an invented name.

prude ● noun a person who is easily shocked by matters relating to sex or nudity.
– DERIVATIVES **prudish** adjective **prudery** noun.
– ORIGIN from French *prudefemme* 'good woman and true'.

prudent ● adjective acting with or showing care and thought for the future.
– DERIVATIVES **prudence** noun **prudently** adverb.
– ORIGIN Latin *prudens*, from *providens* 'foreseeing'.

Thesaurus

try cousin, rustic, yokel, village idiot, peasant; *Irish informal* culchie; *N. Amer. informal* hayseed, hick, rube, hillbilly.
– OPPOSITES sophisticate.

provision ● noun **1** *the provision of weapons to guerrillas* SUPPLYING, supply, providing, giving, presentation, donation; equipping, furnishing. **2** *there has been limited provision for gifted children* FACILITIES, services, amenities, resource(s), arrangements; means, funds, benefits, assistance, allowance(s). **3** *provisions for the trip* SUPPLIES, food and drink, stores, groceries, foodstuff(s), provender, rations; *informal* grub, eats, nosh; *N. Amer. informal* chuck; *formal* comestibles; *poetic/literary* viands; *dated* victuals. **4** *he had made no provision for the future* PREPARATIONS, plans, arrangements, prearrangement, precautions, contingency. **5** *the provisions of the Act* TERM, clause; requirement, specification, stipulation; proviso, condition, qualification, restriction, limitation.

provisional ● adjective INTERIM, temporary, pro tem; transitional, changeover, stopgap, short-term, fill-in, acting, caretaker, TBC (to be confirmed), subject to confirmation; pencilled in, working, tentative, contingent.
– OPPOSITES permanent, definite.

provisionally ● adverb TEMPORARILY, short-term, pro tem, for the interim, for the present, for the time being, for now, for the nonce; subject to confirmation, in an acting capacity, conditionally, tentatively.

proviso ● noun CONDITION, stipulation, provision, clause, rider, qualification, restriction, caveat.

provocation ● noun **1** *he remained calm despite severe provocation* GOADING, prodding, egging on, incitement, pressure; ANNOYANCE, irritation, nettling; harassment, plaguing, molestation; teasing, taunting, torment; affront, insults; *informal* hassle, aggravation. **2** *without provocation, Jones punched Mr Cartwright* JUSTIFICATION, excuse, pretext, occasion, call, motivation, motive, cause, grounds, reason, need.

provocative ● adjective **1** *provocative remarks* ANNOYING, irritating, exasperating, infuriating, maddening, vexing, galling; insulting, offensive, inflammatory, incendiary, controversial; *informal* aggravating, in-your-face. **2** *a provocative pose* SEXY, sexually arousing, sexually exciting, alluring, seductive, suggestive, inviting, tantalizing, titillating; indecent, pornographic, indelicate, immodest, shameless; erotic, sensuous, slinky, coquettish, amorous, flirtatious; *informal* tarty, come-hither.
– OPPOSITES soothing, calming, modest, decorous.

provoke ● verb **1** *the plan has provoked outrage* AROUSE, produce, evoke, cause, give rise to, occasion, call forth, elicit, induce, excite, spark off, touch off, kindle, generate, engender, instigate, result in, lead to, bring on, precipitate, prompt, trigger; *poetic/literary* beget. **2** *he was provoked into replying* GOAD, spur, prick, sting, prod, egg on, incite, rouse, stir, move, stimulate, motivate, excite, inflame, work/fire up, impel. **3** *he wouldn't be provoked* ANNOY, anger, incense, enrage, irritate, infuriate, exasperate, madden, nettle, get/take a rise out of, ruffle, ruffle someone's feathers, make someone's hackles rise; harass, harry, plague, molest; tease, taunt, torment; *Brit.* rub up the wrong way; *informal* peeve, aggravate, hassle, miff, rile, needle, get, bug, hack off, make someone's blood boil, get under someone's skin, get in someone's hair, get/put someone's back up, get up someone's nose, get someone's goat, get across someone; *Brit. informal* wind up, nark; *N. Amer. informal* rankle, ride, gravel.
– OPPOSITES allay, deter, pacify, appease.

prow ● noun BOW(S), stem, front, nose, head, cutwater; *Brit. humorous* sharp end.

prowess ● noun **1** *his prowess as a winemaker* SKILL, expertise, mastery, facility, ability, capability, capacity, savoir faire, talent, genius, adeptness, aptitude, dexterity, deftness, competence, accomplishment, proficiency, finesse; *informal* know-how. **2** *the knights' prowess in battle* COURAGE, bravery, gallantry, valour, heroism, intrepidity, nerve, pluck, pluckiness, boldness, daring, audacity, fearlessness; *informal* bottle, guts, spunk; *N. Amer. informal* moxie, sand.
– OPPOSITES inability, ineptitude, cowardice.

prowl ● verb MOVE STEALTHILY, slink, skulk, steal, nose, pussyfoot, sneak, stalk, creep; *informal* snoop.

proximity ● noun CLOSENESS, nearness, propinquity; accessibility, handiness; *archaic* vicinity.

proxy ● noun DEPUTY, representative, substitute, delegate, agent, surrogate, stand-in, attorney, go-between.

prude ● noun PURITAN, prig, killjoy, moralist, pietist; *informal* goody-goody; *N. Amer. informal* bluenose.

prudence ● noun **1** *you have gone beyond the bounds of prudence* WISDOM, judgement, good judgement, common sense, sense, sagacity, shrewdness, advisability. **2** *financial prudence* CAUTION, care, providence, far-sightedness, foresight, forethought, shrewdness,

prudential ● adjective involving or showing care and forethought.
– DERIVATIVES **prudentially** adverb.

prune[1] ● noun **1** a plum preserved by drying and having a black, wrinkled appearance. **2** informal a disagreeable person.
– ORIGIN Greek *prounon* 'plum'.

prune[2] ● verb **1** trim (a tree, shrub, or bush) by cutting away dead or overgrown branches or stems. **2** remove superfluous or unwanted parts from. ● noun an instance of pruning.
– DERIVATIVES **pruner** noun.
– ORIGIN Old French *proignier*, possibly from Latin *rotundus* 'round'.

prurient /prooriənt/ ● adjective having or encouraging an excessive interest in sexual matters.
– DERIVATIVES **prurience** noun **pruriency** noun **pruriently** adverb.
– ORIGIN originally in the sense 'having a craving': from Latin *prurire* 'itch, long, be wanton'.

pruritus /prooritəss/ ● noun Medicine severe itching of the skin.
– DERIVATIVES **pruritic** adjective.
– ORIGIN Latin, 'itching'.

Prussian ● noun a person from the former German kingdom of Prussia. ● adjective relating to Prussia.

Prussian blue ● noun a deep blue pigment.

prussic acid /prussik/ ● noun old-fashioned term for HYDROCYANIC ACID.
– ORIGIN from French *prussique* 'relating to Prussian blue'.

pry[1] ● verb (**pries**, **pried**) enquire too intrusively into a person's private affairs.
– DERIVATIVES **prying** adjective.
– ORIGIN of unknown origin.

pry[2] ● verb (**pries**, **pried**) chiefly N. Amer. another term for PRISE.
– ORIGIN from PRISE, interpreted as *pries*, third person singular of the present tense.

PS ● abbreviation **1** Police Sergeant. **2** postscript. **3** private secretary.

psalm /saam/ ● noun a religious song or hymn, in particular any of those contained in the biblical Book of Psalms.
– DERIVATIVES **psalmist** noun.
– ORIGIN Greek *psalmos* 'song sung to harp music'.

psalmody /saamədi/ ● noun the singing of psalms or similar religious verses.
– DERIVATIVES **psalmodic** adjective **psalmodist** noun.
– ORIGIN Greek *psalmōidia* 'singing to a harp'.

psalter /sawltər/ ● noun a copy of the biblical Psalms.
– ORIGIN Greek *psaltērion* 'stringed instrument'.

psaltery /sawltəri/ ● noun (pl. **psalteries**) an ancient and medieval musical instrument resembling a dulcimer but played by plucking the strings.

PSBR ● abbreviation Brit. public-sector borrowing requirement.

psephology /sefolləji/ ● noun the statistical study of elections and trends in voting.
– DERIVATIVES **psephologist** noun.
– ORIGIN from Greek *psēphos* 'pebble, vote'.

pseud /syood/ ● noun informal a pretentious person; a poseur.

pseudo /syoodō/ ● adjective not genuine; fake, pretentious, or insincere. ● noun (pl. **pseudos**) a pretentious or insincere person.

pseudo- (also **pseud-** before a vowel) ● combining form **1** false; not genuine: *pseudonym*. **2** resembling or imitating: *pseudohallucination*.
– ORIGIN from Greek *pseudēs* 'false', *pseudos* 'falsehood'.

pseudonym /syoodənim/ ● noun a fictitious name, especially one used by an author.
– ORIGIN from Greek *pseudēs* 'false' + *onoma* 'name'.

pseudonymous /syoodonniməss/ ● adjective writing or written under a false name.
– DERIVATIVES **pseudonymity** /syoodənimmiti/ noun **pseudonymously** adverb.

pseudoscience ● noun beliefs or practices mistakenly regarded as being based on scientific method.
– DERIVATIVES **pseudoscientific** adjective.

psi /psī, sī/ ● noun **1** the twenty-third letter of the Greek alphabet (Ψ, ψ), transliterated as 'ps'. **2** supposed psychic faculties or phenomena.
– ORIGIN Greek.

p.s.i. ● abbreviation pounds per square inch.

psilocybin /sīlōsībin/ ● noun a hallucinogenic compound found in the liberty cap and related toadstools.
– ORIGIN from Greek *psilos* 'bald' + *kubē* 'head'.

psittacine /sittəsīn/ Ornithology ● adjective relating to birds of the parrot family. ● noun a bird of the parrot family.
– ORIGIN from Greek *psittakos* 'parrot'.

psittacosis /sittəkōsiss/ ● noun a contagious disease of birds, transmissible (especially from parrots) to human beings as a form of pneumonia.

psoriasis /sərīəsiss/ ● noun a skin disease marked by red, itchy, scaly patches.
– DERIVATIVES **psoriatic** /soriattik/ adjective.
– ORIGIN Greek, from *psōrian* 'to itch'.

PSV ● abbreviation Brit. public service vehicle.

psych /sīk/ ● verb informal **1** (**psych up**) mentally prepare (someone) for a testing task or occasion. **2** (**psych out**) intimidate (an opponent or rival) by appearing very confident or aggressive.

psyche /sīki/ ● noun the human soul, mind, or spirit.
– ORIGIN Greek *psukhē* 'breath, life, soul'.

psychedelia /sīkədeeliə/ ● noun music, culture, or art based on the experiences produced by psychedelic drugs.

psychedelic /sīkədellik/ ● adjective **1** (of drugs) producing hallucinations and apparent expansion of consciousness. **2** (of rock music) characterized by musical experimentation and drug-related lyrics. **3** having an intense, vivid colour or a swirling abstract pattern.
– DERIVATIVES **psychedelically** adverb.
– ORIGIN from Greek *psyche* 'soul' + *dēlos* 'clear, manifest'.

psychiatrist ● noun a medical practitioner specializing in the diagnosis and treatment of mental illness.

p

Thesaurus

circumspection; thrift, economy.
– OPPOSITES folly, recklessness, extravagance.

prudent ● adjective **1** *it is prudent to obtain consent* WISE, well judged, sensible, politic, judicious, sagacious, sage, shrewd, advisable, well advised. **2** *a prudent approach to borrowing* CAUTIOUS, careful, provident, far-sighted, judicious, shrewd, circumspect; thrifty, economical.
– OPPOSITES unwise, reckless, extravagant.

prudish ● adjective PURITANICAL, priggish, prim, prim and proper, moralistic, pietistic, sententious, censorious, strait-laced, Victorian, old-maidish, stuffy; *informal* goody-goody; *rare* Grundyish, starchy.
– OPPOSITES permissive.

prune ● verb **1** *I pruned the roses* CUT BACK, trim, thin, pinch back, clip, shear, pollard, top, dock. **2** *prune lateral shoots of wisteria* CUT OFF, lop (off), chop off, clip, snip (off), nip off, dock. **3** *staff numbers have been pruned* REDUCE, cut (back/down), pare (down), slim down, make reductions in, make cutbacks in, trim, decrease, diminish, downsize, axe, shrink; *informal* slash.
– OPPOSITES increase.

prurient ● adjective SALACIOUS, licentious, voyeuristic, lascivious, lecherous, lustful, lewd, libidinous, lubricious; *formal* concupiscent.

pry ● verb ENQUIRE IMPERTINENTLY, be inquisitive, be curious, poke about/around, ferret (about/around), spy, be a busybody; eavesdrop, listen in, tap someone's phone, intrude; *informal* stick/poke one's nose in/into, be nosy, nose, snoop; *Austral./NZ informal* stickybeak.
– OPPOSITES mind one's own business.

psalm ● noun SACRED SONG, religious song, hymn, song of praise; chant, plainsong; (**psalms**) psalmody, psalter.

pseud ● noun *(informal)* PRETENTIOUS PERSON, poser, poseur, sham, fraud; *informal* show-off, phoney.

pseudo ● adjective BOGUS, sham, phoney, artificial, mock, ersatz, quasi-, fake, false, spurious, deceptive, misleading, assumed, contrived, affected, insincere; *informal* pretend, put-on; *Brit. informal* cod.
– OPPOSITES genuine.

pseudonym ● noun PEN NAME, nom de plume, assumed name, false name, alias, professional name, sobriquet, stage name, nom de guerre.

psych ● verb *(informal)*
– PHRASES **psych someone out** INTIMIDATE, daunt, browbeat, bully, cow, tyrannize, scare, terrorize, frighten, dishearten, unnerve, subdue; *informal* bulldoze; *N. Amer. informal* buffalo. **psych oneself up** NERVE ONESELF, steel oneself, brace oneself, summon one's courage, prepare oneself, gear oneself up, urge oneself on, gird (up) one's loins.

psyche ● noun SOUL, spirit, (inner) self, ego, true being, inner

psychiatry /sīkīətri/ ● noun the branch of medicine concerned with the study and treatment of mental illness and emotional disturbance.
– DERIVATIVES **psychiatric** /sīkiatrik/ adjective **psychiatrically** adverb.
– ORIGIN from Greek *psukhē* 'soul, mind' + *iatreia* 'healing'.

psychic /sīkik/ ● adjective **1** relating to faculties or phenomena that are apparently inexplicable by natural laws, especially those involving telepathy or clairvoyance. **2** (of a person) appearing or considered to be telepathic or clairvoyant. **3** relating to the soul or mind. ● noun **1** a person considered or claiming to have psychic powers; a medium. **2** (**psychics**) (treated as sing. or pl.) the study of psychic phenomena.
– DERIVATIVES **psychical** adjective **psychically** adverb.

psycho ● noun (pl. **psychos**) informal a psychopath.

psycho- ● combining form relating to the mind or psychology: *psychometrics.*
– ORIGIN from Greek *psukhē* 'breath, soul, mind'.

psychoactive ● adjective affecting the mind.

psychoanalysis ● noun a method of treating mental disorders by investigating the conscious and unconscious elements in the mind and bringing repressed fears and conflicts into the conscious mind.
– DERIVATIVES **psychoanalyse** (US **psychoanalyze**) verb **psychoanalyst** noun **psychoanalytic** adjective.

psychobabble ● noun informal, derogatory jargon used in popular psychology.

psychodrama ● noun **1** a form of psychotherapy in which patients act out events from their past. **2** a play, film, or novel in which psychological elements are the main interest.

psychokinesis /sīkōkineesiss, sīkōkī-/ ● noun the supposed ability to move objects by mental effort alone.
– DERIVATIVES **psychokinetic** adjective.

psycholinguistics ● plural noun (treated as sing.) the study of the relationships between language and psychological processes, including the process of language acquisition.
– DERIVATIVES **psycholinguist** noun **psycholinguistic** adjective.

psychological ● adjective **1** of, affecting, or arising in the mind. **2** relating to psychology.
– DERIVATIVES **psychologically** adverb.

psychological warfare ● noun actions intended to reduce an opponent's morale.

psychology ● noun **1** the scientific study of the human mind and its functions. **2** the mental characteristics or attitude of a person. **3** the mental factors governing a situation or activity.
– DERIVATIVES **psychologist** noun.

psychometrics ● plural noun (treated as sing.) the science of measuring mental capacities and processes.

psychometry /sīkommitri/ ● noun **1** the supposed ability to discover facts about an event or person from inanimate objects associated with them. **2** another term for PSYCHOMETRICS.
– DERIVATIVES **psychometric** /sīkōmetrik/ adjective **psychometrist** noun.

psychopath ● noun a person suffering from chronic mental disorder with abnormal or violent social behaviour.
– DERIVATIVES **psychopathic** adjective.

psychopathology ● noun **1** the scientific study of mental disorders. **2** mental or behavioural disorder.
– DERIVATIVES **psychopathological** adjective **psychopathologist** noun.

psychopathy /sīkoppəthi/ ● noun mental illness or disorder.

psychosexual ● adjective of or involving the psychological aspects of the sexual impulse.
– DERIVATIVES **psychosexually** adverb.

psychosis /sīkōsiss/ ● noun (pl. **psychoses** /sīkōseez/) a severe mental disorder in which thought and emotions are so impaired that contact is lost with external reality.

psychosocial ● adjective of or relating to the interrelation of social factors and individual thought and behaviour.
– DERIVATIVES **psychosocially** adverb.

psychosomatic /sīkōsəmattik/ ● adjective **1** (of a physical illness) caused or aggravated by a mental factor such as internal conflict or stress. **2** relating to the interaction of mind and body.
– DERIVATIVES **psychosomatically** adverb.

psychosurgery ● noun brain surgery used to treat mental disorder.
– DERIVATIVES **psychosurgical** adjective.

psychotherapy ● noun the treatment of mental disorder by psychological rather than medical means.
– DERIVATIVES **psychotherapeutic** adjective **psychotherapist** noun.

psychotic /sīkottik/ ● adjective relating to or suffering from a psychosis. ● noun a psychotic person.
– DERIVATIVES **psychotically** adverb.

psychotropic /sīkətrōpik, -troppik/ ● adjective (of drugs) affecting a person's mental state.

psychrometer /sīkrommitər/ ● noun a hygrometer consisting of wet and dry-bulb thermometers, the difference in the two thermometer readings being used to determine atmospheric humidity.
– ORIGIN from Greek *psukhros* 'cold'.

PT ● abbreviation physical training.

Pt ● abbreviation **1** Part. **2** (**pt**) pint. **3** (in scoring) point. **4** Printing point (as a unit of measurement). **5** (**Pt.**) Point (on maps). **6** (**pt**) port (a side of a ship or aircraft). ● symbol the chemical element platinum.

PTA ● abbreviation **1** parent–teacher association. **2** (in the UK) Passenger Transport Authority.

ptarmigan /taarmigən/ ● noun a grouse of northern mountains and the Arctic, having grey and black plumage which changes to white in winter.
– ORIGIN Scottish Gaelic *tàrmachan.*

Pte ● abbreviation Private (in the army).

pteranodon /terannədon/ ● noun a large tailless pterosaur of the Cretaceous period, with a long toothless beak.
– ORIGIN from Greek *pteron* 'wing' + *an-* 'without' + *odous* 'tooth'.

pterodactyl /terrədaktil/ ● noun a pterosaur of the late Jurassic period, with a long slender head and neck.
– ORIGIN from Greek *pteron* 'wing' + *daktulos* 'finger'.

pterosaur /terrəsawr/ ● noun a fossil warm-blooded flying reptile of the Jurassic and Cretaceous periods, with membranous wings supported by a greatly lengthened fourth finger.
– ORIGIN from Greek *pteron* 'wing' + *sauros* 'lizard'.

PTO ● abbreviation please turn over.

Ptolemaic /tolləmayik/ ● adjective **1** relating to the 2nd-century Greek astronomer Ptolemy. **2** relating to the Ptolemies, rulers of Egypt 304–30 BC.

Ptolemaic system (also **Ptolemaic theory**) ● noun the formerly held theory that the earth is the stationary centre of the universe.

ptomaine /tōmayn/ ● noun any of a group of amine compounds of unpleasant taste and odour formed in putrefying animal and

Thesaurus

man/woman, persona, subconscious, mind, intellect; *technical* anima, pneuma.
– OPPOSITES body.

psychiatrist ● noun PSYCHOTHERAPIST, psychoanalyst; *informal* shrink, head doctor; *Brit. humorous* trick cyclist.

psychic ● adjective **1** *psychic powers* SUPERNATURAL, paranormal, other-worldly, supernormal, preternatural, metaphysical, extrasensory, magic, magical, mystical, mystic, occult. **2** *I'm not psychic* CLAIRVOYANT, telepathic, having second sight, having a sixth sense. **3** *psychic development* EMOTIONAL, spiritual, inner; cognitive, psychological, intellectual, mental, psychiatric, psychogenic.
– OPPOSITES normal, physical.
● noun *she is a psychic* CLAIRVOYANT, fortune teller, crystal-gazer; medium, spiritualist; telepathist, telepath, mind-reader, palmist, palm-reader.

psychological ● adjective **1** *his psychological state* MENTAL, emotional, intellectual, inner, cerebral, brain, rational, cognitive. **2** *her pain was psychological* (ALL) IN THE MIND, psychosomatic, emotional, irrational, subjective, subconscious, unconscious.
– OPPOSITES physical.

psychology ● noun **1** *a degree in psychology* STUDY OF THE MIND, science of the mind. **2** *the psychology of the road user* MINDSET, mind, mental processes, thought processes, way of thinking, cast of mind, mentality, persona, psyche, (mental) attitude(s), make-up, character; *informal* what makes someone tick.

psychopath ● noun MADMAN/MADWOMAN, maniac, lunatic, psychotic, sociopath; *informal* loony, fruitcake, nutcase, nut, psycho, schizo, head case, headbanger, sicko; *Brit. informal* nutter; *N. Amer. informal* screwball, crazy, kook, meshuggener.

psychopathic. ● adjective. See MAD sense 1.

psychosomatic ● adjective (ALL) IN THE MIND, psychological, irrational, stress-related, stress-induced, subjective, subconscious,

vegetable matter and formerly thought to cause food poisoning.
– ORIGIN from Greek *ptōma* 'corpse'.
PTSD ● abbreviation post-traumatic stress disorder.
Pu ● symbol the chemical element plutonium.
pub Brit. ● noun **1** an establishment for the sale and consumption of beer and other drinks. **2** Austral. a hotel.
– ORIGIN abbreviation of PUBLIC HOUSE.
pub crawl ● noun Brit. informal a tour taking in several pubs, with one or more drinks at each.
pube /pyo͞ob/ ● noun informal a pubic hair.
puberty ● noun the period during which adolescents reach sexual maturity and become capable of reproduction.
– DERIVATIVES **pubertal** adjective.
– ORIGIN Latin *pubertas*, from *puber* 'adult', related to *pubes* (see PUBES).
pubes ● noun **1** /pyo͞obeez/ (pl. same) the lower part of the abdomen at the front of the pelvis, covered with hair from puberty. **2** /pyo͞obeez/ plural of PUBIS. **3** /pyo͞obz/ informal plural of PUBE.
– ORIGIN Latin, 'pubic hair, groin, genitals'.
pubescence /pyoobess'nss/ ● noun **1** the time when puberty begins. **2** Botany & Zoology soft down on the leaves and stems of plants or on animals, especially insects.
– DERIVATIVES **pubescent** adjective & noun.
– ORIGIN from Latin *pubescere* 'reach puberty'.
pubic ● adjective relating to the pubes or pubis.
pubis /pyo͞obiss/ ● noun (pl. **pubes** /pyo͞obeez/) either of a pair of bones forming the two sides of the pelvis.
– ORIGIN from Latin *os pubis* 'bone of the pubes'.
public ● adjective **1** of, concerning, or available to the people as a whole. **2** of or involved in the affairs of the community, especially in government or entertainment. **3** done, perceived, or existing in open view. **4** of or provided by the state rather than an independent, commercial company. ● noun **1** (**the public**) (treated as sing. or pl.) ordinary people in general; the community. **2** (**one's public**) the people who watch or are interested in an artist, writer, or performer.
– PHRASES **go public 1** become a public company. **2** reveal details about a previously private concern. **in public** in view of other people; when others are present. **the public eye** the state of being known or of interest to people in general, especially through the media.
– DERIVATIVES **publicly** adverb.
– ORIGIN Latin *publicus*, blend of *poplicus* 'of the people' and *puber* 'adult'.
public address system ● noun a system of microphones, amplifiers, and loudspeakers used to amplify speech or music.
publican ● noun **1** Brit. a person who owns or manages a pub. **2** Austral. a person who owns or manages a hotel. **3** (in ancient Roman and biblical times) a tax collector.
– ORIGIN Latin *publicanus*, from *publicum* 'public revenue'.
public analyst ● noun Brit. a health official who analyses food.
publication ● noun **1** the action or process of publishing something. **2** a book or journal that is published.
public bar ● noun Brit. the more plainly furnished bar in a pub.
public company ● noun a company whose shares are traded freely on a stock exchange.
public defender ● noun US Law a lawyer employed by the state in a criminal trial to represent a defendant who is unable to afford legal assistance.
public enemy ● noun a notorious wanted criminal.
public house ● noun formal term for PUB.
publicist ● noun a person responsible for publicizing a product or celebrity.
publicity ● noun **1** notice or attention given to someone or something by the media. **2** material or information used for advertising or promotional purposes.
publicize (also **publicise**) ● verb **1** make widely known. **2** give out publicity about; advertise or promote.
public lending right ● noun (in the UK) the right of authors to receive payment when their books are lent out by public libraries.
public limited company ● noun (in the UK) a company with shares offered to the public subject to conditions of limited liability.
public nuisance ● noun Brit. **1** an act that is illegal because it interferes with the rights of the public generally. **2** informal an obnoxious or dangerous person or group.
public prosecutor ● noun a law officer who conducts criminal proceedings on behalf of the state or in the public interest.
public relations ● plural noun (treated as sing.) the professional maintenance of a favourable public image by an organization or famous person.
public school ● noun **1** (in the UK) a private fee-paying secondary school. **2** (chiefly in North America) a school supported by public funds.
public sector ● noun the part of an economy that is controlled by the state.
public servant ● noun a person who works for the state or for local government.
public-spirited ● adjective showing a willingness to promote the public good.
public transport ● noun buses, trains, and other forms of transport that are available to the public, charge set fares, and run on fixed routes.
public utility ● noun an organization supplying the community with electricity, gas, water, or sewerage.
publish ● verb **1** prepare and issue (a book, newspaper, piece of music, etc.) for public sale. **2** print in a book, newspaper, or journal so as to make generally known. **3** announce formally. **4** Law communicate (a libel) to a third party.
– DERIVATIVES **publishable** adjective **publishing** noun.
– ORIGIN Latin *publicare* 'make public'.

p

Thesaurus

unconscious.
psychotic ● adjective. See MAD sense 1.
pub ● noun *(Brit.)* BAR, inn, tavern, hostelry, wine bar, taproom, roadhouse; *Brit.* public house; *Austral./NZ* hotel; *informal* watering hole; *Brit. informal* local, boozer; *dated* alehouse; *historical* pot-house, beerhouse; *N. Amer. historical* saloon.
puberty ● noun ADOLESCENCE, pubescence, sexual maturity, growing up; youth, young adulthood, teenage years, teens, the awkward age; *formal* juvenescence.
public ● adjective **1** *public affairs* STATE, national, federal, government; constitutional, civic, civil, official, social, municipal, community, communal, local; nationalized. **2** *by public demand* POPULAR, general, common, communal, collective, shared, joint, universal, widespread. **3** *a public figure* PROMINENT, well known, important, leading, eminent, distinguished, notable, noteworthy, noted, celebrated, household, famous, famed, influential; *N. Amer.* major-league. **4** *public places* OPEN (TO THE PUBLIC), communal, accessible to all, available, free, unrestricted, community. **5** *the news became public* KNOWN, published, publicized, in circulation, exposed, overt, plain, obvious.
– OPPOSITES private, obscure, unknown, restricted, secret.
● noun **1** *the British public* PEOPLE, citizens, subjects, general public, electors, electorate, voters, taxpayers, residents, inhabitants, citizenry, population, populace, community, society, country, nation, world; everyone. **2** *his adoring public* AUDIENCE, spectators, followers, following, fans, devotees, aficionados, admirers; patrons, clientele, market, consumers, buyers, customers, readers.
– PHRASES **in public** PUBLICLY, in full view of people, openly, in the open, for all to see, undisguisedly, blatantly, flagrantly, brazenly, with no attempt at concealment, overtly; *formal* coram populo.
publication ● noun **1** *the author of this publication* BOOK, volume, title, work, tome, opus; newspaper, paper, magazine, periodical, newsletter, bulletin, journal, report; organ, booklet, brochure, catalogue; daily, weekly, monthly, quarterly, annual; *informal* rag, mag, 'zine. **2** *the publication of her new book* ISSUING, announcement, publishing, printing, notification, reporting, declaration, communication, proclamation, broadcasting, publicizing, advertising, distribution, spreading, dissemination, promulgation, issuance, appearance.
publicity ● noun **1** *the blaze of publicity* PUBLIC ATTENTION, public interest, public notice, media attention/interest, exposure, glare, limelight. **2** *publicity should boost sales* PROMOTION, advertising, propaganda; boost, push; *informal* hype, ballyhoo, puff, puffery, build-up, razzmatazz; plug.
publicize ● verb **1** *I never publicize the fact* MAKE KNOWN, make public, publish, announce, report, post, communicate, broadcast, issue, put out, distribute, spread, promulgate, disseminate, circulate, air; disclose, reveal, divulge, leak. **2** *he just wants to publicize his book* ADVERTISE, promote, build up, talk up, push, beat the drum for, boost; *informal* hype, plug, puff (up).
– OPPOSITES conceal, suppress.
public-spirited ● adjective COMMUNITY-MINDED, socially concerned,

publisher ● noun **1** a company or person that prepares and issues books, newspapers, journals, or music for sale. **2** chiefly N. Amer. a newspaper proprietor.

puce /pyōōss/ ● noun a dark red or purple-brown colour.
– ORIGIN French, 'flea, flea-colour'.

puck[1] ● noun a black disc made of hard rubber, used in ice hockey.
– ORIGIN of unknown origin.

puck[2] ● noun a mischievous or evil spirit.
– ORIGIN Old English.

pucker ● verb tightly gather or contract into wrinkles or small folds. ● noun a wrinkle or small fold.
– ORIGIN probably from POKE[2] and POCKET (suggesting the formation of small purse-like gatherings).

puckish ● adjective playful and mischievous.

pud ● noun Brit. informal short for PUDDING.

pudding ● noun **1** a dessert, especially a cooked one. **2** chiefly Brit. the dessert course of a meal. **3** a baked or steamed savoury dish made with suet and flour or batter. **4** the intestines of a pig or sheep stuffed with oatmeal, spices, and meat and boiled. **5** informal a fat person.
– PHRASES **in the pudding club** Brit. informal pregnant.
– DERIVATIVES **puddingy** adjective.
– ORIGIN probably from Old French *boudin* 'black pudding', from Latin *botellus* 'sausage, small intestine'.

pudding basin ● noun **1** a deep round bowl used for cooking steamed puddings. **2** (before another noun) (of a hairstyle) produced or seemingly produced by cutting round the edge of a pudding basin inverted on a person's head.

puddle ● noun **1** a small pool of liquid, especially of rainwater on the ground. **2** clay and sand mixed with water and used as a watertight covering or lining for embankments or canals. ● verb **1** cover with or form puddles. **2** (**puddle about/around**) informal occupy oneself in a disorganized or unproductive way. **3** line or cover with puddle. **4** knead (clay and sand) into puddle. **5** (usu. as noun **puddling**) historical stir (molten iron) with iron oxide in a furnace, to produce wrought iron.
– DERIVATIVES **puddler** noun.
– ORIGIN Old English, 'small ditch'.

pudendum /pyoodendəm/ ● noun (pl. **pudenda** /pyoodendə/) a person's external genitals, especially a woman's.
– ORIGIN from Latin *pudenda membra* 'parts to be ashamed of'.

pudeur /pyoodör/ ● noun a sense of shame or embarrassment, especially with regard to matters of a sexual or personal nature.
– ORIGIN French, 'modesty'.

pudgy ● adjective (**pudgier, pudgiest**) informal fat or flabby.
– ORIGIN of unknown origin.

pueblo /pweblō/ ● noun (pl. **pueblos**) **1** a town or village in Spain, Latin America, or the south-western US, especially an American Indian settlement. **2** (**Pueblo**) (pl. same or **Pueblos**) a member of any of various American Indian peoples living in pueblos chiefly in New Mexico and Arizona.
– ORIGIN Spanish, 'people'.

puerile /pyooril/ ● adjective childishly silly and trivial.
– DERIVATIVES **puerility** /pyoorilliti/ noun (pl. **puerilities**).
– ORIGIN Latin *puerilis*, from *puer* 'boy'.

puerperal fever ● noun fever caused by uterine infection following childbirth.
– ORIGIN from Latin *puer* 'child, boy' + *parus* 'bearing'.

Puerto Rican /pwertō reekən/ ● noun a person from Puerto Rico. ● adjective relating to Puerto Rico.

puff ● noun **1** a short burst of breath or wind, or a small quantity of vapour or smoke sent out by such a burst. **2** an act of drawing quickly on a pipe, cigarette, or cigar. **3** a light pastry case, typically filled with cream or jam. **4** informal breath: *out of puff.* **5** informal an overly enthusiastic review or promotional feature. ● verb **1** breathe in repeated short gasps. **2** move with short, noisy puffs of air or steam. **3** smoke a pipe, cigarette, or cigar. **4** (**be puffed/puffed out**) be out of breath. **5** (**puff out/up**) swell or cause to swell. **6** informal advertise with exaggerated or false praise.
– DERIVATIVES **puffer** noun.
– ORIGIN imitative.

puff adder ● noun a large, sluggish African viper which inflates the upper part of its body and hisses loudly when under threat.

puffa jacket ● noun Brit. a type of thick padded jacket.

puffball ● noun a fungus that produces a large round fruiting body which ruptures when ripe to release a cloud of spores.

pufferfish ● noun a fish with a spiny body which can inflate itself like a balloon when threatened.

puffery ● noun exaggerated praise.

puffin ● noun a northern auk with a large head and a massive brightly coloured triangular bill.
– ORIGIN originally denoting a shearwater: apparently from PUFF, with reference to a shearwater's fat nestlings.

puff pastry ● noun light flaky pastry.

puff sleeve ● noun a short sleeve gathered at the top and cuff and full in the middle.

puffy ● adjective (**puffier, puffiest**) **1** softly rounded: *puffy clouds.* **2** (of a part of the body) swollen and soft.
– DERIVATIVES **puffiness** noun.

pug ● noun a dwarf of dog with a broad flat nose and deeply wrinkled face.
– ORIGIN perhaps Low German.

pugilist /pyōōjilist/ ● noun dated or humorous a boxer.
– DERIVATIVES **pugilism** noun **pugilistic** adjective.
– ORIGIN from Latin *pugil* 'boxer'.

pugnacious /pugnayshəss/ ● adjective eager or quick to argue, quarrel, or fight.
– DERIVATIVES **pugnacity** noun.
– ORIGIN from Latin *pugnare* 'to fight'.

pug nose ● noun a short nose with an upturned tip.

puisne /pyōōni/ ● adjective Law (in the UK and some other coun-

p

Thesaurus

philanthropic, charitable; ALTRUISTIC, humanitarian, generous, unselfish.

publish ● verb **1** *we publish novels* ISSUE, bring out, produce, print. **2** *he ought to publish his views* MAKE KNOWN, make public, publicize, announce, report, post, communicate, broadcast, issue, put out, distribute, spread, promulgate, disseminate, circulate, air; disclose, reveal, divulge, leak.

pucker ● verb *she puckered her forehead* WRINKLE, crinkle, crease, furrow, crumple, rumple, ruck up, scrunch up, corrugate, ruffle, screw up, shrivel; cockle.
● noun *a pucker in the sewing* WRINKLE, crinkle, crumple, corrugation, furrow, line, fold.

puckish ● adjective MISCHIEVOUS, naughty, impish, roguish, playful, arch, prankish; *informal* waggish.

pudding ● noun DESSERT, sweet, second course, last course; *Brit. informal* afters, pud.

puddle ● noun POOL, spill, splash; *poetic/literary* plash.

puerile ● adjective CHILDISH, immature, infantile, juvenile, babyish; silly, inane, fatuous, jejune, asinine, foolish, petty.
– OPPOSITES mature, sensible.

puff ● noun **1** *a puff of wind* GUST, blast, flurry, rush, draught, waft, breeze, breath. **2** *he took a puff at his cigar* PULL; *informal* drag. **3** *(informal) they expected a puff in our review column* FAVOURABLE MENTION, review, recommendation, good word, advertisement, promotion, commercial; *informal* ad; *Brit. informal* advert. **4** *(informal) a salesman's puff* PUBLICITY, advertising, promotion, marketing, propaganda, build-up; patter, line, pitch, sales talk; *informal* spiel.
● verb **1** *he walked fast, puffing a little* BREATHE HEAVILY, pant, blow; gasp, fight for breath. **2** *she puffed at her cigarette* SMOKE, draw on, drag on, suck at/on. **3** *(informal) new ways to puff our products* ADVERTISE, promote, publicize, push, recommend, endorse, beat the drum for; *informal* hype (up), plug.
– PHRASES **puff out/up** BULGE, swell (out), stick out, distend, tumefy, balloon (up/out), expand, inflate, enlarge. **puff something out/up** DISTEND, expand, dilate, inflate, blow up, pump up, enlarge, bloat.

puffed ● adjective OUT OF BREATH, breathless, short of breath; panting, puffing, gasping, wheezing, wheezy, winded; *informal* out of puff.

puffed-up ● adjective SELF-IMPORTANT, conceited, arrogant, bumptious, pompous, overbearing; affected, stiff, vain, proud; *informal* snooty, uppity, uppish.

puffy ● adjective SWOLLEN, puffed up, distended, enlarged, inflated, dilated, bloated, engorged, bulging, tumid, tumescent.

pugilism ● noun *(dated)* BOXING, prizefighting, bare-knuckle boxing, sparring; fisticuffs; the ring.

pugilist ● noun *(dated)* BOXER, fighter, prizefighter; *informal* bruiser, pug.

pugnacious ● adjective COMBATIVE, aggressive, antagonistic, belligerent, bellicose, warlike, quarrelsome, argumentative, contentious, disputatious, hostile, threatening, truculent; fiery, hot-

tries) denoting a judge of a superior court inferior in rank to chief justices.
– ORIGIN originally in the sense 'a junior or inferior person'; from Old French *puis* 'afterwards' + *ne* 'born'.

puissance /pweesənss/ ● noun **1** /also pweesONSS/ a competitive test of a horse's ability to jump large obstacles in showjumping. **2** archaic or literary great power or skill.
– DERIVATIVES **puissant** adjective (archaic or literary).
– ORIGIN Old French, from Latin *posse* 'be able'.

puja /pōōjaa/ ● noun a Hindu ceremonial offering.
– ORIGIN Sanskrit, 'worship'.

puke ● verb & noun informal vomit.
– DERIVATIVES **pukey** adjective.
– ORIGIN probably imitative.

pukka /pukkə/ ● adjective **1** authentic. **2** socially acceptable. **3** informal excellent.
– ORIGIN Hindi, 'cooked, ripe, substantial'.

pul /pōōl/ ● noun (pl. **puls** or **puli**) a monetary unit of Afghanistan, equal to one hundredth of an afghani.
– ORIGIN Pashto, from Persian, 'copper coin'.

pula /pōōlə/ ● noun (pl. same) the basic monetary unit of Botswana, equal to 100 thebe.
– ORIGIN Setswana (a Bantu language), 'rain'.

pulao /pəlow/ ● noun variant spelling of PILAF.

pulchritude /pulkrityōōd/ ● noun literary beauty.
– DERIVATIVES **pulchritudinous** adjective.
– ORIGIN from Latin *pulcher* 'beautiful'.

pule /pyōōl/ ● verb (often as adj. **puling**) literary cry querulously or weakly.
– ORIGIN probably imitative.

pull ● verb **1** exert force on (something) so as to move it towards oneself or the origin of the force. **2** remove by pulling. **3** informal bring out (a weapon) for use. **4** move steadily: *the bus pulled away.* **5** move oneself with effort or against resistance: *she pulled away from him.* **6** attract as a customer. **7** strain (a muscle, ligament, etc.). **8** (**pull at/on**) inhale deeply while drawing on (a cigarette). **9** informal cancel or withdraw (an entertainment or advertisement). **10** check the speed of (a horse) to make it lose a race. **11** informal succeed in attracting sexually. ● noun **1** an act of pulling. **2** a deep draught of a drink or an inhalation on a cigarette, pipe, etc. **3** a force, influence, or compulsion.
– PHRASES **on the pull** informal attempting to attract someone sexually. **pull back 1** retreat or withdraw. **2** improve or restore a team's position in a sporting contest. **pull down** demolish (a building). **pull in 1** succeed in securing or obtaining. **2** informal arrest. **pull someone's leg** deceive someone playfully. **pull off** informal succeed in achieving or winning (something difficult). **pull out** withdraw or retreat. **pull the plug on** informal prevent from happening or continuing. **pull (one's) punches** limit the severity of one's criticism or aggression. **pull round** chiefly Brit. recover from an illness. **pull strings** make use of one's influence to gain an advantage. **pull the strings** be in control of events or of other people's actions. **pull through** get through an illness or other difficult situation. **pull together** cooperate in an undertaking. **pull oneself together** regain one's self-control. **pull up 1** (of a vehicle) come to a halt. **2** cause to stop or pause. **3** reprimand. **pull one's weight** do one's fair share of work.
– DERIVATIVES **puller** noun.
– ORIGIN Old English, 'pluck, snatch'.

pullet ● noun a young hen, especially one less than one year old.
– ORIGIN Old French *poulet*, from Latin *pullus* 'chicken, young animal'.

pulley ● noun (pl. **pulleys**) a wheel with a grooved rim around which a rope, chain, or belt passes, used to raise heavy weights.
– ORIGIN Old French *polie*, probably ultimately from Greek *polos* 'pivot, axis'.

Pullman ● noun (pl. **Pullmans**) a luxurious railway carriage.
– ORIGIN named after its American designer George M. *Pullman* (1831–97).

pull-out ● noun a section of a magazine or newspaper that is designed to be detached and kept for rereading.

pullover ● noun a knitted garment put on over the head and covering the top half of the body.

pullulate /pulyoolayt/ ● verb **1** reproduce or spread so as to become very widespread. **2** teem with life and activity.
– ORIGIN Latin *pullulare* 'to sprout'.

pulmonary /pulmənəri/ ● adjective relating to the lungs.
– ORIGIN from Latin *pulmo* 'lung'.

pulp ● noun **1** a soft, wet mass of crushed or pounded material. **2** the soft fleshy part of a fruit. **3** a soft wet mass of fibres derived from rags or wood, used in papermaking. **4** (before another noun) denoting popular or sensational writing, often regarded as being of poor quality. ● verb **1** crush into a pulp. **2** withdraw (a publication) from the market and recycle the paper.
– DERIVATIVES **pulper** noun **pulpy** adjective.
– ORIGIN Latin *pulpa*; sense 4 is from the printing of such material on cheap paper.

pulpit ● noun a raised enclosed platform in a church or chapel from which the preacher delivers a sermon.

Thesaurus

tempered.
– OPPOSITES peaceable.

puke ● verb *(informal).* See VOMIT verb senses 1, 2.

pukka ● adjective **1** *the pukka thing to do* RESPECTABLE, decorous, proper, genteel, polite; conventional, right, correct, accepted, decent. **2** *pukka racing cars* GENUINE, authentic, proper, actual, real, true, bona fide, veritable, legitimate; *informal* kosher, the real McCoy. **3** *(informal) a pukka meal* EXCELLENT, very good, outstanding, exceptional, marvellous, wonderful, first-class; *informal* A1, ace, great, terrific, fantastic, fabulous, fab, awesome, wicked; *Brit. informal* brilliant, brill.
– OPPOSITES improper, imitation, bad.

pull ● verb **1** *he pulled the box towards him* TUG, haul, drag, draw, tow, heave, lug, jerk, wrench; *informal* yank. **2** *he pulled the bad tooth out* EXTRACT, take out, remove. **3** *she pulled a muscle* STRAIN, sprain, wrench, turn, rick, tear; damage. **4** *race day pulled big crowds* ATTRACT, draw, bring in, pull in, lure, seduce, entice, tempt, beckon, interest, fascinate.
– OPPOSITES push, repel.
● noun **1** *give the chain a pull* TUG, jerk, heave; *informal* yank. **2** *she took a pull on her beer* GULP, draught, drink, swallow, mouthful, slug; *informal* swill, swig. **3** *a pull on a cigarette* PUFF; *informal* drag. **4** *she felt the pull of the sea* ATTRACTION, draw, lure, allurement, enticement, magnetism, temptation, fascination, appeal. **5** *he has a lot of pull in finance* INFLUENCE, sway, power, authority, say, prestige, standing, weight, leverage, muscle, teeth; *informal* clout.
– PHRASES **pull something apart** DISMANTLE, disassemble, take/pull to pieces, take/pull to bits, take apart, strip down; demolish, destroy, break up. **pull back** WITHDRAW, retreat, fall back, back off; pull out, retire, disengage; flee, turn tail. **pull something down** DEMOLISH, knock down, tear down, dismantle, raze (to the ground), level, flatten, bulldoze, destroy. **pull in** STOP, halt, come to a halt, pull over, draw up, brake, park. **pull someone/something in 1** *they pulled in big audiences.* See PULL verb sense 4. **2** *(informal) the police pulled him in* ARREST, apprehend, detain, take into custody, seize, capture, catch; *informal* collar, nab, nick, pinch, run in, bust, feel someone's collar. **pull someone's leg** TEASE, fool, play a trick on, rag, pull the wool over someone's eyes; *informal* kid, rib, lead up the garden path, take for a ride; *Brit. informal* wind up, have on. **pull something off** ACHIEVE, fulfil, succeed in, accomplish, bring off, carry off, perform, discharge, complete, clinch, fix, effect, engineer. **pull out** WITHDRAW, resign, leave, retire, step down, bow out, back out, give up; *informal* quit. **pull through** GET BETTER, get well again, improve, recover, rally, come through, recuperate. **pull something to pieces 1** *don't pull my radio to pieces.* See PULL SOMETHING APART. **2** *they pulled the plan to pieces* CRITICIZE, attack, censure, condemn, find fault with, pillory, maul, savage; *informal* knock, slam, pan, bash, crucify, lay into, roast; *Brit. informal* slate, rubbish, slag off. **pull oneself together** REGAIN ONE'S COMPOSURE, recover, get a grip on oneself, get over it; *informal* snap out of it, get one's act together, buck up. **pull up.** See PULL IN. **pull someone up** REPRIMAND, rebuke, scold, chide, chastise, upbraid, berate, reprove, reproach, censure, take to task, admonish, lecture, read someone the Riot Act, haul over the coals; *informal* tell off, bawl out, dress down, give someone hell, give someone an earful; *Brit. informal* tick off, carpet, give someone a rollicking; *N. Amer. informal* chew out; *Austral. informal* monster; *formal* castigate.

pulp ● noun **1** *he kneaded it into a pulp* MUSH, mash, paste, purée, pomace, pap, slop, slush, mulch; *informal* gloop, goo; *N. Amer. informal* glop. **2** *the sweet pulp on cocoa seeds* FLESH, marrow, meat.
● verb *pulp the gooseberries* MASH, purée, cream, crush, press, liquidize, liquefy, sieve, squash, pound, macerate, grind, mince.

– ORIGIN Latin *pulpitum* 'scaffold, platform'.

pulque /poolkay, -ki/ ● noun an alcoholic Mexican drink made by fermenting sap from the maguey.

– ORIGIN from a Nahuatl word meaning 'decomposed'.

pulsar /pulsaar/ ● noun a celestial object, thought to be a rapidly rotating neutron star, that emits regular rapid pulses of radio waves.

– ORIGIN from *pulsating star*.

pulsate /pulsayt/ ● verb **1** expand and contract with strong regular movements. **2** produce a regular throbbing sensation or sound. **3** (**pulsating**) very exciting.

– DERIVATIVES **pulsation** noun **pulsator** noun.

– ORIGIN Latin *pulsare* 'throb, pulse'.

pulse[1] ● noun **1** the rhythmical throbbing of the arteries as blood is propelled through them. **2** each successive throb of the arteries. **3** a single vibration or short burst of sound, electric current, light, etc. **4** a musical beat or other regular rhythm. **5** the centre of activity in an area or field: *those close to the economic pulse.* ● verb **1** pulsate. **2** convert (a wave or beam) into a series of pulses.

– PHRASES **feel** (or **take**) **the pulse of** ascertain the mood or opinion of.

– ORIGIN Latin *pulsus* 'beating', from *pellere* 'to drive, beat'.

pulse[2] ● noun the edible seeds of various leguminous plants, e.g. lentils or beans.

– ORIGIN Latin *puls* 'porridge of meal or pulse'.

pulverize (also **pulverise**) ● verb **1** reduce to fine particles. **2** informal defeat utterly.

– DERIVATIVES **pulverizer** noun.

– ORIGIN Latin *pulverizare*, from *pulvis* 'dust'.

puma ● noun a large American wild cat with a plain tawny to greyish coat.

– ORIGIN Quechua.

pumice /pummiss/ ● noun a light and porous form of solidified lava, used as a skin abrasive.

– ORIGIN Old French *pomis*, from Latin *pumex*; related to POUNCE[2].

pummel ● verb (**pummelled**, **pummelling**; US **pummeled**, **pummeling**) strike repeatedly, especially with the fists.

– ORIGIN variant of POMMEL.

pummelo ● noun variant spelling of POMELO.

pump[1] ● noun a mechanical device using suction or pressure to raise or move liquids, compress gases, or force air into inflatable objects. ● verb **1** move or force to move by or as if by a pump. **2** fill (something) with (liquid, gas, etc.). **3** move or cause to move vigorously up and down. **4** informal try to obtain information from (someone) by persistent questioning.

– PHRASES **pump iron** informal exercise with weights.

– ORIGIN related to Dutch *pomp* 'ship's pump'.

pump[2] ● noun **1** chiefly N. English a plimsoll. **2** a light shoe for dancing. **3** N. Amer. a court shoe.

– ORIGIN of unknown origin.

pump-action ● adjective denoting a repeating firearm in which a new round is brought into the breech by a slide action in line with the barrel.

pumpernickel /pumpərnikk'l/ ● noun dark, dense German bread made from wholemeal rye.

– ORIGIN German, originally meaning 'lout, bumpkin'.

pumpkin ● noun **1** a large rounded orange-yellow fruit with a thick rind and edible flesh. **2** Brit. another term for SQUASH[2].

– ORIGIN obsolete French *pompon*, from Greek *pepōn* 'large melon'.

pump-priming ● noun **1** the introduction of fluid into a pump to prepare it for working. **2** the stimulation of economic activity by investment.

pun ● noun a joke exploiting the different meanings of a word or the fact that there are words of the same sound and different meanings. ● verb (**punned**, **punning**) make a pun.

– DERIVATIVES **punster** noun.

– ORIGIN perhaps an abbreviation of obsolete *pundigrion*, a fanciful alteration of PUNCTILIO.

punch[1] ● verb **1** strike with the fist. **2** press (a button or key on a machine). **3** N. Amer. drive (cattle) by prodding them with a stick. ● noun **1** a blow with the fist. **2** informal effectiveness; impact.

– PHRASES **punch above one's weight** informal engage in an activity perceived as beyond one's abilities.

– DERIVATIVES **puncher** noun.

– ORIGIN variant of POUNCE[1].

punch[2] ● noun **1** a device or machine for making holes in paper, metal, leather, etc. **2** a tool or machine for impressing a design or stamping a die on a material. ● verb **1** pierce a hole in (a material) with or as if with a punch. **2** pierce (a hole) with or as if with a punch.

– ORIGIN perhaps an abbreviation of PUNCHEON, or from PUNCH[1].

punch[3] ● noun a drink made from wine or spirits mixed with water, fruit juices, spices, etc.

– ORIGIN apparently from a Sanskrit word meaning 'five, five kinds of' (because the drink had five ingredients).

punch[4] ● noun **1** (**Punch**) a grotesque, hook-nosed humpbacked buffoon, the chief male character of the Punch and Judy puppet show. **2** (also **Suffolk punch**) a short-legged thickset breed of draught horse.

– ORIGIN abbreviation of *Punchinello*, a similar character in an Italian puppet show and commedia dell'arte; sense 2 derives from a dialect term denoting a short, fat person.

punchbag ● noun Brit. a stuffed suspended bag used for punching as exercise or training, especially by boxers.

punchball ● noun Brit. a suspended or mounted stuffed or inflated ball, used for punching as exercise or training, especially by boxers.

punchbowl ● noun **1** a deep bowl for mixing and serving punch. **2** chiefly Brit. a deep round hollow in a hilly area.

punch-drunk ● adjective stupefied by or as if by a series of punches.

punched card (also **punchcard**) ● noun a card perforated according to a code, for controlling the operation of a machine, formerly used to program computers.

puncheon /punchən/ ● noun **1** a short post, especially one used for supporting the roof in a coal mine. **2** another term for PUNCH[2].

p

Thesaurus

● adjective *pulp fiction* TRASHY, cheap, sensational, lurid, tasteless; *informal* tacky, rubbishy.

pulpit ● noun STAND, lectern, platform, podium, stage, dais, rostrum.

pulsate ● verb PALPITATE, pulse, throb, pump, undulate, surge, heave, rise and fall; beat, thump, drum, thrum; flutter, quiver.

pulse[1] ● noun **1** *the pulse in her neck* HEARTBEAT, pulsation, pulsing, throbbing, pounding. **2** *the pulse of the train wheels* RHYTHM, beat, tempo, cadence, pounding, thudding, drumming. **3** *pulses of ultrasound* BURST, blast, spurt, impulse, surge.

● verb *music pulsed through the building* THROB, pulsate, vibrate, beat, pound, thud, thump, drum, thrum, reverberate, echo.

pulse[2] ● noun *eat plenty of pulses* LEGUME, pea, bean, lentil.

pulverize ● verb **1** *the seeds are pulverized into flour* GRIND, crush, pound, powder, mill, crunch, squash, press, pulp, mash, sieve, mince, macerate; *technical* comminute. **2** *(informal) he pulverized the opposition.* See TROUNCE.

pummel ● verb BATTER, pound, belabour, drub, beat; punch, strike, hit, thump, thrash; *informal* clobber, wallop, bash, whack, beat the living daylights out of, give someone a (good) hiding, belt, biff, lay into, lam; *Brit. informal* slosh; *N. Amer. informal* bust, slug; *Austral./NZ informal* quilt; *poetic/literary* smite.

pump ● verb **1** *I pumped air out of the tube* FORCE, drive, push; suck, draw, tap, siphon, withdraw, expel, extract, bleed, drain. **2** *she pumped up the tyre* INFLATE, aerate, blow up, fill up; swell, enlarge, distend, expand, dilate, puff up. **3** *blood was pumping from his leg* SPURT, spout, squirt, jet, surge, spew, gush, stream, flow, pour, spill, well, cascade, run, course. **4** *(informal) I pumped them for information* INTERROGATE, cross-examine, ask, question, quiz, probe, sound out, catechize, give someone the third degree; *informal* grill.

pun ● noun PLAY ON WORDS, wordplay, double entendre, innuendo, witticism, quip, bon mot.

punch[1] ● verb *Jim punched him in the face* HIT, strike, thump, jab, smash, welt, cuff, clip; batter, buffet, pound, pummel; *informal* sock, slug, biff, bop, wallop, clobber, bash, whack, thwack, clout, lam, whomp; *Brit. informal* stick one on, dot, slosh; *N. Amer. informal* boff, bust; *Austral./NZ informal* quilt; *poetic/literary* smite.

● noun **1** *a punch on the nose* BLOW, hit, knock, thump, box, jab, clip, welt; uppercut, hook; *informal* sock, slug, biff, bop, wallop, bash, whack, clout, belt; *N. Amer. informal* boff, bust; *dated* buffet. **2** *the album is full of punch* VIGOUR, liveliness, vitality, drive, strength, zest, verve, enthusiasm; impact, bite, kick; *informal* oomph, zing.

– ORIGIN Old French *poinchon*, probably from Latin *pungere* 'puncture'; see also POUNCE[1].

punchline ● noun the culmination of a joke or story, providing the humour or climax.

punch-up ● noun informal, chiefly Brit. a brawl.

punchy ● adjective (**punchier**, **punchiest**) effective; forceful.

punctilio /pungktilliō/ ● noun (pl. **punctilios**) **1** a fine or petty point of conduct or procedure. **2** punctilious behaviour.

– ORIGIN Italian *puntiglio* and Spanish *puntillo* 'small point'.

punctilious /pungktilliəss/ ● adjective showing great attention to detail or correct behaviour.

– DERIVATIVES **punctiliously** adverb **punctiliousness** noun.

punctual ● adjective happening or keeping to the appointed time.

– DERIVATIVES **punctuality** noun **punctually** adverb.

– ORIGIN Latin *punctualis*, from *punctum* 'a point'.

punctuate /pungktyooayt/ ● verb **1** interrupt at intervals throughout. **2** insert punctuation marks in.

– ORIGIN Latin *punctuare* 'bring to a point'.

punctuation ● noun **1** the marks, such as full stop, comma, and brackets, used in writing to separate sentences and their elements and to clarify meaning. **2** the use of such marks.

– DERIVATIVES **punctuational** adjective.

puncture ● noun a small hole caused by a sharp object, especially one in a tyre. ● verb **1** make a puncture in. **2** cause a sudden collapse of (a mood, feeling, etc.).

– ORIGIN Latin *punctura*, from *pungere* 'to prick'.

pundit /pundit/ ● noun **1** an authority who frequently pronounces on a subject in public. **2** variant spelling of PANDIT.

– DERIVATIVES **punditry** noun.

– ORIGIN from a Sanskrit word meaning 'learned'.

pungent ● adjective **1** having a sharply strong taste or smell. **2** (of remarks or humour) sharp and caustic.

– DERIVATIVES **pungency** noun **pungently** adverb.

– ORIGIN from Latin *pungere* 'to prick'.

Punic /pyo͞onik/ ● adjective relating to ancient Carthage. ● noun the language of ancient Carthage.

– ORIGIN Latin *Punicus*, from *Poenus*, from Greek *Phoinix* 'Phoenician'.

punish ● verb **1** impose a penalty on (someone) for an offence. **2** impose a penalty on someone for (an offence). **3** treat harshly or unfairly.

– DERIVATIVES **punishable** adjective.

– ORIGIN Latin *punire*, from *poena* 'penalty'.

punishment ● noun **1** the action of punishing or the state of being punished. **2** the penalty imposed for an offence. **3** informal harsh or rough treatment.

punitive /pyo͞onitiv/ ● adjective inflicting or intended as punishment.

– DERIVATIVES **punitively** adverb **punitiveness** noun.

Punjabi /punjaabi, po͝on-/ (also **Panjabi**) ● noun (pl. **Punjabis**) **1** a person from Punjab, a region of NW India and Pakistan. **2** the language of Punjab. ● adjective relating to Punjab.

punk ● noun **1** (also **punk rock**) a loud, fast form of rock music characterized by aggressive and anarchic lyrics and behaviour. **2** (also **punk rocker**) an admirer or player of punk music. **3** informal, chiefly N. Amer. a worthless person; a thug or criminal. **4** chiefly N. Amer. tinder. ● adjective **1** relating to punk rock and its associated subculture. **2** N. Amer. informal bad; worthless.

– DERIVATIVES **punkish** adjective **punky** adjective.

– ORIGIN perhaps, in some senses, related to archaic *punk* 'prostitute', also to SPUNK.

punkah /pungkə/ ● noun chiefly historical (in India) a large cloth fan on a frame suspended from the ceiling, worked by a cord or electrically.

– ORIGIN Sanskrit, 'wing'.

punnet ● noun Brit. a small light basket or other container for fruit or vegetables.

– ORIGIN perhaps from dialect *pun* 'a pound'.

punt[1] /punt/ ● noun a long, narrow, flat-bottomed boat, square at both ends and propelled with a long pole. ● verb travel or convey in a punt.

– ORIGIN Latin *ponto*, denoting a flat-bottomed ferry boat.

punt[2] /punt/ ● verb **1** American Football & Rugby kick the ball after it has dropped from the hands and before it reaches the ground. **2** Soccer kick (the ball) a long distance upfield. ● noun a kick of this kind.

– ORIGIN probably from dialect *punt*, 'push forcibly'.

punt[3] /punt/ ● verb **1** Brit. informal bet or speculate. **2** (in some gambling card games) lay a stake against the bank. ● noun informal, chiefly Brit. a bet.

– ORIGIN French *ponte* 'player against the bank'.

Thesaurus

punch[2] ● verb *he punched her ticket* MAKE A HOLE IN, perforate, puncture, pierce, prick, hole, spike, skewer; *poetic/literary* transpierce.

punch-up ● noun *(Brit. informal)*. See FIGHT noun sense 1.

punchy ● adjective *punchy dialogue* FORCEFUL, incisive, strong, powerful, vigorous, dynamic, effective, impressive, telling, compelling; dramatic, passionate, graphic, vivid, potent, authoritative, aggressive; *informal* in-your-face.

– OPPOSITES ineffectual.

punctilio ● noun **1** *a stickler for punctilio* CONFORMITY, conscientiousness, punctiliousness; etiquette, protocol, conventions, formalities, propriety, decorum, manners, politesse, good form, the done thing. **2** *the punctilios of court procedure* NICETY, detail, fine point, subtlety, nuance, refinement.

– OPPOSITES informality.

punctilious ● adjective METICULOUS, conscientious, diligent, scrupulous, careful, painstaking, rigorous, perfectionist, methodical, particular, strict; fussy, fastidious, finicky, pedantic; *informal* nit-picking, pernickety; *N. Amer. informal* persnickety; *archaic* nice.

– OPPOSITES careless.

punctual ● adjective ON TIME, prompt, on schedule, in (good) time; *informal* on the dot.

– OPPOSITES late.

punctuate ● verb **1** *how to punctuate direct speech* ADD PUNCTUATION TO, put punctuation marks in, dot, apostrophize. **2** *slides punctuated the talk* BREAK UP, interrupt, intersperse, pepper, sprinkle, scatter.

puncture ● noun **1** *the tyre developed a puncture* HOLE, perforation, rupture; cut, slit; leak. **2** *my car has a puncture* FLAT TYRE; *informal* flat.

● verb **1** *he punctured her balloon* MAKE A HOLE IN, pierce, rupture, perforate, stab, cut, slit, prick, spike, stick, lance; deflate. **2** *she knows how to puncture his speeches* PUT AN END TO, cut short, deflate, reduce.

pundit ● noun EXPERT, authority, specialist, doyen(ne), master, guru, sage, savant; *informal* buff, whizz.

pungent ● adjective **1** *a pungent marinade* STRONG, powerful, pervasive, penetrating; sharp, acid, sour, biting, bitter, tart, vinegary, tangy; highly flavoured, aromatic, spicy, piquant, peppery, hot. **2** *pungent remarks* CAUSTIC, biting, trenchant, cutting, acerbic, sardonic, sarcastic, scathing, acrimonious, barbed, sharp, tart, incisive, bitter, venomous, waspish.

– OPPOSITES bland, mild.

punish ● verb **1** *they punished their children* DISCIPLINE, bring someone to book, teach someone a lesson; tan someone's hide; *informal* murder, wallop, come down on (like a ton of bricks), have someone's guts for garters; *Brit. informal* give someone what for; *dated* chastise. **2** *higher charges would punish the poor* PENALIZE, unfairly disadvantage, handicap, hurt, wrong, ill-use, maltreat. **3** *the strikers punished the defence's mistakes* EXPLOIT, take advantage of, turn to account, profit from, capitalize on, cash in on; *informal* walk all over.

punishable ● adjective ILLEGAL, unlawful, illegitimate, criminal, felonious, actionable, indictable, penal; blameworthy, dishonest, fraudulent, unauthorized, outlawed, banned, forbidden, prohibited, interdicted, proscribed.

punishing ● adjective *a punishing schedule* ARDUOUS, demanding, taxing, onerous, burdensome, strenuous, rigorous, stressful, trying; hard, difficult, tough, exhausting, tiring, gruelling, crippling, relentless; *informal* killing.

– OPPOSITES easy.

punishment ● noun **1** *the punishment of the guilty* PENALIZING, punishing, disciplining; retribution; *dated* chastisement. **2** *the teacher imposed punishments* PENALTY, penance, sanction, sentence, one's just deserts; discipline, correction, vengeance, justice, judgement; *informal* comeuppance. **3** *both boxers took punishment* A BATTERING, a thrashing, a beating, a drubbing; *informal* a hiding. **4** *ovens take continual punishment* MALTREATMENT, mistreatment, abuse, ill-use, manhandling; damage, harm.

– RELATED TERMS punitive, penal.

punitive ● adjective **1** *punitive measures* PENAL, disciplinary, corrective, correctional, retributive. **2** *punitive taxes* HARSH, severe, stiff, stringent, burdensome, demanding, crushing, crippling;

punt[4] /pŏont/ ● **noun** the basic monetary unit of the Republic of Ireland.
– ORIGIN Irish, 'a pound'.

punter ● **noun 1** informal a person who gambles or places a bet. **2** Brit. informal a customer or client.

puny /pyōoni/ ● **adjective** (**punier**, **puniest**) **1** small and weak. **2** meagre.
– DERIVATIVES **punily** adverb **puniness** noun.
– ORIGIN phonetic spelling of PUISNE.

pup ● **noun 1** a young dog. **2** a young wolf, seal, rat, or other mammal. **3** dated, chiefly Brit. a cheeky or arrogant boy or young man. ● **verb** (**pupped**, **pupping**) give birth to a pup or pups.
– PHRASES **sell** (or **buy**) **a pup** Brit. informal swindle (or be swindled) by selling (or buying) something worthless.
– ORIGIN from PUPPY.

pupa /pyōopə/ ● **noun** (pl. **pupae** /pyōopee/) an insect in its inactive immature form between larva and adult, e.g. a chrysalis.
– DERIVATIVES **pupal** adjective.
– ORIGIN Latin, 'girl, doll'.

pupate ● **verb** become a pupa.
– DERIVATIVES **pupation** noun.

pupil[1] ● **noun 1** a person who is taught by another, especially a schoolchild. **2** Brit. a trainee barrister.
– ORIGIN from Latin *pupillus* 'little boy' and *pupilla* 'little girl'.

pupil[2] ● **noun** the dark circular opening in the centre of the iris of the eye, which regulates the amount of light reaching the retina.
– ORIGIN Latin *pupilla* 'little doll' (from the tiny reflected images visible in the eye).

pupillage ● **noun 1** the state of being a pupil. **2** Law (in the UK) apprenticeship to a member of the Bar, which qualifies a barrister to practise independently.

puppet ● **noun 1** a movable model of a person or animal, moved either by strings or by a hand inside it, used to entertain. **2** a person under the control of another.
– DERIVATIVES **puppeteer** noun **puppetry** noun.
– ORIGIN later form of POPPET.

puppy ● **noun** (pl. **puppies**) **1** a young dog. **2** informal, dated a conceited or arrogant young man.
– DERIVATIVES **puppyish** adjective.
– ORIGIN perhaps from Old French *poupee* 'doll, toy'.

puppy fat ● **noun** fat on the body of a child which disappears around adolescence.

puppy love ● **noun** intense but relatively short-lived love, typically associated with adolescents.

purblind /purblīnd/ ● **adjective 1** partially sighted. **2** lacking in discernment or understanding.
– ORIGIN originally in the sense 'completely blind': from PURE 'utterly' + BLIND.

purchase ● **verb** obtain by payment; buy. ● **noun 1** the action of buying. **2** a thing bought. **3** firm contact or grip. **4** a pulley or similar device for moving heavy objects.
– DERIVATIVES **purchasable** adjective **purchaser** noun.
– ORIGIN Old French *pourchacier* 'seek to obtain or bring about'.

purdah /purdə/ ● **noun** the practice in certain Muslim and Hindu societies of screening women from men or strangers by means of a curtain or all-enveloping clothes.
– ORIGIN from Urdu and Persian, 'veil, curtain'.

pure ● **adjective 1** not mixed or adulterated with any other substance or material. **2** free of impurities. **3** innocent or morally good. **4** complete; nothing but: *a shout of pure anger*. **5** theoretical rather than practical: *pure mathematics*. **6** (of a sound) perfectly in tune and with a clear tone.
– DERIVATIVES **purely** adverb.
– ORIGIN Latin *purus*.

pure-bred ● **adjective** (of an animal) bred from parents of the same breed or variety.

purée /pyooray/ ● **noun** a smooth pulp of liquidized, crushed, or sieved fruit or vegetables. ● **verb** (**purées**, **puréed**, **puréeing**) make a purée of.
– ORIGIN French, 'purified'.

purgation /purgaysh'n/ ● **noun 1** purification. **2** evacuation of the bowels brought about by laxatives.
– ORIGIN Latin, from *purgare* 'purify'.

purgative /purgətiv/ ● **adjective** strongly laxative in effect. ● **noun** a laxative.

purgatory /purgətri/ ● **noun** (pl. **purgatories**) **1** (in Catholic doctrine) a place or state of suffering inhabited by the souls of sinners who are atoning for their sins before going to heaven. **2** mental anguish.
– DERIVATIVES **purgatorial** adjective.
– ORIGIN Latin *purgatorium*, from *purgare* 'purge'.

purge ● **verb 1** rid (someone or something) of people or things considered undesirable or harmful. **2** evacuate one's bowels, especially as a result of taking a laxative. **3** Law atone for or wipe out (contempt of court). ● **noun 1** an act of purging. **2** dated a laxative.
– ORIGIN Latin *purgare* 'purify', from *purus* 'pure'.

puri /poori/ ● **noun** (pl. **puris**) (in Indian cookery) a small, round piece of unleavened bread which puffs up when deep-fried.
– ORIGIN Sanskrit.

purify ● **verb** (**purifies**, **purified**) remove contaminants from;

Thesaurus

high, sky-high, inflated, exorbitant, extortionate, excessive, inordinate, unreasonable; *Brit.* swingeing.

punter ● **noun 1** *(informal) each punter has a 1:39 chance* GAMBLER, backer, staker, speculator, bettor; *informal* plunger, high roller. **2** *(Brit. informal) sales bring the punters in* CUSTOMER, client, patron; buyer, purchaser, shopper, consumer; (**punters**) clientele, audience, trade, business; *Brit. informal* bums on seats.

puny ● **adjective 1** *he grew up puny* UNDERSIZED, undernourished, underfed, stunted, slight, small, little; weak, feeble, sickly, delicate, frail, fragile; *informal* weedy, pint-sized. **2** *puny efforts to save their homes* PITIFUL, pitiable, inadequate, insufficient, derisory, miserable, sorry, meagre, paltry, trifling, inconsequential; *informal* pathetic, measly, piddling; *formal* exiguous.
– OPPOSITES sturdy, substantial.

pupil ● **noun 1** *former pupils of the school* STUDENT, scholar; schoolchild, schoolboy, schoolgirl. **2** *the guru's pupils* DISCIPLE, follower, student, protégé, apprentice, trainee, novice.

puppet ● **noun 1** *a show with puppets* MARIONETTE; glove puppet, hand puppet, finger puppet. **2** *a puppet of the government* PAWN, tool, instrument, cat's paw, poodle, creature, dupe; mouthpiece, minion, stooge.

purchase ● **verb** *we purchased the software* BUY, pay for, acquire, obtain, pick up, snap up, take, procure; invest in; *informal* get hold of, score.
– OPPOSITES sell.
● **noun 1** *he's happy with his purchase* ACQUISITION, buy, investment, order, bargain; shopping, goods. **2** *he could get no purchase on the wall* GRIP, grasp, hold, foothold, toehold, anchorage, attachment, support; resistance, friction, leverage.
– OPPOSITES sale.

purchaser ● **noun** BUYER, shopper, customer, consumer, patron; *Law* vendee.

pure ● **adjective 1** *pure gold* UNADULTERATED, uncontaminated, unmixed, undiluted, unalloyed, unblended; sterling, solid, refined, 100%; clarified, clear, filtered; flawless, perfect, genuine, real. **2** *the air is so pure* CLEAN, clear, fresh, sparkling, unpolluted, untainted, uncontaminated; wholesome, natural, healthy; sanitary, uninfected, disinfected, germ-free, sterile, sterilized, aseptic. **3** *pure in body and mind* VIRTUOUS, moral, ethical, good, righteous, saintly, honourable, reputable, wholesome, clean, honest, upright, upstanding, exemplary, irreproachable; chaste, virginal, maidenly; decent, worthy, noble, blameless, guiltless, spotless, unsullied, uncorrupted, undefiled; *informal* squeaky clean. **4** *pure maths* THEORETICAL, abstract, conceptual, academic, hypothetical, speculative, conjectural. **5** *three hours of pure magic* SHEER, utter, absolute, out-and-out, complete, total, perfect, unmitigated.
– OPPOSITES adulterated, polluted, immoral, practical.

pure-bred ● **adjective** PEDIGREE, thoroughbred, full-bred, blooded, pedigreed, pure.
– OPPOSITES hybrid.

purely ● **adverb** ENTIRELY, completely, absolutely, wholly, exclusively, solely, only, just, merely.

purgative ● **adjective** *purgative medicine* LAXATIVE, evacuant; *Medicine* aperient; *Medicine, archaic* lenitive.
● **noun** *orris root is a purgative* LAXATIVE, evacuant; *Medicine* aperient; *Medicine, archaic* lenitive; *dated* purge.

purgatory ● **noun** TORMENT, torture, misery, suffering, affliction, anguish, agony, woe, hell; an ordeal, a nightmare.
– OPPOSITES paradise.

purge ● **verb 1** *he purged them of their doubt* CLEANSE, clear, purify, wash, shrive, absolve; *rare* lustrate. **2** *lawbreakers were purged from the army* REMOVE, get rid of, expel, eject, exclude, dismiss,

make pure.
– DERIVATIVES **purification** noun **purifier** noun.
purism ● noun scrupulous observance of traditional rules or structures, especially in language or style.
– DERIVATIVES **purist** noun & adjective.
puritan ● noun **1** (**Puritan**) a member of a group of English Protestants in the 16th and 17th centuries who sought to simplify and regulate forms of worship. **2** a person with censorious moral beliefs, especially about self-indulgence and sex. ● adjective **1** (**Puritan**) relating to the Puritans. **2** characteristic of a puritan.
– DERIVATIVES **puritanical** adjective **puritanism** (also **Puritanism**) noun.
purity ● noun the state of being pure.
purl[1] ● adjective (of a knitting stitch) made by putting the needle through the front of the stitch from right to left. Compare with PLAIN[1] (in sense 8). ● verb knit with a purl stitch.
– ORIGIN origin uncertain.
purl[2] ● verb literary (of a stream or river) flow with a swirling motion and babbling sound.
– ORIGIN probably imitative.
purler ● noun Brit. informal a headlong fall.
– ORIGIN from dialect *purl* 'upset, overturn'.
purlieu /purlyoō/ ● noun (pl. **purlieus** or **purlieux**) **1** (**purlieus**) the area near or surrounding a place. **2** Brit. historical a tract on the border of a forest.
– ORIGIN probably from Old French *puralee* 'a walk round to settle boundaries'.
purlin /purlin/ ● noun a horizontal beam along the length of a roof, supporting the rafters.
– ORIGIN perhaps French.
purloin /pərloyn/ ● verb formal or humorous steal.
– ORIGIN Old French *purloigner* 'put away'.
purple ● noun **1** a colour intermediate between red and blue. **2** (also **Tyrian purple**) a crimson dye obtained from some molluscs, used for robes worn by an emperor or senior magistrate in ancient Rome or Byzantium. **3** (**the purple**) the scarlet official dress of a cardinal. ● adjective of a colour intermediate between red and blue.
– PHRASES **born in** (or **to**) **the purple** born into a reigning family or privileged class.
– DERIVATIVES **purplish** adjective **purply** adjective.
– ORIGIN from Greek *porphura*, denoting molluscs that yielded a crimson dye, also cloth dyed with this.
purple heart ● noun **1** (**Purple Heart**) (in the US) a decoration for those wounded or killed in action. **2** Brit. informal a mauve heart-shaped stimulant tablet, especially of amphetamine.
purple passage ● noun an excessively ornate passage in a literary work.
purple patch ● noun **1** informal a run of success or good luck. **2** a purple passage.
purple prose ● noun prose that is too ornate.
purport ● verb /pərport/ appear to be or do, especially falsely. ● noun /purport/ **1** the meaning of something. **2** the purpose of something.
– DERIVATIVES **purported** adjective **purportedly** adverb.
– ORIGIN Latin *proportare*, from *pro-* 'forth' + *portare* 'carry, bear'.
purpose ● noun **1** the reason for which something is done or for which something exists. **2** resolve or determination. ● verb formal have as one's objective.
– PHRASES **on purpose** intentionally.
– ORIGIN Old French *porpos*, from *proposer* 'to propose'.
purposeful ● adjective **1** having or showing determination. **2** having a purpose.
– DERIVATIVES **purposefully** adverb **purposefulness** noun.
purposeless ● adjective done with or having no purpose.
– DERIVATIVES **purposelessly** adverb **purposelessness** noun.
purposely ● adverb deliberately; on purpose.
purposive ● adjective having or done with a purpose.
– DERIVATIVES **purposively** adverb **purposiveness** noun.
purr ● verb **1** (of a cat) make a low continuous vibratory sound expressing contentment. **2** (of a vehicle or engine) move or run smoothly while making a similar sound. ● noun a purring sound.
– ORIGIN imitative.
purse ● noun **1** a small pouch for carrying money. **2** N. Amer. a handbag. **3** money for spending; funds. **4** a sum of money given as a prize in a sporting contest. ● verb (with reference to the lips) pucker or contract.
– PHRASES **hold the purse strings** have control of expenditure.
– ORIGIN Latin *bursa*, from Greek *bursa* 'hide, leather'.
purser ● noun a ship's officer who keeps the accounts, especially on a passenger vessel.
purse seine ● noun a seine net which may be drawn into the shape of a bag, used for catching shoal fish.
purslane /purslin/ ● noun a small fleshy-leaved plant of damp or marshy habitats, some kinds of which are edible.
– ORIGIN Old French *porcelaine*, probably from Latin *porcillaca*, variant of *portulaca*.
pursuance ● noun formal the carrying out of a plan or action.
pursuant /pərsyoōənt/ ● adverb (**pursuant to**) formal in accord-

p

Thesaurus

sack, oust, eradicate, clear out, weed out.
● noun *the purge of dissidents* REMOVAL, expulsion, ejection, exclusion, eviction, dismissal, sacking, ousting, eradication.
purify ● verb **1** *trees help to purify the air* CLEAN, cleanse, refine, decontaminate; filter, clarify, clear, freshen, deodorize; sanitize, disinfect, sterilize. **2** *they purify themselves before the ceremony* PURGE, cleanse, unburden, deliver; redeem, shrive, exorcize, sanctify; *rare* lustrate.
purist ● noun PEDANT, perfectionist, formalist, literalist, stickler, traditionalist, doctrinaire, quibbler, dogmatist; *informal* nit-picker; *archaic* precisian.
puritan ● noun MORALIST, pietist, prude, prig, killjoy; ascetic; *informal* goody-goody, Holy Joe; *N. Amer. informal* bluenose.
puritanical ● adjective MORALISTIC, puritan, pietistic, strait-laced, stuffy, prudish, prim, priggish; narrow-minded, sententious, censorious; austere, severe, ascetic, abstemious; *informal* goody-goody, starchy.
– OPPOSITES permissive.
purity ● noun **1** *the purity of our tap water* CLEANNESS, clearness, clarity, freshness; sterility. **2** *they sought purity in a foul world* VIRTUE, morality, goodness, righteousness, saintliness, piety, honour, honesty, integrity, decency, ethicality, impeccability; innocence, chastity.
purloin ● verb (*formal*) STEAL, thieve, rob, take, snatch, pilfer, loot, appropriate; *informal* swipe, nab, rip off, lift, 'liberate', 'borrow', filch, snaffle; *Brit. informal* pinch, half-inch, nick, whip, knock off, nobble; *N. Amer. informal* heist.
purport ● verb *this work purports to be authoritative* CLAIM, profess, pretend; appear, seem; be ostensibly, pose as, impersonate, masquerade as, pass for.
● noun **1** *the purport of his remarks* GIST, substance, drift, implication, intention, meaning, significance, sense, essence, thrust, message. **2** *the purport of the attack* INTENTION, purpose, object, objective, aim, goal, target, end, design, idea.
purpose ● noun **1** *the purpose of his visit* MOTIVE, motivation, grounds, cause, occasion, reason, point, basis, justification. **2** *their purpose was to subvert the economy* INTENTION, aim, object, objective, goal, end, plan, scheme, target; ambition, aspiration. **3** *I cannot see any purpose in it* ADVANTAGE, benefit, good, use, value, merit, worth, profit; *informal* mileage, percentage. **4** *the original purpose of the porch* FUNCTION, role, use. **5** *they started the game with purpose* DETERMINATION, resolution, resolve, steadfastness, backbone, drive, push, enthusiasm, ambition, motivation, commitment, conviction, dedication; *informal* get-up-and-go.
● verb (*formal*) *they purposed to reach the summit* INTEND, mean, aim, plan, design, have the intention; decide, resolve, determine, propose, aspire, set one's sights on.
– PHRASES **on purpose** DELIBERATELY, intentionally, purposely, by design, wilfully, knowingly, consciously, of one's own volition; expressly, specifically, especially, specially.
purposeful ● adjective DETERMINED, resolute, steadfast, single-minded; enthusiastic, motivated, committed, dedicated, persistent, dogged, unfaltering, unshakeable.
– OPPOSITES aimless.
purposely ● adverb. See ON PURPOSE at PURPOSE.
purse ● noun **1** *the money fell out of her purse* WALLET, money bag; *N. Amer.* change purse, billfold. **2** (*N. Amer.*) *a woman's purse.* See HANDBAG. **3** *the public purse* FUND(S), kitty, coffers, pool, bank, treasury, exchequer; money, finances, wealth, reserves, cash, capital, assets. **4** *the fight will net him a $75,000 purse* PRIZE, reward, award; winnings, stake(s).
● verb *he pursed his lips* PRESS TOGETHER, compress, tighten, puck-

ance with.
– ORIGIN from Old French, 'pursuing'; later influenced in spelling by PURSUE.
pursue ● verb (**pursues**, **pursued**, **pursuing**) **1** follow in order to catch or attack. **2** seek to attain (a goal). **3** engage in or continue with (an activity or course of action). **4** continue to investigate or discuss.
– DERIVATIVES **pursuer** noun.
– ORIGIN Old French *pursuer*, from Latin *prosequi* 'prosecute'.
pursuit ● noun **1** the action of pursuing. **2** a recreational or sporting activity.
pursuivant /persivənt/ ● noun Brit. an officer of the College of Arms ranking below a herald.
– ORIGIN Old French *pursivant* 'follower or attendant'.
purulent /pyooroolənt/ ● adjective consisting of, containing, or discharging pus.
– ORIGIN Latin *purulentus*, from *pus* 'pus'.
purvey ● verb provide or supply (food or drink) as one's business.
– DERIVATIVES **purveyor** noun.
– ORIGIN originally also in the senses 'foresee', 'attend to in advance': from Old French *purveier*, from Latin *providere* 'foresee, attend to'.
purview ● noun **1** the scope of the influence or concerns of something. **2** a range of experience or thought.
– ORIGIN from Old French *purveu* 'foreseen', from *purveier* (see PURVEY).
pus ● noun a thick yellowish or greenish opaque liquid produced in infected tissue.
– ORIGIN Latin.
push ● verb **1** exert force on (someone or something) so as to move them away from oneself or from the source of the force. **2** move (one's body or a part of it) forcefully into a specified position. **3** move forward by using force. **4** drive oneself or urge (someone) to greater effort. **5** (**push for**) demand persistently. **6** informal promote the use, sale, or acceptance of. **7** informal sell (a narcotic drug) illegally. **8** (**be pushed**) informal have very little of something, especially time. **9** (**be pushing**) informal be nearly (a particular age). ● noun **1** an act of pushing. **2** a vigorous effort. **3** forcefulness and enterprise.
– PHRASES **at a push** Brit. informal only if necessary or with difficulty. **get** (or **give someone**) **the push** Brit. informal **1** be dismissed (or dismiss someone) from a job. **2** be rejected in (or end) a relationship. **push ahead** proceed with or continue a course of action. **push along** (or **off**) informal go away. **push in** go in front of people who are already queuing. **push one's luck** informal take a risk on the assumption that one will continue to be successful. **when push comes to shove** informal when one must commit oneself to action.
– DERIVATIVES **pusher** noun.
– ORIGIN Old French *pousser*, from Latin *pulsare* 'pulse'.
pushbike ● noun Brit. informal a bicycle.
pushcart ● noun a small handcart or barrow.
pushchair ● noun Brit. a folding chair on wheels, in which a young child can be pushed along.
pushover ● noun informal **1** a person who is easy to influence or defeat. **2** a thing that is easily done.
push technology ● noun Computing a service in which a provider supplies information from the Internet to a subscriber in pre-selected categories of interest.
pushy ● adjective (**pushier**, **pushiest**) excessively self-assertive or ambitious.
– DERIVATIVES **pushiness** noun.
pusillanimous /pyōōsilanniməss/ ● adjective lacking courage; timid.
– DERIVATIVES **pusillanimity** /pyōōsilənimmiti/ noun.
– ORIGIN from Latin *pusillus* 'very small' + *animus* 'mind'.
puss ● noun informal **1** a cat. **2** a coquettish girl or young woman: *a glamour puss*.
– ORIGIN probably from Low German *pūs* or Dutch *poes*.
pussy ● noun (pl. **pussies**) **1** (also **pussy cat**) informal a cat. **2** vulgar slang a woman's genitals. **3** vulgar slang women considered sexually.
pussyfoot ● verb (**pussyfoots**, **pussyfooting**, **pussyfooted**) **1** act very cautiously. **2** move stealthily.
pussy willow ● noun a willow with soft fluffy catkins that appear before the leaves.
pustule /pustyōōl/ ● noun a small blister or pimple containing

Thesaurus

er, pout.
pursuance ● noun *(formal)* **1** *he was arrested in pursuance of this Act* EXECUTION, discharge, implementation, performance, accomplishment, fulfilment, dispatch, prosecution, enforcement. **2** *their pursuance of power* SEARCH FOR, pursuit of, quest for, hunt for.
pursue ● verb **1** *I pursued him down the garden* FOLLOW, run after, chase; hunt, stalk, track, trail, shadow, hound, course; *informal* tail. **2** *pursue the goal of political union* STRIVE FOR, work towards, seek, search for, aim at/for, aspire to. **3** *he had been pursuing her for weeks* WOO, pay court to, chase, run after; *informal* make up to; *dated* court, make love to, romance, set one's cap at. **4** *she pursued a political career* ENGAGE IN, be occupied in, practise, follow, prosecute, conduct, ply, take up, undertake, carry on. **5** *we will not pursue the matter* INVESTIGATE, research, inquire into, look into, examine, scrutinize, analyse, delve into, probe.
– OPPOSITES avoid, shun.
pursuit ● noun **1** *the pursuit of profit* STRIVING TOWARDS, quest after/for, search for; aim, goal, objective, dream. **2** *a worthwhile pursuit* ACTIVITY, hobby, pastime, diversion, recreation, relaxation, divertissement, amusement; occupation, trade, vocation, business, work, job, employment.
purvey ● verb SELL, supply, provide, furnish, cater, retail, deal in, trade, stock, offer; peddle, hawk, tout, traffic in; *informal* flog.
purveyor ● noun SELLER, vendor, retailer, supplier, stockist, trader, pedlar, hawker; *Brit.* tout.
pus ● noun SUPPURATION, matter; discharge, secretion.
– RELATED TERMS purulent.
push ● verb **1** *she tried to push him away* SHOVE, thrust, propel; send, drive, force, prod, poke, nudge, elbow, shoulder; sweep, bundle, hustle, manhandle. **2** *she pushed her way into the flat* FORCE, shove, thrust, squeeze, jostle, elbow, shoulder, bundle, hustle; work, inch. **3** *he pushed the panic button* PRESS, depress, bear down on, hold down, squeeze; operate, activate. **4** *don't push her to join in* URGE, press, pressure, pressurize, force, impel, coerce, nag; prevail on, browbeat into; *informal* lean on, twist someone's arm, bulldoze. **5** *(informal) they push their own products* ADVERTISE, publicize, promote, bang the drum for; sell, market, merchandise; *informal* plug, hype (up), puff, flog; *N. Amer. informal* ballyhoo.
– OPPOSITES pull.
● noun **1** *I felt a push in the back* SHOVE, thrust, nudge, ram, bump, jolt, butt, prod, poke. **2** *the enemy's eastward push* ADVANCE, drive, thrust, charge, attack, assault, onslaught, onrush, offensive, sortie, sally, incursion.
– PHRASES **at a push** *(Brit. informal)* IF NECESSARY, if need be, if needs must, if all else fails, in an emergency. **push someone around** BULLY, domineer, ride roughshod over, trample on, bulldoze, browbeat, tyrannize, intimidate, threaten, victimize, pick on; *informal* lean on, boss about/around. **push for** DEMAND, call for, request, press for, campaign for, lobby for, speak up for; urge, promote, advocate, champion, espouse. **push off** *(informal)* GO AWAY, depart, leave, get out; go, get moving, be off (with you), shoo; *informal* skedaddle, split, scram, run along, beat it, get lost, shove off, buzz off, clear off, on your bike; *Brit. informal* get stuffed, sling your hook, hop it, bog off, naff off; *N. Amer. informal* bug off, take a powder, take a hike; *Austral./NZ informal* rack off, nick off; *poetic/literary* begone. **push on** PRESS ON, continue one's journey, carry on, advance, proceed, go on, progress, make headway, forge ahead.
pushover ● noun **1** *the teacher was a pushover* WEAKLING, feeble opponent, man of straw; *informal* soft touch, easy touch, easy meat. **2** *this course is no pushover* EASY TASK, walkover, five-finger exercise, gift; child's play; *informal* doddle, piece of cake, picnic, money for old rope, cinch, breeze; *Brit. informal* doss; *N. Amer. informal* duck soup, snap; *Austral./NZ informal* bludge; *dated* snip.
pushy ● adjective ASSERTIVE, self-assertive, overbearing, domineering, aggressive, forceful, forward, bold, bumptious, officious; thrusting, ambitious, overconfident, cocky; *informal* bossy; *dated* pushful.
– OPPOSITES submissive.
pusillanimous ● adjective TIMID, timorous, cowardly, fearful, faint-hearted, lily-livered, spineless, craven, shrinking; *informal* chicken, gutless, wimpy, wimpish, sissy, yellow, yellow-bellied.
– OPPOSITES brave.
pussyfoot ● verb **1** *you can't pussyfoot around with this* EQUIVOCATE, tergiversate, be evasive, be non-committal, sidestep the issue, prevaricate, quibble, hedge, beat about the bush; *Brit.* hum and haw; *informal* duck the question, sit on the fence, shilly-shally.

pus.
– DERIVATIVES **pustular** adjective.
– ORIGIN Latin *pustula*.

put ● verb (**putting**; past and past part. **put**) **1** move to or place in a particular position. **2** bring into a particular state or condition: *she tried to put me at ease.* **3** (**put on/on to**) cause to carry or be subject to. **4** assign a value, figure, or limit to. **5** express in a particular way. **6** (of a ship) proceed in a particular direction: *the boat put out to sea.* **7** throw (a shot or weight) as an athletic sport. ● noun a throw of the shot or weight.
– PHRASES **put about 1** spread (information or rumours). **2** (of a ship) turn on the opposite tack. **put away** informal **1** consume (food or drink) in large quantities. **2** confine in a prison or psychiatric hospital. **put down 1** suppress (a rebellion, coup, or riot) by force. **2** kill (a sick, old, or injured animal). **3** pay (a sum) as a deposit. **4** informal humiliate by public criticism. **put down to** attribute (something) to. **put one's hands together** applaud. **put off 1** cancel or postpone an appointment with. **2** postpone. **3** cause to feel dislike or lose enthusiasm. **4** distract. **put on 1** present or provide (a play, service, etc.). **2** become heavier by (a specified amount). **3** assume (an expression, accent, etc.). **put on to** make aware of. **put out 1** inconvenience, upset, or annoy. **2** dislocate (a joint). **put one over on** informal deceive into accepting something false. **put through 1** subject to a gruelling or unpleasant experience. **2** connect (someone) by telephone to another person or place. **put to** submit (something) to (someone) for consideration. **put up 1** present, provide, or offer. **2** accommodate temporarily. **3** propose for election or adoption. **put upon** informal exploit the good nature of. **put up or shut up** informal justify oneself or remain silent. **put up to** informal encourage to do (something wrong or unwise). **put up with** tolerate or endure.
– ORIGIN Old English.

putative /pyo͞otətiv/ ● adjective generally considered or reputed to be.
– DERIVATIVES **putatively** adverb.
– ORIGIN Latin *putativus*, from *putare* 'think'.

put-down ● noun informal a humiliating or critical remark.

put-put /putput/ ● noun & verb another term for PUTTER[2].

putrefy /pyo͞otrifī/ ● verb (**putrefies**, **putrefied**) decay or rot and produce a fetid smell.
– DERIVATIVES **putrefaction** noun.
– ORIGIN Latin *putrefacere*, from *puter* 'rotten'.

putrescent /pyo͞otress'nt/ ● adjective becoming putrid; rotting.

putrid ● adjective **1** decaying or rotting and emitting a fetid smell. **2** informal very unpleasant.
– ORIGIN Latin *putridus*, from *putrere* 'to rot'.

putsch /po͝och/ ● noun a violent attempt to overthrow a government.
– ORIGIN Swiss German, 'thrust, blow'.

putt /put/ ● verb (**putted**, **putting**) strike a golf ball gently so that it rolls into or near a hole. ● noun a stroke of this kind.
– ORIGIN Scots form of PUT.

puttanesca /po͞otənesskə/ ● adjective denoting a pasta sauce of tomatoes, garlic, olives, anchovies, etc.
– ORIGIN Italian, from *puttana* 'a prostitute' (the sauce is said to have been devised by prostitutes as one which could be cooked quickly between clients' visits).

puttee /putti/ ● noun a long strip of cloth wound spirally round the leg from ankle to knee for protection and support.

Thesaurus

2 *I had to pussyfoot over the gravel* CREEP, tiptoe, pad, soft-shoe, steal, sneak, slink.

pustule ● noun PIMPLE, spot, bleb, boil, swelling, eruption, carbuncle, blister, abscess; *informal* whitehead, zit; *Scottish informal* plook; *technical* comedo, papule.

put ● verb **1** *she put the parcel on a chair* PLACE, set (down), lay (down), deposit, position, settle; leave, plant; *informal* stick, dump, bung, park, plonk, pop; *N. Amer. informal* plunk. **2** *he didn't want to be put in a category* ASSIGN TO, consign to, allocate to, place in. **3** *don't put the blame on me* LAY, pin, place, fix; attribute to, impute to, assign to, allocate to, ascribe to. **4** *the proposals put to the committee* SUBMIT, present, tender, offer, proffer, advance, suggest, propose. **5** *she put it bluntly* EXPRESS, word, phrase, frame, formulate, render, convey, couch; state, say, utter. **6** *he put the cost at £8,000* ESTIMATE, calculate, reckon, gauge, assess, evaluate, value, judge, measure, compute, fix, set; *informal* guesstimate.
– PHRASES **put about** *the ship put about* TURN ROUND, come about, change course. **put something about** *the rumour had been put about* SPREAD, circulate, make public, disseminate, broadcast, publicize, pass on, propagate, bandy about. **put something across/over** COMMUNICATE, convey, get across/over, explain, make clear, spell out, clarify; get through to someone. **put something aside 1** *we've got a bit put aside in the bank* SAVE, put by, set aside, deposit, reserve, store, stockpile, hoard, stow, cache; *informal* salt away, squirrel away, stash away. **2** *they put aside their differences* DISREGARD, set aside, ignore, forget, discount, bury. **put someone away** (*informal*) **1** *they put him away for life* JAIL, imprison, put in prison, put behind bars, lock up, incarcerate; *informal* cage; *Brit. informal* bang up, send down; *N. Amer. informal* jug. **2** *you should be put away!* CERTIFY, commit, hospitalize, institutionalize, put in a psychiatric hospital. **put something away 1** *I put away some money.* See PUT SOMETHING ASIDE sense 1. **2** *she never puts her things away* REPLACE, put back, tidy away, tidy up, clear away. **3** (*informal*) *she can put away a lot of food.* See EAT sense 1. **put something back 1** *he put the books back* REPLACE, return, restore, put away, tidy away. **2** *they put back the film's release date.* See PUT SOMETHING OFF. **put someone down 1** (*informal*) *he often puts me down* CRITICIZE, belittle, disparage, deprecate, denigrate, slight, humiliate, shame, crush, squash, deflate; *informal* show up, cut down to size. **2** *I put him down as shy* CONSIDER TO BE, judge to be, reckon to be, take to be; regard, have down, take for. **put something down 1** *he put his ideas down on paper* WRITE DOWN, note down, jot down, take down, set down; list, record, register, log. **2** *they put down the rebellion* SUPPRESS, check, crush, quash, squash, quell, overthrow, stamp out, repress, subdue. **3** *the horse had to be put down* DESTROY, put to sleep, put out of its misery, put to death, kill. **4** *put it down to the heat* ATTRIBUTE, ascribe, chalk up, impute; blame on. **put something forward.** See PUT sense 4. **put in for** APPLY FOR, put in an application for, try for; request, seek, ask for. **put someone off** DETER, discourage, dissuade, daunt, unnerve, intimidate, scare off, repel, repulse; distract, disturb, divert, sidetrack; *informal* turn off. **put something off** POSTPONE, defer, delay, put back, adjourn, hold over, reschedule, shelve, table; *informal* put on ice, put on the back burner. **put it on** PRETEND, play-act, make believe, fake it, go through the motions. **put something on 1** *she put on jeans* DRESS IN, don, pull on, throw on, slip into, change into; *informal* doll oneself up in. **2** *I put the light on* SWITCH ON, turn on, activate. **3** *they put on an extra train* PROVIDE, lay on, supply, make available. **4** *the museum put on an exhibition* ORGANIZE, stage, mount, present, produce. **5** *she put on an American accent* FEIGN, fake, simulate, affect, assume. **6** *he put a fiver on Oxford United* BET, gamble, stake, wager; place, lay; risk, chance, hazard. **put one over on** (*informal*). See HOODWINK. **put someone out 1** *Maria was put out by the slur* ANNOY, anger, irritate, offend, affront, displease, irk, vex, pique, nettle, gall, upset; *informal* rile, miff, peeve; *Brit. informal* nark. **2** *I don't want to put you out* INCONVENIENCE, trouble, bother, impose on, disoblige; *informal* put someone on the spot; *formal* discommode. **put something out 1** *firemen put out the blaze* EXTINGUISH, quench, douse, smother; blow out, snuff out. **2** *he put out a press release* ISSUE, publish, release, bring out, circulate, publicize, post. **put someone up 1** *we can put him up for a few days* ACCOMMODATE, house, take in, lodge, quarter, billet; give someone a roof over their head. **2** *they put up a candidate* NOMINATE, propose, put forward, recommend. **put something up 1** *the building was put up 100 years ago* BUILD, construct, erect, raise. **2** *she put up a poster* DISPLAY, pin up, stick up, hang up, post. **3** *we put up alternative schemes* PROPOSE, put forward, present, submit, suggest, tender. **4** *the chancellor put up taxes* INCREASE, raise; *informal* jack up, hike, bump up. **5** *he put up most of the funding* PROVIDE, supply, furnish, give, contribute, donate, pledge, pay; *informal* fork out, cough up, shell out; *N. Amer. informal* ante up, pony up. **put upon** (*informal*) TAKE ADVANTAGE OF, impose on, exploit, use, misuse; *informal* walk all over. **put someone up to something** (*informal*) PERSUADE TO, encourage to, urge to, egg on to, incite to, goad into. **put up with** TOLERATE, take, stand (for), accept, stomach, swallow, endure, bear, support, take something lying down; *informal* abide, lump it; *Brit. informal* stick, be doing with; *formal* brook; *archaic* suffer.

putative ● adjective SUPPOSED, assumed, presumed; accepted, recognized; commonly regarded, presumptive, alleged, reputed, reported, rumoured.

put-down ● noun (*informal*) SNUB, slight, affront, rebuff, sneer, disparagement, humiliation, barb, jibe, criticism; *informal* dig.

putrefy ● verb DECAY, rot, decompose, go bad, go off, spoil, fester,

– ORIGIN Hindi, 'band, bandage'.
putter[1] /puttər/ ● noun a golf club designed for putting.
putter[2] /puttər/ ● noun the rapid intermittent sound of a small petrol engine. ● verb move with or make such a sound.
– ORIGIN imitative.
putting green ● noun a smooth area of short grass surrounding a hole on a golf course.
putto /puttō/ ● noun (pl. **putti** /putti/) a representation of a naked child, especially a cherub or a cupid in Renaissance art.
– ORIGIN Italian, 'boy'.
putty ● noun a malleable paste that hardens as it sets, used for sealing glass in window frames, filling holes in wood, etc.
– PHRASES **be (like) putty in someone's hands** be easily manipulated by someone.
– ORIGIN French *potée*, 'potful'.
put-up job ● noun informal something devised so as to deceive.
putz /puts/ N. Amer. informal ● noun **1** a stupid or worthless person. **2** vulgar slang a man's penis. ● verb (often **putz around**) engage in inconsequential or unproductive activity.
– ORIGIN Yiddish, 'penis'.
puzzle ● verb **1** confuse because difficult to understand. **2** think hard about something difficult to understand. ● noun **1** a game, toy, or problem designed to test ingenuity or knowledge. **2** a person or thing that is difficult to understand.
– DERIVATIVES **puzzlement** noun **puzzler** noun.
– ORIGIN of unknown origin.
PVA ● abbreviation polyvinyl acetate.
PVC ● abbreviation polyvinyl chloride.
PVS ● abbreviation Medicine persistent vegetative state.
PW ● abbreviation policewoman.
p.w. ● abbreviation per week.
PWA ● abbreviation person with Aids.
PWR ● abbreviation pressurized-water reactor.
pya /pyaa/ ● noun a monetary unit of Burma (Myanmar), equal to one hundredth of a kyat.
– ORIGIN Burmese.
pyaemia /pīeemiə/ (US **pyemia**) ● noun blood poisoning caused by the release of pus-forming bacteria from an abscess.
– ORIGIN Latin, from Greek *puon* 'pus' + *haima* 'blood'.
pye-dog (also **pi-dog**) ● noun (in Asia) a half-wild stray mongrel.
– ORIGIN from a Hindi word meaning 'outsider' + DOG.
pygmy (also **pigmy**) ● noun (pl. **pygmies**) **1** a member of certain peoples of very short stature in equatorial Africa. **2** chiefly derogatory a very small person or thing. **3** a person who is deficient in a particular respect: *intellectual pygmies*. ● adjective very small; dwarf.
– ORIGIN Greek *pugmaios* 'dwarf', from *pugmē* 'the length measured from elbow to knuckles'.
pyjamas (US **pajamas**) ● plural noun **1** a suit of loose trousers and jacket for sleeping in. **2** loose trousers with a drawstring waist, worn by both sexes in some Asian countries.
– ORIGIN from the Persian words for 'leg' + 'clothing'.
pylon ● noun **1** (also **electricity pylon**) a tall tower-like structure for carrying electricity cables. **2** a monumental gateway to an ancient Egyptian temple, formed by two truncated pyramidal towers.
– ORIGIN Greek *pulōn* 'gateway'.
pylorus /pīlorəss/ ● noun (pl. **pylori** /pīlorī/) Anatomy the opening from the stomach into the small intestine.
– DERIVATIVES **pyloric** adjective.
– ORIGIN Greek *pulouros* 'gatekeeper'.
pyracantha /pīrəkanthə/ ● noun a thorny evergreen shrub with white flowers and bright red or yellow berries.
– ORIGIN Latin, from Greek *pur* 'fire' + *akantha* 'thorn'.
pyramid ● noun **1** a monumental stone structure with a square or triangular base and sloping sides that meet in a point at the top, especially one built as a royal tomb in ancient Egypt. **2** Geometry a polyhedron of which one face is a polygon and the other faces are triangles with a common vertex. **3** a pyramid-shaped thing or pile of things. ● verb chiefly N. Amer. heap or stack in a pyramidal shape.
– ORIGIN Greek *puramis*.
pyramidal /pirammid'l/ ● adjective resembling a pyramid in shape.
pyramid selling ● noun a system of selling goods in which agency rights are sold to an increasing number of distributors at successively lower levels.
pyre ● noun a heap of combustible material, especially one for the ritual cremation of a corpse.
– ORIGIN Greek *pur* 'fire'.
pyrethrum /pīreethrəm/ ● noun **1** an aromatic plant of the daisy family, typically with brightly coloured flowers. **2** an insecticide made from the dried flowers of these plants.
– ORIGIN Greek *purethron* 'feverfew'.
pyretic /pīrettik/ ● adjective feverish or inducing fever.
– ORIGIN from Greek *puretos* 'fever'.
Pyrex ● noun trademark a hard heat-resistant type of glass.
pyrexia /pīreksiə/ ● noun Medicine fever.
– ORIGIN Greek *purexis*, from *puressein* 'be feverish'.
pyridoxine /pirridoksin/ ● noun vitamin B_6, a compound present chiefly in cereals, liver oils, and yeast, and important in the metabolism of fats.
– ORIGIN from *pyrid(ine)* (a liquid chemical) + *oxy(gen)*.
pyrites /pīrīteez/ (also **iron pyrites** or **pyrite**) ● noun a shiny yellow mineral consisting of iron disulphide.
– ORIGIN from Greek *puritēs* 'of fire', from *pur* 'fire'.
pyro- ● combining form **1** relating to fire: *pyromania*. **2** Chemistry & Mineralogy formed or affected by heat: *pyroxene*.
– ORIGIN from Greek *pur* 'fire'.
pyroclastic /pīrōklastik/ ● adjective Geology of or relating to rock fragments or ash erupted by a volcano, especially as a hot, dense, destructive flow.
– ORIGIN from Greek *klastos* 'broken in pieces'.
pyrogenic ● adjective **1** Medicine inducing fever. **2** resulting from combustion or heating.
pyrography /pīrogrəfi/ ● noun the art or technique of decorating wood or leather by burning a design on the surface with a heated metallic point.
pyromania ● noun an obsessive desire to set fire to things.
– DERIVATIVES **pyromaniac** noun.
pyrotechnic /pīrōteknik/ ● adjective **1** relating to fireworks. **2** brilliant or spectacular.
– DERIVATIVES **pyrotechnical** adjective.
pyrotechnics ● plural noun **1** a firework display. **2** (treated as sing.) the art of making fireworks or staging firework displays. **3** a spectacular performance or display: *vocal pyrotechnics*.
pyrrhic /pirrik/ ● adjective (of a victory) won at too great a cost to have been worthwhile for the victor.
– ORIGIN named after *Pyrrhus*, a king of Epirus whose victory over the Romans in 279 BC incurred heavy losses.
Pythagoras' theorem ● noun the theorem that the square on the hypotenuse of a right-angled triangle is equal in area to the sum of the squares on the other two sides.
Pythagorean /pīthaggəreeən/ ● adjective relating to the Greek

p

Thesaurus

perish, deteriorate; moulder.
putrid ● adjective DECOMPOSING, decaying, rotting, rotten, bad, off, putrefied, putrescent, rancid, mouldy; foul, fetid, rank.
puzzle ● verb **1** *her decision puzzled me* PERPLEX, confuse, bewilder, bemuse, baffle, mystify, confound, nonplus; *informal* flummox, faze, stump, beat; *N. Amer. informal* discombobulate. **2** *she puzzled over the problem* THINK HARD ABOUT, mull over, muse over, ponder, contemplate, meditate on, consider, deliberate on, chew over. **3** *she tried to puzzle out what he meant* WORK OUT, understand, comprehend, sort out, reason out, solve, make sense of, make head or tail of, unravel, decipher; *informal* figure out, suss out.
● noun *the poem has always been a puzzle* ENIGMA, mystery, paradox, conundrum, poser, riddle, problem; *informal* stumper.
puzzled ● adjective PERPLEXED, confused, bewildered, bemused, baffled, mystified, confounded, nonplussed, at a loss, at sea; *informal* flummoxed, stumped, fazed, clueless; *N. Amer. informal* discombobulated.
puzzling ● adjective BAFFLING, perplexing, bewildering, confusing, complicated, unclear, mysterious, enigmatic, ambiguous, obscure, abstruse, unfathomable, incomprehensible, impenetrable, cryptic.
pygmy ● noun **1** *a Congo pygmy* VERY SMALL PERSON, person of restricted growth, midget, dwarf, homunculus, manikin; Lilliputian; *informal* shrimp. **2** *an intellectual pygmy* LIGHTWEIGHT, mediocrity, nonentity, nobody, cipher; small fry; *informal* pipsqueak, no-hoper; *Brit. informal* squit; *N. Amer. informal* picayune.
– OPPOSITES giant.
pyromaniac ● noun ARSONIST, incendiary; *Brit.* fire-raiser; *informal* firebug, pyro; *N. Amer. informal* torch.

philosopher and mathematician Pythagoras (*c.*580–500 BC) or his philosophy. ● noun a follower of Pythagoras.

python ● noun a large non-venomous snake which kills prey by constriction.
– DERIVATIVES **pythonic** adjective.
– ORIGIN Greek *Puthōn*, a huge serpent killed by Apollo.

pyx /piks/ (also **pix**) ● noun Christian Church the container in which the consecrated bread of the Eucharist is kept.
– ORIGIN Greek *puxis* 'box'.

pzazz ● noun variant spelling of PIZZAZZ.

p

Qq

Q[1] (also **q**) ● noun (pl. **Qs** or **Q's**) the seventeenth letter of the alphabet.

Q[2] ● abbreviation **1** queen (used especially in card games and chess). **2** question.

QA ● abbreviation quality assurance.

Qabalah ● noun variant spelling of KABBALAH.

Qatari /kataari/ ● noun a person from Qatar, a country in the Persian Gulf. ● adjective relating to Qatar.

QB ● abbreviation Law Queen's Bench.

QC ● abbreviation **1** quality control. **2** Quebec. **3** Law Queen's Counsel.

QED ● abbreviation quod erat demonstrandum.

qi /kee/ ● noun variant spelling of CHI[2].

qigong /cheegong/ ● noun a Chinese system of physical exercises and breathing control related to tai chi.
– ORIGIN Chinese.

qintar /kintaar/ ● noun (pl. same, **qintars**, or **qindarka**) a monetary unit of Albania, equal to one hundredth of a lek.
– ORIGIN Albanian.

QPM ● abbreviation (in the UK) Queen's Police Medal.

qt ● abbreviation quart(s).

q.t. ● noun (in phrase **on the q.t.**) informal secretly.
– ORIGIN abbreviation of *quiet*.

qua /kwaa/ ● conjunction formal in the capacity of.
– ORIGIN Latin.

quack[1] ● noun the characteristic harsh sound made by a duck. ● verb make this sound.
– ORIGIN imitative.

quack[2] ● noun **1** an unqualified person who dishonestly claims to have medical knowledge. **2** Brit. informal a doctor.
– DERIVATIVES **quackery** noun.
– ORIGIN abbreviation of earlier *quacksalver*, from Dutch, probably from obsolete *quacken* 'prattle' + *salf* 'salve'.

quad ● noun **1** a quadrangle. **2** a quadruplet. ● adjective quadraphonic.

quad bike ● noun a motorcycle with four large tyres, for off-road use.

quadragenarian /kwodrəjinairiən/ ● noun a person who is between 40 and 49 years old.
– ORIGIN Latin *quadragenarius*, from *quadraginta* 'forty'.

Quadragesima /kwodrəjessimə/ ● noun the first Sunday in Lent.
– ORIGIN from Latin *quadragesimus* 'fortieth' (Lent lasting forty days).

quadrangle ● noun **1** a four-sided geometrical figure, especially a square or rectangle. **2** a square or rectangular courtyard enclosed by buildings.
– DERIVATIVES **quadrangular** adjective.
– ORIGIN from Latin *quadri-* 'four' + *angulus* 'corner, angle'.

quadrant ● noun **1** each of four parts of a circle, plane, body, etc. divided by two lines or planes at right angles. **2** historical an instrument for taking angular measurements of altitude in astronomy and navigation.
– ORIGIN Latin *quadrans* 'quarter', from *quattuor* 'four'.

quadraphonic /kwodrəfonnik/ (also **quadrophonic**) ● adjective (of sound reproduction) transmitted through four channels.
– DERIVATIVES **quadraphony** noun.

quadrate /kwodrət/ ● adjective roughly square or rectangular.
– ORIGIN from Latin *quadrare* 'make square'.

quadratic /kwodrattik/ ● adjective Mathematics involving the second and no higher power of an unknown quantity or variable.

quadrennial /kwodrenniəl/ ● adjective lasting for or recurring every four years.
– ORIGIN from Latin *quadri-* 'four' + *annus* 'year'.

quadri- ● combining form four; having four: *quadriplegia*.
– ORIGIN Latin, from *quattuor* 'four'.

quadriceps /kwodriseps/ ● noun (pl. same) a large muscle at the front of the thigh.
– ORIGIN from Latin, 'four-headed'.

quadrilateral ● noun a four-sided figure. ● adjective having four straight sides.

quadrille[1] /kwodril/ ● noun a square dance performed typically by four couples and containing five figures.
– ORIGIN French, from Spanish *cuadrilla* or Italian *quadriglia* 'troop, company'.

quadrille[2] /kwodril/ ● noun a trick-taking card game for four players, fashionable in the 18th century.
– ORIGIN French, perhaps from Spanish *cuartillo*, from *cuarto* 'fourth'.

quadrillion /kwodrilyən/ ● cardinal number **1** a thousand raised to the power of five (10^{15}); a thousand million million. **2** (also **quadrillions**) informal a very large number or amount.
– DERIVATIVES **quadrillionth** ordinal number.

quadripartite /kwodripaartīt/ ● adjective **1** consisting of four parts. **2** shared by or involving four parties.

quadriplegia /kwodripleejə/ ● noun Medicine paralysis of all four limbs.
– DERIVATIVES **quadriplegic** adjective & noun.

quadroon ● noun archaic a person who is one-quarter black by descent.
– ORIGIN Spanish *cuarterón*, from *cuarto* 'quarter'.

quadrophonic ● adjective variant spelling of QUADRAPHONIC.

quadruped /kwodrooped/ ● noun an animal which has four feet, especially a mammal.
– DERIVATIVES **quadrupedal** /kwodroopeed'l, kwodrōōpid'l/ adjective.
– ORIGIN from Latin *quadru-* 'four' + *pes* 'foot'.

quadruple ● adjective **1** consisting of four parts or elements. **2** four times as much or as many. **3** (of time in music) having four beats in a bar. ● verb increase or be increased fourfold. ● noun a quadruple number or amount.
– ORIGIN Latin *quadruplus*.

quadruplet ● noun each of four children born at one birth.

quadruplicate ● adjective /kwodrōōplikət/ consisting of four parts or elements. ● verb /kwodrōōplikayt/ **1** multiply by four. **2** make four copies of.
– PHRASES **in quadruplicate** in four copies.
– ORIGIN Latin *quadruplicare* 'to quadruple'.

quaff /kwof/ ● verb drink heartily.
– DERIVATIVES **quaffable** adjective **quaffer** noun.
– ORIGIN probably imitative.

quag /kwag, kwog/ ● noun archaic a marshy or boggy place.
– ORIGIN related to dialect *quag* 'to shake'.

quagga /kwaggə/ ● noun an extinct South African zebra with a yellowish-brown coat with darker stripes.
– ORIGIN probably from Khoikhoi.

quagmire /kwagmīr, kwog-/ ● noun **1** a soft boggy area of land that gives way underfoot. **2** a complex or difficult situation.

Thesaurus

quack ● noun **1** *a quack selling fake medicines* SWINDLER, charlatan, mountebank, trickster, fraud, fraudster, impostor, hoaxer, sharper; *informal* con man, shark; *Brit. informal* twister; *N. Amer. informal* grifter; *Austral. informal* shicer. **2** *(Brit. informal) get the quack to examine you.* See DOCTOR noun.

quadrangle ● noun COURTYARD, quad, court, cloister, precinct; square, plaza, piazza.

quaff ● verb DRINK, swallow, gulp (down), guzzle, slurp, down, drain, empty; imbibe, partake of, consume, sup, sip; *informal* sink, kill, glug, swig, swill, slug, knock back, toss off; *Brit. informal* get outside (of), shift, murder, neck; *N. Amer. informal* chug, snarf (down).

quagmire ● noun **1** *the field became a quagmire* SWAMP, morass, bog, marsh, mire, slough; *archaic* quag. **2** *a judicial quagmire* MUD-

quail[1] ● noun (pl. same or **quails**) a small short-tailed game bird, typically with brown camouflaged plumage.
– ORIGIN Old French *quaille*, from Latin *coacula*.
quail[2] ● verb feel or show fear or apprehension.
– ORIGIN originally in the sense 'waste away': of unknown origin.
quaint ● adjective attractively unusual or old-fashioned.
– DERIVATIVES **quaintly** adverb **quaintness** noun.
– ORIGIN originally in the sense 'wise', 'ingenious': from Old French *cointe*, from Latin *cognoscere* 'ascertain'.
quake ● verb **1** (especially of the earth) shake or tremble. **2** shudder with fear. ● noun informal an earthquake.
– ORIGIN Old English.
Quaker ● noun a member of the Religious Society of Friends, a Christian movement devoted to peaceful principles and rejecting both formal ministry and all set forms of worship.
– DERIVATIVES **Quakerism** noun.
– ORIGIN from QUAKE, perhaps alluding to the founder's direction to his followers to 'tremble at the Word of the Lord'.
qualification ● noun **1** the action of qualifying or the fact of becoming qualified. **2** a pass of an examination or an official completion of a course. **3** a quality that makes someone suitable for a job or activity. **4** a condition that must be fulfilled before a right can be acquired. **5** a statement that qualifies another.
qualifier ● noun **1** a person or team that qualifies for a competition or its final rounds. **2** a match or contest to decide which individuals or teams qualify for a competition or its final rounds. **2** Grammar a word or phrase, especially an adjective, used to qualify another word, especially a noun.
qualify ● verb (**qualifies**, **qualified**) **1** (often **qualify for**) meet the necessary standard or conditions to be entitled to or eligible for something. **2** become officially recognized as a practitioner of a profession or activity, typically after study and passing examinations. **3** make competent or knowledgeable enough to do something. **4** modify (a statement) by adding restrictions or reservations. **5** describe or class as being. **6** Grammar (of a word or phrase) attribute a quality to (another word, especially a preceding noun).
– ORIGIN Latin *qualificare*, from *qualis* (see QUALITY).
qualitative /kwollitətiv/ ● adjective **1** of, concerned with, or measured by quality. **2** Grammar (of an adjective) describing the quality of something in size, appearance, etc.
– DERIVATIVES **qualitatively** adverb.
qualitative analysis ● noun Chemistry identification of the constituents present in a substance.
quality ● noun (pl. **qualities**) **1** the degree of excellence of something as measured against other similar things. **2** general excellence. **3** a distinctive attribute or characteristic. **4** archaic high social standing.
– ORIGIN Latin *qualitas*, from *qualis* 'of what kind, of such a kind'.
quality control ● noun a system of maintaining standards in manufactured products by testing a sample against the specification.
quality time ● noun time devoted exclusively to another person in order to strengthen a relationship.
qualm /kwaam/ ● noun **1** a feeling of doubt or unease, especially about one's conduct. **2** archaic a momentary faint or sick feeling.
– ORIGIN perhaps related to an Old English word meaning 'pain'.
quandary /kwondri/ ● noun (pl. **quandaries**) a state of uncertainty.
– ORIGIN perhaps partly from Latin *quando* 'when'.
quango /kwanggō/ ● noun (pl. **quangos**) Brit., chiefly derogatory a semi-public administrative body with financial support from and senior appointments made by the government.
– ORIGIN acronym from *quasi* (or *quasi-autonomous*) *non-governmental organization*.
quant /kwont, kwant/ ● noun Brit. a pole for propelling a barge or punt, with a prong at the bottom to prevent it sinking into the mud.
– ORIGIN perhaps from Greek *kontos* 'boat pole'.
quanta plural of QUANTUM.
quantifier ● noun Grammar a determiner or pronoun indicative of quantity (e.g. *all*).
quantify ● verb (**quantifies, quantified**) express or measure the quantity of.
– DERIVATIVES **quantifiable** adjective **quantification** noun.
quantitative /kwollitətiv/ ● adjective of, concerned with, or measured by quantity.
– DERIVATIVES **quantitatively** adverb.
quantitative analysis ● noun Chemistry measurement of the quantities of particular constituents present in a substance.
quantitive ● adjective another term for QUANTITATIVE.
– DERIVATIVES **quantitively** adverb.
quantity ● noun (pl. **quantities**) **1** a certain amount or number. **2** the property of something that is measurable in number, amount, size, or weight. **3** a considerable number or amount.
– ORIGIN Latin *quantitas*, from *quantus* 'how great, how much'.
quantity surveyor ● noun Brit. a person who calculates the amount and cost of materials needed for building work.
quantize (also **quantise**) ● verb **1** Physics divide into quanta. **2** Electronics approximate (a continuously varying signal) by one whose amplitude is restricted to prescribed values.
– DERIVATIVES **quantization** noun **quantizer** noun.
quantum /kwontəm/ ● noun (pl. **quanta**) **1** Physics an individual quantity of energy corresponding to that involved in the absorption or emission of energy or light by an atom or other particle. **2** a total amount, especially an amount of money legally payable in damages. **3** a share.
– ORIGIN Latin, from *quantus* 'how great'.
quantum computer ● noun a computer which makes use of the quantum states of subatomic particles to store information.
quantum leap (also **quantum jump**) ● noun a sudden large increase or advance.
quantum mechanics ● plural noun (treated as sing.) the branch of

q

Thesaurus

DLE, mix-up, mess, predicament, mare's nest, quandary, tangle, imbroglio; trouble, confusion, difficulty; *informal* sticky situation, pickle, stew, dilemma, fix, bind.
quail ● verb COWER, cringe, flinch, shrink, recoil, shy (away), pull back; shiver, tremble, shake, quake, blench, blanch.
quaint ● adjective **1** *a quaint town* PICTURESQUE, charming, sweet, attractive, old-fashioned, old-world; *Brit.* twee; *N. Amer.* cunning; *pseudo-archaic* olde (worlde). **2** *quaint customs* UNUSUAL, different, out of the ordinary, curious, eccentric, quirky, bizarre, whimsical, unconventional; *informal* offbeat.
– OPPOSITES ugly, ordinary.
quake ● verb **1** *the ground quaked* SHAKE, tremble, quiver, shudder, sway, rock, wobble, move, heave, convulse. **2** *we quaked when we saw the soldiers* TREMBLE, shake, quiver, shiver; blench, blanch, flinch, shrink, recoil, cower, cringe.
qualification ● noun **1** *a teaching qualification* CERTIFICATE, diploma, degree, licence, document, warrant; eligibility, acceptability, adequacy; proficiency, skill, ability, capability, aptitude. **2** *I can't accept it without qualification* MODIFICATION, limitation, reservation, stipulation; alteration, amendment, revision, moderation, mitigation; condition, proviso, caveat.
qualified ● adjective CERTIFIED, certificated, chartered, licensed, professional; trained, fit, competent, accomplished, proficient, skilled, experienced, expert.
qualify ● verb **1** *I qualify for free travel* BE ELIGIBLE, meet the requirements; be entitled to, be permitted. **2** *they qualify as refugees* COUNT, be considered, be designated, be eligible. **3** *she qualified as a solicitor* BE CERTIFIED, be licensed; pass, graduate, make the grade, succeed, pass muster. **4** *the course qualified them to teach* AUTHORIZE, empower, allow, permit, license; equip, prepare, train, educate, teach. **5** *they qualified their findings* MODIFY, limit, restrict, make conditional; moderate, temper, modulate, mitigate.
quality ● noun **1** *a poor quality of signal* STANDARD, grade, class, calibre, condition, character, nature, form, rank, value, level; sort, type, kind, variety. **2** *work of such quality* EXCELLENCE, superiority, merit, worth, value, virtue, calibre, eminence, distinction, incomparability; talent, skill, virtuosity, craftsmanship. **3** *her good qualities* FEATURE, trait, attribute, characteristic, point, aspect, facet, side, property.
qualm ● noun MISGIVING, doubt, reservation, second thought, worry, concern, anxiety; (**qualms**) hesitation, hesitance, hesitancy, demur, reluctance, disinclination, apprehension, trepidation, unease; scruples, remorse, compunction.
quandary ● noun PREDICAMENT, plight, difficult situation, awkward situation; trouble, muddle, mess, confusion, difficulty, mare's nest; *informal* dilemma, sticky situation, pickle, hole, stew, fix, bind, jam.
quantity ● noun **1** *the quantity of food collected* AMOUNT, total, aggregate, sum, quota, mass, weight, volume, bulk; quantum, proportion, portion, part. **2** *a quantity of ammunition* AMOUNT, lot,

physics concerned with describing the behaviour of subatomic particles in terms of quanta, incorporating the idea that particles can also be regarded as waves.

quantum theory ● noun a theory of matter and energy based on the idea of quanta.

quarantine ● noun a state or period of isolation for people or animals that have arrived from elsewhere or been exposed to contagious disease. ● verb put in quarantine.
– ORIGIN originally denoting a period of forty days during which a widow who was entitled to a share of her deceased husband's estate had the right to remain in his house; from Italian *quarantina* 'forty days'.

quark[1] /kwaark, kwawrk/ ● noun Physics any of a group of subatomic particles which carry a fractional electric charge and are believed to be building blocks of protons, neutrons, and other particles.
– ORIGIN invented by the American physicist Murray Gell-Mann and associated by him with the line 'Three quarks for Muster Mark' in James Joyce's *Finnegans Wake* (1939), which seemed appropriate because three kinds of quark were originally proposed.

quark[2] /kwaark/ ● noun a type of low-fat curd cheese.
– ORIGIN German, 'curd, curds'.

quarrel[1] ● noun **1** an angry argument or disagreement. **2** a reason for disagreement. ● verb (**quarrelled**, **quarrelling**; US **quarreled**, **quarreling**) **1** have a quarrel. **2** (**quarrel with**) disagree with.
– ORIGIN Latin *querella* 'complaint', from *queri* 'complain'.

quarrel[2] ● noun historical a short heavy square-headed arrow or bolt for a crossbow or arbalest.
– ORIGIN Old French, from Latin *quadrus* 'square'; compare with QUARRY[3].

quarrelsome ● adjective given to or characterized by quarrelling.

quarry[1] ● noun (pl. **quarries**) an open excavation in the earth's surface from which stone or other materials are extracted. ● verb (**quarries**, **quarried**) **1** extract from a quarry. **2** cut into (rock or ground) to obtain stone or other materials.
– DERIVATIVES **quarrier** noun.
– ORIGIN Old French *quarriere*, from Latin *quadrum* 'a square'.

quarry[2] ● noun (pl. **quarries**) **1** an animal being hunted. **2** a person or thing being chased or sought.
– ORIGIN originally denoting the parts of a deer placed on a hide for the hounds: from Old French *couree*, from Latin *cor* 'heart'.

quarry[3] ● noun (pl. **quarries**) **1** a diamond-shaped pane in a lattice window. **2** (also **quarry tile**) an unglazed floor tile.
– ORIGIN alteration of QUARREL[2], which originally denoted a lattice windowpane.

quart ● noun **1** a unit of liquid capacity equal to a quarter of a gallon or two pints, equivalent in Britain to approximately 1.13 litres and in the US to approximately 0.94 litre. **2** N. Amer. a unit of dry capacity equivalent to approximately 1.10 litres.
– PHRASES **you can't get a quart into a pint pot** Brit. proverb you cannot achieve the impossible.
– ORIGIN from Latin *quarta pars* 'fourth part', from *quartus* 'fourth'.

quarter ● noun **1** each of four equal or corresponding parts into which something is or can be divided. **2** a period of three months, used especially in reference to financial transactions. **3** a quarter-hour. **4** a US or Canadian coin worth 25 cents. **5** one fourth of a pound weight (avoirdupois, equal to 4 ounces). **6** one fourth of a hundredweight (Brit. 28 lb or US 25 lb). **7** a part of a town or city with a specific character or use: *the business quarter*. **8** (**quarters**) rooms or lodgings. **9** a person, area, etc. regarded as the source of something: *help from an unexpected quarter*. **10** pity or mercy shown to an opponent: *they gave the enemy no quarter*. **11** (**quarters**) the haunches or hindquarters of a horse. **12** the direction of one of the points of the compass. ● verb **1** divide into quarters. **2** historical cut the body of (an executed person) into four parts. **3** (**be quartered**) be stationed or lodged. **4** range over (an area) in all directions. **5** Heraldry display (different coats of arms) in the four divisions of a shield.
– ORIGIN Latin *quartarius* 'fourth part of a measure', from *quartus* 'fourth'.

quarterback ● noun American Football a player stationed behind the centre who directs a team's offensive play.

quarter day ● noun Brit. each of four days in the year on which some tenancies begin and end and quarterly payments fall due.

quarterdeck ● noun the part of a ship's upper deck near the stern, traditionally reserved for officers or for ceremonial use.

quarter-final ● noun a match of a knockout competition preceding the semi-final.

quarter-hour ● noun **1** (also **quarter of an hour**) a period of fifteen minutes. **2** a point of time fifteen minutes before or after a full hour of the clock.

quarter-light ● noun Brit. a window in the side of a motor vehicle other than a main door window.

quarterly ● adjective & adverb produced or occurring once every quarter of a year. ● noun (pl. **quarterlies**) a publication produced four times a year.

quartermaster ● noun **1** a regimental officer in charge of quartering and supplies. **2** a naval petty officer responsible for steering and signals.

quarter sessions ● plural noun historical (in England, Wales, and Northern Ireland) a court of limited criminal and civil jurisdiction and of appeal, usually held quarterly.

quarterstaff ● noun a stout pole 6–8 feet long, formerly used as a weapon.

quarter tone ● noun Music half a semitone.

quartet (also **quartette**) ● noun **1** a group of four people playing music or singing together. **2** a composition for a quartet. **3** a set of four.
– ORIGIN Italian *quartetto*, from *quarto* 'fourth'.

quartic /kwortik/ ● adjective Mathematics referring to an equation, curve, etc. involving the fourth and no higher power of an unknown quantity or variable.

quartile /kwawrtīl/ ● noun Statistics each of four equal groups into which a population can be divided according to the distribution of values of a particular variable.
– ORIGIN Latin *quartilis*, from *quartus* 'fourth'.

quarto /kwawrtō/ ● noun (pl. **quartos**) **1** a page or paper size resulting from folding a sheet into four leaves, typically 10 inches × 8 inches (254 × 203 mm). **2** a book of this size.
– ORIGIN from Latin *in quarto* 'in the fourth (of a sheet)'.

quartz ● noun a hard mineral consisting of silica, typically occurring as colourless or white hexagonal prisms.
– ORIGIN German *Quarz*, from Polish dialect *kwardy*, corresponding to Czech *tvrdý* 'hard'.

quartz clock (or **watch**) ● noun a clock (or watch) regulated by vibrations of an electrically driven quartz crystal.

quartzite ● noun compact, hard, granular rock consisting mainly of quartz.

quasar /kwayzaar/ ● noun a massive and extremely remote ce-

q

Thesaurus

great deal, good deal, an abundance, a wealth, a profusion, plenty; *informal* piles, oodles, tons, lots, loads, heaps, masses, stacks, bags; *Brit. informal* shedloads.

quarrel ● noun *they had a quarrel about money* ARGUMENT, disagreement, squabble, fight, dispute, wrangle, clash, altercation, feud, contretemps, disputation, falling-out, war of words, shouting match; *informal* tiff, slanging match, run-in; *Brit. informal* barney, row, bust-up.
● verb *don't quarrel over it* ARGUE, fight, disagree, fall out; differ, be at odds; bicker, squabble, cross swords, lock horns, be at each other's throats; *informal* argufy; *Brit. informal* row.
– PHRASES **quarrel with** *you can't quarrel with the verdict* FAULT, criticize, object to, oppose, take exception to; attack, take issue with, impugn, contradict, dispute, controvert; *informal* knock; *formal* gainsay.

quarrelsome ● adjective ARGUMENTATIVE, disputatious, confrontational, captious, pugnacious, combative, antagonistic, bellicose, belligerent, cantankerous, choleric; *Brit. informal* stroppy; *N. Amer. informal* scrappy.
– OPPOSITES peaceable.

quarry ● noun PREY, victim; object, goal, target; kill, game.

quarter ● noun **1** *the Latin quarter* DISTRICT, area, region, part, side, neighbourhood, precinct, locality, sector, zone; ghetto, community, enclave. **2** *help from an unexpected quarter* SOURCE, direction, place, location; person. **3** *the servants' quarters* ACCOMMODATION, lodgings, rooms, chambers; home; *informal* pad, digs; *formal* abode, residence, domicile. **4** *the riot squads gave no quarter* MERCY, leniency, clemency, lenity, compassion, pity, charity, sympathy, tolerance.
● verb **1** *they were quartered in a villa* ACCOMMODATE, house, board,

lestial object which emits large amounts of energy.
– ORIGIN contraction of *quasi-stellar radio source*: telescope images of quasars are typically star-like.

quash ● verb **1** reject as invalid, especially by legal procedure. **2** put an end to; suppress.
– ORIGIN Old French *quasser* 'annul', from Latin *cassus* 'null, void'.

quasi- /kwayzī/ ● combining form **1** seemingly: *quasi-scientific.* **2** being partly or almost: *quasicrystalline.*
– ORIGIN Latin, 'as if, almost'.

quassia /kwoshə/ ● noun a South American shrub or small tree whose wood, bark, or root yields a bitter medicinal tonic and insecticide.
– ORIGIN named after Graman *Quassi*, the eighteenth-century Surinamese slave who discovered its medicinal properties.

quatercentenary /kwattərsenteenəri, -tennəri/ ● noun (pl. **quatercentenaries**) a four-hundredth anniversary.
– ORIGIN from Latin *quater* 'four times'.

quaternary /kwəternəri/ ● adjective **1** fourth in order or rank. **2** (**Quaternary**) Geology relating to the most recent period in the Cenozoic era, from about 1.64 million years ago to the present.
– ORIGIN Latin *quaternarius*, from *quater* 'four times'.

quatrain /kwətrayn/ ● noun a stanza of four lines, typically with alternate rhymes.
– ORIGIN French, from *quatre* 'four'.

quatrefoil /katrəfoyl/ ● noun an ornamental design of four lobes or leaves, resembling a flower or clover leaf.
– ORIGIN from Old French *quatre* 'four' + *foil* 'leaf'.

quattrocento /kwatrōchentō/ ● noun the 15th century as a period of Italian art or architecture.
– ORIGIN Italian, '400' (shortened from *milquattrocento* '1400').

quaver ● verb (of a voice) tremble. ● noun **1** a tremble in a voice. **2** Music, chiefly Brit. a note having the value of an eighth of a semibreve or half a crotchet, represented by a large dot with a hooked stem.
– DERIVATIVES **quavery** adjective.
– ORIGIN dialect *quave* 'quake, tremble', probably from an Old English word related to QUAKE.

quay ● noun a platform lying alongside or projecting into water for loading and unloading ships.
– ORIGIN Old French *kay*.

quayside ● noun a quay and the area around it.

qubit /kyōōbit/ ● noun a physical structure for information storage in a quantum computer that is capable of existing in either of two quantum states, and hence can represent two different binary values simultaneously.
– ORIGIN blend of QUANTUM and BIT[4]

queasy ● adjective (**queasier**, **queasiest**) **1** feeling sick; nauseous. **2** slightly nervous or uneasy.
– DERIVATIVES **queasily** adverb **queasiness** noun.
– ORIGIN perhaps related to Old French *coisier* 'to hurt'.

q

Quechua /kechwə/ ● noun (pl. same or **Quechuas**) **1** a member of an American Indian people of Peru and neighbouring countries. **2** the language of this people.
– DERIVATIVES **Quechuan** adjective & noun.
– ORIGIN Quechua, 'temperate valleys'.

queen ● noun **1** the female ruler of an independent state, especially one who inherits the position by right of birth. **2** (also **queen consort**) a king's wife. **3** the best or most important woman or thing in a sphere or group. **4** a playing card bearing a representation of a queen, ranking next below a king. **5** the most powerful chess piece, able to move in any direction. **6** a reproductive female in a colony of ants, bees, wasps, or termites. **7** informal a flamboyantly effeminate male homosexual. ● verb **1** (**queen it**) (of a woman) act in an unpleasantly superior way. **2** Chess convert (a pawn) into a queen when it reaches the opponent's end of the board.
– DERIVATIVES **queendom** noun **queenly** adjective **queenship** noun.
– ORIGIN Old English.

Queen Anne ● adjective denoting a style of English furniture or architecture characteristic of the early 18th century.

queen bee ● noun **1** the single reproductive female in a colony of honeybees. **2** informal a dominant woman in a group.

queen dowager ● noun the widow of a king.

queen mother ● noun the widow of a king and mother of the sovereign.

queen post ● noun either of two upright timbers between the tie beam and principal rafters of a roof truss.

Queen's Bench ● noun (in the UK) a division of the High Court of Justice.

Queensberry Rules ● plural noun the standard rules of boxing.
– ORIGIN named after the 8th Marquess of *Queensberry*, who supervised the preparation of the rules in 1867.

Queen's Counsel ● noun a senior barrister appointed on the recommendation of the Lord Chancellor.

Queen's English ● noun the English language as correctly written and spoken in Britain.

Queen's evidence ● noun English Law evidence for the prosecution given by a participant in the crime being tried.

Queen's Guide (or **Queen's Scout**) ● noun (in the UK) a Guide (or Scout) who has reached the highest rank of proficiency.

Queen's highway ● noun Brit. the public road network.

queen-sized (also **queen-size**) ● adjective of a larger size than the standard but smaller than king-sized.

Queen's Messenger ● noun (in the UK) a courier in the diplomatic service.

Queen's Speech ● noun (in the UK) a statement read by the sovereign at the opening of parliament, detailing the government's proposed legislative programme.

queer ● adjective **1** strange; odd. **2** informal, derogatory (of a man) homosexual. **3** Brit. informal, dated slightly ill. ● noun informal, derogatory a homosexual man. ● verb informal spoil or ruin.
– PHRASES **in Queer Street** Brit. informal, dated in difficulty or debt. **queer someone's pitch** Brit. informal spoil someone's plans or chances of doing something.
– DERIVATIVES **queerish** adjective **queerly** adverb **queerness** noun.
– USAGE The word **queer** was first used to mean 'homosexual' in the early 20th century. It was originally, and usually still is, a deliberately derogatory term when used by heterosexual people. In recent years, however, gay people have taken the word **queer** and deliberately used it in place of **gay** or **homosexual**, in an attempt, by using the word positively, to deprive it of its negative power.
– ORIGIN perhaps from German *quer* 'oblique, perverse'.

quell ● verb **1** put an end to (a rebellion or other disorder), typ-

Thesaurus

lodge, put up, take in, install, shelter; Military billet. **2** *I quartered the streets* PATROL, range over, tour, reconnoitre, traverse, survey, scout; Brit. informal recce.

quash ● verb **1** *he may quash the sentence* CANCEL, reverse, rescind, repeal, revoke, retract, countermand, withdraw, overturn, overrule, veto, annul, nullify, invalidate, negate, void; Law vacate; formal abrogate. **2** *we want to quash these rumours* PUT AN END TO, put a stop to, stamp out, crush, put down, check, curb, nip in the bud, squash, quell, subdue, suppress, extinguish, stifle; informal squelch, put the kibosh on.
– OPPOSITES validate.

quasi- ● combining form **1** *quasi-scientific* SUPPOSEDLY, seemingly, apparently, allegedly, ostensibly, on the face of it, on the surface, to all intents and purposes, outwardly, superficially, purportedly, nominally; pseudo-. **2** *a quasi-autonomous organization* PARTLY, partially, part, to a certain extent, to some extent, half, relatively, comparatively, (up) to a point; almost, nearly, just about, all but.

quaver ● verb TREMBLE, waver, quiver, shake, vibrate, oscillate, fluctuate, falter, warble.

quay ● noun WHARF, pier, jetty, landing stage, berth; marina, dock, harbour.

queasy ● adjective NAUSEOUS, nauseated, bilious, sick; ill, unwell, poorly, green about the gills; Brit. off colour.

queen ● noun **1** *the Queen was crowned* MONARCH, sovereign, ruler, head of state; Her Majesty; king's consort, queen consort. **2** *the queen of soul music* DOYENNE, star, superstar, leading light, big name, queen bee, prima donna, idol, heroine, favourite, darling, goddess.

queer ● adjective **1** *it seemed queer to see him here* ODD, strange, unusual, funny, peculiar, curious, bizarre, weird, uncanny, freakish, eerie, unnatural; unconventional, unorthodox, unexpected, unfamiliar, abnormal, anomalous, atypical, untypical, out of the ordinary, incongruous, irregular; puzzling, perplexing, baffling, unaccountable; informal fishy, creepy, spooky, freaky; Brit. informal rum. **2** *(Brit. informal, dated) the pills made her feel queer.* See ILL adjective sense 1.
– OPPOSITES normal, well.
● verb *he queered the whole deal* SPOIL, ruin, wreck, destroy,

ically by force. **2** subdue or suppress.
– ORIGIN Old English, 'kill'.

quench ● **verb** **1** satisfy (thirst) by drinking. **2** satisfy (a desire). **3** extinguish (a fire). **4** stifle (a feeling). **5** rapidly cool (hot metal). **6** Physics & Electronics suppress or damp (luminescence, an oscillation, etc.).
– DERIVATIVES **quencher** noun.
– ORIGIN Old English, 'put out, extinguish'.

quenelle /kənel/ ● **noun** a small seasoned ball of fish or meat.
– ORIGIN French, probably from Alsatian German *knödel*.

quern /kwern/ ● **noun** a simple hand mill for grinding grain, typically consisting of two circular stones.
– ORIGIN Old English.

querulous /kwerrooləss/ ● **adjective** complaining in a petulant or whining manner.
– DERIVATIVES **querulously** adverb **querulousness** noun.
– ORIGIN Latin *querulus*, from *queri* 'complain'.

query ● **noun** (pl. **queries**) **1** a question, especially one expressing doubt. **2** chiefly Printing a question mark. ● **verb** (**queries**, **queried**) **1** ask a query. **2** N. Amer. put a query or queries to.
– ORIGIN from Latin *quaerere* 'ask, seek'.

quesadilla /kayssədeeyə/ ● **noun** a hot tortilla with a spicy cheese filling.
– ORIGIN Spanish.

quest ● **noun** **1** a long or arduous search. **2** (in medieval romance) an expedition by a knight to accomplish a specific task. ● **verb** search for something.
– DERIVATIVES **quester** (also **questor**) noun.
– ORIGIN Old French *queste*, from Latin *quaerere* 'ask, seek'.

question ● **noun** **1** a sentence worded or expressed so as to obtain information. **2** a doubt. **3** the raising of a doubt or objection: *he obeyed without question.* **4** a problem requiring resolution. **5** a matter or issue depending on conditions: *it's only a question of time before something changes.* ● **verb** **1** ask questions of. **2** express doubt about; object to.
– PHRASES **come** (or **bring**) **into question** become (or raise) an issue for further consideration or discussion. **in question** **1** being considered or discussed. **2** in doubt. **no question of** no possibility of. **out of the question** not possible. **put the question** require supporters and opponents of a debated proposal to record their votes.
– DERIVATIVES **questioner** noun.
– ORIGIN Old French, from Latin *quaerere* 'ask, seek'.

questionable ● **adjective** **1** open to doubt. **2** of suspect morality, honesty, etc.
– DERIVATIVES **questionably** adverb.

question mark ● **noun** a punctuation mark (?) indicating a question.

question master ● **noun** Brit. the questioner in a quiz or panel game.

questionnaire /kwess-chənair, kess-/ ● **noun** a set of printed questions, usually with a choice of answers, devised for a survey or statistical study.
– ORIGIN French.

question time ● **noun** (in the UK) a period during proceedings in the House of Commons when MPs may question ministers.

quetzal /kwets'l/ ● **noun** a long-tailed tropical American bird with iridescent green plumage and typically red underparts.
– ORIGIN from an Aztec word meaning 'brightly coloured tail feather'.

queue ● **noun** **1** a line of people or vehicles awaiting their turn to be attended to or to proceed. **2** Computing a list of data items, commands, etc., stored so as to be retrievable in a definite order. ● **verb** (**queues**, **queued**, **queuing** or **queueing**) wait in a queue.
– ORIGIN originally as a heraldic term denoting an animal's tail, later a long plait: from French, from Latin *cauda* 'tail'; compare with CUE².

queue-jump ● **verb** Brit. move forward out of turn in a queue.

quibble ● **noun** **1** a slight objection or criticism. **2** archaic a pun. ● **verb** argue about a trivial matter.
– ORIGIN from obsolete *quib* 'a petty objection', probably from Latin *quibus*, from *qui*, *quae*, *quod* 'who, what, which', frequently used in legal documents and therefore associated with subtle distinctions.

quiche /keesh/ ● **noun** a baked flan with a savoury filling thickened with eggs.
– ORIGIN French, from Alsatian dialect *Küchen*.

Thesaurus

scotch, disrupt, undo, thwart, foil, blight, cripple, jeopardize, threaten, undermine, compromise; *informal* botch, blow, put the kibosh on; *Brit. informal* scupper.

quell ● **verb** **1** *troops quelled the unrest* PUT AN END TO, put a stop to, end, crush, put down, check, crack down on, curb, nip in the bud, squash, quash, subdue, suppress, overcome; *informal* squelch. **2** *he quelled his misgivings* CALM, soothe, pacify, settle, quieten, quiet, silence, allay, assuage, mitigate, moderate; *poetic/literary* stay.

quench ● **verb** **1** *they quenched their thirst* SATISFY, slake, sate, satiate, gratify, relieve, assuage, take the edge off, indulge; lessen, reduce, diminish, check, suppress, extinguish, overcome. **2** *the flames were quenched* EXTINGUISH, put out, snuff out, smother, douse.

querulous ● **adjective** PETULANT, peevish, pettish, complaining, fractious, fretful, irritable, testy, tetchy, cross, snappish, crabby, crotchety, cantankerous, miserable, moody, grumpy, bad-tempered, sullen, sulky, sour, churlish; *informal* snappy, grouchy, whingy; *Brit. informal* ratty, cranky; *N. English informal* mardy; *N. Amer. informal* soreheaded.

query ● **noun** **1** *we are happy to answer any queries* QUESTION, enquiry; *Brit. informal* quiz. **2** *there was a query as to who owned the hotel* DOUBT, uncertainty, question (mark), reservation; scepticism. ● **verb** **1** *'Why do that?' queried Isobel* ASK, enquire, question; *Brit. informal* quiz. **2** *folk may query his credentials* QUESTION, call into question, challenge, dispute, cast aspersions on, doubt, have suspicions about, have reservations about.

quest ● **noun** **1** *their quest for her killer* SEARCH, hunt; pursuance of. **2** *Sir Galahad's quest* EXPEDITION, journey, voyage, trek, travels, odyssey, adventure, exploration, search; crusade, mission, pilgrimage.
– PHRASES **in quest of** IN SEARCH OF, in pursuit of, seeking, looking for, on the lookout for, after.

question ● **noun** **1** *please answer my question* ENQUIRY, query; interrogation; *Brit. informal* quiz. **2** *there is no question that he is ill* DOUBT, dispute, argument, debate, uncertainty, dubiousness, reservation; *formal* dubiety. **3** *the political questions of the day* ISSUE, matter, business, problem, concern, topic, theme, case; debate, argument, dispute, controversy.
– RELATED TERMS interrogative.
– OPPOSITES answer, certainty.
● **verb** **1** *the magistrate questions the suspect* INTERROGATE, cross-examine, cross-question, quiz, catechize; interview, debrief, examine, give the third degree to; *informal* grill, pump. **2** *she questioned his motives* QUERY, call into question, challenge, dispute, cast aspersions on, doubt, suspect, have suspicions about, have reservations about.
– PHRASES **beyond question** **1** *her loyalty is beyond question* UNDOUBTED, beyond doubt, certain, indubitable, indisputable, incontrovertible, unquestionable, undeniable, clear, patent, manifest. **2** *the results demonstrated this beyond question* INDISPUTABLY, irrefutably, incontestably, incontrovertibly, unquestionably, undeniably, undoubtedly, beyond doubt, without doubt, clearly, patently, obviously. **in question** AT ISSUE, under discussion, under consideration, on the agenda, to be decided. **out of the question** IMPOSSIBLE, impracticable, unfeasible, unworkable, inconceivable, unimaginable, unrealizable, unsuitable; *informal* not on.

questionable ● **adjective** **1** *jokes of questionable taste* CONTROVERSIAL, contentious, doubtful, dubious, uncertain, debatable, arguable; unverified, unprovable, unresolved, unconvincing, implausible, improbable; borderline, marginal, moot; *informal* iffy; *Brit. informal* dodgy. **2** *questionable financial dealings* SUSPICIOUS, suspect, dubious, irregular, odd, strange, murky, dark, unsavoury, disreputable; *informal* funny, fishy, shady, iffy; *Brit. informal* dodgy.
– OPPOSITES indisputable, honest.

questionnaire ● **noun** QUESTION SHEET, survey form, opinion poll; test, exam, examination, quiz; *Medicine* questionary.

queue ● **noun** **1** *a queue of people* LINE, row, column, file, chain, string; procession, train, cavalcade; waiting list; *N. Amer.* wait list; *Brit. informal* crocodile. **2** *a traffic queue* (TRAFFIC) JAM, tailback, gridlock; *N. Amer.* back-up; *informal* snarl-up.
● **verb** *we queued for ice creams* LINE UP, form a queue, queue up, wait in line, form a line, fall in.

quibble ● **noun** *I have just one quibble* CRITICISM, objection, complaint, protest, argument, exception, grumble, grouse, cavil; *informal* niggle, moan, gripe, beef, grouch.
● **verb** *no one quibbled with the title* OBJECT TO, find fault with,

quick • adjective **1** moving fast. **2** lasting or taking a short time: *a quick worker*. **3** with little or no delay; prompt. **4** intelligent. **5** (of a person's eye or ear) keenly perceptive. **6** (of temper) easily roused. • noun **1** (**the quick**) the tender flesh below the growing part of a fingernail or toenail. **2** the central or most sensitive part: *his laughter cut us to the quick*. **3** (as plural noun **the quick**) archaic those who are living.
– PHRASES **a quick one** informal a rapidly consumed alcoholic drink. **quick with child** archaic at a stage of pregnancy when the fetus can be felt to move.
– DERIVATIVES **quickly** adverb **quickness** noun.
– ORIGIN Old English, 'alive, animated, alert'.
quicken • verb **1** make or become quicker. **2** stimulate or be stimulated. **3** archaic reach a stage in pregnancy when the fetus can be felt to move. **4** archaic (of a fetus) begin to show signs of life.
quick-fire • adjective **1** unhesitating and rapid. **2** (of a gun) firing shots in rapid succession.
quick fix • noun a speedy but inadequate solution.
quickie informal • noun **1** a rapidly consumed alcoholic drink. **2** a brief act of sexual intercourse. • adjective done or made quickly.
quicklime • noun a white caustic alkaline substance consisting of calcium oxide, obtained by heating limestone.
quick march • noun a brisk military march.
quicksand • noun (also **quicksands**) loose wet sand that sucks in anything resting on it.
quickset • noun Brit. hedging, especially of hawthorn, grown from slips or cuttings.
quicksilver • noun **1** liquid mercury. **2** (before another noun) moving or changing rapidly.
quickstep • noun a fast foxtrot in 4/4 time.
quick-tempered • adjective easily angered.
quickthorn • noun hawthorn.
quick-witted • adjective able to think or respond quickly.
quid[1] • noun (pl. same) Brit. informal one pound sterling.
– PHRASES **not the full quid** Austral./NZ informal not intelligent. **quids in** Brit. informal profiting or likely to profit from something.
– ORIGIN of obscure origin.
quid[2] • noun a lump of chewing tobacco.
– ORIGIN variant of CUD.
quiddity /kwidditi/ • noun (pl. **quiddities**) **1** the inherent nature or essence of a person or thing. **2** a subtle distinction in an argument.
– ORIGIN Latin *quidditas*, from *quid* 'what'.
quidnunc /kwidnungk/ • noun archaic or literary an inquisitive, gossipy person.
– ORIGIN from Latin *quid nunc?* 'what now?'
quid pro quo /kwid prō kwō/ • noun (pl. **quid pro quos**) a favour or advantage given in return for something.
– ORIGIN Latin, 'something for something'.
quiescent /kwiess'nt/ • adjective in a state or period of inactivity.
– DERIVATIVES **quiescence** noun **quiescently** adverb.
– ORIGIN from Latin *quiescere* 'be still', from *quies* 'quiet'.
quiet • adjective (**quieter**, **quietest**) **1** making little or no noise. **2** free from activity, disturbance, or excitement. **3** without being disturbed or interrupted: *a quiet drink*. **4** discreet, moderate, or restrained. **5** (of a person) tranquil and reserved. • noun absence of noise or disturbance. • verb chiefly N. Amer. make or become quiet.
– PHRASES **keep quiet** refrain from speaking or revealing a secret. **on the quiet** informal secretly or unobtrusively.
– DERIVATIVES **quietly** adverb **quietness** noun.
– ORIGIN from Latin *quies* 'repose, quiet'.
quieten • verb chiefly Brit. make or become quiet and calm.
quietism • noun **1** (in the Christian faith) devotional contemplation and abandonment of the will as a form of religious mysticism. **2** calm acceptance of things as they are.
– DERIVATIVES **quietist** noun & adjective.
quietude • noun a state of calmness and quiet.
quietus /kwieetəss/ • noun (pl. **quietuses**) **1** literary death or a cause of death, regarded as a release from life. **2** archaic something calming or soothing.
– ORIGIN from Latin *quietus est* 'he is quit' (see QUIT), originally used as a receipt on payment of a debt.
quiff • noun chiefly Brit. a tuft of hair, brushed upwards and backwards from a man's forehead.
– ORIGIN of unknown origin.
quill • noun **1** a main wing or tail feather of a bird. **2** the hollow shaft of a feather, especially the lower part that lacks barbs.

Thesaurus

complain about, cavil at; split hairs, chop logic; criticize, query, fault, pick holes in; *informal* nit-pick; *archaic* pettifog.
quick • adjective **1** *a quick worker* FAST, swift, rapid, speedy, high-speed, expeditious, brisk, smart; lightning, whirlwind, fast-track, whistle-stop, breakneck; *informal* nippy, zippy; *poetic/literary* fleet. **2** *she took a quick look* HASTY, hurried, cursory, perfunctory, desultory, superficial, summary; brief, short, fleeting, transient, transitory, short-lived, lightning, momentary. **3** *a quick end to the recession* SUDDEN, instantaneous, immediate, instant, abrupt, precipitate. **4** *she isn't as quick as the others* INTELLIGENT, bright, clever, gifted, able, astute, quick-witted, sharp-witted, smart; observant, alert, sharp, perceptive; *informal* brainy, on the ball, quick on the uptake.
– OPPOSITES slow, long.
quicken • verb **1** *she quickened her pace* SPEED UP, accelerate, step up, hasten, hurry (up); *informal* gee up. **2** *the film quickened his interest in nature* STIMULATE, excite, arouse, rouse, stir up, activate, galvanize, whet, inspire, kindle; invigorate, revive, revitalize.
quickly • adverb **1** *he walked quickly* FAST, swiftly, briskly, rapidly, speedily, at the speed of light, at full tilt, as fast as one's legs can carry one, at a gallop, at the double, post-haste, hotfoot; *informal* double quick, p.d.q. (pretty damn quick), like (greased) lightning, hell for leather, like mad, like blazes, like the wind; *Brit. informal* like the clappers, like billy-o; *N. Amer. informal* lickety-split; *poetic/literary* apace. **2** *you'd better leave quickly* IMMEDIATELY, directly, at once, now, straight away, right away, instantly, forthwith, without delay, without further ado; soon, promptly, early; *N. Amer.* momentarily; *informal* like a shot, a.s.a.p. (as soon as possible), pronto, before you can say Jack Robinson, straight off. **3** *he quickly inspected it* BRIEFLY, fleetingly, briskly; hastily, hurriedly, cursorily, perfunctorily, superficially, desultorily.
quick-tempered • adjective IRRITABLE, irascible, hot-tempered, short-tempered, snappish, fiery, touchy, volatile; cross, crabby, crotchety, cantankerous, grumpy, ill-tempered, bad-tempered, testy, tetchy, prickly, choleric; *informal* snappy, chippy, grouchy, cranky, on a short fuse; *Brit. informal* narky, ratty, eggy, like a bear with a sore head; *N. Amer. informal* soreheaded.
– OPPOSITES placid.
quick-witted • adjective INTELLIGENT, bright, clever, gifted, able, astute, quick, smart, sharp-witted; observant, alert, sharp, perceptive; *informal* brainy, on the ball, quick on the uptake.
– OPPOSITES slow.
quid pro quo • noun EXCHANGE, trade, trade-off, swap, switch, barter, substitute, reciprocation, return; amends, compensation, recompense, restitution, reparation.
quiescent • adjective INACTIVE, inert, idle, dormant, at rest, inoperative, deactivated, quiet; still, motionless, immobile, passive.
– OPPOSITES active.
quiet • adjective **1** *the whole pub went quiet* SILENT, still, hushed, noiseless, soundless; mute, dumb, speechless. **2** *a quiet voice* SOFT, low, muted, muffled, faint, indistinct, inaudible, hushed, whispered, suppressed. **3** *a quiet village* PEACEFUL, sleepy, tranquil, calm, still, restful, undisturbed, untroubled; unfrequented. **4** *can I have a quiet word?* PRIVATE, confidential, secret, discreet, unofficial, off the record, between ourselves. **5** *quiet colours* UNOBTRUSIVE, restrained, muted, understated, subdued, subtle, low-key; soft, pale, pastel. **6** *you can't keep it quiet for long* SECRET, confidential, classified, unrevealed, undisclosed, unknown, under wraps; *informal* hush-hush, mum; *formal* sub rosa. **7** *business is quiet* SLOW, stagnant, slack, sluggish, inactive, idle.
– OPPOSITES loud, busy, public.
• noun *the quiet of the countryside* PEACEFULNESS, peace, restfulness, calm, tranquillity, serenity; silence, quietness, stillness, still, quietude, hush, soundlessness.
quieten • verb **1** *quieten the children down* SILENCE, hush, shush, quiet; *informal* shut up. **2** *her companions quietened* FALL SILENT, stop talking, break off, shush, hold one's tongue; *informal* shut up, clam up, shut it, pipe down, shut one's mouth, put a sock in it, button it. **3** *he tried to quieten manic patients* PACIFY, calm (down), soothe, subdue, tranquillize, relax, comfort, compose.
quietly • adverb **1** *she quietly entered the room* SILENTLY, in silence, noiselessly, soundlessly, inaudibly; mutely, dumbly. **2** *he spoke quietly* SOFTLY, in a low voice, in a whisper, in a murmur, under one's breath, in an undertone, sotto voce, gently, faintly, weakly,

3 a pen made from a quill. **4** a hollow sharp spine of a porcupine, hedgehog, etc.
– ORIGIN probably from Low German *quiele*.

quilling ● noun a type of ornamental craftwork involving the shaping of paper or fabric into delicate pleats or folds.

quilt ● noun **1** a warm bed covering made of padding enclosed between layers of fabric and kept in place by lines of decorative stitching. **2** a bedspread of similar design. ● verb (often as adj. **quilted**) join (layers of fabric or padding) with stitching to form a quilt, a garment, or for decorative effect.
– DERIVATIVES **quilter** noun **quilting** noun.
– ORIGIN Old French *cuilte*, from Latin *culcita* 'mattress, cushion'.

quim ● noun Brit. vulgar slang a woman's genitals.
– ORIGIN of unknown origin.

quin ● noun informal, chiefly Brit. a quintuplet.

quince ● noun the hard, acid, pear-shaped fruit of an Asian shrub or small tree, used in preserves or as flavouring.
– ORIGIN Old French *cooin*, from Latin *malum cydonium* 'apple of *Cydonia* (= Chania, in Crete)'.

quincentenary /kwinsenteenəri, -tennəri/ ● noun (pl. **quincentenaries**) a five-hundredth anniversary.
– DERIVATIVES **quincentennial** noun & adjective.
– ORIGIN from Latin *quinque* 'five'.

quincunx /kwinkungks/ ● noun (pl. **quincunxes**) an arrangement of five objects with four at the corners of a square or rectangle and the fifth at its centre.
– DERIVATIVES **quincuncial** adjective.
– ORIGIN Latin, 'five twelfths'.

quinine /kwinneen, kwineen/ ● noun a bitter crystalline compound present in cinchona bark, used as a tonic and formerly to treat malaria.
– ORIGIN from a Quechua word meaning 'bark'.

quinone /kwinnōn/ ● noun Chemistry any of a class of organic compounds related to benzene but having two hydrogen atoms replaced by oxygen.
– ORIGIN from Spanish *quina* 'cinchona bark'.

quinquagenarian /kwingkwəjinairiən/ ● noun a person between 50 and 59 years old.
– ORIGIN Latin *quinquagenarius*, from *quinquaginti* 'fifty'.

Quinquagesima /kwingkwəjessimə/ ● noun the Sunday before the beginning of Lent.
– ORIGIN from Latin *quinquagesimus* 'fiftieth', on the pattern of *Quadragesima* (because it is ten days before the forty days of Lent).

quinque- ● combining form five; having five: *quinquereme*.
– ORIGIN Latin.

quinquennial /kwingkwenniəl/ ● adjective lasting for or recurring every five years.
– DERIVATIVES **quinquennially** adverb.
– ORIGIN from Latin *quinque* 'five' + *annus* 'year'.

quinquennium /kwingkwenniəm/ ● noun (pl. **quinquennia** /kwingkwenniə/ or **quinquenniums**) a period of five years.

quinquereme /kwingkwireem/ ● noun an ancient Roman or Greek galley of a kind believed to have had three banks of oars, the oars in the top two banks being rowed by pairs of oarsmen and the oars in the bottom bank being rowed by single oarsmen.
– ORIGIN from Latin *quinque* 'five' + *remus* 'oar'.

quinsy /kwinzi/ ● noun inflammation of the throat, especially an abscess near the tonsils.
– ORIGIN Greek *kunankhē* 'canine quinsy', from *kun-* 'dog' + *ankhein* 'to strangle'.

quinta /kintə, kwin-/ ● noun **1** (in Spain, Portugal, and Latin America) a large country house. **2** a wine-growing estate, especially in Portugal.
– ORIGIN Spanish and Portuguese, from *quinta parte* 'fifth part' (with reference to the amount of a farm's produce paid in rent).

quintal /kwint'l/ ● noun **1** a unit of weight equal to a hundredweight (112 lb) or, formerly, 100 lb. **2** a unit of weight equal to 100 kg.
– ORIGIN Latin *quintale*, from *centenarius* 'containing a hundred'.

quintessence /kwintess'nss/ ● noun **1** the most perfect or typical example or embodiment of a quality or type. **2** a refined essence or extract of a substance.
– ORIGIN from Latin *quinta essentia* 'fifth essence', from the belief in ancient philosophy that a fifth substance existed in addition to the four elements, which pervaded all things.

quintessential /kwintisensh'l/ ● adjective representing the most perfect or typical example.
– DERIVATIVES **quintessentially** adverb.

quintet ● noun **1** a group of five people playing music or singing together. **2** a composition for a quintet. **3** a set of five.
– ORIGIN Italian *quintetto*, from *quinto* 'fifth'.

quintillion /kwintilyən/ ● cardinal number a thousand raised to the power of six (10^{18}); a million million million.
– DERIVATIVES **quintillionth** ordinal number.

quintuple /kwintyoop'l/ ● adjective **1** consisting of five parts or elements. **2** five times as much or as many. **3** (of time in music) having five beats in a bar. ● verb increase or be increased fivefold. ● noun a quintuple number or amount.
– ORIGIN Latin *quintuplus*.

quintuplet /kwintyooplit/ ● noun each of five children born at one birth.

quintuplicate ● adjective **1** fivefold. **2** of which five copies are made.

quip ● noun a witty remark. ● verb (**quipped**, **quipping**) make a quip.
– DERIVATIVES **quipster** noun.
– ORIGIN perhaps from Latin *quippe* 'indeed'.

quire /kwīr/ ● noun **1** four sheets of paper or parchment folded to form eight leaves, as in medieval manuscripts. **2** 25 (formerly 24) sheets of paper; one twentieth of a ream. **3** any collection of leaves one within another in a manuscript or book.
– ORIGIN Old French *quaier*, from Latin *quaterni* 'set of four'.

quirk ● noun **1** a peculiar behavioural habit. **2** a strange chance occurrence: *a quirk of fate*. **3** a sudden twist, turn, or curve.
– DERIVATIVES **quirkish** adjective **quirky** adjective (**quirkier**, **quirkiest**).
– ORIGIN of unknown origin.

quirt /kwurt/ ● noun a short-handled riding whip with a braided leather lash.
– ORIGIN Spanish *cuerda* 'cord' or Mexican Spanish *cuarta* 'whip'.

quisling /kwizling/ ● noun a traitor collaborating with an occupying enemy force.
– ORIGIN from the Norwegian army officer Major Vidkun *Quisling* (1887–1945), who ruled Norway on behalf of the German occupying forces.

quit ● verb (**quitting**; past and past part. **quitted** or **quit**) **1** leave, especially permanently. **2** informal resign from (a job). **3** informal, chiefly N. Amer. stop or discontinue. **4** (**quit oneself**) archaic behave in a specified way. ● adjective (**quit of**) rid of.
– ORIGIN Old French *quiter*, from Latin *quietus*, from *quiescere* 'be still'.

quitch ● noun another term for COUCH[2].

Thesaurus

feebly. **3** *some bonds were sold quietly* DISCREETLY, privately, confidentially, secretly, unofficially, off the record. **4** *she is quietly confident* CALMLY, patiently, placidly, serenely.

quilt ● noun DUVET, cover(s); *Brit.* eiderdown; *N. Amer.* comforter, puff; *Austral. trademark* Doona.

quintessence ● noun **1** *it's the quintessence of the modern home* PERFECT EXAMPLE, exemplar, prototype, stereotype, picture, epitome, embodiment, ideal; best, pick, prime, acme, crème de la crème. **2** *the quintessence of intelligence* ESSENCE, soul, spirit, nature, core, heart, crux, kernel, marrow, substance; *informal* nitty-gritty; *Philosophy* quiddity, esse.

quintessential ● adjective TYPICAL, prototypical, stereotypical, archetypal, classic, model, standard, stock, representative, conventional; ideal, consummate, exemplary, best, ultimate.

quip ● noun *the quip provoked a smile* JOKE, witty remark, witticism, jest, pun, sally, pleasantry, bon mot; *informal* one-liner, gag, crack, wisecrack, funny.
● verb *'Enjoy your trip?' he quipped* JOKE, jest, pun, sally; *informal* gag, wisecrack.

quirk ● noun **1** *they all know his quirks* IDIOSYNCRASY, peculiarity, oddity, eccentricity, foible, whim, vagary, caprice, fancy, crotchet, habit, characteristic, trait, fad; *informal* hang-up. **2** *a quirk of fate* CHANCE, fluke, freak, anomaly, twist.

quirky ● adjective ECCENTRIC, idiosyncratic, unconventional, unorthodox, unusual, strange, bizarre, peculiar, odd, outlandish, zany; *informal* wacky, freaky, kinky, way-out, far out, kooky, offbeat.
– OPPOSITES conventional.

quisling ● noun COLLABORATOR, fraternizer, colluder, sympathizer; traitor, turncoat, back-stabber, double-crosser, defector, Judas,

– ORIGIN Old English; perhaps related to QUICK (with reference to its vigorous growth).

quite ● adverb **1** to the utmost or most absolute extent or degree; completely. **2** to a certain extent; moderately. **3** US very; really. ● exclamation (also **quite so**) expressing agreement.
– PHRASES **quite a ——** a remarkable or impressive (person or thing). **quite a lot** (or **a bit**) a considerable number or amount. **quite some** a considerable amount of.
– ORIGIN from the obsolete adjective *quite*, variant of QUIT.

quits ● adjective on equal terms by retaliation or repayment.
– PHRASES **call it quits 1** agree that terms are now equal. **2** decide to abandon an activity.
– ORIGIN originally in the sense 'freed from a liability or debt': perhaps an informal abbreviation of Latin *quittus*, from *quietus*, used as a receipt (see QUIETUS).

quittance ● noun archaic or literary a release from a debt or obligation.

quitter ● noun informal a person who gives up easily.

quiver[1] ● verb shake or vibrate with a slight rapid motion. ● noun a quivering movement or sound.
– DERIVATIVES **quivery** adjective.
– ORIGIN from an Old English word meaning 'nimble, quick'.

quiver[2] ● noun an archer's portable case for arrows.
– ORIGIN Old French *quiveir*.

quiverful ● noun **1** as much as a quiver can hold. **2** Brit. humorous a large number of offspring. [ORIGIN with biblical allusion to Psalm 127.]

qui vive /kee veev/ ● noun (in phrase **on the qui vive**) on the alert or lookout.
– ORIGIN French, '(long) live who?', i.e. 'on whose side are you?', used as a sentry's challenge.

quixotic /kwiksottik/ ● adjective impractically idealistic or fanciful.
– DERIVATIVES **quixotically** adverb **quixotism** /**kwik**sətiz'm/ noun.
– ORIGIN from the name of Don *Quixote*, the hero of a romance by the Spanish writer Cervantes (1547–1616)

quiz[1] ● noun (pl. **quizzes**) **1** a test of knowledge, especially as a competition for entertainment. **2** informal, chiefly Brit. a period of questioning. ● verb (**quizzes**, **quizzed**, **quizzing**) question (someone).
– ORIGIN possibly from QUIZ[2], influenced by INQUISITIVE.

quiz[2] archaic ● verb (**quizzes**, **quizzed**, **quizzing**) **1** peer at. **2** make fun of. ● noun (pl. **quizzes**) **1** a hoax. **2** an odd or eccentric person.
– ORIGIN origin uncertain; possibly a deliberately coined nonsense word.

quizmaster ● noun Brit. a question master.

quizzical ● adjective indicating mild or amused puzzlement.
– DERIVATIVES **quizzicality** noun **quizzically** adverb **quizzicalness** noun.

quod erat demonstrandum /kwod errat demmənstrandəm/ ● used, especially at the conclusion of a formal proof, to convey that something demonstrates the truth of one's claim.
– ORIGIN Latin, 'which was to be demonstrated'.

quoin /koyn/ ● noun **1** an external angle of a wall or building. **2** a cornerstone.
– DERIVATIVES **quoining** noun.
– ORIGIN variant of COIN, in the former senses 'cornerstone' and 'wedge'.

quoit /koyt/ ● noun **1** a ring of iron, rope, or rubber thrown in a game to encircle or land as near as possible to an upright peg. **2** (**quoits**) (treated as sing.) a game of aiming and throwing quoits.
– ORIGIN probably French.

quokka /kwokkə/ ● noun a small short-tailed wallaby native to Western Australia.
– ORIGIN from an extinct Aboriginal language.

quoll /kwol/ ● noun a catlike carnivorous marsupial with a white-spotted coat, native to Australia and New Guinea.
– ORIGIN from an Aboriginal language.

quondam /kwondam/ ● adjective formal former.
– ORIGIN Latin, 'formerly'.

Quonset /kwonsit/ (also **Quonset hut**) ● noun N. Amer. trademark a prefabricated building with a semicylindrical corrugated roof.
– ORIGIN named after *Quonset* Point, Rhode Island, where such huts were first made.

quorate /kworət/ ● adjective Brit. (of a meeting) attended by a quorum.

quorum /kworəm/ ● noun (pl. **quorums**) the minimum number of members of an assembly or society that must be present at a meeting to make the proceedings valid.
– ORIGIN used in commissions in which particular people were designated as members of a body (originally of justices of the peace) by the Latin words *quorum vos ... unum* (*duos*, etc.) *esse volumus* 'of whom we wish that you ... be one (two, etc.)'.

quota ● noun **1** a limited quantity of a product which may be produced, exported, or imported. **2** a share that one is entitled to receive or bound to contribute. **3** a fixed number of a group allowed to do something, e.g. immigrants entering a country.
– ORIGIN from Latin *quota pars* 'how great a part'.

quotable ● adjective suitable for or worth quoting.
– DERIVATIVES **quotability** noun.

quotation ● noun **1** a passage or remark repeated by someone other than the originator. **2** the action of quoting. **3** a short musical passage or visual image taken from one piece of music or work of art and used in another. **4** a formal statement of the estimated cost of a job or service. **5** Stock Exchange a registration granted to a company enabling their shares to be officially listed and traded.

quotation mark ● noun each of a set of punctuation marks, single (' ') or double (" "), used either to mark the beginning and end of a title or quotation, or to indicate slang or jargon words.

quote ● verb **1** repeat or copy out (a passage or remark by another). **2** repeat a passage or remark from. **3** (**quote as**) put forward or describe as being. **4** give someone (an estimated price). **5** (**quote at/as**) name (someone or something) at (specified odds). **6** give (a company) a listing on a stock exchange. ● noun **1** a quotation. **2** (**quotes**) quotation marks.
– ORIGIN originally in the sense 'mark a book with numbers or marginal references': from Latin *quotare*, from *quot* 'how many'.

quoth /kwōth/ ● verb archaic or humorous said (used only in first

Thesaurus

snake in the grass, fifth columnist.

quit ● verb **1** *he quit the office at 12.30* LEAVE, vacate, exit, depart from, withdraw from; abandon, desert. **2** *(informal) he's decided to quit his job* RESIGN FROM, leave, give up, hand in one's notice, stand down from, relinquish, vacate, walk out on, retire from; *informal* chuck, pack in. **3** *(informal) quit living in the past* GIVE UP, stop, cease, discontinue, drop, break off, abandon, abstain from, desist from, refrain from, avoid, forgo; *informal* pack (it) in, leave off.

quite ● adverb **1** *two quite different types* COMPLETELY, entirely, totally, wholly, absolutely, utterly, thoroughly, altogether. **2** *red hair was quite common* FAIRLY, rather, somewhat, slightly, relatively, comparatively, moderately, reasonably, to a certain extent; *informal* pretty, kind of, sort of.

quiver ● verb **1** *I quivered with terror* TREMBLE, shake, shiver, quaver, quake, shudder. **2** *the bird quivers its wings* FLUTTER, flap, beat, agitate, vibrate.
● noun *a quiver in her voice* TREMOR, tremble, shake, quaver, flutter, fluctuation, waver.

quixotic ● adjective IDEALISTIC, romantic, visionary, Utopian, extravagant, starry-eyed, unrealistic, unworldly; impracticable, unworkable, impossible.

quiz ● noun **1** *a music quiz* COMPETITION, test of knowledge. **2** *(informal) jockey faces quiz over bribes* INTERROGATION, questioning, interview, examination, the third degree; *informal* grilling.
● verb *a man was being quizzed by police* QUESTION, interrogate, cross-examine, cross-question, interview, sound out, give someone the third degree; *informal* grill, pump.

quizzical ● adjective ENQUIRING, questioning, curious; puzzled, perplexed, baffled, mystified; amused, mocking, teasing.

quota ● noun ALLOCATION, share, allowance, limit, ration, portion, dispensation, slice (of the cake); percentage, commission; proportion, fraction, bit, amount, quantity; *informal* cut, rake-off; *Brit. informal* whack.

quotation ● noun **1** *a quotation from Dryden* CITATION, quote, excerpt, extract, passage, line, paragraph, verse, phrase; reference, allusion; *N. Amer.* cite. **2** *a quotation for the building work* ESTIMATE, quote, price, tender, bid, costing, charge, figure.

quote ● verb **1** *he quoted a sentence from the book* RECITE, repeat, reproduce, retell, echo, iterate; take, extract. **2** *she quoted one case in which a girl died* CITE, mention, refer to, name, instance, specify, identify; relate, recount; allude to, point out, present, offer, advance.

and third person singular before the subject).
– ORIGIN past tense of obsolete *quethe* 'say', of Germanic origin.
quotidian /kwotiddiən/ ● **adjective 1** daily. **2** ordinary or everyday.
– ORIGIN Latin *quotidianus*, from *cotidie* 'daily'.
quotient /kwōsh'nt/ ● **noun 1** Mathematics a result obtained by dividing one quantity by another. **2** a degree or amount of a specified quality.
– ORIGIN from Latin *quotiens* 'how many times', from *quot* 'how many'.
Qur'an /kəraan/ (also **Quran**) ● **noun** Arabic spelling of KORAN.
qursh /koorsh/ ● **noun** (pl. same) a monetary unit of Saudi Arabia, equal to one twentieth of a rial.
– ORIGIN Arabic.
q.v. ● **abbreviation** used to direct a reader to another part of a text for further information.
– ORIGIN from Latin *quod vide*, 'which see'.
qwerty /kwerti/ ● **adjective** denoting the standard layout on English-language typewriters and keyboards, having *q, w, e, r, t,* and *y* as the first keys on the top row of letters.

Thesaurus

● **noun 1** *a Shakespeare quote.* See QUOTATION sense 1. **2** *ask the contractor for a quote.* See QUOTATION sense 2.
quotidian ● **adjective 1** *the quotidian routine* DAILY, everyday, day-to-day, diurnal. **2** *her dreadfully quotidian car* ORDINARY, average, run-of-the-mill, everyday, standard, typical, middle-of-the-road, common, conventional, mainstream, unremarkable, unexceptional, workaday, commonplace, mundane, uninteresting; *informal* bog-standard, nothing to write home about, a dime a dozen; *Brit. informal* common or garden.
– OPPOSITES unusual.

q

Rr

R[1] (also **r**) ● noun (pl. **Rs** or **R's**) the eighteenth letter of the alphabet.
– PHRASES **the three Rs** reading, writing, and arithmetic, regarded as the fundamentals of learning.
R[2] ● abbreviation **1** rand. **2** Regina or Rex. **3** (®) registered as a trademark. **4** (**R.**) River. **5** roentgen(s). **6** rook (in chess). **7** Cricket (on scorecards) run(s).
r ● abbreviation **1** radius. **2** right.
RA ● abbreviation **1** (in the UK) Royal Academician or Royal Academy. **2** (in the UK) Royal Artillery.
Ra ● symbol the chemical element radium.
RAAF ● abbreviation Royal Australian Air Force.
rabbet /rabbit/ ● noun & verb chiefly N. Amer. another term for REBATE[2].
– ORIGIN Old French *rabbat* 'abatement, recess'.
rabbi /rabbī/ ● noun (pl. **rabbis**) **1** a Jewish scholar or teacher, especially of Jewish law. **2** a Jewish religious leader.
– DERIVATIVES **rabbinate** /rabbinət/ noun.
– ORIGIN from a Hebrew word meaning 'my master'.
rabbinic /rəbinnik/ ● adjective relating to rabbis or to Jewish law or teachings.
– DERIVATIVES **rabbinical** adjective.
rabbit ● noun **1** a burrowing plant-eating mammal, with long ears and a short tail. **2** N. Amer. a hare. **3** the fur of the rabbit. **4** informal a poor performer in a sport or game. ● verb (**rabbited**, **rabbiting**) **1** (usu. as noun **rabbiting**) hunt rabbits. **2** Brit. informal chatter. [ORIGIN from *rabbit and pork*, rhyming slang for 'talk'.]
– DERIVATIVES **rabbity** adjective.
– ORIGIN apparently from Old French, perhaps of Dutch origin.
rabbit punch ● noun a sharp chop with the edge of the hand to the back of the neck.
rabble ● noun **1** a disorderly crowd. **2** (**the rabble**) ordinary people regarded as socially inferior or uncouth.
– ORIGIN perhaps related to dialect *rabble* 'to gabble'.
rabble-rouser ● noun a person who stirs up popular opinion, especially for political reasons.
Rabelaisian /rabbəlayziən/ ● adjective of or like the French satirist François Rabelais (*c.*1494–1553) or his writings, especially in being characterized by exuberant imagination and earthy humour.
rabid /rabbid, ray-/ ● adjective **1** extreme; fanatical. **2** relating to or affected with rabies.
– DERIVATIVES **rabidly** adverb.
rabies /raybeez/ ● noun a dangerous disease of dogs and other mammals, caused by a virus transmissible through the saliva to humans and causing madness and convulsions.
– ORIGIN Latin, from *rabere* 'rave'.
RAC ● abbreviation **1** (in the UK) Royal Armoured Corps. **2** (in the UK) Royal Automobile Club.
raccoon /rəko͞on/ (also **racoon**) ● noun a greyish-brown omnivorous American mammal with a black facial mask and a ringed tail.
– ORIGIN from an Algonquian dialect word.
race[1] ● noun **1** a competition between runners, horses, vehicles, etc. to see which is fastest over a set course. **2** (**the races**) a series of races for horses or dogs, held at a fixed time on a set course. **3** a situation in which people compete to be first to achieve something. **4** a strong or rapid current flowing through a narrow channel. **5** a water channel, especially one in a mill or mine. **6** a smooth ring-shaped groove or guide for a ball bearing or roller bearing. ● verb **1** compete in a race. **2** have a race with. **3** prepare and enter (an animal or vehicle) for races. **4** move or progress swiftly. **5** (of machinery) operate at excessive speed.
– ORIGIN Old Norse, 'current'.
race[2] ● noun **1** each of the major divisions of humankind, having distinct physical characteristics. **2** racial origin or distinction: *rights based on race.* **3** a group of people sharing the same culture, language, etc.; an ethnic group. **4** a group of people or things with a common feature. **5** Biology a distinct population within a species; a subspecies.
– USAGE Some people now feel that the word **race** should be avoided, because of its associations with the now discredited theories of 19th-century anthropologists and physiologists about supposed racial superiority. Terms such as **people**, **community**, or **ethnic group** are less emotionally charged.
– ORIGIN French, from Italian *razza*.
racecard ● noun a programme giving information about the races at a race meeting.
racecourse ● noun a ground or track for horse or dog racing.
racehorse ● noun a horse bred and trained for racing.
raceme /rəseem/ ● noun a flower cluster with the separate flowers attached by short stalks along a central stem, the lower flowers developing first. Compare with CYME.
– ORIGIN Latin *racemus* 'bunch of grapes'.
race meeting ● noun Brit. a sporting event consisting of a series of horse races held at one course.
racer ● noun **1** an animal or vehicle used for racing. **2** a person who competes in races.
race relations ● plural noun relations between members of different races within a country.
racetrack ● noun **1** a racecourse. **2** a track for motor racing.
rachitic /rəkittik/ ● adjective Medicine relating to or suffering from rickets.
– ORIGIN from Greek *rhakhitis* 'rickets', from *rhakhis* 'spine'.
Rachmanism /rakməniz'm/ ● noun Brit. the exploitation and intimidation of tenants by unscrupulous landlords.
– ORIGIN named after the notorious London landlord Peter *Rachman* (1919–62).
racial ● adjective **1** of or relating to a race. **2** relating to relations or differences between races.
– DERIVATIVES **racially** adverb.
racialism ● noun racism.
– DERIVATIVES **racialist** noun & adjective **racialize** (also **racialise**)

Thesaurus

rabbit ● noun buck, doe; *Brit.* coney; *informal* bunny.
rabble ● noun **1** *a rabble of noisy youths* MOB, crowd, throng, gang, swarm, horde, pack, mass, group. **2** *rule by the rabble* THE COMMON PEOPLE, the masses, the populace, the multitude, the rank and file, the commonality, the commonalty, the plebeians, the proletariat, the peasantry, the hoi polloi, the lower classes, the riff-raff; *informal* the proles, the plebs.
– OPPOSITES nobility.
rabble-rouser ● noun AGITATOR, troublemaker, instigator, firebrand, revolutionary, demagogue.
rabid ● adjective **1** *a rabid dog* rabies-infected, mad. **2** *a rabid anti-royalist* EXTREME, fanatical, overzealous, extremist, maniacal, passionate, fervent, diehard, uncompromising, illiberal; *informal* gung-ho.
– OPPOSITES moderate.
race[1] ● noun **1** *Dave won the race* CONTEST, competition, event, fixture, heat, trial(s). **2** *the race for naval domination* COMPETITION, rivalry, contention; quest. **3** *the mill race* CHANNEL, waterway, conduit, sluice, spillway.
● verb **1** *he will race in the final* COMPETE, contend; run. **2** *Claire raced after him* HURRY, dash, rush, run, sprint, bolt, dart, gallop, career, charge, shoot, hurtle, hare, fly, speed, scurry; *informal* tear, belt, pelt, scoot, hotfoot it, leg it; *Brit. informal* bomb; *N. Amer. informal* hightail it. **3** *her heart was racing* POUND, beat rapidly, throb, pulsate, thud, thump, hammer, palpitate, flutter, pitter-patter, quiver, pump.
race[2] ● noun **1** *pupils of many different races* ETHNIC GROUP, racial type, (ethnic) origin. **2** *a bloodthirsty race* PEOPLE, nation.

verb.

racing ● noun a sport involving races. ● adjective **1** moving swiftly. **2** (of a person) following horse racing.

racing car ● noun a car built for racing.

racing driver ● noun a driver of racing cars.

racism ● noun **1** the belief that there are characteristics, abilities, or qualities specific to each race. **2** discrimination against or antagonism towards other races.

– DERIVATIVES **racist** noun & adjective.

rack[1] ● noun **1** a framework for holding or storing things. **2** a cogged or toothed bar or rail engaging with a wheel or pinion, or using pegs to adjust the position of something. **3** (**the rack**) historical an instrument of torture consisting of a frame on which the victim was tied by the wrists and ankles and stretched. **4** a vertically barred holder for animal fodder. **5** a triangular frame for positioning pool balls. **6** a single game of pool. ● verb **1** (also **wrack**) cause extreme physical or mental pain to. **2** place in or on a rack. **3** (**rack up**) accumulate or achieve (a score or amount).

– PHRASES **rack** (or **wrack**) **one's brains** make a great mental effort.

– ORIGIN from Dutch *rec*, Low German *rek* 'horizontal bar or shelf', probably from *recken* 'to stretch, reach'.

rack[2] ● noun a joint of meat, especially lamb, including the front ribs.

– ORIGIN of unknown origin.

rack[3] (also **wrack**) ● noun (in phrase **go to rack and ruin**) gradually deteriorate due to neglect.

– ORIGIN Old English, 'vengeance'; related to WREAK.

rack[4] ● verb draw off (wine, beer, etc.) from the sediment in the barrel.

– ORIGIN Provençal *arracar*, from *raca* 'stems and husks of grapes, dregs'.

rack[5] ● noun variant spelling of WRACK[3].

rack-and-pinion ● adjective denoting a mechanism using a fixed cogged or toothed bar or rail engaging with a smaller cog.

racket[1] (also **racquet**) ● noun a bat with a round or oval frame strung with catgut or nylon, used especially in tennis, badminton, and squash.

– ORIGIN French *raquette*, from an Arabic word meaning 'palm of the hand'.

racket[2] ● noun **1** a loud unpleasant noise. **2** informal a fraudulent scheme for obtaining money. **3** informal a person's line of business. ● verb (**racketed**, **racketing**) make a loud unpleasant noise.

– DERIVATIVES **rackety** adjective.

– ORIGIN perhaps imitative of clattering.

racketeer ● noun a person engaging in fraudulent business dealings.

– DERIVATIVES **racketeering** noun.

rackets ● plural noun (treated as sing.) a ball game for two or four people played with rackets and a hard ball in a four-walled court.

rack railway ● noun a railway for steep slopes, having a toothed rail between the bearing rails which engages with a cogwheel under the locomotive.

rack rent ● noun a very high rent.

raclette /raklet/ ● noun a Swiss dish of melted cheese, typically with potatoes.

– ORIGIN French, 'small scraper', from the practice of scraping the cheese on to a plate as it melts.

raconteur /rakkontör/ ● noun (fem. **raconteuse** /rakkontöz/) a skilful teller of anecdotes.

– ORIGIN French, from *raconter* 'relate, recount'.

racoon ● noun variant spelling of RACCOON.

racquet ● noun variant spelling of RACKET[1].

racy ● adjective (**racier**, **raciest**) **1** suggestive; risqué. **2** lively, vigorous, or spirited.

– DERIVATIVES **racily** adverb **raciness** noun.

rad[1] ● abbreviation radian(s).

rad[2] ● noun Physics a unit of absorbed dose of ionizing radiation.

– ORIGIN acronym from *radiation absorbed dose*.

rad[3] ● noun a radiator.

RADA /raadə/ ● abbreviation (in the UK) Royal Academy of Dramatic Art.

radar ● noun a system for detecting the presence, direction, and speed of aircraft, ships, etc., by sending out pulses of radio waves which are reflected back off the object.

– ORIGIN from *radio detection and ranging*.

radar gun ● noun a hand-held radar device used by traffic police to estimate a vehicle's speed.

radar trap ● noun an area of road in which radar is used by the police to detect speeding vehicles.

raddled ● adjective showing signs of age or fatigue.

– ORIGIN originally in the sense 'coloured with rouge so as to imperfectly conceal signs of ageing'; variant of RUDDLE.

radial ● adjective **1** of or arranged like rays or the radii of a circle; diverging in lines from a common centre. **2** (also **radial-ply**) (of a tyre) in which the layers of fabric have their cords running at right angles to the circumference of the tyre. **3** (of an internal-combustion engine) having its cylinders fixed like the spokes of a wheel around a rotating crankshaft. ● noun a radial tyre.

– DERIVATIVES **radially** adverb.

– ORIGIN Latin *radialis*, from *radius* 'spoke, ray'.

radial symmetry ● noun chiefly Biology symmetry about a central axis, as in a starfish.

radian /raydiən/ ● noun a unit of measurement of angles equal to about 57.3°, equivalent to the angle subtended at the centre of a circle by an arc equal in length to the radius.

radiant ● adjective **1** shining or glowing brightly. **2** emanating great joy, love, or health. **3** (of electromagnetic energy, especially heat) transmitted by radiation, rather than conduction or convection. **4** (of an appliance) emitting radiant energy for cooking or heating. ● noun a point or object from which light or heat radiates.

– DERIVATIVES **radiance** noun **radiantly** adverb.

radiate ● verb **1** (with reference to light, heat, or other energy) emit or be emitted in the form of rays or waves. **2** emanate (a strong feeling or quality). **3** diverge from or as if from a central point.

– DERIVATIVES **radiative** adjective.

Thesaurus

racial ● adjective ETHNIC, ethnological, race-related; cultural, national, tribal.

racism ● noun RACIAL DISCRIMINATION, racialism, racial prejudice, xenophobia, chauvinism, bigotry; anti-Semitism.

racist ● noun *he was exposed as a racist* RACIAL BIGOT, racialist, xenophobe, chauvinist; anti-Semite.
● adjective *a racist society* (RACIALLY) DISCRIMINATORY, racialist, prejudiced, bigoted; anti-Semitic.

rack ● noun *put the cake on a wire rack* FRAME, framework, stand, holder, trestle, support, shelf.
● verb *she was racked with guilt* TORMENT, afflict, torture, agonize, harrow; plague, bedevil, persecute, trouble, worry.

– PHRASES **on the rack** UNDER PRESSURE, under stress, under a strain, in distress; in trouble, in difficulties, having problems. **rack one's brains** THINK HARD, concentrate, cudgel one's brains; informal scratch one's head.

racket ● noun **1** *the engine makes such a racket* NOISE, din, hubbub, clamour, uproar, tumult, commotion, rumpus, pandemonium, babel; informal hullabaloo; Brit. informal row. **2** (informal) *a gold-smuggling racket* ILLEGAL SCHEME, fraud, swindle; informal rip-off; N. Amer. informal shakedown.

raconteur ● noun STORYTELLER, narrator, anecdotalist; Austral. informal magsman.

racy ● adjective RISQUÉ, suggestive, naughty, sexy, spicy, ribald; indecorous, indecent, immodest, off colour, dirty, rude, smutty, crude, salacious; N. Amer. gamy; informal raunchy, blue; Brit. informal saucy; euphemistic adult.

– OPPOSITES prim.

raddled ● adjective HAGGARD, gaunt, drawn, tired, fatigued, drained, exhausted, worn out, washed out; unwell, unhealthy; informal the worse for wear.

radiance ● noun **1** *the radiance of the sun* LIGHT, brightness, brilliance, luminosity, beams, rays, illumination, blaze, glow, gleam, lustre, glare; luminescence, incandescence. **2** *her face flooded with radiance* JOY, elation, jubilance, ecstasy, rapture, euphoria, delirium, happiness, delight, pleasure.

radiant ● adjective **1** *the radiant moon* SHINING, bright, illuminated, brilliant, gleaming, glowing, ablaze, luminous, luminescent, lustrous, incandescent, dazzling, shimmering; archaic splendent. **2** *she looked radiant* JOYFUL, elated, thrilled, overjoyed, jubilant, rapturous, ecstatic, euphoric, in seventh heaven, on cloud nine, delighted, very happy; informal on top of the world, over the moon; Austral.

– ORIGIN Latin *radiare* 'emit in rays', from *radius* 'ray, spoke'.
radiation • noun 1 the action or process of radiating. 2 energy emitted as electromagnetic waves or subatomic particles.
radiation sickness • noun illness caused by exposure to X-rays, gamma rays, or other radiation.
radiation therapy • noun radiotherapy.
radiator • noun 1 a thing that radiates light, heat, or sound. 2 a device that radiates heat, consisting of a metal case through which hot water circulates, or a similar one heated by electricity or oil. 3 a cooling device in a vehicle or aircraft engine consisting of a bank of thin tubes in which circulating water is cooled by the surrounding air.
radical • adjective 1 relating to or affecting the fundamental nature of something. 2 advocating thorough political or social reform; politically extreme. 3 departing from tradition; innovative or progressive. 4 (of surgery) thorough and intended to be completely curative. 5 Mathematics of the root of a number or quantity. 6 of or coming from the root or stem base of a plant. 7 informal, chiefly N. Amer. excellent. • noun 1 an advocate of radical political or social reform. 2 Chemistry a group of atoms behaving as a unit in a number of compounds. See also FREE RADICAL.
– DERIVATIVES **radicalism** noun **radicalize** (also **radicalise**) verb **radically** adverb **radicalness** noun.
– ORIGIN Latin *radicalis*, from *radix* 'root'.
radical chic • noun the fashionable affectation of radical left-wing views.
radical sign • noun Mathematics the sign √ which indicates the square root of the number following (or a higher root indicated by a preceding superscript numeral).
radicchio /radeekiō/ • noun (pl. **radicchios**) chicory of a variety with dark red leaves.
– ORIGIN Italian.
radices plural of RADIX.
radicle /raddik'l/ • noun the part of a plant embryo that develops into the primary root.
– ORIGIN Latin *radicula* 'little root'.
radii plural of RADIUS.
radio • noun (pl. **radios**) 1 the transmission and reception of electromagnetic waves having a frequency in the range 10^4 to 10^{11} or 10^{12} hertz, especially those carrying sound messages. 2 broadcasting in sound. 3 a broadcasting station or channel. 4 an apparatus for receiving radio programmes. 5 an apparatus capable of receiving and transmitting radio messages. • verb (**radioes**, **radioed**) 1 send a message by radio. 2 communicate with by radio.
– ORIGIN abbreviation of RADIOTELEPHONE.
radio- • combining form 1 denoting radio waves or broadcasting: *radiogram*. 2 connected with rays, radiation, or radioactivity: *radiograph*. 3 denoting artificially prepared radioisotopes: *radio-cobalt*.
radioactive • adjective emitting or relating to the emission of ionizing radiation or particles.
– DERIVATIVES **radioactively** adverb.
radioactivity • noun 1 the emission of ionizing radiation or particles caused by the spontaneous disintegration of atomic nuclei. 2 radioactive particles.
radio astronomy • noun the branch of astronomy concerned with radio emissions from celestial objects.
radiocarbon • noun a radioactive isotope of carbon, especially carbon-14 used in carbon dating.
radio-controlled • adjective controllable from a distance by radio.
radio-element • noun a radioactive element or isotope.
radiogram • noun 1 Brit. a combined radio and record player. [ORIGIN from RADIO- + GRAMOPHONE.] 2 a radiograph.
radiograph • noun an image produced on a sensitive plate or film by X-rays or other radiation.
– DERIVATIVES **radiographer** noun **radiographic** adjective **radiography** noun.
radioisotope • noun a radioactive isotope.
– DERIVATIVES **radioisotopic** adjective.
radiology • noun the science of X-rays and other high-energy radiation, especially as used in medicine.
– DERIVATIVES **radiologic** adjective **radiological** adjective **radiologist** noun.
radiometer /raydiommitər/ • noun an instrument for detecting or measuring radiation.
– DERIVATIVES **radiometry** noun.
radiometric • adjective relating to the measurement of radioactivity.
– DERIVATIVES **radiometrically** adverb.
radionics /raydionniks/ • plural noun (treated as sing.) a system of alternative medicine based on the study of radiation supposedly emitted by living matter.
– ORIGIN from RADIO-, on the pattern of *electronics*.
radionuclide • noun a radioactive nuclide.
radiophonic • adjective relating to or denoting sound produced electronically.
radioscopy /raydioskəpi/ • noun the examination by X-rays of objects opaque to light.
radiotelephone • noun a telephone using radio transmission.
– DERIVATIVES **radiotelephony** noun.
radio telescope • noun an instrument used to detect radio emissions from space.
radiotherapy • noun the treatment of cancer or other disease using X-rays or similar radiation.
– DERIVATIVES **radiotherapeutic** adjective **radiotherapist** noun.
radio wave • noun an electromagnetic wave of radio frequency.
radish • noun the small, pungent, red root of a plant of the cabbage family, eaten raw.
– ORIGIN Latin *radix* 'root'.
radium /raydiəm/ • noun a reactive, radioactive metallic chemical element, formerly used as a source of radiation for medical treatment.
– ORIGIN from Latin *radius* 'ray'.
radius /raydiəss/ • noun (pl. **radii** /raydi-ī/ or **radiuses**) 1 a straight line from the centre to the circumference of a circle or sphere. 2 a radial line from the focus to any point of a curve. 3 a specified distance from a centre in all directions: *pubs within a two-mile radius*. 4 Anatomy & Zoology a bone of the forearm or forelimb, in humans the thicker and shorter of two. • verb (**radiused**, **radiusing**) (often as adj. **radiused**) make (a corner or edge) rounded.
– ORIGIN Latin, 'spoke, ray'.
radix /raydiks/ • noun (pl. **radices** /raydiseez/) 1 Mathematics the base of a system of numeration. 2 formal a source or origin.
– ORIGIN Latin, 'root'.
radome /raydōm/ • noun a dome or other structure protecting radar equipment and made from material transparent to radio waves.
– ORIGIN blend of RADAR and DOME.
radon /raydon/ • noun a rare radioactive gaseous element produced by the radioactive decay of radium and used as a source of alpha particles in radiotherapy.
– ORIGIN from RADIUM, on the pattern of *argon*.
RAF • abbreviation (in the UK) Royal Air Force.
raffia • noun fibre from the leaves of a tropical palm tree of Africa and Madagascar, used for making hats, baskets, etc.
– ORIGIN Malagasy.
raffish • adjective slightly disreputable, especially in an attractive manner.
– DERIVATIVES **raffishly** adverb **raffishness** noun.
– ORIGIN from RIFF-RAFF.

Thesaurus

informal wrapped.
– OPPOSITES dark, gloomy.
radiate • verb 1 *the stars radiate energy* EMIT, give off, give out, discharge, diffuse; shed, cast. 2 *light radiated from the hall* SHINE, beam, emanate. 3 *their faces radiate hope* DISPLAY, show, exhibit; emanate, breathe, be a picture of. 4 *four spokes radiate from the hub* FAN OUT, spread out, branch out/off, extend, issue.
radical • adjective 1 *radical reform* THOROUGHGOING, thorough, complete, total, comprehensive, exhaustive, sweeping, far-reaching, wide-ranging, extensive, profound, major, stringent, rigorous. 2 *radical differences between the two theories* FUNDAMENTAL, basic, essential, quintessential; structural, deep-seated, intrinsic, organic, constitutive. 3 *a radical political movement* REVOLUTIONARY, progressive, reformist, revisionist, progressivist; extreme, extremist, fanatical, militant, diehard.
– OPPOSITES superficial, minor, conservative.
• noun *the arrested man was a radical* REVOLUTIONARY, progressive, reformer, revisionist; militant, zealot, extremist, fanatic, diehard; *informal* ultra.
– OPPOSITES conservative.

raffle ● noun a lottery with goods as prizes. ● verb offer as a prize in a raffle.
– ORIGIN originally denoting a dice game: from Old French.

raft[1] ● noun **1** a flat buoyant structure of timber or other materials fastened together, used as a boat or floating platform. **2** a small inflatable boat. **3** a floating mass of fallen trees, ice, etc. ● verb travel or transport on or as if on a raft.
– DERIVATIVES **rafting** noun.
– ORIGIN originally in the sense 'rafter': from Old Norse.

raft[2] ● noun a large amount.
– ORIGIN alteration of dialect *raff* 'abundance', by association with RAFT[1] in sense 3.

rafter[1] ● noun a beam forming part of the internal framework of a roof.
– DERIVATIVES **raftered** adjective.
– ORIGIN Old English, related to RAFT[1].

rafter[2] ● noun a person who travels by raft.

rag[1] ● noun **1** a piece of old cloth, especially one torn from a larger piece. **2** (**rags**) old or tattered clothes. **3** informal a low-quality newspaper. ● verb give a decorative effect to (a painted surface) by applying paint with a rag.
– PHRASES **lose one's rag** informal lose one's temper.
– ORIGIN probably from RAGGED or RAGGY.

rag[2] ● noun Brit. **1** a programme of entertainments organized by students to raise money for charity. **2** informal, dated a prank. ● verb (**ragged**, **ragging**) **1** informal make fun of loudly and boisterously. **2** rebuke severely.
– ORIGIN of unknown origin.

rag[3] ● noun a ragtime composition or tune.
– ORIGIN perhaps from RAGGED; compare with RAGTIME.

rag[4] ● noun **1** a large coarse roofing slate. **2** (also **ragstone**) Brit. a hard coarse sedimentary rock that can be broken into thick slabs.
– ORIGIN of unknown origin.

raga /raagə/ ● noun (in Indian music) a characteristic pattern of notes used as a basis for improvisation.
– ORIGIN Sanskrit, 'colour, musical tone'.

ragamuffin (also **raggamuffin**) ● noun **1** a person in ragged, dirty clothes. **2** an exponent or follower of ragga, typically wearing scruffy clothes.
– ORIGIN probably based on RAG[1], with a fanciful suffix.

rag-and-bone man ● noun Brit. a person who goes from door to door, collecting old clothes and other second-hand items for resale.

ragbag ● noun **1** a bag for storing rags and old clothes. **2** a miscellaneous collection.

rage ● noun **1** violent uncontrollable anger. **2** (in combination) violent anger associated with conflict arising from a particular context: *air rage*. **3** a vehement desire or passion. **4** Austral./NZ informal a lively party. ● verb **1** feel or express rage. **2** continue violently or with great force: *the argument raged for days*. **3** Austral./NZ informal enjoy oneself socially.
– PHRASES **all the rage** temporarily very popular or fashionable.
– DERIVATIVES **rager** noun.
– ORIGIN Old French, from a variant of Latin *rabies* 'rabies'.

ragga /raggə/ ● noun chiefly Brit. a style of dance music in which a DJ improvises lyrics over a backing track.
– ORIGIN from RAGAMUFFIN, because of the clothing worn by its followers.

raggamuffin ● noun variant spelling of RAGAMUFFIN.

ragged /raggid/ ● adjective **1** (of cloth or clothes) old and torn. **2** wearing ragged clothes. **3** rough or irregular. **4** lacking finish, smoothness, or uniformity. **5** suffering from exhaustion or stress.
– PHRASES **run someone ragged** exhaust someone.
– DERIVATIVES **raggedly** adverb **raggedness** noun **raggedy** adjective (informal, chiefly N. Amer.).
– ORIGIN Scandinavian.

ragged robin ● noun a pink-flowered campion with divided petals that give it a tattered appearance.

raggle-taggle ● adjective untidy and scruffy.
– ORIGIN apparently a fanciful variant of RAGTAG.

raggy ● adjective (**raggier**, **raggiest**) informal ragged.
– ORIGIN Scandinavian.

raglan ● adjective having or denoting sleeves continuing in one piece up to the neck of a garment.
– ORIGIN named after Lord *Raglan* (1788–1855), a British commander in the Crimean War.

ragout /ragoō/ ● noun a highly seasoned stew of chopped meat and vegetables.
– ORIGIN French, from *ragoûter* 'revive the taste of'.

rag paper ● noun paper made from cotton.

ragpicker ● noun historical a person who collected and sold rags.

rag-roll ● verb create a striped or marbled effect on (a surface) by painting it with a rag crumpled up into a roll.

rag rug ● noun a rug made from small strips of fabric hooked into or pushed through a material such as hessian.

ragstone ● noun see RAG[4] (sense 2).

ragtag ● adjective untidy, disorganized, or incongruously varied: *a ragtag group of idealists*.
– ORIGIN superseding earlier *tag-rag* and *tag and rag* (see RAG[1], TAG[1]).

ragtime ● noun music characterized by a syncopated melodic line and regularly accented accompaniment, played especially on the piano.
– ORIGIN probably from RAG[3] (referring to the 'ragged' syncopation).

rag trade ● noun informal the clothing or fashion industry.

ragworm ● noun a predatory marine bristle worm, often used as bait by fishermen.

ragwort ● noun a yellow-flowered ragged-leaved plant of the daisy family, toxic to livestock.

rai /rī/ ● noun a style of music fusing Arabic and Algerian folk elements with Western rock.
– ORIGIN perhaps from Arabic, 'that's the thinking, here is the view', a phrase frequently found in the songs.

raid ● noun **1** a rapid surprise attack on an enemy or on premises to commit a crime. **2** a surprise visit by police to arrest suspects or seize illicit goods. ● verb **1** make a raid on. **2** quickly and illicitly take something from (a place).
– DERIVATIVES **raider** noun.
– ORIGIN Scots variant of ROAD in the early senses 'journey on

Thesaurus

raffish ● adjective RAKISH, unconventional, bohemian; devil-may-care, casual, careless; louche, disreputable, dissolute, decadent.

raffle ● noun LOTTERY, (prize) draw, sweepstake, sweep, tombola; *N. Amer.* lotto.

rag[1] ● noun **1** *an oily rag* CLOTH, scrap of cloth; *N. Amer. informal* schmatte. **2** *a man dressed in rags* TATTERS, torn clothing, old clothes; cast-offs, hand-me-downs.

rag[2] ● noun *(Brit.) the student rag* FUND-RAISING EVENT, charity event, charitable event.
● verb *(informal) he was ragged mercilessly*. See TEASE.

ragamuffin ● noun URCHIN, waif, guttersnipe; *informal* scarecrow; *dated* gamin(e).

ragbag ● noun JUMBLE, hotchpotch, mishmash, mess, hash; assortment, mixture, miscellany, medley, mixed bag, melange, variety, diversity, pot-pourri; *N. Amer.* hodgepodge.

rage ● noun **1** *his rage is due to frustration* FURY, anger, wrath, outrage, indignation, temper, spleen, resentment, pique, annoyance, vexation, displeasure; pet, tantrum, (bad) mood; *informal* grump, strop; *poetic/literary* ire, choler. **2** *the current rage for DIY* CRAZE, passion, fashion, taste, trend, vogue, fad, enthusiasm, obsession, compulsion, fixation, fetish, mania, preoccupation; *informal* thing.
● verb **1** *she raged silently* BE ANGRY, be furious, be enraged, be incensed, seethe, be beside oneself, rave, storm, fume, spit; *informal* be livid, be wild, foam at the mouth, have a fit, be steamed up. **2** *he raged against the reforms* PROTEST ABOUT, complain about, oppose, denounce; fulminate, storm, rail; *informal* kick up a stink about. **3** *a storm was raging* BE VIOLENT, be turbulent, be tempestuous; thunder, rampage.
– PHRASES **(all) the rage** POPULAR, fashionable, in fashion, in vogue, the (latest) thing, in great demand, sought-after, le dernier cri; *informal* in, the in thing, cool, big, trendy, hot, hip.

ragged ● adjective **1** *ragged jeans* TATTERED, in tatters, torn, ripped, holey, in holes, moth-eaten, frayed, worn (out), falling to pieces, threadbare, scruffy, shabby; *informal* tatty. **2** *a ragged child* SHABBY, scruffy, down at heel, unkempt, dressed in rags. **3** *a ragged coastline* JAGGED, craggy, rugged, uneven, rough, irregular; serrated, sawtooth, indented; *technical* crenulate, crenulated.
– OPPOSITES smart.

raging ● adjective **1** *a raging mob* ANGRY, furious, enraged, incensed, infuriated, irate, seething, fuming, ranting; *informal* livid, wild; *poetic/literary* wrathful. **2** *raging seas* STORMY, violent, wild, turbulent, tempestuous. **3** *a raging headache* EXCRUCIATING, agonizing,

horseback', 'foray'.

rail[1] ● noun **1** a bar or series of bars fixed on upright supports or attached to a wall or ceiling, serving as part of a fence or barrier or used to hang things on. **2** a steel bar or continuous line of bars laid on the ground as one of a pair forming a railway track. **3** railways as a means of transport. ● verb **1** provide or enclose with a rail or rails. **2** convey (goods) by rail.
– PHRASES **go off the rails** informal begin behaving in an uncontrolled way. **on the rails 1** informal functioning normally. **2** (of a racehorse or jockey) in a position on the racetrack nearest the inside fence.
– ORIGIN Old French *reille* 'iron rod', from Latin *regula* 'straight stick, rule'.

rail[2] ● verb **(rail against/at)** complain or protest strongly about or to.
– ORIGIN French *railler*, from Provençal *ralhar* 'to jest', from an alteration of Latin *rugire* 'to bellow'.

rail[3] ● noun a secretive waterside bird with drab grey and brown plumage.
– ORIGIN Old French *raille*, perhaps of imitative origin.

railcar ● noun **1** Brit. a powered railway passenger vehicle designed to operate singly or as part of a multiple unit. **2 (rail car)** N. Amer. any railway carriage or wagon.

railcard ● noun Brit. a pass entitling the holder to reduced rail fares.

railhead ● noun **1** a point on a railway from which roads and other transport routes begin. **2** the furthest point reached in constructing a railway.

railing ● noun a fence or barrier made of rails.

raillery /raylǝri/ ● noun good-humoured teasing.
– ORIGIN from French *railler* (see RAIL[2]).

railroad ● noun N. Amer. a railway. ● verb informal **1** rush or coerce into doing something. **2** cause (a measure) to be approved quickly by applying pressure.

railway ● noun chiefly Brit. **1** a track made of rails along which trains run. **2** a system of such tracks with the trains, organization, and personnel required for its working.

raiment /raymǝnt/ ● noun archaic or literary clothing.
– ORIGIN shortening of obsolete *arrayment* 'dress, outfit'.

rain ● noun **1** the condensed moisture of the atmosphere falling visibly in separate drops. **2 (rains)** falls of rain. **3** a large quantity of things falling or descending: *a rain of blows.* ● verb **1 (it rains, it is raining**, etc.) rain falls. **2 (be rained off)** (of an event) be terminated or cancelled because of rain. **3** fall or cause to fall in large quantities.
– PHRASES **be as right as rain** be perfectly fit and well. **rain cats and dogs** rain heavily.
– DERIVATIVES **rainless** adjective.
– ORIGIN Old English.

rainbow ● noun **1** an arch of colours visible in the sky, caused by the refraction and dispersion of the sun's light by water droplets in the atmosphere. **2** a wide range of things of different colours or kinds.

rainbow coalition ● noun a political alliance of differing groups, especially one comprising minorities and other disadvantaged groups.

rainbow trout ● noun a large trout with reddish sides, native to western North America and introduced widely elsewhere.

rain check ● noun N. Amer. a ticket given for later use when an outdoor event is interrupted or postponed by rain.
– PHRASES **take a rain check** politely refuse an offer, with the implication that one may take it up later.

raincoat ● noun a coat made from waterproofed or water-resistant fabric.

raindrop ● noun a single drop of rain.

rainfall ● noun **1** the fall of rain. **2** the quantity of rain falling within a given area in a given time.

rainforest ● noun a luxuriant, dense forest found in tropical areas with consistently heavy rainfall.

rainmaker ● noun **1** a person who attempts to cause rain to fall. **2** N. Amer. informal a person who is highly successful, especially in business.

rain shadow ● noun a relatively dry region sheltered from prevailing rain-bearing winds by a range of hills.

rainswept ● adjective frequently or recently exposed to rain and wind.

rainy ● adjective **(rainier, rainiest)** having or characterized by considerable rainfall.
– PHRASES **a rainy day** a time in the future when money may be needed.

raise ● verb **1** lift or move to a higher position or level. **2** set upright. **3** increase the amount, level, or strength of. **4** promote to a higher rank. **5** cause to be heard, felt, or considered: *doubts have been raised.* **6** build (a structure). **7** collect or levy (money or resources). **8** generate (an invoice or other document). **9** bring up (a child). **10** breed or grow (animals or plants). **11** wake from sleep or bring back from death. **12** abandon or force to abandon (a blockade, embargo, etc.). **13** drive (an animal) from its lair. **14** Brit. informal establish contact with (someone), especially by telephone or radio. **15 (raise something to)** Mathematics multiply a quantity to (a specified power). ● noun chiefly N. Amer. an increase in salary.
– PHRASES **raise hell** informal make a noisy disturbance. **raise the roof** make a great deal of noise, especially cheering.
– DERIVATIVES **raisable** adjective **raiser** noun.
– ORIGIN Old Norse, related to REAR[2].

Thesaurus

painful, throbbing, acute, bad. **4** *her raging thirst* SEVERE, extreme, great, excessive.

raid ● noun **1** *the raid on Dieppe* ATTACK, assault, descent, blitz, incursion, sortie; onslaught, storming, charge, offensive, invasion, blitzkrieg. **2** *a raid on a shop* ROBBERY, burglary, hold-up, break-in, ram raid; looting, plunder; *informal* smash-and-grab, stick-up; *Brit. informal* blag; *N. Amer. informal* heist. **3** *a police raid on the flat* SWOOP, search; *N. Amer. informal* bust, takedown.
● verb **1** *they raided shipping in the harbour* ATTACK, assault, set upon, descend on, swoop on, blitz, assail, storm, rush. **2** *armed men raided the store* ROB, hold up, break into; plunder, steal from, pillage, loot, ransack, sack; *informal* stick up. **3** *homes were raided by police* SEARCH, swoop on; *N. Amer. informal* bust.

raider ● noun ROBBER, burglar, thief, housebreaker, plunderer, pillager, looter, marauder; attacker, assailant, invader.

rail ● verb *he rails against injustice* PROTEST, fulminate, inveigh, rage, speak out, make a stand; expostulate about, criticize, denounce, condemn; object to, oppose, complain about, challenge; *informal* kick up a fuss about.

railing ● noun FENCE, fencing, rail(s), paling, palisade, balustrade, banister, hurdle.

raillery ● noun TEASING, mockery, chaff, ragging; banter, badinage; *informal* leg-pulling, ribbing, kidding; *N. Amer. informal* josh.

rain ● noun **1** *the rain had stopped* RAINFALL, precipitation, raindrops, wet weather; drizzle, mizzle, shower, rainstorm, cloudburst, torrent, downpour, deluge, storm. **2** *a rain of hot ash* SHOWER, deluge, flood, torrent, avalanche, flurry; storm, hail.
– RELATED TERMS pluvial.
● verb **1** *it rained heavily* POUR (DOWN), pelt down, tip down, teem down, beat down, lash down, sheet down, rain cats and dogs; fall, drizzle, spit; *informal* be chucking it down; *Brit. informal* bucket down. **2** *bombs rained on the city* FALL, hail, drop, shower.

rainy ● adjective WET, showery, drizzly, damp, inclement.

raise ● verb **1** *he raised a hand in greeting* LIFT (UP), hold aloft, elevate, uplift, upraise, upthrust; hoist, haul up, hitch up; *Brit. informal* hoick up. **2** *he raised himself in the bed* SET UPRIGHT, set vertical; sit up, stand up. **3** *they raised prices* INCREASE, put up, push up, up, mark up, escalate, inflate; *informal* hike (up), jack up, bump up. **4** *he raised his voice* AMPLIFY, louden, magnify, intensify, boost, lift, increase, heighten, augment. **5** *the temple was raised in 900 BC* BUILD, construct, erect, assemble, put up. **6** *how will you raise the money?* GET, obtain, acquire; accumulate, amass, collect, fetch, net, make. **7** *the city raised troops to fight for them* RECRUIT, enlist, sign up, conscript, call up, mobilize, rally, assemble; *US* draft. **8** *a tax raised on imports* LEVY, impose, exact, demand, charge. **9** *he raised several objections* BRING UP, air, ventilate; present, table, propose, submit, advance, suggest, moot, put forward. **10** *the disaster raised doubts about safety* GIVE RISE TO, occasion, cause, produce, engender, elicit, create, result in, lead to, prompt, awaken, arouse, induce, kindle, incite, stir up, trigger, spark off, provoke, instigate, foment, whip up; *poetic/literary* beget. **11** *most parents raise their children well* BRING UP, rear, nurture, look after, care for, provide for, mother, parent, tend, cherish; educate, train. **12** *he raised cattle* BREED, rear, nurture, keep, tend; grow, farm, cultivate, produce. **13** *he was raised to the peerage* PROMOTE, advance, upgrade, elevate, ennoble; *informal* kick upstairs; *archaic* prefer. **14** *(Brit. informal) raise them on the radio* CONTACT, get hold of, reach, get in touch with, communicate with, call.

raisin ● noun a partially dried grape.
– DERIVATIVES **raisiny** adjective.
– ORIGIN Old French, 'grape', from an alteration of Latin *racemus* 'bunch of grapes'.

raison d'être /rayzon detrə/ ● noun (pl. **raisons d'être** pronunc. same) the most important reason or purpose for someone or something's existence.
– ORIGIN French, 'reason for being'.

raita /rītə/ ● noun an Indian side dish of spiced yogurt containing chopped cucumber or other vegetables.
– ORIGIN Hindi.

Raj /raaj/ ● noun (**the Raj**) historical British sovereignty in India.
– ORIGIN Hindi, 'reign'.

raja /raajaa/ (also **rajah**) ● noun historical an Indian king or prince.
– ORIGIN from Hindi or Sanskrit.

Rajput /raajpoot/ ● noun a member of a Hindu military caste.
– ORIGIN from the Sanskrit words for 'king' + 'son'.

rake¹ ● noun an implement consisting of a pole with a toothed crossbar or fine tines at the end, used for drawing together leaves, cut grass, etc. or smoothing loose soil or gravel. ● verb **1** draw together with a rake. **2** make smooth with a rake. **3** scratch or scrape with a long sweeping movement. **4** draw or drag (something) through something with a long sweeping movement. **5** sweep with gunfire, a look, or a beam of light. **6** (**rake through**) search or rummage through.
– PHRASES **rake it in** informal make a lot of money. **rake over old coals** (or **rake over the ashes**) chiefly Brit. revive the memory of a past event. **rake up/over** revive the memory of (an incident or period best forgotten).
– DERIVATIVES **raker** noun.
– ORIGIN Old English; the verb is partly from Old Norse.

rake² ● noun a fashionable or wealthy man of dissolute habits.
– ORIGIN abbreviation of archaic *rakehell* in the same sense.

rake³ ● verb **1** set at a sloping angle. **2** (of a ship's mast or funnel) incline from the perpendicular towards the stern. ● noun **1** the angle at which a thing slopes. **2** the angle of the edge or face of a cutting tool.
– ORIGIN probably related to German *ragen* 'to project'.

rake-off ● noun informal a share of the profits from a deal, especially one that is disreputable.

raki /rəkee, rakki/ ● noun a strong alcoholic spirit made in eastern Europe or the Middle East.
– ORIGIN Turkish.

rakish ● adjective **1** having a dashing, jaunty, or slightly disreputable quality or appearance. **2** (of a boat or car) smart and streamlined.
– DERIVATIVES **rakishly** adverb.

rallentando /raləntandō/ ● adverb & adjective Music with a gradual decrease of speed.
– ORIGIN Italian, 'slowing down'.

rally¹ ● verb (**rallies, rallied**) **1** (with reference to troops) bring or come together again so as to continue fighting. **2** bring or come together as support or for united action: *his family rallied round.* **3** recover or cause to recover in health, spirits, or poise. **4** (of share, currency, or commodity prices) increase after a fall. **5** drive in a motor rally. ● noun (pl. **rallies**) **1** a mass meeting held as a protest or in support of a cause. **2** a long-distance competition for motor vehicles over public roads or rough terrain. **3** an open-air event for people who own a particular kind of vehicle. **4** a quick or marked recovery. **5** (in tennis and other racket sports) an extended exchange of strokes between players.
– DERIVATIVES **rallier** noun **rallyist** noun.
– ORIGIN French *rallier*, from *re-* 'again' + *allier* 'to ally'.

rally² ● verb (**rallies, rallied**) archaic tease.
– ORIGIN French *railler* (see RAIL²).

rallycross ● noun Brit. a form of motor racing in which cars are driven in heats over rough terrain and private roads.

rallying ● noun **1** (before another noun) having the effect of calling people to action: *a rallying cry.* **2** the action or sport of participating in a motor rally.

RAM ● abbreviation Computing random-access memory.

ram ● noun **1** an uncastrated male sheep. **2** a battering ram. **3** a striking or plunging device in various machines. **4** historical a projecting part of the bow of a warship, for piercing the sides of other ships. ● verb (**rammed, ramming**) **1** roughly force into place. **2** strike or be struck with force.
– DERIVATIVES **rammer** noun.
– ORIGIN Old English.

Ramadan /rammədan/ (also **Ramadhan** /rammәzan/) ● noun the ninth month of the Muslim year, during which strict fasting is observed from sunrise to sunset.
– ORIGIN from an Arabic word meaning 'be hot'; because the fasting period was originally supposed to be in one of the hot months.

ramble ● verb **1** walk for pleasure in the countryside. **2** (of a plant) grow over walls, fences, etc. **3** (often **ramble on**) talk or write at length in a confused or inconsequential way. ● noun a walk taken for pleasure in the countryside.
– DERIVATIVES **rambler** noun.
– ORIGIN probably related to Dutch *rammelen* (used of animals in the sense 'wander about on heat'), also to RAM.

Rambo /rambō/ ● noun an extremely tough and aggressive man.
– ORIGIN the hero of David Morrell's novel *First Blood* (1972), popularized in the films *First Blood* (1982) and *Rambo: First Blood Part II* (1985).

Thesaurus

– OPPOSITES lower, reduce, demolish.
● noun *the workers wanted a raise* PAY RISE, pay increase, increment.
– PHRASES **raise hell** *(informal).* See HELL.

raised ● adjective EMBOSSED, relief, relievo, die-stamped.

rake¹ ● verb **1** *he raked the leaves into a pile* SCRAPE UP, collect, gather. **2** *she raked the gravel* SMOOTH (OUT), level, even out, flatten, comb. **3** *the cat raked his arm with its claws* SCRATCH, lacerate, scrape, rasp, graze, grate; *Medicine* excoriate. **4** *she raked a hand through her hair* DRAG, pull, scrape, tug, comb. **5** *I raked through my pockets* RUMMAGE, search, hunt, sift, rifle. **6** *machine-gun fire raked the streets* SWEEP, enfilade, pepper, strafe.
– PHRASES **rake something in** *(informal)* EARN, make, get, gain, obtain, acquire, accumulate, bring in, pull in, pocket, realize, fetch, return, yield, raise, net, gross. **rake something up** REMIND PEOPLE OF, recollect, remember, call to mind; drag up, dredge up.

rake² ● noun *he was something of a rake* PLAYBOY, libertine, profligate; degenerate, roué, debauchee; lecher, seducer, womanizer, philanderer, adulterer, Don Juan, Lothario, Casanova; *informal* ladykiller, ladies' man, lech.

rake-off ● noun *(informal).* See CUT noun sense 3.

rakish ● adjective DASHING, debonair, stylish, jaunty, devil-may-care; raffish, disreputable, louche; *informal* sharp.

rally ● verb **1** *the troops rallied and held their ground* REGROUP, reassemble, re-form, reunite. **2** *he rallied an army* MUSTER, marshal, mobilize, raise, call up, recruit, enlist, conscript; assemble, gather, round up; *US* draft; *formal* convoke. **3** *ministers rallied to denounce the rumours* GET TOGETHER, band together, assemble, join forces, unite, ally, collaborate, cooperate, pull together. **4** *share prices rallied* RECOVER, improve, get better, pick up, revive, bounce back, perk up, look up, turn a corner.
– OPPOSITES disperse, disband, slump.
● noun **1** *a rally in support of the strike* (MASS) MEETING, gathering, assembly; demonstration, (protest) march; *informal* demo. **2** *a rally in oil prices* RECOVERY, upturn, improvement, comeback, resurgence; *Stock Exchange* dead cat bounce.
– OPPOSITES slump.

ram ● verb **1** *he rammed his sword into its sheath* FORCE, thrust, plunge, stab, push, sink, dig, stick, cram, jam, stuff, pack. **2** *a van rammed the police car* HIT, strike, crash into, collide with, impact, run into, smash into, bump (into), butt.

ramble ● verb **1** *we rambled around the lanes* WALK, hike, tramp, trek, backpack; wander, stroll, saunter, amble, roam, range, rove, traipse; *Scottish & Irish* stravaig; *informal* mosey, tootle; *Brit. informal* pootle; *formal* perambulate. **2** *she does ramble on* CHATTER, babble, prattle, prate, blather, gabble, jabber, twitter, rattle, maunder; *informal* jaw, gas, gab, yak, yabber; *Brit. informal* witter, chunter, natter, waffle, rabbit.
● noun *a ramble in the hills* WALK, hike, trek; wander, stroll, saunter, amble, roam, traipse, jaunt, promenade; *informal* mosey, tootle; *Brit. informal* pootle; *formal* perambulation.

rambler ● noun WALKER, hiker, backpacker, wanderer, rover; *poetic/literary* wayfarer.

rambling ● adjective **1** *a rambling speech* LONG-WINDED, verbose, wordy, prolix; digressive, maundering, roundabout, circuitous, circumlocutory; disconnected, disjointed, incoherent. **2** *rambling*

r

rambunctious /rambungkshəss/ ● adjective informal, chiefly N. Amer. uncontrollably exuberant.
– DERIVATIVES **rambunctiously** adverb **rambunctiousness** noun.
– ORIGIN of unknown origin.
rambutan /rambōōt'n/ ● noun the red, plum-sized fruit of a tropical Malaysian tree, with soft spines and a slightly acidic taste.
– ORIGIN from a Malay word meaning 'hair' (referring to the fruit's spines).
ramekin /rammikin/ ● noun a small dish for baking and serving an individual portion of food.
– ORIGIN French *ramequin*, of Low German or Dutch origin.
ramie /rammi/ ● noun a vegetable fibre from a tropical Asian plant, used in the manufacture of textiles.
– ORIGIN Malay.
ramification ● noun **1** (**ramifications**) complex consequences of an action or event. **2** a subdivision of a complex structure or process. **3** the action of ramifying or the state of being ramified.
ramify /rammifī/ ● verb (**ramifies**, **ramified**) form branches or cause to branch out.
– ORIGIN Latin *ramificare*, from *ramus* 'branch'.
ramjet ● noun a type of jet engine in which the air drawn in for combustion is compressed solely by the forward motion of the aircraft.
ramp ● noun **1** a sloping surface joining two different levels. **2** a movable set of steps for entering or leaving an aircraft. **3** Brit. a transverse ridge in a road to control the speed of vehicles. **4** N. Amer. an inclined slip road leading to or from a main road or motorway. ● verb **1** provide with a ramp. **2** (**ramp up**) increase (the production of goods). **3** archaic (of an animal) rear up threateningly.
– ORIGIN Old French *ramper* 'creep, crawl'.
rampage /rampayj/ ● verb rush around in a violent and uncontrollable manner. ● noun an instance of rampaging.
– ORIGIN perhaps from RAMP and RAGE.
rampant ● adjective **1** flourishing or spreading unchecked. **2** unrestrained in action or performance. **3** (after a noun) Heraldry (of an animal) represented standing on its left hind foot with its forefeet in the air.
– DERIVATIVES **rampantly** adverb.
– ORIGIN Old French, 'crawling', from *ramper* (see RAMP).
rampart ● noun a defensive wall of a castle or walled city, having a broad top with a walkway.
– ORIGIN French *rempart*, from *remparer* 'fortify, take possession of again'.
ram raid ● noun a robbery in which a shop window is rammed with a vehicle and looted.
ramrod ● noun a rod for ramming down the charge of a muzzle-loading firearm.
ramshackle ● adjective in a state of severe disrepair.
– ORIGIN from obsolete *ransackled* 'ransacked'.
RAN ● abbreviation Royal Australian Navy.
ran past of RUN.
ranch ● noun **1** a large farm, especially in the western US and Canada, where cattle or other animals are bred. **2** (also **ranch house**) N. Amer. a single-storey house. ● verb run a ranch.
– DERIVATIVES **rancher** noun.
– ORIGIN Spanish *rancho* 'group of persons eating together'.
rancid ● adjective (of foods containing fat or oil) smelling or tasting unpleasant as a result of being stale.
– DERIVATIVES **rancidity** noun.
– ORIGIN Latin *rancidus* 'stinking'.
rancour (US **rancor**) ● noun bitterness; resentment.
– DERIVATIVES **rancorous** adjective.
– ORIGIN Latin *rancor* 'rankness', later 'bitter grudge'.
rand /rand/ ● noun the basic monetary unit of South Africa, equal to 100 cents.
– ORIGIN from *the Rand*, a goldfield district near Johannesburg.
random ● adjective **1** made, done, or happening without method or conscious decision. **2** Statistics governed by or involving equal chances for each item.
– DERIVATIVES **randomize** (also **randomise**) verb **randomly** adverb **randomness** noun.
– ORIGIN originally in the sense 'impetuous headlong rush'; from Old French *randon* 'great speed', from *randir* 'gallop'.
random access ● noun Computing the process of transferring information to or from memory in which every memory location can be accessed directly rather than being accessed in a fixed sequence.
randy ● adjective (**randier**, **randiest**) informal, chiefly Brit. sexually aroused or excited.
– ORIGIN perhaps from obsolete Dutch *randen* 'to rant'.
rang past of RING².
rangatira /ranggəteerə/ ● noun NZ a Maori chief or noble.
– ORIGIN Maori.
range ● noun **1** the area of variation between limits on a particular scale: *the car's outside my price range.* **2** a set of different things of the same general type. **3** the scope or extent of a person's or thing's abilities or capacity. **4** the distance within which something is able to operate or be effective. **5** a line or series of mountains or hills. **6** a large area of open land for grazing or hunting. **7** an area used as a testing ground for military equipment. **8** an area with targets for shooting practice. **9** the area over which a plant or animal is distributed. **10** a large cooking stove with several burners or hotplates. ● verb **1** vary or extend between specified limits. **2** place or arrange in a row or rows or in a specified manner. **3** (**range against**) place in opposition to. **4** travel or wander over a wide area. **5** embrace a wide number of different topics.
– ORIGIN Old French, 'row, rank', from *rangier* 'put in order'.
rangefinder ● noun an instrument for estimating the distance

Thesaurus

r

streets WINDING, twisting, twisty, labyrinthine; sprawling. **3** *a rambling rose* TRAILING, creeping, climbing, vining.
– OPPOSITES concise.
ramification ● noun CONSEQUENCE, result, aftermath, outcome, effect, upshot; development, implication; product, by-product.
ramp ● noun SLOPE, bank, incline, gradient, tilt; rise, ascent, acclivity; drop, descent, declivity.
rampage ● verb *mobs rampaged through the streets* RIOT, run riot, go on the rampage, run amok, go berserk; storm, charge, tear.
– PHRASES **go on the rampage** RIOT, rampage, go berserk, get out of control, run amok; *N. Amer. informal* go postal.
rampant ● adjective **1** *rampant inflation* UNCONTROLLED, unrestrained, unchecked, unbridled, widespread; out of control, out of hand, rife. **2** *rampant dislike* VEHEMENT, strong, violent, forceful, intense, passionate, fanatical. **3** *rampant vegetation* LUXURIANT, exuberant, lush, rich, riotous, rank, profuse, vigorous; *informal* jungly. **4** *(Heraldry) a lion rampant* UPRIGHT, erect, standing (up), rearing up.
– OPPOSITES controlled, mild.
rampart ● noun DEFENSIVE WALL, embankment, earthwork, parapet, breastwork, battlement, bulwark, outwork.
ramshackle ● adjective TUMBLEDOWN, dilapidated, derelict, decrepit, neglected, run down, gone to rack and ruin, crumbling, decaying; rickety, shaky, unsound; *informal* shambly; *N. Amer. informal* shacky.
– OPPOSITES sound.
rancid ● adjective SOUR, stale, turned, rank, putrid, foul, rotten, bad, off; gamy, high, fetid, stinking, malodorous, foul-smelling; *poetic/literary* noisome.
– OPPOSITES fresh.
rancorous ● adjective BITTER, spiteful, hateful, resentful, acrimonious, malicious, malevolent, hostile, venomous, vindictive, baleful, vitriolic, vengeful, pernicious, mean, nasty; *informal* bitchy, catty.
– OPPOSITES amicable.
rancour ● noun BITTERNESS, spite, hate, hatred, resentment, malice, ill will, malevolence, animosity, antipathy, enmity, hostility, acrimony, venom, vitriol.
random ● adjective **1** *random spot checks* UNSYSTEMATIC, unmethodical, arbitrary, unplanned, undirected, casual, indiscriminate, non-specific, haphazard, stray, erratic; chance, accidental.
– OPPOSITES systematic.
– PHRASES **at random** UNSYSTEMATICALLY, arbitrarily, randomly, unmethodically, haphazardly.
range ● noun **1** *his range of vision* SPAN, scope, compass, sweep, extent, area, field, orbit, ambit, horizon, latitude; limits, bounds, confines, parameters. **2** *a range of mountains* ROW, chain, sierra, ridge, massif; line, string, series. **3** *a range of quality foods* ASSORTMENT, variety, diversity, mixture, collection, array, selection, choice. **4** *she put the dish into the range* STOVE, cooker; *trademark* Aga. **5** *cows grazed on open range* PASTURE, pasturage, pastureland, grass, grassland, grazing land, bocage, veld; *Scottish* shieling; *poetic/literary* greensward.

of an object.

ranger ● noun **1** a keeper of a park, forest, or area of countryside. **2** a member of a body of armed men. **3** (**Ranger** or **Ranger Guide**) Brit. a senior Guide.

rangy /raynji/ ● adjective (of a person) tall and slim; long-limbed.

rank[1] ● noun **1** a position within a fixed hierarchy, especially that of the armed forces. **2** high social standing. **3** a single line of soldiers or police officers drawn up abreast. **4** (**the ranks**) (in the armed forces) those who are not commissioned officers. **5** (**ranks**) the people belonging to or constituting a group or class: *the ranks of the unemployed.* **6** Chess each of the eight rows of eight squares running from side to side across a chessboard. Compare with FILE[1]. ● verb **1** give (someone or something) a rank within a grading system. **2** hold a specified rank. **3** US take precedence over (someone) in respect to rank. **4** arrange in a row or rows.

– PHRASES **break rank** (or **ranks**) **1** (of soldiers or police officers) fail to remain in line. **2** fail to maintain solidarity. **close ranks 1** (of soldiers or police officers) come closer together in a line. **2** unite in order to defend common interests. **pull rank** take unfair advantage of one's seniority. **rank and file** the ordinary members of an organization as opposed to its leaders. [ORIGIN referring to the 'ranks' and 'files' into which privates and non-commissioned officers form on parade.]

– ORIGIN Old French *ranc*; related to RING[1].

rank[2] ● adjective **1** (of vegetation) growing too thickly. **2** having a foul smell. **3** complete and utter: *a rank amateur.*

– DERIVATIVES **rankly** adverb **rankness** noun.

– ORIGIN Old English, 'proud, rebellious, sturdy', also 'fully grown'.

ranker ● noun **1** chiefly Brit. a soldier in the ranks; a private. **2** a commissioned officer who has been in the ranks.

ranking ● noun **1** a position in a hierarchy or scale. **2** the action of giving a rank or status to someone or something. ● adjective having a specified rank: *high-ranking officers.*

rankle ● verb (of a comment or fact) cause annoyance or resentment.

– ORIGIN originally in the sense 'fester'; from Old French *rancler*, from *rancle* 'festering sore'.

ransack ● verb **1** go hurriedly through (a place) stealing things and causing damage. **2** thoroughly search.

– ORIGIN Old Norse.

ransom ● noun a sum of money demanded or paid for the release of a captive. ● verb **1** obtain the release of (someone) by paying a ransom. **2** detain (someone) and demand a ransom for their release.

– PHRASES **hold to ransom 1** hold (someone) captive and demand payment for release. **2** demand concessions from (someone) by threatening damaging action. **a king's ransom** a huge amount of money.

– ORIGIN Old French *ransoun*, from Latin *redemptio* 'redemption'.

rant ● verb speak or shout at length in a wild, impassioned way. ● noun a spell of ranting.

– DERIVATIVES **ranter** noun.

– ORIGIN Dutch *ranten* 'talk nonsense, rave'.

ranunculus /rənungkyooləss/ ● noun (pl. **ranunculuses** or **ranunculi** /rənungkyoolī/) a plant of the genus that includes the buttercups and water crowfoots.

– ORIGIN Latin, 'little frog'.

rap ● verb (**rapped**, **rapping**) **1** strike (a hard surface) with a series of rapid audible blows. **2** strike sharply. **3** informal rebuke or criticize sharply. **4** (usu. **rap out**) say something sharply or suddenly. **5** perform rap music. ● noun **1** a quick, sharp knock or blow. **2** informal a rebuke or criticism. **3** a type of popular music of US black origin in which words are recited rapidly and rhythmically over an instrumental backing. **4** informal, chiefly N. Amer. an impromptu talk or discussion. **5** informal, chiefly N. Amer. a criminal charge: *a murder rap.*

– PHRASES **beat the rap** N. Amer. informal escape punishment for or be acquitted of a crime. **take the rap** informal be punished or blamed for something.

– DERIVATIVES **rapper** noun.

– ORIGIN probably imitative and Scandinavian.

rapacious /rəpayshəss/ ● adjective aggressively greedy.

– DERIVATIVES **rapaciously** adverb **rapaciousness** noun **rapacity** noun.

– ORIGIN from Latin *rapax*, from *rapere* 'to snatch'.

rape[1] ● verb **1** (of a man) force (another person) to have sexual intercourse with him against their will. **2** spoil or destroy (a place). ● noun an act or the crime of raping someone.

– ORIGIN originally denoting violent seizure of property: from Latin *rapere* 'seize'.

rape[2] ● noun a plant of the cabbage family with bright yellow flowers, especially a variety (**oilseed rape**) grown for its oil-rich seed.

– ORIGIN Latin *rapum, rapa* 'turnip'.

Thesaurus

● verb **1** *charges range from 1% to 5%* VARY, fluctuate, differ; extend, stretch, reach, cover, go, run. **2** *on the stalls are ranged fresh foods* ARRANGE, line up, order, position, dispose, set out, array. **3** *they ranged over the steppes* ROAM, rove, traverse, travel, journey, wander, drift, ramble, meander, stroll, traipse, walk, hike, trek.

rangy ● adjective LONG-LEGGED, long-limbed, leggy, tall; slender, slim, lean, thin, gangling, gangly, lanky, spindly, skinny, spare.

– OPPOSITES squat.

rank[1] ● noun **1** *he was elevated to ministerial rank* POSITION, level, grade, echelon; class, status, standing; dated station. **2** *a family of rank* HIGH STANDING, blue blood, high birth, nobility, aristocracy; eminence, distinction, prestige; prominence, influence, consequence, power. **3** *a rank of riflemen* ROW, line, file, column, string, train, procession.

● verb **1** *the plant is ranked as endangered* CLASSIFY, class, categorize, rate, grade, bracket, group, pigeonhole, designate; catalogue, file, list. **2** *he ranked below the others* HAVE A RANK, be graded, have a status, be classed, be classified, be categorized; belong. **3** *tulips ranked like guardsmen* LINE UP, align, order, arrange, dispose, set out, array, range.

– PHRASES **the rank and file 1** *the officers and the rank and file* OTHER RANKS, soldiers, NCOs, lower ranks; men, troops. **2** *a speech appealing to the rank and file* THE (COMMON) PEOPLE, the proletariat, the masses, the populace, the commonality, the commonalty, the third estate, the plebeians; the hoi polloi, the rabble, the riff-raff, the great unwashed; informal the proles, the plebs.

rank[2] ● adjective **1** *rank vegetation* ABUNDANT, lush, luxuriant, dense, profuse, vigorous, overgrown; informal jungly. **2** *a rank smell* OFFENSIVE, unpleasant, nasty, revolting, sickening, obnoxious, noxious; foul, fetid, smelly, stinking, reeking, high, off, rancid, putrid, malodorous; Brit. informal niffy, pongy, whiffy, humming; poetic/literary noisome. **3** *rank stupidity* DOWNRIGHT, utter, outright, out-and-out, absolute, complete, sheer, arrant, thoroughgoing, unqualified, unmitigated, positive, perfect, patent, pure, total.

– OPPOSITES sparse, pleasant.

rankle ● verb CAUSE RESENTMENT, annoy, upset, anger, irritate, offend, affront, displease, provoke, irk, vex, pique, nettle, gall; informal rile, miff, peeve, aggravate, hack off; Brit. informal nark; N. Amer. informal tick off.

ransack ● verb PLUNDER, pillage, raid, rob, loot, sack, strip, despoil; ravage, devastate, turn upside down; scour, rifle, comb, search.

ransom ● noun *they demanded a huge ransom* PAY-OFF, payment, sum, price.

● verb *the girl was ransomed for £4 million* RELEASE, free, deliver, liberate, rescue; exchange for a ransom, buy the freedom of.

rant ● verb *she ranted on about the unfairness* HOLD FORTH, go on, fulminate, vociferate, sound off, spout, pontificate, bluster, declaim; shout, yell, bellow; informal mouth off.

● noun *he went into a rant about them* TIRADE, diatribe, broadside; poetic/literary philippic.

rap[1] ● verb **1** *she rapped his fingers with a ruler* HIT, strike; informal whack, thwack, bash, wallop; poetic/literary smite. **2** *I rapped on the door* KNOCK, tap, bang, hammer, pound. **3** (informal) *banks were rapped for high charges.* See REPRIMAND verb.

● noun **1** *a rap on the knuckles* BLOW, hit, knock, bang, crack; informal whack, thwack, bash, wallop. **2** *a rap at the door* KNOCK, tap, rat-tat, bang, hammering, pounding.

– PHRASES **take the rap** (informal) BE PUNISHED, take the blame, suffer (the consequences), pay (the price).

rap[2] ● noun *they didn't care a rap* WHIT, iota, jot, hoot, scrap, bit, fig; informal damn, monkey's.

rapacious ● adjective GRASPING, greedy, avaricious, acquisitive, covetous; mercenary, materialistic; insatiable, predatory; informal money-grubbing; N. Amer. informal grabby.

– OPPOSITES generous.

r

rapeseed ● noun seeds of the rape plant, used for oil.

rapid ● adjective happening in a short time or at great speed. ● noun (usu. **rapids**) a fast-flowing and turbulent part of the course of a river.
– DERIVATIVES **rapidity** noun **rapidly** adverb.
– ORIGIN Latin *rapidus*, from *rapere* 'take by force'.

rapid eye movement ● noun the jerky movement of a person's eyes that occurs in REM sleep.

rapier ● noun a thin, light sharp-pointed sword used for thrusting.
– ORIGIN French *rapière*, from *râpe* 'rasp, grater' (because the perforated hilt resembles a rasp or grater).

rapine /rappin/ ● noun literary the violent seizure of property.
– ORIGIN Old French, from Latin *rapere* 'seize'.

rapist ● noun a man who commits rape.

rappel /rapel/ ● noun & verb (**rappelled**, **rappelling**) another term for ABSEIL.
– ORIGIN French, 'a recalling', from *rappeler* in the sense 'bring back to oneself' (with reference to the rope manoeuvre).

rappen /rapp'n/ ● noun (pl. same) a monetary unit of the German-speaking cantons of Switzerland and of Liechtenstein, equal to one hundredth of the Swiss franc.
– ORIGIN German *Rappe* 'raven', with reference to the depiction of a raven's head on a medieval coin.

rapport /rapor/ ● noun a close and harmonious relationship in which there is common understanding.
– ORIGIN French, from *rapporter* 'bring back'.

rapporteur /rapportör/ ● noun a person appointed by an organization to report on its meetings.
– ORIGIN French.

rapprochement /raproshmon/ ● noun the establishment or resumption of harmonious relations.
– ORIGIN French.

rapscallion /rapskalyən/ ● noun archaic or humorous a mischievous person.
– ORIGIN alteration of earlier *rascallion*, perhaps from RASCAL.

rapt ● adjective **1** fully absorbed and intent; fascinated. **2** filled with an intense and pleasurable emotion. **3** Austral. informal another term for WRAPPED.
– DERIVATIVES **raptly** adverb **raptness** noun.
– ORIGIN Latin *raptus* 'seized'.

raptor ● noun **1** a bird of prey. **2** informal a dromaeosaurid dinosaur, such as a velociraptor.
– DERIVATIVES **raptorial** adjective.
– ORIGIN Latin, 'plunderer'.

rapture ● noun **1** intense pleasure or joy. **2** (**raptures**) the expression of intense pleasure or enthusiasm.

rapturous ● adjective characterized by, feeling or expressing great pleasure or enthusiasm.
– DERIVATIVES **rapturously** adverb.

rara avis /rairə ayviss/ ● noun (pl. **rarae aves** /rairee ayveez/) another term for RARE BIRD.
– ORIGIN Latin.

rare[1] ● adjective (**rarer**, **rarest**) **1** occurring very infrequently. **2** remarkable: *a player of rare skill.*
– ORIGIN Latin *rarus*.

rare[2] ● adjective (**rarer**, **rarest**) (of red meat) lightly cooked, so that the inside is still red.
– ORIGIN variant of obsolete *rear* 'half-cooked'.

rare bird ● noun an exceptional person or thing.

rarebit (also **Welsh rarebit** or **Welsh rabbit**) ● noun a dish of melted and seasoned cheese on toast.
– ORIGIN originally as *Welsh rabbit*: the reason for the use of the term *rabbit* is unknown.

rare earth ● noun Chemistry any of a group of chemically similar metallic elements including cerium, lanthanum, and the other lanthanide elements together with (usually) scandium and yttrium.

raree show /rairee/ ● noun archaic a form of street entertainment, especially one carried in a box, such as a peep show.
– ORIGIN apparently representing *rare show*, as pronounced by Savoyard showmen.

rarefaction /rairifaksh'n/ ● noun reduction of the density of something, especially air or a gas.
– ORIGIN Latin, from *rarefacere* 'grow thin, become rare'.

rarefied /rairifīd/ ● adjective **1** (of air) of lower pressure than usual; thin. **2** very esoteric or refined.

rare gas ● noun another term for NOBLE GAS.

rarely ● adverb not often; seldom.

raring ● adjective informal very eager to do something: *she was raring to go.*
– ORIGIN from *rare*, dialect variant of ROAR or REAR[2].

rarity ● noun (pl. **rarities**) **1** the state or quality of being rare. **2** a rare thing.

rascal ● noun a mischievous or cheeky person.
– DERIVATIVES **rascality** noun **rascally** adjective.
– ORIGIN originally in the senses 'a mob' and 'member of the rabble': from Old French *rascaille* 'rabble'.

rase ● verb variant spelling of RAZE.

rash[1] ● adjective acting or done impetuously, without careful consideration.
– DERIVATIVES **rashly** adverb **rashness** noun.

Thesaurus

rape ● noun **1** *he was charged with rape* SEXUAL ASSAULT, sexual abuse; *archaic* ravishment, defilement. **2** *the rape of rainforest* DESTRUCTION, violation, ravaging, pillaging, plundering, desecration, defilement, sacking, sack.
● verb **1** *he raped her at knifepoint* SEXUALLY ASSAULT, sexually abuse, violate, force oneself on; *poetic/literary* ravish; *archaic* defile. **2** *they raped our country* RAVAGE, violate, desecrate, defile, plunder, pillage, despoil; lay waste, ransack, sack.

rapid ● adjective QUICK, fast, swift, speedy, expeditious, express, brisk; lightning, meteoric, whirlwind; sudden, instantaneous, instant, immediate; hurried, hasty, precipitate; *informal* p.d.q. (pretty damn quick); *poetic/literary* fleet.
– OPPOSITES slow.

rapidly ● adverb QUICKLY, fast, swiftly, speedily, at the speed of light, post-haste, hotfoot, at full tilt, briskly; hurriedly, hastily, in haste, in a rush, precipitately; *informal* like a shot, double quick, p.d.q. (pretty damn quick), in a flash, hell for leather, at the double, like a bat out of hell, like (greased) lightning, like mad, like the wind; *Brit. informal* like the clappers, at a rate of knots, like billy-o; *N. Amer. informal* lickety-split; *poetic/literary* apace.
– OPPOSITES slowly.

rapport ● noun AFFINITY, close relationship, (mutual) understanding, bond, empathy, sympathy, accord.

rapt ● adjective FASCINATED, enthralled, spellbound, captivated, riveted, gripped, mesmerized, enchanted, entranced, bewitched; transported, enraptured, thrilled, ecstatic.
– OPPOSITES inattentive.

rapture ● noun *she gazed at him in rapture* ECSTASY, bliss, exaltation, euphoria, elation, joy, enchantment, delight, happiness, pleasure.
– PHRASES **go into raptures** ENTHUSE, rhapsodize, rave, gush, wax lyrical; praise something to the skies.

rapturous ● adjective ECSTATIC, joyful, elated, euphoric, enraptured, on cloud nine, in seventh heaven, transported, enchanted, blissful, happy; enthusiastic, delighted, thrilled, overjoyed, rapt; *informal* over the moon, on top of the world, blissed out; *Austral. informal* wrapped.

rara avis ● noun RARITY, rare bird, wonder, marvel, nonpareil, nonsuch, one of a kind; curiosity, oddity, freak; *Brit. informal* one-off.

rare ● adjective **1** *rare moments of privacy* INFREQUENT, scarce, sparse, few and far between, thin on the ground, like gold dust; occasional, limited, odd, isolated, unaccustomed, unwonted; *Brit.* out of the common. **2** *rare stamps* UNUSUAL, recherché, uncommon, unfamiliar, atypical, singular. **3** *a man of rare talent* EXCEPTIONAL, outstanding, unparalleled, peerless, matchless, unique, unrivalled, inimitable, beyond compare, without equal, second to none, unsurpassed; consummate, superior, superlative, first-class; *informal* A1, top-notch.
– OPPOSITES common, commonplace.

rarefied ● adjective ESOTERIC, exclusive, select; elevated, lofty.

rarely ● adverb SELDOM, infrequently, hardly (ever), scarcely, not often; once in a while, now and then, occasionally; *informal* once in a blue moon.
– OPPOSITES often.

raring ● adjective (*informal*) EAGER, keen, enthusiastic; impatient, longing, desperate; ready; *informal* dying, itching, gagging.

rarity ● noun **1** *the rarity of earthquakes in the UK* INFREQUENCY, rareness, unusualness, uncommonness, scarcity, scarceness. **2** *this book is a rarity* COLLECTOR'S ITEM, rare thing, rare bird, rara avis; wonder, nonpareil, one of a kind; curiosity, oddity; *Brit. informal* one-off.

r

– ORIGIN Germanic.

rash[2] ● noun **1** an area of reddening of a person's skin, sometimes with raised spots. **2** an unwelcome series of things happening within a short space of time: *a rash of strikes.*

– ORIGIN probably related to Old French *rasche* 'eruptive sores, scurf'.

rasher ● noun a thin slice of bacon.

– ORIGIN of unknown origin.

rasp ● noun **1** a coarse file for use on metal, wood, or other hard material. **2** a harsh, grating noise. ● verb **1** file with a rasp. **2** (of a rough surface or object) scrape in a painful or unpleasant way. **3** make a harsh, grating noise.

– DERIVATIVES **raspy** adjective.

– ORIGIN Old French *rasper.*

raspberry ● noun **1** an edible soft fruit related to the blackberry, consisting of a cluster of reddish-pink drupels. **2** informal a sound made with the tongue and lips, expressing derision or contempt. [ORIGIN from *raspberry tart*, rhyming slang for 'fart'.]

– ORIGIN from obsolete *raspis* 'raspberry', of unknown origin.

Rasta /rastə/ ● noun & adjective informal short for RASTAFARIAN.

Rastafarian /rastəfairiən/ ● adjective relating to a religious movement of Jamaican origin holding that Emperor Haile Selassie of Ethiopia was the Messiah and that blacks are the chosen people. ● noun a member of this movement.

– DERIVATIVES **Rastafarianism** noun.

– ORIGIN from *Ras Tafari*, the name by which Haile Selassie was known (1916–30).

raster /rastə/ ● noun a rectangular pattern of parallel scanning lines followed by the electron beam on a television screen or computer monitor.

– ORIGIN German, 'screen'.

rasterize (also **rasterise**) ● verb Computing convert (an image stored as an outline) into pixels that can be displayed on a screen or printed.

– DERIVATIVES **rasterization** noun.

rat ● noun **1** a large, long-tailed rodent, typically considered a serious pest. **2** informal a despicable person. **3** informal an informer. **4** N. Amer. a person who is associated with or frequents a specified place: *a mall rat.* ● exclamation (**rats**) informal expressing mild annoyance. ● verb (**ratted, ratting**) **1** hunt or kill rats. **2** informal desert one's party, side, or cause. **3** (**rat on**) informal inform on. **4** (**rat on**) informal break (an agreement or promise).

– ORIGIN Old English, reinforced by Old French *rat.*

rata /raatə/ ● noun a large New Zealand tree with crimson flowers and hard red wood.

– ORIGIN Maori.

ratable ● adjective variant spelling of RATEABLE.

ratafia /rattəfeeə/ ● noun **1** a liqueur flavoured with almonds or the kernels of peaches, apricots, or cherries. **2** an almond-flavoured biscuit like a small macaroon.

– ORIGIN French.

rat-arsed ● adjective Brit. vulgar slang very drunk.

ratatouille /rattətwee/ ● noun a vegetable dish consisting of onions, courgettes, tomatoes, aubergines, and peppers, stewed in oil.

– ORIGIN French.

ratbag ● noun Brit. informal an unpleasant or disliked person.

ratchet ● noun a device consisting of a bar or wheel with a set of angled teeth in which a pawl, cog, or tooth engages, allowing motion in one direction only. ● verb (**ratcheted, ratcheting**) **1** operate by means of a ratchet. **2** (**ratchet up/down**) cause (something) to rise (or fall) as a step in an irreversible process.

– ORIGIN French *rochet*, originally denoting a blunt lance head.

rate[1] ● noun **1** a measure, quantity, or frequency measured against another quantity or measure: *the crime rate.* **2** the speed with which something moves, happens, or changes. **3** a fixed price paid or charged for something. **4** the amount of a charge or payment expressed as a percentage of some other amount, or as a basis of calculation. **5** (**rates**) (in the UK) a tax on commercial land and buildings paid to a local authority. ● verb **1** assign a standard or value to (something) according to a particular scale. **2** consider to be of a certain quality or standard. **3** be worthy of; merit. **4** informal have a high opinion of.

– PHRASES **at any rate** whatever happens or may have happened. **at this rate** if things continue in this way.

– ORIGIN Latin *rata*, from *pro rata parte* 'according to the proportional share'.

rate[2] ● verb archaic scold angrily.

– ORIGIN of unknown origin.

rateable (also **ratable**) ● adjective able to be rated or estimated.

rateable value ● noun (in the UK) a value ascribed to a commercial property based on its size, location, etc., used to determine the rates payable by its owner.

rate of exchange ● noun another term for EXCHANGE RATE.

ratepayer ● noun **1** (in the UK) a person liable to pay rates. **2** N. Amer. a customer of a public utility.

rather ● adverb **1** (**would rather**) indicating one's preference in a particular matter. **2** to a certain or significant extent or degree. **3** on the contrary. **4** more precisely. **5** instead of; as opposed to. ● exclamation Brit. dated expressing emphatic affirmation, agreement, or acceptance.

– PHRASES **had rather** literary or archaic would rather.

– ORIGIN Old English, 'earlier, sooner'.

rathskeller /raatskellər/ ● noun US a beer hall or restaurant in a basement.

– ORIGIN obsolete German, from *Rathaus* 'town hall' + *Keller* 'cellar'.

ratify ● verb (**ratifies, ratified**) give formal consent to; make officially valid.

– DERIVATIVES **ratification** noun **ratifier** noun.

– ORIGIN Latin *ratificare*, from *ratus* 'fixed'.

Thesaurus

rascal ● noun SCALLYWAG, imp, monkey, mischief-maker, wretch; *informal* scamp, tyke, horror, monster; *Brit. informal* perisher; *N. Amer. informal* varmint; *archaic* rapscallion.

rash[1] ● noun **1** *he broke out in a rash* SPOTS, breakout, eruption; hives; *Medicine* erythema, exanthema, urticaria. **2** *a rash of articles in the press* SERIES, succession, spate, wave, flood, deluge, torrent; outbreak, epidemic, flurry.

rash[2] ● adjective *a rash decision* RECKLESS, impulsive, impetuous, hasty, foolhardy, incautious, precipitate; careless, heedless, thoughtless, imprudent, foolish; ill-advised, injudicious, ill-judged, misguided, hare-brained; *poetic/literary* temerarious.

– OPPOSITES prudent.

rasp ● verb **1** *enamel is rasped off the teeth* SCRAPE, rub, abrade, grate, grind, sand, file, scratch, scour; *Medicine* excoriate. **2** *'Help!' he rasped* CROAK, squawk, caw, say hoarsely.

rasping ● adjective HARSH, grating, jarring; raspy, scratchy, hoarse, rough, gravelly, croaky, gruff, husky, throaty, guttural.

rat *(informal)* ● noun **1** *her rat of a husband* SCOUNDREL, wretch, rogue; *informal* beast, pig, swine, creep, louse, lowlife, scumbag, heel, dog, weasel; *N. Amer. informal* rat fink; *dated* cad; *informal, dated* rotter. **2** *the most famous rat in mob history* INFORMER, betrayer, stool pigeon; *informal* snitch, squealer; *Brit. informal* grass, supergrass, nark, snout; *Scottish & N. Irish informal* tout; *N. Amer. informal* fink, stoolie.

– PHRASES **rat on 1** *we don't rat on our friends* INFORM ON, betray, be unfaithful to, stab in the back; *informal* tell on, sell down the river, blow the whistle on, squeal on, stitch up, peach on, do the dirty on; *Brit. informal* grass on, shop; *N. Amer. informal* rat out, finger. **2** *he ratted on his pledge* BREAK, renege on, go back on, welsh on.

rate ● noun **1** *a fixed rate of interest* PERCENTAGE, ratio, proportion; scale, standard. **2** *an hourly rate of £30* CHARGE, price, cost, tariff, fare, levy, toll; fee, remuneration, payment, wage, allowance. **3** *the rate of change* SPEED, pace, tempo, velocity, momentum. ● verb **1** *they rated their ability at driving* ASSESS, evaluate, appraise, judge, weigh up, estimate, calculate, gauge, measure, adjudge; grade, rank, classify, categorize. **2** *the scheme was rated effective* CONSIDER, judge, reckon, think, hold, deem, find; regard as, look on as, count as. **3** *he rated only a brief mention* MERIT, deserve, warrant, be worthy of, be deserving of. **4** *(informal) Ben doesn't rate him* THINK HIGHLY OF, think much of, set much store by; admire, esteem, value.

– PHRASES **at any rate** IN ANY CASE, anyhow, anyway, in any event, nevertheless; whatever happens, come what may, regardless, notwithstanding.

rather ● adverb **1** *I'd rather you went* SOONER, by preference, preferably, by choice. **2** *it's rather complicated* QUITE, a bit, a little, fairly, slightly, somewhat, relatively, to some degree, comparatively; *informal* pretty, sort of, kind of. **3** *her true feelings—or rather, lack of feelings* MORE PRECISELY, to be precise, to be exact, strictly speaking. **4** *she seemed sad rather than angry* MORE; as opposed to, instead of. **5** *it was not impulsive, but rather a considered decision* ON THE CONTRARY, instead.

ratify ● verb CONFIRM, approve, sanction, endorse, agree to, accept,

rating • noun **1** a classification or ranking based on quality, standard, or performance. **2** (**ratings**) the estimated audience size of a television or radio programme. **3** Brit. a non-commissioned sailor in the navy.

ratio • noun (pl. **ratios**) the quantitative relation between two amounts showing the number of times one value contains or is contained within the other.
– ORIGIN Latin, 'reckoning'.

ratiocinate /rattiossinayt, rashi-/ • verb formal form judgements by a process of logic; reason.
– DERIVATIVES **ratiocination** noun **ratiocinative** adjective.
– ORIGIN Latin *ratiocinari* 'deliberate, calculate', from *ratio* 'reckoning'.

ration • noun **1** a fixed amount of a commodity officially allowed to each person during a time of shortage. **2** (**rations**) an amount of food supplied on a regular basis to members of the armed forces during a war. **3** (**rations**) food; provisions. • verb **1** limit the supply of (a commodity) to fixed rations. **2** limit the amount of a commodity available to.
– ORIGIN Latin, 'reckoning, ratio'.

rational • adjective **1** based on or in accordance with reason or logic. **2** able to think sensibly or logically. **3** having the capacity to reason. **4** Mathematics (of a number or quantity) expressible as a ratio of whole numbers.
– DERIVATIVES **rationality** noun **rationally** adverb.

rationale /rashənaal/ • noun a set of reasons or a logical basis for a course of action or a belief.

rationalism • noun the practice or principle of basing opinions and actions on reason and knowledge rather than on religious belief or emotional response.
– DERIVATIVES **rationalist** noun.

rationalize (also **rationalise**) • verb **1** attempt to justify (an action or attitude) with logical reasoning. **2** reorganize (a process or system) in such a way as to make it more logical and consistent. **3** make (a company or industry) more efficient by dispensing with superfluous personnel or equipment.
– DERIVATIVES **rationalization** noun **rationalizer** noun.

rat-kangaroo • noun a small rat-like Australian marsupial with long hindlimbs used for hopping.

ratlines /ratlinz/ • plural noun a series of small rope lines fastened across a sailing ship's shrouds, used for climbing the rigging.
– ORIGIN of unknown origin.

rat pack • noun informal a group of journalists and photographers perceived as aggressive or relentless in their pursuit of stories.

rat race • noun informal a way of life in which people are caught up in a fiercely competitive struggle for wealth or power.

rat run • noun Brit. informal a minor street used by drivers to avoid congestion on main roads.

rat's tails • plural noun Brit. informal hair hanging in lank, damp, or greasy strands.

rattan /rətan/ • noun a tropical climbing palm which yields thin, jointed stems used to make furniture.
– ORIGIN Malay.

rat-tat (also **rat-tat-tat**) • noun a rapping sound.
– ORIGIN imitative.

ratted • adjective Brit. informal very drunk.

rattle • verb **1** make or cause to make a rapid succession of short, sharp knocking or clinking sounds. **2** move or travel while making such sounds. **3** (**rattle about/around in**) be in or occupy (too large a space). **4** informal make nervous, worried, or irritated. **5** (**rattle off**) say, perform, or produce quickly and effortlessly. **6** (**rattle on/away**) talk rapidly and at length. • noun **1** a rattling sound. **2** a device or plaything designed to make a rattling sound. **3** a gurgling sound in the throat.
– DERIVATIVES **rattler** noun **rattly** adjective.
– ORIGIN related to Dutch and Low German *ratelen*, of imitative origin.

rattlesnake • noun a heavy-bodied American viper with a series of horny rings on the tail that produce a characteristic rattling sound when vibrated as a warning.

rattletrap • noun informal an old or rickety vehicle.

rattling • adjective **1** making a rattle. **2** informal, dated very good of its kind.

ratty • adjective **1** resembling or characteristic of a rat. **2** infested with rats. **3** informal shabby, untidy, or in bad condition. **4** Brit. informal bad-tempered and irritable.

raucous /rawkəss/ • adjective making or constituting a harsh, loud noise.
– DERIVATIVES **raucously** adverb **raucousness** noun.
– ORIGIN Latin *raucus* 'hoarse'.

raunch • noun informal energetic earthiness or vulgarity.

raunchy • adjective (**raunchier**, **raunchiest**) informal energetically earthy and sexually explicit.
– DERIVATIVES **raunchily** adverb **raunchiness** noun.
– ORIGIN of unknown origin.

ravage • verb cause extensive damage to; devastate. • noun (**ravages**) the destructive effects of something.
– ORIGIN French *ravager*, from *ravir* (see RAVISH).

rave • verb **1** talk wildly or incoherently. **2** speak or write about someone or something with great enthusiasm or admiration. **3** informal, chiefly Brit. attend or take part in a rave party. • noun informal **1** chiefly Brit. a very large party or event with dancing to loud, fast electronic music. **2** a person or thing that inspires intense and widely shared enthusiasm. **3** chiefly N. Amer. an extremely enthusiastic appraisal of someone or something.
– ORIGIN originally in the sense 'show signs of madness': probably from Old French *raver*.

ravel • verb (**ravelled**, **ravelling**; US **raveled**, **raveling**) **1** (**ravel**

Thesaurus

r

uphold, authorize, formalize, validate, recognize; sign.
– OPPOSITES reject.

rating • noun GRADE, grading, classification, ranking, rank, category, designation; assessment, evaluation, appraisal; mark, score.

ratio • noun PROPORTION, comparative number, correlation, relationship, correspondence; percentage, fraction, quotient.

ration • noun **1** *a daily ration of chocolate* ALLOWANCE, allocation, quota, quantum, share, portion, helping; amount, quantity, measure, proportion, percentage. **2** *the garrison ran out of rations* SUPPLIES, provisions, food, foodstuffs, eatables, edibles, provender; stores; *informal* grub, eats; *N. Amer. informal* chuck; *formal* comestibles; *dated* victuals.
• verb *fuel supplies were rationed* CONTROL, limit, restrict; conserve.

rational • adjective **1** *a rational approach* LOGICAL, reasoned, sensible, reasonable, cogent, intelligent, judicious, shrewd, commonsense, commonsensical, sound, prudent; down-to-earth, practical, pragmatic. **2** *she was not rational at the time of signing* SANE, compos mentis, in one's right mind, of sound mind; normal, balanced, lucid, coherent; *informal* all there. **3** *man is a rational being* INTELLIGENT, thinking, reasoning; cerebral, logical, analytical; *formal* ratiocinative.
– OPPOSITES illogical, insane.

rationale • noun REASON(S), reasoning, thinking, logic, grounds, sense; principle, theory, argument, case; motive, motivation, explanation, justification, excuse; the whys and wherefores.

rationalize • verb **1** *he tried to rationalize his behaviour* JUSTIFY, explain (away), account for, defend, vindicate, excuse. **2** *an attempt to rationalize the industry* STREAMLINE, reorganize, modernize, update; trim, hone, simplify, downsize, prune.

rattle • verb **1** *hailstones rattled against the window* CLATTER, patter; clink, clunk. **2** *he rattled some coins* JINGLE, jangle, clink, tinkle. **3** *the bus rattled along* JOLT, bump, bounce, jounce, shake, judder. **4** *the government were rattled by the strike* UNNERVE, disconcert, disturb, fluster, shake, perturb, discompose, discomfit, ruffle, throw; *informal* faze.
• noun *the rattle of the bottles* CLATTER, clank, clink, clang; jingle, jangle.
– PHRASES **rattle something off** REEL OFF, recite, list, fire off, run through, enumerate. **rattle on/away** PRATTLE, babble, chatter, gabble, prate, go on, jabber, gibber, blether, ramble; *informal* gab, yak, yap; *Brit. informal* witter, rabbit, chunter, waffle.

ratty • adjective *(Brit. informal)*. See IRRITABLE.

raucous • adjective **1** *raucous laughter* HARSH, strident, screeching, piercing, shrill, grating, discordant, dissonant; noisy, loud, cacophonous. **2** *a raucous hen night* ROWDY, noisy, boisterous, roisterous, wild.
– OPPOSITES soft, quiet.

raunchy • adjective *(informal)*. See SEXY sense 2.

ravage • verb LAY WASTE, devastate, ruin, destroy, wreak havoc on, leave desolate; pillage, plunder, despoil, ransack, sack, loot; *poetic/literary* rape; *archaic* spoil.

ravages • plural noun **1** *the ravages of time* DAMAGING EFFECTS, ill ef-

out) untangle. **2** confuse or complicate (a question or situation). ● noun a tangle or cluster.
– ORIGIN probably from Dutch *ravelen* 'fray out, tangle'.
raven /rayv'n/ ● noun a large heavily built black crow. ● adjective (especially of hair) of a glossy black colour.
– ORIGIN Old English.
ravening ● adjective extremely hungry; voracious.
ravenous ● adjective extremely hungry.
– DERIVATIVES **ravenously** adverb.
– ORIGIN Old French *ravineus*, from *raviner* 'to ravage'.
raver ● noun **1** informal a person who has an exciting and uninhibited social life. **2** informal, chiefly Brit. a person who regularly goes to raves. **3** a person who talks wildly or incoherently.
rave-up ● noun Brit. informal a lively, noisy party.
ravine /rəveen/ ● noun a deep, narrow gorge with steep sides.
– ORIGIN French, 'violent rush'.
raving ● noun (**ravings**) wild or incoherent talk. ● adjective & adverb informal extremely or conspicuously the thing mentioned: *raving mad.*
ravioli /ravviōli/ ● plural noun small pasta envelopes containing minced meat, cheese, or vegetables.
– ORIGIN Italian.
ravish ● verb archaic or literary **1** seize and carry off by force. **2** rape. **3** fill with intense delight; enrapture.
– ORIGIN Old French *ravir*, from Latin *rapere* 'seize'.
ravishing ● adjective causing intense delight; entrancing.
– DERIVATIVES **ravishingly** adverb.
raw ● adjective **1** (of food) uncooked. **2** (of a material or substance) in its natural state; not processed. **3** (of data) not organized, analysed, or evaluated. **4** new and lacking in experience in an activity or job. **5** (of the skin) red and painful, especially as the result of abrasion. **6** (of the nerves) very sensitive. **7** (of an emotion or quality) strong and undisguised. **8** (of the weather) bleak, cold, and damp. **9** (of the edge of a piece of cloth) not having a hem or selvedge.
– PHRASES **in the raw 1** in its true state. **2** informal naked.
– DERIVATIVES **rawly** adverb **rawness** noun.
– ORIGIN Old English.
raw-boned ● adjective having a bony or gaunt physique.
rawhide ● noun **1** stiff untanned leather. **2** N. Amer. a whip or rope made of rawhide.
Rawlplug /rawlplug/ ● noun Brit. trademark a thin plastic or fibre sheath that is inserted into a hole in masonry in order to hold a screw.
– ORIGIN from *Rawlings* (the name of the engineers who introduced it).
raw material ● noun a basic material from which a product is made.
ray[1] ● noun **1** each of the lines in which light seems to stream from the sun or any luminous body. **2** the straight line in which radiation travels to a given point. **3** (**rays**) a specified form of non-luminous radiation: *ultra-violet rays.* **4** an initial or slight indication of a positive or welcome quality: *a ray of hope.* **5** Botany any of the individual strap-shaped florets around the edge of the flower of a daisy or related plant. **6** Zoology each of the long slender bony supports in a fish's fins.
– PHRASES **ray of sunshine** informal a person who brings happiness into the lives of others.
– ORIGIN Old French *rai*, from Latin *radius* 'spoke, ray'.
ray[2] ● noun a broad flat fish with wing-like pectoral fins and a long slender tail.
– ORIGIN Latin *raia.*
ray[3] (also **re**) ● noun Music the second note of a major scale, coming after 'doh' and before 'me'.
– ORIGIN *re*, representing (as an arbitrary name for the note) the first syllable of *resonare*, taken from a Latin hymn.
ray gun ● noun (in science fiction) a gun causing injury or damage by the emission of rays.
rayon ● noun a textile fibre or fabric made from viscose.
– ORIGIN an arbitrary formation.
raze (also **rase**) ● verb tear down and destroy (a building, town, etc.).
– ORIGIN Old French *raser* 'shave closely', from Latin *radere* 'scrape'.
razor ● noun an instrument with a sharp blade, used to shave unwanted hair from the face or body. ● verb cut with a razor.
– ORIGIN Old French *rasor*, from *raser* 'shave closely'.
razorback ● noun a pig of a half-wild breed common in the southern US, with the back formed into a high narrow ridge.
razorbill ● noun a black-and-white auk with a deep bill.
razor shell ● noun a burrowing bivalve mollusc with a long straight shell.
razor wire ● noun metal wire with sharp edges or studded with small sharp blades, used as a defensive barrier.
razz ● verb informal, chiefly N. Amer. tease playfully.
– ORIGIN from informal *razzberry*, alteration of RASPBERRY.
razzle ● noun (in phrase **on the razzle**) informal out celebrating or enjoying oneself.
– ORIGIN abbreviation of RAZZLE-DAZZLE.
razzle-dazzle ● noun another term for RAZZMATAZZ.
– ORIGIN reduplication of DAZZLE.
razzmatazz (also **razzamatazz**) ● noun informal noisy, showy, and exciting activity and display.

Thesaurus

fects. **2** *the ravages of man* (ACTS OF) DESTRUCTION, damage, devastation, ruin, havoc, depredation(s).
rave ● verb **1** *he was raving about the fires of hell* TALK WILDLY, babble, jabber, talk incoherently. **2** *I raved and swore at them* RANT (AND RAVE), rage, lose one's temper, storm, fulminate, fume; shout, roar, thunder, bellow; *informal* fly off the handle, blow one's top, go up the wall, hit the roof; *Brit. informal* go spare; *N. Amer. informal* flip one's wig. **3** *he raved about her talent* PRAISE ENTHUSIASTICALLY, go into raptures about/over, wax lyrical about, sing the praises of, rhapsodize over, enthuse about/over, acclaim, eulogize, extol; *N. Amer. informal* ballyhoo; *formal* laud; *archaic* panegyrize.
– OPPOSITES criticize.
● noun *(informal)* **1** *the imaginative menu won raves from local critics* ENTHUSIASTIC/LAVISH PRAISE, a rapturous reception, tribute, plaudits, acclaim. **2** *a fancy-dress rave.* See PARTY noun sense 1.
– OPPOSITES criticism.
● adjective *(informal) rave reviews* VERY ENTHUSIASTIC, rapturous, glowing, ecstatic, excellent, highly favourable.
raven ● noun.
– RELATED TERMS corvine.
● adjective *raven hair* BLACK, jet-black, ebony; *poetic/literary* sable.
ravenous ● adjective **1** *I'm absolutely ravenous* VERY HUNGRY, starving; *informal* famished; *rare* esurient. **2** *her ravenous appetite* VORACIOUS, insatiable; greedy, gluttonous; *poetic/literary* insatiate.
rave-up ● noun *(Brit. informal).* See PARTY noun sense 1.
ravine ● noun GORGE, canyon, gully, defile, couloir; chasm, abyss, gulf; *S. English* chine; *N. English* clough, gill, thrutch; *N. Amer.* gulch, coulee.
raving ● adjective *(informal)* **1** *she's raving mad.* See MAD sense 1. **2** *a raving beauty* VERY GREAT, remarkable, extraordinary, singular, striking, outstanding, stunning.
ravings ● plural noun WILD/INCOHERENT TALK, gibberish, rambling, babbling.
ravish ● verb **1** *(poetic/literary) he tried to ravish her* RAPE, sexually assault/abuse, violate, force oneself on, molest; *archaic* dishonour, defile. **2** *(poetic/literary) you will be ravished by this wine* ENRAPTURE, enchant, delight, charm, entrance, enthral, captivate. **3** *(archaic) her child was ravished from her breast* SEIZE, snatch, carry off/away, steal, abduct.
ravishing ● adjective VERY BEAUTIFUL, gorgeous, stunning, wonderful, lovely, striking, magnificent, dazzling, radiant, delightful, charming, enchanting; *informal* amazing, sensational, fantastic, fabulous, terrific; *Brit. informal* smashing; *N. Amer. informal* bodacious.
– OPPOSITES hideous.
raw ● adjective **1** *raw carrot* UNCOOKED, fresh. **2** *raw materials* UNPROCESSED, untreated, unrefined, crude, natural. **3** *raw recruits* INEXPERIENCED, new, untrained, untried, untested; callow, immature, green, naive; *informal* wet behind the ears. **4** *his skin is raw* SORE, red, painful, tender; abraded, chafed; *Medicine* excoriated. **5** *a raw morning* BLEAK, cold, chilly, freezing, icy, icy-cold, wintry, bitter; *informal* nippy; *Brit. informal* parky. **6** *raw emotions* STRONG, intense, passionate, fervent, powerful, violent; undisguised, unconcealed, unrestrained, uninhibited. **7** *raw images of Latin America* REALISTIC, unembellished, unvarnished, brutal, harsh.
– OPPOSITES cooked, processed.
– PHRASES **in the raw** *(informal).* See NAKED sense 1.
raw-boned ● adjective THIN, lean, gaunt, bony, skinny, spare.
– OPPOSITES plump.
ray ● noun **1** *rays of light* BEAM, shaft, streak, stream. **2** *a ray of hope* GLIMMER, flicker, spark, hint, suggestion, sign.

– ORIGIN probably an alteration of RAZZLE-DAZZLE.

R & B ● abbreviation rhythm and blues.

Rb ● symbol the chemical element rubidium.

RC ● abbreviation **1** Red Cross. **2** Electronics resistance/capacitance (or resistor/capacitor). **3** Roman Catholic.

R & D ● abbreviation research and development.

RD ● abbreviation (in the UK) Royal Naval Reserve Decoration.

Rd ● abbreviation Road (used in street names).

RDA ● abbreviation recommended daily (or dietary) allowance.

RDS ● abbreviation radio data system.

RE ● abbreviation religious education (as a school subject).

Re ● symbol the chemical element rhenium.

re[1] /ree, ray/ ● preposition **1** in the matter of (used in headings or to introduce a reference). **2** about; concerning.

– ORIGIN Latin, from *res* 'thing'.

re[2] ● noun variant spelling of RAY[3].

re- ● prefix **1** once more; afresh; anew: *reactivate.* **2** with return to a previous state: *restore.* **3** (also **red-**) in return; mutually: *resemble.* **4** in opposition: *repel.* **5** behind or after: *relic.* **6** in a withdrawn state: *reticent.* **7** back and away; down: *recede.* **8** with frequentative or intensive force: *resound.* **9** with negative force: *recant.*

– ORIGIN Latin *re-*, 'again, back'.

're ● abbreviation informal are (usually after the pronouns you, we, and they).

reach ● verb **1** stretch out an arm in order to touch or grasp something. **2** be able to touch (something) with an outstretched arm or leg. **3** arrive at or attain; extend to. **4** make contact with. **5** succeed in influencing or having an effect on. ● noun **1** an act of reaching. **2** the distance to which someone can stretch out their arm. **3** the extent or range of something's application, effect, or influence. **4** (often **reaches**) a continuous extent of land or water, especially a stretch of river between two bends.

– DERIVATIVES **reachable** adjective.

– ORIGIN Old English.

reach-me-down ● noun Brit. informal, dated a second-hand or ready-made garment.

react ● verb **1** respond to something in a particular way. **2** (**react against**) respond with hostility or a contrary course of action to. **3** suffer from adverse physiological effects after ingesting, breathing, or touching a substance. **4** Chemistry & Physics interact and undergo a chemical or physical change. **5** Stock Exchange (of share prices) fall after rising.

reactance ● noun Physics the non-resistive component of impedance in an alternating-current circuit, arising from inductance and/or capacitance.

reactant ● noun Chemistry a substance that takes part in and undergoes change during a reaction.

reaction ● noun **1** an instance of reacting to or against something. **2** (**reactions**) a person's ability to respond physically and mentally to external stimuli. **3** opposition to political or social progress or reform. **4** a process in which substances interact causing chemical or physical change. **5** Physics a force exerted in opposition to an applied force.

reactionary ● adjective opposing political or social progress or reform. ● noun (pl. **reactionaries**) a person holding reactionary views.

reactivate ● verb restore to a state of activity.

– DERIVATIVES **reactivation** noun.

reactive ● adjective **1** showing a response to a stimulus. **2** acting in response to a situation rather than creating or controlling it. **3** having a tendency to react chemically.

– DERIVATIVES **reactivity** noun.

reactor ● noun **1** an apparatus or structure in which fissile material can be made to undergo a controlled, self-sustaining nuclear reaction releasing energy. **2** a container or apparatus in which substances are made to react chemically. **3** Medicine a person who reacts to a drug, antigen, etc.

read ● verb (past and past part. **read** /red/) **1** look at and understand the meaning of (written or printed matter) by interpreting its characters or symbols. **2** speak (written or printed words) aloud. **3** (of a passage, text, or sign) contain or consist of specified words. **4** habitually read (a particular newspaper or journal). **5** discover (information) by reading. **6** understand or interpret the nature or significance of: *her exclusion can be read as a back-handed compliment.* **7** (**read into**) attribute a meaning or significance to (something) that it may not possess. **8** (**read up on**) acquire information about (a subject) by reading. **9** chiefly Brit. study (an academic subject) at a university. **10** present (a bill or other measure) before a legislative assembly. **11** inspect and record the figure indicated on (a measuring instrument). **12** hear and understand the words of (someone speaking on a radio transmitter). **13** (of a computer) copy or transfer (data). ● noun **1** chiefly Brit. a period or act of reading. **2** informal a book considered in terms of its readability: *a good read.*

– PHRASES **read between the lines** look for or discover a meaning that not explicitly stated. **read someone's mind** discern what someone is thinking. **read my lips** N. Amer. informal listen carefully. **take as read** assume without the need for further discussion. **well read** having a high level of knowledge as a result of reading widely.

– DERIVATIVES **readable** adjective.

– ORIGIN Old English; early senses included 'advise' and 'interpret (a riddle or dream)'.

reader ● noun **1** a person who reads. **2** a person who assesses the merits of manuscripts submitted for publication. **3** (**Reader**) Brit. a university lecturer of the highest grade below professor. **4** a book containing extracts of a text or texts for teaching

Thesaurus

● verb *her hair rayed out in the water* SPREAD OUT, fan out.

raze ● verb DESTROY, demolish, raze to the ground, tear down, pull down, knock down, level, flatten, bulldoze, wipe out, lay waste.

re ● preposition ABOUT, concerning, regarding, with regard to, relating to, apropos (of), on the subject of, in respect of, with reference to, in connection with.

reach ● verb **1** *Travis reached out a hand* STRETCH OUT, hold out, extend, outstretch, thrust out, stick out. **2** *reach me that book* PASS, hand, give, let someone have. **3** *soon she reached Helen's house* ARRIVE AT, get to, come to; end up at. **4** *the temperature reached 94 degrees* ATTAIN, get to; rise to, climb to; fall to, sink to, drop to; *informal* hit. **5** *the leaders reached an agreement* ACHIEVE, work out, draw up, put together, negotiate, thrash out, hammer out. **6** *I have been trying to reach you all day* GET IN TOUCH WITH, contact, get through to, get, speak to; *informal* get hold of. **7** *our concern is to reach more people* INFLUENCE, sway, get (through) to, make an impression on, have an impact on.

● noun **1** *Bobby moved out of her reach* GRASP, range. **2** *small goals within your reach* CAPABILITIES, capacity. **3** *beyond the reach of the law* JURISDICTION, authority, influence; scope, range, compass, ambit.

react ● verb **1** *how he would react if she told him the truth?* BEHAVE, act, take it, conduct oneself; respond, reply, answer. **2** *he reacted against the regulations* REBEL AGAINST, oppose, rise up against.

reaction ● noun **1** *his reaction had bewildered her* RESPONSE, answer, reply, rejoinder, retort, riposte; *informal* comeback. **2** *a reaction against modernism* BACKLASH, counteraction. **3** *the forces of reaction* CONSERVATISM, the right (wing), the extreme right.

reactionary ● adjective *a reactionary policy* RIGHT-WING, conservative, rightist, traditionalist, conventional, unprogressive.

– OPPOSITES progressive.

● noun *an extreme reactionary* RIGHT-WINGER, conservative, rightist, traditionalist, conventionalist.

– OPPOSITES radical.

read ● verb **1** *he was reading the newspaper* PERUSE, study, scrutinize, look through; pore over, be absorbed in; run one's eye over, cast an eye over, leaf through, scan, flick through, skim through, thumb through. **2** *he read a passage of the letter* READ OUT/ALOUD, recite, declaim. **3** *I can't read my own writing* DECIPHER, make out, make sense of, interpret, understand. **4** *his remark could be read as a criticism* INTERPRET, take (to mean), construe, see, understand. **5** *the dial read 70mph* INDICATE, register, record, display, show. **6** *he read modern history* STUDY, take; *N. Amer. & Austral./NZ* major in.

– RELATED TERMS legible.

● noun *I settled down for a read* PERUSAL, study, scan; look (at), browse (through), leaf (through), flick (through), skim (through).

– PHRASES **read something into something** INFER FROM, interpolate from, assume from, attribute to; read between the lines. **read up on** STUDY; *informal* bone up on; *Brit. informal* mug up on, swot; *archaic* con.

readable ● adjective **1** *the inscription is perfectly readable* LEGIBLE, easy to read, decipherable, clear, intelligible, comprehensible. **2** *her novels are immensely readable* ENJOYABLE, entertaining,

purposes. **5** a device that produces on a screen a readable image from a microfiche or microfilm.
– DERIVATIVES **readerly** adjective.
readership • noun **1** (treated as sing. or pl.) the readers of a publication regarded collectively. **2** (**Readership**) Brit. the position of Reader at a university.
readily • adverb **1** without hesitation; willingly. **2** without difficulty; easily.
reading • noun **1** the action or skill of reading. **2** an instance of something being read to an audience. **3** an interpretation of a text. **4** a figure recorded on a measuring instrument. **5** a stage of debate in parliament through which a bill must pass before it can become law.
reading age • noun a child's reading ability expressed with reference to an average age at which a comparable ability is found.
readjust • verb **1** set or adjust again. **2** adjust or adapt to a changed situation or environment.
– DERIVATIVES **readjustment** noun.
read-only memory • noun Computing memory read at high speed but not capable of being changed by program instructions.
read-write • adjective Computing capable of reading existing data and accepting alterations or further input.
ready • adjective (**readier**, **readiest**) **1** prepared for an activity or situation. **2** made suitable and available for immediate use. **3** easily available or obtained; within reach. **4** (**ready to/for**) willing to do or having a desire for. **5** immediate, quick, or prompt. • noun (**readies** or **the ready**) Brit. informal available money; cash. • verb (**readies**, **readied**) make (something) ready.
– PHRASES **at the ready** prepared or available for immediate use. **make ready** prepare.
– DERIVATIVES **readiness** noun.
– ORIGIN Old English.
ready-made • adjective **1** made to a standard size or specification rather than to order. **2** easily available: *ready-made answers.*
ready-mixed • adjective (of concrete, paint, food, etc.) having some or all of the constituents already mixed together.
ready money • noun money in the form of cash that is immediately available.
ready reckoner • noun a book, table, etc. listing standard numerical calculations or other kinds of information.
ready-to-wear • adjective (of clothes) sold through shops rather than made to order for an individual customer.
reagent /riayjənt/ • noun a substance or mixture for use in chemical analysis or other reactions.
real¹ /reel/ • adjective **1** actually existing or occurring in fact; not imagined or supposed. **2** significant; serious. **3** not artificial; genuine. **4** rightly so called; proper: *a real man.* **5** adjusted for changes in the value of money; assessed by purchasing power: *real incomes had fallen by 30 per cent.* **6** Mathematics (of a number or quantity) having no imaginary part. • adverb informal, chiefly N. Amer. really; very.
– PHRASES **for real** informal as a serious or actual concern.
– DERIVATIVES **realness** noun.
– ORIGIN Latin *realis*, from *res* 'thing'.
real² /rayaal/ • noun **1** the basic monetary unit of Brazil since 1994, equal to 100 centavos. **2** a former coin and monetary unit of various Spanish-speaking countries.
– ORIGIN Spanish and Portuguese, 'royal'.
real ale • noun chiefly Brit. cask-conditioned beer that is served traditionally, without additional gas pressure.
real estate • noun chiefly N. Amer. real property; land.
realign • verb **1** change or restore to a different or former position or state. **2** (**realign oneself with**) change one's position or attitude with regard to.
– DERIVATIVES **realignment** noun.
realism • noun **1** the practice of accepting a situation as it is and dealing with it accordingly. **2** (in art or literature) the representation of things in a way that is accurate and true to life. **3** Philosophy the doctrine that universals or abstract concepts have an objective or absolute existence. Often contrasted with NOMINALISM.
– DERIVATIVES **realist** noun.
realistic • adjective **1** having a sensible and practical idea of what can be achieved or expected. **2** representing things in a way that is accurate and true to life.
– DERIVATIVES **realistically** adverb.
reality • noun (pl. **realities**) **1** the state of things as they actually exist, as opposed to an idealistic or notional idea of them. **2** a thing that is actually experienced or seen. **3** the quality of being lifelike. **4** the state or quality of having existence or substance.
realize (also **realise**) • verb **1** become fully aware of as a fact;

Thesaurus

interesting, absorbing, gripping, enthralling, engrossing, stimulating; *informal* unputdownable.
– OPPOSITES illegible.
readily • adverb **1** *Durkin readily offered to drive him* WILLINGLY, without hesitation, unhesitatingly, ungrudgingly, gladly, happily, eagerly, promptly. **2** *the island is readily accessible* EASILY, with ease, without difficulty.
– OPPOSITES reluctantly.
readiness • noun **1** *their readiness to accept change* WILLINGNESS, enthusiasm, eagerness, keenness; promptness, quickness, alacrity. **2** *a state of readiness* PREPAREDNESS, preparation. **3** *the readiness of his reply* PROMPTNESS, quickness, rapidity, swiftness, speed, speediness.
– PHRASES **in readiness** (AT THE) READY, available, on hand, accessible, handy; prepared, primed, on standby, standing by, on full alert.
reading • noun **1** *a cursory reading of the financial pages* PERUSAL, study, scan, scanning; browse (through), look (through), glance (through), leaf (through), flick (through), skim (through). **2** *a man of wide reading* (BOOK) LEARNING, scholarship, education, erudition. **3** *readings from the Bible* PASSAGE, lesson; section, piece; recital, recitation. **4** *my reading of the situation* INTERPRETATION, construal, understanding, explanation, analysis. **5** *a meter reading* RECORD, figure, indication, measurement.
ready • adjective **1** *are you ready?* PREPARED, (all) set, organized, primed; *informal* fit, psyched up, geared up. **2** *everything is ready* COMPLETED, finished, prepared, organized, done, arranged, fixed, in readiness. **3** *he's always ready to help* WILLING, prepared, pleased, inclined, disposed, predisposed; eager, keen, happy, glad; *informal* game. **4** *she looked ready to collapse* ABOUT TO, on the point of, on the verge of, close to, liable to, likely to. **5** *a ready supply of food* (EASILY) AVAILABLE, accessible; handy, close/near at hand, to/on hand, convenient, within reach, at the ready, near, at one's fingertips. **6** *a ready answer* PROMPT, quick, swift, speedy, fast, immediate, unhesitating; clever, sharp, astute, shrewd, keen, perceptive, discerning; *poetic/literary* rathe.
• verb *he needed time to ready himself* PREPARE, get/make ready, organize; gear oneself up; *informal* psych oneself up.
– PHRASES **at the ready** IN POSITION, poised, ready for use/action, waiting; *N. Amer.* on deck. **make ready** PREPARE, make preparations, get everything ready, gear up for.
ready-made • adjective **1** *ready-made clothing* READY-TO-WEAR; *Brit.* off the peg; *N. Amer.* off the rack. **2** *ready-made meals* PRE-COOKED, oven-ready, convenience.
– OPPOSITES tailor-made.
real • adjective **1** *is she a fictional character or a real person?* ACTUAL, non-fictional, factual; historical; material, physical, tangible, concrete, palpable. **2** *real gold* GENUINE, authentic, bona fide; *informal* pukka, kosher. **3** *my real name* TRUE, actual. **4** *tears of real grief* SINCERE, genuine, true, unfeigned, heartfelt, unaffected. **5** *a real man* PROPER, true; *informal* regular; *archaic* very. **6** *you're a real idiot* COMPLETE, utter, thorough, absolute, total, prize, perfect; *Brit. informal* right, proper; *Austral./NZ informal* fair.
– OPPOSITES imaginary, imitation.
• adverb (*N. Amer. informal*) *that's real good of you.* See VERY adverb.
realism • noun **1** *optimism tinged with realism* PRAGMATISM, practicality, common sense, level-headedness. **2** *a degree of realism* AUTHENTICITY, fidelity, verisimilitude, truthfulness, faithfulness.
realistic • adjective **1** *you've got to be realistic* PRACTICAL, pragmatic, matter-of-fact, down-to-earth, sensible, commonsensical; rational, reasonable, level-headed, clear-sighted, businesslike; *informal* having both/one's feet on the ground, hard-nosed, no-nonsense. **2** *a realistic aim* ACHIEVABLE, attainable, feasible, practicable, viable, reasonable, sensible, workable; *informal* doable. **3** *a realistic portrayal of war* TRUE (TO LIFE), lifelike, truthful, faithful, real-life, naturalistic, graphic.
– OPPOSITES idealistic, impracticable.
reality • noun **1** *distinguishing fantasy from reality* THE REAL WORLD,

understand clearly. **2** cause (something desired or anticipated) to happen; fulfil. **3** give actual or physical form to (a concept or work). **4** sell for or make a profit of.
– DERIVATIVES **realizable** adjective **realization** noun.
really ● adverb **1** in reality; in actual fact. **2** very; thoroughly. ● exclamation **1** expressing interest, surprise, doubt, or protest. **2** chiefly US expressing agreement.
realm ● noun **1** archaic, literary, or Law a kingdom. **2** a field or domain of activity or interest.
– ORIGIN Old French *reaume*, from Latin *regimen* 'government'.
realpolitik /rayaalpolliteek/ ● noun politics based on practical rather than moral or ideological considerations.
– ORIGIN German, 'practical politics'.
real property ● noun Law property consisting of land or buildings. Compare with PERSONAL PROPERTY.
real tennis ● noun the original form of tennis, played with a solid ball on an enclosed court.
real time ● noun the actual time during which something occurs. ● adjective (**real-time**) Computing (of a system) in which input data is available virtually immediately as feedback to the process from which it is coming, e.g. in a missile guidance system.
realtor /reeəltər/ ● noun N. Amer. an estate agent.
realty /reeəlti/ ● noun Law a person's real property. Compare with PERSONALTY.
ream[1] ● noun **1** 500 (formerly 480) sheets of paper. **2** a large quantity of something, especially paper.
– ORIGIN Old French *raime*, from an Arabic word meaning 'bundle'.
ream[2] ● verb widen (a bore or hole) with a special tool.
– DERIVATIVES **reamer** noun.
– ORIGIN of unknown origin.
reanimate ● verb restore to life or consciousness.
– DERIVATIVES **reanimation** noun.
reap ● verb **1** cut or gather (a crop or harvest). **2** receive as a consequence of one's own or others' actions.
– PHRASES **you reap what you sow** proverb you eventually have to face up to the consequences of your actions.
– ORIGIN Old English.
reaper ● noun **1** a person or machine that harvests a crop. **2** (**the Reaper** or **the Grim Reaper**) a personification of death as a cloaked skeleton wielding a large scythe.
reappear ● verb appear again.
– DERIVATIVES **reappearance** noun.
reappoint ● verb appoint again to a position previously held.
– DERIVATIVES **reappointment** noun.
reappraise ● verb appraise again or differently.
– DERIVATIVES **reappraisal** noun.
rear[1] ● noun **1** the back or hindmost part of something. **2** (also **rear end**) a person's buttocks. ● adjective at the back.
– PHRASES **bring up the rear 1** be at the very end of a queue. **2** come last in a race.
– ORIGIN Old French *rere*, from Latin *retro* 'back'.
rear[2] ● verb **1** bring up and care for (offspring). **2** breed or cultivate (animals or plants). **3** (of an animal) raise itself upright on its hind legs. **4** (of a building, mountain, etc.) extend or appear to extend to a great height. **5** (**rear up**) show anger or irritation.
– ORIGIN Old English, 'set upright, construct, elevate'.
rear admiral ● noun a rank of naval officer, above commodore and below vice admiral.
rearguard ● noun **1** the soldiers at the rear of a body of troops, especially those protecting a retreating army. **2** a reactionary or conservative faction.
rearguard action ● noun a defensive action carried out by a retreating army.
rearm ● verb provide with or acquire a new supply of weapons.
– DERIVATIVES **rearmament** noun.
rearmost ● adjective furthest back.
rearrange ● verb arrange again in a different way.
– DERIVATIVES **rearrangement** noun.
rearrest ● verb arrest again.
rear-view mirror ● noun a mirror fixed inside the windscreen of a motor vehicle enabling the driver to see the vehicle or road behind.
rearward ● adjective directed towards the back. ● adverb (also **rearwards**) towards the back.
rear-wheel drive ● noun a transmission system that provides power to the rear wheels of a motor vehicle.
reason ● noun **1** a cause, explanation, or justification. **2** good or obvious cause to do something: *we have reason to celebrate.* **3** the power of the mind to think, understand, and form judgements logically. **4** (**one's reason**) one's sanity. **5** what is right, practical, or possible: *I'll answer anything, within reason.* ● verb **1** think, understand, and form judgements logically. **2** (**reason out**) find a solution (to a problem) by considering possible options. **3** (**reason with**) persuade with rational argument.
– PHRASES **by reason of** formal because of. **listen to reason** be persuaded to act sensibly. **it stands to reason** it is obvious or logical.
– DERIVATIVES **reasoned** adjective.
– ORIGIN Old French *reisun*, from Latin *reri* 'consider'.

Thesaurus

r

real life, actuality; truth; physical existence. **2** *the harsh realities of life* FACT, actuality, truth. **3** *the reality of the detail* VERISIMILITUDE, authenticity, realism, fidelity, faithfulness.
– OPPOSITES fantasy.
– PHRASES **in reality** IN (ACTUAL) FACT, in point of fact, as a matter of fact, actually, really, in truth; in practice; archaic in sooth.
realization ● noun **1** *a growing realization of the danger* AWARENESS, understanding, comprehension, consciousness, appreciation, recognition, discernment; formal cognizance. **2** *the realization of our dreams* FULFILMENT, achievement, accomplishment, attainment; formal effectuation.
realize ● verb **1** *he suddenly realized what she meant* REGISTER, perceive, discern, be/become aware of (the fact that), be/become conscious of (the fact that), notice; understand, grasp, comprehend, see, recognize, work out, fathom (out), apprehend; informal latch on to, cotton on to, tumble to, savvy, figure out, get (the message); Brit. informal twig, suss; formal be/become cognizant of. **2** *they realized their dream* FULFIL, achieve, accomplish, make a reality, make happen, bring to fruition, bring about/off, carry out/through; formal effectuate. **3** *the company realized significant profits* MAKE, clear, gain, earn, return, produce. **4** *the goods realized £3000* BE SOLD FOR, fetch, go for, make, net. **5** *he realized his assets* CASH IN, liquidate, capitalize.
really ● adverb **1** *he is really very wealthy* IN (ACTUAL) FACT, actually, in reality, in point of fact, as a matter of fact, in truth, to tell the truth; archaic in sooth. **2** *he really likes her* GENUINELY, truly, honestly; undoubtedly, without a doubt, indubitably, certainly, assuredly, unquestionably; archaic verily. **3** *they were really kind to me* VERY, extremely, thoroughly, decidedly, dreadfully, exceptionally, exceedingly, immensely, tremendously, uncommonly, remarkably, eminently, extraordinarily, most, downright; Scottish unco; N. Amer. quite; informal awfully, terribly, terrifically, fearfully, right, devilishly, ultra, too —— for words, seriously, majorly; Brit. informal jolly, ever so, dead, well, fair; N. Amer. informal real, mighty, awful, plumb, powerful, way; informal, dated devilish, frightfully; archaic exceeding.
● exclamation *'They've split up.' 'Really?'* IS THAT SO, is that a fact, well I never (did); informal {well, knock/blow me down with a feather}; Brit. informal {well, I'll be blowed}.
realm ● noun **1** (poetic/literary) *peace in the realm* KINGDOM, country, land, dominion, nation. **2** *the realm of academia* DOMAIN, sphere, area, field, world, province, territory.
reap ● verb **1** *the corn has been reaped* HARVEST, garner, gather in, bring in. **2** *reaping the benefits* RECEIVE, obtain, get, acquire, secure, realize.
rear[1] ● verb **1** *I was reared in Newcastle* BRING UP, care for, look after, nurture, parent; educate; N. Amer. raise. **2** *he reared cattle* BREED, raise, keep. **3** *laboratory-reared plants* GROW, cultivate. **4** *Harry reared his head* RAISE, lift (up), hold up, uplift. **5** *Creagan Hill reared up before them* RISE (UP), tower, soar, loom.
rear[2] ● noun **1** *the rear of the building* BACK (PART), hind part, back end; Nautical stern. **2** *the rear of the queue* (TAIL) END, rear end, back end, tail; N. Amer. tag end. **3** *he slapped her on the rear.* See BOTTOM noun sense 6.
– OPPOSITES front.
● adjective *the rear bumper* BACK, end, rearmost; hind, hinder, hindmost; technical posterior.
rearrange ● verb **1** *the furniture has been rearranged* REPOSITION, move round, change round, arrange differently. **2** *Tony had rearranged his schedule* REORGANIZE, alter, adjust, change (round), reschedule; informal jigger.
reason ● noun **1** *the main reason for his decision* CAUSE, ground(s),

reasonable • adjective **1** fair and sensible. **2** as much as is appropriate or fair; moderate. **3** fairly good; average.
– DERIVATIVES **reasonableness** noun **reasonably** adverb.
reassemble • verb assemble again; put back together.
– DERIVATIVES **reassembly** noun.
reassert • verb assert again.
– DERIVATIVES **reassertion** noun.
reassess • verb assess again, especially differently.
– DERIVATIVES **reassessment** noun.
reassign • verb assign again or differently.
– DERIVATIVES **reassignment** noun.
reassure • verb allay the doubts and fears of.
– DERIVATIVES **reassurance** noun **reassuring** adjective.
reattach • verb attach again.
– DERIVATIVES **reattachment** noun.
reattempt • verb attempt again.
reawaken • verb awaken again.
rebar /reebaar/ • noun reinforcing steel, especially as rods in concrete.
rebarbative /ribaarbətiv/ • adjective formal unattractive and objectionable.
– ORIGIN French *rébarbatif*, from Old French *se rebarber* 'face each other beard to beard' (i.e. aggressively).
rebate[1] /reebayt/ • noun **1** a partial refund to someone who has paid too much for tax, rent, etc. **2** a deduction or discount on a sum due. • verb pay back as a rebate.
– ORIGIN from Old French *rebatre* 'beat back', also 'deduct'.
rebate[2] /reebayt/ • noun a step-shaped recess cut in a piece of wood, typically forming a match to the edge or tongue of another piece. • verb (**rebated**, **rebating**) **1** make a rebate in. **2** join or fix with a rebate.
– ORIGIN alteration of RABBET.
rebec /reebek/ (also **rebeck**) • noun a medieval three-stringed instrument played with a bow.
– ORIGIN French, from Arabic.
rebel • noun /rebb'l/ a person who rebels. • verb /ribel/ (**rebelled**, **rebelling**) **1** rise in opposition or armed resistance to an established government or ruler. **2** resist authority, control, or convention.
– ORIGIN originally denoting a fresh declaration of war by the defeated: from Old French *rebelle*, from Latin *bellum* 'war'.
rebellion • noun **1** an act of rebelling against an established government or ruler. **2** defiance of authority or control.
rebellious • adjective **1** showing a desire to rebel. **2** not easily handled or kept in place; unmanageable.
– DERIVATIVES **rebelliously** adverb **rebelliousness** noun.
rebid • verb (**rebidding**; past and past part. **rebid**) bid again. • noun a further bid.
rebind • verb (past and past part. **rebound**) give a new binding to (a book).
rebirth • noun **1** reincarnation. **2** a revival.
rebirthing • noun a form of therapy involving controlled breathing intended to simulate the trauma of being born.
reboot • verb boot (a computer system) again.
rebore • verb make a new or wider boring in (the cylinders of an internal-combustion engine). • noun **1** an act of reboring. **2** an engine with rebored cylinders.
reborn • adjective **1** brought back to life or activity. **2** born-again.
rebound[1] • verb /ribownd/ **1** bounce back after hitting a hard surface. **2** recover in value, amount, or strength. **3** (**rebound on/upon**) have an unexpected adverse consequence for. • noun /reebownd/ **1** a ball or shot that rebounds. **2** an instance of recovering in value, amount, or strength.
– PHRASES **on the rebound** while still distressed after the ending of a romantic relationship.
– ORIGIN Old French *rebondir*, from *bondir* 'bounce up'.
rebound[2] past and past participle of REBIND.
rebrand • verb change the corporate image of.
rebroadcast • verb (past **rebroadcast** or **rebroadcasted**; past part. **rebroadcast**) broadcast again. • noun a repeated broadcast.
rebuff • verb reject in an abrupt or ungracious manner. • noun an abrupt rejection.
– ORIGIN obsolete French *rebuffer*, from Italian *buffo* 'a gust, puff'.

Thesaurus

basis, rationale; motive, motivation, purpose, point, aim, intention, objective, goal; explanation, justification, argument, defence, vindication, excuse, pretext. **2** *postmodern voices railing against reason* RATIONALITY, logic, logical thought, reasoning, cognition; formal ratiocination. **3** *he was losing his reason* SANITY, mind, mental faculties; senses, wits; informal marbles. **4** *he continues, against reason, to love her* GOOD SENSE, good judgement, common sense, wisdom, sagacity, reasonableness.
• verb **1** *a young child is unable to reason* THINK RATIONALLY, think logically, use one's common sense, use one's head/brain; formal cogitate, ratiocinate. **2** *Scott reasoned that Annabel might be ill* CALCULATE, come to the conclusion, conclude, reckon, think, judge, deduce, infer, surmise; informal figure. **3** *her husband tried to reason with her* TALK ROUND, bring round, win round, persuade, prevail on, convince, make someone see the light.
– PHRASES **by reason of** (formal) BECAUSE OF, on account of, as a result of, owing to, due to, by virtue of, thanks to. **reason something out** WORK OUT, think through, make sense of, get to the bottom of, puzzle out; informal figure out. **reason with someone** TALK ROUND, bring round, persuade, prevail on, convince; make someone see the light. **with reason** JUSTIFIABLY, justly, legitimately, rightly, reasonably.
reasonable • adjective **1** *a reasonable man | a reasonable explanation* SENSIBLE, rational, logical, fair, fair-minded, just, equitable; intelligent, wise, level-headed, practical, realistic; sound, (well) reasoned, valid, commonsensical; tenable, plausible, credible, believable. **2** *you must take all reasonable precautions* WITHIN REASON, practicable, sensible; appropriate, suitable. **3** *cars in reasonable condition* FAIRLY GOOD, acceptable, satisfactory, average, adequate, fair, all right, tolerable, passable; informal OK. **4** *reasonable prices* INEXPENSIVE, moderate, low, cheap, budget, bargain; competitive.
reasoned • adjective LOGICAL, rational, well thought out, clear, lucid, coherent, cogent, well expressed, well presented, considered, sensible.
reasoning • noun THINKING, (train of) thought, thought process, logic, reason, analysis, interpretation, explanation, rationalization; reasons, rationale, arguments; formal ratiocination.
reassure • verb PUT/SET SOMEONE'S MIND AT REST, put someone at ease, encourage, inspirit, hearten, buoy up, cheer up; comfort, soothe.
– OPPOSITES alarm.
rebate • noun (PARTIAL) REFUND, repayment; discount, deduction, reduction, decrease.
rebel • noun **1** *the rebels took control of the capital* REVOLUTIONARY, insurgent, revolutionist, mutineer, insurrectionist, insurrectionary, guerrilla, terrorist, freedom fighter. **2** *the concept of the artist as a rebel* NONCONFORMIST, dissenter, dissident, iconoclast, maverick.
• verb **1** *the citizens rebelled* REVOLT, mutiny, riot, rise up, take up arms, stage/mount a rebellion, be insubordinate. **2** *his stomach rebelled at the thought of food* RECOIL, show/feel repugnance. **3** *teenagers rebelling against their parents* DEFY, disobey, refuse to obey, kick against, challenge, oppose, resist.
– OPPOSITES obey.
• adjective **1** *rebel troops* INSURGENT, revolutionary, mutinous, rebellious, insurrectionary, insurrectionist. **2** *rebel MPs* REBELLIOUS, defiant, disobedient, insubordinate, subversive, resistant, recalcitrant; nonconformist, maverick, iconoclastic; archaic contumacious.
– OPPOSITES compliant.
rebellion • noun **1** *troops suppressed the rebellion* UPRISING, revolt, insurrection, mutiny, revolution, insurgence, insurgency; rioting, riot, disorder, unrest. **2** *an act of rebellion* DEFIANCE, disobedience, rebelliousness, insubordination, subversion, subversiveness, resistance.
rebellious • adjective **1** *rebellious troops* REBEL, insurgent, mutinous, mutinying, rebelling, rioting, riotous, insurrectionary, insurrectionist, revolutionary. **2** *a rebellious adolescent* DEFIANT, disobedient, insubordinate, unruly, mutinous, wayward, obstreperous, recalcitrant, intractable; Brit. informal bolshie; formal refractory; archaic contumacious.
rebirth • noun REVIVAL, renaissance, resurrection, reawakening, renewal, regeneration; revitalization, rejuvenation; formal renascence.
rebound • verb **1** *the ball rebounded off the wall* BOUNCE (BACK), spring back, ricochet, boomerang; N. Amer. carom. **2** *later sterling rebounded* RECOVER, rally, pick up, make a recovery. **3** *Thomas's tactics rebounded on him* BACKFIRE, boomerang, have unwelcome repercussions; archaic redound on.
rebuff • verb *his offer was rebuffed* REJECT, turn down, spurn, ref-

rebuild ● verb (past and past part. **rebuilt**) build again.

rebuke ● verb criticize or reprimand sharply. ● noun a sharp criticism.
– ORIGIN Old French *rebuker* 'beat down'.

rebus /reebəss/ ● noun (pl. **rebuses**) a puzzle in which words are represented by combinations of pictures and letters.
– ORIGIN Latin, 'by things'.

rebut /ribut/ ● verb (**rebutted**, **rebutting**) claim or prove to be false.
– ORIGIN originally in the senses 'rebuke' and 'repulse': from Old French *rebuter*, from *boter* 'to butt'.

rebuttal ● noun a refutation or contradiction.

recalcitrant /rikalsitrənt/ ● adjective obstinately uncooperative. ● noun a recalcitrant person.
– DERIVATIVES **recalcitrance** noun **recalcitrantly** adverb.
– ORIGIN from Latin *recalcitrare* 'kick out with the heels'.

recalculate ● verb calculate again.
– DERIVATIVES **recalculation** noun.

recall /rikawl/ ● verb **1** remember. **2** cause one to remember or think of. **3** officially order to return. **4** (of a manufacturer) request the return of (faulty products). **5** reselect (a sports player) as a member of a team. **6** call up (stored computer data). ● noun /also reekawl/ **1** the action or faculty of remembering. **2** an act of officially recalling someone or something.
– PHRASES **beyond recall** in such a way that restoration is impossible.
– DERIVATIVES **recallable** adjective.

recant /rikant/ ● verb renounce a former opinion or belief.
– DERIVATIVES **recantation** /reekantaysh'n/ noun.
– ORIGIN Latin *recantare* 'revoke', from *cantare* 'sing, chant'.

recap informal ● verb (**recapped**, **recapping**) recapitulate. ● noun a recapitulation.

recapitulate /reekəpityoolayt/ ● verb **1** summarize and state again the main points of. **2** Biology repeat (an evolutionary or other process) during development and growth.
– ORIGIN Latin *recapitulare* 'go through heading by heading', from *capitulum* 'chapter'.

recapitulation /reekəpityoolaysh'n/ ● noun **1** an act or instance of recapitulating. **2** Music a part of a movement in which themes from the exposition are restated.

recapture ● verb **1** capture (an escapee). **2** recover (something taken or lost). **3** recreate (a past time, event, or feeling). ● noun an act of recapturing.

recast ● verb (past and past part. **recast**) **1** cast (metal) again or differently. **2** present in a different form or style. **3** allocate roles in (a play or film) to different actors.

recce /rekki/ informal, chiefly Brit. ● noun reconnaissance. ● verb (**recced**, **recceing**) reconnoitre.

recede ● verb **1** move back or further away. **2** gradually diminish. **3** (of a man's hair) cease to grow at the temples and above the forehead. **4** (**receding**) (of a facial feature) sloping backwards.
– ORIGIN Latin *recedere* 'go back'.

receipt ● noun **1** the action of receiving something or the fact of its being received. **2** a written acknowledgement of receiving something. **3** (**receipts**) an amount of money received over a period by an organization.
– ORIGIN Old French *receite*, from Latin *recipire* 'receive'.

receivable ● adjective able to be received. ● noun (**receivables**) amounts owed to a business, regarded as assets.

receive ● verb **1** be given, presented with, or paid. **2** accept or take delivery of. **3** chiefly Brit. buy or accept (goods known to be stolen). **4** form (an idea or impression) from an experience. **5** detect or pick up (broadcast signals). **6** (in tennis and similar games) be the player to whom the server serves (the ball). **7** serve as a receptacle for. **8** suffer, experience, or be subject to: *the event received wide press coverage*. **9** meet with (a specified reaction). **10** (**received**) widely accepted as authoritative or true. **11** entertain as a guest. **12** admit as a member.
– PHRASES **be at** (or **on**) **the receiving end** informal be subjected to something unpleasant.
– ORIGIN Old French *receivre*, from Latin *recipere*, from *capere* 'take'.

received pronunciation (also **received standard**) ● noun the standard form of British English pronunciation, based on educated speech in southern England.

receiver ● noun **1** a person or thing that receives something. **2** a piece of radio or television apparatus converting broadcast signals into sound or images. **3** a telephone handset, in particular the part that converts electrical signals into sounds. **4** (Brit.

Thesaurus

use, decline, repudiate; snub, slight, repulse, repel, dismiss, brush off, give someone the cold shoulder; *informal* give someone the brush-off; *N. Amer. informal* give someone the bum's rush.
– OPPOSITES accept.
● noun *the rebuff did little to dampen his ardour* REJECTION, snub, slight, repulse; refusal, spurning, cold-shouldering, discouragement; *informal* brush-off, kick in the teeth, slap in the face.

rebuild ● verb RECONSTRUCT, renovate, restore, remodel, remake, reassemble.
– OPPOSITES demolish.

rebuke ● verb *she never rebuked him in front of others* REPRIMAND, reproach, scold, admonish, reprove, chastise, upbraid, berate, take to task, criticize, censure; *informal* tell off, give someone a telling-off, give someone a talking-to, give someone a dressing-down, give someone an earful; *Brit. informal* tick off; *N. Amer. informal* chew out, ream out; *Austral. informal* monster; *formal* castigate.
– OPPOSITES praise.
● noun *Damian was silenced by the rebuke* REPRIMAND, reproach, reproof, scolding, admonishment, admonition, reproval, upbraiding; *informal* telling-off, dressing-down; *Brit. informal* ticking-off; *formal* castigation.
– OPPOSITES compliment.

rebut ● verb REFUTE, deny, disprove; invalidate, negate, contradict, controvert, counter, discredit, give the lie to, explode; *informal* shoot full of holes; *formal* confute.
– OPPOSITES confirm.

rebuttal ● noun REFUTATION, denial, countering, invalidation, negation, contradiction.

recalcitrant ● adjective UNCOOPERATIVE, intractable, insubordinate, defiant, rebellious, wilful, wayward, headstrong, self-willed, contrary, perverse, difficult, awkward; *Brit. informal* bloody-minded, bolshie, stroppy; *formal* refractory; *archaic* contumacious, froward.
– OPPOSITES amenable.

recall ● verb **1** *he recalled his student days* REMEMBER, recollect, call to mind; think back on/to, look back on, reminisce about. **2** *their exploits recall the days of chivalry* BRING TO MIND, call to mind, put one in mind of, call up, conjure up, evoke. **3** *the ambassador was recalled* SUMMON BACK, order back, call back. **4** (*archaic*) *he recalled his earlier communication* REVOKE, rescind, cancel, retract, countermand, withdraw; *formal* abrogate.
– OPPOSITES forget.
● noun **1** *the recall of the ambassador* SUMMONING BACK, ordering back, calling back. **2** *their recall of dreams* RECOLLECTION, memory, remembrance.

recant ● verb **1** *he was forced to recant his political beliefs* RENOUNCE, disavow, deny, repudiate, renege on; *formal* forswear, abjure. **2** *he refused to recant* CHANGE ONE'S MIND, be apostate; *rare* tergiversate. **3** *he recanted his testimony* RETRACT, take back, withdraw.

recantation ● noun RENUNCIATION, renouncement, disavowal, denial, repudiation, retraction, withdrawal.

recapitulate ● verb SUMMARIZE, sum up; restate, repeat, reiterate, go over, review; *informal* recap.

recede ● verb **1** *the flood waters receded* RETREAT, go back/down, move back/away, withdraw, ebb, subside, abate. **2** *the lights receded into the distance* DISAPPEAR FROM VIEW, fade into the distance, be lost to view. **3** *fears of violence have receded* DIMINISH, lessen, decrease, dwindle, fade, abate, subside, ebb, wane.
– OPPOSITES advance, grow.

receipt ● noun **1** *the receipt of a letter* RECEIVING, getting, obtaining, gaining; arrival, delivery. **2** *make sure you get a receipt* PROOF OF PURCHASE, sales ticket, till receipt. **3** *receipts from house sales* PROCEEDS, takings, money/payment received, income, revenue, earnings; profits, (financial) return(s); *N. Amer.* take.

receive ● verb **1** *Tony received an award | they received £650 in damages* BE GIVEN, be presented with, be awarded, collect; get, obtain, gain, acquire; win, be paid, earn, gross, net. **2** *she received a letter* BE SENT, be in receipt of, accept (delivery of). **3** *Alec received the news on Monday* BE TOLD, be informed of, be notified of, hear, discover, find out (about), learn; *informal* get wind of. **4** *he received her suggestion with a complete lack of interest* HEAR, listen to; respond to, react to. **5** *she received a serious injury* EXPERIENCE, sustain, undergo, meet with; suffer, bear. **6** *they received their guests* GREET, welcome, say hello to. **7** *she's not receiving visitors today*

r

also **official receiver**) a person appointed to manage the financial affairs of a bankrupt business.

receivership ● noun the state of being managed by an official receiver.

recension /risensh'n/ ● noun 1 a revised edition of a text. 2 the revision of a text.

– ORIGIN Latin, from *recensere* 'revise'.

recent ● adjective 1 having happened or been done lately; belonging to a period of time not long ago. 2 (**Recent**) Geology another term for HOLOCENE.

– DERIVATIVES **recently** adverb.

– ORIGIN Latin *recens*.

receptacle /riseptək'l/ ● noun 1 an object or space used to contain something. 2 Botany the base of a flower or flower head.

– ORIGIN Latin *receptaculum*, from *receptare* 'receive back'.

reception ● noun 1 the action or process of receiving someone or something. 2 the way in which something is received: *an enthusiastic reception.* 3 a formal social occasion held to welcome someone or celebrate an event. 4 the area in a hotel, office, etc. where visitors are greeted. 5 the quality with which broadcast signals are received.

– ORIGIN Latin, from *recipere* 'receive'.

receptionist ● noun a person who greets and deals with clients and visitors to a surgery, office, hotel, etc.

reception room ● noun 1 a function room in a hotel or other building. 2 Brit. a room in a private house suitable for entertaining visitors.

receptive ● adjective 1 able or willing to receive something. 2 willing to consider new suggestions and ideas.

– DERIVATIVES **receptivity** noun.

receptor /riseptər/ ● noun Physiology an organ or cell that responds to external stimuli such as light or heat and transmits signals to a sensory nerve.

recess /risess, reesess/ ● noun 1 a small space set back in a wall. 2 a hollow in something. 3 (**recesses**) remote, secluded, or secret places. 4 a break between sessions of a parliament, law court, etc. 5 chiefly N. Amer. a break between school classes. ● verb 1 set (a fitment) back into a wall or surface. 2 temporarily suspend (proceedings).

– ORIGIN Latin *recessus*, from *recedere* 'go back'.

recession ● noun a temporary economic decline during which trade and industrial activity are reduced.

– DERIVATIVES **recessionary** adjective.

recessional ● adjective relating to an economic recession. ● noun a hymn sung while the clergy and choir withdraw after a service.

recessive Genetics ● adjective (of a heritable characteristic) controlled by a gene that is expressed in offspring only when inherited from both parents. Compare with DOMINANT. ● noun a recessive trait or gene.

recharge ● verb 1 charge (something, especially a battery) again. 2 return to a normal state of mind or strength after exertion.

– DERIVATIVES **rechargeable** adjective **recharger** noun.

recheck ● verb check again. ● noun an act of rechecking.

recherché /rəshairshay/ ● adjective too unusual or obscure to be easily understood.

– ORIGIN French, 'carefully sought out'.

rechristen ● verb give a new name to.

recidivist /risiddivist/ ● noun a convicted criminal who reoffends.

– DERIVATIVES **recidivism** noun.

– ORIGIN French *récidiviste*, from Latin *recidere* 'fall back'.

recipe /ressipi/ ● noun 1 a list of ingredients and instructions for preparing a dish. 2 something likely to lead to a particular outcome: *a recipe for disaster.*

– ORIGIN Latin, 'receive!' (originally used as an instruction in medical prescriptions).

recipient ● noun a person who receives something.

reciprocal /risiprək'l/ ● adjective 1 given, felt, or done in return. 2 (of an agreement or arrangement) bearing on or binding two parties equally. 3 Grammar (of a pronoun or verb) expressing mutual action or relationship (e.g. *each other, they kissed*). ● noun Mathematics the quantity obtained by dividing the number one by a given quantity.

– DERIVATIVES **reciprocally** adverb.

– ORIGIN Latin *reciprocus*, from *re-* 'back' + *pro-* 'forward'.

reciprocate /risiprəkayt/ ● verb respond to (a gesture, action, or emotion) with a corresponding one.

– DERIVATIVES **reciprocation** noun.

reciprocating engine ● noun a piston engine.

reciprocity /ressiprossiti/ ● noun the practice of exchanging things with others for mutual benefit.

recirculate ● verb circulate again.

– DERIVATIVES **recirculation** noun.

recital ● noun 1 the performance of a programme of music by a soloist or small group. 2 an enumeration of connected names, facts, or elements.

– DERIVATIVES **recitalist** noun.

recitative /ressitəteev/ ● noun musical declamation of the kind usual in the narrative and dialogue parts of opera and oratorio.

recite ● verb 1 repeat aloud or declaim from memory before an audience. 2 state (names, facts, etc.) in order.

– DERIVATIVES **recitation** noun **reciter** noun.

– ORIGIN Latin *recitare* 'read out'.

reck ● verb archaic 1 pay heed to something: *ye reck not of lands*

Thesaurus

ENTERTAIN, be at home to.

– OPPOSITES give, send.

receiver ● noun 1 *the receiver of a gift* RECIPIENT, beneficiary, donee. 2 *a telephone receiver* HANDSET.

– OPPOSITES donor.

recent ● adjective 1 *recent research* NEW, the latest, current, fresh, modern, contemporary, up to date, up to the minute. 2 *his recent visit* NOT LONG PAST, occurring recently, just gone.

– OPPOSITES old.

recently ● adverb NOT LONG AGO, a short time ago, in the past few days/weeks/months, a little while back; lately, latterly, just now.

receptacle ● noun CONTAINER, holder, repository; box, tin, bin, can, canister, case, pot, bag.

reception ● noun 1 *the reception of the goods* RECEIPT, receiving, getting. 2 *the reception of foreign diplomats* GREETING, welcoming, entertaining. 3 *a chilly reception* RESPONSE, reaction, treatment. 4 *a wedding reception* (FORMAL) PARTY, function, social occasion, soirée; N. Amer. levee; informal do, bash; Brit. informal rave-up, knees-up, beanfeast, bunfight, beano.

receptive ● adjective OPEN-MINDED, responsive, amenable, well disposed, flexible, approachable, accessible; archaic susceptive.

– OPPOSITES unresponsive.

recess ● noun 1 *two recesses fitted with bookshelves* ALCOVE, bay, niche, nook, corner, hollow, oriel. 2 *the deepest recesses of Broadcasting House* INNERMOST PARTS/REACHES, remote/secret places, heart, depths, bowels. 3 *the Christmas recess* ADJOURNMENT, break, interlude, interval, rest; holiday, vacation; informal breather. ● verb *let's recess for lunch* ADJOURN, take a recess, stop, (take a) break; informal take five.

recession ● noun ECONOMIC DECLINE, downturn, depression, slump, slowdown.

– OPPOSITES boom.

recherché ● adjective OBSCURE, rare, esoteric, abstruse, arcane, recondite, exotic, strange, unusual, unfamiliar, out of the ordinary.

recipe ● noun 1 *a tasty recipe* cooking instructions/directions; archaic receipt. 2 *a recipe for success* MEANS/WAY OF ACHIEVING, prescription, formula, blueprint.

recipient ● noun RECEIVER, beneficiary, donee.

– OPPOSITES donor.

reciprocal ● adjective 1 *reciprocal love* GIVEN/FELT IN RETURN, requited, reciprocated. 2 *reciprocal obligations and duties* MUTUAL, common, shared, joint, corresponding, complementary.

reciprocate ● verb 1 *I was happy to reciprocate* DO THE SAME (IN RETURN), return the favour. 2 *love that was not reciprocated* REQUITE, return, give back.

recital ● noun 1 *a piano recital* CONCERT, (musical) performance, solo (performance); informal gig. 2 *her recital of Adam's failures* ENUMERATION, list, litany, catalogue, listing, detailing; account, report, description, recapitulation, recounting. 3 *a recital of the Lord's Prayer.* See RECITATION sense 1.

recitation ● noun 1 *the recitation of his poem* RECITAL, saying aloud, declamation, rendering, rendition, delivery, performance. 2 *a recitation of her life story* ACCOUNT, description, narration, narrative, story. 3 *songs and recitations* READING, passage; poem, verse, monologue.

recite ● verb 1 *he began to recite verses of the Koran* REPEAT FROM MEMORY, say aloud, declaim, quote, deliver, render. 2 *he stood up*

r

or goods. **2** (**it recks**) it is important.
– ORIGIN Old English.
reckless ● adjective without thought or care for the consequences of an action.
– DERIVATIVES **recklessly** adverb **recklessness** noun.
– ORIGIN Old English, from a base meaning 'care'.
reckon ● verb **1** calculate. **2** informal be of the opinion. **3** regard in a specified way. **4** (**reckon on**) rely on or be sure of. **5** (**reckon with** or **without**) take (or fail to take) into account.
– PHRASES **to be reckoned with** not to be ignored or underestimated.
– ORIGIN Old English, 'recount, relate', later 'give an account of items received'.
reckoning ● noun **1** the action of calculating or estimating something. **2** an opinion or judgement. **3** punishment or retribution for one's actions.
– PHRASES **into** (or **out of**) **the reckoning** into or out of contention for selection, victory, etc.
reclaim ● verb **1** retrieve or recover. **2** bring (waste land or land formerly under water) under cultivation. **3** redeem from a state of vice. ● noun the action of reclaiming or the process of being reclaimed.
– DERIVATIVES **reclamation** noun.
reclassify ● verb (**reclassifies**, **reclassified**) assign to a different class or category.
– DERIVATIVES **reclassification** noun.
recline ● verb **1** lean or lie back in a relaxed position. **2** (of a seat) have a back able to move into a sloping position.
– DERIVATIVES **reclinable** adjective **recliner** noun.
– ORIGIN Latin *reclinare*, from *clinare* 'to bend'.
recluse /rikloʊss/ ● noun a person who avoids others and lives a solitary life.
– DERIVATIVES **reclusion** noun **reclusive** adjective.
– ORIGIN from Old French *reclus* 'shut up', from Latin *recludere* 'enclose'.
recognition ● noun **1** the action of recognizing or the process of being recognized. **2** appreciation or acknowledgement. **3** (also **diplomatic recognition**) formal acknowledgement by a country that another political entity fulfils the conditions of statehood.
recognizance /rikogniz'nss/ (also **recognisance**) ● noun Law a bond undertaken before a court or magistrate requiring the observation of a condition, for example to appear when summoned.
recognize (also **recognise**) ● verb **1** identify as already known; know again. **2** acknowledge the existence, validity, or legality of. **3** show official appreciation of.
– DERIVATIVES **recognizable** adjective.
– ORIGIN Latin *recognoscere*, from *cognoscere* 'to learn'.
recoil ● verb **1** suddenly spring back or flinch in fear, horror, or disgust. **2** feel such emotions at the thought of something. **3** spring back through force of impact or elasticity. **4** (**recoil on/upon**) have an adverse consequence for (the originator). ● noun the action of recoiling.
– DERIVATIVES **recoilless** adjective.
– ORIGIN Old French *reculer* 'move back', from Latin *culus* 'buttocks'.
recollect /rekkəlekt/ ● verb **1** remember. **2** (**recollect oneself**) compose oneself.
recollection ● noun **1** the action or faculty of remembering. **2** a memory.
recombinant /rikombinənt/ ● adjective Genetics relating to genetic material formed by recombination.
recombination ● noun **1** the process of recombining. **2** Genetics the rearrangement of genetic material, especially by exchange between chromosomes or by the artificial joining of DNA segments.
recombine ● verb combine again or differently.
recommence ● verb begin again.
– DERIVATIVES **recommencement** noun.
recommend ● verb **1** put forward with approval as being suitable for a purpose or role. **2** advise as a course of action. **3** make appealing or desirable: *the house had much to recommend it.*
– DERIVATIVES **recommendable** adjective **recommendation** noun.
recommission ● verb commission again.

Thesaurus

and started reciting GIVE A RECITATION, say a poem. **3** *Sir John recited the facts they knew* ENUMERATE, list, detail, reel off; recount, relate, describe, narrate, give an account of, recapitulate, repeat.
reckless ● adjective RASH, careless, thoughtless, heedless, unheeding, hasty, overhasty, precipitate, precipitous, impetuous, impulsive, daredevil, devil-may-care; irresponsible, foolhardy, overadventurous, audacious; ill-advised, injudicious, madcap, imprudent, unwise, ill-considered; *poetic/literary* temerarious.
– OPPOSITES careful.
reckon ● verb **1** *the cost was reckoned at £6,000* CALCULATE, compute, work out, put a figure on, figure; count (up), add up, total; *Brit.* tot up. **2** *Anselm reckoned Hugh among his friends* INCLUDE, count, consider to be, regard as, look on as. **3** *(informal) I reckon I can manage that* BELIEVE, think, be of the opinion/view, be convinced, dare say, imagine, guess, suppose, consider; *informal* figure. **4** *it was reckoned a failure* REGARD AS, consider, judge, hold to be, think of as; deem, rate, gauge, count. **5** *I reckon to get good value for money* EXPECT, anticipate, hope to, be looking to; count on, rely on, depend on, bank on; *N. Amer. informal* figure on.
– PHRASES **to be reckoned with** IMPORTANT, of considerable importance, significant; influential, powerful, strong, potent, formidable, redoubtable. **reckon with 1** *it's her mother you'll have to reckon with* DEAL WITH, contend with, face (up to). **2** *they hadn't reckoned with her burning ambition* TAKE INTO ACCOUNT, take into consideration, bargain for/on, anticipate, foresee, be prepared for, consider; *formal* take cognizance of. **reckon without** OVERLOOK, fail to take account of, disregard.
reckoning ● noun **1** *by my reckoning, this comes to £2 million* CALCULATION, estimation, computation, working out, summation, addition. **2** *by her reckoning, the train was late* OPINION, view, judgement, evaluation, estimate, estimation. **3** *the terrible reckoning that he deserved* RETRIBUTION, fate, doom, nemesis, punishment.
– PHRASES **day of reckoning** JUDGEMENT DAY, day of retribution, doomsday.
reclaim ● verb **1** *travelling expenses can be reclaimed* GET BACK, claim back, recover, regain, retrieve, recoup. **2** *Henrietta had reclaimed him from a life of vice* SAVE, rescue, redeem; reform.
recline ● verb LIE (DOWN/BACK), lean back; be recumbent; relax, repose, loll, lounge, sprawl, stretch out; *poetic/literary* couch.
recluse ● noun **1** *a religious recluse* HERMIT, ascetic, eremite; *historical* anchorite, anchoress. **2** *a natural recluse* LONER, solitary, lone wolf.
reclusive ● adjective SOLITARY, secluded, isolated, hermit-like, hermitic, eremitic, eremitical, cloistered.
– OPPOSITES gregarious.
recognition ● noun **1** *there was no sign of recognition on his face* IDENTIFICATION, recollection, remembrance. **2** *his recognition of his lack of experience* ACKNOWLEDGEMENT, acceptance, admission; realization, awareness, consciousness, knowledge, appreciation; *formal* cognizance. **3** *official recognition* OFFICIAL APPROVAL, certification, accreditation, endorsement, validation. **4** *you deserve recognition for the tremendous job you are doing* APPRECIATION, gratitude, thanks, congratulations, credit, commendation, acclaim, acknowledgement; *informal* bouquets.
recognizable ● adjective IDENTIFIABLE, noticeable, perceptible, discernible, detectable, distinguishable, observable, perceivable; distinct, unmistakable, clear; *archaic* sensible.
– OPPOSITES imperceptible.
recognize ● verb **1** *Hannah recognized him at once* IDENTIFY, place, know, put a name to; remember, recall, recollect; know by sight; *Scottish & N. English* ken. **2** *they recognized Alan's ability* ACKNOWLEDGE, accept, admit; realize, be aware of, be conscious of, perceive, discern, appreciate; *formal* be cognizant of. **3** *psychotherapists who are recognized* OFFICIALLY APPROVE, certify, accredit, endorse, sanction, validate. **4** *the Trust recognized their hard work* PAY TRIBUTE TO, show appreciation of, appreciate, be grateful for, acclaim, commend.
recoil ● verb **1** *she instinctively recoiled* DRAW BACK, jump back, pull back; flinch, shy away, shrink (back), blench. **2** *he recoiled from the thought* FEEL REVULSION AT, feel disgust at, be unable to stomach, shrink from, baulk at. **3** *his rifle recoiled* KICK (BACK), jerk back, spring back. **4** *this will eventually recoil on him* HAVE AN ADVERSE EFFECT ON, rebound on, affect badly, backfire, boomerang; *archaic* redound on.
● noun *the recoil of the gun* KICKBACK, kick.
recollect ● verb REMEMBER, recall, call to mind, think of; think back to, look back on, reminisce about.
– OPPOSITES forget.

r

recompense /rekkəmpenss/ ● verb **1** make amends to (someone) for loss or harm suffered; compensate. **2** pay or reward for effort or work. ● noun compensation or reward.
– ORIGIN Latin *recompensare*, from *compensare* 'weigh one thing against another'.

recon /rikon/ informal, chiefly N. Amer. ● noun reconnaissance. ● verb (**reconned, reconning**) reconnoitre.

reconcile /rekkənsīl/ ● verb **1** restore friendly relations between. **2** make or show to be compatible. **3** (**reconcile to**) make (someone) accept (a disagreeable thing).
– DERIVATIVES **reconcilable** adjective **reconciliation** noun.
– ORIGIN Latin *reconciliare*, from *conciliare* 'bring together'.

recondite /rekkəndīt, rikon-/ ● adjective (of a subject or knowledge) obscure.
– ORIGIN Latin *reconditus* 'hidden, put away'.

recondition ● verb **1** condition again. **2** Brit. overhaul or renovate.

reconfigure ● verb configure differently.
– DERIVATIVES **reconfiguration** noun.

reconnaissance /rikonnis'nss/ ● noun **1** military observation of a region to locate an enemy or ascertain strategic features. **2** preliminary surveying or research.
– ORIGIN French.

reconnect ● verb connect again.
– DERIVATIVES **reconnection** noun.

reconnoitre /rekkənoytər/ (US **reconnoiter**) ● verb make a military observation of (a region). ● noun informal an act of reconnoitring.
– ORIGIN obsolete French, from Latin *recognoscere* 'know again, recognize'.

reconsider ● verb consider again.
– DERIVATIVES **reconsideration** noun.

reconstitute ● verb **1** reconstruct. **2** change the form and organization of (an institution). **3** restore (something dried) to its original state by adding water.
– DERIVATIVES **reconstitution** noun.

reconstruct ● verb **1** construct again. **2** form an impression, model, or re-enactment of (something) from evidence.
– DERIVATIVES **reconstruction** noun **reconstructive** adjective.

reconvene ● verb convene again.

reconvert ● verb convert back to a former state.
– DERIVATIVES **reconversion** noun.

record ● noun **1** a piece of evidence or information constituting an account of something that has occurred, been said, etc. **2** the previous conduct or performance of a person or thing. **3** (also **criminal record**) a list of a person's previous criminal convictions. **4** the best performance or most remarkable event of its kind officially recognized. **5** a thin plastic disc carrying recorded sound in grooves on each surface, for reproduction by a record player. ● verb **1** make a record of. **2** convert (sound, a broadcast, etc.) into permanent form for later reproduction.
– PHRASES **for the record** so that the true facts are recorded or known. **on record** officially measured and noted. **on** (or **off**) **the record** made (or not made) as an official or attributable statement. **put** (or **set**) **the record straight** correct a misapprehension.
– DERIVATIVES **recordable** adjective **recording** noun **recordist** noun.
– ORIGIN Old French, 'remembrance', from Latin *recordari* 'remember'.

record-breaking ● adjective surpassing a record.

Thesaurus

recollection ● noun MEMORY, remembrance, impression, reminiscence.

recommend ● verb **1** *his former employer recommended him for the post* ADVOCATE, endorse, commend, suggest, put forward, propose, nominate, put up; speak favourably of, speak well of, put in a good word for, vouch for; *informal* plug. **2** *the committee recommended a cautious approach* ADVISE, counsel, urge, exhort, enjoin, prescribe, argue for, back, support; suggest, advocate, propose. **3** *there was little to recommend her* HAVE IN ONE'S FAVOUR, give an advantage to; *informal* have going for one.

recommendation ● noun **1** *the advisory group's recommendations* ADVICE, counsel, guidance, direction, enjoinder; suggestion, proposal. **2** *a personal recommendation* COMMENDATION, endorsement, good word, favourable mention, testimonial; suggestion, tip; *informal* plug. **3** *a place whose only recommendation is that it has very few women* ADVANTAGE, good point/feature, benefit, asset, boon, attraction, appeal.

recompense ● verb **1** *offenders should recompense their victims* COMPENSATE, indemnify, repay, reimburse, make reparation to, make restitution to, make amends to. **2** *she wanted to recompense him* REWARD, pay back; *archaic* guerdon. **3** *nothing could recompense her loss* MAKE UP FOR, compensate for, make amends for, make restitution for, make reparation for, redress, make good.
● noun *damages were paid in recompense* COMPENSATION, reparation, restitution, indemnification, indemnity; reimbursement, repayment, redress; *archaic* guerdon.

reconcilable ● adjective COMPATIBLE, consistent, congruous, congruent.

reconcile ● verb **1** *the news reconciled us* REUNITE, bring (back) together (again), restore friendly relations between, make peace between; pacify, appease, placate, mollify; *formal* conciliate. **2** *her divorced parents have reconciled* SETTLE ONE'S DIFFERENCES, make (one's) peace, (kiss and) make up, bury the hatchet, declare a truce. **3** *trying to reconcile his religious beliefs with his career* MAKE COMPATIBLE, harmonize, square, make congruent, balance. **4** *the quarrel was reconciled* SETTLE, resolve, sort out, mend, remedy, heal, rectify; *informal* patch up. **5** *they had to reconcile themselves to drastic losses* (COME TO) ACCEPT, resign oneself to, come to terms with, learn to live with, get used to.
– OPPOSITES estrange, quarrel.

reconciliation ● noun **1** *the reconciliation of the disputants* REUNITING, reunion, bringing (back) together (again), conciliation, reconcilement; pacification, appeasement, placating, mollification. **2** *a reconciliation of their differences* RESOLUTION, settlement, settling, resolving, mending, remedying. **3** *there was little hope of reconciliation* RESTORATION OF HARMONY, agreement, compromise, understanding, peace; *formal* concord. **4** *the reconciliation of theory with practice* HARMONIZING, harmonization, squaring, balancing.

recondite ● adjective OBSCURE, abstruse, arcane, esoteric, recherché, profound, difficult, complex, complicated, involved; incomprehensible, unfathomable, impenetrable, opaque.

recondition ● verb OVERHAUL, rebuild, renovate, restore, repair, reconstruct, remodel, refurbish; *informal* do up, revamp.

reconnaissance ● noun (PRELIMINARY) SURVEY, exploration, observation, investigation, examination, inspection; patrol, search; reconnoitring; *informal* recce; *N. Amer. informal* recon.

reconnoitre ● verb SURVEY, make a reconnaissance of, explore; investigate, examine, scrutinize, inspect, observe, take a look at; patrol; *informal* recce, make a recce of, check out; *N. Amer. informal* recon.

reconsider ● verb RETHINK, review, revise, re-examine, re-evaluate, reassess, reappraise; change, alter, modify; have second thoughts, change one's mind.

reconsideration ● noun REVIEW, re-examination, reassessment, re-evaluation, reappraisal, rethink.

reconstruct ● verb **1** *the building had to be reconstructed* REBUILD, restore, renovate, recreate, remake, reassemble, remodel, refashion, revamp, recondition, refurbish. **2** *reconstructing the events of that day* RECREATE, build up a picture/impression of, piece together, re-enact.

record ● noun **1** *written records of the past* ACCOUNT(S), document(s), documentation, data, file(s), dossier(s), evidence, report(s); annal(s), archive(s), chronicle(s); minutes, transactions, proceedings, transcript(s); certificate(s), deed(s), instrument(s); register, log, logbook; *Law* muniment(s). **2** *he spent hours listening to records* album, vinyl; *dated* gramophone record, LP, EP, single, forty-five, seventy-eight. **3** *his previous good record* PREVIOUS CONDUCT/PERFORMANCE, track record, (life) history, reputation. **4** *he's got a record* CRIMINAL RECORD, police record; previous; *Brit. informal* form; *N. Amer. informal* rap sheet. **5** *a new British record* BEST PERFORMANCE, highest achievement; best time, fastest time; world record. **6** *a lasting record of what they have achieved* REMINDER, memorial, souvenir, memento, remembrance, testament.
● adjective *record profits* RECORD-BREAKING, best ever, unsurpassed, unparalleled, unequalled, second to none.
● verb **1** *the doctor recorded her blood pressure* WRITE DOWN, put in writing, take down, note, make a note of, jot down, put down on paper; document, put on record, enter, minute, register, log; list, catalogue. **2** *the thermometer recorded a high temperature* INDICATE, register, show, display. **3** *the team recorded their fourth away win* ACHIEVE, accomplish, chalk up, notch up; *informal* clock up. **4** *the recital was recorded live* MAKE A RECORD/RECORDING OF, tape, tape-record; video-record, videotape, video.

r

– DERIVATIVES **record-breaker** noun.
recorded delivery • noun Brit. a service in which the Post Office obtains a signature from the recipient as a record that an item of post has been delivered.
recorder • noun **1** an apparatus for recording sound, pictures, or data. **2** a person who keeps records. **3** (**Recorder**) (in England and Wales) a barrister appointed to serve as a part-time judge. **4** a simple woodwind instrument without keys, played by blowing air through a shaped mouthpiece.
record player • noun an apparatus for reproducing sound from gramophone records, with a turntable and a stylus that picks up sound from the groove.
recount[1] /rikownt/ • verb give an account of something.
– ORIGIN Old French *reconter* 'tell again'.
recount[2] • verb /reekownt/ count again. • noun /reekownt/ an act of counting something again.
recoup • verb regain (a loss).
– DERIVATIVES **recoupable** adjective **recoupment** noun.
– ORIGIN French *recouper* 'retrench, cut back'.
recourse • noun **1** a source of help in a difficult situation. **2** (**recourse to**) the use of (someone or something) as a recourse.
– ORIGIN Latin *recursus*, from *cursus* 'course, running'.
recover • verb **1** return to a normal state of health, mind, or strength. **2** find or regain possession of. **3** regain or secure (compensation). **4** remove or extract (an energy source, chemical, etc.) for use, reuse, or waste treatment.
– DERIVATIVES **recoverable** adjective.
– ORIGIN Old French *recoverer*, from Latin *recuperare* 'get again'.
re-cover • verb put a new cover or covering on.
recovery • noun (pl. **recoveries**) **1** an act or the process of recovering. **2** the action of taking a vehicle that has broken down or crashed for repair.
recovery position • noun Brit. a position used to prevent an unconscious person from choking, the body being placed face downwards and slightly to the side, supported by the bent limbs.
recreant /rekriənt/ archaic • adjective **1** cowardly. **2** disloyal. • noun a recreant person.
– ORIGIN Old French, 'surrendering', from Latin *(se) recredere* 'surrender (oneself)'.
recreate • verb **1** create again. **2** reproduce.
recreation[1] /rekriaysh'n/ • noun enjoyable leisure activity.
– DERIVATIVES **recreational** adjective.
– ORIGIN Latin, from *recreare* 'create again, renew'.
recreation[2] /reekriaysh'n/ • noun the action or an act of recreating something.
recreation ground • noun Brit. a piece of public land used for sports and games.
recriminate /rikrimminayt/ • verb make counter accusations.
recrimination • noun (usu. **recriminations**) an accusation in response to one from someone else.
– ORIGIN Latin, from *recriminari* 'accuse in return'.
recrudesce /reekroodess/ • verb formal break out again; recur.
– DERIVATIVES **recrudescence** noun **recrudescent** adjective.
– ORIGIN Latin *recrudescere* 'become raw again'.
recruit • verb **1** enlist (someone) in the armed forces. **2** enrol (someone) as a member or worker in an organization. **3** informal persuade to do or help with something. • noun a newly recruited person.
– DERIVATIVES **recruiter** noun **recruitment** noun.
– ORIGIN obsolete French *recrute*, from Latin *recrescere* 'grow again'.
recta plural of RECTUM.
rectal • adjective relating to or affecting the rectum.
– DERIVATIVES **rectally** adverb.
rectangle • noun a plane figure with four straight sides and four right angles, and with unequal adjacent sides.
– DERIVATIVES **rectangular** adjective.
– ORIGIN Latin *rectangulum*, from *rectus* 'straight' + *angulus* 'an angle'.
rectifier • noun an electrical device converting an alternating current into a direct one by allowing it to flow in one direction only.
rectify • verb (**rectifies**, **rectified**) **1** put right; correct. **2** convert (alternating current) to direct current.
– DERIVATIVES **rectifiable** adjective **rectification** noun.
– ORIGIN Latin *rectificare*, from *rectus* 'right'.
rectilinear /rektilinniər/ (also **rectilineal** /rektilinniəl/) • adjective contained by, consisting of, or moving in a straight line or lines.
– ORIGIN from Latin *rectus* 'straight' + *linea* 'line'.
rectitude • noun morally correct behaviour.
– ORIGIN Old French, from Latin *rectus* 'right'.
recto • noun (pl. **rectos**) a right-hand page of an open book, or the front of a loose document. Contrasted with VERSO.
– ORIGIN Latin, 'on the right'.
rector • noun **1** (in the Church of England) a priest in charge of a parish where all tithes formerly passed to the incumbent. **2** (in other Anglican Churches) a member of the clergy in charge of a parish. **3** (in the Roman Catholic Church) a priest in charge of a church or a religious institution. **4** the head of certain universities, colleges, and schools. **5** (in Scotland) a person elected to represent students on a university's governing body.
– DERIVATIVES **rectorate** noun **rectorial** adjective **rectorship** noun.

Thesaurus

– PHRASES **off the record 1** *his comments were off the record* UNOFFICIAL, confidential, in (strict) confidence, not to be made public. **2** *they admitted, off the record, that they had made a mistake* UNOFFICIALLY, privately, in (strict) confidence, confidentially, between ourselves.
recorder • noun **1** *he put a tape in the recorder* tape recorder, cassette recorder; video (recorder), VCR, videotape recorder. **2** *a recorder of rural life* RECORD KEEPER, archivist, annalist, diarist, chronicler, historian.
recount • verb TELL, relate, narrate, give an account of, describe, report, outline, delineate, relay, convey, communicate, impart.
recoup • verb GET BACK, regain, recover, win back, retrieve, redeem, recuperate.
recourse • noun *surgery may be the only recourse* OPTION, possibility, alternative, resort, way out, hope, remedy, choice, expedient.
– PHRASES **have recourse to** RESORT TO, make use of, avail oneself of, turn to, call on, look to, fall back on.
recover • verb **1** *he's recovering from a heart attack* RECUPERATE, get better, convalesce, regain one's strength, get stronger, get back on one's feet; be on the mend, be on the road to recovery, pick up, rally, respond to treatment, improve, heal, pull through, bounce back. **2** *later, shares recovered* RALLY, improve, pick up, make a recovery, rebound, bounce back. **3** *the stolen material has been recovered* RETRIEVE, regain (possession of), get back, recoup, reclaim, repossess, redeem, recuperate, find (again), track down. **4** *gold coins recovered from a wreck* SALVAGE, save, rescue, retrieve.
– OPPOSITES deteriorate.
– PHRASES **recover oneself** PULL ONESELF TOGETHER, regain one's composure, regain one's self-control; informal get a grip (on oneself).
recovery • noun **1** *her recovery may be slow* RECUPERATION, convalescence. **2** *the economy was showing signs of recovery* IMPROVEMENT, rallying, picking up, upturn, upswing. **3** *the recovery of the stolen goods* RETRIEVAL, regaining, repossession, getting back, reclamation, recouping, redemption, recuperation.
– OPPOSITES relapse, deterioration.
recreation • noun **1** *she cycles for recreation* PLEASURE, leisure, relaxation, fun, enjoyment, entertainment, amusement; play, sport; informal R and R; N. Amer. informal rec; archaic disport. **2** *his favourite recreations* PASTIME, hobby, leisure activity.
– OPPOSITES work.
recrimination • noun ACCUSATION(S), counter-accusation(s), countercharge(s), retaliation(s).
recruit • verb **1** *more soldiers were recruited* ENLIST, call up, conscript; US draft, muster in; archaic levy. **2** *the king recruited an army* MUSTER, form, raise, mobilize. **3** *the company is recruiting staff* HIRE, employ, take on; enrol, sign up, engage.
– OPPOSITES disband, dismiss.
• noun **1** *new recruits were enlisted* CONSCRIPT, new soldier; US draftee; Brit. informal sprog; N. Amer. informal yardbird. **2** *top-quality recruits* NEW MEMBER, new entrant, newcomer, initiate, beginner, novice; N. Amer. tenderfoot, hire; informal rookie, newbie; N. Amer. informal greenhorn.
rectify • verb CORRECT, (put) right, put to rights, sort out, deal with, amend, remedy, repair, fix, make good, resolve, settle; informal patch up.
rectitude • noun RIGHTEOUSNESS, goodness, virtue, morality, hon-

– ORIGIN Latin, 'ruler'.
rectory ● noun (pl. **rectories**) **1** a rector's house. **2** a Church of England benefice held by a rector.
rectum /rektəm/ ● noun (pl. **rectums** or **recta** /rektə/) the final section of the large intestine, terminating at the anus.
– ORIGIN from Latin *rectum intestinum* 'straight intestine'.
recumbent /rikumbənt/ ● adjective **1** lying down. **2** (of a plant) growing close to the ground.
– DERIVATIVES **recumbency** noun.
– ORIGIN from Latin *recumbere* 'recline'.
recuperate /rikōōpərayt/ ● verb **1** recover from illness or exertion. **2** regain (something lost).
– DERIVATIVES **recuperation** noun **recuperative** adjective.
– ORIGIN Latin *recuperare* 'regain'.
recur ● verb (**recurred**, **recurring**) **1** occur again. **2** (of a thought, image, etc.) come back to one's mind.
– DERIVATIVES **recurrence** noun.
– ORIGIN Latin *recurrere*, from *currere* 'run'.
recurrent ● adjective occurring often or repeatedly.
– DERIVATIVES **recurrently** adverb.
recurring decimal ● noun a decimal fraction in which a figure or group of figures is repeated indefinitely, as in *0.666* ...
recursion /rikursh'n/ ● noun chiefly Mathematics & Linguistics **1** the repeated application of a procedure or rule to successive results of the process. **2** a recursive procedure or rule.
– DERIVATIVES **recursive** adjective.
recusant /rekyooz'nt/ ● noun **1** a person who refuses to submit to authority or comply with a regulation. **2** historical a person who refused to attend services of the Church of England.
– DERIVATIVES **recusancy** noun.
– ORIGIN from Latin *recusare* 'refuse'.
recuse /rikyōōz/ ● verb (**recuse oneself**) chiefly N. Amer. & S. African (of a judge) excuse oneself from a case because of a possible lack of impartiality.
– DERIVATIVES **recusal** noun.
recycle ● verb **1** convert (waste) into reusable material. **2** use again.
– DERIVATIVES **recyclable** adjective **recycler** noun.
red ● adjective (**redder**, **reddest**) **1** of a colour at the end of the spectrum next to orange and opposite violet, as of blood, fire, or rubies. **2** (of a person's face) red due to embarrassment, anger, or heat. **3** (of hair or fur) of a reddish-brown colour. **4** (of wine) made from dark grapes and coloured by their skins. **5** informal, chiefly derogatory communist or socialist. **6** archaic or literary involving bloodshed or violence. ● noun **1** red colour, pigment, or material. **2** informal, chiefly derogatory a communist or socialist. **3** (**the red**) the situation of having spent more than is in one's bank account.
– PHRASES **the red planet** Mars. **see red** informal become very angry suddenly.
– DERIVATIVES **reddish** adjective **reddy** adjective **redly** adverb **redness** noun.
– ORIGIN Old English.
redact /ridakt/ ● verb rare edit for publication.
– DERIVATIVES **redaction** noun **redactor** noun.
– ORIGIN Latin *redigere* 'bring back'.
red admiral ● noun a butterfly having dark wings with red bands and white spots.
redback ● noun a highly venomous Australasian spider with a bright red stripe down the back.
red-blooded ● adjective (of a man) vigorous or virile.
redbreast ● noun informal, chiefly Brit. a robin.
red-brick ● adjective (of a British university) founded in the late 19th or early 20th century and with buildings of red brick as distinct from the older universities which were built of stone.
redcap ● noun **1** Brit. informal a member of the military police. **2** N. Amer. a railway porter.
red card ● noun (especially in soccer) a red card shown by the referee to a player being sent off the field. ● verb (**red-card**) (of a referee) show a red card to.
red carpet ● noun a long, narrow red carpet for a distinguished visitor to walk along.
red cell ● noun less technical term for ERYTHROCYTE.
red cent ● noun N. Amer. **1** a one-cent coin, formerly made of copper. **2** the smallest amount of money: *they don't deserve a single red cent.*
redcoat ● noun **1** historical a British soldier. **2** (in the UK) an organizer and entertainer at a Butlin's holiday camp.
Red Crescent ● noun a national branch in Muslim countries of the International Movement of the Red Cross and the Red Crescent.
Red Cross ● noun the International Movement of the Red Cross and the Red Crescent, an organization bringing relief to victims of war or natural disaster.
redcurrant ● noun a small edible red berry.
red deer ● noun a deer with a rich red-brown summer coat that turns brownish-grey in winter, the male having large antlers.
Red Delicious ● noun a variety of apple with soft flesh and red skin.
redden ● verb **1** make or become red. **2** blush.
reddle ● noun red ochre, used to mark sheep.
– ORIGIN variant of RUDDLE.
red dwarf ● noun Astronomy a small, old, relatively cool star.
redecorate ● verb decorate again or differently.
– DERIVATIVES **redecoration** noun.
rededicate ● verb dedicate again.
– DERIVATIVES **rededication** noun.
redeem ● verb **1** make up for the faults or bad aspects of. **2** (**redeem oneself**) make up for one's poor past performance or behaviour. **3** save from sin, error, or evil. **4** fulfil (a pledge or promise). **5** gain or regain possession of in exchange for payment. **6** exchange (a coupon) for goods or money. **7** repay (a stock, bond, etc.) or clear (a debt). **8** archaic buy the freedom of.
– DERIVATIVES **redeemable** adjective.
– ORIGIN Latin *redimere* 'buy back'.
redeemer ● noun **1** a person who redeems someone or something. **2** (**the Redeemer**) Christ.
redefine ● verb define again or differently.

r

Thesaurus

our, honourableness, integrity, principle, probity, honesty, trustworthiness, uprightness, good character, decency.
recumbent ● adjective LYING, flat, horizontal, stretched out, sprawled (out), reclining, prone, prostrate, supine; lying down.
– OPPOSITES upright.
recuperate ● verb **1** *he went to France to recuperate* GET BETTER, recover, convalesce, get well, regain one's strength/health, get over something. **2** *he recuperated the money* GET BACK, regain, recover, recoup, retrieve, reclaim, repossess, redeem.
recur ● verb HAPPEN AGAIN, reoccur, occur again, repeat (itself); come back (again), return, reappear, appear again; *formal* recrudesce.
recurrent ● adjective REPEATED, recurring, repetitive, periodic, cyclical, seasonal, perennial, regular, frequent; intermittent, sporadic, spasmodic.
recycle ● verb REUSE, reprocess, reclaim, recover; salvage, save.
red ● adjective **1** *a red dress* scarlet, vermilion, ruby, cherry, cerise, cardinal, carmine, wine, blood-red; coral, cochineal, rose; brick-red, maroon, rusty, rufous; reddish; *poetic/literary* damask, vermeil, sanguine. **2** *he was red in the face* FLUSHED, reddish, pink, pinkish, florid, rubicund; ruddy, rosy, glowing; burning, feverish; *poetic/literary* rubescent; *archaic* sanguine. **3** *his eyes were red* BLOODSHOT, swollen, sore. **4** *red hair* reddish, auburn, Titian, chestnut, carroty, ginger.
● noun *(informal, derogatory) the war against the Reds* COMMUNIST, socialist, left-winger, leftist; *informal* Commie, lefty.
– PHRASES **in the red** OVERDRAWN, in debt, in debit, in deficit, in arrears. **see red** *(informal)* BECOME VERY ANGRY, become enraged, lose one's temper; *informal* go mad, go crazy, go wild, go bananas, hit the roof, go up the wall, fly off the handle, blow one's top, flip (one's lid), go ballistic; *Brit. informal* go spare, do one's nut; *N. Amer. informal* flip one's wig, blow one's lid/stack.
red-blooded ● adjective MANLY, masculine, virile, macho.
redden ● verb GO/TURN RED, blush, flush, colour (up), burn.
redeem ● verb **1** *one feature redeems the book* SAVE, compensate for the defects of, vindicate. **2** *he fully redeemed himself next time* VINDICATE, free from blame, absolve. **3** *you cannot redeem their sins* ATONE FOR, make amends for, make restitution for. **4** *redeeming sinners* SAVE, deliver from sin, convert. **5** *Billy redeemed his drums from the pawnbrokers* RETRIEVE, regain, recover, get back, reclaim, repossess; buy back. **6** *this voucher can be redeemed at any branch* (GIVE IN) EXCHANGE, cash in, convert, trade in. **7** *they could not redeem their debts* PAY OFF/BACK, clear, discharge, honour. **8** *he made no effort to redeem his promise* FULFIL, carry out, discharge, make good; keep (to), stick to, hold to, adhere to, abide by, honour.

– DERIVATIVES **redefinition** noun.
redemption • noun **1** the action of redeeming or of being redeemed. **2** a thing that saves someone from error or evil.
– DERIVATIVES **redemptive** adjective.
red ensign • noun a red flag with the Union Jack in the top corner next to the flagstaff, flown by British-registered ships.
redeploy • verb deploy again or differently.
– DERIVATIVES **redeployment** noun.
redesign • verb design again or differently. • noun the action or process of redesigning.
redetermine • verb determine again or differently.
– DERIVATIVES **redetermination** noun.
redevelop • verb develop again or differently.
– DERIVATIVES **redeveloper** noun **redevelopment** noun.
red-eye • noun **1** the effect in photography of people appearing to have red eyes, caused by a reflection from the retina when the flashgun is too near the camera lens. **2** (also **red-eye flight**) informal, chiefly N. Amer. a flight on which one cannot expect much sleep. **3** US informal cheap whisky.
red-faced • adjective embarrassed or ashamed.
red-figure • noun a type of ancient Greek pottery in which the background is painted black, leaving figures in the red colour of the clay.
red flag • noun **1** a warning of danger. **2** the symbol of socialist revolution.
red giant • noun Astronomy a very large luminous star of low surface temperature.
red grouse • noun a British moorland grouse with reddish-brown plumage.
red-handed • adjective in or just after the act of doing something wrong.
redhead • noun a person, especially a woman, with red hair.
red heat • noun the temperature or state of something so hot that it emits red light.
red herring • noun **1** a dried smoked herring. **2** a misleading clue or distraction. [ORIGIN so named from the practice of using the scent of red herring in training hounds.]
red-hot • adjective **1** so hot as to glow red. **2** extremely exciting or popular. **3** very passionate.
red-hot poker • noun a plant with tall erect spikes of tubular flowers, the upper ones of which are red and the lower ones yellow.
redial • verb (**redialled**, **redialling**; US **redialed**, **redialing**) dial (a telephone number) again.
redid past of REDO.
rediffusion • noun Brit. the relaying of broadcast programmes, especially by cable from a central receiver.
Red Indian • noun old-fashioned term for AMERICAN INDIAN.
redingote /reddinggōt/ • noun a woman's long coat with a cutaway or contrasting front.
– ORIGIN French, from English *riding coat*.
redirect • verb direct differently.
– DERIVATIVES **redirection** noun.
rediscover • verb discover again.
– DERIVATIVES **rediscovery** noun.
redistribute • verb distribute again or differently.
– DERIVATIVES **redistribution** noun **redistributive** adjective.
redivide • verb divide again or differently.
– DERIVATIVES **redivision** noun.
redivivus /reddiveevəss/ • adjective (after a noun) literary come back to life; reborn.
– ORIGIN Latin, from *re-* 'again' + *vivus* 'living'.
red lead • noun red lead oxide used as a pigment.
Red Leicester • noun see LEICESTER.
red-letter day • noun a noteworthy or memorable day.
– ORIGIN from the practice of highlighting a festival in red on a calendar.
red light • noun a red light instructing moving vehicles to stop.
red-light district • noun an area with many brothels, strip clubs, etc.
– ORIGIN from the use of a red light as the sign of a brothel.
redline • verb N. Amer. informal **1** drive with (the car engine) at its maximum rpm. **2** refuse (a loan or insurance) to someone due to their area of residence.
– ORIGIN from the use of *red* as a limit marker, in sense 2 a ring marking part of a map.
red meat • noun meat that is red when raw, e.g. beef or lamb.
red mullet • noun an elongated food fish with long barbels on the chin, living in warmer seas.
redneck • noun N. Amer. informal, derogatory a working-class white person from the southern US, especially a politically conservative one.
redo • verb (**redoes**; past **redid**; past part. **redone**) **1** do again or differently. **2** informal redecorate.
redolent /reddələnt/ • adjective **1** (**redolent of/with**) strongly reminiscent or suggestive of. **2** (**redolent of/with**) literary strongly smelling of. **3** archaic or literary fragrant.
– DERIVATIVES **redolence** noun **redolently** adverb.
– ORIGIN from Latin *redolere* 'give out a strong smell'.
redouble • verb make or become much greater, more intense, or more numerous.
redoubt • noun a temporary or supplementary fortification, typically square or polygonal and without flanking defences.
– ORIGIN French *redoute*, from Latin *reductus* 'refuge'.
redoubtable • adjective often humorous (of a person) formidable, especially as an opponent.
– DERIVATIVES **redoubtably** adverb.
– ORIGIN Old French *redoutable*, from *redouter* 'to fear'.
redound /ridownd/ • verb **1** (**redound to**) formal contribute greatly to (a person's credit or honour). **2** (**redound upon**) archaic rebound on.
– ORIGIN Latin *redundare* 'surge', from *unda* 'a wave'.
redox /reedoks, reddoks/ • adjective Chemistry involving both oxidation and reduction.
– ORIGIN blend.
red pepper • noun the ripe red fruit of a sweet pepper.
redpoll /redpōl/ • noun **1** a mainly brown finch with a red forehead, related to the linnet. **2** (**red poll**) an animal of a breed of red-haired polled cattle.
redraft • verb draft differently.
redraw • verb (past **redrew**; past part. **redrawn**) draw or draw up again or differently.
redress • verb **1** remedy or set right. **2** archaic set upright again. • noun remedy or compensation for a wrong or grievance.
– PHRASES **redress the balance** restore equality in a situation.
– ORIGIN Old French *redresser*.
re-dress • verb dress again or differently.
red roan • adjective (of an animal's coat) bay or chestnut mixed with white or grey.
red rose • noun the emblem of Lancashire or the Lancastrians in the Wars of the Roses.
red salmon • noun the sockeye salmon.
red setter • noun less formal term for IRISH SETTER.
redshank • noun a large sandpiper with long red legs.
red shift • noun Astronomy a displacement of the spectrum to longer wavelengths in the light from a distant galaxy or other object moving away from the observer.
redskin • noun dated or offensive an American Indian.

Thesaurus

redeeming • adjective COMPENSATING, compensatory, extenuating, redemptive.
redemption • noun **1** *God's redemption of his people* SAVING, freeing from sin, absolution. **2** *the redemption of their possessions* RETRIEVAL, recovery, reclamation, repossession, return. **3** *the redemption of credit vouchers* EXCHANGE, cashing in, conversion. **4** *the redemption of the mortgage* PAYING OFF/BACK, discharge, clearing, honouring. **5** *the redemption of his obligations* FULFILMENT, carrying out, discharge, performing, honouring, meeting.
red-handed • adjective IN THE ACT, with one's fingers/hand in the till, in flagrante delicto; *Brit. informal* with one's trousers down; *N. Amer. informal* with one's pants down.
redolent • adjective **1** *names redolent of history* EVOCATIVE, suggestive, reminiscent. **2** *(poetic/literary) the air was redolent of incense* SMELLING OF, scented with, fragrant with, perfumed with.
redoubtable • adjective FORMIDABLE, awe-inspiring, fearsome, daunting; impressive, commanding, indomitable, invincible, doughty, mighty.
redound • verb **1** *(formal) his effort will redound to his credit* CONTRIBUTE TO, be conducive to, result in, lead to, have an effect; *formal* conduce to. **2** *(archaic) the consequences redounded upon them* REBOUND ON, have an adverse effect on, backfire.
redress • verb **1** *it is impossible to redress the situation* RECTIFY, correct, right, put to rights, compensate for, amend, remedy, make good, resolve, settle. **2** *we aim to redress the balance* EVEN UP, regulate, equalize.

r

red snapper ● noun a reddish edible marine fish.
red squirrel ● noun a small squirrel with a reddish coat.
redstart ● noun a small songbird of the thrush family with a reddish tail.
– ORIGIN from RED + START in the obsolete sense 'tail'.
red tape ● noun excessive bureaucracy or adherence to rules, especially in public business.
– ORIGIN so named because of the red or pink tape used to bind official documents.
red top ● noun Brit. a tabloid newspaper.
– ORIGIN from the red background on which the titles of certain British newspapers are printed.
reduce ● verb **1** make or become smaller or less in amount, degree, or size. **2** (**reduce to**) change (something) to (a simpler or more basic form). **3** (**reduce to**) bring to (an undesirable state or action). **4** boil (a sauce or other liquid) so that it becomes thicker and more concentrated. **5** Chemistry cause to combine chemically with hydrogen. **6** Chemistry cause to undergo a reaction in which electrons are gained from another substance or molecule. The opposite of OXIDIZE. **7** restore (a dislocated body part) to its proper position. **8** archaic conquer (a place).
– PHRASES **reduced circumstances** poverty after relative prosperity. **reduce to the ranks** demote (a non-commissioned officer) to an ordinary soldier.
– DERIVATIVES **reducer** noun **reducible** adjective.
– ORIGIN originally in the sense 'restore': from Latin *reducere* 'bring or lead back'.
reductio ad absurdum /riduktiō ad absurdəm/ ● noun Philosophy a method of proving that a premise is false by showing that its logical consequence is absurd or contradictory.
– ORIGIN Latin, 'reduction to the absurd'.
reduction ● noun **1** the action of reducing something. **2** the amount by which something is reduced. **3** a smaller copy of a picture or photograph. **4** a thick and concentrated liquid or sauce.
reductionism ● noun often derogatory the analysis and description of a complex phenomenon in terms of its simple or fundamental constituents.
– DERIVATIVES **reductionist** noun & adjective.
reductive ● adjective **1** tending to present a subject or problem in a simplified form, especially one viewed as crude. **2** relating to chemical reduction.
– DERIVATIVES **reductively** adverb **reductiveness** noun.
reductivism ● noun **1** minimalism. **2** reductionism.
redundant ● adjective **1** not or no longer needed or useful; superfluous. **2** chiefly Brit. made unemployed because one's job is superfluous to requirements.
– DERIVATIVES **redundancy** noun (pl. **redundancies**) **redundantly** adverb.
– ORIGIN originally in the sense 'abundant': from Latin *redundare* 'surge'.
reduplicate ● verb **1** repeat or copy so as to form another of the same kind. **2** repeat (a linguistic element) exactly or with a slight change (e.g. *hurly-burly*).
– DERIVATIVES **reduplication** noun.
redux /reeduks/ ● adjective (after a noun) revived; restored.
– ORIGIN Latin, from *reducere* 'bring back'.
redwing ● noun a small migratory thrush of northern Europe, with red underwings.
redwood ● noun a giant coniferous tree with reddish wood, native to California and Oregon.
reebok ● noun variant spelling of RHEBOK.
re-echo ● verb (**re-echoes**, **re-echoed**) echo again or repeatedly.
reed ● noun **1** a tall, slender-leaved plant growing in water or on marshy ground. **2** reeds or straw used for thatching. **3** literary a rustic musical pipe made from reeds or straw. **4** a piece of thin cane or metal which vibrates in a current of air to produce the sound of various musical instruments, as in the mouthpiece of a clarinet or at the base of some organ pipes. **5** a wind instrument played with a reed.
– DERIVATIVES **reeded** adjective.
– ORIGIN Old English.
re-edit ● verb (**re-edited**, **re-editing**) edit again.
reed mace ● noun a tall reed-like water plant with a dark brown velvety cylindrical flower head.
reed organ ● noun a keyboard instrument similar to a harmonium, in which air is drawn upwards past metal reeds.
re-educate ● verb educate or train to behave or think differently.
– DERIVATIVES **re-education** noun.
reedy ● adjective (**reedier**, **reediest**) **1** (of a sound or voice) high and thin in tone. **2** full of or edged with reeds. **3** (of a person) tall and thin.
reef[1] ● noun **1** a ridge of jagged rock or coral just above or below the surface of the sea. **2** a vein of gold or other ore.
– ORIGIN Old Norse, 'rib'; compare with REEF[2].
reef[2] Sailing ● noun each of several strips across a sail which can be taken in or rolled up to reduce the area exposed to the wind. ● verb take in one or more reefs of (a sail).
– ORIGIN Old Norse, 'rib'; compare with REEF[1].
reefer[1] ● noun informal a cannabis cigarette.
– ORIGIN perhaps related to Mexican Spanish *grifo* 'smoker of cannabis'.
reefer[2] ● noun a person who reefs a sail.
reefer[3] ● noun informal a refrigerated truck, railway wagon, or ship.
– ORIGIN abbreviation.
reefer jacket ● noun a thick close-fitting double-breasted jacket.
reef knot ● noun a double knot made symmetrically to hold securely and cast off easily.
reek ● verb **1** have a foul smell. **2** (**reek of**) be suggestive of (something unpleasant). **3** archaic give off smoke, steam, or fumes. ● noun **1** a foul smell. **2** chiefly Scottish smoke.
– DERIVATIVES **reeky** adjective.
– ORIGIN Old English.
reel ● noun **1** a cylinder on which film, wire, thread, etc. can be wound. **2** a part of a film. **3** a lively Scottish or Irish folk dance with music in simple or duple time. ● verb **1** (**reel in**) wind on or bring towards one by turning a reel. **2** (**reel off**) say or recite rapidly and effortlessly. **3** dance a reel. **4** stagger or lurch violently. **5** feel giddy or bewildered.
– DERIVATIVES **reeler** noun.
– ORIGIN Old English.
re-elect ● verb elect again.

r

Thesaurus

● noun *your best hope of redress* COMPENSATION, reparation, restitution, recompense, repayment, indemnity, indemnification, retribution, satisfaction; justice.
reduce ● verb **1** *the aim to reduce pollution* LESSEN, make smaller, lower, bring down, decrease, diminish, minimize; shrink, narrow, contract, shorten; axe, cut (back/down), make cutbacks in, trim, slim (down), prune; informal chop. **2** *he reduced her to tears* BRING TO, bring to the point of, drive to. **3** *he was reduced to the ranks* DEMOTE, downgrade, lower (in rank). **4** *bread has been reduced* MAKE CHEAPER, lower the price of, cut (in price), mark down, discount, put on sale; informal slash, knock down.
– OPPOSITES increase, put up.
– PHRASES **in reduced circumstances** IMPOVERISHED, in straitened circumstances, ruined, bankrupted; poor, indigent, impecunious, in penury, poverty-stricken, destitute; needy, badly off, hard up; informal flat (broke), without two pennies to rub together, strapped for cash; Brit. informal stony broke, skint, in Queer Street; N. Amer. informal stone broke; formal penurious.
reduction ● noun **1** *a reduction in pollution* LESSENING, lowering, decrease, diminution. **2** *a reduction in staff* CUT, cutback, scaling down, trimming, pruning, axing, chopping. **3** *a reduction in inflationary pressure* EASING, lightening, moderation, alleviation. **4** *a reduction in status* DEMOTION, downgrading, lowering. **5** *substantial reductions* DISCOUNT, markdown, deduction, (price) cut, concession.
redundancy ● noun **1** *redundancy in language* SUPERFLUITY, unnecessariness, excess. **2** *redundancies are in the offing* SACKING, dismissal, lay-off, discharge; unemployment.
redundant ● adjective **1** *many churches are now redundant* UNNECESSARY, not required, unneeded, uncalled for, surplus (to requirements), superfluous. **2** *2,000 workers were made redundant* SACKED, dismissed, laid off, discharged; unemployed, jobless, out of work.
– OPPOSITES employed.
reef ● noun SHOAL, bar, sandbar, sandbank, spit; Scottish skerry.
reek ● verb *the whole place reeked* STINK, smell (bad), stink to high heaven.
● noun *the reek of cattle dung* STINK, bad smell, stench, malodour;

– DERIVATIVES **re-election** noun.

reel-to-reel ● adjective (of a tape recorder) in which the tape passes between two reels mounted separately rather than within a cassette.

re-emerge ● verb emerge again.

– DERIVATIVES **re-emergence** noun **re-emergent** adjective.

re-emphasize (also **re-emphasise**) ● verb emphasize again.

– DERIVATIVES **re-emphasis** noun.

re-enact ● verb **1** act out (a past event). **2** enact (a repealed law) once more.

– DERIVATIVES **re-enactment** noun.

re-engineer ● verb **1** redesign (a machine). **2** restructure (a company or its operations).

re-enter ● verb enter again.

– DERIVATIVES **re-entrance** noun.

re-entrant ● adjective (of an angle) pointing inwards. The opposite of SALIENT.

re-entry ● noun (pl. **re-entries**) **1** the action or process of re-entering. **2** the return of a spacecraft or missile into the earth's atmosphere.

reeve[1] ● noun historical a local official, in particular the chief magistrate of a town or district in Anglo-Saxon England.

– ORIGIN Old English.

reeve[2] ● verb (past and past part. **rove** or **reeved**) Nautical thread (a rope or rod) through a ring or other aperture.

– ORIGIN probably from Dutch *reven* 'reef a sail'; related to REEF[2].

reeve[3] ● noun a female ruff (bird).

– ORIGIN of unknown origin.

re-examine ● verb **1** examine again or further. **2** Law examine (a witness) again, after cross-examination by the opposing counsel.

– DERIVATIVES **re-examination** noun.

re-export ● verb /ree-iksport/ export (imported goods), typically after further processing or manufacture. ● noun /ree-eksport/ **1** the action of re-exporting. **2** a thing that has or will be re-exported.

– DERIVATIVES **re-exportation** noun **re-exporter** noun.

ref ● noun informal (in sports) a referee.

ref. ● abbreviation **1** reference. **2** refer to.

reface ● verb put a new facing on (a building).

refection ● noun literary or archaic **1** refreshment by food or drink. **2** a meal or snack.

– ORIGIN Latin, from *reficere* 'refresh, renew'.

refectory ● noun (pl. **refectories**) a room used for communal meals, especially in an educational or religious institution.

refectory table ● noun a long, narrow table.

refer ● verb (**referred**, **referring**) **1** (**refer to**) mention or allude to. **2** (**refer to**) direct the attention of (someone) to. **3** (**refer to**) (of a word or phrase) describe or denote. **4** (**refer to**) pass (a person or matter) to (a higher body) for a decision. **5** fail (a candidate in an examination). **6** (**refer to**) archaic trace or attribute (something) to (a cause or source).

– PHRASES **refer to drawer** Brit. a phrase used by banks when suspending payment of a cheque.

– DERIVATIVES **referable** adjective **referrer** noun.

– ORIGIN Latin *referre* 'carry back'.

referee ● noun **1** an official who supervises a game or match to ensure that the rules are adhered to. **2** a person willing to testify about the character or ability of a job applicant. **3** a person appointed to examine and assess an academic work for publication. ● verb (**referees**, **refereed**, **refereeing**) be a referee of.

reference ● noun **1** the action of referring to something. **2** a mention or citation of a source of information in a book or article. **3** a letter from a previous employer testifying to someone's ability or reliability, used when applying for a new job. ● verb provide (a book or article) with references.

– PHRASES **terms of reference** the scope and limitations of an activity or area of knowledge. **with** (or **in**) **reference to** in relation to; as regards.

reference library ● noun a library in which the books are to be consulted rather than borrowed.

reference point ● noun a basis or standard for evaluation or comparison.

referendum /refférendəm/ ● noun (pl. **referendums** or **referenda** /reffərendə/) a general vote by the electorate on a single political question which has been referred to them for a direct decision.

– ORIGIN Latin, 'something to be referred'.

referent ● noun Linguistics the thing in the world that a word or phrase denotes or stands for.

referential ● adjective **1** containing or of the nature of a reference or references. **2** Linguistics relating to a referent, in particular having the external world rather than a text or language as a referent.

– DERIVATIVES **referentiality** noun **referentially** adverb.

referral ● noun the action of referring someone or something for consultation or review, especially the directing of a patient by a GP to a specialist.

referred pain ● noun Medicine pain felt in a part of the body other than its actual source.

refill ● verb /reefill/ fill or become full again. ● noun /reefill/ an act of refilling or a glass that is refilled.

– DERIVATIVES **refillable** adjective.

refinance ● verb finance again, typically with new loans at a lower rate of interest.

refine ● verb **1** remove impurities or unwanted elements from. **2** make minor changes so as to improve (a theory or method).

– DERIVATIVES **refiner** noun.

refined ● adjective **1** with impurities or unwanted elements having been removed by processing. **2** elegant and cultured.

refinement ● noun **1** the process of refining. **2** an improvement or clarification brought about by the making of small changes. **3** cultured elegance or superior taste.

refinery ● noun (pl. **refineries**) an industrial installation where a substance is refined.

refinish ● verb apply a new finish to (a surface or object).

Thesaurus

Brit. informal niff, pong, whiff; *poetic/literary* miasma.

reel ● verb **1** *he reeled as the ship began to roll* STAGGER, lurch, sway, rock, stumble, totter, wobble, falter. **2** *we were reeling from the crisis* BE SHAKEN, be stunned, be in shock, be shocked, be taken aback, be staggered, be aghast, be upset. **3** *the room reeled* GO ROUND (AND ROUND), whirl, spin, revolve, swirl, twirl, turn, swim.

– PHRASES **reel something off** RECITE, rattle off, list rapidly, run through, enumerate, detail, itemize.

refer ● verb **1** *he referred to errors in the article* MENTION, make reference to, allude to, touch on, speak of/about, talk of/about, write about, comment on, deal with, point out, call attention to. **2** *the matter has been referred to my insurers* PASS, hand on/over, send on, transfer, remit, entrust, assign. **3** *these figures refer only to 2001* APPLY TO, be relevant to, concern, relate to, be connected with, pertain to, appertain to, be pertinent to, have a bearing on, cover. **4** *the name refers to a Saxon village* DENOTE, describe, indicate, mean, signify, designate. **5** *the constable referred to his notes* CONSULT, turn to, look at, have recourse to.

referee ● noun **1** *the referee blew his whistle* UMPIRE, judge; *informal* ref. **2** *include the names of two referees* SUPPORTER, character witness, advocate.

● verb **1** *he refereed the game* UMPIRE, judge. **2** *they asked him to referee in the dispute* ARBITRATE, mediate.

reference ● noun **1** *his journal contains many references to railways* MENTION OF, allusion to, comment on, remark about. **2** *references are given in the bibliography* (INFORMATION) SOURCE, citation, authority, credit; bibliographical data. **3** *reference to a higher court* REFERRAL, transfer, remission. **4** *a glowing reference* TESTIMONIAL, character reference, recommendation; credentials; *dated* character.

– PHRASES **with reference to** APROPOS, with regard to, regarding, with respect to, on the subject of, re; in relation to, relating to, in connection with.

referendum ● noun (POPULAR) VOTE, plebiscite, ballot, poll.

refine ● verb **1** *refining our cereal foods* PURIFY, process, treat. **2** *helping students to refine their language skills* IMPROVE, perfect, polish (up), hone, fine-tune.

refined ● adjective **1** *refined sugar* PURIFIED, processed, treated. **2** *a refined lady* CULTIVATED, cultured, polished, stylish, elegant, sophisticated, urbane; polite, gracious, well mannered, well bred, gentlemanly, ladylike, genteel. **3** *a person of refined taste* DISCRIMINATING, discerning, fastidious, exquisite, impeccable, fine.

– OPPOSITES crude, coarse.

refinement ● noun **1** *the refinement of sugar* PURIFICATION, refining, processing, treatment, treating. **2** *all writing needs endless refinement* IMPROVEMENT, polishing, honing, fine-tuning, touching up, finishing off, revision, editing. **3** *a woman of refinement* STYLE, elegance, finesse, polish, sophistication, urbanity; politeness,

refit • verb (**refitted**, **refitting**) replace or repair machinery, equipment, and fittings in (a ship, building, etc.). • noun an act of refitting.

reflag • verb (**reflagged**, **reflagging**) change the national registration of (a ship).

reflate • verb (of a government) expand the level of output of (an economy).
– DERIVATIVES **reflation** noun **reflationary** noun.

reflect • verb **1** throw back (heat, light, or sound) without absorbing it. **2** (of a mirror or shiny surface) show an image of. **3** represent in a faithful or appropriate way. **4** (**reflect well/badly on**) bring about a good or bad impression of. **5** (**reflect on/upon**) think deeply or carefully about.
– ORIGIN Latin *reflectere* 'bend back'.

reflectance • noun Physics a property of a surface equal to the proportion of the light shining on it which it reflects or scatters.

reflecting telescope • noun a telescope in which a mirror is used to collect and focus light.

reflection • noun **1** the phenomenon of light, heat, sound, etc. being reflected. **2** an image formed by reflection. **3** a consequence or result: *healthy skin is a reflection of good health.* **4** a thing bringing discredit. **5** serious thought or consideration.

reflective • adjective **1** providing or produced by reflection. **2** thoughtful.
– DERIVATIVES **reflectively** adverb **reflectiveness** noun **reflectivity** noun.

reflector • noun **1** a piece of reflective material, e.g. a red one on the back of a motor vehicle or bicycle. **2** an object or device which reflects radio waves, sound, or other waves. **3** a reflecting telescope.

reflex • noun **1** an action performed without conscious thought as a response to a stimulus. **2** a thing that reproduces the essential features or qualities of something else. **3** archaic a reflected source of light. • adjective **1** performed as a reflex. **2** (of an angle) exceeding 180°. **3** archaic (of light) reflected. **4** archaic bent or turned backwards.
– DERIVATIVES **reflexly** adverb.
– ORIGIN Latin *reflexus*, from *reflectere* 'bend back'.

reflex camera • noun a camera with a ground-glass focusing screen on which the image is formed by a combination of lens and mirror, enabling a scene to be correctly composed and focused.

reflexible • adjective chiefly technical capable of being reflected.

reflexion • noun archaic spelling of REFLECTION.

reflexive • adjective **1** Grammar (of a pronoun) referring back to the subject of the clause in which it is used, e.g. *myself*. **2** Grammar (of a verb or clause) having a reflexive pronoun as its object (e.g. *wash oneself*). **3** performed without conscious thought; reflex.
– DERIVATIVES **reflexively** adverb **reflexivity** noun.

reflexology • noun a system of massage used to relieve tension and treat illness, based on the theory that there are points on the feet, hands, and head linked to every part of the body.
– DERIVATIVES **reflexologist** noun.

refloat • verb set afloat again.

refluent /reffloōənt/ • adjective literary flowing back; ebbing.
– DERIVATIVES **refluence** noun.
– ORIGIN from Latin *refluere* 'flow back'.

reflux /reefluks/ • noun **1** Chemistry the process of boiling a liquid so that any vapour is liquefied and returned to the stock. **2** technical the flowing back of a bodily fluid.

refocus • verb (**refocused**, **refocusing** or **refocussed**, **refocussing**) **1** adjust the focus of (a lens or one's eyes). **2** focus (attention or resources) on something new or different.

reforest • verb replant with trees; cover again with forest.
– DERIVATIVES **reforestation** noun.

reform • verb **1** make changes in (something) in order to improve it. **2** cause to abandon an immoral or criminal lifestyle. • noun the action or process of reforming.
– DERIVATIVES **reformable** adjective **reformative** adjective **reformer** noun.
– ORIGIN Latin *reformare* 'form or shape again'.

re-form • verb form or cause to form again.
– DERIVATIVES **re-formation** noun.

reformat • verb (**reformatted**, **reformatting**) chiefly Computing give a new format to.

reformation • noun **1** the action or process of reforming. **2** (**the Reformation**) a 16th-century movement for the reform of abuses in the Roman Church, ending in the establishment of the Reformed and Protestant Churches.

reformatory • noun (pl. **reformatories**) N. Amer. dated an institution to which young offenders are sent as an alternative to prison. • adjective tending or intended to produce reform.

Reformed Church • noun a Church that has accepted the principles of the Reformation, especially a Calvinist Church (as distinct from Lutheran).

reformist • adjective supporting or advocating gradual reform rather than abolition or revolution. • noun a supporter or advocate of such a policy.
– DERIVATIVES **reformism** noun.

Reform Judaism • noun a form of Judaism which has reformed or abandoned aspects of Orthodox Jewish worship and ritual.

reform school • noun historical an institution to which young offenders were sent as an alternative to prison.

reformulate • verb formulate again or differently.
– DERIVATIVES **reformulation** noun.

refract • verb (of water, air, or glass) make (a ray of light) change direction when it enters at an angle.
– ORIGIN Latin *refringere* 'break up'.

refracting telescope • noun a telescope which uses a lens to collect and focus the light.

refraction • noun the fact or phenomenon of being refracted.

refractive • adjective of or involving refraction.
– DERIVATIVES **refractively** adverb.

refractive index • noun the ratio of the velocity of light in a vacuum to its velocity in a specified medium.

refractor • noun **1** a lens or other object which causes refraction. **2** a refracting telescope.

refractory • adjective **1** formal stubborn or unmanageable. **2** Medicine not yielding to treatment. **3** technical heat-resistant; hard to melt or fuse.
– DERIVATIVES **refractoriness** noun.
– ORIGIN Latin *refractarius* 'stubborn'.

refrain[1] • verb (**refrain from**) stop oneself from (doing some-

r

Thesaurus

grace, graciousness, good manners, good breeding, gentility; cultivation, taste, discrimination.

reflect • verb **1** *the snow reflects light* SEND BACK, throw back, cast back. **2** *their expressions reflected their feelings* INDICATE, show, display, demonstrate, be evidence of, register, reveal, betray, disclose; express, communicate; formal evince. **3** *he reflected on his responsibilities* THINK ABOUT, give thought to, consider, give consideration to, review, mull over, contemplate, cogitate about/on, meditate on, muse on, brood on/over, turn over in one's mind; archaic pore on; rare cerebrate.
– PHRASES **reflect badly on** DISCREDIT, disgrace, shame, put in a bad light, damage, tarnish the reputation of, give a bad name to, bring into disrepute.

reflection • noun **1** *the reflection of light* SENDING BACK, throwing back, casting back. **2** *her reflection in the mirror* (MIRROR) IMAGE, likeness. **3** *your hands are a reflection of your well-being* INDICATION, display, demonstration, manifestation; expression, evidence. **4** *a sad reflection on society* SLUR, aspersion, imputation, reproach, shame, criticism. **5** *after some reflection, he turned it down* THOUGHT, thinking, consideration, contemplation, deliberation, pondering, meditation, musing, rumination; formal cogitation; rare cerebration. **6** *write down your reflections* OPINION, thought, view, belief, feeling, idea, impression, conclusion, assessment; comment, observation, remark.

reflex • adjective INSTINCTIVE, automatic, involuntary, reflexive, impulsive, intuitive, spontaneous, unconscious, unconditioned, untaught, unlearned.
– OPPOSITES conscious.

reform • verb **1** *a plan to reform the system* IMPROVE, (make) better, ameliorate, refine; alter, make alterations to, change, adjust, make adjustments to, adapt, amend, revise, reshape, refashion, redesign, restyle, revamp, rebuild, reconstruct, remodel, reorganize. **2** *after his marriage he reformed* MEND ONE'S WAYS, change for the better, turn over a new leaf, improve.
• noun *the reform of the prison system* IMPROVEMENT, amelioration, refinement; alteration, change, adaptation, amendment, revision, reshaping, refashioning, redesigning, restyling, revamp, revamping, renovation, rebuilding, reconstruction, remodelling, reorgan-

thing).
– ORIGIN Latin *refrenare*, from *frenum* 'bridle'.
refrain[2] ● noun a repeated line or section in a poem or song, typically at the end of each verse.
– ORIGIN from Latin *refringere* 'break up' (because the refrain 'broke' the sequence).
refrangible ● adjective able to be refracted.
– DERIVATIVES **refrangibility** noun.
– ORIGIN from Latin *refringere* 'break up'.
refresh ● verb **1** give new strength or energy to. **2** stimulate (someone's memory) by going over previous information. **3** revise or update (skills, knowledge, etc.).
refresher ● noun **1** (before a noun) (of a course or activity) intended to refresh one's skills or knowledge. **2** Law, Brit. an extra fee payable to counsel in a prolonged case.
refreshing ● adjective **1** serving to refresh. **2** welcome or stimulating because new or different.
– DERIVATIVES **refreshingly** adverb.
refreshment ● noun **1** a light snack or drink. **2** the giving of fresh strength or energy.
refried beans ● plural noun (in Mexican cooking) pinto beans boiled and fried in advance and reheated when required.
refrigerant ● noun a substance used for refrigeration. ● adjective causing cooling or refrigeration.
refrigerate ● verb subject (food or drink) to cold in order to chill or preserve it.
– DERIVATIVES **refrigeration** noun.
– ORIGIN Latin *refrigerare* 'make cool', from *frigus* 'cold'.
refrigerator ● noun an appliance or compartment which is artificially kept cool and used to store food and drink.
refuel ● verb (**refuelled**, **refuelling**; US **refueled**, **refueling**) supply or be supplied with more fuel.
refuge ● noun **1** a place or state of safety from danger or trouble. **2** Brit. a traffic island.
– ORIGIN Latin *refugium*, from *fugere* 'flee'.
refugee ● noun a person who has been forced to leave their country in order to escape war, persecution, or natural disaster.
refulgent /rifuljənt/ ● adjective literary shining very brightly.
– DERIVATIVES **refulgence** noun **refulgently** adverb.
– ORIGIN from Latin *refulgere* 'shine out'.
refund ● verb /rifund/ pay back (money) to. ● noun /reefund/ a refunded sum of money.
– DERIVATIVES **refundable** adjective.
– ORIGIN Latin *refundere* 'pour back'.
refurbish ● verb renovate and redecorate.
– DERIVATIVES **refurbishment** noun.
refuse[1] /rifyo͞oz/ ● verb **1** state that one is unwilling to do something. **2** state that one is unwilling to grant or accept (something offered or requested). **3** (of a horse) decline to jump (a fence or other obstacle).
– DERIVATIVES **refusal** noun **refuser** noun.
– ORIGIN Old French *refuser*, probably an alteration of Latin *recusare* 'to refuse'.
refuse[2] /refyo͞os/ ● noun matter thrown away as worthless.
– ORIGIN perhaps from Old French *refusé* 'refused'.
refusenik /rifyo͞oznik/ ● noun **1** a Jew in the former Soviet Union who was refused permission to emigrate to Israel. **2** a person who refuses to comply with orders or the law as a protest.
refute /rifyo͞ot/ ● verb **1** prove (a statement or the person advancing it) to be wrong. **2** deny (a statement or accusation).
– DERIVATIVES **refutable** adjective **refutation** noun.
– USAGE Strictly speaking, **refute** means 'prove (a statement) to be wrong', although it is often now used to mean simply 'deny'.
– ORIGIN Latin *refutare* 'repel, rebut'.
regain ● verb **1** obtain possession or use of (something lost) again. **2** get back to.
regal ● adjective of, resembling, or fit for a monarch, especially in being magnificent or dignified.
– DERIVATIVES **regally** adverb.
– ORIGIN Latin *regalis*, from *rex* 'king'.
regale ● verb **1** entertain with conversation. **2** lavishly supply with food or drink.
– ORIGIN French *régaler*, from Old French *gale* 'pleasure'.
regalia /rigayliə/ ● plural noun (treated as sing. or pl.) **1** the insignia of royalty, especially the crown and other ornaments used at a coronation. **2** the distinctive clothing and trappings of high office, worn at formal occasions.
– USAGE The word **regalia** comes from Latin and is, technically speaking, the plural of the adjective *regalis*. However, in modern English use it behaves as a collective noun, similar to words like **government**, which means that it can be used with either a singular or plural verb.

Thesaurus

izing, reorganization.
refractory ● adjective (formal) OBSTINATE, stubborn, mulish, pigheaded, obdurate, headstrong, self-willed, wayward, wilful, perverse, contrary, recalcitrant, obstreperous, disobedient; *Brit. informal* bloody-minded, bolshie, stroppy; *N. Amer. informal* balky; *archaic* contumacious, froward.
– OPPOSITES obedient.
refrain ● verb ABSTAIN, desist, hold back, stop oneself, forbear, avoid, eschew, shun, renounce; *informal* swear off; *formal* forswear, abjure.
refresh ● verb **1** *the cool air will refresh me* REINVIGORATE, revitalize, revive, restore, fortify, enliven, perk up, stimulate, freshen, energize, exhilarate, reanimate, wake up, revivify, inspirit; blow away the cobwebs; *informal* buck up, pep up. **2** *let me refresh your memory* JOG, stimulate, prompt, prod. **3** (N. Amer.) *I refreshed his glass* REFILL, top up, replenish, recharge.
– OPPOSITES weary.
refreshing ● adjective **1** *a refreshing drink* INVIGORATING, revitalizing, reviving, restoring, bracing, fortifying, enlivening, inspiriting, stimulating, energizing, exhilarating. **2** *a refreshing change of direction* WELCOME, stimulating, fresh, imaginative, innovative, innovatory.
refreshment ● noun **1** *refreshments were available in the interval* FOOD AND DRINK, sustenance, provender; snacks, titbits, eatables; *informal* nibbles, eats, grub, nosh; *formal* comestibles; *poetic/literary* viands; *dated* victuals; *archaic* aliment. **2** *spiritual refreshment* INVIGORATION, revival, stimulation, reanimation, revivification, rejuvenation, regeneration, renewal.
refrigerate ● verb KEEP COLD, cool (down), chill.
– OPPOSITES heat.
refuge ● noun **1** *homeless people seeking refuge in subway stations* SHELTER, protection, safety, security, asylum, sanctuary. **2** *a refuge for mountain gorillas* SANCTUARY, shelter, place of safety, (safe) haven, sanctum; retreat, bolt-hole, hiding place, hideaway, hideout.
refugee ● noun DISPLACED PERSON, DP, fugitive, asylum seeker, exile, émigré, stateless person; *Austral. informal* reffo.
refund ● verb **1** *we will refund your money if you're not satisfied* REPAY, give back, return, pay back. **2** *they refunded the subscribers* REIMBURSE, compensate, recompense, remunerate, indemnify. ● noun *a full refund* REPAYMENT, reimbursement, rebate.
refurbish ● verb RENOVATE, recondition, rehabilitate, revamp, overhaul, restore, renew, redevelop, rebuild, reconstruct; redecorate, spruce up, upgrade, refit; *N. Amer.* bring up to code; *informal* do up; *N. Amer. informal* rehab.
refusal ● noun **1** *we had one refusal to our invitation* NON-ACCEPTANCE, no, dissent, demurral, negation, turndown; regrets. **2** *you can have first refusal* OPTION, choice, opportunity to purchase. **3** *the refusal of planning permission* WITHHOLDING, denial, turndown.
refuse[1] ● verb **1** *he refused their invitation* DECLINE, turn down, say no to; reject, spurn, rebuff, dismiss; send one's regrets; *informal* pass up. **2** *the Council refused planning permission* WITHHOLD, not grant, deny.
– OPPOSITES accept, grant.
refuse[2] ● noun *piles of refuse* RUBBISH, waste, debris, litter, detritus, dross; dregs, leftovers; *N. Amer.* garbage, trash; *Austral./NZ* mullock; *informal* dreck, junk.
refute ● verb **1** *attempts to refute Einstein's theory* DISPROVE, prove wrong/false, controvert, rebut, give the lie to, explode, debunk, discredit, invalidate; *informal* shoot full of holes; *formal* confute. **2** *she refuted the allegation* DENY, reject, repudiate, rebut; contradict; *formal* gainsay.
regain ● verb **1** *government troops regained the capital* RECOVER, get back, win back, recoup, retrieve, reclaim, repossess; take back, retake, recapture, reconquer. **2** *they regained dry land* RETURN TO, get back to, reach again, rejoin.
regal ● adjective **1** *a regal feast.* See SPLENDID sense 1. **2** *his regal forebears* ROYAL, kingly, queenly, princely.
regale ● verb **1** *they were lavishly regaled* ENTERTAIN, wine and

– ORIGIN Latin, 'royal privileges'.

regality ● noun (pl. **regalities**) **1** the state of being a monarch. **2** regal manner or bearing. **3** historical (in Scotland) territorial jurisdiction granted by the king to a powerful subject.

regard ● verb **1** think of in a particular way. **2** gaze at in a specified fashion. **3** archaic pay attention to. ● noun **1** heed or concern: *she rescued him without regard for herself.* **2** high opinion; esteem. **3** a steady look. **4** (**regards**) best wishes (used especially at the end of letters).

– PHRASES **as regards** concerning. **in this** (or **that**) **regard** in connection with the point previously mentioned. **with** (or **in** or **having**) **regard to** as concerns.

– ORIGIN Old French *regarder* 'to watch', from *garder* 'to guard'.

regardful ● adjective (**regardful of**) formal mindful of.

regarding ● preposition about; concerning.

regardless ● adverb despite the prevailing circumstances.

– PHRASES **regardless of** without regard for.

regatta ● noun a sporting event consisting of a series of boat or yacht races.

– ORIGIN Italian, 'a fight or contest'.

regency /reejənsi/ ● noun (pl. **regencies**) **1** the office or period of government by a regent. **2** a commission acting as regent. **3** (**the Regency**) the period of the regency in Britain (1811–20) or France (1715–23). ● adjective (**Regency**) in the neoclassical style of British architecture, clothing, and furniture popular during the late 18th and early 19th centuries.

regenerate ● verb /rijennərayt/ **1** regrow (new tissue). **2** bring new and more vigorous life to (an area or institution). **3** (especially in Christian use) give a new and higher spiritual nature to. ● adjective /rijennərət/ reborn, especially in a spiritual or moral sense.

– DERIVATIVES **regeneration** noun **regenerative** adjective **regenerator** noun.

regent ● noun a person appointed to administer a state because the monarch is a minor or is absent or unfit to rule. ● adjective (after a noun) acting as regent: *Prince Regent.*

– ORIGIN from Latin *regere* 'to rule'.

reggae /reggay/ ● noun a style of popular music with a strongly accented subsidiary beat, originating in Jamaica.

– ORIGIN perhaps related to Jamaican English *rege-rege* 'quarrel, row'.

regicide /rejisīd/ ● noun **1** the killing of a king. **2** a person who kills a king.

– DERIVATIVES **regicidal** adjective.

– ORIGIN from Latin *rex* 'king'.

regime /rayzheem/ ● noun **1** a government, especially an authoritarian one. **2** a systematic or ordered way of doing something. **3** the conditions under which a scientific or industrial process occurs.

– ORIGIN originally in the sense 'regimen': from French, from Latin *regimen* 'rule'.

regimen /rejimən/ ● noun **1** a therapeutic course of medical treatment, often including recommendations as to diet and exercise. **2** archaic a system of government.

– ORIGIN Latin, from *regere* 'to rule'.

regiment ● noun /rejimənt/ **1** a permanent unit of an army, typically divided into several smaller units and often into two battalions. **2** a large number of people or things. **3** archaic rule or government. ● verb /rejiment/ organize according to a strict system.

– DERIVATIVES **regimentation** noun.

– ORIGIN Latin *regimentum* 'rule', from *regere* 'to rule'.

regimental ● adjective relating to a regiment. ● noun (**regimentals**) military uniform, especially that of a particular regiment.

– DERIVATIVES **regimentally** adverb.

Regina /rijīnə/ ● noun the reigning queen (used following a name or in the titles of lawsuits, e.g. *Regina v. Jones*, the Crown versus Jones).

– ORIGIN Latin, 'queen'.

region ● noun **1** an area of a country or the world having definable characteristics but not always fixed boundaries. **2** an administrative district of a city or country. **3** (**the regions**) the parts of a country outside the capital or chief seat of government. **4** a part of the body, especially around or near an organ.

– PHRASES **in the region of** approximately.

– ORIGIN Latin, 'direction, district', from *regere* 'to rule, direct'.

regional ● adjective **1** relating to or characteristic of a region. **2** relating to the regions of a country rather than the capital: *a regional accent.*

– DERIVATIVES **regionalize** (also **regionalise**) verb **regionally** adverb.

regionalism ● noun **1** commitment to regional rather than central systems of administration; loyalty to one's own region in cultural and political terms. **2** a linguistic feature peculiar to a particular region.

– DERIVATIVES **regionalist** noun & adjective.

register ● noun **1** an official list or record. **2** a record of attendance, for example of pupils in a class. **3** a particular part of the range of a voice or instrument. **4** a variety of a language determined by its degree of formality. **5** (in printing and photography) exact correspondence of the position of colour components or of printed matter. **6** a sliding device controlling a set of organ pipes, or a set of organ pipes so controlled. **7** (in electronic devices) a location in a store of data. ● verb **1** enter in or place on a register. **2** put one's name on a register, especially as an eligible voter or as a guest in a hotel. **3** express (an opinion or emotion). **4** (of an emotion) show in a person's face or gestures. **5** become aware of: *he had not even registered her presence.* **6** (of an instrument) detect and show (a reading) automatically.

– DERIVATIVES **registrable** adjective.

– ORIGIN Latin *registrum*, from *regerere* 'enter, record'.

Thesaurus

dine, fête, feast, serve, feed. **2** *he regaled her with colourful stories* ENTERTAIN, amuse, divert, delight, fascinate, captivate.

regard ● verb **1** *we regard these results as encouraging* CONSIDER, look on, view, see, think of, judge, deem, estimate, assess, reckon, adjudge, rate, gauge. **2** *he regarded her coldly* LOOK AT, contemplate, eye, gaze at, stare at; watch, observe, view, study, scrutinize; poetic/literary behold. **3** (archaic) *he seldom regards her advice* HEED, pay heed to, pay attention to, listen to, take notice of.

● noun **1** *he has no regard for human life* CONSIDERATION, care, concern, thought, notice, heed, attention. **2** *doctors are held in high regard* ESTEEM, respect, acclaim, admiration, approval, approbation, estimation. **3** *Jamie sends his regards* BEST WISHES, good wishes, greetings, kind/kindest regards, felicitations, salutations, respects, compliments, best, love. **4** *his steady regard* (FIXED) LOOK, gaze, stare; observation, contemplation, study, scrutiny. **5** *in this regard I disagree with you* RESPECT, aspect, point, item, particular, detail, specific; matter, issue, topic, question.

– PHRASES **with regard to**. See REGARDING.

regarding ● preposition CONCERNING, as regards, with/in regard to, with respect to, with reference to, relating to, respecting, re, about, apropos, on the subject of, in connection with, vis-à-vis.

regardless ● adverb *he decided to go, regardless* ANYWAY, anyhow, in any case, nevertheless, nonetheless, despite everything, in spite of everything, even so, all the same, in any event, come what may; informal irregardless.

– PHRASES **regardless of** IRRESPECTIVE OF, without regard to, without reference to, disregarding, without consideration of, discounting, ignoring, notwithstanding, no matter; informal irregardless of.

regenerate ● verb REVIVE, revitalize, renew, restore, breathe new life into, revivify, rejuvenate, reanimate, resuscitate; informal give a shot in the arm to.

regime ● noun **1** *the former Communist regime* (SYSTEM OF) GOVERNMENT, authorities, rule, authority, control, command, administration, leadership. **2** *a health regime* SYSTEM, arrangement, scheme; order, pattern, method, procedure, routine, course, plan, programme.

regiment ● noun *the regiment was fighting in France* UNIT, outfit, force, corps, division, brigade, battalion, squadron, company, platoon.

● verb *their life is strictly regimented* ORGANIZE, order, systematize, control, regulate, manage, discipline.

regimented ● adjective STRICTLY REGULATED, organized, disciplined, controlled, ordered, systematic, orderly.

region ● noun *the western region of the country* DISTRICT, province, territory, division, area, section, sector, zone, belt, part, quarter; informal parts.

– PHRASES **in the region of.** See APPROXIMATELY.

regional ● adjective **1** *regional variation* GEOGRAPHICAL, territorial; by region. **2** *a regional parliament* LOCAL, localized, provincial, district, parochial.

– OPPOSITES national.

register ● noun **1** *the register of electors* OFFICIAL LIST, listing, roll,

registered post • noun Brit. a postal procedure with special precautions for safety and for compensation in case of loss.

register office • noun (in the UK) a local government building where civil marriages are conducted and births, marriages, and deaths are recorded.
– USAGE The official term is **register office**, although the form **registry office** is commonly used in unofficial and informal contexts.

registrant • noun a person who registers.

registrar /rejistraar, rejistraar/ • noun **1** an official responsible for keeping a register or official records. **2** the chief administrative officer in a university. **3** (in the UK) the judicial and administrative officer of the High Court. **4** Brit. a middle-ranking hospital doctor undergoing training as a specialist.

Registrar General • noun a government official responsible for holding a population census.

registration • noun **1** the action or process of registering or of being registered. **2** (also **registration mark** or **registration number**) Brit. the series of letters and figures identifying a motor vehicle, displayed on a number plate.

registry • noun (pl. **registries**) **1** a place where registers are kept. **2** registration.

registry office • noun another term for REGISTER OFFICE (in informal and non-official use).

Regius professor /reejiəss/ • noun (in the UK) the holder of a university chair founded by a sovereign or filled by Crown appointment.
– ORIGIN from Latin *regius* 'royal'.

regnal /regn'l/ • adjective of a reign or monarch.
– ORIGIN from Latin *regnum* 'kingdom'.

regnant /regnənt/ • adjective **1** reigning. **2** formal dominant.
– ORIGIN from Latin *regnare* 'to reign'.

regrade • verb grade again or differently.

regress • verb /rigress/ **1** return to a former state. **2** return mentally to a former stage of life or a supposed previous life. • noun /reegress/ the action of regressing.
– ORIGIN Latin *regredi* 'go back, return'.

regression • noun **1** the action of regressing to a former state. **2** the action or an act of regressing to an earlier stage of life or a supposed previous life.

regressive • adjective **1** tending to regress or characterized by regression. **2** (of a tax) taking a proportionally greater amount from those on lower incomes.
– DERIVATIVES **regressively** adverb **regressiveness** noun.

regret • verb (**regretted, regretting**) feel or express sorrow, repentance, or disappointment over. • noun **1** a feeling of sorrow, repentance, or disappointment. **2** (often **one's regrets**) used in polite formulas to express apology or sadness.
– ORIGIN Old French *regreter* 'lament the dead'.

regretful • adjective feeling or showing regret.
– DERIVATIVES **regretfulness** noun.

regretfully • adverb **1** in a regretful manner. **2** it is regrettable that.
– USAGE The established sense of **regretfully** is 'in a regretful manner'. However, it is now sometimes used with the meaning 'it is regrettable that, regrettably', although traditionalists object to this use.

regrettable • adjective giving rise to regret; undesirable.
– DERIVATIVES **regrettably** adverb.

regroup • verb reassemble into organized groups, typically after being attacked or defeated.
– DERIVATIVES **regroupment** noun.

regrow • verb (past **regrew**; past part. **regrown**) grow again.
– DERIVATIVES **regrowth** noun.

regular • adjective **1** arranged or recurring in a constant or definite pattern, especially with the same space between individual instances. **2** doing the same thing often or at uniform intervals: *regular worshippers.* **3** done or happening frequently. **4** conforming to or governed by an accepted standard of procedure or convention. **5** usual or customary. **6** Grammar (of a word) following the normal pattern of inflection. **7** (of merchandise) of average size. **8** of or belonging to the permanent professional armed forces of a country. **9** chiefly N. Amer. of an ordinary kind. **10** Geometry (of a figure) having all sides and all angles equal. **11** Christian Church subject to or bound by religious rule. Contrasted with SECULAR. **12** informal, dated rightly so called; absolute: *this place is a regular fisherman's paradise.* • noun **1** a regular customer, member of a team, etc. **2** a regular member of the armed forces.
– DERIVATIVES **regularity** noun (pl. **regularities**) **regularly** adverb.
– ORIGIN Latin *regularis*, from *regula* 'rule'.

regular canon • noun see CANON².

regular guy • noun N. Amer. informal an ordinary, uncomplicated, sociable man.

regularize (also **regularise**) • verb **1** make regular. **2** establish (a hitherto temporary or provisional arrangement) on an official or correct basis.
– DERIVATIVES **regularization** noun.

regulate • verb **1** control or maintain the rate or speed of (a machine or process). **2** control or supervise by means of rules and regulations.
– DERIVATIVES **regulative** adjective **regulator** noun **regulatory** adjective.

regulation • noun **1** a rule or directive made and maintained by an authority. **2** (before another noun) informal of a familiar or predictable type: *regulation blonde hair.* **3** the action or process of regulating or being regulated.

regulo /regyooloˉ/ • noun Brit. trademark used before a numeral to

Thesaurus

roster, index, directory, catalogue, inventory. **2** *the parish register* RECORD, chronicle, log, logbook, ledger, archive; annals, files. **3** *the lower register of the piano* RANGE, reaches; notes, octaves.
• verb **1** *I wish to register a complaint* RECORD, put on record, enter, file, lodge, write down, put in writing, submit, report, note, minute, log. **2** *it is not too late to register* ENROL, put one's name down, enlist, sign on/up, apply. **3** *the dial registered a speed of 100mph* INDICATE, read, record, show, display. **4** *her face registered anger* DISPLAY, show, express, exhibit, betray, evidence, reveal, manifest, demonstrate, bespeak; *formal* evince. **5** *the content of her statement did not register* MAKE AN IMPRESSION, get through, sink in, penetrate, have an effect, strike home.

regress • verb REVERT, retrogress, relapse, lapse, backslide, slip back; deteriorate, decline, worsen, degenerate, get worse; *informal* go downhill.
– OPPOSITES progress.

regret • verb **1** *they came to regret their decision* BE SORRY ABOUT, feel contrite about, feel remorse about/for, be remorseful about, rue, repent (of), feel repentant about, be regretful at/about. **2** *regretting the passing of youth* MOURN, grieve for/over, feel grief at, weep over, sigh over, feel sad about, lament, sorrow for, deplore.
– OPPOSITES welcome.
• noun **1** *both players later expressed regret* REMORSE, sorrow, contrition, contriteness, repentance, penitence, guilt, compunction, remorsefulness, ruefulness. **2** *please give your grandmother my regrets* APOLOGY, apologies; refusal. **3** *they left with genuine regret* SADNESS, sorrow, disappointment, unhappiness, grief.
– OPPOSITES satisfaction.

regretful • adjective SORRY, remorseful, contrite, repentant, rueful, penitent, conscience-stricken, apologetic, guilt-ridden, ashamed, shamefaced.
– OPPOSITES unrepentant.

regrettable • adjective UNDESIRABLE, unfortunate, unwelcome, sorry, woeful, disappointing; deplorable, lamentable, shameful, disgraceful.

regular • adjective **1** *plant them at regular intervals* UNIFORM, even, consistent, constant, unchanging, unvarying, fixed. **2** *a regular beat* RHYTHMIC, steady, even, uniform, constant, unchanging, unvarying. **3** *the subject of regular protests* FREQUENT, repeated, continual, recurrent, periodic, constant, perpetual, numerous. **4** *regular methods of business* ESTABLISHED, conventional, orthodox, proper, official, approved, bona fide, standard, usual, traditional, tried and tested. **5** *a regular procedure* METHODICAL, systematic, structured, well ordered, well organized, orderly, efficient. **6** *his regular route to work* USUAL, normal, customary, habitual, routine, typical, accustomed, established. **7** *(informal, dated) he's a regular charmer* UTTER, real, absolute, complete, thorough, total, out-and-out, perfect; *N. Amer.* full-bore; *Brit. informal* right, proper; *Austral./NZ informal* fair.
– OPPOSITES erratic, occasional.

regulate • verb **1** *the flow of the river has been regulated* CONTROL, adjust, manage. **2** *a new act regulating businesses* SUPERVISE, police, monitor, check (up on), be responsible for; control, manage, direct, guide, govern.

regulation • noun **1** *EC regulations* RULE, ruling, order, directive, act, law, by-law, statute, edict, canon, pronouncement, dictate,

denote a setting on a temperature scale in a gas oven.

regurgitate /rigurjitayt/ • verb **1** bring (swallowed food) up again to the mouth. **2** repeat (information) without analysing or understanding it.
– DERIVATIVES **regurgitation** noun.
– ORIGIN Latin *regurgitare*, from *gurges* 'whirlpool'.

rehab /reehab/ • noun informal rehabilitation.

rehabilitate • verb **1** restore to health or normal life by training and therapy after imprisonment, addiction, or illness. **2** restore the standing or reputation of. **3** restore to a former condition.
– DERIVATIVES **rehabilitation** noun **rehabilitative** adjective.
– ORIGIN Latin *rehabilitare*, from *habilitare* 'make able'.

rehash • verb reuse (old ideas or material) without significant change or improvement. • noun an instance of rehashing.

rehearsal • noun **1** a trial performance of a play or other work for later public performance. **2** the action or process of rehearsing.

rehearse • verb **1** practise (a play, piece of music, or other work) for later public performance. **2** state (a list of points that have been made many times before).
– ORIGIN originally in the sense 'repeat aloud': from Old French *rehercier*, perhaps from *hercer* 'to harrow'.

reheat • verb heat again. • noun the use of the hot exhaust to burn extra fuel in a jet engine and produce extra power.

rehoboam /reehəbōəm/ • noun a wine bottle of about six times the standard size.
– ORIGIN named after *Rehoboam*, a king of ancient Israel.

rehouse • verb provide with new housing.

rehydrate • verb absorb or cause to absorb moisture after dehydration.
– DERIVATIVES **rehydration** noun.

Reich /rīk, rīkh/ • noun the former German state, in particular the **Third Reich** (the Nazi regime, 1933–45).
– ORIGIN German, 'empire'.

reify /reeifī/ • verb (**reifies**, **reified**) formal make (something abstract) more concrete or real.
– DERIVATIVES **reification** noun.
– ORIGIN from Latin *res* 'thing'.

reign • verb **1** rule as monarch. **2** prevail: *confusion reigned.* **3** (**reigning**) (of a sports player or team) currently holding a particular title. • noun **1** the period of rule of a monarch. **2** the period during which someone or something is predominant or pre-eminent.
– ORIGIN Old French *reignier*, from Latin *regnum* 'kingdom, reign'.

reiki /rayki/ • noun a healing technique based on the principle that the therapist can channel energy into the patient by means of touch, to activate the natural healing processes of the patient's body.
– ORIGIN Japanese, 'universal life energy'.

reimburse /ree-imburss/ • verb repay (money) to (a person who has spent or lost it).
– DERIVATIVES **reimbursable** adjective **reimbursement** noun.
– ORIGIN from obsolete *imburse* 'put in a purse', from Latin *bursa* 'purse'.

reimport • verb import (goods processed or made from exported materials). • noun **1** the action of reimporting. **2** a reimported item.
– DERIVATIVES **reimportation** noun.

rein • noun **1** a long, narrow strap attached at one end to a horse's bit, used in pairs to guide or check a horse. **2** (**reins**) the power to direct and control. • verb **1** check or guide (a horse) by pulling on its reins. **2** (often **rein in/back**) restrain.
– PHRASES (**a**) **free rein** freedom of action or expression. **keep a tight rein on** exercise strict control over.
– ORIGIN Old French *rene*, from Latin *retinere* 'retain'.

reincarnate • verb /ree-inkaarnayt/ cause (someone) to undergo rebirth in another body. • adjective /ree-inkaarnət/ (after a noun) reborn in another body.

reincarnation • noun **1** the rebirth of a soul in a new body. **2** a person in whom a soul is believed to have been reborn.

reindeer • noun (pl. same or **reindeers**) a deer with large branching antlers, native to the northern tundra and subarctic.
– ORIGIN Old Norse.

reinfect • verb cause to become infected again.
– DERIVATIVES **reinfection** noun.

reinforce • verb **1** strengthen (a military force) with additional personnel or material. **2** give added strength to.
– DERIVATIVES **reinforcer** noun.
– ORIGIN French *renforcer*, influenced by *inforce*, an obsolete spelling of ENFORCE.

reinforced concrete • noun concrete in which metal bars or wire are embedded to strengthen it.

reinforcement • noun **1** the action or process of reinforcing. **2** (**reinforcements**) extra personnel sent to strengthen an army or similar force.

reinstate • verb restore to a former position or state.
– DERIVATIVES **reinstatement** noun.

reinsure • verb (of an insurer) transfer (all or part of a risk) to

Thesaurus

dictum, decree, fiat, command, precept. **2** *the regulation of blood sugar* ADJUSTMENT, control, management, balancing. **3** *the regulation of financial services* SUPERVISION, policing, superintendence, monitoring, inspection; control, management, responsibility for.
• adjective *regulation dress* OFFICIAL, prescribed, set, fixed, mandatory, compulsory, obligatory.
– OPPOSITES unofficial.

regurgitate • verb **1** *a ruminant continually regurgitates food* DISGORGE, bring up; archaic regorge. **2** *regurgitating facts* REPEAT, say again, restate, reiterate, recite, parrot; informal trot out.

rehabilitate • verb **1** *efforts to rehabilitate patients* RESTORE TO NORMALITY, reintegrate, readapt; N. Amer. informal rehab. **2** *former dissidents were rehabilitated* REINSTATE, restore, bring back; pardon, absolve, exonerate, forgive; formal exculpate. **3** *rehabilitating vacant housing* RECONDITION, restore, renovate, refurbish, revamp, overhaul, redevelop, rebuild, reconstruct; redecorate, spruce up; upgrade, refit, modernize; informal do up; N. Amer. informal rehab.

rehearsal • noun PRACTICE (SESSION), trial performance, read-through, run-through; informal dry run.

rehearse • verb **1** *I rehearsed the role* PREPARE, practise, read through, run through/over, go over. **2** *he rehearsed the Vienna Philharmonic* TRAIN, drill, prepare, coach, put someone through their paces. **3** *the document rehearsed all the arguments* ENUMERATE, list, itemize, detail, spell out, catalogue, recite, rattle off; restate, repeat, reiterate, recapitulate, go over, run through; informal recap.

reign • verb **1** *Robert II reigned for nineteen years* BE KING/QUEEN, be monarch, be sovereign, sit on the throne, wear the crown, rule. **2** *chaos reigned* PREVAIL, exist, be present, be the case, occur, be prevalent, be current, be rife, be rampant, be the order of the day, be in force, be in effect; formal obtain.
• noun **1** *during Henry's reign* RULE, sovereignty, monarchy. **2** *his reign as manager* PERIOD IN OFFICE, incumbency, managership, leadership.

reigning • adjective **1** *the reigning monarch* RULING, regnant; on the throne. **2** *the reigning world champion* INCUMBENT, current. **3** *the reigning legal conventions* PREVAILING, existing, current; usual, common, recognized, established, accepted, popular, widespread.

reimburse • verb **1** *they will reimburse your travel costs* REPAY, refund, return, pay back. **2** *we'll reimburse you* COMPENSATE, recompense, repay.

rein • noun *there is no rein on his behaviour* RESTRAINT, check, curb, constraint, restriction, limitation, control, brake.
• verb *they reined back costs* RESTRAIN, check, curb, constrain, hold back/in, keep under control, regulate, restrict, control, curtail, limit.
– PHRASES **free rein** FREEDOM, a free hand, leeway, latitude, flexibility, liberty, independence, free play, licence, room to manoeuvre, carte blanche. **keep a tight rein on** EXERCISE STRICT CONTROL OVER, regulate, discipline, regiment, keep in line.

reincarnation • noun REBIRTH, transmigration of the soul, metempsychosis.

reinforce • verb **1** *troops reinforced the dam* STRENGTHEN, fortify, bolster up, shore up, buttress, prop up, underpin, brace, support. **2** *reinforcing links between colleges and companies* STRENGTHEN, fortify, support; cement, boost, promote, encourage, deepen, enrich, enhance, intensify, improve. **3** *the need to reinforce NATO troops* AUGMENT, increase, add to, supplement, boost, top up.

reinforcement • noun **1** *the reinforcement of our defences* STRENGTHENING, fortification, bolstering, shoring up, buttressing, bracing. **2** *reinforcement of the bomber force* AUGMENTATION, increase, supplementing, boosting, topping up. **3** *they returned later with reinforcements* ADDITIONAL TROOPS, fresh troops, auxiliaries, reserves; support, back-up, help.

another insurer to provide protection against the risk of the first insurance.
– DERIVATIVES **reinsurance** noun **reinsurer** noun.
reintegrate • verb **1** restore (distinct elements) to unity. **2** integrate back into society.
– DERIVATIVES **reintegration** noun.
reinterpret • verb (**reinterpreted**, **reinterpreting**) interpret in a new or different light.
– DERIVATIVES **reinterpretation** noun.
reintroduce • verb **1** bring into effect again. **2** put (a species of animal or plant) back into a former habitat.
– DERIVATIVES **reintroduction** noun.
reinvent • verb change (something) so much that it appears entirely new.
– PHRASES **reinvent the wheel** waste a great deal of time or effort in creating something that already exists.
– DERIVATIVES **reinvention** noun.
reinvest • verb put (the profit on a previous investment) back into the same scheme.
– DERIVATIVES **reinvestment** noun.
reinvigorate • verb give new energy or strength to.
– DERIVATIVES **reinvigoration** noun.
reissue • verb (**reissues**, **reissued**, **reissuing**) make a new supply or different form of (a book, record, or other product) available for sale. • noun a new issue of such a product.
reiterate • verb say something again or repeatedly.
– DERIVATIVES **reiteration** noun.
– ORIGIN Latin *reiterare* 'go over again'.
reive /reev/ • verb historical (in the Scottish Borders) carry out raids to plunder and steal cattle.
– DERIVATIVES **reiver** noun.
– ORIGIN variant of archaic *reave* 'to plunder'.
reject • verb /rijekt/ **1** dismiss as inadequate or faulty. **2** refuse to consider or agree to. **3** fail to show due affection or concern for. **4** Medicine show a damaging immune response to (a transplanted organ or tissue). • noun /reejekt/ a rejected person or thing.
– DERIVATIVES **rejection** noun.
– ORIGIN Latin *reicere* 'throw back'.
rejig • verb (**rejigged**, **rejigging**) chiefly Brit. **1** rearrange. **2** dated refit.
rejoice • verb feel or show great joy.
– ORIGIN Old French *rejoir*, from *joir* 'experience joy'.
rejoin[1] • verb **1** join together again. **2** return to.
rejoin[2] • verb say in reply; retort.
– ORIGIN Old French *rejoindre*, from *joindre* 'to join'.
rejoinder • noun **1** a sharp or witty reply. **2** Law, dated a defendant's answer to the plaintiff's reply.
rejuvenate /rijoovənayt/ • verb make or cause to appear younger or more vital.
– DERIVATIVES **rejuvenation** noun **rejuvenator** noun.
– ORIGIN from Latin *juvenis* 'young'.
rekindle • verb **1** relight (a fire). **2** revive (something lapsed or lost).
relaid past and past participle of RELAY[2].
relapse /rilaps/ • verb **1** (of a sick or injured person) return to ill health after a period of improvement. **2** (**relapse into**) return to (a worse or less active state). • noun /reelaps/ a return to ill health after a temporary improvement.
– ORIGIN Latin *relabi* 'slip back'.
relate • verb **1** give an account of. **2** (**be related**) be connected by blood or marriage. **3** establish a causal connection between: *many drowning accidents are related to alcohol use.* **4** (**relate to**) have reference to; concern. **5** (**relate to**) feel sympathy with.
– DERIVATIVES **relater** (also **relator**) noun.
– ORIGIN Latin *referre* 'bring back'.
related • adjective belonging to the same family, group, or type; connected.
– DERIVATIVES **relatedness** noun.
relation • noun **1** the way in which two or more people or things are connected or related. **2** (**relations**) the way in which two or more people or groups feel about and behave towards each other. **3** a relative. **4** (**relations**) formal sexual intercourse. **5** the action of telling a story.
– PHRASES **in relation to** in connection with.
– DERIVATIVES **relational** adjective.
relationship • noun **1** the way in which two or more people or things are connected, or the state of being connected. **2** the way in which two or more people or groups regard and behave towards each other. **3** an emotional and sexual association between two people.

Thesaurus

reinstate • verb RESTORE, return to power, put back, bring back, reinstitute, reinstall.
reiterate • verb REPEAT, say again, restate, recapitulate, go over (and over), rehearse.
reject • verb **1** *the miners rejected the offer* TURN DOWN, refuse, decline, say no to, spurn; *informal* give the thumbs down to. **2** *Jamie rejected her* REBUFF, spurn, shun, snub, repudiate, cast off/aside, discard, abandon, desert, turn one's back on, have nothing (more) to do with, wash one's hands of; *informal* give someone the brush-off; *poetic/literary* forsake.
– OPPOSITES accept.
• noun **1** *it is only a reject* SUBSTANDARD ARTICLE, discard, second. **2** *what a reject!* FAILURE, loser, incompetent.
rejection • noun **1** *a rejection of the offer* REFUSAL, declining, turning down, dismissal, spurning. **2** *Madeleine's rejection of him* REPUDIATION, rebuff, spurning, abandonment, desertion; *informal* brush-off; *poetic/literary* forsaking.
rejoice • verb **1** *they rejoiced when she returned* BE JOYFUL, be happy, be pleased, be glad, be delighted, be elated, be ecstatic, be euphoric, be overjoyed, be as pleased as Punch, be cock-a-hoop, be jubilant, be in raptures, be beside oneself with joy, be delirious, be thrilled, be on cloud nine, be in seventh heaven; celebrate, make merry; *informal* be over the moon, be on top of the world; *Austral. informal* be wrapped; *poetic/literary* joy; *archaic* jubilate. **2** *he rejoiced in their success* TAKE DELIGHT, find/take pleasure, feel satisfaction, find joy, enjoy, revel in, glory in, delight in, relish, savour.
– OPPOSITES mourn.
rejoicing • noun HAPPINESS, pleasure, joy, gladness, delight, elation, jubilation, exuberance, exultation, celebration, revelry, merrymaking.
rejoin[1] • verb *the path rejoins the main road further on* RETURN TO, be reunited with, join again, reach again, regain.
rejoin[2] • verb *Eugene rejoined that you couldn't expect much* ANSWER, reply, respond, return, retort, riposte, counter.
rejoinder • noun ANSWER, reply, response, retort, riposte, counter; *informal* comeback.
rejuvenate • verb REVIVE, revitalize, regenerate, breathe new life into, revivify, reanimate, resuscitate, refresh, reawaken, put new life into; *informal* give a shot in the arm to, pep up, buck up.
relapse • verb **1** *a few patients relapse* GET ILL/WORSE AGAIN, have/suffer a relapse, deteriorate, degenerate, take a turn for the worse. **2** *she relapsed into silence* REVERT, lapse; regress, retrogress, slip back, slide back, degenerate.
– OPPOSITES improve.
• noun **1** *one patient suffered a relapse* DETERIORATION, turn for the worse. **2** *a relapse into alcoholism* DECLINE, lapse, deterioration, degeneration, reversion, regression, retrogression, fall, descent, slide.
relate • verb **1** *he related many stories* TELL, recount, narrate, report, chronicle, outline, delineate, retail, recite, repeat, communicate, impart. **2** *mortality is related to unemployment levels* CONNECT (WITH), associate (with), link (with), correlate (with), ally (with), couple (with). **3** *the charges relate to offences committed in August* APPLY, be relevant, concern, pertain to, be pertinent to, have a bearing on, appertain to, involve; *archaic* regard. **4** *she cannot relate to her step-father* HAVE A RAPPORT, get on (well), feel sympathy, feel for, identify with, empathize with, understand; *informal* hit it off with.
related • adjective **1** *related ideas* CONNECTED, interconnected, associated, linked, coupled, allied, affiliated, concomitant, corresponding, analogous, kindred, parallel, comparable, equivalent, homologous. **2** *are you two related?* OF THE SAME FAMILY, kin, akin, kindred, consanguineous; *formal* cognate.
– OPPOSITES unconnected.
relation • noun **1** *the relation between church and state* CONNECTION, relationship, association, link, correlation, correspondence, parallel, alliance, bond, interrelation, interconnection. **2** *this had no relation to national security* RELEVANCE, applicability, reference, pertinence, bearing. **3** *are you a relation of his?* RELATIVE, member of the family, kinsman, kinswoman; (**relations**) family, (kith and) kin, kindred. **4** *improving relations with India* DEALINGS, communi-

relative /rellətiv/ • adjective **1** considered in relation or in proportion to something else. **2** existing or possessing a characteristic only in comparison to something else: *months of relative calm ended in April.* **3** Grammar (of a pronoun, determiner, or adverb) referring to an expressed or implied antecedent and attaching a subordinate clause to it, e.g. *which.* **4** Grammar (of a clause) attached to an antecedent by a relative word. • noun **1** a person connected by blood or marriage. **2** a species related to another by common origin.
– PHRASES **relative to 1** compared with or in relation to. **2** concerning.

relative atomic mass • noun the ratio of the average mass of one atom of an element to one twelfth of the mass of an atom of carbon-12.

relative density • noun the ratio of the density of a substance to a standard density, usually that of water or air.

relative humidity • noun the amount of water vapour present in air, expressed as a percentage of the amount needed for saturation at the same temperature.

relatively • adverb **1** in relation, comparison, or proportion to something else. **2** viewed in comparison with something else rather than absolutely; quite.

relative molecular mass • noun the ratio of the average mass of one molecule of an element or compound to one twelfth of the mass of an atom of carbon-12.

relativism • noun the doctrine that knowledge, truth, and morality exist in relation to culture, society, or historical context, and are not absolute.
– DERIVATIVES **relativist** noun.

relativistic • adjective Physics accurately described only by the theory of relativity.
– DERIVATIVES **relativistically** adverb.

relativity • noun **1** the absence of standards of absolute and universal application. **2** Physics a description of matter, energy, space, and time according to Einstein's theories based on the importance of relative motion and the principle that the speed of light is constant for all observers.

relativize (also **relativise**) • verb **1** make or treat as relative. **2** Physics treat according to the principles of relativity.
– DERIVATIVES **relativization** noun.

relaunch • verb launch again or in a different form. • noun an instance of relaunching.

relax • verb **1** make or become less tense, anxious, or rigid. **2** rest from work or engage in a recreational activity. **3** make (a rule or restriction) less strict.
– ORIGIN Latin *relaxare*, from *laxus* 'lax, loose'.

relaxant • noun a drug or other thing that promotes relaxation or reduces tension. • adjective causing relaxation.

relaxation • noun the action of relaxing or the state of being relaxed.

relay[1] /reelay/ • noun **1** a group of people or animals engaged in a task for a period of time and then replaced by a similar group. **2** a race between teams of runners, each team member in turn covering part of the total distance. **3** an electrical device which opens or closes a circuit in response to a current in another circuit. **4** a device to receive, reinforce, and retransmit a signal. • verb /also rilay/ **1** receive and pass on (information or a message). **2** broadcast by means of a relay.
– ORIGIN Old French *relayer*, from Latin *laxare* 'slacken'.

relay[2] /reelay/ • verb (past and past part. **relaid**) lay again or differently.

release • verb **1** set free from confinement. **2** free from an obligation or duty. **3** allow to move or flow freely. **4** allow (information) to be generally available. **5** make (a film or recording) available to the public. **6** make over (property, money, or a right) to another. • noun **1** the action or process of releasing or being released. **2** a film or other product released to the public. **3** a handle or catch that releases part of a mechanism. **4** a document making over property, money, or a right to another.
– DERIVATIVES **releasable** adjective **releaser** noun.
– ORIGIN Old French *relesser*, from Latin *relaxare* 'slacken, relax'.

relegate • verb **1** place in an inferior rank or position. **2** (usu. **be relegated**) Brit. transfer (a sports team) to a lower division of a league.
– DERIVATIVES **relegation** noun.
– ORIGIN Latin *relegare* 'send away'.

relent • verb **1** abandon or moderate a harsh intention or cruel treatment. **2** become less intense.
– ORIGIN originally in the sense 'dissolve': from Latin *re-* 'back' + *lentare* 'to bend'.

relentless • adjective **1** oppressively constant. **2** harsh or inflexible.
– DERIVATIVES **relentlessly** adverb **relentlessness** noun.

relevant • adjective closely connected or appropriate to the mat-

Thesaurus

cation, relationship, connections, contact, interaction. **5** (formal) *sexual relations.* See SEX sense 1.

relationship • noun **1** *the relationship between diet and diabetes* CONNECTION, relation, association, link, correlation, correspondence, parallel, alliance, bond, interrelation, interconnection. **2** *evidence of their relationship to a common ancestor* FAMILY TIES/CONNECTIONS, blood relationship, kinship, affinity, consanguinity, common ancestry/lineage. **3** *the end of their relationship* ROMANCE, (love) affair, love, liaison, amour.

relative • adjective **1** *the relative importance of each factor* COMPARATIVE, respective, comparable, correlative, parallel, corresponding. **2** *the food required is relative to body weight* PROPORTIONATE, proportional, in proportion, commensurate, corresponding. **3** *relative ease* MODERATE, reasonable, a fair degree of, considerable, comparative.
• noun *he's a relative of mine* RELATION, member of someone's/the family, kinsman, kinswoman; (**relatives**) family, (kith and) kin, kindred, kinsfolk.

relatively • adverb COMPARATIVELY, by comparison; quite, fairly, reasonably, rather, somewhat, to a certain degree/degree, tolerably, passably; informal pretty, kind of, sort of.

relax • verb **1** *yoga is helpful in learning to relax* UNWIND, loosen up, ease up/off, slow down, de-stress, unbend, rest, put one's feet up, take it easy; informal unbutton; N. Amer. informal hang loose, chill out. **2** *a walk will relax you* CALM (DOWN), unwind, loosen up, make less tense/uptight, soothe, pacify, compose. **3** *he relaxed his grip* LOOSEN, loose, slacken, unclench, weaken, lessen. **4** *her muscles relaxed* BECOME LESS TENSE, loosen, slacken, unknot. **5** *they relaxed the restrictions* MODERATE, modify, temper, ease (up on), loosen, lighten, dilute, weaken, reduce, decrease; informal let up on.
– OPPOSITES tense, tighten.

relaxation • noun **1** *a state of relaxation* (MENTAL) REPOSE, calm, tranquillity, peacefulness, loosening up, unwinding. **2** *I just play for relaxation* RECREATION, enjoyment, amusement, entertainment, fun, pleasure, leisure; informal R and R. **3** *muscle relaxation* LOOSENING, slackening, loosing. **4** *relaxation of censorship rules* MODERATION, easing, loosening, lightening; alleviation, mitigation, dilution, weakening, reduction; informal letting up.

relay • noun *a live relay of the performance* BROADCAST, transmission, showing.
• verb *relaying messages through a third party* PASS ON, hand on, transfer, repeat, communicate, send, transmit, disseminate, spread, circulate.

release • verb **1** *all prisoners were released* (SET) FREE, let go/out, allow to leave, liberate, set at liberty. **2** *Burke released the animal* UNTIE, undo, loose, let go, unleash, unfetter. **3** *this released staff for other duties* MAKE AVAILABLE, free (up), put at someone's disposal, supply, furnish, provide. **4** *she released Stephen from his promise* EXCUSE, exempt, discharge, deliver, absolve; informal let off. **5** *police released the news yesterday* MAKE PUBLIC, make known, issue, break, announce, declare, report, reveal, divulge, disclose, publish, broadcast, circulate, communicate, disseminate. **6** *the film has been released on video* LAUNCH, put on the market, put on sale, bring out, make available.
– OPPOSITES imprison, tie up.
• noun **1** *the release of political prisoners* FREEING, liberation, deliverance; freedom, liberty. **2** *the release of the news* ISSUING, announcement, declaration, reporting, revealing, divulging, disclosure, publication, communication, dissemination. **3** *a press release* ANNOUNCEMENT, bulletin, newsflash, dispatch, proclamation. **4** *the group's last release* CD, album, single, record; video, film; book.

relegate • verb DOWNGRADE, lower (in rank/status), put down, move down; demote, degrade.
– OPPOSITES upgrade.

relent • verb **1** *the government finally relented* CHANGE ONE'S MIND, do a U-turn, back-pedal, back down, give way/in, capitulate; become merciful, become lenient, agree to something, allow something, concede something; Brit. do an about-turn; formal accede. **2** *the rain has relented* EASE (OFF/UP), slacken, let up, abate, drop, die down, lessen, decrease, subside, weaken, tail off.

ter in hand.
– DERIVATIVES **relevance** noun **relevancy** noun **relevantly** adverb.
– ORIGIN from Latin *relevare* 'raise up'.
reliable ● adjective able to be relied on.
– DERIVATIVES **reliability** noun **reliably** adverb.
reliance ● noun dependence on or trust in someone or something.
– DERIVATIVES **reliant** adjective.
relic ● noun **1** an object of interest surviving from an earlier time. **2** a surviving but outdated object, custom, or belief. **3** a part of a holy person's body or belongings kept and revered after their death.
– ORIGIN from Latin *reliquiae* 'remains'.
relict /rellikt/ ● noun **1** an organism or other thing which has survived from an earlier period. **2** archaic a widow.
– ORIGIN from Latin *relictus* 'left behind'.
relief ● noun **1** a feeling of reassurance and relaxation following release from anxiety or distress. **2** a cause of relief. **3** the action of relieving. **4** (usu. **light relief**) a temporary break in a generally tense or boring situation. **5** financial or practical assistance given to those in special need or difficulty. **6** a person or group of people replacing others who have been on duty. **7** distinct appearance due to being accentuated in some way: *the sun threw the peaks into relief.* **8** a method of moulding, carving, or stamping in which the design stands out from the surface, to a greater (**high relief**) or lesser (**low relief**) extent.
– PHRASES **on relief** chiefly N. Amer. receiving state assistance because of need.
– ORIGIN from Latin *relevare* 'raise again, alleviate'.
relief map ● noun **1** a map indicating hills and valleys by shading rather than by contour lines alone. **2** a map model with elevations and depressions representing hills and valleys.
relief road ● noun Brit. a road taking traffic around, rather than through, a congested urban area.
relieve ● verb **1** alleviate or remove (pain, distress, or difficulty). **2** (usu. **be relieved**) cause (someone) to stop feeling distressed or anxious. **3** release (someone) from duty by taking their place. **4** (**relieve of**) take (a burden or responsibility) from. **5** bring military support for (a besieged place). **6** make less boring or monotonous. **7** (**relieve oneself**) formal or euphemistic urinate or defecate.
– DERIVATIVES **reliever** noun.
– ORIGIN Old French *relever*, from Latin *relevare* (see RELIEF).
relight ● verb (past and past part. **relighted** or **relit**) light again.
religion ● noun **1** the belief in and worship of a superhuman controlling power, especially a personal God or gods. **2** a particular system of faith and worship. **3** a pursuit or interest followed with devotion.
– ORIGIN originally in the sense 'life under monastic vows': from Latin *religio* 'obligation, reverence'.
religiose /rilijiōss/ ● adjective excessively religious.
– DERIVATIVES **religiosity** noun.
religious ● adjective **1** of, concerned with, or believing in a religion. **2** treated or regarded with care and devotion appropriate to worship. ● noun (pl. same) a person bound by monastic vows.
– DERIVATIVES **religiously** adverb **religiousness** noun.
relinquish ● verb willingly cease to keep or claim; give up.
– DERIVATIVES **relinquishment** noun.
– ORIGIN Latin *relinquere*, from *linquere* 'to leave'.
reliquary /rellikwəri/ ● noun (pl. **reliquaries**) a container for holy relics.
reliquiae /rilikwi-ee/ ● plural noun formal remains.
– ORIGIN Latin, from *reliquus* 'remaining'.
relish ● noun **1** great enjoyment. **2** pleasurable anticipation. **3** a piquant sauce or pickle eaten with plain food to add flavour. **4** archaic an appetizing flavour. ● verb **1** enjoy greatly. **2** anticipate with pleasure. **3** archaic make pleasant to the taste.
– ORIGIN originally in the sense 'odour, taste': from Old French *reles* 'remainder'.
relive ● verb live through (an experience or feeling) again in one's imagination.
reload ● verb load (something, especially a gun) again.
relocate ● verb move to a new place and establish one's home or business there.
– DERIVATIVES **relocation** noun.
reluctance ● noun unwillingness or disinclination to do something.
reluctant ● adjective unwilling and hesitant.

Thesaurus

relentless ● adjective **1** *their relentless pursuit of quality* PERSISTENT, continuing, constant, continual, continuous, non-stop, never-ending, unabating, interminable, incessant, unceasing, endless, unending, unremitting, unrelenting, unrelieved; unfaltering, unflagging, untiring, unwavering, dogged, single-minded, tireless, indefatigable; formal pertinacious. **2** *a relentless taskmaster* HARSH, grim, cruel, severe, strict, remorseless, merciless, pitiless, ruthless, unmerciful, heartless, hard-hearted, unforgiving; inflexible, unbending, uncompromising, obdurate, unyielding.
relevant ● adjective PERTINENT, applicable, apposite, material, apropos, to the point, germane; connected, related, linked.
reliable ● adjective **1** *reliable evidence* DEPENDABLE, good, well founded, authentic, valid, genuine, sound, true. **2** *a reliable friend* TRUSTWORTHY, dependable, good, true, faithful, devoted, steadfast, staunch, constant, loyal, trusty, dedicated, unfailing; truthful, honest. **3** *reliable brakes* DEPENDABLE, safe, fail-safe. **4** *a reliable firm* REPUTABLE, dependable, trustworthy, honest, responsible, established, proven.
– OPPOSITES untrustworthy.
reliance ● noun **1** *reliance on the state* DEPENDENCE, dependency. **2** *reliance on his own judgement* TRUST, confidence, faith, belief, conviction.
relic ● noun **1** *a Viking relic* ARTEFACT, historical object, ancient object, antiquity, antique. **2** *a saint's relics* REMAINS, corpse, bones, reliquiae; Medicine cadaver.
relief ● noun **1** *it was such a relief to share my worries* REASSURANCE, consolation, comfort, solace. **2** *the relief of pain* ALLEVIATION, alleviating, relieving, assuagement, assuaging, palliation, allaying, soothing, easing, lessening, reduction. **3** *relief from her burden* FREEDOM, release, liberation, deliverance. **4** *a little light relief* RESPITE, amusement, diversion, entertainment, jollity, jollification, recreation. **5** *bringing relief to the starving* HELP, aid, assistance, succour, sustenance; charity, gifts, donations. **6** *his relief arrived to take over* REPLACEMENT, substitute, deputy, reserve, cover, stand-in, supply, locum (tenens), understudy.
– OPPOSITES intensification.
– PHRASES **throw something into relief** HIGHLIGHT, spotlight, give prominence to, point up, show up, emphasize, bring out, stress, accent, underline, underscore, accentuate.
relieve ● verb **1** *this helps relieve pain* ALLEVIATE, mitigate, assuage, ease, dull, reduce, lessen, diminish. **2** *relieving the boredom* COUNTERACT, reduce, alleviate, mitigate; interrupt, vary, stop, dispel, prevent. **3** *the helpers relieved us* REPLACE, take over from, stand in for, fill in for, substitute for, deputize for, cover for. **4** *this relieves the teacher of a heavy load* (SET) FREE, release, exempt, excuse, absolve, let off, discharge.
– OPPOSITES aggravate.
relieved ● adjective GLAD, thankful, grateful, pleased, happy, easy/easier in one's mind, reassured.
– OPPOSITES worried.
religion ● noun FAITH, belief, worship, creed; sect, cult, church, denomination.
religious ● adjective **1** *a religious person* DEVOUT, pious, reverent, godly, God-fearing, churchgoing, practising, faithful, devoted, committed. **2** *religious beliefs* SPIRITUAL, theological, scriptural, doctrinal, church, churchly, ecclesiastical, holy, divine, sacred. **3** *religious attention to detail* SCRUPULOUS, conscientious, meticulous, sedulous, punctilious, strict, rigorous, close.
– OPPOSITES atheistic, secular.
relinquish ● verb **1** *he relinquished control of the company* RENOUNCE, give up/away, hand over, let go of. **2** *he relinquished his post* LEAVE, resign from, stand down from, bow out of, give up; informal quit, chuck. **3** *he relinquished his pipe-smoking* DISCONTINUE, stop, cease, give up, desist from; informal quit, leave off, kick; formal forswear. **4** *she relinquished her grip* LET GO, release, loose, loosen, relax.
– OPPOSITES retain, continue.
relish ● noun **1** *he dug into his food with relish* ENJOYMENT, gusto, delight, pleasure, glee, rapture, satisfaction, contentment, appreciation, enthusiasm, appetite; humorous delectation. **2** *a hot relish* CONDIMENT, sauce, dressing, flavouring, seasoning, dip.
– OPPOSITES dislike.
● verb **1** *he was relishing his moment of glory* ENJOY, delight in, love, adore, take pleasure in, rejoice in, appreciate, savour, revel in, luxuriate in, glory in. **2** *I don't relish the drive* LOOK FORWARD TO, fancy, anticipate with pleasure.

r

– DERIVATIVES **reluctantly** adverb.
– ORIGIN originally in the sense 'offering opposition': from Latin *reluctari* 'struggle against'.
rely ● verb (**relies**, **relied**) (**rely on/upon**) **1** depend on with full trust. **2** be dependent on.
– ORIGIN originally in the sense 'gather together', later 'turn to': from Old French *relier* 'bind together', from Latin *religare*.
rem ● noun (pl. same) a unit of effective absorbed dose of radiation in human tissue, approximately equivalent to one roentgen of X-rays.
– ORIGIN acronym from *roentgen equivalent man*.
remade past and past participle of REMAKE.
remain ● verb **1** be in the same place or condition during further time. **2** continue to be: *he remained alert.* **3** be left over after others or other parts have been completed, used, or dealt with.
– ORIGIN Latin *remanere*, from *manere* 'to stay'.
remainder ● noun **1** a part, number, or quantity that is left over. **2** a part that is still to come. **3** the number which is left over in a division in which one quantity does not exactly divide another. **4** a copy of a book left unsold when demand has fallen. ● verb (often **be remaindered**) dispose of (an unsold book) at a reduced price.
remains ● plural noun **1** things remaining. **2** historical or archaeological relics. **3** a person's body after death.
remake ● verb (past and past part. **remade**) make again or differently. ● noun a film or piece of music that has been filmed or recorded again and re-released.
remand Law ● verb place (a defendant) on bail or in custody, especially when a trial is adjourned. ● noun a committal to custody.
– ORIGIN Latin *remandare* 'commit again'.
remark ● verb **1** say as a comment; mention. **2** regard with attention; notice. ● noun **1** a comment. **2** the action of noticing or commenting.
– ORIGIN French *remarquer* 'note again'.
remarkable ● adjective extraordinary or striking.
– DERIVATIVES **remarkably** adverb.
remarry ● verb (**remarries**, **remarried**) marry again.
– DERIVATIVES **remarriage** noun.
remaster ● verb make a new or improved master of (a sound recording).
rematch ● noun a second match or game between two sports teams or players.
remedial ● adjective **1** giving or intended as a remedy. **2** provided or intended for children with learning difficulties.
remediation /rimeediaysh'n/ ● noun **1** the action of remedying something, in particular environmental damage. **2** the giving of remedial teaching or therapy.
– DERIVATIVES **remediate** verb.
remedy ● noun (pl. **remedies**) **1** a medicine or treatment for a disease or injury. **2** a means of counteracting or eliminating something undesirable. **3** a means of legal reparation. ● verb (**remedies**, **remedied**) make good (an undesirable situation); rectify.
– DERIVATIVES **remediable** adjective.
– ORIGIN Latin *remedium*, from *mederi* 'heal'.
remember ● verb **1** have in or be able to bring to one's mind (someone or something from the past). **2** keep something necessary or advisable in mind: *remember to post the letters.* **3** bear (someone) in mind by making them a gift or by mentioning them in prayer: *he remembered the boy in his will.* **4** (**remember oneself**) recover one's manners after a lapse. **5** (**remember to**) convey greetings from (one person) to (another).
– ORIGIN Latin *rememorari* 'call to mind'.
remembrance ● noun **1** the action of remembering. **2** a memory. **3** a thing kept or given as a reminder or in commemoration of someone.
Remembrance Sunday (also **Remembrance Day**) ● noun (in the UK) the Sunday nearest 11 November, when those who were killed in the First and Second World Wars and later conflicts are commemorated.
remind ● verb **1** cause (someone) to remember something or to do something. **2** (**remind of**) cause (someone) to think of (some-

Thesaurus

reluctance ● noun UNWILLINGNESS, disinclination; hesitation, wavering, vacillation; doubts, second thoughts, misgivings; *archaic* disrelish.
reluctant ● adjective **1** *her parents were reluctant* UNWILLING, disinclined, unenthusiastic, resistant, resisting, opposed; hesitant. **2** *a reluctant smile* SHY, bashful, coy, diffident, reserved, timid, timorous. **3** *he was reluctant to leave* LOATH, unwilling, disinclined, indisposed; not in favour of, against, opposed to.
– OPPOSITES willing, eager.
rely ● verb **1** *we can rely on his discretion* DEPEND, count, bank, place reliance, reckon; be confident of, be sure of, believe in, have faith in, trust in; *informal* swear by; *N. Amer. informal* figure on. **2** *we rely on government funding* BE DEPENDENT, depend, be unable to manage without.
remain ● verb **1** *the problem will remain* CONTINUE TO EXIST, endure, last, abide, carry on, persist, stay (around), prevail, survive, live on. **2** *he remained in hospital* STAY (BEHIND/PUT), wait (around), be left, hang on; *informal* hang around/round; *Brit. informal* hang about; *archaic* bide. **3** *union leaders remain sceptical* CONTINUE TO BE, stay, keep, persist in being, carry on being. **4** *the few minutes that remain* BE LEFT (OVER), be still available, be unused; have not yet passed.
remainder ● noun RESIDUE, balance, remaining part/number, rest, others, those left, remnant(s), surplus, extra, excess; *technical* residuum.
remaining ● adjective **1** *the remaining workers* RESIDUAL, surviving, left (over); extra, surplus, spare, superfluous, excess. **2** *his remaining jobs* UNSETTLED, outstanding, unfinished, incomplete, to be done, unattended to. **3** *my only remaining memories* SURVIVING, lasting, enduring, continuing, persisting, abiding, (still) existing.
remains ● plural noun **1** *the remains of her drink* REMAINDER, residue, remaining part/number, rest, remnant(s); *technical* residuum. **2** *Roman remains* ANTIQUITIES, relics, reliquiae. **3** *the saint's remains* CORPSE, (dead) body, carcass; bones, skeleton; *Medicine* cadaver.
remark ● verb **1** *'You're quiet,' he remarked* COMMENT, say, observe, mention, reflect, state, declare, announce, pronounce, assert; *formal* opine. **2** *many critics remarked on their rapport* COMMENT, mention, refer to, speak of, pass comment on. **3** *he remarked the absence of policemen* NOTE, notice, observe, take note of, perceive, discern.
● noun **1** *his remarks have been misinterpreted* COMMENT, statement, utterance, observation, declaration, pronouncement. **2** *worthy of remark* ATTENTION, notice, comment, mention, observation, acknowledgement.
remarkable ● adjective EXTRAORDINARY, exceptional, amazing, astonishing, astounding, marvellous, wonderful, sensational, stunning, incredible, unbelievable, phenomenal, outstanding, momentous; out of the ordinary, unusual, uncommon, surprising; *informal* fantastic, terrific, tremendous, stupendous, awesome; *poetic/literary* wondrous.
– OPPOSITES ordinary.
remediable ● adjective CURABLE, treatable, operable; solvable, reparable, rectifiable, resolvable.
– OPPOSITES incurable.
remedy ● noun **1** *herbal remedies* TREATMENT, cure, medicine, medication, medicament, drug; *archaic* physic. **2** *a remedy for all kinds of problems* SOLUTION, answer, cure, antidote, curative, nostrum, panacea, cure-all; *informal* magic bullet.
● verb **1** *remedying the situation* PUT/SET RIGHT, put/set to rights, right, rectify, solve, sort out, straighten out, resolve, correct, repair, mend, make good. **2** *anaemia can be remedied by iron tablets* CURE, treat, heal, make better; relieve, ease, alleviate, palliate.
remember ● verb **1** *remembering happy times* RECALL, call to mind, recollect, think of; reminisce about, look back on; *archaic* bethink oneself of. **2** *can you remember all that?* MEMORIZE, commit to memory, retain; learn off by heart. **3** *you must remember she's only five* BEAR/KEEP IN MIND, be mindful of the fact; take into account, take into consideration. **4** *remember to feed the cat* BE SURE, be certain; mind that you, make sure that you. **5** *remember me to Alice* SEND ONE'S BEST WISHES TO, send one's regards to, give one's love to, send one's compliments to, say hello to. **6** *the nation remembered those who gave their lives* COMMEMORATE, pay tribute to, honour, salute, pay homage to. **7** *she remembered them in her will* BEQUEATH SOMETHING TO, leave something to, bestow something on.
– OPPOSITES forget.
remembrance ● noun **1** *an expression of remembrance* RECOLLECTION, reminiscence; remembering, recalling, recollecting, reminiscing. **2** *she smiled at the remembrance* MEMORY, recollection, reminiscence, thought. **3** *we sold poppies in remembrance* COMMEMOR-

thing) because of a resemblance.

reminder • noun **1** a thing that causes someone to remember something. **2** a letter sent to remind someone to pay a bill.

reminisce /remminiss/ • verb indulge in reminiscence.

reminiscence • noun **1** a story told about a past event remembered by the narrator. **2** the enjoyable recollection of past events. **3** a characteristic of one thing suggestive of another.
– ORIGIN Latin *reminiscentia*, from *reminisci* 'remember'.

reminiscent • adjective **1** (usu. **reminiscent of**) tending to remind one of something. **2** absorbed in memories.
– DERIVATIVES **reminiscently** adverb.

remiss /rimiss/ • adjective lacking care or attention to duty.
– ORIGIN originally in the senses 'weakened in colour or consistency' and (in describing sound) 'faint': from Latin *remittere* 'slacken'.

remission • noun **1** the cancellation of a debt, charge, or penalty. **2** Brit. the reduction of a prison sentence, especially as a reward for good behaviour. **3** a temporary lessening of the severity of disease or pain. **4** formal forgiveness of sins.

remit • verb /rimit/ (**remitted**, **remitting**) **1** cancel (a debt) or refrain from inflicting (a punishment). **2** send (money) in payment, especially by post. **3** refer (a matter for decision) to an authority. **4** Theology pardon (a sin). **5** archaic diminish. • noun /reemit/ **1** the task or area of activity officially assigned to an individual or organization. **2** an item referred for consideration.
– ORIGIN Latin *remittere* 'send back, restore'.

remittance • noun **1** a sum of money remitted. **2** the action of remitting money.

remittance man • noun chiefly historical an emigrant supported or assisted by money sent from home.

remix • verb **1** mix again. **2** produce a different version of (a musical recording) by altering the balance of the separate tracks. • noun a remixed musical recording.
– DERIVATIVES **remixer** noun.

remnant • noun **1** a small remaining quantity. **2** a piece of cloth left when the greater part has been used or sold. **3** a surviving trace. • adjective remaining.
– ORIGIN Old French *remenant*, from *remenoir*, *remanoir* 'remain'.

remodel • verb (**remodelled**, **remodelling**; US **remodeled**, **remodeling**) **1** change the structure or form of. **2** shape (a figure or object) again or differently.

remold • verb US spelling of REMOULD.

remonstrance /rimonstrənss/ • noun a forcefully reproachful protest.

remonstrate /remmənstrayt/ • verb make a forcefully reproachful protest.
– DERIVATIVES **remonstration** noun.
– ORIGIN originally in the sense 'make plain': from Latin *remonstrare* 'demonstrate'.

remora /remmərə/ • noun a slender sea fish which attaches itself to large fish by means of a sucker on top of the head.
– ORIGIN Latin, 'hindrance' (because of the former belief that the fish slowed down ships).

remorse • noun deep regret or guilt for a wrong committed.
– ORIGIN Latin *remorsus*, from *mordere* 'to bite'.

remorseful • adjective filled with remorse or repentance.
– DERIVATIVES **remorsefully** adverb.

remorseless • adjective **1** without remorse. **2** (of something unpleasant) relentless.
– DERIVATIVES **remorselessly** adverb **remorselessness** noun.

remortgage • verb take out another or a different mortgage on. • noun a different or additional mortgage.

remote • adjective (**remoter**, **remotest**) **1** far away in space or time. **2** situated far from the main centres of population. **3** distantly related. **4** (often **remote from**) having very little connection. **5** (of a chance or possibility) unlikely to occur. **6** aloof and unfriendly in manner. **7** (of an electronic device) operating or operated by means of radio or infrared signals. **8** Computing (of a device) that can only be accessed by means of a network.
– DERIVATIVES **remotely** adverb **remoteness** noun.
– ORIGIN Latin *remotus* 'removed'.

remote control • noun **1** control of a machine or apparatus from a distance by means of signals transmitted from a radio or electronic device. **2** (also **remote controller**) a device that controls an apparatus in this way.
– DERIVATIVES **remote-controlled** adjective.

remote sensing • noun the scanning of the earth by satellite or high-flying aircraft.

remoulade /remmoolaad/ • noun salad or seafood dressing

Thesaurus

ATION, memory, recognition. **4** *a remembrance of my father* MEMENTO, reminder, keepsake, souvenir, token, memorial.

remind • verb **1** *I left a note to remind him* JOG SOMEONE'S MEMORY, help someone remember, prompt. **2** *the song reminded me of my sister* MAKE ONE THINK OF, cause one to remember, put one in mind of, bring/call to mind, evoke.

reminder • noun PROMPT, prompting, aide-memoire.

reminisce • verb REMEMBER (WITH PLEASURE), cast one's mind back to, look back on, be nostalgic about, recall, recollect, reflect on, call to mind.

r

reminiscences • plural noun MEMORIES, recollections, reflections, remembrances.

reminiscent • adjective SIMILAR TO, comparable with, evocative of, suggestive of, redolent of.

remiss • adjective NEGLIGENT, neglectful, irresponsible, careless, thoughtless, heedless, lax, slack, slipshod, lackadaisical; *N. Amer.* derelict; *informal* sloppy; *formal* delinquent.
– OPPOSITES careful.

remission • noun **1** *the remission of all fees* CANCELLATION, setting aside, suspension, revocation; *formal* abrogation. **2** *the cancer is in remission* RESPITE, abeyance. **3** *the wind howled without remission* RESPITE, lessening, abatement, easing, decrease, reduction, diminution, slackening, dying down, lull; *informal* let-up. **4** *the remission of sins* FORGIVENESS, pardoning, absolution, exoneration; *formal* exculpation.

remit • verb **1** *the fines were remitted* CANCEL, set aside, suspend, revoke; *formal* abrogate. **2** *remitting duties to the authorities* SEND, dispatch, forward, hand over; pay. **3** *the case was remitted to the Court of Appeal* PASS (ON), refer, send on, transfer. **4** *(rare) we remitted all further discussion* POSTPONE, defer, put off/back, shelve, delay, suspend; *N. Amer.* table; *informal* put on the back burner, put on ice. **5** *remitting their sins* PARDON, forgive; excuse. **6** *(archaic) the fever remitted* DIMINISH, lessen, decrease, ease (up), abate, moderate, subside.
• noun *that is outside his remit* AREA OF RESPONSIBILITY, sphere, orbit, scope, ambit, province; brief, instructions, orders; *informal* bailiwick.

remittance • noun **1** *send the form with your remittance* PAYMENT, money, fee; cheque; *formal* monies. **2** *a monthly remittance* ALLOWANCE, sum of money.

remnant • noun **1** *the remnants of the picnic* REMAINS, remainder, leftovers, residue, rest; *technical* residuum. **2** *remnants of cloth* SCRAP, piece, bit, fragment, shred, offcut, oddment.

remonstrate • verb **1** *'I'm not a child!' he remonstrated* PROTEST, complain, expostulate; argue with, take issue with. **2** *we remonstrated against this proposal* OBJECT STRONGLY TO, complain vociferously about, protest against, argue against, oppose strongly, make a fuss about, challenge; deplore, condemn, denounce, criticize; *informal* kick up a fuss/stink about.

remorse • noun CONTRITION, deep regret, repentance, penitence, guilt, compunction, remorsefulness, ruefulness, contriteness; pangs of conscience.

remorseful • adjective SORRY, full of regret, regretful, contrite, repentant, penitent, guilt-ridden, conscience-stricken, guilty, chastened, self-reproachful.
– OPPOSITES unrepentant.

remorseless • adjective **1** HEARTLESS, pitiless, merciless, ruthless, callous, cruel, hard-hearted, inhumane, unmerciful, unforgiving, unfeeling. **2** *remorseless cost-cutting* RELENTLESS, unrelenting, unremitting, unabating, inexorable, unstoppable.
– OPPOSITES compassionate.

remote • adjective **1** *areas remote from hospitals* FARAWAY, distant, far (off), far removed. **2** *a remote mountain village* ISOLATED, out of the way, off the beaten track, secluded, lonely, in the back of beyond, godforsaken, inaccessible; *N. Amer.* in the backwoods, lonesome; *Austral./NZ* in the backblocks, in the booay; *informal* in the sticks, in the middle of nowhere; *N. Amer. informal* in the tall timbers; *Austral./NZ informal* beyond the black stump; *archaic* unapproachable. **3** *events remote from modern times* IRRELEVANT TO, unrelated to, unconnected to, unconcerned with, not pertinent to, immaterial to, unassociated with; foreign to, alien to. **4** *a remote possibility* UNLIKELY, improbable, implausible, doubtful, dubious; faint, slight, slim, small, slender. **5** *she seems very remote* ALOOF, distant, detached, withdrawn, reserved, uncommunicative, unforthcom-

made with hard-boiled egg yolks, oil, vinegar, and seasoning.
– ORIGIN French.
remould (US **remold**) ● verb /reemōld/ **1** mould again or differently. **2** Brit. put a new tread on (a worn tyre). ● noun /reemōld/ a remoulded tyre.
remount ● verb /reemownt/ **1** get on (a horse or vehicle) again. **2** attach to a new frame or setting. **3** initiate (a course of action) again. ● noun /reemownt/ a fresh horse for a rider.
removal ● noun **1** the action of removing. **2** chiefly Brit. the transfer of furniture and other contents when moving house.
removalist ● noun Austral. a person or firm engaged in household or business removals.
remove ● verb **1** take off or away from the position occupied. **2** abolish or get rid of. **3** dismiss from a post. **4** (**be removed**) be very different from. **5** (**remove to**) dated relocate to (another place). **6** (**removed**) separated by a particular number of steps of descent: *his second cousin once removed.* ● noun **1** a degree of remoteness or separation: *at this remove, the incident seems insane.* **2** a form or division in some British schools.
– DERIVATIVES **removable** adjective **remover** noun.
– ORIGIN Latin *removere*, from *movere* 'to move'.
REM sleep ● noun a kind of sleep that occurs at intervals during the night and is characterized by rapid eye movement, more dreaming and bodily movement, and faster pulse and breathing.
remunerate /rimyōōnərayt/ ● verb pay (someone) for services rendered or work done.
– DERIVATIVES **remunerative** adjective.
– ORIGIN Latin *remunerari* 'reward, recompense'.
remuneration ● noun money paid for work or a service.
Renaissance /rinaysənss, -sonss/ ● noun **1** the revival of art and literature under the influence of classical models in the 14th–16th centuries. **2** (**renaissance**) a revival of or renewed interest in something.
– ORIGIN French, 'rebirth'.
Renaissance man ● noun a person with a wide range of talents or interests.
renal /reen'l/ ● adjective technical relating to the kidneys.
– ORIGIN Latin *renalis*, from *renes* 'kidneys'.
rename ● verb give a new name to.
renascence /rinass'nss/ ● noun **1** the revival of something that has been dormant. **2** another term for RENAISSANCE.
renascent ● adjective becoming active again.
– ORIGIN Latin, from *renasci* 'be born again'.
rend ● verb (past and past part. **rent**) literary **1** tear to pieces. **2** cause great emotional pain to.
– PHRASES **rend the air** sound piercingly.
– ORIGIN Old English.
render ● verb **1** provide or give (a service, help, etc.). **2** submit for inspection, consideration, or payment. **3** literary hand over; surrender. **4** cause to be or become. **5** represent, interpret, or perform artistically. **6** translate. **7** melt down (fat) so as to clarify it. **8** process (the carcass of an animal) in order to extract proteins, fats, and other usable parts. **9** cover (stone or brick) with a coat of plaster. ● noun a first coat of plaster applied to a brick or stone surface.
– DERIVATIVES **renderer** noun.
– ORIGIN Old French *rendre*, from Latin *reddere* 'give back'.
rendering ● noun **1** a performance of a piece of music or drama. **2** a translation. **3** the action of rendering. **4** a first coat of plaster.
rendezvous /rondayvōō/ ● noun (pl. same or /rondayvōōz/) **1** a meeting at an agreed time and place. **2** a meeting place. ● verb (**rendezvouses** /rondayvōōz/, **rendezvoused** /rondayvōōd/, **rendezvousing** /rondayvōōing/) meet at an agreed time and place.
– ORIGIN French *rendez-vous!* 'present yourselves!'.
rendition ● noun **1** a rendering of a dramatic, musical, or artistic work. **2** a translation.
renegade /rennigayd/ ● noun a person who deserts and betrays an organization, country, or set of principles. ● adjective having treacherously changed allegiance.
– ORIGIN Spanish *renegado*, from Latin *renegare* 'renounce'.
renege /rinayg, -neeg/ (also **renegue**) ● verb go back on a promise, undertaking, or contract.
– DERIVATIVES **reneger** noun.
– ORIGIN Latin *renegare*, from *negare* 'deny'.
renegotiate ● verb negotiate again in order to change the ori-

Thesaurus

ing, unapproachable, unresponsive, unfriendly, unsociable, introspective, introverted; *informal* stand-offish.
– OPPOSITES close, central.
removal ● noun **1** *the removal of heavy artillery* TAKING AWAY, moving, carrying away. **2** *his removal from office* DISMISSAL, ejection, expulsion, ousting, displacement, deposition; *N. Amer.* ouster; *informal* sacking, firing. **3** *the removal of customs barriers* WITHDRAWAL, elimination, taking away. **4** *the removal of errors* DELETION, elimination, erasing, effacing, obliteration. **5** *the removal of weeds* UPROOTING, eradication. **6** *the removal of old branches* CUTTING OFF, chopping off, hacking off. **7** *her removal to France* MOVE, transfer, relocation. **8** *the removal of a rival* KILLING, murder, elimination; *informal* liquidation.
– OPPOSITES installation.
remove ● verb **1** *remove the plug* DETACH, unfasten; pull out, take out, disconnect. **2** *she removed the lid* TAKE OFF, undo, unfasten. **3** *he removed a note from his wallet* TAKE OUT, produce, bring out, get out, pull out, withdraw. **4** *police removed boxes of documents* TAKE AWAY, carry away, move, transport; confiscate; *informal* cart off. **5** *Sheila removed the mud* CLEAN OFF, wash off, wipe off, rinse off, scrub off, sponge out. **6** *Henry removed his coat* TAKE OFF, pull off, slip out of; *Brit. informal* peel off. **7** *he was removed from his post* DISMISS, discharge, get rid of, dislodge, displace, expel, oust, depose; *informal* sack, fire, kick out, boot out; *Brit. informal* turf out. **8** *tax relief was removed* WITHDRAW, abolish, eliminate, get rid of, do away with, stop, cut, axe. **9** *Gabriel removed two words* DELETE, erase, rub out, cross out, strike out, score out. **10** *weeds have to be removed* UPROOT, pull out, eradicate. **11** *removing branches* CUT OFF, chop off, lop off, hack off. **12** *(dated) he removed to Edinburgh* MOVE (HOUSE), relocate, transfer; emigrate; *Brit. informal* up sticks; *N. Amer. informal* pull up stakes.
– OPPOSITES attach, insert, replace.
● noun *it is impossible, at this remove, to reconstruct the accident* DISTANCE, space of time, interval.
removed ● adjective DISTANT, remote, disconnected; unrelated, unconnected, foreign, alien.
remunerate ● verb PAY, reward, reimburse, recompense.
remuneration ● noun PAYMENT, pay, salary, wages; earnings, fee(s), reward, recompense, reimbursement; *formal* emolument(s).
remunerative ● adjective LUCRATIVE, well paid, financially rewarding; profitable.
renaissance ● noun REVIVAL, renewal, resurrection, reawakening, re-emergence, reappearance, resurgence, regeneration, rebirth; *formal* renascence.
rend ● verb *(poetic/literary)* TEAR/RIP APART, tear/rip in two, split, rupture, sever; *poetic/literary* tear/rip asunder, sunder; *rare* dissever; *archaic* rive.
render ● verb **1** *her fury rendered her speechless* MAKE, cause to be/become, leave. **2** *rendering assistance* GIVE, provide, supply, furnish, contribute; offer, proffer. **3** *the invoices rendered by the accountants* SEND IN, present, submit. **4** *the jury rendered their verdict* DELIVER, return, hand down, give, announce. **5** *paintings rendered in vivid colours* PAINT, draw, depict, portray, represent, execute; *poetic/literary* limn. **6** *she rendered all three verses* PERFORM, sing. **7** *the characters are vividly rendered* ACT, perform, play, depict, interpret. **8** *the phrase was rendered into English* TRANSLATE, put, express, rephrase, reword. **9** *he rendered up the stolen money* GIVE BACK, return, restore, pay back, repay, hand over, give up, surrender. **10** *the fat can be rendered* MELT DOWN, clarify.
rendezvous ● noun *Edward was late for their rendezvous* MEETING, appointment, assignation; *informal* date; *poetic/literary* tryst.
● verb *the bar where they had agreed to rendezvous* MEET, come together, gather, assemble.
rendition ● noun **1** *our rendition of Beethoven's Fifth* PERFORMANCE, rendering, interpretation, presentation, execution, delivery. **2** *the artist's rendition of Adam and Eve* DEPICTION, portrayal, representation. **3** *an interpreter's rendition of the message* TRANSLATION, interpretation, version.
renegade ● noun **1** *he was denounced as a renegade* TRAITOR, defector, deserter, turncoat, rebel, mutineer; *rare* tergiversator. **2** *(archaic) a religious renegade* APOSTATE, heretic, dissenter; *archaic* recreant.
● adjective **1** *renegade troops* TREACHEROUS, traitorous, disloyal, treasonous, rebel, mutinous. **2** *a renegade monk* APOSTATE, heretic, heretical, dissident; *archaic* recreant.
– OPPOSITES loyal.

ginal agreed terms.
– DERIVATIVES **renegotiable** adjective **renegotiation** noun.

renew • verb **1** resume or re-establish after an interruption. **2** give fresh life or strength to. **3** extend the period of validity of (a licence, subscription, or contract). **4** replace or restore (something broken or worn out).
– DERIVATIVES **renewal** noun **renewer** noun.

renewable • adjective **1** capable of being renewed. **2** (of energy or its source) not depleted when used.
– DERIVATIVES **renewability** noun.

renminbi /renminbi/ • noun (pl. same) the national currency of the People's Republic of China.
– ORIGIN from the Chinese words for 'people' and 'currency'.

rennet /rennit/ • noun **1** curdled milk from the stomach of an unweaned calf, containing rennin and used in curdling milk for cheese. **2** a preparation containing rennin.
– ORIGIN probably related to RUN.

rennin /rennin/ • noun an enzyme secreted into the stomach of unweaned mammals, causing the curdling of milk.
– ORIGIN from RENNET.

renounce • verb **1** formally declare one's abandonment of (a claim, right, or possession). **2** refuse to recognize any longer. **3** abandon (a cause, bad habit, or way of life).
– DERIVATIVES **renounceable** adjective **renouncement** noun **renouncer** noun.
– ORIGIN Old French *renoncer*, from Latin *renuntiare* 'protest against'.

renovate /rennəvayt/ • verb restore (something old) to a good state of repair.
– DERIVATIVES **renovation** noun **renovator** noun.
– ORIGIN Latin *renovare* 'make new again'.

renown • noun the state of being famous.
– DERIVATIVES **renowned** adjective.
– ORIGIN from Old French *renomer* 'make famous', from *nom* 'name'.

rent[1] • noun **1** a tenant's regular payment to a landlord for the use of property or land. **2** a sum paid for the hire of equipment. • verb **1** pay someone for the use of. **2** let someone use (something) in return for payment.
– DERIVATIVES **rentable** adjective.
– ORIGIN Old French *rente*, from a root shared by RENDER.

rent[2] • noun a large tear in a piece of fabric.
– ORIGIN from REND.

rent[3] past and past participle of REND.

rental • noun **1** an amount paid or received as rent. **2** the action of renting. **3** N. Amer. a rented house or car. • adjective relating to or available for rent.

rent boy • noun Brit. informal a young male prostitute.

renter • noun **1** a person who rents a flat, car, etc. **2** (in the UK) a person who distributes cinema films. **3** US a rented car or video cassette. **4** Brit. informal a male prostitute.

rentier /rontiay/ • noun a person living on income from property or investments.
– ORIGIN French, from *rente* 'dividend'.

renumber • verb change the number or numbers assigned to.

renunciation • noun the action or an act of renouncing.

reoccupy • verb (**reoccupies**, **reoccupied**) occupy again.
– DERIVATIVES **reoccupation** noun.

reoccur • verb (**reoccurred**, **reoccurring**) occur again or repeatedly.
– DERIVATIVES **reoccurrence** noun.

reoffend • verb commit a further offence.
– DERIVATIVES **reoffender** noun.

reopen • verb open again.

reorder • verb **1** order again. **2** arrange again. • noun a renewed or repeated order for goods.

reorganize (also **reorganise**) • verb change the organization of.
– DERIVATIVES **reorganization** noun **reorganizer** noun.

reorient /reeorient/ • verb **1** change the focus or direction of. **2** (**reorient oneself**) find one's bearings again.
– DERIVATIVES **reorientate** verb **reorientation** noun.

Rep. • abbreviation **1** (in the US Congress) Representative. **2** Republic. **3** US a Republican.

rep[1] informal • noun a representative. • verb (**repped**, **repping**) act as a sales representative.

rep[2] • noun informal **1** repertory. **2** a repertory theatre or company.

rep[3] (also **repp**) • noun a fabric with a ribbed surface, used in curtains and upholstery.
– ORIGIN French *reps*.

rep[4] • noun N. Amer. informal short for REPUTATION.

rep[5] • noun (in bodybuilding) a repetition of a set of exercises. • verb (as an instruction in knitting patterns) repeat.

repackage • verb package again or differently.

repaid past and past participle of REPAY.

repaint • verb cover with a new coat of paint.

repair[1] • verb **1** restore (something damaged, worn, or faulty) to a good condition. **2** set right (a rift in relations). • noun **1** the action of repairing. **2** a result of this. **3** the relative physical condition of an object: *the cottages were in good repair.*
– DERIVATIVES **repairable** adjective **repairer** noun.
– ORIGIN Latin *reparare*, from *parare* 'make ready'.

repair[2] • verb (**repair to**) formal or humorous go to (a place).
– ORIGIN Old French *repairer*, from Latin *repatriare* 'return to one's country'.

reparable /reppərəb'l/ • adjective able to be repaired or

Thesaurus

r

renege • verb DEFAULT ON, fail to honour, go back on, break, back out of, withdraw from, retreat from, welsh on, backtrack on; break one's word/promise.
– OPPOSITES honour.

renew • verb **1** *I renewed my search* RESUME, return to, take up again, come back to, begin again, start again, restart, recommence; continue (with), carry on (with). **2** *they renewed their vows* REAFFIRM, reassert; repeat, reiterate, restate. **3** *something to renew her interest in life* REVIVE, regenerate, revitalize, reinvigorate, restore, resuscitate, breathe new life into; *archaic* renovate. **4** *the hotel was completely renewed* RENOVATE, restore, modernize, overhaul, redevelop, rebuild, reconstruct, remodel; *N. Amer.* bring something up to code; *informal* do up; *N. Amer. informal* rehab. **5** *they renewed Jackie's contract* EXTEND, prolong. **6** *I renewed my supply of toilet paper* REPLENISH, restock, resupply, top up, replace.

renewal • noun **1** *the renewal of our friendship* RESUMPTION, recommencement, re-establishment; continuation. **2** *spiritual renewal* REGENERATION, revival, reinvigoration, revitalization; *archaic* renovation. **3** *the renewal of older urban areas* RENOVATION, restoration, modernization, reconditioning, overhauling, redevelopment, rebuilding, reconstruction.

renounce • verb **1** *Edward renounced his claim to the throne* GIVE UP, relinquish, abandon, abdicate, surrender, waive, forego; *Law* disclaim; *formal* abnegate. **2** *Hungary renounced the agreement* REJECT, refuse to abide by, repudiate. **3** *she renounced her family* REPUDIATE, deny, reject, abandon, wash one's hands of, turn one's back on, disown, spurn, shun; *poetic/literary* forsake. **4** *he renounced alcohol* ABSTAIN FROM, give up, desist from, refrain from, keep off, eschew; *informal* quit, pack in, lay off; *formal* forswear.
– OPPOSITES assert, accept.
– PHRASES **renounce the world** BECOME A RECLUSE, turn one's back on society, cloister oneself, hide oneself away.

renovate • verb MODERNIZE, restore, refurbish, revamp, recondition, rehabilitate, overhaul, redevelop; update, upgrade, refit; *N. Amer.* bring something up to code; *informal* do up; *N. Amer. informal* rehab.

renown • noun FAME, distinction, eminence, pre-eminence, prominence, repute, reputation, prestige, acclaim, celebrity, notability.

renowned • adjective FAMOUS, celebrated, famed, eminent, distinguished, acclaimed, illustrious, pre-eminent, prominent, great, esteemed, of note, of repute, well known, well thought of.
– OPPOSITES unknown.

rent[1] • noun *I can't afford to pay the rent* HIRE CHARGE, rental. • verb **1** *she rented a car* HIRE, lease, charter. **2** *why don't you rent it out?* LET (OUT), lease (out), hire (out); sublet, sublease.

rent[2] • noun **1** *the rent in his trousers* RIP, tear, split, hole, slash, slit. **2** *a vast rent in the mountains* GORGE, chasm, fault, rift, fissure, crevasse.

renunciation • noun **1** *Henry's renunciation of his throne* RELINQUISHMENT, giving up, abandonment, abdication, surrender, waiving, foregoing; *Law* disclaimer; *rare* abnegation. **2** *his renunciation of luxury* ABSTENTION, refraining, going without, giving up, eschewal; *formal* forswearing. **3** *their renunciation of terrorism* REPUDIATION, rejection, abandonment.

reorganize • verb RESTRUCTURE, change, alter, adjust, transform, shake up, rationalize, rearrange, reshape, overhaul.

repair[1] • verb **1** *the car was repaired* MEND, fix (up), put/set right, restore (to working order), overhaul, service; *informal* patch up.

rectified.

reparation /reppəraysh'n/ ● noun **1** the making of amends for a wrong. **2** (**reparations**) compensation for war damage paid by a defeated state. **3** archaic the action of repairing.
– DERIVATIVES **reparative** /reppərətiv, riparrətiv/ adjective.
– ORIGIN Latin, from *reparare* (see REPAIR[1]).

repartee /reppaartee/ ● noun conversation or speech characterized by quick, witty comments or replies.
– ORIGIN from French *repartie* 'replied promptly'.

repast /ripaast/ ● noun formal a meal.
– ORIGIN Old French, from Latin *repascere*, from *pascere* 'to feed'.

repatriate /reepatriayt/ ● verb send (someone) back to their own country. ● noun a person who has been repatriated.
– DERIVATIVES **repatriation** noun.
– ORIGIN Latin *repatriare* 'return to one's country'.

repay ● verb (past and past part. **repaid**) **1** pay back (a loan). **2** pay back money owed to. **3** do or give something as recompense for (a favour or kindness received). **4** be worth subjecting to (a specified action): *these sites would repay more detailed investigation.*
– DERIVATIVES **repayable** adjective **repayment** noun.

repayment mortgage ● noun a mortgage in which the borrower repays the capital and interest together in fixed instalments over a fixed period.

repeal ● verb revoke or annul (a law or act of parliament). ● noun the action of repealing.
– DERIVATIVES **repealable** adjective.
– ORIGIN Old French *repeler*, from *apeler* 'to call, appeal'.

repeat ● verb **1** say or do again. **2** (**repeat oneself**) say the same thing again. **3** (**repeat itself**) occur again in the same way or form. **4** (of food) be tasted again after being swallowed, as a result of indigestion. ● noun **1** an instance of repeating or being repeated. **2** a repeated broadcast of a television or radio programme. **3** (before another noun) occurring, done, or used more than once: *a repeat prescription.* **4** Music a passage intended to be repeated.
– DERIVATIVES **repeatable** adjective **repeater** noun.
– ORIGIN Latin *repetere*, from *petere* 'seek'.

repel ● verb (**repelled, repelling**) **1** drive or force back or away. **2** be repulsive or distasteful to. **3** formal refuse to accept; reject. **4** (of a magnetic pole or electric field) force (something similarly magnetized or charged) away. **5** (of a substance) resist mixing with or be impervious to.
– DERIVATIVES **repeller** noun.
– ORIGIN Latin *repellere*, from 'to drive'.

repellent (also **repellant**) ● adjective **1** able to repel or impervious to a particular thing: *water-repellent nylon.* **2** causing disgust or distaste. ● noun **1** a substance that deters insects or other pests. **2** a substance used to treat something to make it impervious to water.
– DERIVATIVES **repellence** noun **repellency** noun **repellently** adverb.

repent ● verb **1** feel or express sincere regret or remorse. **2** feel regret or remorse about.
– DERIVATIVES **repentance** noun **repentant** adjective **repenter** noun.
– ORIGIN Old French *repentir*, from Latin *paenitere* 'cause to repent'.

repercussions ● plural noun the consequences of an event or action.
– DERIVATIVES **repercussive** adjective.
– ORIGIN originally as a medical term meaning 'repressing of infection': from Latin *repercutere* 'cause to rebound, push back'.

repertoire /reppərtwaar/ ● noun the body of pieces known or regularly performed by a performer or company.
– ORIGIN French, from Latin *reperire* 'find, discover'.

repertory /reppərtri/ ● noun (pl. **repertories**) **1** the performance by a company of the plays, operas, or ballets in its repertoire at regular short intervals. **2** another term for REPERTOIRE. **3** a repository or collection.
– ORIGIN originally denoting an index or catalogue: from Latin *repertorium*, from *reperire* 'find, discover'.

Thesaurus

2 *they repaired the costumes* MEND, darn; *informal* patch up. **3** *repairing relations with other countries* PUT/SET RIGHT, mend, fix, straighten out, improve; *informal* patch up. **4** *she sought to repair the wrong she had done* RECTIFY, make good, (put) right, correct, make up for, make amends for, make reparation for.
● noun **1** *in need of repair* RESTORATION, fixing (up), mending, renovation; *archaic* reparation. **2** *an invisible repair* MEND, darn. **3** *in good repair* CONDITION, working order, state, shape, fettle; *Brit. informal* nick.
– PHRASES **beyond repair** IRREPARABLE, irreversible, irretrievable, irremediable, irrecoverable, past hope.

repair[2] ● verb (*formal*) *we repaired to the sitting room* GO TO, head for, adjourn, wend one's way; *formal* remove; *poetic/literary* betake oneself.

reparable ● adjective RECTIFIABLE, remediable, curable, restorable, recoverable, retrievable, salvageable.

reparation ● noun AMENDS, restitution, redress, compensation, recompense, repayment, atonement.

repartee ● noun BANTER, badinage, bantering, raillery, witticism(s), ripostes, sallies, quips, joking, jesting, chaff, chaffing; *formal* persiflage.

repast ● noun (*formal*) MEAL, feast, banquet; *informal* spread, feed, bite (to eat); *Brit. informal* nosh-up; *formal* collation; *poetic/literary* refection.

repay ● verb **1** *repaying customers who have been cheated* REIMBURSE, refund, pay back/off, recompense, compensate, indemnify. **2** *the grants have to be repaid* PAY BACK, return, refund, reimburse. **3** *I'd like to repay her generosity* RECIPROCATE, return, requite, recompense, reward. **4** *interesting books that would repay further study* BE WELL WORTH, be worth one's while.

repayment ● noun **1** *the repayment of tax* REFUND, reimbursement, paying back. **2** *repayment for all they have done* RECOMPENSE, reward, compensation.

repeal ● verb *the Act was repealed* REVOKE, rescind, cancel, reverse, annul, nullify, declare null and void, quash, abolish; *Law* vacate; *formal* abrogate; *archaic* recall.
– OPPOSITES enact.
● noun *the repeal of the law* REVOCATION, rescinding, cancellation, reversal, annulment, nullification, quashing, abolition; *formal* abrogation; *archaic* recall.

repeat ● verb **1** *she repeated her story* SAY AGAIN, restate, reiterate, go/run through again, recapitulate; *informal* recap. **2** *children can repeat large chunks of text* RECITE, quote, parrot, regurgitate; *informal* trot out. **3** *Steele was invited to repeat his work* DO AGAIN, redo, replicate, duplicate. **4** *the episodes were repeated* REBROADCAST, rerun, reshow.
● noun **1** *a repeat of the previous year's final* REPETITION, duplication, replication, duplicate. **2** *repeats of his TV show* RERUN, rebroadcast, reshowing.
– PHRASES **repeat itself** REOCCUR, recur, occur again, happen again.

repeated ● adjective RECURRENT, frequent, persistent, continual, incessant, constant; regular, periodic, numerous, (very) many, a great many.
– OPPOSITES occasional.

repeatedly ● adverb FREQUENTLY, often, again and again, over and over (again), time and (time) again, many times, many a time; persistently, recurrently, constantly, continually, regularly; *N. Amer.* oftentimes; *informal* 24-7; *poetic/literary* oft, oft-times.

repel ● verb **1** *the rebels were repelled* FIGHT OFF, repulse, drive back/away, force back, beat back, push back; hold off, ward off, keep at bay; *Brit.* see off; *archaic* rebut. **2** *the coating will repel water* BE IMPERVIOUS TO, be impermeable to, keep out, resist. **3** *the thought of kissing him repelled me* REVOLT, disgust, repulse, sicken, nauseate, turn someone's stomach, be repulsive, be distasteful, be repugnant; *informal* turn off; *N. Amer. informal* gross out.

repellent ● adjective **1** *a repellent stench* REVOLTING, repulsive, disgusting, repugnant, sickening, nauseating, stomach-turning, nauseous, vile, nasty, foul, horrible, awful, dreadful, terrible, obnoxious, loathsome, offensive, objectionable; abhorrent, despicable, reprehensible, contemptible, odious, hateful, execrable; *N. Amer.* vomitous; *informal* ghastly, horrid, gross, yucky, icky; *poetic/literary* noisome; *archaic* disgustful. **2** *a repellent coating* IMPERMEABLE, impervious, resistant; -proof.
– OPPOSITES delightful.

repent ● verb FEEL REMORSE, regret, be sorry, rue, reproach oneself, be ashamed, feel contrite; be penitent, be remorseful, be repentant.

repentance ● noun REMORSE, contrition, contriteness, penitence, regret, ruefulness, remorsefulness, shame, guilt; *archaic* rue.

repentant ● adjective PENITENT, contrite, regretful, rueful, remorseful, apologetic, ashamed, chastened, shamefaced.
– OPPOSITES impenitent.

repercussion ● noun **1** *political repercussions* CONSEQUENCE, result, effect, outcome; reverberation, backlash, aftermath, fallout. **2** (*archaic*) *a vicious repercussion* REVERBERATION, recoil, kickback.

repertory company ● noun a theatrical company that performs plays from its repertoire for regular, short periods of time, moving on from one play to another.
repetition ● noun **1** the action or an instance of repeating or being repeated. **2** a thing that repeats another.
repetitious ● adjective having too much repetition; repetitive.
– DERIVATIVES **repetitiously** adverb **repetitiousness** noun.
repetitive ● adjective involving or characterized by repetition, especially when boring or unnecessary.
– DERIVATIVES **repetitively** adverb **repetitiveness** noun.
repetitive strain injury ● noun a condition in which the prolonged performance of repetitive actions, typically with the hands, causes pain or impairment of function in the tendons and muscles involved.
rephrase ● verb express in an alternative way.
repine ● verb literary be discontented; fret.
replace ● verb **1** take the place of. **2** provide a substitute for. **3** put back in a previous place or position.
– DERIVATIVES **replaceable** adjective **replacer** noun.
replacement ● noun **1** the action or process of replacing someone or something. **2** a person or thing that takes the place of another.
replant ● verb **1** plant in a new pot or site. **2** provide (an area) with new plants or trees.
replay ● verb **1** play back (a recording). **2** play (a match) again. ● noun **1** the action or an instance of replaying. **2** a replayed match. **3** an occurrence which closely follows the pattern of a previous event: *a replay of the 1988 campaign.*
replenish ● verb **1** fill up again. **2** restore (a stock or supply) to a former level or condition.
– DERIVATIVES **replenisher** noun **replenishment** noun.
– ORIGIN Old French *replenir*, from *plenir* 'fill'.
replete /ripleet/ ● adjective **1** (**replete with**) filled or well-supplied with. **2** very full with food; sated.
– DERIVATIVES **repletion** noun.
– ORIGIN from Latin *replere* 'fill up'.
replica ● noun an exact copy or model of something, especially one on a smaller scale.
– ORIGIN originally as a musical term in the sense 'a repeat': from Italian, from *replicare* 'to reply'.
replicate ● verb /replikayt/ **1** make an exact copy of; reproduce. **2** (**replicate itself**) (of genetic material or a living organism) reproduce or give rise to a copy of itself. **3** repeat (a scientific experiment or trial) to obtain a consistent result. ● noun /replikət/ **1** a close or exact copy; a replica. **2** a replicated experiment or trial. **3** Music a tone one or more octaves above or below the given tone.
– DERIVATIVES **replicable** /replikəb'l/ adjective **replication** noun **replicative** adjective **replicator** noun.
– ORIGIN Latin *replicare*, from *plicare* 'to fold'.
reply ● verb (**replies**, **replied**) **1** say or write something in response to something said or written. **2** respond with a similar action: *they replied to the shelling with a mortar attack.* ● noun (pl. **replies**) **1** the action of replying. **2** a spoken or written response.
– DERIVATIVES **replier** noun.
– ORIGIN Old French *replier*, from Latin *replicare* 'repeat', later 'make a reply'.
repo /reepō/ N. Amer. informal ● noun (pl. **repos**) a car or other item which has been repossessed. ● verb (**repo's, repo'd**) repossess.
repopulate ● verb introduce a population into (an area previously deserted or taken by occupying forces).
– DERIVATIVES **repopulation** noun.
report ● verb **1** give a spoken or written account of something. **2** convey information about an event or situation. **3** make a formal complaint about. **4** present oneself as having arrived somewhere or as ready to do something. **5** (**report to**) be responsible to (a supervisor or manager). **6** Brit. formally announce that a parliamentary committee has dealt with (a bill). ● noun **1** an account given of a matter after investigation or consideration. **2** a piece of information about an event or situation. **3** Brit. a teacher's written assessment of a pupil's work and progress. **4** a sudden loud noise of or like an explosion or gunfire.
– DERIVATIVES **reportable** adjective.
– ORIGIN Latin *reportare* 'bring back'.
reportage /repportaazh/ ● noun **1** the reporting of news by the press and the broadcasting media. **2** factual, journalistic presentation in a book or other text.
reported speech ● noun a speaker's words reported in a subordinate clause, with the required changes of person and tense (e.g. *he said that he would go*, based on *I will go*). Contrasted with DIRECT SPEECH.
reporter ● noun a person who reports news for a newspaper or broadcasting company.
report stage ● noun (in the UK and Canada) the stage in the process of a bill becoming law at which it is debated after being reported.

Thesaurus

repertoire ● noun COLLECTION, stock, range, repertory, reserve, store, repository, supply.
repetition ● noun **1** *the statistics bear repetition* REITERATION, repeating, restatement, retelling. **2** *the repetition the of words* REPEATING, echoing, parroting. **3** *a repetition of the scene in the kitchen* RECURRENCE, reoccurrence, repeat, rerun. **4** *there is some repetition* REPETITIOUSNESS, repetitiveness, redundancy, tautology.
repetitious ● adjective *repetitious work.* See REPETITIVE.
repetitive ● adjective MONOTONOUS, tedious, boring, humdrum, mundane, tiresome, dreary; unvaried, unchanging, unvarying, recurrent, recurring, repeated, repetitious, routine, mechanical, automatic.
rephrase ● verb REWORD, put in other words, express differently, paraphrase.
repine ● verb *(poetic/literary)* FRET, be/feel unhappy, mope, eat one's heart out, brood; lament, grieve, mourn, sorrow, pine.
replace ● verb **1** *Adam replaced the receiver* PUT BACK, return, restore. **2** *a new chairman came in to replace him* TAKE THE PLACE OF, succeed, take over from, supersede; stand in for, substitute for, deputize for, cover for, relieve; *informal* step into someone's shoes/boots. **3** *she replaced the spoon with a fork* SUBSTITUTE, exchange, change, swap.
– OPPOSITES remove.
replacement ● noun **1** *we have to find a replacement* SUCCESSOR; SUBSTITUTE, stand-in, locum, relief, cover. **2** *the wiring was in need of replacement* RENEWAL, replacing.
replenish ● verb **1** *she replenished their glasses* REFILL, top up, fill up, recharge; *N. Amer.* freshen. **2** *their supplies were replenished* STOCK UP, restock, restore, replace.
– OPPOSITES empty, exhaust.
replete ● adjective **1** *the guests were replete* WELL FED, sated, satiated, full (up); glutted, gorged; *informal* stuffed. **2** *a sumptuous environment replete with antiques* FILLED, full, well stocked, well supplied, crammed, packed, jammed, teeming, overflowing, bursting; *informal* jam-packed, chock-a-block.
replica ● noun **1** *is it real or a replica?* (CARBON) COPY, model, duplicate, reproduction, replication; dummy, imitation, facsimile. **2** *a replica of her mother* PERFECT LIKENESS, double, lookalike, (living) image, twin, clone; *informal* spitting image, (dead) ringer.
replicate ● verb COPY, reproduce, duplicate, recreate, repeat, perform again; clone.
reply ● verb **1** *Rachel didn't reply* ANSWER, respond, come back, write back. **2** *he replied defensively* RESPOND, answer, rejoin, retort, riposte, counter, come back.
● noun *he waited for a reply* ANSWER, response, rejoinder, retort, riposte; *informal* comeback.
report ● verb **1** *the government reported a fall in inflation* ANNOUNCE, describe, give an account of, detail, outline, communicate, divulge, disclose, reveal, make public, publish, broadcast, proclaim, publicize. **2** *the newspapers reported on the scandal* INVESTIGATE, look into, inquire into; write about, cover, describe, give details of, commentate on. **3** *I reported him to the police* INFORM ON, tattle on; *informal* shop, tell on, squeal on, rat on, peach on; *Brit. informal* grass on. **4** *Juliet reported for duty* PRESENT ONESELF, arrive, turn up, clock in, sign in; *Brit.* clock on; *N. Amer.* punch in; *informal* show up.
● noun **1** *a full report on the meeting* ACCOUNT, review, record, description, statement; transactions, proceedings, transcripts, minutes. **2** *reports of drug dealing* NEWS, information, word, intelligence; *poetic/literary* tidings. **3** *newspaper reports* STORY, account, article, piece, item, column, feature, bulletin, dispatch. **4** *(Brit.) a school report* ASSESSMENT, evaluation, appraisal; *N. Amer.* report card. **5** *reports of his imminent resignation* RUMOUR, whisper; *informal* buzz; *archaic* bruit. **6** *the report of a gun* BANG, blast, crack, shot, gunshot, explosion, boom. **7** *(archaic) of good report.* See REPUTATION.
reporter ● noun JOURNALIST, correspondent, newspaperman, news-

r

repose[1] /ripōz/ ● noun **1** a state of restfulness or tranquillity. **2** composure. ● verb **1** rest. **2** be situated or kept in a particular place.
– ORIGIN Old French *reposer*, from Latin *pausare* 'to pause'.
repose[2] /ripōz/ ● verb (**repose in**) place (something, especially one's confidence or trust) in.
– ORIGIN originally in the sense 'put back in the same position': from POSE, suggested by Latin *reponere* 'replace'.
reposition ● verb adjust or alter the position of.
repository /ripozzitəri/ ● noun (pl. **repositories**) **1** a place or receptacle for storage. **2** a place where something is found in significant quantities.
– ORIGIN Latin *repositorium*, from *reponere* 'replace'.
repossess ● verb retake possession of (something) when a buyer defaults on payments.
– DERIVATIVES **repossession** noun **repossessor** noun.
repot ● verb (**repotted**, **repotting**) put (a plant) in another pot.
repoussé /rəpōōssay/ ● adjective (of metalwork) hammered into relief from the reverse side. ● noun ornamental metalwork fashioned in this way.
– ORIGIN French, 'pushed back'.
repp ● noun variant spelling of REP[3].
reprehend /reprihend/ ● verb reprimand.
– DERIVATIVES **reprehension** noun.
– ORIGIN Latin *reprehendere* 'seize, check, rebuke'.
reprehensible ● adjective deserving condemnation.
– DERIVATIVES **reprehensibility** noun **reprehensibly** adverb.
represent ● verb **1** be entitled or appointed to act and speak for. **2** be an elected member of a legislature for. **3** constitute; amount to. **4** be a specimen or example of; typify. **5** (**be represented**) be present to a particular degree. **6** portray in a particular way. **7** depict in a work of art. **8** signify, symbolize, or embody.
– ORIGIN Latin *repraesentare*, from *praesentare* 'to present'.
re-present ● verb present again.
– DERIVATIVES **re-presentation** noun.
representation ● noun **1** the action or an instance of representing or being represented. **2** an image, model, or other depiction of something. **3** (**representations**) formal statements made to an authority to communicate an opinion or register a protest.
representational ● adjective **1** relating to or characterized by representation. **2** relating to art which depicts the physical appearance of things.
representative ● adjective **1** typical of a class or group. **2** containing typical examples of many or all types: *a representative sample.* **3** (of a legislative or deliberative assembly) consisting of people chosen to act and speak on behalf of a wider group. **4** serving as a portrayal or symbol of something. ● noun **1** a person chosen to act and speak for another or others. **2** an agent of a firm who travels to potential clients to sell its products. **3** an example of a class or group.
– DERIVATIVES **representatively** adverb **representativeness** noun.
repress ● verb **1** subdue by force. **2** restrain, prevent, or inhibit. **3** suppress (a thought or feeling) in oneself so that it becomes or remains unconscious.
– DERIVATIVES **represser** noun **repressible** adjective **repression** noun.
– ORIGIN Latin *reprimere* 'press back, check'.
repressed ● adjective **1** oppressed. **2** (of a thought or feeling) kept suppressed and unconscious in one's mind. **3** tending to suppress one's feelings and desires.
repressive ● adjective inhibiting or restraining personal freedom; oppressive.
– DERIVATIVES **repressively** adverb **repressiveness** noun.
reprieve ● verb **1** cancel the punishment of. **2** abandon or postpone plans to close: *the threatened pits could be reprieved.* ● noun **1** the cancellation of a punishment. **2** a respite from difficulty or danger.
– ORIGIN Old French *reprendre*, from Latin *prehendere* 'seize'.
reprimand /reprimaand/ ● noun a formal expression of disap-

Thesaurus

paperwoman, newsman, newswoman, columnist; *Brit.* pressman; *N. Amer.* legman, wireman; *Austral.* roundsman; *informal* news hound, hack, stringer, journo; *N. Amer. informal* newsy.
repose ● noun **1** *a face in repose* REST, relaxation, inactivity; sleep, slumber. **2** *they found true repose* PEACE (AND QUIET), peacefulness, quiet, quietness, calm, tranquillity. **3** *he lost his repose* COMPOSURE, serenity, equanimity, poise, self-possession, aplomb.
● verb **1** *the diamond reposed on a bed of velvet* LIE, rest, be placed, be situated. **2** *the trust he had reposed in her* PUT, place, invest, entrust. **3** *the beds where we reposed* LIE (DOWN), recline, rest, sleep; *poetic/literary* slumber.
repository ● noun STORE, storehouse, depository; reservoir, bank, cache, treasury, fund, mine.
reprehensible ● adjective DEPLORABLE, disgraceful, discreditable, despicable, blameworthy, culpable, wrong, bad, shameful, dishonourable, objectionable, opprobrious, repugnant, inexcusable, unforgivable, indefensible, unjustifiable; criminal, sinful, scandalous, iniquitous; *formal* exceptionable.
– OPPOSITES praiseworthy.
represent ● verb **1** *a character representing a single quality* SYMBOLIZE, stand for, personify, epitomize, typify, embody, illustrate. **2** *the initials which represent her qualification* STAND FOR, designate, denote; *poetic/literary* betoken. **3** *Hathor is represented as a woman with cow's horns* DEPICT, portray, render, picture, delineate, show, illustrate; *poetic/literary* limn. **4** *he represented himself as the owner of the factory* DESCRIBE AS, present as, profess to be, claim to be, pass oneself off as, pose as, pretend to be. **5** *ageing represents a threat to one's independence* CONSTITUTE, be, amount to, be regarded as. **6** *a panel representing a cross section of the public* BE A TYPICAL SAMPLE OF, be representative of, typify. **7** *his solicitor represented him in court* APPEAR FOR, act for, speak on behalf of. **8** *the Queen was represented by Lord Lewin* DEPUTIZE FOR, substitute for, stand in for. **9** *(formal) I represented the case as I saw it* POINT OUT, state, present, put forward. **10** *(formal) the vendors represented that the information was accurate* CLAIM, maintain, state, affirm, contend; *rare* asseverate.
representation ● noun **1** *Rossetti's representation of women* PORTRAYAL, depiction, delineation, presentation, rendition. **2** *representations of the human form* LIKENESS, painting, drawing, picture, illustration, sketch, image, model, figure, figurine, statue, statuette. **3** *(formal) making representations to the council* STATEMENT, deposition, allegation, declaration, exposition, report, protestation.
representative ● adjective **1** *a representative sample* TYPICAL, prototypical, characteristic, illustrative, archetypal. **2** *a female figure representative of Britain* SYMBOLIC, emblematic. **3** *representative government* ELECTED, elective, democratic, popular.
– OPPOSITES atypical, totalitarian.
● noun **1** *a representative of the Royal Society* SPOKESPERSON, spokesman, spokeswoman, agent, official, mouthpiece. **2** *a sales representative* (COMMERCIAL) TRAVELLER, (travelling) salesman, saleswoman, agent; *informal* rep; *N. Amer. informal* drummer. **3** *the Cambodian representative at the UN* DELEGATE, commissioner, ambassador, attaché, envoy, emissary, chargé d'affaires, deputy. **4** *our representatives in parliament* MEMBER (OF PARLIAMENT), MP; councillor; *N. Amer.* Member of Congress, senator. **5** *he acted as his father's representative* DEPUTY, substitute, stand-in, proxy. **6** *fossil representatives of lampreys* EXAMPLE, specimen, exemplar, exemplification.
repress ● verb **1** *the rebellion was repressed* SUPPRESS, quell, quash, subdue, put down, crush, extinguish, stamp out, defeat, conquer, rout, overwhelm, contain. **2** *the peasants were repressed* OPPRESS, subjugate, keep down, rule with a rod of iron, intimidate, tyrannize, crush. **3** *these emotions may well be repressed* RESTRAIN, hold back/in, keep back, suppress, keep in check, control, keep under control, curb, stifle, bottle up; *informal* button up, keep the lid on.
repressed ● adjective **1** *a repressed country* OPPRESSED, subjugated, subdued, tyrannized. **2** *repressed feelings* RESTRAINED, suppressed, held back/in, kept in check, stifled, pent up, bottled up. **3** *emotionally repressed* INHIBITED, frustrated, restrained; *informal* uptight, hung up.
– OPPOSITES democratic, uninhibited.
repression ● noun **1** *the repression of the protests* SUPPRESSION, quashing, subduing, crushing, stamping out. **2** *political repression* OPPRESSION, subjugation, suppression, tyranny, despotism, authoritarianism. **3** *the repression of sexual urges* RESTRAINT, restraining, holding back, keeping back, suppression, keeping in check, control, keeping under control, stifling, bottling up.
repressive ● adjective OPPRESSIVE, authoritarian, despotic, tyrannical, dictatorial, fascist, autocratic, totalitarian, undemocratic.
reprieve ● verb **1** *she was reprieved* GRANT A STAY OF EXECUTION TO, pardon, spare, grant an amnesty to, amnesty; *informal* let off (the hook); *archaic* respite. **2** *the project has been reprieved* SAVE, rescue; *informal* take off the hit list.

proval; a rebuke. ● verb address a reprimand to.
– ORIGIN French *réprimande*, from Latin *reprimere* 'press back, check'.
reprint ● verb print again or in a revised form. ● noun **1** an act of reprinting. **2** a copy of a book or other material that has been reprinted.
reprisal ● noun **1** an act of retaliation. **2** historical the forcible seizure of a foreign subject or their goods as an act of retaliation.
– ORIGIN Old French *reprisaille*, from Latin *reprehendere* 'seize, check, rebuke'.
reprise /ripreez/ ● noun **1** a repeated passage in music. **2** a further performance of something. ● verb repeat (a piece of music or a performance).
– ORIGIN French, 'taken up again'.
reproach ● verb **1** express one's disapproval of or disappointment with. **2** (**reproach with**) accuse of. ● noun an expression of disapproval or disappointment.
– PHRASES **above** (or **beyond**) **reproach** such that no criticism can be made; perfect.
– DERIVATIVES **reproachable** adjective.
– ORIGIN Old French *reprochier*, from a base meaning 'bring back close'.
reproachful ● adjective expressing disapproval or disappointment.
– DERIVATIVES **reproachfully** adverb.
reprobate /reprəbayt/ ● noun a person without moral principles. ● adjective unprincipled.
– DERIVATIVES **reprobation** noun.
– ORIGIN from Latin *reprobare* 'disapprove'.
reprocess ● verb process (something, especially spent nuclear fuel) again or differently, in order to reuse it.
reproduce ● verb **1** produce a copy or representation of. **2** recreate in a different medium or context. **3** (of an organism) produce offspring.
– DERIVATIVES **reproducer** noun **reproducible** adjective.
reproduction ● noun **1** the action or process of reproducing. **2** a copy of a work of art, especially a print made of a painting. **3** (before another noun) made to imitate the style of an earlier period or particular craftsman: *reproduction furniture*.
– DERIVATIVES **reproductive** adjective.
reprogram (also **reprogramme**) ● verb (**reprogrammed**, **reprogramming**; US also **reprogramed**, **reprograming**) program (a computer) again.
– DERIVATIVES **reprogrammable** adjective.
reprographics ● plural noun (treated as sing.) reprography.
reprography /reeprografi/ ● noun the science and practice of reproducing documents and graphic material.
– DERIVATIVES **reprographic** adjective.
reproof[1] /riproof/ ● noun a rebuke or reprimand.
– ORIGIN from Old French *reprover* 'reprove'.
reproof[2] /reeproof/ ● verb **1** Brit. make waterproof again. **2** make a fresh proof of (printed matter).
reprove ● verb rebuke or reprimand.
– ORIGIN Old French *reprover*, from late Latin *reprobare* 'disapprove'.
reptile ● noun **1** a cold-blooded vertebrate animal of a class that includes snakes, lizards, crocodiles, turtles, and tortoises, typically having a dry scaly skin and laying soft-shelled eggs on land. **2** informal a person regarded with loathing and contempt.
– DERIVATIVES **reptilian** adjective & noun.
– ORIGIN from Latin *reptilis* 'crawling', from *repere* 'to crawl'.
republic ● noun a state in which supreme power is held by the people and their elected representatives, and which has an elected or nominated president rather than a monarch.
– ORIGIN Latin *respublica*, from *res* 'concern' + *publicus* 'of the people, public'.
republican ● adjective **1** belonging to or characteristic of a republic. **2** advocating republican government. **3** (**Republican**) (in the US) supporting the Republican Party. ● noun **1** a person advocating republican government. **2** (**Republican**) (in the US) a member or supporter of the Republican Party. **3** (**Republican**) an advocate of a united Ireland.
– DERIVATIVES **republicanism** noun.
repudiate /ripyoodiayt/ ● verb **1** refuse to accept or be associated with. **2** deny the truth or validity of. **3** chiefly Law refuse to fulfil or discharge (an agreement, obligation, or debt). **4** archaic disown or divorce (one's wife).

Thesaurus

● noun *a last-minute reprieve* STAY OF EXECUTION, remission, pardon, amnesty; *US Law* continuance; *informal* let-off.
reprimand ● verb *he was publicly reprimanded* REBUKE, admonish, chastise, chide, upbraid, reprove, reproach, scold, berate, take to task, lambaste, give someone a piece of one's mind, haul over the coals, lecture, criticize, censure; *informal* tell off, give someone a telling-off, give someone a talking-to, dress down, give someone a dressing-down, give someone an earful, give someone a roasting, rap over the knuckles, slap someone's wrist, bawl out, pitch into, lay into, lace into, blast; *Brit. informal* tick off, carpet, tear off a strip, give someone what for, give someone a wigging, give someone a rocket, give someone a rollicking; *N. Amer. informal* chew out, ream out; *Austral. informal* monster; *formal* castigate; *dated* give someone a rating; *rare* reprehend, objurgate.
– OPPOSITES praise.
● noun *they received a severe reprimand* REBUKE, reproof, admonishment, admonition, reproach, reproval, scolding, upbraiding, censure; *informal* telling-off, rap over the knuckles, slap on the wrist, flea in one's ear, dressing-down, earful, roasting, tongue-lashing; *Brit. informal* ticking-off, carpeting, wigging, rocket, rollicking; *formal* castigation; *dated* rating.
– OPPOSITES commendation.
reprisal ● noun RETALIATION, counter-attack, comeback; revenge, vengeance, retribution, requital; *informal* a taste of one's own medicine.
reproach ● verb *Albert reproached him for being late.* See REPRIMAND verb.
● noun **1** *an expression of reproach.* See REPRIMAND noun. **2** *this party is a reproach to British politics* DISGRACE, discredit, source of shame, blemish, stain, blot; *poetic/literary* smirch.
– OPPOSITES praise, credit.
– PHRASES **beyond/above reproach** PERFECT, blameless, above suspicion, without fault, faultless, flawless, irreproachable, exemplary, impeccable, immaculate, unblemished, spotless, untarnished, stainless, unsullied, whiter than white; *informal* squeaky clean.
reproachful ● adjective DISAPPROVING, reproving, critical, censorious, disparaging, withering, accusatory, admonitory; *formal* castigatory.
– OPPOSITES approving.
reprobate ● noun *a hardened reprobate* ROGUE, rascal, scoundrel, miscreant, good-for-nothing, villain, wretch, rake, degenerate, debauchee, libertine; *informal, dated* rotter, bounder; *dated* blackguard, cad; *archaic* knave, rapscallion, scapegrace.
● adjective *reprobate behaviour* UNPRINCIPLED, roguish, bad, wicked, rakish, shameless, immoral, degenerate, dissipated, debauched, depraved; *archaic* knavish.
– OPPOSITES upright, virtuous.
● verb *(archaic) they reprobated his conduct* CRITICIZE, condemn, censure, denounce.
reproduce ● verb **1** *each artwork is reproduced in colour* COPY, duplicate, replicate; photocopy, xerox, photostat, print. **2** *this work has not been reproduced in other laboratories* REPEAT, replicate, recreate, redo; simulate, imitate, emulate, mirror, mimic. **3** *some animals reproduce prolifically* BREED, produce offspring, procreate, propagate, multiply.
reproduction ● noun **1** *colour reproduction* COPYING, duplication, duplicating; photocopying, xeroxing, photostatting, printing. **2** *a reproduction of the original* PRINT, copy, reprint, duplicate, facsimile, carbon copy, photocopy; *trademark* Xerox. **3** *the process of reproduction* BREEDING, procreation, multiplying, propagation.
reproductive ● adjective GENERATIVE, procreative, propagative; sexual, genital.
reproof ● noun REBUKE, reprimand, reproach, admonishment, admonition; disapproval, criticism, censure, condemnation; *informal* telling-off, dressing down; *Brit. informal* ticking-off; *dated* rating.
reprove ● verb REPRIMAND, rebuke, reproach, scold, admonish, chastise, chide, upbraid, berate, take to task, haul over the coals, criticize, censure; *informal* tell off, give someone a telling-off, give someone a talking-to, dress down, give someone a dressing-down, give someone an earful, give someone a roasting, rap over the knuckles, slap someone's wrist; *Brit. informal* tick off, carpet, tear off a strip, give someone a rocket, give someone a rollicking; *formal* castigate; *dated* give someone a rating; *rare* reprehend, objurgate.
reptilian ● adjective **1** *reptilian species* REPTILE, reptile-like, saurian; cold-blooded. **2** *a reptilian smirk* UNPLEASANT, distasteful,

r

– DERIVATIVES **repudiation** noun **repudiator** noun.
– ORIGIN from Latin *repudiatus* 'divorced, cast off', from *repudium* 'divorce'.
repugnance /ripugnənss/ ● noun intense disgust.
– DERIVATIVES **repugnancy** noun.
– ORIGIN originally in the sense 'opposition': from Latin *repugnare* 'oppose'.
repugnant ● adjective extremely distasteful; unacceptable.
repulse ● verb **1** drive back (an attacking enemy) by force. **2** rebuff or refuse to accept. **3** cause to feel intense distaste or disgust. ● noun the action or an instance of repulsing or being repulsed.
– ORIGIN from Latin *repellere*, from *pellere* 'to drive'.
repulsion ● noun **1** a feeling of intense distaste or disgust. **2** Physics a force under the influence of which objects tend to move away from each other, e.g. through having the same magnetic polarity or electric charge.
repulsive ● adjective **1** arousing intense distaste or disgust. **2** Physics of or relating to repulsion between physical objects.
– DERIVATIVES **repulsively** adverb **repulsiveness** noun.
repurchase ● verb buy back. ● noun the action of buying back.
reputable ● adjective having a good reputation.
– DERIVATIVES **reputably** adverb.
reputation ● noun **1** the beliefs or opinions that are generally held about someone or something. **2** a widespread belief that someone or something has a particular characteristic: *his reputation as a brainless lad.*
repute ● noun **1** the opinion generally held of someone or something. **2** the state of being highly regarded. ● verb **1** (**be reputed**) be generally regarded as having done something or as having particular characteristics. **2** (**reputed**) generally believed to exist: *the reputed flatness of the country.*
– DERIVATIVES **reputedly** adverb.
– ORIGIN from Latin *reputare* 'think over'.
request ● noun **1** an act of asking politely or formally for something. **2** a thing that is asked for in such a way. ● verb **1** politely or formally ask for. **2** politely or formally ask (someone) to do something.
– DERIVATIVES **requester** noun.
– ORIGIN from Latin *requirere* 'require'.
request stop ● noun Brit. a bus stop at which the bus halts only if requested by a passenger or if hailed.
requiem /rekwiəm/ ● noun **1** (especially in the Roman Catholic Church) a Mass for the repose of the souls of the dead. **2** a musical composition setting parts of such a Mass.
– ORIGIN Latin, from *requies* 'rest'.
require ● verb **1** need for a purpose; depend on. **2** wish to have. **3** instruct or expect (someone) to do something. **4** (**require of**) regard (an action or quality) as due from. **5** specify as compulsory: *the minimum required by law.*
– ORIGIN Latin *requirere*, from *quaerere* 'seek'.
requirement ● noun **1** something required; a need. **2** something specified as compulsory.
requisite /rekwizit/ ● adjective made necessary by particular circumstances or regulations. ● noun a thing that is necessary for the achievement of a specified end.
– ORIGIN Latin *requisitus* 'searched for, deemed necessary', from *requirere* 'require'.
requisition /rekwizish'n/ ● noun **1** an official order laying claim to the use of property or materials. **2** the appropriation

Thesaurus

nasty, disagreeable, unattractive, off-putting, horrible, horrid; unctuous, ingratiating, oily, oleaginous; *informal* smarmy, slimy, creepy.
repudiate ● verb **1** *she repudiated communism* REJECT, renounce, abandon, give up, turn one's back on, disown, cast off, lay aside; *formal* forswear, abjure; *poetic/literary* forsake. **2** *Cranham repudiated the allegations* DENY, refute, contradict, controvert, rebut, dispute, dismiss, brush aside; *formal* gainsay. **3** *Egypt repudiated the treaty* CANCEL, revoke, rescind, reverse, overrule, overturn, invalidate, nullify; disregard, flout, renege on; *Law* disaffirm; *formal* abrogate.
– OPPOSITES embrace, confirm.
repudiation ● noun **1** *the repudiation of one's religion* REJECTION, renunciation, abandonment, forswearing, giving up; *rare* abjuration. **2** *his repudiation of the allegations* DENIAL, refutation, rebuttal, rejection. **3** *a repudiation of the contract* CANCELLATION, revocation, rescindment, reversal, invalidation, nullification; *Law* disaffirmation; *formal* abrogation.
repugnance ● noun REVULSION, disgust, abhorrence, repulsion, loathing, hatred, detestation, aversion, distaste, antipathy, contempt; *archaic* disrelish.
repugnant ● adjective **1** *the idea of cannibalism is repugnant* ABHORRENT, revolting, repulsive, repellent, disgusting, offensive, objectionable, vile, foul, nasty, loathsome, sickening, nauseating, hateful, detestable, execrable, abominable, monstrous, appalling, insufferable, intolerable, unacceptable, contemptible, unsavoury, unpalatable; *informal* ghastly, horrible, horrid, gross; *poetic/literary* noisome. **2** (*formal*) *the restriction is repugnant to the tenancy* INCOMPATIBLE WITH, in conflict with, contrary to, at variance with, inconsistent with.
– OPPOSITES pleasant.
repulse ● verb **1** *the rebels were repulsed* REPEL, drive back/away, fight back/off, put to flight, force back, beat off/back; ward off, hold off; *Brit.* see off; *archaic* rebut. **2** *her advances repulsed* REBUFF, reject, spurn, snub, cold-shoulder; *informal* give someone the brush-off, freeze out; *Brit. informal* knock back; *N. Amer. informal* give someone the bum's rush. **3** *his bid for the company was repulsed* REJECT, turn down, refuse, decline. **4** *the brutality repulsed her* REVOLT, disgust, repel, sicken, nauseate, turn someone's stomach, be repugnant to; *informal* turn off; *N. Amer. informal* gross out.
● noun **1** *the repulse of the attack* REPELLING, driving back; warding off, holding off. **2** *he was mortified by this repulse* REBUFF, rejection, snub, slight; *informal* brush-off, knock-back.
repulsion ● noun DISGUST, revulsion, abhorrence, repugnance, nausea, horror, aversion, abomination, distaste; *archaic* disrelish.
repulsive ● adjective REVOLTING, disgusting, abhorrent, repellent, repugnant, offensive, objectionable, vile, foul, nasty, loathsome, sickening, nauseating, hateful, detestable, execrable, abominable, monstrous, noxious, horrendous, awful, terrible, dreadful, frightful, obnoxious, unsavoury, unpleasant, disagreeable, distasteful; ugly, hideous, grotesque; *informal* ghastly, horrible, horrid, gross; *poetic/literary* noisome; *archaic* disgustful, loathly.
– OPPOSITES attractive.
reputable ● adjective WELL THOUGHT OF, highly regarded, (well) respected, respectable, of (good) repute, prestigious, established; reliable, dependable, trustworthy; *archaic* of good report.
– OPPOSITES untrustworthy.
reputation ● noun (GOOD) NAME, character, repute, standing, stature, status, position, renown, esteem, prestige; *N. Amer. informal* rep, rap; *archaic* honour, report.
repute ● noun **1** *a woman of ill repute* REPUTATION, name, character; *archaic* report. **2** *a firm of international repute* FAME, renown, celebrity, distinction, high standing, stature, prestige.
reputed ● adjective **1** *they are reputed to be very rich* THOUGHT, said, reported, rumoured, believed, held, considered, regarded, deemed, alleged. **2** *his reputed father* SUPPOSED, putative. **3** *a reputed naturalist* WELL THOUGHT OF, (well) respected, highly regarded, of good repute.
reputedly ● adverb SUPPOSEDLY, by all accounts, so I'm told, so people say, allegedly.
request ● noun **1** *requests for assistance* APPEAL, entreaty, plea, petition, application, demand, call; *formal* adjuration; *poetic/literary* behest. **2** *Charlotte spoke, at Ursula's request* BIDDING, entreaty, demand, insistence. **3** *indicate your requests on the form* REQUIREMENT, wish, desire; choice.
● verb **1** *the government requested military aid* ASK FOR, appeal for, call for, seek, solicit, plead for, apply for, demand; *formal* adjure. **2** *I requested him to help* CALL ON, beg, entreat, implore; *poetic/literary* beseech.
require ● verb **1** *the child required hospital treatment* NEED, be in need of. **2** *a situation requiring patience* NECESSITATE, demand, call for, involve, entail. **3** *unquestioning obedience is required* DEMAND, insist on, call for, ask for, expect. **4** *she was required to pay costs* ORDER, instruct, command, enjoin, oblige, compel, force. **5** *do you require anything else?* WANT, wish to have, desire; lack, be short of.
required ● adjective **1** *required reading* ESSENTIAL, vital, indispensable, necessary, compulsory, obligatory, mandatory, prescribed. **2** *cut it to the required length* DESIRED, preferred, chosen; correct, proper, right.
– OPPOSITES optional.
requirement ● noun NEED, wish, demand, want, necessity, essential, prerequisite, stipulation.
requisite ● adjective *he lacks the requisite skills* NECESSARY, required, prerequisite, essential, indispensable, vital.
– OPPOSITES optional.

of goods for military or public use. **3** a formal written demand that something should be performed or put into operation. ● **verb** demand the use, supply, or performance of through the issue of a requisition.

requite /rikwit/ ● **verb** formal **1** make appropriate return for. **2** return a favour to (someone).
– DERIVATIVES **requital** noun.
– ORIGIN from RE- + obsolete *quite* 'behave' (see QUIT).

reran past of RERUN.

reread ● **verb** (past and past part. **reread**) read (a text) again. ● **noun** an act of rereading.

reredos /reerdoss/ ● **noun** (pl. same) an ornamental screen at the back of an altar in a church.
– ORIGIN Old French *areredos*, from *arere* 'behind' + *dos* 'back'.

re-release ● **verb** release (a recording or film) again. ● **noun** a re-released recording or film.

re-route ● **verb** send by or along a different route.

rerun ● **verb** (**rerunning**; past **reran**; past part. **rerun**) show, stage, or perform again. ● **noun** a rerun event, competition, or programme.

resale ● **noun** the sale of a thing previously bought.
– DERIVATIVES **resaleable** (also **resalable**) adjective.

resat past and past participle of RESIT.

reschedule ● **verb** **1** change the time of (a planned event). **2** arrange a new scheme of repayments of (a debt).

rescind /risind/ ● **verb** revoke, cancel, or repeal (a law, order, or agreement).
– DERIVATIVES **rescindable** adjective.
– ORIGIN Latin *rescindere*, from *scindere* 'to divide, split'.

rescission /risizh'n/ ● **noun** formal the rescinding of a law, order, or agreement.

rescue ● **verb** (**rescues**, **rescued**, **rescuing**) save from a dangerous or distressing situation. ● **noun** an act of rescuing or being rescued.
– DERIVATIVES **rescuable** adjective **rescuer** noun.
– ORIGIN Old French *rescoure*, from Latin *excutere* 'shake out, discard'.

reseal ● **verb** seal again.
– DERIVATIVES **resealable** adjective.

research /riserch/ ● **noun** the systematic study of materials and sources in order to establish facts and reach new conclusions. ● **verb** **1** carry out research into. **2** use research to discover or verify information to be presented in (a book, programme, etc.).
– DERIVATIVES **researcher** noun.
– ORIGIN obsolete French *recercher*, from *cerchier* 'to search'.

research and development ● **noun** (in industry) work directed towards innovation in and improvement of products and processes.

reselect ● **verb** select again or differently.
– DERIVATIVES **reselection** noun.

resell ● **verb** (past and past part. **resold**) sell (something one has bought) to someone else.
– DERIVATIVES **reseller** noun.

resemblance ● **noun** **1** the state of resembling. **2** a way in which things resemble each other.

resemble ● **verb** have a similar appearance to or features in common with.
– ORIGIN Old French *resembler*, from Latin *similare*, from *similis* 'like'.

resent ● **verb** feel bitterness or indignation towards.
– ORIGIN originally in the sense 'experience (an emotion or sensation)': from obsolete French *resentir*, from *sentir* 'feel'.

resentful ● **adjective** feeling or expressing bitterness or indignation.
– DERIVATIVES **resentfully** adverb **resentfulness** noun.

resentment ● **noun** bitterness; indignation.

reservation ● **noun** **1** the action of reserving. **2** an arrangement whereby something is reserved. **3** an area of land set aside for occupation by North American Indians or Australian Aboriginals. **4** a qualification or expression of doubt attached to a statement or claim.

reserve ● **verb** **1** keep for future use. **2** arrange for (a seat, ticket, etc.) to be kept for the use of a particular person. **3** retain or hold (a right or entitlement). **4** refrain from delivering (a judgement or decision) without due consideration or evidence. ● **noun** **1** a supply of a commodity available for use if required. **2** funds kept available by a bank, company, or government. **3** a force or body of troops withheld from action to reinforce or protect others, or additional to the regular forces and available in an emergency. **4** an extra player in a team, serving as a possible substitute. **5** (**the reserves**) the second-choice team. **6** an area of land set aside for occupation by a native people. **7** a protected area for wildlife. **8** a lack of warmth or openness. **9** qualification or doubt attached to a statement or claim.

Thesaurus

● **noun** **1** *toilet requisites* REQUIREMENT, need, necessity, essential. **2** *a requisite for a successful career* NECESSITY, essential (requirement), prerequisite, precondition, sine qua non; *informal* must.

requisition ● **noun** **1** *requisitions for staff* ORDER, request, call, application, claim, demand; *Brit.* indent. **2** *the requisition of cultural treasures* APPROPRIATION, commandeering, seizure, confiscation, expropriation.
● **verb** **1** *the house was requisitioned by the army* COMMANDEER, appropriate, take over, take possession of, occupy, seize, confiscate, expropriate. **2** *she requisitioned statements* REQUEST, order, call for, demand.

requital ● **noun** **1** *in requital of your kindness* REPAYMENT, return, payment, recompense. **2** *personal requital* REVENGE, vengeance, retribution, redress.

requite ● **verb** **1** *requiting their hospitality* RETURN, reciprocate, repay. **2** *Drake had requited the wrongs inflicted on them* AVENGE, exact revenge for, revenge, pay someone back for; take reprisals, settle the score, get even. **3** *she did not requite his love* RECIPROCATE, return.

rescind ● **verb** REVOKE, repeal, cancel, reverse, overturn, overrule, annul, nullify, void, invalidate, quash, abolish; *Law* vacate; *formal* abrogate; *archaic* recall.
– OPPOSITES enforce.

rescission ● **noun** *(formal)* REVOCATION, repeal, rescindment, annulment, nullification, invalidation, voiding; *formal* abrogation; *archaic* recall.

rescue ● **verb** **1** *an attempt to rescue the hostages* SAVE (FROM DANGER), save the life of, come to the aid of; (set) free, release, liberate. **2** *Boyd rescued his papers* RETRIEVE, recover, salvage, get back.
● **noun** *the rescue of 10 crewmen* SAVING, rescuing; release, freeing, liberation, deliverance, redemption.
– PHRASES **come to someone's rescue** HELP, assist, lend a (helping) hand to, bail out; *informal* save someone's bacon, save someone's neck, save someone's skin.

research ● **noun** **1** *medical research* INVESTIGATION, experimentation, testing, analysis, fact-finding, examination, scrutiny, scrutinization. **2** *he continued his researches* EXPERIMENTS, experimentation, tests, inquiries, studies.
● **verb** **1** *the phenomenon has been widely researched* INVESTIGATE, study, inquire into, look into, probe, explore, analyse, examine, scrutinize, review. **2** *I researched all the available material* STUDY, read (up on), sift through; *informal* check out.

resemblance ● **noun** SIMILARITY, likeness, similitude, correspondence, congruity, congruence, coincidence, conformity, agreement, equivalence, comparability, parallelism, sameness, uniformity.

resemble ● **verb** LOOK LIKE, be similar to, be like, bear a resemblance to, remind one of, take after, favour, have the look of; approximate to, smack of, have (all) the hallmarks of, correspond to, echo, mirror, parallel.

resent ● **verb** BEGRUDGE, feel aggrieved at/about, feel bitter about, grudge, be annoyed at/about, be resentful of, dislike, take exception to, object to, take amiss, take offence at, take umbrage at, bear/harbour a grudge about.
– OPPOSITES welcome.

resentful ● **adjective** AGGRIEVED, indignant, irritated, piqued, put out, in high dudgeon, dissatisfied, disgruntled, discontented, offended, bitter, jaundiced; envious, jealous; *informal* miffed, peeved; *Brit. informal* narked; *N. Amer. informal* sore.

resentment ● **noun** BITTERNESS, indignation, irritation, pique, dissatisfaction, disgruntlement, discontentment, discontent, resentfulness, bad feelings, hard feelings, ill will, acrimony, rancour, animosity, jaundice; envy, jealousy.

reservation ● **noun** **1** *grave reservations* DOUBT, qualm, scruple; misgivings, scepticism, unease, hesitation, objection. **2** *group reservations* (ADVANCE) BOOKING; *dated* engagement. **3** *the reservation of the room* BOOKING, ordering, securing; *dated* engagement. **4** *Indian reservation* RESERVE, enclave, sanctuary, territory, homeland.
– PHRASES **without reservation** WHOLEHEARTEDLY, unreservedly,

r

– DERIVATIVES **reservable** adjective.
– ORIGIN Latin *reservare* 'keep back'.
re-serve ● verb serve again.
reserve bank ● noun **1** (in the US) a regional bank operating under and implementing the policies of the Federal Reserve. **2** Austral./NZ a central bank.
reserve currency ● noun a strong currency widely used in international trade that a central bank is prepared to hold as part of its foreign exchange reserves.
reserved ● adjective slow to reveal emotion or opinions.
– DERIVATIVES **reservedly** adverb **reservedness** noun.
reserved occupation ● noun Brit. an occupation from which a person will not be taken for military service.
reserve price ● noun the price stipulated as the lowest acceptable by the seller for an item sold at auction.
reservist ● noun a member of a military reserve force.
reservoir ● noun **1** a large natural or artificial lake used as a source of water supply. **2** a place where fluid collects, especially in rock strata or in the body. **3** a receptacle or part of a machine designed to hold fluid. **4** a supply or source of something.
– ORIGIN French, from *réserver* 'to reserve, keep'.
reset ● verb (**resetting**; past and past part. **reset**) **1** set again or differently. **2** set (a counter, clock, etc.) to zero.
– DERIVATIVES **resettable** adjective.
resettle ● verb settle or cause to settle in a different place.
– DERIVATIVES **resettlement** noun.
reshape ● verb shape or form differently or again.
reshuffle ● verb **1** interchange the positions of (members of a team, especially government ministers). **2** rearrange. ● noun an act of reshuffling.
reside ● verb **1** have one's permanent home in a particular place. **2** (of a right or legal power) belong to a person or body. **3** (of a quality) be present or inherent in something.
residence ● noun **1** the fact of residing somewhere. **2** formal the place where a person resides; a person's home. **3** the official house of a government minister or other official figure.
– PHRASES **artist** (or **writer**) **in residence** an artist or writer who is based for a set period within a college or other institution and is available for teaching purposes.
residency ● noun (pl. **residencies**) **1** the fact of living in a place. **2** a residential post held by an artist or writer. **3** Brit. a musician's regular engagement at a club or other venue. **4** N. Amer. a period of specialized medical training in a hospital; the position of a resident. **5** a group or organization of intelligence agents in a foreign country. **6** historical the official residence of a British government agent in a semi-independent state.
resident ● noun **1** a person who lives somewhere on a long-term basis. **2** Brit. a guest in a hotel who stays for one or more nights. **3** US a pupil who boards at a boarding school. **4** N. Amer. a medical graduate engaged in specialized practice under supervision in a hospital. **5** an intelligence agent in a foreign country. **6** historical a British Governor General's representative at the court of an Indian state. **7** a bird, butterfly, or other animal of a species that does not migrate. ● adjective **1** living somewhere on a long-term basis. **2** having living quarters on the premises of one's work. **3** attached to and working regularly for a particular institution. **4** (of a bird, butterfly or other animal) non-migratory.
– ORIGIN from Latin *residere* 'remain'.
residential ● adjective **1** designed for or relating to residence. **2** providing accommodation in addition to other services. **3** occupied by private houses.
– DERIVATIVES **residentially** adverb.
residua plural of RESIDUUM.
residual ● adjective remaining after the greater part or quantity has gone or been subtracted. ● noun **1** a residual quantity. **2** a royalty paid to a performer or writer for a repeat of a play, television show, or advertisement. **3** the resale value of a new car or other item at a specified time after purchase.
– DERIVATIVES **residually** adverb.
residue /rezzidyo͞o/ ● noun **1** a small amount of something that remains after the main part has gone or been taken or used. **2** Law the part of an estate that is left after the payment of charges, debts, and bequests. **3** a substance that remains after a process such as combustion or evaporation.
– ORIGIN Latin *residuum*, from *residere* 'remain'.
residuum /rizidyooəm/ ● noun (pl. **residua** /rizidyooə/) technical a chemical residue.
– ORIGIN Latin.
resign ● verb **1** voluntarily leave a job or position of office. **2** (**be resigned**) accept that something undesirable cannot be avoided.
– ORIGIN Latin *resignare* 'unseal, cancel'.
re-sign ● verb sign (a document or contract) again.
resignation ● noun **1** an act of resigning. **2** a document conveying an intention to resign. **3** acceptance of something undesirable but inevitable.
resilient ● adjective **1** able to recoil or spring back into shape

Thesaurus

without qualification, fully, completely, totally, entirely, wholly, unconditionally.
reserve ● verb **1** *ask your newsagent to reserve you a copy* PUT TO ONE SIDE, put aside, set aside, keep (back), save, hold back, keep in reserve, earmark. **2** *he reserved a table* BOOK, make a reservation for, order, arrange for, secure; *formal* bespeak; *dated* engage. **3** *the management reserves the right to alter the programme* RETAIN, keep, hold. **4** *reserve your judgement until you know him better* DEFER, postpone, put off, delay, withhold.
● noun **1** *reserves of petrol* STOCK, store, supply, stockpile, pool, hoard, cache. **2** *the army are calling up reserves* REINFORCEMENTS, extras, auxiliaries. **3** *a nature reserve* NATIONAL PARK, sanctuary, preserve, conservation area. **4** *his natural reserve* RETICENCE, detachment, distance, remoteness, coolness, aloofness, constraint, formality; shyness, diffidence, timidity, taciturnity, inhibition; *informal* stand-offishness. **5** *she trusted him without reserve* RESERVATION, qualification, condition, limitation, hesitation, doubt.
● adjective *a reserve goalkeeper* SUBSTITUTE, stand-in, relief, replacement, fallback, spare, extra.
– PHRASES **in reserve** AVAILABLE, to/on hand, ready, in readiness, set aside, at one's disposal.
reserved ● adjective **1** *Sewell is rather reserved* RETICENT, quiet, private, uncommunicative, unforthcoming, undemonstrative, unsociable, formal, constrained, cool, aloof, detached, distant, remote, unapproachable, unfriendly, withdrawn, secretive, silent, taciturn; shy, retiring, diffident, timid, self-effacing, inhibited, introverted; *informal* stand-offish. **2** *that table is reserved* BOOKED, taken, spoken for, pre-arranged; *dated* engaged; *formal* bespoken.
– OPPOSITES outgoing.
reservoir ● noun **1** *sailing on the reservoir* lake, pool, pond; water supply; *Scottish* loch. **2** *an ink reservoir* RECEPTACLE, container, holder, repository, tank. **3** *the reservoir of managerial talent* STOCK, store, stockpile, reserve(s), supply, bank, pool, fund.
reshuffle ● verb *the prime minister reshuffled his cabinet* REORGANIZE, restructure, change (around), shake up, rearrange, shuffle.
● noun *a management reshuffle* REORGANIZATION, restructuring, change, rearrangement; *informal* shake-up.
reside ● verb **1** *most students reside in flats* LIVE IN, occupy, inhabit, stay in, lodge in; *formal* dwell in, be domiciled in. **2** *the paintings reside in an air-conditioned vault* BE SITUATED, be found, be located, lie. **3** *executive power resides in the president* BE VESTED IN, be bestowed on, be conferred on, be in the hands of. **4** *the qualities that reside within each individual* BE INHERENT, be present, exist.
residence ● noun **1** *(formal) her private residence* HOME, house, place of residence, address; quarters, lodgings; *informal* pad; *formal* dwelling (place), domicile, abode. **2** *his place of residence* OCCUPANCY, habitation, residency; *formal* abode.
resident ● noun **1** *the residents of New York City* INHABITANT, local, citizen, native; householder, homeowner, occupier, tenant; *formal* denizen. **2** *(Brit.) the bar is open to residents only* GUEST, lodger.
● adjective **1** *resident in the UK* LIVING, residing, in residence; *formal* dwelling. **2** *a resident nanny* LIVE-IN, living in. **3** *the resident registrar in obstetrics* PERMANENT, incumbent.
residential ● adjective SUBURBAN, commuter, dormitory.
residual ● adjective **1** *residual heat* REMAINING, leftover, unused, unconsumed. **2** *residual affection* LINGERING, enduring, abiding, surviving, vestigial.
residue ● noun REMAINDER, remaining part, rest, remnant(s); surplus, extra, excess; remains, leftovers; *technical* residuum.
resign ● verb **1** *the senior manager resigned* LEAVE, hand in one's notice, give notice, stand down, step down; *informal* quit. **2** *19 MPs resigned their seats* GIVE UP, leave, vacate, stand down from; *informal* quit, pack in; *archaic* demit. **3** *he resigned his right to the title* RENOUNCE, relinquish, give up, abandon, surrender, forego, cede; *Law* disclaim; *poetic/literary* forsake. **4** *we resigned ourselves to a long wait* RECONCILE ONESELF TO, become resigned to, come to terms

r

after bending, stretching, or being compressed. **2** (of a person) able to withstand or recover quickly from difficult conditions.
– DERIVATIVES **resilience** noun **resiliently** adverb.
– ORIGIN from Latin *resilire* 'leap back'.
resin /rezzin/ • noun **1** a sticky substance exuded by some trees. **2** a synthetic polymer used as the basis of plastics, adhesives, varnishes, etc. • verb (**resined**, **resining**) rub or treat with resin.
– DERIVATIVES **resinous** adjective.
– ORIGIN Latin *resina*; related to Greek *rhētinē* 'pine resin'.
resinate • verb impregnate or flavour with resin.
– DERIVATIVES **resinated** adjective.
resist • verb **1** withstand the action or effect of. **2** try to prevent by action or argument. **3** refrain from (something tempting). **4** struggle against someone or something. • noun a resistant substance used to protect parts of a surface during the application of dye, glaze, etc.
– DERIVATIVES **resister** noun **resistible** adjective.
– ORIGIN Latin *resistere*, from *sistere* 'stop'.
resistance • noun **1** the action of resisting. **2** (also **resistance movement**) a secret organization resisting political authority. **3** the impeding effect exerted by one material thing on another. **4** the ability not to be affected by something. **5** lack of sensitivity to a drug, insecticide, etc., especially as a result of continued exposure or genetic change. **6** the degree to which a material or device opposes the passage of an electric current.
– PHRASES **the line** (or **path**) **of least resistance** the easiest course of action.
– DERIVATIVES **resistant** adjective.
resistive • adjective **1** technical able to resist something. **2** Physics of or concerning electrical resistance.
– DERIVATIVES **resistivity** noun.
resistor • noun Physics a device having resistance to the passage of an electric current.
resit Brit. • verb (**resitting**; past and past part. **resat**) take (an examination) again after failing. • noun an examination held for this purpose.
resize • verb alter the size of (something, especially a computer window or image).
reskill • verb teach or equip with new skills.
resold past and past participle of RESELL.
re-soluble • adjective able to dissolve or be dissolved again.
resolute /rezzəloot/ • adjective determined; unwavering.
– DERIVATIVES **resolutely** adverb **resoluteness** noun.
– ORIGIN originally in the sense 'paid', describing a rent: from Latin *resolutus* 'loosened, released, paid'.
resolution • noun **1** a firm decision. **2** an expression of opinion or intention agreed on by a legislative body. **3** the quality of being resolute. **4** the resolving of a problem or dispute. **5** the process of reducing or separating something into components. **6** the smallest interval measurable by a telescope or other scientific instrument. **7** the degree of detail visible in a photographic or television image.
resolve • verb **1** settle or find a solution to. **2** decide firmly on a course of action. **3** (of a legislative body) take a decision by a formal vote. **4** (**resolve into**) reduce into (separate elements or a more elementary form). **5** (of something seen at a distance) turn into a different form when seen more clearly. **6** (of optical or photographic equipment) separate or distinguish between (closely adjacent objects). • noun **1** firm determination. **2** US a formal resolution by a legislative body or public meeting.
– DERIVATIVES **resolvable** adjective **resolver** noun.
– ORIGIN Latin *resolvere*, from *solvere* 'loosen'.
resolving power • noun the ability of an optical instrument or type of film to separate or distinguish small or closely adjacent images.
resonance • noun **1** the quality of being resonant. **2** Physics the reinforcement or prolongation of sound by reflection or synchronous vibration.
resonant • adjective **1** (of sound) deep, clear, and continuing to sound or ring. **2** (of a room, musical instrument, or hollow body) tending to reinforce or prolong sounds. **3** (**resonant with**) filled or resounding with. **4** suggesting images, memories, or emotions.
– DERIVATIVES **resonantly** adverb.
– ORIGIN from Latin *resonare* 'sound again, resound'.
resonate • verb **1** be resonant. **2** chiefly US (of an idea or action) meet with someone's agreement.
– DERIVATIVES **resonator** noun.
resorb /risorb/ • verb **1** absorb again. **2** Physiology remove (cells, tissue, etc.) by gradual breakdown and dispersal in the circulation.

Thesaurus

with.
resignation • noun **1** *his resignation from his post* DEPARTURE, leaving, standing down, stepping down; *informal* quitting. **2** *she handed in her resignation* NOTICE (TO QUIT), letter of resignation. **3** *he accepted his fate with resignation* PATIENCE, forbearance, stoicism, fortitude, fatalism, acceptance, acquiescence, compliance, passivity.
resigned • adjective PATIENT, long-suffering, uncomplaining, forbearing, stoical, philosophical, fatalistic, acquiescent, compliant, passive.
resilient • adjective **1** *resilient materials* FLEXIBLE, pliable, supple; durable, hard-wearing, stout, strong, sturdy, tough. **2** *young and resilient* STRONG, tough, hardy; quick to recover, buoyant, irrepressible.
resist • verb **1** *built to resist cold winters* WITHSTAND, be proof against, combat, weather, endure, be resistant to, keep out. **2** *they resisted his attempts to change things* OPPOSE, fight against, refuse to accept, object to, defy, set one's face against, kick against; obstruct, impede, hinder, block, thwart, frustrate; *informal* be anti. **3** *I resisted the urge to retort* REFRAIN FROM, abstain from, forbear from, desist from, not give in to, restrain oneself from, stop oneself from. **4** *she tried to resist him* STRUGGLE WITH/AGAINST, fight (against), stand up to, withstand, hold off; fend off, ward off.
– OPPOSITES welcome, submit.
– PHRASES **cannot resist** LOVE, adore, relish, have a weakness for, be very keen on, like, delight in, enjoy, take great pleasure in; *informal* be mad about, get a kick/thrill out of.
resistance • noun **1** *resistance to change* OPPOSITION, hostility, refusal to accept. **2** *a spirited resistance* OPPOSITION, fight, stand, struggle. **3** *the body's resistance to disease* ABILITY TO FIGHT OFF, immunity from, defences against. **4** *the French resistance* RESISTANCE MOVEMENT, freedom fighters, underground, partisans.
resistant • adjective **1** *resistant to water* IMPERVIOUS, unsusceptible, immune, invulnerable, proof against, unaffected by. **2** *resistant to change* OPPOSED, averse, hostile, inimical, against; *informal* anti.
resolute • adjective DETERMINED, purposeful, resolved, adamant, single-minded, firm, unswerving, unwavering, steadfast, staunch, stalwart, unfaltering, unhesitating, persistent, indefatigable, tenacious, strong-willed, unshakeable; stubborn, dogged, obstinate, obdurate, inflexible, intransigent, implacable, unyielding, unrelenting; spirited, brave, bold, courageous, plucky, indomitable; *N. Amer.* rock-ribbed; *informal* gutsy, spunky; *formal* pertinacious.
– OPPOSITES half-hearted.
resolution • noun **1** *her resolution not to smoke* INTENTION, resolve, decision, intent, aim, plan; commitment, pledge, promise. **2** *the committee passed the resolution* MOTION, proposal, proposition; *N. Amer.* resolve. **3** *she handled the work with resolution* DETERMINATION, purpose, purposefulness, resolve, resoluteness, single-mindedness, firmness (of purpose); steadfastness, staunchness, perseverance, persistence, indefatigability, tenacity, tenaciousness, staying power, dedication, commitment; stubbornness, doggedness, obstinacy, obduracy; spiritedness, braveness, bravery, boldness, courage, pluck, grit, courageousness; *informal* guts, spunk; *formal* pertinacity. **4** *a satisfactory resolution of the problem* SOLUTION, answer, end, ending, settlement, conclusion.
resolve • verb **1** *this matter cannot be resolved overnight* SETTLE, sort out, solve, find a solution to, fix, straighten out, deal with, put right, put to rights, rectify; *informal* hammer out, thrash out, figure out. **2** *Charity resolved not to wait any longer* DETERMINE, decide, make up one's mind, take a decision. **3** *the committee resolved that the project should proceed* VOTE, pass a resolution, rule, decide formally, agree. **4** *the compounds were resolved into their active constituents* BREAK DOWN/UP, separate, reduce, divide. **5** *the ability to resolve facts into their legal categories* ANALYSE, dissect, break down. **6** *the grey smudge resolved into a sandy beach* TURN, change, be transformed.
• noun **1** *their intimidation merely strengthened his resolve.* See RESOLUTION sense 3. **2** *(N. Amer.) he made a resolve not to go there again* DECISION, resolution, commitment.
resolved • adjective DETERMINED, hell bent, intent, set.
resonant • adjective **1** *a resonant voice* DEEP, low, sonorous, full, full-bodied, vibrant, rich, clear, ringing; loud, booming, thunder-

– ORIGIN Latin *resorbere*.
resorption /rizorpsh'n/ ● noun the process or action of resorbing or being resorbed.
– DERIVATIVES **resorptive** adjective.
resort ● verb (**resort to**) turn to and adopt (a strategy or course of action) so as to resolve a difficult situation. ● noun **1** a place frequented for holidays or recreation. **2** the action of resorting to something. **3** a strategy or course of action.
– PHRASES **as a first** (or **last** or **final**) **resort** before anything else is attempted (or when all else has failed).
– ORIGIN Old French *resortir* 'come or go out again'.
resound /rizownd/ ● verb **1** fill or be filled with a ringing, booming, or echoing sound. **2** (of fame, success, etc.) be much talked of. **3** (**resounding**) emphatic; unmistakable: *a resounding success.*
resource /risorss, -zorss/ ● noun **1** (**resources**) a stock or supply of materials or assets that can be drawn on in order to function effectively. **2** (**resources**) a country's collective means of supporting itself or becoming wealthier, as represented by its minerals, land, and other assets. **3** (**resources**) personal attributes and capabilities that sustain one in adverse circumstances. **4** an action or thing resorted to. ● verb provide with resources.
– ORIGIN from Old French dialect *resourdre* 'rise again, recover'.
resourceful ● adjective able to find quick and clever ways to overcome difficulties.
– DERIVATIVES **resourcefully** adverb **resourcefulness** noun.
respect ● noun **1** a feeling of admiration for someone because of their qualities or achievements. **2** due regard for the feelings or rights of others. **3** (**respects**) polite greetings. **4** a particular aspect, point, or detail. ● verb **1** feel or have respect for. **2** avoid harming or interfering with. **3** agree to recognize and abide by.
– PHRASES **in respect of** (or **with respect to**) as regards; with reference to.
– DERIVATIVES **respecter** noun.
– ORIGIN Latin *respectus*, from *respicere* 'look back at, regard'.
respectable ● adjective **1** regarded by society as being proper, correct, and good. **2** of some merit or importance. **3** adequate or acceptable in number, size, or amount.
– DERIVATIVES **respectability** noun **respectably** adverb.
respectful ● adjective feeling or showing deference and respect.
– DERIVATIVES **respectfully** adverb **respectfulness** noun.
respecting ● preposition with reference or regard to.
respective ● adjective belonging or relating separately to each of two or more people or things.
respectively ● adverb separately or individually and in the order already mentioned.
respell ● verb (past and past part. **respelled** or chiefly Brit. **respelt**) spell (a word) differently, especially in order to indicate its pronunciation.
respirate /respirayt/ ● verb Medicine & Biology assist to breathe by means of artificial respiration.
respiration ● noun **1** the action of breathing. **2** a single breath. **3** Biology a process in living organisms involving the production of energy, typically with the intake of oxygen and the release of carbon dioxide from the oxidation of complex organic substances.
respirator ● noun **1** an apparatus worn over the face to prevent the inhalation of dust, smoke, or other harmful substances. **2** an apparatus used to induce artificial respiration.
respiratory /rispirrətri/ ● adjective relating to respiration or the organs of respiration.
respiratory tract ● noun the passage formed by the mouth, nose, throat, and lungs, through which air passes during breathing.
respire ● verb **1** breathe. **2** (of a plant) carry out respiration.
– DERIVATIVES **respirable** adjective.
– ORIGIN Latin *respirare* 'breathe out'.
respite /respīt, rispīt/ ● noun a short period of rest or relief from something difficult or unpleasant.
– ORIGIN Old French *respit*, from Latin *respectus* 'refuge, consideration'.
respite care ● noun temporary care of a sick, elderly, or disabled person, providing relief for their usual carer.
resplendent /risplendənt/ ● adjective attractive and impressive through being richly colourful or sumptuous.
– DERIVATIVES **resplendence** noun **resplendency** noun **resplendently** adverb.
– ORIGIN Latin, from *resplendere* 'shine out'.
respond ● verb say or do something in reply or as a reaction.
– DERIVATIVES **responder** noun.
– ORIGIN Latin *respondere* 'answer, offer in return'.

Thesaurus

ous. **2** *valleys resonant with the sound of church bells* REVERBERATING, reverberant, resounding, echoing, filled. **3** *resonant words* EVOCATIVE, suggestive, expressive, redolent.
resort ● noun **1** *a seaside resort* HOLIDAY DESTINATION, (tourist) centre; *informal* honeypot. **2** *settle the matter without resort to legal proceedings* RECOURSE TO, turning to, the use of, utilizing. **3** *strike action is our last resort* EXPEDIENT, measure, step, recourse, alternative, option, choice, possibility, hope.
– PHRASES **in the last resort** ULTIMATELY, in the end, at the end of the day, in the long run, when all is said and done. **resort to** HAVE RECOURSE TO, fall back on, turn to, make use of, use, employ, avail oneself of; stoop to, descend to, sink to.
resound ● verb **1** *the explosion resounded round the silent street* ECHO, re-echo, reverberate, ring out, boom, thunder, rumble. **2** *resounding with the clang of hammers* REVERBERATE, echo, re-echo, resonate, ring. **3** *nothing will resound like their earlier achievements* BE ACCLAIMED, be celebrated, be renowned, be famed, be glorified, be trumpeted.
resounding ● adjective **1** *a resounding voice* REVERBERANT, reverberating, resonant, resonating, echoing, ringing, sonorous, deep, rich, clear; loud, booming. **2** *a resounding success* ENORMOUS, huge, very great, tremendous, terrific, colossal; emphatic, decisive, conclusive, outstanding, remarkable, phenomenal.
resource ● noun **1** *use your resources efficiently* ASSETS, funds, wealth, money, capital; staff; supplies, materials, store(s), stock(s), reserve(s). **2** *your tutor is there as a resource* FACILITY, amenity, aid, help, support. **3** *tears were her only resource* EXPEDIENT, resort, course, scheme, stratagem; trick, ruse, device. **4** *a person of resource* INITIATIVE, resourcefulness, enterprise, ingenuity, inventiveness; talent, ability, capability; *informal* gumption.
resourceful ● adjective INGENIOUS, enterprising, inventive, creative; clever, talented, able, capable.
respect ● noun **1** *the respect due to a great artist* ESTEEM, regard, high opinion, admiration, reverence, deference, honour. **2** *he spoke to her with respect* DUE REGARD, politeness, courtesy, civility, deference. **3** *paying one's respects* (KIND) REGARDS, compliments, greetings, best/good wishes, felicitations, salutations; *archaic* remembrances. **4** *the report was accurate in every respect* ASPECT, regard, facet, feature, way, sense, particular, point, detail.
– OPPOSITES contempt.
● verb **1** *he is highly respected for his industry* ESTEEM, admire, think highly of, have a high opinion of, hold in high regard, hold in (high) esteem, look up to, revere, reverence, honour. **2** *they respected our privacy* SHOW CONSIDERATION FOR, have regard for, observe, be mindful of, be heedful of; *formal* take cognizance of. **3** *father respected her wishes* ABIDE BY, comply with, follow, adhere to, conform to, act in accordance with, defer to, obey, observe, keep (to).
– OPPOSITES despise, disobey.
– PHRASES **with respect to/in respect of** CONCERNING, regarding, in/with regard to, with reference to, respecting, re, about, apropos, on the subject of, in connection with, vis-à-vis.
respectable ● adjective **1** *a respectable middle-class background* REPUTABLE, of good repute, upright, honest, honourable, trustworthy, decent, good, well bred, clean-living. **2** *a respectable salary* FAIRLY GOOD, decent, fair, reasonable, moderately good; substantial, considerable, sizable.
– OPPOSITES disreputable, paltry.
respectful ● adjective DEFERENTIAL, reverent, reverential, dutiful; polite, well mannered, civil, courteous, gracious.
– OPPOSITES rude.
respective ● adjective SEPARATE, personal, own, particular, individual, specific, special, appropriate, different, various.
respite ● noun **1** *a brief respite* REST, break, breathing space, interval, intermission, interlude, recess, lull, pause, time out; relief, relaxation, repose; *informal* breather, let-up. **2** *respite from debts* POSTPONEMENT, deferment, delay, reprieve; *US Law* continuance.
resplendent ● adjective SPLENDID, magnificent, brilliant, dazzling, glittering, gorgeous, impressive, imposing, spectacular, striking, stunning, majestic; *informal* splendiferous.
respond ● verb **1** *they do not respond to questions* ANSWER, reply, make a response, make a rejoinder. **2** *'No,' she responded* SAY IN

respondent ● noun **1** a defendant in a lawsuit, especially one in an appeal or divorce case. **2** a person who responds to a questionnaire or an advertisement.

response ● noun **1** an instance of responding; an answer or reaction. **2** an excitation of a nerve impulse caused by a change or event.

responsibility ● noun (pl. **responsibilities**) **1** the state or fact of being responsible. **2** the opportunity or ability to act independently and take decisions without authorization. **3** a thing which one is required to do as part of a job, role, or legal obligation.

responsible ● adjective **1** having an obligation to do something, or having control over or care for someone. **2** being the cause of something and so able to be blamed or credited for it. **3** morally accountable for one's behaviour. **4** capable of being trusted. **5** (of a job or position) involving important duties or decisions or control over others. **6** (**responsible to**) having to report to and be answerable to.
– DERIVATIVES **responsibleness** noun **responsibly** adverb.
– ORIGIN from Latin *respondere* 'answer, offer in return'.

responsive ● adjective **1** responding readily and positively. **2** in response; answering.
– DERIVATIVES **responsively** adverb **responsiveness** noun.

respray ● verb /reespray/ spray with a new coat of paint. ● noun /reespray/ an instance of respraying.

res publica /rayz pŏŏbblikə/ ● noun the state, republic, or commonwealth.
– ORIGIN Latin, 'public matter'.

rest¹ ● verb **1** cease work or movement in order to relax or recover strength. **2** allow to be inactive in order to regain or save strength or energy. **3** place or be placed so as to stay in a specified position: *his feet rested on the table.* **4** (**rest on**) depend or be based on. **5** (**rest in/on**) place (trust, hope, or confidence) in or on. **6** (**rest with**) (of power, responsibility, etc.) belong to. **7** (of a problem or subject) be left without further investigation or discussion. **8** N. Amer. conclude the case for the prosecution or defence in a court of law. ● noun **1** the action or a period of resting. **2** a motionless state. **3** Music an interval of silence of a specified duration. **4** an object that is used to hold or support something.
– PHRASES **rest one's case** conclude one's presentation of evidence and arguments in a lawsuit.
– ORIGIN Old English, from a root meaning 'league' or 'mile' (referring to a distance after which one rests).

rest² ● noun **1** the remaining part of something. **2** (treated as pl.) the remaining people or things; the others. ● verb remain or be left in a specified condition.
– ORIGIN from Latin *restare* 'remain'.

restart ● verb start again.

restaurant /rest(ə)ront, -RON/ ● noun a place where people pay to sit and eat meals that are cooked on the premises.
– ORIGIN French, from *restaurer* 'provide food for' (literally 'restore to a former state').

restaurateur /rest(ə)rətör/ ● noun a person who owns and manages a restaurant.
– ORIGIN French.

restful ● adjective having a quiet and soothing quality.
– DERIVATIVES **restfully** adverb.

rest home ● noun a residential institution where old or frail people are cared for.

restitution ● noun **1** the restoration of something lost or stolen to its proper owner. **2** recompense for injury or loss. **3** the restoration of something to its original state.
– DERIVATIVES **restitutive** adjective.
– ORIGIN Latin, from *restituere* 'restore'.

restive ● adjective **1** unable to keep still or silent; restless. **2** (of a horse) stubbornly standing still or moving backwards or sideways.
– DERIVATIVES **restively** adverb **restiveness** noun.
– ORIGIN Old French, from Latin *restare* 'remain'.

restless ● adjective **1** unable to rest or relax as a result of anxiety or boredom. **2** offering no physical or emotional rest: *a restless night.*
– DERIVATIVES **restlessly** adverb **restlessness** noun.

restock ● verb replenish with fresh stock or supplies.

restoration ● noun **1** the action of returning something to a former condition, place, or owner. **2** the process of repairing or renovating a building, work of art, etc. **3** the reinstatement of a previous practice, right, or situation. **4** the return of a monarch to a throne, a head of state to government, or a regime to power. **5** (**the Restoration**) the re-establishment of Charles II as King of England in 1660, or the period following this. **6** a structure provided to replace or repair dental tissue.

restorative ● adjective **1** having the ability to restore health,

Thesaurus

RESPONSE, answer, reply, rejoin, retort, riposte, counter. **3** *they were slow to respond* REACT, make a response, reciprocate, retaliate.

response ● noun **1** *his response to the question* ANSWER, reply, rejoinder, retort, riposte; *informal* comeback. **2** *an angry response* REACTION, reply, retaliation; *informal* comeback.
– OPPOSITES question.

responsibility ● noun **1** *it was his responsibility to find witnesses* DUTY, task, function, job, role, business; *Brit. informal* pigeon. **2** *they denied responsibility for the bomb attack* BLAME, fault, guilt, culpability, liability. **3** *a sense of responsibility* TRUSTWORTHINESS, (common) sense, maturity, reliability, dependability. **4** *managerial responsibility* AUTHORITY, control, power, leadership.

responsible ● adjective **1** *who is responsible for prisons?* IN CHARGE OF, in control of, at the helm of, accountable for, liable for. **2** *I am responsible for the mistake* ACCOUNTABLE, answerable, to blame, guilty, culpable, blameworthy, at fault, in the wrong. **3** *a responsible job* IMPORTANT, powerful, executive. **4** *he is responsible to the president* ANSWERABLE, accountable. **5** *a responsible tenant* TRUSTWORTHY, sensible, mature, reliable, dependable.

responsive ● adjective QUICK TO REACT, reactive, receptive, open to suggestions, amenable, flexible, forthcoming.

rest¹ ● verb **1** *he needed to rest* RELAX, take a rest, ease up/off, let up, slow down, have/take a break, unbend, unwind, recharge one's batteries, be at leisure, take it easy, put one's feet up; lie down, go to bed, have/take a nap, catnap, doze, sleep; *informal* take five, have/take a breather, snatch forty winks, get some shut-eye; *Brit. informal* have a kip; *N. Amer. informal* chill out, catch some Zs. **2** *his hands rested on the rail* LIE, be laid, repose, be placed, be positioned, be supported by. **3** *she rested her basket on the ground* SUPPORT, prop (up), lean, lay, set, stand, position, place, put. **4** *the film script rests on an improbable premise* BE BASED, depend, be dependent, rely, hinge, turn on, be contingent, revolve around.
● noun **1** *get some rest* REPOSE, relaxation, leisure, respite, time off, breathing space; sleep, nap, doze; *informal* shut-eye, snooze, lie-down, forty winks; *Brit. informal* kip. **2** *a short rest from work* HOLIDAY, vacation, break, breathing space, interval, interlude, intermission, time off/out; *informal* breather. **3** *she took the poker from its rest* STAND, base, holder, support, rack, frame, shelf. **4** *we came to rest 100 metres lower* A STANDSTILL, a halt, a stop.

rest² ● noun *the rest of the board are appointees* REMAINDER, residue, balance, remaining part/number/quantity, others, those left, remains, remnant(s), surplus, excess; *technical* residuum.
● verb *you may rest assured that he is there* REMAIN, continue to be, stay, keep, carry on being.

restaurant ● noun EATING PLACE, bistro, cafe, cafeteria, carvery, brasserie; *N. Amer.* diner; *informal* eatery.

restful ● adjective RELAXED, relaxing, quiet, calm, calming, tranquil, soothing, peaceful, placid, reposeful, leisurely, undisturbed, untroubled.
– OPPOSITES exciting.

restitution ● noun **1** *restitution of the land seized* RETURN, restoration, handing back, surrender. **2** *restitution for the damage caused* COMPENSATION, recompense, reparation, damages, indemnification, indemnity, reimbursement, repayment, remuneration, redress; *archaic* guerdon.

restive ● adjective **1** *Edward is getting restive.* See RESTLESS sense 1. **2** *the militants are increasingly restive* UNRULY, disorderly, uncontrollable, unmanageable, wilful, recalcitrant, insubordinate; *Brit. informal* bolshie; *formal* refractory; *archaic* contumacious.

restless ● adjective **1** *Maria was restless* UNEASY, ill at ease, restive, fidgety, edgy, on edge, tense, worked up, nervous, agitated, anxious, on tenterhooks, keyed up; *Brit.* nervy; *informal* jumpy, jittery, twitchy, uptight, like a cat on a hot tin roof; *Brit. informal* like a cat on hot bricks. **2** *a restless night* SLEEPLESS, wakeful; fitful, broken, disturbed, troubled, unsettled; *rare* insomnolent.

restlessness ● noun UNEASE, restiveness, edginess, tenseness, nervousness, agitation, anxiety, fretfulness, apprehension, disquiet; *informal* jitteriness.

restoration ● noun **1** *the restoration of democracy* REINSTATEMENT,

strength, or a feeling of well-being. **2** relating to the restoration of a damaged tooth or other part of the body. ● noun a medicine or drink that restores health, strength, or well-being.
– DERIVATIVES **restoratively** adverb.
restore ● verb **1** return to a former condition, place, or owner. **2** repair or renovate (a building, work of art, etc.). **3** bring back (a previous practice, right, or situation); reinstate.
– DERIVATIVES **restorable** adjective **restorer** noun.
– ORIGIN Latin *restaurare* 'rebuild, restore'.
restrain ● verb **1** keep under control or within limits. **2** deprive of freedom of movement or personal liberty. **3** repress (a strong emotion).
– DERIVATIVES **restrainable** adjective **restrainer** noun.
– ORIGIN Latin *restringere* 'tie back'.
restrained ● adjective **1** reserved, unemotional, or dispassionate. **2** understated and subtle; not ornate or brightly coloured.
restraint ● noun **1** the action of restraining. **2** a measure or condition that restrains. **3** a device which limits or prevents freedom of movement. **4** dispassionate or moderate behaviour; self-control.
restrict ● verb **1** put a limit on; keep under control. **2** deprive of freedom of movement or action.
– ORIGIN Latin *restringere* 'tie back'.
restricted ● adjective **1** limited in extent, number, or scope. **2** not revealed or made open to the public for reasons of national security.
restriction ● noun **1** a limiting condition or measure. **2** the action of restricting or the state of being restricted.
restrictive ● adjective imposing restrictions.
– DERIVATIVES **restrictively** adverb **restrictiveness** noun.
restrictive practice ● noun Brit. **1** an arrangement by a group of workers to limit output or restrict the entry of new workers in order to protect their own interests. **2** an arrangement in industry or trade that restricts or controls competition between firms.
restring ● verb (past and past part. **restrung**) **1** fit new strings to. **2** string (beads) again.
restroom ● noun chiefly N. Amer. a toilet in a public building.
restructure ● verb **1** organize differently. **2** Finance convert (a debt) into another debt that is repayable at a later time.
restyle ● verb **1** rearrange or remake in a new shape or layout. **2** give a new designation to. ● noun an instance of restyling.
result ● noun **1** a consequence, effect, or outcome. **2** an item of information or a quantity or formula obtained by experiment or calculation. **3** a final score, mark, or placing in a sporting event or examination. **4** a satisfactory or favourable outcome: *determination and persistence guarantee results.* **5** the outcome of a business's trading over a given period, expressed as a statement of profit or loss. ● verb **1** occur or follow as a result. **2** (**result in**) have (a specified outcome).
– ORIGIN Latin *resultare* 'spring back', later 'to result'.
resultant ● adjective occurring or produced as a result.
resume ● verb **1** begin again or continue after a pause or interruption. **2** take or put on again; return to the use of.
– DERIVATIVES **resumption** noun.
– ORIGIN Latin *resumere* 'take back'.
résumé /rezyoomay/ ● noun **1** a summary. **2** N. Amer. a curriculum vitae.
– ORIGIN from French, 'resumed'.
resurface ● verb **1** put a new coating on (a surface). **2** come back up to the surface of deep water. **3** arise or become evident again.
resurgent ● adjective increasing or reviving after a period of little activity, popularity, or occurrence.
– DERIVATIVES **resurgence** noun.
– ORIGIN from Latin *resurgere* 'rise again'.
resurrect ● verb **1** restore to life. **2** revive the practice, use, or memory of.
resurrection ● noun **1** the action of resurrecting or the fact of being resurrected. **2** (**the Resurrection**) (in Christian belief) Christ's rising from the dead.
– ORIGIN Latin, from *resurgere* 'rise again'.
resuscitate /risussitayt/ ● verb **1** revive from unconsciousness. **2** make active or vigorous again.
– DERIVATIVES **resuscitation** noun **resuscitative** adjective **resuscitator** noun.

Thesaurus

reinstitution, re-establishment, reimposition, return. **2** *the restoration of derelict housing* REPAIR, repairing, fixing, mending, refurbishment, reconditioning, rehabilitation, rebuilding, reconstruction, overhaul, redevelopment, renovation; *N. Amer. informal* rehab.
restore ● verb **1** *the aim to restore democracy* REINSTATE, bring back, reinstitute, reimpose, reinstall, re-establish. **2** *he restored it to its rightful owner* RETURN, give back, hand back. **3** *the building has been restored* REPAIR, fix, mend, refurbish, recondition, rehabilitate, rebuild, reconstruct, remodel, overhaul, redevelop, renovate; *informal* do up; *N. Amer. informal* rehab. **4** *a good sleep can restore you* REINVIGORATE, revitalize, revive, refresh, energize, fortify, revivify, regenerate, stimulate, freshen.
– OPPOSITES abolish.
restrain ● verb **1** *Charles restrained his anger* CONTROL, keep under control, check, hold/keep in check, curb, suppress, repress, contain, dampen, subdue, smother, choke back, stifle, bottle up, rein back/in; *informal* keep the lid on. **2** *she could barely restrain herself from swearing* PREVENT, stop, keep, hold back. **3** *the insane used to be restrained* TIE UP, bind, tether, chain (up), fetter, shackle, manacle, put in irons.
restrained ● adjective **1** *Julie was quite restrained* SELF-CONTROLLED, self-restrained, not given to excesses, sober, steady, unemotional, undemonstrative. **2** *restrained elegance* MUTED, soft, discreet, subtle, quiet, unobtrusive, unostentatious, understated, tasteful.
restraint ● noun **1** *a restraint on their impulsiveness* CONSTRAINT, check, control, restriction, limitation, curtailment; rein, bridle, brake, damper, impediment, obstacle. **2** *the customary restraint of the police* SELF-CONTROL, self-restraint, self-discipline, control, moderation, prudence, judiciousness. **3** *the room has been decorated with restraint* SUBTLETY, understatedness, taste, tastefulness, discretion, discrimination. **4** *a child restraint* BELT, harness, strap.
restrict ● verb **1** *a busy working life restricted his leisure activities* LIMIT, keep within bounds, regulate, control, moderate, cut down. **2** *the cuff supports the ankle without restricting movement* HINDER, interfere with, impede, hamper, obstruct, block, check, curb. **3** *he restricted himself to a 15-minute speech* CONFINE, limit.
restricted ● adjective **1** *restricted space* CRAMPED, confined, constricted, small, narrow, tight; *archaic* strait. **2** *a restricted calorie intake* LIMITED, controlled, regulated, reduced. **3** *a restricted zone* OUT OF BOUNDS, off limits, private, exclusive. **4** *restricted information* (TOP) SECRET, classified; *informal* hush-hush.
– OPPOSITES unlimited.
restriction ● noun **1** *there is no restriction on the number of places* LIMITATION, limit, constraint, control, check, curb; condition, proviso, qualification. **2** *the restriction of personal freedom* REDUCTION, limitation, diminution, curtailment. **3** *restriction of movement* HINDRANCE, impediment, slowing, reduction, limitation.
result ● noun **1** *stress is the result of overwork* CONSEQUENCE, outcome, upshot, sequel, effect, reaction, repercussion, ramification, conclusion, culmination. **2** *what is your result?* ANSWER, solution; sum, total, product. **3** *exam results* MARK, score, grade. **4** *the result of the trial* VERDICT, decision, outcome, conclusion, judgement, findings, ruling.
– OPPOSITES cause.
● verb **1** *differences between species could result from their habitat* FOLLOW, ensue, develop, stem, spring, arise, derive, evolve, proceed; occur, happen, take place, come about; be caused by, be brought about by, be produced by, originate in, be consequent on. **2** *the shooting resulted in five deaths* END IN, culminate in, finish in, terminate in, lead to, prompt, precipitate, trigger; cause, bring about, occasion, effect, give rise to, produce, engender, generate; *poetic/literary* beget.
resume ● verb **1** *the government resumed negotiations* RESTART, recommence, begin again, start again, reopen; renew, return to, continue with, carry on with. **2** *the priest resumed his kneeling posture* RETURN TO, come back to, take up again, reoccupy.
– OPPOSITES suspend, abandon.
résumé ● noun SUMMARY, precis, synopsis, abstract, outline, summarization, summation, epitome; abridgement, digest, condensation, abbreviation, overview, review.
resumption ● noun RESTART, restarting, recommencement, reopening; continuation, carrying on, renewal, return to.
resurgence ● noun RENEWAL, revival, recovery, comeback, reawakening, resurrection, reappearance, re-emergence, regeneration; resumption, recommencement, continuation; *formal* renascence.
resurrect ● verb **1** *Jesus was resurrected* RAISE FROM THE DEAD, re-

– ORIGIN Latin *resuscitare* 'raise again'.
ret /ret/ (also **rate**) ● verb (**retted**, **retting**) soak (flax or hemp) in water to soften it.
– ORIGIN related to ROT.
retail ● noun the sale of goods to the general public (rather than to a wholesaler). ● adverb being sold to the general public. ● verb **1** sell (goods) by retail. **2** (**retail at/for**) be sold by retail for (a specified price). **3** recount or relate details of.
– DERIVATIVES **retailer** noun.
– ORIGIN Old French *retaillier*, from *tailler* 'to cut'.
retail price index ● noun (in the UK) an index of the variation in the prices of retail goods and other items.
retain ● verb **1** continue to have; keep possession of. **2** absorb and continue to hold (a substance). **3** keep in place; hold fixed. **4** keep engaged in one's service. **5** secure the services of (a barrister) with a preliminary payment.
– DERIVATIVES **retainable** adjective.
– ORIGIN Latin *retinere* 'hold back'.
retainer ● noun **1** a thing that holds something in place. **2** a fee paid in advance to a barrister to secure their services. **3** Brit. a reduced rent paid to retain accommodation during a period of non-occupancy. **4** a servant who has worked for a person or family for a long time.
retaining wall ● noun a wall that holds back earth or water on one side of it.
retake ● verb (past **retook**; past part. **retaken**) **1** take (a test or examination) again. **2** regain possession of. ● noun **1** a test or examination that is retaken. **2** an instance of filming a scene or recording a piece of music again.
retaliate /ritaliayt/ ● verb make an attack or assault in return for a similar attack.
– DERIVATIVES **retaliation** noun **retaliative** adjective **retaliator** noun **retaliatory** adjective.
– ORIGIN Latin *retaliare* 'return in kind'.
retard ● verb /ritaard/ hold back the development or progress of. ● noun /reetaard/ derogatory a mentally handicapped person.
– DERIVATIVES **retardation** noun **retarder** noun.
– ORIGIN Latin *retardare*, from *tardus* 'slow'.
retardant ● adjective preventing or inhibiting: *fire-retardant polymers.* ● noun a fabric or substance that prevents or inhibits the outbreak of fire.
– DERIVATIVES **retardancy** noun.
retardataire /ritaardətair/ ● adjective (of a work of art or architecture) executed in an earlier style.
– ORIGIN French.
retarded ● adjective less advanced in mental, physical, or social development than is usual for one's age.
retch ● verb make the sound and movement of vomiting. ● noun an instance of retching.
– ORIGIN from a Germanic word meaning 'spittle'.
retell ● verb (past and past part. **retold**) tell (a story) again or differently.
retention ● noun **1** the action of retaining or the state of being retained. **2** failure to eliminate a substance from the body.
retentive ● adjective **1** (of a person's memory) effective in retaining facts and impressions. **2** able to retain or hold in place.
– DERIVATIVES **retentively** adverb **retentiveness** noun **retentivity** noun.
rethink ● verb (past and past part. **rethought**) assess or consider (a policy or course of action) again. ● noun an instance of rethinking.
reticent /rettis'nt/ ● adjective not revealing one's thoughts or feelings readily.
– DERIVATIVES **reticence** noun **reticently** adverb.
– ORIGIN from Latin *reticere* 'remain silent'.
reticulated ● adjective constructed, arranged, or marked like a net or network.
– ORIGIN Latin *reticulatus*, from *rete* 'net'.
reticulation /ritikyoolaysh'n/ ● noun a pattern or arrangement of interlacing lines resembling a net.
reticule /rettikyool/ ● noun chiefly historical a woman's small drawstring handbag.
– ORIGIN French, from Latin *reticulum* 'little net'.
retina /rettinə/ ● noun (pl. **retinas** or **retinae** /rettinee/) a layer at the back of the eyeball containing cells that are sensitive to light and from which impulses are sent to the brain, where they are interpreted as visual images.
– DERIVATIVES **retinal** adjective.
– ORIGIN Latin, from *rete* 'net'.
retinitis /rettinītiss/ ● noun inflammation of the retina.
retinitis pigmentosa /pigmentōsə/ ● noun Medicine a hereditary eye disease characterized by black pigmentation and gradual degeneration of the retina.
– ORIGIN *pigmentosa* from Latin *pigmentum* 'pigment'.
retinol /rettinol/ ● noun vitamin A, a yellow compound which is essential for growth and vision in dim light and is found in vegetables, egg yolk, and fish-liver oil.
retinopathy /rettinoppəthi/ ● noun Medicine disease of the retina which results in impairment or loss of vision.
retinue /rettinyoo/ ● noun a group of advisers or assistants accompanying an important person.
– ORIGIN from Old French *retenir* 'keep back, retain'.
retire ● verb **1** leave one's job and cease to work, especially because one has reached a particular age. **2** (of a sports player) cease to play competitively. **3** withdraw from a race or match because of accident or injury. **4** withdraw to or from a particular place. **5** (of a jury) leave the courtroom to decide the verdict of a trial. **6** go to bed.
– DERIVATIVES **retired** adjective.
– ORIGIN French *retirer* 'draw back'.
retirement ● noun **1** the action or fact of retiring. **2** the period of one's life after retiring from work. **3** seclusion.

Thesaurus

store to life, revive. **2** *resurrecting his career* REVIVE, restore, regenerate, revitalize, breathe new life into, reinvigorate, resuscitate, rejuvenate, stimulate, re-establish, relaunch.
resuscitate ● verb **1** *medics resuscitated him* BRING ROUND, revive, bring back to consciousness; give artificial respiration to, give the kiss of life to. **2** *measures to resuscitate the economy* REVIVE, resurrect, restore, regenerate, revitalize, breathe new life into, reinvigorate, rejuvenate, stimulate.
retain ● verb **1** *the government retained a share in the industries* KEEP (POSSESSION OF), keep hold of, hold on to, hang on to. **2** *existing footpaths are to be retained* MAINTAIN, keep, preserve, conserve. **3** *some students retain facts easily* REMEMBER, memorize, keep in one's mind/memory. **4** *solicitors can retain a barrister* EMPLOY, contract, keep on the payroll.
– OPPOSITES give up, abolish.
retainer ● noun **1** *they're paid a retainer* (RETAINING) FEE, periodic payment, advance, standing charge. **2** *a faithful retainer.* See SERVANT sense 1.
retaliate ● verb FIGHT BACK, hit back, respond, react, reply, reciprocate, counter-attack, return like for like, get back at someone, give tit for tat, give someone a taste of their own medicine; have/get/take one's revenge, be revenged, avenge oneself, take reprisals, get even, pay someone back; informal get one's own back; archaic give someone a Roland for an Oliver.
retaliation ● noun REVENGE, vengeance, reprisal, retribution, requital, recrimination, repayment; response, reaction, reply, counter-attack; archaic a Roland for an Oliver.
retard ● verb DELAY, slow down/up, hold back/up, set back, postpone, put back, detain, decelerate; hinder, hamper, obstruct, inhibit, impede, check, restrain, restrict, trammel; poetic/literary stay.
– OPPOSITES accelerate.
retch ● verb **1** *the sour taste made her retch* GAG, heave; informal keck. **2** *he retched all over the table.* See VOMIT verb sense 1.
reticence ● noun RESERVE, restraint, inhibition, diffidence, shyness; unresponsiveness, quietness, taciturnity, secretiveness.
reticent ● adjective RESERVED, withdrawn, introverted, inhibited, diffident, shy; uncommunicative, unforthcoming, unresponsive, tight-lipped, quiet, taciturn, silent, guarded, secretive.
– OPPOSITES expansive.
retinue ● noun ENTOURAGE, escort, company, court, staff, personnel, household, train, suite, following, bodyguard; aides, attendants, servants, retainers.
retire ● verb **1** *he has retired* GIVE UP WORK, stop working, stop work. **2** *we've retired him on full pension* PENSION OFF, force to retire. **3** *Gillian retired to her office* WITHDRAW, go away, take oneself off, decamp, shut oneself away; formal repair; poetic/literary betake oneself. **4** *their forces retired* RETREAT, withdraw, pull back, fall back, disengage, back off, give ground. **5** *everyone retired early* GO TO BED, call it a day, go to sleep; informal turn in, hit the hay/sack.
retired ● adjective *a retired schoolteacher* FORMER, ex-, past, in retirement, elderly.
● noun *apartments for the retired* RETIRED PEOPLE, (old-age) pen-

retiring ● adjective tending to avoid company; shy.
retold past and past participle of RETELL.
retook past of RETAKE.
retool ● verb **1** equip (a factory) with new or adapted tools. **2** chiefly N. Amer. adapt, alter, or prepare for a new purpose or challenge.
retort[1] ● verb say something sharp or witty in answer to a remark or accusation. ● noun a sharp or witty reply.
– ORIGIN Latin *retorquere* 'twist back'.
retort[2] ● noun **1** a container or furnace for carrying out a chemical process on a large or industrial scale. **2** historical a glass container with a long neck, used in distilling liquids and other chemical operations. ● verb heat in a retort.
– ORIGIN Latin *retorta*, from *retorquere* 'twist back' (with reference to the backward-bending neck of the glass container).
retouch ● verb improve or repair (a painting, photograph, etc.) by making slight additions or alterations.
– DERIVATIVES **retoucher** noun.
retrace ● verb **1** go back over (the same route that one has just taken). **2** discover and follow (a route or course taken by someone else). **3** trace (something) back to its source or beginning.
retract ● verb **1** draw or be drawn back. **2** withdraw (a statement or accusation) as untrue or unjustified. **3** withdraw or go back on (an undertaking or promise).
– DERIVATIVES **retractable** adjective **retraction** noun **retractive** adjective.
– ORIGIN Latin *retrahere* 'draw back'.
retractile /ritraktīl/ ● adjective Zoology capable of being retracted.
– DERIVATIVES **retractility** noun.
retractor ● noun **1** a device for retracting something. **2** (also **retractor muscle**) chiefly Zoology a muscle serving to retract a part of the body.
retrain ● verb teach or learn new skills.
retread ● verb **1** (past **retrod**; past part. **retrodden**) go back over (a path or one's steps). **2** (past and past part. **retreaded**) put a new tread on (a worn tyre). ● noun a tyre that has been given a new tread; a remould.
retreat ● verb **1** (of an army) withdraw from confrontation with enemy forces. **2** move back from a difficult situation. **3** withdraw to a quiet or secluded place. ● noun **1** an act of retreating. **2** a quiet or secluded place. **3** a period or place of seclusion for the purposes of prayer and meditation. **4** a military musical ceremony carried out at sunset.
– ORIGIN Latin *retrahere* 'draw back'.
retrench ● verb **1** reduce costs or spending in response to economic difficulty. **2** chiefly Austral. make (an employee) redundant in order to reduce costs.
– DERIVATIVES **retrenchment** noun.
– ORIGIN French *retrancher* 'cut out'.
retrial ● noun Law a second or further trial.
retribution /retribyōōsh'n/ ● noun punishment inflicted in the spirit of moral outrage or personal vengeance.
– DERIVATIVES **retributive** /ritribyootiv/ adjective **retributory** /ritribyootəri/ adjective.
– ORIGIN Latin, from *retribuere* 'assign again'.
retrieve ● verb **1** get or bring back. **2** (of a dog) find and bring back (game that has been shot). **3** find or extract (information stored in a computer). **4** rescue from a state of difficulty or collapse. ● noun an act of retrieving.
– DERIVATIVES **retrievable** adjective **retrieval** noun.
– ORIGIN Old French *retrover* 'find again'.
retriever ● noun a dog of a breed used for retrieving game.
retro ● adjective imitative of a style from the recent past. ● noun retro clothes, music, or style.
– ORIGIN French, from *rétrograde* 'retrograde'.
retro- ● combining form **1** denoting action that is directed backwards or is reciprocal: *retrogress*. **2** denoting location behind: *retrorocket*.
– ORIGIN Latin *retro* 'backwards'.
retroactive ● adjective (especially of legislation) taking effect from a date in the past.
– DERIVATIVES **retroaction** noun **retroactively** adverb.
retrod past of RETREAD (in sense 1).
retrodden past participle of RETREAD (in sense 1).
retrofit ● verb (**retrofitted**, **retrofitting**) fit with a component or accessory not fitted during manufacture. ● noun an act of retrofitting.
– ORIGIN blend of RETROACTIVE and REFIT.
retroflex (also **retroflexed**) ● adjective Anatomy & Medicine turned backwards.
– DERIVATIVES **retroflexion** noun.
– ORIGIN from Latin *retroflectere* 'bend backwards'.
retrograde ● adjective **1** directed or moving backwards. **2** (of the order of something) reversed; inverse. **3** reverting to an earlier and inferior condition. **4** chiefly Astronomy proceeding in a reverse direction from normal, especially (of planetary motion) from east to west. ● verb **1** go back in position or time. **2** Astronomy show retrograde motion.
– DERIVATIVES **retrogradation** noun.
– ORIGIN Latin *retrogradus*, from *gradus* 'a step'.
retrogress /retrəgress/ ● verb go back to an earlier and typically inferior state.
retrogression ● noun the process of retrogressing.
– DERIVATIVES **retrogressive** adjective.
retrorocket ● noun a small auxiliary rocket on a spacecraft or missile, fired in the direction of travel to slow it down.
retrospect ● noun a survey or review of a past course of events or period of time.
– PHRASES **in retrospect** when looking back on a past event; with hindsight.
– DERIVATIVES **retrospection** noun.
retrospective ● adjective **1** looking back on or dealing with past events or situations. **2** (of an exhibition or compilation)

Thesaurus

r

sioners, OAPs, senior citizens, the elderly; *N. Amer.* seniors.
retirement ● noun **1** *they are nearing retirement* GIVING UP WORK, stopping working, stopping work. **2** *retirement in an English village* SECLUSION, retreat, solitude, isolation, obscurity.
retiring ● adjective **1** *the retiring president* DEPARTING, outgoing. **2** *a retiring man* SHY, diffident, self-effacing, unassuming, unassertive, reserved, reticent, quiet, timid, modest; private, secret, secretive, withdrawn, reclusive, unsociable.
– OPPOSITES incoming, outgoing.
retort ● verb *'Oh, sure,' she retorted* ANSWER, reply, respond, say in response, return, counter, rejoin, riposte, retaliate, snap back.
● noun *a sarcastic retort* ANSWER, reply, response, return, counter, rejoinder, riposte, retaliation; *informal* comeback.
retract ● verb **1** *the sea otter can retract its claws* PULL IN/BACK, draw in. **2** *he retracted his allegation* TAKE BACK, withdraw, recant, disavow, disclaim, repudiate, renounce, reverse, revoke, rescind, go back on, backtrack on; *formal* abjure.
– OPPOSITES extend, assert.
retreat ● verb **1** *the army retreated* WITHDRAW, retire, draw back, pull back/out, fall back, give way, give ground, beat a retreat. **2** *the tide was retreating* GO OUT, ebb, recede, fall, go down. **3** *the government had to retreat* CHANGE ONE'S MIND, change one's plans; back down, climb down, do a U-turn, backtrack, back-pedal, give in, concede defeat; *Brit.* do an about-turn.
– OPPOSITES advance.
● noun **1** *the retreat of the army* WITHDRAWAL, pulling back. **2** *the President's retreat* CLIMBDOWN, backdown, about-face; *Brit.* about-turn. **3** *her rural retreat* REFUGE, haven, sanctuary; hideaway, hideout, hiding place; *informal* hidey-hole. **4** *a period of retreat from the world* SECLUSION, withdrawal, retirement, solitude, isolation, sanctuary.
retrench ● verb **1** *we have to retrench* ECONOMIZE, cut back, make cutbacks, make savings, make economies, reduce expenditure, be economical, be frugal, tighten one's belt. **2** *services have to be retrenched* REDUCE, cut (back/down), pare (down), slim down, make reductions in, make cutbacks in, trim, prune; *informal* slash.
retribution ● noun PUNISHMENT, penalty, one's just deserts; revenge, reprisal, requital, retaliation, vengeance, an eye for an eye (and a tooth for a tooth), tit for tat; redress, reparation, restitution, recompense, repayment, indemnification, atonement, amends.
retrieve ● verb **1** *I retrieved our balls from their garden* GET BACK, bring back, recover, regain (possession of), recoup, reclaim, repossess, redeem, recuperate. **2** *they were trying to retrieve the situation* PUT/SET RIGHT, rectify, remedy, restore, sort out, straighten out, resolve.
retrograde ● adjective **1** *a retrograde step* FOR THE WORSE, regressive, negative, downhill, unwelcome. **2** *retrograde motion* BACKWARD(S), reverse, rearward.
– OPPOSITES positive.

showing the development of an artist's work over a period of time. **3** (of a statute or legal decision) taking effect from a date in the past. ● noun a retrospective exhibition or compilation.
– DERIVATIVES **retrospectively** adverb.
retroussé /rətrōōsay/ ● adjective (of a person's nose) turned up at the tip.
– ORIGIN French, 'tucked up'.
retroverted /retrəvertid/ ● adjective Anatomy (of the uterus) tilted backwards.
– DERIVATIVES **retroversion** noun.
– ORIGIN from Latin *retrovertere* 'turn backwards'.
retrovirus /retrōvīrəss/ ● noun Biology any of a group of RNA viruses which insert a DNA copy of their genome into the host cell in order to replicate, e.g. HIV.
– ORIGIN from the initial letters of *reverse transcriptase* + VIRUS.
retsina /retseenə/ ● noun a Greek white wine flavoured with resin.
– ORIGIN modern Greek.
retune ● verb tune again or differently.
return ● verb **1** come or go back to a place. **2** (**return to**) go back to (a particular state or activity). **3** give or send back or put back in place. **4** feel, say, or do (the same feeling, action, etc.) in response. **5** (in tennis) hit or send (the ball) back to an opponent. **6** (of a judge or jury) state or present (a verdict). **7** yield or make (a profit). **8** (of an electorate) elect to office. ● noun **1** an act or the action of returning. **2** a profit from an investment. **3** chiefly Brit. a ticket allowing travel to a place and back again. **4** (in sport) a second contest between the same opponents. **5** a ticket for an event that has been returned because no longer wanted. **6** an official report or statement submitted in response to a formal demand: *census returns.* **7** Architecture a part receding from the line of the front, for example the side of a house or of a window opening.
– PHRASES **by return of post** Brit. in the next available mail delivery to the sender. **many happy returns of the day** a greeting to someone on their birthday.
– DERIVATIVES **returnable** adjective **returner** noun.
– ORIGIN Old French *returner*, from Latin *tornare* 'to turn'.
returnee ● noun **1** a refugee returning from abroad. **2** a person returning to work after an extended absence.
returning officer ● noun Brit. the official in each constituency who conducts an election and announces the result.
retype ● verb type (text) again.
reunify ● verb (**reunifies**, **reunified**) restore political unity to.
– DERIVATIVES **reunification** noun.
reunion ● noun **1** the process or an instance of reuniting. **2** a social gathering of people who have not seen each other for some time.
reunite ● verb bring or come together again after a period of separation or disunity.
reuse ● verb /reeyōōz/ use again or more than once. ● noun /reeyōōss/ the action of using something again.
– DERIVATIVES **reusable** adjective.
Rev. ● abbreviation Reverend.
rev informal ● noun (**revs**) the number of revolutions of an engine per minute. ● verb (**revved**, **revving**) increase the running speed of (an engine) by pressing the accelerator.
revalue ● verb (**revalues**, **revalued**, **revaluing**) **1** value again. **2** Economics adjust the value of (a currency) in relation to other currencies.
– DERIVATIVES **revaluation** noun.
revamp ● verb give new and improved form, structure, or appearance to. ● noun a new and improved version.
revanchism /rivanchiz'm/ ● noun a policy of retaliation, especially to recover lost territory.
– DERIVATIVES **revanchist** adjective & noun.
– ORIGIN from French *revanche* 'revenge'.
rev counter ● noun an instrument that measures the rate of revolutions of an engine.
Revd ● abbreviation Reverend.
reveal[1] ● verb **1** make (previously unknown or secret information) known. **2** cause or allow to be seen.
– DERIVATIVES **revealer** noun.
– ORIGIN Latin *revelare*, from *velum* 'veil'.
reveal[2] ● noun either side surface of an aperture in a wall for a door or window.
– ORIGIN from Old French *revaler* 'to lower'.
revealing ● adjective **1** divulging interesting or significant information. **2** (of a garment) allowing much of the wearer's body to be seen.
– DERIVATIVES **revealingly** adverb.
revegetate ● verb produce new vegetation on (disturbed or barren ground).
– DERIVATIVES **revegetation** noun.
reveille /rivali/ ● noun a military waking signal sounded on a bugle, drum, etc.
– ORIGIN from French *réveillez!* 'wake up!'.
revel ● verb (**revelled**, **revelling**; US **reveled**, **reveling**) **1** engage in lively and noisy festivities. **2** (**revel in**) gain great pleasure from. ● noun (**revels**) lively and noisy festivities.
– DERIVATIVES **reveller** noun **revelry** noun (pl. **revelries**).
– ORIGIN Old French *reveler* 'rise up in rebellion', from Latin *rebellare* 'to rebel'.
revelation ● noun **1** the revealing of something previously unknown. **2** a surprising or remarkable thing. **3** the disclosure of knowledge to humans by divine or supernatural means.
– DERIVATIVES **revelational** adjective.
revelatory /revvəlaytəri/ ● adjective revealing something hitherto unknown.
revenant /revvənənt/ ● noun a person who has returned, espe-

Thesaurus

r

retrospect ● noun
– PHRASES **in retrospect** LOOKING BACK, on reflection, in/with hindsight.
retrospective ● adjective BACKDATED, retroactive, ex post facto.
return ● verb **1** *he returned to London* GO BACK, come back, arrive back, come home. **2** *the symptoms returned* RECUR, reoccur, occur again, repeat (itself); reappear, appear again. **3** *he returned the money* GIVE BACK, hand back; pay back, repay. **4** *Peter returned the book* RESTORE, put back, replace, reinstall. **5** *he returned the volley* HIT BACK, throw back. **6** *she returned his kiss* RECIPROCATE, requite, give in return, repay, give back. **7** *'Later,' returned Isabel* ANSWER, reply, respond, counter, rejoin, retort. **8** *the jury returned a unanimous verdict* DELIVER, bring in, hand down. **9** *the club returned a profit* YIELD, earn, realize, net, gross, clear. **10** *the Labour candidate was returned* ELECT, vote in, choose, select.
– OPPOSITES depart, disappear, keep.
● noun **1** *his return to Paris* HOMECOMING. **2** *the return of hard times* RECURRENCE, reoccurrence, repeat, repetition, reappearance, revival, resurrection, re-emergence, resurgence. **3** *I requested the return of my books* GIVING BACK, handing back, replacement, restoration, reinstatement, restitution. **4** *two returns to London* RETURN TICKET/FARE; *N. Amer.* round trip ticket/fare. **5** *a quick return on investments* YIELD, profit, gain, revenue, interest, dividend. **6** *a census return* STATEMENT, report, submission, record, dossier; document, form.
– OPPOSITES departure, disappearance, single.
– PHRASES **in return for** IN EXCHANGE FOR, as a reward for, as compensation for.
revamp ● verb RENOVATE, redecorate, refurbish, recondition, rehabilitate, overhaul, make over; upgrade, refit, re-equip; remodel, refashion, redesign, restyle; *informal* do up, give something a facelift, vamp up; *Brit. informal* tart up; *N. Amer. informal* rehab.
reveal ● verb **1** *the police can't reveal his whereabouts* DIVULGE, disclose, tell, let slip/drop, give away/out, blurt (out), release, leak; make known, make public, broadcast, publicize, circulate, disseminate; *informal* let on; *archaic* discover. **2** *he revealed his new car* SHOW, display, exhibit, disclose, uncover; *poetic/literary* uncloak. **3** *the data reveal a good deal of information* BRING TO LIGHT, uncover, lay bare, unearth, unveil; *formal* evince; *poetic/literary* uncloak.
– OPPOSITES hide.
revel ● verb **1** *they revelled all night* CELEBRATE, make merry, have a party, carouse, roister, go on a spree; *informal* party, live it up, whoop it up, make whoopee, rave, paint the town red. **2** *he revelled in the applause* ENJOY, delight in, love, like, adore, be pleased by, take pleasure in, appreciate, relish, lap up, savour.
● noun *late-night revels* CELEBRATION, festivity, jollification, merrymaking, carousal, carouse, spree; party, jamboree; *informal* rave, shindig, bash; *Brit. informal* rave-up, knees-up; *N. Amer. informal* wingding, blast; *Austral. informal* rage, ding, jollo.
revelation ● noun **1** *revelations about his personal life* DISCLOSURE, surprising fact, announcement, report; admission, confession. **2** *the revelation of a secret* DIVULGING, divulgence, disclosure, disclosing, letting slip/drop, giving away/out, leaking, leak, betrayal, unveiling, making known, making public, broadcasting, publiciz-

cially supposedly from the dead.
– ORIGIN from French, 'coming back'.
revenge ● noun **1** retaliation for an injury or wrong. **2** the desire to inflict such retaliation. ● verb **1** (**revenge oneself** or **be revenged**) inflict revenge for an injury or wrong done to oneself. **2** inflict revenge on behalf of (someone else) or for (a wrong or injury).
– PHRASES **revenge is a dish best served** (or **eaten**) **cold** proverb vengeance is often more satisfying if it is delayed.
– ORIGIN Old French *revencher*, from Latin *vindicare* 'claim, avenge'.
revengeful ● adjective eager for revenge.
revenue ● noun **1** the income received by an organization. **2** a state's annual income from which public expenses are met.
– ORIGIN from Latin *revenire* 'return'.
reverberate ● verb **1** (of a loud noise) be repeated as an echo. **2** have continuing serious effects.
– DERIVATIVES **reverberant** adjective **reverberation** noun **reverberative** adjective **reverberator** noun **reverberatory** adjective.
– ORIGIN Latin *reverberare* 'strike again'.
revere /riveer/ ● verb respect or admire deeply.
– ORIGIN Latin *revereri*, from *vereri* 'to fear'.
reverence ● noun **1** deep respect. **2** archaic a bow or curtsy. **3** (**His/Your Reverence**) a title given to a member of the clergy, especially a priest in Ireland. ● verb regard or treat with reverence.
reverend ● adjective a title or form of address to members of the clergy. ● noun informal a clergyman.
Reverend Mother ● noun the title of the Mother Superior of a convent.
reverent ● adjective showing reverence.
– DERIVATIVES **reverential** adjective **reverently** adverb.
reverie /revvəri/ ● noun **1** a daydream. **2** Music an instrumental piece suggesting a dreamy or musing state.
– ORIGIN Old French, 'rejoicing, revelry', from *rever* 'be delirious'.
revers /riveer/ ● noun (pl. same or /riveerz/) the turned-back edge of a garment revealing the underside, especially at the lapel.
– ORIGIN French, 'reverse'.
reversal ● noun **1** a change to an opposite direction, position, or course of action. **2** an adverse change of fortune.
reverse ● verb **1** move backwards. **2** make (something) the opposite of what it was. **3** turn the other way round or up or inside out. **4** revoke or annul (a judgement by a lower court or authority). **5** (of an engine) work in a contrary direction. ● adjective **1** going in or turned towards the opposite direction. **2** operating or behaving in a way contrary to that which is usual or expected. ● noun **1** a complete change of direction or action. **2** reverse gear. **3** (**the reverse**) the opposite or contrary. **4** a setback or defeat. **5** the opposite side or face to the observer. **6** the side of a coin or medal bearing the value or secondary design.
– PHRASES **reverse the charges** chiefly Brit. make the recipient of a telephone call responsible for payment.
– DERIVATIVES **reversible** adjective.
– ORIGIN Latin *revertere* 'turn back'.
reverse engineering ● noun the reproduction of another manufacturer's product after detailed examination of its construction or composition.
reverse gear ● noun a gear making a vehicle or piece of machinery move or work backwards.
reverse takeover ● noun a takeover of a public company by a smaller company.
reversing light ● noun Brit. a white light at the rear of a vehicle that shines when the vehicle is reversing.
reversion /riversh'n/ ● noun **1** a return to a previous state, practice, or belief. **2** Biology the action of reverting to a former or ancestral type. **3** Law the right to possess or succeed to property on the death of the present possessor or at the end of a lease. **4** a sum payable on a person's death by way of life insurance.
– DERIVATIVES **reversionary** adjective.
revert ● verb (**revert to**) **1** return to (a previous state, condition, etc.). **2** Biology return to (a former or ancestral type). **3** Law (of property) return or pass to (the original owner) by reversion.
– ORIGIN Latin *revertere* 'turn back'.
revetment /rivetmənt/ ● noun **1** a retaining wall or facing of masonry, supporting or protecting a rampart, wall, etc. **2** a barricade of earth or sandbags providing protection from blast or to prevent aircraft from overrunning when landing.
– ORIGIN French *revêtement*, from Latin *revestire* 'reclothe'.
review ● noun **1** a formal assessment of something with the intention of instituting change if necessary. **2** a critical appraisal of a book, play, or other work. **3** a retrospective survey or report. **4** a ceremonial display and formal inspection of military or naval forces. ● verb **1** carry out or write a review of. **2** view

Thesaurus

ing, dissemination, reporting, report, declaring, declaration.
reveller ● noun MERRYMAKER, partygoer, carouser, roisterer; *archaic* wassailer.
revelry ● noun CELEBRATION(S), parties, revels, festivity, festivities, jollification, merrymaking, carousing, carousal, roistering; *informal* partying.
revenge ● noun **1** *she is seeking revenge* VENGEANCE, retribution, retaliation, reprisal, requital, recrimination, an eye for an eye (and a tooth for a tooth), redress, satisfaction. **2** *they were filled with revenge* VENGEFULNESS, vindictiveness, vitriol, spite, spitefulness, malice, maliciousness, malevolence, ill will, animosity, hate, hatred, rancour, bitterness; *poetic/literary* maleficence.
● verb **1** *he revenged his brother's murder* AVENGE, take/exact revenge for, exact retribution for, take reprisals for, get redress for, get satisfaction for. **2** *I'll be revenged on the whole pack of you* TAKE REVENGE ON, get one's revenge on, avenge oneself on, take vengeance on, get even with, settle a/the score with, pay back, take reprisals against; *informal* get one's own back on; *archaic* give someone a Roland for an Oliver.
revenue ● noun INCOME, takings, receipts, proceeds, earnings; profit(s).
– OPPOSITES expenditure.
reverberate ● verb RESOUND, echo, re-echo, resonate, ring, boom, rumble.
reverberation ● noun **1** *natural reverberation* RESONANCE, echo, echoing, re-echoing, resounding, ringing, booming, rumbling. **2** *political reverberations* REPERCUSSIONS, ramifications, consequences, shock waves; aftermath, fallout, backlash.
revere ● verb RESPECT, admire, think highly of, have a high opinion of, esteem, hold in high esteem/regard, look up to.
– OPPOSITES despise.
reverence ● noun *reverence for the countryside* HIGH ESTEEM, high regard, great respect, acclaim, admiration, appreciation, estimation, favour.
– OPPOSITES scorn.
● verb *they reverence modern jazz.* See REVERE.
reverent ● adjective RESPECTFUL, reverential, admiring, devoted, devout, dutiful, awed, deferential.
reverie ● noun DAYDREAM, daydreaming, trance, musing; inattention, inattentiveness, wool-gathering, preoccupation, absorption, abstraction, lack of concentration.
reversal ● noun **1** *there was no reversal on this issue* TURNAROUND, turnabout, about-face, volte-face, change of heart, U-turn, backtracking; *Brit.* about-turn; *rare* tergiversation. **2** *a reversal of roles* SWAP, exchange, change, swapping, interchange. **3** *the reversal of the decision* ALTERATION, changing; countermanding, undoing, overturning, overthrow, disallowing, overriding, overruling, veto, vetoing, revocation, repeal, rescinding, annulment, nullification, voiding, invalidation; *formal* rescission, abrogation. **4** *they suffered a reversal* SETBACK, reverse, upset, failure, misfortune, mishap, disaster, blow, disappointment, adversity, hardship, affliction, vicissitude, defeat; bad luck.
reverse ● verb **1** *the car reversed into a lamp post* BACK, drive back/backwards, move back/backwards. **2** *reverse the bottle in the ice bucket* TURN UPSIDE DOWN, turn over, upend, upturn, invert; *archaic* overset. **3** *I reversed my jacket* TURN INSIDE OUT. **4** *reverse your roles* SWAP (ROUND), change (round), exchange, interchange, switch (round). **5** *the umpire reversed the decision* ALTER, change; overturn, overthrow, disallow, override, overrule, veto, revoke, repeal, rescind, annul, nullify, void, invalidate; *Brit.* do an about-turn on; *formal* abrogate.
● adjective *in reverse order* BACKWARD(S), reversed, inverted, transposed.
● noun **1** *the reverse is the case* OPPOSITE, contrary, converse, inverse, obverse, antithesis. **2** *successes and reverses.* See REVERSAL sense 4. **3** *the reverse of the page* OTHER SIDE, reverse side, back, underside, wrong side, verso.
revert ● verb **1** *life will soon revert to normal* RETURN, go back,

or inspect again.
– DERIVATIVES **reviewable** adjective **reviewer** noun.
– ORIGIN obsolete French *reveue*, from *revoir* 'see again'.
revile ● verb (usu. **be reviled**) criticize in an abusive or scornful way.
– ORIGIN Old French *reviler*, from *vil* 'vile'.
revise ● verb **1** examine and improve or amend (text). **2** reconsider and alter (an opinion or judgement). **3** Brit. reread work done previously in order to prepare for an examination. ● noun Printing a proof including corrections made in an earlier proof.
– DERIVATIVES **reviser** noun.
– ORIGIN Latin *revisere* 'look at again'.
revision ● noun **1** the action of revising. **2** a revised edition or form.
– DERIVATIVES **revisionary** adjective.
revisionism ● noun often derogatory the revision or modification of accepted theories or principles.
– DERIVATIVES **revisionist** noun & adjective.
revisit ● verb (**revisited, revisiting**) come back to or visit again.
revitalize (also **revitalise**) ● verb give new life and vitality to.
– DERIVATIVES **revitalization** noun.
revival ● noun **1** an improvement in the condition, strength, or popularity of something. **2** a reawakening of religious fervour brought about by evangelistic meetings. **3** a new production of an old play.
revivalism ● noun **1** belief in or the promotion of a revival of religious fervour. **2** a tendency or desire to revive a former custom or practice.
– DERIVATIVES **revivalist** noun & adjective.
revive ● verb **1** restore to or regain life, consciousness, or strength. **2** restore interest in or the popularity of.
– DERIVATIVES **revivable** adjective **reviver** noun.
– ORIGIN Latin *revivere*, from *vivere* 'live'.
revivify /rivivvifi/ ● verb (**revivifies, revivified**) give new life or vigour to.
– DERIVATIVES **revivification** noun.
revoke ● verb end the validity or operation of (a decree, decision, or promise).
– DERIVATIVES **revocable** adjective **revocation** noun **revoker** noun.
– ORIGIN Latin *revocare* 'call back'.
revolt ● verb **1** rebel against or defy an authority. **2** cause to feel disgust. ● noun an act of rebellion or defiance.
– DERIVATIVES **revolting** adjective.
– ORIGIN French *révolter*, from Latin *revolvere* 'roll back'.
revolution ● noun **1** a forcible overthrow of a government or social order, in favour of a new system. **2** a dramatic and far-reaching change. **3** motion in orbit or in a circular course or round an axis or centre. **4** the single completion of an orbit or rotation.
– DERIVATIVES **revolutionist** noun.
– ORIGIN Latin, from *revolvere* 'roll back'.
revolutionary ● adjective **1** involving or causing dramatic change or innovation. **2** engaged in, promoting, or relating to political revolution. ● noun (pl. **revolutionaries**) a person who introduces a major change or who starts or supports a political revolution.
revolutionize (also **revolutionise**) ● verb change radically or fundamentally.

Thesaurus

change back, default; fall back, regress, relapse. **2** *the property reverted to the landlord* BE RETURNED; *historical* escheat.
review ● noun **1** *the Council undertook a review* ANALYSIS, evaluation, assessment, appraisal, examination, investigation, inquiry, probe, inspection, study. **2** *the rent is due for review* RECONSIDERATION, reassessment, re-evaluation, reappraisal; change, alteration, modification, revision. **3** *book reviews* CRITICISM, critique, assessment, evaluation, commentary; *Brit. informal* crit. **4** *a scientific review* JOURNAL, periodical, magazine, publication. **5** *their review of the economy* SURVEY, report, study, account, description, statement, overview. **6** *a military review* INSPECTION, parade, tattoo, procession; *Brit.* march past.
● verb **1** *I reviewed the evidence* SURVEY, study, research, consider, analyse, examine, scrutinize, explore, look into, probe, investigate, inspect, assess, appraise; *informal* size up. **2** *the referee reviewed his decision* RECONSIDER, re-examine, reassess, re-evaluate, reappraise, rethink; change, alter, modify, revise. **3** *he reviewed the day* REMEMBER, recall, reflect on, think through, go over in one's mind, look back on. **4** *reviewing troops* INSPECT, view. **5** *she reviewed the play* COMMENT ON, evaluate, assess, appraise, judge, critique, criticize.
reviewer ● noun CRITIC, COMMENTATOR, judge, observer, pundit, analyst.
revile ● verb CRITICIZE, censure, condemn, attack, inveigh against, rail against, lambaste, denounce; slander, libel, malign, vilify, besmirch, abuse; *informal* knock, slam, pan, crucify, roast, badmouth; *Brit. informal* slate, rubbish, slag off; *N. Amer. informal* pummel; *Austral./NZ informal* bag, monster; *formal* excoriate, calumniate.
– OPPOSITES praise.
revise ● verb **1** *she revised her opinion* RECONSIDER, review, re-examine, reassess, re-evaluate, reappraise, rethink; change, alter, modify. **2** *the editor revised the text* AMEND, emend, correct, alter, change, edit, rewrite, redraft, rephrase, rework. **3** *(Brit.) revise your lecture notes* GO OVER, reread, memorize; cram; *informal* bone up on; *Brit. informal* swot up (on), mug up (on).
revision ● noun **1** *a revision of the Prayer Book* EMENDATION, correction, alteration, adaptation, editing, rewriting, redrafting. **2** *a new revision* VERSION, edition, rewrite. **3** *a major revision of the system* RECONSIDERATION, review, re-examination, reassessment, re-evaluation, reappraisal, rethink; change, alteration, modification. **4** *(Brit.) he was doing some revision* REREADING, memorizing, cramming; *Brit. informal* swotting.
revitalize ● verb REINVIGORATE, re-energize, boost, regenerate, revive, revivify, rejuvenate, reanimate, resuscitate, refresh, stimulate, breathe new life into; *informal* give a shot in the arm to, pep up, buck up.
revival ● noun **1** *a revival in the economy* IMPROVEMENT, rallying, picking up, amelioration, turn for the better, upturn, upswing, resurgence. **2** *the revival of traditional crafts* COMEBACK, re-establishment, reintroduction, restoration, reappearance, resurrection, regeneration, rejuvenation.
– OPPOSITES downturn, disappearance.
revive ● verb **1** *attempts to revive her failed* RESUSCITATE, bring round, bring back to consciousness. **2** *the man soon revived* REGAIN CONSCIOUSNESS, come round, wake up. **3** *a cup of tea revived her* REINVIGORATE, revitalize, refresh, energize, reanimate, resuscitate, revivify, rejuvenate, regenerate, enliven, stimulate. **4** *reviving old traditions* REINTRODUCE, re-establish, restore, resurrect, bring back, regenerate, resuscitate.
revoke ● verb CANCEL, repeal, rescind, reverse, annul, nullify, void, invalidate, countermand, retract, withdraw, overrule, override; *Law* vacate; *formal* abrogate.
revolt ● verb **1** *the people revolted* REBEL, rise (up), take to the streets, riot, mutiny. **2** *the smell revolted him* DISGUST, sicken, nauseate, make someone sick, make someone's gorge rise, turn someone's stomach, be repugnant to, be repulsive to, put off, be offensive to; *informal* turn off; *N. Amer. informal* gross out.
● noun *an armed revolt* REBELLION, revolution, insurrection, mutiny, uprising, riot, rioting, insurgence, seizure of power, coup (d'état).
revolting ● adjective DISGUSTING, sickening, nauseating, stomach-turning, stomach-churning, repulsive, repellent, repugnant, appalling, abominable, hideous, horrible, awful, dreadful, terrible, obnoxious, vile, nasty, foul, loathsome, offensive, objectionable, off-putting, distasteful, disagreeable; *N. Amer.* vomitous; *informal* ghastly, putrid, horrid, gross, gut-churning, yucky, skanky, icky; *formal* rebarbative; *poetic/literary* noisome; *archaic* disgustful, loathly.
– OPPOSITES attractive, pleasant.
revolution ● noun **1** *the French Revolution* REBELLION, revolt, insurrection, mutiny, uprising, riot, rioting, insurgence, seizure of power, coup (d'état). **2** *a revolution in printing techniques* DRAMATIC CHANGE, radical alteration, sea change, metamorphosis, transformation, innovation, reorganization, restructuring; *informal* shake-up; *N. Amer. informal* shakedown. **3** *one revolution of a wheel* (SINGLE) TURN, rotation, circle, spin; circuit, lap. **4** *the revolution of the earth* TURNING, rotation, circling; orbit.
revolutionary ● adjective **1** *revolutionary troops* REBELLIOUS, rebel, insurgent, rioting, mutinous, renegade, insurrectionary, insurrectionist, seditious, subversive, extremist. **2** *revolutionary change* THOROUGHGOING, thorough, complete, total, absolute, utter, comprehensive, sweeping, far-reaching, extensive, profound. **3** *a revolutionary kind of wheelchair* NEW, novel, original, unusual, unconventional, unorthodox, newfangled, innovative, innovatory, innovational, modern, state-of-the-art, futuristic, pioneering.
● noun *political revolutionaries* REBEL, insurgent, revolutionist, mutineer, insurrectionist, agitator, subversive.

r

revolve ● verb **1** move in a circle on a central axis. **2** (**revolve about/around**) move in a circular orbit around. **3** (**revolve around**) treat as the most important point or element.
– ORIGIN Latin *revolvere* 'roll back'.
revolver ● noun a pistol with revolving chambers enabling several shots to be fired without reloading.
revolving door ● noun an entrance to a large building in which four partitions turn about a central axis.
revue ● noun a light theatrical entertainment of short sketches, songs, and dances, typically dealing satirically with topical issues.
– ORIGIN French, 'review'.
revulsion ● noun a sense of disgust and loathing.
– ORIGIN Latin, from *revellere* 'tear out'.
reward ● noun **1** a thing given in recognition of service, effort, or achievement. **2** a fair return for good or bad behaviour. **3** a sum offered for the detection of a criminal, the restoration of lost property, etc. ● verb **1** give a reward to. **2** show one's appreciation of (an action or quality) with a reward. **3** (**be rewarded**) receive what one deserves.
– ORIGIN Old French *reguard* 'regard, heed'.
rewarding ● adjective providing satisfaction.
– DERIVATIVES **rewardingly** adverb.
rewind ● verb (past and past part. **rewound**) wind (a film or tape) back to the beginning. ● noun a mechanism for rewinding a film or tape.
– DERIVATIVES **rewinder** noun.
rewire ● verb provide with new electric wiring.
– DERIVATIVES **rewirable** adjective.
reword ● verb put into different words.
rework ● verb alter, revise, or reshape.
rewound past and past participle of REWIND.
rewrite ● verb (past **rewrote**; past part. **rewritten**) write again in an altered or improved form. ● noun **1** an instance of rewriting. **2** a text that has been rewritten.
Rex ● noun the reigning king (following a name or in the titles of lawsuits, e.g. *Rex v. Jones*: the Crown versus Jones).
– ORIGIN Latin, 'king'.
Rf ● symbol the chemical element rutherfordium.
r.f. ● abbreviation radio frequency.
RFC ● abbreviation Rugby Football Club.
Rh ● abbreviation rhesus (factor).
RHA ● abbreviation (in the UK) regional health authority.
Rhadamanthine /raddəmantīn/ ● adjective literary stern and incorruptible in judgement.
– ORIGIN from *Rhadamanthus*, ruler and judge of the underworld in Greek mythology.
rhapsodize (also **rhapsodise**) ● verb enthuse about someone or something.
rhapsody ● noun (pl. **rhapsodies**) **1** an enthusiastic or ecstatic expression of feeling. **2** a piece of music in one extended movement, typically emotional in character. **3** (in ancient Greece) an epic poem of a suitable length for recitation at one time.
– DERIVATIVES **rhapsodic** adjective.
– ORIGIN Greek *rhapsōidia*, from *rhaptein* 'to stitch' + *ōidē* 'song, ode'.
rhea /reeə/ ● noun a large flightless bird of South American grasslands, resembling a small ostrich with greyish-brown plumage.
– ORIGIN from *Rhea*, the mother of Zeus in Greek mythology.
rhebok /reebok/ (also **reebok**) ● noun a small South African antelope with a brownish-grey coat, a long slender neck, and short straight horns.
– ORIGIN Dutch *reebok* 'roebuck'.
Rhenish /rennish/ ● adjective of the river Rhine and adjacent regions.
– ORIGIN from Latin *Rhenus* 'Rhine'.
rhenium /reeniəm/ ● noun a rare silvery-white metallic element.
– ORIGIN from Latin *Rhenus* 'Rhine'.
rheology /reeolləji/ ● noun the branch of physics concerned with the deformation and flow of matter.
– DERIVATIVES **rheological** adjective **rheologist** noun.
– ORIGIN from Greek *rheos* 'stream'.
rheostat /reeəstat/ ● noun an electrical instrument used to control a current by varying the resistance.
– DERIVATIVES **rheostatic** adjective.
– ORIGIN from Greek *rheos* 'stream'.
rhesus factor ● noun a substance occurring on red blood cells which can cause disease in a newborn baby whose blood contains the factor (i.e. is **rhesus-positive**) while the mother's blood does not (i.e. is **rhesus-negative**).
– ORIGIN from RHESUS MONKEY, in which the antigen was first observed.
rhesus monkey ● noun a small brown macaque with red skin on the face and rump, native to southern Asia.
– ORIGIN Latin *Rhesus*, from Greek *Rhēsos*, a mythical king of Thrace.
rhetoric /rettərik/ ● noun **1** the art of effective or persuasive speaking or writing. **2** language with a persuasive or impressive effect, but often lacking sincerity or meaningful content.
– ORIGIN from Greek *rhētorikē tekhnē* 'art of rhetoric'.
rhetorical /ritorrik'l/ ● adjective **1** relating to or concerned with rhetoric. **2** expressed in terms intended to persuade or impress. **3** (of a question) asked for effect or to make a statement rather than to obtain an answer.
– DERIVATIVES **rhetorically** adverb.
rhetorician ● noun **1** an expert in formal rhetoric. **2** a speaker whose words are intended to impress or persuade.
rheum /rōōm/ ● noun chiefly literary a watery fluid that collects in or drips from the nose or eyes.
– DERIVATIVES **rheumy** adjective.
– ORIGIN Greek *rheuma* 'stream'.
rheumatic /roomattik/ ● adjective relating to, caused by, or suffering from rheumatism. ● noun a person with rheumatism.
– DERIVATIVES **rheumaticky** adjective (informal).
– ORIGIN originally referring to infection characterized by rheum.
rheumatic fever ● noun an acute fever marked by inflammation and pain in the joints, caused by a streptococcal infection.
rheumatics ● plural noun (usu. treated as sing.) informal rheumatism.
rheumatism ● noun any disease marked by inflammation and pain in the joints, muscles, or fibrous tissue, especially rheumatoid arthritis.
– ORIGIN Greek *rheumatismos*, from *rheuma* 'stream' (because it was believed to be caused by the internal flow of 'watery' humours).
rheumatoid /rōōmətoyd/ ● adjective relating to, affected by, or resembling rheumatism.
rheumatoid arthritis ● noun a chronic progressive disease causing inflammation in the joints and resulting in painful deformity and immobility.

r

Thesaurus

revolutionize ● verb TRANSFORM, alter dramatically, shake up, turn upside down, restructure, reorganize, transmute, metamorphose; *humorous* transmogrify.
revolve ● verb **1** *a fan revolved slowly* GO ROUND, turn round, rotate, spin. **2** *the moon revolves around the earth* CIRCLE, travel, orbit. **3** *his life revolves around cars* BE CONCERNED WITH, be preoccupied with, focus on, centre around. **4** *her mind revolved the possibilities* THINK ABOUT/OVER, give thought to, consider, reflect on, mull over, muse on, cogitate about/on, chew over, weigh up; *archaic* pore on.
revulsion ● noun DISGUST, repulsion, abhorrence, repugnance, nausea, horror, aversion, abomination, distaste; *archaic* disrelish.
– OPPOSITES delight.
reward ● noun *a reward for its safe return* RECOMPENSE, prize, award, honour, decoration, bonus, premium, bounty, present, gift, payment; *informal* pay-off, perk; *formal* perquisite.
● verb *they were well rewarded* RECOMPENSE, pay, remunerate, make something worth someone's while; give an award to.
– OPPOSITES punish.
rewarding ● adjective SATISFYING, gratifying, pleasing, fulfilling, enriching, edifying, beneficial, illuminating, worthwhile, productive, fruitful.
reword ● verb REWRITE, rephrase, recast, put in other words, express differently, redraft, revise; paraphrase.
rewrite ● verb REVISE, recast, reword, rephrase, redraft.
rhetoric ● noun **1** *a form of rhetoric* ORATORY, eloquence, command of language, way with words. **2** *empty rhetoric* BOMBAST, turgidity, grandiloquence, magniloquence, pomposity, extravagant language, purple prose; wordiness, verbosity, prolixity; *informal* hot air; *rare* fustian.
rhetorical ● adjective **1** *rhetorical devices* STYLISTIC, oratorical, linguistic, verbal. **2** *rhetorical hyperbole* EXTRAVAGANT, grandiloquent,

rheumatology /rōōmətolləji/ ● noun the study of rheumatism, arthritis, and other disorders of the joints, muscles, and ligaments.
– DERIVATIVES **rheumatological** adjective **rheumatologist** noun.
rhinestone ● noun an imitation diamond.
– ORIGIN translating French *caillou du Rhin* 'pebble of the Rhine'.
rhinitis /rīnītiss/ ● noun inflammation of the mucous membrane of the nose, caused by a viral infection or an allergic reaction.
– ORIGIN from Greek *rhis* 'nose'.
rhino ● noun (pl. same or **rhinos**) informal a rhinoceros.
rhinoceros /rīnossərəss/ ● noun (pl. same or **rhinoceroses**) a large, heavily built plant-eating mammal with one or two horns on the nose and thick folded skin, native to Africa and South Asia.
– ORIGIN from Greek *rhis* 'nose' + *keras* 'horn'.
rhinoplasty /rīnōplasti/ ● noun (pl. **rhinoplasties**) Medicine plastic surgery performed on the nose.
rhizobium /rīzōbiəm/ ● noun (pl. **rhizobia**) a nitrogen-fixing bacterium that is common in the soil, especially in the root nodules of leguminous plants.
– ORIGIN Latin, from Greek *rhiza* 'root' + *bios* 'life'.
rhizome /rīzōm/ ● noun a horizontal underground plant stem with lateral shoots and adventitious roots at intervals.
– ORIGIN Greek *rhizōma*, from *rhiza* 'root'.
rho /rō/ ● noun the seventeenth letter of the Greek alphabet (**Ρ**, ρ), transliterated as 'r' or 'rh'.
– ORIGIN Greek.
Rhodesian /rōdeezhən/ ● noun a person from Rhodesia (now Zimbabwe). ● adjective relating to Rhodesia.
Rhodes Scholarship ● noun any of several scholarships awarded annually and tenable at Oxford University by students from certain Commonwealth countries, the US, and Germany.
– DERIVATIVES **Rhodes Scholar** noun.
– ORIGIN named after the South African statesman Cecil *Rhodes* (1853–1902), who founded the scholarships.
rhodium /rōdiəm/ ● noun a hard, dense silvery-white metallic element.
– ORIGIN from Greek *rhodon* 'rose' (from the colour of its salts).
rhododendron /rōdədendrən/ ● noun a shrub with large clusters of showy trumpet-shaped flowers and typically with large evergreen leaves.
– ORIGIN from Greek *rhodon* 'rose' + *dendron* 'tree'.
rhombi plural of RHOMBUS.
rhombohedron /rombōheedrən/ ● noun (pl. **rhombohedra** /rombōheedrə/ or **rhombohedrons**) a solid figure whose faces are six equal rhombuses.
– DERIVATIVES **rhombohedral** adjective.
rhomboid /romboyd/ ● adjective having or resembling the shape of a rhombus. ● noun a quadrilateral of which only the opposite sides and angles are equal.
– DERIVATIVES **rhomboidal** adjective.
rhombus /rombəss/ ● noun (pl. **rhombuses** or **rhombi** /rombī/) Geometry a parallelogram with oblique angles and equal sides.
– ORIGIN Greek *rhombos* 'thing that can be spun round, a rhombus'.
rhubarb ● noun **1** the thick leaf stalks of a plant of the dock family, which are reddish or green and eaten as a fruit after cooking. **2** Brit. informal noise made by a group of actors to give the impression of indistinct background conversation. **3** nonsense.
– ORIGIN Latin *rheubarbarum*, *rhabarbarum* 'foreign rhubarb', from Greek *rha* (also meaning 'rhubarb') + *barbaros* 'foreign'.
rhumb /rum/ ● noun Nautical **1** (also **rhumb line**) an imaginary line on the earth's surface cutting all meridians at the same angle, used to plot a ship's course on a chart. **2** any of the thirty-two points of the compass.
– ORIGIN French *rumb* (earlier *ryn de vent* 'point of the compass').
rhumba ● noun variant spelling of RUMBA.
rhyme ● noun **1** correspondence of sound between words or the endings of words, especially when used in poetry. **2** a short poem with rhyming lines. **3** rhyming poetry or verse. **4** a word with the same sound as another. ● verb **1** (of a word, syllable, or line) have or end with a sound that corresponds to another. **2** (**rhyme with**) put (a word) together with (another word with a corresponding sound). **3** literary compose verse or poetry.
– PHRASES **rhyme or reason** logical explanation. *there's no rhyme or reason to it.*
– DERIVATIVES **rhymer** noun.
– ORIGIN Old French *rime*, from Greek *rhuthmos* 'rhythm'.
rhymester ● noun a composer of rhymes.
rhyming slang ● noun a type of slang that replaces words with rhyming words or phrases, typically with the rhyming element omitted (e.g. *butcher's*, short for *butcher's hook*, meaning 'look').
rhyolite /rīəlīt/ ● noun a pale fine-grained volcanic rock of granitic composition.
– ORIGIN German *Rhyolit*, from Greek *rhuax* 'lava stream' + *lithos* 'stone'.
rhythm /rithəm/ ● noun **1** a strong, regular repeated pattern of movement or sound. **2** the systematic arrangement of musical sounds, according to duration and periodical stress. **3** a particular pattern formed by such arrangement: *a slow waltz rhythm.* **4** the measured flow of words and phrases in verse or prose as determined by the length of and stress on syllables. **5** a regularly recurring sequence of events or actions.
– DERIVATIVES **rhythmless** adjective.
– ORIGIN French *rhythme*, from Greek *rhuthmos*, related to *rhein* 'to flow'.
rhythm and blues ● noun popular music of US black origin, arising from a combination of blues with jazz rhythms.
rhythmic ● adjective **1** having or relating to rhythm. **2** occurring regularly.
– DERIVATIVES **rhythmical** adjective **rhythmically** adverb **rhythmicity** noun.
rhythm method ● noun a method of birth control involving the avoidance of sexual intercourse when ovulation is likely to occur.
rhythm section ● noun the part of a pop or jazz group supplying the rhythm, in particular the bass and drums.
RI ● abbreviation Rhode Island.
ria /reeə/ ● noun Geography a long narrow inlet formed by the partial submergence of a river valley.
– ORIGIN Spanish, 'estuary'.
rial /reeaal/ (also **riyal**) ● noun **1** the basic monetary unit of Iran and Oman. **2** (usu. **riyal**) the basic monetary unit of Saudi Arabia, Qatar, and Yemen.
– ORIGIN Arabic, from Spanish *real* 'royal'.
rib ● noun **1** each of a series of slender curved bones articulated in pairs to the spine, protecting the thoracic cavity and its organs. **2** Architecture a curved member supporting a vault or defining its form. **3** a curved transverse strut of metal or timber in a ship, forming part of the framework of the hull. **4** each of the hinged rods supporting the fabric of an umbrella. **5** a vein of a leaf or an insect's wing. **6** Knitting alternate plain and purl stitches producing a ridged, slightly elastic fabric. ● verb (**ribbed**, **ribbing**) **1** (usu. **be ribbed**) mark with or form into raised bands or ridges. **2** informal tease good-naturedly.
– ORIGIN Old English.
ribald /ribb'ld/ ● adjective coarsely or irreverently humorous.
– ORIGIN originally denoting a licentious or irreverent person: from Old French *ribauld*, from *riber* 'indulge in licentious pleasures'.
ribaldry ● noun ribald talk or behaviour.
riband /ribb'nd/ ● noun archaic a ribbon.
– ORIGIN Old French *riban*, probably related to BAND[1].
ribbed ● adjective **1** having a pattern of raised bands. **2** Architecture strengthened with ribs.
ribbing ● noun **1** a rib-like structure or pattern. **2** informal good-natured teasing.
ribbon ● noun **1** a long, narrow strip of fabric, used for tying something or for decoration. **2** a ribbon of a special colour or design awarded as a prize or worn to indicate the holding of an honour. **3** a long, narrow strip. **4** a narrow band of inked material wound on a spool and used to produce the characters in

Thesaurus

magniloquent, high-flown, orotund, bombastic, grandiose, pompous, pretentious, overblown, oratorical, turgid, flowery, florid; *informal* highfalutin; *rare* fustian.
rhyme ● noun POEM, piece of poetry, verse; (**rhymes**) poetry, doggerel.
rhythm ● noun **1** *the rhythm of the music* BEAT, cadence, tempo, time, pulse, throb, swing. **2** *poetic features such as rhythm* METRE, measure, stress, accent, cadence. **3** *the rhythm of daily life* PATTERN, flow, tempo.
rhythmic ● adjective RHYTHMICAL, with a steady pulse, measured,

some typewriters and computer printers.
– PHRASES **cut** (or **tear**) **to ribbons** cut (or tear) into ragged strips.
– DERIVATIVES **ribboned** adjective.
– ORIGIN variant of RIBAND.
ribbon development • noun Brit. the building of houses along a main road.
ribby • adjective having prominent ribs.
ribcage • noun the bony frame formed by the ribs.
riboflavin /rībōflayvin/ • noun vitamin B_2, a yellow compound essential for energy production and present especially in milk, liver, and green vegetables.
– ORIGIN from RIBOSE + Latin *flavus* 'yellow'.
ribonucleic acid /rībōnyoōkleeik, -klayik/ • noun see RNA.
– ORIGIN *ribonucleic* from RIBOSE + NUCLEIC ACID.
ribose /rībōz/ • noun a sugar which is a constituent of DNA and several vitamins and enzymes.
– ORIGIN arbitrary alteration of *arabinose*, a related sugar.
ribosome /rībəsōm/ • noun Biochemistry a minute particle of RNA and protein found in cells, involved in the synthesis of polypeptides and proteins.
– DERIVATIVES **ribosomal** adjective.
– ORIGIN from RIBONUCLEIC ACID + Greek *soma* 'body'.
rib-tickler • noun informal a very amusing joke or story.
ribulose /ribyoolōz/ • noun Chemistry a sugar containing five carbon atoms which is important in carbohydrate metabolism and photosynthesis.
rice • noun **1** a swamp grass which is cultivated as a source of food in warm countries. **2** the grains of this cereal used as food. • verb N. Amer. force (cooked potatoes or other vegetables) through a sieve or similar utensil.
– DERIVATIVES **ricer** N. Amer. noun.
– ORIGIN Old French *ris*, from Greek *oruza*.
ricepaper • noun thin edible paper made from the flattened and dried pith of a shrub, used in oriental painting and in baking biscuits and cakes.
rich • adjective **1** having a great deal of money or assets. **2** (of a country or region) having valuable natural resources or a successful economy. **3** of expensive materials or workmanship. **4** plentiful; abundant. **5** having or producing something in large amounts: *fruits rich in vitamins.* **6** (of food) containing much fat, sugar, etc. **7** (of a colour, sound, or smell) pleasantly deep and strong. **8** (of soil or land) fertile. **9** (of the mixture in an internal-combustion engine) containing a high proportion of fuel. **10** informal (of a remark) causing ironic amusement or indignation.
– DERIVATIVES **richen** verb **richness** noun.
– ORIGIN Old English, 'powerful, wealthy'.
riches • plural noun **1** material wealth. **2** valuable natural resources.
richly • adverb **1** in a rich way. **2** fully.
Richter scale /riktər/ • noun a logarithmic scale for expressing the magnitude of an earthquake on the basis of seismograph oscillations.
– ORIGIN named after the American geologist Charles F. *Richter* (1900–85).
ricin /rīsin, rissin/ • noun Chemistry a highly toxic protein obtained from the pressed seeds of the castor oil plant.
– ORIGIN from Latin *Ricinus communis* (denoting the castor oil plant).
rick[1] • noun a stack of hay, corn, or straw, especially one built into a regular shape and thatched.
– ORIGIN Old English.
rick[2] • noun a slight sprain or strain, especially in the neck or back. • verb strain (one's neck or back) slightly.
– ORIGIN dialect.
rickets /rikkits/ • noun (treated as sing. or pl.) a disease of children caused by vitamin D deficiency, characterized by softening and distortion of the bones.
– ORIGIN perhaps an alteration of Greek *rhakhitis* 'rickets'.
rickety • adjective **1** poorly made and likely to collapse. **2** suffering from rickets.
– DERIVATIVES **ricketiness** noun.
rickrack • noun braided trimming in a zigzag pattern, used on clothes.
– ORIGIN of unknown origin.
rickshaw • noun a light two-wheeled hooded vehicle drawn by one or more people, chiefly used in Asian countries.
– ORIGIN Japanese, 'person-strength-vehicle'.
ricochet /rikkəshay, -shet/ • verb (**ricocheted** /rikkəshayd/, **ricocheting** /rikkəshaying/ or **ricochetted** /rikkəshetid/, **ricochetting** /rikkəsheting/) **1** (of a bullet or other projectile) rebound off a surface. **2** move or appear to move in such a way. • noun **1** a shot or hit that ricochets. **2** the ricocheting action of a bullet or other projectile.
– ORIGIN French.
ricotta /rikottə/ • noun a soft white unsalted Italian cheese.
– ORIGIN Italian, 'recooked, cooked twice'.
rictus /riktəss/ • noun a fixed grimace or grin.
– DERIVATIVES **rictal** adjective.
– ORIGIN Latin, 'open mouth', from *ringi* 'to gape'.
rid • verb (**ridding**; past and past part. **rid**) **1** (**rid of**) make (someone or something) free of (an unwanted person or thing). **2** (**be** (or **get**) **rid of**) be freed or relieved of.
– ORIGIN Old Norse.
riddance • noun the action of getting rid of someone or something.
– PHRASES **good riddance** expressing relief at being rid of someone or something.
ridden past participle of RIDE. • adjective (in combination) full of or dominated by a particular thing: *guilt-ridden.*
riddle[1] • noun **1** a question or statement phrased so as to require ingenuity in finding its answer or meaning. **2** a puzzling person or thing. • verb archaic speak in or pose riddles.
– DERIVATIVES **riddler** noun.
– ORIGIN Old English, related to READ.
riddle[2] • verb (usu. **be riddled**) **1** make many holes in, especially with gunshot. **2** fill or permeate with something undesirable:

r

Thesaurus

throbbing, beating, pulsating, regular, steady, even.
– OPPOSITES irregular.
ribald • adjective. See CRUDE sense 3.
rich • adjective **1** *rich people* WEALTHY, affluent, moneyed, well off, well-to-do, prosperous, opulent; *N. Amer.* silk-stocking; *informal* rolling in money, in the money, loaded, stinking rich, filthy rich, well heeled, made of money; *informal, dated* oofy. **2** *rich furnishings* SUMPTUOUS, opulent, luxurious, luxury, de luxe, lavish, gorgeous, splendid, magnificent, costly, expensive, fancy; *informal* posh, plush, ritzy, swanky, classy; *Brit. informal* swish; *N. Amer. informal* swank. **3** *a garden rich in flowers* ABOUNDING, well provided, well stocked, crammed, packed, teeming, bursting; *informal* jam-packed, chock-a-block, chock-full; *Austral./NZ informal* chocker. **4** *a rich supply of restaurants* PLENTIFUL, abundant, copious, ample, profuse, lavish, liberal, generous, bountiful; *poetic/literary* plenteous, bounteous. **5** *rich soil* FERTILE, productive, fecund, fruitful. **6** *a rich sauce* CREAMY, fatty, heavy, full-flavoured. **7** *a rich wine* FULL-BODIED, heavy, fruity. **8** *rich colours* STRONG, deep, full, intense, vivid, brilliant. **9** *her rich contralto voice filled the room* SONOROUS, full, resonant, deep, clear, mellow, mellifluous; *rare* mellifluent. **10** *(informal) that's rich!* PREPOSTEROUS, outrageous, absurd, ridiculous, ludicrous, laughable, risible; *informal* a bit much; *Brit. informal* a bit thick.
– OPPOSITES poor, light.
riches • plural noun **1** *his new-found riches* MONEY, wealth, funds, (hard) cash, (filthy) lucre, wherewithal, means, (liquid) assets, capital, resources, reserves; opulence, affluence, prosperity; *informal* dough, bread, loot, readies, shekels, moolah, the necessary; *Brit. informal* dosh, brass, lolly, spondulicks; *N. Amer. informal* bucks, mazuma, dinero; *US informal* greenbacks, simoleons, jack, rocks; *Austral./NZ informal* Oscar; *Brit. dated* l.s.d.; *archaic* pelf. **2** *underwater riches* RESOURCES, treasure(s), bounty, jewels, gems.
richly • adverb **1** *the richly furnished chamber* SUMPTUOUSLY, opulently, luxuriously, lavishly, gorgeously, splendidly, magnificently; *informal* poshly, plushly, ritzily, swankily, classily; *Brit. informal* swishly. **2** *the joy she richly deserves* FULLY, thoroughly, in full measure, well, completely, wholly, totally, entirely, absolutely, amply, utterly.
– OPPOSITES meanly.
rickety • adjective SHAKY, unsteady, unsound, unsafe, tumbledown, broken-down, dilapidated, ramshackle; *informal* shambly; *N. Amer. informal* shacky.
rid • verb *ridding the building of asbestos* CLEAR, free, purge, empty, strip.
– PHRASES **get rid of 1** *we must get rid of some stuff* DISPOSE OF, throw away/out, clear out, discard, scrap, dump, bin, jettison; *in-*

a policy riddled with inadequacies. **3** pass through a riddle. ● noun a large coarse sieve, especially one for separating ashes from cinders or sand from gravel.
– ORIGIN Old English.
riddling ● adjective speaking or expressed in riddles; enigmatic.
ride ● verb (past **rode**; past part. **ridden**) **1** sit on and control the movement of (a horse, bicycle, or motorcycle). **2** (usu. **ride in/on**) travel in or on a vehicle or horse. **3** travel over on horseback or on a bicycle or motorcycle: *ride the scenic trail.* **4** be carried or supported by: *surfers rode the waves.* **5** sail or float: *a ship rode at anchor in the dock.* **6** (**ride up**) (of a garment) gradually move upwards out of its proper position. **7** (**ride on**) depend on. **8** (**ride out**) come safely through. **9** yield to (a blow) so as to reduce its impact. **10** (**be ridden**) be full of or dominated by: *people ridden by ill health.* ● noun **1** an act of riding. **2** a roller coaster, roundabout, etc. ridden at a fair or amusement park. **3** a path for horse riding. **4** N. Amer. a person giving a lift in a vehicle.
– PHRASES **be riding for a fall** informal be acting in a reckless way that invites failure. **let something ride** take no immediate action over something. **ride high** be successful. **ride to hounds** chiefly Brit. go fox-hunting on horseback. **a rough** (or **easy**) **ride** a difficult (or easy) time. **take someone for a ride** informal deceive someone.
– DERIVATIVES **rideable** (also **ridable**) adjective.
– ORIGIN Old English.
rider ● noun **1** a person who rides a horse, bicycle, motorcycle, etc. **2** an added condition or proviso.
– DERIVATIVES **riderless** adjective.
ridge ● noun **1** a long narrow hilltop, mountain range, or watershed. **2** a narrow raised band on a surface. **3** Meteorology an elongated region of high barometric pressure. **4** the edge formed where the two sloping sides of a roof meet at the top. ● verb (often **ridged**) mark with or form into ridges.
– DERIVATIVES **ridgy** adjective.
– ORIGIN Old English, 'spine, crest'.
ridge tent ● noun a tent with a central ridge supported by a pole or frame at each end.
ridgeway ● noun a road or track along a ridge.
ridicule ● noun mockery or derision. ● verb make fun of; mock.
ridiculous ● adjective inviting mockery or derision; absurd.
– DERIVATIVES **ridiculously** adverb **ridiculousness** noun.
– ORIGIN Latin *ridiculus* 'laughable', from *ridere* 'to laugh'.
riding[1] ● noun **1** the sport or activity of riding horses. **2** a path for horse riding.
riding[2] ● noun **1** (usu. **the East/North/West Riding**) one of three former administrative divisions of Yorkshire. **2** an electoral district of Canada.
– ORIGIN Old Norse, 'third part'.
riding crop ● noun a short flexible whip with a loop for the hand, used when riding horses.
riding habit ● noun a woman's riding dress, consisting of a skirt and a double-breasted jacket.
riel /reeəl/ ● noun the basic monetary unit of Cambodia, equal to 100 sen.
– ORIGIN Khmer.
Riesling /reesling/ ● noun **1** a variety of wine grape grown especially in Germany and Austria. **2** a dry white wine made from this grape.
– ORIGIN German.
rife ● adjective **1** (especially of something undesirable) widespread. **2** (**rife with**) full of.
– DERIVATIVES **rifeness** noun.
– ORIGIN Old English, probably from an Old Norse word meaning 'acceptable'.
riff ● noun a short repeated phrase in popular music or jazz. ● verb play riffs.
– ORIGIN abbreviation of RIFFLE.
riffle ● verb **1** turn over something, especially pages, quickly and casually. **2** (**riffle through**) search quickly through. **3** shuffle (playing cards) by flicking up and releasing the corners of two piles of cards so that they intermingle. ● noun an act of riffling.
– ORIGIN perhaps from a variant of RUFFLE, influenced by RIPPLE.
riff-raff ● noun disreputable or undesirable people.
– ORIGIN from Old French *rif et raf* 'one and all, every bit'.
rifle[1] ● noun **1** a gun, especially one fired from shoulder level, having a long spirally grooved barrel to make a bullet spin and thereby increase accuracy over a long distance. **2** (**rifles**) troops armed with rifles. ● verb **1** (usu. as adj. **rifled**) make spiral grooves in (a gun or its barrel or bore). **2** hit or kick (a ball) hard and straight.
– ORIGIN from French *rifler* 'graze, scratch'.
rifle[2] ● verb **1** search through something hurriedly to find or steal something. **2** steal.
– ORIGIN Old French *rifler* 'graze, plunder'.
rifleman ● noun a soldier armed with a rifle.
rifle range ● noun a place for practising rifle shooting.
rifling ● noun spiral grooves on the inside of a rifle barrel.
rift ● noun **1** a crack, split, or break. **2** a serious break in friendly relations.
– ORIGIN Scandinavian.
rift valley ● noun a steep-sided valley formed by subsidence of the earth's surface between nearly parallel faults.
rig[1] ● verb (**rigged**, **rigging**) **1** provide (a boat) with sails and rigging. **2** assemble and adjust (the equipment of a sailing boat, aircraft, etc.) in readiness for operation. **3** (often **rig up**) set up (a device or structure), typically in a makeshift way. **4** (**rig out**) provide with clothes of a particular type. ● noun **1** the arrangement of a boat's sails and rigging. **2** an apparatus or device for a particular purpose: *a lighting rig.* **3** an oil rig or drilling rig. **4** a person's costume or outfit. **5** chiefly N. Amer. & Austral./NZ a truck.
– DERIVATIVES **rigged** adjective.
– ORIGIN perhaps Scandinavian.

Thesaurus

formal chuck (away), ditch, junk, get shut of; *Brit. informal* get shot of; *N. Amer. informal* trash. **2** *the cats got rid of the rats* DESTROY, eliminate, annihilate, obliterate, wipe out, kill.
riddle[1] ● noun *an answer to the riddle* PUZZLE, conundrum, brainteaser, (unsolved) problem, question, poser, enigma, mystery; *informal* stumper.
riddle[2] ● verb **1** *his car was riddled by gunfire* PERFORATE, hole, pierce, puncture, pepper. **2** *he was riddled with cancer* PERMEATE, suffuse, fill, pervade, spread through, imbue, saturate, overrun, beset. **3** *the soil must be riddled* SIEVE, sift, strain, screen, filter; *archaic* griddle.
ride ● verb **1** *she can ride a horse* SIT ON, mount, bestride; manage, handle, control. **2** *riding round the town on motor bikes* TRAVEL, move, proceed, make one's way; drive, cycle; trot, canter, gallop.
● noun *he took us for a ride* TRIP, journey, drive, run, excursion, outing, jaunt; lift; *informal* spin.
ridicule ● noun *he was subjected to ridicule* MOCKERY, derision, laughter, scorn, scoffing, contempt, jeering, sneering, sneers, jibes, jibing, teasing, taunts, taunting, ragging, chaffing, sarcasm, satire; *informal* kidding, ribbing, joshing; *N. Amer. informal* goofing, razzing; *Austral./NZ informal* chiacking; *dated* sport.
– OPPOSITES respect.
● verb *his theory was ridiculed* DERIDE, mock, laugh at, heap scorn on, jeer at, jibe at, sneer at, treat with contempt, scorn, make fun of, poke fun at, scoff at, satirize, lampoon, burlesque, caricature, parody, tease, taunt, rag, chaff; *informal* kid, rib, josh, take the mickey out of; *N. Amer. informal* goof on, rag on, razz, pull someone's chain; *Austral./NZ informal* chiack, poke mullock at, sling off at; *dated* make sport of, twit.
ridiculous ● adjective **1** *that looks ridiculous* LAUGHABLE, absurd, comical, funny, hilarious, risible, droll, amusing, farcical, silly, ludicrous; *rare* derisible. **2** *a ridiculous suggestion* SENSELESS, silly, foolish, foolhardy, stupid, inane, fatuous, childish, puerile, half-baked, hare-brained, ill-thought-out, crackpot, idiotic. **3** *a ridiculous exaggeration* ABSURD, preposterous, ludicrous, laughable, risible, nonsensical, senseless, outrageous.
– OPPOSITES sensible.
rife ● adjective **1** *violence is rife* WIDESPREAD, general, common, universal, extensive, ubiquitous, omnipresent, endemic, inescapable, insidious, prevalent. **2** *the village was rife with gossip* OVERFLOWING, bursting, alive, teeming, abounding.
– OPPOSITES unknown.
riff-raff ● noun RABBLE, scum, the lowest of the low, good-for-nothings, undesirables; *informal* peasants.
– OPPOSITES elite.
rifle ● verb **1** *she rifled through her wardrobe* RUMMAGE, search, hunt, forage. **2** *a thief rifled her home* BURGLE, rob, steal from, loot, raid, plunder, ransack.
rift ● noun **1** *a deep rift in the ice* CRACK, fault, flaw, split, break, breach, fissure, fracture, cleft, crevice, cavity, opening. **2** *the rift*

rig² ● verb (**rigged**, **rigging**) manage or conduct fraudulently so as to gain an advantage.
– ORIGIN of unknown origin.

rigatoni /riggətōni/ ● plural noun pasta in the form of short hollow fluted tubes.
– ORIGIN Italian.

rigger¹ ● noun **1** (in combination) a ship rigged in a particular way: *a square-rigger*. **2** a person who attends to the rigging of a sailing ship, aircraft, or parachute. **3** a person who erects and maintains scaffolding, cranes, etc. **4** a person who works on an oil rig.

rigger² ● noun a person who rigs something to their advantage.

rigging ● noun **1** the system of ropes or chains supporting a ship's masts and controlling or setting the yards and sails. **2** the ropes and wires supporting the structure of an airship, biplane, hang-glider, or parachute. **3** the cables and fittings controlling the flight surfaces and engines of an aircraft.

right ● adjective **1** on, towards, or relating to the side of a human body or of a thing which is to the east when the person or thing is facing north. **2** morally good, justified, or acceptable. **3** factually correct. **4** most appropriate: *the right man for the job*. **5** in a satisfactory, sound, or normal condition. **6** relating to a right-wing person or group. **7** informal, chiefly Brit. complete; absolute: *I felt a right idiot*. ● adverb **1** on or to the right side. **2** to the furthest or most complete extent or degree. **3** exactly; directly. **4** correctly or satisfactorily. **5** informal immediately. ● noun **1** that which is morally right. **2** a moral or legal entitlement to have or do something. **3** (**rights**) the authority to perform, publish, or film a particular work or event. **4** (**the right**) the right-hand part, side, or direction. **5** a right turn. **6** a person's right fist, or a blow given with it. **7** (often **the Right**) (treated as sing. or pl.) a group or political party favouring conservative views. ● verb **1** restore to a normal or upright position. **2** restore to a normal or correct condition. **3** make amends for (a wrong).
– PHRASES **bang to rights** informal (of a criminal) with positive proof of guilt. **by rights** if things were fair or correct. **in one's own right** as a result of one's own claims, qualifications, or efforts. **put** (or **set**) **right** tell the true facts to. **put** (or **set**) **to rights** restore to the correct or normal state. **right** (or **straight**) **away** immediately. **right on** informal **1** expressing support, approval, or encouragement. **2** (**right-on**) informal, often derogatory in keeping with fashionable liberal or left-wing opinions and values. **a right one** Brit. informal a silly or foolish person. **she's** (or **she'll be**) **right** Austral./NZ informal don't worry.
– DERIVATIVES **righter** noun **rightish** adjective **rightmost** adjective **rightness** noun **rightward** adjective & adverb **rightwards** adverb.
– ORIGIN Old English.

right angle ● noun an angle of 90°, as in a corner of a square.
– PHRASES **at right angles to** forming an angle of 90° with.
– DERIVATIVES **right-angled** adjective.

right ascension ● noun Astronomy position measured along the celestial equator, expressed in hours, minutes, and seconds.

right back ● noun a defender in soccer or field hockey who plays primarily on the right of the field.

right bank ● noun the bank of a river on the right as one faces downstream.

righteous /rīchəss/ ● adjective morally right or justifiable.
– DERIVATIVES **righteously** adverb **righteousness** noun.

rightful ● adjective **1** having a legitimate right to something. **2** legitimately claimed; fitting.
– DERIVATIVES **rightfully** adverb **rightfulness** noun.

right hand ● noun **1** the hand of a person's right side. **2** the region or direction on the right side. **3** the most important position next to someone. ● adjective **1** on or towards the right side. **2** done with or using the right hand.

right-hand drive ● noun a motor-vehicle steering system with the steering wheel and other controls fitted on the right side, for use in countries where vehicles drive on the left.

right-handed ● adjective **1** using or done with the right hand. **2** turning to the right; towards the right. **3** (of a screw) advanced by turning clockwise.

Thesaurus

between them BREACH, division, split; quarrel, squabble, disagreement, falling-out, row, argument, dispute, conflict, feud; estrangement; *informal* spat, scrap; *Brit. informal* bust-up.

rig¹ ● verb **1** *the boats were rigged with a single sail* EQUIP, kit out, fit out, supply, furnish, provide, arm. **2** *I rigged myself out in black* DRESS, clothe, attire, robe, garb, array, deck out, drape, accoutre, outfit, get up, trick out/up; *informal* doll up; *archaic* apparel. **3** *he will rig up a shelter* SET UP, erect, assemble; throw together, cobble together, put together, whip up, improvise, contrive; *Brit. informal* knock up.
● noun **1** *a CB radio rig* APPARATUS, appliance, machine, device, instrument, contraption, system; tackle, gear, kit, outfit. **2** *the rig of the American Army Air Corps* UNIFORM, costume, ensemble, outfit, livery, attire, clothes, clothing, garments, dress, garb, regimentals, regalia, trappings; *Brit.* strip; *informal* get-up, gear, togs; *Brit. informal* kit; *formal* apparel; *archaic* raiment, vestments.

rig² ● verb *they rigged the election* MANIPULATE, engineer, distort, misrepresent, pervert, tamper with, doctor; falsify, fake, trump up; *informal* fix; *Brit. informal* fiddle.

right ● adjective **1** *it wouldn't be right to do that* JUST, fair, proper, good, upright, righteous, virtuous, moral, ethical, honourable, honest; lawful, legal. **2** *the right answer* CORRECT, accurate, exact, precise; proper, valid, conventional, established, official, formal; *Brit. informal* spot on. **3** *the right person for the job* SUITABLE, appropriate, fitting, correct, proper, desirable, preferable, ideal; *archaic* meet. **4** *you've come at the right time* OPPORTUNE, advantageous, favourable, propitious, good, lucky, happy, fortunate, providential, felicitous; timely, seasonable, convenient, expedient, suitable, appropriate. **5** *he's not right in the head* SANE, lucid, rational, balanced, compos mentis; *informal* all there. **6** *he does not look right* HEALTHY, well, (fighting) fit, normal, up to par; *informal* up to scratch, in the pink. **7** *my right hand* DEXTRAL. **8** *(informal) it's a right mess* ABSOLUTE, complete, total, real, thorough, perfect, utter, sheer, unmitigated, veritable.
– OPPOSITES wrong, insane, unhealthy.
● adverb **1** *she was right at the limit of her patience* COMPLETELY, fully, totally, absolutely, utterly, thoroughly, quite. **2** *right in the middle of the village* EXACTLY, precisely, directly, immediately, just, squarely, dead; *informal* (slap) bang, smack, plumb; *N. Amer. informal* smack dab. **3** *keep going right on* STRAIGHT, directly, as the crow flies. **4** *(informal) he'll be right down* STRAIGHT, immediately, instantly, at once, straight away, now, right now, this minute, directly, forthwith, without further ado, promptly, quickly, a.s.a.p., as soon as possible; *N. Amer.* in short order; *informal* straight off, p.d.q. (pretty damn quick), pronto; *N. Amer. informal* lickety-split. **5** *I think I heard right* CORRECTLY, accurately, properly, precisely, aright, rightly, perfectly. **6** *make sure you're treated right* WELL, properly, justly, fairly, equitably, impartially, honourably, lawfully, legally. **7** *things will turn out right* WELL, for the best, favourably, happily, advantageously, profitably, providentially, luckily, conveniently.
– OPPOSITES wrong, badly.
● noun **1** *the difference between right and wrong* GOODNESS, righteousness, virtue, integrity, rectitude, propriety, morality, truth, honesty, honour, justice, fairness, equity; lawfulness, legality. **2** *you have the right to say no* ENTITLEMENT, prerogative, privilege, advantage, due, birthright, liberty, authority, power, licence, permission, dispensation, leave, sanction; *Law, historical* droit.
– OPPOSITES wrong.
● verb **1** *the way to right a capsized dinghy* SET UPRIGHT, turn back over. **2** *we must right the situation* REMEDY, put right, rectify, retrieve, fix, resolve, sort out, settle, square; straighten out, correct, repair, mend, redress, make good, ameliorate, better.
– PHRASES **by rights** PROPERLY, correctly, technically, in fairness; legally, de jure. **in the right** JUSTIFIED, vindicated, right. **put something to rights**. See RIGHT verb sense 2. **right away** AT ONCE, straight away, (right) now, this (very) minute, this instant, immediately, instantly, directly, forthwith, without further ado, promptly, quickly, without delay, a.s.a.p., as soon as possible; *N. Amer.* in short order; *informal* straight off, p.d.q. (pretty damn quick), pronto; *N. Amer. informal* lickety-split. **within one's rights** ENTITLED, permitted, allowed, at liberty, empowered, authorized, qualified, licensed, justified.

righteous ● adjective **1** *righteous living* GOOD, virtuous, upright, upstanding, decent; ethical, principled, moral, high-minded, law-abiding, honest, honourable, blameless, irreproachable, noble; saintly, angelic, pure. **2** *righteous anger* JUSTIFIABLE, justified, legitimate, defensible, supportable, rightful; admissible, allowable, understandable, excusable, acceptable, reasonable.
– OPPOSITES sinful, unjustifiable.

rightful ● adjective **1** *the car's rightful owner* LEGAL, lawful, real, true, proper, correct, recognized, genuine, authentic, acknow-

right-hander • noun **1** a right-handed person. **2** a blow struck with a person's right hand.
right-hand man • noun an indispensable helper or chief assistant.
Right Honourable • adjective Brit. a title given to certain high officials such as government ministers.
rightism • noun the political views or policies of the right.
– DERIVATIVES **rightist** noun & adjective.
rightly • adverb **1** in accordance with what is true or just. **2** with good reason.
right-minded • adjective having sound views and principles.
right of way • noun **1** the legal right to pass along a specific route through another's property. **2** a path subject to such a right. **3** the right of a pedestrian, vehicle, or ship to proceed with precedence over others in a situation or place.
Right Reverend • adjective a title given to a bishop.
right side • noun the side of something intended to be uppermost or foremost.
– PHRASES **on the right side of 1** in favour with. **2** somewhat less than (a specified age).
rights issue • noun an issue of shares offered at a special price by a company to its existing shareholders.
rightsize • verb chiefly US convert to an appropriate or optimum size, in particular shed staff from (an organization).
right-thinking • adjective right-minded.
right-to-life • adjective another term for PRO-LIFE.
right whale • noun a whale with a large head and a deeply curved jaw, of Arctic and temperate waters.
– ORIGIN so named because it was regarded as the 'right' whale to hunt.
right wing • noun **1** the conservative or reactionary section of a political party or system. [ORIGIN see LEFT WING.] **2** the right side of a sports team on the field or of an army.
– DERIVATIVES **right-winger** noun.
rigid • adjective **1** unable to bend or be forced out of shape. **2** (of a person) stiff and unmoving. **3** not able to be changed or adapted.
– DERIVATIVES **rigidify** verb **rigidity** noun **rigidly** adverb.
– ORIGIN Latin *rigidus*, from *rigere* 'be stiff'.
rigmarole /rigmərōl/ • noun **1** a lengthy and complicated procedure. **2** a long, rambling story.
– ORIGIN apparently from obsolete *ragman roll*, originally denoting a legal document recording a list of offences.
rigor mortis /riggər mortiss/ • noun stiffening of the joints and muscles a few hours after death, lasting from one to four days.
– ORIGIN Latin, 'stiffness of death'.
rigorous • adjective **1** extremely thorough or accurate. **2** (of a rule, system, etc.) strictly applied or adhered to. **3** adhering strictly to a belief, opinion, or system. **4** harsh or severe: *rigorous military training.*
– DERIVATIVES **rigorously** adverb **rigorousness** noun.
rigour (US **rigor**) • noun **1** the quality of being rigorous. **2** (**rigours**) demanding, difficult, or extreme conditions.
– ORIGIN Latin *rigor* 'stiffness'.
rig-out • noun informal, chiefly Brit. an outfit of clothes.
rijsttafel /rīsttaaf'l/ • noun a meal of SE Asian food consisting of a selection of spiced rice dishes.
– ORIGIN Dutch, from *rijst* 'rice' + *tafel* 'table'.

rile • verb informal annoy or irritate.
– ORIGIN variant of ROIL.
Riley • noun (in phrase **the life of Riley**) informal a luxurious or carefree existence.
– ORIGIN of unknown origin.
rill • noun a small stream.
– ORIGIN probably Low German.
rillettes /reeyet/ • plural noun (treated as sing. or pl.) pâté of minced pork or other light meat combined with fat.
– ORIGIN French, from Old French *rille* 'strip of pork'.
rim • noun **1** the upper or outer edge of something more or less circular. **2** (also **wheel rim**) the outer edge of a wheel, on which the tyre is fitted. **3** a limit or boundary. **4** an encircling stain or deposit. • verb (**rimmed**, **rimming**) (usu. **be rimmed**) provide or mark with a rim.
– DERIVATIVES **rimless** adjective **rimmed** adjective.
– ORIGIN Old English, 'a border, coast'.
rime[1] /rīm/ • noun technical & literary hoar frost. • verb literary cover with hoar frost.
– DERIVATIVES **rimy** adjective (literary).
– ORIGIN Old English.
rime[2] • noun & verb archaic spelling of RHYME.
rimu /reemoo/ • noun a tall conifer which is the chief native softwood tree of New Zealand.
– ORIGIN Maori.
rind • noun **1** a tough outer layer or covering, especially of fruit, cheese, or bacon. **2** the bark of a tree.
– DERIVATIVES **rinded** adjective **rindless** adjective.
– ORIGIN Old English.
rinderpest /rindərpest/ • noun an infectious disease of ruminants, especially cattle, transmitted by a virus and characterized by fever and dysentery.
– ORIGIN German, from *Rinder* 'cattle' + *Pest* 'plague'.
ring[1] • noun **1** a small circular band, typically of precious metal, worn on a finger. **2** a circular band, object, or mark. **3** an enclosed space in which a sport, performance, or show takes place. **4** a group of people or things arranged in a circle. **5** a group of people with a shared interest or goal, especially one involving illegal activity: *a drug ring.* **6** a flat circular heating device forming part of a gas or electric hob. **7** Chemistry a number of atoms bonded together to form a closed loop in a molecule. • verb **1** surround. **2** draw a circle round.
– PHRASES **hold the ring** monitor a dispute or conflict without becoming involved. **run** (or **make**) **rings round** (or **around**) informal outclass or outwit easily.
– DERIVATIVES **ringed** adjective **ringless** adjective.
– ORIGIN Old English, related to RANK[1].
ring[2] • verb (past **rang**; past part. **rung**) **1** make or cause to make a clear resonant or vibrating sound. **2** (**ring with**) reverberate with (a sound). **3** chiefly Brit. call by telephone. **4** (**ring off**) Brit. end a telephone call by replacing the receiver. **5** call for attention by sounding a bell. **6** sound (the hour, a peal, etc.) on a bell or bells. **7** (**ring in** or **out**) usher (someone or something) in (or out) by or as if by ringing a bell. **8** (of the ears) be filled with a buzzing or humming sound due to a blow or loud noise. **9** (**ring up**) record (an amount) on a cash register. **10** convey a specified impression or quality: *her honesty rings true.* • noun **1** an act or instance of ringing. **2** a loud clear sound or tone.

r

Thesaurus

ledged, approved, licensed, valid, bona fide, de jure; *informal* legit, kosher. **2** *their rightful place in society* DESERVED, merited, due, just, right, fair, proper, fitting, appropriate, suitable.
right-wing • adjective CONSERVATIVE, rightist, ultra-conservative, blimpish, diehard; reactionary, traditionalist, conventional, unprogressive.
– OPPOSITES left-wing.
rigid • adjective **1** *a rigid container* STIFF, hard, firm, inflexible, unbending, unyielding, inelastic. **2** *a rigid routine* FIXED, set, firm, inflexible, unalterable, unchangeable, immutable, unvarying, invariable, hard and fast, cast-iron. **3** *a rigid approach to funding* STRICT, severe, stern, stringent, rigorous, inflexible, uncompromising, intransigent.
– OPPOSITES flexible, lenient.
rigmarole • noun **1** *the rigmarole of dressing up* FUSS, bother, trouble, folderol, ado, pother; *NZ* bobsy-die; *informal* palaver, song and dance, performance, to-do, pantomime, hassle; *Brit. informal* carry-on. **2** *that rigmarole about the house being haunted* TALE, saga, yarn, shaggy-dog story; *informal* spiel.

rigorous • adjective **1** *rigorous attention to detail* METICULOUS, conscientious, punctilious, careful, diligent, attentive, scrupulous, painstaking, exact, precise, accurate, thorough, particular, strict, demanding, exacting; *informal* pernickety. **2** *the rigorous enforcement of rules* STRICT, severe, stern, stringent, tough, harsh, rigid, relentless, unsparing, inflexible, draconian, intransigent, uncompromising, exacting. **3** *rigorous yachting conditions* HARSH, severe, bad, bleak, extreme, inclement; unpleasant, disagreeable, foul, nasty, filthy; stormy, wild, tempestuous.
– OPPOSITES slapdash, lax, mild.
rigour • noun **1** *a mine operated under conditions of rigour* STRICTNESS, severity, stringency, toughness, harshness, rigidity, inflexibility, intransigence. **2** *intellectual rigour* METICULOUSNESS, thoroughness, carefulness, diligence, scrupulousness, exactness, exactitude, precision, accuracy, correctness, strictness. **3** *the rigours of the journey* HARDSHIP, harshness, severity, adversity; ordeal, misery, trial; discomfort, inconvenience, privation.
rile • verb *(informal).* See ANNOY.
rim • noun **1** *the rim of her cup* BRIM, edge, lip. **2** *the rim of the*

3 Brit. informal a telephone call. 4 a quality conveyed by something heard: *the tale had a ring of truth.* 5 a set of bells, especially church bells.
– PHRASES **ring down** (or **up**) **the curtain** 1 lower (or raise) a theatre curtain. 2 mark the end (or beginning) of something.
– ORIGIN Old English.
ring binder • noun a loose-leaf binder with ring-shaped clasps that can be opened to pass through holes in the paper.
ringdove • noun Brit. a wood pigeon.
ringer • noun 1 a person or device that rings. 2 informal a person's or thing's double. 3 informal an athlete or horse fraudulently substituted for another in a competition. 4 Austral./NZ a shearer with the highest tally of sheep shorn. 5 Austral./NZ a person who looks after livestock.
ring fence • noun 1 a fence completely enclosing a piece of land. 2 an effective barrier. • verb (**ring-fence**) 1 enclose with a ring fence. 2 guard securely. 3 guarantee that (funds for a particular purpose) will not be spent on anything else.
ring finger • noun the finger next to the little finger, especially of the left hand, on which the wedding ring is worn.
ringgit /ringgit/ • noun (pl. same or **ringgits**) the basic monetary unit of Malaysia, equal to 100 sen.
– ORIGIN Malay.
ringing • adjective 1 having a clear resonant sound. 2 (of a statement) forceful and unequivocal.
– DERIVATIVES **ringingly** adverb.
ringleader • noun a person who leads an illicit activity.
ringlet • noun a corkscrew-shaped curl of hair.
– DERIVATIVES **ringletted** (also **ringleted**) adjective.
ring main • noun Brit. 1 an electrical supply serving a series of consumers and returning to the original source. 2 an electric circuit serving a number of power points, with one fuse in the supply.
ringmaster • noun the person directing a circus performance.
ring ouzel • noun an upland bird resembling a blackbird, with a white crescent across the breast.
ring pull • noun a ring on a can that is pulled to open it.
ring road • noun a bypass encircling a town.
ringside • noun the area beside a boxing ring or circus ring.
– DERIVATIVES **ringsider** noun.
ringside seat • noun an advantageous position from which to observe something.
ringworm • noun a contagious itching skin disease occurring in small circular patches, caused by various fungi and affecting chiefly the scalp or feet.
rink • noun 1 (also **ice rink**) an enclosed area of ice for skating, ice hockey, or curling. 2 (also **roller rink**) a smooth enclosed floor for roller skating. 3 (also **bowling rink**) the strip of a bowling green used for a match. 4 a team in curling or bowls.
– ORIGIN originally Scots in the sense 'jousting ground': perhaps from Old French *renc* 'rank'.
rinse • verb 1 wash with clean water to remove soap or dirt. 2 (often **rinse off/out**) remove (soap or dirt) by rinsing. • noun 1 an act of rinsing. 2 an antiseptic solution for cleansing the mouth. 3 a preparation for conditioning or tinting the hair.
– DERIVATIVES **rinser** noun.
– ORIGIN Old French *rincer.*
Rioja /riokhə/ • noun a wine produced in La Rioja, Spain.
riot • noun 1 a violent disturbance of the peace by a crowd. 2 a confused or lavish combination or display: *a riot of colour.* 3 (**a riot**) informal a highly amusing or entertaining person or thing. • verb 1 take part in a riot. 2 behave in an unrestrained way.
– PHRASES **read the Riot Act** give a severe warning or reprimand. [ORIGIN from the name of a former act partly read out to disperse rioters.] **run riot** 1 behave in a violent and unrestrained way. 2 proliferate or spread uncontrollably.
– DERIVATIVES **rioter** noun.
– ORIGIN Old French *riote* 'debate', from *rioter* 'to quarrel'.
riotous • adjective 1 marked by or involving public disorder. 2 involving wild and uncontrolled behaviour. 3 having a vivid, varied appearance.
– DERIVATIVES **riotously** adverb **riotousness** noun.
RIP • abbreviation rest in peace (used on graves).
– ORIGIN from Latin *requiescat* (or (plural) *requiescant*) *in pace.*
rip[1] • verb (**ripped**, **ripping**) 1 tear or pull forcibly away from something or someone. 2 tear. 3 move forcefully and rapidly. 4 (**rip off**) informal cheat (someone), especially financially. 5 (**rip off**) informal steal or plagiarize. 6 (**rip into**) informal make a vehement verbal attack on. • noun a long tear or cut.
– PHRASES **let rip** informal 1 proceed vigorously or without restraint. 2 express oneself vehemently.
– ORIGIN of unknown origin.
rip[2] (also **rip tide**) • noun a stretch of fast-flowing and rough water caused by the meeting of currents.
– ORIGIN perhaps related to RIP[1].
rip[3] • noun informal, dated 1 a dissolute immoral man. 2 a worthless horse.
– ORIGIN perhaps from *rep*, an abbreviation of REPROBATE.
riparian /rīpairiən/ • adjective relating to or situated on the banks of a river.
– ORIGIN from Latin *riparius*, from *ripa* 'bank'.
ripcord • noun a cord that is pulled to open a parachute.
ripe • adjective 1 (of fruit or grain) ready for harvesting and eating. 2 (of a cheese or wine) fully matured. 3 (**ripe for**) having reached a fitting time for. 4 (of a person's age) advanced. 5 (**ripe with**) full of.
– DERIVATIVES **ripely** adverb **ripeness** noun.
– ORIGIN Old English.

Thesaurus

crater EDGE, border, side, margin, brink, fringe, boundary, perimeter, limits, periphery; *archaic* skirt.
rind • noun SKIN, peel, zest, integument; *Botany* pericarp.
ring[1] • noun 1 *a ring round the moon* CIRCLE, band, halo, disc. 2 *she wore a ring* WEDDING RING, band. 3 *a circus ring* ARENA, enclosure, field, ground; amphitheatre, stadium. 4 *a ring of onlookers* CIRCLE, group, knot, cluster, bunch, band, throng, crowd, flock, pack. 5 *a spy ring* GANG, syndicate, cartel, mob, band, circle, organization, association, society, alliance, league, coterie, cabal.
• verb *police ringed the building* SURROUND, circle, encircle, encompass, girdle, enclose, hem in, confine, seal off.
ring[2] • verb 1 *church bells rang all day* TOLL, sound, peal, chime, clang, bong, ding, jingle, tinkle; *poetic/literary* knell. 2 *the room rang with laughter* RESOUND, reverberate, resonate, echo. 3 *I'll ring you tomorrow* TELEPHONE, phone (up), call (up); reach, dial; *informal* give someone a buzz; *Brit. informal* give someone a bell, give someone a tinkle, get on the blower to; *N. Amer. informal* get someone on the horn.
• noun 1 *the ring of a bell* CHIME, toll, peal, clang, clink, ding, jingle, tinkle, tintinnabulation, sound; *poetic/literary* knell. 2 *I'll give Chris a ring* CALL, telephone call, phone call; *informal* buzz; *Brit. informal* bell, tinkle.
– PHRASES **ring something in** HERALD, signal, announce, proclaim, usher in, introduce; mark, signify, indicate; *poetic/literary* betoken, knell.
rinse • verb WASH (OUT), clean, cleanse, bathe; dip, drench, splash, swill, sluice, hose down.
riot • noun 1 *a riot in the capital* UPROAR, commotion, upheaval, disturbance, furore, tumult, melee, scuffle, fracas, fray, brawl, free-for-all; violence, fighting, vandalism, mayhem, turmoil, lawlessness, anarchy; *N. Amer. informal* wilding; *Law, dated* affray. 2 *the garden was a riot of colour* MASS, sea, splash, show, exhibition.
• verb *the miners rioted* (GO ON THE) RAMPAGE, run riot, fight in the streets, run wild, run amok, go berserk; *informal* raise hell.
– PHRASES **run riot** 1 *the children ran riot* (GO ON THE) RAMPAGE, riot, run amok, go berserk, go out of control; *informal* raise hell. 2 *the vegetation has run riot* GROW PROFUSELY, spread uncontrolled, grow rapidly, spread like wildfire; burgeon, multiply, rocket.
riotous • adjective 1 *the demonstration turned riotous* UNRULY, rowdy, disorderly, uncontrollable, unmanageable, undisciplined, uproarious, tumultuous; violent, wild, ugly, lawless, anarchic. 2 *a riotous party* BOISTEROUS, lively, loud, noisy, unrestrained, uninhibited, uproarious, unruly, rollicking; *Brit. informal* rumbustious; *N. Amer. informal* rambunctious.
– OPPOSITES peaceable.
rip • verb 1 *he ripped the posters down* TEAR, wrench, wrest, pull, snatch, tug, prise, heave, drag, peel, pluck; *informal* yank. 2 *she ripped Leo's note into pieces* TEAR, claw, hack, slit, cut; *poetic/literary* rend.
• noun *a rip in my sleeve* TEAR, slit, split, rent, laceration, cut, gash, slash.
ripe • adjective 1 *a ripe tomato* MATURE, ripened, full grown, ready to eat; luscious, juicy, tender, sweet. 2 *the dock is ripe for development* READY, fit, suitable, right. 3 *the ripe old age of ninety* ADVANCED, hoary, venerable, old. 4 *the time is ripe for his return* OPPORTUNE, advantageous, favourable, auspicious, propitious, prom-

ripen ● verb become or make ripe.
rip-off ● noun informal **1** an article that is greatly overpriced. **2** an inferior imitation.
riposte /ripost/ ● noun **1** a quick clever reply. **2** a quick return thrust in fencing. ● verb make a riposte.
– ORIGIN French, from Italian *risposta* 'response'.
ripper ● noun **1** a person or thing that rips. **2** informal a thing that is particularly admirable or excellent.
ripping ● adjective Brit. informal, dated excellent.
ripple ● noun **1** a small wave or series of waves. **2** a gentle rising and falling sound that spreads through a group of people. **3** a feeling or effect that spreads through someone or something. **4** a type of ice cream with wavy lines of coloured flavoured syrup running through it. **5** a small periodic variation in voltage. ● verb **1** form or cause to form ripples. **2** (of a sound or feeling) spread through a person or place.
– DERIVATIVES **ripply** adjective.
– ORIGIN of unknown origin.
rip-roaring ● adjective full of energy and vigour.
ripsaw ● noun a coarse saw for cutting wood along the grain.
ripsnorting ● adjective informal showing great vigour or intensity.
– DERIVATIVES **ripsnorter** noun.
ripstop ● noun nylon fabric that is woven so that a tear will not spread.
RISC ● noun reduced instruction set computer (or computing).
rise ● verb (past **rose**; past part. **risen**) **1** come or go up. **2** get up from lying, sitting, or kneeling. **3** increase in number, size, intensity, or quality. **4** (of land) slope upwards. **5** (of the sun, moon, or stars) appear above the horizon. **6** reach a higher social or professional position. **7** (**rise above**) succeed in not being restricted by. **8** (**rise to**) respond adequately to (a challenging situation). **9** (often **rise up**) rebel. **10** (of a river) have its source. **11** be restored to life. **12** chiefly Brit. (of a meeting or a session of a court) adjourn. ● noun **1** an act or instance of rising. **2** an upward slope or hill. **3** Brit. an increase in salary or wages. **4** the vertical height of a step, arch, or incline.
– PHRASES **get** (or **take**) **a rise out of** informal provoke an angry or irritated response from. **on the rise 1** increasing. **2** becoming more successful. **rise and shine** informal wake up and get out of bed promptly.
– ORIGIN Old English, 'make an attack', 'get out of bed'.
riser ● noun **1** a person who habitually gets out of bed at a particular time of the morning: *an early riser.* **2** a vertical section between the treads of a staircase. **3** a vertical pipe for the upward flow of liquid or gas. **4** a low platform on a stage or in an auditorium.
risible /rizzib'l/ ● adjective such as to provoke laughter.
– DERIVATIVES **risibility** noun **risibly** adverb.
– ORIGIN Latin *risibilis*, from *ridere* 'to laugh'.
rising ● adjective approaching a specified age. ● noun a revolt.
rising damp ● noun Brit. moisture absorbed from the ground into a wall.
risk ● noun **1** a situation involving exposure to danger. **2** the possibility that something unpleasant will happen. **3** a person or thing causing a risk or regarded in relation to risk: *a fire risk.* ● verb **1** expose to danger or loss. **2** act in such a way as to incur the risk of. **3** incur risk by engaging in (an action).
– PHRASES **at one's** (**own**) **risk** taking responsibility for one's own safety or possessions. **run** (or **take**) **a risk** (or **risks**) act in such a way as to expose oneself to danger.
– ORIGIN Italian *risco* 'danger'.
risk capital ● noun another term for VENTURE CAPITAL.
risky ● adjective (**riskier, riskiest**) involving risk.
– DERIVATIVES **riskily** adverb **riskiness** noun.
risotto /rizottō/ ● noun (pl. **risottos**) an Italian dish of rice cooked in stock with ingredients such as meat or seafood.
– ORIGIN Italian, from *riso* 'rice'.
risqué /riskay/ ● adjective slightly indecent and liable to shock.
– ORIGIN French, from *risquer* 'to risk'.
rissole ● noun a compressed mixture of meat and spices, coated in breadcrumbs and fried.
– ORIGIN French, ultimately from Latin *russeolus* 'reddish'.
ritardando /rittaardandō/ ● adverb & adjective Music another term for RALLENTANDO.
– ORIGIN Italian.
rite ● noun **1** a religious or other solemn ceremony or act. **2** a body of customary observances characteristic of a Church or a part of it.
– PHRASES **rite of passage** a ceremony or event, e.g. marriage, marking an important stage in someone's life.
– ORIGIN Latin *ritus* '(religious) usage'.
ritual ● noun **1** a religious or solemn ceremony involving a series of actions performed according to a set order. **2** a set order of performing such a ceremony. **3** a series of actions habitually and invariably followed by someone. ● adjective relating to or done as a ritual.
– DERIVATIVES **ritually** adverb.
ritualism ● noun the regular observance or practice of ritual,

Thesaurus

ising, good, right, fortunate, benign, providential, felicitous, seasonable; convenient, suitable, appropriate, apt, fitting.
– OPPOSITES unsuitable, young.
ripen ● verb BECOME RIPE, mature, mellow.
rip-off ● noun *(informal)* FRAUD, swindle, confidence trick; *informal* con, scam, flimflam, gyp; *Brit. informal* swizz, daylight robbery; *N. Amer. informal* rip, shakedown, bunco; *Austral. informal* rort.
riposte ● noun *an indignant riposte* RETORT, counter, rejoinder, sally, return, answer, reply, response; *informal* comeback.
● verb *'Heaven help you,' riposted Sally* RETORT, counter, rejoin, return, retaliate, hurl back, answer, reply, respond, come back.
ripple ● noun *he blew ripples in his coffee* WAVELET, wave, undulation, ripplet, ridge, ruffle.
● verb *a breeze rippled the lake* FORM RIPPLES ON, ruffle, wrinkle.
rise ● verb **1** *the sun rose* MOVE UP/UPWARDS, come up, make one's/its way up, arise, ascend, climb, mount, soar. **2** *the mountains rising above us* LOOM, tower, soar, rise up, rear (up). **3** *prices rose* GO UP, increase, soar, shoot up, surge, leap, jump, rocket, escalate, spiral. **4** *living standards have risen* IMPROVE, get better, advance, go up, soar, shoot up. **5** *his voice rose* GET HIGHER, grow, increase, become louder, swell, intensify. **6** *he rose from his chair* STAND UP, get to one's feet, get up, jump up, leap up; *formal* arise. **7** *he rises at dawn* GET UP, get out of bed, rouse oneself, stir, bestir oneself, be up and about; *informal* rise and shine, shake a leg, surface; *formal* arise. **8** *the court rose at midday* ADJOURN, recess, be suspended, pause, take a break; *informal* knock off, take five. **9** *he rose through the ranks* MAKE PROGRESS, climb, advance, get on, work one's way, be promoted. **10** *he wouldn't rise to the bait* REACT, respond; take. **11** *Christ rose again* COME BACK TO LIFE, be resurrected, revive. **12** *the dough started to rise* SWELL, expand, enlarge, puff up. **13** *the nation rose against its oppressors* REBEL, revolt, mutiny, riot, take up arms. **14** *the Rhine rises in the Alps* ORIGINATE, begin, start, emerge; issue from, spring from, flow from, emanate from. **15** *her spirits rose* BRIGHTEN, lift, cheer up, improve, pick up; *informal* buck up. **16** *the ground rose gently* SLOPE UPWARDS, go uphill, incline, climb.
– OPPOSITES fall, descend, drop, sit, retire, resume, die, shelve.
● noun **1** *a price rise* INCREASE, hike, leap, upsurge, upswing, climb, escalation. **2** *he got a rise of 11%* RAISE, pay increase, wage increase; hike, increment. **3** *a rise in standards* IMPROVEMENT, amelioration, upturn, leap. **4** *his rise to power* PROGRESS, climb, promotion, elevation, aggrandizement. **5** *we walked up the rise* SLOPE, incline, acclivity, hillock, hill; *formal* eminence.
risible ● adjective LAUGHABLE, ridiculous, absurd, comical, comic, amusing, funny, hilarious, humorous, droll, farcical, silly, ludicrous, hysterical; *informal* rib-tickling, priceless; *informal, dated* killing.
risk ● noun **1** *there is a certain amount of risk* CHANCE, uncertainty, unpredictability, precariousness, instability, insecurity, perilousness, riskiness. **2** *the risk of fire* POSSIBILITY, chance, probability, likelihood, danger, peril, threat, menace, fear, prospect.
– OPPOSITES safety, impossibility.
● verb **1** *he risked his life to save them* ENDANGER, imperil, jeopardize, hazard, gamble (with), chance; put on the line, put in jeopardy. **2** *you risk getting cold and wet* CHANCE, stand a chance of.
– PHRASES **at risk** IN DANGER, in peril, in jeopardy, under threat.
risky ● adjective DANGEROUS, hazardous, perilous, fraught with danger, unsafe, insecure, precarious, touch-and-go, treacherous; uncertain, unpredictable; *informal* chancy, dicey, hairy; *N. Amer. informal* gnarly; *archaic* parlous.
risqué ● adjective RIBALD, rude, bawdy, racy, earthy, indecent, suggestive, improper, naughty, locker-room; vulgar, dirty, smutty, crude, coarse, obscene, lewd, X-rated; *informal* blue, raunchy; *Brit. informal* fruity, off colour, saucy; *N. Amer. informal* gamy.
rite ● noun CEREMONY, ritual, ceremonial; service, sacrament, liturgy, worship, office; act, practice, custom, tradition, convention,

especially when excessive or without regard to its function.
– DERIVATIVES **ritualist** noun **ritualistic** adjective.
ritualize (also **ritualise**) ● verb make into a ritual by following a pattern of actions or behaviour.
– DERIVATIVES **ritualization** noun.
ritz ● noun informal ostentatious luxury and glamour.
– ORIGIN from *Ritz*, a name associated with luxury hotels, from the Swiss hotel owner César *Ritz* (1850–1918).
ritzy ● adjective (**ritzier**, **ritziest**) informal expensively stylish.
rival ● noun **1** a person or thing competing with another for superiority or the same objective. **2** a person or thing equal to another in quality: *she has no rivals as a female rock singer*. ● verb (**rivalled**, **rivalling**; US **rivaled**, **rivaling**) be comparable to.
– DERIVATIVES **rivalrous** adjective. **rivalry** noun (pl. **rivalries**).
– ORIGIN Latin *rivalis*, originally in the sense 'person using the same stream as another', from *rivus* 'stream'.
rive /rīv/ ● verb (past **rived**; past part. **riven** /rivv'n/) (usu. **be riven**) tear apart.
– ORIGIN Old Norse.
river ● noun **1** a large natural flow of water travelling along a channel to the sea, a lake, or another river. **2** a large quantity of a flowing substance.
– PHRASES **sell down the river** informal betray. [ORIGIN originally with reference to the sale of a troublesome slave to a plantation owner on the lower Mississippi, where conditions were relatively harsher.]
– ORIGIN Old French, from Latin *riparius*, from *ripa* 'bank of a river'.
riverine /rivvərīn/ ● adjective technical or literary relating to or situated on a river or riverbank.
rivet /rivvit/ ● noun a short metal pin or bolt for holding together two metal plates, its headless end being beaten out or pressed down when in place. ● verb (**riveted**, **riveting**) **1** join or fasten with a rivet or rivets. **2** (usu. **be riveted**) completely engross. **3** (usu. **be riveted**) direct (one's eyes or attention) intently.
– DERIVATIVES **riveter** noun.
– ORIGIN Old French, from *river* 'fix, clinch'.
riviera /rivviairə/ ● noun a coastal region with a subtropical climate and vegetation, especially that of southern France and northern Italy.
– ORIGIN Italian, 'seashore'.
rivulet /rivyoolit/ ● noun a very small stream.
– ORIGIN alteration of obsolete French *riveret*, 'small river', from Latin *rivus* 'stream'.
riyal ● noun variant spelling of RIAL.
RL ● abbreviation rugby league.
RM ● abbreviation (in the UK) Royal Marines.
RN ● abbreviation (in the UK) Royal Navy.
Rn ● symbol the chemical element radon.
RNA ● noun ribonucleic acid, a substance in living cells which carries instructions from DNA for controlling the synthesis of proteins and in some viruses carries genetic information instead of DNA.
RNLI ● abbreviation (in the UK) Royal National Lifeboat Institution.
RNZAF ● abbreviation Royal New Zealand Air Force.
RNZN ● abbreviation Royal New Zealand Navy.
roach[1] ● noun (pl. same) a common freshwater fish of the carp family.
– ORIGIN Old French *roche*.
roach[2] ● noun informal **1** chiefly N. Amer. a cockroach. **2** a roll of card or paper that forms the butt of a cannabis cigarette. [ORIGIN of unknown origin.]
road ● noun **1** a wide way between places, especially one surfaced for use by vehicles. **2** a way to achieving a particular outcome. **3** a partly sheltered stretch of water near the shore in which ships can ride at anchor.
– PHRASES **down the road** informal, chiefly N. Amer. in the future. **in** (or **out of**) **the** (or **one's**) **road** informal in (or out of) someone's way. **one for the road** informal a final alcoholic drink before leaving. **on the road 1** on a long journey or series of journeys. **2** (of a car) able to be driven.
– DERIVATIVES **roadless** adjective.
– ORIGIN Old English, 'journey on horseback', 'foray'; related to RIDE.
roadblock ● noun a barrier put across a road by the police or army to stop and examine traffic.
road fund licence ● noun Brit. a disc displayed on a vehicle certifying payment of road tax.
road hog ● noun informal a reckless or inconsiderate motorist.
roadholding ● noun the ability of a moving vehicle to remain stable, especially when cornering at high speeds.
roadhouse ● noun a pub, club, or restaurant on a country road.
road hump ● noun a hump in the road intended to cause traffic to reduce speed.
roadie ● noun informal a person employed by a touring band of musicians to set up and maintain equipment.
road kill ● noun chiefly N. Amer. **1** animals killed on the road by a vehicle **2** a killing of an animal on the road by a vehicle.
road pricing ● noun the practice of charging motorists to use busy roads at certain times, especially to relieve congestion.
road rage ● noun violent anger arising from conflict with the driver of another motor vehicle.
roadrunner ● noun a fast-running long-tailed bird found chiefly in arid country from the southern US to Central America.
roadshow ● noun **1** each of a series of radio or television programmes broadcast on location from different venues. **2** a touring political or promotional campaign. **3** a touring show of pop musicians.
roadstead ● noun another term for ROAD (in sense 3).
roadster ● noun **1** an open-top car with two seats. **2** a bicycle designed for use on the road.
road tax ● noun Brit. a periodic tax payable on motor vehicles using public roads.
road test ● noun **1** a test of the performance of a vehicle or engine on the road. **2** a test of equipment carried out in working conditions.
roadway ● noun **1** a road. **2** the part of a road intended for vehicles, in contrast to the pavement or verge.

r

Thesaurus

institution, procedure.
ritual ● noun *an elaborate civic ritual* CEREMONY, rite, ceremonial, observance; service, sacrament, liturgy, worship; act, practice, custom, tradition, convention, formality, procedure, protocol.
● adjective *a ritual burial* CEREMONIAL, ritualistic, prescribed, set, formal; sacramental, liturgical; traditional, conventional.
ritzy ● adjective (*informal*). See POSH sense 1.
rival ● noun **1** *his rival for the nomination* OPPONENT, challenger, competitor, contender; adversary, antagonist, enemy; *poetic/literary* foe. **2** *the tool has no rival* EQUAL, match, peer, equivalent, counterpart, like.
– OPPOSITES ally.
● verb *few countries can rival it for scenery* MATCH, compare with, compete with, vie with, equal, measure up to, be in the same league as, be on a par with, touch, challenge; *informal* hold a candle to.
● adjective *rival candidates* COMPETING, opposing, contending.
rivalry ● noun COMPETITIVENESS, competition, contention, vying; opposition, conflict, feuding, antagonism, friction, enmity; *informal* keeping up with the Joneses.
riven ● adjective *a country riven by civil war* TORN APART, split, rent, severed; *poetic/literary* cleft, torn asunder.
river ● noun **1** WATERCOURSE, waterway, stream, tributary, brook, inlet, rill, runnel, freshet; *Scottish & N. English* burn; *N. English* beck; *S. English* bourn; *N. Amer. & Austral./NZ* creek; *Austral.* billabong. **2** *a river of molten lava* STREAM, torrent, flood, deluge, cascade.
– RELATED TERMS fluvial, fluvio-.
– PHRASES **sell someone down the river** (*informal*). See DOUBLE-CROSS.
riveted ● adjective **1** *she stood riveted to the spot* FIXED, rooted, frozen, unable to move; motionless, unmoving, immobile, stock-still. **2** *he was riveted by the newsreels* FASCINATED, engrossed, gripped, captivated, enthralled, spellbound, mesmerized, transfixed. **3** *their eyes were riveted on the teacher* FIXED, fastened, focused, concentrated, locked.
– OPPOSITES bored.
riveting ● adjective FASCINATING, gripping, engrossing, interesting, intriguing, absorbing, captivating, enthralling, compelling, spellbinding, mesmerizing; *informal* unputdownable.
– OPPOSITES boring.
road ● noun **1** *the roads were crowded with traffic* STREET, thoroughfare, roadway, avenue, broadway, bypass, ring road, trunk road, byroad; lane, crescent, drive, parade, row; *Brit.* dual carriageway, clearway, motorway; *N. Amer.* highway, freeway, throughway, parkway, expressway; *US* turnpike, interstate. **2** *a step on the*

roadworks ● plural noun Brit. repairs to roads or to utilities under roads.

roadworthy ● adjective (of a vehicle) fit to be used on the road.
– DERIVATIVES **roadworthiness** noun.

roam ● verb **1** travel aimlessly over a wide area. **2** wander over, through, or about (a place). ● noun an aimless walk.
– DERIVATIVES **roamer** noun.
– ORIGIN of unknown origin.

roan ● adjective (of a horse or cow) having a bay, chestnut, or black coat thickly interspersed with hairs of another colour, typically white. ● noun a roan animal.
– ORIGIN Old French.

roar ● noun **1** a full, deep, prolonged sound as made by a lion, natural force, or engine. **2** a loud, deep sound uttered by a person, especially as an expression of pain, anger, or great amusement. ● verb **1** make or utter a roar. **2** laugh loudly. **3** move, act, or happen very fast.
– DERIVATIVES **roarer** noun.
– ORIGIN Old English.

roaring ● adjective informal complete; unqualified: *a roaring success.*
– PHRASES **do a roaring trade** (or **business**) informal do very good business. **the roaring forties** stormy ocean tracts between latitudes 40° and 50° south. **the roaring twenties** the prosperous years of the 1920s.
– DERIVATIVES **roaringly** adverb.

roast ● verb **1** (with reference to food, especially meat) cook or be cooked by prolonged exposure to heat in an oven or over a fire. **2** process (a foodstuff) by subjecting it to intense heat. **3** make or become very warm. **4** criticize or reprimand severely. ● adjective (of food) having been roasted. ● noun **1** a joint of meat that has been roasted or that is intended for roasting. **2** the process of roasting something, especially coffee. **3** an outdoor party at which meat is roasted: *a pig roast.*
– DERIVATIVES **roaster** noun.
– ORIGIN Old French *rostir.*

roasting informal ● adjective very hot and dry. ● noun a severe criticism or reprimand.

rob ● verb (**robbed**, **robbing**) **1** take property unlawfully from (a person or place) by force or threat of force. **2** deprive of something needed, deserved, or significant. **3** informal overcharge.
– PHRASES **rob Peter to pay Paul** deprive one person of something in order to pay another. [ORIGIN probably with reference to the saints and apostles *Peter* and *Paul*; the allusion is uncertain.]
– DERIVATIVES **robber** noun.
– ORIGIN Old French *rober.*

robbery ● noun (pl. **robberies**) **1** the action of robbing a person or place. **2** informal unashamed swindling or overcharging.

robe ● noun **1** a loose outer garment reaching to the ankles, often worn on formal or ceremonial occasions as an indication of the wearer's rank, office, or profession. **2** a bathrobe or dressing gown. ● verb clothe in or put on a robe or robes.
– ORIGIN Old French, 'garment, booty', from the Germanic base of ROB (because clothing was an important component of booty).

robin ● noun **1** a small European songbird of the thrush family, with a red breast and brown back and wings. **2** (also **American robin**) a large North American thrush with an orange-red breast.
– ORIGIN Old French, familiar form of the given name *Robert.*

robot /rōbot/ ● noun a machine capable of carrying out a complex series of actions automatically, especially one programmable by a computer.
– DERIVATIVES **robotize** (also **robotise**) verb.
– ORIGIN from Czech *robota* 'forced labour'; the term was coined in K. Čapek's play *R.U.R.* 'Rossum's Universal Robots' (1920).

robotic /rōbottik/ ● adjective **1** relating to robots. **2** mechanical, stiff, or unemotional.
– DERIVATIVES **robotically** adverb.

robotics ● plural noun (treated as sing.) the branch of technology concerned with the design, construction, and application of robots.

robust ● adjective **1** sturdy or resilient. **2** strong and healthy. **3** uncompromising and forceful; not subtle: *a robust defence.* **4** (of wine or food) strong and rich in flavour or smell.
– DERIVATIVES **robustly** adverb **robustness** noun.
– ORIGIN Latin *robustus* 'firm and hard'.

robusta ● noun a type of coffee bean from a West African species of coffee plant, used especially in making instant coffee.
– ORIGIN Latin, from *robustus* 'robust'.

roc ● noun a gigantic mythological bird described in the *Arabian Nights.*
– ORIGIN ultimately from Persian.

rock[1] ● noun **1** the hard mineral material of the earth's crust, exposed on the surface or underlying the soil. **2** a mass of rock projecting out of the ground or water. **3** a boulder. **4** Geology any natural material with a distinctive composition of minerals. **5** Brit. a kind of hard confectionery in the form of cylindrical peppermint-flavoured sticks. **6** informal a diamond or other precious stone.
– PHRASES **on the rocks** informal **1** experiencing difficulties and likely to fail. **2** (of a drink) served undiluted and with ice cubes.
– ORIGIN Latin *rocca.*

Thesaurus

r

road to recovery WAY, path, route, course. **3** *oil tankers waiting in the roads* ANCHORAGE, channel, haven, roadstead.
– PHRASES **on the road** ON TOUR, touring, travelling.

roam ● verb WANDER, rove, ramble, drift, walk, traipse; range, travel, tramp, traverse, trek; *Scottish & Irish* stravaig; *informal* cruise, mosey; *formal* perambulate; *archaic* peregrinate.

roar ● noun **1** *the roars of the crowd* SHOUT, bellow, yell, cry, howl; clamour; *informal* holler. **2** *the roar of the sea* BOOM, crash, rumble, roll, thundering. **3** *roars of laughter* GUFFAW, howl, hoot, shriek, gale, peal.
● verb **1** *'Get out!' roared Angus* BELLOW, yell, shout, bawl, howl; *informal* holler. **2** *thunder roared* BOOM, rumble, crash, roll, thunder. **3** *the movie left them roaring* GUFFAW, laugh, hoot; *informal* split one's sides, be rolling in the aisles, be doubled up, crack up, be in stitches, die laughing; *Brit. informal* crease up, fall about. **4** *a motorbike roared past* SPEED, zoom, whizz, flash; *informal* belt, tear, zip; *Brit. informal* bomb.

roaring ● adjective **1** *a roaring fire* BLAZING, burning, flaming. **2** *(informal) a roaring success* ENORMOUS, huge, massive, (very) great, tremendous; complete, out-and-out, thorough; *informal* rip-roaring, whopping, fantastic.

roast ● verb **1** *potatoes roasted in olive oil* COOK, bake, grill; *N. Amer.* broil. **2** *(informal) they roasted him for wasting time.* See CRITICIZE.

roasting *(informal)* ● adjective *a roasting day* HOT, sweltering, scorching, blistering, searing, torrid; *informal* boiling (hot), baking (hot).
● noun *the boss gave him a roasting.* See LECTURE noun sense 2.

rob ● verb **1** *the gang robbed the local bank* BURGLE, steal from, hold up, break into; raid, loot, plunder, pillage; *N. Amer.* burglarize; *informal* do, turn over, knock off, stick up. **2** *he robbed an old woman* STEAL FROM; *informal* mug, jump; *N. Amer. informal* clip. **3** *he was robbed of his savings* CHEAT, swindle, defraud; *informal* do out of, con out of, fleece; *N. Amer. informal* stiff. **4** *(informal) it cost £70 — I was robbed* OVERCHARGE; *informal* rip off, sting, do, diddle; *N. Amer. informal* gouge. **5** *defeat robbed him of his title* DEPRIVE, strip, divest; deny.

robber ● noun BURGLAR, thief, housebreaker, mugger, shoplifter; stealer, pilferer, raider, looter, plunderer, pillager; bandit, highwayman; *informal* crook, cracksman; *Brit. informal* tea leaf; *N. Amer. informal* yegg; *poetic/literary* brigand.

robbery ● noun **1** *they were arrested for robbery* BURGLARY, theft, thievery, stealing, breaking and entering, housebreaking, larceny, shoplifting; embezzlement, fraud; hold-up, break-in, raid; *informal* mugging, smash-and-grab, stick-up; *Brit. informal* blag; *N. Amer. informal* heist. **2** *(informal) Six quid? That's robbery.* A SWINDLE; *informal* a con, a rip-off; *Brit. informal* daylight robbery.

robe ● noun **1** *the women wore black robes* CLOAK, kaftan, djellaba, wrap, mantle, cape; *N. Amer.* wrapper. **2** *coronation robes* GARB, regalia, costume, finery; garments, clothes; *formal* apparel; *archaic* raiment, habiliments, vestments. **3** *priestly robes* VESTMENT, surplice, cassock, rochet, alb, dalmatic, chasuble; canonicals. **4** *a towelling robe* DRESSING GOWN, bathrobe, housecoat; *N. Amer.* wrapper.
● verb *he robed for Mass* DRESS, clothe oneself; *formal* enrobe.

robot ● noun AUTOMATON, android, golem; *informal* bot, droid.

robust ● adjective **1** *a large, robust man* STRONG, vigorous, sturdy, tough, powerful, solid, muscular, sinewy, rugged, hardy, strapping, brawny, burly, husky; healthy, (fighting) fit, hale and hearty, lusty, in fine fettle; *informal* beefy, hunky. **2** *these knives are robust* DURABLE, resilient, tough, hard-wearing, long-lasting, sturdy, strong. **3** *her usual robust view of things* DOWN-TO-EARTH, practical, realistic, pragmatic, common-sense, commonsensical, matter-of-fact, businesslike, sensible, unromantic, unsentimental;

rock² ● verb **1** move gently to and fro or from side to side. **2** shake violently, especially because of an earthquake or explosion. **3** shock or distress greatly. **4** informal dance to or play rock music. **5** informal have an atmosphere of excitement or much social activity. ● noun **1** (also **rock music**) a form of popular music derived from rock and roll and pop music but characterized by a more serious approach. **2** rock and roll. **3** a rocking movement.
– ORIGIN Old English.

rockabilly ● noun a type of popular music, originating in the south-eastern US, combining elements of rock and roll and country music.
– ORIGIN blend of ROCK AND ROLL and HILLBILLY.

rock and roll (also **rock 'n' roll**) ● noun a type of popular dance music originating in the 1950s and characterized by a heavy beat and simple melodies.

rock-bottom ● adjective at the lowest possible level.

rock cake ● noun chiefly Brit. a small currant cake with a hard rough surface.

rock climbing ● noun the sport or pastime of climbing rock faces, especially with the aid of ropes and special equipment.

rock crystal ● noun transparent quartz, typically in the form of colourless hexagonal crystals.

rocker ● noun **1** a person who performs, dances to, or enjoys rock music. **2** Brit. a young person, especially in the 1960s, belonging to a subculture characterized by leather clothing, riding motorcycles, and a liking for rock music. **3** a rocking chair. **4** a curved bar or similar support on which something such as a chair can rock. **5** a rocking device forming part of a mechanism.
– PHRASES **off one's rocker** informal mad.

rockery ● noun (pl. **rockeries**) a heaped arrangement of rocks with soil between them, planted with rock plants.

rocket¹ ● noun **1** a cylindrical projectile that can be propelled to a great height or distance by the combustion of its contents. **2** a missile or spacecraft propelled by an engine providing thrust on the same principle. **3** Brit. informal a severe reprimand. ● verb (**rocketed**, **rocketing**) **1** increase very rapidly and suddenly. **2** move or progress very rapidly. **3** attack with rocket-propelled missiles.
– ORIGIN Italian *rocchetto* 'small distaff (for spinning)', with reference to its cylindrical shape.

rocket² ● noun an edible Mediterranean plant of the cabbage family, eaten in salads.
– ORIGIN French *roquette*, ultimately from Latin *eruca* 'downy-stemmed plant'.

rocketeer ● noun a person who designs or operates space rockets.

rocketry ● noun the branch of science and technology concerned with rockets.

rocket scientist ● noun informal, chiefly N. Amer. a very intelligent person.

rock garden ● noun a rockery.

rocking chair ● noun a chair mounted on rockers or springs.

rocking horse ● noun a model of a horse mounted on rockers or springs for a child to ride on.

rock plant ● noun a plant that grows on or among rocks.

rock pool ● noun a pool of water among rocks, typically along a shoreline.

rock rose ● noun a herbaceous or shrubby plant with rose-like flowers, native to temperate and warm regions.

rock salmon ● noun Brit. dogfish or wolf fish as food.

rock salt ● noun common salt occurring naturally as a mineral.

rock solid ● adjective completely firm or stable.

rock wool ● noun inorganic material made into matted fibre, used especially for insulation or soundproofing.

rocky¹ ● adjective (**rockier**, **rockiest**) **1** consisting or formed of rock. **2** full of rocks.

rocky² ● adjective (**rockier**, **rockiest**) unsteady or unstable.

rococo /rəkōkō/ ● adjective **1** relating to an elaborately ornate late baroque style of European furniture or architecture of the 18th century, characterized by asymmetrical curves, scroll-work, and decorative motifs. **2** (of music or literature) highly ornamented and florid. ● noun the rococo style.
– ORIGIN French, humorous alteration of *rocaille*, an 18th-century style of decoration based on shells and pebbles.

rod ● noun **1** a thin straight bar, especially of wood or metal. **2** a fishing rod. **3** a slender straight stick or shoot growing on or cut from a tree or bush. **4** (**the rod**) the use of a stick for caning or flogging. **5** historical, chiefly Brit. a perch or square perch (see PERCH³). **6** Anatomy one of two types of light-sensitive cell present in the retina of the eye, responsible mainly for monochrome vision in poor light. Compare with CONE.
– PHRASES **make a rod for one's own back** do something likely to cause difficulties for oneself later. **spare the rod and spoil the child** proverb if children are not physically punished when they do wrong their personal development will suffer.
– DERIVATIVES **rodlet** noun.
– ORIGIN Old English.

rode past of RIDE.

rodent ● noun a mammal of a large group (the order Rodentia) including rats, mice, and squirrels and distinguished by strong constantly growing incisors and no canine teeth.
– ORIGIN from Latin *rodere* 'gnaw'.

rodenticide /rōdentisīd/ ● noun a poison used to kill rodents.

rodent ulcer ● noun Medicine a slow-growing cancerous tumour of the face.

rodeo /rōdiō, rədayō/ ● noun (pl. **rodeos**) **1** a contest or entertainment in which cowboys show their skill at riding broncos, roping calves, etc. **2** a competitive display of other skills, such as motorcycle riding. **3** a round-up of cattle on a ranch for branding and counting.
– ORIGIN Spanish, from *rodear* 'go round', from Latin *rotare* 'rotate'.

rodomontade /roddəmon**tayd**/ ● noun boastful or inflated talk or behaviour.
– ORIGIN from Italian *rodomonte* 'boaster', from the name of a boastful character in the medieval *Orlando* epics.

roe¹ ● noun **1** (also **hard roe**) the mass of eggs contained in the ovaries of a female fish or shellfish, especially when ripe and used as food. **2** (**soft roe**) the ripe testes of a male fish, especially when used as food.
– ORIGIN related to Low German, Dutch *roge*.

roe² (also **roe deer**) ● noun (pl. same or **roes**) a small deer with a

r

Thesaurus

informal no-nonsense. **4** *a robust red wine* STRONG, full-bodied, flavourful, flavoursome, rich.
– OPPOSITES frail, fragile, romantic, insipid.

rock¹ ● verb **1** *the ship rocked on the water* MOVE TO AND FRO, move back and forth, sway, see-saw; roll, pitch, plunge, toss, lurch, reel, list; wobble, oscillate. **2** *the building began to rock* SHAKE, vibrate, quake, tremble. **3** *Wall Street was rocked by the news* STUN, shock, stagger, astonish, startle, surprise, shake (up), take aback, throw, unnerve, disconcert.

rock² ● noun **1** *a gully strewn with rocks* BOULDER, stone, pebble; Austral. informal goolie. **2** *a castle built on a rock* CRAG, cliff, outcrop. **3** *he was the rock on which they relied* FOUNDATION, cornerstone, support, prop, mainstay; tower of strength, bulwark, anchor. **4** (informal) *she wore a massive rock* DIAMOND (RING), jewel, precious stone.
– RELATED TERMS litho-, petro-.
– PHRASES **on the rocks** (informal) **1** *her marriage is on the rocks* IN DIFFICULTY, in trouble, breaking up, over; in tatters, in ruins, ruined. **2** *a Scotch on the rocks* WITH ICE, on ice.

rocket ● noun **1** *guerrillas fired rockets at them* MISSILE, projectile. **2** *they lit some colourful rockets* FIREWORK, Roman candle, banger. **3** (Brit. informal) *he got a rocket from the boss.* See LECTURE noun sense 2.
● verb **1** *prices have rocketed* SHOOT UP, soar, increase, rise, escalate, spiral; informal go through the roof. **2** *they rocketed into the alley* SPEED, zoom, shoot, whizz, tear, career; Brit. informal bomb; N. Amer. informal barrel, hightail it.
– OPPOSITES plummet.

rocky¹ ● adjective *a rocky path* STONY, pebbly, shingly; rough, bumpy; craggy, mountainous.

rocky² ● adjective **1** *that table's rocky* UNSTEADY, shaky, unstable, wobbly, tottery, rickety, flimsy. **2** *a rocky marriage* DIFFICULT, problematic, precarious, unstable, unreliable, undependable; informal iffy, up and down.
– OPPOSITES steady, stable.

rococo ● adjective ORNATE, fancy, elaborate, extravagant, baroque; fussy, busy, ostentatious, showy; flowery, florid, flamboyant, high-flown, magniloquent, orotund, bombastic, overwrought, overblown, inflated, turgid; informal highfalutin.
– OPPOSITES plain.

rod ● noun **1** *an iron rod* BAR, stick, pole, baton, staff; shaft, strut,

reddish summer coat that turns greyish in winter.
– ORIGIN Old English.
roebuck ● noun a male roe deer.
roentgen /runtyən/ ● noun a unit of quantity of ionizing radiation.
– ORIGIN named after the German physicist and discoverer of X-rays Wilhelm Conrad *Röntgen* (1845–1923).
rogan josh /rōgən jōsh/ ● noun an Indian dish of curried meat in a rich tomato-based sauce.
– ORIGIN Urdu.
rogations /rōgaysh'nz/ ● plural noun (in the Christian Church) a special litany chanted on the three days before Ascension Day.
– ORIGIN from Latin *rogare* 'ask'.
roger ● exclamation your message has been received and understood (used in radio communication). ● verb Brit. vulgar slang (of a man) have sexual intercourse with.
– ORIGIN from the given name *Roger*; the verb is from an obsolete sense ('penis') of the noun.
rogue ● noun **1** a dishonest or unprincipled man. **2** a mischievous but likeable person. **3** an elephant or other large wild animal with destructive tendencies driven away or living apart from the herd. **4** a person or thing that is defective or unpredictable.
– ORIGIN originally denoting an idle vagrant: probably from Latin *rogare* 'beg, ask'.
roguery ● noun (pl. **rogueries**) behaviour characteristic of a rogue.
rogues' gallery ● noun informal a collection of photographs of known criminals, used by police to identify suspects.
roguish ● adjective characteristic of a rogue, especially in being playfully mischievous: *a roguish smile.*
– DERIVATIVES **roguishly** adverb **roguishness** noun.
roil /royl/ ● verb **1** make (a liquid) muddy by disturbing the sediment. **2** (of a liquid) move in a turbulent manner.
– ORIGIN perhaps from Old French *ruiler* 'mix mortar', from Latin *regulare* 'regulate'.
roister /roystər/ ● verb enjoy oneself or celebrate in a noisy or boisterous way.
– DERIVATIVES **roisterer** noun **roisterous** adjective.
– ORIGIN from obsolete *roister* 'roisterer', from French *rustre* 'ruffian'.
role ● noun **1** an actor's part in a play, film, etc. **2** a person's or thing's function in a particular situation.
– ORIGIN from obsolete French *roule* 'roll', referring originally to the roll of paper on which an actor's part was written.
role model ● noun a person looked to by others as an example to be imitated.
role playing (also **role play**) ● noun the acting out of a particular role, either consciously (as a technique in psychotherapy or training) or unconsciously (in accordance with the perceived expectations of society).
roll ● verb **1** move by turning over and over on an axis. **2** move forward on wheels or with a smooth, undulating motion. **3** (of a moving ship, aircraft, or vehicle) sway on an axis parallel to the direction of motion. **4** (of a machine or device) begin operating. **5** (often **roll up**) turn (something flexible) over and over on itself to form a cylindrical or spherical shape. **6** (**roll up**) curl up tightly. **7** flatten (something) by passing a roller over it or by passing it between rollers. **8** (of a loud, deep sound such as that of thunder) reverberate. **9** pronounce (a consonant, typically an *r*) with a trill. **10** (**rolling**) (of land) extending in gentle undulations. **11** (**rolling**) steady and continuous: *a rolling programme of reforms.* ● noun **1** a cylinder formed by rolling flexible material. **2** a rolling movement. **3** a gymnastic exercise in which the body is rolled into a tucked position and turned in a forward or backward circle. **4** a prolonged, deep, reverberating sound. **5** (in drumming) a sustained, rapid alternation of single or double strokes of each stick. **6** a very small loaf of bread. **7** an official list or register of names. **8** a document in scroll form. **9** N. Amer. & Austral. a quantity of banknotes rolled together.
– PHRASES **a roll in the hay** (or **the sack**) informal an act of sexual intercourse. **be rolling in it** (or **money**) informal be very rich. **on a roll** informal experiencing a prolonged spell of success or good luck. **roll in** informal **1** be received in large amounts. **2** arrive in a casual way in spite of being late. **a rolling stone gathers no moss** proverb a person who does not settle in one place will not accumulate wealth or status, or responsibilities or commitments. **roll of honour** a list of people whose deeds are honoured, especially a list of those who have died in battle. **roll out** officially launch (a new product). **roll over** Finance contrive or extend (a financial arrangement). **roll up** informal arrive. **roll up one's sleeves** prepare to fight or work. **roll with the punches 1** (of a boxer) move one's body away from an opponent's blows so as to lessen the impact. **2** adapt oneself to adverse circumstances.
– ORIGIN Old French *roller*, from Latin *rotulus* 'a roll, little wheel'.
roll bar ● noun a metal bar running up the sides and across the top of a sports car, protecting the occupants if the vehicle overturns.
roll-call ● noun the process of calling out a list of names to establish who is present.
rolled gold ● noun gold in the form of a thin coating applied to a baser metal by rolling.
rolled oats ● plural noun oats that have been husked and crushed.
roller ● noun **1** a cylinder that rotates about a central axis and is used to move, flatten, or spread something. **2** a small cylinder on which hair is rolled to produce curls. **3** a long swelling wave that appears to roll steadily towards the shore. **4** a brightly coloured crow-sized bird with a characteristic tumbling display flight.
rollerball ● noun **1** a ballpoint pen using relatively thin ink. **2** Computing an input device containing a ball which is moved with the fingers to control the cursor.
roller bearing ● noun a bearing similar to a ball bearing but using small cylindrical rollers instead of balls.
Rollerblade ● noun trademark an in-line skate. ● verb skate using Rollerblades.

Thesaurus

rail, spoke. **2** *the ceremonial rod* STAFF, mace, sceptre. **3** *instruction was accompanied by the rod* CORPORAL PUNISHMENT, the cane, the lash, the birch; beating, flogging, caning, birching.
rogue ● noun **1** *a rogue without ethics* SCOUNDREL, villain, miscreant, reprobate, rascal, good-for-nothing, ne'er-do-well, wretch; *informal* rat, dog, louse, crook; *informal, dated* rotter, bounder, blighter; *dated* cad; *archaic* blackguard, knave. **2** *your boy's a little rogue* RASCAL, imp, devil, monkey; *informal* scamp, scallywag, monster, horror, terror, tyke; *Brit. informal* perisher; *N. Amer. informal* hellion.
roguish ● adjective **1** *a roguish character* UNPRINCIPLED, dishonest, deceitful, unscrupulous, untrustworthy, shameless; wicked, villainous; *informal* shady, scoundrelly, rascally; *archaic* knavish. **2** *a roguish grin* MISCHIEVOUS, playful, teasing, cheeky, naughty, wicked, impish, devilish, arch; *informal* waggish.
roister ● verb ENJOY ONESELF, celebrate, revel, carouse, frolic, romp, have fun, make merry, rollick; *informal* party, live it up, whoop it up, have a ball, make whoopee.
role ● noun **1** *a small role in the film* PART; character. **2** *his role as President of the EC* CAPACITY, position, job, post, office, duty, responsibility, mantle, place; function, part.
roll ● verb **1** *the bottle rolled down the table* BOWL, turn over and over, spin, rotate. **2** *waiters rolled in the trolleys* WHEEL, push, trundle. **3** *we rolled past fields* TRAVEL, go, move, pass, cruise, sweep. **4** *the months rolled by* PASS, go by, slip by, fly by, elapse, wear on, march on. **5** *tears rolled down her cheeks* FLOW, run, course, stream, pour, spill, trickle. **6** *the mist rolled in* BILLOW, undulate, tumble. **7** *he rolled his handkerchief into a ball* WIND, coil, fold, curl; twist. **8** *roll out the pastry* FLATTEN, level; even out. **9** *they rolled about with laughter* STAGGER, lurch, reel, totter, teeter, wobble. **10** *the ship began to roll* LURCH, toss, rock, pitch, plunge, sway, reel, list, keel. **11** *thunder rolled* RUMBLE, reverberate, echo, resound, boom, roar, grumble.
● noun **1** *a roll of wrapping paper* CYLINDER, tube, scroll; bolt. **2** *a roll of film* REEL, spool. **3** *a roll of notes* WAD, bundle. **4** *a roll of the dice* THROW, toss, turn, spin. **5** *crusty rolls* BREAD ROLL, bun, bagel; *Brit.* bap, muffin; *N. English* barm; *N. Amer.* hoagie; *Military slang* wad. **6** *the electoral roll* LIST, register, directory, record, file, index, catalogue, inventory; census. **7** *a roll of thunder* RUMBLE, reverberation, echo, boom, clap, crack, roar, grumble.
– PHRASES **roll in** *(informal)* **1** *money has been rolling in* POUR IN, flood in, flow in. **2** *he rolled in at nine o'clock* ARRIVE, turn up, appear, show one's face; *informal* show up, roll up, blow in. **rolling in it** *(informal)*. See RICH sense 1. **roll something out** UNROLL, spread out, unfurl, unfold, open (out), unwind, uncoil. **roll something up**

– DERIVATIVES **rollerblader** noun.
roller blind ● noun a window blind fitted on a roller.
roller coaster ● noun a fairground attraction consisting of a light railway track with many tight turns and steep slopes, on which people ride in small open carriages.
roller skate ● noun each of a pair of boots or metal frames fitted to shoes, having four or more small wheels and used for gliding across a hard surface.
– DERIVATIVES **roller skater** noun **roller skating** noun.
roller towel ● noun a long towel with the ends joined and hung on a roller.
rollicking[1] ● adjective exuberantly lively and amusing.
– ORIGIN perhaps a blend of ROMP and FROLIC.
rollicking[2] (also **rollocking**) ● noun Brit. informal a severe reprimand.
– ORIGIN euphemistic alteration of BOLLOCKING.
rolling hitch ● noun a kind of hitch used to attach a rope to a spar or larger rope.
rolling mill ● noun a factory or machine for rolling steel or other metal into sheets.
rolling pin ● noun a cylinder for rolling out dough.
rolling stock ● noun **1** locomotives, carriages, or other vehicles used on a railway. **2** US the road vehicles of a trucking company.
rollmop ● noun a rolled uncooked pickled herring fillet.
– ORIGIN German *Rollmops*.
roll neck ● noun a high loosely turned-over collar.
rollocking ● noun variant spelling of ROLLICKING[2].
roll-on ● adjective (of a deodorant or cosmetic) applied by means of a rotating ball in the neck of the container.
roll-on roll-off ● adjective referring to a ferry in which vehicles are driven directly on at the start of the voyage and driven off at the end of it.
roll-out ● noun **1** the unveiling or launch of a new aircraft, spacecraft, or product. **2** Aeronautics the stage of an aircraft's landing during which it travels along the runway while losing speed.
rollover ● noun (in a lottery) the accumulative carry-over of prize money to the following draw.
roll-top desk ● noun a writing desk with a semicircular flexible cover sliding in curved grooves.
roll-up ● noun informal **1** Brit. a hand-rolled cigarette. **2** Austral. a gathering of people.
roly-poly ● noun (also **roly-poly pudding**) Brit. a pudding made of a sheet of suet pastry covered with jam or fruit, formed into a roll, and steamed or baked. ● adjective informal round and plump.
– ORIGIN fanciful formation from ROLL.
ROM ● abbreviation Computing read-only memory.
romaine /rəmayn/ ● noun a cos lettuce.
– ORIGIN French, feminine of *romain* 'Roman'.
Roman ● adjective **1** relating to ancient Rome or its empire or people. **2** relating to medieval or modern Rome. **3** referring to the alphabet used for writing Latin, English, and most European languages, developed in ancient Rome. **4** (**roman**) (of type) of a plain upright kind used in ordinary print. ● noun **1** an inhabitant of ancient or modern Rome. **2** (**roman**) roman type.
roman-à-clef /rōmonaaklay/ ● noun (pl. **romans-à-clef** pronunc. same) a novel in which real people or events appear with invented names.
– ORIGIN French, 'novel with a key'.
Roman candle ● noun a firework giving off flaming coloured balls and sparks.
Roman Catholic ● adjective relating to the Roman Catholic Church. ● noun a member of this Church.
– DERIVATIVES **Roman Catholicism** noun.
– ORIGIN translation of Latin *Ecclesia Romana Catholica et Apostolica* 'Roman Catholic and Apostolic Church', apparently first used in place of the earlier *Roman, Romanist*, or *Romish*, which were considered derogatory.
Roman Catholic Church ● noun the part of the Christian Church which acknowledges the Pope as its head, especially as it has developed since the Reformation.
Romance /rəmanss/ ● noun the group of languages descended from Latin, principally French, Spanish, Portuguese, Italian, and Romanian.
– ORIGIN originally denoting the ordinary language of France as opposed to Latin: from Latin *Romanicus* 'Roman'.
romance /rəmanss/ ● noun **1** a pleasurable feeling of excitement and wonder associated with love. **2** a love affair. **3** a book or film dealing with love in a sentimental or idealized way. **4** a quality or feeling of mystery, excitement, and remoteness from everyday life. **5** a medieval tale dealing with a hero of chivalry, of the kind common in the Romance languages. ● verb **1** court or pursue amorously. **2** informal court the favour of. **3** romanticize.
– ORIGIN originally denoting a composition in the vernacular as opposed to works in Latin: from ROMANCE.
romancer /rōmansər/ ● noun **1** a person prone to wild exaggeration or falsehood. **2** a writer of medieval romances.
Roman Empire ● noun the empire under Roman rule established in 27 BC and divided in AD 395 into the Western or Latin and Eastern or Greek Empire.
Romanesque /rōmənesk/ ● adjective relating to a style of architecture which prevailed in Europe *c.*900–1200, with massive vaulting and round arches.
– ORIGIN French, from *roman* 'romance'.
roman-fleuve /rōmonflöv/ ● noun (pl. **romans-fleuves** pronunc. same) a novel or sequence of novels dealing with the lives of a family or other group over a prolonged period of time.
– ORIGIN French, 'river novel'.
Roman holiday ● noun an occasion on which enjoyment or profit is derived from the suffering of others.
– ORIGIN from Byron's poem *Childe Harold* (1818), originally with reference to a holiday given for a gladiatorial combat.
Romanian (also **Rumanian**) ● noun **1** a person from Romania. **2** the language of Romania. ● adjective relating to Romania.
Romanic /rōmannik/ ● noun less common term for ROMANCE.
romanize /rōməniz/ (also **romanise**) ● verb **1** historical bring under Roman influence or authority. **2** make Roman Catholic in character. **3** put (text) into the Roman alphabet or into roman type.
– DERIVATIVES **romanization** noun.
Roman law ● noun the law code of the ancient Romans forming the basis of civil law in many countries today.
Roman nose ● noun a nose with a high bridge.
Roman numeral ● noun any of the letters representing numbers in the Roman numerical system: I = 1, V = 5, X = 10, L = 50, C = 100, D = 500, M = 1,000.
Romansh /rōmansh/ ● noun the language spoken in the Swiss canton of Grisons, an official language of Switzerland.
– ORIGIN from Latin *romanice* 'in the Romanic manner'.
romantic ● adjective **1** inclined towards or suggestive of love or romance. **2** of, characterized by, or suggestive of an idealized view of reality. **3** (**Romantic**) relating to the artistic and literary movement of romanticism. ● noun **1** a person with romantic beliefs or attitudes. **2** (**Romantic**) a writer or artist of the Romantic movement.
– DERIVATIVES **romantically** adverb.

r

Thesaurus

FOLD (UP), furl, wind up, coil (up), bundle up. **roll up** *(informal)*. See ROLL IN sense 2.
rollicking[1] ● noun *(Brit. informal) I got a rollicking for being late.* See LECTURE noun sense 2.
rollicking[2] ● adjective *a rollicking party* LIVELY, boisterous, exuberant, spirited; riotous, noisy, wild, rowdy, roisterous; *Brit. informal* rumbustious; *N. Amer. informal* rambunctious.
roly-poly ● adjective *(informal)* CHUBBY, plump, fat, stout, rotund, round, dumpy, chunky, portly, overweight, fleshy, paunchy, bulky, corpulent; *informal* tubby, pudgy, beefy, porky, blubbery; *Brit. informal* podgy; *N. Amer. informal* zaftig, corn-fed.
– OPPOSITES skinny.
romance ● noun **1** *their romance blossomed* LOVE, passion, ardour, adoration, devotion; affection, fondness, attachment. **2** *he's had many romances* LOVE AFFAIR, relationship, liaison, courtship, attachment; flirtation, dalliance. **3** *an author of historical romances* LOVE STORY, novel; romantic fiction; *informal* tear-jerker. **4** *the romance of the Far East* MYSTERY, glamour, excitement, exoticism, mystique; appeal, allure, charm.
● verb **1** *he was romancing Meg* WOO, chase, pursue; go out with, pay court to; *informal* see, go steady with, date; *dated* court, make love to. **2** *I am romancing the past* ROMANTICIZE, idealize, paint a rosy picture of.
romantic ● adjective **1** *he's so romantic* LOVING, amorous, passionate, tender, affectionate; *informal* lovey-dovey. **2** *romantic songs* SENTIMENTAL, hearts-and-flowers; mawkish, sickly, saccharine, syrupy;

romanticism ● noun a literary and artistic movement which began in the late 18th century and emphasized inspiration and subjectivity.
– DERIVATIVES **romanticist** noun.
romanticize (also **romanticise**) ● verb deal with or describe in an idealized or unrealistic fashion.
– DERIVATIVES **romanticization** noun.
Romany /romməni, rō-/ ● noun (pl. **Romanies**) **1** the language of the gypsies. **2** a gypsy.
– ORIGIN from Romany *Rom* 'man, husband'.
Romeo /rōmiō/ ● noun (pl. **Romeos**) an attractive, passionate male seducer or lover.
– ORIGIN the hero of Shakespeare's romantic tragedy *Romeo and Juliet*.
Romish /rōmish/ ● adjective chiefly derogatory Roman Catholic.
romp ● verb **1** play about roughly and energetically. **2** informal achieve something easily. **3** (**romp home/in**) informal finish as the easy winner of a race or other contest. **4** informal engage in sexual activity. ● noun **1** a spell of romping. **2** a light-hearted film or other work. **3** informal an easy victory.
– ORIGIN perhaps an alteration of RAMP.
rompers (also **romper suit**) ● plural noun a young child's one-piece outer garment.
rondeau /rondō/ ● noun (pl. **rondeaux** pronunc. same or /rondōz/) a poem of ten or thirteen lines with only two rhymes throughout and with the opening words used twice as a refrain.
– ORIGIN French.
rondel /rond'l/ ● noun a rondeau, especially one of three stanzas of thirteen or fourteen lines with a two-line refrain.
– ORIGIN Old French, from *rond* 'round'.
rondo /rondō/ ● noun (pl. **rondos**) a musical form with a recurring leading theme, often found in the final movement of a sonata or concerto.
– ORIGIN Italian, from French *rondeau*.
röntgen ● noun variant spelling of ROENTGEN.
roo ● noun Austral. informal a kangaroo.
rood /ro͝od/ ● noun **1** a crucifix, especially one positioned above the rood screen of a church or on a beam over the entrance to the chancel. **2** chiefly Brit. a former measure of land area equal to a quarter of an acre.
– ORIGIN Old English.
rood screen ● noun a screen of wood or stone separating the nave from the chancel of a church.
roof ● noun (pl. **roofs**) **1** the structure forming the upper covering of a building or vehicle. **2** the top inner surface of a covered area or space. **3** the upper limit or level of prices or wages. ● verb (usu. **be roofed**) cover with or as a roof.
– PHRASES **go through the roof** informal (of prices or figures) reach extreme levels. **hit** (or **go through**) **the roof** informal suddenly become very angry.
– DERIVATIVES **roofless** adjective.
– ORIGIN Old English.
roofer ● noun a person who constructs or repairs roofs.
roofing ● noun **1** material for constructing a building's roof. **2** the process of constructing a roof or roofs.
roof of the mouth ● noun the palate.
roof rack ● noun a framework for carrying luggage on the roof of a vehicle.
roof tree ● noun the ridge piece of a roof.
rook[1] ● noun a crow with black plumage and a bare face, nesting in colonies in treetops. ● verb informal defraud, swindle, or overcharge.
– ORIGIN Old English.
rook[2] ● noun a chess piece, typically with its top in the shape of a battlement, that can move in any direction along a rank or file on which it stands.
– ORIGIN Arabic.
rookery ● noun (pl. **rookeries**) **1** a breeding colony of rooks, typically a collection of nests high in a clump of trees. **2** a breeding colony of seabirds (especially penguins), seals, or turtles.
rookie ● noun informal a new recruit or member, especially in the army or police or a sports team; a novice.
– ORIGIN perhaps an alteration of RECRUIT.
room /ro͞om, ro͝om/ ● noun **1** space viewed in terms of its capacity to accommodate contents or allow action: *there was no room to move.* **2** opportunity or scope: *room for improvement.* **3** a part of a building enclosed by walls, floor, and ceiling. **4** (**rooms**) a set of rooms rented out to lodgers. ● verb chiefly N. Amer. share lodgings, especially at a college or similar institution.
– PHRASES **no room to swing a cat** humorous a very confined space. [ORIGIN *cat* in the sense 'cat-o'-nine-tails'.]
– DERIVATIVES **roomed** adjective.
– ORIGIN Old English.
rooming house ● noun chiefly N. Amer. a lodging house.
room-mate ● noun **1** a person occupying the same room as another. **2** N. Amer. a person occupying the same room, flat, or house as another.
room service ● noun provision of food and drink to hotel guests in their rooms.
room temperature ● noun a comfortable ambient temperature, generally taken as about 20°C.
roomy ● adjective (**roomier**, **roomiest**) having plenty of room; spacious.
– DERIVATIVES **roominess** noun.
roost ● noun a place where birds or bats regularly settle to rest. ● verb (of a bird or bat) settle or gather for rest.
– PHRASES **curses, like chickens, come home to roost** proverb one's past mistakes or wrongdoings will eventually be the cause of present troubles.
– ORIGIN Old English.
rooster ● noun chiefly N. Amer. a male domestic fowl.
root[1] ● noun **1** a part of a plant normally below ground, which acts as a support and collects water and nourishment. **2** the embedded part of a bodily organ or structure such as a hair. **3** (also **root vegetable**) a turnip, carrot, or other vegetable which grows as the root of a plant. **4** the basic cause, source, or origin: *money is the root of all evil.* **5** (**roots**) family, ethnic, or cultural origins. **6** (also **root note**) Music the fundamental note of a chord. **7** Linguistics a form from which words have been made by the addition of prefixes or suffixes or by other modification. **8** Mathematics a number or quantity that when multiplied by itself one or more times gives a specified number or quantity. ● verb **1** cause (a plant or cutting) to establish roots. **2** (usu. **be rooted**) establish deeply and firmly. **3** (**be rooted in**) have as a source or origin. **4** (**be rooted**) stand immobile through fear or amazement. **5** (**root out/up**) find and get rid of. **6** Austral./NZ & Irish vulgar slang have sexual intercourse with.
– PHRASES **at root** fundamentally. **put down roots** begin to have a settled life in a place. **root and branch** (of a process or operation) thorough or radical. **take root** become fixed or estab-

Thesaurus

informal slushy, mushy, sloppy, schmaltzy, gooey, treacly, cheesy, corny; *Brit. informal* soppy; *N. Amer. informal* cornball, sappy. **3** *a romantic setting* IDYLLIC, picturesque, fairy-tale; beautiful, lovely, charming, pretty. **4** *romantic notions of rural communities* IDEALISTIC, idealized, unrealistic, fanciful, impractical; head-in-the-clouds, starry-eyed, optimistic, hopeful, visionary, utopian, fairy-tale.
– OPPOSITES unsentimental, realistic.
● noun *an incurable romantic* IDEALIST, sentimentalist, romanticist; dreamer, visionary, utopian, Don Quixote, fantasist; *N. Amer.* fantast.
– OPPOSITES realist.
Romeo ● noun LADIES' MAN, Don Juan, Casanova, Lothario, womanizer, playboy, lover, seducer, philanderer, flirt; gigolo; *informal* ladykiller, stud.
romp ● verb **1** *two fox cubs romped playfully* PLAY, frolic, frisk, gambol, skip, prance, caper, cavort, rollick; *dated* sport. **2** *(informal) South Africa romped to a win* SAIL, coast, sweep; win hands down, run away with it; *informal* win by a mile, walk it.
roof ● noun
– PHRASES **hit the roof** *(informal)* BE VERY ANGRY, be furious, lose one's temper; *informal* go mad, go crazy, go wild, go bananas, have a fit, blow one's top, do one's nut, go up the wall, go off the deep end, go ape, flip, lose one's rag; *Brit. informal* go spare.
room ● noun **1** *there isn't much room* SPACE; headroom, legroom; area, expanse, extent; *informal* elbow room. **2** *room for improvement* SCOPE, capacity, leeway, latitude, freedom; opportunity, chance. **3** *he wandered around the room* CHAMBER. **4** *he had rooms in the Pepys building* LODGINGS, quarters; accommodation; a suite, an apartment; *informal* a pad, digs.
● verb *he roomed there in September* LODGE, board, live, stay; be quartered, be housed; *formal* dwell, reside, sojourn.

lished.
– DERIVATIVES **rootless** adjective.
– ORIGIN Old English, related to WORT.

root² ● verb **1** (of an animal) turn up the ground with its snout in search of food. **2** rummage. **3** (**root for**) informal support enthusiastically.
– ORIGIN Old English.

root beer ● noun N. Amer. a fizzy drink made from an extract of the roots and bark of certain plants.

root canal ● noun **1** the pulp-filled cavity in the root of a tooth. **2** N. Amer. a procedure to replace infected pulp in a root canal with an inert material.

rootin'-tootin' ● adjective N. Amer. informal boisterous, noisy, or lively.
– ORIGIN reduplication of *rooting* in the sense 'inquisitive', an early dialect sense of the compound.

rootle ● verb Brit. informal root or rummage.
– ORIGIN from ROOT².

root mean square ● noun Mathematics the square root of the arithmetic mean of the squares of a set of values.

root sign ● noun Mathematics the radical sign.

rootstock ● noun **1** a rhizome. **2** a plant on to which another variety is grafted. **3** a primary form or source from which offshoots have arisen.

rootsy ● adjective informal (of music) unpolished and emphasizing its traditional or ethnic origins.

rope ● noun **1** a length of stout cord made by twisting together strands of hemp, sisal, nylon, etc. **2** a quantity of roughly spherical objects strung together: *a rope of pearls.* **3** (**the ropes**) the ropes enclosing a boxing or wrestling ring. **4** (**the ropes**) informal the established procedures in an organization or area of activity: *I showed her the ropes.* ● verb **1** catch, fasten, or secure with rope. **2** (**rope in/into**) persuade (someone) to take part in something.
– PHRASES **give a man enough rope** (or **plenty of rope**) **and he will hang himself** proverb given enough freedom of action a person will bring about their own downfall. **on the ropes 1** Boxing forced against the ropes by the opponent's attack. **2** in state of near collapse. **a rope of sand** literary illusory security.
– ORIGIN Old English.

ropeable /rōpəb'l/ (also **ropable**) ● adjective Austral./NZ informal very angry; furious.
– ORIGIN from the notion that the person requires to be restrained.

rope ladder ● noun two long ropes connected by short crosspieces, used as a ladder.

ropy (also **ropey**) ● adjective (**ropier**, **ropiest**) **1** resembling a rope. **2** Brit. informal poor in quality or health.
– DERIVATIVES **ropily** adverb **ropiness** noun.

Roquefort /rokfor/ ● noun trademark a soft blue cheese made from ewes' milk.
– ORIGIN named after a village in southern France.

ro-ro ● abbreviation Brit. roll-on roll-off.

rorqual /rorkwəl/ ● noun a baleen whale of a small group with pleated skin on the underside, e.g. the blue, fin, and humpback whales.
– ORIGIN Norwegian *røyrkval* 'fin whale'.

Rorschach test /rorshaak/ ● noun a test used in psychoanalysis, in which a standard set of symmetrical ink blots is presented to the subject, who is asked to describe what they suggest or resemble.
– ORIGIN named after the Swiss psychiatrist Hermann *Rorschach* (1884–1922).

rort /rort/ ● noun Austral. informal **1** a fraudulent or dishonest act or practice. **2** a wild party.
– ORIGIN from RORTY.

rorty ● adjective (**rortier**, **rortiest**) Brit. informal boisterous and high-spirited.
– ORIGIN of unknown origin.

rosacea /rōzayshiə/ ● noun a condition in which some facial blood vessels enlarge, giving the cheeks and nose a flushed appearance.
– ORIGIN short for Latin *acne rosacea* 'rose-coloured acne'.

rosaceous /rōzayshəss/ ● adjective Botany relating to plants of the rose family (Rosaceae).

rosary /rōzəri/ ● noun (pl. **rosaries**) **1** (in the Roman Catholic Church) a form of devotion in which five (or fifteen) sets of ten Hail Marys are repeated. **2** a string of beads for keeping count in such a devotion or in the devotions of some other religions.
– ORIGIN originally in the sense 'rose garden': from Latin *rosarium.*

rose¹ ● noun **1** a fragrant flower (typically red, pink, yellow, or white) borne on a prickly bush or shrub. **2** a perforated cap attached to a shower, the spout of a watering can, or the end of a hose to produce a spray. **3** a warm pink or light crimson colour. **4** (**roses**) favourable circumstances or ease of success: *everything was coming up roses.*
– PHRASES **come up** (or **out**) **smelling of roses** emerge from a difficult situation with reputation intact.
– ORIGIN Latin *rosa.*

rose² past of RISE.

rosé /rōzay/ ● noun light pink wine made from red grapes, coloured by only brief contact with the skins.
– ORIGIN French, 'pink'.

roseate /rōziət/ ● adjective rose-coloured.

rosebay ● noun **1** (also **rosebay willowherb**) a tall willowherb with pink flowers. **2** N. Amer. an azalea.

rosebud ● noun **1** the bud of a rose. **2** Brit. dated a pretty young woman.

rose-coloured (also **rose-tinted**) ● adjective **1** of a warm pink colour. **2** referring to a naively optimistic or unfoundedly favourable viewpoint: *looking at the world through rose-coloured spectacles.*

rose hip ● noun fuller form of HIP².

rosella /rəzellə/ ● noun an Australian parakeet with brightly coloured plumage.
– ORIGIN alteration of *Rosehill*, New South Wales, where the bird was first found.

rose madder ● noun a pale shade of pink.

rosemary ● noun an evergreen aromatic shrub of southern Eur-

Thesaurus

roomy ● adjective SPACIOUS, capacious, sizeable, generous, big, large, extensive; voluminous, ample; *formal* commodious.
– OPPOSITES cramped.

root ● noun **1** *a plant's roots* rootstock, tuber, rootlet; *Botany* rhizome, radicle. **2** *the root of the problem* SOURCE, origin, germ, beginnings, genesis; cause, reason, basis, foundation, bottom, seat; core, heart, nub, essence; *formal* radix. **3** *he rejected his roots* ORIGINS, beginnings, family, ancestors, predecessors, heritage; birthplace, homeland.
– RELATED TERMS radical, rhizo-.
● verb **1** *has the shoot rooted?* TAKE ROOT, grow roots, establish, strike, take. **2** *root the cuttings* PLANT, bed out, sow. **3** *he rooted around in the cupboard* RUMMAGE, hunt, search, rifle, delve, forage, dig, nose, poke; *Brit. informal* rootle.
– PHRASES **put down roots** SETTLE, establish oneself, set up home. **root and branch 1** *the firm should be eradicated, root and branch* COMPLETELY, entirely, wholly, totally, thoroughly. **2** *a root-and-branch reform* COMPLETE, total, thorough, radical. **root for** *(informal)* CHEER (ON), applaud, support, encourage. **root something out 1** *the hedge was rooted out* UPROOT, deracinate, pull up, grub out. **2** *root out corruption* ERADICATE, eliminate, weed out, destroy, wipe out, stamp out, extirpate, abolish, end, put a stop to. **3** *he rooted out a dark secret* UNEARTH, dig up, bring to light, uncover, discover, dredge up, ferret out, expose. **take root 1** *leave the plants to take root* GERMINATE, sprout, establish, strike, take. **2** *Christianity took root in Persia* BECOME ESTABLISHED, take hold; develop, thrive, flourish.

rooted ● adjective **1** *views rooted in Indian culture* EMBEDDED, fixed, established, entrenched, ingrained. **2** *Neil was rooted to the spot* FROZEN, riveted, paralysed, glued, fixed; stock-still, motionless, unmoving.

rootless ● adjective ITINERANT, unsettled, drifting, roving, footloose; homeless, of no fixed abode.

rope ● noun CORD, cable, line, hawser; string.
– RELATED TERMS funicular.
● verb *his feet were roped together* TIE, bind, lash, truss; secure, moor, fasten, attach; hitch, tether, lasso.
– PHRASES **know the ropes** *(informal)* KNOW WHAT TO DO, know the routine, know one's way around, know one's stuff, know what's what; be experienced; *informal* know the drill, know the score. **rope someone in/into** PERSUADE TO/INTO, talk into, inveigle into; enlist, engage.

ropy ● adjective **1** *ropy strands of lava* STRINGY, thready, fibrous, filamentous; viscous, sticky, mucilaginous, thick. **2** *(Brit. informal) I*

ope, the leaves of which are used as a herb in cooking.
– ORIGIN from Latin *ros marinus*, from *ros* 'dew' + *marinus* 'of the sea'.

rose of Jericho • noun a desert plant whose dead branches fold inwards to form a ball.

rose of Sharon • noun **1** a low shrub with dense foliage and large golden-yellow flowers. **2** (in biblical use) a flowering plant of unknown identity.
– ORIGIN from *Sharon*, a region of fertile coastal plain in present-day Israel.

roseroot • noun a yellow-flowered stonecrop whose roots smell of roses when dried or bruised.

rosette • noun **1** a rose-shaped decoration made of ribbon, worn by supporters of a team or political party or awarded as a prize. **2** a design or object resembling a rose. **3** a radiating arrangement of spreading leaves at the base of a low-growing plant.
– ORIGIN French, 'little rose'.

rose water • noun scented water made with rose petals.

rose window • noun a circular window with mullions or tracery radiating in a form suggestive of a rose.

rosewood • noun a close-grained tropical timber used for making furniture and musical instruments.

Rosh Hashana /rosh həshaanə/ (also **Rosh Hashanah**) • noun the Jewish New Year festival.
– ORIGIN Hebrew, 'head of the year'.

Rosicrucian /rōzikrōōsh'n/ • noun a member of a secretive 17th- and 18th-century society devoted to the study of metaphysical, mystical, and alchemical lore. • adjective relating to the Rosicrucians.
– DERIVATIVES **Rosicrucianism** noun.
– ORIGIN from the Latin form of the name of Christian *Rosenkreuz*, legendary 15th-century founder of the movement.

rosin /rozzin/ • noun resin, especially the solid amber residue obtained after distilling oil of turpentine and used for treating the bows of stringed instruments. • verb (**rosined**, **rosining**) rub or treat with rosin.
– ORIGIN Latin *rosina*, from *resina* 'resin'.

RoSPA /rospə/ • abbreviation (in the UK) Royal Society for the Prevention of Accidents.

roster /rostər/ • noun **1** a list or plan showing turns of duty or leave in an organization. **2** a list of names, in particular of sports players available for team selection. • verb (usu. **be rostered**) assign according to a duty roster.
– ORIGIN Dutch *rooster* 'list', earlier 'gridiron', with reference to its parallel lines.

rösti /rösti/ • noun a Swiss dish of grated potatoes formed into a small flat cake and fried.
– ORIGIN Swiss German.

rostrum /rostrəm/ • noun (pl. **rostra** /rostrə/ or **rostrums**) **1** a raised platform on which a person stands to make a public speech, play music, or conduct an orchestra. **2** a platform for supporting a film or television camera. **3** chiefly Zoology a beak-like projection.
– DERIVATIVES **rostral** adjective (chiefly Zoology).
– ORIGIN Latin, 'beak'; the word was originally used to denote an orator's platform in the Forum in ancient Rome, which was decorated with the beaks of captured galleys.

rosy • adjective (**rosier**, **rosiest**) **1** (especially of a person's skin) rose-red or pink, typically as an indication of health or youthfulness. **2** promising or suggesting good fortune; hopeful.
– DERIVATIVES **rosily** adverb **rosiness** noun.

rot • verb (**rotted**, **rotting**) **1** decompose by the action of bacteria and fungi; decay. **2** gradually deteriorate or decline. • noun **1** the process of decaying. **2** rotten or decayed matter. **3** (**the rot**) Brit. a process of deterioration or decline in standards. **4** a fungal or bacterial disease that causes tissue deterioration, especially in plants. **5** informal nonsense; rubbish: *don't talk rot.*
– ORIGIN Old English.

rota • noun chiefly Brit. a list showing times and names for people to take their turn to undertake duties.
– ORIGIN Latin, 'wheel'.

Rotarian • noun a member of Rotary. • adjective relating to Rotary.

rotary • adjective **1** revolving around a centre or axis. **2** acting by means of rotation; having a rotating part or parts: *a rotary mower.* • noun (pl. **rotaries**) **1** a rotary machine or device. **2** N. Amer. a traffic roundabout. **3** (**Rotary**) a worldwide charitable society of business and professional people organized into local Rotary clubs.

rotary wing • noun an aerofoil that rotates in an approximately horizontal plane, providing all or most of the lift in a helicopter or autogiro.

rotate /rōtayt/ • verb **1** move in a circle round an axis. **2** move or pass on in a regularly recurring order or succession. **3** grow (different crops) in succession on a particular piece of land.
– DERIVATIVES **rotatable** adjective **rotatory** /rōtətəri, rōtaytəri/ adjective.
– ORIGIN Latin *rotare* 'turn in a circle', from *rota* 'wheel'.

rotation • noun the action or process of rotating.
– DERIVATIVES **rotational** adjective **rotationally** adverb.

rotator • noun **1** a thing which rotates or which causes something to rotate. **2** Anatomy a muscle whose contraction causes or assists in the rotation of a part of the body.

rotavator /rōtəvaytər/ • noun trademark a machine with rotating blades for breaking up or tilling the soil.
– DERIVATIVES **rotavate** verb.
– ORIGIN blend of ROTARY + CULTIVATOR.

rote • noun mechanical or habitual repetition: *a poem learnt by rote.*
– ORIGIN of unknown origin.

rotgut • noun informal poor-quality and potentially harmful alcoholic liquor.

rotisserie /rōtissəri/ • noun **1** a restaurant specializing in roasted or barbecued meat. **2** a rotating spit for roasting and barbecuing meat.
– ORIGIN French, from *rôtir* 'to roast'.

rotogravure /rōtəgrəvyoor/ • noun a printing system using a rotary press with intaglio cylinders.
– ORIGIN German *Rotogravur*, part of the name of a printing company.

rotor • noun **1** the rotating part of a turbine, electric motor, or other device. **2** a hub with a number of radiating blades that is rotated to provide the lift for a helicopter.

rotten • adjective **1** suffering from decay. **2** corrupt. **3** informal very bad or unpleasant. • adverb informal very much: *your mother spoiled you rotten.*
– DERIVATIVES **rottenness** noun.

r

Thesaurus

feel a bit ropy. See ILL adjective sense 1. **3** *(Brit. informal) ropy defending from the home team.* See SUBSTANDARD.

roster • noun SCHEDULE, list, listing, register, agenda, calendar, table; *Brit.* rota.

rostrum • noun DAIS, platform, podium, stage; soapbox.

rosy • adjective **1** *a rosy complexion* PINK, pinkish, roseate, reddish; glowing, healthy, fresh, radiant, blooming; blushing, flushed; ruddy, high-coloured, florid. **2** *his future looks rosy* PROMISING, optimistic, auspicious, hopeful, encouraging, favourable, bright, golden; *informal* upbeat.
– OPPOSITES pale, bleak.

rot • verb **1** *the floorboards rotted* DECAY, decompose, become rotten; disintegrate, crumble, perish. **2** *the meat began to rot* GO BAD, go off, spoil; moulder, putrefy, fester. **3** *poor neighbourhoods have been left to rot* DETERIORATE, degenerate, decline, decay, go to rack and ruin, go to seed, go downhill; *informal* go to pot, go to the dogs.
– RELATED TERMS sapro-.
– OPPOSITES improve.
• noun **1** *the leaves turned black with rot* DECAY, decomposition, mould, mouldiness, mildew, blight, canker; putrefaction, putrescence. **2** *(Brit.) traditionalists said the rot had set in* DETERIORATION, decline; corruption, cancer. **3** *(informal) stop talking rot.* See NONSENSE sense 1.
– OPPOSITES sense.

rota • noun *(Brit.)*. See ROSTER.

rotary • adjective ROTATING, rotatory, rotational, revolving, turning, spinning, gyrating, gyratory.

rotate • verb **1** *the wheels rotate continually* REVOLVE, go round, turn (round), spin, gyrate, whirl, twirl, swivel, circle, pivot. **2** *many nurses rotate jobs* ALTERNATE, take turns, change, switch, interchange, exchange, swap; move around.

rotation • noun **1** *the rotation of the wheels* REVOLVING, turning, spinning, gyration, circling. **2** *a rotation of the Earth* TURN, revolution, orbit, spin. **3** *each member is chair for six months in rotation* SEQUENCE, succession; alternation, cycle.
– RELATED TERMS gyro-.

– ORIGIN Old Norse.

rotten borough ● noun Brit. historical (before the Reform Act of 1832) a borough that was able to elect an MP though having very few voters.

rotter ● noun informal, dated a cruel, mean, or unkind person.

Rottweiler /rotvīlər/ ● noun a large powerful dog of a tall black-and-tan breed.

– ORIGIN from *Rottweil*, a town in SW Germany.

rotund /rōtund/ ● adjective **1** large and plump. **2** round; spherical.

– DERIVATIVES **rotundity** noun **rotundly** adverb.

– ORIGIN Latin *rotundus*, from *rotare* 'rotate'.

rotunda ● noun a round building or room, especially one with a dome.

– ORIGIN from Italian *rotonda camera* 'round chamber'.

rouble /rōtund/ (also **ruble**) ● noun the basic monetary unit of Russia and some other former republics of the USSR, equal to 100 kopeks.

– ORIGIN Russian.

roué /ro͞oay/ ● noun a man who leads an immoral, dissolute life.

– ORIGIN French, 'broken on a wheel', referring to the instrument of torture thought to be deserved by such a person.

rouge /ro͞ozh/ ● noun a red powder or cream used as a cosmetic for colouring the cheeks or lips. ● verb colour with rouge.

– ORIGIN French, 'red'.

rough ● adjective **1** having an uneven or irregular surface; not smooth or level. **2** not gentle; violent or boisterous: *rough treatment.* **3** (of weather or the sea) wild and stormy. **4** lacking sophistication or refinement. **5** not finished tidily; plain and basic. **6** harsh in sound or taste. **7** not worked out or correct in every detail; approximate: *a rough guess.* **8** informal difficult and unpleasant. ● noun **1** a rough, preliminary state: *jot things down in rough first.* **2** chiefly Brit. a disreputable and violent person. **3** (on a golf course) the area of longer grass around the fairway and the green. ● verb **1** work or shape in a rough, preliminary fashion. **2** make uneven. **3** (**rough it**) informal live in discomfort with only basic necessities. **4** (**rough up**) informal beat (someone) up.

– PHRASES **in the rough 1** in a natural state; without decoration or other treatment. **2** in difficulties. **rough and ready 1** crude but effective. **2** unsophisticated or unrefined. **the rough edge** (or **side**) **of one's tongue** a scolding. **rough edges** small imperfections in something that is otherwise satisfactory. **rough justice** treatment that is not scrupulously fair or in accordance with the law. **sleep rough** Brit. sleep in uncomfortable conditions, typically out of doors. **take the rough with the smooth** accept the difficult or unpleasant aspects of life as well as the good.

– DERIVATIVES **roughness** noun.

– ORIGIN Old English.

roughage ● noun fibrous indigestible material in vegetable foodstuffs which aids the passage of food and waste products through the gut.

rough and tumble ● noun a situation without rules or organization.

– ORIGIN originally boxing slang.

roughcast ● noun plaster of lime, cement, and gravel, used on outside walls. ● adjective **1** coated with roughcast. **2** (of a person) lacking refinement. ● verb coat with roughcast.

rough diamond ● noun **1** an uncut diamond. **2** a person who is of good character but lacks manners or education.

roughen ● verb make or become rough.

rough-hewn ● adjective (of a person) uncultivated or uncouth.

rough house informal, chiefly N. Amer. ● noun a violent disturbance. ● verb (**rough-house**) act or treat in a rough, violent manner.

roughly ● adverb **1** in a rough or harsh manner. **2** approximately: *a walk of roughly 13 miles.*

roughneck ● noun **1** informal a rough, uncouth person. **2** an oil-rig worker.

rough-rider ● noun N. Amer. a person who breaks in or can ride unbroken horses.

roughshod ● adjective archaic (of a horse) having shoes with nail

Thesaurus

rote ● noun

– PHRASES **by rote** MECHANICALLY, automatically, parrot-fashion, unthinkingly, mindlessly; from memory, by heart.

rotten ● adjective **1** *rotten meat* DECAYING, rotting, bad, off, decomposing, putrid, putrescent, perished, mouldy, mouldering, mildewy, rancid, festering, fetid; addled; maggoty, wormy, flyblown. **2** *rotten teeth* DECAYING, decayed, carious, black; disintegrating, crumbling. **3** *he's rotten to the core* CORRUPT, unprincipled, dishonest, dishonourable, unscrupulous, untrustworthy, immoral; villainous, bad, wicked, evil, iniquitous, venal; *informal* crooked, warped; *Brit. informal* bent. **4** *(informal) a rotten thing to do* NASTY, unkind, unpleasant, obnoxious, vile, contemptible, despicable, shabby; spiteful, mean, malicious, hateful, hurtful; unfair, uncharitable, uncalled for; *informal* dirty, low-down; *Brit. informal* out of order. **5** *(informal) he was a rotten singer* BAD, poor, dreadful, awful, terrible, frightful, atrocious, hopeless, inadequate, inferior, substandard; *informal* crummy, pathetic, useless, lousy, appalling, abysmal, dire; *Brit. informal* duff, rubbish, a load of pants. **6** *(informal) I feel rotten about it* GUILTY, conscience-stricken, remorseful, ashamed, shamefaced, chastened, contrite, sorry, regretful, repentant, penitent. **7** *(informal) I felt rotten with that cold.* See ILL adjective sense 1.

– OPPOSITES fresh, honourable, kind, good, well.

rotter ● noun *(informal, dated)*. See SCOUNDREL.

rotund ● adjective **1** *a small, rotund man* PLUMP, chubby, fat, stout, portly, dumpy, round, chunky, overweight, heavy, paunchy, ample; flabby, fleshy, bulky, corpulent, obese; *informal* tubby, roly-poly, pudgy, beefy, porky, blubbery; *Brit. informal* podgy; *N. Amer. informal* zaftig, corn-fed. **2** *rotund cauldrons* ROUND, bulbous, spherical, spheric; *poetic/literary* orbicular.

– OPPOSITES thin.

roué ● noun LIBERTINE, rake, debauchee, degenerate, profligate; lecher, seducer, womanizer, philanderer, adulterer, Don Juan, Lothario; *informal* ladykiller, lech, dirty old man.

rough ● adjective **1** *rough ground* UNEVEN, irregular, bumpy, lumpy, knobbly, stony, rocky, rugged, rutted, pitted, rutty. **2** *the terrier's rough coat* COARSE, bristly, scratchy, prickly, shaggy, hairy, bushy. **3** *rough skin* DRY, leathery, weather-beaten; chapped, calloused, scaly, scabrous. **4** *his voice was rough* GRUFF, hoarse, harsh, rasping, raspy, husky, throaty, gravelly, guttural. **5** *rough red wine* SHARP, sour, acidic, acid, vinegary, acidulous. **6** *he gets rough when he's drunk* VIOLENT, brutal, vicious; AGGRESSIVE, belligerent, pugnacious, thuggish; boisterous, rowdy, disorderly, unruly, riotous. **7** *a machine that can take rough handling* CARELESS, clumsy, inept, unskilful. **8** *rough manners* BOORISH, loutish, oafish, brutish, coarse, crude, uncouth, vulgar, unrefined, unladylike, ungentlemanly, uncultured; unmannerly, impolite, discourteous, uncivil, ungracious, rude. **9** *rough seas* TURBULENT, stormy, tempestuous, violent, heavy, heaving, choppy. **10** *(informal) I've had a rough time* DIFFICULT, hard, tough, bad, unpleasant; demanding, arduous. **11** *(informal) you were a bit rough on her* HARSH, hard, tough, stern, severe, unfair, unjust; insensitive, nasty, cruel, unkind, unsympathetic, brutal, heartless, merciless. **12** *(informal) I'm feeling rough.* See ILL adjective sense 1. **13** *a rough draft* PRELIMINARY, hasty, quick, sketchy, cursory, basic, crude, rudimentary, raw, unpolished; incomplete, unfinished. **14** *a rough estimate* APPROXIMATE, inexact, imprecise, vague, estimated, hazy; *N. Amer. informal* ballpark. **15** *the accommodation is rather rough* PLAIN, BASIC, simple, rough and ready, rude, crude, primitive, spartan.

– OPPOSITES smooth, sleek, soft, dulcet, sweet, gentle, careful, refined, calm, easy, kind, well, exact, luxurious.

● noun **1** *the artist's initial roughs* SKETCH, draft, outline, mock-up. **2** *(Brit.) a bunch of roughs attacked him* RUFFIAN, thug, lout, hooligan, hoodlum, rowdy; *informal* tough, roughneck, bruiser, gorilla, yahoo; *Brit. informal* yob, yobbo.

● verb *rough the surface with sandpaper* ROUGHEN.

– PHRASES **rough something out** DRAFT, sketch out, outline, block out, mock up; *formal* adumbrate. **rough someone up** *(informal)* BEAT UP, attack, assault, knock about/around, batter, manhandle; *informal* do over, beat the living daylights out of; *Brit. informal* duff up.

rough and ready ● adjective BASIC, simple, crude, unrefined, unsophisticated; makeshift, provisional, stopgap, improvised, extemporary, ad hoc; hurried, sketchy.

rough and tumble ● noun SCUFFLE, fight, brawl, melee, free-for-all, fracas, rumpus; horseplay; *Law, dated* affray; *informal* scrap, dust-up, punch-up, shindy; *N. Amer. informal* rough house.

roughly ● adverb **1** *he shoved her roughly away* VIOLENTLY, forcefully, forcibly, abruptly, unceremoniously. **2** *they treated him roughly* HARSHLY, unkindly, unsympathetically; brutally, savagely, mercilessly, cruelly, heartlessly. **3** *roughly £2.4 million* APPROXIMATELY, (round) about, around, circa, in the region of, something like, of the order of, or so, or thereabouts, more or less, give or take;

heads projecting to prevent slipping.
– PHRASES **ride roughshod over** arrogantly or inconsiderately disregard.
rough trade • noun informal male homosexual prostitution, especially when involving brutality or sadism.
roughy /ruffi/ • noun (pl. **roughies**) Austral./NZ a marine fish with large rough-edged scales which become spiny on the belly.
roulade /roolaad/ • noun a piece of meat, sponge, or other food, spread with a filling and rolled up.
– ORIGIN French, from *rouler* 'to roll'.
roulette • noun a gambling game in which a ball is dropped on to a revolving wheel with numbered compartments, the players betting on the number at which the ball comes to rest.
– ORIGIN French, 'small wheel'.
Roumanian • adjective & noun old-fashioned variant of ROMANIAN.
round • adjective **1** shaped like a circle or cylinder. **2** shaped like a sphere. **3** having a curved surface with no sharp projections. **4** (of a person's shoulders) bent forward. **5** (of a voice or musical tone) rich and mellow. **6** (of a number) expressed in convenient units rather than exactly, for example to the nearest whole number. **7** (of a figure) completely and exactly reached: *a round 100.* **8** frank and truthful: *she berated him in round terms.* • noun **1** a circular piece or section. **2** a route or sequence by which a number of people or places are visited or inspected in turn: *a newspaper round.* **3** a regularly recurring sequence of activities: *the daily round.* **4** each of a sequence of sessions in a process, especially in a sports contest. **5** a single division of a boxing or wrestling match. **6** a song for three or more unaccompanied voices or parts, each singing the same theme but starting one after another. **7** the amount of ammunition needed to fire one shot. **8** a set of drinks bought for all the members of a group. **9** Brit. a slice of bread. **10** Brit. the quantity of sandwiches made from two slices of bread. • adverb chiefly Brit. **1** so as to rotate or cause rotation. **2** so as to cover the whole area surrounding a particular centre. **3** so as to rotate and face in the opposite direction. **4** used in describing the relative position of something: *it's the wrong way round.* **5** so as to surround or give support. **6** so as to reach a new place or position. • preposition chiefly Brit. **1** on every side of (a focal point). **2** so as to encircle. **3** from or on the other side of. **4** so as to cover the whole of. • verb **1** pass and go round. **2** make (a figure) less exact but more convenient for calculations: *we'll round the weight up to the nearest kilo.* **3** make or become round in shape.
– PHRASES **in the round 1** (of sculpture) standing free, rather than carved in relief. **2** (of theatre) with the audience placed on at least three sides of the stage. **3** with all aspects shown or considered; fully. **round off 1** smooth the edges of. **2** complete in a satisfying or suitable way. **round on** make a sudden attack on. **round up** drive or collect (a number of people or animals) together.
– DERIVATIVES **roundness** noun.
– ORIGIN Old French, from Latin *rotundus* 'rotund'.
roundabout • noun Brit. **1** a road junction at which traffic moves in one direction round a central island to reach one of the roads converging on it. **2** a large revolving device in a playground, for children to ride on. **3** a merry-go-round. • adjective not following a short direct route; circuitous.
round dance • noun **1** a folk dance in which the dancers form one large circle. **2** a ballroom dance such as a waltz or polka in which couples move in circles round the ballroom.
rounded • adjective **1** round or curved. **2** well developed in all aspects; complete and balanced: *a rounded human being.*
roundel /rownd'l/ • noun **1** a small disc, especially a decorative medallion. **2** a circular identifying mark painted on military aircraft.
– ORIGIN Old French *rondel.*
roundelay /rowndəlay/ • noun literary **1** a short simple song with a refrain. **2** a circle dance.
– ORIGIN Old French *rondelet,* from *rondel* 'roundel, circle'.
rounders • plural noun (treated as sing.) a ball game similar to baseball, in which players run round a circuit of bases after hitting the ball with a cylindrical wooden bat, scoring a **rounder** if all four bases are reached before the ball is fielded.
Roundhead • noun historical a member or supporter of the Parliamentary party in the English Civil War.
– ORIGIN with reference to their short-cropped hair.
roundhouse • noun **1** a railway locomotive maintenance shed built around a turntable. **2** informal a blow given with a wide sweep of the arm. **3** a cabin or set of cabins on the quarterdeck of a sailing ship.
roundly • adverb **1** in a vehement, emphatic, or thorough manner. **2** in a circular or roughly circular shape.
round robin • noun **1** a tournament in which each competitor plays in turn against every other. **2** a petition, especially one with signatures written in a circle to conceal the order of writing.
roundsman • noun **1** Brit. a trader's employee who goes round delivering and taking orders. **2** US a police officer in charge of a patrol. **3** Austral. a journalist covering a specified subject.
round table • noun usu. as modifier an assembly where parties meet on equal terms for discussion.
round trip • noun a journey to a place and back again.
round-up • noun **1** a systematic gathering together of people or things. **2** a summary of facts or events.
roundworm • noun a nematode worm, especially a parasitic one found in the intestines of mammals.
rouse /rowz/ • verb **1** bring or come out of sleep; awaken or wake up. **2** bring out of inactivity. **3** excite; provoke: *his eva-*

Thesaurus

r

nearly, close to, approaching; *Brit.* getting on for.
roughneck • noun *(informal).* See RUFFIAN.
round • adjective **1** *a round window* CIRCULAR, disc-shaped, ring-shaped, hoop-shaped; spherical, spheroidal, globular, globe-shaped, orb-shaped; cylindrical; bulbous, rounded, rotund; *technical* annular, discoid, discoidal; *poetic/literary* orbicular. **2** *a short, round man* PLUMP, chubby, fat, stout, rotund, portly, dumpy, chunky, overweight, pot-bellied, paunchy; flabby, fleshy, bulky, corpulent, obese; *informal* tubby, roly-poly, pudgy, beefy, porky, blubbery; *Brit. informal* podgy; *N. Amer. informal* zaftig, corn-fed. **3** *his deep, round voice* SONOROUS, resonant, rich, full, mellow, mellifluous, orotund. **4** *a round dozen* COMPLETE, entire, whole, full. **5** *she berated him in round terms* CANDID, frank, direct, honest, truthful, straightforward, plain, blunt, forthright, bald, explicit, unequivocal.
– OPPOSITES thin, reedy.
• noun **1** *mould the dough into rounds* BALL, sphere, globe, orb, circle, disc, ring, hoop; *technical* annulus. **2** *a policeman on his rounds* CIRCUIT, beat, route, tour. **3** *the first round of the contest* STAGE, level; heat, game, bout, contest. **4** *an endless round of parties* SUCCESSION, sequence, series, cycle. **5** *the gun fires thirty rounds a second* BULLET, cartridge, shell, shot.
• preposition & adverb **1** *the alleys round the station* AROUND, about, encircling; near, in the vicinity of; orbiting. **2** *casinos dotted round France* THROUGHOUT, all over, here and there in.
• verb *the ship rounded the point* GO ROUND, travel round, skirt, circumnavigate, orbit.
– PHRASES **round about** APPROXIMATELY, about, around, circa, roughly, of the order of, something like, more or less, as near as dammit to, close to, near to, practically; or so, or thereabouts, give or take a few; not far off, nearly, almost, approaching; *Brit.* getting on for. **round the bend** *(informal).* See MAD sense 1. **round the clock 1** *we're working round the clock* DAY AND NIGHT, night and day, all the time, {morning, noon, and night}, continuously, non-stop, steadily, unremittingly; *informal* 24-7. **2** *round-the-clock supervision* CONTINUOUS, constant, non-stop, continual, uninterrupted. **round something off 1** *the square edges were rounded off* SMOOTH OFF, plane off, sand off, level off. **2** *the party rounded off a successful year* COMPLETE, finish off, crown, cap, top; conclude, close, end. **round on someone** SNAP AT, attack, turn on, weigh into, let fly at, lash out at, hit out at; *informal* bite someone's head off, jump down someone's throat, lay into, tear into; *Brit. informal* have a go at; *N. Amer. informal* light into. **round someone/something up** GATHER TOGETHER, herd together, muster, marshal, rally, assemble, collect, group; *N. Amer.* corral.
roundabout • adjective **1** *a roundabout route* CIRCUITOUS, indirect, meandering, serpentine, tortuous. **2** *I asked in a roundabout sort of way* INDIRECT, oblique, circuitous, circumlocutory, periphrastic, digressive, long-winded; evasive.
– OPPOSITES direct.
• noun *(Brit.)* **1** *go straight on at the roundabout* *N. Amer.* rotary, traffic circle. **2** *a roundabout with wooden horses* MERRY-GO-ROUND, carousel; *archaic* whirligig.
roundly • adverb **1** *he was roundly condemned* VEHEMENTLY, emphatically, fiercely, forcefully, severely; plainly, frankly, candidly. **2** *she was roundly defeated* UTTERLY, completely, thoroughly, decisively, conclusively, heavily, soundly.

siveness roused my curiosity.
– ORIGIN originally as a hawking and hunting term: probably from Old French.
rouseabout ● noun Austral./NZ an unskilled labourer on a farm.
– ORIGIN originally dialect in the sense 'rough bustling person'; from ROUSE.
rousing ● adjective **1** stirring: *a rousing speech.* **2** archaic (of a fire) blazing strongly.
– DERIVATIVES **rousingly** adverb.
roust /rowst/ ● verb **1** cause to get up or start moving; rouse. **2** N. Amer. informal treat roughly; harass.
– ORIGIN perhaps an alteration of ROUSE.
roustabout /rowstəbowt/ ● noun an unskilled or casual labourer, especially a labourer on an oil rig.
– ORIGIN from ROUST.
rout¹ /rowt/ ● noun **1** a disorderly retreat of defeated troops. **2** a decisive defeat. **3** archaic a disorderly or tumultuous crowd of people. ● verb defeat utterly and force to retreat.
– ORIGIN obsolete French *route* or Old French *rute*, from Latin *rumpere* 'break'.
rout² /rowt/ ● verb **1** cut a groove in (a surface). **2** rummage; root. **3** (**rout out**) root out.
– ORIGIN alteration of ROOT².
route /ro͞ot/ ● noun **1** a way or course taken in getting from a starting point to a destination. **2** N. Amer. a round travelled in delivering, selling, or collecting goods. ● verb (**routeing** or **routing**) send or direct along a specified course.
– ORIGIN Old French *rute* 'road', from Latin *rupta via* 'broken way'.
router /rowtər/ ● noun a power tool with a shaped cutter, used in carpentry.
routine ● noun **1** a sequence of actions regularly followed; a fixed unvarying programme. **2** a set sequence in a theatrical or comic performance. ● adjective **1** performed as part of a regular procedure: *a routine inspection.* **2** characteristic of routine; without variety.
– DERIVATIVES **routinely** adverb.
– ORIGIN French, from *route* 'route'.
roux /ro͞o/ ● noun (pl. same) Cookery a mixture of fat (especially butter) and flour used in making sauces.
– ORIGIN from French *beurre roux* 'browned butter'.
ROV ● abbreviation remotely operated vehicle.
rove¹ ● verb **1** travel constantly without a fixed destination; wander. **2** (of eyes) look around in all directions.
– ORIGIN originally an archery term in the sense 'shoot at a casual mark of undetermined range': perhaps from dialect *rave* 'to stray'.
rove² past of REEVE².
rover¹ ● noun **1** a person who spends their time wandering. **2** a vehicle for driving over rough terrain.
rover² ● noun archaic a pirate.
– ORIGIN Low German and Dutch, from *rōven* 'rob'.
roving commission ● noun Brit. an authorization given to someone conducting an inquiry to travel as is necessary.
row¹ /rō/ ● noun a number of people or things in a more or less straight line.
– PHRASES **in a row** in succession.
– ORIGIN Old English.
row² /rō/ ● verb **1** propel (a boat) with oars. **2** row a boat as a sport. ● noun a spell of rowing.
– DERIVATIVES **rower** noun.
– ORIGIN Old English, related to RUDDER.
row³ /row/ informal, chiefly Brit. ● noun **1** an acrimonious quarrel. **2** a loud noise or uproar. **3** a severe reprimand. ● verb have an acrimonious quarrel.
– ORIGIN of unknown origin.
rowan /rōən, row-/ ● noun a small tree with white flowers and red berries.
– ORIGIN Scandinavian.
rowdy ● adjective (**rowdier**, **rowdiest**) noisy and disorderly. ● noun (pl. **rowdies**) a rowdy person.
– DERIVATIVES **rowdily** adverb **rowdiness** noun **rowdyism** noun.
– ORIGIN originally US in the sense 'lawless backwoodsman': of unknown origin.
rowel /rowəl/ ● noun a spiked revolving disc at the end of a spur.
– ORIGIN Old French *roele*, from Latin *rotella* 'little wheel'.
row house ● noun N. Amer. a terrace house.
rowing machine ● noun an exercise machine with oars and a sliding seat.

Thesaurus

round-up ● noun **1** *a cattle round-up* ASSEMBLY, muster, rally; *N. Amer.* rodeo. **2** *the sports round-up* SUMMARY, synopsis, overview, review, outline, digest, precis; *N. Amer.* wrap-up; *informal* recap.
rouse ● verb **1** *he roused Ralph at dawn* WAKE (UP), awaken, arouse; *Brit. informal* knock up; *formal* waken. **2** *she roused and looked around* WAKE UP, awake, awaken, come to, get up, rise, bestir oneself; *formal* arise. **3** *he roused the crowd* STIR UP, excite, galvanize, electrify, stimulate, inspire, inspirit, move, inflame, agitate, goad, provoke; incite, spur on; *N. Amer.* light a fire under. **4** *he's got a temper when he's roused* PROVOKE, annoy, anger, infuriate, madden, incense, vex, irk; *informal* aggravate. **5** *her disappearance roused my suspicions* AROUSE, awaken, prompt, provoke, stimulate, pique, trigger, spark off, touch off, kindle, elicit.
– OPPOSITES calm, pacify, allay.
rousing ● adjective STIRRING, inspiring, exciting, stimulating, moving, electrifying, invigorating, energizing, exhilarating; enthusiastic, vigorous, spirited; inflammatory.
rout ● noun **1** *the army's ignominious rout* RETREAT, flight. **2** *Newcastle scored 13 tries in the rout* CRUSHING DEFEAT, trouncing, annihilation; debacle, fiasco; *informal* licking, hammering, thrashing, pasting, drubbing, massacre.
– OPPOSITES victory.
● verb **1** *his army was routed* PUT TO FLIGHT, drive off, scatter; defeat, beat, conquer, vanquish, crush, overpower. **2** *he routed the defending champion* BEAT HOLLOW, trounce, defeat, get the better of; *informal* lick, hammer, clobber, thrash, paste, demolish, annihilate, drub, cane, wipe the floor with, walk all over, make mincemeat of, massacre, slaughter; *Brit. informal* stuff; *N. Amer. informal* cream, shellac, skunk.
– OPPOSITES lose.
route ● noun *a different route to the shops* WAY, course, road, path, direction; passage, journey.
● verb *enquiries are routed to the relevant desk* DIRECT, send, convey, dispatch, forward.
routine ● noun **1** *his morning routine* PROCEDURE, practice, pattern, drill, regime, regimen; programme, schedule, plan; formula, method, system; customs, habits; wont. **2** *a stand-up routine* ACT, performance, number, turn, piece; *informal* spiel, patter.
● adjective **1** *a routine health check* STANDARD, regular, customary, normal, usual, ordinary, typical; everyday, common, commonplace, conventional, habitual, wonted. **2** *a routine action movie* BORING, tedious, tiresome, wearisome, monotonous, humdrum, run-of-the-mill, prosaic, dreary, pedestrian; predictable, hackneyed, stock, unimaginative, unoriginal, banal, trite.
– OPPOSITES unusual.
rove ● verb WANDER, roam, ramble, drift, meander; range, travel; *Scottish* stravaig; *archaic* peregrinate.
rover ● noun WANDERER, traveller, globetrotter, drifter, bird of passage, roamer, itinerant, transient; nomad, gypsy, Romany; tramp, vagrant, vagabond; *N. Amer.* hobo.
row¹ ● noun **1** *rows of children* LINE, column, file, queue; procession, chain, string, succession; *informal* crocodile. **2** *the middle row of seats* TIER, line, rank, bank.
– PHRASES **in a row** *three days in a row* CONSECUTIVELY, in succession; running, straight; *informal* on the trot.
row² *(Brit. informal)* ● noun **1** *have you two had a row?* ARGUMENT, quarrel, squabble, fight, contretemps, falling-out, disagreement, dispute, clash, altercation, shouting match; *informal* tiff, set-to, run-in, slanging match, spat; *Brit. informal* barney, bust-up. **2** *the row the crowd was making* DIN, noise, racket, clamour, uproar, tumult, hubbub, commotion, brouhaha, rumpus, pandemonium, babel; *informal* hullabaloo. **3** *Mum give me a row* REPRIMAND, rebuke, reproof, admonition, reproach, remonstration, lecture, criticism; *informal* telling-off, slap on the wrist, dressing-down, roasting, tongue-lashing; *Brit. informal* ticking-off, carpeting, rollicking, rocket.
● verb *they rowed about money* ARGUE, quarrel, squabble, bicker, fight, fall out, disagree, have words, dispute, wrangle, cross swords, lock horns, be at loggerheads; *informal* scrap, argufy.
rowdy ● adjective *rowdy youths* UNRULY, disorderly, obstreperous, riotous, undisciplined, uncontrollable, ungovernable, disruptive, out of control, rough, wild, lawless; boisterous, uproarious, noisy, loud, clamorous; *Brit. informal* rumbustious; *N. Amer. informal* rambunctious.
– OPPOSITES peaceful.

rowlock /rollək/ ● noun a fitting on the gunwale of a boat which serves as a fulcrum for an oar and keeps it in place.
– ORIGIN alteration of OARLOCK, influenced by ROW².

royal ● adjective **1** relating to or having the status of a king or queen or a member of their family. **2** of a quality or size suitable for a king or queen; splendid. ● noun informal a member of the royal family.
– PHRASES **royal 'we'** the use of 'we' instead of 'I' by a single person, as traditionally used by a sovereign.
– DERIVATIVES **royally** adverb.
– ORIGIN Old French *roial*, from Latin *regalis* 'regal'.

royal assent ● noun assent of the sovereign to a bill which has been passed by Parliament, and which thus becomes an Act of Parliament.

royal blue ● noun a deep, vivid blue.

Royal Commission ● noun (in the UK) a commission of inquiry appointed by the Crown on the recommendation of the government.

royal flush ● noun the highest straight flush in poker, including ace, king, queen, jack, and ten all in the same suit.

royal icing ● noun chiefly Brit. hard white icing, typically used to decorate fruit cakes.

royalist ● noun **1** a person who supports the principle of monarchy. **2** historical a supporter of the King against Parliament in the English Civil War.
– DERIVATIVES **royalism** noun.

royal jelly ● noun a substance secreted by honeybee workers and fed by them to larvae which are being raised as potential queen bees.

royal tennis ● noun another term for REAL TENNIS.

royalty ● noun (pl. **royalties**) **1** people of royal blood or status. **2** the status or power of a king or queen. **3** a sum paid for the use of a patent or to an author or composer for each copy of a work sold or for each public performance. **4** a royal right (now especially over minerals) granted by the sovereign. **5** a payment made by a producer of minerals, oil, or natural gas to the owner of the site.

royal warrant ● noun a warrant issued by the sovereign, in particular one authorizing a company to display the royal arms, indicating that goods or services are supplied to the royal family.

rozzer ● noun Brit. informal a police officer.
– ORIGIN of unknown origin.

RP ● abbreviation received pronunciation.

RPG ● abbreviation rocket-propelled grenade.

RPI ● abbreviation retail price index.

rpm ● abbreviation revolutions per minute.

RPV ● abbreviation remotely piloted vehicle.

R & R ● abbreviation informal rest and recreation.

RRP ● abbreviation Brit. recommended retail price.

Rs ● abbreviation rupee(s).

RSA ● abbreviation **1** Republic of South Africa. **2** Royal Scottish Academy; Royal Scottish Academician. **3** Royal Society of Arts.

RSC ● abbreviation Royal Shakespeare Company.

RSI ● abbreviation repetitive strain injury.

RSJ ● abbreviation rolled steel joist.

RSM ● abbreviation (in the British army) Regimental Sergeant Major.

RSPB ● abbreviation (in the UK) Royal Society for the Protection of Birds.

RSPCA ● abbreviation (in the UK) Royal Society for the Prevention of Cruelty to Animals.

RSV ● abbreviation Revised Standard Version (of the Bible).

RSVP ● abbreviation répondez s'il vous plaît; please reply (used at the end of invitations).
– ORIGIN from French.

RTE ● abbreviation Radio Telefís Éireann (the broadcasting authority of the Republic of Ireland).

RTF ● abbreviation Computing rich text format.

Rt Hon. ● abbreviation Brit. Right Honourable.

Rt Revd (also **Rt Rev.**) ● abbreviation Right Reverend.

RU ● abbreviation rugby union.

Ru ● symbol the chemical element ruthenium.

rub ● verb (**rubbed**, **rubbing**) **1** apply firm pressure to (a surface) with a repeated back and forth motion. **2** move to and fro against a surface while pressing or grinding against it. **3** apply with a rubbing action. **4** (**rub down**) dry, smooth, or clean by rubbing. **5** (**rub in/into**) work (fat) into (a mixture) by breaking and blending it with the fingertips. **6** reproduce the design of (a sepulchral brass or a stone) by rubbing paper laid on it with pencil or chalk. ● noun **1** an act of rubbing. **2** an ointment designed to be rubbed on the skin. **3** (**the rub**) the central or most important difficulty. [ORIGIN from Shakespeare's *Hamlet* (III. i. 65).]
– PHRASES **rub along** Brit. informal cope or get along without undue difficulty. **the rub of the green 1** Golf an accidental or unpredictable influence on the course or position of the ball. **2** good fortune. **rub one's hands** rub one's hands together to show keen satisfaction. **rub it in** (or **rub someone's nose in something**) informal emphatically draw someone's attention to an embarrassing or painful fact. **rub noses** rub one's nose against someone else's in greeting (as is traditional among Maoris and some other peoples). **rub off** be transferred by contact or association. **rub out 1** erase (pencil marks) with a rubber. **2** N. Amer. informal kill. **rub shoulders** (or N. Amer. **elbows**) associate or come into contact. **rub (up) the wrong way** Brit. anger or irritate.
– ORIGIN perhaps from Low German *rubben*, of unknown origin.

rubato /roobaatō/ (also **tempo rubato**) ● noun (pl. **rubatos** or **rubati** /roobaati/) Music temporary disregard for strict tempo to allow an expressive quickening or slackening.
– ORIGIN Italian, 'robbed'.

rubber¹ ● noun **1** a tough elastic substance made from the latex of a tropical plant or synthetically. **2** Brit. a piece of such material used for erasing pencil marks. **3** N. Amer. informal a condom. **4** (**rubbers**) N. Amer. rubber boots; galoshes.
– DERIVATIVES **rubberize** (also **rubberise**) verb **rubbery** adjective.
– ORIGIN from RUB; an early use of the substance rubber was to rub out pencil marks.

rubber² ● noun **1** a contest consisting of a series of matches between the same sides in cricket, tennis, and other games. **2** Bridge a unit of play in which one side scores bonus points for winning the best of three games.
– ORIGIN originally used as a term in bowls: of unknown origin.

rubber band ● noun a loop of rubber for holding things together.

rubber bullet ● noun a bullet made of rubber, used especially in riot control.

rubberneck informal ● noun a person who turns their head to stare at something in a foolish manner. ● verb stare in such a way.
– DERIVATIVES **rubbernecker** noun.

rubber plant ● noun an evergreen tree with large dark green shiny leaves, native to SE Asia and formerly grown as a source of rubber.

rubber stamp ● noun **1** a hand-held device for imprinting dates, addresses, etc. **2** a person who automatically authorizes another's actions. ● verb (**rubber-stamp**) **1** apply a rubber stamp to. **2** approve automatically without proper consideration.

Thesaurus

● noun *the pub filled up with rowdies* RUFFIAN, troublemaker, lout, hooligan, thug, hoodlum; *Brit.* tearaway; *informal* tough, bruiser, yahoo; *Brit. informal* rough, yob, yobbo.

royal ● adjective **1** *the royal prerogative* REGAL, kingly, queenly, princely; sovereign, monarchical. **2** *a royal welcome* EXCELLENT, fine, magnificent, splendid, superb, wonderful, first-rate, first-class; *informal* fantastic, great, tremendous.

rub ● verb **1** *Polly rubbed her arm* MASSAGE, knead; stroke, pat. **2** *he rubbed sun lotion on her back* APPLY, smear, spread, work in. **3** *my shoes rub painfully* CHAFE, pinch; hurt, be painful.
● noun **1** *she gave his back a rub* MASSAGE, rub-down. **2** *I gave my shoes a rub* POLISH, wipe, clean. **3** *it's too complicated — that's the rub* PROBLEM, difficulty, trouble, drawback, hindrance, impediment; snag, hitch, catch.
– PHRASES **rub along** *(Brit. informal)* MANAGE, cope, get by, make do, muddle along/through; *informal* make out. **rub something down** CLEAN, sponge, wash; groom. **rub it in** *(informal)* EMPHASIZE, stress, underline, highlight; go on, harp on; *informal* rub someone's nose in it. **rub off on** BE TRANSFERRED TO, be passed on to, be transmitted to, be communicated to; affect, influence. **rub something out** ERASE, delete, remove, efface, obliterate, expunge. **rub shoulders with** ASSOCIATE WITH, mingle with, fraternize with, socialize with, mix with, keep company with, consort with; *N. Amer.* rub elbows with; *informal* hang around/out with, hobnob with, knock

rubber tree ● noun a tree that produces the latex from which rubber is manufactured, native to the Amazonian rainforest.

rubbing ● noun **1** the action of rubbing. **2** an impression of a design on brass or stone, made by rubbing.

rubbing alcohol ● noun denatured alcohol used as an antiseptic or in massage.

rubbish ● noun chiefly Brit. **1** waste material; refuse or litter. **2** unimportant or valueless material. **3** nonsense; worthless talk or ideas. ● verb Brit. informal criticize and reject as worthless. ● adjective Brit. informal very bad.
– DERIVATIVES **rubbishy** adjective (informal).
– ORIGIN Old French *rubbous*, perhaps related to *robe* 'spoils'; compare with RUBBLE.

rubble ● noun rough fragments of stone, brick, concrete, etc., especially as the debris from the demolition of buildings.
– DERIVATIVES **rubbly** adjective.
– ORIGIN perhaps from Old French *robe* 'spoils'; compare with RUBBISH.

rube /ro͞ob/ ● noun N. Amer. informal a country bumpkin.
– ORIGIN abbreviation of the given name *Reuben*.

rubella /roobellə/ ● noun a contagious disease transmitted by a virus and with symptoms like mild measles; German measles.
– ORIGIN Latin, 'reddish things'.

rubescent /roobess'nt/ ● adjective literary reddening; blushing.
– ORIGIN from Latin *rubescere* 'redden'.

Rubicon /ro͞obikon/ ● noun a point of no return.
– ORIGIN a stream in NE Italy marking the ancient boundary between Italy and Cisalpine Gaul, which Julius Caesar crossed in 49 BC, breaking the law and so causing a civil war.

rubicund /ro͞obikənd/ ● adjective having a ruddy complexion.
– ORIGIN Latin *rubicundus*, from *rubere* 'be red'.

rubidium /roobiddiəm/ ● noun a rare soft silvery reactive metallic element.
– ORIGIN from Latin *rubidus* 'red' (with reference to lines in its spectrum).

Rubik's cube /ro͞obiks/ ● noun trademark a puzzle in the form of a plastic cube covered with multicoloured squares, which the player attempts to turn so that all the squares on each face are of the same colour.
– ORIGIN named after its Hungarian inventor Erno *Rubik* (born 1944).

ruble ● noun variant spelling of ROUBLE.

rubric /ro͞obrik/ ● noun **1** a heading on a document. **2** a set of instructions or rules. **3** a direction in a liturgical book as to how a church service should be conducted.
– ORIGIN originally referring to text written in red for emphasis: from Latin *rubrica terra* 'red earth or ochre as writing material'.

ruby ● noun (pl. **rubies**) **1** a precious stone consisting of corundum in colour varieties varying from deep crimson or purple to pale rose. **2** an intense deep red colour.
– ORIGIN Latin *rubinus*, from *rubeus* 'red'.

ruby wedding ● noun the fortieth anniversary of a wedding.

RUC ● abbreviation Royal Ulster Constabulary.

ruche /ro͞osh/ ● noun a frill or pleat of fabric.
– DERIVATIVES **ruched** adjective **ruching** noun.
– ORIGIN French, from Latin *rusca* 'tree bark'.

ruck[1] ● noun **1** Rugby a loose scrum formed around a player with the ball on the ground. **2** Australian Rules a group of three players who follow the play without fixed positions. **3** a tightly packed crowd of people. ● verb Rugby & Australian Rules take part in a ruck.
– ORIGIN originally in the sense 'stack of fuel, heap': probably of Scandinavian origin.

ruck[2] ● verb (often **ruck up**) make or form wrinkles, creases, or folds. ● noun a crease or wrinkle.
– ORIGIN Old Norse.

ruck[3] ● noun Brit. informal a brawl.
– ORIGIN perhaps a shortened form of RUCTION or RUCKUS.

ruckle ● verb & noun Brit. another term for RUCK[2].

rucksack /ruksak/ ● noun a bag with two shoulder straps which allow it to be carried on the back, used by hikers.
– ORIGIN German, from dialect *rucken* 'back' + *Sack* 'bag, sack'.

ruckus /rukkəss/ ● noun a row or commotion.
– ORIGIN perhaps related to RUCTION and RUMPUS.

ruction ● noun informal **1** a disturbance or quarrel. **2** (**ructions**) trouble.
– ORIGIN perhaps from INSURRECTION.

rudbeckia /rudbekkiə/ ● noun a North American plant of the daisy family, with yellow or orange flowers and a dark cone-like centre.
– ORIGIN named after the Swedish botanist Olaf *Rudbeck* (1660–1740).

rudd ● noun (pl. same) a freshwater fish of the carp family with a silvery body and red fins.
– ORIGIN probably from obsolete *rud* 'red colour'.

rudder ● noun **1** a flat piece hinged vertically near the stern of a boat for steering. **2** a vertical aerofoil pivoted from the tailplane of an aircraft, for controlling movement about the vertical axis.
– ORIGIN Old English, 'paddle, oar'.

rudderless ● adjective **1** lacking a rudder. **2** lacking direction.

ruddle ● noun another term for REDDLE.
– ORIGIN related to obsolete *rud* 'red colour' and RED.

ruddy ● adjective (**ruddier, ruddiest**) **1** reddish. **2** (of a person's face) having a healthy red colour. **3** Brit. informal, dated used as a euphemism for 'bloody'.
– DERIVATIVES **ruddiness** noun.
– ORIGIN Old English, related to RUDDLE and RED.

ruddy duck ● noun a duck with a broad bill, the male having mainly deep red-brown plumage and white cheeks.

rude ● adjective **1** offensively impolite or ill-mannered. **2** referring to sex in a way considered improper and offensive. **3** very abrupt: *a rude awakening*. **4** chiefly Brit. vigorous or hearty: *rude health*. **5** dated roughly made or done; lacking sophistication. **6** archaic ignorant and uneducated.
– DERIVATIVES **rudely** adverb **rudeness** noun **rudery** noun.
– ORIGIN Latin *rudis* 'unwrought, uncultivated'.

rude boy ● noun (in Jamaica) a lawless urban youth who likes ska or reggae music.

rudiment /ro͞odimənt/ ● noun **1** (**rudiments**) the first principles of a subject. **2** (**rudiments**) an elementary or primitive form of something. **3** Biology an undeveloped or immature part or organ.
– ORIGIN Latin *rudimentum*, from *rudis* 'unwrought'.

rudimentary /ro͞odimentri/ ● adjective **1** involving or limited to basic principles. **2** immature, undeveloped, or basic.
– DERIVATIVES **rudimentarily** adverb.

r

Thesaurus

about/around with. **rub something up** POLISH, buff up, burnish, shine, wax; clean, wipe. **rub someone up the wrong way** (*Brit.*). See ANNOY.

rubbish ● noun **1** *throw away that rubbish* REFUSE, waste, litter, debris, detritus, scrap, dross; flotsam and jetsam, lumber; sweepings, scraps, dregs; *N. Amer.* garbage, trash; *informal* dreck, junk. **2** *she's talking rubbish* NONSENSE, balderdash, gibberish, claptrap, blarney, moonshine, garbage; *informal* hogwash, baloney, tripe, drivel, bilge, bunk, piffle, poppycock, phooey, twaddle, gobbledegook; *Brit. informal* codswallop, cobblers, tosh, cack; *Scottish & N. English informal* havers; *N. Amer. informal* bushwa, applesauce.
● verb (*Brit. informal*) *they often rubbish trade unions.* See CRITICIZE.
● adjective (*Brit. informal*) *a rubbish team.* See HOPELESS sense 3.

rubbishy ● adjective (*informal*) WORTHLESS, trashy, inferior, substandard, second-rate, third-rate, poor-quality, cheap, shoddy; bad, poor, dreadful, awful, terrible; *informal* crummy, appalling, lousy, dire, tacky; *Brit. informal* duff, chronic, rubbish.

rubble ● noun DEBRIS, remains, ruins, wreckage.

ruction ● noun (*informal*) DISTURBANCE, noise, racket, din, commotion, fuss, uproar, furore, hue and cry, rumpus, fracas; (**ructions**) trouble, hell to pay; *informal* to-do, hullabaloo, hoo-ha, ballyhoo, stink, kerfuffle; *Brit. informal* row, carry-on.

ruddy ● adjective **1** *a ruddy complexion* ROSY, red, pink, roseate, rubicund; healthy, glowing, fresh; flushed, blushing; florid, high-coloured; *poetic/literary* rubescent. **2** (*Brit. informal, dated*) *you ruddy idiot!* See DAMNED sense 2.
– OPPOSITES pale.

rude ● adjective **1** *a rude man* ILL-MANNERED, bad-mannered, impolite, discourteous, uncivil, unmannerly, mannerless; impertinent, insolent, impudent, disrespectful, cheeky; churlish, curt, brusque, brash, offhand, short, sharp; offensive, insulting, derogatory, disparaging, abusive; tactless, undiplomatic, uncomplimentary. **2** *rude jokes* VULGAR, coarse, smutty, dirty, filthy, crude, lewd, obscene, off colour, offensive, indelicate, tasteless; risqué, naughty, ribald, bawdy, racy; *informal* blue; *Brit. informal* near the knuckle; *N. Amer. informal* gamy; *euphemistic* adult. **3** *a rude awakening* ABRUPT, sudden, sharp, startling; unpleasant, nasty, harsh. **4** (*dated*) *a rude cabin* PRIMITIVE, crude, rudimentary, rough, simple, basic. **5** (*archaic*)

rue[1] ● verb (**rues**, **rued**, **rueing** or **ruing**) bitterly regret (a past event or action). ● noun archaic **1** repentance; regret. **2** compassion; pity.
– ORIGIN Old English.
rue[2] ● noun a perennial evergreen shrub with bitter strong-scented lobed leaves which are used in herbal medicine.
– ORIGIN Greek *rhutē*.
rueful ● adjective expressing regret, especially in a wry or humorous way.
– DERIVATIVES **ruefully** adverb **ruefulness** noun.
ruff[1] ● noun **1** a projecting starched frill worn round the neck, characteristic of Elizabethan and Jacobean costume. **2** a ring of feathers or hair round the neck of a bird or mammal. **3** (pl. same or **ruffs**) a wading bird, the male of which has a large ruff and ear tufts in the breeding season.
– ORIGIN probably from a variant of ROUGH.
ruff[2] ● verb (in bridge and whist) play a trump in a trick which was led in a different suit. ● noun an act of ruffing or opportunity to ruff.
– ORIGIN originally the name of a card game: from Old French *rouffle*, perhaps an alteration of Italian *trionfo* 'a trump'.
ruffian ● noun a violent or lawless person.
– DERIVATIVES **ruffianism** noun **ruffianly** adjective.
– ORIGIN Old French, from Italian *ruffiano*, perhaps from dialect *rofia* 'scab, scurf'.
ruffle ● verb **1** make or become disarranged; disrupt the smooth surface of. **2** disconcert or upset the composure of. **3** (**ruffled**) ornamented with or gathered into a frill. ● noun an ornamental gathered frill on a garment.
– ORIGIN of unknown origin.
rufiyaa /ro͞ofeeyaa/ ● noun (pl. same) the basic monetary unit of the Maldives, equal to 100 laris.
– ORIGIN Maldivian.
rufous /ro͞ofəss/ ● adjective reddish brown in colour. ● noun a reddish-brown colour.
– ORIGIN Latin *rufus* 'red, reddish'.
rug ● noun **1** a small carpet. **2** chiefly Brit. a thick woollen blanket. **3** informal, chiefly N. Amer. a toupee or wig.
– PHRASES **pull the rug out from under** abruptly expose or withdraw support from.
– ORIGIN probably Scandinavian; related to RAG[1].
rugby (also **rugby football**) ● noun a team game played with an oval ball that may be kicked, carried, and passed by hand, in which points are won by scoring a try or by kicking the ball over the crossbar of the opponents' goal.
– ORIGIN named after *Rugby* School in central England, where the game was first played.
rugby league ● noun a form of rugby played in teams of thirteen, in which professionalism has always been allowed.
rugby union ● noun a form of rugby played in teams of fifteen, traditionally strictly amateur but opened to professionalism in 1995.
rugged /ruggid/ ● adjective **1** having a rocky and uneven surface. **2** having or requiring toughness and determination. **3** (of a man) having attractively masculine, rough-hewn features.
– DERIVATIVES **ruggedly** adverb **ruggedness** noun.
– ORIGIN originally in the sense 'shaggy': probably of Scandinavian origin.
ruggedized (also **ruggedised**) ● adjective chiefly N. Amer. designed or improved to be hard-wearing.
rugger ● noun Brit. informal rugby.
rugose /ro͞ogōss/ ● adjective chiefly Biology wrinkled; corrugated.
– ORIGIN Latin *rugosus*, from *ruga* 'wrinkle'.
ruin ● noun **1** physical destruction or collapse. **2** a building (or the remains of a building) that has suffered much damage. **3** a dramatic decline; a downfall. **4** the complete loss of a person's money and other assets. ● verb **1** damage irreparably; reduce to a state of ruin. **2** reduce to poverty or bankruptcy.
– ORIGIN Latin *ruina*, from *ruere* 'to fall'.
ruination ● noun the action or fact of ruining or the state of being ruined.
ruinous ● adjective **1** disastrous or destructive. **2** in ruins; dilapidated.
– DERIVATIVES **ruinously** adverb.
rule ● noun **1** a regulation or principle governing conduct or procedure within a particular sphere. **2** control or government: *British rule*. **3** a code of practice and discipline for a religious community. **4** (**the rule**) the normal or customary state of things. **5** a straight strip of rigid material used for measuring; a ruler. **6** a thin printed line or dash. ● verb **1** exercise ultimate power over (a people or nation). **2** exert a powerful and restricting influence on. **3** pronounce authoritatively and legally to be the case. **4** make parallel lines on (paper).
– PHRASES **as a rule** usually, but not always. **rule of thumb** a

Thesaurus

a rude and barbarous people UNEDUCATED, ignorant, illiterate; uncultured, uncivilized, unrefined; rough, coarse, uncouth, boorish.
– OPPOSITES polite, clean, luxurious, civilized.
rudimentary ● adjective **1** *rudimentary carpentry skills* BASIC, elementary, primary, fundamental, essential. **2** *the equipment was rudimentary* PRIMITIVE, crude, simple, unsophisticated, rough (and ready), makeshift. **3** *a rudimentary thumb* VESTIGIAL, undeveloped, incomplete; *Biology* abortive, primitive.
– OPPOSITES advanced, sophisticated, developed.
rudiments ● plural noun BASICS, fundamentals, essentials, first principles, foundation; *informal* nuts and bolts, ABC.
rue ● verb REGRET, be sorry about, feel remorseful about, repent of, reproach oneself for; deplore, lament, bemoan, bewail.
rueful ● adjective REGRETFUL, apologetic, sorry, remorseful, shamefaced, sheepish, hangdog, contrite, repentant, penitent, self-reproachful, conscience-stricken; sorrowful, sad.
ruffian ● noun THUG, lout, hooligan, hoodlum, vandal, delinquent, rowdy, scoundrel, villain, rogue, bully boy, brute; *informal* tough, bruiser, heavy, yahoo; *Brit. informal* rough, yob, yobbo; *N. Amer. informal* goon.
ruffle ● verb **1** *he ruffled her hair* DISARRANGE, tousle, dishevel, rumple, riffle, disorder, mess up, tangle; *N. Amer. informal* muss up. **2** *the wind ruffled the water* RIPPLE, riffle. **3** *don't let him ruffle you* ANNOY, irritate, vex, nettle, anger, exasperate; disconcert, unnerve, fluster, agitate, harass, upset, disturb, discomfit, put off, perturb, unsettle, bother, worry, trouble; *informal* rattle, faze, throw, get to, rile, needle, aggravate, bug, peeve; *Brit. informal* wind up, nark.
– OPPOSITES smooth, soothe.
● noun *a shirt with ruffles* FRILL, flounce, ruff, ruche, jabot, furbelow.
rug ● noun **1** *they sat on the rug* MAT, carpet, drugget, runner; hearthrug; *N. Amer.* floorcloth. **2** *he was wrapped in a tartan rug* BLANKET, coverlet, throw, wrap; *N. Amer.* lap robe. **3** *(informal) he's wearing a ridiculous rug* TOUPEE, wig, hairpiece.
rugged ● adjective **1** *the rugged coast path* ROUGH, uneven, bumpy, rocky, stony, pitted, jagged, craggy. **2** *a rugged vehicle* ROBUST, durable, sturdy, strong, tough, resilient. **3** *rugged manly types* WELL BUILT, burly, strong, muscular, muscly, brawny, strapping, husky, hulking; tough, hardy, robust, sturdy, lusty, solid; *informal* hunky, beefy. **4** *his rugged features* STRONG, craggy, rough-hewn; manly, masculine; irregular, weathered.
– OPPOSITES smooth, flimsy, weedy, delicate.
ruin ● noun **1** *the buildings were saved from ruin* DISINTEGRATION, decay, disrepair, dilapidation, ruination; destruction, demolition, wreckage. **2** *the ruins of a church* REMAINS, remnants, fragments, relics; rubble, debris, wreckage. **3** *electoral ruin for Labour* DOWNFALL, collapse, defeat, undoing, failure, breakdown, ruination; Waterloo. **4** *shopkeepers are facing ruin* BANKRUPTCY, insolvency, penury, poverty, destitution, impoverishment, indigence; failure.
– OPPOSITES preservation, triumph, wealth.
● verb **1** *don't ruin my plans* WRECK, destroy, spoil, mar, blight, shatter, dash, torpedo, scotch, mess up; sabotage; *informal* screw up, foul up, put the kibosh on, do for, nix, queer; *Brit. informal* scupper. **2** *the bank's collapse ruined them all* BANKRUPT, make insolvent, impoverish, pauperize, wipe out, break, cripple; bring someone to their knees. **3** *a country ruined by civil war* DESTROY, devastate, lay waste, ravage; raze, demolish, wreck, wipe out, flatten.
– OPPOSITES save, rebuild.
– PHRASES **in ruins 1** *the abbey is in ruins* DERELICT, ruined, in disrepair, falling to pieces, dilapidated, tumbledown, ramshackle, decrepit, decaying, ruinous. **2** *his career is in ruins* DESTROYED, ruined, in pieces, in ashes; over, finished; *informal* in tatters, on the rocks, done for.
ruined ● adjective DERELICT, in ruins, dilapidated, ruinous, tumbledown, ramshackle, decrepit, falling to pieces, crumbling, decaying, disintegrating; *informal* shambly.
ruinous ● adjective **1** *a ruinous trade war* DISASTROUS, devastating, catastrophic, calamitous, crippling, crushing, damaging, destructive, harmful; costly. **2** *ruinous interest rates* EXTORTIONATE, exorbi-

broadly accurate guide or principle, based on practice rather than theory. **rule out/in** exclude (or include) as a possibility. **rule the roost** be in complete control. **run the rule over** Brit. examine cursorily.
– ORIGIN Old French *reule*, from Latin *regula* 'straight stick'.
ruler • noun **1** a person who rules a people or nation. **2** a straight-edged strip of rigid material, marked at regular intervals and used to draw straight lines or measure distances.
ruling • noun an authoritative decision or pronouncement. • adjective exercising rule.
rum[1] • noun **1** an alcoholic spirit distilled from sugar-cane residues or molasses. **2** N. Amer. any intoxicating liquor.
– ORIGIN perhaps an abbreviation of obsolete *rumbullion*.
rum[2] • adjective (**rummer**, **rummest**) Brit. informal, dated odd; peculiar.
– ORIGIN of unknown origin.
Rumanian • adjective & noun variant spelling of ROMANIAN.
rumba /rumbə/ (also **rhumba**) • noun **1** a rhythmic dance with Spanish and African elements, originating in Cuba. **2** a ballroom dance based on this. • verb (**rumbas**, **rumbaed** /rumbəd/ or **rumba'd**, **rumbaing** /rumbəing/) dance the rumba.
– ORIGIN Latin American Spanish.
rum baba • noun see BABA[1].
rumble • verb **1** make a continuous deep, resonant sound. **2** move with such a sound. **3** (**rumble on**) (of a dispute) continue in a low-key way. **4** Brit. informal discover (an illicit activity or its perpetrator). • noun **1** a continuous deep, resonant sound like distant thunder. **2** US informal a street fight between rival gangs.
– DERIVATIVES **rumbler** noun.
– ORIGIN probably from Dutch *rommelen*, *rummelen*, of imitative origin.
rumble seat • noun N. Amer. an uncovered folding seat in the rear of a motor car.
rumble strip • noun one of a series of raised strips set in a road to warn drivers of speed restrictions or an approaching hazard.
rumbustious /rumbusschəss/ • adjective informal, chiefly Brit. boisterous or unruly.
– ORIGIN probably an alteration of archaic *robustious* 'boisterous, robust'.
rum butter • noun a rich, sweet, rum-flavoured sauce made with butter and sugar.
ruminant • noun a mammal of a type that chews the cud, comprising cattle, sheep, antelopes, deer, giraffes, and their relatives. • adjective relating to ruminants.
– ORIGIN from Latin *ruminari* 'chew over again', from *rumen* 'throat, first stomach of a ruminant'.
ruminate /roominayt/ • verb **1** think deeply about something. **2** (of a ruminant) chew the cud.
– DERIVATIVES **rumination** noun **ruminative** adjective.
rummage • verb search unsystematically and untidily for something. • noun an act of rummaging.
– ORIGIN originally referring to the arranging of items in the hold of a ship: from Old French *arrumer* 'stow in a hold'.
rummage sale • noun chiefly N. Amer. a jumble sale.
rummy • noun a card game in which the players try to form sets and sequences of cards.
– ORIGIN of unknown origin.
rumour (US **rumor**) • noun a currently circulating story or report of unverified or doubtful truth. • verb (**be rumoured**) be circulated as a rumour.
– ORIGIN Latin *rumor* 'noise'.
rump • noun **1** the hind part of the body of a mammal or the lower back of a bird. **2** a small or unimportant remnant.
– ORIGIN probably Scandinavian.
rumple • verb give a ruffled or dishevelled appearance to. • noun an untidy state.
– DERIVATIVES **rumpled** adjective.
– ORIGIN originally in the sense 'wrinkle': from Dutch *rompel*.
rumpus • noun (pl. **rumpuses**) a noisy disturbance.
– ORIGIN probably fanciful.
rumpus room • noun N. Amer. & Austral./NZ a room for playing games or other noisy activities.
rumpy pumpy • noun informal, humorous sexual relations.
– ORIGIN reduplication of RUMP.
run • verb (**running**; past **ran**; past part. **run**) **1** move at a speed faster than a walk, never having both or all feet on the ground at the same time. **2** move about in a hurried and hectic way. **3** pass or cause to pass: *Helen ran her fingers through her hair.* **4** move forcefully: *the tanker ran aground.* **5** (of a bus, train, etc.) make a regular journey on a particular route. **6** be in charge of; manage or organize. **7** continue, operate, or proceed. **8** function or cause to function. **9** pass into or reach a specified state or level: *inflation is running at 11 per cent.* **10** (**run in**) (of a quality or trait) be common or inherent in. **11** (of a liquid) flow. **12** emit or exude a liquid. **13** (of dye or colour) dissolve and spread when wet. **14** stand as a candidate. **15** enter or be

Thesaurus

tant, excessive, sky-high, outrageous, inflated; *Brit.* over the odds; *informal* criminal, steep. **3** *a ruinous chapel.* See RUINED.
rule • noun **1** *health and safety rules* REGULATION, ruling, directive, order, act, law, statute, edict, canon, mandate, command, dictate, decree, fiat, injunction, commandment, stipulation, requirement, guideline, direction; *formal* ordinance. **2** *church attendance on Sunday was the general rule* PROCEDURE, practice, protocol, convention, norm, routine, custom, habit, wont; *formal* praxis. **3** *moderation is the golden rule* PRECEPT, principle, standard, axiom, truth, maxim. **4** *Punjab came under British rule* CONTROL, jurisdiction, command, power, dominion; government, administration, sovereignty, leadership, supremacy, authority; raj.
– RELATED TERMS hegemonic, -cracy, -archy.
• verb **1** *El Salvador was ruled by Spain* GOVERN, preside over, control, lead, dominate, run, head, administer, manage. **2** *Mary ruled for six years* BE IN POWER, be in control, be in command, be in charge, govern; reign, be monarch, be sovereign. **3** *the judge ruled that they be set free* DECREE, order, pronounce, judge, adjudge, ordain; decide, find, determine, resolve, settle. **4** *subversion ruled* PREVAIL, predominate, be the order of the day, reign supreme; *formal* obtain.
– PHRASES **as a rule** USUALLY, generally, in general, normally, ordinarily, customarily, for the most part, on the whole, by and large, in the main, mainly, mostly, commonly, typically. **rule something out** EXCLUDE, eliminate, disregard; preclude, prohibit, prevent, disallow.
ruler • noun LEADER, sovereign, monarch, potentate, king, queen, emperor, empress, prince, princess; crowned head, head of state, president, premier, governor; overlord, chief, chieftain, lord; dictator, autocrat.
– OPPOSITES subject.
ruling • noun *the judge's ruling* JUDGEMENT, decision, adjudication, finding, verdict; pronouncement, resolution, decree, injunction.
• adjective **1** *the ruling monarch* REIGNING, sovereign, regnant. **2** *Japan's ruling party* GOVERNING, controlling, commanding, supreme, leading, dominant, ascendant. **3** *football was their ruling passion* MAIN, chief, principal, major, prime, dominating, foremost; predominant, central, focal; *informal* number-one.
rum • adjective *(Brit. informal, dated)*. See PECULIAR sense 1.
rumble • verb BOOM, thunder, roll, roar, resound, reverberate, echo, grumble.
rumbustious • adjective *(Brit. informal)*. See BOISTEROUS sense 1.
ruminate • verb **1** *we ruminated on life* THINK ABOUT, contemplate, consider, meditate on, muse on, mull over, ponder on/over, deliberate about/on, chew over, puzzle over; *formal* cogitate about. **2** *cows ruminating* CHEW THE CUD.
rummage • verb SEARCH, hunt, root about/around, ferret about/around, fish about/around, poke around in, dig, delve, go through, explore, sift through, rifle through; *Brit. informal* rootle around.
rumour • noun GOSSIP, hearsay, talk, tittle-tattle, speculation, word, on dit; (**rumours**) reports, stories, whispers, canards; *informal* the grapevine, the word on the street, the buzz; *N. Amer. informal* scuttlebutt.
rump • noun **1** *a smack on the rump* REAR (END), backside, seat; buttocks, cheeks; *Brit.* bottom; *informal* behind, BTM, sit-upon, derrière; *Brit. informal* bum, botty, jacksie; *N. Amer. informal* butt, fanny, tush, tail, buns, booty, heinie; *humorous* fundament, posterior, stern; *Anatomy* nates. **2** *the rump of the army* REMAINDER, rest, remnant, remains.
rumple • verb **1** *the sheet was rumpled* CRUMPLE, crease, wrinkle, crinkle, ruck (up), scrunch up; *Brit.* ruckle. **2** *Ian rumpled her hair* RUFFLE, disarrange, tousle, dishevel, riffle; mess up; *N. Amer. informal* muss up.
– OPPOSITES smooth.
rumpus • noun DISTURBANCE, commotion, uproar, furore, brouhaha,

entered in a race. **16** publish or be published in a newspaper or magazine. **17** transport in a car. **18** smuggle (goods). **19** chiefly N. Amer. (of a stocking or pair of tights) develop a ladder. ● **noun 1** an act or spell of running. **2** a running pace. **3** a journey or route. **4** a short excursion made in a car. **5** a course or track made or regularly used: *a ski run.* **6** a length, spell, or stretch of something: *a run of bad luck.* **7** an enclosed area in which animals or birds may run freely in the open. **8** Austral./NZ a large open stretch of land used for pasture or livestock. **9** a rapid series of musical notes. **10** a sequence of cards of the same suit. **11** (**the run**) the average or usual type. **12** (**the run of**) free and unrestricted use of or access to somewhere. **13** Cricket a unit of scoring achieved by hitting the ball so that both batsmen are able to run between the wickets. **14** Baseball a point scored by the batter returning to the home plate after touching the bases. **15** a ladder in stockings or tights. **16** (**the runs**) informal diarrhoea.

– PHRASES **be run off one's feet** be extremely busy. **a (good) run for one's money 1** challenging competition or opposition. **2** reward or enjoyment in return for one's efforts. **on the run 1** escaping from arrest. **2** while running or moving. **run across** meet or find by chance. **run after** informal pursue persistently. **run along** informal go away. **run away 1** take flight; escape. **2** try to avoid facing up to danger or difficulty. **run away with 1** escape the control of. **2** win (a competition or prize) easily. **run before one can walk** attempt something difficult before one has grasped the basic skills. **run by** (or **past**) tell (someone) about (something) to find out their opinion. **run down 1** knock down with a vehicle. **2** criticize unfairly or unkindly. **3** reduce or become reduced in size or resources. **4** lose or cause to lose power; stop functioning. **5** gradually deteriorate. **run in 1** Brit. use (something new) in such a way as not to make maximum demands upon it. **2** informal arrest (someone). **run into 1** collide with. **2** meet by chance. **3** experience (a problem or difficult situation). **run off 1** produce (a copy) on a machine. **2** write or recite quickly and with little effort. **run on** continue without stopping; go on longer than is expected. **run out 1** use up or be used up. **2** become no longer valid. **3** extend; project. **4** Cricket dismiss (a batsman) by dislodging the bails with the ball while the batsman is still running. **run over 1** knock down with a vehicle. **2** overflow. **3** exceed (a limit). **run through 1** stab so as to kill. **2** (also **run over**) go over quickly or briefly as a rehearsal or reminder. **run to 1** extend to or reach. **2** show a tendency towards. **run up 1** allow (a bill, score, etc.) to accumulate. **2** make quickly or hurriedly. **3** raise (a flag). **run up against** experience or meet (a difficulty or problem). **you can't run with the hares and hunt with the hounds** proverb you can't be loyal to both sides in a conflict or dispute.

– DERIVATIVES **runnable** adjective.

– ORIGIN Old English.

Thesaurus

hue and cry, ruckus; fracas, melee, tumult, noise, racket, din; *informal* to-do, hullabaloo, hoo-ha, kerfuffle, ballyhoo; *Brit. informal* row, carry-on; *Scottish informal* stushie.

run ● **verb 1** *she ran across the road* SPRINT, race, dart, rush, dash, hasten, hurry, scurry, scamper, hare, bolt, fly, gallop, career, charge, shoot, hurtle, speed, zoom, go like lightning, go hell for leather, go like the wind; jog, trot; *informal* tear, pelt, scoot, hotfoot it, leg it, belt, zip, whip; *Brit. informal* bomb; *N. Amer. informal* hightail it, barrel. **2** *the robbers turned and ran* FLEE, run away, run off, run for it, take flight, make off, take off, take to one's heels, make a break for it, bolt, make one's getaway, escape; *informal* beat it, clear off/out, vamoose, skedaddle, split, leg it, scram; *Brit. informal* do a runner, scarper, do a bunk; *N. Amer. informal* light out, take a powder, skidoo; *Austral. informal* shoot through. **3** *he ran in the marathon* COMPETE, take part, participate. **4** *a shiver ran down my spine* GO, pass, slide, move, travel. **5** *he ran his eye down the list* CAST, pass, skim, flick. **6** *the road runs the length of the valley* EXTEND, stretch, reach, continue. **7** *water ran from the eaves* FLOW, pour, stream, gush, flood, cascade, roll, course, spill, trickle, drip, dribble, leak. **8** *a bus runs to Sorrento* TRAVEL, shuttle, go. **9** *I'll run you home* DRIVE, take, bring, ferry, chauffeur, give someone a lift. **10** *he runs a transport company* BE IN CHARGE OF, manage, direct, control, head, govern, supervise, superintend, oversee; operate, conduct, own. **11** *it's expensive to run a car* MAINTAIN, keep, own, possess, have; drive. **12** *they ran some tests* CARRY OUT, do, perform, execute. **13** *he left the engine running* OPERATE, function, work, go; tick over, idle. **14** *the lease runs for twenty years* BE VALID, last, be in effect, be operative, continue, be effective. **15** *the show ran for two years* BE STAGED, be performed, be on, be mounted, be screened. **16** *he ran for president* STAND FOR, be a candidate for, be a contender for. **17** *the paper ran the story* PUBLISH, print, feature, carry, put out, release, issue. **18** *they run drugs* SMUGGLE, traffic in, deal in. **19** *they were run out of town* CHASE, drive, hound.

● **noun 1** *his morning run* SPRINT, jog, dash, gallop, trot. **2** *she did the school run* ROUTE, journey; circuit, round, beat. **3** *a run in the car* DRIVE, ride, turn; trip, excursion, outing, jaunt, airing; *informal* spin, tootle; *Scottish informal* hurl. **4** *an unbeaten run of victories* SERIES, succession, sequence, string, chain, streak, spell, stretch, spate. **5** *a run on sterling* DEMAND FOR, rush on. **6** *they had the run of her home* FREE USE OF, unrestricted access to. **7** *the usual run of cafes* TYPE, kind, sort, variety, class. **8** *against the run of play, he scored again* TREND, tendency, course, direction, movement, drift, tide. **9** *a chicken run* ENCLOSURE, pen, coop. **10** *a ski run* SLOPE, track, piste; *N. Amer.* trail. **11** *a run in her tights* LADDER, rip, tear, snag, hole.

– PHRASES **in the long run** EVENTUALLY, in the end, ultimately, when all is said and done, in the fullness of time; *Brit. informal* at the end of the day. **on the run** ON THE LOOSE, at large, loose; running away, fleeing, fugitive; *informal* AWOL; *N. Amer. informal* on the lam. **run across** MEET (BY CHANCE), come across, run into, chance on, stumble on, happen on; *informal* bump into. **run after** *(informal)* PURSUE, chase; make advances to, flirt with; *informal* make up to, come on to, be all over, vamp; *dated* set one's cap at. **run along** *(informal)* GO AWAY, be off with you, shoo; *informal* scram, buzz off, skedaddle, scat, beat it, get lost, shove off, clear off; *Brit. informal* hop it; *poetic/literary* begone. **run around** *(informal)* BE UNFAITHFUL, have affairs, philander; *informal* play the field, sleep around; *Brit. informal* play away; *N. Amer. informal* fool around. **run away 1** *her attacker ran away.* See RUN verb sense 2. **2** *she ran away with the championship* WIN EASILY, win hands down; *informal* win by a mile, walk it, romp home. **run down** DECLINE, degenerate, go downhill, go to seed, decay, go to rack and ruin; *informal* go to pot, go to the dogs. **run someone down 1** *he was run down by joyriders* RUN OVER, knock down/over; hit, strike. **2** *she ran him down in front of other people* CRITICIZE, denigrate, belittle, disparage, deprecate, find fault with; *informal* put down, knock, bad-mouth; *Brit. informal* rubbish, slag off; *formal* derogate. **run something down 1** *she finally ran a copy of the book down* FIND, discover, locate, track down, trace, unearth. **2** *employers ran down their workforces gradually* REDUCE, cut back on, downsize, decrease, trim; phase out, wind down/up. **run for it.** See RUN verb sense 2. **run high** *feelings were running high* BE STRONG, be fervent, be passionate, be intense. **run in** *heart disease runs in the family* BE COMMON IN, be inherent in. **run someone in** *(informal).* See ARREST verb sense 1. **run into 1** *a car ran into his van* COLLIDE WITH, hit, strike, crash into, smash into, plough into, ram, impact. **2** *I ran into Hugo the other day* MEET (BY CHANCE), run across, chance on, stumble on, happen on; *informal* bump into. **3** *we ran into a problem* EXPERIENCE, encounter, meet with, be faced with, be confronted with. **4** *his debts run into six figures* REACH, extend to, be as much as. **run low** *supplies were running low* DWINDLE, diminish, become depleted, be used up, be in short supply, be tight. **run off 1** *the youths ran off.* See RUN verb sense 2. **2** *(informal) he ran off with her money.* See STEAL verb sense 1. **run something off 1** *would you run off that list for me?* COPY, photocopy, xerox, duplicate, print, produce, do. **2** *run off some of the excess water* DRAIN, bleed, draw off, pump out. **run on 1** *the call ran on for hours* CONTINUE, go on, carry on, last, keep going, stretch. **2** *your mother does run on* TALK INCESSANTLY, talk a lot, go on, chatter on, ramble on; *informal* yak, gab, yabber; *Brit. informal* rabbit on, witter on, chunter on, talk the hind leg off a donkey; *N. Amer. informal* run off at the mouth. **run out 1** *supplies ran out* BE USED UP, dry up, be exhausted, be finished, peter out. **2** *they ran out of cash* BE OUT OF; use up, consume, eat up; *informal* be fresh out of, be cleaned out of. **3** *her contract ran out* EXPIRE, end, terminate, finish; lapse. **run out on someone** *(informal).* See ABANDON verb sense 3. **run over 1** *the bathwater ran over* OVERFLOW, spill over, brim over; *archaic* overbrim. **2** *the project ran over budget* EXCEED, go over, overshoot, overreach. **3** *he quickly ran over the story* RECAPITULATE, repeat, run through, go over, reiterate, review; look over, read through; *informal* recap on. **run someone over.** See RUN SOMEONE DOWN sense 1. **run the show** *(informal)* BE IN CHARGE, be in control, be at the helm, be in the driving seat, be at the wheel; *informal* be the boss, call the shots. **run through 1** *they quickly ran*

runabout • noun a small car or light aircraft, especially one used for short journeys.

runaround • noun informal **1** (**the runaround**) evasive treatment. **2** a runabout.

runaway • noun a person who has run away from their home or an institution. • adjective **1** (of an animal or vehicle) running out of control. **2** happening or done quickly or uncontrollably: *runaway success.*

runcible spoon /runsib'l/ • noun a fork curved like a spoon, with three broad prongs, one of which has a sharpened outer edge for cutting.

– ORIGIN used by the English humorist Edward Lear (1812–88), perhaps suggested by obsolete *rouncival,* denoting a large variety of pea.

rundown • noun a brief analysis or summary. • adjective (**run-down**) **1** in a poor or neglected state. **2** tired and rather unwell, especially through overwork.

rune /roōn/ • noun **1** a letter of an ancient Germanic alphabet used especially in Scandinavia. **2** a mysterious symbol, especially in a spell or incantation. **3** an ancient Scandinavian poem or part of one.

– DERIVATIVES **runic** adjective.

– ORIGIN Old English, 'secret, mystery'.

rung[1] • noun **1** a horizontal support on a ladder for a person's foot. **2** a strengthening crosspiece in the structure of a chair. **3** a level in a hierarchical structure.

– ORIGIN Old English.

rung[2] past participle of RING[2].

run-in • noun **1** the approach to an action or event. **2** informal a disagreement or fight.

runnel • noun **1** a gutter. **2** a brook or stream.

– ORIGIN from dialect *rindle,* influenced by RUN.

runner • noun **1** a person or animal that runs. **2** a messenger, collector, or agent for a bank, bookmaker, etc. **3** an orderly in the army. **4** a rod, groove, blade, or roller on which something slides. **5** a ring capable of sliding or being drawn along a strap or rod. **6** a shoot which grows along the ground and can take root at points along its length. **7** a climbing plant, or one that spreads by means of runners. **8** a long, narrow rug or strip of carpet.

– PHRASES **do a runner** Brit. informal leave hastily to escape or avoid something.

runner bean • noun chiefly Brit. a climbing bean plant with scarlet flowers and long green edible pods.

runner-up • noun (pl. **runners-up**) a competitor or team taking second place in a contest.

running • noun **1** the activity or movement of a runner. **2** the action or business of managing or operating. • adjective **1** (of water) flowing naturally or supplied through pipes and taps. **2** exuding liquid or pus. **3** continuous or recurring: *a running joke.* **4** done while running. **5** (after a noun) consecutive; in succession: *the third week running.*

– PHRASES **in** (or **out of**) **the running** in (or no longer in) contention. **make** (or **take up**) **the running** set the pace.

running back • noun American Football an offensive player who specializes in carrying the ball.

running battle • noun a military engagement which does not occur at a fixed location.

running board • noun a footboard extending along the side of a vehicle.

running commentary • noun a verbal description of events, given as they occur.

running dog • noun informal a servile follower, especially of a political system.

running head • noun a heading printed at the top of each page of a book or chapter.

running knot • noun a knot that slips along the rope and changes the size of a noose.

running lights • plural noun **1** another term for NAVIGATION LIGHTS. **2** small lights on a motor vehicle that remain illuminated while the vehicle is running.

running mate • noun **1** chiefly US an election candidate for the lesser of two closely associated political offices. **2** chiefly N. Amer. a horse entered in a race in order to set the pace for another horse which is intended to win.

running repairs • plural noun minor or temporary repairs carried out on machinery while it is in use.

running stitch • noun a simple needlework stitch consisting of a line of small even stitches which run back and forth through the cloth.

running total • noun a total that is continually adjusted to take account of further items.

runny • adjective (**runnier**, **runniest**) **1** more liquid in consistency than is usual or expected. **2** (of a person's nose) producing or discharging mucus.

run-off • noun **1** a further contest after a tie or inconclusive result. **2** rainfall or other liquid that drains away from the surface of an area.

run-of-the-mill • adjective lacking unusual or special aspects; ordinary.

run-out • noun **1** Cricket the dismissal of a batsman by being run out. **2** informal a short session of play or practice in a sport.

runt • noun a small pig or other animal, especially the smallest in a litter.

– DERIVATIVES **runtish** adjective **runty** adjective.

– ORIGIN originally in the sense 'old or decayed tree stump', later 'small ox or cow': of unknown origin.

run-through • noun **1** a rehearsal. **2** a brief outline or sum-

Thesaurus

through their money SQUANDER, spend, fritter away, dissipate, waste, go through, consume, use up; *informal* blow. **2** *the attitude that runs through his writing* PERVADE, permeate, suffuse, imbue, inform. **3** *he ran through his notes.* See RUN OVER sense 3. **4** *let's run through scene three* REHEARSE, practise, go over, repeat; *N. Amer.* run down; *informal* recap on. **run someone through** STAB, pierce, transfix, impale. **run to 1** *the bill ran to £22,000* AMOUNT TO, add up to, total, come to, equal, reach, be as much as. **2** *we can't run to champagne* AFFORD, stretch to, manage. **3** *he was running to fat* TEND TO, become, get, grow.

runaway • noun *a teenage runaway* FUGITIVE, escaper, escapee; refugee; truant; absconder, deserter.

• adjective **1** *a runaway horse* OUT OF CONTROL, escaped, loose, on the loose. **2** *a runaway victory* EASY, effortless; *informal* as easy as pie. **3** *runaway inflation* RAMPANT, out of control, unchecked, unbridled.

rundown • noun SUMMARY, synopsis, precis, run-through, summarization, summation, review, overview, briefing, sketch, outline; *informal* low-down, recap.

run down • adjective **1** *a run-down area of London* DILAPIDATED, tumbledown, ramshackle, derelict, ruinous, in ruins, crumbling, decaying; neglected, uncared-for, depressed, seedy, shabby, slummy, squalid; *informal* shambly; *Brit. informal* grotty. **2** *she was feeling rather run down* UNWELL, ill, poorly, unhealthy, peaky; tired, drained, exhausted, fatigued, worn out, below par, washed out; *Brit.* off colour; *informal* under the weather; *Brit. informal* off, ropy, knackered; *Scottish informal* wabbit; *Austral./NZ informal* crook; *dated* seedy.

run-in • noun *(informal)* DISAGREEMENT, argument, dispute, altercation, confrontation, contretemps, quarrel; brush, encounter, tangle, fight, clash; *informal* set-to, spat, scrap; *Brit. informal* row.

runner • noun **1** *the runners were limbering up* ATHLETE, sprinter, hurdler, racer, jogger. **2** *a strawberry runner* SHOOT, offshoot, sprout, tendril; *Botany* stolon. **3** *the bookmaker employed runners* MESSENGER, courier, errand boy; *informal* gofer.

– PHRASES **do a runner** *(Brit. informal).* See ABSCOND.

running • noun **1** *his running was particularly fast* SPRINTING, sprint, racing, jogging, jog. **2** *the running of the school* ADMINISTRATION, management, organization, coordination, orchestration, handling, direction, control, regulation, supervision. **3** *the smooth running of her department* OPERATION, working, function, performance.

• adjective **1** *running water* FLOWING, gushing, rushing, moving. **2** *a running argument* ONGOING, sustained, continuous, incessant, ceaseless, constant, perpetual; recurrent, recurring. **3** *she was late two days running* IN SUCCESSION, in a row, in sequence, consecutively; straight, together; *informal* on the trot.

– PHRASES **in the running** *he's in the running for a prize* LIKELY TO GET, a candidate for, in line for, on the shortlist for, up for.

runny • adjective LIQUEFIED, liquid, fluid, melted, molten; watery, thin.

– OPPOSITES solid.

run-of-the-mill • adjective ORDINARY, average, middle-of-the-road, commonplace, humdrum, mundane, standard, nondescript, characterless, conventional; unremarkable, unexceptional, uninteresting, dull, boring, routine, bland, lacklustre; *N. Amer.* garden-

mary.

run-up ● noun **1** the preparatory period before a notable event. **2** an act of running briefly to gain momentum before bowling, performing a jump, etc.

runway ● noun **1** a strip of hard ground along which aircraft take off and land. **2** a raised gangway extending into an auditorium, especially as used for fashion shows. **3** an animal run. **4** a chute down which logs are slid.

rupee /roopee/ ● noun the basic monetary unit of India, Pakistan, Sri Lanka, Nepal, Mauritius, and the Seychelles.
– ORIGIN Sanskrit, 'wrought silver'.

rupiah /ro͞opeeə/ ● noun the basic monetary unit of Indonesia, equal to 100 sen.
– ORIGIN Indonesian, from Hindi (see RUPEE).

rupture ● verb **1** break or burst suddenly. **2** (**be ruptured** or **rupture oneself**) suffer an abdominal hernia. **3** breach or disturb (a harmonious situation). ● noun **1** an instance of rupturing. **2** an abdominal hernia.
– ORIGIN Latin *ruptura*, from *rumpere* 'to break'.

rural ● adjective relating to or characteristic of the countryside rather than the town.
– DERIVATIVES **ruralism** noun **ruralist** noun **rurality** noun **ruralize** (also **ruralise**) verb **rurally** adverb.
– ORIGIN Latin *ruralis*, from *rus* 'country'.

Ruritanian /rooritaynian/ ● adjective relating to or characteristic of romantic adventure or its setting.
– ORIGIN from *Ruritania*, the imaginary setting for the novels of courtly intrigue and romance written by the English novelist Anthony Hope (1863–1933).

ruse /ro͞oz/ ● noun a stratagem or trick.
– ORIGIN from Old French *ruser* 'use trickery', earlier 'drive back', perhaps from Latin *rursus* 'backwards'.

rush[1] ● verb **1** move or act with urgent haste. **2** transport or produce with urgent haste. **3** deal with hurriedly. **4** (of air or a liquid) flow strongly. **5** dash towards in an attempt to attack or capture. ● noun **1** the action or an instance of rushing. **2** a flurry of hasty activity. **3** a sudden strong demand for a commodity. **4** a sudden intensity of feeling. **5** a sudden thrill experienced after taking certain drugs. **6** (**rushes**) the first prints made of a film after a period of shooting.
– PHRASES **rush one's fences** Brit. act with undue haste. **a rush of blood to the head** a sudden attack of wild irrationality.
– ORIGIN Old French *ruser* 'drive back'; related to RUSE.

rush[2] ● noun a marsh or waterside plant with slender pith-filled leaves, some kinds of which are used for matting, baskets, etc.
– DERIVATIVES **rushy** adjective.
– ORIGIN Old English.

rush hour ● noun a time at the start and end of the working day when traffic is at its heaviest.

rushlight ● noun historical a candle made by dipping the pith of a rush in tallow.

rusk ● noun a dry biscuit or piece of rebaked bread.
– ORIGIN Spanish or Portuguese *rosca* 'twist, coil, roll of bread'.

russet ● adjective reddish brown. ● noun **1** a reddish-brown colour. **2** a variety of dessert apple with a slightly rough greenish-brown skin. **3** historical a coarse homespun reddish-brown or grey cloth.
– DERIVATIVES **russety** adjective.
– ORIGIN Old French *rousset*, from Latin *russus* 'red'.

Russian ● noun **1** a person from Russia. **2** the Slavic language of Russia, written in the Cyrillic alphabet. ● adjective relating to Russia.

Russian doll ● noun each of a set of brightly painted hollow wooden dolls that fit inside each other.

Russian Orthodox Church ● noun the national Church of Russia.

Russian roulette ● noun a dangerous game of chance in which a single bullet is loaded into the chamber of a revolver, the cylinder is spun, and people take it in turns to hold the gun to their own head and fire it.

Russian vine ● noun a fast-growing Asian climbing plant of the dock family, with long clusters of white or pink flowers.

Russki /ruski/ (also **Russky**) ● noun (pl. **Russkis** or **Russkies**) informal, chiefly derogatory a Russian.

rust ● noun **1** a reddish- or yellowish-brown flaky coating of iron oxide that is formed on iron or steel by oxidation, especially in the presence of moisture. **2** a fungal disease of plants which results in reddish or brownish patches. **3** a reddish-brown colour. ● verb be affected with rust.
– DERIVATIVES **rustless** adjective.
– ORIGIN Old English, related to RED.

rust belt ● noun informal (especially in the American Midwest and NE states) a region characterized by declining industry and a falling population.

rust bucket ● noun informal a vehicle or ship which is old and badly rusted.

rustic ● adjective **1** of or characteristic of life in the country. **2** having a simplicity and charm that is considered typical of the countryside. **3** (of furniture) made of rough branches or timber. ● noun often derogatory an unsophisticated country person.
– DERIVATIVES **rustically** adverb **rusticity** noun.
– ORIGIN Latin *rusticus*, from *rus* 'the country'.

rusticate /rustikayt/ ● verb **1** Brit. suspend (a student) from a university as a punishment (used chiefly at Oxford and Cambridge). **2** fashion (masonry) in large blocks with sunken joints and a roughened surface.
– DERIVATIVES **rustication** noun.
– ORIGIN originally in the sense 'make countrified': from Latin *rusticus* 'rustic'.

rustle ● verb **1** make a soft crackling sound like that caused by the movement of dry leaves or paper. **2** move with such a sound. **3** round up and steal (cattle, horses, or sheep). **4** (**rustle up**) informal produce (food or a drink) quickly. **5** N. Amer. informal move or act quickly or energetically. ● noun a rustling sound.
– DERIVATIVES **rustler** noun.
– ORIGIN imitative.

r

Thesaurus

variety; *informal* bog-standard, nothing to write home about, nothing special, a dime a dozen; *Brit. informal* common or garden.
– OPPOSITES exceptional.

rupture ● noun **1** *pipeline ruptures* BREAK, fracture, crack, burst, split, fissure. **2** *a rupture due to personal differences* RIFT, estrangement, falling-out, break-up, breach, split, separation, parting, division, schism; *informal* bust-up. **3** *an abdominal rupture* HERNIA.
● verb **1** *the reactor core might rupture* BREAK, fracture, crack, breach, burst, split; *informal* bust. **2** *the problem ruptured their relationships* SEVER, break off, breach, disrupt; *poetic/literary* sunder.

rural ● adjective COUNTRY, countryside, bucolic, rustic, pastoral; agricultural, agrarian; *poetic/literary* sylvan, georgic.
– OPPOSITES urban.

ruse ● noun PLOY, stratagem, tactic, scheme, trick, gambit, cunning plan, dodge, subterfuge, machination, wile; *Brit. informal* wheeze.

rush ● verb **1** *she rushed home* HURRY, dash, run, race, sprint, bolt, dart, gallop, career, charge, shoot, hurtle, hare, fly, speed, zoom, scurry, scuttle, scamper, hasten; *informal* tear, belt, pelt, scoot, zip, whip, hotfoot it, leg it; *Brit. informal* bomb; *N. Amer. informal* hightail it. **2** *water rushed along gutters* FLOW, pour, gush, surge, stream, cascade, run, course. **3** *the tax was rushed through parliament* PUSH, hurry, hasten, speed, hustle, press, force. **4** *they rushed the cordon of troops* ATTACK, charge, run at, assail, storm.
● noun **1** *Tim made a rush for the exit* DASH, run, sprint, dart, bolt, charge, scramble, break. **2** *the lunchtime rush* HUSTLE AND BUSTLE, commotion, hubbub, hurly-burly, stir. **3** *a last minute rush for flights* DEMAND, clamour, call, request; run on. **4** *he was in no rush to leave* HURRY, haste, urgency. **5** *a rush of adrenalin* SURGE, flow, flood, spurt, stream; dart, thrill, flash. **6** *a rush of cold air* GUST, draught, flurry. **7** *I made a sudden rush at him* CHARGE, onslaught, attack, assault, onrush.
● adjective *a rush job* URGENT, high-priority, emergency; hurried, hasty, fast, quick, swift; *N. Amer. informal* hurry-up.

rushed ● adjective **1** *a rushed divorce* HASTY, fast, speedy, quick, swift, rapid, hurried. **2** *he was too rushed to enjoy his stay* PUSHED FOR TIME, pressed for time, busy, in a hurry, run off one's feet.

rust ● verb CORRODE, oxidize, become rusty, tarnish.
– RELATED TERMS ferruginous.

rustic ● adjective **1** *a rustic setting* RURAL, country, countryside, countrified, pastoral, bucolic; agricultural, agrarian; *poetic/literary* sylvan, georgic. **2** *rustic wooden tables* PLAIN, simple, homely, unsophisticated; rough, rude, crude. **3** *rustic peasants* UNSOPHISTICATED, uncultured, unrefined, simple; artless, unassuming, guileless, naive, ingenuous; coarse, rough, uncouth, boorish; *N. Amer. informal* hillbilly, hick.
– OPPOSITES urban, ornate, sophisticated.
● noun *the rustics were carousing* PEASANT, countryman, countrywoman, bumpkin, yokel, country cousin; *N. Amer. informal* hillbilly,

rustproof ● adjective not susceptible to corrosion by rust. ● verb make rustproof.

rusty ● adjective (**rustier**, **rustiest**) **1** affected by rust. **2** (of knowledge or a skill) impaired by lack of recent practice.
– DERIVATIVES **rustily** adverb **rustiness** noun.

rut[1] ● noun **1** a long deep track made by the repeated passage of the wheels of vehicles. **2** a routine or pattern of behaviour or activity that has become dull but is hard to change.
– DERIVATIVES **rutted** adjective **rutty** adjective.
– ORIGIN probably from Old French *rute* (see ROUTE).

rut[2] ● noun an annual period of sexual activity in deer and some other mammals, during which the males fight each other for access to the females. ● verb (**rutted**, **rutting**) engage in such activity.
– DERIVATIVES **ruttish** adjective.
– ORIGIN Old French, from Latin *rugire* 'to roar'.

rutabaga /rōotəbaygə/ ● noun chiefly N. Amer. a swede.
– ORIGIN Swedish dialect *rotabagge*.

ruth ● noun archaic a feeling of pity, distress, or grief.
– ORIGIN from RUE[1].

ruthenium /rootheeniəm/ ● noun a hard silvery-white metallic chemical element.
– ORIGIN from *Ruthenia*, a region of central Europe, because the element was discovered in ores from the Urals.

rutherfordium /ruthərfordiəm/ ● noun a very unstable chemical element made by high-energy atomic collisions.
– ORIGIN named after the New Zealand physicist Ernest *Rutherford* (1871–1937).

ruthless ● adjective having or showing no compassion.
– DERIVATIVES **ruthlessly** adverb **ruthlessness** noun.

RV ● abbreviation N. Amer. recreational vehicle (especially a motorized caravan).

Rwandan /rōoandən/ (also **Rwandese** /rōoandeez/) ● noun a person from Rwanda, a country in central Africa. ● adjective relating to Rwanda.

rye ● noun **1** a wheat-like cereal plant which tolerates poor soils and low temperatures. **2** whisky in which a significant amount of the grain used in distillation is fermented rye.
– ORIGIN Old English.

rye bread ● noun a dense, chewy bread made with rye flour.

ryegrass ● noun a grass used for fodder and lawns.
– ORIGIN alteration of obsolete *ray-grass*, of unknown origin.

Thesaurus

hayseed, hick; *Austral./NZ informal* bushy; *archaic* swain, cottier.

rustle ● verb **1** *her dress rustled as she moved* SWISH, whoosh, whisper, sigh. **2** *he was rustling cattle* STEAL, thieve, take; abduct, kidnap.
● noun *the rustle of the leaves* SWISH, whisper, rustling; *poetic/literary* susurration, susurrus.
– PHRASES **rustle something up** *(informal)* PREPARE HASTILY, throw together, make; *informal* fix; *Brit. informal* knock up.

rusty ● adjective **1** *rusty wire* RUSTED, rust-covered, corroded, oxidized; tarnished, discoloured. **2** *his hair was a rusty colour* REDDISH-BROWN, chestnut, auburn, tawny, russet, coppery, copper, Titian, red. **3** *my French is a little rusty* OUT OF PRACTICE, below par; unpractised, deficient, impaired, weak.

rut ● noun **1** *the car bumped across the ruts* FURROW, groove, trough, ditch, hollow, pothole, crater. **2** *he was stuck in a rut* BORING ROUTINE, humdrum existence, groove, dead end.

ruthless ● adjective MERCILESS, pitiless, cruel, heartless, hard-hearted, cold-hearted, cold-blooded, harsh, callous, unmerciful, unforgiving, uncaring, unsympathetic, uncharitable; remorseless, unbending, inflexible, implacable; brutal, inhuman, inhumane, barbarous, barbaric, savage, sadistic, vicious.
– OPPOSITES merciful.

Ss

S¹ (also **s**) ● **noun** (pl. **Ss** or **S's**) the nineteenth letter of the alphabet.
S² ● **abbreviation** **1** (chiefly in Catholic use) Saint. **2** siemens. **3** small (as a clothes size). **4** South or Southern. ● **symbol** the chemical element sulphur.
s ● **abbreviation** **1** second or seconds. **2** shilling or shillings. **3** Grammar singular. **4** (in genealogies) son or sons.
's /ss, z after a vowel sound or voiced consonant/ ● **contraction** informal **1** is. **2** has. **3** us. **4** does.
-s¹ /ss, z after a vowel sound or voiced consonant/ ● **suffix** denoting the plurals of nouns (as in *wagons*).
-s² /ss, z after a vowel sound or voiced consonant/ ● **suffix** forming the third person singular of the present of verbs (as in *sews*).
-'s¹ /ss, z after a vowel sound or voiced consonant, iz after a sibilant/ ● **suffix** denoting possession in singular nouns, also in plural nouns not having a final *-s*: *John's book*.
-'s² /ss, z after a vowel sound or voiced consonant, iz after a sibilant/ ● **suffix** denoting the plural of a letter or symbol: *9's*.
SA ● **abbreviation** **1** Salvation Army. **2** South Africa. **3** South America. **4** South Australia.
saag /saag/ (also **sag**) ● **noun** Indian term for SPINACH.
– ORIGIN Hindi.
sabbatarian /sabbətairiən/ ● **noun** a strict observer of the sabbath. ● **adjective** relating to or upholding the observance of the sabbath.
– DERIVATIVES **sabbatarianism** noun.
sabbath ● **noun** **1** (often **the Sabbath**) a day of religious observance and abstinence from work, kept by Jews from Friday evening to Saturday evening, and by most Christians on Sunday. **2** (also **witches' sabbath**) a midnight pagan ritual held by witches.
– ORIGIN from Hebrew, 'to rest'.
sabbatical /səbattik'l/ ● **noun** a period of paid leave granted to a university teacher for study or travel (traditionally one year for every seven years worked). ● **adjective** **1** relating to a sabbatical. **2** archaic of or appropriate to the sabbath.
– ORIGIN from Greek *sabbatikos* 'of the sabbath'.
saber ● **noun & verb** US spelling of SABRE.
Sabine /sabbīn/ ● **noun** a member of an ancient people of the central Apennines in Italy.
– ORIGIN Latin *Sabinus*.
sable¹ /sayb'l/ ● **noun** **1** a marten with a short tail and dark brown fur, native to Japan and Siberia. **2** the fur of the sable.
– ORIGIN Old French, from Latin *sabelum*.
sable² /sayb'l/ ● **adjective & noun** literary or Heraldry black.
– ORIGIN Old French, and generally taken to be identical with SABLE¹, although sable fur is dark brown.
sabot /sabbō/ ● **noun** a kind of simple shoe, shaped and hollowed out from a single block of wood.
– ORIGIN French, blend of *savate* 'shoe' and *botte* 'boot'.
sabotage /sabbətaazh/ ● **verb** deliberately destroy or obstruct, especially for political or military advantage. ● **noun** the action of sabotaging.
– ORIGIN French, from *saboter* 'kick with sabots, wilfully destroy'.
saboteur /sabbətör/ ● **noun** a person who engages in sabotage.
– ORIGIN French.
sabra /sabrə/ ● **noun** a Jew born in Israel (or before 1948 in Palestine).
– ORIGIN Hebrew, 'opuntia fruit' (opuntias being common in coastal regions of Israel).
sabre /saybər/ (US **saber**) ● **noun** **1** a heavy cavalry sword with a curved blade and a single cutting edge. **2** a light fencing sword with a tapering, typically curved blade.
– ORIGIN French, from Hungarian *szablya*.
sabre-rattling ● **noun** the display or threat of military force.
sabretooth ● **noun** a large extinct carnivore of the cat family with massive curved upper canine teeth.
– DERIVATIVES **sabre-toothed** adjective.
sac /sak/ ● **noun** **1** a hollow, flexible structure resembling a bag or pouch. **2** a cavity enclosed by a membrane within a living organism.
– ORIGIN Latin *saccus* 'sack, bag'.
saccharide /sakkərid/ ● **noun** Biochemistry another term for SUGAR (in sense 2).
saccharin /sakkərin/ ● **noun** a sweet-tasting synthetic compound used as a low-calorie substitute for sugar.
– ORIGIN Greek *sakkharon* 'sugar'.
saccharine /sakkərīn, -rin/ ● **adjective** **1** excessively sweet or sentimental. **2** relating to or containing sugar. ● **noun** saccharin.
sacerdotal /sakkərdōt'l/ ● **adjective** relating to priests or the priesthood.
– DERIVATIVES **sacerdotalism** noun.
– ORIGIN Latin *sacerdotalis*, from *sacerdos* 'priest'.
sachem /saychem/ ● **noun** **1** (among some American Indian peoples) a chief. **2** N. Amer. informal a boss or leader.
– ORIGIN Narragansett.
Sachertorte /zakhərtortə/ ● **noun** (pl. **Sachertorten** /zakhərtortən/) a chocolate gateau with chocolate icing and an apricot jam filling.
– ORIGIN German, from the name of the pastry chef Franz *Sacher* + *Torte* 'tart, pastry'.
sachet /sashay/ ● **noun** chiefly Brit. a small sealed bag or packet containing a small quantity of something.
– ORIGIN French, 'little bag', from Latin *saccus* 'sack, bag'.
sack¹ ● **noun** **1** a large bag made of a material such as hessian or thick paper, used for storing and carrying goods. **2** (**the sack**) informal dismissal from employment. **3** (**the sack**) informal bed. ● **verb** informal **1** dismiss from employment. **2** (**sack out**) chiefly N. Amer. go to sleep or bed.
– PHRASES **hit the sack** informal go to bed.
– DERIVATIVES **sackable** adjective.
– ORIGIN Greek *sakkos* 'sack, sackcloth'.
sack² ● **verb** plunder and destroy (used chiefly in historical contexts). ● **noun** the sacking of a town or city.
– ORIGIN French *sac*, from *mettre à sac* 'put to sack', on the model of Italian *mettere a sacco*, which perhaps originally referred to filling a sack with plunder.
sack³ ● **noun** historical a dry white wine formerly imported into Britain from Spain and the Canaries.
– ORIGIN from French *vin sec* 'dry wine'.

Thesaurus

sable ● **adjective** *(poetic/literary)* BLACK, jet-black, pitch-black, ebony, raven, sooty, dusky, inky, coal-black.
sabotage ● **noun** VANDALISM, wrecking, destruction, impairment, incapacitation, damage; subversion, obstruction, disruption, spoiling, undermining; *Brit. informal* a spanner in the works.
● **verb** VANDALIZE, wreck, damage, destroy, cripple, impair, incapacitate; obstruct, disrupt, spoil, ruin, undermine, threaten, subvert.
sac ● **noun** BAG, pouch; *Medicine* blister, cyst; *Anatomy* bladder, bursa, saccule, vesicle.
saccharine ● **adjective** SENTIMENTAL, sickly, mawkish, cloying, sugary, sickening, nauseating; *informal* mushy, slushy, schmaltzy, weepy, gooey, drippy, cheesy, corny, toe-curling; *Brit. informal* soppy, twee; *N. Amer. informal* cornball, sappy.
sack¹ ● **noun** **1** *a sack of flour* BAG, pouch, pocket, pack. **2** *(informal) work hard or you'll get the sack* DISMISSAL, discharge, redundancy; *informal* the boot, the bullet, the axe, the heave-ho, one's marching orders, the elbow, the push; *Brit. informal* one's cards. **3** *(informal) she stayed in the sack* BED; *informal* kip; *Brit. informal* pit.
● **verb** *(informal) she was sacked for stealing* DISMISS, discharge, lay

sackbut /sakbut/ ● noun an early form of trombone used in Renaissance music.
– ORIGIN French *saquebute*, from obsolete *saqueboute* 'hook for pulling a man off a horse'.
sackcloth ● noun a coarse fabric woven from flax or hemp.
– PHRASES **sackcloth and ashes** an expression of extreme sorrow or remorse. [ORIGIN with allusion to the wearing of sackcloth and having ashes sprinkled on the head as a sign of penitence or mourning (Gospel of Matthew, chapter 11).]
sack dress ● noun a woman's loose unwaisted dress, originally fashionable in the 1950s.
sacking ● noun **1** an act of dismissing someone from employment. **2** coarse material for making sacks; sackcloth.
sack race ● noun a children's race in which each competitor stands in a sack and moves forward by jumping.
sacra plural of SACRUM.
sacral /saykrəl/ ● adjective **1** Anatomy relating to the sacrum. **2** relating to sacred rites or symbols.
sacrament /sakrəmənt/ ● noun **1** (in the Christian Church) a religious ceremony or ritual regarded as imparting divine grace, such as baptism and the Eucharist. **2** (also **the Blessed Sacrament** or **the Holy Sacrament**) (in Catholic use) the consecrated elements of the Eucharist, especially the bread. **3** a thing of sacred significance.
– ORIGIN Latin *sacramentum* 'solemn oath'.
sacramental ● adjective relating to or constituting a sacrament. ● noun (in the Christian Church) an observance that is comparable to but not itself considered to be a sacrament, such as the use of holy water or the sign of the cross.
– DERIVATIVES **sacramentalism** noun **sacramentalize** (also **sacramentalise**) verb **sacramentally** adverb.
sacré bleu /sakray blö/ ● exclamation a French expression of surprise, exasperation, or dismay.
– ORIGIN alteration of *sacré Dieu* 'holy God'.
sacred /saykrid/ ● adjective **1** connected with a deity and so deserving veneration; holy. **2** (of a text) embodying the doctrines of a religion. **3** religious rather than secular.
– DERIVATIVES **sacredly** adverb **sacredness** noun.
– ORIGIN from Latin *sacrare* 'consecrate', from *sacer* 'holy'.
sacred cow ● noun an idea, custom, or institution held to be above criticism (with reference to the respect of Hindus for the cow as a sacred animal).
sacrifice ● noun **1** the practice or an act of killing an animal or person or surrendering a possession as an offering to a deity. **2** an animal, person, or object offered in this way. **3** an act of giving up something one values for the sake of something that is of greater importance. ● verb offer or give up as a sacrifice.
– DERIVATIVES **sacrificial** adjective.
– ORIGIN Latin *sacrificium*, from *sacer* 'holy'.
sacrilege /sakrilij/ ● noun violation or misuse of something regarded as sacred or as having great value.
– DERIVATIVES **sacrilegious** adjective.
– ORIGIN Latin *sacrilegium*, from *sacrilegus* 'stealer of sacred things'.
sacristan /sakristən/ ● noun a person in charge of a sacristy.
sacristy /sakristi/ ● noun (pl. **sacristies**) a room in a church where a priest prepares for a service, and where vestments and other things used in worship are kept.
– ORIGIN Latin *sacristia*, from *sacer* 'sacred'.
sacroiliac /saykrōilliak/ ● adjective Anatomy **1** relating to the sacrum and the ilium. **2** denoting the rigid joint at the back of the pelvis between the sacrum and the ilium.
sacrosanct /sakrōsankt/ ● adjective regarded as too important or valuable to be interfered with.
– DERIVATIVES **sacrosanctity** noun.
– ORIGIN Latin *sacrosanctus*, from *sacro* 'by a sacred rite' + *sanctus* 'holy'.
sacrum /saykrəm/ ● noun (pl. **sacra** /saykrə/ or **sacrums**) Anatomy a triangular bone in the lower back formed from fused vertebrae and situated between the two hip bones of the pelvis.
– ORIGIN from Latin *os sacrum* 'sacred bone' (from the belief that the soul resides in it).
SAD ● abbreviation seasonal affective disorder.
sad ● adjective (**sadder**, **saddest**) **1** feeling sorrow; unhappy. **2** causing or characterized by sorrow or regret. **3** informal pathetically inadequate or unfashionable.
– DERIVATIVES **sadness** noun.
– ORIGIN Old English 'sated, weary', also 'weighty, dense'.
sadden ● verb make unhappy.
saddle ● noun **1** a seat with a raised ridge at the front and back, fastened on the back of a horse for riding. **2** a seat on a bicycle or motorcycle. **3** a low part of a hill or mountain ridge between two higher points or peaks. **4** the lower part of the back in a mammal or fowl. **5** a joint of meat consisting of the two loins. ● verb **1** put a saddle on (a horse). **2** (**be saddled with**) be burdened with (a responsibility or task).
– PHRASES **in the saddle 1** on horseback. **2** in a position of control or responsibility.
– ORIGIN Old English.
saddleback ● noun **1** a hill with a ridge along the top that dips in the middle. **2** a pig of a black breed with a white stripe across the back.
– DERIVATIVES **saddlebacked** adjective.
saddlebag ● noun a bag attached to a saddle.
saddle horse ● noun **1** a wooden stand on which saddles are cleaned or stored. **2** chiefly N. Amer. a horse kept for riding only.
saddler ● noun a person who makes, repairs, or deals in saddlery.
saddlery ● noun (pl. **saddleries**) **1** saddles, bridles, and other equipment for horses. **2** the making or repairing of such equipment. **3** a saddler's business or premises.
saddle soap ● noun soft soap containing neat's-foot oil, used

Thesaurus

off, make redundant, let go, throw out; *Military* cashier; *informal* fire, kick out, boot out, give someone the bullet, give someone the sack, give someone their marching orders, show someone the door, send packing; *Brit. informal* give someone their cards.
– PHRASES **hit the sack** (*informal*) GO TO BED, retire, go to sleep; *informal* turn in, hit the hay.
sack² ● verb *raiders sacked the town* RAVAGE, lay waste, devastate, raid, ransack, strip, plunder, despoil, pillage, loot, rob.
sackcloth ● noun HESSIAN, sacking, hopsack, burlap; *N. Amer.* gunny.
– PHRASES **wearing sackcloth and ashes** PENITENT, contrite, regretful, sorrowful, rueful, remorseful, apologetic, ashamed, guilt-ridden, chastened, shamefaced, self-reproachful, guilty.
sacred ● adjective **1** *the priest entered the sacred place* HOLY, hallowed, blessed, consecrated, sanctified, venerated, revered; *archaic* blest. **2** *sacred music* RELIGIOUS, spiritual, devotional, church, ecclesiastical. **3** *the hill is sacred to the tribe* SACROSANCT, inviolable, inviolate, invulnerable, untouchable, protected, defended, secure.
– RELATED TERMS hiero-.
– OPPOSITES secular, profane.
sacrifice ● noun **1** *the sacrifice of animals* RITUAL SLAUGHTER, offering, oblation, immolation. **2** *the calf was a sacrifice* (VOTIVE) OFFERING, burnt offering, gift, oblation. **3** *the sacrifice of sovereignty* SURRENDER, giving up, abandonment, renunciation, forfeiture, relinquishment, resignation, abdication.
● verb **1** *two goats were sacrificed* OFFER UP, immolate, slaughter. **2** *he sacrificed his principles* GIVE UP, abandon, surrender, forgo, renounce, forfeit, relinquish, resign, abdicate; betray.
sacrificial ● adjective VOTIVE, oblatory, oblational; expiatory, propitiatory.
sacrilege ● noun DESECRATION, profanity, profanation, blasphemy, impiety, irreligion, unholiness, irreverence, disrespect.
– OPPOSITES piety.
sacrilegious ● adjective PROFANE, blasphemous, impious, sinful, irreverent, irreligious, unholy, disrespectful.
sacrosanct ● adjective SACRED, hallowed, respected, inviolable, inviolate, unimpeachable, invulnerable, untouchable, inalienable; protected, defended, secure, safe.
sad ● adjective **1** *we felt sad when we left* UNHAPPY, sorrowful, dejected, depressed, downcast, miserable, down, despondent, despairing, disconsolate, desolate, wretched, glum, gloomy, doleful, dismal, melancholy, mournful, woebegone, forlorn, crestfallen, heartbroken, inconsolable; *informal* blue, down in the mouth, down in the dumps. **2** *they knew her sad story* TRAGIC, unhappy, unfortunate, awful, miserable, wretched, sorry, pitiful, pathetic, traumatic, heartbreaking, heart-rending, harrowing. **3** *a sad state of affairs* UNFORTUNATE, regrettable, sorry, deplorable, lamentable, pitiful, shameful, disgraceful.
– OPPOSITES happy, cheerful, fortunate.
sadden ● verb DEPRESS, dispirit, deject, dishearten, grieve, desolate, discourage, upset, get down, bring down, break someone's heart.

for cleaning leather.
saddle-sore ● adjective chafed by a saddle.
saddle stitch ● noun **1** a stitch of thread or a wire staple passed through the fold of a magazine or booklet. **2** (in needlework) a decorative stitch made with long stitches on the upper side of the cloth alternated with short stitches on the underside.
saddo ● noun (pl. **saddos**) Brit. informal a person perceived as pathetically inadequate.
Sadducee /sadyosee/ ● noun a member of an ancient Jewish sect that denied the resurrection of the dead and the existence of spirits, and that emphasized acceptance of the written Law rather than oral tradition.
– DERIVATIVES **Sadducean** /sadyooseeən/ adjective.
– ORIGIN Hebrew, 'descendant of Zadok' (high priest in the time of kings David and Solomon).
sadhu /saadoo/ ● noun Indian a holy man, sage, or ascetic.
– ORIGIN Sanskrit.
sadism ● noun the tendency to derive sexual gratification or general pleasure from inflicting pain, suffering, or humiliation on others.
– DERIVATIVES **sadist** noun **sadistic** adjective **sadistically** adverb.
– ORIGIN French *sadisme*, from the name of the French writer the Marquis de *Sade* (1740–1814).
sadly ● adverb **1** in a sad manner. **2** it is sad or regrettable that; regrettably.
sadomasochism /saydōmassəkiz'm/ ● noun psychological tendency or sexual practice characterized by a combination of sadism and masochism.
– DERIVATIVES **sadomasochist** noun **sadomasochistic** adjective.
sae ● abbreviation Brit. stamped addressed envelope.
safari ● noun (pl. **safaris**) (especially in East Africa) an expedition to observe or hunt animals in their natural habitat.
– ORIGIN Kiswahili, from Arabic, 'to travel'.
safari park ● noun an area of parkland where wild animals are kept in the open and may be observed by visitors driving through.
safari suit ● noun a lightweight suit consisting of a belted jacket with patch pockets and matching trousers, shorts, or skirt.
safe ● adjective **1** protected from danger or risk. **2** not causing or leading to harm or injury. **3** (of a place) affording security or protection. **4** often derogatory cautious and unenterprising: *a safe choice.* **5** (of an assertion, verdict, bet, etc.) based on good reasons or evidence and not likely to be proved wrong. **6** informal excellent. ● noun **1** a strong fireproof cabinet with a complex lock, used for the storage of valuables. **2** N. Amer. informal a condom.
– PHRASES **safe and sound** uninjured; with no harm done. **to be on the safe side** in order to have a margin of security against risks.
– DERIVATIVES **safely** adverb **safeness** noun.
– ORIGIN Old French *sauf*, from Latin *salvus* 'uninjured'.
safe conduct ● noun immunity from arrest or harm when passing through an area.
safe deposit (also **safety deposit**) ● noun a strongroom or safe in a bank or hotel.
safeguard ● noun a measure taken to protect or prevent something. ● verb protect with a safeguard.
safe house ● noun a house in a secret location, used by spies or criminals in hiding.
safekeeping ● noun preservation in a safe place.
safe period ● noun the time during and near a woman's menstrual period when conception is least likely.
safe seat ● noun a parliamentary seat that is likely to be retained with a large majority in an election.
safe sex ● noun sexual activity engaged in by people who have taken precautions to protect themselves against sexually transmitted diseases such as Aids.
safety ● noun (pl. **safeties**) **1** the condition of being safe. **2** (before another noun) denoting something designed to prevent injury or damage: *a safety barrier.* **3** US informal a condom.
– PHRASES **there's safety in numbers** proverb being in a group of people makes you feel more confident or secure about taking action.
safety belt ● noun a belt or strap securing a person to their seat in a vehicle or aircraft.
safety catch ● noun a device that prevents a gun being fired or a machine being operated accidentally.
safety curtain ● noun a fireproof curtain that can be lowered between the stage and the main part of a theatre to prevent the spread of fire.
safety deposit ● noun a safe deposit.
safety glass ● noun glass that has been toughened or laminated so that it is less likely to splinter when broken.
safety match ● noun a match that ignites only when struck on a specially prepared surface, such as that on the side of a matchbox.
safety net ● noun **1** a net placed to catch an acrobat in case of a fall. **2** a safeguard against adversity.
safety pin ● noun a pin with a point that is bent back to the head and is held in a guard when closed.
safety razor ● noun a razor with a guard to reduce the risk of cutting the skin.
safety valve ● noun **1** a valve that opens automatically to relieve excessive pressure. **2** a means of giving harmless vent to feelings of tension or stress.
safflower ● noun an orange-flowered thistle-like plant with seeds that yield an edible oil and petals that were formerly used to produce a red or yellow dye.
– ORIGIN Dutch *saffloer* or German *Saflor*, from Arabic, 'yellow'.
saffron ● noun an orange-yellow spice used for flavouring and colouring food, made from the dried stigmas of a crocus.
– ORIGIN Arabic.
sag[1] ● verb (**sagged**, **sagging**) **1** sink or bulge downwards gradually under weight or pressure or through weakness. **2** hang down loosely or unevenly. ● noun an instance of sagging.
– DERIVATIVES **saggy** adjective.
– ORIGIN probably related to Low German *sacken*, Dutch *zakken* 'subside'.
sag[2] ● noun variant spelling of SAAG.
saga ● noun **1** a long story of heroic achievement, especially a medieval prose narrative in Old Norse or Old Icelandic. **2** a long, involved account or series of incidents.
– ORIGIN Old Norse, 'narrative'.
sagacious /səgayshəss/ ● adjective having or showing good judgement.

S

Thesaurus

saddle ● verb *they were saddled with the children* BURDEN, encumber, lumber, hamper; land, charge; impose something on, thrust something on, fob something off on to.
sadism ● noun CALLOUSNESS, schadenfreude, barbarity, brutality, cruelty, cold-bloodedness, inhumanity, ruthlessness, heartlessness; perversion.
sadistic ● adjective CALLOUS, barbarous, vicious, brutal, cruel, fiendish, cold-blooded, inhuman, ruthless, heartless; perverted.
sadness ● noun UNHAPPINESS, sorrow, dejection, depression, misery, despondency, despair, desolation, wretchedness, gloom, gloominess, dolefulness, melancholy, mournfulness, woe, heartache, grief.
safe ● adjective **1** *the jewels are safe in the bank* SECURE, protected, shielded, sheltered, guarded, out of harm's way. **2** *the lost children are all safe* UNHARMED, unhurt, uninjured, unscathed, all right, well, in one piece, out of danger; *informal* OK. **3** *a safe place to hide* SECURE, sound, impregnable, unassailable, invulnerable. **4** *a safe driver* CAUTIOUS, circumspect, prudent, attentive; unadventurous, conservative, unenterprising. **5** *the drug is safe* HARMLESS, innocuous, benign, non-toxic, non-poisonous; wholesome.
– OPPOSITES insecure, dangerous, reckless, harmful.
● noun *I keep the ring in a safe* STRONGBOX, safety-deposit box, safe-deposit box, coffer, casket; strongroom, vault.
safeguard ● noun *a safeguard against crises* PROTECTION, defence, guard, screen, buffer, preventive, precaution, provision, security; surety, cover, insurance, indemnity.
● verb *the contract will safeguard 1000 jobs* PROTECT, preserve, conserve, save, secure, shield, guard, keep safe.
– OPPOSITES jeopardize.
safety ● noun **1** *the safety of the residents* WELFARE, well-being, protection, security. **2** *the safety of ferries* SECURITY, soundness, dependability, reliability. **3** *we reached the safety of the shore* SHELTER, sanctuary, refuge.
sag ● verb **1** *he sagged back in his chair* SINK, slump, loll, flop, crumple. **2** *the floors all sag* DIP, droop; bulge, bag. **3** *production has sagged* DECLINE, fall (off), drop, decrease, diminish, slump, plummet; *informal* nosedive.
saga ● noun **1** *Celtic tribal sagas* EPIC, chronicle, legend, folk tale,

– DERIVATIVES **sagaciously** adverb **sagacity** noun.
– ORIGIN from Latin *sagax* 'wise'.

sage[1] ● noun an aromatic Mediterranean plant with greyish-green leaves that are used as a herb in cookery.
– ORIGIN Old French *sauge*, from Latin *salvia* 'healing plant'.

sage[2] ● noun (especially in ancient history or legend) a man recognized for his wisdom. ● adjective wise; judicious.
– DERIVATIVES **sagely** adverb **sageness** noun.
– ORIGIN Old French, from Latin *sapere* 'be wise'.

sagebrush ● noun **1** a shrubby aromatic North American plant of the daisy family. **2** semi-arid country dominated by this plant.

sage green ● noun a greyish-green colour like that of sage leaves.

Sagittarius /sajitairiəss/ ● noun **1** Astronomy a large constellation (the Archer), said to represent a centaur carrying a bow and arrow. **2** Astrology the ninth sign of the zodiac, which the sun enters about 22 November.
– DERIVATIVES **Sagittarian** noun & adjective.
– ORIGIN Latin, 'archer'.

sago /saygō/ ● noun **1** edible starch obtained from a palm, dried and processed to produce a flour or granules. **2** (also **sago pudding**) a sweet dish made from sago and milk.
– ORIGIN Malay.

Saharan /səhaarən/ ● adjective relating to the Sahara Desert in North Africa.

Sahelian /səheeliən/ ● adjective relating to the Sahel, a semi-arid region bordering the southern Sahara Desert in North Africa.

sahib /saab, saahib/ ● noun Indian a polite title or form of address for a man.
– ORIGIN Arabic, 'friend, lord'.

said past and past participle of SAY. ● adjective denoting someone or something already mentioned: *the said agreement.*

sail ● noun **1** a piece of material extended on a mast to catch the wind and propel a boat or ship. **2** a wind-catching apparatus attached to the arm of a windmill. **3** a voyage or excursion in a sailing boat or ship. ● verb **1** travel in a sailing boat as a sport or for recreation. **2** travel in a ship or boat using sails or engine power. **3** begin a voyage. **4** travel by ship on or across (a sea) or on (a route). **5** navigate or control (a boat or ship). **6** move smoothly or confidently. **7** (**sail through**) informal succeed easily at.
– PHRASES **sail close to the wind 1** sail as nearly against the wind as possible. **2** behave or operate in a risky way. **under sail** with the sails hoisted.
– ORIGIN Old English.

sailboard ● noun a board with a mast and a sail, used in windsurfing.
– DERIVATIVES **sailboarder** noun **sailboarding** noun.

sailcloth ● noun **1** canvas or other strong fabric used for making sails. **2** a similar fabric used for making durable clothes.

sailfish ● noun an edible marine fish with a high sail-like dorsal fin.

sailing boat ● noun (N. Amer. **sailboat**) a boat propelled by sails.

sailing ship ● noun a ship propelled by sails.

sailor ● noun **1** a person who works as a member of the crew of a commercial or naval ship or boat. **2** a person who sails as a sport or for recreation. **3** (**a good/bad sailor**) a person who rarely (or often) becomes seasick.

sailor collar ● noun a collar cut deep and square at the back, tapering to a V-neck at the front, resembling the collar in the uniform traditionally worn by sailors.

sailor suit ● noun a suit of blue and white material resembling the traditional uniform of a sailor.

sailplane ● noun a glider designed for sustained flight.

sainfoin /saynfoyn/ ● noun a pink-flowered Asian plant, grown for fodder.
– ORIGIN obsolete French *saintfoin*, from Latin *sanum foenum* 'wholesome hay'.

saint /saynt, before a name usually sənt/ ● noun **1** a person who is acknowledged as holy or virtuous and regarded in Christian faith as being in heaven after death. **2** a person of exalted virtue who is canonized by the Church after death and who may be the object of veneration and prayers for intercession. **3** informal a very virtuous person. ● verb **1** formally recognize as a saint; canonize. **2** (**sainted**) worthy of being a saint; very virtuous.
– DERIVATIVES **sainthood** noun **saintliness** noun **saintly** adjective.
– ORIGIN Old French *seint*, from Latin *sanctus* 'holy'.

saintpaulia /səntpawliə/ ● noun an African violet.
– ORIGIN from the name of the German explorer Baron W. von *Saint Paul* (1860–1910), who discovered it.

saint's day ● noun (in the Christian Church) a day on which a saint is particularly commemorated.

saith /seth/ archaic third person singular present of SAY.

saithe /sayth/ ● noun a North Atlantic food fish of the cod family.
– ORIGIN Old Norse.

sake[1] /sayk/ ● noun **1** (**for the sake of**) for the purpose of or in the interest of. **2** (**for the sake of**) out of consideration for or in order to help. **3** (**for old times' sake**) in memory of former times. **4** (**for God's/goodness sake**) expressing impatience or desperation.
– ORIGIN Old English, 'contention, crime'.

sake[2] /saaki, sakkay/ ● noun a Japanese alcoholic drink made from fermented rice.
– ORIGIN Japanese.

Sakti ● noun variant spelling of SHAKTI.

salaam /səlaam/ ● noun a gesture of greeting or respect in Arabic-speaking and Muslim countries, consisting of a low bow of the head and body with the hand or fingers touching the forehead. ● verb make a salaam.
– ORIGIN from an Arabic phrase meaning 'peace be upon you'.

salable ● adjective variant spelling of SALEABLE.

salacious /səlayshəss/ ● adjective having or conveying undue or indecent interest in sexual matters.
– DERIVATIVES **salaciously** adverb **salaciousness** noun.
– ORIGIN from Latin *salax*, from *salire* 'to leap'.

salad ● noun a cold dish of raw vegetables.
– ORIGIN Old French *salade*, from Latin *sal* 'salt'.

salad cream ● noun Brit. a creamy dressing resembling mayon-

Thesaurus

romance, history, narrative, adventure, myth, fairy story. **2** *the saga of how they met* LONG STORY, rigmarole; chain of events; *informal* spiel.

sagacious ● adjective WISE, clever, intelligent, knowledgeable, sensible, sage; discerning, judicious, canny, perceptive, astute, shrewd, prudent, thoughtful, insightful, perspicacious; *informal* streetwise; *formal* sapient.
– OPPOSITES foolish.

sage ● noun *the Chinese sage Confucius* WISE MAN/WOMAN, learned person, philosopher, thinker, scholar, savant; authority, expert, guru.
● adjective *some very sage comments.* See SAGACIOUS.

sail ● noun *the ship's sails* canvas.
● verb **1** *we sailed across the Atlantic* VOYAGE, travel by water, steam, navigate, cruise. **2** *you can learn to sail here* YACHT, boat, go sailing; crew, helm. **3** *we sail tonight* SET SAIL, put to sea, leave port, hoist sail, weigh anchor, shove off. **4** *he is sailing the ship* STEER, pilot, navigate, con, helm, captain; *informal* skipper. **5** *clouds were sailing past* GLIDE, drift, float, flow, sweep, skim, coast, flit. **6** *a pencil sailed past his ear* WHIZZ, speed, streak, shoot, whip, buzz, zoom, flash; fly, wing, soar; *informal* zip.
– PHRASES **sail into** ATTACK, set upon, set about, fall on, assault, assail, lay into, pitch into, hit out at, thump, batter, pummel, beat, thrash, belabour; berate, abuse, round on; *informal* let someone have it; *Brit. informal* have a go at; *N. Amer. informal* light into. **sail through** *(informal)* SUCCEED EASILY AT, pass easily, romp through, walk through.

sailor ● noun SEAMAN, seafarer; boatman, yachtsman, yachtswoman; hand; *informal* (old) salt, sea dog, bluejacket; *Brit. informal* matelot; *Brit. informal, dated* Jack tar; *poetic/literary* mariner.

saintly ● adjective HOLY, godly, pious, religious, devout, spiritual, prayerful; virtuous, righteous, good, moral, innocent, sinless, guiltless, irreproachable, spotless, uncorrupted, pure, angelic.
– OPPOSITES ungodly.

sake ● noun **1** *this is simplified for the sake of clarity* PURPOSE, reason, aim, end, objective, object, goal, motive. **2** *she had to be brave for the her daughter's sake* BENEFIT, advantage, good, well-being, welfare, interest, profit.

salacious ● adjective **1** *salacious writing* PORNOGRAPHIC, obscene, indecent, crude, lewd, vulgar, dirty, filthy; erotic, titillating, arousing, suggestive, sexy, risqué, ribald, smutty, bawdy; X-rated; *informal* porn, porno, blue; *euphemistic* adult. **2** *salacious women* LUST-

naise.

salad days ● plural noun (**one's salad days**) **1** the period when one is young and inexperienced. **2** the peak or heyday of something.
– ORIGIN from Shakespeare's *Antony and Cleopatra* (I. v. 72).

salamander /saləmandər/ ● noun **1** a long-tailed amphibian resembling a newt, typically with bright markings. **2** a mythical lizard-like creature said to live in fire or to be able to withstand its effects. **3** a metal plate heated and placed over food to brown it.
– DERIVATIVES **salamandrine** /saləmandrin/ adjective.
– ORIGIN Greek *salamandra.*

salami /səlaami/ ● noun (pl. same or **salamis**) a type of highly seasoned preserved sausage, originally from Italy.
– ORIGIN Italian, from Latin *salare* 'to salt'.

sal ammoniac /sal əmōniak/ ● noun dated ammonium chloride, a white crystalline salt.
– ORIGIN Latin *sal ammoniacus* 'salt of Ammon', from Greek *ammōniakos* 'of Ammon', used as a name for the salt and gum obtained near the temple of Jupiter *Ammon* at Siwa in Egypt.

salaried ● adjective earning or offering a salary: *a salaried job.*

salary ● noun (pl. **salaries**) a fixed regular payment made by an employer to an employee, especially a professional or white-collar worker.
– ORIGIN Latin *salarium,* originally denoting a Roman soldier's allowance to buy salt, from *sal* 'salt'.

salchow /salkō/ ● noun a jump in figure skating from the backward inside edge of one skate to the backward outside edge of the other, with one or more full turns in the air.
– ORIGIN named after the Swedish skater Ulrich *Salchow* (1877–1949).

sale ● noun **1** the exchange of a commodity for money. **2** (**sales**) the activity or profession of selling. **3** a period in which goods are sold at reduced prices. **4** a public event at which goods are sold or auctioned.
– PHRASES **for** (or **on**) **sale** offered for purchase. **sale or return** Brit. an arrangement by which a retailer takes a quantity of goods with the right to return unsold items without payment.
– ORIGIN Old English.

saleable (also **salable**) ● adjective fit or able to be sold.
– DERIVATIVES **saleability** noun.

saleroom (also **salesroom**) ● noun chiefly Brit. a room in which auctions are held.

sales clerk ● noun N. Amer. a shop assistant.

salesman (or **saleswoman**) ● noun a person whose job involves selling or promoting commercial products.
– DERIVATIVES **salesmanship** noun.

salesperson ● noun a salesman or saleswoman.

salicylic acid /salisillik/ ● noun Chemistry a bitter compound present in certain plants, used as a fungicide and in the manufacture of aspirin and dyestuffs.
– DERIVATIVES **salicylate** /səlissilayt/ noun.
– ORIGIN from Latin *salix* 'willow' (salicylic acid was originally derived from willow bark).

salient /saylіənt/ ● adjective **1** most noticeable or important. **2** (of an angle) pointing outwards. ● noun **1** a piece of land or section of fortification that juts out to form an angle. **2** an outward bulge in a military line.
– DERIVATIVES **salience** noun **saliency** noun **saliently** adverb.
– ORIGIN from Latin *salire* 'to leap'.

saline /saylīn/ ● adjective **1** containing or impregnated with salt. **2** chiefly Medicine (of a solution) containing sodium chloride and/or other salts, especially in the same concentration as in the body. ● noun a saline solution.
– DERIVATIVES **salinity** noun **salinization** (also **salinisation**) noun.
– ORIGIN from Latin *sal* 'salt'.

Salish /saylish/ ● noun (pl. same) a member of a group of American Indian peoples of the north-western US and the west coast of Canada.
– DERIVATIVES **Salishan** adjective.
– ORIGIN a local name, literally 'Flatheads'.

saliva /səlīvə/ ● noun a watery liquid secreted into the mouth by glands, providing lubrication for chewing and swallowing, and aiding digestion.
– DERIVATIVES **salivary** /səlīvəri, salivəri/ adjective.
– ORIGIN Latin.

salivate /salivayt/ ● verb **1** produce saliva, especially in anticipation of food. **2** display great relish at the sight or prospect of something.
– DERIVATIVES **salivation** noun.
– ORIGIN Latin *salivare.*

sallow[1] ● adjective (**sallower**, **sallowest**) (of a person's face or complexion) of a yellowish or pale brown colour.
– DERIVATIVES **sallowish** adjective **sallowness** noun.
– ORIGIN Old English, 'dusky'.

sallow[2] ● noun chiefly Brit. a willow tree of a low-growing or shrubby kind.
– ORIGIN Old English, related to Latin *salix* 'willow'.

sally ● noun (pl. **sallies**) **1** a sudden charge out of a besieged place against the enemy. **2** a witty or lively retort. ● verb (**sallies, sallied**) set forth.
– ORIGIN French *saillie,* from Latin *salire* 'to leap'.

Sally Lunn ● noun a sweet, light teacake.
– ORIGIN said to be from the name of a woman selling such cakes in Bath *c.*1800.

salmagundi /salməgundi/ ● noun (pl. **salmagundis**) **1** a dish of chopped meat, anchovies, eggs, onions, and seasoning. **2** a miscellaneous collection or mixture.
– ORIGIN French *salmigondis.*

salmon /sammən/ ● noun (pl. same or **salmons**) a large fish with edible pink flesh, that matures in the sea and migrates to freshwater streams to spawn.
– DERIVATIVES **salmony** adjective.
– ORIGIN Latin *salmo.*

salmonella /salmənellə/ ● noun (pl. **salmonellae** /salmənellee/) **1** a bacterium that occurs mainly in the gut and can cause food poisoning. **2** food poisoning caused by this.
– DERIVATIVES **salmonellosis** /salmənelōsiss/ noun.
– ORIGIN named after the American veterinary surgeon Daniel E. *Salmon* (1850–1914).

salmon pink ● noun a pale orange-pink colour like that of the flesh of salmon.

salmon trout ● noun a sea trout or other fish resembling a small salmon.

salon ● noun **1** an establishment where a hairdresser, beautician, or couturier conducts their trade. **2** a reception room in a large house. **3** chiefly historical a regular gathering of writers, artists, etc., held in a fashionable household. **4** (**Salon**) an annual exhibition of the work of living artists held by the Royal Academy of Painting and Sculpture in Paris (originally in the Salon d'Apollon in the Louvre).
– ORIGIN French, from Italian *salone* 'large hall'.

Thesaurus

FUL, lecherous, licentious, lascivious, libidinous, prurient, lewd; debauched, wanton, loose, fast, impure, unchaste, degenerate, sinful, depraved, promiscuous; *informal* randy, horny, raunchy, pervy.

salary ● noun PAY, wages, earnings, payment, remuneration, fee(s), stipend, income; *formal* emolument.

sale ● noun **1** *the sale of firearms* SELLING, vending; dealing, trading. **2** *they make a sale every minute* DEAL, transaction, bargain.
– OPPOSITES purchase.
– PHRASES **for sale** ON THE MARKET, on sale, on offer, available, purchasable, obtainable.

salesperson ● noun SALES ASSISTANT, salesman, saleswoman, shop assistant, seller, agent; shopkeeper, trader, merchant, dealer, pedlar, hawker; *N. Amer.* clerk; *informal* counter-jumper, rep.

salient ● adjective IMPORTANT, main, principal, major, chief, primary; notable, noteworthy, outstanding, conspicuous, striking, noticeable, obvious, remarkable, prominent, predominant, dominant; key, crucial, vital, essential, pivotal, prime, central, paramount.
– OPPOSITES minor.

saliva ● noun SPIT, spittle, dribble, drool, slaver, slobber, sputum.

sallow ● adjective YELLOWISH, jaundiced, pallid, wan, pale, anaemic, bloodless, pasty; unhealthy, sickly, washed out, peaky; *informal* like death warmed up.

sally ● noun **1** *the garrison made a sally against us* SORTIE, charge, foray, thrust, drive, offensive, attack, assault, raid, incursion, invasion, onset, onslaught. **2** *a fruitless sally into Wales* EXPEDITION, excursion, trip, outing, jaunt, visit. **3** *he was delighted with his sally* WITTICISM, smart remark, quip, barb, pleasantry; joke, pun, jest, bon mot; retort, riposte, counter, rejoinder; *informal* gag, wisecrack, comeback.

salon ● noun **1** *a hairdressing salon* SHOP, parlour, establishment, premises; boutique, store. **2** *the chateau's mirrored salon* RECEP-

S

saloon ● noun **1** a public room or building used for a specified purpose. **2** Brit. another term for LOUNGE BAR. **3** a large public room for use as a lounge on a ship. **4** N. Amer. historical or humorous a place where alcoholic drinks may be bought and drunk. **5** Brit. a car having a closed body and separate boot. **6** (also **saloon car**) Brit. a luxurious railway carriage used as a lounge or restaurant.
– ORIGIN originally in the sense 'drawing room': from French *salon*, from Italian *salone* 'large hall'.

saloon deck ● noun a deck on the same level as a ship's saloon, for the use of passengers.

salopettes /salәpets/ ● plural noun padded or fleecy trousers with a high waist and shoulder straps, worn for skiing.
– ORIGIN French *salopette*.

salsa /salsә/ ● noun **1** a type of Latin American dance music incorporating elements of jazz and rock. **2** a dance performed to this music. **3** (especially in Latin American cookery) a spicy tomato sauce.
– ORIGIN Spanish, 'sauce'.

salsa verde /salsә verdi/ ● noun **1** an Italian sauce made with olive oil, garlic, capers, anchovies, vinegar or lemon juice, and parsley. **2** a Mexican sauce of chopped onion, garlic, coriander, parsley, and hot peppers.
– ORIGIN Spanish, 'green sauce'.

salsify /salsifi/ ● noun a plant of the daisy family, with a long edible root like that of a parsnip.
– ORIGIN French *salsifis*.

SALT /sawlt/ ● abbreviation Strategic Arms Limitation Talks.

salt ● noun **1** (also **common salt**) sodium chloride, a white crystalline substance which gives seawater its characteristic taste and is used for seasoning or preserving food. **2** Chemistry any compound formed by the reaction of an acid with a base, with the hydrogen of the acid replaced by a metal or equivalent group. **3** (**old salt**) informal an experienced sailor. ● adjective **1** impregnated or treated with salt. **2** (of a plant) growing on the coast or in salt marshes. ● verb **1** season or preserve with salt. **2** sprinkle (a road or path) with salt in order to melt snow or ice. **3** (**salt away**) informal put by (money) secretly. **4** make piquant or more interesting.
– PHRASES **rub salt into the wound** make a painful experience even more painful. **the salt of the earth** a person of great goodness and strength of character. [ORIGIN with reference to the Gospel of Matthew, chapter 5.] **sit below the salt** be of lower social standing. [ORIGIN from the former custom of placing a salt cellar in the middle of a dining table with the host at one end.] **take with a pinch** (or **grain**) **of salt** regard as exaggerated. **worth one's salt** good or competent at one's job or allotted task.
– DERIVATIVES **saltless** adjective **saltness** noun.
– ORIGIN Old English.

saltbush ● noun a salt-tolerant plant, sometimes planted on saline soils.

salt cellar ● noun a dish or container for storing salt.
– ORIGIN *cellar* is from Old French *salier* 'salt-box'.

salt flats ● plural noun areas of flat land covered with a layer of salt.

salt glaze ● noun a hard glaze with a pitted surface, produced on stoneware by adding salt to the kiln during firing.

saltimbocca /saltimbokkә/ ● noun a dish consisting of rolled pieces of veal or poultry cooked with herbs, bacon, and other flavourings.
– ORIGIN Italian, 'leap into the mouth'.

salting ● noun (usu. **saltings**) Brit. an area of coastal land that is regularly covered by the tide.

saltire /sawltīr/ ● noun Heraldry a diagonal cross as a heraldic ordinary.
– ORIGIN Old French *saultoir* 'stirrup cord, stile, saltire', from Latin *saltare* 'to dance'.

salt lick ● noun **1** a place where animals go to lick salt from the ground. **2** a block of salt provided for animals to lick.

salt marsh ● noun an area of coastal grassland that is regularly flooded by seawater.

salt pan ● noun a shallow container or depression in the ground in which salt water evaporates to leave a deposit of salt.

saltpetre /sawltpeetәr/ (US **saltpeter**) ● noun potassium nitrate or (**Chile saltpetre**) sodium nitrate.
– ORIGIN Latin *salpetra*, probably representing *sal petrae* 'salt of rock'.

saltwater ● adjective of or found in salt water; living in the sea.

salty ● adjective (**saltier**, **saltiest**) **1** tasting of, containing, or preserved with salt. **2** (of language or humour) down-to-earth; coarse.
– DERIVATIVES **saltily** adverb **saltiness** noun.

salubrious /sәlo͞obriәss/ ● adjective **1** health-giving; healthy. **2** (of a place) pleasant; not dirty or run-down.
– DERIVATIVES **salubriously** adverb **salubriousness** noun **salubrity** noun.
– ORIGIN Latin *salubris*, from *salus* 'health'.

saluki /sәlo͞oki/ ● noun (pl. **salukis**) a tall, swift, slender breed of dog with a silky coat and large drooping ears.
– ORIGIN Arabic.

salutary /salyootәri/ ● adjective **1** (of something disadvantageous) beneficial in providing an opportunity for learning from experience. **2** archaic health-giving.
– ORIGIN Latin *salutaris*, from *salus* 'health'.

salutation ● noun a greeting.
– DERIVATIVES **salutational** adjective **salutatory** adjective.

salute ● noun **1** a gesture of respect and recognition. **2** a raising of a hand to the head, made as a formal gesture of respect by a member of a military or similar force. **3** the discharge of a gun or guns as a formal or ceremonial sign of respect or celebration. ● verb **1** make a formal salute to. **2** greet. **3** show or express admiration and respect for.
– DERIVATIVES **saluter** noun.
– ORIGIN from Latin *salutare* 'greet, pay one's respects to', from *salus* 'health, welfare, greeting'.

Salvadorean /salvәdoriәn/ ● noun a person from El Salvador, a country in Central America. ● adjective relating to El Salvador.

salvage ● verb **1** rescue (a ship or its cargo) from loss at sea. **2** retrieve or preserve from loss or destruction. ● noun **1** the action of salvaging. **2** cargo salvaged. **3** Law payment made or due to a person who has salvaged a ship or its cargo.
– DERIVATIVES **salvageable** adjective **salvager** noun.
– ORIGIN Latin *salvagium*, from *salvare* 'to save'.

S

Thesaurus

TION ROOM, drawing room, sitting room, living room, lounge; *dated* parlour.

salt ● noun **1** *the potatoes need salt* SODIUM CHLORIDE. **2** *(poetic/literary) danger is the salt of pleasure* ZEST, spice, piquancy, bite, edge; vitality, spirit, sparkle; *informal* zing, punch.
– RELATED TERMS saline.
● adjective *salt water* SALTY, salted, saline, briny, brackish.
– PHRASES **salt something away** *(informal)* SAVE, put aside, put by, set aside, reserve, keep, store, stockpile, hoard, stow away; *informal* squirrel away, stash away. **with a pinch of salt** WITH RESERVATIONS, with misgivings, sceptically, cynically, doubtfully, doubtingly, suspiciously, quizzically, incredulously.

salty ● adjective **1** *salty water* SALT, salted, saline, briny, brackish. **2** *a salty sense of humour* EARTHY, colourful, spicy, racy, naughty, vulgar, rude; piquant, biting.

salubrious ● adjective **1** *I found the climate salubrious* HEALTHY, health-giving, healthful, beneficial, wholesome; *archaic* salutary. **2** *a salubrious area of London* PLEASANT, agreeable, nice, select, high-class; *Brit.* upmarket; *informal* posh, swanky, classy; *Brit. informal* swish; *N. Amer. informal* swank.
– OPPOSITES unhealthy, unpleasant.

salutary ● adjective **1** *a salutary lesson on the fragility of nature* BENEFICIAL, advantageous, good, profitable, productive, helpful, useful, valuable, worthwhile; timely. **2** *(archaic) the salutary Atlantic air* HEALTHY, health-giving, healthful, salubrious, beneficial.
– OPPOSITES unwelcome, unhealthy.

salutation ● noun GREETING, salute, address, welcome.

salute ● noun **1** *he gave the Brigadier a salute* GREETING, salutation, gesture of respect, obeisance, acknowledgement, welcome, address. **2** *a salute to British courage* TRIBUTE, testimonial, homage, toast, honour, eulogy; celebration of, acknowledgement of.
● verb **1** *he saluted the ambassadors* GREET, address, hail, welcome, acknowledge, toast; make obeisance to. **2** *we salute a great photographer* PAY TRIBUTE TO, pay homage to, honour, celebrate, acknowledge, take one's hat off to.

salvage ● verb **1** *an attempt to salvage the vessel* RESCUE, save, recover, retrieve, raise, reclaim. **2** *he salvaged a precious point for his club* RETAIN, preserve, conserve; regain, recoup, redeem,

salvage yard • noun a place where disused machinery, vehicles, etc. are broken up and parts salvaged.

salvation • noun **1** Theology deliverance from sin and its consequences, believed by Christians to be brought about by faith in Christ. **2** preservation or deliverance from harm, ruin, or loss. **3** (**one's salvation**) a source or means of being saved in this way.
– ORIGIN Latin, from *salvare* 'to save'.

salvationist • noun (**Salvationist**) a member of the Salvation Army, a Christian evangelical organization. • adjective **1** relating to salvation. **2** (**Salvationist**) relating to the Salvation Army.
– DERIVATIVES **salvationism** noun.

salve • noun **1** an ointment used to soothe or promote healing of the skin. **2** something that soothes wounded feelings or an uneasy conscience. • verb alleviate (guilty feelings): *charity salves our conscience.*
– ORIGIN Old English.

salver • noun a tray, typically one made of silver and used in formal circumstances.
– ORIGIN French *salve* 'tray for presenting food to the king', from Spanish *salva* 'sampling of food'.

salvia • noun a plant of a large group that includes sage, especially one cultivated for its spikes of bright flowers.
– ORIGIN Latin, 'sage'.

salvo • noun (pl. **salvos** or **salvoes**) **1** a simultaneous discharge of artillery or other guns in a battle. **2** a sudden vigorous series of aggressive statements or acts.
– ORIGIN Italian *salva* 'salutation'.

sal volatile /sal vəlattili/ • noun a scented solution of ammonium carbonate in alcohol, used as smelling salts.
– ORIGIN Latin, 'volatile salt'.

salwar /sulwaar/ (also **shalwar**) • noun a pair of light, loose trousers tapering to a tight fit around the ankles, worn by women from the Indian subcontinent, typically with a kameez.
– ORIGIN Persian and Urdu.

SAM • abbreviation surface-to-air missile.

Samaritan • noun **1** a member of a people inhabiting Samaria, an ancient city and region of Palestine, in biblical times. **2** (**good Samaritan**) a charitable or helpful person. [ORIGIN with biblical reference to the story of the Samaritan who helped a man in need whom others had passed by, in the Gospel of Luke.] **3** (**the Samaritans**) (in the UK) an organization which counsels those in distress, mainly through a telephone service.
– DERIVATIVES **Samaritanism** noun.

samarium /səmairiəm/ • noun a hard silvery-white metallic chemical element of the lanthanide series.
– ORIGIN from *samarskite*, a mineral in which its spectrum was first observed (named after a 19th-century Russian official called *Samarsky*).

samba /sambə/ • noun a Brazilian dance of African origin. • verb (**sambas, sambaed** /sambəd/ or **samba'd, sambaing** /sambə(r)ing/) dance the samba.
– ORIGIN Portuguese, of African origin.

sambal /sambal/ • noun (in oriental cookery) relish made with vegetables or fruit and spices.
– ORIGIN Malay.

Sam Browne • noun a leather belt with a supporting strap that passes over the right shoulder, worn by army and police officers.
– ORIGIN named after the British military commander Sir *Sam*uel J. *Brown(e)* (1824–1901).

sambuca /sambo͞okə/ • noun an Italian aniseed-flavoured liqueur.
– ORIGIN Italian, from Latin *sambucus* 'elder tree'.

same • adjective **1** (**the same**) exactly alike; not different or changed. **2** (**this/that same**) referring to a person or thing just mentioned. • pronoun **1** (**the same**) the same thing as previously mentioned. **2** (**the same**) identical people or things. **3** the person or thing just mentioned. • adverb in the same way.
– PHRASES **all** (or **just**) **the same 1** nevertheless. **2** anyway. **at the same time** nevertheless.
– DERIVATIVES **sameness** noun.
– ORIGIN Old Norse.

samey • adjective (**samier, samiest**) Brit. informal lacking in variety.

Samhain /sown, sowin/ • noun a festival held by the ancient Celts on 1 November, marking the beginning of winter and the Celtic new year.
– ORIGIN Old Irish *samain*.

Sami /saami/ • plural noun the Lapps of northern Scandinavia.
– USAGE **Sami** is the term by which the Lapps themselves prefer to be known.
– ORIGIN Lappish.

samite /sammīt, saymīt/ • noun a rich silk fabric interwoven with gold and silver threads, made in the Middle Ages.
– ORIGIN Old French *samit*, from Greek *hexa-* 'six' + *mitos* 'thread'.

samizdat /sammizdat/ • noun (especially in the former Soviet Union) the clandestine copying and distribution of literature banned by the state.
– ORIGIN Russian, 'self-publishing house'.

Samoan • noun **1** a person from Samoa. **2** the Polynesian language of Samoa. • adjective relating to Samoa.

samosa /səmōsə/ • noun a triangular fried pastry containing spiced vegetables or meat.
– ORIGIN Persian and Urdu.

samovar /samməvaar/ • noun a highly decorated Russian tea urn.
– ORIGIN Russian, 'self-boiler'.

Samoyed /samməyed/ • noun **1** a member of a group of mainly nomadic peoples of northern Siberia. **2** a dog of a white Arctic breed.
– ORIGIN Russian *samoed*.

sampan /sampan/ • noun a small boat propelled with an oar at the stern, used in the Far East.
– ORIGIN from Chinese words meaning 'three' and 'board'.

samphire /samfīr/ • noun a fleshy-leaved plant which grows on rocks near the sea.
– ORIGIN from French *herbe de Saint Pierre* 'St Peter's herb'.

sample • noun **1** a small part or quantity intended to show what the whole is like. **2** Statistics a portion of a population, serving as a basis for estimates of the attributes of the whole population. **3** a specimen taken for scientific testing or analysis. **4** a sound created by sampling. • verb **1** take a sample or samples of. **2** get a representative experience of. **3** Electronics ascertain the momentary value of (an analogue signal) many times a second so as to convert the signal to digital form.
– ORIGIN Old French *essample* 'example'.

Thesaurus

snatch.
• noun *the salvage is taking place off the coast* RESCUE, recovery, reclamation.

salvation • noun **1** *salvation by way of repentance* REDEMPTION, deliverance, reclamation. **2** *that conviction was her salvation* LIFELINE, preservation; means of escape, help.
– OPPOSITES damnation.

salve • noun *lip salve* OINTMENT, cream, balm, unguent, emollient; embrocation, liniment; archaic unction.
• verb *she did it to salve her conscience* SOOTHE, assuage, ease, allay, lighten, alleviate, comfort, mollify.

salver • noun PLATTER, plate, dish, paten, tray; archaic charger.

same • adjective **1** *we stayed at the same hotel* IDENTICAL, selfsame, very same, one and the same. **2** *they had the same symptoms* MATCHING, identical, alike, duplicate, carbon-copy, twin; indistinguishable, interchangeable, corresponding, equivalent, parallel, like, comparable, similar, congruent, concordant, consonant. **3** *it happened that same month* SELFSAME; aforesaid, aforementioned. **4** *they provide the same menu worldwide* UNCHANGING, unvarying, unvaried, invariable, consistent, uniform, regular.
– RELATED TERMS homo-.
– OPPOSITES another, different, dissimilar, varying.
• noun *Louise said the same* THE SAME THING, the aforementioned, the aforesaid, the above-mentioned.
– PHRASES **all the same 1** *I was frightened all the same* IN SPITE OF EVERYTHING, despite that, nevertheless, nonetheless, even so, however, but, still, yet, though, be that as it may, just the same, at the same time, in any event, notwithstanding, regardless, anyway, anyhow; informal still and all. **2** *it's all the same to me* IMMATERIAL, of no importance, of no consequence, inconsequential, unimportant, of little account, irrelevant, insignificant, trivial, petty.

sample • noun **1** *a sample of the fabric* SPECIMEN, example, bit, snippet, swatch, exemplification, representative piece; prototype, test piece, dummy, pilot, trial, taste, taster, tester. **2** *a sample of*

sampler ● noun **1** a piece of embroidery worked in various stitches as a specimen of skill. **2** a representative collection or example of something. **3** a device for sampling music and sound.

sampling ● noun **1** the taking of a sample or samples. **2** Statistics a sample. **3** the technique of digitally encoding music or sound and reusing it as part of a composition or recording.

samurai /samyoori/ ● noun (pl. same) historical a member of a powerful military caste in feudal Japan.
– ORIGIN Japanese.

San /saan/ ● noun (pl. same) **1** a member of the Bushmen (a number of aboriginal peoples) of southern Africa. **2** the languages spoken by these peoples.
– ORIGIN Nama, 'aboriginals, settlers'.

sanatorium /sannətoriəm/ ● noun (pl. **sanatoriums** or **sanatoria** /sannətoriə/) **1** an establishment for the care of convalescent or chronically ill people. **2** Brit. a place in a boarding school for children who are unwell.
– ORIGIN Latin, from *sanare* 'heal'.

Sancerre /sonsair/ ● noun a light white wine produced in Sancerre, in the upper Loire region of France.

sanctify /sangktifī/ ● verb (**sanctifies**, **sanctified**) **1** make or declare holy; consecrate. **2** make legitimate or binding by religious sanction. **3** free from sin. **4** give the appearance of being right or good.
– DERIVATIVES **sanctification** noun **sanctifier** noun.
– ORIGIN Latin *sanctificare*, from *sanctus* 'holy'.

sanctimonious /sangktimōniəss/ ● adjective derogatory making a show of being morally superior.
– DERIVATIVES **sanctimoniously** adverb **sanctimoniousness** noun **sanctimony** /sangktiməni/ noun.
– ORIGIN from Latin *sanctimonia* 'sanctity'.

sanction ● noun **1** a threatened penalty for disobeying a law or rule. **2** (**sanctions**) measures taken by a state to coerce another to conform to an international agreement or norms of conduct. **3** official permission or approval. ● verb **1** give official permission for. **2** impose a sanction or penalty on.
– DERIVATIVES **sanctionable** adjective.
– ORIGIN Latin, from *sancire* 'ratify'.

sanctity ● noun (pl. **sanctities**) **1** holiness; saintliness. **2** ultimate importance and inviolability: *the sanctity of human life.*
– ORIGIN Old French *saincteé*, from Latin *sanctus* 'holy'.

sanctuary ● noun (pl. **sanctuaries**) **1** a place of refuge or safety. **2** a nature reserve. **3** a place where injured or unwanted animals are cared for. **4** a holy place. **5** the part of the chancel of a church containing the high altar.
– ORIGIN originally denoting a church or sacred place in which, by law, a fugitive was immune from arrest: from Latin *sanctuarium*, from *sanctus* 'holy'.

sanctum /sangktəm/ ● noun (pl. **sanctums**) **1** a sacred place, especially a shrine in a temple or church. **2** a private place.
– ORIGIN Latin, from *sanctus* 'holy'.

Sanctus /sangktəss/ ● noun Christian Church a hymn beginning *Sanctus, sanctus, sanctus* (Holy, holy, holy) forming a set part of the Mass.
– ORIGIN Latin.

sand ● noun **1** a substance consisting of fine particles of eroded rocks, forming a major constituent of beaches, river beds, the seabed, and deserts. **2** (**sands**) an expanse of sand. ● verb **1** smooth with sandpaper or a sander. **2** sprinkle or overlay with sand.
– PHRASES **the sands (of time) are running out** the allotted time is nearly at an end. [ORIGIN with reference to the sand of an hourglass.]
– ORIGIN Old English.

sandal ● noun a shoe with an openwork upper or straps attaching the sole to the foot.
– DERIVATIVES **sandalled** (US **sandaled**) adjective.
– ORIGIN Greek *sandalon* 'wooden shoe'.

sandalwood ● noun the fragrant wood of an Indian or SE Asian tree.
– ORIGIN *sandal* from Latin *sandalum*, from Sanskrit.

sandbag ● noun a bag of sand, used for defensive purposes or as ballast in a boat. ● verb (**sandbagged**, **sandbagging**) **1** protect or reinforce with sandbags. **2** hit with or as if with a blow from a sandbag. **3** N. Amer. bully.
– DERIVATIVES **sandbagger** noun.

sandbank ● noun a deposit of sand forming a shallow area in the sea or a river.

sandbar ● noun a long, narrow sandbank.

sandblast ● verb roughen or clean with a jet of sand driven by compressed air or steam.
– DERIVATIVES **sandblaster** noun.

sandboy ● noun (in phrase **as happy as a sandboy**) extremely happy or carefree.
– ORIGIN probably originally denoting a boy going around selling sand.

sandcastle ● noun a model of a castle built out of sand.

sander ● noun a power tool used for smoothing a surface with sandpaper or other abrasive material.

sanderling /sandərling/ ● noun a small migratory sandpiper, typically seen running after receding waves on the beach.
– ORIGIN of unknown origin.

sandfly ● noun **1** a small hairy biting fly of tropical and subtropical regions, which transmits a number of diseases. **2** Austral./NZ another term for BLACKFLY (in sense 2).

sandglass ● noun an hourglass.

Sandinista /sandəneestə/ ● noun a member of a left-wing Nicaraguan political organization, in power from 1979 until 1990.
– ORIGIN named after a similar organization founded by the nationalist leader Augusto César *Sandino* (1893–1934).

sandlot ● noun N. Amer. **1** a piece of unoccupied land used by children for games. **2** (before another noun) denoting sport played by amateurs.

sandman ● noun (**the sandman**) a fictional man supposed to make children sleep by sprinkling sand in their eyes.

sand martin ● noun a small gregarious swallow with dark brown and white plumage, excavating nest holes in sandy

Thesaurus

S

10,000 people nationwide CROSS SECTION, variety, sampling, test.
● verb *we sampled the culinary offerings* TRY (OUT), taste, test, put to the test, experiment with; appraise, evaluate; *informal* check out.
● adjective **1** *the sample group is small* REPRESENTATIVE, illustrative, selected, specimen, test, trial, typical. **2** *a sample copy can be obtained* SPECIMEN, test, trial, pilot, dummy.

sanatorium ● noun INFIRMARY, clinic, hospital, medical centre, hospice; sickbay, sickroom; *N. Amer.* sanitarium; *informal* san.

sanctify ● verb **1** *he came to sanctify the site* CONSECRATE, bless, make holy, hallow, make sacred, dedicate to God. **2** *they sanctified themselves* PURIFY, cleanse, free from sin, absolve, unburden, redeem; *rare* lustrate. **3** *we must not sanctify this outrage* APPROVE, sanction, condone, vindicate, endorse, support, back, permit, allow, authorize, legitimize, legitimatize.

sanctimonious ● adjective SELF-RIGHTEOUS, holier-than-thou, pious, pietistic, churchy, moralizing, smug, superior, priggish, hypocritical, insincere; *informal* goody-goody, pi.

sanction ● noun **1** *trade sanctions* PENALTY, punishment, deterrent; punitive action, discipline, penalization, restriction; embargo, ban, prohibition, boycott. **2** *the scheme has the sanction of the court* AUTHORIZATION, consent, leave, permission, authority, warrant, licence, dispensation, assent, acquiescence, agreement, approval, approbation, endorsement, accreditation, ratification, validation, blessing, imprimatur; *informal* the go-ahead, the thumbs up, the OK, the green light.
– OPPOSITES reward, prohibition.
● verb **1** *the rally was sanctioned by the government* AUTHORIZE, permit, allow, warrant, accredit, license, endorse, approve, accept, back, support; *informal* OK. **2** *the penalties available to sanction crime* PUNISH, discipline someone for.
– OPPOSITES prohibit.

sanctity ● noun **1** *the sanctity of St Francis* HOLINESS, godliness, blessedness, saintliness, spirituality, piety, piousness, devoutness, righteousness, goodness, virtue, purity; *formal* sanctitude. **2** *the sanctity of the family meal* SACROSANCTITY, inviolability; importance, paramountcy.

sanctuary ● noun **1** *the sanctuary at Delphi* HOLY PLACE, temple; shrine, altar; sanctum, sacrarium, holy of holies, sanctum sanctorum. **2** *the island is our sanctuary* REFUGE, haven, harbour, port in a storm, oasis, shelter, retreat, bolt-hole, hideaway, fastness. **3** *he was given sanctuary in the embassy* SAFETY, protection, shelter, immunity, asylum. **4** *a bird sanctuary* RESERVE, park, reservation, preserve.

sanctum ● noun **1** *the sanctum in the temple* HOLY PLACE, shrine, sanctuary, holy of holies, sanctum sanctorum. **2** *a private sanctum for the bar's regulars* REFUGE, retreat, bolt-hole, hideout, hide-

banks near water.

sandpaper ● noun paper with sand or another abrasive stuck to it, used for smoothing wooden or other surfaces. ● verb smooth with sandpaper.
– DERIVATIVES **sandpapery** adjective.

sandpiper ● noun a wading bird with a long bill and long legs, frequenting coastal areas.

sandpit ● noun **1** Brit. a shallow box or hollow, partly filled with sand for children to play in. **2** a quarry from which sand is excavated.

sandshoe ● noun chiefly Scottish & Austral./NZ a plimsoll.

sandstone ● noun sedimentary rock consisting of sand or quartz grains cemented together, typically red, yellow, or brown in colour.

sandstorm ● noun a strong wind in a desert carrying clouds of sand.

sandwich ● noun **1** an item of food consisting of two pieces of bread with a filling between them. **2** Brit. a sponge cake of two or more layers with jam or cream between them. ● verb **1** (**sandwich between**) insert between (two people or things). **2** (**sandwich together**) squeeze (two things) together.
– ORIGIN named after the 4th Earl of *Sandwich* (1718–92), an English nobleman said to have eaten food in this form.

sandwich board ● noun a pair of advertisement boards connected by straps by which they are hung over a person's shoulders.

sandwich course ● noun Brit. a training course with alternate periods of formal instruction and practical experience.

sandy ● adjective (**sandier, sandiest**) **1** covered in or consisting of sand. **2** light yellowish brown.
– DERIVATIVES **sandiness** noun.

sane ● adjective **1** of sound mind; not mad. **2** reasonable; sensible.
– DERIVATIVES **sanely** adverb **saneness** noun.
– ORIGIN Latin *sanus* 'healthy'.

sang past of SING.

sangfroid /sONfrwaa/ ● noun composure or coolness under trying circumstances.
– ORIGIN French, 'cold blood'.

Sangiovese /sanjiəvayzi/ ● noun a variety of black wine grape used to make Chianti and other Italian red wines.
– ORIGIN Italian.

sangria /sanggreeə/ ● noun a Spanish drink of red wine, lemonade, fruit, and spices.
– ORIGIN Spanish, 'bleeding'.

sanguinary /sanggwinəri/ ● adjective chiefly archaic involving or causing much bloodshed.

sanguine /sanggwin/ ● adjective **1** cheerfully optimistic. **2** (in medieval medicine) having a predominance of blood among the bodily humours, supposedly marked by a ruddy complexion and an optimistic disposition.
– ORIGIN Old French, 'blood red', from Latin *sanguis* 'blood'.

Sanhedrin /sannidrin/ (also **Sanhedrim** /sannidrim/) ● noun the highest court of justice and the supreme council in ancient Jerusalem.
– ORIGIN Hebrew, from Greek *sunedrion* 'council'.

sanitarium /sannitairiəm/ ● noun (pl. **sanitariums** or **sanitaria** /sannitairiə/) North American term for SANATORIUM.

sanitary ● adjective **1** relating to sanitation. **2** hygienic.
– ORIGIN from Latin *sanitas* 'health'.

sanitary protection ● noun sanitary towels and tampons collectively.

sanitary towel (N. Amer. **sanitary napkin**) ● noun a pad worn by women to absorb menstrual blood.

sanitaryware ● noun toilet bowls, cisterns, and other fittings.

sanitation ● noun arrangements to protect public health, especially the provision of clean drinking water and the disposal of sewage.

sanitize (also **sanitise**) ● verb **1** make hygienic. **2** derogatory make more acceptable.
– DERIVATIVES **sanitizer** noun.

sanity ● noun **1** the condition of being sane. **2** reasonable and rational behaviour.

sank past of SINK[1].

sans /sanz/ ● preposition literary or humorous without: *she plays her role sans accent.*
– ORIGIN Old French *sanz*, from Latin *sine*.

sans-culotte /sanzkyoolot, sON-/ ● noun **1** a lower-class Parisian republican in the French Revolution. **2** an extreme republican or revolutionary.
– ORIGIN French, 'without knee breeches'.

Sanskrit /sanskrit/ ● noun an ancient language of India, still used as a language of religion and scholarship, and the source of many Indian languages.
– ORIGIN from Sanskrit, 'composed, elaborated'.

sans serif /san serrif/ (also **sanserif**) ● noun Printing a style of type without serifs.

Santa Claus (also informal **Santa**) ● noun Father Christmas.
– ORIGIN originally a US usage: alteration of Dutch *Sante Klaas* 'St Nicholas'.

santim /santeem/ ● noun a monetary unit of Latvia, equal to one hundredth of a lat.
– ORIGIN Latvian, from French *centime*.

sap[1] ● noun **1** the fluid, chiefly water with nutrients, circulating in the vascular system of a plant. **2** vigour or energy. ● verb (**sapped, sapping**) **1** gradually weaken (a person's strength or power). **2** (**sap of**) drain (someone) of (strength or power).
– ORIGIN Old English; the verb is derived originally from SAP[2] in the sense 'undermine'.

sap[2] historical ● noun a tunnel or trench to conceal an assailant's approach to a fortified place. ● verb (**sapped, sapping**) dig a sap.
– ORIGIN from French *saper*, from Italian *zappa* 'spade, spadework'.

sap[3] ● noun informal, chiefly N. Amer. a foolish and gullible person.
– ORIGIN abbreviation of *sapskull* 'person with a head like sapwood'.

sapele /səpeeli/ ● noun a large tropical African hardwood tree, with reddish-brown wood resembling mahogany.
– ORIGIN named after a port in Nigeria.

sapid /sappid/ ● adjective chiefly N. Amer. **1** flavoursome. **2** pleasant or interesting.
– ORIGIN Latin *sapidus*, from *sapere* 'to taste'.

sapient /saypiənt/ ● adjective formal wise, or attempting to appear wise.
– ORIGIN from Latin *sapere* 'be wise'.

sapling ● noun **1** a young, slender tree. **2** literary a young and slender or inexperienced person.

S

Thesaurus

away, den.

sand ● noun *she ran across the sand* BEACH, sands, shore, seashore; (sand) dunes; *poetic/literary* strand.

sane ● adjective **1** *the accused is presumed to be sane* OF SOUND MIND, in one's right mind, compos mentis, lucid, rational, balanced, stable, normal; *informal* all there. **2** *it isn't sane to use nuclear weapons* SENSIBLE, practical, advisable, responsible, realistic, prudent, wise, reasonable, rational, level-headed, commonsensical, judicious, politic.
– OPPOSITES mad, foolish.

sangfroid ● noun COMPOSURE, equanimity, self-possession, equilibrium, aplomb, poise, self-assurance, self-control, nerve, calm, presence of mind; *informal* cool, unflappability.

sanguine ● adjective **1** *he is sanguine about the advance of technology* OPTIMISTIC, bullish, hopeful, buoyant, positive, confident, cheerful, cheery; *informal* upbeat. **2** *(archaic) a sanguine complexion.* See FLORID sense 1.
– OPPOSITES gloomy.

sanitary ● adjective HYGIENIC, clean, antiseptic, aseptic, sterile, uninfected, disinfected, unpolluted, uncontaminated; salubrious, healthy, wholesome.

sanitize ● verb **1** *the best way to sanitize a bottle* STERILIZE, disinfect, clean, cleanse, purify, fumigate, decontaminate. **2** *the diaries have not been sanitized* MAKE PRESENTABLE, make acceptable, make palatable, clean up; expurgate, bowdlerize, censor.

sanity ● noun **1** *she was losing her sanity* MENTAL HEALTH, faculties, reason, rationality, saneness, stability, lucidity; sense, wits, mind. **2** *sanity has prevailed* (COMMON) SENSE, wisdom, prudence, judiciousness, rationality, soundness, sensibleness.

sap[1] ● noun **1** *sap from the roots of trees* JUICE, secretion, fluid, liquid. **2** *they're full of youthful sap* VIGOUR, energy, drive, dynamism, life, spirit, liveliness, sparkle, verve, ebullience, enthusiasm, gusto, vitality, vivacity, fire, zest, zeal, exuberance; *informal* get-up-and-go, oomph, vim.
● verb *they sapped the will of the troops* ERODE, wear away/down, deplete, reduce, lessen, attenuate, undermine, exhaust, drain,

sapodilla /sappədillə/ ● noun **1** a large evergreen tropical American tree which has hard durable wood and yields chicle. **2** (also **sapodilla plum**) the sweet brownish bristly fruit of this tree.
– ORIGIN Spanish *zapotillo*, from Nahuatl.

saponify /səponnifī/ ● verb (**saponifies**, **saponified**) Chemistry turn (fat or oil) into soap by reaction with an alkali.
– DERIVATIVES **saponification** noun.
– ORIGIN from Latin *sapo* 'soap'.

sapper ● noun **1** a military engineer who lays or detects and disarms mines. **2** Brit. a soldier in the Corps of Royal Engineers.
– ORIGIN from SAP².

sapphic /saffik/ ● adjective **1** (**Sapphic**) relating to the Greek lyric poet Sappho (early 7th century BC), or her poetry expressing love and affection for women. **2** formal or humorous relating to lesbians or lesbianism.

sapphire /saffīr/ ● noun **1** a transparent blue precious stone which is a form of corundum. **2** a bright blue colour.
– ORIGIN Greek *sappheiros*, probably denoting lapis lazuli.

sapphism /saffiz'm/ ● noun formal or humorous lesbianism.

sappy ● adjective (**sappier**, **sappiest**) **1** informal, chiefly N. Amer. over-sentimental. **2** (of a plant) containing a lot of sap.

saprophyte /saprəfīt/ ● noun Biology a plant, fungus, or micro-organism that lives on decaying matter.
– DERIVATIVES **saprophytic** adjective.
– ORIGIN from Greek *sapros* 'putrid' + *phuton* 'plant'.

sapwood ● noun the soft outer layers of new wood between the heartwood and the bark.

saraband /sarrəband/ (also **sarabande**) ● noun a slow, stately Spanish dance in triple time.
– ORIGIN Spanish and Italian *zarabanda*.

Saracen /sarrəs'n/ ● noun **1** an Arab or Muslim, especially at the time of the Crusades. **2** a nomad of the Syrian and Arabian desert at the time of the Roman Empire.
– ORIGIN Greek *Sarakēnos*, perhaps from an Arabic word meaning 'eastern'.

sarape /saraapay/ ● noun variant of SERAPE.

sarcasm ● noun the use of irony to mock or convey contempt.
– ORIGIN Greek *sarkasmos*, from *sarkazein* 'tear flesh', later 'gnash the teeth, speak bitterly'.

sarcastic ● adjective marked by or given to using irony in order to mock or convey contempt.
– DERIVATIVES **sarcastically** adverb.

sarcenet ● noun variant spelling of SARSENET.

sarcoma /saarkōmə/ ● noun (pl. **sarcomas** or **sarcomata** /saarkōmətə/) Medicine a malignant tumour of a kind found chiefly in connective tissue.
– ORIGIN Greek *sarkōma*, from *sarkoun* 'become fleshy'.

sarcophagus /saarkoffəgəss/ ● noun (pl. **sarcophagi** /saarkoffəgī/) a stone coffin.
– ORIGIN Latin, from Greek *sarkophagos* 'flesh-consuming'.

sard /saard/ ● noun a yellow or brownish-red variety of chalcedony.
– ORIGIN Greek *sardios*, probably from *Sardō* 'Sardinia'.

sardar /serdaar/ (also **sirdar**) ● noun chiefly Indian **1** a leader. **2** a Sikh.
– ORIGIN Persian and Urdu.

sardine ● noun a young pilchard or other young or small herring-like fish. ● verb informal pack closely together.
– PHRASES **packed like sardines** crowded close together, as sardines in tins.
– ORIGIN Latin *sardina*, probably from Greek *Sardō* 'Sardinia'.

Sardinian ● noun **1** a person from Sardinia. **2** the language of Sardinia. ● adjective relating to Sardinia.

sardonic /saardonnik/ ● adjective grimly mocking or cynical.
– DERIVATIVES **sardonically** adverb **sardonicism** noun.
– ORIGIN French *sardonique*, from Greek *sardonios* 'of Sardinia', alteration of *sardanios*, used by Homer to describe bitter or scornful laughter.

sardonyx /saardəniks/ ● noun onyx in which white layers alternate with sard.
– ORIGIN Greek *sardonux*.

sargassum /saargassəm/ (also **sargasso**) ● noun a brown seaweed with berry-like air bladders, typically floating in large masses.
– ORIGIN Latin, from Portuguese *sargaço*.

sarge ● noun informal sergeant.

sari /saari/ (also **saree**) ● noun (pl. **saris** or **sarees**) a garment consisting of a length of cotton or silk elaborately draped around the body, traditionally worn by women from the Indian subcontinent.
– ORIGIN Hindi.

sarin /saarin/ ● noun a nerve gas developed during the Second World War.
– ORIGIN German.

sarky ● adjective (**sarkier**, **sarkiest**) Brit. informal sarcastic.
– DERIVATIVES **sarkily** adverb **sarkiness** noun.

sarnie ● noun Brit. informal a sandwich.

sarong /sərong/ ● noun a garment consisting of a long piece of cloth wrapped round the body and tucked at the waist or under the armpits.
– ORIGIN Malay, 'sheath'.

sarsaparilla /saasəpərillə/ ● noun **1** a preparation of the dried roots of various plants, used to flavour drinks and medicines and formerly as a tonic. **2** a sweet drink flavoured with this.
– ORIGIN Spanish *zarzaparilla*, from *zarza* 'bramble' + *parra* 'vine'.

sarsen /saars'n/ ● noun a silicified sandstone boulder of a kind used at Stonehenge and in other prehistoric monuments in southern England.
– ORIGIN probably a variant of SARACEN.

sarsenet /saarsənit/ (also **sarcenet**) ● noun a fine soft silk fabric.
– ORIGIN Old French *sarzinett*, perhaps from *sarzin* 'Saracen', suggested by *drap sarrasinois* 'Saracen cloth'.

sartorial /saartoriəl/ ● adjective relating to tailoring, clothes, or style of dress.
– DERIVATIVES **sartorially** adverb.
– ORIGIN from Latin *sartor* 'tailor'.

SAS ● abbreviation Special Air Service.

sash¹ ● noun a long strip or loop of cloth worn over one shoulder or round the waist.
– ORIGIN earlier as *shash*, denoting fabric worn as a turban, from Arabic.

sash² ● noun a frame holding the glass in a window.
– ORIGIN alteration of CHASSIS.

sashay /sashay/ ● verb informal, chiefly N. Amer. walk ostentatiously, with exaggerated hip and shoulder movements.
– ORIGIN alteration of CHASSÉ.

sashimi /sashimi/ ● noun a Japanese dish of bite-sized pieces of raw fish eaten with soy sauce and horseradish paste.
– ORIGIN Japanese.

sash window ● noun a window with one or two sashes which can be slid vertically to open it.

Sasquatch /saskwach/ ● noun another name for BIGFOOT.
– ORIGIN Salish.

sass N. Amer. informal ● noun impudence. ● verb be impudent to.
– ORIGIN variant of SAUCE.

sassafras /sassəfrass/ ● noun an extract of the aromatic leaves or bark of a North American tree, used medicinally or in perfumery.
– ORIGIN Spanish *sasafrás*, from Latin *saxifraga* 'saxifrage'.

Sassenach /sassənak/ Scottish & Irish derogatory ● noun an English person. ● adjective English.
– ORIGIN Scottish Gaelic *Sasunnoch*, Irish *Sasanach*, from Latin *Saxones* 'Saxons'.

sassy ● adjective (**sassier**, **sassiest**) informal, chiefly N. Amer. bold and spirited; impudent.

SAT ● abbreviation standard assessment task.

sat past and past participle of SIT.

Satan ● noun the Devil; Lucifer.
– ORIGIN Hebrew, 'adversary'.

S

Thesaurus

bleed.

sap² ● noun (*N. Amer. informal*) *he fell for it — what a sap!* See IDIOT.

sarcasm ● noun DERISION, mockery, ridicule, scorn, sneering, scoffing; irony.

sarcastic ● adjective SARDONIC, ironic, ironical; derisive, snide, scornful, contemptuous, mocking, sneering, jeering; caustic, scathing, trenchant, cutting, sharp, acerbic; *Brit. informal* sarky; *N. Amer. informal* snarky.

sardonic ● adjective MOCKING, satirical, sarcastic, ironical, ironic; cynical, scornful, contemptuous, derisive, derisory, sneering, jeering; scathing, caustic, trenchant, cutting, sharp, acerbic; *Brit. informal* sarky.

satang /sattang/ • noun (pl. same or **satangs**) a monetary unit of Thailand, equal to one hundredth of a baht.
– ORIGIN Thai.
satanic • adjective **1** characteristic of Satan. **2** connected with satanism.
satanism • noun the worship of Satan, typically involving a travesty of Christian symbols and practices.
– DERIVATIVES **satanist** noun & adjective.
satay /sattay/ (also **saté**) • noun an Indonesian and Malaysian dish consisting of small pieces of meat grilled on a skewer and served with spiced sauce.
– ORIGIN Malay and Indonesian.
satchel • noun a shoulder bag with a long strap, used especially for school books.
– ORIGIN Old French *sachel*, from Latin *saccellus* 'small bag'.
sate • verb **1** satisfy fully. **2** supply with as much as or more than is desired or can be managed.
– ORIGIN Old English, 'become sated or weary'; related to SAD.
saté • noun variant spelling of SATAY.
sateen /sateen/ • noun a cotton fabric woven like satin with a glossy surface.
– ORIGIN alteration of SATIN.
satellite • noun **1** an artificial body placed in orbit round the earth or another planet to collect information or for communication. **2** Astronomy a celestial body orbiting a planet. **3** a thing separate from something else but dependent on or controlled by it.
– ORIGIN Latin *satelles* 'attendant'.
satellite dish • noun a bowl-shaped aerial with which signals are transmitted to or received from a communications satellite.
satellite television • noun television in which the signals are broadcast via satellite.
sati • noun (pl. **satis**) variant spelling of SUTTEE.
satiate /sayshiayt/ • verb another term for SATE.
– DERIVATIVES **satiation** noun.
– ORIGIN Latin *satiare*, from *satis* 'enough'.
satiety /sətīəti/ • noun the feeling or state of being satiated.
satin • noun **1** a smooth, glossy fabric, usually of silk. **2** (before a noun) denoting or having a smooth, glossy surface or finish.
– DERIVATIVES **satiny** adjective.
– ORIGIN from an Arabic word meaning 'of *Tsinkiang*', a town in China.
satin stitch • noun a long straight embroidery stitch, giving the appearance of satin.
satinwood • noun the glossy yellowish wood of a tropical tree, valued for cabinetwork.
satire /sattīr/ • noun **1** the use of humour, irony, exaggeration, or ridicule to expose and criticize people's stupidity or vices. **2** a play, novel, etc. using satire. **3** (in Latin literature) a literary miscellany, especially a poem ridiculing prevalent vices or follies.
– DERIVATIVES **satirist** noun.
– ORIGIN Latin *satira* 'poetic medley'.
satirical (also **satiric**) • adjective **1** containing or using satire. **2** sarcastic; humorously critical.
– DERIVATIVES **satirically** adverb.
satirize /sattirīz/ (also **satirise**) • verb mock and criticize by means of satire.
satisfaction • noun **1** the state of being satisfied. **2** Law the payment of a debt or fulfilment of an obligation or claim. **3** what is felt to be due to one to make up for an injustice: *the work will stop if they don't get satisfaction.*
satisfactory • adjective fulfilling expectations or needs; acceptable.
– DERIVATIVES **satisfactorily** adverb.
satisfied • adjective contented; pleased: *satisfied customers.*
satisfy • verb (**satisfies**, **satisfied**) **1** meet the expectations, needs, or desires of. **2** fulfil (a desire or need). **3** provide with adequate information about or proof of something. **4** comply with (a condition, obligation, or demand).
– ORIGIN Latin *satisfacere* 'to content', from *satis* 'enough' + *facere* 'make'.
satori /sətori/ • noun Buddhism sudden enlightenment.
– ORIGIN Japanese, 'awakening'.
satrap /satrap/ • noun **1** a provincial governor in the ancient Persian empire. **2** a subordinate or local ruler.
– ORIGIN Latin *satrapa*, from a Persian word meaning 'country-protector'.
satsuma /satsoomə/ • noun a tangerine of a loose-skinned variety, originally grown in Japan.
– ORIGIN named after the former Japanese province of *Satsuma*.
saturate • verb /sachərayt/ **1** soak thoroughly with water or other liquid. **2** cause (a substance) to combine with, dissolve, or hold the greatest possible quantity of another substance. **3** magnetize or charge (a substance or device) fully. **4** supply (a market) beyond the point at which the demand for a product is satisfied. **5** overwhelm (an enemy target) by concentrated bombing. • noun /sachərət/ a saturated fat.
– ORIGIN Latin *saturare* 'fill, glut', from *satur* 'full'.
saturated • adjective **1** Chemistry (of a solution) containing the

Thesaurus

sash • noun BELT, cummerbund, waistband, girdle, obi; *poetic/literary* cincture.
Satan • noun. See DEVIL sense 1.
satanic • adjective DIABOLICAL, fiendish, devilish, demonic, demoniacal, ungodly, hellish, infernal, wicked, evil, sinful, iniquitous, nefarious, vile, foul, abominable, unspeakable, loathsome, monstrous, heinous, hideous, horrible, horrifying, shocking, appalling, dreadful, awful, terrible, ghastly, abhorrent, despicable, damnable.
sate • verb. See SATIATE.
satellite • noun **1** *the European Space Agency's ERS-1 satellite* SPACE STATION, space capsule, spacecraft; sputnik. **2** *the two small satellites of Mars* MOON, secondary planet. **3** *Bulgaria was then a Russian satellite* DEPENDENCY, colony, protectorate, possession, holding; *historical* fief, vassal.
• adjective *a satellite state* DEPENDENT, subordinate, subsidiary; puppet.
satiate • verb FILL, satisfy, sate; slake, quench; gorge, stuff, surfeit, glut, cloy, sicken, nauseate.
satiety • noun SATIATION, satisfaction, repleteness, repletion, fullness; surfeit.
satiny • adjective SMOOTH, shiny, glossy, shining, gleaming, lustrous, sleek, silky.
satire • noun **1** *a satire on American politics* PARODY, burlesque, caricature, lampoon, skit, pasquinade; *informal* spoof, take-off, send-up. **2** *he has become the subject of satire* MOCKERY, ridicule, derision, scorn, caricature; irony, sarcasm.
satirical • adjective MOCKING, ironic, ironical, satiric, sarcastic, sardonic; caustic, trenchant, mordant, biting, cutting, stinging, acerbic; critical, irreverent, disparaging, disrespectful.
satirize • verb MOCK, ridicule, deride, make fun of, poke fun at, parody, lampoon, burlesque, caricature, take off; criticize; *informal* send up, take the mickey out of.
satisfaction • noun **1** *he derived great satisfaction from his work* CONTENTMENT, content, pleasure, gratification, fulfilment, enjoyment, happiness, pride; self-satisfaction, smugness, complacency. **2** *the satisfaction of consumer needs* FULFILMENT, gratification; appeasement, assuaging. **3** *investors turned to the courts for satisfaction* COMPENSATION, recompense, redress, reparation, restitution, repayment, payment, settlement, reimbursement, indemnification, indemnity.
satisfactory • adjective ADEQUATE, all right, acceptable, good enough, sufficient, reasonable, quite good, competent, fair, decent, average, passable; fine, in order, up to scratch, up to the mark, up to standard, up to par; *informal* OK, so-so.
– OPPOSITES inadequate, poor.
satisfied • adjective **1** *a satisfied smile* PLEASED, well pleased, content, contented, happy, proud, triumphant; smug, self-satisfied, pleased with oneself, complacent; *Brit. informal* like the cat that's got the cream. **2** *the pleasure of satisfied desire* FULFILLED, gratified. **3** *I am satisfied that she is happy with the decision* CONVINCED, certain, sure, positive, persuaded, easy in one's mind.
– OPPOSITES discontented, unhappy.
satisfy • verb **1** *a last chance to satisfy his hunger for romance* FULFIL, gratify, meet, fill; indulge, cater to, pander to; appease, assuage; quench, slake, satiate, sate, take the edge off. **2** *she satisfied herself that it had been an accident* CONVINCE, persuade, assure; reassure, put someone's mind at rest. **3** *products which satisfy the EC's criteria* COMPLY WITH, meet, fulfil, answer, conform to; measure up to, come up to; suffice, be good enough, fit/fill the bill. **4** *there was insufficient collateral to satisfy the loan* REPAY, pay (off), settle, make good, discharge, square, liquidate, clear.
– OPPOSITES frustrate.
satisfying • adjective FULFILLING, rewarding, gratifying, pleasing,

largest possible amount of solute. **2** Chemistry (of an organic molecule) containing the greatest possible number of hydrogen atoms, without double or triple bonds. **3** (of colour) bright and rich.

saturation • noun **1** the action of saturating or the state of being saturated. **2** (before another noun) to the fullest extent: *saturation bombing.*

saturation point • noun the stage beyond which no more can be absorbed or accepted.

Saturday • noun the day of the week before Sunday and following Friday.
– ORIGIN Old English, translation of Latin *Saturni dies* 'day of Saturn'.

Saturnalia /sattərnayliə/ • noun (treated as sing. or pl.) **1** the ancient Roman festival of the god Saturn in December, a period of unrestrained merrymaking. **2** (**saturnalia**) an occasion of wild revelry.
– DERIVATIVES **saturnalian** adjective.
– ORIGIN Latin, 'matters relating to Saturn'.

Saturnian • adjective relating to the planet Saturn.

saturnine /sattərnīn/ • adjective **1** gloomy. **2** (of looks, temperament, etc.) dark and brooding.
– ORIGIN from Latin *Saturninus* 'of Saturn' (associated with slowness and gloom by astrologers).

satyr /sattər/ • noun **1** Greek Mythology one of a class of lustful, drunken woodland gods, represented as a man with a horse's ears and tail or (in Roman representations) with a goat's ears, tail, legs, and horns. **2** a man with strong sexual desires.
– DERIVATIVES **satyric** adjective.
– ORIGIN Greek *saturos.*

satyriasis /sattirīəsiss/ • noun excessive sexual desire in a man.

sauce • noun **1** thick liquid served with food to add moistness and flavour. **2** N. Amer. stewed fruit, especially apples. **3** informal, chiefly Brit. impertinence. • verb **1** (usu. **be sauced**) season with a sauce. **2** make more interesting and exciting. **3** informal be impudent to.
– PHRASES **what's sauce for the goose is sauce for the gander** proverb what is appropriate in one case is also appropriate in the other case in question.
– ORIGIN Old French, from Latin *salsus* 'salted'.

sauce boat • noun a long, narrow jug for serving sauce.

saucepan • noun a deep cooking pan, with one long handle and a lid.

saucer • noun a shallow dish with a central circular indentation, on which a cup is placed.
– ORIGIN Old French *saussier* 'sauce boat'.

saucy • adjective (**saucier**, **sauciest**) informal **1** chiefly Brit. sexually suggestive in a light-hearted way. **2** chiefly N. Amer. bold, lively, and spirited.
– DERIVATIVES **saucily** adverb **sauciness** noun.

Saudi /sowdi/ • noun (pl. **Saudis**) a citizen of Saudi Arabia, or a member of its ruling dynasty. • adjective relating to Saudi Arabia or its ruling dynasty.
– ORIGIN from the name of Abdul-Aziz ibn *Saud* (1880–1953), first king of Saudi Arabia.

Saudi Arabian • noun a person from Saudi Arabia. • adjective relating to Saudi Arabia.

sauerkraut /sowərkrowt/ • noun a German dish of chopped pickled cabbage.
– ORIGIN German, from *sauer* 'sour' + *Kraut* 'vegetable'.

sauna /sawnə/ • noun **1** a small room used as a hot-air or steam bath for cleaning and refreshing the body. **2** a session in a sauna.
– ORIGIN Finnish.

saunter • verb walk in a slow, relaxed manner. • noun a leisurely stroll.
– ORIGIN of unknown origin.

-saur • combining form forming names of reptiles, especially extinct ones: *ichthyosaur.*
– ORIGIN from Greek *sauros* 'lizard'.

saurian /sawriən/ • adjective of or like a lizard.

saurischian /sawriskiən/ • noun Palaeontology a dinosaur of a group with pelvic bones resembling that of lizards. Compare with ORNITHISCHIAN.
– ORIGIN from Greek *sauros* 'lizard' + *iskhion* 'hip joint'.

sauropod /sawrəpod/ • noun an apatosaurus, brachiosaurus, or similar huge herbivorous dinosaur with a long neck and tail.
– ORIGIN from Greek *sauros* 'lizard' + *pous* 'foot'.

-saurus • combining form forming genus names of reptiles, especially extinct ones: *stegosaurus.*

sausage • noun **1** a short tube of raw minced meat encased in a skin, that is grilled or fried before eating. **2** a tube of seasoned minced meat that is cooked or preserved and eaten cold in slices. **3** a cylindrical object.
– PHRASES **not a sausage** Brit. informal nothing at all.
– ORIGIN Old French *saussiche*, from Latin *salsus* 'salted'.

sausage dog • noun Brit. informal a dachshund.

sausage meat • noun minced meat with spices and a binder such as cereal, used in sausages or as a stuffing.

sausage roll • noun a piece of sausage meat baked in a roll of pastry.

sauté /sōtay/ • adjective fried quickly in a little hot fat. • noun a dish cooked in such a way. • verb (**sautés**, **sautéed** or **sautéd**, **sautéing**) cook in such a way.
– ORIGIN French, 'jumped'.

Sauternes /sōtern/ • noun a sweet white wine from Sauternes in the Bordeaux region of France.

Sauvignon /sōvinyON/ (also **Sauvignon Blanc**) • noun a variety of white wine grape.
– ORIGIN French.

savage • adjective **1** fierce, violent, and uncontrolled. **2** cruel and vicious. **3** primitive; uncivilized. **4** (of a place) wild; uncultivated. • noun **1** a member of a people regarded as primitive and uncivilized. **2** a brutal or vicious person. • verb **1** (especially of a dog) attack ferociously. **2** criticize brutally.
– DERIVATIVES **savagely** adverb **savagery** noun.
– ORIGIN Old French *sauvage* 'wild', from Latin *silvaticus* 'of the woods'.

savannah (also **savanna**) • noun a grassy plain in tropical and

Thesaurus

S

enjoyable, pleasurable, to one's liking.

saturate • verb **1** *heavy rain saturated the ground* SOAK, drench, waterlog, wet through; souse, steep, douse. **2** *the air was saturated with the stench of joss sticks* PERMEATE, suffuse, imbue, pervade, charge, infuse, fill. **3** *the company has saturated the market* FLOOD, glut, oversupply, overfill, overload.

saturated • adjective **1** *his trousers were saturated* SOAKED, soaking (wet), wet through, sopping (wet), sodden, dripping, wringing wet, drenched; soaked to the skin, like a drowned rat. **2** *the saturated ground* WATERLOGGED, soggy, squelchy, heavy, muddy, boggy.
– OPPOSITES dry.

saturnine • adjective **1** *a saturnine temperament* GLOOMY, sombre, melancholy, moody, lugubrious, dour, glum, morose, unsmiling, humourless. **2** *his saturnine good looks* SWARTHY, dark, dark-skinned, dark-complexioned; mysterious, mercurial, moody.
– OPPOSITES cheerful.

sauce • noun **1** *a piquant sauce* RELISH, condiment, ketchup; dip, dressing; jus, coulis. **2** (*Brit. informal*) *'I'll have less of your sauce,' said Aunt Edie* IMPUDENCE, impertinence, cheek, cheekiness, effrontery, forwardness, brazenness; insolence, rudeness, disrespect; *informal* mouth, lip; *N. Amer. informal* sassiness.

saucepan • noun PAN, pot, casserole, skillet, stockpot, stewpot; billy, billycan.

saucy • adjective (*informal*) **1** (*Brit.*) *saucy postcards* SUGGESTIVE, titillating, risqué, rude, bawdy, racy, ribald, spicy; *informal* raunchy, smutty, nudge-nudge; *Brit. informal* fruity; *N. Amer. informal* gamy. **2** *you saucy little minx!* CHEEKY, impudent, impertinent, irreverent, forward, disrespectful, bold, as bold as brass, brazen; *informal* fresh, lippy, mouthy; *N. Amer. informal* sassy; *archaic* malapert. **3** (*N. Amer.*) *the cap sat at a saucy angle on her black hair* JAUNTY, rakish, sporty, raffish.
– OPPOSITES demure, polite.

saunter • verb STROLL, amble, wander, meander, drift, walk; stretch one's legs, take the air; *informal* mosey, tootle; *Brit. informal* pootle; *formal* promenade.

savage • adjective **1** *savage dogs* FEROCIOUS, fierce; wild, untamed, undomesticated, feral. **2** *a savage assault* VICIOUS, brutal, cruel, sadistic, ferocious, fierce, violent, bloody, murderous, homicidal, bloodthirsty; *poetic/literary* fell; *archaic* sanguinary. **3** *a savage attack on European free-trade policy* FIERCE, blistering, scathing, searing, stinging, devastating, mordant, trenchant, caustic, cutting, biting, withering, virulent, vitriolic. **4** *a savage race* PRIMITIVE, uncivilized, unenlightened, non-literate, in a state of nature. **5** *a savage landscape* RUGGED, rough, wild, inhospitable, uninhabitable. **6** *a*

subtropical regions, with few trees.
– ORIGIN Spanish *sabana*, from Taino (an extinct Caribbean language).

savant /savv'nt/ (or **savante** /savv'nt/) ● noun a learned person.
– ORIGIN French, 'knowing'.

save[1] ● verb **1** keep safe or rescue from harm or danger. **2** prevent from dying. **3** (in Christian use) preserve (a soul) from damnation. **4** store up for future use. **5** Computing keep (data) by moving a copy to a storage location. **6** avoid the need to use up or spend: *computers save time.* **7** avoid, lessen, or guard against. **8** prevent an opponent from scoring (a goal or point). ● noun chiefly Soccer an act of preventing an opponent's scoring.
– PHRASES **save one's breath** not bother to say something pointless. **save the day** (or **situation**) provide a solution to a problem. **save someone's skin** (or **neck** or **bacon**) rescue someone from difficulty.
– ORIGIN Latin *salvare*, from *salvus* 'safe'.

save[2] ● preposition & conjunction formal or literary except; other than.
– ORIGIN from Latin *salvus* 'safe', used in phrases such as *salvo jure, salva innocentia* 'with no violation of right or innocence'.

saveloy /savvəloy/ ● noun Brit. a seasoned red pork sausage, dried and smoked and sold ready to eat.
– ORIGIN Italian *cervellata*.

saver ● noun **1** a person who regularly saves money through a bank or recognized scheme. **2** something that prevents a particular resource from being used up: *space-saver.*

saving ● noun **1** an economy of or reduction in money, time, etc. **2** (**savings**) money saved. ● adjective (in combination) preventing waste of a particular resource: *energy-saving.* ● preposition **1** except. **2** archaic with due respect to.

saving grace ● noun **1** the redeeming grace of God. **2** a redeeming quality or characteristic.

savings account ● noun a deposit account.

savings and loan (also **savings and loan association**) ● noun (in the US) an institution which accepts savings at interest and lends money to savers.

savings bank ● noun a non-profit-making financial institution receiving small deposits at interest.

Savings Bond ● noun a Premium Bond.

saviour (US **savior**) ● noun **1** a person who saves someone or something from danger or harm. **2** (**the/our Saviour**) (in Christianity) God or Jesus Christ.
– ORIGIN Old French *sauveour*, from Latin *salvare* 'to save'.

savoir faire /savwaar fair/ ● noun the ability to act appropriately in social situations.
– ORIGIN French, 'know how to do'.

savory[1] ● noun an aromatic plant of the mint family, used as a herb in cookery.
– ORIGIN Latin *satureia*.

savory[2] ● adjective & noun US spelling of SAVOURY.

savour (US **savor**) ● verb **1** appreciate and enjoy the taste of (food or drink). **2** enjoy or appreciate to the full. **3** (**savour of**) have a suggestion or trace of. ● noun **1** a characteristic taste, flavour, or smell. **2** a suggestion or trace.
– ORIGIN Old French, from Latin *sapere* 'to taste'.

savoury (US **savory**) ● adjective **1** (of food) salty or spicy rather than sweet. **2** morally wholesome or acceptable: *the less savoury aspects of the story.* ● noun (pl. **savouries**) chiefly Brit. a savoury snack.

savoy ● noun a cabbage of a hardy variety with densely wrinkled leaves.
– ORIGIN from *Savoy*, an area of SE France.

savvy informal ● noun shrewdness. ● verb (**savvies**, **savvied**) know or understand. ● adjective (**savvier**, **savviest**) shrewd and knowledgeable.
– ORIGIN originally black and pidgin English imitating Spanish *sabe usted* 'you know'.

saw[1] ● noun **1** a hand tool for cutting wood or other hard materials, having a long, thin serrated blade and operated using a backwards and forwards movement. **2** a mechanical power-driven cutting tool with a toothed rotating disc or moving band. **3** Zoology a serrated organ or part, e.g. the toothed snout of a sawfish. ● verb (past part. chiefly Brit. **sawn** or chiefly N. Amer. **sawed**) **1** cut or form with a saw. **2** cut roughly. **3** move something back and forward as if cutting with a saw.
– ORIGIN Old English.

saw[2] past of SEE[1].

saw[3] ● noun a proverb or maxim.
– ORIGIN Old English, related to SAY and SAGA.

sawbones ● noun (pl. same) informal, dated a doctor or surgeon.

sawbuck ● noun N. Amer. a sawhorse.
– ORIGIN Dutch *zaagbok*, from *zaag* 'saw' + *bok* 'vaulting horse'.

sawdust ● noun powdery particles of wood produced by sawing.

sawfish ● noun a large tropical fish with a long flattened snout bearing large blunt teeth along each side.

Thesaurus

savage blow for the town SEVERE, crushing, devastating, crippling, terrible, awful, dreadful, dire, catastrophic, calamitous, ruinous.
– OPPOSITES tame, mild, civilized.
● noun **1** *she'd expected mud huts and savages* BARBARIAN, wild man, wild woman, primitive. **2** *she described her son's assailants as savages* BRUTE, beast, monster, barbarian, sadist, animal.
● verb **1** *he was savaged by a dog* MAUL, attack, tear to pieces, lacerate, claw, bite. **2** *critics savaged the film* CRITICIZE SEVERELY, attack, lambaste, condemn, denounce, pillory, revile; *informal* pan, tear to pieces, hammer, slam, do a hatchet job on, crucify; *Brit. informal* slate, rubbish; *N. Amer. informal* trash; *Austral./NZ informal* bag, monster; *formal* excoriate.

savant ● noun INTELLECTUAL, scholar, sage, philosopher, thinker, wise/learned person; guru, master, pandit.
– OPPOSITES ignoramus.

save ● verb **1** *the captain was saved by his crew* RESCUE, come to someone's rescue, save someone's life; set free, free, liberate, deliver, extricate; bail out; *informal* save someone's bacon/neck/skin. **2** *the farmhouse has been saved from demolition* PRESERVE, keep safe, keep, protect, safeguard; salvage, retrieve, reclaim, rescue. **3** *start saving old newspapers for wrapping china* PUT ASIDE, set aside, put by, put to one side, save up, keep, retain, reserve, conserve, stockpile, store, hoard, save for a rainy day; *informal* salt away, squirrel away, stash away, hang on to. **4** *asking me first would have saved a lot of trouble* PREVENT, obviate, forestall, spare; stop; avoid, avert.
● preposition & conjunction *(formal) no one needed to know save herself* EXCEPT, apart from, but, other than, besides, aside from, bar, barring, excluding, leaving out, saving; *informal* outside of.

saving ● noun **1** *a considerable saving in development costs* REDUCTION, cut, decrease, economy. **2** *I'll have to use some of my savings* NEST EGG, money put by for a rainy day, life savings; capital, assets, funds, resources, reserves.

saving grace ● noun REDEEMING FEATURE, good point, thing in its/one's favour, advantage, asset, selling point.

saviour ● noun **1** *the country's saviour* RESCUER, liberator, deliverer, emancipator; champion, knight in shining armour, friend in need, good Samaritan. **2** *the Saviour is depicted with two archangels* CHRIST, Jesus (Christ), the Redeemer, the Messiah, Our Lord, the Lamb of God, the Son of God, the Son of Man, the Prince of Peace.

savoir faire ● noun SOCIAL SKILL, social grace(s), urbanity, suavity, finesse, sophistication, poise, aplomb, adroitness, polish, style, smoothness, tact, tactfulness, diplomacy, discretion, delicacy, sensitivity; *informal* savvy.
– OPPOSITES gaucheness.

savour ● verb **1** *she wanted to savour every moment* RELISH, enjoy (to the full), appreciate, delight in, revel in, smack one's lips over, luxuriate in, bask in. **2** *such a declaration savoured of immodesty* SUGGEST, smack of, have the hallmarks of, seem like, have the air of, show signs of.
● noun **1** *the subtle savour of wood smoke* SMELL, aroma, fragrance, scent, perfume, bouquet; TASTE, flavour, tang, smack. **2** *a savour of bitterness seasoned my feelings for him* TRACE, hint, suggestion, touch, smack. **3** *her usual diversions had lost their savour* PIQUANCY, interest, attraction, flavour, spice, zest, excitement, enjoyment; *informal* zing.

savoury ● adjective **1** *sweet or savoury dishes* SALTY, spicy, piquant, tangy. **2** *a rich, savoury aroma* APPETIZING, mouth-watering, delicious, delectable, luscious; tasty, flavoursome, flavourful, palatable, toothsome; *informal* scrumptious, finger-licking, yummy, scrummy, moreish. **3** *one of the less savoury aspects of the affair* ACCEPTABLE, pleasant, respectable, wholesome, honourable, proper, seemly.
– OPPOSITES sweet, unappetizing.
● noun *cocktail savouries* CANAPÉ, hors d'oeuvre, appetizer, titbit.

savvy *(informal)* ● noun *his political savvy.* See ACUMEN.
● adjective *a savvy investor.* See SHREWD.

S

sawfly ● noun an insect related to the wasps, with a saw-like tube used in laying eggs in plant tissues.
sawhorse ● noun N. Amer. a rack supporting wood for sawing.
sawmill ● noun a factory in which logs are sawn by machine.
sawn past participle of SAW[1].
sawn-off (N. Amer. **sawed-off**) ● adjective **1** (of a gun) having a shortened barrel for ease of handling and a wider field of fire. **2** informal (of a garment) having been cut short.
sawtooth (also **sawtoothed**) ● adjective shaped like the teeth of a saw.
sawyer ● noun a person who saws timber.
sax ● noun informal **1** a saxophone. **2** a saxophone player.
– DERIVATIVES **saxist** noun.
saxe ● noun a light blue colour with a greyish tinge.
– ORIGIN French, 'Saxony', the source of a dye of this colour.
saxhorn ● noun a brass instrument with valves and a funnel-shaped mouthpiece, used mainly in military and brass bands.
– ORIGIN named after the Belgian instrument-makers Charles J. *Sax* (1791– 1865) and his son Antoine-Joseph 'Adolphe' *Sax* (1814–94).
saxifrage /saksifrayj/ ● noun a low-growing plant of rocky or stony ground, bearing small white, yellow, or red flowers.
– ORIGIN Latin *saxifraga*, from *saxum* 'rock' + *frangere* 'to break'.
Saxon ● noun **1** a member of a Germanic people that conquered and settled in much of southern England in the 5th–6th centuries. **2** a native of modern Saxony in Germany. **3** (**Old Saxon**) the language of the ancient Saxons. **4** another term for OLD ENGLISH. ● adjective **1** relating to the Anglo-Saxons, their language, or their period of dominance in England (5th–11th centuries). **2** relating to Saxony or the continental Saxons.
– ORIGIN Greek *Saxones*, perhaps from the base of Old English *seax* 'knife'.
saxophone /saksəfōn/ ● noun a member of a family of metal wind instruments with a reed like a clarinet, used especially in jazz and dance music.
– DERIVATIVES **saxophonic** /saksəfonnik/ adjective **saxophonist** /saksoffənist/ noun.
– ORIGIN named after the Belgian instrument-maker Adolphe *Sax* (1814–94).
say ● verb (**says**; past and past part. **said**) **1** utter words so as to convey information, an opinion, an instruction, etc. **2** (of a text or symbol) convey information or instructions. **3** (of a clock or watch) indicate (a time). **4** (**be said**) be asserted or reported. **5** (**say for**) present (a consideration) in favour of or excusing: *he had nothing to say for himself.* **6** assume as a hypothesis. ● noun **1** an opportunity to state one's opinion or feelings. **2** an opportunity to influence events.
– PHRASES **go without saying** be obvious. **how say you?** Law how do you find? (used to request a jury's verdict). **say the word** give permission or instructions. **there is no saying** it is impossible to know. **they say** it is rumoured. **when all is said and done** when everything is taken into account.
– DERIVATIVES **sayable** adjective **sayer** noun.
– ORIGIN Old English.
saying ● noun a short, commonly known expression containing advice or wisdom.
say-so ● noun (usu. **on someone's say-so**) informal **1** the power to decide or allow something. **2** an arbitrary assertion or command.
Sb ● symbol the chemical element antimony.
– ORIGIN from Latin *stibium*.
SBS ● abbreviation Special Boat Service.
SC ● abbreviation South Carolina.
sc. ● abbreviation scilicet.
scab ● noun **1** a dry, rough protective crust that forms over a cut or wound during healing. **2** mange or a similar skin disease in animals. **3** any of a number of fungal diseases of plants in which rough patches develop. **4** informal a person or thing regarded with contempt. **5** derogatory a person who refuses to strike or who takes the place of a striking worker. ● verb (**scabbed**, **scabbing**) **1** (**scabbed**) encrusted with a scab or scabs. **2** derogatory work as a scab.
– DERIVATIVES **scabby** adjective.
– ORIGIN Old Norse.
scabbard /skabbərd/ ● noun **1** a sheath for the blade of a sword or dagger. **2** a sheath for a gun or other weapon or tool.
– ORIGIN Old French *escalberc*.
scabies /skaybeez/ ● noun a contagious skin disease marked by itching and small raised red spots, caused by the itch mite.
– ORIGIN Latin, from *scabere* 'to scratch'.
scabious /skaybiəss/ ● noun a plant with blue, pink, or white pincushion-shaped flowers.
– ORIGIN from Latin *scabiosa herba* 'rough, scabby plant'; it was formerly regarded as a cure for skin disease.
scabrous /skaybrəss/ ● adjective **1** rough and covered with scabs. **2** salacious or sordid.
– ORIGIN Latin *scabrosus*, from *scaber* 'rough'.
scads ● plural noun informal, chiefly N. Amer. a large number or quantity.
– ORIGIN of unknown origin.
scaffold ● noun **1** a raised wooden platform used formerly for public executions. **2** a structure made using scaffolding. ● verb attach scaffolding to.
– DERIVATIVES **scaffolder** noun.
– ORIGIN Old French *eschaffaut*; related to CATAFALQUE.
scaffolding ● noun **1** a temporary structure on the outside of a building, made of wooden planks and metal poles, used while building, repairing, or cleaning. **2** the materials used in such a structure.
scag ● noun variant spelling of SKAG.
scalable ● adjective **1** able to be scaled or climbed. **2** able to be changed in size or scale. **3** technical able to be graded according to a scale.
– DERIVATIVES **scalability** noun.
scalar /skaylər/ Mathematics & Physics ● adjective having only magnitude, not direction. ● noun a scalar quantity (especially as opposed to a vector).
– ORIGIN Latin *scalaris*, from *scala* 'ladder'.
scalawag ● noun variant spelling of SCALLYWAG.
scald ● verb **1** injure with very hot liquid or steam. **2** heat (a liquid) to near boiling point. **3** immerse briefly in boiling water. ● noun a burn or other injury caused by hot liquid or steam.
– PHRASES **like a scalded cat** very fast.
– ORIGIN Latin *excaldare*, from *calidus* 'hot'.
scale[1] ● noun **1** each of the small overlapping plates protecting the skin of fish and reptiles. **2** a thick dry flake of skin. **3** a

S

Thesaurus

saw ● noun SAYING, maxim, proverb, aphorism, axiom, adage, apophthegm, epigram, gnome.
say ● verb **1** *she felt her stomach flutter as he said her name* SPEAK, utter, voice, pronounce, give voice to, vocalize. **2** *'I must go,' she said* DECLARE, state, announce, remark, observe, mention, comment, note, add; reply, respond, answer, rejoin; *informal* come out with. **3** *Newall says he's innocent* CLAIM, maintain, assert, hold, insist, contend; allege, profess; *formal* opine, aver; *rare* asseverate. **4** *I can't conjure up the words to say how I feel* EXPRESS, put into words, phrase, articulate, communicate, make known, put/get across, convey, verbalize; reveal, divulge, impart, disclose; imply, suggest. **5** *they sang hymns and said a prayer* RECITE, repeat, utter, deliver, perform, declaim, orate. **6** *the dial of her watch said one twenty* INDICATE, show, read. **7** *I'd say it's about five miles* ESTIMATE, judge, guess, hazard a guess, predict, speculate, surmise, conjecture, venture; *informal* reckon. **8** *let's say you'd just won a million pounds* SUPPOSE, assume, imagine, presume, hypothesize, postulate, posit.
● noun **1** *everyone is entitled to their say* CHANCE TO SPEAK, turn to speak, opinion, view, voice; *informal* twopence worth, twopenn'orth. **2** *don't I have any say in the matter?* INFLUENCE, sway, weight, voice, input, share, part.
– PHRASES **that is to say** IN OTHER WORDS, to put it another way; i.e., that is, to wit, viz, namely. **to say the least** TO PUT IT MILDLY, putting it mildly, without any exaggeration, at the very least.
saying ● noun PROVERB, maxim, aphorism, axiom, adage, saw, tag, motto, apophthegm, epigram, dictum, gnome; expression, phrase, formula; slogan, catchphrase; platitude, cliché, commonplace, truism.
– PHRASES **it goes without saying** OF COURSE, naturally, needless to say, it's taken for granted, it's understood/assumed, it's taken as read, it's an accepted fact; obviously, self-evidently, manifestly; *informal* natch.
say-so ● noun *(informal)* AUTHORIZATION, (seal of) approval, agreement, consent, assent, permission, endorsement, sanction, ratification, approbation, acquiescence, blessing, leave; *informal* the OK, the go-ahead, the green light, the thumbs up.
– OPPOSITES refusal, denial.

white deposit formed in a kettle, boiler, etc. by the evaporation of water containing lime. **4** tartar formed on teeth. ● **verb 1** remove scale or scales from. **2** (often as noun **scaling**) (especially of the skin) form or flake off in scales.
– PHRASES **the scales fall from someone's eyes** someone is no longer deceived. [ORIGIN with biblical reference to Acts of the Apostles, chapter 9.]
– ORIGIN Old French *escale*.

scale² ● **noun 1** (usu. **scales**) an instrument or device for weighing. **2** either of the dishes on a simple scale balance. ● **verb** have a weight of (a specified amount).
– PHRASES **throw on** (or **into**) **the scale** contribute (something) to one side of an argument or debate. **tip** (or **turn**) **the scales** (or **balance**) be the deciding factor; make the critical difference.
– ORIGIN Old Norse, 'bowl'.

scale³ ● **noun 1** a graduated range of values forming a standard system for measuring or grading something: *a pay scale*. **2** a measuring instrument based on such a system. **3** relative size or extent: *he operated on a grand scale*. **4** a ratio of size in a map, model, drawing, or plan. **5** Music an arrangement of the notes in any system of music in ascending or descending order of pitch. ● **verb 1** climb up or over (something high and steep). **2** represent or draw according to a common scale. **3** (of a quantity or property) be variable according to a particular scale. **4** (**scale back/down** or **up**) reduce (or increase) in size, number, or extent.
– PHRASES **to scale** with a uniform reduction or enlargement. **in scale** in proportion to the surroundings.
– ORIGIN Latin *scala* 'ladder'.

scale insect ● **noun** a small bug which secretes a protective shield-like scale and spends its life attached to a single plant.

scalene /skayleen/ ● **adjective** (of a triangle) having sides unequal in length.
– ORIGIN Greek *skalēnos* 'unequal'.

scallion /skalyən/ ● **noun** a long-necked onion with a small bulb, in particular a shallot or spring onion.
– ORIGIN Old French *scaloun*, from Latin *Ascalonia caepa* 'onion of *Ascalon*', a port in ancient Palestine.

scallop /skolləp, skaləp/ ● **noun 1** an edible bivalve mollusc with a ribbed fan-shaped shell. **2** each of a series of small curves resembling the edge of a scallop shell, forming a decorative edging. ● **verb** (**scalloped, scalloping**) **1** (**scalloped**) decorated with scallops. **2** (usu. as noun **scalloping**) N. Amer. gather or dredge for scallops.
– ORIGIN Old French *escalope*.

scally ● **noun** (pl. **scallies**) informal (in NW English dialect) a rascal; a rogue.
– ORIGIN abbreviation of SCALLYWAG.

scallywag (US also **scalawag**) ● **noun** informal a mischievous person; a rascal.
– ORIGIN of unknown origin.

scalp ● **noun 1** the skin covering the top and back of the head. **2** historical the scalp with the hair cut away from an enemy's head as a battle trophy, a former practice among American Indians. ● **verb 1** take the scalp of (an enemy). **2** informal punish severely. **3** informal, chiefly N. Amer. resell (shares or tickets) at a large or quick profit.
– DERIVATIVES **scalper** noun.
– ORIGIN probably Scandinavian.

scalpel ● **noun** a knife with a small sharp blade, as used by a surgeon.
– ORIGIN Latin *scalpellum* 'small chisel', from *scalpere* 'to scratch'.

scaly ● **adjective** (**scalier, scaliest**) **1** covered in scales. **2** (of skin) dry and flaking.

scam informal ● **noun** a dishonest scheme; a fraud. ● **verb** (**scammed, scamming**) swindle.
– DERIVATIVES **scammer** noun.
– ORIGIN of unknown origin.

scamp¹ ● **noun** informal a mischievous person, especially a child.
– DERIVATIVES **scampish** adjective.
– ORIGIN originally denoting a highwayman: from obsolete *scamp* 'rob on the highway', probably from Dutch *schampen* 'slip away'.

scamp² ● **verb** dated perform in a perfunctory or inadequate way.
– ORIGIN perhaps from SCAMP¹, but associated in sense with SKIMP.

scamper ● **verb** run with quick light steps, especially through fear or excitement. ● **noun** an act of scampering.
– ORIGIN probably from SCAMP¹.

scampi ● **noun** (treated as sing. or pl.) a kind of small lobster prepared for eating, especially fried in breadcrumbs.
– ORIGIN Italian.

scan ● **verb** (**scanned, scanning**) **1** look at quickly in order to identify relevant features or information. **2** traverse with a detector or an electromagnetic beam, especially to obtain an image. **3** convert (a document or picture) into digital form for storage or processing on a computer. **4** analyse the metre of a line of verse. **5** (of verse) conform to metrical principles. ● **noun 1** an act of scanning. **2** a medical examination using a scanner. **3** an image obtained by scanning or with a scanner.
– DERIVATIVES **scannable** adjective.
– ORIGIN Latin *scandere* 'climb' (later 'scan verses', by analogy with the raising and lowering of one's foot when marking rhythm).

scandal ● **noun 1** an action or event regarded as morally or legally wrong and causing general public outrage. **2** outrage, rumour, or gossip arising from this.
– ORIGIN Latin *scandalum* 'cause of offence', from Greek *skandalon* 'snare, stumbling block'.

scandalize (also **scandalise**) ● **verb** shock or horrify by a violation of propriety or morality.

scandalous ● **adjective 1** causing general public outrage by a perceived offence against morality or law. **2** (of a state of affairs) disgracefully bad.
– DERIVATIVES **scandalously** adverb.

Thesaurus

S

scalding ● **adjective** EXTREMELY HOT, burning, blistering, searing, red-hot; piping hot; *informal* boiling (hot), sizzling.

scale¹ ● **noun 1** *the reptile's scales* plate; *technical* lamella, lamina, squama, scute, scutum. **2** *scales on the skin* FLAKE; (**scales**) scurf, dandruff. **3** *scale in kettles* LIMESCALE, deposit, incrustation; *Brit.* fur.

scale² ● **noun 1** *the Celsius scale of temperature* CALIBRATED SYSTEM, graduated system, system of measurement. **2** *opposite ends of the social scale* HIERARCHY, ladder, ranking, pecking order, order, spectrum; succession, sequence, series. **3** *the scale of the map* RATIO, proportion, relative size. **4** *no one foresaw the scale of the disaster* EXTENT, size, scope, magnitude, dimensions, range, breadth, compass, degree, reach.
● **verb** *thieves scaled an 8ft high fence* CLIMB, ascend, clamber up, shin (up), scramble up, mount; *N. Amer.* shinny (up).
– PHRASES **scale something down** REDUCE, cut down, cut back, cut, decrease, lessen, lower, trim, slim down, prune. **scale something up** INCREASE, expand, augment, build up, add to; step up, boost, escalate.

scaly ● **adjective 1** *the dragon's scaly hide technical* squamous, squamulose, squamate, lamellate. **2** *scaly patches of dead skin* DRY, flaky, flaking, scurfy, rough, scabrous, mangy, scabious; *technical* furfuraceous.

scam ● **noun** *(informal)* FRAUD, swindle, racket, trick, diddle; *informal* con (trick); *Brit. informal* ramp; *N. Amer. informal* hustle, grift, bunco.

scamp ● **noun** *(informal)* RASCAL, monkey, devil, imp, wretch, mischief-maker; *informal* scallywag, horror, monster, tyke; *Brit. informal* perisher; *N. English informal* scally; *N. Amer. informal* varmint; *archaic* rapscallion, scapegrace.

scamper ● **verb** SCURRY, scuttle, dart, run, rush, race, dash, hurry, hasten; *informal* scoot; *dated* make haste.

scan ● **verb 1** *Adam scanned the horizon* SCRUTINIZE, examine, study, inspect, survey, search, scour, sweep, rake; look at, stare at, gaze at, eye, watch; *informal* check out; *N. Amer. informal* scope. **2** *I scanned the papers* GLANCE THROUGH, look through, have a look at, run/cast one's eye over, skim through, flick through, flip through, leaf through, thumb through.
● **noun 1** *a careful scan of the terrain* INSPECTION, scrutiny, examination, survey. **2** *a quick scan through the report* GLANCE, look, flick, browse. **3** *a brain scan* EXAMINATION, screening.

scandal ● **noun 1** *revelation of the sex scandal forced him to resign* WRONGDOING, impropriety, misconduct, immoral behaviour, unethical behaviour; offence, transgression, crime, sin; skeleton in the closet; *informal* -gate. **2** *it's a scandal that the disease is not adequately treated* DISGRACE, outrage, injustice; (crying) shame. **3** *no scandal attached to her name* MALICIOUS GOSSIP, malicious rumour(s), slander, libel, calumny, defamation, aspersions, muckraking; *informal* dirt.

scandalize ● **verb** SHOCK, appal, outrage, horrify, disgust; offend,

Scandinavian ● adjective relating to Scandinavia. ● noun **1** a person from Scandinavia. **2** the northern branch of the Germanic languages, comprising Danish, Norwegian, Swedish, Icelandic, and Faroese, all descended from Old Norse.

scandium /skandiəm/ ● noun a soft silvery-white metallic chemical element resembling the rare-earth elements.
– ORIGIN Latin, from *Scandinavia* (where minerals are found containing this element).

scanner ● noun **1** Medicine a machine that examines the body through the use of radiation, ultrasound etc., used to aid diagnosis. **2** a device that scans documents and converts them into digital data.

scansion /skansh'n/ ● noun **1** the action of scanning a line of verse to determine its rhythm. **2** the rhythm of a line of verse.

scant ● adjective **1** barely sufficient or adequate. **2** barely amounting to the amount specified. ● verb chiefly N. Amer. provide or deal with insufficiently.
– DERIVATIVES **scantly** adverb **scantness** noun.
– ORIGIN Old Norse, 'short'.

scantling ● noun **1** a timber beam of small cross section. **2** (often **scantlings**) a set of standard dimensions for parts of a structure, especially in shipbuilding.
– ORIGIN Old French *escantillon* 'sample'.

scanty ● adjective (**scantier**, **scantiest**) small or insufficient in quantity or amount.
– DERIVATIVES **scantily** adverb.

scapegoat ● noun **1** a person who is blamed for the wrongdoings or mistakes of others. **2** (in the Bible) a goat sent into the wilderness after the Jewish chief priest had symbolically laid the sins of the people upon it (Leviticus, chapter 16). ● verb make a scapegoat of.
– ORIGIN from archaic *scape* 'escape' + GOAT.

scapegrace ● noun archaic a mischievous person; a rascal.
– ORIGIN from archaic *scape* 'escape' + GRACE, i.e. a person who lacks the grace of God.

scapula /skapyoolə/ ● noun (pl. **scapulae** /skapyoolee/ or **scapulas**) Anatomy technical term for SHOULDER BLADE.
– ORIGIN Latin.

scapular ● adjective Anatomy & Zoology relating to the shoulder or shoulder blade. ● noun a short monastic cloak covering the shoulders.

scar[1] ● noun **1** a mark left on the skin or within body tissue after the healing of a wound or burn. **2** a mark left at the point of separation of a leaf, frond, or other part from a plant. **3** a lasting effect left following an unpleasant experience. ● verb (**scarred**, **scarring**) mark or be marked with a scar or scars.
– ORIGIN Greek *eskhara* 'scab'.

scar[2] ● noun a steep high cliff or rock outcrop.
– ORIGIN Old Norse, 'low reef'.

scarab /skarrəb/ ● noun **1** a large dung beetle, regarded as sacred in ancient Egypt. **2** an ancient Egyptian gem in the form of a scarab beetle, engraved with hieroglyphs on the flat underside.
– ORIGIN Greek *skarabeios*.

scarce ● adjective **1** (of a resource) insufficient for the demand. **2** rarely found.
– PHRASES **make oneself scarce** informal leave a place, especially so as to avoid a difficult situation.
– DERIVATIVES **scarcity** noun.
– ORIGIN Old French *escars*, from a Romance word meaning 'selected'.

scarcely ● adverb **1** only just. **2** only a very short time before. **3** used to suggest that something is unlikely to be or certainly not the case: *they could scarcely all be wrong*.

scare ● verb **1** cause great fear or nervousness in; frighten. **2** (**scare away/off**) drive or keep (someone) away by fear. **3** become frightened. ● noun **1** a sudden attack of fright. **2** a period of general anxiety or alarm about something.
– ORIGIN Old Norse.

scarecrow ● noun an object made to resemble a human figure, set up to scare birds away from a field where crops are growing.

scared ● adjective feeling or showing fear or nervousness.

scarf[1] ● noun (pl. **scarves** or **scarfs**) a length or square of fabric worn around the neck or head.
– DERIVATIVES **scarfed** (also **scarved**) adjective.
– ORIGIN probably from Old French *escharpe* 'pilgrim's pouch'.

scarf[2] ● verb join the ends of (two pieces of timber or metal) by bevelling or notching them so that they fit together. ● noun a joint made by scarfing.
– ORIGIN Old Norse.

scarf[3] ● verb N. Amer. informal eat or drink hungrily or enthusiastically.
– ORIGIN variant of SCOFF[2].

scarifier /skarrifiər, skairifiər/ ● noun **1** a tool with spikes or prongs used for breaking up matted vegetation in the surface of

Thesaurus

affront, insult, cause raised eyebrows.
– OPPOSITES impress.

scandalous ● adjective **1** *a scandalous waste of taxpayers' money* DISGRACEFUL, shocking, outrageous, monstrous, criminal, wicked, shameful, appalling, deplorable, reprehensible, inexcusable, intolerable, insupportable, unforgivable, unpardonable. **2** *a series of scandalous liaisons* DISCREDITABLE, disreputable, dishonourable, improper, unseemly, sordid. **3** *scandalous rumours* SCURRILOUS, malicious, slanderous, libellous, defamatory.

scant ● adjective LITTLE, little or no, minimal, limited, negligible, meagre; insufficient, inadequate, deficient; *formal* exiguous.
– OPPOSITES abundant, ample.

scanty ● adjective **1** *their scanty wages* MEAGRE, scant, minimal, limited, modest, restricted, sparse; tiny, small, paltry, negligible, insufficient, inadequate, deficient; scarce, in short supply, thin on the ground, few and far between; *informal* measly, piddling, mingy, pathetic; *formal* exiguous. **2** *her scanty nightdress* SKIMPY, revealing, short, brief; low, low-cut; indecent.
– OPPOSITES ample, plentiful.

scapegoat ● noun WHIPPING BOY, Aunt Sally; *informal* fall guy; *N. Amer. informal* patsy.

scar ● noun **1** *the scar on his left cheek* CICATRIX, mark, blemish, disfigurement, discoloration; pockmark, pock, pit; lesion, stigma; birthmark, naevus. **2** *deep psychological scars* TRAUMA, damage, injury.
● verb **1** *he's likely to be scarred for life* DISFIGURE, mark, blemish; pockmark, pit; *Christianity* stigmatize. **2** *a landscape which has been scarred by strip mining* DAMAGE, spoil, mar, deface, injure. **3** *she was profoundly scarred by the incident* TRAUMATIZE, damage, injure; distress, disturb, upset.

scarce ● adjective **1** *food was scarce* IN SHORT SUPPLY, scant, scanty, meagre, sparse, hard to find, hard to come by, insufficient, deficient, inadequate; at a premium, like gold dust; paltry, negligible; *informal* not to be had for love nor money; *formal* exiguous. **2** *birds that prefer dense forest are becoming scarcer* RARE, few and far between, thin on the ground; uncommon, unusual; *Brit.* out of the common.
– OPPOSITES plentiful.

scarcely ● adverb **1** *she could scarcely hear what he was saying* HARDLY, barely, only just; almost not. **2** *I scarcely ever see him* RARELY, seldom, infrequently, not often, hardly ever, every once in a while; *informal* once in a blue moon. **3** *this could scarcely be accidental* SURELY NOT, not, hardly, certainly not, not at all, on no account, under no circumstances, by no means; *N. Amer.* noway.
– OPPOSITES often.

scarcity ● noun SHORTAGE, dearth, lack, undersupply, insufficiency, paucity, scantness, meagreness, sparseness, poverty; deficiency, inadequacy; unavailability, absence; *formal* exiguity.

scare ● verb *stop it, you're scaring me* FRIGHTEN, startle, alarm, terrify, petrify, unnerve, intimidate, terrorize, cow; strike terror into, put the fear of God into, chill someone to the bone/marrow, make someone's blood run cold; *informal* frighten/scare the living daylights out of, scare stiff, frighten/scare someone out of their wits, scare witless, frighten/scare to death, scare the pants off, make someone's hair stand on end, throw into a blue funk, make someone jump out of their skin; *Brit. informal* put the wind up, make someone's hair curl; *N. Amer. informal* spook; *Irish informal* scare the bejesus out of; *archaic* affright.
● noun *you gave me a scare—how did you get here?* FRIGHT, shock, start, turn, jump.

scared ● adjective FRIGHTENED, afraid, fearful, nervous, panicky; terrified, petrified, horrified, panic-stricken, scared stiff, frightened/scared out of one's wits, frightened/scared to death, scared witless; *Scottish* feart; *informal* in a cold sweat, in a (blue) funk; *Brit. informal* funky, windy; *N. Amer. informal* spooked; *dialect* frit; *archaic* afeared, affrighted.

scaremonger ● noun ALARMIST, prophet of doom, Cassandra,

S

a lawn. **2** a machine with spikes used for breaking up the surface of a road.

scarify[1] /skarrifī, skair-/ ● verb (**scarifies**, **scarified**) **1** cut and remove debris from (a lawn) with a scarifier. **2** break up the surface of (soil or a road or pavement). **3** make shallow incisions in (the skin). **4** criticize severely and hurtfully.
– DERIVATIVES **scarification** noun.
– ORIGIN Old French *scarifier*, from Greek *skariphasthai* 'scratch an outline'.

scarify[2] /skairifī/ ● verb (**scarifies**, **scarified**) informal frighten.
– ORIGIN from SCARE.

scarlatina /skaarləteenə/ (also **scarletina**) ● noun another term for SCARLET FEVER.
– ORIGIN Latin.

scarlet ● noun a brilliant red colour.
– ORIGIN originally denoting any brightly coloured cloth: from Latin *scarlata*, from *sigillatus* 'decorated with small images'.

scarlet fever ● noun an infectious bacterial disease affecting especially children, and causing fever and a scarlet rash.

scarlet woman ● noun a notoriously promiscuous or immoral woman.

scarp ● noun a very steep bank or slope; an escarpment. ● verb cut or erode so as to form a scarp.
– ORIGIN Italian *scarpa*.

scarper ● verb Brit. informal run away.
– ORIGIN probably from Italian *scappare* 'to escape', influenced by rhyming slang *Scapa Flow* 'go'.

Scart (also **SCART**) ● noun a 21-pin socket used to connect video equipment.
– ORIGIN acronym from French *Syndicat des Constructeurs des Appareils Radiorécepteurs et Téléviseurs*, the committee which designed the connector.

scarves plural of SCARF[1].

scary ● adjective (**scarier**, **scariest**) informal frightening; causing fear.
– DERIVATIVES **scarily** adverb.

scat[1] ● verb (**scatted**, **scatting**) informal go away; leave.
– ORIGIN perhaps an abbreviation of SCATTER, or perhaps from the sound of a hiss + *-cat*.

scat[2] ● noun improvised jazz singing in which the voice is used in imitation of an instrument. ● verb (**scatted**, **scatting**) sing in such a way.
– ORIGIN probably imitative.

scathing ● adjective witheringly scornful; severely critical.
– DERIVATIVES **scathingly** adverb.
– ORIGIN from obsolete *scathe* 'harm, injure', from Old Norse.

scatology /skatolləji/ ● noun a preoccupation with excrement and excretion.
– DERIVATIVES **scatological** adjective.
– ORIGIN from Greek *skōr* 'dung'.

scatter ● verb **1** throw in various random directions. **2** separate and move off in different directions. **3** (**be scattered**) occur or be found at various places rather than all together. **4** Physics deflect or diffuse (electromagnetic radiation or particles). ● noun a small, dispersed amount of something.
– ORIGIN probably a variant of SHATTER.

scatterbrained ● adjective disorganized and lacking in concentration.

scatter cushion ● noun a small cushion placed randomly so as to create a casual effect.

scattergun ● noun **1** chiefly N. Amer. a shotgun. **2** (also **scattershot**) (before another noun) covering a broad range in a random and unsystematic way: *the scattergun approach.*

scatty ● adjective (**scattier**, **scattiest**) informal absent-minded and disorganized.
– ORIGIN abbreviation of *scatterbrained.*

scaup /skawp/ ● noun a diving duck, the male of which has a black head with a green or purple gloss.
– ORIGIN Scots and northern English *scalp* 'mussel-bed', a feeding ground of the duck.

scavenge /skavvinj/ ● verb **1** search for and collect (anything usable) from discarded waste. **2** search for (carrion) as food. **3** technical combine with and remove (a substance) from a medium.

scavenger ● noun **1** a person or animal that scavenges. **2** Chemistry a substance that combines with and removes particular molecules, radicals, etc.
– ORIGIN originally denoting an official who collected *scavage*, a toll on foreign merchants' goods, later a person who kept the streets clean: from Old French *escauwer* 'inspect'.

SCE ● abbreviation Scottish Certificate of Education.

scenario /sinaariō/ ● noun (pl. **scenarios**) **1** a written outline of a film, novel, or stage work giving details of the plot and individual scenes. **2** a suggested sequence or development of events.
– ORIGIN Italian, from Latin *scena* 'scene'.

scene ● noun **1** the place where a real or fictional incident occurs or occurred. **2** a view or landscape as seen by a spectator. **3** an incident or representation of an incident of a specified nature: *scenes of violence.* **4** a sequence of continuous action in a play, film, opera, etc. **5** the scenery used in a play or opera. **6** a public display of emotion or anger. **7** a specified area of activity or interest: *the literary scene.*
– PHRASES **behind the scenes** out of public view. **change of scene** a move to different surroundings. **come** (or **appear** or **arrive**) **on the scene** arrive; appear. **not one's scene** informal not something one enjoys or is interested in.
– ORIGIN Latin *scena*, from Greek *skēnē* 'tent, stage'.

scenery ● noun **1** the natural features of a landscape considered in terms of their appearance. **2** the painted background used to represent a place on a stage or film set.

scenic ● adjective **1** relating to impressive or beautiful natural scenery. **2** relating to theatrical scenery. **3** (of a picture) representing an incident.

Thesaurus

voice of doom, doom-monger; *informal* doom (and gloom) merchant.

scarf ● noun MUFFLER, headscarf, headsquare, square; mantilla, stole, tippet; *N. Amer.* babushka.

scarper ● verb *(Brit. informal).* See RUN verb sense 2.

scary ● adjective *(informal)* FRIGHTENING, alarming, terrifying, hair-raising, spine-chilling, blood-curdling, horrifying, nerve-racking, unnerving; eerie, sinister; *informal* creepy, spine-tingling, spooky, hairy.

scathing ● adjective WITHERING, blistering, searing, devastating, fierce, ferocious, savage, severe, stinging, biting, cutting, mordant, trenchant, virulent, caustic, vitriolic, scornful, sharp, bitter, harsh, unsparing; *formal* mordacious.
– OPPOSITES mild.

scatter ● verb **1** *scatter the seeds as evenly as possible* THROW, strew, toss, fling; sprinkle, spread, distribute, sow, broadcast, disseminate. **2** *the crowd scattered | onlookers were scattered in all directions* DISPERSE, break up, disband, separate, go separate ways, dissolve; drive, send, put to flight, chase. **3** *the sky was scattered with stars* FLECK, stud, dot, cover, sprinkle, stipple, spot, pepper; *poetic/literary* bestrew.
– OPPOSITES gather, assemble.

scatterbrained ● adjective ABSENT-MINDED, forgetful, disorganized; dreamy, wool-gathering, with one's head in the clouds, featherbrained, giddy; *informal* scatty, with a mind/memory like a sieve, dizzy, dippy.

scavenge ● verb SEARCH, hunt, look, forage, rummage, root about/around, grub about/around.

scenario ● noun **1** *Walt wrote scenarios for a major Hollywood studio* PLOT, outline, storyline, framework; screenplay, script; *formal* diegesis. **2** *every possible scenario must be explored* SEQUENCE OF EVENTS, course of events, chain of events, situation. **3** *this film has a more contemporary scenario* SETTING, background, context, scene, milieu.

scene ● noun **1** *the scene of the accident* LOCATION, site, place, position, point, spot; locale, whereabouts; *technical* locus. **2** *the scene is London, in the late 1890s* BACKGROUND, setting, context, milieu, backdrop, mise en scène. **3** *terrible scenes of violence* INCIDENT, event, episode, happening. **4** *an impressive mountain scene* VIEW, vista, outlook, panorama, sight; landscape, scenery. **5** *she made an embarrassing scene* FUSS, exhibition of oneself, performance, tantrum, commotion, disturbance, row, upset, furore, brouhaha; *informal* to-do; *Brit. informal* carry-on. **6** *the political scene* ARENA, stage, sphere, world, milieu, realm, domain; area of interest, field, province, preserve. **7** *a scene from a Laurel and Hardy film* CLIP, section, segment, part, sequence.
– PHRASES **behind the scenes** SECRETLY, in secret, privately, in private, behind closed doors, surreptitiously; *informal* on the quiet, on the q.t.; *formal* sub rosa.

scenery ● noun **1** *the beautiful scenery of west Wales* LANDSCAPE, countryside, country, terrain, topography, setting, surroundings,

– DERIVATIVES **scenically** adverb.

scenic railway ● noun a miniature railway at a fair or amusement park that goes past natural features and artificial scenery.

scent ● noun **1** a distinctive smell, especially one that is pleasant. **2** pleasant-smelling liquid worn on the skin; perfume. **3** a trail indicated by the characteristic smell of an animal. ● verb **1** give a pleasant scent to. **2** discern by the sense of smell. **3** sense the presence or approach of.

– DERIVATIVES **scented** adjective.

– ORIGIN from Latin *sentire* 'perceive, smell'.

scent gland ● noun an animal gland that secretes an odorous pheromone or defensive substance.

sceptic (US **skeptic**) ● noun **1** a person inclined to question or doubt accepted opinions. **2** a person who doubts the truth of Christianity and other religions; an atheist.

– DERIVATIVES **scepticism** noun.

– ORIGIN Greek *skeptikos*, from *skepsis* 'inquiry, doubt'.

sceptical ● adjective not easily convinced; having doubts or reservations.

sceptre (US **scepter**) ● noun a staff carried by rulers on ceremonial occasions as a symbol of sovereignty.

– DERIVATIVES **sceptred** adjective.

– ORIGIN Greek *skēptron*, from *skēptein* 'lean on'.

Schadenfreude /shaadənfroydə/ ● noun pleasure derived from another's misfortune.

– ORIGIN German, from *Schaden* 'harm' + *Freude* 'joy'.

schedule /shedyool, sked-/ ● noun **1** a plan for carrying out a process or procedure, giving lists of intended events and times. **2** a timetable. **3** chiefly Law an appendix to a formal document or statute, especially as a list, table, or inventory. ● verb **1** arrange or plan for (something) to happen or for (someone) to do something. **2** Brit. include (a building) in a list for legal preservation or protection.

– PHRASES **to** (or **on** or **according to**) **schedule** on time; as planned.

– DERIVATIVES **scheduler** noun.

– ORIGIN Latin *schedula* 'slip of paper', from Greek *skhedē* 'papyrus leaf'.

scheduled ● adjective **1** forming part of or included on a schedule. **2** (of an airline or flight) forming part of a regular service rather than specially chartered.

scheduled caste ● noun the official name given in India to the untouchable caste, who are given special concessions in recognition of their disadvantaged status.

schema /skeemə/ ● noun (pl. **schemata** /skeemətə/ or **schemas**) technical a representation of a plan or theory in the form of an outline or model.

– ORIGIN Greek *skhēma* 'form, figure'.

schematic ● adjective **1** (of a diagram or representation) symbolic and simplified. **2** (of thought, ideas, etc.) simplistic or formulaic in character.

– DERIVATIVES **schematically** adverb.

schematize (also **schematise**) ● verb arrange or represent in a schematic form.

scheme ● noun **1** a systematic plan or arrangement for achieving a particular object or effect. **2** a secret or underhand plan; a plot. **3** a particular ordered system or pattern: *a classical rhyme scheme*. ● verb **1** make plans in an underhand way; plot. **2** arrange according to a colour scheme.

– DERIVATIVES **schemer** noun.

– ORIGIN Greek *skhēma* 'form, figure'.

schemozzle ● noun variant spelling of SHEMOZZLE.

scherzo /skairtsō/ ● noun (pl. **scherzos** or **scherzi** /skairtsi/) Music a vigorous, light, or playful composition, typically comprising a movement in a symphony or sonata.

– ORIGIN Italian, 'jest'.

schilling /shilling/ ● noun the basic monetary unit of Austria, equal to 100 groschen.

– ORIGIN German *Schilling*.

schism /sizz'm, skizz'm/ ● noun **1** a division between strongly opposed parties, caused by differences in opinion or belief. **2** the formal separation of a Church into two Churches or the secession of a group owing to doctrinal and other differences.

– ORIGIN Greek *skhisma* 'cleft', from *skhizein* 'to split'.

schismatic ● adjective characterized by or favouring schism. ● noun chiefly historical (especially in the Christian Church) a person who promotes schism.

schist /shist/ ● noun Geology a coarse-grained metamorphic rock which consists of layers of different minerals and can be split into thin irregular plates.

– ORIGIN from Greek *skhistos* 'split'.

schistosome /shistəsōm/ ● noun a parasitic flatworm which causes bilharzia, infesting freshwater snails when immature and the blood vessels of birds and mammals when adult.

– ORIGIN from Greek *skhistos* 'divided' + *sōma* 'body'.

schistosomiasis /shistəmīəsiss/ ● noun another term for BILHARZIA.

schizo ● adjective & noun (pl. **schizos**) informal schizophrenic.

schizoid /skitzoyd/ ● adjective **1** Psychiatry denoting a personality type characterized by emotional aloofness and solitary habits. **2** informal resembling schizophrenia in having contradictory elements; mad or crazy. ● noun a schizoid person.

schizophrenia /skitsəfreeniə/ ● noun a long-term mental disorder involving faulty perception, inappropriate actions and feelings, and withdrawal from reality into fantasy and delusion.

– ORIGIN Latin, from Greek *skhizein* 'to split' + *phrēn* 'mind'.

Thesaurus

environment; view, vista, panorama. **2** *we all helped with the scenery and costumes* STAGE SET, set, mise en scène, flats, backdrop, drop curtain; *Brit.* backcloth.

scenic ● adjective PICTURESQUE, pretty, pleasing, attractive, lovely, beautiful, charming, pretty as a picture, easy on the eye; impressive, striking, spectacular, breathtaking; panoramic.

scent ● noun **1** *the scent of freshly cut hay* SMELL, fragrance, aroma, perfume, redolence, savour, odour; bouquet, nose. **2** *a bottle of scent* PERFUME, fragrance, toilet water, eau de toilette, cologne; eau de cologne. **3** *the hounds picked up the scent of a hare* SPOOR, trail, track; *Hunting* foil, wind.

● verb **1** *a shark can scent blood from over half a kilometre away* SMELL, detect the smell of, get a whiff of. **2** *Rose looked at him, scenting a threat* SENSE, become aware of, detect, discern, recognize, get wind of.

scented ● adjective PERFUMED, fragranced, perfumy; sweet-smelling, fragrant, aromatic.

sceptic ● noun **1** *sceptics said the marriage wouldn't last* CYNIC, doubter; pessimist, prophet of doom. **2** *sceptics who have found faith* AGNOSTIC, atheist, unbeliever, non-believer, disbeliever, doubting Thomas; *rare* nullifidian.

sceptical ● adjective DUBIOUS, doubtful, taking something with a pinch of salt, doubting; cynical, distrustful, mistrustful, suspicious, disbelieving, unconvinced, incredulous, scoffing; pessimistic, defeatist.

– OPPOSITES certain, convinced.

scepticism ● noun **1** *his ideas were met with scepticism* DOUBT, doubtfulness, a pinch of salt; disbelief, cynicism, distrust, mistrust, suspicion, incredulity; pessimism, defeatism; *formal* dubiety. **2** *he passed from scepticism to religious belief* AGNOSTICISM, doubt; atheism, unbelief, non-belief.

schedule ● noun **1** *we need to draw up a production schedule* PLAN, programme, timetable, scheme. **2** *I have a very busy schedule* TIMETABLE, agenda, diary, calendar; itinerary.

● verb *another meeting was scheduled for April 20* ARRANGE, organize, plan, programme, timetable, set up, line up; *N. Amer.* slate.

– PHRASES **behind schedule** LATE, running late, overdue, behind time, behind, behindhand.

scheme ● noun **1** *adventurous fund-raising schemes* PLAN, project, plan of action, programme, strategy, stratagem, tactic, game plan, course/line of action; system, procedure, design, formula, recipe; *Brit. informal* wheeze; *archaic* shift. **2** *police uncovered a scheme to steal the paintings* PLOT, intrigue, conspiracy; ruse, ploy, stratagem, manoeuvre, subterfuge; machinations; *informal* game, racket. **3** *the sonnet's rhyme scheme* ARRANGEMENT, system, organization, configuration, pattern, format; *technical* schema.

● verb *he schemed to bring about the collapse of the government* PLOT, hatch a plot, conspire, intrigue, connive, manoeuvre, plan.

scheming ● adjective CUNNING, crafty, calculating, devious, designing, conniving, wily, sly, tricky, artful, guileful, slippery, slick, manipulative, Machiavellian, unscrupulous, disingenuous; duplicitous, deceitful, underhand, treacherous.

– OPPOSITES ingenuous, honest.

schism ● noun DIVISION, split, rift, breach, rupture, break, separation, severance; chasm, gulf; discord, disagreement, dissension.

schismatic ● adjective SEPARATIST, heterodox, dissident, dissen-

S

schizophrenic /skitsəfrennik/ ● adjective **1** suffering from schizophrenia. **2** (in general use) characterized by inconsistent or contradictory elements. ● noun a schizophrenic person.

schlep /shlep/ (also **schlepp**) informal, chiefly N. Amer. ● verb (**schlepped**, **schlepping**) **1** haul or carry with difficulty. **2** go or move reluctantly or with effort. ● noun **1** a tedious or difficult journey. **2** (also **schlepper**) an inept or stupid person.
– ORIGIN Yiddish, 'drag'.

schlock /shlok/ ● noun informal, chiefly N. Amer. cheap or inferior goods; trash.
– DERIVATIVES **schlocky** adjective.
– ORIGIN apparently from Yiddish words for 'an apoplectic stroke' and 'wretch, untidy person'.

schloss /shloss/ ● noun (in Germany, Austria, or their former territories) a castle.
– ORIGIN German.

schmaltz /shmolts/ ● noun informal excessive sentimentality.
– DERIVATIVES **schmaltzy** adjective.
– ORIGIN Yiddish, from German *Schmalz* 'dripping, lard'.

schmooze /shmo͞oz/ informal, chiefly N. Amer. ● verb **1** chat; gossip. **2** chat to (someone) in order to gain an advantage. ● noun an intimate conversation.
– DERIVATIVES **schmoozer** noun **schmoozy** adjective.
– ORIGIN Yiddish.

schmuck /shmuk/ ● noun N. Amer. informal a foolish or contemptible person.
– ORIGIN Yiddish, 'penis'.

schnapps /shnaps/ ● noun a strong alcoholic drink resembling gin.
– ORIGIN German *Schnaps* 'dram of liquor'.

schnauzer /shnowzər/ ● noun a German breed of dog with a close wiry coat and heavy whiskers round the muzzle.
– ORIGIN German, from *Schnauze* 'muzzle, snout'.

schnitzel /shnitz'l/ ● noun a thin slice of veal or other pale meat, coated in breadcrumbs and fried.
– ORIGIN German, 'slice'.

schnozz /shnoz/ (also **schnozzle** or **schnozzola**) ● noun N. Amer. informal a person's nose.
– ORIGIN Yiddish, from German *Schnauze* 'snout'.

scholar ● noun **1** a specialist in a particular branch of study, especially the humanities; a distinguished academic. **2** chiefly archaic a person who is highly educated or has an aptitude for study. **3** a university student holding a scholarship.
– ORIGIN Latin *scholaris*, from Greek *skholē* (see SCHOOL).

scholarly ● adjective **1** relating to serious academic study. **2** having or showing knowledge, learning, or devotion to academic pursuits.

scholarship ● noun **1** academic achievement; learning of a high level. **2** a grant made to support a student's education, awarded on the basis of achievement.

scholastic ● adjective **1** concerning schools and education. **2** relating to medieval scholasticism. ● noun an adherent of medieval scholasticism.

scholasticism ● noun the system of theology and philosophy taught in medieval European universities, based on Aristotelian logic and the writings of the early Christian Fathers.

school[1] ● noun **1** an institution for educating children. **2** a day's work at school; lessons. **3** any institution at which instruction is given in a particular discipline. **4** a department or faculty of a university. **5** N. Amer. informal a university. **6** a group of artists, philosophers, etc. sharing similar ideas, methods, or style. **7** Brit. a group of people gambling together. ● verb **1** formal or N. Amer. send to school; educate. **2** train in a particular skill or activity. **3** Riding train (a horse) on the flat or over fences.
– PHRASES **school of thought** a particular way of thinking.
– ORIGIN Greek *skholē* 'leisure, philosophy, lecture-place'.

school[2] ● noun a large group of fish or sea mammals. ● verb (of fish or sea mammals) form a school.
– ORIGIN Low German, Dutch *schōle*; compare with SHOAL[1].

schoolhouse ● noun **1** a building used as a school, especially in a rural community. **2** Brit., chiefly historical a house adjoining a school, lived in by the schoolteacher.

schooling ● noun **1** education received at school. **2** Riding the training of a horse on the flat or over fences.

schoolmarm ● noun chiefly N. Amer. a schoolmistress, especially one regarded as prim and strict.

schoolmaster ● noun a male teacher in a school.

schoolmate ● noun informal a fellow pupil.

schoolmistress ● noun a female teacher in a school.

schoolteacher ● noun a person who teaches in a school.

schooner /sko͞onər/ ● noun **1** a sailing ship with two or more masts, typically with the foremast smaller than the mainmast. **2** Brit. a large glass for sherry. **3** N. Amer. & Austral./NZ a tall beer glass.
– ORIGIN perhaps from dialect *scun* 'skim along'.

schottische /shoteesh/ ● noun a dance resembling a slow polka.
– ORIGIN from German *der schottische Tanz* 'the Scottish dance'.

schtuck ● noun variant spelling of SHTOOK.

schtum /shto͝om/ ● adjective variant spelling of SHTUM.

schuss /sho͝oss/ ● noun a straight downhill run on skis. ● verb perform a schuss.
– ORIGIN German, 'shot'.

sciatic /sīattik/ ● adjective **1** relating to the hip. **2** affecting the sciatic nerve. **3** suffering from or liable to sciatica.
– ORIGIN French *sciatique*, from Greek *iskhiadikos* 'relating to the hips'.

sciatica ● noun pain affecting the back, hip, and outer side of the leg, caused by compression of a spinal nerve root in the lower back.

sciatic nerve ● noun Anatomy a major nerve extending from the lower end of the spinal cord down the back of the thigh.

science ● noun **1** the intellectual and practical activity encompassing the systematic study of the structure and behaviour of the physical and natural world through observation and experiment. **2** a systematically organized body of knowledge on any subject.
– ORIGIN Latin *scientia*, from *scire* 'know'.

science fiction ● noun fiction based on imagined future worlds portraying scientific or technological changes.

science park ● noun an area devoted to scientific research or the development of science-based industries.

S

Thesaurus

tient, dissenting, heretical; breakaway, splinter.
– OPPOSITES orthodox.

schmaltzy ● adjective *(informal)*. See SENTIMENTAL sense 2.

scholar ● noun **1** *a leading biblical scholar* ACADEMIC, intellectual, learned person, man/woman of letters, mind, intellect, savant, polymath, highbrow, bluestocking; authority, expert; *informal* egghead; *N. Amer. informal* pointy-head; *archaic* bookman. **2** *(archaic) the school had 28 scholars* PUPIL, student, schoolchild, schoolboy, schoolgirl.

scholarly ● adjective **1** *an earnest, scholarly man* LEARNED, erudite, academic, well read, widely read, intellectual, literary, lettered, educated, knowledgeable, highbrow; studious, bookish, donnish, bluestocking, cerebral; *N. Amer. informal* pointy-headed; *archaic* clerkly. **2** *a scholarly career* ACADEMIC, scholastic, pedagogic.
– OPPOSITES uneducated, illiterate.

scholarship ● noun **1** *a centre of medieval scholarship* LEARNING, book learning, knowledge, erudition, education, letters, culture, academic study, academic achievement. **2** *a scholarship of £200 per term* GRANT, award, endowment, payment; *Brit.* bursary, exhibition.

scholastic ● adjective ACADEMIC, educational, school, scholarly.

school ● noun **1** *their children went to the village school* EDUCATIONAL INSTITUTION; academy, college; seminary; alma mater. **2** *the university's School of English* DEPARTMENT, faculty, division. **3** *the Barbizon school* GROUP, set, circle; followers, following, disciples, apostles, admirers, devotees, votaries; proponents, adherents. **4** *the school of linguistics associated with his ideas* WAY OF THINKING, school of thought, persuasion, creed, credo, doctrine, belief, faith, opinion, point of view; approach, method, style.
– RELATED TERMS scholastic.
● verb **1** *he was born in Paris and schooled in Lyon* EDUCATE, teach, instruct. **2** *he schooled her in horsemanship* TRAIN, teach, tutor, coach, instruct, drill, discipline, direct, guide, prepare, groom; prime, verse.

schooling ● noun **1** *his parents paid for his schooling* EDUCATION, teaching, tuition, instruction, tutoring, tutelage; lessons; (book) learning. **2** *the schooling of horses* TRAINING, coaching, instruction, drill, drilling, discipline, disciplining.

schoolteacher ● noun TEACHER, schoolmaster, schoolmistress, tutor, educationist; *Brit.* master, mistress; *N. Amer. informal* schoolmarm; *Austral./NZ informal* chalkie, schoolie; *formal* pedagogue.

science ● noun **1** *a science teacher* physics, chemistry, biology;

scientific ● adjective **1** relating to or based on science. **2** systematic; methodical.
– DERIVATIVES **scientifically** adverb.
scientism ● noun **1** thought or expression regarded as characteristic of scientists. **2** excessive belief in the power of scientific knowledge and techniques.
scientist ● noun a person who has expert knowledge of one or more of the natural or physical sciences.
Scientology ● noun trademark a religious system based on the seeking of self-knowledge and spiritual fulfilment through courses of study and training.
– DERIVATIVES **Scientologist** noun.
– ORIGIN from Latin *scientia* 'knowledge'.
sci-fi ● noun informal short for SCIENCE FICTION.
scilicet /sīliset, skeeliket/ ● adverb that is to say; namely.
– ORIGIN from Latin *scire licet* 'one is permitted to know'.
scilla /sillə/ ● noun a plant of the lily family which typically bears small blue star- or bell-shaped flowers and glossy leaves.
– ORIGIN Greek *skilla* 'sea onion'.
scimitar /simmitər/ ● noun a short sword with a curved blade that broadens towards the point, used originally in Eastern countries.
– ORIGIN French *cimeterre* or Italian *scimitarra*.
scintilla /sintillə/ ● noun a tiny trace or amount: *not a scintilla of doubt*.
– ORIGIN Latin, 'spark'.
scintillate /sintilayt/ ● verb emit flashes of light; sparkle.
– DERIVATIVES **scintillant** adjective & noun **scintillation** noun.
– ORIGIN Latin *scintillare* 'to sparkle'.
scintillating ● adjective **1** sparkling or shining brightly. **2** brilliant and exciting.
scion /sīən/ ● noun **1** a young shoot or twig of a plant, especially one cut for grafting or rooting. **2** a descendant of a notable family.
– ORIGIN Old French *ciun* 'shoot, twig'.
scissor ● verb **1** cut with scissors. **2** move in a way resembling the action of scissors.
scissors ● plural noun **1** (also **a pair of scissors**) an instrument used for cutting cloth and paper, consisting of two crossing blades pivoted in the middle and operated by thumb and fingers inserted in rings at each end. **2** (also **scissor**) (before another noun) referring to an action in which two things cross each other or open and close like a pair of scissors: *a scissor kick*.
– ORIGIN Old French *cisoires*, from Latin *cisorium* 'cutting instrument'.
sclera /skleerə/ ● noun Anatomy the white outer layer of the eyeball.
– DERIVATIVES **scleral** adjective.
– ORIGIN Latin, from Greek *sklēros* 'hard'.
scleroderma /skleerədermə/ ● noun Medicine a chronic hardening and contraction of the skin and connective tissue.
sclerose /skleerōss/ ● verb Medicine (usu. as adj. **sclerosed** or **sclerosing**) affect with sclerosis.
sclerosis /sklərōsiss/ ● noun Medicine **1** abnormal hardening of body tissue. **2** (in full **multiple sclerosis**) a chronic, typically progressive disease involving damage to the sheaths of nerve cells in the brain and spinal cord.
– ORIGIN Greek *sklērōsis*, from *sklēroun* 'harden'.
sclerotic /sklərottik/ ● adjective **1** Medicine of or having sclerosis. **2** rigid; unable to adapt.
scoff¹ ● verb speak about something in a scornfully derisive way. ● noun an expression of scornful derision.
– DERIVATIVES **scoffer** noun.
– ORIGIN perhaps Scandinavian.
scoff² ● verb informal, chiefly Brit. eat quickly and greedily.
– ORIGIN from Dutch *schoft* 'quarter of a day, meal'.
scold ● verb angrily remonstrate with or rebuke. ● noun archaic a woman who nags or grumbles constantly.
– ORIGIN probably from an Old Norse word meaning 'a person who writes and recites epic poems'.
sconce ● noun a candle holder attached to a wall with an ornamental bracket.
– ORIGIN Old French *esconse* 'lantern', from Latin *absconsa laterna* 'dark lantern'.
scone /skon, skōn/ ● noun a small unsweetened or lightly sweetened cake made from flour, fat, and milk.
– ORIGIN perhaps from Dutch *schoonbroot* 'fine bread'.
scoop ● noun **1** a utensil resembling a spoon, having a short handle and a deep bowl. **2** the bowl-shaped part of a digging machine or dredger. **3** informal a piece of news published or broadcast in advance of being released by other newspapers or broadcast stations. ● verb **1** pick up with a scoop. **2** create (a hollow) with or as if with a scoop. **3** pick or gather up in a swift, fluid movement. **4** informal publish a scoop before (a rival). **5** informal win.
– ORIGIN Low German *schōpe* 'waterwheel bucket'.
scoop neck ● noun a deeply curved wide neckline on a woman's garment.
scoot ● verb informal go or leave somewhere quickly.
– ORIGIN of unknown origin.
scooter ● noun **1** (also **motor scooter**) a light two-wheeled motorcycle. **2** any small light vehicle able to travel quickly across water or snow. **3** a child's toy consisting of a footboard mounted on two wheels and a long steering handle, propelled

Thesaurus

physical sciences, life sciences. **2** *the science of criminology* BRANCH OF KNOWLEDGE, body of knowledge/information, area of study, discipline, field.
scientific ● adjective **1** *scientific research* technological, technical; research-based, knowledge-based, empirical. **2** *you need to approach it in a more scientific way* SYSTEMATIC, methodical, organized, well organized, ordered, orderly, meticulous, rigorous; exact, precise, accurate, mathematical; analytical, rational.
scintilla ● noun PARTICLE, iota, jot, whit, atom, speck, bit, trace, ounce, shred, crumb, fragment, grain, drop, spot, mite, modicum, hint, touch, suggestion, whisper, suspicion; *informal* smidgen, tad; *archaic* scantling.
scintillate ● verb SPARKLE, shine, gleam, glitter, flash, shimmer, twinkle, glint, glisten, wink; *poetic/literary* glister, coruscate.
scintillating ● adjective **1** *a scintillating diamond necklace* SPARKLING, shining, bright, brilliant, gleaming, glittering, twinkling, shimmering. **2** *a scintillating second-half performance* BRILLIANT, dazzling, exciting, exhilarating, stimulating; sparkling, lively, vivacious, vibrant, animated, ebullient, effervescent; witty, clever; *poetic/literary* coruscating.
– OPPOSITES dull, boring.
scion ● noun **1** *a scion of the tree* CUTTING, graft, slip; shoot, offshoot, twig. **2** *the scion of an aristocratic family* DESCENDANT; heir, successor; child, offspring; *Law* issue.
scoff¹ ● verb *they scoffed at her article* MOCK, deride, ridicule, sneer at, jeer at, jibe at, taunt, make fun of, poke fun at, laugh at, scorn, laugh to scorn, dismiss, make light of, belittle; *informal* pooh-pooh.
scoff² ● verb *(Brit. informal) the bears scoffed our packed lunch* EAT, devour, consume, guzzle, gobble, wolf down, bolt; *informal* put away, nosh, polish off, demolish, shovel down, stuff one's face with, pig oneself on, pig out on; *Brit. informal* gollop, shift; *N. Amer. informal* scarf (down/up), snarf (down/up).
scold ● verb *Mum took Anna away, scolding her for her bad behaviour* REBUKE, reprimand, reproach, reprove, admonish, remonstrate with, chastise, chide, upbraid, berate, take to task, read someone the Riot Act, give someone a piece of one's mind, haul over the coals; *informal* tell off, dress down, give someone an earful, give someone a roasting, rap over the knuckles, let someone have it, bawl out, give someone hell; *Brit. informal* tick off, have a go at, carpet, tear someone off a strip, give someone what for, give someone some stick, give someone a rollicking/rocket/row; *N. Amer. informal* chew out, ream out; *Austral. informal* monster; *formal* castigate.
– OPPOSITES praise.
● noun *(archaic) she is turning into a scold* NAG, shrew, fishwife, harpy, termagant, harridan; complainer, moaner, grumbler; *N. Amer. informal* kvetch.
scolding ● noun REBUKE, reprimand, reproach, reproof, admonishment, reproval, remonstration, lecture, upbraiding; *informal* telling-off, talking-to, rap over the knuckles, dressing-down, earful, roasting; *Brit. informal* ticking-off, carpeting, rocket, rollicking; *formal* castigation.
scoop ● noun **1** *a measuring scoop* SPOON, ladle, dipper; bailer. **2** *a scoop of vanilla ice cream* SPOONFUL, ladleful, portion, lump, ball; *informal* dollop. **3** *(informal) reporters competed for scoops* EXCLUSIVE (STORY), inside story, exposé, revelation.
● verb **1** *a hole was scooped out in the floor* HOLLOW OUT, gouge out, dig, excavate, cut out. **2** *cut the tomatoes in half and scoop out the flesh* REMOVE, take out, spoon out, scrape out. **3** *she scooped up*

S

by pushing one foot against the ground. ● verb travel or ride on a scooter.

scope[1] ● noun **1** the extent of the area or subject matter that something deals with or to which it is relevant. **2** the opportunity or possibility for doing something.
– ORIGIN originally denoting a target for shooting at: from Greek *skopos* 'target'.

scope[2] ● noun informal a telescope, microscope, or other device having a name ending in *-scope*.

-scope ● combining form denoting an instrument for observing or examining: *telescope*.
– DERIVATIVES **-scopic** combining form in corresponding adjectives.
– ORIGIN from Greek *skopein* 'look at'.

scopolamine /skəpolləmeen/ ● noun another term for HYOSCINE.
– ORIGIN from *Scopolia* (genus name of the plants yielding the substance) + AMINE.

-scopy ● combining form indicating observation or examination: *microscopy*.
– ORIGIN from Greek *skopia* 'observation'.

scorbutic /skorbyōōtik/ ● adjective relating to or affected with scurvy.
– ORIGIN from Latin *scorbutus* 'scurvy'.

scorch ● verb **1** burn or become burnt on the surface or edges. **2** (**scorched**) dried out and withered as a result of extreme heat. **3** informal move very fast: *a car scorching along the motorway*. ● noun the burning or charring of the surface of something.
– ORIGIN perhaps related to an Old Norse word meaning 'be shrivelled'.

scorched earth policy ● noun a military strategy of burning or destroying all crops and resources that might be of use to an invading enemy force.

scorcher ● noun informal **1** a day or period of very hot weather. **2** Brit. a remarkable or powerful example of something.

score ● noun **1** the number of points, goals, runs, etc. achieved by an individual or side in a game. **2** (pl. same) a group or set of twenty. **3** (**scores of**) a large amount or number of. **4** a written representation of a musical composition showing all the vocal and instrumental parts. **5** a notch or line cut or scratched into a surface. **6** (**the score**) informal the state of affairs; the real facts. ● verb **1** gain (a point, goal, run, etc.) in a competitive game. **2** be worth (a number of points). **3** record the score during a game. **4** cut or scratch a mark on (a surface). **5** (**score out/through**) delete (text) by drawing a line through it. **6** orchestrate or arrange (a piece of music). **7** informal succeed in obtaining (illegal drugs). **8** informal succeed in attracting a sexual partner.
– PHRASES **on that** (or **this**) **score** so far as that (or this) is concerned. **settle a score** take revenge on someone.
– DERIVATIVES **scoreless** adjective **scorer** noun.
– ORIGIN Old Norse, 'notch, tally, twenty'; related to SHEAR.

scorecard ● noun **1** (also **scoresheet** or **scorebook**) a card, sheet, or book in which scores are entered. **2** a card listing the names and positions of players in a team.

scoreline ● noun the number of points or goals scored in a match.

scoria /skoriə/ ● noun (pl. **scoriae** /skori-ee/) **1** basaltic lava ejected as fragments from a volcano. **2** slag separated from molten metal during smelting.
– DERIVATIVES **scoriaceous** adjective.
– ORIGIN Greek *skōria* 'refuse', from *skōr* 'dung'.

scorn ● noun open contempt or disdain. ● verb **1** express scorn for. **2** reject in a contemptuous way.
– DERIVATIVES **scorner** noun **scornful** adjective **scornfully** adverb.
– ORIGIN Old French *escarn*.

Scorpio ● noun Astrology the eighth sign of the zodiac (the Scorpion), which the sun enters about 23 October.
– DERIVATIVES **Scorpian** noun & adjective.
– ORIGIN Latin.

scorpion ● noun an arachnid with lobster-like pincers and a poisonous sting at the end of its tail.
– ORIGIN Greek *skorpios* 'scorpion'.

scorzonera /skorzəneerə/ ● noun a plant with tapering purple-brown edible roots, which can be eaten as a vegetable.
– ORIGIN Italian, from an alteration of Latin *curtio* 'venomous snake' (against whose venom the plant may have been regarded as an antidote).

Scot ● noun **1** a person from Scotland. **2** a member of a Gaelic people that migrated from Ireland to Scotland around the late 5th century.
– ORIGIN Latin *Scottus*.

Scotch ● adjective old-fashioned term for SCOTTISH. ● noun **1** short for SCOTCH WHISKY. **2** dated the form of English spoken in Scotland.
– ORIGIN contraction of SCOTTISH.

scotch ● verb **1** decisively put an end to. **2** archaic injure and render harmless.
– ORIGIN perhaps related to SKATE[1].

Thesaurus

armfuls of clothes PICK UP, gather up, lift, take up; snatch up, grab.

scoot ● verb *(informal)*. See DASH verb sense 1.

scope ● noun **1** *the scope of the investigation* EXTENT, range, breadth, width, reach, sweep, purview, span, horizon; area, sphere, field, realm, compass, orbit, ambit, terms/field of reference, jurisdiction, remit; confine, limit; gamut. **2** *the scope for change is limited by political realities* OPPORTUNITY, freedom, latitude, leeway, capacity, liberty, room (to manoeuvre), elbow room; possibility, chance.

scorch ● verb **1** *the buildings were scorched by the fire* BURN, sear, singe, char, blacken, discolour. **2** *grass scorched by the sun* DRY UP, desiccate, parch, wither, shrivel; burn, bake.

scorching ● adjective **1** *the scorching July sun* EXTREMELY HOT, red-hot, blazing, flaming, fiery, burning, blistering, searing, sweltering, torrid; *N. Amer.* broiling; *informal* boiling (hot), baking (hot), sizzling. **2** *scorching criticism* FIERCE, savage, scathing, withering, blistering, searing, devastating, stringent, severe, harsh, stinging, biting, mordant, trenchant, caustic, virulent, vitriolic.
– OPPOSITES freezing, mild.

score ● noun **1** *the final score was 4–3* RESULT, outcome; total, sum total, tally, count. **2** *an IQ score of 161* RATING, grade, mark, percentage. **3** *I've got a score to settle with you* GRIEVANCE, bone to pick, axe to grind, grudge, complaint; dispute, bone of contention. **4** *(informal) he knew the score before he got here* THE SITUATION, the position, the facts, the truth of the matter, the (true) state of affairs, the picture, how things stand, the lie of the land; *Brit.* the state of play; *N. Amer.* the lay of the land; *informal* the set-up, what's what. **5** *scores of complaints* A GREAT MANY, a lot, a great/good deal, large quantities, plenty; *informal* lots, umpteen, a slew, loads, masses, stacks, scads, heaps, piles, bags, tons, oodles, dozens, hundreds, thousands, millions, billions; *Brit. informal* shedloads; *N. Amer. informal* a bunch, gazillions; *Austral./NZ informal* a swag.
● verb **1** *he's already scored 13 goals this season* GET, gain, chalk up, achieve, make; record, rack up, notch up; *informal* bag, knock up. **2** *(informal) his new movie really scored* BE SUCCESSFUL, be a success, triumph, make an impression, go down well; *informal* be a hit, be a winner, be a sell-out, go down a storm. **3** *the piece was scored for flute, violin, and continuo* ORCHESTRATE, arrange, set, adapt; write, compose. **4** *score the wood in criss-cross patterns* SCRATCH, cut, notch, incise, scrape, nick, snick, chip, gouge; mark; *archaic* scotch.
– PHRASES **score points off** GET THE BETTER OF, gain the advantage over, outdo, worst, have the edge over; have the last laugh on, make a fool of, humiliate; *informal* get/be one up on, get one over on, best. **score something out/through** CROSS OUT, strike out, put a line through, ink out, blue-pencil, scratch out; delete, obliterate, expunge.

scorn ● noun *he was unable to hide the scorn in his voice* CONTEMPT, derision, contemptuousness, disdain, derisiveness, mockery, sneering; *archaic* contumely, despite.
– OPPOSITES admiration, respect.
● verb **1** *critics scorned the painting* DERIDE, hold in contempt, treat with contempt, pour/heap scorn on, look down on, look down one's nose at, disdain, curl one's lip at, mock, scoff at, sneer at, jeer at, laugh at, laugh out of court; disparage, slight; dismiss, cock a snook at, spit in the eye/face of, thumb one's nose at; *informal* turn one's nose up at; *archaic* contemn. **2** *'I am a woman scorned,' she thought* SPURN, rebuff, reject, ignore, shun, snub. **3** *she would have scorned to stoop to such tactics* REFUSE TO, refrain from, not lower oneself to; be above, consider it beneath one.
– OPPOSITES admire, respect.

scornful ● adjective CONTEMPTUOUS, derisive, withering, mocking, scoffing, sneering, jeering, scathing, snide, disparaging, supercilious, disdainful, superior; *archaic* contumelious.
– OPPOSITES admiring, respectful.

scotch ● verb PUT AN END TO, put a stop to, nip in the bud, put the

S

Scotch bonnet ● noun W. Indian & N. Amer. a small chilli pepper which is the hottest variety available.
Scotch broth ● noun a traditional Scottish soup made from meat stock with pearl barley and vegetables.
Scotch egg ● noun a hard-boiled egg enclosed in sausage meat, rolled in breadcrumbs, and fried.
Scotchgard ● noun trademark a preparation for giving a waterproof stain-resistant finish to textiles and other materials.
Scotch mist ● noun a thick drizzly mist of a kind common in the Scottish Highlands.
Scotch pancake ● noun a drop scone.
Scotch tape ● noun trademark, chiefly N. Amer. transparent adhesive tape.
Scotch whisky ● noun whisky distilled in Scotland.
scoter /skōtər/ ● noun a northern diving duck, the male of which has mainly black plumage.
– ORIGIN of unknown origin.
scot-free ● adverb without suffering any punishment or injury.
– ORIGIN from obsolete *scot* 'a tax', from an Old Norse word meaning 'a shot'.
scotoma /skotōmə/ ● noun (pl. **scotomas** or **scotomata** /skotōmətə/) Medicine a partial loss of vision or blind spot in an otherwise normal visual field.
– ORIGIN Greek *skotōma*, from *skotos* 'darkness'.
Scots ● adjective another term for SCOTTISH. ● noun the form of English used in Scotland.
Scots pine ● noun a pine tree, now widely planted for commercial use, forming the dominant tree of the old Caledonian pine forest of the Scottish Highlands.
Scotticism /skottisiz'm/ (also **Scoticism**) ● noun a characteristically Scottish phrase, word, or idiom.
Scottie (also **Scottie dog**) ● noun informal a Scottish terrier.
Scottish ● adjective relating to Scotland or its people. ● noun (as pl. n. **the Scottish**) the people of Scotland.
– DERIVATIVES **Scottishness** noun.
Scottish Nationalist ● noun a member or supporter of Scottish nationalism or of the Scottish National Party.
Scottish terrier ● noun a small rough-haired breed of terrier.
scoundrel ● noun a dishonest or unscrupulous person.
– DERIVATIVES **scoundrelism** noun **scoundrelly** adjective.
– ORIGIN of unknown origin.
scour[1] ● verb **1** clean or brighten by vigorous rubbing with an abrasive or detergent. **2** (of running water) erode (a channel or pool). ● noun **1** the action of scouring or the state of being scoured. **2** (also **scours**) diarrhoea in livestock, especially cattle and pigs.
– DERIVATIVES **scourer** noun.
– ORIGIN Old French *escurer*, from Latin *excurare* 'clean (off)'.
scour[2] ● verb **1** subject to a thorough search. **2** move rapidly.
– ORIGIN related to obsolete *scour* 'moving hastily', of unknown origin.
scourge ● noun **1** historical a whip used as an instrument of punishment. **2** a person or thing causing great trouble or suffering. ● verb **1** historical whip with a scourge. **2** cause great suffering to.
– ORIGIN Old French *escorge*, from Latin *ex-* 'thoroughly' + *corrigia* 'thong, whip'.
Scouse Brit. informal ● noun **1** the dialect or accent of people from Liverpool. **2** (also **Scouser**) a person from Liverpool. ● adjective relating to Liverpool.
– ORIGIN abbreviation of *lobscouse*, a stew formerly eaten by sailors.
scout ● noun **1** a soldier or other person sent ahead of a main force to gather information about the enemy. **2** (also **Scout**) a member of the Scout Association, a boys' organization with the aim of developing their character through outdoor and other activities. **3** a talent scout. **4** an instance of scouting. ● verb **1** make a detailed search of a place. **2** explore or examine so as to gather information. **3** act as a scout.
– DERIVATIVES **scouter** noun **scouting** noun.
– ORIGIN Old French *escouter* 'listen', from Latin *auscultare*.
scow /skow/ ● noun a wide-beamed sailing dinghy.
– ORIGIN Dutch *schouw* 'ferry boat'.
scowl ● noun an angry or bad-tempered expression. ● verb frown in an angry or bad-tempered way.
– ORIGIN probably Scandinavian.
SCR ● abbreviation Brit. Senior Common (or Combination) Room.
scrabble ● verb **1** scratch or grope around with one's fingers to find or hold on to something. **2** move quickly and in a disorderly manner; scramble. ● noun **1** an act of scrabbling. **2** (**Scrabble**) trademark a board game in which players build up words from small lettered squares or tiles.
– ORIGIN Dutch *schrabbelen*, from *schrabben* 'to scrape'.
scrag ● verb (**scragged**, **scragging**) informal, chiefly Brit. handle roughly; beat up. ● noun **1** an unattractively thin person or animal. **2** archaic, informal the neck.
– ORIGIN perhaps an alteration of Scots and northern English *crag* 'neck'.
scrag-end ● noun Brit. the inferior end of a neck of mutton.
scraggy ● adjective (**scraggier**, **scraggiest**) **1** thin and bony. **2** (also chiefly N. Amer. **scraggly**) ragged or untidy in form or appearance.
scram ● verb (**scrammed**, **scramming**) informal go away or leave quickly.
– ORIGIN probably from SCRAMBLE.
scramble ● verb **1** move or make one's way quickly and awkwardly, typically by using one's hands as well as one's feet.

Thesaurus

lid on; ruin, wreck, destroy, smash, shatter, demolish, queer; frustrate, thwart; *informal* put paid to, put the kibosh on; *Brit. informal* scupper.
scot-free ● adverb UNPUNISHED, without punishment; unscathed, unhurt, unharmed, without a scratch.
Scotland ● noun Caledonia; *Brit.* north of the border; *informal* the land of cakes.
scoundrel ● noun ROGUE, rascal, miscreant, good-for-nothing, reprobate; cheat, swindler, fraudster, trickster, charlatan; *informal* villain, bastard, beast, son of a bitch, SOB, rat, louse, swine, dog, skunk, heel, snake (in the grass), wretch, scumbag; *Irish informal* sleeveen, spalpeen; *N. Amer. informal* rat fink; *informal, dated* rotter, hound, bounder, blighter; *dated* blackguard, cad; *archaic* knave, varlet, whoreson.
scour[1] ● verb *she scoured the cooker and cleaned out the cupboards* SCRUB, rub, clean, wash, cleanse, wipe; polish, buff (up), shine, burnish; abrade.
scour[2] ● verb *Chris scoured the shops for a gift* SEARCH, comb, hunt through, rummage through, go through with a fine-tooth comb, root through, rake through, leave no stone unturned, look high and low in; ransack, turn upside-down; *Austral./NZ informal* fossick through.
scourge ● noun **1** *(historical) he was beaten with a scourge* WHIP, horsewhip, lash, strap, birch, switch; *N. Amer.* bullwhip, rawhide; *historical* cat-o'-nine-tails. **2** *inflation was the scourge of the mid-1970s* AFFLICTION, bane, curse, plague, menace, evil, misfortune, burden, cross to bear; blight, cancer, canker.
– OPPOSITES blessing, godsend.
● verb **1** *(historical) he was publicly scourged* FLOG, whip, beat, horsewhip, lash, flagellate, strap, birch, cane, thrash, belt, leather; *informal* tan someone's hide, take a strap to. **2** *a disease which scourged the English for centuries* AFFLICT, plague, torment, torture, curse, oppress, burden, bedevil, beset.
scout ● noun **1** *scouts reported that the enemy were massing ahead* LOOKOUT, outrider, advance guard, vanguard; spy. **2** *a lengthy scout round the area* RECONNAISSANCE, reconnoitre; exploration, search, expedition; *informal* recce; *Brit. informal* shufti; *N. Amer. informal* recon. **3** *a record company scout* TALENT SPOTTER, talent scout; *N. Amer. informal* bird dog.
● verb **1** *I scouted around for some logs* SEARCH, look, hunt, ferret about/around, root about/around. **2** *a night patrol was sent to scout out the area* RECONNOITRE, explore, make a reconnaissance of, inspect, investigate, spy out, survey; examine, scan, study, observe; *informal* make a recce of, check out, case; *Brit. informal* take a shufti round; *N. Amer. informal* recon.
scowl ● verb GLOWER, frown, glare, grimace, lour, look daggers at, give someone a black look; make a face, pull a face, turn the corner's of one's mouth down, pout; *informal* give someone a dirty look.
– OPPOSITES smile, grin.
scraggy ● adjective SCRAWNY, thin, as thin as a rake, skinny, skin-and-bones, gaunt, bony, angular, gawky, raw-boned; *dated* spindle-shanked.
– OPPOSITES fat.
scram ● verb *(informal) scram or I'll call the police* GO AWAY, leave, get out; go, get moving, be off (with you), shoo; *informal* skedaddle, split, run along, beat it, get lost, shove off, buzz off, push off, clear off, on your bike; *Brit. informal* get stuffed, sling your hook,

S

2 make or become jumbled or muddled. **3** make (a broadcast transmission or telephone conversation) unintelligible unless received by an appropriate decoding device. **4** cook (beaten eggs with a little liquid) in a pan. **5** (with reference to fighter aircraft) take off or cause to take off immediately in an emergency or for action. **6** act in a hurried, disorderly, or undignified manner: *firms scrambled to win contracts.* ● noun **1** an act of scrambling. **2** Brit. a motorcycle race over rough and hilly ground. **3** a disordered mixture.
– ORIGIN imitative.

scrambler ● noun **1** a device for scrambling a broadcast transmission or telephone conversation. **2** Brit. a motorcycle for racing over rough ground.

scrap[1] ● noun **1** a small piece or amount of something, especially one that is left over after the greater part has been used. **2** (**scraps**) bits of uneaten food left after a meal. **3** material discarded for reprocessing. ● verb (**scrapped**, **scrapping**) **1** remove from use or service, especially for conversion to scrap metal. **2** abolish or cancel (a plan, policy, or law).
– ORIGIN Old Norse.

scrap[2] informal ● noun a fight or quarrel, especially a minor or spontaneous one. ● verb (**scrapped**, **scrapping**) **1** engage in such a fight or quarrel. **2** compete fiercely.
– DERIVATIVES **scrapper** noun.
– ORIGIN perhaps from SCRAPE.

scrapbook ● noun a book of blank pages for sticking cuttings, drawings, or pictures in.

scrape ● verb **1** drag or pull a hard or sharp implement across (a surface or object) to remove dirt or waste matter. **2** use a sharp or hard implement to remove (dirt or unwanted matter). **3** rub against a rough or hard surface. **4** just manage to achieve, succeed, or pass. **5** (**scrape by/along**) manage to live with difficulty. **6** (**scrape together/up**) collect or accumulate with difficulty. ● noun **1** an act or sound of scraping. **2** an injury or mark caused by scraping. **3** informal an embarrassing or difficult predicament. **4** archaic an obsequious bow in which one foot is drawn backwards along the ground.
– PHRASES **scrape the barrel** (or **the bottom of the barrel**) informal be reduced to using the last and poorest resources.
– DERIVATIVES **scraper** noun.
– ORIGIN Old English, 'scratch with the fingernails'.

scrapie ● noun a disease of sheep involving the central nervous system, characterized by a lack of coordination causing affected animals to rub against objects for support.
– ORIGIN from SCRAPE.

scrappy ● adjective (**scrappier**, **scrappiest**) disorganized, untidy, or incomplete.
– DERIVATIVES **scrappily** adverb **scrappiness** noun.

scrapyard ● noun Brit. a place where scrap is collected before being discarded, reused, or recycled.

scratch ● verb **1** make a long mark or wound on (a surface) with something sharp or pointed. **2** rub (a part of one's body) with one's fingernails to relieve itching. **3** (of a bird or mammal) rake the ground with the beak or claws in search of food. **4** cancel or strike out (writing). **5** withdraw from a competition. **6** cancel or abandon (an undertaking or project). **7** (**scratch around/along**) make a living or find resources with difficulty. **8** (**scratching**) the technique, used in rap music, of stopping a record by hand and moving it back and forwards to give a rhythmic scratching effect. ● noun **1** a mark or wound made by scratching. **2** an act or spell of scratching. **3** informal a slight or insignificant wound or injury. ● adjective assembled or made from whatever is available.
– PHRASES **from scratch** from the very beginning. **scratch the surface** deal with a matter only in the most superficial way. **up to scratch** up to the required standard; satisfactory. **you scratch my back and I'll scratch yours** proverb if you do me a favour, I'll return it.
– DERIVATIVES **scratcher** noun.
– ORIGIN probably a blend of the synonymous dialect words *scrat* and *cratch*, of uncertain origin.

scratch card ● noun a card with a section or sections coated in an opaque waxy substance which may be scraped away to reveal whether a prize has been won.

scratchy ● adjective (**scratchier**, **scratchiest**) **1** causing or characterized by scratching. **2** (of a voice or sound) rough; grating. **3** (of a record) making a crackling sound because of scratches on the surface.

scrawl ● verb write in a hurried, careless way. ● noun hurried, careless handwriting.
– ORIGIN apparently an alteration of CRAWL.

scrawny ● adjective (**scrawnier**, **scrawniest**) unattractively

Thesaurus

hop it, bog off, naff off; *N. Amer. informal* bug off, take a powder, take a hike; *Austral./NZ informal* rack off; *poetic/literary* begone.

scramble ● verb **1** *we scrambled over the boulders* CLAMBER, climb, crawl, claw one's way, scrabble, grope one's way, struggle; *N. Amer.* shinny. **2** *small children scrambled for the scattered coins* JOSTLE, scuffle, tussle, struggle, strive, compete, contend, vie, jockey. **3** *the alcohol has scrambled his brains* MUDDLE, confuse, mix up, jumble (up), disarrange, disorganize, disorder, disturb, mess up.
● noun **1** *a short scramble over the rocks* CLAMBER, climb, trek. **2** *I lost Tommy in the scramble for a seat* TUSSLE, jostle, scrimmage, scuffle, struggle, free-for-all, competition, contention, vying, jockeying; muddle, confusion, melee.

scrap[1] ● noun **1** *a scrap of paper* FRAGMENT, piece, bit, snippet, shred; offcut, oddment, remnant. **2** *there wasn't a scrap of evidence* BIT, speck, iota, particle, ounce, whit, jot, atom, shred, scintilla, tittle, jot or tittle; *informal* smidgen, tad. **3** *he slept rough and lived on scraps* LEFTOVERS, leavings, crumbs, scrapings, remains, remnants, residue, odds and ends, bits and pieces. **4** *the whole thing was made from bits of scrap* WASTE, rubbish, refuse, litter, debris, detritus; flotsam and jetsam; *N. Amer.* garbage, trash; *informal* junk.
● verb **1** *old cars which are due to be scrapped* THROW AWAY, throw out, dispose of, get rid of, toss out, throw on the scrap heap, discard, remove, dispense with, lose, bin; decommission, recycle, break up, demolish; *informal* chuck (away/out), ditch, dump, junk, get shut of; *Brit. informal* get shot of; *N. Amer. informal* trash. **2** *campaigners called for the plans to be scrapped* ABANDON, drop, abolish, withdraw, throw out, do away with, put an end to, cancel, axe, jettison; *informal* ditch, dump, junk.
– OPPOSITES keep, preserve.

scrap[2] (*informal*) ● noun *he and Joe had several scraps* QUARREL, argument, row, fight, disagreement, difference of opinion, falling-out, dispute, squabble, contretemps, clash, altercation, brawl, tussle, conflict, shouting match; *informal* tiff, set-to, run-in, slanging match, shindy, spat, dust-up, ruction; *Brit. informal* barney, ding-dong, bust-up.
● verb *the older boys started scrapping with me* QUARREL, argue, row, fight, squabble, brawl, bicker, spar, wrangle, lock horns, be at each other's throats.

scrape ● verb **1** *we scraped all the paint off the windows* ABRADE, grate, sand, sandpaper, scour, scratch, rub, file, rasp. **2** *their boots scraped along the floor* GRATE, creak, rasp, grind, scratch. **3** *she scraped her hair back behind her ears* RAKE, drag, pull, tug, draw. **4** *he scraped a hole in the ground* SCOOP OUT, hollow out, dig (out), excavate, gouge out. **5** *Ellen had scraped her shins on the wall* GRAZE, scratch, abrade, scuff, rasp, skin, rub raw, cut, lacerate, bark, chafe; *Medicine* excoriate.
● noun **1** *the scrape of her key in the lock* GRATING, creaking, grinding, rasp, rasping, scratch, scratching. **2** *there was a long scrape on his shin* GRAZE, scratch, abrasion, cut, laceration, wound. **3** (*informal*) *he's always getting into scrapes* PREDICAMENT, plight, tight corner/spot, ticklish/tricky situation, problem, crisis, mess, muddle; *informal* jam, fix, stew, bind, hole, hot water, a pretty/fine kettle of fish; *Brit. informal* spot of bother.
– PHRASES **scrape by** MANAGE, cope, survive, muddle through/along, make ends meet, get by/along, make do, keep the wolf from the door, keep one's head above water, eke out a living; *informal* make out.

scrappy ● adjective DISORGANIZED, untidy, disjointed, unsystematic, uneven, bitty, sketchy; piecemeal; fragmentary, incomplete, unfinished.

scratch ● verb **1** *the paintwork was scratched* SCORE, abrade, scrape, scuff. **2** *thorns scratched her skin* GRAZE, scrape, abrade, skin, rub raw, cut, lacerate, bark, chafe; wound; *Medicine* excoriate. **3** *many names had been scratched out* CROSS OUT, strike out, score out, delete, erase, remove, eliminate, expunge, obliterate. **4** *she was forced to scratch from the race* WITHDRAW, pull out of, back out of, bow out of, stand down.
● noun **1** *he had two scratches on his cheek* GRAZE, scrape, abrasion, cut, laceration, wound. **2** *a scratch on the paintwork* SCORE, mark, line, scrape.

S

thin and bony.

– ORIGIN variant of dialect *scranny*.

scream ● verb **1** make a long, loud, piercing cry or sound expressing extreme emotion or pain. **2** move very rapidly with or as if with such a sound. **3** present in an urgent or obvious way: *the headlines screamed 'he offered me sex'*. ● noun **1** a screaming cry or sound. **2** (**a scream**) informal an irresistibly funny person or thing.

– ORIGIN origin uncertain; perhaps Dutch.

screamer ● noun **1** a person or thing that makes a screaming sound. **2** informal a thing remarkable for speed or impact.

screamingly ● adverb to a very great extent; extremely: *screamingly obvious.*

scree ● noun a mass of small loose stones that form or cover a slope on a mountain.

– ORIGIN probably from Old Norse, 'landslip'.

screech ● noun a loud, harsh, piercing cry or sound. ● verb **1** make a screech. **2** move rapidly with a screech.

– DERIVATIVES **screecher** noun **screechy** adjective (**screechier**, **screechiest**).

– ORIGIN imitative.

screech owl ● noun Brit. another term for BARN OWL.

screed ● noun **1** a long speech or piece of writing. **2** a levelled layer of material applied to a floor or other surface.

– DERIVATIVES **screeding** noun.

– ORIGIN probably a variant of SHRED.

screen ● noun **1** an upright partition used to divide a room, give shelter, or provide concealment. **2** something that provides shelter or concealment. **3** the surface of a cathode ray tube or similar electronic device, especially that of a television, VDU, or monitor, on which images and data are displayed. **4** a blank surface on which a photographic image is projected. **5** (**the screen**) films or television. **6** a frame with fine wire netting used in a window or doorway to keep out flying insects. ● verb **1** conceal, protect, or shelter with a screen. **2** show (a film or video) or broadcast (a television programme). **3** protect from something dangerous or unpleasant. **4** test for the presence or absence of a disease. **5** investigate (someone), typically to ascertain their suitability for a job.

– DERIVATIVES **screener** noun **screenful** noun.

– ORIGIN Old French *escren*.

screenager ● noun a person in their teens or twenties who has an aptitude for computers and the Internet.

screenplay ● noun the script of a film, including acting instructions and scene directions.

screen-print ● verb force ink on to (a surface) through a prepared screen of fine material so as to create a picture or pattern. ● noun (**screen print**) a picture or design produced by screen-printing.

screen saver ● noun Computing a program which replaces an unchanging screen display with a moving image to prevent damage to the phosphor.

screen test ● noun a filmed test to ascertain whether an actor is suitable for a film role. ● verb (**screen-test**) give such a test to.

screenwriter ● noun a person who writes a screenplay.

– DERIVATIVES **screenwriting** noun.

screw ● noun **1** a thin, sharp-pointed metal pin with a raised spiral thread running around it and a slotted head, used to join things together by being rotated in under pressure. **2** a cylinder with a spiral ridge or thread running round the outside that can be turned to seal an opening, apply pressure, adjust position, etc. **3** (also **screw propeller**) a ship's or aircraft's propeller. **4** informal, derogatory a prison warder. **5** vulgar slang an act of sexual intercourse. ● verb **1** fasten or tighten with a screw or screws. **2** rotate (something) so as to attach or remove it by means of a spiral thread. **3** informal cheat or swindle. **4** vulgar slang have sexual intercourse with.

– PHRASES **have one's head screwed on** (**the right way**) informal have common sense. **have a screw loose** informal be slightly eccentric or mentally disturbed. **screw up 1** crush into a tight mass. **2** informal cause to fail or go wrong. **3** informal make emotionally or mentally disturbed. **4** summon up (one's courage).

– ORIGIN Old French *escroue* 'female screw, nut', from Latin *scrofa*, 'sow', later 'screw'.

screwball informal, chiefly N. Amer. ● noun a crazy or eccentric person. ● adjective **1** crazy; absurd. **2** referring to a style of fast-moving comedy film involving eccentric characters or ridiculous situations.

screwdriver ● noun **1** a tool with a shaped tip that fits into the head of a screw to turn it. **2** a cocktail made from vodka and orange juice.

screwy ● adjective (**screwier**, **screwiest**) informal, chiefly N. Amer. rather odd or eccentric.

scribble ● verb **1** write or draw carelessly or hurriedly. **2** informal write for a living or as a hobby. ● noun a piece of writing or a picture produced carelessly or hurriedly.

– DERIVATIVES **scribbler** noun.

– ORIGIN Latin *scribillare*, from *scribere* 'write'.

scribe ● noun **1** historical a person who copied out documents. **2** informal, often humorous a writer, especially a journalist. **3** Jewish History a Jewish record-keeper or, later, a professional theologian and jurist. **4** (also **scriber** or **scribe awl**) a pointed instrument used for making marks to guide a saw or in signwriting. ● verb **1** literary write. **2** mark with a pointed instrument.

– DERIVATIVES **scribal** adjective.

– ORIGIN Latin *scriba*, from *scribere* 'write'.

scrim ● noun **1** strong, coarse fabric used for heavy-duty lining

Thesaurus

– PHRASES **up to scratch** GOOD ENOUGH, up to the mark, up to standard, up to par, satisfactory, acceptable, adequate, passable, sufficient, all right; *informal* OK, up to snuff.

scrawl ● verb *he scrawled his name at the bottom of the page* SCRIBBLE, write hurriedly, write untidily, dash off.

● noun *pages of handwritten scrawl* SCRIBBLE, squiggle(s), hieroglyphics; *rare* cacography.

scrawny ● adjective SKINNY, thin, as thin as a rake, skin-and-bones, gaunt, bony, angular, gawky, scraggy, raw-boned; *dated* spindle-shanked.

– OPPOSITES fat.

scream ● verb *he screamed in pain* SHRIEK, screech, yell, howl, shout, bellow, bawl, cry out, call out, yelp, squeal, wail, squawk; *informal* holler.

● noun **1** *a scream of pain* SHRIEK, screech, yell, howl, shout, bellow, bawl, cry, yelp, squeal, wail, squawk; *informal* holler. **2** *(informal) the whole thing's a scream* LAUGH, hoot; *informal* gas, giggle, riot, bundle of fun/laughs. **3** *(informal) he's an absolute scream* WIT, hoot, comedian, comic, entertainer, joker, clown, character; *informal* gas, giggle, riot; *informal, dated* caution, case, card.

screech ● verb. See SCREAM verb.

screen ● noun **1** *he dressed hurriedly behind the screen* PARTITION, (room) divider; windbreak. **2** *a computer with a 15-inch screen* DISPLAY, monitor, visual display unit, VDU; cathode-ray tube, CRT. **3** *every window has a screen because of mosquitoes* MESH, net, netting. **4** *the hedge acts as a screen against the wind* BUFFER, protection, shield, shelter, guard. **5** *the earth must be put through a screen* SIEVE, riddle, strainer, colander, filter.

● verb **1** *the end of the hall had been screened of* PARTITION OFF, divide off, separate off, curtain off. **2** *the cottage was screened by the trees* CONCEAL, hide, veil; shield, shelter, shade, protect, guard, safeguard. **3** *the prospective candidates will have to be screened* VET, check, check up on, investigate; *informal* check out. **4** *all donated blood is screened for the virus* CHECK, test, examine, investigate. **5** *coal used to be screened by hand* SIEVE, riddle, sift, strain, filter, winnow. **6** *the programme is screened on Thursday evenings* SHOW, broadcast, transmit, televise, put out, put on the air.

screw ● noun **1** *stainless steel screws* bolt, fastener; nail, pin, tack, spike, rivet, brad. **2** *the handle needs a couple of screws to tighten it* TURN, twist, wrench. **3** *the ship's twin screws* PROPELLER, rotor.

● verb **1** *he screwed the lid back on the jar* TIGHTEN, turn, twist, wind. **2** *the bracket was screwed in place* FASTEN, secure, fix, attach. **3** *(informal) she intended to screw money out of them* EXTORT, force, extract, wrest, wring, squeeze; *informal* bleed.

– PHRASES **put the screws on** *(informal)* PRESSURIZE, put pressure on, pressure, coerce, browbeat, use strong-arm tactics on; hold a gun to someone's head; *informal* put the heat on, lean on. **screw something up 1** *Christina screwed up her face in disgust* WRINKLE (UP), pucker, crumple, crease, furrow, contort, distort, twist, purse. **2** *(informal) they'll screw up the whole economy* WRECK, ruin, destroy, wreak havoc on, damage, spoil, mar; dash, shatter, scotch, make a mess of, mess up; *informal* louse up, foul up, put the kibosh on, banjax, do for, nix, queer; *Brit. informal* scupper, cock up.

scribble ● verb *he scribbled a few lines on a piece of paper* SCRAWL, write hurriedly, write untidily, scratch, dash off, jot (down); doodle.

or upholstery. **2** Theatre a piece of gauze cloth that appears opaque until lit from behind, used as a screen or backcloth. **3** chiefly N. Amer. something that conceals or obscures.
– ORIGIN of unknown origin.
scrimmage ● noun **1** a confused struggle or fight. **2** American Football a sequence of play beginning with the placing of the ball on the ground with its longest axis at right angles to the goal line. ● verb American Football engage in a scrimmage.
– ORIGIN variant of SKIRMISH.
scrimp ● verb be thrifty or parsimonious; economize.
– ORIGIN Scots, 'meagre'.
scrimshank ● verb Brit. informal shirk one's duty.
– DERIVATIVES **scrimshanker** noun.
– ORIGIN of unknown origin.
scrimshaw /skrimshaw/ ● verb adorn (shells, ivory, or other materials) with carved designs. ● noun work done in such a way.
– ORIGIN of unknown origin; perhaps influenced by the surname *Scrimshaw*.
scrip ● noun **1** a provisional certificate of money subscribed to a bank or company, entitling the holder to a formal certificate and dividends. **2** certificates of this type collectively. **3** an issue of additional shares to shareholders in proportion to the shares already held.
– ORIGIN abbreviation of *subscription receipt*.
script ● noun **1** the written text of a play, film, or broadcast. **2** handwriting as distinct from print. **3** writing using a particular alphabet. **4** Brit. a candidate's written answers in an examination. ● verb write a script for.
– ORIGIN Latin *scriptum*, from *scribere* 'write'.
scriptural ● adjective of or relating to the Bible.
scripture (also **scriptures**) ● noun **1** the sacred writings of Christianity contained in the Bible. **2** the sacred writings of another religion.
– ORIGIN Latin *scriptura* 'writings', from *scribere* 'write'.
scriptwriter ● noun a person who writes a script for a play, film, or broadcast.
– DERIVATIVES **scriptwriting** noun.
scrivener /skrivvənər/ ● noun historical a clerk, scribe, or notary.
– ORIGIN Old French *escrivein*, from Latin *scriba* (see SCRIBE).
scrofula /skrofyoolə/ ● noun chiefly historical a disease with glandular swellings, probably a form of tuberculosis.
– DERIVATIVES **scrofulous** adjective.
– ORIGIN from Latin *scrofa* 'breeding sow' (said to be subject to the disease).
scroll ● noun **1** a roll of parchment or paper for writing or painting on. **2** an ornamental design or carving resembling a partly unrolled scroll of parchment. ● verb move displayed text or graphics on a computer screen in order to view different parts of them.
– DERIVATIVES **scrollable** adjective **scroller** noun.
– ORIGIN from obsolete *scrow* 'roll', shortening of ESCROW.
scroll bar ● noun a long thin section at the edge of a computer display by which material can be scrolled using a mouse.
scrolled ● adjective having an ornamental design or carving resembling a scroll.
scrollwork ● noun decoration consisting of spiral lines or patterns.
Scrooge ● noun a person who is mean with money.
– ORIGIN from Ebenezer *Scrooge*, a miser in Charles Dickens's story *A Christmas Carol* (1843).
scrotum /skrōtəm/ ● noun (pl. **scrota** /skrōtə/ or **scrotums**) the pouch of skin containing the testicles.
– DERIVATIVES **scrotal** adjective.
– ORIGIN Latin.
scrounge informal ● verb seek to obtain (something) from others without having to pay or work for it. ● noun an act or the action of scrounging.
– DERIVATIVES **scrounger** noun.
– ORIGIN variant of dialect *scrunge* 'steal'.
scrub[1] ● verb (**scrubbed**, **scrubbing**) **1** rub hard so as to clean. **2** (**scrub up**) thoroughly clean one's hands and arms before performing surgery. **3** informal cancel or abandon. ● noun **1** an act of scrubbing. **2** a semi-abrasive cosmetic lotion used to cleanse the skin. **3** (**scrubs**) hygienic clothing worn by surgeons during operations.
– ORIGIN probably from Low German or Dutch *schrobben*, *schrubben*.
scrub[2] ● noun **1** vegetation consisting mainly of brushwood or stunted forest growth. **2** (also **scrubs**) land covered with such vegetation. **3** (before another noun) denoting a shrubby or small form of a plant.
– DERIVATIVES **scrubby** adjective.
– ORIGIN from SHRUB[1].
scrubber ● noun **1** a person or thing that scrubs. **2** an apparatus using water or a solution for purifying gases or vapours. **3** Brit. informal, derogatory a sexually promiscuous woman.
scruff[1] ● noun the back of a person's or animal's neck.
– ORIGIN from dialect *scuff*, of obscure origin.
scruff[2] ● noun Brit. informal a scruffy person.
– ORIGIN variant of SCURF.
scruffy ● adjective (**scruffier**, **scruffiest**) shabby and untidy or dirty.
– DERIVATIVES **scruffily** adverb **scruffiness** noun.
scrum ● noun **1** Rugby an ordered formation of players in which the forwards of each team push against each other with heads down and the ball is thrown in. **2** Brit. informal a disorderly crowd. ● verb (**scrummed**, **scrumming**) Rugby form or take part in a scrum.
– ORIGIN abbreviation of SCRUMMAGE.
scrummage ● noun & verb fuller form of SCRUM.
– ORIGIN variant of SCRIMMAGE.
scrummy ● adjective (**scrummier**, **scrummiest**) informal delicious.
– ORIGIN from SCRUMPTIOUS.
scrump ● verb Brit. informal steal (fruit) from an orchard or garden.
– ORIGIN from dialect, 'withered apple'.
scrumptious ● adjective informal extremely delicious or attractive.
– ORIGIN of unknown origin.

S

Thesaurus

● noun *a page of scribble* SCRAWL, squiggle(s), jottings; doodle, doodlings; *rare* cacography.
scribe ● noun **1** *(historical) a medieval scribe* CLERK, secretary, copyist, transcriber, amanuensis; *historical* penman, scrivener. **2** *(informal) a local cricket scribe* WRITER, author, penman; journalist, reporter; *informal* hack.
scrimmage ● noun FIGHT, tussle, brawl, struggle, fracas, free-for-all, rough and tumble; *Law, dated* affray; *informal* scrap, dust-up, punch-up, set-to, shindy; *Brit. informal* scrum; *N. Amer. informal* rough house.
scrimp ● verb ECONOMIZE, skimp, scrimp and save, save; be thrifty, be frugal, tighten one's belt, cut back, husband one's resources, draw in one's horns, watch one's pennies; *N. Amer.* pinch the pennies.
script ● noun **1** *her neat, tidy script* HANDWRITING, writing, hand, pen, penmanship, calligraphy. **2** *the script of the play* TEXT, screenplay; libretto, score; lines, dialogue, words.
scripture ● noun THE BIBLE, the Holy Bible, Holy Writ, the Gospel, the Good Book, the Word of God, the Book of Books; sacred text(s).
Scrooge ● noun MISER, penny-pincher, pinchpenny, niggard; *informal* skinflint, meanie, money-grubber, cheapskate; *N. Amer. informal* tightwad.
– OPPOSITES spendthrift.
scrounge ● verb *(informal)* BEG, borrow; *informal* cadge, sponge, bum, touch someone for; *Brit. informal* scab; *N. Amer. informal* mooch; *Austral./NZ informal* bludge.
scrounger ● noun *(informal)* BEGGAR, borrower, parasite, cadger; *informal* sponger, freeloader; *N. Amer. informal* mooch, moocher, schnorrer; *Austral./NZ informal* bludger.
scrub[1] ● verb **1** *he scrubbed the kitchen floor* SCOUR, rub; clean, cleanse, wash, wipe. **2** *(informal) the plans were scrubbed* ABANDON, scrap, drop, cancel, call off, axe, jettison, discard, discontinue, abort; *informal* ditch, dump, junk.
scrub[2] ● noun *there the buildings ended and the scrub began* BRUSH, brushwood, scrubland, undergrowth.
scruffy ● adjective SHABBY, worn, down at heel, ragged, tattered, mangy, dirty; untidy, unkempt, bedraggled, messy, dishevelled, ill-groomed; *informal* tatty, the worse for wear; *N. Amer. informal* raggedy.
– OPPOSITES smart, tidy.
scrumptious ● adjective *(informal)* DELICIOUS, delectable, mouth-

scrumpy • noun Brit. rough strong cider, especially as made in the West Country of England.

scrunch • verb **1** make a loud crunching noise. **2** crush or squeeze into a compact mass. • noun a loud crunching noise.
– ORIGIN probably imitative.

scrunchy • adjective making a loud crunching noise when crushed or compressed. • noun (also **scrunchie**) (pl. **scrunchies**) chiefly Brit. a circular band of fabric-covered elastic used for fastening the hair.

scruple • noun **1** a feeling of doubt as to whether an action is morally right. **2** historical a unit of weight used by apothecaries, equal to 20 grains. • verb hesitate to do something that one thinks may be wrong.
– ORIGIN from Latin *scrupus*, literally 'rough pebble', (figuratively) 'anxiety'.

scrupulous • adjective **1** diligent and thorough. **2** very concerned to avoid doing wrong.
– DERIVATIVES **scrupulosity** noun **scrupulously** adverb **scrupulousness** noun.

scrutineer • noun **1** a person who examines something closely and thoroughly. **2** chiefly Brit. a person who supervises the conduct of an election or competition.

scrutinize (also **scrutinise**) • verb examine closely and thoroughly.

scrutiny • noun (pl. **scrutinies**) close and critical observation or examination.
– ORIGIN Latin *scrutinium*, from *scrutari* 'sort rubbish', later 'to search'.

scry /skrī/ • verb (**scries**, **scried**) foretell the future, especially using a crystal ball.
– ORIGIN shortening of DESCRY.

SCSI • abbreviation Computing small computer system interface.

scuba /skōōbə/ • noun an aqualung.
– ORIGIN acronym from *self-contained underwater breathing apparatus*.

scuba-diving • noun the sport or pastime of swimming underwater using a scuba.

scud • verb (**scudded**, **scudding**) move fast in a straight line because or as if driven by the wind. • noun literary **1** clouds or spray driven fast by the wind. **2** the action of scudding.
– ORIGIN perhaps from SCUT, reflecting the sense 'race like a hare'.

scuff • verb **1** scrape (a shoe or other object) against something. **2** mark by scuffing. **3** drag (one's feet) when walking. • noun a mark made by scuffing.
– ORIGIN perhaps imitative.

scuffle • noun a short, confused fight or struggle. • verb **1** engage in a scuffle. **2** move in a hurried, confused, or shuffling way.
– ORIGIN probably Scandinavian.

scull • noun **1** each of a pair of small oars used by a single rower. **2** an oar placed over the stern of a boat to propel it with a side to side motion. **3** a light, narrow boat propelled with a scull or a pair of sculls. • verb propel a boat with sculls.
– DERIVATIVES **sculler** noun.
– ORIGIN of unknown origin.

scullery • noun (pl. **sculleries**) a small kitchen or room at the back of a house used for washing dishes and other dirty household work.
– ORIGIN Old French *escuelerie*, from Latin *scutella* 'salver'.

scullion • noun archaic a servant assigned the most menial kitchen tasks.
– ORIGIN perhaps influenced by SCULLERY.

sculpt • verb create or represent by sculpture.

sculptor • noun (fem. **sculptress**) an artist who makes sculptures.

sculpture • noun **1** the art of making three-dimensional figures and shapes, especially by carving stone or wood or casting metal. **2** a work of such a kind. • verb **1** make or represent by sculpture. **2** (**sculptured**) formed or shaped as if by sculpture, especially with strong, smooth curves.
– DERIVATIVES **sculptural** adjective.
– ORIGIN from Latin *sculpere* 'carve'.

scum • noun **1** a layer of dirt or froth on the surface of a liquid. **2** informal a worthless or contemptible person or group of people. • verb (**scummed**, **scumming**) cover or become covered with a layer of scum.
– DERIVATIVES **scummy** adjective (**scummier**, **scummiest**).
– ORIGIN Low German or Dutch *schūm*.

scumbag • noun informal a contemptible person.

scumble Art • verb give a softer or duller effect to (a picture or colour) by applying a very thin coat of opaque paint. • noun paint applied in this way.
– ORIGIN perhaps from SCUM.

scunge /skunj/ • noun Austral./NZ informal a disagreeable person.
– DERIVATIVES **scungy** adjective (**scungier**, **scungiest**).
– ORIGIN originally Scots in the sense 'scrounger': of unknown origin.

scupper[1] • noun a hole in a ship's side to allow water to run away from the deck.
– ORIGIN perhaps from Old French *escopir* 'to spit'.

scupper[2] • verb chiefly Brit. **1** sink (a ship) deliberately. **2** informal prevent from working or succeeding; thwart.
– ORIGIN originally as military slang in the sense 'ambush and kill'; of unknown origin.

scurf • noun flakes on the surface of the skin that form as fresh skin develops below, occurring especially as dandruff.
– DERIVATIVES **scurfy** adjective.
– ORIGIN from Old English, 'cut to shreds'.

scurrilous /skurriləss/ • adjective making scandalous claims about someone in order to damage their reputation.
– DERIVATIVES **scurrility** noun (pl. **scurrilities**).
– ORIGIN Latin *scurrilus*, from *scurra* 'buffoon'.

scurry • verb (**scurries**, **scurried**) move hurriedly with short quick steps. • noun a situation of hurried and confused move-

Thesaurus

watering, tasty, appetizing, rich, savoury, flavoursome, flavourful, toothsome; succulent, luscious; *informal* scrummy, yummy; *Brit. informal* moreish; *N. Amer. informal* finger-licking, nummy.
– OPPOSITES unpalatable.

scrunch • verb CRUMPLE, crunch, crush, rumple, screw up, squash, squeeze, compress; *informal* squidge.

scruple • verb *she would not scruple to ask them for money* HESITATE, be reluctant, be loath, have qualms, have scruples, have misgivings, have reservations, think twice, baulk, demur; recoil from, shrink from, shy away from, flinch from.

scruples • plural noun *he had no scruples about eavesdropping* QUALMS, compunction, pangs/twinges of conscience, hesitation, reservations, second thoughts, doubt(s), misgivings, uneasiness, reluctance.

scrupulous • adjective **1** *scrupulous attention to detail* CAREFUL, meticulous, painstaking, thorough, assiduous, sedulous, attentive, conscientious, punctilious, searching, close, minute, rigorous, particular, strict. **2** *a scrupulous man* HONEST, honourable, upright, upstanding, high-minded, right-minded, moral, ethical, good, virtuous, principled, incorruptible.
– OPPOSITES careless, dishonest.

scrutinize • verb EXAMINE, inspect, survey, study, look at, peruse; investigate, explore, probe, inquire into, go into, check.

scrutiny • noun EXAMINATION, inspection, survey, study, perusal; investigation, exploration, probe, inquiry; *informal* going-over.

scud • verb SPEED, race, rush, sail, shoot, sweep, skim, whip, whizz, flash, fly, scurry, flit, scutter.

scuff • verb SCRAPE, scratch, rub, abrade; mark.

scuffle • noun *there was a scuffle outside the pub* FIGHT, struggle, tussle, brawl, fracas, free-for-all, rough and tumble, scrimmage; *Law, dated* affray; *informal* scrap, dust-up, punch-up, set-to, shindy; *N. Amer. informal* rough house.
• verb *demonstrators scuffled with police* FIGHT, struggle, tussle, exchange blows, come to blows, brawl, clash; *informal* scrap.

sculpt • verb CARVE, model, chisel, sculpture, fashion, form, shape, cast, cut, hew.

sculpture • noun *a bronze sculpture* MODEL, carving, statue, statuette, figure, figurine, effigy, bust, head, likeness.
• verb *the choir stalls were carefully sculptured.* See SCULPT.

scum • noun **1** *the water was covered with a thick green scum* FILM, layer, covering, froth; filth, dross, dirt. **2** *(informal) drug dealers are scum* DESPICABLE PEOPLE, the lowest of the low, the dregs of society, vermin, riff-raff; *informal* the scum of the earth, dirt.

scupper *(Brit.)* • verb **1** *the captain decided to scupper the ship* SINK, scuttle, submerge, send to the bottom. **2** *(informal) he denied trying to scupper the agreement* RUIN, wreck, destroy, sabotage, torpedo, spoil, ruin, mess up; *informal* screw up, foul up, put the kibosh on, banjax, do for; *archaic* bring to naught.

scurrilous • adjective DEFAMATORY, slanderous, libellous, scandal-

ment.

– ORIGIN abbreviation of *hurry-scurry*, from HURRY.

scurvy ● noun a disease caused by a deficiency of vitamin C, characterized by bleeding gums and the opening of previously healed wounds. ● adjective (**scurvier, scurviest**) archaic worthless or contemptible.

– ORIGIN from SCURF.

scut ● noun the short tail of a hare, rabbit, or deer.

– ORIGIN of unknown origin.

scutter chiefly Brit. ● verb move hurriedly with short steps. ● noun an act or sound of scuttering.

– ORIGIN perhaps from SCUTTLE².

scuttle¹ ● noun **1** a lidded metal container with a handle, used to store coal for a domestic fire. **2** Brit. the part of a car's bodywork between the windscreen and the bonnet.

– ORIGIN Latin *scutella* 'dish'.

scuttle² ● verb run hurriedly or furtively with short quick steps. ● noun an act or sound of scuttling.

– ORIGIN probably related to SCUD.

scuttle³ ● verb **1** sink (one's own ship) deliberately. **2** deliberately cause (a scheme) to fail. ● noun an opening with a lid in a ship's deck or side.

– ORIGIN perhaps from Spanish *escotilla* 'hatchway'.

scuttlebutt ● noun informal, chiefly N. Amer. rumour; gossip.

– ORIGIN originally denoting a water butt on the deck of a ship: from *scuttled butt*.

scuzz ● noun informal, chiefly N. Amer. a disgusting person or thing.

– DERIVATIVES **scuzzy** adjective.

– ORIGIN probably an abbreviation of *disgusting*.

scythe ● noun a tool used for cutting crops such as grass or corn, with a long curved blade at the end of a long pole. ● verb **1** cut with a scythe. **2** move through or penetrate rapidly and forcefully.

– ORIGIN Old English.

Scythian /sithiən/ ● noun a person from Scythia, an ancient region of SE Europe and Asia. ● adjective relating to Scythia.

SD ● abbreviation South Dakota.

SDI ● abbreviation Strategic Defense Initiative.

SDLP ● abbreviation (in Northern Ireland) Social Democratic and Labour Party.

SE ● abbreviation **1** south-east. **2** south-eastern.

Se ● symbol the chemical element selenium.

sea ● noun **1** the expanse of salt water that covers most of the earth's surface and surrounds its land masses. **2** a roughly definable area of this. **3** a vast expanse or quantity: *a sea of faces*.

– PHRASES **at sea 1** sailing on the sea. **2** confused; uncertain. **one's sea legs** one's ability to keep one's balance and not feel seasick on board a ship.

– DERIVATIVES **seaward** adjective & adverb **seawards** adverb.

– ORIGIN Old English.

sea anchor ● noun an object dragged in the water behind a boat in order to keep its bows pointing into the waves or to lessen leeway.

sea anemone ● noun a marine animal with a tube-shaped body which bears a ring of stinging tentacles around the mouth.

sea bass ● noun a marine fish with a spiny dorsal fin, resembling the freshwater perch.

seabed ● noun the ground under the sea; the ocean floor.

seabird ● noun a bird that frequents the sea or coast.

seaboard ● noun a region bordering the sea; the coastline.

seaborgium /seeborgiəm/ ● noun a very unstable chemical element made by high-energy atomic collisions.

– ORIGIN named after the American nuclear chemist Glenn *Seaborg* (1912–99).

sea bream ● noun a deep-bodied marine fish that resembles the freshwater bream.

sea breeze ● noun a breeze blowing towards the land from the sea.

SeaCat ● noun trademark a large, high-speed catamaran used as a passenger and car ferry on short sea crossings.

sea change ● noun a profound or notable transformation.

– ORIGIN from Shakespeare's *Tempest*.

sea cow ● noun a sirenian, especially a manatee.

sea cucumber ● noun a marine invertebrate animal having a thick worm-like body with tentacles around the mouth.

sea dog ● noun informal an old or experienced sailor.

seafaring ● adjective travelling by sea. ● noun travel by sea.

– DERIVATIVES **seafarer** noun.

seafood ● noun shellfish and sea fish served as food.

seafront ● noun the part of a coastal town next to and directly facing the sea.

seagoing ● adjective **1** (of a ship) suitable for voyages on the sea. **2** relating to sea travel.

seagrass ● noun eelgrass or a similar grass-like plant that grows near the sea.

sea green ● noun a pale bluish green colour.

seagull ● noun a gull.

sea horse ● noun a small marine fish with an upright posture and a head and neck suggestive of a horse.

seakale ● noun a maritime plant of the cabbage family, cultivated for its edible young shoots.

seal¹ ● noun **1** a device or substance used to join two things together or make something impervious. **2** a piece of wax or lead with an individual design stamped into it, attached to a document as a guarantee of authenticity. **3** a confirmation or guarantee: *a seal of approval*. **4** an engraved device used for stamping a seal. ● verb **1** fasten or close securely. **2** (**seal off**) isolate (an area) by preventing entrance to and exit from it. **3** apply a non-porous coating to (a surface) to make it impervious. **4** conclude, establish, or secure definitively. **5** authenticate (a document) with a seal.

– PHRASES **my lips are sealed** I will not discuss or reveal a particular secret. **put** (or **set**) **the seal on** finally confirm or conclude. **set** (or **put**) **one's seal to** (or **on**) mark with one's distinctive character.

– DERIVATIVES **sealable** adjective.

– ORIGIN Old French *seel*, from Latin *sigillum* 'small picture'.

seal² ● noun a fish-eating aquatic mammal with a streamlined body and feet developed as flippers. ● verb hunt for seals.

– ORIGIN Old English.

sealant ● noun material used to make something airtight or watertight.

sealer¹ ● noun a device or substance used to seal something.

sealer² ● noun a ship or person engaged in hunting seals.

sea level ● noun the level of the sea's surface, used in reckoning the height of geographical features and as a barometric

S

Thesaurus

ous, insulting, offensive, gross; abusive, vituperative, malicious; *informal* bitchy.

scurry ● verb *pedestrians scurried for cover* HURRY, hasten, run, rush, dash; scamper, scuttle, scramble; *Brit.* scutter; *informal* scoot, beetle; *dated* make haste.

– OPPOSITES amble.

● noun *there was a scurry to get out* RUSH, race, dash, run, hurry; scramble, bustle.

scuttle ● verb. See SCURRY verb.

sea ● noun **1** *the sea sparkled in the sun* (THE) OCEAN, the waves; *informal* the drink; *Brit. informal* the briny; *poetic/literary* the deep, the main, the foam. **2** *the boat overturned in the heavy seas* WAVES, swell, breakers, rollers, combers; *informal* boomers. **3** *a sea of roofs and turrets* EXPANSE, stretch, area, tract, sweep, blanket, sheet, carpet, mass; multitude, host, profusion, abundance, plethora.

– RELATED TERMS marine, maritime, nautical.

– OPPOSITES land.

● adjective *sea creatures* MARINE, ocean, oceanic; saltwater, seawater; ocean-going, seagoing, seafaring; maritime, naval, nautical; *technical* pelagic, thalassic.

– PHRASES **at sea** CONFUSED, perplexed, puzzled, baffled, mystified, bemused, bewildered, nonplussed, disconcerted, disoriented, dumbfounded, at a loss, at sixes and sevens; *informal* flummoxed, bamboozled, fazed; *N. Amer. informal* discombobulated; *archaic* wildered, mazed.

seafaring ● adjective MARITIME, nautical, naval, seagoing, sea.

seal ● noun **1** *the seal round the bath* SEALANT, sealer, adhesive. **2** *the king put his seal on the letter* EMBLEM, symbol, insignia, device, badge, crest, coat of arms, mark, monogram, stamp. **3** *the Minister gave his seal of approval to the project* RATIFICATION, approval, blessing, consent, agreement, permission, sanction, endorsement, clearance.

● verb **1** *she quietly sealed the door behind her* FASTEN, secure, shut, close, lock, bolt. **2** *seal each bottle while it is hot* STOP UP, seal up, make airtight/watertight, cork, stopper, plug. **3** *police sealed off the High Street* CLOSE OFF, shut off, cordon off, fence off, isolate.

standard.

sealing wax ● noun a mixture of shellac and rosin with turpentine and pigment, softened by heating and used to make seals.

sea lion ● noun a large seal of the Pacific Ocean, the male of which has a mane on the neck and shoulders.

Sea Lord ● noun either of two senior officers in the Royal Navy (**First Sea Lord**, **Second Sea Lord**) serving originally as members of the Admiralty Board (now of the Ministry of Defence).

Sealyham /seeliəm/ ● noun a terrier of a wire-haired short-legged breed.
– ORIGIN from *Sealyham*, a village in SW Wales, where the dog was first bred.

seam ● noun **1** a line where two pieces of fabric are sewn together in a garment or other article. **2** a line where the edges of two pieces of wood or other material touch each other. **3** an underground layer of a mineral such as coal or gold. ● verb join with a seam.
– ORIGIN Old English.

seaman ● noun **1** a sailor, especially one below the rank of officer. **2** the lowest rank in the US navy, below petty officer.
– DERIVATIVES **seamanlike** adjective **seamanship** noun.

seam bowler ● noun Cricket a bowler who makes the ball deviate by causing it to bounce on its seam.

sea mile ● noun a unit of distance equal to a minute of arc of a great circle, varying between approximately 2,014 yards (1,842 metres) at the equator and 2,035 yards (1,861 metres) at the pole.

seamless ● adjective smooth and without seams or obvious joins.
– DERIVATIVES **seamlessly** adverb.

seamstress ● noun a woman who sews, especially as a job.
– ORIGIN from archaic *seamster* 'tailor, seamstress'.

seamy ● adjective (**seamier**, **seamiest**) sordid and disreputable.

seance /sayonss/ ● noun a meeting at which people attempt to make contact with the dead.
– ORIGIN French, from Latin *sedere* 'sit'.

seaplane ● noun an aircraft with floats or skis instead of wheels, designed to land on and take off from water.

seaport ● noun a town or city with a harbour for seagoing ships.

sear ● verb **1** burn or scorch with a sudden intense heat. **2** (of pain) be experienced as a sudden burning sensation. **3** brown (food) quickly at a high temperature. ● adjective (also **sere**) literary withered.
– ORIGIN Old English.

search ● verb **1** try to find something by looking or otherwise seeking carefully and thoroughly. **2** examine (a place, vehicle, or person) thoroughly in order to find something or someone. **3** (**searching**) investigating very deeply: *searching questions.* ● noun an act of searching.
– PHRASES **search me!** informal I do not know.
– DERIVATIVES **searchable** adjective **searcher** noun.
– ORIGIN Old French *cerchier*, from Latin *circare* 'go round'.

search engine ● noun Computing a program for the retrieval of data, files, or documents from a database or network, especially the Internet.

searchlight ● noun a powerful outdoor electric light with a concentrated beam that can be turned in the required direction.

search party ● noun a group of people organized to look for someone or something.

search warrant ● noun a legal document authorizing a police officer or other official to enter and search premises.

sea salt ● noun salt produced by the evaporation of seawater.

seascape ● noun a view or picture of an expanse of sea.

seashell ● noun the shell of a marine mollusc.

seashore ● noun **1** an area of sandy, stony, or rocky land bordering and level with the sea. **2** Law the land between high- and low-water marks.

seasick ● adjective suffering from nausea caused by the motion of a ship at sea.
– DERIVATIVES **seasickness** noun.

seaside ● noun a place by the sea, especially a beach area or holiday resort.

sea slug ● noun a shell-less marine mollusc with external gills and a number of appendages on the upper surface.

season ● noun **1** each of the four divisions of the year (spring, summer, autumn, and winter) marked by particular weather patterns and daylight hours. **2** a period of the year characterized by a climatic feature, sport, or event. **3** the time of year when a particular fruit, vegetable, etc., is plentiful and in good condition. **4** (usu. in phrase **in season**) a period when a female mammal is ready to mate. **5** (**the season**) the time of year traditionally marked by fashionable upper-class social events. **6** archaic a proper or suitable time. ● verb **1** add salt, herbs, or spices to (food). **2** add an enlivening quality or feature to. **3** keep (wood) so as to dry it for use as timber. **4** (**seasoned**) accustomed to particular conditions; experienced: *a seasoned traveller.*
– ORIGIN Old French *seson*, from Latin *serere* 'to sow'.

seasonable ● adjective usual for or appropriate to a particular season of the year.

seasonal ● adjective **1** relating to or characteristic of a particular season of the year. **2** fluctuating according to the season.
– DERIVATIVES **seasonality** noun **seasonally** adverb.

seasonal affective disorder ● noun depression associated with late autumn and winter and thought to be caused by a

Thesaurus

4 *he held out his hand to seal the bargain* CLINCH, secure, settle, conclude, complete, establish, set the seal on, confirm, guarantee; *informal* sew up.

seam ● noun **1** *the seam was coming undone* JOIN, stitching; *Surgery* suture. **2** *a seam of coal* LAYER, stratum, vein, lode. **3** *the seams of his face* WRINKLE, line, crow's foot, furrow, crease, corrugation, crinkle, pucker, groove, ridge.

seaman ● noun SAILOR, seafarer, boatman, hand; *informal* (old) salt, sea dog, bluejacket; *Brit. informal* matelot; *informal, dated* tar, Jack Tar; *poetic/literary* mariner.
– OPPOSITES landlubber.

seamy ● adjective SORDID, disreputable, seedy, sleazy, squalid, insalubrious, unwholesome, unsavoury, rough, unpleasant.
– OPPOSITES salubrious.

sear ● verb **1** *the heat of the blast seared his face* SCORCH, burn, singe, char. **2** *sear the meat before adding the other ingredients* FLASH-FRY, seal, brown. **3** *his betrayal had seared her terribly* HURT, wound, pain, cut to the quick, sting; distress, grieve, upset, trouble, harrow, torment, torture.

search ● verb **1** *I searched for the key in my handbag* HUNT, look, seek, forage, fish about/around, look high and low, cast about/around, ferret about/around, root about/around, rummage about/around; *Brit. informal* rootle about/around. **2** *he searched the house thoroughly* LOOK THROUGH, hunt through, explore, scour, rifle through, go through, sift through, comb, go through with a fine-tooth comb; turn upside down, turn inside out, leave no stone unturned in; *Austral./NZ informal* fossick through. **3** *the guards searched him for weapons* EXAMINE, inspect, check, frisk.
● noun *we continued our search for a hotel* HUNT, look, quest; pursuit.
– PHRASES **in search of** SEARCHING FOR, hunting for, seeking, looking for, on the lookout for, in pursuit of. **search me!** *(informal)* I DON'T KNOW, how should I know?, it's a mystery, I haven't a clue, I haven't the least idea, I've no idea; *informal* dunno, don't ask me, I haven't the faintest/foggiest (idea/notion), it beats me, ask me another.

searching ● adjective PENETRATING, piercing, probing, penetrative, keen, shrewd, sharp, intent.

searing ● adjective **1** *the searing heat* SCORCHING, blistering, sweltering, blazing (hot), burning, fiery, torrid; *informal* boiling (hot), baking (hot), sizzling, roasting. **2** *searing pain* INTENSE, excruciating, agonizing, sharp, stabbing, shooting, stinging, severe, extreme, racking. **3** *a searing attack* FIERCE, savage, blistering, scathing, stinging, devastating, mordant, trenchant, caustic, cutting, biting, withering.

seaside ● noun COAST, shore, seashore, waterside; beach, sand, sands; *poetic/literary* strand.
– RELATED TERMS littoral.

season ● noun *the rainy season* | *the opera season* PERIOD, time, time of year, spell, term.
● verb **1** *season the casserole to taste* FLAVOUR, add flavouring to, add salt/pepper to, spice. **2** *his albums include standard numbers seasoned with a few of his own tunes* ENLIVEN, leaven, spice (up), liven up; *informal* pep up.
– PHRASES **in season** AVAILABLE, obtainable, to be had, on offer, on the market; plentiful, abundant.

lack of light.

seasoning ● noun salt, herbs, or spices added to food to enhance the flavour.

season ticket ● noun a ticket allowing travel within a particular period or admission to a series of events.

sea squirt ● noun a marine animal which has a bag-like body with orifices through which water flows in and out.

seat ● noun **1** a thing made or used for sitting on. **2** the horizontal part of a chair. **3** a sitting place for a passenger in a vehicle or for a member of an audience. **4** a person's buttocks. **5** chiefly Brit. a place in an elected parliament or council. **6** Brit. a parliamentary constituency. **7** a site or location. **8** a large country house and estate belonging to an aristocratic family. **9** a part of a machine that supports or guides another part. **10** a manner of sitting on a horse. ● verb **1** arrange for (someone) to sit somewhere. **2** (**seat oneself** or **be seated**) sit down. **3** (of a place) have sufficient seats for.
– DERIVATIVES **seating** noun **seatless** adjective.
– ORIGIN Old Norse, related to SIT.

seat belt ● noun a belt used to secure someone in the seat of a motor vehicle or aircraft.

sea trout ● noun Brit. a brown trout of a salmon-like migratory race.

sea urchin ● noun a marine animal which has a shell covered in mobile spines.

sea wall ● noun a wall or embankment erected to prevent the sea encroaching on an area of land.

seaway ● noun a waterway or channel used by or capable of accommodating ships.

seaweed ● noun large algae growing in the sea or on rocks below the high-water mark.

seaworthy ● adjective (of a boat) in a good enough condition to sail on the sea.
– DERIVATIVES **seaworthiness** noun.

sebaceous /sibayshəss/ ● adjective technical **1** relating to oil or fat. **2** relating to a sebaceous gland or its secretion.
– ORIGIN Latin *sebaceus*, from *sebum* 'tallow'.

sebaceous gland ● noun a gland in the skin which secretes oily matter (sebum) into the hair follicles to lubricate the skin and hair.

sebum /seebəm/ ● noun an oily secretion of the sebaceous glands.
– ORIGIN Latin, 'grease'.

sec[1] ● abbreviation secant.

sec[2] ● noun informal a second or a very short space of time.

sec[3] ● adjective (of wine) dry.
– ORIGIN French, from Latin *siccus*.

secant /seekənt/ ● noun **1** Mathematics (in a right-angled triangle) the ratio of the hypotenuse to the shorter side adjacent to an acute angle. **2** Geometry a straight line that cuts a curve in two or more parts.
– ORIGIN from Latin *secare* 'to cut'.

secateurs /sekkəturz/ ● plural noun chiefly Brit. a pair of pruning clippers for use with one hand.
– ORIGIN French, 'cutters', from Latin *secare* 'to cut'.

secede /siseed/ ● verb withdraw formally from membership of a federal union or a political or religious organization.
– DERIVATIVES **seceder** noun.
– ORIGIN Latin *secedere* 'withdraw'.

secession /sisesh'n/ ● noun the action of seceding from a federation or organization.
– DERIVATIVES **secessionism** noun.

seclude ● verb keep (someone) away from other people.
– ORIGIN Latin *secludere*, from *claudere* 'to shut'.

secluded ● adjective (of a place) not seen or visited by many people; sheltered and private.

seclusion ● noun the state of being private and away from other people.

second[1] /sekkənd/ ● ordinal number **1** constituting number two in a sequence; 2nd. **2** subordinate or inferior in position, rank, or importance. **3** (**seconds**) goods of an inferior quality. **4** (**seconds**) informal a second course or second helping of food at a meal. **5** secondly. **6** Brit. a place in the second highest grade in an examination for a degree. **7** an attendant assisting a combatant in a duel or boxing match. ● verb **1** formally support or endorse (a nomination or resolution) before adoption or further discussion. **2** express agreement with.
– DERIVATIVES **seconder** noun.
– ORIGIN Latin *secundus* 'following, second', from *sequi* 'follow'.

second[2] /sekkənd/ ● noun **1** the unit of time in the SI system, equal to one-sixtieth of a minute. **2** informal a very short time. **3** (also **arc second** or **second of arc**) a sixtieth of a minute of angular distance.
– ORIGIN from Latin *secunda minuta* 'second minute', from *secundus*, referring to the 'second' operation of dividing an hour by sixty.

second[3] /sikond/ ● verb Brit. temporarily transfer (a worker) to another position.
– DERIVATIVES **secondee** noun **secondment** noun.
– ORIGIN from French *en second* 'in the second rank (of officers)'.

secondary ● adjective **1** coming after, less important than, or resulting from something primary. **2** relating to education for children from the age of eleven to sixteen or eighteen.
– DERIVATIVES **secondarily** adverb.

Thesaurus

seasonable ● adjective USUAL, expected, predictable, normal for the time of year.

seasoned ● adjective EXPERIENCED, practised, well versed, knowledgeable, established, habituated, veteran, hardened, battle-scarred.
– OPPOSITES inexperienced.

S

seasoning ● noun FLAVOURING, salt and pepper, herbs, spices, condiments.

seat ● noun **1** *a wooden seat* CHAIR, bench, stool, settle, stall; (**seats**) seating, room; *Brit. informal* pew. **2** *the seat of government* HEADQUARTERS, base, centre, nerve centre, hub, heart; location, site, whereabouts, place. **3** *the family's country seat* RESIDENCE, ancestral home, mansion, stately home; *formal* abode.
● verb **1** *they seated themselves round the table* POSITION, put, place; ensconce, install, settle; *informal* plonk, park. **2** *the hall seats 500* HAVE ROOM FOR, contain, take, sit, hold, accommodate.

seating ● noun SEATS, room, places, chairs, accommodation.

secede ● verb *the Kingdom of Belgium seceded from the Netherlands in 1830* WITHDRAW FROM, break away from, break with, separate (oneself) from, leave, split with, split off from, disaffiliate from, resign from, pull out of; *informal* quit.
– OPPOSITES join.

secluded ● adjective SHELTERED, private, concealed, hidden, unfrequented, sequestered, tucked away.
– OPPOSITES busy.

seclusion ● noun ISOLATION, solitude, retreat, privacy, retirement, withdrawal, purdah, concealment, hiding, secrecy.

second[1] ● adjective **1** *the second day of the trial* NEXT, following, subsequent, succeeding. **2** *he keeps a second pair of glasses in his office* ADDITIONAL, extra, alternative, another, spare, back-up, relief, fallback; *N. Amer.* alternate. **3** *he dropped down to captain the second team* SECONDARY, lower, subordinate, subsidiary, lesser, inferior. **4** *the conflict could turn into a second Vietnam* ANOTHER, new; repeat of, copy of, carbon copy of.
– OPPOSITES first.
● noun **1** *Eva had been working as his second* ASSISTANT, attendant, helper, aide, supporter, auxiliary, right-hand man/woman, second in command, number two, deputy, understudy, subordinate; *informal* sidekick. **2** *(informal) he enjoyed the pie and asked for seconds* A SECOND HELPING, a further helping, more.
● verb *George Beale seconded the motion* FORMALLY SUPPORT, give one's support to, vote for, back, approve, endorse.
– PHRASES **second to none** INCOMPARABLE, matchless, unrivalled, inimitable, beyond compare/comparison, unparalleled, without parallel, unequalled, without equal, in a class of its own, peerless, unsurpassed, unsurpassable, nonpareil, unique; perfect, consummate, transcendent, surpassing, superlative, supreme; *formal* unexampled.

second[2] ● noun *I'll only be gone for a second* MOMENT, bit, little while, short time, instant, split second; *informal* sec, jiffy; *Brit. informal* mo, tick, two ticks.
– PHRASES **in a second** VERY SOON, in a minute, in a moment, in a trice, shortly, any minute (now), in the twinkling of an eye, in (less than) no time, in no time at all; *N. Amer.* momentarily; *informal* in a jiffy, in two shakes (of a lamb's tail), before you can say Jack Robinson, in the blink of an eye; *Brit. informal* in a tick, in two ticks, in a mo; *N. Amer. informal* in a snap; *poetic/literary* ere long.

second[3] ● verb *(Brit.) he was seconded to their Welsh office* ASSIGN TEMPORARILY, lend; transfer, move, shift, relocate, assign, reassign, send.

secondary industry • noun Economics industry that converts raw materials into commodities and products; manufacturing industry.

secondary modern school • noun chiefly historical (in the UK) a secondary school for children not selected for grammar or technical schools.

secondary picketing • noun Brit. picketing of a firm not directly involved in a particular dispute.

secondary sexual characteristics • plural noun physical characteristics developed at puberty which distinguish between the sexes but are not involved in reproduction.

second best • adjective next after the best. • noun a less adequate or less desirable alternative.

second chamber • noun the upper house of a parliament with two chambers.

second class • noun **1** a set of people or things grouped together as the second best. **2** the second-best accommodation in an aircraft, train, or ship. **3** Brit. the second-highest division in the results of the examinations for a university degree. • adjective & adverb relating to the second class.

Second Coming • noun Christian Theology the prophesied return of Christ to Earth at the Last Judgement.

second-degree • adjective **1** Medicine (of burns) that cause blistering but not permanent scars. **2** Law, chiefly N. Amer. (of a crime, especially a murder) less serious than a first-degree crime.

second-generation • adjective **1** referring to the offspring of parents who have immigrated to a particular country. **2** of a more advanced stage of technology than previous models or systems.

second-guess • verb **1** anticipate or predict (someone's actions or thoughts) by guesswork. **2** judge (someone) with hindsight.

second-hand • adjective & adverb **1** (of goods) having had a previous owner; not new. **2** accepted on another's authority and not from original investigation.

– PHRASES **at second hand** by hearsay rather than direct observation or experience.

second hand • noun an extra hand in some watches and clocks which moves round to indicate the seconds.

second in command • noun the officer next in authority to the commanding or chief officer.

second lieutenant • noun a rank of officer in the army and the US air force, above warrant officer or chief warrant officer and below lieutenant or first lieutenant.

secondly • adverb in the second place; second.

second mate • noun another term for SECOND OFFICER.

second name • noun Brit. a surname.

second nature • noun a tendency or habit that has become instinctive.

second officer • noun an assistant mate on a merchant ship.

second person • noun see PERSON (sense 3).

second-rate • adjective of mediocre or inferior quality.

– DERIVATIVES **second-rater** noun.

second reading • noun a second presentation of a bill to a legislative assembly.

second sight • noun the supposed ability to perceive future or distant events; clairvoyance.

second string • noun an alternative resource or course of action in case another one fails.

second thoughts • plural noun a change of opinion or resolve reached after reconsideration.

second wind • noun regained ability to breathe freely during exercise, after having been out of breath.

secret • adjective **1** not known or seen or not meant to be known or seen by others. **2** fond of having or keeping secrets; secretive. • noun **1** something secret. **2** a method of achieving something that is not commonly known or recognized: *the secret of a happy marriage is compromise.* **3** something not properly understood; a mystery: *the secrets of the universe.*

– DERIVATIVES **secrecy** noun **secretly** adverb.

– ORIGIN Latin *secretus* 'separate, set apart', from *secernere* 'move apart'.

secret agent • noun a spy acting for a country.

secretaire /sekritair/ • noun a small writing desk.

– ORIGIN French, 'secretary'.

secretariat /sekritairiət/ • noun a governmental administrative office or department.

secretary • noun (pl. **secretaries**) **1** a person employed to assist with correspondence, keep records, etc. **2** an official of a society or other organization who conducts its correspondence and keeps its records. **3** the principal assistant of a UK government minister or ambassador.

– DERIVATIVES **secretarial** adjective.

– ORIGIN originally in the sense 'person entrusted with a secret': from Latin *secretarius* 'confidential officer', from *secretum* 'a secret'.

secretary bird • noun a slender long-legged African bird of prey that feeds on snakes, having a crest likened to a quill pen stuck behind the ear.

Secretary General • noun (pl. **Secretaries General**) the title of the principal administrator of some organizations.

Secretary of State • noun **1** (in the UK) the head of a major government department. **2** (in the US) the head of the State Department, responsible for foreign affairs.

secrete[1] /sikreet/ • verb (of a cell, gland, or organ) produce and discharge (a substance).

– DERIVATIVES **secretor** noun **secretory** adjective.

secrete[2] /sikreet/ • verb conceal; hide.

– ORIGIN from the obsolete verb *secret* 'keep secret'.

secretion • noun **1** a process by which substances are produced

Thesaurus

secondary • adjective **1** *a secondary issue* LESS IMPORTANT, subordinate, lesser, minor, peripheral, incidental, ancillary, subsidiary, non-essential, inessential, of little account, unimportant. **2** *secondary infections* ACCOMPANYING, attendant, concomitant, consequential, resulting, resultant.

– OPPOSITES primary, main.

second-class • adjective SECOND-RATE, second-best, inferior, lesser, unimportant.

second-hand • adjective **1** *second-hand clothes* USED, old, worn, pre-owned, handed-down, hand-me-down, cast-off; *Brit. informal* reach-me-down. **2** *second-hand information* INDIRECT, derivative; vicarious.

– OPPOSITES new, direct.

• adverb *I was discounting anything I heard second-hand* INDIRECTLY, at second-hand, on the bush telegraph; *informal* on the grapevine.

– OPPOSITES directly.

second in command • noun DEPUTY, number two, subordinate, right-hand man/woman; understudy.

secondly • adverb FURTHERMORE, also, moreover; second, in the second place, next; secondarily.

second-rate • adjective INFERIOR, substandard, low-quality, below par, bad, poor, deficient, defective, faulty, imperfect, shoddy, inadequate, insufficient, unacceptable; *Brit. informal* ropy, duff, rubbish.

– OPPOSITES first-rate, excellent.

secrecy • noun **1** *the secrecy of the material* CONFIDENTIALITY, classified nature. **2** *a government which thrived on secrecy* SECRETIVENESS, covertness, furtiveness, surreptitiousness, stealth, stealthiness.

secret • adjective **1** *a secret plan* CONFIDENTIAL, top secret, classified, undisclosed, unknown, private, under wraps; *informal* hush-hush; *formal* sub rosa. **2** *a secret drawer in the table* HIDDEN, concealed, disguised; invisible. **3** *a secret operation to infiltrate terrorist groups* CLANDESTINE, covert, undercover, underground, surreptitious, stealthy, furtive, cloak-and-dagger, hole-and-corner, closet; *informal* hush-hush. **4** *a secret message* | *a secret code* CRYPTIC, encoded, coded; mysterious, abstruse, recondite, arcane, esoteric, cabbalistic. **5** *a secret place* SECLUDED, private, concealed, hidden, unfrequented, out of the way, tucked away. **6** *a very secret person.* See SECRETIVE.

– OPPOSITES public, open.

• noun **1** *he just can't keep a secret* CONFIDENTIAL MATTER, confidence, private affair; skeleton in the cupboard. **2** *the secrets of the universe* MYSTERY, enigma, paradox, puzzle, conundrum, poser, riddle. **3** *the secret of their success* RECIPE, (magic) formula, blueprint, key, answer, solution.

– PHRASES **in secret** SECRETLY, in private, privately, behind closed doors, behind the scenes, in camera, under cover, under the counter, discreetly, behind someone's back, furtively, stealthily, on the sly, on the quiet, conspiratorially, covertly, clandestinely, on the side; *informal* on the q.t.; *formal* sub rosa.

secret agent • noun SPY, double agent, counterspy, undercover agent, operative, plant, mole; *N. Amer. informal* spook.

S

and discharged from a cell, gland, or organ for a particular function in the organism or for excretion. **2** a substance discharged in such a way.
– ORIGIN Latin, 'separation', from *secernere* 'move apart'.

secretive ● adjective inclined to conceal feelings and intentions or not to disclose information.
– DERIVATIVES **secretively** adverb **secretiveness** noun.

secret police ● noun (treated as pl.) a police force working in secret against a government's political opponents.

secret service ● noun **1** a government department concerned with espionage. **2** (**Secret Service**) (in the US) a branch of the Treasury Department dealing with counterfeiting and providing protection for the President.

secret society ● noun an organization whose members are sworn to secrecy about its activities.

sect ● noun **1** a group of people with different religious beliefs (typically regarded as heretical) from those of a larger group to which they belong. **2** a group with extreme or dangerous philosophical or political ideas.
– ORIGIN Latin *secta* 'following, faction', from *sequi* 'follow'.

sectarian ● adjective **1** concerning or deriving from a sect or sects. **2** carried out on the grounds of membership of a sect or other group: *sectarian killings.* ● noun a member or follower of a sect.
– DERIVATIVES **sectarianism** noun.

section ● noun **1** any of the more or less distinct parts into which something is divided or from which it is made up. **2** a distinct group within a larger body of people or things. **3** the shape resulting from cutting a solid by or along a plane. **4** a representation of the internal structure of something as if it has been cut through. **5** Biology a thin slice of plant or animal tissue prepared for microscopic examination. **6** Surgery a separation by cutting. **7** NZ a building plot. ● verb **1** divide into sections. **2** Surgery divide by cutting. **3** Brit. (often **be sectioned**) commit compulsorily to a psychiatric hospital (in accordance with a section of the Mental Health Act).
– DERIVATIVES **sectional** adjective.
– ORIGIN Latin, from *secare* 'to cut'.

sectionalism ● noun **1** restriction of interest to parochial rather than general concerns. **2** undue concern with petty distinctions.
– DERIVATIVES **sectionalist** noun & adjective.

sector ● noun **1** an area or portion that is distinct from others. **2** a distinct part of an economy, society, or sphere of activity. **3** a subdivision of an area for military operations. **4** the plane figure enclosed by two radii of a circle or ellipse and the arc between them. **5** a mathematical instrument consisting of two arms hinged at one end and marked with sines, tangents, etc. for making diagrams.
– DERIVATIVES **sectoral** adjective.
– ORIGIN Latin, 'cutter'.

secular /sekyoolər/ ● adjective **1** not religious, sacred, or spiritual. **2** (of clergy) not subject to or bound by religious rule. **3** Astronomy denoting slow changes in the motion of the sun or planets. **4** Economics (of a fluctuation or trend) occurring or persisting over an indefinitely long period. ● noun a secular priest.
– DERIVATIVES **secularism** noun **secularist** noun **secularity** noun **secularize** (also **secularise**) verb **secularly** adverb.
– ORIGIN Latin *saecularis* 'relating to an age or period', from *saeculum* 'generation', used in Christian Latin to mean 'the world'.

secure ● adjective **1** certain to remain safe and unthreatened. **2** fixed or fastened so as not to give way, become loose, or be lost. **3** feeling free from fear or anxiety. **4** protected against attack, burglary, etc. **5** (of a place of detention) having provisions against the escape of inmates. ● verb **1** protect against danger or threat. **2** fix or fasten securely. **3** succeed in obtaining. **4** seek to guarantee repayment of (a loan) by having a right to take possession of an asset in the event of non-payment.
– DERIVATIVES **securable** adjective **securely** adverb **securement** noun **secureness** noun.
– ORIGIN Latin *securus*, from *cura* 'care'.

securitize (also **securitise**) ● verb convert (an asset, especially a loan) into marketable securities, typically for the purpose of raising cash.
– DERIVATIVES **securitization** noun.

security ● noun (pl. **securities**) **1** the state of being or feeling secure. **2** the safety of a state or organization against criminal activity such as terrorism or espionage. **3** a thing deposited or pledged as a guarantee of the fulfilment of an undertaking or the repayment of a loan, to be forfeited in case of default. **4** a certificate attesting credit, the ownership of stocks or bonds, etc.

security blanket ● noun **1** a blanket or other familiar object which is a comfort to a child. **2** Brit. an official sanction imposed on information in order to maintain complete secrecy.

sedan /sidan/ ● noun **1** an enclosed chair carried between two horizontal poles, common in the 17th and 18th centuries. **2** chiefly N. Amer. a car for four or more people.
– ORIGIN perhaps from an Italian dialect word, from Latin *sella* 'saddle'.

sedate[1] ● adjective **1** calm and unhurried. **2** staid and rather

Thesaurus

secretary ● noun ASSISTANT, personal assistant, PA, administrator, amanuensis, girl/man Friday.

secrete[1] ● verb *a substance secreted by the prostate gland* PRODUCE, discharge, emit, excrete, release, send out.
– OPPOSITES absorb.

secrete[2] ● verb *we secreted ourselves in the bushes* CONCEAL, hide, cover up, veil, shroud, screen, stow away; bury, cache; *informal* stash away.
– OPPOSITES reveal.

secretive ● adjective UNCOMMUNICATIVE, secret, unforthcoming, playing one's cards close to one's chest, reticent, reserved, silent, non-communicative, quiet, tight-lipped, close-mouthed, taciturn.
– OPPOSITES open, communicative.

secretly ● adverb **1** *they met secretly for a year* IN SECRET, in private, privately, behind closed doors, in camera, behind the scenes, under cover, under the counter, behind someone's back, furtively, stealthily, on the sly, on the quiet, conspiratorially, covertly, clandestinely, on the side; *informal* on the q.t.; *formal* sub rosa. **2** *he was secretly jealous of Bartholomew* PRIVATELY, in one's heart (of hearts), deep down.

sect ● noun (RELIGIOUS) CULT, religious group, denomination, persuasion, religious order; splinter group, faction.

sectarian ● adjective FACTIONAL, separatist, partisan, parti pris; doctrinaire, dogmatic, extreme, fanatical, rigid, inflexible, bigoted, hidebound, narrow-minded.
– OPPOSITES tolerant, liberal.

section ● noun **1** *the separate sections of a train* PART, piece, bit, segment, component, division, portion, element, unit, constituent. **2** *the last section of the questionnaire* SUBDIVISION, part, subsection, division, portion, bit, chapter, passage, clause. **3** *the reference section of the library* DEPARTMENT, area, part, division. **4** *a residential section of the capital.* See SECTOR sense 2.

sector ● adjective **1** *every sector of the industry is affected* PART, branch, arm, division, area, department, field, sphere. **2** *the north-eastern sector of the town* DISTRICT, quarter, part, section, zone, region, area, belt.

secular ● adjective NON-RELIGIOUS, lay, temporal, worldly, earthly, profane; *formal* laic.
– OPPOSITES holy, religious.

secure ● adjective **1** *check to ensure that all bolts are secure* FASTENED, fixed, secured, done up; closed, shut, locked. **2** *an environment in which children can feel secure* SAFE, protected from harm/danger, out of from danger, sheltered, safe and sound, out of harm's way, in a safe place, in safe hands, invulnerable; at ease, unworried, relaxed, happy, confident. **3** *a secure future* CERTAIN, assured, reliable, dependable, settled, fixed.
– OPPOSITES loose, vulnerable, uncertain.
● verb **1** *pins secure the handle to the main body* FIX, attach, fasten, affix, connect, couple. **2** *the doors had not been properly secured* FASTEN, close, shut, lock, bolt, chain, seal. **3** *he leapt out to secure the boat* TIE UP, moor, make fast; anchor. **4** *they sought to secure the country against attack* PROTECT, make safe, fortify, strengthen. **5** *a written constitution would secure the rights of the individual* ASSURE, ensure, guarantee, protect, confirm, establish. **6** *the division secured a major contract* OBTAIN, acquire, gain, get, get possession of; *informal* get hold of, land.

security ● noun **1** *the security of the nation's citizens* SAFETY, freedom from danger, protection, invulnerability. **2** *he could give her the security she needed* PEACE OF MIND, feeling of safety, stability, certainty, happiness, confidence. **3** *security at the court was tight* SAFETY MEASURES, safeguards, surveillance, defence, protection. **4** *additional security for your loan may be required* GUARANTEE, col-

S

dull.
– DERIVATIVES **sedately** adverb **sedateness** noun.
– ORIGIN originally used also as a medical term in the sense 'not sore or painful': from Latin *sedare* 'settle'.
sedate² ● verb put under sedation.
sedation ● noun the administering of a sedative drug to produce a state of calm or sleep.
– ORIGIN Latin, from *sedare* 'settle'.
sedative ● adjective promoting calm or inducing sleep. ● noun a sedative drug.
sedentary /seddəntri/ ● adjective **1** sitting; seated. **2** tending to sit down a lot; taking little physical exercise. **3** tending to stay in the same place for much of the time.
– ORIGIN originally in the sense 'not migratory': from Latin *sedentarius*, from *sedere* 'sit'.
sedge ● noun a grass-like plant with triangular stems and inconspicuous flowers, growing typically in wet ground.
– ORIGIN Old English.
sedge warbler ● noun a common migratory songbird with streaky brown plumage, frequenting marshes and reed beds.
sediment ● noun **1** matter that settles to the bottom of a liquid. **2** Geology material carried in particles by water or wind and deposited on the land surface or seabed. ● verb settle or deposit as sediment.
– DERIVATIVES **sedimentation** noun.
– ORIGIN Latin *sedimentum* 'settling'.
sedimentary ● adjective **1** of or relating to sediment. **2** Geology (of rock) that has formed from sediment deposited by water or wind.
sedition ● noun conduct or speech inciting rebellion against the authority of a state or monarch.
– DERIVATIVES **seditious** adjective **seditiously** adverb.
– ORIGIN Latin, from *sed-* 'apart' + *itio* 'going'.
seduce ● verb **1** persuade to do something inadvisable. **2** entice into sexual activity.
– DERIVATIVES **seducer** noun **seducible** adjective **seduction** noun **seductress** noun.
– ORIGIN Latin *seducere* 'lead aside or away'.
seductive ● adjective tempting and attractive.
– DERIVATIVES **seductively** adverb **seductiveness** noun.
sedulous /sedyooləss/ ● adjective showing dedication and diligence.
– DERIVATIVES **sedulity** /sidyōōliti/ noun **sedulously** adverb **sedulousness** noun.
– ORIGIN Latin *sedulus* 'zealous'.
sedum /seedəm/ ● noun a plant of a large group having fleshy leaves and small star-shaped flowers.
– ORIGIN Latin.
see¹ ● verb (**sees**, **seeing**; past **saw**; past part. **seen**) **1** perceive with the eyes. **2** experience or witness. **3** deduce after reflection or from information. **4** regard in a specified way. **5** regard as a possibility; envisage. **6** meet (someone one knows) socially or by chance. **7** meet regularly as a boyfriend or girlfriend. **8** consult (a specialist or professional). **9** give an interview or consultation to. **10** escort to a specified place. **11** (**see to**) attend to. **12** (**see that**) ensure that.
– PHRASES **see about** attend to; deal with. **see off 1** accompany (a person who is leaving) to their point of departure. **2** Brit. repel or deter (an intruder, aggressor, etc.). **see out** Brit. **1** last longer than the life of. **2** come to the end of (a period of time or undertaking). **see over** tour and examine. **see right** Brit. informal reward or look after appropriately. **see through 1** support (a person) for the duration of a difficult time. **2** persist with (an undertaking) until it is completed. **3** detect the true nature of.
– DERIVATIVES **seeable** adjective.
– ORIGIN Old English.
see² ● noun the seat of authority of a bishop or archbishop, centred on a cathedral church.
– ORIGIN Latin *sedes* 'seat'.
seed ● noun **1** a flowering plant's unit of reproduction, capable of developing into another such plant. **2** the beginning of a feeling, process, or condition. **3** archaic a man's semen. **4** archaic (chiefly in biblical use) offspring or descendants. **5** any of a number of stronger competitors in a sports tournament who have been assigned a position in an ordered list to ensure they do not play each other in the early rounds. ● verb **1** sow (land) with seeds. **2** produce or drop seeds. **3** remove the seeds from. **4** initiate the development or growth of. **5** give (a competitor)

Thesaurus

lateral, surety, pledge, bond; *archaic* gage.
– OPPOSITES vulnerability, danger.
sedate¹ ● verb *the patient had to be sedated* TRANQUILLIZE, put under sedation, drug.
sedate² ● adjective **1** *a sedate pace* SLOW, steady, dignified, unhurried, relaxed, measured, leisurely, slow-moving, easy, easy-going, gentle. **2** *he had lived a sedate and straightforward life* CALM, placid, tranquil, quiet, uneventful; boring, dull.
– OPPOSITES exciting, fast.
sedative ● adjective *sedative drugs* TRANQUILLIZING, calming, calmative, relaxing, soporific; depressant; *Medicine* neuroleptic.
● noun *the doctor gave him a sedative* TRANQUILLIZER, calmative, sleeping pill, narcotic, opiate; depressant; *informal* trank, sleeper, downer.
sedentary ● adjective SITTING, seated, desk-bound; inactive.
– OPPOSITES active.
sediment ● noun DREGS, lees, precipitate, deposit, grounds, settlings, residue, remains; silt, alluvium; *technical* residuum; *archaic* grouts.
sedition ● noun RABBLE-ROUSING, incitement to rebel, subversion, troublemaking, provocation; rebellion, insurrection, mutiny, insurgence, civil disorder.
seditious ● adjective RABBLE-ROUSING, provocative, inflammatory, subversive, troublemaking; rebellious, insurrectionist, mutinous, insurgent.
seduce ● verb **1** *he took her to his hotel room and tried to seduce her* persuade to have sex; *euphemistic* have one's (wicked) way with, take advantage of; *dated* debauch. **2** *a firm which had seduced customers into buying worthless products* ATTRACT, allure, lure, tempt, entice, beguile, inveigle, manoeuvre.
seducer ● noun WOMANIZER, philanderer, Romeo, Don Juan, Lothario, Casanova, playboy, ladies' man; *informal* ladykiller, wolf, skirt-chaser.
seductive ● adjective SEXY, alluring, tempting, exciting, provocative, sultry, slinky; coquettish, flirtatious; *informal* vampish, come-hither, come-to-bed.
seductress ● noun TEMPTRESS, siren, femme fatale, Mata Hari; flirt, coquette; *informal* vamp.
sedulous ● adjective DILIGENT, careful, meticulous, thorough, assiduous, attentive, industrious, conscientious, ultra-careful, punctilious, scrupulous, painstaking, minute, rigorous, particular.
see¹ ● verb **1** *he saw her running across the road* DISCERN, spot, notice, catch sight of, glimpse, catch/get a glimpse of, make out, pick out, spy, distinguish, detect, perceive, note; *informal* clap/lay/set eyes on, clock; *poetic/literary* behold, descry, espy. **2** *I saw a documentary about it last week* WATCH, look at, view; catch. **3** *would you like to see over the house?* INSPECT, view, look round, tour, survey, examine, scrutinize; *informal* give something a/the once-over. **4** *I finally saw what she meant* UNDERSTAND, grasp, comprehend, follow, take in, realize, appreciate, recognize, work out, get the drift of, perceive, fathom (out); *informal* get, latch on to, cotton on to, catch on to, tumble to, savvy, figure out, get a fix on; *Brit. informal* twig, suss (out). **5** *I must go and see what Victor is up to* FIND OUT, discover, learn, ascertain, determine, establish. **6** *see that no harm comes to him* ENSURE, make sure/certain, see to it, take care, mind. **7** *I see trouble ahead* FORESEE, predict, forecast, prophesy, anticipate, envisage, picture, visualize. **8** *about a year later, I saw him in town* ENCOUNTER, meet, run into/across, come across, stumble on/across, happen on, chance on; *informal* bump into; *archaic* run against. **9** *they see each other from time to time* MEET, meet up with, get together with, socialize with. **10** *you'd better see a doctor* CONSULT, confer with, talk to, speak to, have recourse to, call on, call in, turn to, ask. **11** *he's seeing someone else now* GO OUT WITH, date, take out, be involved with; *informal* go steady with; *Brit. informal, dated* walk out with; *N. Amer. informal, dated* step out with; *dated* court. **12** *he saw her to her car* ESCORT, accompany, show, walk, conduct, lead, take, usher, attend.
– PHRASES **see about** ARRANGE, see to, deal with, take care of, look after, attend to, sort out. **see through** UNDERSTAND, get/have the measure of, read like a book; *informal* be wise to, have someone's number, know someone's (little) game. **see someone through** SUSTAIN, encourage, buoy up, keep going, support, be a tower of strength to, comfort, help (out), stand by, stick by. **see something through** PERSEVERE WITH, persist with, continue (with), carry on with, keep at, follow through, stay with; *informal* stick at, stick it out, hang in there. **see to** ATTEND TO, deal with, see about, take

S

the status of seed in a tournament.
– PHRASES **go** (or **run**) **to seed 1** cease flowering as the seeds develop. **2** deteriorate.
– DERIVATIVES **seedless** adjective.
– ORIGIN Old English, related to sow[1].
seedbed • noun a bed of fine soil in which seedlings are germinated.
seed cake • noun cake containing caraway seeds.
seed corn • noun **1** good-quality corn kept for seed. **2** Brit. assets set aside for the generation of future profit.
seeder • noun **1** a machine for sowing seed. **2** a plant that produces seeds in a particular way or under particular conditions.
seed head • noun a flower head in seed.
seed leaf • noun Botany a cotyledon.
seedling • noun a young plant raised from seed.
seed money (also **seed capital**) • noun money allocated to initiate a project.
seed pearl • noun a very small pearl.
seed potato • noun a potato intended for replanting to produce a new plant.
seedsman • noun a person who deals in seeds as a profession.
seedy • adjective (**seedier**, **seediest**) **1** sordid or squalid. **2** dated unwell.
– DERIVATIVES **seedily** adverb **seediness** noun.
seeing • conjunction because; since.
– PHRASES **seeing is believing** proverb you need to see something before you can accept that it really exists or occurs.
seek • verb (past and past part. **sought**) **1** try to find or obtain. **2** (**seek out**) search for and find. **3** (**seek to do**) try or want to do. **4** ask for.
– DERIVATIVES **seeker** noun.
– ORIGIN Old English.
seem • verb **1** give the impression of being. **2** (**cannot seem to do**) appear to be unable to do, despite having tried.
– ORIGIN originally also in the sense 'be appropriate': from an Old Norse word meaning 'fitting'.
seeming • adjective appearing to be real or true; apparent.
– DERIVATIVES **seemingly** adverb.
seemly • adjective conforming to propriety or good taste.
– DERIVATIVES **seemliness** noun.
– ORIGIN Old Norse, 'fitting'; related to SEEM.
seen past participle of SEE[1].
seep • verb (of a liquid) flow or leak slowly through porous material or small holes.
– DERIVATIVES **seepage** noun.
– ORIGIN perhaps a dialect form of an Old English word meaning 'to soak'.
seer /seer/ • noun a person of supposed supernatural insight who sees visions of the future.
seersucker • noun a fabric with a puckered surface.
– ORIGIN from a Persian phrase meaning 'milk and sugar' (with reference to the alternating stripes in which the fabric was originally woven).
see-saw • noun **1** a long plank balanced on a fixed support, on each end of which children sit and move up and down by pushing the ground with their feet. **2** a situation characterized by repeated alternation between two states or positions. • verb repeatedly change from one state or position to another and back again.
– ORIGIN from SAW[1].
seethe • verb **1** (of a liquid) boil or be turbulent as if boiling. **2** be filled with intense but unexpressed anger. **3** be crowded with people or things.
– ORIGIN Old English.
see-through • adjective transparent or translucent.
segment /segmənt/ • noun **1** each of the parts into which something is divided. **2** Geometry a part of a circle cut off by a chord, or a part of a sphere cut off by a plane not passing through the centre. **3** Zoology each of a series of similar anatomical units of which the body and appendages of some animals are composed. • verb /segment/ divide into segments.
– DERIVATIVES **segmental** adjective **segmentary** adjective **segmentation** noun.
– ORIGIN Latin *segmentum*, from *secare* 'to cut'.
segregate /segrigayt/ • verb **1** set apart from the rest or from each other. **2** separate along racial, sexual, or religious lines.
– ORIGIN Latin *segregare* 'separate from the flock'.
segregation • noun **1** the action of segregating or the state of being segregated. **2** the enforced separation of different racial groups in a country, community, or establishment.
– DERIVATIVES **segregational** adjective **segregationist** adjective & noun.
segue /segway/ • verb (**segues**, **segued**, **seguing**) (in music and film) move without interruption from one song, melody, or

Thesaurus

care of, look after, sort out, fix, organize, arrange.
see[2] • noun *a bishop's see* DIOCESE, bishopric.
seed • noun **1** *sow the seeds in trays or pots* pip, stone, kernel; ovule. **2** *each war contains within it the seeds of a fresh war* GENESIS, source, origin, root, starting point, germ, beginnings, potential (for); cause, reason, motivation, motive, grounds. **3** (*archaic*) *Abraham and his seed* DESCENDANTS, heirs, successors, scions; offspring, children, sons and daughters, progeny, family; *Law* issue; *derogatory* spawn; *archaic* fruit of someone's loins.
– RELATED TERMS seminal.
– PHRASES **go/run to seed** DETERIORATE, degenerate, decline, decay, fall into decay, go to rack and ruin, go downhill, moulder, rot; *informal* go to pot, go to the dogs, go down the toilet.
seedy • adjective **1** *the seedy world of prostitution* SORDID, disreputable, seamy, sleazy, squalid, unwholesome, unsavoury. **2** *a seedy block of flats* DILAPIDATED, tumbledown, ramshackle, falling to pieces, decrepit, gone to rack and ruin, run down, down at heel, shabby, dingy, slummy, insalubrious, squalid; *informal* crummy; *Brit. informal* grotty.
– OPPOSITES high-class.
seek • verb **1** *they sought shelter from the winter snows* SEARCH FOR, try to find, look for, be on the lookout for, be after, hunt for, be in quest of. **2** *the company is seeking a judicial review of the decision* TRY TO OBTAIN, work towards, be intent on, aim at/for. **3** *he sought help from the police* ASK FOR, request, solicit, call for, entreat, beg for, petition for, appeal for, apply for, put in for. **4** *we constantly seek to improve the service* TRY, attempt, endeavour, strive, work, do one's best; *formal* essay.
seem • verb APPEAR (TO BE), have the appearance/air of being, give the impression of being, look, look as though one is, look like, show signs of, look to be; come across as, strike someone as, sound.
seeming • adjective APPARENT, ostensible, supposed, outward, surface, superficial; pretended, feigned.
– OPPOSITES actual, genuine.
seemingly • adverb APPARENTLY, on the face of it, to all appearances, as far as one can see/tell, on the surface, to all intents and purposes, outwardly, superficially, supposedly.
seemly • adjective DECOROUS, proper, decent, becoming, fitting, suitable, appropriate, apt, apposite, meet, in good taste, genteel, polite, the done thing, right, correct, acceptable, comme il faut.
– OPPOSITES unseemly, unbecoming.
seep • verb OOZE, trickle, exude, drip, dribble, flow, issue, escape, leak, drain, bleed, filter, percolate, soak.
seer • noun SOOTHSAYER, oracle, augur, prophet(ess), prognosticator, diviner, fortune teller, crystal-gazer, clairvoyant, psychic; *Scottish* spaewife; *poetic/literary* sibyl.
see-saw • verb FLUCTUATE, swing, go up and down, rise and fall, oscillate, alternate, yo-yo, vary.
seethe • verb **1** *the brew seethed* BOIL, bubble, simmer, foam, froth, fizz, effervesce. **2** *the water seethed with fish* TEEM, swarm, boil, swirl, churn, surge. **3** *I seethed at the injustice of it all* BE ANGRY, be furious, be enraged, be incensed, be beside oneself, boil, simmer, rage, rant, rave, storm, fume, smoulder; *informal* be livid, be wild, foam at the mouth, be steamed up, be hot under the collar; *Brit. informal* do one's nut, throw a wobbly.
see-through • adjective TRANSPARENT, translucent, clear, limpid, pellucid; thin, lightweight, flimsy, sheer, diaphanous, filmy, gossamer, chiffony, gauzy.
– OPPOSITES opaque.
segment • noun **1** *orange segments* PIECE, bit, section, part, chunk, portion, division, slice; fragment, wedge, lump, tranche. **2** *all segments of society* PART, section, sector, division, portion, constituent, element, unit, compartment; branch, wing.
• verb *they plan to segment their market share* DIVIDE (UP), subdivide, separate, split, cut up, carve up, slice up, break up; segregate, divorce, partition, section.
– OPPOSITES amalgamate.
segregate • verb SEPARATE, set apart, keep apart, isolate, quarantine, closet; partition, divide, detach, disconnect, sever, dissoci-

S

scene to another. ● noun an instance of this.
– ORIGIN Italian, 'follows'.

seicento /saychentō/ ● noun the style of Italian art and literature of the 17th century.
– DERIVATIVES **seicentist** noun.
– ORIGIN Italian, '600', shortened from *mille seicento* '1600'.

seigneur /saynyör/ (also **seignior** /saynyər/) ● noun a feudal lord; the lord of a manor.
– DERIVATIVES **seigneurial** adjective.
– ORIGIN Old French, from Latin *senior* 'older, elder'.

seine /sayn/ ● noun a fishing net which hangs vertically in the water with floats at the top and weights at the bottom edge, the ends being drawn together to encircle the fish. ● verb fish or catch with a seine.
– DERIVATIVES **seiner** noun.
– ORIGIN Greek *sagēnē*.

seismic /sīzmik/ ● adjective **1** relating to earthquakes or other vibrations of the earth and its crust. **2** of enormous proportions or effect.
– DERIVATIVES **seismical** adjective **seismically** adverb.
– ORIGIN from Greek *seismos* 'earthquake'.

seismicity /sīzmissiti/ ● noun Geology the occurrence or frequency of earthquakes in a region.

seismogram /sīzməgram/ ● noun a record produced by a seismograph.

seismograph /sīzməgraaf/ ● noun an instrument that measures and records details of earthquakes, such as force and duration.
– DERIVATIVES **seismographic** adjective.

seismology /sīzmolləji/ ● noun the branch of science concerned with earthquakes and related phenomena.
– DERIVATIVES **seismological** adjective **seismologist** noun.

seismometer /sīzmommitər/ ● noun a seismograph.

seismosaurus /sīzməsawrəss/ ● noun a huge late Jurassic plant-eating dinosaur with a long neck and tail.
– ORIGIN from Greek *seismos* 'earthquake' + *sauros* 'lizard'.

seize ● verb **1** take hold of suddenly and forcibly. **2** take forcible possession of. **3** (of the police or another authority) take possession of by warrant or legal right. **4** take (an opportunity) eagerly and decisively. **5** (**seize on/upon**) take eager advantage of. **6** (of a machine or part in a machine) become jammed.
– DERIVATIVES **seizable** adjective **seizer** noun.
– ORIGIN Latin *sacire*, in the phrase *ad proprium sacire* 'claim as one's own'.

seizure ● noun **1** the action of seizing. **2** a sudden attack of illness, especially a stroke or an epileptic fit.

seldom ● adverb not often. ● adjective dated infrequent: *a great but seldom pleasure.*
– ORIGIN Old English.

select ● verb carefully choose as being the best or most suitable. ● adjective **1** carefully chosen as being among the best. **2** used by or consisting of a wealthy or sophisticated elite.
– DERIVATIVES **selectable** adjective **selectness** noun.
– ORIGIN Latin *seligere* 'choose'.

select committee ● noun a small parliamentary committee appointed for a special purpose.

selection ● noun **1** the action or fact of selecting. **2** a number of selected things. **3** a range of things from which a choice may be made. **4** a horse or horses tipped as worth bets in a race or meeting. **5** Biology the evolutionary process which determines which types of organism thrive; natural selection.

selective ● adjective **1** relating to or involving selection. **2** tending to choose carefully. **3** (of a process or agent) affecting some things and not others.
– DERIVATIVES **selectively** adverb **selectiveness** noun **selectivity** noun.

selector ● noun **1** a person appointed to select a team in a sport. **2** a device for selecting a particular gear or other setting of a machine or device.

selenite /sellinīt/ ● noun a form of gypsum occurring as transparent crystals or thin plates.
– ORIGIN from Greek *selēnitēs lithos* 'moonstone'.

selenium /sileeniəm/ ● noun a grey crystalline non-metallic chemical element with semiconducting properties.
– DERIVATIVES **selenide** noun.
– ORIGIN from Greek *selēnē* 'moon'.

self ● noun (pl. **selves**) **1** a person's essential being that distinguishes them from others. **2** a person's particular nature or personality: *he was back to his old self.* ● pronoun (pl. **selves**) **1** oneself. **2** used on counterfoils, cheques, and other papers to refer to the holder or person who has signed. ● adjective (of a trimming, woven design, etc.) of the same material or colour as the rest.
– ORIGIN Old English.

self- /self-/ ● combining form **1** of or directed towards oneself or itself: *self-hatred.* **2** by one's own efforts; by its own action: *self-adjusting.* **3** on, in, for, or relating to oneself or itself: *self-adhesive.*

self-abandonment (also **self-abandon**) ● noun the complete surrender of oneself to a desire or impulse.

self-absorption ● noun preoccupation with one's own emotions, interests, or situation.
– DERIVATIVES **self-absorbed** adjective.

self-abuse ● noun **1** behaviour which causes damage or harm to oneself. **2** euphemistic masturbation.

self-addressed ● adjective (of an envelope) bearing one's own address.

self-adhesive ● adjective adhering without requiring moistening.

self-adjusting ● adjective (chiefly of machinery) adjusting itself to meet varying requirements.
– DERIVATIVES **self-adjustment** noun.

self-advertisement ● noun the active publicizing of oneself.

self-affirmation ● noun the recognition and assertion of the existence and value of one's individual self.

self-appointed ● adjective having assumed a position or role without the endorsement of others.

self-assembly ● noun the construction of a piece of furniture from materials sold in kit form.
– DERIVATIVES **self-assemble** verb.

Thesaurus

S

ate; ghettoize.
– OPPOSITES amalgamate.

seize ● verb **1** *she seized the microphone* GRAB, grasp, snatch, take hold of, get one's hands on; grip, clutch; Brit. informal nab. **2** *rebels seized the air base* CAPTURE, take, overrun, occupy, conquer, take over. **3** *the drugs were seized by customs* CONFISCATE, impound, commandeer, requisition, appropriate, expropriate, take away; Law distrain; Scottish Law poind. **4** *terrorists seized his wife* KIDNAP, abduct, take captive, take prisoner, take hostage, hold to ransom; informal snatch.
– OPPOSITES relinquish, release.
– PHRASES **seize on** *they seized on the opportunity* TAKE ADVANTAGE OF, exploit, grasp with both hands, leap at, jump at, pounce on.

seizure ● noun **1** *Napoleon's seizure of Spain* CAPTURE, takeover, annexation, invasion, occupation, colonization. **2** *the seizure of defaulters' property* CONFISCATION, appropriation, expropriation, sequestration; Law distraint; Scottish Law poind. **3** *the seizure of UN staff by rebels* KIDNAPPING, kidnap, abduction. **4** *the baby suffered a seizure* CONVULSION, fit, spasm, paroxysm; Medicine ictus; dated apoplexy.

seldom ● adverb RARELY, infrequently, hardly (ever), scarcely (ever), almost never; now and then, occasionally, sporadically; informal once in a blue moon.
– OPPOSITES often.

select ● verb *select the correct tool for the job* CHOOSE, pick (out), single out, sort out, take; opt for, decide on, settle on, determine, nominate, appoint, elect.
● adjective **1** *a select group of SAS members* CHOICE, hand-picked, prime, first-rate, first-class, superior, finest, best, top-class, supreme, superb, excellent; informal A1, top-notch. **2** *a select clientele* EXCLUSIVE, elite, favoured, privileged; wealthy; informal posh.
– OPPOSITES inferior.

selection ● noun **1** *Jim made his selection of toys* CHOICE, pick; option, preference. **2** *a wide selection of dishes* RANGE, array, diversity, variety, assortment, mixture. **3** *a selection of his poems* ANTHOLOGY, assortment, collection, assemblage; miscellany, medley, pot-pourri.

selective ● adjective DISCERNING, discriminating, discriminatory, critical, exacting, demanding, particular; fussy, fastidious, faddish; informal choosy, pernickety, picky; Brit. informal faddy.

self ● noun EGO, I, oneself, persona, person, identity, character, personality, psyche, soul, spirit, mind, inner self.
– OPPOSITES other.

self-assembly ● noun *kits for self-assembly* DO-IT-YOURSELF, DIY.

self-assertion • noun the confident and forceful expression or promotion of oneself or one's views.
– DERIVATIVES **self-assertive** adjective **self-assertiveness** noun.

self-assessment • noun **1** assessment of oneself or one's performance in relation to an objective standard. **2** calculation of one's own taxable liability.

self-assurance • noun confidence in one's own abilities or character.
– DERIVATIVES **self-assured** adjective.

self-awareness • noun conscious knowledge of one's own character, feelings, motives, and desires.
– DERIVATIVES **self-aware** adjective.

self-cancelling • adjective **1** having elements which contradict or negate one another. **2** (of a mechanical device) designed to stop working automatically when no longer required.

self-catering Brit. • adjective (of a holiday or accommodation) offering facilities for people to cook their own meals. • noun the action of catering for oneself.

self-censorship • noun the exercising of control over what one says and does.

self-centred • adjective preoccupied with oneself and one's affairs.
– DERIVATIVES **self-centredly** adverb **self-centredness** noun.

self-certification • noun **1** the practice of attesting something about oneself in a formal statement, rather than asking a disinterested party to do so. **2** the practice, for the purpose of claiming sick pay, by which an employee rather than a doctor declares in writing that an absence was due to illness.

self-certify • verb Brit. **1** attest (one's financial standing) in a formal statement. **2** (**self-certified**) (of a loan or mortgage) obtained as a result of such self-certification.

self-colour • noun **1** a single uniform colour. **2** the natural colour of something.

self-confessed • adjective openly admitting to having certain characteristics.

self-confidence • noun a feeling of trust in one's abilities, qualities, and judgement.
– DERIVATIVES **self-confident** adjective **self-confidently** adverb.

self-congratulation • noun undue pride regarding one's achievements or qualities.
– DERIVATIVES **self-congratulatory** adjective.

self-conscious • adjective **1** nervous or awkward because unduly aware of oneself or one's actions. **2** (especially of an action) deliberate and with full awareness.
– DERIVATIVES **self-consciously** adverb **self-consciousness** noun.

self-consistent • adjective not having conflicting parts or aspects; consistent.
– DERIVATIVES **self-consistency** noun.

self-contained • adjective **1** complete, or having all that is needed, in itself. **2** chiefly Brit. (of accommodation) having its own kitchen and bathroom, and typically its own private entrance. **3** not depending on or influenced by others.

self-contradiction • noun inconsistency between aspects or parts of a whole.

self-control • noun the ability to control one's emotions or behaviour in difficult situations.
– DERIVATIVES **self-controlled** adjective.

self-deception • noun the action or practice of deceiving oneself into believing that a false or unfounded feeling, idea, or situation is true.

self-defeating • adjective (of an action or policy) unable to achieve the end it is designed to bring about.

self-defence • noun the defence of oneself or one's interests, especially the defence of one's person through physical force, permitted in certain cases as an answer to a charge of violent crime.
– DERIVATIVES **self-defensive** adjective.

self-denial • noun the denial of one's own interests and needs.
– DERIVATIVES **self-denying** adjective.

self-deprecating • adjective modest about or critical of oneself.
– DERIVATIVES **self-deprecation** noun **self-deprecatory** adjective.

self-depreciatory • adjective another term for SELF-DEPRECATING.
– DERIVATIVES **self-depreciation** noun.

self-destruct • verb explode or disintegrate automatically, having been preset to do so.

self-destructive • adjective destroying or causing harm to oneself.
– DERIVATIVES **self-destruction** noun **self-destructively** adverb.

self-determination • noun **1** the process by which a country determines its own statehood and forms its own allegiances and government. **2** the process by which a person controls their own life.

self-directed • adjective **1** (of an emotion, statement, or activity) directed at one's self. **2** (of an activity) under one's own control.
– DERIVATIVES **self-direction** noun.

self-discipline • noun the ability to control one's feelings and overcome one's weaknesses.
– DERIVATIVES **self-disciplined** adjective.

self-doubt • noun lack of confidence in oneself and one's abilities.

self-drive • adjective **1** Brit. (of a hired vehicle) driven by the hirer. **2** (of a holiday) involving use of one's own car rather than transport arranged by the operator.

self-educated • adjective educated largely through one's own efforts, rather than by formal instruction.
– DERIVATIVES **self-education** noun.

self-effacing • adjective not claiming attention for oneself.
– DERIVATIVES **self-effacement** noun.

self-employed • adjective working for oneself as a freelance or the owner of a business rather than for an employer.
– DERIVATIVES **self-employment** noun.

self-enclosed • adjective (of a person, community, or system) not choosing or able to communicate with others or with external systems.

self-esteem • noun confidence in one's own worth or abilities.

self-evaluation • noun another term for SELF-ASSESSMENT.

self-evident • adjective not needing to be demonstrated or explained; obvious.

self-examination • noun **1** the study of one's behaviour and motivations. **2** the examination of one's body for signs of illness.

self-explanatory • adjective not needing explanation; clearly

Thesaurus

• adjective *self-assembly furniture* FLAT-PACK, kit, self-build, do-it-yourself, DIY.

self-assurance • noun SELF-CONFIDENCE, confidence, assertiveness, self-reliance, self-possession, composure, presence of mind, aplomb.
– OPPOSITES diffidence.

self-assured • adjective SELF-CONFIDENT, confident, assertive, assured, authoritative, commanding, self-reliant, self-possessed, poised.

self-centred • adjective EGOCENTRIC, egotistic, egotistical, egomaniacal, self-absorbed, self-obsessed, self-seeking, self-interested, self-serving; narcissistic, vain; inconsiderate, thoughtless; *informal* looking after number one.

self-confidence • noun MORALE, confidence, self-assurance, assurance, assertiveness, self-reliance, self-possession, composure.

self-conscious • adjective EMBARRASSED, uncomfortable, uneasy, nervous; unnatural, inhibited, gauche, awkward; modest, shy, diffident, bashful, retiring, shrinking.
– OPPOSITES confident.

self-contained • adjective **1** *each train was a self-contained unit* COMPLETE, independent, separate, free-standing, enclosed. **2** *a very self-contained child* INDEPENDENT, self-sufficient, self-reliant; introverted, quiet, private, aloof, insular, reserved, reticent, secretive.

self-control • noun SELF-DISCIPLINE, restraint, self-possession, will power, composure, coolness; moderation, temperance, abstemiousness; *informal* cool.

self-denial • noun SELF-SACRIFICE, selflessness, unselfishness; self-discipline, asceticism, self-deprivation, abstemiousness, abstinence, abstention; moderation, temperance.
– OPPOSITES self-indulgence.

self-discipline • noun SELF-CONTROL; restraint, self-restraint; will power, purposefulness, strong-mindedness, resolve, moral fibre; doggedness, persistence, determination, grit.

self-employed • adjective FREELANCE, independent, casual; consultant, consulting; temporary, jobbing, visiting, outside, external, extramural, peripatetic.

self-esteem • noun SELF-RESPECT, pride, dignity, self-regard, faith in oneself; morale, self-confidence, confidence, self-assurance.

self-evident • adjective OBVIOUS, clear, plain, evident, apparent, manifest, patent; distinct, transparent, overt, conspicuous, palp-

understood.

self-expression ● noun the expression of one's feelings or thoughts, especially in writing, art, music, or dance.

self-fertile ● adjective Botany (of a plant) capable of self-fertilization.
– DERIVATIVES **self-fertility** noun.

self-fertilization (also **self-fertilisation**) ● noun Biology the fertilization of plants and some invertebrate animals by their own pollen or sperm.
– DERIVATIVES **self-fertilize** verb.

self-financing ● adjective (of an organization or enterprise) having or generating enough income to finance itself.
– DERIVATIVES **self-financed** adjective.

self-fulfilling ● adjective (of an opinion or prediction) bound to be proved correct or to come true as a result of behaviour caused by its being expressed.

self-governing ● adjective **1** (of a British hospital or school) having opted out of local authority control. **2** (of a former colony or dependency) administering its own affairs.
– DERIVATIVES **self-governed** adjective **self-government** noun.

self-heal ● noun a purple-flowered plant of the mint family, formerly used for healing wounds.

self-help ● noun the use of one's own efforts and resources to achieve things without relying on others.

selfhood ● noun the quality that constitutes one's individuality.

self-identification ● noun the attribution of certain characteristics or qualities to oneself.

self-image ● noun the idea one has of one's abilities, appearance, and personality.

self-immolation ● noun the offering of oneself as a sacrifice, especially by burning.

self-importance ● noun an exaggerated sense of one's own value or importance.
– DERIVATIVES **self-important** adjective.

self-improvement ● noun the improvement of one's knowledge, status, or character by one's own efforts.

self-induced ● adjective brought about by oneself.

self-indulgent ● adjective indulging or tending to indulge one's desires.
– DERIVATIVES **self-indulgence** noun.

self-inflicted ● adjective (of a wound or other harm) inflicted on oneself by one's own actions.

self-interest ● noun one's personal interest or advantage, especially when pursued without regard for others.
– DERIVATIVES **self-interested** adjective.

self-involved ● adjective wrapped up in oneself or one's own thoughts.
– DERIVATIVES **self-involvement** noun.

selfish ● adjective concerned chiefly with one's own personal profit or pleasure at the expense of consideration for others.
– DERIVATIVES **selfishly** adverb **selfishness** noun.

selfless ● adjective concerned more with the needs and wishes of others than with one's own.
– DERIVATIVES **selflessly** adverb **selflessness** noun.

self-limiting ● adjective Medicine (of a condition) ultimately resolving itself without treatment.

self-love ● noun regard for one's own well-being and happiness.

self-made ● adjective **1** having become successful or rich by one's own efforts. **2** made by oneself.

self-management ● noun **1** management of or by oneself. **2** the distribution of political control to individual regions of a state, especially as a form of socialism.
– DERIVATIVES **self-managing** adjective.

self-motivated ● adjective motivated to do something because of one's own enthusiasm or interest, without needing pressure from others.
– DERIVATIVES **self-motivating** adjective **self-motivation** noun.

self-mutilation ● noun deliberate injury to one's own body.

self-opinionated ● adjective having an arrogantly high regard for oneself or one's own opinions.

self-parody ● noun the intentional or inadvertent parodying of one's own behaviour, style, etc.

self-perpetuating ● adjective perpetuating itself without external agency or intervention.
– DERIVATIVES **self-perpetuation** noun.

self-pity ● noun excessive concern with and unhappiness over one's own troubles.
– DERIVATIVES **self-pitying** adjective.

self-policing ● noun the process of keeping order or maintaining control within a community without accountability or reference to an external authority.

self-pollination ● noun Botany the pollination of a flower by pollen from the same plant.
– DERIVATIVES **self-pollinate** verb **self-pollinator** noun.

self-portrait ● noun a portrait by an artist of himself or herself.

self-possessed ● adjective calm, confident, and in control of one's feelings.
– DERIVATIVES **self-possession** noun.

self-preservation ● noun the protection of oneself from harm or death, regarded as a basic instinct in human beings and animals.

self-proclaimed ● adjective proclaimed to be such by oneself, without endorsement by others.

self-propelled ● adjective moving or able to move without external propulsion or agency.
– DERIVATIVES **self-propelling** adjective.

self-raising flour ● noun Brit. flour that has a raising agent already added.

self-realization (also **self-realisation**) ● noun fulfilment of one's own potential.

self-referential ● adjective (especially of a literary or other creative work) making reference to itself, its creator, or their other work.

self-regard ● noun **1** consideration for oneself. **2** vanity.
– DERIVATIVES **self-regarding** adjective.

self-regulating ● adjective regulating itself without intervention from external bodies.
– DERIVATIVES **self-regulation** noun **self-regulatory** adjective.

self-reliance ● noun reliance on one's own powers and resources rather than those of others.
– DERIVATIVES **self-reliant** adjective.

self-respect ● noun pride and confidence in oneself.

Thesaurus

S

able, unmistakable, undeniable.
– OPPOSITES unclear.

self-explanatory ● adjective EASILY UNDERSTOOD, comprehensible, intelligible, straightforward, unambiguous, accessible, crystal clear, user-friendly, simple, self-evident, obvious.
– OPPOSITES impenetrable.

self-governing ● noun INDEPENDENT, sovereign, autonomous, free; self-legislating, self-determining.
– OPPOSITES dependent.

self-important ● adjective CONCEITED, arrogant, bumptious, full of oneself, puffed up, swollen-headed, pompous, overbearing, opinionated, cocky, presumptuous, sententious, vain, overweening, proud, egotistical; *informal* snooty, uppity, uppish.
– OPPOSITES humble.

self-indulgent ● adjective HEDONISTIC, pleasure-seeking, sybaritic, indulgent, luxurious, lotus-eating, epicurean; intemperate, immoderate, overindulgent, excessive, extravagant, licentious, dissolute, decadent.
– OPPOSITES abstemious.

self-interest ● noun SELF-SEEKING, self-serving, self-obsession, self-absorption, self-regard, egocentrism, egotism, egomania, selfishness; *informal* looking after number one.
– OPPOSITES altruism.

self-interested ● adjective SELF-SEEKING, self-serving, self-obsessed, self-absorbed, wrapped up in oneself, egocentric, egotistic, egotistical, egomaniacal, selfish.

selfish ● adjective EGOCENTRIC, egotistic, egotistical, egomaniacal, self-centred, self-absorbed, self-obsessed, self-seeking, self-serving, wrapped up in oneself; inconsiderate, thoughtless, unthinking, uncaring, uncharitable; mean, miserly, grasping, greedy, mercenary, acquisitive, opportunistic; *informal* looking after number one.
– OPPOSITES altruistic.

selfless ● adjective UNSELFISH, altruistic, self-sacrificing, self-denying; considerate, compassionate, kind, noble, generous, magnanimous, ungrudging, charitable, benevolent, open-handed.
– OPPOSITES inconsiderate.

self-possessed ● adjective ASSURED, self-assured, calm, cool, composed, at ease, unperturbed, unruffled, confident, self-confident, poised, imperturbable; *informal* together, unfazed, unflappable.
– OPPOSITES unsure.

self-possession ● noun COMPOSURE, assurance, self-assurance, self-control, imperturbability, impassivity, equanimity, noncha-

– DERIVATIVES **self-respecting** adjective.

self-restraint ● noun self-control.

– DERIVATIVES **self-restrained** adjective.

self-revealing ● adjective revealing one's character or motives, especially inadvertently.

self-righteous ● adjective certain that one is totally correct or morally superior.

– DERIVATIVES **self-righteously** adverb **self-righteousness** noun.

self-righting ● adjective (of a boat) designed to right itself when capsized.

self-rule ● noun self-government.

self-sacrifice ● noun the giving up of one's own interests or wishes in order to help others or advance a cause.

– DERIVATIVES **self-sacrificial** adjective **self-sacrificing** adjective.

selfsame ● adjective (**the selfsame**) the very same.

self-satisfied ● adjective smugly complacent.

– DERIVATIVES **self-satisfaction** noun.

self-seed ● verb (of a plant) propagate itself by seed.

– DERIVATIVES **self-seeder** noun.

self-seeking ● adjective pursuing one's own welfare and interests before those of others.

– DERIVATIVES **self-seeker** noun.

self-selection ● noun **1** the action of putting oneself forward for something. **2** the action of selecting something for oneself.

self-service ● adjective denoting a shop, restaurant, or other outlet where customers select goods for themselves and pay at a checkout.

self-serving ● adjective another term for SELF-SEEKING.

self-starter ● noun a self-motivated and ambitious person who acts on their own initiative.

self-styled ● adjective using a description or title that one has given oneself: *self-styled experts.*

self-sufficient ● adjective **1** able to satisfy one's basic needs without outside help, especially with regard to the production of food. **2** emotionally and intellectually independent.

– DERIVATIVES **self-sufficiency** noun.

self-supporting ● adjective **1** having the resources to be able to survive without outside assistance. **2** staying up or upright without being supported by something else.

self-surrender ● noun the surrender of oneself or one's will to an emotion or to some external influence.

self-sustaining ● adjective able to continue in a healthy state without outside assistance.

– DERIVATIVES **self-sustained** adjective.

self-tapping ● adjective (of a screw) able to cut a thread in the material into which it is inserted.

self-taught ● adjective having acquired knowledge or skill on one's own initiative rather than through formal instruction or training.

self-timer ● noun a mechanism in a camera that introduces a delay between the operation of the shutter release and the opening of the shutter, enabling the photographer to be included in the photograph.

self-willed ● adjective determinedly pursuing one's own wishes.

self-worth ● noun another term for SELF-ESTEEM.

sell ● verb (past and past part. **sold**) **1** hand over in exchange for money. **2** deal in (goods or property). **3** (of goods) attain sales. **4** (**sell out**) sell all of one's stock of something. **5** (**sell up**) sell all of one's property or assets. **6** persuade someone of the merits of. **7** (**sell out**) betray (someone) for one's own financial or material benefit. **8** (**sell out**) abandon one's principles for reasons of expedience.

– PHRASES **sell short** fail to recognize or state the true value of. **sell one's soul** (**to the devil**) be willing to do anything, no matter how wrong it is, in order to achieve one's objective.

– DERIVATIVES **sellable** adjective.

– ORIGIN Old English.

sell-by date ● noun **1** chiefly Brit. a date marked on a perishable product indicating the recommended time by which it should be sold. **2** informal a time after which something or someone is no longer considered desirable or effective.

seller ● noun **1** a person who sells. **2** a product that sells in a specified way.

– PHRASES **seller's** (or **sellers'**) **market** an economic situation in which goods or shares are scarce and sellers can ask high prices.

selling point ● noun a feature of a product for sale that makes it attractive to customers.

sell-off ● noun a sale of assets at a low price, carried out in order to dispose of them rather than as normal trade.

Sellotape Brit. ● noun trademark transparent adhesive tape. ● verb fasten or stick with Sellotape.

– ORIGIN from an alteration of CELLULOSE + TAPE.

sell-out ● noun **1** the selling of an entire stock of something. **2** an event for which all tickets are sold. **3** a sale of a business or company. **4** a betrayal.

seltzer /seltsər/ ● noun dated carbonated mineral water.

– ORIGIN from German *Selterser*, from *Niederselters* in Germany, where a medicinal mineral water was produced.

selvedge /selvij/ (chiefly N. Amer. also **selvage**) ● noun an edge produced on woven fabric during manufacture that prevents it from unravelling.

– ORIGIN from SELF + EDGE, on the pattern of Dutch *selfegghe*.

selves plural of SELF.

Thesaurus

lance, confidence, self-confidence, poise, aplomb, presence of mind, nerve, sangfroid; *informal* cool.

self-reliant ● adjective SELF-SUFFICIENT, self-supporting, self-sustaining, able to stand on one's own two feet; independent, autarkic.

S

self-respect ● noun SELF-ESTEEM, self-regard, amour propre, faith in oneself, pride, dignity, morale, self-confidence.

self-restraint ● noun SELF-CONTROL, restraint, self-discipline, self-possession, will power, moderation, temperance, abstemiousness, abstention.

– OPPOSITES self-indulgence.

self-righteous ● adjective SANCTIMONIOUS, holier-than-thou, self-satisfied, smug, priggish, complacent, pious, moralizing, superior, hypocritical; *informal* goody-goody.

– OPPOSITES humble.

self-sacrifice ● noun SELF-DENIAL, selflessness, unselfishness; self-discipline, asceticism, abnegation, self-deprivation, abstinence, moderation, austerity, temperance, abstention.

self-satisfied ● adjective COMPLACENT, self-congratulatory, smug, superior, puffed up, pleased with oneself; *informal* goody-goody, I'm-all-right-Jack; *Brit. informal* like the cat that's got the cream.

self-seeking ● adjective SELF-INTERESTED, self-serving, selfish; self-obsessed, self-absorbed, egocentric, egotistic, egotistical; inconsiderate, thoughtless, unthinking; *informal* looking after number one.

– OPPOSITES altruistic.

self-styled ● adjective WOULD-BE, self-appointed, so-called, self-titled, professed, self-confessed, soi-disant.

self-sufficient ● adjective SELF-SUPPORTING, self-reliant, self-sustaining, able to stand on one's own two feet; independent, autarkic.

self-willed ● adjective WILFUL, contrary, perverse, uncooperative, wayward, headstrong, stubborn, obstinate, obdurate, pig-headed, mulish, intransigent, recalcitrant, intractable; *Brit. informal* bloody-minded; *formal* refractory.

– OPPOSITES biddable.

sell ● verb **1** *they are selling their house* PUT UP FOR SALE, offer for sale, put on sale, dispose of, vend, auction (off); trade, barter. **2** *he sells cakes* TRADE IN, deal in, traffic in, stock, carry, offer for sale, peddle, hawk, retail, market. **3** *the book should sell well* GO, be bought, be purchased; move, be in demand. **4** *it sells for £79.95* COST, be priced at, retail at, go for, be. **5** *he still has to sell the deal to Congress* PROMOTE; persuade someone to accept, talk someone into, bring someone round to, win someone over to, win approval for.

– OPPOSITES buy.

– PHRASES **sell someone down the river** (*informal*). See DOUBLE-CROSS. **sell out 1** *we've sold out of petrol* HAVE NONE LEFT, be out of stock, have run out; *informal* be fresh out, be cleaned out. **2** *the edition sold out quickly* BE BOUGHT UP, be depleted, be exhausted. **3** *they say the band has sold out* ABANDON ONE'S PRINCIPLES, prostitute oneself, sell one's soul, betray one's ideals, be untrue to oneself; debase oneself, degrade oneself, demean oneself. **sell someone out** BETRAY, inform on; be disloyal to, be unfaithful to, double-cross, break faith with, stab in the back; *informal* tell on, sell down the river, blow the whistle on, squeal on, stitch up, peach on, do the dirty on; *Brit. informal* grass on, shop; *N. Amer. informal* finger. **sell someone short** UNDERVALUE, underrate, underestimate, disparage, deprecate, belittle; *formal* derogate.

seller ● noun VENDOR, retailer, purveyor, supplier, stockist, trader, merchant, dealer; shopkeeper, salesperson, salesman, sales-

semantic /simantik/ ● adjective relating to meaning in language or logic.
– DERIVATIVES **semantically** adverb **semanticity** noun.
– ORIGIN Greek *sēmantikos* 'significant'.
semantics ● plural noun (usu. treated as sing.) **1** the branch of linguistics and logic concerned with meaning. **2** the meaning of a word, phrase, sentence, or text.
– DERIVATIVES **semanticist** noun.
semaphore ● noun **1** a system of sending messages by holding the arms or two flags or poles in certain positions according to an alphabetic code. **2** an apparatus for signalling in this way, consisting of an upright with movable parts. ● verb send by semaphore.
– DERIVATIVES **semaphoric** adjective.
– ORIGIN French *sémaphore*, from Greek *sēma* 'sign' + *-phoros* 'bearing'.
semblance ● noun the outward appearance or apparent form of something.
– ORIGIN from Old French *sembler* 'seem', from Latin *similare* 'simulate'.
semen /seemən/ ● noun the male reproductive fluid, containing spermatozoa in suspension.
– ORIGIN Latin, 'seed'.
semester /simestər/ ● noun a half-year term in a school or university, especially in North America, typically lasting for fifteen to eighteen weeks.
– ORIGIN from Latin *semestris* 'six-monthly'.
semi ● noun (pl. **semis**) informal **1** Brit. a semi-detached house. **2** a semi-final.
semi- ● prefix **1** half: *semicircular*. **2** partly; in some degree: *semi-conscious*.
– ORIGIN Latin.
semiaquatic ● adjective **1** (of an animal) living partly on land and partly in water. **2** (of a plant) growing in very wet or waterlogged ground.
semi-automatic ● adjective **1** partially automatic. **2** (of a firearm) having a mechanism for automatic loading but not for continuous firing.
semi-autonomous ● adjective **1** having a degree of self-government. **2** acting independently to some degree.
semi-basement ● noun a storey of a building partly below ground level.
semibreve /semmibreev/ ● noun Music, chiefly Brit. a note having the time value of two minims or four crotchets, represented by a ring with no stem.
semicircle ● noun a half of a circle or of its circumference.
– DERIVATIVES **semicircular** adjective.
semicircular canals ● plural noun a system of three fluid-filled bony channels in the inner ear, involved in sensing and maintaining balance.
semicolon /semmikōlən/ ● noun a punctuation mark (;) indicating a more pronounced pause than that indicated by a comma.
semiconductor ● noun a solid, e.g. silicon, whose conductivity is between that of an insulator and a conductive metal and increases with temperature.
– DERIVATIVES **semi-conducting** adjective.
semi-conscious ● adjective partially conscious.
semi-detached ● adjective (of a house) joined to another house on one side by a common wall.
semi-double ● adjective (of a flower) intermediate between single and double in having only the outer stamens converted to petals.
semi-final ● noun (in sport) a match or round immediately preceding the final.
– DERIVATIVES **semi-finalist** noun.
semi-fluid ● adjective having a thick consistency between solid and liquid. ● noun a semi-fluid substance.
semi-invalid ● noun a partially disabled or somewhat infirm person.
semi-liquid ● adjective & noun another term for SEMI-FLUID.
Semillon /semmiyon/ ● noun a variety of white wine grape grown in France, Australia, and South America.
– ORIGIN French, from Latin *semen* 'seed'.
semilunar ● adjective chiefly Anatomy shaped like a half-moon or crescent.
seminal ● adjective **1** (of a work, event, or idea) strongly influencing later developments. **2** relating to or denoting semen. **3** Botany relating to or derived from the seed of a plant.
– DERIVATIVES **seminally** adverb.
– ORIGIN Latin *seminalis*, from *semen* 'seed'.
seminar /semminaar/ ● noun **1** a conference or other meeting for discussion or training. **2** a small group of students at university, meeting to discuss topics with a teacher.
– ORIGIN German, from Latin *seminarium* 'seed plot, seminary'.
seminary /semminəri/ ● noun (pl. **seminaries**) a training college for priests or rabbis.
– DERIVATIVES **seminarian** /semminairiən/ noun **seminarist** noun.
– ORIGIN Latin *seminarium* 'seed plot, seminary', from *semen* 'seed'.
Seminole /seminōl/ ● noun (pl. same or **Seminoles**) a member of an American Indian people of the Creek confederacy.
– ORIGIN from American Spanish *cimarrón* 'wild'.
semiology /seemiolləji, semmi-/ ● noun another term for SEMIOTICS.
– DERIVATIVES **semiological** adjective **semiologist** noun.
– ORIGIN from Greek *sēmeion* 'sign'.
semiotics /seemiottiks, sem-/ ● plural noun (treated as sing.) the study of signs and symbols and their use or interpretation.
– DERIVATIVES **semiotic** adjective **semiotician** /seemiətish'n, sem-/ noun.
– ORIGIN from Greek *sēmeiotikos* 'of signs'.
semipermeable ● adjective permeable only to certain substances, especially allowing the passage of a solvent but not of the solute.
semi-precious ● adjective denoting minerals which can be used as gems but are considered to be less valuable than precious stones.
semiquaver /semmikwayvər/ ● noun Music, chiefly Brit. a note having the time value of a sixteenth of a semibreve or half a quaver, represented by a large dot with a two-hooked stem.
semi-retired ● adjective having retired from employment or an occupation but continuing to work part-time or occasionally.
– DERIVATIVES **semi-retirement** noun.
semi-skilled ● adjective (of work or a worker) having or needing some, but not extensive, training.
semi-skimmed ● adjective Brit. (of milk) having had some of the cream removed.
semi-solid ● adjective highly viscous; slightly thicker than semi-fluid.
semi-submersible ● adjective denoting an oil or gas drilling platform or barge with submerged hollow pontoons able to be flooded with water when the vessel is anchored on site in order to provide stability.
Semite /seemit/ ● noun a member of a people speaking a Semitic language, in particular the Jews and Arabs.
– ORIGIN from Greek *Sēm* 'Shem', son of Noah in the Bible, from whom these people are traditionally descended.
Semitic /simittik/ ● noun a family of languages that includes Hebrew, Arabic, and Aramaic and certain ancient languages such as Phoenician. ● adjective relating to these languages or their speakers.
semitone ● noun Music the smallest interval used in classical Western music, equal to a twelfth of an octave or half a tone.
semolina ● noun the hard grains left after the milling of flour, used in puddings and in pasta.
– ORIGIN Italian *semolino*, from *semola* 'bran'.
sempiternal /sempitern'l/ ● adjective eternal and unchanging; everlasting.
– DERIVATIVES **sempiternally** adverb **sempiternity** noun.
– ORIGIN Latin *sempiternus*, from *semper* 'always' + *aeternus* 'eternal'.
sempre /sempray/ ● adverb Music throughout; always.
– ORIGIN Italian.

S

Thesaurus

woman, sales assistant, shop assistant, travelling salesperson, pedlar, hawker; auctioneer; *N. Amer.* clerk; *informal* counter-jumper.
semblance ● noun (OUTWARD) APPEARANCE, air, show, facade, front, veneer, guise, pretence.
seminal ● adjective INFLUENTIAL, formative, ground-breaking, pioneering, original, innovative; major, important.
seminar ● noun **1** *a seminar for education officials* CONFERENCE, symposium, meeting, convention, forum, summit, discussion, consultation. **2** *teaching in the form of seminars* STUDY GROUP, workshop, tutorial, class, lesson.

sempstress /sem(p)striss/ ● noun another term for SEAMSTRESS.
Semtex ● noun a pliable, odourless plastic explosive.
– ORIGIN probably a blend of *Semtin* (a village in the Czech Republic near the place of production) and EXPLOSIVE.
SEN ● abbreviation (in the UK) State Enrolled Nurse.
sen ● noun (pl. same) a monetary unit of Brunei, Cambodia, Indonesia, and Malaysia, equal to one hundredth of the basic unit.
– ORIGIN representing CENT.
senate ● noun **1** a legislative or governing body, especially the smaller upper assembly in the US, US states, France, and other countries. **2** the governing body of a university or college. **3** the state council of the ancient Roman republic and empire.
– ORIGIN Latin *senatus*, from *senex* 'old man'.
senator ● noun a member of a senate.
– DERIVATIVES **senatorial** adjective **senatorship** noun.
send ● verb (past and past part. **sent**) **1** cause to go or be taken to a destination. **2** cause to move sharply or quickly; propel. **3** cause to be in a specified state: *it nearly sent me crazy.*
– PHRASES **send down** Brit. **1** expel (a student) from a university. **2** informal sentence to imprisonment. **send for 1** order (someone) to come. **2** order by post. **send off** (of a soccer or rugby referee) order (a player) to leave the field and take no further part in the game. **send to Coventry** chiefly Brit. refuse to associate with or speak to. [ORIGIN perhaps from the unpopularity of royalist soldiers or prisoners quartered in *Coventry* (sympathetic to parliament) during the English Civil war.] **send up 1** informal ridicule (someone) by imitating them in an exaggerated manner. **2** US sentence to imprisonment. **send word** send a message.
– DERIVATIVES **sender** noun.
– ORIGIN Old English.
send-off ● noun a celebratory demonstration of goodwill at a person's departure.
send-up ● noun informal an exaggerated imitation of someone or something.
sene /senni/ ● noun (pl. same or **senes**) a monetary unit of Samoa, equal to one hundredth of a tala.
– ORIGIN Samoan.
Seneca /sennikə/ ● noun (pl. same or **Senecas**) a member of an American Indian people forming part of the Iroquois confederacy.
– ORIGIN Algonquian.
Senegalese /sennigəleez/ ● noun a person from Senegal, a country on the coast of West Africa. ● adjective relating to Senegal.
senesce /siness/ ● verb (of a living organism) deteriorate with age.
– DERIVATIVES **senescence** noun **senescent** adjective.
– ORIGIN Latin *senescere*, from *senex* 'old'.
seneschal /sennish'l/ ● noun **1** historical the steward or major-domo of a medieval great house. **2** chiefly historical a governor or other administrative or judicial officer.
– ORIGIN Latin *seniscalus*, from a Germanic compound of words meaning 'old' and 'servant'.
senile /seenīl/ ● adjective having the weaknesses or diseases of old age, especially a loss of mental faculties. ● noun a senile person.
– DERIVATIVES **senility** noun.
– ORIGIN Latin *senilis*, from *senex* 'old man'.
senile dementia ● noun severe mental deterioration in old age, characterized by loss of memory and lack of control of bodily functions.
senior ● adjective **1** of or relating to a more advanced age. **2** Brit. for or referring to schoolchildren above a certain age, typically eleven. **3** US of the final year at a university or high school. **4** (after a name) denoting the elder of two with the same name in a family. **5** high or higher in rank or status. ● noun **1** a person who is a specified number of years older than someone else: *she was two years his senior.* **2** a student in one of the higher forms of a senior school. **3** (in sport) a competitor of above a certain age or of the highest status. **4** an elderly person, especially an old-age pensioner.
– DERIVATIVES **seniority** noun.
– ORIGIN Latin, from *senex* 'old man, old'.
senior aircraftman (or **senior aircraftwoman**) ● noun a rank in the RAF, above leading aircraftman (or leading aircraftwoman) and below junior technician.
senior citizen ● noun an elderly person, especially an old-age pensioner.
senior common room ● noun Brit. a room used for social purposes by fellows, lecturers, and other senior members of a college.
senior nursing officer ● noun Brit. the person in charge of nursing services in a hospital.
senior registrar ● noun Brit. a hospital doctor undergoing specialist training, one grade below that of consultant.
Senior Service ● noun Brit. the Royal Navy.
seniti /senniti/ ● noun (pl. same) a monetary unit of Tonga, equal to one hundredth of a pa'anga.
– ORIGIN Tongan.
senna ● noun a laxative prepared from the dried pods of the cassia tree.
– ORIGIN Arabic.
señor /senyor/ ● noun (pl. **señores** /senyorayz/) (in Spanish-speaking countries) a form of address for a man, corresponding to *Mr* or *sir*.
– ORIGIN Spanish, from Latin *senior* 'older, older man'.
señora /senyorə/ ● noun (in Spanish-speaking countries) a form of address for a woman, corresponding to *Mrs* or *madam.*
señorita /senyəreetə/ ● noun (in Spanish-speaking countries) a form of address for an unmarried woman, corresponding to *Miss*.
sensate /sensayt/ ● adjective perceiving or perceived with the senses.
sensation ● noun **1** a physical feeling or perception resulting from something that happens to or comes into contact with the body. **2** the capacity to have such feelings or perceptions: *gradual loss of sensation.* **3** a general awareness or impression not caused by anything that can be seen or defined. **4** a widespread reaction of interest and excitement, or a person or thing causing it.
sensational ● adjective **1** causing or seeking to cause great pub-

S

Thesaurus

seminary ● noun THEOLOGICAL COLLEGE, rabbinical college, Talmudical college; academy, training college, training institute, school.
send ● verb **1** *they sent a message to HQ* DISPATCH, post, mail, address, consign, direct, forward; transmit, convey, communicate; telephone, phone, broadcast, radio, fax, e-mail; *dated* telegraph, wire, cable. **2** *we sent for a doctor* CALL, summon, contact; ask for, request, order. **3** *the pump sent out a jet of petrol* PROPEL, project, eject, deliver, discharge, spout, fire, shoot, release; throw, let fly; *informal* chuck. **4** *the barrels send off nasty fumes* EMIT, give off, discharge, exude, send out, release, leak. **5** *it's enough to send one mad* MAKE, drive, turn. **6** *(informal) it's the music that sends us* EXCITE, stimulate, move, rouse, stir, thrill, electrify, intoxicate, enrapture, enthral, grip; charm, delight; *informal* blow away, give someone a kick.
– OPPOSITES receive.
– PHRASES **send someone down 1** *(Brit.) she was sent down from Cambridge* EXPEL, exclude; *Brit.* rusticate. **2** *(informal) he was sent down for life* SEND TO PRISON, imprison, jail, incarcerate, lock up, confine, detain, intern; *informal* put away; *Brit. informal* bang up. **send someone off** *(Sport)* ORDER OFF, dismiss; show someone the red card; *informal* red-card, send for an early bath, sin-bin. **send someone/something up** *(informal)* SATIRIZE, ridicule, make fun of, parody, lampoon, mock, caricature, imitate, ape; *informal* take off, spoof, take the mickey out of.
send-off ● noun FAREWELL, goodbye, adieu, leave-taking, valediction; funeral; *archaic* vale.
– OPPOSITES welcome.
send-up ● noun *(informal)* SATIRE, burlesque, lampoon, pastiche, caricature, imitation, impression, impersonation; mockery, mimicry, travesty; *informal* spoof, take-off, mickey-take.
senile ● adjective DODDERING, doddery, decrepit, senescent, declining, infirm, feeble; aged, long in the tooth, in one's dotage; mentally confused, having Alzheimer's (disease), having senile dementia; *informal* past it, gaga.
senior ● adjective **1** *senior school pupils* OLDER, elder. **2** *a senior officer* SUPERIOR, higher-ranking, high-ranking, more important; top, chief; *N. Amer.* ranking. **3** *Albert Stone Senior* THE ELDER; *Brit.* major; *N. Amer.* I.
– OPPOSITES junior, subordinate.
senior citizen ● noun RETIRED PERSON, (old-age) pensioner, OAP; old person, elderly person, geriatric, dotard, Methuselah; *N. Amer.* senior, retiree, golden ager; *informal* old stager, old-timer, oldie,

lic interest and excitement. **2** informal very impressive or attractive.

– DERIVATIVES **sensationalize** (also **sensationalise**) verb **sensationally** adverb.

sensationalism ● noun (in the media) the use of exciting or shocking stories or language at the expense of accuracy, in order to provoke public interest or excitement.

– DERIVATIVES **sensationalist** noun & adjective **sensationalistic** adjective.

sense ● noun **1** any of the faculties of sight, smell, hearing, taste, and touch, by which the body perceives an external stimulus. **2** a feeling that something is the case. **3** (**sense of**) awareness or appreciation of or sensitivity to: *a sense of direction.* **4** a sane and practical attitude to situations. **5** reason or purpose; good judgement: *there's no sense in standing in the rain.* **6** a meaning of a word or expression or the way in which a word or expression can be interpreted. ● verb **1** perceive by a sense or senses. **2** be vaguely aware of. **3** (of a machine or similar device) detect.

– PHRASES **come to one's senses 1** regain consciousness. **2** regain one's sound judgement. **make sense** be intelligible, justifiable, or practicable. **make sense of** find meaning or coherence in.

– ORIGIN Latin *sensus* 'faculty of feeling, thought, meaning', from *sentire* 'feel'.

sensei /sensay/ ● noun (pl. same) (in martial arts) a teacher.

– ORIGIN Japanese, from *sen* 'previous' + *sei* 'birth'.

senseless ● adjective **1** unconscious or incapable of sensation. **2** lacking meaning, purpose, or common sense.

– DERIVATIVES **senselessly** adverb **senselessness** noun.

sense organ ● noun an organ of the body which responds to external stimuli by conveying impulses to the sensory nervous system.

sensibility ● noun (pl. **sensibilities**) **1** the ability to appreciate and respond to complex emotional or aesthetic influences. **2** (**sensibilities**) the tendency to be easily offended of shocked.

sensible ● adjective **1** wise and prudent; having or showing common sense. **2** practical and functional rather than decorative. **3** (**sensible of/to**) formal or dated aware of: *I am very sensible to your concerns.*

– DERIVATIVES **sensibleness** noun **sensibly** adverb.

sensitive ● adjective **1** quick to detect, respond to, or be affected by slight changes, signals, or influences. **2** delicately appreciating the feelings of others. **3** easily offended or upset. **4** kept secret or with restrictions on disclosure.

– DERIVATIVES **sensitively** adverb **sensitiveness** noun.

– ORIGIN Latin *sensitivus*, from *sentire* 'feel'.

sensitive plant ● noun a tropical American plant of the pea family, whose leaflets fold together and leaves bend down when touched.

sensitivity ● noun (pl. **sensitivities**) **1** the quality or condition of being sensitive. **2** (**sensitivities**) a person's feelings which might be easily offended or hurt.

sensitize (also **sensitise**) ● verb cause to respond to certain stimuli; make sensitive.

– DERIVATIVES **sensitization** noun **sensitizer** noun.

sensor ● noun a device which detects or measures a physical property.

sensory ● adjective relating to sensation or the senses.

– DERIVATIVES **sensorily** adverb.

sensual /senshooəl, -syoo-/ ● adjective relating to the physical senses as a source of pleasure, especially sexual pleasure.

– DERIVATIVES **sensualist** noun **sensuality** noun **sensually** adverb.

– USAGE Strictly speaking there is a difference between **sensual** and **sensuous. Sensual** is used in relation to gratification of the senses, especially sexual gratification, while **sensuous** is a more neutral term, meaning 'relating to the senses rather than the intellect'.

Thesaurus

oldster, wrinkly, crumbly; *Brit. informal* buffer, josser.

seniority ● noun RANK, superiority, standing, primacy, precedence, priority; age.

sensation ● noun **1** *a sensation of light* FEELING, sense, awareness, consciousness, perception, impression. **2** *I caused a sensation by donating £1m* COMMOTION, stir, uproar, furore, scandal, impact; interest, excitement; *informal* splash, to-do, hullabaloo. **3** *the new cars were a sensation* TRIUMPH, success, sell-out; talking point; *informal* smash (hit), hit, winner, crowd-puller, wow, knockout.

sensational ● adjective **1** *a sensational murder trial* SHOCKING, scandalous, appalling; amazing, startling, astonishing, staggering; stirring, exciting, thrilling, electrifying; fascinating, interesting, noteworthy, significant, remarkable, momentous, historic, newsworthy. **2** *sensational stories* OVER-DRAMATIZED, dramatic, melodramatic, exaggerated, sensationalist, sensationalistic; graphic, explicit, lurid; *informal* shock-horror, juicy. **3** *(informal) she looked sensational* GORGEOUS, stunning, wonderful, exquisite, lovely, radiant, delightful, charming, enchanting, captivating; striking, spectacular, remarkable, outstanding, arresting, eye-catching; marvellous, superb, excellent, fine, first-class; *informal* great, terrific, tremendous, super, fantastic, fabulous, fab, heavenly, divine, knockout, delectable, scrumptious, awesome, magic, wicked, out of this world; *Brit. informal* smashing, brilliant, brill.

– OPPOSITES dull, understated, unremarkable.

sense ● noun **1** *the sense of touch* SENSORY FACULTY, feeling, sensation, perception; sight, hearing, touch, taste, smell. **2** *a sense of guilt* FEELING, awareness, sensation, consciousness, recognition. **3** *a sense of humour* APPRECIATION, awareness, understanding, comprehension, discernment. **4** *she had the sense to press the panic button* WISDOM, common sense, sagacity, discernment, perception; wit, intelligence, cleverness, shrewdness, judgement, reason, logic, brain(s); *informal* gumption, nous, horse sense, savvy; *Brit. informal* loaf, common; *N. Amer. informal* smarts. **5** *I can't see the sense in this* PURPOSE, point, reason, object, motive; use, value, advantage, benefit. **6** *the different senses of 'well'* MEANING, definition, import, signification, significance, purport, implication, nuance; drift, gist, thrust, tenor, message.

– OPPOSITES stupidity.

● verb *she sensed their hostility* DISCERN, feel, observe, notice, recognize, pick up, be aware of, distinguish, make out, identify; comprehend, apprehend, see, appreciate, realize; suspect, have a funny feeling about, have a hunch, divine, intuit; *informal* catch on to; *Brit. informal* twig.

senseless ● adjective **1** *they found him senseless on the floor* UNCONSCIOUS, stunned, insensible, insensate, comatose, knocked out, out cold, out for the count; numb; *informal* KO'd, dead to the world; *Brit. informal* spark out. **2** *a senseless waste* POINTLESS, futile, useless, needless, unavailing, in vain, purposeless, meaningless, unprofitable; absurd, foolish, insane, stupid, idiotic, ridiculous, ludicrous, mindless, illogical.

– OPPOSITES conscious, wise.

sensibility ● noun **1** *study leads to the growth of sensibility* SENSITIVITY, finer feelings, delicacy, taste, discrimination, discernment; understanding, insight, empathy, appreciation; feeling, intuition, responsiveness, receptiveness, perceptiveness, awareness. **2** *the wording might offend their sensibilities* (FINER) FEELINGS, emotions, sensitivities, moral sense.

sensible ● adjective PRACTICAL, realistic, responsible, reasonable, commonsensical, rational, logical, sound, balanced, sober, no-nonsense, pragmatic, level-headed, thoughtful, down-to-earth, wise, prudent, judicious, sagacious, shrewd.

– OPPOSITES foolish.

sensitive ● adjective **1** *she's sensitive to changes in temperature* RESPONSIVE TO, reactive to, sentient of, sensitized to; aware of, conscious of, alive to; susceptible to, affected by, vulnerable to; attuned to. **2** *sensitive skin* DELICATE, fragile; tender, sore, raw. **3** *the matter needs sensitive handling* TACTFUL, careful, thoughtful, diplomatic, delicate, subtle, kid-glove; sympathetic, compassionate, understanding, intuitive, responsive, insightful. **4** *he's sensitive about his bald patch* TOUCHY, oversensitive, hypersensitive, easily offended, easily upset, easily hurt, thin-skinned, defensive; paranoid, neurotic; *informal* twitchy, uptight. **5** *a sensitive issue* DIFFICULT, delicate, tricky, awkward, problematic, ticklish, precarious; controversial, emotive; *informal* sticky.

– OPPOSITES impervious, resilient, clumsy, thick-skinned, uncontroversial.

sensitivity ● noun **1** *the sensitivity of the skin* RESPONSIVENESS, sensitiveness, reactivity; susceptibility, vulnerability. **2** *the job calls for sensitivity* CONSIDERATION, care, thoughtfulness, tact, diplomacy, delicacy, subtlety, finer feelings; understanding, empathy, sensibility, feeling, intuition, responsiveness, receptiveness; perception, discernment, insight; savoir faire. **3** *her sensitivity on the subject of boyfriends* TOUCHINESS, oversensitivity, hypersensitivity, defensiveness. **4** *the sensitivity of the issue* DELICACY, trickiness, awkwardness, ticklishness.

sensual ● adjective **1** *sensual pleasure* PHYSICAL, carnal, bodily,

sensuous /senshooəss, -syoo-/ ● adjective **1** relating to or affecting the senses rather than the intellect. **2** attractive or gratifying physically, especially sexually.
– DERIVATIVES **sensuously** adverb **sensuousness** noun.
– ORIGIN from Latin *sensus* 'sense'.

sent[1] past and past participle of SEND[1].

sent[2] /sent/ ● noun a monetary unit of Estonia, equal to one hundredth of a kroon.
– ORIGIN respelling of CENT.

sente /senti/ ● noun (pl. **lisente** /lisenti/) a monetary unit of Lesotho, equal to one hundredth of a loti.
– ORIGIN Sesotho, a Bantu language.

sentence ● noun **1** a set of words that is complete in itself, conveying a statement, question, exclamation, or command and typically containing a subject and predicate. **2** the punishment assigned to someone found guilty by a court. ● verb declare the punishment decided for (an offender).
– ORIGIN originally also in the sense 'way of thinking, opinion': from Latin *sententia* 'opinion'.

sentence adverb ● noun Grammar an adverb that expresses an attitude to the content of the sentence in which it occurs or that places the sentence in a particular context.

sententious /sentenshəss/ ● adjective given to moralizing in a pompous or affected manner.
– DERIVATIVES **sententiously** adverb **sententiousness** noun.
– ORIGIN originally in the sense 'full of meaning or wisdom': from Latin *sententia* 'opinion'.

sentient /sensh'nt/ ● adjective able to perceive or feel things.
– DERIVATIVES **sentience** noun **sentiently** adverb.
– ORIGIN from Latin *sentire* 'to feel'.

sentiment ● noun **1** a view, opinion, or feeling. **2** exaggerated and self-indulgent feelings of tenderness, sadness, or nostalgia.
– ORIGIN Latin *sentimentum*, from *sentire* 'feel'.

sentimental ● adjective **1** deriving from or prone to feelings of tenderness, sadness, or nostalgia. **2** having or arousing such feelings in an exaggerated and self-indulgent way.
– PHRASES **sentimental value** value of an object deriving from personal or emotional associations rather than material worth.
– DERIVATIVES **sentimentalism** noun **sentimentalist** noun **sentimentality** noun **sentimentalize** (also **sentimentalise**) verb **sentimentally** adverb.

sentinel /sentin'l/ ● noun a soldier or guard whose job is to stand and keep watch. ● verb (**sentinelled**, **sentinelling**; US **sentineled**, **sentineling**) station a sentinel to keep watch over.
– ORIGIN Italian *sentinella*.

sentry ● noun (pl. **sentries**) a soldier stationed to keep guard or to control access to a place.
– ORIGIN perhaps from obsolete *centrinel*, from SENTINEL.

sentry box ● noun a structure providing shelter for a standing sentry.

sepal /sepp'l/ ● noun Botany each of the leaf-like parts of a flower that surround the petals, enclosing them when the flower is in bud.
– ORIGIN from Greek *skepē* 'covering', influenced by French *pétale* 'petal'.

separable ● adjective able to be separated or treated separately.
– DERIVATIVES **separability** noun.

separate ● adjective /sepparət/ **1** forming or viewed as a unit apart or by itself; not joined or united with others. **2** different; distinct. ● verb /sepparayt/ **1** move or come apart. **2** stop living together as a couple. **3** divide into constituent or distinct elements. **4** extract or remove for use or rejection. **5** distinguish between or from another; consider individually. **6** form a distinction or boundary between: *six years separated the brothers.* ● noun /sepparət/ (**separates**) individual items of clothing that may be worn in different combinations.
– DERIVATIVES **separately** adverb **separateness** noun **separative** adjective **separator** noun.
– ORIGIN from Latin *separare* 'disjoin, divide'.

separation ● noun **1** the action of separating or the state of being separated. **2** the state in which a husband and wife remain married but live apart.

separatism ● noun the advocacy or practice of separation of a group of people from a larger body on the basis of ethnicity, religion, or gender.
– DERIVATIVES **separatist** noun & adjective.

Sephardi /sifaardi/ ● noun (pl. **Sephardim** /sifaardim/) a Jew of Spanish or Portuguese descent. Compare with ASHKENAZI.
– DERIVATIVES **Sephardic** adjective.
– ORIGIN Hebrew, from the name of a country mentioned in the Bible (Obadiah 20) and taken to be Spain.

sepia /seepiə/ ● noun **1** a reddish-brown colour, associated particularly with early monochrome photographs. **2** a brown pigment prepared from cuttlefish ink, used in drawing and in

Thesaurus

fleshly, animal; hedonistic, epicurean, sybaritic, voluptuary. **2** *a beautiful, sensual woman* SEXUALLY ATTRACTIVE, sexy, voluptuous, sultry, seductive, passionate; sexually arousing, erotic, sexual.
– OPPOSITES spiritual, passionless.

sensualist ● noun HEDONIST, pleasure-seeker, sybarite, voluptuary; epicure, gastronome; bon vivant, bon viveur.

sensuality ● noun SEXINESS, sexual attractiveness, sultriness, seductiveness; sexuality, eroticism; physicality, carnality.

sensuous ● adjective **1** *big sensuous canvases* AESTHETICALLY PLEASING, gratifying, rich, sumptuous, luxurious; sensory, sensorial. **2** *sensuous lips* SEXUALLY ATTRACTIVE, sexy, seductive, voluptuous, luscious, lush.

S

sentence ● noun PRISON TERM, prison sentence; punishment; *informal* time, stretch, stint; *Brit. informal* porridge, bird.
● verb *they were sentenced to death* PASS JUDGEMENT ON, punish, convict; condemn, doom.

sententious ● adjective MORALISTIC, moralizing, sanctimonious, self-righteous, pietistic, pious, priggish, judgemental; pompous, pontifical, self-important; *informal* preachy, preachifying; *Brit. informal* pi.

sentient ● adjective (CAPABLE OF) FEELING, living, live; conscious, aware, responsive, reactive.

sentiment ● noun **1** *the comments echo my own sentiments* VIEW, feeling, attitude, thought, opinion, belief. **2** *there's no room for sentiment in sport* SENTIMENTALITY, sentimentalism, mawkishness, emotionalism; emotion, sensibility, soft-heartedness, tenderheartedness; *informal* schmaltz, mush, slushiness, corniness, cheese; *Brit. informal* soppiness; *N. Amer. informal* sappiness.

sentimental ● adjective **1** *she kept the vase for sentimental reasons* NOSTALGIC, tender, emotional, affectionate. **2** *the film is too sentimental* MAWKISH, over-emotional, cloying, sickly, saccharine, sugary; romantic, hearts-and-flowers, touching; *Brit.* twee; *informal* slushy, mushy, weepy, tear-jerking, schmaltzy, lovey-dovey, gooey, drippy, cheesy, corny; *Brit. informal* soppy; *N. Amer. informal* cornball, sappy, hokey. **3** *she is sentimental about animals* SOFT-HEARTED, tender-hearted, soft; *informal* soppy.
– OPPOSITES practical, gritty.

sentry ● noun GUARD, sentinel, lookout, watch, watchman, patrol.

separable ● adjective DIVISIBLE, distinct, independent, distinguishable; detachable, removable.

separate ● adjective **1** *his personal life was separate from his job* UNCONNECTED, unrelated, different, distinct, discrete; detached, divorced, disconnected, independent, autonomous. **2** *the infirmary was separate from the school* SET APART, detached, disjoined; fenced off, cut off, segregated, isolated; free-standing, self-contained.
– OPPOSITES linked, attached.
● verb **1** *they separated two rioting mobs* SPLIT (UP), break up, part, pull apart, divide; *poetic/literary* sunder. **2** *the connectors can be separated* DISCONNECT, detach, disengage, uncouple, unyoke, disunite, disjoin; split, divide, sever; disentangle. **3** *the wall that separated the two estates* PARTITION, divide, come between, keep apart; bisect, intersect. **4** *the south aisle was separated off* ISOLATE, partition off, section off; close off, shut off, cordon off, fence off, screen off. **5** *they separated at the airport* PART (COMPANY), go their separate ways, split up; say goodbye; disperse, disband, scatter. **6** *the road separated* FORK, divide, branch, bifurcate, diverge. **7** *her parents separated* SPLIT UP, break up, part, be estranged, divorce. **8** *separate fact from fiction* ISOLATE, set apart, segregate; distinguish, differentiate, dissociate; sort out, sift out, filter out, remove, weed out. **9** *those who separate themselves from society* BREAK AWAY FROM, break with, secede from, withdraw from, leave, quit, dissociate oneself from, resign from, drop out of, repudiate, reject.
– OPPOSITES unite, join, link, meet, merge, marry.

separately ● adverb INDIVIDUALLY, one by one, one at a time, singly, severally; apart, independently, alone, by oneself, on one's own.

separation ● noun **1** *the separation of the two companies* DISCONNECTION, detachment, severance, dissociation, disunion, disaffiliation, segregation, partition. **2** *her parent's separation* BREAK-UP, split, parting (of the ways), estrangement, rift, rupture, breach; divorce; *Brit. informal* bust-up. **3** *the separation between art*

watercolours. 3 cuttlefish ink.
– ORIGIN Greek, 'cuttlefish'.
sepoy /seepoy/ • noun historical an Indian soldier serving under British or other European orders.
– ORIGIN Urdu and Persian, 'soldier'.
seppuku /sepookoo/ • noun another term for HARA-KIRI.
– ORIGIN Japanese, from words meaning 'to cut' and 'abdomen'.
sepsis /sepsiss/ • noun Medicine the presence in tissues of harmful bacteria, typically through infection of a wound.
– ORIGIN Greek, from *sēpein* 'make rotten'.
Sept. • abbreviation September.
sept- • combining form variant spelling of SEPTI-.
septa plural of SEPTUM.
septal • adjective 1 Anatomy & Biology relating to a septum or septa. 2 Archaeology (of a stone or slab) separating compartments in a burial chamber.
September • noun the ninth month of the year.
– ORIGIN from Latin *septem* 'seven' (being originally the seventh month of the Roman year).
septennial • adjective lasting for or recurring every seven years.
– ORIGIN from Latin *septem* 'seven' + *annus* 'year'.
septet /septet/ • noun a group of seven people playing music or singing together.
– ORIGIN from Latin *septem* 'seven'.
septi- (also **sept-**) • combining form seven; having seven: *septillion.*
– ORIGIN from Latin *septem* 'seven'.
septic /septik/ • adjective 1 (of a wound or a part of the body) infected with bacteria. 2 denoting a drainage system incorporating a septic tank.
– DERIVATIVES **septically** adverb **septicity** /septissiti/ noun.
– ORIGIN Greek *sēptikos*, from *sēpein* 'make rotten'.
septicaemia /septiseemiə/ (US **septicemia**) • noun blood poisoning caused by bacteria.
– DERIVATIVES **septicaemic** adjective.
septic tank • noun a underground tank in which sewage is allowed to decompose through bacterial activity before draining by means of a soakaway.
septillion /septilyən/ • cardinal number a thousand raised to the eighth power (10^{24}); a million million million million.
– DERIVATIVES **septillionth** ordinal number.
septimal /septim'l/ • adjective relating to the number seven.
– ORIGIN from Latin *septimus* 'seventh'.
septuagenarian /septyooəjinairiən/ • noun a person who is between 70 and 79 years old.
– ORIGIN Latin *septuagenarius*, from *septuaginta* 'seventy'.
Septuagesima /septyooəjessimə/ • noun the Sunday before Sexagesima.
– ORIGIN from Latin *septuagesimus* 'seventieth'.
Septuagint /septyooəjint/ • noun a Greek version of the Hebrew Bible (or Old Testament), including the Apocrypha, produced in the 3rd and 2nd centuries BC.
– ORIGIN from Latin *septuaginta* 'seventy', because of the tradition that it was produced by seventy-two translators working independently.
septum /septəm/ • noun (pl. **septa** /septə/) chiefly Anatomy & Biology a partition separating two chambers, such as that between the nostrils or the chambers of the heart.
– ORIGIN Latin, from *sepire* 'enclose'.
septuple /septyoop'l/ • adjective 1 consisting of seven parts or elements. 2 (of time in music) having seven beats in a bar. 3 consisting of seven times as much or as many as usual. • verb multiply by seven; increase sevenfold.
– ORIGIN from Latin *septem* 'seven'.
septuplet /septyooplit/ • noun 1 each of seven children born at one birth. 2 Music a group of seven notes to be performed in the time of four or six.
sepulchral /sipulkrəl/ • adjective 1 of or relating to a tomb or burial. 2 gloomy; dismal.
– DERIVATIVES **sepulchrally** adverb.
sepulchre /seppəlkər/ (US **sepulcher**) • noun a stone tomb or monument in which a dead person is laid or buried.
– ORIGIN Latin *sepulcrum* 'burial place', from *sepelire* 'bury'.
seq. (also **seqq.**) • adverb short for ET SEQ.
sequel • noun 1 a published, broadcast, or recorded work that continues the story or develops the theme of an earlier one. 2 something that takes place after or as a result of an earlier event.
– ORIGIN Latin *sequella*, from *sequi* 'follow'.
sequela /sikwaylə/ • noun (pl. **sequelae** /sikwaylee/) Medicine a condition which is the consequence of a previous disease or injury.
– ORIGIN Latin, from *sequi* 'follow'.
sequence • noun 1 a particular order in which related things follow each other. 2 a set of related things that follow each other in a particular order. 3 a part of a film dealing with one particular event or topic. 4 Music a repetition of a phrase or melody at a higher or lower pitch. • verb 1 arrange in a sequence. 2 play or record (music) with a sequencer.
– ORIGIN Latin *sequentia*, from *sequi* 'to follow'.
sequencer • noun a programmable electronic device for storing sequences of musical notes, chords, or rhythms and transmitting them to an electronic musical instrument.
sequential • adjective forming or following in a logical order or sequence.
– DERIVATIVES **sequentiality** noun **sequentially** adverb.
sequester /sikwestər/ • verb 1 isolate or hide away. 2 another term for SEQUESTRATE.
– ORIGIN Latin *sequestrare* 'commit for safekeeping', from *sequester* 'trustee'.
sequestrate /sikwestrayt, seekwi-/ • verb 1 take legal possession of (assets) until a debt has been paid or other claims have been met. 2 take forcible possession of; confiscate.
– DERIVATIVES **sequestration** noun **sequestrator** /seekwistraytər/ noun.
sequin • noun a small, shiny disc sewn on to clothing for decoration.
– DERIVATIVES **sequinned** (also **sequined**) adjective.
– ORIGIN originally denoting a former Venetian gold coin: from Italian *zecchino*, from an Arabic word meaning 'a die for coining'.
sequoia /sikwoyə/ • noun a redwood tree, especially the California redwood.
– ORIGIN named after *Sequoya*, a Cherokee Indian scholar.
sera plural of SERUM.
seraglio /səraaliō/ • noun (pl. **seraglios**) 1 the women's apartments in a Muslim house or palace. 2 a harem.
– ORIGIN Italian *serraglio*, from a Persian word meaning 'palace'.
serai /səri/ • noun a caravanserai.
serape /seraapay/ (also **sarape**) • noun a shawl or blanket worn as a cloak by people from Latin America.
– ORIGIN Mexican Spanish.
seraph /serrəf/ • noun (pl. **seraphim** /serrəfim/ or **seraphs**) an angelic being associated with light, ardour, and purity.
– DERIVATIVES **seraphic** adjective **seraphically** adverb.
– ORIGIN Hebrew.
Serb • noun a person from Serbia.
Serbian • noun 1 the language of the Serbs. 2 a Serb. • adjective relating to Serbia.

S

Thesaurus

and life DISTINCTION, difference, differentiation, division, dividing line; gulf, gap, chasm.
septic • adjective INFECTED, festering, suppurating, pus-filled, putrid, putrefying, poisoned, diseased; *Medicine* purulent.
sepulchral • adjective GLOOMY, lugubrious, sombre, melancholy, melancholic, sad, sorrowful, mournful, doleful, dismal, cheerless; *poetic/literary* dolorous.
– OPPOSITES cheerful.
sepulchre • noun TOMB, vault, burial chamber, mausoleum, crypt, undercroft, catacomb; grave.
sequel • noun 1 *the film inspired a sequel* FOLLOW-UP, continuation. 2 *the sequel was an armed uprising* CONSEQUENCE, result, upshot, outcome, development, issue, postscript; effect, after-effect, aftermath; *informal* pay-off.
sequence • noun 1 *the sequence of events* SUCCESSION, order, course, series, chain, train, string, progression, chronology; pattern, flow; *formal* concatenation. 2 *a sequence from his film* EXCERPT, clip, extract, episode, section.
sequester • verb 1 *he sequestered himself from the world* ISOLATE ONESELF, hide away, shut oneself away, seclude oneself, cut oneself off, segregate oneself; closet oneself, withdraw, retire. 2 *the government sequestered his property.* See SEQUESTRATE.
sequestrate • verb CONFISCATE, seize, take, sequester, appropriate, expropriate, impound, commandeer; *Law* distrain; *Scottish Law*

Serbo-Croat /serbōkrōat/ (also **Serbo-Croatian** /serbōkrō-aysh'n/) • noun the language spoken in Serbia, Croatia, and elsewhere in the former Yugoslavia.
sere • adjective variant spelling of SEAR.
serenade • noun a piece of music sung or played in the open air at night, especially by a man under the window of his beloved. • verb entertain with a serenade.
– DERIVATIVES **serenader** noun.
– ORIGIN Italian *serenata*, from *sereno* 'serene'.
serendipity /serrəndippiti/ • noun the occurrence and development of events by chance in a happy or beneficial way.
– DERIVATIVES **serendipitous** adjective **serendipitously** adverb.
– ORIGIN from *Serendip* (a former name for Sri Lanka): coined by the English politican and writer Horace Walpole (1717–97), after *The Three Princes of Serendip*, a fairy tale in which the heroes were always making fortunate discoveries.
serene • adjective calm, peaceful, and untroubled; tranquil.
– DERIVATIVES **serenely** adverb **serenity** noun.
– ORIGIN Latin *serenus*.
serf • noun (in the feudal system) an agricultural labourer who was tied to working on a particular estate.
– DERIVATIVES **serfdom** noun.
– ORIGIN Latin *servus* 'slave'.
serge /serj/ • noun a durable twilled woollen or worsted fabric.
– ORIGIN Old French *sarge*, from a variant of Latin *serica lana* 'silken wool'.
sergeant /saarjənt/ • noun **1** a rank of non-commissioned officer in the army or air force, above corporal and below staff sergeant. **2** Brit. a police officer ranking below an inspector.
– ORIGIN originally in the senses 'servant' and 'common soldier': from Old French *sergent*, from Latin *servire* 'serve'.
sergeant-at-arms • noun variant spelling of SERJEANT-AT-ARMS.
sergeant major • noun a warrant officer in the British army whose job is to assist the adjutant of a regiment or battalion or a subunit commander.
serial • adjective **1** consisting of, forming part of, or taking place in a series. **2** repeatedly committing the same offence or following a characteristic behaviour pattern: *a serial killer*. **3** Computing (of a device) involving the transfer of data as a single sequence of bits. • noun **1** a story or play published or broadcast in regular instalments. **2** (in a library) a periodical.
– DERIVATIVES **seriality** noun **serially** adverb.
serialism • noun a technique of musical composition using the twelve notes of the chromatic scale in a fixed order which is subject to change only in specific ways.
– DERIVATIVES **serialist** adjective & noun.
serialize (also **serialise**) • verb **1** publish or broadcast (a story or play) in regular instalments. **2** arrange in a series.
– DERIVATIVES **serialization** noun.
serial number • noun an identification number showing the position of a manufactured or printed item in a series.
sericulture /serrikulchər/ • noun the production of silk and the rearing of silkworms for this purpose.
– ORIGIN from Latin *sericum* 'silk'.
series • noun (pl. same) **1** a number of similar or related things coming one after another. **2** a sequence of related television or radio programmes. **3** Geology a range of strata corresponding to an epoch in time. **4** Mathematics a set of quantities constituting a progression or having values determined by a common relation.
– PHRASES **in series** (of electrical components or circuits) arranged so that the current passes through each successively.
– ORIGIN Latin, 'row, chain', from *serere* 'join, connect'.
serif /serrif/ • noun a slight projection finishing off a stroke of a letter, as in T contrasted with T.
– ORIGIN perhaps from Dutch *schreef* 'dash, line'.
serine /serreen/ • noun Biochemistry an amino acid which is a constituent of most proteins.
– ORIGIN from Latin *sericum* 'silk'.
serio-comic /seeriō/ • adjective combining the serious and the comic.
serious • adjective **1** demanding or characterized by careful consideration or application. **2** solemn or thoughtful. **3** sincere and in earnest, rather than joking or half-hearted. **4** significant or worrying in terms of danger or risk: *serious injury*. **5** informal substantial in terms of size, number, or quality: *serious money*.
– DERIVATIVES **seriousness** noun.
– ORIGIN Latin *serius* 'earnest, serious'.
seriously • adverb in a serious manner or to a serious extent.
serjeant • noun (in official lists) a sergeant in the Foot Guards.
– ORIGIN variant of SERGEANT.
serjeant-at-arms (also **sergeant-at-arms**) • noun (pl. **serjeants-at-arms**) an official of a legislative assembly whose duties include maintaining order and security.
serjeant-at-law • noun (pl. **serjeants-at-law**) historical a barrister of the highest rank.
sermon • noun **1** a talk on a religious or moral subject, especially one given during a church service. **2** informal a long or tedious moralizing or admonitory talk.
– DERIVATIVES **sermonic** adjective **sermonize** (also **sermonise**) verb.
– ORIGIN Latin, 'discourse, talk'.
serology /seerolləji/ • noun the scientific study or diagnostic examination of blood serum.
– DERIVATIVES **serologic** adjective **serological** adjective **serologist** noun.
seropositive (or **seronegative**) • adjective giving a positive (or negative) result in a test of blood serum, especially for the presence of a virus.
serotonin /serrətōnin/ • noun a compound present in blood which constricts the blood vessels and acts as a neurotransmitter.
– ORIGIN from SERUM + TONIC.
serous /seerəss/ • adjective of, resembling, or producing serum.
serpent • noun **1** literary a large snake. **2** a sly or treacherous person. **3** historical a bass wind instrument made of leather-

Thesaurus

S

poind.
seraphic • adjective BLISSFUL, beatific, sublime, rapturous, ecstatic, joyful, rapt; serene, ethereal; cherubic, saintly, angelic.
serendipitous • adjective CHANCE, accidental, coincidental; lucky, fluky, fortuitous; unexpected, unforeseen.
serendipity • noun (HAPPY) CHANCE, (happy) accident, fluke; luck, good luck, good fortune, fortuity, providence; happy coincidence.
serene • adjective **1** *on the surface she seemed serene* CALM, composed, tranquil, peaceful, untroubled, relaxed, at ease, unperturbed, unruffled, unworried; placid, equable; *N. Amer.* centered; *informal* together, unflappable. **2** *serene valleys* PEACEFUL, tranquil, quiet, still, restful, relaxing, undisturbed.
– OPPOSITES agitated, turbulent.
series • noun **1** *a series of lectures* SUCCESSION, sequence, string, chain, run, round; spate, wave, rash; set, course, cycle; row, line; *formal* concatenation. **2** *a new drama series* SERIAL, programme; soap opera; *informal* soap.
serious • adjective **1** *a serious expression* SOLEMN, earnest, grave, sombre, sober, unsmiling, poker-faced, stern, grim, dour, humourless, stony-faced; thoughtful, preoccupied, pensive. **2** *serious decisions* IMPORTANT, significant, consequential, momentous, weighty, far-reaching, major, grave; urgent, pressing, crucial, critical, vital, life-and-death, high-priority. **3** *give serious consideration to this* CAREFUL, detailed, in-depth, deep, profound, meaningful. **4** *a serious play* INTELLECTUAL, highbrow, heavyweight, deep, profound, literary, learned, scholarly; *informal* heavy. **5** *serious injuries* SEVERE, grave, bad, critical, acute, terrible, dire, dangerous, perilous; *formal* grievous; *archaic* parlous. **6** *we're serious about equality* IN EARNEST, earnest, sincere, wholehearted, genuine; committed, resolute, determined.
– OPPOSITES light-hearted, trivial, superficial, lowbrow, minor, half-hearted.
seriously • adverb **1** *Faye nodded seriously* SOLEMNLY, earnestly, gravely, soberly, sombrely, sternly, grimly, dourly, humourlessly; thoughtfully, pensively. **2** *she was seriously injured* SEVERELY, gravely, badly, critically, acutely, dangerously; *formal* grievously. **3** *do you seriously expect me to come?* REALLY, actually, honestly. **4** *seriously, I'm very pleased* JOKING ASIDE, to be serious, honestly, truthfully, truly, I mean it; *informal* Scout's honour; *Brit. informal* straight up; *dated* honest Injun. **5** *'I've resigned.' 'Seriously?'* REALLY, is that so, is that a fact, you're joking, well I never, go on, you don't say; *informal* you're kidding; *Brit. informal* {well, I'll be blowed}. **6** *(informal) he was seriously rich.* See EXTREMELY.
sermon • noun **1** *he preached a sermon* HOMILY, address, speech, talk, discourse, oration; lesson. **2** *the headmaster gave them a lengthy sermon* LECTURE, tirade, harangue, diatribe; speech, disquisition, monologue; reprimand, reproach, reproof, admonishment, admonition, reproval, remonstration, criticism; *informal*

covered wood in three U-shaped turns.
– ORIGIN from Latin *serpere* 'to creep'.

serpentine /serpəntīn/ ● adjective **1** of or like a serpent or snake, especially in being winding or twisting. **2** complex, cunning, or treacherous. ● noun a dark green mineral consisting of a silicate of magnesium, sometimes mottled or spotted like a snake's skin.

SERPS /serps/ ● abbreviation (in the UK) state earnings-related pension scheme.

serrated ● adjective having or denoting a jagged edge like the teeth of a saw.
– ORIGIN Latin *serratus*, from *serra* 'saw'.

serration ● noun a tooth or point of a serrated edge or surface.

serried ● adjective (of rows of people or things) standing close together.
– ORIGIN from archaic *serry* 'press close', probably from French *serré* 'close together'.

serum /seerəm/ ● noun (pl. **sera** /seerə/ or **serums**) the amber-coloured, protein-rich liquid which separates out when blood coagulates.
– ORIGIN Latin, 'whey'.

servant ● noun **1** a person employed to perform domestic duties in a household or as a personal attendant. **2** a person regarded as providing support or service for an organization or person: *a government servant.*
– ORIGIN Old French, 'person serving', from *servir* 'to serve'.

serve ● verb **1** perform duties or services for. **2** be employed as a member of the armed forces. **3** spend (a period) in office, in an apprenticeship, or in prison. **4** present food or drink to. **5** attend to (a customer in a shop). **6** be of use in fulfilling (a purpose). **7** treat in a specified way. **8** (of food or drink) be enough for. **9** Law formally deliver (a summons or writ) to the person to whom it is addressed. **10** (in tennis and other racket sports) hit the ball or shuttlecock to begin play for each point of a game. **11** (of a male breeding animal) copulate with (a female). ● noun **1** an act of serving in tennis, badminton, etc. **2** Austral. informal a reprimand.
– PHRASES **serve someone right** be someone's deserved punishment or misfortune. **serve one's** (or **its**) **turn** be useful.
– ORIGIN Latin *servire*, from *servus* 'slave'.

server ● noun **1** a person or thing that serves. **2** a computer or computer program which manages access to a centralized resource or service in a network.

servery ● noun (pl. **serveries**) Brit. a counter, hatch, or room from which meals are served.

service ● noun **1** the action or process of serving. **2** a period of employment with an organization. **3** an act of assistance. **4** a ceremony of religious worship according to a prescribed form. **5** a system supplying a public need such as transport, or utilities such as water. **6** a public department or organization run by the state: *the probation service.* **7** (**the services**) the armed forces. **8** (often in phrase **in service**) employment as a servant. **9** a set of matching crockery used for serving a particular meal. **10** (in tennis, badminton, etc.) a serve. **11** a periodic routine inspection and maintenance of a vehicle or other machine. ● verb **1** perform routine maintenance or repair work on. **2** provide a service or services for. **3** pay interest on (a debt). **4** (of a male animal) mate with (a female animal).
– PHRASES **be at someone's service** be ready to assist someone whenever required. **be of service** be available to assist someone. **in** (or **out of**) **service** available (or not available) for use.
– ORIGIN Latin *servitium* 'slavery'.

serviceable ● adjective **1** fulfilling its function adequately; usable or in working order. **2** functional and durable rather than attractive.
– DERIVATIVES **serviceability** noun.

service area ● noun chiefly Brit. a roadside area where services are available to motorists.

service charge ● noun **1** a charge added to a bill for service in a restaurant. **2** a charge made for banking or other services.

service flat ● noun Brit. a rented flat in which domestic service and sometimes meals are provided by the management.

service industry ● noun a business that provides a service for a customer, but is not involved in manufacturing.

serviceman (or **servicewoman**) ● noun **1** a person serving in the armed forces. **2** a person providing maintenance for machinery.

service provider ● noun Computing a company which gives its subscribers access to the Internet.

service road ● noun a subsidiary road running parallel to a main road and giving access to houses, shops, or businesses.

service station ● noun a roadside establishment selling petrol and oil and sometimes offering vehicle maintenance.

service tree ● noun a tree resembling a rowan, with brown berries.
– ORIGIN from the plural of obsolete *serve*, from Latin *sorbus*.

serviette ● noun Brit. a table napkin.
– ORIGIN Old French, from *servir* 'to serve'.

servile ● adjective **1** excessively willing to serve or please others. **2** of or characteristic of a slave or slaves.
– DERIVATIVES **servilely** adverb **servility** noun.
– ORIGIN Latin *servilis*, from *servus* 'slave'.

Thesaurus

telling-off, talking-to, dressing-down, earful; *Brit. informal* ticking-off, row, rocket, rollicking; *formal* castigation.

serpentine ● adjective **1** *a serpentine path* WINDING, windy, zigzag, twisty, twisting and turning, meandering, sinuous, snaky, tortuous. **2** *serpentine election rules* COMPLICATED, complex, intricate, involved, tortuous, convoluted, elaborate, knotty, confusing, bewildering, baffling, impenetrable.
– OPPOSITES straight, simple.

serrated ● adjective JAGGED, sawtoothed, sawtooth, zigzag, notched, indented, toothed, denticulate, denticulated; *Botany* serrate; *technical* crenulated.
– OPPOSITES smooth.

serried ● adjective CLOSE TOGETHER, packed together, close-set, dense, tight, compact.

servant ● noun **1** *servants were cleaning the hall* ATTENDANT, retainer; domestic (worker), (hired) help, cleaner; lackey, flunkey, minion; maid, housemaid, footman, page (boy), valet, butler, batman, manservant; housekeeper, steward; drudge, menial, slave; *Brit. informal* Mrs Mop, daily (woman), skivvy, scout; *Brit. dated* charwoman, charlady, boots; *archaic* abigail, scullion. **2** *a servant of the Labour Party* HELPER, supporter, follower.

serve ● verb **1** *they served their masters faithfully* WORK FOR, be in the service of, be employed by; obey. **2** *this job serves the community* BE OF SERVICE TO, be of use to, help, assist, aid, make a contribution to, do one's bit for, do something for, benefit. **3** *she served on the committee for years* BE A MEMBER OF, work on, be on, sit on, have a place on. **4** *he served his apprenticeship in Scotland* CARRY OUT, perform, do, fulfil, complete, discharge; spend. **5** *serve the soup hot* DISH UP/OUT, give out, distribute; present, provide, supply; eat. **6** *she served another customer* ATTEND TO, deal with, see to; ASSIST, help, look after. **7** *they served him with a writ* PRESENT, deliver, give, hand over. **8** *a saucer serving as an ashtray* ACT AS, function as, do the work of, be a substitute for. **9** *official forms will serve in most cases* SUFFICE, be adequate, be good enough, fit/fill the bill, do, answer, be useful, meet requirements, suit.

service ● noun **1** *your conditions of service* WORK, employment, employ, labour. **2** *he has done us a service* FAVOUR, kindness, good turn, helping hand; (**services**) ASSISTANCE, help, aid, offices, ministrations. **3** *the food and service were excellent* WAITING, waitressing, serving, attendance. **4** *products which give reliable service* USE, usage; functioning. **5** *he took his car in for a service* OVERHAUL, maintenance check, servicing. **6** *a marriage service* CEREMONY, ritual, rite, observance; liturgy, sacrament; *formal* ordinance. **7** *a range of local services* AMENITY, facility, resource, utility. **8** *soldiers leaving the services* (ARMED) FORCES, armed services, military; army, navy, air force.
● verb *the appliances are serviced regularly* OVERHAUL, check, go over, maintain; repair, mend, recondition.
– PHRASES **be of service** HELP, assist, benefit, be of assistance, be beneficial, serve, be useful, be of use, be valuable; do someone a good turn. **out of service** OUT OF ORDER, broken, broken-down, out of commission, unserviceable, faulty, defective, inoperative, in disrepair; down; *informal* conked out, bust, kaput, on the blink, acting up, shot; *Brit. informal* knackered.

serviceable ● adjective **1** *a serviceable heating system* IN WORKING ORDER, working, functioning, functional, operational, operative; usable, workable, viable. **2** *serviceable lace-up shoes* FUNCTIONAL, utilitarian, sensible, practical; HARD-WEARING, durable, tough, robust.
– OPPOSITES unusable, impractical.

servile ● adjective OBSEQUIOUS, sycophantic, deferential, subservient, fawning, ingratiating, unctuous, grovelling, toadyish, slav-

S

serving ● noun a quantity of food suitable for or served to one person.
servitor /servitər/ ● noun archaic a servant or attendant.
servitude /servityo͞od/ ● noun **1** the state of being a slave. **2** the state of being completely subject to someone more powerful.
– ORIGIN Latin *servitudo*, from *servus* 'slave'.
servo ● noun (pl. **servos**) short for SERVOMECHANISM or SERVOMOTOR.
– ORIGIN from Latin *servus* 'slave'.
servomechanism ● noun a powered mechanism producing motion or forces at a higher level of energy than the input level, e.g. in the brakes and steering of large motor vehicles.
servomotor ● noun the motive element in a servomechanism.
sesame /sessəmi/ ● noun a tall herbaceous plant of tropical and subtropical areas, cultivated for its oil-rich seeds.
– PHRASES **open sesame** a free or unrestricted means of admission or access. [ORIGIN from the magic formula in the tale of Ali Baba and the Forty Thieves.]
– ORIGIN Greek *sēsamon, sēsamē*.
sesqui- ● combining form denoting one and a half: *sesquicentenary.*
– ORIGIN from Latin *semi-* 'half' + *que* 'and'.
sesquicentenary /seskwisenteenəri, -tenn-/ ● noun (pl. **sesquicentenaries**) the one-hundred-and-fiftieth anniversary of a significant event.
– DERIVATIVES **sesquicentennial** adjective & noun.
sesquipedalian /seskwipidaylian/ ● adjective formal **1** (of a word) having many syllables; long. **2** characterized by long words; long-winded.
– ORIGIN from Latin *sesquipedalis* 'a foot and a half long'.
sessile /sessīl/ ● adjective **1** (of an organism) fixed in one place; immobile. **2** (of a structure) attached directly by its base without a stalk or peduncle.
– ORIGIN Latin *sessilis*, from *sedere* 'sit'.
session ● noun **1** a period devoted to a particular activity: *a training session.* **2** a meeting of a council, court, or legislative body to conduct its business. **3** a period during which such meetings are regularly held. **4** an academic year. **5** informal a period of heavy or sustained drinking.
– DERIVATIVES **sessional** adjective.
– ORIGIN Latin, from *sedere* 'sit'.
session musician ● noun a freelance musician hired to play on recording sessions.
sestet /sestet/ ● noun the last six lines of a sonnet.
– ORIGIN Italian *sestetto*, from Latin *sextus* 'a sixth'.
set[1] ● verb (**setting**; past and past part. **set**) **1** put, lay, or stand in a specified place or position. **2** put, bring, or place into a specified state. **3** cause or instruct (someone) to do something. **4** give someone (a task). **5** decide on or fix (a time, value, or limit). **6** establish as (an example or record). **7** adjust (a device) as required. **8** prepare (a table) for a meal by placing cutlery, crockery, etc., on it. **9** harden into a solid, semi-solid, or fixed state. **10** arrange (damp hair) into the required style. **11** put (a broken or dislocated bone or limb) into the correct position for healing. **12** (of the sun, moon, etc.) appear to move towards and below the earth's horizon as the earth rotates. **13** Printing arrange (type or text) as required. **14** (**set something to**) provide (music) so that a written work can be produced in a musical form. **15** (of a tide or current) take or have a specified direction or course. **16** (of blossom or a tree) form into or produce (fruit).
– PHRASES **set about 1** start doing something with vigour or determination. **2** Brit. informal attack. **set apart** give (someone) an air of unusual superiority. **set aside 1** save or keep for a particular purpose. **2** annul (a legal decision or process). **set back** informal cost (someone) a particular amount of money. **set down** record in writing or as an authoritative rule or principle. **set forth 1** begin a journey or trip. **2** state or describe in writing or speech. **set in** (of something unwelcome) begin and seem likely to continue. **set off 1** begin a journey. **2** cause (a bomb or alarm) to go off. **3** serve as decorative embellishment to. **set on** (or **upon**) attack or urge to attack violently. **set out 1** begin a journey. **2** aim or intend to do something. **3** arrange or display in a particular order or position. **set out one's stall** display one's abilities or attributes. **set sail 1** hoist the sails of a boat. **2** begin a voyage. **set one's teeth** become resolute. **set to** begin doing something vigorously. **set up 1** place or erect in position. **2** establish (a business, institution, etc.). **3** establish (someone) in a particular capacity or role. **4** begin making (a loud sound). **5** informal make (an innocent person) appear guilty. **set the wheels in motion** begin a process or put a plan into action.
– ORIGIN Old English, related to SIT.
set[2] ● noun **1** a number of things or people grouped together as similar or forming a unit. **2** a group of people with common interests or occupations: *the literary set.* **3** the way in which something is set, disposed, or positioned: *that cold set of his jaw.* **4** a radio or television receiver. **5** (in tennis, darts, and other games) a group of games counting as a unit towards a match. **6** a collection of scenery, stage furniture, etc., used for a scene in a play or film. **7** (in jazz or popular music) a sequence of songs or pieces constituting or forming part of a live show or recording. **8** Mathematics a collection of distinct entities satisfying specified conditions and regarded as a unit. **9** a cutting, young plant, or bulb used in the propagation of new plants: *an onion set.* **10** (also **dead set**) a setter's pointing in the presence of game. **11** variant spelling of SETT.
– PHRASES **make a dead set at** Brit. make a determined attempt to win the affections of. [ORIGIN by association with hunting (see sense 10 above).]
– ORIGIN partly from Old French *sette*, from Latin *secta* 'sect', partly from SET[1].
set[3] ● adjective **1** fixed or arranged in advance. **2** firmly fixed and unchanging. **3** having a conventional or predetermined wording. **4** ready, prepared, or likely to do something. **5** (**set on**) determined to do.

Thesaurus

S

ish, humble, self-abasing; *informal* slimy, bootlicking, smarmy, sucky; *N. Amer. informal* apple-polishing.
– OPPOSITES assertive.
serving ● noun PORTION, helping, plateful, plate, bowlful; amount, quantity, ration.
servitude ● noun SLAVERY, enslavement, bondage, subjugation, subjection, domination; *historical* serfdom.
– OPPOSITES liberty.
session ● noun **1** *a special session of the committee* MEETING, sitting, assembly, conclave, plenary; hearing; conference, discussion, forum, symposium; *Scottish* sederunt, diet; *N. Amer. & NZ* caucus. **2** *training sessions* PERIOD, time, spell, stretch, bout. **3** *the next college session begins in August* ACADEMIC YEAR, school year; term, semester; *N. Amer.* trimester.
set[1] ● verb **1** *Beth set the bag on the table* PUT (DOWN), place, lay, deposit, position, settle, leave, stand, plant, posit; *informal* stick, dump, bung, park, plonk, pop; *N. Amer. informal* plunk. **2** *the cottage is set on a hill* BE SITUATED, be located, lie, stand, be sited, be perched. **3** *the fence is set in concrete* FIX, embed, insert; mount. **4** *a ring set with precious stones* ADORN, ornament, decorate, embellish; *poetic/literary* bejewel. **5** *I'll go and set the table* LAY, prepare, arrange. **6** *we set them some easy tasks* ASSIGN, allocate, give, allot, prescribe. **7** *just set your mind to it* APPLY, address, direct, aim, turn, focus, concentrate. **8** *they set a date for the election* DECIDE ON, select, choose, arrange, schedule; fix (on), settle on, determine, designate, name, appoint, specify, stipulate. **9** *he set his horse towards her* DIRECT, steer, orientate, point, aim, train. **10** *his jump set a national record* ESTABLISH, create, institute. **11** *he set his watch* ADJUST, regulate, synchronize; calibrate; put right, correct; programme, activate, turn on. **12** *the adhesive will set in an hour* SOLIDIFY, harden, stiffen, thicken, gel, gelatinize; cake, congeal, coagulate, clot; freeze, crystallize. **13** *the sun was setting* GO DOWN, sink, dip; vanish, disappear.
– OPPOSITES melt, rise.
– PHRASES **set about 1** *Mike set about raising £5000* BEGIN, start, commence, go about, get to work on, get down to, embark on, tackle, address oneself to, undertake. **2** *the youths set about him* ATTACK, assail, assault, hit, strike, beat, thrash, pummel, wallop, tear into, set upon, fall on; *informal* lay into, lace into, pitch into, let someone have it, do over, work over, rough up, knock about/around; *Brit. informal* duff up, have a go at; *N. Amer. informal* beat up on. **set someone against someone else** ALIENATE FROM, estrange from; drive a wedge between, sow dissension, set at odds. **set someone apart** DISTINGUISH, differentiate, mark out, single out, separate, demarcate. **set something apart** ISOLATE, separate, segregate, put to one side. **set something aside 1** *set aside some money each month* SAVE, put by, put aside, put away, lay by, keep, reserve; store, stockpile, hoard, stow away, cache, withhold; *informal* salt away, squirrel away, stash away. **2** *he set aside his cup* PUT DOWN, cast aside, discard, abandon, dispense with. **3** *set aside*

set-aside ● noun **1** the policy of taking land out of production to reduce crop surpluses. **2** land taken out of production in this way.
setback ● noun a reversal or check in progress.
SETI ● abbreviation search for extraterrestrial intelligence.
set phrase ● noun an unvarying phrase having a specific meaning or being the only context in which a word appears.
set piece ● noun **1** a formal or elaborate arrangement, especially part of a novel, film, etc., arranged for maximum effect. **2** a carefully organized and practised move in a team game.
set point ● noun (in tennis and other sports) a point which if won by one of the players will also win them a set.
set square ● noun a right-angled triangular plate for drawing lines, especially at 90°, 45°, 60°, or 30°.
sett (also **set**) ● noun **1** the earth or burrow of a badger. **2** a granite paving block.
– ORIGIN variant of SET².
settee ● noun a long upholstered seat for more than one person, typically with a back and arms.
– ORIGIN perhaps a variant of SETTLE².
setter ● noun **1** a dog of a large long-haired breed trained to stand rigid when scenting game. **2** a person or thing that sets something.
set theory ● noun the branch of mathematics concerned with the formal properties and applications of sets.
setting ● noun **1** the way or place in which something is set. **2** a piece of metal in which a precious stone or gem is fixed to form a piece of jewellery. **3** a piece of vocal or choral music composed for particular words. **4** (also **place setting**) a complete set of crockery and cutlery for one person at a meal.
settle¹ ● verb **1** reach an agreement or decision about (an argument or problem). **2** (often **settle down**) adopt a more steady or secure life, especially through establishing a permanent home. **3** sit, come to rest, or arrange comfortably or securely. **4** become or make calmer or quieter. **5** (often **settle in**) begin to feel comfortable or established in a new situation. **6** (**settle down to**) apply oneself to. **7** pay (a debt or account). **8** (**settle for**) accept or agree to (something less than satisfactory). **9** (**settle something on**) give money or property to (someone) through a deed of settlement or a will. **10** fall or sink down. **11** (of suspended particles) sink slowly in a liquid to form sediment.
– DERIVATIVES **settleable** adjective.
– ORIGIN Old English, 'to seat, place', from SETTLE².
settle² ● noun a wooden bench with a high back and arms, typically incorporating a box under the seat.
– ORIGIN Old English, related to SIT.
settlement ● noun **1** the action or process of settling. **2** an official agreement intended to settle a dispute or conflict. **3** a place where people establish a community. **4** Law an arrangement whereby property passes to a person or succession of people as dictated by the settlor.

Thesaurus

your differences DISREGARD, put aside, ignore, forget, discount, shrug off, bury. **4** *the Appeal Court set aside the decision* OVERRULE, overturn, reverse, revoke, countermand, nullify, annul, cancel, quash, dismiss, reject, repudiate; *Law* disaffirm; *formal* abrogate. **set someone back** *(informal).* See COST verb sense 1. **set someone/something back** DELAY, hold up, hold back, slow down/up, retard, check, decelerate; hinder, impede, obstruct, hamper, inhibit, frustrate, thwart. **set something down 1** *he set down his thoughts* WRITE DOWN, put in writing, jot down, note down, make a note of; record, register, log. **2** *we set down a code of practice* FORMULATE, draw up, establish, frame; lay down, determine, fix, stipulate, specify, prescribe, impose, ordain. **3** *I set it down to the fact that he was drunk* ATTRIBUTE, put down, ascribe, assign, chalk up; blame on, impute. **set something forth** PRESENT, describe, set out, detail, delineate, explain, expound; state, declare, announce; submit, offer, put forward, advance, propose, propound. **set someone free** RELEASE, free, let go, turn loose, let out, liberate, deliver, emancipate. **set in** *bad weather set in* BEGIN, start, arrive, come, develop. **set off** SET OUT, start out, sally forth, leave, depart, embark, set sail; *informal* hit the road. **set something off 1** *the bomb was set off* DETONATE, explode, blow up, touch off, trigger; ignite. **2** *it set off a wave of protest* GIVE RISE TO, cause, lead to, set in motion, occasion, bring about, initiate, precipitate, prompt, trigger (off), spark (off), touch off, provoke, incite. **3** *the blue dress set off her auburn hair* ENHANCE, bring out, emphasize, show off, throw into relief; complement. **set on/upon** ATTACK, assail, assault, hit, strike, beat, thrash, pummel, wallop, set about, fall on; *informal* lay into, lace into, let someone have it, get stuck into, work over, rough up, knock about/around; *Brit. informal* duff up, have a go at; *N. Amer. informal* beat up on, light into. **set one's heart on** WANT DESPERATELY, wish for, desire, long for, yearn for, hanker after, ache for, hunger for, thirst for, burn for; *informal* be itching for, be dying for. **set out 1** *he set out early.* See SET OFF. **2** *you've done what you set out to achieve* AIM, intend, mean, seek; hope, aspire, want. **set something out 1** *the gifts were set out on tables* ARRANGE, lay out, put out, array, dispose, display, exhibit. **2** *they set out some guidelines* PRESENT, set forth, detail; state, declare, announce; submit, put forward, advance, propose, propound. **set someone up 1** *his father set him up in business* ESTABLISH, finance, fund, back, subsidize. **2** *(informal) she set him up for Newley's murder* FALSELY INCRIMINATE, frame, entrap; *Brit. informal* fit up. **set something up 1** *a monument to her memory was set up* ERECT, put up, construct, build, raise, elevate. **2** *she set up her own business* ESTABLISH, start, begin, initiate, institute, found, create. **3** *set up a meeting* ARRANGE, organize, fix (up), schedule, timetable, line up.
set² ● noun **1** *a set of colour postcards* GROUP, collection, series; assortment, selection, compendium, batch, number; arrangement, array. **2** *the literary set* CLIQUE, coterie, circle, crowd, group, crew, band, company, ring, camp, fraternity, school, faction, league; *informal* gang, bunch. **3** *a chemistry set* KIT, apparatus, equipment, outfit. **4** *a set of cutlery* CANTEEN, box, case. **5** *a set of china* SERVICE. **6** *he's in the bottom set at school* CLASS, form, group; stream, band. **7** *the set of his shoulders* POSTURE, position, cast, attitude; bearing, carriage. **8** *a stage set* SCENERY, setting, backdrop, flats; mise en scène.
set³ ● adjective **1** *a set routine* FIXED, established, predetermined, hard and fast, pre-arranged, prescribed, specified, defined; unvarying, unchanging, invariable, unvaried, rigid, inflexible, cast-iron, strict, settled, predictable; routine, standard, customary, regular, usual, habitual, accustomed, wonted. **2** *she had set ideas* INFLEXIBLE, rigid, fixed, firm, deep-rooted, deep-seated, ingrained, entrenched. **3** *he had a set speech for such occasions* STOCK, standard, routine, rehearsed, well worn, formulaic, conventional. **4** *I was all set for the evening* READY, prepared, organized, equipped, primed; *informal* geared up, psyched up. **5** *he's set on marrying her* DETERMINED TO, intent on, (hell) bent on, resolute about, insistent about. **6** *you were dead set against the idea* OPPOSED TO, averse to, hostile to, resistant to, antipathetic to, unsympathetic to; *informal* anti.
– OPPOSITES variable, flexible, original, unprepared, uncertain.
setback ● noun PROBLEM, difficulty, hitch, complication, upset, disappointment, misfortune, mishap, reversal; blow, stumbling block, hindrance, impediment, obstruction; delay, hold-up; *informal* glitch, hiccup.
– OPPOSITES breakthrough.
settee ● noun SOFA, couch, divan, chaise longue, chesterfield; *Brit.* put-you-up; *N. Amer.* davenport, day bed.
setting ● noun **1** *a rural setting* SURROUNDINGS, position, situation, environment, background, backdrop, milieu, environs, habitat; spot, place, location, locale, site, scene; area, region, district. **2** *a garnet in a gold setting* MOUNT, fixture, surround.
settle ● verb **1** *they settled the dispute* RESOLVE, sort out, solve, clear up, end, fix, work out, iron out, straighten out, set right, rectify, remedy, reconcile; *informal* patch up. **2** *she settled their affairs* PUT IN ORDER, sort out, tidy up, arrange, organize, order, clear up. **3** *they settled on a date for the wedding* DECIDE ON, set, fix, agree on, name, establish, arrange, appoint, designate, assign; choose, select, pick. **4** *she went down to the lobby to settle her bill* PAY, settle up, square, clear, defray. **5** *they settled for a 4.2% pay rise* ACCEPT, agree to, assent to; *formal* accede to. **6** *he settled in London* MAKE ONE'S HOME, set up home, take up residence, put down roots, establish oneself; live, move to, emigrate to. **7** *immigrants settled much of Australia* COLONIZE, occupy, inhabit, people, populate. **8** *Catherine settled down to her work* APPLY ONESELF TO, get down to, set about, attack; concentrate on, focus on, devote oneself to. **9** *the class wouldn't settle down* CALM DOWN, quieten down, be quiet, be still; *informal* shut up. **10** *a brandy will settle your nerves* CALM, quieten, quiet, soothe, pacify, quell; sedate, tranquillize. **11** *he settled into an armchair* SIT DOWN, seat oneself, install oneself, ensconce oneself, plant oneself; *informal* park oneself, plonk oneself. **12** *a butterfly settled on the flower* LAND, come to

settler • noun a person who settles in an area, especially one with no or few previous inhabitants.
settlor /setlər/ • noun Law a person who makes a settlement, especially of a property.
set-to • noun (pl. **set-tos**) informal a fight or argument.
set-up • noun informal **1** the way in which something is organized or arranged. **2** an organization or arrangement. **3** a scheme or trick intended to incriminate or deceive someone.
seven • cardinal number one more than six; 7. (Roman numeral: **vii** or **VII**.)
– PHRASES **the seven deadly sins** (in Christian tradition) the sins of pride, covetousness, lust, anger, gluttony, envy, and sloth. **the seven seas** all the oceans of the world (conventionally the Arctic, Antarctic, North Pacific, South Pacific, North Atlantic, South Atlantic, and Indian Oceans). **the Seven Wonders of the World** the seven most spectacular man-made structures of the ancient world. **the seven year itch** a supposed tendency to infidelity after seven years of marriage.
– DERIVATIVES **sevenfold** adjective & adverb.
– ORIGIN Old English.
seventeen • cardinal number one more than sixteen; 17. (Roman numeral: **xvii** or **XVII**.)
– DERIVATIVES **seventeenth** adjective & noun.
seventh • ordinal number **1** constituting number seven in a sequence; 7th. **2** (**a seventh/one seventh**) each of seven equal parts into which something is or may be divided. **3** Music an interval spanning seven consecutive notes in a diatonic scale. **4** Music the note which is higher by this interval than the tonic of a diatonic scale or root of a chord.
– DERIVATIVES **seventhly** adverb.
Seventh-Day Adventist • noun a member of a strict Protestant sect which preaches the imminent return of Christ to Earth and observes Saturday as the sabbath.
seventy • cardinal number (pl. **seventies**) ten less than eighty; 70. (Roman numeral: **lxx** or **LXX**.)
– DERIVATIVES **seventieth** ordinal number.
seventy-eight • noun an old gramophone record designed to be played at 78 rpm.
sever • verb **1** divide by cutting or slicing. **2** put an end to (a connection or relationship).
– DERIVATIVES **severable** adjective.
– ORIGIN Old French *severer*, from Latin *separare* 'disjoin, divide'.
several • determiner & pronoun more than two but not many. • adjective separate or respective.
– DERIVATIVES **severally** adverb.
– ORIGIN Old French, from Latin *separ* 'separate, different'.
severance • noun **1** the action of ending a connection or relationship. **2** the state of being separated or cut off.
severance pay • noun money paid to an employee on the early termination of a contract.
severe • adjective **1** (of something bad, undesirable, or difficult) very great; intense. **2** strict or harsh. **3** very plain in style or appearance.
– DERIVATIVES **severely** adverb **severity** noun.
– ORIGIN Latin *severus*.
Seville orange /sevvil/ • noun a bitter orange used for marmalade.
– ORIGIN from *Seville* in Spain.
Sèvres /sevrə/ • noun a type of fine porcelain characterized by elaborate decoration on backgrounds of intense colour.
– ORIGIN from *Sèvres* in the suburbs of Paris, the place of manufacture.
sew • verb (past part. **sewn** or **sewed**) **1** join, fasten, or repair by making stitches with a needle and thread or a sewing machine. **2** (**sew up**) informal bring to a favourable state or conclusion.
– ORIGIN Old English.
sewage /so͞oij/ • noun waste water and excrement conveyed in sewers.
– ORIGIN from SEWER[1].
sewage farm (also **sewage works**) • noun a place where sewage is treated, especially for use as fertilizer.
sewer[1] /so͞oər/ • noun an underground conduit for carrying off drainage water and waste matter.
– ORIGIN Old French *seuwiere* 'channel to drain the overflow from a fish pond', from Latin *ex-* 'out of' + *aqua* 'water'.
sewer[2] /sōər/ • noun a person who sews.
sewerage • noun **1** the provision of drainage by sewers. **2** US term for SEWAGE.
sewing machine • noun a machine with a mechanically driven needle for sewing or stitching cloth.
sewn past participle of SEW.
sex • noun **1** either of the two main categories (male and female) into which humans and most other living things are divided on the basis of their reproductive functions. **2** the fact of belonging to one of these categories. **3** the group of all members of either sex. **4** sexual activity, specifically sexual intercourse. • verb determine the sex of.
– DERIVATIVES **sexer** noun.

Thesaurus

rest, alight, descend, perch; archaic light. **13** *sediment settles at the bottom* SINK, subside, fall, gravitate.
– OPPOSITES agitate, rise.
settlement • noun **1** *a pay settlement* AGREEMENT, deal, arrangement, resolution, bargain, understanding, pact. **2** *the settlement of the dispute* RESOLUTION, settling, solution, reconciliation. **3** *a frontier settlement* COMMUNITY, colony, outpost, encampment, post; village, commune; historical plantation. **4** *the settlement of the area* COLONIZATION, settling, populating; historical plantation. **5** *the settlement of his debt* PAYMENT, discharge, defrayal, liquidation, clearance.
settler • noun COLONIST, colonizer, frontiersman, frontierswoman, pioneer; immigrant, newcomer, incomer; N. Amer. historical homesteader.
– OPPOSITES native.
set-up • noun (informal) **1** *a telecommunications set-up* SYSTEM, structure, organization, arrangement, framework, layout, configuration. **2** *a set-up called Film International* ORGANIZATION, group, body, agency, association, operation; company, firm; informal outfit. **3** *the whole thing was a set-up* TRICK, trap; conspiracy; informal put-up job, frame-up.
seven • cardinal number SEPTET, septuplets; technical heptad.
– RELATED TERMS hepta-, septi-.
sever • verb **1** *the head was severed from the body* CUT OFF, chop off, detach, disconnect, dissever, separate, part; amputate, dock; poetic/literary sunder. **2** *a knife had severed the artery* CUT (THROUGH), rupture, split, pierce. **3** *they severed diplomatic relations* BREAK OFF, discontinue, suspend, end, terminate, cease, dissolve.
– OPPOSITES join, maintain.
several • adjective **1** *several people* SOME, a number of, a few; various, assorted, sundry, diverse; poetic/literary divers. **2** *they sorted out their several responsibilities* RESPECTIVE, individual, own, particular, specific; separate, different, disparate, distinct; various.
severe • adjective **1** *severe injuries* ACUTE, very bad, serious, grave, critical, dreadful, terrible, awful; dangerous, life-threatening; formal grievous; archaic parlous. **2** *severe storms* FIERCE, violent, strong, powerful, intense; tempestuous, turbulent. **3** *a severe winter* HARSH, bitter, cold, bleak, freezing, icy, arctic, extreme. **4** *a severe headache* EXCRUCIATING, agonizing, intense, dreadful, awful, terrible, unbearable, intolerable; informal splitting, pounding. **5** *a severe test of their stamina* DIFFICULT, demanding, tough, arduous, formidable, exacting, rigorous, punishing, onerous, gruelling. **6** *severe criticism* HARSH, scathing, sharp, strong, fierce, savage, scorching, devastating, trenchant, caustic, biting, withering. **7** *severe tax penalties* EXTORTIONATE, excessive, unreasonable, inordinate, outrageous, sky-high, harsh, stiff; punitive; Brit. swingeing. **8** *they received severe treatment* HARSH, stern, hard, inflexible, uncompromising, unrelenting, merciless, pitiless, ruthless, draconian, oppressive, repressive, punitive; brutal, cruel, savage. **9** *his severe expression* STERN, dour, grim, forbidding, disapproving, unsmiling, unfriendly, sombre, grave, serious, stony, steely; cold, frosty. **10** *a severe style of architecture* PLAIN, simple, austere, unadorned, unembellished, unornamented, stark, spartan, ascetic; clinical, uncluttered.
– OPPOSITES minor, gentle, mild, easy, lenient, friendly, ornate.
severely • adjective **1** *he was severely injured* BADLY, seriously, critically; fatally; formal grievously. **2** *she was severely criticized* SHARPLY, roundly, soundly, fiercely, savagely. **3** *murderers should be treated more severely* HARSHLY, strictly, sternly, rigorously, mercilessly, pitilessly, roughly, sharply; with a rod of iron; brutally, cruelly, savagely. **4** *she looked severely at Harriet* STERNLY, grimly, dourly, disapprovingly; coldly, frostily. **5** *she dressed severely in black* PLAINLY, simply, austerely, starkly.
sew • verb *she sewed the seams of the tunic* STITCH, tack, baste, seam, hem; embroider.
– PHRASES **sew something up 1** *the tear was sewn up* DARN, mend, repair, patch. **2** (informal) *the company sewed up a deal with IBM* SE-

– ORIGIN Latin *sexus*.
sexagenarian /seksəjinairiən/ ● noun a person between 60 and 69 years old.
– ORIGIN Latin *sexagenarius*, from *sexaginta* 'sixty'.
Sexagesima /seksəjessimə/ ● noun the Sunday before Quinquagesima.
– ORIGIN Latin, 'sixtieth (day)'.
sexagesimal /seksəjessim'l/ ● adjective relating to or based on sixtieths.
– ORIGIN from Latin *sexagesimus* 'sixtieth'.
sex appeal ● noun the quality of being attractive in a sexual way.
sex bomb ● noun informal a woman who is very sexually attractive.
sex chromosome ● noun a chromosome concerned in determining the sex of an organism (in mammals the X and Y chromosomes).
sexed ● adjective having specified sexual appetites: *highly sexed.*
sexennial /seksenniəl/ ● adjective lasting for or recurring every six years.
– ORIGIN from Latin *sex* 'six' + *annus* 'year'.
sex hormone ● noun a hormone affecting sexual development or reproduction, such as oestrogen or testosterone.
sexi- (also **sex-**) ● combining form six; having six: *sextuplet.*
– ORIGIN from Latin *sex* 'six'.
sexism ● noun prejudice, stereotyping, or discrimination, typically against women, on the basis of sex.
– DERIVATIVES **sexist** adjective & noun.
sex kitten ● noun informal a young woman who asserts or exploits her sexual attractiveness.
sexless ● adjective **1** not sexually desirable, attractive, or active. **2** neither male nor female.
– DERIVATIVES **sexlessly** adverb **sexlessness** noun.
sex life ● noun a person's sexual activity and relationships considered as a whole.
sex object ● noun a person regarded purely in terms of their sexual attractiveness or availability.
sexology ● noun the study of human sexual behaviour.
– DERIVATIVES **sexological** adjective **sexologist** noun.
sexpot ● noun informal a sexy person.
sex symbol ● noun a person widely noted for their sexual attractiveness.
sext ● noun a service forming part of the Divine Office of the Western Christian Church, traditionally said at the sixth hour of the day (i.e. noon).
– ORIGIN from Latin *sexta hora* 'sixth hour'.
sextant /sekstənt/ ● noun an instrument with a graduated arc of 60° and a sighting mechanism, used for measuring the angular distances between objects and especially for taking altitudes in navigation and surveying.
– ORIGIN originally denoting the sixth part of a circle: from Latin *sextans* 'sixth part'.
sextet (also **sextette**) ● noun **1** a group of six people playing music or singing together. **2** a composition for a sextet. **3** a set of six.
– ORIGIN alteration of SESTET, suggested by Latin *sex* 'six'.
sextillion /sekstilyən/ ● cardinal number a thousand raised to the seventh power (10^{21}); a thousand million million million.
– DERIVATIVES **sextillionth** ordinal number.
sexton ● noun a person who looks after a church and churchyard, typically acting as bell-ringer and gravedigger.
– ORIGIN Old French *segrestein*, from Latin *sacristanus* 'sacristan'.
sex tourism ● noun travel abroad with the aim of taking advantage of the lack of restrictions on sexual activity and prostitution in some countries.
sextuple /sekstyoop'l/ ● adjective **1** consisting of six parts or elements. **2** six times as much or as many.
– ORIGIN Latin *sextuplus*, from *sex* 'six'.
sextuplet /sekstyooplit/ ● noun **1** each of six children born at one birth. **2** Music a group of six notes to be performed in the time of four.
sexual ● adjective **1** relating to the instincts and activities connected with physical attraction or intimate physical contact between individuals. **2** relating to the sexes or to gender. **3** (of reproduction) involving the fusion of gametes. **4** Biology being of one sex or the other; capable of sexual reproduction.
– DERIVATIVES **sexualize** (also **sexualise**) verb **sexually** adverb.
sexual harassment ● noun the repeated making of unwanted sexual advances or obscene remarks to a person, especially in a workplace.
sexual intercourse ● noun sexual contact between individuals involving penetration, especially the insertion of a man's erect penis into a woman's vagina culminating in orgasm and the ejaculation of semen.
sexuality ● noun (pl. **sexualities**) **1** capacity for sexual feelings. **2** a person's sexual orientation or preference.
sexual politics ● plural noun (treated as sing.) relations between the sexes regarded in terms of power.
sex worker ● noun euphemistic a prostitute.
sexy ● adjective (**sexier**, **sexiest**) **1** sexually attractive or exciting. **2** sexually aroused. **3** informal very exciting or appealing.
– DERIVATIVES **sexily** adverb **sexiness** noun.
Seychellois /sayshelwaa/ ● noun a person from the Seychelles. ● adjective relating to the Seychelles.
SF ● abbreviation science fiction.
sforzando /sfortsandō/ (also **sforzato** /sfortsaatō/) ● adverb & adjective Music with sudden emphasis.
– ORIGIN Italian, 'using force'.
SFX ● abbreviation special effects.
– ORIGIN *FX* representing a pronunciation of *effects.*
SG ● abbreviation Physics specific gravity.
Sg ● symbol the chemical element seaborgium.
SGML ● abbreviation Computing Standard Generalized Mark-up Language, a system for encoding electronic texts so that they can be displayed in any desired format.
shabby ● adjective (**shabbier**, **shabbiest**) **1** worn out or dilapidated. **2** dressed in old or worn clothes. **3** mean and unfair: *a shabby trick.*
– DERIVATIVES **shabbily** adverb **shabbiness** noun.
– ORIGIN from dialect *shab* 'scab', from Germanic.

Thesaurus

CURE, clinch, pull off, bring off, settle, conclude, complete, finalize, tie up; *informal* swing.
sewing ● noun STITCHING, needlework, needlecraft, fancy-work.
sex ● noun **1** *the men talked about sex* SEXUAL INTERCOURSE, intercourse, lovemaking, making love, sex act, (sexual) relations; mating, copulation; *informal* nooky; *Brit. informal* bonking, rumpy pumpy, how's your father; *formal* fornication; *technical* coitus, coition; *dated* carnal knowledge. **2** *teach your children about sex* THE FACTS OF LIFE, reproduction; *informal* the birds and the bees. **3** *adults of both sexes* GENDER.
– PHRASES **have sex** HAVE SEXUAL INTERCOURSE, make love, sleep with, go to bed; mate, copulate; seduce, rape; *informal* do it, go all the way, know in the biblical sense; *Brit. informal* bonk; *N. Amer. informal* get it on; *euphemistic* be intimate; *poetic/literary* ravish; *formal* fornicate.
sex appeal ● noun SEXINESS, seductiveness, sexual attractiveness, desirability, sensuality, sexuality; *informal* it, SA.
sexism ● noun SEXUAL DISCRIMINATION, chauvinism, prejudice, bias.
sexless ● adjective ASEXUAL, non-sexual, neuter; androgynous, epicene.
sexual ● adjective **1** *the sexual organs* REPRODUCTIVE, genital, sex, procreative. **2** *sexual activity* CARNAL, erotic; *formal* venereal; *technical* coital.
sexual intercourse ● noun. See SEX sense 1.
sexuality ● noun **1** *she had a powerful sexuality* SENSUALITY, sexiness, seductiveness, desirability, eroticism, physicality; sexual appetite, passion, desire, lust. **2** *I'm open about my sexuality* SEXUAL ORIENTATION, sexual preference, leaning, persuasion; heterosexuality, homosexuality, lesbianism, bisexuality. **3** *sexuality within holy matrimony* SEXUAL ACTIVITY, sexual relations, sexual intercourse, sex, procreation.
sexy ● adjective **1** *she's so sexy* SEXUALLY ATTRACTIVE, seductive, desirable, alluring, sensual, sultry, slinky, provocative, tempting, tantalizing; nubile, voluptuous, luscious, lush; *informal* fanciable, beddable; *Brit. informal* fit; *N. Amer. informal* foxy, cute; *Austral. informal* spunky. **2** *sexy videos* EROTIC, sexually explicit, arousing, exciting, stimulating, hot, titillating, racy, naughty, risqué, adult, X-rated; rude, pornographic, crude, lewd; *informal* raunchy, steamy, porno, blue, skin. **3** *they weren't feeling sexy* (SEXUALLY) AROUSED, sexually excited, amorous, lustful, passionate; *informal* horny, hot, turned on, sexed up; *Brit. informal* randy. **4** *(informal) a sexy sales promotion* EXCITING, stimulating, interesting, appealing, intriguing.
shabby ● adjective **1** *a shabby little bar* RUN DOWN, down at heel, scruffy, dilapidated, ramshackle, tumbledown; seedy, slummy, in-

shack ● noun a roughly built hut or cabin. ● verb (**shack up**) informal live with someone as a lover.
– ORIGIN perhaps from the Mexican or Nahuatl words for 'wooden hut'.
shackle ● noun **1** (**shackles**) a pair of fetters connected by a chain, used to fasten a prisoner's wrists or ankles together. **2** (**shackles**) restraints or impediments. **3** a metal link or loop, closed by a bolt and used to secure a chain or rope to something. ● verb **1** chain with shackles. **2** restrain; limit.
– ORIGIN Old English.
shad ● noun (pl. same or **shads**) an edible herring-like marine fish that enters rivers to spawn.
– ORIGIN Old English.
shaddock /shaddək/ ● noun another term for POMELO.
– ORIGIN named after Captain *Shaddock*, who introduced it to the West Indies in the 17th century.
shade ● noun **1** comparative darkness and coolness caused by shelter from direct sunlight. **2** a colour, especially with regard to how light or dark it is. **3** a position of relative inferiority or obscurity: *your bravery puts me in the shade.* **4** a slightly differing variety. **5** a slight amount: *a shade anxious.* **6** a lampshade. **7** (**shades**) informal sunglasses. **8** literary a ghost. ● verb **1** screen from direct light. **2** cover or moderate the light of. **3** darken or colour with parallel pencil lines or a block of colour. **4** pass or change by degrees: *outrage began to shade into dismay.*
– PHRASES **shades of ——** suggestive or reminiscent of.
– DERIVATIVES **shadeless** adjective **shader** noun.
– ORIGIN Old English.
shading ● noun **1** the representation of light and shade on a drawing or map. **2** a very slight variation. **3** something providing shade.
shadow ● noun **1** a dark area or shape produced by an object coming between light rays and a surface. **2** partial or complete darkness. **3** a position of relative inferiority or obscurity. **4** sadness or gloom. **5** the slightest trace: *without a shadow of a doubt.* **6** a weak or inferior remnant or version: *a shadow of her former self.* **7** an inseparable attendant or companion. **8** a person secretly following and observing another. **9** (before another noun) Brit. denoting the opposition counterpart of a government minister. ● verb **1** cast a shadow over. **2** follow and observe secretly. **3** accompany (a worker) in their daily activities for experience of or insight into a job.
– DERIVATIVES **shadower** noun **shadowless** adjective.
– ORIGIN Old English.
shadow-box ● verb spar with an imaginary opponent as a form of training.
shadowland ● noun literary **1** a place in shadow. **2** an indeterminate borderland between places or states.
shadowy ● adjective (**shadowier**, **shadowiest**) **1** full of shadows. **2** of uncertain identity or nature.
– DERIVATIVES **shadowiness** noun.
shady ● adjective (**shadier**, **shadiest**) **1** situated in or full of shade. **2** giving shade. **3** informal of doubtful honesty or legality.
– DERIVATIVES **shadiness** noun.
shaft ● noun **1** a long, narrow part forming the handle of a tool or club, the body of a spear or arrow, or similar. **2** a ray of light or bolt of lightning. **3** a long, narrow, typically vertical hole giving access to a mine, accommodating a lift, etc. **4** each of the pair of poles between which a horse is harnessed to a vehicle. **5** a long cylindrical rotating rod for the transmission of motive power in a machine. **6** a column, especially the part between the base and capital. **7** a sudden flash of a quality or feeling. **8** a witty, wounding, or provoking remark. ● verb **1** (of light) shine in beams. **2** informal treat harshly or unfairly. **3** vulgar slang (of a man) have sexual intercourse with.
– DERIVATIVES **shafted** adjective.
– ORIGIN Old English.
shag[1] ● noun **1** a carpet or rug with a long, rough pile. **2** (before another noun) (of pile) long and rough. **3** a thick, tangled hairstyle. **4** coarse cut tobacco.
– ORIGIN Old English.
shag[2] ● noun a cormorant with greenish-black plumage and a long curly crest in the breeding season.
– ORIGIN perhaps from SHAG[1], with reference to the bird's 'shaggy' crest.
shag[3] Brit. vulgar slang ● verb (**shagged**, **shagging**) have sexual intercourse with. ● noun an act of sexual intercourse.
– DERIVATIVES **shagger** noun.
– ORIGIN of unknown origin.
shag[4] ● noun a dance originating in the US, characterized by

Thesaurus

salubrious, squalid, sordid; *informal* crummy, scuzzy, shambly; *Brit. informal* grotty; *N. Amer. informal* shacky. **2** *a shabby grey coat* SCRUFFY, old, worn out, threadbare, moth-eaten, mangy, ragged, frayed, tattered, battered, faded; *informal* tatty, ratty, the worse for wear; *N. Amer. informal* raggedy. **3** *her shabby treatment of Ben* CONTEMPTIBLE, despicable, dishonourable, discreditable, mean, low, dirty, hateful, shameful, sorry, ignoble, unfair, unworthy, unkind, shoddy, nasty; *informal* rotten, low-down; *Brit. informal* beastly.
– OPPOSITES smart, honourable.
shack ● noun HUT, shanty, cabin, lean-to, shed; hovel; *Scottish* bothy, shieling.
– PHRASES **shack up with** *(informal)* COHABIT, live with; *informal, dated* live in sin.
shackle ● verb **1** *he was shackled to the wall* CHAIN, fetter, manacle; secure, tie (up), bind, tether, hobble; put in chains, clap in irons, handcuff. **2** *journalists were shackled by a new law* RESTRAIN, restrict, limit, constrain, handicap, hamstring, hamper, hinder, impede, obstruct, inhibit, check, curb.
shackles ● plural noun **1** *the men filed through their shackles* CHAINS, fetters, irons, leg-irons, manacles, handcuffs; bonds; *informal* cuffs, bracelets. **2** *the shackles of bureaucracy* RESTRICTIONS, restraints, constraints, impediments, hindrances, obstacles, barriers, obstructions, checks, curbs; *poetic/literary* trammels.
shade ● noun **1** *they sat in the shade* SHADOW(S), shadiness, shelter, cover; cool. **2** *shades of blue* COLOUR, hue, tone, tint, tinge. **3** *shades of meaning* NUANCE, gradation, degree, difference, variation, variety; nicety, subtlety; undertone, overtone. **4** *her skirt was a shade too short* A LITTLE, a bit, a trace, a touch, a modicum, a tinge; slightly, rather, somewhat; *informal* a tad, a smidgen. **5** *the window shade* BLIND, curtain, screen, cover, covering; awning, canopy. **6** *(informal) he was wearing shades* SUNGLASSES, dark glasses; *Austral. informal* sunnies.
– OPPOSITES light.
● verb **1** *vines shaded the garden* CAST A SHADOW OVER, shadow, shelter, cover, screen; darken. **2** *she shaded in the picture* DARKEN, colour in, pencil in, block in, fill in; cross-hatch. **3** *the sky shaded from turquoise to blue* CHANGE, transmute, turn, go; merge, blend.
– PHRASES **put someone/something in the shade** SURPASS, outshine, outclass, overshadow, eclipse, transcend, cap, top, outstrip, outdo, put to shame, beat, outperform, upstage; *informal* run rings around, be a cut above, leave standing. **shades of** ECHOES OF, a reminder of, memories of, suggestions of, hints of.
shadow ● noun **1** *he saw her shadow in the doorway* SILHOUETTE, outline, shape, contour, profile. **2** *he emerged from the shadows* SHADE, darkness, twilight; gloom, murkiness; *archaic* umbrage. **3** *the shadow of war* (BLACK) CLOUD, pall; gloom, blight; threat. **4** *she knew without any shadow of doubt* TRACE, scrap, shred, crumb, iota, scintilla, jot, whit, grain; *informal* smidgen, smidge, tad. **5** *a shadow of a smile* TRACE, hint, suggestion, suspicion, ghost, glimmer. **6** *he's a shadow of his former self* INFERIOR VERSION, poor imitation, apology, travesty; remnant. **7** *the dog became her shadow* CONSTANT COMPANION, alter ego, second self; close friend, bosom friend, fidus Achates; *informal* Siamese twin.
● verb **1** *the market is shadowed by the church* OVERSHADOW, shade; darken, dim. **2** *he is shadowing a poacher* FOLLOW, trail, track, stalk, pursue, hunt; *informal* tail, keep tabs on.
shadowy ● adjective **1** *a shadowy corridor* DARK, dim, gloomy, murky, crepuscular, shady, shaded; *poetic/literary* tenebrous. **2** *a shadowy figure* INDISTINCT, hazy, indefinite, vague, nebulous, ill-defined, faint, blurred, blurry, unclear, indistinguishable, unrecognizable; ghostly, spectral, wraithlike.
– OPPOSITES bright, clear.
shady ● adjective **1** *a shady garden* SHADED, shadowy, dim, dark; sheltered, screened, shrouded; leafy; *poetic/literary* bosky, tenebrous. **2** *(informal) shady deals* SUSPICIOUS, suspect, questionable, dubious, doubtful, disreputable, untrustworthy, dishonest, dishonourable, devious, underhand, unscrupulous, irregular, unethical; *N. Amer.* snide; *informal* fishy, murky; *Brit. informal* dodgy; *Austral./NZ informal* shonky.
– OPPOSITES bright, honest.
shaft ● noun **1** *the shaft of a golf club* POLE, shank, stick, rod, staff; handle, hilt, stem. **2** *the shaft of a feather* QUILL; *Ornithology* rachis. **3** *shafts of sunlight* RAY, beam, gleam, streak, finger. **4** *he directs his shafts against her* CUTTING REMARK, barb, gibe, taunt; *informal* dig.

S

vigorous hopping from one foot to the other.
– ORIGIN perhaps from obsolete *shag* 'waggle'.

shagged ● adjective Brit. vulgar slang **1** exhausted. **2** damaged or ruined.

shaggy ● adjective (**shaggier**, **shaggiest**) **1** (of hair or fur) long, thick, and unkempt. **2** having shaggy hair or fur.
– PHRASES **shaggy-dog story** a long, rambling story or joke, amusing only because it is absurdly inconsequential.
– DERIVATIVES **shaggily** adverb **shagginess** noun.

shagreen /shagreen/ ● noun **1** sharkskin used for decoration or as an abrasive. **2** untanned leather with a rough granulated surface.
– ORIGIN variant of CHAGRIN in the literal sense 'rough skin'.

shah /shaa/ ● noun historical a title of the former monarch of Iran.
– ORIGIN Persian, 'king'.

shake ● verb (past **shook**; past part. **shaken**) **1** move quickly and jerkily up and down or to and fro. **2** tremble uncontrollably with strong emotion. **3** make a threatening gesture with: *he shook his fist*. **4** remove or dislodge by shaking. **5** shock or astonish. **6** weaken (confidence, a belief, etc.). **7** get rid of or put an end to: *old habits he couldn't shake off*. ● noun **1** an act of shaking. **2** an amount sprinkled from a container. **3** informal a milkshake. **4** (**the shakes**) informal a fit of trembling or shivering.
– PHRASES **in two shakes (of a lamb's tail)** informal very quickly. **no great shakes** informal not very good. **shake down 1** settle down. **2** N. Amer. informal extort money from. **shake the dust off one's feet** leave indignantly or disdainfully. **shake hands (with someone)** clasp someone's right hand in one's own at meeting or parting, in reconciliation or congratulation, or as a sign of agreement. **shake a leg** informal make a start; rouse oneself. **shake on** informal confirm (an agreement) by shaking hands. **shake up 1** rouse from lethargy or apathy. **2** make radical changes to (an institution or system).
– ORIGIN Old English.

shakedown ● noun informal, chiefly N. Amer. **1** a radical change or restructuring. **2** a thorough search. **3** a swindle. **4** a makeshift bed.

shaker ● noun **1** a container used for mixing ingredients by shaking. **2** a container with a pierced top from which a powder is poured by shaking. **3** (**Shaker**) a member of an American Christian sect living simply in celibate mixed communities. [ORIGIN so named from the wild, ecstatic movements engaged in during worship.] **4** (**Shaker**) (before another noun) denoting a style of elegantly functional furniture traditionally produced by Shakers.
– DERIVATIVES **Shakerism** noun.

Shakespearean /shaykspeeriən/ (also **Shakespearian**) ● adjective relating to or in the style of William Shakespeare or his works. ● noun an expert in or student of Shakespeare's works.

shake-up (also **shake-out**) ● noun informal a radical reorganization.

shako /shaykō/ ● noun (pl. **shakos**) a peaked cylindrical military hat with a plume or pompom.
– ORIGIN Hungarian *csákó (süveg)* 'peaked (cap)'.

Shakti /shuktee/ (also **Sakti**) ● noun Hinduism the female principle of divine energy.
– ORIGIN Sanskrit.

shaky ● adjective (**shakier**, **shakiest**) **1** shaking or trembling. **2** unstable. **3** not safe or reliable.
– DERIVATIVES **shakily** adverb **shakiness** noun.

shale ● noun soft stratified sedimentary rock formed from consolidated mud or clay.
– DERIVATIVES **shaly** (also **shaley**) adjective.
– ORIGIN probably from German *Schale*.

shall ● modal verb (3rd sing. present **shall**) **1** (in the first person) expressing the future tense. **2** expressing a strong assertion or intention. **3** expressing an instruction or command. **4** used in questions indicating offers or suggestions.
– USAGE Strictly speaking **shall** should be used with **I** and **we** to form the future tense, as in *I shall be late*, while **will** should be used with **you**, **he**, **she**, **it**, and **they**, as in *she will not be there*. This, however, is reversed when strong determination is being expressed, as in *I will not tolerate this*, and *you shall go to school*. In speech the distinction tends to be obscured, through the use of the contracted forms **I'll**, **she'll**, etc.
– ORIGIN Old English, from a base meaning 'owe'.

shallot /shəlot/ ● noun the small bulb of a plant of the onion family, used in cookery and pickling.
– ORIGIN French *eschalotte*, alteration of Old French *eschaloigne*, *scaloun* 'scallion'.

shallow ● adjective **1** of little depth. **2** not showing, requiring, or capable of serious thought. ● noun (**shallows**) a shallow area of water.
– DERIVATIVES **shallowly** adverb **shallowness** noun.
– ORIGIN related to SHOAL².

shalom /shəlom/ ● exclamation used as salutation by Jews at meeting or parting.
– ORIGIN Hebrew, 'peace'.

shalt archaic second person singular of SHALL.

shalwar /shulwaar/ ● noun variant spelling of SALWAR.

sham ● noun **1** a person or thing that is not what they are claimed to be. **2** pretence. ● adjective pretended; not genuine. ● verb (**shammed**, **shamming**) pretend or pretend to be.
– DERIVATIVES **shammer** noun.
– ORIGIN perhaps a northern English dialect variant of SHAME.

Thesaurus

5 *a ventilation shaft* MINESHAFT, tunnel, passage, pit, adit, downcast, upcast; borehole, bore; duct, well, flue, vent.

shaggy ● adjective HAIRY, bushy, thick, woolly, hirsute; tangled, tousled, unkempt, dishevelled, untidy, matted.
– OPPOSITES sleek.

shake ● verb **1** *the whole building shook* VIBRATE, tremble, quiver, quake, shiver, shudder, judder, jiggle, wobble, rock, sway; convulse. **2** *she shook the bottle* JIGGLE, joggle, agitate, waggle. **3** *he shook his stick at them* BRANDISH, wave, flourish, swing, wield; *informal* waggle. **4** *the look in his eyes really shook her* UPSET, distress, disturb, unsettle, disconcert, discompose, disquiet, unnerve, trouble, throw off balance, agitate, fluster; shock, alarm, frighten, scare, worry; *informal* rattle. **5** *this will shake their confidence* WEAKEN, undermine, damage, impair, harm; reduce, diminish, decrease.
– OPPOSITES soothe, strengthen.
● noun **1** *he gave his coat a shake* JIGGLE, joggle; *informal* waggle. **2** *a shake of his fist* FLOURISH, brandish, wave. **3** *it gives me the shakes* TREMORS, delirium tremens; *informal* DTs, jitters, willies, heebie-jeebies, yips; *Austral. informal* Joe Blakes.
– PHRASES **in two shakes (of a lamb's tail)** *(informal)*. See IN A MOMENT at MOMENT. **no great shakes** *(informal)* NOT VERY GOOD, unexceptional, unmemorable, forgettable, uninspired, uninteresting, indifferent, unimpressive, lacklustre; *informal* nothing to write home about, nothing special, not up to much. **shake a leg** *(informal)*. See HURRY verb sense 1. **shake someone off** GET AWAY FROM, escape, elude, dodge, lose, leave behind, get rid of, give someone the slip, throw off the scent; *Brit. informal* get shot of. **shake something off** RECOVER FROM, get over; get rid of, free oneself from; *Brit. informal* get shot of; *N. Amer. informal* shuck off. **shake someone/something up 1** *the accident shook him up*. See SHAKE verb sense 4. **2** *plans to shake up the legal profession* REORGANIZE, restructure, revolutionize, alter, change, transform, reform, overhaul.

shake-up ● noun *(informal)* REORGANIZATION, restructuring, reshuffle, change, overhaul, makeover; upheaval; *N. Amer. informal* shakedown.

shaky ● adjective **1** *shaky legs* TREMBLING, shaking, tremulous, quivering, quivery, unsteady, wobbly, weak; tottering, tottery, teetering, doddery; *informal* trembly. **2** *I feel a bit shaky* FAINT, dizzy, light-headed, giddy; weak, wobbly, quivery, groggy, muzzy; *informal* trembly, woozy. **3** *a shaky table* UNSTEADY, unstable, wobbly, precarious, rocky, rickety, ramshackle; *Brit. informal* wonky. **4** *the evidence is shaky* UNRELIABLE, untrustworthy, questionable, dubious, doubtful, tenuous, suspect, flimsy, weak, unsound, unsupported, unsubstantiated, unfounded; *informal* iffy; *Brit. informal* dodgy.
– OPPOSITES steady, stable, sound.

shallow ● adjective SUPERFICIAL, facile, simplistic, oversimplified; flimsy, insubstantial, lightweight, empty, trivial, trifling; surface, skin-deep; frivolous, foolish, silly.
– OPPOSITES profound.

sham ● noun **1** *his tenderness had been a sham* PRETENCE, fake, act, fiction, simulation, fraud, feint, lie, counterfeit; humbug. **2** *the doctor was a sham* CHARLATAN, fake, fraud, impostor, pretender; quack, mountebank; *informal* phoney.
● adjective *sham togetherness* FAKE, pretended, feigned, simulated, false, artificial, bogus, insincere, contrived, affected, make-believe, fictitious; imitation, mock, counterfeit, fraudulent; *informal* pretend, put-on, phoney, pseudo; *Brit. informal* cod.

shaman /shaymən, shammən/ • noun (pl. **shamans**) (especially among some peoples of northern Asia and North America) a person regarded as having access to, and influence in, the world of good and evil spirits.
– DERIVATIVES **shamanic** /shəmannik/ adjective **shamanism** noun **shamanistic** adjective.
– ORIGIN Tungus (a language of Siberia).

shamateur • noun derogatory a sports player who makes money from sporting activities though classified as amateur.
– ORIGIN blend of SHAM and AMATEUR.

shamble • verb move with a slow, shuffling, awkward gait. • noun a shambling gait.
– ORIGIN probably from dialect *shamble* 'ungainly', perhaps from *shamble legs*, with reference to the legs of trestle tables typical of meat markets (see SHAMBLES).

shambles • noun **1** informal a state of complete disorder. **2** archaic a butcher's slaughterhouse.
– ORIGIN originally in the sense 'meat market': plural of earlier *shamble* 'stool, stall', from Latin *scamellum* 'little bench'.

shambolic • adjective informal, chiefly Brit. chaotic or disorganized.
– ORIGIN from SHAMBLES, probably on the pattern of *symbolic*.

shame • noun **1** a feeling of humiliation or distress caused by awareness of wrong or foolish behaviour. **2** loss or respect or esteem. **3** a cause of shame. **4** a regrettable or unfortunate thing. • verb cause to feel ashamed.
– PHRASES **put to shame** shame (someone) by outdoing or surpassing them. **shame on you!** you should be ashamed.
– ORIGIN Old English.

shamefaced • adjective showing shame.
– DERIVATIVES **shamefacedly** adverb **shamefacedness** noun.

shameful • adjective worthy of or causing shame.
– DERIVATIVES **shamefully** adverb **shamefulness** noun.

shameless • adjective showing a lack of shame.
– DERIVATIVES **shamelessly** adverb **shamelessness** noun.

shammy (also **shammy leather**) • noun (pl. **shammies**) informal chamois leather.
– ORIGIN a phonetic spelling.

shampoo • noun **1** a liquid preparation for washing the hair. **2** a similar substance for cleaning a carpet, car, etc. **3** an act of washing with shampoo. • verb (**shampoos**, **shampooed**) wash or clean with shampoo.
– ORIGIN originally in the sense 'massage': from a Hindi word meaning 'to press'.

shamrock • noun a clover-like plant with three-lobed leaves, the national emblem of Ireland.
– ORIGIN Irish *seamróg* 'trefoil'.

shamus /shayməss/ • noun N. Amer. informal a private detective.
– ORIGIN of unknown origin.

shandy • noun (pl. **shandies**) beer mixed with lemonade or ginger beer.
– ORIGIN abbreviation of *shandygaff*, of unknown origin.

shanghai[1] /shanghī/ • verb (**shanghais**, **shanghaied**, **shanghaiing**) **1** historical force to join a ship's crew by underhand means. **2** informal coerce or trick into doing something.
– ORIGIN from *Shanghai*, a major Chinese seaport.

shanghai[2] /shanghī/ Austral./NZ • noun (pl. **shanghais**) a catapult. • verb (**shanghais**, **shanghaied**, **shanghaiing**) shoot with or as with a catapult.
– ORIGIN probably an alteration of Scots dialect *shangan* 'a stick cleft at one end'.

Shangri-La /shanggrilaa/ • noun an earthly paradise.
– ORIGIN named after a Tibetan utopia in James Hilton's *Lost Horizon* (1933), from *Shangri* (an invented name) + Tibetan *la* 'mountain pass'.

shank • noun **1** a person's leg, especially the lower part. **2** the lower part of an animal's foreleg, especially as a cut of meat. **3** the shaft or stem of a tool or implement. **4** the band of a ring.
– DERIVATIVES **shanked** adjective.
– ORIGIN Old English.

Shanks's pony (also **Shanks's mare**) • noun one's own legs as a means of conveyance.

shan't • contraction shall not.

shantung /shantung/ • noun a type of soft silk with a coarse surface.
– ORIGIN from *Shantung* in China, where it was originally made.

shanty[1] • noun (pl. **shanties**) a small, crudely built shack.
– ORIGIN perhaps from Canadian French *chantier* 'lumberjack's cabin, logging camp'.

shanty[2] (also **chanty** or **sea shanty**) • noun (pl. **shanties**) a song with alternating solo and chorus, of a kind originally sung by sailors working together.
– ORIGIN probably from French *chantez!* 'sing!'.

shanty town • noun an impoverished area consisting of large numbers of shanty dwellings.

shape • noun **1** the external form or appearance of someone or something as produced by their outline. **2** a piece of material, paper, etc., made or cut in a particular form. **3** a particular condition or state: *the house was in poor shape*. **4** a specific form or guise assumed by someone or something: *a fiend in human shape*. **5** definite or orderly arrangement. • verb **1** give a shape or form to. **2** determine the nature of. **3** (often **shape up**) develop in a particular way. **4** (**shape up**) become physically fit. **5** (**shape up**) informal improve (something).
– PHRASES **in (good) shape** in good physical condition. **in the shape of** by way of. **lick** (or **knock**) **into shape** act forcefully to bring into a better state. **out of shape 1** not having its usual or original shape. **2** in poor physical condition. **take shape** assume a distinct form.
– DERIVATIVES **shaped** adjective **shaper** noun.
– ORIGIN Old English.

Thesaurus

– OPPOSITES genuine.
• verb **1** *she shams indifference* FEIGN, fake, pretend, put on, simulate, affect. **2** *was he ill or just shamming?* PRETEND, fake, dissemble; malinger; *informal* put it on; *Brit. informal* swing the lead.

shaman • noun WITCH DOCTOR, medicine man/woman, healer, kahuna.

shamble • verb SHUFFLE, drag one's feet, lumber, totter, dodder; hobble, limp.

shambles • plural noun **1** *we have to sort out this shambles* CHAOS, mess, muddle, confusion, disorder, havoc, mare's nest; *Brit. informal* dog's dinner/breakfast. **2** *the room was a shambles* MESS, pigsty; *informal* disaster area; *Brit. informal* tip.

shambolic • adjective *(Brit. informal)*. See CHAOTIC.

shame • noun **1** *her face was scarlet with shame* HUMILIATION, mortification, chagrin, ignominy, embarrassment, indignity, abashment, discomfort. **2** *I felt shame at telling a lie* GUILT, remorse, contrition, compunction. **3** *he brought shame on the family* DISGRACE, dishonour, discredit, degradation, ignominy, disrepute, infamy, scandal, opprobrium, contempt; *dated* disesteem. **4** *it's a shame she never married* PITY, misfortune, sad thing; bad luck; *informal* bummer, crime, sin.
– OPPOSITES pride, honour.
• verb **1** *you shamed your family's name* DISGRACE, dishonour, discredit, degrade, debase; stigmatize, taint, sully, tarnish, besmirch, blacken, drag through the mud. **2** *he was shamed in public* HUMILIATE, mortify, chagrin, embarrass, abash, chasten, humble, take down a peg or two, cut down to size; *informal* show up; *N. Amer. informal* make someone eat crow.
– OPPOSITES honour.
– PHRASES **put someone/something to shame** OUTSHINE, outclass, eclipse, surpass, excel, outstrip, outdo, put in the shade, upstage; *informal* run rings around, leave standing; *Brit. informal* knock spots off.

shamefaced • adjective ASHAMED, abashed, sheepish, guilty, conscience-stricken, guilt-ridden, contrite, sorry, remorseful, repentant, penitent, regretful, rueful, apologetic; embarrassed, mortified, red-faced, chagrined, humiliated; *informal* with one's tail between one's legs.
– OPPOSITES unrepentant.

shameful • adjective **1** *shameful behaviour* DISGRACEFUL, deplorable, despicable, contemptible, dishonourable, discreditable, reprehensible, low, unworthy, ignoble, shabby; shocking, scandalous, outrageous, abominable, atrocious, appalling, vile, odious, heinous, egregious, loathsome, bad; inexcusable, unforgivable; *informal* low-down, hateful. **2** *a shameful secret* EMBARRASSING, mortifying, humiliating, degrading, ignominious.
– OPPOSITES admirable.

shameless • adjective FLAGRANT, blatant, barefaced, overt, brazen, brash, audacious, outrageous, undisguised, unconcealed, transparent; immodest, indecorous; unabashed, unashamed, unblushing, unrepentant.
– OPPOSITES modest.

shanty • noun SHACK, hut, cabin, lean-to, shed; hovel; *Scottish* bothy, shieling.

shapeless ● adjective lacking definite or attractive shape.
– DERIVATIVES **shapelessly** adverb **shapelessness** noun.
shapely ● adjective (**shapelier**, **shapeliest**) having an attractive or well-proportioned shape.
– DERIVATIVES **shapeliness** noun.
shape-shifter ● noun an imaginary being who is able to change their physical form at will.
shard ● noun a sharp piece of broken ceramic, metal, glass, etc.
– ORIGIN Old English, 'gap, notch, potsherd'; related to SHEAR.
share¹ ● noun **1** a part of a larger amount which is divided among or contributed by a number of people. **2** any of the equal parts into which a company's capital is divided, entitling the holder to a proportion of the profits. **3** the allotted or due amount expected to be had or done: *more than their fair share of problems.* **4** a person's contribution to an enterprise. ● verb **1** have or give a share of. **2** possess or use in common with others. **3** (**share in**) participate in. **4** tell someone about.
– DERIVATIVES **shareable** (also **sharable**) adjective **sharer** noun.
– ORIGIN Old English, related to SHEAR.
share² ● noun a ploughshare.
sharecropper ● noun chiefly N. Amer. a tenant farmer who gives a part of each crop as rent.
shareholder ● noun an owner of shares in a company.
– DERIVATIVES **shareholding** noun.
share option ● noun an option for an employee to buy shares in their company at a discount or at a stated fixed price.
shareware ● noun computer software that is available free of charge and often distributed informally for evaluation.
sharia /shəreeə/ ● noun Islamic canonical law based on the teachings of the Koran and the traditions of Muhammad.
– ORIGIN Arabic.
shark¹ ● noun a long-bodied cartilaginous marine fish, typically predatory and voracious, with a prominent dorsal fin.
– ORIGIN of unknown origin.
shark² ● noun informal a person who exploits or swindles others.
– ORIGIN perhaps from German *Schurke* 'worthless rogue', influenced by SHARK¹.
sharkskin ● noun a stiff, slightly lustrous synthetic fabric.
sharon fruit /sharrən/ ● noun a persimmon, especially one of an orange variety grown in Israel.
– ORIGIN from *Sharon*, a fertile coastal plain in Israel.
sharp ● adjective **1** having a cutting or piercing edge or point. **2** tapering to a point or edge. **3** sudden and marked: *a sharp increase.* **4** making a sudden change of direction. **5** clearly defined. **6** producing a sudden, piercing sensation or effect: *a sharp pain.* **7** quick to understand, notice, or respond. **8** quick to take advantage, especially in a dishonest way. **9** (of a food, taste, or smell) acidic and intense. **10** (of a sound) sudden and penetrating. **11** critical or hurtful. **12** informal smart and stylish. **13** (of musical sound) above true or normal pitch. **14** (after a noun) (of a note or key) higher by a semitone than a specified note or key. ● adverb **1** precisely: *at 7.30 sharp.* **2** suddenly or abruptly. **3** above the true or normal pitch of musical sound. ● noun **1** a musical note raised a semitone above natural pitch. **2** the sign (♯) indicating this. **3** a thing with a sharp edge or point.
– DERIVATIVES **sharply** adverb **sharpness** noun.
– ORIGIN Old English.
sharpen ● verb make or become sharp.
– DERIVATIVES **sharpener** noun.
sharper ● noun informal a swindler, especially at cards.
sharpish informal ● adjective fairly sharp. ● adverb chiefly Brit. quickly; soon.
sharp practice ● noun dishonest or barely honest dealings.
sharpshooter ● noun a person skilled in shooting.
sharp-tongued ● adjective given to using harsh or critical language.
sharp-witted ● adjective perceptive or intelligent.
shashlik /shashlik/ ● noun (pl. same or **shashliks**) (in Asia and eastern Europe) a mutton kebab.
– ORIGIN Russian *shashlyk*, from Turkish *şiş* 'spit, skewer'.
shat past and past participle of SHIT.
shatter ● verb **1** break suddenly and violently into pieces. **2** damage or destroy. **3** upset greatly. **4** (**shattered**) informal completely exhausted.
– DERIVATIVES **shatterer** noun.
– ORIGIN perhaps imitative.
shave ● verb **1** cut the hair off one's face with a razor. **2** cut the

Thesaurus

shape ● noun **1** *the shape of the dining table* FORM, appearance, configuration, formation, structure; figure, build, physique, body; contours, lines, outline, silhouette, profile. **2** *a spirit in the shape of a fox* GUISE, likeness, semblance, form, appearance, image. **3** *you're in pretty good shape* CONDITION, health, trim, fettle, order; Brit. informal nick.
– RELATED TERMS morpho-.
● verb **1** *the metal is shaped into tools* FORM, fashion, make, mould, model, cast; sculpt, sculpture, carve, cut, whittle. **2** *attitudes were shaped by his report* DETERMINE, form, fashion, mould, define, develop; influence, affect.
– PHRASES **shape up 1** *her work is shaping up nicely* IMPROVE, get better, progress, show promise; develop, take shape, come on, come along. **2** *a regime to help you shape up* GET FIT, get into shape, tone up; slim, lose weight. **take shape** BECOME CLEAR, become definite, become tangible, crystallize, come together, fall into place.
shapeless ● adjective **1** *shapeless lumps* FORMLESS, amorphous, unformed, indefinite. **2** *a shapeless dress* BAGGY, saggy, ill-fitting, sack-like, oversized, unshapely, formless.
shapely ● adjective WELL PROPORTIONED, clean-limbed, curvaceous, voluptuous, full-figured, Junoesque; attractive, sexy; informal curvy; archaic comely.
shard ● noun FRAGMENT, sliver, splinter, shiver, chip, piece, bit, particle.
share ● noun *her share of the profits* PORTION, part, division, quota, quantum, allowance, ration, allocation, measure, due; percentage, commission, dividend; helping, serving; informal cut, slice, rake-off; Brit. informal whack, divvy.
● verb **1** *we share the bills* SPLIT, divide, go halves on; informal go fifty-fifty, go Dutch. **2** *they shared out the peanuts* APPORTION, divide up, allocate, portion out, ration out, parcel out, measure out; carve up; Brit. informal divvy up. **3** *we all share in the learning process* PARTICIPATE IN, take part in, play a part in, be involved in, contribute to, have a hand in, partake in.
sharp ● adjective **1** *a sharp knife* KEEN, razor-edged; sharpened, honed. **2** *a sharp pain* EXCRUCIATING, agonizing, intense, stabbing, shooting, severe, acute, keen, fierce, searing; exquisite. **3** *a sharp taste* TANGY, piquant, strong; ACIDIC, acid, sour, tart, pungent, acrid, bitter, acidulous. **4** *a sharp cry of pain* LOUD, piercing, shrill, high-pitched, penetrating, harsh, strident, ear-splitting, deafening. **5** *a sharp wind* COLD, chilly, chill, brisk, keen, penetrating, biting, icy, bitter, freezing, raw; informal nippy; Brit. informal parky. **6** *sharp words* HARSH, bitter, cutting, scathing, caustic, barbed, trenchant, acrimonious, acerbic, sarcastic, sardonic, spiteful, venomous, malicious, vitriolic, vicious, hurtful, nasty, cruel, abrasive; informal bitchy, catty. **7** *a sharp sense of loss* INTENSE, acute, keen, strong, bitter, fierce, heartfelt, overwhelming. **8** *her nose is sharp* POINTED, tapering, tapered; spiky; informal pointy. **9** *the lens brings it into sharp focus* DISTINCT, clear, crisp; stark, obvious, marked, definite, pronounced. **10** *a sharp increase* SUDDEN, abrupt, rapid; steep, precipitous. **11** *a sharp corner* HAIRPIN, tight. **12** *a sharp drop* STEEP, sheer, abrupt, precipitous, vertical. **13** *sharp eyes* KEEN, perceptive, observant, acute, beady, hawklike. **14** *she was sharp and witty* PERCEPTIVE, percipient, perspicacious, incisive, sensitive, keen, acute, quick-witted, clever, shrewd, canny, astute, intelligent, intuitive, bright, alert, smart, quick off the mark, insightful, knowing; informal on the ball, quick on the uptake, savvy; Brit. informal suss; Scottish & N. English informal pawky; N. Amer. informal heads-up. **15** (informal) *a sharp suit* SMART, stylish, fashionable, chic, modish, elegant; informal trendy, cool, snazzy, classy, flash, snappy, natty, nifty; N. Amer. informal fly, spiffy.
– OPPOSITES blunt, mild, sweet, soft, kind, rounded, indistinct, gradual, slow, weak, stupid, naive, untidy.
● adverb **1** *nine o'clock sharp* PRECISELY, exactly, on the dot; promptly, prompt, punctually, dead on; informal on the nose; N. Amer. informal on the button. **2** *the recession pulled people up sharp* ABRUPTLY, suddenly, sharply, unexpectedly.
– OPPOSITES roughly.
sharpen ● verb **1** *sharpen the carving knife* HONE, whet, strop, grind, file. **2** *the players are sharpening up their skills* IMPROVE, brush up, polish up, better, enhance; hone, fine-tune, perfect.
sharp-eyed ● adjective OBSERVANT, perceptive, eagle-eyed, hawk-eyed, keen-eyed, gimlet-eyed; watchful, vigilant, alert, on the lookout; informal beady-eyed.
shatter ● verb **1** *the glasses shattered* SMASH, break, splinter,

S

hair off (part of the body) with a razor. **3** cut (a thin slice or slices) off something. **4** reduce by a small amount. **5** pass or send something very close to. ● **noun 1** an act of shaving. **2** a tool for shaving very thin slices or layers from wood.
– ORIGIN Old English.
shaven ● **adjective** shaved.
shaver ● **noun 1** an electric razor. **2** informal, dated a young lad.
Shavian /shayviən/ ● **adjective** relating to or in the style of the Irish dramatist George Bernard Shaw (1856–1950) or his works or ideas. ● **noun** an admirer of Shaw or his work.
– ORIGIN from *Shavius*, the Latinized form of *Shaw*.
shaving ● **noun 1** a thin strip cut off a surface. **2** (before another noun) used when shaving: *shaving foam.*
shawl ● **noun** a large piece of fabric worn by women over the shoulders or head or wrapped round a baby.
– DERIVATIVES **shawled** adjective.
– ORIGIN Urdu and Persian, probably from *Shāliāt*, a town in India.
shawl collar ● **noun** a rounded collar without lapel notches that extends down the front of a garment.
shawm /shawm/ ● **noun** a medieval and Renaissance wind instrument, forerunner of the oboe, with a double reed in a wooden mouthpiece.
– ORIGIN Old French *chalemel*, from Greek *kalamos* 'reed'.
Shawnee /shawnee/ ● **noun** (pl. same or **Shawnees**) a member of an American Indian people formerly living in the eastern US.
– ORIGIN the name in Delaware.
shaykh ● **noun** variant spelling of SHEIKH.
she ● **pronoun** (third person sing.) **1** used to refer to a woman, girl, or female animal previously mentioned or easily identified. **2** used to refer to a ship, country, or other inanimate thing regarded as female. **3** any female person (in modern use, now largely replaced by 'anyone' or 'the person'). **4** Austral./NZ informal it; the state of affairs. ● **noun** a female; a woman.
– ORIGIN Old English.
sheaf ● **noun** (pl. **sheaves**) **1** a bundle of grain stalks laid lengthways and tied together after reaping. **2** a bundle of objects, especially papers. ● **verb** bundle into sheaves.
– ORIGIN Old English, related to SHOVE.
shear ● **verb** (past part. **shorn** or **sheared**) **1** cut the wool off (a sheep or other animal). **2** cut off with scissors or shears. **3** (**be shorn of**) be deprived or stripped of. **4** break off or cause to break off, owing to a structural strain. ● **noun** a strain produced by pressure in the structure of a substance, when its layers are laterally shifted in relation to each other.
– DERIVATIVES **shearer** noun.
– ORIGIN Old English, from a base meaning 'divide, shear, shave'.
shears (also **a pair of shears**) ● **plural noun** a cutting instrument in which two blades move past each other, like very large scissors.
shearwater ● **noun** a long-winged seabird related to the petrels, often flying low over the water.
sheath ● **noun** (pl. **sheaths** /sheethz, sheeths/) **1** a cover for the blade of a knife or sword. **2** a condom. **3** a structure in living tissue which closely envelops another. **4** a protective covering around an electric cable. **5** (also **sheath dress**) a close-fitting dress.
– ORIGIN Old English, related to SHED².
sheathe /sheeth/ ● **verb 1** put (a knife or sword) into a sheath. **2** (often **be sheathed in**) encase in a close-fitting or protective covering.
sheathing /sheething/ ● **noun** protective casing or covering.
sheath knife ● **noun** a short knife similar to a dagger, carried in a sheath.
sheave¹ ● **verb** make into sheaves.
sheave² ● **noun** a wheel with a groove for a rope to run on, as in a pulley block.
– ORIGIN Germanic.
sheaves plural of SHEAF.
shebang /shibang/ ● **noun** informal a matter, operation, or situation: *the whole shebang.*
– ORIGIN originally US, in the sense 'a rough hut or shelter'; of unknown origin.
shebeen /shibeen/ ● **noun** (especially in Ireland, Scotland, and South Africa) an unlicensed establishment or private house selling alcoholic liquor.
– ORIGIN Anglo-Irish *síbín*, from *séibe* 'mugful'.
shed¹ ● **noun 1** a simple roofed structure, typically of wood and used for storage or to shelter animals. **2** a larger structure, typically with one or more sides open, for storing vehicles or machinery.
– ORIGIN apparently a variant of SHADE.
shed² ● **verb** (**shedding**; past and past part. **shed**) **1** allow (leaves, hair, skin, etc.) to fall off naturally. **2** discard; get rid of. **3** take off (clothes). **4** cast or give off (light). **5** accidentally drop or spill. **6** resist the absorption of.
– PHRASES **shed tears** cry.
– DERIVATIVES **shedder** noun.
– ORIGIN Old English, 'separate out, divide', also 'scatter'; related to SHEATH.
she'd ● **contraction** she had; she would.
she-devil ● **noun** a malicious or spiteful woman.
shedload ● **noun** Brit. informal a large amount or number.
sheen ● **noun** a soft lustre on a surface.
– DERIVATIVES **sheeny** adjective.
– ORIGIN from obsolete *sheen* 'beautiful, resplendent'; apparently related to SHINE.
sheep ● **noun** (pl. same) **1** a domesticated ruminant mammal with a thick woolly coat, kept in flocks for its wool or meat. **2** a person who is too easily influenced or led. **3** a member of a minister's congregation.
– PHRASES **make sheep's eyes at** look at in a foolishly amorous way.
– DERIVATIVES **sheeplike** adjective.
– ORIGIN Old English; sense 3 with allusion to the Gospel of Luke, chapter 15.
sheep dip ● **noun 1** a liquid preparation for cleansing sheep of parasites or preserving their wool. **2** a place where sheep are dipped in this liquid.
sheepdog ● **noun 1** a dog trained to guard and herd sheep. **2** a breed of dog suitable for this.
sheepish ● **adjective** embarrassed from shame or shyness.
– DERIVATIVES **sheepishly** adverb **sheepishness** noun.

Thesaurus

crack, fracture, fragment, disintegrate, shiver; *informal* bust. **2** *the announcement shattered their hopes* DESTROY, wreck, ruin, dash, crush, devastate, demolish, torpedo, scotch; *informal* put the kibosh on, banjax, do for, put paid to; *Brit. informal* scupper. **3** *we were shattered by the news* DEVASTATE, shock, stun, daze, traumatize, crush, distress; *informal* knock sideways; *Brit. informal* knock for six.
shattered ● **adjective 1** *he was shattered by the reviews* DEVASTATED, shocked, stunned, dazed, traumatized, crushed; heartbroken. **2** *(informal) I feel too shattered to move.* See EXHAUSTED sense 1.
– OPPOSITES thrilled.
shave ● **verb 1** *he shaved his beard* CUT OFF, snip off; crop, trim, barber. **2** *shave off excess wood* PLANE, pare, whittle, scrape. **3** *shave parmesan over the top* GRATE, shred. **4** *he shaved the MP's majority to 2,000* REDUCE, cut, lessen, decrease, pare down, shrink, slim down. **5** *his shot shaved the post* GRAZE, brush, touch, glance off, kiss.
sheaf ● **noun** BUNDLE, bunch, stack, pile, heap, mass; *Brit. informal* wodge.
sheath ● **noun 1** *put the sword in its sheath* SCABBARD, case. **2** *the wire has a plastic sheath* COVERING, cover, case, casing, envelope, sleeve, wrapper, capsule. **3** *a contraceptive sheath.* See CONDOM.
shed¹ ● **noun** *the rabbit lives in the shed* HUT, lean-to, outhouse, outbuilding; shack; potting shed, woodshed; *Brit.* lock-up.
shed² ● **verb 1** *the trees shed their leaves* DROP, scatter, spill. **2** *the caterpillar shed its skin* SLOUGH OFF, cast off, moult; *technical* exuviate. **3** *we shed our jackets* TAKE OFF, remove, shrug off, discard, doff, climb out of, slip out of, divest oneself of; *Brit. informal* peel off. **4** *much blood has been shed* SPILL, discharge. **5** *the firm is to shed ten workers* MAKE REDUNDANT, dismiss, let go, discharge, get rid of, discard; *informal* sack, fire, give someone their marching orders, send packing, give someone the push, boot out. **6** *they must shed their illusions* DISCARD, get rid of, dispose of, do away with, drop, abandon, jettison, scrap, cast aside, dump, reject, repudiate; *informal* ditch, junk, get shut of; *Brit. informal* get shot of. **7** *the moon shed a watery light* CAST, radiate, diffuse, disperse, give out.
– OPPOSITES don, hire, keep.
– PHRASES **shed tears** WEEP, cry, sob; lament, grieve, mourn; *Scottish* greet; *informal* blub, blubber, boohoo.
sheen ● **noun** SHINE, lustre, gloss, patina, shininess, burnish, polish, shimmer, brilliance, radiance.

sheepshank ● noun a knot used to shorten a rope temporarily.

sheepskin ● noun a sheep's skin with the wool on, especially when made into a garment or rug.

sheer[1] ● adjective **1** nothing but; absolute: *sheer hard work*. **2** (of a cliff, wall, etc.) perpendicular or nearly so. **3** (of a fabric) very thin. ● adverb perpendicularly.
– DERIVATIVES **sheerly** adverb **sheerness** noun.
– ORIGIN probably from dialect *shire* 'pure, clear', from the Germanic base of SHINE.

sheer[2] ● verb **1** (especially of a boat) swerve or change course quickly. **2** avoid or move away from an unpleasant topic.
– ORIGIN perhaps from Low German *scheren* 'to shear'.

sheet[1] ● noun **1** a large rectangular piece of cotton or other fabric, used on a bed to cover the mattress or as a layer beneath blankets. **2** a broad flat piece of metal or glass. **3** a rectangular piece of paper. **4** an extensive layer or moving mass of water, ice, flame, etc. ● verb **1** cover with or wrap in a sheet or sheeting. **2** (of rain) fall heavily.
– ORIGIN Old English, related to SHOOT.

sheet[2] ● noun **1** a rope attached to the lower corner of a sail. **2** (**sheets**) the space at the bow or stern of an open boat.
– PHRASES **two** (or **three**) **sheets to the wind** informal drunk.
– ORIGIN Old English, 'lower corner of a sail'; related to SHEET[1].

sheet anchor ● noun **1** an additional anchor for use in emergencies. **2** a person or thing that can be relied on if all else fails.
– ORIGIN perhaps related to obsolete *shot*, denoting two cables spliced together, later influenced by SHEET[2].

sheeting ● noun material formed into or used as a sheet.

sheet lightning ● noun lightning with its brightness diffused by reflection within clouds.

sheet metal ● noun metal formed into thin sheets.

sheet music ● noun **1** printed music, as opposed to performed or recorded music. **2** music published in single or interleaved sheets.

sheikh /shayk/ (also **shaykh** or **sheik**) ● noun **1** an Arab leader, especially the chief or head of a tribe, family, or village. **2** a leader in a Muslim community or organization.
– DERIVATIVES **sheikhdom** noun.
– ORIGIN Arabic, 'old man, sheikh'.

sheila ● noun Austral./NZ informal a girl or woman.
– ORIGIN originally as *shaler*: of unknown origin, later assimilated to the given name *Sheila*.

shekel /shekk'l/ ● noun **1** the basic monetary unit of modern Israel, equal to 100 agora. **2** (**shekels**) informal money; wealth.
– ORIGIN Hebrew.

shelduck /shelduk/ ● noun (pl. same or **shelducks**) a large goose-like duck with boldly marked plumage.
– ORIGIN probably from dialect *sheld* 'pied' (related to Dutch *schillede* 'variegated') + DUCK[1].

shelf ● noun (pl. **shelves**) **1** a flat length of wood or other rigid material attached to a wall or forming part of a piece of furniture, providing a surface for storage or display. **2** a ledge of rock or protruding strip of land.
– PHRASES **off the shelf** taken from existing stock, not designed or made to order. **on the shelf 1** no longer useful or desirable. **2** past an age when one might expect to be married.
– ORIGIN Low German *schelf*.

shelf life ● noun the length of time for which an item remains usable, edible, or saleable.

shell ● noun **1** the hard protective outer case of an animal such as a snail, shellfish, or turtle. **2** the outer covering of an egg, nut kernel, or seed. **3** an explosive artillery projectile or bomb. **4** a hollow metal or paper case used as a container for fireworks, explosives, or cartridges. **5** N. Amer. a cartridge. **6** something resembling or likened to a shell, especially a hollow case. **7** the walls of an unfinished or gutted building. **8** a light racing boat. **9** (also **shell program**) Computing a program providing an interface between the user and the operating system. ● verb **1** bombard with shells. **2** remove the shell or pod from. **3** (**shell out**) informal pay (an amount of money).
– PHRASES **come out of one's shell** cease to be shy.
– DERIVATIVES **shelled** adjective **shell-less** adjective **shell-like** adjective **shelly** adjective.
– ORIGIN Old English, related to SCALE[1].

she'll ● contraction she shall; she will.

shellac /shəlak/ ● noun lac resin melted into thin flakes, used for making varnish. ● verb (**shellacked**, **shellacking**) varnish with shellac.
– ORIGIN from SHELL + LAC[1], translating French *laque en écailles* 'lac in thin plates'.

shell company ● noun a non-trading company used as a vehicle for various financial manoeuvres.

shellfire ● noun bombardment by shells.

shellfish ● noun an aquatic shelled mollusc or crustacean, especially an edible one.

shell pink ● noun a delicate pale pink.

shell shock ● noun psychological disturbance caused by prolonged exposure to active warfare.

shell suit ● noun a casual outfit consisting of a loose jacket and trousers with a soft lining and a shiny polyester outer shell.

Shelta /sheltə/ ● noun an ancient secret language used by Irish and Welsh tinkers and gypsies, based on altered Irish or Gaelic words.
– ORIGIN of unknown origin.

shelter ● noun **1** a place giving protection from bad weather or danger. **2** a place providing food and accommodation for the homeless. **3** a shielded condition; protection. ● verb **1** provide with shelter. **2** find refuge or take cover. **3** (**sheltered**) protected from having to do or face something difficult.
– ORIGIN perhaps from obsolete *sheltron* 'phalanx', from an Old English word meaning 'shield troop'.

sheltered housing (also **sheltered accommodation**) ● noun Brit. accommodation for elderly or handicapped people consist-

Thesaurus

sheep ● noun ram, ewe, lamb, wether, bellwether, tup; *Austral. informal* jumbuck, woolly.
– RELATED TERMS ovine.

sheepish ● adjective EMBARRASSED, uncomfortable, hangdog, self-conscious; shamefaced, ashamed, abashed, mortified, chastened, remorseful, contrite, apologetic, rueful, regretful, penitent, repentant.

sheer[1] ● adjective **1** *the sheer audacity of the plan* UTTER, complete, absolute, total, pure, downright, out-and-out, arrant, thorough, thoroughgoing, patent, veritable, unmitigated, plain; *Austral./NZ informal* fair. **2** *a sheer drop* PRECIPITOUS, steep, vertical, perpendicular, abrupt, bluff, sharp. **3** *a sheer dress* DIAPHANOUS, gauzy, filmy, floaty, gossamer, thin, translucent, transparent, see-through, insubstantial.
– OPPOSITES gradual, thick.

sheer[2] ● verb **1** *the boat sheered off along the coast* SWERVE, veer, slew, skew, swing, change course. **2** *her mind sheered away from his image* TURN AWAY, flinch, recoil, shy away; avoid.

sheet ● noun **1** *she changed the sheets* BED LINEN, linen, bedclothes. **2** *a sheet of ice* LAYER, stratum, covering, blanket, coating, coat, film, skin. **3** *a sheet of glass* PANE, panel, piece, plate; slab. **4** *she put a fresh sheet in the typewriter* PIECE OF PAPER, leaf, page, folio. **5** *a sheet of water* EXPANSE, area, stretch, sweep.

shelf ● noun **1** *the plant on the shelf* LEDGE, sill, bracket, rack; mantelpiece; shelving. **2** *the waters above the shelf* SANDBANK, sandbar, bank, bar, reef, shoal.
– PHRASES **on the shelf** UNMARRIED, single, unattached; lonely, unloved, neglected.

shell ● noun **1** *a crab shell* CARAPACE, exterior; armour; *Zoology* exoskeleton. **2** *peanut shells* POD, husk, hull, casing, case, covering, integument; *N. Amer.* shuck. **3** *shells passing overhead* PROJECTILE, bomb, explosive; grenade; bullet, cartridge. **4** *the metal shell of the car* FRAMEWORK, frame, chassis, skeleton; hull, exterior.
– RELATED TERMS conchoidal, concho-.
● verb **1** *they were shelling peas* HULL, pod, husk; *N. Amer.* shuck. **2** *rebel artillery shelled the city* BOMBARD, fire on, shoot at, attack, bomb, blitz, strafe.
– PHRASES **shell something out** *(informal)*. See PAY verb sense 2.

shellfish ● noun CRUSTACEAN, bivalve, mollusc.

shelter ● noun **1** *the trees provide shelter for animals* PROTECTION, cover, screening, shade; safety, security, refuge, sanctuary, asylum. **2** *a shelter for abandoned cats* SANCTUARY, refuge, home, haven, safe house; harbour, port in a storm.
– OPPOSITES exposure.
● verb **1** *the hut sheltered him from the wind* PROTECT, shield, screen, cover, shade, save, safeguard, preserve, defend, cushion, guard, insulate. **2** *the anchorage where the convoy sheltered* TAKE SHELTER, take refuge, seek sanctuary, take cover; *informal* hole up.
– OPPOSITES expose.

sheltered ● adjective **1** *a sheltered stretch of water* PROTECTED,

ing of private independent units with some shared facilities and a warden.

shelve[1] ● verb **1** place on a shelf. **2** abandon or defer (a plan or project). **3** fit with shelves.
– DERIVATIVES **shelver** noun.
– ORIGIN from *shelves*, plural of SHELF.

shelve[2] ● verb (of ground) slope downwards.
– ORIGIN perhaps from SHELF.

shelves plural of SHELF.

shelving ● noun shelves collectively.

shemozzle /shimozz'l/ (also **schemozzle**) ● noun informal a muddle.
– ORIGIN Yiddish, suggested by a Hebrew word meaning 'of no luck'.

shenanigans /shinannigənz/ ● plural noun informal **1** secret or dishonest activity. **2** mischief.
– ORIGIN of unknown origin.

Sheol /sheeōl/ ● noun the Hebrew underworld, abode of the dead.
– ORIGIN Hebrew.

shepherd ● noun **1** a person who tends sheep. **2** a member of the clergy providing spiritual care and guidance for a congregation. ● verb **1** tend (sheep). **2** guide or direct somewhere. **3** give spiritual or other guidance to.
– DERIVATIVES **shepherdess** noun.
– ORIGIN Old English, from SHEEP + obsolete *herd* 'herdsman'.

shepherd's pie ● noun a dish of minced meat under a layer of mashed potato.

shepherd's purse ● noun a white-flowered weed with triangular or heart-shaped seed pods.

Sheraton /sherrət'n/ ● adjective (of furniture) designed by or in the simple, graceful style of the English furniture-maker Thomas Sheraton (1751–1806).

sherbet ● noun **1** Brit. a flavoured sweet fizzing powder eaten alone or made into a drink. **2** (especially in Arab countries) a drink of sweet diluted fruit juices. **3** N. Amer. water ice; sorbet. **4** Austral. humorous beer.
– ORIGIN Arabic, 'drink'; related to SYRUP.

sherd /sherd/ ● noun another term for POTSHERD.
– ORIGIN variant of SHARD.

sheriff ● noun **1** (also **high sheriff**) (in England and Wales) the chief executive officer of the Crown in a county. **2** an honorary officer elected annually in some English towns. **3** (in Scotland) a judge. **4** US an elected officer in a county, responsible for keeping the peace.
– ORIGIN Old English, 'shire reeve'.

sheriff court ● noun (in Scotland) a court for civil cases, equivalent to a county court.

Sherpa /sherpə/ ● noun (pl. same or **Sherpas**) a member of a Himalayan people living on the borders of Nepal and Tibet.
– ORIGIN Tibetan, 'inhabitant of an Eastern country'.

sherry ● noun (pl. **sherries**) a fortified wine originally and mainly from southern Spain.
– ORIGIN from Spanish *vino de Xeres* 'Xeres wine' (Xeres being the former name of the city of *Jerez de la Frontera*).

she's ● contraction she is; she has.

Shetlander /shetləndər/ ● noun a person from the Shetland Islands.

Shetland pony ● noun a small, hardy rough-coated breed of pony.

shew ● verb old-fashioned variant of SHOW.

Shia /sheeə/ (also **Shi'a**) ● noun (pl. same or **Shias**) **1** one of the two main branches of Islam, regarding Ali, the fourth caliph, as Muhammad's first true successor. Compare with SUNNI. **2** a Muslim who adheres to this branch of Islam.
– ORIGIN Arabic, 'party (of Ali)'.

shiatsu /shiatsoo/ ● noun a Japanese therapy in which pressure is applied with the hands to points on the body.
– ORIGIN Japanese, 'finger pressure'.

shibboleth /shibbəleth/ ● noun a custom, principle, or belief distinguishing a particular class or group of people.
– ORIGIN originally in the sense 'a word or sound which a foreigner is unable to pronounce': from Hebrew, 'ear of corn' (according to the Book of Judges, chapter 12, the word was used as a test of nationality because of its difficult pronunciation).

shied past and past participle of SHY[2].

shield ● noun **1** a broad piece of armour held for protection against blows or missiles. **2** a sporting trophy consisting of an engraved metal plate mounted on a piece of wood. **3** Heraldry a stylized representation of a shield used for displaying a coat of arms. **4** a US police officer's badge. **5** a protective plate, screen, etc. **6** a source of protection. ● verb **1** protect from a danger, risk, etc. **2** prevent from being seen. **3** enclose or screen (machinery or a source of sound, light, radiation) to protect the user.
– ORIGIN Old English, from a base meaning 'divide, separate'.

shift ● verb **1** move or change from one position to another. **2** Brit. informal move quickly. **3** (**shift oneself**) Brit. informal move or rouse oneself. **4** Brit. remove (a stain). **5** informal sell (goods) quickly or in large quantities. **6** chiefly N. Amer. change gear. ● noun **1** a slight change in position, direction, or tendency. **2** a key used to switch between two sets of characters or functions on a keyboard. **3** each of two or more periods in which different groups of workers do the same jobs in relay. **4** N. Amer. a gear lever or gear-changing mechanism. **5** a straight unwaisted dress. **6** historical a long, loose undergarment. **7** archaic an ingenious or devious device or stratagem.
– PHRASES **make shift** dated manage or contrive to do something. **shift for oneself** manage alone as best one can. **shift one's ground** change one's position in an argument.
– DERIVATIVES **shifter** noun.
– ORIGIN Old English, 'arrange, divide, apportion'.

shiftless ● adjective lazy, indolent, and lacking ambition.
– DERIVATIVES **shiftlessness** noun.

shifty ● adjective (**shiftier**, **shiftiest**) informal deceitful or evasive.
– DERIVATIVES **shiftily** adverb **shiftiness** noun.

shigella /shigellə/ ● noun (pl. same or **shigellae** /shigellee/) a bacterium of a genus including some kinds responsible for dys-

Thesaurus

S

screened, shielded, covered; shady; cosy. **2** *she led a sheltered life* SECLUDED, cloistered, isolated, protected, withdrawn, sequestered, reclusive; privileged, secure, safe, quiet.

shelve ● verb POSTPONE, put off, delay, defer, put back, reschedule, hold over/off, put to one side, suspend, stay, keep in abeyance, mothball; abandon, drop, give up, stop, cancel, jettison, axe; *N. Amer.* put over, table, take a rain check on; *informal* put on ice, put on the back burner, ditch, dump, junk.
– OPPOSITES execute.

shepherd ● noun *he worked as a shepherd* shepherdess, herdsman, herder, sheepman.
● verb *we shepherded them away* USHER, steer, herd, lead, take, escort, guide, conduct, marshal, walk; show, see, chaperone.

shield ● noun **1** *he used his shield to fend off blows Heraldry* escutcheon; *historical* buckler, target; *archaic* targe. **2** *a shield against dirt* PROTECTION, guard, defence, cover, screen, security, shelter, safeguard, protector.
● verb *he shielded his eyes* PROTECT, cover, screen, shade; save, safeguard, preserve, defend, secure, guard; cushion, insulate.
– OPPOSITES expose.

shift ● verb **1** *he shifted some chairs* MOVE, carry, transfer, transport, convey, lug, haul, fetch, switch, relocate, reposition, rearrange; *informal* cart. **2** *she shifted her position* CHANGE, alter, adjust, vary; modify, revise, reverse, retract; do a U-turn. **3** *the cargo has shifted* MOVE, slide, slip, be displaced. **4** *the wind shifted* VEER, alter, change, turn, swing round. **5** *(Brit.) this brush really shifts the dirt* GET RID OF, remove, get off, budge, lift, expunge.
– OPPOSITES keep.
● noun **1** *the southward shift of people* MOVEMENT, move, transference, transport, transposition, relocation. **2** *a shift in public opinion* CHANGE, alteration, adjustment, amendment, variation, modification, revision, reversal, retraction, U-turn; *Brit.* about-turn. **3** *they worked three shifts* STINT, stretch, spell of work. **4** *the night shift went home* WORKERS, crew, gang, team, squad, patrol. **5** *(archaic) dubious shifts to make money* STRATAGEM, scheme, subterfuge, expedient, dodge, trick, ruse, wile, strategy, device, plan.
– PHRASES **shift for oneself** COPE, manage, survive, make it, fend for oneself, take care of oneself, make do, get by/along, scrape by/along, muddle through; stand on one's own two feet; *informal* make out.

shiftless ● adjective LAZY, idle, indolent, slothful, lethargic, lackadaisical; spiritless, apathetic, feckless, good-for-nothing, worthless; unambitious, unenterprising.

shifty ● adjective *(informal)* DEVIOUS, evasive, slippery, duplicitous, false, deceitful, underhand, untrustworthy, dishonest, shady, wily, crafty, tricky, sneaky, treacherous, artful, sly, scheming; *N.*

entery.
– ORIGIN from the name of the Japanese bacteriologist Kiyoshi *Shiga* (1870–1957).

shih-tzu /sheetsōō/ ● noun a breed of dog with long silky erect hair and short legs.
– ORIGIN Chinese, 'lion'.

shiitake /shitaakay/ ● noun an edible mushroom cultivated in Japan and China.
– ORIGIN Japanese, from words meaning 'an oak' and 'mushroom'.

Shiite /sheeīt/ (also **Shi'ite**) ● noun an adherent of the Shia branch of Islam. ● adjective relating to Shia.
– DERIVATIVES **Shiism** /sheeiz'm/ (also **Shi'ism**) noun.

shiksa /shiksə/ ● noun derogatory (in Jewish use) a gentile girl or woman.
– ORIGIN Hebrew, 'detested thing'.

shill ● noun N. Amer. informal an accomplice of a hawker, gambler, or swindler who acts as an enthusiastic customer to entice others.
– ORIGIN of unknown origin.

shillelagh /shilayli/ ● noun (In Ireland) a cudgel of blackthorn or oak.
– ORIGIN named after the town of *Shillelagh*, in County Wicklow, Ireland.

shilling ● noun **1** a former British coin and monetary unit equal to one twentieth of a pound or twelve pence. **2** the basic monetary unit of Kenya, Tanzania, and Uganda.
– PHRASES **not the full shilling** Brit. informal not very clever. **take the King's** (or **Queen's**) **shilling** Brit. enlist as a soldier. [ORIGIN with reference to the former practice of paying a shilling to a new recruit.]
– ORIGIN Old English.

shilly-shally ● verb (**shilly-shallies**, **shilly-shallied**) be indecisive. ● noun indecisive behaviour.
– ORIGIN originally as *shill I, shall I*, reduplication of *shall I?*

shim ● noun a washer or thin strip of material used to align parts, make them fit, or reduce wear. ● verb (**shimmed**, **shimming**) wedge or fill up with a shim.
– ORIGIN of unknown origin.

shimmer ● verb shine with a soft wavering light. ● noun a light with such qualities.
– DERIVATIVES **shimmery** adjective.
– ORIGIN Old English, related to SHINE.

shimmy ● noun (pl. **shimmies**) **1** a kind of ragtime dance in which the whole body shakes or sways. **2** abnormal vibration of the wheels of a motor vehicle. ● verb (**shimmies**, **shimmied**) **1** dance the shimmy. **2** shake or vibrate abnormally. **3** move swiftly and effortlessly.
– ORIGIN of unknown origin.

shin ● noun **1** the front of the leg below the knee. **2** a cut of beef from the lower part of a cow's leg. ● verb (**shinned**, **shinning**) (**shin up/down**) climb quickly up or down by gripping with one's arms and legs.
– ORIGIN Old English, probably from a Germanic base meaning 'narrow or thin piece'.

shin bone ● noun the tibia.

shindig ● noun informal **1** a large, lively party. **2** a noisy disturbance or quarrel.
– ORIGIN probably from SHIN and DIG, influenced later by SHINDY.

shindy ● noun (pl. **shindies**) informal **1** a noisy disturbance or quarrel. **2** a large, lively party.
– ORIGIN perhaps an alteration of SHINTY.

shine ● verb (past and past part. **shone** or **shined**) **1** give out a bright light, or glow with reflected light. **2** direct (a torch or other light) somewhere. **3** (of a person's eyes) be bright with the expression of emotion. **4** excel at something. **5** (**shine through**) (of a quality or skill) be clearly evident. **6** (past and past part. **shined**) polish. ● noun **1** a quality of brightness, especially through reflecting light. **2** an act of polishing.
– PHRASES **take the shine off** spoil the brilliance or excitement of. **take a shine to** informal develop a liking for.
– ORIGIN Old English.

shiner ● noun informal a black eye.

shingle[1] ● noun a mass of small rounded pebbles, especially on a seashore.
– DERIVATIVES **shingly** adjective.
– ORIGIN of unknown origin.

shingle[2] ● noun **1** a rectangular wooden tile used on walls or roofs. **2** dated a woman's short haircut, tapering from the back of the head to the nape of the neck. **3** N. Amer. a small signboard, especially one outside an office. ● verb **1** roof or clad with shingles. **2** dated cut (hair) in a shingle.
– ORIGIN probably from Latin *scindula* 'a split piece of wood'.

shingles ● plural noun (treated as sing.) an acute painful inflammation of nerve endings, with a skin eruption often forming a girdle around the body.
– ORIGIN from Latin *cingulum* 'girdle'.

shinny[1] ● verb (**shinnies**, **shinnied**) (**shinny up/down**) N. Amer. shin up or down.

shinny[2] ● noun N. Amer. an informal form of ice hockey played on the street or on ice.
– ORIGIN variant of SHINTY.

Shinola /shīnōlə/ ● noun US trademark a brand of boot polish.
– PHRASES **not know shit from Shinola** vulgar slang be ignorant or innocent.

shin pad ● noun a protective pad worn on the shins when playing soccer and other sports.

shin splints ● plural noun (treated as sing. or pl.) acute pain in the shin and lower leg caused by prolonged running on hard surfaces.

Shinto /shintō/ ● noun a Japanese religion incorporating the worship of ancestors and nature spirits.
– DERIVATIVES **Shintoism** noun **Shintoist** noun.
– ORIGIN Japanese, from Chinese words meaning 'way of the gods'.

shinty ● noun a Scottish game resembling hockey, played with curved sticks and taller goalposts and derived from hurling.
– ORIGIN apparently from the cry *shin ye, shin you, shin t' ye*, used in the game, of unknown origin.

shiny ● adjective (**shinier**, **shiniest**) reflecting light because very smooth, clean, or polished.
– DERIVATIVES **shinily** adverb **shininess** noun.

ship ● noun **1** a large seagoing boat. **2** a sailing vessel with a bowsprit and three or more square-rigged masts. **3** a spaceship. **4** N. Amer. an aircraft. ● verb (**shipped**, **shipping**) **1** transport on a ship or by other means. **2** make (a product) available for purchase. **3** (of a sailor) take service on a ship. **4** (of a boat) take in (water) over the side. **5** take (oars) from the rowlocks and lay

S

Thesaurus

Amer. snide; *Brit. informal* dodgy; *Austral./NZ informal* shonky.
– OPPOSITES honest.

shilly-shally ● verb DITHER, be indecisive, be irresolute, vacillate, waver, hesitate, blow hot and cold, falter, drag one's feet; *Brit.* haver, hum and haw; *Scottish* swither; *informal* dilly-dally.

shimmer ● verb *the lake shimmered in the moonlight* GLINT, glisten, twinkle, sparkle, flash, scintillate, gleam, glow, glimmer, glitter, wink; *poetic/literary* coruscate.
● noun *the shimmer of lights from the traffic* GLINT, twinkle, sparkle, flash, gleam, glow, glimmer, lustre, glitter; *poetic/literary* coruscation.

shin ● verb CLIMB, clamber, scramble, swarm, shoot, go; mount, ascend, scale; descend; *N. Amer.* shinny.

shine ● verb **1** *the sun shone* EMIT LIGHT, beam, radiate, gleam, glow, glint, glimmer, sparkle, twinkle, glitter, glisten, shimmer, flash, flare, glare, fluoresce, luminesce; *poetic/literary* glister, coruscate. **2** *she shone his shoes* POLISH, burnish, buff, wax, gloss, rub up. **3** *they shone at university* EXCEL, be outstanding, be brilliant, be successful, stand out.
● noun **1** *the shine of the moon on her face* LIGHT, brightness, gleam, glow, glint, glimmer, sparkle, twinkle, glitter, glisten, shimmer, beam, glare, radiance, illumination, luminescence, luminosity, incandescence. **2** *linseed oil restores the shine* POLISH, burnish, gleam, gloss, lustre, sheen, patina.

shining ● adjective **1** *a shining expanse of water* GLEAMING, bright, brilliant, illuminated, lustrous, glowing, glinting, sparkling, twinkling, glittering, glistening, shimmering, dazzling, luminous, luminescent, incandescent; *poetic/literary* glistering, coruscating. **2** *a shining face* GLOWING, beaming, radiant, happy. **3** *shining chromium tubes* SHINY, bright, polished, gleaming, glossy, glassy, sheeny, lustrous.
– PHRASES **a shining example** PARAGON, model, epitome, archetype, ideal, exemplar, nonpareil, paradigm, quintessence, the crème de la crème, the beau idéal, acme, jewel, flower, treasure; *informal* one in a million, the bee's knees.

shiny ● adjective GLOSSY, glassy, bright, polished, gleaming, satiny,

them inside a boat. **6** fix (a rudder, mast, etc.) in place on a ship.
– PHRASES **a sinking ship** a failing organization or endeavour. **when one's ship comes in** when one's fortune is made.
– DERIVATIVES **shipload** noun **shipper** noun.
– ORIGIN Old English.
-ship • suffix forming nouns: **1** denoting a quality or condition: *companionship.* **2** denoting status, office, or honour: *citizenship.* **3** denoting a skill in a certain capacity: *workmanship.* **4** denoting the collective individuals of a group: *membership.*
– ORIGIN Old English.
shipboard • noun (before another noun) used or occurring on board a ship.
shipbroker • noun a broker who arranges charters, cargo space, and passenger bookings on ships.
shipbuilder • noun a person or company that designs and builds ships.
– DERIVATIVES **shipbuilding** noun.
ship canal • noun a canal large enough for use by ships.
shiplap • verb fit (boards) together by halving so that each overlaps the one below. • noun shiplapped boards, used for cladding.
shipmate • noun a fellow member of a ship's crew.
shipment • noun **1** the action of shipping goods. **2** a consignment of goods shipped.
ship money • noun historical a tax raised in medieval England to provide ships for the navy.
ship of the desert • noun literary a camel.
ship of the line • noun historical a warship of the largest size, used in the line of battle.
shipping • noun **1** ships collectively. **2** the transport of goods by sea or other means.
shippon /shippən/ (also **shippen**) • noun dialect a cattle shed.
– ORIGIN Old English.
ship's biscuit • noun a hard, coarse kind of biscuit formerly taken on sea voyages.
ship's company • noun the crew of a ship.
shipshape (also **shipshape and Bristol fashion**) • adjective orderly and neat.
– ORIGIN *Bristol fashion* refers to the commercial prosperity of Bristol when its shipping trade was thriving.
shipway • noun a slope on which a ship is built and down which it slides to be launched.
shipworm • noun another term for TEREDO.
shipwreck • noun **1** the destruction of a ship at sea by sinking or breaking up. **2** a ship so destroyed. • verb (**be shipwrecked**) suffer a shipwreck.
shipwright • noun a shipbuilder.
shipyard • noun a place where ships are built and repaired.
shiralee /shirrəlee/ • noun Austral. informal a bundle of belongings carried by a tramp.
– ORIGIN of unknown origin.
Shiraz /shiraz/ • noun a variety of black wine grape.
– ORIGIN from *Shiraz* in Iran, apparently an alteration of French *syrah*, influenced by the belief that the vine was brought from Iran by the Crusades.
shire /shīr/ • noun **1** Brit. a county, especially in England. **2** (**the Shires**) the parts of England regarded as strongholds of traditional rural culture, especially the rural Midlands. **3** a medieval administrative district ruled jointly by an alderman and a sheriff. **4** Austral. a rural area with its own elected council.
– ORIGIN Old English, 'care, official charge, county'.
shire county • noun (in the UK since 1974) a non-metropolitan county.
shire horse • noun a heavy powerful breed of draught horse, originally from the English Midlands.
shirk • verb avoid or neglect (a duty or responsibility).
– DERIVATIVES **shirker** noun.
– ORIGIN from obsolete *shirk* 'sponger', perhaps from German *Schurke* 'scoundrel'.
shirr /shur/ • verb **1** gather (fabric) by means of drawn or elasticized threads in parallel rows. **2** US bake (an egg without its shell).
– ORIGIN of unknown origin.
shirt • noun **1** a garment for the upper body, with a collar and sleeves and buttons down the front. **2** a similar garment of light material without full fastenings, worn for sports and leisure.
– PHRASES **keep your shirt on** informal stay calm. **lose one's shirt** informal lose all one's possessions. **put one's shirt on** Brit. informal bet all one has on. **the shirt off one's back** informal one's last remaining possessions.
– DERIVATIVES **shirted** adjective.
– ORIGIN Old English, related to SKIRT and SHORT.
shirt dress • noun a dress with a collar and button fastening in the style of a shirt, without a seam at the waist.
shirtsleeve • noun the sleeve of a shirt.
– PHRASES **in (one's) shirtsleeves** wearing a shirt with nothing over it.
– DERIVATIVES **shirtsleeved** adjective.
shirtwaist • noun N. Amer. **1** a woman's blouse resembling a shirt. **2** a shirtwaister.
shirtwaister • noun a shirt dress with a seam at the waist.
shirty • adjective (**shirtier, shirtiest**) Brit. informal bad-tempered or annoyed.
– DERIVATIVES **shirtily** adverb **shirtiness** noun.
shish kebab /shish kibab/ • noun a dish of pieces of marinated meat and vegetables cooked and served on skewers.
– ORIGIN Turkish *şiş kebap.*
shit vulgar slang • verb (**shitting**; past and past part. **shitted** or **shit** or **shat**) **1** defecate. **2** (**shit oneself**) be very frightened. • noun **1** faeces. **2** something worthless; rubbish. **3** a contemptible person. • exclamation expressing disgust or annoyance.
– PHRASES **be scared shitless** vulgar slang be extremely frightened. **not give a shit** not care at all. **be up shit creek (without a paddle)** be in an awkward predicament. **when the shit hits the fan** when the disastrous consequences of something become known.
– ORIGIN Old English, 'diarrhoea'.
shite • noun & exclamation vulgar slang another term for SHIT.
shit-hot • adjective vulgar slang excellent.
shit-stirrer • noun vulgar slang a person who takes pleasure in causing trouble or discord.
– DERIVATIVES **shit-stirring** noun.
shitty • adjective (**shittier, shittiest**) vulgar slang **1** contemptible or awful. **2** covered with excrement.
shive /shīv/ • noun a broad bung hammered into a hole in the top of a cask when the cask has been filled.
– ORIGIN originally in the sense 'slice of bread', later 'piece of split wood': related to SHEAVE[2].
shiver[1] • verb shake slightly and uncontrollably as a result of being cold, frightened, or excited. • noun **1** a momentary trembling movement. **2** (**the shivers**) a spell or attack of shivering.
– DERIVATIVES **shivery** adjective.
– ORIGIN perhaps from dialect *chavele* 'to chatter', from an Old English word meaning 'jaw'.
shiver[2] • noun a splinter. • verb break into shivers.
– PHRASES **shiver my timbers** a mock oath attributed to sailors.
– ORIGIN from a Germanic base meaning 'to split'.
Shoah /shōə/ • noun (in Jewish use) the Holocaust.
– ORIGIN modern Hebrew, 'catastrophe'.
shoal[1] • noun **1** a large number of fish swimming together. **2** informal, chiefly Brit. a large number of people. • verb (of fish) form shoals.
– ORIGIN probably from Dutch *schōle* 'troop'.

Thesaurus

sheeny, lustrous.
– OPPOSITES matt.
ship • noun BOAT, vessel, craft.
– RELATED TERMS marine, maritime, naval.
shirk • verb **1** *she didn't shirk any task* EVADE, dodge, avoid, get out of, sidestep, shrink from, shun, slide out of, skip, miss; neglect; *informal* duck (out of), cop out of; *Brit. informal* skive off; *N. Amer. informal* cut; *Austral./NZ informal* duck-shove. **2** *no one shirked* AVOID ONE'S DUTY, be remiss, be negligent, play truant; *Brit. informal* skive (off), swing the lead, scrimshank, slack off; *N. Amer. informal* goof off, play hookey.
shirker • noun DODGER, truant, absentee, layabout, loafer, idler; *informal* slacker; *Brit. informal* skiver, scrimshanker; *archaic* shirk.
shiver[1] • verb *she was shivering with fear* TREMBLE, quiver, shake, shudder, quaver, quake.
• noun *she gave a shiver as the door opened* TREMBLE, quiver, shake, shudder, quaver, quake, tremor, twitch.
shiver[2] • noun *a shiver of glass* SPLINTER, sliver, shard, fragment, chip, shaving, smithereen, particle, bit, piece.
• verb *the window shivered into thousands of pieces* SHATTER, splin-

shoal² ● noun **1** an area of shallow water. **2** a submerged sandbank visible at low water. ● verb (of water) become shallower.
– ORIGIN Old English, related to SHALLOW.
shock¹ ● noun **1** a sudden upsetting or surprising event or experience, or the resulting feeling. **2** an acute medical condition associated with a fall in blood pressure, caused by loss of blood, severe burns, sudden emotional stress, etc. **3** a violent shaking movement caused by an impact, explosion, or tremor. **4** an electric shock. ● verb **1** cause to feel surprised and upset. **2** offend the moral feelings of; outrage. **3** affect with physiological shock, or with an electric shock.
– DERIVATIVES **shockable** adjective **shockproof** adjective.
– ORIGIN French *choc.*
shock² ● noun a group of twelve sheaves of grain placed upright and supporting each other to allow the grain to dry and ripen.
– ORIGIN perhaps from Dutch, Low German *schok.*
shock³ ● noun an unkempt or thick mass of hair.
– ORIGIN origin uncertain.
shock absorber ● noun a device for absorbing jolts and vibrations, especially on a vehicle.
shocker ● noun informal **1** a person or thing that shocks, especially through being unacceptable or sensational. **2** Brit. a shock absorber.
shock-headed ● adjective having thick, shaggy, and unkempt hair.
shocking ● adjective **1** causing shock or disgust. **2** Brit. informal very bad.
– DERIVATIVES **shockingly** adverb.
shocking pink ● noun a vibrant shade of pink.
shock tactics ● plural noun the use of sudden violent or extreme action to shock someone into doing something.
shock therapy (also **shock treatment**) ● noun treatment of chronic mental conditions by electroconvulsive therapy or by inducing physiological shock.
shock troops ● plural noun troops trained for carrying out sudden assaults.
shock wave ● noun an intense travelling pressure wave caused by explosion or by a body moving faster than sound.
shod past and past participle of SHOE.
shoddy ● adjective (**shoddier**, **shoddiest**) **1** badly made or done. **2** lacking moral principle; sordid. ● noun an inferior yarn or fabric made from shredded woollen waste.
– DERIVATIVES **shoddily** adverb **shoddiness** noun.
– ORIGIN of unknown origin.
shoe ● noun **1** a covering for the foot having a sturdy sole and not reaching above the ankle. **2** a horseshoe. **3** a brake shoe or a drag for a wheel. **4** a socket on a camera for fitting a flash unit. **5** a metal rim or ferrule, especially on the runner of a sledge. **6** a step for a mast. ● verb (**shoes**, **shoeing**; past and past part. **shod**) **1** fit (a horse) with a shoe or shoes. **2** (**be shod**) be wearing shoes of a specified kind. **3** protect with a metal shoe.
– PHRASES **be** (or **put oneself**) **in another person's shoes** imagine oneself in another's situation or predicament. **dead men's shoes** property or a position coveted by a prospective successor but available only on a person's death or departure.
– ORIGIN Old English.
shoeblack ● noun dated a person who cleans the shoes of passers-by for payment.
shoebox ● noun **1** a box in which a pair of shoes is delivered or sold. **2** informal a very cramped room or space.
shoehorn ● noun a curved instrument used for easing one's heel into a shoe. ● verb force into an inadequate space.
shoelace ● noun a cord or leather strip passed through eyelets or hooks on opposite sides of a shoe and pulled tight and fastened.
shoemaker ● noun a person who makes shoes and other footwear as a profession.
shoeshine ● noun chiefly N. Amer. an act of polishing someone's shoes.
shoestring ● noun **1** N. Amer. a shoelace. **2** informal a small or inadequate budget: *living on a shoestring.*
shoe tree ● noun a shaped block inserted into a shoe when it is not being worn to keep it in shape.
shogun /shōgoon/ ● noun (in feudal Japan) a hereditary commander-in-chief.
– DERIVATIVES **shogunate** /shōgoonət/ noun.
– ORIGIN Japanese, from a Chinese word meaning 'general'.
Shona /shōnə/ ● noun (pl. same or **Shonas**) a member of a group of peoples inhabiting parts of southern Africa, particularly Zimbabwe.
– ORIGIN the name in Shona.
shone past and past participle of SHINE.
shonky Austral./NZ informal ● adjective (**shonkier**, **shonkiest**) dishonest, unreliable, or illegal. ● noun (also **shonk**) a person engaged in suspect business activities.
– ORIGIN perhaps from English dialect *shonk* 'smart'.
shoo-in ● noun chiefly N. Amer. a person or thing that is certain to succeed or win.
shook past of SHAKE.
shoot ● verb (past and past part. **shot**) **1** kill or wound (a person or animal) with a bullet or arrow. **2** cause (a gun) to fire. **3** move suddenly and rapidly. **4** direct (a glance, question, or remark) at someone. **5** film or photograph (a scene, film, etc.). **6** (**shooting**) (of a pain) sudden and piercing. **7** (of a boat) sweep swiftly down or under (rapids, a waterfall, or a bridge). **8** move (a door bolt) to fasten or unfasten a door. **9** send out buds or shoots; germinate. **10** informal drive past (a traffic light at red). **11** (in sport) kick, hit, or throw the ball or puck in an attempt to score a goal. **12** informal make (a specified score) for a round of golf. ● noun **1** a young branch or sucker springing from the main stock of a tree or other plant. **2** an occasion when a group of people hunt and shoot game for sport. **3** Brit. land used for shooting game. **4** an occasion of taking photographs professionally or making a film or video: *a fashion shoot.* **5** variant spelling of CHUTE¹. ● exclamation N. Amer. informal used as a euphemism for 'shit'.
– PHRASES **shoot the breeze** (or **the bull**) N. Amer. informal have a casual conversation. **shoot one's cuffs** pull one's shirt cuffs out to project beyond the cuffs of one's jacket or coat. **shoot down** bring down (an aircraft or person) by shooting. **shoot oneself in the foot** informal inadvertently make a situation worse for oneself. **shoot a line** Brit. informal describe something in an exaggerated, untruthful, or boastful way. **shoot one's mouth off** informal talk boastfully or indiscreetly. **the whole shooting match** informal everything. **shoot through** Austral./NZ informal depart, especially hurriedly. **shoot up** informal inject oneself with a narcotic drug.
– ORIGIN Old English.

Thesaurus

ter, smash, fragment, crack, break.
shivery ● adjective TREMBLING, trembly, quivery, shaky, shuddering, shuddery, quavery, quaking; cold, chilly.
shoal ● noun SANDBANK, bank, mudbank, bar, sandbar, tombolo, shelf, cay.
shock¹ ● noun **1** *the news came as a shock* BLOW, upset, disturbance; surprise, revelation, a bolt from the blue, thunderbolt, bombshell, rude awakening, eye-opener; *informal* whammy. **2** *you gave me a shock* FRIGHT, scare, jolt, start; *informal* turn. **3** *she was suffering from shock* TRAUMA, traumatism, prostration; collapse, breakdown. **4** *the first shock of the earthquake* VIBRATION, reverberation, shake, jolt, jar, jerk; impact, blow.
● verb *the murder shocked the nation* APPAL, horrify, outrage, revolt, disgust, nauseate, sicken; traumatize, distress, upset, disturb, disquiet, unsettle; stun, rock, stagger, astound, astonish, amaze, startle, surprise, dumbfound, shake, take aback, throw, unnerve.
shock² ● noun *a shock of red hair* MASS, mane, mop, thatch, head, crop, bush, frizz, tangle, cascade, halo.
shocking ● adjective APPALLING, horrifying, horrific, dreadful, awful, frightful, terrible; scandalous, outrageous, disgraceful, vile, abominable, abhorrent, atrocious; odious, repugnant, disgusting, nauseating, sickening, loathsome; distressing, upsetting, disturbing, disquieting, unsettling; staggering, amazing, astonishing, startling, surprising.
shoddy ● adjective **1** *shoddy goods* POOR-QUALITY, inferior, second-rate, third-rate, cheap, cheapjack, trashy, jerry-built; *informal* tacky, rubbishy, junky; *Brit. informal* duff, rubbish. **2** *shoddy workmanship* CARELESS, slapdash, sloppy, slipshod, scrappy, crude; negligent, cursory.
– OPPOSITES quality, careful.
shoemaker ● noun COBBLER, bootmaker, clogger; *Scottish & N. English* souter.
shoot ● verb **1** *they shot him in the street* GUN DOWN, mow down, hit, wound, injure; put a bullet in, pick off, bag, fell, kill; *informal* pot, blast, pump full of lead, plug. **2** *they shot at the enemy* FIRE, open

shooter ● noun **1** a person who uses a gun. **2** informal a gun. **3** (in netball, basketball, etc.) a player whose role is to attempt to score goals.
shooting box ● noun Brit. a lodge used by hunters in the shooting season.
shooting brake ● noun Brit. dated an estate car.
shooting gallery ● noun a room or fairground booth for recreational shooting at targets.
shooting iron ● noun informal, chiefly US a firearm.
shooting star ● noun a small, rapidly moving meteor that burns up on entering the earth's atmosphere.
shooting stick ● noun a walking stick with a handle that unfolds to form a seat and a sharpened end which can be stuck firmly in the ground.
shoot-out ● noun **1** informal a decisive gun battle. **2** Soccer a tie-breaker decided by each side taking a specified number of penalty kicks.
shop ● noun **1** a building or part of a building where goods or services are sold. **2** a place where things are manufactured or repaired; a workshop. ● verb (**shopped**, **shopping**) **1** go to a shop or shops to buy goods. **2** (**shop around**) look for the best available price or rate for something. **3** informal, chiefly Brit. inform on.
– PHRASES **talk shop** discuss matters concerning one's work, especially at an inappropriate time.
– ORIGIN shortening of Old French *eschoppe* 'lean-to booth'.
shopaholic ● noun informal a compulsive shopper.
shop assistant ● noun Brit. a person who serves customers in a shop.
shopfitter ● noun a person whose job it is to fit the counters, shelves, etc. with which a shop is equipped.
shop floor ● noun Brit. the part of a workshop or factory where production as distinct from administrative work is carried out.
shopfront ● noun the facade of a shop.
shopkeeper ● noun the owner and manager of a shop.
shoplifting ● noun the theft of goods from a shop by someone pretending to be a customer.
– DERIVATIVES **shoplift** verb **shoplifter** noun.
shopper ● noun **1** a person who is shopping. **2** Brit. a bag for holding shopping, attached to wheels and pushed or pulled along. **3** a small-wheeled bicycle with a basket.
shopping ● noun **1** the purchasing of goods from shops. **2** goods bought from shops, especially food and household goods.
shopping centre ● noun an area or complex of shops.
shopping list ● noun **1** a list of purchases to be made. **2** a list of items to be considered or acted on.
shop-soiled (N. Amer. **shopworn**) ● adjective Brit. (of an article) made dirty or imperfect by being displayed or handled in a shop.
shop steward ● noun a person elected by workers in a factory to represent them in dealings with management.
shopwalker ● noun Brit. dated a senior employee in a large shop who supervises assistants and directs customers.
shop window ● noun **1** a display window of a shop. **2** a position that allows a person or organization to demonstrate their strengths.
shore[1] ● noun **1** the land along the edge of a sea, lake, etc. **2** (also **shores**) literary a country or other geographic area bounded by a coast: *distant shores.*
– PHRASES **in shore** on the water near land or nearer to land. **on shore** ashore; on land.
– DERIVATIVES **shoreward** adjective & adverb **shorewards** adverb.
– ORIGIN Dutch, Low German *schōre.*
shore[2] ● noun a prop or beam set up against something weak or unstable as a support. ● verb (often **shore up**) support or hold up with or as if with shores.
– DERIVATIVES **shoring** noun.
– ORIGIN Dutch, Low German *schore* 'prop'.
shore leave ● noun leisure time spent ashore by a sailor.
shoreline ● noun the line along which a large body of water meets the land.
shorn past participle of SHEAR.
short ● adjective **1** of a small length or duration. **2** relatively small in extent. **3** (of a person) small in height. **4** (**short of/on**) not having enough of. **5** in insufficient supply. **6** (of a person) terse; uncivil. **7** (of a ball in sport) travelling only a small distance, or not far enough. **8** (of odds or a chance) reflecting or representing a high level of probability. **9** Phonetics (of a vowel) categorized as short with regard to quality and length (e.g. in standard British English the vowel sound in *good*). **10** (of pastry) containing a high proportion of fat to flour and therefore crumbly. ● adverb (in sport) at, to, or over a short distance, or not as far as the point aimed at. ● noun **1** Brit. informal a strong alcoholic drink, especially spirits, served in small measures. **2** a short film as opposed to a feature film. **3** a short circuit. ● verb short-circuit.
– PHRASES **be caught short 1** be put at a disadvantage. **2** Brit. informal urgently need to urinate or defecate. **bring** (or **pull**) **up short** cause (someone) to stop or pause abruptly. **for short** as an abbreviation or nickname. **get** (or **have**) **by the short and curlies** informal have complete control of. **go short** not have enough of something. **in short** to sum up; briefly. **in the short run** (or **term**) in the near future. **in short supply** (of a commodity) scarce. **make short work of** accomplish, consume, or destroy quickly. **short for** an abbreviation or nickname for. **short of 1** less than. **2** not reaching as far as. **3** without going so far as (some extreme action). **stop short** stop suddenly or abruptly.
– DERIVATIVES **shortish** adjective **shortness** noun.
– ORIGIN Old English, related to SHIRT, SKIRT.

Thesaurus

fire, aim, snipe, let fly; bombard, shell. **3** *faster than a gun can shoot bullets* DISCHARGE, fire, launch, loose off, let fly, emit. **4** *a car shot past* RACE, speed, flash, dash, dart, rush, hurtle, streak, whizz, go like lightning, go hell for leather, zoom, charge; career, sweep, fly, wing; *informal* belt, scoot, scorch, tear, zip, whip, step on it, burn rubber; *Brit. informal* bomb, bucket, shift; *N. Amer. informal* clip, hightail it, barrel. **5** *the plant failed to shoot* SPROUT, bud, burgeon, germinate. **6** *the film was shot in Tunisia* FILM, photograph, take, snap, capture, record; televise, video.
● noun *nip off the new shoots* SPROUT, bud, offshoot, scion, sucker, spear, runner, tendril, sprig.
shop ● noun **1** *a shop selling clothes* STORE, (retail) outlet, boutique, cash and carry, emporium, department store, supermarket, hypermarket, superstore, chain store, concession, market, mart, trading post; *N. Amer.* minimart. **2** *he works in the machine shop* WORKSHOP, workroom, plant, factory, works, industrial unit, mill, foundry, yard.
● verb **1** *he was shopping for spices* GO SHOPPING, go to the shops; buy, purchase, get, acquire, obtain, pick up, snap up, procure, stock up on; *humorous* indulge in retail therapy. **2** *(Brit. informal) he shopped his fellow robbers.* See BETRAY sense 1.
shopkeeper ● noun SHOP-OWNER, shop manager, vendor, retailer, dealer, seller, trader, wholesaler, salesperson, tradesman, distributor; *N. Amer.* storekeeper.
shopper ● noun BUYER, purchaser, customer, consumer, client, patron; *Law* vendee.
shopping centre ● noun SHOPPING PRECINCT, (shopping) mall, (shopping) arcade, galleria, parade; marketplace, mart; *N. Amer.* plaza.
shore[1] ● noun *he swam out from the shore* SEASHORE, beach, foreshore, sand(s), shoreline, waterside, front, coast, seaboard, shoreside; *poetic/literary* strand.
– RELATED TERMS littoral.
shore[2] ● verb *we had to shore up the building* PROP UP, hold up, bolster, support, brace, buttress, strengthen, fortify, reinforce, underpin.
short ● adjective **1** *a short piece of string* SMALL, little, tiny; *informal* teeny. **2** *short people* SMALL, little, petite, tiny, diminutive, stubby, elfin, dwarfish, midget, pygmy, Lilliputian, minuscule, miniature; *Scottish* wee; *informal* pint-sized, teeny, knee-high to a grasshopper. **3** *a short report* CONCISE, brief, succinct, compact, summary, economical, crisp, pithy, epigrammatic, laconic, thumbnail, abridged, abbreviated, condensed, synoptic, summarized, contracted, truncated; *formal* compendious. **4** *a short time* BRIEF, momentary, temporary, short-lived, impermanent, cursory, fleeting, passing, fugitive, lightning, transitory, transient, ephemeral, quick. **5** *money is a bit short* SCARCE, in short supply, scant, meagre, sparse, insufficient, deficient, inadequate, lacking, wanting. **6** *he was rather short with her* CURT, sharp, abrupt, blunt, brusque, terse, offhand, gruff, surly, testy, rude, uncivil; *informal* snappy.
– OPPOSITES long, tall, plentiful, courteous.
● adverb *she stopped short* ABRUPTLY, suddenly, sharply, all of a sudden, all at once, unexpectedly, without warning, out of the

shortage ● noun a situation in which something needed cannot be obtained in sufficient amounts.
short back and sides ● noun Brit. a haircut in which the hair is cut short at the back and the sides.
shortbread ● noun a crisp, rich, crumbly type of biscuit made with butter, flour, and sugar.
shortcake ● noun **1** another term for SHORTBREAD. **2** N. Amer. a rich dessert made from short pastry and topped with fruit and whipped cream.
short change ● noun insufficient money given as change. ● verb (**short-change**) **1** cheat by giving short change. **2** treat unfairly by withholding something of value.
short circuit ● noun an electrical circuit of lower than usual resistance, especially one formed unintentionally. ● verb (**short-circuit**) **1** cause or suffer a short circuit. **2** shorten (a process or activity) by using a more direct but irregular method.
shortcoming ● noun a failure to meet a certain standard; a fault or defect.
shortcrust pastry ● noun Brit. crumbly pastry made with flour, fat, and a little water.
short cut ● noun **1** an alternative route that is shorter than the one usually taken. **2** an accelerated but somewhat irregular way of doing something.
short-dated ● adjective (of a stock or bond) due for early payment or redemption.
short division ● noun division in which the quotient is written directly without a succession of intermediate workings.
shorten ● verb **1** make or become shorter. **2** Sailing reduce the amount of (sail spread).
shortening ● noun fat used for making pastry.
shortfall ● noun a deficit of something required or expected.
short fuse ● noun informal a quick temper.
shorthand ● noun **1** a method of rapid writing by means of abbreviations and symbols, used for taking dictation. **2** a short and simple way of expressing or referring to something.
short-handed ● adjective & adverb without enough or the usual number of staff or crew.
short haul ● noun a relatively short distance in terms of travel or the transport of goods.
short head ● noun Brit. Horse Racing a distance less than the length of a horse's head.
shorthold ● adjective English Law (of a tenancy) whereby the tenant agrees to rent a property for a stated term, at the end of which the landlord may recover it.
shorthorn ● noun a breed of cattle with short horns.
shortlist ● noun a list of selected candidates from which a final choice is made. ● verb put on a shortlist.
short-lived ● adjective lasting only a short time.
shortly ● adverb **1** in a short time; soon. **2** in a few words; briefly. **3** abruptly, sharply, or curtly.
short measure ● noun an amount less than that which is declared or paid for.
short-order ● adjective N. Amer. relating to food dishes which can be quickly prepared and served: *a short-order cook.*
short-range ● adjective **1** able to be used or be effective only over short distances. **2** of or over a short period of future time.
shorts ● plural noun **1** short trousers that reach only to the knees or thighs. **2** N. Amer. men's underpants.
short shrift ● noun rapid and unsympathetic dismissal; curt treatment.
– ORIGIN originally in sense 'little time allowed for making confession between being condemned and executed or punished'.
short sight ● noun the inability to see things clearly unless they are relatively close to the eyes; myopia.
short-sighted ● adjective **1** having short sight. **2** lacking imagination or foresight.
– DERIVATIVES **short-sightedly** adverb **short-sightedness** noun.
short-staffed ● adjective not having enough or the usual number of staff.
shortstop ● noun Baseball a fielder positioned between second and third base.
short story ● noun a story with a fully developed theme but significantly shorter and less elaborate than a novel.
short-tempered ● adjective having a tendency to lose one's temper quickly.
short-termism ● noun concentration on immediate profit or advantage at the expense of long-term security.
short time ● noun the condition of working fewer than the regular hours per day or days per week.
short-waisted ● adjective (of a dress or a person's body) having a high waist.
short wave ● noun **1** a radio wave of a wavelength between about 10 and 100 metres (and a frequency of about 3 to 30 megahertz). **2** broadcasting using radio waves of this wavelength.
short weight ● noun weight that is less than that declared.
short-winded ● adjective out of breath, or tending to run out of breath quickly.
shorty (also **shortie**) ● noun (pl. **shorties**) informal **1** a short person. **2** a short dress, nightdress, or raincoat.
Shoshone /shəshōni/ ● noun (pl. same or **Shoshones**) a member of an American Indian people living chiefly in Wyoming, Idaho, and Nevada.
– ORIGIN of unknown origin.
shot[1] ● noun **1** the firing of a gun or cannon. **2** a person with a specified level of ability in shooting: *he was an excellent shot.* **3** a hit, stroke, or kick of the ball in sports, in particular an attempt to score. **4** informal an attempt to do something. **5** (pl. same) a ball of stone or metal fired from a large gun or cannon. **6** (also **lead shot**) tiny lead pellets used in a single charge or cartridge in a shotgun. **7** a heavy ball thrown by a shot-putter. **8** a photograph. **9** a film sequence photographed continuously by one camera. **10** the launch of a rocket: *a moon shot.* **11** informal a small drink of spirits. **12** informal an injection of a drug or vaccine.
– PHRASES **give it one's best shot** informal do the best that one can. **like a shot** informal without hesitation. **a shot in the arm** informal an encouraging stimulus.
– ORIGIN Old English, from the base of SHOOT.
shot[2] past and past participle of SHOOT. ● adjective **1** (of coloured cloth) woven with different colours, giving a contrasting effect when looked at from different angles. **2** informal ruined or worn

Thesaurus

S

blue.
– PHRASES **in short** BRIEFLY, in a word, in a nutshell, in precis, in essence, to come to the point; in conclusion, in summary, to sum up. **short of 1** *we are short of nurses* DEFICIENT IN, lacking, wanting, in need of, low on, short on, missing; *informal* strapped for, pushed for, minus. **2** *short of searching everyone, there is nothing we can do* APART FROM, other than, aside from, besides, except (for), excepting, without, excluding, not counting, save (for).
shortage ● noun SCARCITY, sparseness, sparsity, dearth, paucity, poverty, insufficiency, deficiency, inadequacy, famine, lack, want, deficit, shortfall, rarity.
– OPPOSITES abundance.
shortcoming ● noun DEFECT, fault, flaw, imperfection, deficiency, limitation, failing, drawback, weakness, weak point, foible, frailty, vice.
– OPPOSITES strength.
shorten ● verb MAKE SHORTER, abbreviate, abridge, condense, precis, synopsize, contract, compress, reduce, shrink, diminish, cut (down); dock, trim, crop, pare down, prune; curtail, truncate.
– OPPOSITES extend.
short-lived ● adjective BRIEF, short, momentary, temporary, impermanent, cursory, fleeting, passing, fugitive, lightning, transitory, transient, ephemeral, quick.
shortly ● adverb **1** *she will be with you shortly* SOON, presently, in a little while, at any moment, in a minute, in next to no time, before long, by and by; *N. Amer.* momentarily; *informal* anon, any time now, pretty soon, before one can say Jack Robinson, in a jiffy; *Brit. informal* in a mo, sharpish; *dated* directly. **2** *'I know,' he replied shortly* CURTLY, sharply, abruptly, bluntly, brusquely, tersely, gruffly, snappily, testily, rudely.
short-sighted ● adjective **1** *I'm a little short-sighted* MYOPIC, near-sighted; *informal* as blind as a bat. **2** *short-sighted critics* NARROW-MINDED, unimaginative, improvident, small-minded, insular, parochial, provincial.
– OPPOSITES long-sighted, imaginative.
short-staffed ● adjective UNDERSTAFFED, short-handed, undermanned, below strength.
short-tempered ● adjective IRRITABLE, irascible, hot-tempered, quick-tempered, snappish, fiery, touchy, volatile; cross, crabby, crotchety, cantankerous, grumpy, ill-tempered, bad-tempered, testy, tetchy, prickly, choleric; *informal* snappy, chippy, grouchy, cranky, on a short fuse; *Brit. informal* narky, ratty, eggy, like a bear

out. **3** US & Austral./NZ informal drunk.
– PHRASES **get** (or **be**) **shot of** Brit. informal get (or be) rid of. **shot through with** suffused with.
shot[3] • noun Brit. informal, dated a bill or one's share of it, especially in a pub.
– ORIGIN from SHOT[1].
shot-blast • verb clean or strip (a surface) by directing a high-speed stream of steel particles at it.
shot glass • noun N. Amer. a small glass used for serving spirits.
shotgun • noun a smooth-bore gun for firing small shot at short range.
shotgun marriage (also **shotgun wedding**) • noun informal an enforced or hurried wedding, especially because the bride is pregnant.
shot put • noun an athletic contest in which a very heavy round ball is thrown as far as possible.
– DERIVATIVES **shot-putter** noun **shot-putting** noun.
should • modal verb (3rd sing. **should**) **1** used to indicate obligation, duty, or correctness. **2** used to indicate what is probable. **3** formal expressing the conditional mood. **4** used in a clause with 'that' after a main clause describing feelings. **5** used in a clause with 'that' expressing purpose. **6** (in the first person) expressing a polite request or acceptance. **7** (in the first person) expressing a conjecture or hope.
– USAGE Strictly speaking **should** is used with **I** and **we**, as in *I should be grateful if you would let me know*, while **would** is used with **you**, **he**, **she**, **it**, and **they**, as in *you didn't say you would be late*; in practice **would** is normally used instead of **should** in reported speech and conditional clauses, such as *I said I would be late*. In speech the distinction tends to be obscured, through the use of the contracted forms **I'd**, **we'd**, etc.
– ORIGIN past of SHALL.
shoulder • noun **1** the joint between the upper arm or forelimb and the main part of the body. **2** a joint of meat from the upper foreleg and shoulder blade of an animal. **3** a part of something resembling a shoulder, in particular a point at which a steep slope descends from a plateau or highland area. • verb **1** put (something heavy) over one's shoulder or shoulders to carry. **2** take on (a burden or responsibility). **3** push out of one's way with one's shoulder.
– PHRASES **put one's shoulder to the wheel** set to work vigorously. **shoulder arms** hold a rifle against the right side of the body, barrel upwards. **shoulder to shoulder** side by side or acting together.
– DERIVATIVES **shouldered** adjective.
– ORIGIN Old English.
shoulder bag • noun a bag with a long strap that is hung over the shoulder.
shoulder blade • noun either of the large, flat, triangular bones which lie against the ribs in the upper back; the scapula.
shoulder pad • noun a pad sewn into the shoulder of a garment to provide shape or give protection.
shoulder strap • noun **1** a narrow strip of material going over the shoulder from front to back of a garment. **2** a long strap attached to a bag for carrying it over the shoulder. **3** a strip of cloth from shoulder to collar on a military uniform or coat.
shouldn't • contraction should not.
shout • verb **1** speak or call out very loudly. **2** (**shout at**) reprimand loudly. **3** (**shout down**) prevent (someone) from speaking or being heard by shouting. **4** Austral./NZ informal treat (someone) to (something, especially a drink). • noun **1** a loud cry or call. **2** (**one's shout**) Brit. informal one's turn to buy a round of drinks.
– PHRASES **all over bar the shouting** informal (of a contest) almost finished and therefore virtually decided. **give someone a shout** informal call on or get in touch with someone. **in with a shout** informal having a good chance. **shout the odds** talk loudly and in an opinionated way.
– ORIGIN perhaps related to SHOOT.
shove • verb **1** push roughly. **2** put somewhere carelessly or roughly. • noun a strong push.
– PHRASES **shove off 1** informal go away. **2** push away from the shore in a boat. **shove up** informal move oneself to make room for someone.
– ORIGIN Old English, related to SHUFFLE.
shove-halfpenny • noun a game in which coins are struck so that they slide across a marked board on a table.
shovel • noun a tool resembling a spade with a broad blade and upturned sides, used for moving coal, earth, snow, etc. • verb (**shovelled**, **shovelling**; US **shoveled**, **shoveling**) **1** move with a shovel. **2** (**shovel down/in**) informal eat (food) quickly and in large quantities.
– ORIGIN Old English, related to SHOVE.
shovelboard • noun Brit. a game played by pushing discs with the hand or with a long-handled shovel over a marked surface.
– ORIGIN alteration of obsolete *shoveboard*.
shoveler (also **shoveller**) • noun a dabbling duck with a long broad bill.
shovel hat • noun a black felt hat with a low round crown and a broad brim turned up at the sides, formerly worn by clergymen.
show • verb (past part. **shown** or **showed**) **1** be, allow, or make visible. **2** exhibit or produce for inspection or viewing. **3** represent or depict in art. **4** display or allow to be perceived (a quality, emotion, or characteristic). **5** demonstrate or prove. **6** treat (someone) with (a specified quality). **7** explain or demonstrate something to. **8** conduct or lead: *show them in, please.* **9** (also **show up**) informal arrive for an appointment or at a gathering. **10** N. Amer. finish third or in the first three in a race. • noun **1** a

Thesaurus

with a sore head; *N. Amer. informal* soreheaded.
– OPPOSITES placid.
shot[1] • noun **1** *a shot rang out* report of a gun, crack, bang, blast; (**shots**) gunfire. **2** *the cannon have run out of shot* BULLETS, cannonballs, pellets, ammunition. **3** *a winning shot* STROKE, hit, strike; kick, throw, pitch, lob. **4** *Mike was an excellent shot* MARKSMAN, markswoman, shooter. **5** *a shot of us on holiday* PHOTOGRAPH, photo, snap, snapshot, picture, print, slide, still; *Brit.* enprint. **6** *(informal) it's nice to get a shot at driving* ATTEMPT, try; turn, chance, opportunity; *informal* go, stab, crack, bash; *formal* essay. **7** *(informal) tetanus shots* INJECTION, inoculation, immunization, vaccination, booster; *informal* jab.
– PHRASES **a shot in the arm** *(informal)* BOOST, fillip, tonic, stimulus, spur, impetus, encouragement. **a shot in the dark** (WILD) GUESS, surmise, supposition, conjecture, speculation. **like a shot** *(informal)* WITHOUT HESITATION, unhesitatingly, eagerly, enthusiastically; immediately, at once, right away/now, straight away, instantly, instantaneously, without delay; *informal* in/like a flash, before one can say Jack Robinson. **not by a long shot** BY NO (MANNER OF) MEANS, not at all, in no way, certainly not, absolutely not, definitely not; *Brit.* not by a long chalk.
shot[2] • adjective *shot silk* VARIEGATED, mottled; multicoloured, varicoloured; iridescent, opalescent.
shoulder • verb **1** *Britain shouldered the primary responsibility* TAKE ON (ONESELF), undertake, accept, assume; bear, carry. **2** *another lad shouldered him aside* PUSH, shove, thrust, jostle, force, bulldoze, bundle.
– PHRASES **give someone the cold shoulder** SNUB, shun, cold-shoulder, ignore, cut (dead), rebuff, spurn, ostracize; *informal* give someone the brush-off, freeze out; *Brit. informal* send to Coventry; *N. Amer. informal* give someone the brush. **put one's shoulder to the wheel** GET (DOWN) TO WORK, apply oneself, set to work, buckle down, roll up one's sleeves; work hard, be diligent, be industrious, exert oneself. **shoulder to shoulder 1** *the regiment lined up shoulder to shoulder* SIDE BY SIDE, abreast, alongside (each other). **2** *he fought shoulder to shoulder with the others* UNITED, (working) together, jointly, in partnership, in collaboration, in cooperation, side by side, in alliance.
shout • verb *'Help,' he shouted* YELL, cry (out), call (out), roar, howl, bellow, bawl, call at the top of one's voice, clamour, shriek, scream; raise one's voice, vociferate; *informal* holler.
– OPPOSITES whisper.
• noun *a shout of pain* YELL, cry, call, roar, howl, bellow, bawl, clamour, vociferation, shriek, scream; *informal* holler.
shove • verb **1** *she shoved him back into the chair* PUSH, thrust, propel, drive, force, ram, knock, elbow, shoulder; jostle, bundle, hustle, manhandle. **2** *she shoved past him* PUSH (ONE'S WAY), force one's way, barge (one's way), elbow (one's way), shoulder one's way.
• noun *a hefty shove* PUSH, thrust, bump, jolt.
– PHRASES **shove off** *(informal) shove off!* GO AWAY, get out (of my sight); go (your way), get going, take oneself off, be off (with you), shoo; *informal* scram, make yourself scarce, be on your way, beat it, get lost, push off, buzz off, clear off, go (and) jump in the lake; *Brit. informal* hop it, bog off, naff off; *N. Amer. informal* bug off, haul off, take a hike; *Austral. informal* nick off; *Austral./NZ informal* rack off;

spectacle or display. **2** a play or other stage performance, especially a musical. **3** a light entertainment programme on television or radio. **4** an event or competition involving the public display of animals, plants, or products. **5** informal an undertaking, project, or organization: *I run the show.* **6** an outward appearance or display of a quality or feeling. **7** (often in phrase **for show**) an outward display intended to give a false impression.

– PHRASES **get the show on the road** informal begin an undertaking or enterprise. **good** (or **bad** or **poor**) **show!** informal, dated used to express approval (or disapproval or dissatisfaction). **on show** being exhibited. **show someone a clean pair of heels** informal run away from someone extremely fast. **show someone the door** dismiss or eject someone. **show one's hand** (or **cards**) disclose one's plans. **show off 1** boastfully display one's abilities or accomplishments. **2** display (something) that is a source of pride. **show of force** a demonstration of the forces at one's command and of one's readiness to use them. **show of hands** a vote by the raising of hands. **show oneself** (or **one's face**) allow oneself to be seen; appear in public. **show round** point out interesting features in a place or building to. **show one's teeth** Brit. use one's power or authority in an aggressive or intimidating way. **show up 1** expose as being bad or faulty. **2** informal embarrass or humiliate. **show willing** display a willingness to help.

– ORIGIN Old English, 'look at, inspect'.

showband ● noun **1** a band which plays cover versions of popular songs. **2** a jazz band which performs with theatrical extravagance.

showbiz ● noun informal show business.

– DERIVATIVES **showbizzy** adjective.

showboat ● noun **1** (in the US) a river steamer on which theatrical performances are given. **2** N. Amer. informal a show-off. ● verb N. Amer. informal show off.

show business ● noun the theatre, films, television, and pop music as a profession or industry.

showcase ● noun **1** a glass case used for displaying articles in a shop or museum. **2** a place or occasion for presenting something to general attention. ● verb exhibit; display.

showdown ● noun **1** a final test or confrontation intended to settle a dispute. **2** (in poker or brag) the requirement at the end of a round that the players should show their cards to determine which is the strongest hand.

shower /showr/ ● noun **1** a brief and usually light fall of rain or snow. **2** a mass of small things falling or moving at once. **3** a large number of things happening or given at the same time: *a shower of awards.* **4** a cubicle or bath in which a person stands under a spray of water to wash. **5** an act of washing oneself in a shower. **6** Brit. informal an incompetent or worthless group of people. **7** N. Amer. a party at which presents are given to a woman who is about to get married or have a baby. ● verb **1** fall, throw, or be thrown in a shower. **2** (**shower on/upon/with**) give (a great number of things) to. **3** wash oneself in a shower.

– ORIGIN Old English.

showerproof ● adjective (of a garment) resistant to light rain. ● verb make showerproof.

showery ● adjective characterized by frequent showers of rain.

showgirl ● noun an actress who sings and dances in musicals, variety acts, etc.

showground ● noun an area of land on which a show takes place.

show house (also **show home**) ● noun Brit. a house on a newly built estate which is furnished and decorated to be shown to prospective buyers.

showing ● noun **1** a presentation of a cinema film or television programme. **2** a performance of a specified quality: *poor opinion poll showings.*

showjumping ● noun the competitive sport of riding horses over a course of fences and other obstacles in an arena.

– DERIVATIVES **showjumper** noun.

showman ● noun **1** the manager or presenter of a circus, fair, etc. **2** a person skilled at entertaining, theatrical presentation, or performance.

– DERIVATIVES **showmanship** noun.

shown past participle of SHOW.

show-off ● noun informal a person who boastfully displays their abilities or accomplishments.

showpiece ● noun **1** an outstanding example of its type. **2** an item of work presented for exhibition or display.

showplace ● noun a place of beauty or interest attracting many visitors.

showroom ● noun a room used to display cars, furniture, or other goods for sale.

show-stopper ● noun informal a performance or item receiving prolonged applause.

– DERIVATIVES **show-stopping** adjective.

show trial ● noun a judicial trial held in public with the intention of influencing or satisfying public opinion, rather than of ensuring justice.

showy ● adjective (**showier, showiest**) strikingly bright, colourful, or ostentatious.

– DERIVATIVES **showily** adverb **showiness** noun.

shrank past of SHRINK.

shrapnel /shrapnəl/ ● noun **1** small metal fragments thrown out by the explosion of a shell, bomb, etc. **2** shells designed to

Thesaurus

poetic/literary begone.

shovel ● noun *a pick and shovel* SPADE; *Austral./NZ* banjo.
● verb *shovelling snow* SCOOP (UP), dig, excavate.

show ● verb **1** *the stitches do not show* BE VISIBLE, be seen, be in view, be obvious. **2** *he wouldn't show the picture* DISPLAY, exhibit, put on show/display, put on view, parade, uncover, reveal. **3** *Frank showed his frustration* MANIFEST, exhibit, reveal, convey, communicate, make known; express, proclaim, make plain, make obvious, disclose, betray; *formal* evince. **4** *I'll show you how to make a daisy chain* DEMONSTRATE, explain, describe, illustrate; teach, instruct, give instructions. **5** *recent events show this to be true* PROVE, demonstrate, confirm, show beyond doubt; substantiate, corroborate, verify, establish, attest, certify, testify, bear out; *formal* evince. **6** *a young woman showed them to their seats* ESCORT, accompany, take, conduct, lead, usher, guide, direct, steer, shepherd. **7** *(informal) they never showed* APPEAR, arrive, come, get here/there, put in an appearance, materialize, turn up; *informal* show up.

– OPPOSITES conceal.

● noun **1** *a spectacular show of bluebells* DISPLAY, array, exhibition, presentation, exposition, spectacle. **2** *the motor show* EXHIBITION, exposition, fair, extravaganza, spectacle; *N. Amer.* exhibit. **3** *they took in a show* (THEATRICAL) PERFORMANCE, musical, play. **4** *she's only doing it for show* APPEARANCE, display, impression, ostentation, image. **5** *Drew made a show of looking busy* PRETENCE, outward appearance, (false) front, guise, semblance, pose, parade. **6** *(informal) I don't run the show* UNDERTAKING, affair, operation, proceedings, enterprise, business, venture.

– PHRASES **show off** BEHAVE AFFECTEDLY, put on airs, put on an act, swagger around, swank, strut, strike an attitude, posture; draw attention to oneself; *N. Amer. informal* cop an attitude. **show something off** DISPLAY, show to advantage, exhibit, demonstrate, parade, draw attention to, flaunt. **show up 1** *cancers show up on X-rays* BE VISIBLE, be obvious, be seen, be revealed. **2** *(informal) only two waitresses showed up.* See SHOW verb sense 7. **show someone/something up 1** *the sun showed up the shabbiness of the room* EXPOSE, reveal, make visible, make obvious, highlight. **2** *(informal) they showed him up in front of his friends.* See HUMILIATE.

showdown ● noun CONFRONTATION, clash, face-off.

shower ● noun **1** *a shower of rain* (LIGHT) FALL, drizzle, sprinkling, mizzle. **2** *a shower of arrows* VOLLEY, hail, salvo, bombardment, barrage, fusillade, cannonade. **3** *a shower of awards* AVALANCHE, deluge, flood, spate, flurry; profusion, abundance, plethora.
● verb **1** *confetti showered down on us* RAIN, fall, hail. **2** *she showered them with gifts* DELUGE, flood, inundate, swamp, engulf; overwhelm, overload, snow under. **3** *showering honours on his cronies* LAVISH, heap, bestow freely.

showing ● noun **1** *another showing of the series* PRESENTATION, broadcast, airing, televising. **2** *the party's present showing* PERFORMANCE, (track) record, results, success, achievement.

showman ● noun **1** *a travelling showman* IMPRESARIO, stage manager; ringmaster, host, compère, master of ceremonies, MC; presenter; *N. Amer. informal* emcee. **2** *he is a great showman* ENTERTAINER, performer, virtuoso.

show-off ● noun *(informal)* EXHIBITIONIST, extrovert, poser, poseur, peacock, swaggerer, self-publicist; *informal* pseud.

showy ● adjective OSTENTATIOUS, conspicuous, pretentious, flamboyant, gaudy, garish, brash, vulgar, loud, extravagant,

S

burst short of the target and shower it with shrapnel.
– ORIGIN named after the British soldier General Henry *Shrapnel* (1761–1842), inventor of shrapnel shells.

shred ● noun **1** a strip of material that has been torn, cut, or scraped from something larger. **2** a very small amount: *not a shred of evidence.* ● verb (**shredded**, **shredding**) tear or cut into shreds.
– ORIGIN Old English, related to SHROUD.

shredder ● noun a device for shredding something, especially documents.

shrew ● noun **1** a small insect-eating mammal resembling a mouse, with a long pointed snout and tiny eyes. **2** a bad-tempered or aggressively assertive woman.
– ORIGIN Old English.

shrewd ● adjective having or showing sharp powers of judgement; astute.
– DERIVATIVES **shrewdly** adverb **shrewdness** noun.
– ORIGIN originally in the sense 'evil in nature or character': from SHREW in the obsolete sense 'evil person or thing', or as the past participle of obsolete *shrew* 'to curse'.

shrewish ● adjective (of a woman) bad-tempered or nagging.
– DERIVATIVES **shrewishly** adverb **shrewishness** noun.

shriek ● verb utter a high-pitched piercing sound, cry, or words. ● noun a high-pitched piercing cry or sound.
– DERIVATIVES **shrieker** noun.
– ORIGIN imitative.

shrift ● noun archaic **1** confession, especially to a priest. **2** absolution by a priest.
– ORIGIN Old English, 'penance imposed after confession', from SHRIVE.

shrike ● noun a predatory songbird with a hooked bill, often impaling its prey on thorns.
– ORIGIN imitative.

shrill ● adjective **1** (of a voice or sound) high-pitched and piercing. **2** derogatory (of a complaint or demand) loud and forceful. ● verb make a shrill noise.
– DERIVATIVES **shrillness** noun **shrilly** adverb.
– ORIGIN Germanic.

shrimp ● noun **1** (pl. same or **shrimps**) a small, mainly marine edible crustacean with ten legs. **2** informal, derogatory a small, physically weak person. ● verb fish for shrimps.
– DERIVATIVES **shrimper** noun.
– ORIGIN probably related to Low German *schrempen* 'to wrinkle'.

shrine ● noun **1** a place regarded as holy because of its associations with a divinity or a sacred person. **2** a casket containing sacred relics; a reliquary. **3** a niche or enclosure containing a religious statue or other object. ● verb literary enshrine.
– ORIGIN Old English, 'cabinet, chest, reliquary'.

shrink ● verb (past **shrank**; past part. **shrunk** or (especially as adj.) **shrunken**) **1** become or make smaller in size or amount; contract. **2** (of clothes or material) become smaller as a result of being immersed in water. **3** move back or away in fear or disgust. **4** (**shrink from**) be averse to or unwilling to do. ● noun informal a psychiatrist. [ORIGIN from *headshrinker*.]
– DERIVATIVES **shrinkable** adjective.
– ORIGIN Old English.

shrinkage ● noun **1** the process or amount of shrinking. **2** an allowance made for reduction in the takings of a business due to wastage or theft.

shrinking violet ● noun informal an exaggeratedly shy person.

shrink wrap ● noun clinging transparent plastic film used to enclose an article as packaging. ● verb (**shrink-wrap**) enclose in shrink wrap.

shrive /shrīv/ ● verb (past **shrove**; past part. **shriven**) archaic **1** (of a priest) hear the confession of, assign penance to, and absolve (someone). **2** (**shrive oneself**) present oneself to a priest for confession, penance, and absolution.
– ORIGIN Old English, related to Latin *scribere* 'write'.

shrivel ● verb (**shrivelled**, **shrivelling**; US **shriveled**, **shriveling**) wrinkle and contract through loss of moisture.
– ORIGIN perhaps Scandinavian.

shroud ● noun **1** a length of cloth or an enveloping garment in which a dead person is wrapped for burial. **2** a thing that envelops or obscures. **3** technical a protective casing or cover. **4** (**shrouds**) a set of ropes forming part of the rigging of a sailing boat and supporting the mast or topmast. ● verb **1** wrap or dress in a shroud. **2** cover or envelop so as to conceal from view.
– ORIGIN Old English, 'garment, clothing'; related to SHRED.

shrove past of SHRIVE.

Shrove Tuesday ● noun the day before Ash Wednesday, traditionally marked by feasting before the Lenten fast.

shrub[1] ● noun a woody plant which is smaller than a tree and has several main stems arising at or near the ground.
– DERIVATIVES **shrubby** adjective.
– ORIGIN Old English.

shrub[2] ● noun **1** a drink made of sweetened fruit juice and rum or brandy. **2** N. Amer. a slightly acid cordial made from fruit juice and water.
– ORIGIN Arabic, related to SHERBET and SYRUP.

shrubbery ● noun (pl. **shrubberies**) an area in a garden planted with shrubs.

shrug ● verb (**shrugged**, **shrugging**) **1** raise (one's shoulders) slightly and momentarily to express doubt, ignorance, or indifference. **2** (**shrug off**) dismiss as unimportant. ● noun **1** an act of shrugging one's shoulders. **2** a woman's close-fitting cardigan or jacket cut short at the front and back so that only the arms and shoulders are covered.
– ORIGIN originally in the sense 'fidget': of unknown origin.

shrunk (also **shrunken**) past participle of SHRINK.

shtick /shtik/ ● noun informal an attention-getting or theatrical routine, gimmick, or talent.

Thesaurus

S

fancy, ornate, over-elaborate, kitsch; *informal* flash, flashy, glitzy, ritzy, swanky; *N. Amer. informal* superfly.
– OPPOSITES restrained.

shred ● noun **1** *her dress was torn to shreds* TATTER, scrap, strip, ribbon, rag, fragment, sliver, (tiny) bit/piece. **2** *not a shred of evidence* SCRAP, bit, speck, iota, particle, ounce, whit, jot, crumb, morsel, fragment, grain, drop, trace, scintilla, spot; *informal* smidgen.
● verb *shredding vegetables* CHOP FINELY, cut up, tear up, grate, mince, macerate, grind.

shrew ● noun VIRAGO, dragon, termagant, fishwife, witch, tartar, hag; *informal* battleaxe, old bag, old bat; *archaic* scold.

shrewd ● adjective ASTUTE, sharp-witted, sharp, smart, acute, intelligent, clever, canny, perceptive, perspicacious, sagacious, wise; *informal* on the ball, savvy; *N. Amer. informal* heads-up; *formal* sapient.
– OPPOSITES stupid.

shrewdness ● noun ASTUTENESS, sharp-wittedness, acuteness, acumen, acuity, intelligence, cleverness, smartness, wit, canniness, common sense, discernment, insight, understanding, perception, perceptiveness, perspicacity, perspicaciousness, discrimination, sagacity, sageness; *informal* nous, horse sense, savvy; *formal* sapience.

shrewish ● adjective BAD-TEMPERED, quarrelsome, spiteful, sharp-tongued, scolding, nagging; venomous, rancorous, bitchy.

shriek ● verb *she shrieked with laughter* SCREAM, screech, squeal, squawk, roar, howl, shout, yelp; *informal* holler.
● noun *a shriek of laughter* SCREAM, screech, squeal, squawk, roar, howl, shout, yelp; *informal* holler.

shrill ● adjective HIGH-PITCHED, piercing, high, sharp, ear-piercing, ear-splitting, penetrating, screeching, shrieking, screechy.
– OPPOSITES low, soft.

shrine ● noun **1** *the shrine of St James* HOLY PLACE, temple, church, chapel, tabernacle, sanctuary, sanctum. **2** *a shrine to the Beatles* MEMORIAL, monument.

shrink ● verb **1** *the sweater shrank in the wash* GET SMALLER, become/grow smaller, contract, diminish, lessen, reduce, decrease, dwindle, decline, fall off, drop off. **2** *he shrank back against the wall* DRAW BACK, recoil, back away, retreat, withdraw, cringe, cower, quail. **3** *he doesn't shrink from naming names* RECOIL, shy away, demur, flinch, have scruples, have misgivings, have qualms, be loath, be reluctant, be unwilling, be averse, fight shy of, be hesitant, be afraid, hesitate, baulk at; *archaic* disrelish something.
– OPPOSITES expand, increase.

shrivel ● verb WITHER, shrink; wilt; dry up, desiccate, dehydrate, parch, frazzle.

shroud ● noun **1** *the Turin Shroud* WINDING SHEET; *historical* cerements. **2** *a shroud of mist | a shroud of secrecy* COVERING, cover, cloak, mantle, blanket, layer, cloud, veil.
● verb *a mist shrouded the jetties* COVER, envelop, veil, cloak, blanket, screen, conceal, hide, mask, obscure; *poetic/literary* enshroud.

shrub ● noun BUSH, woody plant.

– ORIGIN Yiddish, from German *Stück* 'piece'.
shtook /shto͝ok/ (also **schtuck**) ● **noun** informal trouble.
– ORIGIN of unknown origin.
shtum /shto͝om/ (also **schtum**) ● **adjective** informal silent; non-communicative.
– ORIGIN Yiddish, from German *stumm*.
shubunkin /sho͞obungkin/ ● **noun** an ornamental variety of goldfish with black spots, red patches, and long fins and tail.
– ORIGIN Japanese.
shuck /shuk/ chiefly N. Amer. ● **noun 1** a husk or pod, especially the husk of an ear of maize. **2** the shell of an oyster or clam. ● **verb 1** remove the shucks from. **2** informal get rid of. **3** informal take off (a garment).
– ORIGIN of unknown origin.
shucks ● **exclamation** informal, chiefly N. Amer. used to express surprise, regret, etc.
shudder ● **verb** tremble or shake convulsively, especially as a result of fear or repugnance. ● **noun** an act of shuddering.
– DERIVATIVES **shuddery** adjective.
– ORIGIN Dutch *schūderen*.
shuffle ● **verb 1** walk by dragging one's feet along or without lifting them fully from the ground. **2** restlessly shift one's position. **3** rearrange (a pack of cards) by sliding them over each other quickly. **4** (**shuffle through**) sort or look through (a number of things) hurriedly. **5** move (people or things) around into different positions or a different order. **6** (**shuffle off/out of**) get out of or avoid (a responsibility or obligation). ● **noun 1** a shuffling movement, walk, or sound. **2** a quick dragging or scraping movement of the feet in dancing. **3** an act of shuffling a pack of cards. **4** a change of order or relative positions; a reshuffle. **5** a facility on a CD player for playing tracks in an arbitrary order.
– DERIVATIVES **shuffler** noun.
– ORIGIN perhaps from Low German *schuffeln* 'walk clumsily', also 'deal dishonestly, shuffle (cards)'.
shuffleboard ● **noun** North American term for SHOVELBOARD.
shufti /sho͝ofti/ ● **noun** (pl. **shuftis**) Brit. informal a quick look or reconnoitre.
– ORIGIN World War Two military slang: from an Arabic word meaning 'try to see'.
shun ● **verb** (**shunned**, **shunning**) persistently avoid, ignore, or reject.
– ORIGIN Old English, 'abhor, shrink back with fear, seek safety from an enemy'.
shunt ● **verb 1** slowly push or pull (a railway vehicle or vehicles) so as to make up or remove from a train. **2** push or shove. **3** direct or divert to a less important place or position. ● **noun 1** an act of shunting. **2** Brit. informal a motor accident, especially a collision of vehicles travelling one close behind the other. **3** an electrical conductor joining two points of a circuit.
– ORIGIN perhaps from SHUN.
shunter ● **noun 1** a small locomotive used for shunting. **2** a railway worker engaged in such work.
shut ● **verb** (**shutting**; past and past part. **shut**) **1** move into position to block an opening. **2** (**shut in/out**) confine or exclude by closing something such as a door. **3** fold or bring together the sides or parts of. **4** chiefly Brit. make or become unavailable for business or service.
– PHRASES **be** (or **get**) **shut of** informal be (or get) rid of. **shut down** cease business or operation. **shut off** stop flowing or working. **shut out** prevent (an opponent) from scoring in a game. **shut up** informal stop talking.
– ORIGIN Old English, 'put (a bolt) in position to hold fast'; related to SHOOT.
shutdown ● **noun** a closure of a factory or instance of turning off a machine or computer.
shut-eye ● **noun** informal sleep.
shutout ● **noun** a match or period in which the opposition is prevented from scoring.
shutter ● **noun 1** each of a pair of hinged panels fixed inside or outside a window that can be closed for security or privacy or to keep out the light. **2** a device that opens and closes to expose the film in a camera. **3** the blind enclosing the swell box in an organ, used for controlling the volume of sound. ● **verb** close the shutters of (a window or building).
shuttle ● **noun 1** a form of transport that travels regularly between two places. **2** (in weaving) a bobbin with two pointed ends used for carrying the weft thread across the cloth, between the warp threads. **3** a bobbin carrying the lower thread in a sewing machine. **4** short for SHUTTLECOCK. ● **verb 1** travel regularly between two or more places. **2** transport in a shuttle.
– ORIGIN Old English, 'dart, missile'; related to SHOOT.
shuttlecock ● **noun** a light cone-shaped object struck with rackets in the games of badminton and battledore, traditionally of cork with feathers attached.
shuttle diplomacy ● **noun** negotiations conducted by a mediator who travels between two or more parties that are reluctant to hold direct discussions.
shy[1] ● **adjective** (**shyer**, **shyest**) **1** nervous or timid in the company of other people. **2** (**shy of/about**) slow or reluctant to do. **3** (in combination) having a specified dislike or aversion: *camera-shy*. **4** (**shy of**) informal less than; short of. ● **verb** (**shies**, **shied**) **1** (especially of a horse) start suddenly aside in fright. **2** (**shy from**) avoid through nervousness or lack of confidence.
– DERIVATIVES **shyly** adverb **shyness** noun.
– ORIGIN Old English.
shy[2] ● **verb** (**shies**, **shied**) throw at a target. ● **noun** (pl. **shies**) an act of shying.
– ORIGIN of unknown origin.
shyster ● **noun** informal a person, especially a lawyer, who uses unscrupulous methods.
– ORIGIN said to be from *Scheuster*, the name of a lawyer.

Thesaurus

shrug ● **verb**
– PHRASES **shrug something off** DISREGARD, dismiss, take no notice of, ignore, pay no heed to, play down, make light of.
shudder ● **verb** *she shuddered at the thought* SHAKE, shiver, tremble, quiver, vibrate, palpitate.
● **noun** *a shudder racked his body* SHAKE, shiver, tremor, tremble, trembling, quiver, quivering, vibration, palpitation.
shuffle ● **verb 1** *they shuffled along the passage* SHAMBLE, drag one's feet, totter, dodder. **2** *she shuffled her feet* SCRAPE, drag, scuffle, scuff. **3** *he shuffled the cards* MIX (UP), mingle, rearrange, jumble.
shun ● **noun** AVOID, evade, eschew, steer clear of, shy away from, fight shy of, keep one's distance from, give a wide berth to, have nothing to do with; snub, give someone the cold shoulder, cold-shoulder, ignore, cut (dead), look right through; reject, rebuff, spurn, ostracize; *informal* give someone the brush-off, freeze out, stiff-arm; *Brit. informal* send to Coventry; *N. Amer. informal* give someone the bum's rush, give someone the brush.
shut ● **verb** *please shut the door* CLOSE, pull/push to, slam, fasten; put the lid on, bar, lock, secure.
– OPPOSITES open, unlock.
– PHRASES **shut down** CEASE ACTIVITY, close (down), cease operating, cease trading, be shut (down); *informal* fold. **shut someone/something in** CONFINE, enclose, impound, shut up, pen (in/up), fence in, immure, lock up/in, cage, imprison, intern, incarcerate; *N. Amer.* corral. **shut someone/something out 1** *he shut me out of the house* LOCK OUT, keep out, refuse entrance to. **2** *she shut out the memories* BLOCK, suppress. **3** *the bamboo shut out the light* KEEP OUT, block out, screen, veil. **shut up** *(informal)* BE QUIET, keep quiet, hold one's tongue, keep one's lips sealed; stop talking, quieten (down); *informal* keep mum, button it, cut the cackle, shut it, shut your face/mouth/trap, belt up, put a sock in it, give it a rest; *Brit. informal* shut your gob; *N. Amer. informal* save it. **shut someone/something up 1** *I haven't shut the hens up yet.* See SHUT SOMEONE/SOMETHING IN. **2** *(informal) that should shut them up* QUIETEN (DOWN), silence, hush, shush, quiet, gag, muzzle.
shuttle ● **verb** PLY, run, commute, go/travel back and forth, go/travel to and fro; ferry.
shy[1] ● **adjective** *I was painfully shy* BASHFUL, diffident, timid, sheepish, reserved, reticent, introverted, retiring, self-effacing, withdrawn, timorous, mousy, nervous, insecure, unconfident, inhibited, repressed, self-conscious, embarrassed.
– OPPOSITES confident.
– PHRASES **shy away from** FLINCH, demur, recoil, hang back, have scruples, have misgivings, have qualms, be chary, be diffident, be bashful, fight shy, be coy; be loath, be reluctant, be unwilling, be disinclined, be hesitant, hesitate, baulk at; *informal* boggle at; *archaic* disrelish.
shy[2] ● **verb** *they began shying stones* THROW, toss, fling, hurl, cast, lob, launch, pitch; *informal* chuck, heave, sling, bung.
shyness ● **noun** BASHFULNESS, diffidence, sheepishness, reserve, reservedness, introversion, reticence, timidity, timidness, timor-

SI • abbreviation **1** Système International, the international system of units of measurement based on the metre, kilogram, second, ampere, kelvin, candela, and mole. **2** Law statutory instrument.
Si • symbol the chemical element silicon.
Siamese • noun (pl. same) **1** dated a native of Siam (now Thailand) in SE Asia. **2** (also **Siamese cat**) a lightly built short-haired breed of cat characterized by slanting blue eyes and pale fur with darker points. • adjective dated relating to Siam.
Siamese twins • plural noun twins that are physically joined at birth, in some cases sharing organs.
– ORIGIN with reference to the *Siamese* men Chang and Eng (1811–74), who were joined at the waist.
sib • noun chiefly Zoology a brother or sister; a sibling.
– ORIGIN from Old English, 'related by birth or descent'.
Siberian /sɪbeeriən/ • noun a person from Siberia. • adjective relating to Siberia.
sibilant • adjective **1** making or characterized by a hissing sound. **2** Phonetics (of a speech sound) sounded with a hissing effect, for example *s, sh*. • noun Phonetics a sibilant speech sound.
– DERIVATIVES **sibilance** noun.
– ORIGIN from Latin *sibilare* 'hiss'.
siblicide /siblisid/ • noun Zoology the killing of a sibling or siblings.
sibling • noun each of two or more children or offspring having one or both parents in common; a brother or sister.
– ORIGIN Old English, 'relative'.
sibyl • noun **1** (in ancient times) a woman supposedly able to utter the oracles and prophecies of a god. **2** literary a woman able to foretell the future.
– DERIVATIVES **sibylline** adjective.
– ORIGIN Greek *Sibulla*.
sic /sik/ • adverb (after a copied or quoted word that appears odd or wrong) written exactly as it stands in the original.
– ORIGIN Latin, 'so, thus'.
Sicilian • noun a person from Sicily. • adjective relating to Sicily.
sick[1] • adjective **1** affected by physical or mental illness. **2** feeling nauseous and wanting to vomit. **3** informal disappointed, embarrassed, or miserable. **4** (**sick of**) bored by or annoyed with through excessive exposure. **5** informal having abnormal or unnatural tendencies; perverted. **6** informal (of humour) dealing offensively with unpleasant subjects. **7** archaic pining or longing. • noun Brit. informal vomit. • verb (**sick up**) Brit. informal bring up by vomiting.
– PHRASES **be sick 1** be ill. **2** Brit. vomit. **get sick 1** be ill. **2** N. Amer. vomit.
– ORIGIN Old English.
sick[2] • verb (**sick on**) **1** set (a dog) on. **2** set (someone) to pursue, keep watch on, or accompany.
– ORIGIN dialect variant of SEEK.
sickbay • noun a room or building set aside for sick people, especially on a ship or in a school.
sickbed • noun an invalid's bed.
sick building syndrome • noun a condition marked by headaches, respiratory problems, etc. affecting office workers, attributed to factors such as poor ventilation in the working environment.
sicken • verb **1** make disgusted or appalled. **2** become ill. **3** (**sicken for**) begin to show symptoms of (an illness). **4** (**sickening**) informal very irritating or annoying.
– DERIVATIVES **sickeningly** adverb.
sickener • noun informal something which causes disgust or severe disappointment.
sick headache • noun a headache accompanied by nausea, particularly a migraine.
sickie • noun informal **1** chiefly Brit. a period of sick leave taken when one is not actually ill. **2** another word for SICKO.
sickle • noun a short-handled farming tool with a semicircular blade, used for cutting corn, lopping, or trimming.
– ORIGIN Latin *secula*, from *secare* 'to cut'.
sick leave • noun leave of absence granted because of illness.
sickle-cell anaemia (also **sickle-cell disease**) • noun a severe hereditary form of anaemia in which a mutated form of haemoglobin distorts the red blood cells into a crescent shape at low oxygen levels.
sickly • adjective (**sicklier, sickliest**) **1** often ill; in poor health. **2** causing, characterized by, or indicative of poor health. **3** (of flavour, colour, etc.) so garish or sweet as to induce nausea. **4** excessively sentimental or mawkish.
– DERIVATIVES **sickliness** noun.
sickness • noun **1** the state of being ill. **2** a particular type of illness or disease. **3** nausea or vomiting.
sickness benefit • noun (in the UK) benefit paid weekly by the state to an individual for sickness which interrupts paid employment.
sicko • noun (pl. **sickos**) informal a mentally ill or perverted person, especially a dangerous one.
sickroom • noun a room occupied by or set apart for people who are unwell.
side • noun **1** a position to the left or right of an object, place, or central point. **2** either of the two halves of something regarded as divided by an imaginary central line. **3** an upright or sloping surface of a structure or object that is not the top or bottom and generally not the front or back. **4** each of the flat surfaces of a solid object. **5** each of the lines forming the boundary of a plane rectilinear figure. **6** each of the two surfaces of something flat and thin, e.g. paper. **7** each of the two faces of a record or of the two separate tracks on a cassette tape. **8** a part or region near the edge and away from the middle of something. **9** (before another noun) subsidiary or less important: *a side dish.* **10** a person or group opposing another or others in a dispute or contest. **11** a particular aspect: *he had a disagreeable side.* **12** a person's kinship or line of descent as traced through either their father or mother. **13** a sports team. **14** Brit. informal a television channel. **15** Brit. informal boastful or pretentious manner or attitude. • verb (**side with/against**) support or oppose in a conflict or dispute.
– PHRASES **from side to side 1** alternately left and right from a central point. **2** across the entire width; right across. **no side** Rugby the end of a game. **on the side 1** informal in addition to one's regular job. **2** informal secretly, especially as an illicit sex-

Thesaurus

ousness, mousiness, lack of confidence, inhibitedness, self-consciousness, embarrassment, coyness, demureness.
sibling • noun brother, sister; *Zoology* sib.
sick • adjective **1** *the children are sick* ILL, unwell, poorly, ailing, indisposed, not oneself; *Brit.* off colour; *informal* laid up, under the weather; *Austral./NZ informal* crook. **2** *he was feeling sick* NAUSEOUS, nauseated, queasy, about to throw up, bilious, green about the gills; seasick, carsick, airsick, travel-sick. **3** *(informal) we're sick about the plans* DISAPPOINTED, depressed, dejected, despondent, downcast, unhappy; angry, cross, annoyed, displeased, disgruntled, fed up; *Brit. informal* cheesed off. **4** *I'm sick of this music* FED UP, bored, tired, weary. **5** *(informal) a sick joke* MACABRE, black, ghoulish, morbid, perverted, gruesome, sadistic, cruel.
– OPPOSITES well.
– PHRASES **be sick** *(Brit.)* VOMIT, throw up, retch, heave, gag; *informal* chunder, chuck up, hurl, spew, keck; *Brit. informal* honk; *N. Amer. informal* spit up, barf, upchuck, toss one's cookies.
sicken • verb **1** *the stench sickened him* CAUSE TO FEEL SICK/NAUSEOUS, make sick, turn someone's stomach, revolt, disgust, make someone want to throw up; *N. Amer. informal* gross out. **2** *she sickened and died* BECOME ILL, fall ill, be taken ill/sick, catch something. **3** *I'm sickening for something* BECOME ILL WITH, fall ill with, be taken ill with, show symptoms of, develop, come down with; *Brit.* go down with; *N. Amer. informal* take sick with.
– OPPOSITES recover.
sickening • adjective NAUSEATING, stomach-turning, stomach-churning, repulsive, revolting, disgusting, repellent, repugnant, appalling, obnoxious, nauseous, vile, nasty, foul, loathsome, offensive, objectionable, off-putting, distasteful, obscene, gruesome, grisly; *N. Amer.* vomitous; *informal* gross; *formal* rebarbative; *archaic* disgustful.
sickly • adjective **1** *a sickly child* UNHEALTHY, in poor health, delicate, frail, weak. **2** *sickly faces* PALE, wan, pasty, sallow, pallid, ashen, anaemic. **3** *a sickly green* INSIPID, pale, light, light-coloured, washed out, faded. **4** *sickly love songs* SENTIMENTAL, mawkish, cloying, sugary, syrupy, saccharine; *informal* mushy, slushy, schmaltzy, weepy, lovey-dovey, corny; *Brit. informal* soppy; *N. Amer. informal* cornball, sappy, hokey, three-hankie.
– OPPOSITES healthy.
sickness • noun **1** *she was absent through sickness* ILLNESS, disease, ailment, complaint, infection, malady, infirmity, indisposition; *informal* bug, virus; *Brit. informal* lurgy; *Austral. informal* wog. **2** *a wave of sickness* NAUSEA, biliousness, queasiness. **3** *he suffered sickness and diarrhoea* VOMITING, retching, gagging; travel-

ual relationship. **3** N. Amer. served separately from the main dish. **side by side** close together and facing the same way. **take sides** support one person or cause against another or others.

– DERIVATIVES **sided** adjective **sideward** adjective & adverb **sidewards** adverb.

– ORIGIN Old English.

side arms • plural noun weapons worn at a person's side, such as pistols.

sidebar • noun a short note or supplement placed alongside a main article of text.

sideboard • noun **1** a flat-topped piece of furniture with cupboards and drawers, used for storing crockery, glasses, etc. **2** Brit. a sideburn.

sideburn • noun a strip of hair grown by a man down each side of the face in front of his ears.

– ORIGIN originally *burnside*, named after the American General Ambrose *Burnside* (1824–81), who had sideburns.

sidecar • noun a small, low vehicle attached to the side of a motorcycle for carrying passengers.

side drum • noun a small drum with a membrane at each end, the upper one being struck with sticks and the lower one often fitted with rattling cords or wires (snares).

side effect • noun a secondary, typically undesirable effect of a drug or medical treatment.

side issue • noun a subsidiary point or topic connected to some other issue.

sidekick • noun informal a person's assistant or junior associate.

sidelight • noun **1** Brit. a small supplementary light on either side of a motor vehicle's headlights. **2** (**sidelights**) a ship's navigation lights. **3** a narrow pane of glass alongside a door or larger window.

sideline • noun **1** an activity done in addition to one's main job. **2** either of the two lines bounding the longer sides of a football field, basketball court, etc. **3** (**the sidelines**) a position of observing a situation rather than being directly involved in it. • verb remove or bar from a team, game, or influential position.

sidelong • adjective & adverb directed to or from one side; sideways.

sideman • noun a supporting musician in a jazz band or rock group.

side-on • adjective & adverb on, from, or towards a side.

sidereal /sīdeeriəl/ • adjective relating to the distant stars or their apparent positions in the sky.

– ORIGIN from Latin *sidus* 'star'.

sidereal day • noun Astronomy the time between consecutive meridional transits of the First Point of Aries, almost four minutes shorter than the solar day.

sidereal time • noun Astronomy time reckoned from the motion of the earth (or a planet) relative to the distant stars (rather than with respect to the sun).

side road • noun a minor or subsidiary road joining or diverging from a main road.

side-saddle • adverb (**side-saddle**) (of a woman rider) sitting with both feet on the same side of the horse.

sideshow • noun **1** a small show or stall at an exhibition, fair, or circus. **2** a minor but diverting incident or issue.

sidesman • noun Brit. a churchwarden's assistant.

side-splitting • adjective informal extremely amusing.

sidestep • verb (**sidestepped**, **sidestepping**) **1** avoid by stepping sideways. **2** avoid dealing with or discussing. • noun an instance of sidestepping.

side street • noun a minor or subsidiary street.

sidestroke • noun a swimming stroke similar to the breaststroke in which the swimmer lies on their side.

sideswipe • noun **1** a passing critical remark. **2** chiefly N. Amer. a glancing blow from or on the side, especially of a motor vehicle. • verb chiefly N. Amer. strike with a glancing blow.

sidetrack • verb **1** distract from an immediate or important issue. **2** chiefly N. Amer. direct (a train) into a branch line or siding. • noun chiefly N. Amer. a railway branch line or siding.

sidewalk • noun N. Amer. a pavement.

sidewall • noun the side of a tyre.

sideways • adverb & adjective **1** to, towards, or from the side. **2** unconventional or unorthodox: *a sideways look at life.*

– DERIVATIVES **sidewise** adverb & adjective.

side whiskers • plural noun whiskers or sideburns on a man's cheeks.

side wind • noun a wind blowing predominantly from one side.

sidewinder /sīdwindər/ • noun a nocturnal burrowing rattlesnake that moves sideways over sand by throwing its body into S-shaped curves.

siding • noun **1** a short track at the side of and opening on to a railway line, where trains are shunted or left. **2** N. Amer. cladding material for the outside of a building.

sidle • verb walk in a furtive or stealthy manner, especially sideways or obliquely. • noun an instance of sidling.

– ORIGIN from obsolete *sideling* 'sidelong'.

SIDS • abbreviation sudden infant death syndrome.

siege • noun **1** a military operation in which enemy forces surround a town or building, cutting off essential supplies, with the aim of compelling those inside to surrender. **2** a similar operation by a police team to compel an armed person to surrender.

– PHRASES **lay siege to** conduct a siege of. **under siege** undergoing a siege.

– ORIGIN originally denoting a chair or seat: from Old French *sege*, from Latin *sedes* 'seat'.

siege mentality • noun a defensive or paranoid attitude based on the belief that others are hostile towards one.

siemens /seemənz/ • noun Physics the SI unit of conductance, equal to the reciprocal of one ohm of resistance.

Thesaurus

sickness, seasickness, carsickness, airsickness, motion sickness; *informal* throwing up, puking.

side • noun **1** *the side of the road* EDGE, border, verge, boundary, margin, fringe(s), flank, bank, perimeter, extremity, periphery, (outer) limit, limits, bounds; *poetic/literary* marge, bourn. **2** *the wrong side of the road* HALF, part; carriageway, lane. **3** *the east side of the city* DISTRICT, quarter, area, region, part, neighbourhood, sector, section, zone, ward. **4** *one side of the paper* SURFACE, face, plane. **5** *his side of the argument* POINT OF VIEW, viewpoint, perspective, opinion, way of thinking, standpoint, position, outlook, slant, angle. **6** *the losing side in the war* FACTION, camp, bloc, party, wing. **7** *the players in their side* TEAM, squad, line-up. **8** *(Brit. informal) there's absolutely no side about her.* See AFFECTATION sense 1.

– RELATED TERMS lateral.

– OPPOSITES centre, end.

• adjective **1** *elaborate side pieces* LATERAL, wing, flanking. **2** *a side issue* SUBORDINATE, lesser, lower-level, secondary, minor, peripheral, incidental, ancillary, subsidiary, of little account, extraneous.

– OPPOSITES front, central.

• verb *siding with the underdog.* See TAKE SOMEONE'S SIDE.

– PHRASES **side by side 1** *they cycled along side by side* ALONGSIDE (EACH OTHER), beside each other, abreast, shoulder to shoulder, close together. **2** *most transactions proceed side by side* AT (ONE AND) THE SAME TIME, simultaneously, contemporaneously. **take someone's side** SUPPORT, take someone's part, side with, be on someone's side, stand by, back, give someone one's backing, be loyal to, defend, champion, ally (oneself) with, sympathize with, favour.

sideline • noun *he founded the company as a sideline* SECONDARY OCCUPATION, second job; hobby, leisure activity/pursuit, recreation.

– PHRASES **on the sidelines** WITHOUT TAKING PART, without getting involved.

sidelong • adjective *a sidelong glance* INDIRECT, oblique, sideways, sideward; surreptitious, furtive, covert, sly.

– OPPOSITES overt.

• adverb *he looked sidelong at her* INDIRECTLY, obliquely, sideways, out of the corner of one's eye; surreptitiously, furtively, covertly, slyly.

side-splitting • adjective *(informal).* See FUNNY sense 1.

sidestep • verb AVOID, evade, dodge, circumvent, skirt round, bypass; *informal* duck.

sidetrack • verb DISTRACT, divert, deflect, draw away.

sideways • adverb **1** *I slid off sideways* TO THE SIDE, laterally. **2** *the expansion slots are mounted sideways* EDGEWISE, sidewards, side first, edgeways, end on. **3** *he looked sideways at her.* See SIDELONG adverb.

• adjective **1** *sideways force* LATERAL, sideward, on the side, side to side. **2** *a sideways look.* See SIDELONG adjective.

sidle • verb CREEP, sneak, slink, slip, slide, steal, edge, inch, move furtively.

– ORIGIN named after the German-born British engineer Sir Charles William *Siemens* (1823–83).

sienna ● noun a kind of earth used as a pigment in painting, normally yellowish-brown (**raw sienna**) or deep reddish-brown when roasted (**burnt sienna**).
– ORIGIN from Italian *terra di Sienna* 'earth of *Siena*' (an Italian city).

sierra /sierrə/ ● noun (in Spanish-speaking countries or the western US) a long jagged mountain chain.
– ORIGIN Spanish, from Latin *serra* 'saw'.

Sierra Leonean /sierrə liōniən/ ● noun a person from Sierra Leone, a country in West Africa. ● adjective relating to Sierra Leone.

siesta /siestə/ ● noun an afternoon rest or nap, especially one habitually taken in a hot climate.
– ORIGIN Spanish, from Latin *sexta hora* 'sixth hour'.

sieve /siv/ ● noun a utensil consisting of a wire or plastic mesh held in a frame, used for straining solids from liquids or separating coarser from finer particles. ● verb **1** put through a sieve. **2** (**sieve through**) examine in detail.
– ORIGIN Old English.

sievert /seevərt/ ● noun Physics the SI unit of dose equivalent, defined as a dose which delivers a joule of energy per kilogram of recipient mass.
– ORIGIN named after the Swedish physicist Rolf M. *Sievert* (1896–1966).

sift ● verb **1** put (a dry substance) through a sieve so as to remove lumps or large particles. **2** examine thoroughly to isolate what is important or useful. **3** (**sift down**) (of snow, ash, etc.) descend lightly or sparsely. ● noun an act of sifting.
– DERIVATIVES **sifter** noun.
– ORIGIN Old English, related to SIEVE.

sigh ● verb **1** let out a long, deep, audible breath expressing sadness, relief, tiredness, etc. **2** (**sigh for**) literary yearn for. ● noun an act of sighing, or a sound resembling this.
– ORIGIN Old English.

sight ● noun **1** the faculty or power of seeing. **2** the action or fact of seeing someone or something. **3** the area or distance within which someone can see or something can be seen. **4** a thing that one sees or that can be seen. **5** (**sights**) places of interest to tourists and other visitors. **6** (**a sight**) informal a person or thing having a ridiculous or unattractive appearance. **7** (also **sights**) a device on a gun or optical instrument used for assisting in precise aim or observation. ● verb **1** manage to see or briefly observe. **2** take aim by looking through the sights of a gun. **3** take a detailed visual measurement with a sight. **4** adjust the sight of (a gun or optical instrument).
– PHRASES **at first sight** at the first glimpse; on the first impression. **catch sight of** glimpse for a moment. **in sight 1** visible. **2** close to being achieved or realized. **in** (or **within**) **sight of 1** so as to see or be seen from. **2** close to attaining. **in** (or **within**) **one's sights 1** visible through the sights of one's gun. **2** within the scope of one's ambitions or expectations. **lose sight of 1** be no longer able to see. **2** fail to consider, be aware of, or remember. **on** (or **at**) **sight** as soon as someone or something has been seen. **out of sight 1** not visible. **2** informal excellent. **out of sight, out of mind** proverb you soon forget people or things that are no longer visible or present. **raise** (or **lower**) **one's sights** increase (or lower) one's expectations. **set one's sights on** hope strongly to achieve or reach. **a sight —** informal considerably: *she is a sight cleverer than Sarah.* **a sight for sore eyes** informal a person or thing that one is extremely pleased or relieved to see.
– DERIVATIVES **sighter** noun **sighting** noun.
– ORIGIN Old English.

sighted ● adjective **1** having the ability to see; not blind. **2** having a specified kind of sight: *keen-sighted.*

sightless ● adjective unable to see; blind.

sight line ● noun a hypothetical line from someone's eye to what is seen.

sight-read ● verb read and perform (music) at sight, without preparation.

sight screen ● noun Cricket a large white screen placed near the boundary in line with the wicket to help the batsman see the ball.

sightseeing ● noun the activity of visiting places of interest in a particular location.
– DERIVATIVES **sightseer** noun.

sight unseen ● adverb without the opportunity to look at the object in question beforehand.

sigil /sijil/ ● noun a sign or symbol.
– ORIGIN Latin *sigillum* 'sign'.

sigma /sigmə/ ● noun the eighteenth letter of the Greek alphabet (Σ, σ, or at the end of a word ς), transliterated as 's'.
– ORIGIN Greek.

sign ● noun **1** a thing whose presence or occurrence indicates the probable presence, occurrence, or advent of something else. **2** a signal, gesture, or notice conveying information or an instruction. **3** a symbol or word used to represent something in algebra, music, or other subjects. **4** Astrology each of the twelve equal sections into which the zodiac is divided. ● verb **1** write one's name on (something) for the purposes of identification or authorization. **2** engage for or commit oneself to work by signing a contract. **3** use gestures to convey information or instructions.
– PHRASES **sign off 1** conclude a letter, broadcast, or other message. **2** authorize (someone) to miss work. **sign on 1** commit oneself to something. **2** Brit. register as unemployed. **3** employ (someone). **sign out** sign to indicate that one has borrowed or hired (something). **sign up** commit oneself to a course, job, etc.
– DERIVATIVES **signer** noun.
– ORIGIN Latin *signum* 'mark, token'.

Thesaurus

S

siege ● noun BLOCKADE, encirclement; *archaic* investment.
– OPPOSITES relief.

siesta ● noun AFTERNOON SLEEP, nap, catnap, doze, rest; *informal* snooze, lie-down, forty winks, a bit of shut-eye; *Brit. informal* kip, zizz.

sieve ● noun *use a sieve to strain the mixture* STRAINER, sifter, filter, riddle, screen.
● verb **1** *sieve the mixture into a bowl* STRAIN, sift, screen, filter, riddle; *archaic* bolt. **2** *the coins were sieved from the ash* SEPARATE OUT, filter out, sift, sort out, divide, segregate, extract.

sift ● verb **1** *sift the flour into a large bowl* SIEVE, strain, screen, filter, riddle; *archaic* bolt. **2** *we sift out unsuitable applications* SEPARATE OUT, filter out, sort out, put to one side, weed out, get rid of, remove. **3** *investigators are sifting through the wreckage* SEARCH THROUGH, look through, examine, inspect, scrutinize, pore over, investigate, analyse, dissect, review.

sigh ● verb **1** *she sighed with relief* BREATHE OUT, exhale; groan, moan. **2** *the wind sighed in the trees* RUSTLE, whisper, murmur, sough. **3** *he sighed for days gone by* YEARN, long, pine, ache, grieve, cry for/over, weep for/over, rue, miss, mourn, lament, hanker for/after.

sight ● noun **1** *she has excellent sight* EYESIGHT, vision, eyes, faculty of sight, visual perception. **2** *her first sight of it* VIEW, glimpse, glance, look. **3** *within sight of the enemy* RANGE OF VISION, field of vision, view. **4** *(dated) we are all equal in the sight of God* PERCEPTION, judgement, belief, opinion, point of view, view, viewpoint, mind, perspective, standpoint. **5** *historic sights* LANDMARK, place of interest, monument, spectacle, view, marvel, wonder. **6** *(informal) I must look a sight* EYESORE, spectacle, mess; *informal* fright.
– RELATED TERMS optical, visual.
● verb *one of the helicopters sighted wreckage* GLIMPSE, catch/get a glimpse of, catch sight of, see, spot, spy, notice, observe; *poetic/literary* espy, descry.
– PHRASES **catch sight of** GLIMPSE, catch/get a glimpse of, see, spot, spy, make out, pick out, sight, have sight of; *poetic/literary* espy, descry. **set one's sights on** ASPIRE TO, aim at/for, try for, strive for/towards, work towards.

sightseer ● noun **1** *sightseers to the city* TOURIST, visitor, tripper, holidaymaker; *Brit. informal* grockle. **2** *gawping sightseers* BUSYBODY gawker; *informal* rubberneck; *Brit. informal* gawper.

sign ● noun **1** *a sign of affection* INDICATION, signal, symptom, pointer, suggestion, intimation, mark, manifestation, demonstration, token, evidence; *poetic/literary* sigil. **2** *a sign of things to come* PORTENT, omen, warning, forewarning, augury, presage; promise, threat. **3** *at his sign the soldiers followed* GESTURE, signal, wave, gesticulation, cue, nod. **4** *signs saying 'keep out'* NOTICE, signpost, signboard, warning sign, road sign, traffic sign. **5** *the dancers were daubed with signs* SYMBOL, mark, cipher, letter, character, figure, hieroglyph, ideogram, rune, emblem, device, logo.
● verb **1** *he signed the letter* WRITE ONE'S NAME ON, autograph, endorse, initial, countersign; *formal* subscribe. **2** *the government signed the agreement* ENDORSE, validate, certify, authenticate, au-

signage ● noun chiefly N. Amer. signs collectively, especially commercial or public display signs.
signal[1] ● noun **1** a gesture, action, or sound conveying information or an instruction. **2** an indication of a state of affairs. **3** an event or statement that provides the impulse or occasion for something to happen. **4** a light or semaphore on a railway, giving indications to train drivers of whether or not to proceed. ● verb (**signalled**, **signalling**; US **signaled**, **signaling**) **1** transmit a signal. **2** instruct or indicate by means of a signal.
– DERIVATIVES **signaller** noun.
– ORIGIN Latin *signalis*, from *signum* 'mark, token'.
signal[2] ● adjective noteworthy; striking.
– DERIVATIVES **signally** adverb.
– ORIGIN Italian *segnalato* 'distinguished', from *segnale* 'a signal'.
signal box ● noun Brit. a building beside a railway track from which signals, points, and other equipment are controlled.
signalize (also **signalise**) ● verb mark or indicate.
signalman ● noun **1** a railway worker responsible for operating signals and points. **2** a person responsible for sending and receiving naval or military signals.
signal-to-noise ratio ● noun the ratio of the strength of an electrical or other signal carrying information to that of unwanted interference, generally expressed in decibels.
signatory /signətri/ ● noun (pl. **signatories**) a party that has signed an agreement.
– ORIGIN from Latin *signatorius* 'of sealing', from *signare* 'to sign, mark'.
signature ● noun **1** a person's name written in a distinctive way as a form of identification or authorization. **2** the action of signing something. **3** a distinctive product or characteristic by which someone or something can be identified. **4** Music a key signature or time signature.
– ORIGIN Latin *signatura* 'sign manual', from *signare* 'to sign, mark'.
signature tune ● noun chiefly Brit. a distinctive piece of music associated with a particular programme or performer on television or radio.
signboard ● noun a board displaying the name or logo of a business or product.
signet ● noun historical a small seal, especially one set in a ring, used to give authentication to an official document.
– ORIGIN Latin *signetum* 'small token, seal'.
signet ring ● noun a ring with letters or a design set into it.
significance ● noun **1** the quality of being significant; importance. **2** the unstated meaning to be found in words or events.
– ORIGIN Latin *significantia*, from *significare* 'indicate, portend'.
significant ● adjective **1** extensive or important enough to merit attention. **2** having an unstated meaning; indicative of something.
– DERIVATIVES **significantly** adverb.
significant figure ● noun Mathematics each of the digits of a number that are used to express it to the required degree of accuracy.
signified ● noun Linguistics the meaning or idea expressed by a sign, as distinct from the physical form in which it is expressed.
signifier ● noun Linguistics a sign's physical form (such as a sound, printed word, or image) as distinct from its meaning.
signify ● verb (**signifies**, **signfied**) **1** be an indication of. **2** be a symbol of; have as meaning. **3** indicate or declare (a feeling or intention). **4** be of importance: *the locked door doesn't necessarily signify.*
– DERIVATIVES **signification** noun.
– ORIGIN Latin *significare* 'indicate, portend', from *signum* 'token'.
signing ● noun **1** Brit. a person who has recently been signed to join a sports team, record company, etc. **2** an event at which an author signs copies of their book to gain publicity and sales. **3** sign language.
sign language ● noun a system of communication used among and with deaf people, consisting of gestures and signs made by the hands and face.
signor /seenyor/ ● noun (pl. **signori** /seenyoree/) a title or form of address used of or to an Italian-speaking man, corresponding to *Mr* or *sir*.
– ORIGIN Italian, from Latin *senior* 'older man'.
signora /seenyorə/ ● noun a title or form of address used of or to an Italian-speaking married woman, corresponding to *Mrs* or *madam*.
– ORIGIN Italian, feminine of SIGNOR.
signorina /seenyəreenə/ ● noun a title or form of address used of or to an Italian-speaking unmarried woman, corresponding to *Miss*.
– ORIGIN Italian, from SIGNORA.
signpost ● noun a sign on a post, giving information such as the direction and distance to a nearby town. ● verb **1** provide (an area) with a signpost or signposts. **2** chiefly Brit. indicate (a place or feature) with a signpost.
signwriter ● noun a person who paints commercial signs and advertisements.
– DERIVATIVES **signwriting** noun.
sika /seekə/ ● noun a deer with a greyish coat that turns yellowish-brown with white spots in summer, native to Japan and SE Asia.
– ORIGIN Japanese.
Sikh /seek/ ● noun an adherent of Sikhism. ● adjective relating to Sikhs or Sikhism.
– ORIGIN Punjabi, 'disciple'.
Sikhism /seekiz'm/ ● noun a monotheistic religion founded in Punjab in the 15th century by Guru Nanak.
Siksika /siksikə/ ● plural noun the northernmost of the three peoples forming the Blackfoot confederacy.
– ORIGIN Blackfoot, 'black foot'.
silage /sīlij/ ● noun green fodder that is compacted and stored in airtight conditions without first being dried, used as animal

Thesaurus

thorize, sanction; agree to, approve, ratify, adopt, give one's approval to; *informal* give something the go-ahead, give something the green light, give something the thumbs up. **3** *he signed his name* WRITE, inscribe, pen. **4** *we have signed a new player* RECRUIT, hire, engage, employ, take on, appoint, sign on/up, enlist. **5** *she signed to Susan to leave* GESTURE, signal, give a sign to, motion; wave, beckon, nod.
– PHRASES **sign on/up** ENLIST, take a job, join (up), enrol, register, volunteer. **sign someone on/up** *they signed on a new player.* See SIGN verb sense 4. **sign something over** TRANSFER, make over, hand over, bequeath, pass on, transmit, cede; *Law* devolve, convey.
signal[1] ● noun **1** *a signal to stop* GESTURE, sign, wave, gesticulation, cue, indication, warning, motion. **2** *a clear signal that the company is in trouble* INDICATION, sign, symptom, hint, pointer, intimation, clue, demonstration, evidence, proof. **3** *the encroaching dark is a signal for people to emerge* CUE, prompt, impetus, stimulus; *informal* go-ahead.
● verb **1** *the driver signalled to her to cross* GESTURE, sign, give a sign to, direct, motion; wave, beckon, nod. **2** *they signalled displeasure by refusing to cooperate* INDICATE, show, express, communicate, proclaim, declare. **3** *his death signals the end of an era* MARK, signify, mean, be a sign of, be evidence of, herald; *poetic/literary* betoken, foretoken.
signal[2] ● adjective *a signal failure* NOTABLE, noteworthy, remarkable, striking, glaring, significant, momentous, memorable, unforgettable, obvious, special, extraordinary, exceptional, conspicuous.
significance ● noun **1** *a matter of considerable significance* IMPORTANCE, import, consequence, seriousness, gravity, weight, magnitude, momentousness; *formal* moment. **2** *the significance of his remarks* MEANING, sense, signification, import, thrust, drift, gist, implication, message, essence, substance, point.
significant ● adjective **1** *a significant increase* NOTABLE, noteworthy, worthy of attention, remarkable, important, of importance, of consequence; serious, crucial, weighty, momentous, uncommon, unusual, rare, extraordinary, exceptional, special; *formal* of moment. **2** *a significant look* MEANINGFUL, expressive, eloquent, suggestive, knowing, telling.
significantly ● adverb **1** *significantly better* NOTABLY, remarkably, outstandingly, importantly, crucially, materially, appreciably; markedly, considerably, obviously, conspicuously, strikingly, signally. **2** *he paused significantly* MEANINGFULLY, expressively, eloquently, revealingly, suggestively, knowingly.
signify ● verb **1** *this signified a fundamental change* BE EVIDENCE OF, be a sign of, mark, signal, mean, spell, be symptomatic of, herald, indicate; *poetic/literary* betoken. **2** *the egg signifies life* MEAN, denote, designate, represent, symbolize, stand for; *poetic/literary* betoken. **3** *signify your agreement by signing below* EXPRESS, indicate, show, proclaim, declare. **4** *the locked door doesn't signify* MEAN ANYTHING,

S

feed in the winter.
– ORIGIN from Spanish *ensilar* 'put into a silo'.
silence ● noun **1** complete absence of sound. **2** the fact or state of abstaining from speech. ● verb **1** make silent. **2** (**silenced**) fitted with a silencer.
– PHRASES **silence is golden** proverb it is often wise to say nothing.
– ORIGIN Latin *silentium*, from *silere* 'be silent'.
silencer ● noun a device for reducing the noise emitted by a mechanism, especially a gun or exhaust system.
silent ● adjective **1** not making or accompanied by any sound. **2** not speaking or not spoken aloud. **3** (of a film) without an accompanying soundtrack. **4** (of a letter) written but not pronounced, e.g. *b* in *doubt*. **5** not prone to speak much.
– DERIVATIVES **silently** adverb.
silent partner ● noun North American term for SLEEPING PARTNER.
silhouette /sillooet/ ● noun **1** the dark shape and outline of someone or something visible in restricted light against a brighter background. **2** a representation of someone or something showing the shape and outline only. ● verb cast or show as a silhouette.
– ORIGIN named after the French author and politician Étienne de *Silhouette* (1709–67).
silica /sillikə/ ● noun silicon dioxide, a hard, unreactive, colourless compound which occurs as quartz and in sandstone and many other rocks.
– DERIVATIVES **siliceous** /silishəss/ adjective.
– ORIGIN from Latin *silex* 'flint', on the pattern of words such as *alumina*.
silica gel ● noun hydrated silica in a hard granular hygroscopic form used as a drying agent.
silicate /sillikayt, -kət/ ● noun a salt or mineral containing silica combined with a base.
silicic /silissik/ ● adjective Geology (of rocks) rich in silica.
silicon ● noun a grey non-metallic chemical element with semiconducting properties, used in making electronic circuits.
– ORIGIN from Latin *silex* 'flint', on the pattern of *carbon* and *boron*.
silicon carbide ● noun a hard refractory compound of silicon and carbon; carborundum.
silicon chip ● noun a microchip.
silicone ● noun a durable synthetic resin with a structure based on chains of silicon and oxygen atoms with organic side chains.
silicosis /sillikōsiss/ ● noun Medicine lung fibrosis caused by the inhalation of dust containing silica.
silk ● noun **1** a fine, soft lustrous fibre produced by silkworms. **2** thread or fabric made from silk. **3** (**silks**) garments made from silk, especially as worn by a jockey. **4** Brit. informal a Queen's (or King's) Counsel. [ORIGIN so named because of the right accorded to wear a gown made of silk.]
– PHRASES **take silk** Brit. become a Queen's (or King's) Counsel.
– DERIVATIVES **silken** adjective.
– ORIGIN Latin *sericus*, from Greek *Sēres*, the name given to the inhabitants of the Far Eastern countries from which silk first came overland to Europe.
silk screen ● noun a screen of fine mesh used in screen printing. ● verb (**silk-screen**) print, decorate, or reproduce using a silk screen.
silkworm ● noun a caterpillar of a domesticated silk moth, which spins a silk cocoon that is processed to yield silk fibre.
silky ● adjective (**silkier**, **silkiest**) **1** of or resembling silk. **2** suave and smooth.
– DERIVATIVES **silkily** adverb **silkiness** noun.
sill (also chiefly Building **cill**) ● noun **1** a shelf or slab of stone, wood, or metal at the foot of a window or doorway. **2** a strong horizontal member at the base of any structure. **3** Geology a sheet of igneous rock intruded between and parallel with existing strata. Compare with DYKE[1].
– ORIGIN Old English.
silly ● adjective (**sillier**, **silliest**) **1** lacking in common sense or judgement; foolish. **2** trivial or frivolous. **3** Cricket denoting fielding positions very close to the batsman: *silly mid-on.* ● noun (pl. **sillies**) informal a silly person.
– DERIVATIVES **sillily** adverb **silliness** noun.
– ORIGIN originally in the sense 'happy', later 'innocent, feeble, ignorant': from dialect *seely*, from Germanic.
silo /sīlō/ ● noun (pl. **silos**) **1** a tall tower or pit on a farm, used to store grain. **2** a pit or other airtight structure in which green crops are stored as silage. **3** an underground chamber in which a guided missile is kept ready for firing.
– ORIGIN Spanish, from Greek *siros* 'corn pit'.
silt ● noun fine sand, clay, or other material carried by running water and deposited as a sediment. ● verb fill or block with silt.
– DERIVATIVES **siltation** noun **silty** adjective.
– ORIGIN probably originally denoting a salty deposit; related to SALT.
siltstone ● noun fine-grained sedimentary rock consisting of consolidated silt.
Silurian /sīlyooriən/ ● adjective Geology referring to the third period of the Palaeozoic era (between the Ordovician and Devonian periods, about 439 to 409 million years ago), a time when the first fish and land plants appeared.
– ORIGIN from *Silures*, the Latin name of a people of ancient Wales.
silver ● noun **1** a precious greyish-white metallic chemical element. **2** a shiny grey-white colour or appearance like that of silver. **3** coins made from silver or from a metal that resembles silver. **4** silver dishes, containers, or cutlery. **5** household cutlery of any material. ● verb **1** coat or plate with silver. **2** provide (mirror glass) with a backing of a silver-coloured material in order to make it reflective. **3** (with reference to hair) turn or cause to turn grey or white.

Thesaurus

S

be of importance, be important, be significant, be of significance, be of account, count, matter, be relevant.
silence ● noun **1** *the silence of the night* QUIETNESS, quiet, quietude, still, stillness, hush, tranquillity, noiselessness, soundlessness, peacefulness, peace (and quiet). **2** *she was reduced to silence* SPEECHLESSNESS, wordlessness, dumbness, muteness, taciturnity. **3** *the politicians kept their silence* SECRETIVENESS, secrecy, reticence, taciturnity, uncommunicativeness.
– OPPOSITES sound.
● verb **1** *he silenced her with a kiss* QUIETEN, quiet, hush, shush; gag, muzzle, censor. **2** *silencing outside noises* MUFFLE, deaden, soften, mute, smother, dampen, damp down, mask, suppress, reduce. **3** *this would silence their complaints* STOP, put an end to, put a stop to.
silent ● adjective **1** *the night was silent* COMPLETELY QUIET, still, hushed, inaudible, noiseless, soundless. **2** *the right to remain silent* SPEECHLESS, quiet, unspeaking, dumb, mute, taciturn, uncommunicative, tight-lipped; *informal* mum. **3** *silent thanks* UNSPOKEN, wordless, unsaid, unexpressed, unvoiced, tacit, implicit, understood.
– OPPOSITES audible, noisy.
silently ● adverb **1** *Nancy crept silently up the stairs* QUIETLY, inaudibly, noiselessly, soundlessly, in silence. **2** *they drove on silently* WITHOUT A WORD, saying nothing, in silence. **3** *I silently said goodbye* WITHOUT WORDS, wordlessly, in one's head, tacitly, implicitly.
silhouette ● noun *the silhouette of the dome* OUTLINE, contour(s), profile, form, shape, figure, shadow.
● verb *the castle was silhouetted against the sky* OUTLINE, delineate, define; stand out.
silky ● adjective SMOOTH, soft, sleek, fine, glossy, satiny, silken.
silly ● adjective **1** *don't be so silly* FOOLISH, stupid, unintelligent, idiotic, brainless, mindless, witless, imbecilic, doltish; imprudent, thoughtless, rash, reckless, foolhardy, irresponsible; mad, scatterbrained, feather-brained; frivolous, giddy, inane, immature, childish, puerile, empty-headed; *informal* crazy, dotty, scatty, loopy, screwy, thick, thickheaded, birdbrained, pea-brained, dopey, dim, dim-witted, half-witted, dippy, blockheaded, boneheaded, lamebrained; *Brit. informal* daft, divvy; *N. Amer. informal* chowderheaded; *dated* tomfool. **2** *that was a silly thing to do* UNWISE, imprudent, thoughtless, foolish, stupid, idiotic, senseless, mindless; rash, reckless, foolhardy, irresponsible, injudicious, misguided, irrational; *informal* crazy; *Brit. informal* daft. **3** *he would brood about silly things* TRIVIAL, trifling, frivolous, footling, petty, small, insignificant, unimportant; *informal* piffling, piddling; *N. Amer. informal* small-bore. **4** *he drank himself silly* SENSELESS, insensible, unconscious, stupid, into a stupor, into senselessness, stupefied.
– OPPOSITES sensible.
● noun *(informal) you are a silly!* See FOOL noun sense 1.
silt ● noun *the flooding brought more silt* SEDIMENT, deposit, allu-

– PHRASES **be born with a silver spoon in one's mouth** be born into a wealthy family of high social standing. **every cloud has a silver lining** proverb every difficult or sad situation has a comforting or more hopeful aspect, even though this may not be immediately apparent. **the silver screen** the cinema industry.
– DERIVATIVES **silveriness** noun **silvery** adjective.
– ORIGIN Old English.
silver birch ● noun a birch with silver-grey bark.
silver fern ● noun **1** another term for PONGA. **2** a stylized fern leaf in silver, as an emblem of New Zealand.
silverfish ● noun a small silvery wingless insect that lives in buildings.
silver jubilee ● noun the twenty-fifth anniversary of a significant event.
silver medal ● noun a medal made of or coloured silver, customarily awarded for second place in a race or competition.
silver plate ● noun **1** a thin layer of silver applied as a coating to another metal. **2** plates, dishes, etc. made of or plated with silver.
silver sand ● noun Brit. a fine, white sand used in gardening.
silver service ● noun a style of serving food at formal meals in which the server uses a silver spoon and fork in one hand to place food on the diner's plate.
silverside ● noun Brit. the upper side of a round of beef from the outside of the leg.
silversmith ● noun a person who makes silver articles.
– DERIVATIVES **silversmithing** noun.
silver tongue ● noun an ability to be eloquent and persuasive in speaking.
– DERIVATIVES **silver-tongued** adjective.
silver wedding ● noun the twenty-fifth anniversary of a wedding.
silviculture /silvikulchər/ ● noun the growing and cultivation of trees.
– DERIVATIVES **silvicultural** adjective.
– ORIGIN from Latin *silva* 'wood'.
sim ● noun informal a video game that simulates an activity such as flying an aircraft or playing a sport.
simian /simmiən/ ● adjective relating to or resembling apes or monkeys. ● noun an ape or monkey.
– ORIGIN from Latin *simia* 'ape', perhaps from Greek *simos* 'flat-nosed'.
similar ● adjective **1** of the same kind in appearance, character, or quantity, without being identical. **2** (of geometrical figures) having the same angles and proportions, though of different sizes.
– DERIVATIVES **similarity** noun **similarly** adverb.
– USAGE Use the construction **similar to**, as in *I've had problems similar to yours*; it is not good English to say **similar as**, as in *I've had similar problems as yourself.*

– ORIGIN Latin *similaris*, from *similis* 'like'.
simile /simmili/ ● noun a figure of speech involving the comparison of one thing with another thing of a different kind (e.g. *as solid as a rock*).
– ORIGIN Latin, from *similis* 'like'.
similitude /simillityo͞od/ ● noun the quality or state of being similar.
SIMM ● abbreviation Computing single in-line memory module.
simmer ● verb **1** stay or cause to stay just below boiling point while bubbling gently. **2** be in a state of suppressed anger or excitement. **3** (**simmer down**) become calmer and quieter. ● noun a state or temperature just below boiling point.
– ORIGIN from dialect *simper* in the same sense; perhaps imitative.
simnel cake ● noun chiefly Brit. a rich fruit cake with a layer of marzipan on top, eaten especially at Easter or during Lent.
– ORIGIN from Latin *simila* or Greek *semidalis* 'fine flour'.
simony /sīməni, sim-/ ● noun chiefly historical the buying or selling of pardons, benefices, and other ecclesiastical privileges.
– ORIGIN Latin *simonia*, from *Simon* Magus in the Bible, in allusion to his offer of money to the Apostles.
simoom /simo͞om/ (also **simoon** /simo͞on/) ● noun a hot, dry, dust-laden wind blowing in the desert.
– ORIGIN from an Arabic word meaning 'to poison'.
simpatico /simpattikō/ ● adjective likeable; congenial.
– ORIGIN Italian and Spanish.
simper ● verb smile in an ingratiating or coy manner. ● noun a smile of this kind.
– DERIVATIVES **simpering** adjective.
– ORIGIN of unknown origin.
simple ● adjective (**simpler**, **simplest**) **1** easily understood or done. **2** plain and uncomplicated in form, nature, or design. **3** humble and unpretentious. **4** of very low intelligence. **5** composed of a single element; not compound. **6** (in English grammar) denoting a tense formed without an auxiliary. **7** (of interest) payable on the sum loaned only. Compare with COMPOUND¹. **8** Botany (of a leaf or stem) not divided or branched. **9** (of a lens, microscope, etc.) consisting of a single lens or component. ● noun chiefly historical a medicinal herb, or a medicine made from one.
– DERIVATIVES **simpleness** noun.
– ORIGIN Latin *simplus*.
simple eye ● noun a small eye of an insect or other arthropod which has only one lens.
simple fracture ● noun a fracture of the bone only, without damage to the surrounding tissues or breaking of the skin.
simple-minded ● adjective having or showing very little intelligence or judgement.
simple time ● noun musical rhythm or metre in which each beat in a bar may be subdivided simply into halves or quar-

Thesaurus

vium, mud.
● verb *the harbour had silted up* BECOME BLOCKED, become clogged, fill up (with silt).
silver ● noun **1** *freshly polished silver* SILVERWARE, (silver) plate; cutlery, {knives, forks, and spoons}. **2** *a handful of silver* COINS, coinage, specie; (small) change, loose change. **3** *she won three silvers* SILVER MEDAL, second prize.
● adjective **1** *silver hair* GREY, greyish, white. **2** *the silver water* SILVERY, shining, lustrous, gleaming; poetic/literary argent.
similar ● adjective **1** *you two are very similar* ALIKE, (much) the same, indistinguishable, almost identical, homogeneous; informal much of a muchness. **2** *northern India and similar areas* COMPARABLE, like, corresponding, homogeneous, equivalent, analogous. **3** *other parts were similar to Wales* LIKE, much the same as, comparable to.
– OPPOSITES different, unlike.
– PHRASES **be similar to** RESEMBLE, look like, have the appearance of.
similarity ● noun RESEMBLANCE, likeness, sameness, similitude, comparability, correspondence, parallel, equivalence, homogeneity, indistinguishability, uniformity; archaic semblance.
similarly ● adverb LIKEWISE, in similar fashion, in like manner, comparably, correspondingly, uniformly, indistinguishably, analogously, homogeneously, equivalently, in the same way, the same, identically.
similitude ● noun. See SIMILARITY.
simmer ● verb **1** *the soup was simmering on the stove* BOIL GENTLY, cook gently, bubble. **2** *she was simmering with resentment* BE FURIOUS, be enraged, be angry, be incensed, be infuriated, seethe, fume, smoulder; informal be steamed up, be hot under the collar.
– PHRASES **simmer down** BECOME LESS ANGRY, cool off/down, be placated, control oneself, become calmer, calm down, become quieter, quieten down.
simper ● verb SMILE AFFECTEDLY, smile coquettishly, look coy.
simple ● adjective **1** *it's really pretty simple* STRAIGHTFORWARD, easy, uncomplicated, uninvolved, effortless, painless, undemanding, elementary, child's play; informal as easy as falling off a log, as easy as pie, as easy as ABC, a piece of cake, a cinch, no sweat, a doddle, a pushover, money for old rope, kids' stuff, a breeze; Brit. informal easy-peasy, a doss; N. Amer. informal duck soup, a snap; Austral./NZ informal a bludge, a snack. **2** *simple language* CLEAR, plain, straightforward, intelligible, comprehensible, uncomplicated, in words of one syllable, accessible; informal user-friendly. **3** *a simple white blouse* PLAIN, unadorned, undecorated, unembellished, unornamented, unelaborate, basic, unsophisticated, no-frills; classic, understated, uncluttered, restrained. **4** *the simple truth* CANDID, frank, honest, sincere, plain, absolute, unqualified, bald, stark, unadorned, unvarnished, unembellished. **5** *simple country people* UNPRETENTIOUS, unsophisticated, ordinary, unaffected, unassuming, natural, honest-to-goodness; N. Amer. cracker-barrel. **6** *he's a bit simple* HAVING LEARNING DIFFICULTIES, having special (educational) needs; of low intelligence, simple-minded, unintelligent, backward, (mentally) retarded; dated (mentally) subnormal, educationally subnormal, ESN. **7** *simple chemical substances* NON-COMPOUND,

ters. Compare with COMPOUND TIME.

simpleton • noun a foolish or gullible person.

simplex • adjective technical composed of or characterized by a single part or structure.
– ORIGIN Latin, 'single', from *simplus* 'simple'.

simplicity • noun the quality or condition of being simple.

simplify • verb (**simplifies**, **simplified**) make more simple.
– DERIVATIVES **simplification** noun.

simplistic • adjective treating complex issues and problems as simpler they really are.
– DERIVATIVES **simplistically** adverb.

simply • adverb **1** in a simple manner. **2** merely; just. **3** absolutely; completely.

simulacrum /simyoolaykrəm/ • noun (pl. **simulacra** / simyoolaykrə/ or **simulacrums**) **1** an image or representation of someone or something. **2** an unsatisfactory imitation or substitute.
– ORIGIN Latin, from *simulare* 'copy, represent'.

simulate • verb imitate or reproduce the appearance, character, or conditions of.
– DERIVATIVES **simulant** noun **simulation** noun.
– ORIGIN Latin *simulare* 'copy, represent'.

simulator • noun a machine that simulates the controls and conditions of a real vehicle, process, etc., used for training or testing.

simulcast /simməlkaast/ • noun **1** a simultaneous transmission of the same programme on radio and television, or on two or more channels. **2** N. Amer. a live transmission of a public celebration or sports event. • verb broadcast (such a transmission).
– ORIGIN blend of SIMULTANEOUS and BROADCAST.

simultaneous /simməltayniəss/ • adjective occurring, operating, or done at the same time.
– DERIVATIVES **simultaneity** /simməltənayiti/ noun **simultaneously** adverb **simultaneousness** noun.
– ORIGIN from Latin *simul* 'at the same time'.

simultaneous equations • plural noun equations involving two or more unknowns that are to have the same values in each equation.

sin[1] /sin/ • noun **1** an immoral act considered to violate divine law. **2** an act regarded as a serious offence. • verb (**sinned**, **sinning**) commit a sin.
– PHRASES **live in sin** informal, dated (of an unmarried couple) live together.
– DERIVATIVES **sinless** adjective.
– ORIGIN Old English, probably related to Latin *sons* 'guilty'.

sin[2] /sīn/ • abbreviation sine.

sin bin • noun informal **1** (in sport) a box or bench to which offending players can be sent as a penalty during a game. **2** Brit. a detention centre for offenders.

since • preposition in the period between (the time mentioned) and the time under consideration. • conjunction **1** during or in the time after. **2** for the reason that; because. • adverb **1** from the time mentioned until the present or the time under consideration. **2** ago.
– ORIGIN Old English.

sincere • adjective (**sincerer**, **sincerest**) proceeding from or characterized by genuine feelings; free from deceit.
– DERIVATIVES **sincerely** adverb **sincerity** noun.
– ORIGIN Latin *sincerus* 'clean, pure'.

sine /sīn/ • noun Mathematics (in a right-angled triangle) the ratio of the side opposite a particular acute angle to the hypotenuse.
– ORIGIN Latin *sinus* 'curve'.

sinecure /sīnikyoor, sin-/ • noun a position requiring little or no work but giving the holder status or financial benefit.
– ORIGIN from Latin *sine cura* 'without care'.

sine curve (also **sine wave**) • noun a curve representing periodic oscillations of constant amplitude, as given by a graph of the value of the sine plotted as a function of angle.

sine die /seenay deeay, sīni dīee/ • adverb (with reference to an adjournment) with no appointed date for resumption.
– ORIGIN Latin, 'without a day'.

sine qua non /seenay kwaa nōn/ • noun a thing that is absolutely essential.
– ORIGIN Latin, 'without which not'.

sinew • noun **1** a piece of tough fibrous tissue uniting muscle to bone; a tendon or ligament. **2** (**sinews**) the parts of a structure or system that give it strength or bind it together.
– DERIVATIVES **sinewy** adjective.
– ORIGIN Old English.

sinfonia /sinfōniə, sinfəneeə/ • noun Music **1** a symphony. **2** (in baroque music) an orchestral piece used as an introduction to an opera, cantata, or suite. **3** a small symphony orchestra.
– ORIGIN Italian.

sinful • adjective **1** wicked and immoral. **2** highly reprehensible: *a sinful waste.*
– DERIVATIVES **sinfully** adverb **sinfulness** noun.

Thesaurus

non-complex, uncombined, unblended, unalloyed, pure, single.
– OPPOSITES difficult, complex, fancy, compound.

simpleton • noun. See FOOL noun sense 1.

simplicity • noun **1** *the simplicity of the recipes* STRAIGHTFORWARDNESS, ease, easiness, simpleness, effortlessness. **2** *the simplicity of the language* CLARITY, clearness, plainness, simpleness, intelligibility, comprehensibility, understandability, straightforwardness, accessibility. **3** *the building's simplicity* PLAINNESS, lack/absence of adornment, lack/absence of decoration, austerity, spareness, clean lines. **4** *the simplicity of their lifestyle* UNPRETENTIOUSNESS, ordinariness, lack of sophistication, lack of affectation, naturalness.

S

simplify • verb MAKE SIMPLE/SIMPLER, make easy/easier to understand, make plainer, clarify, make more intelligible, make more comprehensible; paraphrase, put in words of one syllable.
– OPPOSITES complicate.

simplistic • adjective FACILE, superficial, oversimple, oversimplified; shallow, jejune, naive; *N. Amer. informal* dime-store.

simply • adverb **1** *he spoke simply and forcefully* STRAIGHTFORWARDLY, directly, clearly, plainly, intelligibly, lucidly, unambiguously. **2** *she was dressed simply* PLAINLY, without adornment, without decoration, without ornament/ornamentation, soberly, unfussily, unelaborately, classically. **3** *they lived simply* UNPRETENTIOUSLY, modestly, quietly. **4** *they are welcomed simply because they have plenty of money* MERELY, just, purely, solely, only. **5** *Mrs Marks was simply livid* UTTERLY, absolutely, completely, positively, really; *informal* plain. **6** *it's simply the best thing ever written* WITHOUT DOUBT, unquestionably, undeniably, incontrovertibly, certainly, categorically.

simulate • verb **1** *they simulated pleasure* FEIGN, pretend, fake, sham, affect, put on, give the appearance of. **2** *simulating conditions in space* IMITATE, reproduce, replicate, duplicate, mimic.

simulated • adjective **1** *simulated fear* FEIGNED, fake, mock, affected, sham, insincere, false, bogus; *informal* pretend, put-on, phoney. **2** *simulated leather* ARTIFICIAL, imitation, fake, mock, synthetic, man-made, ersatz.
– OPPOSITES real.

simultaneous • adjective CONCURRENT, happening at the same time, contemporaneous, concomitant, coinciding, coincident, synchronous, synchronized.

simultaneously • adverb AT (ONE AND) THE SAME TIME, at the same instant/moment, at once, concurrently, concomitantly; (all) together, in unison, in concert, in chorus.

sin • noun **1** *a sin in the eyes of God* IMMORAL ACT, wrong, wrongdoing, act of evil/wickedness, transgression, crime, offence, misdeed, misdemeanour; *archaic* trespass. **2** *the human capacity for sin* WICKEDNESS, wrongdoing, wrong, evil, evil-doing, sinfulness, immorality, vice, crime, iniquity. **3** *(informal) wasting money—it's a sin* SCANDAL, crime, disgrace, outrage.
– OPPOSITES virtue.
• verb *I have sinned* COMMIT A SIN, commit an offence, transgress, do wrong, commit a crime, break the law, misbehave, go astray; *archaic* trespass.

sincere • adjective **1** *our sincere gratitude* HEARTFELT, wholehearted, profound, deep; genuine, real, unfeigned, unaffected, true, honest, bona fide. **2** *a sincere person* HONEST, genuine, truthful, unhypocritical, straightforward, direct, frank, candid; *informal* straight, upfront, on the level; *N. Amer. informal* on the up and up.

sincerely • adverb GENUINELY, honestly, really, truly, truthfully, wholeheartedly, earnestly, fervently.

sincerity • noun HONESTY, genuineness, truthfulness, integrity, probity, trustworthiness; straightforwardness, openness, candour, candidness.

sinecure • noun EASY JOB, soft option; *informal* cushy number, money for old rope, picnic, doddle, cinch; *Austral. informal* bludge.

sinewy • adjective MUSCULAR, muscly, brawny, powerfully built, burly, strapping, sturdy, rugged, strong, powerful, athletic, muscle-bound; *informal* hunky, beefy; *dated* stalwart; *poetic/literary*

sing ● verb (past **sang**; past part. **sung**) **1** make musical sounds with the voice, especially words with a set tune. **2** perform (a song) in this way. **3** (of a bird) make characteristic melodious whistling and twittering sounds. **4** (**sing along**) sing in accompaniment to a song or piece of music. **5** make a high-pitched sound. **6** recount or celebrate: *they sang his praises.*
– DERIVATIVES **singable** adjective **singer** noun.
– ORIGIN Old English.

singalong ● noun an informal occasion when people sing together in a group.

Singaporean /singəporiən/ ● noun a person from Singapore. ● adjective relating to Singapore.

singe ● verb (**singeing**) **1** burn or be burnt lightly or superficially. **2** burn the bristles or down off (the carcass of a pig or fowl) to prepare it for cooking. ● noun a light or superficial burn.
– ORIGIN Old English.

Singhalese /singgəleez/ ● noun & adjective variant spelling of SINHALESE.

single ● adjective **1** only one; not one of several. **2** designed or suitable for one person. **3** consisting of one part. **4** regarded as distinct from others in a group. **5** even one: *not a single mention.* **6** not involved in an established romantic or sexual relationship. **7** Brit. (of a ticket) valid for an outward journey only. ● noun **1** a single person or thing. **2** a short record or CD with one song on each side. **3** (**singles**) a game or competition for individual players. **4** Cricket one run. ● verb (**single out**) choose (someone or something) from a group for special treatment.
– DERIVATIVES **singleness** noun **singly** adverb.
– ORIGIN Latin *singulus.*

single-action ● adjective (of a gun) needing to be cocked by hand before it can be fired.

single bond ● noun a chemical bond in which one pair of electrons is shared between two atoms.

single-breasted ● adjective (of a jacket or coat) fastened by one row of buttons at the centre of the front.

single combat ● noun fighting between two people.

single cream ● noun Brit. thin cream with a relatively low fat content.

single file ● noun a line of people or things arranged one behind another. ● adverb one behind another.

single-handed ● adverb & adjective **1** done without help from others. **2** done or designed to be used with one hand.
– DERIVATIVES **single-handedly** adverb.

single-lens reflex ● adjective denoting a reflex camera in which the lens that forms the image on the film also provides the image in the viewfinder.

single malt ● noun whisky that has not been blended with any other malt.

single market ● noun an association of countries trading with each other without restrictions or tariffs.

single-minded ● adjective concentrating purposefully on one particular thing.
– DERIVATIVES **single-mindedly** adverb **single-mindedness** noun.

single parent ● noun a person bringing up a child or children without a partner.

singlet ● noun chiefly Brit. a vest or similar sleeveless garment.
– ORIGIN originally denoting a man's short jacket: from SINGLE (because the garment was unlined).

singleton ● noun **1** a single person or thing of the kind under consideration. **2** informal a person who is not in a long-term relationship. **3** (in card games) a card that is the only one of its suit in a hand.

single transferable vote ● noun an electoral system of proportional representation in which a person's vote can be transferred to a further choice of candidate.

sing-song ● adjective (of a person's voice) having a repeated rising and falling rhythm. ● noun Brit. informal an informal gathering for singing.

singular ● adjective **1** exceptionally good or great; remarkable. **2** single; unique. **3** Grammar (of a word or form) denoting or referring to just one person or thing. **4** strange or eccentric. ● noun Grammar the singular form of a word.
– DERIVATIVES **singularly** adverb.
– ORIGIN Latin *singularis*, from *singulus* 'single'.

singularity ● noun (pl. **singularities**) **1** the state or quality of being singular. **2** Physics a point of infinite density at the centre of a black hole.

Sinhalese /sinhəleez, sinnə-/ (also **Singhalese**, **Sinhala** /sinhaalə/) ● noun (pl. same) **1** a member of an Indian people now forming the majority of the population of Sri Lanka. **2** an Indic language spoken by this people. ● adjective relating to the Sinhalese.
– ORIGIN from Sanskrit, 'Sri Lanka'.

sinister ● adjective **1** suggestive of evil or harm. **2** archaic & Heraldry on or towards the left-hand side and the observer's right of a coat of arms. The opposite of DEXTER.
– DERIVATIVES **sinisterly** adverb.
– ORIGIN Latin, 'left'.

sinistral /sinnistrəl/ technical ● adjective **1** of or on the left side or the left hand. **2** left-handed. ● noun a left-handed person.

sink[1] ● verb (past **sank**; past part. **sunk**) **1** become submerged in liquid. **2** (with reference to a ship) go or cause to go to the bottom of the sea. **3** disappear and not be seen or heard of again.

Thesaurus

thewy.
– OPPOSITES puny.

sinful ● adjective **1** *sinful conduct* IMMORAL, wicked, (morally) wrong, wrongful, evil, bad, iniquitous, corrupt, criminal, nefarious, depraved, degenerate; *rare* peccable. **2** *a sinful waste of money* REPREHENSIBLE, scandalous, disgraceful, deplorable, shameful, criminal.
– OPPOSITES virtuous.

sinfulness ● noun IMMORALITY, wickedness, sin, wrongdoing, evil, evil-doing, iniquitousness, corruption, depravity, degeneracy, vice; *formal* turpitude; *rare* peccability.
– OPPOSITES virtue.

sing ● verb **1** *Miguelito began to sing* croon, carol, trill, troll, chant, intone, chorus. **2** *the birds were singing* WARBLE, trill, chirp, chirrup, cheep, peep. **3** *he sang out a greeting* CALL (OUT), cry (out), shout, yell; *informal* holler. **4** (*informal*) *he's going to sing to the police* INFORM (ON SOMEONE); *informal* squeal, rat on someone, blow the whistle on someone, peach (on someone), snitch (on someone); *Brit. informal* grass (on someone), shop someone; *N. Amer. informal* finger someone, fink on someone, drop a/the dime on someone; *Austral. informal* pimp on someone.

singe ● verb SCORCH, burn, sear, char.

singer ● noun VOCALIST, soloist, songster, songstress, cantor.

single ● adjective **1** *a single red rose* ONE (ONLY), sole, lone, solitary, by itself/oneself, unaccompanied, alone. **2** *she wrote down every single word* INDIVIDUAL, separate, distinct, particular. **3** *is she single?* UNMARRIED, unwed, unwedded, unattached, free, a bachelor, a spinster; *archaic* sole.
– OPPOSITES double, married.
– PHRASES **single someone/something out** SELECT, pick out, choose, decide on; target, earmark, mark out, separate out, set apart/aside.

single-handed ● adverb BY ONESELF, alone, on one's own, solo, unaided, unassisted, without help.

single-minded ● adjective DETERMINED, committed, unswerving, unwavering, resolute, purposeful, devoted, dedicated, uncompromising, tireless, tenacious, persistent, indefatigable, dogged; *formal* pertinacious.
– OPPOSITES half-hearted.

singly ● adverb ONE BY ONE, one at a time, one after the other, individually, separately, by oneself, on one's own.
– OPPOSITES together.

singular ● adjective **1** *the gallery's singular capacity to attract sponsors* REMARKABLE, extraordinary, exceptional, outstanding, signal, notable, noteworthy; rare, unique, unparalleled, unprecedented, amazing, astonishing, phenomenal, astounding; *informal* fantastic, terrific. **2** *why was Betty was behaving in so singular a fashion?* STRANGE, unusual, odd, peculiar, funny, curious, extraordinary, bizarre, eccentric, weird, queer, unexpected, unfamiliar, abnormal, atypical, unconventional, out of the ordinary, untypical, puzzling, mysterious, perplexing, baffling, unaccountable.

singularity ● noun **1** *the singularity of their concerns* UNIQUENESS, distinctiveness. **2** *his singularities* IDIOSYNCRASY, quirk, foible, peculiarity, oddity, eccentricity.

singularly ● adverb. See EXTREMELY.

sinister ● adjective **1** *there was a sinister undertone in his words* MENACING, threatening, ominous, forbidding, baleful, frightening, alarming, disturbing, disquieting, dark, black; *formal* minatory; *poetic/literary* direful. **2** *a sinister motive* EVIL, wicked, criminal, corrupt, nefarious, villainous, base, vile, malevolent, malicious; *infor-*

S

4 drop downwards. **5** lower oneself or drop down gently. **6** (**sink in**) become fully understood. **7** insert beneath a surface. **8** (**sink into**) cause (something sharp) to penetrate (a surface). **9** gradually decrease or decline in amount or intensity. **10** pass or fall into a particular state or condition: *she sank into sleep.* **11** (**sink in/into**) put (money or energy) into.
– PHRASES **a sinking feeling** an unpleasant bodily sensation caused by apprehension or dismay. **sink or swim** fail or succeed by one's own efforts.
– ORIGIN Old English.

sink² ● noun **1** a fixed basin with a water supply and outflow pipe. **2** a sinkhole. **3** (before another noun) denoting a school or estate situated in a socially deprived area: *a sink school.* **4** a body or process by which energy or a component is removed from a system: *a heat sink.*
– ORIGIN from SINK¹.

sinker ● noun a weight used to sink a fishing line or sounding line.

sinkhole ● noun a cavity in the ground caused by water erosion and providing a route for surface water to disappear underground.

sinking fund ● noun a fund formed by periodically setting aside money for the gradual repayment of a debt.

sinner ● noun a person who sins.

Sino- /sīnō/ ● combining form Chinese; Chinese and ...: *Sino-American.*
– ORIGIN from Latin *Sinae*, from Arabic.

sinology /sīnolləji, sin-/ ● noun the study of Chinese language, history, and culture.
– DERIVATIVES **sinologist** noun.

sinter ● noun Geology a hard siliceous or calcareous deposit precipitated from mineral springs. ● verb cause (a powdered material) to coalesce by heating (and usually also by compression), without melting.
– ORIGIN German, 'cinder'.

sinuous /sinyooəss/ ● adjective **1** having many curves and turns. **2** lithe and supple.
– DERIVATIVES **sinuosity** noun **sinuously** adverb.
– ORIGIN Latin *sinuosus*, from *sinus* 'a bend'.

sinus /sīnəss/ ● noun Anatomy & Zoology a cavity within a bone or other tissue, especially one in the bones of the face or skull connecting with the nasal cavities.
– ORIGIN Latin, 'a recess, bend'.

sinusitis /sīnəsītiss/ ● noun Medicine inflammation of a nasal sinus.

Sioux /sōō/ ● noun (pl. same) the Dakota people of North America or their language.
– ORIGIN Ojibwa.

sip ● verb (**sipped**, **sipping**) drink (something) by taking small mouthfuls. ● noun a small mouthful of liquid.
– DERIVATIVES **sipper** noun.
– ORIGIN perhaps from SUP¹.

siphon (also **syphon**) ● noun a tube used to convey liquid upwards from a container and then down to a lower level, the flow being maintained by atmospheric pressure. ● verb **1** draw off or convey (liquid) by means of a siphon. **2** draw off (small amounts of money) over a period of time, especially illicitly.
– DERIVATIVES **siphonage** noun **siphonic** adjective.
– ORIGIN Greek, 'pipe'.

sir (also **Sir**) ● noun **1** a polite or respectful form of address to a man. **2** used to address a man at the beginning of a formal letter. **3** used as a title before the forename of a knight or baronet.
– ORIGIN reduced form of SIRE.

sire /sīr/ ● noun **1** the male parent of an animal. **2** literary a father or other male forebear. **3** archaic a respectful form of address to someone of high social status, especially a king. ● verb be the sire of.
– ORIGIN Old French, from Latin *senior* 'older, older man'.

siren ● noun **1** a device that makes a loud prolonged signal or warning sound. **2** Greek Mythology each of a number of women or winged creatures whose singing lured unwary sailors on to rocks. **3** a woman who is considered to be alluring but also dangerous.
– ORIGIN originally denoting an imaginary type of snake: from Greek *Seirēn.*

sirenian /sīreeniən/ ● noun Zoology a large aquatic plant-eating mammal of a group (the order Sirenia) including the dugong and manatee.
– ORIGIN Latin, from SIREN.

sirloin ● noun the choicer part of a loin of beef.
– ORIGIN Old French, 'above the loin'.

sirocco /sirokkō/ ● noun (pl. **siroccos**) a hot wind blowing from North Africa across the Mediterranean to southern Europe.
– ORIGIN Arabic, 'east wind'.

sirrah /sirrə/ ● noun archaic a term of address to a man or boy, especially one of lower status than the speaker.
– ORIGIN probably from SIRE.

sirup ● noun US spelling of SYRUP.

SIS ● abbreviation (in the UK) Secret Intelligence Service.

sis ● noun informal sister.

sisal /sīs'l/ ● noun **1** a Mexican agave with large fleshy leaves, cultivated for the fibre it yields. **2** fibre made from the sisal plant, used especially for ropes or matting.
– ORIGIN named after the port of *Sisal* in Yucatán, Mexico.

siskin ● noun a small yellowish-green finch.
– ORIGIN Dutch *siseken.*

sissy (also **cissy**) informal ● noun (pl. **sissies**) a person regarded as feeble or effeminate. ● adjective (**sissier**, **sissiest**) feeble or effeminate.
– DERIVATIVES **sissified** adjective.
– ORIGIN from SIS.

sister ● noun **1** a woman or girl in relation to other children of her parents. **2** a female friend or associate. **3** (before another noun) denoting an organization or a place which bears a relationship to another of common origin or allegiance. **4** (often **Sister**) a member of a religious order of women. **5** (often **Sister**) Brit. a senior female nurse.

Thesaurus

S

mal shady.
– OPPOSITES innocent.

sink ● verb **1** *the coffin sank below the waves* BECOME SUBMERGED, be engulfed, go down, drop, fall, descend. **2** *the cruise liner sank yesterday* FOUNDER, go under, submerge. **3** *they sank their ships* SCUTTLE, send to the bottom; *Brit.* scupper. **4** *the announcement sank hopes of a recovery* DESTROY, ruin, wreck, put an end to, demolish, smash, shatter, dash; *informal* put the kibosh on, put paid to; *Brit. informal* scupper; *archaic* bring to naught. **5** *they agreed to sink their differences* IGNORE, overlook, disregard, forget, put aside, set aside, bury. **6** *I sank myself in student life* IMMERSE, plunge, lose, bury. **7** *the plane sank towards the airstrip* DESCEND, drop, go down/downwards. **8** *the sun was slowly sinking* SET, go down/downwards. **9** *Loretta sank into an armchair* LOWER ONESELF, flop, collapse, drop down, slump; *informal* plonk oneself. **10** *her voice sank to a whisper* FALL, drop, become/get quieter, become/get softer. **11** *she would never sink to your level* STOOP, lower oneself, descend. **12** *he was sinking fast* DETERIORATE, decline, fade, grow weak, flag, waste away; be at death's door, be on one's deathbed, be slipping away; *informal* go downhill, be on one's last legs, be giving up the ghost. **13** *sink the pots into the ground* EMBED, insert, drive, plant. **14** *sinking a gold mine* DIG, excavate, bore, drill. **15** (*informal*) *he sank five pints of lager* DRINK, quaff; *informal* down, knock back, polish off; *N. Amer. informal* chug, scarf down. **16** *they sank their life savings in the company* INVEST, venture, risk.
– OPPOSITES float, rise.
● noun *he washed himself at the sink* BASIN, washbasin, handbasin; *dated* lavabo.
– PHRASES **sink in** REGISTER, be understood, be comprehended, be grasped, get through.

sinless ● adjective INNOCENT, pure, virtuous, as pure as the driven snow, uncorrupted, faultless, blameless, guiltless, immaculate.
– OPPOSITES wicked.

sinner ● noun WRONGDOER, evil-doer, transgressor, miscreant, offender, criminal; *archaic* trespasser.

sinuous ● adjective **1** *a sinuous river* WINDING, windy, serpentine, curving, twisting, meandering, snaking, zigzag, curling, coiling. **2** *sinuous grace* LITHE, supple, agile, graceful, loose-limbed, limber, lissom.

sip ● verb *Amanda sipped her coffee* DRINK (SLOWLY); *dated* sup.
● noun *a sip of whisky* MOUTHFUL, swallow, drink, drop, dram, nip; *informal* swig; *dated* sup.

siren ● noun **1** *an air-raid siren* ALARM (BELL), warning bell, danger signal; *archaic* tocsin. **2** *the siren's allure* SEDUCTRESS, temptress, femme fatale; flirt, coquette; *informal* mantrap, vamp.

sissy (*informal*) ● noun *he's a real sissy.* See DRIP noun sense 2.

– DERIVATIVES **sisterly** adjective.
– ORIGIN Old English.
sisterhood ● noun **1** the relationship between sisters. **2** a feeling of kinship with and closeness to a group of women or all women. **3** an association or community of women linked by a common interest, religion, or trade.
sister-in-law ● noun (pl. **sisters-in-law**) **1** the sister of one's wife or husband. **2** the wife of one's brother or brother-in-law.
Sisyphean /sissifeeən/ ● adjective (of a task) unending.
– ORIGIN from *Sisyphus* in Greek mythology who was condemned to the eternal task of rolling a large stone to the top of a hill, from which it always rolled down again.
sit ● verb (**sitting**; past and past part. **sat**) **1** be or cause to be in a position in which one's weight is supported by one's buttocks and one's back is upright. **2** be or remain in a particular position or state: *the fridge was sitting in a pool of water*. **3** (of an animal) rest with the hind legs bent and the body close to the ground. **4** (of a parliament, committee, court of law, etc.) be engaged in its business. **5** serve as a member of a council, jury, or other official body. **6** Brit. take (an examination). **7** (of a table or room) have enough seats for. **8** (**sit for**) pose for (an artist or photographer). ● noun a period of sitting.
– PHRASES **sit in** occupy a place as a form of protest. **sit in for** temporarily carry out the duties of. **sit on** informal **1** fail to deal with. **2** subdue or suppress. **sit out** not take part in. **sit tight** informal **1** remain firmly in one's place. **2** refrain from taking action or changing one's mind. **sit up** refrain from going to bed until later than usual.
– USAGE It is good English to use the participle **sitting** rather than **sat** with the verb 'to be': *we were sitting there for hours* rather than *we were sat there for hours*.
– ORIGIN Old English.
sitar /sittaar, sitaar/ ● noun a large, long-necked Indian lute played with a wire pick.
– DERIVATIVES **sitarist** noun.
– ORIGIN from the Persian words for 'three' and 'string'.
sitcom ● noun informal a situation comedy.
sit-down ● adjective **1** (of a meal) eaten sitting at a table. **2** (of a protest) in which demonstrators occupy their workplace or sit down on the ground in a public place. ● noun **1** a period of sitting down. **2** a sit-down protest.
site ● noun **1** an area of ground on which something is located. **2** a place where a particular event or activity is occurring or has occurred. ● verb fix or build in a particular place.
– ORIGIN Latin *situs* 'local position'.
Sitka /sitkə/ ● noun a fast-growing North American spruce tree, cultivated for its strong lightweight wood.
– ORIGIN named after the town of *Sitka* in Alaska.
sitter ● noun **1** a person who sits, especially for a portrait or examination. **2** (usu. in combination) a person who looks after children, pets, or a house while the parents or owners are away. **3** informal (in sport) an easy catch or shot.
sitting ● noun **1** a period or spell of sitting. **2** a period of time when a group of people are served a meal. **3** a period of time during which a committee or parliament is engaged in its normal business. ● adjective **1** in a seated position. **2** (of an elected representative) currently present or in office.
sitting duck ● noun informal a person or thing with no protection against attack.
sitting room ● noun chiefly Brit. a room that is furnished for sitting and relaxing in.
sitting tenant ● noun Brit. a tenant already in occupation of premises.
situate ● verb **1** place in a particular location or context. **2** (**be situated**) be in a specified financial or marital position.
– ORIGIN Latin *situare* 'place', from *situs* 'site'.
situation ● noun **1** a set of circumstances in which one finds oneself. **2** the location and surroundings of a place. **3** a job.
– PHRASES **situations vacant** (or **wanted**) chiefly Brit. jobs currently available (or sought).
– DERIVATIVES **situational** adjective.
situation comedy ● noun a television or radio series in which the same set of characters are involved in amusing situations.
situationism ● noun **1** the theory that human behaviour is determined by surrounding circumstances rather than by personal qualities. **2** a revolutionary political theory which regards modern industrial society as being inevitably oppressive and exploitative.
– DERIVATIVES **situationist** noun & adjective.
sit-up ● noun a physical exercise designed to strengthen the abdominal muscles, in which a person sits up from a supine position without using the arms for leverage.
sitz bath /sits/ ● noun a bath in which only the buttocks and hips are immersed in water.
– ORIGIN partial translation of German *Sitzbad*, from *sitzen* 'sit' + *Bad* 'bath'.
six ● cardinal number **1** one more than five; 6. (Roman numeral: **vi** or **VI**.) **2** Cricket a hit that reaches the boundary without first striking the ground, scoring six runs.
– PHRASES **at sixes and sevens** in a state of confusion or disarray. **knock for six** Brit. informal utterly surprise. **six feet under** informal dead and buried. **six of one and half a dozen of the other** a situation in which there is little difference between two alternatives.
– DERIVATIVES **sixfold** adjective & adverb.
– ORIGIN Old English.
sixer ● noun the leader of a group of six Brownies or Cubs.
six-pack ● noun **1** a pack of six cans of beer. **2** informal a set of well-developed abdominal muscles.
sixpence ● noun Brit. a small coin worth six old pence (2½ p), withdrawn in 1980.
sixpenny ● adjective Brit. costing or worth six pence, especially before decimalization (1971).
six-shooter ● noun a revolver with six chambers.
sixteen ● cardinal number one more than fifteen; 16. (Roman numeral: **xvi** or **XVI**.)
– DERIVATIVES **sixteenth** ordinal number.
sixth ● ordinal number **1** constituting number six in a sequence;

Thesaurus

S

● adjective *don't be so sissy* COWARDLY, weak, feeble, spineless, effeminate, effete, unmanly; *informal* wet, weedy, wimpish, wimpy.
sister ● noun **1** *I have two sisters* SIBLING. **2** *our European sisters* COMRADE, partner, colleague. **3** *the sisters in the convent* NUN, novice, abbess, prioress.
– RELATED TERMS sororal.
sit ● verb **1** *you'd better sit down* TAKE A SEAT, seat oneself, be seated, perch, ensconce oneself, plump oneself, flop; *informal* take the load/weight off one's feet, plonk oneself; *Brit. informal* take a pew. **2** *she sat the package on the table* PUT (DOWN), place, set (down), lay, deposit, rest, stand; *informal* stick, bung, dump, park, plonk. **3** *the chapel sat about 3,000 people* HOLD, seat, have seats for, have space/room for, accommodate. **4** *she sat for Picasso* POSE, model. **5** *a hotel sitting on the bank of the River Dee* BE SITUATED, be located, be sited, stand. **6** *the committee sits on Saturday* BE IN SESSION, meet, be convened. **7** *women jurists sit on the tribunal* SERVE ON, have a seat on, be a member of. **8** *his shyness doesn't sit easily with Hollywood tradition* BE HARMONIOUS, go, fit in, harmonize. **9** *Mrs Hillman will sit for us* BABYSIT, childmind.
– OPPOSITES stand.
– PHRASES **sit back** RELAX, unwind, lie back; *informal* let it all hang out, veg out; *N. Amer. informal* hang loose, chill out. **sit in for** STAND IN FOR, fill in for, cover for, substitute for, deputize for; *informal* sub for. **sit in on** ATTEND, be present at, be an observer at, observe; *N. Amer.* audit. **sit tight** *(informal)* **1** *just sit tight* STAY PUT, wait there, remain in one's place. **2** *we're advising our clients to sit tight* TAKE NO ACTION, wait, hold back, bide one's time; *informal* hold one's horses.
site ● noun *the site of the battle* LOCATION, place, position, situation, locality, whereabouts; *technical* locus.
● verb *bins sited at police stations* PLACE, put, position, situate, locate.
sitting ● noun *all-night sittings* SESSION, meeting, assembly; hearing.
● adjective *a sitting position* SEDENTARY, seated.
– OPPOSITES standing.
sitting room ● noun LIVING ROOM, lounge, front room, drawing room, reception room, family room; *dated* parlour.
situate ● verb LOCATE, site, position, place, station, build.
situation ● noun **1** *their financial situation* CIRCUMSTANCES, (state of) affairs, state, condition. **2** *I'll fill you in on the situation* THE FACTS, how things stand, the lie of the land, what's going on; *Brit.* the state of play; *N. Amer.* the lay of the land; *informal* the score. **3** *the hotel's pleasant situation* LOCATION, position, spot, site, setting, environment; *technical* locus. **4** *he was offered a situation in America* JOB, post, position, appointment; employment; *archaic* em-

6th. **2** (**a sixth/one sixth**) each of six equal parts into which something is or may be divided. **3** chiefly Brit. the sixth form of a school. **4** Music an interval spanning six consecutive notes in a diatonic scale.

sixth-form college • noun Brit. a college for pupils in their final years of secondary education, starting at the age of 16.

sixth sense • noun a supposed intuitive faculty giving awareness not explicable in terms of normal perception.

sixty • cardinal number (pl. **sixties**) ten more than fifty; 60. (Roman numeral: **lx** or **LX**.)
– DERIVATIVES **sixtieth** ordinal number.

sixty-four thousand dollar question • noun informal something that is not known and on which a great deal depends.
– ORIGIN originally *sixty-four dollar question*, from a question posed for the top prize in a broadcast quiz show.

sizable • adjective variant spelling of SIZEABLE.

size[1] • noun **1** the overall dimensions or extent of something. **2** each of the classes into which articles are divided according to how large they are. • verb **1** alter or sort in terms of size or according to size. **2** (**size up**) informal make an assessment of.
– PHRASES **that's the size of it** informal that is the truth about a situation, however unpalatable. **to size** to the dimensions wanted.
– DERIVATIVES **sized** adjective.
– ORIGIN Old French *assise* 'ordinance', or a shortening of ASSIZE.

size[2] • noun a gelatinous solution used in glazing paper, stiffening textiles, and preparing plastered walls for decoration. • verb treat with size.
– ORIGIN perhaps the same word as SIZE[1].

sizeable (also **sizable**) • adjective fairly large.
– DERIVATIVES **sizeably** adverb.

sizzle • verb **1** (of food) make a hissing sound when frying or roasting. **2** (**sizzling**) informal very hot or exciting. • noun an instance or the sound of sizzling.
– DERIVATIVES **sizzler** noun.
– ORIGIN imitative.

sjambok /shambok/ • noun (in South Africa) a long, stiff whip, originally made of rhinoceros hide. • verb flog with a sjambok.
– ORIGIN South African Dutch *tjambok*, from Urdu.

SK • abbreviation Saskatchewan.

ska /skaa/ • noun a style of fast popular music having a strong offbeat and originating in Jamaica in the 1960s.
– ORIGIN of unknown origin.

skag (also **scag**) • noun informal, chiefly N. Amer. heroin.
– ORIGIN of unknown origin.

skank /skangk/ • noun **1** a dance performed to reggae music, characterized by rhythmically bending forward, raising the knees, and extending the hands palms-downwards. **2** informal, chiefly N. Amer. a sleazy or unpleasant person. • verb **1** play reggae music or dance in this style. **2** informal walk or move in a sexually suggestive way.
– ORIGIN of unknown origin.

skanky • adjective informal, chiefly N. Amer. very unpleasant.

skate[1] • noun **1** an ice skate or roller skate. **2** a wheeled device used to move a heavy or unwieldy object. • verb **1** move on ice skates or roller skates in a gliding fashion. **2** ride on a skateboard. **3** (**skate over/round/around**) pass over or refer only fleetingly to (a subject or problem). **4** (**skate through**) make quick and easy progress through.
– PHRASES **get one's skates on** Brit. informal hurry up.
– DERIVATIVES **skater** noun **skating** noun.
– ORIGIN Dutch *schaats*, from Old French *eschasse* 'stilt'.

skate[2] • noun (pl. same or **skates**) an edible marine fish with a diamond-shaped body.
– ORIGIN Old Norse.

skateboard • noun a short narrow board with two small wheels fixed to the bottom of either end, on which a person can ride. • verb ride on a skateboard.
– DERIVATIVES **skateboarder** noun.

skatepark • noun an area designated and equipped for skateboarding.

skean-dhu /skeeən do͞o/ • noun a dagger worn in the stocking as part of Highland dress.
– ORIGIN from Irish and Scottish Gaelic *sgian* 'knife' + Scottish Gaelic *dubh* 'black'.

skedaddle • verb informal depart hurriedly.
– ORIGIN of unknown origin.

skeet (also **skeet shooting**) • noun a shooting sport in which a clay target is thrown from a trap.
– ORIGIN apparently a pseudo-archaic alteration of SHOOT.

skein /skayn/ • noun **1** a length of thread or yarn, loosely coiled and knotted. **2** a flock of wild geese or swans in flight.
– ORIGIN Old French *escaigne*.

skeletal /skellit'l/ • adjective **1** relating to or functioning as a skeleton. **2** existing only in outline or as a framework. **3** very thin; emaciated.
– DERIVATIVES **skeletally** adverb.

skeleton • noun **1** an internal or external framework of bone, cartilage, or other rigid material supporting or containing the body of an animal or plant. **2** a very thin or emaciated person or animal. **3** a supporting framework, basic structure, or essential part. **4** (before another noun) denoting an essential or minimum number of people or things: *a skeleton staff.*
– PHRASES **skeleton in the cupboard** a discreditable fact that someone wishes to keep secret.
– DERIVATIVES **skeletonize** (also **skeletonise**) verb.
– ORIGIN Greek, from *skeletos* 'dried up'.

skeleton key • noun a key designed to fit many locks by having the interior of the bit hollowed.

skep (also **skip**) • noun **1** a straw or wicker beehive. **2** archaic a wooden or wicker basket.
– ORIGIN Old Norse, 'basket, bushel'.

skeptic • noun US spelling of SCEPTIC.

skerrick • noun Austral./NZ informal the smallest bit: *there's not a skerrick of food in the house.*
– ORIGIN of unknown origin.

skerry • noun (pl. **skerries**) Scottish a reef or rocky island.
– ORIGIN Old Norse.

sketch • noun **1** a rough or unfinished drawing or painting. **2** a short humorous play or performance. **3** a brief written or spoken account or description. • verb **1** make a sketch of. **2** give a brief account or general outline of.
– DERIVATIVES **sketcher** noun.
– ORIGIN Italian *schizzo*, from Greek *skhedios* 'done extempore'.

Thesaurus

ploy.

six • cardinal number SEXTET, sextuplets; *technical* hexad.
– RELATED TERMS hexa-, sexi-.

size • noun *the room was of medium size* DIMENSIONS, measurements, proportions, magnitude, largeness, bigness, area, expanse; breadth, width, length, height, depth; immensity, hugeness, vastness.
• verb *the drills are sized in millimetres* SORT, categorize, classify.
– PHRASES **size someone/something up** (*informal*) ASSESS, appraise, form an estimate of, take the measure of, judge, take stock of, evaluate; *Brit. informal* suss out.

sizeable • adjective FAIRLY LARGE, substantial, considerable, respectable, significant, largish, biggish, goodly.
– OPPOSITES small.

sizzle • verb CRACKLE, frizzle, sputter, spit.

sizzling • adjective (*informal*) **1** *sizzling temperatures* EXTREMELY HOT, unbearably hot, blazing, burning, scorching, sweltering; *N. Amer.* broiling; *informal* boiling (hot), baking (hot). **2** *a sizzling affair* PASSIONATE, torrid, ardent, lustful, erotic; *informal* steamy, hot.
– OPPOSITES freezing.

skedaddle • verb (*informal*). See RUN verb sense 2.

skeletal • adjective **1** *a skeletal man* EMACIATED, very thin, as thin as a rake, cadaverous, skin-and-bones, skinny, bony, gaunt; *informal* anorexic. **2** *a skeletal account* LACKING IN DETAIL, incomplete, outline, fragmentary, sketchy; thumbnail.
– OPPOSITES fat, detailed.

skeleton • noun **1** *the human skeleton* BONES. **2** *she was no more than a skeleton* SKIN AND BONE; *informal* bag of bones. **3** *a concrete skeleton* FRAMEWORK, frame, shell. **4** *the skeleton of a report* OUTLINE, (rough) draft, abstract, (bare) bones.
• adjective *a skeleton staff* MINIMUM, minimal, basic; essential.

sketch • noun **1** *a sketch of the proposed design* (PRELIMINARY) DRAWING, outline; diagram, design, plan; *informal* rough. **2** *she gave a rough sketch of what had happened* OUTLINE, brief description, rundown, main points, thumbnail sketch, (bare) bones; summary, synopsis, summarization, precis, résumé; *N. Amer.* wrap-up. **3** *a biographical sketch* DESCRIPTION, portrait, profile, portrayal, depiction. **4** *a hilarious sketch* SKIT, scene, piece, act, item, routine.
• verb **1** *he sketched the garden* DRAW, make a drawing of, draw a picture of, pencil, rough out, outline. **2** *the company sketched out*

sketchbook (also **sketch pad**) ● noun a pad of drawing paper for sketching on.

sketchy ● adjective (**sketchier**, **sketchiest**) not thorough or detailed.
– DERIVATIVES **sketchily** adverb **sketchiness** noun.

skew ● adjective neither parallel nor at right angles to a specified or implied line; askew. ● noun **1** an oblique angle; a slant. **2** a bias towards one particular group or subject. ● verb **1** suddenly change direction or move at an angle. **2** make biased or distorted.
– DERIVATIVES **skewness** noun.
– ORIGIN from Old French *eschiver* 'eschew'.

skewbald ● adjective (of a horse) with irregular patches of white and another colour (properly not black). ● noun a skewbald horse.
– ORIGIN from obsolete *skewed* 'skewbald', on the pattern of *piebald*.

skewer ● noun a long piece of wood or metal used for holding pieces of food together during cooking. ● verb fasten together or pierce with a pin or skewer.
– ORIGIN of unknown origin.

skew-whiff ● adverb & adjective informal, chiefly Brit. not straight; askew.

ski ● noun (pl. **skis**) **1** each of a pair of long, narrow pieces of hard flexible material fastened under the feet for travelling over snow. **2** a similar device attached beneath a vehicle or aircraft. ● verb (**skis**, **skied**, **skiing**) travel over snow on skis.
– DERIVATIVES **skiable** adjective **skiing** noun.
– ORIGIN Norwegian, from an Old Norse word meaning 'snowshoe'.

skid ● verb (**skidded**, **skidding**) **1** (of a vehicle) slide sideways on slippery ground or as a result of stopping or turning too quickly. **2** slip; slide. ● noun **1** an act of skidding. **2** a runner attached to the underside of an aircraft for use when landing on snow or grass. **3** a braking device consisting of a wooden or metal shoe that prevents a wheel from revolving.
– PHRASES **hit the skids** informal begin a rapid decline. **on the skids** informal in a bad state; failing. **put the skids under** informal hasten the decline or failure of.
– ORIGIN perhaps related to SKI.

skidoo /skidōō/ trademark, chiefly N. Amer. ● noun a motorized toboggan. ● verb (**skidoos**, **skidooed**) ride on a skidoo.
– ORIGIN an arbitrary formation from SKI.

skidpan ● noun a slippery road surface prepared for drivers to practise control of skidding.

skid road ● noun N. Amer. a road formed of wooden rollers along which logs are hauled.

skid row ● noun informal, chiefly N. Amer. a run-down part of a town frequented by vagrants and alcoholics.
– ORIGIN alteration of SKID ROAD.

skier ● noun a person who skis.

skiff ● noun a light rowing boat, typically for one person.
– ORIGIN Italian *schifo*; related to SHIP.

skiffle ● noun Brit. a kind of folk music popular in the 1950s, often incorporating improvised instruments such as washboards.
– ORIGIN perhaps imitative.

ski jump ● noun **1** a steep slope levelling off before a sharp drop to allow a skier to leap through the air. **2** a leap made from such a slope.

skilful (also chiefly N. Amer. **skillful**) ● adjective having or showing skill.
– DERIVATIVES **skilfully** adverb **skilfulness** noun.

ski lift ● noun a system used to transport skiers up a slope to the top of a run, typically consisting of moving seats attached to an overhead cable.

skill ● noun **1** the ability to do something well; expertise or dexterity. **2** a particular ability. ● verb (usu. as noun **skilling**) train (a worker) to do a particular task.
– ORIGIN Old Norse, 'discernment, knowledge'.

skilled ● adjective **1** having or showing skill. **2** (of work) requiring special abilities or training.

skillet ● noun **1** a frying pan. **2** historical a small metal cooking pot with a long handle.
– ORIGIN perhaps from Latin *scutella* 'dish, platter'.

skim ● verb (**skimmed**, **skimming**) **1** remove (a substance) from the surface of a liquid. **2** move quickly and lightly over or on a surface or through the air. **3** read through quickly, noting only the important points. **4** (**skim over**) deal with or treat briefly or superficially. **5** throw (a flat stone) so that it bounces several times on the surface of water. ● noun **1** a thin layer of a substance on the surface of a liquid. **2** an act of reading something quickly or superficially.
– DERIVATIVES **skimmer** noun.
– ORIGIN Old French *escumer* 'skim'.

ski mask ● noun a protective covering for the head and face, with holes for the eyes, nose, and mouth.

skimmed milk (N. Amer. also **skim milk**) ● noun milk from which the cream has been removed.

skimp ● verb expend fewer resources on something than are necessary in an attempt to economize.
– ORIGIN of unknown origin.

skimpy ● adjective (**skimpier**, **skimpiest**) **1** providing or consisting of less than is necessary; meagre. **2** (of clothes) short and revealing.

skin ● noun **1** the thin layer of tissue forming the natural outer covering of the body of a person or animal. **2** the skin of a dead animal used as material for clothing or other items. **3** the peel or outer layer of a fruit or vegetable. **4** an outer layer. **5** (before another noun) informal referring to pornography: *the skin trade.* **6** Brit. informal a skinhead. ● verb (**skinned**, **skinning**) **1** remove the skin from. **2** graze (a part of one's body).
– PHRASES **by the skin of one's teeth** by a very narrow margin. **get under someone's skin** informal **1** annoy someone intensely. **2** reach or display a deep understanding of someone. **have a thick** (or **thin**) **skin** be insensitive (or oversensitive) to criticism or insults. **it's no skin off one's nose** informal one is not offended or adversely affected. **there's more than one way to skin a cat** proverb there's more than one way of achieving one's aim.
– DERIVATIVES **skinless** adjective **skinned** adjective **skinner** noun.
– ORIGIN Old English.

Thesaurus

S

its plans DESCRIBE, outline, give a brief idea of, rough out; summarize, precis.

sketchily ● adverb PERFUNCTORILY, cursorily, incompletely, patchily, vaguely, imprecisely; hastily, hurriedly.

sketchy ● adjective INCOMPLETE, patchy, fragmentary, cursory, perfunctory, scanty, vague, imprecise; hurried, hasty.
– OPPOSITES detailed.

skew-whiff ● adjective *(Brit. informal).* See CROOKED sense 3.

skilful ● adjective EXPERT, accomplished, skilled, masterly, master, virtuoso, consummate, proficient, talented, gifted, adept, adroit, deft, dexterous, able, good, competent, capable, brilliant, handy; *informal* mean, wicked, crack, ace, wizard; *N. Amer. informal* crackerjack.

skill ● noun **1** *his skill as a politician* EXPERTISE, skilfulness, expertness, adeptness, adroitness, deftness, dexterity, ability, prowess, mastery, competence, capability, aptitude, artistry, virtuosity, talent. **2** *bringing up a family gives you many skills* ACCOMPLISHMENT, strength, gift.
– OPPOSITES incompetence.

skilled ● adjective EXPERIENCED, trained, qualified, proficient, practised, accomplished, expert, skilful, talented, gifted, adept, adroit, deft, dexterous, able, good, competent; *informal* crack; *N. Amer. informal* crackerjack.
– OPPOSITES inexperienced.

skim ● verb **1** *skim off the scum* REMOVE, cream off, scoop off. **2** *the boat skimmed over the water* GLIDE, move lightly, slide, sail, skate, float. **3** *he skimmed the pebble across the water* THROW, toss, cast, pitch; bounce. **4** *she skimmed through the newspaper* GLANCE, flick, flip, leaf, thumb, read quickly, scan, run one's eye over. **5** *Hannah skimmed over this part of the story* MENTION BRIEFLY, pass over quickly, skate over, gloss over.
– OPPOSITES elaborate on.

skimp ● verb **1** *don't skimp on the quantity* STINT ON, scrimp on, economize on, cut back on, be sparing, be frugal, be mean, be parsimonious, cut corners; *informal* be stingy, be mingy, be tight. **2** *the process cannot be skimped* DO HASTILY, do carelessly.

skimpy ● adjective **1** *a skimpy black dress* REVEALING, short, low, low-cut; flimsy, thin, see-through, indecent. **2** *my information is rather skimpy* MEAGRE, scanty, sketchy, limited, paltry, deficient, sparse.

skin ● noun **1** *these chemicals could damage the skin* EPIDERMIS, dermis, derma. **2** *Mary's fair skin* COMPLEXION, colouring, skin

skin-deep ● adjective not deep or lasting; superficial.

skin diving ● noun the action or sport of swimming under water without a diving suit, typically using an aqualung and flippers.
– DERIVATIVES **skin-diver** noun.

skinflint ● noun informal a miser.

skinful ● noun Brit. informal enough alcoholic drink to make one drunk.

skinhead ● noun a young person of a subculture characterized by close-cropped hair and heavy boots, often perceived as aggressive and racist.

skink ● noun a smooth-bodied lizard with short or absent limbs.
– ORIGIN Greek *skinkos.*

skinny ● adjective (**skinnier**, **skinniest**) **1** (of a person) unattractively thin. **2** (of an article of clothing) tight-fitting.
– DERIVATIVES **skinniness** noun.

skinny-dip informal ● verb swim naked. ● noun a naked swim.

skint ● adjective Brit. informal having little or no money available.
– ORIGIN variant of informal *skinned*, in the same sense.

skin test ● noun a test to determine whether an immune reaction is produced when a substance is applied to or injected into the skin.

skintight ● adjective (of a garment) very close-fitting.

skip[1] ● verb (**skipped**, **skipping**) **1** move along lightly, stepping from one foot to the other with a hop or bounce. **2** jump repeatedly over a rope which is held at both ends and turned over the head and under the feet. **3** jump lightly over. **4** omit or move quickly over (a stage or point). **5** fail to attend or deal with; miss. ● noun a skipping movement.
– ORIGIN probably Scandinavian.

skip[2] ● noun **1** Brit. a large transportable open-topped container for bulky refuse. **2** a cage or bucket in which workers or materials are lowered and raised in mines and quarries.
– ORIGIN variant of SKEP.

ski pants ● plural noun women's trousers made of stretchy fabric with tapering legs and an elastic stirrup under each foot.

skipjack ● noun (also **skipjack tuna**) a small tuna with dark horizontal stripes.
– ORIGIN from SKIP[1] + JACK (with reference to the fish's habit of jumping out of the water).

skipper informal ● noun **1** the captain of a ship, boat, or aircraft. **2** the captain of a side in a game or sport. ● verb act as captain of.
– ORIGIN Dutch, Low German *schipper*, from *schip* 'ship'.

skirl ● noun a shrill sound, especially that of bagpipes. ● verb (of bagpipes) make such a sound.
– ORIGIN probably Scandinavian.

skirmish ● noun an episode of irregular or unpremeditated fighting. ● verb engage in a skirmish.
– DERIVATIVES **skirmisher** noun.
– ORIGIN from Old French *eskirmir*, from a Germanic verb meaning 'defend'.

skirt ● noun **1** a woman's outer garment fastened around the waist and hanging down around the legs. **2** the part of a coat or dress that hangs below the waist. **3** a surface that conceals or protects the wheels or underside of a vehicle or aircraft. **4** an animal's diaphragm and other membranes as food. **5** Brit. a cut of meat from the lower flank of an animal. **6** informal women regarded as objects of sexual desire. ● verb (also **skirt along/around**) **1** go round or past the edge of. **2** avoid dealing with.
– ORIGIN Old Norse, 'shirt'.

skirting (also **skirting board**) ● noun Brit. a wooden board running along the base of an interior wall.

skit ● noun a short comedy sketch or piece of humorous writing, especially a parody.
– ORIGIN related to archaic *skit* 'move lightly and rapidly'.

skite /skīt/ informal ● verb **1** Austral./NZ boast. **2** Scottish & dialect move or glance off quickly and forcefully. ● noun Austral./NZ **1** a boaster. **2** boasting or boastfulness.
– ORIGIN perhaps from Old Norse.

skitter ● verb move lightly and quickly or hurriedly.
– ORIGIN perhaps related to SKITE.

skittery ● adjective restless; skittish.

skittish ● adjective **1** (of a horse) nervous; inclined to shy. **2** lively and unpredictable; playful.
– DERIVATIVES **skittishly** adverb **skittishness** noun.
– ORIGIN perhaps related to SKIT.

skittle ● noun **1** (**skittles**) (treated as sing.) a game played with wooden pins set up at the end of an alley to be bowled down with a wooden ball. **2** a pin used in the game of skittles. **3** (also **table skittles**) a game played with similar pins set up on a board to be knocked down by swinging a suspended ball. ● verb knock over as if in a game of skittles.
– ORIGIN of unknown origin.

skive /skīv/ Brit. informal ● verb avoid work or a duty; shirk. ● noun an instance of shirking.
– DERIVATIVES **skiver** noun.
– ORIGIN perhaps from French *esquiver* 'slink away'.

skivvy ● noun (pl. **skivvies**) **1** Brit. informal a low-ranking female domestic servant. **2** a person doing menial work. ● verb (**skivvies, skivvied**) informal do menial household tasks.
– ORIGIN of unknown origin.

skua /skyo͞oə/ ● noun a large predatory seabird which pursues other birds to make them disgorge fish.
– ORIGIN Faroese.

skulduggery (also **skullduggery**) ● noun underhand or unscrupulous behaviour; trickery.
– ORIGIN alteration of Scots *sculduddery*, of unknown origin.

skulk ● verb hide or move around secretly, typically with a sin-

Thesaurus

colour/tone, pigmentation. **3** *leopard skins* HIDE, pelt, fleece; archaic fell. **4** *a banana skin* PEEL, rind, integument. **5** *milk with a skin on it* FILM, layer, membrane. **6** *the plane's skin was damaged* CASING, exterior.
– RELATED TERMS cutaneous.
● verb **1** *skin the tomatoes* PEEL, pare, hull; technical decorticate. **2** *he skinned his knee* GRAZE, scrape, abrade, bark, rub something raw, chafe; Medicine excoriate. **3** (informal) *Dad would skin me alive if I forgot it* PUNISH SEVERELY; informal murder, come down on someone (like a ton of bricks); Brit. informal give someone what for.
– PHRASES **by the skin of one's teeth** (ONLY) JUST, narrowly, by a hair's breadth, by a very small margin; informal by a whisker. **get under someone's skin** (informal) **1** *the children really got under my skin.* See IRRITATE sense 1. **2** *she got under my skin* OBSESS, intrigue, captivate, charm; enthral, enchant, entrance. **it's no skin off my nose** (informal) I DON'T CARE, I don't mind, I'm not bothered, it doesn't bother me, it doesn't matter to me; informal I don't give a damn, I don't give a monkey's.

skin-deep ● adjective SUPERFICIAL, (on the) surface, external, outward, shallow.

skinflint ● noun (informal). See MISER.

skinny ● adjective. See THIN adjective sense 3.

skip ● verb **1** *skipping down the path* CAPER, prance, trip, dance, bound, bounce, gambol, frisk, romp, cavort. **2** *we skipped the boring stuff* OMIT, leave out, miss out, dispense with, pass over, skim over, disregard; informal give something a miss. **3** *I skipped school* PLAY TRUANT FROM, miss; N. Amer. cut; Brit. informal skive off; N. Amer. informal play hookey from; Austral./NZ informal play the wag from. **4** *I skipped through the magazine* HAVE A QUICK LOOK AT, flick through, flip through, leaf through. **5** (informal) *they skipped off again* RUN OFF/AWAY, take off; informal beat it, clear off, cut and run; Brit. informal do a runner, do a bunk, scarper; N. Amer. informal light out, cut out; Austral. informal shoot through.

skirmish ● noun **1** *the unit was caught up in a skirmish* FIGHT, battle, clash, conflict, encounter, engagement, fray, combat. **2** *there was a skirmish over the budget* ARGUMENT, quarrel, squabble, contretemps, disagreement, difference of opinion, falling-out, dispute, clash, altercation; informal tiff, spat; Brit. informal row, barney, dingdong.
● verb *they skirmished with enemy soldiers* FIGHT, (do) battle with, engage with, close with, combat, clash with.

skirt ● verb **1** *he skirted the city* GO ROUND, walk round, circle. **2** *the fields that skirt the highway* BORDER, edge, flank, line, lie alongside. **3** *he carefully skirted round the subject* AVOID, evade, sidestep, dodge, pass over, gloss over; informal duck; Austral./NZ informal duckshove.

skit ● noun COMEDY SKETCH, comedy act, parody, pastiche, burlesque, satire, pasquinade; informal spoof, take-off, send-up.

skittish ● adjective **1** *she grew increasingly skittish* PLAYFUL, lively, high-spirited, sportive, frisky; poetic/literary frolicsome, wanton. **2** *Cranston's mount was skittish* RESTIVE, excitable, nervous, skittery, jumpy, highly strung.

skive ● verb (Brit. informal) MALINGER, play truant, truant, shirk, idle; N. Amer. cut; Brit. informal bunk off, swing the lead, scrimshank; N.

S

ister or cowardly motive.
– DERIVATIVES **skulker** noun.
– ORIGIN Scandinavian.

skull ● noun **1** a bone framework enclosing the brain of a person or animal. **2** informal a person's head or brain.
– PHRASES **out of one's skull** informal **1** insane. **2** very drunk. **skull and crossbones** a representation of a skull with two thigh bones crossed below it as an emblem of piracy or death.
– ORIGIN of unknown origin.

skullcap ● noun a small close-fitting peakless cap or protective helmet.

skunk ● noun a black-and-white striped American mammal able to spray foul-smelling irritant liquid at attackers.
– ORIGIN Abnaki (an American Indian language).

sky ● noun (pl. **skies**) **1** the region of the upper atmosphere seen from the earth. **2** literary heaven; heavenly power. ● verb (**skies, skied**) informal hit (a ball) high into the air.
– PHRASES **the sky is the limit** there is practically no limit. **to the skies** very highly; enthusiastically.
– DERIVATIVES **skyward** adjective & adverb **skywards** adverb.
– ORIGIN Old Norse, 'cloud'.

sky blue ● noun a bright clear blue.

skybox ● noun N. Amer. a luxurious enclosed seating area high up in a sports arena.

skydiving ● noun the sport of jumping from an aircraft and performing acrobatic manoeuvres in the air before landing by parachute.
– DERIVATIVES **skydiver** noun.

sky-high ● adverb & adjective **1** as if reaching the sky; very high. **2** at or to a very high level.

skyjack ● verb hijack (an aircraft). ● noun an act of skyjacking.
– DERIVATIVES **skyjacker** noun.

skylark ● noun a common lark of open country, noted for its prolonged song given in hovering flight. ● verb play practical jokes or indulge in horseplay.

skylight ● noun a window set in a roof or ceiling at the same angle.

skyline ● noun an outline of land and buildings defined against the sky.

skyrocket ● noun a rocket designed to explode high in the air as a signal or firework. ● verb (**skyrocketed, skyrocketing**) informal (of a price or amount) increase very rapidly.

skyscape ● noun a view or picture of an expanse of sky.

skyscraper ● noun a very tall building of many storeys.

skyway ● noun chiefly N. Amer. **1** a recognized route followed by aircraft. **2** (also **skywalk**) a covered overhead walkway between buildings.

skywriting ● noun words in the form of smoke trails made by an aircraft.

slab ● noun **1** a large, thick, flat piece of solid material, in particular stone, concrete, or heavy food. **2** Brit. a table used for laying a body on in a mortuary. **3** an outer piece of timber sawn from a log.
– ORIGIN of unknown origin.

slabber chiefly Scottish & Irish ● verb dribble at the mouth; slaver. ● noun a dribble of saliva.
– ORIGIN related to dialect *slab* 'muddy place, puddle'.

slack[1] ● adjective **1** not taut or held tightly in position; loose. **2** (of business or trade) not busy; quiet. **3** careless, lazy, or negligent. **4** (of a tide) neither ebbing nor flowing. ● noun **1** the part of a rope or line which is not held taut. **2** (**slacks**) casual trousers. **3** informal a spell of inactivity or laziness. ● verb **1** loosen or reduce the intensity or speed of; slacken. **2** (**slack off/up**) decrease in intensity or speed. **3** Brit. informal work slowly or lazily.
– PHRASES **cut some slack** N. Amer. informal allow (someone) some leeway in conduct. **take** (or **pick**) **up the slack 1** improve the use of resources to avoid an undesirable lull in business. **2** pull on the loose part of a rope to make it taut.
– DERIVATIVES **slacken** verb **slackly** adverb **slackness** noun.
– ORIGIN Old English, 'inclined to be lazy, unhurried'.

slack[2] ● noun coal dust or small pieces of coal.
– ORIGIN probably Low German or Dutch.

slacker ● noun informal **1** a person who avoids work or effort. **2** chiefly N. Amer. a young person of a subculture characterized by apathy and aimlessness.

slack water ● noun the state of the tide when it is turning.

slag ● noun **1** stony waste matter separated from metals during the smelting or refining of ore. **2** Brit. informal, derogatory a promiscuous woman. ● verb (**slagged, slagging**) **1** (usu. as noun **slagging**) produce deposits of slag. **2** (often **slag off**) Brit. informal criticize abusively.
– ORIGIN Low German *slagge*, perhaps from *slagen* 'strike', with reference to fragments formed by hammering.

slag heap ● noun a hill or area of refuse from a mine or industrial site.

slain past participle of SLAY.

slainte /slaanchə/ ● exclamation used as a toast before drinking.
– ORIGIN Scottish Gaelic, 'health'.

slake ● verb **1** satisfy (a desire, thirst, etc.). **2** combine (quicklime) with water to produce calcium hydroxide.
– ORIGIN Old English, 'become less eager'.

slaked lime ● noun calcium hydroxide.

slalom /slaaləm/ ● noun a skiing, canoeing, or sailing race following a winding course marked out by poles. ● verb move or race in a winding path, avoiding obstacles.
– ORIGIN Norwegian, 'sloping track'.

slam[1] ● verb (**slammed, slamming**) **1** shut forcefully and loudly. **2** push or put somewhere with great force. **3** (often **slam into**) crash or strike heavily into. **4** put into action suddenly or forcefully. **5** informal criticize severely. **6** informal, chiefly N. Amer. easily score points against or defeat. ● noun a loud bang caused by the forceful shutting of something.
– ORIGIN probably Scandinavian.

slam[2] ● noun Bridge a grand slam (all thirteen tricks) or small slam (twelve tricks), for which bonus points are scored if bid and made.
– ORIGIN perhaps from obsolete *slampant* 'trickery'.

slam-bang ● adjective informal, chiefly N. Amer. **1** exciting and ener-

Thesaurus

Amer. *informal* gold-brick, play hookey, goof off; *Austral./NZ informal* play the wag.

skulduggery ● noun TRICKERY, fraudulence, sharp practice, unscrupulousness, underhandedness, chicanery; *informal* shenanigans, funny business, monkey business; *Brit. informal* monkey tricks, jiggery-pokery; *N. Amer. informal* monkeyshines.

skulk ● verb LURK, loiter, hide; creep, sneak, slink, prowl, pussyfoot.

sky ● noun *the sun was shining in the sky* the upper atmosphere; *poetic/literary* the heavens, the firmament, the blue, the (wide) blue yonder, the welkin, the azure, the empyrean.
– RELATED TERMS celestial.
– PHRASES **to the skies** *he praised Lizzie to the skies* EFFUSIVELY, profusely, very highly, very enthusiastically, unreservedly, fervently, fulsomely, extravagantly.

slab ● noun PIECE, block, hunk, chunk, lump; cake, tablet, brick, wodge.

slack ● adjective **1** *the rope went slack* LOOSE, limp, hanging, flexible. **2** *slack skin* FLACCID, flabby, loose, sagging, saggy. **3** *business is slack* SLUGGISH, slow, quiet, slow-moving, flat, depressed, stagnant. **4** *slack accounting procedures* LAX, negligent, remiss, careless, slapdash, slipshod, lackadaisical, inefficient, casual; *informal* sloppy, slap-happy.
– OPPOSITES tight, taut.
● noun **1** *the rope had some slack in it* LOOSENESS, play, give. **2** *foreign demand will help pick up the slack* SURPLUS, excess, residue, spare capacity. **3** *a little slack in the daily routine* LULL, pause, respite, break, hiatus, breathing space; *informal* let-up, breather.
● verb **1** *the horse slacked his pace* REDUCE, lessen, slacken, slow. **2** *(Brit. informal) no slacking!* IDLE, shirk, be lazy, be indolent, waste time, lounge about; *Brit. informal* skive; *N. Amer. informal* goof off.
– PHRASES **slack off 1** *the rain has slacked off* DECREASE, subside, let up, ease off, abate, diminish, die down, fall off. **2** *slack off a bit!* RELAX, take things easy, let up, ease up/off, loosen up, slow down; *N. Amer. informal* hang loose, chill out. **slack up** *the horse slacked up* SLOW (DOWN), decelerate, reduce speed.

slacken ● verb **1** *he slackened his grip* LOOSEN, release, relax, loose, lessen, weaken. **2** *he slackened his pace* SLOW (DOWN), become/get/make slower, decelerate, slack (up). **3** *the rain is slackening* DECREASE, lessen, subside, ease up/off, let up, abate, slack off, diminish, die down, fall off.
– OPPOSITES tighten.

slacker ● noun *(informal).* See LAYABOUT.

slag ● verb
– PHRASES **slag someone/something off** *(Brit. informal).* See CRITICIZE.

slake ● verb QUENCH, satisfy, sate, satiate, relieve, assuage.

getic. **2** direct and forceful.

slam-dancing • noun chiefly N. Amer. a form of dancing to rock music in which the dancers deliberately collide with one another.

slam dunk • noun **1** Basketball a shot thrust down through the basket. **2** N. Amer. informal a foregone conclusion or certainty. • verb (**slam-dunk**) **1** Basketball thrust (the ball) down through the basket. **2** N. Amer. informal defeat or dismiss decisively.

slammer • noun **1** informal prison. **2** (also **tequila slammer**) a cocktail made with tequila and champagne or another fizzy drink, which is covered, slammed on the table, and then drunk in one.

slander • noun Law **1** the action or crime of making a false spoken statement damaging to a person's reputation. Compare with LIBEL. **2** a false and malicious spoken statement. • verb make such statements about.
– DERIVATIVES **slanderer** noun **slanderous** adjective.
– ORIGIN Old French *esclandre*, from Latin *scandalum* 'cause of offence'.

slang • noun informal language that is more common in speech than in writing and is typically restricted to a particular context or group. • verb informal attack using abusive language.
– DERIVATIVES **slangy** adjective.
– ORIGIN of unknown origin.

slanging match • noun informal, chiefly Brit. a prolonged exchange of insults.

slant • verb **1** diverge from the vertical or horizontal; slope or lean. **2** present or view (information) from a particular angle, especially in a biased or unfair way. • noun **1** a sloping position. **2** a point of view. • adjective sloping.
– DERIVATIVES **slantwise** adjective & adverb.
– ORIGIN Scandinavian.

slap • verb (**slapped**, **slapping**) **1** hit or strike with the palm of one's hand or a flat object. **2** hit against with a slapping sound. **3** (**slap down**) informal reprimand forcefully. **4** (**slap on**) apply quickly, carelessly, or forcefully. **5** (**slap on**) informal impose (a fine or penalty) on. • noun **1** an act or sound of slapping. **2** informal make-up. • adverb (also **slap bang**) informal suddenly and directly, especially with great force.
– PHRASES **slap and tickle** Brit. informal physical amorous play. **slap in the face** an unexpected rejection or affront. **slap on the back** a congratulation or commendation. **slap on the wrist** a mild reprimand or punishment.
– ORIGIN probably imitative.

slapdash • adjective & adverb done too hurriedly and carelessly.

slap-happy • adjective informal **1** cheerfully casual or flippant. **2** slapdash.

slaphead • noun Brit. informal, derogatory a bald or balding man.

slapper • noun Brit. informal, derogatory a promiscuous or vulgar woman.

slapstick • noun **1** comedy based on deliberately clumsy actions and humorously embarrassing events. **2** a device consisting of two flexible pieces of wood joined together at one end, used by clowns and in pantomime to produce a loud slapping sound.

slap-up • adjective informal, chiefly Brit. (of a meal) large and sumptuous.

slash • verb **1** cut with a violent sweeping movement. **2** informal reduce (a price, quantity, etc.) greatly. **3** archaic lash, whip, or thrash severely. • noun **1** a cut made with a wide, sweeping stroke. **2** a bright patch or flash of colour or light. **3** an oblique stroke (/) used between alternatives, in fractions and ratios, or between separate elements of a text. **4** Brit. informal an act of urinating.
– DERIVATIVES **slasher** noun.
– ORIGIN Old French *esclachier* 'break in pieces'.

slash-and-burn • adjective (of agriculture) in which vegetation is cut down and burned off before new seeds are sown.

slashed • adjective (of a garment) having slits to show the lining material or skin beneath.

slat • noun a thin, narrow piece of wood or other material, especially one of a series which overlap or fit into each other.
– DERIVATIVES **slatted** adjective.
– ORIGIN shortening of Old French *esclat* 'splinter'.

slate • noun **1** a fine-grained grey, green, or bluish-purple rock easily split into smooth, flat plates, used as roofing material. **2** a plate of slate formerly used in schools for writing on. **3** a bluish-grey colour. **4** a list of candidates for election to a post or office. **5** Brit. a record of a person's debt or credit. **6** a board showing the identifying details of a take of a film, held in front of the camera at the beginning and end of the take. • verb **1** cover (a roof) with slates. **2** Brit. informal criticize severely. **3** chiefly N. Amer. schedule; plan.
– ORIGIN shortening of Old French *esclate* 'splinter'.

slather /slathər/ • verb informal spread or smear thickly or liberally.

Thesaurus

slam • verb **1** *he slammed the door behind him* BANG, shut/close with a bang, shut/close noisily, shut/close with force. **2** *the car slammed into a lamp post* CRASH INTO, smash into, collide with, hit, strike, ram, plough into, run into, bump into; *N. Amer.* impact. **3** *(informal) he was slammed by the critics.* See CRITICIZE.

slander • noun *he could sue us for slander* DEFAMATION (OF CHARACTER), character assassination, calumny, libel; scandalmongering, malicious gossip, disparagement, denigration, aspersions, vilification, traducement, obloquy; lie, slur, smear, false accusation; *informal* mud-slinging, bad-mouthing; *archaic* contumely.
• verb *they were accused of slandering the minister* DEFAME (SOMEONE'S CHARACTER), blacken someone's name, tell lies about, speak ill/evil of, sully someone's reputation, libel, smear, cast aspersions on, spread scandal about, besmirch, tarnish, taint; malign, traduce, vilify, disparage, denigrate, run down; *N. Amer.* slur; *formal* derogate, calumniate.

slanderous • adjective DEFAMATORY, denigratory, disparaging, libellous, pejorative, false, misrepresentative, scurrilous, scandalous, malicious, abusive, insulting; *informal* mud-slinging.

slang • noun INFORMAL LANGUAGE, colloquialisms, patois, argot, cant.

slanging match • noun *(informal).* See QUARREL noun.

slant • verb **1** *the floor was slanting* SLOPE, tilt, incline, be at an angle, tip, cant, lean, dip, pitch, shelve, list, bank. **2** *their findings were slanted in our favour* BIAS, distort, twist, skew, weight, give a bias to.
• noun **1** *the slant of the roof* SLOPE, incline, tilt, gradient, pitch, angle, cant, camber, inclination. **2** *a feminist slant* POINT OF VIEW, viewpoint, standpoint, stance, angle, perspective, approach, view, attitude, position; bias, leaning.

slanting • adjective OBLIQUE, sloping, at an angle, on an incline, inclined, tilting, tilted, slanted, aslant, diagonal, canted, cambered.

slap • verb **1** *he slapped her hard* HIT, strike, smack, clout, cuff, thump, punch, spank; *informal* whack, thwack, wallop, biff, bash; *Brit. informal* slosh; *N. Amer. informal* boff, slug, bust; *Austral./NZ informal* dong, quilt; *archaic* smite. **2** *he slapped down a £10 note* FLING, throw, toss, slam, bang; *informal* plonk. **3** *slap on a coat of paint* DAUB, plaster, spread. **4** *(informal) they slapped a huge tax on imports* IMPOSE, levy, put on.
• noun *a slap across the cheek* SMACK, blow, thump, cuff, clout, punch, spank; *informal* whack, thwack, wallop, clip, biff, bash.
• adverb *(informal) the bypass goes slap through the green belt* STRAIGHT, right, directly, plumb; *informal* smack, (slap) bang; *N. Amer. informal* spang, smack dab.
– PHRASES **a slap in the face** REBUFF, rejection, snub, insult, putdown, humiliation. **a slap on the back** CONGRATULATIONS, commendation, approbation, approval, accolades, compliments, tributes, a pat on the back, praise, acclaim, acclamation; *formal* laudation. **a slap on the wrist** REPRIMAND, rebuke, reproof, scolding, admonishment; *informal* telling-off, rap over the knuckles, dressing-down; *Brit. informal* ticking-off, wigging; *Austral./NZ informal* serve. **slap someone down** *(informal).* See BERATE.

slapdash • adjective CARELESS, slipshod, hurried, haphazard, unsystematic, untidy, messy, hit-or-miss, negligent, neglectful; *informal* sloppy, slap-happy; *Brit. informal* shambolic.
– OPPOSITES meticulous.

slap-happy • adverb *(informal)* **1** *his slap-happy friend* HAPPY-GO-LUCKY, devil-may-care, carefree, easy-going, nonchalant, insouciant, blithe, airy, casual. **2** *slap-happy work.* See SLAPDASH. **3** *she's a bit slap-happy after such a narrow escape* DAZED, stupefied, punch-drunk.

slap-up • adjective *(Brit. informal)* LAVISH, sumptuous, elaborate, expensive, fit for a king, princely, splendid.
– OPPOSITES meagre.

slash • verb **1** *her tyres had been slashed* CUT (OPEN), gash, slit, split open, lacerate, knife, make an incision in. **2** *(informal) the company slashed prices* REDUCE, cut, lower, bring down, mark down. **3** *(informal) they have slashed 10,000 jobs* GET RID OF, axe, cut, shed.
• noun **1** *a slash across his temple* CUT, gash, laceration, slit, inci-

– PHRASES **open slather** Austral./NZ informal freedom to act without restriction.
– ORIGIN of unknown origin.
slattern /slattərn/ ● **noun** dated a dirty, untidy woman.
– DERIVATIVES **slatternly** adjective.
– ORIGIN related to dialect *slatter* 'to spill or slop', of unknown origin.
slaughter /slawtər/ ● **noun** **1** the killing of farm animals for food. **2** the killing of a large number of people in a cruel or violent way. **3** informal a thorough defeat. ● **verb** **1** kill (animals) for food. **2** kill (people) in a cruel or violent way. **3** informal defeat (an opponent) thoroughly.
– DERIVATIVES **slaughterer** noun.
– ORIGIN Old Norse, 'butcher's meat'.
slaughterhouse ● **noun** a place where animals are slaughtered for food.
Slav /slaav/ ● **noun** a member of a group of peoples in central and eastern Europe speaking Slavic languages.
– ORIGIN Greek *Sklabos*.
slave ● **noun** **1** historical a person who is the legal property of another and is forced to obey them. **2** a person who is excessively dependent upon or controlled by something: *a slave to fashion.* ● **verb** work excessively hard.
– ORIGIN Old French *esclave*, from Latin *sclava* 'Slavonic captive': the Slavonic peoples had been reduced to a servile state by conquest in the 9th century.
slave-driver ● **noun** informal a person who works others very hard.
slave labour ● **noun** labour which is coerced and inadequately rewarded.
slaver[1] /slayvər/ ● **noun** historical **1** a person dealing in or owning slaves. **2** a ship used for transporting slaves.
slaver[2] /slavvər/ ● **noun** **1** saliva running from the mouth. **2** archaic excessive or obsequious flattery. ● **verb** **1** let saliva run from the mouth. **2** (usu. **slaver over**) show excessive desire.
– ORIGIN probably from Low German.
slavery ● **noun** **1** the state of being a slave. **2** the practice or system of owning slaves.
slave state ● **noun** historical any of the Southern states of the US in which slavery was legal before the Civil War.
slave trade ● **noun** historical the procuring, transporting, and selling of human beings, especially African blacks, as slaves.
Slavic /slaavik/ ● **noun** the branch of the Indo-European language family that includes Russian, Polish, Czech, Bulgarian, and Serbo-Croat. ● **adjective** relating to this branch of languages or their speakers.
slavish ● **adjective** **1** showing no attempt at originality. **2** servile or submissive.
– DERIVATIVES **slavishly** adverb.
Slavonic /sləvonnik/ ● **noun & adjective** another term for SLAVIC.
slaw ● **noun** N. Amer. coleslaw.
– ORIGIN Dutch *sla*, from *salade* 'salad'.
slay ● **verb** (past **slew**; past part. **slain**) **1** archaic or literary kill in a violent way. **2** N. Amer. murder.
– DERIVATIVES **slayer** noun.
– ORIGIN Old English.
sleaze informal ● **noun** **1** immoral, sordid, and corrupt behaviour or material. **2** informal, chiefly N. Amer. a sordid, corrupt, or immoral person. ● **verb** behave in an immoral, corrupt, or sordid way.
sleazy ● **adjective** (**sleazier**, **sleaziest**) **1** sordid, corrupt, or immoral. **2** (of a place) squalid and seedy.
– DERIVATIVES **sleazily** adverb **sleaziness** noun.
– ORIGIN originally in the sense 'thin or flimsy': of unknown origin.
sled ● **noun & verb** (**sledded**, **sledding**) North American term for SLEDGE.
– ORIGIN Low German *sledde*.
sledge[1] ● **noun** **1** a vehicle on runners for travelling over snow or ice, either pushed, pulled, or allowed to slide downhill. **2** Brit. a toboggan. ● **verb** ride or carry on a sledge.
– DERIVATIVES **sledging** noun.
– ORIGIN Dutch *sleedse*.
sledge[2] ● **noun** a sledgehammer. ● **verb** (**sledging**) Cricket offensive remarks made by a fielder to a batsman in order to break their concentration.
– ORIGIN Old English, from a base meaning 'to strike'; related to SLAY.
sledgehammer ● **noun** **1** a large, heavy hammer used for breaking rocks, driving in posts, etc. **2** (before another noun) very powerful, forceful, or unsubtle: *sledgehammer blows.*
sleek ● **adjective** **1** (of hair or fur) smooth, glossy, and healthy-looking. **2** wealthy and well-groomed in appearance. **3** elegant and streamlined. ● **verb** make (the hair) sleek by applying pressure or moisture.
– DERIVATIVES **sleekly** adverb **sleekness** noun.
– ORIGIN variant of SLICK.
sleep ● **noun** **1** a regularly recurring condition of body and mind in which the nervous system is inactive, the eyes closed, the postural muscles relaxed, and consciousness practically suspended. **2** a gummy secretion found in the corners of the eyes after sleep. ● **verb** (past and past part. **slept**) **1** be asleep. **2** (**sleep off**) recover from (something) by going to sleep. **3** (**sleep in**) remain asleep or in bed later than usual in the morning. **4** provide (a specified number of people) with beds or bedrooms. **5** (**sleep with**) have sexual intercourse or be involved in a sexual relationship with. **6** (**sleep around**) have many casual sexual partners.

Thesaurus

sion; wound. **2** *sentence breaks are indicated by slashes* SOLIDUS, oblique, backslash.
slate ● **verb** *(Brit. informal).* See CRITICIZE.
slatternly ● **adjective** SLOVENLY, untidy, messy, scruffy, unkempt, ill-groomed, dishevelled, frowzy; *N. Amer. informal* raggedy.
slaughter ● **verb** **1** *the animals were slaughtered* KILL, butcher. **2** *innocent civilians are being slaughtered* MASSACRE, murder, butcher, kill (off), annihilate, exterminate, liquidate, eliminate, destroy, decimate, wipe out, put to death; *poetic/literary* slay. **3** *(informal) their team were slaughtered.* See DEFEAT verb sense 1.
● **noun** **1** *the slaughter of 20 demonstrators* MASSACRE, murdering, (mass) murder, mass killing, mass execution, annihilation, extermination, liquidation, decimation, carnage, butchery, genocide; *poetic/literary* slaying. **2** *a scene of slaughter* CARNAGE, bloodshed, bloodletting, bloodbath. **3** *(informal) their electoral slaughter.* See DEFEAT noun sense 1.
slaughterhouse ● **noun** ABATTOIR; *Brit.* butchery; *archaic* shambles.
slave ● **noun** **1** *the work was done by slaves* *historical* serf, vassal, thrall; *archaic* bondsman, bondswoman. **2** *Anna was his willing slave* DRUDGE, servant, man/maid of all work, lackey; *informal* gofer; *Brit. informal* skivvy, dogsbody, poodle.
– RELATED TERMS servile.
– OPPOSITES freeman, master.
● **verb** *slaving away for a pittance* TOIL, labour, grind, sweat, work one's fingers to the bone, work like a Trojan/dog; *informal* work one's socks off, kill oneself, sweat blood, slog away; *Brit. informal* graft; *Austral./NZ informal* bullock; *poetic/literary* travail; *archaic* drudge, moil.
slaver ● **verb** DROOL, slobber, dribble, salivate; *archaic* drivel.
slavery ● **noun** **1** *thousands were sold into slavery* BONDAGE, enslavement, servitude, thraldom, thrall, serfdom, vassalage. **2** *this work is sheer slavery* DRUDGERY, toil, (hard) slog, hard labour, grind; *poetic/literary* travail; *archaic* moil.
– OPPOSITES freedom.
slavish ● **adjective** **1** *slavish lackeys of the government* SERVILE, subservient, fawning, obsequious, sycophantic, toadying, unctuous; *informal* bootlicking, forelock-tugging; *N. Amer. informal* apple-polishing. **2** *slavish copying* UNORIGINAL, uninspired, unimaginative, uninventive, imitative.
slay ● **verb** **1** *(poetic/literary) 8,000 men were slain* KILL, murder, put to death, butcher, cut down, cut to pieces, slaughter, massacre, shoot down, gun down, mow down, eliminate, annihilate, exterminate, liquidate; *informal* wipe out, bump off, do in/for. **2** *(informal) you slay me, you really do* AMUSE GREATLY, entertain greatly, make someone laugh; *informal* have people rolling in the aisles, kill, knock dead, be a hit with.
slaying ● **noun** *(poetic/literary)* MURDER, killing, butchery, slaughter, massacre, extermination, liquidation.
sleazy ● **adjective** **1** *sleazy arms dealers* CORRUPT, immoral, unsavoury, disreputable; *informal* shady, sleazoid. **2** *a sleazy bar* SQUALID, seedy, seamy, sordid, insalubrious, mean, cheap, low-class, run down; *informal* scruffy, scuzzy, crummy, skanky; *Brit. informal* grotty.
– OPPOSITES reputable, upmarket.
sledge ● **noun** TOBOGGAN, bobsleigh, sleigh; *N. Amer.* sled.
sleek ● **adjective** **1** *his sleek dark hair* SMOOTH, glossy, shiny, shin-

– PHRASES **let sleeping dogs lie** proverb avoid interfering in a situation that is currently causing no problems but may well do so as a result of such interference. **put to sleep** kill (an animal) painlessly.
– DERIVATIVES **sleepless** adjective.
– ORIGIN Old English.
sleeper • noun **1** a sleeping car or a train carrying sleeping cars. **2** a film, book, play, etc. that suddenly achieves success after initially attracting little attention. **3** Brit. a ring or bar worn in a pierced ear to keep the hole from closing. **4** chiefly Brit. a wooden or concrete beam laid transversely under railway track to support it.
sleeping bag • noun a warm lined padded bag to sleep in, especially when camping.
sleeping car (Brit. also **sleeping carriage**) • noun a railway carriage provided with beds or berths.
sleeping draught • noun Brit. dated a drink or drug intended to induce sleep.
sleeping partner • noun Brit. a partner not sharing in the actual work of a firm.
sleeping pill • noun a tablet of a sleep-inducing drug.
sleeping policeman • noun Brit. a road hump.
sleeping sickness • noun a tropical disease transmitted by the bite of the tsetse fly, marked by extreme lethargy.
sleepover • noun chiefly N. Amer. an occasion of spending the night away from home.
sleepwalk • verb walk around and sometimes perform other actions while asleep.
– DERIVATIVES **sleepwalker** noun.
sleepy • adjective (**sleepier**, **sleepiest**) **1** needing or ready for sleep. **2** (of a place) without much activity. **3** not dynamic or able to respond to change.
– DERIVATIVES **sleepily** adverb **sleepiness** noun.
sleepyhead • noun informal a sleepy or inattentive person.
sleet • noun **1** rain containing some ice, or snow melting as it falls. **2** US a thin coating of ice formed by sleet or rain freezing on coming into contact with a cold surface. • verb (**it sleets, it is sleeting**, etc.) sleet falls.
– DERIVATIVES **sleety** adjective.
– ORIGIN Germanic.
sleeve • noun **1** the part of a garment that wholly or partly covers a person's arm. **2** a protective paper or cardboard cover for a record. **3** a protective or connecting tube fitting over a rod, spindle, or smaller tube. **4** a windsock.
– PHRASES **up one's sleeve** kept secret and in reserve for use when needed.
– DERIVATIVES **sleeved** adjective **sleeveless** adjective.
– ORIGIN Old English.
sleigh • noun a sledge drawn by horses or reindeer. • verb ride on a sleigh.
– ORIGIN Dutch *slee*; related to SLED.
sleigh bell • noun a tinkling bell attached to the harness of a sleigh horse.
sleight /slīt/ • noun literary the use of dexterity or cunning, especially so as to deceive.
– PHRASES **sleight of hand 1** manual dexterity, typically in performing conjuring tricks. **2** skilful deception.
– ORIGIN from Old Norse, 'sly'.
slender • adjective (**slenderer**, **slenderest**) **1** gracefully thin. **2** barely sufficient: *a slender majority*.
– DERIVATIVES **slenderly** adverb **slenderness** noun.
– ORIGIN of unknown origin.
slept past and past participle of SLEEP.
sleuth /slōōth/ informal • noun a detective. • verb carry out a search or investigation in the manner of a detective.
– ORIGIN originally in the sense 'track': from Old Norse.
S level • noun (in the UK except Scotland) an examination taken together with an A level in the same subject but having a more advanced syllabus.
– ORIGIN abbreviation of *Special level* or (formerly) *Scholarship level*.
slew[1] (also **slue**) • verb turn or slide violently or uncontrollably. • noun a slewing movement.
– ORIGIN of unknown origin.
slew[2] past of SLAY.
slew[3] • noun informal, chiefly N. Amer. a large number or quantity.
– ORIGIN Irish *sluagh*.
slice • noun **1** a thin, broad piece of food cut from a larger portion. **2** a portion or share. **3** a utensil with a broad, flat blade for lifting foods such as cake and fish. **4** (in sports) a sliced stroke or shot. • verb **1** cut into slices. **2** cut with or as if with a sharp implement. **3** (often **slice through**) move easily and quickly. **4** Golf strike (the ball) so that it curves away to the right (for a left-handed player, the left). **5** (in other sports) propel (the ball) with a glancing contact so that it travels forward spinning.
– DERIVATIVES **slicer** noun.
– ORIGIN shortening of Old French *esclice* 'splinter'.
slick • adjective **1** done or operating in an impressively smooth and efficient way. **2** glibly assured. **3** (of skin or hair) smooth and glossy. **4** (of a surface) smooth, wet, and slippery. • noun a smooth patch of oil, especially on the sea. • verb **1** make (hair) flat and slick with water, oil, or cream. **2** (**slick up**) N. Amer. make smart, tidy, or stylish.
– DERIVATIVES **slickly** adverb **slickness** noun.
– ORIGIN probably related to an Old Norse word meaning 'smooth'.
slicker • noun chiefly N. Amer. **1** informal a convincing rogue. **2** a raincoat made of smooth material.
slide • verb (past and past part. **slid**) **1** move along a smooth sur-

Thesaurus

ing, lustrous, silken, silky. **2** *the car's sleek lines* STREAMLINED, trim, elegant, graceful. **3** *sleek young men in city suits* WELL GROOMED, stylish, wealthy-looking.
sleep • noun *go and have a sleep* NAP, doze, siesta, catnap, beauty sleep; *informal* snooze, forty winks, a bit of shut-eye; *Brit. informal* kip, zizz; *children's language* bye-byes; *poetic/literary* slumber.
• verb *she slept for about an hour* BE ASLEEP, doze, take a siesta, take a nap, catnap, sleep like a log/top; *informal* snooze, snatch forty winks, get some shut-eye; *Brit. informal* (have a) kip, get one's head down, (get some) zizz; *N. Amer. informal* catch some Zs; *humorous* be in the land of Nod; *poetic/literary* slumber.
– OPPOSITES wake up.
– PHRASES **go to sleep** FALL ASLEEP, get to sleep; *informal* drop off, nod off, drift off, crash out, flake out; *N. Amer. informal* sack out, zone out. **put something to sleep** PUT DOWN, destroy.
sleepiness • noun DROWSINESS, tiredness, somnolence, languor, languidness, doziness; lethargy, sluggishness, lassitude, enervation.
sleepless • adjective WAKEFUL, restless, without sleep, insomniac; (wide) awake, unsleeping, tossing and turning; *archaic* watchful.
sleeplessness • noun INSOMNIA, wakefulness.
sleepwalker • noun SOMNAMBULIST; *rare* noctambulist.
sleepy • adjective **1** *she felt very sleepy* DROWSY, tired, somnolent, languid, languorous, heavy-eyed, asleep on one's feet; lethargic, sluggish, enervated, torpid; *informal* dopey; *poetic/literary* slumberous. **2** *the sleepy heat of the afternoon* SOPORIFIC, sleep-inducing, somnolent. **3** *a sleepy little village* QUIET, peaceful, tranquil, placid, slow-moving; dull, boring.
– OPPOSITES awake, alert.
sleight of hand • noun **1** *impressive sleight of hand* DEXTERITY, adroitness, deftness, skill. **2** *financial sleight of hand* DECEPTION, deceit, dissimulation, chicanery, trickery, sharp practice.
slender • adjective **1** *her tall slender figure* SLIM, lean, willowy, sylphlike, svelte, lissom, graceful; slight, slightly built, thin, skinny. **2** *slender evidence* MEAGRE, limited, slight, scanty, scant, sparse, paltry, insubstantial, insufficient, deficient, negligible; *formal* exiguous. **3** *the chances seemed slender* FAINT, remote, flimsy, tenuous, fragile, slim; unlikely, improbable.
– OPPOSITES plump.
sleuth • noun *(informal)* (PRIVATE) DETECTIVE, (private) investigator; *informal* private eye, snoop, sleuth-hound; *N. Amer. informal* shamus, gumshoe.
slice • noun **1** *a slice of fruitcake* PIECE, portion, slab, rasher, sliver, wafer, shaving. **2** *a huge slice of public spending* SHARE, part, portion, tranche, piece, proportion, allocation, percentage.
• verb **1** *slice the cheese thinly* CUT (UP), carve. **2** *one man had his ear sliced off* CUT OFF, sever, chop off, shear off.
slick • adjective **1** *a slick advertising campaign* EFFICIENT, smooth, smooth-running, polished, well organized, well run, streamlined. **2** *his slick use of words* GLIB, smooth, fluent, plausible. **3** *a slick salesman* SUAVE, urbane, polished, assured, self-assured, smooth-talking, glib; *informal* smarmy. **4** *her slick brown hair* SHINY, glossy, shining, sleek, smooth, oiled. **5** *the pavements were slick with rain* SLIPPERY, slithery, wet, greasy; *informal* slippy.

face while maintaining continuous contact with it. **2** move smoothly, quickly, or unobtrusively. **3** change gradually to a worse condition or lower level. ● **noun 1** a structure with a smooth sloping surface for children to slide down. **2** a smooth stretch of ice or packed snow for sliding or tobogganing on. **3** an act of sliding. **4** a rectangular piece of glass on which an object is mounted or placed for examination under a microscope. **5** a mounted transparency, especially one placed in a projector for viewing on a screen. **6** Brit. a hairslide.
– ORIGIN Old English, related to SLED and SLEDGE.

slide guitar ● **noun** a style of guitar playing in which a glissando effect is produced by moving a bottleneck or similar device over the strings.

slide rule ● **noun** a ruler with a sliding central strip, marked with logarithmic scales and used for making rapid calculations.

sliding scale ● **noun** a scale of fees, wages, etc., that varies in accordance with the variation of some standard.

slight ● **adjective 1** small in degree; inconsiderable. **2** not profound or substantial. **3** not sturdy and strongly built. ● **verb** insult (someone) by treating them without proper respect or attention. ● **noun** an insult.
– DERIVATIVES **slightness** noun.
– ORIGIN Old Norse, 'smooth'.

slightly ● **adverb 1** to a small degree. **2** (of a person's build) in a slender way.

slily ● **adverb** variant spelling of slyly (see SLY).

slim ● **adjective** (**slimmer**, **slimmest**) **1** gracefully thin; slenderly built. **2** small in width and long and narrow in shape. **3** very small: *a slim chance.* ● **verb** (**slimmed**, **slimming**) **1** make or become thinner, especially by dieting. **2** reduce (a business) to a smaller size in the interests of efficiency.
– DERIVATIVES **slimmer** noun **slimness** noun.
– ORIGIN Low German or Dutch.

slime ● **noun** an unpleasantly moist, soft, and slippery substance. ● **verb** cover with slime.
– ORIGIN Old English.

slimeball ● **noun** informal a repulsive or despicable person.

slimline ● **adjective 1** slender in design or build. **2** (of food or drink) low in calories.

slimy ● **adjective** (**slimier**, **slimiest**) **1** covered by or having the feel or consistency of slime. **2** informal repulsively obsequious.

sling[1] ● **noun 1** a flexible strap, bandage, pouch, etc. used in the form of a loop to support or raise a hanging weight. **2** a simple weapon in the form of a strap or loop, used to hurl stones or other small missiles. **3** Austral./NZ informal a bribe or gratuity. ● **verb** (past and past part. **slung**) **1** suspend or carry loosely with or as with a sling or strap. **2** informal throw; fling. **3** hurl from a sling or similar weapon. **4** Austral./NZ informal pay a bribe or gratuity. **5** (**sling off**) Austral./NZ informal mock; make fun.
– PHRASES **put someone's** (or **have one's**) **ass in a sling** N. Amer. vulgar slang cause someone to be (or be) in trouble.
– DERIVATIVES **slinger** noun.
– ORIGIN probably from Low German.

sling[2] ● **noun** a sweetened drink of spirits, especially gin, and water.
– ORIGIN of unknown origin.

slingback ● **noun** a shoe held in place by a strap around the ankle above the heel.

slingshot ● **noun** a hand-held catapult.

slink ● **verb** (past and past part. **slunk**) **1** move quietly with gliding steps, in a stealthy or sensuous manner. **2** come or go unobtrusively or furtively. ● **noun** an act of slinking.
– ORIGIN Old English, 'crawl, creep'.

slinky ● **adjective** (**slinkier**, **slinkiest**) informal graceful and sinuous in movement or form.

slip[1] ● **verb** (**slipped**, **slipping**) **1** lose one's balance or footing and slide unintentionally for a short distance. **2** accidentally slide or move out of position or from someone's grasp. **3** fail to grip or make proper contact with a surface. **4** pass gradually to a worse condition. **5** (usu. **slip up**) informal make a careless error. **6** move or place quietly, quickly, or stealthily. **7** escape or get loose from. **8** fail to be remembered by. **9** release (the clutch of a motor vehicle) slightly or for a moment. **10** Knitting move (a stitch) to the other needle without knitting it. ● **noun 1** an act or instance of slipping. **2** a minor or careless mistake. **3** a loose-fitting garment, especially a short petticoat. **4** Cricket a fielding position close behind the batsman on the off side. **5** (usu. **slips**) a leash that enables a dog to be released quickly.
– PHRASES **give someone the slip** informal evade or escape from someone. **let slip** reveal inadvertently in conversation. **slip of the pen** (or **the tongue**) a minor mistake in writing (or speech). **there's many a slip 'twixt cup and lip** proverb many things can go wrong between the start of a project and its completion.
– DERIVATIVES **slippage** noun.
– ORIGIN probably from Low German *slippen.*

slip[2] ● **noun 1** a small piece of paper for writing on or that gives printed information. **2** a cutting taken from a plant for grafting or planting.
– PHRASES **a slip of a boy/girl/thing** a small, slim young person.
– ORIGIN probably from Dutch or Low German *slippe* 'cut, strip'.

slip[3] ● **noun** a creamy mixture of clay, water, and typically a pigment, used for decorating earthenware.
– ORIGIN of obscure origin.

Thesaurus

● **verb** *his hair was slicked down* SMOOTH, sleek, grease, oil, gel; *informal* smarm.

slide ● **verb 1** *the glass slid across the table* GLIDE, move smoothly, slip, slither, skim, skate; skid, slew. **2** *tears slid down her cheeks* TRICKLE, run, flow, pour, stream. **3** *four men slid out of the shadows* CREEP, steal, slink, slip, tiptoe, sidle. **4** *the country is sliding into recession* SINK, fall, drop, descend; decline, degenerate.
● **noun 1** *the current slide in house prices* FALL, decline, drop, slump, downturn, downswing. **2** *a slide show* TRANSPARENCY, diapositive.
– OPPOSITES rise.
– PHRASES **let something slide** NEGLECT, pay little/no attention to, not attend to, be remiss about, let something go downhill.

slight ● **adjective 1** *the chance of success is slight* SMALL, modest, tiny, minute, inappreciable, negligible, insignificant, minimal, remote, slim, faint; *informal* minuscule; *formal* exiguous. **2** *the book is a slight work* MINOR, inconsequential, trivial, unimportant, lightweight, superficial, shallow. **3** *Elizabeth's slight figure* SLIM, slender, petite, diminutive, small, delicate, dainty.
– OPPOSITES considerable.
● **verb** *he had been slighted* INSULT, snub, rebuff, repulse, spurn, treat disrespectfully, give someone the cold shoulder, cut (dead), scorn; *informal* give someone the brush-off, freeze out, stiff-arm.
– OPPOSITES respect.
● **noun** *an unintended slight* INSULT, affront, snub, rebuff; *informal* put-down, dig.
– OPPOSITES compliment.

slighting ● **adjective** INSULTING, disparaging, derogatory, disrespectful, denigratory, pejorative, abusive, offensive, defamatory, slanderous, scurrilous; disdainful, scornful, contemptuous; *archaic* contumelious.

slightly ● **adverb** A LITTLE, a bit, somewhat, rather, moderately, to a certain extent, faintly, vaguely, a shade.
– OPPOSITES very.

slim ● **adjective 1** *she was tall and slim* SLENDER, lean, thin, willowy, sylphlike, svelte, lissom, trim, slight, slightly built. **2** *a slim silver bracelet* NARROW, slender, slimline. **3** *a slim chance of escape* SLIGHT, small, slender, faint, poor, remote, unlikely, improbable.
– OPPOSITES plump.
● **verb 1** *I'm trying to slim* LOSE WEIGHT, get thinner, lose some pounds/inches, get into shape; *N. Amer.* slenderize. **2** *the number of staff had been slimmed down* REDUCE, cut (down/back), scale down, decrease, diminish, pare down.

slime ● **noun** OOZE, sludge, muck, mud, mire; *informal* goo, gunk, gook, gloop; *Brit. informal* gunge; *N. Amer. informal* guck, glop.

slimy ● **adjective 1** *the floor was slimy* SLIPPERY, slithery, greasy, muddy, mucky, sludgy, wet, sticky; *informal* slippy, gunky, gooey, gloopy. **2** *(informal) her slimy press agent.* See OBSEQUIOUS.

sling ● **noun 1** *she had her arm in a sling* (SUPPORT) BANDAGE, support, strap. **2** *armed only with a sling* CATAPULT, slingshot; *Austral./NZ* shanghai.
● **verb 1** *a hammock was slung between two trees* HANG, suspend, string, swing. **2** *(informal) she slung her jacket on the sofa.* See THROW verb sense 1.

slink ● **verb** CREEP, sneak, steal, slip, slide, sidle, tiptoe, pussyfoot.

slinky ● **adjective** *(informal)* **1** *a slinky black dress* TIGHT-FITTING, close-fitting, figure-hugging, sexy. **2** *her slinky elegance* SINUOUS, willowy, graceful, sleek.

slip[1] ● **verb 1** *she slipped on the ice* SLIDE, skid, slither, glide; fall (over), lose one's balance, tumble. **2** *the envelope slipped through*

S

slip case ● noun a close-fitting case open at one side or end for an object such as a book.
slip cover ● noun **1** a detachable cover for a chair or sofa. **2** a jacket or slip case for a book.
slip knot ● noun **1** a knot that can be undone by a pull. **2** a running knot.
slip-on ● adjective (of shoes or clothes) having no fastenings and therefore able to be put on and taken off quickly.
slipover ● noun a pullover, typically one without sleeves.
slipped disc ● noun a cartilaginous disc between vertebrae in the spine that is displaced or partly protruding, pressing on nearby nerves and causing back pain or sciatica.
slipper ● noun **1** a comfortable slip-on shoe that is worn indoors. **2** a light slip-on shoe, especially one used for dancing.
– DERIVATIVES **slippered** adjective.
slipper orchid ● noun another term for LADY'S SLIPPER.
slippery ● adjective **1** difficult to hold firmly or stand on through being smooth, wet, or slimy. **2** (of a person) evasive and unpredictable. **3** (of a word or concept) changing in meaning according to context or point of view.
– DERIVATIVES **slipperiness** noun.
slippery elm ● noun a North American elm with slimy inner bark, used medicinally.
slippery slope ● noun a course of action likely to lead to something bad.
slippy ● adjective (**slippier, slippiest**) informal slippery.
– PHRASES **look** (or **be**) **slippy** Brit. dated be quick.
slip road ● noun Brit. a road entering or leaving a motorway or dual carriageway.
slipshod ● adjective **1** lacking in care, thought, or organization. **2** archaic (of shoes) worn down at the heel.
slip stitch ● noun **1** (in sewing) a loose stitch joining layers of fabric and not visible externally. **2** Knitting a type of stitch in which the stitches are moved from one needle to the other without being knitted.
slipstream ● noun **1** a current of air or water driven back by a revolving propeller or jet engine. **2** the partial vacuum created in the wake of a moving vehicle. **3** an assisting force regarded as drawing something along in its wake. ● verb follow in the slipstream of a vehicle, especially in motor racing.
slip-up ● noun informal a mistake or blunder.
slipway ● noun a slope leading into water, used for launching and landing boats and ships or for building and repairing them.
slit ● noun a long, narrow cut or opening. ● verb (**slitting**; past and past part. **slit**) **1** make a slit in. **2** (past and past part. **slitted**) form (one's eyes) into slits.
– ORIGIN Old English.
slither ● verb **1** move smoothly over a surface with a twisting or oscillating motion. **2** slide or slip unsteadily on a loose or slippery surface. ● noun **1** a slithering movement. **2** a sliver.
– DERIVATIVES **slithery** adjective.
– ORIGIN alteration of dialect *slidder*; related to SLIDE.
slitty ● adjective (**slittier, slittiest**) chiefly derogatory (of the eyes) long and narrow.
sliver /slivər, slī-/ ● noun a small, narrow, sharp piece cut or split off a larger piece. ● verb cut or break into slivers.
– ORIGIN from dialect *slive* 'cleave'.
slivovitz /slivvəvits/ ● noun a type of plum brandy made chiefly in the former Yugoslavia and in Romania.
– ORIGIN Serbo-Croat.
Sloane (also **Sloane Ranger**) ● noun Brit. informal a fashionable upper-class young woman.
– DERIVATIVES **Sloaney** adjective.
– ORIGIN from *Sloane* Square, London + Lone *Ranger*, a fictitious cowboy hero.
slob informal ● noun a lazy and slovenly person. ● verb behave in a lazy and slovenly manner.
– DERIVATIVES **slobbish** adjective **slobby** adjective.
– ORIGIN Irish *slab* 'mud'.
slobber ● verb **1** have saliva dripping copiously from the mouth. **2** (**slobber over**) show excessive enthusiasm for. ● noun saliva dripping copiously from the mouth.
– DERIVATIVES **slobbery** adjective.
– ORIGIN probably from Dutch *slobberen* 'walk through mud', also 'feed noisily'.
sloe ● noun **1** another term for BLACKTHORN. **2** the small bluish-black fruit of the blackthorn, with a sharp sour taste.
– ORIGIN Old English.
sloe-eyed ● adjective having attractive dark almond-shaped eyes.
sloe gin ● noun a liqueur made by steeping sloes in gin.
slog ● verb (**slogged, slogging**) **1** work hard over a period of time. **2** walk or move with difficulty or effort. **3** hit or strike forcefully. **4** (**slog it out**) fight or compete fiercely. ● noun **1** a spell of difficult, tiring work or travelling. **2** a forceful hit or strike.
– DERIVATIVES **slogger** noun.
– ORIGIN of unknown origin.
slogan ● noun **1** a short, memorable phrase used in advertising

Thesaurus

Luke's fingers FALL, drop, slide. **3** *we slipped out by a back door* CREEP, steal, sneak, slide, sidle, slope, slink, tiptoe. **4** *standards have slipped* DECLINE, deteriorate, degenerate, worsen, get worse, fall (off), drop; *informal* go downhill, go to the dogs, go to pot. **5** *the bank's shares slipped 1.5p* DROP, go down, sink, slump, decrease, depreciate. **6** *the hours slipped by* PASS, elapse, go by/past, roll by/past, fly by/past, tick by/past. **7** *she slipped the map into her pocket* PUT, tuck, shove; *informal* pop, stick, stuff. **8** *Sarah slipped into a black skirt* PUT ON, pull on, don, dress/clothe oneself in; change into. **9** *she slipped out of her clothes* TAKE OFF, remove, pull off, doff; *Brit. informal* peel off. **10** *he slipped the knot of his tie* UNTIE, unfasten, undo.
● noun **1** *a single slip could send them plummeting downwards* FALSE STEP, misstep, slide, skid, fall, tumble. **2** *a careless slip* MISTAKE, error, blunder, gaffe, slip of the tongue/pen; oversight, omission, lapse, inaccuracy; *informal* slip-up, boo-boo, howler; *Brit. informal* boob, clanger, bloomer; *N. Amer. informal* goof, blooper, bloop. **3** *a silk slip* UNDERSKIRT, petticoat, underslip.
– PHRASES **give someone the slip** (*informal*) ESCAPE FROM, get away from, evade, dodge, elude, lose, shake off, throw off (the scent), get clear of. **let something slip** REVEAL, disclose, divulge, let out, give away, blurt out; give the game away; *informal* let on, blab, let the cat out of the bag, spill the beans; *Brit. informal* blow the gaff. **slip away 1** *they managed to slip away* ESCAPE, get away, break free; *informal* fly the coop; *Brit. informal* do a bunk, do a runner; *N. Amer. informal* take a powder. **2** *she slipped away in her sleep.* See DIE sense 1. **slip up** (*informal*) MAKE A MISTAKE, (make a) blunder, get something wrong, make an error, err; *informal* make a bloomer, make a boo-boo; *Brit. informal* boob, drop a clanger; *N. Amer. informal* goof up.
slip² ● noun **1** *a slip of paper* PIECE OF PAPER, scrap of paper, sheet, note; chit; *informal* stickie. **2** *they took slips from rare plants* CUTTING, graft; scion, shoot, offshoot.
– PHRASES **a slip of a ——** SMALL, slender, slim, slight, slightly built, petite, little, tiny, diminutive; *informal* pint-sized.
slipper ● noun **1** *he pulled on his slippers* carpet slipper, bedroom slipper, house shoe; *N. Amer.* slipperette. **2** *satin slippers* pump, mule.
slippery ● adjective **1** *the roads are slippery* SLITHERY, greasy, oily, icy, glassy, smooth, slimy, wet; *informal* slippy. **2** *a slippery customer* EVASIVE, unreliable, unpredictable; devious, crafty, cunning, wily, tricky, artful, slick, sly, sneaky, scheming, untrustworthy, deceitful, duplicitous, dishonest, treacherous, two-faced; *N. Amer.* snide; *informal* shady, shifty; *Brit. informal* dodgy; *Austral./NZ informal* shonky.
slipshod ● adjective CARELESS, lackadaisical, slapdash, disorganized, haphazard, hit-or-miss, untidy, messy, unsystematic, unmethodical, casual, negligent, neglectful, remiss, lax, slack; *informal* sloppy, slap-happy.
– OPPOSITES meticulous.
slip-up ● noun (*informal*) MISTAKE, slip, error, blunder, oversight, omission, gaffe, slip of the tongue/pen, inaccuracy; *informal* boo-boo, howler; *Brit. informal* boob, clanger, bloomer; *N. Amer. informal* goof, blooper, bloop.
slit ● noun **1** *three diagonal slits* CUT, incision, split, slash, gash, laceration. **2** *a slit in the curtains* OPENING, gap, chink, crack, aperture, slot.
● verb *he threatened to slit her throat* CUT, slash, split open, slice open, gash, lacerate, make an incision in.
slither ● verb SLIDE, slip, glide, wriggle, crawl; skid.
sliver ● noun SPLINTER, shard, shiver, chip, flake, shred, scrap, slither, shaving, paring, piece, fragment.
slob ● noun (*informal*) LAYABOUT, good-for-nothing, sluggard, laggard; *informal* slacker, couch potato; *archaic* sloven.

or associated with a political party or group. **2** historical a Scottish Highland war cry.
– ORIGIN from Scottish Gaelic *sluagh* 'army' + *gairm* 'shout'.

sloganeer chiefly N. Amer. ● **verb** employ or invent slogans, especially in a political context. ● **noun** a person who does this.

slo-mo ● **noun** short for SLOW MOTION.

sloop ● **noun** **1** a single-masted sailing boat with a mainsail and jib rigged fore and aft. **2** a small anti-submarine warship used for convoy escort in the Second World War.
– ORIGIN Dutch *sloep*.

sloosh Brit. informal ● **noun** a rushing of water or energetic rinsing. ● **verb** flow, pour, or rinse with a rush.
– ORIGIN imitative.

slop ● **verb** (**slopped**, **slopping**) **1** (of a liquid) spill or flow over the edge of a container. **2** apply casually or carelessly. **3** (**slop out**) (especially in prison) empty the contents of a chamber pot. **4** (**slop about/around**) chiefly Brit. spend time lazily and in scruffy clothes. **5** chiefly N. Amer. speak or write in a sentimentally gushing manner. ● **noun** **1** (**slops**) waste water or liquid that has to be emptied by hand. **2** (**slops**) unappetizing weak, semi-liquid food. **3** chiefly N. Amer. sentimental language or material.
– ORIGIN probably related to SLIP[3].

slope ● **noun** **1** a surface of which one end or side is at a higher level than another. **2** a part of the side of a hill or mountain, especially as a place for skiing. ● **verb** **1** be inclined from a horizontal or vertical line; slant up or down. **2** informal move in an idle or aimless manner. **3** (**slope off**) informal leave unobtrusively, typically in order to evade work or duty.
– ORIGIN from archaic *aslope* 'in a sloping position', of uncertain origin.

sloppy ● **adjective** (**sloppier**, **sloppiest**) **1** (of semi-fluid matter) containing too much liquid; watery. **2** careless and unsystematic. **3** (of a garment) casual and loose-fitting. **4** weakly or foolishly sentimental.
– DERIVATIVES **sloppily** adverb **sloppiness** noun.

slosh ● **verb** **1** (of liquid in a container) move irregularly with a splashing sound. **2** move through liquid with a splashing sound. **3** pour (liquid) clumsily. **4** Brit. informal hit hard. ● **noun** **1** an act or sound of splashing. **2** Brit. informal a heavy blow.
– ORIGIN variant of SLUSH.

sloshed ● **adjective** informal drunk.

sloshy ● **adjective** (**sloshier**, **sloshiest**) **1** wet and sticky; slushy. **2** excessively sentimental; sloppy.

slot ● **noun** **1** a long, narrow aperture or slit into which something may be fitted or inserted. **2** an allotted place in an arrangement or scheme. ● **verb** (**slotted**, **slotting**) **1** place or be placed into a slot. **2** (**slot in/into**) fit easily into (a new role or situation).
– DERIVATIVES **slotted** adjective.
– ORIGIN Old French *esclot*.

sloth /slōth/ ● **noun** **1** reluctance to work or make an effort; laziness. **2** a slow-moving tropical American mammal that hangs upside down from branches using its long limbs and hooked claws.
– DERIVATIVES **slothful** adjective.
– ORIGIN Old English, from SLOW.

slot machine ● **noun** a fruit machine or (Brit.) vending machine.

slouch ● **verb** **1** stand, move, or sit in a lazy, drooping way. **2** dated bend one side of the brim of (a hat) downwards. ● **noun** **1** a lazy, drooping posture or movement. **2** informal an incompetent person: *he was no slouch at making a buck.*
– DERIVATIVES **slouchy** adjective.
– ORIGIN of unknown origin.

slouch hat ● **noun** a hat with a wide flexible brim.

slough[1] /slow/ ● **noun** **1** a swamp. **2** a situation characterized by lack of progress or activity.
– DERIVATIVES **sloughy** adjective.
– ORIGIN Old English.

slough[2] /sluf/ ● **verb** (of an animal, especially a snake) cast off or shed (an old skin). ● **noun** the dropping off of dead tissue from living flesh.
– ORIGIN perhaps related to Low German *sluwe* 'husk, peel'.

Slovak /slōvak/ ● **noun** **1** a person from Slovakia. **2** the language of Slovakia.
– ORIGIN from a Slavic root shared with SLOVENE and perhaps related to *slovo* 'word'.

Slovakian /sləvakkiən/ ● **noun** a person from Slovakia. ● **adjective** relating to Slovakia.

sloven /sluvv'n/ ● **noun** dated a person who is habitually untidy or careless.
– ORIGIN perhaps from Flemish *sloef* 'dirty' or Dutch *slof* 'careless, negligent'.

Slovene /slōveen/ ● **noun** **1** a person from Slovenia. **2** the language of Slovenia.
– DERIVATIVES **Slovenian** noun & adjective.

slovenly ● **adjective** **1** untidy and dirty. **2** careless; excessively casual.
– DERIVATIVES **slovenliness** noun.

slow ● **adjective** **1** moving or capable of moving only at a low

Thesaurus

slobber ● **verb** DROOL, slaver, dribble, salivate; *archaic* drivel.

slog ● **verb** **1** *they were all slogging away* WORK HARD, toil, labour, work one's fingers to the bone, work like a Trojan/dog, exert oneself, grind, slave, grub, plough, plod, peg; *informal* beaver, plug, work one's guts out, work one's socks off, sweat blood; *Brit. informal* graft; *Austral./NZ informal* bullock; *poetic/literary* travail; *archaic* drudge, moil. **2** *they slogged around the streets* TRUDGE, tramp, traipse, toil, plod, trek, footslog, drag oneself.
– OPPOSITES relax.
● **noun** **1** *10 months' hard slog* HARD WORK, toil, toiling, labour, effort, exertion, grind, drudgery; *informal* sweat; *Brit. informal* graft; *Austral./NZ informal* (hard) yakka; *poetic/literary* travail; *archaic* moil. **2** *a steady uphill slog* TRUDGE, tramp, traipse, plod, trek, footslog.
– OPPOSITES leisure.

slogan ● **noun** CATCHPHRASE, catchline, jingle; *N. Amer. informal* tag line.

slop ● **verb** *water slopped over the edge* SPILL, flow, overflow, run, slosh, splash.
– PHRASES **slop around/about** *(Brit. informal)* LAZE (AROUND/ABOUT), lounge (around/about), loll (around/about), loaf (around/about), slouch (about/around); *informal* hang around; *Brit. informal* hang about, mooch about/around; *N. Amer. informal* bum around, lollygag.

slope ● **noun** **1** *the slope of the roof* GRADIENT, incline, angle, slant, inclination, pitch, decline, ascent, declivity, acclivity, rise, fall, tilt, tip, downslope, upslope; *N. Amer.* grade, downgrade, upgrade. **2** *a grassy slope* HILL, hillside, hillock, bank, escarpment, scarp; *poetic/literary* steep. **3** *the ski slopes* PISTE, nursery slope, dry slope.
● **verb** *the garden sloped down to a stream* SLANT, incline, tilt; drop away, fall away, decline, descend, shelve, lean; rise, ascend, climb.
– PHRASES **slope off** *(informal)* LEAVE, go away, slip away, steal away, slink off, creep off, sneak off; *informal* push off, clear off.

sloping ● **adjective** AT A SLANT, on the slant, at an angle, slanting, slanted, leaning, inclining, inclined, angled, cambered, canted, tilting, tilted, dipping, declivitous, acclivitous.
– OPPOSITES level.

sloppy ● **adjective** **1** *sloppy chicken curry* RUNNY, watery, thin, liquid, semi-liquid, mushy; *informal* gloopy. **2** *their defending was sloppy* CARELESS, slapdash, slipshod, lackadaisical, haphazard, lax, slack, slovenly; *informal* slap-happy; *Brit. informal* shambolic. **3** *sloppy T-shirts* BAGGY, loose-fitting, loose, generously cut; shapeless, sack-like, oversized. **4** *sloppy letters* SENTIMENTAL, mawkish, cloying, saccharine, sugary, syrupy; romantic, hearts-and-flowers; *informal* slushy, schmaltzy, lovey-dovey; *Brit. informal* soppy; *N. Amer. informal* cornball, sappy, hokey, three-hankie.

slosh ● **verb** **1** *beer sloshed over the side of the glass* SPILL, slop, splash, flow, overflow. **2** *workers sloshed round in boots* SPLASH, swash, squelch, wade; *informal* splosh. **3** *she sloshed more wine into her glass* POUR, slop, splash. **4** *(Brit. informal) Gary sloshed him.* See HIT verb sense 1.

slot ● **noun** **1** *he slid a coin into the slot* APERTURE, slit, crack, hole, opening. **2** *a mid-morning slot* SPOT, time, period, niche, space; *informal* window.
● **verb** *he slotted a cassette into the machine* INSERT, put, place, slide, slip.

sloth ● **noun** LAZINESS, idleness, indolence, slothfulness, inactivity, inertia, sluggishness, apathy, accidie, listlessness, lassitude, lethargy, languor, torpidity; *poetic/literary* hebetude.
– OPPOSITES industriousness.

slothful ● **adjective** LAZY, idle, indolent, work-shy, inactive, sluggish, apathetic, lethargic, listless, languid, torpid; *informal* bone idle; *archaic* otiose.

slouch ● **verb** SLUMP, hunch; loll, droop.

slovenly ● **adjective** **1** *his slovenly appearance* SCRUFFY, untidy,

speed. **2** lasting or taking a long time. **3** (of a clock or watch) showing a time earlier than the correct time. **4** not prompt to understand, think, or learn. **5** uneventful; showing little activity. **6** Photography (of a film) needing long exposure. **7** (of a fire or oven) burning or giving off heat gently. ● **verb** (often **slow down/up**) **1** reduce one's speed or the speed of a vehicle or process. **2** live or work less actively or intensely.

– PHRASES **slow but sure** not quick but achieving the required result eventually.

– DERIVATIVES **slowly** noun **slowness** noun.

– ORIGIN Old English.

slowcoach ● **noun** Brit. informal a person who acts or moves slowly.

slow cooker ● **noun** a large electric pot used for cooking food very slowly.

slow handclap ● **noun** a slow, rhythmic clapping by an audience as a sign of displeasure or impatience.

slow march ● **noun** a military marching pace approximately half the speed of the quick march.

slow motion ● **noun** the action of showing film or video more slowly than it was made or recorded, so that the action appears much slower than in real life.

slowpoke ● **noun** informal North American term for SLOWCOACH.

slow puncture ● **noun** chiefly Brit. a puncture causing only gradual deflation of a tyre.

slow-worm ● **noun** a small snake-like legless lizard that gives birth to live young.

– ORIGIN Old English, from an unexplained first element + *wyrm* 'snake'.

SLR ● **abbreviation** **1** self-loading rifle. **2** single-lens reflex.

slub ● **noun** **1** a lump or thick place in yarn or thread. **2** fabric woven from yarn with such a texture. ● **adjective** (of fabric) having an irregular appearance caused by uneven thickness of the warp.

– DERIVATIVES **slubbed** adjective.

– ORIGIN of unknown origin.

sludge ● **noun** **1** thick, soft, wet mud or a similar viscous mixture. **2** dirty oil or industrial waste. **3** a muddy shade of brown or green.

– DERIVATIVES **sludgy** adjective.

– ORIGIN origin uncertain.

slue ● **verb & noun** variant spelling of SLEW[1].

slug[1] ● **noun** **1** a tough-skinned terrestrial mollusc which lacks a shell and secretes a film of mucus for protection. **2** an amount of alcoholic liquor that is gulped or poured. **3** a bullet. ● **verb** (**slugged, slugging**) gulp (something, typically alcohol).

– ORIGIN originally in the sense 'a sluggard': probably Scandinavian.

slug[2] informal, chiefly N. Amer. ● **verb** (**slugged, slugging**) **1** strike with a hard blow. **2** (**slug it out**) settle a dispute or contest by fighting or competing fiercely. ● **noun** a hard blow.

– DERIVATIVES **slugger** noun.

– ORIGIN of unknown origin.

sluggard ● **noun** a lazy, sluggish person.

– DERIVATIVES **sluggardly** adjective.

– ORIGIN from rare or obsolete *slug* 'be lazy or slow'.

sluggish ● **adjective** **1** slow-moving or inactive. **2** lacking energy or alertness.

– DERIVATIVES **sluggishly** adverb **sluggishness** noun.

slug pellet ● **noun** a pellet containing a substance poisonous to slugs, placed among growing plants to prevent them being damaged.

sluice /slo͞os/ ● **noun** **1** (also **sluice gate**) a sliding gate or other device for controlling the flow of water. **2** (also **sluiceway**) an artificial water channel for carrying off overflow or surplus water. **3** an act of rinsing or showering with water. ● **verb** wash or rinse freely with a stream or shower of water.

– ORIGIN Old French *escluse*, from Latin *excludere* 'exclude'.

slum ● **noun** **1** a squalid and overcrowded urban area inhabited by very poor people. **2** a house or building unfit for human habitation. ● **verb** (**slummed, slumming**) (often **slum it**) informal voluntarily spend time in uncomfortable conditions or at a lower social level than one's own.

– DERIVATIVES **slummer** noun **slummy** adjective.

– ORIGIN of unknown origin.

slumber literary ● **verb** sleep. ● **noun** a sleep.

– DERIVATIVES **slumberous** (also **slumbrous**) adjective.

– ORIGIN alteration of Scots and northern English *sloom*, in the same sense.

slump ● **verb** **1** sit, lean, or fall heavily and limply. **2** fail or decline substantially or over a prolonged period. ● **noun** **1** an instance of slumping. **2** a prolonged period of abnormally low economic activity.

– DERIVATIVES **slumped** adjective.

– ORIGIN probably imitative and related to Norwegian *slumpe* 'to fall'.

slung past and past participle of SLING[1].

slunk past and past participle of SLINK.

slur ● **verb** (**slurred, slurring**) **1** speak indistinctly. **2** pass over (a fact or aspect) so as to conceal or minimize it. **3** Music perform (a group of two or more notes) legato. **4** chiefly US make in-

Thesaurus

messy, unkempt, ill-groomed, slatternly, dishevelled, bedraggled, tousled, rumpled, frowzy; *informal* slobbish, slobby; *N. Amer. informal* raggedy, raunchy. **2** *his work is slovenly* CARELESS, slapdash, slipshod, haphazard, hit-or-miss, untidy, messy, negligent, lax, lackadaisical, slack; *informal* sloppy, slap-happy.

– OPPOSITES tidy, careful.

slow ● **adjective** **1** *their slow walk home* UNHURRIED, leisurely, steady, sedate, slow-moving, plodding, dawdling, sluggish, sluggardly. **2** *a slow process* LONG-DRAWN-OUT, time-consuming, lengthy, protracted, prolonged, gradual. **3** *he can be so slow* OBTUSE, stupid, unperceptive, insensitive, bovine, stolid, slow-witted, dull-witted, unintelligent, doltish, witless; *informal* dense, dim, dim-witted, thick, slow on the uptake, dumb, dopey, boneheaded; *Brit. informal* dozy; *N. Amer. informal* chowderheaded. **4** *they were slow to voice their opinions* RELUCTANT, unwilling, disinclined, loath, hesitant, afraid, chary, shy. **5** *the slow season* SLUGGISH, slack, quiet, inactive, flat, depressed, stagnant, dead. **6** *a slow narrative* DULL, boring, uninteresting, unexciting, uneventful, tedious, tiresome, wearisome, monotonous, dreary, lacklustre.

– OPPOSITES fast.

● **verb** **1** *the traffic forced him to slow down* REDUCE SPEED, go slower, decelerate, brake. **2** *you need to slow down* TAKE IT EASY, relax, ease up/off, take a break, slack off, let up; *N. Amer. informal* chill out, hang loose. **3** *this would slow down economic growth* HOLD BACK/UP, delay, retard, set back; restrict, check, curb, inhibit, impede, obstruct, hinder, hamper; *archaic* stay.

– OPPOSITES accelerate.

slowly ● **adverb** **1** *Rose walked off slowly* AT A SLOW PACE, without hurrying, unhurriedly, steadily, at a leisurely pace, at a snail's pace; *Music* adagio, lento, largo. **2** *her health is improving slowly* GRADUALLY, bit by bit, little by little, slowly but surely, step by step.

– OPPOSITES quickly.

sludge ● **noun** MUD, muck, mire, ooze, silt, alluvium; *informal* gunk, crud, gloop, gook, goo; *Brit. informal* gunge, grot; *N. Amer. informal* guck, glop.

sluggish ● **adjective** **1** *Alex felt tired and sluggish* LETHARGIC, listless, lacking in energy, lifeless, inert, inactive, slow, torpid, languid, apathetic, weary, tired, fatigued, sleepy, drowsy, enervated; lazy, idle, indolent, slothful, sluggardly; *Medicine* asthenic; *N. Amer.* logy; *informal* dozy, dopey. **2** *the economy is sluggish* INACTIVE, quiet, slow, slack, flat, depressed, stagnant.

– OPPOSITES vigorous.

sluice ● **verb** **1** *crews sluiced down the decks* WASH (DOWN), rinse, clean, cleanse. **2** *the water sluiced out* POUR, flow, run, gush, stream, course, flood, surge, spill.

slum ● **noun** HOVEL; (**slums**) ghetto, shanty town.

slumber (*poetic/literary*) ● **verb** *the child slumbered fitfully.* See SLEEP verb.

● **noun** *an uneasy slumber.* See SLEEP noun.

slummy ● **adjective** SEEDY, insalubrious, squalid, sleazy, run down, down at heel, shabby, dilapidated; *informal* scruffy, skanky; *Brit. informal* grotty; *N. Amer. informal* shacky.

– OPPOSITES upmarket.

slump ● **verb** **1** *he slumped into a chair* SIT HEAVILY, flop, flump, collapse, sink, fall; *informal* plonk oneself. **2** *houses prices slumped* FALL STEEPLY, plummet, tumble, drop, go down; *informal* crash, nosedive. **3** *reading standards have slumped* DECLINE, deteriorate, degenerate, worsen, slip; *informal* go downhill.

● **noun** **1** *a slump in profits* STEEP FALL, drop, tumble, downturn, downswing, slide, decline, decrease; *informal* nosedive. **2** *an economic slump* RECESSION, economic decline, depression, slowdown,

sinuations or allegations about. ● noun **1** an insinuation or allegation. **2** an indistinct utterance. **3** Music a curved line indicating that notes are to be slurred.
– ORIGIN originally in the sense 'thin mud', later 'to smear': of unknown origin.

slurp ● verb eat or drink with a loud sucking sound. ● noun an act or sound of slurping.
– ORIGIN Dutch *slurpen*.

slurry ● noun (pl. **slurries**) a semi-liquid mixture, especially of fine particles of manure, cement, or coal and water.
– ORIGIN related to dialect *slur* 'thin mud', of unknown origin.

slush ● noun **1** partially melted snow or ice. **2** watery mud. **3** informal excessive sentiment. ● verb make a soft splashing sound.
– DERIVATIVES **slushy** adjective.
– ORIGIN probably imitative.

slush fund ● noun a reserve of money used for illicit purposes, especially political bribery.
– ORIGIN originally nautical slang denoting money collected to buy luxuries, from the sale of watery food known as *slush*.

slut ● noun a slovenly or promiscuous woman.
– DERIVATIVES **sluttish** adjective.
– ORIGIN of unknown origin.

sly ● adjective (**slyer**, **slyest**) **1** having a cunning and deceitful nature. **2** (of a remark, glance, or expression) insinuating. **3** (of an action) surreptitious.
– PHRASES **on the sly** in a surreptitious fashion.
– DERIVATIVES **slyly** (also **slily**) adverb **slyness** noun.
– ORIGIN Old Norse, 'cunning'.

SM ● abbreviation **1** sadomasochism. **2** Sergeant Major.

Sm ● symbol the chemical element samarium.

smack[1] ● noun **1** a sharp blow given with the palm of the hand. **2** a loud, sharp sound made by such a blow. **3** informal a loud kiss. ● verb **1** hit with a smack. **2** smash, drive, or put forcefully into or on to something. **3** part (one's lips) noisily. ● adverb (Brit. also **smack bang**) informal **1** in a sudden and violent way. **2** (N. Amer. also **smack dab**) exactly; precisely.
– ORIGIN Dutch *smacken*.

smack[2] ● verb (**smack of**) **1** have a flavour or smell of. **2** suggest the presence or effects of. ● noun (**a smack of**) a flavour, smell, or suggestion of.
– ORIGIN Old English.

smack[3] ● noun a single-masted sailing boat used for coasting or fishing.
– ORIGIN Dutch *smak*.

smack[4] ● noun informal heroin.
– ORIGIN probably an alteration of a Yiddish word meaning 'a sniff'.

smacker (also **smackeroo**) ● noun informal **1** a loud kiss. **2** Brit. one pound sterling. **3** N. Amer. one dollar.

small ● adjective **1** of less than normal or usual size. **2** not great in amount, number, strength, or power. **3** not fully grown or developed; young. **4** insignificant; unimportant. **5** (of a business or its owner) operating on a modest scale. ● noun (**smalls**) Brit. informal underwear. ● adverb **1** into small pieces. **2** in a small manner or size.
– PHRASES **feel** (or **look**) **small** feel (or look) contemptibly weak or insignificant. **small beer** chiefly Brit. something unimportant. **the small of the back** the part of a person's back where the spine curves in at the level of the waist. **the small screen** television as a medium.
– DERIVATIVES **smallness** noun.
– ORIGIN Old English.

small arms ● plural noun portable firearms.

small-bore ● adjective (of a firearm) having a narrow bore.

small change ● noun **1** money in the form of coins of low value. **2** something trivial.

small claims court ● noun a local court in which claims for small sums of money can be heard and decided quickly and cheaply, without legal representation.

small end ● noun (in a piston engine) the end of the connecting rod connected to the piston.

small fry ● plural noun **1** young or small fish. **2** young or insignificant people or things.

smallholding ● noun Brit. an agricultural holding that is smaller than a farm.
– DERIVATIVES **smallholder** noun.

small hours ● plural noun (**the small hours**) the early hours of the morning after midnight.

small intestine ● noun the part of the intestine that runs between the stomach and the large intestine.

small-minded ● adjective having a narrow outlook; petty.

smallpox ● noun an acute contagious disease spread by a virus, with fever and pustules usually leaving permanent scars.

small print ● noun **1** printed matter in small type. **2** inconspicuous but binding details or conditions printed in an agreement or contract.

small-scale ● adjective of limited size or extent.

small talk ● noun polite conversation about trivial or uncontro-

Thesaurus

stagnation.
– OPPOSITES rise, boom.

slur ● verb *she was slurring her words* MUMBLE, speak unclearly, garble.
● noun *a gross slur* INSULT, slight, slander, slanderous statement, aspersion, smear, allegation.

slush ● noun **1** *he wiped the slush off his shoes* MELTING SNOW, wet snow, mush, sludge. **2** *(informal) the slush of romantic films* SENTIMENTALITY, mawkishness, sentimentalism; *informal* schmaltz, mush, slushiness, corniness; *Brit. informal* soppiness; *N. Amer. informal* sappiness, hokeyness.

slut ● noun PROMISCUOUS WOMAN, prostitute, whore; *informal* tart, floozie, pro; *Brit. informal* scrubber, slag, slapper; *N. Amer. informal* tramp, hooker, hustler, roundheel; *dated* scarlet woman, loose woman, hussy, trollop; *archaic* harlot, strumpet, wanton.

sly ● adjective **1** *she's rather sly* CUNNING, crafty, clever, wily, artful, guileful, tricky, scheming, devious, deceitful, duplicitous, dishonest, underhand, sneaky; *archaic* subtle. **2** *a sly grin* ROGUISH, mischievous, impish, playful, wicked, arch, knowing. **3** *she took a sly sip of water* SURREPTITIOUS, furtive, stealthy, covert.
– PHRASES **on the sly** IN SECRET, secretly, furtively, surreptitiously, covertly, clandestinely, on the quiet, behind someone's back.

smack[1] ● noun **1** *she gave him a smack* SLAP, clout, cuff, blow, spank, rap, swat, crack, thump, punch; *informal* whack, thwack, clip, biff, wallop, swipe, bop, belt, bash, sock. **2** *the parcel landed with a smack* BANG, crash, crack, thud, thump. **3** *(informal) a smack on the lips* KISS, peck; *informal* smacker.
● verb **1** *he tried to smack her* SLAP, hit, strike, spank, cuff, clout, thump, punch, swat; box someone's ears; *informal* whack, clip, wallop, biff, swipe, bop, belt, bash, sock; *Scottish & N. English informal* skelp; *N. Amer. informal* boff, slug, bust. **2** *the waiter smacked a plate down* BANG, slam, crash, thump; sling, fling; *informal* plonk; *N. Amer. informal* plunk.
● adverb *(informal) smack in the middle* EXACTLY, precisely, straight, right, directly, squarely, dead, plumb, point-blank; *informal* slap, bang; *N. Amer. informal* smack dab.

smack[2] ● noun **1** *the beer has a smack of hops* TASTE, flavour, savour. **2** *a smack of bitterness in his words* TRACE, tinge, touch, suggestion, hint, overtone, suspicion, whisper.
– PHRASES **smack of 1** *the tea smacked of tannin* TASTE OF, have the flavour of. **2** *the plan smacked of self-promotion* SUGGEST, hint at, have overtones of, give the impression of, have the stamp of, seem like; smell of, reek of.

small ● adjective **1** *a small flat* LITTLE, compact, bijou, tiny, miniature, mini; minute, microscopic, minuscule; toy, baby; poky, cramped, boxy; *Scottish* wee; *informal* tiddly, teeny, teensy, itsy-bitsy, itty-bitty, pocket-sized, half-pint, dinky, ickle; *Brit. informal* titchy; *N. Amer. informal* little-bitty. **2** *a very small man* SHORT, little, petite, diminutive, elfin, tiny; puny, undersized, stunted, dwarfish, midget, pygmy, Lilliputian; *Scottish* wee; *informal* teeny, pint-sized. **3** *a few small changes* SLIGHT, minor, unimportant, trifling, trivial, insignificant, inconsequential, negligible, nugatory, infinitesimal; *informal* minuscule, piffling, piddling. **4** *small helpings* INADEQUATE, meagre, insufficient, ungenerous; *informal* measly, stingy, mingy, pathetic. **5** *they made him feel small* FOOLISH, stupid, insignificant, unimportant; embarrassed, humiliated, uncomfortable, mortified, ashamed; crushed. **6** *a small farmer* SMALL-SCALE; modest, unpretentious, humble; *informal* small-time.
– RELATED TERMS micro-, mini-, nano-.
– OPPOSITES big, tall, major, ample, substantial.

small change ● noun COINS, change, coppers, silver, cash, specie.

small-minded ● adjective NARROW-MINDED, petty, mean-spirited, uncharitable; close-minded, short-sighted, myopic, blinkered, inward-looking, unimaginative, parochial, provincial, insular, small-town; intolerant, illiberal, conservative, hidebound, dyed-in-the-wool, set in one's ways, inflexible; prejudiced, bigoted; *Brit.*

versial matters.

small-time ● adjective informal unimportant; minor.

smarm informal ● verb **1** chiefly Brit. behave in an ingratiating way. **2** smooth down (one's hair), especially with oil or gel. ● noun ingratiating behaviour.
– ORIGIN of unknown origin.

smarmy ● adjective informal ingratiating and wheedling in an insincere or excessive way.
– DERIVATIVES **smarmily** adverb **smarminess** noun.

smart ● adjective **1** clean, tidy, and stylish. **2** bright and fresh in appearance. **3** (of a place) fashionable and upmarket. **4** informal having a quick intelligence. **5** chiefly N. Amer. impertinently clever or sarcastic. **6** quick; brisk. ● verb **1** give a sharp, stinging pain. **2** feel upset and annoyed. ● noun **1** a smarting pain. **2** (**smarts**) N. Amer. informal intelligence; acumen. ● adverb archaic in a quick or brisk manner.
– PHRASES **look smart** chiefly Brit. be quick.
– DERIVATIVES **smartly** adverb **smartness** noun.
– ORIGIN Old English.

smart alec (also **smart aleck**) ● noun informal a person considered irritating in always having a clever answer to a question.

smart-arse (US **smart-ass**) ● noun informal another term for SMART ALEC.

smart card ● noun a plastic card with a built-in microprocessor, used for financial transactions and personal identification.

smarten ● verb (usu. **smarten up**) make or become smarter.

smartish ● adverb informal, chiefly Brit. quickly; briskly.

smart-mouth ● verb N. Amer. informal make impudent remarks.
– DERIVATIVES **smart-mouthed** adjective.

smash ● verb **1** break violently into pieces. **2** hit or collide with forcefully. **3** crash and severely damage (a vehicle). **4** (in sport) strike (the ball) with great force. **5** completely defeat, destroy, or foil. ● noun **1** an act, instance, or sound of smashing. **2** (also **smash hit**) informal a very successful song, film, or show.
– ORIGIN probably imitative.

smash-and-grab ● adjective (of a robbery) in which the thief smashes a shop window and seizes goods.

smashed ● adjective informal very drunk.

smasher ● noun **1** a person or device that smashes something. **2** Brit. informal a very attractive or impressive person or thing.

smashing ● adjective informal, chiefly Brit. excellent; wonderful.

smattering (also **smatter**) ● noun **1** a small amount. **2** a slight knowledge of a language or subject.
– ORIGIN from *smatter* 'talk ignorantly' (now only Scots), of unknown origin.

smear ● verb **1** coat or mark with a greasy or sticky substance. **2** blur or smudge. **3** damage the reputation of (someone) by false accusations. ● noun **1** a greasy or sticky mark. **2** a false or unwarranted accusation. **3** a sample thinly spread on a microscopic slide.
– DERIVATIVES **smeary** adjective.
– ORIGIN Old English.

smear test ● noun a test to detect signs of cervical cancer, conducted by taking a cervical smear.

smegma /smegmə/ ● noun an oily secretion in the folds of the skin, especially under a man's foreskin.
– ORIGIN Greek, 'soap'.

smell ● noun **1** the faculty of perceiving odours by means of the organs in the nose. **2** a quality that is perceived by this faculty; an odour. **3** an act of inhaling in order to perceive an odour. ● verb (past and past part. **smelt** or **smelled**) **1** perceive the odour of. **2** sniff at (something) in order to ascertain its odour. **3** emit an odour of a specified kind. **4** have a strong or unpleasant odour. **5** detect or suspect by means of instinct or intuition. **6** be suggestive of something: *it smells like a hoax to me.*
– PHRASES **smell a rat** informal suspect trickery.
– DERIVATIVES **smeller** noun.
– ORIGIN of unknown origin.

smelling salts ● plural noun chiefly historical ammonium carbonate mixed with perfume, sniffed by someone who feels faint.

smelly ● adjective (**smellier**, **smelliest**) having a strong or unpleasant smell.
– DERIVATIVES **smelliness** noun.

smelt[1] ● verb extract (metal) from its ore by a process involving heating and melting.
– DERIVATIVES **smelter** noun.
– ORIGIN Dutch, Low German *smelten*.

Thesaurus

parish-pump, blimpish.
– OPPOSITES tolerant.

small-time ● adjective *(informal)* MINOR, small-scale; petty, unimportant, insignificant, inconsequential; *N. Amer.* minor-league; *informal* penny-ante, piddling; *N. Amer. informal* two-bit, bush-league, picayune.
– OPPOSITES major.

smarmy ● adjective *(informal)* UNCTUOUS, ingratiating, slick, oily, greasy, obsequious, sycophantic, fawning; *informal* slimy, sucky.

smart ● adjective **1** *you look very smart* WELL DRESSED, stylish, chic, fashionable, modish, elegant, neat, spruce, trim, dapper; *N. Amer.* trig; *informal* snazzy, natty, snappy, sharp, cool; *N. Amer. informal* sassy, spiffy, fly, kicky. **2** *a smart restaurant* FASHIONABLE, stylish, high-class, exclusive, chic, fancy; *Brit.* upmarket; *N. Amer.* high-toned; *informal* trendy, posh, ritzy, plush, classy, swanky, glitzy; *Brit. informal* swish; *N. Amer. informal* swank. **3** *(informal) he's the smart one* CLEVER, bright, intelligent, sharp-witted, quick-witted, shrewd, astute, able; perceptive, percipient; *informal* brainy, savvy, quick on the uptake. **4** *a smart pace* BRISK, quick, fast, rapid, swift, lively, spanking, energetic, vigorous; *informal* snappy, cracking. **5** *a smart blow on the snout* SHARP, severe, forceful, violent.
– OPPOSITES untidy, downmarket, stupid, slow, gentle.
● verb **1** *her eyes were smarting* STING, burn, tingle, prickle; hurt, ache. **2** *she smarted at the accusations* FEEL ANNOYED, feel upset, take offence, feel aggrieved, feel indignant, be put out, feel hurt.
– PHRASES **look smart** *(Brit.)* BE QUICK, hurry up, speed up; *informal* make it snappy, get cracking, get moving, step on it; *Brit. informal* get one's skates on, stir one's stumps; *N. Amer. informal* get a wiggle on.

smarten ● verb SPRUCE UP, clean up, tidy up, neaten, tidy; groom, freshen, preen, primp, beautify; redecorate, refurbish, modernize; *informal* do up, titivate, doll up; *Brit. informal* tart up, posh up; *N. Amer. informal* gussy up.

smash ● verb **1** *he smashed a window* BREAK, shatter, splinter, crack, shiver; *informal* bust. **2** *she's smashed the car* CRASH, wreck; *Brit.* write off; *Brit. informal* prang; *N. Amer. informal* total. **3** *they smashed into a wall* CRASH INTO, collide with, hit, strike, ram, smack into, slam into, plough into, run into, bump into; *N. Amer.* impact. **4** *Don smashed him over the head* HIT, strike, thump, punch, smack; *informal* whack, bash, biff, bop, clout, wallop, crown; *Brit. informal* slosh, dot; *N. Amer. informal* slug. **5** *he smashed their hopes of glory* DESTROY, wreck, ruin, shatter, dash, crush, devastate, demolish, overturn, scotch; *informal* put the kibosh on, do for, put paid to, queer; *Brit. informal* scupper.
● noun **1** *the smash of glass* BREAKING, shattering, crash. **2** *a motorway smash* CRASH, collision, accident, bump; *Brit.* RTA; *N. Amer.* wreck; *informal* pile-up, smash-up; *Brit. informal* prang, shunt. **3** *(informal) a box-office smash* SUCCESS, sensation, sell-out, triumph; *informal* (smash) hit, winner, crowd-puller, knockout, wow, biggie.

smashing ● adjective *(Brit. informal)*. See MARVELLOUS sense 2.

smattering ● noun BIT, little, modicum, touch, soupçon; nodding acquaintance; rudiments, basics; *informal* smidgen, smidge, tad.

smear ● verb **1** *the table was smeared with grease* STREAK, smudge, mark, soil, dirty; *informal* splotch, splodge; *poetic/literary* besmear. **2** *smear the meat with olive oil* COVER, coat, grease; *poetic/literary* bedaub. **3** *she smeared sunblock on her skin* SPREAD, rub, daub, slap, slather, smother, plaster, cream, slick; apply; *poetic/literary* besmear. **4** *they are trying to smear our reputation* SULLY, tarnish, blacken, drag through the mud, taint, damage, defame, discredit, malign, slander, libel; *N. Amer.* slur; *informal* do a hatchet job on; *formal* calumniate; *poetic/literary* besmirch.
● noun **1** *smears of blood* STREAK, smudge, daub, dab, spot, patch, blotch, mark; *informal* splotch, splodge. **2** *press smears about his closest aides* FALSE ACCUSATION, lie, untruth, slur, slander, libel, defamation, calumny.

smell ● noun *the smell of the kitchen* ODOUR, aroma, fragrance, scent, perfume, redolence; bouquet, nose; stench, stink, reek; *Brit. informal* pong, niff, whiff, hum; *Scottish informal* guff; *N. Amer. informal* funk; *poetic/literary* miasma.
– RELATED TERMS osmic, olfactory.
● verb **1** *he smelled her perfume* SCENT, get a sniff of, detect. **2** *the dogs smelled each other* SNIFF, nose. **3** *the cellar smells* STINK, reek, have a bad smell; *Brit. informal* pong, hum, niff, whiff. **4** *it smells like a hoax to me* SMACK OF, have the hallmarks of, seem like, have the air of, suggest.

smelly ● adjective FOUL-SMELLING, stinking, reeking, fetid, malodor-

smelt[2] past and past participle of SMELL.
smelt[3] ● noun (pl. same or **smelts**) a small silvery fish of both marine and fresh water.
– ORIGIN Old English.
smew /smyoō/ ● noun a small northern diving duck, the male of which is white with black markings.
– ORIGIN obscurely related to Dutch *smient* 'wigeon' and German *Schmeiente* 'small wild duck'.
smidgen (also **smidgeon** or **smidgin**) ● noun informal a tiny amount.
– ORIGIN perhaps from Scots *smitch* in the same sense.
smile ● verb **1** form one's features into a pleased, friendly, or amused expression, with the corners of the mouth turned up. **2** (**smile at/on/upon**) regard favourably or indulgently. ● noun an act of smiling; a smiling expression.
– ORIGIN perhaps Scandinavian; related to SMIRK.
smiley ● adjective informal smiling; cheerful.
smirch /smurch/ ● verb **1** make dirty. **2** discredit; taint. ● noun **1** a dirty mark or stain. **2** a flaw.
– ORIGIN probably symbolic.
smirk ● verb smile in an irritatingly smug or silly way. ● noun a smug or silly smile.
– DERIVATIVES **smirker** noun **smirky** adjective.
– ORIGIN Old English, related to SMILE.
smite ● verb (past **smote**; past part. **smitten**) **1** archaic or literary strike with a firm blow. **2** archaic or literary defeat or conquer. **3** (**be smitten**) be affected severely by a disease. **4** (**be smitten**) be strongly attracted to someone or something.
– ORIGIN Old English, 'to smear, blemish'.
smith ● noun **1** a worker in metal. **2** a blacksmith. ● verb treat (metal) by heating, hammering, and forging it.
– ORIGIN Old English.
-smith ● combining form denoting a person skilled in creating something with a specified material: *goldsmith*.
smithereens /smithəreenz/ ● plural noun informal small pieces.
– ORIGIN probably from Irish *smidirín*.
smithy /smithi/ ● noun (pl. **smithies**) a blacksmith's workshop; a forge.
– ORIGIN Old Norse.
smitten past participle of SMITE.
smock ● noun **1** a loose dress or blouse having the upper part closely gathered in smocking. **2** a loose overall worn to protect one's clothes. ● verb decorate with smocking.
– ORIGIN Old English.
smocking ● noun decoration on a garment created by gathering a section of the material into tight pleats and holding them together with parallel stitches in an ornamental pattern.
smog ● noun fog or haze intensified by smoke or other atmospheric pollutants.
– DERIVATIVES **smoggy** adjective.
– ORIGIN blend of SMOKE and FOG.
smoke ● noun **1** a visible suspension of carbon or other particles in the air, emitted from a burning substance. **2** an act of smoking tobacco. **3** informal a cigarette or cigar. **4** (**the Smoke** or **the Big Smoke**) Brit. a big city, especially London. ● verb **1** emit smoke. **2** inhale and exhale the smoke of tobacco or a drug. **3** cure or preserve (meat or fish) by exposure to smoke. **4** treat (glass) so as to darken it. **5** (**smoke out**) drive out of a place by using smoke.
– PHRASES **go up in smoke** informal **1** be destroyed by fire. **2** (of a plan) come to nothing. **there is no smoke without fire** rumours usually have some basis in fact. **smoke and mirrors** N. Amer. the use of misleading or irrelevant information to obscure or embellish the truth.
– DERIVATIVES **smokable** (also **smokeable**) adjective **smokeless** adjective.
– ORIGIN Old English.
smoke alarm ● noun a device that detects and gives a warning of the presence of smoke.
smokehouse ● noun a shed or room for smoking fish or meat.
smokeless zone ● noun Brit. a district in which it is illegal to create smoke and where only smokeless fuel may be used.
smoker ● noun **1** a person who smokes tobacco regularly. **2** a person or device that smokes fish or meat. **3** chiefly N. Amer. an informal social gathering for men.
smokescreen ● noun **1** a cloud of smoke created to conceal military operations. **2** a thing designed to disguise someone's real intentions or activities.
smoke signal ● noun a column of smoke used to convey a message to a distant person.
smokestack ● noun a chimney or funnel for discharging smoke from a locomotive, ship, factory, etc.
smoking gun ● noun a piece of undeniable incriminating evidence.
smoking jacket ● noun a man's comfortable jacket, formerly worn while smoking after dinner.
smoky ● adjective (**smokier**, **smokiest**) **1** producing, filled with, or resembling smoke. **2** having the taste or aroma of smoked food.
– DERIVATIVES **smokily** adverb **smokiness** noun.
smolder ● verb US spelling of SMOULDER.
smolt /smōlt/ ● noun a young salmon or trout after the parr stage, when it becomes silvery and migrates to the sea for the first time.
– ORIGIN of unknown origin.
smooch informal ● verb **1** kiss and cuddle amorously. **2** Brit. dance slowly in a close embrace. ● noun a spell of smooching.
– DERIVATIVES **smoocher** noun **smoochy** adjective (**smoochier**, **smoochiest**).
– ORIGIN imitative.
smoodge (also **smooge**) Austral./NZ informal ● verb **1** behave amorously. **2** behave in an ingratiating manner. ● noun **1** a display of amorous affection. **2** an act or instance of being ingratiating.
– DERIVATIVES **smoodger** noun.
– ORIGIN probably from SMOOCH.
smooth ● adjective **1** having an even and regular surface; free from projections or indentations. **2** (of a liquid) having an even consistency; without lumps. **3** (of movement) without jerks. **4** without problems or difficulties. **5** charming in a suave or excessively ingratiating way. **6** (of a flavour) without harshness or bitterness. ● verb (also **smoothe**) **1** make smooth. **2** (often **smooth over**) deal successfully with (a problem).
– DERIVATIVES **smoothly** adverb **smoothness** noun.
– ORIGIN Old English.

S

Thesaurus

ous, pungent, rank, noxious; off, gamy, high; musty, fusty; *informal* stinky; *Brit. informal* pongy, whiffy, humming; *N. Amer. informal* funky; *poetic/literary* miasmic, noisome.
smile ● verb *he smiled at her* BEAM, grin (from ear to ear), dimple, twinkle; smirk, simper; leer.
– OPPOSITES frown.
● noun *the smile on her face* BEAM, grin, twinkle; smirk, simper; leer.
smirk ● verb SMILE SMUGLY, simper, snigger; leer.
smitten ● adjective **1** *he was smitten with cholera* STRUCK DOWN, laid low, suffering, affected, afflicted, plagued, stricken. **2** *Jane's smitten with you* INFATUATED, besotted, in love, obsessed, head over heels; enamoured of, attracted to, taken with; captivated, enchanted, under someone's spell; *informal* bowled over, swept off one's feet, crazy about, mad about, keen on, gone on, sweet on; *Brit. informal* potty about.
smog ● noun FOG, haze; fumes, smoke, pollution; *Brit. informal* pea-souper.
smoke ● verb **1** *the fire was smoking* SMOULDER, emit smoke; *archaic* reek. **2** *he smoked his cigarette* PUFF ON, draw on, pull on; inhale; light; *informal* drag on. **3** *they smoke their salmon* CURE, preserve, dry.
● noun *the smoke from the bonfire* FUMES, exhaust, gas, vapour; smog.
smoky ● adjective **1** *the smoky atmosphere* SMOKE-FILLED, sooty, smoggy, hazy, foggy, murky, thick; *Brit. informal* fuggy. **2** *her smoky eyes* GREY, sooty, dark, black.
smooth ● adjective **1** *the smooth flat rocks* EVEN, level, flat, plane; unwrinkled, featureless; glassy, glossy, silky, polished. **2** *his face was smooth* CLEAN-SHAVEN, hairless. **3** *a smooth sauce* CREAMY, velvety, blended. **4** *a smooth sea* CALM, still, tranquil, undisturbed, unruffled, even, flat, waveless, like a millpond. **5** *the smooth running of the equipment* STEADY, regular, uninterrupted, unbroken, fluid, fluent; straightforward, easy, effortless, trouble-free. **6** *a smooth wine* MELLOW, mild, agreeable, pleasant. **7** *the smooth tone of the clarinet* DULCET, soft, soothing, mellow, sweet, silvery, honeyed, mellifluous, melodious, lilting, lyrical, harmonious. **8** *a smooth, confident man* SUAVE, urbane, sophisticated, polished, debonair; courteous, gracious, glib, slick, ingratiating, unctuous; *informal* smarmy.

smooth-bore • noun a gun with an unrifled barrel.
smoothie • noun **1** informal a man with a smooth, suave manner. **2** N. Amer. & Austral./NZ a thick, smooth drink of fresh fruit puréed with milk, yogurt, or ice cream.
smoothing iron • noun historical a flat iron.
smooth snake • noun a harmless snake which is grey to reddish in colour, typically living in heathy country where it feeds on lizards.
smooth-talk • verb informal address or persuade with persuasively charming or flattering language.
– DERIVATIVES **smooth-talker** noun **smooth-talking** adjective.
smooth-tongued • adjective insincerely flattering.
smorgasbord /smorgəsbord/ • noun a range of open sandwiches and savoury delicacies served as hors d'oeuvres or a buffet.
– ORIGIN Swedish, from *smörgås* 'slice of bread and butter' + *bord* 'table'.
smorzando /smortsandō/ • adverb & adjective Music dying away.
– ORIGIN Italian, 'extinguishing'.
smote past of SMITE.
smother • verb **1** suffocate by covering the nose and mouth. **2** extinguish (a fire) by covering it. **3** (**smother in/with**) cover entirely with. **4** cause to feel trapped and oppressed. **5** suppress (a feeling or action). • noun a mass of something that stifles or obscures.
– ORIGIN Old English.
smoulder (US also **smolder**) • verb **1** burn slowly with smoke but no flame. **2** feel intense and barely suppressed anger, hatred, lust, etc. • noun an instance of smouldering.
– ORIGIN related to Dutch *smeulen*.
SMS • abbreviation Short Messaging (or Message) Service, a system of abbreviations for use in electronic communication via mobile phones.
smudge • verb make or become blurred or smeared. • noun a smudged mark or image.
– DERIVATIVES **smudgy** adjective (**smudgier, smudgiest**).
– ORIGIN of unknown origin.
smudging • noun N. Amer. a ceremony or ritual, allegedly of North American Indian origin, involving the burning of sage, cedar, etc., intended to purify or sanctify a person or place.
– ORIGIN related to obsolete *smudge* 'cure (herring) by smoking', of unknown origin.
smug • adjective (**smugger, smuggest**) irritatingly pleased with oneself; self-satisfied.
– DERIVATIVES **smugly** adverb **smugness** noun.
– ORIGIN originally in the sense 'neat, spruce'; from Low German *smuk* 'pretty'.
smuggle • verb **1** move (goods) illegally into or out of a country. **2** convey secretly and illicitly.
– DERIVATIVES **smuggler** noun **smuggling** noun.
– ORIGIN Low German *smuggelen*.
smut • noun **1** a small flake of soot or dirt. **2** indecent or obscene talk, writing, or pictures. **3** a disease of cereals caused by a fungus, in which parts of the ear change to black powder. • verb (**smutted, smutting**) **1** mark with smuts. **2** infect with smut.
– ORIGIN related to German *schmutzen*.
smutty • adjective **1** indecent or obscene. **2** soiled with or characterized by smut or soot.
Sn • symbol the chemical element tin.
– ORIGIN from Latin *stannum* 'tin'.
snack • noun **1** a small quantity of food eaten between meals or in place of a meal. **2** Austral. informal a thing that is easy to accomplish. • verb eat a snack.
– ORIGIN Dutch, from *snacken* 'to bite'.
snaffle • noun a simple bit on a bridle, used with a single set of reins. • verb informal illicitly take for oneself.
– ORIGIN probably Low German or Dutch.
snafu /snafōō/ informal, chiefly N. Amer. • noun a confused or chaotic state; a mess. • verb throw into confusion or chaos.
– ORIGIN acronym from *situation normal: all fouled* (or *fucked*) *up*.
snag[1] • noun **1** an unexpected or hidden obstacle or drawback. **2** a sharp, angular, or jagged projection. **3** a small rent or tear. • verb (**snagged, snagging**) **1** catch or tear on a snag. **2** N. Amer. informal catch; obtain.
– DERIVATIVES **snaggy** adjective.
– ORIGIN probably Scandinavian.
snag[2] • noun Austral./NZ informal a sausage.
– ORIGIN of unknown origin.
snaggle • noun a tangled or knotted mass. • verb become knotted or tangled.
– ORIGIN from SNAG[1].
snaggle-toothed • adjective having irregular or projecting teeth.
snail • noun a slow-moving mollusc with a spiral shell into which the whole body can be withdrawn.
– ORIGIN Old English.
snail mail • noun informal the ordinary post as opposed to email.
snake • noun **1** a predatory reptile with a long slender limbless body, many kinds of which have a venomous bite. **2** (also **snake in the grass**) a treacherous or deceitful person. • verb move or extend with the twisting motion of a snake.
– ORIGIN Old English.
snakebite • noun Brit. a drink consisting of draught cider and

Thesaurus

– OPPOSITES uneven, rough, hairy, lumpy, irregular, raucous, gauche.
• verb **1** *she smoothed the soil* FLATTEN, level (out/off), even out/off; press, roll, steamroll, iron, plane. **2** *a plan to smooth the way for the agreement* EASE, facilitate, clear the way for, pave the way for, expedite, assist, aid, help, oil the wheels of, lubricate.
smoothly • adverb **1** *her hair was combed smoothly back* EVENLY, level, flat, flush. **2** *the door closed smoothly* FLUIDLY, fluently, steadily, frictionlessly, easily; quietly. **3** *the plan had gone smoothly* WITHOUT A HITCH, like clockwork, without difficulty, easily, effortlessly, according to plan, swimmingly, satisfactorily, very well; informal like a dream.
smooth-talking • adjective (informal) PERSUASIVE, glib, plausible, silver-tongued, slick, eloquent, fast-talking; ingratiating, flattering, unctuous, obsequious, sycophantic; informal smarmy.
– OPPOSITES blunt.
smother • verb **1** *she tried to smother her baby* SUFFOCATE, asphyxiate, stifle, choke. **2** *we smothered the flames* EXTINGUISH, put out, snuff out, dampen, douse, stamp out, choke. **3** *we smothered ourselves with suncream* SMEAR, daub, spread, cover; poetic/literary besmear, bedaub. **4** *their granny always smothers them* OVERWHELM, inundate, envelop, cocoon; Brit. wrap someone in cotton wool. **5** *she smothered a sigh* STIFLE, muffle, strangle, repress, suppress, hold back, fight back, bite back, swallow, contain, bottle up, conceal, hide; bite one's lip; informal keep a/the lid on.
smoulder • verb **1** *the bonfire still smouldered* SMOKE, glow, burn; archaic reek. **2** *she was smouldering with resentment* SEETHE, boil, fume, burn, simmer, be boiling over, be beside oneself; informal be livid.
smudge • noun *a smudge of blood* STREAK, smear, mark, stain, blotch, stripe, blob, dab; informal splotch, splodge.
• verb **1** *her face was smudged with dust* STREAK, mark, dirty, soil, blotch, blacken, smear, blot, daub, stain; informal splotch, splodge; poetic/literary bedaub, besmirch. **2** *she smudged her make-up* SMEAR, streak, mess up.
smug • adjective SELF-SATISFIED, self-congratulatory, complacent, superior, pleased with oneself, self-approving; Brit. informal like the cat that got the cream, I'm-all-right-Jack.
smuggle • verb IMPORT/EXPORT ILLEGALLY, traffic in, run.
smuggler • noun CONTRABANDIST, runner, courier; informal mule, moonshiner.
smutty • adjective VULGAR, rude, crude, dirty, filthy, salacious, coarse, obscene, lewd, pornographic, X-rated; risqué, racy, earthy, bawdy, suggestive, naughty, ribald, off colour; informal blue, raunchy; Brit. informal near the knuckle, saucy; N. Amer. informal gamy; euphemistic adult.
snack • noun *she made herself a snack* LIGHT MEAL, sandwich, treat, refreshments, nibbles, titbit(s); informal bite (to eat); Brit. informal elevenses.
• verb *don't snack on sugary foods* EAT BETWEEN MEALS, nibble, munch; informal graze.
snaffle • verb (informal). See STEAL verb sense 1.
snag • noun **1** *the snag is that this might affect inflation* COMPLICATION, difficulty, catch, hitch, obstacle, stumbling block, pitfall, problem, impediment, hindrance, inconvenience, setback, hurdle, disadvantage, downside, drawback. **2** *smooth rails with no snags* SHARP PROJECTION, jag; thorn, spur. **3** *a snag in her tights* TEAR, rip, hole, gash, slash; ladder, run.
• verb **1** *she snagged her tights* TEAR, rip, ladder. **2** *the zip snagged on the fabric* CATCH, get caught, hook.

S

lager in equal proportions.

snake charmer • noun an entertainer who appears to make snakes move by playing music.

snake oil • noun informal, chiefly N. Amer. a substance with no real medicinal value sold as a cure-all.

snakes and ladders • plural noun (treated as sing.) a board game in which players proceed up ladders or fall back down snakes depicted on the board.

snaky • adjective (**snakier**, **snakiest**) **1** long and sinuous like a snake. **2** cold and cunning. **3** Austral./NZ informal angry; irritable.

snap • verb (**snapped**, **snapping**) **1** break with a sharp cracking sound. **2** (of an animal) make a sudden audible bite. **3** open or close with a brisk movement or sharp sound. **4** (**snap up**) quickly secure (something that is in short supply). **5** suddenly lose one's self-control. **6** say something quickly and irritably. **7** (**snap out of**) informal get out of (a bad mood) by a sudden effort. **8** take a snapshot of. • noun **1** an act or sound of snapping. **2** a brief spell of cold or otherwise distinctive weather. **3** vigour; liveliness. **4** informal a snapshot. **5** Brit. a card game in which players compete to call 'snap' as soon as two cards of the same type are exposed. **6** a crisp, brittle biscuit. • adjective done or taken on the spur of the moment: *a snap decision*.
– ORIGIN probably from Dutch or Low German *snappen* 'seize'.

snap-brim • adjective (of a hat) having a brim that can be turned up and down at opposite sides.

snapdragon • noun a plant bearing spikes of brightly coloured two-lobed flowers which gape like a mouth when a bee lands on the curved lip.

snap fastener • noun another term for PRESS STUD.

snap-lock • adjective (of a device or component) fastened automatically when pushed into position.

snapper • noun a marine fish noted for snapping its toothed jaws.

snappish • adjective **1** (of a dog) irritable and inclined to bite. **2** (of a person) irritable; curt.
– DERIVATIVES **snappishly** adverb **snappishness** noun.

snappy • adjective (**snappier**, **snappiest**) informal **1** irritable and sharp. **2** cleverly concise. **3** neat and stylish: *a snappy dresser*.
– PHRASES **make it snappy** do it quickly.
– DERIVATIVES **snappily** adverb.

snapshot • noun an informal photograph, taken quickly.

snare • noun **1** a trap for catching small animals, consisting of a loop of wire or cord that pulls tight. **2** a thing likely to lure someone into harm or error. **3** a length of wire, gut, or hide stretched across a drumhead to produce a rattling sound. **4** (also **snare drum**) a side drum. • verb catch in a snare or trap.
– ORIGIN Old Norse; sense 3 is probably from Low German or Dutch, 'harp string'.

snarf • verb informal, chiefly N. Amer. consume quickly or greedily.
– ORIGIN perhaps imitative.

snarky • adjective (**snarkier**, **snarkiest**) N. Amer. informal sharply critical.
– ORIGIN from dialect *snark* 'snore, snort', 'find fault'.

snarl[1] • verb **1** growl with bared teeth. **2** say something aggressively. • noun an act or sound of snarling.
– DERIVATIVES **snarly** adjective.
– ORIGIN Germanic.

snarl[2] • verb (**snarl up**) entangle or become entangled. • noun a knot or tangle.
– ORIGIN from SNARE.

snarl-up • noun informal **1** a traffic jam. **2** a muddle.

snatch • verb **1** seize quickly and deftly. **2** informal steal or kidnap by seizing suddenly. **3** quickly take when the chance presents itself: *snatching a few hours' sleep*. • noun **1** an act of snatching. **2** a fragment of music or talk. **3** Weightlifting the rapid raising of a weight from the floor to above the head in one movement.
– ORIGIN perhaps related to SNACK.

snazzy • adjective (**snazzier**, **snazziest**) informal smart; stylish.
– ORIGIN of unknown origin.

sneak • verb (past and past part. **sneaked** or informal, chiefly N. Amer. **snuck**) **1** move, go, or convey in a furtive manner. **2** stealthily acquire or obtain: *she sneaked a glance at her watch*. **3** Brit. informal inform someone in authority of a person's misdeeds. • noun informal **1** a furtive person. **2** Brit. a telltale. • adjective acting or done surreptitiously or unofficially: *a sneak preview*.
– ORIGIN perhaps related to obsolete *snike* 'to creep'.

Thesaurus

snake • noun *the snake shed its skin* poetic/literary serpent; Zoology ophidian; Austral./NZ rhyming slang Joe Blake.
– RELATED TERMS colubrine, serpentine.
• verb *the road snakes inland* TWIST, wind, meander, zigzag, curve.
– PHRASES **snake in the grass** TRAITOR, turncoat, betrayer, informer, back-stabber, double-crosser, quisling, Judas; fraudster, trickster, charlatan; informal two-timer, rat.

snap • verb **1** *the ruler snapped* BREAK, fracture, splinter, come apart, split, crack; informal bust. **2** *she snapped after years of violence* FLARE UP, lose one's self-control, freak out, go to pieces, get worked up; informal crack up, lose one's cool, blow one's top, fly off the handle; Brit. informal throw a wobbly. **3** *a dog was snapping at his heels* BITE; gnash its teeth. **4** *'shut up!' Anna snapped* SAY ROUGHLY, say brusquely, say abruptly, say angrily, bark, snarl, growl; retort, rejoin, retaliate; round on someone; informal jump down someone's throat. **5** *photographers snapped the royals* PHOTOGRAPH, picture, take, shoot, film, capture.
• noun **1** *she closed her purse with a snap* CLICK, crack, pop. **2** *a cold snap* PERIOD, spell, time, interval, stretch; Brit. informal patch. **3** (informal) *holiday snaps* PHOTOGRAPH, picture, photo, shot, snapshot, print, slide, frame, still; Brit. enprint.
– PHRASES **snap out of it** (informal) RECOVER, get a grip, pull oneself together, get over it, get better, cheer up, perk up; informal buck up. **snap something up** BUY EAGERLY, accept eagerly, jump at, take advantage of, grab, seize (on), grasp with both hands, pounce on.

snappy • adjective (informal) **1** *a snappy mood* IRRITABLE, irascible, short-tempered, hot-tempered, quick-tempered, snappish, fiery, touchy, volatile; cross, crabby, crotchety, cantankerous, grumpy, bad-tempered, testy, tetchy; informal chippy, grouchy, cranky, on a short fuse; Brit. informal narky, ratty, eggy, like a bear with a sore head; N. Amer. informal soreheaded. **2** *a snappy catchphrase* CONCISE, succinct, memorable, catchy, neat, clever, crisp, pithy, witty, incisive, brief, short. **3** *a snappy dresser* SMART, fashionable, stylish, chic, modish, elegant, neat, spruce, trim, dapper; informal snazzy, natty, sharp, nifty, cool; N. Amer. informal sassy, spiffy, fly.
– OPPOSITES peaceable, long-winded, slovenly.
– PHRASES **make it snappy** HURRY (UP), be quick (about it), get a move on, look lively, speed up; informal get cracking, step on it, move it, buck up, shake a leg; Brit. informal get your skates on; N. Amer. informal get a wiggle on; dated make haste.

snare • noun **1** *the hare was caught in a snare* TRAP, gin, net, noose. **2** *avoid the snares of the new law* PITFALL, trap, catch, danger, hazard, peril; web, mesh; poetic/literary toils.
• verb **1** *game birds were snared* TRAP, catch, net, bag, ensnare, entrap. **2** *he managed to snare an heiress* ENSNARE, catch, get hold of, bag, hook, land.

snarl[1] • verb **1** *the wolves are snarling* GROWL, gnash one's teeth. **2** *'Shut it!' he snarled* SAY ROUGHLY, say brusquely, say nastily, bark, snap, growl; informal jump down someone's throat.

snarl[2] • verb **1** *the rope got snarled up in a bush* TANGLE, entangle, entwine, enmesh, ravel, knot, foul. **2** *this case has snarled up the court process* COMPLICATE, confuse, muddle, jumble; informal mess up.

snarl-up • noun (informal) **1** *a snarl-up in Edinburgh* TRAFFIC JAM, tailback, gridlock. **2** *a snarl-up in terminology* MUDDLE, mess, tangle, jumble; misunderstanding, misinterpretation, misconception, confusion; mistake, mix-up, bungle; informal hash, foul-up, screw-up; N. Amer. informal snafu.

snatch • verb **1** *she snatched the sandwich* GRAB, seize, take hold of, get one's hands on, take, pluck; grasp at, clutch at. **2** (informal) *someone snatched my bag*. See STEAL verb sense 1. **3** (informal) *she snatched the newborn from the hospital*. See ABDUCT. **4** *he snatched victory* SEIZE, pluck, wrest, achieve, secure, obtain; scrape.
• noun **1** *brief snatches of sleep* PERIOD, spell, time, fit, bout, interval, stretch. **2** *a snatch of conversation* FRAGMENT, snippet, bit, scrap, part, extract, excerpt, portion.

snazzy • adjective (informal). See STYLISH.

sneak • verb **1** *I sneaked out* CREEP, slink, steal, slip, slide, sidle, edge, move furtively, tiptoe, pussyfoot, pad, prowl. **2** *she sneaked a camera in* BRING/TAKE SURREPTITIOUSLY, bring/take secretly, bring/take illicitly, smuggle, spirit, slip. **3** *he sneaked a doughnut* TAKE FURTIVELY, take surreptitiously; steal; informal snatch. **4** (Brit. informal) *the little squirt sneaked on me* INFORM, tell tales; report, give someone away, be disloyal, sell out, stab in the back; informal squeal, rat, blow the whistle, peach, snitch, stitch up; Brit. informal grass, split, shop; Scottish informal clype; N. Amer. informal finger; Austral./NZ informal dob.

S

sneaker ● noun chiefly N. Amer. a soft shoe worn for sports or casual occasions.
sneaking ● adjective (of a feeling) persistent in one's mind but reluctantly held; nagging.
sneaky ● adjective furtive or sly.
– DERIVATIVES **sneakily** adverb **sneakiness** noun.
sneck Scottish & N. English ● noun a latch on a door or window. ● verb close or fasten with a latch.
– ORIGIN related to SNATCH.
sneer ● noun a contemptuous or mocking smile, remark, or tone. ● verb smile or speak in a contemptuous or mocking manner.
– ORIGIN probably imitative.
sneeze ● verb make a sudden involuntary expulsion of air from the nose and mouth due to irritation of one's nostrils. ● noun an act or the sound of sneezing.
– PHRASES **not to be sneezed at** informal not to be rejected without careful consideration.
– DERIVATIVES **sneezer** noun **sneezy** adjective.
– ORIGIN Old English.
snib chiefly Scottish & Irish ● noun **1** a lock, latch, or fastening for a door or window. **2** a small catch on a lock which holds the bolt in or out. ● verb (**snibbed**, **snibbing**) fasten or lock.
– ORIGIN perhaps from Low German *snibbe* 'beak-like point'.
snick ● verb **1** cut a small notch or incision in. **2** make or cause to make a clicking sound. ● noun **1** a small notch or cut. **2** a sharp click.
– ORIGIN probably from obsolete *snick or snee* 'fight with knives'.
snicker ● verb **1** snigger. **2** (of a horse) whinny. ● noun an act or sound of snickering.
– ORIGIN imitative.
snicket ● noun chiefly N. English a narrow alley between houses.
– ORIGIN of unknown origin.
snide ● adjective **1** derogatory or mocking in an indirect way. **2** chiefly N. Amer. devious and underhand. **3** informal counterfeit or inferior. ● noun a snide person or remark.
– DERIVATIVES **snidely** adverb **snidey** adjective.
– ORIGIN of unknown origin.
sniff ● verb **1** draw in air audibly through the nose. **2** (**sniff at**) show contempt or dislike for: *the price is not to be sniffed at.* **3** (**sniff around/round**) informal investigate something secretly. **4** (**sniff out**) informal discover by secret or hidden investigation. ● noun **1** an act or sound of sniffing. **2** informal a hint or sign. **3** informal a slight chance.
– DERIVATIVES **sniffer** noun.
– ORIGIN imitative.
sniffer dog ● noun informal a dog trained to find drugs or explosives by smell.
sniffle ● verb sniff slightly or repeatedly, typically because of a cold or fit of crying. ● noun **1** an act of sniffling. **2** a slight head cold.
– DERIVATIVES **sniffly** adjective.
– ORIGIN imitative.
sniffy ● adjective (**sniffier**, **sniffiest**) informal scornful; contemptuous.
– DERIVATIVES **sniffily** adverb.
snifter ● noun informal **1** a small quantity of an alcoholic drink. **2** chiefly N. Amer. a balloon glass for brandy.
– ORIGIN imitative.
snigger ● noun a smothered or half-suppressed laugh. ● verb give such a laugh.
– ORIGIN variant of SNICKER.
snip ● verb (**snipped**, **snipping**) cut with small, quick strokes with scissors or shears. ● noun **1** an act of snipping. **2** a small piece that has been cut off. **3** Brit. informal a bargain. **4** informal a thing that is easily achieved. **5** (**snips**) hand shears for cutting metal.
– ORIGIN from Low German, 'small piece'.
snipe /snīp/ ● noun (pl. same or **snipes**) a wading bird with brown camouflaged plumage and a long straight bill. ● verb **1** shoot at someone from a hiding place at long range. **2** make a sly or petty verbal attack.
– DERIVATIVES **sniper** noun.
– ORIGIN probably Scandinavian.
snippet ● noun a small piece or brief extract.
snippy ● adjective (**snippier**, **snippiest**) informal curt or sharp.
snit ● noun N. Amer. informal a fit of irritation or pique.
– ORIGIN of unknown origin.
snitch informal ● verb **1** steal. **2** inform on someone. ● noun an informer.
– ORIGIN of unknown origin.
snivel ● verb (**snivelled**, **snivelling**; US **sniveled**, **sniveling**) **1** cry and sniffle. **2** complain in a whining or tearful way. ● noun a spell of snivelling.
– DERIVATIVES **sniveller** noun.
– ORIGIN from Old English, 'mucus'.
snob ● noun **1** a person who has an exaggerated respect for high social position or wealth and who looks down on those regarded as socially inferior. **2** a person who believes that their tastes in a particular area are superior to others: *a wine snob.*
– DERIVATIVES **snobbery** noun (pl. **snobberies**) **snobbism** noun **snobby** adjective (**snobbier**, **snobbiest**).
– ORIGIN originally dialect in the sense 'cobbler', later denoting a person lacking high rank or status.

Thesaurus

● noun *(Brit. informal) Ethel was the class sneak* INFORMER, traitor; *informal* snitch, squealer, rat, whistle-blower; *Brit. informal* grass; *Scottish informal* clype; *N. Amer. informal* fink; *Austral./NZ informal* dobber.
● adjective *a sneak preview* FURTIVE, secret, stealthy, sly, surreptitious, clandestine, covert; private, quick.
sneaking ● adjective **1** *she had a sneaking admiration for him* SECRET, private, hidden, concealed, unvoiced, undisclosed, undeclared, unavowed. **2** *a sneaking feeling* NIGGLING, nagging, lurking, insidious, lingering, gnawing, persistent.
sneaky ● adjective SLY, crafty, cunning, wily, artful, scheming, devious, guileful, deceitful, duplicitous, underhand, unscrupulous; furtive, secretive, secret, stealthy, surreptitious, clandestine, covert; *informal* foxy, shifty, dirty.
– OPPOSITES honest.
sneer ● noun **1** *she had a sneer on her face* SMIRK, curl of the lip, disparaging smile, contemptuous smile, cruel smile. **2** *the sneers of others* JIBE, barb, jeer, taunt, insult, slight, affront, slur; *informal* dig.
● verb **1** *he looked at me and sneered* SMIRK, curl one's lip, smile disparagingly, smile contemptuously, smile cruelly. **2** *it is easy to sneer at them* SCOFF AT, scorn, disdain, mock, jeer at, hold in contempt, ridicule, deride, insult, slight; *N. Amer.* slur.
snicker ● verb *they all snickered at her* SNIGGER, titter, giggle, chortle, simper.
● noun *he could not suppress a snicker* SNIGGER, titter, giggle, chortle, simper.
snide ● adjective DISPARAGING, derogatory, deprecating, denigratory, insulting, contemptuous; mocking, taunting, sneering, scornful, derisive, sarcastic, spiteful, nasty, mean; *Brit. informal* sarky.
sniff ● verb **1** *she sniffed and blew her nose* INHALE, breathe in; snuffle. **2** *Tom sniffed the fruit* SMELL, scent, get a whiff of.
● noun **1** *she gave a loud sniff* SNUFFLE, inhalation. **2** *a sniff of fresh air* SMELL, scent, whiff; lungful. **3** *(informal) the first sniff of trouble* INDICATION, hint, whiff, inkling, suggestion, whisper, trace, sign, suspicion.
– PHRASES **sniff at** SCORN, disdain, hold in contempt, look down one's nose at, treat as inferior, look down on, sneer at, scoff at; *informal* turn one's nose up at. **sniff something out** *(informal)* DETECT, find, discover, bring to light, track down, dig up, hunt out, ferret out, root out, uncover, unearth, run to earth/ground.
snigger ● verb *they snigger at him behind his back* SNICKER, titter, giggle, chortle, laugh; sneer, smirk.
● noun *the joke got hardly a snigger* SNICKER, titter, giggle, chortle, laugh; sneer, smirk.
snip ● verb **1** *an usher snipped our tickets* CUT, clip, snick, slit, nick, notch. **2** *snip off the faded flowers* CUT OFF, trim (off), clip, prune, chop off, lop (off), dock, crop, sever, detach, remove, take off.
● noun **1** *make snips along the edge* CUT, slit, snick, nick, notch, incision. **2** *snips of wallpaper* SCRAP, snippet, cutting, shred, remnant, fragment, sliver, bit, piece. **3** *(Brit. informal) the book was a snip.* See BARGAIN noun sense 2. **4** *(informal) the job was a snip.* See CINCH sense 1.
snippet ● noun PIECE, bit, scrap, fragment, particle, shred; excerpt, extract.
snivel ● verb **1** *he slumped in a chair, snivelling* SNIFFLE, snuffle, whimper, whine, weep, cry; *Scottish* greet; *informal* blub, blubber, boohoo; *Brit. informal* grizzle. **2** *don't snivel about what you get* COMPLAIN, mutter, grumble, grouse, groan, carp, bleat, whine; *informal* gripe, moan, grouch, beef, bellyache, whinge, sound off; *Brit. infor-*

S

snobbish ● adjective characteristic of or like a snob.
– DERIVATIVES **snobbishly** adverb.
snog Brit. informal ● verb (**snogged**, **snogging**) kiss and caress amorously. ● noun an act or spell of kissing and caressing.
– ORIGIN of unknown origin.
snood /sno͝od/ ● noun **1** an ornamental hairnet or pouch worn over the hair at the back of a woman's head. **2** a wide ring of knitted material worn as a hood or scarf.
– ORIGIN Old English.
snook /sno͝ok/ ● noun (in phrase **cock a snook**) informal, chiefly Brit. **1** place one's hand so that the thumb touches one's nose and the fingers are spread out, as a gesture of contempt. **2** openly show contempt or a lack of respect for someone or something.
– ORIGIN of unknown origin.
snooker ● noun **1** a game played with cues on a billiard table, in which the players use a white cue ball to pocket the other balls in a set order. **2** a position in a game of snooker or pool in which a player cannot make a direct shot at any permitted ball. ● verb **1** subject to a snooker. **2** (**be snookered**) informal be ruined or placed in an impossible position.
– ORIGIN of unknown origin.
snoop informal ● verb investigate or look around furtively in an attempt to find out something. ● noun **1** an act of snooping. **2** a person who snoops.
– DERIVATIVES **snooper** noun.
– ORIGIN Dutch *snœpen* 'eat on the sly'.
snoot ● noun informal **1** a person's nose. **2** a snob.
– ORIGIN variant of SNOUT.
snooty ● adjective (**snootier**, **snootiest**) informal showing disapproval of or contempt towards others, especially those considered to be socially inferior.
– DERIVATIVES **snootily** adverb **snootiness** noun.
snooze informal ● noun a short, light sleep. ● verb have a snooze.
– DERIVATIVES **snoozer** noun **snoozy** adjective.
– ORIGIN of unknown origin.
snooze button ● noun a control on a clock which sets an alarm to repeat after a short interval.
snore ● noun a snorting or grunting sound in a person's breathing while they are asleep. ● verb make such a sound while asleep.
– DERIVATIVES **snorer** noun.
– ORIGIN probably imitative.
snorkel /snork'l/ ● noun a tube for a swimmer to breathe through while under water. ● verb (**snorkelled**, **snorkelling**; US **snorkeled**, **snorkeling**) swim using a snorkel.
– DERIVATIVES **snorkeller** noun **snorkelling** noun.
– ORIGIN German *Schnorchel*.
snort ● noun **1** an explosive sound made by the sudden forcing of breath through the nose. **2** informal an inhaled dose of cocaine. **3** informal a measure of an alcoholic drink. ● verb **1** make a snort, especially to express anger or derision. **2** informal inhale (cocaine).
– DERIVATIVES **snorter** noun.
– ORIGIN probably imitative.
snot ● noun informal **1** nasal mucus. **2** a contemptible person.
– ORIGIN probably from Dutch, Low German; related to SNOUT.
snot-nosed ● adjective informal **1** childish and inexperienced. **2** considering oneself superior; snobbish.
snotty ● adjective (**snottier**, **snottiest**) informal **1** full of or covered with nasal mucus. **2** having a superior or conceited attitude.
– DERIVATIVES **snottily** adverb **snottiness** noun.
snout ● noun **1** the projecting nose and mouth of an animal, especially a mammal. **2** the projecting front or end of something such as a pistol. **3** Brit. informal tobacco or a cigarette. **4** Brit. informal a police informer.
– DERIVATIVES **snouted** adjective.
– ORIGIN Dutch, Low German *snūt*; related to SNOT.
snow ● noun **1** atmospheric water vapour frozen into ice crystals and falling in light white flakes or lying on the ground as a white layer. **2** (**snows**) falls of snow. **3** a mass of flickering white spots on a television or radar screen, caused by interference or a poor signal. ● verb **1** (**it snows**, **it is snowing**, etc.) snow falls. **2** (**be snowed in/up**) be confined or blocked by a large quantity of snow. **3** (**be snowed under**) be overwhelmed with a large quantity of something, especially work.
– DERIVATIVES **snowless** adjective.
– ORIGIN Old English.
snowball ● noun **1** a ball of packed snow. **2** a cocktail containing advocaat and lemonade. ● verb **1** throw snowballs at. **2** increase rapidly in size, intensity, or importance.
snow-blindness ● noun temporary blindness caused by the glare of light reflected by a large expanse of snow.
snowboard ● noun a board resembling a short, broad ski, used for sliding downhill on snow.
– DERIVATIVES **snowboarder** noun **snowboarding** noun.
snowbound ● adjective **1** prevented from travelling or going out by snow. **2** cut off or inaccessible because of snow.
snowcat (also US trademark **Sno-Cat**) ● noun a tracked vehicle for travelling over snow.
– ORIGIN from SNOW + CATERPILLAR.
snowdrift ● noun a bank of deep snow heaped up by the wind.
snowdrop ● noun a plant which bears drooping white flowers during the late winter.
snowfall ● noun **1** a fall of snow. **2** the quantity of snow falling within a given area in a given time.
snowfield ● noun a permanent wide expanse of snow in mountainous or polar regions.
snowflake ● noun each of the many feathery ice crystals that fall as snow.
snow goose ● noun a goose that breeds in Arctic Canada and Greenland, typically having white plumage with black wing tips.
snow leopard ● noun a rare large cat which has pale grey fur patterned with dark blotches and rings, living in mountainous parts of central Asia.
snowline ● noun the altitude above which some snow remains on the ground throughout the year.
snowman ● noun a representation of a human figure created with compressed snow.
snowmobile ● noun a motor vehicle, especially one with runners or caterpillar tracks, for travelling over snow.
snowplough (US **snowplow**) ● noun **1** an implement or vehicle for clearing roads of snow. **2** Skiing an act of turning the points of one's skis inwards in order to slow down or turn.
snowshoe ● noun a flat device resembling a racket, which is attached to the sole of a boot and used for walking on snow.
snowstorm ● noun a heavy fall of snow accompanied by a high wind.

S

Thesaurus

mal create; *N. Amer. informal* kvetch.
snobbery ● noun AFFECTATION, pretension, pretentiousness, arrogance, haughtiness, airs and graces, elitism; disdain, condescension, superciliousness; *informal* snootiness, uppitiness; *Brit. informal* side.
snobbish ● adjective ELITIST, snobby, superior, supercilious; arrogant, haughty, disdainful, condescending; pretentious, affected; *informal* snooty, uppity, high and mighty, la-di-da, stuck-up, hoity-toity, snotty; *Brit. informal* toffee-nosed.
snoop *(informal)* ● verb **1** *don't snoop into our affairs* PRY, inquire, be inquisitive, be curious, poke about/around, be a busybody, poke one's nose into; interfere (in/with), meddle (in/with), intrude (on); *informal* be nosy; *Austral./NZ informal* stickybeak. **2** *they snooped around the building* INVESTIGATE, explore, search, nose, have a good look; prowl around.
● noun **1** *he went for a snoop around* SEARCH, nose, look, prowl, ferret, poke, investigation. **2** *radio snoops.* See SNOOPER.
snooper ● noun MEDDLER, busybody, eavesdropper; investigator, detective; *informal* snoop, nosy parker, Paul Pry, private eye, PI, sleuth; *N. Amer. informal* gumshoe; *Austral./NZ informal* stickybeak.
snooty ● adjective *(informal)* ARROGANT, proud, haughty, conceited, aloof, superior, self-important, disdainful, supercilious, snobbish, snobby, patronizing, condescending; *informal* uppity, high and mighty, la-di-da, stuck-up, hoity-toity; *Brit. informal* toffee-nosed.
– OPPOSITES modest.
snooze *(informal)* ● noun *a good place for a snooze* NAP, doze, sleep, rest, siesta, catnap; *informal* forty winks; *Brit. informal* kip; *poetic/literary* slumber.
● verb *she gently snoozed* NAP, doze, sleep, rest, take a siesta, catnap; *informal* snatch forty winks, get some shut-eye; *Brit. informal* kip, get one's head down; *N. Amer. informal* catch some Zs; *poetic/literary* slumber.
snout ● noun MUZZLE, nose, proboscis, trunk; *Scottish & N. English* neb.
snow ● noun SNOWFLAKES, flakes, snowfall, snowstorm, blizzard,

snowy ● adjective (**snowier**, **snowiest**) **1** covered with snow. **2** (of weather or a period of time) characterized by snowfall. **3** of or like snow, especially in being pure white.
– DERIVATIVES **snowily** adverb.
snowy owl ● noun a large northern owl that breeds mainly in the Arctic tundra, the male being entirely white.
snub ● verb (**snubbed**, **snubbing**) ignore or spurn disdainfully. ● noun an act of snubbing. ● adjective (of a person's nose) short and turned up at the end.
– ORIGIN Old Norse, 'chide, check the growth of'.
snuck informal, chiefly N. Amer. past and past participle of SNEAK.
snuff[1] ● verb **1** extinguish (a candle). **2** (**snuff out**) abruptly put an end to. **3** (**snuff it**) Brit. informal die. ● noun the charred part of a candle wick.
– ORIGIN of unknown origin.
snuff[2] ● noun powdered tobacco that is sniffed up the nostril. ● verb inhale or sniff at.
– PHRASES **up to snuff** informal **1** up to the required standard. **2** in good health.
– ORIGIN probably an abbreviation of Dutch *snuftabak*; the verb is from Dutch *snuffen* 'to snuffle'.
snuffer ● noun a small hollow metal cone on the end of a handle, used to extinguish a candle by smothering the flame.
snuffle ● verb **1** breathe noisily through a partially blocked nose. **2** (of an animal) make repeated sniffing sounds. ● noun **1** a snuffling sound. **2** (**the snuffles**) informal a cold.
– DERIVATIVES **snuffly** adjective.
– ORIGIN probably from Low German and Dutch *snuffelen*.
snuff movie ● noun informal a pornographic film or video recording of an actual murder.
snug ● adjective (**snugger**, **snuggest**) **1** warm and cosy. **2** close-fitting. ● noun Brit. a small, cosy public room in a pub or small hotel.
– DERIVATIVES **snugly** adverb **snugness** noun.
– ORIGIN originally in nautical use in the sense 'shipshape, compact, prepared for bad weather': probably from Low German or Dutch.
snuggery ● noun (pl. **snuggeries**) a cosy place, especially someone's private room.
snuggle ● verb settle into a warm, comfortable position.
– ORIGIN from SNUG.
so[1] ● adverb **1** to such a great extent. **2** extremely; very much. **3** to the same extent: *he isn't so bad as you'd think* **4** referring back to something previously mentioned. **5** similarly. **6** in the way described or demonstrated; thus. ● conjunction **1** and for this reason; therefore. **2** (**so that**) with the result or aim that. **3** and then. **4** introducing a question or concluding statement. **5** in the same way; correspondingly.
– PHRASES **and so on** (or **forth**) and similar things; et cetera. **or so** approximately. **so be it** an expression of acceptance or resignation. **so long!** informal goodbye. **so much as** even: *without so much as a word.* **so to speak** (or **say**) indicating that one is talking in an exaggerated or metaphorical way.
– ORIGIN Old English.
so[2] ● noun variant spelling of SOH.
soak ● verb **1** make or become thoroughly wet by immersion in liquid. **2** (of a liquid) penetrate or permeate completely. **3** (**soak up**) absorb (a liquid). **4** (**soak up**) expose oneself to (something beneficial or enjoyable). **5** (**soak oneself in**) immerse oneself in (a particular experience). **6** informal impose heavy charges or taxation on. ● noun **1** an act or spell of soaking. **2** informal a heavy drinker. **3** Austral. a hollow where rainwater collects.
– ORIGIN Old English.
soakaway ● noun Brit. a pit through which waste water drains slowly out into the surrounding soil.
so-and-so ● noun (pl. **so-and-sos**) informal **1** a person or thing whose name the speaker does not know, remember, or need to specify. **2** euphemistic a person who is disliked or considered to have an objectionable characteristic (used instead of a vulgar word): *a nosy so-and-so.*
soap ● noun **1** a substance used with water for washing and cleaning, made of natural oils or fats combined with an alkali, and typically perfumed. **2** informal a soap opera. ● verb wash with soap.
– DERIVATIVES **soapless** adjective.
– ORIGIN Old English.
soapbox ● noun **1** a box or crate used as a makeshift stand for public speaking. **2** an opportunity for someone to air their views publicly.
soap opera ● noun a television or radio drama serial dealing with daily events in the lives of the same group of characters.
– ORIGIN so named because such serials were originally sponsored in the US by soap manufacturers.
soapstone ● noun a soft rock consisting largely of talc.
soapy ● adjective (**soapier**, **soapiest**) **1** containing or covered with soap. **2** of or like soap. **3** unpleasantly flattering and ingratiating. **4** informal characteristic of a soap opera.
soar ● verb **1** fly or rise high into the air. **2** maintain height in the air by gliding. **3** increase rapidly above the usual level.
– ORIGIN shortening of Old French *essorer*, from Latin *ex-* 'out of' + *aura* 'breeze'.
Soave /sōaavay/ ● noun a dry white wine produced in the region of northern Italy around Soave.
sob ● verb (**sobbed**, **sobbing**) **1** cry making loud, convulsive gasps. **2** say while sobbing. ● noun an act or sound of sobbing.
– ORIGIN perhaps Dutch or Low German.
s.o.b. ● abbreviation N. Amer. informal son of a bitch.
sober ● adjective (**soberer**, **soberest**) **1** not affected by alcohol; not drunk. **2** serious; thoughtful. **3** (of a colour) not bright or conspicuous. ● verb **1** (usu. **sober up**) make or become sober after drinking alcohol. **2** make or become serious.
– DERIVATIVES **soberly** adverb.
– ORIGIN Latin *sobrius*.
sobriety /səbrīəti/ ● noun the state of being sober.
sobriquet /sōbrikay/ (also **soubriquet**) ● noun a person's nick-

Thesaurus

S

sleet; snowdrift, avalanche.
– RELATED TERMS niveous, nival.
snub ● verb *they snubbed their hosts* REBUFF, spurn, repulse, cold-shoulder, brush off, give the cold shoulder to, keep at arm's length; cut (dead), ignore; insult, slight, affront, humiliate; *informal* freeze out, knock back; *N. Amer. informal* stiff.
● noun *a very public snub* REBUFF, repulse, slap in the face; humiliation, insult, slight, affront; *informal* brush-off, put-down.
snuff ● verb EXTINGUISH, put out, douse, smother, choke, blow out, quench, stub out.
snug ● adjective **1** *our tents were snug* COSY, comfortable, warm, homely, welcoming, restful, reassuring, intimate, sheltered, secure; *informal* comfy. **2** *a snug dress* TIGHT, skintight, close-fitting, figure-hugging, slinky.
– OPPOSITES bleak, loose.
snuggle ● verb NESTLE, curl up, huddle (up), cuddle up, nuzzle, settle; *N. Amer.* snug down.
soak ● verb **1** *soak the beans in water* IMMERSE, steep, submerge, submerse, dip, dunk, bathe, douse, marinate, souse. **2** *we got soaked outside* DRENCH, wet through, saturate, waterlog, deluge, inundate, submerge, drown, swamp. **3** *the sweat soaked through his clothes* PERMEATE, penetrate, percolate, seep into, spread through, infuse, impregnate. **4** *use towels to soak up the water* ABSORB, suck up, blot (up), mop (up), sponge up, sop up.
soaking ● adjective DRENCHED, soaked (through), wet (through), sodden, soggy, waterlogged, saturated, sopping wet, dripping wet, wringing wet.
– OPPOSITES parched.
soar ● verb **1** *the bird soared into the air* FLY, wing, ascend, climb, rise; take off, take flight. **2** *the gulls soared on the winds* GLIDE, plane, float, drift, wheel, hover. **3** *the cost of living soared* INCREASE, escalate, shoot up, rise, spiral; *informal* go through the roof, skyrocket.
– OPPOSITES plummet.
sob ● verb WEEP, cry, shed tears, snivel, whimper; howl, bawl; *Scottish* greet; *informal* blub, blubber, boohoo; *Brit. informal* grizzle.
sober ● adjective **1** *the driver was clearly sober* NOT DRUNK, clear-headed; teetotal, abstinent, abstemious, dry; *informal* on the wagon. **2** *a sober view of life* SERIOUS, solemn, sensible, thoughtful, grave, sombre, staid, level-headed, businesslike, down-to-earth, commonsensical, pragmatic, conservative; unemotional, dispassionate, objective, matter-of-fact, no-nonsense, rational, logical, straightforward; *Scottish* douce. **3** *a sober suit* SOMBRE, subdued, severe; conventional, traditional, quiet, drab, plain.
– OPPOSITES drunk, frivolous, sensational, flamboyant.
● verb **1** *I ought to sober up* BECOME SOBER; *informal* dry out. **2** *his expression sobered her* MAKE SERIOUS, subdue, calm down, quieten, steady; bring down to earth, make someone stop and think, give

name.
– ORIGIN French, originally in the sense 'a tap under the chin'.
sob story ● noun informal a story intended to arouse sympathy.
soca /sōkə/ ● noun calypso music with elements of soul, originally from Trinidad.
– ORIGIN blend of SOUL and CALYPSO.
so-called ● adjective called by the name or term specified (often in the speaker's view, inappropriately).
soccer ● noun a form of football played with a round ball which may not be handled during play except by the goalkeepers, the object being to score goals by kicking or heading the ball into the opponents' goal.
– ORIGIN shortening of *Assoc* from ASSOCIATION FOOTBALL.
sociable ● adjective **1** willing to talk and engage in activities with others. **2** marked by friendliness.
– DERIVATIVES **sociability** noun **sociably** adverb.
– ORIGIN Latin *sociabilis*, from *sociare* 'unite'.
social ● adjective **1** relating to society, its organization, or hierarchy. **2** needing companionship; suited to living in communities. **3** relating to or designed for activities in which people meet each other for pleasure. **4** (of birds, insects, or mammals) breeding or living in colonies or organized communities. ● noun an informal social gathering organized by the members of a club or group.
– DERIVATIVES **sociality** noun **socially** adverb.
– ORIGIN Latin *socialis* 'allied', from *socius* 'friend'.
social climber ● noun derogatory a person who is anxious to gain a higher social status.
social contract (also **social compact**) ● noun an implicit agreement among the members of a society to cooperate for mutual benefit, for example by sacrificing some individual freedom for state protection.
social democracy ● noun a socialist system of government achieved by democratic means.
social fund ● noun (in the UK) a social security fund from which loans or grants are made to people in need.
socialism ● noun a political and economic theory of social organization which advocates that the means of production, distribution, and exchange should be owned or regulated by the community as a whole.
– DERIVATIVES **socialist** noun & adjective **socialistic** adjective.
socialite ● noun a person who mixes in fashionable society.
socialize (also **socialise**) ● verb **1** mix socially with others. **2** make (someone) behave in a way that is acceptable to society. **3** organize according to the principles of socialism.
– DERIVATIVES **socialization** noun.
social market economy (also **social market**) ● noun an economic system based on a free market operated in conjunction with state provision for those unable to sell their labour, such as the elderly or unemployed.
social realism ● noun the realistic depiction in art of contemporary life, as a means of social or political comment.
social science ● noun **1** the scientific study of human society and social relationships. **2** a subject within this field, such as economics.
social security ● noun (in the UK) state financial assistance for people with an inadequate or no income.
social service ● noun **1** (**social services**) services provided by the state for the community, such as education and medical care. **2** activity aiming to promote the welfare of others.
social studies ● plural noun (treated as sing.) the study of human society.
social work ● noun work carried out by trained personnel with the aim of alleviating the conditions of those people suffering from social deprivation.
– DERIVATIVES **social worker** noun.
society ● noun (pl. **societies**) **1** the aggregate of people living together in a more or less ordered community. **2** a particular community of people living in a country or region, and having shared customs, laws, and organizations. **3** (also **high society**) people who are fashionable, wealthy, and influential, regarded as a distinct social group. **4** an organization or club formed for a particular purpose or activity. **5** the situation of being in the company of other people.
– DERIVATIVES **societal** adjective.
– ORIGIN Latin *societas*, from *socius* 'companion'.
sociobiology ● noun the scientific study of the biological (especially ecological and evolutionary) aspects of social behaviour in animals and humans.
– DERIVATIVES **sociobiological** adjective **sociobiologist** noun.
socio-economic ● adjective relating to or concerned with the interaction of social and economic factors.
sociolinguistics ● plural noun (treated as sing.) the study of language in relation to social factors.
– DERIVATIVES **sociolinguist** noun **sociolinguistic** adjective.
sociology ● noun the study of the development, structure, and functioning of human society.
– DERIVATIVES **sociological** adjective **sociologist** noun.
sociopath /sōsiōpath, sōshi-/ ● noun a person with a personality disorder manifesting itself in extreme antisocial attitudes and behaviour.
– DERIVATIVES **sociopathic** adjective **sociopathy** noun.
sock ● noun **1** a knitted garment for the foot and lower part of the leg. **2** an insole. **3** informal a hard blow. ● verb informal hit forcefully.
– PHRASES **knock** (or **blow**) **someone's socks off** informal amaze or impress someone. **knock the socks off** informal surpass or beat. **pull one's socks up** informal make an effort to improve. **put a sock in it** Brit. informal stop talking. **sock it to** informal make a forceful impression on.
– ORIGIN Greek *sukkhos* 'comic actor's shoe, light low-heeled slipper'.
socket ● noun **1** a hollow in which something fits or revolves. **2** an electrical device receiving a plug or light bulb to make a connection. ● verb (**socketed, socketing**) place in or fit with a socket.

Thesaurus

someone pause for thought.
sobriety ● noun **1** *she noted his sobriety* SOBERNESS, clear-headedness; abstinence, teetotalism, non-indulgence, abstemiousness, temperance. **2** *the mayor is a model of sobriety* SERIOUSNESS, solemnity, gravity, dignity, level-headedness, common sense, pragmatism, practicality, self-control, self-restraint, conservatism.
so-called ● adjective INAPPROPRIATELY NAMED, supposed, alleged, presumed, ostensible, reputed; nominal, titular, self-styled, professed, would-be, self-appointed, soi-disant.
sociable ● adjective FRIENDLY, affable, companionable, gregarious, convivial, clubbable, amicable, cordial, warm, genial; communicative, responsive, forthcoming, open, outgoing, extrovert, hail-fellow-well-met, approachable; *informal* chummy, clubby; *Brit. informal* matey.
– OPPOSITES unfriendly.
social ● adjective **1** *a major social problem* COMMUNAL, community, collective, group, general, popular, civil, public, societal. **2** *a social club* RECREATIONAL, leisure, entertainment, amusement. **3** *a uniquely social animal* GREGARIOUS, interactional; organized.
– OPPOSITES individual.
● noun *the club has a social once a month* PARTY, gathering, function, get-together; celebration, reunion, jamboree; *informal* bash, shindig, do; *Brit. informal* rave-up, knees-up, beano, bunfight, jolly.
socialism ● noun LEFTISM, Fabianism, labourism, welfarism; radicalism, progressivism, social democracy; communism, Marxism, Leninism, Maoism; *historical* Bolshevism.
socialist ● adjective *the socialist movement* LEFT-WING, leftist, Labour, Labourite, labourist, Fabian, progressive, reform; radical, revolutionary, militant, red; communist, Marxist, Leninist, Maoist; *informal, derogatory* lefty, Bolshie, Commie.
– OPPOSITES conservative.
● noun *a well-known socialist* LEFT-WINGER, leftist, Fabian, Labourite, labourist, progressive, progressivist, reformer; radical, revolutionary, militant, red; communist, Marxist, Leninist, Maoist; *informal, derogatory* lefty, Bolshie, Commie.
– OPPOSITES conservative.
socialize ● verb INTERACT, converse, be sociable, mix, mingle, get together, meet, fraternize, consort; entertain, go out; *informal* hobnob.
society ● noun **1** *a danger to society* THE COMMUNITY, the (general) public, the people, the population; civilization, humankind, mankind, humanity. **2** *an industrial society* CULTURE, community, civilization, nation, population. **3** *Lady Angela will help you enter society* HIGH SOCIETY, polite society, the upper classes, the elite, the county set, the smart set, the beautiful people, the beau monde, the haut monde; *informal* the upper crust, the top drawer. **4** *a local history society* ASSOCIATION, club, group, circle, fellowship, guild,

– ORIGIN Old French *soket* 'small ploughshare'.
sockeye ● noun a commercially valuable salmon of the North Pacific region.
– ORIGIN Salish, 'fish of fishes'.
socking ● adverb Brit. informal very: *a socking great diamond.*
Socratic /səkrattik/ ● adjective relating to the Athenian philosopher Socrates (469–399 BC) or his philosophy or methods.
sod[1] ● noun **1** grass-covered ground; turf. **2** a piece of turf.
– PHRASES **under the sod** dead and buried.
– ORIGIN Dutch or Low German *sode.*
sod[2] vulgar slang, chiefly Brit. ● noun **1** an unpleasant person. **2** a person of a specified kind. **3** a difficult or problematic thing. ● verb (**sodded, sodding**) **1** used to express anger or annoyance. **2** (**sod off**) go away. **3** (**sodding**) used as a general term of contempt.
– PHRASES **sod all** absolutely nothing.
– ORIGIN abbreviation of SODOMITE.
soda ● noun **1** (also **soda water**) carbonated water (originally made with sodium bicarbonate). **2** N. Amer. a sweet carbonated drink. **3** sodium carbonate. **4** sodium in chemical combination.
– ORIGIN Latin, from an Arabic word meaning 'saltwort'.
soda bread ● noun bread leavened with baking soda.
soda fountain ● noun N. Amer. **1** a device dispensing soda water or soft drinks. **2** a shop or counter selling drinks from such a device.
sodality /sōdaliti/ ● noun (pl. **sodalities**) a fraternity or association, especially a Roman Catholic religious guild or brotherhood.
– ORIGIN Latin *sodalitas,* from *sodalis* 'comrade'.
soda siphon ● noun a bottle from which carbonated water is dispensed by allowing the gas pressure to force it out.
soda water ● noun see SODA (sense 1).
sodden ● adjective **1** soaked through. **2** (in combination) having drunk an excessive amount of an alcoholic drink: *whisky-sodden.*
– DERIVATIVES **soddenly** adverb **soddenness** noun.
– ORIGIN originally in the sense 'boiled': from SEETHE.
sodium ● noun a soft silver-white reactive metallic chemical element of which common salt and soda are compounds.
– ORIGIN from SODA.
sodium bicarbonate ● noun a soluble white powder used chiefly in effervescent drinks and as a raising agent in baking.
sodium chloride ● noun the chemical name for common salt.
sodium hydroxide ● noun a strongly alkaline white compound used in many industrial processes; caustic soda.
sodium-vapour lamp (also **sodium lamp**) ● noun a lamp in which an electrical discharge in sodium vapour gives a yellow light.
sodomite /soddəmīt/ ● noun a person who engages in sodomy.
– DERIVATIVES **sodomitic** adjective **sodomitical** adjective.
sodomy ● noun anal intercourse.
– DERIVATIVES **sodomize** (also **sodomise**) verb.
– ORIGIN from Latin *peccatum Sodomiticum* 'sin of Sodom' (after the Book of Genesis chapter 19, which implies that the men of the town of Sodom in ancient Palestine practised homosexual rape).
Sod's Law ● noun another name for MURPHY'S LAW.
sofa ● noun a long upholstered seat with a back and arms, for two or more people.
– ORIGIN French, from Arabic.
sofa bed ● noun a sofa that can be converted into a bed.
soffit /soffit/ ● noun the underside of an arch, a balcony, overhanging eaves, etc.
– ORIGIN Italian *soffitto,* from Latin *suffixus* 'fastened below'.
soft ● adjective **1** easy to mould, cut, compress, or fold. **2** not rough or coarse in texture. **3** quiet and gentle. **4** (of light or colour) pleasingly subtle; not harsh. **5** sympathetic or lenient, especially excessively so. **6** informal (of a job or way of life) requiring little effort. **7** informal foolish. **8** (**soft on**) informal infatuated with. **9** (of a drink) not alcoholic. **10** (of a drug) not likely to cause addiction. **11** (of water) free from mineral salts. **12** (of a faction within a political party) willing to compromise. **13** (also **soft-core**) (of pornography) suggestive but not explicit.
– PHRASES **have a soft spot for** be fond of. **a soft** (or **easy**) **touch** informal a person who is easily persuaded or imposed upon.
– DERIVATIVES **softish** adjective **softly** adverb **softness** noun.
– ORIGIN Old English.
softback ● adjective & noun another term for PAPERBACK.
softball ● noun a modified form of baseball played on a smaller field with a larger, softer ball.
soft-boiled ● adjective (of an egg) lightly boiled, leaving the yolk soft or liquid.
soft copy ● noun a legible version of a piece of information, stored or displayed on a computer.
soften ● verb **1** make or become soft or softer. **2** (often **soften up**) undermine the resistance of.
– DERIVATIVES **softener** noun.
soft focus ● noun deliberate slight blurring or lack of definition in a photograph or film.
soft fruit ● noun Brit. a small stoneless fruit, e.g. a strawberry.
soft furnishings ● plural noun Brit. curtains, chair coverings, and other cloth items used to decorate a room.
soft-headed ● adjective not intelligent.
soft-hearted ● adjective kind and compassionate.
softie (also **softy**) ● noun (pl. **softies**) informal a weak or soft-hearted person.
softly-softly ● adjective cautious and patient.
soft palate ● noun the fleshy, flexible part towards the back of the roof of the mouth.
soft pedal ● noun a pedal on a piano that can be pressed to soften the tone. ● verb (**soft-pedal**) play down the unpleasant aspects of.
soft sell ● noun subtly persuasive selling.
soft soap ● noun **1** a semi-fluid soap. **2** informal persuasive flattery. ● verb (**soft-soap**) informal use flattery to persuade.
soft target ● noun a relatively vulnerable person or thing.
soft-top ● noun a motor vehicle with a roof that can be folded back.
software ● noun programs and other operating information used by a computer. Compare with HARDWARE.
softwood ● noun the wood from a conifer as distinguished from

S

Thesaurus

lodge, fraternity, brotherhood, sisterhood, sorority, league, union, alliance. **5** *the society of others* COMPANY, companionship, fellowship, friendship, comradeship, camaraderie.
sodden ● adjective **1** *his clothes were sodden* SOAKING, soaked (through), wet (through), saturated, drenched, sopping wet, wringing wet. **2** *sodden fields* WATERLOGGED, soggy, saturated, boggy, swampy, miry, marshy; heavy, squelchy, soft.
– OPPOSITES arid.
sofa ● noun SETTEE, couch, divan, chaise longue, chesterfield; *Brit.* put-you-up; *N. Amer.* davenport, day bed.
soft ● adjective **1** *soft fruit* MUSHY, squashy, pulpy, pappy, slushy, squelchy, squishy, doughy; *informal* gooey; *Brit. informal* squidgy. **2** *soft ground* SWAMPY, marshy, boggy, miry, oozy; heavy, squelchy. **3** *a soft cushion* SQUASHY, spongy, compressible, supple, springy, pliable, pliant, resilient, malleable. **4** *soft fabric* VELVETY, smooth, fleecy, downy, furry, silky, silken, satiny. **5** *a soft wind* GENTLE, light, mild, moderate. **6** *soft light* DIM, low, faint, subdued, muted, mellow. **7** *soft colours* PALE, pastel, muted, understated, restrained, subdued, subtle. **8** *soft voices* QUIET, low, faint, muted, subdued, muffled, hushed, whispered, stifled, murmured, gentle, dulcet; indistinct, inaudible. **9** *soft outlines* BLURRED, vague, hazy, misty, foggy, nebulous, fuzzy, blurry, indistinct, unclear. **10** *he seduced her with soft words* KIND, gentle, sympathetic, soothing, tender, sensitive, affectionate, loving, warm, sweet, sentimental; *informal* mushy, slushy, schmaltzy. **11** *she's too soft with her pupils* LENIENT, easy-going, tolerant, forgiving, forbearing, indulgent, clement, permissive, liberal, lax. **12** *(informal) he's soft in the head* FOOLISH, stupid, simple, brainless, mindless; mad, scatterbrained, feather-brained; slow, weak, feeble; *informal* dopey, dippy, dotty, scatty, loopy; *Brit. informal* daft; *Scottish & N. English informal* glaikit.
– OPPOSITES hard, firm, rough, strong, harsh, lurid, strident, sharp, strict, sensible.
soften ● verb **1** *he tried to soften the blow of new taxes* ALLEVIATE, ease, relieve, soothe, take the edge off, assuage, cushion, moderate, mitigate, palliate, diminish, blunt, deaden. **2** *the winds softened* DIE DOWN, abate, subside, moderate, let up, calm, diminish, slacken, weaken.
– PHRASES **soften someone up** CHARM, win over, persuade, influence, weaken, disarm, sweeten, butter up, soft-soap.
soft-hearted ● adjective KIND, kindly, tender-hearted, tender, gentle, sympathetic, compassionate, humane; generous, indulgent, lenient, merciful, benevolent.

that of broadleaved trees.
softy • noun variant spelling of SOFTIE.
soggy • adjective (**soggier**, **soggiest**) very wet and soft.
– DERIVATIVES **soggily** adverb **sogginess** noun.
– ORIGIN from dialect *sog* 'a swamp'.
soh /sō/ (also **so** or **sol**) • noun Music the fifth note of a major scale, coming after 'fah' and before 'lah'.
– ORIGIN representing (as an arbitrary name for the note) the first syllable of *solve*, taken from a Latin hymn.
soi-disant /swaadeezoN/ • adjective self-styled.
– ORIGIN French, from *soi* 'oneself' + *disant* 'saying'.
soigné /swaanyay/ • adjective (fem. **soignée** pronunc. same) elegant and well groomed.
– ORIGIN French, from *soigner* 'take care of'.
soil[1] • noun **1** the upper layer of earth in which plants grow, typically consisting of organic remains, clay, and rock particles. **2** the territory of a particular nation.
– DERIVATIVES **soil-less** adjective.
– ORIGIN Old French, perhaps from Latin *solium* 'seat', by association with *solum* 'ground'.
soil[2] • verb **1** make dirty. **2** bring discredit to. • noun waste matter, especially sewage.
– ORIGIN Old French *soiller*, from Latin *sucula* 'little pig'.
soirée /swaaray/ • noun an evening social gathering, typically in a private house, for conversation or music.
– ORIGIN French, from *soir* 'evening'.
sojourn /sojurn/ formal • noun a temporary stay. • verb stay temporarily.
– DERIVATIVES **sojourner** noun.
– ORIGIN from Old French *sojourner*, from Latin *sub-* 'under' + *diurnum* 'day'.
sol[1] • noun variant of SOH.
sol[2] • noun Chemistry a fluid suspension of a colloidal solid in a liquid.
– ORIGIN abbreviation of SOLUTION.
sol[3] /sol/ • noun (pl. **soles**) the basic monetary unit of Peru, equal to 100 cents.
– ORIGIN Spanish, 'sun'.
sola /sōlə/ • noun an Indian swamp plant with pithy stems.
– ORIGIN Hindi.
solace /solləss/ • noun comfort or consolation in time of distress. • verb give solace to.
– ORIGIN Old French *solas*, from Latin *solari* 'to console'.
solar /sōlər/ • adjective relating to or determined by the sun or its rays.
– ORIGIN from Latin *sol* 'sun'.
solar battery (also **solar cell**) • noun a device converting solar radiation into electricity.
solar eclipse • noun an eclipse in which the sun is obscured by the moon.
solar energy • noun radiant energy emitted by the sun.
solar flare • noun a brief eruption of intense high-energy radiation from the sun's surface.
solarium /səlairiəm/ • noun (pl. **solariums** or **solaria** /səlairiə/) **1** a room equipped with sunlamps or sunbeds. **2** a room with extensive areas of glass to admit sunlight.
– ORIGIN Latin, 'sundial, place for sunning oneself'.
solar panel • noun a panel designed to absorb the sun's rays as a source of energy for generating electricity or heating.
solar plexus • noun a complex of ganglia and radiating nerves at the pit of the stomach.
solar power • noun power obtained by harnessing the energy of the sun's rays.
solar system • noun the sun together with the planets, asteroids, comets, etc. in orbit around it.
solar wind • noun a continuous flow of charged particles from the sun, permeating the solar system.
solar year • noun the time between successive spring or autumn equinoxes, or winter or summer solstices (365 days, 5 hours, 48 minutes, and 46 seconds).
sola topi • noun an Indian sun hat made from the pith of the sola plant.
– ORIGIN Hindi, 'sola hat'.
sold past and past participle of SELL.
solder /sōldər, sol-/ • noun a low-melting alloy, especially one based on lead and tin, used for joining less fusible metals. • verb join with solder.
– ORIGIN Old French *soudure*, from Latin *solidare* 'fasten together'.
soldering iron • noun an electrical tool for melting and applying solder.
soldi plural of SOLDO.
soldier • noun **1** a person who serves in an army. **2** (also **common soldier** or **private soldier**) a private in an army. **3** Brit. informal a strip of bread or toast, dipped into a soft-boiled egg. • verb **1** serve as a soldier. **2** (**soldier on**) informal persevere.
– PHRASES **soldier of fortune** a mercenary.
– DERIVATIVES **soldierly** adjective.
– ORIGIN Old French, from *soulde* '(soldier's) pay', from Latin *solidus* 'solid, solidus'.
soldiery • noun **1** soldiers collectively. **2** military training or knowledge.
soldo /soldō/ • noun (pl. **soldi** /soldi/) a former Italian coin and monetary unit worth the twentieth part of a lira.
– ORIGIN Italian, from Latin *solidus* 'solid'.
sole[1] • noun **1** the underside of a person's foot. **2** the section forming the underside of a piece of footwear. **3** the underside of a tool or implement, e.g. a plane. • verb (usu. **be soled**) put a new sole on (a shoe).
– ORIGIN Latin *solea* 'sandal, sill'.
sole[2] • noun an edible marine flatfish.
– ORIGIN Latin *solea* (see SOLE[1]), named from its shape.
sole[3] • adjective **1** one and only. **2** belonging or restricted to one person or group.
– DERIVATIVES **solely** adverb.
– ORIGIN Latin *sola*, feminine of *solus* 'alone'.
solecism /sollisiz'm/ • noun **1** a grammatical mistake. **2** an instance of bad manners or incorrect behaviour.
– DERIVATIVES **solecistic** /sollisistik/ adjective.
– ORIGIN Greek *soloikismos*, from *soloikos* 'speaking incorrectly'.
solemn • adjective **1** formal and dignified. **2** not cheerful; serious. **3** deeply sincere.
– DERIVATIVES **solemnly** adverb.
– ORIGIN originally in the sense 'associated with religious rites': from Latin *sollemnis* 'customary, celebrated at a fixed date'.
solemnity /səlemniti/ • noun (pl. **solemnities**) **1** the state or

S

Thesaurus

softly-softly • adjective CAUTIOUS, circumspect, discreet, gentle, patient, tactful, diplomatic.
soggy • adjective MUSHY, squashy, pulpy, slushy, squelchy, squishy; swampy, marshy, boggy, miry; soaking, soaked through, wet, saturated, drenched; Brit. informal squidgy.
soil[1] • noun **1** *acid soil* EARTH, loam, dirt, clay, sod, turf; ground. **2** *British soil* TERRITORY, land, domain, dominion, region, country.
soil[2] • verb **1** *he soiled his tie* DIRTY, stain, splash, spot, spatter, splatter, smear, smudge, sully, spoil, foul; informal muck up; poetic/literary begrime. **2** *our reputation is being soiled* DISHONOUR, damage, sully, stain, blacken, tarnish, taint, blemish, defile, blot, smear, drag through the mud; poetic/literary besmirch.
sojourn (formal) • noun *a sojourn in France* STAY, visit, stop, stopover; holiday, vacation.
• verb *they sojourned in the monastery* STAY, live, put up, stop (over), lodge, room, board; holiday, vacation.
solace • noun *they found solace in each other* COMFORT, consolation, cheer, support, relief.
• verb *she was solaced with tea and sympathy* COMFORT, console, cheer, support, soothe, calm.
soldier • noun FIGHTER, trooper, serviceman, servicewoman; warrior; US GI; Brit. informal squaddie; archaic man-at-arms.
– PHRASES **soldier on** (informal). See PERSEVERE.
sole • adjective ONLY, one (and only), single, solitary, lone, unique, exclusive.
solecism • noun **1** *a poem marred by solecisms* (GRAMMATICAL) MISTAKE, error, blunder; informal howler, blooper; Brit. informal boob. **2** *it would have been a solecism to answer* FAUX PAS, gaffe, impropriety, social indiscretion, infelicity, slip, error, blunder, lapse; informal slip-up, boo-boo; Brit. informal boob, clanger, bloomer; N. Amer. informal goof, blooper.
solely • adverb ONLY, simply, just, merely, uniquely, exclusively, entirely, wholly; alone.
solemn • adjective **1** *a solemn occasion* DIGNIFIED, ceremonious, ceremonial, formal, stately, courtly, majestic; imposing, awe-inspiring, splendid, magnificent, grand. **2** *he looked very solemn* SERIOUS, grave, sober, sombre, unsmiling, stern, grim, dour, humourless; pensive, meditative. **3** *a solemn promise* SINCERE, earn-

quality of being solemn. **2** a solemn rite or ceremony.

solemnize /solləmnīz/ (also **solemnise**) ● verb **1** duly perform (a ceremony, especially that of marriage). **2** mark with a formal ceremony.
– DERIVATIVES **solemnization** noun.

solenoid /sōlənoyd, sol-/ ● noun a cylindrical coil of wire acting as a magnet when carrying electric current.
– DERIVATIVES **solenoidal** adjective.
– ORIGIN from Greek *sōlēn* 'channel, pipe'.

soleplate ● noun **1** a metal plate forming the base of an electric iron, machine saw, or other machine. **2** a horizontal timber at the base of a wall frame.

sol-fa /solfaa/ ● noun short for TONIC SOL-FA.

soli plural of SOLO.

solicit ● verb (**solicited**, **soliciting**) **1** ask for or try to obtain (something) from someone. **2** ask for something from. **3** accost someone and offer one's or someone else's services as a prostitute.
– DERIVATIVES **solicitation** noun.
– ORIGIN Latin *sollicitare* 'agitate'.

solicitor ● noun **1** Brit. a lawyer qualified to deal with conveyancing, draw up wills, advise clients and instruct barristers, and represent clients in lower courts. Compare with BARRISTER. **2** N. Amer. the chief law officer of a city, town, or government department.

Solicitor General ● noun (pl. **Solicitors General**) (in the UK) the Crown law officer below the Attorney General or (in Scotland) below the Lord Advocate.

solicitous ● adjective showing interest or concern about a person's well-being.
– DERIVATIVES **solicitously** adverb **solicitousness** noun.

solicitude ● noun care or concern.

solid ● adjective (**solider**, **solidest**) **1** firm and stable in shape; not liquid or fluid. **2** strongly built or made. **3** not hollow or having spaces or gaps. **4** consisting of the same substance throughout. **5** (of time) continuous. **6** able to be relied on; dependable or sound. **7** Geometry three-dimensional. ● noun **1** a solid substance or object. **2** (**solids**) food that is not liquid. **3** a three-dimensional body or geometric figure.
– DERIVATIVES **solidity** noun **solidly** adverb **solidness** noun.
– ORIGIN Latin *solidus*.

solidarity ● noun unity resulting from common interests, feelings, or sympathies.

solidi plural of SOLIDUS.

solidify ● verb (**solidifies**, **solidified**) make or become hard or solid.
– DERIVATIVES **solidification** noun **solidifier** noun.

solid-state ● adjective (of an electronic device) employing solid semiconductors, e.g. transistors, as opposed to valves.

solidus /sollidəss/ ● noun (pl. **solidi** /sollidī/) chiefly Brit. another term for SLASH (in sense 3).
– ORIGIN Latin, 'solid', also denoting a coin of the later Roman Empire.

soliloquy /səlilləkwi/ ● noun (pl. **soliloquies**) an act of speaking one's thoughts aloud when alone or regardless of hearers, especially in a play.
– DERIVATIVES **soliloquist** noun **soliloquize** (also **soliloquise**) verb.
– ORIGIN from Latin *solus* 'alone' + *loqui* 'speak'.

solipsism /sollipsiz'm/ ● noun the view that the self is all that can be known to exist.
– DERIVATIVES **solipsist** noun **solipsistic** adjective.
– ORIGIN from Latin *solus* 'alone' + *ipse* 'self'.

solitaire /sollitair, sollitair/ ● noun **1** a game for one player played by removing pegs from a board one at a time by jumping others over them from adjacent holes, the object being to be left with only one peg. **2** the card game patience. **3** a single diamond or other gem in a piece of jewellery.
– ORIGIN French.

solitary ● adjective **1** done or existing alone. **2** secluded or isolated. **3** single; only. **4** (of a bee, wasp, etc.) not social or colonial. ● noun (pl. **solitaries**) **1** a recluse or hermit. **2** informal solitary confinement.
– DERIVATIVES **solitarily** adverb **solitariness** noun.
– ORIGIN Latin *solitarius*, from *solus* 'alone'.

solitary confinement ● noun the isolation of a prisoner in a separate cell as a punishment.

solitude ● noun **1** the state of being alone. **2** a lonely or uninhabited place.

solmization /solmizaysh'n/ (also **solmisation**) ● noun Music a system of associating each note of a scale with a particular syllable (typically the sequence doh, ray, me, fah, so, la, te), especially to teach singing.
– ORIGIN French, from *sol* 'soh' + *mi* (see ME²).

solo ● noun (pl. **solos**) **1** (pl. **solos** or **soli**) a piece of music, song, or dance for one performer. **2** an unaccompanied flight by a pilot. **3** (also **solo whist**) a card game resembling whist in which the players make bids and the highest bidder plays against the others. ● adjective & adverb for or done by one person. ● verb (**soloes**, **soloed**) **1** perform a solo. **2** fly an aircraft unaccompanied.
– ORIGIN from Latin *solus* 'alone'.

soloist ● noun a performer of a solo.

Thesaurus

est, honest, genuine, firm, heartfelt, wholehearted, sworn.
– OPPOSITES frivolous, light-hearted, insincere.

solemnize ● verb PERFORM, celebrate; formalize, officiate at.

solicit ● verb **1** *Phil tried to solicit his help* ASK FOR, request, seek, apply for, put in for, call for, press for, beg, plead for; *dated* crave. **2** *they are solicited for their opinions* ASK, beg, implore, plead with, entreat, appeal to, lobby, petition, importune, supplicate, call on, press; *poetic/literary* beseech. **3** *the girls gathered to solicit* WORK AS A PROSTITUTE, make sexual advances, tout (for business); *N. Amer. informal* hustle.

solicitor ● noun *(Brit.)* LAWYER, legal representative, legal practitioner, notary (public), advocate, attorney; *Brit.* articled clerk; *Scottish* law agent; *informal* brief.

solicitous ● adjective CONCERNED, caring, considerate, attentive, mindful, thoughtful, interested; anxious, worried.

solid ● adjective **1** *the ice cream was solid* HARD, rock-hard, rigid, firm, solidified, set, frozen, concrete. **2** *solid gold* PURE, 24-carat, unalloyed, unadulterated, genuine. **3** *a solid line* CONTINUOUS, uninterrupted, unbroken, non-stop, undivided. **4** *solid houses* WELL BUILT, sound, substantial, strong, sturdy, durable. **5** *a solid argument* WELL FOUNDED, valid, sound, reasonable, logical, authoritative, convincing, cogent, plausible, credible, reliable. **6** *a solid friendship* DEPENDABLE, reliable, firm, unshakeable, trustworthy, stable, steadfast, staunch, constant. **7** *solid citizens* SENSIBLE, dependable, trustworthy, decent, law-abiding, upright, upstanding, worthy. **8** *the company is very solid* FINANCIALLY SOUND, secure, creditworthy, profit-making, solvent, in credit, in the black; *Finance* ungeared, unlevered. **9** *solid support from their colleagues* UNANIMOUS, united, consistent, undivided.
– OPPOSITES liquid, alloyed, broken, flimsy, untenable, unreliable.

solidarity ● noun UNANIMITY, unity, like-mindedness, agreement, accord, harmony, consensus, concurrence, cooperation, cohesion; *formal* concord.

solidify ● verb HARDEN, set, freeze, thicken, stiffen, congeal, cake, dry, bake; ossify, fossilize, petrify.
– OPPOSITES liquefy.

soliloquy ● noun MONOLOGUE, speech, address, lecture, oration, sermon, homily, aside.

solitary ● adjective **1** *a solitary life* LONELY, companionless, unaccompanied, by oneself, on one's own, alone, friendless; antisocial, unsociable, withdrawn, reclusive, cloistered, hermitic; *N. Amer.* lonesome. **2** *solitary farmsteads* ISOLATED, remote, lonely, out of the way, in the back of beyond, outlying, off the beaten track, godforsaken, obscure, inaccessible, cut-off; secluded, private, sequestered, desolate; *N. Amer.* in the backwoods; *Austral./NZ* in the backblocks; *informal* in the sticks, in the middle of nowhere; *N. Amer. informal* in the boondocks; *Austral./NZ informal* beyond the black stump; *poetic/literary* lone. **3** *a solitary piece of evidence* SINGLE, lone, sole, unique; only, one, individual; odd.
– OPPOSITES sociable, accessible.
● noun *he became a solitary* RECLUSE, loner, hermit, eremite; *historical* anchorite.

solitude ● noun **1** *she savoured her solitude* LONELINESS, solitariness, isolation, seclusion, sequestration, withdrawal, privacy, peace. **2** *solitudes like the area around the loch* WILDERNESS, rural area, wilds, backwoods; desert, emptiness, wasteland; *Austral.* the bush, the outback; *N. Amer. & Austral./NZ* backcountry; *informal* the sticks; *N. Amer. informal* the boondocks.

solo ● adjective *a solo flight* UNACCOMPANIED, single-handed, companionless, unescorted, unattended, unchaperoned, independent, solitary; alone, on one's own, by oneself.
– OPPOSITES accompanied.

Solomon /solləmən/ ● **noun** a very wise person.
– DERIVATIVES **Solomonic** /solləmonnik/ adjective.
– ORIGIN the name of a king of ancient Israel *c.*970–*c.*930 BC, famed for his wisdom.

Solomon's seal ● **noun** a plant with arching stems bearing a double row of broad leaves and drooping green and white flowers.

solstice /solstiss/ ● **noun** each of the two times in the year, respectively at midsummer and midwinter, when the sun reaches its highest or lowest point in the sky at noon, marked by the longest and shortest days.
– DERIVATIVES **solstitial** adjective.
– ORIGIN Latin *solstitium*, from *sol* 'sun' + *sistere* 'stop, be stationary'.

soluble ● **adjective 1** (of a substance) able to be dissolved, especially in water. **2** able to be solved.
– DERIVATIVES **solubility** noun.
– ORIGIN Latin *solubilis*, from *solvere* 'loosen'.

solute /solyoot/ ● **noun** the minor component in a solution, dissolved in the solvent.

solution ● **noun 1** a means of solving a problem. **2** the correct answer to a puzzle. **3** a liquid mixture in which the minor component (the solute) is uniformly distributed within the major component (the solvent). **4** the process of dissolving or the state of being dissolved.
– ORIGIN Latin, from *solvere* 'loosen'.

solve ● **verb** find an answer to, explanation for, or way of dealing with (a problem or mystery).
– DERIVATIVES **solvable** adjective **solver** noun.
– ORIGIN Latin *solvere* 'loosen, unfasten'.

solvent ● **adjective 1** having assets in excess of liabilities. **2** able to dissolve other substances. ● **noun** the liquid in which another substance is dissolved to form a solution.
– DERIVATIVES **solvency** noun.

solvent abuse ● **noun** the use of certain volatile solvents as intoxicants by inhalation, e.g. glue-sniffing.

Som. ● **abbreviation** Somerset.

som /sōm/ ● **noun** (pl. same) the basic monetary unit of Kyrgyzstan, equal to 100 tiyin.

soma /sōmə/ ● **noun 1** Biology the parts of an organism other than the reproductive cells. **2** the body as distinct from the soul, mind, or psyche.
– ORIGIN Greek, 'body'.

Somali /səmaali/ ● **noun** (pl. same or **Somalis**) **1** a member of a mainly Muslim people of Somalia. **2** the language of this people. **3** a person from Somalia. ● **adjective** relating to Somalia.
– DERIVATIVES **Somalian** adjective & noun.
– ORIGIN the name in Somali.

somatic /səmattik/ ● **adjective** relating to the body, especially as distinct from the mind.
– DERIVATIVES **somatically** adverb.
– ORIGIN Greek *sōmatikos*, from *sōma* 'body'.

somatotrophin /sōmətətrōfin/ ● **noun** a growth hormone secreted by the pituitary gland.

sombre (US also **somber**) ● **adjective 1** dark or dull. **2** oppressively solemn or sober.
– DERIVATIVES **sombrely** adverb **sombreness** noun.
– ORIGIN French, from Latin *sub* 'under' + *umbra* 'shade'.

sombrero /sombrairō/ ● **noun** (pl. **sombreros**) a broad-brimmed felt or straw hat, typically worn in Mexico and the southwestern US.
– ORIGIN Spanish.

some ● **determiner 1** an unspecified amount or number of. **2** referring to an unknown or unspecified person or thing. **3** (used with a number) approximately. **4** a considerable amount or number of. **5** at least a small amount or number of. **6** expressing admiration. ● **pronoun 1** an unspecified number or amount of people or things. **2** at least a small number or amount of people or things.
– ORIGIN Old English.

-some[1] ● **suffix** forming adjectives meaning: **1** productive of: *loathsome.* **2** characterized by being: *wholesome.* **3** apt to: *tiresome.*
– ORIGIN Old English.

-some[2] ● **suffix** (forming nouns) denoting a group of a specified number: *foursome.*
– ORIGIN Old English, 'some'.

somebody ● **pronoun** someone.

some day (also **someday**) ● **adverb** at some time in the future.

somehow ● **adverb 1** by one means or another. **2** for an unknown or unspecified reason.

someone ● **pronoun 1** an unknown or unspecified person. **2** a person of importance or authority.

someplace ● **adverb & pronoun** informal, chiefly N. Amer. somewhere.

somersault ● **noun 1** an acrobatic movement in which a person turns head over heels in the air or on the ground and finishes on their feet. **2** a dramatic upset or reversal of policy or opinion. ● **verb** perform a somersault.
– ORIGIN Old French *sombresault*, from Latin *supra* 'above' + *saltus* 'a leap'.

something ● **pronoun 1** an unspecified or unknown thing. **2** an unspecified or unknown amount or degree. ● **adverb** informal used for emphasis with a following adjective: *my back hurts something terrible.*
– PHRASES **quite** (or **really**) **something** informal something impressive or notable. **something else** informal an exceptional person or thing. **something of** to some degree. **thirty-something** (**forty-something**, etc.) informal an unspecified age between thirty and forty (forty and fifty, etc.).

sometime ● **adverb** at some unspecified or unknown time. ● **adjective** former.

sometimes ● **adverb** occasionally.

somewhat ● **adverb** to some extent.
– PHRASES **somewhat of** something of.

Thesaurus

● **adverb** *she sailed solo* UNACCOMPANIED, alone, on one's own, single-handed(ly), by oneself, unescorted, unattended, unchaperoned, unaided, independently.
– OPPOSITES accompanied.

solution ● **noun 1** *an easy solution to the problem* ANSWER, result, resolution, way out, panacea; key, formula, explanation, interpretation. **2** *a solution of ammonia in water* MIXTURE, mix, blend, compound, suspension, tincture, infusion, emulsion.

solve ● **verb** RESOLVE, answer, work out, find a solution to, find the key to, puzzle out, fathom, decipher, decode, clear up, straighten out, get to the bottom of, unravel, piece together, explain; *informal* figure out, crack; *Brit. informal* suss out.

solvent ● **adjective** FINANCIALLY SOUND, debt-free, not in debt, in the black, in credit, creditworthy, solid, secure, profit-making; *Finance* ungeared, unlevered.

sombre ● **adjective 1** *sombre clothes* DARK, drab, dull, dingy; restrained, subdued, sober, funereal. **2** *a sombre expression* SOLEMN, earnest, serious, grave, sober, unsmiling, stern, grim, dour, humourless; gloomy, depressed, sad, melancholy, dismal, doleful, mournful, lugubrious.
– OPPOSITES bright, cheerful.

somebody ● **noun** *she wanted to be a somebody* IMPORTANT PERSON, VIP, public figure, notable, dignitary, worthy; someone, (big/household) name, celebrity, star, superstar; grandee, luminary; *informal* celeb, bigwig, big shot, big cheese, hotshot, megastar.
– OPPOSITES nonentity.

some day ● **adverb** SOMETIME, one day, one of these (fine) days, at a future date, sooner or later, by and by, in due course, in the fullness of time, in the long run.
– OPPOSITES never.

somehow ● **adverb** BY SOME MEANS, by any means, in some way, one way or another, no matter how, by fair means or foul, by hook or by crook, come what may.

sometime ● **adverb 1** *I'll visit sometime* SOME DAY, one day, one of these (fine) days, at a future date, sooner or later, by and by, in due course, in the fullness of time, in the long run. **2** *it happened sometime on Sunday* AT SOME TIME, at some point; during, in the course of.
– OPPOSITES never.
● **adjective** *the sometime editor of the paper* FORMER, past, previous, prior, foregoing, late, erstwhile, one-time, ex-; *formal* quondam.

sometimes ● **adverb** OCCASIONALLY, from time to time, now and then, every so often, once in a while, on occasion, at times, off and on, at intervals, periodically, sporadically, spasmodically, intermittently.

somewhat ● **adverb 1** *matters have improved somewhat* A LITTLE, a bit, to some extent, (up) to a point, in some measure, rather, quite; *N. Amer. informal* some; *informal* kind of, sort of. **2** *a somewhat thicker book* SLIGHTLY, relatively, comparatively, moderately, fair-

somewhere ● adverb **1** in or to an unspecified or unknown place. **2** used to indicate an approximate amount. ● pronoun some unspecified place.
– PHRASES **get somewhere** informal make progress.
sommelier /somməlyay, səmelyay/ ● noun a waiter who serves wine.
– ORIGIN French, 'butler'.
somnambulism /somnambyooliz'm/ ● noun sleepwalking.
– DERIVATIVES **somnambulant** adjective **somnambulist** noun **somnambulistic** adjective.
– ORIGIN from Latin *somnus* 'sleep' + *ambulare* 'to walk'.
somnolent /somnələnt/ ● adjective **1** sleepy; drowsy. **2** inducing drowsiness.
– DERIVATIVES **somnolence** noun **somnolently** adverb.
– ORIGIN Latin *somnolentus,* from *somnus* 'sleep'.
son ● noun **1** a boy or man in relation to his parents. **2** a male descendant. **3** (**the Son**) (in Christian belief) the second person of the Trinity; Christ. **4** (also **my son**) used as a form of address for a boy or younger man.
– PHRASES **son of a bitch** (pl. **sons of bitches**) informal used as a general term of abuse. **son of a gun** (pl. **sons of guns**) informal a jocular way of addressing or referring to someone. [ORIGIN with reference to the guns carried on ships: said to have been applied originally to babies born at sea to women allowed to accompany their husbands.] **Son of Man** Jesus Christ.
– DERIVATIVES **sonship** noun.
– ORIGIN Old English.
sonar /sōnaar/ ● noun **1** a system for the detection of objects under water based on the emission and measured reflection of sound pulses. **2** an apparatus used for this.
– ORIGIN from *so(und) na(vigation and) r(anging),* on the pattern of *radar*.
sonata /sənaatə/ ● noun a classical composition for an instrumental soloist, often with a piano accompaniment.
– ORIGIN Italian, 'sounded'.
son et lumière /son ay loomyair/ ● noun an entertainment held by night at a historic monument or building, telling its history by the use of lighting effects and recorded sound.
– ORIGIN French, 'sound and light'.
song ● noun **1** a poem or other set of words set to music. **2** singing or vocal music. **3** the musical phrases uttered by some birds, whales, and insects. **4** a poem, especially one in rhymed stanzas.
– PHRASES **for a song** informal very cheaply. **on song** Brit. informal performing well. **a song and dance** informal a fuss.
– ORIGIN Old English, related to SING.
songbird ● noun a bird with a musical song.
song cycle ● noun a set of related songs forming a single musical entity.
songsmith ● noun informal a writer of popular songs.
songster ● noun (fem. **songstress**) **1** a person who sings. **2** a songbird.
song thrush ● noun a thrush with a buff spotted breast and a song in which phrases are repeated two or three times.
songwriter ● noun a writer of songs or the music for them.
sonic ● adjective relating to or using sound waves.
– DERIVATIVES **sonically** adverb.
– ORIGIN from Latin *sonus* 'sound'.
sonicate /sonnikayt/ ● verb Biochemistry subject to fragmentation by ultrasonic vibration.
– DERIVATIVES **sonication** noun.
sonic boom ● noun an explosive noise caused by the shock wave from an aircraft or other object travelling faster than the speed of sound.
sonics ● plural noun musical sounds artificially produced or reproduced.
son-in-law ● noun (pl. **sons-in-law**) the husband of one's daughter.
sonnet ● noun a poem of fourteen lines using any of a number of formal rhyme schemes, in English typically having ten syllables per line.
– ORIGIN Italian *sonetto* 'little sound'.
sonneteer /sonniteer/ ● noun a writer of sonnets.
sonny ● noun informal **1** a familiar form of address to a young boy. **2** (also **Sonny Jim**) a humorous or patronizing way of addressing a man.
sonogram ● noun **1** a graph showing the distribution of energy at different frequencies in a sound. **2** a visual image produced from an ultrasound examination.
– DERIVATIVES **sonograph** noun **sonographic** adjective **sonography** noun.
– ORIGIN from Latin *sonus* 'sound'.
sonorous /sonnərəss, sənorəss/ ● adjective **1** (of a sound) deep and full. **2** (of speech) using imposing or grandiose language.
– DERIVATIVES **sonority** noun **sonorously** adverb **sonorousness** noun.
– ORIGIN from Latin *sonor* 'sound'.
sool /sōōl/ ● verb chiefly Austral./NZ **1** (of a dog) attack or worry. **2** urge or goad into doing something.
– ORIGIN variant of dialect *sowl* 'seize by the ears', of unknown origin.
soon ● adverb **1** in or after a short time. **2** early. **3** used to indicate a preference: *I'd just as soon Tim did it.*
– PHRASES **no sooner than** at the very moment that. **sooner or later** eventually.
– DERIVATIVES **soonish** adverb.
– ORIGIN Old English.
soot ● noun a black powdery or flaky substance produced by the incomplete burning of organic matter.
– ORIGIN Old English.
sooth /sooth/ ● noun archaic truth.
– PHRASES **in sooth** truly.
– ORIGIN Old English.
soothe ● verb **1** gently calm. **2** relieve (pain or discomfort).
– DERIVATIVES **soother** noun **soothing** adjective.
– ORIGIN Old English, 'verify, show to be true', from SOOTH.
soothsayer ● noun a person supposed to be able to foresee the future.
– DERIVATIVES **soothsaying** noun.
– ORIGIN originally in the sense 'person who speaks the truth': see SOOTH.
sooty ● adjective (**sootier**, **sootiest**) covered with or coloured

S

Thesaurus

ly, rather, quite, marginally.
– OPPOSITES greatly.
somnolent ● adjective **1** *he felt somnolent after lunch* SLEEPY, drowsy, tired, languid, dozy, groggy, lethargic, sluggish, enervated, torpid; *informal* snoozy, dopey, yawny; *poetic/literary* slumberous. **2** *a somnolent village* QUIET, restful, tranquil, calm, peaceful, relaxing, soothing, undisturbed, untroubled.
son ● noun MALE CHILD, boy, heir; descendant, offspring; *informal* lad.
– RELATED TERMS filial.
song ● noun **1** *a beautiful song* AIR, strain, ditty, melody, tune, number, track. **2** *the song of the birds* CALL(S), chirping, cheeping, peeping, chirruping, warble(s), warbling, trilling, twitter; birdsong.
– PHRASES **song and dance** *(informal).* See FUSS noun sense 1.
songster, songstress ● noun SINGER, vocalist, soloist, crooner, chorister, choirboy, choirgirl; alto, bass, baritone, contralto, tenor, soprano; balladeer; *informal* warbler, popster, soulster, folkie; *historical* minstrel, troubadour; *archaic* melodist.
sonorous ● adjective **1** *a sonorous voice* RESONANT, rich, full, round, booming, deep, clear, mellow, orotund, fruity, strong, resounding, reverberant. **2** *sonorous words of condemnation* IMPRESSIVE, imposing, grandiloquent, magniloquent, high-flown, lofty, orotund, bombastic, grandiose, pompous, pretentious, overblown, turgid; oratorical, rhetorical; *informal* highfalutin.
soon ● adverb **1** *we'll be there soon* SHORTLY, presently, in the near future, before long, in a little while, in a minute, in a moment, in an instant, in the twinkling of an eye, in no time, before you know it, any minute (now), any day (now), by and by; *informal* pronto, in a jiffy, before you can say Jack Robinson, anon; *Brit. informal* sharpish, in a tick, in two ticks; *dated* directly. **2** *how soon can you get here?* EARLY, quickly, promptly, speedily, punctually.
sooner ● adverb **1** *he should have done it sooner* EARLIER, before, beforehand, in advance, ahead of time; already. **2** *I would sooner stay* RATHER, preferably, by preference, by choice, more willingly, more readily.
soothe ● verb **1** *Rachel tried to soothe him* CALM (DOWN), pacify, comfort, hush, quiet, subdue, settle (down), lull, tranquillize; appease, conciliate, mollify; *Brit.* quieten (down). **2** *an anaesthetic to soothe the pain* ALLEVIATE, ease, relieve, take the edge off, assuage, allay, lessen, palliate, diminish, decrease, dull, blunt, deaden.
– OPPOSITES agitate, aggravate.
soothing ● adjective **1** *soothing music* RELAXING, restful, calm, calm-

like soot.

sop ● noun **1** a thing given or done to appease or bribe someone. **2** a piece of bread dipped in gravy, soup, or sauce. ● verb (**sopped**, **sopping**) (**sop up**) soak up (liquid).
– ORIGIN Old English.

sophism /soffiz'm/ ● noun a false argument, especially one used to deceive.
– ORIGIN Greek *sophisma* 'clever device', from *sophizesthai* 'devise, become wise'.

sophist /soffist/ ● noun a person who uses clever but false arguments.
– DERIVATIVES **sophistic** /səfistik/ adjective **sophistical** /səfistik'l/ adjective.

sophisticate ● verb **1** make more discerning and aware of complex issues through education or experience. **2** make more complex or refined. ● noun a sophisticated person.
– DERIVATIVES **sophistication** noun.
– ORIGIN Latin *sophisticare* 'tamper with', from *sophisticus* 'sophistic'.

sophisticated ● adjective **1** (of a machine, system, or technique) highly developed and complex. **2** having or showing worldly experience and taste in matters of culture or fashion. **3** appealing to sophisticated people.
– DERIVATIVES **sophisticatedly** adverb.

sophistry /soffistri/ ● noun (pl. **sophistries**) **1** the use of false arguments, especially to deceive. **2** a false argument.

sophomore /soffəmor/ ● noun N. Amer. a second-year university or high-school student.
– DERIVATIVES **sophomoric** adjective.
– ORIGIN probably from *sophum*, *sophom* (obsolete variants of SOPHISM).

soporific /soppəriffik/ ● adjective inducing drowsiness or sleep. ● noun a soporific drug or other agent.
– DERIVATIVES **soporifically** adverb.
– ORIGIN from Latin *sopor* 'sleep'.

sopping ● adjective wet through.

soppy ● adjective (**soppier**, **soppiest**) Brit. informal **1** self-indulgently sentimental. **2** lacking spirit.
– DERIVATIVES **soppily** adverb **soppiness** noun.
– ORIGIN originally in the sense 'soaked with water': from SOP.

soprano /səpraanō/ ● noun (pl. **sopranos**) **1** the highest singing voice. **2** (before another noun) denoting an instrument of a high or the highest pitch in its family: *a soprano saxophone*.
– ORIGIN Italian, from *sopra* 'above'.

sorbet /sorbay, -bit/ ● noun a water ice.
– ORIGIN French, from an Arabic word meaning 'to drink'; compare with SHERBET.

sorcerer ● noun (fem. **sorceress**) a person believed to practise magic; a wizard.
– DERIVATIVES **sorcerous** adjective **sorcery** noun.
– ORIGIN Old French *sorcier*, from Latin *sors* 'lot'.

sordid ● adjective **1** involving ignoble actions and motives. **2** dirty or squalid.
– DERIVATIVES **sordidly** adverb **sordidness** noun.
– ORIGIN Latin *sordidus*, from *sordere* 'be dirty'.

sore ● adjective **1** painful or aching. **2** suffering pain. **3** severe; urgent: *in sore need*. **4** informal, chiefly N. Amer. upset and angry. ● noun **1** a raw or painful place on the body. **2** a source of distress or annoyance. ● adverb archaic extremely; severely: *sore afraid*.
– PHRASES **sore point** an issue about which someone feels distressed or annoyed. **stand** (or **stick**) **out like a sore thumb** be quite obviously different.
– DERIVATIVES **soreness** noun.
– ORIGIN Old English.

sorely ● adverb extremely; badly.

sorghum /sorgəm/ ● noun a cereal native to warm regions, grown for grain and animal feed.
– ORIGIN Italian *sorgo*, perhaps from a variant of Latin *syricum* 'Syrian'.

sororal /sərorəl/ ● adjective formal of or like a sister or sisters.
– ORIGIN from Latin *soror* 'sister'.

sorority /sərorriti/ ● noun (pl. **sororities**) N. Amer. a society for female students in a university or college.
– ORIGIN from Latin *soror* 'sister', on the pattern of *fraternity*.

sorrel[1] /sorrəl/ ● noun an edible plant of the dock family with arrow-shaped leaves and a bitter flavour.
– ORIGIN Old French *sorele*; related to SOUR.

sorrel[2] /sorrəl/ ● noun **1** a light reddish-brown colour. **2** a horse with a sorrel coat.
– ORIGIN Old French *sorel*, from *sor* 'yellowish'.

sorrow ● noun **1** deep distress caused by loss or disappointment. **2** a cause of sorrow. ● verb feel sorrow.
– ORIGIN Old English.

sorrowful ● adjective **1** feeling or showing sorrow. **2** causing sorrow.
– DERIVATIVES **sorrowfully** adverb **sorrowfulness** noun.

sorry ● adjective (**sorrier**, **sorriest**) **1** feeling distress or pity

Thesaurus

ing, tranquil, peaceful, reposeful, tranquillizing, soporific. **2** *soothing ointment* PALLIATIVE, mild, calmative.

soothsayer ● noun SEER, oracle, augur, prophet(ess), sage, prognosticator, diviner, fortune teller, crystal-gazer, clairvoyant, psychic; Scottish spaewife; poetic/literary sibyl.

sophisticated ● adjective **1** *sophisticated techniques* ADVANCED, modern, state of the art, the latest, new, up to the minute; innovatory, trailblazing, revolutionary, futuristic, avant-garde; complex, complicated, intricate. **2** *a sophisticated woman* WORLDLY, worldly-wise, experienced, enlightened, cosmopolitan, knowledgeable; urbane, cultured, cultivated, civilized, polished, refined; elegant, stylish; informal cool.
– OPPOSITES crude, naive.

sophistication ● noun WORLDLINESS, experience; urbanity, culture, civilization, polish, refinement; elegance, style, poise, finesse, savoir faire; informal cool.

sophistry ● noun **1** *to claim this is pure sophistry* SPECIOUS REASONING, fallacy, sophism, casuistry. **2** *he went along with her sophistry* FALLACIOUS ARGUMENT, sophism, fallacy; Logic paralogism.

soporific ● adjective *soporific drugs* SLEEP-INDUCING, sedative, somnolent, calmative, tranquillizing, narcotic, opiate; drowsy, sleepy, somniferous; Medicine hypnotic.
– OPPOSITES invigorating.
● noun *she was given a soporific* SLEEPING PILL, sedative, calmative, tranquillizer, narcotic, opiate; Medicine hypnotic.
– OPPOSITES stimulant.

soppy ● adjective (Brit. informal) **1** *the songs are really soppy.* See SENTIMENTAL sense 2. **2** *they were too soppy for our games.* See FEEBLE sense 3.

sorcerer, sorceress ● noun WIZARD, witch, magician, warlock, enchanter, enchantress, magus; shaman, witch doctor; archaic mage.

sorcery ● noun (BLACK) MAGIC, the black arts, witchcraft, wizardry, enchantment, spells, incantation, witching, witchery, thaumaturgy; shamanism; Irish pishogue.

sordid ● adjective **1** *a sordid love affair* SLEAZY, seedy, seamy, unsavoury, tawdry, cheap, debased, degenerate, dishonourable, disreputable, discreditable, contemptible, ignominious, shameful, wretched, abhorrent. **2** *a sordid little street* SQUALID, slummy, dirty, filthy, mucky, grimy, shabby, messy, soiled, scummy, unclean; informal cruddy, grungy, crummy, scuzzy; Brit. informal grotty.
– OPPOSITES respectable, immaculate.

sore ● adjective **1** *a sore leg* PAINFUL, hurting, hurt, aching, throbbing, smarting, stinging, agonizing, excruciating; inflamed, sensitive, tender, raw, bruised, wounded, injured. **2** *we are in sore need of you* DIRE, urgent, pressing, desperate, critical, crucial, acute, grave, serious, drastic, extreme, life-and-death, great, terrible; formal exigent; archaic parlous. **3** (N. Amer. informal) *they were sore at us* UPSET, angry, annoyed, cross, furious, vexed, displeased, disgruntled, dissatisfied, exasperated, irritated, galled, irked, put out, aggrieved, offended, affronted, piqued, nettled; informal aggravated, miffed, peeved, hacked off, riled; Brit. informal narked, cheesed off, brassed off; N. Amer. informal teed off, ticked off.
● noun *a sore on his leg* INFLAMMATION, swelling, lesion; wound, scrape, abrasion, cut, laceration, graze, contusion, bruise; ulcer, boil, abscess, carbuncle.

sorrow ● noun **1** *he felt sorrow at her death* SADNESS, unhappiness, misery, despondency, regret, depression, despair, desolation, dejection, wretchedness, gloom, dolefulness, melancholy, woe, heartache, grief; poetic/literary dolour. **2** *the sorrows of life* TROUBLE, difficulty, problem, adversity, misery, woe, affliction, trial, tribulation, misfortune, setback, reverse, blow, failure, tragedy.
– OPPOSITES joy.
● verb *they sorrowed over her grave* MOURN, lament, grieve, be sad, be miserable, be despondent, despair, suffer, ache, agonize, anguish, pine, weep, wail.

S

through sympathy with someone else's misfortune. **2** feeling or expressing regret or penitence. **3** in a poor or pitiful state. **4** unpleasant and regrettable: *a sorry business.*
– DERIVATIVES **sorriness** noun.
– ORIGIN Old English, 'pained, distressed'; related to SORE.

sort ● noun **1** a category of people or things with a common feature or features. **2** informal a person with a specified nature: *a friendly sort.* **3** Computing the arrangement of data in a prescribed sequence. ● verb **1** arrange systematically in groups. **2** (often **sort out**) separate from a mixed group. **3** (**sort out**) resolve (a problem or difficulty). **4** (**sort out**) informal deal with (a troublesome person).
– PHRASES **in some sort** to some extent. **it takes all sorts to make a world** proverb people vary greatly in character, tastes, and abilities (implying that one should be tolerant of strange behaviour). **of a sort** (or **of sorts**) of a somewhat unusual or inferior kind. **out of sorts** slightly unwell or unhappy. **sort of** informal to some extent.
– DERIVATIVES **sortable** adjective **sorter** noun.
– ORIGIN Old French *sorte*, from Latin *sors* 'lot, condition'.

sorted ● adjective Brit. informal **1** organized; arranged. **2** emotionally well balanced.

sortie ● noun **1** an attack by troops coming out from a position of defence. **2** an operational flight by a single military aircraft. **3** a short trip. ● verb (**sorties**, **sortied**, **sortieing**) make a sortie.
– ORIGIN French, from *sortir* 'go out'.

SOS ● noun **1** an international coded signal of extreme distress, used especially by ships at sea. **2** an urgent appeal for help.
– ORIGIN letters chosen as being easily transmitted and recognized in Morse code; by folk etymology an abbreviation of *save our souls.*

so-so ● adjective informal neither very good nor very bad.

sot ● noun a habitual drunkard.
– DERIVATIVES **sottish** adjective.
– ORIGIN Latin *sottus* 'foolish person'.

sotto voce /sottō vōchay/ ● adverb & adjective in a quiet voice.
– ORIGIN from Italian *sotto* 'under' + *voce* 'voice'.

sou /so͞o/ ● noun **1** a former French coin of low value. **2** informal a very small amount of money.
– ORIGIN French, from Old French *sout*, from Latin *solidus* 'solid'.

soubrette /so͞obret/ ● noun a pert maidservant or similar minor female role in a comedy.
– ORIGIN Provençal *soubreto*, feminine of *soubret* 'coy'.

soubriquet /so͞obrikay/ ● noun variant spelling of SOBRIQUET.

soufflé ● noun a light, spongy baked dish made by mixing egg yolks and another ingredient such as cheese or fruit with stiffly beaten egg whites.
– ORIGIN French, 'blown'.

sough /sow, suf/ ● verb literary (of the wind, sea, etc.) make a moaning, whistling, or rushing sound.
– ORIGIN Old English.

sought past and past participle of SEEK.

sought after ● adjective much in demand.

souk /so͝ok/ (also **suq**) ● noun an Arab market.
– ORIGIN Arabic.

soukous /so͞oko͞os/ ● noun a style of African popular music with syncopated rhythms and intricate contrasting guitar melodies.
– ORIGIN perhaps from French *secouer* 'to shake'.

soul ● noun **1** the spiritual element of a person, regarded as immortal. **2** a person's moral or emotional nature. **3** emotional or intellectual energy or integrity. **4** a person regarded as the embodiment of a particular quality. **5** an individual, often of a specified type: *poor soul.* **6** (also **soul music**) a kind of music incorporating elements of gospel music and rhythm and blues, popularized by American blacks.
– PHRASES **lost soul** a soul that is damned. **upon my soul** dated an exclamation of surprise.
– ORIGIN Old English.

soul-destroying ● adjective unbearably monotonous.

soul food ● noun food traditionally associated with black people of the southern US.

soulful ● adjective expressing deep and typically sorrowful feeling.
– DERIVATIVES **soulfully** adverb **soulfulness** noun.

soulless ● adjective **1** lacking character and individuality. **2** (of an activity) tedious and uninspiring. **3** lacking human feelings.
– DERIVATIVES **soullessly** adverb **soullessness** noun.

soulmate ● noun a person ideally suited to another.

soul-searching ● noun close examination of one's emotions and motives.

Thesaurus

– OPPOSITES rejoice.

sorrowful ● adjective **1** *sorrowful eyes* SAD, unhappy, dejected, regretful, downcast, miserable, downhearted, despondent, despairing, disconsolate, desolate, glum, gloomy, doleful, dismal, melancholy, mournful, woeful, woebegone, forlorn, crestfallen, heartbroken; *informal* blue, down in the mouth, down in the dumps. **2** *sorrowful news* TRAGIC, sad, unhappy, awful, miserable, sorry, pitiful; traumatic, upsetting, depressing, distressing, dispiriting, heartbreaking, harrowing; *formal* grievous.

sorry ● adjective **1** *I was sorry to hear about his accident* SAD, unhappy, sorrowful, distressed, upset, downcast, downhearted, disheartened, despondent; heartbroken, inconsolable, grief-stricken. **2** *he felt sorry for her* FULL OF PITY, sympathetic, compassionate, moved, consoling, empathetic, concerned. **3** *I'm sorry if I was brusque* REGRETFUL, remorseful, contrite, repentant, rueful, penitent, apologetic, abject, guilty, self-reproachful, ashamed, shamefaced, sheepish. **4** *he looks a sorry sight* PITIFUL, pitiable, heartrending, distressing; unfortunate, wretched, unhappy, unlucky, regrettable, shameful, awful.
– OPPOSITES glad, unsympathetic, unrepentant.

sort ● noun **1** *what sort of book is it?* TYPE, kind, nature, manner, variety, class, category, style; calibre, quality, form, group, set, bracket, genre, species, family, order, generation, vintage, make, model, brand, stamp, ilk, kidney, cast, grain, mould; *N. Amer.* stripe. **2** *(informal) he's a good sort* PERSON, individual, soul, creature, human being; character, customer; *informal* fellow, type, beggar, cookie; *Brit. informal* bod; *informal, dated* body, dog, cove.
● verb **1** *they sorted things of similar size* CLASSIFY, class, categorize, catalogue, grade, group; organize, arrange, order, marshal, assemble, systematize, systemize, pigeonhole. **2** *the problem was soon sorted* RESOLVE, settle, solve, fix, work out, straighten out, deal with, put right, set right, rectify, iron out; answer, explain, fathom, unravel, clear up; *informal* sew up, hammer out, thrash out, patch up, figure out.
– PHRASES **out of sorts 1** *I'm feeling out of sorts* UNWELL, ill, poorly, sick, queasy, nauseous, peaky, run down, below par; *Brit.* off colour; *informal* under the weather, funny, rough, lousy, rotten, awful; *Brit. informal* off, ropy; *Scottish informal* wabbit, peely-wally; *Austral./NZ informal* crook; *dated* seedy. **2** *I've been out of sorts and I'd like a chat* UNHAPPY, sad, miserable, down, depressed, melancholy, gloomy, glum, dispirited, despondent, forlorn, woebegone, fed up, low, in the doldrums; *informal* blue, down in the dumps, down in the mouth. **sort of** *(informal)* **1** *you look sort of familiar* SLIGHTLY, faintly, remotely, vaguely; somewhat, moderately, quite, rather, fairly, reasonably, relatively; *informal* pretty, kind of. **2** *he sort of pirouetted* AS IT WERE, kind of, somehow. **sort something out 1** *she sorted out the clothes.* See SORT verb sense 1. **2** *they must sort out their problems.* See SORT verb sense 2.

sortie ● noun **1** *a sortie against their besiegers* FORAY, sally, charge, offensive, attack, assault, onset, onslaught, thrust, drive. **2** *a bomber sortie* RAID, flight, mission, operation.

so-so ● adjective *(informal)* MEDIOCRE, indifferent, average, middle-of-the-road, middling, moderate, ordinary, adequate, fair; uninspired, undistinguished, unexceptional, unremarkable, run-of-the-mill, lacklustre; *informal* bog-standard, no great shakes, not up to much; *NZ informal* half-pie.

soul ● noun **1** *seeing the soul through the eyes* SPIRIT, psyche, (inner) self, inner being, life force, vital force; individuality, make-up, subconscious, anima; *Philosophy* pneuma; *Hinduism* atman. **2** *he is the soul of discretion* EMBODIMENT, personification, incarnation, epitome, quintessence, essence; model, exemplification, exemplar, image, manifestation. **3** *not a soul in sight* PERSON, human being, individual, man, woman, mortal, creature. **4** *their music lacked soul* INSPIRATION, feeling, emotion, passion, animation, intensity, fervour, ardour, enthusiasm, warmth, energy, vitality, spirit.

soulful ● adjective EMOTIONAL, deep, profound, fervent, heartfelt, sincere, passionate; meaningful, significant, eloquent, expressive; moving, stirring; sad, mournful, doleful.

soulless ● adjective **1** *a soulless room* CHARACTERLESS, featureless, bland, dull, colourless, lacklustre, dreary, drab, uninspiring, undistinguished, anaemic, insipid. **2** *it was soulless work* BORING, dull, tedious, dreary, humdrum, tiresome, wearisome, uninterest-

S

sound[1] ● noun **1** vibrations which travel through the air or another medium and are sensed by the ear. **2** a thing that can be heard. **3** music, speech, and sound effects accompanying a film or broadcast. **4** an idea or impression conveyed by words. ● verb **1** emit or cause to emit sound. **2** utter. **3** convey a specified impression: *the job sounds great.* **4** (**sound off**) express one's opinions loudly or forcefully.
– DERIVATIVES **soundless** adjective.
– ORIGIN Latin *sonus*.
sound[2] ● adjective **1** in good condition. **2** based on reason or judgement. **3** financially secure. **4** competent or reliable. **5** (of sleep) deep and unbroken. **6** severe or thorough: *a sound thrashing.* ● adverb soundly.
– DERIVATIVES **soundly** adverb **soundness** noun.
– ORIGIN Old English.
sound[3] ● verb **1** ascertain the depth of water in (the sea, a lake, etc.) by means of a line or pole or using sound echoes. **2** (**sound out**) question (someone) discreetly or cautiously as to their opinions or feelings. **3** Medicine examine (the bladder or other internal cavity) with a long surgical probe.
– DERIVATIVES **sounder** noun.
– ORIGIN Old French *sonder*, from Latin *sub-* 'below' + *unda* 'wave'.
sound[4] ● noun a narrow stretch of water forming an inlet or connecting two larger bodies of water.
– ORIGIN Old Norse, 'swimming, strait'; related to SWIM.
sound barrier ● noun the speed of sound, regarded as presenting problems of drag, controllability, etc. for aircraft.
sound bite ● noun a short extract from a recorded interview, chosen for its pungency or aptness.
soundboard (also **sounding board**) ● noun a thin board under the strings of a piano or similar instrument to increase the sound produced.
soundbox ● noun the hollow chamber forming the body of a stringed instrument and providing resonance.
soundcheck ● noun a test of sound equipment before a musical performance or recording.
sound effect ● noun a sound other than speech or music made artificially for use in a play, film, etc.
sounding[1] ● noun **1** the action of sounding the depth of water. **2** a measurement taken by sounding. **3** (**soundings**) information or evidence ascertained before taking action.
sounding[2] ● adjective archaic producing sound, especially of a loud or resonant nature.
sounding board ● noun **1** a board over or behind a pulpit or stage to reflect a speaker's voice forward. **2** a soundboard. **3** a person or group whose reactions to ideas or opinions are used as a test of their validity or likely success.
sounding line ● noun a weighted line used to measure the depth of water under a boat.
soundproof ● adjective preventing the passage of sound. ● verb make soundproof.
soundscape ● noun a piece of music considered in terms of its component sounds.
sound system ● noun a set of equipment for the reproduction and amplification of sound.
soundtrack ● noun the sound accompaniment to a film.
sound wave ● noun a wave of alternate compression and rarefaction by which sound travels through a medium.
soup ● noun a savoury liquid dish made by boiling meat, fish, or vegetables in stock or water. ● verb (**soup up**) informal **1** increase the power and efficiency of (an engine). **2** make more elaborate or impressive.
– PHRASES **in the soup** informal in trouble.
– ORIGIN Old French *soupe* 'sop, broth (poured on slices of bread)', from Latin *suppa*.
soupçon /so͞opsoN/ ● noun a very small quantity.
– ORIGIN French, from Latin *suspectio* 'suspicion'.
soup kitchen ● noun a place where free food is served to the homeless or destitute.
soupy ● adjective (**soupier**, **soupiest**) **1** having the appearance or consistency of soup. **2** informal mawkishly sentimental.
– DERIVATIVES **soupily** adverb **soupiness** noun.
sour ● adjective **1** having a sharp taste like lemon or vinegar. **2** tasting or smelling rancid from fermentation or staleness. **3** resentful, bitter, or angry. ● noun a cocktail made by mixing a spirit with lemon or lime juice. ● verb make or become sour.
– PHRASES **go** (or **turn**) **sour** become less pleasant; turn out badly. **sour grapes** an attitude in which someone pretends to despise something because they cannot have it themselves. [ORIGIN with allusion to Aesop's fable *The Fox and the Grapes*.]
– DERIVATIVES **sourish** adjective **sourly** adverb **sourness** noun.
– ORIGIN Old English.
source ● noun **1** a place, person, or thing from which something originates. **2** a spring or other place from which a river or stream issues. **3** a person, book, or document that provides information or evidence. ● verb obtain from a particular source.
– ORIGIN Old French *sourse*, from Latin *surgere* 'to rise'.
sour cream ● noun cream deliberately fermented by adding certain bacteria.
sourdough ● noun **1** leaven for making bread, consisting of fermenting dough, originally that left over from a previous baking. **2** bread made using such leaven.
sourpuss ● noun informal a bad-tempered or sullen person.

Thesaurus

ing, uninspiring, unexciting, soul-destroying, mind-numbing, dry; monotonous, repetitive.
– OPPOSITES exciting.
sound[1] ● noun **1** *the sound of the car* NOISE, note; din, racket, row, hubbub; resonance, reverberation. **2** *she did not make a sound* UTTERANCE, cry, word, noise, peep; *informal* cheep. **3** *the sound of the flute* MUSIC, tone, notes. **4** *I don't like the sound of that* IDEA, thought, concept, prospect, description. **5** *we're within sound of the sea* EARSHOT, hearing (distance), range.
– RELATED TERMS acoustic, sonic, aural, audio-, sono-.
– OPPOSITES silence.
● verb **1** *the buzzer sounded* MAKE A NOISE, resonate, resound, reverberate, go off, blare; ring, chime, peal. **2** *drivers must sound their horns* BLOW, blast, toot, blare; operate, set off; ring. **3** *do you sound the 'h'?* PRONOUNCE, verbalize, voice, enunciate, articulate, vocalize, say. **4** *she sounded a warning* UTTER, voice, deliver, express, speak, announce, pronounce. **5** *it sounds a crazy idea* APPEAR, look (like), seem, strike someone as being, give every indication of being.
sound[2] ● adjective **1** *your heart is sound* HEALTHY, in good condition, in good shape, fit, hale and hearty, in fine fettle; undamaged, unimpaired. **2** *a sound building* WELL BUILT, solid, substantial, strong, sturdy, durable, stable, intact, unimpaired. **3** *sound advice* WELL FOUNDED, valid, reasonable, logical, weighty, authoritative, reliable. **4** *a sound judge of character* RELIABLE, dependable, trustworthy, fair; good, sensible, wise, judicious, sagacious, shrewd, perceptive. **5** *financially sound* SOLVENT, debt-free, in the black, in credit, creditworthy, secure. **6** *a sound sleep* DEEP, undisturbed, uninterrupted, untroubled, peaceful. **7** *a sound thrashing* THOROUGH, proper, real, complete, unqualified, out-and-out, thoroughgoing, severe; *informal* right (royal).
– OPPOSITES unhealthy, unsafe, unreliable, insolvent, light.
sound[3] ● verb *sound the depth of the river* MEASURE, gauge, determine, test, investigate, survey, plumb, fathom, probe.
– PHRASES **sound someone/something out** INVESTIGATE, test, check, examine, probe, research, look into; canvass, survey, poll, question, interview, sample; *informal* pump.
sound[4] ● noun *an oil spill in Prince William Sound* CHANNEL, (sea) passage, strait(s), narrows, waterway; inlet, arm (of the sea), fjord, creek, bay; estuary, firth.
soup ● noun BROTH, potage, consommé, bouillon, chowder, bisque.
sour ● adjective **1** *sour wine* ACID, acidic, acidy, acidulated, tart, bitter, sharp, vinegary, pungent; *N. Amer.* acerb; *technical* acerbic. **2** *sour milk* BAD, off, turned, curdled, rancid, high, rank, foul, fetid. **3** *a sour old man* EMBITTERED, resentful, rancorous, jaundiced, bitter; nasty, spiteful, irritable, peevish, fractious, cross, crabby, crotchety, cantankerous, disagreeable, petulant, querulous, grumpy, bad-tempered, ill-humoured, sullen, surly, sulky, churlish; *informal* snappy, grouchy; *Brit. informal* ratty, stroppy, shirty; *N. Amer. informal* cranky, soreheaded.
– OPPOSITES sweet, fresh, amiable.
● verb **1** *the war had soured him* EMBITTER, disillusion, disenchant, poison, alienate; dissatisfy, frustrate. **2** *the dispute soured relations* SPOIL, mar, damage, harm, impair, wreck, upset, poison, blight, tarnish.
– OPPOSITES improve.
source ● noun **1** *the source of the river* SPRING, origin, (well) head, headspring, headwater(s); *poetic/literary* wellspring. **2** *the source of the rumour* ORIGIN, birthplace, spring, fountainhead, fount, starting point; history, provenance, derivation, root, beginning, gen-

soursop ● noun a large acidic custard apple with white fibrous flesh.
sousaphone /so͞ozəfōn/ ● noun an American form of tuba with a wide bell pointing forward above the player's head.
– ORIGIN named after the American composer J. P. *Sousa* (1854–1932), on the pattern of *saxophone*.
souse /sowss/ ● verb **1** soak in or drench with liquid. **2** (**soused**) (of gherkins, fish, etc.) pickled or marinaded: *soused herring*. **3** (**soused**) informal drunk. ● noun **1** liquid used for pickling. **2** informal a drunkard.
– ORIGIN Old French *sous* 'pickle'; related to SALT.
soutane /so͞otaan/ ● noun a type of cassock worn by Roman Catholic priests.
– ORIGIN Italian *sottana*, from *sotto* 'under'.
south ● noun **1** the direction towards the point of the horizon 90° clockwise from east. **2** the southern part of a country, region, or town. ● adjective **1** lying towards, near, or facing the south. **2** (of a wind) blowing from the south. ● adverb to or towards the south.
– PHRASES **south by east** (or **west**) between south and south-south-east (or south-south-west).
– DERIVATIVES **southbound** adjective & adverb.
– ORIGIN Old English.
South African ● noun a person from South Africa. ● adjective relating to South Africa.
South American ● noun a person from South America. ● adjective relating to South America.
south-east ● noun **1** the point of the horizon midway between south and east. **2** the south-eastern part of a country, region, or town. ● adjective **1** lying towards, near, or facing the south-east. **2** (of a wind) from the south-east. ● adverb to or towards the south-east.
– DERIVATIVES **south-eastern** adjective.
south-easterly ● adjective & adverb in a south-eastward position or direction. ● noun a wind blowing from the south-east.
south-eastward ● adverb (also **south-eastwards**) towards the south-east. ● adjective situated in, directed toward, or facing the south-east.
southerly ● adjective & adverb **1** in a southward position or direction. **2** (of a wind) blowing from the south. ● noun a wind blowing from the south.
southern ● adjective **1** situated in, directed towards, or facing the south. **2** (usu. **Southern**) living in, coming from, or characteristic of the south.
– DERIVATIVES **southernmost** adjective.
southerner ● noun a person from the south of a particular region or country.
Southern Lights ● plural noun the aurora australis.
southing ● noun **1** distance travelled or measured southward. **2** a figure or line representing southward distance on a map.
southpaw ● noun **1** a left-handed boxer who leads with the right hand. **2** informal, chiefly N. Amer. a left-hander in any sphere.
south-south-east ● noun the compass point or direction midway between south and south-east.
south-south-west ● noun the compass point or direction midway between south and south-west.
southward /sowthwərd/ Nautical /suthərd/ ● adjective in a southerly direction. ● adverb (also **southwards**) towards the south.
south-west ● noun **1** the point of the horizon midway between south and west. **2** the south-western part of a country, region, or town. ● adjective **1** lying towards, near, or facing the south-west. **2** (of a wind) from the south-west. ● adverb to or towards the south-west.
– DERIVATIVES **south-western** adjective.
south-westerly ● adjective & adverb in a south-westward position or direction. ● noun a wind blowing from the south-west.
south-westward ● adverb (also **south-westwards**) towards the south-west. ● adjective situated in, directed towards, or facing the south-west.
souvenir /so͞ovəneer/ ● noun a thing that is kept as a reminder of a person, place, or event.
– ORIGIN French, from Latin *subvenire* 'occur to the mind'.
sou'wester /sowwestər/ ● noun a waterproof hat with a broad brim or flap covering the back of the neck.
sovereign ● noun **1** a king or queen who is the supreme ruler of a country. **2** a former British gold coin worth one pound sterling. ● adjective **1** possessing supreme or ultimate power. **2** (of a nation or its affairs) acting or done independently and without outside interference.
– ORIGIN Old French *soverain*, from Latin *super* 'above'.
sovereignty ● noun (pl. **sovereignties**) **1** supreme power or authority. **2** a self-governing state.
soviet /sōviet, sov-/ ● noun **1** (**Soviet**) a citizen of the former Soviet Union. **2** an elected council in the former Soviet Union. **3** a revolutionary council of workers or peasants in Russia before 1917. ● adjective (**Soviet**) of or concerning the former Soviet Union.
– DERIVATIVES **Sovietism** noun **Sovietize** (also **Sovietise**) verb
– ORIGIN Russian *sovet* 'council'.
Sovietologist /sōviətolləjist, sov-/ ● noun an expert on the former Soviet Union.
– DERIVATIVES **Sovietological** adjective **Sovietology** noun.
sow[1] /sō/ ● verb (past **sowed** /sōd/; past part. **sown** /sōn/ or **sowed**) **1** plant (seed) by scattering it on or in the earth. **2** plant (an area) with seed. **3** spread or introduce (something unwelcome).
– DERIVATIVES **sower** noun.
– ORIGIN Old English.
sow[2] /sow/ ● noun an adult female pig.
– PHRASES **you can't make a silk purse out of a sow's ear** proverb you can't create a fine product from inferior materials.
– ORIGIN Old English.
sown past participle of sow[1].
soy ● noun **1** (also **soy sauce**) a sauce made with fermented soya beans, used in Chinese and Japanese cooking. **2** another term for SOYA.
– ORIGIN Chinese, from two words meaning 'salted beans' and 'oil'.
soya ● noun a plant of the pea family which produces an edible bean that is high in protein.
– ORIGIN Malay; related to SOY.
soya milk ● noun a suspension of soya bean flour in water, used as a fat-free substitute for milk.
sozzled ● adjective informal very drunk.
– ORIGIN from dialect *sozzle* 'mix sloppily', probably of imitative origin.
SP ● abbreviation starting price.
spa ● noun **1** a mineral spring considered to have health-giving properties. **2** a place or resort with a mineral spring.
– ORIGIN from *Spa*, a small town in eastern Belgium noted for its mineral springs.
space ● noun **1** unoccupied ground or area. **2** a free or unoccu-

Thesaurus

esis, start, rise; author, originator, initiator, inventor; N. Amer. provenience. **3** *a historian uses primary and secondary sources* REFERENCE, authority, informant; document.
souse ● verb DRENCH, douse, soak, steep, saturate, plunge, immerse, submerge, dip, sink, dunk.
soused ● adjective **1** *a soused herring* PICKLED, marinated, soaked, steeped. **2** (informal) *he was well and truly soused.* See DRUNK adjective.
south ● adjective SOUTHERN, southerly, meridional, austral.
souvenir ● noun MEMENTO, keepsake, reminder, remembrance, token, memorial; trophy, relic.
sovereign ● noun RULER, monarch, crowned head, head of state, potentate, suzerain, overlord, dynast, leader; king, queen, emperor, empress, prince, princess, tsar, royal duke, regent, mogul, emir, sheikh, sultan, maharaja, raja.
– RELATED TERMS regal.
● adjective **1** *sovereign control* SUPREME, absolute, unlimited, unrestricted, boundless, ultimate, total, unconditional, full; principal, chief, dominant, predominant, ruling; royal, regal, monarchical. **2** *a sovereign state* INDEPENDENT, autonomous, self-governing, self-determining; non-aligned, free. **3** (dated) *a sovereign remedy for all ills* EFFECTIVE, effectual, efficient, powerful, potent; useful, helpful, valuable, worthwhile; excellent, reliable, unfailing; informal sure-fire; formal efficacious.
sovereignty ● noun **1** *their sovereignty over the islands* JURISDICTION, rule, supremacy, dominion, power, ascendancy, suzerainty, hegemony, domination, authority, control, influence. **2** *full sovereignty was achieved in 1955* AUTONOMY, independence, self-government, self-rule, home rule, self-determination, freedom.
sow ● verb **1** *sow the seeds in rows* PLANT, scatter, spread, broadcast, disperse, strew, disseminate, distribute; drill, dibble, seed. **2** *the new policy has sown confusion* CAUSE, bring about, occasion,

pied area or expanse. **3** the dimensions of height, depth, and width within which all things exist and move. **4** a blank between typed or written words or characters. **5** (also **outer space**) the physical universe beyond the earth's atmosphere. **6** an interval of time (indicating that it is short): *forty men died in the space of two days.* **7** the freedom and scope to live and develop as one wishes. ● verb **1** position (two or more items) at a distance from one another. **2** (**be spaced out** or chiefly N. Amer. **space out**) informal be or become euphoric or disorientated, especially from taking drugs.
– DERIVATIVES **spacer** noun **spacing** noun.
– ORIGIN Old French *espace*, from Latin *spatium*.
space age ● noun (**the space age**) the era starting when the exploration of space became possible. ● adjective (**space-age**) very modern; technologically advanced.
space bar ● noun a long key on a typewriter or computer keyboard for making a space between words.
space cadet ● noun **1** a trainee astronaut. **2** informal a person perceived as being out of touch with reality.
space capsule ● noun a small spacecraft or the part of a larger one that contains the instruments or crew, designed to be returned to earth.
spacecraft ● noun (pl. same or **spacecrafts**) a vehicle used for travelling in space.
spaceman ● noun a male astronaut.
space probe ● noun an unmanned exploratory spacecraft.
spaceship ● noun a manned spacecraft.
space shuttle ● noun a rocket-launched spacecraft able to land like an unpowered aircraft, used for journeys between earth and craft orbiting the earth.
space station ● noun a large artificial satellite used as a long-term base for manned operations in space.
spacesuit ● noun a sealed and pressurized suit designed to allow an astronaut to survive in space.
space–time ● noun Physics the concepts of time and three-dimensional space regarded as fused in a four-dimensional continuum.
space walk ● noun an excursion by an astronaut outside a spacecraft.
spacey (also **spacy**) ● adjective (**spacier**, **spaciest**) informal **1** out of touch with reality. **2** (of popular music) drifting and ethereal.
spacial ● adjective variant spelling of SPATIAL.
spacious ● adjective (of a room or building) having plenty of space.
– DERIVATIVES **spaciously** adverb **spaciousness** noun.
spade[1] ● noun a tool with a rectangular metal blade and a long handle, used for digging. ● verb dig over or move with a spade.
– PHRASES **call a spade a spade** speak plainly and frankly.
– ORIGIN Old English.
spade[2] ● noun (**spades**) one of the four suits in a pack of playing cards, denoted by a black inverted heart-shaped figure with a small stalk.
– PHRASES **in spades** informal in large amounts or to a high degree.
– ORIGIN Italian *spade* 'swords', from Greek *spathē* 'blade, paddle'.
spadework ● noun hard or routine preparatory work.
spadix /spaydiks/ ● noun (pl. **spadices** /**spay**diseez/) Botany a spike of minute flowers closely arranged round a fleshy axis and typically enclosed in a spathe, characteristic of the arums.
– ORIGIN Greek, 'palm branch'.
spaghetti /spəgetti/ ● plural noun pasta made in solid strings, between macaroni and vermicelli in thickness.
– ORIGIN Italian, 'little strings'.
spaghetti Bolognese /bollənayz/ ● noun a dish of spaghetti with a sauce of minced beef, tomato, onion, and herbs.
– ORIGIN Italian, 'spaghetti of Bologna'.
spaghetti western ● noun informal a western film made in Europe by an Italian director.
spake archaic or literary past of SPEAK.
spall /spawl/ ● noun a splinter or chip of rock. ● verb break into spalls.
– ORIGIN of unknown origin.
spam ● noun **1** trademark a canned meat product made mainly from ham. **2** irrelevant or inappropriate messages sent on the Internet to a large number of users. ● verb (**spammed**, **spamming**) send the same email message indiscriminately to (large numbers of users).
– DERIVATIVES **spammer** noun.
– ORIGIN apparently from the first two and last two letters of *spiced ham*; the Internet sense apparently derives from a sketch by the British 'Monty Python' comedy group, set in a cafe in which every item on the menu includes spam.
span ● noun **1** the full extent of something from end to end; the amount of space covered. **2** the length of time for which something lasts. **3** a wingspan. **4** a part of a bridge between piers or supports. **5** the maximum distance between the tips of the thumb and little finger, taken as the basis of a measurement equal to 9 inches. ● verb (**spanned**, **spanning**) extend across or over.
– ORIGIN Old English.
spandex ● noun trademark a type of stretchy polyurethane fabric.
– ORIGIN an arbitrary formation from EXPAND.
spandrel /spandril/ ● noun Architecture the almost triangular space between the curve of an arch, a wall or an adjoining arch, and the ceiling or framework above.
– ORIGIN perhaps from Old French *espaundre* 'expand'.
spangle ● noun **1** a small thin piece of glittering material, used to ornament a garment; a sequin. **2** a spot of bright colour or light. ● verb cover with spangles.
– DERIVATIVES **spangly** adjective.
– ORIGIN from obsolete *spang* 'glittering ornament', from Dutch *spange* 'buckle'.
Spaniard /spanyərd/ ● noun a person from Spain.
spaniel ● noun a breed of dog with a long silky coat and drooping ears.
– ORIGIN Old French *espaigneul* 'Spanish (dog)', from Latin *Hispaniolus* 'Spanish'.
Spanish ● noun the main language of Spain and of much of Central and South America. ● adjective relating to Spain or Spanish.
– DERIVATIVES **Spanishness** noun.
Spanish-American ● noun a person from the Spanish-speaking countries of Central and South America. ● adjective relating to the Spanish-speaking countries of Central and South America.
Spanish fly ● noun a toxic preparation of the dried bodies of a bright green blister beetle (*Lytta vesicatoria*), formerly used in medicine as a counterirritant and sometimes taken as an aphrodisiac.
Spanish guitar ● noun the standard six-stringed acoustic guitar, used especially for classical and folk music.
Spanish omelette ● noun an omelette containing potatoes and onions, served open rather than folded.
Spanish onion ● noun a large onion with a mild flavour.
spank ● verb slap with one's open hand or a flat object, especially on the buttocks as a punishment. ● noun a slap or series of slaps of this type.

Thesaurus

create, lead to, produce, engender, generate, prompt, initiate, precipitate, trigger, provoke; culminate in, entail, necessitate; foster, foment; *poetic/literary* beget.
space ● noun **1** *there was not enough space* ROOM, capacity, area, volume, expanse, extent, scope, latitude, margin, leeway, play, clearance. **2** *green spaces in London* AREA, expanse, stretch, sweep, tract. **3** *the space between the timbers* GAP, interval, opening, aperture, cavity, cranny, fissure, crack, interstice, lacuna. **4** *write your name in the appropriate space* BLANK, gap, box. **5** *a space of seven years* PERIOD, span, time, duration, stretch, course, interval. **6** *the first woman in space* OUTER SPACE, deep space; the universe, the galaxy, the solar system; infinity.
● verb *the chairs were spaced widely* POSITION, arrange, range, array, dispose, lay out, locate, situate, set, stand.
spaceman, spacewoman ● noun ASTRONAUT, cosmonaut, space traveller, space cadet; *N. Amer. informal* jock.
spacious ● adjective ROOMY, capacious, palatial, airy, sizable, generous, large, big, vast, immense; extensive, expansive, sweeping, rolling, rambling, open; *formal* commodious.
– OPPOSITES cramped.
spadework ● noun GROUNDWORK, preliminary work, preliminaries, preparatory measures, preparations, planning, foundations; hard work, donkey work, labour, drudgery, toil; *informal* grind; *Brit. informal* graft.
span ● noun **1** *a six-foot wing span* EXTENT, length, width, reach, stretch, spread, distance, range. **2** *the span of one working day* PERIOD, space, time, duration, course, interval.
● verb **1** *an arch spanned the stream* BRIDGE, cross, traverse, pass

– ORIGIN perhaps imitative.

spanking ● adjective **1** lively; brisk. **2** informal very good; impressive or pleasing. ● noun a series of spanks.

spanner ● noun chiefly Brit. a tool with a shaped opening or jaws for gripping and turning a nut or bolt.
– PHRASES **spanner in the works** a person or thing that prevents the successful implementation of a plan.
– ORIGIN from German *spannen* 'draw tight'.

spar[1] ● noun a thick, strong pole such as is used for a mast or yard on a ship.
– ORIGIN shortening of Old French *esparre*, or from Old Norse.

spar[2] ● verb (**sparred**, **sparring**) **1** make the motions of boxing without landing heavy blows, as a form of training. **2** engage in argument without marked hostility. ● noun a period or bout of sparring.
– ORIGIN Old English, 'strike out'.

spar[3] ● noun a crystalline translucent or transparent mineral that is easily broken apart.
– ORIGIN Low German.

spare ● adjective **1** additional to what is required for ordinary use. **2** not currently in use or occupied. **3** with no excess fat; thin. **4** elegantly simple. ● noun an item kept in case another item of the same type is lost, broken, or worn out. ● verb **1** give (something of which one has enough) to. **2** make free or available. **3** refrain from killing or harming. **4** refrain from inflicting (harm) on.
– PHRASES **go spare** Brit. informal become extremely angry or distraught. **spare no expense** (or **no expense spared**) be prepared to pay any amount. **to spare** left over.
– DERIVATIVES **sparely** adverb **spareness** noun.
– ORIGIN Old English, 'not plentiful, meagre'.

spare rib ● noun (usu. **spare ribs**) a trimmed rib of pork.
– ORIGIN probably a transposition of Low German *ribbesper*; also associated with SPARE.

spare tyre ● noun **1** an extra tyre carried in a motor vehicle for use in case of puncture. **2** informal a roll of fat round a person's waist.

sparing ● adjective moderate; economical.
– DERIVATIVES **sparingly** adverb.

spark ● noun **1** a small fiery particle thrown off from a fire, alight in ashes, or caused by friction. **2** a light produced by a sudden disrupted electrical discharge through the air. **3** a discharge such as this serving to ignite the explosive mixture in an internal-combustion engine. **4** a small bright object or point. **5** a small but concentrated amount or trace: *a tiny spark of anger*. **6** a sense of liveliness and excitement. ● verb **1** emit or produce sparks. **2** ignite. **3** (usu. **spark off**) provide the stimulus for; trigger.
– PHRASES **bright spark** a lively person. **spark out** Brit. informal unconscious.
– DERIVATIVES **sparky** adjective.
– ORIGIN Old English.

sparkle ● verb **1** shine brightly with flashes of light. **2** be vivacious and witty. **3** (**sparkling**) (of drink) effervescent. ● noun **1** a glittering flash of light. **2** vivacity and wit.
– DERIVATIVES **sparkly** adjective.

sparkler ● noun a hand-held firework that emits sparks.

spark plug (also **sparking plug**) ● noun a device for firing the explosive mixture in an internal-combustion engine.

sparrow ● noun a small bird with brown and grey plumage.
– ORIGIN Old English.

sparrowhawk ● noun **1** a small hawk that preys on small birds. **2** N. Amer. the American kestrel.

sparse ● adjective thinly dispersed.
– DERIVATIVES **sparsely** adverb **sparseness** noun **sparsity** noun.
– ORIGIN Latin *sparsus*, from *spargere* 'scatter'.

Spartan ● adjective **1** of or relating to Sparta, a city state in ancient Greece. **2** (**spartan**) lacking in comfort or luxury; austere. ● noun a citizen of Sparta.

spasm ● noun **1** a sudden involuntary muscular contraction or convulsive movement. **2** a sudden brief spell of an activity or sensation.
– ORIGIN Greek *spasmos*, from *span* 'pull'.

spasmodic ● adjective **1** occurring or done in brief, irregular bursts. **2** of or caused by a spasm or spasms.
– DERIVATIVES **spasmodically** adverb.

spastic ● adjective **1** relating to or affected by muscle spasm. **2** of or having a form of muscular weakness typical of cerebral palsy, involving reflex resistance to passive movement of the limbs and difficulty in initiating and controlling muscular movement. **3** informal, offensive incompetent or uncoordinated. ● noun **1** a person with cerebral palsy. **2** informal, offensive an incompetent or uncoordinated person.
– DERIVATIVES **spastically** adverb **spasticity** noun.
– USAGE In modern use the term **spastic** is likely to cause offence. It is preferable to use phrasing such as *people with cerebral palsy* instead.
– ORIGIN Greek *spastikos* 'pulling'.

spat[1] past and past participle of SPIT[1].

spat[2] ● noun a short cloth gaiter covering the instep and ankle.

Thesaurus

over. **2** *his career spanned twenty years* LAST, cover, extend, spread over, comprise.

spank ● verb SMACK, slap, hit, cuff; *informal* wallop, belt, whack, give someone a hiding; *Scottish & N. English* skelp.

spar ● verb QUARREL, argue, fight, disagree, differ, be at odds, be at variance, fall out, dispute, squabble, wrangle, bandy words, cross swords, lock horns, be at loggerheads; *informal* scrap, argufy, spat; *Brit. informal* row.

S

spare ● adjective **1** *a spare set of keys* EXTRA, supplementary, additional, second, other, alternative; emergency, reserve, back-up, relief, fallback, substitute; fresh; *N. Amer.* alternate. **2** *they sold off the spare land* SURPLUS, superfluous, excessive; redundant, unnecessary, inessential, unessential, unneeded, uncalled for, dispensable, disposable, expendable, unwanted; *informal* going begging. **3** *your spare time* FREE, leisure, own. **4** *a spare woman* SLENDER, lean, willowy, svelte, lissom, rangy, clean-limbed, trim, slight; thin, skinny, gaunt, lanky, spindly; *informal* skin and bone.
● verb **1** *he could not spare any money* AFFORD, do without, manage without, dispense with, part with, give, provide. **2** *they were spared by their captors* PARDON, let off, forgive, reprieve, release, free; leave uninjured, leave unhurt; be merciful to, show mercy to, have mercy on, be lenient to, have pity on.
– PHRASES **go spare** (*Brit. informal*). See GET ANGRY at ANGRY. **to spare** LEFT (OVER), remaining, unused, unneeded, not required, still available, surplus (to requirements), superfluous, extra; *informal* going begging.

sparing ● adjective THRIFTY, economical, frugal, canny, careful, prudent, cautious; mean, miserly, niggardly, parsimonious, close-fisted, penny-pinching, cheese-paring, ungenerous, close, grasping; *informal* stingy, tight-fisted, tight, mingy, money-grubbing; *N. Amer. informal* cheap.
– OPPOSITES lavish.

spark ● noun **1** *a spark of light* FLASH, glint, twinkle, flicker, flare, pinprick. **2** *not a spark of truth in the story* PARTICLE, iota, jot, whit, glimmer, atom, bit, trace, vestige, ounce, shred, crumb, grain, mite, hint, touch, suggestion, whisper, scintilla; *informal* smidgen, tad.
● verb *the trial sparked a furious row* CAUSE, give rise to, lead to, occasion, bring about, start, initiate, precipitate, prompt, trigger (off), provoke, stimulate, stir up.

sparkle ● verb **1** *her earrings sparkled* GLITTER, glint, glisten, twinkle, flash, blink, wink, shimmer, shine, gleam; *poetic/literary* coruscate, glister. **2** *she sparkled as the hostess* BE LIVELY, be vivacious, be animated, be ebullient, be exuberant, be bubbly, be effervescent, be witty, be full of life.
● noun *the sparkle of the pool* GLITTER, glint, twinkle, flicker, shimmer, flash, shine, gleam; *poetic/literary* coruscation.

sparkling ● adjective **1** *sparkling wine* EFFERVESCENT, fizzy, carbonated, aerated, gassy, bubbly, frothy; mousseux, spumante. **2** *a sparkling performance* BRILLIANT, dazzling, scintillating, exciting, exhilarating, stimulating, invigorating; vivacious, lively, vibrant, animated.
– OPPOSITES still, dull.

sparse ● adjective SCANT, scanty, scattered, scarce, infrequent, few and far between; meagre, paltry, skimpy, limited, in short supply.
– OPPOSITES abundant.

spartan ● adjective AUSTERE, harsh, hard, frugal, stringent, rigorous, strict, stern, severe; ascetic, abstemious; bleak, joyless, grim, bare, stark, plain.
– OPPOSITES luxurious.

spasm ● noun **1** *a muscle spasm* CONTRACTION, convulsion, cramp; twitch, jerk, tic, shudder, shiver, tremor. **2** *a spasm of coughing* FIT, paroxysm, attack, burst, bout, seizure, outburst, outbreak, access; *informal* splurt; *formal* boutade.

– ORIGIN from *spatterdash*, a long gaiter or legging formerly worn when riding.

spat[3] informal ● **noun** a petty quarrel. ● **verb** (**spatted**, **spatting**) quarrel pettily.
– ORIGIN probably imitative.

spatchcock ● **noun** a chicken or game bird split open and grilled or roasted. ● **verb** prepare (a chicken or game bird) in this way.
– ORIGIN perhaps related to DISPATCH + COCK.

spate ● **noun** **1** a large number of similar things or events coming in quick succession. **2** chiefly Brit. a sudden flood in a river.
– ORIGIN of unknown origin.

spathe /spayth/ ● **noun** Botany a large sheathing bract enclosing the flower cluster of certain plants, especially the spadix of arums and palms.
– ORIGIN Greek, 'broad blade'.

spatial /spaysh'l/ (also **spacial**) ● **adjective** of or relating to space.
– DERIVATIVES **spatiality** noun **spatialize** (also **spatialise**) verb **spatially** adverb.
– ORIGIN from Latin *spatium* 'space'.

spatter ● **verb** **1** cover with drops or spots. **2** splash or be splashed over a surface. ● **noun** **1** a spray or splash. **2** a short outburst of sound.
– ORIGIN originally in the sense 'splutter': related to Dutch, Low German *spatten* 'burst, spout'.

spatula ● **noun** an implement with a broad, flat, blunt blade, used especially for mixing or spreading.
– ORIGIN Latin, from *spathula* 'small spathe'.

spatulate /spatyoolət/ ● **adjective** having a broad, rounded end.

spavin /spavvin/ ● **noun** a disorder of a horse's hock.
– DERIVATIVES **spavined** adjective.
– ORIGIN Old French *espavin*.

spawn ● **verb** **1** (of a fish, frog, etc.) release or deposit eggs. **2** produce or generate; give rise to. ● **noun** **1** the eggs of fish, frogs, etc. **2** the mycelium of a fungus, especially a cultivated mushroom.
– DERIVATIVES **spawner** noun.
– ORIGIN Old French *espaundre* 'to shed roe', from Latin *expandere* 'expand'.

spay ● **verb** sterilize (a female animal) by removing the ovaries.
– ORIGIN Old French *espeer* 'cut with a sword', from Latin *spatha* 'spathe'.

speak ● **verb** (past **spoke**; past part. **spoken**) **1** say something. **2** (**speak to**) talk to in order to advise, pass on information, etc. **3** communicate in or be able to communicate in (a specified language). **4** (**speak for**) express the views or position of. **5** (**speak out/up**) express one's opinions frankly and publicly. **6** (**speak up**) speak more loudly. **7** (of behaviour, an event, etc.) serve as evidence for something. **8** (**speak to**) appeal or relate to. **9** make a speech.
– PHRASES **speak in tongues** speak in an unknown language during religious worship, regarded as one of the gifts of the Holy Spirit (Acts 2). **speak one's mind** express one's opinions frankly. **speak volumes** convey a great deal without using words.
– ORIGIN Old English.

speakeasy ● **noun** (pl. **speakeasies**) informal (in the US during Prohibition) an illicit liquor shop or drinking club.

speaker ● **noun** **1** a person who speaks. **2** a person who speaks a specified language. **3** a person who makes a speech at a formal occasion. **4** (**Speaker**) the presiding officer in a legislative assembly, especially the House of Commons. **5** a loudspeaker.

speaking ● **adjective** **1** used for or engaged in speech. **2** able to communicate in a specified language.
– PHRASES **on speaking terms** slightly acquainted; moderately friendly.

speaking clock ● **noun** Brit. a telephone service giving the correct time in recorded speech.

spear ● **noun** **1** a weapon with a pointed metal tip and a long shaft, used for thrusting or throwing. **2** a plant shoot, especially a pointed stem of asparagus or broccoli. **3** (before another noun) denoting the male side or members of a family. Compare with DISTAFF. ● **verb** pierce or strike with a spear or other pointed object.
– ORIGIN Old English.

speargun ● **noun** a gun used to propel a spear in underwater fishing.

spearhead ● **noun** **1** the point of a spear. **2** an individual or group leading an attack or movement. ● **verb** lead (an attack or movement).

spearmint ● **noun** the common garden mint, which is used in cooking as a herb and in flavouring.

spec[1] ● **noun** (in phrase **on spec**) informal in the hope of success but without any specific preparation or plan.
– ORIGIN abbreviation of *speculation*.

spec[2] ● **noun** informal a detailed working description; a specification.

special ● **adjective** **1** better, greater, or otherwise different from what is usual. **2** designed for or belonging to a particular person, place, or event. **3** (of a subject) studied in particular depth. **4** (of education) for children with particular needs, especially those with learning difficulties. ● **noun** **1** something designed or organized for a particular occasion or purpose. **2** a dish not on the regular menu but served on a particular day. **3** a person assigned to a special duty.
– DERIVATIVES **specialness** noun.
– ORIGIN Latin *specialis*, from *species* 'appearance'.

special constable ● **noun** (in the UK) a person who is trained

Thesaurus

spasmodic ● **adjective** INTERMITTENT, fitful, irregular, sporadic, erratic, occasional, infrequent, scattered, patchy, isolated, periodic, periodical, on and off.

spate ● **noun** SERIES, succession, run, cluster, string, rash, epidemic, outbreak, wave, flurry, rush, flood, deluge, torrent.

spatter ● **verb** SPLASH, bespatter, splatter, spray, sprinkle, shower, speck, speckle, fleck, mottle, blotch, mark, cover; *informal* splotch; *Brit. informal* splodge.

spawn ● **verb** GIVE RISE TO, bring about, occasion, generate, engender, originate; lead to, result in, effect, induce, initiate, start, set off, precipitate, trigger; breed, bear; *poetic/literary* beget.

speak ● **verb** **1** *she refused to speak about it* TALK, say anything/something; utter, state, declare, tell, voice, express, pronounce, articulate, enunciate, vocalize, verbalize. **2** *we spoke the other day* CONVERSE, have a conversation, talk, communicate, chat, pass the time of day, have a word, gossip; *informal* have a confab, chew the fat; *Brit. informal* natter; *N. Amer. informal* shoot the breeze; *formal* confabulate. **3** *the Minister spoke for two hours* GIVE A SPEECH, talk, lecture, hold forth, discourse, expound, expatiate, orate, sermonize, pontificate; *informal* spout, spiel, speechify, jaw, sound off. **4** *he was spoken of as a promising student* MENTION, talk about, discuss, refer to, remark on, allude to. **5** *his expression spoke disbelief* INDICATE, show, display, register, reveal, betray, exhibit, manifest, express, convey, impart, bespeak, communicate, evidence; suggest, denote, reflect; *formal* evince. **6** *you must speak to him about his rudeness* REPRIMAND, rebuke, admonish, chastise, chide, upbraid, reprove, reproach, scold, remonstrate with, take to task, pull up; *informal* tell off, dress down, rap over the knuckles, come down on; *Brit. informal* tick off, have a go at, tear someone off a strip, give someone what for; *formal* castigate.
– PHRASES **speak for** **1** *she speaks for the Liberal Democrats* REPRESENT, act for, appear for, express the views of, be spokesperson for. **2** *I spoke for the motion* ADVOCATE, champion, uphold, defend, support, promote, recommend, back, endorse, sponsor, espouse. **speak out** SPEAK PUBLICLY, speak openly, speak frankly, speak one's mind, sound off, stand up and be counted. **speak up** SPEAK LOUDLY, speak clearly, raise one's voice; shout, yell, bellow; *informal* holler.

speaker ● **noun** SPEECH-MAKER, lecturer, talker, speechifier, orator, declaimer, rhetorician; spokesperson, spokesman/woman, mouthpiece; reader, lector, commentator, broadcaster, narrator; *informal* tub-thumper, spieler; *historical* demagogue, rhetor.

spear ● **noun** JAVELIN, lance, assegai, harpoon, bayonet; gaff, leister; *historical* pike.

spearhead ● **noun** **1** *a Bronze Age spearhead* SPEAR TIP, spear point. **2** *the spearhead of the struggle against Fascism* LEADER(S), driving force; forefront, front runner(s), front line, vanguard, van, cutting edge.
● **verb** *she spearheaded the campaign* LEAD, head, front; lead the way, be in the van, be in the vanguard.

special ● **adjective** **1** *a very special person* EXCEPTIONAL, unusual, singular, uncommon, notable, noteworthy, remarkable, outstanding, unique. **2** *our town's special character* DISTINCTIVE, distinct, individual, particular, specific, peculiar. **3** *a special occasion* MOMENTOUS, significant, memorable, signal, important, historic, festive, gala, red-letter. **4** *a special tool for cutting tiles* SPECIFIC, particular,

to act as a police officer on particular occasions, especially in times of emergency.

special effects ● plural noun illusions created for films and television by props, camerawork, computer graphics, etc.

specialist ● noun a person who is highly skilled or knowledgeable in a particular field. ● adjective relating to or involving detailed knowledge or a specific focus within a field.
– DERIVATIVES **specialism** noun.

speciality /speshialiti/ (chiefly N. Amer. & Medicine also **specialty**) ● noun (pl. **specialities**) **1** a pursuit, area of study, or skill to which someone has devoted themselves and in which they are expert. **2** a product for which a person or region is famous. **3** (usu. **specialty**) a branch of medicine or surgery.

specialize (also **specialise**) ● verb **1** concentrate on and become expert in a particular skill or area. **2** make a habit of engaging in a particular activity. **3** (**be specialized**) Biology (of an organ or part) be adapted or set apart to serve a special function.
– DERIVATIVES **specialization** noun.

specially ● adverb for a special purpose.

special needs ● plural noun particular educational requirements resulting from learning difficulties, physical disability, or emotional and behavioural difficulties.

special pleading ● noun argument in which the speaker deliberately ignores aspects that are unfavourable to their point of view.

specialty /spesh'lti/ ● noun (pl. **specialties**) chiefly N. Amer. & Medicine another term for SPECIALITY.

speciation /speeshiaysh'n, speessi-/ ● noun Biology the formation of new and distinct species in the course of evolution.
– DERIVATIVES **speciate** verb.

specie /speeshi, -see/ ● noun money in the form of coins rather than notes.
– ORIGIN originally used in the phrase *in specie* 'in kind', later 'in the coin specified': from Latin *species* 'form, kind'.

species /speesheez, -seez/ ● noun (pl. same) **1** Biology a group of living organisms consisting of similar individuals capable of exchanging genes or interbreeding. **2** (before another noun) denoting a plant belonging to a distinct species rather than to one of the many varieties produced by hybridization. **3** a kind or sort.
– ORIGIN Latin, 'appearance, form, beauty', from *specere* 'to look'.

speciesism ● noun the assumption of human superiority over other creatures, leading to the exploitation of animals.
– DERIVATIVES **speciesist** adjective & noun.

specific /spəsiffik/ ● adjective **1** clearly defined or identified. **2** precise and clear. **3** (**specific to**) belonging or relating uniquely to. **4** Biology relating to species or a species. ● noun (**specifics**) precise details.
– DERIVATIVES **specifically** adverb **specificity** /spessifissiti/ noun **specificness** noun.
– ORIGIN Latin *specificus*, from *species* 'appearance, form'.

specification ● noun **1** the action of specifying. **2** (usu. **specifications**) a detailed description of the design and materials used to make something. **3** a standard of workmanship, materials, etc. required to be met in a piece of work.

specific gravity ● noun another term for RELATIVE DENSITY.

specify ● verb (**specifies**, **specified**) **1** make specific; state or identify clearly and definitely. **2** include in an architect's or engineer's specifications.
– DERIVATIVES **specifiable** adjective **specifier** noun.

specimen ● noun **1** an individual animal, plant, object, etc. used as an example of its species or type for scientific study or display. **2** a sample for medical testing, especially of urine. **3** an example of something regarded as typical of its class or group. **4** informal a person or animal of a specific type: *he was confronted by a sorrier specimen than himself.*
– ORIGIN originally in the sense 'pattern, model': from Latin, from *specere* 'to look'.

specious /speeshəss/ ● adjective **1** superficially plausible, but actually wrong. **2** misleading in appearance.
– DERIVATIVES **speciously** adverb **speciousness** noun.
– ORIGIN originally in the sense 'beautiful': from Latin *speciosus* 'fair, plausible'.

speck ● noun a tiny spot or particle. ● verb mark with small spots.
– ORIGIN Old English.

speckle ● noun a small spot or patch of colour. ● verb mark with speckles.
– DERIVATIVES **speckled** adjective.
– ORIGIN Dutch *spekkel*.

specs ● plural noun informal a pair of spectacles.

spectacle ● noun a visually striking performance or display.
– PHRASES **make a spectacle of oneself** draw attention to oneself by behaving in a ridiculous way in public.
– ORIGIN Latin *spectaculum* 'public show', from *specere* 'to look'.

spectacled ● adjective wearing spectacles.

spectacles ● plural noun Brit. a pair of glasses.

spectacular ● adjective very impressive, striking, or dramatic. ● noun a performance or event produced on a large scale and with striking effects.
– DERIVATIVES **spectacularly** adverb.

spectate ● verb be a spectator.

spectator ● noun a person who watches at a show, game, or other event.
– ORIGIN Latin, from *specere* 'to look'.

specter ● noun US spelling of SPECTRE.

spectra plural of SPECTRUM.

spectral ● adjective **1** of or like a spectre. **2** of or concerning spectra or the spectrum.
– DERIVATIVES **spectrally** adverb.

Thesaurus

purpose-built, tailor-made, custom-built.
– OPPOSITES ordinary, general.

S

specialist ● noun EXPERT, authority, pundit, professional; connoisseur; master, maestro, adept, virtuoso; *informal* pro, buff, ace, whizz, hotshot; *Brit. informal* dab hand; *N. Amer. informal* maven.
– OPPOSITES amateur.

speciality ● noun **1** *his speciality was watercolours* FORTE, strong point, strength, métier, strong suit, talent, skill, bent, gift; *informal* bag, thing, cup of tea. **2** *a speciality of the region* DELICACY, specialty, fine food/product, traditional food/product.

species ● noun TYPE, kind, sort; genus, family, order, breed, strain, variety, class, classification, category, set, bracket; style, manner, form, genre; generation, vintage.

specific ● adjective **1** *a specific purpose* PARTICULAR, specified, fixed, set, determined, distinct, definite; single, individual, peculiar, discrete, express, precise. **2** *I gave specific instructions* DETAILED, explicit, express, clear-cut, unequivocal, precise, exact, meticulous, strict, definite.
– OPPOSITES general, vague.

specification ● noun **1** *clear specification of objectives* STATEMENT, identification, definition, description, setting out, framing, designation, detailing, enumeration; stipulation, prescription. **2** *a shelter built to their specifications* INSTRUCTIONS, guidelines, parameters, stipulations, requirements, conditions, provisions, restrictions, order; description, details.

specify ● verb STATE, name, identify, define, describe, set out, frame, itemize, detail, list, spell out, enumerate, particularize, cite, instance; stipulate, prescribe.

specimen ● noun SAMPLE, example, instance, illustration, demonstration, exemplification; bit, snippet; model, prototype, pattern, dummy, pilot, trial, taster, tester.

specious ● adjective MISLEADING, deceptive, false, fallacious, unsound, casuistic, sophistic; plausible.

speck ● noun **1** *a mere speck in the distance* DOT, pinprick, spot, fleck, speckle. **2** *a speck of dust* PARTICLE, grain, atom, molecule; bit, trace.

speckled ● adjective FLECKED, speckly, specked, freckled, freckly, spotted, spotty, dotted, mottled, dappled.

spectacle ● noun **1** *a spectacle fit for a monarch* DISPLAY, show, pageant, parade, performance, exhibition, extravaganza, spectacular. **2** *they were rather an odd spectacle* SIGHT, vision, scene, prospect, vista, picture. **3** *don't make a spectacle of yourself* EXHIBITION, laughing stock, fool, curiosity.

spectacles ● plural noun GLASSES, eyewear; *N. Amer.* eyeglasses; *informal* specs.

spectacular ● adjective **1** *a spectacular victory* IMPRESSIVE, magnificent, splendid, dazzling, sensational, dramatic, remarkable, outstanding, memorable, unforgettable. **2** *a spectacular view* STRIKING, picturesque, eye-catching, breathtaking, arresting, glorious; *informal* out of this world.
– OPPOSITES unimpressive, dull.
● noun *a spectacular put on for the tourists.* See SPECTACLE sense 1.

spectator ● noun WATCHER, viewer, observer, onlooker, bystander, witness; commentator, reporter, monitor; *poetic/literary* beholder.

spectre (US **specter**) ● noun **1** a ghost. **2** something unpleasant or dangerous that is imagined or expected.
– ORIGIN French, from Latin *spectrum* 'image, apparition'.
spectrogram ● noun a visual or electronic record of a spectrum.
spectrograph ● noun an apparatus for photographing or otherwise recording spectra.
– DERIVATIVES **spectrographic** adjective.
spectrometer ● noun an apparatus used for recording and measuring spectra, especially as a method of analysis.
– DERIVATIVES **spectrometric** adjective **spectrometry** noun.
spectroscope ● noun an apparatus for producing and recording spectra for examination.
spectroscopy ● noun the branch of science concerned with the investigation and measurement of spectra produced when matter interacts with or emits electromagnetic radiation.
– DERIVATIVES **spectroscopic** adjective **spectroscopist** noun.
spectrum /spektrəm/ ● noun (pl. **spectra** /spektrə/) **1** a band of colours produced by separation of the components of light by their different degrees of refraction, e.g. in a rainbow. **2** the entire range of wavelengths of electromagnetic radiation. **3** a characteristic series of frequencies of electromagnetic radiation emitted or absorbed by a substance. **4** the components of a sound or other phenomenon arranged according to frequency, energy, etc. **5** a scale extending between two points; a range: *the political spectrum.*
– ORIGIN Latin, 'image, apparition', from *specere* 'to look'.
specula plural of SPECULUM.
speculate /spekyoolayt/ ● verb **1** form a theory or conjecture without firm evidence. **2** invest in stocks, property, or other ventures in the hope of financial gain but with the risk of loss.
– DERIVATIVES **speculation** noun **speculator** noun.
– ORIGIN Latin *speculari* 'observe', from *specula* 'watchtower'.
speculative ● adjective **1** engaged in or based on conjecture rather than knowledge. **2** (of an investment) involving a high risk of loss.
– DERIVATIVES **speculatively** adverb **speculativeness** noun.
speculum /spekyooləm/ ● noun (pl. **specula** /spekyoolə/) Medicine a metal instrument that is used to dilate an orifice or canal in the body to allow inspection.
– ORIGIN Latin, 'mirror', from *specere* 'to look'.
sped past and past participle of SPEED.
speech ● noun **1** the expression of thoughts and feelings by articulate sounds. **2** a formal address delivered to an audience. **3** a sequence of lines written for one character in a play.
– ORIGIN Old English.
speech day ● noun Brit. an annual event held at some schools, at which speeches are made and prizes are presented.
speechify ● verb (**speechifies**, **speechified**) deliver a speech, especially in a tedious or pompous way.
– DERIVATIVES **speechification** noun **speechifier** noun.
speechless ● adjective unable to speak, especially as the temporary result of shock or strong emotion.
– DERIVATIVES **speechlessly** adverb **speechlessness** noun.
speech recognition ● noun the process of enabling a computer to identify and respond to the sounds produced in human speech.
speech therapy ● noun treatment to help people with speech and language problems.
– DERIVATIVES **speech therapist** noun.
speed ● noun **1** the rate at which someone or something moves or operates. **2** rapidity of movement or action. **3** each of the possible gear ratios of a bicycle. **4** the light-gathering power or f-number of a camera lens. **5** the duration of a photographic exposure. **6** the sensitivity of photographic film to light. **7** informal an amphetamine drug, especially methamphetamine. **8** archaic success; prosperity. ● verb (past and past part. **speeded** or **sped**) **1** move quickly. **2** (**speed up**) move or work more quickly. **3** (of a motorist) travel at a speed greater than the legal limit. **4** archaic make prosperous or successful.
– PHRASES **at speed** quickly. **up to speed 1** operating at full speed or capacity. **2** fully informed or up to date.
– DERIVATIVES **speeder** noun.
– ORIGIN Old English.
speedball ● noun informal a mixture of cocaine with heroin.
speedboat ● noun a motor boat designed for high speed.
speed bump (Brit. also **speed hump**) ● noun a ridge set in a road to control the speed of vehicles.
speed camera ● noun a roadside camera designed to catch speeding vehicles by taking video footage or a photograph.
speed limit ● noun the maximum speed at which a vehicle may legally travel on a particular stretch of road.
speedo ● noun (pl. **speedos**) informal a speedometer.
speedometer /speedommitər/ ● noun an instrument on a vehicle's dashboard indicating its speed.
speedster ● noun informal a person or thing that operates well at high speed.
speedway ● noun **1** a form of motorcycle racing in which the riders race laps around an oval dirt track. **2** N. Amer. a highway for fast motor traffic.
speedwell ● noun a small creeping plant with blue or pink flowers.
speedy ● adjective (**speedier**, **speediest**) **1** done or occurring quickly. **2** moving quickly.
– DERIVATIVES **speedily** adverb **speediness** noun.
speleology /speeliolləji/ ● noun the study or exploration of

Thesaurus

– OPPOSITES participant.
spectral ● adjective GHOSTLY, phantom, wraithlike, shadowy, incorporeal, insubstantial, disembodied, unearthly, other-worldly; *informal* spooky.
spectre ● noun **1** *the spectres in the crypt* GHOST, phantom, apparition, spirit, wraith, shadow, presence; *informal* spook; *poetic/literary* phantasm, shade. **2** *the looming spectre of war* THREAT, menace, shadow, cloud; prospect; danger, peril, fear, dread.
spectrum ● noun RANGE, gamut, sweep, scope, span; compass, orbit, ambit.
speculate ● verb **1** *they speculated about my private life* CONJECTURE, theorize, hypothesize, guess, surmise; think, wonder, muse. **2** *investors speculate on the stock market* GAMBLE, take a risk, venture, wager; invest, play the market; *Brit. informal* have a flutter, punt.
speculative ● adjective **1** *any discussion is largely speculative* CONJECTURAL, suppositional, theoretical, hypothetical, putative, academic, notional, abstract; tentative, unproven, unfounded, groundless, unsubstantiated. **2** *a speculative investment* RISKY, hazardous, unsafe, uncertain, unpredictable; *informal* chancy, dicey, iffy; *Brit. informal* dodgy.
speech ● noun **1** *he doesn't have the power of speech* SPEAKING, talking, verbal expression, verbal communication. **2** *her speech was slurred* DICTION, elocution, articulation, enunciation, pronunciation; utterance, words. **3** *an after-dinner speech* TALK, address, lecture, discourse, oration, disquisition, peroration, deliverance, presentation; sermon, homily; monologue, soliloquy; *informal* spiel. **4** *Spanish popular speech* LANGUAGE, tongue, parlance, idiom, dialect, vernacular, patois; *informal* lingo, patter, -speak, -ese.
– RELATED TERMS lingual, oral, phono-, -phone, -phasia.
speechless ● adjective LOST FOR WORDS, dumbstruck, bereft of speech, tongue-tied, inarticulate, mute, dumb, voiceless, silent; *informal* mum; *archaic* mumchance.
– OPPOSITES verbose.
speed ● noun **1** *the speed of their progress* RATE, pace, tempo, momentum. **2** *the speed with which they responded* RAPIDITY, swiftness, speediness, quickness, dispatch, promptness, immediacy, briskness, sharpness; haste, hurry, precipitateness; acceleration, velocity; *informal* lick, clip; *poetic/literary* celerity.
– RELATED TERMS tacho-, tachy-.
● verb **1** *I sped home* HURRY, rush, dash, run, race, sprint, bolt, dart, gallop, career, charge, shoot, hurtle, hare, fly, zoom, scurry, scuttle, scamper, hasten; *informal* tear, belt, pelt, scoot, zip, whip, hotfoot it, leg it; *Brit. informal* bomb; *N. Amer. informal* hightail it. **2** *he was caught speeding* DRIVE TOO FAST, exceed the speed limit. **3** *a holiday will speed his recovery* HASTEN, expedite, speed up, accelerate, advance, further, promote, boost, stimulate, aid, assist, facilitate.
– OPPOSITES slow, hinder.
– PHRASES **speed up** HURRY UP, accelerate, go faster, get a move on, put a spurt on, pick up speed, gather speed; *informal* get cracking, get moving, step on it, shake a leg; *Brit. informal* get one's skates on; *N. Amer. informal* get a wiggle on.
speedily ● adverb RAPIDLY, swiftly, quickly, fast, post-haste, at the speed of light, at full tilt; promptly, immediately, briskly; hastily, hurriedly, precipitately; *informal* p.d.q. (pretty damn quick), double quick, hell for leather, at the double, like the wind, like (greased) lightning; *Brit. informal* like the clappers, like billy-o; *N. Amer. informal*

caves.
– DERIVATIVES **speleological** adjective **speleologist** noun.
– ORIGIN from Greek *spēlaion* 'cave'.

spell[1] ● verb (past and past part. **spelled** or chiefly Brit. **spelt**) **1** write or name the letters that form (a word) in correct sequence. **2** (of letters) make up or form (a word). **3** be a sign of; lead to: *the plans would spell disaster.* **4** (**spell out**) explain clearly and in detail.
– ORIGIN Old French *espeller*; related to SPELL[2].

spell[2] ● noun **1** a form of words used as a magical charm or incantation. **2** a state of enchantment or influence induced by a spell.
– ORIGIN Old English, 'narration'.

spell[3] ● noun **1** a short period of time. **2** Austral./NZ a period of rest from work. ● verb **1** allow (someone) to rest briefly by taking over from them in an activity. **2** Austral./NZ take a brief rest.
– ORIGIN from dialect *spele* 'take the place of', of unknown origin.

spellbind ● verb (past and past part. **spellbound**) hold the complete attention of, as if by a spell; entrance.
– DERIVATIVES **spellbinder** noun.

spellchecker (also **spelling checker**) ● noun a computer program which checks the spelling of words in files of text by comparing them with a stored list of words.
– DERIVATIVES **spellcheck** verb & noun.

speller ● noun **1** a person of a specified spelling ability. **2** a spellchecker.

spelling ● noun **1** the process or activity of spelling a word. **2** the way in which a word is spelled. **3** a person's ability to spell.

spelt past and past participle of SPELL[1].

spencer ● noun **1** a short, close-fitting jacket worn by women and children in the early 19th century. **2** a thin woollen vest.
– ORIGIN probably named after the second Earl *Spencer* (1758–1834), English politician.

spend ● verb (past and past part. **spent**) **1** pay out (money) in buying or hiring goods or services. **2** use or use up (energy or resources); exhaust. **3** pass (time) in a specified way. ● noun informal an amount of money paid out.
– PHRASES **spend a penny** Brit. informal, euphemistic urinate. [ORIGIN with reference to the coin-operated locks of public toilets.]
– DERIVATIVES **spendable** adjective **spender** noun.
– ORIGIN Latin *expendere* 'pay out'.

spendthrift ● noun a person who spends money in an extravagant, irresponsible way.

spent past and past participle of SPEND. ● adjective used up; exhausted.

sperm ● noun (pl. same or **sperms**) **1** semen. **2** a spermatozoon.
– ORIGIN Greek *sperma* 'seed'.

spermaceti /spermәseeti, -setti/ ● noun a white waxy substance obtained from an organ in the head of the sperm whale, which focuses acoustic signals and aids in the control of buoyancy, and was formerly used in candles and ointments.
– ORIGIN from Latin *sperma* 'sperm' + *ceti* 'of a whale', from the belief that it was whale spawn.

spermatozoon /spermәtәzōon/ ● noun (pl. **spermatozoa** /spermәtәzōә/) Biology the motile male sex cell of an animal by which the ovum is fertilized, typically having a compact head and one or more long flagella for swimming.
– DERIVATIVES **spermatozoal** adjective **spermatozoan** adjective.
– ORIGIN from Greek *sperma* 'seed' + *zōion* 'animal'.

sperm bank ● noun a place where semen is kept in cold storage for use in artificial insemination.

sperm count ● noun the number of spermatozoa in a measured amount of semen, used as an indication of a man's fertility.

spermicide ● noun a substance that kills spermatozoa, used as a contraceptive.
– DERIVATIVES **spermicidal** adjective.

sperm oil ● noun an oil found with spermaceti in the head of the sperm whale, used formerly as a lubricant.

sperm whale ● noun a toothed whale with a massive head, feeding at great depths largely on squid.
– ORIGIN abbreviation of SPERMACETI.

spew ● verb **1** expel or be expelled in large quantities rapidly and forcibly. **2** informal vomit. ● noun informal vomit.
– DERIVATIVES **spewer** noun.
– ORIGIN Old English.

SPF ● abbreviation sun protection factor.

sphagnum /sfagnәm/ ● noun a plant of a genus that comprises the peat mosses.
– ORIGIN Latin, from Greek *sphagnos*, denoting a kind of moss.

sphere ● noun **1** a round solid figure in which every point on the surface is equidistant from the centre. **2** each of a series of revolving concentrically arranged spherical shells in which celestial bodies were formerly thought to be set in a fixed relationship. **3** an area of activity, interest, or expertise: *political reforms to match those in the economic sphere.*
– ORIGIN Greek *sphaira* 'ball'.

spheric /sferrik/ ● adjective spherical.
– DERIVATIVES **sphericity** noun.

spherical ● adjective **1** shaped like a sphere. **2** of or relating to the properties of spheres.
– DERIVATIVES **spherically** adverb.

spheroid /sfeeroyd/ ● noun a sphere-like but not perfectly spherical body.
– DERIVATIVES **spheroidal** adjective.

spherule /sferrōōl/ ● noun a small sphere.

Thesaurus

lickety-split; *poetic/literary* apace.

speedy ● adjective **1** *a speedy reply* RAPID, swift, quick, fast; prompt, immediate, expeditious, express, brisk, sharp; whirlwind, lightning, meteoric; hasty, hurried, precipitate, breakneck, rushed; *informal* p.d.q. (pretty damn quick), snappy, quickie. **2** *a speedy hatchback* FAST, high-speed; *informal* nippy, zippy; *poetic/literary* fleet.
– OPPOSITES slow.

S

spell[1] ● verb *the drought spelled disaster for them* SIGNAL, signify, mean, amount to, add up to, constitute; portend, augur, herald, bode, promise; involve; *poetic/literary* betoken, foretoken, forebode.
– PHRASES **spell something out** EXPLAIN, make clear, make plain, elucidate, clarify; specify, itemize, detail, enumerate, list, expound, particularize, catalogue.

spell[2] ● noun **1** *the witch recited a spell* INCANTATION, charm, conjuration, formula; (**spells**) magic, sorcery, witchcraft; *N. Amer.* hex. **2** *she surrendered to his spell* INFLUENCE, (animal) magnetism, charisma, allure, lure, charm, attraction, enticement; magic, romance, mystique.
– PHRASES **cast a spell on** BEWITCH, enchant, entrance; curse, jinx, witch; *N. Amer.* hex.

spell[3] ● noun **1** *a spell of dry weather* PERIOD, time, interval, season, stretch, run, course, streak; *Brit. informal* patch. **2** *a spell of dizziness* BOUT, fit, attack.

spellbinding ● adjective FASCINATING, enthralling, entrancing, bewitching, captivating, riveting, engrossing, gripping, absorbing, compelling, compulsive, mesmerizing, hypnotic; *informal* unputdownable.
– OPPOSITES boring.

spellbound ● adjective ENTHRALLED, fascinated, rapt, riveted, transfixed, gripped, captivated, bewitched, enchanted, mesmerized, hypnotized; *informal* hooked.

spend ● verb **1** *she spent £185 on shoes* PAY OUT, dish out, expend, disburse; squander, waste, fritter away; lavish; *informal* fork out, lay out, shell out, cough up, blow, splash out, splurge; *Brit. informal* stump up, blue; *N. Amer. informal* pony up. **2** *the morning was spent gardening* PASS, occupy, fill, take up, while away. **3** *I've spent hours on this essay* PUT IN, devote; waste. **4** *the storm had spent its force* USE UP, consume, exhaust, deplete, drain.

spendthrift ● noun *he is such spendthrift* PROFLIGATE, prodigal, squanderer, waster; *informal* big spender.
– OPPOSITES miser.
● adjective *his spendthrift father* PROFLIGATE, improvident, thriftless, wasteful, extravagant, prodigal.
– OPPOSITES frugal.

spent ● adjective **1** *a spent force* USED UP, consumed, exhausted, finished, depleted, drained; *informal* burnt out. **2** *that's enough — I'm spent* EXHAUSTED, tired (out), weary, worn out, dog-tired, on one's last legs, drained, fatigued, ready to drop; *informal* done in, all in, dead on one's feet, dead beat, bushed, wiped out, frazzled; *Brit. informal* knackered, whacked; *N. Amer. informal* pooped, tuckered out.

spew ● verb **1** *factories spewed out yellow smoke* EMIT, discharge, eject, expel, belch out, pour out, spout, gush, spurt, disgorge. **2** (*informal*) *he wanted to spew.* See VOMIT verb sense 1.

sphere ● noun **1** *a glass sphere* GLOBE, ball, orb, spheroid, globule, round; bubble. **2** *our sphere of influence* AREA, field, compass, orbit; range, scope, extent. **3** *the sphere of foreign affairs* DOMAIN,

– DERIVATIVES **spherular** adjective.
sphincter /sfingktər/ ● noun Anatomy a ring of muscle surrounding and serving to guard or close an opening such as the anus.
– ORIGIN Greek *sphinktēr*, from *sphingein* 'bind tight'.
sphinx ● noun **1** an ancient Egyptian stone figure having a lion's body and a human or animal head. **2** an enigmatic or inscrutable person.
– ORIGIN originally denoting a winged monster in Greek mythology, having a woman's head and a lion's body, who propounded a riddle and killed those who failed to solve it: from Greek, apparently from *sphingein* 'draw tight'.
sphygmomanometer /sfigmōmənommitər/ ● noun an instrument for measuring blood pressure, consisting of an inflatable rubber cuff which is applied to the arm and connected to a column of mercury next to a graduated scale.
– DERIVATIVES **sphygmomanometry** noun.
– ORIGIN from Greek *sphugmos* 'pulse'.
spic ● noun US informal, offensive a Spanish-speaking person from Central or South America or the Caribbean, especially a Mexican.
– ORIGIN perhaps from *speak the* in 'no speak the English'.
spic and span ● adjective variant spelling of SPICK AND SPAN.
spiccato /spikaatō/ ● noun Music a style of staccato playing on stringed instruments involving bouncing the bow on the strings.
– ORIGIN Italian, 'detailed, distinct'.
spice ● noun **1** an aromatic or pungent vegetable substance used to flavour food. **2** an element providing interest and excitement. ● verb **1** flavour with spice. **2** (**spice up**) make more exciting or interesting.
– ORIGIN Old French *espice*, from Latin *species* 'sort, kind', later 'wares'.
spick and span (also **spic and span**) ● adjective neat, clean, and well looked after.
– ORIGIN originally in the sense 'brand new': from *spick and span new*, from Old Norse words meaning 'chip' + 'new'; also influenced by Dutch *spiksplinternieuw* 'splinter new'.
spicule /spikyōōl/ ● noun **1** chiefly Zoology a small needle-like structure, in particular any of those making up the skeleton of a sponge. **2** Astronomy a short-lived jet of gas in the sun's corona.
– DERIVATIVES **spicular** adjective.
– ORIGIN Latin *spicula* 'little ear of grain'.
spicy (also **spicey**) ● adjective (**spicier**, **spiciest**) **1** strongly flavoured with spice. **2** mildly indecent.
– DERIVATIVES **spicily** adverb **spiciness** noun.
spider ● noun **1** an eight-legged predatory arachnid with an unsegmented body consisting of a fused head and thorax and a rounded abdomen, most kinds of which spin webs in which to capture insects. **2** Billiards & Snooker a long-legged rest for a cue that can be placed over a ball without touching it. ● verb **1** move in a scuttling manner suggestive of a spider. **2** form a pattern suggestive of a spider or its web.
– ORIGIN Old English, from a word meaning 'to spin'.
spider crab ● noun a crab with long thin legs and a compact pear-shaped body.
spider mite ● noun a plant-feeding mite resembling a minute spider.
spider monkey ● noun a South American monkey with very long limbs and a long prehensile tail.
spider plant ● noun a plant of the lily family having long narrow leaves with a central yellow stripe, popular as a house plant.
spidery ● adjective resembling a spider, especially having long, thin, angular lines like a spider's legs.
spiel /shpeel, speel/ informal ● noun an elaborate and glib speech or story, such as that used by a salesperson. ● verb speak or reel off at length or glibly.
– ORIGIN German, 'a game'.
spieler ● noun informal **1** a glib or voluble speaker. **2** Austral./NZ a gambler or swindler. **3** a gambling club.
spiff ● verb (**spiff up**) informal make smart or stylish.
– ORIGIN perhaps from dialect *spiff* 'well dressed, a well-dressed man'.
spiffing ● adjective Brit. informal, dated excellent; splendid.
– ORIGIN of unknown origin.
spiffy ● adjective (**spiffier**, **spiffiest**) N. Amer. informal smart or stylish.
– DERIVATIVES **spiffily** adverb.
spigot /spiggət/ ● noun **1** a small peg or plug, especially for insertion into the vent of a cask. **2** US a tap. **3** the plain end of a section of a pipe fitting into the socket of the next one.
– ORIGIN perhaps from Provençal *espigou*, from Latin *spiculum* 'little ear of corn'.
spike[1] ● noun **1** a thin, pointed piece of metal or wood. **2** each of several metal points set into the sole of a sports shoe to prevent slipping. **3** chiefly Brit. a pointed metal rod fixed to a base, used for impaling and storing notes or papers. **4** a sharp increase in magnitude or intensity. ● verb **1** impale on or pierce with or as with a spike. **2** form into or cover with sharp points. **3** put an end to (a plan or undertaking). **4** informal surreptitiously lace (drink or food) with alcohol or a drug. **5** increase and then decrease sharply.
– ORIGIN perhaps from Low German, Dutch *spiker*, related to SPOKE[1]; sense 3 of the verb derives from the editorial practice of rejecting submitted news stories by filing them on a spike.
spike[2] ● noun Botany a flower cluster formed of many flower heads attached directly to a long stem.
– ORIGIN originally denoting an ear of corn: from Latin *spica*.
spikelet ● noun Botany the basic unit of a grass flower, consisting of two outer bracts at the base and one or more florets above.
spikenard /spīknaard/ ● noun a Himalayan plant of which the rhizome was used in ancient times to make a highly valued perfumed ointment.
– ORIGIN from Latin *spica* 'spike' + Greek *nardos* 'spikenard'.
spiky ● adjective (**spikier**, **spikiest**) **1** like a spike or spikes or having many spikes. **2** informal easily annoyed; irritable.
– DERIVATIVES **spikily** adverb **spikiness** noun.
spile /spīl/ ● noun **1** a small wooden peg or spigot. **2** a large, heavy timber driven into the ground to support a superstructure.
– ORIGIN Dutch, Low German; sense 2 is apparently from PILE[2].
spill[1] ● verb (past and past part. **spilt** or **spilled**) **1** flow or cause to flow over the edge of a container. **2** move or empty out from a place. **3** informal reveal (confidential information). ● noun **1** an instance of a liquid spilling or the quantity spilt. **2** a fall from a horse or bicycle. **3** Austral. a vacating of posts in a cabinet or parliamentary party to allow reorganization after one important change of office.
– PHRASES **spill the beans** informal reveal secret information unintentionally or indiscreetly. **spill blood** kill or wound people.
– DERIVATIVES **spillage** noun **spiller** noun.
– ORIGIN Old English, 'kill, waste, shed (blood)'.
spill[2] ● noun a thin strip of wood or paper used for lighting a fire.
– ORIGIN originally in the sense 'sharp fragment of wood': related to SPILE.

Thesaurus

realm, province, field, area, territory, arena, department.
spherical ● adjective ROUND, globular, globose, globoid, globe-shaped, spheroidal, spheric; *poetic/literary* orbicular.
spice ● noun **1** *the spices in curry powder* SEASONING, flavouring, condiment. **2** *the risk added spice to their affair* EXCITEMENT, interest, colour, piquancy, zest; an edge; *informal* a kick; *poetic/literary* salt.
– PHRASES **spice something up** ENLIVEN, make more exciting, vitalize, perk up, put some life into, ginger up, galvanize, electrify, boost; *informal* pep up, jazz up, buck up.
spick and span ● adjective NEAT, tidy, orderly, well kept, shipshape (and Bristol fashion), in apple-pie order; immaculate, uncluttered, trim, spruce; spotless.
– OPPOSITES untidy.
spicy ● adjective **1** *a spicy casserole* PIQUANT, tangy, peppery, hot, picante; spiced, seasoned; tasty, flavoursome, zesty, strong, pungent. **2** *spicy stories* ENTERTAINING, colourful, lively, spirited, exciting, piquant, zesty; risqué, racy, scandalous, ribald, titillating, bawdy, naughty, salacious, dirty, smutty; *informal* raunchy, juicy; *Brit. informal* saucy, fruity; *N. Amer. informal* gamy.
– OPPOSITES bland, boring.
spiel ● noun *(informal)* SPEECH, patter, (sales) pitch, talk; monologue; rigmarole, story, saga.
spike ● noun **1** *a metal spike* PRONG, barb, point; skewer, stake, spit; tine, pin; spur; *Mountaineering* piton. **2** *the spikes of a cactus* THORN, spine, prickle, bristle; *Zoology* spicule.
● verb **1** *she spiked an oyster* IMPALE, spear, skewer; pierce, penetrate, perforate, stab, stick, transfix; *poetic/literary* transpierce. **2** *(informal) his drink was spiked with drugs* ADULTERATE, contaminate,

spillikin /spillikin/ ● noun **1** (**spillikins**) (treated as sing.) a game played with a heap of small rods of wood, bone, or plastic, in which players try to remove one at a time without disturbing the others. **2** a splinter or fragment.
– ORIGIN from SPILL².

spilt past and past participle of SPILL¹.

spin ● verb (**spinning**; past and past part. **spun**) **1** turn round quickly. **2** (of a person's head) give a sensation of dizziness. **3** (with reference to a ball) move through the air with a revolving motion. **4** draw out and twist (the fibres of wool, cotton, etc.) to convert them into yarn. **5** (of a spider or a silkworm or other insect) produce (gossamer or silk) or construct (a web or cocoon) by extruding a fine thread from a special gland. **6** (**spin out**) make (something) last as long as possible. ● noun **1** a spinning motion. **2** informal a brief trip in a vehicle for pleasure. **3** a favourable bias or slant given to a news story. **4** Austral./NZ informal a piece of good or bad luck.
– PHRASES **flat spin 1** a spin in which an aircraft descends in tight circles while remaining horizontal. **2** Brit. informal a state of agitation. **spin a yarn** tell a far-fetched story.
– ORIGIN Old English.

spina bifida /spinə biffidə/ ● noun a congenital defect in which part of the spinal cord is exposed through a gap in the backbone, and which can cause paralysis and other problems.
– ORIGIN Latin, from *spina* 'backbone, thorn' + *bifidus* 'doubly split'.

spinach ● noun a plant with large dark green leaves which are eaten as a vegetable.
– ORIGIN probably from Old French *espinache*, from Persian.

spinach beet ● noun beet of a variety cultivated for its spinach-like leaves.

spinal ● adjective relating to the spine.
– DERIVATIVES **spinally** adverb.

spinal column ● noun the spine.

spinal cord ● noun the cylindrical bundle of nerve fibres which is enclosed in the spine and connected to the brain, with which it forms the central nervous system.

spinal tap ● noun North American term for LUMBAR PUNCTURE.

spindle ● noun **1** a slender rounded rod with tapered ends, used in hand spinning to twist and wind fibres from a mass of wool, flax, etc. held on a distaff. **2** a rod or pin serving as an axis that revolves or on which something revolves. **3** a turned piece of wood used as a banister or chair leg.
– ORIGIN Old English, from SPIN.

spindle-shanks ● plural noun informal, dated **1** long thin legs. **2** (treated as sing.) a person with such legs.

spindly ● adjective long or tall and thin.

spin doctor ● noun informal a spokesperson for a political party or politician employed to give a favourable interpretation of events to the media.

spindrift ● noun **1** spray blown from the crests of waves by the wind. **2** driving snow.
– ORIGIN from archaic *spoondrift*, from *spoon* 'run before wind or sea' + DRIFT.

spin dryer ● noun a machine for extracting water from wet clothes by spinning them in a revolving perforated drum.

spine ● noun **1** a series of vertebrae extending from the skull to the small of the back, enclosing the spinal cord and providing support for the thorax and abdomen; the backbone. **2** a central feature or main source of strength. **3** the part of a book that encloses the inner edges of the pages. **4** chiefly Zoology & Botany a prickle or other hard pointed projection or structure.
– ORIGIN Latin *spina* 'thorn, backbone'.

spine-chiller ● noun a story or film that inspires terror and excitement.
– DERIVATIVES **spine-chilling** adjective.

spinel /spinel/ ● noun a hard glassy mineral consisting chiefly of magnesium and aluminium oxides.
– ORIGIN Italian *spinella* 'little thorn'.

spineless ● adjective **1** having no spine; invertebrate. **2** (of an animal or plant) lacking spines. **3** lacking courage and determination.
– DERIVATIVES **spinelessly** adverb **spinelessness** noun.

spinet /spinet, spinnit/ ● noun **1** a small harpsichord with the strings set obliquely to the keyboard, popular in the 18th century. **2** US a type of small upright piano.
– ORIGIN Italian *spinetta* 'virginal, spinet', from Latin *spina* 'thorn, spine, quill' (the strings of the instrument being plucked by quills).

spine-tingling ● adjective informal thrilling or pleasurably frightening.

spinifex /spinnifeks/ ● noun a grass with spiny flower heads which break off and are blown about, occurring from east Asia to Australia.
– ORIGIN Latin, from *spina* 'thorn'.

spinnaker /spinnikər/ ● noun a large three-cornered sail set forward of the mainsail of a racing yacht when running before the wind.
– ORIGIN apparently from *Sphinx*, the yacht first using such a sail, perhaps influenced by *spanker*, a fore-and-aft sail.

spinner ● noun **1** a person occupied in spinning thread. **2** Cricket a bowler who is expert in spinning the ball. **3** (also **spinnerbait**) Fishing a lure designed to revolve when pulled through the water.

spinneret /spinnəret/ ● noun **1** Zoology any of a number of different organs through which the silk, gossamer, or thread of spiders, silkworms, and certain other insects is produced. **2** (in the production of man-made fibres) a cap or plate with a number of small holes through which a fibre-forming solution is forced.

spinney ● noun (pl. **spinneys**) Brit. a small area of trees and bushes.
– ORIGIN Old French *espinei*, from Latin *spinetum* 'thicket'.

spinning jenny ● noun historical a machine for spinning with more than one spindle at a time.

spinning top ● noun see TOP².

Thesaurus

S

drug, lace; *informal* dope, doctor, cut.

spill ● verb **1** *Kevin spilled his drink* KNOCK OVER, tip over, upset, overturn. **2** *the bath water spilled on to the floor* OVERFLOW, flow, pour, run, slop, slosh, splash; leak, escape; *archaic* overbrim. **3** *students spilled out of the building* STREAM, pour, surge, swarm, flood, throng, crowd. **4** *the horse spilled his rider* UNSEAT, throw, dislodge, unhorse. **5** *(informal) he's spilling out his troubles to her* REVEAL, disclose, divulge, blurt out, babble, betray, tell; *informal* blab.
● noun **1** *an oil spill* SPILLAGE, leak, leakage, overflow, flood. **2** *he took a spill in the opening race* FALL, tumble; *informal* header, cropper, nosedive.
– PHRASES **spill the beans** *(informal)* REVEAL ALL, tell all, give the game away, talk; *informal* let the cat out of the bag, blab, come clean.

spin ● verb **1** *the bike wheels are spinning* REVOLVE, rotate, turn, go round, whirl, gyrate, circle. **2** *she spun round to face him* WHIRL, wheel, twirl, turn, swing, twist, swivel, pirouette, pivot. **3** *her head was spinning* REEL, whirl, go round, swim. **4** *she spun me a yarn* TELL, recount, relate, narrate; weave, concoct, invent, fabricate, make up.
– RELATED TERMS rotary.
● noun **1** *a spin of the wheel* ROTATION, revolution, turn, whirl, twirl, gyration. **2** *a positive spin on the campaign* SLANT, angle, twist, bias. **3** *(informal) a spin in the car* TRIP, jaunt, outing, excursion, journey; drive, ride, run, turn, airing; *informal* tootle; *Scottish informal* hurl.
– PHRASES **in a flat spin** *(Brit. informal)*. See AGITATED. **spin something out** PROLONG, protract, draw out, drag out, string out, extend, carry on, continue; fill out, pad out; *archaic* wire-draw.

spindle ● noun pivot, pin, rod, axle, capstan; axis.

spindly ● adjective **1** *he was pale and spindly* LANKY, thin, skinny, lean, spare, gangling, gangly, scrawny, bony, rangy, angular; *dated* spindle-shanked. **2** *spindly chairs* RICKETY, flimsy, wobbly, shaky.
– OPPOSITES stocky.

spine ● noun **1** *he injured his spine* BACKBONE, spinal column, vertebral column; back; *technical* rachis. **2** *the spine of his philosophy* CORE, centre, cornerstone, foundation, basis. **3** *the spines of a hedgehog* NEEDLE, quill, bristle, barb, spike, prickle; thorn; *technical* spicule.
– RELATED TERMS vertebral.

spine-chilling ● adjective TERRIFYING, blood-curdling, petrifying, hair-raising, frightening, scaring, chilling, horrifying, fearsome; eerie, sinister, ghostly; *Scottish* eldritch; *informal* scary, creepy, spooky.
– OPPOSITES comforting, reassuring.

spineless ● adjective WEAK, weak-willed, weak-kneed, feeble, soft, ineffectual, irresolute, indecisive; COWARDLY, timid, timorous, fearful, faint-hearted, pusillanimous, craven, unmanly, namby-pamby, lily-livered, chicken-hearted; *informal* wimpish, wimpy,

spinning wheel ● noun an apparatus for spinning yarn or thread with a spindle driven by a wheel attached to a crank or treadle.
spin-off ● noun **1** a product or incidental benefit produced during or after a primary activity. **2** a subsidiary of a parent company that has been sold off, creating a new company.
spinster ● noun chiefly derogatory an unmarried woman, typically an older woman beyond the usual age for marriage.
– DERIVATIVES **spinsterhood** noun **spinsterish** adjective.
– ORIGIN originally in the sense 'woman who spins'.
spiny ● adjective (**spinier**, **spiniest**) **1** full of or covered with prickles. **2** informal difficult to understand or handle.
– DERIVATIVES **spininess** noun.
spiny anteater ● noun another term for ECHIDNA.
spiracle /spīrək'l/ ● noun Zoology an external respiratory opening in insects, cartilaginous fish, and other animals.
– DERIVATIVES **spiracular** adjective.
– ORIGIN Latin *spiraculum*, from *spirare* 'breathe'.
spiraea /spīreeə/ (chiefly US also **spirea**) ● noun a shrub with clusters of small white or pink flowers.
– ORIGIN Greek *speiraia*, from *speira* 'a coil'.
spiral ● adjective winding in a continuous curve around a central point or axis. ● noun **1** a spiral curve, shape, or pattern. **2** a progressive rise or fall of prices, wages, etc., each responding to an upward or downward stimulus provided by a previous one. **3** a process of progressive deterioration. ● verb (**spiralled**, **spiralling**; US **spiraled**, **spiraling**) **1** take or cause to follow a spiral course. **2** show a continuous and dramatic increase or decrease.
– DERIVATIVES **spirally** adverb.
– ORIGIN Latin *spiralis*, from Greek *speira* 'a coil'.
spiral-bound ● adjective (of a book or notepad) bound with a spiral wire threaded through a row of holes along one edge.
spire ● noun a tapering conical or pyramidal structure on the top of a building, especially a church tower.
– ORIGIN Old English, 'tall slender stem of a plant'.
spirea ● noun chiefly US variant spelling of SPIRAEA.
spirit ● noun **1** a person's non-physical being, composed of their character and emotions. **2** this regarded as surviving after the death of the body, often manifested as a ghost. **3** a supernatural being. **4** the prevailing or typical character, quality, or mood: *the nation's egalitarian spirit.* **5** (**spirits**) a person's mood. **6** courage, energy, and determination. **7** the real meaning or intention of something as opposed to its strict verbal interpretation. **8** chiefly Brit. strong distilled liquor such as rum. **9** a volatile liquid, especially a fuel, prepared by distillation. ● verb (**spirited**, **spiriting**) (**spirit away**) convey rapidly and secretly.
– PHRASES **in spirit** in thought or intention though not physically. **when the spirit moves someone** when someone feels inclined to do something.
– ORIGIN Latin *spiritus* 'breath, spirit', from *spirare* 'breathe'.
spirited ● adjective **1** full of energy, enthusiasm, and determination. **2** having a specified character or mood: *a generous-spirited man.*
– DERIVATIVES **spiritedly** adverb **spiritedness** noun.
spirit gum ● noun a quick-drying solution of gum, chiefly used by actors to attach false hair to their faces.
spirit lamp ● noun a lamp burning methylated or other volatile spirits instead of oil.
spiritless ● adjective lacking courage, energy, or determination.
– DERIVATIVES **spiritlessly** adverb **spiritlessness** noun.
spirit level ● noun a device consisting of a sealed glass tube partially filled with alcohol or other liquid, containing an air bubble whose position reveals whether a surface is perfectly level.
spiritual /spirrityooəl/ ● adjective **1** relating to or affecting the human spirit as opposed to material or physical things. **2** relating to religion or religious belief. ● noun (also **negro spiritual**) a religious song of a kind associated with black Christians of the southern US.
– DERIVATIVES **spirituality** noun **spiritualize** (also **spiritualise**) verb **spiritually** adverb.
spiritualism ● noun a system of belief and practice based on supposed communication with the spirits of the dead, especially through mediums.
– DERIVATIVES **spiritualist** noun **spiritualistic** adjective.
spirituous /spirrityooəss/ ● adjective formal or archaic containing much alcohol.
spirogyra /spīrəjīrə/ ● noun Botany algae of a genus found in blanket weed, consisting of long green filaments.
– ORIGIN from Greek *speira* 'coil' + *guros* 'round'.
spirometer /spīrommitər/ ● noun an instrument for measuring the air capacity of the lungs.
– DERIVATIVES **spirometry** noun.
spit[1] ● verb (**spitting**; past and past part. **spat** or **spit**) **1** eject saliva forcibly from one's mouth. **2** forcibly eject (food or liquid) from one's mouth. **3** say in a hostile way. **4** (of a fire or something being cooked) emit small bursts of sparks or hot fat with a series of explosive noises. **5** (**it spits, it is spitting**, etc.) Brit. light rain falls. ● noun **1** saliva. **2** an act of spitting.
– PHRASES **be the spitting image of** (or **be the spit of**) informal look exactly like. [ORIGIN originally as *the spit of* or *the spit and image of*: perhaps from the idea of a person apparently being formed from the spit of another, so great is the similarity be-

Thesaurus

sissy, chicken, yellow, yellow-bellied, gutless; *Brit. informal* wet.
– OPPOSITES bold, brave, strong-willed.
spiny ● adjective PRICKLY, spiky, thorny, bristly, bristled, spiked, barbed, scratchy, sharp; *technical* spinose, spinous.
spiral ● adjective *a spiral column of smoke* COILED, helical, corkscrew, curling, winding, twisting, whorled; *technical* voluted, helicoid, helicoidal.
● noun *a spiral of smoke* COIL, helix, corkscrew, curl, twist, gyre, whorl, scroll; *technical* volute, volution.
● verb **1** *smoke spiralled up* COIL, wind, swirl, twist, wreathe, snake, gyrate; *poetic/literary* gyre. **2** *prices spiralled* SOAR, shoot up, rocket, increase rapidly, rise rapidly, escalate, climb; *informal* skyrocket, go through the roof. **3** *the economy is spiralling downward* DETERIORATE, decline, degenerate, worsen, get worse; *informal* go downhill, take a nosedive, go to pot, go to the dogs, hit the skids, go down the tubes.
– OPPOSITES fall, improve.
spire ● noun STEEPLE, flèche.
spirit ● noun **1** *harmony between body and spirit* SOUL, psyche, (inner) self, inner being, inner man/woman, mind, ego, id; *Philosophy* pneuma. **2** *a spirit haunts the island* GHOST, phantom, spectre, apparition, wraith, presence; *informal* spook; *poetic/literary* shade. **3** *that's the spirit* ATTITUDE, frame of mind, way of thinking, point of view, outlook, thoughts, ideas. **4** *she was in good spirits when I left* MOOD, frame of mind, state of mind, emotional state, humour, temper. **5** *team spirit* MORALE, esprit de corps. **6** *the spirit of the age* ETHOS, prevailing tendency, motivating force, essence, quintessence; atmosphere, mood, feeling, climate; attitudes, beliefs, principles, standards, ethics. **7** *his spirit never failed him* COURAGE, bravery, pluck, valour, strength of character, fortitude, backbone, mettle, stout-heartedness, determination, resolution, resolve, fight, grit; *informal* guts, spunk; *Brit. informal* bottle; *N. Amer. informal* sand, moxie. **8** *they played with great spirit* ENTHUSIASM, eagerness, keenness, liveliness, vitality, vivaciousness, animation, energy, verve, vigour, dynamism, zest, dash, elan, panache, sparkle, exuberance, gusto, brio, pep, fervour, zeal, fire, passion; *informal* get-up-and-go. **9** *the spirit of the law* REAL/TRUE MEANING, true intention, essence, substance. **10** *he drinks spirits* STRONG LIQUOR/DRINK; *informal* hard stuff, firewater, hooch; *Brit. informal* short.
– OPPOSITES body, flesh.
– PHRASES **spirit someone/something away** WHISK AWAY/OFF, vanish with, make off with, make someone/something disappear, run away with, abscond with, carry off, steal someone/something away, abduct, kidnap, snatch, seize.
spirited ● adjective LIVELY, vivacious, vibrant, full of life, vital, animated, high-spirited, sparkling, sprightly, energetic, active, vigorous, dynamic, dashing, enthusiastic, passionate; determined, resolute, purposeful; *informal* feisty, spunky, have-a-go, gutsy; *N. Amer. informal* peppy.
– OPPOSITES timid, apathetic, lifeless.
spiritless ● adjective APATHETIC, passive, unenthusiastic, lifeless, listless, weak, feeble, spineless, languid, bloodless, insipid, characterless, submissive, meek, irresolute, indecisive; lacklustre, flat, colourless, passionless, uninspired, wooden, dry, anaemic, vapid, dull, boring, wishy-washy.
– OPPOSITES spirited, lively.
spiritual ● adjective **1** *your spiritual self* NON-MATERIAL, incorporeal, intangible; inner, mental, psychological; transcendent, ethereal, other-worldly, mystic, mystical, metaphysical; *rare* extramundane. **2** *spiritual writings* RELIGIOUS, sacred, divine, holy, non-secular,

tween them.] **spit and polish** thorough cleaning and polishing. **spit-and-sawdust** Brit. informal (of a pub) that appears dirty or run-down. **spit blood** (or Austral. **chips**) feel or express vehement anger. **spit in the eye** (or **face**) **of** show contempt or scorn for. **spit it out** informal (as a command) say it quickly; stop hesitating.
– DERIVATIVES **spitter** noun.
– ORIGIN Old English.
spit² ● noun **1** a long, thin metal rod pushed through meat in order to hold and turn it while it is roasted. **2** a narrow point of land projecting into the sea. ● verb (**spitted, spitting**) put a spit through (meat).
– ORIGIN Old English.
spit³ ● noun (pl. same or **spits**) a layer of earth whose depth is equal to the length of the blade of a spade.
– ORIGIN Dutch and Low German; probably related to SPIT².
spitball N. Amer. ● noun a ball of chewed paper used as a missile. ● verb informal throw out (a suggestion) for discussion.
– DERIVATIVES **spitballer** noun.
spite ● noun a desire to hurt, annoy, or offend. ● verb deliberately hurt, annoy, or offend.
– PHRASES **in spite of** without being affected by. **in spite of oneself** although one did not want or expect to do so.
– ORIGIN Old French *despit* 'contempt'.
spiteful ● adjective showing or caused by malice.
– DERIVATIVES **spitefully** adverb **spitefulness** noun.
spitfire ● noun a person with a fierce temper.
spit-roasted ● adjective cooked on a spit.
spittle ● noun saliva, especially as ejected from the mouth.
– ORIGIN dialect *spattle*, altered by association with SPIT¹.
spittoon /spitoon/ ● noun a container for spitting into.
spiv ● noun Brit. informal a flashily dressed man who makes a living by disreputable dealings.
– DERIVATIVES **spivvish** adjective **spivvy** adjective.
– ORIGIN perhaps related to SPIFFY.
splash ● verb **1** (with reference to a liquid) fall or cause to fall in scattered drops. **2** make wet or cover with scattered drops. **3** strike or move around in water, causing it to fly about. **4** (**splash down**) (of a spacecraft) land on water. **5** display (a story or photograph) in a prominent place in a newspaper or magazine. **6** (**splash out**) Brit. informal spend money freely. ● noun **1** an instance or sound of splashing. **2** a small quantity of liquid that has splashed on to a surface. **3** a small quantity of liquid added to a drink. **4** a bright patch of colour. **5** informal a prominent news feature or story.
– PHRASES **make a splash** informal attract a great deal of attention.
– DERIVATIVES **splashy** adjective (**splashier, splashiest**).
– ORIGIN from PLASH.
splashback ● noun Brit. a panel behind a sink or cooker that protects the wall from splashes.
splat¹ ● noun a piece of thin wood in the centre of a chair back.
– ORIGIN from obsolete *splat* 'split up'.
splat² informal ● noun a sound of something soft and wet or heavy striking a surface. ● verb (**splatted, splatting**) hit or land with a splat.
– ORIGIN from SPLATTER.
splatter ● verb splash with a sticky or viscous liquid. ● noun **1** a splash of a sticky or viscous liquid. **2** (before another noun) informal (of a film or genre of film) featuring many violent and gruesome deaths.
– ORIGIN imitative.
splatterpunk ● noun informal a literary genre characterized by the explicit description of horrific, violent, or pornographic scenes.
splay ● verb **1** spread or be spread out or further apart. **2** construct (a window, doorway, or other aperture) so that it is wider at one side of the wall than the other. ● noun **1** a tapered widening. **2** a surface making an oblique angle with another. ● adjective turned outward or widened.
– ORIGIN originally in the sense 'unfold to view': shortening of DISPLAY.
splay-footed ● adjective having a broad flat foot turned outward.
spleen ● noun **1** an abdominal organ involved in the production and removal of blood cells and forming part of the immune system. **2** bad temper; spite.
– ORIGIN Greek *splēn*; sense 2 derives from the former belief that the spleen was the seat of bad temper.
splendid ● adjective **1** magnificent; very impressive. **2** informal excellent.
– DERIVATIVES **splendidly** adverb.
– ORIGIN Latin *splendidus*, from *splendere* 'shine'.
splendiferous ● adjective informal, humorous splendid.
splendour (US **splendor**) ● noun magnificent and impressive appearance.
splenetic /splinettik/ ● adjective bad-tempered or spiteful.

Thesaurus

church, ecclesiastical, devotional.
– OPPOSITES physical, secular.
spit¹ ● verb **1** *Cranston coughed and spat* EXPECTORATE, hawk; *Brit. informal* gob. **2** *'Go to hell,' she spat* SNAP, say angrily, hiss. **3** *the fat began to spit* SIZZLE, hiss; crackle, sputter. **4** *(Brit.) it began to spit* RAIN LIGHTLY, drizzle, spot; *N. English* mizzle; *N. Amer.* sprinkle.
● noun **1** *spit dribbled from his mouth* SPITTLE, saliva, sputum, slobber, dribble; *Brit. informal* gob. **2** *(informal) he is the spit of his father* EXACT LIKENESS, image, very/living image, double, twin, lookalike, duplicate, copy, Doppelgänger; *informal* spitting image, ringer, dead ringer.
spit² ● noun *chicken cooked on a spit* SKEWER, brochette, rotisserie.
spite ● noun *he said it out of spite* MALICE, malevolence, ill will, vindictiveness, vengefulness, revenge, malignity, evil intentions, animus, enmity; *informal* bitchiness, cattiness; *poetic/literary* maleficence.
– OPPOSITES benevolence.
● verb *he did it to spite me* UPSET, hurt, make miserable, grieve, distress, wound, pain, torment, injure.
– OPPOSITES please.
– PHRASES **in spite of** DESPITE, notwithstanding, regardless of, for all; undeterred by, in defiance of, in the face of; even though, although.
spiteful ● adjective MALICIOUS, malevolent, evil-intentioned, vindictive, vengeful, malign, mean, nasty, hurtful, mischievous, wounding, cruel, unkind; *informal* bitchy, catty; *poetic/literary* malefic, maleficent.
– OPPOSITES benevolent.
splash ● verb **1** *splash your face with cool water* SPRINKLE, spray, shower, splatter, slosh, slop, squirt; daub; wet. **2** *his boots were splashed with mud* SPATTER, bespatter, splatter, speck, speckle, blotch, smear, stain, mark; *Scottish & Irish* slabber; *informal* splotch, splodge; *poetic/literary* bedabble. **3** *waves splashed on the beach* SWASH, wash, break, lap; dash, beat, lash, batter, crash, buffet; *poetic/literary* plash. **4** *children splashed in the water* PADDLE, wade, slosh; wallow; *informal* splosh. **5** *the story was splashed across the front pages* BLAZON, display, spread, plaster, trumpet, publicize; *informal* splatter.
● noun **1** *a splash of fat on his shirt* SPOT, blob, dab, daub, smudge, smear, speck, fleck; mark, stain; *informal* splotch, splodge. **2** *a splash of lemonade* DROP, dash, bit, spot, soupçon, dribble, driblet; *Scottish informal* scoosh. **3** *a splash of colour* PATCH, burst, streak.
– PHRASES **make a splash** *(informal)* CAUSE A SENSATION, cause a stir, attract attention, draw attention to oneself/itself, get noticed, make an impression, make an impact. **splash out** *(Brit. informal)* BE EXTRAVAGANT, go on a spending spree, spare no expense, spend lavishly; *informal* lash out, splurge; *Brit. informal* push the boat out.
spleen ● noun BAD TEMPER, bad mood, ill temper, ill humour, anger, wrath, vexation, annoyance, irritation, displeasure, dissatisfaction, resentment, rancour; spite, ill feeling, malice, maliciousness, bitterness, animosity, antipathy, hostility, malevolence, venom, gall, malignance, malignity, acrimony, bile, hatred, hate; *poetic/literary* ire, choler.
– OPPOSITES good humour.
splendid ● adjective **1** *splendid costumes* MAGNIFICENT, sumptuous, grand, impressive, imposing, superb, spectacular, resplendent, opulent, luxurious, de luxe, rich, fine, costly, expensive, lavish, ornate, gorgeous, glorious, dazzling, elegant, handsome, beautiful; stately, majestic, princely, noble, proud, palatial; *informal* plush, posh, swanky, ritzy, splendiferous; *Brit. informal* swish; *N. Amer. informal* swank; *poetic/literary* brave. **2** *(informal) we had a splendid holiday* EXCELLENT, wonderful, marvellous, superb, glorious, sublime, lovely, delightful, first-class, first-rate; *informal* super, great, amazing, fantastic, terrific, tremendous, phenomenal, sensational, heavenly, gorgeous, dreamy, grand, fabulous, fab, awesome, magic, ace, cool, mean, bad, wicked, mega, crucial, far out, A1, sound, out of this world; *Brit. informal* smashing, brilliant, brill; *N. Amer. informal* dandy, neat; *Austral./NZ informal* beaut, bonzer; *black English* def; *informal, dated* divine, capital; *Brit. informal, dated* champion, wizard, rip-

S

– ORIGIN Latin *spleneticus*, from Greek *splēn* 'spleen'.
splenic /splennik, spleenik/ ● adjective relating to the spleen.
splice ● verb **1** join (a rope or ropes) by interweaving the strands at the ends. **2** join (pieces of timber, film, or tape) at the ends. **3** Genetics join or insert (a gene or gene fragment). ● noun a spliced join.
– PHRASES **get spliced** informal get married. **splice the main brace** Brit. historical (in the navy) serve out an extra tot of rum.
– DERIVATIVES **splicer** noun.
– ORIGIN probably from Dutch *splissen*.
spliff ● noun informal a cannabis cigarette.
– ORIGIN of unknown origin.
spline ● noun a rectangular key fitting into grooves in the hub and shaft of a wheel. ● verb secure by means of a spline.
– ORIGIN perhaps related to SPLINTER.
splint ● noun **1** a strip of rigid material for supporting a broken bone when it has been set. **2** a long, thin strip of wood used in basketwork or to light a fire. ● verb secure with a splint or splints.
– ORIGIN Dutch, Low German *splinte* 'metal plate or pin'.
splinter ● noun a small, thin, sharp piece of wood, glass, etc. broken off from a larger piece. ● verb break into splinters.
– DERIVATIVES **splintery** adjective.
– ORIGIN Dutch.
splinter group ● noun a small organization that has broken away from a larger one.
split ● verb (**splitting**; past and past part. **split**) **1** break forcibly into parts. **2** divide into parts or groups. **3** (often **split up**) end a marriage or other relationship. **4** (**be splitting**) informal (of one's head) suffering great pain from a headache. **5** (**split on**) Brit. informal betray the secrets of or inform on. ● noun **1** a tear, crack, or fissure. **2** an instance of splitting or being split. **3** (**the splits**) (in gymnastics and dance) an act of leaping in the air or sitting down with the legs straight and at right angles to the body. **4** the time taken to complete a recognized part of a race, or the point in the race where such a time is measured.
– PHRASES **split the difference** take the average of two proposed amounts. **split one's sides** informal be convulsed with laughter.
– DERIVATIVES **splitter** noun.
– ORIGIN Dutch *splitten* '(of a storm or rock) break up (a ship)'.
split end ● noun a tip of a person's hair which has split from dryness or ill-treatment.
split infinitive ● noun a construction consisting of an infinitive with an adverb or other word inserted between *to* and the verb, e.g. *she seems to really like it*.
– USAGE It is still widely held that splitting infinitives is wrong, a view based on an analogy with Latin. In that language, infinitives consist of only one word (e.g. *amare* 'to love'), which makes them impossible to split. It is therefore maintained that they should not be split in English either. But English is not the same as Latin. In particular, the placing of an adverb in English is extremely important in giving the appropriate emphasis: *you really have to watch him* and *to go boldly where no man has gone before*, examples where the infinitive is not split, convey a different emphasis or sound awkward. Therefore, although still held by some to be incorrect, in standard English the use of split infinitives is broadly accepted as both normal and useful.
split-level ● adjective **1** (of a room or building) having the floor level of one part about half a storey above or below the floor level of an adjacent part. **2** (of a cooker) having the oven and hob in separately installed units.
split pea ● noun a pea dried and split in half for cooking.
split pin ● noun a metal cotter pin with two arms passed through a hole, held in place by the springing apart of the arms.
split screen ● noun a cinema, television, or computer screen on which two or more separate images are displayed.
split second ● noun a very brief moment of time. ● adjective (**split-second**) very rapid or accurate.
splodge ● noun & verb Brit. another term for SPLOTCH.
splosh informal ● verb move with a soft splashing sound. ● noun a splash or splashing sound.
– ORIGIN imitative.
splotch informal ● noun a spot, splash, or smear. ● verb make a splotch on.
– DERIVATIVES **splotchy** adjective.
– ORIGIN perhaps a blend of SPOT and obsolete *plotch* 'blotch'.
splurge informal ● noun **1** a sudden burst of extravagance. **2** a large or excessive amount. ● verb spend extravagantly.
– ORIGIN probably imitative.
splutter ● verb **1** make a series of short explosive spitting or choking sounds. **2** say in a rapid indistinct way. ● noun a spluttering sound.
– DERIVATIVES **splutterer** noun.
– ORIGIN imitative.
spoil ● verb (past and past part. **spoilt** (chiefly Brit.) or **spoiled**) **1** diminish or destroy the value or quality of. **2** (of food) become unfit for eating. **3** harm the character of (a child) by being too indulgent. **4** treat with great or excessive kindness. **5** (**be spoiling for**) be extremely or aggressively eager for. **6** mark (a ballot paper) incorrectly so as to invalidate one's vote. ● noun **1** (**spoils**) stolen goods. **2** waste material brought up during the course of an excavation or a dredging or mining operation.
– PHRASES **be spoilt for choice** Brit. have so many options that it is difficult to make a choice.
– DERIVATIVES **spoilage** noun.
– ORIGIN Latin *spoliare*, from *spolium* 'plunder, skin stripped from an animal', or a shortening of DESPOIL.

Thesaurus

ping, cracking, spiffing, top-hole; *N. Amer. informal, dated* swell; *archaic* goodly.
– OPPOSITES modest, awful.
splendour ● noun MAGNIFICENCE, sumptuousness, grandeur, impressiveness, resplendence, opulence, luxury, richness, fineness, lavishness, ornateness, glory, beauty, elegance; majesty, stateliness; *informal* ritziness, splendiferousness.
– OPPOSITES ordinariness, simplicity, modesty.
splenetic ● adjective BAD-TEMPERED, ill-tempered, angry, cross, peevish, petulant, pettish, irritable, irascible, choleric, dyspeptic, testy, tetchy, snappish, waspish, crotchety, crabby, querulous, resentful, rancorous, bilious; SPITEFUL, malicious, ill-natured, hostile, acrimonious, sour, bitter, malevolent, malignant, malign; *informal* bitchy.
– OPPOSITES good-humoured.
splice ● verb *the ropes are spliced together* INTERWEAVE, braid, plait, entwine, intertwine, interlace, knit, mesh; *Nautical* marry.
– PHRASES **get spliced** *(informal)*. See MARRY sense 1.
splinter ● noun *a splinter of wood* SLIVER, shiver, chip, shard; fragment, piece, bit, shred; *Scottish* skelf; (**splinters**) matchwood, flinders.
● verb *the windscreen splintered* SHATTER, break into tiny pieces, smash, smash into smithereens, fracture, split, crack, disintegrate, crumble.
split ● verb **1** *the axe split the wood* BREAK, chop, cut, hew, lop, cleave; snap, crack. **2** *the ice cracked and split* BREAK APART, fracture, rupture, fissure, snap, come apart, splinter. **3** *her dress was split* TEAR, rip, slash, slit; *poetic/literary* rend. **4** *the issue could split the Party* DIVIDE, disunite, separate, sever; bisect, partition; *poetic/literary* tear asunder. **5** *they split the money between them* SHARE (OUT), divide (up), apportion, allocate, allot, distribute, dole out, parcel out, measure out; carve up, slice up; *informal* divvy up. **6** *the path split* FORK, divide, bifurcate, diverge, branch. **7** *they split up last year* BREAK UP, separate, part, part company, become estranged; divorce, get divorced; *Brit. informal* bust up. **8** *(informal) let's split.* See LEAVE[1] sense 1.
– RELATED TERMS fissile, schizo-.
– OPPOSITES mend, join, unite, pool, converge, get together, marry.
● noun **1** *a split in the rock face* CRACK, fissure, cleft, crevice, break, fracture, breach. **2** *a split in the curtain* RIP, tear, cut, rent, slash, slit. **3** *a split in the Party* DIVISION, rift, breach, schism, rupture, partition, separation, severance, scission, break-up. **4** *the acrimonious split with his wife* BREAK-UP, split-up, separation, parting, estrangement, rift; divorce; *Brit. informal* bust-up.
– OPPOSITES marriage.
– PHRASES **split hairs** QUIBBLE, cavil, carp, niggle, chop logic; *informal* nit-pick; *archaic* pettifog. **split on someone** *(Brit. informal)*. See BETRAY sense 1.
split-up ● noun BREAK-UP, separation, split, parting, estrangement, rift; divorce; *Brit. informal* bust-up.
spoil ● verb **1** *too much sun spoils the complexion* MAR, damage, impair, blemish, disfigure, blight, flaw, deface, scar, injure, harm; ruin, destroy, wreck; be a blot on the landscape; *rare* disfeature. **2** *rain spoiled my plans* RUIN, wreck, destroy, upset, undo, mess

spoiler ● noun **1** a person or thing that spoils. **2** a flap on an aircraft wing which can be projected to create drag and so reduce speed. **3** a similar device on a motor vehicle intended to improve road-holding at high speeds. **4** a news story published with the intention of reducing the impact of a related item published in a rival paper.

spoilsport ● noun a person who spoils the pleasure of others.

spoilt chiefly Brit. past and past participle of SPOIL.

spoke[1] ● noun **1** each of the bars or wire rods connecting the centre of a wheel to its rim. **2** each of a set of radial handles projecting from a ship's wheel. **3** each of the metal rods in an umbrella to which the material is attached.
– PHRASES **put a spoke in someone's wheel** Brit. prevent someone from carrying out a plan.
– ORIGIN Old English, related to SPIKE[1].

spoke[2] past of SPEAK.

spoken past participle of SPEAK. ● adjective (in combination) speaking in a specified way: *a soft-spoken man.*
– PHRASES **be spoken for 1** be already claimed or reserved. **2** already have a romantic commitment.

spokeshave ● noun a small plane with a handle on each side of its blade, used for shaping curved surfaces.

spokesman (or **spokeswoman**) ● noun a person who makes statements on behalf of a group.

spokesperson ● noun (pl. **spokespersons** or **spokespeople**) a spokesman or spokeswoman (used as a neutral alternative).

spoliation /spōliaysh'n/ ● noun **1** the action of spoiling. **2** the action of plundering.

spondee /spondee/ ● noun Poetry a foot consisting of two long (or stressed) syllables.
– ORIGIN from Greek *spondeios pous* 'foot of a libation', from *spondē* 'libation' (being characteristic of music accompanying libations).

spondulicks /spondoōliks/ ● plural noun Brit. informal money.
– ORIGIN of unknown origin.

spondylitis /spondilītiss/ ● noun Medicine arthritis in the backbone, especially (**ankylosing spondylitis**) a form in which vertebrae become fused.
– ORIGIN from Latin *spondylus* 'vertebra'.

sponge ● noun **1** an aquatic invertebrate with a soft porous body. **2** a piece of a light, absorbent substance originally consisting of the fibrous skeleton of a sponge but now usually made of synthetic material, used for washing, as padding, etc. **3** a very light cake made with eggs, sugar, and flour but little or no fat. **4** a piece of sponge impregnated with spermicide and inserted into a woman's vagina as a form of barrier contraceptive. **5** informal a person who lives at someone else's expense. ● verb (**sponging** or **spongeing**) **1** wipe or clean with a wet sponge or cloth. **2** informal obtain money or food from others without giving anything in return.
– DERIVATIVES **sponge-like** adjective.
– ORIGIN Greek *spongos*.

sponge bag ● noun Brit. a toilet bag.

sponge pudding ● noun Brit. a steamed or baked pudding of fat, flour, and eggs.

sponger ● noun informal a person who lives at others' expense.

spongiform /spunjiform/ ● adjective technical having a porous structure or consistency like that of a sponge.

spongy ● adjective (**spongier**, **spongiest**) like a sponge, especially in being porous, compressible, or absorbent.
– DERIVATIVES **sponginess** noun.

sponsor ● noun **1** a person or organization that pays for or contributes to the costs of a sporting or artistic event or a radio or television programme in return for advertising. **2** a person who pledges an amount of money to a charity after another person has participated in a fund-raising event. **3** a person who introduces and supports a proposal for legislation. **4** a person taking official responsibility for the actions of another. **5** a godparent at a child's baptism. ● verb be a sponsor for.
– DERIVATIVES **sponsorship** noun.
– ORIGIN Latin, from *spondere* 'promise solemnly'.

spontaneous ● adjective **1** performed or occurring as a result of an unpremeditated impulse and without external stimulus. **2** open, natural, and uninhibited. **3** (of a process or event) occurring without apparent external cause. **4** Biology (of movement or activity) instinctive or involuntary.
– DERIVATIVES **spontaneity** noun **spontaneously** adverb.
– ORIGIN Latin *spontaneus*, from *sua sponte* 'of one's own accord'.

spontaneous combustion ● noun the ignition of organic matter without apparent cause.

spoof informal ● noun **1** an imitation of something, especially a film, in which its characteristic features are exaggerated for comic effect; a parody. **2** a trick played on someone as a joke. ● verb **1** parody. **2** trick or hoax.
– DERIVATIVES **spoofer** noun **spoofery** noun.
– ORIGIN coined by the English comedian Arthur Roberts (1852–1933).

spook informal ● noun **1** a ghost. **2** chiefly N. Amer. a spy. ● verb frighten or become frightened.
– ORIGIN Dutch.

spooky ● adjective (**spookier**, **spookiest**) informal sinister or ghostly.

Thesaurus

up, make a mess of, dash, sabotage, scotch, torpedo; *informal* foul up, louse up, muck up, screw up, put the kibosh on, banjax, do for; *Brit. informal* cock up, scupper, throw a spanner in the works of; *archaic* bring to naught. **3** *his sisters spoil him* OVERINDULGE, pamper, indulge, mollycoddle, cosset, coddle, baby, wait on hand and foot, kill with kindness; nanny; *archaic* cocker. **4** *stockpiled food may spoil* GO BAD, go off, go rancid, turn, go sour, go mouldy, go rotten, rot, perish.
– OPPOSITES improve, enhance, further, help, neglect, be strict with, keep.
– PHRASES **spoiling for** EAGER FOR, itching for, looking for, keen to have, after, bent on, longing for.

spoils ● plural noun **1** *the spoils of war* BOOTY, loot, stolen goods, plunder, ill-gotten gains, haul, pickings; *informal* swag, boodle. **2** *the spoils of office* BENEFITS, advantages, perks, prize; *formal* perquisites.

spoilsport ● noun KILLJOY, dog in the manger, misery, damper; *informal* wet blanket, party-pooper.

spoken ● adjective *spoken communication* VERBAL, oral, vocal, viva voce, uttered, said, stated; unwritten; by word of mouth.
– OPPOSITES non-verbal, written.
– PHRASES **spoken for 1** *the money is spoken for* RESERVED, set aside, claimed, owned, booked. **2** *Claudine is spoken for* ATTACHED, going out with someone, in a relationship; *informal* going steady; *dated* courting.

spokesman, spokeswoman ● noun SPOKESPERSON, representative, agent, mouthpiece, voice, official; *informal* spin doctor.

sponge ● verb **1** *I'll sponge your face* WASH, clean, wipe, swab; mop, rinse, sluice, swill. **2** *(informal) he lived by sponging off others* SCROUNGE, be a parasite, beg; live off; *informal* freeload, cadge, bum; *N. Amer. informal* mooch; *Austral./NZ* bludge.

sponger ● noun *(informal)* PARASITE, hanger-on, leech, scrounger, beggar; *informal* freeloader, cadger, bum, bloodsucker; *N. Amer. informal* mooch, moocher, schnorrer; *Austral./NZ informal* bludger.

spongy ● adjective SOFT, squashy, cushioned, cushiony, compressible, yielding; springy, resilient, elastic; porous, absorbent, permeable; *technical* spongiform; *Brit. informal* squidgy.
– OPPOSITES hard, solid.

sponsor ● noun *the money came from sponsors* BACKER, patron, promoter, benefactor, benefactress, supporter, contributor, subscriber, friend, guarantor, underwriter; *informal* angel.
● verb *a bank sponsored the event* FINANCE, put up the money for, fund, subsidize, back, promote, support, contribute to, be a patron of, guarantee, underwrite; *informal* foot the bill for, pick up the tab for; *N. Amer. informal* bankroll.

sponsorship ● noun BACKING, support, promotion, patronage, subsidy, funding, financing, aid, financial assistance.

spontaneous ● adjective **1** *a spontaneous display of affection* UNPLANNED, unpremeditated, unrehearsed, impulsive, impetuous, unstudied, impromptu, spur-of-the-moment, extempore, extemporaneous; unforced, voluntary, unconstrained, unprompted, unbidden, unsolicited; *informal* off-the-cuff. **2** *a spontaneous reaction to danger* REFLEX, automatic, mechanical, natural, knee-jerk, involuntary, unthinking, unconscious, instinctive, instinctual; *informal* gut. **3** *a spontaneous kind of person* NATURAL, uninhibited, relaxed, unselfconscious, unaffected, open, genuine, easy, free and easy; impulsive, impetuous.
– OPPOSITES planned, calculated, conscious, voluntary, inhibited.

spontaneously ● adverb **1** *they applauded spontaneously* WITHOUT BEING ASKED, of one's own accord, voluntarily, on impulse, impulsively, on the spur of the moment, extempore, extemporaneously; *informal* off the cuff. **2** *he reacted spontaneously* WITHOUT THINKING,

– DERIVATIVES **spookily** adverb **spookiness** noun.

spool ● noun a cylindrical device on which thread, film, fishing line, etc. can be wound. ● verb **1** wind or be wound on to a spool. **2** Computing send (data for printing or peripheral processing) to an intermediate store.
– ORIGIN Old French *espole* or Low German *spōle*; sense 2 of the verb is an acronym from *simultaneous peripheral operation online*.

spoon ● noun an implement consisting of a small, shallow bowl on a long handle, used for eating, stirring, and serving food. ● verb **1** transfer with a spoon. **2** informal, dated (of a couple) behave in an amorous way.
– DERIVATIVES **spoonful** noun.
– ORIGIN Old English, 'chip of wood'.

spoonbill ● noun a tall wading bird having a long bill with a very broad flat tip.

spoonerism ● noun an error in speech in which the initial sounds or letters of two or more words are accidentally transposed, often to humorous effect, as in *you have hissed the mystery lectures*.
– ORIGIN named after the English scholar Revd W. A. *Spooner* (1844–1930), who reputedly made such errors in speaking.

spoon-feed ● verb **1** feed (a baby or infirm adult) using a spoon. **2** provide (someone) with so much help or information that they do not need to think for themselves.

spoor ● noun the track or scent of an animal.
– ORIGIN Dutch *spor*.

sporadic /spəraddik/ ● adjective occurring at irregular intervals or only in a few places.
– DERIVATIVES **sporadically** adverb.
– ORIGIN Greek *sporadikos*, from *sporas* 'scattered'.

sporangium /spəranjiəm/ ● noun (pl. **sporangia** /spəranjiə/) Botany (in ferns and fungi) a receptacle in which asexual spores are formed.
– ORIGIN Latin, from Greek *spora* 'spore' + *angeion* 'vessel'.

spore ● noun Biology a minute, typically single-celled, reproductive unit characteristic of lower plants, fungi, and protozoans.
– ORIGIN Greek *spora* 'sowing, seed'.

sporran /sporrən/ ● noun a small pouch worn around the waist so as to hang in front of the kilt as part of men's Scottish Highland dress.
– ORIGIN Scottish Gaelic *sporan*.

sport ● noun **1** an activity involving physical exertion and skill in which an individual or team competes against another or others. **2** informal a person who behaves in a good or specified way in response to teasing, defeat, etc. **3** success or pleasure derived from an activity such as hunting. **4** dated entertainment; fun. **5** chiefly Austral./NZ a friendly form of address, especially between unacquainted men. **6** Biology an animal or plant showing abnormal or striking variation from the parent type as a result of spontaneous mutation. ● verb **1** wear or display (a distinctive item). **2** amuse oneself or play in a lively way.
– PHRASES **the sport of kings** horse racing.
– DERIVATIVES **sporter** noun.
– ORIGIN shortening of DISPORT.

sporting ● adjective **1** connected with or interested in sport. **2** fair and generous in one's behaviour.
– DERIVATIVES **sportingly** adverb.

sporting chance ● noun a reasonable chance of winning or succeeding.

sportive ● adjective playful; light-hearted.

sports bar ● noun a bar where televised sport is shown continuously.

sports car ● noun a low-built car designed for performance at high speeds.

sports jacket ● noun a man's jacket resembling a suit jacket, for informal wear.

sportsman (or **sportswoman**) ● noun **1** a person who takes part in a sport, especially as a professional. **2** a person who behaves sportingly.
– DERIVATIVES **sportsmanlike** adjective **sportsmanship** noun.

sportsperson ● noun (pl. **sportspersons** or **sportspeople**) a sportsman or sportswoman (used as a neutral alternative).

sportster ● noun a sports car.

sportswear ● noun clothes worn for sport or for casual outdoor use.

sporty ● adjective (**sportier**, **sportiest**) informal **1** fond of or good at sport. **2** (of clothing) suitable for wearing for sport or for casual use. **3** (of a car) compact and with fast acceleration.
– DERIVATIVES **sportiness** noun.

spot ● noun **1** a small round mark differing in colour or texture from the surface around it. **2** a pimple. **3** a particular place, point, or position. **4** a place for an individual item in a show. **5** informal, chiefly Brit. a small amount: *a spot of lunch*. ● verb (**spotted**, **spotting**) **1** notice or recognize (someone or something) that is difficult to detect or that one is searching for. **2** mark with spots. **3** (**it spots, it is spotting**, etc.) rain slightly.
– PHRASES **in a spot** informal in a difficult situation. **on the spot** **1** immediately. **2** at the scene of an action or event. **put on the spot** informal force (someone) into a situation in which they must respond or act.
– DERIVATIVES **spotted** adjective.
– ORIGIN perhaps from Dutch *spotte*.

spot check ● noun a test made without warning on a randomly selected subject. ● verb (**spot-check**) subject to a spot check.

spotless ● adjective absolutely clean or pure.
– DERIVATIVES **spotlessly** adverb **spotlessness** noun.

spotlight ● noun **1** a lamp projecting a narrow, intense beam of light directly on to a place or person. **2** (**the spotlight**) intense public attention. ● verb (past and past part. **spotlighted** or **spotlit**)

Thesaurus

automatically, mechanically, unthinkingly, involuntarily, instinctively, naturally, by oneself/itself.

spooky ● adjective *(informal)* EERIE, sinister, ghostly, uncanny, weird, unearthly, mysterious; FRIGHTENING, spine-chilling, hair-raising; *informal* creepy, scary, spine-tingling.

sporadic ● adjective OCCASIONAL, infrequent, irregular, periodic, scattered, patchy, isolated, odd; INTERMITTENT, spasmodic, fitful, desultory, erratic, unpredictable.
– OPPOSITES frequent, steady, continuous.

sport ● noun **1** *we did a lot of sport* (COMPETITIVE) GAME(S), physical recreation, physical activity, physical exercise; pastime. **2** *(dated) they were rogues out for a bit of sport* FUN, pleasure, enjoyment, entertainment, amusement, diversion.
● verb *he sported a beard* WEAR, have on, dress in; DISPLAY, exhibit, show off, flourish, parade, flaunt.

sporting ● adjective SPORTSMANLIKE, generous, gentlemanly, considerate; fair, just, honourable; *Brit. informal* decent.
– OPPOSITES dirty, unfair.

sporty ● adjective *(informal)* **1** *he's quite a sporty type* ATHLETIC, fit, active, energetic. **2** *a sporty outfit* STYLISH, smart, jaunty; CASUAL, informal; *informal* trendy, cool, snazzy; *N. Amer. informal* sassy. **3** *a sporty car* FAST, speedy; *informal* nippy, zippy.
– OPPOSITES unfit, lazy, formal, sloppy, slow.

spot ● noun **1** *a grease spot on the wall* MARK, patch, dot, fleck, smudge, smear, stain, blotch, blot, splash; *informal* splotch, splodge. **2** *a spot on his nose* PIMPLE, pustule, blackhead, boil, swelling, eruption, wen, sty; (**spots**) acne; *technical* comedo, papule; *informal* zit, whitehead; *Scottish informal* plook. **3** *a secluded spot* PLACE, location, site, position, point, situation, scene, setting, locale, locality, area, neighbourhood, region; venue; *technical* locus. **4** *social policy has a regular spot on the agenda* POSITION, place, slot, space. **5** *a spot to eat or drink* BIT, little, some, small amount, morsel, bite, mouthful; drop, splash; *informal* smidgen, tad. **6** *(informal) in a tight spot* PREDICAMENT, mess, difficulty, trouble, plight, corner, quandary, dilemma; *informal* fix, jam, hole, sticky situation, pickle, scrape, hot water.
● verb **1** *she spotted him in his car* NOTICE, see, observe, note, discern, detect, perceive, make out, recognize, identify, locate; catch sight of, glimpse; *Brit. informal* clock; *poetic/literary* behold, espy. **2** *her clothes were spotted with grease* STAIN, mark, fleck, speckle, smudge, streak, splash, spatter; *informal* splotch, splodge. **3** *it was spotting with rain* RAIN LIGHTLY, drizzle; *Brit.* spit; *N. English* mizzle; *N. Amer.* sprinkle.
– PHRASES **on the spot** IMMEDIATELY, at once, straight away, right away, without delay, without hesitation, that instant, directly, there and then, then and there, forthwith, instantly, summarily; *N. Amer.* in short order; *archaic* straightway, instanter. **spot on** *(Brit. informal)* ACCURATE, correct, right, perfect, exact, unerring; *Brit. informal* bang on; *N. Amer. informal* on the money, on the nose.

spotless ● adjective **1** *the kitchen was spotless* PERFECTLY CLEAN, ultra-clean, pristine, immaculate, shining, shiny, gleaming, spick and span. **2** *a spotless reputation* UNBLEMISHED, unsullied, untarnished, untainted, unstained, pure, whiter than white, innocent, impeccable, blameless, irreproachable, above reproach; *informal*

S

1 illuminate with a spotlight. 2 direct attention to.
spot on ● adjective & adverb Brit. informal completely accurate or accurately.
spotted dick ● noun Brit. a suet pudding containing currants.
spotted dog ● noun 1 a Dalmatian dog. 2 Brit. another term for SPOTTED DICK.
spotted fever ● noun a disease characterized by fever and skin spots, especially (also **Rocky Mountain spotted fever**) a rickettsial disease transmitted by ticks.
spotter ● noun 1 (usu. in combination) a person who observes or looks for a particular thing as a hobby or job. 2 an aviator or aircraft employed in spotting enemy positions.
spotty ● adjective (**spottier**, **spottiest**) 1 marked with or having spots. 2 chiefly N. Amer. of uneven quality.
spot-weld ● verb join by welding at a number of separate points.
spousal /spowz'l/ ● adjective Law, chiefly N. Amer. relating to marriage or to a husband or wife.
spouse ● noun a husband or wife.
– ORIGIN Latin *sponsus*, from *spondere* 'betroth'.
spout ● noun 1 a projecting tube or lip through or over which liquid can be poured from a container. 2 a stream of liquid issuing with great force. 3 a pipe, trough, or chute for conveying liquid, grain, etc. ● verb 1 send out or flow forcibly in a stream. 2 express (one's views) in a lengthy or declamatory way.
– PHRASES **up the spout** Brit. informal 1 useless or ruined. 2 (of a woman) pregnant.
– DERIVATIVES **spouted** adjective **spouter** noun.
– ORIGIN related to an Old Norse word meaning 'to spit'.
sprain ● verb wrench the ligaments of (a joint) violently so as to cause pain and swelling but not dislocation. ● noun the result of such a wrench.
– ORIGIN of unknown origin.
sprang past of SPRING.
sprat ● noun 1 a small marine fish of the herring family, caught for food and fish products. 2 informal any small sea fish.
– PHRASES **a sprat to catch a mackerel** Brit. a small outlay or risk ventured in the hope of a significant return.
– ORIGIN Old English.
sprawl ● verb 1 sit, lie, or fall with one's limbs spread out in an ungainly way. 2 (often as adj. **sprawling**) spread out irregularly over a large area. ● noun 1 a sprawling position or movement. 2 a sprawling group or mass, especially the disorganized expansion of an urban or industrial area into the adjoining countryside.
– ORIGIN Old English, 'move the limbs convulsively'.
spray[1] ● noun 1 liquid sent through the air in tiny drops. 2 a liquid preparation which can be forced out of an aerosol or other container in a spray. ● verb 1 apply (liquid) in a spray. 2 cover or treat with a spray. 3 (of liquid) be sent through the air in a spray. 4 scatter over an area with force.
– DERIVATIVES **sprayer** noun.
– ORIGIN related to Dutch *sprayen* 'sprinkle'.
spray[2] ● noun 1 a stem or small branch of a tree or plant, bearing flowers and foliage. 2 a bunch of cut flowers arranged in an attractive way.
– ORIGIN Old English.
spray gun ● noun a device resembling a gun which is used to spray a liquid such as paint under pressure.
spread ● verb (past and past part. **spread**) 1 open out so as to increase in surface area, width, or length. 2 stretch out (limbs, hands, fingers, or wings) so that they are far apart. 3 extend or distribute over a wide area or a specified period of time. 4 reach or cause to reach a larger area or more and more people: *panic spread*. 5 apply (a substance) in an even layer. ● noun 1 the fact or action of spreading. 2 the extent, width, or area covered by something. 3 the range of something. 4 a soft paste that can be spread on bread. 5 an article or advertisement covering several columns or pages of a newspaper or magazine. 6 informal a large and elaborate meal. 7 N. Amer. a large farm or ranch.
– DERIVATIVES **spreadable** adjective.
– ORIGIN Old English.
spread betting ● noun a form of betting in which money is won or lost according to the degree by which the score or result of a sporting fixture varies from the spread of expected values quoted by the bookmaker.
spreadeagle ● verb (usu. **be spreadeagled**) stretch (someone) out with their arms and legs extended.
spreader ● noun 1 a device for spreading. 2 a person who disseminates something.
spreadsheet ● noun a computer program used chiefly for accounting, in which figures arranged in a grid can be manipulated and used in calculations.
spree ● noun a spell of unrestrained activity of a particular kind.
– ORIGIN of unknown origin.
sprezzatura /spretsətyoorə/ ● noun studied carelessness, especially in art or literature.
– ORIGIN Italian.
sprig[1] ● noun 1 a small stem bearing leaves or flowers, taken from a bush or plant. 2 a descendant or younger member of a family or social class. 3 a small moulded decoration applied to a piece of pottery before firing. ● verb decorate with sprigs.

Thesaurus

squeaky clean.
– OPPOSITES dirty, tarnished, impure.
spotlight ● noun *she was constantly in the spotlight* PUBLIC EYE, glare of publicity, limelight; focus of public/media attention.
● verb *this article spotlights the problem* FOCUS ATTENTION ON, highlight, point up, draw/call attention to, give prominence to, throw into relief, turn the spotlight on, bring to the fore.
spotted ● adjective 1 *the spotted leaves* MOTTLED, dappled, speckled, flecked, freckled, freckly, dotted, stippled, brindle(d); *informal* splotchy. 2 *a black-and-white spotted dress* POLKA-DOT, spotty, dotted.
– OPPOSITES plain.
spotty ● adjective 1 *a spotty dog* SPOTTED, mottled, speckled, speckly, flecked, specked, stippled; *informal* splodgy, splotchy. 2 *a spotty dress* POLKA-DOT, spotted, dotted. 3 *(Brit.) his spotty face* PIMPLY, pimpled, acned; *Scottish informal* plooky.
spouse ● noun PARTNER, mate, consort; *informal* better half; *Brit. informal* other half. See also HUSBAND, WIFE.
spout ● verb 1 *lava was spouting from the crater* SPURT, gush, spew, erupt, shoot, squirt, spray; disgorge, discharge, emit, belch forth. 2 *he spouts on foreign affairs* HOLD FORTH, sound off, go on, talk at length, expatiate; *informal* mouth off, speechify, spiel.
● noun *a can with a spout* NOZZLE, lip, rose.
– PHRASES **up the spout** *(Brit. informal)* 1 *my computer's up the spout.* See BROKEN sense 3. 2 *his daughter's up the spout.* See PREGNANT sense 1.
sprawl ● verb 1 *he sprawled on a sofa* STRETCH OUT, lounge, loll, lie, recline, drape oneself, slump, flop, slouch. 2 *the town sprawled ahead of them* SPREAD, stretch, extend, be strung out, be scattered, straggle, spill.
spray[1] ● noun 1 *a spray of water* SHOWER, sprinkling, sprinkle, jet, mist, drizzle; spume, spindrift; foam, froth. 2 *a perfume spray* ATOMIZER, vaporizer, aerosol, sprinkler; nebulizer.
● verb 1 *water was sprayed all around* SPRINKLE, shower, spatter; scatter, disperse, diffuse; mist; douche; *poetic/literary* besprinkle. 2 *water sprayed into the air* SPOUT, jet, gush, spurt, shoot, squirt.
spray[2] ● noun 1 *a spray of holly* SPRIG, twig. 2 *a spray of flowers* BOUQUET, bunch, posy, nosegay; corsage, buttonhole, boutonnière.
spread ● verb 1 *he spread the map out* LAY OUT, open out, unfurl, unroll, roll out; straighten out, fan out; stretch out, extend; *poetic/literary* outspread. 2 *the landscape spread out below* EXTEND, stretch, open out, be displayed, be exhibited, be on show; sprawl. 3 *papers were spread all over his desk* SCATTER, strew, disperse, distribute. 4 *he's been spreading rumours* DISSEMINATE, circulate, pass on, put about, communicate, diffuse, make public, make known, purvey, broadcast, publicize, propagate, promulgate; repeat; *poetic/literary* bruit about/abroad. 5 *she spread cold cream on her face* SMEAR, daub, plaster, slather, lather, apply, put; smooth, rub. 6 *he spread the toast with butter* COVER, coat, layer, daub, smother; butter.
– OPPOSITES fold up, suppress.
● noun 1 *the spread of learning* EXPANSION, proliferation, extension, growth; dissemination, diffusion, transmission, propagation. 2 *a spread of six feet* SPAN, width, extent, stretch, reach. 3 *the immense spread of the heavens* EXPANSE, area, sweep, stretch. 4 *a wide spread of subjects* RANGE, span, spectrum, sweep; variety. 5 *(informal) his mother laid on a huge spread* LARGE/ELABORATE MEAL, feast, banquet; *informal* blowout, nosh; *Brit. informal* nosh-up, slap-up meal.
spree ● noun 1 *a shopping spree* UNRESTRAINED BOUT, orgy; *informal* binge, splurge; *humorous* retail therapy. 2 *a drinking spree* DRINKING

S

– ORIGIN from or related to Low German *sprick*.
sprig[2] ● noun a small tapering tack with no head, used chiefly to hold glass in a window frame until the putty dries.
– ORIGIN of unknown origin.
sprightly (also **spritely**) ● adjective (**sprightlier**, **sprightliest**) (especially of an old person) lively; energetic.
– DERIVATIVES **sprightliness** noun.
– ORIGIN from *spright*, a rare variant of SPRITE.
spring ● verb (past **sprang** or chiefly N. Amer. **sprung**; past part. **sprung**) **1** move suddenly or rapidly upwards or forwards. **2** move suddenly by or as if by the action of a spring. **3** operate by or as if means of a spring mechanism: *spring a trap.* **4** (**spring from**) originate or appear from. **5** (**spring up**) suddenly develop or appear. **6** (**sprung**) (of a vehicle or item of furniture) provided with springs. **7** (**spring on**) present (something) suddenly or unexpectedly to. **8** informal bring about the escape or release of (a prisoner). **9** cause (a game bird) to rise from cover. ● noun **1** the season after winter and before summer. **2** an elastic device, typically a spiral metal coil, that can be pressed or pulled but returns to its former shape when released. **3** a sudden jump upwards or forwards. **4** a place where water wells up from an underground source. **5** elastic quality.
– PHRASES **spring a leak** (of a boat or container) develop a leak. [ORIGIN originally in nautical use, referring to timbers springing out of position.]
– DERIVATIVES **springless** adjective **springlike** adjective.
– ORIGIN Old English.
spring balance ● noun a balance that measures weight by the tension of a spring.
springboard ● noun **1** a strong, flexible board from which a diver or gymnast may jump in order to gain impetus. **2** a thing providing impetus to an action or enterprise.
springbok ● noun **1** a southern African gazelle with a characteristic habit of leaping when disturbed. **2** (**Springbok**) a member of a sports team selected to represent South Africa.
– ORIGIN Afrikaans, from Dutch *springen* 'to spring' + *bok* 'antelope'.
spring chicken ● noun **1** informal a young person: *I'm no spring chicken.* **2** a young chicken for eating (originally available only in spring).
spring clean ● noun Brit. a thorough cleaning of a house or room, typically undertaken in spring. ● verb (**spring-clean**) clean thoroughly.
springer ● noun (also **springer spaniel**) a small spaniel of a breed originally used to spring game.
spring fever ● noun a feeling of restlessness and excitement felt at the beginning of spring.
spring greens ● plural noun the leaves of young cabbage plants of a variety that does not develop a heart.
spring-loaded ● adjective containing a compressed or stretched spring pressing one part against another.
spring onion ● noun chiefly Brit. an onion taken from the ground before the bulb has formed.
spring roll ● noun a Chinese snack consisting of a pancake filled with vegetables and sometimes meat, rolled into a cylinder and fried.
spring tide ● noun a tide just after a new or full moon, when there is the greatest difference between high and low water.
springy ● adjective (**springier**, **springiest**) **1** springing back quickly when squeezed or stretched. **2** (of movements) light and confident.
– DERIVATIVES **springily** adverb **springiness** noun.
sprinkle ● verb **1** scatter or pour small drops or particles over. **2** scatter or pour (small drops or particles) over an object or surface. **3** distribute something randomly throughout. ● noun a small amount that is sprinkled.
– ORIGIN perhaps from Dutch *sprenkelen*.
sprinkler ● noun **1** a device for watering lawns. **2** an automatic fire extinguisher installed in a ceiling.
sprinkling ● noun a small, thinly distributed amount.
sprint ● verb run at full speed over a short distance. ● noun **1** an act or spell of sprinting. **2** a short, fast race.
– DERIVATIVES **sprinter** noun.
– ORIGIN related to Swedish *spritta*.
sprit ● noun Sailing a small spar reaching diagonally from a mast to the upper outer corner of a sail.
– ORIGIN Old English, 'punting pole'; related to SPROUT.
sprite ● noun **1** an elf or fairy. **2** Computing a graphical figure which can be moved and manipulated as a single entity.
– ORIGIN a contraction of SPIRIT.
spritely ● adjective variant spelling of SPRIGHTLY.
spritsail ● noun **1** a sail extended by a sprit. **2** a sail extended by a yard set under a ship's bowsprit.
spritz chiefly N. Amer. ● verb squirt or spray in quick short bursts at or on to. ● noun an act or instance of spritzing.
– ORIGIN German *spritzen* 'to squirt'.
spritzer ● noun a mixture of wine and soda water.
– ORIGIN German, 'a splash'.
sprocket ● noun **1** each of several projections on the rim of a wheel that engage with the links of a chain or with holes in film, tape, or paper. **2** (also **sprocket wheel**) a wheel with projections of this kind.
– ORIGIN originally denoting a triangular piece of timber used in a roof: of unknown origin.
sprog ● noun Brit. informal, chiefly derogatory a child.
– ORIGIN perhaps from obsolete *sprag* 'lively young man', of unknown origin.
sprout ● verb **1** produce shoots. **2** grow (plant shoots or hair). **3** start to grow or develop. ● noun **1** a shoot of a plant. **2** a Brussels sprout.
– ORIGIN Germanic.
spruce[1] ● adjective neat and smart. ● verb (**spruce up**) make smarter.
– ORIGIN perhaps from SPRUCE[2] in the obsolete sense 'Prussian', in the phrase *spruce leather jerkin.*
spruce[2] ● noun a widespread coniferous tree which has a distinctive conical shape and hanging cones.
– ORIGIN originally referring to Prussia or something originating

Thesaurus

S

BOUT, debauch; *informal* binge, bender, session, booze-up, blind; *Scottish informal* skite; *N. Amer. informal* jag, toot; *poetic/literary* bacchanal, bacchanalia; *archaic* wassail.
sprig ● noun SMALL STEM, spray, twig.
sprightly ● adjective SPRY, lively, agile, nimble, energetic, active, full of energy, vigorous, spirited, animated, vivacious, frisky; *informal* full of vim and vigour; *N. English informal* wick.
– OPPOSITES doddery, lethargic.
spring ● verb **1** *the cat sprang off her lap* LEAP, jump, bound, vault, hop. **2** *the branch sprang back* FLY, whip, flick, whisk, kick, bounce. **3** *all art springs from feelings* ORIGINATE, derive, arise, stem, emanate, proceed, issue, evolve, come. **4** *fifty men sprang from nowhere* APPEAR SUDDENLY, appear unexpectedly, materialize, pop up, shoot up, sprout, develop quickly; proliferate, mushroom. **5** *he sprang the truth on me* ANNOUNCE SUDDENLY/UNEXPECTEDLY, reveal suddenly/unexpectedly, surprise someone with.
● noun **1** *with a sudden spring he leapt on to the table* LEAP, jump, bound, vault, hop; pounce. **2** *the mattress has lost its spring* SPRINGINESS, bounciness, bounce, resilience, elasticity, flexibility, stretch, stretchiness, give. **3** *there was a spring in his step* BUOYANCY, bounce, energy, liveliness, jauntiness, sprightliness, confidence. **4** *a mineral spring* WELL HEAD, source; spa, geyser; *poetic/literary* wellspring, fount. **5** *the springs of his own emotions* ORIGIN, source, fountainhead, root, roots, basis.
– RELATED TERMS vernal.
springy ● adjective ELASTIC, stretchy, stretchable, tensile; flexible, pliant, pliable, whippy; bouncy, resilient, spongy.
– OPPOSITES rigid, squashy.
sprinkle ● verb **1** *he sprinkled water over the towel* SPLASH, trickle, spray, shower; spatter. **2** *sprinkle sesame seeds over the top* SCATTER, strew; drizzle. **3** *sprinkle the cake with icing sugar* DREDGE, dust. **4** *the sky was sprinkled with stars* DOT, stipple, stud, fleck, speckle, spot, pepper; scatter, cover; *poetic/literary* besprinkle.
sprinkling ● noun **1** *a sprinkling of nutmeg* SCATTERING, sprinkle, scatter, dusting; pinch, dash. **2** *mainly women, but a sprinkling of men* FEW, one or two, couple, handful, small number, trickle, scattering.
sprint ● verb RUN, race, dart, rush, dash, hasten, hurry, scurry, scamper, hare, bolt, fly, gallop, career, charge, shoot, hurtle, speed, zoom, go like lightning, go hell for leather, go like the wind; jog, trot; *informal* tear, pelt, scoot, hotfoot it, leg it, belt, zip, whip; *Brit. informal* bomb; *N. Amer. informal* hightail it, barrel.
– OPPOSITES walk.
sprite ● noun FAIRY, elf, pixie, imp, brownie, puck, peri, kelpie, leprechaun; nymph, nixie, sylph, naiad.
sprout ● verb **1** *the weeds begin to sprout* GERMINATE, put/send out

in Prussia: from obsolete *Pruce* 'Prussia'.

sprue[1] ● noun **1** a channel through which metal or plastic is poured into a mould. **2** a piece of metal or plastic which has solidified in a sprue.
– ORIGIN of unknown origin.

sprue[2] ● noun a disease characterized by ulceration of the mouth and chronic enteritis, suffered by visitors to tropical regions.
– ORIGIN Dutch *spruw* 'thrush'.

spruik /sproo͝k/ ● verb Austral. informal speak in public, especially to advertise a show.
– DERIVATIVES **spruiker** noun.
– ORIGIN of unknown origin.

sprung past participle and (especially in North America) past of SPRING.

spry ● adjective (**spryer**, **spryest**) (especially of an old person) lively.
– ORIGIN of unknown origin.

spud ● noun **1** informal a potato. **2** a small, narrow spade for cutting the roots of weeds. ● verb (**spudded**, **spudding**) **1** dig up or cut (weeds) with a spud. **2** make the initial drilling for (an oil well).
– ORIGIN originally denoting a short knife: of unknown origin.

spumante /spoomanti/ ● noun an Italian sparkling white wine.
– ORIGIN Italian, 'sparkling'.

spume /spyo͞om/ literary ● noun froth or foam, especially that found on waves. ● verb froth or foam.
– ORIGIN Latin *spuma*.

spun past and past participle of SPIN.

spunk ● noun **1** informal courage and determination. **2** Brit. vulgar slang semen. **3** Austral. informal a sexually attractive person.
– DERIVATIVES **spunky** adjective (**spunkier**, **spunkiest**).
– ORIGIN perhaps a blend of SPARK and obsolete *funk* 'spark'.

spur ● noun **1** a device with a small spike or a spiked wheel, worn on a rider's heel for urging a horse forward. **2** an incentive. **3** a projection from a mountain or mountain range. **4** Botany a slender tubular projection from the base of a flower. **5** a short branch road or railway line. ● verb (**spurred**, **spurring**) **1** urge (a horse) forward with spurs. **2** give an incentive to; encourage.
– PHRASES **on the spur of the moment** on a momentary impulse.
– ORIGIN Old English, related to SPURN.

spurge ● noun a plant or shrub with milky latex and small greenish flowers.
– ORIGIN Old French *espurge*, from Latin *expurgare* 'cleanse' (because of the purgative properties of the milky latex).

spur gear ● noun another term for SPUR WHEEL.

spurious /spyooriəss/ ● adjective **1** false or fake. **2** (of a line of reasoning) apparently but not actually valid.
– DERIVATIVES **spuriously** adverb **spuriousness** noun.
– ORIGIN Latin *spurius* 'false'.

spurn ● verb reject with contempt.
– ORIGIN originally in the sense 'strike or push away with the foot': from Old English.

spurt ● verb **1** gush out or cause to gush out in a sudden stream. **2** move with a sudden burst of speed. ● noun **1** a sudden gushing stream. **2** a sudden burst of activity or speed.
– ORIGIN of unknown origin.

spur wheel ● noun a gearwheel with teeth projecting parallel to the wheel's axis.

sputnik /sputnik, spoo͝t-/ ● noun each of a series of Soviet satellites, the first of which was the first artificial satellite to be placed in orbit.
– ORIGIN Russian, 'fellow-traveller'.

sputter ● verb **1** make a series of soft explosive sounds. **2** speak in a series of incoherent bursts. ● noun a sputtering sound.
– ORIGIN Dutch *sputteren*.

sputum ● noun a mixture of saliva and mucus coughed up from the respiratory tract.
– ORIGIN Latin, from *spuere* 'to spit'.

spy ● noun (pl. **spies**) **1** a person employed to collect and report secret information on an enemy or competitor. **2** a person or device that observes others secretly. ● verb (**spies**, **spied**) **1** be a spy. **2** (**spy on**) observe furtively. **3** observe or notice. **4** (**spy out**) collect information about (something) before deciding how to act.
– ORIGIN from Old French *espier* 'espy'.

spyglass ● noun a small telescope.

spyhole ● noun Brit. a peephole.

sq ● abbreviation square.

SQL ● abbreviation Computing Structured Query Language, an international standard for database manipulation.

squab /skwob/ ● noun **1** a young unfledged pigeon. **2** Brit. the padded back or side of a vehicle seat. **3** a thick cushion, especially one covering the seat of a chair or sofa.
– ORIGIN originally in the sense 'inexperienced person': of unknown origin.

squabble ● noun a trivial noisy quarrel. ● verb engage in a squabble.
– ORIGIN probably imitative.

Thesaurus

shoots, bud, burgeon. **2** *he had sprouted a beard* GROW, develop, put/send out. **3** *parsley sprouted from the pot* SPRING UP, shoot up, come up, grow, burgeon, develop, appear.

spruce ● adjective *the Captain looked very spruce* NEAT, well groomed, well turned out, well dressed, smart, trim, dapper, elegant, chic; *informal* natty, snazzy; *N. Amer. informal* spiffy, trig.
– OPPOSITES untidy.
● verb **1** *the cottage had been spruced up* SMARTEN, tidy, neaten, put in order, clean; *informal* do up; *Brit. informal* tart up, posh up; *N. Amer. informal* gussy up. **2** *Sarah had spruced herself up* GROOM, tidy, smarten, preen, primp, prink; *N. Amer.* trig; *informal* titivate, doll up; *Brit. informal* tart up.

spry ● adjective SPRIGHTLY, lively, agile, nimble, energetic, active, full of energy, vigorous, spirited, animated, vivacious, frisky; *informal* full of vim and vigour; *N. English informal* wick.
– OPPOSITES doddery, lethargic.

spume ● noun FOAM, froth, surf, spindrift, bubbles.

spunk ● noun (*informal*) COURAGE, bravery, valour, nerve, confidence, daring, audacity, pluck, spirit, grit, mettle, spine, backbone; *informal* guts, gumption; *Brit. informal* bottle; *N. Amer. informal* moxie.

spur ● noun **1** *competition can be a spur* STIMULUS, incentive, encouragement, inducement, fillip, impetus, prod, motivation, inspiration; *informal* kick up the backside, shot in the arm. **2** *a spur of bone* PROJECTION, spike, point; *technical* process.
– OPPOSITES disincentive, discouragement.
● verb *the thought spurred him into action* STIMULATE, encourage, prompt, propel, prod, induce, impel, motivate, move, galvanize, inspire, incentivize, urge, drive, egg on, stir; incite, goad, provoke, prick, sting; *N. Amer.* light a fire under.
– OPPOSITES discourage.
– PHRASES **on the spur of the moment** IMPULSIVELY, on impulse, impetuously, without thinking, without premeditation, unpremeditatedly, impromptu, extempore, spontaneously; *informal* off the cuff.

spurious ● adjective BOGUS, fake, false, counterfeit, forged, fraudulent, sham, artificial, imitation, simulated, feigned, deceptive, misleading; *informal* phoney, pretend; *Brit. informal* cod.
– OPPOSITES genuine.

spurn ● verb REJECT, rebuff, scorn, turn down, treat with contempt, disdain, look down one's nose at, despise; snub, slight, jilt, dismiss, brush off, turn one's back on; give someone the cold shoulder, cold-shoulder; *informal* turn one's nose up at, give someone the brush-off, kick in the teeth; *Brit. informal* knock back; *N. Amer. informal* give someone the bum's rush.
– OPPOSITES welcome, accept.

spurt ● verb *water spurted from the tap* SQUIRT, shoot, jet, erupt, gush, pour, stream, pump, surge, spew, course, well, spring, burst; disgorge, discharge, emit, belch forth, expel, eject; *Brit. informal* sloosh.
● noun **1** *a spurt of water* SQUIRT, jet, spout, gush, stream, rush, surge, flood, cascade, torrent. **2** *a spurt of courage* BURST, fit, bout, rush, spate, surge, attack, outburst, blaze. **3** *Daisy put on a spurt* BURST OF SPEED, turn of speed, sprint, rush, burst of energy.

spy ● noun *a foreign spy* SECRET AGENT, intelligence agent, double agent, counterspy, mole, plant, scout; *informal* snooper; *N. Amer. informal* spook; *archaic* intelligencer.
● verb **1** *he spied for the West* BE A SPY, gather intelligence, work for the secret service; *informal* snoop. **2** *investigators spied on them* OBSERVE FURTIVELY, keep under surveillance/observation, watch, keep a watch on, keep an eye on. **3** *she spied a coffee shop* NOTICE, observe, see, spot, sight, catch sight of, glimpse, make out, discern, detect; *informal* clap/lay/set eyes on; *poetic/literary* espy, behold, descry.

spying ● noun ESPIONAGE, intelligence gathering, surveillance, infiltration, undercover work, cloak-and-dagger activities.

S

squad • noun (treated as sing. or pl.) **1** a small number of soldiers assembled for drill or assigned to a particular task. **2** a group of sports players from which a team is chosen. **3** a division of a police force dealing with a particular type of crime.
– ORIGIN Italian *squadra* 'square'.
squad car • noun a police patrol car.
squaddie • noun (pl. **squaddies**) Brit. informal a private soldier.
squadron • noun **1** an operational unit in an air force consisting of two or more flights of aircraft. **2** a principal division of an armoured or cavalry regiment, consisting of two or more troops. **3** a group of warships detached on a particular duty or under the command of a flag officer.
– ORIGIN originally denoting a group of soldiers in square formation: from Italian *squadrone*, from *squadra* 'square'.
squadron leader • noun a rank of officer in the RAF, above flight lieutenant and below wing commander.
squalid • adjective **1** extremely dirty and unpleasant. **2** showing a contemptible lack of moral standards: *a squalid attempt to buy votes*.
– ORIGIN Latin *squalidus*, from *squalere* 'be rough or dirty'.
squall • noun **1** a sudden violent gust of wind or localized storm. **2** a loud cry. • verb (of a baby or small child) cry noisily and continuously.
– DERIVATIVES **squally** adjective.
– ORIGIN probably an alteration of SQUEAL.
squalor • noun the state of being squalid.
squamous /skwayməss/ • adjective **1** technical covered with or characterized by scales. **2** Anatomy referring to a layer of epithelium consisting of very thin flattened cells.
– ORIGIN Latin *squamosus*, from *squama* 'scale'.
squander • verb waste in a reckless or foolish manner.
– ORIGIN of unknown origin.
square • noun **1** a plane figure with four equal straight sides and four right angles. **2** an open, typically four-sided, area surrounded by buildings. **3** an area within a military barracks or camp used for drill. **4** the product of a number multiplied by itself. **5** an L-shaped or T-shaped instrument used for obtaining or testing right angles. **6** informal an old-fashioned or boringly conventional person. • adjective **1** having the shape of a square. **2** having or forming a right angle. **3** referring to a unit of measurement equal to the area of a square whose side is of the unit specified. **4** (after a noun) denoting the length of each side of a square shape or object: *the room was ten metres square*. **5** at right angles. **6** level or parallel. **7** broad and solid in shape. **8** fair and honest. **9** informal old-fashioned or boringly conventional. • adverb directly; straight. • verb **1** make square or rectangular. **2** (**squared**) marked out in squares. **3** multiply (a number) by itself. **4** (**square with**) make or be compatible. **5** settle (a bill or debt). **6** make the score of (a match or game) even. **7** informal secure the co-operation of (someone) by offering an inducement. **8** bring (one's shoulders) into a position in which they appear square and broad.
– PHRASES **back to square one** informal back to where one started. **square the circle 1** construct a square equal in area to a given circle (a problem incapable of a purely geometrical solution). **2** do something considered to be impossible. **a square deal** see DEAL[1]. **a square peg in a round hole** see PEG. **square up 1** assume the attitude of a person about to fight. **2** (**square up to**) face and tackle (a difficulty) resolutely.
– DERIVATIVES **squareness** noun **squarer** noun **squarish** adjective.
– ORIGIN Old French *esquare*, from Latin *quadra* 'square'.
square-bashing • noun Brit. informal military drill performed repeatedly on a barrack square.
square dance • noun a country dance that starts with four couples facing one another in a square, with the steps and movements shouted out by a caller.
square eyes • plural noun Brit. humorous eyes supposedly affected by excessive television viewing.
square leg • noun Cricket a fielding position level with the batsman approximately halfway towards the boundary on the leg side.
squarely • adverb without deviation or equivocation; directly.
square meal • noun a substantial and balanced meal.
– ORIGIN said to derive from nautical use, with reference to the square platters on which meals were served.
square measure • noun a unit of measurement relating to area.
square number • noun the product of a number multiplied by itself, e.g. 1, 4, 9, 16.
square-rigged • adjective (of a sailing ship) having the principal sails at right angles to the length of the ship.
square root • noun a number which produces a specified quantity when multiplied by itself.
square wave • noun Electronics a periodic wave that varies abruptly in amplitude between two fixed values.
squash[1] • verb **1** crush or squeeze (something) so that it becomes flat, soft, or out of shape. **2** squeeze or force into a restricted space. **3** suppress, subdue, or reject. • noun **1** a state of being squashed. **2** Brit. a concentrated liquid made from fruit juice and sugar, diluted to make a drink. **3** (also **squash rackets**) a game in which two players use rackets to hit a small rubber ball against the walls of a closed court. **4** dated a social

Thesaurus

squabble • noun *there was a squabble over which way they should go* QUARREL, disagreement, row, argument, contretemps, falling-out, dispute, clash, altercation, shouting match, exchange, war of words; *informal* tiff, set-to, run-in, slanging match, shindig, shindy, stand-up, spat, scrap, dust-up; *Brit. informal* barney, ding-dong; *N. Amer. informal* rhubarb.
• verb *the boys were squabbling over a ball* QUARREL, row, argue, bicker, fall out, disagree, have words, dispute, spar, cross swords, lock horns, be at loggerheads; *informal* scrap, argufy.
squad • noun **1** *an assassination squad* TEAM, crew, gang, band, cell, body, mob, outfit, force. **2** *a firing squad* DETACHMENT, detail, unit, platoon, battery, troop, patrol, squadron, cadre, commando.
squalid • adjective **1** *a squalid prison* DIRTY, filthy, grubby, grimy, mucky, slummy, foul, vile, poor, sorry, wretched, miserable, mean, seedy, shabby, sordid, insalubrious; NEGLECTED, uncared-for, broken-down, run down, down at heel, depressed, dilapidated, ramshackle, tumbledown, gone to rack and ruin, crumbling, decaying; *informal* scruffy, crummy, shambly, ratty; *Brit. informal* grotty; *N. Amer. informal* shacky. **2** *a squalid deal with the opposition* IMPROPER, sordid, unseemly, unsavoury, sleazy, seedy, seamy, shoddy, cheap, base, low, corrupt, dishonest, dishonourable, disreputable, despicable, discreditable, disgraceful, contemptible, shameful; *informal* sleazoid.
– OPPOSITES clean, pleasant, smart, upmarket, proper, decent.
squall • noun GUST, storm, blast, flurry, shower, gale, blow, rush.
squally • adjective STORMY, gusty, gusting, blustery, blustering, windy, blowy; wild, tempestuous, rough.
squalor • noun DIRT, filth, grubbiness, grime, muck, foulness, vileness, poverty, wretchedness, meanness, seediness, shabbiness, sordidness, sleaziness, insalubrity; NEGLECT, decay, dilapidation; *informal* scruffiness, crumminess, grunge, rattiness; *Brit. informal* grottiness.
– OPPOSITES cleanliness, pleasantness, smartness.
squander • verb WASTE, misspend, misuse, throw away, fritter away, spend recklessly, spend unwisely, spend like water; *informal* blow, go through, splurge, pour down the drain; *Brit. informal* blue.
– OPPOSITES manage, make good use of, save.
square • noun **1** *a shop in the square* market square, marketplace, plaza, piazza. **2** *(informal) you're such a square!* (OLD) FOGEY, conservative, traditionalist, conventionalist, conformist, bourgeois, fossil; *Brit.* museum piece; *informal* stick-in-the-mud, fuddy-duddy, back number, stuffed shirt.
– OPPOSITES trendy.
• adjective **1** *a square table* QUADRILATERAL, rectangular, oblong, right-angled, at right angles, perpendicular; straight, level, parallel, horizontal, upright, vertical, true, plane. **2** *the sides were square at half-time* LEVEL, even, drawn, equal, tied; neck and neck, level pegging, nip and tuck, side by side, evenly matched; *informal* even-steven(s). **3** *I'm going to be square with you* FAIR, honest, just, equitable, straight, true, upright, above board, ethical, decent, proper; *informal* on the level. **4** *(informal) don't be square!* OLD-FASHIONED, behind the times, out of date, conservative, traditionalist, conventional, conformist, bourgeois, strait-laced, fogeyish, stuffy; *informal* stick-in-the-mud, fuddy-duddy.
– OPPOSITES crooked, uneven, underhand, trendy.
• verb **1** *the theory does not square with the data* AGREE, tally, be in agreement, be consistent, match up, correspond, fit, coincide, accord, conform, be compatible. **2** *his goal squared the match 1–1* LEVEL, even, make equal. **3** *would you square up the bill?* PAY, settle, discharge, clear, meet. **4** *(informal) they tried to square the press* BRIBE, buy off, buy, corrupt, suborn; *informal* grease someone's palm, give a backhander to. **5** *Tom squared things with his boss*

S

gathering or informal meeting.
– DERIVATIVES **squashy** adjective (**squashier**, **squashiest**).
– ORIGIN from QUASH.

squash[2] ● noun (pl. same or **squashes**) a gourd with flesh that can be cooked and eaten as a vegetable.
– ORIGIN Narragansett.

squat ● verb (**squatted**, **squatting**) **1** crouch or sit with the knees bent and the heels close to the bottom or thighs. **2** unlawfully occupy an uninhabited building or area of land. ● adjective (**squatter**, **squattest**) short or low, and disproportionately broad or wide. ● noun **1** a squatting position or movement. **2** a building occupied by squatters. **3** an act of squatting in an uninhabited building.
– ORIGIN Old French *esquatir* 'flatten', from Latin *cogere* 'compel'.

squatter ● noun **1** a person who squats in a building or on unused land. **2** Austral./NZ a large-scale sheep or cattle farmer.

squat thrust ● noun an exercise in which the legs are thrust backwards to their full extent from a squatting position with the hands on the floor.

squaw /skwaw/ ● noun offensive an American Indian woman or wife.
– ORIGIN Narragansett, 'woman'.

squawk ● verb **1** (of a bird) make a loud, harsh noise. **2** say something in a loud, discordant tone. ● noun an act of squawking.
– DERIVATIVES **squawker** noun.
– ORIGIN imitative.

squawk box ● noun informal, chiefly N. Amer. a loudspeaker.

squeak ● noun **1** a short, high-pitched sound or cry. **2** a single remark or communication: *I didn't hear a squeak from him.* ● verb **1** make a squeak. **2** say something in a high-pitched tone. **3** informal succeed in achieving something by a very narrow margin.
– PHRASES **a narrow squeak** Brit. informal something that is only narrowly achieved.
– DERIVATIVES **squeaker** noun **squeaky** adjective (**squeakier**, **squeakiest**).
– ORIGIN imitative.

squeaky clean ● adjective informal **1** completely clean. **2** beyond reproach.

squeal ● noun a long, high-pitched cry or noise. ● verb **1** make a squeal. **2** say something in a high-pitched, excited tone. **3** complain. **4** (often **squeal on**) informal inform on someone.
– DERIVATIVES **squealer** noun.
– ORIGIN imitative.

squeamish ● adjective **1** easily nauseated or disgusted. **2** having fastidious moral views.
– DERIVATIVES **squeamishly** adverb **squeamishness** noun.
– ORIGIN Old French *escoymos*.

squeegee /skweejee/ ● noun a scraping implement with a rubber-edged blade, typically used for cleaning windows. ● verb (**squeegees**, **squeegeed**, **squeegeeing**) clean or scrape with a squeegee.
– ORIGIN from archaic *squeege* 'to press', from SQUEEZE.

squeeze ● verb **1** firmly press from opposite or all sides. **2** extract (liquid or a soft substance) from something by squeezing. **3** (**squeeze in/into/through**) manage to get into or through (a restricted space). **4** (**squeeze in**) manage to find time for. **5** obtain from someone with difficulty. **6** (**squeeze off**) informal shoot (a round or shot) from a gun. ● noun **1** an act of squeezing or the state of being squeezed. **2** a hug. **3** a small amount of liquid extracted by squeezing. **4** a strong financial demand or pressure. **5** (often **main squeeze**) N. Amer. informal a person's girlfriend or boyfriend.
– PHRASES **put the squeeze on** informal coerce or pressurize.
– DERIVATIVES **squeezable** adjective **squeezer** noun.
– ORIGIN from obsolete *queise*, of unknown origin.

squeeze box ● noun informal an accordion or concertina.

squeezy ● adjective (especially of a container) flexible and able to be squeezed to force out the contents.

squelch ● verb **1** make a soft sucking sound such as that of treading in thick mud. **2** informal forcefully silence or suppress. ● noun a squelching sound.
– DERIVATIVES **squelchy** adjective.
– ORIGIN imitative.

squib ● noun **1** a small firework that hisses before exploding. **2** a short piece of satirical writing.
– ORIGIN of unknown origin; perhaps imitative of a small explosion.

squid ● noun (pl. same or **squids**) an elongated cephalopod mollusc with eight arms and two long tentacles.
– ORIGIN of unknown origin.

squidge ● verb informal **1** squash or crush. **2** squelch.
– ORIGIN perhaps imitative.

squidgy ● adjective (**squidgier**, **squidgiest**) informal, chiefly Brit. soft and moist.

squiffy ● adjective (**squiffier**, **squiffiest**) informal **1** chiefly Brit. slightly drunk. **2** askew; awry.
– ORIGIN of unknown origin.

squiggle ● noun a short line that curls and loops irregularly.
– DERIVATIVES **squiggly** adjective.
– ORIGIN perhaps a blend of SQUIRM and WIGGLE or WRIGGLE.

squill ● noun **1** (also **sea squill**) a Mediterranean plant with broad leaves and white flowers. **2** a small plant resembling a hyacinth, with clusters of violet-blue or blue-striped flowers.
– ORIGIN Greek *skilla*.

squillion ● cardinal number informal an indefinite very large number.

Thesaurus

RESOLVE, sort out, settle, clear up, work out, iron out, smooth over, straighten out, deal with, put right, set right, put to rights, rectify, remedy; *informal* patch up.

squash ● verb **1** *the fruit got squashed* CRUSH, squeeze, flatten, compress, press, smash, distort, pound, trample, stamp on; pulp, mash, cream, liquidize, beat, pulverize. **2** *she squashed her clothes inside the bag* FORCE, ram, thrust, push, cram, jam, stuff, pack, compress, squeeze, wedge, press. **3** *the proposal was immediately squashed* REJECT, block, cancel, scotch, frustrate, thwart, suppress, put a stop to, nip in the bud, put the lid on; *informal* put paid to, put the kibosh on, stymie; *Brit. informal* dish, scupper.

squashy ● adjective **1** *a squashy pillow* SPRINGY, resilient, spongy, soft, pliant, pliable, yielding, elastic, cushiony, compressible. **2** *squashy pears* MUSHY, pulpy, pappy, slushy, squelchy, squishy, oozy, doughy, soft; *Brit. informal* squidgy.
– OPPOSITES firm, hard.

squat ● verb *I was squatting on the floor* CROUCH (DOWN), hunker (down), sit on one's haunches, sit on one's heels.
● adjective *he was muscular and squat* STOCKY, thickset, dumpy, stubby, stumpy, short, small; *Brit. informal* fubsy.

squawk ● verb & noun *a pheasant squawked | the gull gave a squawk* SCREECH, squeal, shriek, scream, croak, crow, caw, cluck, cackle, hoot, cry, call.

squeak ● noun & verb **1** *the vole's dying squeak | the rat squeaked* PEEP, cheep, pipe, piping, squeal, tweet, yelp, whimper. **2** *the squeak of the hinge | the hinges of the gate squeaked* SCREECH, creak, scrape, grate, rasp, jar, groan.

squeal ● noun *the harsh squeal of a fox* SCREECH, scream, shriek, squawk.
● verb **1** *a dog squealed* SCREECH, scream, shriek, squawk. **2** *the bookies only squealed because we beat them* COMPLAIN, protest, object, grouse, grumble, whine, wail, carp, squawk; *informal* kick up a fuss, kick up a stink, gripe, grouch, bellyache, moan, bitch, beef, whinge; *N. English informal* mither. **3** *(informal) he squealed on the rest of the gang to the police* INFORM, tell tales, sneak; report, give away, be disloyal, sell out, stab in the back; *informal* rat, peach, snitch, put the finger on, sell down the river, stitch up; *Brit. informal* grass, split, shop; *N. Amer. informal* rat out, finger, drop a/the dime on; *Austral. informal* dob, pimp on, pool.

squeamish ● adjective **1** *I'm too squeamish to gut fish* EASILY NAUSEATED, nervous; (**be squeamish about**) BE PUT OFF BY, cannot stand the sight of, —— makes one feel sick. **2** *less squeamish nations will sell them arms* SCRUPULOUS, principled, fastidious, particular, punctilious, honourable, upright, upstanding, high-minded, righteous, right-minded, moral, ethical.

squeeze ● verb **1** *I squeezed the bottle* COMPRESS, press, crush, squash, pinch, nip, grasp, grip, clutch, flatten. **2** *squeeze the juice from both oranges* EXTRACT, press, force, express. **3** *Sally squeezed her feet into the sandals* FORCE, thrust, cram, ram, jam, stuff, pack, wedge, press, squash. **4** *we all squeezed into Steve's van* CROWD, crush, cram, pack, jam, squash, wedge oneself, shove, push, force one's way. **5** *he would squeeze more money out of Bill* EXTORT, force, extract, wrest, wring, milk; *informal* bleed someone of something.
● noun **1** *he gave her hand a squeeze* PRESS, pinch, nip; grasp, grip, clutch, hug, clasp; compression. **2** *it was a tight squeeze in the*

– DERIVATIVES **squillionth** ordinal number.
– ORIGIN fanciful formation on the pattern of *billion* and *trillion*.
squinch ● verb chiefly N. Amer. tense up the muscles of (one's eyes or face).
– ORIGIN perhaps a blend of SQUEEZE and PINCH.
squint ● verb **1** look at someone or something with partly closed eyes. **2** partly close (one's eyes). **3** have a squint affecting one eye. ● noun **1** a permanent deviation in the direction of the gaze of one eye. **2** informal a quick or casual look.
– DERIVATIVES **squinty** adjective.
– ORIGIN perhaps related to Dutch *schuinte* 'slant'.
squire ● noun **1** a country gentleman, especially the chief landowner in an area. **2** Brit. informal used as a friendly form of address by one man to another. **3** historical a young nobleman acting as an attendant to a knight before becoming a knight himself. ● verb **1** (of a man) accompany or escort (a woman). **2** dated (of a man) have a romantic relationship with (a woman).
– ORIGIN Old French *esquier* 'esquire'.
squirearchy ● noun (pl. **squirearchies**) landowners collectively.
– ORIGIN from SQUIRE, on the pattern of words such as *hierarchy*.
squirm ● verb **1** wriggle or twist the body from side to side, especially due to nervousness or discomfort. **2** be embarrassed or ashamed. ● noun a wriggling movement.
– DERIVATIVES **squirmy** adjective.
– ORIGIN probably associated with WORM.
squirrel ● noun an agile tree-dwelling rodent with a bushy tail, typically feeding on nuts and seeds. ● verb (**squirrelled**, **squirrelling**; US also **squirreled**, **squirreling**) **1** (**squirrel away**) hide (money or valuables) in a safe place. **2** move about inquisitively or busily.
– ORIGIN Old French *esquireul*, from Greek *skia* 'shade' + *oura* 'tail'.
squirrelly ● adjective **1** relating to or resembling a squirrel. **2** informal, chiefly N. Amer. restless or nervous.
squirrel monkey ● noun a small South American monkey with a non-prehensile tail.
squirt ● verb **1** (with reference to a liquid) be or cause to be ejected in a thin jet from a small opening. **2** wet with a jet of liquid. ● noun **1** a thin jet of liquid. **2** a device from which liquid may be squirted. **3** informal a puny or insignificant person.
– ORIGIN imitative.
squish ● verb **1** make a soft squelching sound. **2** informal squash. ● noun a soft squelching sound.
– DERIVATIVES **squishy** adjective (**squishier**, **squishiest**).
– ORIGIN imitative.
squiz ● noun Austral./NZ informal a look or glance.
– ORIGIN probably a blend of QUIZ² and SQUINT.
Sr ● symbol the chemical element strontium.
sr ● abbreviation steradian(s).
SRAM ● abbreviation Electronics static random-access memory.
Sri Lankan /sri langkən, shri/ ● noun a person from Sri Lanka. ● adjective relating to Sri Lanka.
SRN ● abbreviation State Registered Nurse.
SS¹ ● abbreviation **1** Saints. **2** steamship.
SS² ● noun the Nazi special police force.
– ORIGIN abbreviation of German *Schutzstaffel* 'defence squadron'.
SSE ● abbreviation south-south-east.
SSP ● abbreviation (in the UK) statutory sick pay.
SSSI ● abbreviation (in the UK) Site of Special Scientific Interest.
SSW ● abbreviation south-south-west.
St ● abbreviation **1** Saint. **2** Street.
st ● abbreviation stone (in weight).
stab ● verb (**stabbed**, **stabbing**) **1** thrust a knife or other pointed weapon into. **2** thrust a pointed object at. **3** (of a pain or painful thing) cause a sudden sharp sensation. ● noun **1** an act of stabbing. **2** a sudden sharp feeling or pain. **3** (**a stab at**) informal an attempt to do.
– PHRASES **stab in the back** betray.
– DERIVATIVES **stabber** noun.
– ORIGIN of unknown origin.
stability ● noun the state of being stable.
stabilize (also **stabilise**) ● verb make or become stable.
– DERIVATIVES **stabilization** noun.
stabilizer (also **stabiliser**) ● noun **1** the horizontal tailplane of an aircraft. **2** a gyroscopic device used to reduce the rolling of a ship. **3** (**stabilizers**) Brit. a pair of small supporting wheels fitted on a child's bicycle. **4** a substance preventing the breakdown of emulsions, especially in food or paint.
stable¹ ● adjective (**stabler**, **stablest**) **1** not likely to give way or overturn; firmly fixed. **2** not deteriorating in health after an injury or operation. **3** emotionally well-balanced. **4** not likely to change or fail. **5** not liable to undergo chemical decomposition or radioactive decay.
– DERIVATIVES **stably** adverb.
– ORIGIN Latin *stabilis*, from *stare* 'to stand'.
stable² ● noun **1** a building for housing horses. **2** an establishment where racehorses are kept and trained. **3** an establishment producing particular types of people or things. ● verb put or keep (a horse) in a stable.
– ORIGIN Old French *estable* 'stable, pigsty', from Latin *stabulum*.
stable boy (or **stable girl**) ● noun a boy or man (or girl or

Thesaurus

tiny hall CRUSH, jam, squash, press, huddle; congestion. **3** *a squeeze of lemon juice* FEW DROPS, dash, splash, dribble, trickle, spot, hint, touch.
squint ● verb **1** *the sun made them squint* SCREW UP ONE'S EYES, narrow one's eyes, peer, blink. **2** *he has squinted from birth* BE CROSS-EYED, have a squint, suffer from strabismus; Scottish be skelly; Brit. informal be boss-eyed.
● noun **1** (informal) *we must have another squint at his record card* LOOK, glance, peep, peek, glimpse; view, examination, study, inspection, scan, sight; informal eyeful, dekko, butcher's, gander, look-see, once-over, shufti. **2** *does he have a squint?* CROSS-EYES, strabismus; Brit. informal boss-eye.
squire ● noun **1** *the squire of the village* LANDOWNER, landholder, landlord, lord of the manor, country gentleman. **2** (historical) *his squire carried a banner* ATTENDANT, courtier, equerry, aide, steward, page boy.
squirm ● verb **1** *I tried to squirm away* WRIGGLE, wiggle, writhe, twist, slide, slither, turn, shift, fidget, jiggle, twitch, thresh, flounder, flail, toss and turn. **2** *he squirmed as everyone laughed* WINCE, shudder, feel embarrassed, feel ashamed.
squirrel
– RELATED TERMS sciurine.
– PHRASES **squirrel something away** SAVE, put aside, put by, lay by, set aside, lay aside, keep in reserve, stockpile, accumulate, stock up with/on, hoard; informal salt away, stash away.
squirt ● verb **1** *a jet of ink squirted out of the tube* SPURT, shoot, spray, fountain, jet, erupt; gush, rush, pump, surge, stream, spew, well, spring, burst, issue, emanate; emit, belch forth, expel, eject; Brit. informal sloosh. **2** *she squirted me all over with scent* SPLASH, wet, spray, shower, spatter, splatter, sprinkle; Scottish & Irish slabber; poetic/literary besprinkle.
● noun **1** *a squirt of water* SPURT, jet, spray, fountain, gush, stream, surge. **2** (informal) *he was just a little squirt* IMPUDENT PERSON, insignificant person, gnat, insect; informal pipsqueak, whippersnapper; Brit. informal squit; Scottish informal nyaff; N. Amer. informal bozo, picayune, pisher.
stab ● verb **1** *he stabbed him in the stomach* KNIFE, run through, skewer, spear, bayonet, gore, spike, stick, impale, transfix, pierce, prick, puncture; poetic/literary transpierce. **2** *she stabbed at the earth with a fork* LUNGE, thrust, jab, poke, prod, dig.
● noun **1** *a stab in the leg* KNIFE WOUND, puncture, incision, prick, cut, perforation. **2** *they made stabs into the air* LUNGE, thrust, jab, poke, prod, dig, punch. **3** *a stab of pain* TWINGE, pang, throb, spasm, cramp, dart, blaze, prick, flash, thrill. **4** (informal) *he had a stab at writing* ATTEMPT, try, effort, endeavour; guess; informal go, shot, crack, bash, whack; formal essay.
– PHRASES **stab someone in the back** BETRAY, be disloyal to, be unfaithful to, desert, break one's promise to, double-cross, break faith with, sell out, play false, inform on/against; informal tell on, sell down the river, squeal on, stitch up, peach on, do the dirty on; Brit. informal grass on, shop; N. Amer. informal rat out, finger, drop a/the dime on; Austral. informal pimp on, pool, put someone's pot on.
stability ● noun **1** *the stability of play equipment* FIRMNESS, solidity, steadiness, strength, security, safety. **2** *his mental stability* BALANCE OF MIND, mental health, sanity, normality, soundness, rationality, reason, sense. **3** *the stability of their relationship* STEADINESS, firmness, solidity, strength, durability, lasting nature, enduring nature, permanence, changelessness, invariability, immutability, indestructibility, reliability, dependability.
stable ● adjective **1** *a stable tent* FIRM, solid, steady, secure, fixed, fast, safe, moored, anchored, stuck down, immovable. **2** *a stable person* WELL BALANCED, of sound mind, compos mentis, sane, nor-

S

woman) employed in a stable.

stable door ● noun a door of a kind found in a stable, divided into two parts horizontally.

stable lad ● noun Brit. a person employed in a stable.

stablemate ● noun **1** a horse from the same stable as another. **2** a person or product from the same organization or background as another.

stabling ● noun accommodation for horses.

staccato /stəkaatō/ ● adverb & adjective Music with each sound or note sharply separated from the others. ● noun (pl. **staccatos**) **1** Music a staccato passage or performance. **2** a series of short, detached sounds or words.
– ORIGIN Italian, 'detached'.

stack ● noun **1** a neat pile of objects. **2** a rectangular or cylindrical pile of hay, straw, etc. **3** informal a large quantity. **4** a chimney or vertical exhaust pipe. **5** (also **sea stack**) Brit. a column of rock standing in the sea. **6** a number of aircraft flying in circles at different altitudes around the same point while waiting to land at an airport. ● verb **1** arrange in a stack. **2** fill or cover with stacks of things. **3** cause (aircraft) to fly in stacks. **4** shuffle or arrange (a pack of cards) dishonestly. **5** (**be stacked against/in favour of**) (of a situation) be overwhelmingly likely to produce an unfavourable or favourable outcome for.
– DERIVATIVES **stackable** adjective **stacker** noun.
– ORIGIN Old Norse, 'haystack'.

stacked ● adjective **1** arranged in a stack or stacks. **2** filled or covered with goods. **3** (of a pack of cards) shuffled or arranged dishonestly.

stadium /staydiəm/ ● noun (pl. **stadiums** or **stadia** /staydiə/) **1** an athletic or sports ground with tiers of seats for spectators. **2** (in ancient Rome or Greece) a racing track.
– ORIGIN Greek *stadion*.

staff ● noun **1** (treated as sing. or pl.) the employees of an organization. **2** (treated as sing. or pl.) a group of officers assisting an officer in command of an army formation or administration headquarters. **3** a long stick used as a support or weapon. **4** a rod or sceptre held as a sign of office or authority. **5** Music another term for STAVE (in sense 3). ● verb provide with staff.
– PHRASES **the staff of life** a staple food or usual sustenance.
– ORIGIN Old English.

staff college ● noun a college at which military officers are trained for staff duties.

staffer ● noun chiefly N. Amer. a member of a staff, especially of a newspaper.

staff nurse ● noun Brit. an experienced nurse less senior than a sister or charge nurse.

staff officer ● noun a military officer serving on the staff of a headquarters or government department.

Staffordshire bull terrier ● noun a small, stocky breed of terrier with a short, broad head and dropped ears.

staffroom ● noun chiefly Brit. a common room for teachers in a school or college.

Staffs. ● abbreviation Staffordshire.

staff sergeant ● noun a rank of non-commissioned officer in the army, above sergeant and below warrant officer.

stag ● noun **1** a fully adult male deer. **2** an adult male turkey. **3** (before another noun) (of a social gathering) attended by men only. **4** Brit. Stock Exchange a person who applies for shares in a new issue with a view to selling at once for a profit. ● verb (**stagged**, **stagging**) Brit. Stock Exchange buy (shares in a new issue) and sell them at once for a profit.
– ORIGIN related to an Old Norse word meaning 'male bird'.

stag beetle ● noun a large dark beetle, the male of which has large branched jaws resembling antlers.

stage ● noun **1** a point, period, or step in a process or development. **2** a raised floor or platform on which actors, entertainers, or speakers perform. **3** (**the stage**) the acting or theatrical profession. **4** a scene of action or forum of debate. **5** a floor of a building. **6** each of two or more sections of a rocket or spacecraft that are jettisoned in turn when their propellant is exhausted. **7** Electronics a part of a circuit containing a single amplifying transistor or valve. **8** Geology a range of strata corresponding to an age in time, forming a subdivision of a series. **9** archaic a stagecoach. ● verb **1** present a performance of (a play or other show). **2** organize and participate in (a public event). **3** cause (something dramatic or unexpected) to happen.
– PHRASES **hold the stage** dominate a scene of action or forum of debate. **set the stage for** prepare the conditions for.
– DERIVATIVES **stageable** adjective.
– ORIGIN Old French *estage* 'dwelling', from Latin *stare* 'to stand'.

stagecoach ● noun a large closed horse-drawn vehicle formerly used to carry passengers and often mail along a regular route.

stagecraft ● noun skill in writing or staging plays.

stage direction ● noun an instruction in a play script indicating the position or tone of an actor, or specifying sound effects, lighting, etc.

stage door ● noun an actors' and workmen's entrance from the street to the backstage area of a theatre.

stage fright ● noun nervousness before or during a performance.

stagehand ● noun a person dealing with scenery or props during a play.

stage-manage ● verb **1** be the stage manager of. **2** arrange carefully to create a certain effect.
– DERIVATIVES **stage management** noun.

stage manager ● noun the person responsible for lighting and other technical arrangements for a stage play.

stage name ● noun a name assumed for professional purposes by an actor.

stage-struck ● adjective having a passionate love of the theatre and wishing to become an actor.

stage whisper ● noun a loud whisper by an actor on stage, intended to be heard by the audience.

stagey ● adjective variant spelling of STAGY.

stagflation ● noun Economics persistent high inflation combined with high unemployment and stagnant demand in a country's economy.
– ORIGIN blend of *stagnation* and *inflation*.

stagger ● verb **1** walk or move unsteadily, as if about to fall. **2** astonish. **3** spread over a period of time. **4** arrange (objects or parts) so that they are not in line. ● noun an act of staggering or a staggered arrangement.
– ORIGIN Old Norse.

staggers ● plural noun (usu. treated as sing.) **1** a diseased condition

S

Thesaurus

mal, right in the head, rational, steady, reasonable, sensible, sober, down-to-earth, matter-of-fact, having both one's feet on the ground; *informal* all there. **3** *a stable relationship* SECURE, solid, strong, steady, firm, sure, steadfast, unwavering, unvarying, unfaltering, unfluctuating; established, abiding, durable, enduring, lasting, permanent, reliable, dependable.
– OPPOSITES loose, wobbly, unbalanced, rocky, lasting, changeable.

stack ● noun **1** *a stack of boxes* HEAP, pile, mound, mountain, pyramid, tower. **2** *a stack of hay* HAYSTACK, rick, hayrick, stook, mow, shock; *dated* cock. **3** *(informal) a stack of money*. See LOT pronoun. **4** CHIMNEY, smokestack, funnel, exhaust pipe.
– OPPOSITES few, little.
● verb **1** *Leo was stacking plates* HEAP (UP), pile (up), make a heap/pile/stack of; assemble, put together, collect, hoard, store, stockpile. **2** *they stacked the shelves* LOAD, fill (up), lade, pack, charge, stuff, cram; stock.
– OPPOSITES empty.

stadium ● noun ARENA, field, ground, pitch; bowl, amphitheatre, coliseum, ring, dome, manège; track, course, racetrack, racecourse, speedway, velodrome; *(in ancient Rome)* circus.

staff ● noun **1** *there is a reluctance to take on new staff* EMPLOYEES, workers, workforce, personnel, human resources, manpower, labour; *informal* liveware. **2** *he carried a wooden staff* STICK, stave, pole, crook. **3** *a staff of office* ROD, tipstaff, cane, mace, wand, sceptre, crozier, verge; *Greek Mythology* caduceus.
● verb *the centre is staffed by teachers* MAN, people, crew, work, operate, occupy.

stage ● noun **1** *this stage of the development* PHASE, period, juncture, step, point, time, moment, instant, level. **2** *the last stage of the race* PART, section, portion, stretch, leg, lap, circuit. **3** *a theatre stage* PLATFORM, dais, stand, grandstand, staging, apron, rostrum, podium. **4** *she has written for the stage* THEATRE, drama, dramatics, dramatic art, thespianism; *informal* the boards. **5** *the political stage* SCENE, setting; context, frame, sphere, field, realm, arena, backdrop; affairs.
● verb **1** *they staged two plays* PUT ON, put before the public, present, produce, mount, direct; perform, act, give. **2** *workers staged a protest* ORGANIZE, arrange, coordinate, lay on, put together, get to-

of farm animals manifested by staggering or loss of balance. **2** (**the staggers**) the inability to stand or walk steadily.
staghorn (also **stag's horn**) ● noun the material of a stag's antler, used chiefly to make handles for cutlery.
staghound ● noun a large breed of dog used for hunting deer.
staging ● noun **1** an instance or method of staging something. **2** a stage or set of stages or platforms for performers or between levels of scaffolding. **3** Brit. shelving for plants in a greenhouse.
staging area ● noun a stopping place or assembly point en route to a destination.
staging post ● noun a place at which people or vehicles regularly stop during a journey.
stagnant ● adjective **1** (of water or air) motionless and often having an unpleasant smell as a consequence. **2** showing little activity.
– DERIVATIVES **stagnancy** noun.
– ORIGIN from Latin *stagnare* 'form a pool of standing water', from *stagnum* 'pool'.
stagnate ● verb become stagnant.
– DERIVATIVES **stagnation** noun.
stag night (also **stag party**) ● noun an all-male celebration, especially one held for a man about to be married.
stagy (also **stagey**) ● adjective (**stagier**, **stagiest**) excessively theatrical or exaggerated.
– DERIVATIVES **stagily** adverb **staginess** noun.
staid ● adjective respectable and unadventurous.
– ORIGIN archaic past participle of STAY[1].
stain ● verb **1** mark or discolour with something that is not easily removed. **2** damage (someone's or something's reputation). **3** colour with a penetrative dye or chemical. ● noun **1** a stubborn discoloured patch or dirty mark. **2** a thing that damages a reputation. **3** a dye or chemical used to colour materials. **4** Biology a dye used to colour organic tissue so as to make the structure visible for microscopic examination.
– DERIVATIVES **stainable** adjective **stainer** noun.
– ORIGIN from Old French *desteindre* 'tinge with a different colour'.
stained glass ● noun coloured glass used to form decorative or pictorial designs, typically used for church windows.
stainless ● adjective unmarked by or resistant to stains.
stainless steel ● noun a form of steel containing chromium, resistant to tarnishing and rust.
stair ● noun **1** each of a set of fixed steps. **2** (**stairs**) a set of such steps leading from one floor of a building to another.
– ORIGIN from a Germanic word meaning 'climb'.
staircase ● noun a set of stairs and its surrounding structure.
stairlift ● noun a lift in the form of a chair that can be raised or lowered at the edge of a domestic staircase.
stairway ● noun a staircase.
stairwell ● noun a shaft in which a staircase is built.
staithe /stayth/ ● noun (in the north and east of England) a landing stage for loading or unloading cargo boats.
– ORIGIN Old Norse.
stake[1] ● noun **1** a strong post with a point at one end, driven into the ground to support a tree, form part of a fence, etc. **2** (**the stake**) historical a wooden post to which a person was tied before being burned alive. ● verb **1** support (a plant) with a stake. **2** (**stake out**) mark (an area) with stakes so as to claim ownership. **3** (**stake out**) informal keep (a place or person) under surveillance.
– PHRASES **stake a claim** assert one's right to something.
– ORIGIN Old English, related to STICK[2].
stake[2] ● noun **1** a sum of money gambled on a risky game or venture. **2** a share or interest in a business or situation. **3** (**stakes**) prize money. **4** (**stakes**) a competitive situation: *one step ahead in the fashion stakes.* ● verb gamble (money or something of value).
– PHRASES **at stake 1** at risk. **2** at issue or in question.
– ORIGIN perhaps from STAKE[1], from the notion of an object being placed as a wager on a post or stake.
stakeholder ● noun **1** an independent party with whom money or counters wagered are deposited. **2** a person with an interest or concern in something.
stake-out ● noun informal a period of secret surveillance.
Stakhanovite /stəkaanəvīt/ ● noun a worker, especially in the former USSR, who is exceptionally productive or zealous.
– ORIGIN from the name of the Russian coal miner Aleksei Grigorevich *Stakhanov* (1906–77).
stalactite /staləktīt/ ● noun a tapering structure hanging from the roof of a cave, formed of calcium salts deposited by dripping water.
– ORIGIN from Greek *stalaktos* 'dripping', from *stalassein* 'to drip'.
stalagmite /staləgmīt/ ● noun a mound or tapering column rising from the floor of a cave, formed of calcium salts deposited by dripping water.
– ORIGIN from Greek *stalagma* 'a drop', from *stalassein* 'to drip'.
stale ● adjective (**staler**, **stalest**) **1** (of food) no longer fresh or pleasant to eat. **2** no longer new and interesting. **3** no longer performing well because of having done something for too long. ● verb make or become stale.
– DERIVATIVES **stalely** adverb **staleness** noun.
– ORIGIN originally describing beer in the sense 'clear from long standing': probably from Old French *estaler* 'to halt'.

Thesaurus

gether, set up; orchestrate, choreograph, mastermind, engineer; take part in, participate in, join in.
stagger ● verb **1** *he staggered to the door* LURCH, walk unsteadily, reel, sway, teeter, totter, stumble, wobble. **2** *I was absolutely staggered* AMAZE, astound, astonish, surprise, startle, stun, confound, dumbfound, stupefy, daze, nonplus, take aback, leave open-mouthed, leave aghast; *informal* flabbergast, bowl over; *Brit. informal* knock for six. **3** *meetings are staggered throughout the day* SPREAD (OUT), space (out), time at intervals, overlap. **4** *stagger the screws at each joint* ALTERNATE, step, arrange in a zigzag.
stagnant ● adjective **1** *stagnant water* STILL, motionless, static, stationary, standing, dead, slack; FOUL, stale, putrid, smelly. **2** *a stagnant economy* INACTIVE, sluggish, slow-moving, lethargic, static, flat, depressed, declining, moribund, dying, dead, dormant.
– OPPOSITES flowing, fresh, active, vibrant.
stagnate ● verb **1** *obstructions allow water to stagnate* STOP FLOWING, become stagnant, become trapped; stand; become foul, become stale; fester, putrefy. **2** *exports stagnated* LANGUISH, decline, deteriorate, fall, become stagnant, do nothing, stand still, be sluggish.
– OPPOSITES flow, rise, boom.
staid ● adjective SEDATE, respectable, quiet, serious, serious-minded, steady, conventional, traditional, unadventurous, unenterprising, set in one's ways, sober, proper, decorous, formal, stuffy, stiff; *informal* starchy, stick-in-the-mud.
– OPPOSITES frivolous, daring, informal.
stain ● verb **1** *her clothing was stained with blood* DISCOLOUR, blemish, soil, mark, muddy, spot, spatter, splatter, smear, splash, smudge, blotch, blacken. **2** *the report stained his reputation* DAMAGE, injure, harm, sully, blacken, tarnish, taint, smear, bring discredit to, dishonour, drag through the mud; *poetic/literary* besmirch. **3** *the wood was stained* COLOUR, tint, dye, tinge, pigment, colourwash.
● noun **1** *a mud stain* MARK, spot, spatter, splatter, blotch, smudge, smear. **2** *a stain on his character* BLEMISH, injury, taint, blot, smear, discredit, dishonour; damage. **3** *dark wood stain* TINT, colour, dye, tinge, pigment, colourant, colour wash.
stake[1] ● noun *a stake in the ground* POST, pole, stick, spike, upright, support, prop, strut, pale, paling, picket, pile, piling, cane.
● verb **1** *the plants have to be staked* PROP UP, tie up, tether, support, hold up, brace, truss. **2** *he staked his claim* ASSERT, declare, proclaim, state, make, lay, put in.
– PHRASES **stake something out 1** *builders staked out the plot* MARK OFF/OUT, demarcate, measure out, delimit, fence off, section off, close off, shut off, cordon off. **2** *(informal) the police staked out his flat* OBSERVE, watch, keep an eye on, keep under observation, keep watch on, monitor, keep under surveillance, surveil; *informal* keep tabs on, keep a tab on, case.
stake[2] ● noun **1** *playing dice for high stakes* BET, wager, ante. **2** *they are racing for record stakes* PRIZE MONEY, purse, pot, winnings. **3** *low down in the popularity stakes* COMPETITION, contest, battle, challenge, rivalry, race, running, struggle, scramble. **4** *a 40% stake in the business* SHARE, interest, ownership, involvement.
● verb *he staked all his week's pay* BET, wager, lay, put on, gamble, chance, venture, risk, hazard.
stale ● adjective **1** *stale food* OLD, past its best, past its sell-by date; off, dry, hard, musty, rancid. **2** *stale air* STUFFY, close, musty, fusty, stagnant, frowzy; *Brit.* frowsty, fuggy. **3** *stale beer* FLAT, turned, spoiled, off, insipid, tasteless. **4** *stale jokes* HACKNEYED, tired, worn out, overworked, threadbare, warmed-up, banal, trite,

stalemate ● noun **1** Chess a position counting as a draw, in which a player is not in check but can only move into check. **2** a situation in which further progress by opposing parties seems impossible. ● verb bring to stalemate.
– ORIGIN from Old French *estale* 'position' + MATE².

Stalinism ● noun the ideology and policies adopted by the Soviet Communist Party leader and head of state Joseph Stalin (1879–1953), based on centralization, totalitarianism, and the pursuit of communism.
– DERIVATIVES **Stalinist** noun & adjective.

stalk¹ ● noun **1** the main stem of a herbaceous plant. **2** the attachment or support of a leaf, flower, or fruit. **3** a slender support or stem.
– DERIVATIVES **stalk-like** adjective **stalky** adjective.
– ORIGIN probably from an Old English word meaning 'rung of a ladder, long handle'.

stalk² ● verb **1** pursue or approach stealthily. **2** harass or persecute with unwanted and obsessive attention. **3** stride in a proud, stiff, or angry manner. **4** chiefly literary move silently or threateningly through. ● noun **1** a stealthy pursuit. **2** a stiff, striding gait.
– DERIVATIVES **stalker** noun.
– ORIGIN Old English.

stalking horse ● noun **1** a false pretext concealing someone's real intentions. **2** a candidate for the leadership of a political party who stands only in order to provoke an election and thus allow a stronger candidate to come forward.
– ORIGIN from the former practice of using a horse trained to allow a fowler to hide behind it until within easy range of prey.

stall ● noun **1** a stand, booth, or compartment for the sale of goods in a market. **2** an individual compartment for an animal in a stable or cowshed, enclosed on three sides. **3** a stable or cowshed. **4** (also **starting stall**) a cage-like compartment in which a horse is held prior to the start of a race. **5** a compartment for one person in a set of toilets, shower cubicles, etc. **6** (**stalls**) Brit. the ground-floor seats in a theatre. **7** a seat in the choir or chancel of a church, enclosed at the back and sides. ● verb **1** (with reference to a motor vehicle or its engine) stop running. **2** (of an aircraft) be moving at a speed too low to allow effective operation of the controls. **3** stop making progress. **4** prevaricate or delay by prevaricating: *she was stalling for time.*
– ORIGIN Old English, related to STAND.

stallholder ● noun Brit. a person in charge of a market stall.

stallion ● noun an uncastrated adult male horse.
– ORIGIN Old French *estalon*.

stalwart /stawlwərt/ ● adjective **1** loyal, reliable, and hard-working. **2** dated sturdy. ● noun a stalwart supporter or member of an organization.
– ORIGIN Scots, from Old English words meaning 'place' + 'worth'.

stamen /staymən/ ● noun Botany a male fertilizing organ of a flower, typically consisting of a pollen-containing anther and a filament.
– ORIGIN Latin, 'warp in an upright loom, thread'.

stamina ● noun the ability to sustain prolonged physical or mental effort.
– ORIGIN originally in the sense 'rudiments': from Latin, plural of STAMEN in the sense 'threads spun by the Fates'.

stammer ● verb **1** speak with sudden involuntary pauses and a tendency to repeat the initial letters of words. **2** say in such a way. ● noun a tendency to stammer.
– DERIVATIVES **stammerer** noun.
– ORIGIN Old English, related to STUMBLE.

stamp ● verb **1** bring down (one's foot) heavily on the ground or an object. **2** walk with heavy, forceful steps. **3** (**stamp out**) suppress or put an end to by taking decisive action. **4** impress with a device that leaves a mark or pattern. **5** impress (a pattern or mark). **6** (**stamp on**) fix in the mind: *the date was stamped on his memory.* **7** cut out using a die or mould. **8** fix a postage stamp to. ● noun **1** a small adhesive piece of paper recording payment of postage. **2** an instrument for stamping a pattern or mark. **3** a mark or pattern made by a stamp. **4** a characteristic or distinctive impression or quality. **5** a particular class or type: *he went around with men of his own stamp.* **6** an act or sound of stamping the foot.
– DERIVATIVES **stamper** noun.
– ORIGIN Germanic.

stamp duty ● noun a duty levied on the legal recognition of certain documents.

stampede ● noun **1** a sudden panicked rush of a number of horses, cattle, etc. **2** a sudden rapid movement or reaction of a mass of people due to interest or panic. ● verb take part or cause to take part in a stampede.
– DERIVATIVES **stampeder** noun.
– ORIGIN Spanish *estampida* 'crash, uproar'.

stamping ground (N. Amer. also **stomping ground**) ● noun a place one regularly frequents.

stance /staanss, stanss/ ● noun **1** the way in which someone stands. **2** an attitude or standpoint. **3** Scottish a street site for a market, stall, or taxi rank.
– ORIGIN French, from Italian *stanza*.

stanch /stawnch, staanch/ ● verb chiefly US variant spelling of STAUNCH².

Thesaurus

clichéd, platitudinous, unoriginal, unimaginative, uninspired, flat; out of date, outdated, outmoded, passé, archaic, obsolete; *N. Amer.* warmed-over; *informal* old hat, corny, out of the ark, played out.
– OPPOSITES fresh, original.

S

stalemate ● noun DEADLOCK, impasse, stand-off; draw, tie, dead heat.

stalk¹ ● noun *the stalk of a plant* STEM, shoot, trunk, stock, cane, bine, bent, haulm, straw, reed.
– RELATED TERMS cauline.

stalk² ● verb **1** *a stoat was stalking a rabbit* CREEP UP ON, trail, follow, shadow, track down, go after, be after, course, hunt; *informal* tail. **2** *she stalked out* STRUT, stride, march, flounce, storm, stomp, sweep.

stall ● noun **1** *a market stall* STAND, table, counter, booth, kiosk. **2** *stalls for larger animals* PEN, coop, sty, corral, enclosure, compartment. **3** *(Brit.) theatre stalls N. Amer.* orchestra, parterre.
● verb **1** *the Government has stalled the project* OBSTRUCT, impede, interfere with, hinder, hamper, block, interrupt, hold up, hold back, thwart, baulk, sabotage, delay, stonewall, check, stop, halt, derail, put a brake on; *informal* stymie; *N. Amer. informal* bork. **2** *quit stalling* USE DELAYING TACTICS, play for time, temporize, gain time, procrastinate, hedge, beat about the bush, drag one's feet, delay, filibuster, stonewall. **3** *stall him for a bit* DELAY, divert, distract; HOLD OFF, stave off, fend off, keep off, ward off, keep at bay.

stalwart ● adjective STAUNCH, loyal, faithful, committed, devoted, dedicated, dependable, reliable, steady, constant, trusty, hard-working, steadfast, redoubtable, unwavering.
– OPPOSITES disloyal, unfaithful, unreliable.

stamina ● noun ENDURANCE, staying power, tirelessness, fortitude, strength, energy, toughness, determination, tenacity, perseverance, grit.

stammer ● verb *he began to stammer* STUTTER, stumble over one's words, hesitate, falter, pause, halt, splutter.
● noun *he had a stammer* STUTTER, speech impediment, speech defect.

stamp ● verb **1** *he stamped on my toe* TRAMPLE, step, tread, tramp; CRUSH, squash, flatten. **2** *John stamped off, muttering* STOMP, stump, clomp, clump. **3** *the name is stamped on the cover* IMPRINT, print, impress, punch, inscribe, emboss, brand, frank. **4** *his face was stamped on Martha's memory* FIX, inscribe, etch, carve, imprint, impress. **5** *his style stamps him as a player to watch* IDENTIFY, characterize, brand, distinguish, classify, mark out, set apart, single out.
● noun **1** *the stamp of authority* MARK, hallmark, indication, sign, seal, sure sign, telltale sign, quality, smack, smell, savour, air. **2** *he was of a very different stamp* TYPE, kind, sort, variety, class, category, classification, style, description, condition, calibre, status, quality, nature, ilk, kidney, cast, grain, mould; *N. Amer.* stripe.
– PHRASES **stamp something out** PUT AN END/STOP TO, end, stop, crush, put down, crack down on, curb, nip in the bud, scotch, squash, quash, quell, subdue, suppress, extinguish, stifle, abolish, get rid of, eliminate, eradicate, beat, overcome, defeat, destroy, wipe out; *informal* put the kibosh on.

stamp collecting ● noun PHILATELY.

stampede ● noun *the noise caused a stampede* CHARGE, panic, rush, flight, rout.
● verb *the sheep stampeded* BOLT, charge, flee, take flight; race, rush, career, sweep, run.

stance ● noun **1** *a natural golfer's stance* POSTURE, body position,

stanchion /stansh'n/ ● noun an upright bar, post, or frame forming a support or barrier.
– ORIGIN Old French *stanchon*, from *estance* 'a support'.

stand ● verb (past and past part. **stood**) **1** be in or rise to an upright position, supported by one's feet. **2** place or be situated in a particular position. **3** move in a standing position to a specified place: *stand aside*. **4** remain stationary or without disturbance. **5** be in a specified state or condition. **6** remain valid or unaltered. **7** adopt a particular attitude towards an issue. **8** be likely to do something: *investors stood to lose heavily*. **9** act in a specified capacity. **10** tolerate, withstand, or like: *I can't stand it*. **11** Brit. be a candidate in an election. **12** provide (food or drink) for (someone) at one's expense. **13** (of a ship) remain on a specified course. ● noun **1** an attitude towards a particular issue. **2** a determined effort to hold one's ground or resist something. **3** a stopping of motion or progress. **4** a large raised tiered structure for spectators. **5** a raised platform for a band, orchestra, or speaker. **6** a rack, base, or item of furniture for holding or displaying something. **7** a small temporary stall or booth from which promotional goods are sold or displayed. **8** (**the stand**) a witness box. **9** a place where vehicles wait for passengers. **10** a group of trees or other plants. **11** Cricket a partnership.
– PHRASES **stand alone** be unequalled. **stand and deliver!** a highwayman's order to hand over money and valuables. **stand by 1** look on without intervening. **2** support, remain loyal to, or abide by. **3** be ready to take action if required. **stand down 1** (also **stand aside**) resign from or leave a position or office. **2** relax after a state of readiness. **stand for 1** be an abbreviation of or symbol for. **2** endure or tolerate. **stand in** deputize. **stand off** move or keep away. **stand on** be scrupulous in the observance of. **stand on one's own (two) feet** be or become self-reliant or independent. **stand out 1** project or be easily noticeable. **2** be clearly better. **stand to** Military stand ready for an attack. **stand trial** be tried in a court of law. **stand up** informal fail to keep a date with (someone). **stand up and be counted** state publicly one's support for someone or something. **stand up for** speak or act in support of. **stand up to 1** make a spirited defence against. **2** be resistant to the harmful effects of.
– USAGE it is not good English to use the past participle **stood** with the verb 'to be', as in *we were stood in a line for hours*; the correct form is *we were standing in a line for hours*.
– ORIGIN Old English, related to STEAD.

stand-alone ● adjective (of computer hardware or software) able to operate independently of other hardware or software.

standard ● noun **1** a level of quality or attainment. **2** a required or agreed level of quality or attainment. **3** something used as a measure, norm, or model in comparative evaluations. **4** (**standards**) principles of honourable, decent behaviour. **5** a military or ceremonial flag. **6** an upright water or gas pipe. **7** a tree that grows on an erect stem of full height. **8** a shrub grafted on an erect stem and trained in tree form. ● adjective **1** used or accepted as normal or average. **2** (of a size, measure, etc.) regularly used or produced. **3** (of a work, writer, etc.) viewed as authoritative and so widely read.
– DERIVATIVES **standardly** adverb.
– ORIGIN Old French *estendart*, from *estendre* 'extend'.

standard assessment task ● noun (in the UK) a standard test given to schoolchildren to assess their progress in a core subject of the national curriculum.

standard-bearer ● noun **1** a soldier carrying the standard of a unit, regiment, or army. **2** a leading figure in a cause or movement.

standard deviation ● noun Statistics a quantity calculated to indicate the extent of deviation for a group as a whole.

Standard Grade ● noun (in Scotland) an examination equivalent to the GCSE.

standardize (also **standardise**) ● verb **1** cause to conform to a standard. **2** determine the properties of by comparison with a standard.
– DERIVATIVES **standardization** noun.

standard lamp ● noun chiefly Brit. a lamp with a tall stem whose base stands on the floor.

standard of living ● noun the degree of material comfort available to a person or community.

standard time ● noun a uniform time for places in approximately the same longitude.

standby ● noun (pl. **standbys**) **1** readiness for duty or immedi-

Thesaurus

pose, attitude. **2** *a liberal stance* ATTITUDE, stand, point of view, viewpoint, opinion, way of thinking, outlook, standpoint, position, angle, perspective, approach, line, policy.

stand ● verb **1** *Lionel stood in the doorway* BE ON ONE'S FEET, be upright, be erect, be vertical. **2** *the men stood up* RISE, get/rise to one's feet, get up, straighten up, pick oneself up, find one's feet, be upstanding; *formal* arise. **3** *today a house stands on the site* BE, be situated, be located, be positioned, be sited, have been built. **4** *he stood the book on the shelf* PUT, set, set up, erect, up-end, place, position, locate, prop, lean, stick, install, arrange; *informal* park. **5** *my decision stands* REMAIN IN FORCE, remain valid/effective/operative, remain in operation, hold, hold good, apply, be the case, exist; *formal* obtain. **6** *his heart could not stand the strain* WITHSTAND, endure, bear, put up with, take, cope with, handle, sustain, resist, stand up to. **7** *I can't stand it any longer* ENDURE, tolerate, bear, put up with, take, abide, support, countenance; *Scottish* thole; *informal* swallow, stomach; *Brit. informal* stick, wear; *formal* brook.
– OPPOSITES sit, lie, sit down, lie down.
● noun **1** *the party's stand on immigration* ATTITUDE, stance, point of view, viewpoint, opinion, way of thinking, outlook, standpoint, position, approach, thinking, policy, line. **2** *a stand against tyranny* OPPOSITION, resistance, objection, hostility, animosity. **3** *a large mirror on a stand* BASE, support, mounting, platform, rest, plinth, bottom; tripod, rack, trivet. **4** *a beer stand* STALL, counter, booth, kiosk, tent. **5** *a taxi stand* RANK, station, park, bay. **6** *the train drew to a stand* STOP, halt, standstill, dead stop. **7** *a stand of trees* COPSE, spinney, thicket, grove.
– PHRASES **stand by** WAIT, be prepared, be in (a state of) readiness, be ready for action, be on full alert, wait in the wings. **stand by someone/something 1** *she stood by her husband* REMAIN/BE LOYAL TO, stick with/by, remain/be true to, stand up for, support, back up, defend, stick up for. **2** *the government must stand by its pledges* ABIDE BY, keep (to), adhere to, hold to, stick to, observe, comply with. **stand down** RELAX, stand easy, come off full alert. **stand for 1** *V stands for volts* MEAN, be an abbreviation of, represent, signify, denote, indicate, symbolize. **2** *I won't stand for any nonsense* PUT UP WITH, endure, tolerate, accept, take, abide, stand, support, countenance; *informal* swallow, stomach; *Brit. informal* stick, wear; *formal* brook. **3** *we stand for animal welfare* ADVOCATE, champion, uphold, defend, stand up for, support, back, endorse, be in favour of, promote, recommend, urge. **stand in** DEPUTIZE, act, act as deputy, substitute, fill in, sit in, do duty, take over, act as locum, be a proxy, cover, hold the fort, step into the breach; replace, relieve, take over from; *informal* sub, fill someone's shoes, step into someone's shoes; *N. Amer.* pinch-hit. **stand out 1** *his veins stood out* PROJECT, stick out, bulge (out), be proud, jut (out). **2** *she stood out in the crowd* BE NOTICEABLE, be visible, be obvious, be conspicuous, stick out, be striking, be distinctive, be prominent, attract attention, catch the eye, leap out, show up; *informal* stick/stand out a mile, stick/stand out like a sore thumb. **stand up** REMAIN/BE VALID, be sound, be plausible, hold water, hold up, stand questioning, survive investigation, bear examination, be verifiable. **stand up for someone/something** SUPPORT, defend, back, back up, stick up for, champion, promote, uphold, take someone's part, take the side of, side with, be loyal to, come to the defence of. **stand up to someone/something 1** *she stood up to her parents* DEFY, confront, challenge, resist, take on, put up a fight against, argue with, take a stand against. **2** *the old house has stood up to the war* WITHSTAND, survive, come through (unscathed), outlast, outlive, weather, ride out, ward off.

standard ● noun **1** *the standard of her work* QUALITY, level, grade, calibre, merit, excellence. **2** *a safety standard* GUIDELINE, norm, yardstick, benchmark, measure, criterion, guide, touchstone, model, pattern, example, exemplar. **3** *a standard to live by* PRINCIPLE, ideal; (**standards**) code of behaviour, code of honour, morals, scruples, ethics. **4** *the regiment's standard* FLAG, banner, pennant, ensign, colour(s), banderole, guidon; *Brit.* pendant; *Nautical* burgee.
● adjective **1** *the standard way of doing it* NORMAL, usual, typical, stock, common, ordinary, customary, conventional, wonted, established, settled, set, fixed, traditional, prevailing. **2** *the standard work on the subject* DEFINITIVE, established, classic, recognized, accepted, authoritative, most reliable, exhaustive.
– OPPOSITES unusual, special.

ate action. **2** a person or thing ready to be deployed in an emergency. ● adjective (of tickets for a journey or performance) unreserved and sold only at the last minute if still available.
standee /standee/ ● noun chiefly N. Amer. a person who is standing.
stand-in ● noun a substitute.
standing ● noun **1** position, status, or reputation. **2** duration: *a problem of long standing.* ● adjective **1** (of a jump or start of a race) performed from rest or an upright position. **2** remaining in force or use: *a standing invitation.* **3** (of water) stagnant or still. **4** (of corn) not yet reaped.
– PHRASES **leave standing** informal be much better or faster than.
standing committee ● noun a permanent committee meeting regularly.
standing joke ● noun something regularly causing amusement or provoking ridicule.
standing order ● noun **1** Brit. an instruction to a bank to make regular fixed payments to someone. **2** Brit. an order placed on a regular basis with a retailer. **3** (**standing orders**) rulings governing the procedures of a parliament, council, etc.
standing ovation ● noun a period of prolonged applause during which the audience rise to their feet.
standing stone ● noun another term for MENHIR.
standing wave ● noun Physics a vibration of a system in which some particular points remain fixed while others between them vibrate with the maximum amplitude.
stand-off ● noun **1** a deadlock between two equally matched opponents. **2** short for STAND-OFF HALF.
stand-off half ● noun Rugby a halfback who forms a link between the scrum half and the three-quarters.
stand-offish ● adjective informal distant and cold in manner.
standout ● noun informal, chiefly N. Amer. an outstanding person or thing.
standpipe ● noun a vertical pipe extending from a water supply, especially one connecting a temporary tap to the mains.
standpoint ● noun **1** an attitude towards a particular issue. **2** the position from which a scene or an object is viewed.
standstill ● noun a situation or condition without movement or activity.
stand-to ● noun Military **1** the action or state of standing to. **2** the beginning of a spell of duty.
stand-up ● adjective **1** involving or used by people standing up. **2** (of comedy or a comedian) performed or performing by standing in front of an audience and telling jokes. **3** (of a fight or argument) involving direct confrontation; loud or violent. **4** designed to stay upright or erect.
stank past of STINK.
Stanley knife ● noun Brit. trademark a utility knife with a short, strong replaceable blade.
stannary /stannəri/ ● noun (pl. **stannaries**) Brit., chiefly historical a tin-mining district in Cornwall or Devon.
– ORIGIN Latin *stannaria* (plural), from *stannum* 'tin'.
St Anthony's fire ● noun **1** another term for ERYSIPELAS. **2** another term for ERGOTISM.
stanza /stanzə/ ● noun a group of lines forming the basic recurring metrical unit in a poem; a verse.
– ORIGIN Italian, 'standing place, stanza'.
staphylococcus /staffiləkokkəss/ ● noun (pl. **staphylococci** /staffiləkokkī/) a bacterium of a genus including many kinds that cause pus to be formed.
– DERIVATIVES **staphylococcal** adjective.
– ORIGIN from Greek *staphulē* 'bunch of grapes' + *kokkos* 'berry'.
staple[1] ● noun **1** a small flattened U-shaped piece of wire used to fasten papers together. **2** a small U-shaped metal bar with pointed ends for driving into wood to hold things in place. ● verb secure with a staple or staples.
– ORIGIN Old English, 'pillar'.
staple[2] ● noun **1** a main item of trade or production. **2** a main or important element of something. **3** the fibre of cotton or wool considered with regard to its length and fineness. ● adjective main or important: *a staple food.*
– ORIGIN originally denoting a centre of trade in a specified commodity: from Low German, Dutch *stapel* 'pillar, emporium'; related to STAPLE[1].
stapler ● noun a device for fastening papers together with staples.
star ● noun **1** a fixed luminous point in the night sky which is a large, remote incandescent body like the sun. **2** a stylized representation of a star, often used to indicate a category of excellence. **3** a famous or talented entertainer or sports player. **4** an outstanding person or thing in a group. **5** Astrology a planet, constellation, or configuration regarded as influencing one's fortunes or personality. ● verb (**starred**, **starring**) **1** (of a film, play, etc.) have (someone) as a principal performer. **2** (of a performer) have a principal role in a film, play, etc. **3** mark, decorate, or cover with star-shaped marks or objects.
– PHRASES **see stars** seem to see flashes of light as a result of a blow on the head.
– ORIGIN Old English.
star anise ● noun a small star-shaped fruit with an aniseed flavour, used in Asian cookery.
starboard /staarbərd/ ● noun the side of a ship or aircraft on the right when one is facing forward. The opposite of PORT[3]. ● verb turn (a ship or its helm) to starboard.
– ORIGIN Old English, 'rudder side', because early Teutonic sailing vessels were steered with a paddle on the right side; related to STEER[1].
starburst ● noun **1** a pattern of lines or rays radiating from a central point. **2** an explosion producing such an effect. **3** Astronomy an intense episode of star formation.
starch ● noun **1** an odourless, tasteless carbohydrate which is obtained chiefly from cereals and potatoes and is an important constituent of the human diet. **2** powder or spray made from this substance, used to stiffen fabric. **3** stiffness of manner.

Thesaurus

standardize ● verb SYSTEMATIZE, make consistent, make uniform, make comparable, regulate, normalize, bring into line, equalize, homogenize, regiment.
stand-in ● noun *a stand-in for the minister* SUBSTITUTE, replacement, deputy, surrogate, proxy, understudy, locum, supply, fill-in, cover, relief, stopgap; *informal* temp; *N. Amer. informal* pinch-hitter.
● adjective *a stand-in goalkeeper* SUBSTITUTE, replacement, deputy, fill-in, stopgap, supply, surrogate, relief, acting, temporary, provisional, caretaker; *N. Amer. informal* pinch-hitting.
standing ● noun **1** *his standing in the community* STATUS, rank, ranking, position; reputation, estimation, stature; *dated* station. **2** *a person of some standing* SENIORITY, rank, eminence, prominence, prestige, repute, stature, esteem, importance, account, consequence, influence, distinction; *informal* clout; *dated* mark. **3** *a squabble of long standing* DURATION, existence, continuance, endurance, life.
● adjective **1** *standing stones* UPRIGHT, erect, vertical, plumb, upended, on end, perpendicular; on one's feet; not yet reaped; *Heraldry* rampant. **2** *standing water* STAGNANT, still, motionless, static, stationary, dead, slack. **3** *a standing invitation* PERMANENT, perpetual, everlasting, continuing, abiding, indefinite, open-ended; regular, repeated.
– OPPOSITES flat, lying down, seated, flowing, temporary, occasional.
stand-off ● noun DEADLOCK, stalemate, impasse; draw, tie, dead heat; suspension of hostilities, lull.
stand-offish ● adjective *(informal)* ALOOF, distant, remote, detached, withdrawn, reserved, uncommunicative, unforthcoming, unapproachable, unresponsive, unfriendly, unsociable, introspective, introverted.
– OPPOSITES friendly, approachable, sociable.
standpoint ● noun POINT OF VIEW, viewpoint, vantage point, attitude, stance, view, opinion, position, way of thinking, outlook, perspective.
standstill ● noun HALT, stop, dead stop, stand.
staple ● adjective MAIN, principal, chief, major, primary, leading, foremost, first, most important, predominant, dominant, (most) prominent, basic, standard, prime, premier; *informal* number-one.
star ● noun **1** *the sky was full of stars* CELESTIAL BODY, heavenly body, sun; asteroid, planet. **2** *the stars of the film* PRINCIPAL, leading lady/man, lead, female/male lead, hero, heroine. **3** *a star of the world of chess* CELEBRITY, superstar, big name, famous name, household name, someone, somebody, lion, leading light, VIP, personality, personage, luminary; *informal* celeb, big shot, big noise, megastar.
– RELATED TERMS astral, astro-, sidereal, sidero-, stellar.
– OPPOSITES nobody.
● adjective **1** *a star pupil* BRILLIANT, talented, gifted, able, exceptional, outstanding, bright, clever, masterly, consummate, precocious, prodigious. **2** *the star attraction* TOP, leading, best, greatest,

• verb stiffen with starch.
– ORIGIN from Old English, 'stiffened', related to STARK.
starchy • adjective (**starchier**, **starchiest**) **1** (of food) containing a lot of starch. **2** (of clothing) stiff with starch. **3** informal very stiff, formal, or prim in manner or character.
– DERIVATIVES **starchily** adverb **starchiness** noun.
star-crossed • adjective literary ill-fated.
stardom • noun the state or status of being a famous or talented entertainer or sports player.
stardust • noun magical or charismatic quality or feeling.
stare • verb **1** look fixedly at someone or something with the eyes wide open. **2** (**stare out/down**) look fixedly at (someone) until they feel forced to look away. • noun an act of staring.
– PHRASES **be staring someone in the face** be glaringly obvious.
– DERIVATIVES **starer** noun.
– ORIGIN Old English.
starfish • noun a marine echinoderm having a flattened body with five or more radiating arms bearing tube feet.
starfruit • noun **1** another term for CARAMBOLA. **2** a small aquatic plant with tiny white flowers and six-pointed star-shaped fruit.
stargazer • noun informal an astronomer or astrologer.
stark • adjective **1** severe or bare in appearance. **2** unpleasantly or sharply clear. **3** complete; sheer: *stark terror*.
– PHRASES **stark naked** completely naked. **stark raving** (or **staring**) **mad** informal completely mad.
– DERIVATIVES **starkly** adverb **starkness** noun.
– ORIGIN Old English, 'unyielding, severe'.
starkers • adjective informal, chiefly Brit. completely naked.
starlet • noun informal a promising young actress or performer.
starlight • noun light coming from the stars.
starling • noun a gregarious songbird with dark lustrous or iridescent plumage.
– ORIGIN Old English.
starlit • adjective lit by stars.
Star of David • noun a six-pointed figure consisting of two interlaced equilateral triangles, used as a Jewish and Israeli symbol.
starry • adjective (**starrier**, **starriest**) **1** full of or lit by stars. **2** informal relating to stars in entertainment.
starry-eyed • adjective naively enthusiastic or idealistic.
Stars and Bars • plural noun (treated as sing.) historical the flag of the Confederate States of America.
Stars and Stripes • plural noun (treated as sing.) the national flag of the US.
star shell • noun an explosive projectile which bursts in the air to light up an enemy's position.
starship • noun (in science fiction) a large manned spaceship for interstellar travel.
star sign • noun a sign of the zodiac.
star-spangled • adjective **1** literary covered or decorated with stars. **2** informal very successful or celebrated.
star-struck • adjective fascinated and greatly impressed by famous people.
star-studded • adjective **1** (of the sky) filled with stars. **2** informal featuring a number of famous people.
START • abbreviation Strategic Arms Reduction Talks.
start • verb **1** begin to do, be, happen, or engage in. **2** begin to operate or work. **3** cause to happen or operate. **4** begin to move or travel. **5** jump or jerk from surprise. **6** literary move or appear suddenly. **7** rouse (game) from its lair. **8** (of eyes) bulge. **9** displace or be displaced by pressure or shrinkage. • noun **1** an act of beginning or the point at which something begins. **2** an advantage given at the beginning of a race. **3** a sudden movement of surprise.
– PHRASES **for a start** in the first place. **start at** cost at least (a specified amount). **start off** begin (or cause someone or something to begin) working, operating, etc. **start on 1** begin to work on or deal with. **2** informal begin to talk in a critical or hostile way to. **start over** N. Amer. make a new beginning. **start out** (or **up**) embark on a venture or undertaking. **start something** informal cause trouble. **to start with** as the first thing to be taken into account.
– ORIGIN Old English, 'to caper, leap'.
starter • noun **1** a person or thing that starts. **2** chiefly Brit. the first course of a meal. **3** an automatic device for starting a machine. **4** a competitor taking part in a race or game at the start. **5** a topic or question with which to start a discussion or course of study.
– PHRASES **for starters** informal first of all. **under starter's orders** waiting for the signal to start a race.
starting block • noun a shaped rigid block for bracing the feet of a runner at the start of a race.
starting gate • noun a barrier raised at the start of a horse race to ensure a simultaneous start.
starting pistol • noun a pistol used to signal the start of a race.
starting price • noun the final odds at the start of a horse race.
startle • verb cause to feel sudden shock or alarm.
– DERIVATIVES **startled** adjective.
– ORIGIN Old English, 'kick, struggle'; related to START.
startling • adjective **1** alarming. **2** very surprising or remarkable.
– DERIVATIVES **startlingly** adverb.

Thesaurus

foremost, major, pre-eminent, champion.
– OPPOSITES poor, minor.
starchy • adjective *(informal)*. See STAID.
stare • verb GAZE, gape, goggle, glare, ogle, peer; *informal* gawk, rubberneck; *Brit. informal* gawp.
stark • adjective **1** *a stark silhouette* SHARP, sharply defined, well focused, crisp, distinct, obvious, evident, clear, clear-cut, graphic, striking. **2** *a stark landscape* DESOLATE, bare, barren, arid, vacant, empty, forsaken, godforsaken, bleak, sombre, depressing, cheerless, joyless; *poetic/literary* drear. **3** *a stark room* AUSTERE, severe, bleak, plain, simple, bare, unadorned, unembellished, undecorated. **4** *stark terror* SHEER, utter, complete, absolute, total, pure, downright, out-and-out, outright; thorough, consummate, rank, unqualified, unmitigated, unalloyed. **5** *the stark facts* BLUNT, bald, bare, simple, basic, plain, unvarnished, harsh, grim.
– OPPOSITES fuzzy, indistinct, pleasant, ornate, disguised.
• adverb *stark naked* COMPLETELY, totally, utterly, absolutely, downright, dead, entirely, wholly, fully, quite, altogether, thoroughly, truly.
start • verb **1** *the meeting starts at 7.45* BEGIN, commence, get under way, go ahead, get going; *informal* kick off. **2** *this was how her illness had started* COME INTO BEING, begin, commence, be born, come into existence, appear, arrive, come forth, emerge, erupt, burst out, arise, originate, develop. **3** *she started her own charity* ESTABLISH, set up, found, create, bring into being, institute, initiate, inaugurate, introduce, open, launch, float, kick-start, get something off the ground, pioneer, organize, mastermind; *informal* kick something off. **4** *we had better start on the work* MAKE A START, begin, commence, take the first step, make the first move, get going, go ahead, set things moving, start/get/set the ball rolling, buckle to/down, turn to; *informal* get moving, get cracking, get stuck in, get down to it, get to it, get down to business, get one's finger out, get the show on the road, take the plunge, kick off, get off one's backside, fire away; *Brit. informal* get weaving. **5** *he started across the field* SET OFF, set out, start out, set forth, begin one's journey, get on the road, depart, leave, get under way, make a start, sally forth, embark, sail; *informal* hit the road. **6** *you can start the machine* ACTIVATE, set in motion, switch on, start up, turn on, fire up; energize, actuate, set off, start off, set something going/moving. **7** *the machine started* BEGIN WORKING, start up, get going, spring into life. **8** *'Oh my!' she said, starting* FLINCH, jerk, jump, twitch, recoil, shy, shrink, blench, wince.
– OPPOSITES finish, stop, clear up, wind up, hang about, give up, arrive, stay, close down.
• noun **1** *the start of the event* BEGINNING, commencement, inception. **2** *the start of her illness* ONSET, commencement, emergence, (first) appearance, arrival, eruption, dawn, birth. **3** *a quarter of an hour's start* LEAD, head start, advantage. **4** *a start in life* ADVANTAGEOUS BEGINNING, flying start, helping hand, lift, assistance, support, encouragement, boost, kick-start; *informal* break, leg up. **5** *she awoke with a start* JERK, twitch, flinch, wince, spasm, convulsion, jump.
– OPPOSITES end, finish, handicap.
startle • verb SURPRISE, frighten, scare, alarm, give someone a shock/fright/jolt, make someone jump; PERTURB, unsettle, agitate, disturb, disconcert, disquiet; *informal* give someone a turn, make someone jump out of their skin.
– OPPOSITES put at ease.
startling • adjective SURPRISING, astonishing, amazing, unexpected, unforeseen, staggering, shocking, stunning; extraordinary, re-

star turn • noun the principal act or performer in a programme.
starve • verb **1** suffer or die from hunger. **2** cause to starve. **3** (**be starving** or **starved**) informal feel very hungry. **4** (**be starved of** or US **for**) be deprived of.
– DERIVATIVES **starvation** noun.
– ORIGIN Old English, 'to die'.
starveling /staarvling/ archaic • adjective starving or emaciated. • noun an emaciated person or animal.
stash informal • verb store safely in a secret place. • noun **1** a secret store of something. **2** dated a hiding place.
– ORIGIN of unknown origin.
stasis /staysiss, sta-/ • noun **1** formal or technical a period or state of inactivity or equilibrium. **2** Medicine a stoppage of flow of a body fluid.
– ORIGIN Greek, 'standing, stoppage'.
state • noun **1** the condition of someone or something at a particular time. **2** a nation or territory considered as an organized political community under one government. **3** a community or area forming part of a federal republic. **4** (**the States**) the United States of America. **5** the civil government of a country. **6** pomp and ceremony associated with monarchy or government. **7** (**a state**) informal an agitated, disorderly, or dirty condition. • verb express definitely or clearly in speech or writing.
– PHRASES **state of affairs** (or **things**) a situation. **state-of-the-art** incorporating the newest ideas and most up-to-date features. **state of emergency** a situation of national danger or disaster in which a government suspends normal constitutional procedures. **state of grace** a state of being free from sin. **the state of play** Brit. **1** the score at a particular time in a cricket or football match. **2** the current situation.
– DERIVATIVES **statehood** noun.
– ORIGIN partly a shortening of ESTATE, partly from Latin *status* (see STATUS).
state capitalism • noun a political system in which the state has control of production and the use of capital.
statecraft • noun the skilful management of state affairs.
State Department • noun (in the US) the department of foreign affairs.
state house • noun **1** (in the US) the building where the legislature of a state meets. **2** NZ a private house owned and let by the government.
stateless • adjective not recognized as a citizen of any country.
– DERIVATIVES **statelessness** noun.
stately • adjective (**statelier**, **stateliest**) dignified, imposing, or grand.
– DERIVATIVES **stateliness** noun.
stately home • noun Brit. a large and fine house occupied or formerly occupied by an aristocratic family.
statement • noun **1** a definite or clear expression of something in speech or writing. **2** a formal account of facts or events, especially one given to the police or in court. **3** a document setting out items of debit and credit between a bank or other organization and a customer.
stateroom • noun **1** a large room in a palace or public building, for use on formal occasions. **2** a private compartment on a ship.
state school • noun Brit. a school funded and controlled by the state.
state's evidence • noun US Law evidence for the prosecution given by a participant in or accomplice to the crime being tried.
stateside • adjective & adverb informal, chiefly US of, in, or towards the US.
statesman (or **stateswoman**) • noun a skilled, experienced, and respected political leader or figure.
– DERIVATIVES **statesmanlike** adjective **statesmanship** noun.
state socialism • noun a political system in which the state has control of industries and services.
static /stattik/ • adjective **1** lacking movement, action, or change. **2** Physics concerned with bodies at rest or forces in equilibrium. Often contrasted with DYNAMIC. **3** (of an electric charge) acquired by objects that cannot conduct a current. • noun **1** static electricity. **2** crackling or hissing on a telephone, radio, etc.
– DERIVATIVES **statically** adverb.
– ORIGIN Greek *statikos* 'causing to stand', from *histanai* 'to stand'.
statics • plural noun **1** (usu. treated as sing.) the branch of mechanics concerned with bodies at rest and forces in equilibrium. **2** another term for STATIC (in sense 2).
station • noun **1** a place where passenger trains stop on a railway line, typically with platforms and buildings. **2** a place where a specified activity or service is based: *a radar station.* **3** a broadcasting company of a specified kind. **4** the place where someone or something stands or is placed for a particular purpose or duty. **5** dated one's social rank or position. **6** Austral./NZ a large sheep or cattle farm. • verb assign to a station.
– ORIGIN Latin, from *stare* 'to stand'.
stationary • adjective **1** not moving. **2** not changing in quantity

Thesaurus

markable, dramatic; disturbing, unsettling, perturbing, disconcerting, disquieting; frightening, alarming, scary.
– OPPOSITES predictable, ordinary.
starvation • noun EXTREME HUNGER, lack of food, famine, undernourishment, malnourishment, fasting; deprivation of food; death from lack of food.
starving • adjective DYING OF HUNGER, deprived of food, undernourished, malnourished, starved, half-starved; very hungry, ravenous, empty, hollow; *informal* famished.
– OPPOSITES full.
stash (informal) • verb *he stashed his things away* STORE, stow, pack, load, cache, hide, conceal, secrete; hoard, save, stockpile; *informal* salt away, squirrel away.
• noun *a stash of money* CACHE, hoard, stock, stockpile, store, supply, accumulation, collection, reserve.
state[1] • noun **1** *the state of the economy* CONDITION, shape, situation, circumstances, position; predicament, plight. **2** (informal) *don't get into a state* FLUSTER, frenzy, fever, fret, panic, state of agitation/anxiety; *informal* flap, tizzy, tiz-woz, dither, stew, sweat; *N. Amer. informal* twit. **3** (informal) *your room is in a state* MESS, chaos, disorder, disarray, confusion, muddle, heap, shambles; clutter, untidiness, disorganization. **4** *an autonomous state* COUNTRY, nation, land, sovereign state, nation state, kingdom, realm, power, republic, confederation, federation. **5** *the country is divided into thirty-two states* PROVINCE, federal state, region, territory, canton, department, county, district; *Brit.* shire. **6** *the power of the state* GOVERNMENT, parliament, administration, regime, authorities.
• adjective *a state visit to China* CEREMONIAL, official, formal, governmental, national, public.
– OPPOSITES unofficial, private, informal.
state[2] • verb *I stated my views* EXPRESS, voice, utter, put into words, declare, affirm, assert, announce, make known, put across/over, communicate, air, reveal, disclose, divulge, proclaim, present, expound; set out, set down; *informal* come out with.
stated • adjective SPECIFIED, fixed, settled, set, agreed, declared, designated, laid down.
– OPPOSITES undefined, irregular, tacit.
stately • adjective DIGNIFIED, majestic, ceremonious, courtly, imposing, impressive, solemn, awe-inspiring, regal, elegant, grand, glorious, splendid, magnificent, resplendent; slow-moving, measured, deliberate.
statement • noun DECLARATION, expression of views/facts, affirmation, assertion, announcement, utterance, communication, proclamation, presentation, expounding; account, testimony, evidence, report, bulletin, communiqué.
state-of-the-art • adjective MODERN, ultra-modern, the latest, new, the newest, up to the minute; advanced, highly developed, innovatory, trailblazing, revolutionary; sophisticated.
statesman, stateswoman • noun SENIOR POLITICIAN, respected political figure, elder statesman, political leader, national leader.
static • adjective **1** *static prices* UNCHANGED, fixed, stable, steady, unchanging, changeless, unvarying, invariable, constant, consistent. **2** *a static display* STATIONARY, motionless, immobile, unmoving, still, stock-still, at a standstill, at rest, not moving a muscle, like a statue, rooted to the spot, frozen, inactive, inert, lifeless, inanimate.
– OPPOSITES variable, mobile, active, dynamic.
station • noun **1** *a railway station* STOPPING PLACE, stop, halt, stage; terminus, terminal, depot. **2** *a research station* ESTABLISHMENT, base, camp; post, depot; mission; site, facility, installation, yard. **3** *a police station* OFFICE, depot, base, headquarters; *N. Amer.* precinct, station house; *informal* cop shop; *Brit. informal* nick. **4** *a local radio station* CHANNEL, broadcasting organization; wavelength. **5** (Austral./NZ) *a sheep station* RANCH, range; farm. **6** *the lookout re-*

S

or condition.

– USAGE Take care to distinguish between **stationary** and **stationery**: **stationary** is an adjective meaning 'not moving or changing', whereas **stationery** is a noun meaning 'paper and other writing materials'.

stationer ● noun a seller of stationery.

– ORIGIN Latin *stationarius* 'tradesman at a fixed location'.

stationery ● noun paper and other materials needed for writing.

station hand ● noun Austral./NZ a worker on a large sheep or cattle farm.

station house ● noun N. Amer. a police or fire station.

stationmaster ● noun an official in charge of a railway station.

Station of the Cross ● noun each of a series of fourteen pictures representing incidents during Jesus' progress from Pilate's house to his crucifixion at Calvary.

station wagon ● noun N. Amer. & Austral./NZ an estate car.

statism /staytiz'm/ ● noun a political system in which the state has substantial central control over social and economic affairs.

– DERIVATIVES **statist** noun & adjective.

statistic ● noun a fact or piece of data obtained from a study of a large quantity of numerical data.

– ORIGIN German *Statistik*.

statistical ● adjective relating to statistics.

– DERIVATIVES **statistically** adverb.

statistics ● plural noun (treated as sing.) the collection and analysis of numerical data in large quantities.

– DERIVATIVES **statistician** noun.

statoscope ● noun an aneroid barometer measuring minute variations of pressure, used especially to indicate aircraft altitude.

– ORIGIN from Greek *statos* 'standing'.

stats ● plural noun informal statistics.

statuary /statyooəri/ ● noun statues collectively.

statue ● noun a carved or cast figure of a person or animal, especially one that is life-size or larger.

– ORIGIN Latin *statua*, from *stare* 'to stand'.

statuesque /statyooesk/ ● adjective (especially of a woman) attractively tall, graceful, and dignified.

– DERIVATIVES **statuesquely** adverb.

statuette ● noun a small statue.

– ORIGIN French.

stature ● noun **1** a person's natural height when standing. **2** importance or reputation gained by ability or achievement.

– ORIGIN Latin *statura*, from *stare* 'to stand'.

status ● noun **1** relative social or professional standing. **2** high rank or social standing. **3** the position of affairs at a particular time. **4** official classification.

– ORIGIN Latin, 'standing'.

status quo /staytəss kwō/ ● noun the existing state of affairs.

– ORIGIN Latin, 'the state in which'.

status symbol ● noun a possession taken to indicate a person's wealth or high status.

statute /statyoot/ ● noun **1** a written law passed by a legislative body. **2** a rule of an organization or institution.

– ORIGIN Latin *statutum* 'thing set up'.

statute book ● noun **1** a book in which laws are written. **2** (**the statute book**) a nation's laws collectively.

statute law ● noun the body of principles and rules of law laid down in statutes.

statute of limitations ● noun Law a statute limiting the period for the bringing of certain kinds of actions.

statutory ● adjective **1** required, permitted, or enacted by statute. **2** having come to be required or expected due to being done regularly.

– DERIVATIVES **statutorily** adverb.

statutory instrument ● noun Law a government or executive order of subordinate legislation.

statutory rape ● noun US Law the offence of having sexual intercourse with a minor.

staunch[1] /stawnch/ ● adjective **1** very loyal and committed. **2** archaic strong or watertight.

– DERIVATIVES **staunchly** adverb **staunchness** noun.

– ORIGIN Old French *estanche* 'watertight'.

staunch[2] /stawnch, staanch/ (US also **stanch**) ● verb stop or restrict (a flow of blood from a wound); stop from bleeding.

– ORIGIN Old French *estanchier*; related to STAUNCH[1].

stave ● noun **1** any of the lengths of wood fixed side by side to make a barrel, bucket, etc. **2** a strong stick, post, or pole. **3** (also **staff**) Music a set of five parallel lines on or between any of which a note is written to indicate its pitch. **4** a verse or stanza of a poem. ● verb **1** (past and past part. **staved** or **stove**) (**stave in**) break (something) by forcing it inwards or piercing it roughly with a hole. **2** (past and past part. **staved**) (**stave off**) avert or delay (something bad or dangerous).

– ORIGIN from *staves*, variant plural form of STAFF.

stay[1] ● verb **1** remain in the same place. **2** remain in a specified state or position. **3** live somewhere temporarily as a visitor or guest. **4** Scottish & S. African live permanently. **5** stop, delay, or prevent. **6** literary support or prop up. ● noun **1** a period of staying somewhere. **2** a suspension or postponement of judicial proceedings: *a stay of execution.* **3** a device used as a brace or support. **4** (**stays**) historical a corset made of two pieces laced together and stiffened by strips of whalebone.

– PHRASES **stay the course** (or **distance**) **1** keep going to the end of a race or contest. **2** pursue a difficult task or activity to the end. **stay on** continue to study, work, or be somewhere after others have left. **stay over** stay for the night as a visitor or guest. **stay put** remain somewhere without moving. **stay up** not go to bed. **stay with** continue, persevere, or keep up with (an activity or person).

– DERIVATIVES **stayer** noun.

– ORIGIN Old French *ester*, from Latin *stare* 'to stand'.

stay[2] ● noun **1** a large rope, wire, or rod used to support a ship's mast or other upright pole. **2** a supporting wire or cable on an aircraft. ● verb secure or steady with a stay.

– ORIGIN Old English.

staying power ● noun informal endurance or stamina.

Thesaurus

S

sumed his station POST, position, place. **7** *(dated) Karen was getting ideas above her station* RANK, place, status, position in society, social class, stratum, level, grade; caste; archaic condition, degree.

● verb *the regiment was stationed at Woolwich* PUT ON DUTY, post, position, place; establish, install; deploy, base, garrison.

stationary ● adjective **1** *a stationary car* STATIC, parked, stopped, motionless, immobile, unmoving, still, stock-still, at a standstill, at rest; not moving a muscle, like a statue, rooted to the spot, frozen, inactive, inert, lifeless, inanimate. **2** *a stationary population* UNCHANGING, unvarying, invariable, constant, consistent, unchanged, changeless, fixed, stable, steady.

– OPPOSITES moving, shifting.

statue ● noun SCULPTURE, figure, effigy, statuette, figurine, idol; carving, bronze, graven image, model; bust, head.

statuesque ● adjective TALL AND DIGNIFIED, imposing, striking, stately, majestic, noble, magnificent, splendid, impressive, regal.

stature ● noun **1** *she was small in stature* HEIGHT, tallness; size, build. **2** *an architect of international stature* REPUTATION, repute, standing, status, position, prestige, distinction, eminence, pre-eminence, prominence, importance, influence, note, fame, celebrity, renown, acclaim.

status ● noun **1** *the status of women* STANDING, rank, ranking, position, social position, level, place, estimation; dated station. **2** *wealth and status* PRESTIGE, kudos, cachet, standing, stature, regard, fame, note, renown, honour, esteem, image, importance, prominence, consequence, distinction, influence, authority, eminence.

statute ● noun LAW, regulation, enactment, act, bill, decree, edict, rule, ruling, resolution, dictum, command, order, directive, pronouncement, proclamation, dictate, diktat, fiat, by-law; N. Amer. formal ordinance.

staunch[1] ● adjective *a staunch supporter* STALWART, loyal, faithful, committed, devoted, dedicated, dependable, reliable, steady, constant, trusty, hard-working, steadfast, redoubtable, unwavering.

– OPPOSITES disloyal, unfaithful, unreliable.

staunch[2] ● verb *she tried to staunch the flow of blood* STEM, stop, halt, check, hold back, restrain, restrict, control, contain, curb; block, dam; slow, lessen, reduce, diminish, retard; N. Amer. stanch; archaic stay.

stave ● verb

– PHRASES **stave something in** BREAK IN, smash in, put a hole in, push in, kick in, cave in. **stave something off** AVERT, prevent, avoid, counter, preclude, forestall, nip in the bud; ward off, fend off, head off, keep off, keep at bay.

staysail /staysayl, stays'l/ ● noun a triangular fore-and-aft sail extended on a stay.

stay stitching ● noun stitching placed along a bias or curved seam to prevent the fabric of a garment from stretching while the garment is being made.

St Bernard ● noun a breed of very large dog originally kept to rescue travellers by the monks of the hospice on the Great St Bernard, a pass across the Alps.

STD ● abbreviation **1** sexually transmitted disease. **2** Brit. subscriber trunk dialling.

stead ● noun the place or role that someone or something should have or fill: *she was appointed in his stead.*
– PHRASES **stand in good stead** be advantageous to (someone) over time or in the future.
– ORIGIN Old English.

steadfast ● adjective resolutely or dutifully firm and unwavering.
– DERIVATIVES **steadfastly** adverb **steadfastness** noun.
– ORIGIN Old English, 'standing firm' (see STEAD, FAST[1]).

steading ● noun Scottish & N. English a farmstead.

steady ● adjective (**steadier**, **steadiest**) **1** firmly fixed, supported, or balanced. **2** not faltering or wavering; controlled. **3** sensible and reliable. **4** regular, even, and continuous in development, frequency, or intensity. ● verb (**steadies**, **steadied**) make or become steady. ● exclamation (also **steady on!**) a warning to keep calm or take care.
– PHRASES **go steady** informal have a regular romantic or sexual relationship with someone.
– DERIVATIVES **steadier** noun **steadily** adverb **steadiness** noun.

steak ● noun **1** high-quality beef from the hindquarters of the animal, cut into thick slices for grilling or frying. **2** a thick slice of other meat or fish. **3** poorer-quality beef for braising or stewing.
– ORIGIN Old Norse.

steak tartare ● noun a dish consisting of raw minced steak mixed with raw egg.

steal ● verb (past **stole**; past part. **stolen**) **1** take (something) without permission or legal right and without intending to return it. **2** give or take surreptitiously or without permission: *I stole a look at my watch.* **3** move somewhere quietly or surreptitiously. **4** (in various sports) gain (a point, advantage, etc.) unexpectedly or by exploiting the temporary distraction of an opponent. ● noun **1** informal a bargain. **2** chiefly N. Amer. an act of stealing.
– PHRASES **steal a march on** gain an advantage over by taking early action. **steal the show** attract the most attention and praise. **steal someone's thunder** win praise or attention for oneself by pre-empting someone else's attempt to impress.
– DERIVATIVES **stealer** noun.
– ORIGIN Old English.

stealth ● noun **1** cautious and surreptitious action or movement. **2** (before another noun) (of aircraft) designed to make detection by radar or sonar difficult: *a stealth bomber.*
– ORIGIN originally in the sense 'theft': probably related to STEAL.

stealthy ● adjective (**stealthier**, **stealthiest**) characterized by stealth.
– DERIVATIVES **stealthily** adverb **stealthiness** noun.

steam ● noun **1** the hot vapour into which water is converted when heated, which condenses in the air into a mist of minute water droplets. **2** the expansive force of this vapour used as a source of power for machines. **3** momentum; impetus: *the dispute gathered steam.* ● verb **1** give off or produce steam. **2** (**steam up**) mist over with steam. **3** cook (food) by heating it in steam from boiling water. **4** clean or otherwise treat with steam. **5** (of a ship or train) travel somewhere under steam power. **6** informal move somewhere rapidly or forcefully. **7** (**be/get steamed up**) informal be or become extremely agitated or angry.
– PHRASES **get up steam 1** generate enough pressure to drive a steam engine. **2** gradually gain impetus. **have steam coming out of one's ears** informal be extremely angry. **let off steam** informal get rid of pent-up energy or strong emotion. **run out of steam** informal lose impetus or enthusiasm. **under one's own steam** without assistance from others.
– ORIGIN Old English.

steam bath ● noun a room filled with hot steam for cleaning

Thesaurus

stay[1] ● verb **1** *he stayed where he was* REMAIN (BEHIND), stay behind, stay put; wait, linger, stick, be left, hold on, hang on, lodge; *informal* hang around/round; *Brit. informal* hang about; *archaic* bide, tarry. **2** *they won't stay hidden* CONTINUE (TO BE), remain, keep, persist in being, carry on being, go on being. **3** *our aunt is staying with us* VISIT, spend time, put up, stop (off/over); holiday; lodge, room, board, have rooms, be housed, be accommodated, be quartered, be billeted; *N. Amer.* vacation; *formal* sojourn; *archaic* bide. **4** *legal proceedings were stayed* POSTPONE, put off, delay, defer, put back, hold over/off; adjourn, suspend, prorogue; *N. Amer.* put over, table, lay on the table, take a rain check on; *US Law* continue; *informal* put on ice, put on the back burner. **5** *(poetic/literary) we must stay the enemy's advance* DELAY, slow down/up, hold back/up, set back, keep back, put back, put a brake on, retard; hinder, hamper, obstruct, inhibit, impede, curb, check, restrain, restrict, arrest; *Brit. informal* throw a spanner in the works of; *N. Amer. informal* throw a monkey wrench in the works of.
– OPPOSITES leave, advance, promote.
● noun **1** *a stay at a hotel* VISIT, stop, stop-off, stopover, break, holiday; *N. Amer.* vacation; *formal* sojourn. **2** *a stay of judgement* POSTPONEMENT, putting off, delay, deferment, deferral, putting back; adjournment, suspension, prorogation; *N. Amer.* tabling; *US Law* continuance.

stay[2] ● noun *the stays holding up the mast* STRUT, WIRE, brace, tether, guy, prop, rod, support, truss; *Nautical* shroud.
● verb *her masts were well stayed* BRACE, tether, strut, wire, guy, prop, support, truss.

steadfast ● adjective **1** *a steadfast friend* LOYAL, faithful, committed, devoted, dedicated, dependable, reliable, steady, true, constant, staunch, trusty. **2** *a steadfast refusal to yield to pressure* FIRM, determined, resolute, relentless, implacable, single-minded; unchanging, unwavering, unhesitating, unfaltering, unswerving, unyielding, unflinching, uncompromising.
– OPPOSITES disloyal, irresolute.

steady ● adjective **1** *the ladder must be steady* STABLE, firm, fixed, secure, fast, safe, immovable, unshakeable, dependable; anchored, moored, jammed, rooted, braced. **2** *keep the camera steady* MOTIONLESS, still, unshaking, static, stationary, unmoving. **3** *a steady gaze* FIXED, intent, unwavering, unfaltering. **4** *a steady young man* SENSIBLE, level-headed, rational, settled, mature, down-to-earth, full of common sense, reliable, dependable, sound, sober, serious-minded, responsible, serious. **5** *a steady income* CONSTANT, unchanging, regular, consistent, invariable; continuous, continual, unceasing, ceaseless, perpetual, unremitting, unwavering, unfaltering, unending, endless, round-the-clock, all-year-round. **6** *a steady boyfriend* REGULAR, usual, established, settled, firm, devoted, faithful.
– OPPOSITES unstable, loose, shaky, darting, flighty, immature, fluctuating, sporadic, occasional.
● verb **1** *he steadied the rifle* STABILIZE, hold steady; brace, support; balance, poise; secure, fix, make fast. **2** *she needed to steady her nerves* CALM, soothe, quieten, compose, settle; subdue, quell, control, get a grip on.

steal ● verb **1** *the raiders stole a fax machine* PURLOIN, thieve, take, take for oneself, help oneself to, loot, pilfer, run off with, carry off, shoplift; embezzle, misappropriate; have one's fingers/hand in the till; *informal* walk off with, rob, swipe, nab, rip off, lift, 'liberate', 'borrow', filch, snaffle, snitch; *Brit. informal* nick, pinch, half-inch, whip, knock off, nobble; *N. Amer. informal* heist; *formal* peculate. **2** *his work was stolen by his tutor* PLAGIARIZE, copy, pass off as one's own, pirate, poach, borrow; *informal* rip off, lift, pinch, nick, crib. **3** *he stole a kiss* SNATCH, sneak, get stealthily/surreptitiously. **4** *he stole out of the room* CREEP, sneak, slink, slip, slide, glide, tiptoe, sidle, slope, edge.
● noun *(informal) at £30 it's a steal.* See BARGAIN noun sense 2.

stealing ● noun THEFT, thieving, thievery, robbery, larceny, burglary, shoplifting, pilfering, pilferage, looting, misappropriation; embezzlement; *formal* peculation.

stealth ● noun FURTIVENESS, secretiveness, secrecy, surreptitiousness, sneakiness, slyness.
– OPPOSITES openness.

stealthy ● adjective FURTIVE, secretive, secret, surreptitious, sneaking, sly, clandestine, covert, conspiratorial.
– OPPOSITES open.

steam ● noun **1** *steam from the kettle* WATER VAPOUR, condensation, mist, haze, fog, moisture. **2** *he ran out of steam* ENERGY, vigour, vitality, stamina, enthusiasm; MOMENTUM, impetus, force, strength, thrust, impulse, push, drive; speed, pace.

S

and refreshing the body.

steamboat ● noun a boat propelled by a steam engine, especially (in the US) a paddle-wheel craft of a type used on rivers in the 19th century.

steamed ● adjective informal **1** Brit. very drunk. **2** chiefly N. Amer. angry; upset.

steam engine ● noun **1** an engine that uses the expansion or rapid condensation of steam to generate power. **2** a steam locomotive.

steamer ● noun **1** a ship or boat powered by steam. **2** a type of saucepan in which food can be steamed.

steam hammer ● noun a large steam-powered hammer used in forging.

steaming ● adjective **1** giving off steam. **2** Brit. informal extremely drunk. **3** Brit. informal very angry.

steam iron ● noun an electric iron that emits steam from holes in its flat surface.

steamroller ● noun a heavy, slow-moving vehicle with a roller, used to flatten the surfaces of roads during construction. ● verb (also **steamroll**) **1** forcibly pass (a measure) by restricting debate or otherwise overriding opposition. **2** force into doing or accepting something.

steam turbine ● noun a turbine in which a high-velocity jet of steam rotates a bladed disc or drum.

steamy ● adjective (**steamier**, **steamiest**) **1** producing, filled with, or clouded with steam. **2** hot and humid. **3** informal of or involving passionate sexual activity.
– DERIVATIVES **steamily** adverb **steaminess** noun.

stearic acid /steerik/ ● noun Chemistry a solid saturated fatty acid obtained from animal or vegetable fats.
– ORIGIN from Greek *stear* 'tallow'.

stearin /steerin/ ● noun a white crystalline substance which is the main constituent of tallow and suet.

steatite /steeətīt/ ● noun the mineral talc occurring in bulk form, especially as soapstone.
– ORIGIN Greek *steatītēs*, from *stear* 'tallow'.

steatopygia /steeətəpijiə/ ● noun accumulation of large amounts of fat on the buttocks, especially as a normal condition in the Khoikhoi and other peoples of arid parts of southern Africa.
– DERIVATIVES **steatopygous** /steeətəpigəss, steeətoppigəss/ adjective.
– ORIGIN from Greek *stear* 'tallow' + *pugē* 'rump'.

steed ● noun archaic or literary a horse.
– ORIGIN Old English, related to STUD².

steel ● noun **1** a hard, strong grey or bluish-grey alloy of iron with carbon and usually other elements, used as a structural material and in manufacturing. **2** a rod of roughened steel on which knives are sharpened. **3** strength and determination: *nerves of steel.* ● verb mentally prepare (oneself) to do or face something difficult.
– ORIGIN Old English.

steel band ● noun a band that plays music on steel drums.

steel drum (also **steel pan**) ● noun a percussion instrument originating in Trinidad, made out of an oil drum with one end beaten down and divided into sections to give different notes.

steel wool ● noun fine strands of steel matted together into a mass, used as an abrasive.

steelworks ● plural noun (usu. treated as sing.) a factory where steel is manufactured.

steely ● adjective (**steelier**, **steeliest**) **1** resembling steel in colour, brightness, or strength. **2** coldly determined; severe.
– DERIVATIVES **steeliness** noun.

steelyard ● noun an apparatus for weighing that has a short arm taking the item to be weighed and a long graduated arm along which a weight is moved until it balances.
– ORIGIN from STEEL + YARD¹ in obsolete sense 'rod, measuring stick'.

steep¹ ● adjective **1** rising or falling sharply; almost perpendicular. **2** (of a rise or fall in an amount) very large or rapid. **3** informal (of a price or demand) not reasonable; excessive. **4** informal (of a claim or account) exaggerated. ● noun chiefly literary a steep mountain slope.
– DERIVATIVES **steeply** adverb **steepness** noun.
– ORIGIN Old English, 'extending to a great height'; related to STEEPLE and STOOP¹.

steep² ● verb **1** soak or be soaked in water or other liquid. **2** (usu. **be steeped in**) fill or imbue with a particular quality or influence.
– ORIGIN Germanic, related to STOUP.

steepen ● verb become or cause to become steeper.

steeple ● noun **1** a church tower and spire. **2** a spire on the top of a church tower or roof.
– DERIVATIVES **steepled** adjective.
– ORIGIN Old English, related to STEEP¹.

steeplechase ● noun **1** a horse race run on a racecourse having ditches and hedges as jumps. **2** a running race in which runners must clear hurdles and water jumps.
– DERIVATIVES **steeplechaser** noun **steeplechasing** noun.
– ORIGIN so named because originally the race was run across country, with a steeple marking the finishing point.

steeplejack ● noun a person who climbs tall structures such as chimneys and steeples in order to carry out repairs.

steer¹ ● verb **1** guide or control the movement of (a vehicle, ship, etc.). **2** direct or guide in a particular direction. ● noun informal a piece of advice or information.
– PHRASES **steer clear of** take care to avoid.
– DERIVATIVES **steerable** adjective **steerer** noun.
– ORIGIN Old English.

steer² ● noun a bullock.
– ORIGIN Old English.

steerage ● noun **1** historical the part of a ship providing accommodation for passengers with the cheapest tickets. **2** archaic or literary the action of steering a boat.

steerage way ● noun the rate of headway required if a ship is to be controlled by the helm.

steering ● noun the mechanism in a vehicle, vessel, or aircraft which allows it to be steered.

Thesaurus

S

● verb (informal) *he steamed into the shop.* See RUN verb sense 1.
– PHRASES **steamed up** (informal) **1** *he got steamed up about forgetting his papers.* See AGITATED. **2** *they get steamed up about the media.* See ANGRY sense 1. **let off steam** (informal) GIVE VENT TO ONE'S FEELINGS, speak one's mind, speak out, sound off, lose one's inhibitions, let oneself go; use up surplus energy. **steam up** MIST (UP/OVER), fog (up), become misty/misted.

steamy ● adjective **1** *the steamy jungle* HUMID, muggy, sticky, dripping, moist, damp, clammy, sultry, sweaty, steaming. **2** (informal) *a steamy love scene.* See EROTIC. **3** (informal) *they had a steamy affair* PASSIONATE, torrid, amorous, ardent, lustful; informal sizzling, hot, red-hot.

steel ● verb
– PHRASES **steel oneself** BRACE ONESELF, nerve oneself, summon (up) one's courage, screw up one's courage, gear oneself up, prepare oneself, get in the right frame of mind; fortify oneself, harden oneself; informal psych oneself up; poetic/literary gird (up) one's loins.

steely ● adjective **1** *steely light* BLUE-GREY, grey, steel-coloured, steel-grey, iron-grey. **2** *steely muscles* HARD, firm, toned, rigid, stiff, tense, tensed, taut. **3** *steely eyes* CRUEL, unfeeling, merciless, ruthless, pitiless, heartless, hard-hearted, hard, stony, cold-blooded, cold-hearted, harsh, callous, severe, unrelenting, unpitying, unforgiving, uncaring, unsympathetic; poetic/literary adamantine. **4** *steely determination* RESOLUTE, firm, steadfast, dogged, single-minded; bitter, burning, ferocious, fanatical; ruthless, iron, grim, gritty; unquenchable, unflinching, unswerving, unfaltering, untiring, unwavering.
– OPPOSITES flabby, kind, half-hearted.

steep¹ ● adjective **1** *steep cliffs* PRECIPITOUS, sheer, abrupt, sharp, perpendicular, vertical, bluff, vertiginous. **2** *a steep increase* SHARP, sudden, precipitate, precipitous, rapid. **3** (informal) *steep prices* EXPENSIVE, dear, costly, high, stiff; unreasonable, excessive, exorbitant, extortionate, outrageous, prohibitive; Brit. over the odds.
– OPPOSITES gentle, gradual, reasonable.

steep² ● verb **1** *the ham is then steeped in brine* MARINADE, marinate, soak, souse, macerate; pickle. **2** *winding sheets were steeped in mercury sulphate* SOAK, saturate, immerse, wet through, drench; technical ret. **3** *a city steeped in history* IMBUE WITH, fill with, permeate with, pervade with, suffuse with, infuse with, soak in.

steeple ● noun SPIRE, tower; bell tower, belfry, campanile; minaret.

steer ● verb **1** *he steered the boat* GUIDE, direct, manoeuvre, drive, pilot, navigate; Nautical con, helm. **2** *Luke steered her down the path* GUIDE, conduct, direct, lead, take, usher, shepherd, marshal, herd.

steering column ● noun a shaft that connects the steering wheel of a vehicle to the rest of the steering mechanism.
steering committee (also **steering group**) ● noun a committee that decides on the priorities or order of business of an organization.
steering wheel ● noun a wheel that a driver rotates in order to steer a vehicle.
steersman ● noun a person who steers a boat or ship.
stegosaur /steggəsawr/ (also **stegosaurus** /steggəsawrəss/) ● noun a plant-eating dinosaur with a double row of large bony plates along the back.
– ORIGIN from Greek *stegē* 'covering' + *sauros* 'lizard'.
stein /stīn/ ● noun a large earthenware beer mug.
– ORIGIN German, 'stone'.
stela /steelə/ (also **stele** /steel, steeli/) ● noun (pl. **stelae** /steelee/) Archaeology an upright stone slab or column bearing an inscription or design.
– ORIGIN Greek.
stellar /stellə/ ● adjective **1** relating to a star or stars. **2** informal of or having the quality of a star performer.
– ORIGIN Latin *stellaris*, from *stella* 'star'.
stellate /stellayt/ ● adjective arranged in a radiating pattern like that of a star.
– DERIVATIVES **stellated** adjective.
St Elmo's fire /elmōz/ ● noun a phenomenon in which a luminous electrical discharge appears on a ship or aircraft during a storm.
– ORIGIN regarded as a sign of protection given by *St Elmo*, the patron saint of sailors.
stem[1] ● noun **1** the main body or stalk of a plant or shrub. **2** the stalk supporting a fruit, flower, or leaf. **3** a long, thin supportive or main section of something, such as that of a wine glass or tobacco pipe. **4** a rod or cylinder in a mechanism. **5** a vertical stroke in a letter or musical note. **6** Grammar the root or main part of a word, to which inflections or formative elements are added. **7** the main upright timber or metal piece at the bow of a ship. ● verb (**stemmed**, **stemming**) **1** (**stem from**) originate in or be caused by. **2** remove the stems from (fruit or tobacco leaves). **3** (of a boat) make headway against (the tide or current).
– PHRASES **from stem to stern** from one end to the other, especially of a ship.
– DERIVATIVES **stemmed** adjective.
– ORIGIN Old English.
stem[2] ● verb (**stemmed**, **stemming**) **1** stop or restrict (the flow or progress of something). **2** Skiing slide the tail of one ski or both skis outwards in order to turn or slow down.
– ORIGIN Old Norse.
stem ginger ● noun pieces of crystallized or preserved ginger.
stem stitch ● noun an embroidery stitch forming a continuous line of long, overlapped stitches.
stemware ● noun N. Amer. goblets and stemmed glasses regarded collectively.
stench ● noun a strong and very unpleasant smell.
– ORIGIN Old English, related to STINK.
stencil ● noun a thin sheet of card, plastic, or metal with a pattern or letters cut out of it, used to produce the cut design on the surface below by the application of ink or paint through the holes. ● verb (**stencilled**, **stencilling**; US **stenciled**, **stenciling**) decorate or form with a stencil.
– ORIGIN from earlier *stansel* 'ornament with various colours', from Latin *scintilla* 'spark'.
Sten gun ● noun a type of lightweight British sub-machine gun.
– ORIGIN from the initials of the inventors' surnames, *S*hepherd and *T*urpin, suggested by BREN GUN.
stenography /stenogrəfi/ ● noun N. Amer. the action or process of writing in shorthand and transcribing the shorthand on a typewriter.
– DERIVATIVES **stenographer** noun **stenographic** adjective.
– ORIGIN from Greek *stenos* 'narrow'.
stentorian /stentoriən/ ● adjective (of a person's voice) loud and powerful.
– ORIGIN from *Stentor*, a herald in the Trojan War.
step ● noun **1** an act of lifting and setting down the foot or alternate feet, as in walking. **2** the distance covered by a step. **3** informal a short and easily walked distance. **4** a flat surface on which to place one's foot when moving from one level to another. **5** a position or grade in a scale or hierarchy. **6** a measure or action taken to deal with or achieve something. **7** (**steps** or **a pair of steps**) Brit. a stepladder. **8** a block fixed to a boat's keel to take the base of a mast or other fitting. **9** Music, chiefly US an interval in a scale; a tone (whole step) or semitone (half step). ● verb (**stepped**, **stepping**) **1** lift and set down one's foot or alternate feet. **2** set up (a mast) in its step.
– PHRASES **in** (or **out of**) **step 1** walking, marching, or dancing in the same (or a different) rhythm and pace as others. **2** conforming (or not conforming) to what others are doing or thinking. **3** Physics in (or out of) synchrony. **follow in someone's steps** do as someone else did before. **mind** (or **watch**) **one's step** walk or act carefully. **step down** (or **aside**) withdraw or resign from a position or office. **step forward** offer one's help or services. **step in 1** become involved in a difficult situation, especially in order to help. **2** act as a substitute for someone. **step on it** informal go faster. **step out 1** leave a room or building briefly. **2** N. Amer. informal have a romantic or sexual relationship. **3** walk with long or vigorous steps. **step out of line** behave inappropriately or disobediently. **step up** increase the amount, speed, or intensity of.
– DERIVATIVES **stepped** adjective **stepper** noun **stepwise** adjective.
– ORIGIN Old English.
step- ● combining form denoting a relationship resulting from a remarriage: *stepmother*.
– ORIGIN Old English, from a base meaning 'bereaved, orphaned'.
step aerobics ● plural noun a type of aerobics that involves

Thesaurus

– PHRASES **steer clear of** KEEP AWAY FROM, keep one's distance from, keep at arm's length, give a wide berth to, avoid, avoid dealing with, have nothing to do with, shun, eschew.
stem[1] ● noun *a plant stem* STALK, shoot, trunk, stock, cane, bine.
– RELATED TERMS cauline.
– PHRASES **stem from** HAVE ITS ORIGINS IN, arise from, originate from, spring from, derive from, come from, emanate from, flow from, proceed from; BE CAUSED BY, be brought on/about by, be produced by.
stem[2] ● verb *he stemmed the flow of blood* STAUNCH, stop, halt, check, hold back, restrict, control, contain, curb; block, dam; slow, lessen, reduce, diminish; *N. Amer.* stanch; *archaic* stay.
stench ● noun STINK, reek; *Brit. informal* niff, pong, whiff, hum; *Scottish informal* guff; *N. Amer. informal* funk; *poetic/literary* miasma.
stentorian ● adjective LOUD, thundering, thunderous, ear-splitting, deafening; powerful, strong, carrying; booming, resonant; strident.
– OPPOSITES quiet, soft.
step ● noun **1** *Frank took a step forward* PACE, stride. **2** *she heard a step on the stairs* FOOTSTEP, footfall, tread. **3** *she left the room with a springy step* GAIT, walk, tread. **4** *it is only a step to the river* SHORT DISTANCE, stone's throw, spitting distance; *informal* {a hop, skip, and jump}. **5** *the top step* STAIR, tread; (**steps**) STAIRS, staircase, stairway. **6** *each step of the ladder* RUNG, tread. **7** *resigning is a very serious step* COURSE OF ACTION, measure, move, act, action, initiative, manoeuvre, operation. **8** *a significant step towards a ceasefire* ADVANCE, development, move, movement; breakthrough. **9** *the first step on the managerial ladder* STAGE, level, grade, rank, degree; notch.
● verb **1** *she stepped forward* WALK, move, tread, pace, stride. **2** *the bull had stepped on his hat* TREAD, stamp, trample; squash, crush, flatten.
– PHRASES **in step** *he is in step with mainstream thinking* IN ACCORD, in harmony, in agreement, in tune, in line, in keeping, in conformity. **mind/watch one's step** BE CAREFUL, take care, step/tread carefully, exercise care/caution, mind how one goes, look out, watch out, be wary, be on one's guard, be on the qui vive. **out of step** *the paper was often out of step with public opinion* AT ODDS, at variance, in disagreement, out of tune, out of line, not in keeping, out of harmony. **step by step** ONE STEP AT A TIME, bit by bit, gradually, in stages, by degrees, slowly, steadily. **step down** RESIGN, stand down, give up one's post/job, bow out, abdicate; *informal* quit. **step in 1** *nobody stepped in to save the bank* INTERVENE, intercede, involve oneself, become/get involved, take a hand. **2** *I stepped in for a sick colleague* STAND IN, sit in, fill in, cover, substitute, take over; replace, take someone's place; *informal* sub. **step on it** (*informal*) HURRY UP, get a move on, speed up, go faster, be quick; *informal* get cracking, get moving, step on the gas; *Brit. informal* get one's skates on; *N. Amer. informal* get a wiggle on; *dated* make haste. **step something up 1** *the army stepped up its offensive* INCREASE,

S

stepping up on to and down from a portable block.

stepbrother • noun a son of one's step-parent, by a marriage other than that with one's own father or mother.

stepchild • noun a child of one's husband or wife by a previous marriage.

stepdaughter • noun a daughter of one's husband or wife by a previous marriage.

stepfather • noun a man who is married to one's mother after the divorce of one's parents or the death of one's father.

stephanotis /steffənōtiss/ • noun a climbing plant with fragrant waxy white flowers.
– ORIGIN Greek, 'fit for a wreath'.

stepladder • noun a short folding ladder with flat steps and a small platform.

stepmother • noun a woman who is married to one's father after the divorce of one's parents or the death of one's mother.

steppe /step/ • noun a large area of flat unforested grassland in SE Europe or Siberia.
– ORIGIN Russian *step'*.

stepping stone • noun **1** a raised stone on which to step when crossing a stream or muddy area. **2** an action that helps one to make progress towards a goal.

stepsister • noun a daughter of one's step-parent by a marriage other than with one's own father or mother.

stepson • noun a son of one's husband or wife by a previous marriage.

-ster • suffix **1** denoting a person engaged in or associated with a particular activity or thing: *songster*. **2** denoting a person having a particular quality: *youngster*.
– ORIGIN Old English.

steradian /stəraydiən/ • noun the unit of solid angle in the SI system, equal to the angle at the centre of a sphere subtended by a part of the surface equal in area to the square of the radius.
– ORIGIN from Greek *stereos* 'solid' + RADIAN.

stereo /sterriō, steeriō/ • noun (pl. **stereos**) **1** stereophonic sound. **2** a stereophonic CD player, record player, etc. • adjective **1** stereophonic. **2** stereoscopic.

stereographic • adjective representing three-dimensional things on a two-dimensional surface, as in cartography.

stereophonic • adjective (of sound reproduction) using two or more channels so that the reproduced sound seems to surround the listener and to come from more than one source. Compare with MONOPHONIC.
– DERIVATIVES **stereophonically** adverb **stereophony** noun.
– ORIGIN from Greek *stereos* 'solid'.

stereoscope • noun a device by which two photographs of the same object taken at slightly different angles are viewed together, creating an impression of depth and solidity.
– DERIVATIVES **stereoscopic** adjective.

stereotype • noun **1** a preconceived and over-simplified idea of the characteristics which typify a person or thing. **2** a relief printing plate cast in a mould made from composed type or an original plate. • verb view or represent as a stereotype.
– DERIVATIVES **stereotypy** noun.

stereotypical • adjective relating to or resembling a stereotype.
– DERIVATIVES **stereotypic** adjective **stereotypically** adverb.

sterile • adjective **1** not able to produce children, young, crops, or fruit. **2** lacking in imagination, creativity, or excitement. **3** free from bacteria or other living micro-organisms.
– DERIVATIVES **sterilely** adverb **sterility** noun.
– ORIGIN Latin *sterilis*, related to Greek *steira* 'barren cow'.

sterilize (also **sterilise**) • verb **1** make sterile. **2** deprive of the ability to produce offspring by removing or blocking the sex organs.
– DERIVATIVES **sterilization** noun.

sterling • noun British money. • adjective chiefly Brit. excellent; of great value.
– ORIGIN probably from Old English *steorra* 'star' (because some early Norman pennies bore a small star).

sterling silver • noun silver of at least 92¼ per cent purity.

stern[1] • adjective **1** grimly serious or strict, especially in the exercise of discipline. **2** severe; demanding.
– DERIVATIVES **sternly** adverb **sternness** noun.
– ORIGIN Old English.

stern[2] • noun the rearmost part of a ship or boat.
– DERIVATIVES **sternmost** adjective **sternwards** adverb.
– ORIGIN probably from an Old Norse word meaning 'steering'.

sternal • adjective relating to the sternum.

sternpost • noun the central upright support at the stern of a boat, traditionally bearing the rudder.

sternum /sternəm/ • noun (pl. **sternums** or **sterna** /sternə/) the breastbone.
– ORIGIN Greek *sternon* 'chest'.

sternutation /sternyootaysh'n/ • noun formal the action of sneezing.
– ORIGIN Latin, from *sternutare* 'to sneeze'.

steroid /steeroyd, sterroyd/ • noun **1** any of a large class of organic compounds that includes certain hormones and vitamins, with a molecule containing four rings of carbon atoms. **2** an anabolic steroid.
– DERIVATIVES **steroidal** adjective.
– ORIGIN from STEROL.

sterol /steerol, sterrol/ • noun Biochemistry any of a group of naturally occurring unsaturated steroid alcohols, typically waxy solids.
– ORIGIN independent usage of the ending of words such as CHOLESTEROL.

stertorous /stertərəss/ • adjective (of breathing) noisy and laboured.
– DERIVATIVES **stertorously** adverb.
– ORIGIN from Latin *stertere* 'to snore'.

stet • verb let it stand (used as an instruction on a printed proof to ignore a correction).
– ORIGIN Latin.

stethoscope /stethəskōp/ • noun a medical instrument for listening to the action of someone's heart or breathing, having a small disc that is placed against the chest and two tubes connected to earpieces.
– ORIGIN from Greek *stēthos* 'breast' + *skopein* 'look at'.

Stetson /stetsən/ • noun (trademark in the US) a hat with a high crown and a very wide brim, traditionally worn by cowboys

Thesaurus

S

intensify, strengthen, augment, escalate; *informal* up, crank up. **2** *I stepped up my pace* SPEED UP, increase, accelerate, quicken, hasten.

stereotype • noun *the stereotype of the rancher* CONVENTIONAL IMAGE, standard image, received idea, cliché, hackneyed idea, formula.
• verb *women are often stereotyped as scheming* TYPECAST, pigeonhole, conventionalize, categorize, label, tag.

stereotyped • adjective STOCK, conventional, stereotypical, standard, formulaic, predictable; hackneyed, clichéd, cliché-ridden, banal, trite, unoriginal; typecast; *informal* corny, old hat.
– OPPOSITES unconventional, original.

sterile • adjective **1** *mules are sterile* INFERTILE, unable to reproduce/conceive, unable to have children/young, barren; *technical* infecund. **2** *sterile desert* UNPRODUCTIVE, infertile, unfruitful, uncultivatable, barren. **3** *a sterile debate* POINTLESS, unproductive, unfruitful, unrewarding, useless, unprofitable, profitless, futile, vain, idle; *archaic* bootless. **4** *sterile academicism* UNIMAGINATIVE, uninspired, uninspiring, unoriginal, stale, lifeless, musty. **5** *sterile conditions* ASEPTIC, sterilized, germ-free, antiseptic, disinfected; uncontaminated, unpolluted, pure, clean; sanitary, hygienic.
– OPPOSITES fertile, productive, creative, original, septic.

sterilize • verb **1** *the scalpel was first sterilized* DISINFECT, fumigate, decontaminate, sanitize; pasteurize; clean, cleanse, purify; *technical* autoclave. **2** *well over 6.5 million people were sterilized* MAKE UNABLE TO HAVE CHILDREN, make infertile, hysterectomize, vasectomize. **3** *stray pets are usually sterilized* NEUTER, castrate, spay, geld, cut, fix, desex; *N. Amer. & Austral.* alter; *Brit. informal* doctor.
– OPPOSITES contaminate.

sterling • adjective *(Brit.)* EXCELLENT, first-rate, first-class, exceptional, outstanding, splendid, superlative, praiseworthy, laudable, commendable, admirable, valuable, worthy, deserving.
– OPPOSITES poor, unexceptional.

stern[1] • adjective **1** *a stern expression* SERIOUS, unsmiling, frowning, severe, forbidding, grim, unfriendly, austere, dour, stony, flinty, steely, unrelenting, unforgiving, unbending, unsympathetic, disapproving. **2** *stern measures* STRICT, severe, stringent, harsh, drastic, hard, tough, extreme, rigid, ruthless, rigorous, exacting, demanding, uncompromising, unsparing, inflexible, authoritarian, draconian.
– OPPOSITES genial, friendly, lenient, lax.

stern[2] • noun *the stern of the ship* REAR (END), back, after end, poop,

and ranchers in the US.
– ORIGIN named after the American hat manufacturer John B. *Stetson* (1830–1906).
stevedore /steevədor/ ● noun a person employed at a dock to load and unload ships.
– ORIGIN Spanish *estivador*, from *estivar* 'stow a cargo'.
stew[1] ● noun **1** a dish of meat and vegetables cooked slowly in liquid in a closed dish or pan. **2** informal a state of anxiety or agitation. **3** archaic a public steam bath. **4** archaic a brothel. ● verb **1** cook slowly in liquid in a closed dish or pan. **2** Brit. (of tea) become strong and bitter with prolonged brewing. **3** informal be in a heated or stifling atmosphere. **4** informal be in an anxious or agitated state.
– PHRASES **stew in one's own juice** informal be left to suffer the consequences of one's own actions.
– ORIGIN Old French *estuve*, related to *estuver* 'heat in steam'.
stew[2] ● noun Brit. **1** a pond or large tank for keeping fish for eating. **2** an artificial oyster bed.
– ORIGIN Old French *estui*, from *estoier* 'confine'.
steward ● noun **1** a person who looks after the passengers on a ship or aircraft. **2** a person responsible for supplies of food to a college, club, etc. **3** an official who supervises arrangements at a large public event. **4** a person employed to manage a large house or estate. **5** chiefly historical an officer of the British royal household, especially an administrator of Crown estates. ● verb act as a steward of.
– DERIVATIVES **stewardship** noun.
– ORIGIN Old English.
stewardess ● noun a woman who looks after the passengers on a ship or aircraft.
stewed ● adjective informal drunk.
St George's cross ● noun a +-shaped cross, red on a white background (especially as a national emblem of England).
stick[1] ● noun **1** a thin piece of wood that has fallen or been cut off a tree. **2** a piece of trimmed wood used for support in walking or as a weapon. **3** (in hockey, polo, etc.) a long, thin implement used to hit or direct the ball or puck. **4** a long, thin object or piece: *a stick of dynamite.* **5** a group of bombs or paratroopers dropped from an aircraft. **6** the threat of punishment as a means of persuasion (as contrasted with the 'carrot' or enticement). **7** Brit. informal severe criticism or treatment. **8** (**the sticks**) informal, derogatory rural areas. **9** informal, dated a person of a specified kind: *Janet's not a bad old stick.*
– PHRASES **up sticks** Brit. informal go to live elsewhere. [ORIGIN from nautical slang *to up sticks* 'set up a boat's mast' (ready for departure).]
– ORIGIN Old English.
stick[2] ● verb (past and past part. **stuck**) **1** insert or push (something pointed) into or through something. **2** (**stick in/into/through**) be or remain fixed with its point embedded in. **3** stab or pierce with a sharp object. **4** protrude or extend in a certain direction. **5** informal put somewhere in a quick or careless way. **6** adhere or cause to adhere. **7** (**be stuck**) be fixed in a particular position or unable to move or be moved. **8** (**be stuck**) be unable to progress with a task or find the answer or solution. **9** Brit. informal accept; tolerate; endure: *I can't stick Geoff.*
– PHRASES **be stuck for** be at a loss for or in need of. **be stuck on** informal be infatuated with. **be stuck with** informal be unable to get rid of or escape from. **get stuck in** (or **into**) Brit. informal start doing something with determination. **stick around** informal remain in or near a place. **stick at** informal persevere with. **stick by** continue to support or be loyal to. **stick in one's throat** (or **craw**) be difficult or impossible to accept. **stick it out** informal put up with or persevere with something difficult or disagreeable. **stick one's neck out** informal risk criticism or anger by acting or speaking boldly. **stick out** be extremely noticeable. **stick out for** refuse to accept less than. **stick to** continue or confine oneself to doing, using, or practising. **stick together** informal remain united or mutually loyal. **stick up** informal, chiefly N. Amer. rob at gunpoint. **stick up for** support or defend. **stick with** informal persevere or continue with.
– ORIGIN Old English.
sticker ● noun **1** an adhesive label or notice. **2** informal a determined or persistent person.
stick insect ● noun a long, slender, slow-moving insect that resembles a twig.
stick-in-the-mud ● noun informal a person who resists change.
stickleback ● noun a small freshwater or coastal fish with sharp spines along its back.
– ORIGIN from Old English words meaning 'thorn, sting' + 'back'.
stickler ● noun a person who insists on a certain quality or type of behaviour.
– ORIGIN originally in the sense 'umpire': from Old English, 'set in order'.
stickpin ● noun N. Amer. a straight pin with an ornamental head, worn to keep a tie in place or as a brooch.
stick shift ● noun N. Amer. a gear lever or manual transmission.
stick-up ● noun informal, chiefly US an armed robbery in which a gun is used to threaten people.

Thesaurus

transom, tail.
– OPPOSITES bow.
stew ● noun **1** *a beef stew* CASSEROLE, hotpot, ragout, goulash, carbonnade, daube, grillade; *N. Amer.* burgoo. **2** *(informal) she's in a right old stew* PANIC, fluster, fret, fuss, fever; *informal* flap, sweat, lather, tizzy, dither, twitter, state; *N. Amer. informal* twit; *poetic/literary* pother.
● verb **1** *stew the meat for an hour* BRAISE, casserole, simmer, boil; jug; *archaic* seethe. **2** *(informal) there's no point stewing over it.* See WORRY verb sense 1. **3** *(informal) the girls sat stewing in the heat* SWELTER, be very hot, perspire, sweat; *informal* roast, bake, be boiling.
steward ● noun **1** *an air steward* FLIGHT ATTENDANT, cabin attendant; stewardess, air hostess; *N. Amer. informal* stew. **2** *the race stewards* OFFICIAL, marshal, organizer. **3** *the steward of the estate* (ESTATE) MANAGER, agent, overseer, custodian, caretaker; *Brit.* land agent, bailiff; *Scottish* factor; *historical* reeve.
stick[1] ● noun **1** *a fire made of sticks* PIECE OF WOOD, twig, small branch. **2** *he walks with a stick* WALKING STICK, cane, staff, alpenstock, crook, crutch; *trademark* Zimmer frame. **3** *the plants need supporting on sticks* CANE, pole, post, stake, upright. **4** *he beat me with a stick* CLUB, cudgel, bludgeon, shillelagh; truncheon, baton; cane, birch, switch, rod; *Brit. informal* cosh. **5** *(Brit. informal) he'll get stick for this.* See CRITICISM sense 1.
– OPPOSITES praise, commendation.
– PHRASES **the sticks** *(informal)* THE COUNTRY, the countryside, rural areas, the provinces; the backwoods, the back of beyond, the wilds, the hinterland, a backwater; *N. Amer.* the backcountry, the backland; *Austral./NZ* the backblocks, the booay; *S. African* the backveld, the platteland; *informal* the middle of nowhere; *N. Amer. informal* the boondocks, the boonies; *Austral./NZ informal* Woop Woop, beyond the black stump.
stick[2] ● verb **1** *he stuck his fork into the sausage* THRUST, push, insert, jab, poke, dig, plunge. **2** *the bristles stuck into his skin* PIERCE, penetrate, puncture, prick, stab. **3** *the cup stuck to its saucer* ADHERE, cling, be fixed, be glued. **4** *stick the stamp there* AFFIX, attach, fasten, fix; paste, glue, gum, tape, sellotape, pin, tack. **5** *the wheels stuck fast* BECOME TRAPPED, become jammed, jam, catch, become wedged, become lodged, become fixed, become embedded. **6** *that sticks in his mind* REMAIN, stay, linger, dwell, persist, continue, last, endure. **7** *the charges won't stick* BE UPHELD, hold, be believed; *informal* hold water. **8** *(informal) just stick that sandwich on my desk* PUT (DOWN), place, set (down), lay (down), deposit, position; leave, stow; *informal* dump, bung, park, plonk, pop; *N. Amer. informal* plunk. **9** *(Brit. informal) I can't stick it any longer* TOLERATE, put up with, take, stand, stomach, endure, bear; *Scottish* thole; *informal* abide.
– PHRASES **stick at** *(informal)* PERSEVERE WITH, persist with, keep at, work at, continue with, carry on with, not give up with, hammer away at, stay with; go the distance, stay the course; *informal* soldier on with, hang in there. **stick by** BE LOYAL TO, be faithful to, be true to, stand by, keep faith with, keep one's promise to. **stick it out** *(informal)* PUT UP WITH IT, grin and bear it, keep at it, keep going, stay with it, see it through; persevere, persist, carry on, struggle on; *informal* hang in there, soldier on, tough it out. **stick out 1** *his front teeth stuck out* PROTRUDE, jut (out), project, stand out, extend, poke out; bulge, overhang. **2** *they stuck out in their strange clothes* BE NOTICEABLE, be visible, be obvious, be conspicuous, stand out, be obtrusive, be prominent, attract attention, catch the eye, leap out, show up; *informal* stick/stand out a mile, stick/stand out like a sore thumb. **stick to** *he stuck to his promise* ABIDE BY, keep, adhere to, hold to, comply with, fulfil, make good, stand by. **stick up for** SUPPORT, take someone's side, side with, be on the side of, stand by, stand up for, take someone's part, defend, come to the defence of, champion, speak up for, fight for.

sticky ● adjective (**stickier**, **stickiest**) **1** tending or designed to stick; adhesive. **2** glutinous; viscous. **3** (of the weather) hot and humid; muggy. **4** informal difficult; awkward. **5** informal (of a website) attracting a long visit or repeat visits from users.
– PHRASES **come to a sticky end** informal be led by one's own actions to ruin or an unpleasant death. **sticky fingers** informal a tendency to steal.
– DERIVATIVES **stickily** adverb **stickiness** noun.
stickybeak Austral./NZ informal ● noun an inquisitive person. ● verb pry.
stiction /stiksh'n/ ● noun Physics the friction which tends to prevent stationary surfaces from being set in motion.
stiff ● adjective **1** not easily bent; rigid. **2** not moving freely; difficult to turn or operate. **3** unable to move easily and without pain. **4** not relaxed or friendly; constrained. **5** severe or strong: *stiff fines.* **6** (**stiff with**) informal full of. **7** (—— **stiff**) informal having a specified unpleasant feeling to an extreme extent: *scared stiff.* ● noun informal **1** a dead body. **2** chiefly N. Amer. a boring, conventional person. ● verb N. Amer. informal kill.
– DERIVATIVES **stiffly** adverb **stiffness** noun.
– ORIGIN Old English.
stiffen ● verb **1** make or become stiff. **2** make or become stronger or more steadfast.
– DERIVATIVES **stiffener** noun.
stiff-necked ● adjective haughty and stubborn.
stiff upper lip ● noun a quality of uncomplaining endurance.
stifle[1] ● verb **1** prevent from breathing freely; suffocate. **2** smother or suppress. **3** prevent or constrain (an activity or idea).
– ORIGIN perhaps from Old French *estouffer* 'smother, stifle'.
stifle[2] ● noun a joint in the legs of horses and other animals, equivalent to the knee in humans.
– ORIGIN of unknown origin.
stifling ● adjective unpleasantly hot and stuffy.
– DERIVATIVES **stiflingly** adverb.
stigma /stigmə/ ● noun (pl. **stigmas** or especially in sense 2 **stigmata** /stigmaatə, stigmətə/) **1** a mark or sign of disgrace or discredit. **2** (**stigmata**) (in Christian tradition) marks corresponding to those left on Christ's body by the Crucifixion, said to have been impressed by divine favour on the bodies of St Francis of Assisi and others. **3** Medicine a visible sign or characteristic of a disease. **4** Botany the part of a pistil that receives the pollen during pollination.
– ORIGIN Greek, 'a mark made by a pointed instrument, a dot'.
stigmatic ● adjective relating to a stigma or stigmas. ● noun a person bearing stigmata.
stigmatize (also **stigmatise**) ● verb **1** regard as worthy of disgrace. **2** mark with stigmata.
– DERIVATIVES **stigmatization** noun.
stile ● noun an arrangement of steps set into a fence or wall that allows people to climb over.
– ORIGIN Old English.
stiletto ● noun (pl. **stilettos**) **1** chiefly Brit. a thin, high tapering heel on a woman's shoe. **2** a short dagger with a tapering blade. **3** a sharp-pointed tool for making eyelet holes.
– ORIGIN Italian, 'little dagger'.
still[1] ● adjective **1** not moving. **2** (of air or water) undisturbed by wind, sound, or current. **3** (of a drink) not fizzy. ● noun **1** a state of deep and quiet calm. **2** a photograph or a single shot from a cinema film. ● adverb **1** even now or at a particular time. **2** nevertheless. **3** even: *better still.* ● verb make or become still.
– DERIVATIVES **stillness** noun.
– ORIGIN Old English.
still[2] ● noun an apparatus for distilling alcoholic drinks such as whisky.
– ORIGIN from DISTIL.
stillbirth ● noun the birth of an infant that has died in the womb.
stillborn ● adjective **1** (of an infant) born dead. **2** (of a proposal or plan) having failed to develop or succeed; unrealized.
still life ● noun a painting or drawing of an arrangement of objects such as flowers or fruit.
stilly literary ● adverb /stilli/ quietly and with little movement. ● adjective /stilli/ still and quiet.
stilt ● noun **1** either of a pair of upright poles with supports for the feet enabling the user to walk raised above the ground. **2** each of a set of posts or piles supporting a building. **3** a long-billed wading bird with very long slender legs.
– ORIGIN Germanic.
stilted ● adjective **1** (of speech or writing) stiff and self-conscious or unnatural. **2** standing on stilts.
– DERIVATIVES **stiltedly** adverb **stiltedness** noun.

Thesaurus

stick-in-the-mud ● noun *(informal)* (OLD) FOGEY, conservative, fossil, troglodyte; *Brit.* museum piece; *informal* fuddy-duddy, square, stuffed shirt.
sticky ● adjective **1** *sticky tape* (SELF-)ADHESIVE, gummed; *technical* adherent. **2** *sticky clay* GLUTINOUS, viscous, viscid, ropy; gluey, tacky, gummy, treacly, syrupy; mucilaginous; *Brit.* claggy; *informal* gooey, gloopy, icky; *Brit. informal* gungy; *N. Amer. informal* gloppy. **3** *sticky weather* HUMID, muggy, close, sultry, steamy, sweaty. **4** *(informal) a sticky situation* AWKWARD, difficult, tricky, ticklish, problematic, delicate, touch-and-go, embarrassing, sensitive, uncomfortable; *informal* hairy.
– OPPOSITES dry, fresh, cool, easy.
stiff ● adjective **1** *stiff cardboard* RIGID, hard, firm, inelastic, inflexible. **2** *a stiff paste* SEMI-SOLID, viscous, viscid, thick, stiffened, firm. **3** *I'm stiff all over* ACHING, achy, painful; arthritic, rheumatic; *informal* creaky, rheumaticky, rusty. **4** *a rather stiff manner* FORMAL, reserved, unfriendly, chilly, cold, frigid, icy, austere, wooden, forced, strained, stilted; *informal* starchy, uptight, stand-offish. **5** *a stiff fine* HARSH, severe, heavy, crippling, punishing, stringent, drastic, draconian; *Brit.* swingeing. **6** *stiff resistance* VIGOROUS, determined, full of determination, strong, spirited, resolute, tenacious, steely, four-square, unflagging, unyielding, dogged, stubborn, obdurate; *N. Amer.* rock-ribbed. **7** *a stiff climb* DIFFICULT, hard, arduous, tough, strenuous, laborious, uphill, exacting, tiring, demanding, formidable, challenging, punishing, gruelling; *informal* killing, hellish; *Brit. informal* knackering. **8** *a stiff breeze* STRONG, fresh, brisk. **9** *a stiff drink* STRONG, potent, alcoholic.
– OPPOSITES flexible, plastic, limp, runny, supple, limber, relaxed, informal, lenient, mild, half-hearted, easy, gentle, weak.
stiffen ● verb **1** *stir until the mixture stiffens* BECOME STIFF, thicken; set, become solid, solidify, harden, gel, congeal, coagulate, clot. **2** *she stiffened her muscles | without exercise, joints will stiffen* MAKE/BECOME STIFF, tense (up), tighten, tauten. **3** *intimidation stiffened their resolve* STRENGTHEN, harden, toughen, fortify, reinforce, give a boost to.
– OPPOSITES soften, liquefy, relax, weaken.
stifle ● verb **1** *she stifled him with a bolster* SUFFOCATE, choke, asphyxiate, smother. **2** *Eleanor stifled a giggle* SUPPRESS, smother, restrain, fight back, choke back, gulp back, check, swallow, curb, silence. **3** *cartels stifle competition* CONSTRAIN, hinder, hamper, impede, hold back, curb, check, restrain, prevent, inhibit, suppress.
– OPPOSITES let out, encourage.
stifling ● adjective AIRLESS, suffocating, oppressive; very hot, sweltering; humid, close, muggy; *informal* boiling.
– OPPOSITES fresh, airy, cold.
stigma ● noun SHAME, disgrace, dishonour, ignominy, opprobrium, humiliation.
– OPPOSITES honour, credit.
stigmatize ● verb CONDEMN, denounce; brand, label, mark out; disparage, vilify, pillory, pour scorn on, defame.
still ● adjective **1** *Polly lay still* MOTIONLESS, unmoving, not moving a muscle, stock-still, immobile, like a statue, as if turned to stone, rooted to the spot, transfixed, static, stationary. **2** *a still night* QUIET, silent, hushed, soundless, noiseless, undisturbed; CALM, peaceful, serene, windless; *poetic/literary* stilly. **3** *the lake was still* CALM, flat, even, smooth, placid, tranquil, pacific, waveless, glassy, like a millpond, unruffled.
– OPPOSITES moving, active, noisy, rough.
● noun *the still of the night* QUIETNESS, quiet, quietude, silence, stillness, hush, soundlessness; calm, tranquillity, peace, serenity.
– OPPOSITES noise, disturbance, hubbub.
● adverb **1** *he's still here* UP TO THIS TIME, up to the present time, until now, even now, yet. **2** *He's crazy. Still, he's harmless* NEVERTHELESS, nonetheless, all the same, just the same, anyway, anyhow, even so, yet, but, however, notwithstanding, despite that, in spite of that, for all that, be that as it may, in any event, at any rate; *informal* still and all.
● verb **1** *he stilled the crowd* QUIETEN, quiet, silence, hush; calm, settle, pacify, soothe, lull, allay, subdue. **2** *the wind stilled* ABATE, die down, lessen, subside, ease up/off, let up, moderate, slacken, weaken.
– OPPOSITES stir up, get stronger, get up.

Stilton • noun trademark a kind of strong, rich blue cheese originally made in Leicestershire.
– ORIGIN so named because it was formerly sold at a coaching inn in *Stilton*, Cambridgeshire.

stimulant • noun **1** a substance that acts to increase physiological or nervous activity in the body. **2** something that promotes activity, interest, or enthusiasm. • adjective acting as a stimulant.

stimulate • verb **1** apply or act as a stimulus to. **2** animate or excite.
– DERIVATIVES **stimulation** noun **stimulator** noun **stimulatory** adjective.
– ORIGIN Latin *stimulare* 'urge, goad'.

stimulus /stimyooləss/ • noun (pl. **stimuli** /stimyoolī/) **1** something that evokes a specific reaction in an organ or tissue. **2** something that promotes activity, interest, or enthusiasm.
– ORIGIN Latin, 'goad, spur, incentive'.

sting • noun **1** a small sharp-pointed organ of an insect, capable of inflicting a painful wound by injecting poison. **2** any of a number of minute hairs on certain plants, causing inflammation if touched. **3** a wound from a sting. **4** a sharp tingling sensation or hurtful effect. **5** informal a carefully planned undercover operation. • verb (past and past part. **stung**) **1** wound with a sting. **2** produce a stinging sensation. **3** hurt; upset. **4** (**sting into**) provoke (someone) to do (something) by causing annoyance or offence. **5** informal swindle or exorbitantly overcharge.
– PHRASES **sting in the tail** an unexpected and unpleasant end to something.
– DERIVATIVES **stinger** noun.
– ORIGIN Old English.

stinging nettle • noun a nettle covered in stinging hairs.

stingray • noun a marine ray with a long poisonous serrated spine at the base of the tail.

stingy /stinji/ • adjective (**stingier**, **stingiest**) informal mean; ungenerous.
– DERIVATIVES **stingily** adverb **stinginess** noun.
– ORIGIN perhaps a dialect variant of STING.

stink • verb (past **stank** or **stunk**; past part. **stunk**) **1** have a strong unpleasant smell. **2** informal be contemptible or scandalous. • noun **1** a strong, unpleasant smell. **2** informal a row or fuss.
– PHRASES **like stink** informal extremely hard or intensely.
– ORIGIN Old English, related to STENCH.

stink bomb • noun a small container holding a sulphurous compound that is released when the container is broken, emitting a very unpleasant smell.

stinker • noun informal **1** a person or thing that stinks. **2** a contemptible or very unpleasant person or thing.

stinkhorn • noun a fungus with a rounded head that turns into a foul-smelling slime containing the spores.

stinking • adjective **1** foul-smelling. **2** informal contemptible or very unpleasant. • adverb informal extremely: *stinking rich.*

stinky • adjective (**stinkier**, **stinkiest**) informal having a strong unpleasant smell.

stint[1] • verb (also **stint on**) be restrictive or ungenerous towards (someone) or in providing (something). • noun **1** an allotted period of work. **2** limited supply or effort.
– ORIGIN Old English, 'make blunt'.

stint[2] • noun a very small short-legged northern sandpiper.
– ORIGIN of unknown origin.

stipend /stīpend/ • noun a fixed regular sum paid as a salary or as expenses to a clergyman, teacher, or public official.
– ORIGIN Latin *stipendium*, from *stips* 'wages' + *pendere* 'to pay'.

stipendiary /stīpendiəri/ • adjective **1** receiving a stipend; working for pay rather than voluntarily. **2** relating to or of the nature of a stipend.

stipple • verb **1** mark (a surface) with numerous small dots or specks. **2** produce a decorative effect on (paint or other material) by roughening its surface when wet. • noun the process, technique, or effect of stippling.
– ORIGIN Dutch *stippelen* 'to prick'.

stipulate /stipyoolayt/ • verb demand or specify as part of a bargain or agreement.
– DERIVATIVES **stipulation** noun.
– ORIGIN Latin *stipulari* 'demand as a formal promise'.

stir[1] • verb (**stirred**, **stirring**) **1** move an implement round and

Thesaurus

stilted • adjective STRAINED, forced, contrived, constrained, laboured, stiff, self-conscious, awkward, unnatural, wooden.
– OPPOSITES natural, effortless, spontaneous.

stimulant • noun **1** *caffeine is a stimulant* TONIC, restorative; antidepressant; *informal* pep pill, upper, pick-me-up, bracer; *Medicine* analeptic. **2** *a stimulant to discussion* STIMULUS, incentive, encouragement, impetus, inducement, fillip, boost, spur, prompt; *informal* shot in the arm.
– OPPOSITES sedative, downer, deterrent.

stimulate • verb ENCOURAGE, act as a stimulus/incentive/impetus/fillip/spur to, prompt, prod, move, motivate, trigger, spark, spur on, galvanize, activate, kindle, fire, fire with enthusiasm, fuel, whet, nourish; inspire, incentivize, inspirit, rouse, excite, animate, electrify; *N. Amer.* light a fire under, spirit someone up.
– OPPOSITES discourage.

stimulating • adjective **1** *a stimulating effect on the circulation* RESTORATIVE, tonic, invigorating, bracing, energizing, reviving, refreshing, revitalizing, revivifying; *Medicine* analeptic. **2** *a stimulating lecture* THOUGHT-PROVOKING, interesting, fascinating, inspiring, inspirational, lively, sparkling, exciting, stirring, rousing, intriguing, giving one food for thought, refreshing; provocative, challenging.
– OPPOSITES sedative, uninspiring, uninteresting, boring.

stimulus • noun SPUR, stimulant, encouragement, impetus, boost, prompt, prod, incentive, inducement, inspiration, fillip; motivation, impulse; *informal* shot in the arm.
– OPPOSITES deterrent, discouragement.

sting • noun **1** *a bee sting* PRICK, wound, injury, puncture. **2** *this cream will take the sting away* SMART, pricking; pain, soreness, hurt, irritation. **3** *the sting of his betrayal* HEARTACHE, heartbreak, agony, torture, torment, hurt, pain, anguish. **4** *there was a sting in her words* SHARPNESS, severity, bite, edge, pointedness, asperity; sarcasm, acrimony, malice, spite, venom. **5** *(informal) the victim of a sting* SWINDLE, fraud, deception; trickery, sharp practice; *informal* rip-off, con, con trick, fiddle; *N. Amer. informal* bunco.
• verb **1** *she was stung by a scorpion* PRICK, wound; poison. **2** *the smoke made her eyes sting* SMART, burn, hurt, be irritated, be sore. **3** *the criticism stung her* UPSET, wound, cut to the quick, sear, grieve, hurt, pain, torment, mortify. **4** *he was stung into action* PROVOKE, goad, incite, spur, prick, prod, rouse, drive, galvanize. **5** *(informal) they stung a bank for thousands* SWINDLE, defraud, cheat, fleece, gull; *informal* rip off, screw, shaft, bilk, do, rook, diddle, take for a ride, skin; *N. Amer. informal* chisel, gouge; *Brit. informal, dated* rush.
– OPPOSITES deter.

stingy • adjective *(informal)* MEAN, miserly, niggardly, close-fisted, parsimonious, penny-pinching, cheese-paring, Scrooge-like; *informal* tight-fisted, tight, mingy, money-grubbing; *N. Amer. informal* cheap; *formal* penurious; *archaic* near, niggard.
– OPPOSITES generous, liberal.

stink • verb **1** *his clothes stank of stale sweat* REEK, smell (foul/bad/disgusting), stink/smell to high heaven. **2** *(informal) the whole idea stinks* BE VERY UNPLEASANT, be abhorrent, be despicable, be contemptible, be disgusting, be vile, be foul; *N. Amer. informal* suck. **3** *(informal) the whole affair stinks of a set-up* SMACK, reek, give the impression, have all the hallmarks; strongly suggest.
• noun **1** *the stink of sweat* STENCH, reek, foul/bad smell, malodour; *Brit. informal* pong, niff, hum; *Scottish informal* guff; *N. Amer. informal* funk; *poetic/literary* miasma. **2** *(informal) she kicked up a stink* FUSS, commotion, rumpus, ruckus, trouble, outcry, uproar, brouhaha, furore; *informal* song and dance, to-do, kerfuffle, hoo-ha; *Brit. informal* row, carry-on.

stinking • adjective **1** *stinking rubbish* FOUL-SMELLING, smelly, reeking, fetid, malodorous, rank, putrid, noxious; *informal* stinky, reeky; *Brit. informal* niffing, niffy, pongy, whiffy, humming; *N. Amer. informal* funky; *poetic/literary* miasmic, noisome. **2** *(informal) a stinking cold* DREADFUL, awful, terrible, frightful, ghastly, nasty, foul, vile; *Brit. informal* rotten, shocking.
– OPPOSITES sweet-smelling, aromatic, mild, slight.

stint • verb *we saved by stinting on food* SKIMP, scrimp, be economical, economize, be sparing, hold back, be frugal; be mean, be parsimonious; limit, restrict; *informal* be stingy, be mingy, be tight.
• noun *a two-week stint in the office* SPELL, stretch, turn, session, term, shift, tour of duty.

stipulate • verb SPECIFY, set down, set out, lay down; demand, require, insist on, make a condition of, prescribe, impose; *Law* provide.

S

round in (a liquid or other substance) to mix it thoroughly. **2** move slightly or begin to be active. **3** wake or rise from sleep. **4** (often **stir up**) arouse (a strong feeling) in someone. **5** Brit. informal deliberately cause trouble by spreading rumours or gossip. ● noun **1** an act of stirring or being stirred. **2** a disturbance or commotion.
– DERIVATIVES **stirrer** noun.
– ORIGIN Old English.

stir² ● noun informal prison.
– ORIGIN perhaps from Romany *sturbin* 'jail'.

stir-crazy ● adjective informal psychologically disturbed as a result of being confined or imprisoned.

stir-fry ● verb fry rapidly over a high heat while stirring briskly.

stirring ● adjective causing great excitement or strong emotion; rousing. ● noun an initial sign of activity, movement, or emotion.
– DERIVATIVES **stirringly** adverb.

stirrup ● noun **1** each of a pair of devices attached at either side of a horse's saddle, in the form of a loop with a flat base to support the rider's foot. **2** (also **lithotomy stirrups**) a pair of metal supports for the ankles used during gynaecological examinations and childbirth.
– ORIGIN Old English.

stirrup cup ● noun an alcoholic drink offered to a person on horseback who is about to depart.

stirrup pump ● noun a hand-operated water pump with a footrest resembling a stirrup, used to extinguish small fires.

stitch ● noun **1** a loop of thread or yarn resulting from a single pass of the needle in sewing, knitting, or crocheting. **2** a method of sewing, knitting, or crocheting producing a particular pattern. **3** informal the smallest item of clothing: *swimming with not a stitch on.* **4** a sudden sharp pain in the side of the body, caused by strenuous exercise. ● verb make or mend with stitches.
– PHRASES **in stitches** informal laughing uncontrollably. **a stitch in time saves nine** proverb if you sort out a problem immediately it may save a lot of extra work later. **stitch up** Brit. informal **1** manipulate (a situation) to someone's disadvantage. **2** cheat or falsely incriminate.
– DERIVATIVES **stitcher** noun **stitchery** noun **stitching** noun.
– ORIGIN Old English, related to STICK².

St John's wort ● noun a herbaceous plant or shrub with yellow flowers and paired oval leaves.
– ORIGIN so named because some species come into flower near the feast day of St John the Baptist (24 June).

St Lucian /lo͞osh'n/ ● noun a person from the Caribbean island of St Lucia. ● adjective relating to St Lucia.

stoa /stōə/ ● noun (in ancient Greek architecture) a portico or roofed colonnade.
– ORIGIN Greek.

stoat ● noun a small carnivorous mammal of the weasel family, with chestnut fur (white in northern animals in winter), white underparts, and a black-tipped tail.
– ORIGIN of unknown origin.

stochastic /stəkastik/ ● adjective having a random probability distribution or pattern that can be analysed statistically but not predicted precisely.
– DERIVATIVES **stochastically** adverb.
– ORIGIN Greek *stokhastikos*, from *stokhazesthai* 'aim at, guess'.

stock ● noun **1** a supply of goods or materials available for sale or use. **2** farm animals bred and kept for their meat or milk; livestock. **3** the capital of a company raised through the issue and subscription of shares. **4** (**stocks**) a portion of a company's stock held by an individual or group as an investment. **5** securities issued by the government in fixed units with a fixed rate of interest. **6** water in which bones, meat, fish, or vegetables have been slowly simmered. **7** the raw material from which a specified commodity can be manufactured. **8** a person's ancestry. **9** a breed, variety, or population of an animal or plant. **10** the trunk or woody stem of a tree or shrub. **11** a plant cultivated for its fragrant flowers, typically lilac, pink, or white. **12** (**the stocks**) (treated as sing. or pl.) historical a wooden structure with holes for securing a person's feet and hands, in which criminals were locked as a method of public punishment. **13** the part of a firearm to which the barrel and firing mechanism are attached. **14** a band of material worn round the neck. ● adjective **1** usually kept in stock and thus regularly available for sale. **2** constantly recurring, common, or conventional: *stock characters.* ● verb **1** have or keep a stock of. **2** provide or fill with a stock of something. **3** (**stock up**) amass stocks of something.
– PHRASES **in** (or **out of**) **stock** available (or unavailable) for immediate sale or use. **put stock in** have a specified amount of belief or faith in. **take stock** make an overall assessment of a particular situation.
– ORIGIN Old English, 'trunk, block of wood, post'.

stockade ● noun **1** a barrier or enclosure formed from upright wooden posts. **2** chiefly N. Amer. a military prison. ● verb enclose with a stockade.
– ORIGIN obsolete French *estocade*, related to STAKE¹.

stockbreeder ● noun a farmer who breeds livestock.

stockbroker ● noun a broker who buys and sells securities on a stock exchange on behalf of clients.
– DERIVATIVES **stockbroking** noun.

stockbroker belt ● noun Brit. an affluent residential area outside a large city.

stock car ● noun an ordinary car that has been strengthened

Thesaurus

stipulation ● noun CONDITION, precondition, proviso, provision, prerequisite, specification; demand, requirement; rider, caveat, qualification.

stir ● verb **1** *stir the mixture well* MIX, blend, agitate; beat, whip, whisk, fold in; *N. Amer.* muddle. **2** *Travis stirred in his sleep* MOVE SLIGHTLY, change one's position, shift. **3** *a breeze stirred the leaves* DISTURB, rustle, shake, move, flutter, agitate. **4** *he finally stirred at ten o'clock* GET UP, get out of bed, rouse oneself, rise; WAKE (UP), awaken; *informal* rise and shine, surface, show signs of life; *formal* arise; *poetic/literary* waken. **5** *I never stirred from here* MOVE, budge, make a move, shift, go away; leave. **6** *symbolism can stir the imagination* AROUSE, rouse, fire, kindle, inspire, stimulate, excite, awaken, quicken; *poetic/literary* waken. **7** *the war stirred him to action* SPUR, drive, rouse, prompt, propel, prod, motivate, encourage; urge, impel; provoke, goad, prick, sting, incite; *N. Amer.* light a fire under.
– OPPOSITES go to bed, retire, go to sleep, stultify, stay, stay put.
● noun *the news caused a stir* COMMOTION, disturbance, fuss, excitement, turmoil, sensation; *informal* to-do, hoo-ha, hullabaloo, flap, splash.
– PHRASES **stir something up** WHIP UP, work up, foment, fan the flames of, trigger, spark off, precipitate, excite, provoke, incite.

stirring ● adjective EXCITING, thrilling, rousing, stimulating, moving, inspiring, inspirational, passionate, impassioned, emotional, heady.
– OPPOSITES boring, pedestrian.

stitch ● noun *he was panting and had a stitch* SHARP PAIN, stabbing pain, shooting pain, stab of pain, pang, twinge, spasm.
● verb *the seams are stitched by hand* SEW, baste, tack; seam, hem; darn.
– PHRASES **stitch someone up** *(Brit. informal)* FALSELY INCRIMINATE, get someone into trouble; *informal* frame, set up; *Brit. informal* fit someone up, drop someone in it.

stock ● noun **1** *the shop carries little stock* MERCHANDISE, goods, wares, items/articles for sale, inventory. **2** *a stock of fuel* STORE, supply, stockpile, reserve, hoard, cache, bank, accumulation, quantity, collection. **3** *farm stock* ANIMALS, livestock, beasts; flocks, herds. **4** *blue-chip stocks* SHARES, securities, equities, bonds. **5** *his stock is low with most voters* POPULARITY, favour, regard, estimation, standing, status, reputation, name, prestige. **6** *his mother was of French stock* DESCENT, ancestry, origin(s), parentage, pedigree, lineage, line (of descent), heritage, birth, extraction, family, blood, bloodline. **7** *chicken stock* BOUILLON, broth. **8** *the stock of a weapon* HANDLE, butt, haft, grip, shaft, shank.
● adjective **1** *a stock size* STANDARD, regular, normal, established, set; common, readily/widely available; staple. **2** *the stock response* USUAL, routine, predictable, set, standard, staple, customary, familiar, conventional, traditional, stereotyped, clichéd, hackneyed, unoriginal, formulaic.
– OPPOSITES non-standard, original, unusual.
● verb **1** *we do not stock GM food* SELL, carry, keep (in stock), offer, have (for sale), retail, supply. **2** *the fridge was well stocked with milk* SUPPLY, provide, furnish, provision, equip, fill, load.
– PHRASES **in stock** FOR/ON SALE, (immediately) available, on the shelf. **stock up on/with** AMASS SUPPLIES OF, stockpile, hoard, cache, lay in, buy up/in, put away/by, put/set aside, collect, accumulate,

S

for use in a race in which competing cars collide with each other.

stock cube ● noun a cube of concentrated dehydrated meat, vegetable, or fish stock for use in cooking.

stock exchange ● noun a market in which securities are bought and sold.

stockholder ● noun chiefly N. Amer. a shareholder.

stockinet (also **stockinette**) ● noun a soft, loosely knitted stretch fabric.
– ORIGIN probably an alteration of *stocking-net*.

stocking ● noun **1** either of a pair of separate close-fitting nylon garments covering the foot and leg, worn especially by women. **2** US or archaic a long sock worn by men. **3** a real or ornamental stocking hung up by children on Christmas Eve for Father Christmas to fill with presents. **4** a white marking of the lower part of a horse's leg.
– DERIVATIVES **stockinged** adjective.
– ORIGIN from *stock* in the dialect sense 'stocking'.

stocking cap ● noun a knitted hat with a long tapered end that hangs down.

stocking filler (N. Amer. **stocking stuffer**) ● noun Brit. a small present suitable for putting in a Christmas stocking.

stocking stitch ● noun a knitting stitch consisting of alternate rows of plain and purl stitch.

stock-in-trade ● noun the typical subject or commodity a person, company, or profession uses or deals in.

stockist ● noun Brit. a retailer that stocks goods of a particular type for sale.

stockman ● noun **1** a person who looks after livestock. **2** US an owner of livestock.

stock market ● noun a stock exchange.

stockpile ● noun a large accumulated stock of goods or materials. ● verb accumulate a large stock of.

stockpot ● noun a pot in which stock is prepared by long, slow cooking.

stock-still ● adverb without any movement; completely still.

stocktaking ● noun the action or process of recording the amount of stock held by a business.

stocky ● adjective (**stockier**, **stockiest**) (especially of a person) short and sturdy.
– DERIVATIVES **stockily** adverb **stockiness** noun.

stockyard ● noun N. Amer. a large yard containing pens and sheds in which livestock is kept and sorted.

stodge ● noun informal, chiefly Brit. **1** food that is heavy, filling, and high in carbohydrates. **2** dull and uninspired material or work.
– DERIVATIVES **stodginess** noun **stodgy** adjective.
– ORIGIN originally a verb in the sense 'stuff to stretching point': suggested by STUFF and PODGE.

stoep /sto͞op/ ● noun S. African a terraced veranda in front of a house.
– ORIGIN Afrikaans, from Dutch; related to STEP.

stogy /stōgi/ (also **stogie**) ● noun (pl. **stogies**) N. Amer. a long, thin, cheap cigar.
– ORIGIN originally as *stoga*: short for *Conestoga* in Pennsylvania.

stoic /stōik/ ● noun **1** a stoical person. **2** (**Stoic**) a member of the ancient philosophical school of Stoicism. ● adjective **1** stoical. **2** (**Stoic**) relating to the Stoics or Stoicism.
– ORIGIN Greek *stōïkos*, from STOA (with reference to the teaching of the ancient Greek philosopher Zeno, in the *Stoa Poikilē* or Painted Porch, at Athens).

stoical /stōik'l/ ● adjective enduring pain and hardship without showing one's feelings or complaining.
– DERIVATIVES **stoically** adverb.

stoicism /stōisiz'm/ ● noun **1** stoical behaviour. **2** (**Stoicism**) an ancient Greek school of philosophy which taught that it is wise to remain indifferent to changes of fortune and to pleasure and pain.

stoke ● verb **1** add coal to (a fire, furnace, etc.). **2** encourage or incite (a strong emotion). **3** (**stoke up**) informal consume a large quantity of food to give one energy.

stoker ● noun **1** a person who tends the furnace on a steamship or steam train. **2** a mechanical device for supplying fuel to a furnace.
– ORIGIN Dutch, from *stoken* 'stoke (a furnace)' (earlier 'push, poke').

STOL ● abbreviation Aeronautics short take-off and landing.

stole[1] ● noun **1** a woman's long scarf or shawl, worn loosely over the shoulders. **2** a priest's vestment worn over the shoulders.
– ORIGIN Greek, 'clothing'.

stole[2] past of STEAL.

stolen past participle of STEAL.

stolid ● adjective calm, dependable, and showing little emotion or animation.
– DERIVATIVES **stolidity** noun **stolidly** adverb.
– ORIGIN Latin *stolidus*, perhaps related to *stultus* 'foolish'.

stollen /shtollən, stollən/ ● noun a rich German fruit and nut loaf.
– ORIGIN German.

stoma /stōmə/ ● noun (pl. **stomas** or **stomata** /stōmətə/) **1** Botany a minute pore in the epidermis of the leaf or stem of a plant, allowing movement of gases in and out. **2** Zoology a small mouth-like opening in some lower animals. **3** Medicine an artificial opening made into a hollow organ, especially the gut or trachea.
– ORIGIN Greek, 'mouth'.

stomach ● noun **1** the internal organ in which the first part of digestion occurs. **2** the abdominal area of the body; the belly. **3** an appetite or desire for something: *they had no stomach for a fight.* ● verb **1** consume (food or drink) without feeling or being sick: *he cannot stomach milk.* **2** endure or accept: *what I won't stomach is thieving.*
– PHRASES **a strong stomach** an ability to see or do unpleasant things without feeling sick or squeamish.
– ORIGIN Greek *stomakhos* 'gullet'.

stomacher ● noun historical a V-shaped ornamental panel worn over the chest and stomach by men and women in the 16th century, later only by women.

stomach pump ● noun a syringe attached to a long tube, used for extracting the contents of a person's stomach (for example,

S

Thesaurus

save; *informal* squirrel away, salt away, stash away. **take stock of** REVIEW, assess, weigh up, appraise, evaluate; *informal* size up.

stockings ● plural noun NYLONS, stay-ups; tights; hosiery, hose; *N. Amer.* pantyhose.

stockpile ● noun *a stockpile of weapons* STOCK, store, supply, accumulation, collection, reserve, hoard, cache; *informal* stash.
● verb *food had been stockpiled* STORE UP, amass, accumulate, store (up), stock up on, hoard, cache, collect, lay in, put away, put/set aside, put by, put away for a rainy day, stow away, save; *informal* salt away, stash away.

stock-still ● adjective MOTIONLESS, completely still, unmoving, not moving a muscle, immobile, like a statue, as if turned to stone, rooted to the spot, transfixed, static, stationary.
– OPPOSITES moving, active.

stocky ● adjective THICKSET, sturdy, heavily built, chunky, burly, strapping, brawny, solid, heavy, hefty, beefy.
– OPPOSITES slender, skinny.

stodgy ● adjective **1** *a stodgy pudding* SOLID, substantial, filling, hearty, heavy, starchy, indigestible. **2** *stodgy writing* BORING, dull, uninteresting, dreary, turgid, tedious, dry, heavy going, unimaginative, uninspired, unexciting, unoriginal, monotonous, humdrum, prosaic, staid; *informal* deadly, square.
– OPPOSITES light, interesting, lively.

stoical ● adjective LONG-SUFFERING, uncomplaining, patient, forbearing, accepting, tolerant, resigned, phlegmatic, philosophical.
– OPPOSITES complaining, intolerant.

stoicism ● noun PATIENCE, forbearance, resignation, fortitude, endurance, acceptance, tolerance, philosophicalness, phlegm.
– OPPOSITES intolerance.

stoke ● verb ADD FUEL TO, mend, keep burning, tend.

stolid ● adjective IMPASSIVE, phlegmatic, unemotional, cool, calm, placid, unexcitable; dependable; unimaginative, dull.
– OPPOSITES emotional, lively, imaginative.

stomach ● noun **1** *a stomach pain* ABDOMEN, belly, gut, middle; *informal* tummy, tum, breadbasket, insides. **2** *his fat stomach* PAUNCH, pot belly, beer belly, girth; *informal* beer gut, pot, tummy, spare tyre, middle-aged spread; *N. Amer. informal* bay window; *dated, humorous* corporation. **3** *he had no stomach for it* APPETITE, taste, hunger, thirst; inclination, desire, relish, fancy.
– RELATED TERMS gastric.
● verb **1** *I can't stomach butter* DIGEST, keep down, manage to eat/consume, tolerate, take. **2** *they couldn't stomach the sight* TOLERATE, put up with, take, stand, endure, bear; *Scottish* thole; *informal* hack, abide; *Brit. informal* stick.

if they have taken poison).

stomata plural of STOMA.

stomp ● verb **1** tread heavily and noisily. **2** dance with heavy stamping steps.
– ORIGIN variant of STAMP.

stomping ground ● noun N. Amer. another term for STAMPING GROUND.

stone ● noun **1** hard, solid non-metallic mineral matter of which rock is made. **2** a small piece of stone found on the ground. **3** a piece of stone shaped for a purpose, especially to commemorate something or to mark out a boundary. **4** a gem. **5** a hard seed in certain fruits. **6** (pl. same) Brit. a unit of weight equal to 14 lb (6.35 kg). **7** a whitish or brownish-grey colour. ● verb **1** throw stones at in order to injure or kill. **2** remove the stone from (a fruit). **3** build, face, or pave with stone. ● adverb extremely or totally: *stone cold.*
– PHRASES **leave no stone unturned** try every possible course of action in order to achieve something. **a stone's throw** a short distance. **stone me!** (or **stone the crows!**) Brit. informal an exclamation of surprise or shock.
– ORIGIN Old English.

Stone Age ● noun a prehistoric period when weapons and tools were made of stone, preceding the Bronze Age.

stonechat ● noun a small heathland bird with a call like two stones being knocked together.

stone circle ● noun a megalithic monument consisting of stones arranged in a circle.

stonecrop ● noun a plant with star-shaped yellow or white flowers which grows among rocks or on walls.

stoned ● adjective informal under the influence of drugs or alcohol.

stone-faced ● adjective informal revealing no emotions through the expressions of the face.

stoneground ● adjective (of flour) ground with millstones.

stonemason ● noun a person who cuts, prepares, and builds with stone.

stonewall ● verb **1** delay or block by refusing to answer questions or by giving evasive replies, especially in politics. **2** Cricket bat extremely defensively.

stoneware ● noun a type of pottery which is impermeable and partly vitrified but opaque.

stonewashed (also **stonewash**) ● adjective (of a garment or fabric) washed with abrasives to produce a worn or faded appearance.

stonework ● noun **1** the parts of a building that are made of stone. **2** the work of a mason.

stonker ● noun Brit. informal something very large or impressive of its kind.
– DERIVATIVES **stonking** adjective.
– ORIGIN from military slang *stonk* 'a concentrated artillery bombardment'.

stonkered ● adjective Austral./NZ informal **1** utterly exhausted or defeated. **2** drunk.
– ORIGIN from Scots and northern English *stonk* 'game of marbles'.

stony ● adjective (**stonier**, **stoniest**) **1** full of stones. **2** of or resembling stone. **3** cold and unfeeling.
– PHRASES **fall on stony ground** (of words or a suggestion) be ignored or badly received. [ORIGIN with biblical reference to the parable of the sower in the Gospel of Matthew.]
– DERIVATIVES **stonily** adverb.

stony broke ● adjective Brit. informal entirely without money.

stood past and past participle of STAND.

stooge ● noun **1** derogatory a subordinate used by another to do routine or unpleasant work. **2** a performer whose act involves being the butt of a comedian's jokes. ● verb **1** informal move about aimlessly. **2** be a comedian's stooge.
– ORIGIN of unknown origin.

stook /stŏŏk, stōōk/ Brit. ● noun a group of sheaves of grain stood on end in a field. ● verb arrange in stooks.
– ORIGIN Low German *stūke.*

stool ● noun **1** a seat without a back or arms. **2** chiefly Medicine a piece of faeces. **3** a root or stump of a tree or plant from which shoots spring. **4** US a decoy bird in hunting.
– PHRASES **fall between two stools** Brit. fail to be or take either of two satisfactory alternatives.
– ORIGIN Old English, related to STAND.

stool pigeon ● noun **1** a police informer. **2** a person acting as a decoy.
– ORIGIN so named from the original use of a pigeon fixed to a stool as a decoy.

stoop¹ ● verb **1** bend one's head or body forwards and downwards. **2** have the head and shoulders habitually bent forwards. **3** lower one's standards so far as to do something morally wrong. ● noun a stooping posture.
– ORIGIN Old English, related to STEEP¹.

stoop² ● noun N. Amer. a porch with steps in front of a building.
– ORIGIN Dutch *stoep.*

stoor ● noun variant of STOUR.

stop ● verb (**stopped**, **stopping**) **1** come or bring to an end. **2** prevent from happening or from doing something. **3** cease or cause to cease moving or operating. **4** (of a bus or train) call at a designated place to pick up or set down passengers. **5** Brit. informal stay somewhere for a short time. **6** withhold or deduct. **7** (in full **stop payment of** or **on**) instruct a bank to withhold payment on (a cheque). **8** block or close up (a hole or leak). **9** obtain the required pitch from (the string of a musical instrument) by pressing at the appropriate point with the finger. ● noun **1** an act of stopping. **2** a place designated for a bus or train to stop. **3** an object or part of a mechanism which prevents movement. **4** a set of organ pipes of a particular tone and range of pitch. **5** a knob or lever in an organ or harpsichord which activates a set of pipes or strings of a particular tone and range of pitch. **6** Photography the effective diameter of a lens.
– PHRASES **pull out all the stops** make a very great effort to achieve something. [ORIGIN with reference to the stops of an organ.] **put a stop to** cause to end. **stop dead** (or **short**) suddenly cease moving, speaking, or acting. **stop off** (or **over**) pay a short visit en route to one's ultimate destination. **stop up** Brit. informal refrain from going to bed; stay up.
– ORIGIN Old English.

Thesaurus

stomach ache ● noun INDIGESTION, dyspepsia; colic, gripe; *informal* bellyache, tummy ache, gut ache, collywobbles.

stone ● noun **1** *someone threw a stone at me* ROCK, pebble, boulder. **2** *a commemorative stone* TABLET, monument, monolith, obelisk; gravestone, headstone, tombstone. **3** *paving stones* SLAB, flagstone, flag, sett. **4** *a precious stone* GEM, gemstone, jewel, semi-precious stone, brilliant; *informal* rock, sparkler. **5** *a peach stone* KERNEL, seed, pip, pit.
– RELATED TERMS lithic, lapidary.

stony ● adjective **1** *a stony path* ROCKY, pebbly, gravelly, shingly; rough, hard. **2** *a stony stare* UNFRIENDLY, hostile, cold, chilly, frosty, icy; hard, flinty, steely, stern, severe; fixed, expressionless, blank, poker-faced, deadpan; unfeeling, uncaring, unsympathetic, indifferent, cold-hearted, callous, heartless, hard-hearted, stony-hearted, merciless, pitiless.
– OPPOSITES smooth, friendly, sympathetic.

stooge ● noun **1** *a government stooge* UNDERLING, minion, lackey, subordinate; henchman; PUPPET, pawn, cat's paw; *informal* sidekick; *Brit. informal* dogsbody, poodle. **2** *a comedian's stooge* BUTT, foil, straight man.

stoop ● verb **1** *she stooped to pick up the pen* BEND (OVER/DOWN), lean over/down, crouch (down). **2** *he stooped his head* LOWER, bend, incline, bow, duck. **3** *he stoops when he walks* HUNCH ONE'S SHOULDERS, walk with a stoop, be round-shouldered. **4** *Davis would stoop to crime* LOWER ONESELF, sink, descend, resort; go as far as, sink as low as.
● noun *a man with a stoop* HUNCH, round shoulders; curvature of the spine; *Medicine* kyphosis.

stop ● verb **1** *we can't stop the decline* PUT AN END/STOP/HALT TO, bring to an end/stop/halt/close/standstill, end, halt; finish, terminate, wind up, discontinue, cut short, interrupt, nip in the bud; deactivate, shut down. **2** *he stopped running* CEASE, discontinue, desist from, break off; give up, abandon, abstain from, cut out; *informal* quit, leave off, knock off, pack in, lay off, give over; *Brit. informal* jack in. **3** *the car stopped* PULL UP, draw up, come to a stop/halt, come to rest, pull in, pull over; park. **4** *the music stopped* COME TO AN END/STOP/STANDSTILL, cease, end, finish, draw to a close, be over, conclude, terminate; pause, break off; peter out, fade away. **5** *divers stopped the flow of oil* STEM, staunch, hold back, check, curb, block, dam; *N. Amer.* stanch; *archaic* stay. **6** *the police stopped her leaving* PREVENT, hinder, obstruct, impede, block, bar, preclude; dissuade from. **7** *the council stopped the Kilmarnock scheme* THWART, baulk, foil, frustrate, stand in the way of; scotch, derail; *informal* put paid to, put the kibosh on, do for, stymie; *Brit. informal*

stopcock • noun an externally operated valve regulating the flow of a liquid or gas through a pipe.
stopgap • noun a temporary solution or substitute.
stop light • noun a red traffic signal.
stop-motion • noun a technique of film animation whereby the camera is repeatedly stopped and started to give the impression of movement.
stoppage • noun **1** an instance of stopping. **2** an instance of industrial action. **3** a blockage. **4** (**stoppages**) Brit. deductions from wages by an employer for the payment of tax, National Insurance, etc.
stoppage time • noun another term for INJURY TIME.
stopper • noun **1** a plug for sealing a hole. **2** a person or thing that stops something. • verb seal with a stopper.
stop press • noun Brit. late news inserted in a newspaper or periodical either just before printing or after printing has begun.
stopwatch • noun a special watch with buttons that start and stop the display, used to time races.
storage • noun **1** the action of storing. **2** space available for storing. **3** a charge for storing things in a warehouse.
storage battery (also **storage cell**) • noun a battery (or cell) used for storing electrical energy.
storage heater • noun Brit. an electric heater that stores up heat during the night and releases it during the day.
store • noun **1** a quantity or supply kept for use as needed. **2** (**stores**) supplies of equipment and food kept for use by members of an army, navy, or other institution. **3** a place where things are kept for future use or sale. **4** chiefly N. Amer. a shop. **5** Brit. a large shop selling different types of goods. **6** Brit. a computer memory. • verb **1** keep or accumulate for future use. **2** retain or enter (information) in the memory of a computer. **3** (**be stored with**) have a useful supply of.
– PHRASES **in store** about to happen. **set** (or **lay** or **put**) **store by** (or **on**) consider to be of a particular degree of importance.
– ORIGIN Old French *estore*, from Latin *instaurare* 'renew'.
storefront • noun chiefly N. Amer. **1** another term for SHOPFRONT. **2** a room or rooms facing the street on the ground floor of a commercial building, typically used as a shop.
storehouse • noun **1** a building used for storing goods. **2** a repository: *an enormous storehouse of facts.*
storey (N. Amer. also **story**) • noun (pl. **storeys** or **stories**) a part of a building comprising all the rooms that are on the same level.
– ORIGIN from Latin *historia* 'history': perhaps originally referring to a tier of painted windows or sculptures on a building, representing a historical subject.
storied • adjective literary celebrated in or associated with stories or legends.
stork • noun a tall long-legged bird with a long heavy bill and white and black plumage.
– ORIGIN Old English.
storm • noun **1** a violent disturbance of the atmosphere with strong winds and usually rain, thunder, lightning, or snow. **2** an uproar or controversy: *the book caused a storm in America.* **3** a violent or noisy outburst of a specified feeling or reaction: *a storm of protest.* • verb **1** move angrily or forcefully in a specified direction. **2** (of troops) suddenly attack and capture (a place). **3** shout angrily.
– PHRASES **go down a storm** be enthusiastically received. **a storm in a teacup** Brit. great anger or excitement about a trivial matter. **take by storm 1** capture (a place) by a sudden and violent attack. **2** have great and rapid success in (a place).
– ORIGIN Old English.
stormbound • adjective prevented by storms from starting or continuing a journey.
storm cloud • noun **1** a heavy, dark rain cloud. **2** (**storm clouds**) an ominous state of affairs.
storm door (or **storm window**) • noun chiefly N. Amer. an additional outer door or window for protection in bad weather or winter.
storm drain (US **storm sewer**) • noun a drain built to carry away excess water in times of heavy rain.
stormer • noun Brit. informal a thing which is particularly impressive of its kind.
– DERIVATIVES **storming** adjective.
storm lantern • noun chiefly Brit. a hurricane lamp.
storm petrel • noun a small petrel with blackish plumage, formerly believed to be a sign of bad weather to come.
storm troops • plural noun shock troops.
– DERIVATIVES **storm trooper** noun.
stormy • adjective (**stormier**, **stormiest**) **1** affected or disturbed by a storm. **2** full of angry or violent outbursts of feeling.
– DERIVATIVES **stormily** adverb **storminess** noun.
story[1] • noun (pl. **stories**) **1** an account of imaginary or real people and events told for entertainment. **2** an account of past events, experiences, etc. **3** an item of news. **4** a storyline. **5** informal a lie.

Thesaurus

scupper. **8** *the firm stops your tax* WITHHOLD, keep back, hold back, deduct, take away, refuse to pay. **9** *just stop the bottle with your thumb* BLOCK (UP), plug, close (up), fill (up); seal, caulk, bung up; *technical* occlude.
– OPPOSITES start, begin, continue, allow, encourage, expedite, pay, open.
• noun **1** *all business came to a stop* HALT, end, finish, close, standstill; cessation, conclusion, stoppage, discontinuation. **2** *a brief stop in the town* BREAK, stopover, stop-off, stay, visit; *formal* sojourn. **3** *the next stop is Oxford Street* STOPPING PLACE, halt, station, stage. **4** *a full stop* (FULL) POINT; *N. Amer.* period.
– OPPOSITES start, beginning, continuation.
– PHRASES **put a stop to**. See STOP verb senses 1, 7. **stop off/over** BREAK ONE'S JOURNEY, take a break, pause; stay, remain, put up, lodge, rest; *formal* sojourn.
stopgap • noun *that old plane was merely a stopgap* TEMPORARY SOLUTION, expedient, makeshift; substitute, stand-in.
• adjective *a stopgap measure* TEMPORARY, provisional, interim, pro tem, short-term, working, makeshift, emergency; caretaker, acting, stand-in, fill-in.
– OPPOSITES permanent.
stopover • noun BREAK, stop, stop-off, visit, stay; *formal* sojourn.
stoppage • noun **1** *the stoppage of production* DISCONTINUATION, stopping, halting, cessation, termination, end, finish; interruption, suspension, breaking off. **2** *a stoppage of the blood supply* OBSTRUCTION, blocking, blockage, block; *Medicine* occlusion, stasis. **3** *a stoppage over pay* STRIKE, walkout; industrial action. **4** *(Brit.) she was paid £3.40 an hour before stoppages* DEDUCTION, subtraction.
– OPPOSITES start, continuation.
stopper • noun BUNG, plug, cork, spigot, spile, seal; *N. Amer.* stopple.
store • noun **1** *a store of food* STOCK, supply, stockpile, hoard, cache, reserve, bank, pool. **2** *a grain store* STOREROOM, storehouse, repository, depository, stockroom, depot, warehouse, magazine; *informal* lock-up. **3** *ship's stores* SUPPLIES, provisions, stocks, necessities; food, rations, provender; materials, equipment, hardware; *Military* materiel, accoutrements; *Nautical* chandlery. **4** *a DIY store* SHOP, (retail) outlet, boutique, department store, chain store, emporium; supermarket, hypermarket, superstore, megastore.
• verb *rabbits don't store food* KEEP, keep in reserve, stockpile, lay in, put/set aside, put away/by, put away for a rainy day, save, collect, accumulate, hoard, cache; *informal* squirrel away, salt away, stash away.
– OPPOSITES use, discard.
– PHRASES **set (great) store by** VALUE, attach great importance to, put a high value on, put a premium on; THINK HIGHLY OF, hold in (high) regard, have a high opinion of; *informal* rate.
storehouse • noun WAREHOUSE, depository, repository, store, storeroom, depot.
storey • noun FLOOR, level, deck.
storm • noun **1** *battered by a storm* TEMPEST, squall; gale, hurricane, tornado, cyclone, typhoon; thunderstorm, rainstorm, monsoon, hailstorm, snowstorm, blizzard; *N. Amer.* williwaw, windstorm. **2** *a storm of bullets* VOLLEY, salvo, fusillade, barrage, cannonade; shower, spray, hail, rain. **3** *there was a storm over his remarks* UPROAR, outcry, fuss, furore, brouhaha, rumpus, trouble, hue and cry, controversy; *informal* to-do, hoo-ha, hullabaloo, ballyhoo, ructions, stink; *Brit. informal* row. **4** *a storm of protest* OUTBURST, outbreak, explosion, eruption, outpouring, surge, blaze, flare-up, wave.
• verb **1** *she stormed out* STRIDE ANGRILY, stomp, march, stalk, flounce, stamp, fling. **2** *his mother stormed at him* RANT, rave, shout, bellow, roar, thunder, rage. **3** *police stormed the building* ATTACK, charge, rush, assail, descend on, swoop on.
stormy • adjective **1** *stormy weather* BLUSTERY, squally, windy, gusty, blowy; rainy, thundery; wild, tempestuous, turbulent, vio-

S

– ORIGIN Old French *estorie*, from Latin *historia* 'history'.

story² ● noun N. Amer. variant spelling of STOREY.

storyboard ● noun a sequence of drawings representing the shots planned for a film or television production.

storybook ● noun **1** a book containing a story or stories for children. **2** (before another noun) idyllically perfect: *a storybook romance.*

storyline ● noun the plot of a novel, play, film, etc.

stotin /stoteen/ ● noun a monetary unit of Slovenia, equal to one hundredth of a tolar.

– ORIGIN Slovene.

stotinka /stotingkə/ ● noun (pl. **stotinki** /stotingki/) a monetary unit of Bulgaria, equal to one hundredth of a lev.

– ORIGIN Bulgarian, 'one hundredth'.

stoup /sto͞op/ ● noun a basin for holy water in a church.

– ORIGIN Old Norse, related to STEEP².

stour /sto͞or/ (also **stoor**) ● noun Scottish & N. English dust forming a cloud or deposited in a mass.

– DERIVATIVES **stoury** adjective.

– ORIGIN origin uncertain.

stout ● adjective **1** rather fat or heavily built. **2** (of an object) sturdy and thick. **3** brave and determined. ● noun a kind of strong, dark beer brewed with roasted malt or barley.

– DERIVATIVES **stoutly** adverb **stoutness** noun.

– ORIGIN Old French.

stove¹ ● noun an apparatus for cooking or heating that operates by burning fuel or using electricity.

– ORIGIN Dutch or Low German.

stove² past and past participle of STAVE.

stovepipe ● noun a pipe taking the smoke and gases from a stove up through a roof or to a chimney.

stovepipe hat ● noun a type of tall top hat.

stovies /stōviz/ ● plural noun Scottish a dish of stewed potatoes.

– ORIGIN from Scots *stove* 'stew (meat or vegetables)'.

stow ● verb **1** pack or store (an object) tidily in an appropriate place. **2** (**stow away**) conceal oneself on a ship, aircraft, etc. so as to travel secretly or without paying.

– DERIVATIVES **stowage** noun.

– ORIGIN shortening of BESTOW.

stowaway ● noun a person who stows away.

strabismus /strəbizməss/ ● noun the condition of having a squint.

– ORIGIN Greek *strabismos*, from *strabizein* 'to squint'.

straddle ● verb **1** sit or stand with one leg on either side of. **2** extend across both sides of. ● noun an act of straddling.

– ORIGIN from dialect *striddling* 'astride'.

Stradivarius /straddivairiəss/ ● noun a violin or other stringed instrument made by the Italian violin-maker Antonio Stradivari (*c.*1644–1737) or his followers.

strafe /straaf, strayf/ ● verb attack with machine-gun fire or bombs from low-flying aircraft. ● noun an act of strafing.

– ORIGIN humorous adaptation of the German First World War catchphrase *Gott strafe England* 'may God punish England'.

straggle ● verb **1** trail slowly behind the person or people in front. **2** grow or spread out in an irregular, untidy way. ● noun an irregular and untidy group.

– DERIVATIVES **straggler** noun **straggly** adjective.

– ORIGIN perhaps from dialect *strake* 'go'.

straight ● adjective **1** extending uniformly in one direction only; without a curve or bend. **2** properly positioned so as to be level, upright, or symmetrical. **3** in proper order or condition. **4** honest and direct. **5** (of thinking) clear and logical. **6** in continuous succession: *his fourth straight win.* **7** (of an alcoholic drink) undiluted. **8** (of drama) serious as opposed to comic or musical. **9** informal conventional or respectable. **10** informal heterosexual. ● adverb **1** in a straight line or in a straight manner. **2** without delay or diversion. ● noun **1** the straight part of something. **2** Poker a continuous sequence of five cards. **3** informal a conventional person. **4** informal a heterosexual.

– PHRASES **go straight** live an honest life after being a criminal. **keep a straight face** keep a blank or serious facial expression when trying not to laugh. **the straight and narrow** the honest and morally acceptable way of living. **straight away** immediately. **a straight fight** Brit. a contest between just two opponents. **straight from the shoulder 1** dated (of a blow) swift and well delivered. **2** (of words) frank or direct. **straight off** (or **out**) informal without hesitation or deliberation. **straight up** informal **1** Brit. honestly. **2** chiefly N. Amer. undiluted or unadulterated.

– DERIVATIVES **straightly** adverb **straightness** noun.

– ORIGIN archaic past participle of STRETCH.

Thesaurus

lent, rough, foul. **2** *a stormy debate* ANGRY, heated, fiery, fierce, furious, passionate, 'lively'.

– OPPOSITES calm, fine, peaceful.

story ● noun **1** *an adventure story* TALE, narrative, account, anecdote; *informal* yarn, spiel. **2** *the novel has a good story* PLOT, storyline, scenario; *formal* diegesis. **3** *the story appeared in the papers* NEWS ITEM, news report, article, feature, piece. **4** *there have been a lot of stories going round* RUMOUR, piece of gossip, whisper; speculation; *Austral./NZ informal* furphy. **5** *Harper changed his story* TESTIMONY, statement, report, account, version. **6** *(informal) Ellie never told stories.* See FALSEHOOD sense 1.

storyteller ● noun NARRATOR, teller of tales, raconteur, raconteuse, fabulist, anecdotalist; *Austral. informal* magsman.

stout ● adjective **1** *a short stout man* FAT, plump, portly, rotund, dumpy, chunky, corpulent; stocky, burly, bulky, hefty, solidly built, thickset; *informal* tubby, pudgy; *Brit. informal* podgy, fubsy; *N. Amer. informal* zaftig, corn-fed; *archaic* pursy. **2** *stout leather shoes* STRONG, sturdy, solid, substantial, robust, tough, durable, hard-wearing. **3** *stout resistance* DETERMINED, vigorous, forceful, spirited; staunch, steadfast, stalwart, firm, resolute, unyielding, dogged; brave, bold, courageous, valiant, valorous, gallant, fearless, doughty, intrepid; *informal* gutsy, spunky.

– OPPOSITES thin, flimsy, feeble.

stout-hearted ● adjective BRAVE, determined, courageous, bold, plucky, spirited, valiant, valorous, gallant, fearless, doughty, intrepid, stalwart; *informal* gutsy, spunky.

stove ● noun OVEN, range, cooker.

stow ● verb *Barney stowed her luggage in the boot* PACK, load, store, place, put (away), deposit, stash.

– OPPOSITES unload.

– PHRASES **stow away** HIDE, conceal oneself, travel secretly.

straddle ● verb **1** *she straddled the motorbike* SIT/STAND ASTRIDE, bestride, mount, get on. **2** *a mountain range straddling the border* LIE ON BOTH SIDES OF, extend across, span. **3** *(N. Amer.) he straddled the issue of taxes* BE EQUIVOCAL ABOUT, be undecided about, equivocate about, vacillate about, waver about; *informal* sit on the fence.

strafe ● verb BOMB, shell, bombard, fire on, machine-gun, rake with gunfire, enfilade; *archaic* fusillade.

straggle ● verb TRAIL, lag, dawdle, walk slowly; fall behind, bring up the rear.

straggly ● adjective UNTIDY, messy, unkempt, straggling, dishevelled.

straight ● adjective **1** *a long, straight road* UNSWERVING, undeviating, linear, as straight as an arrow, uncurving, unbending. **2** *that picture isn't straight* LEVEL, even, in line, aligned, square; vertical, upright, perpendicular; horizontal. **3** *we must get the place straight* IN ORDER, (neat and) tidy, neat, shipshape (and Bristol fashion), orderly, spick and span, organized, arranged, sorted out, straightened out. **4** *a straight answer* HONEST, direct, frank, candid, truthful, sincere, forthright, straightforward, plain-spoken, blunt, straight from the shoulder, unequivocal, unambiguous; *informal* upfront. **5** *straight thinking* LOGICAL, rational, clear, lucid, sound, coherent. **6** *three straight wins* SUCCESSIVE, in succession, consecutive, in a row, running; *informal* on the trot. **7** *straight brandy* UNDILUTED, neat, pure; *N. Amer. informal* straight up. **8** *(informal) she's very straight* RESPECTABLE, conventional, conservative, traditional, old-fashioned, strait-laced; *informal* stuffy, square, fuddy-duddy.

– OPPOSITES winding, crooked, untidy, evasive.

● adverb **1** *he looked me straight in the eyes* RIGHT, directly, squarely, full; *informal* smack, (slap) bang; *N. Amer. informal* spang, smack dab. **2** *she drove straight home* DIRECTLY, right, by a direct route. **3** *I'll call you straight back* RIGHT AWAY, straight away, immediately, directly, at once; *archaic* straightway. **4** *I told her straight* FRANKLY, directly, candidly, honestly, forthrightly, plainly, point-blank, bluntly, flatly, straight from the shoulder, without beating about the bush, without mincing words, unequivocally, unambiguously, in plain English, to someone's face; *Brit. informal* straight up. **5** *he can't think straight* LOGICALLY, rationally, clearly, lucidly, coherently, cogently.

– PHRASES **go straight** REFORM, mend one's ways, turn over a new leaf, get back on the straight and narrow. **straight away** AT ONCE, right away, (right) now, this/that (very) minute, this/that instant, immediately, instantly, directly, forthwith, without further/more

straight angle ● noun Mathematics an angle of 180°.
straight edge ● noun a bar with one edge accurately straight, used for testing straightness.
straighten ● verb **1** make or become straight. **2** stand or sit erect after bending.
straight flush ● noun (in poker or brag) a hand of cards all of one suit and in a continuous sequence.
straightforward ● adjective **1** easy to do or understand. **2** honest and open.
– DERIVATIVES **straightforwardly** adverb **straightforwardness** noun.
straightjacket ● noun variant spelling of STRAITJACKET.
straight-laced ● adjective variant spelling of STRAIT-LACED.
straight man ● noun a comedian's stooge.
straight shooter ● noun informal, chiefly N. Amer. an honest and forthright person.
straight-up ● adjective N. Amer. informal honest; trustworthy.
strain[1] ● verb **1** force (a part of one's body or oneself) to make an unusually great effort. **2** injure (a limb, muscle, or organ) by overexertion. **3** make severe or excessive demands on. **4** pull or push forcibly at something. **5** pour (a mainly liquid substance) through a sieve or similar device to separate out any solid matter. ● noun **1** a force tending to strain something to an extreme degree. **2** an injury caused by straining a muscle, limb, etc. **3** a severe demand on strength or resources. **4** a state of tension or exhaustion caused by severe demands or pressures. **5** the sound of a piece of music as it is played or performed.
– ORIGIN Old French *estreindre*, from Latin *stringere* 'draw tight'.
strain[2] ● noun **1** a distinct breed or variety of an animal, plant, or other organism. **2** a tendency in a person's character.
– ORIGIN Old English, 'acquisition, gain'.
strained ● adjective **1** not relaxed or comfortable; showing signs of strain. **2** produced by deliberate effort; artificial or laboured.
strainer ● noun a device for straining liquids, having holes punched in it or made of crossed wire.
strait ● noun **1** (also **straits**) a narrow passage of water connecting two seas or other large areas of water. **2** (**straits**) a situation characterized by a specified degree of trouble or difficulty: *the economy is in dire straits.* ● adjective archaic **1** narrow or cramped. **2** strict or rigorous.
– ORIGIN Old French *estreit* 'tight, narrow', from Latin *strictus* 'tightened'.
straiten ● verb **1** (**straitened**) restricted in range. **2** (**straitened**) restricted because of poverty: *they lived in straitened circumstances.* **3** archaic make or become narrow.
straitjacket (also **straightjacket**) ● noun **1** a strong garment with long sleeves which can be tied together to confine the arms of a violent prisoner or mental patient. **2** a severe restriction.
strait-laced (also **straight-laced**) ● adjective having or showing very strict moral attitudes.
strake ● noun **1** a continuous line of planking or plates from the stem to the stern of a ship or boat. **2** a protruding ridge fitted to an aircraft or other structure to improve aerodynamic stability.
– ORIGIN Latin *stracus*.
stramash /strəmash/ ● noun Scottish & N. English an uproar; a row.
– ORIGIN apparently imitative.
strand[1] ● verb **1** drive or leave aground on a shore. **2** leave without the means to move from a place. ● noun literary the shore of a sea, lake, or large river.
– ORIGIN Old English.
strand[2] ● noun **1** a single thin length of thread, wire, etc. **2** an element that forms part of a complex whole.
– ORIGIN of unknown origin.
strange ● adjective **1** unusual or surprising. **2** not previously visited, seen, or encountered. **3** (**strange to/at/in**) archaic unaccustomed to or unfamiliar with. **4** Physics denoting one of the six flavours of quark.
– DERIVATIVES **strangely** adverb **strangeness** noun.
– ORIGIN Old French *estrange*, from Latin *extraneus* 'external, strange'.
stranger ● noun **1** a person whom one does not know. **2** a per-

Thesaurus

ado, promptly, quickly, without delay, then and there, here and now, a.s.a.p., as soon as possible, as quickly as possible; *N. Amer.* in short order; *informal* straight off, in double quick time, p.d.q., pretty damn quick, pronto, before you can say Jack Robinson; *N. Amer. informal* lickety-split; *archaic* straight, straightway. **straight from the shoulder.** See STRAIGHT adverb sense 4.
straighten ● verb **1** *Rory straightened his tie* MAKE STRAIGHT, adjust, arrange, rearrange, (make) tidy, spruce up. **2** *we must straighten things out with Viola* PUT/SET RIGHT, sort out, clear up, settle, resolve, put in order, regularize, rectify, remedy; *informal* patch up. **3** *he straightened up* STAND UP (STRAIGHT), stand upright.
straightforward ● adjective **1** *the process was remarkably straightforward* UNCOMPLICATED, simple, easy, effortless, painless, undemanding, plain sailing, child's play; *informal* as easy as falling off a log, as easy as pie, a piece of cake, a cinch, a snip, a doddle, a breeze, a cakewalk; *Brit. informal* easy-peasy, a doss; *N. Amer. informal* duck soup, a snap; *Austral./NZ informal* a bludge, a snack. **2** *a straightforward man* HONEST, frank, candid, open, truthful, sincere, on the level; forthright, plain-speaking, direct, unambiguous; *informal* upfront; *N. Amer. informal* on the up and up.
– OPPOSITES complicated.
strain[1] ● verb **1** *take care that you don't strain yourself* OVERTAX, overwork, overextend, overreach, drive too far, overdo it; exhaust, wear out; *informal* knacker, knock oneself out. **2** *you have strained a muscle* INJURE, damage, pull, wrench, twist, sprain. **3** *we strained to haul the guns up the slope* STRUGGLE, labour, toil, make every effort, try very hard, break one's back, push/drive oneself to the limit; *informal* pull out all the stops, go all out, bust a gut; *Austral. informal* go for the doctor. **4** *the flood of refugees is straining the relief services* MAKE EXCESSIVE DEMANDS ON, overtax, be too much for, test, tax, put a strain on. **5** *the bear strained at the chain* PULL, tug, heave, haul, jerk; *informal* yank. **6** *(archaic) she strained the infant to her bosom* CLASP, press, clutch, hold tight; embrace, hug, enfold, envelop. **7** *strain the mixture* SIEVE, sift, filter, screen, riddle; *rare* filtrate.
● noun **1** *the rope snapped under the strain* TENSION, tightness, tautness. **2** *muscle strain* INJURY, sprain, wrench, twist. **3** *the strain of her job* PRESSURE, demands, burdens; stress; *informal* hassle. **4** *Melissa was showing signs of strain* STRESS, (nervous) tension; exhaustion, fatigue, pressure of work, overwork. **5** *the strains of Brahms's lullaby* SOUND, music; melody, tune.
strain[2] ● noun **1** *a different strain of flu* VARIETY, kind, type, sort; breed, genus. **2** *Hawthorne was of Puritan strain* DESCENT, ancestry, origin(s), parentage, lineage, extraction, family, roots. **3** *there was a strain of insanity in the family* TENDENCY, susceptibility, propensity, proneness; trait, disposition. **4** *a strain of solemnity* ELEMENT, strand, vein, note, trace, touch, suggestion, hint.
strained ● adjective **1** *relations between them were strained* AWKWARD, tense, uneasy, uncomfortable, edgy, difficult, troubled. **2** *Jean's strained face* DRAWN, careworn, worn, pinched, tired, exhausted, drained, haggard. **3** *a strained smile* FORCED, constrained, unnatural; artificial, insincere, false, affected, put-on.
– OPPOSITES friendly.
strainer ● noun SIEVE, colander, filter, sifter, riddle, screen; *archaic* griddle.
strait ● noun **1** *a strait about six miles wide* CHANNEL, sound, inlet, stretch of water. **2** *the company is in desperate straits* A BAD/DIFFICULT SITUATION, difficulty, trouble, crisis, a mess, a predicament, a plight; *informal* hot/deep water, a jam, a hole, a bind, a fix, a scrape.
straitened ● adjective IMPOVERISHED, poverty-stricken, poor, destitute, penniless, on one's beam-ends, as poor as a church mouse, in penury, impecunious, unable to make ends meet, in reduced circumstances; *Brit.* on the breadline; *informal* (flat) broke, strapped for cash, on one's uppers; *Brit. informal* stony broke, skint, in Queer Street; *N. Amer. informal* stone broke; *formal* penurious.
strait-laced ● adjective PRIM (AND PROPER), prudish, puritanical, prissy, mimsy, niminy-piminy; conservative, old-fashioned, stuffy, staid, narrow-minded; *informal* starchy, square, fuddy-duddy.
– OPPOSITES broad-minded.
strand[1] ● noun **1** *strands of wool* THREAD, filament, fibre; length, ply. **2** *the various strands of the ecological movement* ELEMENT, component, factor, ingredient, aspect, feature, strain.
strand[2] ● noun *(poetic/literary) a walk along the strand* SEASHORE, shore, beach, sands, foreshore, shoreline, seaside, waterfront, front, waterside.
stranded ● adjective **1** *a stranded ship* BEACHED, grounded, run aground, high and dry; shipwrecked, wrecked, marooned. **2** *she was stranded in a strange city* HELPLESS, without resources, in

son who does not know, or is not known in, a particular place. **3** (**stranger to**) a person entirely unaccustomed to (a feeling, experience, or situation).

strangle • verb **1** squeeze or constrict the neck of, especially so as to cause death. **2** suppress or hinder (an impulse, action, or sound).
– DERIVATIVES **strangler** noun.
– ORIGIN Old French *estrangler*, from Greek *strangalē* 'halter'.

stranglehold • noun **1** a grip around the neck of a person that can kill by asphyxiation if held for long enough. **2** complete or overwhelming control.

strangulate /stranggyoolayt/ • verb Medicine prevent blood circulation through (a part of the body) by constriction.
– ORIGIN Latin *strangulare* 'choke'.

strangulation • noun **1** the action of strangling or the state of being strangled. **2** Medicine the condition in which circulation of blood to a part of the body is cut off by constriction.

strap • noun **1** a strip of flexible material used for fastening, securing, carrying, or holding on to. **2** a strip of metal, often hinged, used for fastening or securing. **3** (**the strap**) punishment by beating with a leather strap. • verb (**strapped**, **strapping**) **1** fasten or secure with a strap. **2** Brit. bind (an injured part of the body) with adhesive plaster. **3** beat with a leather strap. **4** (**strapped**) informal short of money.
– DERIVATIVES **strapless** adjective **strappy** adjective.
– ORIGIN dialect form of STROP[1].

strapline • noun a subheading or caption in a newspaper or magazine.

strapping[1] • adjective (of a person) big and strong.

strapping[2] • noun **1** adhesive plaster for strapping injuries. **2** leather or metal straps.

strata plural of STRATUM.

stratagem /strattəjəm/ • noun **1** a plan or scheme intended to outwit an opponent. **2** archaic cunning.
– ORIGIN Greek *stratēgēma*, from *stratēgein* 'be a general'.

strategic /strəteejik/ • adjective **1** forming part of a long-term plan or aim to achieve a specific purpose. **2** relating to the gaining of overall or long-term military advantage. **3** (of bombing or weapons) done or for use against industrial areas and communication centres in enemy territory. Often contrasted with TACTICAL.
– DERIVATIVES **strategically** adverb.

strategy /strattiji/ • noun (pl. **strategies**) **1** a plan designed to achieve a particular long-term aim. **2** the art of planning and directing military activity in a war or battle. Often contrasted with **tactics** (see TACTIC).
– DERIVATIVES **strategist** noun.
– ORIGIN Greek *stratēgia* 'generalship'.

strath /strath/ • noun Scottish a broad river valley.
– ORIGIN Scottish Gaelic *srath*.

strathspey /strathspay/ • noun a slow Scottish dance.
– ORIGIN named after *Strathspey* in Scotland.

stratify /strattifī/ • verb (**stratifies**, **stratified**) **1** form or arrange into strata. **2** arrange or classify.
– DERIVATIVES **stratification** noun.

stratigraphy /strətigrəfi/ • noun **1** the branch of geology concerned with the order and relative dating of strata. **2** the analysis of the order and position of layers of archaeological remains. **3** the structure of a particular set of strata.
– DERIVATIVES **stratigrapher** noun **stratigraphic** adjective **stratigraphical** adjective.

stratocumulus /strattōkyōōmyooləss/ • noun cloud forming a low layer of clumped or broken grey masses.

stratosphere /strattəsfeer/ • noun **1** the layer of the earth's atmosphere above the troposphere and below the mesosphere. **2** informal the very highest levels of something.
– DERIVATIVES **stratospheric** /strattəsferrik/ adjective.

stratum /straatəm, stray-/ • noun (pl. **strata** /straatə, stray-/) **1** a layer or a series of layers of rock. **2** a thin layer within any structure. **3** a level or class of society.
– DERIVATIVES **stratal** adjective.
– USAGE It is incorrect to use **strata** as a singular or to create the form **stratas** as the plural. In this case English follows Latin, in which one layer is a **stratum** and more than one are **strata**.
– ORIGIN Latin, 'something spread or laid down'.

stratus /straatəss, stray-/ • noun cloud forming a continuous horizontal grey sheet, often with rain or snow.
– ORIGIN Latin, 'strewn'.

straw • noun **1** dried stalks of grain, used as fodder or for thatching, packing, or weaving. **2** a single dried stalk of grain. **3** a thin hollow tube of paper or plastic for sucking drink from a container. **4** a pale yellow colour.
– PHRASES **clutch at straws** resort in desperation to unlikely or inadequate means of salvation. [ORIGIN from the proverb *a drowning man will clutch at a straw.*] **draw the short straw** be chosen to perform an unpleasant task. **the last** (or **final**) **straw** a further minor difficulty that comes after a series of difficulties and makes a situation unbearable. [ORIGIN from the proverb *the last straw breaks the (laden) camel's back.*] **a straw in the wind** a slight hint of future developments.
– ORIGIN Old English, related to STREW.

strawberry • noun **1** a sweet soft red fruit with a seed-studded surface. **2** a deep pinkish-red colour.

strawberry blonde • adjective (of hair) having a light reddish-blonde colour.

strawberry mark • noun a soft red birthmark.

straw man • noun another term for **man of straw**.

straw poll (N. Amer. also **straw vote**) • noun an unofficial ballot conducted as a test of opinion.

stray • verb **1** move away aimlessly from a group or from the right course or place. **2** (of the eyes or a hand) move idly in a specified direction. **3** informal be unfaithful to a spouse or partner. • adjective **1** not in the right place; separated from a group. **2** (of a domestic animal) having no home or having wandered away from home. • noun a stray person or thing, especially a domestic animal.

Thesaurus

difficulties; in the lurch, abandoned, deserted.

strange • adjective **1** *strange things have been happening* UNUSUAL, odd, curious, peculiar, funny, bizarre, weird, uncanny, queer, unexpected, unfamiliar, atypical, anomalous, out of the ordinary, extraordinary, puzzling, mystifying, mysterious, perplexing, baffling, unaccountable, inexplicable, singular, freakish; suspicious, questionable; eerie, unnatural; *informal* fishy, creepy, spooky. **2** *strange clothes* WEIRD, eccentric, odd, peculiar, funny, bizarre, unusual; unconventional, outlandish, freakish, quirky, zany; *informal* wacky, way out, freaky, kooky, offbeat, off the wall; *N. Amer. informal* screwy, wacko. **3** *visiting a strange house* UNFAMILIAR, unknown, new. **4** *Jean was feeling strange* ILL, unwell, poorly, peaky; *Brit.* off colour; *informal* under the weather, funny, peculiar, lousy; *Brit. informal* off, ropy, grotty; *Austral./NZ informal* crook; *dated* queer. **5** *she felt strange with him* ILL AT EASE, uneasy, uncomfortable, awkward, self-conscious. **6** (*archaic*) *I am strange to the work.* See A STRANGER TO at STRANGER.
– OPPOSITES ordinary, familiar.

strangeness • noun ODDITY, eccentricity, peculiarity, curiousness, bizarreness, weirdness, queerness, unusualness, abnormality, unaccountability, inexplicability, incongruousness, outlandishness, singularity.

stranger • noun NEWCOMER, new arrival, visitor, outsider; *Austral. informal* blow-in.
– PHRASES **a stranger to** UNACCUSTOMED TO, unfamiliar with, unused to, new to, fresh to, inexperienced in; *archaic* strange to.

strangle • verb **1** *the victim was strangled with a scarf* THROTTLE, choke, garrotte; *informal* strangulate. **2** *she strangled a sob* SUPPRESS, smother, stifle, repress, restrain, fight back, choke back. **3** *bureaucracy is strangling commercial activity* HAMPER, hinder, impede, restrict, inhibit, curb, check, constrain, squash, crush, suppress, repress.

strap • noun *thick leather straps* THONG, tie, band, belt.
• verb **1** *a bag was strapped to the bicycle* FASTEN, secure, tie, bind, make fast, lash, truss. **2** *his knee was strapped up* BANDAGE, bind. **3** *his father strapped him.* See LASH verb sense 1.

strapping • adjective BIG, strong, well built, brawny, burly, broad-shouldered, muscular, rugged; *informal* hunky, beefy; *dated* stalwart.
– OPPOSITES weedy.

stratagem • noun PLAN, scheme, tactic, manoeuvre, ploy, device, trick, ruse, plot, machination, dodge; subterfuge, artifice; *Brit. informal* wheeze; *Austral. informal* lurk; *archaic* shift.

strategic • adjective PLANNED, calculated, tactical, politic, judicious, prudent, shrewd.

strategy • noun **1** *the government's economic strategy* MASTER PLAN, grand design, game plan, plan (of action), policy, programme; tactics. **2** *military strategy* THE ART OF WAR, (military) tactics.

stratum • noun **1** *a stratum of flint* LAYER, vein, seam, lode, bed.

– ORIGIN Old French *estrayer*, from Latin *extra* 'out of bounds' + *vagari* 'wander'.

streak ● noun **1** a long, thin mark of a different substance or colour from its surroundings. **2** an element of a specified kind in someone's character: *a ruthless streak*. **3** a spell of specified success or luck: *a winning streak*. ● verb **1** mark with streaks. **2** move very fast in a specified direction. **3** informal run naked in a public place so as to shock or amuse.
– DERIVATIVES **streaker** noun **streaking** noun.
– ORIGIN Old English, related to STRIKE.

streaky ● adjective (**streakier**, **streakiest**) **1** having streaks. **2** Brit. (of bacon) from the belly, thus having alternate strips of fat and lean.
– DERIVATIVES **streakily** adverb **streakiness** noun.

stream ● noun **1** a small, narrow river. **2** a continuous flow of liquid, air, gas, people, etc. **3** Brit. a group in which schoolchildren of the same age and ability are taught. ● verb **1** run or move in a continuous flow. **2** (usu. **be streaming**) run with tears, sweat, or other liquid. **3** float at full extent in the wind. **4** Brit. put (schoolchildren) in streams.
– PHRASES **against** (or **with**) **the stream** against (or with) the prevailing view or tendency. **on stream** in or into operation or existence.
– ORIGIN Old English.

streamer ● noun **1** a long, narrow strip of material used as a decoration or flag. **2** a banner headline in a newspaper. **3** Fishing a fly with feathers attached.

streaming ● adjective (of a cold) accompanied by copious running of the nose and eyes. ● noun a method of relaying data (especially video and audio material) over a computer network as a steady continuous stream.

streamline ● verb **1** design or form in a way that presents very little resistance to a flow of air or water. **2** make (an organization or system) more efficient by employing faster or simpler working methods.

stream of consciousness ● noun **1** Psychology a person's thoughts and reactions to events, perceived as a continuous flow. **2** a literary style which records as a continuous flow the thoughts and reactions in the mind of a character.

street ● noun **1** a public road in a city, town, or village. **2** (before another noun) relating to the subculture of fashionable urban youth: *street style*. **3** (before another noun) homeless: *street children*.
– PHRASES **not in the same street** Brit. informal far inferior in terms of ability. **on the streets 1** homeless. **2** working as a prostitute. **streets ahead** Brit. informal greatly superior. **up** (or **right up**) **one's street** (or N. Amer. **alley**) informal well suited to one's tastes, interests, or abilities.
– ORIGIN from Latin *strāta via* 'paved way'.

streetcar ● noun N. Amer. a tram.

street-smart ● adjective chiefly N. Amer. another term for STREETWISE.

street value ● noun the price a commodity would fetch if sold illicitly.

streetwalker ● noun a prostitute who seeks clients in the street.

streetwise ● adjective informal having the skills and knowledge necessary for dealing with modern urban life.

Strega /straygə/ ● noun trademark an orange-flavoured Italian liqueur.
– ORIGIN Italian, 'witch'.

strelitzia /strəlitsiə/ ● noun a southern African plant of a genus including the bird of paradise flower.
– ORIGIN named after Charlotte of Mecklenburg-*Strelitz* (1744–1818), queen of George III.

strength /strength, strengkth/ ● noun **1** the quality or state of being strong. **2** a good or beneficial quality or attribute. **3** literary a source of mental or emotional support. **4** the number of people comprising a group. **5** a full complement of people: *100 staff below strength*.
– PHRASES **go from strength to strength** progress with increasing success. **in strength** in large numbers. **on the strength of** on the basis or with the justification of. **tower** (or **pillar**) **of strength** a person who can be relied upon to support and comfort others.
– ORIGIN Old English.

strengthen ● verb make or become stronger.
– DERIVATIVES **strengthener** noun.

strenuous /strenyooəss/ ● adjective requiring or using great ex-

Thesaurus

2 *this stratum of society* LEVEL, class, echelon, rank, grade, group, set; caste; dated station, estate.

stray ● verb **1** *the gazelle had strayed from the herd* WANDER OFF, go astray, get separated, get lost. **2** *we strayed from our original topic* DIGRESS, deviate, wander, get sidetracked, go off at a tangent; get off the subject. **3** *the young men were likely to stray* BE UNFAITHFUL, have affairs, philander; informal play around, play the field. **4** *he strayed from the path of righteousness* SIN, transgress, err, go astray; archaic trespass. **5** (poetic/literary) *straying about in a strange place* ROAM, rove, wander, drift.
● adjective **1** *a stray dog* HOMELESS, lost, strayed, gone astray, abandoned. **2** *a stray bullet* RANDOM, chance, freak, unexpected, isolated, lone, single.
● noun *wardens who deal with strays* HOMELESS ANIMAL, stray dog/cat, waif.

S

streak ● noun **1** *a streak of orange light* BAND, line, strip, stripe, vein, slash, ray. **2** *green streaks on her legs* MARK, smear, smudge, stain, blotch; informal splotch. **3** *a streak of self-destructiveness* ELEMENT, vein, touch, strain; trait, characteristic. **4** *a winning streak* PERIOD, spell, stretch, run; Brit. informal patch.
● verb **1** *the sky was streaked with red* STRIPE, band, fleck; archaic freak. **2** *overalls streaked with paint* MARK, daub, smear; informal splotch. **3** *Miranda streaked across the road.* See RUN verb sense 1.

streaky ● adjective STRIPED, stripy, streaked, banded, veined, brindled.

stream ● noun **1** *a mountain stream* BROOK, rivulet, rill, runnel, streamlet, freshet; tributary; Scottish & N. English burn; N. English beck; S. English bourn; N. Amer. & Austral./NZ creek; Austral. billabong. **2** *a stream of boiling water* JET, flow, rush, gush, surge, torrent, flood, cascade, outpouring, outflow; technical efflux. **3** *a steady stream of visitors* SUCCESSION, series, string.
● verb **1** *tears were streaming down her face* FLOW, pour, course, run, gush, surge, flood, cascade, spill. **2** *children streamed out of the classrooms* POUR, surge, flood, swarm, pile, crowd. **3** *a flag streamed from the mast* FLUTTER, float, flap, fly, blow, waft, wave.

streamer ● noun PENNANT, pennon, flag, banderole, banner.

streamlined ● adjective **1** *streamlined cars* AERODYNAMIC, smooth, sleek, elegant. **2** *a streamlined organization* EFFICIENT, smooth-running, well run, slick; time-saving, labour-saving.

street ● noun *Amsterdam's narrow cobbled streets* ROAD, thoroughfare, avenue, drive, boulevard, parade; side street/road, lane; N. Amer. highway.
– PHRASES **the man/woman in the street** AN ORDINARY PERSON, Mr/Mrs Average; Brit. informal Joe Bloggs, Joe Public, the man on the Clapham omnibus; N. Amer. informal John Doe, Joe Sixpack. **on the streets** HOMELESS, sleeping rough, down and out.

strength ● noun **1** *enormous physical strength* POWER, brawn, muscle, muscularity, burliness, sturdiness, robustness, toughness, hardiness; vigour, force, might; informal beef; poetic/literary thew. **2** *Oliver began to regain his strength* HEALTH, fitness, vigour, stamina. **3** *her inner strength* FORTITUDE, resilience, backbone, spirit, strength of character; courage, bravery, pluck, pluckiness, courageousness, grit; informal guts, spunk. **4** *the strength of the retaining wall* ROBUSTNESS, sturdiness, firmness, toughness, soundness, solidity, durability. **5** *Europe's military strength* POWER, influence, dominance, ascendancy, supremacy; informal clout; poetic/literary puissance. **6** *the strength of feeling against the president* INTENSITY, vehemence, force, forcefulness, depth, ardour, fervour. **7** *the strength of their argument* COGENCY, forcefulness, force, weight, power, potency, persuasiveness, soundness, validity. **8** *what are your strengths?* STRONG POINT, advantage, asset, forte, aptitude, talent, skill; speciality. **9** (poetic/literary) *my strength and shield* SUPPORT, mainstay, anchor. **10** *the strength of the army* SIZE, extent, magnitude.
– OPPOSITES weakness.
– PHRASES **on the strength of** BECAUSE OF, by virtue of, on the basis of.

strengthen ● verb **1** *calcium strengthens growing bones* MAKE STRONG/STRONGER, build up, give strength to. **2** *engineers strengthened the walls* REINFORCE, make stronger, buttress, shore up, underpin. **3** *strengthened glass* TOUGHEN, temper, anneal. **4** *the wind had strengthened* BECOME STRONG/STRONGER, gain strength, intensify, pick up. **5** *his insistence strengthened her determination* FORTIFY, bolster, make stronger, boost, reinforce, harden, stiffen, toughen, fuel. **6** *they strengthened their efforts* STEP UP, increase, escalate; informal up, crank up, beef up. **7** *the argument is strength-*

ertion.
– DERIVATIVES **strenuously** adverb **strenuousness** noun.
– ORIGIN Latin *strenuus* 'brisk'.

streptococcus /streptəkokkəss/ ● noun (pl. **streptococci** /streptəkokkī/) a bacterium of a large genus including those causing scarlet fever, pneumonia, souring of milk, and dental decay.
– DERIVATIVES **streptococcal** adjective.
– ORIGIN from Greek *streptos* 'twisted'.

streptomycin /streptəmīsin/ ● noun Medicine an antibiotic used against tuberculosis.
– ORIGIN from Greek *streptos* 'twisted' + *mukēs* 'fungus'.

stress ● noun **1** pressure or tension exerted on a material object. **2** a state of mental, emotional, or other strain. **3** particular emphasis. **4** emphasis given to a syllable or word in speech. ● verb **1** emphasize. **2** give emphasis to (a syllable or word) when pronouncing it. **3** subject to pressure, tension, or strain.
– ORIGIN shortening of DISTRESS, or partly from Old French *estresse* 'narrowness, oppression'; related to STRICT.

stressful ● adjective causing mental or emotional stress.

stretch ● verb **1** (of something soft or elastic) be made or be able to be made longer or wider without tearing or breaking. **2** pull (something) tightly from one point to another. **3** extend one's body or a part of one's body to its full length. **4** last longer than expected. **5** extend over an area or period of time. **6** (of finances or resources) be sufficient for a particular purpose. **7** make demands on. ● noun **1** an act of stretching. **2** the fact or condition of being stretched. **3** the capacity to stretch or be stretched; elasticity. **4** a continuous expanse or period. **5** informal a period of time spent in prison. **6** (before another noun) informal a motor vehicle or aircraft modified with extended seating or storage capacity: *a stretch limo.* **7** a difficult or demanding task.
– PHRASES **at full stretch** using the maximum amount of one's resources or energy. **at a stretch 1** in one continuous period. **2** just possible but with difficulty. **stretch one's legs** go for a short walk. **stretch a point** allow or do something not usually acceptable.
– DERIVATIVES **stretchy** adjective (**stretchier**, **stretchiest**).
– ORIGIN Old English.

stretcher ● noun **1** a framework of two poles with a long piece of canvas slung between them, used for carrying sick, injured, or dead people. **2** a wooden frame over which a canvas is stretched ready for painting. **3** a brick or stone laid with its long side along the face of a wall. ● verb carry on a stretcher.

stretch marks ● plural noun marks on the skin, especially on the abdomen, caused by stretching of the skin from obesity or during pregnancy.

strew ● verb (past part. **strewn** or **strewed**) **1** (usu. **be strewn**) scatter untidily over a surface or area. **2** (usu. **be strewn with**) cover (a surface or area) with untidily scattered things.
– ORIGIN Old English.

strewth (also **struth**) ● exclamation informal used to express surprise or dismay.
– ORIGIN contraction of *God's truth*.

stria /strīə/ ● noun (pl. **striae** /strīee/) **1** technical a linear mark, ridge, or groove, especially one of a number of similar parallel features. **2** Anatomy a longitudinal collection of nerve fibres in the brain.
– ORIGIN Latin, 'furrow'.

striate technical ● adjective /strīət/ marked with striae. ● verb /strīayt/ (**striated**) marked with striae.
– DERIVATIVES **striation** noun.

stricken North American or archaic past participle of STRIKE. ● adjective **1** seriously affected by an undesirable condition or unpleasant feeling. **2** (of a face or look) showing great distress.

strict ● adjective **1** demanding that rules concerning behaviour are obeyed. **2** (of a rule) demanding total compliance; rigidly enforced. **3** following rules or beliefs exactly. **4** not allowing deviation or relaxation.
– DERIVATIVES **strictly** adverb **strictness** noun.
– ORIGIN Latin *strictus* 'tightened'.

stricture /strikchər/ ● noun **1** a rule restricting behaviour or action. **2** a sternly critical remark. **3** Medicine abnormal narrowing of a canal or duct in the body: *a colonic stricture.*

stride ● verb (past **strode**; past part. **stridden**) **1** walk with long, decisive steps. **2** (**stride across/over**) cross (an obstacle) with one long step. ● noun **1** a long, decisive step. **2** the length of a step or manner of taking steps in running or walking. **3** a step in progress towards an aim. **4** (**one's stride**) a good or regular rate of progress, especially after a slow start. **5** (**strides**) Brit. informal trousers.
– PHRASES **take something in one's stride** deal with something difficult in a calm way.
– ORIGIN Old English.

Thesaurus

ened by this evidence REINFORCE, lend more weight to; support, back up, confirm, bear out, corroborate.
– OPPOSITES weaken.

strenuous ● adjective **1** *a strenuous climb* ARDUOUS, difficult, hard, tough, taxing, demanding, exacting, exhausting, tiring, gruelling, back-breaking; *informal* killing; *Brit. informal* knackering; *archaic* toilsome. **2** *strenuous efforts* VIGOROUS, energetic, zealous, forceful, strong, spirited, intense, determined, resolute, tenacious, tireless, indefatigable, dogged; *formal* pertinacious.
– OPPOSITES easy, half-hearted.

stress ● noun **1** *he's under a lot of stress* STRAIN, pressure, (nervous) tension, worry, anxiety, trouble, difficulty; *informal* hassle. **2** *laying greater stress on education* EMPHASIS, importance, weight. **3** *the stress falls on the first syllable* EMPHASIS, accent, accentuation; beat; *Prosody* ictus. **4** *the stress is uniform across the bar* PRESSURE, tension, strain.
● verb **1** *they stressed the need for reform* EMPHASIZE, draw attention to, underline, underscore, point up, place emphasis on, lay stress on, highlight, accentuate, press home. **2** *the last syllable is stressed* PLACE THE EMPHASIS ON, emphasize, place the accent on. **3** *all the staff were stressed* OVERSTRETCH, overtax, push to the limit, pressurize, pressure, make tense, worry, harass; *informal* hassle.
– OPPOSITES play down.

stressful ● adjective DEMANDING, trying, taxing, difficult, hard, tough; fraught, traumatic, pressured, tense, frustrating.
– OPPOSITES relaxing.

stretch ● verb **1** *this material stretches* BE ELASTIC, be stretchy, be tensile. **2** *he stretched the elastic* PULL (OUT), draw out, extend, lengthen, elongate, expand. **3** *stretch your weekend into a vacation* PROLONG, lengthen, make longer, extend, spin out. **4** *my budget won't stretch to a new car* BE SUFFICIENT FOR, be enough for, cover; afford, have the money for. **5** *the court case stretched their finances* PUT A STRAIN ON, overtax, overextend, drain, sap. **6** *stretching the truth* BEND, strain, distort, exaggerate, embellish. **7** *she stretched out her hand to him* REACH OUT, hold out, extend, outstretch, proffer; *poetic/literary* outreach. **8** *he stretched his arms* EXTEND, straighten (out). **9** *she stretched out on the sofa* LIE DOWN, recline, lean back, be recumbent, sprawl, lounge, loll. **10** *the desert stretches for miles* EXTEND, spread, continue.
– OPPOSITES shorten.
● noun **1** *magnificent stretches of forest* EXPANSE, area, tract, belt, sweep, extent. **2** *a four-hour stretch* PERIOD, time, spell, run, stint, session, shift. **3** *(informal) a ten-year stretch* (PRISON) SENTENCE; *N. Amer. informal* rap.
● adjective *stretch fabrics* STRETCHY, stretchable, elastic.

strew ● verb SCATTER, spread, disperse, litter, toss; *poetic/literary* bestrew.

stricken ● adjective TROUBLED, (deeply) affected, afflicted, struck, hit.

strict ● adjective **1** *a strict interpretation of the law* PRECISE, exact, literal, faithful, accurate, careful, meticulous, rigorous. **2** *strict controls on spending* STRINGENT, rigorous, severe, harsh, hard, rigid, tough. **3** *strict parents* STERN, severe, harsh, uncompromising, authoritarian, firm, austere. **4** *this will be treated in strict confidence* ABSOLUTE, utter, complete, total. **5** *a strict Roman Catholic* ORTHODOX, devout, conscientious.
– OPPOSITES loose, liberal.

strictness ● noun **1** *the strictness of the laws* SEVERITY, harshness, rigidity, rigidness, stringency, rigorousness, sternness. **2** *the provision has been interpreted with strictness* PRECISION, preciseness, accuracy, exactness, faithfulness; meticulousness, scrupulousness.
– OPPOSITES imprecision.

stricture ● noun **1** *the constant strictures of the nuns* CRITICISM, censure, condemnation, reproof, reproach, admonishment. **2** *the strictures on Victorian women* CONSTRAINT, restriction, limitation, restraint, curb, impediment, barrier, obstacle. **3** *an intestinal stricture* NARROWING, constriction.
– OPPOSITES praise, freedom.

strident ● adjective **1** loud and harsh. **2** presenting a point of view in an excessively forceful way.
– DERIVATIVES **stridency** noun **stridently** adverb.
– ORIGIN from Latin *stridere* 'creak'.
stridulate /**strid**yoolayt/ ● verb (of a grasshopper or similar insect) make a shrill sound by rubbing the legs, wings, or other parts of the body together.
– DERIVATIVES **stridulation** noun.
– ORIGIN from Latin *stridulus* 'creaking'.
strife ● noun **1** angry or bitter disagreement; conflict. **2** Austral./NZ trouble or difficulty of any kind.
– ORIGIN Old French *estrif*.
strike ● verb (past and past part. **struck**) **1** deliver a blow to. **2** come into forcible contact with. **3** (in sport) hit or kick (a ball) so as to score a run, point, or goal. **4** ignite (a match) by rubbing it briskly against an abrasive surface. **5** (of a disaster, disease, etc.) occur suddenly and have harmful effects on. **6** attack suddenly. **7** (**strike into**) cause (a strong emotion) in. **8** cause to become suddenly: *he was struck dumb*. **9** suddenly come into the mind of. **10** (**strike on/upon**) discover or think of, especially unexpectedly. **11** (**be struck by/with**) find particularly interesting or impressive. **12** (of employees) refuse to work as a form of organized protest. **13** cancel or remove by crossing out with a pen. **14** (**strike off**) officially remove (someone) from membership of a professional group. **15** move or proceed vigorously or purposefully. **16** (**strike out**) start out on a new or independent course. **17** reach (an agreement, balance, or compromise). **18** (of a clock) indicate the time by sounding a chime or stroke. **19** make (a coin or medal) by stamping metal. **20** discover (gold, minerals, or oil) by drilling or mining. **21** take down or dismantle (a tent, camp, or theatrical scenery). ● noun **1** an act of striking by employees. **2** a refusal to do something as an organized protest: *a rent strike*. **3** a sudden attack. **4** (in sport) an act of striking a ball. **5** (in tenpin bowling) an act of knocking down all the pins with one's first ball. **6** an act of striking gold, minerals, or oil.
– PHRASES **strike an attitude** (or **pose**) hold one's body in a particular position to create an impression. **strike a blow for** (or **against**) do something to help (or hinder) a cause, belief, or principle. **strike up 1** begin to play a piece of music. **2** begin (a friendship or conversation) with someone. **strike while the iron is hot** make use of an opportunity immediately. [ORIGIN with reference to smithing.]
– ORIGIN Old English, 'go, flow' and 'rub lightly'.
strike-breaker ● noun a person who works or is employed in place of others who are on strike.
strike pay ● noun money paid to strikers by their trade union.
striker ● noun **1** an employee on strike. **2** the player who is to strike the ball in a game. **3** (chiefly in soccer) a forward or attacker.
strike rate ● noun the success rate of a sports team in scoring goals or runs.
striking ● adjective **1** noticeable. **2** dramatically good-looking or beautiful.
– DERIVATIVES **strikingly** adverb.
strimmer ● noun trademark an electrically powered grass trimmer with a cutting cord which rotates rapidly on a spindle.
Strine /strīn/ ● noun informal Australian English or the Australian accent.
– ORIGIN representing *Australian* in Strine.
string ● noun **1** material consisting of threads twisted together to form a thin length. **2** a piece of such material. **3** a length of catgut or wire on a musical instrument, producing a note by vibration. **4** (**strings**) the stringed instruments in an orchestra. **5** a piece of catgut, nylon, etc., interwoven with others to form the head of a sports racket. **6** a set of things tied or threaded together on a thin cord. **7** a sequence of similar items or events. **8** a tough piece of fibre in vegetables, meat, or other food. ● verb (past and past part. **strung**) **1** arrange on a string. **2** (**be strung** or **be strung out**) be arranged in a long line. **3** fit a string or strings to (a musical instrument, a racket, or a bow).
– PHRASES **no strings attached** informal there are no special conditions or restrictions. **second string** a reserve team or player. **string along** informal **1** stay with a person or group as long as it is convenient. **2** mislead deliberately over a length of time. **string out** prolong. **string up** informal **1** kill by hanging. **2** (**be strung up**) Brit. be tense or nervous.
– DERIVATIVES **stringed** adjective.
– ORIGIN Old English, related to STRONG.
string bass ● noun (especially among jazz musicians) a double bass.
string bean ● noun any of various beans eaten in their pods.
stringent /strinjənt/ ● adjective (of regulations or requirements) strict, precise, and exacting.
– DERIVATIVES **stringency** noun **stringently** adverb.
– ORIGIN from Latin *stringere* 'draw tight'.

Thesaurus

stride ● verb *she came striding down the path* MARCH, pace, step.
● noun *long swinging strides* (LONG/LARGE) STEP, pace.
– PHRASES **take something in one's stride** DEAL WITH EASILY, cope with easily, not bat an eyelid.
strident ● adjective HARSH, raucous, rough, grating, rasping, jarring, loud, shrill, screeching, piercing, ear-piercing.
– OPPOSITES soft.
strife ● noun CONFLICT, friction, discord, disagreement, dissension, dispute, argument, quarrelling, wrangling, bickering, controversy; ill/bad feeling, falling-out, bad blood, hostility, animosity.
– OPPOSITES peace.

S

strike ● verb **1** *the teacher struck Mary* HIT, slap, smack, beat, thrash, spank, thump, punch, cuff; cane, lash, whip, club; *Austral./NZ informal* quilt; *informal* clout, wallop, belt, whack, thwack, bash, clobber, bop, biff; *poetic/literary* smite. **2** *he struck the gong* BANG, beat, hit; *informal* bash, wallop. **3** *the car struck a tree* CRASH INTO, collide with, hit, run into, bump into, smash into; *N. Amer.* impact. **4** *Jennifer struck the ball* HIT, drive, propel; *informal* clout, wallop, swipe. **5** *he struck a match* IGNITE, light. **6** *she was asleep when the killer struck* ATTACK, set upon someone, fall on someone, assault someone. **7** *the disease is striking 3,000 people a year* AFFECT, afflict, attack, hit. **8** *striking a balance* ACHIEVE, reach, arrive at, find, attain, establish. **9** *we have struck a bargain* AGREE (ON), come to an agreement on, settle on; *informal* clinch. **10** *he struck a heroic pose* ASSUME, adopt, take on/up, affect; *N. Amer. informal* cop. **11** *they have struck oil* DISCOVER, find, come upon. **12** *a thought struck her* OCCUR TO, come to (mind), dawn on one, hit, spring to mind, enter one's head. **13** *you strike me as intelligent* SEEM TO, appear to, give the impression to. **14** *train drivers are striking* TAKE INDUSTRIAL ACTION, go on strike, down tools, walk out. **15** *they struck the big tent* TAKE DOWN, pull down. **16** *Lord Bridport struck his flag* LOWER, take down, bring down. **17** *we should strike south* GO, make one's way, head.
● noun **1** *a 48-hour strike* INDUSTRIAL ACTION, walkout. **2** *a military strike* (AIR) ATTACK, assault, bombing. **3** *a gold strike* FIND, discovery.
– PHRASES **strike something out** DELETE, cross out, erase, rub out. **strike something up 1** *the band struck up another tune* BEGIN TO PLAY, start playing. **2** *we struck up a friendship* BEGIN, start, commence, embark on, establish.
striking ● adjective **1** *Lizzie bears a striking resemblance to her sister* NOTICEABLE, obvious, conspicuous, evident, marked, notable, unmistakable, strong; remarkable, extraordinary, incredible, amazing, astounding, astonishing, staggering. **2** *Kenya's striking landscape* IMPRESSIVE, imposing, grand, splendid, magnificent, spectacular, breathtaking, superb, marvellous, wonderful, stunning, staggering, sensational, dramatic. **3** *striking good looks* STUNNING, attractive, good-looking, beautiful, glamorous, gorgeous, prepossessing, ravishing, handsome, pretty; *informal* knockout; *archaic* fair, comely.
– OPPOSITES unremarkable.
string ● noun **1** *a ball of string* TWINE, cord, yarn, thread, strand. **2** *a string of brewers* CHAIN, group, firm, company. **3** *a string of convictions* SERIES, succession, chain, sequence, run, streak. **4** *a string of wagons* QUEUE, procession, line, file, column, convoy, train, cavalcade. **5** *a string of pearls* STRAND, rope, necklace. **6** *a guaranteed loan with no strings* CONDITIONS, qualifications, provisions, provisos, caveats, stipulations, riders, prerequisites, limitations, limits, constraints, restrictions; *informal* catches.
● verb **1** *lights were strung across the promenade* HANG, suspend, sling, stretch, run; thread, loop, festoon. **2** *beads strung on a silver chain* THREAD, loop, link.
– PHRASES **string along** *(informal)* GO ALONG, come too, accompany, join (up with). **string someone along** *(informal)* MISLEAD, deceive, take advantage of, dupe, hoax, fool, make a fool of, play with, toy with, dally with, trifle with; *informal* lead up the garden path, take for a ride. **string something out 1** *stringing out a story* SPIN OUT, drag out, lengthen. **2** *airfields strung out along the Gulf* SPREAD OUT, space out, distribute, scatter. **string someone up** *(informal)*

stringer ● noun **1** a structural piece running lengthwise in a framework, especially that of a ship or aircraft. **2** informal a journalist who is not on the regular staff of a newspaper, but who reports part-time on a particular place.

string quartet ● noun a chamber music ensemble consisting of first and second violins, viola, and cello.

string vest ● noun a man's undergarment made of a meshed fabric.

stringy ● adjective (**stringier**, **stringiest**) **1** resembling string. **2** tall, wiry, and thin. **3** (of food) tough and fibrous.

stringybark ● noun Austral. a eucalyptus with tough fibrous bark.

strip[1] ● verb (**stripped**, **stripping**) **1** remove all coverings or clothes from. **2** take off one's clothes. **3** leave bare of accessories or fittings. **4** remove (paint) from a surface with solvent. **5** (**strip of**) deprive (someone) of (rank, power, or property). **6** sell off (the assets of a company) for profit. **7** tear the thread or teeth from (a screw, gearwheel, etc.). ● noun **1** an act of undressing, especially in a striptease. **2** Brit. the identifying outfit worn by the members of a sports team while playing.
– ORIGIN Germanic; sense 2 of the noun is perhaps from the notion of clothing to which a player 'strips' down.

strip[2] ● noun **1** a long, narrow piece of cloth, paper, etc. **2** a long, narrow area of land. **3** chiefly N. Amer. a main road lined with shops and other facilities.
– ORIGIN Low German *strippe* 'strap, thong'.

stripe ● noun **1** a long narrow band or strip of a different colour or texture from the surface on either side of it. **2** a chevron sewn on to a uniform to denote military rank. **3** chiefly N. Amer. a type or category. ● verb (usu. **be striped**) mark with stripes.
– DERIVATIVES **striped** adjective **stripy** (also **stripey**) adjective.
– ORIGIN perhaps from Dutch or Low German.

strip light ● noun Brit. a tubular fluorescent lamp.

stripling ● noun archaic or humorous a young man.
– ORIGIN probably from STRIP[2] (from the notion of 'narrowness', i.e. slimness).

strip mine ● noun chiefly N. Amer. an opencast mine.

stripper ● noun **1** a device or substance for stripping. **2** a striptease performer.

strippergram ● noun a novelty greetings message delivered by a man or woman who accompanies it with a striptease act.

strip poker ● noun a form of poker in which a player with a losing hand takes off an item of clothing as a forfeit.

strip-search ● verb search (someone) for concealed drugs, weapons, or other items, by stripping off their clothes.

striptease ● noun a form of entertainment in which a performer gradually undresses to music in a sexually exciting way.

strive ● verb (past **strove** or **strived**; past part. **striven** or **strived**) **1** make great efforts. **2** (**strive against**) fight vigorously against.
– DERIVATIVES **striver** noun.
– ORIGIN Old French *estriver*.

strobe informal ● noun **1** a stroboscope. **2** a stroboscopic lamp. **3** N. Amer. an electronic flash for a camera. ● verb **1** flash intermittently. **2** show or cause strobing.

strobing ● noun **1** irregular movement and loss of continuity of lines and stripes in a television picture. **2** jerkiness in what should be a smooth movement of a cinematographic image.

stroboscope /strōbəskōp/ ● noun Physics an instrument which shines a bright light at rapid intervals so that a moving or rotating object appears stationary.
– DERIVATIVES **stroboscopic** adjective.
– ORIGIN from Greek *strobos* 'whirling'.

strode past of STRIDE.

stroganoff /stroggənof/ ● noun a dish in which the central ingredient, typically strips of beef, is cooked in a sauce containing sour cream.
– ORIGIN named after the Russian diplomat Count Pavel *Stroganov* (1772–1817).

stroke ● noun **1** an act of hitting. **2** Golf an act of hitting the ball with a club, as a unit of scoring. **3** a sound made by a striking clock. **4** an act of stroking with the hand. **5** a mark made by drawing a pen, pencil, or paintbrush once across paper or canvas. **6** a line forming part of a written or printed character. **7** a short diagonal line separating characters or figures. **8** one of a series of repeated movements. **9** a style of moving the arms and legs in swimming. **10** the mode or action of moving the oar in rowing. **11** a sudden disabling attack or loss of consciousness caused by an interruption in the flow of blood to the brain. ● verb move one's hand with gentle pressure over.
– PHRASES **at a stroke** by a single action having immediate effect. **not do a stroke of work** do no work at all. **put someone off their stroke** disconcert someone so that they make a mistake or hesitate. **stroke of genius** an outstandingly original idea. **stroke of luck** a fortunate unexpected occurrence.
– ORIGIN Old English, related to STRIKE.

stroke play ● noun play in golf in which the score is reckoned by counting the number of strokes taken overall. Compare with MATCH PLAY.

stroll ● verb **1** walk in a leisurely way. **2** informal achieve a sporting victory easily. ● noun **1** a short leisurely walk. **2** informal a victory easily achieved.
– ORIGIN originally in the sense 'roam as a vagrant': probably from German *strollen*, from *Strolch* 'vagabond'.

stroller ● noun N. Amer. a pushchair.

stroma /strōmə/ ● noun (pl. **stromata** /strōmətə/) Biology **1** the supportive tissue or matrix of an organ, tumour, cell, etc. **2** a cushion-like mass of fungal tissue containing spore-bearing structures.
– ORIGIN Greek, 'coverlet'.

stromatolite /strəmattəlīt/ ● noun Biology a mound built up of layers of blue-green algae and lime-rich sediment, especially as fossilized in Precambrian rocks.

strong ● adjective (**stronger**, **strongest**) **1** physically powerful. **2** done with or exerting great force. **3** able to withstand great force or pressure. **4** secure, stable, or firmly established.

Thesaurus

S

HANG, lynch, gibbet.

stringent ● adjective STRICT, firm, rigid, rigorous, severe, harsh, tough, tight, exacting, demanding, inflexible, hard and fast.

stringy ● adjective **1** *stringy hair* STRAGGLY, lank, thin. **2** *a stringy brunette* LANKY, gangling, gangly, rangy, wiry, bony, skinny, scrawny, thin, spare, gaunt. **3** *stringy meat* FIBROUS, gristly, sinewy, chewy, tough, leathery.

strip[1] ● verb **1** *he stripped and got into bed* UNDRESS, strip off, take one's clothes off, unclothe, disrobe, strip naked. **2** *stripping off paint* PEEL, remove, take off, scrape, rub, clean. **3** *they stripped him of his doctorate* TAKE AWAY FROM, dispossess, deprive, confiscate, divest, relieve. **4** *they stripped down my engine* DISMANTLE, disassemble, take to bits/pieces, take apart. **5** *the house had been stripped* EMPTY, clear, clean out, plunder, rob, burgle, loot, pillage, ransack, despoil, sack; archaic spoil.
– OPPOSITES dress.
● noun *the team's new strip* OUTFIT, clothes, clothing, garments, dress, garb; Brit. kit; informal gear, get-up; Brit. informal rig-out.

strip[2] ● noun *a strip of paper* (NARROW) PIECE, bit, band, belt, ribbon, slip, shred.

stripe ● noun LINE, band, strip, belt, bar, streak, vein, flash, blaze; technical stria, striation.

striped ● adjective. See STRIPY.

stripling ● noun (archaic) YOUTH, adolescent, youngster, boy, schoolboy, lad, teenager, juvenile, minor, young man; Scottish laddie; informal kid, young 'un, nipper, whippersnapper, shaver.

stripy ● adjective STRIPED, barred, lined, banded; streaky, variegated; technical striated.

strive ● verb **1** *I shall strive to be virtuous* TRY (HARD), attempt, endeavour, aim, venture, make an effort, exert oneself, do one's best, do all one can, do one's utmost, labour, work; informal go all out, give it one's best shot, pull out all the stops; formal essay. **2** *scholars must strive against bias* STRUGGLE, fight, battle, combat; campaign, crusade.

stroke ● noun **1** *five strokes of the axe* BLOW, hit, thump, punch, slap, smack, cuff, knock; informal wallop, clout, whack, thwack, bash, biff, swipe; archaic smite. **2** *cricket strokes* SHOT, hit, strike. **3** *light upward strokes* MOVEMENT, action, motion. **4** *a stroke of genius* FEAT, accomplishment, achievement, master stroke. **5** *broad brush strokes* MARK, line. **6** *the budget was full of bold strokes* DETAIL, touch, point. **7** *he suffered a stroke* THROMBOSIS, seizure; Medicine ictus.
● verb *she stroked the cat* CARESS, fondle, pat, pet, touch, rub, massage, soothe.

stroll ● verb *they strolled along the river* SAUNTER, amble, wander, meander, ramble, promenade, walk, go for a walk, stretch one's legs, get some air; informal mosey; formal perambulate.
● noun *a stroll in the park* SAUNTER, amble, wander, walk, turn,

5 great in power, influence, or ability. **6** great in intensity or degree. **7** (of language or actions) forceful and extreme. **8** (of something seen or heard) not soft or muted. **9** pungent and full-flavoured. **10** (of a solution or drink) containing a large proportion of a substance. **11** used after a number to indicate the size of a group: *a crowd several thousands strong*. **12** Grammar (of verbs) forming the past tense and past participle by a change of vowel within the stem rather than by addition of a suffix (e.g. *swim, swam, swum*).
– PHRASES **come on strong** informal behave aggressively or assertively. **going strong** informal continuing to be healthy, vigorous, or successful. **strong on 1** good at. **2** possessing large quantities of. **strong meat** Brit. ideas or language likely to be found unacceptably forceful or extreme.
– DERIVATIVES **strongly** adverb.
– ORIGIN Old English, related to STRING.
strong-arm ● adjective using or characterized by force or violence.
strongbox ● noun a small lockable metal box in which valuables may be kept.
stronghold ● noun **1** a place that has been fortified against attack. **2** a place of strong support for a cause or political party.
strongman ● noun **1** a man of great physical strength, especially one who performs feats of strength for entertainment. **2** a leader who rules by the exercise of threats, force, or violence.
strong point ● noun **1** a specially fortified defensive position. **2** a thing at which one excels.
strongroom ● noun a room, typically one in a bank, designed to protect valuable items against fire and theft.
strong suit ● noun **1** (in bridge or whist) a holding of a number of high cards of one suit in a hand. **2** a thing at which a person excels.
strontia /stronshə/ ● noun Chemistry strontium oxide, a white solid resembling quicklime.
– ORIGIN from *Strontian*, a village in Scotland, where strontium carbonate was discovered.
strontium /strontiəm/ ● noun a soft silver-white metallic chemical element.
strop¹ ● noun **1** a strip of leather for sharpening razors. **2** Nautical a collar of leather, spliced rope, or iron, used for handling cargo. ● verb (**stropped**, **stropping**) sharpen on or with a strop.
– ORIGIN probably from Latin *stroppus* 'thong'.
strop² ● noun Brit. informal a temper.
stroppy ● adjective (**stroppier**, **stroppiest**) Brit. informal bad-tempered; argumentative.
– ORIGIN perhaps from OBSTREPEROUS.
strove past of STRIVE.
struck past and past participle of STRIKE.
structural ● adjective relating to or forming part of a structure.
– DERIVATIVES **structurally** adverb.
structuralism ● noun a method of interpretation and analysis of human cognition, behaviour, culture, and experience, which focuses on relationships of contrast between elements in a conceptual system.
– DERIVATIVES **structuralist** noun & adjective.
structure ● noun **1** the arrangement of and relations between the parts of something complex. **2** a building or other object constructed from several parts. **3** the quality of being well organized. ● verb give structure to.
– ORIGIN Latin *structura*, from *struere* 'to build'.
strudel /stroōd'l/ ● noun a dessert of thin pastry rolled up round a fruit filling and baked.
– ORIGIN German, 'whirlpool'.
struggle ● verb **1** make forceful efforts to get free. **2** strive under difficult circumstances to do something. **3** make one's way with difficulty. **4** have difficulty in gaining recognition or a living. ● noun **1** an act of struggling. **2** a very difficult task.
– DERIVATIVES **struggler** noun.
– ORIGIN perhaps of imitative origin.
strum ● verb (**strummed**, **strumming**) play (a guitar or similar instrument) by sweeping the thumb or a plectrum up or down the strings. ● noun an instance or the sound of strumming.
– ORIGIN imitative.
strumpet ● noun archaic or humorous a female prostitute or a promiscuous woman.
– ORIGIN of unknown origin.
strung past and past participle of STRING.
strut ● noun **1** a bar used to support or strengthen a structure. **2** a strutting gait. ● verb (**strutted**, **strutting**) **1** walk with a stiff, erect, and conceited gait. **2** brace with a strut or struts.
– ORIGIN from Old English, 'protrude stiffly'.
struth ● exclamation variant spelling of STREWTH.

Thesaurus

promenade; *informal* mosey; *dated* constitutional; *formal* perambulation.
strong ● adjective **1** *a strong lad* POWERFUL, muscular, brawny, powerfully built, strapping, sturdy, burly, meaty, robust, athletic, tough, rugged, lusty, strong as an ox/horse; *informal* beefy, hunky, husky; *dated* stalwart. **2** *she isn't very strong* WELL, healthy, in good health, (fighting) fit, robust, vigorous, blooming, thriving, hale and hearty, in fine fettle; *informal* in the pink. **3** *a strong character* FORCEFUL, determined, spirited, self-assertive, tough, tenacious, formidable, redoubtable, strong-minded; *informal* gutsy, feisty. **4** *a strong fortress* SECURE, well built, indestructible, well fortified, well protected, impregnable, solid. **5** *strong cotton bags* DURABLE, hard-wearing, heavy-duty, tough, sturdy, well made, long-lasting. **6** *the current is very strong* FORCEFUL, powerful, vigorous, fierce, intense. **7** *a strong interest in literature* KEEN, eager, passionate, fervent. **8** *strong feelings* INTENSE, forceful, passionate, ardent, fervent, fervid, deep-seated; *poetic/literary* perfervid. **9** *a strong supporter* KEEN, eager, enthusiastic, dedicated, staunch, loyal, steadfast. **10** *strong arguments* COMPELLING, cogent, forceful, powerful, potent, weighty, convincing, sound, valid, well founded, persuasive, influential. **11** *a need for strong action* FIRM, forceful, drastic, extreme. **12** *she bore a very strong resemblance to Vera* MARKED, noticeable, pronounced, distinct, definite, unmistakable, notable. **13** *a strong voice* LOUD, powerful, forceful, resonant, sonorous, rich, deep, booming. **14** *strong language* BAD, foul, obscene, profane. **15** *a strong blue colour* INTENSE, deep, rich, bright, brilliant, vivid. **16** *strong lights* BRIGHT, brilliant, dazzling, glaring. **17** *strong black coffee* CONCENTRATED, undiluted. **18** *strong cheese* HIGHLY FLAVOURED, flavourful, flavoursome; piquant, tangy, spicy. **19** *strong drink* ALCOHOLIC, intoxicating, hard, stiff; *formal* spirituous.
– OPPOSITES weak, gentle, mild.
strong-arm ● adjective AGGRESSIVE, forceful, bullying, coercive, threatening, intimidatory; *informal* bully-boy.
strongbox ● noun SAFE, safe-deposit box, cash/money box.
stronghold ● noun **1** *the enemy stronghold* FORTRESS, fort, castle, citadel, garrison. **2** *a Tory stronghold* BASTION, centre, hotbed.
strong-minded ● adjective DETERMINED, firm, resolute, purposeful, strong-willed, uncompromising, unbending, forceful, persistent, tenacious, dogged; *informal* gutsy, spunky.
strong point ● noun STRENGTH, strong suit, forte, speciality.
– OPPOSITES weakness.
strong-willed ● adjective DETERMINED, resolute, stubborn, obstinate, wilful, headstrong, strong-minded, self-willed, unbending, unyielding, intransigent, intractable, obdurate, recalcitrant; *formal* refractory.
stroppy ● adjective *(Brit. informal)*. See BAD-TEMPERED.
structure ● noun **1** *a vast Gothic structure* BUILDING, edifice, construction, erection, pile. **2** *the structure of local government* CONSTRUCTION, form, formation, shape, composition, anatomy, make-up, constitution; organization, system, arrangement, design, framework, configuration, pattern.
● verb *the programme is structured around periods of residential study* ARRANGE, organize, design, shape, construct, build, put together.
struggle ● verb **1** *they struggled to do better* STRIVE, try hard, endeavour, make every effort, do one's best/utmost, bend over backwards, put oneself out; *informal* go all out, give it one's best shot; *formal* essay. **2** *James struggled with the raiders* FIGHT, grapple, wrestle, scuffle, brawl, spar; *informal* scrap. **3** *the teams struggled to be first* COMPETE, contend, vie, fight, battle, jockey. **4** *she struggled over the dunes* SCRAMBLE, flounder, stumble, fight/battle one's way, labour.
● noun **1** *the struggle for justice* ENDEAVOUR, striving, effort, exertion, labour; campaign, battle, crusade, drive, push. **2** *they were arrested without a struggle* FIGHT, scuffle, brawl, tussle, wrestling bout, skirmish, fracas, melee; breach of the peace; *informal* scrap, dust-up, punch-up; *Brit. informal* bust-up, ding-dong; *Law, dated* affray. **3** *many perished in the struggle* CONFLICT, fight, battle, confrontation, clash, skirmish; hostilities, fighting, war, warfare, campaign. **4** *a struggle within the leadership* CONTEST, competition, fight, clash; rivalry, friction, feuding, conflict. **5** *life has been a*

S

strychnine /strikneen/ ● noun a bitter and highly poisonous substance obtained from nux vomica and related plants.
– ORIGIN from Greek *strukhnos*, denoting a kind of nightshade.

St Swithin's day ● noun 15 July, a Church festival commemorating St Swithin and popularly believed to be a day on which, if it rains, it will continue raining for the next forty days.

Stuart (also **Stewart**) ● adjective belonging or relating to the royal family ruling Scotland 1371–1714 and Britain 1603–1714 (interrupted by the Commonwealth 1649–60). ● noun a member of this family.

stub ● noun **1** the remnant of a pencil, cigarette, or similar-shaped object after use. **2** a shortened or unusually short thing. **3** the counterfoil of a cheque, ticket, or other document. ● verb (**stubbed**, **stubbing**) **1** accidentally strike (one's toe) against something. **2** (often **stub out**) extinguish (a cigarette) by pressing the lighted end against something.
– ORIGIN Old English, 'stump of a tree'.

stubble ● noun **1** the cut stalks of cereal plants left in the ground after harvesting. **2** short, stiff hairs growing on a man's face when he has not shaved for a while.
– DERIVATIVES **stubbly** adjective.
– ORIGIN Old French *stuble*, from Latin *stipula* 'straw'.

stubborn ● adjective **1** determined not to change one's attitude or position. **2** difficult to move, remove, or cure.
– DERIVATIVES **stubbornly** adverb **stubbornness** noun.
– ORIGIN of unknown origin.

stubby ● adjective (**stubbier**, **stubbiest**) short and thick. ● noun (pl. **stubbies**) Austral./NZ informal a small squat bottle of beer.

stucco ● noun fine plaster used for coating wall surfaces or moulding into architectural decorations. ● verb (**stuccoes**, **stuccoed**) (usu. as adj. **stuccoed**) coat or decorate with stucco.
– ORIGIN Italian.

stuck past participle of STICK².

stuck-up ● adjective informal snobbishly aloof.

stud¹ ● noun **1** a large-headed piece of metal that pierces and projects from a surface, especially for decoration. **2** a small projection fixed to the base of a shoe or boot to provide better grip. **3** a small piece of jewellery which is pushed through a pierced ear or nostril. **4** a fastener consisting of two buttons joined with a bar, used to fasten a shirt front or to fasten a collar to a shirt. ● verb (**studded**, **studding**) (usu. **be studded**) **1** decorate with studs or similar small objects. **2** strew or scatter: *the sky was studded with stars.*
– DERIVATIVES **studding** noun.
– ORIGIN Old English, 'post, upright prop'.

stud² ● noun **1** an establishment where horses or other domesticated animals are kept for breeding. **2** (also **stud horse**) a stallion. **3** informal a sexually active or virile young man. **4** (also **stud poker**) a form of poker in which the first card of a player's hand is dealt face down and the others face up, with betting after each round of the deal.
– ORIGIN Old English, related to STAND.

student ● noun **1** a person studying at a university or other place of higher education. **2** chiefly N. Amer. a school pupil. **3** (before another noun) denoting someone who is studying to enter a particular profession: *a student nurse.* **4** a person who takes a particular interest in a subject.
– DERIVATIVES **studentship** noun (Brit.) **studenty** adjective (Brit. informal).
– ORIGIN from Latin *studere* 'apply oneself to'.

studio ● noun (pl. **studios**) **1** a room where an artist works or where dancers practise. **2** a room from which television or radio programmes are broadcast, or in which they are recorded. **3** a place where film or sound recordings are made. **4** a film production company.
– ORIGIN Italian, from Latin *studium* 'zeal, painstaking application'.

studio flat ● noun Brit. a flat containing one main room.

studious ● adjective **1** spending a lot of time studying or reading. **2** done deliberately or with great care.
– DERIVATIVES **studiously** adverb **studiousness** noun.

study ● noun (pl. **studies**) **1** the devotion of time and attention to acquiring knowledge. **2** a detailed investigation and analysis of a subject or situation. **3** a room for reading, writing, or academic work. **4** a piece of work done for practice or as an experiment. ● verb (**studies**, **studied**) **1** acquire knowledge on. **2** make a study of. **3** apply oneself to study. **4** look at closely in order to observe or read. **5** (**studied**) done with deliberate and careful effort.
– PHRASES **a study in** a good example of (a quality or emotion). **in a brown study** absorbed in one's thoughts. [ORIGIN apparently originally from *brown* in the sense 'gloomy'.]
– ORIGIN Latin *studium* 'zeal, painstaking application'.

stuff ● noun **1** matter, material, articles, or activities of a specified or indeterminate kind. **2** basic characteristics; substance: *Helen was made of sterner stuff.* **3** (**one's stuff**) informal one's area of expertise. **4** Brit. dated woollen fabric, especially as distinct from silk, cotton, and linen. **5** Brit. informal, dated nonsense; rubbish. ● verb **1** fill tightly with something. **2** force tightly or hastily into a receptacle or space. **3** fill out the skin

Thesaurus

struggle for me EFFORT, trial, trouble, stress, strain, battle; informal grind, hassle.

strumpet ● noun (archaic). See PROSTITUTE noun.

strut ● verb SWAGGER, swank, parade, stride, sweep; N. Amer. informal sashay.

stub ● noun **1** *a cigarette stub* BUTT, (tail) end; informal dog-end. **2** *a ticket stub* COUNTERFOIL, ticket slip, tab. **3** *a stub of pencil* STUMP, remnant, (tail) end.

stubble ● noun **1** *a field of stubble* STALKS, straw. **2** *grey stubble* BRISTLES, whiskers, facial hair; informal five o'clock shadow.

stubbly ● adjective BRISTLY, unshaven, whiskered; prickly, rough, coarse, scratchy.

stubborn ● adjective **1** *you're too stubborn to admit it* OBSTINATE, stubborn as a mule, headstrong, wilful, strong-willed, pig-headed, obdurate, difficult, contrary, perverse, recalcitrant, inflexible, iron-willed, uncompromising, unbending; informal stiff-necked; Brit. informal bolshie, bloody-minded; N. Amer. informal balky; formal pertinacious, refractory; archaic contumacious, froward. **2** *stubborn stains* INDELIBLE, permanent, persistent, tenacious, resistant.
– OPPOSITES compliant.

stubby ● adjective DUMPY, stocky, chunky, chubby, squat; short, stumpy, dwarfish.
– OPPOSITES slender, tall.

stuck ● adjective **1** *a message was stuck to his screen* FIXED, fastened, attached, glued, pinned. **2** *the gate was stuck* IMMOVABLE, stuck fast, jammed. **3** *if you get stuck, leave a blank* BAFFLED, beaten, at a loss, at one's wits' end; informal stumped, bogged down, flummoxed, fazed, bamboozled.
– PHRASES **get stuck into** (informal) GET DOWN TO, make a start on, commence, embark on, get to work at, tackle, throw oneself into. **stuck on** (informal) INFATUATED WITH, besotted with, smitten with, (head over heels) in love with, obsessed with; informal struck on, crazy about, mad about, wild about, carrying a torch for. **stuck with** LUMBERED WITH, left with, made responsible for.

stuck-up ● adjective (informal). See CONCEITED.

studded ● adjective DOTTED, scattered, sprinkled, covered, spangled; poetic/literary bespangled, bejewelled.

student ● noun **1** *a university student* UNDERGRADUATE, postgraduate, scholar; freshman, freshwoman, finalist; N. Amer. sophomore; Brit. informal fresher. **2** *a former student* PUPIL, schoolchild, schoolboy, schoolgirl, scholar. **3** *a nursing student* TRAINEE, apprentice, probationer, recruit, novice; informal rookie.

studied ● adjective DELIBERATE, careful, considered, conscious, calculated, intentional; affected, forced, strained, artificial.

studio ● noun WORKSHOP, workroom, atelier.

studious ● adjective **1** *a studious nature* SCHOLARLY, academic, bookish, intellectual, erudite, learned, donnish. **2** *studious attention* DILIGENT, careful, attentive, assiduous, painstaking, thorough, meticulous. **3** *his studious absence from public view* DELIBERATE, wilful, conscious, intentional.

study ● noun **1** *two years of study* LEARNING, education, schooling, academic work, scholarship, tuition, research; informal swotting, cramming. **2** *a study of global warming* INVESTIGATION, enquiry, research, examination, analysis, review, survey. **3** *Father was in his study* OFFICE, workroom, studio. **4** *a critical study* ESSAY, article, work, review, paper, dissertation, disquisition.
● verb **1** *Anne studied hard* WORK, revise; informal swot, cram, mug up; archaic con. **2** *he studied electronics* LEARN, read, be taught. **3** *Thomas was studying child development* INVESTIGATE, inquire into, research, look into, examine, analyse, explore, review, appraise, conduct a survey of. **4** *she studied her friend thoughtfully* SCRUTINIZE, examine, inspect, consider, regard, look at, eye, observe, watch, survey; informal check out; N. Amer. informal eyeball.
– PHRASES **in a brown study** LOST IN THOUGHT, in a reverie, musing,

of (a dead animal or bird) with material to restore the original shape and appearance. **4** (**be stuffed up**) have one's nose blocked up with catarrh. **5** (**stuff oneself**) informal eat greedily. **6** Brit. informal defeat heavily in sport.
– PHRASES **get stuffed** Brit. informal said to express dismissal or contempt.
– ORIGIN Old French *estoffe* 'material, furniture', from Greek *stuphein* 'draw together'.
stuffed shirt ● noun informal a conservative, pompous person.
stuffing ● noun **1** a mixture used to stuff poultry or meat before cooking. **2** padding used to stuff cushions, furniture, or soft toys.
– PHRASES **knock** (or **take**) **the stuffing out of** informal severely damage the confidence or strength of.
stuffy ● adjective (**stuffier**, **stuffiest**) **1** lacking fresh air or ventilation. **2** conventional and narrow-minded. **3** (of a person's nose) blocked up.
– DERIVATIVES **stuffily** adverb **stuffiness** noun.
stultify /stultifī/ ● verb (**stultifies**, **stultified**) **1** (usu. as adj. **stultifying**) cause to feel bored or drained of energy. **2** cause to appear foolish or absurd.
– DERIVATIVES **stultification** noun.
– ORIGIN Latin *stultificare*, from *stultus* 'foolish'.
stumble ● verb **1** trip or momentarily lose one's balance. **2** walk unsteadily. **3** make a mistake or repeated mistakes in speaking. **4** (**stumble across/on/upon**) find by chance. ● noun an act of stumbling.
– ORIGIN Old Norse.
stumbling block ● noun an obstacle.
stump ● noun **1** the part of a tree trunk left projecting from the ground after the rest has fallen or been felled. **2** a projecting remnant of something worn away or cut or broken off. **3** Cricket each of the three upright pieces of wood which form a wicket. ● verb **1** informal baffle. **2** Cricket dismiss (a batsman) by dislodging the bails with the ball while the batsman is out of the crease but not running. **3** walk stiffly and noisily. **4** (**stump up**) Brit. informal pay (a sum of money).
– PHRASES **on the stump** informal engaged in political campaigning. [ORIGIN from the use of a tree stump as a platform for a speaker.]
– ORIGIN Low German *stumpe* or Dutch *stomp*.
stumper ● noun informal a puzzling question.
stumpy ● adjective (**stumpier**, **stumpiest**) short and thick; squat.
stun ● verb (**stunned**, **stunning**) **1** knock unconscious or into a dazed or semi-conscious state. **2** astonish or shock (someone) so that they are temporarily unable to react.
– ORIGIN Old French *estoner* 'astonish'.
stung past and past participle of STING.
stun gun ● noun a device used to immobilize an attacker without causing serious injury.
stunk past and past participle of STINK.
stunner ● noun informal **1** a strikingly beautiful or impressive person or thing. **2** an astonishing turn of events.
stunning ● adjective extremely impressive or attractive.
– DERIVATIVES **stunningly** adverb.
stunt[1] ● verb retard the growth or development of.
– ORIGIN from dialect *stunt* 'foolish, stubborn', from Germanic.
stunt[2] ● noun **1** an action displaying spectacular skill and daring. **2** something unusual done to attract attention.
– ORIGIN of unknown origin.
stuntman (or **stuntwoman**) ● noun a person taking an actor's place in performing dangerous stunts.
stupa /stōōpə/ ● noun a dome-shaped building erected as a Buddhist shrine.
– ORIGIN Sanskrit.
stupefy /styōōpifī/ ● verb (**stupefies**, **stupefied**) **1** make (someone) unable to think or feel properly. **2** astonish and shock.
– DERIVATIVES **stupefaction** noun.
– ORIGIN Latin *stupefacere*, from *stupere* 'be struck senseless'.
stupendous /styoopendəss/ ● adjective extremely impressive.
– DERIVATIVES **stupendously** adverb.
– ORIGIN from Latin *stupendus* 'to be wondered at'.
stupid ● adjective (**stupider**, **stupidest**) **1** lacking intelligence or

Thesaurus

ruminating, cogitating, dreaming, daydreaming; *informal* miles away.
stuff ● noun **1** *suede is tough stuff* MATERIAL, fabric, cloth, textile; matter, substance. **2** *first-aid stuff* ITEMS, articles, objects, goods; *informal* things, bits and pieces, odds and ends. **3** *all my stuff is in the suitcase* BELONGINGS, (personal) possessions, effects, goods (and chattels), paraphernalia; *informal* gear, things, kit; *Brit. informal* clobber, gubbins. **4** *he knows his stuff* FACTS, information, data, subject; *informal* onions.
● verb **1** *stuffing pillows* FILL, pack, pad, upholster. **2** *Robyn stuffed her clothes into a bag* SHOVE, thrust, push, ram, cram, squeeze, force, jam, pack, pile, stick. **3** *(informal) they stuffed themselves with chocolate* FILL, gorge, overindulge; gobble, devour, wolf; *informal* pig (out), make a pig of oneself. **4** *my nose was stuffed up* BLOCK, bung, congest, obstruct. **5** *(Brit. informal) Scotland stuffed Chile.* See TROUNCE.
– PHRASES **stuff and nonsense** *(Brit. informal).* See NONSENSE sense 1.
stuffing ● noun **1** *the stuffing is coming out of the armchair* PADDING, wadding, filling, upholstery, packing, filler. **2** *sage and onion stuffing* FILLING, forcemeat, salpicon; *N. Amer.* dressing.
– PHRASES **knock the stuffing out of** *(informal)* DEVASTATE, shatter, crush, shock; *informal* knock sideways; *Brit. informal* knock for six.
stuffy ● adjective **1** *a stuffy atmosphere* AIRLESS, close, musty, stale; *Brit.* frowsty; *Brit. informal* fuggy. **2** *a stuffy young man* STAID, sedate, sober, prim, priggish, strait-laced, conformist, conservative, old-fashioned; *informal* square, straight, starchy, fuddy-duddy. **3** *a stuffy nose* BLOCKED, stuffed up, bunged up.
– OPPOSITES airy, clear.
stultify ● verb **1** *the free market was stultified by the welfare state* HAMPER, impede, thwart, frustrate, foil, suppress, smother. **2** *he stultifies her with too much gentleness* BORE, make bored, dull, numb, benumb, stupefy.
stumble ● verb **1** *he stumbled and fell heavily* TRIP (OVER/UP), lose one's balance, lose/miss one's footing, slip. **2** *he stumbled back home* STAGGER, totter, teeter, dodder, blunder, hobble, move clumsily. **3** *he stumbled through his speech* STAMMER, stutter, hesitate, falter, speak haltingly; *informal* fluff one's lines.
– PHRASES **stumble across/on** COME ACROSS/UPON, chance on, happen on, light on; discover, find, unearth, uncover; *informal* dig up.
stumbling block ● noun OBSTACLE, hurdle, barrier, bar, hindrance, impediment, handicap, disadvantage; snag, hitch, catch, drawback, difficulty, problem, weakness, defect, pitfall; *informal* fly in the ointment, hiccup.
stump ● verb **1** *(informal) they were stumped by the question* BAFFLE, perplex, puzzle, confuse, confound, nonplus, defeat, put at a loss; *informal* flummox, fox, throw, floor; *N. Amer. informal* discombobulate. **2** *she stumped along the landing* STOMP, stamp, clomp, clump, lumber, thump, thud.
– PHRASES **stump something up** *(Brit. informal)* PAY (UP), dish out, contribute; *informal* fork out, shell out, lay out, cough up, chip in; *N. Amer. informal* ante up, pony up.
stumpy ● adjective SHORT, stubby, squat, stocky, chunky.
– OPPOSITES long, thin.
stun ● verb **1** *a glancing blow stunned Gary* DAZE, stupefy, knock unconscious, knock out, lay out. **2** *she was stunned by the news* ASTOUND, amaze, astonish, dumbfound, stupefy, stagger, shock, take aback; *informal* flabbergast, knock sideways, bowl over; *Brit. informal* knock for six.
stunner ● noun *(informal).* See BEAUTY sense 2.
stunning ● adjective **1** *a stunning win* REMARKABLE, extraordinary, staggering, incredible, outstanding, amazing, astonishing, marvellous, phenomenal, splendid; *informal* fabulous, fantastic, tremendous. **2** *she was looking stunning.* See BEAUTIFUL.
– OPPOSITES ordinary.
stunt[1] ● verb *a disease that stunts growth* INHIBIT, impede, hamper, hinder, restrict, retard, slow, curb, check.
– OPPOSITES encourage.
stunt[2] ● noun *acrobatic stunts* FEAT, exploit, trick.
stunted ● adjective SMALL, undersize(d), diminutive.
stupefaction ● noun **1** *alcoholic stupefaction* OBLIVION, obliviousness, unconsciousness, insensibility, stupor, daze. **2** *Don shook his head in stupefaction* BEWILDERMENT, confusion, perplexity, wonder, amazement, astonishment.
stupefy ● verb **1** *the blow had stupefied her* STUN, daze, knock unconscious, knock out, lay out. **2** *they were stupefied* DRUG, sedate, tranquillize, intoxicate, inebriate; *informal* dope. **3** *the amount stupefied us* SHOCK, stun, astound, dumbfound, overwhelm, stagger, amaze, astonish, take aback, take someone's breath away; *informal* flabbergast, knock sideways, bowl over, floor; *Brit. informal* knock for six.

S

common sense. **2** informal used to express exasperation or boredom: *you and your stupid paintings!* **3** dazed and unable to think clearly.
– DERIVATIVES **stupidity** noun **stupidly** adverb.
– ORIGIN Latin *stupidus*, from *stupere* 'be amazed or stunned'.

stupor /styo͞opər/ ● noun a state of near-unconsciousness or insensibility.
– DERIVATIVES **stuporous** adjective.
– ORIGIN Latin, from *stupere* 'be amazed or stunned'.

sturdy ● adjective (**sturdier**, **sturdiest**) **1** strongly and solidly built or made. **2** confident and determined: *a sturdy independence.*
– DERIVATIVES **sturdily** adverb **sturdiness** noun.
– ORIGIN originally in the senses 'reckless, violent' and 'intractable, obstinate': from Old French *esturdi* 'stunned, dazed'.

sturgeon /sturjən/ ● noun a very large fish with bony plates on the body, found in seas and rivers and commercially important for its caviar and flesh.
– ORIGIN Old French.

Sturm und Drang /shtoorm o͝ont drang/ ● noun an 18th-century German literary and artistic movement characterized by the expression of emotional unrest.
– ORIGIN German, 'storm and stress'.

stutter ● verb **1** talk with continued involuntary repetition of sounds, especially initial consonants. **2** (of a machine or gun) produce a series of short, sharp sounds. ● noun a tendency to stutter while speaking.
– DERIVATIVES **stutterer** noun.
– ORIGIN from dialect *stut*, from Germanic.

St Vitus's dance /vītəsiz/ ● noun old-fashioned term for SYDENHAM'S CHOREA.
– ORIGIN so named because a visit to the shrine of the Christian martyr *St Vitus* (died *c.*300) was believed to alleviate the disease.

sty[1] ● noun (pl. **sties**) a pigsty.
– ORIGIN from an Old English word found in the combination 'sty pig'.

sty[2] (also **stye**) ● noun (pl. **sties** or **styes**) an inflamed swelling on the edge of an eyelid.
– ORIGIN dialect *styany*, from an Old English word meaning 'riser' + EYE.

Stygian /stijiən/ ● adjective literary very dark.
– ORIGIN from the River *Styx*, an underworld river in Greek mythology.

style ● noun **1** a manner of doing something. **2** a distinctive appearance, design, or arrangement. **3** a way of painting, writing, etc., characteristic of a particular period, person, etc. **4** elegance and sophistication. **5** an official or legal title. **6** Botany a narrow extension of the ovary, bearing the stigma. ● verb **1** design, make, or arrange in a particular form. **2** designate with a particular name, description, or title.
– DERIVATIVES **styleless** adjective **styler** noun.
– ORIGIN Latin *stilus* 'stylus, stake, style of speaking or writing'.

styli plural of STYLUS.

stylish ● adjective **1** having or displaying a good sense of style. **2** fashionably elegant.
– DERIVATIVES **stylishly** adverb **stylishness** noun.

stylist ● noun **1** a person who designs fashionable clothes or cuts hair. **2** a writer noted for their literary style.

stylistic ● adjective of or concerning style, especially literary style.
– DERIVATIVES **stylistically** adverb.

stylistics ● plural noun (treated as sing.) the study of the literary styles of particular genres or writers.

stylized (also **stylised**) ● adjective depicted or treated in a mannered and non-realistic style.
– DERIVATIVES **stylization** noun.

stylus /stīləs/ ● noun (pl. **styli** /stīlī/) **1** a hard point following a groove in a gramophone record and transmitting the recorded sound for reproduction. **2** an ancient writing implement for scratching letters on wax-covered tablets.
– ORIGIN an erroneous spelling of Latin *stilus* (see STYLE).

stymie /stīmi/ ● verb (**stymies**, **stymied**, **stymying** or **stymieing**) informal prevent or hinder the progress of.
– ORIGIN originally a golfing term, denoting a situation on the green where a ball obstructs the shot of another player; of unknown origin.

styptic /stiptik/ Medicine ● adjective capable of causing bleeding to stop. ● noun a styptic substance.
– ORIGIN Greek *stuptikos*, from *stuphein* 'to contract'.

styrene /stīreen/ ● noun Chemistry an unsaturated liquid hydrocarbon obtained as a petroleum by-product and used to make plastics and resins.
– ORIGIN from *styrax*, a gum resin.

styrofoam ● noun (trademark in the US) a kind of expanded polystyrene, used especially for making food containers.
– ORIGIN from POLYSTYRENE + FOAM.

suasion /swayzh'n/ ● noun formal persuasion as opposed to force or compulsion.
– ORIGIN Latin, from *suadere* 'to urge'.

suave /swaav/ ● adjective (**suaver**, **suavest**) (of a man) charming, confident, and elegant.
– DERIVATIVES **suavely** adverb **suaveness** noun **suavity** noun.
– ORIGIN Latin *suavis* 'agreeable'.

Thesaurus

stupendous ● adjective **1** *stupendous achievements* AMAZING, astounding, astonishing, extraordinary, remarkable, phenomenal, staggering, breathtaking; *informal* fantastic, mind-boggling, awesome; *poetic/literary* wondrous. **2** *a building of stupendous size* COLOSSAL, immense, vast, gigantic, massive, mammoth, huge, enormous.
– OPPOSITES ordinary.

stupid ● adjective **1** *they're rather stupid* UNINTELLIGENT, ignorant, dense, foolish, dull-witted, slow, simple-minded, vacuous, vapid, idiotic, imbecilic, imbecile, obtuse, doltish; *informal* thick (as two short planks), dim, dumb, dopey, dozy, moronic, cretinous, pea-brained, half-witted, soft in the head, boneheaded, thickheaded, wooden-headed, muttonheaded; *Brit. informal* barmy, daft, not the full shilling. **2** *a stupid mistake* FOOLISH, silly, unintelligent, idiotic, scatterbrained, nonsensical, senseless, unthinking, ill-advised, ill-considered, unwise, injudicious; inane, absurd, ludicrous, ridiculous, laughable, risible, fatuous, asinine, mad, insane, lunatic; *informal* crazy, dopey, cracked, half-baked, cock-eyed, hare-brained, nutty, dotty, batty, gormless, cuckoo, loony, loopy, off one's head, off one's trolley; *Brit. informal* potty. **3** *he drank himself stupid* INTO A STUPOR, into a daze, into oblivion; stupefied, dazed, unconscious.
– OPPOSITES intelligent, sensible.

stupidity ● noun **1** *he cursed their stupidity* LACK OF INTELLIGENCE, foolishness, denseness, brainlessness, ignorance, dull-wittedness, slow-wittedness, doltishness, slowness; *informal* thickness, dimness, dopiness, doziness. **2** *she blushed at her stupidity* FOOLISHNESS, folly, silliness, idiocy, brainlessness, senselessness, injudiciousness, ineptitude, inaneness, inanity, absurdity, ludicrousness, ridiculousness, fatuousness, madness, insanity, lunacy; *informal* craziness; *Brit. informal* daftness.

stupor ● noun DAZE, state of unconsciousness, torpor, insensibility, oblivion.

sturdy ● adjective **1** *a sturdy lad* STRAPPING, well built, muscular, athletic, strong, hefty, brawny, powerful, solid, burly, rugged, robust, tough, hardy, lusty; *informal* husky, beefy, meaty; *dated* stalwart; *poetic/literary* thewy, stark. **2** *sturdy boots* ROBUST, strong, strongly made, well built, solid, stout, tough, resilient, durable, long-lasting, hard-wearing. **3** *sturdy resistance* VIGOROUS, strong, stalwart, firm, determined, resolute, staunch, steadfast.
– OPPOSITES weak.

stutter ● verb *he stuttered over a word* STAMMER, stumble, falter.
● noun *a bad stutter* STAMMER, speech impediment, speech defect.

Stygian ● adjective (*poetic/literary*). See DARK adjective sense 1.

style ● noun **1** *differing styles of management* MANNER, way, technique, method, methodology, approach, system, mode, form, modus operandi; *informal* MO. **2** *a non-directive style of counselling* TYPE, kind, variety, sort, genre, school, brand, pattern, model. **3** *wearing clothes with style* FLAIR, stylishness, elegance, grace, gracefulness, poise, polish, suaveness, sophistication, urbanity, chic, dash, panache, elan; *informal* class, pizzazz. **4** *Laura travelled in style* COMFORT, luxury, elegance, opulence, lavishness. **5** *modern styles* FASHION, trend, vogue, mode.
● verb **1** *sportswear styled by Karl* DESIGN, fashion, tailor. **2** *men who were styled 'knight'* CALL, name, title, entitle, dub, designate, term, label, tag, nickname; *formal* denominate.

stylish ● adjective FASHIONABLE, modish, voguish, modern, up to date; smart, sophisticated, elegant, chic, dapper, dashing; *informal* trendy, natty, classy, nifty, ritzy, snazzy; *N. Amer. informal* fly, kicky, tony, spiffy.

sub informal ● noun **1** a submarine. **2** a subscription. **3** a substitute, especially in a sporting team. **4** a subeditor. **5** Brit. an advance or loan against expected income. ● verb (**subbed**, **subbing**) **1** act as a substitute. **2** Brit. lend or advance a sum to. **3** subedit.

sub- (also **suc-** before *c*; **suf-** before *f*; **sug-** before *g*; **sup-** before *p*; **sur-** before *r*; **sus-** before *c, p, t*) ● prefix **1** at, to, or from a lower level or position: *subalpine*. **2** lower in rank or importance: *subdeacon*. **3** somewhat; nearly: *subantarctic*. **4** denoting subsequent or secondary action of the same kind: *subdivision*. **5** denoting support: *subsidy*.
– ORIGIN from Latin *sub* 'under, close to'.

subacute ● adjective Medicine between acute and chronic.

subadult ● noun Zoology an animal that is not fully adult.

subalpine ● adjective of or situated on the higher slopes of mountains just below the treeline.

subaltern /subbəltərn/ ● noun an officer in the British army below the rank of captain, especially a second lieutenant. ● adjective of lower status.
– ORIGIN from Latin *sub-* 'next below' + *alternus* 'every other'.

subantarctic ● adjective relating to the region immediately north of the Antarctic Circle.

sub-aqua ● adjective relating to swimming or exploring under water, especially with an aqualung.

subaqueous ● adjective existing, formed, or taking place under water.

subarctic ● adjective relating to the region immediately south of the Arctic Circle.

sub-assembly ● noun (pl. **sub-assemblies**) a unit assembled separately but designed to be incorporated with other units into a larger manufactured product.

subatomic ● adjective smaller than or occurring within an atom.

subcategory ● noun (pl. **subcategories**) a secondary or subordinate category.

sub-clause ● noun chiefly Law a subsidiary section of a clause of a bill, contract, or treaty.

subconscious ● adjective of or concerning the part of the mind of which one is not fully aware but which influences one's actions and feelings. ● noun (**one's/the subconscious**) this part of the mind.
– DERIVATIVES **subconsciously** adverb **subconsciousness** noun.

subcontinent ● noun a large distinguishable part of a continent, such as North America or southern Africa.
– DERIVATIVES **subcontinental** adjective.

subcontract ● verb /subkəntrakt/ **1** employ a firm or person outside one's company to do (work). **2** work as a subcontractor. ● noun /sub**kon**trakt/ a contract to do work for another company as part of a larger project.

subcontractor ● noun a firm or person that carries out work for a company as part of a larger project.

subcostal ● adjective Anatomy beneath a rib; below the ribs.

subculture ● noun a cultural group within a larger culture, often having beliefs or interests at variance with those of the larger culture.
– DERIVATIVES **subcultural** adjective.

subcutaneous ● adjective Anatomy & Medicine situated or applied under the skin.
– DERIVATIVES **subcutaneously** adverb.

subdeacon ● noun (in some Christian Churches) a minister of an order ranking below deacon.

subdivide ● verb divide (something that has already been divided or that is a separate unit).

subdivision ● noun **1** the action of subdividing or the state of being subdivided. **2** a secondary or subordinate division. **3** N. Amer. & Austral./NZ an area of land divided into plots for sale.

subduction ● noun Geology the sideways and downward movement of the edge of a plate of the earth's crust into the mantle beneath another plate.
– DERIVATIVES **subduct** verb.
– ORIGIN Latin, from *subducere* 'draw from below'.

subdue ● verb (**subdues**, **subdued**, **subduing**) **1** overcome, quieten, or bring under control. **2** bring (a country) under control by force.
– ORIGIN Latin *subducere* 'draw from below'.

subdued ● adjective **1** quiet and rather reflective or depressed. **2** (of colour or lighting) soft; muted.

subedit ● verb (**subedited**, **subediting**) chiefly Brit. check and correct (newspaper or magazine text) before printing.
– DERIVATIVES **subeditor** noun.

subfloor ● noun the foundation for a floor in a building.

subframe ● noun a supporting frame.

subfusc /subfusk/ ● adjective literary dull or gloomy. ● noun Brit. the formal clothing worn for examinations and formal occasions at some universities.
– ORIGIN from Latin *sub-* 'somewhat' + *fuscus* 'dark brown'.

subgroup ● noun a subdivision of a group.

sub-heading (also **sub-head**) ● noun a heading given to a subsection of a piece of writing.

subhuman ● adjective **1** of a lower order of being than the human. **2** Zoology (of a primate) closely related to humans. **3** derogatory not worthy of a human being; debased or depraved. ● noun a subhuman creature or person.

subject ● noun /subjikt/ **1** a person or thing that is being discussed, studied, or dealt with. **2** a branch of knowledge studied or taught. **3** Grammar the word or words in a sentence that name who or what performs the action of the verb. **4** a member of a state owing allegiance to its monarch or supreme ruler. **5** Music a theme, leading phrase, or motif. **6** Philosophy a thinking or feeling entity; the conscious mind or ego. ● adjective /subjikt/ (**subject to**) **1** likely or prone to be affected by (something bad). **2** dependent or conditional upon. **3** under the control or authority of. ● adverb /subjikt/ (**subject to**) conditionally upon. ● verb /səbjekt/ (usu. **subject to**) **1** cause to undergo. **2** bring under one's control or jurisdiction.
– DERIVATIVES **subjection** noun.
– ORIGIN from Latin *subicere* 'bring under'.

subjective ● adjective **1** based on or influenced by personal feelings, tastes, or opinions. **2** dependent on the mind for existence. **3** Grammar relating to or denoting a case of nouns and pronouns used for the subject of a sentence.
– DERIVATIVES **subjectively** adverb **subjectivity** noun.

S

Thesaurus

– OPPOSITES unfashionable.

stymie ● verb *(informal)*. See HAMPER².

suave ● adjective CHARMING, sophisticated, debonair, urbane, polished, refined, poised, self-possessed, dignified, civilized, gentlemanly, gallant; smooth, polite, well mannered, civil, courteous, affable, tactful, diplomatic.
– OPPOSITES unsophisticated.

suavity ● noun CHARM, sophistication, polish, urbanity, suaveness, refinement, poise; politeness, courtesy, courteousness, civility, tact.

subconscious ● adjective *subconscious desires* UNCONSCIOUS, latent, suppressed, repressed, subliminal, dormant, underlying, innermost; informal bottled up.
● noun *the creative powers of the subconscious* (UNCONSCIOUS) MIND, imagination, inner(most) self, psyche.

subdue ● verb **1** *he subdued all his enemies* CONQUER, defeat, vanquish, overcome, overwhelm, crush, quash, beat, trounce, subjugate, suppress, bring someone to their knees; informal lick, thrash, hammer. **2** *she could not subdue her longing* CURB, restrain, hold back, constrain, contain, repress, suppress, stifle, smother, keep in check, rein in, control, master, quell; informal keep a/the lid on.

subdued ● adjective **1** *Lewis's subdued air* SOMBRE, low-spirited, downcast, sad, dejected, depressed, gloomy, despondent, dispirited, disheartened, forlorn, woebegone; withdrawn, preoccupied; informal down in the mouth, down in the dumps, in the doldrums. **2** *subdued voices* HUSHED, muted, quiet, low, soft, faint, muffled, indistinct. **3** *subdued light* DIM, muted, softened, soft, lowered, subtle.
– OPPOSITES cheerful, bright.

subject ● noun **1** *the subject of this chapter* THEME, subject matter, topic, issue, question, concern, point; substance, essence, gist. **2** *popular university subjects* BRANCH OF STUDY, discipline, field. **3** *six subjects did the trials* PARTICIPANT, volunteer; informal guinea pig. **4** *British subjects* CITIZEN, national; taxpayer, voter. **5** *a loyal subject* LIEGE, liegeman, vassal, henchman, follower.
● verb *they were subjected to violence* PUT THROUGH, treat with, expose to.
– PHRASES **subject to 1** *it is subject to budgetary approval* CONDITIONAL ON, contingent on, dependent on. **2** *horses are subject to coughs* SUSCEPTIBLE TO, liable to, prone to, vulnerable to, predisposed to, at risk of; archaic susceptive of. **3** *we are all subject to the law* BOUND BY, constrained by, accountable to.

subjectivism • noun Philosophy the doctrine that knowledge is merely subjective and that there is no external or objective truth.
– DERIVATIVES **subjectivist** noun & adjective.

subject matter • noun the topic dealt with or the subject represented in a debate, exposition, or work of art.

sub judice /sub jo͞odisi/ • adjective Law under judicial consideration and therefore prohibited from public discussion elsewhere.
– ORIGIN Latin, 'under a judge'.

subjugate /subjoogayt/ • verb bring under domination or control, especially by conquest.
– DERIVATIVES **subjugation** noun.
– ORIGIN Latin *subjugare* 'bring under a yoke', from *jugum* 'yoke'.

subjunctive /subjungktiv/ Grammar • adjective (of a form of a verb) expressing what is imagined or wished or possible. • noun a verb in the subjunctive mood.
– ORIGIN Latin *subjunctivus*, from *subjungere* 'add to, join in addition'.

sublet • verb /sublet/ (**subletting**; past and past part. **sublet**) lease (a property) to a subtenant. • noun /**sub**let/ a lease of a property by a tenant to a subtenant.

sub lieutenant • noun a rank of officer in the Royal Navy, above midshipman and below lieutenant.

sublimate /sublimayt/ • verb **1** (in psychoanalytic theory) divert or modify (an instinctual impulse) into a culturally higher or socially more acceptable activity. **2** transform into a purer or idealized form. **3** Chemistry another term for SUBLIME. • noun /also sublimət/ Chemistry a solid deposit of a substance which has sublimed.
– DERIVATIVES **sublimation** noun.
– ORIGIN Latin *sublimare* 'raise up'.

sublime • adjective (**sublimer**, **sublimest**) **1** of such excellence, grandeur, or beauty as to inspire great admiration or awe. **2** extreme or unparalleled: *sublime confidence.* • verb Chemistry (with reference to a solid substance) change directly into vapour when heated, typically forming a solid deposit again on cooling.
– DERIVATIVES **sublimely** adverb **sublimity** noun.
– ORIGIN Latin *sublimis*, from *sub-* 'up to' + a second element perhaps related to *limen* 'threshold' or *limus* 'oblique'.

subliminal /səblimmin'l/ • adjective Psychology (of a stimulus or mental process) perceived by or affecting someone's mind without their being aware of it.
– DERIVATIVES **subliminally** adverb.
– ORIGIN from SUB- + Latin *limen* 'threshold'.

sublunary • adjective literary belonging to this world rather than a better or more spiritual one.
– ORIGIN from Latin *sublunaris*, from *luna* 'moon'.

sub-machine gun • noun a hand-held lightweight machine gun.

submarine • noun a streamlined warship designed to operate completely submerged in the sea for long periods. • adjective existing, occurring, done, or used under the surface of the sea.
– DERIVATIVES **submariner** noun.

submerge • verb **1** cause to be under water. **2** descend below the surface of water. **3** completely cover or obscure.
– DERIVATIVES **submergence** noun.
– ORIGIN Latin *submergere*, from *mergere* 'to dip'.

submerse • verb technical submerge.

submersible • adjective designed to operate while submerged. • noun a small boat or craft that is submersible.

submersion • noun the action of submerging or the state of being submerged.

submicroscopic • adjective too small to be seen by an ordinary light microscope.

submission • noun **1** the action or fact of submitting. **2** a proposal or application submitted for consideration.

submissive • adjective meekly obedient or passive.
– DERIVATIVES **submissively** adverb **submissiveness** noun.

submit • verb (**submitted**, **submitting**) **1** accept or yield to a superior force or stronger person. **2** subject to a particular process, treatment, or condition. **3** present (a proposal or application) for consideration or judgement. **4** (especially in judicial contexts) suggest; argue.
– ORIGIN Latin *submittere*, from *mittere* 'send, put'.

submodifier • noun Grammar an adverb used in front of an adjective or another adverb to modify its meaning, e.g. *very* in *very cold*.

subnormal • adjective not reaching a level regarded as usual, especially with respect to intelligence or development.
– DERIVATIVES **subnormality** noun.

suboptimal • adjective technical of less than the highest standard or quality.

suborder • noun Biology a taxonomic category that ranks below order and above family.

subordinate • adjective /sə**bor**dinət/ **1** lower in rank or position. **2** of less or secondary importance. • noun /sə**bor**dinət/ a person under the authority or control of another. • verb /sə**bor**dinayt/ **1** treat or regard as subordinate. **2** make subservient or dependent.
– DERIVATIVES **subordinately** adverb **subordination** noun.
– ORIGIN Latin *subordinatus* 'placed in an inferior rank'.

subordinate clause • noun a clause that forms part of and is dependent on a main clause (e.g. 'when it rang' in 'she answered the phone when it rang').

Thesaurus

subjection • noun SUBJUGATION, domination, oppression, mastery, repression, suppression.

subjective • adjective PERSONAL, individual, emotional, instinctive, intuitive.
– OPPOSITES objective.

subjugate • verb CONQUER, vanquish, defeat, crush, quash, bring someone to their knees, enslave, subdue, suppress.
– OPPOSITES liberate.

sublimate • verb CHANNEL, control, divert, transfer, redirect, convert.

sublime • adjective **1** *sublime music* EXALTED, elevated, noble, lofty, awe-inspiring, majestic, magnificent, glorious, superb, wonderful, marvellous, splendid; *informal* fantastic, fabulous, terrific, heavenly, divine, out of this world. **2** *the sublime confidence of youth* SUPREME, total, complete, utter, consummate.

subliminal • adjective SUBCONSCIOUS; hidden, concealed.
– OPPOSITES explicit.

submerge • verb **1** *the U-boat submerged* GO UNDER WATER, dive, sink. **2** *submerge the bowl in water* IMMERSE, plunge, sink. **3** *the farmland was submerged* FLOOD, inundate, deluge, swamp. **4** *she was submerged in work* OVERWHELM, inundate, deluge, swamp, bury, engulf, snow under.
– OPPOSITES surface.

submission • noun **1** *submission to authority* YIELDING, capitulation, acceptance, consent, compliance. **2** *Tim raised his hands in submission* SURRENDER, capitulation, resignation, defeat. **3** *he wanted her total submission* COMPLIANCE, submissiveness, acquiescence, passivity, obedience, docility, deference, subservience, servility, subjection. **4** *a report for submission to the Board* PRESENTATION, presenting, proffering, tendering, proposal, proposing. **5** *his original submission* PROPOSAL, suggestion, proposition, recommendation. **6** *the judge rejected his submission* ARGUMENT, assertion, contention, statement, claim, allegation.
– OPPOSITES defiance, resistance.

submissive • adjective COMPLIANT, yielding, acquiescent, unassertive, passive, obedient, biddable, dutiful, docile, pliant; *informal* under someone's thumb.

submit • verb **1** *she submitted under duress* GIVE IN/WAY, yield, back down, cave in, capitulate; surrender, knuckle under. **2** *he refused to submit to their authority* BE GOVERNED BY, abide by, be regulated by, comply with, accept, adhere to, be subject to, agree to, consent to, conform to. **3** *we submitted an unopposed bid* PUT FORWARD, present, offer, proffer, tender, propose, suggest; put in, send in, register. **4** *they submitted that the judgement was inappropriate* CONTEND, assert, argue, state, claim, posit, postulate.
– OPPOSITES resist, withdraw.

subnormal • adjective **1** *subnormal trade activity* BELOW AVERAGE, below normal, low, poor. **2** (*dated*) *subnormal children* HAVING LEARNING DIFFICULTIES, having special (educational) needs, of low intelligence, backward; *dated* ESN.

subordinate • adjective **1** *subordinate staff* LOWER-RANKING, junior, lower, supporting. **2** *a subordinate rule* SECONDARY, lesser, minor, subsidiary, subservient, ancillary, auxiliary, peripheral, marginal; supplementary, accessory.
– OPPOSITES senior.
• noun *the manager and his subordinates* JUNIOR, assistant, second (in command), number two, right-hand man/woman, deputy, aide, underling, minion; *informal* sidekick.

suborn /səborn/ ● **verb** bribe or otherwise induce (someone) to commit an unlawful act such as perjury.
– ORIGIN Latin *subornare* 'incite secretly'.
sub-plot ● **noun** a subordinate plot in a play, novel, etc.
subpoena /səpeenə/ Law ● **noun** a writ ordering a person to attend a court. ● **verb** (**subpoenas**, **subpoenaed** or **subpoena'd**, **subpoenaing**) summon with a subpoena.
– ORIGIN from Latin *sub poena* 'under penalty' (the first words of the writ).
sub-post office ● **noun** (in the UK) a small local post office offering fewer services than a main post office.
sub rosa /sub rōzə/ ● **adjective & adverb** formal happening or done in secret.
– ORIGIN Latin, 'under the rose' (the rose being an emblem of secrecy).
subroutine ● **noun** Computing a set of instructions designed to perform a frequently used operation within a program.
sub-Saharan ● **adjective** from or forming part of the African regions south of the Sahara desert.
subscribe ● **verb** **1** (often **subscribe to**) arrange to receive something, especially a periodical regularly by paying in advance. **2** (**subscribe to**) contribute (a sum of money) to a project or cause. **3** apply to participate in. **4** (**subscribe to**) express agreement with (an idea or proposal).
– DERIVATIVES **subscriber** noun.
– ORIGIN Latin *subscribere* 'write below'.
subscriber trunk dialling ● **noun** Brit. the automatic connection of trunk calls by dialling without the assistance of an operator.
subscript ● **adjective** (of a letter, figure, or symbol) written or printed below the line. ● **noun** a subscript letter, figure, or symbol.
subscription ● **noun** **1** the action or fact of subscribing. **2** a payment to subscribe to something. **3** formal a signature or short piece of writing at the end of a document.
subsection ● **noun** a division of a section.
subsequent ● **adjective** coming after something in time.
– DERIVATIVES **subsequently** adverb.
– ORIGIN from Latin *subsequi* 'follow after'.
subserve ● **verb** formal help to further or promote.
subservient ● **adjective** **1** prepared to obey others unquestioningly; obsequious. **2** less important; subordinate.
– DERIVATIVES **subservience** noun.
subset ● **noun** **1** a part of a larger group of related things. **2** Mathematics a set of which all the elements are contained in another set.
subside ● **verb** **1** become less intense, violent, or severe. **2** (of water) go down to a lower or the normal level. **3** (of a building) sink lower into the ground. **4** (of the ground) cave in; sink. **5** (**subside into**) give way to (an overwhelming feeling).
– ORIGIN Latin *subsidere*, from *sidere* 'settle'.
subsidence /səbsīd'nss, subsid'nss/ ● **noun** the gradual caving in or sinking of an area of land.
subsidiarity /səbsiddiarriti/ ● **noun** (in politics) the principle that a central authority should perform only those tasks which cannot be performed at a more local level.
subsidiary ● **adjective** **1** less important than but related or supplementary to. **2** (of a company) controlled by a holding or parent company. ● **noun** (pl. **subsidiaries**) a subsidiary company.
– ORIGIN Latin *subsidiarius*, from *subsidium* 'assistance'.
subsidize (also **subsidise**) ● **verb** **1** support (an organization or activity) financially. **2** pay part of the cost of producing (something) to reduce its price.
– DERIVATIVES **subsidization** noun.
subsidy ● **noun** (pl. **subsidies**) **1** a sum of money granted from public funds to help an industry or business keep the price of a commodity or service low. **2** a sum of money granted to support an undertaking held to be in the public interest. **3** a grant or contribution of money. **4** historical a parliamentary grant to the sovereign for state needs.
– ORIGIN Latin *subsidium* 'assistance'.
subsist ● **verb** **1** maintain or support oneself, especially at a minimal level. **2** chiefly Law remain in being, force, or effect. **3** (**subsist in**) be attributable to.
– ORIGIN Latin *subsistere* 'stand firm'.
subsistence ● **noun** **1** the action or fact of subsisting. **2** the means of doing this. **3** (before another noun) referring to production at a level sufficient only for one's own use, without any surplus for trade: *subsistence agriculture.*
subsistence level (also **subsistence wage**) ● **noun** a standard of living (or wage) that provides only the bare necessities of life.
subsoil ● **noun** the soil lying immediately under the surface soil.
subsonic ● **adjective** relating to or flying at a speed or speeds less than that of sound.
subspace ● **noun** **1** Mathematics a space that is wholly contained in another space. **2** (in science fiction) a hypothetical space–time continuum used for communication at a speed faster than that of light.
subspecies ● **noun** (pl. same) Biology a subdivision of a species, usually a geographically isolated variety.
substance ● **noun** **1** a particular kind of matter with uniform properties. **2** the real physical matter of which a person or

Thesaurus

– OPPOSITES superior.
subordination ● **noun** INFERIORITY, subjection, subservience, submission, servitude.
sub rosa ● **adverb** *(formal)* IN SECRET, secretly, in private, privately, behind closed doors, in camera.
– OPPOSITES openly.
subscribe ● **verb** **1** *we subscribe to 'Punch'* PAY A SUBSCRIPTION, take, buy regularly. **2** *millions subscribe to the NSPCC* DONATE, make a donation, make a subscription, give (money), contribute towards. **3** *I can't subscribe to that theory* AGREE WITH, accept, believe in, endorse, back, support, champion; *formal* accede to. **4** *(formal) he subscribed the document* SIGN, countersign, initial, autograph, witness.
subscriber ● **noun** (REGULAR) READER, member, patron, supporter, backer, contributor.
subscription ● **noun** **1** *the club's subscription* MEMBERSHIP FEE, dues, annual payment, charge. **2** *we put your subscription to good use* DONATION, contribution, gift, grant; *formal* benefaction. **3** *their subscription to capitalism* AGREEMENT, belief, endorsement, backing, support. **4** *(formal) the subscription was witnessed* SIGNATURE, initials; addition, appendage.
subsequent ● **adjective** *the subsequent months* FOLLOWING, ensuing, succeeding, later, future, coming, to come, next.
– OPPOSITES previous.
– PHRASES **subsequent to** FOLLOWING, after, at the close/end of.
subsequently ● **adverb** LATER (ON), at a later date, afterwards, in due course, following this/that, eventually; *informal* after a bit; *formal* thereafter.
subservient ● **adjective** **1** *subservient women* SUBMISSIVE, deferential, compliant, obedient, dutiful, biddable, docile, passive, unassertive, subdued, downtrodden; *informal* under someone's thumb. **2** *individual rights are subservient to the interests of the state* SUBORDINATE, secondary, subsidiary, peripheral, ancillary, auxiliary, less important.
– OPPOSITES independent.
subside ● **verb** **1** *wait until the storm subsides* ABATE, let up, quieten down, calm, slacken (off), ease (up), relent, die down, recede, lessen, soften, diminish, decline, dwindle, weaken, fade, wane, ebb; *archaic* remit. **2** *the flood has subsided* RECEDE, ebb, fall, go down, get lower, abate. **3** *the volcano is gradually subsiding* SINK, settle, cave in, collapse, crumple, give way. **4** *Sarah subsided into a chair* SLUMP, flop, sink, collapse; *informal* flump, plonk oneself.
– OPPOSITES intensify, rise.
subsidiary ● **adjective** *a subsidiary company* SUBORDINATE, secondary, ancillary, auxiliary, subservient, supplementary, peripheral.
– OPPOSITES principal.
● **noun** *two major subsidiaries* SUBORDINATE COMPANY, branch, division, subdivision, derivative, offshoot.
subsidize ● **verb** GIVE MONEY TO, pay a subsidy to, contribute to, invest in, sponsor, support, fund, finance, underwrite; *informal* shell out for, fork out for, cough up for; *N. Amer. informal* bankroll.
subsidy ● **noun** GRANT, allowance, endowment, contribution, donation, bursary, handout; backing, support, sponsorship, finance, funding; *formal* benefaction.
subsist ● **verb** **1** *he subsists on his pension* SURVIVE, live, stay alive, exist, eke out an existence; support oneself, manage, get along/by, make (both) ends meet. **2** *the tenant's rights of occupation subsist* CONTINUE, last, persist, endure, prevail, carry on, remain.
subsistence ● **noun** **1** *they depend on fish for subsistence* SURVIVAL, existence, living, life, sustenance, nourishment. **2** *the money*

thing consists. **3** solid basis in reality or fact: *the claim has no substance.* **4** the quality of being important, valid, or significant. **5** the most important or essential part or meaning. **6** the subject matter of a text or work of art. **7** an intoxicating or narcotic drug.
– PHRASES **in substance** essentially.
– ORIGIN Latin *substantia* 'being, essence', from *substare* 'stand firm'.

substandard ● adjective below the usual or required standard.

substantial ● adjective **1** of considerable importance, size, or worth. **2** strongly built or made. **3** concerning the essentials of something. **4** real and tangible rather than imaginary.
– DERIVATIVES **substantiality** noun.

substantially ● adverb **1** to a great or significant extent. **2** for the most part; essentially.

substantiate /səbstanshiayt/ ● verb provide evidence to support or prove the truth of.
– DERIVATIVES **substantiation** noun.
– ORIGIN Latin *substantiare* 'give substance'.

substantive /substəntiv/ ● adjective /also səbstantiv/ **1** having a firm basis in reality and so important or meaningful. **2** having a separate and independent existence. **3** (of law) defining rights and duties as opposed to giving the rules by which such things are established. ● noun Grammar, dated a noun.
– DERIVATIVES **substantively** adverb.

substation ● noun **1** a set of equipment reducing the high voltage of electrical power transmission to that suitable for supply to consumers. **2** a subordinate police station or fire station.

substituent /səbstityooənt/ ● noun Chemistry an atom or group of atoms taking the place of another or occupying a specified position in a molecule.

substitute ● noun **1** a person or thing acting or serving in place of another. **2** a sports player eligible to replace another after a match has begun. ● verb **1** use, add, or serve in place of. **2** replace with another. **3** replace (a sports player) with a substitute during a match.
– DERIVATIVES **substitutable** adjective **substitution** noun **substitutive** adjective.
– USAGE Traditionally, **substitute** is followed by **for** and means 'put (someone or something) in place of another', as in *she substituted the fake vase for the real one.* It may also be used with **with** or **by** to mean 'replace (something) with something else', as in *she substituted the real vase with the fake one.* This can be confusing, since the two sentences shown above mean the same thing, yet the object of the verb and the object of the preposition have swapped positions. Despite the potential confusion, the second, newer use is acceptable, although still disapproved of by some people.
– ORIGIN Latin *substituere* 'put in place of'.

substrate /substrayt/ ● noun **1** the surface or material on which an organism lives, grows, or feeds. **2** the substance on which an enzyme acts.
– ORIGIN anglicized form of SUBSTRATUM.

substratum ● noun (pl. **substrata**) **1** an underlying layer or substance, in particular a layer of rock or soil beneath the surface of the ground. **2** a foundation or basis.

substructure ● noun an underlying or supporting structure.

subsume ● verb include or absorb in something else.
– DERIVATIVES **subsumable** adjective.
– ORIGIN Latin *subsumere*, from *sumere* 'take'.

subtenant ● noun a person who leases property from a tenant.

subtend ● verb (of a line, arc, etc.) form (an angle) at a particular point when straight lines from its extremities meet.
– ORIGIN Latin *subtendere*, from *tendere* 'stretch'.

subterfuge /subtərfyooj/ ● noun a trick or deception used in order to achieve one's goal.
– ORIGIN from Latin *subterfugere* 'escape secretly'.

subterranean /subtəraynian/ ● adjective existing or occurring under the earth's surface.
– ORIGIN Latin *subterraneus*, from *terra* 'earth'.

subtext ● noun an underlying theme in a piece of writing or speech.

subtitle ● noun **1** (**subtitles**) captions displayed at the bottom of a cinema or television screen that translate or transcribe the dialogue or narrative. **2** a subordinate title of a published work. ● verb provide with a subtitle or subtitles.

subtle ● adjective (**subtler**, **subtlest**) **1** so delicate or precise as to be difficult to analyse or describe. **2** capable of making fine distinctions. **3** delicately complex and understated: *subtle lighting.* **4** making use of clever and indirect methods to achieve something.
– DERIVATIVES **subtlety** noun **subtly** adverb.
– ORIGIN Latin *subtilis*.

subtotal ● noun the total of one set of a larger group of figures

Thesaurus

needed for his subsistence MAINTENANCE, keep, upkeep, livelihood, board (and lodging), nourishment, food.

substance ● noun **1** *an organic substance* MATERIAL, matter, stuff. **2** *ghostly figures with no substance* SOLIDITY, body, corporeality; density, mass, weight, shape, structure. **3** *none of the objections has any substance* MEANINGFULNESS, significance, importance, import, validity, foundation; *formal* moment. **4** *the substance of the tale is very thin* CONTENT, subject matter, theme, message, essence. **5** *Rangers are a team of substance* CHARACTER, backbone, mettle. **6** *independent men of substance* WEALTH, fortune, riches, affluence, prosperity, money, means.

substandard ● adjective INFERIOR, second-rate, low-quality, poor, below par, imperfect, faulty, defective, shoddy, shabby, unsound, unsatisfactory; *informal* tenth-rate, crummy, lousy; *Brit. informal* duff, ropy, rubbish, chronic.

substantial ● adjective **1** *substantial beings* REAL, true, actual; physical, solid, material, concrete, corporeal. **2** *substantial progress had been made* CONSIDERABLE, real, significant, important, notable, major, valuable, useful. **3** *substantial damages* SIZEABLE, considerable, significant, large, ample, appreciable, goodly. **4** *substantial Victorian villas* STURDY, solid, stout, strong, well built, durable, long-lasting, hard-wearing. **5** *substantial country gentlemen* HEFTY, stout, sturdy, large, solid, bulky, burly, well built, portly. **6** *substantial City companies* SUCCESSFUL, profitable, prosperous, wealthy, affluent, moneyed, well-to-do, rich; *informal* loaded, stinking rich. **7** *substantial agreement* FUNDAMENTAL, essential, basic.

substantially ● adverb **1** *the cost has fallen substantially* CONSIDERABLY, significantly, greatly, to a great/large extent, markedly, appreciably. **2** *the draft was substantially accepted* LARGELY, for the most part, by and large, on the whole, in the main, mainly, in essence, basically, fundamentally, to all intents and purposes.
– OPPOSITES slightly.

substantiate ● verb PROVE, show to be true, give substance to, support, uphold, bear out, justify, vindicate, validate, corroborate, verify, authenticate, confirm, endorse, give credence to.
– OPPOSITES disprove.

substitute ● noun *substitutes for permanent employees* REPLACEMENT, deputy, relief, proxy, reserve, surrogate, cover, stand-in, locum (tenens), understudy; *informal* sub.
● adjective *a substitute teacher* ACTING, replacement, deputy, relief, reserve, surrogate, stand-in, temporary, caretaker, interim, provisional.
– OPPOSITES permanent.
● verb **1** *curd cheese can be substituted for yogurt* EXCHANGE, replace with, use instead of, use as an alternative to, use in place of, swap. **2** *the Senate was empowered to substitute for the President* DEPUTIZE, act as deputy, act as a substitute, stand in, cover; replace, relieve, take over from; *informal* fill someone's boots/shoes, sub.

substitution ● noun EXCHANGE, change; replacement, replacing, swapping, switching.

subterfuge ● noun **1** *the use of subterfuge by journalists* TRICKERY, intrigue, deviousness, deceit, deception, dishonesty, cheating, duplicity, guile, cunning, craftiness, chicanery, pretence, fraud, fraudulence. **2** *a disreputable subterfuge* TRICK, hoax, ruse, wile, ploy, stratagem, artifice, dodge, bluff, pretence, deception, fraud, blind, smokescreen; *informal* con, scam.

subtle ● adjective **1** *subtle colours* UNDERSTATED, muted, subdued; delicate, faint, pale, soft, indistinct. **2** *subtle distinctions* FINE, fine-drawn, nice, overnice, hair-splitting. **3** *a subtle mind* ASTUTE, keen, quick, fine, acute, sharp, shrewd, perceptive, discerning, discriminating, penetrating, sagacious, wise, clever, intelligent. **4** *a subtle plan* INGENIOUS, clever, cunning, crafty, wily, artful, devious.

subtlety ● noun **1** *the subtlety of the flavour* DELICACY, delicateness, subtleness; understatedness, mutedness, softness. **2** *classification is fraught with subtlety* FINENESS, subtleness, niceness, nicety, nuance. **3** *the subtlety of the human mind* ASTUTENESS, keenness, acuteness, sharpness, canniness, shrewdness, perceptiveness, discernment, discrimination, percipience, perspicacity, wisdom,

to be added.
subtract ● verb take away (a number or amount) from another to calculate the difference.
– DERIVATIVES **subtraction** noun **subtractive** adjective.
– ORIGIN Latin *subtrahere* 'draw away'.
subtropics ● plural noun the regions adjacent to or bordering on the tropics.
– DERIVATIVES **subtropical** adjective.
subunit ● noun a distinct component of something.
suburb ● noun an outlying residential district of a city.
– DERIVATIVES **suburban** adjective **suburbanite** noun **suburbanize** (also **suburbanise**) verb.
– ORIGIN from Latin *sub-* 'near to' + *urbs* 'city'.
suburbia ● noun the suburbs viewed collectively.
subvention ● noun a grant of money, especially from a government.
– ORIGIN Latin, from *subvenire* 'assist'.
subversive ● adjective seeking or intended to subvert an established system or institution. ● noun a subversive person.
– DERIVATIVES **subversively** adverb **subversiveness** noun.
subvert ● verb undermine the power and authority of (an established system or institution).
– DERIVATIVES **subversion** noun **subverter** noun.
– ORIGIN Latin *subvertere*, from *vertere* 'to turn'.
subway ● noun **1** Brit. a tunnel under a road for use by pedestrians. **2** chiefly N. Amer. an underground railway.
subwoofer ● noun a loudspeaker component designed to reproduce very low bass frequencies.
sub-zero ● adjective (of temperature) lower than zero; below freezing.
suc- ● prefix variant spelling of SUB- before *c*.
succeed ● verb **1** achieve an aim or purpose. **2** attain fame, wealth, or social status. **3** take over an office, title, etc., from (someone). **4** become the new rightful holder of an office, title, etc. **5** come after and take the place of.
– ORIGIN Latin *succedere* 'come close after'.
succès d'estime /sōōksay desteem/ ● noun (pl. same) a success in terms of critical appreciation, as opposed to popularity or commercial gain.
– ORIGIN French, 'success of opinion'.
success ● noun **1** the accomplishment of an aim or purpose. **2** the attainment of fame, wealth, or social status. **3** a person or thing that achieves success.
– ORIGIN Latin *successus*, from *succedere* 'come close after'.
successful ● adjective **1** accomplishing an aim or purpose. **2** having achieved fame, wealth, or social status.
– DERIVATIVES **successfully** adverb.
succession ● noun **1** a number of people or things following one after the other. **2** the action, process, or right of inheriting an office, title, etc. **3** Ecology the process by which a plant community successively gives way to another until stability is reached.
– PHRASES **in quick succession** following one another at short intervals. **in succession** following one after the other without interruption.
– DERIVATIVES **successional** adjective.
successive ● adjective following one another or following others.
– DERIVATIVES **successively** adverb.
successor ● noun a person or thing that succeeds another.
success story ● noun informal a successful person or thing.
succinct /səksingkt/ ● adjective briefly and clearly expressed.
– DERIVATIVES **succinctly** adverb **succinctness** noun.
– ORIGIN from Latin *succingere* 'tuck up'.
succotash /sukkətash/ ● noun US a dish of maize and lima beans boiled together.
– ORIGIN Narragansett.
succour /sukkər/ (US **succor**) ● noun assistance and support in times of hardship and distress. ● verb give assistance to.
– ORIGIN Latin *succursus*, from *succurrere* 'run to the help of'.
succubus /sukyoobəss/ ● noun (pl. **succubi** /sukyoobī/) a female demon believed to have sexual intercourse with sleeping men.
– ORIGIN Latin, 'prostitute', from *sub-* 'under' + *cubare* 'to lie'.
succulent ● adjective **1** (of food) tender, juicy, and tasty. **2** Botany (of a plant) having thick fleshy leaves or stems adapted to storing water. ● noun Botany a succulent plant.
– DERIVATIVES **succulence** noun **succulently** adverb.
– ORIGIN Latin *succulentus*, from *succus* 'juice'.
succumb ● verb **1** fail to resist (pressure, temptation, etc.).

Thesaurus

cleverness, intelligence. **4** *the subtlety of their tactics* INGENUITY, cleverness, skilfulness, adroitness, cunning, guile, craftiness, wiliness, artfulness, deviousness.
subtract ● verb TAKE AWAY/OFF, deduct, debit, dock; *informal* knock off, minus.
– OPPOSITES add.
suburb ● noun RESIDENTIAL AREA, dormitory area, commuter belt; suburbia.
suburban ● adjective **1** *a suburban area* RESIDENTIAL, commuter, dormitory. **2** *her drab suburban existence* DULL, boring, uninteresting, conventional, ordinary, commonplace, unremarkable, unexceptional; provincial, unsophisticated, parochial, bourgeois, middle-class.

S

subversive ● adjective *subversive activities* DISRUPTIVE, troublemaking, inflammatory, insurrectionary; seditious, revolutionary, rebellious, rebel, renegade, dissident.
● noun *a dangerous subversive* TROUBLEMAKER, dissident, agitator, revolutionary, renegade, rebel.
subvert ● verb **1** *a plot to subvert the state* DESTABILIZE, unsettle, overthrow, overturn; bring down, topple, depose, oust; disrupt, wreak havoc on, sabotage, ruin, undermine, weaken, damage. **2** *attempts to subvert Soviet youth* CORRUPT, pervert, deprave, contaminate, poison, embitter.
subway ● noun **1** *he walked through the subway* UNDERPASS, (pedestrian) tunnel. **2** *Tokyo's subway* UNDERGROUND (RAILWAY), metro; *Brit. informal* tube.
succeed ● verb **1** *Darwin succeeded where others had failed* TRIUMPH, achieve success, be successful, do well, flourish, thrive; *informal* make it, make the grade, make a name for oneself. **2** *the plan succeeded* BE SUCCESSFUL, turn out well, work (out), be effective; *informal* come off, pay off. **3** *Rosebery succeeded Gladstone as Prime Minister* REPLACE, take the place of, take over from, follow, supersede; *informal* step into someone's shoes. **4** *he succeeded to the throne* INHERIT, assume, acquire, attain; *formal* accede to. **5** *embarrassment was succeeded by fear* FOLLOW, come after, follow after.
– OPPOSITES fail, precede.
succeeding ● adjective SUBSEQUENT, successive, following, ensuing, later, future, coming.
success ● noun **1** *the success of the scheme* FAVOURABLE OUTCOME, successfulness, successful result, triumph. **2** *the trappings of success* PROSPERITY, prosperousness, affluence, wealth, riches, opulence. **3** *a West End success* TRIUMPH, best-seller, box-office success, sell-out; *informal* (smash) hit, winner. **4** *an overnight success* STAR, superstar, celebrity, big name, household name; *informal* celeb, megastar.
– OPPOSITES failure.
successful ● adjective **1** *a successful campaign* VICTORIOUS, triumphant; fortunate, lucky. **2** *a successful designer* PROSPEROUS, affluent, wealthy, rich; doing well, famous, eminent, top; *informal* on the up and up. **3** *successful companies* FLOURISHING, thriving, booming, buoyant, doing well, profitable, moneymaking, lucrative; *informal* on the up and up.
succession ● noun **1** *a succession of exciting events* SEQUENCE, series, progression, chain, cycle, round, string, train, line, run, flow, stream. **2** *his succession to the throne* ACCESSION, elevation, assumption.
– PHRASES **in succession** ONE AFTER THE OTHER, in a row, consecutively, successively, in sequence; running; *informal* on the trot.
successive ● adjective CONSECUTIVE, in a row, straight, sequential, in succession, running; *informal* on the trot.
successor ● noun HEIR (APPARENT), inheritor, next-in-line.
– OPPOSITES predecessor.
succinct ● adjective CONCISE, short (and sweet), brief, compact, condensed, crisp, laconic, terse, to the point, pithy, epigrammatic, synoptic, gnomic; *formal* compendious.
– OPPOSITES verbose.
succour ● noun *providing succour in times of need* AID, help, a helping hand, assistance; comfort, ease, relief, support.
● verb *the prisoners were succoured* HELP, aid, bring aid to, give/render assistance to, assist, lend a (helping) hand to; minister to, care for, comfort, bring relief to, support, take care of, look after, attend to.
succulent ● adjective JUICY, moist, luscious, soft, tender; choice, mouth-watering, appetizing, flavoursome, tasty, delicious; *informal*

2 die from the effect of a disease or injury.
– ORIGIN Latin *succumbere*, from *sub-* 'under' + a verb related to *cubare* 'to lie'.

such ● determiner, predeterminer, & pronoun **1** of the type previously mentioned. **2** (**such —— as/that**) of the type about to be mentioned. **3** to so high a degree; so great.
– PHRASES **as such** in the exact sense of the word. **such-and-such** an unspecified person or thing. **such as 1** for example. **2** of a kind that; like. **such as it is** what little there is; for what it's worth. **such that** to the extent that.
– ORIGIN Old English, related to so[1] and ALIKE.

suchlike ● pronoun things of the type mentioned. ● determiner of the type mentioned.

suck ● verb **1** draw into the mouth by contracting the lip muscles to make a partial vacuum. **2** hold (something) in the mouth and draw at it by contracting the lip and cheek muscles. **3** draw in a specified direction by creating a vacuum. **4** (**suck in/into**) involve (someone) in something without their choosing. **5** (**suck up to**) informal attempt to gain advantage by behaving obsequiously towards. **6** N. Amer. informal be very bad or disagreeable. ● noun an act or sound of sucking. ● exclamation (**sucks**) Brit. informal used to express derision and defiance.
– PHRASES **give suck** archaic suckle. **suck someone dry** exhaust someone's physical, material, or emotional resources.
– ORIGIN Old English, related to SOAK.

sucker ● noun **1** a rubber cup that adheres to a surface by suction. **2** a flat or concave organ enabling an animal to cling to a surface by suction. **3** informal a gullible person. **4** (**a sucker for**) informal a person especially susceptible to or fond of (a specified thing). **5** a shoot springing from the base of a tree or other plant, especially one arising from the root at some distance from the trunk. ● verb **1** (of a plant) produce suckers. **2** N. Amer. informal fool or trick.

sucker punch ● noun an unexpected punch or blow. ● verb (**sucker-punch**) hit with a sucker punch.

suckle ● verb (with reference to a baby or young animal) feed from the breast or teat.
– DERIVATIVES **suckler** noun.

suckling ● noun an unweaned child or animal.

sucre /so͞okray/ ● noun the basic monetary unit of Ecuador, equal to 100 centavos.
– ORIGIN named after the Venezuelan revolutionary Antonio José de *Sucre* (1795–1830).

sucrose /so͞okrōz, syo͞o-/ ● noun Chemistry a compound which is the chief component of cane or beet sugar.
– ORIGIN from French *sucre* 'sugar'.

suction ● noun the production of a partial vacuum by the removal of air in order to force fluid into a vacant space or produce adhesion. ● verb remove using suction.
– ORIGIN Latin, from *sugere* 'suck'.

suction pump ● noun a pump for drawing liquid through a pipe into a chamber emptied by a piston.

Sudanese /so͞odəneez/ ● noun a person from the Sudan. ● adjective relating to the Sudan.

sudarium /so͞odairiəm, syoo-/ ● noun (pl. **sudaria** /so͞odairiə, syoo-/) (in the Roman Catholic Church) another term for VERONICA (in sense 2).
– ORIGIN Latin, 'napkin'.

sudden ● adjective occurring or done quickly and unexpectedly.
– PHRASES (**all**) **of a sudden** suddenly.
– DERIVATIVES **suddenness** noun.
– ORIGIN Old French *sudein*, from Latin *subitus*.

sudden death ● noun a means of deciding the winner in a tied match, in which play continues and the winner is the first side or player to score.

sudden infant death syndrome ● noun technical term for COT DEATH.

suddenly ● adverb quickly and unexpectedly.

sudorific /syo͞odəriffik, so͞o-/ Medicine ● adjective relating to or causing sweating. ● noun a sudorific drug.
– ORIGIN from Latin *sudor* 'sweat'.

Sudra /so͞odrə/ ● noun a member of the worker caste, lowest of the four Hindu castes.
– ORIGIN Sanskrit.

suds ● plural noun **1** froth made from soap and water. **2** N. Amer. informal beer. ● verb chiefly N. Amer. cover or wash in soapy water.
– DERIVATIVES **sudsy** adjective.
– ORIGIN perhaps originally denoting the flood water of the fens; probably related to SEETHE.

sue ● verb (**sues**, **sued**, **suing**) **1** institute legal proceedings against (a person or institution), typically for redress. **2** (**sue for**) formal appeal formally to a person for.
– ORIGIN Old French *suer*, from Latin *sequi* 'follow'.

suede ● noun leather, especially the skin of a young goat, with the flesh side rubbed to make a velvety nap.
– ORIGIN from French *gants de Suède* 'gloves of Sweden'.

suet ● noun the hard white fat on the kidneys and loins of cattle, sheep, and other animals, used in making puddings, pastry, etc.
– DERIVATIVES **suety** adjective.
– ORIGIN Old French, from Latin *sebum* 'tallow'.

suet pudding ● noun a boiled or steamed pudding of suet and flour.

suf- ● prefix variant spelling of SUB- before *f*.

suffer ● verb **1** experience or be subjected to (something bad or unpleasant). **2** (**suffer from**) be affected by or subject to (an illness or ailment). **3** become or appear worse in quality. **4** archaic tolerate. **5** archaic allow (someone) to do something.
– DERIVATIVES **sufferer** noun.
– ORIGIN Latin *sufferre*, from *ferre* 'to bear'.

sufferance ● noun absence of objection rather than genuine approval; toleration.

suffice /səfīss/ ● verb **1** be enough or adequate. **2** meet the needs of.
– PHRASES **suffice** (**it**) **to say** used to indicate that one is withholding something for reasons of discretion or brevity.
– ORIGIN Latin *sufficere* 'put under, meet the need of'.

sufficiency ● noun (pl. **sufficiencies**) **1** the condition or quality of being sufficient. **2** an adequate amount, especially of something essential.

sufficient ● adjective & determiner enough; adequate.

Thesaurus

S

scrumptious, scrummy.
– OPPOSITES dry.

succumb ● verb **1** *she succumbed to temptation* YIELD, give in/way, submit, surrender, capitulate, cave in. **2** *he succumbed to the disease* DIE FROM/OF; catch, develop, contract, fall ill with; *informal* come/go down with.
– OPPOSITES resist.

suck ● verb **1** *they sucked orange juice through straws* SIP, sup, siphon, slurp, draw, drink. **2** *Fran sucked in a deep breath* DRAW, pull, breathe, gasp; inhale, inspire. **3** *they got sucked into petty crime* IMPLICATE IN, involve in, draw into; *informal* mix up in. **4** *(N. Amer. informal) the weather sucks* BE VERY BAD, be awful, be terrible, be dreadful, be horrible; *informal* stink.
– PHRASES **suck up** *(informal) they suck up to him, hanging on to his every word* GROVEL, creep, toady, be obsequious, be sycophantic, kowtow, bow and scrape, truckle; fawn on; *informal* lick someone's boots, be all over.

suckle ● verb BREASTFEED, feed, nurse.

sudden ● adjective UNEXPECTED, unforeseen, unanticipated, unlooked-for; immediate, instantaneous, instant, precipitous, precipitate, abrupt, rapid, swift, quick.

suddenly ● adverb IMMEDIATELY, instantaneously, instantly, straight away, all of a sudden, all at once, promptly, abruptly, swiftly; unexpectedly, without warning, without notice, out of the blue; *informal* straight off, in a flash, like a shot.
– OPPOSITES gradually.

suds ● plural noun LATHER, foam, froth, bubbles, soap.

sue ● verb **1** *he sued for negligence* TAKE LEGAL ACTION, take to court, bring an action/suit, proceed against; *informal* have the law on. **2** *suing for peace* APPEAL, petition, ask, solicit, request, seek.

suffer ● verb **1** *I hate to see him suffer* HURT, ache, be in pain, feel pain; be in distress, be upset, be miserable. **2** *he suffers from asthma* BE AFFLICTED BY, be affected by, be troubled with, have. **3** *England suffered a humiliating defeat* UNDERGO, experience, be subjected to, receive, endure, face. **4** *the school's reputation has suffered* BE IMPAIRED, be damaged, deteriorate, decline. **5** *(archaic) he was obliged to suffer her intimate proximity* TOLERATE, put up with, bear, stand, abide, endure; *formal* brook. **6** *(archaic) my conscience would not suffer me to accept* ALLOW, permit, let, give leave to, sanction.

suffering ● noun HARDSHIP, distress, misery, wretchedness, adversity, tribulation; pain, agony, anguish, trauma, torment, torture, hurt, affliction, sadness, unhappiness, sorrow, grief, woe, angst, heartache, heartbreak, stress; *poetic/literary* dolour.

– DERIVATIVES **sufficiently** adverb.

suffix /suffiks/ ● noun an element added at the end of a word to form a derivative (e.g. *-ation*). ● verb /səfiks/ append, especially as a suffix.

suffocate ● verb **1** die or cause to die from lack of air or inability to breathe. **2** feel or cause to feel trapped or oppressed.
– DERIVATIVES **suffocation** noun.
– ORIGIN Latin *suffocare* 'stifle', from *fauces* 'throat'.

suffragan /sufrəgən/ (also **suffragan bishop**) ● noun a bishop appointed to help a diocesan bishop.
– ORIGIN Latin *suffraganeus* 'assistant'.

suffrage /sufrij/ ● noun the right to vote in political elections.
– ORIGIN originally in the sense 'intercessory prayers', also 'assistance': from Latin *suffragium*.

suffragette /sufrəjet/ ● noun historical a woman seeking the right to vote through organized protest.

suffragist ● noun chiefly historical a person advocating the extension of suffrage, especially to women.

suffuse /səfyoōz/ ● verb gradually spread through or over.
– DERIVATIVES **suffusion** noun.
– ORIGIN Latin *suffundere* 'pour into'.

Sufi /soōfi/ ● noun (pl. **Sufis**) a Muslim ascetic and mystic.
– DERIVATIVES **Sufic** adjective **Sufism** noun.
– ORIGIN Arabic, perhaps from a word meaning 'wool', referring to the woollen garment worn by Sufis.

sug- ● prefix variant spelling of SUB- before *g*.

sugar ● noun **1** a sweet crystalline substance obtained especially from sugar cane and sugar beet. **2** Biochemistry any of the class of soluble crystalline sweet-tasting carbohydrates, including sucrose and glucose. **3** informal, chiefly N. Amer. used as a term of endearment. ● verb **1** sweeten, sprinkle, or coat with sugar. **2** make more agreeable or palatable.
– DERIVATIVES **sugarless** adjective.
– ORIGIN Old French *sukere*, from Arabic.

sugar beet ● noun beet of a variety from which sugar is extracted.

sugar cane ● noun a tropical grass with tall stout stems from which sugar is extracted.

sugar-coated ● adjective superficially attractive or excessively sentimental.

sugarcraft ● noun the art of creating confectionery or cake decorations from sugar paste.

sugar daddy ● noun informal a rich older man who lavishes gifts on a young woman.

sugarloaf ● noun a conical moulded mass of sugar.

sugar maple ● noun a North American maple, the sap of which is used to make maple sugar and maple syrup.

sugar snap (also **sugar snap pea**) ● noun mangetout, especially of a variety with thicker and more rounded pods.

sugar soap ● noun Brit. an alkaline preparation containing washing soda and soap, used for cleaning or removing paint.

sugary ● adjective **1** containing much sugar. **2** coated in sugar. **3** excessively sentimental.

suggest ● verb **1** put forward for consideration. **2** cause one to think that (something) exists or is the case. **3** state or express indirectly. **4** (**suggest itself**) (of an idea) come into one's mind.
– ORIGIN Latin *suggerere* 'suggest, prompt'.

suggestible ● adjective open to suggestion; easily swayed.
– DERIVATIVES **suggestibility** noun.

suggestion ● noun **1** an idea or plan put forward for consideration. **2** the action of suggesting. **3** something that implies or indicates a certain fact or situation. **4** a slight trace or indication: *a suggestion of a smile.* **5** Psychology the influencing of a person to accept a belief or impulse uncritically.

suggestive ● adjective **1** tending to suggest or evoke something. **2** hinting at or bringing to mind sexual matters; mildly indecent.
– DERIVATIVES **suggestively** adverb **suggestiveness** noun.

suicide ● noun **1** the action of killing oneself intentionally. **2** a person who does this. **3** (before another noun) referring to a military operation carried out by people who do not expect to survive it: *a suicide bomber.* **4** a course of action which is disastrously damaging to one's own interests. ● verb intentionally kill oneself.
– DERIVATIVES **suicidal** adjective **suicidally** adverb.
– ORIGIN from Latin *sui* 'of oneself' + *caedere* 'kill'.

suicide pact ● noun an agreement between two or more people to commit suicide together.

sui generis /soō-i jennəriss/ ● adjective unique.
– ORIGIN Latin, 'of its own kind'.

suit ● noun **1** a set of outer clothes made of the same fabric and designed to be worn together, typically consisting of a jacket and trousers or a jacket and skirt. **2** a set of clothes for a particular activity. **3** any of the sets into which a pack of playing cards is divided (spades, hearts, diamonds, and clubs). **4** a lawsuit. **5** informal a high-ranking business executive. **6** the process of trying to win a woman's affection with a view to marriage. **7** literary a petition or entreaty made to a person in authority. ● verb **1** be convenient for or acceptable to. **2** go well with or enhance the features, figure, or character of. **3** (**suit oneself**) act entirely according to one's own wishes. **4** (**suited**) appropriate or fitting.
– PHRASES **suit down to the ground** Brit. be extremely convenient or appropriate for.
– DERIVATIVES **suiting** noun.
– ORIGIN Old French *siwte*, from Latin *sequi* 'follow'.

suitable ● adjective right or appropriate for a particular person, purpose, or situation.
– DERIVATIVES **suitability** noun **suitably** adverb.

suitcase ● noun a case with a handle and a hinged lid, used for

Thesaurus

suffice ● verb BE ENOUGH, be sufficient, be adequate, do, serve, meet requirements, satisfy demands, answer/meet one's needs, answer/serve the purpose; *informal* fit/fill the bill, hit the spot.

sufficient ● adjective & determiner ENOUGH, adequate, plenty of, ample.
– OPPOSITES inadequate.

suffocate ● verb **1** *she suffocated her victim* SMOTHER, asphyxiate, stifle; choke, strangle. **2** *she was suffocating in the heat* BE BREATHLESS, be short of air, struggle for air; be too hot, swelter; *informal* roast, bake, boil.

suffrage ● noun FRANCHISE, right to vote, the vote, enfranchisement, ballot.

suffuse ● verb PERMEATE, spread over, spread throughout, cover, bathe, pervade, wash, saturate, imbue.

sugary ● adjective **1** *sugary snacks* SWEET, sugared, sickly. **2** *sugary romance* SENTIMENTAL, mawkish, cloying, sickly (sweet), saccharine, syrupy; *informal* soppy, schmaltzy, slushy, mushy, sloppy, cutesy, corny.
– OPPOSITES sour.

suggest ● verb **1** *Ruth suggested a holiday* PROPOSE, put forward, recommend, advocate; advise, urge, encourage, counsel. **2** *evidence suggests that teenagers are responsive to price increases* INDICATE, lead to the belief, argue, demonstrate, show; *formal* evince. **3** *sources suggest that the Prime Minister will change his cabinet* HINT, insinuate, imply, intimate, indicate. **4** *the seduction scenes suggest his guilt and her loneliness* CONVEY, express, impart, imply, intimate, smack of, evoke, conjure up; *formal* evince.

suggestion ● noun **1** *some suggestions for tackling this problem* PROPOSAL, proposition, motion, submission, recommendation; advice, counsel, hint, tip, clue, idea. **2** *the suggestion of a smirk* HINT, trace, touch, suspicion, dash, soupçon; ghost, semblance, shadow, glimmer, impression, whisper. **3** *there is no suggestion that he was party to a conspiracy* INSINUATION, hint, implication, intimation, innuendo, imputation.

suggestive ● adjective **1** *suggestive remarks* INDECENT, indelicate, improper, unseemly, sexual, sexy, smutty, dirty, ribald, bawdy, racy, risqué, lewd, vulgar, coarse, salacious. **2** *an odour suggestive of a brewery* REDOLENT, evocative, reminiscent; characteristic, indicative, typical.

suicide ● noun SELF-DESTRUCTION, taking one's own life, self-murder; *informal* topping oneself.

suit ● noun **1** *a pinstriped suit* OUTFIT, set of clothes, ensemble. **2** (*informal*) *suits in faraway boardrooms* BUSINESSMAN, BUSINESSWOMAN, executive, bureaucrat, administrator, manager. **3** *a medical malpractice suit* LEGAL ACTION, lawsuit, (court) case, action, (legal/judicial) proceedings, litigation. **4** *they spurned his suit* ENTREATY, request, plea, appeal, petition, supplication, application. **5** *his suit came to nothing* COURTSHIP, wooing, attentions.
● verb **1** *blue really suits you* LOOK ATTRACTIVE ON, enhance the appearance of, look good on, become, flatter. **2** *savings schemes to suit all pockets* BE CONVENIENT FOR, be acceptable to, be suitable for, meet the requirements of; *informal* fit the bill. **3** *recipes ideally suited to students* MAKE APPROPRIATE TO/FOR, tailor, fashion, adjust, adapt, modify, fit, gear, design.

carrying clothes and other personal possessions.

suite /sweet/ • noun **1** a set of rooms for one person's or family's use or for a particular purpose. **2** a set of furniture of the same design. **3** Music a set of instrumental compositions to be played in succession. **4** a set of pieces from an opera or musical arranged as one instrumental work.
– ORIGIN French, from Old French *siwte* (see SUIT).

suitor /so͞otər, syo͞o-/ • noun **1** a man who pursues a relationship with a woman with a view to marriage. **2** a prospective buyer of a business or corporation.

sukiyaki /so͝okiyaaki/ • noun a Japanese dish of sliced meat fried rapidly with vegetables and sauce.
– ORIGIN Japanese.

sulfur etc. • noun US spelling of SULPHUR etc.

sulk • verb be silent, morose, and bad-tempered through annoyance or disappointment. • noun a period of sulking.
– DERIVATIVES **sulker** noun.

sulky • adjective (**sulkier**, **sulkiest**) morose, bad-tempered, and resentful.
– DERIVATIVES **sulkily** adverb **sulkiness** noun.
– ORIGIN perhaps from obsolete *sulke* 'hard to dispose of', of unknown origin.

sullen • adjective bad-tempered and sulky.
– DERIVATIVES **sullenly** adverb **sullenness** noun.
– ORIGIN originally in the senses 'averse to company' and 'unusual': from Old French *sulein*, from *sol* 'sole'.

sully • verb (**sullies**, **sullied**) damage the purity or integrity of; defile.
– ORIGIN perhaps from French *souiller* 'to soil'.

sulpha /sulfə/ (US **sulfa**) • noun short for SULPHONAMIDE.

sulphate (US **sulfate**) • noun Chemistry a salt or ester of sulphuric acid.

sulphide /sulfīd/ (US **sulfide**) • noun Chemistry a compound of sulphur with another element or group.

sulphite /sulfīt/ (US **sulfite**) • noun Chemistry a salt of sulphurous acid.

sulphonamide /sulfonnəmīd/ (US **sulfonamide**) • noun Medicine any of a class of sulphur-containing drugs which are able to prevent the multiplication of some pathogenic bacteria.

sulphonic acid (US **sulfonic**) • noun Chemistry an organic acid containing the group $-SO_2OH$.

sulphur (US & Chemistry **sulfur**) • noun **1** a combustible nonmetallic chemical element which typically occurs as yellow crystals. **2** the material of which hellfire and lightning were formerly believed to consist.
– ORIGIN Latin *sulfur*, *sulphur*.

sulphur dioxide • noun Chemistry a colourless pungent toxic gas formed by burning sulphur.

sulphuric /sulfyoorik/ (US **sulfuric**) • adjective containing sulphur or sulphuric acid.

sulphuric acid • noun a strong acid made by oxidizing solutions of sulphur dioxide.

sulphurous (US **sulfurous**) • adjective **1** containing or derived from sulphur. **2** pale yellow.

sulphurous acid • noun Chemistry an unstable weak acid formed when sulphur dioxide dissolves in water.

sultan • noun a Muslim sovereign.
– DERIVATIVES **sultanate** noun.
– ORIGIN Arabic, 'power, ruler'.

sultana • noun **1** a small light brown seedless raisin. **2** a wife or concubine of a sultan.
– ORIGIN Italian, feminine of *sultano* 'sultan'.

sultry • adjective (**sultrier**, **sultriest**) **1** (of the weather) hot and humid. **2** displaying or suggesting passion; provocative.
– ORIGIN from obsolete *sulter* 'swelter'.

sum • noun **1** a particular amount of money. **2** the total amount resulting from the addition of two or more numbers or amounts. **3** an arithmetical problem, especially at an elementary level. • verb (**summed**, **summing**) (**sum up**) **1** concisely describe the nature or character of. **2** summarize briefly. **3** Law (of a judge) review the evidence at the end of a case, and direct the jury regarding points of law.
– PHRASES **in sum** to sum up.
– ORIGIN Latin *summa* 'main part, sum total', from *summus* 'highest'.

sumac /so͞omak, sho͞o-/ (also **sumach**) • noun a shrub or small tree with conical clusters of fruits and bright autumn colours.
– ORIGIN Arabic.

Sumatran /so͝omaatrən/ • noun a person from the Indonesian island of Sumatra. • adjective relating to Sumatra.

Sumerian /soomeeriən/ • noun a member of a people of ancient Sumer in Babylonia. • adjective relating to Sumer.

summa cum laude /so͝ommə ko͝om lowday/ • adverb & adjective chiefly N. Amer. (of a degree, diploma, etc.) with the highest distinction.
– ORIGIN Latin, 'with highest praise'.

summary • noun (pl. **summaries**) a brief statement of the main points of something. • adjective **1** dispensing with needless details or formalities. **2** Law (of a judicial process) conducted without the customary legal formalities.
– DERIVATIVES **summarily** adverb **summarize** (also **summarise**) verb.
– ORIGIN Latin *summarius*, from *summa* (see SUM).

summation /səmaysh'n/ • noun **1** the process of adding things

Thesaurus

suitable • adjective **1** *suitable employment opportunities* ACCEPTABLE, satisfactory, fitting; *informal* right up someone's street. **2** *a drama suitable for all ages* APPROPRIATE, fitting, fit, acceptable, right. **3** *music suitable for a lively dinner party* APPROPRIATE, suited, befitting, in keeping with; *informal* cut out for. **4** *they treated him with suitable respect* PROPER, seemly, decent, appropriate, fitting, befitting, correct, due. **5** *suitable candidates* WELL QUALIFIED, well suited, appropriate, fitting.
– OPPOSITES inappropriate.

suitcase • noun TRAVELLING BAG, travel bag, case, valise, overnight case, portmanteau, vanity case; (**suitcases**) luggage, baggage.

suite • noun **1** *a penthouse suite* APARTMENT, flat, (set of) rooms. **2** *the Queen and her suite* RETINUE, entourage, train, escort, royal household, court; attendants, retainers, servants.

suitor • noun ADMIRER, wooer, boyfriend, sweetheart, lover; *poetic/literary* swain; *dated* beau.

sulk • verb *Dad was sulking* MOPE, brood, be sullen, have a long face, be in a bad mood, be in a huff, be grumpy, be moody; *informal* be down in the dumps.
• noun *he sank into a deep sulk* (BAD) MOOD, fit of ill humour, fit of pique, pet, huff, (bad) temper, the sulks, the blues; *informal* grump.

sulky • adjective *sulky faces* SULLEN, surly, moping, pouting, moody, sour, piqued, petulant, disgruntled, ill-humoured, in a bad mood, having a fit of the sulks, out of humour, fed up, put out; bad-tempered, grumpy, huffy, glum, gloomy, morose; *informal* grouchy.
– OPPOSITES cheerful.

sullen • adjective SURLY, sulky, pouting, sour, morose, resentful, glum, moody, gloomy, grumpy, bad-tempered, ill-tempered; unresponsive, uncommunicative, uncivil, unfriendly.
– OPPOSITES cheerful.

sully • verb TAINT, defile, soil, tarnish, stain, blemish, pollute, spoil, mar; *poetic/literary* besmirch, befoul.

sultry • adjective **1** *a sultry day* HUMID, close, airless, stifling, oppressive, muggy, sticky, sweltering, tropical, heavy; hot; *informal* boiling, roasting. **2** *a sultry film star* PASSIONATE, attractive, sensual, sexy, voluptuous, erotic, seductive.
– OPPOSITES refreshing.

sum • noun **1** *a large sum of money* AMOUNT, quantity, volume. **2** *just a small sum* AMOUNT OF MONEY, price, charge, fee, cost. **3** *the sum of two numbers* (SUM) TOTAL, grand total, tally, aggregate, summation. **4** *the sum of his wisdom* ENTIRETY, totality, total, whole, aggregate, summation, beginning and end. **5** *we did sums at school* (ARITHMETICAL) PROBLEM, calculation; (**sums**) arithmetic, mathematics, computation; *Brit. informal* maths; *N. Amer. informal* math.
– OPPOSITES difference.
– PHRASES **sum up** SUMMARIZE THE EVIDENCE, review the evidence, give a summing-up. **sum someone/something up 1** *one reviewer summed it up as 'compelling'* EVALUATE, assess, appraise, rate, weigh up, gauge, judge, deem, adjudge, estimate, form an opinion of. **2** *he summed up his reasons* SUMMARIZE, make/give a summary of, precis, outline, give an outline of, recapitulate, review; *informal* recap.

summarily • adverb IMMEDIATELY, instantly, right away, straight away, at once, on the spot, promptly; speedily, swiftly, rapidly, without delay; arbitrarily, without formality, peremptorily, without due process.

summarize • verb SUM UP, abridge, condense, encapsulate, outline, give an outline of, put in a nutshell, recapitulate, give/make a summary of, give a synopsis of, precis, give a résumé of, give the gist of; *informal* recap; *archaic* epitomize.

together. **2** the action of summing up. **3** a summary.
– DERIVATIVES **summative** adjective.
summer • noun the season after spring and before autumn, when the weather is warmest. • verb spend the summer in a particular place.
– DERIVATIVES **summery** adjective.
– ORIGIN Old English.
summer house • noun a small building in a garden, used for relaxation during fine weather.
summer pudding • noun Brit. a pudding of soft summer fruit encased in bread or sponge.
summer school • noun a course of lectures held during school and university summer vacations.
summer season • noun the summer period when most people take holidays.
summertime • noun **1** the season or period of summer. **2** (**summer time**) Brit. time as advanced one hour ahead of standard time to achieve longer evening daylight in summer.
summing-up • noun **1** a summary. **2** Law a judge's review of evidence at the end of a case, with a direction to the jury regarding points of law.
summit • noun **1** the highest point of a hill or mountain. **2** the highest attainable level of achievement. **3** a meeting between heads of government.
– ORIGIN Old French *somete*, from Latin *summus* 'highest'.
summiteer • noun a participant in a government summit.
summon • verb **1** authoritatively call on (someone) to be present, especially to appear in a law court. **2** urgently demand (help). **3** call people to attend (a meeting). **4** cause (a quality or reaction) to emerge from within oneself: *she managed to summon up a smile.*
– ORIGIN Latin *summonere* 'give a hint', from *monere* 'warn'.
summons • noun (pl. **summonses**) **1** an order to appear in a law court. **2** an act of summoning. • verb chiefly Law serve with a summons.
sumo /sōōmō/ • noun (pl. **sumos**) a Japanese form of heavyweight wrestling in which a wrestler must not go outside a circle or touch the ground with any part of his body except the soles of his feet.
– ORIGIN Japanese.
sump • noun **1** the base of an internal-combustion engine, which serves as a reservoir of oil for the lubrication system. **2** a depression in the floor of a mine or cave in which water collects. **3** a cesspool.
– ORIGIN originally denoting a marsh: from Dutch or Low Geramn *sump*, or (in the mining sense) from German *Sumpf*.
sumptuary /sumptyoori/ • adjective chiefly historical referring to laws that limit private expenditure on food and personal items.
– ORIGIN Latin *sumptuarius*, from *sumptus* 'cost'.
sumptuous • adjective splendid and expensive-looking.
– DERIVATIVES **sumptuously** adverb **sumptuousness** noun.
– ORIGIN Latin *sumptuosus*, from *sumptus* 'cost'.
sum total • noun another term for SUM (in sense 2).
sun • noun **1** (also **Sun**) the star round which the earth orbits. **2** any similar star, with or without planets. **3** the light or warmth received from the sun. • verb (**sunned**, **sunning**) (**sun oneself**) sit or lie in the sun.
– PHRASES **under the sun** in existence.
– DERIVATIVES **sunless** adjective **sunlike** adjective **sunward** adjective & adverb **sunwards** adverb.
– ORIGIN Old English.
sun-baked • adjective exposed to the heat of the sun.
sunbathe • verb sit or lie in the sun to get a suntan.
– DERIVATIVES **sunbather** noun.
sunbeam • noun a ray of sunlight.
sunbed • noun Brit. **1** a lounger used for sunbathing. **2** an apparatus for acquiring a tan, consisting of two banks of sunlamps between which one lies or stands.
sunbelt • noun a strip of territory receiving a high amount of sunshine, especially the southern US from California to Florida.
sunblock • noun a cream or lotion for protecting the skin from sunburn.
sunburn • noun reddening and inflammation of the skin caused by overexposure to the ultraviolet rays of the sun. • verb (past and past part. **sunburned** or **sunburnt**) (**be sunburned**) suffer from sunburn.
sunburst • noun **1** a sudden brief appearance of the full sun from behind clouds. **2** a design or ornament representing the sun and its rays.
suncream • noun a creamy preparation for protecting the skin from sunburn.
sundae • noun a dish of ice cream with added ingredients such as fruit, nuts, and syrup.
– ORIGIN perhaps from SUNDAY, either because the dish was made with ice cream left over from Sunday, or because it was sold only on Sundays.
sun dance • noun a dance performed by North American Indians in honour of the sun.
Sunday • noun the day of the week before Monday and following Saturday, observed by Christians as a day of rest and religious worship.
– ORIGIN Old English, 'day of the sun'.
Sunday best • noun a person's best clothes.
Sunday school • noun a class held on Sundays to teach children about Christianity.
sun deck • noun the deck of a yacht or cruise ship that is open to the sky.
sunder • verb literary split apart.
– ORIGIN Old English.
sundew • noun a small carnivorous plant of boggy places, with leaves bearing sticky hairs for trapping insects.
sundial • noun an instrument showing the time by the shadow cast by a pointer.
sundown • noun chiefly N. Amer. sunset.
sundowner • noun Brit. informal an alcoholic drink taken at sun-

Thesaurus

S

summary • noun *a summary of the findings* SYNOPSIS, precis, résumé, abstract, digest, encapsulation, abbreviated version; outline, sketch, rundown, review, summing-up, overview, recapitulation, epitome, conspectus; *informal* recap.
• adjective **1** *a summary financial statement* ABRIDGED, abbreviated, shortened, condensed, concise, succinct, short, brief, pithy; *formal* compendious. **2** *summary execution* IMMEDIATE, instant, instantaneous, on-the-spot; speedy, swift, rapid, without delay, sudden; arbitrary, without formality, peremptory.
summer house • noun GAZEBO, pavilion, belvedere; *poetic/literary* bower.
summit • noun **1** *the summit of Mont Blanc* (MOUNTAIN) TOP, peak, crest, crown, apex, tip, cap, hilltop. **2** *the summits of world literature* ACME, peak, height, pinnacle, zenith, climax, high point/spot, highlight, crowning glory, best, finest, nonpareil. **3** *the next superpower summit* MEETING, negotiation, conference, talk(s), discussion.
– OPPOSITES base, nadir.
summon • verb **1** *he was summoned to the Embassy* SEND FOR, call for, request the presence of; ask, invite. **2** *they were summoned as witnesses* SERVE WITH A SUMMONS, summons, subpoena, cite, serve with a citation. **3** *the chair summoned a meeting* CONVENE, assemble, order, call, announce; *formal* convoke. **4** *he summoned the courage to move closer* MUSTER, gather, collect, rally, screw up. **5** *summoning up their memories of home* CALL TO MIND, call up/forth, conjure up, evoke, recall, revive, arouse, kindle, awaken, spark (off). **6** *they summoned spirits of the dead* CONJURE UP, call up, invoke.
summons • noun **1** *the court issued a summons* WRIT, subpoena, warrant, court order; *Law* citation. **2** *a summons to go to the boss's office* ORDER, directive, command, instruction, demand, decree, injunction, edict, call, request.
• verb *he was summonsed to appear in court* SERVE WITH A SUMMONS, summon, subpoena, cite, serve with a citation.
sumptuous • adjective LAVISH, luxurious, opulent, magnificent, resplendent, gorgeous, splendid, grand, lavishly appointed, palatial, rich; *informal* plush, ritzy; *Brit. informal* swish.
– OPPOSITES plain.
sun • noun SUNSHINE, sunlight, daylight, light, warmth; beams, rays.
– RELATED TERMS solar, helio-.
– PHRASES **sun oneself.** See SUNBATHE.
sunbathe • verb SUN ONESELF, bask, get a tan, tan oneself; *informal* catch some rays.
sunburnt • adjective **1** *his sunburnt shoulders* BURNT, sunburned, red, scarlet. **2** *a handsome sunburnt face* TANNED, suntanned, brown, bronzed, bronze.
– OPPOSITES pale.
Sunday • noun THE LORD'S DAY, the Sabbath.
– RELATED TERMS dominical.

set.

sundress ● noun a light, loose sleeveless dress, typically having a wide neckline and thin shoulder straps.

sun-dried ● adjective dried in the sun, as opposed to by artificial heat.

sundry ● adjective of various kinds. ● noun (pl. **sundries**) (**sundries**) various items not important enough be mentioned individually.
– ORIGIN Old English, 'distinct, separate'.

sunfish ● noun a large, short-tailed sea fish with tall dorsal and anal fins near the rear of the body.

sunflower ● noun a tall plant with very large golden-rayed flowers, grown for its edible seeds which yield oil.

sung past participle of SING.

sunglasses ● plural noun glasses tinted to protect the eyes from sunlight or glare.

sunk past and past participle of SINK[1].

sunken past participle of SINK[1]. ● adjective **1** having sunk. **2** at a lower level than the surrounding area. **3** (of a person's eyes or cheeks) deeply recessed.

sun-kissed ● adjective made warm or brown by the sun.

sunlamp ● noun a lamp emitting ultraviolet rays, used chiefly to produce an artificial suntan or in therapy.

sunlight ● noun light from the sun.
– DERIVATIVES **sunlit** adjective.

Sunna /so͝onnə, sunnə/ ● noun the traditional portion of Muslim law based on Muhammad's words or acts, accepted as authoritative by Muslims.
– ORIGIN Arabic, 'form, way, rule'.

Sunni /so͝onni, sunni/ ● noun (pl. same or **Sunnis**) **1** one of the two main branches of Islam, differing from Shia in its understanding of the Sunna and in its acceptance of the first three caliphs. Compare with SHIA. **2** a Muslim who adheres to this branch of Islam.
– ORIGIN Arabic, 'custom, normative rule'.

sunny ● adjective (**sunnier**, **sunniest**) **1** bright with or receiving much sunlight. **2** cheerful.
– PHRASES **sunny side up** N. Amer. (of an egg) fried on one side only.

sunray ● noun a radiating line or broadening stripe resembling a ray of the sun.

sunrise ● noun **1** the time in the morning when the sun rises. **2** the colours and light visible in the sky at sunrise.

sunrise industry ● noun a new and growing industry.

sunroof ● noun a panel in the roof of a car that can be opened for extra ventilation.

sunscreen ● noun a cream or lotion rubbed on to the skin to protect it from the sun.

sunset ● noun **1** the time in the evening when the sun sets. **2** the colours and light visible in the sky at sunset. **3** the final declining phase of something.

sunshade ● noun a parasol, awning, or other device giving protection from the sun.

sunshine ● noun **1** sunlight unbroken by cloud. **2** cheerfulness or happiness. **3** Brit. informal used as a familiar form of address.
– DERIVATIVES **sunshiny** adjective.

sunspot ● noun Astronomy a temporary darker and cooler patch on the sun's surface, associated with the sun's magnetic field.

sunstroke ● noun heatstroke brought about by excessive exposure to the sun.

suntan ● noun a golden-brown colouring of the skin caused by exposure to the sun.
– DERIVATIVES **suntanned** adjective.

suntrap ● noun Brit. a place sheltered from the wind and positioned to receive much sunshine.

sunup ● noun chiefly N. Amer. sunrise.

sun visor ● noun a small hinged screen above a vehicle's windscreen that can be lowered to protect the occupants' eyes from bright sunlight.

sup[1] ● verb (**supped**, **supping**) dated or N. English take (drink or liquid food) by sips or spoonfuls. ● noun a sip.
– ORIGIN Old English.

sup[2] ● verb (**supped**, **supping**) dated eat supper.
– PHRASES **he who sups with the devil should have a long spoon** proverb a person who has dealings with a dangerous or wily person should be cautious.
– ORIGIN Old French *super*; related to SUP[1].

sup- ● prefix variant spelling of SUB- before *p*.

super ● adjective informal excellent. ● noun informal a superintendent.

super- ● combining form **1** above; over; beyond: *superstructure.* **2** to a great or extreme degree: *superabundant.* **3** extra large of its kind: *supercontinent.* **4** of a higher kind (especially in names of classificatory divisions): *superfamily.*
– ORIGIN from Latin *super* 'above, beyond'.

superabundant ● adjective formal excessive in quantity.
– DERIVATIVES **superabundance** noun.

superadd ● verb add to what has already been added.

superannuate ● verb **1** retire (someone) with a pension. **2** (**superannuated**) belonging to a superannuation scheme. **3** (**superannuated**) too old to be effective or useful.
– ORIGIN from Latin *super-* 'over' + *annus* 'year'.

superannuation ● noun regular payment made into a fund by an employee towards a future pension.

superb ● adjective **1** excellent. **2** magnificent or splendid.
– DERIVATIVES **superbly** adverb.
– ORIGIN Latin *superbus* 'proud, magnificent'.

superbike ● noun a high-performance motorcycle.

superbug ● noun informal a bacterium, insect, etc. regarded as having enhanced qualities, especially of resistance to antibiotics or pesticides.

supercar ● noun a high-performance sports car.

supercargo ● noun (pl. **supercargoes** or **supercargos**) a representative of the ship's owner on board a merchant ship, responsible for the cargo.
– ORIGIN Spanish *sobrecargo*, from *sobre* 'over' + *cargo* 'cargo'.

supercede ● verb variant spelling of SUPERSEDE.
– USAGE See the note at SUPERSEDE.

supercharge ● verb **1** provide with a supercharger. **2** (**super-**

Thesaurus

sunder ● verb (*poetic/literary*) DIVIDE, split, cleave, separate, rend, sever, rive.

sundry ● adjective VARIOUS, varied, miscellaneous, assorted, mixed, diverse, diversified; several, numerous, many, manifold, multifarious, multitudinous; *poetic/literary* divers.

sunken ● adjective **1** *sunken eyes* HOLLOWED, hollow, depressed, deep-set, concave, indented. **2** *a sunken garden* BELOW GROUND LEVEL, at a lower level, lowered.

sunless ● adjective **1** *a cold sunless day* DARK, overcast, cloudy, grey, gloomy, dismal, murky, dull. **2** *the sunless side of the house* SHADY, shadowy, dark, gloomy.

sunlight ● noun DAYLIGHT, sun, sunshine, sun's rays, (natural) light.

sunny ● adjective **1** *a sunny day* BRIGHT, sunshiny, sunlit, clear, fine, cloudless, without a cloud in the sky. **2** *a sunny disposition* CHEERFUL, cheery, happy, light-hearted, bright, merry, joyful, bubbly, blithe, jolly, jovial, animated, buoyant, ebullient, upbeat, vivacious. **3** *look on the sunny side* OPTIMISTIC, rosy, bright, hopeful, auspicious, favourable.
– OPPOSITES dull, miserable.

sunrise ● noun (CRACK OF) DAWN, daybreak, break of day, first light, (early) morning, cockcrow; *N. Amer.* sunup; *poetic/literary* aurora, dayspring.

sunset ● noun NIGHTFALL, close of day, twilight, dusk, evening; *N. Amer.* sundown; *poetic/literary* eventide, gloaming.

sunshine ● noun **1** *relaxing in the sunshine* SUNLIGHT, sun, sun's rays, daylight, (natural) light. **2** *his smile was all sunshine* HAPPINESS, cheerfulness, cheer, gladness, laughter, gaiety, merriment, joy, joyfulness, blitheness, joviality, jollity. **3** (*Brit. informal*) *hello, sunshine* MY FRIEND; *informal* pal, chum; *Brit. informal* mate, matey, squire, mush; *N. Amer. informal* bud, buddy, buster.

super ● adjective (*informal*) EXCELLENT, superb, superlative, first-class, outstanding, marvellous, magnificent, wonderful, splendid, glorious; *informal* great, fantastic, fabulous, terrific, ace, divine, A1, wicked, cool; *Brit. informal* smashing, brilliant, brill.
– OPPOSITES rotten.

superannuated ● adjective **1** *a superannuated civil servant* PENSIONED (OFF), retired; elderly, old. **2** *superannuated computing equipment* OLD, old-fashioned, antiquated, out of date, outmoded, broken-down, obsolete, disused, defunct; *informal* clapped out.

superb ● adjective **1** *he scored a superb goal* EXCELLENT, superlative, first-rate, first-class, outstanding, remarkable, marvellous, magnificent, wonderful, splendid, admirable, noteworthy, impressive, fine, exquisite, exceptional, glorious; *informal* great, fantastic, fabulous, terrific, super, awesome, ace, cool, A1; *Brit. informal* brilliant, brill, smashing. **2** *a superb diamond necklace* MAGNIFICENT,

charged) having powerful emotional associations.

supercharger ● noun a device that increases the pressure of the fuel-air mixture in an internal-combustion engine, thereby giving greater efficiency.

supercilious ● adjective having an air of contemptuous superiority.
– DERIVATIVES **superciliously** adverb **superciliousness** noun.
– ORIGIN Latin *superciliosus* 'haughty', from *supercilium* 'eyebrow'.

supercomputer ● noun a particularly powerful mainframe computer.

superconductivity ● noun Physics the property of zero electrical resistance in some substances at very low temperatures.
– DERIVATIVES **superconducting** adjective **superconductive** adjective **superconductor** noun.

supercontinent ● noun a large land mass believed to have divided in the geological past to form some of the present continents.

supercool ● verb Chemistry cool (a liquid) below its freezing point without solidification or crystallization.

supercritical ● adjective Physics greater than or above a critical threshold such as critical mass or temperature.

super-duper ● adjective informal, humorous excellent; super.

superego ● noun (pl. **superegos**) Psychoanalysis the part of the mind that acts as a self-critical conscience, reflecting social standards that have been learned. Compare with EGO and ID.

supererogation /soopərerrəgaysh'n/ ● noun the performance of more work than duty requires.
– PHRASES **works of supererogation** (in the Roman Catholic Church) actions believed to form a reserve fund of merit that can be drawn on by prayer in favour of sinners.
– DERIVATIVES **supererogatory** /soopərirroggətəri/ adjective.
– ORIGIN Latin, from *supererogare* 'pay in addition'.

superficial ● adjective **1** existing or occurring at or on the surface. **2** apparent rather than actual. **3** not thorough or deep; cursory. **4** lacking depth of character or understanding.
– DERIVATIVES **superficiality** noun (pl. **superficialities**) **superficially** adverb.
– ORIGIN Latin *superficialis*, from *superficies* 'top, surface'.

superfluidity ● noun Physics the property of flowing without friction or viscosity, as shown by liquid helium close to absolute zero.
– DERIVATIVES **superfluid** noun & adjective.

superfluous ● adjective unnecessary, especially through being more than enough.
– DERIVATIVES **superfluity** noun (pl. **superfluities**) **superfluously** adverb.
– ORIGIN Latin *superfluus*, from *fluere* 'to flow'.

supergiant ● noun Astronomy a star that is greater and more luminous than a giant.

superglue ● noun a very strong quick-setting adhesive.

supergrass ● noun Brit. informal a police informer who implicates a large number of people.

superheat ● verb Physics **1** heat (a liquid) under pressure above its boiling point without vaporization. **2** heat (steam or other vapour) above the temperature of the liquid from which it was formed.

superhero ● noun (pl. **superheroes**) a benevolent fictional character with superhuman powers.

superhighway ● noun N. Amer. a dual carriageway with controlled access.

superhuman ● adjective having or showing exceptional ability or powers.
– DERIVATIVES **superhumanly** adverb.

superimpose ● verb place or lay (one thing) over another.
– DERIVATIVES **superimposition** noun.

superintend ● verb manage or oversee.
– DERIVATIVES **superintendence** noun.

superintendent ● noun **1** a person who supervises or is in charge of an organization, department, etc. **2** (in the UK) a police officer ranking above chief inspector. **3** (in the US) the chief of a police department. **4** N. Amer. the caretaker of a building.
– ORIGIN from Latin *superintendere*.

superior ● adjective **1** higher in status, quality, or power. **2** of high standard or quality. **3** (**superior to**) above yielding to or being influenced by. **4** conceited. **5** (of a letter, figure, or symbol) written or printed above the line. **6** chiefly Anatomy further above or out; higher in position. ● noun **1** a person of superior rank. **2** the head of a monastery or other religious institution. **3** Printing a superior letter, figure, or symbol.
– ORIGIN Latin, 'higher', from *super* 'above'.

superiority ● noun the state of being superior.

superiority complex ● noun an attitude of superiority which conceals actual feelings of inferiority and failure.

superlative /soopərlətiv, syoo-/ ● adjective **1** of the highest quality or degree. **2** Grammar (of an adjective or adverb) expressing the highest or a very high degree of a quality (e.g. *bravest, most fiercely*). Contrasted with POSITIVE and COMPARATIVE. ● noun an exaggerated expression of praise.
– DERIVATIVES **superlatively** adverb.
– ORIGIN Latin *superlativus*, from *superferre* 'carry beyond'.

Thesaurus

majestic, splendid, grand, impressive, imposing, awe-inspiring, breathtaking; gorgeous.
– OPPOSITES poor, inferior.

supercilious ● adjective ARROGANT, haughty, conceited, disdainful, overbearing, pompous, condescending, superior, patronizing, imperious, proud, snobbish, snobby, smug, scornful, sneering; *informal* hoity-toity, high and mighty, uppity, snooty, stuck-up, snotty, jumped up, too big for one's boots.

S

superficial ● adjective **1** *superficial burns* SURFACE, exterior, external, outer, outside, slight. **2** *a superficial friendship* SHALLOW, surface, skin-deep, artificial; empty, hollow, meaningless. **3** *a superficial investigation* CURSORY, perfunctory, casual, sketchy, desultory, token, slapdash, offhand, rushed, hasty, hurried. **4** *a superficial resemblance* APPARENT, seeming, outward, ostensible, cosmetic, slight. **5** *a superficial biography* TRIVIAL, lightweight. **6** *a superficial person* FACILE, shallow, flippant, empty-headed, trivial, frivolous, silly, inane.
– OPPOSITES deep, thorough.

superficially ● adverb APPARENTLY, seemingly, ostensibly, outwardly, on the surface, on the face of it, to all intents and purposes, at first glance, to the casual eye.

superfluity ● noun SURPLUS, excess, overabundance, glut, surfeit, profusion, plethora.
– OPPOSITES shortage.

superfluous ● adjective **1** *superfluous material* SURPLUS (TO REQUIREMENTS), redundant, unneeded, excess, extra, (to) spare, remaining, unused, left over, in excess, waste. **2** *words seemed superfluous* UNNECESSARY, unneeded, redundant, uncalled for, unwarranted.
– OPPOSITES necessary.

superhuman ● adjective **1** *a superhuman effort* EXTRAORDINARY, phenomenal, prodigious, stupendous, exceptional, immense, heroic. **2** *superhuman power* DIVINE, holy, heavenly. **3** *superhuman beings* SUPERNATURAL, preternatural, paranormal, other-worldly, unearthly; *rare* extramundane.
– OPPOSITES mundane.

superintend ● verb SUPERVISE, oversee, be in charge of, be in control of, preside over, direct, administer, manage, run, be responsible for.

superintendent ● noun **1** *the superintendent of the museum* MANAGER, director, administrator, supervisor, overseer, controller, chief, head, governor; *informal* boss. **2** *(N. Amer.) the building's superintendent* CARETAKER, janitor, warden, porter.

superior ● adjective **1** *a superior officer* HIGHER-RANKING, higher-level, senior, higher, higher-up. **2** *the superior candidate* BETTER, more expert, more skilful; worthier, fitter, preferred. **3** *superior workmanship* FINER, better, higher-grade, of higher quality, greater; accomplished, expert. **4** *superior chocolate* GOOD-QUALITY, high-quality, first-class, first-rate, top-quality; choice, select, exclusive, prime, prize, fine, excellent, best, choicest, finest. **5** *a superior hotel* HIGH-CLASS, upper-class, select, exclusive; *Brit.* upmarket; *informal* classy, posh. **6** *Jake regarded her with superior amusement* CONDESCENDING, supercilious, patronizing, haughty, disdainful, pompous, snobbish; *informal* high and mighty, hoity-toity, snooty, stuck-up.
– OPPOSITES junior, inferior.
● noun *my immediate superior* MANAGER, chief, supervisor, senior, controller, foreman; *informal* boss.
– OPPOSITES subordinate.

superiority ● noun SUPREMACY, advantage, lead, dominance, primacy, ascendancy, eminence.

superlative ● adjective EXCELLENT, magnificent, wonderful, marvellous, supreme, consummate, outstanding, remarkable, fine,

superlunary /sōōpərlōōnəri, syōō-/ ● **adjective** literary belonging to a higher world; celestial.
– ORIGIN Latin *superlunaris*, from *luna* 'moon'.
superman ● **noun** **1** another term for ÜBERMENSCH. **2** informal a man with exceptional physical or mental ability.
– ORIGIN coined by the Irish playwright G. B. Shaw in imitation of German *Übermensch* (used by Nietzsche).
supermarket ● **noun** a large self-service shop selling foods and household goods.
supermodel ● **noun** a very successful and famous fashion model.
supernal /sōōpern'l/ ● **adjective** literary **1** relating to the sky or the heavens. **2** supremely excellent.
– ORIGIN Latin *supernalis*, from *super* 'above'.
supernatural ● **adjective** **1** attributed to some force beyond scientific understanding or the laws of nature. **2** exceptionally or extraordinarily great. ● **noun** (**the supernatural**) supernatural manifestations or events.
– DERIVATIVES **supernaturally** adverb.
supernormal ● **adjective** beyond what is normal.
supernova /sōōpərnōvə, syōō-/ ● **noun** (pl. **supernovae** /sōōpərnōvee, syōō-/ or **supernovas**) Astronomy a star that undergoes a catastrophic explosion, becoming suddenly very much brighter.
supernumerary /sōōpərnyōōmərəri, syōō-/ ● **adjective** **1** present in excess of the normal or required number. **2** not belonging to a regular staff but engaged for extra work. ● **noun** (pl. **supernumeraries**) a supernumerary person or thing.
– ORIGIN Latin *supernumerarius* 'soldier added to a legion after it is complete'.
superordinate /sōōpərordinət, syōō-/ ● **noun** **1** a thing that represents a higher order or category within a system of classification. **2** a person of higher rank or status. ● **adjective** higher in status.
superpose ● **verb** place (something) on or above something else, especially so that they coincide.
– DERIVATIVES **superposition** noun.
– ORIGIN French *superposer*.
superpower ● **noun** any of the few most powerful and influential nations of the world.
supersaturate ● **verb** Chemistry increase the concentration of (a solution) beyond saturation point.
– DERIVATIVES **supersaturation** noun.
superscribe ● **verb** **1** write or print (an inscription) at the top of or on the outside of a document. **2** write or print (a character or word) above an existing one.
– DERIVATIVES **superscription** noun.
– ORIGIN Latin *superscribere* 'write above'.
superscript ● **adjective** (of a letter, figure, or symbol) written or printed above the line.
supersede /sōōpərseed/ ● **verb** take the place of; supplant.
– USAGE The standard spelling is **supersede** rather than **supercede**.
– ORIGIN Latin *supersedere* 'be superior to'.
supersonic ● **adjective** involving or referring to a speed greater than that of sound.
– DERIVATIVES **supersonically** adverb.
supersonics ● **plural noun** (treated as sing.) another term for ULTRASONICS.
superstar ● **noun** an extremely famous and successful performer or sports player.
– DERIVATIVES **superstardom** noun.
superstate ● **noun** a large and powerful state formed from a federation or union of nations.
superstition ● **noun** **1** excessively credulous belief in the supernatural. **2** a widely held but irrational belief in supernatural influences, especially as bringing good or bad luck.
– ORIGIN Latin, from *super-* 'over' + *stare* 'to stand'.
superstitious ● **adjective** characterized or influenced by superstition.
– DERIVATIVES **superstitiously** adverb.
superstore ● **noun** a very large out-of-town supermarket.
superstructure ● **noun** **1** a structure built on top of something else. **2** the part of a building above its foundations. **3** the parts of a ship, other than masts and rigging, above its hull and main deck. **4** a concept or idea based on others.
supertanker ● **noun** a very large oil tanker.
supertax ● **noun** an additional tax on something already taxed.
supervene /sōōpərveen, syōō-/ ● **verb** occur as an interruption or change to an existing situation.
– DERIVATIVES **supervenient** adjective **supervention** noun.
– ORIGIN Latin *supervenire* 'come in addition'.
supervise ● **verb** observe and direct the performance of (a task or activity) or the work of (a person).
– DERIVATIVES **supervision** noun **supervisor** noun **supervisory** adjective.
– ORIGIN Latin *supervidere* 'survey, supervise'.
superwoman ● **noun** informal a woman with exceptional physical or mental ability.
supinate /sōōpinayt, syōō-/ ● **verb** technical put or hold (a hand, foot, or limb) with the palm or sole turned upwards. Compare with PRONATE.
– DERIVATIVES **supination** noun.
– ORIGIN Latin *supinare* 'lay backwards'.
supinator ● **noun** Anatomy a muscle involved in supination.
supine /sōōpīn, syōō-/ ● **adjective** **1** lying face upwards. **2** failing to act as a result of laziness or lack of courage; passive.
– DERIVATIVES **supinely** adverb **supineness** noun.
– ORIGIN Latin *supinus* 'bent backwards'.
supper ● **noun** **1** a light or informal evening meal. **2** Scottish & N. English a meal consisting of the specified food with chips: *a fish supper*.
– PHRASES **sing for one's supper** provide a service in return for a benefit.
– ORIGIN from Old French *super* 'to sup'.
supplant ● **verb** supersede and replace.
– DERIVATIVES **supplanter** noun.
– ORIGIN Latin *supplantare* 'trip up'.
supple ● **adjective** (**suppler**, **supplest**) flexible or pliant.
– DERIVATIVES **suppleness** noun.
– ORIGIN Latin *supplex* 'submissive'.
supplement ● **noun** **1** a thing added to something else to en-

Thesaurus

choice, first-rate, first-class, premier, prime, unsurpassed, unequalled, unparalleled, unrivalled, pre-eminent; *informal* crack, ace, wicked; *Brit. informal* brilliant.
– OPPOSITES mediocre.
supernatural ● **adjective** **1** *supernatural powers* PARANORMAL, psychic, magic, magical, occult, mystic, mystical, superhuman, supernormal; *rare* extramundane. **2** *a supernatural being* GHOSTLY, phantom, spectral, other-worldly, unearthly, unnatural.
supersede ● **verb** REPLACE, take the place of, take over from, succeed; supplant, displace, oust, overthrow, remove, unseat; *informal* fill someone's shoes/boots.
superstition ● **noun** **1** *the old superstitions held by sailors* MYTH, belief, old wives' tale; legend, story. **2** *medicine was riddled with superstition* UNFOUNDED BELIEF, credulity, fallacy, delusion, illusion; magic, sorcery.
superstitious ● **adjective** **1** *superstitious beliefs* MYTHICAL, irrational, illusory, groundless, unfounded; traditional. **2** *he's incredibly superstitious* CREDULOUS, naive, gullible.
– OPPOSITES factual, sceptical.
supervise ● **verb** **1** *he had to supervise the loading* SUPERINTEND, oversee, be in charge of, preside over, direct, manage, run, look after, be responsible for, govern, organize, handle. **2** *you may need to supervise the patient* WATCH, oversee, keep an eye on, observe, monitor, mind.
supervision ● **noun** **1** *the supervision of the banking system* ADMINISTRATION, management, control, charge; superintendence, regulation, government, governance. **2** *keep your children under supervision* OBSERVATION, guidance, custody, charge, safe keeping, care, guardianship; control.
supervisor ● **noun** MANAGER, director, overseer, controller, superintendent, governor, chief, head; steward, foreman; *Brit.* ganger; *informal* boss; *Brit. informal* gaffer.
supine ● **adjective** **1** *she lay supine on the sand* FLAT ON ONE'S BACK, face upwards, flat, horizontal, recumbent, stretched out. **2** *a supine media* WEAK, spineless, yielding, effete; docile, acquiescent, pliant, submissive, passive, inert, spiritless.
– OPPOSITES prostrate, strong.
supper ● **noun** DINNER, evening meal, main meal; snack, bite to eat; *Brit.* tea; *formal* repast; *poetic/literary* refection.
supplant ● **verb** **1** *motorways supplanted the network of A-roads* REPLACE, supersede, displace, take over from, substitute for, override. **2** *the man he supplanted as Prime Minister* OUST, usurp,

hance or complete it. **2** a separate section added to a newspaper or periodical. **3** an additional charge payable for an extra service or facility. ● verb provide a supplement for.
– DERIVATIVES **supplemental** adjective **supplementation** noun.
– ORIGIN Latin *supplementum*, from *supplere* 'fill up'.
supplementary ● adjective completing or enhancing something.
supplementary benefit ● noun (in the UK) payment made by the state to those on a low income, now replaced by income support.
suppliant /supliənt/ ● noun a person who makes a humble or earnest request. ● adjective making or expressing a humble or earnest request.
supplicate /suplikayt/ ● verb ask or beg for something earnestly or humbly.
– DERIVATIVES **supplicant** adjective & noun **supplication** noun **supplicatory** adjective.
– ORIGIN Latin *supplicare* 'implore'.
supply ● verb (**supplies**, **supplied**) **1** make (something needed) available to someone. **2** provide with something needed. **3** be adequate to satisfy (a requirement or demand). ● noun (pl. **supplies**) **1** a stock or amount of something supplied or available. **2** the action of supplying. **3** (**supplies**) provisions and equipment necessary for an army or expedition. **4** (before another noun) acting as a temporary substitute for another: *a supply teacher.*
– PHRASES **supply and demand** the amount of goods or services available and the desire of buyers for them, considered as factors regulating its price.
– DERIVATIVES **supplier** noun.
– ORIGIN Latin *supplere* 'fill up'.
supply-side ● adjective Economics (of a policy) designed to increase output and employment by reducing taxation and other forms of restriction.
support ● verb **1** bear all or part of the weight of. **2** give assistance, encouragement, or approval to. **3** be actively interested in (a sports team). **4** provide with a home and the necessities of life. **5** be capable of sustaining (life). **6** confirm or back up. **7** endure; tolerate. **8** (**supporting**) of secondary importance to the leading roles in a play or film. **9** (of a pop or rock group or performer) function as a secondary act to (another) at a concert. ● noun **1** a person or thing that supports. **2** the action of supporting or the state of being supported. **3** assistance, encouragement, or approval.
– DERIVATIVES **supportable** adjective.
– ORIGIN Latin *supportare*, from *portare* 'carry'.
supporter ● noun a person who supports a sports team, policy, etc.
supportive ● adjective providing encouragement or emotional help.
– DERIVATIVES **supportively** adverb **supportiveness** noun.
suppose ● verb **1** think or assume that something is true or probable, but without proof. **2** (of a theory or argument) assume or require that something is the case as a precondition. **3** (**be supposed to do**) be required or expected to do.
– ORIGIN Latin *supponere*, from *ponere* 'to place'.
supposedly ● adverb according to what is generally believed or supposed.
supposition ● noun an assumption or hypothesis.

Thesaurus

overthrow, remove, topple, unseat, depose, dethrone; succeed, come after; *informal* fill someone's shoes/boots.
supple ● adjective **1** *her supple body* LITHE, limber, lissom(e), willowy, flexible, loose-limbed, agile, acrobatic, nimble, double-jointed. **2** *supple leather* PLIANT, pliable, flexible, soft, bendable, workable, malleable, stretchy, elastic, springy, yielding, rubbery.
– OPPOSITES stiff, rigid.
supplement ● noun **1** *a mouse is a keyboard supplement* ADDITION, supplementation, supplementary, extra, add-on, accessory, adjunct, appendage; *Computing* peripheral. **2** *a single room supplement* SURCHARGE, addition, increase. **3** *a supplement to the essay* APPENDIX, addendum, end matter, tailpiece, codicil, postscript, addition, coda. **4** *a special supplement with today's paper* PULL-OUT, insert, extra section.
● verb *they supplemented their incomes by spinning* AUGMENT, increase, add to, boost, swell, amplify, enlarge, top up.
supplementary ● adjective **1** *supplementary income* ADDITIONAL, supplemental, extra, more, further; add-on, subsidiary, auxiliary, ancillary. **2** *a supplementary index* APPENDED, attached, added, extra, accompanying.
suppliant ● noun *they were not mere suppliants* PETITIONER, supplicant, pleader, beggar, applicant.
● adjective *those around her were suppliant* PLEADING, begging, imploring, entreating, supplicating; on bended knee.
supplicate ● verb ENTREAT, beg, plead with, implore, petition, appeal to, call on, urge, enjoin, importune, sue, ask, request; *poetic/literary* beseech.
supply ● verb **1** *they supplied money to rebels* GIVE, contribute, provide, furnish, donate, bestow, grant, endow, impart; dispense, disburse, allocate, assign; *informal* fork out, shell out. **2** *the lake supplies the city with water* PROVIDE, furnish, endow, serve, confer; equip, arm. **3** *windmills supply their power needs* SATISFY, meet, fulfil, cater for.
● noun **1** *a limited supply of food* STOCK, store, reserve, reservoir, stockpile, hoard, cache; storehouse, repository; fund, mine, bank. **2** *the supply of alcoholic liquor* PROVISION, dissemination, distribution, serving. **3** *go to a supermarket for supplies* PROVISIONS, stores, stocks, rations, food, foodstuffs, eatables, produce, necessities; *informal* eats; *formal* comestibles.
● adjective *a supply teacher* SUBSTITUTE, stand-in, fill-in, locum, temporary, stopgap.
support ● verb **1** *a roof supported by pillars* HOLD UP, bear, carry, prop up, keep up, brace, shore up, underpin, buttress, reinforce. **2** *he struggled to support his family* PROVIDE FOR, maintain, sustain, keep, take care of, look after. **3** *she supported him to the end* COMFORT, encourage, sustain, buoy up, hearten, fortify, console, solace, reassure; *informal* buck up. **4** *evidence to support the argument* SUBSTANTIATE, back up, bear out, corroborate, confirm, attest to, verify, prove, validate, authenticate, endorse, ratify. **5** *the money supports charitable projects* HELP, aid, assist; contribute to, back, subsidize, fund, finance; *N. Amer. informal* bankroll. **6** *an independent candidate supported by locals* BACK, champion, help, assist, aid, abet, favour, encourage; vote for, stand behind, defend; sponsor, second, promote, endorse, sanction; *informal* throw one's weight behind. **7** *they support human rights* ADVOCATE, promote, champion, back, espouse, be in favour of, recommend, defend, subscribe to. **8** *I could not support the grief* ENDURE, bear, tolerate, stand, put up with, abide, stomach, sustain; *formal* brook; *archaic* suffer.
– OPPOSITES neglect, contradict, oppose.
● noun **1** *bridge supports* PILLAR, post, prop, upright, crutch, plinth, brace, buttress; base, substructure, foundation, underpinning. **2** *he pays support for his wife* MAINTENANCE, keep, sustenance, subsistence. **3** *I was lucky to have their support* ENCOURAGEMENT, friendship, strength, consolation, solace, succour, relief. **4** *he was a great support* COMFORT, help, assistance, tower of strength, prop, mainstay. **5** *support for community services* CONTRIBUTIONS, backing, donations, money, subsidy, funding, funds, finance, capital. **6** *they voiced their support for him* BACKING, help, assistance, aid, endorsement, approval; votes, patronage. **7** *a surge in support for decentralization* ADVOCACY, backing, promotion, championship, espousal, defence, recommendation.
supporter ● noun **1** *supporters of gun control* ADVOCATE, backer, adherent, promoter, champion, defender, upholder, crusader, proponent, campaigner, apologist. **2** *Labour supporters* BACKER, helper, adherent, follower, ally, voter, disciple; member. **3** *the charity relies on its supporters* CONTRIBUTOR, donor, benefactor, sponsor, backer, patron, subscriber, well-wisher. **4** *the team's supporters* FAN, follower, enthusiast, devotee, admirer; *informal* buff, addict.
supportive ● adjective **1** *a supportive teacher* ENCOURAGING, caring, sympathetic, reassuring, understanding, concerned, helpful, kind, kindly. **2** *we are supportive of the proposal* IN FAVOUR OF, favourable to, pro, on the side of, sympathetic to, well disposed to, receptive to.
suppose ● verb **1** *I suppose he's used to this* ASSUME, presume, expect, dare say, take it (as read); believe, think, fancy, suspect, sense, trust; guess, surmise, reckon, conjecture, deduce, infer, gather; *formal* opine. **2** *suppose you had a spacecraft* ASSUME, imagine, (let's) say; hypothesize, theorize, speculate. **3** *the theory supposes rational players* REQUIRE, presuppose, imply, assume; call for, need.
supposed ● adjective **1** *the supposed phenomena* APPARENT, ostensible, seeming, alleged, putative, reputed, rumoured, claimed, purported; professed, declared, assumed, presumed. **2** *I'm supposed to meet him at 8.30* MEANT, intended, expected; required, obliged.
supposition ● noun BELIEF, surmise, idea, notion, suspicion, con-

suppositious ● adjective based on assumption rather than fact.

supposititious /səpozzitiəsssh/ ● adjective substituted for the real thing; counterfeit.

– ORIGIN Latin *supposititius*, from *supponere* 'to substitute'.

suppository ● noun (pl. **suppositories**) a solid medical preparation in a roughly conical or cylindrical shape, designed to dissolve after insertion into the rectum or vagina.

– ORIGIN Latin *suppositorium* 'thing placed underneath'.

suppress ● verb **1** forcibly put an end to. **2** prevent from being expressed or published. **3** Psychoanalysis consciously avoid thinking of (an unpleasant idea or memory).

– DERIVATIVES **suppression** noun **suppressive** adjective **suppressor** noun.

– ORIGIN Latin *supprimere* 'press down'.

suppressant ● noun a drug or other substance which acts to suppress something.

suppurate /supyərayt/ ● verb form or discharge pus.

– DERIVATIVES **suppuration** noun **suppurative** /supyərətiv/ adjective.

– ORIGIN from Latin *sub-* 'below' + *pus* 'pus'.

supra- /so͞oprə/ ● prefix **1** above: *suprarenal*. **2** beyond; transcending: *supranational*.

– ORIGIN from Latin *supra* 'above, beyond, before in time'.

supranational ● adjective having power or influence that transcends national boundaries or governments.

supremacist ● noun an advocate of the supremacy of a particular group, especially one determined by race or sex. ● adjective relating to or advocating such supremacy.

– DERIVATIVES **supremacism** noun.

supremacy /so͞opremməsi, syo͞o-/ ● noun the state or condition of being superior to all others in authority, power, or status.

supreme ● adjective **1** highest in authority or rank. **2** very great or greatest; most important. ● noun (also **suprême**) a rich cream sauce or a dish served in this.

– DERIVATIVES **supremely** adverb

– ORIGIN Latin *supremus* 'highest'.

Supreme Being ● noun (**the Supreme Being**) a name for God.

supreme court ● noun the highest judicial court in a country or state.

Supreme Soviet ● noun the governing council of the former USSR or one of its constituent republics.

supremo /so͞opreemō, syo͞o-/ ● noun (pl. **supremos**) Brit. informal **1** a person in overall charge. **2** a person with great authority or skill in a certain area.

– ORIGIN Spanish, 'supreme'.

suq ● noun variant spelling of SOUK.

sur-[1] ● prefix equivalent to SUPER-.

– ORIGIN French.

sur-[2] ● prefix variant spelling of SUB- before *r*.

surcease ● noun archaic or N. Amer. **1** cessation. **2** relief. ● verb archaic cease.

– ORIGIN from Old French *surseoir* 'refrain, delay', from Latin *supersedere* (see SUPERSEDE).

surcharge ● noun **1** an additional charge or payment. **2** a mark printed on a postage stamp changing its value. ● verb **1** exact a surcharge from. **2** mark (a postage stamp) with a surcharge.

surcoat /surkōt/ ● noun historical an outer coat or garment worn over armour, in particular a short sleeveless garment worn as part of the insignia of an order of knighthood.

surd /surd/ ● noun **1** Mathematics a number which is not expressible as a ratio of two whole numbers. **2** Phonetics a speech sound uttered with the breath and not the voice (e.g. *f*, *k*, *p*).

– ORIGIN from Latin *surdus* 'deaf, mute'.

sure /shoor, shor/ ● adjective **1** completely confident that one is right. **2** (**sure of/to do**) certain to receive, get, or do. **3** undoubtedly true; completely reliable. **4** steady and confident. ● adverb informal certainly.

– PHRASES **be sure to do** do not fail to do. **for sure** informal without doubt. **make sure** confirm or ensure. **sure thing** informal **1** a certainty. **2** chiefly N. Amer. certainly. **to be sure** certainly; it must be admitted.

– DERIVATIVES **sureness** noun.

– ORIGIN Old French *sur*, from Latin *securus* 'free from care'.

sure-fire ● adjective informal certain to succeed.

sure-footed ● adjective **1** unlikely to stumble or slip. **2** confident and competent.

surely ● adverb **1** it must be true that. **2** certainly. **3** with assurance. **4** N. Amer. informal of course.

surety /shooriti, shor-/ ● noun (pl. **sureties**) **1** a person who takes responsibility for another's performance of an undertaking, e.g. the payment of a debt. **2** money given as a guarantee that someone will do something. **3** the state of being sure.

surf ● noun the mass or line of foam formed by waves breaking on a seashore or reef. ● verb **1** stand or lie on a surfboard and ride on the crest of a wave towards the shore. **2** occupy oneself by moving from site to site on (the Internet).

– DERIVATIVES **surfer** noun **surfing** noun.

– ORIGIN apparently from obsolete *suff*, of unknown origin.

surface ● noun **1** the outside part or uppermost layer of something. **2** the upper limit of a body of liquid. **3** outward appearance as distinct from less obvious aspects. ● adjective **1** relating to or occurring on the surface. **2** (of transportation) by sea or overland as contrasted with by air. **3** outward or superficial: *surface politeness*. ● verb **1** rise or come up to the surface. **2** become apparent. **3** provide (something, especially a road) with a particular surface. **4** informal appear after having been asleep.

Thesaurus

jecture, speculation, inference, theory, hypothesis, postulation, guess, feeling, hunch, assumption, presumption.

suppress ● verb **1** *they could suppress the rebellion* SUBDUE, repress, crush, quell, quash, squash, stamp out; defeat, conquer, overpower, put down, crack down on; end, stop, terminate, halt. **2** *she suppressed her irritation* CONCEAL, restrain, stifle, smother, bottle up, hold back, control, check, curb, contain, bridle, inhibit, keep a rein on, put a lid on. **3** *the report was suppressed* CENSOR, keep secret, conceal, hide, hush up, gag, withhold, cover up, stifle; ban, proscribe, outlaw; sweep under the carpet.

– OPPOSITES incite, reveal.

suppurate ● verb FESTER, form pus, discharge, run, weep, become septic; *Medicine* maturate.

supremacy ● noun ASCENDANCY, predominance, primacy, dominion, hegemony, authority, mastery, control, power, rule, sovereignty, influence; dominance, superiority, advantage, the upper hand, the whip hand, the edge; distinction, greatness.

supreme ● adjective **1** *the supreme commander* HIGHEST RANKING, chief, head, top, foremost, principal, superior, premier, first, prime; greatest, dominant, predominant, pre-eminent. **2** *a supreme achievement* EXTRAORDINARY, remarkable, incredible, phenomenal, rare, exceptional, outstanding, great, incomparable, unparalleled, peerless. **3** *the supreme sacrifice* ULTIMATE, final, last; utmost, extreme, greatest, highest.

– OPPOSITES subordinate, insignificant.

sure ● adjective **1** *I am sure that they didn't* CERTAIN, positive, convinced, confident, definite, assured, satisfied, persuaded; unhesitating, unwavering, unshakeable. **2** *someone was sure to be blamed* BOUND, likely, destined, fated. **3** *a sure winner with the children* GUARANTEED, unfailing, infallible, unerring, assured, certain, inevitable, as sure as eggs is eggs; *informal* sure-fire. **4** *he entered in the sure knowledge that he would win* UNQUESTIONABLE, indisputable, irrefutable, incontrovertible, undeniable, indubitable, undoubted, absolute, categorical, true, certain; obvious, evident, plain, clear, conclusive, definite. **5** *a sure sign that he's worried* RELIABLE, dependable, trustworthy, unfailing, infallible, certain, unambiguous, true, foolproof, established, effective; *informal* sure-fire; *formal* efficacious. **6** *the sure hand of the soloist* FIRM, steady, stable, secure, confident, steadfast, unfaltering, unwavering.

– OPPOSITES uncertain, unlikely.

● exclamation *'Can I come too?' 'Sure.'* YES, all right, of course, indeed, certainly, absolutely, agreed; *informal* OK, yeah, yep, uh-huh, you bet, I'll say, sure thing.

– PHRASES **be sure to** REMEMBER TO, don't forget to, see that you, mind that you, take care to, be certain to. **for sure** *(informal)* DEFINITELY, surely, certainly, without doubt, without question, undoubtedly, indubitably, absolutely, undeniably, unmistakably. **make sure** CHECK, confirm, make certain, ensure, assure; verify, corroborate, substantiate.

surely ● adverb **1** *surely you remembered?* IT MUST BE THE CASE THAT, assuredly, without question. **2** *I will surely die* CERTAINLY, for sure, definitely, undoubtedly, without doubt, doubtless, indubitably, unquestionably, without fail, inevitably, unavoidably. **3** *slowly but surely manipulating the public* FIRMLY, steadily, confidently, assuredly, unhesitatingly, unfalteringly, unswervingly, determinedly, doggedly.

surety ● noun **1** *she's a surety for her his obligations* GUARANTOR, sponsor. **2** *bail of £10,000 with a further £10,000 surety* PLEDGE, col-

S

– ORIGIN French, from *sur-* 'above' + *face* 'form, appearance, face'.

surface tension ● noun the tension of the surface film of a liquid, which tends to minimize surface area.

surface-to-air ● adjective (of a missile) designed to be fired from the ground or a vessel at an aircraft.

surfactant /surfaktənt/ ● noun a substance which tends to reduce the surface tension of a liquid in which it is dissolved.
– ORIGIN from *surface-active*.

surfboard ● noun a long, narrow board used in surfing.

surfeit ● noun **1** an excess. **2** archaic an illness caused by excessive eating or drinking. ● verb (**surfeited**, **surfeiting**) **1** cause to be wearied of something through excess. **2** archaic overeat.
– ORIGIN Old French, from Latin *super-* 'above, in excess' + *facere* 'do'.

surge ● noun **1** a sudden powerful forward or upward movement. **2** a sudden large temporary increase. **3** a powerful rush of an emotion or feeling. ● verb **1** move in a surge. **2** increase suddenly and powerfully.
– ORIGIN from Latin *surgere* 'to rise'.

surgeon ● noun **1** a medical practitioner qualified to practise surgery. **2** a doctor in the navy.
– ORIGIN Old French *serurgien*, from Greek *kheirourgia* 'handiwork, surgery'.

surgeon general ● noun (pl. **surgeons general**) (in the US) the head of a public health service or of the medical service of the armed forces.

surgery ● noun (pl. **surgeries**) **1** the branch of medicine concerned with treatment of bodily injuries or disorders by incision or manipulation. **2** Brit. a place where a medical practitioner treats or advises patients. **3** Brit. an occasion on which an MP, lawyer, or other professional person gives advice.

surgical ● adjective **1** relating to or used in surgery. **2** worn to correct or relieve an injury, illness, or deformity. **3** done with great precision.
– DERIVATIVES **surgically** adverb.

surgical spirit ● noun Brit. methylated spirit used for cleansing the skin before injections or surgery.

suricate /soorikayt/ ● noun a gregarious burrowing meerkat native to southern Africa.
– ORIGIN from a local African word.

surly ● adjective (**surlier**, **surliest**) bad-tempered and unfriendly.
– DERIVATIVES **surlily** adverb **surliness** noun.
– ORIGIN originally in the sense 'lordly, haughty': from obsolete *sirly*, from SIR.

surmise /sərmīz/ ● verb suppose without having evidence. ● noun a supposition or guess.
– ORIGIN originally in the sense 'allege formally': from Old French, 'accused', from Latin *supermittere* 'put in afterwards'.

surmount ● verb **1** overcome (a difficulty or obstacle). **2** stand or be placed on top of.
– DERIVATIVES **surmountable** adjective.

surname ● noun a hereditary name common to all members of a family, as distinct from a forename.

surpass ● verb **1** be greater or better than. **2** (**surpassing**) archaic or literary incomparable or outstanding.
– DERIVATIVES **surpassable** adjective.

surplice /surpliss/ ● noun a loose white linen robe worn over a cassock by clergy and choristers at Christian church services.
– ORIGIN Old French *sourpelis*, from Latin *super-* 'above' + *pellicia* 'fur garment'.

surplus ● noun **1** an amount left over when requirements have been met. **2** an excess of income or assets over expenditure or liabilities in a given period. ● adjective more than what is needed or used; extra.
– ORIGIN from Latin *super-* 'in addition' + *plus* 'more'.

surprise ● noun **1** a feeling of mild astonishment or shock caused by something unexpected. **2** an unexpected or astonishing thing. ● verb **1** cause to feel surprise. **2** capture, attack, or discover suddenly and unexpectedly.
– PHRASES **take by surprise 1** attack or capture unexpectedly. **2** happen unexpectedly to.
– DERIVATIVES **surprised** adjective **surprising** adjective.
– ORIGIN Old French, from Latin *superprehendere* 'seize'.

surreal ● adjective having the qualities of surrealism; bizarre.

Thesaurus

lateral, guaranty, guarantee, bond, assurance, insurance, deposit; security, indemnity, indemnification; earnest.

surface ● noun **1** *the surface of the door* OUTSIDE, exterior; top, side; finish, veneer. **2** *the surface of police culture* OUTWARD APPEARANCE, facade. **3** *a floured surface* WORKTOP, top, work surface, counter, table.
– OPPOSITES inside, interior.
● adjective *surface appearances* SUPERFICIAL, external, exterior, outward, ostensible, apparent, cosmetic, skin deep.
– OPPOSITES underlying.
● verb **1** *a submarine surfaced* COME TO THE SURFACE, come up, rise. **2** *the idea first surfaced in the sixties* EMERGE, arise, appear, come to light, crop up, materialize, spring up. **3** (*informal*) *she eventually surfaces for breakfast* GET UP, get out of bed, rise, wake, awaken, appear.
– OPPOSITES dive.
– PHRASES **on the surface** AT FIRST GLANCE, to the casual eye, outwardly, to all appearances, apparently, ostensibly, superficially, externally.

S

surfeit ● noun *a surfeit of apples* EXCESS, surplus, abundance, oversupply, superabundance, superfluity, glut, avalanche, deluge; overdose; too much; *informal* bellyful.
– OPPOSITES lack.
● verb *we'll all be surfeited with food* SATIATE, gorge, overfeed, overfill, glut, cram, stuff, overindulge, fill.

surge ● noun **1** *a surge of water* GUSH, rush, outpouring, stream, flow. **2** *a surge in oil production* INCREASE, rise, growth, upswing, upsurge, escalation, leap. **3** *a sudden surge of anger* RUSH, storm, torrent, blaze, outburst, eruption. **4** *the surge of sea* SWELL, heaving, rolling, roll, swirling; tide.
● verb **1** *the water surged into people's homes* GUSH, rush, stream, flow, burst, pour, cascade, spill, overflow, sweep, roll. **2** *the Dow Jones index surged 47.63 points* INCREASE, rise, grow, escalate, leap. **3** *the sea surged* SWELL, heave, rise, roll.

surly ● adjective SULLEN, sulky, moody, sour, unfriendly, unpleasant, scowling, unsmiling; bad-tempered, grumpy, crotchety, prickly, cantankerous, irascible, testy, short-tempered; abrupt, brusque, curt, gruff, churlish, ill-humoured, crabby, uncivil; *informal* grouchy.
– OPPOSITES pleasant.

surmise ● verb GUESS, conjecture, suspect, deduce, infer, conclude, theorize, speculate, divine; assume, presume, suppose, understand, gather, feel, sense, think, believe, imagine, fancy, reckon; *formal* opine.

surmount ● verb **1** *his reputation surmounts language barriers* OVERCOME, conquer, prevail over, triumph over, beat, vanquish; clear, cross, pass over; resist, endure. **2** *they surmounted the ridge* CLIMB OVER, top, ascend, scale, mount. **3** *the dome is surmounted by a statue* CAP, top, crown, finish.
– OPPOSITES descend.

surname ● noun FAMILY NAME, last name; patronymic.

surpass ● verb EXCEL, exceed, transcend; outdo, outshine, outstrip, outclass, overshadow, eclipse; improve on, top, trump, cap, beat, better, outperform.

surplus ● noun *a surplus of grain* EXCESS, surfeit, superabundance, superfluity, oversupply, glut, profusion, plethora; remainder, residue, remains, leftovers.
– OPPOSITES dearth.
● adjective *surplus adhesive* EXCESS, leftover, unused, remaining, extra, additional, spare; superfluous, redundant, unwanted, unneeded, dispensable, expendable.
– OPPOSITES insufficient.

surprise ● noun **1** *Kate looked at me in surprise* ASTONISHMENT, amazement, wonder, incredulity, bewilderment, stupefaction, disbelief. **2** *the test came as a big surprise* SHOCK, bolt from the blue, bombshell, revelation, rude awakening, eye-opener; *informal* turn up for the books, shocker.
● verb **1** *I was so surprised that I dropped it* ASTONISH, amaze, startle, astound, stun, stagger, shock; leave open-mouthed, take someone's breath away, dumbfound, daze, take aback, shake up; *informal* bowl over, floor, flabbergast; *Brit. informal* knock for six. **2** *she surprised a burglar* TAKE BY SURPRISE, catch unawares, catch off guard, catch red-handed, catch in the act, catch out; *Brit. informal* catch on the hop.

surprised ● adjective ASTONISHED, amazed, astounded, startled, stunned, staggered, shocked, nonplussed, taken aback, stupefied, dumbfounded, dumbstruck, speechless, thunderstruck, confounded, shaken up; *informal* bowled over, flabbergasted, floored, flummoxed.

surprising ● adjective UNEXPECTED, unforeseen, unpredictable; as-

– DERIVATIVES **surreally** adverb.

surrealism ● noun an avant-garde 20th-century movement in art and literature which sought to release the creative potential of the unconscious mind, for example by the irrational juxtaposition of images.

– DERIVATIVES **surrealist** noun & adjective **surrealistic** adjective.

surrender ● verb **1** stop resisting an opponent and submit to their authority. **2** give up (a person, right, or possession) on compulsion or demand. **3** (**surrender to**) abandon oneself entirely to (a powerful emotion or influence). **4** cancel (a life insurance policy) and receive back a proportion of the premiums paid. ● noun the action or an act of surrendering.

– ORIGIN Old French *surrendre*, from RENDER.

surreptitious /surrəptishəss/ ● adjective done secretly or furtively.

– DERIVATIVES **surreptitiously** adverb.

– ORIGIN originally in the sense 'obtained by suppression of the truth': from Latin *surreptitius* 'obtained secretly'.

surrey ● noun (pl. **surreys**) historical (in the US) a light four-wheeled carriage with two seats facing forwards.

– ORIGIN from *Surrey cart*, first made in *Surrey*, England.

surrogate /surrəgət/ ● noun **1** a substitute, especially a person deputizing for another in a role or office. **2** (in the Christian Church) a bishop's deputy who grants marriage licences.

– DERIVATIVES **surrogacy** noun.

– ORIGIN from Latin *surrogare* 'elect as a substitute'.

surrogate mother ● noun a woman who bears a child on behalf of another woman, either from her own egg or from having a fertilized egg from the other woman implanted in her womb.

surround ● verb **1** be all round; encircle. **2** be associated with. ● noun **1** a border or edging. **2** (**surrounds**) surroundings.

– ORIGIN originally in the sense 'overflow': from Latin *superundare*, from *undare* 'to flow'.

surroundings ● plural noun the conditions or area around a person or thing.

surtax ● noun an additional tax on something already taxed, especially a higher rate of tax on incomes above a certain level.

surtitle ● noun a caption projected on a screen above the stage in an opera, translating the text being sung. ● verb provide with surtitles.

surveillance /survaylənss/ ● noun close observation, especially of a suspected spy or criminal.

– ORIGIN French, from *sur-* 'over' + *veiller* 'watch'.

survey ● verb /sərvay/ **1** look carefully and thoroughly at. **2** examine and record the features of (an area of land) to produce a map or description. **3** Brit. examine and report on the condition of (a building), especially for a prospective buyer. **4** conduct a survey among (a group of people). ● noun /survay/ **1** a general view, examination, or description. **2** an investigation of the opinions or experience of a group of people, based on a series of questions. **3** an act of surveying. **4** a map or report obtained by surveying.

– ORIGIN Old French *surveier*, from Latin *super-* 'over' + *videre* 'to see'.

surveyor ● noun **1** a person who surveys land, buildings, etc. as a profession. **2** Brit. an official inspector of something for purposes of measurement and valuation.

survival ● noun **1** the state or fact of surviving. **2** an object or practice that has survived from an earlier time.

– PHRASES **survival of the fittest** Biology the continued existence of the organisms best adapted to their environment; natural selection.

survivalism ● noun **1** the policy of trying to ensure one's own survival or that of one's social or national group. **2** the practising of outdoor survival skills as a sport or hobby.

– DERIVATIVES **survivalist** noun & adjective.

survive ● verb **1** continue to live or exist. **2** continue to live or exist in spite of (an accident or ordeal). **3** remain alive after the death of.

– DERIVATIVES **survivable** adjective.

– ORIGIN Old French *sourvivre*, from Latin *super-* 'in addition' + *vivere* 'live'.

survivor ● noun a person who has survived.

sus- ● prefix variant spelling of SUB- before *c*, *p*, *t*.

susceptibility ● noun (pl. **susceptibilities**) **1** the state or fact of being susceptible. **2** (**susceptibilities**) a person's feelings, regarded as being easily hurt.

susceptible /səseptib'l/ ● adjective **1** (often **susceptible to**) likely to be influenced or harmed by a particular thing. **2** easily influenced by feelings or emotions. **3** (**susceptible of**) capable or admitting of.

– DERIVATIVES **susceptibly** adverb.

– ORIGIN Latin *susceptibilis*, from *suscipere* 'take up, sustain'.

sushi /sooshi/ ● noun a Japanese dish consisting of small balls or rolls of cold rice with vegetables, egg, or raw seafood.

– ORIGIN Japanese.

suspect ● verb /səspekt/ **1** believe to be probable or possible. **2** believe to be guilty of a crime or offence, without certain proof. **3** doubt the genuineness or truth of. ● noun /suspekt/ a person suspected of a crime or offence. ● adjective /suspekt/ possibly dangerous or false.

Thesaurus

tonishing, amazing, startling, astounding, staggering, incredible, extraordinary, breathtaking, remarkable; *informal* mind-blowing.

surrender ● verb **1** *the army surrendered* CAPITULATE, give in, give (oneself) up, give way, yield, concede (defeat), submit, climb down, back down, cave in, relent, crumble; lay down one's arms, raise the white flag, throw in the towel/sponge. **2** *they surrendered power to the government* GIVE UP, relinquish, renounce, forgo, forswear; cede, abdicate, waive, forfeit, sacrifice; hand over, turn over, yield, resign, transfer, grant. **3** *surrender all hope of changing things* ABANDON, give up, cast aside.

– OPPOSITES resist, seize.

● noun **1** *the surrender of the hijackers* CAPITULATION, submission, yielding, succumbing, acquiescence; fall, defeat. **2** *a surrender of power to the shop floor* RELINQUISHMENT, renunciation, cession, abdication, resignation, transfer.

surreptitious ● adjective SECRET, secretive, stealthy, clandestine, sneaky, sly, furtive; concealed, hidden, undercover, covert, veiled, cloak-and-dagger.

– OPPOSITES blatant.

surrogate ● noun SUBSTITUTE, proxy, replacement; deputy, representative, stand-in, standby, stopgap, relief, understudy.

surround ● verb *we were surrounded by cops* ENCIRCLE, enclose, encompass, ring; fence in, hem in, confine, bound, circumscribe, cut off; besiege, trap.

● noun *a fireplace with a wood surround* BORDER, edging, edge, perimeter, boundary, margin, skirting, fringe.

surrounding ● adjective NEIGHBOURING, nearby, near, neighbourhood, local; adjoining, adjacent, bordering, abutting; encircling, encompassing.

surroundings ● plural noun ENVIRONMENT, setting, milieu, background, backdrop; conditions, circumstances, situation, context; vicinity, locality, habitat.

surveillance ● noun OBSERVATION, scrutiny, watch, view, inspection, supervision; spying, espionage, infiltration, reconnaissance; *informal* bugging, wiretapping, recon.

survey ● verb **1** *he surveyed his work* LOOK AT, look over, observe, view, contemplate, regard, gaze at, stare at, eye; scrutinize, examine, inspect, scan, study, consider, review, take stock of; *informal* size up; *poetic/literary* behold. **2** *they surveyed 4000 drug users* INTERVIEW, question, canvass, poll, cross-examine, investigate, research, study, probe, sample. **3** *he was asked to survey the house* APPRAISE, assess, prospect; make a survey of, value.

● noun **1** *a survey of the current literature* STUDY, review, consideration, overview; scrutiny, examination, inspection, appraisal. **2** *a survey of sexual behaviour* POLL, review, investigation, inquiry, study, probe, questionnaire, census, research. **3** *a thorough survey of the property* APPRAISAL, assessment, valuation, estimate, estimation.

survive ● verb **1** *he survived by escaping through a hole* REMAIN ALIVE, live, sustain oneself, pull through, get through, hold on/out, make it, keep body and soul together. **2** *the theatre must survive* CONTINUE, remain, persist, endure, live on, persevere, abide, go on, carry on, be extant, exist. **3** *he was survived by his sons* OUTLIVE, outlast; live longer than.

susceptible ● adjective **1** *susceptible children* IMPRESSIONABLE, credulous, gullible, innocent, ingenuous, naive, easily led; defenceless, vulnerable; persuadable, tractable; sensitive, responsive, thin-skinned. **2** *people susceptible to blackmail* OPEN TO, receptive to, vulnerable to; an easy target for. **3** *he is susceptible to ulcers* LIABLE TO, prone to, subject to, inclined to, predisposed to, disposed to, given to, at risk of; *archaic* susceptive of. **4** *the database will be susceptible of exploitation* OPEN TO, capable of, admit-

– ORIGIN Latin *suspicere* 'mistrust'.

suspend ● verb **1** halt temporarily. **2** temporarily remove (someone) from a post as a punishment or during investigation. **3** defer or delay (an action, event, or judgement). **4** (**suspended**) Law (of a sentence) not enforced as long as no further offence is committed within a specified period. **5** hang from somewhere. **6** (**be suspended**) be dispersed in a suspension.

– ORIGIN Latin *suspendere*, from *pendere* 'hang'.

suspended animation ● noun temporary stopping of most vital functions, without death.

suspended ceiling ● noun a ceiling with a space between it and the floor above from which it hangs.

suspender ● noun **1** Brit. an elastic strap attached to a belt or garter, fastened to the top of a stocking to hold it up. **2** (**suspenders**) N. Amer. braces for holding up trousers.

suspender belt ● noun Brit. a woman's undergarment consisting of a decorative belt and suspenders.

suspense ● noun a state or feeling of excited or anxious uncertainty about what may happen.

– DERIVATIVES **suspenseful** adjective.

– ORIGIN Old French *suspens* 'abeyance', from Latin *suspendere* 'suspend'.

suspension ● noun **1** the action of suspending or the condition of being suspended. **2** the system of springs and shock absorbers by which a vehicle is supported on its wheels. **3** a mixture in which particles are dispersed throughout a fluid.

suspension bridge ● noun a bridge in which the deck is suspended from cables running between towers.

suspicion ● noun **1** a feeling or belief that something is possible or probable or that someone is guilty of a crime or offence. **2** cautious distrust. **3** a very slight trace: *a suspicion of a smile.*

– PHRASES **above suspicion** too good or honest to be thought capable of wrongdoing. **under suspicion** suspected of wrongdoing.

– ORIGIN Old French *suspeciun*, from Latin *suspicere* 'mistrust'.

suspicious ● adjective **1** having or showing suspicion. **2** giving an impression of dishonest or dangerous character.

– DERIVATIVES **suspiciously** adverb **suspiciousness** noun.

suss Brit. informal ● verb (**sussed**, **sussing**) **1** (often **suss out**) realize or understand the true character or nature of. **2** (**sussed**) clever and well informed. ● noun knowledge or awareness of a specified kind: *business suss.*

– ORIGIN abbreviation of SUSPECT.

sustain ● verb **1** strengthen or support physically or mentally. **2** bear (the weight of an object). **3** suffer (something unpleasant). **4** keep (something) going over time or continuously. **5** confirm that (something) is just or valid.

– DERIVATIVES **sustainer** noun **sustainment** noun.

– ORIGIN Latin *sustinere*, from *tenere* 'hold'.

sustainable ● adjective **1** able to be sustained. **2** (of industry, development, or agriculture) avoiding depletion of natural resources.

– DERIVATIVES **sustainability** noun **sustainably** adverb.

sustenance ● noun **1** food and drink regarded as sustaining life. **2** the process of sustaining or keeping alive.

susurration /sōōssəraysh'n, syōō-/ (also **susurrus** /soosurrəss, syoo-/) ● noun literary whispering or rustling.

– ORIGIN Latin, from *susurrare* 'to murmur, hum'.

sutler /sutlər/ ● noun historical a person who followed an army and sold provisions to the soldiers.

– ORIGIN from obsolete Dutch *soetelen* 'perform mean duties'.

sutra /sōōtrə/ ● noun **1** a rule or aphorism in Sanskrit literature, or a set of these on grammar or Hindu law or philosophy. **2** a Buddhist or Jainist scripture.

– ORIGIN Sanskrit, 'thread, rule'.

suttee /sutee, sutti/ (also **sati**) ● noun (pl. **suttees**) the former Hindu practice of a widow burning herself to death on her husband's funeral pyre.

– ORIGIN Sanskrit, 'faithful wife'.

suture /sōōchər/ ● noun **1** a stitch or row of stitches holding together the edges of a wound or surgical incision. **2** a thread or wire used for this. **3** a seam-like junction between two parts, especially between bones of the skull. ● verb stitch up with a suture.

– ORIGIN Latin *sutura*, from *suere* 'sew'.

suzerain /sōōzərayn/ ● noun **1** a sovereign or state having some control over another state that is internally autonomous. **2** a feudal overlord.

– DERIVATIVES **suzerainty** noun.

– ORIGIN French, from *sus* 'above' and *souverain* 'sovereign'.

Sv ● abbreviation sievert(s).

s.v. ● abbreviation (in textual references) under the word or heading given.

– ORIGIN from Latin *sub voce* or *sub verbo* 'under the word or voice'.

svelte ● adjective slender and elegant.

Thesaurus

ting of, receptive of, responsive to.

– OPPOSITES sceptical, immune, resistant.

suspect ● verb **1** *I suspected she'd made a mistake* HAVE A SUSPICION, have a feeling, feel, (be inclined to) think, fancy, reckon, guess, surmise, conjecture, conclude, have a hunch; suppose, presume, deduce, infer, sense, imagine; fear. **2** *he had no reason to suspect my honesty* DOUBT, distrust, mistrust, have misgivings about, be sceptical about, have qualms about, be suspicious of, be wary of, harbour reservations about; *informal* smell a rat.

● noun *a murder suspect* SUSPECTED PERSON, accused, defendant.

● adjective *a suspect package* SUSPICIOUS, dubious, doubtful, untrustworthy; odd, queer; *informal* fishy, funny, shady; *Brit. informal* dodgy.

S

suspend ● verb **1** *the court case was suspended* ADJOURN, interrupt, break off, postpone, delay, defer, shelve, put off, intermit, prorogue, hold over, hold in abeyance; cut short, discontinue, dissolve, disband, terminate; *N. Amer.* table; *informal* put on ice, put on the back burner, mothball; *N. Amer. informal* take a rain check on. **2** *he was suspended from his duties* EXCLUDE, debar, remove, eliminate, expel, eject. **3** *lights were suspended from the ceiling* HANG, sling, string; swing, dangle.

suspense ● noun *I can't bear the suspense* TENSION, uncertainty, doubt, anticipation, expectation, expectancy, excitement, anxiety, apprehension, strain.

– PHRASES **in suspense** EAGERLY, agog, with bated breath, on tenterhooks; on edge, anxious, edgy, jumpy, keyed up, uneasy; *informal* uptight, jittery.

suspension ● noun **1** *the suspension of army operations* ADJOURNMENT, interruption, postponement, delay, deferral, deferment, stay, prorogation; armistice; cessation, end, halt, stoppage, dissolution, disbandment, termination. **2** *his suspension from school* EXCLUSION, debarment, removal, elimination, expulsion, ejection; *Brit.* rustication.

suspicion ● noun **1** *she had a suspicion that he didn't like her* INTUITION, feeling, impression, inkling, hunch, fancy, notion, supposition, belief, idea, theory; presentiment, premonition; *informal* gut feeling, sixth sense. **2** *I confronted him with my suspicions* MISGIVING, doubt, qualm, reservation, hesitation, question; scepticism, uncertainty, distrust, mistrust. **3** *wine with a suspicion of soda* TRACE, touch, suggestion, hint, soupçon, tinge, shade, whiff, bit, drop, dash, taste, jot, mite.

suspicious ● adjective **1** *she gave him a suspicious look* DOUBTFUL, unsure, dubious, wary, chary, sceptical, distrustful, mistrustful, disbelieving, cynical. **2** *a highly suspicious character* DISREPUTABLE, unsavoury, dubious, suspect, dishonest-looking, funny-looking, slippery; *informal* shifty, shady; *Brit. informal* dodgy. **3** *she disappeared in suspicious circumstances* QUESTIONABLE, odd, strange, dubious, irregular, queer, funny, doubtful, mysterious, murky; *informal* fishy; *Brit. informal* dodgy.

– OPPOSITES trusting, honest, innocent.

sustain ● verb **1** *the balcony might not sustain the weight* BEAR, support, carry, stand, keep up, prop up, shore up, underpin. **2** *her memories sustained her* COMFORT, help, assist, encourage, succour, support, give strength to, buoy up, carry, cheer up, hearten; *informal* buck up. **3** *they were unable to sustain a coalition* CONTINUE, carry on, keep up, keep alive, maintain, preserve, conserve, perpetuate, retain. **4** *she had bread and cheese to sustain her* NOURISH, feed, nurture; maintain, preserve, keep alive, keep going, provide for. **5** *she sustained slight injuries* UNDERGO, experience, suffer, endure. **6** *the allegation was not sustained* UPHOLD, validate, ratify, vindicate, confirm, endorse; verify, corroborate, substantiate, bear out, prove, authenticate, back up, evidence, justify.

sustained ● adjective CONTINUOUS, ongoing, steady, continual, constant, prolonged, persistent, non-stop, perpetual, unabating, relentless, unrelieved, unbroken, never-ending, incessant, unceasing, ceaseless, round the clock.

– OPPOSITES sporadic.

sustenance ● noun **1** *the creature needs sustenance* NOURISHMENT, food, nutriment, nutrition, provisions, provender, rations; *informal*

– ORIGIN Italian *svelto*.

Svengali /svengaali/ ● noun a person who exercises a controlling influence on another, especially for a sinister purpose.

– ORIGIN from *Svengali*, a musician in George du Maurier's novel *Trilby* (1894) who controls Trilby's stage singing hypnotically.

S-VHS ● abbreviation super video home system, an improved version of VHS.

SW ● abbreviation **1** south-west. **2** south-western.

swab ● noun **1** an absorbent pad used for cleaning wounds or applying medication. **2** a specimen of a bodily secretion taken with a swab. **3** a mop or other absorbent device for cleaning or mopping up. **4** archaic a contemptible person. ● verb (**swabbed**, **swabbing**) clean or absorb with a swab.

– ORIGIN from archaic *swabber* 'sailor detailed to swab decks', from Dutch *zwabber*.

swaddle ● verb wrap in garments or cloth.

– ORIGIN from SWATHE².

swaddling clothes ● plural noun cloth bands formerly wrapped round a newborn child to calm it.

swag ● noun **1** an ornamental festoon of flowers, fruit, and greenery. **2** a curtain or drape fastened to hang in a drooping curve. **3** informal money or goods taken by a thief or burglar. **4** Austral./NZ a traveller's or miner's bundle of personal belongings. ● verb (**swagged**, **swagging**) **1** arrange in or decorate with swags. **2** chiefly literary hang or sway heavily.

– ORIGIN probably Scandinavian.

swagger ● verb walk or behave in a very confident or arrogant manner. ● noun a swaggering gait or manner. ● adjective (of a coat or jacket) cut with a loose flare from the shoulders.

– ORIGIN apparently from SWAG.

swagger stick ● noun a short cane carried by a military officer.

swagman ● noun Austral./NZ a tramp or itinerant worker carrying a bundle of belongings.

Swahili /swəheeli/ ● noun (pl. same) **1** a Bantu language widely used as a lingua franca in East Africa. **2** a member of a people of Zanzibar and nearby coastal regions.

– ORIGIN from an Arabic word meaning 'coasts'.

swain ● noun **1** archaic a country youth. **2** literary a young lover or suitor.

– ORIGIN Old Norse, 'lad'.

swallow¹ ● verb **1** cause or allow (food, drink, etc.) to pass down the throat. **2** use the throat muscles as if doing this, especially through fear or nervousness. **3** (often **swallow up**) take in and cause to disappear; engulf. **4** believe (an untrue or unlikely statement) unquestioningly. **5** put up with or meekly accept. **6** resist expressing: *he swallowed his pride.* ● noun an act of swallowing.

– DERIVATIVES **swallower** noun.

– ORIGIN Old English.

swallow² ● noun a swift-flying migratory songbird with a forked tail, feeding on insects in flight.

– PHRASES **one swallow does not make a summer** proverb a single fortunate event doesn't mean that what follows will also be good.

– ORIGIN Old English.

swallow dive ● noun Brit. a dive performed with one's arms outspread until close to the water.

swallow hole ● noun another term for SINKHOLE.

swallowtail ● noun **1** a deeply forked tail. **2** a large brightly coloured butterfly with tail-like projections on the hindwings.

swam past of SWIM.

swami /swaami/ ● noun (pl. **swamis**) a male Hindu religious teacher.

– ORIGIN Hindi, 'master, prince'.

swamp ● noun a bog or marsh. ● verb **1** overwhelm or flood with water. **2** overwhelm with too much of something; inundate.

– DERIVATIVES **swampy** adjective.

– ORIGIN probably ultimately from a Germanic base meaning 'sponge' or 'fungus'.

swan ● noun a large waterbird, typically white, with a long flexible neck, short legs, and webbed feet. ● verb (**swanned**, **swanning**) Brit. informal move or go in a casual, irresponsible, or ostentatious way.

– ORIGIN Old English.

swan dive ● noun N. Amer. a swallow dive.

swank informal ● verb display one's wealth, knowledge, or achievements in an attempt to impress others. ● noun behaviour, talk, or display intended to impress others.

– ORIGIN of unknown origin.

swanky ● adjective (**swankier**, **swankiest**) informal **1** stylishly luxurious and expensive. **2** inclined to show off.

swannery ● noun (pl. **swanneries**) Brit. a place where swans are kept or bred.

swansdown ● noun **1** the fine down of a swan, used for trimmings and powder puffs. **2** a thick cotton fabric with a soft nap on one side.

swansong ● noun the final performance or activity of a person's career.

– ORIGIN suggested by German *Schwanengesang*, denoting a song fabled to be sung by a dying swan.

swan-upping ● noun Brit. the annual practice of catching swans on the River Thames and marking them to indicate ownership by the Crown or a corporation.

swap (also **swop**) ● verb (**swapped**, **swapping**) exchange or substitute. ● noun an act of exchanging one thing for another.

– ORIGIN originally in the sense 'throw forcibly', later 'strike hands as a token of agreement': probably imitative.

SWAPO /swaapō/ ● abbreviation South West Africa People's Organization.

sward /swawrd/ ● noun **1** an expanse of short grass. **2** the upper layer of soil, especially when covered with grass.

– ORIGIN Old English, 'skin'.

swarf /swaarf/ ● noun fine chips or filings produced by machining.

– ORIGIN Old English or Old Norse.

swarm ● noun **1** a large or dense group of flying insects. **2** a large number of honeybees that leave a hive with a queen in order to establish a new colony. **3** a large group of people or things. ● verb **1** move in or form a swarm. **2** (**swarm with**) be crowded or overrun with. **3 swarm up** climb rapidly by gripping with one's hands and feet.

– ORIGIN Old English.

swart /swawrt/ ● adjective archaic or literary swarthy.

S

Thesaurus

grub, chow; *Brit. informal* scoff; *formal* comestibles; *poetic/literary* viands; *dated* victuals. **2** *the sustenance of his family* SUPPORT, maintenance, keep, living, livelihood, subsistence, income.

swagger ● verb **1** *we swaggered into the arena* STRUT, parade, stride; walk confidently; *informal* sashay. **2** *he likes to swagger about his kindness* BOAST, brag, bluster, crow, gloat; strut, posture, blow one's own trumpet, lord it; *informal* show off, swank.

● noun **1** *a slight swagger in his stride* STRUT; confidence, arrogance, ostentation. **2** *he was full of swagger* BLUSTER, braggadocio, bumptiousness, vainglory; *informal* swank.

swallow ● verb **1** *she couldn't swallow anything* EAT, gulp down, consume, devour, put away; ingest, assimilate; drink, guzzle, quaff, imbibe, sup, slug; *informal* polish off, swig, swill, down; *Brit. informal* scoff. **2** *I can't swallow any more of your insults* TOLERATE, endure, stand, put up with, bear, abide, countenance, stomach, take, accept; *informal* hack; *Brit. informal* stick; *formal* brook. **3** *he swallowed my story* BELIEVE, credit, accept, trust; *informal* fall for, buy, go for, {swallow hook, line, and sinker}. **4** *she swallowed her pride* RESTRAIN, repress, suppress, hold back, fight back; overcome, check, control, curb, rein in; silence, muffle, stifle, smother, hide, bottle up; *informal* keep a/the lid on.

– PHRASES **swallow someone/something up 1** *the darkness swallowed them up* ENGULF, swamp, devour, overwhelm, overcome. **2** *the colleges were swallowed up by universities* TAKE OVER, engulf, absorb, assimilate, incorporate.

swamp ● noun *his horse got stuck in a swamp* MARSH, bog, quagmire, mire, morass, fen; quicksand; *N. Amer.* bayou; *archaic* quag.

● verb **1** *the rain was swamping the dry roads* FLOOD, inundate, deluge, immerse; soak, drench, saturate. **2** *he was swamped by media attention* OVERWHELM, inundate, flood, deluge, engulf, snow under, overload, overpower, weigh down, besiege, beset.

swampy ● adjective MARSHY, boggy, fenny, miry; soft, soggy, muddy, spongy, heavy, squelchy, waterlogged, sodden, wet; *archaic* quaggy.

swap ● verb **1** *I swapped some toys for a set of dice* EXCHANGE, trade, barter, interchange, bargain; switch, change, replace. **2** *we swapped jokes* BANDY, exchange, trade, reciprocate.

● noun *a job swap* EXCHANGE, interchange, trade, switch, trade-off, substitution.

swarm ● noun **1** *a swarm of bees* HIVE, flock, collection. **2** *a swarm*

– ORIGIN Old English.
swarthy ● adjective (**swarthier**, **swarthiest**) dark-complexioned.
– DERIVATIVES **swarthiness** noun.
– ORIGIN from obsolete *swarty*, from Old English.
swash ● verb **1** (of water) move with a splashing sound. **2** archaic flamboyantly swagger about or wield a sword. ● noun the rush of seawater up the beach after the breaking of a wave.
– ORIGIN imitative.
swashbuckling ● adjective engaging in daring and romantic adventures with bravado or flamboyance.
– DERIVATIVES **swashbuckler** noun.
swastika /swostikə/ ● noun an ancient symbol in the form of an equal-armed cross with each arm continued at a right angle, used (in clockwise form) as the emblem of the German Nazi party.
– ORIGIN from a Sanskrit word meaning 'well-being'.
swat ● verb (**swatted**, **swatting**) hit or crush with a sharp blow from a flat object.
– ORIGIN originally in the sense 'sit down': northern English dialect and US variant of SQUAT.
swatch ● noun **1** a piece of fabric used as a sample. **2** a number of fabric samples bound together.
– ORIGIN of unknown origin.
swathe[1] /swayth/ (chiefly N. Amer. also **swath** /swawth/) ● noun (pl. **swathes** or **swaths** /swaytthz, swawths/) **1** a row or line of grass, corn, etc. as it falls when mown or reaped. **2** a broad strip or area: *vast swathes of countryside.*
– ORIGIN Old English, 'track, trace'.
swathe[2] /swayth/ ● verb wrap in several layers of fabric. ● noun a strip of material in which something is wrapped.
– ORIGIN Old English.
sway ● verb **1** move slowly and rhythmically backwards and forwards or from side to side. **2** cause (someone) to change their opinion; influence. **3** literary rule; govern. ● noun **1** a swaying movement. **2** influence; rule.
– PHRASES **hold sway** have great power or influence.
– ORIGIN perhaps related to Low German *swājen* 'be blown to and fro' and Dutch *zwaaien* 'swing, walk totteringly'.
Swazi /swaazi/ ● noun (pl. same or **Swazis**) a person from Swaziland.
– ORIGIN named after *Mswati*, a 19th-century king of the Swazis.
swear ● verb (past **swore**; past part. **sworn**) **1** state or promise solemnly or on oath. **2** compel to observe a certain course of action: *I am sworn to secrecy.* **3** use offensive or obscene language, especially to express anger.
– PHRASES **swear blind** Brit. informal affirm something emphatically. **swear by** informal have or express great confidence in. **swear in** admit (someone) to a position or office by directing them to take a formal oath. **swear off** informal promise to abstain from. **swear to** give an assurance that something is the case.
– DERIVATIVES **swearer** noun.
– ORIGIN Old English, related to ANSWER.
swear word ● noun an offensive or obscene word.
sweat ● noun **1** moisture exuded through the pores of the skin, especially as a reaction to heat, physical exertion, or anxiety. **2** informal a state of anxiety or distress. **3** informal hard work or a laborious undertaking. ● verb (past and past part. **sweated** or N. Amer. **sweat**) **1** exude sweat. **2** exert a great deal of strenuous effort. **3** be in a state of extreme anxiety. **4** (of a substance) exude moisture. **5** cook (chopped vegetables) slowly in a pan with a small amount of fat.
– PHRASES **break sweat** informal exert oneself physically. **by the sweat of one's brow** by one's own hard labour. **no sweat** informal all right; no problem. **sweat blood** informal make an extremely strenuous effort.
– ORIGIN Old English.
sweatband ● noun a band of absorbent material worn to soak up sweat.
sweated ● adjective (of goods or workers) produced by or subjected to long hours under poor conditions.
sweater ● noun a pullover with long sleeves.
sweatpants ● plural noun loose, warm trousers with an elasticated or drawstring waist, worn for exercise or leisure.
sweatshirt ● noun a loose knitted cotton sweater worn for exercise or leisure.
sweatshop ● noun a factory or workshop employing workers for long hours in poor conditions.
sweaty ● adjective (**sweatier**, **sweatiest**) exuding, soaked in, or inducing sweat.
– DERIVATIVES **sweatily** adverb **sweatiness** noun.
Swede ● noun a person from Sweden.
swede ● noun Brit. a large, round yellow-fleshed root vegetable originally introduced into Scotland from Sweden; rutabaga.
Swedish ● noun the Scandinavian language of Sweden. ● adjective relating to Sweden.
sweep ● verb (past and past part. **swept**) **1** clean (an area) by brushing away dirt or litter. **2** move or push with great force. **3** (**sweep away/aside**) remove or abolish swiftly and suddenly. **4** search or survey (an area). **5** pass or traverse swiftly and smoothly. **6** affect swiftly and widely: *violence swept the coun-*

Thesaurus

of gendarmes CROWD, multitude, horde, host, mob, gang, throng, mass, army, troop, herd, pack; poetic/literary myriad.
● verb *reporters were swarming all over the place* FLOCK, crowd, throng, surge, stream.
– PHRASES **be swarming with** BE CROWDED WITH, be thronged with, be overrun with, be full of, abound in, be teeming with, bristle with, be alive with, be crawling with, be infested with, overflow with, be prolific in, be abundant in; informal be thick with.
swarthy ● adjective DARK-SKINNED, olive-skinned, dusky, tanned, saturnine, black; archaic swart.
– OPPOSITES pale.
swashbuckling ● adjective DARING, heroic, daredevil, dashing, adventurous, bold, valiant, valorous, fearless, lionhearted, dauntless, devil-may-care; gallant, chivalrous, romantic.
– OPPOSITES timid.
swathe ● verb WRAP, envelop, bind, swaddle, bandage, cover, shroud, drape, wind, enfold, sheathe.
sway ● verb **1** *the curtains swayed in the breeze* SWING, shake, oscillate, undulate, move to and fro, move back and forth. **2** *she swayed on her feet* STAGGER, wobble, rock, lurch, reel, roll, list, stumble, pitch. **3** *we are swayed by the media* INFLUENCE, affect, bias, persuade, talk round, win over; manipulate, bend, mould. **4** *you must not be swayed by emotion* RULE, govern, dominate, control, guide.
● noun **1** *the sway of her hips* SWING, roll, shake, oscillation, undulation. **2** *a province under the sway of the Franks* JURISDICTION, rule, government, sovereignty, dominion, control, command, power, authority, ascendancy, domination, mastery.
– PHRASES **hold sway** HOLD POWER, wield power, exercise power, rule, be in control, predominate; have the upper hand, have the edge, have the whip hand; informal run the show, be in the driving seat, be in the saddle.
swear ● verb **1** *they swore to marry each other* PROMISE, VOW, pledge, give one's word, take an oath, undertake, guarantee; Law depose; formal aver. **2** *she swore she would never go back* INSIST, avow, pronounce, declare, proclaim, assert, profess, maintain, contend, emphasize, stress; formal aver. **3** *Kate spilled wine and swore* CURSE, blaspheme, utter profanities, utter oaths, use bad language, take the Lord's name in vain; informal cuss, eff and blind; archaic execrate.
– PHRASES **swear by** (informal) EXPRESS CONFIDENCE IN, have faith in, trust, believe in; set store by, value; informal rate. **swear off** (informal) RENOUNCE, forswear, forgo, abstain from, go without, shun, avoid, eschew, steer clear of; give up, dispense with, stop, discontinue, drop; informal kick, quit; Brit. informal jack in.
swearing ● noun BAD LANGUAGE, strong language, cursing, blaspheming, blasphemy; profanities, obscenities, curses, oaths, expletives, swear words; informal cussing, effing and blinding, four-letter words; formal imprecation.
sweat ● noun **1** *he was drenched with sweat* PERSPIRATION, moisture, dampness, wetness; Medicine diaphoresis, hidrosis. **2** (informal) *he got into such a sweat about that girl* FLUSTER, panic, frenzy, fever, pother; informal state, flap, tizzy, dither, stew, lather; N. Amer. informal twit. **3** (informal) *the sweat of the working classes* LABOUR, hard work, toil(s), effort(s), exertion(s), industry, drudgery, slog; informal graft, grind, elbow grease.
– RELATED TERMS sudatory.
● verb **1** *she was sweating heavily* PERSPIRE, swelter, glow; be damp, be wet; secrete. **2** *I've sweated over this for six months* WORK (HARD), work like a Trojan, labour, toil, slog, slave, work one's fingers to the bone; informal graft, plug away; archaic drudge. **3** (N. Amer. informal) *I sweated over my mistakes* WORRY, agonize, fuss, panic, fret, dither, lose sleep; informal be on pins and needles, be in a state, be in a flap, be in a stew, torture oneself, torment oneself.

try. **7** extend continuously in an arc or curve. **8** (**swept** or **swept back**) (of an aircraft's wings) directed backwards from the fuselage. **9** N. Amer. be victorious in (a series of games). ● **noun 1** an act of sweeping. **2** a long, swift, curving movement. **3** a long curved stretch of road, river, etc. **4** the range or scope of something. **5** (also **chimney sweep**) a person whose job is cleaning out the soot from chimneys. **6** informal a sweepstake. **7** N. Amer. a victory in every event, award, or place in a contest.
– PHRASES **sweep the board** win every event or prize in a contest.
– ORIGIN Old English.

sweeper ● **noun 1** a person or device that cleans by sweeping. **2** Soccer a player stationed behind the other defenders, free to defend at any point across the field.

sweeping ● **adjective 1** extending or performed in a long, continuous curve. **2** wide in range or effect. **3** (of a statement) too general. ● **noun** (**sweepings**) dirt or refuse collected by sweeping.
– DERIVATIVES **sweepingly** adverb.

sweepstake ● **noun** (also **sweepstakes**) a form of gambling, especially on sporting events, in which all the stakes are divided among the winners.

sweet ● **adjective 1** having the pleasant taste characteristic of sugar or honey; not salt, sour, or bitter. **2** fragrant. **3** (of air, water, etc.) fresh and pure. **4** working, moving, or done smoothly or easily. **5** pleasing; delightful. **6** pleasant and kind or thoughtful. **7** charming and endearing. **8** dear; beloved. **9** (**sweet on**) informal, dated infatuated or in love with. ● **noun 1** Brit. a small shaped piece of confectionery made with sugar. **2** Brit. a sweet dish forming a course of a meal; a dessert. **3** (**sweets**) literary the pleasures or delights found in something.
– PHRASES **she's sweet** Austral./NZ informal all is well.
– DERIVATIVES **sweetish** adjective **sweetly** adverb.
– ORIGIN Old English.

sweet-and-sour ● **adjective** cooked with both sugar and a sour substance, such as vinegar or lemon.

sweetbread ● **noun** the thymus gland or pancreas of an animal, used for food.

sweetbriar ● **noun** a wild rose with fragrant leaves and flowers.

sweetcorn ● **noun** maize of a variety with kernels that have a high sugar content, eaten as a vegetable.

sweeten ● **verb 1** make or become sweet or sweeter. **2** make more agreeable or acceptable.

sweetener ● **noun 1** a substance used to sweeten food or drink. **2** informal, chiefly Brit. an inducement or bribe.

sweetheart ● **noun 1** a person that one is in a romantic relationship with. **2** (before another noun) informal agreed privately by two sides in their own interests: *a sweetheart deal.*

sweetheart neckline ● **noun** a low neckline shaped like the top of a heart.

sweetie ● **noun** informal **1** Brit. a sweet. **2** (also **sweetie-pie**) used as a term of endearment.

sweetmeal ● **noun** Brit. sweetened wholemeal.

sweetmeat ● **noun** archaic an item of confectionery or sweet food.

sweetness ● **noun** the quality of being sweet.
– PHRASES **sweetness and light** good-natured benevolence or harmony.

sweet pea ● **noun** a climbing plant of the pea family with colourful fragrant flowers.

sweet pepper ● **noun** a large green, yellow, orange, or red variety of capsicum with a mild or sweet flavour.

sweet potato ● **noun** the edible tuber of a tropical climbing plant, with pinkish-orange slightly sweet flesh.

sweet-talk ● **verb** informal persuade to do something by insincere flattery or kind words.

sweet tooth ● **noun** (pl. **sweet tooths**) a great liking for sweet-tasting foods.

sweet william ● **noun** a fragrant plant with flattened clusters of vivid red, pink, or white flowers.

swell ● **verb** (past part. **swollen** or **swelled**) **1** become larger or rounder in size. **2** increase in intensity, amount, or volume. ● **noun 1** a full or gently rounded form. **2** a gradual increase in sound, amount, or intensity. **3** a slow, regular movement of the sea in rolling waves that do not break. **4** a mechanism for producing a crescendo or diminuendo in an organ or harmonium. **5** informal, dated a fashionable person of high social position. ● **adjective 1** N. Amer. informal, dated excellent; very good. **2** archaic smart; fashionable.
– ORIGIN Old English.

swelling ● **noun** an abnormal enlargement of a part of the body

Thesaurus

sweaty ● **adjective** PERSPIRING, sweating, clammy, sticky, glowing; moist, damp.

sweep ● **verb 1** *she swept the floor* BRUSH, clean, scrub, wipe, mop, dust, scour; *informal* do. **2** *I swept the crumbs off* REMOVE, brush, clean, clear, whisk. **3** *he was swept out to sea* CARRY, pull, drag, tow. **4** *riots swept the country* ENGULF, overwhelm, flood. **5** *he swept down the stairs* GLIDE, sail, breeze, drift, flit, flounce; stride, stroll, swagger. **6** *a limousine swept past* GLIDE, sail, rush, race, streak, speed, fly, zoom, whizz, hurtle; *informal* tear, whip. **7** *police swept the conference room* SEARCH, probe, check, explore, go through, scour, comb.
● **noun 1** *a great sweep of his hand* GESTURE, stroke, wave, movement. **2** *a security sweep* SEARCH, hunt, exploration, probe. **3** *a long sweep of golden sand* EXPANSE, tract, stretch, extent, plain. **4** *the broad sweep of our interests* RANGE, span, scope, compass, reach, spread, ambit, remit, gamut, spectrum, extent.
– PHRASES **sweep something aside** DISREGARD, ignore, take no notice of, dismiss, shrug off, forget about, brush aside. **sweep something under the carpet** HIDE, conceal, suppress, hush up, keep quiet about, censor, gag, withhold, cover up, stifle.

sweeping ● **adjective 1** *sweeping changes* EXTENSIVE, wide-ranging, global, broad, comprehensive, all-inclusive, all-embracing, far-reaching, across the board; thorough, radical; *informal* wall-to-wall. **2** *a sweeping victory* OVERWHELMING, decisive, thorough, complete, total, absolute, out-and-out, unqualified. **3** *sweeping statements* WHOLESALE, blanket, generalized, all-inclusive, unqualified, indiscriminate, universal, oversimplified, imprecise. **4** *sweeping banks of heather* BROAD, extensive, expansive, vast, spacious, boundless, panoramic.
– OPPOSITES limited, narrow, focused, small.

sweet ● **adjective 1** *sweet biscuits* SUGARY, sweetened, saccharine; sugared, honeyed, candied, glacé; sickly, cloying. **2** *the sweet scent of roses* FRAGRANT, aromatic, perfumed; *poetic/literary* ambrosial. **3** *her sweet voice* DULCET, melodious, lyrical, mellifluous, musical, tuneful, soft, harmonious, silvery, honeyed, mellow, rich, golden. **4** *life was still sweet* PLEASANT, pleasing, agreeable, delightful, nice, satisfying, gratifying, good, acceptable, fine; *informal* lovely, great. **5** *the sweet March air* PURE, wholesome, fresh, clean, clear. **6** *she has a sweet nature* LIKEABLE, appealing, engaging, amiable, pleasant, agreeable, genial, friendly, nice, kind, thoughtful, considerate; charming, enchanting, captivating, delightful, lovely. **7** *she looks quite sweet* CUTE, lovable, adorable, endearing, charming, attractive, dear. **8** *my sweet Lydia* DEAR, dearest, darling, beloved, loved, cherished, precious, treasured.
– OPPOSITES sour, savoury, harsh, disagreeable.
● **noun 1** *(Brit.) sweets for the children* CONFECTIONERY, chocolate, bonbon, fondant, toffee; *N. Amer.* candy; *informal* sweetie; *archaic* sweetmeat. **2** *(Brit.) a delicious sweet for the guests* DESSERT, pudding, second course, last course; *Brit. informal* afters, pud. **3** *happy birthday my sweet!* DEAR, darling, dearest, love, sweetheart, beloved, honey, pet, treasure, angel.
– PHRASES **sweet on** *(informal)* FOND OF, taken with, attracted to, in love with, enamoured of, captivated by, infatuated with, keen on, devoted to, smitten with; *informal* gone on, mad about, bowled over by; *Brit. informal* daft about.

sweeten ● **verb 1** *sweeten the milk with honey* MAKE SWEET, add sugar to, sugar, sugar-coat. **2** *he chewed gum to sweeten his breath* FRESHEN, refresh, purify, deodorize, perfume. **3** *try to sweeten the bad news* SOFTEN, ease, alleviate, mitigate, temper, cushion; embellish, embroider. **4** *(informal) a bigger dividend to sweeten shareholders* MOLLIFY, placate, soothe, soften up, pacify, appease, win over.

sweetheart ● **noun 1** *you look lovely, sweetheart* DARLING, dear, dearest, love, beloved, sweet; *informal* honey, sweetie, sugar, baby, babe, poppet. **2** *my high-school sweetheart* LOVER, love, girlfriend, boyfriend, beloved, significant other, lady love, loved one, suitor, admirer; *informal* steady, flame; *poetic/literary* swain; *dated* beau; *archaic* paramour.

swell ● **verb 1** *her lip swelled up* EXPAND, bulge, distend, inflate, dilate, bloat, puff up, balloon, fatten, fill out, tumefy; *rare* intumesce. **2** *the population swelled* GROW, enlarge, increase, expand, rise, escalate, multiply, proliferate, snowball, mushroom. **3** *she swelled*

as a result of an accumulation of fluid.

swelter • verb be uncomfortably hot. • noun an uncomfortably hot atmosphere.
– ORIGIN from dialect *swelt* 'perish', from Germanic.

swept past and past participle of SWEEP.

swerve • verb abruptly diverge from a straight course. • noun an abrupt change of course.
– ORIGIN Old English, 'leave, turn aside'.

swift • adjective **1** happening quickly or promptly. **2** moving or capable of moving at high speed. • noun a fast-flying insect-eating bird with long, slender wings, spending most of its life on the wing.
– DERIVATIVES **swiftly** adverb **swiftness** noun.
– ORIGIN Old English, from a base meaning 'move in a course, sweep'.

swig informal • verb (**swigged**, **swigging**) drink in large draughts. • noun a large draught of drink.
– ORIGIN of unknown origin.

swill • verb **1** Brit. rinse out with large amounts of water. **2** Brit. (of liquid) swirl round in a container or cavity. **3** informal drink greedily or in large quantities. • noun **1** kitchen refuse and waste food mixed with water for feeding to pigs. **2** informal alcohol of inferior quality.
– ORIGIN Old English.

swim • verb (**swimming**; past **swam**; past part. **swum**) **1** propel oneself through water by bodily movement. **2** be immersed in or covered with liquid. **3** experience a dizzily confusing sensation. • noun **1** an act or period of swimming. **2** a pool in a river which is a particularly good spot for fishing.
– PHRASES **in the swim** involved in or aware of current affairs or events.
– DERIVATIVES **swimmer** noun.
– ORIGIN Old English.

swim bladder • noun a gas-filled sac in a fish's body, used to maintain buoyancy.

swimming costume • noun Brit. a woman's one-piece swimsuit.

swimmingly • adverb informal smoothly and satisfactorily.

swimming trunks • plural noun shorts worn by men for swimming.

swimsuit • noun a woman's one-piece swimming costume.

swimwear • noun clothing worn for swimming.

swindle • verb use deception to obtain (money) or deprive (someone) of money or possessions. • noun a fraudulent scheme or action.
– DERIVATIVES **swindler** noun.
– ORIGIN German *schwindeln* 'be giddy', also 'tell lies'.

swine • noun **1** (pl. same) formal or N. Amer. a pig. **2** (pl. same or **swines**) informal a contemptible or disgusting person.
– DERIVATIVES **swinish** adjective.
– ORIGIN Old English, related to SOW².

swine fever • noun an intestinal disease of pigs, caused by a virus.

swineherd • noun chiefly historical a person who tends pigs.

swine vesicular disease • noun an infectious disease of pigs, causing blisters around the mouth and feet.

swing • verb (past and past part. **swung**) **1** move back and forth or from side to side while or as if suspended. **2** move by grasping a support and leaping. **3** move in a smooth, curving line. **4** (**swing at**) attempt to hit or punch. **5** shift from one opinion, mood, or state of affairs to another. **6** have a decisive influence on (a vote, judgement, etc.). **7** informal succeed in bringing about. **8** play music with an easy flowing but vigorous rhythm. **9** informal be lively, exciting, or fashionable. **10** informal swap sexual partners or engage in group sex. **11** informal be executed by hanging. • noun **1** a seat suspended by ropes or chains, on which someone can sit and swing back and forth. **2** an act of swinging. **3** a discernible change in public opinion, especially in an election. **4** a style of jazz or dance music with an easy flowing but vigorous rhythm. **5** the manner in which a golf club or a bat is swung.
– PHRASES **get into the swing of things** informal become accustomed to an activity or routine. **go with a swing** informal be lively and enjoyable. **in full swing** at the height of activity. **swing the lead** Brit. informal shirk one's duty. [ORIGIN with nautical allusion to using a lead to ascertain the depth of water.] **swings and roundabouts** Brit. a situation in which different actions result in no eventual gain or loss.
– DERIVATIVES **swinger** noun **swingy** adjective.
– ORIGIN Old English, 'to beat, whip', also 'rush'.

Thesaurus

with pride BE FILLED, be bursting, brim, overflow. **4** *the graduate scheme swelled entry numbers* INCREASE, enlarge, augment, boost, top up, step up, multiply. **5** *loud music swelled from inside* GROW LOUD, grow louder, amplify, intensify, heighten.
– OPPOSITES shrink, decrease, quieten.

• noun **1** *a brief swell in the volume* INCREASE, rise, escalation, surge, boost. **2** *a heavy swell on the sea* SURGE, wave, undulation, roll. **3** *(informal, dated) he was an elegant swell* DANDY, fop, beau, poseur; *informal* trendsetter; *Brit. informal* toff; *dated* popinjay; *archaic* coxcomb.
– OPPOSITES decrease, dip.

• adjective *(N. Amer. informal, dated) a swell idea* EXCELLENT, marvellous, wonderful, splendid, magnificent, superb; *informal* super, great, fantastic.
– OPPOSITES bad.

S

swelling • noun BUMP, lump, bulge, protuberance, enlargement, distension, prominence, protrusion, node, nodule, tumescence; boil, blister, bunion, carbuncle.

sweltering • adjective HOT, stifling, humid, sultry, sticky, muggy, close, stuffy; tropical, torrid, searing, blistering; *informal* boiling (hot), baking, roasting, sizzling.
– OPPOSITES freezing.

swerve • verb *a car swerved into her path* VEER, deviate, skew, diverge, sheer, weave, zigzag, change direction; *Sailing* tack.
• noun *the bowler regulated his swerve* CURVE, curl, deviation, twist; *N. Amer.* English.

swift • adjective **1** *a swift decision* PROMPT, rapid, sudden, immediate, instant, instantaneous; abrupt, hasty, hurried, precipitate, headlong. **2** *swift runners* FAST, rapid, quick, speedy, high-speed, brisk, lively; express, breakneck; fleet-footed; *informal* nippy, supersonic.
– OPPOSITES slow, leisurely.

swill • verb **1** *(informal) she was swilling pints* DRINK, quaff, swallow, down, gulp, drain, imbibe, sup, slurp, consume, slug; *informal* swig, knock back, toss off, put away; *Brit. informal* bevvy; *N. Amer. informal* chug. **2** *he swilled out a glass* WASH, rinse, sluice, clean, flush.
• noun **1** *(informal) he took a swill of coffee* GULP, swallow, drink, draught, mouthful, slug; *informal* swig. **2** *swill for the pigs* PIGSWILL, mash, slops, scraps, refuse, scourings, leftovers; *archaic* hogwash.

swim • verb **1** *they swam in the pool* BATHE, take a dip, splash around; float, tread water. **2** *his food was swimming in gravy* BE SATURATED IN, be drenched in, be soaked in, be steeped in, be immersed in, be covered in, be full of.

swimmingly • adverb WELL, smoothly, easily, effortlessly, like clockwork, without a hitch, as planned, to plan; *informal* like a dream, like magic.

swimming pool • noun POOL, baths, lido, piscina; *Brit.* swimming bath(s); *N. Amer.* natatorium.

swimsuit • noun BATHING SUIT, bathing dress, (swimming) trunks, bikini; swimwear; *Brit.* bathing costume, swimming costume; *informal* cossie; *Austral./NZ informal* bathers.

swindle • verb *I was swindled out of money* DEFRAUD, cheat, trick, dupe, deceive, fool, hoax, hoodwink, bamboozle; *informal* fleece, do, con, sting, diddle, swizzle, rip off, take for a ride, pull a fast one on, put one over on, take to the cleaners, gull; *N. Amer. informal* stiff, euchre; *poetic/literary* cozen; *archaic* sharp.
• noun *an insurance swindle* FRAUD, trick, deception, deceit, cheat, sham, artifice, ruse, dodge, racket, wile; sharp practice; *informal* con, fiddle, diddle, rip-off, flimflam, swizzle, swizz; *N. Amer. informal* bunco.

swindler • noun FRAUDSTER, fraud, (confidence) trickster, cheat, rogue, mountebank, charlatan, impostor, hoaxer; *informal* con man, con artist, shark, sharp, hustler, phoney, crook.

swing • verb **1** *the sign swung in the wind* SWAY, oscillate, move back and forth, move to and fro, wave, wag, rock, flutter, flap. **2** *Helen swung the bottle* BRANDISH, wave, flourish, wield, shake, wag, twirl. **3** *this road swings off to the north* CURVE, bend, veer, turn, bear, wind, twist, deviate, slew, skew, drift, head. **4** *the balance swung from one party to the other* CHANGE, fluctuate, shift, alter, oscillate, waver, alternate, see-saw, yo-yo, vary. **5** *(informal) their persistence finally swung it for him* ACCOMPLISH, achieve, obtain, acquire, get, secure, net, win, attain, bag, hook; *informal* wangle, land, fix (up).
• noun **1** *a swing of the pendulum* OSCILLATION, sway, wave. **2** *the*

swing bridge ● noun a bridge that can be be swung to one side to allow ships to pass.
swing door ● noun a door that can be opened in either direction and swings back when released.
swingeing ● adjective chiefly Brit. severe or otherwise extreme.
– ORIGIN from archaic *swinge* 'strike hard', from Old English, 'shake, shatter'.
swinging ● adjective informal **1** lively, exciting, and fashionable. **2** sexually liberated or promiscuous.
swingle ● noun **1** a wooden tool for beating flax and removing the woody parts. **2** the swinging part of a flail.
– ORIGIN Dutch *swinghel*; related to SWING.
swingletree /swingg'ltree/ ● noun a pivoted crossbar to which the traces are attached in a horse-drawn cart or plough.
swing-wing ● noun an aircraft wing that can move from a right-angled to a swept-back position.
swipe informal ● verb **1** hit or try to hit with a swinging blow. **2** steal. **3** pass (a swipe card) through an electronic reader. ● noun **1** a sweeping blow. **2** an attack or criticism.
– ORIGIN perhaps a variant of SWEEP.
swipe card ● noun a plastic card bearing magnetically encoded information which is read when the card is slid through an electronic device.
swirl ● verb move in a twisting or spiralling pattern. ● noun a swirling movement or pattern.
– DERIVATIVES **swirly** adjective.
– ORIGIN perhaps Low German or Dutch.
swish ● verb move with a hissing or rushing sound. ● noun a swishing sound or movement. ● adjective Brit. informal impressively smart and fashionable.
– ORIGIN imitative.
Swiss ● adjective relating to Switzerland or its people. ● noun (pl. same) a person from Switzerland.
Swiss cheese plant ● noun a house plant with perforated leaves (supposedly resembling the holes in a Swiss cheese).
Swiss roll ● noun Brit. a flat thin rectangular sponge cake spread with jam or cream and rolled up.
switch ● noun **1** a device for making and breaking an electrical connection. **2** a change or exchange. **3** a slender, flexible shoot cut from a tree. **4** N. Amer. a set of points on a railway track. **5** a tress of hair used in hairdressing to supplement natural hair. ● verb **1** change in position, direction, or focus. **2** exchange. **3** (**switch off/on**) turn an electrical device off (or on). **4** (**switch off**) informal cease to pay attention. **5** archaic beat with a stick.
– DERIVATIVES **switchable** adjective.
– ORIGIN probably Low German.
switchback ● noun **1** Brit. a road, railway, etc. with alternate sharp ascents and descents. **2** a roller coaster. **3** N. Amer. a hairpin bend.
switchblade ● noun chiefly N. Amer. a flick knife.
switchboard ● noun **1** an installation for the manual control of telephone connections. **2** an apparatus for varying connections between electric circuits.
switched-on ● adjective Brit. informal aware of what is going on or what is up to date.
switcher ● noun **1** US a shunting engine. **2** a device used to select or combine different video and audio signals.
switchgear ● noun electrical switching equipment.
swive /swīv/ ● verb archaic or humorous have sexual intercourse with.
swivel ● noun a coupling between two parts enabling one to revolve without turning the other. ● verb (**swivelled**, **swivelling**; US **swiveled**, **swiveling**) turn on or as if on a swivel.
– ORIGIN Old English, 'move (along a course), sweep'.
swizz ● noun Brit. informal an instance of being mildly cheated or disappointed.
– ORIGIN from SWIZZLE².
swizzle¹ ● noun a mixed alcoholic drink, especially a frothy one of rum or gin and bitters. ● verb stir with a swizzle stick.
– ORIGIN of unknown origin.
swizzle² ● noun Brit. informal another term for SWIZZ.
– ORIGIN probably an alteration of SWINDLE.
swizzle stick ● noun a stick used for frothing up or taking the fizz out of drinks.
swollen past participle of SWELL.
swoon ● verb faint, especially from extreme emotion. ● noun an occurrence of swooning.
– ORIGIN Old English, 'overcome'.
swoop ● verb **1** move rapidly downwards through the air. **2** carry out a sudden raid. **3** (often **swoop up**) informal seize with a sweeping motion. ● noun an act of swooping.
– PHRASES **at** (or **in**) **one fell swoop** see FELL⁴.
– ORIGIN perhaps a dialect variant of SWEEP.
swoosh ● noun the sound produced by a sudden rush of air or liquid. ● verb move with such a sound.
– ORIGIN imitative.
swop ● verb & noun variant spelling of SWAP.
sword ● noun **1** a weapon with a long metal blade and a hilt with a handguard, used for thrusting or striking. **2** (**the sword**) literary military power; violence.
– PHRASES **beat** (or **turn**) **swords into ploughshares** devote resources to peaceful rather than warlike ends. [ORIGIN with biblical allusion to the books of Isaiah (chapter 2) and Micah (chapter 4).] **he who lives by the sword dies by the sword** proverb those who commit violent acts must expect to suffer violence themselves. **put to the sword** kill, especially in war.
– ORIGIN Old English.
swordfish ● noun a large marine fish with a streamlined body and a long sword-like snout.
sword of Damocles /damməkleez/ ● noun an impending danger.
– ORIGIN with reference to *Damocles*, a courtier who flattered the ancient Greek ruler Dionysius I so much that the king made him feast sitting under a sword suspended by a single hair, to show him how precarious the king's good fortune was.
swordplay ● noun fencing with swords or foils.
swordsman ● noun a man who fights with a sword.
– DERIVATIVES **swordsmanship** noun.
swordstick ● noun a hollow walking stick containing a blade that can be used as a sword.
swore past of SWEAR.

Thesaurus

S

swing to the Conservatives CHANGE, move; turnaround, turnabout, reversal, about turn, about face, volte face, change of heart, U-turn, sea change. **3** *a swing towards plain food* TREND, tendency, drift, movement. **4** *a mood swing* FLUCTUATION, change, shift, variation, oscillation.
swingeing ● adjective *(Brit.)* SEVERE, extreme, serious, substantial, drastic, harsh, punishing, excessive, heavy.
– OPPOSITES minor.
swipe *(informal)* ● verb **1** *he swiped at her head* SWING, lash out; strike, hit, slap, cuff; *informal* belt, wallop, sock, biff, clout. **2** *they're always swiping sweets* STEAL, thieve, take, pilfer, purloin, snatch, shoplift; *informal* filch, lift, snaffle, rob, nab; *Brit. informal* nick, pinch, whip; *N. Amer. informal* glom.
● noun *she took a swipe at his face* SWING, stroke, strike, hit, slap, cuff, clip; *informal* belt, wallop.
swirl ● verb WHIRL, eddy, billow, spiral, circulate, revolve, spin, twist; flow, stream, surge, seethe.
switch ● noun **1** *the switch on top of the telephone* BUTTON, lever, control, dial. **2** *a switch from direct to indirect taxation* CHANGE, move, shift, transition, transformation; reversal, turnaround, U-turn, changeover, transfer, conversion; substitution, exchange. **3** *a switch of willow* BRANCH, twig, stick, rod.
● verb **1** *he switched sides* CHANGE, shift; reverse; *informal* chop and change. **2** *he managed to switch envelopes* EXCHANGE, swap, interchange, trade, substitute, replace, rotate.
– PHRASES **switch something on** TURN ON, put on, activate, start, set going, set in motion, operate, initiate, actuate, initialize, energize. **switch something off** TURN OFF, shut off, stop, cut, halt, deactivate.
swivel ● verb TURN, rotate, revolve, pivot, swing; spin, twirl, whirl, wheel, gyrate, pirouette.
swollen ● adjective DISTENDED, expanded, enlarged, bulging, inflated, dilated, bloated, puffed up, puffy, tumescent; inflamed.
swoop ● verb **1** *pigeons swooped down after the grain* DIVE, descend, sweep, pounce, plunge, pitch, nosedive; rush, dart, speed, zoom. **2** *police swooped on the flat* RAID, search; pounce on, attack, assault, assail, charge; *N. Amer. informal* bust.
● noun *an early morning swoop by police* RAID; attack, assault; *N. Amer. informal* bust, takedown.
sword ● noun *a ceremonial sword* BLADE, foil, épée, cutlass, rapier, sabre, scimitar; *poetic/literary* brand.
– PHRASES **cross swords** QUARREL, disagree, dispute, wrangle,

sworn past participle of SWEAR. ● adjective **1** given under oath. **2** determined to remain the specified thing: *sworn enemies.*

swot Brit. informal, derogatory ● verb (**swotted**, **swotting**) (also **swot up**) study intensively. ● noun a person who spends a lot of time studying.
– DERIVATIVES **swotty** adjective.
– ORIGIN dialect variant of SWEAT.

swum past participle of SWIM.

swung past and past participle of SWING.

sybarite /sibbərīt/ ● noun a person who is self-indulgently fond of sensuous luxury.
– DERIVATIVES **sybaritic** adjective.
– ORIGIN originally denoting an inhabitant of Sybaris, an ancient Greek city in southern Italy, noted for its luxury.

sycamore ● noun **1** a large maple native to central and southern Europe. **2** N. Amer. a plane tree.
– ORIGIN Greek *sukomoros*, from *sukon* 'fig' + *moron* 'mulberry'.

sycophant /sikkəfant/ ● noun a person who flatters someone important in a servile way.
– DERIVATIVES **sycophancy** noun **sycophantic** adjective.
– ORIGIN originally denoting an informer: from Greek *sukophantēs*, from *sukon* 'fig' + *phainein* 'to show', perhaps with reference to making the insulting gesture of the 'fig' (sticking the thumb between two fingers) to informers.

Sydenham's chorea ● noun a form of chorea chiefly affecting children, associated with rheumatic fever.
– ORIGIN named after the English physician Thomas *Sydenham* (*c.*1624–89).

syl- ● prefix variant spelling of SYN- before *l*.

syllabary /silləbəri/ ● noun (pl. **syllabaries**) a set of written characters representing syllables, serving the purpose of an alphabet.

syllabic /silabbik/ ● adjective **1** relating to or based on syllables. **2** (of a consonant) constituting a whole syllable.
– DERIVATIVES **syllabically** adverb.

syllabify ● verb (**syllabifies**, **syllabified**) divide words into syllables.
– DERIVATIVES **syllabification** noun.

syllable /silləb'l/ ● noun a unit of pronunciation having one vowel sound, with or without surrounding consonants, and forming all or part of a word.
– ORIGIN Greek *sullabē*, from *sun-* 'together' + *lambanein* 'take'.

syllabub /silləbub/ ● noun a whipped cream dessert, typically flavoured with white wine or sherry.
– ORIGIN of unknown origin.

syllabus /silləbəss/ ● noun (pl. **syllabuses** or **syllabi** /silləbī/) the topics in a course of study or teaching, especially for an examination.
– ORIGIN Latin, from Greek *sittuba* 'title slip, label'.

syllepsis /silepsiss/ ● noun (pl. **syllepses** /silepseez/) a figure of speech in which a word is applied to two others of which it grammatically suits only one (e.g. *neither they nor it is working*).
– ORIGIN Greek *sullēpsis* 'taking together'.

syllogism /sillәjiz'm/ ● noun a form of reasoning in which a conclusion is drawn from two given or assumed propositions (premises); a common or middle term is present in the two premises but not in the conclusion, which may be invalid (e.g. *all dogs are animals; all animals have four legs; therefore all dogs have four legs*).
– DERIVATIVES **syllogistic** adjective.
– ORIGIN Greek *sullogismos*, from *sullogizesthai* 'to reason with'.

sylph /silf/ ● noun **1** an imaginary spirit of the air. **2** a slender woman or girl.
– DERIVATIVES **sylphlike** adjective.
– ORIGIN Latin *sylphes* (plural), perhaps from *sylvestris* 'of the woods' + *nympha* 'nymph'.

sylvan ● adjective chiefly literary **1** consisting of or associated with woods; wooded. **2** pleasantly rural or pastoral.
– ORIGIN from Latin *silva* 'a wood'.

sym- ● prefix variant spelling of SYN- before *b, m, p*.

symbiont /simbiənt/ ● noun Biology an organism living in symbiosis with another.

symbiosis /simbiōsiss, simbī-/ ● noun (pl. **symbioses** /simbiōseez, simbī-/) Biology interaction between two different organisms living in close physical association, especially to the advantage of both.
– DERIVATIVES **symbiotic** /simbiottik, simbī-/ adjective.
– ORIGIN Greek *sumbiōsis* , from *sumbioun* 'live together'.

symbol ● noun **1** a thing that represents or stands for something else, especially a material object representing something abstract. **2** a mark or character used as a conventional representation of something, e.g. a letter standing for a chemical element.
– ORIGIN Greek *sumbolon* 'mark, token'.

symbolic ● adjective **1** serving as a symbol. **2** involving the use of symbols or symbolism.
– DERIVATIVES **symbolically** adverb.

symbolic logic ● noun the use of symbols to denote propositions, terms, and relations in order to assist reasoning.

symbolism ● noun **1** the use of symbols to represent ideas or qualities. **2** symbolic meaning attached to material objects. **3** (**Symbolism**) an artistic and poetic movement or style using symbolic images and indirect suggestion to express mystical ideas, emotions, and states of mind.
– DERIVATIVES **symbolist** noun & adjective.

symbolize (also **symbolise**) ● verb **1** be a symbol of. **2** represent by means of symbols.
– DERIVATIVES **symbolization** noun.

symbology ● noun **1** the study or use of symbols. **2** symbols collectively.

symmetrical ● adjective made up of exactly similar parts facing each other or around an axis; showing symmetry.
– DERIVATIVES **symmetric** adjective **symmetrically** adverb.

symmetry /simmətri/ ● noun (pl. **symmetries**) **1** the quality of being made up of exactly similar parts facing each other or around an axis. **2** correct or pleasing proportion of parts. **3** similarity or exact correspondence.
– ORIGIN Latin *symmetria*, from Greek *sun-* 'with' + *metron* 'measure'.

sympathetic ● adjective **1** feeling, showing, or expressing sympathy. **2** showing approval of an idea or action. **3** pleasing, likeable, or sensitively designed. **4** Physiology referring to the part of the autonomic nervous system supplying the internal organs, blood vessels, and glands, and balancing the action of the parasympathetic nerves. **5** arising in response to a similar action

S

Thesaurus

bicker, be at odds, be at loggerheads, lock horns; fight, contend; *informal* scrap. **put to the sword** KILL, execute, put to death, murder, butcher, slaughter, massacre, cut down; *poetic/literary* slay.

sybarite ● noun HEDONIST, sensualist, voluptuary, libertine, pleasure-seeker, epicure, bon vivant, bon viveur.
– OPPOSITES puritan.

sybaritic ● adjective LUXURIOUS, extravagant, lavish, self-indulgent, pleasure-seeking, sensual, voluptuous, hedonistic, epicurean, lotus-eating, libertine, debauched, decadent.
– OPPOSITES ascetic.

sycophant ● noun TOADY, creep, crawler, fawner, flatterer, truckler, groveller, doormat, lickspittle, kowtower, Uriah Heep; *informal* bootlicker, yes-man.

sycophantic ● adjective OBSEQUIOUS, servile, subservient, deferential, grovelling, toadying, fawning, flattering, ingratiating, cringing, unctuous, slavish; *informal* bootlicking, smarmy.

syllabus ● noun CURRICULUM, course (of study), programme of study, course outline; timetable, schedule.

symbol ● noun **1** *the lotus is the symbol of purity* EMBLEM, token, sign, representation, figure, image; metaphor, allegory. **2** *the chemical symbol for helium* SIGN, character, mark, letter, ideogram. **3** *the Red Cross symbol* LOGO, emblem, badge, stamp, trademark, crest, insignia, coat of arms, seal, device, monogram, hallmark, flag, motif.

symbolic ● adjective **1** *the Colosseum is symbolic of the Roman Empire* EMBLEMATIC, representative, typical, characteristic, symptomatic. **2** *symbolic language* FIGURATIVE, representative, illustrative, emblematic, metaphorical, allegorical, parabolic, allusive, suggestive; meaningful, significant.
– OPPOSITES literal.

symbolize ● verb REPRESENT, stand for, be a sign of, exemplify; denote, signify, mean, indicate, convey, express, imply, suggest, allude to; embody, epitomize, encapsulate, personify, typify; *poetic/literary* betoken.

symmetrical ● adjective REGULAR, uniform, consistent; evenly shaped, aligned, equal; mirror-image; balanced, proportional, regular, even.

symmetry ● noun REGULARITY, evenness, uniformity, consistency,

elsewhere.
– DERIVATIVES **sympathetically** adverb.
sympathetic magic ● noun occult rituals using objects or actions to represent the event or person over which influence is sought.
sympathize (also **sympathise**) ● verb **1** feel or express sympathy. **2** agree with a sentiment or opinion.
– DERIVATIVES **sympathizer** noun.
sympathy ● noun (pl. **sympathies**) **1** feelings of pity and sorrow for someone else's misfortune. **2** understanding between people; common feeling. **3** support for or approval of something. **4** (**in sympathy**) relating harmoniously to something else; in keeping. **5** the state or fact of responding in a way corresponding to an action elsewhere.
– ORIGIN Greek *sumpatheia*, from *sun-* 'with' + *pathos* 'feeling'.
symphonic ● adjective relating to or having the form or character of a symphony.
symphonist ● noun a composer of symphonies.
symphony ● noun (pl. **symphonies**) an elaborate musical composition for full orchestra, typically in four movements.
– ORIGIN Greek *sumphōnia*, from *sumphōnos* 'harmonious'.
symphony orchestra ● noun a large classical orchestra, including string, woodwind, brass, and percussion instruments.
symposium /simpōziəm/ ● noun (pl. **symposia** /simpōziə/ or **symposiums**) **1** a conference or meeting to discuss a particular academic or specialist subject. **2** a collection of related papers by a number of contributors.
– ORIGIN originally denoting a drinking party: from Greek *sumposion*, from *sumpotēs* 'fellow drinker'.
symptom ● noun Medicine **1** a feature which indicates a condition of disease, in particular one apparent to the patient. Compare with SIGN. **2** an indication of an undesirable situation.
– ORIGIN Greek *sumptōma* 'chance, symptom'.
symptomatic ● adjective acting as a symptom of something.
– DERIVATIVES **symptomatically** adverb.
syn- ● prefix united; acting together: *synchrony*.
– ORIGIN from Greek *sun* 'with'.
synaesthesia /sinnisstheeziə/ (US **synesthesia**) ● noun Physiology & Psychology the production of a sense impression relating to one sense or part of the body by stimulation of another sense or part of the body.
– DERIVATIVES **synaesthetic** adjective.
– ORIGIN Latin, on the pattern of *anaesthesia*.
synagogue /sinnəgog/ ● noun a building where a Jewish assembly or congregation meets for religious observance and instruction.
– ORIGIN Greek *sunagōgē* 'meeting'.
synapse /sīnaps, sin-/ ● noun a gap between two nerve cells, across which impulses are conducted through the agency of a neurotransmitter.
– DERIVATIVES **synaptic** adjective.
– ORIGIN Greek *sunapsis*, from *sun-* 'together' + *hapsis* 'joining'.
sync (also **synch**) informal ● noun synchronization. ● verb synchronize.
– PHRASES **in** (or **out of**) **sync** working well (or badly) together.
synchro /singkrō/ ● noun synchronized or synchronization.
synchromesh ● noun a system of gear changing in which the driving and driven gearwheels are made to revolve at the same speed during engagement.
– ORIGIN contraction of *synchronized mesh*.
synchronic /singkronnik/ ● adjective concerned with something (especially a language) as it exists at one point in time. Often contrasted with DIACHRONIC.
– DERIVATIVES **synchronically** adverb.
synchronicity ● noun the simultaneous occurrence of events which appear significantly related but have no discernible causal connection.
synchronism ● noun another term for SYNCHRONY.
synchronize (also **synchronise**) ● verb cause to occur or operate at the same time or rate.
– DERIVATIVES **synchronization** noun **synchronizer** noun.
synchronized swimming ● noun a sport in which teams of swimmers perform coordinated movements in time to music.
synchronous /singkrənəss/ ● adjective **1** existing or occurring at the same time. **2** referring to a satellite which revolves in its orbit in exactly the same time as the primary body rotates on its axis.
– DERIVATIVES **synchronously** adverb.
– ORIGIN Greek *sunkhronos*, from *sun-* 'together' + *khronos* 'time'.
synchrony /singkrəni/ ● noun simultaneous action, development, or occurrence.
syncline ● noun Geology a trough or fold of stratified rock in which the strata slope upwards from the axis. Compare with ANTICLINE.
– ORIGIN from SYN- + Greek *klinein* 'to lean'.
syncopate /singkəpayt/ ● verb (usu. as adj. **syncopated**) (of music or a rhythm) having the beats or accents displaced so that strong beats become weak and vice versa.
– DERIVATIVES **syncopation** noun.
– ORIGIN from SYNCOPE.
syncope /singkəpi/ ● noun **1** Medicine temporary loss of consciousness caused by low blood pressure. **2** Grammar the omission of sounds or letters from within a word, for example when *library* is pronounced /lībri/.
– ORIGIN Greek *sunkopē*, from *sun-* 'together' + *koptein* 'strike, cut off'.
syncretism /singkritiz'm/ ● noun the amalgamation of different religions, cultures, or schools of thought.
– DERIVATIVES **syncretic** adjective **syncretist** noun & adjective **syncretistic** adjective.
– ORIGIN from Greek *sunkrētizein* 'unite against a third party', from *krēs* 'Cretan' (originally with reference to ancient Cretan communities).
syncretize (also **syncretise**) ● verb attempt to amalgamate (differing religious beliefs, schools of thought, etc.).
– DERIVATIVES **syncretization** noun.
syndic ● noun **1** a government official in various countries. **2** (in the UK) a business agent of certain universities and corporations.
– ORIGIN Greek *sundikos*, from *dikē* 'justice'.
syndicalism ● noun historical a movement for transferring the ownership and control of the means of production and distribution to workers' unions.
– DERIVATIVES **syndicalist** noun & adjective.
syndicate ● noun /sindikət/ **1** a group of individuals or organizations combined to promote a common interest. **2** an agency supplying material simultaneously to a number of news media. ● verb /sindikayt/ **1** control or manage by a syndicate. **2** publish or broadcast simultaneously in a number of media.
– DERIVATIVES **syndication** noun.

S

Thesaurus

conformity, correspondence, equality; balance, proportions; *formal* concord.
sympathetic ● adjective **1** *a sympathetic listener* COMPASSIONATE, caring, concerned, solicitous, empathetic, understanding, sensitive; commiserative, pitying, consoling, comforting, supportive, encouraging; considerate, kind, tender-hearted. **2** *the most sympathetic character in the book* LIKEABLE, pleasant, agreeable, congenial, friendly, genial. **3** *I was sympathetic to his cause* IN FAVOUR OF, in sympathy with, pro, on the side of, supportive of, encouraging of; well disposed to, favourably disposed to, receptive to.
– OPPOSITES unfeeling, opposed.
sympathize ● verb **1** *he sympathized with his wife* PITY, feel sorry for, show compassion for, commiserate, offer condolences to, feel for, show concern, show interest; console, comfort, solace, soothe, support, encourage; empathize with, identify with, understand, relate to. **2** *they sympathize with the critique* AGREE WITH, support, be in favour of, go along with, favour, approve of, back, side with.
sympathizer ● noun SUPPORTER, backer, well-wisher, advocate, ally, partisan; collaborator, fraternizer, conspirator, quisling.
sympathy ● noun **1** *he shows sympathy for the poor* COMPASSION, caring, concern, solicitude, empathy; commiseration, pity, condolence, comfort, solace, support, encouragement; consideration, kindness. **2** *sympathy with a fellow journalist* RAPPORT, fellow feeling, affinity, empathy, harmony, accord, compatibility; fellowship, camaraderie. **3** *their sympathy with the Republicans* AGREEMENT, favour, approval, approbation, support, encouragement, partiality; association, alignment, affiliation.
– OPPOSITES indifference, hostility.
symptom ● noun **1** *the symptoms of the disease* MANIFESTATION, indication, indicator, sign, mark, feature, trait; *Medicine* prodrome. **2** *a symptom of the country's present turmoil* EXPRESSION, sign, indication, mark, token, manifestation; portent, warning, clue, hint; testimony, evidence, proof.

syndrome ● noun **1** a group of symptoms which consistently occur together. **2** a characteristic combination of opinions, emotions, or behaviour.
– ORIGIN Greek *sundromē*, from *dramein* 'to run'.
syne /sīn/ ● adverb Scottish ago.
– ORIGIN contraction of dialect *sithen* 'ever since'.
synecdoche /sinekdəki/ ● noun a figure of speech in which a part is made to represent the whole or vice versa, as in *England lost by six wickets* (meaning 'the English cricket team').
– ORIGIN Greek *sunekdokhē*, from *sun-* 'together' + *ekdekhesthai* 'take up'.
synergist ● noun a substance or other agent that participates in synergy.
– DERIVATIVES **synergistic** adjective.
synergy /sinnərji/ (also **synergism**) ● noun interaction or cooperation of two or more agents to produce a combined effect greater than the sum of their separate effects.
– DERIVATIVES **synergetic** adjective.
– ORIGIN from Greek *sunergos* 'working together'.
synesthesia ● noun US spelling of SYNAESTHESIA.
synod /sinnəd/ ● noun an assembly of the clergy (and sometimes also the laity) in a division of a Christian Church.
– DERIVATIVES **synodal** adjective.
– ORIGIN Greek *sunodos* 'meeting'.
synodic /sinoddik/ ● adjective Astronomy relating to or involving a conjunction.
– ORIGIN Greek *sunodikos*, from *sunodos* (see SYNOD).
synodical ● adjective Christian Church relating to or constituted as a synod.
synonym /sinnənim/ ● noun a word or phrase that means the same as another word or phrase in the same language.
– DERIVATIVES **synonymy** /sinonnimi/ noun.
– ORIGIN Greek *sunōnumon*, from *onoma* 'name'.
synonymous /sinonniməss/ ● adjective **1** (of a word or phrase) having the same meaning as another word or phrase in the same language. **2** closely associated with something: *his name was synonymous with victory*.
– DERIVATIVES **synonymously** adverb.
synopsis /sinopsiss/ ● noun (pl. **synopses** /sinopseez/) a brief summary or general survey.
– DERIVATIVES **synopsize** (also **synopsise**) verb.
– ORIGIN Greek, from *sun-* 'together' + *opsis* 'seeing'.
synoptic ● adjective **1** of, forming, or involving a synopsis. **2** (**Synoptic**) referring to the Gospels of Matthew, Mark, and Luke, which describe events from a similar point of view, as contrasted with that of John.
synovial /sīnōviəl, si-/ ● adjective relating to joints of the body enclosed in a thick flexible membrane containing a lubricating fluid (**synovial fluid**).
– ORIGIN from Latin *synovia*, probably coined by the Swiss physician Paracelsus (*c.* 1493–1541).
syntax ● noun **1** the arrangement of words and phrases to create well-formed sentences. **2** a set of rules for or an analysis of this. **3** the structure of statements in a computer language.
– DERIVATIVES **syntactic** adjective **syntactical** adjective **syntactically** adverb.
– ORIGIN Greek *suntaxis*, from *sun-* 'together' + *tassein* 'arrange'.
synth ● noun informal a synthesizer.
– DERIVATIVES **synthy** adjective.
synthesis /sinthəsiss/ ● noun (pl. **syntheses** /sinthəseez/) **1** the combination of components to form a connected whole. Often contrasted with ANALYSIS. **2** the production of chemical compounds by reaction from simpler materials.
– DERIVATIVES **synthesist** noun.
– ORIGIN Greek *sunthesis*, from *suntithenai* 'place together'.
synthesize /sinthəsīz/ (also **synthesise**, **synthetize**, **synthetise**) ● verb **1** make by synthesis. **2** combine into a coherent whole. **3** produce (sound) electronically.
synthesizer ● noun an electronic musical instrument producing sounds by generating and combining signals of different frequencies.
synthetic /sinthettik/ ● adjective **1** made by chemical synthesis, especially to imitate a natural product. **2** not genuine. ● noun a synthetic substance, especially a textile fibre.
– DERIVATIVES **synthetically** adverb.
syphilis ● noun a sexually transmitted disease, spread by bacteria and progressing if untreated from infection of the genitals to the bones, muscles, and brain.
– DERIVATIVES **syphilitic** adjective & noun.
– ORIGIN Latin, from *Syphilus*, the subject of a poem of 1530 who was the supposed first sufferer of the disease.
syphon ● noun & verb variant spelling of SIPHON.
Syrah /seerə/ ● noun another term for SHIRAZ.
Syrian ● noun a person from Syria. ● adjective relating to Syria.
syringe /sirinj/ ● noun a tube with a nozzle and piston for sucking in and ejecting liquid in a thin stream, often one fitted with a hollow needle for injecting or withdrawing bodily fluids. ● verb (**syringing**) spray liquid into or over with a syringe.
– ORIGIN Latin *syringa*, from *syrinx* (see SYRINX).
syrinx /sirringks/ ● noun (pl. **syrinxes**) **1** a set of pan pipes. **2** the lower larynx or voice organ in birds, especially in songbirds.
– ORIGIN Greek *surinx* 'pipe, channel'.
syrup (US also **sirup**) ● noun **1** a thick sweet liquid made by dissolving sugar in boiling water, used for preserving fruit. **2** a thick sweet liquid containing medicine or used as a drink.
– ORIGIN Arabic, 'beverage'; related to SHERBET and SHRUB².
syrupy (US also **sirupy**) ● adjective **1** having the consistency or sweetness of syrup. **2** excessively sentimental.
sysop /sissop/ ● noun Computing a system operator.
system ● noun **1** a set of things working together as a mechanism or interconnecting network. **2** a person's body or mind. **3** Computing a group of related hardware units or programs or both, especially when dedicated to a single application. **4** an organized scheme or method. **5** orderliness; method. **6** the prevailing political or social order, especially when regarded as oppressive. **7** Geology a major range of strata corresponding to a period in time.
– ORIGIN Greek *sustēma*, from *sun-* 'with' + *histanai* 'set up'.
systematic ● adjective done or acting according to a fixed plan or system; methodical.
– DERIVATIVES **systematically** adverb **systematist** noun.
systematics ● plural noun (treated as sing.) the branch of biology concerned with classification and nomenclature; taxonomy.
systematize (also **systematise**) ● verb arrange according to an organized system.
– DERIVATIVES **systematization** noun.
systemic /sistemmik, -steem-/ ● adjective **1** relating to a system as a whole. **2** Physiology referring to the non-pulmonary part of the circulatory system. **3** (of an insecticide, fungicide, etc.) entering the plant via the roots or shoots and passing through the tissues.
– DERIVATIVES **systemically** adverb.
systems analyst ● noun a person who analyses a complex process or operation in order to improve its efficiency, especially by applying a computer system.

Thesaurus

symptomatic ● adjective INDICATIVE, characteristic, suggestive, typical, representative, symbolic.
synopsis ● noun SUMMARY, summarization, precis, abstract, outline, digest, rundown, round-up, abridgement.
synthesis ● noun COMBINATION, union, amalgam, blend, mixture, compound, fusion, composite, alloy; unification, amalgamation, marrying.
synthetic ● adjective ARTIFICIAL, fake, imitation, mock, simulated, ersatz, substitute; pseudo, so-called; man-made, manufactured, fabricated; *informal* phoney, pretend.
– OPPOSITES natural.
syrupy ● adjective **1** *syrupy medicine* OVERSWEET, sweet, sugary, treacly, honeyed, saccharine; thick, sticky, gluey, viscid, glutinous; *informal* gooey. **2** *syrupy romantic drivel* SENTIMENTAL, mawkish, cloying, sickly, saccharine, trite; *informal* soppy, schmaltzy, mushy, slushy, sloppy, lovey-dovey, cheesy, corny.
system ● noun **1** *a system of canals* STRUCTURE, organization, arrangement, complex, network; *informal* set-up. **2** *a system for regulating sales* METHOD, methodology, technique, process, procedure, approach, practice; means, way, mode, framework, modus operandi; scheme, plan, policy, programme, regimen, formula, routine. **3** *there was no system in his work* ORDER, method, orderliness, systematization, planning, logic, routine. **4** *youngsters have no faith in the system* THE ESTABLISHMENT, the administration, the authorities, the powers that be; the status quo.
systematic ● adjective STRUCTURED, methodical, organized, orderly, planned, systematized, regular, routine, standardized, standard; logical, coherent, consistent; efficient, businesslike, practical.

S

– DERIVATIVES **systems analysis** noun.

systole /sistəli/ ● noun the phase of the heartbeat when the heart muscle contracts and pumps blood into the arteries. Often contrasted with DIASTOLE.
– DERIVATIVES **systolic** /sistollik/ adjective.
– ORIGIN Greek *sustolē*, from *sustellein* 'to contract'.

syzygy /sizziji/ ● noun (pl. **syzygies**) **1** Astronomy conjunction or opposition, especially of the moon with the sun. **2** a pair of connected or corresponding things.
– ORIGIN Greek *suzugia*, from *suzugos* 'yoked, paired'.

Tt

T[1] (also **t**) ● noun (pl. **Ts** or **T's**) the twentieth letter of the alphabet.
– PHRASES **to a T** informal exactly; to perfection.
T[2] ● abbreviation **1** tera- (10^{12}). **2** tesla.
t ● abbreviation ton(s).
TA ● abbreviation (in the UK) Territorial Army.
Ta ● symbol the chemical element tantalum.
ta ● exclamation Brit. informal thank you.
– ORIGIN a child's word.
tab[1] ● noun **1** a small flap or strip of material attached to something, for holding, manipulation, identification, etc. **2** Brit. Military a collar marking distinguishing an officer of high rank. **3** informal, chiefly N. Amer. a restaurant bill. **4** N. Amer. a ring pull. **5** N. English & informal a cigarette. ● verb (**tabbed**, **tabbing**) mark with a tab.
– PHRASES **keep tabs on** informal monitor the activities of. **pick up the tab** informal pay for something.
– ORIGIN perhaps related to TAG[1].
tab[2] ● noun short for TABULATOR. ● verb (**tabbed**, **tabbing**) short for TABULATE.
tab[3] ● noun informal a tablet, especially one containing an illicit drug.
tabard /tabbərd/ ● noun **1** a sleeveless jerkin consisting only of front and back pieces with a hole for the head. **2** a herald's official coat emblazoned with the arms of the sovereign.
– ORIGIN Old French *tabart*.
Tabasco /təbaskō/ ● noun trademark a pungent sauce made from capsicums.
– ORIGIN named after the state of *Tabasco* in Mexico.
tabbouleh /tabboolay, təbo͞olay/ ● noun a Middle Eastern salad of cracked wheat mixed with finely chopped tomatoes, onions, parsley, etc.
– ORIGIN Arabic.
tabby ● noun (pl. **tabbies**) **1** a grey or brownish cat with dark stripes. **2** silk or other fabric with a watered pattern.
– ORIGIN originally referring to a striped silk taffeta: from French *tabis*, from the Arabic name of a part of Baghdad where it was manufactured.
tabernacle /tabbərnakk'l/ ● noun **1** (in the Bible) a tent used as a sanctuary for the Ark of the Covenant by the Israelites during the Exodus. **2** a receptacle or cabinet in which a pyx containing the reserved sacrament may be placed in Catholic churches. **3** a meeting place for Nonconformist or Mormon worship.
– ORIGIN Latin *tabernaculum* 'tent', from *taberna* 'hut, tavern'.
tabla /tablə/ ● noun a pair of small hand drums fixed together, used in Indian music.
– ORIGIN Arabic, 'drum'.
tablature /tabləchər/ ● noun a form of musical notation indicating fingering rather than the pitch of notes.
– ORIGIN French, probably from Italian *tavolare* 'set to music'.
table ● noun **1** a piece of furniture with a flat top and one or more legs, for eating, writing, or working at. **2** a set of facts or figures systematically displayed. **3** (**tables**) multiplication tables. **4** food provided in a restaurant or household: *food includes a lunchtime buffet table.* ● verb Brit. present formally for discussion or consideration at a meeting.
– PHRASES **on the table** available for discussion. **turn the tables** reverse a situation disadvantageous to oneself so that it becomes advantageous.
– ORIGIN Latin *tabula* 'plank, tablet, list'.
tableau /tablō/ ● noun (pl. **tableaux** /tablōz/) a group of models or motionless figures representing a scene.
– ORIGIN French, 'picture', from *table* 'table'.
tableau vivant /tablō veevON/ ● noun (pl. **tableaux vivants** pronunc. same) a silent and motionless group of people arranged to represent a scene.
– ORIGIN French, 'living picture'.
tablecloth ● noun a cloth spread over a table, especially during meals.
table d'hôte /taablə dōt/ ● noun a restaurant menu or meal offered at a fixed price and with limited choices.
– ORIGIN French, 'host's table'.
tableland ● noun a broad, high, level region; a plateau.
table manners ● plural noun behaviour that is conventionally required while eating at table.
tablespoon ● noun **1** a large spoon for serving food. **2** the amount held by such a spoon, in the UK considered to be 15 millilitres when used as a measurement in cookery.
tablet ● noun **1** a slab of stone, clay, or wood on which an inscription is written. **2** a pill in the shape of a disc or cylinder, containing a compressed drug or medicine. **3** Brit. a small flat piece of soap.
– ORIGIN Old French *tablete*, from Latin *tabula* 'plank, tablet, list'.
table tennis ● noun an indoor game played with small bats and a small, hollow ball hit across a table divided by a net.
tableware ● noun crockery, cutlery, and glassware used for serving and eating meals at a table.
table wine ● noun wine of moderate quality considered suitable for drinking with a meal.
tabloid ● noun a newspaper having pages half the size of those of the average broadsheet, typically popular in style.
– ORIGIN originally a proprietary term for a medicinal tablet: the current sense reflects the notion of information being presented in a form that is concentrated and easily assimilable.
taboo (also **tabu**) ● noun (pl. **taboos** or **tabus**) a social or religious custom placing prohibition or restriction on a particular thing or person. ● adjective **1** prohibited or restricted by social custom. **2** designated as sacred and prohibited. ● verb (**taboos**, **tabooed** or **tabus**, **tabued**) place under such prohibition.
– ORIGIN from Tongan, 'set apart, forbidden'.
tabor /taybər/ ● noun historical a small drum, especially one used simultaneously by the player of a simple pipe.
– ORIGIN Old French *tabour* 'drum'.
tabular /tabyoolər/ ● adjective **1** (of data) consisting of or presented in columns or tables. **2** broad and flat like the top of a table.
– ORIGIN Latin *tabularis*, from *tabula* 'plank, tablet, list'.

Thesaurus

tab ● noun **1** *his name is on the tab of his jacket* TAG, label, flap. **2** (*informal*) *the company will pick up the tab* BILL, invoice, account, charge, expense, cost; *N. Amer.* check.
table ● noun **1** *put the plates on the table* bench, buffet, stand, counter, work surface, worktop; desk, bar. **2** *he provides an excellent table* MEAL, food, fare, menu, nourishment; eatables, provisions; *informal* spread, grub, chow, eats, nosh; *poetic/literary* viands; *dated* victuals. **3** *the report has numerous tables* CHART, diagram, figure, graph, plan; list, tabulation, index.
● verb *she tabled a question in parliament* SUBMIT, put forward, propose, suggest, move, lodge, file, introduce, air, moot.
tableau ● noun **1** *mythic tableaux* PICTURE, painting, representation, illustration, image. **2** *the first act consists of a series of tableaux* PAGEANT, tableau vivant, parade, diorama, scene. **3** *a domestic tableau around the fireplace* SCENE, arrangement, grouping, group; picture, spectacle, image, vignette.
tablet ● noun **1** *a carved tablet* SLAB, stone, panel, plaque, plate, sign. **2** *a headache tablet* PILL, capsule, lozenge, caplet, pastille, drop, pilule; *informal* tab. **3** *a tablet of soap* BAR, cake, slab, brick, block, chunk, piece.
taboo ● noun *the taboo against healing on the sabbath* PROHIBITION, proscription, veto, interdiction, interdict, ban, restriction.
● adjective *taboo language* FORBIDDEN, prohibited, banned, proscribed, interdicted, non licet, outlawed, illegal, illicit, unlawful,

tabula rasa /tabyoolə raazə/ ● noun (pl. **tabulae rasae** /tabyoolee raazee/) **1** an absence of preconceived ideas or predetermined goals. **2** the human mind, especially at birth, viewed as having no innate ideas.
– ORIGIN Latin, 'scraped tablet', i.e. a tablet with the writing erased.

tabulate /tabyoolayt/ ● verb arrange (data) in tabular form.
– DERIVATIVES **tabulation** noun.

tabulator ● noun a facility in a word-processing program, or a device on a typewriter, for advancing to set positions in tabular work.

tach /tak/ ● noun N. Amer. informal short for TACHOMETER.

tache ● noun variant spelling of TASH.

tachistoscope /təkistəskōp/ ● noun an instrument used for exposing objects to the eye for a very brief measured period of time.
– DERIVATIVES **tachistoscopic** adjective.
– ORIGIN from Greek *takhistos* 'swiftest'.

tacho /takkō/ ● noun (pl. **tachos**) Brit. short for TACHOGRAPH or TACHOMETER.

tachograph ● noun a tachometer used in commercial road vehicles to provide a record of engine speed over a period.
– ORIGIN from Greek *takhos* 'speed'.

tachometer /takommitər/ ● noun an instrument which measures the working speed of an engine, typically in revolutions per minute.

tachycardia /takkikaardiə/ ● noun an abnormally rapid heart rate.
– ORIGIN from Greek *takhus* 'swift' + *kardia* 'heart'.

tachyon /takkion/ ● noun Physics a hypothetical particle that travels faster than light.

tacit /tassit/ ● adjective understood or implied without being stated.
– DERIVATIVES **tacitly** adverb.
– ORIGIN Latin *tacitus* 'silent', from *tacere* 'be silent'.

taciturn /tassiturn/ ● adjective reserved or uncommunicative in speech; saying little.
– DERIVATIVES **taciturnity** noun **taciturnly** adverb.
– ORIGIN Latin *taciturnus*, from *tacitus* 'silent'.

tack[1] ● noun **1** a small, sharp broad-headed nail. **2** N. Amer. a drawing pin. **3** a long stitch used to fasten fabrics together temporarily. **4** a course of action. **5** Sailing an act of tacking. **6** a boat's course relative to the direction of the wind: *the ketch swung to the opposite tack*. ● verb **1** fasten or fix with tacks. **2** (**tack on**) add (something) to something already existing. **3** change course by turning a boat's head into and through the wind. **4** make a series of such changes of course while sailing.
– ORIGIN probably related to Old French *tache* 'clasp, large nail'.

tack[2] ● noun equipment used in horse riding, including the saddle and bridle.
– ORIGIN from TACKLE.

tack[3] ● noun informal cheap, shoddy, or tasteless material.
– ORIGIN from TACKY[2].

tackle ● noun **1** the equipment required for a task or sport. **2** a mechanism consisting of ropes, pulley blocks, and hooks for lifting heavy objects. **3** the running rigging and pulleys used to work a boat's sails. **4** (in sport) an act of tackling an opponent. **5** Brit. vulgar slang a man's genitals. ● verb **1** make determined efforts to deal with (a difficult task). **2** initiate discussion with (someone) about a sensitive issue. **3** (in soccer, hockey, rugby, etc.) intercept (an opponent in possession of the ball).
– DERIVATIVES **tackler** noun.
– ORIGIN probably from Low German *takel*, from *taken* 'lay hold of'.

tacky[1] ● adjective (**tackier**, **tackiest**) (of glue, paint, etc.) slightly sticky because not fully dry.
– DERIVATIVES **tackiness** noun.

tacky[2] ● adjective (**tackier**, **tackiest**) informal showing poor taste and quality.
– DERIVATIVES **tackiness** noun.
– ORIGIN originally denoting a horse of little value: of unknown origin.

taco /takkō/ ● noun (pl. **tacos**) a Mexican dish consisting of a folded tortilla filled with seasoned meat or beans.
– ORIGIN Spanish, 'plug, wad'.

tact ● noun adroitness and sensitivity in dealing with others or with difficult issues.
– ORIGIN Latin *tactus* 'touch, sense of touch', from *tangere* 'to touch'.

Tactel /taktel/ ● noun trademark a polyamide fabric or fibre with a soft, silky feel.
– ORIGIN an invented word: perhaps influenced by TACTILE.

tactful ● adjective having or showing tact.
– DERIVATIVES **tactfully** adverb **tactfulness** noun.

tactic ● noun **1** an action or strategy planned to achieve a specific end. **2** (**tactics**) the art of disposing armed forces in order of battle and of organizing operations. Often contrasted with STRATEGY.
– DERIVATIVES **tactician** noun.
– ORIGIN from Greek *taktikē tekhnē* 'art of tactics', from *taktos* 'ordered, arranged'.

tactical ● adjective **1** done or planned to gain a specific military end. **2** (of bombing or weapons) done or for use in immediate support of military or naval operations. Often contrasted with STRATEGIC. **3** planned in order to achieve an end beyond the immediate action. **4** (of voting) aimed at preventing the strongest candidate from winning by supporting the next strongest, without regard to one's true political allegiance.

Thesaurus

restricted, off limits; unmentionable, unspeakable, unutterable, ineffable; rude, impolite; *Islam* haram; *NZ* tapu; *informal* no go.
– OPPOSITES acceptable.

tabulate ● verb CHART, arrange, order, organize, systematize, systemize, catalogue, list, index, classify, class, codify; compile, group, log, grade, rate.

tacit ● adjective IMPLICIT, understood, implied, inferred, hinted, suggested; unspoken, unstated, unsaid, unexpressed, unvoiced; taken for granted, taken as read.
– OPPOSITES explicit.

taciturn ● adjective UNTALKATIVE, uncommunicative, reticent, unforthcoming, quiet, secretive, tight-lipped, close-mouthed; silent, mute, dumb, inarticulate; reserved, withdrawn.
– OPPOSITES talkative.

tack ● noun **1** *tacks held the carpet down* PIN, drawing pin, nail, staple, rivet, stud. **2** *the brig bowled past on the opposite tack* HEADING, bearing, course, track, path, line. **3** *the defender changed his tack* APPROACH, way, method; policy, procedure, technique, tactic, plan, strategy, stratagem; path, line, angle, direction, course.
● verb **1** *a photo tacked to the wall* PIN, nail, staple, fix, fasten, attach, secure, affix. **2** *the dress was roughly tacked together* STITCH, baste, sew, bind. **3** *the yachts tacked back and forth* CHANGE COURSE, change direction, swerve, zigzag, veer; *Nautical* go/come about, beat. **4** *poems tacked on at the end of the book* ADD, append, join, tag.

tackle ● noun **1** *fishing tackle* GEAR, equipment, apparatus, kit, hardware; implements, instruments, accoutrements, paraphernalia, trappings, appurtenances; *informal* things, stuff, clobber, bits and pieces; *archaic* equipage. **2** *lifting tackle* PULLEYS, gear, hoist, crane, winch, davit, windlass, sheave. **3** *a tackle by the scrum half* INTERCEPTION, challenge, block, attack.
● verb **1** *we must tackle environmental problems* GET TO GRIPS WITH, address, get to work on, set one's hand to, approach, take on, attend to, see to, try to sort out; deal with, take care of, handle, manage; *informal* get stuck into, have a crack at, have a go at. **2** *I tackled Nina about it* CONFRONT, speak to, interview, question, cross-examine; accost, waylay; remonstrate with. **3** *he tackled a masked intruder* CONFRONT, face up to, take on, contend with, challenge; seize, grab, grapple with, intercept, block, stop; bring down, floor, fell; *informal* have a go at. **4** *the winger got tackled* INTERCEPT, challenge, block, stop, attack.

tacky[1] ● adjective *the paint was still tacky* STICKY, wet, gluey, gummy, adhesive, viscous, viscid, treacly; *informal* gooey.

tacky[2] ● adjective *(informal) a tacky game show* TAWDRY, tasteless, kitsch, vulgar, crude, garish, gaudy, showy, trashy, cheap, common, second-rate; *Brit. informal* naff.
– OPPOSITES tasteful.

tact ● noun DIPLOMACY, tactfulness, sensitivity, understanding, thoughtfulness, consideration, delicacy, discretion, prudence, judiciousness, subtlety, savoir faire; *informal* savvy.

tactful ● adjective DIPLOMATIC, discreet, considerate, sensitive, understanding, thoughtful, delicate, judicious, politic, perceptive, subtle; courteous, polite, decorous, respectful; *informal* savvy.

tactic ● noun **1** *a tax-saving tactic* STRATEGY, scheme, stratagem, plan, manoeuvre; method, expedient, gambit, move, approach, tack; device, trick, ploy, dodge, ruse, machination, contrivance;

– DERIVATIVES **tactically** adverb.

tactile ● adjective **1** of or connected with the sense of touch. **2** perceptible or designed to be perceived by touch. **3** given to touching others in a friendly or sympathetic way.
– DERIVATIVES **tactility** noun.
– ORIGIN Latin *tactilis*, from *tangere* 'to touch'.

tactless ● adjective having or showing a lack of tact.
– DERIVATIVES **tactlessly** adverb **tactlessness** noun.

tad informal ● adverb (**a tad**) to a minor extent; somewhat. ● noun a small amount.
– ORIGIN originally denoting a small child: perhaps related to TADPOLE.

Tadjik (also **Tadzhik**) ● noun & adjective variant spelling of TAJIK.

tadpole ● noun the aquatic larva of an amphibian such as a frog or toad, having gills and a tail and lacking legs until the later stages of its development.
– ORIGIN from an Old English word meaning 'toad' + POLL (probably because the tadpole seems to consist of a large head and a tail).

tae-bo ● noun trademark an exercise system combining elements of aerobics and kick-boxing.
– ORIGIN Korean, 'leg' + *bo* (short for boxing).

tae kwon do /tī kwon dō/ ● noun a modern Korean martial art similar to karate.
– ORIGIN Korean, 'art of hand and foot fighting'.

taffeta ● noun a fine lustrous silk or similar synthetic fabric.
– ORIGIN Latin, from a Persian word meaning 'to shine'.

taffrail ● noun a rail round a ship's stern.
– ORIGIN from obsolete *tafferel* 'panel', used to denote the flat part of a ship's stern above the transom, from Dutch *tafereel*.

Taffy (also **Taff**) ● noun (pl. **Taffies**) Brit. informal, often offensive a Welshman.
– ORIGIN representing a supposed Welsh pronunciation of the given name *Davy* or *David* (Welsh *Dafydd*).

taffy ● noun (pl. **taffies**) N. Amer. a sweet similar to toffee.
– ORIGIN earlier form of TOFFEE.

tag[1] ● noun **1** a label providing identification or giving other information. **2** an electronic device attached to someone or something for monitoring purposes. **3** a nickname or description by which someone or something is popularly known. **4** a frequently repeated quotation or stock phrase. **5** a small piece or part that is attached to a main body. **6** a metal or plastic point at the end of a shoelace. **7** Computing a character or set of characters appended to an item of data in order to identify it. ● verb (**tagged**, **tagging**) **1** attach a tag to. **2** (**tag on/to**) add to as an afterthought. **3** (**tag along/on**) accompany someone without invitation.
– ORIGIN originally denoting a narrow hanging section of a decoratively slashed garment: of unknown origin.

tag[2] ● noun a children's game in which one chases the rest, and anyone who is caught then becomes the pursuer.
– ORIGIN perhaps a variant of TIG.

Tagalog /təgaalog/ ● noun **1** a member of a people from the Philippine Islands. **2** the language of this people, the basis of the national language of the Philippines (Filipino).
– ORIGIN from the Tagalog words for 'native' + 'river'.

tag end ● noun chiefly N. Amer. the last remaining part of something.

tagine /tazheen/ ● noun a North African stew of spiced meat and vegetables prepared by slow cooking in a shallow earthenware dish.
– ORIGIN Arabic, 'frying pan'.

tagliatelle /talyətelli/ ● plural noun pasta in narrow ribbons.
– ORIGIN Italian, from *tagliare* 'to cut'.

tag line ● noun informal, chiefly N. Amer. a catchphrase, slogan, or punchline.

tag team ● noun a pair of wrestlers who fight as a team, taking the ring alternately.

tag wrestling ● noun a form of wrestling involving tag teams.

tahini /taaheeni/ ● noun a Middle Eastern paste or spread made from ground sesame seeds.
– ORIGIN modern Greek *takhini*, from an Arabic word meaning 'to crush'.

Tahitian /təheesh'n/ ● noun **1** a person from Tahiti. **2** the language of Tahiti. ● adjective relating to Tahiti.

t'ai chi ch'uan /tī chee **chwaan**/ (also **t'ai chi**) ● noun a Chinese martial art and system of callisthenics, consisting of sequences of very slow controlled movements.
– ORIGIN Chinese, 'great ultimate boxing'.

Taig /tayg/ ● noun informal, offensive (in Northern Ireland) a Protestant name for a Catholic.
– ORIGIN variant of *Teague*, anglicized spelling of the Irish name *Tadhg*, a nickname for an Irishman.

taiga /tīgə/ ● noun swampy coniferous forest of high northern latitudes, especially that between the tundra and steppes of Siberia.
– ORIGIN Mongolian.

tail[1] ● noun **1** the hindmost part of an animal, especially when extended beyond the rest of the body. **2** something extending downwards, outwards, or back like an animal's tail. **3** the rear part of an aircraft, with the tailplane and rudder. **4** the final, more distant, or weaker part. **5** (**tails**) the side of a coin without the image of a head on it. **6** (**tails**) informal a tailcoat, or a man's formal evening suit with such a coat. **7** informal a person secretly following another to observe their movements. ● verb **1** informal secretly follow and observe. **2** (**tail off/away**) gradual-

Thesaurus

informal wangle; *archaic* shift. **2** *our fleet's superior tactics* STRATEGY, policy, campaign, battle plans, game plans, manoeuvres, logistics; generalship, organization, planning, direction, orchestration.

tactical ● adjective CALCULATED, planned, strategic; prudent, politic, diplomatic, judicious, shrewd, cunning, artful.

tactless ● adjective INSENSITIVE, inconsiderate, thoughtless, indelicate, undiplomatic, impolitic, indiscreet, unsubtle, clumsy, heavy-handed, graceless, awkward, inept, gauche; blunt, frank, outspoken, abrupt, gruff, rough, crude, coarse; imprudent, injudicious, unwise; rude, impolite, uncouth, discourteous, crass, tasteless, disrespectful, boorish.

t

tag ● noun **1** *a price tag* LABEL, ticket, badge, mark, marker, tab, sticker, docket, stub, counterfoil, flag. **2** *his jacket was hung up by its tag* TAB, loop, label. **3** *he gained a 'bad boy' tag* DESIGNATION, label, description, characterization, identity; nickname, name, epithet, title, sobriquet; *informal* handle, moniker; *formal* denomination, appellation. **4** *tags from Shakespeare* QUOTATION, quote, phrase, platitude, cliché, excerpt; saying, proverb, maxim, adage, aphorism, motto, epigram; slogan, catchphrase.
● verb **1** *bottles tagged with coloured stickers* LABEL, mark, ticket, identify, flag, indicate. **2** *he is tagged as a 'thinking' actor* LABEL, class, categorize, characterize, designate, describe, identify, classify; mark, stamp, brand, pigeonhole, stereotype, typecast, compartmentalize, typify; name, call, title, entitle, dub, term, style. **3** *a poem tagged on as an afterthought* ADD, tack, join; attach, append. **4** *he was tagging along behind her* FOLLOW, trail; come after, go after, shadow, dog; accompany, attend, escort; *informal* tail.

tail ● noun **1** *the dog's tail* brush, scut, dock; tailpiece, tail feathers; hindquarters. **2** *the tail of the queue* REAR, end, back, extremity; bottom; *Brit. informal* fag end. **3** *the tail of the hunting season* CLOSE, end, conclusion, tail end. **4** *(informal) put a tail on that man* DETECTIVE, investigator, shadow; *informal* sleuth, private eye, tec; *N. Amer. informal* gumshoe.
– RELATED TERMS caudal, cercal.
– OPPOSITES head, front, start.
● verb *(informal) the paparazzi tailed them* FOLLOW, shadow, stalk, trail, track, hunt, hound, dog, pursue, chase.
– PHRASES **on someone's tail** *(informal)* CLOSE BEHIND, following closely, (hard) on someone's heels. **tail off/away** FADE, wane, ebb, dwindle, decrease, lessen, diminish, decline, subside, abate, drop off, peter out, taper off; let up, ease off, die away, die down, come to an end. **turn tail** RUN AWAY, flee, bolt, make off, take to one's heels, cut and run, beat a (hasty) retreat; *informal* scram, scarper, skedaddle, vamoose.

tailback ● noun TRAFFIC JAM, queue, line; congestion.

tailor ● noun OUTFITTER, dressmaker, couturier, (fashion) designer; clothier, costumier, seamstress; *dated* modiste.
– RELATED TERMS sartorial.
● verb *services can be tailored to customer requirements* CUSTOMIZE, adapt, adjust, modify, change, convert, alter, attune, mould, gear, fit, cut, shape, tune.

taint ● noun *the taint of corruption* TRACE, touch, suggestion, hint, tinge; stain, blot, blemish, stigma, black mark, blot on one's escutcheon; discredit, dishonour, disgrace, shame.
● verb **1** *a wilderness tainted by pollution* CONTAMINATE, pollute, adulterate, infect, blight, spoil, soil, ruin, destroy; *poetic/literary* befoul. **2** *fraudulent firms taint our firm's reputation* TARNISH, sully, blacken, stain, blot, blemish, stigmatize, mar, corrupt, defile, soil,

ly diminish in amount, strength, or intensity. **3** (**tail back**) Brit. (of traffic) become congested and form a tailback.
– PHRASES **on someone's tail** informal following someone closely. **with one's tail between one's legs** informal in a state of dejection or humiliation. **with one's tail up** informal in a confident or cheerful mood.
– DERIVATIVES **tailed** adjective **tailless** adjective.
– ORIGIN Old English.

tail² ● noun Law, chiefly historical limitation of ownership, especially of an estate or title limited to a person and their heirs.
– ORIGIN originally referring to a form of taxation: from Old French *taille* 'notch, tax', from *taillier* 'to cut'.

tailback ● noun Brit. a long queue of traffic extending back from a junction or obstruction.

tailboard ● noun Brit. a tailgate.

tailcoat ● noun Brit. a man's formal morning or evening coat,

Thesaurus

muddy, damage, harm, hurt; drag through the mud; *poetic/literary* besmirch.
– OPPOSITES clean, improve.

take ● verb **1** *she took his hand* LAY HOLD OF, get hold of; grasp, grip, clasp, clutch, grab. **2** *he took an envelope from his pocket* REMOVE, pull, draw, withdraw, extract, fish. **3** *a passage taken from my book* EXTRACT, quote, cite, excerpt, derive, abstract, copy, cull. **4** *she took a little wine* DRINK, imbibe; consume, swallow, eat, ingest. **5** *many prisoners were taken* CAPTURE, seize, catch, arrest, apprehend, take into custody; carry off, abduct. **6** *someone's taken my car* STEAL, remove, appropriate, make off with, pilfer, purloin; *informal* filch, swipe, snaffle; *Brit. informal* pinch, nick. **7** *take four from the total* SUBTRACT, deduct, remove; discount; *informal* knock off, minus. **8** *all the seats had been taken* OCCUPY, use, utilize, fill, hold; reserve, engage; *informal* bag. **9** *I have taken a room nearby* RENT, lease, hire, charter; reserve, book, engage. **10** *I took the job* ACCEPT, undertake. **11** *I'd take this over the other option* PICK, choose, select; prefer, favour, opt for, plump for, vote for. **12** *take, for instance, the English* CONSIDER, contemplate, ponder, think about, weigh up, mull over, examine, study, meditate over, ruminate about. **13** *he takes 'The Observer'* SUBSCRIBE TO, buy, read. **14** *she took his temperature* ASCERTAIN, determine, establish, measure, find out, discover; calculate, compute, evaluate, rate, assess, appraise, gauge. **15** *he took notes* WRITE, note (down), jot (down), scribble, scrawl, record, register, document, minute. **16** *I took it back to London* BRING, carry, bear, transport, convey, move, transfer, shift, ferry; *informal* cart, tote. **17** *the priest took her home* ESCORT, accompany, help, assist, show, lead, guide, see, usher, convey. **18** *he took the train* TRAVEL ON/BY, journey on, go via; use. **19** *the town takes its name from the lake* DERIVE, get, obtain, come by, acquire, pick up. **20** *she took the prize for best speaker* RECEIVE, obtain, gain, get, acquire, collect, accept, be awarded; secure, come by, win, earn, pick up, carry off; *informal* land, bag, net, scoop. **21** *I took the chance to postpone it* ACT ON, take advantage of, capitalize on, use, exploit, make the most of, leap at, jump at, pounce on, seize, grasp, grab, accept. **22** *he took great pleasure in painting* DERIVE, draw, acquire, obtain, get, gain, extract, procure; experience, undergo, feel. **23** *Liz took the news badly* RECEIVE, respond to, react to, meet, greet; deal with, cope with. **24** *do you take me for a fool?* REGARD AS, consider to be, view as, see as, believe to be, reckon to be, imagine to be, deem to be. **25** *I take it that you are hungry* ASSUME, presume, suppose, imagine, expect, reckon, gather, dare say, trust, surmise, deduce, guess, conjecture, fancy, suspect. **26** *I take your point* UNDERSTAND, grasp, get, comprehend, apprehend, see, follow; accept, appreciate, acknowledge, sympathize with, agree with. **27** *Shirley was rather taken with him* CAPTIVATE, enchant, charm, delight, attract, beguile, enthral, entrance, infatuate, dazzle; amuse, divert, entertain; *informal* tickle someone's fancy. **28** *I can't take much more* ENDURE, bear, tolerate, stand, put up with, stomach, abide, accept, allow, countenance, support, shoulder; *formal* brook; *archaic* suffer. **29** *applicants must take a test* CARRY OUT, do, complete, conduct, perform, execute, discharge, accomplish, fulfil. **30** *I took English and French* STUDY, learn, have lessons in; take up, pursue; *Brit.* read; *informal* do. **31** *the journey took six hours* LAST, continue for, go on for, carry on for; require, call for, need, necessitate, entail, involve. **32** *it would take an expert to know that* REQUIRE, need, necessitate, demand, call for, entail, involve. **33** *I take size three shoes* WEAR, use; require, need. **34** *the dye did not take* BE EFFECTIVE, take effect, hold, root, be productive, be effectual, be useful; work, operate, succeed, function; *formal* be efficacious.
– OPPOSITES give, free, add, refuse, miss.
● noun **1** *the whalers' commercial take* CATCH, haul, bag, yield, net. **2** *the state's tax take* REVENUE, income, gain, profit; takings, proceeds, returns, receipts, winnings, pickings, earnings, spoils; purse. **3** *a clapperboard for the start of each take* SCENE, sequence, (film) clip. **4** *a wry take on gender issues* VIEW OF, reading of, version of, interpretation of, understanding of, account of, analysis of, approach to.
– PHRASES **take after** RESEMBLE, look like; remind one of, make one think of, recall, conjure up, suggest, evoke; *informal* favour, be a chip off the old block, be the spitting image of. **take against** TAKE A DISLIKE TO, feel hostile towards, view with disfavour, look askance at. **take something apart 1** *we took the machine apart* DISMANTLE, pull to pieces, pull apart, disassemble, break up; tear down, demolish, destroy, wreck. **2** (*informal*) *the scene was taken apart by the director.* See CRITICIZE. **take someone back 1** *the dream took me back to Vienna* EVOKE, remind one of, conjure up, summon up; echo, suggest. **2** *I will never take that girl back* BE RECONCILED TO, forgive, pardon, excuse, exonerate, absolve; let bygones be bygones, bury the hatchet. **take something back 1** *I take back every word* RETRACT, withdraw, renounce, disclaim, unsay, disavow, recant, repudiate; *formal* abjure. **2** *I must take the keys back* RETURN, bring back, give back, restore. **take something down** WRITE DOWN, note down, jot down, set down, record, commit to paper, register, draft, document, minute, pen. **take someone in 1** *she took in paying guests* ACCOMMODATE, board, house, feed, put up, admit, receive; harbour. **2** *you were taken in by a hoax* DECEIVE, delude, hoodwink, mislead, trick, dupe, fool, cheat, defraud, swindle, outwit, gull, hoax, bamboozle; *informal* con, put one over on. **take something in 1** *she could hardly take in the news* COMPREHEND, understand, grasp, follow, absorb; *informal* get. **2** *this route takes in some great scenery* INCLUDE, encompass, embrace, contain, comprise, cover, incorporate, comprehend, hold. **take someone in hand** CONTROL, be in charge of, dominate, master; reform, improve, correct, change, rehabilitate. **take something in hand** DEAL WITH, apply oneself to, get to grips with, set one's hand to, grapple with, take on, attend to, see to, sort out, take care of, handle, manage; *informal* get stuck into. **take it out of someone** EXHAUST, drain, enervate, tire, fatigue, wear out, weary, debilitate; *informal* knacker, poop. **take off 1** *the horse took off at great speed* RUN AWAY/OFF, flee, abscond, take flight, decamp, leave, go, depart, make off, bolt, take to one's heels, escape; *informal* split, clear off, skedaddle, vamoose. **2** *the plane took off* BECOME AIRBORNE, take to the air, take wing; lift off, blast off. **3** *the idea really took off* SUCCEED, do well, become popular, catch on, prosper, flourish, thrive, boom. **take someone off** MIMIC, impersonate, imitate, ape, parody, mock, caricature, satirize, burlesque, lampoon, ridicule; *informal* spoof, send up. **take oneself off** WITHDRAW, retire, leave, exit, depart, go away, quit; *informal* clear off. **take on** (*Brit. informal*) *don't take on so!* GET UPSET, make a fuss, get excited, overreact; *informal* lose one's cool. **take someone on 1** *there was no challenger to take him on* COMPETE AGAINST, oppose, challenge, confront, face, fight, vie with, contend with, stand up to. **2** *we took on extra staff* ENGAGE, hire, employ, enrol, enlist, sign up; *informal* take on board. **take something on 1** *he took on more responsibility* UNDERTAKE, accept, assume, shoulder, acquire, carry, bear. **2** *the study took on political meaning* ACQUIRE, assume, come to have. **take one's time** GO SLOWLY, dally, dawdle, delay, linger, drag one's feet, waste time, kill time; *informal* dilly-dally; *archaic* tarry. **take someone out 1** *he asked if he could take her out* GO OUT WITH, escort, partner, accompany, go with; romance, woo; *informal* date, see, go steady with; *dated* court. **2** (*informal*) *the sniper took them all out* KILL, murder, assassinate, dispatch, execute, finish off, eliminate, exterminate, terminate; *informal* do in, do away with, bump off, rub out, mow down, top; *poetic/literary* slay. **take something over** ASSUME CONTROL OF, take charge of, take command of. **take to 1** *he took to carrying his money in his sock* MAKE A HABIT OF, resort to, turn to, have recourse to; start, commence. **2** *Ruth took to him instantly* LIKE, get on with, be friendly towards; *informal* take a shine to. **3** *the dog has really taken to racing* BECOME GOOD AT, develop an ability for; like, enjoy. **take something up 1** *he took up abstract painting* ENGAGE IN, practise; begin, start, commence. **2** *the meetings took up all her time* CONSUME, fill, absorb, use, occupy; waste, squander. **3** *her cousin took up the story* RESUME, recommence, restart, carry on, continue, pick up, return to. **4** *he took up their offer of a job* ACCEPT, say yes to, agree to, adopt; *formal* accede to. **5** *take the skirt up an inch* SHORTEN, turn up; raise, lift. **take up with** BECOME

with a long skirt divided at the back into tails and cut away in front.

tail end ● noun the last or hindmost part of something, in particular the batting order in cricket.

tail fin ● noun **1** Zoology a fin at the posterior end of a fish's body. **2** a projecting vertical surface on the tail of an aircraft, housing the rudder and providing stability. **3** an upswept projection on each rear corner of a motor car, popular in the 1950s.

tailgate ● noun **1** a hinged flap giving access to the back of a truck. **2** the door at the back of an estate or hatchback car. ● verb informal, chiefly N. Amer. drive too closely behind (another vehicle).
– DERIVATIVES **tailgater** noun.

tail light ● noun a red light at the rear of a vehicle.

tailor ● noun a person whose occupation is making men's outer garments for individual customers. ● verb **1** make (clothes) to fit individual customers. **2** make or adapt for a particular purpose or person.
– ORIGIN Old French *taillour* 'cutter', from Latin *taliare* 'to cut'.

tailored ● adjective (of clothes) smart, fitted, and well cut.

tailoring ● noun **1** the activity or trade of a tailor. **2** the style or cut of a garment or garments.

tailor-made ● adjective **1** (of clothes) made by a tailor for a particular customer. **2** made or adapted for a particular purpose or person.

tailpiece ● noun **1** the final or end part of something. **2** a part added to the end of a piece of writing. **3** a small decorative design at the foot of a page or the end of a chapter or book.

tailpipe ● noun the rear section of the exhaust pipe of a motor vehicle.

tailplane ● noun Brit. a horizontal aerofoil at the tail of an aircraft.

tailspin ● noun a spin by an aircraft.

tailwind ● noun a wind blowing in the direction of travel of a vehicle or aircraft.

taimen /tīmən/ ● noun (pl. same) a large food fish found in Siberia and east Asia.
– ORIGIN Russian.

taint ● noun **1** a trace of a bad or undesirable quality or substance. **2** a contaminating influence or effect. ● verb **1** contaminate or pollute. **2** affect with a bad or undesirable quality.
– ORIGIN Old French *teint* 'tinged', from Latin *tingere* 'to dye, tinge'.

taipan /tīpan/ ● noun a foreigner who is head of a business in China.
– ORIGIN Chinese.

Taiwanese /tīwəneez/ ● noun (pl. same) a person from Taiwan. ● adjective relating to Taiwan.

Tajik /tajeek/ (also **Tadjik** or **Tadzhik**) ● noun **1** a member of a mainly Muslim people inhabiting Tajikistan and parts of neighbouring countries. **2** a person from the republic of Tajikistan.
– ORIGIN Persian, 'a Persian, someone who is neither an Arab nor a Turk'.

taka /taakaa/ ● noun (pl. same) the basic monetary unit of Bangladesh, equal to 100 poisha.
– ORIGIN Bengali.

takahe /taakəhi/ ● noun a large, rare flightless rail found in New Zealand.
– ORIGIN Maori.

take ● verb (past **took**; past part. **taken**) **1** lay hold of with one's hands; reach for and hold. **2** occupy (a place or position). **3** capture or gain possession of by force. **4** carry or bring with one; convey. **5** remove from a place. **6** subtract. **7** consume as food, drink, medicine, or drugs. **8** bring into a specified state. **9** experience or be affected by. **10** use as a route or a means of transport. **11** accept or receive. **12** acquire or assume (a position, state, or form). **13** require or use up. **14** hold or accommodate. **15** act on (an opportunity). **16** regard, view, or deal with in a specified way: *he took it as an insult.* **17** submit to, tolerate, or endure. **18** make, undertake, or perform (an action or task). **19** be taught or examined in (a subject). ● noun **1** a sequence of sound or vision photographed or recorded continuously. **2** a particular version of or approach to something: *his whimsical take on life.* **3** an amount gained or acquired from one source or in one session.
– PHRASES **be on the take** informal take bribes. **take after** resemble (a parent or ancestor). **take as read** Brit. assume. **take back** retract (a statement). **take five** informal, chiefly N. Amer. have a short break. **take in 1** cheat or deceive. **2** make (a garment) tighter by altering its seams. **3** encompass, understand, or absorb. **take in hand 1** undertake to control or reform (someone). **2** start doing or dealing with (a task). **take it on one** (or **oneself**) **to do** decide to do without asking for permission or advice. **take it out of** exhaust the strength of. **take off 1** become airborne. **2** remove (clothing). **3** mimic (someone). **4** depart hastily. **take on 1** engage (an employee). **2** undertake (a task). **3** acquire (a particular meaning or quality). **take something out on** relieve frustration or anger by mistreating. **take over** assume control of or responsibility for. **take one's time** not hurry. **take to 1** fall into the habit of. **2** form a liking or develop an ability for. **3** go to (a place) to escape danger. **take up 1** become interested or engaged in (a pursuit). **2** occupy (time, space, or attention). **3** pursue (a matter) further. **take up on** accept an offer or challenge from. **take up with** begin to associate with.
– DERIVATIVES **taker** noun.
– ORIGIN Old Norse.

takeaway ● noun **1** Brit. a restaurant or shop selling cooked food to be eaten elsewhere. **2** a meal or dish of such food.

take-home pay ● noun the pay received by an employee after the deduction of tax and insurance.

take-off ● noun **1** an act or the action of becoming airborne. **2** informal an act of mimicking.

takeout ● noun chiefly N. Amer. a takeaway.

takeover ● noun an act of assuming control of something, especially the buying-out of one company by another.

taking ● noun **1** the action or process of taking. **2** (**takings**) the amount of money earned by a business from the sale of goods or services. ● adjective dated captivating in manner; charming.
– PHRASES **for the taking** ready or available to take advantage of.

tala /taalə/ ● noun (pl. same or **talas**) the basic monetary unit of Samoa, equal to 100 sene.
– ORIGIN Samoan.

talc ● noun **1** talcum powder. **2** a soft mineral consisting of a hydrated silicate of magnesium.

talcum powder ● noun a preparation for the body and face consisting of the mineral talc in powdered form. ● verb (**talcumed**, **talcuming**) powder with this substance.
– ORIGIN Latin, from Persian.

tale ● noun **1** a narrative or story, especially one that is imaginatively recounted. **2** a lie.
– ORIGIN Old English, 'telling, something told'.

taleggio /talejiō/ ● noun a soft Italian cheese made from cows' milk.
– ORIGIN named after the *Taleggio* valley in Lombardy.

talent ● noun **1** natural aptitude or skill. **2** people possessing such aptitude or skill. **3** informal people regarded as sexually attractive or as prospective sexual partners. **4** an ancient weight and unit of currency.
– DERIVATIVES **talentless** adjective.
– ORIGIN Greek *talanton* 'weight, sum of money': sense 1 is a figurative use with biblical allusion to the parable of the talents (Gospel of Matthew, chapter 25).

talented ● adjective having a natural aptitude or skill for some-

t

Thesaurus

FRIENDS WITH, go around with, fall in with, string along with, get involved with, start seeing; *informal* knock around with, hang out with.

take-off ● noun **1** *the plane crashed on take-off* DEPARTURE, lift-off, launch, blast-off; ascent, flight. **2** *(informal) a take-off of a talent show* PARODY, pastiche, mockery, caricature, travesty, satire, lampoon, mimicry, imitation, impersonation, impression; *informal* send-up, spoof.
– OPPOSITES touchdown.

takeover ● noun BUYOUT, merger, amalgamation; purchase, acquisition.

taking ● adjective *(dated)*. See WINNING sense 2.

takings ● plural noun PROCEEDS, returns, receipts, earnings, winnings, pickings, spoils; profit, gain, income, revenue; gate, purse.

tale ● noun **1** *a tale of witches* STORY, narrative, anecdote, report, account, history; legend, fable, myth, parable, allegory, saga; *informal* yarn. **2** *she told tales to her mother* LIE, fib, falsehood, story, untruth, fabrication, fiction; *informal* tall story, fairy story/tale, cock-and-bull story.

talent ● noun FLAIR, aptitude, facility, gift, knack, technique, touch,

thing.

talent scout ● noun a person whose job is searching for talented performers, especially in sport and entertainment.

talisman /talizmən/ ● noun (pl. **talismans**) an object thought to have magic powers and to bring good luck.
– DERIVATIVES **talismanic** /talizmannik/ adjective.
– ORIGIN Arabic, apparently from Greek *telesma* 'completion, religious rite'.

talk ● verb **1** speak in order to give information or express ideas or feelings. **2** have the power of speech. **3** (**talk over/through**) discuss (something) thoroughly. **4** (**talk back**) reply defiantly or insolently. **5** (**talk down to**) speak patronizingly or condescendingly to. **6** (**talk round**) convince (someone) that they should adopt a particular point of view. **7** (**talk into/out of**) persuade or dissuade (someone) to or from. **8** reveal secret or private information. ● noun **1** conversation; discussion. **2** an address or lecture. **3** (**talks**) formal discussions or negotiations over a period. **4** rumour, gossip, or speculation.
– PHRASES **you can't** (or **can**) **talk** informal used to convey that a criticism made applies equally well to the person making it. **look who's talking** another way of saying **you can't talk**. **now you're talking** informal expressing enthusiastic agreement or approval.
– DERIVATIVES **talker** noun.
– ORIGIN related to TALE or TELL[1].

talkative ● adjective fond of or given to talking.
– DERIVATIVES **talkatively** adverb **talkativeness** noun.

talkback ● noun **1** a system of two-way communication by loudspeaker. **2** another term for PHONE-IN.

talkfest ● noun informal, chiefly N. Amer. a lengthy discussion or debate, especially as part of a television chat show.

talkie ● noun informal a film with a soundtrack, as distinct from a silent film.

talking book ● noun a recorded reading of a book.

talking drum ● noun each of a set of West African drums which are beaten to transmit a tonal language.

talking head ● noun informal, chiefly derogatory a presenter or reporter on television who addresses the camera and is viewed in close-up.

talking point ● noun a topic that invites discussion or argument.

talking shop ● noun Brit. a place or group regarded as a centre for unproductive talk rather than action.

talking-to ● noun informal a sharp reprimand.

talk radio ● noun chiefly N. Amer. a type of radio broadcast in which topical issues are discussed by the presenter and by listeners who phone in.

talk show ● noun a chat show.

tall ● adjective **1** of great or more than average height. **2** measuring a specified distance from top to bottom. **3** fanciful and difficult to believe; unlikely: *a tall story*.
– PHRASES **a tall order** an unreasonable or difficult demand.
– DERIVATIVES **tallish** adjective **tallness** noun.
– ORIGIN probably from Old English, 'swift, prompt'.

tallboy ● noun Brit. a tall chest of drawers in two sections, one standing on the other.

tallow /talō/ ● noun a hard fatty substance made from rendered animal fat, used in making candles and soap.
– DERIVATIVES **tallowy** adjective.
– ORIGIN perhaps from Low German.

tallow tree ● noun a tree with fatty seeds from which vegetable tallow or other oils are extracted.

tall ship ● noun a sailing ship with a high mast or masts.

tally ● noun (pl. **tallies**) **1** a current score or amount. **2** a record of a score or amount. **3** a particular number taken as a group or unit to facilitate counting. **4** a mark registering such a number. **5** (also **tally stick**) historical a piece of wood scored across with notches for the items of an account. ● verb (**tallies, tallied**) **1** agree or correspond. **2** calculate the total number of.
– ORIGIN Old French *tallie*, from Latin *talea* 'twig, cutting'.

tally-ho ● exclamation a huntsman's cry to the hounds on sighting a fox.
– ORIGIN apparently from French *taïaut*.

tallyman ● noun Brit. dated a person who sells goods on credit, especially from door to door.

Talmud /talmŏŏd/ ● noun the body of Jewish civil and ceremonial law and legend.
– DERIVATIVES **Talmudic** adjective **Talmudist** noun.
– ORIGIN Hebrew, 'instruction'.

talon ● noun a claw, especially one belonging to a bird of prey.
– DERIVATIVES **taloned** adjective.
– ORIGIN Old French, 'heel', from Latin *talus* 'ankle bone, heel'.

talus[1] /tayləss/ ● noun (pl. **tali** /tayli/) Anatomy the bone in the ankle that forms a movable joint with the shin bone.
– ORIGIN Latin, 'ankle, heel'.

talus[2] /tayləss/ ● noun (pl. **taluses**) **1** a sloping mass of rock

Thesaurus

bent, ability, expertise, capacity, faculty; strength, forte, genius, brilliance; dexterity, skill, artistry.

talented ● adjective GIFTED, skilful, skilled, accomplished, brilliant, expert, consummate, masterly, adroit, dexterous, able, competent, capable, apt, deft, adept, proficient; *informal* crack, ace.
– OPPOSITES inept.

talisman ● noun (LUCKY) CHARM, fetish, amulet, mascot, totem, juju.

talk ● verb **1** *I was talking to a friend* SPEAK, chat, chatter, gossip, prattle, babble, rattle on, blather; *informal* yak, gab, jaw, chew the fat; *Brit. informal* natter, rabbit, witter, chunter; *N. Amer. informal* rap; *Austral./NZ informal* mag. **2** *you're talking rubbish* UTTER, speak, say, voice, express, articulate, pronounce, verbalize, vocalize. **3** *they were able to talk in peace* CONVERSE, communicate, speak, confer, consult; negotiate, parley; *informal* have a confab, chew the fat/rag, rap; *formal* confabulate. **4** *he talked of suicide* MENTION, refer to, speak about, discuss. **5** *I was able to talk English* SPEAK (IN), talk in, communicate in, converse in, express oneself in; use. **6** *nothing would make her talk* CONFESS, speak out/up, reveal all, tell tales, give the game away, open one's mouth; *informal* come clean, blab, squeal, let the cat out of the bag, spill the beans, grass, sing, rat. **7** *people will talk* GOSSIP, pass comment, make remarks; criticize.

● noun **1** *he was bored with all this talk* CHATTER, gossip, prattle, jabbering, babbling, gabbling; *informal* yakking, gabbing; *Brit. informal* nattering, rabbit. **2** *she needed a talk with Vi* CONVERSATION, chat, discussion, tête-à-tête, heart-to-heart, dialogue, parley, powwow, consultation, conference, meeting; *informal* confab, jaw, chit-chat, gossip; *formal* colloquy, confabulation. **3** *peace talks* NEGOTIATIONS, discussions; conference, summit, meeting, consultation, dialogue, symposium, seminar, conclave, parley; mediation, arbitration; *informal* powwow. **4** *she gave a talk on her travels* LECTURE, speech, address, discourse, oration, presentation, report, sermon; *informal* spiel. **5** *there was talk of a takeover* GOSSIP, rumour, hearsay, tittle-tattle; news, report. **6** *baby talk* SPEECH, language, slang, idiom, idiolect; words; *informal* lingo.
– PHRASES **talk back** ANSWER BACK, be impertinent, be cheeky, be rude; contradict, argue with, disagree with. **talk big** *(informal)*. See BOAST verb sense 1. **talk something down** DENIGRATE, deprecate, disparage, belittle, diminish, criticize; *informal* knock, put down. **talk down to** CONDESCEND TO, patronize, look down one's nose at, put down. **talk someone into something** PERSUADE INTO, argue into, cajole into, coax into, bring round to, inveigle into, wheedle into, sweet-talk into, prevail on someone to; *informal* hustle, fast-talk.

talkative ● adjective CHATTY, loquacious, garrulous, voluble, conversational, communicative; gossipy, babbling, blathering; long-winded, wordy, verbose; *informal* gabby, mouthy.
– OPPOSITES taciturn.

talker ● noun CONVERSATIONALIST, speaker, communicator; chatterbox, gossip.

talking-to ● noun *(informal)*. See REPRIMAND noun.

tall ● adjective **1** *a tall man* BIG, large, huge, towering, colossal, gigantic, giant, monstrous; leggy; *informal* long. **2** *tall buildings* HIGH, big, lofty, towering, elevated, sky-high; multi-storey. **3** *she's five feet tall* IN HEIGHT, high, from head to toe; from top to bottom. **4** *a tall tale* UNLIKELY, improbable, exaggerated, far-fetched, implausible, dubious, unbelievable, incredible, absurd, untrue; *informal* cock-and-bull. **5** *a tall order* DEMANDING, exacting, difficult; unreasonable, impossible.
– OPPOSITES short, low, wide, credible, easy.

tally ● noun **1** *he keeps a tally of the score* RUNNING TOTAL, count, record, reckoning, register, account, roll; census, poll. **2** *his tally of 1,816 wickets* TOTAL, score, count, sum.

● verb **1** *these statistics tally with government figures* CORRESPOND, agree, accord, concur, coincide, match, fit, be consistent, conform, equate, harmonize, be in tune, dovetail, correlate, parallel; *informal* square; *N. Amer. informal* jibe. **2** *votes were tallied with abacuses* COUNT, calculate, add up, total, compute; figure out, work

t

fragments at the foot of a cliff. **2** the sloping side of an earthwork or tapering wall.
– ORIGIN French.
tam ● noun a tam-o'-shanter.
tamagotchi /tamməgochi/ ● noun trademark an electronic toy displaying a digital image of a creature, which has to be looked after as if it were a pet.
– ORIGIN Japanese.
tamale /təmaali/ ● noun a Mexican dish of seasoned meat and maize flour steamed or baked in maize husks.
– ORIGIN Mexican Spanish *tamal*, from Nahuatl.
tamari /təmaari/ ● noun a variety of rich, naturally fermented soy sauce.
– ORIGIN Japanese.
tamarillo /tammərillō/ ● noun (pl. **tamarillos**) the red egg-shaped fruit of a tropical South American plant.
– ORIGIN an invented name, perhaps suggested by Spanish *tomatillo* 'little tomato'.
tamarin /tammərin/ ● noun a small forest-dwelling South American monkey.
– ORIGIN Carib.
tamarind /tammərind/ ● noun sticky brown acidic pulp from the pod of a tropical African tree, used as a flavouring in Asian cookery.
– ORIGIN Arabic, 'Indian date'.
tamarisk /tammərisk/ ● noun a shrub or small tree with tiny scale-like leaves borne on slender branches.
– ORIGIN Latin *tamariscus*, variant of *tamarix*.
tambala /tambaalə/ ● noun (pl. same or **tambalas**) a monetary unit of Malawi, equal to one hundredth of a kwacha.
– ORIGIN from a word in a Bantu language meaning 'cockerel'.
tambour /tamboor/ ● noun **1** historical a small drum. **2** a circular frame for holding fabric taut while it is being embroidered.
– ORIGIN French, 'drum'.
tambourine /tambəreen/ ● noun a percussion instrument resembling a shallow drum with metal discs around the edge, played by being shaken or hit with the hand.
– ORIGIN French *tambourin* 'small tambour'.
tame ● adjective **1** (of an animal) not dangerous or frightened of people; domesticated. **2** not exciting, adventurous, or controversial. **3** informal (of a person) willing to cooperate. ● verb **1** domesticate (an animal). **2** make less powerful and easier to control.
– DERIVATIVES **tamely** adverb **tameness** noun **tamer** noun.
– ORIGIN Old English.
Tamil /tammil/ ● noun **1** a member of a people inhabiting parts of South India and Sri Lanka. **2** the language of the Tamils.
– ORIGIN Tamil.
Tammany /tamməni/ (also **Tammany Hall**) ● noun N. Amer. a corrupt political organization or situation.
– ORIGIN named after a powerful organization within the US Democratic Party that was widely associated with corruption and had headquarters at *Tammany* Hall, New York.
tam-o'-shanter /tamməshantər/ ● noun a round Scottish cap with a bobble in the centre.
– ORIGIN named after the hero of Robert Burns's poem *Tam o' Shanter* (1790).
tamoxifen /təmoksifen/ ● noun a synthetic drug used to treat breast cancer and infertility in women.
– ORIGIN an arbitrary formation based on elements of the drug's chemical name.
tamp ● verb **1** pack (a blast hole) full of clay or sand to concentrate the force of the explosion. **2** firmly ram or pack (a substance) down or into something.
– ORIGIN probably from French *tampon* 'tampon, plug'.
Tampax ● noun (pl. same) trademark a sanitary tampon.
– ORIGIN an arbitrary formation from TAMPON.
tamper ● verb (**tamper with**) interfere with (something) without authority or so as to cause damage.
– DERIVATIVES **tamperer** noun.
– ORIGIN alteration of TEMPER.
tampon ● noun a plug of soft material inserted into the vagina to absorb menstrual blood.
– ORIGIN French, from *tapon* 'plug, stopper'.
tam-tam ● noun a large metal gong.
– ORIGIN perhaps from Hindi (see TOM-TOM).
tan[1] ● noun **1** a yellowish-brown colour. **2** a golden-brown shade of skin developed by pale-skinned people after exposure to the sun. **3** (also **tanbark**) bark of oak or other trees, used as a source of tannin for converting hides into leather. ● verb (**tanned**, **tanning**) **1** give or acquire a tan after exposure to the sun. **2** convert (animal skin) into leather, especially by soaking in a liquid containing tannic acid. **3** informal beat (someone) as a punishment.
– ORIGIN Old English.
tan[2] ● abbreviation tangent.
tanager /tannəjər/ ● noun a brightly coloured American songbird of the bunting family.
– ORIGIN Tupi.
tanbark ● noun see TAN[1] (sense 3).
tandem ● noun **1** a bicycle with seats and pedals for two riders, one behind the other. **2** a carriage driven by two animals harnessed one in front of the other. ● adverb one behind another.
– PHRASES **in tandem 1** alongside each other; together. **2** one behind another.
– ORIGIN from Latin, 'at length'.
tandoor /tandoor/ ● noun a clay oven of a type used originally in northern India and Pakistan.
– ORIGIN Arabic.
tandoori /tandoori/ ● adjective referring to a style of Indian cooking based on the use of a tandoor.
tang ● noun **1** a strong taste, flavour, or smell. **2** the projection on the blade of a knife or other tool by which the blade is held firmly in the handle.
– ORIGIN Old Norse 'point, tang of a knife'.
tanga /tanggə/ ● noun Brit. a pair of briefs consisting of small panels connected by strings at the sides.
– ORIGIN originally denoting a loincloth worn by indigenous peoples in tropical America: from Bantu.
tangelo /tanjəlō/ ● noun (pl. **tangelos**) a hybrid of the tangerine and grapefruit.
– ORIGIN blend of TANGERINE and POMELO.
tangent /tanjənt/ ● noun **1** a straight line or plane that touches a curve or curved surface at a point, but if extended does not cross it at that point. **2** Mathematics the trigonometric function that is equal to the ratio of the sides (other than the hypotenuse) opposite and adjacent to an angle in a right-angled triangle. **3** a completely different line of thought or action: *her mind went off at a tangent.* ● adjective (of a line or plane) touching, but not intersecting, a curve or curved surface.
– DERIVATIVES **tangency** noun.
– ORIGIN from Latin *tangere* 'to touch'.
tangential /tanjensh'l/ ● adjective **1** relating to or along a tangent. **2** having only a slight connection or relevance; peripheral. **3** diverging from a previous course; erratic.
– DERIVATIVES **tangentially** adverb.
tangerine ● noun **1** a small citrus fruit with a loose skin, especially one of a variety with deep orange-red skin. **2** a deep orange-red colour.

Thesaurus

out, reckon, measure, quantify; Brit. tot up; formal enumerate.
– OPPOSITES disagree.
tame ● adjective **1** *a tame elephant* DOMESTICATED, domestic, docile, tamed, broken, trained; gentle, mild; pet; Brit. house-trained; N. Amer. housebroken. **2** *(informal) he has a tame lawyer* AMENABLE, biddable, cooperative, willing, obedient, tractable, acquiescent, docile, submissive, compliant, meek. **3** *it was a pretty tame affair* UNEXCITING, uninteresting, uninspiring, dull, bland, flat, insipid, spiritless, pedestrian, colourless, run-of-the-mill, mediocre, ordinary, humdrum, boring; harmless, safe, inoffensive.
– OPPOSITES wild, uncooperative, exciting.
● verb **1** *wild rabbits can be tamed* DOMESTICATE, break, train, master, subdue. **2** *she learned to tame her emotions* SUBDUE, curb, control, calm, master, moderate, overcome, discipline, suppress, repress, mellow, temper, soften, bridle, get a grip on; informal lick.
tamper ● verb **1** *she saw them tampering with her car* INTERFERE, monkey around, meddle, tinker, fiddle, fool around, play around; doctor, alter, change, adjust, damage, deface, vandalize; informal mess about/around; Brit. informal muck about/around. **2** *the defendant tampered with the jury* INFLUENCE, get at, rig, manipulate, bribe, corrupt, bias; informal fix; Brit. informal nobble.
tan ● adjective *a tan waistcoat* YELLOWISH-BROWN, light brown, pale brown, tawny.
● verb **1** *use a sunscreen to help you tan* BECOME SUNTANNED, get a suntan, (go) brown, bronze. **2** *(informal) I'll tan his hide.* See THRASH sense 1.

– ORIGIN from *Tanger*, the former name of *Tangier* in Morocco, from where the fruit was exported.

tangible /tanjib'l/ • adjective **1** perceptible by touch. **2** clear and definite; real.
– DERIVATIVES **tangibility** noun **tangibly** adverb.
– ORIGIN Latin *tangibilis*, from *tangere* 'to touch'.

tangle • verb **1** twist (strands) together into a confused mass. **2** (**tangle with**) informal become involved in a conflict with. • noun **1** a confused mass of something twisted together. **2** a confused or complicated state; a muddle.
– DERIVATIVES **tangly** adjective.
– ORIGIN probably Scandinavian.

tango • noun (pl. **tangos**) **1** a ballroom dance originating in Buenos Aires, characterized by marked rhythms and postures and abrupt pauses. **2** a piece of music in the style of this dance. • verb (**tangoes**, **tangoed**) dance the tango.
– ORIGIN Latin American Spanish.

tangy • adjective (**tangier**, **tangiest**) having a strong, piquant flavour or smell.
– DERIVATIVES **tanginess** noun.

tank • noun **1** a large container or storage chamber, especially for liquid or gas. **2** the container holding the fuel supply in a motor vehicle. **3** a container with transparent sides in which to keep fish; an aquarium. **4** a heavy armoured fighting vehicle carrying guns and moving on a continuous metal track. • verb **1** (**be/get tanked up**) informal drink heavily or become drunk. **2** US informal fail completely or disastrously.
– DERIVATIVES **tankful** noun **tankless** adjective.
– ORIGIN perhaps from Gujarati or Marathi (a central Indian language), 'underground cistern'.

tankard • noun a tall beer mug, typically made of silver or pewter, with a handle and sometimes a hinged lid.
– ORIGIN perhaps related to Dutch *tanckaert*.

tank engine • noun a steam locomotive carrying fuel and water receptacles in its own frame, not in a tender.

tanker • noun a ship, road vehicle, or aircraft for carrying liquids, especially mineral oils, in bulk.

tank top • noun a close-fitting sleeveless top worn over a shirt or blouse.

tanner[1] • noun a person employed to tan animal hides.

tanner[2] • noun Brit. informal, historical a sixpence.
– ORIGIN of unknown origin.

tannery • noun (pl. **tanneries**) a place where animal hides are tanned.

tannic acid • noun another term for TANNIN.

tannin • noun a yellowish or brownish bitter-tasting organic substance present in tea, some barks, grapes, etc.
– DERIVATIVES **tannic** adjective.
– ORIGIN French *tanin*, from *tan* 'tanbark'.

tannoy • noun Brit. trademark a type of public address system.
– ORIGIN contraction of *tantalum alloy*, which is used as a rectifier in the system.

tansy • noun a plant with yellow flat-topped button-like flower heads.
– ORIGIN Old French *tanesie*, probably from Greek *athanasia* 'immortality'.

tantalize (also **tantalise**) • verb torment or tease with the sight or promise of something that is unobtainable or withheld.
– DERIVATIVES **tantalization** noun **tantalizing** adjective.
– ORIGIN from *Tantalus* in Greek mythology, who was punished for his crimes by being provided with fruit and water which receded when he reached for them.

tantalum /tantələm/ • noun a hard silver-grey metallic chemical element.
– ORIGIN from *Tantalus* (see TANTALIZE), with reference to its frustrating insolubility in acids.

tantalus /tantələss/ • noun Brit. a stand in which spirit decanters may be locked up though still visible.
– ORIGIN from *Tantalus* (see TANTALIZE).

tantamount • adjective (**tantamount to**) equivalent in seriousness to; virtually the same as.
– ORIGIN from earlier *tantamount* 'amount to as much', from Italian *tanto montare*.

tantra /tantrə/ • noun **1** a Hindu or Buddhist mystical or magical text. **2** adherence to the doctrines or principles of the tantras, involving mantras, meditation, yoga, and ritual.
– DERIVATIVES **tantric** adjective **tantrism** noun.
– ORIGIN Sanskrit, 'loom, groundwork, doctrine'.

tantrum • noun an uncontrolled outburst of anger and frustration, typically in a young child.
– ORIGIN of unknown origin.

Tanzanian /tanzəneeən/ • noun a person from Tanzania, a country in East Africa. • adjective relating to Tanzania.

Taoiseach /teeshəkh/ • noun the Prime Minister of the Irish Republic.
– ORIGIN Irish, 'chief, leader'.

Taoism /towiz'm/ • noun a Chinese philosophy based on the interpretation of the writer Lao-Tzu (6th century BC) of the Tao, or fundamental principle underlying the universe, incorporating the principles of yin and yang and advocating humility and religious piety.
– DERIVATIVES **Taoist** noun & adjective **Taoistic** adjective.
– ORIGIN from Chinese, 'the right way'.

tap[1] • noun **1** a device by which a flow of liquid or gas from a pipe or container can be controlled. **2** an instrument for cutting a threaded hole in a material. **3** a device connected to a telephone for listening secretly to conversations. **4** Brit. a taproom. • verb (**tapped**, **tapping**) **1** draw liquid through the tap or spout of (a cask, barrel, etc.). **2** draw sap from (a tree) by cutting into it. **3** exploit or draw a supply from (a resource). **4** informal obtain money or information from. **5** connect a device to (a telephone) so that conversations can be listened to secretly. **6** cut a thread in (something) to accept a screw.
– PHRASES **on tap 1** ready to be poured from a tap. **2** informal freely available whenever needed. **3** N. Amer. informal on schedule to occur.
– DERIVATIVES **tappable** adjective.
– ORIGIN Old English, 'stopper for a cask'.

tap[2] • verb (**tapped**, **tapping**) **1** strike or knock with a quick light blow or blows. **2** strike lightly and repeatedly against something else. **3** US informal designate or select for a task or honour. • noun **1** a quick light blow. **2** tap dancing. **3** a piece of metal attached to the toe and heel of a tap dancer's shoe to make a tapping sound.
– DERIVATIVES **tapper** noun.
– ORIGIN Old French *taper*, or imitative.

Thesaurus

t

tang • noun FLAVOUR, taste, savour; sharpness, zest, bite, edge, smack, piquancy, spice; smell, odour, aroma, fragrance, perfume, redolence; *informal* kick, pep.

tangible • adjective TOUCHABLE, palpable, material, physical, real, substantial, corporeal, solid, concrete; visible, noticeable; actual, definite, clear, clear-cut, distinct, manifest, evident, unmistakable, perceptible, discernible.
– OPPOSITES abstract.

tangle • verb **1** *the wool got tangled up* ENTANGLE, snarl, catch, entwine, twist, ravel, knot, enmesh, coil, mat, jumble, muddle. **2** *he tangled with his old rival* COME INTO CONFLICT, dispute, argue, quarrel, fight, wrangle, squabble, contend, cross swords, lock horns. • noun **1** *a tangle of branches* SNARL, mass, knot, mesh, mishmash. **2** *the defence got into an awful tangle* MUDDLE, jumble, mix-up, confusion, shambles.

tangled • adjective **1** *tangled hair* KNOTTED, knotty, ravelled, entangled, snarled (up), twisted, matted, tangly, messy; tousled, unkempt, ratty; *informal* mussed up. **2** *a tangled bureaucratic mess* CONFUSED, jumbled, mixed up, messy, chaotic, complicated, involved, complex, intricate, knotty, tortuous.
– OPPOSITES simple.

tangy • adjective ZESTY, sharp, acid, acidic, tart, sour, bitter, piquant, spicy, tasty, flavoursome, pungent.
– OPPOSITES bland.

tank • noun **1** *a hot water tank* CONTAINER, receptacle, vat, cistern, repository, reservoir, basin. **2** *a tank full of fish* AQUARIUM, bowl. **3** *the army's use of tanks* ARMOURED VEHICLE, armoured car, combat vehicle; Panzer.

tantalize • verb TEASE, torment, torture, bait; tempt, entice, lure, allure, beguile; excite, fascinate, titillate, intrigue.

tantamount • adjective *this is tantamount to mutiny* EQUIVALENT TO, equal to, as good as, more or less, much the same as, comparable to, on a par with, commensurate with.

tantrum • noun FIT OF TEMPER, fit of rage, fit, outburst, pet, paroxysm, frenzy, (bad) mood, huff, scene; *informal* paddy, wax, wobbly; *Brit. informal, dated* bate; *N. Amer. informal* hissy fit.

tap[1] • noun **1** *she turned the tap on* VALVE, stopcock, cock, spout; *N. Amer.* faucet, spigot, spile. **2** *a phone tap in the embassy* LISTENING

tapas /tappəss/ ● plural noun small Spanish savoury dishes, typically served with drinks at a bar.
– ORIGIN Spanish, 'cover, lid' (because the dishes were given free with the drink, served on a dish balanced on the glass).

tap dance ● noun a dance performed wearing shoes fitted with metal taps, characterized by rhythmical tapping of the toes and heels. ● verb (**tap-dance**) perform such a dance.
– DERIVATIVES **tap dancer** noun **tap-dancing** noun.

tape ● noun **1** light, flexible material in a narrow strip, used to hold, fasten, or mark off something. **2** (also **adhesive tape**) a strip of paper or plastic coated with adhesive, used to stick things together. **3** long, narrow material with magnetic properties, used for recording sound, pictures, or computer data. **4** a cassette or reel containing such material. ● verb **1** record (sound or pictures) on audio or video tape. **2** fasten, attach, or mark off with tape.
– ORIGIN Old English; perhaps related to Low German *teppen* 'pluck, tear'.

tape deck ● noun a piece of equipment for playing audio tapes, as part of a stereo system.

tape measure ● noun a length of tape marked at graded intervals for measuring.

tapenade /tappənaad/ ● noun a Provençal savoury paste or dip, made from black olives, capers, and anchovies.
– ORIGIN Provençal.

taper ● verb **1** diminish or reduce in thickness towards one end. **2** (**taper off**) gradually lessen. ● noun a slender tapered candle, used for conveying a flame.
– ORIGIN Old English, formed, by alteration of *p-* to *t-*, from Latin *papyrus* 'papyrus plant', the pith of which was used for candle wicks.

tape recorder ● noun an apparatus for recording sounds on magnetic tape and afterwards reproducing them.
– DERIVATIVES **tape-record** verb **tape recording** noun.

tapestry ● noun (pl. **tapestries**) a piece of thick textile fabric with pictures or designs formed by weaving coloured weft threads or by embroidering on canvas.
– DERIVATIVES **tapestried** adjective.
– ORIGIN Old French *tapisserie*, from *tapis* 'carpet'.

tapeworm ● noun a parasitic flatworm with a long ribbon-like body, the adult of which lives in the intestines.

tapioca /tappiōkə/ ● noun a starchy substance in the form of hard white grains, obtained from cassava and used for puddings and other dishes.
– ORIGIN Tupi-Guarani, 'squeezed-out dregs'.

tapir /taypər, -peer/ ● noun a hoofed mammal with a short flexible proboscis, native to tropical America and Malaysia.
– ORIGIN Tupi.

tappet ● noun a lever or projecting part on a machine which intermittently makes contact with a cam or other part so as to give or receive motion.
– ORIGIN from TAP[2].

taproom ● noun a room in which beer is available on tap.

taproot ● noun a straight tapering root growing vertically downwards and forming the centre from which subsidiary rootlets spring.

tar[1] ● noun **1** a dark, thick flammable liquid distilled from wood or coal, used in road-making and for coating and preserving timber. **2** a similar substance formed by burning tobacco or other material. ● verb (**tarred**, **tarring**) cover with tar.
– PHRASES **tar and feather** smear with tar and then cover with feathers as a punishment. **tar with the same brush** consider to have the same faults.
– ORIGIN Old English.

tar[2] ● noun informal, dated a sailor.
– ORIGIN perhaps an abbreviation of TARPAULIN, used as a nickname for a sailor in the 17th century.

taramasalata /tarrəməsəlaatə/ (also **tarama** /tarrəmə/) ● noun a paste or dip made from the roe of certain fish, mixed with olive oil and seasoning.
– ORIGIN from modern Greek *taramas* 'roe' + *salata* 'salad'.

tarantella /tarrəntellə/ (also **tarantelle** /tarrəntel/) ● noun a rapid whirling dance originating in southern Italy.
– ORIGIN Italian, from the seaport of *Taranto*.

tarantula /tərantyoolə/ ● noun **1** a very large hairy spider found chiefly in tropical and subtropical America. **2** a large black wolf spider of southern Europe.
– ORIGIN Italian *tarantola*, from the Italian seaport of *Taranto*.

tar baby ● noun informal a difficult problem which is only aggravated by attempts to solve it.
– ORIGIN with allusion to the doll smeared with tar as a trap for Brer Rabbit, in J. C. Harris's *Uncle Remus: His Songs and His Sayings* (1880).

tarboosh /taarbōōsh/ ● noun a man's cap similar to a fez.
– ORIGIN Egyptian Arabic.

tardy ● adjective (**tardier**, **tardiest**) **1** delaying or delayed beyond the right or expected time; late. **2** slow in action or response.
– DERIVATIVES **tardily** adverb **tardiness** noun.
– ORIGIN Latin *tardus* 'slow'.

tare[1] /tair/ ● noun the common vetch.
– ORIGIN of unknown origin.

tare[2] /tair/ ● noun **1** an allowance made for the weight of the packaging in determining the net weight of goods. **2** the weight of a vehicle without its fuel or load.
– ORIGIN French, 'deficiency, tare', from Arabic, 'reject, deduct'.

target ● noun **1** a person, object, or place selected as the aim of an attack. **2** a board marked with concentric circles, aimed at in archery or shooting. **3** an objective or result towards which efforts are directed: *a sales target*. ● verb (**targeted**, **targeting**) **1** select as an object of attention or attack. **2** aim or direct.
– PHRASES **on** (or **off**) **target** succeeding (or not succeeding) in hitting or achieving the thing aimed at.
– DERIVATIVES **targetable** adjective.
– ORIGIN originally denoting a small round shield: from Old English.

tariff ● noun **1** a tax or duty to be paid on a particular class of imports or exports. **2** a table of the fixed charges made by a business, especially in a hotel or restaurant. **3** Law a scale of sentences and damages for crimes and injuries of different severities. ● verb fix the price of (something) according to a tariff.
– ORIGIN Italian *tariffa*, from Arabic, 'notify'.

tarmac ● noun **1** (trademark in the UK) material used for surfacing

Thesaurus

DEVICE, wiretap, wire, bug, bugging device, microphone, receiver.
● verb **1** *several barrels were tapped* DRAIN, bleed, milk; broach, open. **2** *butlers were tapping ale* POUR (OUT), draw off, siphon off, pump out, decant. **3** *their telephones were tapped* BUG, wiretap, monitor, overhear, eavesdrop on, spy on. **4** *the resources were to be tapped for our benefit* DRAW ON, exploit, milk, mine, use, utilize, turn to account.
– PHRASES **on tap 1** *beers on tap* ON DRAUGHT, cask-conditioned, real-ale, from barrels. **2** (informal) *trained staff are on tap* ON HAND, at hand, available, ready, handy, accessible, standing by.

tap[2] ● verb **1** *she tapped on the door* KNOCK, rap, strike, beat, drum. **2** *Dad tapped me on the knee* PAT, hit, strike, slap, jab, poke, dig.
● noun **1** *a sharp tap at the door* KNOCK, rap, drumming. **2** *a tap on the shoulder* PAT, blow, slap, jab, poke, dig.

tape ● noun **1** *a package tied with tape* BINDING, ribbon, string, braid. **2** *secure the bandage with tape* ADHESIVE TAPE, sticky tape, masking tape; trademark Sellotape. **3** *they listened to tapes* (AUDIO) CASSETTE, (tape) recording, audio tape, reel, spool; video.
● verb **1** *a card was taped to the box* BIND, stick, fix, fasten, secure, attach; tie, strap. **2** *they taped off the area* CORDON, seal, close, shut, mark, fence; isolate, segregate. **3** *police taped his confession* RECORD, tape-record; video.

taper ● verb **1** *the leaves taper at the tip* NARROW, thin (out), come to a point, attenuate. **2** *the meetings soon tapered off* DECREASE, lessen, dwindle, diminish, reduce, decline, die down, peter out, wane, ebb, slacken (off), fall off, let up, thin out.
– OPPOSITES thicken, increase.
● noun *a lighted taper* CANDLE, spill, sconce; historical rushlight.

tardy ● adjective LATE, unpunctual, behind schedule, running late; behind, overdue, belated, delayed; slow, dilatory.
– OPPOSITES punctual.

target ● noun **1** *targets at a ranges of 200 yards* MARK, bullseye, goal. **2** *eagles can spot their targets from half a mile* PREY, quarry, game, kill. **3** *their profit target* OBJECTIVE, goal, aim, end; plan, intention, intent, design, aspiration, ambition, ideal, desire, wish. **4** *she was the target for a wave of abuse* VICTIM, butt, recipient, focus, object, subject.
● verb **1** *he was targeted by a gunman* PICK OUT, single out, earmark, fix on; attack, aim at, fire at. **2** *the product is targeted at a specific market* AIM, direct, level, intend, focus.
– PHRASES **on target 1** *the striker was bang on target* ACCURATE, precise, unerring, sure, on the mark; Brit. informal spot on. **2** *the project*

roads or other outdoor areas, consisting of broken stone mixed with tar. **2** (**the tarmac**) a runway or other area surfaced with such material. ● verb (**tarmacked, tarmacking**) surface with tarmac.
– ORIGIN abbreviation of earlier *tarmacadam*, from TAR[1] + MACADAM.

tarn ● noun a small mountain lake.
– ORIGIN Old Norse.

tarnation ● noun & exclamation chiefly N. Amer. used as a euphemism for 'damnation'.

tarnish ● verb **1** lose or cause to lose lustre, especially as a result of exposure to air or moisture. **2** make or become less valuable or respected. ● noun **1** a film or stain formed on an exposed surface of a mineral or metal. **2** dullness of colour; loss of brightness.
– DERIVATIVES **tarnishable** adjective.
– ORIGIN from French *ternir*, from *terne* 'dark, dull'.

taro /taarō/ ● noun a tropical Asian plant with edible starchy corms and fleshy leaves, grown as a staple in the Pacific.
– ORIGIN Polynesian.

tarot /tarrō/ ● noun a set of special playing cards used for fortune telling.
– ORIGIN French, from Italian *tarocchi*.

tarpaulin /taarpawlin/ ● noun **1** heavy-duty waterproof cloth, originally of tarred canvas. **2** a sheet or covering of this.
– ORIGIN probably from TAR[1] + PALL[1] + -ING[1].

tarpon /taarpon/ ● noun a large tropical marine fish of herring-like appearance.
– ORIGIN probably from Dutch *tarpoen*.

tarragon /tarrəgən/ ● noun a plant with narrow aromatic leaves, used as a herb in cooking.
– ORIGIN from Latin *tragonia* and *tarchon*, perhaps ultimately from Greek *drakōn* 'dragon'.

tarry[1] /taari/ ● adjective of, like, or covered with tar.
– DERIVATIVES **tarriness** noun.

tarry[2] /tarri/ ● verb (**tarries, tarried**) archaic stay longer than intended; delay leaving a place.
– ORIGIN of unknown origin.

tarsal /taars'l/ Anatomy & Zoology ● adjective relating to the tarsus. ● noun a bone of the tarsus.

tarsier /taarsiər/ ● noun a small tree-dwelling primate with very large eyes, a long tufted tail, and very long hindlimbs, native to the islands of SE Asia.
– ORIGIN French, from *tarse* 'tarsus', with reference to the animal's long tarsal bones.

tarsus /taarsəss/ ● noun (pl. **tarsi** /taarsī/) **1** the group of small bones in the ankle and upper foot. **2** Zoology the shank of the leg of a bird or reptile.
– ORIGIN Greek *tarsos* 'flat of the foot, the eyelid'.

tart[1] ● noun an open pastry case containing a sweet or savoury filling.
– DERIVATIVES **tartlet** noun.
– ORIGIN Old French *tarte*.

tart[2] ● noun informal, derogatory a prostitute or promiscuous woman. ● verb informal **1** (**tart oneself up**) chiefly Brit. dress or make oneself up in order to look attractive. **2** (**tart up**) decorate or improve the appearance of.
– DERIVATIVES **tarty** adjective (**tartier, tartiest**).
– ORIGIN probably from SWEETHEART.

tart[3] ● adjective **1** sharp or acid in taste. **2** (of a remark or tone of voice) cutting, bitter, or sarcastic.
– DERIVATIVES **tartly** adverb **tartness** noun.
– ORIGIN Old English, 'harsh, severe'.

tartan ● noun a woollen cloth woven in one of several patterns of coloured checks and intersecting lines, especially of a design associated with a particular Scottish clan.
– ORIGIN perhaps from Old French *tertaine*, denoting a kind of cloth; compare with *tartarin*, a rich fabric formerly imported from the east through the ancient region of Tartary.

Tartar /taartər/ ● noun **1** historical a member of the combined forces of central Asian peoples, including Mongols and Turks, who conquered much of Asia and eastern Europe in the early 13th century. **2** (**tartar**) a harsh, fierce, or intractable person.
– DERIVATIVES **Tartarian** /taartairiən/ adjective.
– ORIGIN from *Tatar*, the local name of a tribe formerly living in parts of Russia and Ukraine.

tartar /taartər/ ● noun **1** a hard calcified deposit that forms on the teeth and contributes to their decay. **2** a deposit of impure cream of tartar formed during the fermentation of wine.
– PHRASES **cream of tartar** potassium hydrogen tartrate, an acidic crystalline compound used in baking powder.
– ORIGIN Greek *tartaron*.

tartare /taartaar/ ● adjective (of fish or meat) served raw, typically seasoned and shaped into small cakes: *steak tartare*.
– ORIGIN French, 'Tartar'.

tartare sauce (also **tartar sauce**) ● noun a cold sauce, typically eaten with fish, consisting of mayonnaise mixed with chopped onions, gherkins, and capers.

tartaric acid ● noun Chemistry a crystalline organic acid present especially in unripe grapes and used in baking powders and as a food additive.
– ORIGIN from TARTAR.

tartrate /taartrayt/ ● noun Chemistry a salt or ester of tartaric acid.

tartrazine /taartrəzeen/ ● noun Chemistry a brilliant yellow synthetic dye derived from tartaric acid and used to colour food, drugs, and cosmetics.

Tarzan ● noun a man of great agility and powerful physique.
– ORIGIN named after a fictitious character created by the American writer Edgar Rice Burroughs (1875–1950).

tash (also **tache**) ● noun informal a moustache.

task ● noun a piece of work to be done. ● verb **1** (**task with**) assign (a task) to. **2** make great demands on.
– PHRASES **take to task** reprimand or criticize.
– ORIGIN Old French *tasche*, from Latin *taxare* 'censure, charge'.

task force ● noun **1** an armed force organized for a special operation. **2** a unit specially organized for a task.

taskmaster ● noun a person who imposes a demanding workload on someone.

Tasmanian /tazmayniən/ ● noun a person from the Australian state of Tasmania. ● adjective relating to Tasmania.

Tasmanian devil ● noun a heavily built aggressive marsupial with a large head, powerful jaws, and mainly black fur, found only in Tasmania.

tassel ● noun **1** a tuft of hanging threads, knotted together at one end and used for decoration in soft furnishing and clothing. **2** the tufted head of some plants.
– DERIVATIVES **tasselled** adjective.
– ORIGIN Old French, 'clasp'.

taste ● noun **1** the sensation of flavour perceived in the mouth on contact with a substance. **2** the faculty of perceiving this. **3** a small portion of food or drink taken as a sample. **4** a brief

Thesaurus

was on target ON SCHEDULE, on track, on course, on time.

tariff ● noun TAX, duty, toll, excise, levy, charge, rate, fee; price list.

tarnish ● verb **1** *gold does not tarnish easily* DISCOLOUR, rust, oxidize, corrode, stain, dull, blacken. **2** *it tarnished his reputation* SULLY, blacken, stain, blemish, blot, taint, soil, ruin, disgrace, mar, damage, harm, hurt, undermine, dishonour, stigmatize; *poetic/literary* besmirch.
– OPPOSITES polish, enhance.
● noun **1** *the tarnish on the candlesticks* DISCOLORATION, oxidation, rust; film. **2** *the tarnish on his reputation* SMEAR, stain, blemish, blot, taint, stigma.

tarry ● verb *(archaic)* LINGER, loiter, procrastinate, delay, wait, dawdle; *informal* hang around/round.
– OPPOSITES hurry.

tart[1] ● noun *a jam tart* PASTRY, flan, tartlet, quiche, pie.

tart[2] *(informal)* ● noun *a tart on a street corner.* See PROSTITUTE noun.
● verb **1** *she tarted herself up* DRESS UP, make up, smarten up, preen oneself, beautify oneself, groom oneself; *informal* doll oneself up, titivate oneself. **2** *we must tart this place up a bit* DECORATE, renovate, refurbish, redecorate; smarten up; *informal* do up, fix up.

tart[3] ● adjective **1** *a tart apple* SOUR, sharp, acid, acidic, zesty, tangy, piquant; lemony, acetic. **2** *a tart reply* ACERBIC, sharp, biting, cutting, astringent, caustic, trenchant, incisive, barbed, scathing, sarcastic, acrimonious, nasty, rude, vicious, spiteful, venomous.
– OPPOSITES sweet, kind.

task ● noun *a daunting task* JOB, duty, chore, charge, assignment, detail, mission, engagement, occupation, undertaking, exercise, business, responsibility, burden, endeavour, enterprise, venture.
– PHRASES **take someone to task** REBUKE, reprimand, reprove, reproach, remonstrate with, upbraid, scold, berate, lecture, cen-

experience of something. **5** a person's liking for something. **6** the ability to discern what is of good quality or of a high aesthetic standard. **7** conformity to a specified degree with generally held views on what is acceptable or offensive: *a joke in bad taste.* ● verb **1** perceive or experience the flavour of. **2** have a specified flavour. **3** sample or test the flavour of. **4** eat or drink a small portion of. **5** have a brief experience of.
– PHRASES **to taste** according to personal liking.
– ORIGIN from Old French *taster* 'touch, try, taste', perhaps from a blend of Latin *tangere* 'to touch' and *gustare* 'to taste'.

taste bud ● noun any of the clusters of nerve endings on the tongue and in the lining of the mouth which provide the sense of taste.

tasteful ● adjective showing good aesthetic judgement or appropriate behaviour.
– DERIVATIVES **tastefully** adverb **tastefulness** noun.

tasteless ● adjective **1** lacking flavour. **2** lacking in aesthetic judgement or constituting inappropriate behaviour: *a tasteless remark.*
– DERIVATIVES **tastelessly** adverb **tastelessness** noun.

tastemaker ● noun a person who decides or influences what is or will become fashionable.

taster ● noun **1** a person who tests food or drink by tasting it. **2** a sample or brief experience of something.

tasty ● adjective (**tastier**, **tastiest**) **1** (of food) having a pleasant, distinct flavour. **2** informal, chiefly Brit. attractive; appealing.
– DERIVATIVES **tastily** adverb **tastiness** noun.

tat ● noun Brit. informal tasteless or shoddy articles.
– ORIGIN probably from TATTY.

tatami /tətaami/ ● noun (pl. same or **tatamis**) a rush-covered straw mat forming a traditional Japanese floor covering.
– ORIGIN Japanese.

tater /taytər/ (Brit. also **tatie** /tayti/) ● noun informal a potato.
– ORIGIN alteration.

tatterdemalion /tatərdimayliən/ ● adjective tattered or dilapidated. ● noun a person in tattered clothing.
– ORIGIN from TATTERS or TATTERED: the ending is unexplained.

tattered ● adjective **1** old and torn. **2** ruined; in tatters.

tatters ● plural noun irregularly torn pieces of cloth, paper, etc.
– PHRASES **in tatters 1** torn; in shreds. **2** destroyed; ruined.
– ORIGIN Old Norse, 'rags'.

tattersall /tattərsawl/ ● noun a woollen fabric with a pattern of coloured checks and intersecting lines, resembling a tartan.
– ORIGIN named after *Tattersalls*, the firm of horse auctioneers, by association with the traditional design of horse blankets.

tatting ● noun **1** a kind of knotted lace made by hand with a small shuttle. **2** the process of making such lace.
– ORIGIN of unknown origin.

tattle ● noun gossip; idle talk. ● verb engage in tattle.
– DERIVATIVES **tattler** noun.
– ORIGIN Flemish *tatelen, tateren.*

tattletale US ● noun a telltale. ● verb tell tales.

tattoo[1] ● noun (pl. **tattoos**) **1** an evening drum or bugle signal recalling soldiers to their quarters. **2** a military display consisting of music, marching, and exercises. **3** a rhythmic tapping or drumming.
– ORIGIN from Dutch *taptoe!* 'close the tap of the cask!'.

tattoo[2] ● verb (**tattoos**, **tattooed**) mark with an indelible design by inserting pigment into punctures in the skin. ● noun (pl. **tattoos**) a design made in such a way.
– DERIVATIVES **tattooer** noun **tattooist** noun.
– ORIGIN Polynesian.

tatty ● adjective (**tattier**, **tattiest**) informal worn and shabby; in poor condition.
– DERIVATIVES **tattily** adverb **tattiness** noun.
– ORIGIN from Old English, 'rag'; related to TATTERED.

tau /tow, taw/ ● noun the nineteenth letter of the Greek alphabet (Τ, τ), transliterated as 't'.
– ORIGIN Greek.

taught past and past participle of TEACH.

taunt ● noun a jeering or mocking remark made in order to wound or provoke. ● verb provoke or wound with taunts.
– DERIVATIVES **taunter** noun.
– ORIGIN from French *tant pour tant* 'like for like, tit for tat'.

taupe /tōp/ ● noun a grey tinged with brown.
– ORIGIN French, 'mole, moleskin', from Latin *talpa.*

taurine[1] /tawreen/ ● noun Biochemistry a sulphur-containing amino acid important in the metabolism of fats.
– ORIGIN from Greek *tauros* 'bull' (because it was originally obtained from ox bile).

taurine[2] /tawrīn/ ● adjective **1** of or like a bull. **2** of or relating to bullfighting.
– ORIGIN Latin *taurinus*, from *taurus* 'bull'.

Taurus /tawrəss/ ● noun **1** Astronomy a constellation (the Bull), said to represent a bull tamed by Jason (a hero of Greek mythology). **2** Astrology the second sign of the zodiac, which the sun enters about 21 April.
– DERIVATIVES **Taurean** /tawreeən/ noun & adjective.
– ORIGIN Latin.

taut ● adjective **1** stretched or pulled tight. **2** (of muscles or nerves) tense. **3** (of writing, music, etc.) concise and controlled. **4** (of a ship) having a disciplined crew.
– DERIVATIVES **tauten** verb **tautly** adverb **tautness** noun.
– ORIGIN from obsolete *tought* 'distended', perhaps originally a variant of TOUGH.

tautology /tawtolləji/ ● noun (pl. **tautologies**) the saying of the

Thesaurus

sure, criticize, admonish, chide, chasten, arraign; *informal* tell off, bawl out, give someone a dressing-down; *Brit. informal* tick off, carpet; *formal* castigate.

taste ● noun **1** *a distinctive sharp taste* FLAVOUR, savour, relish, tang, smack. **2** *a taste of brandy* MOUTHFUL, drop, bit, sip, nip, swallow, touch, soupçon, dash, modicum. **3** *it's too sweet for my taste* PALATE, taste buds, appetite, stomach. **4** *a taste for adventure* LIKING, love, fondness, fancy, desire, preference, penchant, predilection, inclination, partiality; hankering, appetite, hunger, thirst, relish. **5** *my first taste of prison* EXPERIENCE, impression; exposure to, contact with, involvement with. **6** *the house was furnished with taste* JUDGEMENT, discrimination, discernment, tastefulness, refinement, finesse, elegance, grace, style. **7** *the photo was rejected on grounds of taste* DECORUM, propriety, etiquette, politeness, delicacy, nicety, sensitivity, discretion, tastefulness.
– RELATED TERMS gustative, gustatory.
– OPPOSITES dislike.
● verb **1** *Adam tasted the wine* SAMPLE, test, try, savour; sip, sup. **2** *he could taste blood* PERCEIVE, discern, make out, distinguish. **3** *a beer that tasted of cashews* HAVE A FLAVOUR, savour, smack, be reminiscent; suggest. **4** *it'll be good to taste real coffee again* CONSUME, drink, partake of; eat, devour. **5** *he tasted defeat* EXPERIENCE, encounter, come face to face with, come up against, undergo; know.

tasteful ● adjective **1** *the decor is simple and tasteful* AESTHETICALLY PLEASING, in good taste, refined, cultured, elegant, stylish, smart, chic, attractive, exquisite. **2** *this video is erotic but tasteful* DECOROUS, proper, seemly, respectable, appropriate, modest.
– OPPOSITES tasteless, improper.

tasteless ● adjective **1** *the vegetables were tasteless* FLAVOURLESS, bland, insipid, unappetizing, savourless, watery, weak. **2** *tasteless leather panelling* VULGAR, crude, tawdry, garish, gaudy, loud, trashy, showy, ostentatious, cheap, inelegant; *informal* flash, flashy, tacky, kitsch; *Brit. informal* naff. **3** *a tasteless remark* CRUDE, vulgar, indelicate, uncouth, crass, tactless, undiplomatic, indiscreet, inappropriate, offensive.
– OPPOSITES tasty, tasteful, seemly.

tasty ● adjective DELICIOUS, palatable, luscious, mouth-watering, delectable, ambrosial, toothsome, dainty, flavoursome, flavourful; appetizing, tempting; *informal* scrumptious, yummy, scrummy, finger-licking, moreish; *dated* flavorous.
– OPPOSITES bland.

tatters ● plural noun *the satin had frayed to tatters* RAGS, scraps, shreds, bits, pieces, ribbons.
– PHRASES **in tatters 1** *his clothes were in tatters* RAGGED, tattered, torn, ripped, frayed, in pieces, worn out, moth-eaten, falling to pieces, threadbare. **2** *her marriage is in tatters* IN RUINS, on the rocks, destroyed, finished, devastated.

tattle ● verb **1** *we were tattling about him* GOSSIP, tittle-tattle, chatter, chat, prattle, babble, jabber, gabble, rattle on; *informal* chinwag, jaw, yak, gab; *Brit. informal* natter, chit-chat. **2** *I would tattle on her if I had evidence* INFORM; report, talk, tell all, spill the beans; *informal* squeal, sing, let the cat out of the bag.
● noun *tabloid tattle* GOSSIP, rumour, tittle-tattle, hearsay, scandal.

taunt ● noun *the taunts of his classmates* JEER, gibe, sneer, insult, barb, catcall; (**taunts**) teasing, provocation, goading, derision, mockery; *informal* dig, put-down.
● verb *she taunted him about his job* JEER AT, sneer at, scoff at, poke fun at, make fun of, get at, insult, tease, chaff, torment,

same thing over again in different words, considered as a fault of style (e.g. *they arrived one after the other in succession*).
– DERIVATIVES **tautological** adjective **tautologous** adjective.
– ORIGIN from Greek *tauto-* 'same' + *logos* 'word, telling'.
tavern • noun chiefly archaic or N. Amer. an inn or public house.
– ORIGIN Old French *taverne*, from Latin *taberna* 'hut, tavern'.
taverna /təvernə/ • noun a small Greek restaurant.
– ORIGIN modern Greek.
tawdry • adjective (**tawdrier**, **tawdriest**) **1** showy but cheap and of poor quality. **2** sordid; sleazy.
– DERIVATIVES **tawdriness** noun.
– ORIGIN short for *tawdry lace*, a fine silk lace or ribbon, contraction of *St Audrey's lace*: *Audrey* was the patron saint of Ely where tawdry laces, along with cheap imitations, were traditionally sold.
tawny • adjective (**tawnier**, **tawniest**) of an orange-brown or yellowish-brown colour.
– DERIVATIVES **tawniness** noun.
– ORIGIN Old French *tane*, from *tan* 'tanbark'; related to TAN[1].
tawny owl • noun a common owl with either reddish-brown or grey plumage, and a familiar quavering hoot.
tax • noun **1** a compulsory contribution to state revenue, levied by the government on personal income and business profits or added to the cost of some goods, services, and transactions. **2** a strain or heavy demand. • verb **1** impose a tax on. **2** pay tax on (a vehicle). **3** make heavy demands on. **4** charge with a fault or wrongdoing.
– DERIVATIVES **taxable** adjective.
– ORIGIN from Latin *taxare* 'to censure, charge, compute'.
taxa plural of TAXON.
taxation • noun **1** the levying of tax. **2** money paid as tax.
tax avoidance • noun Brit. the arrangement of one's financial affairs to minimize tax liability within the law.
tax break • noun informal a tax concession or advantage allowed by government.
tax-deductible • adjective permitted to be deducted from taxable income.
tax disc • noun Brit. a circular label displayed on the windscreen of a vehicle, certifying payment of road tax.
tax evasion • noun the illegal non-payment or underpayment of tax.
tax exile • noun a person with a high taxable income who chooses to live in a country or area with low rates of taxation.
tax haven • noun a country or autonomous area where taxes are levied at a low rate.
taxi • noun (pl. **taxis**) a motor vehicle licensed to transport passengers in return for payment of a fare. • verb (**taxies**, **taxied**, **taxiing** or **taxying**) **1** (with reference to an aircraft) move or guide slowly along the ground before take-off or after landing. **2** travel in a taxi.
– ORIGIN abbreviation of *taxicab* or *taximeter cab* (see TAXIMETER).
taxicab • noun a taxi.
taxidermy /taksidermi/ • noun the art of preparing, stuffing, and mounting the skins of animals so that they appear lifelike.
– DERIVATIVES **taxidermic** adjective **taxidermist** noun.
– ORIGIN from Greek *taxis* 'arrangement' + *derma* 'skin'.
taximeter • noun a device used in taxis that automatically records the distance travelled and the fare payable.
– ORIGIN French *taximètre*, from *taxe* 'tariff' + *mètre* 'meter'.
taxing • adjective physically or mentally demanding.
taxi rank (N. Amer. **taxi stand**) • noun a place where taxis park while waiting to be hired.
taxiway • noun a route along which an aircraft taxies when moving to or from a runway.
taxman • noun informal an inspector or collector of taxes.
taxon /taksən/ • noun (pl. **taxa** /taksə/) Biology a taxonomic group of any rank.
taxonomy /taksonnəmi/ • noun chiefly Biology **1** the branch of science concerned with classification. **2** a scheme of classification.
– DERIVATIVES **taxonomic** adjective **taxonomical** adjective **taxonomist** noun.
– ORIGIN from Greek *taxis* 'arrangement' + *-nomia* 'distribution'.
tax return • noun a form on which a taxpayer makes a statement of income and personal circumstances, used to assess liability for tax.
tax year • noun a year as reckoned for taxation (in Britain from 6 April).
tayberry • noun (pl. **tayberries**) a dark red soft fruit produced by crossing a blackberry and a raspberry.
– ORIGIN named after the River *Tay* in Scotland, near where it was introduced in 1977.
TB • abbreviation tubercle bacillus; tuberculosis.
Tb • symbol the chemical element terbium.
t.b.a. • abbreviation to be announced.
T-bar • noun a type of ski lift in the form of a series of inverted T-shaped bars for towing two skiers at a time uphill.
T-bone • noun a large choice piece of loin steak containing a T-shaped bone.
tbsp (also **tbs**) (pl. same or **tbsps**) • abbreviation tablespoonful.
Tc • symbol the chemical element technetium.
TCP/IP • abbreviation Computing, trademark transmission control protocol/Internet protocol, used to govern the connection of computer systems to the Internet.
TD • abbreviation **1** (in the Republic of Ireland) Teachta Dála, Member of the Dáil. **2** technical drawing. **3** (in the UK) Territorial (Officer's) Decoration.
Te • symbol the chemical element tellurium.
te (N. Amer. **ti**) • noun Music the seventh note of a major scale, coming after 'lah'.
– ORIGIN alteration of obsolete *si*, adopted to avoid having two notes (*soh* and *si*) beginning with the same letter.
tea • noun **1** a hot drink made by infusing the dried, crushed leaves of the tea plant in boiling water. **2** the dried leaves of an evergreen shrub or small tree native to south and east Asia, used to make tea. **3** a drink made from the leaves, fruits, or flowers of other plants. **4** chiefly Brit. a light afternoon meal consisting of sandwiches, cakes, etc., with tea to drink. **5** Brit. a cooked evening meal.
– ORIGIN Chinese.
tea bag • noun a small porous sachet containing tea leaves, on to which boiling water is poured in order to make tea.
tea bread • noun a type of cake containing dried fruit that has been soaked in tea before baking.
tea break • noun Brit. a short rest period during the working day.
teacake • noun Brit. a light yeast-based sweet bun containing dried fruit, typically served toasted and buttered.
tea ceremony • noun an elaborate Japanese ritual of serving and drinking tea, as an expression of Zen Buddhist philosophy.
teach • verb (past and past part. **taught**) **1** impart knowledge to or instruct in how to do something, especially in a school or as part of a recognized programme. **2** give instruction in (a subject or skill). **3** cause to learn by example or experience. **4** advocate as a practice or principle.

Thesaurus

goad, ridicule, deride, mock, heckle; *N. Amer.* ride; *informal* rib, needle, rag, guy.
taut • adjective **1** *the rope is taut* TIGHT, stretched, rigid. **2** *his muscles remained taut* FLEXED, tense, hard, solid, firm, rigid, stiff. **3** *a taut expression* FRAUGHT, strained, stressed, tense; *informal* uptight. **4** *a taut tale of gang life* CONCISE, controlled, crisp, pithy, sharp, succinct, compact, terse. **5** *he ran a taut ship* ORDERLY, tight, trim, neat, disciplined, tidy, spruce, smart, shipshape (and Bristol fashion).
– OPPOSITES slack, relaxed.
tavern • noun BAR, inn, hostelry, taphouse; *Brit.* pub, public house; *informal* watering hole; *Brit. informal* local, boozer; *dated* alehouse; *N. Amer. historical* saloon.
tawdry • adjective GAUDY, flashy, showy, garish, loud; tasteless, vulgar, trashy, junky, cheap (and nasty), cheapjack, shoddy, shabby, gimcrack; *informal* rubbishy, tacky, kitsch.
– OPPOSITES tasteful.
tax • noun **1** *they have to pay tax on the interest* DUTY, excise, customs, dues; levy, tariff, toll, impost, tithe, charge, fee. **2** *a heavy tax on one's attention* BURDEN, load, weight, demand, strain, pressure, stress, drain, imposition.
– RELATED TERMS fiscal.
– OPPOSITES rebate.
• verb **1** *they tax foreign companies more harshly* CHARGE (DUTY ON), tithe; *formal* mulct. **2** *his whining taxed her patience* STRAIN, stretch, overburden, overload, encumber, push too far; overwhelm, try, wear out, exhaust, sap, drain, weary, weaken.
taxing • adjective DEMANDING, exacting, challenging, burdensome, arduous, onerous, difficult, hard, tough, laborious, back-breaking, strenuous, rigorous, punishing; tiring, exhausting, enervating,

– DERIVATIVES **teachable** adjective **teaching** noun.
– ORIGIN Old English, 'show, present, point out'.
teacher ● noun a person who teaches in a school.
– DERIVATIVES **teacherly** adjective.
tea chest ● noun a light metal-lined wooden box in which tea is transported.
teaching hospital ● noun a hospital affiliated to a medical school, in which medical students receive training.
Teachta Dála /tyokhtə dawlə/ ● noun (pl. **Teachti** /tyokhti/) (in the Republic of Ireland) a member of the Dáil or lower House of Parliament.
– ORIGIN Irish.
tea cloth ● noun a tea towel.
tea cosy ● noun a thick or padded cover placed over a teapot to keep the tea hot.
teacup ● noun a cup from which tea is drunk.
tea dance ● noun an afternoon tea with dancing.
teak ● noun hard durable wood used in shipbuilding and for making furniture, obtained from a large deciduous tree native to India and SE Asia.
– ORIGIN Portuguese *teca*, from Tamil.
teal ● noun (pl. same or **teals**) **1** a small freshwater duck, typically with a bright blue-green patch on the wing plumage. **2** (also **teal blue**) a dark greenish-blue colour.
– ORIGIN of unknown origin.
tea lady ● noun Brit. a woman employed to make and serve tea in a workplace.
tea leaf ● noun **1** (**tea leaves**) dried leaves of tea. **2** Brit. rhyming slang a thief.
team ● noun **1** a group of players forming one side in a competitive game or sport. **2** two or more people working together. **3** two or more horses in harness together to pull a vehicle. ● verb **1** (**team up**) come together as a team to achieve a common goal. **2** (**team with**) match or coordinate with.
– ORIGIN Old English, related to TEEM[1] and TOW[1].
teammate ● noun a fellow member of a team.
team player ● noun a person who plays or works well as a member of a team.
team spirit ● noun feelings of camaraderie among the members of a team.
teamster ● noun **1** N. Amer. a truck driver. **2** a driver of a team of animals.
teamwork ● noun the combined effective action of a group.
teapot ● noun a pot with a handle, spout, and lid, in which tea is prepared.
tear[1] /tair/ ● verb (past **tore**; past part. **torn**) **1** rip a hole or split in. **2** (usu. **tear up**) pull or rip apart or to pieces. **3** damage (a muscle or ligament) by overstretching it. **4** (usu. **tear down**) energetically demolish or destroy. **5** (**tear apart**) disrupt and force apart. **6** (**be torn**) be in a state of conflict and uncertainty between two opposing options or parties. **7** (**tear oneself away**) leave despite a strong desire to stay. **8** informal move very quickly and in a reckless or excited manner. **9** (**tear into**) attack verbally. ● noun a hole or split caused by tearing.
– PHRASES **tear one's hair out** informal feel extreme desperation. **tear someone off a strip** (or **tear a strip off someone**) Brit. informal rebuke someone angrily. **that's torn it** Brit. informal expressing dismay when something has happened to disrupt someone's plans.
– DERIVATIVES **tearable** adjective.
– ORIGIN Old English.
tear[2] /teer/ ● noun a drop of clear salty liquid secreted from glands in a person's eye when they are crying or when the eye is irritated.
– PHRASES **in tears** crying.
– DERIVATIVES **teary** adjective.
– ORIGIN Old English.
tearaway ● noun Brit. a person who behaves in a wild or reckless manner.
teardrop ● noun **1** a single tear. **2** (before another noun) shaped like a tear.
tear duct ● noun a passage through which tears pass from the lachrymal glands to the eye or from the eye to the nose.
tearful ● adjective **1** crying or inclined to cry. **2** causing tears; sad.
– DERIVATIVES **tearfully** adverb **tearfulness** noun.
tear gas ● noun gas that causes severe irritation to the eyes, used in warfare and riot control.
tearing /tairing/ ● adjective violent; extreme: *a tearing hurry.*
tear jerker ● noun informal a story, film, or song that is intended to evoke sadness or sympathy.
tearless ● adjective not crying.
tea room ● noun a small restaurant or cafe where tea and other light refreshments are served.
tea rose ● noun a garden rose having flowers that are pale yellow tinged with pink, and a delicate scent resembling that of tea.
tear sheet ● noun a page that can be removed from a magazine, book, etc. for use separately.
tease ● verb **1** playfully make fun of or attempt to provoke. **2** tempt sexually. **3** (**tease out**) find out by searching through a mass of information. **4** gently pull or comb (tangled wool, hair, etc.) into separate strands. **5** archaic comb (the surface of woven cloth) to raise a nap. ● noun informal **1** an act of teasing. **2** a person who teases.
– ORIGIN Old English, related to TEASEL.
teasel (also **teazle** or **teazel**) ● noun **1** a tall prickly plant with spiny purple flower heads. **2** a dried head from a teasel, or a similar man-made device, used to raise a nap on woven cloth.
– ORIGIN Old English, related to TEASE.

Thesaurus

wearing, stressful; *informal* murderous.
– OPPOSITES easy.
teach ● verb **1** *she teaches small children* EDUCATE, instruct, school, tutor, coach, train; enlighten, illuminate, verse, edify, indoctrinate; drill, discipline. **2** *I taught English* GIVE LESSONS IN, lecture in, be a teacher of. **3** *teach your teenager how to negotiate* TRAIN, show, guide, instruct, demonstrate; instil, inculcate.
– RELATED TERMS didactic, pedagogic.
teacher ● noun EDUCATOR, tutor, instructor, master, mistress, schoolmarm, governess, educationist, preceptor; coach, trainer; lecturer, professor, don; guide, mentor, guru, counsellor; *informal* teach; *Brit. informal* beak; *Austral./NZ informal* chalkie, schoolie; *formal* pedagogue; *historical* schoolman.
team ● noun **1** *the sales team* GROUP, squad, company, party, crew, troupe, band, side, line-up; *informal* bunch, gang, posse. **2** *a team of horses* PAIR, span, yoke, duo, set, tandem.
● verb **1** *the horses are teamed in pairs* HARNESS, yoke, hitch, couple. **2** *team a T-shirt with matching shorts* MATCH, coordinate, complement, pair up. **3** *team up with another artist for an exhibition* JOIN (FORCES), collaborate, get together, work together; unite, combine, cooperate, link, ally, associate, club together.
tear[1] ● verb **1** *I tore up the letter* RIP UP, rip in two, pull to pieces, shred. **2** *his flesh was torn* LACERATE, cut (open), gash, slash, scratch, hack, pierce, stab; injure, wound. **3** *the traumas tore her family apart* DIVIDE, split, sever, break up, disunite, rupture; *poetic/literary* rend, sunder, cleave. **4** *Gina tore the book from his hands* SNATCH, grab, seize, rip, wrench, wrest, pull, pluck; *informal* yank. **5** *(informal) Jack tore down the street* SPRINT, race, run, dart, rush, dash, hasten, hurry, hare, bolt, fly, career, charge, shoot, hurtle, speed, whizz, zoom, go like lightning, go like the wind; *informal* pelt, scoot, hotfoot it, leg it, belt, zip, whip; *Brit. informal* go like the clappers, bomb, bucket; *N. Amer. informal* hightail it.
– OPPOSITES unite.
● noun *a tear in her dress* RIP, hole, split, slash, slit; ladder, snag.
– PHRASES **tear something down** DEMOLISH, knock down, raze (to the ground), flatten, level, bulldoze; dismantle, disassemble.
tear[2] ● noun *tears in her eyes* TEARDROP.
– RELATED TERMS lachrymal, lachrymose.
– PHRASES **in tears** CRYING, weeping, sobbing, wailing, howling, bawling, whimpering; tearful, upset; *informal* weepy, teary, blubbing, blubbering.
tearaway ● noun HOOLIGAN, hoodlum, ruffian, lout, rowdy, roughneck; *Austral.* larrikin; *informal* yahoo; *Brit. informal* yob, yobbo; *Scottish informal* ned; *Austral./NZ informal* roughie.
tearful ● adjective **1** *Georgina was tearful* CLOSE TO TEARS, emotional, upset, distressed, sad, unhappy; in tears, crying, weeping, sobbing, snivelling; *informal* weepy, teary; *formal* lachrymose. **2** *a tearful farewell* EMOTIONAL, upsetting, distressing, sad, heartbreaking, sorrowful; poignant, moving, touching, tear-jerking; *poetic/literary* dolorous.
– OPPOSITES cheerful.
tease ● verb MAKE FUN OF, poke fun at, chaff, laugh at, guy, make a monkey (out) of; taunt, bait, goad, pick on; deride, mock, ridicule; *informal* take the mickey out of, rag, send up, rib, josh, have on,

t

teaser ● noun **1** a person who teases others. **2** informal a tricky question or task.
tea set ● noun a set of crockery for serving tea.
teaspoon ● noun **1** a small spoon used for adding sugar to and stirring hot drinks or for eating some foods. **2** the amount held by such a spoon, in the UK considered to be 5 millilitres when used as a measurement in cookery.
teat ● noun **1** a nipple of the mammary gland of a female mammal. **2** Brit. a perforated plastic nipple-shaped device by which an infant or young animal can suck milk from a bottle.
– ORIGIN Old French *tete*.
tea towel ● noun chiefly Brit. a cloth for drying washed crockery, cutlery, and glasses.
tea tree ● noun an Australasian flowering shrub or small tree with leaves that are sometimes used for tea.
tea-tree oil ● noun an oil obtained from a species of tea tree, used in soaps and other products for its refreshing fragrance and antiseptic properties.
teazle (also **teazel**) ● noun variant spelling of TEASEL.
TEC ● abbreviation (in the UK) Training and Enterprise Council.
tech (also **tec**) ● noun informal **1** Brit. a technical college. **2** technology. **3** a technician.
techie /tekki/ (also **techy**) ● noun (pl. **techies**) informal a person who is an expert in technology, especially computing.
technetium /tekneeshiəm/ ● noun an unstable radioactive metallic element made by high-energy collisions.
– ORIGIN from Greek *tekhnētos* 'artificial'.
technic /teknik/ ● noun **1** /also **tekneek**/ chiefly US technique. **2** (**technics**) (treated as sing. or pl.) technical terms, details, and methods; technology.
– DERIVATIVES **technicist** noun.
– ORIGIN originally in the sense 'to do with art': from Greek *tekhnē* 'art'.
technical ● adjective **1** of or relating to a particular subject, art, or craft, or its techniques. **2** requiring specialized knowledge in order to be understood. **3** of or concerned with applied and industrial sciences. **4** according to a strict application or interpretation of the law or rules.
– DERIVATIVES **technically** adverb.
technical college ● noun a college of further education providing courses in applied sciences and other practical subjects.
technicality ● noun (pl. **technicalities**) **1** a small formal detail specified within a set of rules. **2** (**technicalities**) details of theory or practice within a particular field. **3** the use of technical terms or methods.
technical knockout ● noun Boxing the ending of a fight by the referee on the grounds of a contestant's inability to continue, the opponent being declared the winner.
technician ● noun **1** a person employed to look after technical equipment or do practical work in a laboratory. **2** an expert in the practical application of a science. **3** a person skilled in the technique of an art or craft.
Technicolor ● noun trademark **1** a process of colour cinematography using synchronized monochrome films, each of a different colour, to produce a colour print. **2** (**technicolor** or Brit. also **technicolour**) informal vivid colour.
– DERIVATIVES **technicolored** (Brit. also **technicoloured**) adjective.
technique ● noun **1** a way of carrying out a particular task, especially the execution of an artistic work or a scientific procedure. **2** a procedure that is effective in achieving an aim.
– ORIGIN French, from Greek *tekhnē* 'art'.
techno ● noun a style of fast, heavy electronic dance music, with few or no vocals.
– ORIGIN abbreviation of **technological** (see TECHNOLOGY).
technobabble ● noun informal incomprehensible technical jargon.
technocracy /teknokrəsi/ ● noun (pl. **technocracies**) the control of society or industry by an elite of technical experts.
– DERIVATIVES **technocrat** noun **technocratic** adjective.
technology ● noun (pl. **technologies**) **1** the application of scientific knowledge for practical purposes. **2** the branch of knowledge concerned with applied sciences.
– DERIVATIVES **technological** adjective **technologically** adverb **technologist** noun.
– ORIGIN Greek *tekhnologia* 'systematic treatment'.
technology transfer ● noun the transfer of new technology from the originator to a secondary user, especially from developed to underdeveloped countries.
technophile ● noun a person who is enthusiastic about new technology.
– DERIVATIVES **technophilia** noun **technophilic** adjective.
technophobe ● noun a person who dislikes or fears new technology.
– DERIVATIVES **technophobia** noun **technophobic** adjective.
technospeak ● noun technobabble.
techy ● noun variant spelling of TECHIE.
tectonic /tektonnik/ ● adjective **1** Geology of or relating to the structure of the earth's crust and the large-scale processes which take place within it. **2** of or relating to building or construction.
– DERIVATIVES **tectonically** adverb.
– ORIGIN Greek *tektonikos*, from *tektōn* 'carpenter, builder'.
tectonics ● plural noun (treated as sing. or pl.) Geology large-scale processes affecting the structure of the earth's crust.
teddy ● noun (pl. **teddies**) **1** (also **teddy bear**) a soft toy bear. **2** a woman's all-in-one undergarment.
– ORIGIN from *Teddy*, familiar form of the given name *Theodore*: in sense 1 alluding to the US President *Theodore* Roosevelt (1858–1919), an enthusiastic bear-hunter.
Teddy boy ● noun Brit. (in the 1950s) a young man of a subculture characterized by a style of dress based on Edwardian fashion, by hair slicked up in a quiff, and by a liking for rock-and-roll music.
– ORIGIN from *Teddy*, familiar form of the given name *Edward* (with reference to the Edwardian style of dress).
Te Deum /tay dayəm, tee deeəm/ ● noun a hymn beginning *Te Deum laudamus*, 'We praise Thee, O God', sung at matins or on special occasions such as a thanksgiving.
– ORIGIN Latin.
tedious ● adjective too long, slow, or dull.
– DERIVATIVES **tediously** adverb **tediousness** noun.
– ORIGIN from Latin *taedium* 'tedium', from *taedere* 'be weary of'.
tedium ● noun the state of being tedious.
tee[1] ● noun **1** a cleared space on a golf course, from which the ball is struck at the beginning of play for each hole. **2** a small peg with a concave head which is placed in the ground to support a golf ball before it is struck from a tee. **3** a mark aimed at in bowls, quoits, curling, and other similar games. ● verb (**tees, teed, teeing**) Golf **1** (**tee up**) place the ball on a tee ready to make the first stroke of the round or hole. **2** (**tee off**) begin a round or hole by playing the ball from a tee.
– ORIGIN of unknown origin.
tee[2] ● noun informal, chiefly N. Amer. a T-shirt.
tee-hee ● noun a titter or giggle. ● verb (**tee-hees, tee-heed, tee-heeing**) titter or giggle.
– ORIGIN imitative.
teem[1] ● verb (**teem with**) be full of or swarming with.
– ORIGIN Old English, 'give birth to' or 'be or become pregnant'; related to TEAM.
teem[2] ● verb (especially of rain) pour down; fall heavily.
– ORIGIN Old Norse, 'to empty'.
teen informal ● adjective relating to teenagers. ● noun a teenager.

t

Thesaurus

pull someone's leg; *Brit. informal* wind up; *N. Amer. informal* pull someone's chain, razz; *Austral./NZ informal* poke mullock at; *dated* twit.
technical ● adjective **1** *an important technical achievement* practical, scientific, technological, high-tech. **2** *this might seem very technical* SPECIALIST, specialized, scientific; complex, complicated, esoteric. **3** *a technical fault* MECHANICAL.
technique ● noun **1** *different techniques for solving the problem* METHOD, approach, procedure, system, modus operandi, MO, way; means, strategy, tack, tactic, line; routine, practice. **2** *I was impressed with his technique* SKILL, ability, proficiency, expertise, mastery, talent, genius, artistry, craftsmanship; aptitude, adroitness, deftness, dexterity, facility, competence; performance, delivery; *informal* know-how.
tedious ● adjective BORING, dull, monotonous, repetitive, unrelieved, unvaried, uneventful; characterless, colourless, lifeless, insipid, uninteresting, unexciting, uninspiring, flat, bland, dry, stale, tired, lacklustre, stodgy, dreary, humdrum, mundane; mind-numbing, soul-destroying, wearisome, tiring, tiresome, irksome, trying, frustrating; *informal* deadly, not up to much; *Brit. informal* samey; *N. Amer. informal* dullsville.
– OPPOSITES exciting.

-teen • suffix forming the names of numerals from 13 to 19.
– ORIGIN Old English, inflected form of TEN.
teenage • adjective denoting, relating to, or characteristic of a teenager or teenagers.
– DERIVATIVES **teenaged** adjective.
teenager • noun a person aged between 13 and 19 years.
teens • plural noun the years of a person's age from 13 to 19.
teensy • adjective (**teensier**, **teensiest**) informal very tiny.
– ORIGIN probably from TEENY.
teeny • adjective (**teenier**, **teeniest**) informal tiny.
– ORIGIN variant of TINY.
teeny-bopper • noun informal a young teenager who follows the latest fashions in clothes and pop music.
teeny-weeny (also **teensy-weensy**) • adjective informal very tiny.
teepee • noun variant spelling of TEPEE.
tee shirt • noun variant spelling of T-SHIRT.
teeter • verb **1** move or balance unsteadily. **2** waver between different courses.
– ORIGIN Old Norse, 'shake, shiver'.
teeth plural of TOOTH.
teethe • verb cut one's milk teeth.
teething ring • noun a small ring for an infant to bite on while teething.
teething troubles (also **teething problems**) • plural noun short-term problems that occur in the early stages of a new project.
teetotal • adjective choosing or characterized by abstinence from alcohol.
– DERIVATIVES **teetotalism** noun **teetotaller** noun.
– ORIGIN emphatic extension of TOTAL, apparently first used by Richard Turner, a worker from Preston, in a speech (1833) urging total abstinence from all alcohol.
teetotum /tee tōtəm/ • noun a small four-sided spinning top used as a die in games of chance.
– ORIGIN originally as *T totum*: from *T* (representing *totum*, inscribed on one side of the toy) + Latin *totum* 'the whole' (stake).
TEFL /teff'l/ • abbreviation teaching of English as a foreign language.
Teflon /teflon/ • noun **1** trademark a tough synthetic resin used to make seals and bearings and to coat non-stick cooking utensils. **2** (before another noun) (especially of a politician) having an undamaged reputation, in spite of scandal or misjudgement.
tein /tayin/ • noun (pl. same or **teins**) a monetary unit of Kazakhstan, equal to one hundredth of a tenge.
tektite /tektīt/ • noun Geology a small black glassy object believed to have been formed in numbers as molten debris in a meteorite impact and scattered through the air.
– ORIGIN from Greek *tēktos* 'molten'.
tele- /telli/ • combining form **1** to or at a distance: *telecommunication*. **2** relating to television: *telegenic*. **3** done by means of the telephone: *telemarketing*.
– ORIGIN Greek, 'far off'.
telecast • noun a television broadcast. • verb transmit by television.
– DERIVATIVES **telecaster** noun.
telecentre • noun another term for TELECOTTAGE.
telecommunication • noun **1** communication over a distance by cable, telegraph, telephone, or broadcasting. **2** (**telecommunications**) (treated as sing.) the branch of technology concerned with this.
telecommute • verb work from home, communicating with a central workplace using equipment such as telephones, fax machines, and modems.
– DERIVATIVES **telecommuter** noun **telecommuting** noun.
telecomputer • noun a device which combines the capabilities of a computer with those of a television and a telephone.
– DERIVATIVES **telecomputing** noun.
telecoms (also **telecomms**) • plural noun (treated as sing.) telecommunications.
teleconference • noun a conference with participants in different locations linked by telecommunication devices.
– DERIVATIVES **teleconferencing** noun.
telecottage • noun a place, especially in a rural area, where computer equipment is available for communal use.
tele-evangelist • noun variant of TELEVANGELIST.
telegenic /tellijennik/ • adjective having an appearance or manner that is attractive on television.
telegram • noun a message sent by telegraph and delivered in written or printed form, used in the UK only for international messages since 1981.
telegraph • noun a system or device for transmitting messages from a distance along a wire, especially one creating signals by making and breaking an electrical connection. • verb **1** send a message to by telegraph. **2** send (a message) by telegraph. **3** convey (an intentional or unconscious message) with facial expression or body language.
– DERIVATIVES **telegrapher** noun **telegraphist** noun **telegraphy** noun.
telegraphese • noun informal the terse, abbreviated style of language used in telegrams.
telegraphic • adjective **1** of or by telegraphs or telegrams. **2** (of language) omitting inessential words; concise.
– DERIVATIVES **telegraphically** adverb.
telegraph pole • noun a tall pole used to carry telegraph or telephone wires above the ground.
telekinesis /tellikineesiss, telliki-/ • noun the supposed ability to move objects at a distance by mental power or other non-physical means.
– DERIVATIVES **telekinetic** adjective.
– ORIGIN from Greek *kinēsis* 'motion'.
telemarketing • noun the marketing of goods or services by telephone calls to potential customers.
– DERIVATIVES **telemarketer** noun.
telematics • plural noun (treated as sing.) the branch of information technology which deals with the long-distance transmission of computerized information.
– DERIVATIVES **telematic** adjective.
– ORIGIN blend of TELECOMMUNICATION and INFORMATICS.
telemedicine • noun the remote diagnosis and treatment of patients by means of telecommunications technology.
telemessage • noun a message sent by telephone or telex and delivered in written form, which replaced the telegram for inland messages in the UK in 1981.
telemeter • noun an apparatus for recording the readings of an instrument and transmitting them by radio. • verb transmit (readings) to a distant receiving set or station.
– DERIVATIVES **telemetric** adjective **telemetry** noun.
teleology /telliolləji, teel-/ • noun (pl. **teleologies**) **1** Philosophy the doctrine that the existence of phenomena may be explained with reference to the purpose they serve. **2** Theology the doctrine that there is evidence of design and purpose in the natural world.
– DERIVATIVES **teleologic** adjective **teleological** adjective.
– ORIGIN from Greek *telos* 'end' + *logos* 'account, reason'.
telepathy • noun the supposed communication of thoughts or ideas by means other than the known senses.
– DERIVATIVES **telepath** noun **telepathic** adjective.
telephone • noun **1** a system for transmitting voices over a dis-

t

Thesaurus

tedium • noun MONOTONY, boredom, ennui, uniformity, routine, dreariness, dryness, banality, vapidity, insipidity.
– OPPOSITES variety.
teem[1] • verb *the pond was teeming with fish* BE FULL OF, be filled with, be alive with, be brimming with, abound in, be swarming with; be packed with, be crawling with, be overrun by, bristle with, seethe with, be thick with; *informal* be jam-packed with, be chock-a-block with, be chock-full with.
teem[2] • verb *the rain was teeming down* POUR, pelt, tip, beat, lash, sheet; come down in torrents, rain cats and dogs; *informal* be chucking it down; *Brit. informal* bucket down.
teenage • adjective ADOLESCENT, teenaged, youthful, young, juvenile; *informal* teen.
teenager • noun ADOLESCENT, youth, young person, minor, juvenile; *informal* teen, teeny-bopper.
teeny • adjective *(informal)*. See TINY.
teeter • verb **1** *Daisy teetered towards them* TOTTER, wobble, toddle, sway, stagger, stumble, reel, lurch, pitch. **2** *the situation teetered between tragedy and farce* SEE-SAW, veer, fluctuate, oscillate, swing, alternate, waver.
teetotal • adjective ABSTINENT, abstemious; sober, dry; *informal* on the wagon.
– OPPOSITES alcoholic.
telegram • noun TELEMESSAGE, telex; *informal* wire; *dated* radiogram;

tance using wire or radio, by converting acoustic vibrations to electrical signals. **2** an instrument used as part of such a system, typically including a handset with a transmitting microphone and a set of numbered buttons by which a connection can be made to another such instrument. ● verb **1** call or speak to using the telephone. **2** make a telephone call.
– DERIVATIVES **telephonic** adjective **telephonically** adverb.
telephone box ● noun chiefly Brit. a public booth or enclosure housing a payphone.
telephone directory ● noun a book listing the names, addresses, and telephone numbers of the people in a particular area.
telephone exchange ● noun a set of equipment that connects telephone lines during a call.
telephone number ● noun a number assigned to a particular telephone and used in making connections to it.
telephonist ● noun Brit. an operator of a telephone switchboard.
telephony /tileffəni/ ● noun the working or use of telephones.
telephoto lens ● noun a lens with a longer focal length than standard, giving a narrow field of view and a magnified image.
teleport ● noun a centre providing interconnections between different forms of telecommunications, especially one which links satellites to ground-based communications. ● verb (especially in science fiction) transport or be transported across space and distance instantly.
– DERIVATIVES **teleportation** noun.
– ORIGIN from TELE- + a shortened form of *transportation*.
telepresence ● noun the use of virtual reality technology, especially for remote control of machinery or for apparent participation in distant events.
teleprinter ● noun Brit. a device for transmitting telegraph messages as they are keyed, and for printing messages received.
teleprompter ● noun North American term for AUTOCUE.
telescope ● noun an optical instrument designed to make distant objects appear nearer, containing an arrangement of lenses, or of curved mirrors and lenses, by which rays of light are collected and focused and the resulting image magnified. ● verb **1** (with reference to an object made of concentric tubular parts) slide or cause to slide into itself, so that it becomes smaller. **2** condense or conflate so as to occupy less space or time.
– DERIVATIVES **telescopic** adjective **telescopically** adverb.
teletext ● noun a news and information service transmitted to televisions with appropriate receivers.
telethon ● noun a long television programme broadcast to raise money for a charity.
– ORIGIN from TELE- + *-thon* on the pattern of *marathon*.
teletype ● noun **1** trademark a kind of teleprinter. **2** a message received and printed by a teleprinter. ● verb send (a message) by means of a teleprinter.
televangelist (also **tele-evangelist**) ● noun chiefly N. Amer. an evangelical preacher who appears regularly on television.
televise ● verb record for or transmit by television.
– DERIVATIVES **televisable** adjective.
television ● noun **1** a system for converting visual images (with sound) into electrical signals, transmitting them by radio or other means, and displaying them electronically on a screen. **2** the activity, profession, or medium of broadcasting on television. **3** (also **television set**) a device with a screen for receiving television signals.
televisual ● adjective relating to or suitable for television.
– DERIVATIVES **televisually** adverb.
telework ● verb another term for TELECOMMUTE.
– DERIVATIVES **teleworker** noun.
telex ● noun **1** an international system of telegraphy with printed messages transmitted and received by teleprinters using the public telecommunications network. **2** a device used for this. **3** a message sent by this system. ● verb **1** communicate with by telex. **2** send (a message) by telex.
– ORIGIN blend of TELEPRINTER and EXCHANGE.
tell ● verb (past and past part. **told**) **1** communicate information to. **2** instruct to do something. **3** relate (a story). **4** (**tell on**) informal inform on. **5** (**tell off**) informal reprimand. **6** determine correctly or with certainty. **7** perceive (a distinction). **8** (of an experience or period of time) have a noticeable effect on someone.
– PHRASES **tell tales** gossip about another person's secrets or faults. **tell the time** (or N. Amer. **tell time**) be able to ascertain the time from reading the face of a clock or watch. **tell someone where to get off** informal angrily dismiss or rebuke someone. **there is no telling** it is not possible to know what has happened or will happen. **you're telling me** informal I am in complete agreement.
– ORIGIN Old English, 'relate, count, estimate'; related to TALE.
teller ● noun **1** a person who deals with customers' transactions in a bank. **2** a person appointed to count votes. **3** a person who tells something.
telling ● adjective having a striking or revealing effect; significant.
– DERIVATIVES **tellingly** adverb.
telling-off ● noun (pl. **tellings-off**) informal a reprimand.
telltale ● adjective revealing or betraying something. ● noun a person who tells tales.
telluric /telyoorik/ ● adjective **1** of the earth as a planet. **2** of the soil.
– ORIGIN from Latin *tellus* 'earth'.
tellurium /telyooriəm/ ● noun a silvery-white crystalline non-metallic element with semiconducting properties, resembling selenium.
– DERIVATIVES **telluride** /telyoorīd/ noun.
– ORIGIN from Latin *tellus* 'earth'.
telly ● noun (pl. **tellies**) Brit. informal term for TELEVISION.
telnet Computing ● noun a network protocol or program that allows a user on one computer to log in to another computer that is part of the same network. ● verb (**telnetted**, **telnetting**) infor-

Thesaurus

historical cable, cablegram.
telepathic ● adjective PSYCHIC, clairvoyant.
telepathy ● noun MIND-READING, thought transference; extrasensory perception, ESP; clairvoyance, sixth sense; psychometry.
telephone ● noun *Sophie picked up the telephone* PHONE, handset, receiver; *informal* blower; *N. Amer. informal* horn.
● verb *he telephoned me last night* PHONE, call, dial; get, reach; *Brit.* ring (up); *informal* call up, give someone a buzz, get on the blower to; *Brit. informal* give someone a bell, give someone a tinkle; *N. Amer. informal* get someone on the horn.
telescope ● noun SPYGLASS; *informal* scope.
● verb **1** *the front of the car was telescoped* CONCERTINA, compact, compress, crush, squash. **2** *his experience can be telescoped into a paragraph* CONDENSE, shorten, reduce, abbreviate, abridge, summarize, precis, abstract, shrink, consolidate; truncate, curtail.
televise ● verb BROADCAST, screen, air, telecast; transmit, relay.
television ● noun TV; *informal* the small screen; *Brit. informal* telly, the box; *N. Amer. informal* the tube.
tell ● verb **1** *why didn't you tell me before?* INFORM, notify, apprise, let know, make aware, acquaint with, advise, put in the picture, brief, fill in; alert, warn; *informal* clue in/up. **2** *she told the story slowly* RELATE, recount, narrate, unfold, report, recite, describe, sketch, weave, spin; utter, voice, state, declare, communicate, impart, divulge. **3** *she told him to leave* INSTRUCT, order, command, direct, charge, enjoin, call on, require; *poetic/literary* bid. **4** *I tell you, I did nothing wrong* ASSURE, promise, give one's word, swear, guarantee. **5** *the figures tell a different story* REVEAL, show, indicate, be evidence of, disclose, convey, signify. **6** *promise you won't tell?* GIVE THE GAME AWAY, talk, tell tales, tattle; *informal* spill the beans, let the cat out of the bag, blab; *Brit. informal* blow the gaff. **7** *she was bound to tell on him* INFORM ON, tell tales on, give away, denounce, sell out; *informal* split on, blow the whistle on, rat on, peach on, squeal on; *Brit. informal* grass on, sneak on, shop; *N. Amer. informal* finger; *Austral./NZ informal* dob on. **8** *it was hard to tell what he said* ASCERTAIN, determine, work out, make out, deduce, discern, perceive, see, identify, recognize, understand, comprehend; *informal* figure out; *Brit. informal* suss out. **9** *he couldn't tell one from the other* DISTINGUISH, differentiate, discriminate. **10** *the strain began to tell on him* TAKE ITS TOLL, leave its mark; affect.
– PHRASES **tell someone off** *(informal)*. See REPRIMAND verb.
teller ● noun **1** *a bank teller* CASHIER, clerk. **2** *a teller of tales* NARRATOR, raconteur; storyteller, anecdotalist.
telling ● adjective REVEALING, significant, weighty, important, meaningful, influential, striking, potent, powerful, compelling.
– OPPOSITES insignificant.
telling-off ● noun *(informal)*. See REPRIMAND noun.
telltale ● adjective *the telltale blush on her face* REVEALING, revelatory, suggestive, meaningful, significant, meaning; *informal* give-away.
● noun *'Sue did it,' said a telltale* INFORMER, whistle-blower; *N. Amer.*

mal log into a remote computer using a telnet program.

telos /telloss/ ● noun (pl. **teloi** /telloy/) Philosophy or literary an ultimate object or aim.
– ORIGIN Greek.

temazepam /təmazzipam/ ● noun Medicine a tranquillizing drug of the benzodiazepine group.

temblor /temblor/ ● noun US an earthquake.
– ORIGIN American Spanish.

temerity /timerriti/ ● noun excessive confidence or boldness.
– ORIGIN Latin *temeritas*, from *temere* 'rashly'.

temp informal ● noun an employee, especially an office worker, who is employed on a temporary basis. ● verb work as a temp.

tempeh /tempay/ ● noun an Indonesian dish consisting of deep-fried fermented soya beans.
– ORIGIN Indonesian.

temper ● noun **1** a person's state of mind in terms of their being angry or calm. **2** a tendency to become angry easily. **3** an angry state of mind. **4** the degree of hardness and elasticity in steel or other metal. ● verb **1** improve the temper of (a metal) by reheating and then cooling it. **2** (often **be tempered with**) serve as a neutralizing or counterbalancing force to.
– PHRASES **keep** (or **lose**) **one's temper** retain (or fail to retain) composure or restraint when angry.
– DERIVATIVES **temperer** noun.
– ORIGIN Latin *temperare* 'mingle, restrain oneself'; the noun originally denoted a proportionate mixture of elements, also the combination of the four bodily humours, formerly believed to be the basis of temperament.

tempera /tempərə/ ● noun **1** a method of painting with pigments dispersed in an emulsion that mixes with water, typically egg yolk. **2** emulsion used in tempera.
– ORIGIN from Italian *pingere a tempera* 'paint in distemper'.

temperament ● noun a person's nature with regard to the effect it has on their behaviour.
– ORIGIN Latin *temperamentum* 'correct mixture', from *temperare* 'mingle'.

temperamental ● adjective **1** relating to or caused by temperament. **2** liable to unreasonable changes of mood.
– DERIVATIVES **temperamentally** adverb.

temperance ● noun abstinence from alcoholic drink.
– ORIGIN Old French *temperaunce*, from Latin *temperare* 'restrain'.

temperate ● adjective **1** relating or referring to a region or climate characterized by mild temperatures. **2** showing moderation or self-restraint.
– DERIVATIVES **temperately** adverb.
– ORIGIN Latin *temperatus*, from *temperare* 'mingle, restrain'.

temperate zone ● noun each of the two belts of latitude between the torrid zone and the northern and southern frigid zones.

temperature ● noun **1** the degree or intensity of heat present in a substance or object. **2** informal a body temperature above the normal. **3** the degree of excitement or tension present in a situation or discussion.
– ORIGIN originally in the sense 'the state of being tempered or mixed': from Latin *temperatura*, from *temperare* 'restrain'.

tempest ● noun a violent windy storm.
– ORIGIN Latin *tempestas* 'season, weather, storm'.

tempestuous /tempestyooəss/ ● adjective **1** very stormy. **2** characterized by strong and turbulent emotion.
– DERIVATIVES **tempestuously** adverb **tempestuousness** noun.

tempi plural of TEMPO.

Templar /templər/ ● noun historical a member of the Knights Templars, a powerful religious and military order.
– ORIGIN Latin *templarius*, from *templum* (see TEMPLE[1]).

template /templit, -playt/ (also **templet**) ● noun **1** a shaped piece of rigid material used as a pattern for processes such as cutting out, shaping, or drilling. **2** something serving as a model or example.
– ORIGIN probably from *temple* 'a device in a loom for keeping the cloth stretched', from Old French.

temple[1] ● noun a building devoted to the worship of a god or gods.
– ORIGIN Latin *templum* 'open or consecrated space'.

temple[2] ● noun the flat part either side of the head between the forehead and the ear.
– ORIGIN Old French, from Latin *tempus* 'temple of the head'.

templet ● noun variant spelling of TEMPLATE.

tempo /tempō/ ● noun (pl. **tempos** or **tempi** /tempi/) **1** Music the speed at which a passage of music is played. **2** the pace of an activity or process.
– ORIGIN Italian, from Latin *tempus* 'time'.

temporal[1] /tempərəl/ ● adjective **1** relating to time. **2** relating to worldly affairs; secular.
– DERIVATIVES **temporally** adverb.
– ORIGIN Latin *temporalis*, from *tempus* 'time'.

temporal[2] /tempərəl/ ● adjective Anatomy of or situated in the temples of the head.

temporal bone ● noun Anatomy either of a pair of bones which form part of the side of the skull on each side and enclose the middle and inner ear.

temporality ● noun (pl. **temporalities**) the state of existing within or having some relationship with time.

temporal lobe ● noun each of the paired lobes of the brain lying beneath the temples, including areas concerned with the understanding of speech.

Thesaurus

tattletale; informal snitch, squealer; Brit. informal sneak; Scottish informal clype; dated talebearer.

temerity ● noun AUDACITY, nerve, effrontery, impudence, impertinence, cheek, gall, presumption, front; daring; informal face, (brass) neck, chutzpah.

temper ● noun **1** *he walked out in a temper* (FIT OF) RAGE, fury, fit of pique, tantrum, (bad) mood, pet, sulk, huff; informal grump, snit; Brit. informal strop, paddy; Brit. informal, dated bate, wax; N. Amer. informal hissy fit. **2** *a display of temper* ANGER, fury, rage, annoyance, vexation, irritation, irritability, ill humour, spleen, pique, petulance, testiness, tetchiness, crabbiness; Brit. informal stroppiness; poetic/literary ire, choler. **3** *she struggled to keep her temper* COMPOSURE, equanimity, self-control, self-possession, sangfroid, calm, good humour; informal cool.
● verb **1** *the steel is tempered by heat* HARDEN, strengthen, toughen, fortify, anneal. **2** *their idealism is tempered with realism* MODERATE, modify, modulate, mitigate, alleviate, reduce, weaken, lighten, soften.
– PHRASES **lose one's temper** GET ANGRY, fly into a rage, erupt, lose control, go berserk, breathe fire, flare up, boil over; informal go mad, go crazy, go bananas, have a fit, see red, fly off the handle, blow one's top, do one's nut, hit the roof, go off the deep end, go ape, flip, lose one's rag, freak out; Brit. informal go spare, go crackers, throw a wobbly.

temperament ● noun DISPOSITION, nature, character, personality, make-up, constitution, mind, spirit; stamp, mettle, mould; mood, frame of mind, attitude, outlook, humour.

temperamental ● adjective **1** *a temperamental chef* VOLATILE, excitable, emotional, mercurial, capricious, erratic, unpredictable, changeable, inconsistent; hot-headed, fiery, quick-tempered, irritable, irascible, impatient; touchy, moody, sensitive, oversensitive, highly strung, neurotic, melodramatic. **2** *a temperamental dislike of conflict* INHERENT, innate, natural, inborn, constitutional, deep-rooted, ingrained, congenital.
– OPPOSITES placid.

temperance ● noun TEETOTALISM, abstinence, abstention, sobriety, self-restraint; prohibition.
– OPPOSITES alcoholism.

temperate ● adjective **1** *temperate climates* MILD, clement, benign, gentle, balmy. **2** *he was temperate in his consumption* SELF-RESTRAINED, restrained, moderate, self-controlled, disciplined; abstemious, self-denying, austere, ascetic; teetotal, abstinent.
– OPPOSITES extreme.

tempest ● noun STORM, gale, hurricane; tornado, whirlwind, cyclone, typhoon.

tempestuous ● adjective **1** *the day was tempestuous* STORMY, blustery, squally, wild, turbulent, windy, gusty, blowy, rainy; foul, nasty, inclement. **2** *the tempestuous political environment* TURBULENT, stormy, tumultuous, wild, lively, heated, explosive, feverish, frenetic, frenzied. **3** *a tempestuous woman* EMOTIONAL, passionate, impassioned, fiery, intense; temperamental. volatile, excitable, mercurial, capricious, unpredictable, quick-tempered.
– OPPOSITES calm, peaceful, placid.

temple ● noun HOUSE OF GOD, shrine, sanctuary; church, cathedral, mosque, synagogue, shul; archaic fane.

tempo ● noun **1** *the tempo of the music* CADENCE, speed, rhythm, beat, time, pulse; measure, metre. **2** *the tempo of life in Western society* PACE, rate, speed, velocity.

temporal power • noun the power of a bishop or cleric, especially the Pope, in secular matters.

temporary • adjective lasting for only a limited period. • noun (pl. **temporaries**) a person employed on a temporary basis.
– DERIVATIVES **temporarily** adverb **temporariness** noun.
– ORIGIN Latin *temporarius*, from *tempus* 'time'.

temporize (also **temporise**) • verb act in an evasive or delaying way to gain time before committing oneself.
– ORIGIN French *temporiser* 'bide one's time'.

tempo rubato • noun see RUBATO.

Tempranillo /temprəneeyō/ • noun a variety of black wine grape grown in Spain, used to make Rioja wine.
– ORIGIN named after a village in northern Spain.

tempt • verb **1** entice (someone) to do something against their better judgement. **2** (**be tempted to do**) have an urge or inclination to do. **3** attract; charm.
– PHRASES **tempt fate** (or **providence**) do something risky or dangerous.
– DERIVATIVES **tempting** adjective.
– ORIGIN Latin *temptare* 'handle, test, try'.

temptation • noun **1** the action of tempting or the state of being tempted. **2** a tempting thing.

tempter • noun a person or thing that tempts.

temptress • noun a woman who tempts, especially one who is sexually alluring.

tempura /tempŏŏrə/ • noun a Japanese dish of fish, shellfish, or vegetables, fried in batter.
– ORIGIN Japanese, probably from Portuguese *tempêro* 'seasoning'.

ten • cardinal number one more than nine; 10. (Roman numeral: **x** or **X**.)
– PHRASES **ten out of ten** denoting an excellent performance. **ten to one** very probably.
– DERIVATIVES **tenfold** adjective & adverb.
– ORIGIN Old English.

tenable • adjective **1** able to be maintained or defended against attack or objection. **2** (of a post, grant, etc.) able to be held or used for a specified period: *a scholarship tenable for three years*.
– ORIGIN French, from Latin *tenere* 'to hold'.

tenacious /tinayshəss/ • adjective **1** holding firmly to something. **2** persisting in existence or in a course of action.
– DERIVATIVES **tenaciously** adverb **tenacity** /tinassiti/ noun.
– ORIGIN from Latin *tenere* 'to hold'.

tenancy • noun (pl. **tenancies**) possession of land or property as a tenant.

tenant • noun **1** a person who rents land or property from a landlord. **2** Law a person holding real property by private ownership. • verb (usu. **be tenanted**) occupy (property) as a tenant.
– ORIGIN Old French, 'holding', from Latin *tenere* 'to hold'.

tenant farmer • noun a person who farms rented land.

tench • noun (pl. same) a freshwater fish of the carp family, popular with anglers.
– ORIGIN Old French *tenche*, from Latin *tinca*.

Ten Commandments • plural noun (in the Bible) the divine rules of conduct given by God to Moses on Mount Sinai.

tend[1] • verb **1** frequently behave in a particular way or have a certain characteristic. **2** go or move in a particular direction.
– ORIGIN Latin *tendere* 'stretch, tend'.

tend[2] • verb **1** care for or look after. **2** US direct or manage.
– ORIGIN from ATTEND.

tendency • noun (pl. **tendencies**) **1** an inclination towards a particular characteristic or type of behaviour. **2** a group within a larger political party or movement.

tendentious /tendenshəss/ • adjective calculated to promote a particular cause or point of view.
– DERIVATIVES **tendentiously** adverb **tendentiousness** noun.
– ORIGIN suggested by German *tendenziös*.

tender[1] • adjective (**tenderer**, **tenderest**) **1** gentle and sympathetic. **2** (of food) easy to cut or chew. **3** (of a part of the body) sensitive. **4** young and vulnerable. **5** requiring tact or careful handling.
– PHRASES **tender mercies** ironic attention or treatment not in the best interests of its recipients.
– DERIVATIVES **tenderly** adverb **tenderness** noun.
– ORIGIN Old French *tendre*, from Latin *tener* 'tender, delicate'.

tender[2] • verb **1** offer or present formally. **2** make a formal written offer to carry out work, supply goods, etc. for a stated fixed price. **3** offer as payment. • noun a tendered offer.

Thesaurus

temporal • adjective SECULAR, non-spiritual, worldly, profane, material, mundane, earthly, terrestrial; non-religious, lay.
– OPPOSITES spiritual.

temporarily • adverb **1** *the girl was temporarily placed with a foster-family* FOR THE TIME BEING, for the moment, for now, for the present, in the interim, for the nonce, in/for the meantime, in the meanwhile; provisionally, pro tem; *informal* for the minute. **2** *he was temporarily blinded by the light* BRIEFLY, for a short time, momentarily, fleetingly.
– OPPOSITES permanently.

temporary • adjective **1** *temporary accommodation | the temporary captain* NON-PERMANENT, short-term, interim; provisional, pro tem, makeshift, stopgap; acting, fill-in, stand-in, caretaker. **2** *a temporary loss of self-control* BRIEF, short-lived, momentary, fleeting, passing.
– OPPOSITES permanent, lasting.

temporize • verb EQUIVOCATE, procrastinate, play for time, play a waiting game, stall, use delaying tactics, delay, hang back, prevaricate; *Brit.* hum and haw; *rare* tergiversate.

tempt • verb **1** *the manager tried to tempt him to stay* ENTICE, persuade, convince, inveigle, induce, cajole, coax, woo; *informal* sweet-talk. **2** *more customers are being tempted by credit* ALLURE, attract, appeal to, whet the appetite of; lure, seduce, beguile, tantalize, draw.
– OPPOSITES discourage, deter.

temptation • noun **1** *Mary resisted the temptation to answer back* DESIRE, urge, itch, impulse, inclination. **2** *the temptations of London* LURE, allurement, enticement, seduction, attraction, draw, pull; siren song. **3** *the temptation of travel to exotic locations* ALLURE, appeal, attraction, fascination.

tempting • adjective **1** *the tempting shops of the Via Nazionale* ENTICING, alluring, attractive, appealing, inviting, captivating, seductive, beguiling, fascinating, tantalizing; irresistible. **2** *a plate of tempting cakes* APPETIZING, mouth-watering, delicious, toothsome; *informal* scrummy, scrumptious, yummy.
– OPPOSITES off-putting, uninviting.

temptress • noun SEDUCTRESS, siren, femme fatale, Mata Hari; *informal* vamp.

ten • cardinal number DECADE.
– RELATED TERMS decimal, deca-, deci-.

tenable • adjective DEFENSIBLE, justifiable, supportable, sustainable, arguable, able to hold water, reasonable, rational, sound, viable, plausible, credible, believable, conceivable.
– OPPOSITES indefensible.

tenacious • adjective **1** *his tenacious grip* FIRM, tight, fast, clinging; strong, forceful, powerful, unshakeable, immovable, iron. **2** *a tenacious man* PERSEVERING, persistent, determined, dogged, strong-willed, tireless, indefatigable, resolute, patient, purposeful, unflagging, staunch, steadfast, untiring, unwavering, unswerving, unshakeable, unyielding, insistent; stubborn, intransigent, obstinate, obdurate, stiff-necked; *N. Amer.* rock-ribbed; *formal* pertinacious.
– OPPOSITES weak, irresolute.

tenacity • noun PERSISTENCE, determination, perseverance, doggedness, strength of purpose, bulldog spirit, tirelessness, indefatigability, resolution, resoluteness, resolve, firmness, patience, purposefulness, staunchness, steadfastness, staying power, application; stubbornness, intransigence, obstinacy, obduracy; *formal* pertinacity.

tenancy • noun OCCUPANCY, occupation, residence, period of occupancy/occupation, habitation, holding, possession; tenure, lease, rental, leasehold.

tenant • noun OCCUPANT, resident, inhabitant; leaseholder, lessee, renter; *Brit.* occupier, sitting tenant.
– OPPOSITES owner, freeholder.

tend[1] • verb **1** *I tend to get very involved in my work* BE INCLINED, be apt, be disposed, be prone, be liable, have a tendency, have a propensity. **2** *younger voters tended towards the tabloid press* INCLINE, lean, gravitate, move; prefer, favour; *N. Amer.* trend.

tend[2] • verb *she tended her cattle* LOOK AFTER, take care of, care for, minister to, attend to, see to, wait on; watch over, keep an eye on, mind, protect, watch, guard; nurse, nurture, cherish.
– OPPOSITES neglect.

tendency • noun **1** *his tendency to take the law into his own hands* PROPENSITY, proclivity, proneness, aptness, likelihood, inclination, disposition, predisposition, bent, leaning, penchant,

– PHRASES **put something out to tender** seek tenders to carry out work, supply goods, etc.
– DERIVATIVES **tenderer** noun.
– ORIGIN Latin *tendere* 'stretch, strive, hold forth'.
tender³ ● noun **1** a vehicle used by a fire service or the armed forces for carrying supplies or fulfilling a specified role. **2** a wagon closely coupled to a steam locomotive to carry fuel and water. **3** a boat used to ferry people and supplies to and from a ship.
– ORIGIN originally in the sense 'attendant, nurse': from TEND² or ATTEND.
tenderfoot ● noun (pl. **tenderfoots** or **tenderfeet**) chiefly N. Amer. a newcomer or novice.
tender-hearted ● adjective having a kind, gentle, or sentimental nature.
tenderize (also **tenderise**) ● verb make (meat) more tender by beating or slow cooking.
– DERIVATIVES **tenderizer** noun.
tenderloin ● noun **1** the tenderest part of a loin of beef, pork, etc., taken from under the short ribs in the hindquarters. **2** US the undercut of a sirloin. **3** N. Amer. informal a district of a city where vice and corruption are prominent. [ORIGIN originally applied to a district of New York, seen as a 'choice' assignment by police because of the bribes offered to them.]
tendinitis /tendinītiss/ (also **tendonitis** /tendə-/) ● noun inflammation of a tendon.
tendon /tendən/ ● noun **1** a flexible but inelastic cord of strong fibrous tissue attaching a muscle to a bone. **2** the hamstring of a four-legged mammal.
– ORIGIN Greek *tenōn* 'sinew', from *teinein* 'to stretch'.
tendril ● noun **1** a slender thread-like appendage of a climbing plant, which stretches out and twines round any suitable support. **2** a slender ringlet of hair.
– ORIGIN probably from Old French *tendron* 'young shoot', from Latin *tener* 'tender'.
tenebrous /tennibrəss/ ● adjective literary dark; shadowy.
– ORIGIN Latin *tenebrosus*, from *tenebrae* 'darkness'.
tenement /tennəmənt/ ● noun **1** (especially in Scotland or the US) a separate residence within a house or block of flats. **2** (also **tenement house**) a house divided into several separate residences. **3** a piece of land held by an owner.
– ORIGIN Latin *tenementum*, from *tenere* 'to hold'.
tenet /tennit/ ● noun a central principle or belief.
– ORIGIN Latin, 'he holds'.
ten-gallon hat ● noun a large, broad-brimmed hat, traditionally worn by cowboys.
tenge /tenggay/ ● noun (pl. same or **tenges**) **1** the basic monetary unit of Kazakhstan, equal to 100 teins. **2** a monetary unit of Turkmenistan, equal to one hundredth of a manat.
tenner ● noun Brit. informal a ten-pound note.
tennis ● noun a game for two or four players, who use rackets to strike a ball over a net stretched across a grass or clay court. See also REAL TENNIS.
– ORIGIN originally denoting real tennis: apparently from Old French *tenez* 'take, receive' (called by the server to an opponent), from *tenir* 'take, hold'.
tennis elbow ● noun inflammation of the tendons of the elbow caused by overuse of the forearm muscles.
tennis shoe ● noun a light canvas or leather soft-soled shoe suitable for tennis or casual wear.
tenon ● noun a projecting piece of wood made for insertion into a mortise in another piece of wood.
– ORIGIN French, from *tenir* 'to hold'.
tenon saw ● noun a small saw with a strong brass or steel back for precise work.
tenor¹ ● noun **1** a singing voice between baritone and alto or countertenor, the highest of the ordinary adult male range. **2** (before another noun) referring to an instrument of the second or third lowest pitch in its family: *a tenor sax.*
– ORIGIN from Latin *tenere* 'to hold'; so named because the tenor part 'held' the melody.
tenor² ● noun **1** the general meaning or content of something. **2** a prevailing character or direction: *the even tenor of her marriage.*
– ORIGIN Latin *tenor* 'course, substance', from *tenere* 'to hold'.
tenor clef ● noun Music a clef placing middle C on the second-highest line of the stave, used chiefly for cello and bassoon music.
tenosynovitis /tennōsīnəvītiss/ ● noun Medicine inflammation and swelling of a tendon, especially in the wrist and typically caused by repetitive movement.
– ORIGIN from Greek *tenōn* 'tendon' + *synovitis*, 'inflammation of a synovial membrane'.
tenpin ● noun **1** a skittle used in tenpin bowling. **2** (**tenpins**) (treated as sing.) N. Amer. tenpin bowling.
tenpin bowling ● noun a game in which ten skittles are set up at the end of a track and bowled down with hard balls.
tenrec /tenrek/ ● noun a small insect-eating mammal of Madagascar and the Comoro Islands.
– ORIGIN Malagasy.
TENS ● abbreviation transcutaneous electrical nerve stimulation, a technique for relieving pain by applying electrodes to the skin.
tense¹ ● adjective **1** stretched tight or rigid. **2** feeling, causing, or showing anxiety and nervousness. ● verb make or become tense.
– DERIVATIVES **tensely** adverb **tenseness** noun.
– ORIGIN Latin *tensus*, from *tendere* 'stretch'.
tense² ● noun Grammar a set of forms taken by a verb to indicate the time, continuance, or completeness of the action.
– ORIGIN from Latin *tempus* 'time'.
tensile /tensīl/ ● adjective **1** relating to tension. **2** capable of

Thesaurus

predilection, susceptibility, liability; readiness; habit. **2** *this tendency towards cohabitation* TREND, movement, drift, swing, gravitation, direction, course; orientation, bias.
tender¹ ● adjective **1** *a gentle, tender man* CARING, kind, kindly, kind-hearted, soft-hearted, tender-hearted, compassionate, sympathetic, warm, warm-hearted, fatherly, motherly, maternal, gentle, mild, benevolent, generous, giving, humane. **2** *a tender kiss* AFFECTIONATE, fond, loving, emotional, warm, gentle, soft; amorous, adoring; informal lovey-dovey. **3** *tender love songs* ROMANTIC, sentimental, emotional, emotive, touching, moving, poignant; Brit. informal soppy. **4** *simmer until the meat is tender* EASILY CHEWED, chewable, soft; succulent, juicy; tenderized. **5** *tender plants* DELICATE, easily damaged, fragile. **6** *her ankle was swollen and tender* SORE, painful, sensitive, inflamed, raw, red, chafed, bruised; hurting, aching, throbbing, smarting. **7** *the tender age of fifteen* YOUNG, youthful; impressionable, inexperienced, immature, unsophisticated, unseasoned, juvenile, callow, green, raw; informal wet behind the ears. **8** *the issue of conscription was a particularly tender one* DIFFICULT, delicate, tricky, awkward, problematic, troublesome, ticklish; controversial, emotive; informal sticky.
– OPPOSITES hard-hearted, callous, tough.
tender² ● verb **1** *she tendered her resignation* OFFER, proffer, present, put forward, propose, suggest, advance, submit, extend, give, render; hand in. **2** *firms of interior decorators tendered for the work* PUT IN A BID, bid, quote, give an estimate.
● noun *six contractors were invited to submit tenders* BID, offer, quotation, quote, estimate, price; proposal, submission.
tender-hearted ● adjective. See TENDER¹ sense 1.
tenderness ● noun **1** *I felt an enormous tenderness for her* AFFECTION, fondness, love, devotion, loving kindness, emotion, sentiment. **2** *with unexpected tenderness, he told her what had happened* KINDNESS, kindliness, kind-heartedness, tender-heartedness, compassion, care, concern, sympathy, warmth, fatherliness, motherliness, gentleness, benevolence, generosity. **3** *abdominal tenderness* SORENESS, pain, inflammation, bruising; ache, aching, smarting, throbbing.
tenet ● noun PRINCIPLE, belief, doctrine, precept, creed, credo, article of faith, dogma, canon; theory, thesis, conviction, idea, view, opinion, position, hypothesis, postulation; (**tenets**) ideology, code of belief, teaching(s).
tenor ● noun **1** *the general tenor of his speech* SENSE, meaning, theme, drift, thread, import, purport, intent, intention, burden, thrust, significance, message; gist, essence, substance, spirit. **2** *the even tenor of life in the village* COURSE, direction, movement, drift, current, trend.
tense ● adjective **1** *the tense muscles of his neck* TAUT, tight, rigid, stretched, strained, stiff. **2** *Loretta was feeling tense and irritable* ANXIOUS, nervous, on edge, edgy, strained, stressed, under pressure, agitated, ill at ease, uneasy, restless, worked up, keyed up, overwrought, jumpy, on tenterhooks, with one's stomach in knots, worried, apprehensive, panicky; Brit. nervy; informal a bundle of nerves, jittery, twitchy, uptight, stressed out; N. Amer. informal

being drawn out or stretched.

tensile strength ● noun the resistance of a material to breaking under tension.

tension ● noun **1** the state of being tense. **2** mental or emotional strain. **3** a situation in which there is conflict or strain because of differing views, aims, or elements. **4** the degree of stitch tightness in knitting and machine sewing. **5** voltage of specified magnitude: *high tension.* ● verb subject to tension.
– DERIVATIVES **tensional** adjective.

tent ● noun a portable shelter made of cloth, supported by one or more poles and stretched tight by cords attached to pegs driven into the ground. ● verb **1** cover with or as if with a tent. **2** (**tented**) composed of or provided with tents.
– ORIGIN Old French *tente*, from Latin *tendere* 'stretch'.

tentacle ● noun a long slender flexible appendage of an animal, used for grasping or moving about, or bearing sense organs.
– DERIVATIVES **tentacled** adjective **tentacular** adjective.
– ORIGIN Latin *tentaculum*, from *temptare* 'to feel, try'.

tentage ● noun tents collectively.

tentative ● adjective **1** done without confidence; hesitant. **2** not certain or fixed; provisional.
– DERIVATIVES **tentatively** adverb **tentativeness** noun.
– ORIGIN Latin *tentativus*, from *temptare* 'handle, try'.

tenterhook ● noun (in phrase **on tenterhooks**) in a state of agitated suspense.
– ORIGIN originally denoting a hook used to fasten cloth on a *tenter* (from Latin *tendere* 'to stretch'), a framework on which fabric was held taut during manufacture.

tenth ● ordinal number **1** constituting number ten in a sequence; 10th. **2** (**a tenth/one tenth**) each of ten equal parts into which something is divided. **3** Music an interval spanning an octave and a third in the diatonic scale.
– DERIVATIVES **tenthly** adverb.

tent stitch ● noun a series of parallel diagonal stitches.

tenuous ● adjective **1** very slight or insubstantial: *a tenuous distinction.* **2** very slender or fine.
– DERIVATIVES **tenuously** adverb **tenuousness** noun.
– ORIGIN Latin *tenuis* 'thin'.

tenure /tenyər/ ● noun **1** the conditions under which land or buildings are held or occupied. **2** the holding of an office.
– PHRASES **security of tenure 1** the right of a tenant of property to occupy it after the lease expires (unless a court should order otherwise). **2** guaranteed permanent employment after a probationary period.
– ORIGIN Old French, from Latin *tenere* 'to hold'.

tenured ● adjective (especially of a teacher or lecturer) having a permanent post.

tenurial ● adjective relating to the tenure of land.

tepee /teepee/ (also **teepee** or **tipi**) ● noun a conical tent made of skins or cloth on a frame of poles, used by American Indians.
– ORIGIN Sioux, 'dwelling'.

tephra /tefrə/ ● noun rock fragments and particles ejected by a volcanic eruption.
– ORIGIN Greek, 'ash, ashes'.

tepid ● adjective **1** (especially of a liquid) lukewarm. **2** unenthusiastic.
– DERIVATIVES **tepidity** noun **tepidly** adverb.
– ORIGIN Latin *tepidus*, from *tepere* 'be warm'.

tequila /təkeelə/ ● noun a Mexican liquor made from an agave.
– ORIGIN named after the town of *Tequila* in Mexico.

tequila sunrise ● noun a cocktail of tequila, orange juice, and grenadine.

ter- ● combining form three; having three: *tercentenary.*
– ORIGIN Latin *ter* 'thrice'.

tera- /terrə/ ● combining form **1** denoting a factor of one million million (10^{12}): *terawatt.* **2** Computing denoting a factor of 2^{40}: *terabyte.*
– ORIGIN from Greek *teras* 'monster'.

terabyte ● noun Computing a unit of information equal to one million million (10^{12}) or (strictly) 2^{40} bytes.

teraflop ● noun a unit of computing speed equal to one million million floating-point operations per second.

terai /təri/ ● noun a wide-brimmed felt hat, typically with a double crown, worn chiefly by travellers in subtropical regions.
– ORIGIN from *Terai*, a belt of marshy jungle near the Himalayan foothills.

teratogen /tərattəjən/ ● noun an agent or factor causing malformation of an embryo.
– DERIVATIVES **teratogenic** adjective.
– ORIGIN from Greek *teras* 'monster'.

teratology /tərattəjən/ ● noun **1** the branch of medicine concerned with congenital abnormalities. **2** mythology relating to fantastic creatures and monsters.
– DERIVATIVES **teratological** adjective **teratologist** noun.

terbium /terbiəm/ ● noun a silvery-white metallic chemical element.
– ORIGIN from *Ytterby*, a Swedish quarry where it was first found.

terce /terss/ ● noun a service forming part of the Divine Office of the Western Christian Church, traditionally said at the third hour of the day (9 a.m.).
– ORIGIN Old French, from Latin *tertius* 'third'.

tercel /ters'l/ (also **tiercel**) ● noun Falconry a male hawk, especially a peregrine or a goshawk. Compare with FALCON.
– ORIGIN Old French, from Latin *tertius* 'third', perhaps from the belief that the third egg of a clutch produced a male.

tercentenary ● noun (pl. **tercentenaries**) a three-hundredth anniversary.
– DERIVATIVES **tercentennial** adjective & noun.

terebinth /terrəbinth/ ● noun a small tree which was formerly a source of turpentine.
– ORIGIN Greek *terebinthos*.

teredo /təreedō/ ● noun (pl. **teredos**) a worm-like marine bivalve mollusc which bores into wood.
– ORIGIN Greek *terēdōn*, related to *teirein* 'rub hard, wear away'.

tergiversate /terjiversayt/ ● verb **1** use ambiguous or evasive language. **2** change one's loyalties.
– DERIVATIVES **tergiversation** noun.
– ORIGIN Latin *tergiversari* 'turn one's back'.

teriyaki /terriyaaki/ ● noun a Japanese dish of fish or meat marinated in soy sauce and grilled.
– ORIGIN Japanese.

Thesaurus

spooky, squirrelly. **3** *a tense moment* NERVE-RACKING, stressful, anxious, worrying, fraught, charged, strained, nail-biting, difficult, uneasy, uncomfortable; exciting, cliffhanging, knife-edge.
– OPPOSITES slack, calm.
● verb *Hebden tensed his muscles* TIGHTEN, tauten, tense up, flex, contract, brace, stiffen; screw up, knot, strain, stretch; *N. Amer.* squinch up.
– OPPOSITES relax.

tension ● noun **1** *the tension of the rope* TIGHTNESS, tautness, rigidity; pull, traction. **2** *the tension was unbearable* STRAIN, stress, anxiety, pressure; worry, apprehensiveness, apprehension, agitation, nerves, nervousness, jumpiness, edginess, restlessness; suspense, uncertainty, anticipation, excitement; *informal* butterflies (in one's stomach), collywobbles. **3** *months of tension between the military and the government* STRAINED RELATIONS, strain; ill feeling, friction, antagonism, antipathy, hostility, enmity.

tentative ● adjective **1** *tentative arrangements | a tentative conclusion* PROVISIONAL, unconfirmed, pencilled in, preliminary, to be confirmed, TBC, subject to confirmation; speculative, conjectural, untried, unproven, exploratory, experimental, trial, test, pilot. **2** *he took a few tentative steps* HESITANT, uncertain, cautious, timid, hesitating, faltering, shaky, unsteady, halting; wavering, unsure.
– OPPOSITES definite, confident.

tenterhooks ● plural noun
– PHRASES **on tenterhooks** IN SUSPENSE, waiting with bated breath; anxious, nervous, nervy, apprehensive, worried, worried sick, on edge, edgy, tense, strained, stressed, agitated, restless, worked up, keyed up, jumpy, with one's stomach in knots, with one's heart in one's mouth, like a cat on a hot tin roof; *informal* with butterflies in one's stomach, jittery, twitchy, in a state, uptight; *N. Amer. informal* spooky, squirrelly.

tenuous ● adjective **1** *a tenuous connection* SLIGHT, insubstantial, flimsy, weak, doubtful, dubious, questionable, suspect; vague, nebulous, hazy. **2** *a tenuous thread* FINE, thin, slender, delicate, gossamer, fragile.
– OPPOSITES convincing, strong.

tenure ● noun **1** *residents should have security of tenure* TENANCY, occupancy, holding, occupation, residence; possession, title, ownership. **2** *his tenure as Secretary of State for Industry* INCUMBENCY, term (of office), period (of/in office), time (in office).

tepid ● adjective **1** *tepid water* LUKEWARM, warmish, slightly warm; at room temperature. **2** *a tepid response* UNENTHUSIASTIC, apathetic,

term • noun **1** a word or phrase used to describe a thing or to express a concept. **2** (**terms**) language used on a particular occasion: *a protest in the strongest possible terms.* **3** (**terms**) stipulated or agreed requirements or conditions. **4** (**terms**) relationship or footing: *we're on good terms.* **5** a period for which something lasts or is intended to last. **6** each of the periods in the year during which instruction is given in a school or college or during which a law court holds sessions. **7** (also **full term**) the completion of a normal length of pregnancy. **8** Logic a word or words that may be the subject or predicate of a proposition. **9** Mathematics each of the quantities in a ratio, series, or mathematical expression. • verb call by a specified term.
– PHRASES **come to terms with** reconcile oneself to. **in terms of** (or **in —— terms**) with regard to the aspect or subject specified. **the —— term** a period that is a specified way into the future: *in the long term.* **on terms 1** in a state of friendship or equality. **2** (in sport) level in score. **terms of reference** Brit. the scope of an inquiry or discussion.
– DERIVATIVES **termly** adjective & adverb.
– ORIGIN Latin *terminus* 'end, boundary, limit'.

termagant /termәgәnt/ • noun a bad-tempered or overbearing woman.
– ORIGIN originally denoting a violent imaginary deity often appearing in medieval morality plays: from Italian *Trivagante* 'thrice-wandering'.

terminable • adjective **1** able to be terminated. **2** coming to an end after a certain time.

terminal • adjective **1** of, forming, or situated at the end. **2** (of a disease) predicted to lead to death. **3** informal extreme and irreversible. **4** done or occurring each school or college term. • noun **1** the station at the end of a railway or other transport route. **2** a departure and arrival building for passengers at an airport. **3** a point of connection for closing an electric circuit. **4** a device at which to enter data or commands for a computer and which displays the received output. **5** an installation where oil or gas is stored.
– DERIVATIVES **terminally** adverb.
– ORIGIN Latin *terminalis*, from *terminus* 'end, boundary'.

terminal velocity • noun Physics the constant speed that a freely falling object reaches when the resistance of the medium through which it is falling prevents further acceleration.

terminate • verb **1** bring to an end. **2** (**terminate in**) have an end at or resolution in. **3** (of a train or bus service) end its journey. **4** end (a pregnancy) before term by artificial means. **5** chiefly N. Amer. end the employment of. **6** euphemistic, chiefly N. Amer. assassinate.
– DERIVATIVES **termination** noun **terminator** noun.

terminological inexactitude • noun humorous a lie.
– ORIGIN first used by Winston Churchill in 1906.

terminology • noun (pl. **terminologies**) the body of terms used in a subject of study, profession, etc.
– DERIVATIVES **terminological** adjective.

terminus • noun (pl. **termini** or **terminuses**) **1** chiefly Brit. a railway or bus terminal. **2** an end or extremity.
– ORIGIN Latin, 'end, limit, boundary'.

terminus ad quem /terminәss ad **kwem**/ • noun an end or goal.
– ORIGIN Latin, 'end to which'.

terminus ante quem /terminәss anti **kwem**/ • noun the latest possible date.
– ORIGIN Latin, 'end before which'.

termite /termīt/ • noun a small, soft-bodied insect which feeds on wood and lives in complex colonies in large nests of earth.
– ORIGIN Latin *termes* 'woodworm'.

term paper • noun N. Amer. a long essay on a subject studied during a school or college term.

terms of trade • plural noun Economics the ratio of an index of a country's export prices to an index of its import prices.

tern /tern/ • noun a seabird resembling a gull but smaller and more slender, with long pointed wings and a forked tail.
– ORIGIN Scandinavian.

ternary /ternәri/ • adjective **1** composed of three parts. **2** Mathematics using three as a base.
– ORIGIN Latin *ternarius*, from *terni* 'three at once'.

terpene /terpeen/ • noun Chemistry any of a large group of volatile unsaturated hydrocarbons with cyclic molecules, found in the essential oils of conifers and other plants.
– DERIVATIVES **terpenoid** noun & adjective.
– ORIGIN from German *Terpentin* 'turpentine'.

terpsichorean /terpsikәreeәn/ formal or humorous • adjective relating to dancing. • noun a dancer.
– ORIGIN from *Terpsichore*, the ancient Greek and Roman Muse of dance.

terrace • noun **1** each of a series of flat areas on a slope, used for cultivation. **2** a patio. **3** chiefly Brit. a row of houses built in one block in a uniform style. **4** Brit. a flight of wide, shallow steps providing standing room for spectators in a stadium. • verb make or form (sloping land) into terraces.
– DERIVATIVES **terracing** noun.
– ORIGIN Old French, 'rubble, platform', from Latin *terra* 'earth'.

terraced • adjective **1** (of a house) forming part of a terrace. **2** (of land) having been formed into terraces.

terracotta /terrә**kott**ә/ • noun **1** unglazed, typically brownish-red earthenware, used as an ornamental building material and in modelling. **2** a strong brownish-red colour.
– ORIGIN from Italian *terra cotta* 'baked earth'.

terra firma /terrә **furm**ә/ • noun dry land; the ground.
– ORIGIN Latin, 'firm land'.

terraform • verb (especially in science fiction) transform (a planet) so as to resemble the earth.
– DERIVATIVES **terraformer** noun.
– ORIGIN from Latin *terra* 'earth'.

terrain /terayn/ • noun a stretch of land, especially with regard to its physical features.
– ORIGIN French, from Latin *terrenus* 'of or like earth'.

terra incognita /terrә in**kog**nitә, inkog**neet**ә/ • noun unknown

Thesaurus

half-hearted, indifferent, cool, lukewarm, uninterested; *informal* unenthused.
– OPPOSITES hot, cold, enthusiastic.

t

term • noun **1** *scientific and technical terms* WORD, expression, phrase, turn of phrase, idiom, locution; name, title, designation, label; *formal* appellation, denomination. **2** *a protest in the strongest terms* LANGUAGE, mode of expression, manner of speaking, phraseology, terminology; words, phrases, expressions. **3** *the terms of the contract* CONDITIONS, stipulations, specifications, provisions, provisos; restrictions, qualifications; particulars, details, points. **4** *a policy offering more favourable terms* RATES, prices, charges, costs, fees; tariff. **5** *the President is elected for a four-year term* PERIOD, period of time, time, length of time, spell, stint, duration; stretch, run; period of office, incumbency. **6** *(archaic) the whole term of your natural life* DURATION, length, span. **7** *the summer term* SESSION; *N. Amer.* semester, trimester, quarter.
• verb *he has been termed the father of modern theology* CALL, name, entitle, title, style, designate, describe as, dub, label, tag; nickname; *formal* denominate.
– PHRASES **come to terms 1** *the two sides came to terms* REACH AN AGREEMENT/UNDERSTANDING, make a deal, reach a compromise, meet each other halfway. **2** *she eventually came to terms with her situation* ACCEPT, come to accept, reconcile oneself to, learn to live with, become resigned to, make the best of; face up to.

terminal • adjective **1** *a terminal illness* INCURABLE, untreatable, inoperable; fatal, mortal, deadly. **2** *terminal patients* DYING, near death; incurable. **3** *a terminal bonus may be payable when a policy matures* FINAL, last, concluding, closing, end. **4** *(informal) you're making a terminal ass of yourself* COMPLETE, utter, absolute, total, real, thorough, out-and-out, downright, perfect; *Brit. informal* right, proper; *Austral./NZ informal* fair.
• noun **1** *a railway terminal* STATION, last stop, end of the line; depot; *Brit.* terminus. **2** *a computer terminal* WORKSTATION, VDU, visual display unit.

terminate • verb **1** *treatment was terminated* BRING TO AN END, end, bring to a close/conclusion, close, conclude, finish, stop, put an end to, wind up, discontinue, cease, cut short, abort, axe; *informal* pull the plug on. **2** *the train will terminate in Stratford* END ITS JOURNEY, finish up, stop. **3** *the pregnancy was terminated* ABORT, end.
– OPPOSITES begin, start, continue.

termination • noun **1** *the termination of a contract* ENDING, end, closing, close, conclusion, finish, stopping, winding up, discontinuance, discontinuation; cancellation, dissolution; *informal* wind-up. **2** *she had a termination* ABORTION; *rare* feticide.
– OPPOSITES start, beginning.

terminology • noun PHRASEOLOGY, terms, expressions, words, language, parlance, vocabulary, nomenclature; usage, idiom; jargon,

territory.
– ORIGIN Latin, 'unknown land'.
terrapin ● noun a small freshwater turtle.
– ORIGIN Algonquian.
terrarium /terairiəm/ ● noun (pl. **terrariums** or **terraria** /terairiə/) **1** a glass-fronted case for keeping smaller land animals, e.g. reptiles or amphibians. **2** a sealed transparent globe or similar container in which plants are grown.
– ORIGIN from Latin *terra* 'earth', on the pattern of *aquarium*.
terrazzo /teratsō/ ● noun flooring material consisting of chips of marble or granite set in concrete and polished smooth.
– ORIGIN Italian, 'terrace'.
terrene /tereen/ ● adjective archaic **1** of or like earth. **2** occurring on or inhabiting dry land. **3** worldly.
terrestrial /tərestriəl/ ● adjective **1** of, on, or relating to the earth or dry land. **2** (of an animal or plant) living on or in the ground. **3** (of television broadcasting) using ground-based equipment rather than a satellite. ● noun an inhabitant of the earth.
– DERIVATIVES **terrestrially** adverb.
– ORIGIN Latin *terrestris*, from *terra* 'earth'.
terrible ● adjective **1** extremely bad, serious, or unpleasant. **2** troubled or guilty. **3** causing terror.
– DERIVATIVES **terribleness** noun.
– ORIGIN Latin *terribilis*, from *terrere* 'frighten'.
terribly ● adverb **1** informal extremely. **2** very badly.
terrier ● noun **1** a small breed of dog originally used for turning out foxes and other animals from their earths. **2** a tenacious or eager person.
– ORIGIN from Old French *chien terrier* 'earth dog'.
terrific ● adjective **1** of great size, amount, or intensity. **2** informal excellent. **3** archaic causing terror.
– DERIVATIVES **terrifically** adverb.
– ORIGIN Latin *terrificus*, from *terrere* 'frighten'.
terrify ● verb (**terrifies**, **terrified**) cause to feel terror.
– DERIVATIVES **terrifying** adjective.
terrine /təreen/ ● noun **1** a meat, fish, or vegetable mixture prepared in advance and allowed to cool or set in a container. **2** an earthenware container for such a dish.
– ORIGIN French, 'large earthenware pot'; related to TUREEN.
territorial ● adjective **1** relating to the ownership of an area of land or sea. **2** relating to a territory or area. **3** (of an animal) tending to defend a territory. ● noun (**Territorial**) (in the UK) a member of the Territorial Army.
– DERIVATIVES **territoriality** noun **territorially** adverb.
Territorial Army ● noun (in the UK) a volunteer force locally organized to provide a trained reserve for use in an emergency.
territorial waters ● plural noun the waters under the jurisdiction of a state, especially those within a stated distance from its coast.
territory ● noun (pl. **territories**) **1** an area under the jurisdiction of a ruler or state. **2** (**Territory**) an organized division of a country not having the full rights of a state. **3** an area defended by an animal against others of the same sex or species. **4** an area defended by a team or player in a game or sport. **5** an area in which one has certain rights or responsibilities. **6** an area of knowledge or experience.
– ORIGIN Latin *territorium*, from *terra* 'land'.
terror ● noun **1** extreme fear. **2** a cause of terror. **3** the use of terror to intimidate people. **4** (also **holy terror**) informal a person causing trouble or annoyance.
– ORIGIN Latin, from *terrere* 'frighten'.
terrorist ● noun a person who uses violence and intimidation in the pursuit of political aims.
– DERIVATIVES **terrorism** noun.
terrorize (also **terrorise**) ● verb create and maintain a feeling of terror in (a person or area).
terry ● noun (pl. **terries**) fabric with raised uncut loops of thread

Thesaurus

cant, argot; *informal* lingo, -speak, -ese.
terminus ● noun *(Brit.) the bus terminus* STATION, last stop, end of the line, terminal; depot, garage.
terrain ● noun LAND, ground, territory; topography, landscape, countryside, country.
terrestrial ● adjective EARTHLY, worldly, mundane, earthbound; *poetic/literary* sublunary.
terrible ● adjective **1** *a terrible crime | terrible injuries* DREADFUL, awful, appalling, horrific, horrifying, horrible, horrendous, atrocious, abominable, abhorrent, frightful, shocking, hideous, ghastly, grim, dire, unspeakable, gruesome, monstrous, sickening, heinous, vile; serious, grave, acute; *formal* grievous. **2** *a terrible smell* NASTY, disgusting, awful, dreadful, ghastly, horrid, horrible, vile, foul, abominable, frightful, loathsome, revolting, repulsive, odious, nauseating, repellent, horrendous, hideous, appalling, offensive, objectionable, obnoxious; *informal* gruesome, putrid, diabolical, yucky, sick-making, God-awful, gross; *Brit. informal* beastly; *archaic* disgustful. **3** *he was in terrible pain* SEVERE, extreme, intense, excruciating, agonizing, unbearable, intolerable, unendurable. **4** *that's a terrible thing to say* UNKIND, nasty, unpleasant, foul, obnoxious, vile, contemptible, despicable, wretched, shabby; spiteful, mean, malicious, poisonous, mean-spirited, cruel, hateful, hurtful; unfair, uncharitable, uncalled for, below the belt, unwarranted; *Brit. informal* beastly. **5** *the film was terrible* VERY BAD, dreadful, awful, frightful, atrocious, hopeless, poor; *informal* pathetic, pitiful, useless, lousy, appalling, abysmal, dire; *Brit. informal* duff, chronic, poxy, rubbish, a load of pants. **6** *(informal) you're a terrible flirt* INCORRIGIBLE, outrageous; real, awful, dreadful, frightful, shocking; *informal* impossible, fearful; *Brit. informal* right, proper. **7** *I feel terrible—I've been in bed all day* ILL, poorly, sick, queasy, nauseous, nauseated, green about the gills; faint, dizzy; *informal* rough, lousy, awful, dreadful; *Brit. informal* grotty, ropy. **8** *he still feels terrible about what he did to John* GUILTY, conscience-stricken, remorseful, guilt-ridden, sorry, ashamed, chastened, contrite.
– OPPOSITES minor, slight, pleasant, wonderful.
terribly ● adverb **1** *(informal) she's terribly upset* VERY, extremely, really, terrifically, tremendously, immensely, thoroughly, dreadfully, exceptionally, remarkably, extraordinarily, exceedingly; *N. English* right; *informal* awfully, devilishly, seriously, majorly; *Brit. informal* jolly, ever so, dead, well; *N. Amer. informal* real, mighty, awful; *informal, dated* frightfully; *archaic* exceeding. **2** *he played terribly* VERY BADLY, atrociously, awfully, dreadfully, appallingly, execrably; *informal* abysmally, pitifully, diabolically. **3** *(informal) I shall miss you terribly* VERY MUCH, greatly, a great deal, a lot; *informal* loads.
terrific ● adjective **1** *a terrific bang* TREMENDOUS, huge, massive, gigantic, colossal, mighty, great, prodigious, formidable, sizeable, considerable; intense, extreme, extraordinary; *informal* mega, whopping great, humongous; *Brit. informal* whacking great, ginormous. **2** *(informal) a terrific game of top-quality football* MARVELLOUS, wonderful, sensational, outstanding, superb, excellent, first-rate, first-class, dazzling, out of this world, breathtaking; *informal* great, fantastic, fabulous, fab, mega, super, ace, magic, cracking, cool, wicked, awesome; *Brit. informal* brilliant, brill, smashing; *Austral./NZ informal* bonzer; *Brit. informal, dated* spiffing. **3** *(archaic) terrific scenes of slaughter and destruction* DREADFUL, terrible, appalling, awful, horrific, horrible, horrendous, horrifying, hideous, grim, ghastly, gruesome, frightful, fearful.
terrified ● adjective PETRIFIED, frightened, scared, scared/frightened to death, scared stiff, scared/frightened out of one's wits, scared witless, horrified, with one's heart in one's mouth, shaking in one's shoes.
terrify ● verb PETRIFY, horrify, frighten, scare, scare/frighten to death, scare/frighten the living daylights out of, scare/frighten the life out of, scare/frighten someone out of their wits, scare witless, strike terror into, put the fear of God into; paralyse, transfix; *informal* scare the pants off; *Irish informal* scare the bejesus out of.
territory ● noun **1** *British overseas territories* AREA OF LAND, area, region, enclave; country, state, land, dependency, colony, dominion, protectorate, fief, possession, holding. **2** *mountainous territory* TERRAIN, land, ground, countryside. **3** *the territory of biblical scholarship* DOMAIN, area of concern/interest/knowledge, province, department, field, preserve, sphere, arena, realm, world. **4** *Sheffield was his territory* SPHERE OF OPERATIONS, area, section; *informal* turf; *Brit. informal* patch, manor.
terror ● noun **1** *she screamed in terror* EXTREME FEAR, dread, horror, fear and trembling, fright, alarm, panic, shock. **2** *the terrors of her own mind* DEMON, fiend, devil, monster; horror, nightmare. **3** *(informal) he turned out to be a right little terror* RASCAL, devil, imp, monkey, scallywag, mischief-maker; *informal* scamp, horror; *Brit. informal* perisher; *N. English informal* scally; *N. Amer. informal* varmint.
terrorist ● noun bomber, arsonist, incendiary; gunman, assassin; hijacker; revolutionary, radical, guerrilla, urban guerrilla, anarchist, freedom fighter.
terrorize ● verb PERSECUTE, victimize, torment, tyrannize, intimi-

on both sides, used especially for towels.
– ORIGIN of unknown origin.
terse • adjective (**terser**, **tersest**) sparing in the use of words; abrupt.
– DERIVATIVES **tersely** adverb **terseness** noun.
– ORIGIN originally in the sense 'polished, trim': from Latin *tersus* 'wiped, polished'.
tertiary /tershəri/ • adjective **1** third in order or level. **2** chiefly Brit. (of education) at a level beyond that provided by schools. **3** (of medical treatment) provided at a specialist institution. **4** (**Tertiary**) Geology relating to the first period of the Cenozoic era, about 65 to 1.64 million years ago.
– ORIGIN Latin *tertiarius* 'of the third part or rank'.
tertiary industry • noun Economics the service industry of a country.
terylene • noun Brit. trademark a polyester fibre used to make clothing, bed linen, etc.
TESL • abbreviation teaching of English as a second language.
tesla /teslə/ • noun Physics the SI unit of magnetic flux density.
– ORIGIN named after the American electrical engineer Nikola *Tesla* (1856–1943).
TESOL /tessol/ • abbreviation teaching of English to speakers of other languages.
TESSA • noun (in the UK) a tax-exempt special savings account allowing savers to invest a certain amount without paying tax on the interest (replaced in 1999 by the ISA).
tessellate /tessəlayt/ • verb **1** (often as adj. **tessellated**) decorate (a floor) with mosaics. **2** Mathematics cover (a plane surface) by repeated use of a single shape.
– DERIVATIVES **tessellation** noun.
– ORIGIN Latin *tessellare*, from *tessera*.
tessera /tessərə/ • noun (pl. **tesserae** /tessəree/) **1** a small block of stone, tile, etc. used in a mosaic. **2** (in ancient Greece and Rome) a small tablet of wood or bone used as a token.
– ORIGIN Greek, from *tessares* 'four'.
tessitura /tessityoorə/ • noun Music the range within which most notes of a vocal part fall.
– ORIGIN Italian, 'texture'.
test[1] • noun **1** a procedure intended to establish the quality, performance, or reliability of something. **2** a short examination of proficiency or knowledge. **3** a means of testing something. **4** a difficult situation that reveals the strength or quality of someone or something. **5** an examination of part of the body or a body fluid for medical purposes. **6** Chemistry a procedure for identifying a substance or revealing whether it is present. **7** a test match. • verb **1** subject to a test. **2** touch or taste before proceeding further. **3** try severely; tax (a person's endurance or patience).
– PHRASES **test the water** ascertain feelings or opinions before proceeding further.
– DERIVATIVES **testable** adjective.
– ORIGIN originally denoting a container used for treating gold or silver alloys or ore: from Latin *testum* 'earthen pot'.
test[2] • noun Zoology the shell of some invertebrates and protozoans.
– ORIGIN Latin *testa* 'tile, jug, shell'.
testa /testə/ • noun (pl. **testae** /testee/) Botany the protective outer covering of a seed.
– ORIGIN Latin, 'tile, shell'.
testament • noun **1** a person's will. **2** evidence or proof of a fact, event, or quality. **3** (in biblical use) a covenant or dispensation. **4** (**Testament**) a division of the Bible (see OLD TESTAMENT, NEW TESTAMENT).
– ORIGIN Latin *testamentum* 'a will', from *testis* 'a witness'.
testamentary • adjective of, in, or through a will.
testate /testayt/ • adjective having made a valid will before one dies. • noun a person who dies testate.
– ORIGIN Latin *testatus* 'testified, witnessed'.
testator /testaytər/ • noun (fem. **testatrix** /testaytriks/, pl. **testatrices** /testaytriseez/ or **testatrixes**) Law a person who has made a will or given a legacy.
– ORIGIN Latin.
test bed • noun a piece of equipment for testing new machinery, especially aircraft engines.
test card • noun Brit. a still television picture transmitted outside normal programme hours to aid in judging the quality of the image.
test case • noun Law a case setting a precedent for other cases.
test-drive • verb drive (a motor vehicle) to determine its qualities.
tester[1] • noun **1** a person or device that tests. **2** a sample of a product allowing customers to try it before purchase.
tester[2] • noun a canopy over a four-poster bed.
– ORIGIN Latin *testerium*.
testicle • noun either of the two oval organs that produce sperm in male mammals, enclosed in the scrotum behind the penis.
– DERIVATIVES **testicular** adjective.
– ORIGIN Latin *testiculus*, from *testis* 'a witness' (from the idea of a testicle being a 'witness' to virility).
testify • verb (**testifies**, **testified**) **1** give evidence as a witness in a law court. **2** serve as evidence or proof: *luxurious villas testify to the wealth here*.
– ORIGIN Latin *testificari*, from *testis* 'a witness'.
testimonial /testimōniəl/ • noun **1** a formal statement testifying to someone's character and qualifications. **2** a public tribute to someone and to their achievements.
testimony • noun (pl. **testimonies**) **1** a formal statement, especially one given in a court of law. **2** evidence or proof of something.
– ORIGIN Latin *testimonium*.
testis /testiss/ • noun (pl. **testes** /testeez/) Anatomy & Zoology an organ which produces sperm.
– ORIGIN Latin (see TESTICLE).
test match • noun an international cricket or rugby match played between teams representing two different countries.
testosterone /testostərōn/ • noun a steroid hormone stimulating development of male secondary sexual characteristics.
– ORIGIN from TESTIS.
test pilot • noun a pilot who flies new or modified aircraft to test their performance.
test tube • noun a thin glass tube closed at one end, used to hold material for laboratory testing or experiments.
test-tube baby • noun informal a baby conceived by in vitro fer-

Thesaurus

t

date, menace, threaten, bully, browbeat; scare, frighten, terrify, petrify; *Brit. informal* put the frighteners on.
terse • adjective BRIEF, short, to the point, concise, succinct, crisp, pithy, incisive, short and sweet, laconic, elliptical; BRUSQUE, abrupt, curt, clipped, blunt, ungracious.
– OPPOSITES long-winded, polite.
test • noun **1** *a series of scientific tests* TRIAL, experiment, pilot study, try-out; check, examination, assessment, evaluation, appraisal, investigation, inspection, analysis, scrutiny, study, probe, exploration; screening; *technical* assay. **2** *candidates may be required to take a test* EXAM, examination; *N. Amer.* quiz. **3** *the test of a good sparkling wine* CRITERION, proof, indication, yardstick, touchstone, standard, measure, litmus test, acid test.
• verb **1** *a small-scale prototype was tested* TRY OUT, trial, put to the test, put through its paces, experiment with, pilot; check, examine, assess, evaluate, appraise, investigate, analyse, scrutinize, study, probe, explore; sample; screen; *technical* assay. **2** *such behaviour would test any marriage* PUT A STRAIN ON, strain, tax, try; make demands on, stretch, challenge.
testament • noun *an achievement which is a testament to his professionalism and dedication* TESTIMONY, witness, evidence, proof, attestation; demonstration, indication, exemplification; monument, tribute.
testify • verb **1** *you may be required to testify in court* GIVE EVIDENCE, bear witness, be a witness, give one's testimony, attest; *Law* make a deposition. **2** *he testified that he had been threatened by a fellow officer* ATTEST, swear, state on oath, state, declare, assert, affirm; allege, submit, claim; *Law* depose. **3** *the exhibits testify to the talents of the local sculptors* BE EVIDENCE/PROOF OF, attest to, confirm, prove, corroborate, substantiate, bear out; show, demonstrate, bear witness to, indicate, reveal, bespeak.
testimonial • noun REFERENCE, character reference, letter of recommendation, commendation.
testimony • noun **1** *Smith was in court to hear her testimony* EVIDENCE, sworn statement, attestation, affidavit; statement, declaration, assertion, affirmation; allegation, submission, claim; *Law* deposition. **2** *the work is a testimony to his professional commitment* TESTAMENT, proof, evidence, attestation, witness; confirmation, corroboration; demonstration, indication.
testing • adjective DIFFICULT, challenging, tough, hard, demanding,

tilization.

testy ● adjective easily irritated; irritable.
– DERIVATIVES **testily** adverb **testiness** noun.
– ORIGIN originally in the sense 'headstrong, impetuous': from Old French *teste* 'head'.

tetanic /titannik/ ● adjective of or characteristic of tetanus.

tetanus /tettənəss/ ● noun a disease causing muscle rigidity and spasms, spread by bacteria.
– ORIGIN Latin, from Greek *tetanos* 'muscular spasm'.

tetany /tettəni/ ● noun a condition of intermittent muscular spasms, caused by parathyroid malfunction and consequent calcium deficiency.
– ORIGIN French *tétanie*, from Latin *tetanus* 'tetanus'.

tetchy ● adjective bad-tempered and irritable.
– DERIVATIVES **tetchily** adverb **tetchiness** noun.
– ORIGIN probably from Scots *tache* 'blotch, fault', from Old French *teche*.

tête-à-tête /tetaatet/ ● noun (pl. same or **tête-à-têtes** pronunc. same) a private conversation between two people. ● adjective & adverb involving or happening privately between two people.
– ORIGIN French, 'head-to-head'.

tether ● noun a rope or chain with which an animal is tied to restrict its movement. ● verb tie with a tether.
– ORIGIN Old Norse.

tetra- (also **tetr-** before a vowel) ● combining form **1** four; having four: *tetragram*. **2** Chemistry (in names of compounds) containing four atoms or groups of a specified kind: *tetracycline*.
– ORIGIN from Greek *tettares* 'four'.

tetrad /tetrad/ ● noun technical a group or set of four.
– ORIGIN Greek *tetras*.

tetraethyl lead /tetrəeethīl/ ● noun Chemistry an oily organic compound of lead, used as an anti-knock agent in leaded petrol.

Tetragrammaton /tetrəgrammətón/ ● noun the Hebrew name of God transliterated in four letters as *YHWH* or *JHVH* and articulated as *Yahweh* or *Jehovah*.
– ORIGIN Greek, 'thing having four letters'.

tetrahedron /tetrəheedrən/ ● noun (pl. **tetrahedra** /tetrəheedrə/ or **tetrahedrons**) a solid having four plane triangular faces.
– DERIVATIVES **tetrahedral** adjective.

tetralogy /titraləji/ ● noun (pl. **tetralogies**) a group of four related literary or operatic works.

tetrameter /titrammitər/ ● noun Poetry a verse of four measures.

tetraplegia /tetrəpleejə/ ● noun another term for QUADRIPLEGIA.
– DERIVATIVES **tetraplegic** adjective & noun.

tetrapod ● noun **1** Zoology an animal of a group which includes all vertebrates apart from fishes. **2** an object or structure with four feet, legs, or supports.
– ORIGIN from Greek *tetrapous* 'four-footed'.

tetrarch /tetraark/ ● noun (in the Roman Empire) the governor of one of four divisions of a country or province.
– DERIVATIVES **tetrarchy** noun (pl. **tetrarchies**).
– ORIGIN Greek *tetrarkhēs*, from *tetra-* 'four' + *arkhein* 'to rule'.

tetrathlon /tetrathlən/ ● noun a sporting contest in which participants compete in four events, typically riding, shooting, swimming, and running.
– ORIGIN from TETRA- + Greek *athlon* 'contest', on the pattern of *pentathlon*.

tetrode /tetrōd/ ● noun a thermionic valve with four electrodes.
– ORIGIN from TETRA- + Greek *hodos* 'way'.

Teuton /tyoōt'n/ ● noun **1** a member of an ancient Germanic people who lived in Jutland. **2** often derogatory a German.
– ORIGIN from Latin *Teutones* (plural).

Teutonic /tyootonnik/ ● adjective **1** relating to the Teutons. **2** informal, often derogatory displaying characteristics popularly attributed to Germans.

Texan ● noun a person from the US state of Texas. ● adjective relating to Texas.

Tex-Mex ● adjective having a blend of Mexican and southern American features. ● noun Tex-Mex music or food.

text ● noun **1** a written or printed work regarded in terms of content rather than form. **2** the main body of a book or other work as distinct from appendices, illustrations, etc. **3** written or printed words or computer data. **4** a written work chosen as a subject of study. **5** a passage from the Bible, especially as the subject of a sermon. ● verb send (someone) a text message.
– ORIGIN Latin *textus* 'tissue, literary style', from *texere* 'weave'.

textbook ● noun a book used as a standard work for the study of a subject. ● adjective conforming to an established standard; exemplary.

textile ● noun **1** a type of cloth or woven fabric. **2** informal (among nudists) a person who wears clothes. ● adjective relating to fabric or weaving.
– ORIGIN Latin *textilis*, from *texere* 'weave'.

text message ● noun an electronic message sent and received via mobile phone.

textual ● adjective relating to a text or texts.
– DERIVATIVES **textually** adverb.

textual criticism ● noun the process of attempting to ascertain the original wording of a text.

textuality ● noun the quality or use of language characteristic of written works as opposed to spoken usage.

texture ● noun **1** the feel, appearance, or consistency of a surface, substance, or fabric. **2** the quality created by the combination of elements in a work of music or literature. ● verb give a rough or raised texture to.
– DERIVATIVES **textural** adjective.
– ORIGIN Latin *textura* 'weaving', from *texere* 'weave'.

textured vegetable protein ● noun a protein obtained from soya beans and made to resemble minced meat.

texturize (also **texturise**) ● verb give a particular texture to.

T-group ● noun Psychology a group of people observing and seeking to improve their own interpersonal behaviour.
– ORIGIN *T* for *training*.

TGV ● noun a French high-speed passenger train.
– ORIGIN abbreviation of French *train à grande vitesse*.

Th ● symbol the chemical element thorium.

-th[1] (also **-eth**) ● suffix forming ordinal and fractional numbers from *fourth* onwards.
– ORIGIN Old English.

-th[2] ● suffix forming nouns: **1** (from verbs) denoting an action or process: *growth*. **2** (from adjectives) denoting a state: *filth*.
– ORIGIN Old English.

Thai /tī/ ● noun (pl. same or **Thais**) **1** a person from Thailand. **2** the official language of Thailand.
– ORIGIN Thai, 'free'.

thalamus /thaləməss/ ● noun (pl. **thalami** /thaləmī/) Anatomy each of two masses of grey matter in the forebrain, relaying sensory information.
– ORIGIN Greek *thalamos*.

thalassaemia /thaləseemiə/ (US **thalassemia**) ● noun a hereditary disease in which the body produces abnormal haemoglobin, widespread in Mediterranean, African, and Asian countries.
– ORIGIN from Greek *thalassa* 'sea' (because the disease was first

t

Thesaurus

taxing, stressful.
– OPPOSITES easy.

testy ● adjective. See TETCHY.

tetchy ● adjective IRRITABLE, cantankerous, irascible, bad-tempered, grumpy, grouchy, crotchety, crabby, testy, crusty, curmudgeonly, ill-tempered, ill-humoured, peevish, cross, fractious, pettish, crabbed, prickly, waspish; *informal* snappish, snappy, chippy; *Brit. informal* shirty, stroppy, narky, ratty; *N. Amer. informal* cranky, ornery.
– OPPOSITES good-humoured.

tête-à-tête ● noun CONVERSATION, chat, talk, heart-to-heart, one-on-one, one-to-one; *informal* confab, chinwag; *Brit. informal* natter; *formal* confabulation.

tether ● verb *the horse had been tethered to a post* TIE (UP), hitch, rope, chain; fasten, secure.
– OPPOSITES unleash.
● noun *a dog on a tether* ROPE, chain, cord, lead, leash; restraint; halter.
– PHRASES **at the end of one's tether** AT ONE'S WITS' END, desperate, not knowing which way to turn, unable to cope; *N. Amer.* at the end of one's rope.

text ● noun **1** *a text which explores pain and grief* BOOK, work, written/printed work. **2** *the pictures are clear and relate well to the text* WORDS, wording; content, body, main body. **3** *academic texts* TEXTBOOK, book; set book. **4** *a text from the First Book of Samuel* PASSAGE, extract, quotation, verse, line; reading. **5** *he took as his text the fact that Australia is a paradise* THEME, subject, topic, motif; thesis, argument.

textiles ● plural noun FABRICS, cloths, materials.

known around the Mediterranean).

thalassic /thəlassik/ ● adjective literary or technical relating to the sea.

thalassotherapy /thəlassōtherrəpi/ ● noun the use of seawater in cosmetic and health treatment.

thali /taali/ ● noun (pl. **thalis**) a set meal at an Indian restaurant consisting of a variety of dishes and accompaniments.
– ORIGIN Sanskrit.

thalidomide /thəliddəmīd/ ● noun a drug formerly used as a sedative, but found to cause malformation of the fetus when taken in early pregnancy.

thallium /thaliəm/ ● noun a soft silvery-white metallic chemical element whose compounds are very poisonous.
– ORIGIN from Greek *thallos* 'green shoot', because of a green line in its spectrum.

thallus /thaləss/ ● noun (pl. **thalli** /thalī/) Botany a simple plant body not differentiated into stem, leaves, and roots and without a vascular system, typical of algae, fungi, lichens, and some liverworts.
– ORIGIN Greek *thallos* 'green shoot'.

than ● conjunction & preposition **1** introducing the second element in a comparison. **2** used to introduce an exception or contrast. **3** used in expressions indicating one thing happening immediately after another.
– USAGE Traditionally, it has been regarded as wrong to use *me* and *us* rather than *I* and *we* following the word **than**: *she's younger than I* rather than *she's younger than me*. In modern English, however, the use with *me* and *us* is quite acceptable, while *I* and *we* are generally only used in formal situations.
– ORIGIN Old English, originally the same word as THEN.

thanatology /thannətolləji/ ● noun the scientific study of death and practices associated with it.
– ORIGIN from Greek *thanatos* 'death'.

thane /thayn/ ● noun **1** (in Anglo-Saxon England) a man granted land by the king or a nobleman, ranking between a freeman and a hereditary noble. **2** (in Scotland) a man who held land from a Scottish king and ranked with an earl's son.
– ORIGIN Old English, 'servant, soldier'.

thank ● verb **1** express gratitude to. **2** ironic blame or hold responsible: *you have only yourself to thank*.
– PHRASES **thank goodness** (or **God** or **heavens**) an expression of relief. **thank one's lucky stars** feel grateful for one's good fortune. **thank you** a polite expression of gratitude.
– ORIGIN Old English.

thankful ● adjective **1** pleased and relieved. **2** expressing gratitude.
– DERIVATIVES **thankfulness** noun.

thankfully ● adverb **1** in a thankful manner. **2** fortunately.

thankless ● adjective **1** (of a job or task) unpleasant and unlikely to gain the appreciation of others. **2** not showing or feeling gratitude.

thank-offering ● noun an offering made as an act of thanksgiving.

thanks ● plural noun **1** an expression of gratitude. **2** another way of saying **thank you** (see THANK).
– PHRASES **no thanks to** despite the unhelpfulness of. **thanks to** due to.
– ORIGIN Old English, related to THINK.

thanksgiving ● noun **1** the expression of gratitude, especially to God. **2** (**Thanksgiving**) (in North America) an annual national holiday commemorating a harvest festival celebrated by the Pilgrim Fathers in 1621, held in the US on the fourth Thursday in November and in Canada usually on the second Monday in October.

that ● pronoun & determiner (pl. **those**) **1** used to identify a specific person or thing observed or heard by the speaker. **2** referring to the more distant of two things near to the speaker. **3** referring to a specific thing previously mentioned or known. **4** used in singling out someone or something with a particular feature. **5** (as pronoun) (pl. **that**) used instead of which, who, when, etc. to introduce a defining clause. ● adverb **1** to such a degree. **2** informal very: *he wasn't that far away*. ● conjunction **1** introducing a subordinate clause. **2** literary expressing a wish or regret.
– PHRASES **and all that** (or **and that**) informal and so on. **like that** informal instantly or effortlessly. **that is** (or **that is to say**) a formula introducing or following an explanation or further clarification. **that said** even so. **that's that** there is nothing more to do or say about the matter.
– ORIGIN Old English, related to THE.

thatch ● noun **1** a roof covering of straw, reeds, or similar material. **2** informal the hair on a person's head. ● verb cover with thatch.
– DERIVATIVES **thatcher** noun.
– ORIGIN Old English, 'cover'.

Thatcherism ● noun the political and economic policies advocated by the British Conservative politician Margaret Thatcher, Prime Minister 1979–90.
– DERIVATIVES **Thatcherite** noun & adjective.

thaumaturge /thawmət urj/ ● noun a person who works wonders or miracles.
– DERIVATIVES **thaumaturgical** adjective **thaumaturgy** noun.
– ORIGIN Greek *thaumatourgos*, from *thauma* 'marvel' + *-ergos* '-working'.

thaw ● verb **1** become or make liquid or soft after being frozen. **2** (**it thaws, it is thawing**, etc.) the weather becomes warmer and causes snow and ice to melt. **3** (of a part of the body) become warm enough to stop feeling numb. **4** make or become friendlier or more cordial. ● noun **1** a period of warmer weather that thaws ice and snow. **2** an increase in friendliness or cordiality.
– ORIGIN Old English.

the ● determiner **1** denoting one or more people or things already mentioned or assumed to be common knowledge; the definite article. **2** used to refer to a person, place, or thing that is unique. **3** used to point forward to a following qualifying or defining clause or phrase. **4** used to make a generalized reference rather than identifying a particular instance. **5** enough of. **6** (pronounced stressing 'the') used to indicate that someone or something is the best known or most important of that name or type. **7** used with comparatives to indicate how one amount or degree of something varies in relation to another.
– ORIGIN Old English.

theatre (US **theater**) ● noun **1** a building in which plays and other dramatic performances are given. **2** the writing and production of plays. **3** a play or other activity considered in terms of its dramatic quality. **4** (also **lecture theatre**) a room for lectures with seats in tiers. **5** Brit. an operating theatre. **6** the area in which something happens: *a theatre of war*. **7** (before another noun) (of weapons) intermediate between tactical and strategic.
– ORIGIN Greek *theatron*, from *theasthai* 'behold'.

theatric /thiatrik/ ● adjective theatrical. ● noun (**theatrics**) theatricals.

theatrical ● adjective **1** of, for, or relating to acting, actors, or the theatre. **2** exaggerated and excessively dramatic. ● noun **1** a professional actor or actress. **2** (**theatricals**) theatrical performances or behaviour.

t

Thesaurus

texture ● noun FEEL, touch; appearance, finish, surface, grain; quality, consistency; weave, nap.

thank ● verb EXPRESS (ONE'S) GRATITUDE TO, express one's thanks to, offer/extend thanks to, say thank you to, show one's appreciation to.

thankful ● adjective GRATEFUL, filled with gratitude, relieved, pleased, glad.

thankless ● adjective **1** *a thankless task* UNENVIABLE, difficult, unpleasant, unrewarding; unappreciated, unrecognized, unacknowledged. **2** *her thankless children* UNGRATEFUL, unappreciative, unthankful.
– OPPOSITES rewarding, grateful.

thanks ● plural noun *they expressed their thanks and wished her well* GRATITUDE, appreciation; acknowledgement, recognition, credit.
● exclamation *thanks for being so helpful* THANK YOU, many thanks, thanks very much, thanks a lot, thank you kindly, much obliged, much appreciated, bless you; *informal* cheers, thanks a million; *Brit. informal* ta.
– PHRASES **thanks to** AS A RESULT OF, owing to, due to, because of, through, as a consequence of, on account of, by virtue of, by dint of; *formal* by reason of.

thaw ● verb MELT, unfreeze, soften, liquefy, dissolve; defrost; *N. Amer.* unthaw.
– OPPOSITES freeze.

theatre ● noun **1** *the local theatre* PLAYHOUSE, auditorium, amphitheatre. **2** *what made you want to go into the theatre?* ACTING, performing, the stage; drama, the dramatic arts, dramaturgy, the

– DERIVATIVES **theatricality** noun **theatrically** adverb.

thebe /thaybay/ ● noun (pl. same) a monetary unit of Botswana, equal to one hundredth of a pula.
– ORIGIN from a word in a Bantu language meaning 'shield'.

theca /theekə/ ● noun (pl. **thecae** /theesee/) Anatomy **1** the loose sheath enclosing the spinal cord. **2** the outer layer of cells of an ovarian follicle.
– ORIGIN Greek *thēkē* 'case'.

thecodont /theekədont/ ● noun Palaeontology a Triassic fossil reptile thought to be an evolutionary ancestor of the dinosaurs.
– ORIGIN from Greek *thēkē* 'case' + *odous* 'tooth' (because the teeth were fixed in sockets in the jaw).

thee ● pronoun (second person sing.) archaic or dialect form of YOU, as the singular object of a verb or preposition.
– ORIGIN Old English.

theft ● noun the action or crime of stealing.
– ORIGIN Old English.

thegn /thayn/ ● noun historical an English thane.
– ORIGIN modern representation of an Old English word, adopted to distinguish the Old English use of THANE from the Scots use made familiar by Shakespeare.

their ● possessive determiner **1** belonging to or associated with the people or things previously mentioned or easily identified. **2** belonging to or associated with a person of unspecified sex (used in place of either 'his' or 'his or her'). **3** (**Their**) used in titles.
– USAGE On the use of **their** in the singular to mean 'his or her', see note at THEY.
– ORIGIN Old Norse.

theirs ● possessive pronoun used to refer to something belonging to or associated with two or more people or things previously mentioned.

theism /theeiz'm/ ● noun belief in the existence of a god or gods, specifically of a creator who intervenes in the universe. Compare with DEISM.
– DERIVATIVES **theist** noun **theistic** /theeistik/ adjective.
– ORIGIN from Greek *theos* 'god'.

them ● pronoun (third person pl.) **1** used as the object of a verb or preposition to refer to two or more people or things previously mentioned or easily identified. **2** referring to a person of unspecified sex (used in place of either 'him' or 'him or her'). **3** archaic themselves.
– ORIGIN Old Norse.

thematic ● adjective having or relating to subjects or a particular subject. ● noun (**thematics**) (treated as sing. or pl.) a body of topics for study or discussion.
– DERIVATIVES **thematically** adverb.

thematize (also **thematise**) ● verb present or select as a theme.
– DERIVATIVES **thematization** noun.

theme ● noun **1** a subject or topic on which a person speaks, writes, or thinks. **2** Music a prominent or frequently recurring melody or group of notes in a composition. **3** an idea that recurs in or pervades a work of art or literature. **4** (before another noun) (of music) accompanying the beginning and end of a film or programme. **5** (before another noun) (of a restaurant or pub) designed to be suggestive of a particular country, historical period, etc. **6** US an essay on a set subject. ● verb give a particular setting or ambience to.
– ORIGIN Greek *thema* 'proposition'.

theme park ● noun an amusement park with a unifying setting or idea.

themself ● pronoun (third person sing.) informal used instead of 'himself' or 'herself' to refer to a person of unspecified sex.
– USAGE The standard reflexive form corresponding to **they** and **them** is **themselves**, as in *they can do it themselves*. The singular form **themself**, first recorded in the 14th century, has re-emerged in recent years to correspond to the singular gender-neutral use of **they**, as in *this is the first step in helping someone to help themself*. It is not generally accepted as good English, however.

themselves ● pronoun (third person pl.) **1** used as the object of a verb or preposition to refer to a group of people or things previously mentioned as the subject of the clause. **2** used to emphasize a particular group of people or things mentioned. **3** used instead of 'himself' or 'herself' to refer to a person of unspecified sex.

then ● adverb **1** at that time. **2** after that; next. **3** also. **4** therefore.
– PHRASES **but then (again)** on the other hand. **then and there** immediately.
– ORIGIN Old English.

thence (also **from thence**) ● adverb formal **1** from a place or source previously mentioned. **2** as a consequence.
– USAGE **Thence** means 'from that place', as in *he travelled across France to Spain and thence to England*. Strictly speaking, the preposition **from**, as in *they proceeded from thence to Sunderland*, is redundant, but nevertheless **from thence** is usually accepted as good English.

thenceforth (also **from thenceforth**) ● adverb archaic or literary from that time, place, or point onward.

thenceforward ● adverb thenceforth.

theocentric /thee-ōsentrik/ ● adjective having God as a central focus.

theocracy /thiokrəsi/ ● noun (pl. **theocracies**) a system of government in which priests rule in the name of God or a god.
– DERIVATIVES **theocratic** adjective.
– ORIGIN from Greek *theos* 'god'.

theodicy /thioddisi/ ● noun (pl. **theodicies**) the justification of God and divine providence in view of the existence of evil.
– ORIGIN from Greek *theos* 'god' + *dikē* 'justice'.

theodolite /thioddəlīt/ ● noun a surveying instrument with a rotating telescope for measuring horizontal and vertical angles.
– ORIGIN Latin *theodelitus*.

theogony /thioggəni/ ● noun (pl. **theogonies**) the genealogy of a group or system of gods.
– ORIGIN from Greek *theos* 'god' + *-gonia* '-begetting'.

theologian /thiəlōjən/ ● noun a person expert in or studying theology.

theology ● noun (pl. **theologies**) **1** the study of God and religious belief. **2** religious beliefs and theory when systematically developed.
– DERIVATIVES **theological** adjective **theologically** adverb **theologist** noun.

theophany /thioffəni/ ● noun (pl. **theophanies**) a visible manifestation to humankind of God or a god.
– ORIGIN from Greek *theos* 'god' + *phainein* 'to show'.

theorem /theeərəm/ ● noun **1** Physics & Mathematics a general proposition not self-evident but proved by a chain of reasoning. **2** Mathematics a rule expressed by symbols or formulae.
– ORIGIN Greek *theōrēma* 'speculation, proposition'.

theoretical (also **theoretic**) ● adjective **1** concerned with or involving theory rather than its practical application. **2** based on or calculated through theory.
– DERIVATIVES **theoretically** adverb.

t

Thesaurus

thespian art; show business; *informal* the boards, show biz. **3** *the lecture theatre* HALL, room, auditorium. **4** *the theatre of war* SCENE, arena, field/sphere/place of action.

theatrical ● adjective **1** *a theatrical career* STAGE, dramatic, thespian, dramaturgical; show-business; *informal* showbiz; *formal* histrionic. **2** *Henry looked over his shoulder with theatrical caution* EXAGGERATED, ostentatious, actressy, stagy, showy, melodramatic, overacted, overdone, histrionic, affected, mannered; *informal* hammy, ham, camp.

theft ● noun ROBBERY, stealing, thieving, larceny, thievery, shoplifting, burglary, misappropriation, embezzlement; raid, hold-up; *informal* smash and grab; *N. Amer. informal* heist, stick-up; *formal* peculation.
– RELATED TERMS kleptomania.

theme ● noun **1** *the theme of her speech* SUBJECT, topic, subject matter, matter, thesis, argument, text, burden, thrust; thread, motif, keynote. **2** *the first violin takes up the theme* MELODY, tune, air; motif, leitmotif.

then ● adverb **1** *I was living in Cairo then* AT THAT TIME, in those days; at that point (in time), at that moment, on that occasion. **2** *she won the first and then the second game* NEXT, after that, afterwards, subsequently. **3** *and then there's another problem* IN ADDITION, also, besides, as well, additionally, on top of that, over and above that, moreover, furthermore, what's more, to boot; too. **4** *well, if that's what he wants, then he should leave* IN THAT CASE, that being so, it follows that.

theological ● adjective RELIGIOUS, scriptural, ecclesiastical, doctrinal; divine, holy.

theoretical ● adjective HYPOTHETICAL, conjectural, academic, suppositional, speculative, notional, postulatory, assumed, presumed,

theoretician /theeərətish'n/ ● noun a person who develops or studies the theoretical framework of a subject.
theorist ● noun a theoretician.
theorize (also **theorise**) ● verb form a theory or theories about something.
– DERIVATIVES **theorization** noun.
theory ● noun (pl. **theories**) **1** a supposition or a system of ideas intended to explain something, especially one based on general principles independent of the thing to be explained. **2** an idea accounting for or justifying something. **3** a set of principles on which an activity is based.
– PHRASES **in theory** in an ideal or hypothetical situation.
– ORIGIN Greek *theōria* 'contemplation, speculation'.
theosophy /thiossəfi/ ● noun a philosophy maintaining that a knowledge of God may be achieved through spiritual ecstasy, direct intuition, or special individual relations.
– DERIVATIVES **theosophical** adjective **theosophist** noun.
– ORIGIN from Greek *theosophos* 'wise concerning God'.
therapeutic /therrəpyōōtik/ ● adjective **1** relating to the healing of disease. **2** having a good effect on the body or mind.
– DERIVATIVES **therapeutically** adverb **therapeutics** plural noun.
therapsid /therapsid/ ● noun Palaeontology a fossil reptile of a large group including the cynodonts, related to the evolutionary ancestors of mammals.
– ORIGIN from Greek *thēr* 'beast' + *hapsis* 'arch' (referring to the structure of the skull).
therapy ● noun (pl. **therapies**) **1** treatment intended to relieve or heal a disorder. **2** the treatment of mental or psychological disorders by psychological means.
– DERIVATIVES **therapist** noun.
– ORIGIN Greek *therapeia* 'healing', from *therapeuein* 'minister to, treat medically'.
Theravada /therrəvaadə/ ● noun the more conservative of the two major traditions of Buddhism (the other being Mahayana), practised mainly in Sri Lanka, Burma (Myanmar), Thailand, Cambodia, and Laos.
– ORIGIN Pali (an ancient language related to Sanskrit), 'doctrine of the elders'.
there ● adverb **1** in, at, or to that place or position. **2** in that respect; on that issue. **3** used in attracting attention to someone or something. **4** (usu. **there is/are**) used to indicate the fact or existence of something. ● exclamation **1** used to focus attention. **2** used to comfort someone.
– PHRASES **here and there** in various places. **so there** informal used to express defiance. **there and then** immediately.
– ORIGIN Old English.
thereabouts (also **thereabout**) ● adverb **1** near that place. **2** used to indicate that a date or figure is approximate.
thereafter ● adverb formal after that time.
thereat ● adverb archaic or formal **1** at that place. **2** on account of or after that.
thereby ● adverb by that means; as a result of that.
therefore ● adverb for that reason; consequently.
therefrom ● adverb archaic or formal from that or that place.
therein ● adverb archaic or formal in that place, document, or respect.
thereinafter ● adverb archaic or formal in a later part of that document.
thereinbefore ● adverb archaic or formal in an earlier part of that document.
theremin /therrəmin/ ● noun an electronic musical instrument in which the tone is generated by two high-frequency oscillators and the pitch controlled by the movement of the performer's hand towards and away from the circuit.
– ORIGIN named after its Russian inventor Lev *Theremin* (1896–1993).
thereof ● adverb formal of the thing just mentioned; of that.
thereon ● adverb formal on or following from the thing just mentioned.
there's ● contraction **1** there is. **2** there has.
thereto ● adverb archaic or formal to that or that place.
thereunto ● adverb archaic or formal to that.
thereupon ● adverb formal immediately or shortly after that.
therewith ● adverb archaic or formal **1** with or in the thing mentioned. **2** soon or immediately after that; forthwith.
therm ● noun a unit of heat, especially as the former statutory unit of gas supplied in the UK equivalent to 100,000 British thermal units or 1.055×10^8 joules.
– ORIGIN from Greek *thermē* 'heat'.
thermal ● adjective **1** relating to heat. **2** (of a garment) made of a fabric that provides good insulation to keep the body warm. ● noun **1** an upward current of warm air, used by birds, gliders, and balloonists to gain height. **2** (**thermals**) thermal garments, especially underwear.
– DERIVATIVES **thermally** adverb.
thermal capacity ● noun the quantity of heat needed to raise the temperature of a body by one degree.
thermal imaging ● noun the technique of using the heat given off by an object to produce an image of it or locate it.
thermal spring ● noun a spring of naturally hot water.
thermic ● adjective relating to heat.
thermionic ● adjective relating to the emission of electrons from substances heated to very high temperatures.
thermionic valve ● noun Electronics a vacuum tube giving a flow of thermionic electrons in one direction, used in rectifying a current and in radio reception.
thermistor /thermistər/ ● noun an electrical resistor whose resistance is greatly reduced by heating, used for measurement and control.
– ORIGIN contraction of *thermal resistor*.
thermochromic ● adjective undergoing a reversible change of colour when heated or cooled.
thermocline /thermōklīn/ ● noun a temperature gradient in a lake or other body of water, separating layers at different temperatures.
thermocouple ● noun a device for measuring or sensing a temperature difference, consisting of two wires of different metals connected at two points, between which a voltage is developed in proportion to any temperature difference.
thermodynamics ● plural noun (treated as sing.) the branch of science concerned with the relations between heat and other forms of energy involved in physical and chemical processes.
– DERIVATIVES **thermodynamic** adjective **thermodynamically** adverb.
thermoelectric ● adjective producing electricity by a difference of temperatures.
thermogenesis /thermōjennisiss/ ● noun Physiology the production of bodily heat.
– DERIVATIVES **thermogenic** adjective.
thermogram ● noun a record made by a thermograph.
thermograph ● noun an instrument that produces a record of the varying temperature or infrared radiation over an area or during a period of time.
– DERIVATIVES **thermographic** adjective **thermography** noun.
thermoluminescence ● noun the property of some materials of becoming luminescent when treated and heated, used as a

Thesaurus

untested, unproven, unsubstantiated.
– OPPOSITES actual, real.
theorize ● verb SPECULATE, conjecture, hypothesize, postulate, propose, posit, suppose.
theory ● noun **1** *I reckon that confirms my theory* HYPOTHESIS, thesis, conjecture, supposition, speculation, postulation, postulate, proposition, premise, surmise, assumption, presupposition; opinion, view, belief, contention. **2** *modern economic theory* PRINCIPLES, ideas, concepts; philosophy, ideology, system of ideas, science.
– PHRASES **in theory** IN PRINCIPLE, on paper, in the abstract, all things being equal, in an ideal world; hypothetically.
therapeutic ● adjective HEALING, curative, remedial, medicinal, restorative, health-giving, tonic, reparative, corrective, beneficial, good, salutary; *archaic* sanative.
– OPPOSITES harmful.
therapist ● noun PSYCHOLOGIST, psychotherapist, analyst, psychoanalyst, psychiatrist; *informal* shrink; *Brit. humorous* trick cyclist.
therapy ● noun **1** *a wide range of complementary therapies* TREATMENT, remedy, cure. **2** *he's currently in therapy* PSYCHOTHERAPY, psychoanalysis, analysis.
thereabouts ● adverb **1** *the land thereabouts* NEAR THERE, around there. **2** *they sold it for five million or thereabouts* APPROXIMATELY, or so, give or take a bit, plus or minus a bit, in round numbers, not far off; *Brit.* getting on for; *N. Amer. informal* in the ballpark of.
thereafter ● adverb AFTER THAT, following that, afterwards, subsequently, then, next.
therefore ● adverb CONSEQUENTLY, so, as a result, hence, thus, ac-

means of dating ancient artefacts.
– DERIVATIVES **thermoluminescent** adjective.
thermometer • noun an instrument for measuring and indicating temperature, typically consisting of a graduated glass tube containing mercury or alcohol which expands when heated.
thermonuclear • adjective relating to or using nuclear fusion reactions that occur at very high temperatures.
thermopile /thermōpīl/ • noun a set of thermocouples arranged for measuring small quantities of radiant heat.
thermoplastic • adjective (of a substance) becoming plastic when heated.
thermoregulation • noun Physiology the regulation of bodily temperature.
Thermos • noun trademark a vacuum flask.
– ORIGIN from Greek, 'hot'.
thermosetting • adjective (of a substance) setting permanently when heated.
thermosphere • noun the upper region of the atmosphere above the mesosphere.
thermostat /therməstat/ • noun a device that automatically regulates temperature or activates a device at a set temperature.
– DERIVATIVES **thermostatic** adjective **thermostatically** adverb.
theropod /theerəpod/ • noun a dinosaur of a group including bipedal carnivores such as the carnosaurs and dromaeosaurs.
– ORIGIN from Greek *thēr* 'beast' + *pous* 'foot'.
thesaurus /thəsawrəss/ • noun (pl. **thesauri** /thisawri/ or **thesauruses**) a book that lists words in groups of synonyms and related concepts.
– ORIGIN Greek *thēsauros* 'storehouse, treasure'.
these plural of THIS.
thesis /theesiss/ • noun (pl. **theses** /theeseez/) **1** a statement or theory put forward to be maintained or proved. **2** a long essay or dissertation involving personal research, written as part of a university degree.
– ORIGIN Greek, 'placing, a proposition'.
thespian /thespiən/ • adjective relating to drama and the theatre. • noun an actor or actress.
– ORIGIN from the Greek dramatic poet *Thespis* (6th century BC).
theta /theetə/ • noun the eighth letter of the Greek alphabet (Θ, θ), transliterated as 'th'.
– ORIGIN Greek.
thew /thyoo/ • noun (also **thews**) literary muscle or muscular strength.
– ORIGIN Old English, 'usage, custom', later 'good quality'.
they • pronoun (third person pl.) **1** used to refer to two or more people or things previously mentioned or easily identified. **2** people in general. **3** informal people in authority regarded collectively. **4** used to refer to a person of unspecified sex (in place of either 'he' or 'he or she').
– USAGE In recent years many people have come to dislike the traditional use of **he** to refer to a person of either sex, and **they** (or **their**) has increasingly been used to refer to a single person of unspecified sex. **They** is now generally accepted in contexts where it follows an indefinite pronoun such as **anyone**, **no one**, **someone**, or **a person**, as in *each to their own*. However, **they** is still often criticized for being ungrammatical when it comes after a singular noun, as in *ask a friend if they could help*.
– ORIGIN Old Norse.
they'd • contraction **1** they had. **2** they would.
they'll • contraction **1** they shall. **2** they will.
they're • contraction they are.
they've • contraction they have.
thiamine /thīəmeen/ (also **thiamin**) • noun vitamin B_1, a compound found in unrefined cereals, beans, and liver, a deficiency of which causes beriberi.
– ORIGIN from Greek *theion* 'sulphur'.
thick • adjective **1** with opposite sides or surfaces relatively far apart. **2** (of a garment or fabric) made of heavy material. **3** made up of a large number of things or people close together: *thick forest*. **4** (**thick with**) densely filled or covered with. **5** (of the air or atmosphere) opaque, heavy, or dense. **6** (of a liquid or a semi-liquid substance) relatively firm in consistency; not flowing freely. **7** informal of low intelligence; stupid. **8** (of a voice) not clear or distinct; hoarse or husky. **9** (of an accent) very marked and difficult to understand. **10** informal having a very close, friendly relationship. • noun (**the thick**) the middle or the busiest part: *in the thick of battle*.
– PHRASES **a bit thick** Brit. informal unfair or unreasonable. **thick and fast** rapidly and in great numbers. **(as) thick as thieves** informal very close or friendly. **(as) thick as two short planks** (or **as a plank**) Brit. informal very stupid. **the thick end of** Brit. the greater part of. **through thick and thin** under all circumstances, no matter how difficult.
– DERIVATIVES **thickly** adverb.
– ORIGIN Old English.
thicken • verb make or become thick or thicker.
– PHRASES **the plot thickens** the situation is becoming more complicated and puzzling.
– DERIVATIVES **thickener** noun.
thickening • noun **1** the process or result of becoming thicker. **2** a thicker area or part. **3** a substance added to a liquid to make it thicker.
thicket • noun a dense group of bushes or trees.
– ORIGIN Old English, related to THICK.
thickheaded (also **thick-skulled** or **thick-witted**) • noun informal dull and stupid.
thickness • noun **1** the distance through an object, as distinct from width or height. **2** the state or quality of being thick. **3** a layer of material. **4** a thicker part of something.
thickset • adjective heavily or solidly built; stocky.
thief • noun (pl. **thieves**) a person who steals another person's property.
– ORIGIN Old English.

Thesaurus

cordingly, for that reason, ergo, that being the case, on that account; *formal* whence; *archaic* wherefore.
thesis • noun **1** *the central thesis of his lecture* THEORY, contention, argument, line of argument, proposal, proposition, premise, assumption, hypothesis, postulation, surmise, supposition. **2** *a doctoral thesis* DISSERTATION, essay, paper, treatise, disquisition, composition, monograph, study; *N. Amer.* theme.
thick • adjective **1** *the walls are five feet thick* IN EXTENT/DIAMETER, across, wide, broad, deep. **2** *his short, thick legs* STOCKY, sturdy, chunky, hefty, thickset, beefy, meaty, big, solid; fat, stout, plump. **3** *a thick Aran sweater* CHUNKY, bulky, heavy, cable-knit; woollen, woolly. **4** *the station was thick with people* CROWDED, full, filled, packed, teeming, seething, swarming, crawling, crammed, thronged, bursting at the seams, solid, overflowing, choked, jammed, congested; *informal* jam-packed, chock-a-block, stuffed; *Austral./NZ informal* chocker. **5** *the thick summer vegetation* PLENTIFUL, abundant, profuse, luxuriant, bushy, rich, riotous, exuberant; rank, rampant; dense, close-packed, impenetrable, impassable; serried; *informal* jungly. **6** *a thick paste* SEMI-SOLID, firm, stiff, stiffened, heavy; clotted, coagulated, viscid, viscous, gelatinous; concentrated. **7** *thick fog* DENSE, heavy, opaque, impenetrable, soupy, murky. **8** *(informal) he's a bit thick.* See STUPID sense 1. **9** *Guy's voice was thick with desire* HUSKY, hoarse, throaty, guttural, gravelly, rough. **10** *a thick Scottish accent* OBVIOUS, pronounced, marked, broad, strong, rich, decided, distinct. **11** *(informal) she's very thick with him* FRIENDLY, intimate, familiar, on the best of terms, hand in glove; close to, devoted to, inseparable from; *informal* pally, chummy, matey, buddy-buddy, as thick as thieves, well in.
– OPPOSITES thin, slender, sparse.
• noun *in the thick of the crisis* MIDST, centre, hub, middle, core, heart.
– PHRASES **a bit thick** *(Brit. informal)* UNREASONABLE, unfair, unjust, unjustified, uncalled for, unwarranted, unnecessary, excessive; *informal* below the belt, a bit much; *Brit. informal* out of order.
thicken • verb BECOME THICK/THICKER, stiffen, condense; solidify, set, gel, congeal, clot, coagulate, cake, inspissate.
thicket • noun COPSE, coppice, grove, brake, covert, clump; wood; *Brit.* spinney; *archaic* hurst.
thickhead • noun *(informal)*. See FOOL noun sense 1.
thickness • noun **1** *the gateway is several feet in thickness* WIDTH, breadth, depth, diameter. **2** *several thicknesses of limestone* LAYER, stratum, stratification, seam, vein; sheet, lamina.
thickset • adjective STOCKY, sturdy, heavily built, well built, chunky, burly, strapping, brawny, solid, heavy, hefty, beefy, meaty; *Physiology* pyknic.
– OPPOSITES slight.
thick-skinned • adjective INSENSITIVE, unfeeling, tough, impervious, hardened, case-hardened; *informal* hard-boiled.
– OPPOSITES sensitive.
thief • noun ROBBER, burglar, housebreaker, cat burglar, shoplifter,

thieve ● verb be a thief; steal things.
– DERIVATIVES **thievery** noun **thievish** adjective.
thigh ● noun the part of the leg between the hip and the knee.
– ORIGIN Old English.
thigh bone ● noun the femur.
thigh-slapper ● noun informal a very funny joke or anecdote.
thimble ● noun a metal or plastic cap with a closed end, worn to protect the finger and push the needle in sewing.
– ORIGIN Old English, related to THUMB.
thimbleful ● noun a small quantity of something.
thimblerig ● noun a game involving sleight of hand, in which three inverted thimbles or cups are moved about, contestants having to spot which is the one with a pea or other object underneath.
– DERIVATIVES **thimblerigger** noun.
– ORIGIN from THIMBLE + RIG[2] in the sense 'trick, dodge'.
thin ● adjective (**thinner**, **thinnest**) **1** having opposite surfaces or sides close together. **2** (of a garment or fabric) made of light material. **3** having little flesh or fat on the body. **4** having few parts or members relative to the area covered or filled: *a thin crowd.* **5** not dense or heavy. **6** containing much liquid and not much solid substance. **7** (of a sound) faint and high-pitched. **8** lacking substance; weak and inadequate. ● verb (**thinned**, **thinning**) **1** make or become less thick. **2** (often **thin out**) remove some plants from (a row or area) to allow the others more room to grow.
– PHRASES **have a thin time** Brit. informal have a miserable or uncomfortable time. **into thin air** so as to become invisible or non-existent.
– DERIVATIVES **thinly** adverb **thinness** noun.
– ORIGIN Old English.
thine ● possessive pronoun archaic form of YOURS. ● possessive determiner form of THY used before a vowel.
– ORIGIN Old English.
thing ● noun **1** an inanimate material object. **2** an unspecified object. **3** (**things**) personal belongings or clothing. **4** an action, activity, concept, or thought. **5** (**things**) unspecified circumstances or matters: *how are things?* **6** (**the thing**) informal what is needed, required, acceptable, or fashionable. **7** (**one's thing**) informal one's special interest or concern.
– ORIGIN Old English (also in the senses 'meeting' and 'matter, concern').
thingamabob /thingəməbob/ (also **thingamajig** or **thingumajig** /thingəməjig/) ● noun another term for THINGUMMY.
thingummy /thingəmi/ (also **thingamy**) ● noun (pl. **thingummies**) informal a person or thing whose name one has forgotten, does not know, or does not wish to mention.
thingy ● noun (pl. **thingies**) another term for THINGUMMY.
think ● verb (past and past part. **thought**) **1** have a particular opinion, belief, or idea about someone or something. **2** direct one's mind towards someone or something; use one's mind actively to form connected ideas. **3** (**think of/about**) take into account or consideration. **4** (**think of/about**) consider the possibility or advantages of. **5** (**think of**) have a particular opinion of. **6** call something to mind; remember. ● noun an act of thinking.
– PHRASES **think better of** decide not to do (something) after reconsideration. **think nothing** (or **little**) **of** consider (an activity others regard as odd, wrong, or difficult) as straightforward or normal. **think over** consider carefully. **think through** consider every aspect of before taking action. **think twice** consider a course of action carefully before embarking on it. **think up** invent or devise.
– DERIVATIVES **thinkable** adjective **thinker** noun.
– ORIGIN Old English.
thinking ● adjective using thought or rational judgement; intelligent. ● noun a person's ideas or opinions.

Thesaurus

pickpocket, sneak thief, mugger; embezzler, swindler; criminal, villain; kleptomaniac; bandit, pirate, highwayman; *informal* crook, cracksman; *Brit. rhyming slang* tea leaf; *poetic/literary* brigand.
thieve ● verb STEAL, take, purloin, help oneself to, snatch, pilfer; embezzle, misappropriate; have one's fingers/hand in the till; *informal* rob, swipe, nab, rip off, lift, 'liberate', 'borrow', filch, snaffle; *Brit. informal* nick, pinch, half-inch, whip, knock off, nobble; *N. Amer. informal* heist; *formal* peculate.
thievery ● noun. See THIEVING.
thieving ● noun THEFT, stealing, thievery, robbery, larceny, pilfering; burglary, shoplifting, embezzlement; *formal* peculation.
thin ● adjective **1** *a thin white line* NARROW, fine, attenuated. **2** *a thin cotton nightdress* LIGHTWEIGHT, light, fine, delicate, floaty, flimsy, diaphanous, gossamer, insubstantial; sheer, gauzy, filmy, chiffony, transparent, see-through. **3** *a tall, thin woman* SLIM, lean, slender, rangy, willowy, svelte, sylphlike, spare, slight; SKINNY, underweight, scrawny, scraggy, bony, angular, raw-boned, hollow-cheeked, gaunt, as thin as a rake/reed, stick-like, skin-and-bones, emaciated, skeletal, wasted, pinched, undernourished, underfed; lanky, spindly, gangly, gangling, weedy; *informal* anorexic, like a bag of bones; *dated* spindle-shanked; *archaic* starveling. **4** *his thin grey hair* SPARSE, scanty, wispy, thinning. **5** *a bowl of thin soup* WATERY, weak, dilute, diluted; runny, sloppy. **6** *her thin voice* WEAK, faint, feeble, small, soft; reedy, high-pitched. **7** *the plot is very thin* INSUBSTANTIAL, flimsy, slight, feeble, lame, poor, weak, tenuous, inadequate, insufficient, unconvincing, unbelievable, implausible.
– OPPOSITES thick, broad, fat, abundant.
● verb **1** *some paint must be thinned down before use* DILUTE, water down, weaken. **2** *the crowds were beginning to thin out* DISPERSE, dissipate, scatter; become less dense/numerous, decrease, diminish, dwindle.
thing ● noun **1** *the room was full of strange things* OBJECT, article, item, artefact, commodity; device, gadget, instrument, utensil, tool, implement; entity, body; *informal* doodah, whatsit, whatchamacallit, thingummy, thingy, thingamabob, thingamajig; *Brit. informal* gubbins; *N. Amer. informal* doodad, dingus. **2** *I'll come back tomorrow to collect my things* BELONGINGS, possessions, stuff, property, worldly goods, (personal) effects, paraphernalia, bits and pieces, bits and bobs; luggage, baggage, bags; *Law* goods and chattels; *informal* gear, junk; *Brit. informal* clobber. **3** *his gardening things* EQUIPMENT, apparatus, gear, kit, tackle, stuff; implements, tools, utensils; accoutrements. **4** *I've got several things to do today* ACTIVITY, act, action, deed, undertaking, exploit, feat; task, job, chore. **5** *I've got other things on my mind just now* THOUGHT, notion, idea; concern, matter, worry, preoccupation. **6** *I keep remembering things he said* REMARK, statement, comment, utterance, observation, declaration, pronouncement. **7** *quite a few odd things happened* INCIDENT, episode, event, happening, occurrence, phenomenon. **8** *how are things with you?* MATTERS, affairs, circumstances, conditions, relations; state of affairs, situation, life. **9** *one of the things I like about you is your optimism* CHARACTERISTIC, quality, attribute, property, trait, feature, point, aspect, facet. **10** *there's another thing you should know* FACT, piece of information, point, detail, particular, factor. **11** *the thing is, I'm not sure if it's what I want* FACT OF THE MATTER, fact, point, issue, problem. **12** *you lucky thing!* PERSON, soul, creature, wretch; *informal* devil, beggar, bastard. **13** *Dora developed a thing about noise* PHOBIA, fear, dislike, aversion; obsession, fixation; complex, neurosis; *informal* hang-up, bee in one's bonnet. **14** *she had a thing about men who wore glasses* PENCHANT, preference, taste, inclination, partiality, predilection, soft spot, weakness, fancy, fondness, liking, love; fetish, obsession, fixation. **15** *(informal) books aren't really my thing* WHAT ONE LIKES, what interests one; *informal* one's cup of tea, one's bag, what turns one on. **16** *(informal) it's the latest thing* FASHIONABLE, in fashion, popular, all the rage; *informal* trendy, cool, big, hip, happening.
think ● verb **1** *I think he's gone home* BELIEVE, be of the opinion, be of the view, be under the impression; expect, imagine, anticipate; surmise, suppose, conjecture, guess, fancy; conclude, determine, reason; *informal* reckon, figure; *formal* opine; *archaic* ween. **2** *his family was thought to be enormously rich* DEEM, judge, hold, reckon, consider, presume, estimate; regard as, view as. **3** *Jack thought for a moment* PONDER, reflect, deliberate, consider, meditate, contemplate, muse, ruminate, be lost in thought, be in a brown study, brood; concentrate, rack one's brains; *informal* put on one's thinking cap, sleep on it; *formal* cogitate. **4** *she thought of all the visits she had made to her father* RECALL, remember, recollect, call to mind, think back to. **5** *she forced herself to think of how he must be feeling* IMAGINE, picture, visualize, envisage; dream about, fantasize about.
– PHRASES **think better of** HAVE SECOND THOUGHTS ABOUT, think twice about, think again about, change one's mind about; reconsider, decide against; *informal* get cold feet about. **think something over** CONSIDER, contemplate, deliberate about, weigh up, consider the pros and cons of, mull over, ponder, reflect on, muse on, ruminate on. **think something up** DEVISE, dream up, come up with, invent, create, concoct, make up; hit on.

t

– PHRASES **put on one's thinking cap** informal meditate on a problem.

think tank ● noun a body of experts providing advice and ideas on specific political or economic problems.

thinner ● noun a volatile solvent used to make paint or other solutions less viscous.

thinnings ● plural noun seedlings, trees, or fruit which have been thinned out to improve the growth of those remaining.

thiosulphate (US **thiosulfate**) /thīōsulfayt/ ● noun Chemistry a salt containing the anion $S_2O_3^{2-}$, i.e. a sulphate with one oxygen atom replaced by sulphur.

third ● ordinal number **1** constituting number three in a sequence; 3rd. **2** (**a third/one third**) each of three equal parts into which something is or may be divided. **3** Music an interval spanning three consecutive notes in a diatonic scale, e.g. C to E. **4** Brit. a place in the third grade in the examinations for a university degree.
– DERIVATIVES **thirdly** adverb.
– ORIGIN Old English.

third age ● noun Brit. the period in life of active retirement, following middle age.

third class ● noun **1** a set of people or things considered together as the third best. **2** Brit. the third-highest division in the results of the examinations for a university degree. **3** US a cheap class of mail for unsealed printed material. **4** chiefly historical the cheapest and least comfortable accommodation in a train or ship. ● adjective & adverb relating to the third class.

third-degree ● adjective **1** (of burns) being of the most severe kind, affecting tissue below the skin. **2** Law, chiefly N. Amer. (of a crime, especially murder) in the least serious category. ● noun (**the third degree**) long and harsh questioning to obtain information or a confession.

third estate ● noun (treated as sing. or pl.) the third order or class in a country or society, made up of the common people.

third eye ● noun Hinduism & Buddhism the 'eye of insight' in the forehead of an image of a deity.

third man ● noun Cricket a fielding position near the boundary behind the slips.

third party ● noun a person or group besides the two primarily involved in a situation or dispute. ● adjective Brit. (of insurance) covering damage or injury suffered by a person other than the insured.

third person ● noun **1** a third party. **2** see PERSON (sense 3).

third rail ● noun an additional rail supplying electric current, used in some electric railway systems.

third-rate ● adjective of inferior or very poor quality.

third reading ● noun a third presentation of a bill to a legislative assembly, in the UK to debate committee reports and in the US to consider it for the last time.

third way ● noun any option regarded as an alternative to two extremes, especially a political agenda which is moderate and based on general agreement rather than left- or right-wing.

Third World ● noun the developing countries of Asia, Africa, and Latin America.
– ORIGIN first used to distinguish the developing countries from the capitalist and Communist blocs.

thirst ● noun **1** a feeling of needing or wanting to drink. **2** lack of the liquid needed to sustain life. **3** (**thirst for**) a strong desire for. ● verb **1** archaic feel a need to drink. **2** (**thirst for/after**) have a strong desire for.
– ORIGIN Old English.

thirsty ● adjective (**thirstier**, **thirstiest**) **1** feeling thirst. **2** (of an engine, plant, or crop) consuming a lot of fuel or water. **3** causing thirst: *modelling is thirsty work.* **4** (**thirsty for**) having or showing a strong desire for.
– DERIVATIVES **thirstily** adverb **thirstiness** noun.

thirteen ● cardinal number one more than twelve; 13. (Roman numeral: **xiii** or **XIII**.)
– DERIVATIVES **thirteenth** ordinal number.
– ORIGIN Old English.

thirty ● cardinal number (pl. **thirties**) ten less than forty; 30. (Roman numeral: **xxx** or **XXX**.)
– DERIVATIVES **thirtieth** ordinal number.
– ORIGIN Old English.

this ● pronoun & determiner (pl. **these**) **1** used to identify a specific person or thing close at hand or being indicated or experienced. **2** referring to the nearer of two things close to the speaker. **3** referring to a specific thing or situation just mentioned. **4** (as determiner) used with periods of time related to the present. ● adverb to the degree or extent indicated.
– ORIGIN Old English.

thistle ● noun a plant with a prickly stem and leaves and rounded heads of purple flowers.
– ORIGIN Old English.

thistledown ● noun the light fluffy down of thistle seeds, which enable them to be blown about in the wind.

thither ● adverb archaic or literary to or towards that place.
– ORIGIN Old English.

thixotropic /thiksətroppik/ ● adjective Chemistry becoming less viscous when subjected to an applied stress, such as being shaken or stirred.
– ORIGIN from Greek *thixis* 'touching' + *tropē* 'turning'.

tho' (also **tho**) ● conjunction & adverb informal spelling of THOUGH.

thole[1] /thōl/ (also **thole pin**) ● noun a pin fitted to the gunwale of a rowing boat to act as the fulcrum for an oar.
– ORIGIN Old English.

thole[2] /thōl/ ● verb Scottish or archaic endure without complaint; tolerate.
– ORIGIN Old English.

thong ● noun **1** a narrow strip of leather or other material, used as a fastening or as the lash of a whip. **2** a skimpy bathing garment or pair of knickers like a G-string. **3** chiefly N. Amer. another term for FLIP-FLOP (in sense 1).
– ORIGIN Old English.

thoracic /thorassik/ ● adjective Anatomy & Zoology relating to the thorax.

thorax /thoraks/ ● noun (pl. **thoraces** /thorəseez/ or **thoraxes**) **1** Anatomy & Zoology the part of the body between the neck and the abdomen. **2** the middle section of the body of an insect, bearing the legs and wings.
– ORIGIN Greek.

thorium /thoriəm/ ● noun a white radioactive metallic chemical element of the actinide series.
– ORIGIN named after *Thor*, the Scandinavian god of thunder.

thorn ● noun **1** a stiff, sharp-pointed woody projection on the stem or other part of a plant. **2** a thorny bush, shrub, or tree. **3** an Old English and Icelandic runic letter, þ or Þ, eventually superseded by *th*.
– PHRASES **a thorn in someone's side** (or **flesh**) a source of continual annoyance or trouble.
– ORIGIN Old English.

thorny ● adjective (**thornier**, **thorniest**) **1** having many thorns or

t

Thesaurus

thinker ● noun THEORIST, ideologist, philosopher, scholar, savant, sage, intellectual, intellect, mind; *informal* brain.

thinking ● adjective *he seemed a thinking man* INTELLIGENT, sensible, reasonable, rational; logical, analytical; thoughtful, reflective, meditative, contemplative, pensive, philosophical.
– OPPOSITES stupid, irrational.
● noun *the thinking behind the campaign* REASONING, idea(s), theory, thoughts, line of thought, philosophy, beliefs; opinion(s), view(s), position, judgement, assessment, evaluation.

thin-skinned ● adjective SENSITIVE, oversensitive, hypersensitive, easily offended/hurt, touchy, defensive.
– OPPOSITES insensitive.

third-rate ● adjective SUBSTANDARD, bad, inferior, poor, poor-quality, low-grade, inadequate, unsatisfactory, unacceptable; appalling, abysmal, atrocious, awful, terrible, dreadful, execrable, frightful, miserable, wretched, pitiful; jerry-built, shoddy, tinny, trashy; *N. Amer.* cheapjack; *informal* lousy, diabolical, rotten, dire, bum, crummy, rubbishy; *Brit. informal* ropy, duff.
– OPPOSITES excellent.

thirst ● noun **1** *I need a drink—I'm dying of thirst* THIRSTINESS, dryness; dehydration; *Medicine* polydipsia; *archaic* drought. **2** *his thirst for knowledge* CRAVING, desire, longing, yearning, hunger, hankering, keenness, eagerness, lust, appetite; *informal* yen, itch; *archaic* appetency.
● verb *she thirsted for power* CRAVE, want, covet, desire, hunger for, lust after, hanker after, have one's heart set on; wish, long.

thirsty ● adjective **1** *the boys were hot and thirsty* LONGING FOR A DRINK, dry, dehydrated; *informal* parched, gasping; *Brit. informal* spitting feathers; *Austral./NZ informal* spitting chips. **2** *the thirsty soil* DRY, arid, dried up/out, as dry as a bone, parched, baked, desiccated. **3** *she was thirsty for power* EAGER, hungry, greedy, thirsting, craving, longing, yearning, lusting, burning, desirous, hankering; *infor-*

thorn bushes. **2** causing distress, difficulty, or trouble.

thorough ● adjective **1** complete with regard to every detail. **2** performed with or showing great care and completeness. **3** absolute; utter: *he is a thorough nuisance.*

– DERIVATIVES **thoroughly** adverb **thoroughness** noun.

– ORIGIN Old English, 'through'.

thoroughbred ● adjective **1** of pure breed, especially of a breed of horse originating from English mares and Arab stallions. **2** informal of outstanding quality. ● noun a thoroughbred animal.

thoroughfare ● noun a road or path forming a route between two places.

thoroughgoing ● adjective **1** involving or attending to every detail or aspect. **2** complete; absolute.

thorp (also **thorpe**) ● noun (in place names) a village or hamlet.

– ORIGIN Old English.

those plural of THAT.

thou[1] ● pronoun (second person sing.) archaic or dialect form of YOU, as the singular subject of a verb.

– ORIGIN Old English.

thou[2] ● noun (pl. same or **thous**) **1** informal a thousand. **2** one thousandth of an inch.

though ● conjunction **1** despite the fact that; although. **2** however; but. ● adverb however: *he was able to write, though.*

– ORIGIN Old English.

thought[1] ● noun **1** an idea or opinion produced by thinking or occurring suddenly in the mind. **2** the action or process of thinking. **3** (**one's thoughts**) one's mind or attention. **4** an act of considering or remembering. **5** careful consideration or attention: *I haven't given it much thought.* **6** (**thought of**) an intention, hope, or idea of: *they had no thought of surrender.* **7** the formation of opinions, especially as a philosophy or system of ideas, or the opinions so formed.

– PHRASES **not give a second thought** fail to give more than the slightest consideration to.

– ORIGIN Old English.

thought[2] past and past participle of THINK.

thoughtful ● adjective **1** absorbed in or involving thought. **2** showing careful consideration or attention. **3** showing regard for other people.

– DERIVATIVES **thoughtfully** adverb **thoughtfulness** noun.

thoughtless ● adjective **1** not showing consideration for other people. **2** without consideration of the consequences.

– DERIVATIVES **thoughtlessly** adverb **thoughtlessness** noun.

thought police ● noun (treated as pl.) a group of people who aim to suppress ideas that deviate from the way of thinking that they believe to be correct.

thousand ● cardinal number **1** (**a/one thousand**) the number equivalent to the product of a hundred and ten; 1,000. (Roman numeral: **m** or **M.**) **2** (**thousands**) informal an unspecified large number.

– DERIVATIVES **thousandfold** adjective & adverb **thousandth** ordinal number.

– ORIGIN Old English.

Thousand Island dressing ● noun a dressing for salad or seafood consisting of mayonnaise with ketchup and chopped pickles.

– ORIGIN named after large group of islands in the St Lawrence River between the US and Canada.

Thracian /thraysh'n/ ● noun a person from Thrace, an ancient country lying west of the Black Sea and north of the Aegean. ● adjective relating to Thrace.

thrall /thrawl/ ● noun the state of being in another's power: *she was in thrall to her husband.*

– DERIVATIVES **thraldom** (also **thralldom**) noun.

– ORIGIN Old Norse, 'slave'.

thrash ● verb **1** beat repeatedly and violently with a stick or whip. **2** move in a violent or uncontrolled way. **3** informal defeat heavily. **4** (**thrash out**) discuss frankly and thoroughly so as to reach a decision. ● noun **1** a violent or noisy movement of beating or thrashing. **2** Brit. informal a loud or lavish party. **3** (also **thrash metal**) a style of fast, loud, harsh-sounding rock music.

– DERIVATIVES **thrasher** noun.

– ORIGIN Old English, variant of THRESH.

thread ● noun **1** a long, thin strand of cotton, nylon, or other

Thesaurus

mal itching, dying.

thorn ● noun PRICKLE, spike, barb, spine.

thorny ● adjective **1** *dense thorny undergrowth* PRICKLY, spiky, barbed, spiny, sharp; *technical* spinose, spinous. **2** *the thorny subject of confidentiality* PROBLEMATIC, tricky, ticklish, delicate, controversial, awkward, difficult, knotty, tough, taxing, trying, troublesome; complicated, complex, involved, intricate; vexed; *informal* sticky.

thorough ● adjective **1** *a thorough investigation* RIGOROUS, in-depth, exhaustive, thoroughgoing, minute, detailed, close, meticulous, methodical, careful, complete, comprehensive, full, extensive, widespread, sweeping, all-embracing, all-inclusive. **2** *he is slow but thorough* METICULOUS, scrupulous, assiduous, conscientious, painstaking, punctilious, methodical, careful, diligent, industrious, hard-working. **3** *the child is being a thorough nuisance* UTTER, downright, thoroughgoing, absolute, complete, total, out-and-out, arrant, real, perfect, proper, sheer, unqualified, unmitigated; *Brit. informal* right; *Austral./NZ informal* fair.

– OPPOSITES superficial, cursory, careless.

thoroughbred ● adjective PURE-BRED, pedigree, pure, pure-blooded.

thoroughfare ● noun **1** *the park is being used as a thoroughfare* THROUGH ROUTE, access route; *Brit. informal* rat run. **2** *the teeming thoroughfares of central London* STREET, road, roadway, avenue, boulevard, main road, high road, A road, B road; *N. Amer.* highway, freeway, throughway.

thoroughly ● adverb **1** *we will investigate every complaint thoroughly* RIGOROUSLY, in depth, exhaustively, from top to bottom, minutely, closely, in detail, meticulously, scrupulously, assiduously, conscientiously, painstakingly, methodically, carefully, comprehensively, fully. **2** *she is thoroughly spoilt* UTTERLY, downright, absolutely, completely, totally, entirely, really, perfectly, positively, in every respect, through and through; *informal* plain, clean.

though ● conjunction *though she smiled bravely, she looked pale and tired* ALTHOUGH, even though/if, in spite of the fact that, despite the fact that, notwithstanding (the fact) that, for all that. ● adverb *You can't always do that. You can try, though* NEVERTHELESS, nonetheless, even so, however, be that as it may, for all that, despite that, having said that; *informal* still and all.

thought ● noun **1** *what are your thoughts on the matter?* IDEA, notion, opinion, view, impression, feeling, theory; judgement, assessment, conclusion. **2** *he gave up any thought of taking a degree* HOPE, aspiration, ambition, dream; intention, idea, plan, design, aim. **3** *it only took a moment's thought* THINKING, contemplation, musing, pondering, consideration, reflection, introspection, deliberation, rumination, meditation, brooding, reverie, brown study, concentration; *formal* cogitation. **4** *have you no thought for others?* COMPASSION, sympathy, care, concern, regard, solicitude, empathy; consideration, understanding, sensitivity, thoughtfulness, charity.

thoughtful ● adjective **1** *a thoughtful expression* PENSIVE, reflective, contemplative, musing, meditative, introspective, philosophical, ruminative, absorbed, engrossed, rapt, preoccupied, deep/lost in thought, in a brown study, brooding; *formal* cogitative. **2** *how very thoughtful of you!* CONSIDERATE, caring, attentive, understanding, sympathetic, solicitous, concerned, helpful, friendly, obliging, accommodating, neighbourly, unselfish, kind, compassionate, charitable.

– OPPOSITES vacant, inconsiderate.

thoughtless ● adjective **1** *I'm so sorry—how thoughtless of me* INCONSIDERATE, uncaring, insensitive, uncharitable, unkind, tactless, undiplomatic, indiscreet, careless. **2** *a few minutes of thoughtless pleasure* UNTHINKING, heedless, careless, unmindful, absent-minded, injudicious, ill-advised, ill-considered, imprudent, unwise, foolish, silly, stupid, reckless, rash, precipitate, negligent, neglectful, remiss.

– OPPOSITES considerate, careful.

thousand ● cardinal number *informal* K.

– RELATED TERMS millenary, kilo-, milli-.

thrall ● noun POWER, clutches, hands, control, grip, yoke, enslavement, subjection, subjugation, tyranny.

thrash ● verb **1** *she thrashed him across the head and shoulders* HIT, beat, strike, batter, thump, hammer, pound, rain blows on; assault, attack; cudgel, club, birch; *informal* wallop, belt, bash, whack, thwack, clout, clobber, slug, tan, biff, bop, sock, beat the living daylights out of, give someone a good hiding. **2** *(informal) Newcastle were thrashed 8–1.* See TROUNCE. **3** *he was thrashing around in pain* FLAIL, writhe, thresh, jerk, toss, twist, twitch.

– PHRASES **thrash something out** **1** *it's better if we can thrash out our difficulties first* RESOLVE, settle, sort out, straighten out, iron out, clear up; talk through, discuss, debate, air, ventilate. **2** *they*

t

fibres used in sewing or weaving. **2** a long thin line or piece of something. **3** (also **screw thread**) a spiral ridge on the outside of a screw, bolt, etc. or on the inside of a cylindrical hole, to allow two parts to be screwed together. **4** a theme or characteristic running throughout a situation or piece of writing. **5** (**threads**) informal, chiefly N. Amer. clothes. ● verb **1** pass a thread through. **2** move or weave in and out of obstacles. **3** (**threaded**) (of a hole, screw, etc) having a screw thread.
– DERIVATIVES **threader** noun.
– ORIGIN Old English.

threadbare ● adjective thin and tattered with age; worn out.

threadworm ● noun a very slender parasitic nematode worm.

thready ● adjective (**threadier**, **threadiest**) **1** relating to or resembling a thread. **2** Medicine (of a person's pulse) scarcely perceptible.

threat ● noun **1** a stated intention to inflict injury, damage, or other hostile action on someone. **2** a person or thing likely to cause damage or danger. **3** the possibility of trouble or danger.
– ORIGIN Old English, 'oppression'.

threaten ● verb **1** make or express a threat to (someone) or to do (something). **2** put at risk; endanger. **3** (of a situation or the weather) seem likely to produce (an unwelcome result).
– DERIVATIVES **threatening** adjective.

three ● cardinal number one more than two; 3. (Roman numeral: **iii** or **III**.)
– PHRASES **three parts** three out of four equal parts; three quarters.
– DERIVATIVES **threefold** adjective & adverb.
– ORIGIN Old English.

three-dimensional ● adjective **1** having or appearing to have length, breadth, and depth. **2** having depth; lifelike or real.

three-legged race ● noun a race run by pairs of people, one member of each pair having their left leg tied to the right leg of the other.

three-line whip ● noun (in the UK) a written notice, underlined three times to stress its urgency, to members of a political party to attend a parliamentary vote.

threepence /threppənss, thrŏopp-/ ● noun Brit. the sum of three pence, especially before decimalization (1971).

threepenny bit /thrippəni, thrŏoppəni/ ● noun Brit. historical a coin worth three old pence (1¼ p).

three-piece ● adjective **1** consisting of three matching items. **2** (of a set of furniture) consisting of a sofa and two armchairs. **3** (of a set of clothes) consisting of trousers or a skirt with a waistcoat and jacket.

three-point turn ● noun a method of turning a vehicle round in a narrow space by moving forwards, backwards, and forwards again in a sequence of arcs.

three-quarter ● adjective consisting of three quarters of something in terms of length, angle, time, etc. ● noun Rugby each of four players in a team positioned across the field behind the halfbacks.

three-ring circus ● noun chiefly US **1** a circus with three rings for simultaneous performances. **2** a confused situation; a shambles.

threescore ● cardinal number literary sixty.

threesome ● noun a group of three people.

threnody /thrennədi/ ● noun (pl. **threnodies**) a lament.
– ORIGIN Greek *thrēnōidia*, from *thrēnos* 'wailing' + *ōidē* 'song'.

threonine /threeəneen/ ● noun Biochemistry an amino acid which is found in most proteins and is essential in the diet.
– ORIGIN from *threose* (the name of a sugar).

thresh ● verb **1** /thresh/ separate grain from (corn or other crops). **2** /thrash/ variant spelling of THRASH.

thresher /threshər/ ● noun **1** a person or machine that threshes. **2** a shark with a long upper lobe to the tail, used to lash the water to guide its prey.

threshold /threshōld, threshhōld/ ● noun **1** a strip of wood or stone forming the bottom of a doorway and crossed on entering a house or room. **2** a level or point at which something would start or cease to happen or come into effect.
– ORIGIN Old English, related to THRESH (in the sense 'tread').

threw past of THROW.

thrice /thrīss/ ● adverb archaic or literary **1** three times. **2** extremely; very: *I was thrice blessed.*
– ORIGIN Old English.

thrift ● noun **1** carefulness and prudence in the use of money and other resources. **2** a plant which forms low-growing tufts of slender leaves with rounded pink flower heads, growing chiefly on sea cliffs and mountains.
– ORIGIN from Old Norse, 'grasp, get hold of'.

thriftless ● adjective spending money in an extravagant and wasteful way.

thrift shop (also **thrift store**) ● noun N. Amer. a shop selling second-hand clothes and other household goods.

thrifty ● adjective (**thriftier**, **thriftiest**) careful and prudent with money.
– DERIVATIVES **thriftily** adverb.

thrill ● noun **1** a sudden feeling of excitement and pleasure. **2** an exciting or pleasurable experience. **3** a wave or nervous tremor of emotion or sensation. ● verb **1** have or cause to have a thrill. **2** (of an emotion or sensation) pass with a nervous tremor.
– ORIGIN alteration of dialect *thirl* 'pierce, bore', from Old English.

Thesaurus

tried to thrash out an agreement WORK OUT, negotiate, agree on, bring about, hammer out, produce, effect.

thread ● noun **1** *a needle and thread* COTTON, yarn, filament, fibre. **2** *the Thames was a thread of silver below them* STREAK, strand, stripe, line, strip, seam, vein. **3** *she lost the thread of the conversation* TRAIN OF THOUGHT, drift, direction, theme, motif, tenor; storyline, plot.
● verb **1** *he threaded the rope through a pulley* PASS, string, work, ease, push, poke. **2** *she threaded her way through the tables* WEAVE ONE'S WAY, inch one's way, wind one's way, squeeze one's way, make one's way.

threadbare ● adjective WORN, well worn, old, thin, worn out, holey, moth-eaten, mangy, ragged, frayed, tattered, battered; decrepit, shabby, scruffy, unkempt; having seen better days, falling apart at the seams, falling to pieces; *informal* tatty, ratty, the worse for wear; *N. Amer. informal* raggedy.

threat ● noun **1** *Maggie ignored his threats* THREATENING REMARK, warning, ultimatum. **2** *a possible threat to aircraft* DANGER, peril, hazard, menace, risk. **3** *the company faces the threat of liquidation proceedings* POSSIBILITY, chance, probability, likelihood, risk.

threaten ● verb **1** *how dare you threaten me?* MENACE, intimidate, browbeat, bully, terrorize; make/issue threats to. **2** *these events could threaten the stability of Europe* ENDANGER, be a danger/threat to, jeopardize, imperil, put at risk, put in jeopardy. **3** *the grey skies threatened snow* HERALD, bode, warn of, presage, augur, portend, foreshadow, be a harbinger of, indicate, point to, be a sign of, signal, spell; *poetic/literary* foretoken. **4** *as rain threatened, the party moved indoors* SEEM LIKELY, seem imminent, be on the horizon, be brewing, be gathering, be looming, be on the way, be impending; hang over someone.

threatening ● adjective **1** *a threatening letter* MENACING, intimidating, bullying, frightening, hostile; *formal* minatory. **2** *banks of threatening clouds* OMINOUS, sinister, menacing, dark, black, thunderous.

three ● cardinal number TRIO, threesome, triple, triad, trinity, troika, triumvirate, trilogy, triptych, trefoil, three-piece, triplets.
– RELATED TERMS triple, treble, ter-, tri-.

threesome ● noun TRIO, triumvirate, triad, trinity, troika; triplets.

threnody ● noun LAMENT, dirge, requiem, elegy, monody; *Irish* keen; *Irish & Scottish* coronach.

threshold ● noun **1** *the threshold of the church* DOORSTEP, doorway, entrance, entry, door, gate, gateway, portal. **2** *the threshold of a new era* START, beginning, commencement, brink, verge, dawn, inception, day one, opening, debut; *informal* kick-off. **3** *the human threshold of pain* LOWER LIMIT, minimum; *Psychology* limen.
– RELATED TERMS liminal.

thrift ● noun FRUGALITY, economy, economizing, thriftiness, providence, prudence, good management, good husbandry, saving, scrimping and saving, abstemiousness, parsimony, penny-pinching.
– OPPOSITES extravagance.

thriftless ● adjective EXTRAVAGANT, profligate, spendthrift, wasteful, improvident, imprudent, free-spending, prodigal, lavish; immoderate, excessive, reckless, irresponsible.

thrifty ● adjective FRUGAL, economical, sparing, careful with money, provident, prudent, abstemious, parsimonious, penny-pinching; *N. Amer.* forehanded.
– OPPOSITES extravagant.

thrill ● noun **1** *the thrill of jumping out of an aeroplane* (FEELING OF)

thriller • noun a novel, play, or film with an exciting plot, typically involving crime or espionage.
thrips /thrips/ (also **thrip**) • noun (pl. same) a minute black insect which sucks plant sap, noted for swarming on warm still summer days.
– ORIGIN Greek, 'woodworm'.
thrive • verb (past **thrived** or **throve**; past part. **thrived** or **thriven**) **1** grow or develop well or vigorously. **2** prosper; flourish.
– ORIGIN Old Norse, 'grasp, get hold of'; related to THRIFT.
thro' • preposition, adverb, & adjective literary or informal spelling of THROUGH.
throat • noun **1** the passage which leads from the back of the mouth of a person or animal, through which food passes to the oesophagus and air passes to the lungs. **2** the front part of the neck. **3** literary a voice of a person or a songbird.
– PHRASES **be at each other's throats** quarrel or fight persistently. **force something down someone's throat** force something on a person's attention. **stick in one's throat** be unwelcome or unacceptable.
– ORIGIN Old English.
throaty • adjective (**throatier**, **throatiest**) (of a voice or other sound) deep and husky.
– DERIVATIVES **throatily** adverb **throatiness** noun.
throb • verb (**throbbed**, **throbbing**) **1** beat or sound with a strong, regular rhythm. **2** feel pain in a series of pulsations. • noun a strong, regular beat or sound.
– ORIGIN probably imitative.
throes /thrōz/ • plural noun intense or violent pain and struggle.
– PHRASES **in the throes of** struggling in the midst of.
– ORIGIN perhaps related to an Old English word meaning 'calamity'.
thrombosis /thrombōsiss/ • noun (pl. **thromboses** /thrombōseez/) local coagulation or clotting of the blood in a part of the circulatory system.
– DERIVATIVES **thrombotic** adjective.
– ORIGIN Greek, 'curdling'.
thrombus /thrombəss/ • noun (pl. **thrombi** /thrombī/) a blood clot formed within the vascular system of the body and impeding blood flow.
– ORIGIN Greek *thrombos*.
throne • noun **1** a ceremonial chair for a sovereign, bishop, or similar figure. **2** (**the throne**) the power or rank of a sovereign. • verb literary place on a throne.
– ORIGIN Greek *thronos* 'elevated seat'.
throng • noun a large, densely packed crowd. • verb gather in large numbers in (a place).
– ORIGIN Old English.
throstle /thross'l/ • noun Brit. old-fashioned term for SONG THRUSH.
– ORIGIN Old English.
throttle • noun **1** a device controlling the flow of fuel or power to an engine. **2** archaic a person's throat, gullet, or windpipe. • verb **1** attack or kill by choking or strangling. **2** control (an engine or vehicle) with a throttle.
– ORIGIN perhaps from THROAT, but the history of the word is unclear.
through • preposition & adverb **1** moving in one side and out of the other side of (an opening or location). **2** so as to make a hole or passage in. **3** (preposition) expressing the position or location of something beyond (an opening or an obstacle). **4** expressing the extent of changing orientation. **5** continuing in time to or towards completion of. **6** so as to inspect all or part of. **7** (preposition) N. Amer. up to and including (a particular point in a sequence). **8** by means of. **9** (adverb) so as to be connected by telephone. • adjective **1** (of public transport or a ticket) continuing or valid to the final destination. **2** (of traffic, roads, etc.) passing continuously from one side and out of the other side. **3** having successfully passed to the next stage of a competition. **4** informal, chiefly N. Amer. having finished an activity, relationship, etc.
– PHRASES **through and through** thoroughly or completely.
– ORIGIN Old English.
throughout • preposition & adverb all the way through.
throughput • noun the amount of material or items passing

Thesaurus

EXCITEMENT, stimulation, pleasure, tingle; fun, enjoyment, amusement, delight, joy; *informal* buzz, kick; *N. Amer. informal* charge. **2** *a thrill of excitement ran through her* WAVE, rush, surge, flash, blaze, stab, dart, throb, tremor, quiver, flutter, shudder.
• verb **1** *his words thrilled her* EXCITE, stimulate, arouse, rouse, inspire, delight, exhilarate, intoxicate, stir, electrify, galvanize, move, fire (with enthusiasm), fire someone's imagination; *informal* give someone a buzz, give someone a kick; *N. Amer. informal* give someone a charge. **2** *he thrilled at the sound of her voice* BE/FEEL EXCITED, tingle; *informal* get a buzz out of, get a kick out of; *N. Amer. informal* get a charge out of. **3** *shivers of anticipation thrilled through her* RUSH, race, surge, course, flood, flow, wash, sweep, flash, blaze.
– OPPOSITES bore.
thrilling • adjective EXCITING, stirring, action-packed, rip-roaring, gripping, riveting, fascinating, dramatic, hair-raising; rousing, stimulating, moving, inspiring, inspirational, electrifying, heady, soul-stirring.
– OPPOSITES boring.
thrive • verb FLOURISH, prosper, burgeon, bloom, blossom, do well, advance, make strides, succeed, boom.
– OPPOSITES decline, wither.
thriving • adjective FLOURISHING, prosperous, prospering, growing, developing, burgeoning, blooming, healthy, successful, booming, profitable, expanding; *informal* going strong.
– OPPOSITES moribund.
throat • noun GULLET, oesophagus; windpipe, trachea; maw; *informal, dated* the red lane; *archaic* throttle, gorge.
– RELATED TERMS guttural, jugular.
throaty • adjective GRAVELLY, husky, rough, guttural, deep, thick, gruff, growly, growling, hoarse, croaky, croaking; rasping, raspy.
– OPPOSITES high-pitched.
throb • verb *her arms and legs throbbed with tiredness* PULSATE, beat, pulse, palpitate, pound, thud, thump, drum, thrum, vibrate, pitter-patter, go pit-a-pat, quiver.
• noun *the throb of the ship's engines* PULSATION, beat, beating, pulse, palpitation, pounding, thudding, thumping, drumming, thrumming, pit-a-pat, pitter-patter.
throes • plural noun *the throes of childbirth* AGONY, pain, pangs, suffering, torture; *poetic/literary* travail.
– PHRASES **in the throes of** IN THE MIDDLE OF, in the process of, in the midst of, busy with, occupied with, taken up with/by, involved in; struggling with, wrestling with, grappling with.
thrombosis • noun BLOOD CLOT, embolism, embolus, thrombus, infarction.
throne • noun **1** *a golden throne* seat of state, royal seat. **2** *the tsar risked losing his throne* SOVEREIGN POWER, sovereignty, rule, dominion.
throng • noun *throngs of people blocked her way* CROWD, horde, mass, multitude, host, army, herd, flock, drove, swarm, sea, troupe, pack, press, crush; collection, company, gathering, assembly, assemblage, congregation; *informal* gaggle, bunch, gang; *archaic* rout.
• verb **1** *the pavements were thronged with tourists* FILL, crowd. pack, cram, jam. **2** *people thronged to see the play* FLOCK, stream, swarm, troop. **3** *visitors thronged round him* CROWD, cluster, mill, swarm, congregate, gather.
throttle • verb **1** *he tried to throttle her* CHOKE, strangle, strangulate, garrotte. **2** *attempts to throttle the criminal supply of drugs* SUPPRESS, inhibit, stifle, control, restrain, check, contain, put a/the lid on; stop, put an end to, end, stamp out.
through • preposition **1** *we drove through the tunnel* INTO AND OUT OF, to the other/far side of, from one side to the other of. **2** *he got the job through an advertisement* BY MEANS OF, by way of, by dint of, via, using, thanks to, by virtue of, as a result of, as a consequence of, on account of, owing to, because of. **3** *he worked through the night* THROUGHOUT, all through, for the duration of, until/to the end of.
• adverb **1** *as soon as we opened the gate they came streaming through* FROM ONE SIDE TO THE OTHER, from one end to another, in and out the other side. **2** *I woke up, but Anthony slept through* THE WHOLE TIME, all the time, from start to finish, without a break, without an interruption, non-stop, continuously, throughout.
• adjective *a through train* DIRECT, non-stop.
– PHRASES **through and through** IN EVERY RESPECT, to the core; thoroughly, utterly, absolutely, completely, totally, wholly, fully, entirely, unconditionally, unreservedly, altogether, out-and-out.
throughout • preposition **1** *it had repercussions throughout Europe* ALL OVER, in every part of, everywhere in, all through, right through, all round. **2** *Rose had generally been very fit throughout*

t

through a system or process.

throve past of THRIVE.

throw ● verb (past **threw**; past part. **thrown**) **1** propel with force through the air by a rapid movement of the arm and hand. **2** move or put into place quickly, hurriedly, or roughly. **3** project, direct, or cast (light, an expression, etc.) in a particular direction. **4** send suddenly into a particular position or condition: *the country was thrown into chaos.* **5** disconcert or confuse. **6** have (a fit or tantrum). **7** informal give or hold (a party). **8** form (ceramic ware) on a potter's wheel. **9** (of a horse) unseat (its rider). **10** project (one's voice) so that it appears to come from somewhere else. **11** informal lose (a race or contest) intentionally. ● noun **1** an act of throwing. **2** a small rug or light cover for furniture. **3** (**a throw**) informal a single turn, round, or item.

– PHRASES **be thrown back on** be forced to rely on (something) because there is no alternative. **throw away 1** discard as useless or unwanted. **2** waste or fail to make use of (an opportunity or advantage). **throw good money after bad** incur further loss in a hopeless attempt to recoup a previous loss. **throw one's hand in 1** withdraw from a card game because one has a poor hand. **2** withdraw; give up. **throw in 1** include (something extra) with something that is being sold or offered. **2** make (a remark) casually as an interjection in a conversation. **throw in the towel** (or **sponge**) **1** (in boxing) throw a towel (or sponge) into the ring as a token of defeat. **2** admit defeat. **throw oneself into** start to do with enthusiasm and vigour. **throw open** make generally accessible. **throw out 1** discard as unwanted. **2** expel unceremoniously. **3** (of a court, legislature, or other body) dismiss or reject. **4** cause numbers or calculations to become inaccurate. **throw over** abandon or reject (a lover). **throw together 1** bring (people) into contact, especially by chance. **2** make or produce hastily or without careful planning. **throw up** vomit. **throw up one's hands** raise both hands in the air as an indication of one's exasperation.

– DERIVATIVES **thrower** noun.

– ORIGIN Old English, 'to twist, turn'.

throwaway ● adjective **1** intended to be discarded after being used once or a few times. **2** (of a remark) expressed in a casual or understated way.

throwback ● noun a reversion to an earlier ancestral type or characteristic.

throw-in ● noun Soccer & Rugby the act of throwing the ball from the sideline to restart the game after the ball has gone out of play.

throw-over ● adjective (of a bedspread or cloth) used as a loose-fitting decorative cover.

thru ● preposition, adverb, & adjective chiefly US informal spelling of THROUGH.

thrum[1] ● verb (**thrummed**, **thrumming**) **1** make a continuous rhythmic humming sound. **2** strum (the strings of a musical instrument) in a rhythmic way. ● noun a continuous rhythmic humming sound.

– ORIGIN imitative.

thrum[2] ● noun (in weaving) an unwoven end of a warp thread, or a fringe of such ends, left in the loom when the finished cloth is cut away.

– ORIGIN Old English.

thrush[1] ● noun a small or medium-sized songbird with a brown back and spotted breast.

– ORIGIN Old English, related to THROSTLE.

thrush[2] ● noun infection of the mouth and throat or the female genitals by a yeast-like fungus of the genus *Candida.*

– ORIGIN origin uncertain.

thrust ● verb (past and past part. **thrust**) **1** push suddenly or violently. **2** make one's way forcibly. **3** project conspicuously: *the jetty thrust out into the water.* **4** (**thrust on/upon**) impose (something) unwelcome on. ● noun **1** a sudden or violent lunge or attack. **2** the principal purpose or theme of a course of action or line of reasoning. **3** the force which propels a jet or rocket engine.

– DERIVATIVES **thruster** noun.

– ORIGIN Old Norse.

thrusting ● adjective **1** aggressively ambitious. **2** projecting in a conspicuous way.

thud ● noun a dull, heavy sound. ● verb (**thudded**, **thudding**) move, fall, or strike something with a thud.

– ORIGIN originally in the sense 'a sudden gust of wind', later 'a thunderclap': probably from Old English, 'to thrust, push'.

thug ● noun **1** a violent and uncouth man, especially a criminal. **2** (**Thug**) a member of a religious organization of robbers and assassins in India, suppressed by the British in the 1830s.

– DERIVATIVES **thuggery** noun **thuggish** adjective.

– ORIGIN Hindi, 'swindler, thief'.

thuggee /thugee/ ● noun historical the robbery and murder practised by the Thugs in accordance with their ritual.

– DERIVATIVES **thuggism** noun.

– ORIGIN Hindi.

thulium /thyo͞oliəm/ ● noun a soft silvery-white metallic chemical element of the lanthanide series.

Thesaurus

her life ALL THROUGH, all, for the duration of, for the whole of, until the end of.

throw ● verb **1** *she threw the ball back* HURL, toss, fling, pitch, cast, lob, launch, catapult, project, propel; bowl; *informal* chuck, heave, sling, bung; *N. Amer. informal* peg; *Austral. informal* hoy; *NZ informal* bish; *dated* shy. **2** *he threw the door open* PUSH, thrust, fling, bang, force. **3** *a chandelier threw its light over the walls* CAST, send, give off, emit, radiate, project. **4** *he threw another punch* DELIVER, give, land. **5** *she threw a withering glance at him* DIRECT, cast, send, dart, shoot. **6** *the horse threw his rider* UNSEAT, dislodge. **7** *his question threw me* DISCONCERT, unnerve, fluster, ruffle, agitate, discomfit, put off, throw off balance, discountenance, unsettle, confuse; *informal* rattle, faze; *N. Amer. informal* discombobulate. **8** *the pots were thrown on a wheel* SHAPE, form, mould, fashion. **9** *(informal) he threw a farewell party for them* GIVE, host, hold, have, provide, put on, lay on, arrange, organize.

● noun **1** *we were allowed two throws each* LOB, pitch; go; bowl, ball. **2** *(informal) drinks are only £1 a throw* EACH, apiece, per item.

– PHRASES **throw something away 1** *she hated throwing old clothes away* DISCARD, throw out, dispose of, get rid of, do away with, toss out, scrap, throw on the scrap heap, clear out, dump, jettison; *informal* chuck (away/out), ditch, bin, junk, get shut of; *Brit. informal* get shot of. **2** *Cambridge threw away a 15–0 lead* SQUANDER, waste, fritter away, fail to exploit, lose, let slip; *informal* blow, throw something down the drain. **throw someone off** SHAKE OFF, get away from, escape, elude, give someone the slip, throw off the scent, dodge, lose. **throw someone out** EXPEL, eject, evict, drive out, force out, oust, remove; get rid of, depose, topple, unseat, overthrow, bring down, overturn, dislodge, displace, supplant, show someone the door; banish, deport, exile; *informal* boot out, kick out, give someone the boot; *Brit. informal* turf out. **throw something out 1** *throw out food that's past its sell-by date.* See THROW SOMETHING AWAY sense 1. **2** *his case was thrown out by the magistrate* REJECT, dismiss, turn down, refuse, disallow, veto; *informal* give the thumbs down to. **3** *a thermal light bulb throws out a lot of heat* RADIATE, emit, give off, send out, diffuse. **throw someone over** ABANDON, leave, desert, discard, turn one's back on, cast aside/off; jilt, break up with, finish with, leave in the lurch, leave high and dry; *informal* dump, ditch, chuck, drop, walk out on, run out on, leave flat, give someone the push/elbow, give someone the big E; *poetic/literary* forsake. **throw up**. See VOMIT verb sense 1. **throw something up** GIVE UP, abandon, relinquish, resign (from), leave; *informal* quit, chuck, pack in; *Brit. informal* jack in.

throwaway ● adjective **1** *throwaway packaging* DISPOSABLE, non-returnable; biodegradable, photodegradable. **2** *throwaway remarks* CASUAL, passing, careless, unthinking, unstudied, unconsidered, offhand.

thrust ● verb **1** *she thrust her hands into her pockets* SHOVE, push, force, plunge, stick, drive, propel, ram, poke. **2** *fame had been thrust on him* FORCE, foist, impose, inflict. **3** *he thrust his way past her* PUSH, shove, force, elbow, shoulder, barge.

● noun **1** *a hard thrust* SHOVE, push, lunge, poke. **2** *a thrust by the Third Army* ADVANCE, push, drive, attack, assault, onslaught, offensive, charge, sortie, foray, raid, sally, invasion, incursion. **3** *only one engine is producing thrust* FORCE, propulsive force, propulsion, power, impetus, momentum. **4** *the thrust of the speech* GIST, substance, drift, burden, meaning, significance, signification, sense, theme, message, import, tenor.

thrusting ● adjective AMBITIOUS, pushy, forceful, aggressive, assertive, self-assertive, full of oneself, determined, power-hungry.

– OPPOSITES meek.

thud ● noun & verb THUMP, clunk, clonk, crash, smack, bang; stomp, stamp, clump, clomp; *informal* wham.

thug ● noun RUFFIAN, lout, hooligan, bully boy, vandal, hoodlum,

– ORIGIN Latin, from *Thule*, a country identified by the ancients as the northernmost part of the world.
thumb ● noun the short, thick first digit of the hand, set lower and apart from the other four and opposable to them. ● verb **1** press, touch, or indicate with one's thumb. **2** turn over (pages) with one's thumb. **3** (**thumbed**) (of a book's pages) worn or soiled by repeated handling. **4** request or obtain (a free ride in a passing vehicle) by signalling with one's thumb.
– PHRASES **thumb one's nose at** informal show disdain or contempt for. [ORIGIN with reference to the gesture of putting one's thumb on one's nose and spreading the fingers.] **thumbs up** (or **down**) informal an indication of satisfaction or approval (or of rejection or failure). [ORIGIN with reference to the signal of approval or disapproval used by spectators at a Roman amphitheatre (although the Romans used the symbols in reverse).] **under someone's thumb** completely under someone's influence or control.
– ORIGIN Old English.
thumb index ● noun a set of lettered indentations cut down the side of a book for easy reference.
thumbnail ● noun **1** the nail of the thumb. **2** (before another noun) brief or concise: *a thumbnail sketch.*
thumbscrew ● noun an instrument of torture that crushes the thumbs.
thumbtack ● noun N. Amer. a drawing pin.
thump ● verb **1** hit heavily with the fist or a blunt implement. **2** put down forcefully, noisily, or decisively. **3** (of a person's heart or pulse) beat or pulsate strongly. **4** (**thump out**) play (a tune) enthusiastically but heavy-handedly. **5** informal defeat heavily. ● noun a heavy dull blow or noise.
– DERIVATIVES **thumper** noun.
– ORIGIN imitative.
thumping ● adjective **1** pounding; throbbing. **2** informal impressively large: *a thumping 64 per cent majority.*
thunder ● noun **1** a loud rumbling or crashing noise heard after a lightning flash due to the expansion of rapidly heated air. **2** a resounding loud deep noise. ● verb **1** (**it thunders, it is thundering**, etc.) thunder sounds. **2** move heavily and forcefully. **3** speak loudly, angrily, and forcefully.
– DERIVATIVES **thundery** adjective.
– ORIGIN Old English.
thunderbolt ● noun a flash of lightning with a simultaneous crash of thunder.
thunderbug (also **thunderfly**) ● noun another term for THRIPS.
thunderclap ● noun a crash of thunder.
thundercloud ● noun a cumulus cloud with a towering or spreading top, charged with electricity and producing thunder and lightning.
thunderflash ● noun a noisy but harmless pyrotechnic device used especially in military exercises.
thunderhead ● noun a rounded, projecting head of a cumulus cloud.
thundering ● adjective **1** making a resounding, loud, deep noise. **2** informal extremely great, severe, or impressive: *a thundering bore.*
thunderous ● adjective **1** relating to or resembling thunder. **2** (of a person's expression or behaviour) very angry or menacing.
– DERIVATIVES **thunderously** adverb.
thunderstorm ● noun a storm with thunder and lightning.
thunderstruck ● adjective extremely surprised or shocked.
thurible /thyoorib'l/ ● noun a container in which incense is burnt; a censer.
– ORIGIN Latin *thuribulum*, from *thus* 'incense'.
Thursday ● noun the day of the week before Friday and following Wednesday.
– ORIGIN Old English, 'day of thunder' (named after the Germanic thunder god *Thor*), translation of Latin *Jovis dies* 'day of Jupiter'.
thus ● adverb literary or formal **1** as a result or consequence of this; therefore. **2** in this way. **3** to this point; so.
– ORIGIN Old English.
thwack informal ● verb strike forcefully with a sharp blow. ● noun a sharp blow.
– ORIGIN imitative.
thwaite /thwayt/ ● noun (in place names) a piece of wild land cleared or reclaimed for cultivation.
– ORIGIN Old Norse, 'paddock'.
thwart /thwawrt/ ● verb prevent from succeeding in or accomplishing something. ● noun a crosspiece forming a seat for a

Thesaurus

gangster, villain, criminal; *informal* tough, bruiser, heavy, hired gun; *Brit. informal* rough, bovver boy; *N. Amer. informal* hood, goon.
thumb ● noun *technical* pollex, opposable digit.
● verb **1** *he thumbed through his notebook* LEAF, flick, flip, riffle, skim, browse, look. **2** *his dictionaries were thumbed and ink-stained* SOIL, mark, make dog-eared. **3** *he was thumbing his way across France* HITCH-HIKE; *informal* hitch, hitch/thumb a lift.
– PHRASES **all thumbs** *(Brit. informal)* CLUMSY, awkward, maladroit, inept, unskilful, heavy-handed, inexpert; *informal* butterfingered, cack-handed, ham-fisted, having two left feet; *Brit. informal* all fingers and thumbs; *N. Amer. informal* klutzy. **thumbs down** *(informal)* REJECTION, refusal, veto, no, negation, rebuff; *informal* red light, knock-back. **thumbs up** *(informal)* APPROVAL, seal of approval, endorsement; permission, authorization, consent, yes, leave, authority, sanction, ratification, licence, dispensation, nod, assent, blessing, rubber stamp, clearance; *informal* go-ahead, OK, green light, say-so.
thumbnail ● adjective CONCISE, short, brief, succinct, to the point, compact, crisp, short and sweet, quick, rapid; potted.
thump ● verb **1** *the two men kicked and thumped him* HIT, strike, smack, cuff, punch; beat, thrash, batter, belabour, pound, pummel, box someone's ears; *informal* whack, wallop, bash, biff, bop, lam, clout, clobber, sock, swipe, crown, beat the living daylights out of, give someone a (good) hiding, belt, tan, lay into, let someone have it; *Brit. informal* stick one on, slosh; *N. Amer. informal* slug, boff; *poetic/literary* smite. **2** *her heart thumped with fright* THROB, pound, thud, hammer, pulsate, pulse, pump, palpitate, race, beat heavily.
● noun **1** *a well-aimed thump on the jaw* BLOW, punch, box, cuff, smack; thrashing, hiding; *informal* whack, thwack, wallop, bash, belt, biff, clout, swipe; *Brit. informal* slosh; *N. Amer. informal* boff, slug. **2** *she put the box down with a thump* THUD, clunk, clonk, crash, smack, bang.
thumping ● adjective **1** *the thumping beat of her heart* THUDDING, pounding, throbbing, pulsating, banging, hammering, drumming. **2** *(informal) a thumping 64 per cent majority* | *a thumping victory* ENORMOUS, huge, massive, vast, tremendous, substantial, prodigious, gigantic, giant, terrific, fantastic, colossal, immense, mammoth, monumental, stupendous; emphatic, decisive, conclusive, striking, impressive, outstanding, notable, memorable, remarkable, extraordinary, resounding, phenomenal; *informal* whopping, thundering; *Brit. informal* whacking.
● adverb *(informal) a thumping good read.* See VERY adverb.
thunder ● noun **1** *thunder and lightning* THUNDERCLAP, roll/rumble of thunder, crack/crash of thunder; *poetic/literary* thunderbolt. **2** *the ceaseless thunder of the traffic* RUMBLE, rumbling, boom, booming, roar, roaring, pounding, thud, thudding, crash, crashing, reverberation.
● verb **1** *below me the surf thrashed and thundered* RUMBLE, boom, roar, pound, thud, thump, bang; resound, reverberate, beat. **2** *he thundered against the evils of the age* RAIL, fulminate, inveigh, rage; condemn, denounce. **3** *'Answer me!' he thundered* ROAR, bellow, bark, yell, shout, bawl; *informal* holler.
thundering ● adjective *a thundering noise.* See THUNDEROUS.
● adverb *(informal) a thundering good read.* See VERY adverb.
thunderous ● adjective VERY LOUD, tumultuous, booming, roaring, resounding, reverberating, reverberant, ringing, deafening, ear-splitting, noisy.
thunderstruck ● adjective ASTONISHED, amazed, astounded, staggered, surprised, startled, stunned, shocked, aghast, taken aback, dumbfounded, dumbstruck, stupefied, dazed, speechless; *informal* flabbergasted; *Brit. informal* gobsmacked, knocked for six.
thus ● adverb *(formal)* **1** *the studio handled production, thus cutting its costs* CONSEQUENTLY, as a consequence, in consequence, so, that being so, therefore, ergo, accordingly, hence, as a result, for that reason, because of that, on that account. **2** *legislation forbids such data being held thus* LIKE THAT, in that way, so, like so.
– PHRASES **thus far** SO FAR, (up) until now, up to now, up to this point, hitherto.
thwack ● verb *(informal)* HIT, strike, slap, smack, cuff, punch, thump; beat, thrash, batter, belabour, pound, pummel, box someone's ears; whip, flog, cane; *informal* whack, wallop, bash, biff, bop, lam, clout, clobber, sock, swipe, crown, beat the living daylights out of, give someone a (good) hiding, belt, tan, lay into, let someone

t

rower in a boat.
– ORIGIN from Old Norse, 'transverse'.
thy (also **thine** before a vowel) ● **possessive determiner** archaic or dialect form of YOUR.
– ORIGIN Old English.
thyme /tīm/ ● **noun** a low-growing aromatic plant of the mint family, used in cooking.
– ORIGIN Greek *thumon*, from *thuein* 'burn, sacrifice'.
thymine /thīmeen/ ● **noun** Biochemistry a compound which is one of the four constituent bases of DNA.
– ORIGIN from THYMUS.
thymol /thīmol/ ● **noun** Chemistry a white crystalline compound present in oil of thyme and used as a flavouring and preservative.
– ORIGIN from Greek *thumon* 'thyme'.
thymus /thīməss/ ● **noun** (pl. **thymi** /tīmī/) a gland situated in the neck which produces white blood cells for the immune system.
– DERIVATIVES **thymic** adjective.
– ORIGIN Greek *thumos* 'excrescence like a thyme bud, thymus gland'.
thyristor /thīristər/ ● **noun** Electronics a kind of solid-state rectifier containing four layers of semiconductor material.
– ORIGIN blend of *thyratron*, denoting a kind of thermionic valve (from Greek *thura* 'gate') and TRANSISTOR.
thyroid /thīroyd/ ● **noun** (also **thyroid gland**) a large gland in the neck which secretes hormones regulating growth and development through the rate of metabolism.
– ORIGIN from Greek *khondros thureoeidēs* 'shield-shaped cartilage'.
thyroid-stimulating hormone ● **noun** another term for THYROTROPIN.
thyrotoxicosis /thīrōtoksikōsiss/ ● **noun** another term for HYPERTHYROIDISM.
thyrotropin /thīrətrōpin/ ● **noun** Biochemistry a hormone secreted by the pituitary gland which regulates the production of thyroid hormones.
thyroxine /thīrokseen/ ● **noun** Biochemistry the main hormone produced by the thyroid gland, acting to increase metabolic rate and so regulating growth and development.
thyself ● **pronoun** (second person sing.) archaic or dialect form of YOURSELF, corresponding to the subject THOU[1].
Ti ● **symbol** the chemical element titanium.
ti ● **noun** North American form of TE.
Tia Maria /teeə məreeə/ ● **noun** trademark a coffee-flavoured liqueur based on rum.
– ORIGIN Spanish, 'Aunt Mary'.
tiara ● **noun** 1 a jewelled ornamental band worn on the front of a woman's hair. 2 a three-crowned diadem worn by a pope.
– ORIGIN Greek.
Tibetan ● **noun** 1 a person from Tibet. 2 the language of Tibet. ● **adjective** relating to Tibet.
tibia /tibbiə/ ● **noun** (pl. **tibiae** /**tibb**i-ee/) Anatomy the inner and typically larger of the two bones between the knee and the ankle, parallel with the fibula.
– DERIVATIVES **tibial** adjective.
– ORIGIN Latin, 'shin bone'.
tic ● **noun** a habitual contraction of the muscles caused by spasm, most often in the face.
– ORIGIN Italian *ticchio*.
tich /tich/ ● **noun** variant spelling of TITCH.
tick[1] ● **noun** 1 a mark (✓) used to indicate that an item in a text is correct or has been chosen or checked. 2 a regular short, sharp sound. 3 Brit. informal a moment. ● **verb** 1 mark with a tick. 2 make regular ticking sounds. 3 (**tick away/by/past**) (of time) pass inexorably. 4 (**tick over**) (of an engine) run slowly in neutral. 5 (**tick off**) Brit. informal reprimand or rebuke.
– PHRASES **make someone tick** informal motivate someone.
– ORIGIN probably Germanic.
tick[2] ● **noun** 1 a parasitic arachnid which attaches itself to the skin, from which it sucks blood. 2 informal a parasitic louse fly, especially the sheep ked.
– ORIGIN Old English.
tick[3] ● **noun** (in phrase **on tick**) on credit.
– ORIGIN apparently short for TICKET in the phrase *on the ticket*, referring to a promise to pay.
tick[4] ● **noun** 1 a fabric case stuffed to form a mattress or pillow. 2 short for TICKING.
– ORIGIN probably from Greek *thēkē* 'case'.
ticker ● **noun** 1 informal a watch. 2 informal a person's heart. 3 N. Amer. a telegraphic or electronic machine that prints out data on a strip of paper.
ticker tape ● **noun** a paper strip on which messages are recorded in a telegraphic tape machine.
ticket ● **noun** 1 a piece of paper or card giving the holder a right to admission to a place or event or to travel on public transport. 2 an official notice of a traffic offence. 3 a label attached to a retail product, giving its price, size, etc. 4 chiefly N. Amer. a set of principles supported by a party in an election. 5 (**the ticket**) informal the desirable thing. ● **verb** (**ticketed, ticketing**) issue with a ticket.
– ORIGIN Old French *estiquet*, from Dutch *steken* 'to fix'.
tickety-boo ● **adjective** Brit. informal, dated in good order.
– ORIGIN perhaps from a Hindi phrase meaning 'all right'.
ticking ● **noun** a strong, durable material used to cover mattresses.
– ORIGIN from TICK[4].
tickle ● **verb** 1 lightly touch in a way that causes itching or twitching and often laughter. 2 be appealing or amusing to. 3 catch (a trout) by lightly rubbing it so that it moves backwards into the hand. ● **noun** an act of tickling or sensation of being tickled.
– PHRASES **be tickled pink** informal be extremely amused or pleased. **tickle the ivories** informal play the piano.
– DERIVATIVES **tickler** noun **tickly** adjective.
– ORIGIN perhaps from TICK[1], or an alteration of Scots and dialect *kittle* 'to tickle'.
ticklish ● **adjective** 1 sensitive to being tickled. 2 (of a cough) characterized by persistent irritation in the throat. 3 (of a situation or problem) sensitive or difficult to deal with.
tic-tac (also **tick-tack**) ● **noun** (in the UK) a kind of manual semaphore used by racecourse bookmakers to exchange information.
– ORIGIN imitative.
tic-tac-toe (also **tick-tack-toe**) ● **noun** N. Amer. noughts and crosses.
– ORIGIN from *tick-tack*, used earlier to denote games in which the pieces made clicking sounds.
tidal ● **adjective** relating to or affected by tides.
– DERIVATIVES **tidally** adverb.
tidal basin ● **noun** a basin accessible or navigable only at high tide.

Thesaurus

have it, deck, floor; *Brit. informal* stick one on, slosh; *N. Amer. informal* slug, boff; *poetic/literary* smite.
thwart ● **verb** FOIL, frustrate, baulk, stand in the way of, forestall, derail, dash; stop, check, block, prevent, defeat, impede, obstruct, snooker, hinder, hamper; spike someone's guns; *informal* put paid to, put the kibosh on, do for, stymie; *Brit. informal* scupper, queer someone's pitch.
– OPPOSITES facilitate.
tic ● **noun** TWITCH, spasm, jerk, tremor.
tick ● **noun** 1 *put a tick against the item of your choice* mark, stroke; *N. Amer.* check, check mark. 2 *the tick of his watch* TICKING, tick-tock, click, clicking, tap, tapping. 3 *(Brit. informal) I won't be a tick* MOMENT, second, minute, bit, little while, instant; *informal* sec, jiffy; *Brit. informal* mo, two ticks.
● **verb** 1 *tick the appropriate box* PUT A TICK IN/AGAINST, mark, check off, indicate; *N. Amer.* check. 2 *I could hear the clock ticking* TICK-TOCK, click; tap.
– PHRASES **in a tick** *(Brit. informal)* (VERY) SOON, in a second, in a minute, in a moment, in a trice, in a flash, shortly, any second, any minute, in no time (at all); *N. Amer.* momentarily; *informal* in a sec, in a jiffy, in two shakes (of a lamb's tail), before you can say Jack Robinson; *Brit. informal* in two ticks, in a mo; *N. Amer. informal* in a snap; *dated* directly. **tick someone off** *(Brit. informal)*. See REPRIMAND verb.
ticket ● **noun** 1 *can I see your ticket?* PASS, authorization, permit; token, coupon, voucher. 2 *a price ticket* LABEL, tag, sticker, tab, marker, docket.
tickle ● **verb** 1 *he tried to tickle her under the chin* STROKE, pet, chuck. 2 *he found something that tickled his imagination* STIMULATE, interest, appeal to, arouse, excite. 3 *the idea tickled Lewis* AMUSE, entertain, divert, please, delight; *informal* tickle someone pink.

tidal bore ● noun a large wave caused by the constriction of the spring tide as it enters a long, narrow, shallow inlet.

tidal wave ● noun **1** an exceptionally large ocean wave, especially one caused by an underwater earthquake or volcanic eruption. **2** a widespread manifestation of an emotion or phenomenon.

tidbit ● noun US spelling of TITBIT.

tiddledywinks ● plural noun US spelling of TIDDLYWINKS.

tiddler ● noun Brit. informal **1** a small fish. **2** a young or unusually small person or thing.
– ORIGIN perhaps related to TIDDLY[2] or *tittlebat*, a childish form of *stickleback*.

tiddly[1] ● adjective (**tiddlier**, **tiddliest**) informal, chiefly Brit. slightly drunk.
– ORIGIN perhaps from slang *tiddlywink*, denoting an unlicensed public house.

tiddly[2] ● adjective (**tiddlier**, **tiddliest**) Brit. informal little; tiny.
– ORIGIN variant of colloquial *tiddy*, of unknown origin.

tiddlywinks (US **tiddledywinks**) ● plural noun (treated as sing.) a game in which small plastic counters are flicked into a central receptacle, using a larger counter.
– ORIGIN originally denoting an unlicensed public house, also a game of dominoes: of unknown origin.

tide ● noun **1** the alternate rising and falling of the sea due to the attraction of the moon and sun. **2** a powerful surge of feeling or trend of events. ● verb (**tide over**) help (someone) through a difficult period.
– DERIVATIVES **tidal** adjective.
– ORIGIN Old English, 'time, period, era'.

-tide ● combining form **1** literary denoting a specified time or season: *springtide*. **2** denoting a festival of the Christian Church: *Shrovetide*.

tideline ● noun a line left or reached by the sea on a shore at the highest point of a tide.

tidemark ● noun **1** a tideline. **2** Brit. a grimy mark left around the inside of a bath or washbasin at the level reached by the water.

tidewater ● noun water brought or affected by tides.

tideway ● noun a channel in which a tide runs.

tidings ● plural noun literary news; information.
– ORIGIN Old English.

tidy ● adjective (**tidier**, **tidiest**) **1** arranged neatly and in order. **2** inclined to keep oneself and one's possessions neat and in order. **3** informal (of an amount) considerable. ● noun (pl. **tidies**) **1** (also **tidy-up**) an act or spell of tidying. **2** a receptacle for holding small objects. ● verb (**tidies**, **tidied**) **1** (often **tidy up**) make tidy. **2** (**tidy away**) put away for the sake of tidiness.
– DERIVATIVES **tidily** adverb **tidiness** noun.

– ORIGIN originally in the sense 'timely, opportune': from TIDE.

tie ● verb (**tying**) **1** attach or fasten with string, cord, etc. **2** form into a knot or bow. **3** restrict or limit to a particular situation or place. **4** connect; link. **5** achieve the same score or ranking as another competitor. **6** hold together by a crosspiece or tie. **7** Music unite (written notes) by a tie. ● noun (pl. **ties**) **1** a thing that ties. **2** a strip of material worn beneath a collar, tied in a knot at the front. **3** a result in a game or match in which two or more competitors have tied. **4** Brit. a sports match in which the winners proceed to the next round of the competition. **5** Cricket a game in which the scores are level and both sides have completed their innings. Compare with DRAW. **6** a rod or beam holding parts of a structure together. **7** Music a curved line above or below two notes of the same pitch indicating that they are to be played for the combined duration of their time values.
– PHRASES **tie down** restrict to a particular situation or place. **tie in** be or cause to be in harmony with something. **tie up 1** restrict the movement of (someone) by binding their limbs or binding them to something. **2** bring to a satisfactory conclusion. **3** informal occupy (someone) to the exclusion of other activity. **4** invest or reserve (capital) so that it is not immediately available for use.
– ORIGIN Old English.

tie-back ● noun a decorative strip of fabric or cord used for holding an open curtain back from the window.

tie-break (also **tie-breaker**) ● noun a means of deciding a winner from competitors who have tied.

tied ● adjective **1** Brit. (of accommodation) occupied subject to the tenant's working for its owner. **2** (of a public house) owned and controlled by a brewery.

tie-dye ● noun a method of producing textile patterns by tying parts of the fabric to shield it from the dye.

tie-in ● noun **1** a connection or association. **2** a product produced to take commercial advantage of a related work in another medium.

tiepin ● noun an ornamental pin for holding a tie in place.

tier ● noun **1** one of a series of rows or levels placed one above and behind the other. **2** a level or grade within a hierarchy.
– DERIVATIVES **tiered** adjective.
– ORIGIN French *tire* 'sequence, order'.

tierce /teerss/ ● noun another term for TERCE.

tiercel /teers'l/ ● noun variant spelling of TERCEL.

tie-up ● noun a link or connection.

TIFF ● abbreviation Computing tagged image file format.

tiff ● noun informal a trivial quarrel.
– ORIGIN probably dialect.

tiffin ● noun (in India) a light midday meal.

Thesaurus

ticklish ● adjective DIFFICULT, problematic, tricky, delicate, sensitive, awkward, prickly, thorny, tough; vexed; *informal* sticky.

tide ● noun **1** *ships come up the river with the tide* TIDAL FLOW, ebb and flow, tidewater, ebb, current. **2** *the tide of history* COURSE, movement, direction, trend, current, drift, run, turn, tendency, tenor.
– PHRASES **tide someone over** SUSTAIN, keep someone going, keep someone's head above water, see someone through; keep the wolf from the door; help out, assist, aid.

t

tidings ● plural noun *(poetic/literary)* NEWS, information, intelligence, word, reports, notification, communication, the latest; *informal* info, the low down.

tidy ● adjective **1** *a tidy room* NEAT, neat and tidy, as neat as a new pin, orderly, well ordered, in (good) order, well kept, shipshape (and Bristol fashion), in apple-pie order, immaculate, spick and span, uncluttered, straight, trim, spruce. **2** *he's a very tidy person* NEAT, trim, spruce, dapper, well groomed, well turned out; organized, well organized, methodical, meticulous; fastidious; *informal* natty. **3** *(informal) a tidy sum* LARGE, sizeable, considerable, substantial, generous, significant, appreciable, handsome, respectable, decent, goodly; *informal* not to be sneezed at.
– OPPOSITES messy.
● verb **1** *I'd better tidy up the living room* PUT IN ORDER, clear up, sort out, straighten (up), clean up, spruce up. **2** *she tidied herself up in the bathroom* GROOM ONESELF, spruce oneself up, freshen oneself up, smarten oneself up; *informal* titivate oneself.

tie ● verb **1** *they tied Max to a chair* BIND, tie up, tether, hitch, strap, truss, fetter, rope, chain, make fast, moor, lash, attach, fasten, fix, secure, join, connect, link, couple. **2** *he bent to tie his shoelaces* DO UP, lace, knot. **3** *women can feel tied by childcare responsibilities* RESTRICT, restrain, limit, tie down, constrain, trammel, confine, cramp, hamper, handicap, hamstring, shackle, encumber, inhibit; cramp someone's style. **4** *a pay deal tied to a productivity agreement* LINK, connect, couple, relate, join, marry; make conditional on, bind up with. **5** *they tied for second place* DRAW, be equal, be even, be neck and neck.
● noun **1** *he tightened the ties of his robe* LACE, string, cord, fastening, fastener. **2** *a collar and tie* NECKTIE, bow tie, string tie; *Brit.* bootlace tie. **3** *family ties* BOND, connection, link, relationship, attachment, affiliation, allegiance, friendship; kinship, interdependence. **4** *pets can be a tremendous tie* RESTRICTION, constraint, curb, limitation, restraint, hindrance, encumbrance, handicap; obligation, commitment. **5** *there was a tie for first place* DRAW, dead heat, deadlock. **6** *(Brit.) Turkey's World Cup tie against Holland* MATCH, game, contest, fixture, event.
– PHRASES **tie someone down** *she was afraid of being tied down.* See TIE verb sense 3. **tie in** BE CONSISTENT, tally, agree, be in agreement, accord, concur, fit in, harmonize, be in tune, dovetail, correspond, match; *informal* square; *N. Amer. informal* jibe. **tie someone/something up 1** *robbers tied her up and ransacked her home* BIND, bind hand and foot, fasten together, truss (up), fetter, chain up. **2** *(informal) he is tied up in meetings all morning* OCCUPY, engage, keep busy. **3** *they were anxious to tie up the contract* FINALIZE, conclude, complete, finish off, seal, set the seal on, settle, secure, clinch; *informal* wrap up.

tie-in ● noun CONNECTION, link, association, correlation, tie-up, interrelation, relationship, relation, interconnection; parallel, similarity.

– ORIGIN apparently from dialect *tiffing* 'sipping', of unknown origin.
tig ● noun & verb chiefly Brit. another term for TAG².
– ORIGIN perhaps a variant of TICK¹.
tiger ● noun **1** a large solitary cat with a yellow-brown coat striped with black, native to the forests of Asia. **2** (also **tiger economy**) a dynamic economy of one of the smaller East Asian countries, especially that of Singapore, Taiwan, or South Korea.
– ORIGIN Greek *tigris*.
tiger lily ● noun a tall Asian lily which has orange flowers spotted with black or purple.
tiger moth ● noun a moth which has boldly spotted and streaked wings and a hairy caterpillar.
tiger prawn (also **tiger shrimp**) ● noun a large edible prawn marked with dark bands.
tight ● adjective **1** fixed, closed, or fastened firmly. **2** (of clothes) close-fitting. **3** well sealed against something such as water or air. **4** (of a rope, fabric, or surface) stretched so as to leave no slack. **5** (of an area or space) allowing little room for manoeuvre. **6** (of people or things) closely or densely packed together. **7** (of an organization or group) disciplined and well coordinated. **8** (of a form of control) strictly imposed: *security was tight*. **9** (of money or time) limited. **10** (of a bend, turn, or angle) changing direction sharply. **11** informal miserly. **12** informal drunk. ● adverb very firmly, closely, or tensely.
– PHRASES **a tight ship** a strictly controlled and disciplined organization or operation. **a tight corner** (or **spot**) a difficult situation.
– DERIVATIVES **tighten** verb **tightly** adverb **tightness** noun.
– ORIGIN originally in the sense 'healthy, vigorous', later 'firm, solid': probably of Germanic origin.
tight-fisted ● adjective informal not willing to spend or give much money; miserly.
tight-knit (also **tightly knit**) ● adjective (of a group of people) bound together by strong relationships and common interests.
tight-lipped ● adjective with the lips firmly closed, as a sign of suppressed emotion or unwillingness to divulge information.
tightrope ● noun a rope or wire stretched high above the ground, on which acrobats balance.
tights ● plural noun a close-fitting garment made of a knitted yarn, covering the legs, hips, and bottom.
tightwad ● noun informal, chiefly N. Amer. a miserly person.
tigress ● noun a female tiger.
tike ● noun variant spelling of TYKE.
tikka /tikkə, teekə/ ● noun an Indian dish of small pieces of meat or vegetables marinated in a spice mixture.
– ORIGIN Punjabi.
tilapia /tilaypiə/ ● noun an African freshwater fish, introduced in other parts of the world for food.
– ORIGIN Latin genus name.
tilde /tildə/ ● noun an accent (˜) placed over Spanish *n* when pronounced *ny* (as in *señor*) or Portuguese *a* or *o* when nasalized (as in *São Paulo*).
– ORIGIN Spanish, from Latin *titulus* 'inscription, title'.
tile ● noun **1** a thin square or rectangular piece of baked clay, concrete, cork, etc., used for covering roofs, floors, or walls. **2** a thin, flat piece used in Scrabble, mah-jong, and other games. ● verb cover with tiles.
– PHRASES **on the tiles** informal, chiefly Brit. having a lively night out.
– DERIVATIVES **tiler** noun.
– ORIGIN Latin *tegula*.
tiling ● noun **1** the action of laying tiles. **2** a surface covered by tiles.
till¹ ● preposition & conjunction less formal way of saying UNTIL.
– ORIGIN Old English (not a shortened form of *until*).
till² ● noun a cash register or drawer for money in a shop, bank, or restaurant.
– ORIGIN originally in the sense 'drawer or compartment for valuables': of unknown origin.
till³ ● verb prepare and cultivate (land) for crops.
– DERIVATIVES **tillable** adjective **tillage** noun **tiller** noun.
– ORIGIN Old English, 'strive for, obtain by effort'; ultimately related to TILL¹.
till⁴ ● noun Geology boulder clay or other unstratified sediment deposited by melting glaciers or ice sheets.
– ORIGIN of unknown origin.
tiller ● noun a horizontal bar fitted to the head of a boat's rudder post and used for steering.
– ORIGIN Old French *telier* 'weaver's beam, stock of a crossbow', from Latin *tela* 'web'.
tilt ● verb **1** move into a sloping position. **2** incline towards a particular opinion: *he is tilting towards a new economic course.* **3** (**tilt at**) historical (in jousting) thrust at with a lance or other weapon. ● noun **1** a tilting position or movement. **2** an inclination or bias. **3** historical a joust. **4** (**tilt at**) an attempt at (winning something).
– PHRASES **(at) full tilt** with maximum speed or force. **tilt at windmills** attack imaginary enemies. [ORIGIN with allusion to the story of Don Quixote tilting at windmills, believing they were giants.]
– DERIVATIVES **tilter** noun.
– ORIGIN perhaps related to an Old English word meaning 'unsteady', or perhaps of Scandinavian origin.

Thesaurus

tier ● noun **1** *tiers of empty seats* ROW, rank, bank, line; layer, level. **2** *the most senior tier of management* GRADE, gradation, echelon, rung on the ladder.
tiff ● noun *(informal)* QUARREL, squabble, argument, disagreement, fight, falling-out, difference of opinion, dispute, wrangle, altercation, contretemps, disputation, shouting match; *informal* slanging match, run-in, spat, set-to; *Brit. informal* barney, row, bust-up.
tight ● adjective **1** *a tight grip* FIRM, fast, secure, fixed, clenched. **2** *the rope was pulled tight* TAUT, rigid, stiff, tense, stretched, strained. **3** *tight jeans* TIGHT-FITTING, close-fitting, narrow, figure-hugging, skintight; *informal* sprayed on. **4** *a tight mass of fibres* COMPACT, compacted, compressed, dense, solid. **5** *a tight space* SMALL, tiny, narrow, limited, restricted, confined, cramped, constricted, uncomfortable. **6** *the joint will be perfectly tight against petrol leaks* IMPERVIOUS, impenetrable, sealed, sound, hermetic; watertight, airtight. **7** *tight limits on the use of pesticides* STRICT, rigorous, stringent, tough, rigid, firm, uncompromising. **8** *he's in a tight spot* DIFFICULT, tricky, delicate, awkward, problematic, worrying, precarious; *informal* sticky; *Brit. informal* dodgy. **9** *a tight piece of writing* SUCCINCT, concise, pithy, incisive, crisp, condensed, well structured, to the point. **10** *a tight race* CLOSE, even, evenly matched, well matched; hard-fought, neck and neck. **11** *money is a bit tight just now* LIMITED, restricted, in short supply, scarce, depleted, diminished, low, inadequate, insufficient. **12** *(informal) he's tight with his money* MEAN, miserly, parsimonious, niggardly, close-fisted, penny-pinching, cheese-paring, Scrooge-like, close; *informal* stingy, tight-fisted; *N. Amer. informal* cheap; *formal* penurious; *archaic* near. **13** *(informal) he came home tight from the pub.* See DRUNK adjective.
– OPPOSITES slack, loose, generous.
tighten ● verb **1** *I tightened up the screws* MAKE TIGHTER, make fast, screw up. **2** *he tightened his grip* STRENGTHEN, make stronger, harden. **3** *she tightened the rope* TAUTEN, make/draw taut, make/draw tight, stretch, strain, stiffen, tense. **4** *he tightened his lips* NARROW, constrict, contract, compress, screw up, pucker, purse; *N. Amer.* squinch. **5** *security in the area has been tightened up* INCREASE, make stricter, toughen up, heighten, scale up.
– OPPOSITES loosen, slacken, relax.
tight-fisted ● adjective *(informal)* MEAN, miserly, parsimonious, niggardly, close-fisted, penny-pinching, cheese-paring, Scrooge-like, close; *informal* stingy, tight; *N. Amer. informal* cheap; *formal* penurious; *archaic* near.
– OPPOSITES generous.
tight-lipped ● adjective RETICENT, uncommunicative, unforthcoming, playing one's cards close to one's chest, close-mouthed, silent, taciturn; *informal* mum.
– OPPOSITES forthcoming.
till¹ ● preposition & conjunction *he stayed in bed till 7* | *I'll stay here till you get back.* See UNTIL senses 1, 2.
till² ● noun *she counted the money in the till* CASH REGISTER, cash box, cash drawer, strongbox; checkout, cash desk.
till³ ● verb *he went back to tilling the land* CULTIVATE, work, farm, plough, dig, turn over, prepare.
tilt ● verb **1** *the ground seemed to tilt* SLOPE, tip, lean, list, bank, slant, incline, pitch, cant, careen, angle. **2** *(historical) he tilts at his prey* CHARGE, rush, run; lunge, thrust, jab. **3** *(historical) knights tilting at a tournament* JOUST, tourney, enter the lists; contend, spar, fight.
● noun **1** *a tilt of some 45°* SLOPE, list, camber, gradient, bank, slant, incline, pitch, cant, bevel, angle. **2** *(historical) knights would*

t

tilth ● noun **1** cultivation of land; tillage. **2** the condition of tilled soil.
– ORIGIN Old English, related to TILL[3].

timbale /tambaal/ ● noun a dish of finely minced meat or fish cooked with other ingredients in a pastry shell or in a mould.
– ORIGIN French, 'drum'.

timber ● noun **1** wood prepared for use in building and carpentry. **2** informal, chiefly US suitable quality or character: *she is hailed as presidential timber.* ● exclamation used to warn that a tree is about to fall after being cut.
– DERIVATIVES **timbered** adjective **timbering** noun.
– ORIGIN Old English, 'a building', also 'building material'.

timberline ● noun chiefly N. Amer. another term for TREELINE.

timber wolf ● noun a wolf of a large variety found mainly in northern North America, with grey brindled fur.

timbre /tambər/ ● noun the character or quality of a musical sound or voice as distinct from its pitch and intensity.
– ORIGIN French, from Greek *tumpanon* 'drum'.

timbrel /timbrəl/ ● noun archaic a tambourine or similar instrument.
– ORIGIN perhaps from Old French and related to TIMBRE.

time ● noun **1** the indefinite continued progress of existence and events in the past, present, and future, regarded as a whole. **2** a point of time as measured in hours and minutes past midnight or noon. **3** the favourable or appropriate moment to do something. **4** (**a time**) an indefinite period. **5** (also **times**) a portion of time characterized by particular events or circumstances: *Victorian times.* **6** (**one's time**) a period regarded as characteristic of a particular stage of one's life. **7** the length of time taken to complete an activity. **8** time as allotted, available, or used: *a waste of time.* **9** an instance of something happening or being done. **10** Brit. the moment at which the opening hours of a public house end. **11** informal a prison sentence. **12** an apprenticeship. **13** the normal rate of pay for time spent working. **14** (**times**) (following a number) expressing multiplication. **15** the rhythmic pattern or tempo of a piece of music. ● verb **1** arrange a time for. **2** perform at a particular time. **3** measure the time taken by. **4** (**time out**) Computing (of a computer or a program) cancel (an operation) automatically because a predefined interval of time has passed. **5** (**times**) informal multiply (a number).
– PHRASES **about time** conveying that something should have happened earlier. **all the time 1** at all times. **2** very frequently or regularly. **at the same time 1** simultaneously. **2** nevertheless. **at a time** separately in the specified groups or numbers. **behind the times** not aware of or using the latest ideas or techniques. **for the time being** until some other arrangement is made. **have no time for 1** be unable or unwilling to spend time on. **2** dislike or disapprove of. **in time 1** not late. **2** eventually. **3** in accordance with the appropriate musical rhythm or tempo. **keep good** (or **bad**) **time 1** (of a clock or watch) record time accurately (or inaccurately). **2** be habitually punctual (or not punctual). **keep time** play or accompany music in time. **on time** punctual; punctually. **pass the time of day** exchange greetings or casual remarks. **time and tide wait for no man** proverb if you don't make use of a favourable opportunity, you may never get the same chance again. **time immemorial** a point of time in the distant past beyond recall or knowledge. **time is money** proverb time is a valuable resource, therefore it's better to do things as quickly as possible. **the time of one's life** a period or occasion of exceptional enjoyment. **time out of mind** another way of saying **time immemorial**. **time will tell** the truth about something will be established in the future.
– ORIGIN Old English; related to TIDE, which it superseded in temporal senses.

time-and-motion study ● noun an evaluation of the efficiency of an industrial or other operation.

time bomb ● noun a bomb designed to explode at a preset time.

time capsule ● noun a container storing a selection of objects chosen as being typical of the present time, buried for discov-

Thesaurus

take part in a tilt JOUST, tournament, tourney, lists, combat, contest, fight, duel. **3** *another tilt at the European Cup* ATTEMPT, bid; *informal* go, crack, shot.
– PHRASES **(at) full tilt 1** *they charged full tilt down the side of the hill* (AT) FULL SPEED, (at) full pelt, as fast as one's legs can carry one, at a gallop, helter-skelter, headlong, pell-mell, at breakneck speed; *informal* hell for leather, at the double, a mile a minute, like the wind, like a bat out of hell, like a scalded cat, like (greased) lightning; *Brit. informal* like the clappers, at a rate of knots, like billy-o; *N. Amer. informal* lickety-split; *poetic/literary* apace. **2** *the marketing blitz has raged at full tilt for some time now* WITH GREAT FORCE, with full force, full blast, with all the stops out, all out, with a vengeance; *informal* like crazy, like mad.

timber ● noun **1** *houses built of timber* WOOD; *N. Amer.* lumber. **2** *the timbers of wrecked ships* BEAM, spar, plank, batten, lath, board, joist, rafter.

timbre ● noun TONE, sound, sound quality, voice, voice quality, colour, tone colour, tonality, resonance.

time ● noun **1** *what time is it?* HOUR; *dated* o'clock. **2** *late at night was the best time to leave* MOMENT, point (in time), occasion, hour, minute, second, instant, juncture, stage. **3** *he worked there for a time* WHILE, spell, stretch, stint, span, season, interval, period (of time), length of time, duration, run, space, phase, stage, term; *Brit. informal* patch. **4** *the time of the dinosaurs* ERA, age, epoch, period, years, days; generation, date. **5** *I've known a lot of women in my time* LIFETIME, life, life span, days, time on earth, existence, threescore years and ten. **6** *he had been a professional actor in his time* HEYDAY, day, best days/years, prime. **7** *times are hard at the moment* CONDITIONS, circumstances, life, state of affairs, experiences. **8** *tunes in waltz time* RHYTHM, tempo, beat; metre, measure, cadence, pattern.
– RELATED TERMS chronological, temporal.
● verb *the meeting was timed for three o'clock* SCHEDULE, set, set up, arrange, organize, fix, fix up, book, line up, slot in, pre-arrange, timetable, plan; *N. Amer.* slate.
– PHRASES **ahead of time** EARLY, in good time, with time to spare, in advance. **ahead of one's/its time** REVOLUTIONARY, avant-garde, futuristic, innovatory, innovative, trailblazing, pioneering, ground-breaking, advanced. **all the time** CONSTANTLY, the entire time, around the clock, day and night, night and day, {morning, noon, and night}, {day in, day out}, at all times, always, without a break, ceaselessly, endlessly, incessantly, perpetually, permanently, interminably, continuously, continually, eternally, unremittingly, remorselessly, relentlessly; *N. Amer.* without surcease; *informal* 24-7. **at one time** FORMERLY, previously, once, in the past, at one point, once upon a time, time was when, in days/times gone by, in times past, in the (good) old days, long ago; *poetic/literary* in days/times of yore; *archaic* erstwhile, whilom. **at the same time 1** *they arrived at the same time* SIMULTANEOUSLY, at the same instant/moment, together, all together, as a group, at once, at one and the same time; in unison, in concert, in chorus, as one. **2** *I can't really explain it, but at the same time I'm not convinced* NONETHELESS, even so, however, but, still, yet, though; in spite of that, despite that, be that as it may, for all that, that said; notwithstanding, regardless, anyway, anyhow; *informal* still and all. **at times** OCCASIONALLY, sometimes, from time to time, now and then, every so often, once in a while, on occasion, off and on, at intervals, periodically, sporadically. **behind time** LATE, behind, behind schedule, behindhand, running late, overdue. **behind the times** OLD-FASHIONED, out of date, outmoded, outdated, dated, old, passé; *informal* square, not with it, out of the ark; *N. Amer. informal* horse-and-buggy, clunky. **for the time being** FOR NOW, for the moment, for the present, in the interim, for the nonce, in/for the meantime, in the meanwhile, for a short time, briefly; temporarily, provisionally, pro tem; *informal* for the minute. **from time to time** OCCASIONALLY, sometimes, now and then, every so often, once in a while, on occasion, off and on, at intervals, periodically, sporadically. **in no time** (VERY) SOON, in a second, in a minute, in a moment, in a trice, in a flash, shortly, any second, any minute (now); *N. Amer.* momentarily; *informal* in a sec, in a jiffy, in two shakes (of a lamb's tail), before you can say Jack Robinson; *Brit. informal* in a tick, in two ticks, in a mo; *N. Amer. informal* in a snap; *dated* directly. **in good time** PUNCTUALLY, on time, early, with time to spare, ahead of time/schedule. **in time 1** *I came back in time for the party* EARLY ENOUGH, in good time, punctually, on time, not too late, with time to spare, on schedule. **2** *in time, she forgot about it* EVENTUALLY, in the end, in due course, by and by, finally; one day, some day, sometime, sooner or later. **many a time** FREQUENTLY, regularly, often, very often, all the time, habitually, customarily, routinely; again and again, time and again, over and over again, repeatedly, recurrently, continually; *N. Amer.* oftentimes; *poetic/literary* oft, oft-times. **on time** PUNCTUALLY, in good time, to/on schedule, when expected; *informal* on the dot, bang on time. **time after time** REPEATEDLY, frequently, often, again and again,

ery in the future.

time frame ● noun a specified period of time.

time-honoured ● adjective (of a custom or tradition) respected or valued because it has existed for a long time.

timekeeper ● noun **1** a person who records the amount of time taken by a process or activity. **2** a person regarded in terms of their punctuality. **3** a watch or clock regarded in terms of its accuracy.
– DERIVATIVES **timekeeping** noun.

time-lapse ● adjective (of a photographic technique) taking a sequence of frames at set intervals to record changes that take place slowly over time.

timeless ● adjective not affected by the passage of time or changes in fashion.
– DERIVATIVES **timelessly** adverb **timelessness** noun.

time lock ● noun a lock fitted with a device that prevents it from being unlocked until a set time.

timely ● adjective done or occurring at a favourable or appropriate time.
– DERIVATIVES **timeliness** noun.

time machine ● noun (in science fiction) a machine capable of time travel.

time off ● noun time for rest or recreation away from one's usual work or studies.

timeous /tīməss/ ● adjective chiefly Scottish in good time; sufficiently early.

time out ● noun chiefly N. Amer. **1** time for rest or recreation. **2** (**timeout**) a brief break from play in a game or sport.

timepiece ● noun an instrument for measuring time; a clock or watch.

timer ● noun **1** an automatic mechanism for activating a device at a preset time. **2** a person or device that records the amount of time taken by a process or activity. **3** indicating how many times someone has done something: *a first-timer*.

time-release ● adjective (of a drug preparation) releasing an active substance gradually.

timescale ● noun the time allowed for or taken by a process or sequence of events.

time-server ● noun **1** a person who changes their views to suit the prevailing circumstances or fashion. **2** a person who makes very little effort at work because they are waiting to leave or retire.

timeshare ● noun an arrangement whereby joint owners use a property as a holiday home at different specified times.

time sheet ● noun a piece of paper for recording the number of hours worked.

time signature ● noun Music an indication of rhythm following a clef.

times table ● noun informal a multiplication table.

time switch ● noun a switch automatically activated at a preset time.

timetable ● noun a list or plan of times at which events are scheduled to take place. ● verb schedule to take place at a particular time.

time travel ● noun (in science fiction) travel through time into the past or the future.

time trial ● noun (in various sports) a test of a competitor's individual speed over a set distance.

time warp ● noun an imaginary distortion of space in relation to time whereby people or objects of one period can be moved to another.

time-wasting ● noun the tactic of slowing down play towards the end of a match to prevent the opposition scoring.

time-worn ● adjective impaired or made less striking as a result of age or long use.

timid ● adjective (**timider**, **timidest**) lacking in courage or confidence.
– DERIVATIVES **timidity** noun **timidly** adverb **timidness** noun.
– ORIGIN Latin *timidus*, from *timere* 'to fear'.

timing ● noun **1** the choice, judgement, or control of when something should be done. **2** a particular time when something happens.

Timorese /teemoreez/ ● noun (pl. same) a person from Timor, an island in the southern Malay Archipelago. ● adjective relating to Timor.

timorous ● adjective lacking in courage or confidence; nervous.
– DERIVATIVES **timorously** adverb **timorousness** noun.
– ORIGIN Latin *timorosus*, from *timor* 'fear'.

timothy ● noun a grass which is widely grown for grazing and hay.
– ORIGIN named after the American farmer *Timothy* Hanson, who introduced it to Carolina from New York (*c.*1720).

timpani /timpəni/ (also **tympani**) ● plural noun kettledrums.
– DERIVATIVES **timpanist** noun.
– ORIGIN Italian, from Latin *tympanum* 'drum'.

tin ● noun **1** a silvery-white metallic chemical element. **2** a lidded airtight container made of tinplate or aluminium. **3** chiefly Brit. a sealed tinplate or aluminium container for preserving food; a can. **4** an open metal container for baking food. ● verb (**tinned**, **tinning**) **1** cover with a thin layer of tin. **2** (**tinned**) chiefly Brit. preserved in a tin.
– PHRASES **have a tin ear** informal be tone-deaf.
– ORIGIN Old English.

tinamou /tinnəmoo/ ● noun a grouse-like tropical American bird related to the rhea.
– ORIGIN Carib.

tincture /tingkchər/ ● noun **1** a medicine made by dissolving a drug in alcohol. **2** a slight trace. **3** Heraldry any of the conventional colours used in coats of arms. ● verb (**be tinctured**) be tinged or flavoured with a slight trace of.
– ORIGIN Latin *tinctura* 'dyeing'.

tinder ● noun dry, flammable material used for lighting a fire.
– ORIGIN Old English.

tinderbox ● noun historical a box containing tinder, flint, a steel, and other items for kindling fires.

tine /tīn/ ● noun a prong or sharp point.
– DERIVATIVES **tined** adjective.
– ORIGIN Old English.

tinea /tinniə/ ● noun technical term for RINGWORM.
– ORIGIN Latin, 'worm'.

tinfoil ● noun metal foil used for covering or wrapping food.

ting ● noun a sharp, clear ringing sound. ● verb emit a ting.
– ORIGIN imitative.

tinge ● verb (**tinging** or **tingeing**) (often **be tinged**) **1** colour slightly. **2** impart a small amount of a quality to: *a visit tinged with sadness.* ● noun a slight trace of a colour, feeling, or quality.
– ORIGIN Latin *tingere* 'to dip or colour'.

Thesaurus

t

over and over (again), time and (time) again, many times, many a time; persistently, recurrently, constantly, continually; *N. Amer.* oftentimes; *poetic/literary* oft, oft-times.

time-honoured ● adjective TRADITIONAL, established, age-old, long-established, long-standing, long-lived, enduring, lasting, tried and tested.

timeless ● adjective LASTING, enduring, classic, ageless, permanent, perennial, abiding, unfailing, unchanging, never-changing, changeless, unfading, unending, undying, deathless, immortal, eternal, everlasting, immutable.
– OPPOSITES ephemeral.

timely ● adjective OPPORTUNE, well timed, at the right time, convenient, appropriate, expedient, seasonable, felicitous.
– OPPOSITES ill-timed.

timetable ● noun *a bus timetable | I have a very full timetable* SCHEDULE, programme, agenda, calendar; list, itinerary.
● verb *German lessons were timetabled on Wednesday* SCHEDULE, set, arrange, organize, fix, time, line up; *N. Amer.* slate.

time-worn ● adjective **1** *the carpet was old and time-worn* WORN OUT, worn, well worn, old, tattered, battered, dog-eared, shabby, having seen better days; *informal* tatty. **2** *time-worn faces* OLD, aged, weathered, lined, wrinkled, hoary. **3** *a time-worn aphorism* HACKNEYED, trite, banal, platitudinous, clichéd, stock, conventional, unoriginal, overused, overworked, tired, stale; *informal* old hat.
– OPPOSITES new, fresh.

timid ● adjective EASILY FRIGHTENED, fearful, afraid, faint-hearted, timorous, nervous, scared, frightened, cowardly, pusillanimous, lily-livered, spineless; shy, diffident, self-effacing; *informal* wimpish, wimpy, chicken, gutless.
– OPPOSITES bold.

timorous ● adjective. See TIMID.

tincture ● noun **1** *tincture of iodine* SOLUTION, suspension, infusion, elixir. **2** *a tincture of bitterness* TRACE, note, tinge, touch, suggestion, hint, bit, element, suspicion, soupçon.

tinge ● verb **1** *a mass of white blossom tinged with pink* TINT, colour, stain, shade, wash. **2** *his optimism is tinged with realism* IN-

tingle ● noun a slight prickling or stinging sensation. ● verb experience or cause to experience a tingle.
– DERIVATIVES **tingly** adjective.
– ORIGIN perhaps a variant of TINKLE.

tin god ● noun **1** a person who is pompous and self-important. **2** an object of unjustified veneration or respect.

tin hat ● noun informal, chiefly Brit. a soldier's steel helmet.

tinker ● noun **1** a travelling mender of pots, kettles, etc. **2** Brit., chiefly derogatory a gypsy or other person living in a travelling community. **3** Brit. informal a mischievous child. **4** an act of tinkering with something. ● verb (**tinker with**) attempt to repair or improve in a casual manner.
– PHRASES **not give a tinker's curse** informal not care at all.
– DERIVATIVES **tinkerer** noun.
– ORIGIN of unknown origin.

tinkle ● verb **1** make or cause to make a light, clear ringing sound. **2** informal urinate. ● noun **1** a tinkling sound. **2** informal an act of urinating.
– DERIVATIVES **tinkly** adjective.
– ORIGIN imitative.

tinnitus /tinītəss, tinnitəss/ ● noun Medicine ringing or buzzing in the ears.
– ORIGIN Latin, from *tinnire* 'to ring, tinkle'.

tinny ● adjective **1** having a thin, metallic sound. **2** made of thin or poor-quality metal. **3** having an unpleasantly metallic taste. **4** Austral./NZ informal lucky. [ORIGIN from *tin* in the sense 'luck', literally 'money, cash'.] ● noun (pl. **tinnies**) Austral./NZ informal a can of beer.
– DERIVATIVES **tinnily** adverb **tinniness** noun.

tin-opener ● noun chiefly Brit. a tool for opening tins of food.

tinplate ● noun sheet steel or iron coated with tin. ● verb coat with tin.
– DERIVATIVES **tin-plated** adjective.

tinpot ● adjective informal of inferior quality; worthless.

tinsel ● noun **1** a form of decoration consisting of thin strips of shiny metal foil attached to a length of thread. **2** superficial attractiveness or glamour.
– DERIVATIVES **tinselled** adjective **tinselly** adjective.
– ORIGIN Old French *estincele* 'spark', from Latin *scintilla*.

Tinseltown ● noun derogatory the superficially glamorous world of Hollywood and its film industry.

tinsmith ● noun a person who makes or repairs articles of tin or tinplate.

tinsnips ● plural noun a pair of clippers for cutting sheet metal.

tint ● noun **1** a shade or variety of colour. **2** a dye for colouring the hair. **3** Printing an area of faint colour printed as a half-tone. **4** a trace of something. ● verb **1** colour slightly; tinge. **2** dye (hair) with a tint.
– ORIGIN Latin *tinctus* 'dyeing', from *tingere* 'to dye or colour'.

tintinnabulation /tintinabyoolaysh'n/ ● noun a ringing or tinkling sound.
– ORIGIN from Latin *tintinnabulum* 'tinkling bell'.

tin whistle ● noun a small flute-like instrument made from a thin metal tube, with six finger holes of varying size.

tiny ● adjective (**tinier**, **tiniest**) very small. ● noun (pl. **tinies**) informal a very young child.
– DERIVATIVES **tinily** adverb **tininess** noun.
– ORIGIN of unknown origin.

-tion ● suffix forming nouns of action, condition, etc. such as *completion*.
– ORIGIN from Latin.

tip[1] ● noun **1** the pointed or rounded extremity of something slender or tapering. **2** a small part fitted to the end of an object. ● verb (**tipped**, **tipping**) attach to or cover the tip of.
– PHRASES **on the tip of one's tongue** almost but not quite spoken or coming to mind.
– DERIVATIVES **tipped** adjective.
– ORIGIN Old Norse.

tip[2] ● verb (**tipped**, **tipping**) **1** overbalance so as to fall or turn over. **2** be or put in a sloping position. **3** empty out (the contents of a container) by holding it at an angle. **4** (**it tips down**, **it is tipping down**, etc.) Brit. informal rain heavily. **5** strike or touch lightly. ● noun **1** Brit. a place where rubbish is left. **2** informal a dirty or untidy place.
– PHRASES **tip one's hand** N. Amer. informal reveal one's intentions inadvertently. **tip one's hat** raise or touch one's hat as a greeting or mark of respect.
– ORIGIN perhaps Scandinavian.

tip[3] ● noun **1** a small sum of money given as a reward for services rendered. **2** a piece of practical advice. **3** a prediction or piece of expert information about the likely winner of a race or contest. ● verb (**tipped**, **tipping**) **1** give a tip to. **2** Brit. predict as likely to win or achieve something. **3** (**tip off**) informal give (someone) confidential information.
– PHRASES **tip the wink** Brit. informal secretly give confidential information to.
– ORIGIN probably from TIP[1].

tipi ● noun variant spelling of TEPEE.

tip-off ● noun informal a piece of confidential information.

tipper ● noun **1** a truck having a rear platform which can be raised at its front end, thus enabling a load to be discharged. **2** a person who leaves a tip of a specified amount: *a good tipper*.

tippet ● noun **1** a woman's fur cape or woollen shawl. **2** a ceremonial garment worn by the clergy.
– ORIGIN probably from an Old French derivative of TIP[1].

Thesaurus

FLUENCE, affect, touch, flavour, colour, modify.
● noun **1** *the light had a blue tinge to it* TINT, colour, shade, tone, hue. **2** *a tinge of cynicism* TRACE, note, touch, suggestion, hint, bit, scintilla, savour, flavour, element, streak, vein, suspicion, soupçon, tincture.

tingle ● verb *her flesh still tingled from the shock* PRICKLE, sting; tremble, quiver, shiver.
● noun *she felt a tingle of anticipation* PRICKLING, tingling, pricking, sting, stinging; tremor, thrill, quiver, shiver; goose pimples; N. Amer. goosebumps.

tinker ● verb *a workman was tinkering with the engine* FIDDLE WITH, adjust, try to mend, play about with; tamper with, interfere with, mess about with, meddle with; informal rearrange the deckchairs on the Titanic; Brit. informal muck about with.

tinkle ● verb **1** *the bell tinkled* RING, jingle, jangle, chime, peal, ding, ping. **2** *cool water tinkled in the stone fountain* SPLASH, purl, babble, burble; poetic/literary plash.
● noun **1** *the tinkle of the doorbell* RING, chime, peal, ding, ping, jingle, jangle, tintinnabulation. **2** *the faint tinkle of water* SPLASH, purl, babble, burble; poetic/literary plash. **3** (Brit. informal) *I'll give them a tinkle* TELEPHONE CALL, phone call, call; informal buzz; Brit. informal ring, bell.

tinny ● adjective **1** *tinny music* JANGLY, jangling, jingling, jingly. **2** *a tinny little car* CHEAP, cheapjack, poor-quality, inferior, low-grade, gimcrack, shoddy, jerry-built; informal tacky, tatty, rubbishy.

tinsel ● noun *the tinsel of Hollywood* OSTENTATION, showiness, show, glitter, flamboyance, gaudiness; attractiveness, glamour; informal flashiness, glitz, glitziness, razzle-dazzle, razzmatazz.
● adjective *tinsel stardom* OSTENTATIOUS, showy, glittering, flamboyant, gaudy; informal flash, flashy, over the top, OTT, glitzy, ritzy; N. Amer. informal superfly.

tint ● noun **1** *the sky was taking on an apricot tint* SHADE, colour, tone, hue, tinge, cast, tincture, flush, blush. **2** *a hair tint* DYE, colourant, colouring, wash; highlights, lowlights.

tiny ● adjective MINUTE, minuscule, microscopic, very small, little, mini, diminutive, miniature, scaled down, baby, toy, dwarf, pygmy, Lilliputian; Scottish wee; informal teeny, teeny-weeny, teensy, teensy-weensy, itsy-bitsy, eensy, eensy-weensy, tiddly, pint-sized; Brit. informal titchy; N. Amer. informal little-bitty.
– OPPOSITES huge.

tip[1] ● noun **1** *the tip of the spear* POINT, end, extremity, head, sharp end, spike, prong, tine, nib. **2** *the tips of the mountains* PEAK, point, top, summit, apex, crown, crest, pinnacle. **3** *the sticks have tips fitted to protect them* CAP, cover, ferrule.
● verb *mountains tipped with snow* CAP, top, crown.

tip[2] ● verb **1** *the boat tipped over* OVERTURN, turn over, topple (over), fall (over); keel over, capsize, turn turtle; Nautical pitchpole. **2** *a whale could tip over a small boat* UPSET, overturn, topple over, turn over, knock over, push over, upend, capsize; informal roll; archaic overset. **3** *the car tipped to one side* LEAN, tilt, list, slope, bank, slant, incline, pitch, cant, heel, careen. **4** *she tipped the water into the trough* POUR, empty, drain, unload, dump, discharge; decant.
● noun (Brit.) *rubbish must be taken to the tip* DUMP, rubbish dump; Canadian nuisance grounds.

tip[3] ● noun **1** *a generous tip* GRATUITY, baksheesh; present, gift, reward; Brit. informal dropsy. **2** *useful tips* PIECE OF ADVICE, suggestion, word of advice, pointer, recommendation; clue, hint; informal wrinkle, tip-off.

t

Tipp-Ex (also **Tippex**) • noun Brit. trademark a type of correction fluid. • verb delete with correction fluid.
– ORIGIN German, from *tippen* 'to type' and Latin *ex* 'out'.
tipple • verb drink alcohol regularly. • noun informal an alcoholic drink.
tippler • noun a habitual drinker of alcohol.
– ORIGIN of unknown origin.
tippy • adjective N. Amer. inclined to tilt or overturn; unsteady.
tippy-toe • verb informal, chiefly N. Amer. tiptoe.
tipstaff • noun a sheriff's officer; a bailiff.
– ORIGIN from *tipped staff*, a metal-tipped staff carried by a bailiff.
tipster • noun a person who gives tips as to the likely winner of a race or contest.
tipsy • adjective (**tipsier**, **tipsiest**) slightly drunk.
– DERIVATIVES **tipsily** adverb **tipsiness** noun.
– ORIGIN from TIP².
tiptoe • verb (**tiptoes**, **tiptoed**, **tiptoeing**) walk quietly and carefully with one's heels raised and one's weight on the balls of the feet.
– PHRASES **on tiptoe** (or **tiptoes**) with one's heels raised and one's weight on the balls of the feet.
tip-top • adjective of the very best quality; excellent. • noun the highest part or point of excellence.
tirade /tīrayd, ti-/ • noun a long speech of angry criticism or accusation.
– ORIGIN French, from Italian *tirato* 'volley'.
tiramisu /tirrəmisōō/ • noun an Italian dessert consisting of layers of sponge cake soaked in coffee and brandy or liqueur, with powdered chocolate and mascarpone cheese.
– ORIGIN Italian, from *tira mi sù* 'pick me up'.
tire¹ • verb **1** become or cause to become in need of rest or sleep. **2** exhaust the patience or interest of. **3** (**tire of**) become impatient or bored with.
– ORIGIN Old English.
tire² • noun US spelling of TYRE.
tired • adjective **1** in need of sleep or rest; weary. **2** (**tired of**) bored with. **3** (of a statement or idea) boring or uninteresting because overfamiliar..
– PHRASES **tired and emotional** humorous drunk.
– DERIVATIVES **tiredly** adverb **tiredness** noun.
tireless • adjective having or showing great effort or energy.
– DERIVATIVES **tirelessly** adverb **tirelessness** noun.
tiresome • adjective causing one to feel bored or impatient.
– DERIVATIVES **tiresomely** adverb **tiresomeness** noun.
tiro • noun variant spelling of TYRO.
'tis • contraction chiefly literary it is.
tisane /tizan/ • noun a herb tea.
– ORIGIN French.
tissue /tishōō, tisyōō/ • noun **1** any of the distinct types of material of which animals or plants are made, consisting of specialized cells and their products. **2** tissue paper. **3** a piece of absorbent paper used as a disposable handkerchief. **4** delicate gauzy fabric. **5** a web-like structure or network: *a tissue of lies.*
– DERIVATIVES **tissuey** adjective.
– ORIGIN from Old French *tissu* 'woven', from Latin *texere* 'to weave'.
tissue culture • noun Biology & Medicine the growth in an artificial medium of cells derived from living tissue.
tissue paper • noun very thin, soft paper.
tissue type • noun a class of tissues which are immunologically compatible with one another. • verb (**tissue-type**) determine the tissue type of.
tit¹ • noun a titmouse.
– ORIGIN probably Scandinavian.
tit² • noun **1** vulgar slang a woman's breast. **2** Brit. informal a foolish or ineffectual person.
– ORIGIN Old English, 'teat, nipple'.
tit³ • noun (in phrase **tit for tat**) the infliction of an injury or insult in retaliation for one received.
– ORIGIN variant of obsolete *tip for tap*, from TIP².
Titan /tītən/ • noun **1** any of a family of giant gods in Greek mythology. **2** (**titan**) a person or thing of very great strength, intellect, or importance.
titanic • adjective of exceptional strength, size, or power.
– DERIVATIVES **titanically** adverb.
titanium /titayniəm, tī-/ • noun a hard silver-grey metal used in strong, light, corrosion-resistant alloys.
– ORIGIN from TITAN, on the pattern of *uranium.*
titbit (N. Amer. **tidbit**) • noun **1** a small piece of tasty food. **2** a small and particularly interesting item of gossip or information.
– ORIGIN from dialect *tid* 'tender' (of unknown origin) + BIT¹.
titch (also **tich**) • noun Brit. informal a small person.
– ORIGIN from *Little Tich*, stage name of Harry Relph (1868–1928), an English music-hall comedian of small stature, given the nickname because he resembled Arthur Orton, the unsuccessful claimant to the valuable Tichborne estate.
titchy • adjective (**titchier**, **titchiest**) Brit. informal very small.
titer • noun US spelling of TITRE.
titfer • noun Brit. informal a hat.

Thesaurus

tip-off • noun *(informal)* PIECE OF INFORMATION, warning, lead, forewarning; hint, clue; advice, information, notification.
tipple • verb *boys discovered tippling were punished* DRINK ALCOHOL, drink; *informal* booze, wet one's whistle, hit the bottle, take to the bottle; *Brit. informal* bevvy; *N. Amer. informal* bend one's elbow; *archaic* tope.
• noun *(informal) their favourite tipple was claret* ALCOHOLIC DRINK, drink, liquor; *informal* booze, poison.
tippler • noun DRINKER, imbiber; alcoholic, drunk, drunkard, dipsomaniac, inebriate, sot; *informal* boozer, alky, lush, barfly, sponge, dipso, wino, soak; *Austral./NZ informal* hophead; *archaic* toper.
– OPPOSITES teetotaller.
tipsy • adjective MERRY, mellow, slightly drunk; *Brit. informal* tiddly, squiffy.
– OPPOSITES sober.
tirade • noun DIATRIBE, harangue, rant, onslaught, attack, polemic, denunciation, broadside, fulmination, condemnation, censure, criticism, tongue-lashing; *informal* blast; *poetic/literary* philippic.
tire • verb **1** *the ascent grew steeper and he began to tire* GET TIRED, weaken, grow weak, flag, droop. **2** *the journey had tired him* FATIGUE, tire out, exhaust, wear out, drain, weary, wash out, overtire, enervate; *informal* knock out, take it out of, do in, fag out, wear to a frazzle; *Brit. informal* knacker. **3** *they tired of his difficult behaviour* WEARY, get tired, get fed up, get sick, get bored; *informal* have had something up to here.
tired • adjective **1** *you're just tired from travelling* EXHAUSTED, worn out, weary, fatigued, dog-tired, bone-tired, ready to drop, drained, enervated, jaded; *informal* done in, all in, dead beat, shattered, bushed, knocked out, wiped out, bushwhacked; *Brit. informal* knackered, whacked (out), jiggered; *N. Amer. informal* pooped, tuckered out; *Austral./NZ informal* stonkered. **2** *are you tired of having him here?* FED UP WITH, weary of, bored with/by, sick (and tired) of; *informal* up to here with. **3** *tired jokes* HACKNEYED, overused, overworked, worn out, stale, clichéd, hoary, stock, stereotyped, predictable, unimaginative, unoriginal, uninspired, dull, boring, routine; *informal* old hat, corny, played out.
– OPPOSITES energetic, lively, fresh.
tiredness • noun FATIGUE, weariness, exhaustion, enervation, inertia; sleepiness, drowsiness, somnolence.
– OPPOSITES energy.
tireless • adjective VIGOROUS, energetic, industrious, determined, enthusiastic, keen, zealous, spirited, dynamic, dogged, tenacious, persevering, stout, untiring, unwearying, indefatigable, unflagging.
– OPPOSITES lazy.
tiresome • adjective BORING, dull, tedious, wearisome, wearing, uninteresting, uneventful, humdrum; annoying, irritating, trying, irksome, vexatious, troublesome; *informal* aggravating, pesky.
– OPPOSITES interesting, pleasant.
tiring • adjective EXHAUSTING, wearying, taxing, fatiguing, wearing, enervating, draining; hard, heavy, arduous, strenuous, onerous, uphill, demanding, gruelling; *informal* killing, murderous; *Brit. informal* knackering.
tissue • noun **1** *living tissue* MATTER, material, substance; flesh. **2** *a box of tissues* PAPER HANDKERCHIEF, paper towel; *trademark* Kleenex. **3** *a tissue of lies* WEB, network, nexus, complex, mass, set, series, chain.
titanic • adjective HUGE, great, enormous, gigantic, massive, colossal, monumental, mammoth, immense, tremendous, terrific, mighty, stupendous, prodigious, gargantuan, Herculean; *informal* humongous, whopping, thumping, mega; *Brit. informal* whacking, ginormous.
titbit • noun **1** *tasty titbits* DELICACY, tasty morsel, dainty, bonne bouche, treat; snack, nibble, savoury, appetizer; *informal* goody; *N.*

– ORIGIN abbreviation of rhyming slang *tit for tat*.

tithe /tīth/ ● noun **1** one tenth of annual produce or earnings, formerly taken as a tax for the support of the Church and clergy. **2** archaic a tenth of a specified thing. ● verb subject to or pay as a tithe.

– ORIGIN Old English, 'tenth'.

tithe barn ● noun a barn built to hold produce made over as tithes.

Titian /tish'n/ ● adjective (of hair) bright golden auburn.

– ORIGIN from the 16th-century Italian painter *Titian*, by association with the bright auburn hair portrayed in many of his works.

titillate /tittillayt/ ● verb **1** arouse (someone) to mild excitement or interest. **2** archaic lightly touch; tickle.

– DERIVATIVES **titillation** noun.

– ORIGIN Latin *titillare* 'tickle'.

titivate /tittivayt/ ● verb informal make smarter or more attractive.

– DERIVATIVES **titivation** noun.

– ORIGIN originally also spelt *tidivate*: perhaps from TIDY.

title ● noun **1** the name of a book, musical composition, or other artistic work. **2** a name that describes someone's position or job. **3** a word, such as *Dr*, *Mrs*, or *Lord*, used before or instead of someone's name to indicate rank, profession, or status. **4** a name or description that is earned or chosen. **5** the position of being the champion of a major sports competition. **6** a caption or credit in a film or broadcast. **7** Law a right or claim to the ownership of property or to a rank or throne. ● verb give a title to.

– ORIGIN Latin *titulus* 'inscription, title'.

titled ● adjective having a title indicating nobility or rank.

title deed ● noun a legal document constituting evidence of a right, especially to ownership of property.

title music ● noun music played during the credits at the beginning or end of a television programme or film.

title role ● noun the part in a play or film from which the work's title is taken.

titmouse ● noun (pl. **titmice**) a small songbird, typically foraging acrobatically among foliage and branches.

– ORIGIN from TIT[1] + obsolete *mose* 'titmouse'.

titrate /tītrayt/ ● verb Chemistry ascertain the amount of a substance in (a solution) by measuring the volume of a standard reagent required to react with it.

– DERIVATIVES **titration** noun.

– ORIGIN from French *titre* 'fineness of alloyed gold or silver'.

titre /tīter/ (US **titer**) ● noun Chemistry the concentration of a solution as determined by titration.

titter ● noun a short, half-suppressed laugh. ● verb give a titter.

– ORIGIN imitative.

tittle ● noun a tiny amount or part of something.

– ORIGIN Latin *titulus* 'title', later 'small stroke, accent'.

tittle-tattle ● noun gossip. ● verb engage in gossip.

– ORIGIN reduplication of TATTLE.

tittup /tittəp/ ● verb (**tittuped**, **tittuping** or **tittupped**, **tittupping**) (in horse riding) proceed with jerky or exaggerated movements.

– ORIGIN perhaps imitative of hoof-beats.

titular /tityoolər/ ● adjective **1** relating to a title. **2** holding or constituting a formal position or title without any real authority.

– DERIVATIVES **titularly** adverb.

tiyin /teeyin/ ● noun (pl. same or **tiyins**) a monetary unit of Kyrgyzstan, equal to one hundredth of a som.

tizzy (also **tizz**) ● noun (pl. **tizzies**) informal a state of nervous excitement or agitation.

– ORIGIN of unknown origin.

T-junction ● noun a road junction at which one road joins another at right angles without crossing it.

TKO ● abbreviation Boxing technical knockout.

Tl ● symbol the chemical element thallium.

TLC ● abbreviation informal tender loving care.

TM ● abbreviation (trademark in the US) Transcendental Meditation.

Tm ● symbol the chemical element thulium.

TN ● abbreviation Tennessee.

TNT ● abbreviation trinitrotoluene, a high explosive.

to ● preposition **1** expressing direction or position in relation to a particular location, point, or condition. **2** chiefly Brit. (in telling the time) before (the hour specified). **3** identifying the person or thing affected. **4** identifying a particular relationship between one person or thing and another. **5** indicating a rate of return on something. **6** indicating that two things are attached. **7** governing a phrase expressing someone's reaction to something: *to her astonishment, he smiled.* **8** used to introduce the second element in a comparison. ● infinitive marker used with the base form of a verb to indicate that the verb is in the infinitive. ● adverb so as to be closed or nearly closed.

– ORIGIN Old English.

toad ● noun **1** a tailless amphibian with a short stout body and short legs, typically having dry warty skin that can exude poison. **2** a detestable person.

– ORIGIN Old English.

toadflax ● noun a plant with yellow or purplish snapdragon-like flowers and slender leaves.

toad-in-the-hole ● noun Brit. a dish consisting of sausages baked in batter.

toadstool ● noun the spore-bearing fruiting body of a fungus, typically in the form of a rounded cap on a stalk.

– ORIGIN a fanciful name.

toady ● noun (pl. **toadies**) a person who behaves obsequiously towards others. ● verb (**toadies**, **toadied**) act obsequiously.

– ORIGIN said to be from *toad-eater*, a charlatan's assistant who ate toads (regarded as poisonous) as a demonstration of the power of the charlatan's remedy.

to and fro ● adverb in a constant movement backwards and forwards or from side to side.

– DERIVATIVES **toing and froing** noun.

toast ● noun **1** sliced bread browned on both sides by exposure to radiant heat. **2** an act of raising glasses at a gathering and

Thesaurus

Amer. tidbit. **2** *a fascinating titbit* PIECE OF GOSSIP, bit of scandal, piece of information.

tit for tat ● noun RETALIATION, reprisal, counter-attack, counterstroke, comeback; revenge, vengeance, retribution, an eye for an eye, a tooth for a tooth, as good as one gets, payback; *informal* a taste of someone's own medicine.

titillate ● verb AROUSE, excite, tantalize, stimulate, stir, thrill, interest, attract, fascinate; *informal* turn on.

– OPPOSITES bore.

titillating ● adjective AROUSING, exciting, stimulating, sexy, thrilling, provocative, tantalizing, interesting, fascinating; suggestive, salacious, lurid; *Brit. informal* saucy.

– OPPOSITES boring.

titivate ● verb (*informal*) *she titivated herself in front of the hall mirror* GROOM, smarten (up), spruce up, freshen up, preen, primp, prink; tidy, arrange; *informal* doll up, tart up; *N. Amer. informal* gussy up.

title ● noun **1** *the title of the book* NAME. **2** *the cartoon title* CAPTION, legend, inscription, label, heading, sub-heading; credit. **3** *the company publishes 400 titles a year* PUBLICATION, work, book, newspaper, paper, magazine, periodical. **4** *the title of Duke of Marlborough* DESIGNATION, name, form of address; epithet, style; rank, office, position; *informal* moniker, handle; *formal* appellation, denomination. **5** *an Olympic title* CHAMPIONSHIP, crown, first place; laurels, bays, palm. **6** *the vendor is obliged to prove his title to the land* OWNERSHIP, proprietorship, possession, holding, freehold, entitlement, right, claim.

● verb *a policy paper titled 'Law and Order'* CALL, entitle, name, dub, designate, style, term; *formal* denominate.

titter ● verb & noun GIGGLE, snigger, snicker, tee-hee, chuckle, laugh; *informal* chortle.

tittle ● noun. See IOTA.

tittle-tattle ● noun *she would never listen to tittle-tattle* GOSSIP, rumour(s), idle talk, hearsay, whispers, titbits; scandal; *informal* dirt, buzz; *Brit. informal* goss; *N. Amer. informal* scuttlebutt.

● verb *he was tittle-tattling all over the village* GOSSIP, spread rumours, spread gossip, tattle, talk, whisper, tell tales.

titular ● adjective **1** *the titular head of a university* NOMINAL, in title/name only, ceremonial; token, puppet. **2** *the work's titular song* EPONYMOUS, identifying.

toady ● noun *a conniving little toady* SYCOPHANT, fawner, flatterer, creep, crawler, lickspittle; *informal* bootlicker, yes-man; *archaic* toadeater.

● verb *she imagined him toadying to his rich clients* GROVEL TO, ingratiate oneself with, be obsequious to, kowtow to, pander to, crawl to, truckle to, bow and scrape to, dance attendance on,

drinking together in honour of a person or thing. **3** a person who is toasted or held in high regard. ● **verb 1** cook or brown by exposure to radiant heat. **2** drink a toast to. **3** (of a DJ) accompany reggae music with improvised rhythmic speech.
– PHRASES **be toast** informal, chiefly N. Amer. be finished, defunct, or dead.
– ORIGIN from Old French *toster* 'roast', from Latin *torrere* 'parch'; sense 2 originated in the idea that the name of the lady whose health was being drunk flavoured the drink like the pieces of spiced toast formerly placed in wine.

toaster ● **noun** an electrical device for making toast.

toastie ● **noun** Brit. informal a toasted sandwich or snack.

toasting fork ● **noun** a long-handled fork for making toast in front of a fire.

toastmaster (or **toastmistress**) ● **noun** an official responsible for proposing toasts and making other formal announcements at a large social event.

tobacco ● **noun** (pl. **tobaccos**) a preparation of the dried and fermented nicotine-rich leaves of an American plant, used for smoking or chewing.
– ORIGIN Spanish *tabaco*.

tobacconist ● **noun** chiefly Brit. a shopkeeper who sells cigarettes and tobacco.

toboggan ● **noun** a light, narrow vehicle on runners, used for sliding downhill over snow or ice. ● **verb** ride on a toboggan.
– DERIVATIVES **tobogganist** noun.
– ORIGIN Micmac.

toby jug ● **noun** a beer jug or mug in the form of a stout old man wearing a three-cornered hat.
– ORIGIN said to come from an 18th-century poem about *Toby Philpot* (with a pun on *fill pot*), a soldier who liked to drink.

toccata /təkaatə/ ● **noun** a musical composition for a keyboard instrument designed to exhibit the performer's touch and technique.
– ORIGIN Italian, 'touched'.

tocopherol /tokoffərōl/ ● **noun** vitamin E, a compound found in wheatgerm oil, egg yolk, and leafy vegetables and important in stabilizing cell membranes.
– ORIGIN from Greek *tokos* 'offspring' + *pherein* 'to bear'.

tocsin /toksin/ ● **noun** archaic an alarm bell or signal.
– ORIGIN Provençal *tocasenh*, from *tocar* 'to touch' + *senh* 'signal bell'.

tod ● **noun** (in phrase **on one's tod**) Brit. informal on one's own.
– ORIGIN from rhyming slang *Tod Sloan*, an American jockey (1873–1933).

today ● **adverb 1** on or in the course of this present day. **2** at the present period of time; nowadays. ● **noun 1** this present day. **2** the present period of time.
– ORIGIN Old English, 'on this day'.

toddle ● **verb 1** (of a young child) move with short unsteady steps while learning to walk. **2** informal walk or go in a casual or leisurely way. ● **noun** an act of toddling.
– ORIGIN of unknown origin.

toddler ● **noun** a young child who is just beginning to walk.

toddy ● **noun** (pl. **toddies**) **1** a drink made of spirits with hot water and sugar. **2** the sap of some kinds of palm, fermented to produce arrack.
– ORIGIN Sanskrit.

todger ● **noun** Brit. vulgar slang a man's penis.
– ORIGIN of unknown origin.

to-do ● **noun** informal a commotion or fuss.
– ORIGIN from *much to do*, originally meaning 'much needing to be done' but later interpreted as the adjective *much* and a noun.

toe ● **noun 1** any of the five digits at the end of the foot. **2** the lower end, tip, or point of something. ● **verb** (**toes, toed, toeing**) push, touch, or kick with one's toes.
– PHRASES **make someone's toes curl** informal bring about an extreme reaction of delight or disgust in someone. **on one's toes** ready and alert. **toe the line** comply with authority. **turn up one's toes** informal die.
– DERIVATIVES **toed** adjective **toeless** adjective.
– ORIGIN Old English.

toea /tōayə/ ● **noun** (pl. same) a monetary unit of Papua New Guinea, equal to one hundredth of a kina.
– ORIGIN from a word in a Melanesian language meaning 'cone-shaped shell'.

toecap ● **noun** a piece of steel or leather on the front part of a boot or shoe.

toehold ● **noun** a small foothold.

toenail ● **noun** a nail on the upper surface of the tip of each toe.

toerag ● **noun** Brit. informal a contemptible person.
– ORIGIN originally denoting a rag wrapped round the foot as a sock or the wearer of such a rag, such as a vagrant.

toe-tapping ● **adjective** informal (of music) lively.

toff ● **noun** Brit. informal, derogatory a rich or upper-class person.
– ORIGIN perhaps an alteration of TUFT, used to denote a gold tassel worn on the cap by titled undergraduates at Oxford and Cambridge.

toffee ● **noun** a kind of firm or hard sweet which softens when sucked or chewed, made by boiling together sugar and butter.
– ORIGIN alteration of TAFFY.

toffee apple ● **noun** Brit. an apple coated with a thin layer of toffee and fixed on a stick.

toffee-nosed ● **adjective** informal, chiefly Brit. pretentiously superior; snobbish.

tofu /tōfoo/ ● **noun** curd made from mashed soya beans, used in Asian and vegetarian cookery.
– ORIGIN Chinese, 'rotten beans'.

tog[1] informal ● **noun** (**togs**) clothes. ● **verb** (**togged, togging**) (**be togged up/out**) be fully dressed for a particular occasion or activity.
– ORIGIN apparently an abbreviation of obsolete criminals' slang *togeman* 'light cloak', from Latin *toga* 'toga'.

tog[2] ● **noun** Brit. a unit of thermal resistance used to express the insulating properties of clothes and quilts.
– ORIGIN from TOG[1], on the pattern of an earlier unit called the *clo* (first element of *clothes*).

toga /tōgə/ ● **noun** a loose flowing outer garment worn by the citizens of ancient Rome, made of a single piece of cloth and covering the whole body apart from the right arm.
– ORIGIN Latin.

together ● **adverb 1** with or in proximity to another person or people. **2** so as to touch, combine, or be united. **3** in combination; collectively. **4** (of two people) married or in a sexual relationship. **5** at the same time. **6** without interruption. ● **adjective** informal level-headed and well organized.
– PHRASES **together with** as well as.
– DERIVATIVES **togetherness** noun.
– ORIGIN Old English.

Thesaurus

curry favour with, make up to, fawn on/over; *informal* suck up to, lick someone's boots, butter up.

toast ● **noun 1** *he raised his glass in a toast* TRIBUTE, salute, salutation; *archaic* pledge. **2** *he was the toast of the West End* DARLING, favourite, pet, heroine, hero; talk; *Brit. informal* blue-eyed boy/girl; *N. Amer. informal* fair-haired boy/girl.
● **verb 1** *she toasted her hands in front of the fire* WARM (UP), heat, heat (up). **2** *we toasted the couple with champagne* DRINK (TO) THE HEALTH OF, drink to, salute, honour, pay tribute to; *archaic* pledge.

today ● **adverb 1** *the work must be finished today* THIS (VERY) DAY, this morning, this afternoon, this evening. **2** *the complex tasks demanded of computers today* NOWADAYS, these days, at the present time, in these times, in this day and age, now, currently, at the moment, at present, at this moment in time; in the present climate; *N. Amer.* presently.

toddle ● **verb 1** *the child toddled towards him* TOTTER, teeter, wobble, falter, waddle, stumble. **2** *(informal) I toddled down to the quay* AMBLE, potter, wander, meander, stroll, saunter; *informal* mosey, tootle; *N. Amer. informal* putter.

to-do ● **noun** *(informal)* COMMOTION, fuss, ado, excitement, agitation, bother, stir, palaver, confusion, disturbance, brouhaha, uproar, furore, storm in a teacup, much ado about nothing; *informal* hoo-ha, ballyhoo, kerfuffle, song and dance, performance, pantomime; *Brit. informal* carry-on; *N. Amer. informal* fuss and feathers.

together ● **adverb 1** *friends who work together* WITH EACH OTHER, in conjunction, jointly, in cooperation, in collaboration, in partnership, in combination, in league, side by side, hand in hand, shoulder to shoulder, cheek by jowl; in collusion, hand in glove; *informal* in cahoots. **2** *they both spoke together* SIMULTANEOUSLY, at the same time, at one and the same time, at once, all together, as a group, in unison, in concert, in chorus, as one, with one accord. **3** *I was not able to get up for days together* IN SUCCESSION, in a row, at a time, successively, consecutively, running, straight, on end, one after the other, continuously, without a break, without inter-

toggle ● noun **1** a narrow piece of wood or plastic attached to a garment, pushed through a loop to act as a fastener. **2** Computing a key or command that is operated the same way but with opposite effect on successive occasions. ● verb Computing switch from one effect, feature, or state to another by using a toggle.
– ORIGIN of unknown origin.
toggle switch ● noun an electric switch operated by means of a projecting lever that is moved up and down.
Togolese /tōgəleez/ ● noun (pl. same) a person from Togo, a country in West Africa. ● adjective relating to Togo.
toil ● verb **1** work extremely hard or incessantly. **2** move somewhere slowly and with difficulty. ● noun exhausting work.
– DERIVATIVES **toiler** noun.
– ORIGIN Old French *toiler* 'strive, dispute', from Latin *tudiculare* 'stir about'.
toile /twaal/ ● noun **1** an early version of a finished garment made up in cheap material so that the design can be tested. **2** a translucent fabric.
– ORIGIN French, 'cloth, web'.
toilet ● noun **1** a large bowl for urinating or defecating into, typically plumbed into a sewage system. **2** the process of washing oneself, dressing, and attending to one's appearance.
– ORIGIN originally denoting a cloth cover for a dressing table, later a dressing room, and, in the US, one with washing facilities: from French *toilette* 'cloth, wrapper'.
toilet bag ● noun Brit. a waterproof bag for holding toothpaste, soap, etc. when travelling.
toiletries ● plural noun articles used in washing and taking care of one's body, such as soap and shampoo.
toilette /twaalet/ ● noun old-fashioned term for TOILET (in sense 2).
– ORIGIN French (see TOILET).
toilet-train ● verb teach (a young child) to use the toilet.
toilet water ● noun a dilute form of perfume.
toils ● plural noun literary a situation regarded as a trap.
– ORIGIN originally denoting a net into which a hunted animal is driven: from Old French *toile* (see TOILE).
toilsome ● adjective archaic or literary involving hard work.
Tokay /tōkī/ ● noun a sweet aromatic wine, originally made near Tokaj in Hungary.
toke informal ● noun a pull on a cigarette or pipe, especially one containing cannabis. ● verb smoke cannabis or tobacco.
– ORIGIN of unknown origin.
token ● noun **1** a thing serving to represent a fact, quality, feeling, etc. **2** a voucher that can be exchanged for goods or services. **3** a disc used to operate a machine or in exchange for particular goods or services. ● adjective **1** done for the sake of appearances or as a symbolic gesture. **2** chosen by way of tokenism to represent a particular group.
– PHRASES **by the same** (or **that** or **this**) **token** in the same way or for the same reason. **in token of** as a sign or symbol of.
– ORIGIN Old English, related to TEACH.
tokenism ● noun the making of a perfunctory or symbolic effort to do a particular thing, especially by recruiting a small number of people from under-represented groups to give the appearance of sexual or racial equality within a workforce.
– DERIVATIVES **tokenistic** adjective.
tolar /tollaar/ ● noun the basic monetary unit of Slovenia, equal to 100 stotins.
– ORIGIN Slovene.
told past and past participle of TELL.
tolerable ● adjective **1** able to be tolerated. **2** fairly good.
– DERIVATIVES **tolerability** noun **tolerably** adverb.
tolerance ● noun **1** the ability, willingness, or capacity to tolerate something. **2** an allowable amount of variation of a specified quantity, especially in the dimensions of a machine or part.
tolerant ● adjective **1** showing tolerance. **2** able to endure specified conditions or treatment.
– DERIVATIVES **tolerantly** adverb.
tolerate ● verb **1** allow (something that one dislikes or disagrees with) to exist or occur without interference. **2** patiently endure (something unpleasant). **3** be capable of continued exposure to (a drug, toxin, etc.) without adverse reaction.
– DERIVATIVES **toleration** noun.
– ORIGIN Latin *tolerare* 'endure'.
toll[1] /tōl/ ● noun **1** a charge payable to use a bridge or road or (N. Amer.) for a long-distance telephone call. **2** the number of deaths or casualties arising from an accident, disaster, etc. **3** the cost or damage resulting from something.
– PHRASES **take its toll** (or **take a heavy toll**) have an adverse effect.
– ORIGIN Greek *telōnion* 'toll house', from *telos* 'tax'.
toll[2] /tōl/ ● verb **1** (of a bell) sound with a slow, uniform succession of strokes. **2** announce (the time, a service, or a person's death) in this way. ● noun a single ring of a bell.
– ORIGIN probably a special use of dialect *toll* 'drag, pull'.
tollbooth ● noun **1** a roadside kiosk where tolls are paid. **2** Scot-

Thesaurus

ruption; *informal* on the trot.
– OPPOSITES separately.
● adjective *(informal) a very together young woman.* See LEVEL-HEADED.
toil ● verb **1** *she toiled all night* WORK HARD, labour, exert oneself, slave (away), grind away, strive, work one's fingers to the bone, work like a Trojan/slave, keep one's nose to the grindstone; *informal* slog away, plug away, peg away, beaver away, work one's guts out, work one's socks off, sweat blood; *Brit. informal* graft; *poetic/literary* travail; *archaic* moil. **2** *she began to toil up the cliff path* STRUGGLE, trudge, tramp, traipse, slog, plod, trek, footslog, drag oneself; *Brit. informal* yomp; *N. Amer. informal* schlep.
– OPPOSITES rest, relax.
● noun *a life of toil* HARD WORK, labour, exertion, slaving, drudgery, effort, industry, {blood, sweat, and tears}; *informal* slog, elbow grease; *Brit. informal* graft; *poetic/literary* travail; *archaic* moil.
toilet ● noun **1** *he had to go to the toilet* LAVATORY, WC, water closet, (public) convenience, cloakroom, powder room, urinal, privy, latrine, jakes; *N. Amer.* men's/ladies' room, washroom, bathroom, rest room, commode, comfort station; *Nautical* head; *informal* little girls'/boys' room, smallest room; *Brit. informal* loo, bog, the Ladies, the Gents, khazi, lav; *N. Amer. informal* can, john; *Austral./NZ informal* dunny; *archaic* closet, garderobe. **2** *she had always taken a long time over her toilet* WASHING, bathing, showering; grooming, dressing, make-up; *formal or humorous* ablutions; *dated* toilette.
toils ● plural noun *(poetic/literary)* TRAP, net, snare.
token ● noun **1** *a token of our appreciation* SYMBOL, sign, emblem, badge, representation, indication, mark, manifestation, expression, pledge, demonstration, recognition; evidence, proof. **2** *he kept the menu as a token of their golden wedding* MEMENTO, souvenir, keepsake, reminder, remembrance, memorial. **3** *a book token* VOUCHER, coupon. **4** *a telephone token* COUNTER, disc, jetton, chip, piece, man.
● adjective **1** *a one-day token strike* SYMBOLIC, emblematic, indicative; peppercorn. **2** *the practice now meets only token resistance* PERFUNCTORY, slight, nominal, minimal, minor, mild, superficial, inconsequential.
tolerable ● adjective **1** *a tolerable noise level* BEARABLE, endurable, supportable, acceptable. **2** *he had a tolerable voice* FAIRLY GOOD, passable, adequate, all right, acceptable, satisfactory, not (too) bad, average, fair; mediocre, middling, ordinary, indifferent, unremarkable, unexceptional; *informal* OK, so-so, nothing to write home about, no great shakes.
– OPPOSITES intolerable, unacceptable.
tolerance ● noun **1** *an attitude of tolerance towards other people* ACCEPTANCE, toleration; open-mindedness, broad-mindedness, forbearance, liberality, liberalism; patience, charity, indulgence, understanding. **2** *the plant's tolerance of pollution* ENDURANCE, resilience, resistance, immunity. **3** *a 1% maximum tolerance in measurement* DEVIATION, variation, play; inaccuracy, imprecision.
tolerant ● adjective OPEN-MINDED, broad-minded, forbearing, liberal, unprejudiced, unbiased; patient, long-suffering, understanding, charitable, lenient, indulgent, permissive, free and easy, easy-going, lax.
– OPPOSITES intolerant.
tolerate ● verb **1** *a regime unwilling to tolerate serious dissent* ALLOW, permit, condone, accept, swallow, countenance; *formal* brook; *archaic* suffer. **2** *he couldn't tolerate her moods any longer* ENDURE, put up with, bear, take, stand, support, stomach; *informal* hack, abide; *Brit. informal* stick, wear, be doing with.
toleration ● noun ACCEPTANCE, tolerance, endurance; forbearance, liberality, open-mindedness, broad-mindedness, liberalism; patience, charity, indulgence, understanding.
toll[1] ● noun **1** *a motorway toll* CHARGE, fee, payment, levy, tariff, tax. **2** *the toll of dead and injured* NUMBER, count, tally, total, sum total, grand total, sum; record, list, listing. **3** *the toll on the environment has been high* ADVERSE EFFECT(S), detriment, harm, damage,

tish archaic a town hall or town jail.

toll gate ● noun a barrier across a road where a toll must be paid to proceed further.

Toltec /toltek/ ● noun a member of an American Indian people that flourished in Mexico before the Aztecs.
– DERIVATIVES **Toltecan** adjective.
– ORIGIN Nahuatl, 'person from *Tula* (a town and former Toltec site in central Mexico)'.

toluene /tolyooeen/ ● noun Chemistry a colourless liquid hydrocarbon resembling benzene, present in coal tar and petroleum.
– ORIGIN from *tolu*, a fragrant balsam obtained from a South American tree, named after *Santiago de Tolú* in Colombia.

tom ● noun the male of various animals, especially a domestic cat.
– ORIGIN originally denoting an ordinary man: abbreviation of the given name *Thomas*.

tomahawk /tomməhawk/ ● noun **1** a light axe formerly used as a tool or weapon by American Indians. **2** Austral./NZ a hatchet. ● verb strike or cut with a tomahawk.
– ORIGIN from an Algonquian language.

tomato ● noun (pl. **tomatoes**) a glossy red or yellow edible fruit, eaten as a vegetable or in salads.
– ORIGIN Nahuatl.

tomb ● noun **1** a burial place, especially a large underground vault. **2** a monument to a dead person, erected over their burial place. **3** (**the tomb**) literary death.
– ORIGIN Greek *tumbos*.

tombola /tombōlə/ ● noun Brit. a game in which tickets are drawn from a revolving drum to win prizes.
– ORIGIN Italian, from *tombolare* 'turn a somersault'.

tomboy ● noun a girl who enjoys rough, noisy activities traditionally associated with boys.
– DERIVATIVES **tomboyish** adjective.

tombstone ● noun a large, flat inscribed stone standing or laid over a grave.

tomcat ● noun a male domestic cat.

Tom Collins ● noun a cocktail made from gin mixed with soda, sugar, and lemon or lime juice.
– ORIGIN said to have been named after a 19th-century London bartender.

Tom, Dick, and Harry ● noun ordinary people in general.

tome ● noun chiefly humorous a book, especially a large, scholarly one.
– ORIGIN Greek *tomos* 'section, roll of papyrus, volume'.

tomfoolery ● noun foolish or silly behaviour.

Tommy ● noun (pl. **Tommies**) informal a British private soldier.
– ORIGIN familiar form of the given name *Thomas*; from a use of the name *Thomas Atkins* in specimens of completed official forms in the British army.

tommy gun ● noun informal a type of sub-machine gun.
– ORIGIN contraction of *Thompson gun*, named after John T. *Thompson* (1860–1940), the American army officer who conceived it.

tommyrot ● noun informal, dated nonsense.

tomography /təmogrəfi/ ● noun a technique for displaying a cross section through a human body or other solid object using X-rays or ultrasound.
– DERIVATIVES **tomogram** noun **tomographic** adjective.
– ORIGIN from Greek *tomos* 'slice, section'.

tomorrow ● adverb **1** on the day after today. **2** in the near future. ● noun **1** the day after today. **2** the near future.
– PHRASES **like there was no tomorrow** informal completely without restraint.

tomtit ● noun a small, active titmouse or similar bird, especially (Brit.) the blue tit.

tom-tom ● noun **1** a medium-sized cylindrical drum, of which one to three may be used in a drum kit. **2** a drum beaten with the hands, associated with North American Indian, African, or Eastern cultures.
– ORIGIN Hindi.

-tomy ● combining form cutting, especially as part of a surgical process: *hysterectomy*.
– ORIGIN from Greek *-tomia* 'cutting'.

ton /tun/ ● noun **1** (also **long ton**) a unit of weight equal to 2,240 lb avoirdupois (1016.05 kg). **2** (also **short ton**) chiefly N. Amer. a unit of weight equal to 2,000 lb avoirdupois (907.19 kg). **3** a metric ton. **4** (also **displacement ton**) a unit of measurement of a ship's weight equal to 2,240 lb or 35 cu. ft (0.99 cubic metres). **5** informal a large number or amount. **6** informal, chiefly Brit. a hundred, in particular a speed of 100 mph, a score of 100 or more, or a sum of £100. ● adverb (**tons**) Brit. informal much; a lot.
– ORIGIN variant of TUN.

tonal /tōn'l/ ● adjective **1** relating to tone. **2** (of music) written using conventional keys and harmony.
– DERIVATIVES **tonally** adverb.

tonality ● noun (pl. **tonalities**) **1** the character of a piece of music as determined by the key in which it is played or the relations between the notes of a scale or key. **2** the use of conventional keys and harmony as the basis of musical composition. **3** the range of tones used in a picture.

tondo /tondō/ ● noun (pl. **tondi** /tondi/) a circular painting or relief.
– ORIGIN Italian, 'round object'.

tone ● noun **1** a musical or vocal sound with reference to its pitch, quality, and strength. **2** the sound of a person's voice, expressing a feeling or mood. **3** general character: *trust her to lower the tone of the conversation.* **4** (also **whole tone**) a basic interval in classical Western music, equal to two semitones; a major second. **5** the particular quality of brightness, deepness, or hue of a colour. **6** the general effect of colour or of light and shade in a picture. **7** the normal level of firmness or slight contraction in a resting muscle. ● verb **1** (often **tone up**) give greater strength or firmness to (the body or a muscle). **2** (**tone down**) make less harsh, extreme, or intense. **3** (**tone with**) harmonize with in terms of colour.
– DERIVATIVES **toned** adjective **toneless** adjective.
– ORIGIN Greek *tonos* 'tension, tone', from *teinein* 'to stretch'.

tone arm ● noun the movable arm supporting the pickup of a record player.

tone-deaf ● adjective unable to perceive differences of musical pitch accurately.

tonepad ● noun a device generating specific tones to control another device at the other end of a telephone line.

tone poem ● noun a piece of orchestral music, typically in one movement, on a descriptive or rhapsodic theme.

toner ● noun **1** a liquid applied to the skin to reduce oiliness and improve its condition. **2** a powder used in xerographic copying processes. **3** a chemical bath for changing the tone of a photographic print.

tone row ● noun Music a particular sequence of the twelve notes of the chromatic scale used as a basis for twelve-note (serial) music.

tong ● noun a Chinese association or secret society associated with organized crime.
– ORIGIN Chinese, 'meeting place'.

Tongan /tonggən, tongən/ ● noun **1** a person from Tonga, an island group in the South Pacific. **2** the Polynesian language spoken in Tonga. ● adjective relating to Tonga.

tongs ● plural noun **1** a tool with two movable arms that are joined at one end, used for picking up and holding things.

t

Thesaurus

injury, hurt; cost, price, loss, disadvantage, suffering, penalty.

toll[2] ● verb *I heard the bell toll* RING (OUT), chime, strike, peal; sound, clang, resound, reverberate; *poetic/literary* knell.

tomb ● noun BURIAL CHAMBER, sepulchre, mausoleum, vault, crypt, undercroft, catacomb; last/final resting place, grave, barrow, burial mound; *historical* charnel house.
– RELATED TERMS sepulchral.

tombstone ● noun GRAVESTONE, headstone, stone; memorial, monument.

tome ● noun VOLUME, book, work, opus, publication, title.

tomfoolery ● noun SILLINESS, fooling around, clowning, capers, antics, pranks, tricks, buffoonery, skylarking, nonsense, horseplay, mischief, foolishness, foolery; *informal* larks, shenanigans.

tone ● noun **1** *the tone of the tuba* TIMBRE, sound, sound quality, voice, voice quality, colour, tone colour, tonality. **2** *his friendly tone* INTONATION, tone of voice, modulation, accentuation. **3** *the somewhat impatient tone of his letter* MOOD, air, feel, flavour, note, attitude, character, temper; tenor, vein, drift, gist. **4** *a dialling tone* NOTE, signal, beep, bleep. **5** *tones of primrose, lavender, and rose* SHADE, colour, hue, tint, tinge.
● verb *the caramel shirt toned well with her cream skirt* HARMONIZE, go, blend, coordinate, team; match, suit, complement.
– PHRASES **tone something down 1** *the colour needs to be toned down a bit* SOFTEN, lighten, mute, subdue. **2** *the papers refused to*

2 curling tongs.
– ORIGIN Old English.

tongue ● noun **1** the fleshy muscular organ in the mouth, used for tasting, licking, swallowing, and (in humans) articulating speech. **2** the tongue of an ox or lamb as food. **3** a person's style or manner of speaking: *a debater with a caustic tongue.* **4** a particular language. **5** a strip of leather or fabric under the laces in a shoe. **6** the free-swinging metal piece inside a bell which strikes the bell to produce the sound. **7** a long, low promontory of land. **8** a projecting strip on a wooden board fitting into a groove on another. **9** the vibrating reed of a musical instrument or organ pipe. ● verb (**tongues**, **tongued**, **tonguing**) **1** Music sound (a note) distinctly on a wind instrument by interrupting the air flow with the tongue. **2** lick or caress with the tongue.
– PHRASES **find** (or **lose**) **one's tongue** be able (or unable) to express oneself after a shock. **the gift of tongues** the power of speaking in unknown languages, regarded as one of the gifts of the Holy Spirit. **give tongue 1** (of hounds) bark, especially on finding a scent. **2** express one's feelings or opinions freely. **hold one's tongue** informal remain silent. (**with**) **tongue in cheek** insincerely or ironically. **one's tongue is hanging out** one is very eager for something.
– ORIGIN Old English.

tongue and groove ● noun wooden planking in which adjacent boards are joined by means of interlocking ridges and hollows down their sides.

tongue-lashing ● noun a loud or severe scolding.

tongue-tied ● adjective too shy or embarrassed to speak.

tongue-twister ● noun a sequence of words that are difficult to pronounce quickly and correctly.

tonic ● noun **1** a medicinal substance taken to give a feeling of vigour or well-being. **2** something with an invigorating effect. **3** tonic water. **4** Music the first note in a scale which, in conventional harmony, provides the keynote of a piece of music. ● adjective Music referring to the first note of a scale.
– ORIGIN Greek *tonikos* 'of or for stretching', from *tonos* 'tension, tone'.

tonicity /tənissiti/ ● noun muscle tone.

tonic sol-fa ● noun a system of naming the notes of the scale used to teach singing, with doh as the keynote of all major keys and lah as the keynote of all minor keys.

tonic water ● noun a carbonated soft drink with a bitter flavour, used as a mixer with gin or other spirits.

tonight ● adverb on the present or approaching evening or night. ● noun the evening or night of the present day.

tonnage ● noun **1** weight in tons. **2** the size or carrying capacity of a ship measured in tons.

tonne /tun/ ● noun another term for METRIC TON.
– ORIGIN French.

tonneau /tonnō/ ● noun **1** the part of an open car occupied by the back seats. **2** a protective cover for the seats in an open car or cabin cruiser when they are not in use.
– ORIGIN originally denoting a unit of capacity for French wine: from French, 'cask, tun'.

tonsil ● noun either of two small masses of tissue in the throat, one on each side of the root of the tongue.
– ORIGIN from Latin *tonsillae* (plural).

tonsillectomy /tonsilektəmi/ ● noun (pl. **tonsillectomies**) a surgical operation to remove the tonsils.

tonsillitis ● noun inflammation of the tonsils.

tonsorial /tonsoriəl/ ● adjective formal or humorous relating to hairdressing.

tonsure /tonsyər/ ● noun a part of a monk's or priest's head left bare on top by shaving off the hair. ● verb give a tonsure to.
– ORIGIN Latin *tonsura*, from *tondere* 'shear, clip'.

ton-up ● adjective Brit. informal achieving a speed of 100 mph or a score of 100 or more.

Tony ● noun (pl. **Tonys**) (in the US) any of a number of awards given annually for outstanding achievement in the theatre.
– ORIGIN from the nickname of the American actress and director Antoinette Perry (1888–1946).

tony ● adjective (**tonier**, **toniest**) N. Amer. informal fashionable, stylish, or high-class.
– ORIGIN from TONE.

too ● adverb **1** to a higher degree than is desirable, permissible, or possible. **2** in addition. **3** informal very.
– PHRASES **none too** —— not very.
– ORIGIN Old English, stressed form of TO.

toodle-oo ● exclamation informal, dated goodbye.
– ORIGIN perhaps an alteration of French *à tout à l'heure* 'see you soon'.

took past of TAKE.

tool ● noun **1** a device or implement used to carry out a particular function. **2** a thing used to help perform a job. **3** a person used by another. ● verb **1** (usu. **be tooled**) impress a design on (a leather book cover) with a heated tool. **2** equip with tools for industrial production. **3** (**tool up** or **be tooled up**) Brit. informal be or become armed. **4** informal drive or ride in a casual or leisurely manner.
– ORIGIN Old English.

toolbar ● noun Computing a strip of icons used to perform certain functions.

toolmaker ● noun a person who makes and maintains tools for use in a manufacturing process.

toot ● noun **1** a short, sharp sound made by a horn, trumpet, or similar instrument. **2** informal, chiefly N. Amer. a snort of a drug, especially cocaine. ● verb **1** make or cause to make a toot. **2** informal, chiefly N. Amer. snort (cocaine).
– ORIGIN imitative or from Low German *tūten*.

tooth ● noun (pl. **teeth**) **1** each of a set of hard, bony enamel-coated structures in the jaws, used for biting and chewing. **2** a projecting part, especially a cog on a gearwheel or a point on a saw or comb. **3** (**teeth**) genuine force or effectiveness.
– PHRASES **armed to the teeth** formidably armed. **fight tooth and nail** fight very fiercely. **get** (or **sink**) **one's teeth into** work energetically and productively on. **in the teeth of 1** directly against (the wind). **2** in spite of (opposition or difficulty).
– DERIVATIVES **toothed** adjective.
– ORIGIN Old English.

toothache ● noun pain in a tooth or teeth.

toothbrush ● noun a small brush with a long handle, used for cleaning the teeth.

toothcomb ● noun Brit. used with reference to a very thorough search: *the police went over the area with a fine toothcomb.*
– USAGE The forms **toothcomb** and **fine toothcomb** arose from a misreading of the compound noun *fine-tooth comb*, i.e. a comb with narrow, closely-spaced teeth.

toothed whale ● noun any of the large group of predatory whales with teeth, including sperm whales, killer whales, dolphins, porpoises, etc.

tooth fairy ● noun a fairy said to take children's milk teeth after they fall out and leave a coin under their pillow.

toothless ● adjective **1** having no teeth. **2** lacking genuine force or effectiveness.
– DERIVATIVES **toothlessly** adverb **toothlessness** noun.

toothpaste ● noun a paste used on a brush for cleaning the teeth.

toothpick ● noun a short pointed piece of wood or plastic used for removing bits of food lodged between the teeth.

Thesaurus

tone down their criticism MODERATE, modify, modulate, mitigate, temper, dampen, soften, subdue.

tongue ● noun **1** *a foreign tongue* LANGUAGE, dialect, patois, vernacular, mother tongue, native tongue; *informal* lingo. **2** *her sharp tongue* WAY/MANNER OF SPEAKING, speech, parlance.

tongue-tied ● adjective LOST FOR WORDS, speechless, unable to get a word out, struck dumb, dumbstruck; mute, dumb, silent; *informal* mum.
– OPPOSITES loquacious.

tonic ● noun **1** *ginseng can be used as a natural tonic* STIMULANT, restorative, refresher; *informal* pick-me-up, bracer; *Medicine* analeptic. **2** *we found the change of scene a tonic* STIMULANT, boost, fillip; *informal* shot in the arm, pick-me-up.

too ● adverb **1** *invasion would be too risky* EXCESSIVELY, overly, over, unduly, immoderately, inordinately, unreasonably, extremely, very; *informal* too-too. **2** *he was unhappy, too, you know* ALSO, as well, in addition, additionally, into the bargain, besides, furthermore, moreover, on top of that, to boot.

tool ● noun **1** *garden tools* IMPLEMENT, utensil, instrument, device, apparatus, gadget, appliance, machine, contrivance, contraption; *informal* gizmo. **2** *the beautiful Estella is Miss Havisham's tool* PUPPET, pawn, creature, cat's paw; minion, lackey; *informal* stooge. ● verb *red leather, tooled in gold* ORNAMENT, embellish, decorate, work, cut, chase.

t

toothsome ● adjective **1** (of food) temptingly tasty. **2** informal attractive; alluring.

toothy ● adjective (**toothier**, **toothiest**) having or showing numerous or prominent teeth.
– DERIVATIVES **toothily** adverb.

tootle ● verb **1** casually make a series of sounds on a horn, trumpet, etc. **2** informal go or travel in a leisurely way. ● noun **1** an act or sound of tootling. **2** informal a leisurely journey.
– ORIGIN from TOOT.

tootsie (also **tootsy**) ● noun (pl. **tootsies**) informal **1** a person's foot. **2** a young woman.
– ORIGIN humorous, from FOOT.

top[1] ● noun **1** the highest or uppermost point, part, or surface. **2** a thing placed on, fitted to, or covering the upper part of something. **3** (**the top**) the highest or most important rank, level, or position. **4** the utmost degree: *she shouted at the top of her voice.* **5** chiefly Brit. the end that is furthest from the speaker or a point of reference. **6** a garment covering the upper part of the body. **7** (**tops**) informal a particularly good person or thing. **8** the high-frequency component of reproduced sound. **9** a platform at the head of a ship's mast. ● adjective **1** highest in position, rank, or degree. **2** chiefly Brit. furthest away from the speaker or a point of reference. ● verb (**topped**, **topping**) **1** be more, better, or taller than. **2** be at the highest place or rank in. **3** reach the top of (a hill, rise, etc.). **4** (usu. **be topped**) provide with a top or topping. **5** informal kill. **6** Golf mishit (the ball) by hitting above the centre of the ball. ● adverb (**tops**) informal at the most.
– PHRASES **get on top of** be more than (someone) can bear or cope with. **on top** in addition. **on top of 1** so as to cover. **2** in close proximity to. **3** in command or control of. **4** in addition to. **on top of the world** informal happy and elated. **over the top 1** informal, chiefly Brit. to an excessive or exaggerated degree. **2** chiefly historical over the parapet of a trench and into battle. **top and tail** Brit. remove the top and bottom of (a fruit or vegetable) while preparing it as food. **top off** finish (something) in a memorable way. **top out 1** put the highest structural feature on (a building). **2** reach an upper limit. **top up 1** add to (a number or amount) to bring it up to a certain level. **2** fill up (a partly full container).
– DERIVATIVES **topmost** adjective.
– ORIGIN Old English.

top[2] ● noun a conical, spherical, or pear-shaped toy that may be set to spin.
– ORIGIN Old English.

topaz ● noun **1** a colourless, yellow, or pale blue precious stone. **2** a dark yellow colour.
– ORIGIN Greek *topazos*.

top boot ● noun chiefly historical a high boot with a broad band of a different material or colour at the top.

top brass ● noun see BRASS (sense 5).

topcoat ● noun **1** an overcoat. **2** an outer coat of paint.

top dog ● noun informal a person who is successful or dominant in their field.

top drawer ● noun informal high social position or class. ● adjective informal of the highest quality or social class.

top dressing ● noun an application of manure or fertilizer to the surface layer of soil or a lawn.

tope[1] ● verb archaic or literary habitually drink alcohol to excess.
– DERIVATIVES **toper** noun.
– ORIGIN perhaps from obsolete *top* 'overbalance'.

tope[2] ● noun a small shark of inshore waters.
– ORIGIN perhaps Cornish.

tope[3] ● noun another term for STUPA.
– ORIGIN Punjabi, 'barrow, mound'.

top flight ● noun the highest rank or level.

top fruit ● noun Brit. fruit grown on trees rather than bushes.

topgallant /topgalənt, təgal-/ ● noun **1** the section of a square-rigged sailing ship's mast immediately above the topmast. **2** a sail set on such a mast.

top hat ● noun a man's formal hat with a high cylindrical crown.

top-heavy ● adjective **1** disproportionately heavy at the top so as to be unstable. **2** (of an organization) having a disproportionately large number of senior executives.

Tophet /tōfit/ ● noun literary hell.
– ORIGIN from the Hebrew name of a place near Jerusalem used in biblical times for the worship of idols, including the sacrifice of children.

top-hole ● adjective Brit. informal, dated excellent.

topiary /tōpiəri/ ● noun (pl. **topiaries**) **1** the art of clipping shrubs or trees into ornamental shapes. **2** shrubs or trees clipped in such a way.
– ORIGIN Latin *topiarius* 'ornamental gardener'.

topic ● noun a subject of a text, speech, conversation, etc.
– ORIGIN from Greek *ta topika*, 'matters concerning commonplaces' (the title of a treatise by Aristotle).

topical ● adjective **1** relating to or dealing with current affairs. **2** relating to a particular subject.
– DERIVATIVES **topicality** noun **topically** adverb.

topknot ● noun **1** a knot of hair arranged on the top of the head. **2** a decorative knot or bow of ribbon worn on the top of the head, popular in the 18th century. **3** a tuft or crest of hair or feathers on the head of an animal or bird.

topless ● adjective having or leaving the breasts uncovered.

top-level (also **top-line**) ● adjective of the highest quality or ranking.

topmast /topmaast, -məst/ ● noun the second section of a square-rigged sailing ship's mast, immediately above the lower mast.

top-notch ● adjective informal of the highest quality.

topography /təpografi/ ● noun **1** the arrangement of the nat-

Thesaurus

tooth ● noun FANG, tusk; *Zoology* denticle; *informal* gnasher; *Brit. informal* pearly white.
– RELATED TERMS dental.

toothsome ● adjective TASTY, delicious, luscious, mouth-watering, delectable, succulent; tempting, appetizing, inviting; *informal* scrumptious, yummy, scrummy, finger-licking; *Brit. informal* moreish.

top ● noun **1** *the top of the cliff* SUMMIT, peak, pinnacle, crest, crown, brow, head, tip, apex, vertex. **2** *the top of the table* UPPER PART, upper surface, upper layer. **3** *the carrots' green tops* LEAVES, shoots, stem, stalk. **4** *the top of the coffee jar* LID, cap, cover, stopper, cork. **5** *a short-sleeved top* SWEATER, jumper, jersey, sweat shirt; T-shirt, shirt; blouse. **6** *by 1981 he was at the top of his profession* HIGH POINT, height, peak, pinnacle, zenith, acme, culmination, climax, crowning point; prime.
– OPPOSITES bottom, base.
● adjective **1** *the top floor* HIGHEST, topmost, uppermost, upmost. **2** *the world's top scientists* FOREMOST, leading, principal, pre-eminent, greatest, best, finest, elite; *informal* top-notch. **3** *the organization's top management* CHIEF, principal, main, leading, highest, highest-ranking, ruling, commanding, most powerful, most important. **4** *a top Paris hotel* PRIME, excellent, superb, superior, choice, select, top-quality, top-grade, first-rate, first-class, grade A, best, finest, premier, superlative, second to none; *informal* A1, top-notch. **5** *they are travelling at top speed* MAXIMUM, maximal, greatest, utmost.
– OPPOSITES bottom, lowest, minimum.
● verb **1** *sales are expected to top £1.3 billion* EXCEED, surpass, go beyond, better, best, beat, outstrip, outdo, outshine, eclipse, go one better than. **2** *their debut CD is currently topping the charts* LEAD, head, be at the top of. **3** *they topped the rise of a mist-shrouded valley* REACH THE TOP OF, crest, climb, scale, ascend, mount. **4** *chocolate mousse topped with cream* COVER, cap, coat, smother; finish, garnish.
– PHRASES **over the top** *(informal)* EXCESSIVE, immoderate, inordinate, extreme, exaggerated, extravagant, overblown, too much, unreasonable, disproportionate, undue, unwarranted, uncalled for, unnecessary, going too far; *informal* a bit much, OTT. **top something up** FILL, refill, refresh, freshen, replenish, recharge, resupply; supplement, add to, augment.

topcoat ● noun OVERCOAT, coat, greatcoat.

topic ● noun SUBJECT, subject matter, theme, issue, matter, point, talking point, question, concern, argument, thesis, text, keynote.

topical ● adjective CURRENT, up to date, up to the minute, contemporary, recent, relevant; newsworthy, in the news.
– OPPOSITES out of date.

topmost ● adjective **1** *the tree's topmost branches* HIGHEST, top, uppermost, upmost. **2** *the topmost authority on the subject* FOREMOST, leading, principal, premier, prime, top, greatest, best, supreme, pre-eminent, outstanding, most important, main, chief; *N. Amer.* ranking; *informal* number-one.

top-notch ● adjective *(informal)* FIRST-CLASS, first-rate, top-quality,

ural and artificial physical features of an area. **2** a detailed description or representation on a map of such features.
– DERIVATIVES **topographer** noun **topographic** adjective **topographical** adjective.
– ORIGIN from Greek *topos* 'place'.
topoi plural of TOPOS.
topology /təpolləji/ ● noun **1** Mathematics the study of geometrical properties and spatial relations which remain unaffected by smooth changes in shape or size of figures. **2** the way in which constituent parts are interrelated or arranged.
– DERIVATIVES **topological** adjective **topologist** noun.
toponym /toppənim/ ● noun a place name, especially one derived from a topographical feature.
– DERIVATIVES **toponymic** adjective **toponymy** noun.
topos /topposs/ ● noun (pl. **topoi** /toppoy/) a traditional theme or formula in literature.
– ORIGIN Greek, 'place'.
topper ● noun informal **1** a top hat. **2** Brit. dated an exceptionally good person or thing.
topping ● noun a layer of food poured or spread over another food. ● adjective Brit. informal, dated excellent.
topple ● verb overbalance and fall or push over.
– ORIGIN from TOP[1].
topsail /topsayl, -s'l/ ● noun **1** a sail set on a ship's topmast. **2** a fore-and-aft sail set above the gaff.
top secret ● adjective of the highest secrecy.
topside ● noun **1** Brit. the outer side of a round of beef. **2** the upper part of a ship's side, above the waterline.
topsoil ● noun the top layer of soil.
topspin ● noun a fast forward spin given to a moving ball, often resulting in a curved path or a strong forward motion on rebounding.
topsy-turvy ● adjective & adverb **1** upside down. **2** in a state of confusion.
– ORIGIN apparently from TOP[1] and obsolete *terve* 'overturn'.
toque /tōk/ ● noun **1** a woman's small hat, typically having a narrow, closely turned-up brim. **2** a tall white hat with a full pouched crown, worn by chefs.
– ORIGIN French.
tor ● noun a hill or rocky peak.
– ORIGIN perhaps Celtic.
Torah /torə/ ● noun (in Judaism) the law of God as revealed to Moses and recorded in the Pentateuch.
– ORIGIN Hebrew, 'instruction, doctrine, law'.
torc /tork/ (also **torque**) ● noun a neck ornament consisting of a band of twisted metal, worn by the ancient Gauls and Britons.
– ORIGIN Latin *torques* (see TORCH).
torch ● noun **1** Brit. a portable battery-powered electric lamp. **2** chiefly historical a piece of wood or cloth soaked in tallow and ignited. **3** something valuable which needs to be protected and maintained: *the torch of freedom.* **4** chiefly N. Amer. a blowlamp. ● verb informal set fire to.
– PHRASES **carry a torch for** suffer from unrequited love for. **put to the torch** (or **put a torch to**) destroy by burning.
– ORIGIN Latin *torqua, torques* 'necklace, wreath', from *torquere* 'to twist'.
torch song ● noun a sad or sentimental song of unrequited love.
tore past of TEAR[1].
toreador /torriədor/ ● noun a bullfighter, especially one on horseback.
– ORIGIN Spanish, from *toro* 'bull'.
toreador pants ● plural noun chiefly N. Amer. women's tight-fitting calf-length trousers.
torero /torairō/ ● noun (pl. **toreros**) a bullfighter, especially one on foot.
– ORIGIN Spanish.
tori plural of TORUS.
toric /torrik/ ● adjective Geometry having the form of a torus or part of a torus.
torment ● noun **1** severe physical or mental suffering. **2** a cause of torment. ● verb **1** subject to torment. **2** annoy or tease unkindly.
– DERIVATIVES **tormentor** noun.
– ORIGIN Latin *tormentum* 'instrument of torture', from *torquere* 'to twist'.
torn past participle of TEAR[1].
tornado /tornaydō/ ● noun (pl. **tornadoes** or **tornados**) a violently rotating wind storm having the appearance of a funnel-shaped cloud.
– ORIGIN perhaps from Spanish *tronada* 'thunderstorm'.
toroid /toroyd/ ● noun Geometry a figure having the shape of a torus.
– DERIVATIVES **toroidal** adjective.
torpedo ● noun (pl. **torpedoes**) a cigar-shaped self-propelled underwater missile designed to be fired from a ship, submarine, or an aircraft. ● verb (**torpedoes, torpedoed**) **1** attack with a torpedo or torpedoes. **2** ruin (a plan or project).
– ORIGIN originally denoting an electric ray: from Latin, 'stiffness, numbness', also 'electric ray' (with reference to the effects of its shock).
torpedo boat ● noun a small, fast, light warship armed with torpedoes.
torpedo net ● noun a net made of steel wire, formerly hung round an anchored ship to intercept torpedoes.
torpedo ray ● noun an electric ray (fish).
torpid ● adjective **1** mentally or physically inactive. **2** (of an animal) dormant, especially during hibernation.
– DERIVATIVES **torpidity** noun **torpidly** adverb.
– ORIGIN Latin *torpidus*, from *torpere* 'be numb or sluggish'.
torpor /torpər/ ● noun physical or mental inactivity; lethargy.
– ORIGIN Latin.
torque /tork/ ● noun **1** Mechanics a force that tends to cause rotation. **2** variant spelling of TORC. ● verb apply torque to.
– DERIVATIVES **torquey** adjective.
– ORIGIN from Latin *torquere* 'to twist'.
torque converter ● noun a device that transmits or multiplies torque generated by an engine.
torr /tor/ ● noun (pl. same) a unit of pressure equivalent to 1 mm of mercury in a barometer and equal to 133.32 pascals.
– ORIGIN named after the Italian mathematician and physicist Evangelista *Torricelli* (1608–47).
torrent ● noun **1** a strong and fast-moving stream of water or other liquid. **2** an overwhelmingly copious outpouring: *a torrent of abuse.*
– ORIGIN French, from Latin *torrere* 'scorch, boil, roar'.

t

Thesaurus

five-star; superior, prime, premier, premium, grade A, superlative, best, finest, select, exclusive, excellent, superb, outstanding, splendid; *informal* tip-top, A1.
topple ● verb **1** *she toppled over* FALL, tumble, overbalance, overturn, tip, keel; lose one's balance. **2** *protesters toppled a huge statue* KNOCK OVER, upset, push over, tip over, upend. **3** *a plot to topple the government* OVERTHROW, oust, unseat, overturn, bring down, defeat, get rid of, dislodge, eject.
topsy-turvy ● adjective **1** *a topsy-turvy flag* UPSIDE DOWN, the wrong way/side up, inverted. **2** *everything in the flat was topsy-turvy* IN DISARRAY, in a mess, in a muddle, in disorder, disordered, in chaos, chaotic, disorganized, awry, upside down, at sixes and sevens; *informal* every which way, higgledy-piggledy.
torch ● noun **1** *an electric torch* LAMP, light, flashlight. **2** *(historical) a flaming torch* FIREBRAND, brand; *historical* cresset, flambeau.
● verb *(informal) one of the shops had been torched* BURN, set fire to, set on fire, set light to, set alight, incinerate, put/set a match to.
torment ● noun **1** *months of mental and emotional torment* AGONY, suffering, torture, pain, anguish, misery, distress, affliction, trauma, wretchedness; hell, purgatory. **2** *it was a torment to see him like that* ORDEAL, affliction, scourge, curse, plague, bane, thorn in someone's side/flesh, cross to bear; sorrow, tribulation, trouble.
● verb **1** *she was tormented by shame* TORTURE, afflict, rack, harrow, plague, haunt, distress, agonize. **2** *she began to torment the two younger boys* TEASE, taunt, bait, harass, provoke, goad, plague, bother, trouble, persecute; *informal* needle.
torn ● adjective **1** *a torn shirt* RIPPED, rent, cut, slit; ragged, tattered, in tatters, in ribbons. **2** *she was torn between the two options* WAVERING, vacillating, irresolute, dithering, uncertain, unsure, undecided, in two minds.
tornado ● noun WHIRLWIND, windstorm, cyclone, typhoon, storm, hurricane; *N. Amer. informal* twister.
torpid ● adjective LETHARGIC, sluggish, inert, inactive, slow, lifeless; languid, listless, lazy, idle, indolent, slothful, supine, passive, apathetic, somnolent, sleepy, weary, tired.
– OPPOSITES energetic.
torpor ● noun LETHARGY, sluggishness, inertia, inactivity, lifeless-

torrential • adjective (of rain) falling rapidly and heavily.
– DERIVATIVES **torrentially** adverb.

torrid • adjective **1** very hot and dry. **2** full of intense emotions arising from sexual love. **3** full of difficulty.
– DERIVATIVES **torridly** adverb.
– ORIGIN Latin *torridus*, from *torrere* 'parch, scorch'.

torrid zone • noun the hot central belt of the earth bounded by the tropics of Cancer and Capricorn.

torsion /torsh'n/ • noun the action of twisting or the state of being twisted, especially of one end of an object relative to the other.
– DERIVATIVES **torsional** adjective
– ORIGIN Latin, from *torquere* 'to twist'.

torsion bar • noun a bar forming part of a vehicle suspension, twisting in response to the motion of the wheels and absorbing their vertical movement.

torso • noun (pl. **torsos** or US also **torsi**) **1** the trunk of the human body. **2** an unfinished or mutilated thing, especially a work of art or literature.
– ORIGIN Italian, 'stalk, stump'.

tort • noun Law a wrongful act or an infringement of a right (other than under contract) leading to legal liability.
– ORIGIN Latin *tortum* 'wrong, injustice'.

torte /tortə/ • noun (pl. **torten** /tortən/ or **tortes**) a sweet cake or tart.
– ORIGIN German, from Latin *torta* 'round loaf, cake'.

tortellini /tortəleeni/ • noun small stuffed pasta parcels rolled and formed into small rings.
– ORIGIN Italian, from *tortello* 'small cake, fritter'.

tortilla /torteeyə/ • noun **1** (in Mexican cookery) a thin, flat maize pancake. **2** (in Spanish cookery) a thick omelette containing potato.
– ORIGIN Spanish, 'little cake'.

tortious /torshəss/ • adjective Law constituting a tort; wrongful.

tortoise /tortəss, -toyz/ • noun a slow-moving land reptile with a scaly or leathery domed shell into which it can retract its head and legs.
– ORIGIN Latin *tortuca*.

tortoiseshell • noun **1** the semi-transparent mottled yellow and brown shell of certain turtles, used to make jewellery or ornaments. **2** a domestic cat with markings resembling tortoiseshell. **3** a butterfly with mottled orange, yellow, and black markings.

tortuous /tortyooəss, -choo-/ • adjective **1** full of twists and turns. **2** excessively lengthy and complex.
– DERIVATIVES **tortuosity** noun **tortuously** adverb **tortuousness** noun.
– ORIGIN Latin *tortuosus*, from *torquere* 'to twist'.

torture • noun **1** the infliction of severe pain as a punishment or a forcible means of persuasion. **2** great suffering or anxiety. • verb subject to torture.
– DERIVATIVES **torturer** noun.
– ORIGIN Latin *tortura* 'twisting, torment', from *torquere* 'to twist'.

torturous • adjective characterized by pain or suffering.
– DERIVATIVES **torturously** adverb.

torus /torəss/ • noun (pl. **tori** /torī/ or **toruses**) **1** Geometry a surface or solid resembling a ring doughnut, formed by rotating a closed curve about a line which lies in the same plane but does not intersect it. **2** a ring-shaped object or chamber. **3** Architecture a large convex moulding with a semicircular cross section.
– ORIGIN Latin, 'swelling, round moulding'.

Tory • noun (pl. **Tories**) **1** a member or supporter of the British Conservative Party. **2** a member of the English political party that opposed the exclusion of James II from the succession and later gave rise to the Conservative Party. **3** US a colonist who supported the British side during the American Revolution.
– DERIVATIVES **Toryism** noun.
– ORIGIN originally denoting Irish peasants dispossessed by English settlers and living as robbers, and extended to other marauders, especially in the Scottish Highlands: probably from Irish *toraidhe* 'outlaw, highwayman'.

tosh • noun Brit. informal rubbish; nonsense.
– ORIGIN of unknown origin.

Tosk /tosk/ • noun (pl. same or **Tosks**) **1** a member of one of the main ethnic groups of Albania, living chiefly in the south of the country. Compare with GHEG. **2** the dialect of Albanian spoken by this people.
– ORIGIN Albanian.

toss • verb **1** throw lightly or casually. **2** move from side to side or back and forth. **3** jerk (one's head or hair) sharply backwards. **4** throw (a coin) into the air so as to make a choice, based on which side of the coin faces uppermost when it lands. **5** shake or turn (food) in a liquid to coat it lightly. • noun an act of tossing.
– PHRASES **give** (or **care**) **a toss** Brit. informal care at all. **toss off 1** drink (something) rapidly or all at once. **2** produce rapidly or without thought or effort. **3** Brit. vulgar slang masturbate.
– DERIVATIVES **tosser** noun.
– ORIGIN of unknown origin.

toss-up • noun informal **1** the tossing of a coin to make a choice. **2** a situation in which any of two or more outcomes or options is equally possible.

tostada /tostaadə/ (also **tostado** /tostaadō/) • noun (pl. **tostadas** or **tostados**) a Mexican deep-fried maize flour pancake topped with a seasoned mixture of beans, mincemeat, and vegetables.
– ORIGIN Spanish, 'toasted'.

tot[1] • noun **1** a very young child. **2** chiefly Brit. a small drink of spirits.
– ORIGIN of unknown origin.

tot[2] • verb (**totted**, **totting**) (**tot up**) chiefly Brit. **1** add up (numbers or amounts). **2** accumulate over time.
– ORIGIN from archaic *tot* 'set of figures to be added up', abbreviation of TOTAL or of Latin *totum* 'the whole'.

tot[3] • verb (**totted**, **totting**) Brit. informal salvage saleable items from dustbins or rubbish heaps.
– DERIVATIVES **totter** noun.
– ORIGIN from slang *tot* 'bone', of unknown origin.

total • adjective **1** comprising the whole number or amount. **2** complete; absolute. • noun a total number or amount. • verb (**totalled**, **totalling**; US **totaled**, **totaling**) **1** amount to (a total number). **2** find the total of. **3** informal, chiefly N. Amer. destroy or kill.
– DERIVATIVES **totally** adverb.

Thesaurus

ness, listlessness, languor, lassitude, laziness, idleness, indolence, sloth, accidie, passivity, somnolence, weariness, sleepiness.

torrent • noun **1** *a torrent of water* FLOOD, deluge, inundation, spate, cascade, rush, stream, current, flow, overflow, tide. **2** *a torrent of abuse* OUTBURST, outpouring, stream, flood, volley, barrage, tide, spate.
– OPPOSITES trickle.

torrential • adjective COPIOUS, heavy, teeming, severe, relentless, violent.

torrid • adjective **1** *a torrid summer* HOT, dry, scorching, searing, blazing, blistering, sweltering, burning; *informal* boiling (hot), baking (hot), sizzling. **2** *a torrid affair* PASSIONATE, ardent, lustful, amorous; *informal* steamy, sizzling, hot.
– OPPOSITES cold.

tortuous • adjective **1** *a tortuous route* TWISTING, twisty, twisting and turning, winding, windy, zigzag, sinuous, snaky, meandering, serpentine. **2** *a tortuous argument* CONVOLUTED, complicated, complex, labyrinthine, involved, confusing, difficult to follow, lengthy, overlong.
– OPPOSITES straight, straightforward.

torture • noun **1** *the torture of political prisoners* INFLICTION OF PAIN, abuse; ill-treatment, maltreatment, persecution. **2** *the torture of losing a loved one* TORMENT, agony, suffering, pain, anguish, misery, distress, heartbreak, affliction, trauma, wretchedness; hell, purgatory.
• verb **1** *the security forces routinely tortured suspects* INFLICT PAIN ON, ill-treat, abuse, mistreat, maltreat, persecute; *informal* work over, give someone the works. **2** *he was tortured by grief* TORMENT, rack, afflict, harrow, plague, agonize, crucify.

toss • verb **1** *he tossed his tools into the boot* THROW, hurl, fling, sling, cast, pitch, lob, propel, project, launch; *informal* heave, chuck, bung; *dated* shy. **2** *he tossed a coin and it landed heads up* FLIP, flick, spin. **3** *the ship tossed about on the waves* PITCH, lurch, rock, roll, plunge, reel, list, keel, sway, wallow, make heavy weather. **4** *toss the salad ingredients together* SHAKE, stir, turn, mix, combine.

tot[1] • noun **1** *the tot looks just like her mum* INFANT, baby, toddler, tiny tot, child, little one, mite; *Scottish* bairn, wean. **2** *a tot of rum* DRAM, drink, nip, drop, slug; *informal* shot, finger, snifter.

tot[2] • verb **1** *he totted up some figures* ADD, total, count, calculate,

– ORIGIN Latin *totalis*, from *totum* 'the whole'.
total eclipse • noun an eclipse in which the whole of the disc of the sun or moon is obscured.
totalitarian /tōtalitairiən/ • adjective (of government) centralized, dictatorial, and requiring complete subservience to the state. • noun a person advocating such a system.
– DERIVATIVES **totalitarianism** noun.
totality • noun **1** the whole of something. **2** Astronomy the time during which the sun or moon is totally obscured during an eclipse.
totalizator (also **totalisator** or **totalizer**) • noun **1** a device showing the number and amount of bets staked on a race. **2** another term for TOTE[1].
totalize (also **totalise**) • verb **1** combine into a total. **2** calculate the total of.
– DERIVATIVES **totalization.**
total war • noun a war which is unrestricted in terms of the weapons used, the territory or combatants involved, or the objectives pursued.
tote[1] • noun **(the tote)** informal a system of betting based on the use of the totalizator, in which dividends are calculated according to the amount staked rather than odds offered.
tote[2] • verb informal, chiefly N. Amer. carry.
– DERIVATIVES **toter** noun.
– ORIGIN probably dialect.
tote bag • noun a large bag for carrying a number of items.
totem /tōtəm/ • noun a natural object or animal believed by a particular society to have spiritual significance and adopted by it as an emblem.
– DERIVATIVES **totemic** /tōtemmik/ adjective.
– ORIGIN Ojibwa.
totem pole • noun a pole on which totems are hung or on which the images of totems are carved.
totter • verb **1** move in an unsteady way. **2** shake or rock as if about to collapse. **3** be insecure or on the point of failure. • noun a tottering gait.
– DERIVATIVES **tottery** adjective.
– ORIGIN Dutch *touteren* 'to swing'.
totty • noun Brit. informal girls or women collectively regarded as sexually desirable.
– ORIGIN from TOT[1].
toucan /to͞okən/ • noun a tropical American fruit-eating bird with a massive bill and brightly coloured plumage.
– ORIGIN Tupi.
touch • verb **1** come into or be in contact with. **2** come or bring into mutual contact. **3** bring one's hand or another part of one's body into contact with. **4** harm or interfere with. **5** use or consume. **6** have an effect on. **7** (often **be touched**) produce feelings of affection, gratitude, or sympathy in. **8** have any dealings with. **9** informal approach in excellence: *no one can touch him at judo.* **10** **(touched)** informal slightly mad. • noun **1** an act or manner of touching. **2** the faculty of perception through physical contact, especially with the fingers. **3** a small amount. **4** a distinctive detail or feature. **5** a distinctive or skilful manner or method of dealing with something: *a sure political touch.* **6** Rugby & Soccer the area beyond the sidelines, out of play.
– PHRASES **in touch 1** in or into communication. **2** possessing up-to-date knowledge. **lose touch 1** cease to be in communication. **2** cease to be informed. **out of touch** lacking up-to-date knowledge or awareness. **touch at** (of a ship) call briefly at (a port). **touch down 1** (of an aircraft or spacecraft) land. **2** Rugby touch the ground with the ball behind the opponents' goal line, scoring a try. **3** American Football score six points by being in possession of the ball behind the opponents' goal line. **touch for** informal ask (someone) for (money) as a loan or gift. **touch in** lightly mark in (details) with a brush or pencil. **touch off 1** cause (something) to ignite or explode by touching it with a match. **2** cause to happen suddenly. **touch on** (or **upon**) **1** deal briefly with (a subject). **2** come near to being. **touch up 1** make small improvements to. **2** Brit. informal caress (someone) without their consent for sexual pleasure.
– DERIVATIVES **touchable** adjective.
– ORIGIN Old French *tochier*.
touch-and-go • adjective (of an outcome) possible but very uncertain.
touchdown • noun **1** the moment at which an aircraft touches down. **2** Rugby & American Football an act of touching down.
touché /to͞oshay/ • exclamation **1** (in fencing) used to acknowledge a hit by one's opponent. **2** used to acknowledge a good or clever point made at one's expense.
– ORIGIN French, 'touched'.

Thesaurus

compute, reckon, tally. **2** *we've totted up 89 victories* ACCUMULATE, build up, amass, accrue.
total • adjective **1** *the total cost* ENTIRE, complete, whole, full, comprehensive, combined, aggregate, gross, overall. **2** *a total disaster* COMPLETE, utter, absolute, thorough, perfect, downright, out-and-out, outright, thoroughgoing, all-out, sheer, arrant, positive, prize, rank, unmitigated, unqualified; *Brit. informal* right, proper.
– OPPOSITES partial.
• noun *a total of £160,000* SUM, sum total, grand total, aggregate; whole, entirety, totality.
• verb **1** *the prize money totalled £33,050* ADD UP TO, amount to, come to, run to, make, work out as. **2** *he totalled up his score* ADD (UP), count, reckon, tot up, compute, work out.
totalitarian • adjective AUTOCRATIC, undemocratic, one-party, dictatorial, tyrannical, despotic, fascist, oppressive, repressive, illiberal; authoritarian, autarchic, absolute, absolutist; dystopian.
– OPPOSITES democratic.
totality • noun ENTIRETY, whole, total, aggregate, sum, sum total; all, everything.
totally • adverb COMPLETELY, entirely, wholly, thoroughly, fully, utterly, absolutely, perfectly, unreservedly, unconditionally, quite, altogether, downright; in every way, in every respect, one hundred per cent, every inch, to the hilt; *informal* dead, deadly.
– OPPOSITES partly.
totter • verb **1** *he tottered off down the road* TEETER, walk unsteadily, stagger, wobble, stumble, shuffle, shamble, toddle; reel, sway, roll, lurch. **2** *the foundations began to heave and totter* SHAKE, sway, tremble, quiver, teeter, shudder, judder, rock, quake.
touch • verb **1** *his shoes were touching the end of the bed* BE IN CONTACT WITH, come into contact with, meet, join, connect with, converge with, be contiguous with, be against. **2** *he touched her cheek* PRESS LIGHTLY, tap, pat; feel, stroke, fondle, caress, pet; brush, graze. **3** *sales touched twenty grand last year* REACH, attain, come to, make; rise to, soar to; sink to, plummet to; *informal* hit. **4** *(informal) nobody can touch him when he's on form* COMPARE WITH, be on a par with, equal, match, be a match for, be in the same class/league as, parallel, rival, come/get close to, measure up to; better, beat; *informal* hold a candle to. **5** *you're not supposed to touch the computer* HANDLE, hold, pick up, move; meddle with, play about with, fiddle with, interfere with, tamper with, disturb, lay a finger on; use, employ, make use of. **6** *state companies which have been touched by privatization* AFFECT, have an effect/impact on, make a difference to. **7** *Lisa felt touched by her kindness* AFFECT, move, tug at someone's heartstrings; leave an impression on, have an effect on.
• noun **1** *her touch on his shoulder* TAP, pat; stroke, caress; brush, graze. **2** *his political touch* SKILL, skilfulness, expertise, dexterity, deftness, adroitness, adeptness, ability, talent, flair, facility, proficiency, knack, technique, approach, style. **3** *there was a touch of bitterness in her voice | add a touch of vinegar* TRACE, bit, suggestion, suspicion, hint, scintilla, tinge, overtone, undertone; dash, taste, spot, drop, dab, pinch, speck, soupçon. **4** *the gas lights are a nice touch* DETAIL, feature, point; addition, accessory. **5** *have you been in touch with him?* CONTACT, communication, correspondence; connection, association.
– RELATED TERMS tactile.
– PHRASES **touch down** LAND, alight, come down, put down, arrive. **touch something off 1** *he touched off two of the bombs* DETONATE, set off, trigger, explode. **2** *the plan touched off a major political storm* CAUSE, spark off, trigger (off), start, set in motion, ignite, stir up, provoke, give rise to, lead to, generate. **touch on/upon 1** *many television programmes have touched on the subject* REFER TO, mention, comment on, remark on, bring up, raise, broach, allude to; cover, deal with. **2** *a self-confident manner touching on the arrogant* COME CLOSE TO, verge on, border on, approach. **touch someone up** *(Brit. informal)* FONDLE, molest, feel up; *informal* grope, paw, maul, goose; *N. Amer. informal* cop a feel. **touch something up 1** *these paints are handy for touching up small areas* REPAINT, retouch, patch up, fix up; renovate, refurbish, revamp; *informal* do up. **2** *touch up your CV and improve your interview skills* IMPROVE, enhance, make better, refine; *informal* tweak.
touch-and-go • adjective UNCERTAIN, precarious, risky, hazardous,

touch football ● noun a form of American football in which a ball-carrier is downed by touching instead of tackling.
touching ● adjective arousing strong emotion; moving. ● preposition concerning.
– DERIVATIVES **touchingly** adverb.
touch judge ● noun Rugby a linesman.
touchline ● noun Rugby & Soccer the boundary line on each side of the field.
touchpaper ● noun a strip of paper impregnated with nitre, for setting light to fireworks or gunpowder.
touch screen ● noun a display device which allows the user to interact with a computer by touching areas on the screen.
touchstone ● noun **1** a piece of fine-grained dark schist or jasper formerly used for testing alloys of gold by observing the colour of the mark which they made on it. **2** a standard or criterion.
touch-tone ● adjective (of a telephone) generating tones to dial rather than pulses.
touch-type ● verb type using all of one's fingers and without looking at the keys.
touchy ● adjective (**touchier**, **touchiest**) **1** quick to take offence; oversensitive. **2** (of a situation or issue) requiring careful handling.
– DERIVATIVES **touchily** adverb **touchiness** noun.
– ORIGIN perhaps an alteration of TETCHY, influenced by TOUCH.
touchy-feely ● adjective informal, often derogatory openly expressing affection or other emotions, especially through physical contact.
tough ● adjective **1** strong enough to withstand wear and tear. **2** able to endure hardship, adversity, or pain. **3** strict and uncompromising. **4** involving considerable difficulty or hardship. **5** rough or violent. **6** used to express a lack of sympathy. ● noun informal a rough and violent man.
– PHRASES **tough it out** informal endure a period of hardship or difficulty.
– DERIVATIVES **toughly** adverb **toughness** noun.
– ORIGIN Old English.
toughen ● verb make or become tough.
tough love ● noun promotion of a person's welfare by enforcing certain constraints on them or requiring them to take responsibility for their actions.
tough-minded ● adjective strong, realistic, and unsentimental.
toupee /to͞opay/ ● noun a small wig or artificial hairpiece worn to cover a bald spot.
– ORIGIN French, from Old French *toup* 'tuft'.
tour ● noun **1** a journey for pleasure in which several different places are visited. **2** a short trip to view or inspect something. **3** a series of performances or matches in several different places by performers or sports players. **4** (also **tour of duty**) a spell of duty on military or diplomatic service. ● verb make a tour of.
– ORIGIN Old French, 'turn', from Greek *tornos* 'lathe'.
tour de force /toor də forss/ ● noun (pl. **tours de force** pronunc. same) a performance or achievement accomplished with great skill.
– ORIGIN French, 'feat of strength'.
tourer ● noun a car, caravan, or bicycle designed for touring.
Tourette's syndrome /to͝orets/ ● noun Medicine a neurological disorder characterized by involuntary tics and often the compulsive utterance of obscenities.
– ORIGIN named after the French neurologist Gilles de la *Tourette* (1857–1904).
tourism ● noun the commercial organization and operation of holidays and visits to places of interest.
tourist ● noun **1** a person who travels for pleasure. **2** a member of a touring sports team.
– DERIVATIVES **touristic** adjective.
tourist class ● noun the cheapest accommodation or seating in a ship, aircraft, or hotel.
touristy ● adjective informal, often derogatory relating to, appealing to, or visited by tourists.
tourmaline /toormәleen/ ● noun a brittle grey or black mineral with piezoelectric and polarizing properties.
– ORIGIN Sinhalese, 'carnelian'.
tournament ● noun **1** a series of contests between a number of competitors, competing for an overall prize. **2** a medieval sporting event in which knights jousted with blunted weapons for a prize.
– ORIGIN Old French *torneiement*; related to TOURNEY.
tournedos /toornədō/ ● noun (pl. same or /toornədōz/) a small round thick cut from a fillet of beef.
– ORIGIN French, from *tourner* 'to turn' + *dos* 'back'.
tourney /toorni/ ● noun (pl. **tourneys**) a medieval joust. ● verb (**tourneys**, **tourneyed**) take part in a tourney.
– ORIGIN Old French *tornei*, from Latin *tornus* 'a turn'.
tourniquet /toornikay/ ● noun a device for stopping the flow of blood through an artery, typically by compressing a limb with a cord or tight bandage.
– ORIGIN French, probably from Old French *tournicle* 'coat of mail'.
tour operator ● noun a travel agent specializing in package holidays.
tousle /towz'l/ ● verb make (something, especially a person's hair) untidy.
– ORIGIN from dialect *touse* 'handle roughly', of Germanic origin.
tout /towt/ ● verb **1** attempt to sell (something), typically by a direct or persistent approach. **2** attempt to persuade people of the merits of. **3** Brit. sell (a ticket) for a popular event at a price

Thesaurus

dangerous, critical, suspenseful, cliffhanging, hanging by a thread.
– OPPOSITES certain.
touched ● adjective **1** *he was visibly touched by her terrible plight* AFFECTED, moved. **2** (informal) *her mother was a bit touched.* See MAD sense 1.
touching ● adjective MOVING, affecting, heart-warming, emotional, emotive, tender, sentimental; poignant, sad, tear-jerking.
touchstone ● noun CRITERION, standard, yardstick, benchmark, barometer, litmus test; measure, point of reference, norm, gauge, test, guide, exemplar, model, pattern.
touchy ● adjective **1** *she can be so touchy* SENSITIVE, oversensitive, hypersensitive, easily offended, thin-skinned, highly strung, tense; irritable, tetchy, testy, crotchety, peevish, querulous, bad-tempered, petulant, pettish; informal snappy, ratty; N. Amer. informal cranky. **2** *a touchy subject* DELICATE, sensitive, tricky, ticklish, embarrassing, awkward, difficult; contentious, controversial.
– OPPOSITES affable.
tough ● adjective **1** *tough leather gloves* DURABLE, strong, resilient, sturdy, rugged, solid, stout, hard-wearing, long-lasting, heavy-duty, well built, made to last. **2** *the steak was tough* CHEWY, leathery, gristly, stringy, fibrous. **3** *he'll survive—he's pretty tough* ROBUST, resilient, strong, hardy, rugged, fit; informal hard, (as) tough as old boots; dated stalwart. **4** *tough sentencing for persistent offenders* STRICT, stern, severe, stringent, rigorous, hard, firm, hard-hitting, uncompromising; unsentimental, unsympathetic. **5** *the training was pretty tough* ARDUOUS, onerous, strenuous, gruelling, exacting, difficult, demanding, hard, heavy, taxing, tiring, exhausting, punishing, laborious, stressful, Herculean; archaic toilsome. **6** *these are tough questions for American policy-makers* DIFFICULT, hard, knotty, thorny, tricky.
– OPPOSITES soft, weak, easy.
● noun (informal) *a gang of toughs* RUFFIAN, thug, hoodlum, hooligan, bully boy; Brit. rough; informal roughneck, heavy, bruiser, gorilla, yahoo; Brit. informal yob, yobbo.
toughen ● verb **1** *the process toughens the wood fibres* STRENGTHEN, fortify, reinforce, harden, temper, anneal. **2** *measures to toughen up prison discipline* MAKE STRICTER, make more severe, stiffen, tighten up; informal beef up.
tour ● noun **1** *a three-day walking tour* TRIP, excursion, journey, expedition, jaunt, outing; trek, safari; archaic peregrination. **2** *a tour of the factory* VISIT, inspection, guided tour, walkabout. **3** *his tour of duty in Ulster* STINT, stretch, spell, turn, assignment, period of service.
● verb **1** *this hotel is well placed for touring Somerset* TRAVEL ROUND, explore, holiday in; informal do. **2** *the prince toured a local factory* VISIT, go round, walk round, inspect.
tourist ● noun HOLIDAYMAKER, traveller, sightseer, visitor, backpacker, globetrotter, day tripper, tripper; N. Amer. vacationer, vacationist, out-of-towner; Brit. informal grockle.
– OPPOSITES local.
tournament ● noun **1** *a golf tournament* COMPETITION, contest, championship, meeting, meet, event, match, fixture. **2** (historical) *a knight preparing for a tournament* JOUST, tourney, tilt; the lists.
tousled ● adjective UNTIDY, dishevelled, wind-blown, messy, disordered, disarranged, messed up, rumpled, uncombed, un-

higher than the official one. ● **noun** (also **ticket tout**) Brit. a person who buys up tickets for an event to resell them at a profit.
– ORIGIN from obsolete *tute* 'look out', of Germanic origin.
tout court /too koor/ ● **adverb** briefly; simply.
– ORIGIN French, 'very short'.
tout de suite /too də sweet/ ● **adverb** at once.
– ORIGIN French, 'quite in sequence'.
tow[1] ● **verb** use a vehicle or boat to pull (another vehicle or boat) along. ● **noun** an act of towing.
– PHRASES **in tow 1** (also **on tow**) being towed. **2** accompanying or following someone.
– DERIVATIVES **towable** adjective **towage** noun.
– ORIGIN Old English.
tow[2] ● **noun 1** the coarse and broken part of flax or hemp prepared for spinning. **2** a bundle of untwisted natural or manmade fibres.
– ORIGIN Old English.
toward ● **preposition** variant of TOWARDS.
towards (chiefly N. Amer. also **toward**) ● **preposition 1** in the direction of. **2** getting nearer to (a time or goal). **3** in relation to. **4** contributing to the cost of.
– ORIGIN Old English.
tow bar ● **noun** a bar fitted to the back of a vehicle, used in towing a trailer or caravan.
towel ● **noun** a piece of thick absorbent cloth or paper used for drying. ● **verb** (**towelled**, **towelling**; US **toweled**, **toweling**) dry with a towel.
– ORIGIN Old French *toaille*.
towelling (US **toweling**) ● **noun** thick absorbent cloth, typically cotton with uncut loops, used for towels and bathrobes.
tower ● **noun 1** a tall, narrow building, either free-standing or forming part of a building such as a church or castle. **2** a tall structure that houses machinery, operators, etc. **3** a tall structure used as a receptacle or for storage. ● **verb 1** rise to or reach a great height. **2** (**towering**) very important or influential. **3** (**towering**) very intense: *a towering rage*.
– ORIGIN Old English, reinforced by Old French *tour*, from Greek *turris*.
tower block ● **noun** Brit. a tall modern building containing numerous floors of offices or flats.
tow-headed ● **adjective** having very light blonde or untidy hair.
towline ● **noun** a tow rope.
town ● **noun 1** a settlement larger than a village and generally smaller than a city, with defined boundaries and local government. **2** the central part of a town or city, with its business or shopping area. **3** densely populated areas, especially as contrasted with the country or suburbs. **4** the permanent residents of a university town. Often contrasted with GOWN.
– PHRASES **go to town** informal do something thoroughly or enthusiastically. **on the town** informal enjoying the nightlife of a city or town.
– ORIGIN Old English, 'enclosed piece of land, homestead, village'.
town car ● **noun** US a limousine.
town clerk ● **noun 1** N. Amer. a public official in charge of the records of a town. **2** (in the UK, until 1974) the secretary and legal adviser of a town corporation.
town council ● **noun** (especially in the UK) the elected governing body in a municipality.
– DERIVATIVES **town councillor** noun.
town crier ● **noun** historical a person employed to make public announcements in the streets.
townee ● **noun** variant spelling of TOWNIE.
town hall ● **noun** a building used for the administration of local government.
town house ● **noun 1** a tall, narrow traditional terrace house, generally having three or more floors. **2** an urban residence of a person owning another property in the country.
townie (also **townee**) ● **noun** informal a person who lives in a town (used especially with reference to their supposed ignorance of rural affairs).
townland ● **noun** (especially in Ireland) a territorial division of land; a township.
town meeting ● **noun** US a meeting of the voters of a town for the transaction of public business.
town planning ● **noun** the planning and control of the construction, growth, and development of a town or other urban area.
– DERIVATIVES **town planner** noun.
townscape ● **noun** an urban landscape.
township ● **noun 1** (in South Africa) a suburb or city of predominantly black occupation, formerly officially designated for black occupation by apartheid legislation. **2** S. African a new area being developed for residential or industrial use by speculators. **3** N. Amer. a division of a county with some corporate powers. **4** Brit. historical a manor or parish as a territorial division. **5** Austral./NZ a small town.
– ORIGIN Old English.
townsman (or **townswoman**) ● **noun** a person living in a particular town or city.
townspeople (also **townsfolk**) ● **plural noun** the people living in a particular town or city.
towpath ● **noun** a path beside a river or canal, originally used as a pathway for horses towing barges.
tow rope ● **noun** a rope, cable, etc. used in towing.
toxaemia /tokseemiə/ (US **toxemia**) ● **noun** Medicine **1** blood poisoning by toxins from a local bacterial infection. **2** preeclampsia.
– ORIGIN from Latin *toxicum* 'poison'.
toxic ● **adjective 1** poisonous. **2** relating to or caused by poison. ● **noun** (**toxics**) poisonous substances.
– DERIVATIVES **toxicity** noun.
– ORIGIN from Latin *toxicum* 'poison'.
toxicant ● **noun** a toxic substance introduced into the environment, e.g. a pesticide.
– ORIGIN variant of INTOXICANT, differentiated in sense.
toxicology /toksikolləji/ ● **noun** the branch of science concerned with the nature, effects, and detection of poisons.
– DERIVATIVES **toxicological** adjective **toxicologist** noun.
toxic shock syndrome ● **noun** acute septicaemia in women, typically caused by bacterial infection from a retained tampon or IUD.
toxin ● **noun** a poison produced by a micro-organism or other organism and acting as an antigen in the body.
toxocara /toksəkaarə/ ● **noun** a nematode worm which is a parasite of dogs, cats, and other animals and can be transmitted to humans.

Thesaurus

groomed, tangled, wild, unkempt; *informal* mussed up.
– OPPOSITES neat, tidy.
tout ● **verb 1** *street merchants were touting their wares* PEDDLE, sell, hawk, offer for sale; *informal* flog. **2** *minicab drivers were touting for business* SOLICIT, seek, drum up; ask, petition, appeal, canvas. **3** *he's being touted as the next Scotland manager* RECOMMEND, speak of, talk of; predict; *Brit.* tip.
tow ● **verb** *the car was towed back to the garage* PULL, haul, drag, draw, tug, lug.
– PHRASES **in tow** *he arrived with his new girlfriend in tow* IN ATTENDANCE, by one's side, in one's charge; accompanying, following.
towards ● **preposition 1** *they were driving towards her flat* IN THE DIRECTION OF, to; on the way to, on the road to, en route for. **2** *towards evening dark clouds gathered* JUST BEFORE, shortly before, near, nearing, around, approaching, close to, coming to, getting on for. **3** *her attitude towards politics* WITH REGARD TO, as regards, regarding, in/with regard to, respecting, in relation to, concerning, about, apropos. **4** *a grant towards the cost of new buses* AS A CONTRIBUTION TO, for, to help with.
tower ● **noun** *a church tower* STEEPLE, spire; minaret; turret; bell tower, belfry, campanile.
● **verb 1** *snow-capped peaks towered over the valley* SOAR, rise, rear; overshadow, overhang, hang over, dominate. **2** *he towered over most other theologians of his generation* DOMINATE, overshadow, outshine, outclass, eclipse, be head and shoulders above, put someone/something in the shade.
towering ● **adjective 1** *a towering skyscraper* HIGH, tall, lofty, soaring, sky-high, sky-scraping, multi-storey; giant, gigantic, enormous, huge, massive; *informal* ginormous. **2** *a towering intellect* OUTSTANDING, pre-eminent, leading, foremost, finest, top, surpassing, supreme, great, incomparable, unrivalled, unsurpassed, peerless. **3** *a towering rage* EXTREME, fierce, terrible, intense, overpowering, mighty, violent, vehement, passionate.
town ● **noun** URBAN AREA, conurbation, municipality; city, metropolis, megalopolis; *Brit.* borough; *Scottish* burgh.
– RELATED TERMS municipal, urban.
– OPPOSITES country.
toxic ● **adjective** POISONOUS, virulent, noxious, dangerous, harmful,

– DERIVATIVES **toxocariasis** noun.
– ORIGIN from Latin *toxicum* 'poison' + Greek *kara* 'head'.
toxophilite /toksoffilīt/ rare ● noun a student or lover of archery. ● adjective relating to archers and archery.
– ORIGIN from *Toxophilus*, a name invented by the English scholar Roger Ascham, used as the title of his treatise on archery (1545), from Greek *toxon* 'bow' + *-philos* 'loving'.
toxoplasmosis /toksōplazmōsiss/ ● noun Medicine a disease caused by a parasitic protozoan, transmitted chiefly through undercooked meat, soil, or in cat faeces.
– ORIGIN from *Toxoplasma* (genus name) + -OSIS.
toy ● noun **1** an object for a child to play with, typically a model or miniature replica of something. **2** a gadget or machine regarded as providing amusement for an adult. **3** (before another noun) (of a breed or variety of dog) much smaller than is normal for the breed. ● verb (**toy with**) **1** consider casually or indecisively. **2** move or handle absent-mindedly or nervously. **3** eat or drink in an unenthusiastic or restrained way.
– DERIVATIVES **toylike** adjective.
– ORIGIN originally referring to a funny story or remark: of unknown origin.
toy boy ● noun Brit. informal a male lover who is much younger than his partner.
toytown ● adjective **1** resembling a model of a town in being seemingly in miniature. **2** having no real value or substance.
TQM ● abbreviation Total Quality Management.
trace[1] ● verb **1** find by investigation. **2** find or describe the origin or development of. **3** follow the course or position of with one's eye, mind, or finger. **4** copy (a drawing, map, or design) by drawing over its lines on a superimposed piece of transparent paper. **5** draw (a pattern or outline). ● noun **1** a mark or other indication of the existence or passing of something. **2** a very small quantity. **3** a barely discernible indication: *a trace of a smile touched his lips.* **4** a line or pattern corresponding to something which is being recorded or measured. **5** a procedure to trace something.
– DERIVATIVES **traceable** adjective.
– ORIGIN Old French *tracier*, from Latin *tractus* 'drawing, draught'.
trace[2] ● noun each of the two side straps, chains, or ropes by which a horse is attached to a vehicle that it is pulling.
– PHRASES **kick over the traces** become insubordinate or reckless.
– ORIGIN Old French *trais*, plural of *trait* 'trait'.
trace element ● noun a chemical element present or required only in minute amounts.
tracer ● noun **1** a bullet or shell whose course is made visible by a trail of flames or smoke, used to assist in aiming. **2** a substance introduced into a system so that its subsequent distribution can be followed from its colour, radioactivity, or other distinctive property.
tracery ● noun (pl. **traceries**) **1** Architecture ornamental stone openwork. **2** a delicate branching pattern.
– DERIVATIVES **traceried** adjective.
trachea /trəkeeə, traykiə/ ● noun (pl. **tracheae** /trəkee-ee, trayki-ee/ or **tracheas**) Anatomy the tube conveying air between the larynx and the bronchial tubes; the windpipe.
– DERIVATIVES **tracheal** /traykiəl/ adjective.
– ORIGIN from Greek *trakheia artēria* 'rough artery'.
tracheotomy /trakkiottəmi/ (also **tracheostomy** /trakkiostəmi/) ● noun (pl. **tracheotomies**) Medicine an incision in the windpipe made to relieve an obstruction to breathing.
trachoma /trəkōmə/ ● noun a contagious infection transmitted by a bacterium and causing inflammation of the inner surface of the eyelids.
– ORIGIN Greek *trakhōma* 'roughness'.
tracing ● noun **1** a copy of a drawing, map, etc. made by tracing. **2** a faint or delicate mark or pattern.
track ● noun **1** a rough path or minor road. **2** a prepared course or circuit for racing. **3** a mark or line of marks left by a person, animal, or vehicle in passing. **4** a continuous line of rails on a railway. **5** a section of a record, compact disc, or cassette tape containing one song or piece of music. [ORIGIN originally referring to a groove on a gramophone record.] **6** a strip or rail along which something (e.g. a curtain) may be moved. **7** a continuous articulated metal band around the wheels of a heavy vehicle. **8** the transverse distance between a vehicle's wheels. ● verb **1** follow the course or movements of. **2** (**track down**) find after a thorough or difficult search. **3** follow a particular course. **4** (of a film or television camera) move in relation to the subject being filmed. [ORIGIN with reference to early filming when a camera was moved along a track.]
– PHRASES **keep** (or **lose**) **track of** keep (or fail to keep) fully aware of or informed about. **make tracks** (**for**) informal leave (for a place). **on the right** (or **wrong**) **track** following a course likely to result in success (or failure). **stop** (or **be stopped**) **in one's tracks** informal be brought to a sudden and complete halt. **the wrong side of the tracks** informal a poor or less prestigious part of town. [ORIGIN with reference to the railway tracks of American towns, once serving as a line of demarcation between rich and poor quarters.]
– DERIVATIVES **trackless** adjective.
– ORIGIN Old French *trac*, perhaps from Low German or Dutch *trek* 'draught, drawing'.
trackball ● noun a small ball set in a holder that can be rotated by hand to move a cursor on a computer screen.
trackbed ● noun the foundation structure on which railway tracks are laid.
tracker ● noun a person who tracks.
track events ● plural noun athletic events that take place on a running track.
tracking ● noun **1** Electronics the maintenance of a constant difference in frequency between connected circuits or components. **2** the formation of an electrically conducting path over the surface of an insulator.
track record ● noun the past achievements or performance of a person, organization, or product.
tracksuit ● noun a loose, warm outfit consisting of a sweatshirt and trousers.
trackway ● noun a path formed by the repeated treading of people or animals.
tract[1] ● noun **1** a large area of land. **2** a major passage in the body or other continuous elongated anatomical structure.
– ORIGIN Latin *tractus* 'drawing, draught', from *trahere* 'draw, pull'.
tract[2] ● noun a short treatise in pamphlet form, typically on a religious subject.
– ORIGIN apparently an abbreviation of Latin *tractatus* 'treatise'.

Thesaurus

injurious, pernicious.
– OPPOSITES harmless.
toy ● noun **1** *a cuddly toy* PLAYTHING, game. **2** *an executive toy* GADGET, device; trinket, knick-knack; informal gizmo.
● adjective **1** *a toy gun* MODEL, imitation, replica; miniature. **2** *a toy poodle* MINIATURE, small, tiny, diminutive, dwarf, midget, pygmy.
– PHRASES **toy with 1** *I was toying with the idea of writing a book* THINK ABOUT, consider, flirt with, entertain the possibility of; informal kick around. **2** *Adam toyed with his glasses* FIDDLE WITH, play with, fidget with, twiddle; finger. **3** *she toyed with her food* NIBBLE, pick at, peck at, eat listlessly, eat like a bird.
trace ● verb **1** *police hope to trace the owner of the jewellery* TRACK DOWN, find, discover, detect, unearth, turn up, hunt down, ferret out, run to ground. **2** *she traced a pattern in the sand with her toe* DRAW, outline, mark. **3** *the analysis traces out the consequences of such beliefs* OUTLINE, map out, sketch out, delineate, depict, show, indicate.
● noun **1** *no trace had been found of the missing plane* VESTIGE, sign, mark, indication, evidence, clue; remains, remnant, relic, survival. **2** *a trace of bitterness crept into her voice* BIT, touch, hint, suggestion, suspicion, shadow, whiff; drop, dash, tinge, speck, shred, jot, iota; informal smidgen, tad. **3** *the ground was hard and they left no traces* TRAIL, tracks, marks, prints, footprints; spoor.
track ● noun **1** *a gravel track* PATH, pathway, footpath, lane, trail, route, way, course. **2** *the final lap of the track* COURSE, racecourse, racetrack; velodrome; Brit. circuit. **3** *he found the tracks of a grey fox* TRACES, marks, prints, footprints, trail, spoor. **4** *Orkney lies on the track of the Atlantic winds* COURSE, path, line, route, way, trajectory. **5** *commuters had to walk along the tracks* RAIL, line, railway line. **6** *the album's title track* SONG, recording, number, piece.
● verb *he tracked a bear for 40 km* FOLLOW, trail, trace, pursue, shadow, stalk, keep an eye on, keep in sight; informal tail.
– PHRASES **keep track of** MONITOR, follow, keep up with, keep an eye on; keep in touch with, keep up to date with; informal keep tabs on. **track someone/something down** DISCOVER, find, detect, hunt down/out, unearth, uncover, turn up, dig up, ferret out, bring to

tractable • adjective **1** easy to control or influence. **2** (of a situation or problem) easy to deal with.
– DERIVATIVES **tractability** noun.
– ORIGIN Latin *tractabilis*, from *tractare* 'to handle'.

tractate /traktayt/ • noun formal a treatise.
– ORIGIN Latin *tractatus*, from *tractare* 'to handle'.

traction • noun **1** the action of pulling a thing along a surface. **2** the motive power used for pulling. **3** Medicine the application of a sustained pull on a limb or muscle, especially to maintain the position of a fractured bone or to correct a deformity. **4** the grip of a tyre on a road or a wheel on a rail.
– ORIGIN Latin, from *trahere* 'draw, pull'.

traction engine • noun a steam or diesel-powered road vehicle used (especially formerly) for pulling very heavy loads.

tractor • noun a powerful motor vehicle with large rear wheels, used chiefly on farms for hauling equipment and trailers.
– ORIGIN Latin, from *trahere* 'to pull'.

trad informal • adjective (especially of music) traditional. • noun traditional jazz or folk music.

trade • noun **1** the buying and selling of goods and services. **2** a commercial activity of a particular kind: *the tourist trade*. **3** a job requiring manual skills and special training. **4** (**the trade**) (treated as sing. or pl.) the people engaged in a particular area of business. **5** dated, chiefly derogatory the practice of making one's living in business. **6** a trade wind. • verb **1** buy and sell goods and services. **2** buy or sell (a particular item or product). **3** exchange, typically as a commercial transaction. **4** (**trade in**) exchange (a used article) in part payment for another. **5** (**trade on**) take advantage of. **6** (**trade off**) exchange (something of value).
– DERIVATIVES **tradable** (or **tradeable**) adjective.
– ORIGIN Low German, 'track'; related to TREAD.

trade deficit • noun the amount by which the cost of a country's imports exceeds the value of its exports.

trade gap • noun another term for TRADE DEFICIT.

trademark • noun **1** a symbol, word, or words, legally registered or established by use as representing a company or product. **2** a distinctive characteristic or object. • verb provide with a trademark.

trade name • noun **1** a name that has the status of a trademark. **2** a name by which something is known in a particular trade or profession.

trade-off • noun a balance achieved between two desirable but incompatible features; a compromise.

trade plates • plural noun Brit. temporary number plates used by car dealers or manufacturers on unlicensed cars.

trade price • noun the price paid for goods by a retailer to a manufacturer or wholesaler.

trader • noun **1** a person who trades goods, currency, or shares. **2** a merchant ship.

tradescantia /traddiskantiə/ • noun an American plant with triangular three-petalled flowers.
– ORIGIN named in honour of the English botanist John *Tradescant* (1570–1638).

tradesman • noun a person engaged in trading or a trade, typically on a small scale.

trade surplus • noun the amount by which the value of a country's exports exceeds the cost of its imports.

trade union (Brit. also **trades union**) • noun an organized association of workers formed to protect and further their rights and interests.
– DERIVATIVES **trade unionism** noun **trade unionist** noun.

trade wind • noun a wind blowing steadily towards the equator from the north-east in the northern hemisphere or the south-east in the southern hemisphere, especially at sea.
– ORIGIN from the obsolete phrase *blow trade* 'blow steadily', from a former meaning of *trade* which was 'regular course of action'.

trading estate • noun Brit. a specially designed industrial and commercial area.

trading post • noun a store or small settlement established for trading, typically in a remote place.

tradition • noun **1** the transmission of customs or beliefs from generation to generation. **2** a long-established custom or belief passed on in this way. **3** an artistic or literary method or style established by an artist, writer, or movement, and subsequently followed by others.
– ORIGIN Latin, from *tradere* 'deliver, betray'.

traditional • adjective **1** of, relating to, or following tradition. **2** (of jazz) in the style of the early 20th century.
– DERIVATIVES **traditionally** adverb.

traditionalism • noun the upholding of tradition, especially so as to resist change.
– DERIVATIVES **traditionalist** noun & adjective.

traduce /trədyo͞os/ • verb speak badly of or tell lies about.
– ORIGIN Latin *traducere* 'lead in front of others, expose to ridicule'.

traffic • noun **1** vehicles moving on public roads. **2** the movement of ships or aircraft. **3** the commercial transportation of goods or passengers. **4** the messages or signals transmitted through a communications system. **5** the action of trading in something illegal. • verb (**trafficked**, **trafficking**) deal or trade in something illegal.
– DERIVATIVES **trafficker** noun.
– ORIGIN from French *traffique*, Spanish *tráfico*, or Italian *traffico*.

traffic calming • noun the deliberate slowing of traffic in residential areas, by building road humps or other obstructions.

Thesaurus

light, run to earth, run to ground.

tract¹ • noun *large tracts of land* AREA, region, expanse, sweep, stretch, extent, belt, swathe, zone.

tract² • noun *a political tract* TREATISE, essay, article, paper, work, monograph, disquisition, dissertation, thesis, homily; pamphlet, booklet, leaflet.

tractable • adjective MALLEABLE, manageable, amenable, pliable, governable, yielding, complaisant, compliant, persuadable, accommodating, docile, biddable, obedient, submissive, meek.
– OPPOSITES recalcitrant.

traction • noun GRIP, purchase, friction, adhesion.

trade • noun **1** *the illicit trade in stolen cattle* COMMERCE, buying and selling, dealing, traffic, trafficking, business, marketing, merchandising; dealings, transactions. **2** *the glazier's trade* CRAFT, occupation, job, career, profession, business, line (of work), métier, vocation, calling, walk of life, field; work, employment.
– RELATED TERMS mercantile.
• verb **1** *he made his fortune trading in beaver pelts* DEAL, buy and sell, traffic, market, merchandise, peddle; informal hawk, flog. **2** *the business is trading at a loss* OPERATE, run, do business. **3** *I traded the old machine for a newer model* SWAP, exchange, switch; barter.
– PHRASES **trade on** EXPLOIT, take advantage of, capitalize on, profit from, use, make use of; milk; informal cash in on.

trademark • noun **1** *the company's trademark* LOGO, emblem, sign, mark, stamp, symbol, device, badge, crest, monogram, colophon; trade name, brand name, proprietary name. **2** *it had all the trademarks of a Mafia hit* CHARACTERISTIC, hallmark, telltale sign, sign, trait, quality, attribute, feature, peculiarity, idiosyncrasy.

trader • noun DEALER, merchant, buyer, seller, buyer and seller, marketeer, merchandiser, broker, agent; distributor, vendor, purveyor, supplier, trafficker; shopkeeper, retailer, wholesaler.

tradesman, tradeswoman • noun **1** *tradesmen standing nonchalantly outside their stores* SHOPKEEPER, retailer, vendor, wholesaler; N. Amer. storekeeper. **2** *a qualified tradesman* CRAFTSMAN, workman, artisan.

tradition • noun **1** *during a maiden speech, by tradition, everyone keeps absolutely silent* HISTORICAL CONVENTION, unwritten law; oral history, lore, folklore. **2** *an age-old tradition* CUSTOM, practice, convention, ritual, observance, way, usage, habit, institution; formal praxis.

traditional • adjective **1** *traditional Christmas dishes* LONG-ESTABLISHED, customary, time-honoured, established, classic, wonted, accustomed, standard, regular, normal, conventional, usual, orthodox, habitual, set, fixed, routine, ritual; old, age-old. **2** *traditional beliefs* HANDED-DOWN, folk, unwritten, oral.

traduce • verb DEFAME, slander, speak ill of, misrepresent, malign, vilify, denigrate, disparage, slur, impugn, smear, besmirch, run down, blacken the name of, cast aspersions on; informal bad-mouth; formal calumniate.

traffic • noun **1** *the bridge is not open to traffic* VEHICLES, cars, lorries, trucks. **2** *they might be stuck in traffic* TRAFFIC JAMS, congestion, gridlock, tailbacks, hold-ups, queues; informal snarl-ups. **3** *the increased use of railways for goods traffic* TRANSPORT, transportation, freight, conveyancing, shipping. **4** *the illegal traffic in stolen art* TRADE, trading, trafficking, dealing, commerce, business, buying and selling; smuggling, bootlegging, black market; dealings, transactions. **5** (archaic) *he has little traffic with his neighbours* CONTACT, communication, intercourse, dealings, relations.

t

– ORIGIN translation of German *Verkehrsberuhigung*.
traffic island • noun a small raised area in the middle of a road which provides a safe place for pedestrians to stand.
traffic jam • noun a line or lines of traffic at or virtually at a standstill.
traffic lights (also **traffic light** or **traffic signal**) • plural noun a set of automatically operated coloured lights for controlling traffic.
traffic warden • noun Brit. a uniformed official who locates and reports on infringements of parking regulations.
tragedian /trəjeediən/ • noun **1** (fem. **tragedienne** /trəjeedien/) a tragic actor or actress. **2** a writer of tragedies.
tragedy • noun (pl. **tragedies**) **1** an event causing great suffering, destruction, and distress. **2** a serious play with an unhappy ending, especially one concerning the downfall of the main character.
– ORIGIN Greek *tragōidia*, apparently from *tragos* 'goat' (the reason remains unexplained) + *ōidē* 'song, ode'.
tragic • adjective **1** extremely distressing or sad. **2** suffering extreme distress or sadness. **3** relating to tragedy in a literary work.
– DERIVATIVES **tragical** adjective **tragically** adverb.
tragicomedy • noun (pl. **tragicomedies**) a play or novel containing elements of both comedy and tragedy.
– DERIVATIVES **tragicomic** adjective.
trail • noun **1** a mark or a series of signs left behind by the passage of someone or something. **2** a track or scent used in following someone or hunting an animal. **3** a long thin part stretching behind or hanging down from something. **4** a beaten path through rough country. **5** a route planned or followed for a particular purpose: *the tourist trail*. • verb **1** draw or be drawn along behind. **2** follow the trail of. **3** walk or move slowly or wearily. **4** (**trail away/off**) (of the voice or a speaker) fade gradually before stopping. **5** be losing to an opponent in a contest. **6** (of a plant) grow along the ground or so as to hang down. **7** advertise with a trailer.
– ORIGIN from Old French *traillier* 'to tow' or Low German *treilen* 'haul (a boat)', from Latin *trahere* 'to pull'.
trail bike • noun a light motorcycle for use in rough terrain.
trailblazer • noun **1** a person who makes a new track through wild country. **2** an innovator.
– DERIVATIVES **trailblazing** noun & adjective.
trailer • noun **1** an unpowered vehicle towed by another. **2** the rear section of an articulated truck. **3** N. Amer. a caravan. **4** an extract from a film or programme used for advance advertising. • verb **1** advertise with a trailer. **2** transport by trailer.
trailer park • noun **1** N. Amer. a caravan site. **2** (before another noun) US lacking refinement, taste, or quality: *a trailer-park floozy*.
trailer truck • noun US an articulated truck.
trailing edge • noun the rear edge of a moving body, especially an aircraft wing or propeller blade.
trail mix • noun a mixture of dried fruit and nuts eaten as a snack food.
train • verb **1** teach (a person or animal) a particular skill or type of behaviour through regular practice and instruction. **2** be taught in such a way. **3** make or become physically fit through a course of exercise and diet. **4** (**train on**) point (something) at. **5** make (a plant) grow in a particular direction or into a required shape. • noun **1** a series of railway carriages or wagons moved as a unit by a locomotive or by integral motors. **2** a number of vehicles or pack animals moving in a line. **3** a series of connected events, thoughts, etc. **4** a long piece of trailing material attached to the back of a formal dress or robe. **5** a retinue of attendants accompanying an important person.
– PHRASES **in train** in progress.
– DERIVATIVES **trainable** adjective **training** noun **trainload** noun.
– ORIGIN originally in the sense 'a delay': from Old French *trahiner*, from Latin *trahere* 'pull, draw'.
trainee • noun a person undergoing training for a particular job or profession.
– DERIVATIVES **traineeship** noun.
trainer • noun **1** a person who trains people or animals. **2** Brit. a soft shoe, suitable for sports or casual wear.
training college • noun (in the UK) a college where people, especially prospective teachers, are trained.
training shoe • noun another term for TRAINER (in sense 2).
trainspotter • noun Brit. **1** a person who collects locomotive numbers as a hobby. **2** often derogatory a person who obsessively studies the minutiae of any minority interest or specialized hobby.
– DERIVATIVES **trainspotting** noun.
traipse • verb walk or move wearily, reluctantly, or aimlessly. • noun a tedious or tiring walk.
– ORIGIN of unknown origin.
trait /tray, trayt/ • noun **1** a distinguishing quality or characteristic. **2** a genetically determined characteristic.
– USAGE **Trait** has two pronunciations. The first, sounding like **tray**, is the traditional one (corresponding to its sound in French), but the newer one, rhyming with **rate**, is becoming the commoner one and is generally used in the US.
– ORIGIN French, from Latin *tractus* 'drawing, draught'.
traitor • noun a person who betrays their country, a cause, etc.
– DERIVATIVES **traitorous** adjective.
– ORIGIN Old French *traitour*, from Latin *tradere* 'hand over'.

Thesaurus

• verb *he confessed to trafficking in gold and ivory* TRADE, deal, do business, buy and sell; smuggle, bootleg; *informal* run.
tragedy • noun DISASTER, calamity, catastrophe, cataclysm, misfortune, reverse, vicissitude, trial, tribulation, affliction, adversity.
tragic • adjective **1** *a tragic accident* DISASTROUS, calamitous, catastrophic, cataclysmic, devastating, terrible, dreadful, awful, appalling, horrendous; fatal, deadly, mortal, lethal. **2** *a tragic tale* SAD, unhappy, pathetic, moving, distressing, painful, harrowing, heart-rending, piteous, wretched, sorry; melancholy, doleful, mournful. **3** *a tragic waste of talent* DREADFUL, terrible, awful, deplorable, lamentable, regrettable; *formal* grievous.
– OPPOSITES fortunate, happy.
trail • noun **1** *he left a trail of clues | a trail of devastation* SERIES, string, chain, succession, sequence; aftermath. **2** *wolves on the trail of their prey* TRACK, spoor, path, scent; traces, marks, signs, prints, footprints. **3** *the plane's vapour trail* WAKE, tail, stream. **4** *a trail of ants* LINE, column, train, file, procession, string, chain, convoy; queue. **5** *country parks with nature trails* PATH, pathway, way, footpath, track, course, route.
• verb **1** *her robe trailed along the ground* DRAG, sweep, be drawn; dangle, hang (down), droop. **2** *the roses grew wild, their stems trailing over the banks* HANG, droop, fall, spill, cascade. **3** *Sharpe suspected that they were trailing him* FOLLOW, pursue, track, shadow, stalk, hunt (down); run to earth, run to ground; *informal* tail. **4** *the defending champions were trailing 10–5 at half time* LOSE, be down, be behind, lag behind. **5** *I hate trailing round the shops* TRUDGE, plod, drag oneself, traipse, trek; *N. Amer. informal* schlep. **6** *her voice trailed off* FADE, tail off/away, grow faint, die away, dwindle, subside, peter out, fizzle out.
train • verb **1** *an engineer trained in remote-sensing techniques* INSTRUCT, teach, coach, tutor, school, educate, prime, drill, ground; inculcate, indoctrinate. **2** *she's training to be a hairdresser* STUDY, learn, prepare, take instruction. **3** *with the Olympics in mind, athletes are training hard* EXERCISE, do exercises, work out, get into shape, practise. **4** *she trained the gun on his chest* AIM, point, direct, level, focus; take aim, zero in on.
• noun **1** *the train for London* locomotive, railway train; *baby talk* choo choo. **2** *a minister and his train of attendants* RETINUE, entourage, cortège, following, staff, household, court, suite, attendants, retainers, followers, bodyguards. **3** *a train of elephants* PROCESSION, line, file, column, convoy, cavalcade, caravan, queue, string, succession. **4** *a bizarre train of events* CHAIN, string, series, sequence, succession, set, course, cycle, concatenation.
trainer • noun COACH, instructor, teacher, tutor; handler.
training • noun **1** *in-house training for staff* INSTRUCTION, teaching, coaching, tuition, tutoring, schooling, education; indoctrination, inculcation. **2** *four months' hard training before the match* EXERCISE, exercises, working out; practice, preparation.
traipse • verb TRUDGE, trek, tramp, trail, plod, drag oneself, slog; *Brit. informal* trog; *N. Amer. informal* schlep.
trait • noun CHARACTERISTIC, attribute, feature, (essential) quality, property; mannerism, habit, custom, idiosyncrasy, peculiarity, quirk, oddity, foible.
traitor • noun BETRAYER, back-stabber, double-crosser, double-dealer, renegade, Judas, quisling, fifth columnist; turncoat, defector, deserter; collaborator, informer, double agent; *informal* snake in the grass, two-timer.
traitorous • adjective TREACHEROUS, disloyal, treasonous, back-stabbing; double-crossing, double-dealing, faithless, unfaithful, two-faced, false-hearted, duplicitous, deceitful, false; *informal* two-

trajectory /trəjektəri/ ● noun (pl. **trajectories**) the path described by a projectile flying or an object moving under the action of given forces.
– ORIGIN Latin *trajectoria*, from *traicere* 'throw across'.

tram (also **tramcar**) ● noun Brit. a passenger vehicle powered by electricity conveyed by overhead cables, and running on rails laid in a public road.
– ORIGIN Low German and Dutch *trame* 'beam, barrow shaft', the original sense in English; the word also denoted a barrow or cart used in coal mines, later the tracks on which such carts ran.

tramlines ● plural noun Brit. **1** rails for a tramcar. **2** informal a pair of parallel lines at the sides of a tennis court or at the side or back of a badminton court.

trammel ● noun **1** (**trammels**) literary restrictions or impediments to freedom of action. **2** (also **trammel net**) a three-layered net, designed so that a pocket forms when fish attempt to swim through, thus trapping them. ● verb (**trammelled**, **trammelling**; US **trammeled**, **trammeling**) literary constrain or impede.
– ORIGIN Old French *tramail*, from Latin *trimaculum*, perhaps from *tri-* 'three' + *macula* 'mesh'.

tramontana /traamontaanə/ ● noun a cold north wind blowing in Italy or the adjoining regions of the Adriatic and Mediterranean.
– ORIGIN Italian, 'north wind, Pole Star'.

tramp ● verb **1** walk heavily or noisily. **2** walk wearily or reluctantly over a long distance. ● noun **1** an itinerant homeless person who lives by begging or doing casual work. **2** the sound of heavy steps. **3** a long walk. **4** a cargo vessel running between many different ports rather than sailing a fixed route. **5** N. Amer. informal a promiscuous woman.
– DERIVATIVES **tramper** noun.
– ORIGIN probably Low German.

trample ● verb **1** tread on and crush. **2** (**trample on/upon/over**) treat with contempt.
– ORIGIN from TRAMP.

trampoline ● noun a strong fabric sheet connected by springs to a frame, used as a springboard and landing area in doing acrobatic or gymnastic exercises. ● verb (**trampolining**) use a trampoline.
– ORIGIN Italian *trampolino*, from *trampoli* 'stilts'.

tramway ● noun **1** Brit. a set of rails for a tram. **2** a tram system.

trance /traanss/ ● noun **1** a half-conscious state characterized by an absence of response to external stimuli, typically as induced by hypnosis. **2** a state of inattention. **3** (also **trance music**) a type of electronic dance music characterized by hypnotic rhythms.
– ORIGIN from Old French *transir* 'depart, fall into a trance', from Latin *transire* 'go across'.

tranche /traansh/ ● noun a portion, especially of money.
– ORIGIN Old French, 'slice'.

trank ● noun informal a tranquillizing drug.

tranny (also **trannie**) ● noun (pl. **trannies**) informal **1** chiefly Brit. a transistor radio. **2** a transvestite.

tranquil ● adjective free from disturbance; calm.
– DERIVATIVES **tranquillity** (also **tranquility**) noun **tranquilly** adverb.
– ORIGIN Latin *tranquillus*.

tranquillize (also **tranquillise**; US **tranquilize**) ● verb **1** (usu. as adj. **tranquillizing**) (of a drug) have a calming or sedative effect on. **2** administer such a drug to.

tranquillizer (also **tranquilliser**; US also **tranquilizer**) ● noun a medicinal drug taken to reduce tension or anxiety.

trans- ● prefix **1** across; beyond: *transcontinental*. **2** on or to the other side of: *transatlantic*. **3** into another state or place: *translate*.
– ORIGIN from Latin *trans* 'across'.

transact ● verb conduct or carry out (business).
– DERIVATIVES **transactor** noun.

transaction ● noun **1** an instance of buying or selling. **2** the action of conducting business. **3** an exchange or interaction between people.
– DERIVATIVES **transactional** adjective.
– ORIGIN Latin, from *transigere* 'drive through'.

transatlantic ● adjective **1** crossing the Atlantic. **2** concerning countries on both sides of the Atlantic, typically Britain and the US. **3** relating to or situated on the other side of the Atlantic; Brit. American; N. Amer. British or European.

transaxle ● noun an integral driving axle and differential gear in a motor vehicle.

transceiver ● noun a combined radio transmitter and receiver.

transcend ● verb **1** be or go beyond the range or limits of. **2** be superior to; surpass.
– ORIGIN Latin *transcendere*, from *scandere* 'climb'.

transcendent ● adjective **1** transcending normal or physical human experience. **2** (of God) existing apart from and not subject to the limitations of the material universe.
– DERIVATIVES **transcendence** noun **transcendently** adverb.

transcendental ● adjective **1** relating to a spiritual realm. **2** relating to or denoting Transcendentalism.
– DERIVATIVES **transcendentally** adverb.

Transcendentalism ● noun a 19th-century idealistic philo-

Thesaurus

timing; *poetic/literary* perfidious.
– OPPOSITES loyal.

trajectory ● noun COURSE, path, route, track, line, orbit.

trammel (*poetic/literary*) ● noun *the trammels of tradition* RESTRAINT, constraint, curb, check, impediment, obstacle, barrier, handicap, bar, hindrance, encumbrance, disadvantage, drawback, snag, stumbling block; shackles, fetters, bonds.
● verb *those less trammelled by convention than himself* RESTRICT, restrain, constrain, hamper, confine, hinder, handicap, obstruct, impede, hold back, hamstring, shackle, fetter.

tramp ● verb **1** *men were tramping through the shrubbery* TRUDGE, plod, stamp, trample, lumber, clump, clomp, stump, stomp; *informal* traipse, galumph. **2** *he spent ten days tramping through the jungle* TREK, slog, footslog, trudge, drag oneself, walk, hike, march; *informal* traipse; *Brit. informal* yomp; *N. Amer. informal* schlep.
● noun **1** *a dirty old tramp* VAGRANT, vagabond, homeless person, down-and-out; traveller, drifter, beachcomber; beggar, mendicant; *N. Amer.* hobo; *Austral./NZ* bagman; *informal* bag lady; *N. Amer. informal* bum. **2** *the regular tramp of the sentry's boots* FOOTSTEP, step, footfall, tread, stamp, stomp. **3** *a tramp round Norwich* TREK, slog, trudge, hike, march, walk; *Brit. informal* yomp; *N. Amer. informal* schlep.

trample ● verb **1** *someone had trampled on the tulips* TREAD, tramp, stamp, stomp, walk over; squash, crush, flatten. **2** *we do nothing but trample over their feelings* TREAT WITH CONTEMPT, ride roughshod over, disregard, set at naught, show no consideration for, abuse; encroach on, infringe.

trance ● noun DAZE, stupor, hypnotic state, half-conscious state, dream; *Scottish* dwam.

tranquil ● adjective **1** *a wonderfully tranquil village* PEACEFUL, calm, restful, quiet, still, relaxing, undisturbed. **2** *Martha smiled, perfectly tranquil* CALM, serene, relaxed, unruffled, unperturbed, unflustered, untroubled, composed, {cool, calm, and collected}; equable, even-tempered, placid, phlegmatic; *informal* unflappable.
– OPPOSITES busy, excitable.

tranquillity ● noun **1** *the tranquillity of the Norfolk countryside* PEACE, peacefulness, restfulness, repose, calm, calmness, quiet, quietness, stillness. **2** *the incident jolted her out of her tranquillity* COMPOSURE, calmness, serenity; equanimity, equability, placidity; *informal* cool, unflappability.

tranquillize ● verb SEDATE, put under sedation, narcotize, drug.

tranquillizer ● noun SEDATIVE, barbiturate, calmative, sleeping pill, narcotic, opiate; *informal* trank, downer.
– OPPOSITES stimulant.

transact ● verb CONDUCT, carry out, negotiate, do, perform, execute, take care of; settle, conclude, finish, clinch, accomplish.

transaction ● noun **1** *property transactions* DEAL, business deal, undertaking, arrangement, bargain, negotiation, agreement, settlement; proceedings. **2** *the transactions of the Historical Society* PROCEEDINGS, report, record(s), minutes, account; archives. **3** *the transaction of government business* CONDUCT, carrying out, negotiation, performance, execution.

transcend ● verb **1** *an issue that transcended party politics* GO BEYOND, rise above, cut across. **2** *his military exploits far transcended those of his predecessors* SURPASS, exceed, beat, top, cap, outdo, outclass, outstrip, leave behind, outshine, eclipse, overshadow, throw into the shade, upstage.

transcendence ● noun EXCELLENCE, supremacy, incomparability, matchlessness, peerlessness, magnificence.

transcendent ● adjective **1** *the search for a transcendent level of knowledge* MYSTICAL, mystic, transcendental, spiritual; metaphysical. **2** *a transcendent genius* INCOMPARABLE, matchless, peerless, unrivalled, inimitable, beyond compare/comparison, unparalleled,

sophical and social movement which taught that divinity pervades all nature and humanity.
– DERIVATIVES **transcendentalist** noun & adjective.
Transcendental Meditation ● noun (trademark in the US) a technique for detaching oneself from anxiety and promoting harmony and self-realization by meditation and repetition of a mantra.
transcontinental ● adjective crossing or extending across a continent or continents.
transcribe ● verb **1** put (thoughts, speech, or data) into written or printed form. **2** make a copy of, especially in another alphabet or language. **3** arrange (a piece of music) for a different instrument, voice, etc.
– DERIVATIVES **transcriber** noun.
– ORIGIN Latin *transcribere*, from *scribere* 'write'.
transcript ● noun a written or printed version of material originally presented in another medium.
– ORIGIN Latin *transcriptum*, from *transcribere* 'transcribe'.
transcriptase /transkriptayz/ ● noun Biochemistry an enzyme which catalyses the formation of RNA from a DNA template, or (**reverse transcriptase**), the formation of DNA from an RNA template.
transcription ● noun **1** a transcript. **2** the action or process of transcribing. **3** a piece of music transcribed for a different instrument, voice, etc.
transcutaneous /tranzkyootayniəss/ ● adjective existing, applied, or measured across the depth of the skin.
transdermal /tranzderm'l/ ● adjective relating to or denoting the application of a medicine or drug through the skin, especially by means of an adhesive patch.
transducer /tranzdyo͞osər/ ● noun a device that converts variations in a physical quantity (such as pressure or brightness) into an electrical signal, or vice versa.
– DERIVATIVES **transduction** noun.
– ORIGIN from Latin *transducere* 'lead across'.
transect technical ● verb cut across or make a transverse section in. ● noun a straight line or narrow cross section along which observations or measurements are made.
– DERIVATIVES **transection** noun.
– ORIGIN from TRANS- + Latin *secare* 'divide by cutting'.
transept /transept/ ● noun (in a cross-shaped church) either of the two parts forming the arms of the cross shape, projecting at right angles from the nave.
– ORIGIN Latin *transeptum*, from *septum* 'partition'
transfer ● verb (**transferred**, **transferring**) **1** move from one place to another. **2** move to another department, occupation, etc. **3** change to another place, route, or means of transport during a journey. **4** make over the possession of (property, a right, or a responsibility) to another. **5** (**transferred**) (of the sense of a word or phrase) changed by extension or metaphor. ● noun **1** an act or the action of transferring. **2** Brit. a small coloured picture or design on paper, which can be transferred to another surface by being pressed or heated.
– DERIVATIVES **transferable** adjective **transferee** noun **transferor** noun (chiefly Law) **transferral** noun.
– ORIGIN Latin *transferre*, from *ferre* 'to bear'.
transference ● noun **1** the action of transferring or the process of being transferred. **2** Psychoanalysis the redirection to a substitute of emotions originally felt in childhood.
transfer fee ● noun Brit. a fee paid by one soccer or rugby club to another for the transfer of a player.
transfiguration ● noun **1** a complete transformation into a more beautiful or spiritual state. **2** (**the Transfiguration**) Christ's appearance in radiant glory to three of his disciples (in the gospels of Matthew and Mark).
transfigure ● verb (**be transfigured**) be transformed into something more beautiful or spiritual.
– ORIGIN Latin *transfigurare*, from *figura* 'figure'.
transfix ● verb **1** make motionless with horror, wonder, or astonishment. **2** pierce with a sharp implement.
– ORIGIN Latin *transfigere* 'pierce through'.
transform ● verb **1** subject to or undergo transformation. **2** change the voltage of (an electric current) by electromagnetic induction.
– DERIVATIVES **transformative** adjective.
transformation ● noun a marked change in nature, form, or appearance.
– DERIVATIVES **transformational** adjective.
transformer ● noun a device for changing the voltage of an alternating current by electromagnetic induction.
transfuse ● verb **1** Medicine transfer (blood or its components) from one person or animal to another. **2** permeate or infuse.
– DERIVATIVES **transfusion** noun.
– ORIGIN Latin *transfundere* 'pour from one container to another'.
transgender (also **transgendered**) ● adjective transsexual.
transgenic /tranzjennik/ ● adjective Biology containing genetic material into which DNA from a different organism has been artificially introduced.
– DERIVATIVES **transgenics** plural noun.
transgress ● verb go beyond the limits set by (a moral principle, standard, law, etc.).
– DERIVATIVES **transgression** noun **transgressive** adjective **transgressor** noun.
– ORIGIN Latin *transgredi* 'step across'.
tranship ● verb variant spelling of TRANS-SHIP.
transhumance /tranzhyo͞omənss/ ● noun the action or practice of moving livestock seasonally from one grazing ground to another.
– DERIVATIVES **transhumant** adjective.
– ORIGIN French, from Latin *trans-* 'across' + *humus* 'ground'.
transient /tranziənt/ ● adjective **1** lasting only for a short time. **2** staying or working in a place for a short time only. ● noun a transient person.
– DERIVATIVES **transience** noun **transiency** noun **transiently** adverb.
– ORIGIN from Latin *transire* 'go across'.
transistor ● noun **1** a semiconductor device with three connec-

Thesaurus

unequalled, without equal, second to none, unsurpassed, unsurpassable, nonpareil; exceptional, unique, consummate, perfect, rare, surpassing, magnificent; *formal* unexampled.
transcendental ● adjective. See TRANSCENDENT sense 1.
transcribe ● verb **1** *each interview was taped and transcribed* WRITE OUT, copy out, put in writing, put on paper. **2** *a person who can take and transcribe shorthand* TRANSLITERATE, interpret, translate.
transcript ● noun WRITTEN VERSION, printed version, text, transliteration, record, reproduction.
transfer ● verb **1** *the hostages were transferred to a safe house* MOVE, convey, take, bring, shift, remove, carry, transport; transplant, relocate, resettle. **2** *the property was transferred to his wife* HAND OVER, pass on, make over, turn over, sign over, consign, devolve, assign, delegate.
● noun *he died shortly after his transfer to hospital* MOVE, conveyance, transferral, transference, relocation, removal, transplantation.
transfigure ● verb TRANSFORM, transmute, change, alter, metamorphose; *humorous* transmogrify.
transfix ● verb **1** *he was transfixed by the images on the screen* MESMERIZE, hypnotize, spellbind, bewitch, captivate, entrance, enthral, fascinate, enrapture, grip, rivet; root to the spot, paralyse. **2** *a field mouse is transfixed by the owl's curved talons* IMPALE, stab, spear, pierce, spike, skewer, gore, stick, run through; *poetic/literary* transpierce.
transform ● verb CHANGE, alter, convert, metamorphose, transfigure, transmute; revolutionize, overhaul; remodel, reshape, remould, redo, reconstruct, rebuild, reorganize, rearrange, rework, renew, revamp, remake; *humorous* transmogrify.
transformation ● noun CHANGE, alteration, conversion, metamorphosis, transfiguration, transmutation, sea change; revolution, overhaul; remodelling, reshaping, remoulding, redoing, reconstruction, rebuilding, reorganization, rearrangement, reworking, renewal, revamp, remaking; *humorous* transmogrification.
transgress ● verb **1** *if they transgress the punishment is harsh* MISBEHAVE, behave badly, break the law, err, fall from grace, stray from the straight and narrow, sin, do wrong, go astray; *archaic* trespass. **2** *she had transgressed an unwritten social law* INFRINGE, breach, contravene, disobey, defy, violate, break, flout.
transgression ● noun **1** *a punishment for past transgressions* OFFENCE, crime, sin, wrong, wrongdoing, misdemeanour, misdeed, lawbreaking; error, lapse, fault; *archaic* trespass. **2** *Adam's transgression of God's law* INFRINGEMENT, breach, contravention, violation, defiance, disobedience, non-observance.
transgressor ● noun WRONGDOER, offender, miscreant, lawbreaker, criminal, villain, felon, malefactor, guilty party, culprit; sinner, evil-doer; *archaic* trespasser.

tions, capable of amplification and rectification. **2** (also **transistor radio**) a portable radio using circuits containing transistors.
– DERIVATIVES **transistorize** (also **transistorise**) verb.
– ORIGIN from TRANSFER + RESISTOR.

transit ● noun **1** the carrying of people or things from one place to another. **2** an act of passing through or across a place. ● verb (**transited, transiting**) pass across or through.
– ORIGIN Latin *transitus*, from *transire* 'go across'.

transition ● noun **1** the process of changing from one state or condition to another. **2** a period of such change.
– DERIVATIVES **transitional** adjective.

transition metal ● noun Chemistry any of the set of metallic elements occupying the central block in the periodic table, e.g. iron, manganese, chromium, and copper.

transitive /tranzitiv/ ● adjective Grammar (of a verb) able to take a direct object, e.g. *saw* in *he saw the donkey*. The opposite of INTRANSITIVE.
– DERIVATIVES **transitively** adverb **transitivity** noun.
– ORIGIN originally in the sense 'transitory': from Latin *transitivus*, from *transire* 'go across'.

transitory /tranzitəri/ ● adjective not permanent; short-lived.
– DERIVATIVES **transitorily** adverb **transitoriness** noun.
– ORIGIN Latin *transitorius*, from *transire* 'go across'.

translate ● verb **1** express the sense of (words or text) in another language. **2** be expressed or be capable of being expressed in another language. **3** (**translate into**) convert or be converted into another form or medium.
– DERIVATIVES **translatable** adjective.
– ORIGIN from Latin *translatus* 'carried across', from *transferre* 'transfer'.

translation ● noun **1** the action or process of translating. **2** a text or word that is translated.

translator ● noun **1** a person who translates from one language into another. **2** a program that translates from one programming language into another.

transliterate ● verb write or print (a letter or word) using the closest corresponding letters of a different alphabet or language.
– DERIVATIVES **transliteration** noun.
– ORIGIN from TRANS- + Latin *littera* 'letter'.

translocate ● verb chiefly technical move from one place to another.
– DERIVATIVES **translocation** noun.

translucent /tranzloōsənt/ ● adjective allowing light to pass through partially; semi-transparent.
– DERIVATIVES **translucence** noun **translucency** noun.
– ORIGIN from Latin *translucere* 'shine through'.

transmigrate ● verb (of the soul) pass into a different body after death.
– DERIVATIVES **transmigration** noun.

transmission ● noun **1** the action or process of transmitting or the state of being transmitted. **2** a programme or signal that is transmitted. **3** the mechanism by which power is transmitted from an engine to the axle in a motor vehicle.

transmission line ● noun a conductor or conductors carrying electricity over large distances with minimum losses.

transmit ● verb (**transmitted, transmitting**) **1** cause to pass on from one place or person to another. **2** broadcast or send out (an electrical signal or a radio or television programme). **3** allow (heat, light, etc.) to pass through a medium. **4** communicate (an idea or emotion).
– DERIVATIVES **transmissible** adjective (chiefly Medicine) **transmittal** noun.
– ORIGIN Latin *transmittere*, from *mittere* 'send'.

transmitter ● noun a device used to generate and transmit electromagnetic waves carrying messages or signals, especially those of radio or television.

transmogrify /tranzmogrifi/ ● verb (**transmogrifies, transmogrified**) chiefly humorous transform in a surprising or magical manner.
– DERIVATIVES **transmogrification** noun.
– ORIGIN of unknown origin.

transmutation /tranzmyootaysh'n/ ● noun **1** the action of transmuting or the state of being transmuted. **2** the changing of one chemical element into another, either by a nuclear process or as a supposed operation in alchemy.

transmute /tranzmyoōt/ ● verb **1** change in form, nature, or substance. **2** change (a chemical element) into another, either by a nuclear process or as a supposed operation in alchemy.
– DERIVATIVES **transmutable** adjective.
– ORIGIN Latin *transmutare*, from *mutare* 'to change'.

transnational ● adjective extending or operating across national boundaries. ● noun a multinational company.
– DERIVATIVES **transnationalism** noun.

transoceanic ● adjective crossing an ocean.

transom /transəm/ ● noun **1** the flat surface forming the stern of a boat. **2** a strengthening crossbar, in particular one set above a window or door.
– ORIGIN Old French *traversin*, from *traverser* 'to cross'.

transonic ● adjective referring to speeds close to that of sound.

trans-Pacific ● adjective **1** crossing the Pacific. **2** relating to an area beyond the Pacific.

transparency ● noun (pl. **transparencies**) **1** the condition of being transparent. **2** a positive transparent photograph printed on plastic or glass, and viewed using a slide projector.

transparent /transparrənt, -**spair**-/ ● adjective **1** allowing light to pass through so that objects behind can be distinctly seen. **2** obvious or evident.
– DERIVATIVES **transparently** adverb.
– ORIGIN from Latin *transparere* 'shine through'.

transpersonal ● adjective relating to or dealing with states of

Thesaurus

transient ● adjective TRANSITORY, temporary, short-lived, short-term, ephemeral, impermanent, brief, short, momentary, fleeting, passing, fugitive, here today and gone tomorrow; poetic/literary evanescent.
– OPPOSITES permanent.

t

transit ● noun *the transit of goods between states* TRANSPORT, transportation, movement, conveyance, shipment, haulage, freightage, carriage, transfer.
– PHRASES **in transit** EN ROUTE, on the journey, on the way, along/on the road, during transport.

transition ● noun CHANGE, passage, move, transformation, conversion, metamorphosis, alteration, changeover, shift, switch, jump, leap, progression, progress, development, evolution.

transitional ● adjective **1** *a transitional period* INTERMEDIATE, interim, changeover; changing, fluid, unsettled. **2** *the transitional government* INTERIM, temporary, provisional, pro tem, acting, caretaker.

transitory ● adjective TRANSIENT, temporary, brief, short, short-lived, short-term, impermanent, ephemeral, momentary, fleeting, passing, fugitive, here today and gone tomorrow; poetic/literary evanescent.
– OPPOSITES permanent.

translate ● verb **1** *the German original had been translated into English* RENDER, put, express, convert, change; transcribe, transliterate. **2** *be prepared to translate the jargon into normal English* RENDER, paraphrase, reword, rephrase, convert, decipher, decode, gloss, explain. **3** *interesting ideas cannot always be translated into effective movies* CHANGE, convert, transform, alter, adapt, turn, transmute; humorous transmogrify. **4** *in 1228 the bishop was translated from Salisbury to Durham* RELOCATE, transfer, move, remove, shift, transplant.

translation ● noun **1** *the translation of the Bible into English* RENDITION, rendering, conversion; transcription, transliteration. **2** *the translation of these policies into practice* CONVERSION, change, transformation, alteration, adaptation, transmutation; humorous transmogrification.

translucent ● adjective SEMI-TRANSPARENT, pellucid, limpid, clear; diaphanous, gossamer, sheer.
– OPPOSITES opaque.

transmission ● noun **1** *the transmission of knowledge and culture* TRANSFERENCE, transferral, communication, conveyance; dissemination, spreading, circulation. **2** *the transmission of the film* BROADCASTING, relaying, airing, televising. **3** *a live transmission* BROADCAST, programme, show.

transmit ● verb **1** *the use of computers to transmit information* TRANSFER, pass on, hand on, communicate, convey, impart, channel, carry, relay, dispatch; disseminate, spread, circulate. **2** *the programme will be transmitted on Sunday* BROADCAST, relay, send out, air, televise.

transmute ● verb CHANGE, alter, adapt, transform, convert, metamorphose, translate; humorous transmogrify.

transparency ● noun **1** *the transparency of the ice* TRANSLUCENCY,

consciousness beyond the limits of personal identity.

transpire ● verb **1** come to be known; prove to be so. **2** happen. **3** Botany (of a plant or leaf) give off water vapour through the stomata.
– DERIVATIVES **transpiration** noun.
– ORIGIN Latin *transpirare*, from *spirare* 'breathe'.

transplant ● verb /trans**plaant**, traans-/ **1** transfer to another place or situation. **2** take (living tissue or an organ) and implant it in another part of the body or in another body. ● noun /**trans**plaant, **traans**-/ **1** an operation in which an organ or tissue is transplanted. **2** a person or thing that has been transplanted.
– DERIVATIVES **transplantable** adjective **transplantation** noun.
– ORIGIN Latin *transplantare*, from *plantare* 'to plant'.

transponder /transpondər/ ● noun a device for receiving a radio signal and automatically transmitting a different signal.
– ORIGIN blend of TRANSMIT and RESPOND.

transport ● verb **1** take or carry from one place to another by means of a vehicle, aircraft, or ship. **2** (**be transported**) be overwhelmed with a strong emotion, especially joy. **3** historical send (a convict) to a penal colony. ● noun **1** a system or means of transporting. **2** the action of transporting or the state of being transported. **3** a large vehicle, ship, or aircraft for carrying troops or stores. **4** (**transports**) overwhelmingly strong emotions.
– DERIVATIVES **transportation** noun.
– ORIGIN Latin *transportare* 'carry across'.

transportable ● adjective able to be carried or moved.
– DERIVATIVES **transportability** noun.

transport cafe ● noun Brit. a roadside cafe for drivers of haulage vehicles.

transporter ● noun a large vehicle used to carry heavy objects.

transpose ● verb **1** cause to exchange places. **2** transfer to a different place or context. **3** write or play (music) in a different key from the original.
– DERIVATIVES **transposable** adjective **transposition** noun.
– ORIGIN Old French *transposer*, from *poser* 'to place'.

transputer ● noun a microprocessor with integral memory designed for parallel processing.
– ORIGIN blend of TRANSISTOR and COMPUTER.

transsexual (also **transexual**) ● noun a person born with the physical characteristics of one sex who emotionally and psychologically feels that they belong to the opposite sex. ● adjective relating to such a person.
– DERIVATIVES **transsexualism** noun **transsexuality** noun.

trans-ship ● verb (**trans-shipped**, **trans-shipping**) transfer (cargo) from one ship or other form of transport to another.
– DERIVATIVES **trans-shipment** noun.

transubstantiation ● noun Christian Theology the doctrine that the bread and wine of the Eucharist are converted into the body and blood of Christ at consecration.
– ORIGIN from Latin *transubstantiare* 'change in substance'.

transuranic /tranzyoorannik/ ● adjective Chemistry (of an element) having a higher atomic number than uranium (92).

transverse ● adjective situated or extending across something.
– DERIVATIVES **transversely** adverb.
– ORIGIN from Latin *transvertere* 'turn across'.

transvestite ● noun a person, typically a man, who derives pleasure from dressing in clothes considered appropriate to the opposite sex.
– DERIVATIVES **transvestism** noun.
– ORIGIN German *Transvestit*, from Latin *trans-* 'across' + *vestire* 'clothe'.

Transylvanian /transilvayniən/ ● adjective relating to Transylvania, a large region of Romania.

trap[1] ● noun **1** a device or enclosure designed to catch and retain animals. **2** an unpleasant situation from which it is hard to escape. **3** a trick causing someone to act contrary to their interests or intentions. **4** a container or device used to collect a specified thing. **5** a curve in the waste pipe from a bath, basin, or toilet that is always full of liquid to prevent the upward passage of gases. **6** a bunker or other hollow on a golf course. **7** the compartment from which a greyhound is released at the start of a race. **8** a device for hurling an object such as a clay pigeon into the air. **9** chiefly historical a light, two-wheeled carriage pulled by a horse or pony. **10** informal a person's mouth. ● verb (**trapped**, **trapping**) **1** catch or hold in or as in a trap. **2** trick into doing something.
– ORIGIN Old English; related to Latin *trappa*.

trap[2] ● verb (**trapped**, **trapping**) archaic put trappings on (a horse).
– ORIGIN from obsolete *trap* 'trappings', from Old French *drap* 'drape'.

trap[3] (also **traprock**) ● noun N. Amer. basalt or a similar dark, fine-grained igneous rock.
– ORIGIN Swedish *trapp*, from *trappa* 'stair' (because of the often stair-like appearance of its outcroppings).

trapdoor ● noun a hinged or removable panel in a floor, ceiling, or roof.

trapeze ● noun (also **flying trapeze**) a horizontal bar hanging by two ropes and free to swing, used by acrobats in a circus.
– ORIGIN French, from Latin *trapezium*.

trapezium /trəpeeziəm/ ● noun (pl. **trapezia** /trəpeeziə/ or **trapeziums**) Geometry **1** Brit. a quadrilateral with one pair of sides parallel. **2** N. Amer. a quadrilateral with no sides parallel.
– ORIGIN Latin, from Greek *trapeza* 'table'.

trapezius /trəpeeziəss/ ● noun (pl. **trapezii** /trəpeezii/) Anatomy either of a pair of large triangular muscles extending over the back of the neck and shoulders and moving the head and shoulder blade.
– ORIGIN Latin, from Greek *trapezion* 'trapezium' (because of the shape formed by the muscles).

trapezoid /trappizoyd/ ● noun Geometry **1** Brit. a quadrilateral with no sides parallel. **2** N. Amer. a quadrilateral with one pair of sides parallel.
– DERIVATIVES **trapezoidal** adjective.

Thesaurus

limpidity, glassiness, clearness, clarity. **2** *colour transparencies* SLIDE, diapositive.

transparent ● adjective **1** *transparent blue water* CLEAR, crystal clear, see-through, translucent, pellucid, limpid, glassy. **2** *fine transparent fabrics* SEE-THROUGH, sheer, filmy, gauzy, diaphanous. **3** *the symbolism of this myth is transparent* OBVIOUS, unambiguous, unequivocal, clear, crystal clear, plain, (as) plain as the nose on your face, apparent, unmistakable, manifest, conspicuous, patent, palpable, indisputable, evident, self-evident, undisguised, unconcealed.
– OPPOSITES opaque, obscure.

transpire ● verb **1** *it transpired that her family had moved away* BECOME KNOWN, emerge, come to light, be revealed, turn out, come out, be discovered, prove to be the case. **2** *I'm going to find out exactly what transpired* HAPPEN, occur, take place, arise, come about, turn up, chance, befall; poetic/literary come to pass.

transplant ● verb **1** *it was proposed to transplant the club to the vacant site* TRANSFER, move, remove, shift, relocate, take. **2** *the seedlings should be transplanted in larger pots* REPLANT, repot, relocate. **3** *kidneys must be transplanted within 48 hours of removal* TRANSFER, implant.

transport ● verb **1** *the concrete blocks were transported by lorry* CONVEY, carry, take, transfer, move, shift, send, deliver, bear, ship, ferry; informal cart. **2** *he was convicted of theft and transported* BANISH, exile, deport, expatriate, extradite. **3** *she was completely transported by the excitement* THRILL, delight, carry away, enrapture, entrance, enchant, enthral, electrify, captivate, bewitch, fascinate, spellbind, charm; informal send; poetic/literary ravish.
● noun **1** *alternative forms of transport* CONVEYANCE, transportation; vehicle, car, lorry, truck. train. **2** *the transport of crude oil* TRANSPORTATION, conveyance, carriage, freight, freightage, shipment, shipping, haulage; transit. **3** *transports of delight* RAPTURE, ecstasy, elation, exaltation, exhilaration, euphoria, bliss, seventh heaven, heaven, paradise, high; passion, strong feeling/emotion; informal cloud nine.

transpose ● verb **1** *the blue and black plates were transposed* INTERCHANGE, exchange, switch, swap (round), reverse, invert. **2** *the themes are transposed from the sphere of love to that of work* TRANSFER, shift, relocate, transplant, move, displace.

transverse ● adjective CROSSWISE, crossways, cross, horizontal, diagonal, oblique.

trap ● noun **1** *an animal caught in a trap* SNARE, net, mesh, gin, springe; N. Amer. deadfall. **2** *the question was set as a trap* TRICK, ploy, ruse, deception, subterfuge; booby trap; informal set-up. **3** (*informal*) *shut your trap!* See MOUTH noun sense 1.
● verb **1** *police trapped the two men, who admitted blackmail* SNARE, entrap, ensnare, lay a trap for; capture, catch, corner, ambush; archaic ambuscade. **2** *a rat trapped in a barn* CONFINE, cut off,

trapper • noun a person who traps wild animals, especially for their fur.

trappings • plural noun **1** the visible signs or objects associated with a particular situation or role: *the trappings of success*. **2** a horse's ornamental harness.
– ORIGIN from TRAP².

Trappist • adjective of or referring to a branch of the Cistercian order of monks noted for an austere rule including a vow of silence. • noun a member of this order.
– ORIGIN French *trappiste*, from *La Trappe* in Normandy, where the order was founded.

trash • noun chiefly N. Amer. **1** waste material; refuse. **2** informal worthless writing, art, etc. **3** informal a person or people regarded as being of very low social standing. • verb informal, chiefly N. Amer. wreck or destroy.
– DERIVATIVES **trashy** adjective (**trashier**, **trashiest**).
– ORIGIN of unknown origin.

trash can • noun N. Amer. a dustbin.

trash talk US informal • noun insulting or boastful speech intended to demoralize, intimidate, or humiliate. • verb (**trash-talk**) use such speech.
– DERIVATIVES **trash talker** noun.

trattoria /trattəreeə/ • noun an Italian restaurant.
– ORIGIN Italian.

trauma /trawmə/ • noun (pl. **traumas**) **1** a deeply distressing experience. **2** Medicine physical injury. **3** emotional shock following a stressful event.
– DERIVATIVES **traumatic** adjective **traumatically** adverb **traumatize** (also **traumatise**) verb.
– ORIGIN Greek, 'wound'.

travail /travvayl/ literary • noun (also **travails**) **1** painful or laborious effort. **2** labour pains. • verb undergo such effort.
– ORIGIN Old French, from Latin *trepalium* 'instrument of torture'.

travel • verb (**travelled**, **travelling**; US also **traveled**, **traveling**) **1** make a journey. **2** journey along (a road) or through (a region). **3** move or go from one place to another. **4** withstand a journey without adverse effects. • noun **1** the action of travelling. **2** (**travels**) journeys, especially abroad. **3** (before another noun) (of a device) sufficiently compact for use when travelling: *a travel iron*. **4** the range, rate, or mode of motion of a part of a machine.
– ORIGIN variant of TRAVAIL and originally in the same sense.

travel agency • noun an agency that makes the necessary arrangements for travellers.
– DERIVATIVES **travel agent** noun.

travelator (also **travolator**) • noun a moving walkway, typically at an airport.
– ORIGIN from TRAVEL, suggested by ESCALATOR.

travelled • adjective **1** having travelled to many places. **2** used by people travelling: *a well-travelled route*.

traveller (US also **traveler**) • noun **1** a person who is travelling or who often travels. **2** a gypsy. **3** (also **New Age traveller**) a person who holds New Age values and leads an itinerant and unconventional lifestyle.

traveller's cheque • noun a cheque for a fixed amount that may be cashed or used in payment abroad after endorsement by the holder's signature.

traveller's joy • noun a tall wild clematis with small flowers and tufts of grey hairs around the seeds.

travelling salesman • noun a representative of a firm who visits businesses to show samples and gain orders.

travelogue • noun a film, book, or illustrated lecture about a person's travels.

travel-sick • adjective suffering from nausea caused by the motion of a moving vehicle, boat, or aircraft.
– DERIVATIVES **travel-sickness** noun.

traverse /travvərss, trəverss/ • verb **1** travel or extend across or through. **2** move back and forth or sideways. • noun **1** an act of traversing. **2** a part of a structure that extends or is fixed across something.
– DERIVATIVES **traversable** adjective **traversal** noun.
– ORIGIN Latin *traversare*.

travertine /travvərteen/ • noun white or light-coloured calcareous rock deposited from mineral springs, used in building.
– ORIGIN Italian *travertino*, from Latin *tiburtinus* 'of Tibur' (now Tivoli, near Rome).

travesty /travvisti/ • noun (pl. **travesties**) an absurd or grotesque misrepresentation. • verb (**travesties**, **travestied**) represent in such a way.
– ORIGIN from French *travestir* 'to disguise'.

travois /trəvoy/ • noun (pl. same or /trəvoyz/) a V-shaped frame of poles pulled by a horse, formerly used by North American Indians to carry goods.
– ORIGIN French.

travolator • noun variant spelling of TRAVELATOR.

trawl • verb **1** fish or catch with a trawl net or seine. **2** search thoroughly. • noun **1** an act of trawling. **2** (also **trawl net**) a large wide-mouthed fishing net dragged by a boat along the bottom of the sea or a lake.
– ORIGIN probably from Dutch *traghelen* 'to drag'.

trawler • noun a fishing boat used for trawling.

tray • noun a flat, shallow container with a raised rim, typically used for carrying or holding things.
– ORIGIN Old English, related to TREE.

treacherous • adjective **1** guilty of or involving betrayal. **2** hav-

Thesaurus

corner, shut in, pen in, hem in; imprison, hold captive. **3** *I hoped to trap him into an admission* TRICK, dupe, deceive, lure, inveigle, beguile, fool, hoodwink; catch out, trip up.

trappings • plural noun ACCESSORIES, accoutrements, appurtenances, trimmings, frills, accompaniments, extras, ornamentation, adornment, decoration; regalia, panoply, paraphernalia, apparatus, finery, equipment, gear, effects, things.

t

trash • noun **1** *(N. Amer.) the subway entrance was blocked with trash* RUBBISH, refuse, waste, litter, junk, detritus; *N. Amer.* garbage. **2** *(informal) if they read at all, they read trash* RUBBISH, nonsense, trivia, pulp (fiction), pap; *N. Amer.* garbage; *informal* drivel, dreck. **3** *(informal) they're just trash* SCUM, vermin, the dregs of society, the scum of the earth, the lowest of the low; *informal* dirt.
• verb *(N. Amer. informal)* **1** *the apartment had been totally trashed* WRECK, ruin, destroy, wreak havoc on, devastate; vandalize; *informal* total. **2** *his play was trashed by the critics.* See LAMBASTE.

trauma • noun **1** *the trauma of divorce* SHOCK, upheaval, distress, stress, strain, pain, anguish, suffering, upset, agony, misery, sorrow, grief, heartache, heartbreak, torture; ordeal, trial, tribulation, trouble, worry, anxiety; nightmare. **2** *the trauma to the liver* INJURY, damage, wound; cut, laceration, lesion, abrasion, contusion.

traumatic • adjective DISTURBING, shocking, distressing, upsetting, heartbreaking, painful, agonizing, hurtful, stressful, damaging, injurious, harmful, awful, terrible, devastating, harrowing.

travail *(poetic/literary)* • noun **1** *years of bitter travail* ORDEALS, trials, tribulations, trials and tribulations, trouble, hardship, privation, stress; drudgery, toil, slog, effort, exertion, labour, work, endeavour, sweat, struggle. **2** *a woman in travail* LABOUR, childbirth; contractions, labour pains; *archaic* childbed.

travel • verb **1** *he spent much of his time travelling abroad* JOURNEY, tour, take a trip, voyage, go sightseeing, globetrot, backpack; *informal* gallivant; *archaic* peregrinate. **2** *we travelled the length and breadth of the island* JOURNEY THROUGH, cross, traverse, cover; roam, rove, range, trek. **3** *light travels faster than sound* MOVE, be transmitted.
• noun *he amassed great wealth during his travels* JOURNEYS, expeditions, trips, tours, excursions, voyages, treks, safaris, explorations, wanderings, odysseys, pilgrimages, jaunts; travelling, touring, sightseeing, backpacking, globetrotting; *informal* gallivanting; *archaic* peregrinations.

traveller • noun **1** *thousands of travellers were left stranded* TOURIST, tripper, holidaymaker, sightseer, visitor, globetrotter, backpacker; pilgrim; passenger, commuter, fare; *N. Amer.* vacationer, vacationist. **2** *a travellers' site* GYPSY, Romany, tzigane; nomad, migrant, wanderer, itinerant, drifter; tramp, vagrant; *dialect* didicoi; *Brit. derogatory* tinker.

travelling • adjective **1** *the travelling population* NOMADIC, itinerant, peripatetic, wandering, roaming, roving, wayfaring, migrant, vagrant, of no fixed address/abode; gypsy, Romany. **2** *a little travelling clock* PORTABLE, easily carried, easy to carry, lightweight, compact.

traverse • verb **1** *he traversed the deserts of Persia* TRAVEL OVER/ACROSS, cross, journey over/across, pass over; cover; ply; wander, roam, range. **2** *a ditch traversed by a wooden bridge* CROSS, bridge, span; extend across, lie across, stretch across.

travesty • noun *a travesty of justice* MISREPRESENTATION, distortion, perversion, corruption, poor imitation, poor substitute, mockery,

ing hidden or unpredictable dangers: *treacherous currents.*
– DERIVATIVES **treacherously** adverb **treacherousness** noun **treachery** noun.
– ORIGIN Old French *trecherous*, from *trechier* 'to cheat'.
treacle • noun chiefly Brit. **1** molasses. **2** golden syrup.
– DERIVATIVES **treacly** adjective.
– ORIGIN originally referring to an antidote against venom: from Greek *thēriakē* 'antidote against venom', from *thērion* 'wild beast'.
tread • verb (past **trod**; past part. **trodden** or **trod**) **1** walk in a specified way. **2** press down or crush with the feet. **3** walk on or along. • noun **1** a manner or the sound of walking. **2** (also **tread board**) the top surface of a step or stair. **3** the thick moulded part of a vehicle tyre that grips the road. **4** the part of the sole of a shoe that rests on the ground.
– PHRASES **tread on someone's toes** offend someone by encroaching on their area of responsibility. **tread water 1** maintain an upright position in deep water by moving the feet with a walking movement and the hands with a downward circular motion. **2** fail to make progress.
– ORIGIN Old English.
treadle • noun a lever worked by the foot and imparting motion to a machine. • verb operate by a treadle.
– ORIGIN Old English, 'stair, step'.
treadmill • noun **1** a large wheel turned by the weight of people or animals treading on steps fitted into its inner surface, formerly used to drive machinery. **2** a device used for exercise consisting of a continuous moving belt on which to walk or run. **3** a job or situation that is tiring, boring, or unpleasant.
treason (also **high treason**) • noun the crime of betraying one's country, especially by attempting to kill or overthrow the sovereign or government.
– DERIVATIVES **treasonable** adjective **treasonous** adjective.
– ORIGIN Old French *treisoun*, from Latin *tradere* 'hand over'.
treasure • noun **1** a quantity of precious metals, gems, or other valuable objects. **2** a very valuable object. **3** informal a much loved or highly valued person. • verb **1** keep carefully (a valuable or valued item). **2** value highly.
– ORIGIN Old French *tresor*, from Greek *thēsauros* 'storehouse, treasure'.
treasure hunt • noun a game in which players search for hidden objects by following a trail of clues.
treasurer • noun a person appointed to administer or manage the financial assets and liabilities of a society, company, etc.
treasure trove • noun **1** English Law (abolished in 1996) valuables of unknown ownership that are found hidden and declared the property of the Crown. **2** a hidden store of valuable or delightful things.
– ORIGIN from Old French *tresor trové* 'found treasure'.
treasury • noun (pl. **treasuries**) **1** the funds or revenue of a state, institution, or society. **2** (**Treasury**) (in some countries) the government department responsible for the overall management of the economy. **3** a place where treasure is stored. **4** a collection of valuable or delightful things.
Treasury bill • noun a short-dated UK or US government security, yielding no interest but issued at a discount on its redemption price.
treat • verb **1** behave towards or deal with in a certain way. **2** give medical care or attention to. **3** apply a process or a substance to. **4** present or discuss (a subject). **5** (**treat to**) provide (someone) with (food, drink, or entertainment) at one's expense. **6** (**treat oneself**) do or have something very pleasurable. **7** (**treat with**) negotiate terms with. • noun **1** a surprise gift, event, etc. that gives great pleasure. **2** (**one's treat**) an act of treating someone to something.
– PHRASES —— **a treat** Brit. informal doing something specified very well: *their tactics worked a treat.*
– DERIVATIVES **treatable** adjective **treater** noun.
– ORIGIN Old French *traitier*, from Latin *trahere* 'draw, pull'.
treatise /treetiss/ • noun a written work dealing formally and systematically with a subject.
– ORIGIN Old French *tretis*, from *traitier* (see TREAT).
treatment • noun **1** the process or manner of treating someone or something. **2** medical care for an illness or injury. **3** the use of a substance or process to preserve or give particular properties to something. **4** the presentation or discussion of a subject.
treaty • noun (pl. **treaties**) a formally concluded and ratified agreement between states.
– ORIGIN Old French *traite*, from Latin *tractatus* 'treatise'.
treble[1] • adjective **1** consisting of three parts. **2** multiplied or occurring three times. • predeterminer three times as much or as many. • noun **1** Brit. three sporting victories or championships in the same season, event, etc. **2** Darts a hit on the narrow ring enclosed by the two large inner circles of a dartboard, scoring

Thesaurus

parody, caricature; farce, charade, pantomime, sham; *informal* apology for, excuse for.
treacherous • adjective **1** *her treacherous brother betrayed her* TRAITOROUS, disloyal, faithless, unfaithful, duplicitous, false-hearted, deceitful, false, back-stabbing, double-crossing, double-dealing, two-faced, untrustworthy, unreliable; apostate, renegade; *informal* two-timing; *poetic/literary* perfidious. **2** *treacherous driving conditions* DANGEROUS, hazardous, perilous, unsafe, precarious, risky, deceptive, unreliable; *informal* dicey, hairy.
– OPPOSITES loyal, faithful, reliable.
treachery • noun BETRAYAL, disloyalty, faithlessness, unfaithfulness, infidelity, breach of trust, duplicity, deceit, deception, stab in the back, back-stabbing, double-dealing, untrustworthiness; treason; *informal* two-timing; *poetic/literary* perfidy.
tread • verb **1** *he trod purposefully down the hall* WALK, step, stride, pace, go; march, tramp, plod, stomp, trudge. **2** *the snow had been trodden down by the horses* CRUSH, flatten, press down, squash; trample on, tramp on, stamp on, stomp on.
• noun *we heard his heavy tread on the stairs* STEP, footstep, footfall, tramp.
treason • noun TREACHERY, lese-majesty; disloyalty, betrayal, faithlessness; sedition, subversion, mutiny, rebellion; high treason; *poetic/literary* perfidy.
– OPPOSITES allegiance, loyalty.
treasonable • adjective TRAITOROUS, treacherous, disloyal; seditious, subversive, mutinous, rebellious; *poetic/literary* perfidious.
– OPPOSITES loyal.
treasure • noun **1** *a casket of treasure* RICHES, valuables, jewels, gems, gold, silver, precious metals, money, cash; wealth, fortune; *Brit.* treasure trove. **2** *art treasures* VALUABLE OBJECT, valuable, work of art, objet of virtu, masterpiece. **3** *(informal) she's a real treasure* PARAGON, gem, angel, nonpareil; find, prize; *informal* star, one of a kind, one in a million, the tops.
• verb *I treasure the photographs I took of Jack* CHERISH, hold dear, prize, set great store by, value greatly; adore, dote on, love dearly, be devoted to, worship.
treasury • noun **1** *the national treasury* EXCHEQUER, purse; bank, coffers; revenues, finances, funds, moneys. **2** *the area is a treasury of early fossils* RICH SOURCE, repository, storehouse, treasure house; fund, mine, bank. **3** *a treasury of stories* ANTHOLOGY, collection, miscellany, compilation, compendium.
treat • verb **1** *Charlotte treated him very badly* BEHAVE TOWARDS, act towards, use; deal with, handle. **2** *police are treating the fires as arson* REGARD, consider, view, look on; put down as. **3** *the book treats its subject with insight and responsibility* DEAL WITH, tackle, handle, discuss, explore, investigate; consider, study, analyse. **4** *she was treated at Addenbrooke's Hospital* GIVE MEDICAL CARE TO, nurse, tend, attend to; medicate. **5** *the plants may prove useful in treating cancer* CURE, heal, remedy. **6** *he treated her to a slap-up lunch* BUY, take out for, stand, give; pay for; entertain, wine and dine; *informal* foot the bill for. **7** *delegates were treated to authentic Indonesian dance performances* REGALE WITH, entertain with/by, fête with, amuse with, divert with. **8** *(formal) propagandists claimed that he was treating with the enemy* NEGOTIATE, discuss terms, have talks, consult, parley, talk, confer.
• noun **1** *a birthday treat* CELEBRATION, entertainment, amusement; surprise; party, excursion, outing. **2** *I bought you some chocolate as a treat* PRESENT, gift; titbit, delicacy, luxury, indulgence, extravagance; *informal* goodie. **3** *it was a real treat to see them* PLEASURE, delight, thrill, joy.
treatise • noun DISQUISITION, essay, paper, work, exposition, discourse, dissertation, thesis, monograph, study, critique; tract, pamphlet.
treatment • noun **1** *the company's treatment of its workers* BEHAVIOUR TOWARDS, conduct towards; handling of, dealings with. **2** *she's responding well to treatment* MEDICAL CARE, therapy, nursing; medication, drugs, medicaments; cure, remedy. **3** *her treatment of the topic* DISCUSSION, handling, investigation, exploration, consideration, study, analysis, critique.
treaty • noun AGREEMENT, settlement, pact, deal, entente, con-

treble. ● pronoun an amount which is three times as large as usual. ● verb make or become treble.
– ORIGIN from Latin *triplus* 'triple'.
treble² ● noun **1** a high-pitched voice, especially a boy's singing voice. **2** the high-frequency output of a radio or audio system.
– ORIGIN from TREBLE¹, because a part written for such a voice was the highest in a three-part contrapuntal composition.
treble clef ● noun Music a clef placing G above middle C on the second-lowest line of the stave.
trebly ● adjective (of sound, especially recorded music) having too much treble. ● adverb three times as much.
tree ● noun **1** a woody perennial plant, typically with a single stem or trunk growing to a considerable height and bearing lateral branches. **2** a wooden structure or part of a structure. **3** (also **tree diagram**) a diagram with a structure of branching connecting lines. **4** archaic or literary the cross on which Christ was crucified.
– DERIVATIVES **treeless** adjective.
– ORIGIN Old English.
treecreeper ● noun a small brown bird which creeps about on the trunks of trees to search for insects.
tree fern ● noun a large palm-like fern with a trunk-like stem.
tree house ● noun a structure built in the branches of a tree for children to play in.
tree-hugger ● noun informal, chiefly derogatory an environmental campaigner (used in reference to the practice of embracing a tree to prevent it from being felled).
– DERIVATIVES **tree-hugging** noun.
treeline ● noun the altitude above which no trees grow on a mountain.
treen ● noun (treated as pl.) small domestic wooden antiques.
– ORIGIN from Old English, 'wooden'.
tree of knowledge ● noun (in the Bible) the tree in the Garden of Eden bearing the forbidden fruit which Adam and Eve disobediently ate.
Tree of Life ● noun (in the Bible) the tree in the Garden of Eden whose fruit imparts eternal life.
tree ring ● noun each of a number of concentric rings in the cross section of a tree trunk, representing a single year's growth.
tree surgeon ● noun a person who prunes and treats old or damaged trees in order to preserve them.
– DERIVATIVES **tree surgery** noun.
trefoil /treffoyl, tree-/ ● noun **1** a small plant with yellow flowers and three-lobed clover-like leaves. **2** architectural tracery in the form of three rounded lobes like a clover leaf. **3** a thing having three parts.
– ORIGIN Latin *trifolium*, from *tri-* 'three' + *folium* 'leaf'.
trek ● noun a long difficult journey, especially one made on foot. ● verb (**trekked, trekking**) go on a trek.
– DERIVATIVES **trekker** noun.
– ORIGIN from South African Dutch *trekken* 'to pull, travel'.
Trekkie ● noun (pl. **Trekkies**) informal a fan of the US science-fiction television programme *Star Trek*.
trellis ● noun a framework of light wooden or metal bars used as a support for trees or creepers. ● verb (**trellised, trellising**) provide or support with a trellis.
– ORIGIN Old French *trelis*, from Latin *trilix* 'three-ply'.
trematode /tremmətōd/ ● noun Zoology a kind of parasitic flatworm.
– ORIGIN from Greek *trēmatōdēs* 'perforated', from *trēma* 'hole'.
tremble ● verb **1** shake involuntarily, typically as a result of anxiety, excitement, or frailty. **2** be in a state of extreme apprehension. **3** (of a thing) shake slightly. ● noun a trembling feeling, movement, or sound.
– DERIVATIVES **trembly** adjective (informal).
– ORIGIN Old French *trembler*, from Latin *tremere* 'tremble'.
trembler ● noun Brit. an automatic vibrator for making and breaking an electric circuit.
tremendous ● adjective **1** very great in amount, scale, or intensity. **2** informal extremely good or impressive.
– DERIVATIVES **tremendously** adverb.
– ORIGIN Latin *tremendus*, from *tremere* 'tremble'.
tremolo ● noun (pl. **tremolos**) Music **1** a wavering effect in singing or playing some musical instruments. **2** (also **tremolo arm**) a lever on an electric guitar used to produce such an effect.
– ORIGIN Italian.
tremor ● noun **1** an involuntary quivering movement. **2** (also **earth tremor**) a slight earthquake. **3** a sudden feeling of fear or excitement.
– ORIGIN Latin, from *tremere* 'to tremble'.
tremulous ● adjective **1** shaking or quivering slightly. **2** timid; nervous.
– DERIVATIVES **tremulously** adverb **tremulousness** noun.
– ORIGIN Latin *tremulus*, from *tremere* 'tremble'.
trench ● noun **1** a long, narrow ditch. **2** a ditch dug by troops to provide shelter from enemy fire. **3** (also **ocean trench**) a long, narrow, deep depression in the ocean bed. ● verb dig a trench or trenches in.
– ORIGIN Old French *trenche*, from Latin *truncare* 'maim'.
trenchant /trenchənt/ ● adjective **1** vigorous or incisive in expression or style. **2** archaic or literary (of a weapon or tool) having a sharp edge.
– DERIVATIVES **trenchancy** noun **trenchantly** adverb.
– ORIGIN Old French, 'cutting', from Latin *truncare* 'truncate, maim'.
trench coat ● noun **1** a belted double-breasted raincoat. **2** a lined or padded waterproof coat worn by soldiers.

Thesaurus

cordat, accord, protocol, compact, convention, contract, covenant, bargain, pledge; *formal* concord.
tree ● noun sapling, conifer, evergreen.
– RELATED TERMS arboreal.
trek ● noun *a three-day trek across the desert* JOURNEY, trip, expedition, safari, odyssey; hike, march, slog, footslog, tramp, walk; long haul; *Brit. informal* yomp, trog.
● verb *we trekked through the jungle* HIKE, tramp, march, slog, footslog, trudge, traipse, walk; travel, journey; *Brit. informal* yomp, trog.
trellis ● noun LATTICE, framework, espalier; network, mesh, tracery; grille, grid, grating; latticework, trelliswork; *technical* reticulation.
tremble ● verb **1** *Joe's hands were trembling* SHAKE, shake like a leaf, quiver, twitch; quaver, waver. **2** *the entire building trembled* SHAKE, shudder, judder, wobble, rock, vibrate, move, sway, totter, teeter. **3** *she trembled at the thought of what he had in store for her* BE AFRAID, be frightened, be apprehensive, worry, shake in one's shoes; quail, shrink, blench; *informal* be in a blue funk, be all of a tremble.
● noun *the slight tremble in her hands* TREMOR, shake, shakiness, trembling, quiver, twitch.
– OPPOSITES steadiness.
tremendous ● adjective **1** *tremendous sums of money* HUGE, enormous, immense, colossal, massive, prodigious, stupendous, monumental, mammoth, vast, gigantic, giant, mighty, epic, titanic, towering, king-size(d), gargantuan, Herculean; substantial, considerable; *informal* whopping, thumping, astronomical, humongous; *Brit. informal* whacking, ginormous. **2** *a tremendous explosion* VERY LOUD, deafening, ear-splitting, booming, thundering, thunderous, resounding. **3** *(informal) I've seen him play and he's tremendous* EXCELLENT, splendid, wonderful, marvellous, magnificent, superb, glorious, sublime, lovely, delightful, too good to be true; *informal* super, great, amazing, fantastic, terrific, sensational, heavenly, divine, gorgeous, grand, fabulous, fab, awesome, to die for, magic, ace, wicked, mind-blowing, far out, out of this world; *Brit. informal* smashing, brilliant, brill; *N. Amer. informal* boss; *Austral./NZ informal* beaut, bonzer; *Brit. informal, dated* champion, wizard, corking, ripping, spiffing, top-hole; *N. Amer. informal, dated* swell.
– OPPOSITES tiny, small, slight, poor.
tremor ● noun **1** *the sudden tremor of her hands* TREMBLING, shaking, shakiness, tremble, shake, quivering, quiver, twitching, twitch, tic; quavering, quaver. **2** *a tremor of fear ran through her* FRISSON, shiver, spasm, thrill, tingle, stab, dart, shaft; wave, surge, rush, ripple. **3** *the epicentre of the tremor* EARTHQUAKE, earth tremor, shock; *informal* quake; *N. Amer. informal* tremblor.
tremulous ● adjective **1** *a tremulous voice* SHAKY, trembling, shaking, unsteady, quavering, wavering, quivering, quivery, quaking, weak; *informal* trembly, all of a tremble. **2** *a tremulous smile* TIMID, diffident, shy, hesitant, uncertain, nervous, timorous, fearful, frightened, scared, anxious, apprehensive.
– OPPOSITES steady, confident.
trench ● noun DITCH, channel, trough, excavation, furrow, rut, conduit, cut, drain, waterway, watercourse; earthwork, entrenchment, moat; *Archaeology* fosse.
trenchant ● adjective INCISIVE, penetrating, sharp, keen, acute, shrewd, razor-sharp, rapier-like, piercing; vigorous, forceful,

t

trencher¹ ● noun historical a wooden plate or platter.
– ORIGIN Old French *trenchour*, from *trenchier* 'to cut' (because meat was cut and served on a trencher).
trencher² ● noun a machine or attachment used in digging trenches.
trencherman ● noun humorous a person who eats heartily.
trench fever ● noun a highly contagious bacterial disease transmitted by lice, that infested soldiers in the trenches in the First World War.
trench foot ● noun a painful condition of the feet caused by long immersion in cold water or mud and marked by blackening and death of surface tissue.
trench warfare ● noun a type of combat in which opposing troops fight from trenches facing each other.
trend ● noun **1** a general direction in which something is developing or changing. **2** a fashion. ● verb turn in a specified direction.
– ORIGIN Old English, 'revolve, rotate'; related to TRUNDLE.
trendsetter ● noun a person who leads the way in fashion or ideas.
– DERIVATIVES **trendsetting** adjective.
trendy informal ● adjective (**trendier**, **trendiest**) very fashionable or up to date. ● noun (pl. **trendies**) a person of this type.
– DERIVATIVES **trendily** adverb **trendiness** noun.
trepan /tripan/ ● noun chiefly historical a saw used by surgeons for perforating the skull. ● verb (**trepanned**, **trepanning**) perforate (a person's skull) with a trepan.
– DERIVATIVES **trepanation** /treppənaysh'n/ noun.
– ORIGIN from Greek *trupan* 'to bore', from *trupē* 'hole'.
trephine /trifīn, -feen/ ● noun a cylindrical saw used in surgery to remove a circle of tissue or bone. ● verb operate on with a trephine.
– DERIVATIVES **trephination** /treffinaysh'n/ noun.
– ORIGIN from Latin *tres fines* 'three ends', apparently influenced by TREPAN.
trepidation ● noun a feeling of fear or agitation about something that may happen.
– ORIGIN Latin, from *trepidare* 'be agitated, tremble'.
trespass ● verb **1** enter someone's land or property without their permission. **2** (**trespass on**) make unfair claims on or take advantage of (something). **3** (**trespass against**) archaic or literary commit an offence against. ● noun **1** Law entry to a person's land or property without their permission. **2** archaic or literary a sin; an offence.
– DERIVATIVES **trespasser** noun.
– ORIGIN Old French *trespasser* 'pass over, trespass', from Latin *transpassare*.
tress ● noun a long lock of a woman's hair.
– ORIGIN Old French *tresse*, perhaps from Greek *trikha* 'threefold'.
trestle ● noun **1** a framework consisting of a horizontal beam supported by two pairs of sloping legs, used in pairs to support a flat surface such as a table top. **2** (also **trestlework**) an open braced framework used to support an elevated structure such as a bridge.
– ORIGIN Old French *trestel*, from Latin *transtrum* 'beam'.
trestle table ● noun a table consisting of a board or boards laid on trestles.
trews /trōōz/ ● plural noun chiefly Brit. trousers.
– ORIGIN Irish *triús*, Scottish Gaelic *triubhas*; related to TROUSERS.
tri- /trī/ ● combining form **1** three; having three: *triathlon*. **2** Chemistry (in names of compounds) containing three atoms or groups of a specified kind: *triacetate*.
– ORIGIN from Latin *tres*, Greek *treis* 'three'.
triable /trīəb'l/ ● adjective Law (of an offence or case) liable to a judicial trial.
triacetate /triassitayt/ (also **cellulose triacetate**) ● noun a form of cellulose acetate containing three acetate groups per glucose monomer, used as a basis for man-made fibres.
triad /trīad/ ● noun **1** a group or set of three connected people or things. **2** (also **Triad**) a Chinese secret society involved in organized crime.
– DERIVATIVES **triadic** adjective.
– ORIGIN Greek *trias*, from *treis* 'three'.
triage /triaazh/ ● noun **1** the action of sorting according to quality. **2** Medicine the assignment of degrees of urgency to wounds or illnesses to decide the order of treatment of a large number of patients.
– ORIGIN French, from *trier* 'separate out'.
trial ● noun **1** a formal examination of evidence in order to decide guilt in a case of criminal or civil proceedings. **2** a test of performance, qualities, or suitability. **3** (**trials**) an event in which horses or dogs compete or perform. **4** something that tests a person's endurance or forbearance. ● verb (**trialled**, **trialling**; US **trialed**, **trialing**) **1** test (something) to assess its suitability or performance. **2** (of a horse or dog) compete in trials.
– PHRASES **on trial 1** being tried in a court of law. **2** undergoing tests or scrutiny. **trial and error** the process of experimenting with various methods until one finds the most successful.
– ORIGIN Latin *triallum*.
trial court ● noun chiefly N. Amer. a court of law where cases are first tried, as opposed to an appeal court.
trialist (Brit. also **triallist**) ● noun a person who participates in a sports trial or a trial of a new product.
trial run ● noun a first use of a new system or product.
triangle ● noun **1** a plane figure with three straight sides and three angles. **2** something in the form of a triangle. **3** a musical

Thesaurus

strong, telling, emphatic, forthright; mordant, cutting, biting, pungent.
– OPPOSITES vague.
trend ● noun **1** *an upward trend in unemployment* TENDENCY, movement, drift, swing, shift, course, current, direction, inclination, leaning; bias, bent. **2** *the latest trend in dance music* FASHION, vogue, style, mode, craze, mania, rage; *informal* fad, thing.
● verb *interest rates are trending up* MOVE, go, head, drift, gravitate, swing, shift, turn, incline, tend, lean, veer.
trendy ● adjective *(informal)* FASHIONABLE, in fashion, in vogue, popular, (bang) up to date, up to the minute, modern, all the rage, modish, à la mode, trendsetting; stylish, chic, designer; *informal* cool, funky, in, the in thing, hot, big, hip, happening, sharp, groovy, snazzy, with it; *N. Amer. informal* tony, kicky.
– OPPOSITES unfashionable.
trepidation ● noun FEAR, apprehension, dread, fearfulness, agitation, anxiety, worry, nervousness, tension, misgivings, unease, uneasiness, foreboding, disquiet, dismay, consternation, alarm, panic; *informal* butterflies, jitteriness, the jitters, a cold sweat, a blue funk, the heebie-jeebies, the willies, the shakes, the jim-jams, collywobbles, cold feet; *Brit. informal* the (screaming) abdabs/habdabs.
– OPPOSITES equanimity, composure.
trespass ● verb **1** *there is no excuse for trespassing on railway property* INTRUDE ON, encroach on, enter without permission, invade. **2** *I must not trespass on your good nature* TAKE ADVANTAGE OF, impose on, play on, exploit, abuse; encroach on, infringe. **3** *(archaic) he would be the last among us to trespass* SIN, transgress, offend, do wrong, err, go astray, fall from grace, stray from the straight and narrow.
● noun **1** *his alleged trespass on council land* UNLAWFUL ENTRY, intrusion, encroachment, invasion. **2** *(archaic) he asked forgiveness for his trespasses* SIN, wrong, wrongdoing, transgression, crime, offence, misdeed, misdemeanour, error, lapse, fall from grace.
trespasser ● noun **1** *a high stone wall discouraged would-be trespassers* INTRUDER, interloper, unwelcome visitor, encroacher. **2** *(archaic) trespassers asking for forgiveness* SINNER, transgressor, wrongdoer, evil-doer, malefactor, offender, criminal.
tresses ● plural noun HAIR, head of hair, mane, mop of hair, shock of hair; locks, curls, ringlets.
trial ● noun **1** *the trial is expected to last several weeks* COURT CASE, case, lawsuit, suit, hearing, inquiry, tribunal, litigation, (legal/judicial) proceedings, legal action; court martial; appeal, retrial. **2** *the drug is undergoing clinical trials* TEST, try-out, experiment, pilot study; examination, check, assessment, evaluation, appraisal; trial/test period, trial/test run, dummy run; *informal* dry run. **3** *she could be a bit of a trial at times* NUISANCE, pest, bother, irritant, problem, inconvenience, plague, thorn in one's flesh, the bane of one's life, one's cross to bear; bore; *informal* pain, pain in the neck/backside, headache, drag, nightmare; *Scottish informal* skelf; *N. Amer. informal* pain in the butt, nudnik, burr under/in someone's saddle. **4** *a long account of her trials and tribulations* TROUBLE, worry, anxiety, burden, affliction, ordeal, tribulation, adversity, hardship, tragedy, trauma, reverse, setback, difficulty, problem, misfortune, bad luck, mishap, misadventure; *informal* hassle; *poetic/literary* travails.
● adjective *a three-month trial period* TEST, experimental, pilot, exploratory, probationary, provisional.

instrument consisting of a steel rod bent into a triangle, sounded with a rod. **4** an emotional relationship involving a couple and a third person with whom one of them is involved.
– ORIGIN Latin *triangulum*, from *tri-* 'three' + *angulus* 'corner'.

triangular • adjective **1** shaped like a triangle. **2** involving three people or parties. **3** (of a pyramid) having a three-sided base.
– DERIVATIVES **triangularity** noun **triangularly** adverb.

triangulate • verb /trīanggyoolayt/ **1** divide (an area) into triangles for surveying purposes. **2** measure and map (an area) by the use of triangles with a known base length and base angles. **3** determine (a height, distance, or location) in this way. **4** form into a triangle or triangles.

triangulation • noun **1** (in surveying) the tracing and measurement of a series or network of triangles in order to determine the distances and relative positions of points spread over a territory or region. **2** formation of or division into triangles.

triangulation point • noun another term for TRIG POINT.

Triassic /trīassik/ • adjective Geology relating to or denoting the earliest period of the Mesozoic era (between the Permian and Jurassic periods, about 245 to 208 million years ago), a time when the first dinosaurs, ammonites, and primitive mammals appeared.
– ORIGIN from Latin *trias* 'set of three', because the strata are divisible into three groups.

triathlon /trīathlən/ • noun an athletic contest consisting of three different events, typically swimming, cycling, and long-distance running.
– DERIVATIVES **triathlete** noun.
– ORIGIN from TRI-, on the pattern of *decathlon*.

triatomic /trīətommik/ • adjective Chemistry consisting of three atoms.

tribal • adjective of or characteristic of a tribe or tribes. • noun (**tribals**) members of tribal communities.
– DERIVATIVES **tribalism** noun **tribalist** noun **tribally** adverb.

tribe • noun **1** a social division in a traditional society consisting of linked families or communities with a common culture and dialect. **2** derogatory a distinctive close-knit social or political group. **3** (**tribes**) informal large numbers of people. **4** (in ancient Rome) each of several (originally three) political divisions. **5** Biology a taxonomic category that ranks above genus and below family or subfamily.
– USAGE It is best to avoid using the word **tribe** to refer to traditional societies in contemporary contexts, as it is associated with past attitudes of white colonialists towards so-called primitive or uncivilized peoples; alternative terms such as **community** or **people** are better. In historical contexts, as in *the area was inhabited by Slavic tribes*, it is perfectly acceptable.
– ORIGIN Latin *tribus*, perhaps related to *tri-* 'three' and referring to the three divisions of the early people of Rome.

tribesman (or **tribeswoman**) • noun a member of a tribe in a traditional society.

tribology /trībolləji/ • noun the branch of science and technology concerned with surfaces in relative motion, as in bearings.
– DERIVATIVES **tribological** adjective **tribologist** noun.
– ORIGIN from Greek *tribos* 'rubbing'.

tribulation /tribyoolaysh'n/ • noun **1** a state of great trouble or suffering. **2** a cause of this.
– ORIGIN Latin, from *tribulare* 'press, oppress'.

tribunal /trībyoōnl/ • noun **1** Brit. a body established to settle certain types of dispute. **2** a court of justice.
– ORIGIN Latin, 'raised platform provided for a magistrate's seat', from *tribunus* 'tribune, head of a tribe'.

tribune[1] • noun **1** (in ancient Rome) an official chosen by the plebeians to protect their interests. **2** a popular leader; a champion of the people.
– DERIVATIVES **tribunate** noun **tribuneship** noun.
– ORIGIN Latin *tribunus* 'head of a tribe', from *tribus* 'tribe'.

tribune[2] • noun **1** an apse in a basilica. **2** a dais or rostrum, especially in a church.
– ORIGIN originally denoting the principal room in an Italian mansion: from Latin *tribunal* (see TRIBUNAL).

tributary /tribyootri/ • noun (pl. **tributaries**) **1** a river or stream flowing into a larger river or lake. **2** historical a person or state that pays tribute to another state or ruler.
– ORIGIN Latin *tributarius*, from *tributum* (see TRIBUTE).

tribute • noun **1** an act, statement, or gift that is intended to show gratitude, respect, or admiration. **2** something resulting from and indicating the worth of something else: *his victory was a tribute to his persistence.* **3** historical payment made periodically by a state to another on which it is dependent.
– ORIGIN Latin *tributum*, from *tribuere* 'assign, divide between tribes'.

trice /trīss/ • noun (in phrase **in a trice**) in a moment; very quickly.
– ORIGIN originally as *a trice* in the sense 'a tug', also 'an instant': from Dutch *trīsen* 'pull sharply'.

tricentenary • noun (pl. **tricentenaries**) another term for TERCENTENARY.
– DERIVATIVES **tricentennial** adjective & noun.

triceps /trīseps/ • noun (pl. same) Anatomy the large muscle at the back of the upper arm.
– ORIGIN Latin, 'three-headed', because the muscle has three points of attachment at one end.

triceratops /trīserrətops/ • noun a large quadrupedal herbivorous dinosaur living at the end of the Cretaceous period, having a massive head with two large horns, a smaller horn on the beaked snout, and a bony frill above the neck.
– ORIGIN from Greek *trikeratos* 'three-horned' + *ōps* 'face'.

trichina /trikeenə/ • noun (pl. **trichinae** /trikeenee/) a parasitic nematode worm of humans and other mammals, the adults of which live in the small intestine.
– ORIGIN from Greek *trikhinos* 'of hair'.

trichinosis /trikkinōsiss/ • noun a disease caused by trichinae, typically from infected meat, characterized by digestive disturbance, fever, and muscular rigidity.

trichology /trikolləji/ • noun the branch of medical and cosmetic study and practice concerned with the hair and scalp.
– DERIVATIVES **trichological** adjective **trichologist** noun.
– ORIGIN from Greek *thrix* 'hair'.

trichromatic /trīkrəmattik/ • adjective **1** having or using three colours. **2** having normal colour vision, which is sensitive to all three primary colours.
– DERIVATIVES **trichromatism** noun.

trick • noun **1** a cunning or skilful act or scheme intended to deceive or outwit someone. **2** a skilful act performed for entertainment. **3** an illusion: *a trick of the light.* **4** (before another noun)

t

Thesaurus

• verb *the electronic cash card has been trialled by several banks* TEST, try out, put to the test, put through its paces; pilot.

tribe • noun **1** *the nomadic tribes of the Sahara* ETHNIC GROUP, people; family, dynasty, house; clan, sept. **2** *a tribe of children trailed after her* GROUP, crowd, gang, company, body, band, host, bevy, party, pack, army, herd, flock, drove, horde; informal bunch, crew, gaggle, posse.

tribulation • noun **1** *the tribulations of her personal life* TROUBLE, difficulty, problem, worry, anxiety, burden, cross to bear, ordeal, trial, adversity, hardship, tragedy, trauma, affliction; reverse, setback, blow; informal hassle. **2** *his time of tribulation was just beginning* SUFFERING, distress, trouble, misery, wretchedness, unhappiness, sadness, heartache, woe, grief, pain, anguish, agony; poetic/literary travail.

tribunal • noun **1** *a rent tribunal* ARBITRATION BOARD/PANEL, board, panel, committee. **2** *an international war-crimes tribunal* COURT, court of justice, court of law, law court; court of inquiry; N. Amer. forum.

tributary • noun HEADWATER, branch, feeder, side stream, influent; N. Amer. & Austral./NZ creek.

tribute • noun **1** *tributes flooded in from friends and colleagues* ACCOLADE, praise, commendation, salute, testimonial, homage, eulogy, paean, panegyric; congratulations, compliments, plaudits; gift, present, offering; informal bouquet; formal laudation, encomium. **2** *it is a tribute to his determination that he ever played again* TESTIMONY, indication, manifestation, evidence, proof, attestation. **3** *the Vikings demanded tributes in silver* PAYMENT, contribution, dues, levy, tax, duty, impost.
– OPPOSITES criticism, condemnation.
– PHRASES **pay tribute to** PRAISE, sing the praises of, speak highly of, commend, acclaim, take one's hat off to, applaud, salute, honour, show appreciation of, recognize, acknowledge, pay homage to, extol; formal laud.

trice • noun
– PHRASES **in a trice** VERY SOON, in a moment/second/instant, shortly, any minute (now), in a short time, in (less than) no time, in the twinkling of an eye, in a flash, before you know it, before long; N. Amer. momentarily; informal anon, in a jiffy, in two shakes

intended to mystify or trick: *a trick question.* **5** a peculiar or characteristic habit or mannerism. **6** (in bridge, whist, etc.) a sequence of cards forming a single round of play. ● **verb 1** deceive or outwit with cunning or skill. **2** (**trick into/out of**) deceive (someone) into doing or parting with.
– PHRASES **do the trick** informal achieve the required result. **trick or treat** chiefly N. Amer. a children's custom of calling at houses at Halloween with the threat of pranks if they are not given a small gift. **tricks of the trade** special ingenious techniques used in a profession or craft. **turn a trick** informal (of a prostitute) have a session with a client. **up to one's (old) tricks** informal misbehaving in a characteristic way.
– DERIVATIVES **tricker** noun **trickery** noun.
– ORIGIN Old French *triche*, from *trichier* 'deceive'.

trickle ● **verb 1** (of a liquid) flow in a small stream. **2** (**trickle down**) (of wealth) gradually benefit the poorest as a result of the increasing wealth of the richest. **3** come or go slowly or gradually. ● **noun 1** a small flow of liquid. **2** a small group or number of people or things moving slowly.
– ORIGIN imitative.

trickster ● **noun** a person who cheats or deceives people.

tricksy ● **adjective** (**tricksier**, **tricksiest**) **1** clever in an ingenious or deceptive way. **2** playful or mischievous.

tricky ● **adjective** (**trickier**, **trickiest**) **1** requiring care and skill because difficult or awkward. **2** deceitful, crafty, or skilful.
– DERIVATIVES **trickily** adverb **trickiness** noun.

tricolour /trikkələr, trīkuller/ (US **tricolor**) ● **noun** a flag with three bands or blocks of different colours, especially the French national flag with equal upright bands of blue, white, and red. ● **adjective** (also **tricoloured**) having three colours.

tricorne /trīkorn/ (also **tricorn**) ● **adjective** (of a hat) having a brim turned up on three sides. ● **noun** a tricorne hat.
– ORIGIN Latin *tricornis*, from *tri-* 'three' + *cornu* 'horn'.

tricot /trikkō, tree-/ ● **noun** a fine knitted fabric made of a natural or man-made fibre.
– ORIGIN French, 'knitting'.

tricuspid /trīkuspid/ ● **adjective 1** denoting a tooth with three cusps or points. **2** denoting a valve formed of three triangular segments situated between the right atrium and ventricle of the heart.
– ORIGIN from Latin *tri-* 'three' + *cuspis* 'sharp point'.

tricycle ● **noun** a vehicle similar to a bicycle, but having three wheels, two at the back and one at the front.

tricyclic /trīsīklik/ ● **adjective** Chemistry (of a compound) having three rings of atoms in its molecule. ● **noun** Medicine any of a class of antidepressant drugs having molecules with three fused rings.

trident ● **noun** a three-pronged spear.
– ORIGIN Latin, from *tri-* 'three' + *dens* 'tooth'.

tried past and past participle of TRY.

triennial /trīenniəl/ ● **adjective** lasting for or recurring every three years.
– DERIVATIVES **triennially** adverb.

triennium /trīenniəm/ ● **noun** (pl. **triennia** /trīenniə/ or **trienniums**) a period of three years.
– ORIGIN Latin, from *tri-* 'three' + *annum* 'year'.

trier ● **noun 1** a person who always makes an effort, however unsuccessful they may be. **2** a person or body responsible for trying a judicial case.

trifid /trīfid/ ● **adjective** chiefly Biology partly or wholly split into three divisions or lobes.
– ORIGIN Latin *trifidus*, from *tri-* 'three' + *findere* 'split, divide'.

trifle ● **noun 1** a thing of little value or importance. **2** a small amount. **3** Brit. a cold dessert of sponge cake and fruit covered with layers of custard, jelly, and cream. ● **verb 1** (**trifle with**) treat without seriousness or respect. **2** archaic talk or act frivolously.
– DERIVATIVES **trifler** noun.
– ORIGIN from Old French *truffler* 'mock, deceive'.

trifling ● **adjective** unimportant or trivial.
– DERIVATIVES **triflingly** adverb.

trifocal ● **adjective** (of a pair of glasses) having lenses with three parts with different focal lengths. ● **noun** (**trifocals**) a pair of trifocal glasses.

trifoliate /trīfōliət/ ● **adjective** (of a compound leaf) having three leaflets.

triforium /trīforiəm/ ● **noun** (pl. **triforia** /trīforiə/) a gallery or arcade above the arches of the nave, choir, and transepts of a church.
– ORIGIN Latin.

triform ● **adjective** technical composed of three parts.

trifurcate ● **verb** /trīfərkayt/ divide into three branches or forks. ● **adjective** /trīfurkət/ divided in this way.
– DERIVATIVES **trifurcation** noun.

Thesaurus

(of a lamb's tail), before you can say Jack Robinson; *Brit. informal* in a tick, in a mo, in two ticks; *N. Amer. informal* in a snap; *dated* directly.

trick ● **noun 1** *he's capable of any mean trick* STRATAGEM, ploy, ruse, scheme, device, manoeuvre, contrivance, machination, artifice, wile, dodge; deceit, deception, trickery, subterfuge, chicanery, sharp practice; swindle, hoax, fraud, confidence trick; *informal* con (trick), set-up, game, scam, sting, flimflam; *Brit. informal* wheeze; *N. Amer. informal* bunco; *archaic* shift. **2** *I think he's playing a trick on us* PRACTICAL JOKE, joke, prank, jape; *informal* leg-pull, spoof, put-on; *Brit. informal* cod. **3** *conjuring tricks* FEAT, stunt; (**tricks**) SLEIGHT OF HAND, legerdemain, prestidigitation; magic. **4** *it was probably a trick of the light* ILLUSION, optical illusion, figment of the imagination; mirage. **5** *the tricks of the trade* KNACK, art, skill, technique; secret. **6** *he sat biting his fingernails, a trick of his when he was excited* MANNERISM, habit, quirk, idiosyncrasy, peculiarity, foible, way; characteristic, trait.
● **verb** *many people have been tricked by villains with false identity cards* DECEIVE, delude, hoodwink, mislead, take in, dupe, fool, double-cross, cheat, defraud, swindle, catch out, gull, hoax, bamboozle; *informal* con, diddle, rook, put one over on, pull a fast one on, pull the wool over someone's eyes, take for a ride, lead up the garden path, shaft, do, flimflam; *N. Amer. informal* sucker, snooker, gold-brick; *Austral. informal* pull a swifty on; *poetic/literary* cozen.
– PHRASES **do the trick** *(informal)* BE EFFECTIVE, work, solve the problem, fill/fit the bill; *N. Amer.* turn the trick; *informal* do the necessary. **trick someone/something out** DRESS (UP), attire, array, rig out, garb, get up; adorn, decorate, deck (out), bedeck, embellish, ornament, festoon; *poetic/literary* bedizen, caparison; *archaic* apparel.

trickery ● **noun** DECEPTION, deceit, dishonesty, cheating, duplicity, double-dealing, legerdemain, sleight of hand, guile, deviousness, craftiness, subterfuge, skulduggery, chicanery, fraud, fraudulence, swindling, sharp practice; *informal* monkey business, funny business, jiggery-pokery.
– OPPOSITES honesty.

trickle ● **verb** *blood was trickling from two cuts in his lip* DRIP, dribble, ooze, leak, seep, spill.
– OPPOSITES pour, gush.
● **noun** *trickles of water* DRIBBLE, drip, thin stream, rivulet.

trickster ● **noun** SWINDLER, cheat, fraud, fraudster; charlatan, mountebank, quack, impostor, sham, hoaxer; rogue, villain, scoundrel; *informal* con man, sharp, flimflammer; *Brit. informal* twister; *N. Amer. informal* grifter, bunco artist; *Austral. informal* illywhacker, magsman; *dated* confidence man.

tricky ● **adjective 1** *a tricky situation* DIFFICULT, awkward, problematic, delicate, ticklish, sensitive, embarrassing, touchy; risky, uncertain, precarious, touch-and-go; thorny, knotty; *informal* sticky, dicey; *N. Amer. informal* gnarly. **2** *a tricky and unscrupulous politician* CUNNING, crafty, wily, guileful, artful, devious, sly, scheming, calculating, designing, sharp, shrewd, astute, canny; duplicitous, dishonest, deceitful; *informal* foxy.
– OPPOSITES straightforward, honest.

tried and trusted ● **adjective** RELIABLE, dependable, trustworthy, trusted, certain, sure; proven, proved, tested, tried and tested, put to the test, established, fail-safe; reputable.

trifle ● **noun 1** *we needn't bother the headmaster over such trifles* UNIMPORTANT THING, trivial thing, triviality, inessential, thing of no importance/consequence, bagatelle, nothing; technicality; (**trifles**) trivia, minutiae. **2** *he bought it for a trifle* NEXT TO NOTHING, very small amount; pittance; *informal* peanuts; *N. Amer. informal* chump change. **3** *he went to buy a few trifles for Christmas* BAUBLE, trinket, knick-knack, gimcrack, gewgaw, toy.
– PHRASES **a trifle** A LITTLE, a bit, somewhat, a touch, a spot, a mite, a whit; *informal* a tad. **trifle with** PLAY WITH, amuse oneself with, toy with, dally with, flirt with, play fast and loose with; *informal* mess about with; *dated* sport with.

trifling ● **adjective** TRIVIAL, unimportant, insignificant, inconsequential, petty, minor, of little/no account, of little/no consequence, footling, pettifogging, incidental; silly, idle, superficial, small, tiny, inconsiderable, nominal, negligible, nugatory; *informal*

– ORIGIN Latin *trifurcus* 'three-forked'.

trigger ● noun **1** a device that releases a spring or catch and so sets off a mechanism, especially in order to fire a gun. **2** an event that causes something to happen. ● verb **1** cause (a device) to function. **2** cause to happen or exist.
– ORIGIN Dutch *trekker*, from *trekken* 'to pull'.

trigger-happy ● adjective apt to fire a gun or take other drastic action on the slightest provocation.

triglyceride /triglissərīd/ ● noun Chemistry a compound formed from glycerol and three fatty acid groups, e.g. the main constituents of natural fats and oils.

triglyph /trīglif/ ● noun Architecture a tablet in a Doric frieze with three vertical grooves alternating with metopes.
– ORIGIN Greek *trigluphos*, from *tri-* 'three' + *gluphē* 'carving'.

trigonometry /triggənommitri/ ● noun the branch of mathematics concerned with the relations of the sides and angles of triangles and with the relevant functions of any angles.
– DERIVATIVES **trigonometric** /triggənəmetrik/ adjective **trigonometrical** adjective.
– ORIGIN from Greek *trigōnos* 'three-cornered'.

trig point ● noun Brit. a reference point on high ground used in surveying, typically marked by a small pillar.

trigram /trīgram/ ● noun **1** a trigraph. **2** each of the eight figures formed of three parallel lines that combine to form the sixty-four hexagrams of the I Ching.

trigraph /trīgraaf/ ● noun a group of three letters representing one sound, for example German *sch-*.

trihedron /trīheedrən/ ● noun (pl. **trihedra** /trīheedrə/ or **trihedrons**) a solid figure having three sides or faces (in addition to the base or ends).
– DERIVATIVES **trihedral** adjective & noun.

trike ● noun informal **1** a tricycle. **2** a kind of ultralight aircraft.

trilateral ● adjective **1** shared by or involving three parties. **2** Geometry of, on, or with three sides. ● noun a triangle.

trilby ● noun (pl. **trilbies**) chiefly Brit. a soft felt hat with a narrow brim and indented crown.
– ORIGIN from the heroine of George du Maurier's novel *Trilby* (1894), in the stage version of which such a hat was worn.

trilingual ● adjective **1** speaking three languages fluently. **2** written or conducted in three languages.
– DERIVATIVES **trilingualism** noun.

trill ● noun a quavering or vibratory sound, especially a rapid alternation of sung or played notes. ● verb produce a quavering or warbling sound.
– DERIVATIVES **triller** noun.
– ORIGIN Italian *trillo*.

trillion ● cardinal number **1** a million million (1,000,000,000,000 or 10^{12}). **2** dated, chiefly Brit. a million million million (1,000,000,000,000,000,000 or 10^{18}).
– DERIVATIVES **trillionth** ordinal number.

trilobite /trīləbīt/ ● noun a fossil marine arthropod of the Palaeozoic era, with a segmented hindpart divided longitudinally into three lobes.
– ORIGIN from Greek *tri-* 'three' + *lobos* 'lobe'.

trilogy ● noun (pl. **trilogies**) a group of three related novels, plays, or films.

trim ● verb (**trimmed**, **trimming**) **1** make (something) neat by cutting away irregular or unwanted parts. **2** cut off (irregular or unwanted parts). **3** reduce the size, amount, or number of. **4** decorate (something), especially along its edges. **5** adapt one's views to the prevailing political trends for personal advancement. **6** adjust (a sail) to take advantage of the wind. ● noun **1** additional decoration, especially along the edges. **2** the upholstery or interior lining of a car. **3** an act of trimming. **4** the state of being in good order. ● adjective (**trimmer**, **trimmest**) neat and smart; in good order.
– PHRASES **in trim 1** slim and fit. **2** Nautical in good order. **trim one's sails** (**to the wind**) make changes to suit one's new circumstances.
– DERIVATIVES **trimly** adverb **trimmer** noun **trimness** noun.
– ORIGIN Old English, 'make firm, arrange'.

trimaran /trīməran/ ● noun a yacht with three hulls in parallel.
– ORIGIN from TRI- + CATAMARAN.

trimer /trīmər/ ● noun Chemistry a polymer comprising three monomer units.
– DERIVATIVES **trimeric** adjective.

trimester /trīmestər/ ● noun **1** a period of three months, especially as a division of the duration of pregnancy. **2** N. Amer. each of the three terms in an academic year.
– DERIVATIVES **trimestral** adjective **trimestrial** adjective.
– ORIGIN Latin *trimestris*, from *tri-* 'three' + *mensis* 'month'.

trimming ● noun **1** (**trimmings**) small pieces trimmed off. **2** ornamentation or decoration, especially for clothing or furniture. **3** (**the trimmings**) informal the traditional accompaniments to something.

Trinidadian /trinnidaydiən, -dadd-/ ● noun a person from the Caribbean island of Trinidad. ● adjective relating to Trinidad.

Trinitarian /trinnitairiən/ ● adjective referring to belief in the doctrine of the Trinity. ● noun a person who believes in the doctrine of the Trinity.
– DERIVATIVES **Trinitarianism** noun.

trinitrotoluene /trīnītrōtolyooeen/ ● noun fuller form of TNT.

trinity ● noun (pl. **trinities**) **1** (**the Trinity** or **the Holy Trinity**) the three persons of the Christian Godhead; Father, Son, and Holy Spirit. **2** a group of three people or things.
– ORIGIN Latin *trinitas* 'triad', from *trinus* 'threefold'.

trinket ● noun a small ornament or item of jewellery that is of little value.
– DERIVATIVES **trinketry** noun.
– ORIGIN of unknown origin.

trinomial /trīnōmiəl/ ● adjective technical consisting of three terms or names. ● noun a trinomial expression or name.
– ORIGIN from TRI-, on the pattern of *binomial*.

trio ● noun (pl. **trios**) **1** a set or group of three. **2** a group of three musicians.
– ORIGIN Italian, from Latin *tres* 'three'.

triode /trīōd/ ● noun **1** a thermionic valve having three electrodes. **2** a semiconductor rectifier having three connections.
– ORIGIN from TRI- + ELECTRODE.

trioxide /trīoksīd/ ● noun Chemistry an oxide containing three

Thesaurus

t

piffling, piddling, fiddling; *formal* exiguous.
– OPPOSITES important.

trigger ● verb **1** *the incident triggered an acrimonious debate* PRECIPITATE, prompt, trigger off, set off, spark (off), touch off, provoke, stir up; cause, give rise to, lead to, set in motion, occasion, bring about, generate, engender, begin, start, initiate; *poetic/literary* enkindle. **2** *burglars triggered the alarm* ACTIVATE, set off, set going, trip.

trill ● verb WARBLE, sing, chirp, chirrup, tweet, twitter, cheep, peep.

trim ● verb **1** *his hair had been washed and trimmed* CUT, barber, crop, bob, shorten, clip, snip, shear; neaten, shape, tidy up. **2** *trim off the lower leaves using a sharp knife* CUT OFF, remove, take off, chop off, lop off; prune, pollard. **3** *production costs need to be trimmed* REDUCE, decrease, cut down, cut back on, scale down, prune, slim down, pare down, dock. **4** *the story was severely trimmed for the film version* SHORTEN, abridge, condense, abbreviate, telescope, truncate. **5** *a pair of black leather gloves trimmed with fake fur* DECORATE, adorn, ornament, embellish; edge, pipe, border, hem, fringe.
● noun **1** *white curtains with a blue trim* DECORATION, trimming, ornamentation, adornment, embellishment; border, edging, piping, rickrack, hem, fringe, frill; *archaic* purfle. **2** *an unruly mop in desperate need of a trim* HAIRCUT, cut, barbering, clip, snip; pruning; tidy-up.
● adjective **1** *a cropped, fitted jacket looks trim with a long-line skirt* SMART, stylish, chic, spruce, dapper, elegant, crisp; *N. Amer.* trig; *informal* natty, sharp; *N. Amer. informal* spiffy. **2** *a trim little villa* NEAT, tidy, neat and tidy, as neat as a new pin, orderly, in (good) order, uncluttered, well kept, well maintained, shipshape (and Bristol fashion), in apple-pie order, immaculate, spick and span. **3** *her trim figure* SLIM, slender, lean, clean-limbed, sleek, willowy, lissom, sylphlike, svelte; streamlined.
– OPPOSITES untidy, messy.
– PHRASES **in trim** FIT, fighting fit, as fit as a fiddle, in good health, in fine fettle; slim, in shape.

trimming ● noun **1** *a black party dress with lace trimming* DECORATION, trim, ornamentation, adornment, passementerie, embroidery; border, edging, piping, rickrack, fringes, fringing, frills; *archaic* purfles. **2** *roast turkey with all the trimmings* ACCOMPANIMENTS, extras, frills, accessories, accoutrements, trappings, paraphernalia; garnishing, garnish. **3** *hedge trimmings* CUTTINGS, clippings, parings, shavings.

trinket ● noun KNICK-KNACK, bauble, ornament, bibelot, curio, trifle, toy, novelty, gimcrack, gewgaw; *N. Amer.* kickshaw; *N. Amer. informal* tchotchke; *archaic* whim-wham, bijou, gaud.

atoms of oxygen.

trip ● verb (**tripped**, **tripping**) **1** catch one's foot on something and stumble or fall. **2** (**trip up**) make a mistake. **3** walk, run, or dance with quick light steps. **4** activate (a mechanism), especially by contact with a switch. **5** (of part of an electric circuit) disconnect automatically as a safety measure. **6** informal experience hallucinations induced by taking a psychedelic drug, especially LSD. ● noun **1** a journey or excursion. **2** an instance of tripping or falling. **3** informal a hallucinatory experience caused by taking a psychedelic drug. **4** informal a self-indulgent attitude or activity: *a power trip.* **5** a device that trips a mechanism, circuit, etc.

– PHRASES **trip the light fantastic** humorous dance. [ORIGIN from 'Trip it as you go On the light fantastic toe' (Milton's *L'Allegro*).]

– ORIGIN Dutch *trippen* 'to skip, hop'.

tripartite /trīpaartīt/ ● adjective **1** consisting of three parts. **2** shared by or involving three parties.

tripe ● noun **1** the first or second stomach of a cow or other ruminant used as food. **2** informal nonsense; rubbish.

– ORIGIN Old French, 'entrails of an animal'.

trip hammer ● noun a large, heavy pivoted hammer used in forging.

triphthong /trifthong/ ● noun **1** a union of three vowels (letters or sounds) pronounced in one syllable (as in *fire*). **2** three written vowel characters representing the sound of a single vowel (as in b*eau*).

– ORIGIN French *triphtongue*, after DIPHTHONG.

triplane ● noun an early type of aircraft with three pairs of wings, one above the other.

triple ● adjective **1** consisting of or involving three parts, things, or people. **2** having three times the usual size, quality, or strength. ● predeterminer three times as much or as many. ● noun a thing that is three times as large as usual or is made up of three parts. ● verb make or become three times as much or as many.

– DERIVATIVES **triply** adverb.

– ORIGIN Old French, from Greek *triplous*.

triple bond ● noun Chemistry a chemical bond in which three pairs of electrons are shared between two atoms.

triple crown ● noun **1** (**Triple Crown**) an award or honour for winning a group of three important events in a sport. **2** the papal tiara.

triple jump ● noun **1** an athletic event in which competitors attempt to jump as far as possible by performing a hop, a step, and a jump from a running start. **2** Skating a jump in which the skater makes three full turns while in the air.

triplet ● noun **1** one of three children or animals born at the same birth. **2** Music a group of three equal notes to be performed in the time of two or four. **3** a set of three rhyming lines of verse.

triple time ● noun musical time with three beats to the bar.

triplex /tripleks/ ● noun N. Amer. a residential building divided into three apartments. ● adjective having three parts.

– ORIGIN Latin, from *tri-* 'three' + *plicare* 'to fold'.

triplicate ● adjective /triplikət/ existing in three copies or examples. ● verb /triplikayt/ **1** make three copies of. **2** multiply by three.

– DERIVATIVES **triplication** /triplikaysh'n/ noun **triplicity** /tri**plis**siti/ noun.

– ORIGIN from Latin *triplicare* 'make three'.

triploid /triployd/ ● adjective Genetics (of a cell or nucleus) containing three complete sets of chromosomes.

tripmeter ● noun a vehicle instrument that can be set to record the distance of individual journeys.

tripod /trīpod/ ● noun **1** a three-legged stand for supporting a camera or other apparatus. **2** archaic a stool, table, or cauldron set on three legs.

– ORIGIN Greek, from *tri-* 'three' + *pous* 'foot'.

tripos /trīposs/ ● noun the final honours examination for a BA degree at Cambridge University.

– ORIGIN from Latin *tripus* 'tripod', with reference to the stool on which a designated graduate sat to deliver a satirical speech at the degree ceremony.

tripper ● noun Brit. informal a person who goes on a pleasure trip or excursion.

triptych /triptik/ ● noun **1** a picture or carving on three panels, typically hinged together vertically and used as an altarpiece. **2** a set of three associated artistic, literary, or musical works.

– ORIGIN originally denoting a set of three writing tablets hinged or tied together: from TRI-, on the pattern of *diptych*.

tripwire ● noun a wire that is stretched close to the ground and activates a trap, explosion, or alarm when disturbed.

trireme /trīreem/ ● noun an ancient Greek or Roman war galley with three banks of oars.

– ORIGIN Latin *triremis*, from *tri-* 'three' + *remus* 'oar'.

trisect /trīsekt/ ● verb divide into three parts.

– DERIVATIVES **trisection** noun.

– ORIGIN from TRI- + Latin *secare* 'divide, cut'.

trishaw /trīshaw/ ● noun a light three-wheeled vehicle with pedals, used in the Far East.

– ORIGIN from TRI- + RICKSHAW.

trisyllable /trīsilləb'l/ ● noun a word or metrical foot of three syllables.

– DERIVATIVES **trisyllabic** adjective.

trite ● adjective (of a remark or idea) lacking originality or freshness; dull on account of overuse.

– DERIVATIVES **tritely** adverb **triteness** noun.

– ORIGIN Latin *tritus* 'rubbed'.

triticale /trittikayli/ ● noun a hybrid cereal produced by crossing wheat and rye, grown as a fodder crop.

– ORIGIN Latin, from a blend of the genus names *Triticum* 'wheat' and *Secale* 'rye'.

tritium /trittiəm/ ● noun Chemistry a radioactive isotope of hydrogen with a mass approximately three times that of the usual isotope.

– ORIGIN from Greek *tritos* 'third'.

triturate /trityoorayt/ ● verb technical **1** grind to a fine powder. **2** chew or grind (food) thoroughly.

– DERIVATIVES **trituration** noun.

– ORIGIN from Latin *tritura* 'rubbing'.

triumph ● noun **1** a great victory or achievement. **2** the state of being victorious or successful. **3** joy or satisfaction resulting from a success or victory. **4** a highly successful example: *their marriage was a triumph of togetherness.* **5** the processional entry of a victorious general into ancient Rome. ● verb **1** achieve a triumph. **2** rejoice or exult at a triumph.

– DERIVATIVES **triumphal** adjective.

– ORIGIN Latin *triumphus*, probably from Greek *thriambos* 'hymn to Bacchus'.

t

Thesaurus

trio ● noun THREESOME, three, triumvirate, triad, troika, trinity; trilogy, triptych; triplets.

trip ● verb **1** *he tripped on the loose stones* STUMBLE, lose one's footing, catch one's foot, slip, lose one's balance, fall (down), tumble, topple, take a spill. **2** *taxpayers often trip up by not declaring taxable income* MAKE A MISTAKE, miscalculate, make a blunder, blunder, go wrong, make an error, err; *informal* slip up, screw up, make a boo-boo; *Brit. informal* boob; *N. Amer. informal* goof up. **3** *the question was intended to trip him up* CATCH OUT, trick, outwit, outsmart; throw off balance, disconcert, unsettle, discountenance, discomfit; *informal* throw, wrong-foot; *Brit. informal* catch on the hop. **4** *they tripped up the terrace steps* SKIP, run, dance, prance, bound, spring, scamper. **5** *Hoffman tripped the alarm* SET OFF, activate, trigger; turn on, switch on, throw.

● noun **1** *a trip to Paris* EXCURSION, outing, jaunt; HOLIDAY, visit, tour, journey, expedition, voyage; drive, run, day out, day trip; *informal* junket, spin. **2** *trips and falls cause nearly half such accidents* STUMBLE, slip, misstep, false step; fall, tumble, spill.

tripe ● noun *(informal).* See NONSENSE sense 1.

triple ● adjective **1** *a triple alliance* THREE-WAY, tripartite; threefold. **2** *they paid him triple the going rate* THREE TIMES, treble.

tripper ● noun *(Brit. informal)* TOURIST, holidaymaker, sightseer, day tripper, visitor, traveller; *N. Amer.* vacationer, vacationist, out-of-towner; *Brit. informal* grockle.

trite ● adjective BANAL, hackneyed, clichéd, platitudinous, vapid, commonplace, stock, conventional, stereotyped, overused, overdone, overworked, stale, worn out, time-worn, tired, hoary, hack, unimaginative, unoriginal, uninteresting, dull; *informal* old hat, corny, played out; *N. Amer. informal* cornball.

– OPPOSITES original, imaginative.

triumph ● noun **1** *Napoleon's many triumphs* VICTORY, win, conquest, success; achievement. **2** *his eyes shone with triumph* JUBILATION, exultation, elation, delight, joy, happiness, glee, pride, satisfaction. **3** *a triumph of Victorian engineering* TOUR DE FORCE, mas-

triumphalism ● noun excessive exultation over one's success or achievements.
– DERIVATIVES **triumphalist** adjective & noun.
triumphant ● adjective **1** having won a battle or contest; victorious. **2** jubilant after a victory or achievement.
– DERIVATIVES **triumphantly** adverb.
triumvir /trīumvər, trīəmvər/ ● noun (pl. **triumvirs** or **triumviri** /trīumvəri, trīəmvəri/) (in ancient Rome) each of three public officers jointly responsible for overseeing any of the administrative departments.
– DERIVATIVES **triumviral** adjective.
– ORIGIN Latin, from *trium virorum* 'of three men'.
triumvirate /trīumvirət/ ● noun **1** a group of three powerful or notable people or things. **2** (in ancient Rome) a group of three men holding power.
triune /trīyoon/ ● adjective (especially with reference to the Trinity) consisting of three in one.
– ORIGIN from TRI- + Latin *unus* 'one'.
trivet ● noun **1** an iron tripod placed over a fire for a cooking pot or kettle to stand on. **2** a metal stand on which hot dishes are placed.
– ORIGIN apparently from Latin *tripes* 'three-legged'.
trivia ● plural noun unimportant details or pieces of information.
– ORIGIN Latin, plural of *trivium* 'place where three roads meet', influenced by TRIVIAL.
trivial ● adjective of little value or importance.
– DERIVATIVES **triviality** noun (pl. **trivialities**) **trivially** adverb.
– ORIGIN originally in the sense 'belonging to the trivium' (an introductory course at a medieval university involving the study of grammar, rhetoric, and logic): from Latin *trivium*, literally 'place where three roads meet'.
trivialize (also **trivialise**) ● verb make (something) seem less important or complex than it really is.
– DERIVATIVES **trivialization** noun.
trochaic /trōkayik/ Poetry ● adjective consisting of or featuring trochees. ● noun (**trochaics**) trochaic verse.
trochee /trōkee/ ● noun Poetry a foot consisting of one long or stressed syllable followed by one short or unstressed syllable.
– ORIGIN from Greek *trokhaios pous* 'running foot'.
trod past and past participle of TREAD.
trodden past participle of TREAD.
trog ● verb (**trogged**, **trogging**) Brit. informal walk heavily or laboriously; trudge.
– ORIGIN perhaps a blend of TRUDGE, SLOG, TROLL², and JOG.
troglodyte /trogləd̄it/ ● noun **1** a cave-dweller. **2** a person who is deliberately ignorant or old-fashioned.
– DERIVATIVES **troglodytic** adjective.
– ORIGIN Greek *trōglodutēs*, from the name of an Ethiopian people, influenced by *trōglē* 'hole'.
troika /troykə/ ● noun **1** a Russian vehicle pulled by a team of three horses abreast. **2** a team of three horses. **3** a group of three people working together, especially as administrators or managers.
– ORIGIN Russian, from *troe* 'set of three'.
troilism /troyliz'm/ ● noun sexual activity involving three participants.
– ORIGIN perhaps from French *trois* 'three'.
Trojan ● noun an inhabitant of ancient Troy in Asia Minor. ● adjective relating to Troy.
– PHRASES **work like a Trojan** work extremely hard.
Trojan Horse ● noun something intended to undermine or secretly overthrow an enemy or opponent.
– ORIGIN from the hollow wooden statue of a horse in which the ancient Greeks are said to have concealed themselves in order to enter Troy.
troll¹ /trōl, trol/ ● noun (in folklore) an ugly cave-dwelling being depicted as either a giant or a dwarf.
– ORIGIN originally in the sense 'witch': from Old Norse and Swedish *troll*, Danish *trold*.
troll² /trōl, trol/ ● verb **1** fish by trailing a baited line along behind a boat. **2** chiefly Brit. walk; stroll. ● noun **1** an act or instance of trolling. **2** a line or bait used in trolling.
– DERIVATIVES **troller** noun.
– ORIGIN origin uncertain; probably related to Old French *troller* 'wander in search of game' and High German *trollen* 'stroll'.
trolley ● noun (pl. **trolleys**) **1** Brit. a large wheeled metal basket or frame used for transporting heavy or unwieldy items such as luggage or supermarket purchases. **2** a small table on wheels or castors, used especially to convey food and drink. **3** (also **trolley wheel**) a wheel attached to a pole, used for collecting current from an overhead electric wire to drive a tram. **4** a trolleybus or trolley car.
– PHRASES **off one's trolley** Brit. informal mad; insane.
– ORIGIN perhaps from TROLL².
trolleybus ● noun a bus powered by electricity obtained from overhead wires by means of a trolley wheel.
trolley car ● noun US a tram powered by electricity obtained from overhead wires by means of a trolley wheel.
trollop ● noun dated or humorous a sexually disreputable or promiscuous woman.
– ORIGIN perhaps related to archaic *trull* 'prostitute', from German *Trulle*.
trombone ● noun a large brass wind instrument having an extendable slide with which different notes are made.
– DERIVATIVES **trombonist** noun.
– ORIGIN French or Italian, from Italian *tromba* 'trumpet'.
trompe l'œil /tromp loy/ ● noun (pl. **trompe l'œils** pronunc. same) a painting or method of painting that creates the illusion of a three-dimensional object or space.
– ORIGIN French, 'deceives the eye'.
troop ● noun **1** (**troops**) soldiers or armed forces. **2** a unit of an armoured or cavalry division. **3** a group of three or more Scout patrols. **4** a group of people or animals of a particular kind. ● verb come or go as a group.
– PHRASES **troop the colour** Brit. perform the ceremony of parading a regiment's flag along ranks of soldiers.
– ORIGIN French *troupe*, from Latin *troppus* 'flock'.
troop carrier ● noun a large aircraft or armoured vehicle designed for transporting troops.
trooper ● noun **1** a private soldier in a cavalry or armoured unit. **2** chiefly Brit. a ship used for transporting troops. **3** Austral./NZ & US a mounted police officer. **4** US a state police officer.

Thesaurus

terpiece, crowning example, coup, wonder, sensation, master stroke.
– OPPOSITES defeat, disappointment.
● verb **1** *he triumphed in the British Grand Prix* WIN, succeed, come first, be victorious, carry the day, carry all before one, prevail, take the honours, come out on top. **2** *they had no chance of triumphing over the Nationalists* DEFEAT, beat, conquer, trounce, vanquish, worst, overcome, overpower, overwhelm, get the better of; bring someone to their knees, prevail against, subdue, subjugate; *informal* lick, best. **3** *'you can't touch me,' she triumphed* CROW, gloat; rejoice, exult.
– OPPOSITES lose.
triumphant ● adjective **1** *the triumphant British team* VICTORIOUS, successful, winning, conquering; undefeated, unbeaten. **2** *a triumphant expression* JUBILANT, exultant, elated, rejoicing, joyful, joyous, delighted, gleeful, proud, cock-a-hoop; gloating.
– OPPOSITES unsuccessful, despondent.
trivia ● plural noun (PETTY) DETAILS, minutiae, niceties, technicalities, trivialities, trifles, non-essentials.
trivial ● adjective **1** *trivial problems* UNIMPORTANT, insignificant, inconsequential, minor, of no account, of no consequence, of no importance; incidental, inessential, non-essential, petty, trifling, pettifogging, footling, small, slight, little, inconsiderable, negligible, paltry, nugatory; *informal* piddling, piffling, fiddling, penny-ante. **2** *I used to be quite a trivial person* FRIVOLOUS, superficial, shallow, unthinking, empty-headed, feather-brained, lightweight, foolish, silly.
– OPPOSITES important, significant, serious.
triviality ● noun **1** *the triviality of the subject matter* UNIMPORTANCE, insignificance, inconsequence, inconsequentiality, pettiness. **2** *he need not concern himself with such trivialities* MINOR DETAIL, petty detail, thing of no importance/consequence, trifle, non-essential, nothing; technicality; (**trivialities**) trivia, minutiae.
trivialize ● verb TREAT AS UNIMPORTANT, minimize, play down, underestimate, underplay, make light of, treat lightly, dismiss; *informal* pooh-pooh.
troop ● noun **1** *a troop of tourists* GROUP, party, band, gang, bevy, body, company, troupe, crowd, throng, horde, pack, drove, flock, swarm, multitude, host, army; *informal* bunch, gaggle, crew, posse. **2** *British troops were stationed here* SOLDIERS, armed forces, service men/women; the services, the army, the military, soldiery.
● verb **1** *we trooped out of the hall* WALK, march, file; flock, crowd,

– PHRASES **swear like a trooper** swear a great deal.

troopship ● noun a ship for transporting troops.

trope /trōp/ ● noun a figurative or metaphorical use of a word or expression.

– ORIGIN Greek *tropos* 'turn, way, trope'.

trophic /trōfik, troffik/ ● adjective **1** Ecology of or relating to feeding and nutrition. **2** (also **tropic**) Physiology (of a hormone or its effect) stimulating the activity of another endocrine gland.

– ORIGIN Greek *trophikos*, from *trophē* 'nourishment'.

trophy ● noun (pl. **trophies**) **1** a cup or other decorative object awarded as a prize for a victory or success. **2** a souvenir of an achievement, especially a head of an animal taken when hunting.

– ORIGIN French *trophée*, from Greek *tropē* 'a rout'.

tropic[1] /troppik/ ● noun **1** the parallel of latitude 23°26′ north (**tropic of Cancer**) or south (**tropic of Capricorn**) of the equator. **2** (**the tropics**) the region between the tropics of Cancer and Capricorn. **3** Astronomy each of two corresponding circles on the celestial sphere where the sun appears to turn after reaching its greatest declination, marking the northern and southern limits of the ecliptic. ● adjective tropical.

– ORIGIN Greek *tropikos*, from *trepein* 'to turn'.

tropic[2] /trōpik/ ● adjective **1** Biology relating to, consisting of, or exhibiting tropism. **2** Physiology variant spelling of TROPHIC.

tropical ● adjective **1** of or relating to the tropics. **2** very hot and humid.

– DERIVATIVES **tropically** adverb.

tropical storm (also **tropical cyclone**) ● noun a localized, very intense low-pressure wind system with winds of hurricane force, forming over tropical oceans.

tropism /trōpiz'm/ ● noun Biology the turning of all or part of an organism in response to an external stimulus.

– ORIGIN from Greek *tropos* 'turning'.

troposphere /troppəsfeer, trōp-/ ● noun the lowest region of the atmosphere, extending from the earth's surface to a height of about 6–10 km (the lower boundary of the stratosphere).

– DERIVATIVES **tropospheric** adjective.

– ORIGIN from Greek *tropos* 'turning'.

troppo[1] /troppō/ ● adverb Music too much; excessively.

– ORIGIN Italian.

troppo[2] /troppō/ ● adjective Austral./NZ informal mentally disturbed, supposedly as a result of spending too much time in a tropical climate.

Trot ● noun informal, chiefly derogatory a Trotskyist or supporter of extreme left-wing views.

trot ● verb (**trotted**, **trotting**) **1** (of a horse) proceed at a pace faster than a walk, lifting each diagonal pair of legs alternately. **2** (of a person) run at a moderate pace with short steps. **3** informal go or walk briskly. **4** (**trot out**) informal produce (an account that has been produced many times before). ● noun **1** a trotting pace. **2** an act or period of trotting. **3** (**the trots**) informal diarrhoea. **4** informal, chiefly Austral./NZ a run of good or bad luck.

– PHRASES **on the trot** informal **1** Brit. in succession. **2** continually busy.

– ORIGIN Latin *trottare*.

troth /trōth, troth/ ● noun **1** archaic or formal faith or loyalty when pledged in a solemn agreement or undertaking. **2** archaic truth.

– PHRASES **pledge** (or **plight**) **one's troth** make a solemn pledge of commitment or loyalty, especially in marriage.

– ORIGIN variant of TRUTH.

Trotskyism ● noun the political or economic principles of the Russian revolutionary Leon Trotsky (1879–1940), especially the theory that socialism should be established throughout the world by continuing revolution.

– DERIVATIVES **Trotskyist** noun & adjective **Trotskyite** noun & adjective (derogatory).

trotter ● noun **1** a horse bred or trained for the sport of trotting. **2** a pig's foot.

trotting ● noun racing for trotting horses pulling a two-wheeled vehicle and driver.

troubadour /troobədor/ ● noun (in medieval France) a performing poet who composed and sang in Provençal, especially on the theme of courtly love.

– ORIGIN French, from Provençal *trobar* 'find, invent, compose in verse'.

trouble ● noun **1** difficulty or problems. **2** effort or exertion. **3** a cause of worry or inconvenience. **4** (**in trouble**) in a situation in which one is liable to incur punishment or blame. **5** public unrest or disorder. ● verb **1** cause distress, pain, or inconvenience to. **2** (**troubled**) showing or experiencing problems or anxiety. **3** (**trouble about/over/with**) be distressed or anxious about. **4** (**trouble to do**) make the effort required to do.

– PHRASES **ask for trouble** informal act in a way that is likely to incur problems or difficulties. **look for trouble** informal behave in a way that is likely to provoke an argument or fight. **trouble and strife** Brit. rhyming slang one's wife. **a trouble shared is a trouble halved** proverb talking to someone else about one's problems helps to alleviate them.

– ORIGIN Old French *truble*, from Latin *turba* 'crowd, disturbance'.

troublemaker ● noun a person who habitually causes trouble, especially by inciting others to defy those in authority.

troubleshoot ● verb **1** analyse and solve problems for an organization. **2** trace and correct faults in a mechanical or electronic system.

– DERIVATIVES **troubleshooter** noun.

Thesaurus

throng, stream, swarm, surge, spill. **2** *Caroline trooped wearily home* TRUDGE, plod, traipse, trail, drag oneself, tramp; *N. Amer. informal* schlep.

trophy ● noun **1** *a swimming trophy* CUP, medal; prize, award. **2** *a cabinet full of trophies from his travels* SOUVENIR, memento, keepsake; spoils, booty.

tropical ● adjective *tropical weather* VERY HOT, sweltering, humid, sultry, steamy, sticky, oppressive, stifling, suffocating, heavy; *informal* boiling.

– OPPOSITES cold, arctic.

trot ● verb *Doyle trotted across the patio* RUN, jog, jogtrot, dogtrot; scuttle, scurry, bustle, scamper.

– PHRASES **on the trot** *(Brit. informal)* IN SUCCESSION, one after the other, in a row, consecutively, successively; running, straight. **trot something out** *(informal)* RECITE, repeat, regurgitate, churn out; come out with, produce.

troubadour ● noun *(historical)* MINSTREL, singer, balladeer, poet; *historical* jongleur, trouvère.

trouble ● noun **1** *you've caused enough trouble already* PROBLEMS, difficulty, bother, inconvenience, worry, anxiety, distress, stress, agitation, harassment, unpleasantness; *informal* hassle. **2** *she poured out all her troubles* PROBLEM, misfortune, difficulty, trial, tribulation, trauma, burden, pain, woe, grief, heartache, misery, affliction, suffering. **3** *he's gone to a lot of trouble to help you* BOTHER, inconvenience, fuss, effort, exertion, work, labour; pains, care, attention, thought. **4** *I wouldn't want to be a trouble to her* NUISANCE, bother, inconvenience, irritation, irritant, problem, trial, pest, thorn in someone's flesh/side; *informal* headache, pain, pain in the neck/backside, drag; *N. Amer. informal* pain in the butt, burr in/under someone's saddle, nudnik. **5** *you're too gullible, that's your trouble* SHORTCOMING, weakness, weak point, failing, fault, imperfection, defect, blemish; problem, difficulty. **6** *he had a history of heart trouble* DISEASE, illness, sickness, ailments, complaints, problems; disorder, disability. **7** *the crash was due to engine trouble* MALFUNCTION, dysfunction, failure, breakdown. **8** *a match marred by serious crowd trouble* DISTURBANCE, disorder, unrest, fighting, ructions, fracas, breach of the peace; *Law, dated* affray.

● verb **1** *this matter had been troubling her for some time* WORRY, bother, concern, disturb, upset, agitate, distress, perturb, annoy, irritate, vex, irk, nag, niggle, prey on someone's mind, weigh down, burden; *informal* bug. **2** *he was troubled by bouts of ill health* AFFLICT, burden; suffer from, be cursed with; *informal* be a martyr to. **3** *there is nothing you need trouble about* WORRY, upset oneself, fret, be anxious, be concerned, concern oneself. **4** *don't trouble to see me out* BOTHER, take the trouble, go to the trouble, exert oneself, go out of one's way. **5** *I'm sorry to trouble you* INCONVENIENCE, bother, impose on, disturb, put out, disoblige; *informal* hassle; *formal* discommode.

– PHRASES **in trouble** IN DIFFICULTY, in difficulties, in a mess, in a bad way, in a predicament; *informal* in a tight corner/spot, in a fix, in a hole, in hot water, in a pickle, in the soup, up against it; *Brit. informal* up a gum tree.

troubled ● adjective **1** *Joanna looked troubled* ANXIOUS, worried, concerned, perturbed, disturbed, bothered, ill at ease, uneasy, unsettled, agitated; distressed, upset, dismayed. **2** *we live in troubled times* DIFFICULT, problematic, full of problems, unsettled, hard, tough, stressful, dark.

t

troublesome • adjective causing difficulty or annoyance.
– DERIVATIVES **troublesomeness** noun.

trouble spot • noun a place where difficulties or conflict regularly occur.

troublous • adjective archaic or literary full of troubles.

trough • noun **1** a long, narrow open container for animals to eat or drink out of. **2** a channel used to convey a liquid. **3** an elongated region of low barometric pressure. **4** a hollow between two wave crests in the sea. **5** a point of low activity or achievement.
– ORIGIN Old English; related to TREE.

trounce • verb **1** defeat heavily in a contest. **2** rebuke or punish severely.
– ORIGIN of unknown origin.

troupe • noun a group of dancers, actors, or other entertainers who tour to different venues.
– ORIGIN French, from Latin *troppus* 'flock'; related to TROOP.

trouper • noun **1** an actor or other entertainer with long experience. **2** a reliable and uncomplaining person.

trouser • noun (before another noun) relating to trousers: *his trouser pocket.* • verb Brit. informal receive or take for oneself; pocket.

trousers • plural noun an outer garment covering the body from the waist to the ankles, with a separate part for each leg.
– PHRASES **wear the trousers** informal be the dominant partner in a relationship.
– DERIVATIVES **trousered** adjective.
– ORIGIN from Irish *triús* and Scottish Gaelic *triubhas*; related to TREWS.

trouser suit • noun Brit. a pair of trousers and a matching jacket worn by women.

trousseau /tro͞osō/ • noun (pl. **trousseaux** or **trousseaus** /tro͞osōz/) the clothes, linen, and other belongings collected by a bride for her marriage.
– ORIGIN French, 'small bundle'.

trout • noun (pl. same or **trouts**) an edible fish of the salmon family, chiefly inhabiting fresh water.
– PHRASES **old trout** informal an annoying or bad-tempered old woman.
– ORIGIN Old English, from Greek *trōgein* 'gnaw'.

trove • noun a store of valuable or delightful things.
– ORIGIN from TREASURE TROVE.

trow /trō/ • verb archaic think or believe.
– ORIGIN Old English, 'to trust'; related to TRUCE.

trowel • noun **1** a small hand-held tool with a curved scoop for lifting plants or earth. **2** a small hand-held tool with a flat, pointed blade, used to apply and spread mortar or plaster. • verb (**trowelled**, **trowelling**; US **troweled**, **troweling**) apply or spread with or as if with a trowel.
– ORIGIN Latin *truella*, from *trulla* 'scoop'.

troy (also **troy weight**) • noun a system of weights used mainly for precious metals and gems, with a pound of 12 ounces or 5,760 grains. Compare with AVOIRDUPOIS.
– ORIGIN from a weight used at the fair of *Troyes* in France.

truant • noun a pupil who stays away from school without permission or explanation. • adjective wandering; straying. • verb (also **play truant**) (of a pupil) stay away from school without permission or explanation.
– DERIVATIVES **truancy** noun.
– ORIGIN originally denoting a person begging through choice rather than necessity: from Old French.

truce • noun an agreement between enemies to stop fighting for a certain time.
– ORIGIN Old English, 'belief, trust'; related to TRUE.

truck[1] • noun **1** a large road vehicle, used for carrying goods, materials, or troops. **2** Brit. an open railway vehicle for carrying freight. • verb chiefly N. Amer. **1** convey by truck. **2** informal go or proceed in a casual or leisurely way.
– ORIGIN originally denoting a solid wooden wheel: perhaps from TRUCKLE in the sense 'wheel, pulley'.

truck[2] • noun **1** archaic barter. **2** chiefly archaic small wares. **3** N. Amer. market-garden produce, especially vegetables. • verb archaic barter or exchange.
– PHRASES **have no truck with** choose to avoid dealings or association with.
– ORIGIN probably from Old French; compare with Latin *trocare* 'to barter'.

trucker • noun a long-distance truck driver.

truckle • noun a small barrel-shaped cheese, especially cheddar.
– ORIGIN originally denoting a wheel or pulley: from Old French *trocle*, from Latin *trochlea* 'sheaf of a pulley'.

truckle bed • noun chiefly Brit. a low bed on wheels that can be stored under a larger bed.

truck stop • noun N. Amer. a transport cafe.

truculent /trukyoolənt/ • adjective quick to argue or fight; defiant.
– DERIVATIVES **truculence** noun **truculently** adverb.
– ORIGIN Latin *truculentus*, from *trux* 'fierce'.

trudge • verb walk slowly and with heavy steps. • noun a difficult or laborious walk.
– ORIGIN of unknown origin.

true • adjective (**truer**, **truest**) **1** in accordance with fact or reality. **2** rightly or strictly so called; genuine: *true love.* **3** real or actual. **4** accurate and exact. **5** (of a note) exactly in tune. **6** correctly positioned or aligned; upright or level. **7** loyal or faithful. **8** (**true to**) accurately conforming to (a standard or expectation). • verb (**trues**, **trued**, **truing** or **trueing**) bring into the exact shape or position required.
– PHRASES **come true** actually happen or become the case. **out of true** not in the correct or exact shape or alignment. **many a true word is spoken in jest** proverb a humorous remark not intended to be taken seriously may turn out to be accurate after all. **true to form** (or **type**) being or behaving as expected. **true to life** accurately representing real events or objects.
– DERIVATIVES **trueness** noun.
– ORIGIN Old English, 'steadfast, loyal'; related to TRUCE.

true-blue • adjective **1** Brit. staunchly loyal to the Conservative

Thesaurus

troublemaker • noun MISCHIEF-MAKER, rabble-rouser, firebrand, agitator, agent provocateur, ringleader, incendiary; demagogue; scandalmonger, gossipmonger, meddler; *informal* stirrer.

troublesome • adjective **1** *a troublesome problem* ANNOYING, irritating, exasperating, maddening, infuriating, irksome, vexatious, vexing, bothersome, tiresome, worrying, worrisome, disturbing, upsetting, niggling, nagging; difficult, awkward, problematic, taxing; *informal* aggravating; *N. Amer. informal* pesky. **2** *a troublesome child* DIFFICULT, awkward, trying, demanding, uncooperative, rebellious, unmanageable, unruly, obstreperous, disruptive, badly behaved, disobedient, naughty, recalcitrant; *formal* refractory.
– OPPOSITES simple, cooperative.

trough • noun **1** *a large feeding trough* MANGER, feedbox, feeder, fodder rack, crib. **2** *a thirty-yard trough* CHANNEL, conduit, trench, ditch, gully, drain, culvert, cut, flume, gutter.

trounce • verb DEFEAT UTTERLY, beat hollow, rout, crush, overwhelm; *informal* hammer, clobber, thrash, drub, pulverize, massacre, crucify, demolish, destroy, annihilate, wipe the floor with, make mincemeat of, murder; *Brit. informal* stuff; *N. Amer. informal* shellac, cream, skunk.

troupe • noun GROUP, company, band, ensemble, set; cast.

trousers • plural noun SLACKS, chinos, jeans; *N. Amer.* pants; *Brit. informal* trews, strides, kecks, breeches; *Austral. informal* daks.

truant • noun ABSENTEE; *Brit. informal* skiver; *Austral./NZ informal* wag. • verb *pupils who truant.* See PLAY TRUANT.
– PHRASES **play truant** stay away from school, truant; *Brit. informal* skive (off), bunk off; *Irish informal* mitch (off); *N. Amer. informal* play hookey, goof off; *Austral./NZ informal* play the wag.

truce • noun CEASEFIRE, armistice, suspension of hostilities, peace; respite, lull; *informal* let-up.

truck[1] • noun *a heavily laden truck* LORRY, heavy goods vehicle, juggernaut; van, pickup (truck); *Brit.* HGV; *dated* pantechnicon.

truck[2] • noun *we are to have no truck with him* DEALINGS, association, contact, communication, connection, relations; business, trade.

truckle • verb *an ambitious woman who truckled to no man* KOWTOW, submit, defer, yield, bow and scrape, be obsequious, pander, toady, prostrate oneself, grovel; fawn on, dance attendance on, curry favour with, ingratiate oneself with; *informal* suck up, crawl, lick someone's boots; *Austral./NZ informal* smoodge.

truculent • adjective DEFIANT, aggressive, antagonistic, belligerent, pugnacious, confrontational, ready for a fight, obstreperous, argumentative, quarrelsome, uncooperative; bad-tempered, short-tempered, cross, snappish; *informal* feisty, spoiling for a fight; *Brit. informal* stroppy, bolshie.
– OPPOSITES cooperative, amiable.

trudge • verb PLOD, tramp, drag oneself, walk heavily/slowly, plough, slog, footslog, toil, trek; *informal* traipse, galumph; *Brit. infor-*

Party. **2** N. Amer. extremely loyal or orthodox.

true-born ● adjective of a specified kind by birth; genuine.

true north ● noun north according to the earth's axis, not magnetic north.

truffle ● noun **1** an underground fungus that resembles a rough-skinned potato, eaten as a delicacy. **2** a soft chocolate sweet. ● verb (as noun **truffling**) hunting for truffles.
– ORIGIN obsolete French, perhaps from Latin *tuber* 'hump, swelling'.

trug ● noun Brit. a shallow oblong wooden basket, traditionally used for carrying garden flowers and produce.
– ORIGIN originally denoting a basin: perhaps a dialect form of TROUGH.

truism ● noun a statement that is obviously true and says nothing new or interesting.

truly ● adverb **1** in a truthful way. **2** to the fullest degree; absolutely or completely. **3** genuinely or properly. **4** in actual fact; really.
– PHRASES **yours truly 1** used as a formula for ending a letter. **2** humorous used to refer to oneself.

trump[1] ● noun **1** (in bridge, whist, etc.) a playing card of the suit chosen to rank above the others, which can win a trick where a card of a different suit has been led. **2** a valuable resource that may be used, especially as a surprise, to gain an advantage. **3** informal, dated a helpful or admirable person. **4** Austral./NZ informal a person in authority. ● verb **1** play a trump on (a card of another suit). **2** beat by saying or doing something better. **3** (**trump up**) invent (a false accusation or excuse).
– PHRASES **come** (or **turn**) **up trumps** informal, chiefly Brit. **1** have a better performance or outcome than expected. **2** be especially generous or helpful.
– ORIGIN from TRIUMPH, once used in card games in the same sense.

trump[2] ● noun archaic a trumpet or a trumpet blast.
– ORIGIN Old French *trompe*.

trumpery ● noun archaic (pl. **trumperies**) articles, practices, or beliefs of superficial appeal but little real value or worth. ● adjective showy but worthless; illusory.
– ORIGIN Old French *tromperie*, from *tromper* 'deceive'.

trumpet ● noun **1** a brass musical instrument with a flared bell and a bright, penetrating tone. **2** something shaped like a trumpet, especially the tubular central part of a daffodil flower. **3** the loud cry of an elephant. ● verb (**trumpeted**, **trumpeting**) **1** play a trumpet. **2** (of an elephant) make its characteristic loud cry. **3** proclaim widely or loudly.
– PHRASES **blow one's own trumpet** talk openly and boastfully about one's achievements.
– ORIGIN Old French *trompette*.

trumpeter ● noun a person who plays a trumpet.

trumpet major ● noun the chief trumpeter of a cavalry regiment.

truncate /trungkayt/ ● verb shorten by cutting off the top or the end.
– DERIVATIVES **truncation** noun.
– ORIGIN Latin *truncare* 'maim'.

truncheon /trunchən/ ● noun chiefly Brit. a short thick stick carried as a weapon by a police officer.
– ORIGIN Old French *tronchon* 'stump', from Latin *truncus* 'trunk'.

trundle ● verb move slowly and unevenly on or as if on wheels. ● noun an act of trundling.
– ORIGIN originally denoting a small wheel or roller: related to obsolete or dialect *trendle* 'revolve', and to TREND.

trundle bed ● noun chiefly N. Amer. a truckle bed.

trunk ● noun **1** the main woody stem of a tree as distinct from its branches and roots. **2** a person's or animal's body apart from the limbs and head. **3** the elongated, prehensile nose of an elephant. **4** a large box with a hinged lid for storing or transporting clothes and other articles. **5** N. Amer. the boot of a car. **6** (before another noun) of or relating to the main routes of a transport or communication network: *a trunk road*.
– ORIGIN Latin *truncus*.

trunk call ● noun dated, chiefly Brit. a long-distance telephone call made within the same country.

trunking ● noun a system of shafts or conduits for cables or ventilation.

trunks ● plural noun men's shorts, worn especially for swimming or boxing.

trunnion /trunyən/ ● noun a pin or pivot forming one of a pair on which something is supported.
– ORIGIN French *trognon* 'core, tree trunk'.

truss ● noun **1** a framework of rafters, posts, and struts which supports a roof, bridge, or other structure. **2** a padded belt worn against the skin to support a hernia. **3** a large projection of stone or timber, typically one supporting a cornice. **4** Brit., chiefly historical a bundle of old hay (56 lb), new hay (60 lb), or straw (36 lb). **5** a compact cluster of flowers or fruit growing on one stalk. ● verb **1** support with a truss or trusses. **2** bind or tie up tightly. **3** tie up the wings and legs of (a chicken or other

Thesaurus

mal trog.

true ● adjective **1** *you'll see that what I say is true* CORRECT, accurate, right, verifiable, in accordance with the facts, what actually/really happened, the case, so; faithful, literal, factual, unelaborated, unvarnished. **2** *people are still willing to pay for true craftsmanship* GENUINE, authentic, real, actual, bona fide, proper; *informal* honest-to-goodness, kosher, pukka, legit, the real McCoy; *Austral./NZ informal* dinkum. **3** *the true owner of the goods* RIGHTFUL, legitimate, legal, lawful, authorized, bona fide, de jure. **4** *the necessity for true repentance* SINCERE, genuine, real, unfeigned, heartfelt, from the heart. **5** *a true friend* LOYAL, faithful, constant, devoted, staunch, steadfast, unswerving, unwavering; trustworthy, trusty, reliable, dependable. **6** *a true reflection of life in the 50s* ACCURATE, true to life, faithful, telling it like it is, fact-based, realistic, close, lifelike.
– OPPOSITES untrue, false, disloyal, inaccurate.

true-blue ● adjective STAUNCH, loyal, faithful, stalwart, committed, card-carrying, confirmed, dyed-in-the-wool, devoted, dedicated, firm, steadfast, unswerving, unwavering, unfaltering; *informal* deep-dyed.

truism ● noun PLATITUDE, commonplace, cliché, stock phrase, banality, old chestnut, old saw, bromide.

truly ● adverb **1** *tell me truly what you want* TRUTHFULLY, honestly, frankly, candidly, openly, to someone's face, laying one's cards on the table; *informal* pulling no punches. **2** *I'm truly grateful to them* SINCERELY, genuinely, really, indeed, from the bottom of one's heart, heartily, profoundly; very, extremely, dreadfully, immensely, tremendously, incredibly, most; *informal* awfully, terribly, terrifically, fearfully; *Brit. informal* jolly, ever so; *informal, dated* frightfully. **3** *a truly dreadful song* REALLY, absolutely, simply, utterly, totally, perfectly, thoroughly, positively, completely. **4** *this is truly a miracle* WITHOUT (A) DOUBT, unquestionably, undoubtedly, certainly, surely, definitely, beyond doubt/question, indubitably, undeniably, beyond the shadow of a doubt; in truth, really, in reality, actually, in fact; *archaic* forsooth, in sooth, verily. **5** *the streaming system does not truly reflect children's ability* ACCURATELY, correctly, exactly, precisely, faithfully.

trump ● verb *by wearing the simplest of dresses, she had trumped them all* OUTSHINE, outclass, upstage, put in the shade, eclipse, surpass, outdo, outperform; beat, better, top, cap; *informal* be a cut above, be head and shoulders above, leave standing; *Brit. informal* knock spots off; *archaic* outrival.
– PHRASES **trump something up** INVENT, make up, fabricate, concoct, contrive, manufacture, devise, hatch; fake, falsify; *informal* cook up.

trumped-up ● adjective BOGUS, spurious, specious, false, fabricated, invented, manufactured, contrived, made-up, fake, factitious; *informal* phoney.
– OPPOSITES genuine.

trumpery ● noun *(archaic)* TRINKETS, baubles, knick-knacks, ornaments, bibelots, gewgaws, gimcracks.

trumpet ● verb **1** *'come on!' he trumpeted* SHOUT, bellow, roar, yell, cry out, call out; *informal* holler. **2** *companies trumpeted their enthusiasm for the multimedia revolution* PROCLAIM, announce, declare, noise abroad, shout from the rooftops.
– PHRASES **blow one's own trumpet** BOAST, brag, sing one's own praises, show off, swank, congratulate oneself; *N. Amer. informal* blow/toot one's own horn; *Austral./NZ informal* skite.

truncate ● verb SHORTEN, cut, cut short, curtail, bring to an untimely end; abbreviate, condense, reduce.
– OPPOSITES lengthen, extend.

truncheon ● noun *(Brit.)* CLUB, baton, cudgel, bludgeon; stick, staff; *Brit.* life preserver; *N. Amer.* billy, blackjack, nightstick; *Brit. informal* cosh.

trunk ● noun **1** *the trunk of a tree* MAIN STEM, bole, stock. **2** *his powerful trunk* TORSO, body. **3** *an elephant's trunk* PROBOSCIS, nose,

bird) before cooking.
– ORIGIN Old French *trusser* 'pack up, bind in', from Latin *torquere* 'twist'.

trust • noun **1** firm belief in the reliability, truth, ability, or strength of someone or something. **2** acceptance of the truth of a statement without evidence or investigation. **3** the state of being responsible for someone or something. **4** Law an arrangement whereby a person (a trustee) is made the nominal owner of property to be held or used for the benefit of one or more others. **5** a body of trustees, or an organization or company managed by trustees. • verb **1** have trust in. **2** (**trust with**) have the confidence to allow (someone) to have, use, or look after. **3** (**trust to**) commit (someone or something) to the safekeeping of. **4** (**trust to**) place reliance on (luck, fate, etc.). **5** have confidence; hope: *I trust that you have enjoyed this book.*
– DERIVATIVES **trustable** adjective **trusted** adjective.
– ORIGIN from Old Norse, 'strong'.

trust company • noun a company formed to act as a trustee or to deal with trusts.

trustee • noun **1** Law an individual or member of a board given powers of administration of property in trust with a legal obligation to administer it solely for the purposes specified. **2** a state made responsible for the government of an area by the United Nations.
– DERIVATIVES **trusteeship** noun.

trustful • adjective having or showing total trust in someone.
– DERIVATIVES **trustfully** adverb **trustfulness** noun.

trust fund • noun a fund consisting of assets belonging to a trust, held by the trustees for the beneficiaries.

trusting • adjective tending to trust others; not suspicious.
– DERIVATIVES **trustingly** adverb **trustingness** noun.

trust territory • noun a territory under the trusteeship of the United Nations or of a state designated by them.

trustworthy • adjective able to be relied on as honest, truthful, or reliable.
– DERIVATIVES **trustworthiness** noun.

trusty • adjective (**trustier**, **trustiest**) archaic or humorous reliable or faithful.

truth • noun (pl. **truths** /troōths, troōthz/) **1** the quality or state of being true. **2** (also **the truth**) that which is true as opposed to false. **3** a fact or belief that is accepted as true.
– PHRASES **in truth** really; in fact. **to tell the truth** (or **truth to tell** or **if truth be told**) to be frank.
– ORIGIN Old English.

truth drug • noun a drug supposedly able to induce a state in which a person answers questions truthfully.

truthful • adjective **1** telling or expressing the truth; honest. **2** (of a representation) true to life.
– DERIVATIVES **truthfully** adverb **truthfulness** noun.

try • verb (**tries**, **tried**) **1** make an attempt or effort to do something. **2** (also **try out**) test (something new or different) in order to see if it is suitable, effective, or pleasant. **3** attempt to open (a door), contact (someone), etc. **4** (**try on**) put on (an item of clothing) to see if it fits or suits one. **5** make severe demands on. **6** subject (someone) to trial. **7** investigate and decide (a case or issue) in a formal trial. • noun (pl. **tries**) **1** an effort to do something; an attempt. **2** an act of testing something new or different. **3** Rugby an act of touching the ball down behind the opposing goal line, scoring points and entitling the scoring side to a kick at goal.
– PHRASES **tried and tested** (or **true**) having proved effective or reliable before. **try one's hand at** attempt to do for the first time. **try it on** Brit. informal deliberately test or attempt to deceive or seduce someone.
– USAGE The constructions **try to** and **try and** (as in *we should try to* (or *try and*) *help them*) mean the same thing, but **try and** is more informal: use **try to** in formal writing or speech.
– ORIGIN Old French *trier* 'sift'.

trying • adjective difficult or annoying; hard to endure.

trypanosome /trippənəsōm, tripannə-/ • noun Medicine & Zoology a single-celled parasitic protozoan with a trailing flagellum, infesting the blood.
– ORIGIN from Greek *trupanon* 'borer' + *sōma* 'body'.

trypanosomiasis /trippənōsəmīəsiss/ • noun Medicine any tropical disease caused by trypanosomes, especially sleeping sickness or Chagas' disease.

tryptophan /triptəfan/ • noun Biochemistry an amino acid which is a constituent of most proteins and is an essential nutrient in

Thesaurus

snout. **4** *an enormous tin trunk* CHEST, box, crate, coffer; case, portmanteau. **5** *(N. Amer.) the trunk of his car* LUGGAGE COMPARTMENT; *Brit.* boot.

truss • noun **1** *the bridge is supported by three steel trusses* SUPPORT, buttress, joist, brace, prop, strut, stay, stanchion, pier. **2** *a hernia truss* SURGICAL APPLIANCE, support, pad.
• verb *they trussed us up with ropes and chains* TIE UP, bind, chain up; pinion, fetter, tether, secure.

trust • noun **1** *good relationships have to built on trust* CONFIDENCE, belief, faith, certainty, assurance, conviction, credence; reliance. **2** *a position of trust* RESPONSIBILITY, duty, obligation. **3** *the money is to be held in trust for his son* SAFE KEEPING, keeping, protection, charge, care, custody; trusteeship, guardianship.
– OPPOSITES distrust, mistrust, doubt.
• verb **1** *I should never have trusted her* PUT ONE'S TRUST IN, have faith in, have (every) confidence in, believe in, pin one's hopes/faith on. **2** *he can be trusted to carry out an impartial investigation* RELY ON, depend on, bank on, count on, be sure of. **3** *I trust we shall meet again* HOPE, expect, take it, assume, presume. **4** *they don't like to trust their money to anyone outside the family* ENTRUST, consign, commit, give, hand over, turn over, assign; *formal* commend.
– OPPOSITES distrust, mistrust, doubt.

trustee • noun ADMINISTRATOR, agent; custodian, keeper, steward, depositary; executor, executrix; *Law* fiduciary, feoffee.

trustful • adjective. See TRUSTING.

trusting • adjective TRUSTFUL, unsuspecting, unquestioning, unguarded, unwary; naive, innocent, childlike, ingenuous, wide-eyed, credulous, gullible, easily taken in.
– OPPOSITES distrustful, suspicious.

trustworthy • adjective RELIABLE, dependable, honest, honourable, upright, principled, true, truthful, as good as one's word, ethical, virtuous, incorruptible, unimpeachable, above suspicion; responsible, sensible, level-headed; loyal, faithful, staunch, steadfast, trusty; safe, sound, reputable; *informal* on the level; *N. Amer. informal* straight-up.
– OPPOSITES unreliable.

trusty • adjective *(archaic or humorous)* RELIABLE, dependable, trustworthy, never-failing, unfailing, trusted; loyal, faithful, true, staunch, steadfast, constant, unswerving, unwavering.
– OPPOSITES unreliable.

truth • noun **1** *he doubted the truth of her statement* VERACITY, truthfulness, verity, sincerity, candour, honesty; accuracy, correctness, validity, factuality, authenticity. **2** *it's the truth, I swear it* WHAT ACTUALLY HAPPENED, the case, so; gospel (truth), the honest truth. **3** *truth is stranger than fiction* FACT(S), reality, real life, actuality. **4** *scientific truths* FACT, verity, certainty, certitude; law, principle.
– OPPOSITES lies, fiction, falsehood.
– PHRASES **in truth** IN (ACTUAL) FACT, in point of fact, in reality, really, actually, to tell the truth, if truth be told.

truthful • adjective **1** *a truthful answer* HONEST, sincere, trustworthy, genuine; candid, frank, open, forthright, straight; *informal* upfront, on the level; *N. Amer. informal* on the up and up. **2** *a truthful account* TRUE, accurate, correct, factual, faithful, reliable; unvarnished, unembellished; *formal* veracious, veridical.
– OPPOSITES deceitful, untrue.

try • verb **1** *try to help him* ATTEMPT, endeavour, make an effort, exert oneself, strive, do one's best, do one's utmost, move heaven and earth; undertake, aim, take it on oneself; *informal* have a go, give it one's best shot, bend over backwards, bust a gut, do one's damnedest, pull out all the stops, go all out, knock oneself out; *formal* essay; *archaic* assay. **2** *try it and see what you think* TEST, put to the test, sample, taste, inspect, investigate, examine, appraise, evaluate, assess; *informal* check out, give something a whirl. **3** *Mary tried everyone's patience* TAX, strain, test, stretch, sap, drain, exhaust, wear out. **4** *the case is to be tried by a jury* ADJUDICATE, consider, hear, adjudge, examine.
• noun *I'll have one last try* ATTEMPT, go, effort, endeavour; *informal* shot, crack, stab, bash, whack; *formal* essay.
– PHRASES **try something out** TEST, trial, experiment with, pilot; put through its paces; assess, evaluate.

trying • adjective **1** *a trying day* STRESSFUL, taxing, demanding, difficult, tough, hard, pressured, frustrating, fraught; arduous, gruelling, tiring, exhausting; *informal* hellish. **2** *Steve was very trying* ANNOYING, irritating, exasperating, maddening, infuriating;

the diet of vertebrates.
– ORIGIN from *tryptic* 'relating to trypsin' (a digestive enzyme) + Greek *phainein* 'appear'.

try square • noun an implement used to check and mark right angles in constructional work.

tryst /trist/ literary • noun a private, romantic rendezvous between lovers. • verb keep or arrange a tryst.
– ORIGIN Latin *trista* 'an appointed place in hunting'.

tsar /zaar/ (also **czar** or **tzar**) • noun an emperor of Russia before 1917.
– DERIVATIVES **tsardom** noun **tsarism** noun **tsarist** noun & adjective.
– ORIGIN Russian, representing Latin *Caesar*.

tsarevich /zaarivich/ (also **czarevich** or **tzarevich**) • noun historical the eldest son of a Russian tsar.
– ORIGIN Russian, 'son of a tsar'.

tsarina /zaareenə/ (also **czarina** or **tzarina**) • noun an empress of Russia before 1917.

tsetse /tetsi, tsetsi/ (also **tsetse fly**) • noun an African blood-sucking fly which transmits sleeping sickness and other diseases.
– ORIGIN from a southern African language.

T-shirt (also **tee shirt**) • noun a short-sleeved casual top, having the shape of a T when spread out flat.

tsp • abbreviation (pl. same or **tsps**) teaspoonful.

T-square • noun a T-shaped instrument for drawing or testing right angles.

TSR • abbreviation Computing terminate and stay resident, denoting a type of program that remains in the memory of a microcomputer after it has finished running.

TSS • abbreviation toxic shock syndrome.

tsubo /tsoobō/ • noun (pl. same or **tsubos**) (in complementary medicine) a point on the face or body to which pressure or other stimulation is applied during treatment.
– ORIGIN Japanese.

tsunami /tsoonaami/ • noun (pl. same or **tsunamis**) a long high sea wave caused by an earthquake or other disturbance.
– ORIGIN Japanese, 'harbour wave'.

TT • abbreviation **1** teetotal or teetotaller. **2** Tourist Trophy.

TTL • abbreviation **1** Electronics transistor transistor logic, a widely used technology for making integrated circuits. **2** Photography (of a camera focusing system) through-the-lens.

Tuareg /twaareg/ • noun (pl. same or **Tuaregs**) a member of a Berber people of the western and central Sahara.
– ORIGIN the name in Berber.

tub • noun **1** a low, wide, open container with a flat bottom. **2** a small lidded plastic or cardboard container for food. **3** informal, chiefly N. Amer. a bath. **4** informal, derogatory a short, broad boat that handles awkwardly.
– ORIGIN probably Low German or Dutch.

tuba • noun a large low-pitched brass wind instrument with a broad bell.
– ORIGIN Latin, 'trumpet'.

tubal • adjective relating to or occurring in a tube, especially the Fallopian tubes.

tubby • adjective (**tubbier**, **tubbiest**) informal (of a person) short and rather fat.
– DERIVATIVES **tubbiness** noun.

tube • noun **1** a long, hollow cylinder for conveying or holding liquids or gases. **2** a flexible metal or plastic container sealed at one end and having a cap at the other. **3** a hollow cylindrical organ or structure in an animal or plant. **4** Brit. informal (**the tube**) the underground railway system in London. **5** a sealed container containing two electrodes between which an electric current can be made to flow. **6** a cathode ray tube, especially in a television set. **7** (**the tube**) N. Amer. informal television. **8** N. Amer. a thermionic valve. **9** Austral. informal a can of beer. • verb **1** provide with a tube or tubes. **2** convey in a tube.
– PHRASES **go down the tube** (or **tubes**) informal be completely lost or wasted; fail utterly.
– ORIGIN Latin *tubus*.

tubectomy • noun (pl. **tubectomies**) surgical removal of the Fallopian tubes.

tuber • noun **1** a thickened underground part of a stem or rhizome, e.g. that of the potato, bearing buds from which new plants grow. **2** a thickened fleshy root, e.g. of the dahlia.
– ORIGIN Latin, 'hump, swelling'.

tubercle /tyoobərk'l/ • noun **1** a small rounded projection or protuberance on a bone or on the surface of an animal or plant. **2** a small rounded swelling in the lungs or other tissues, characteristic of tuberculosis.
– ORIGIN Latin *tuberculum* 'small lump or swelling'.

tubercle bacillus • noun the bacterium that causes tuberculosis.

tubercular /tyooberkyoolər/ • adjective **1** relating to or affected with tuberculosis. **2** having or covered with tubercles.

tuberculin /tyooberkyoolin/ • noun a sterile protein extract from cultures of tubercle bacillus, used to test for tuberculosis.

tuberculosis /tyooberkyoolōsiss/ • noun an infectious bacterial disease characterized by the growth of tubercles in the tissues, especially the lungs.

tuberculous /tyooberkyooləss/ • adjective another term for TUBERCULAR.

tuberose • noun /tyoobərōz/ a Mexican plant with heavily scented white waxy flowers and a bulb-like base, formerly cultivated as a flavouring for chocolate. • adjective /tyoobərōss/ variant spelling of TUBEROUS.

tuberous /tyoobərəss/ (also **tuberose** /tyoobərōss/) • adjective **1** resembling, forming, or having a tuber or tubers. **2** Medicine characterized by or affected by rounded swellings.

tubifex /tyoobifeks/ • noun a small red worm that lives in fresh water, partly buried in the mud.
– ORIGIN from Latin *tubus* 'tube' + *-fex* '-making'.

tubing • noun a length or lengths of material in tubular form.

tub-thumping informal, derogatory • adjective expressing opinions in a loud and violent or dramatic manner. • noun the expression of opinions in such a way.
– DERIVATIVES **tub-thumper** noun.

tubular • adjective **1** long, round, and hollow like a tube. **2** made from a tube or tubes.

tubular bells • plural noun an orchestral instrument consisting of a row of vertically suspended metal tubes struck with a mallet.

tubule /tyoobyool/ • noun a minute tube, especially in an animal or plant.
– ORIGIN Latin *tubulus*.

TUC • abbreviation (in the UK) Trades Union Congress.

tuck • verb **1** push, fold, or turn under or between two surfaces. **2** draw (part of one's body) together into a small space. **3** (often **tuck away**) store in a secure or secret place. **4** (**tuck in/up**) settle (someone) in bed by pulling the edges of the bedclothes firmly under the mattress. **5** (**tuck in/into**) informal eat food heartily. **6** make a flattened, stitched fold in (a garment or material). • noun **1** a flattened, stitched fold in a garment or material. **2** Brit. informal food eaten by children at school as a snack.
– ORIGIN Old English, 'punish, ill-treat'.

tucker • noun **1** Austral./NZ informal food. **2** historical a piece of lace or linen worn on a bodice or as an insert at the front of a low-cut dress. • verb (**be tuckered out**) N. Amer. informal be exhausted or worn out.

-tude • suffix forming abstract nouns such as *solitude*.
– ORIGIN from Latin *-tudo*.

Tudor • adjective **1** relating or belonging to the English royal dynasty which held the throne from the accession of Henry VII in 1485 until the death of Elizabeth I in 1603. **2** referring to the

t

Thesaurus

tiresome, irksome, troublesome, bothersome; *informal* aggravating.
– OPPOSITES easy, accommodating.

tub • noun **1** *a wooden tub* CONTAINER, butt, barrel, cask, drum, keg. **2** *a tub of yogurt* POT, carton. **3** *a soak in the tub* BATH, bathtub; hot tub.

tubby • adjective *(informal)* CHUBBY, plump, stout, dumpy, chunky, portly, rotund, round, fat, overweight, fleshy, paunchy, pot-bellied, corpulent; *informal* pudgy, beefy, porky, roly-poly, blubbery; *Brit. informal* podgy; *N. Amer. informal* corn-fed.
– OPPOSITES skinny.

tuck • verb **1** *he tucked his shirt into his trousers* PUSH, insert, slip; thrust, stuff, stick, cram; *informal* pop. **2** *the dress was tucked all over* PLEAT, gather, fold, ruffle. **3** *he tucked the knife behind his seat* HIDE, conceal, secrete; store, stow; *informal* stash.
• noun **1** *a dress with tucks* PLEAT, gather, fold, ruffle. **2** *(Brit. informal) they pinched his tuck* FOOD; *informal* eats, grub, nosh, chow; *Brit. informal* scoff; *N. Amer. informal* chuck; *poetic/literary* viands; *dated* victuals.
– PHRASES **tuck someone in/up** MAKE COMFORTABLE, settle down, cover up; put to bed. **tuck in/into** *(informal)* EAT HEARTILY, devour, consume, gobble up, wolf down; *informal* get stuck into, dispose of,

prevalent architectural style of the Tudor period, characterized by half-timbering. ● noun a member of the Tudor dynasty.

Tudor rose ● noun a stylized figure of a rose used in architectural decoration in the Tudor period, especially one combining the red and white roses of Lancaster and York.

Tuesday ● noun the day of the week before Wednesday and following Monday.
– ORIGIN Old English, named after the Germanic god *Tiw* (associated with the Roman god Mars); translation of Latin *dies Marti* 'day of Mars'.

tufa /tyōōfə/ ● noun **1** a porous rock composed of calcium carbonate and formed by precipitation from water, e.g. around mineral springs. **2** another term for TUFF.
– ORIGIN Italian.

tuff /tuf/ ● noun a light, porous rock formed by consolidation of volcanic ash.
– ORIGIN Latin *tofus*.

tuffet ● noun **1** a tuft or clump. **2** a footstool or low seat.
– ORIGIN alteration of TUFT.

tuft ● noun a bunch of threads, grass, or hair, held or growing together at the base.
– DERIVATIVES **tufted** adjective **tufty** adjective.
– ORIGIN probably from Old French *tofe*.

tufted duck ● noun a freshwater diving duck with a drooping crest and black and white (or brown) plumage.

tug ● verb (**tugged**, **tugging**) pull hard or suddenly. ● noun **1** a hard or sudden pull. **2** (also **tugboat**) a small, powerful boat for towing larger boats and ships, especially in harbour.
– ORIGIN from the base of TOW[1].

tug of war ● noun a contest in which two teams pull at opposite ends of a rope until one drags the other over a central line.

tugrik /tōōgrik/ ● noun (pl. same or **tugriks**) the basic monetary unit of Mongolia, equal to 100 mongos.
– ORIGIN Mongolian.

tuition ● noun teaching or instruction, especially of individuals or small groups.
– ORIGIN Latin, from *tueri* 'to watch, guard'.

tulip ● noun a spring-flowering plant with boldly coloured cup-shaped flowers.
– ORIGIN French *tulipe*, from Persian, 'turban' (from the shape of the flower).

tulip tree ● noun **1** a North American tree with large distinctively lobed leaves and insignificant tulip-like flowers. **2** informal term for MAGNOLIA (in sense 1).

tulle /tyōōl/ ● noun a soft, fine net material, used for making veils and dresses.
– ORIGIN from *Tulle*, a town in SW France.

tumble ● verb **1** fall suddenly, clumsily, or headlong. **2** move in a headlong manner. **3** decrease rapidly in amount or value. **4** rumple; disarrange. **5** (**tumble to**) informal come to understand; realize. ● noun **1** an instance of tumbling. **2** an untidy or confused arrangement or state. **3** a handspring or other acrobatic feat.
– ORIGIN Low German *tummelen*.

tumbledown ● adjective falling or fallen into ruin; dilapidated.

tumble-dryer ● noun a machine that dries washed clothes by spinning them in hot air inside a rotating drum.

tumblehome ● noun the inward slope of the upper part of a boat's sides.

tumbler ● noun **1** a drinking glass with straight sides and no handle or stem. [ORIGIN formerly having a rounded bottom so as not to stand upright.] **2** an acrobat. **3** a pivoted piece in a lock that holds the bolt until lifted by a key. **4** an electrical switch worked by pushing a small sprung lever. **5** a tumbling barrel.

tumbleweed ● noun N. Amer. & Austral./NZ a plant of dry regions which breaks off near the ground in late summer, forming light masses blown about by the wind.

tumbling barrel ● noun a revolving device containing an abrasive substance, in which castings, gemstones, or other hard objects can be cleaned.

tumbril /tumbril/ (also **tumbrel**) ● noun historical an open cart that tilted backwards to empty out its load, in particular one used to convey prisoners to the guillotine during the French Revolution.
– ORIGIN Old French *tomberel*, from *tomber* 'to fall'.

tumefy /tyōōmifī/ ● verb (**tumefies**, **tumefied**) become swollen.
– DERIVATIVES **tumefaction** noun.
– ORIGIN Latin *tumefacere*, from *tumere* 'to swell'.

tumescent /tyōōmess'nt/ ● adjective swollen or becoming swollen.
– DERIVATIVES **tumescence** noun.

tumid /tyōōmid/ ● adjective **1** (of a part of the body) swollen or bulging. **2** (of language) pompous or bombastic.
– ORIGIN Latin *tumidus*, from *tumere* 'to swell'.

tummy ● noun (pl. **tummies**) informal a person's stomach or abdomen.
– ORIGIN a child's pronunciation of STOMACH.

tummy button ● noun informal a person's navel.

tumour (US **tumor**) ● noun a swelling of a part of the body caused by an abnormal growth of tissue, whether benign or malignant.
– DERIVATIVES **tumorous** adjective.
– ORIGIN Latin *tumor*, from *tumere* 'to swell'.

tump ● noun chiefly dialect **1** a small rounded hill. **2** a clump of trees or grass.
– ORIGIN of unknown origin.

tumult ● noun **1** a loud, confused noise, as caused by a large mass of people. **2** confusion or disorder.
– ORIGIN Latin *tumultus*.

tumultuous /tyoomultyooəss/ ● adjective **1** very loud or uproarious. **2** excited, confused, or disorderly.
– DERIVATIVES **tumultuously** adverb.

tumulus /tyōōmyooləss/ ● noun (pl. **tumuli** /tyōōmyoolī/) an an-

Thesaurus

polish off, get outside of, put away, scoff (down); *Brit. informal* shift; *N. Amer. informal* scarf (down/up), snarf (down/up).

tuft ● noun CLUMP, bunch, knot, cluster, tussock, tuffet; lock, wisp; crest, topknot; tassel.

tug ● verb **1** *Ben tugged at her sleeve* PULL, pluck, tweak, twitch, jerk, wrench; catch hold of; *informal* yank. **2** *she tugged him towards the door* DRAG, pull, lug, draw, haul, heave, tow, trail.
● noun *one good tug would loosen it* PULL, jerk, wrench, heave; *informal* yank.

tuition ● noun INSTRUCTION, teaching, coaching, tutoring, tutelage, lessons, education, schooling; training, drill, preparation, guidance.

tumble ● verb **1** *he tumbled over* FALL (OVER/DOWN), topple over, lose one's balance, keel over, take a spill, go headlong, go head over heels, trip (up), stumble; *informal* come a cropper. **2** *they all tumbled from the room* HURRY, rush, scramble, scurry, bound, pile, bundle. **3** *a brook tumbled over the rocks* CASCADE, fall, flow, pour, spill, stream. **4** *oil prices tumbled* PLUMMET, plunge, fall, dive, nosedive, drop, slump, slide, decrease, decline; *informal* crash. **5** *(informal) I tumbled to what was happening.* See REALIZE sense 1.
– OPPOSITES rise.
● noun **1** *I took a tumble in the nettles* FALL, trip, spill; *informal* nosedive, header, cropper. **2** *a tumble in share prices* DROP, fall, plunge, dive, nosedive, slump, decline, collapse; *informal* crash.
– OPPOSITES rise.

tumbledown ● adjective DILAPIDATED, ramshackle, decrepit, neglected, run down, gone to rack and ruin, falling to pieces, decaying, derelict, crumbling; rickety, shaky; *N. Amer. informal* shacky.

tumbler ● noun (DRINKING) GLASS, beaker, highball glass.

tumid ● adjective **1** *her tumid belly* SWOLLEN, distended, tumescent, engorged, enlarged, bloated, bulging, protuberant, bulbous. **2** *tumid oratory* BOMBASTIC, pompous, turgid, overblown, inflated, high-flown, pretentious, grandiose, florid, flowery, magniloquent, grandiloquent, orotund; *informal* highfalutin, purple, windy.
– OPPOSITES shrunken, simple.

tummy ● noun *(informal)* STOMACH, abdomen, belly, gut, middle; *informal* tum, insides; *Austral. informal* bingy.

tumour ● noun CANCEROUS GROWTH, malignant growth, cancer, malignancy; lump, growth, swelling; *Medicine* carcinoma, sarcoma.
– RELATED TERMS onco-, -oma.

tumult ● noun **1** *she added her voice to the tumult* CLAMOUR, din, noise, racket, uproar, commotion, ruckus, rumpus, hubbub, pandemonium, babel, bedlam, brouhaha, furore, fracas, melee, frenzy; *Scottish & N. English* stramash; *informal* hullabaloo; *Brit. informal* row. **2** *years of political tumult* TURMOIL, confusion, disorder, disarray, unrest, chaos, turbulence, mayhem, havoc, upheaval, ferment, agitation, trouble.
– OPPOSITES tranquillity.

tumultuous ● adjective **1** *tumultuous applause* LOUD, deafening, thunderous, uproarious, noisy, clamorous, vociferous. **2** *a tumul-*

cient burial mound; a barrow.
– ORIGIN Latin.
tun ● noun 1 a large beer or wine cask. **2** a brewer's fermenting-vat.
– ORIGIN Latin *tunna*.
tuna ● noun (pl. same or **tunas**) a large predatory fish of warm seas, fished commercially.
– ORIGIN Spanish *atún*.
tundish ● noun Brit. a broad open container or large funnel with one or more holes at the bottom, used especially in plumbing or metal-founding.
tundra /tundrə/ ● noun a vast, flat, treeless Arctic region of Europe, Asia, and North America in which the subsoil is permanently frozen.
– ORIGIN Lappish.
tune ● noun a melody or melodious piece of music. ● verb **1** adjust (a musical instrument) to the correct or uniform pitch. **2** adjust (a radio or television) to the frequency of the required signal. **3** adjust (an engine) or balance (mechanical parts) so that they run smoothly and efficiently. **4** (often **be tuned to**) adjust or adapt to a purpose or situation.
– PHRASES **in** (or **out of**) **tune 1** with correct (or incorrect) pitch or intonation. **2** (of a motor engine) properly (or poorly) adjusted. **there's many a good tune played on an old fiddle** proverb someone's abilities do not depend on their being young. **to the tune of** informal amounting to or involving.
– DERIVATIVES **tunable** (also **tuneable**) adjective.
– ORIGIN alteration of TONE.
tuneful ● adjective having a pleasing tune; melodious.
– DERIVATIVES **tunefully** adverb **tunefulness** noun.
tuneless ● adjective not having a pleasing tune; unmelodious.
– DERIVATIVES **tunelessly** adverb **tunelessness** noun.
tuner ● noun **1** a person who tunes musical instruments, especially pianos. **2** an electronic device used for tuning. **3** a unit for detecting and preamplifying a broadcast radio signal and supplying it to an audio amplifier.
tunesmith ● noun informal a composer of popular music or songs.
tungsten /tungstən/ ● noun a hard steel-grey metallic element with a very high melting point, used to make electric light filaments.
– ORIGIN Swedish, from *tung* 'heavy' + *sten* 'stone'.
tungsten carbide ● noun a very hard grey compound used in making engineering dies, cutting and drilling tools, etc.
tunic ● noun **1** a loose sleeveless garment reaching to the thigh or knees. **2** a close-fitting short coat worn as part of a uniform.
– ORIGIN Latin *tunica*.
tunicate /tyoonikət, -kayt/ ● noun a marine invertebrate of a group which includes the sea squirts, with a rubbery or hard outer coat.
tuning fork ● noun a two-pronged steel device used for tuning instruments, which vibrates when struck to give a note of specific pitch.
Tunisian /tyoonizziən/ ● noun a person from Tunisia. ● adjective relating to Tunisia.
tunnel ● noun an artificial underground passage, built through a hill or under a building or by a burrowing animal. ● verb (**tunnelled**, **tunnelling**; US **tunneled**, **tunneling**) dig or force a passage underground or through something.
– DERIVATIVES **tunneller** noun.
– ORIGIN originally denoting a flue of a chimney and a tunnel-shaped net: from Old French *tonel* 'small cask'.
tunnel vision ● noun **1** defective sight in which things cannot be seen properly if they are not close to the centre of the field of view. **2** informal the tendency to focus exclusively on a single or limited objective or view.
tunny ● noun (pl. same or **tunnies**) a tuna.
– ORIGIN Greek *thunnos*.
tup /tup/ chiefly Brit. ● noun a ram. ● verb (**tupped**, **tupping**) (of a ram) copulate with (a ewe).
– ORIGIN of unknown origin.
Tupi /toopi/ ● noun (pl. same or **Tupis**) **1** a member of a group of American Indian peoples of the Amazon valley. **2** any of the languages of these peoples.
– DERIVATIVES **Tupian** adjective.
– ORIGIN a local name.
Tupi-Guarani ● noun a South American Indian language family whose principal members are Guarani and the Tupian languages.
tuppence ● noun Brit. variant spelling of TWOPENCE.
tuppenny ● adjective Brit. variant spelling of TWOPENNY.
turban ● noun a man's headdress consisting of a long length of material wound round a cap or the head, worn especially by Muslims and Sikhs.
– DERIVATIVES **turbaned** (also **turbanned**) adjective.
– ORIGIN Persian.
turbid /turbid/ ● adjective **1** (of a liquid) cloudy, opaque, or thick with suspended matter. **2** obscure or confused in meaning or thought.
– DERIVATIVES **turbidity** noun.
– ORIGIN Latin *turbidus*, from *turba* 'a crowd, a disturbance'.
turbine /turbīn/ ● noun a machine for producing power in which a wheel or rotor is made to revolve by a fast-moving flow of water, steam, gas, or air.
– ORIGIN Latin *turbo* 'spinning top, whirl'.
turbo /turbō/ ● noun (pl. **turbos**) short for TURBOCHARGER.
turbocharge ● verb (often as adj. **turbocharged**) equip with a turbocharger.
turbocharger ● noun a supercharger driven by a turbine powered by the engine's exhaust gases.
turbofan ● noun a jet engine in which a turbine-driven fan provides additional thrust.
turbojet ● noun a jet engine in which the jet gases also operate a turbine-driven compressor for compressing the air drawn into the engine.
turboprop ● noun a jet engine in which a turbine is used to drive a propeller.
turboshaft ● noun a gas turbine engine in which the turbine drives a shaft other than a propeller shaft.
turbot ● noun (pl. same or **turbots**) a flatfish of inshore waters, which has large bony tubercles on the body and is prized as food.
– ORIGIN Scandinavian.
turbulence ● noun **1** violent or unsteady movement of air or water, or of some other fluid. **2** conflict or confusion.
turbulent /turbyoolənt/ ● adjective **1** characterized by conflict, disorder, or confusion. **2** technical (of the flow of fluids) irregularly fluctuating.
– DERIVATIVES **turbulently** adverb.
– ORIGIN Latin *turbulentus* 'full of commotion', from *turba* 'crowd'.
turd ● noun vulgar slang **1** a lump of excrement. **2** an obnoxious or contemptible person.
– ORIGIN Old English.
tureen /tyooreen/ ● noun a deep covered dish from which soup is served.
– ORIGIN French *terrine* (see TERRINE).

t

Thesaurus

tuous crowd DISORDERLY, unruly, rowdy, turbulent, boisterous, excited, agitated, restless, wild, riotous, frenzied; *Brit. informal* rumbustious.
– OPPOSITES soft, orderly.
tune ● noun *she hummed a cheerful tune* MELODY, air, strain, theme; song, jingle, ditty.
● verb **1** *they tuned their guitars* ADJUST, fine-tune. **2** *a body clock tuned to the tides* ATTUNE, adapt, adjust, fine-tune; regulate, modulate.
– PHRASES **change one's tune** CHANGE ONE'S MIND, do a U-turn, have a change of heart; *Brit.* do an about-turn. **in tune** IN ACCORD, in keeping, in accordance, in agreement, in harmony, in step, in line, in sympathy.
tuneful ● adjective MELODIOUS, melodic, musical, mellifluous, dulcet, euphonious, harmonious, lyrical, lilting, sweet.
– OPPOSITES discordant.
tuneless ● adjective DISCORDANT, unmelodious, dissonant, harsh, cacophonous.
– OPPOSITES melodious.
tunnel ● noun *a tunnel under the hills* UNDERGROUND PASSAGE, underpass, subway; shaft; burrow, hole; *historical* mine, sap.
● verb *he tunnelled under the fence* DIG, burrow, mine, bore, drill.
turbid ● adjective MURKY, opaque, cloudy, muddy, thick; *N. Amer.* roily.
– OPPOSITES clear.
turbulent ● adjective **1** *the country's turbulent past* TEMPESTUOUS, stormy, unstable, unsettled, tumultuous, chaotic; violent, anarchic, lawless. **2** *turbulent seas* ROUGH, stormy, tempestuous, storm-

turf • noun (pl. **turfs** or **turves**) **1** grass and the surface layer of earth held together by its roots. **2** a piece of such grass and earth cut from the ground. **3** (**the turf**) horse racing or racecourses generally. **4** (**one's turf**) informal one's territory or sphere of influence. • verb **1** (**turf off/out**) informal, chiefly Brit. force to leave somewhere. **2** cover with turf.
– ORIGIN Old English.

turf accountant • noun Brit. formal a bookmaker.

turgescent /turjess'nt/ • adjective chiefly technical becoming or seeming swollen or distended.
– DERIVATIVES **turgescence** noun.

turgid /turjid/ • adjective **1** swollen and distended or congested. **2** (of language or style) tediously pompous or bombastic.
– DERIVATIVES **turgidity** noun **turgidly** adverb.
– ORIGIN Latin *turgidus*, from *turgere* 'to swell'.

Turk • noun **1** a person from Turkey or of Turkish descent. **2** a member of any of the ancient peoples who spoke Turkic languages, such as the Ottomans.

turkey • noun (pl. **turkeys**) **1** a large mainly domesticated game bird native to North America, having a bald head and (in the male) red wattles. **2** informal, chiefly N. Amer. something extremely unsuccessful, especially a play or film. **3** informal, chiefly N. Amer. a stupid or inept person.
– PHRASES **talk turkey** N. Amer. informal talk frankly and openly.
– ORIGIN short for TURKEYCOCK or *turkeyhen*, originally applied to the guineafowl (which was imported through Turkey), and then erroneously to the American bird because it was considered to be a related species.

turkeycock • noun a male turkey.

turkey trot • noun a kind of ballroom dance to ragtime music, popular in the early 20th century.

Turkic /terkik/ • adjective relating or referring to a large group of languages of western and central Asia, including Turkish and Azerbaijani.

Turkish • noun the language of Turkey. • adjective relating to Turkey or its language.

Turkish bath • noun **1** a cleansing treatment that involves sitting in a room filled with very hot air or steam, followed by washing and massage. **2** a building or room where such a treatment is available.

Turkish coffee • noun very strong black coffee served with the fine grounds in it.

Turkish delight • noun a sweet consisting of flavoured gelatin coated in icing sugar.

Turkmen /turkmən/ • noun (pl. same or **Turkmens**) a member of a group of peoples inhabiting the region east of the Caspian Sea and south of the Aral Sea.
– ORIGIN Turkish.

turmeric /turmərik/ • noun a bright yellow powder obtained from a plant of the ginger family, used for flavouring and colouring in Asian cookery.
– ORIGIN perhaps from French *terre mérite* 'deserving earth'.

turmoil • noun a state of great disturbance, confusion, or uncertainty.
– ORIGIN of unknown origin.

turn • verb **1** move in a circular direction wholly or partly around an axis. **2** move into a different position, especially so as to face or move in the opposite direction. **3** change in nature, state, form, or colour; make or become. **4** shape on a lathe. **5** give a graceful or elegant form to. **6** make (a profit). **7** (of the tide) change from flood to ebb or vice versa. **8** twist or sprain (an ankle). **9** (of leaves) change colour in the autumn. **10** (of milk) become sour. • noun **1** an act of turning. **2** a bend or curve in a road, path, river, etc. **3** a place where a road meets or branches off another; a turning. **4** a time when one period of time ends and another begins. **5** a development or change in circumstances. **6** a short walk or ride. **7** a brief feeling or experience of illness: *a funny turn.* **8** an opportunity or obligation to do something that comes successively to each of a number of people. **9** a short performance, especially one of a number given by different performers. **10** one round in a coil of rope or other material.
– PHRASES **at every turn** on every occasion; continually. **by turns** alternately. **do someone a good** (or **bad**) **turn** do something that is helpful (or unhelpful) for someone. **in turn** one after the other. **one good turn deserves another** proverb if someone does you a favour, you should take the chance to repay it. **out of turn** at a time when it is inappropriate or not one's turn. **take turns** (or **take it in turns**) (of two or more people) do something alternately or in succession. **to a turn** to exactly the right degree. **turn against** become or make hostile towards. **turn away** refuse admittance to. **turn and turn about** chiefly Brit. one after another; in succession. **turn down 1** reject an offer or application of or from. **2** adjust a control on (a device) to reduce the volume, heat, etc. **turn in 1** hand over to the authorities. **2** informal go to bed in the evening. **turn off 1** stop (something) operating by means of a tap, switch, or button. **2** leave one road in order to join another. **3** informal cause to feel bored or repelled. **turn of mind** a particular way of thinking. **turn of speed** the ability to go fast when necessary. **turn on 1** start (something) operating by means of a tap, switch, or button. **2** suddenly attack. **3** have as the main focus. **4** informal excite or stimulate, especially sexually. **turn out 1** extinguish (an electric light). **2** produce (something). **3** empty (one's pockets). **4** prove to be the case. **5** eject or expel from a place. **6** go somewhere to attend a meeting, vote, play in a game, etc. **7** (**be turned out**) be dressed in the manner specified. **turn over 1** (of an engine) start or continue to run properly. **2** (of a business) have a turnover of. **3** change or transfer custody or control of. **turn round** (or **around**) reverse the previously poor performance of. **turn tail** informal turn round and run away. **turn to 1** start doing or becoming involved with. **2** go to for help, support, or information. **turn up 1** increase the volume or strength of (a device) by turning a knob or switch. **2** be found, especially by chance. **3** put in an appearance; arrive. **4** reveal or discover.
– DERIVATIVES **turner** noun.
– ORIGIN Latin *tornare*, from Greek *tornos* 'lathe, circular movement'.

Thesaurus

t

tossed, heavy, violent, wild, seething, choppy, agitated, boisterous.
– OPPOSITES peaceful, calm.

turf • noun **1** *they walked across the turf* GRASS, lawn, sod; *poetic/literary* sward, greensward. **2** *devotees of the turf* HORSE RACING; racecourses, racetracks. **3** *(informal) he was keen to protect his turf* TERRITORY, domain, province, preserve, sphere of influence; stamping ground; *informal* bailiwick; *Brit. informal* patch, manor.
• verb *the lawns have been turfed* GRASS (OVER).
– PHRASES **turf someone/something out** *(informal)*. See EJECT sense 3.

turgid • adjective **1** *his turgid prose* BOMBASTIC, pompous, overblown, inflated, tumid, high-flown, affected, pretentious, grandiose, florid, ornate, magniloquent, grandiloquent, orotund; *informal* highfalutin, purple, windy. **2** *the tissues become turgid* SWOLLEN, distended, tumescent, engorged, bloated.
– OPPOSITES simple.

turmoil • noun *political turmoil* CONFUSION, upheaval, turbulence, tumult, disorder, disturbance, agitation, ferment, unrest, trouble, disruption, chaos, mayhem; uncertainty; *N. Amer. informal* tohubohu.
– OPPOSITES peace.
– PHRASES **in turmoil** CONFUSED, in a whirl, at sixes and sevens; reeling, disorientated; *informal* all over the place.

turn • verb **1** *the wheels were still turning* GO ROUND, revolve, rotate, spin, roll, circle, wheel, whirl, gyrate, swivel, pivot. **2** *I turned and headed back* CHANGE DIRECTION, change course, make a U-turn, turn about/round, wheel round. **3** *the car turned the corner* GO ROUND, round, negotiate, take. **4** *the path turned to right and left* BEND, curve, wind, twist, meander, snake, zigzag. **5** *he turned his pistol on Liam* AIM AT, point at, level at, direct at, train on. **6** *he turned his ankle* SPRAIN, twist, wrench; hurt. **7** *their honeymoon turned into a nightmare* BECOME, develop into, turn out to be; be transformed into, metamorphose into. **8** *Emma turned red* BECOME, go, grow, get. **9** *he turned the house into flats* CONVERT, change, transform, make; adapt, modify, rebuild, reconstruct. **10** *I've just turned forty* REACH, get to, become; *informal* hit. **11** *the milk had turned* (GO) SOUR, go off, curdle, become rancid, go bad, spoil. **12** *he turned to politics* TAKE UP, become involved in, go in for, enter, undertake. **13** *we can now turn to another topic* MOVE ON TO, go on to, consider, attend to, address; take up. **14** *she turned a somersault* PERFORM, execute, do, carry out. **15** *an object turned on a lathe* FASHION, make, shape, form.
• noun **1** *a turn of the wheel* ROTATION, revolution, spin, whirl, gyration, swivel. **2** *a turn to the left* CHANGE OF DIRECTION, veer, divergence. **3** *we're approaching the turn* BEND, corner, dog-leg; turning, junction, crossroads; *N. Amer.* turnout; *Brit.* hairpin bend. **4** *you'll get your turn in a minute* OPPORTUNITY, chance, say; stint, time; try;

turnaround (also **turnround**) ● noun **1** an abrupt or unexpected change. **2** the process of completing or the time needed to complete a task.
turnbuckle ● noun a coupling with internal screw threads used to connect two rods, lengths of boat's rigging, etc. lengthwise or to regulate their length or tension.
turncoat ● noun a person who deserts one party or cause in order to join an opposing one.
turnery ● noun **1** the action or skill of turning objects on a lathe. **2** objects made on a lathe.
turning ● noun **1** a place where a road branches off another. **2** the action or skill of using a lathe. **3** (**turnings**) shavings of wood resulting from turning wood on a lathe.
turning circle ● noun the smallest circle in which a vehicle or vessel can turn without reversing.
turnip ● noun a round root with white or cream flesh which is eaten as a vegetable.
– ORIGIN from a first element of unknown origin + NEEP.
turnkey ● noun (pl. **turnkeys**) archaic a jailer.
turn-off ● noun **1** a junction at which a road branches off. **2** informal a person or thing that causes one to feel bored or repelled.
turn-on ● noun informal a person or thing that causes one to feel excited or sexually aroused.
turnout ● noun the number of people attending or taking part in an event.
turnover ● noun **1** the amount of money taken by a business in a particular period. **2** the rate at which employees leave a workforce and are replaced. **3** the rate at which goods are sold and replaced in a shop. **4** a small pie made by folding a piece of pastry over on itself to enclose a filling.
turnpike ● noun **1** historical a toll gate. **2** historical a road on which a toll was collected. **3** US a motorway on which a toll is charged.
– ORIGIN originally denoting a spiked barrier fixed across a road as a defence against sudden attack: from PIKE².
turnstile ● noun a mechanical gate with revolving horizontal arms that allow only one person at a time to pass through.
turnstone ● noun a small short-billed sandpiper noted for turning over stones to find small animals.
turntable ● noun **1** a circular revolving plate supporting a gramophone record as it is played. **2** a circular revolving platform for turning a railway locomotive.
turn-up ● noun Brit. **1** the end of a trouser leg folded upwards on the outside. **2** informal an unusual or unexpected event.
turpentine /turpətīn/ ● noun **1** (also **crude** or **gum turpentine**) a resinous oily substance secreted by certain pines and other trees and distilled to make rosin and oil of turpentine. **2** (also **oil of turpentine**) a volatile pungent oil distilled from this, used in mixing paints and varnishes and in liniment.
– ORIGIN Old French *terebentine*, from Latin *terebinthina resina* 'resin of the terebinth'.
turpitude /turpityood/ ● noun formal depravity; wickedness.
– ORIGIN Latin *turpitudo*, from *turpis* 'disgraceful, base'.
turps ● noun informal turpentine.
turquoise /turkwoyz, -kwaaz/ ● noun **1** a semi-precious stone, typically opaque and of a greenish-blue or sky-blue colour. **2** a greenish-blue colour.
– ORIGIN Old French *turqueise* 'Turkish stone'.
turret ● noun **1** a small tower at the corner of a building or wall, especially of a castle. **2** an armoured, usually revolving tower for a gun and gunners in a ship, aircraft, fort, or tank. **3** a rotating holder for tools, especially on a lathe.
– DERIVATIVES **turreted** adjective.
– ORIGIN Old French *tourete* 'small tower'.
turtle ● noun **1** a marine or freshwater reptile with a bony or leathery shell and flippers or webbed toes. **2** Computing a directional cursor in a computer graphics system which can be instructed to move around a screen.
– PHRASES **turn turtle** (chiefly of a boat) turn upside down.
– ORIGIN apparently an alteration of French *tortue* 'tortoise'.
turtle dove ● noun a small dove with a soft purring call, noted for the apparent affection shown for its mate.

Thesaurus

informal go, shot, stab, crack. **5** *a comic turn* ACT, routine, performance, number, piece. **6** *a turn around the garden* STROLL, walk, saunter, amble, wander, airing, promenade; outing, excursion, jaunt; *informal* mosey, tootle, spin; *Brit. informal* pootle. **7** *you gave me quite a turn!* SHOCK, start, surprise, jolt; fright, scare. **8** *she did me some good turns* SERVICE, deed, act; favour, kindness; disservice, wrong.
– PHRASES **at every turn** REPEATEDLY, recurrently, all the time, always, constantly, again and again. **in turn** ONE AFTER THE OTHER, one by one, one at a time, in succession, successively, sequentially. **take a turn for the better** IMPROVE, pick up, look up, perk up, rally, turn the corner; recover, revive. **take a turn for the worse** DETERIORATE, worsen, decline; *informal* go downhill. **to a turn** PERFECTLY, just right, to perfection; *informal* to a T. **turn of events** DEVELOPMENT, incident, occurrence, happening, circumstance. **turn against someone** BECOME HOSTILE TO, take a dislike to. **turn someone away** SEND AWAY, reject, rebuff, repel, cold-shoulder; *informal* send packing. **turn back** RETRACE ONE'S STEPS, go back, return; retreat. **turn someone/something down 1** *his novel was turned down* REJECT, spurn, rebuff, refuse, decline; *Brit. informal* knock back. **2** *Pete turned the sound down* REDUCE, lower, decrease, lessen; muffle, mute. **turn in** *(informal)* GO TO BED, retire, call it a day; *informal* hit the hay, hit the sack. **turn someone in** BETRAY, inform on, denounce, sell out, stab someone in the back; *informal* split on, blow the whistle on, rat on, peach on, squeal on; *Brit. informal* grass on, shop; *N. Amer. informal* finger; *Austral./NZ informal* dob on. **turn something in 1** *your documents must be turned in* HAND IN/OVER, give in, submit, surrender, give up; deliver, return. **2** *he turned in a score of 199* ACHIEVE, attain, reach, make; notch up, chalk up, rack up, record. **turn of mind** DISPOSITION, inclination, tendency, propensity, bias, bent. **turn off** *they turned off the road* LEAVE, branch off; *informal* take a left/right; *N. Amer. informal* hang a left/right. **turn someone off** *(informal)* PUT OFF, leave cold, repel, disgust, revolt, offend; disenchant, alienate; bore; *N. Amer. informal* gross out. **turn something off** SWITCH OFF, shut off, put off, extinguish, deactivate; *informal* kill, cut. **turn on** *the decision turned on the law* DEPEND ON, rest on, hinge on, be contingent on, be decided by. **turn someone on** *(informal)*. See AROUSE sense 3. **turn something on** SWITCH ON, put on, start up, activate, trip. **turn on someone** ATTACK, set on, fall on, let fly at, lash out at, hit out at, round on; *informal* lay into, tear into, let someone have it, bite someone's head off, jump down someone's throat; *Brit. informal* have a go at; *N. Amer. informal* light into. **turn out 1** *a huge crowd turned out* COME, be present, attend, appear, turn up, arrive; assemble, gather; *informal* show up. **2** *it turned out that she had been abroad* TRANSPIRE, emerge, come to light, become apparent. **3** *things didn't turn out as I'd intended* HAPPEN, occur, come about; develop, work out, come out, end up; *informal* pan out; *formal* eventuate. **turn someone out** THROW OUT, eject, evict, expel, oust, drum out, banish; *informal* kick out, send packing, boot out, show someone the door, turf out. **turn something out 1** *turn out the light*. See TURN SOMETHING OFF. **2** *they turn out a million engines a year* PRODUCE, make, manufacture, fabricate, put out, churn out. **3** *she turned out the cupboards* CLEAR OUT, clean out, empty (out). **turn over** OVERTURN, upturn, capsize, keel over, turn turtle, be upended. **turn something over 1** *I turned over a few pages* FLIP OVER, flick through, leaf through. **2** *she turned the proposal over in her mind* THINK ABOUT/OVER, consider, weigh up, ponder, contemplate, reflect on, chew over, mull over, muse on, ruminate on. **3** *he turned over the business to his brother* TRANSFER, hand over, pass on, consign, commit. **turn of phrase** EXPRESSION, idiom, phrase, term, word. **turn someone's stomach** NAUSEATE, sicken, make sick, make someone's gorge rise. **turn to someone/something** SEEK HELP FROM, have recourse to, approach, apply to, appeal to; take to, resort to. **turn up 1** *the missing documents turned up* BE FOUND, be discovered, be located, reappear. **2** *the police turned up* ARRIVE, appear, present oneself; *informal* show (up), show one's face. **3** *something better will turn up* PRESENT ITSELF, occur, happen, crop up. **turn something up 1** *she turned up the volume* INCREASE, raise, amplify, intensify. **2** *they turned up lots of information* DISCOVER, uncover, unearth, find, dig up, ferret out, root out, expose. **3** *I turned up the hem* TAKE UP, raise; shorten.
turncoat ● noun TRAITOR, renegade, defector, deserter, betrayer, Judas; fifth columnist, quisling; *informal* rat.
turning ● noun TURN-OFF, turn, side road, exit; *N. Amer.* turnout.
turning point ● noun WATERSHED, critical moment, decisive moment, crossroads, crisis.
turnout ● noun **1** *the lecture attracted a good turnout* ATTENDANCE, audience, house; crowd, gathering, throng, assembly, assemblage, congregation. **2** *his turnout was very elegant* OUTFIT, clothes, clothing, dress, garb, attire, ensemble; *informal* get-up, gear, togs; *Brit. informal* clobber, kit; *formal* apparel.
turnover ● noun **1** *an annual turnover of £2.25 million* (GROSS) REV-

– ORIGIN from Latin *turtur*.
turtleneck ● noun **1** Brit. a high, round, close-fitting neck on a knitted garment. **2** North American term for POLO NECK.
turves plural of TURF.
Tuscan /tuskən/ ● adjective **1** relating to Tuscany in central Italy. **2** referring to a classical order of architecture resembling the Doric but lacking all ornamentation. ● noun a person from Tuscany.
– ORIGIN Latin *Tuscanus*, from *Tuscus* 'an Etruscan'.
Tuscarora /tuskərorə/ ● noun (pl. same or **Tuscaroras**) an American Indian people forming part of the Iroquois confederacy.
– ORIGIN Iroquois.
tush[1] /tush/ ● exclamation archaic or humorous expressing disapproval, impatience, or dismissal.
tush[2] /tush/ ● noun a long pointed tooth, in particular a canine tooth of a male horse.
– ORIGIN Old English, related to TUSK.
tush[3] /tŏosh/ ● noun informal, chiefly N. Amer. a person's buttocks.
– ORIGIN Yiddish, from a Hebrew word meaning 'beneath'.
tusk ● noun a long, pointed tooth, especially one which protrudes from the closed mouth, as in the elephant, walrus, or wild boar.
– DERIVATIVES **tusked** adjective.
– ORIGIN Old English, related to TUSH[2].
tusker ● noun an elephant or wild boar with well-developed tusks.
tussle ● noun a vigorous struggle or scuffle. ● verb engage in a tussle.
– ORIGIN perhaps from dialect *touse* 'handle roughly', the root also of TOUSLE.
tussock /tussək/ ● noun a dense clump or tuft of grass.
– DERIVATIVES **tussocky** adjective.
– ORIGIN perhaps from dialect *tusk* 'tuft', of unknown origin.
tussock grass ● noun a coarse grass which grows in tussocks.
tussore /tussor, tussər/ ● noun a strong but coarse kind of silk.
– ORIGIN Hindi, from a Sanskrit word meaning 'shuttle'.
tutee /tyōotee/ ● noun a student or pupil of a tutor.
tutelage /tyōotilij/ ● noun **1** protection of or authority over someone or something; guardianship. **2** instruction; tuition.
– ORIGIN from Latin *tutela* 'keeping', from *tueri* 'watch'.
tutelary /tyōotiləri/ (also **tutelar** /tyōotilər/) ● adjective **1** serving as a protector, guardian, or patron. **2** relating to protection or a guardian.
tutor ● noun **1** a private teacher, typically one who teaches a single pupil or a very small group. **2** chiefly Brit. a university or college teacher responsible for assigned students. **3** Brit. a book of instruction in a particular subject. ● verb act as a tutor to.
– ORIGIN Latin, from *tueri* 'to watch, guard'.
tutorial ● noun **1** a period of tuition given by a university or college tutor. **2** an account or explanation of a subject, intended for private study. ● adjective relating to a tutor or a tutor's tuition.
Tutsi /tŏotsi/ ● noun (pl. same or **Tutsis**) a member of a people forming a minority of the population of Rwanda and Burundi.
– ORIGIN a local name.
tutti /tŏotti/ ● adverb & adjective Music with all voices or instruments together.
– ORIGIN Italian, from *tutto* 'all', from Latin *totus*.
tutti-frutti /tōotifrōoti/ ● noun (pl. **tutti-fruttis**) a type of ice cream or confectionery containing mixed fruits.
– ORIGIN Italian, 'all fruits'.
tutu /tōotōo/ ● noun a female ballet dancer's costume consisting of a bodice and a very short, stiff attached skirt incorporating numerous layers of fabric and projecting horizontally from the waist.
– ORIGIN French, child's alteration of *cucu*, informal word for *cul* 'buttocks'.
Tuvaluan /tōovəlōoən, tōovalōoən/ ● noun a person from Tuvalu, a country made up of a number of islands in the SW Pacific. ● adjective relating to Tuvalu.
tux ● noun informal, chiefly N. Amer. a tuxedo.
tuxedo /tukseedō/ ● noun (pl. **tuxedos** or **tuxedoes**) chiefly N. Amer. **1** a man's dinner jacket. **2** a formal evening suit including such a jacket.
– DERIVATIVES **tuxedoed** adjective.
– ORIGIN from *Tuxedo* Park, the site of a country club in New York.
TV ● abbreviation television.
TVP ● abbreviation trademark textured vegetable protein.
twaddle ● noun informal trivial or foolish speech or writing.
– ORIGIN of unknown origin.
twain ● cardinal number archaic term for TWO.
– PHRASES **never the twain shall meet** the two things in question are too different to exist alongside each other. [ORIGIN from Rudyard Kipling's 'Oh, East is East, and West is West, and never the twain shall meet'. (*Barrack-room Ballads* (1892)).]
– ORIGIN Old English.
twang ● noun **1** a strong ringing sound such as that made by the plucked string of a musical instrument or a released bowstring. **2** a distinctive nasal pronunciation characteristic of the speech of an individual or region. ● verb make or cause to make a twang.
– DERIVATIVES **twangy** adjective.
– ORIGIN imitative.
'twas ● contraction archaic or literary it was.
twat /twat, twot/ ● noun vulgar slang **1** a woman's genitals. **2** a stupid or obnoxious person. ● verb Brit. informal hit; punch.
– ORIGIN of unknown origin.
tweak ● verb **1** twist or pull with a small but sharp movement. **2** informal improve by making fine adjustments. ● noun an act of tweaking.
– ORIGIN probably from dialect *twick* 'pull sharply'; related to TWITCH.
twee ● adjective (**tweer**, **tweest**) Brit. excessively or affectedly quaint, pretty, or sentimental.
– ORIGIN representing a child's pronunciation of SWEET.
tweed ● noun **1** a rough-surfaced woollen cloth, typically of mixed flecked colours. **2** (**tweeds**) clothes made of tweed.
– ORIGIN a misreading of *tweel*, Scots form of TWILL, influenced by association with the river *Tweed*.
tweedy ● adjective (**tweedier**, **tweediest**) **1** made of tweed cloth. **2** informal of a robust conservative or rural character.
– DERIVATIVES **tweediness** noun.
'tween ● contraction archaic or literary between.
tweet ● noun the chirp of a small or young bird. ● verb make a chirping noise.
– ORIGIN imitative.
tweeter ● noun a loudspeaker designed to reproduce high frequencies.
tweeze ● verb pluck or pull with or as if with tweezers.
tweezers ● plural noun (also **pair of tweezers**) a small instrument like a pair of pincers for plucking out hairs and picking up small objects.
– ORIGIN from obsolete *tweeze* 'case of surgical instruments'.
twelfth /twelfth/ ● ordinal number **1** constituting number twelve in a sequence; 12th. **2** (**a twelfth/one twelfth**) each of twelve equal parts into which something is or may be divided. **3** Music an interval spanning an octave and a fifth in the diatonic scale. **4** (**the (Glorious) Twelfth**) (in the UK) 12 August, the day on

t

Thesaurus

ENUE, income, yield; sales. **2** *a high turnover of staff* rate of replacement, change, movement.
turpitude ● noun *(formal)*. See DEPRAVITY.
tussle ● noun *his glasses were smashed in the tussle* SCUFFLE, fight, struggle, skirmish, brawl, scrum, rough and tumble, free-for-all, fracas, fray, rumpus, melee; *Irish, N. Amer., & Austral.* donnybrook; *informal* scrap, dust-up, punch-up, spat, ruck; *Brit. informal* ding-dong, bust-up; *Scottish informal* rammy; *Law, dated* affray.
● verb *demonstrators tussled with police* SCUFFLE, fight, struggle, brawl, grapple, wrestle, clash; *informal* scrap; *N. Amer. informal* roughhouse.
tutor ● noun *a history tutor* TEACHER, instructor, educator, educationalist, lecturer, trainer, mentor; *informal* teach; *formal* pedagogue.
● verb *he was tutored at home* TEACH, instruct, educate, school, coach, train, drill.
tutorial ● noun LESSON, class, seminar.
twaddle ● noun *(informal)*. See NONSENSE sense 1.
tweak ● verb **1** *he tweaked the boy's ear* PULL, jerk, tug, twist, twitch, pinch, squeeze. **2** *(informal) the programme can be tweaked to suit your needs* ADJUST, modify, alter, change, adapt; refine.
● noun **1** *he gave her hair a tweak* PULL, jerk, tug, twist, pinch, twitch, squeeze. **2** *(informal) a few minor tweaks were required* ADJUSTMENT, modification, alteration, change; refinement.
twee ● adjective *(Brit.)* **1** *twee little shops* QUAINT, sweet, dainty,

which the grouse-shooting season begins.
– DERIVATIVES **twelfthly** adverb.
twelfth man ● noun Cricket a player acting as a reserve in a game.
Twelfth Night ● noun **1** 6 January, the feast of the Epiphany. **2** the evening of 5 January, formerly the twelfth and last day of Christmas festivities.
twelve ● cardinal number two more than ten; 12. (Roman numeral: **xii** or **XII**.)
– ORIGIN Old English, from the base of TWO + a second element probably expressing the sense 'left over'.
twelvemonth ● noun archaic a year.
twelve-note (also **twelve-tone**) ● adjective (of musical composition) using the twelve chromatic notes of the octave on an equal basis without dependence on a key system, a technique central to serialism.
twenty ● cardinal number (pl. **twenties**) ten less than thirty; 20. (Roman numeral: **xx** or **XX**.)
– DERIVATIVES **twentieth** ordinal number.
– ORIGIN Old English.
24-7 (also **24/7**) ● adverb informal, chiefly N. Amer. twenty-four hours a day, seven days a week; all the time.
twenty-twenty (also **20/20**) ● adjective (of vision) of normal sharpness.
– ORIGIN with reference to the fraction for normal visual acuity in eyesight tests.
'twere ● contraction archaic or literary it were.
twerp ● noun informal a silly or annoying person.
– ORIGIN of unknown origin.
twice ● adverb **1** two times. **2** double in degree or quantity.
– ORIGIN Old English.
twiddle ● verb play or fiddle with (something) in a purposeless or nervous way. ● noun **1** an act of twiddling. **2** a rapid or intricate series of musical notes.
– PHRASES **twiddle one's thumbs** be idle; have nothing to do.
– DERIVATIVES **twiddler** noun **twiddly** adjective.
– ORIGIN apparently imitative, combining *twirl* or *twist* with *fiddle*.
twig[1] ● noun a slender woody shoot growing from a branch or stem of a tree or shrub.
– DERIVATIVES **twigged** adjective **twiggy** adjective.
– ORIGIN Old English, related to TWAIN and TWO.
twig[2] ● verb (**twigged**, **twigging**) Brit. informal come to understand or realize something.
– ORIGIN of unknown origin.
twilight ● noun **1** the soft glowing light from the sky when the sun is below the horizon. **2** a period or state of obscurity or gradual decline: *the twilight of his career*.
– ORIGIN from an Old English base meaning 'two' (probably here used in sense 'half-') + LIGHT[1].
twilight zone ● noun **1** an undefined, ambiguous, or intermediate state or area. **2** a dilapidated urban area.
twilit (also **twilighted**) ● adjective dimly illuminated by or as if by twilight.
twill ● noun a fabric so woven as to have a surface of diagonal parallel ridges.
– DERIVATIVES **twilled** adjective.
– ORIGIN from obsolete *twilly*, from an Old English base meaning 'two'.
'twill ● contraction archaic or literary it will.
twin ● noun **1** one of two children or animals born at the same birth. **2** something containing or consisting of two matching or corresponding parts. ● adjective forming or being one of a pair of twins or matching things. ● verb (**twinned**, **twinning**) **1** link or combine as a pair. **2** Brit. link (a town) with another in a different country, for the purposes of cultural exchange.
– ORIGIN Old English.
twine ● noun strong thread or string consisting of strands of hemp or cotton twisted together. ● verb wind round something.
– ORIGIN Old English, 'thread, linen', from a base meaning 'two' (with reference to the number of strands).
twinge ● noun **1** a sudden, sharp localized pain. **2** a brief, sharp pang of emotion. ● verb (**twingeing** or **twinging**) suffer a twinge.
– ORIGIN Old English, 'pinch, wring'.
twinkle ● verb **1** (of a star or light) shine with a gleam that changes constantly from bright to faint. **2** (of a person's eyes) sparkle with amusement or vivacity. **3** move lightly and rapidly. ● noun a twinkling sparkle or gleam.
– PHRASES **in a twinkling (of an eye)** in an instant.
– DERIVATIVES **twinkly** adjective.
– ORIGIN Old English.
twinkle-toed ● adjective informal nimble and quick on one's feet.
twinset ● noun chiefly Brit. a woman's matching cardigan and jumper.
twin-tub ● noun a type of washing machine having two top-loading drums, one for washing and the other for spin-drying.
twirl ● verb spin quickly and lightly round. ● noun **1** an act of twirling. **2** a spiralling or swirling shape, especially a flourish made with a pen.
– DERIVATIVES **twirler** noun **twirly** adjective.
– ORIGIN probably from archaic *trill* 'twiddle, spin', altered by association with WHIRL.
twist ● verb **1** form into a bent, curled, or distorted shape. **2** force out of the natural position by a twisting action: *he twisted his ankle*. **3** turn or bend round or into a different direction. **4** take or have a winding course. **5** distort or misrepresent the meaning of. **6** (**twisted**) unpleasantly or unhealthily abnormal. **7** Brit. informal cheat; defraud. **8** dance the twist. **9** (in pontoon) request, deal, or be dealt a card face upwards. ● noun

Thesaurus

pretty; *informal* cute, cutesy. **2** *the lyrics are too twee in places* SENTIMENTAL, over-sentimental, mawkish, sickly; *Brit. informal* soppy.
twelve ● cardinal number DOZEN, zodiac.
– RELATED TERMS duodecimal, dodeca-.
twenty ● cardinal number SCORE.
– RELATED TERMS icos-.
twiddle ● verb *she twiddled the dials* TURN, twist, swivel, twirl; adjust, move, jiggle; fiddle with, play with.
– PHRASES **twiddle one's thumbs** BE IDLE, kick one's heels, kill time, waste time; *informal* hang around/round; *Brit. informal* hang about.
twig[1] ● noun *leafy twigs* STICK, sprig, withy, shoot, stem, branchlet.
twig[2] ● verb (*Brit. informal*) *she finally twigged what I was on about* REALIZE, understand, grasp, comprehend, take in, fathom, see, recognize; *informal* latch on to, cotton on to, tumble to, get, get wise to, figure out; *Brit. informal* suss.
twilight ● noun **1** *we arrived at twilight* DUSK, sunset, sundown, nightfall, evening, close of day; *poetic/literary* eventide. **2** *it was scarcely visible in the twilight* HALF-LIGHT, semi-darkness, gloom. **3** *the twilight of his career* DECLINE, waning, ebb; autumn, final years.
– RELATED TERMS crepuscular.
– OPPOSITES dawn.
● adjective *a twilight world* SHADOWY, dark, shady, dim, gloomy, obscure.
twin ● noun *a sitting room that was the twin of her own* DUPLICATE, double, carbon-copy, exact likeness, mirror image, replica, lookalike, clone; counterpart, match, pair; *informal* spitting image, dead ringer.
● adjective **1** *the twin towers of the stadium* MATCHING, identical, matched, paired. **2** *the twin aims of conservation and recreation* TWOFOLD, double, dual; related, linked, connected; corresponding, parallel, complementary, equivalent.
● verb *the company twinned its brewing with distilling* COMBINE, join, link, couple, pair.
twine ● noun *a ball of twine* STRING, cord, thread, yarn.
● verb **1** *she twined her arms around him* WIND, entwine, wrap, wreathe. **2** *convolvulus twined around the tree* ENTWINE ITSELF, coil, loop, twist, spiral, curl. **3** *a bloom was twined in her hair* WEAVE, interlace, intertwine, braid, twist.
twinge ● noun **1** *twinges in her stomach* PAIN, spasm, ache, throb; cramp, stitch. **2** *a twinge of guilt* PANG, prick, dart; qualm, scruple, misgiving.
twinkle ● verb **1** *the lights of the city twinkled* GLITTER, sparkle, shine, glimmer, shimmer, glint, gleam, glisten, flicker, flash, wink; *poetic/literary* coruscate, glister. **2** *his feet twinkled over the ground* DART, dance, skip, flit, glide.
● noun *the twinkle of the lights* GLITTER, sparkle, glimmer, shimmer, glint, gleam, flicker, flash, wink; *poetic/literary* coruscation.
twinkling ● adjective SPARKLING, glistening, glittering, glimmering, glinting, gleaming, flickering, winking, shining, scintillating; *poetic/literary* coruscating.
twirl ● verb **1** *she twirled her parasol* SPIN, whirl, turn, gyrate, pivot, swivel, twist, revolve, rotate. **2** *she twirled her hair round*

t

1 an act or instance of twisting. **2** a thing with a spiral shape. **3** Brit. a paper packet with twisted ends. **4** force producing twisting; torque. **5** a new or unexpected development or treatment. **6** a fine strong thread consisting of twisted fibres. **7** a carpet with a tightly curled pile. **8** (**the twist**) a dance with a twisting movement of the body, popular in the 1960s.
– PHRASES **round the twist** Brit. informal crazy. **twist someone's arm** informal forcefully persuade someone to do something that they are reluctant to do.
– DERIVATIVES **twisty** adjective.
– ORIGIN Old English, probably related to TWIN and TWINE.

twister ● noun **1** Brit. informal a swindler or dishonest person. **2** N. Amer. a tornado.

twit[1] ● noun informal, chiefly Brit. a silly or foolish person.
– DERIVATIVES **twittish** adjective.
– ORIGIN originally dialect in the sense 'tale-bearer'.

twit[2] ● verb (**twitted**, **twitting**) informal tease good-humouredly.
– ORIGIN Old English, 'reproach with'.

twitch ● verb make a short, sudden jerking movement. ● noun **1** a twitching movement. **2** a pang: *he felt a twitch of annoyance.*
– ORIGIN Germanic.

twitcher ● noun Brit. informal a birdwatcher devoted to spotting rare birds.

twitchy ● adjective (**twitchier**, **twitchiest**) **1** informal nervous. **2** given to twitching.

twite /twīt/ ● noun a moorland finch with streaky brown plumage and a pink rump.
– ORIGIN imitative of its call.

twitter ● verb **1** (of a bird) make a series of light tremulous sounds. **2** talk rapidly in a nervous or trivial way. ● noun **1** a twittering sound. **2** informal an agitated or excited state.
– DERIVATIVES **twittery** adjective.
– ORIGIN imitative.

'twixt ● contraction betwixt.

twizzle informal or dialect ● verb spin or cause to spin around. ● noun a twisting or spinning movement.
– ORIGIN probably imitative, influenced by TWIST.

two ● cardinal number one less than three; 2. (Roman numeral: **ii** or **II**.)
– PHRASES **put two and two together** draw an obvious conclusion from what is known or evident. **two by two** (or **two and two**) side by side in pairs. **two heads are better than one** proverb it's helpful to have the advice or opinion of a second person. **two-horse race** a contest in which only two of the competitors are likely winners. **two's company, three's a crowd** proverb the presence of a third person is not welcomed by two lovers.
– DERIVATIVES **twofold** adjective & adverb.
– ORIGIN Old English.

two-bit ● adjective N. Amer. informal insignificant, cheap, or worthless.

two-by-four ● noun a length of wood with a rectangular cross section approximately two inches by four inches.

twoc /twok/ ● verb (**twocced**, **twoccing**) Brit. informal steal (a car).
– ORIGIN acronym from *taken without owner's consent.*

two-dimensional ● adjective **1** having or appearing to have length and breadth but no depth. **2** lacking depth; superficial.

two-faced ● adjective insincere and deceitful.

twopence /tuppənss/ (also **tuppence**) ● noun Brit. **1** the sum of two pence, especially before decimalization (1971). **2** informal anything at all: *he didn't care twopence.*

twopenn'orth /to͞opennərth/ ● noun **1** an amount that is worth or costs twopence. **2** a paltry or insignificant amount.
– PHRASES **add** (or **put in**) **one's twopenn'orth** informal contribute one's opinion.

twopenny /tuppəni/ (also **tuppeny**) ● adjective Brit. costing two pence, especially before decimalization (1971).

twopenny-halfpenny ● adjective Brit. informal insignificant or worthless.

two-piece ● adjective consisting of two matching items.

two shot ● noun a cinema or television shot of two people together.

twosome ● noun a set of two people or things.

two-step ● noun a round dance with a sliding step in march or polka time.

two-stroke ● adjective (of an internal-combustion engine) having its power cycle completed in one up-and-down movement of the piston.

two-time ● verb informal be unfaithful to (a lover or husband or wife).

'twould ● contraction archaic it would.

two-up ● noun (in Australia and New Zealand) a gambling game in which two coins are tossed in the air and bets are laid as to whether both will fall heads or tails uppermost.

two-up two-down ● noun Brit. informal a house with two reception rooms downstairs and two bedrooms upstairs.

two-way ● adjective **1** involving movement or communication in opposite directions. **2** (of a switch) permitting a current to be switched on or off from either of two points.
– PHRASES **two-way street** a situation involving mutual or recip-

Thesaurus

her fingers WIND, twist, coil, curl, wrap.
● noun *she did a quick twirl* PIROUETTE, spin, whirl, turn, twist, rotation, revolution, gyration.

twist ● verb **1** *the impact twisted the chassis* CRUMPLE, crush, buckle, mangle, warp, deform, distort. **2** *her face twisted with rage* CONTORT, screw up. **3** *Ma anxiously twisted a handkerchief* WRING, squeeze. **4** *he twisted round in his seat* TURN (ROUND), swivel (round), spin (round), pivot, rotate, revolve. **5** *she twisted out of his grasp* WRIGGLE, squirm, worm, wiggle. **6** *I twisted my ankle* SPRAIN, wrench, turn, rick, crick. **7** *you are twisting my words* DISTORT, misrepresent, change, alter, pervert, falsify, warp, skew, misinterpret, misconstrue, misstate, misquote; garble. **8** *he twisted the radio knob* TWIDDLE, adjust, turn, rotate, swivel. **9** *she twisted her hair round her finger* WIND, twirl, coil, curl, wrap. **10** *the wires were twisted together* INTERTWINE, twine, interlace, weave, plait, braid, coil, wind. **11** *the road twisted and turned* WIND, bend, curve, turn, meander, weave, zigzag, swerve, snake.
● noun **1** *the twist of a dial* TURN, twirl, spin. **2** *a personality twist* QUIRK, idiosyncrasy, foible, eccentricity, peculiarity, oddity, kink; aberration, fault, flaw, imperfection, defect, failing, weakness. **3** *(Brit.) a twist of tobacco* WAD, quid, plug, chew; *Brit.* screw. **4** *long twists of black hair* RINGLET, curl, corkscrew, coil; lock, hank. **5** *the twists of the road* BEND, curve, turn, zigzag, kink, dog-leg; *Brit.* hairpin bend. **6** *the twists of the plot* CONVOLUTION, complication, complexity, intricacy; surprise, revelation. **7** *a new twist on an old theme* INTERPRETATION, slant, outlook, angle, approach, treatment; variation.
– PHRASES **twist someone's arm** *(informal)* PRESSURIZE, coerce, force; persuade; *informal* lean on, bulldoze, railroad, put the screws on.

twisted ● adjective **1** *twisted metal* CRUMPLED, bent, crushed, buckled, warped, misshapen, distorted, deformed. **2** *a twisted smile* CROOKED, lopsided; contorted, wry. **3** *his twisted mind* PERVERTED, warped, deviant, depraved, corrupt, abnormal, unhealthy, aberrant, distorted, corrupted, debauched, debased; *informal* sick, kinky, pervy.

twisty ● adjective WINDING, windy, twisting, bendy, zigzag, meandering, curving, sinuous, snaky.
– OPPOSITES straight.

twit ● noun *(Brit. informal).* See FOOL noun sense 1.

twitch ● verb **1** *he twitched and then lay still* JERK, convulse, have a spasm, quiver, tremble, shiver, shudder. **2** *he twitched the note out of my hand* SNATCH, tweak, pluck, pull, tug; *informal* yank.
● noun **1** *a twitch of her lips* SPASM, convulsion, quiver, tremor, shiver, shudder; tic. **2** *he gave a twitch at his moustache* PULL, tug, tweak; *informal* yank. **3** *he felt a twitch of annoyance* PANG, twinge, dart, stab, prick.

twitter ● verb **1** *sparrows twittered under the eaves* CHIRP, chirrup, cheep, tweet, peep, chatter, trill, warble, sing. **2** *stop twittering about Francis* PRATTLE, babble, chatter, gabble, jabber, go on, yap, blether, blither, ramble; *informal* yak, yabber; *Brit. informal* witter, rabbit, chunter, waffle.
● noun **1** *a bird's twitter* CHIRP, chirrup, cheep, tweet, peep, trill, warble, song. **2** *her non-stop twitter* PRATTLE, chatter, babble, talk, gabble, blether; *informal* yackety-yak; *Brit. informal* wittering, nattering, chuntering. **3** *(informal) she got into a real twitter.* See STEW noun sense 2.

two ● cardinal number PAIR, duo, duet, double, dyad, duplet, tandem; *archaic* twain.
– RELATED TERMS binary, dual, bi-, di-, duo-.

two-faced ● adjective DECEITFUL, insincere, double-dealing, hypocritical, back-stabbing, false, untrustworthy, duplicitous, deceiving, dissembling, dishonest; disloyal, treacherous, faithless;

rocal action or obligation.

two-way mirror ● noun a panel of glass that can be seen through from one side and is a mirror on the other.

TX ● abbreviation Texas.

-ty[1] ● suffix forming nouns denoting quality or condition such as *beauty*.
– ORIGIN from Latin *-tas*.

-ty[2] ● suffix denoting specified groups of ten: *forty*.
– ORIGIN Old English.

tycoon ● noun a wealthy, powerful person in business or industry.
– ORIGIN originally a title applied by foreigners to the shogun of Japan: from Japanese, 'great lord'.

tying present participle of TIE.

tyke (also **tike**) ● noun **1** informal a small child, especially a mischievous one. **2** a dog, especially a mongrel. **3** Brit. informal a person from Yorkshire.
– ORIGIN Old Norse, 'bitch'.

tympani ● plural noun variant spelling of TIMPANI.

tympanum /timpənəm/ ● noun (pl. **tympanums** or **tympana** /timpənə/) **1** Anatomy & Zoology the eardrum. **2** Architecture a vertical recessed triangular space forming the centre of a pediment or over a door.
– DERIVATIVES **tympanic** adjective.
– ORIGIN Greek *tumpanon* 'drum'.

Tynwald /tinwəld/ ● noun the parliament of the Isle of Man.
– ORIGIN Old Norse, 'place of assembly'.

type ● noun **1** a category of people or things having common characteristics. **2** a person or thing symbolizing or exemplifying the defining characteristics of something. **3** informal a person of a specified character or nature: *a sporty type*. **4** printed characters or letters. **5** pieces of metal with raised letters or characters on their upper surface, for use in letterpress printing. ● verb **1** write using a typewriter or computer. **2** Medicine determine the type to which (a person or their blood or tissue) belongs.
– DERIVATIVES **typing** noun.
– ORIGIN Greek *tupos* 'impression, figure, type'.

typecast ● verb (past and past part. **typecast**) (usu. **be typecast**) **1** repeatedly cast (an actor) in the same type of role because their appearance is appropriate or they are known for such roles. **2** regard as fitting a stereotype.

typeface ● noun Printing a particular design of type.

typescript ● noun a typed copy of a text.

typeset ● verb (**typesetting**; past and past part. **typeset**) arrange or generate the type for (text to be printed).
– DERIVATIVES **typesetter** noun **typesetting** noun.

type site ● noun Archaeology a site where objects or materials regarded as typical of a particular period are found.

typewriter ● noun an electric, electronic, or manual machine with keys for producing print-like characters.
– DERIVATIVES **typewriting** noun **typewritten** adjective.

typhoid (also **typhoid fever**) ● noun an infectious bacterial fever with an eruption of red spots on the chest and abdomen and severe intestinal irritation.
– ORIGIN from TYPHUS.

typhoon /tīfo͞on/ ● noun a tropical storm in the region of the Indian or western Pacific oceans.
– ORIGIN partly from Arabic, partly from a Chinese dialect word meaning 'big wind'.

typhus /tīfəss/ ● noun an infectious bacterial disease characterized by a purple rash, headaches, fever, and usually delirium.
– ORIGIN Greek *tuphos* 'smoke, stupor'.

typical ● adjective **1** having the distinctive qualities of a particular type. **2** characteristic of a particular person or thing.
– DERIVATIVES **typicality** noun **typically** adverb.

typify ● verb (**typifies**, **typified**) be typical of.
– DERIVATIVES **typification** noun.

typist ● noun a person skilled in typing, especially one who is employed for this purpose.

typo /tīpō/ ● noun (pl. **typos**) informal a typographical error.

typography /tīpogrəfi/ ● noun **1** the art or process of setting and arranging types and printing from them. **2** the style and appearance of printed matter.
– DERIVATIVES **typographer** noun **typographic** adjective **typographical** adjective.

typology /tīpolləji/ ● noun (pl. **typologies**) **1** classification according to general type. **2** the study and interpretation of types and symbols.
– DERIVATIVES **typological** adjective **typologist** noun.

tyrannical ● adjective exercising power in a cruel or arbitrary way.
– DERIVATIVES **tyrannically** adverb.

tyrannicide /tirannisīd, tī-/ ● noun **1** the killing of a tyrant. **2** the killer of a tyrant.
– DERIVATIVES **tyrannicidal** adjective.

tyrannize /tirrənīz/ (also **tyrannise**) ● verb rule or treat despotically or cruelly.

tyrannosaurus /tirannəsorəss/ (also **tyrannosaurus rex**, **tyrannosaur** /tirannəsor/) ● noun a very large carnivorous dinosaur with powerful jaws and small claw-like front legs.
– ORIGIN from Greek *turannos* 'tyrant' + *sauros* 'lizard'.

tyranny ● noun (pl. **tyrannies**) **1** cruel and oppressive government or rule. **2** a state under such rule. **3** cruel and arbitrary exercise of power or control.
– DERIVATIVES **tyrannous** adjective.

tyrant ● noun **1** a cruel and oppressive ruler. **2** a person exercising power or control in a cruel and arbitrary way. **3** (especially in ancient Greece) a ruler who seized absolute power without legal right.
– ORIGIN Greek *turannos*.

tyre (US **tire**) ● noun **1** a rubber covering, typically inflated or surrounding an inflated inner tube, placed round a wheel to form a soft contact with the road. **2** a strengthening band of metal fitted around the rim of a wheel, especially of a railway vehicle.
– ORIGIN probably a shortening of ATTIRE (because the tyre was the 'clothing' of the wheel).

tyre gauge ● noun a portable pressure gauge for measuring the air pressure in a tyre.

tyro /tīrō/ (also **tiro**) ● noun (pl. **tyros**) a beginner or novice.
– ORIGIN Latin, 'recruit'.

tyrosine /tīrəseen/ ● noun Biochemistry an amino acid which is a

Thesaurus

poetic/literary perfidious.
– OPPOSITES sincere.

twosome ● noun COUPLE, pair, duo.

tycoon ● noun MAGNATE, mogul, businessman, captain of industry, industrialist, financier, entrepreneur; millionaire, multimillionaire; *informal* big shot, bigwig, honcho; *Brit. informal* supremo; *N. Amer. informal* big wheel, kahuna; *derogatory* fat cat.

type ● noun **1** *a curate of the old-fashioned type* KIND, sort, variety, class, category, set, genre, species, order, breed, race; style, nature, manner, rank; generation, vintage; stamp, ilk, kidney, cast, grain, mould; *N. Amer.* stripe. **2** *(informal) sporty types* PERSON, individual, character, sort; *Brit. informal* bod. **3** *his sayings are the type of modern wisdom* EPITOME, quintessence, essence, archetype, paradigm, model, embodiment. **4** *italic type* PRINT, typeface, face, characters, lettering, letters; font; *Brit.* fount.

typhoon ● noun CYCLONE, tropical storm, storm, tornado, hurricane, whirlwind; *N. Amer. informal* twister.

typical ● adjective **1** *a typical example of art deco* REPRESENTATIVE, classic, quintessential, archetypal, model, prototypical, stereotypical. **2** *a fairly typical day* NORMAL, average, ordinary, standard, regular, routine, run-of-the-mill, conventional, unremarkable, unexceptional; *informal* bog-standard. **3** *it's typical of him to forget* CHARACTERISTIC, in keeping, usual, normal, par for the course, predictable, true to form; customary, habitual.
– OPPOSITES unusual, exceptional, uncharacteristic.

typify ● verb **1** *he typified the civil servant* EPITOMIZE, exemplify, characterize, be representative of; personify, embody. **2** *the sun typified the Greeks* SYMBOLIZE, represent, stand for, be emblematic of.

tyrannical ● adjective DICTATORIAL, despotic, autocratic, oppressive, repressive, totalitarian, undemocratic, illiberal; authoritarian, high-handed, imperious, harsh, strict, iron-handed, severe, cruel, brutal, ruthless.
– OPPOSITES liberal.

tyrannize ● verb DOMINATE, dictate to, browbeat, intimidate, bully, lord it over; persecute, victimize, torment; oppress, rule with a rod of iron, repress, crush, subjugate; *informal* push around.

tyranny ● noun DESPOTISM, absolute power, autocracy, dictatorship, totalitarianism, Fascism; oppression, repression, subjugation, enslavement; authoritarianism, bullying, severity, cruelty,

constituent of most proteins and is important in the synthesis of some hormones.
– ORIGIN from Greek *turos* 'cheese'.

tzar ● noun variant spelling of TSAR.

tzarevich ● noun variant spelling of TSAREVICH.

tzarina ● noun variant spelling of TSARINA.

tzatziki /tsatseeki/ ● noun a Greek side dish of yogurt with cucumber, garlic, and often mint.
– ORIGIN modern Greek.

tzigane /tsigaan/ ● noun (pl. same or **tziganes**) a Hungarian gypsy.
– ORIGIN Hungarian.

Thesaurus

brutality, ruthlessness.

tyrant ● noun DICTATOR, despot, autocrat, authoritarian, oppressor; slave-driver, martinet, bully.

tyro ● noun NOVICE, beginner, learner, neophyte, newcomer, initiate, fledgling; apprentice, trainee, probationer, new/raw recruit; *N. Amer.* tenderfoot; *informal* rookie, newie, newbie; *N. Amer. informal* greenhorn.
– OPPOSITES veteran.

t

Uu

U[1] /yōō/ (also **u**) ● noun (pl. **Us** or **U's**) the twenty-first letter of the alphabet.
U[2] /yōō/ ● abbreviation **1** (in names of sports clubs) United. **2** Brit. universal (denoting films classified as suitable without restriction). ● symbol the chemical element uranium.
U[3] /yōō/ ● adjective informal, chiefly Brit. characteristic of or appropriate to the upper social classes.
– ORIGIN abbreviation of UPPER CLASS; coined in 1954 by Alan S. C. Ross, a professor of linguistics, and popularized by Nancy Mitford's *Noblesse Oblige* (1956).
U[4] /ōō/ ● noun a Burmese title of respect before a man's name, equivalent to Mr.
UAE ● abbreviation United Arab Emirates.
UB40 ● noun (in the UK) a card issued to a person registered as unemployed.
U-bend ● noun a section of a pipe, in particular of a waste pipe, shaped like a U.
Übermensch /ōōbərmensh/ ● noun the ideal superior man of the future who could rise above conventional Christian morality to create and impose his own values, originally described by Nietzsche in *Thus Spake Zarathustra* (1883–5).
– ORIGIN German, 'superhuman person'.
ubiquitous /yōōbikwitəss/ ● adjective present, appearing, or found everywhere.
– DERIVATIVES **ubiquitously** adverb **ubiquitousness** noun **ubiquity** noun.
– ORIGIN from Latin *ubique* 'everywhere'.
U-boat ● noun a German submarine of the First or Second World War.
– ORIGIN German *U-boot*, abbreviation of *Unterseeboot* 'undersea boat'.
UBR ● abbreviation uniform business rate (a tax on business property in England and Wales).
UCAS /yōōkass/ ● abbreviation (in the UK) Universities and Colleges Admissions Service.
UDA ● abbreviation Ulster Defence Association.
udder ● noun the mammary gland of female cattle, sheep, goats, horses, etc., hanging near the hind legs as a bag-like organ with two or more teats.
– ORIGIN Old English.
UDI ● abbreviation unilateral declaration of independence.
UDR ● abbreviation Ulster Defence Regiment.
UEFA /yōōeefə, -ayfə/ ● abbreviation Union of European Football Associations.
UFO ● noun (pl. **UFOs**) a mysterious object seen in the sky for which it is claimed no orthodox scientific explanation can be found, popularly said to be a vehicle carrying extraterrestrials.
– DERIVATIVES **ufologist** noun **ufology** noun.
– ORIGIN abbreviation of *unidentified flying object.*
Ugandan /yōōgandən/ ● noun a person from Uganda. ● adjective relating to Uganda.
Ugli fruit /ugli/ ● noun (pl. same) trademark a mottled green and yellow citrus fruit which is a hybrid of a grapefruit and tangerine.
– ORIGIN alteration of UGLY.
ugly ● adjective (**uglier**, **ugliest**) **1** unpleasant or repulsive in appearance. **2** hostile or threatening; likely to involve unpleasantness.
– DERIVATIVES **uglify** verb **ugliness** noun.
– ORIGIN from Old Norse, 'to be dreaded'.
ugly duckling ● noun a person who turns out to be beautiful or talented against all expectations.
– ORIGIN from the title of one of Hans Christian Andersen's fairy tales, in which the 'ugly duckling' becomes a swan.
UHF ● abbreviation ultra-high frequency.
uhlan /ōōlaan/ ● noun historical (in various European armies) a cavalryman armed with a lance.
– ORIGIN Turkish *oğlan* 'youth, servant'.
UHT ● abbreviation ultra heat treated (a process used to extend the shelf life of milk).
uillean pipes /illin/ ● plural noun Irish bagpipes played using bellows worked by the elbow.
– ORIGIN from Irish *píob uilleann* 'pipe of the elbow'.
UK ● abbreviation United Kingdom.
ukase /yōōkayz/ ● noun **1** (in tsarist Russia) a decree with the force of law. **2** an arbitrary or peremptory command.
– ORIGIN Russian *ukaz* 'ordinance, edict'.
ukiyo-e /ōōkeeyō ay/ ● noun a school of Japanese art depicting subjects from everyday life.
– ORIGIN Japanese, from words meaning 'fleeting world' and 'picture'.
Ukrainian ● noun **1** a person from Ukraine. **2** the language of Ukraine. ● adjective relating to Ukraine.
ukulele /yōōkəlayli/ ● noun a small four-stringed guitar of Hawaiian origin.
– ORIGIN Hawaiian, 'jumping flea'.
ulama ● noun variant spelling of ULEMA.
ulcer ● noun an open sore on the body, caused by a break in the skin or mucous membrane which fails to heal.
– DERIVATIVES **ulcered** adjective **ulcerous** adjective.
– ORIGIN Latin *ulcus.*
ulcerate ● verb develop into or become affected by an ulcer.
– DERIVATIVES **ulceration** noun **ulcerative** adjective.
-ule ● suffix forming diminutive nouns such as *capsule.*
– ORIGIN from Latin *-ulus, -ula, -ulum.*
ulema /ōōlimə/ (also **ulama**) ● noun **1** (treated as sing. or pl.) a body of Muslim scholars recognized as expert in Islamic sacred law and theology. **2** a member of an ulema.
– ORIGIN Arabic, ultimately from a word meaning 'know'.
ullage /ullij/ ● noun **1** the amount by which a container falls short of being full. **2** loss of liquid by evaporation or leakage.
– ORIGIN from Old French *euillier* 'fill up', from Latin *oculus* 'eye' (with reference to a container's bunghole).
ulna /ulnə/ ● noun (pl. **ulnae** /ulnee/ or **ulnas**) a bone of the forearm or forelimb, in humans the thinner and longer of the two.
– DERIVATIVES **ulnar** adjective.
– ORIGIN Latin, related to ELL.
U-lock ● noun another term for D-LOCK.
ulster ● noun a man's long, loose overcoat of rough cloth.
– ORIGIN from *Ulster* in Ireland, where it was originally sold.
Ulsterman (or **Ulsterwoman**) ● noun a native or inhabitant of Northern Ireland or Ulster.
ulterior ● adjective **1** other than what is obvious or admitted: *she had some ulterior motive in coming.* **2** beyond what is immediate or present.
– ORIGIN Latin, 'further, more distant'.

Thesaurus

ubiquitous ● adjective OMNIPRESENT, ever-present, everywhere, all over the place, all-pervasive; universal, worldwide, global; rife, prevalent, far-reaching, inescapable.
– OPPOSITES rare.
ugly ● adjective **1** *an ugly face* UNATTRACTIVE, ill-favoured, hideous, plain, unlovely, unprepossessing, unsightly, horrible, frightful, awful, ghastly, unpleasant, vile, revolting, repellent, repugnant; grotesque, monstrous, reptilian, misshapen, deformed, disfigured; *N. Amer.* homely; *informal* not much to look at; *Brit. informal* no oil painting. **2** *things got pretty ugly* UNPLEASANT, nasty, disagreeable, alarming, tense, charged, serious, grave; dangerous, perilous, threatening, menacing, hostile, ominous, sinister. **3** *an ugly rumour* HORRIBLE, despicable, reprehensible, nasty, appalling, objectionable, offensive, obnoxious, vile, dishonourable, rotten, vicious, spiteful.
– OPPOSITES beautiful, pleasant.

ultimate ● adjective **1** being or happening at the end of a process. **2** being the best or most extreme example of its kind: *the ultimate accolade.* **3** basic or fundamental. ● noun **1** (**the ultimate**) the best achievable or imaginable of its kind. **2** a final or fundamental fact or principle.
– DERIVATIVES **ultimacy** noun **ultimately** adverb.
– ORIGIN Latin *ultimatus*, from *ultimare* 'come to an end'.

ultima Thule ● noun a distant unknown region; the extreme limit of travel and discovery.
– ORIGIN Latin, 'furthest Thule', a country to the north of Britain (probably Norway) believed by ancient Greeks and Romans to be the northernmost part of the world.

ultimatum /ultimaytəm/ ● noun (pl. **ultimatums** or **ultimata** /ultimaytə/) a final demand or statement of terms, the rejection of which will result in retaliation or a breakdown in relations.
– ORIGIN Latin, 'thing that has come to an end'.

ultra informal ● adverb very. ● noun an extremist.

ultra- ● prefix **1** beyond; on the other side of: *ultramontane.* **2** extreme; to an extreme degree: *ultramicroscopic.*
– ORIGIN Latin *ultra* 'beyond'.

ultra-high frequency ● noun a radio frequency in the range 300 to 3,000 megahertz.

ultramarine ● noun **1** a brilliant deep blue pigment originally obtained from lapis lazuli. **2** a brilliant deep blue colour.
– ORIGIN from obsolete Italian *azzurro oltramarino* 'azure from overseas' (because the lapis lazuli was imported), from Latin *ultramarinus* 'beyond the sea'.

ultramicroscope ● noun an optical microscope used to detect very small particles by observing light scattered from them.

ultramicroscopic ● adjective **1** too small to be seen by an ordinary optical microscope. **2** relating to an ultramicroscope.

ultramontane /ultrəmontayn/ ● adjective **1** advocating supreme papal authority in matters of faith and discipline. **2** situated on the other side of the Alps from the point of view of the speaker. ● noun an advocate of supreme papal authority.
– DERIVATIVES **ultramontanism** noun.
– ORIGIN originally referring to a representative of the Roman Catholic Church north of the Alps: from Latin *ultra* 'beyond' + *mons* 'mountain'.

ultrasonic ● adjective involving sound waves with a frequency above the upper limit of human hearing.
– DERIVATIVES **ultrasonically** adverb.

ultrasonics ● plural noun **1** (treated as sing.) the science and application of ultrasonic waves. **2** (treated as sing. or pl.) ultrasound.

ultrasound ● noun sound or other vibrations having an ultrasonic frequency, particularly as used in medical imaging.

ultraviolet ● noun electromagnetic radiation having a wavelength just shorter than that of violet light but longer than that of X-rays. ● adjective denoting such radiation.

ultra vires /ultrə vīreez/ ● adjective & adverb Law beyond one's legal power or authority.
– ORIGIN Latin, 'beyond the powers'.

ululate /yoolyoolayt, ul-/ ● verb howl or wail.
– DERIVATIVES **ululation** noun.
– ORIGIN Latin *ululare* 'howl, shriek'.

umbel /umb'l/ ● noun Botany a flower cluster in which stalks spring from a common centre and form a flat or curved surface.
– DERIVATIVES **umbellate** adjective.
– ORIGIN Latin *umbella* 'sunshade'.

umbellifer /umbellifər/ ● noun Botany a plant of the parsley family (Umbelliferae).
– DERIVATIVES **umbelliferous** adjective.

umber /umbər/ ● noun a natural pigment, normally dark yellowish-brown in colour (**raw umber**) or dark brown when roasted (**burnt umber**).
– ORIGIN from French *terre d'ombre*, 'earth of shadow', from Latin *umbra* 'shadow' or *Umbra* 'Umbrian'

umbilical /umbillik'l, umbilīk'l/ ● adjective relating to or affecting the navel or umbilical cord.
– DERIVATIVES **umbilically** adverb.

umbilical cord ● noun a flexible cord-like structure containing blood vessels, attaching a fetus to the placenta during gestation.

umbilicus /umbillikəss, umbilīkəss/ ● noun (pl. **umbilici** /umbillisī, umbilīsī/ or **umbilicuses**) **1** Anatomy the navel. **2** Zoology a central depression or hole in the whorl of some gastropod molluscs and many ammonites.
– ORIGIN Latin.

umbra /umbrə/ ● noun (pl. **umbras** or **umbrae** /umbree/) **1** the fully shaded inner region of a shadow, especially the area on the earth or moon experiencing totality in an eclipse. **2** Astronomy the dark central part of a sunspot.
– DERIVATIVES **umbral** adjective.
– ORIGIN Latin, 'shade'.

umbrage /umbrij/ ● noun (in phrase **take umbrage**) offence or annoyance.
– ORIGIN originally in the sense 'shade or shadow', later 'shadowy outline' and 'ground for suspicion': from Latin *umbra* 'shade'.

umbrageous /umbrayjəss/ ● adjective literary full of shadow; shady.

umbrella ● noun **1** a device consisting of a circular fabric canopy on a folding metal frame supported by a central rod, used as protection against rain. **2** a protecting force or influence. **3** (before another noun) including or containing many different parts: *an umbrella organization.*
– ORIGIN Italian *ombrella*, from Latin *umbra* 'shade'.

Umbrian ● noun a person from Umbria, a region of central Italy. ● adjective relating to Umbria.

umlaut /oomlowt/ ● noun Linguistics a mark (¨) used over a vowel, especially in German, to indicate a different vowel quality.
– ORIGIN German, from *um* 'about' + *Laut* 'sound'.

umma /oomə/ (also **ummah**) ● noun the whole community of Muslims bound together by ties of religion.
– ORIGIN Arabic, 'people, community'.

umph ● noun variant spelling of OOMPH.

umpire ● noun **1** (in certain sports) an official who enforces the rules of a game and settles disputes arising from the play. **2** a person chosen to settle a dispute between contending parties. ● verb act as an umpire.
– ORIGIN originally as *noumpere*, from Old French *nonper* 'not equal': the *n* was lost by wrong division of *a noumpere.*

Thesaurus

ulcer ● noun SORE, ulceration, abscess, boil, carbuncle, blister, gumboil, wen; *Medicine* aphtha, chancre, furuncle.

ulterior ● adjective UNDERLYING, undisclosed, undivulged, concealed, hidden, covert, secret, personal, private, selfish.
– OPPOSITES overt.

ultimate ● adjective **1** *the ultimate collapse of the Empire* EVENTUAL, final, concluding, terminal, end; resulting, ensuing, consequent, subsequent. **2** *ultimate truths about civilization* FUNDAMENTAL, basic, primary, elementary, elemental, absolute, central, key, crucial, essential, pivotal. **3** *the ultimate gift for cat lovers* BEST, ideal, greatest, supreme, paramount, superlative, highest, utmost, optimum, quintessential.
● noun *the ultimate in luxury living* UTMOST, optimum, last word, height, epitome, peak, pinnacle, acme, zenith, nonpareil, dernier cri, ne plus ultra; *informal* the cat's pyjamas/whiskers, the bee's knees.

ultimately ● adverb **1** *the cost will ultimately fall on us* EVENTUALLY, in the end, in the long run, at length, finally, sooner or later, in time, in the fullness of time, when all is said and done, one day, some day, sometime; *informal* when push comes to shove; *Brit. informal* at the end of the day. **2** *two ultimately contradictory reasons* FUNDAMENTALLY, basically, primarily, essentially, at heart, deep down.

ultra- ● combining form *an ultra-conservative view* EXTREMELY, exceedingly, excessively, immensely, especially, exceptionally; *N. English* right; *informal* mega, mucho, majorly, oh-so; *Brit. informal* dead, ever so, well; *N. Amer. informal* real; *informal, dated* devilish; *archaic* exceeding.
● noun *ultras in the animal rights movement* EXTREMIST, radical, fanatic, zealot, diehard, militant.

umbrage ● noun
– PHRASES **take umbrage** TAKE OFFENCE, take exception, be aggrieved, be affronted, be annoyed, be angry, be indignant, be put out, be insulted, be hurt, be piqued, be resentful, be disgruntled, go into a huff; *informal* be miffed, have one's nose put out of joint; *Brit. informal* get the hump.

umbrella ● noun **1** *they huddled under the umbrella* parasol, sunshade; *Brit. informal* brolly; *Brit. informal, dated* gamp. **2** *the groups worked under the umbrella of the Liberal Party* AEGIS, auspices, patronage, protection, guardianship, support, backing, agency, guidance, care, charge, responsibility, cover.

umpire ● noun *the umpire reversed his decision* REFEREE, linesman,

umpteen ● cardinal number informal indefinitely many.
– DERIVATIVES **umpteenth** ordinal number.
– ORIGIN humorous formation.
UN ● abbreviation United Nations.
un-[1] ● prefix **1** (added to adjectives, participles, and their derivatives) denoting the absence of a quality or state; not: *unacademic.* **2** the reverse of: *unselfish.* **3** (added to nouns) a lack of: *untruth.*
– USAGE The prefixes **un-** and **non-** both mean 'not', but are used with a difference of emphasis, **un-** being stronger and less neutral than **non-**. Compare, for example, **unacademic** and **non-academic** in *his language was refreshingly unacademic* and *a non-academic life suits him.*
– ORIGIN Old English.
un-[2] ● prefix added to verbs: **1** denoting the reversal or cancellation of an action or state: *unsettle.* **2** denoting deprivation, separation, or reduction to a lesser state: *unmask.* **3** denoting release: *unhand.*
– ORIGIN Old English.
'un ● contraction informal one.
unabashed ● adjective not embarrassed, disconcerted, or ashamed.
– DERIVATIVES **unabashedly** adverb.
unabated ● adjective without any reduction in intensity or strength.
unable ● adjective lacking the skill, means, or opportunity to do something.
unabridged ● adjective (of a text) not cut or shortened; complete.
unaccented ● adjective having no accent, stress, or emphasis.
unacceptable ● adjective not satisfactory or allowable.
– DERIVATIVES **unacceptability** noun **unacceptably** adverb.
unaccompanied ● adjective **1** having no companion or escort. **2** without instrumental accompaniment. **3** without something occurring at the same time.
unaccountable ● adjective **1** unable to be explained. **2** not responsible for or required to justify consequences.
– DERIVATIVES **unaccountability** noun **unaccountably** adverb.
unaccounted ● adjective (**unaccounted for**) not taken into consideration or explained.
unaccustomed ● adjective **1** not customary; unusual. **2** (**unaccustomed to**) not familiar with or used to.
– DERIVATIVES **unaccustomedly** adverb.
unacknowledged ● adjective **1** existing or having taken place but not accepted or admitted to. **2** deserving but not receiving recognition.
unacquainted ● adjective **1** (**unacquainted with**) having no experience of or familiarity with. **2** not having met before.
unadjusted ● adjective (especially of statistics) not adjusted or refined.
unadopted ● adjective Brit. (of a road) not taken over for maintenance by a local authority.
unadulterated ● adjective **1** complete; utter. **2** having no inferior added substances.
unadventurous ● adjective not offering, involving, or eager for new or stimulating things.
– DERIVATIVES **unadventurously** adverb.
unadvisable ● adjective inadvisable.
unadvisedly ● adverb in an unwise or rash manner.
unaffected ● adjective **1** feeling or showing no effects. **2** sincere and genuine.
– DERIVATIVES **unaffectedly** adverb **unaffectedness** noun.
unaffiliated ● adjective not officially attached to or connected with an organization.
unaffordable ● adjective too expensive to be afforded by the average person.
unafraid ● adjective feeling no fear.
unaided ● adjective needing or having no assistance.
unalienable ● adjective inalienable.
unaligned ● adjective **1** not placed or arranged in a straight line or in correct relative positions. **2** not allied with or supporting an organization or cause.
unalike ● adjective differing from each other.
unalloyed ● adjective **1** (of metal) not alloyed. **2** complete and unreserved: *unalloyed delight.*
unalterable ● adjective not able to be changed.
– DERIVATIVES **unalterably** adverb.
unaltered ● adjective remaining the same.
unambiguous ● adjective without ambiguity.
– DERIVATIVES **unambiguously** adverb.
unambitious ● adjective **1** not motivated by a strong desire to succeed. **2** not involving anything new, exciting, or demanding.
un-American ● adjective **1** not in accordance with American characteristics. **2** US, chiefly historical against the interests of the US and therefore treasonable.
unanimous /yoonanniməss/ ● adjective **1** fully in agreement. **2** (of an opinion, decision, or vote) held or carried by everyone involved.

Thesaurus

adjudicator, arbitrator, judge, moderator; *informal* ref; *N. Amer. informal* ump.
● **verb** *he umpired a boat race* REFEREE, adjudicate, arbitrate, judge, moderate, oversee; *Cricket* stand; *informal* ref.
umpteen ● adjective *(informal).* See COUNTLESS.
unabashed ● adjective UNASHAMED, shameless, unembarrassed, brazen, audacious, barefaced, blatant, flagrant, bold, cocky, unrepentant, undaunted, unconcerned, fearless.
– OPPOSITES sheepish.
unable ● adjective POWERLESS, impotent, at a loss, inadequate, incompetent, unfit, unqualified, incapable.
unabridged ● adjective COMPLETE, entire, whole, intact, uncut, unshortened, unexpurgated.
unacceptable ● adjective INTOLERABLE, insufferable, unsatisfactory, inadmissible, inappropriate, unsuitable, undesirable, unreasonable, insupportable; offensive, obnoxious, disagreeable, disgraceful, deplorable, beyond the pale, bad; *informal* not on, a bit much, too much, out of order; *Brit. informal* a bit thick, a bit off, not cricket; *formal* exceptionable.
– OPPOSITES satisfactory.
unaccompanied ● adjective ALONE, on one's own, by oneself, solo, lone, solitary, single-handed; unescorted, unattended, unchaperoned; *informal* by one's lonesome; *Brit. informal* on one's tod, on one's Jack Jones; *Austral./NZ informal* on one's Pat Malone.
unaccomplished ● adjective **1** *unaccomplished works* UNCOMPLETED, incomplete, unfinished, undone, half-done, unfulfilled, neglected. **2** *an unaccomplished poet* INEXPERT, unskilful, unskilled, amateur, amateurish, unqualified, untrained; incompetent, maladroit.
– OPPOSITES complete, skilful.
unaccountable ● adjective **1** *for some unaccountable reason* INEXPLICABLE, insoluble, incomprehensible, unfathomable, impenetrable, puzzling, perplexing, baffling, bewildering, mystifying, mysterious, inscrutable, peculiar, strange, queer, odd, obscure; *informal* weird, freaky; *Brit. informal* rum. **2** *the Council is unaccountable to anyone* UNANSWERABLE, not liable; free, exempt, immune; unsupervised.
unaccustomed ● adjective **1** *she was unaccustomed to being bossed about* UNUSED, new, fresh; unfamiliar with, inexperienced in, unconversant with, unacquainted with. **2** *he showed unaccustomed emotion* UNUSUAL, unfamiliar, uncommon, unwonted, exceptional, extraordinary, rare, surprising, abnormal, atypical.
– OPPOSITES habitual.
unacquainted ● adjective UNFAMILIAR, unaccustomed, unused; inexperienced, ignorant, uninformed, unenlightened, unconversant, in the dark; *poetic/literary* nescient.
– OPPOSITES familiar.
unadorned ● adjective UNEMBELLISHED, unornamented, undecorated, unfussy, no-nonsense, no-frills; plain, basic, restrained; bare, bald, austere, stark, spartan, clinical.
– OPPOSITES ornate.
unadventurous ● adjective CAUTIOUS, careful, circumspect, wary, hesitant, timid; conservative, conventional, unenterprising, unexciting, unimaginative; boring, strait-laced, stuffy, narrow-minded; *informal* square, straight, stick-in-the-mud.
– OPPOSITES enterprising.
unaffected ● adjective **1** *they are unaffected by the cabinet reshuffle* UNCHANGED, unaltered, uninfluenced; untouched, unmoved, unresponsive to; proof against, impervious to, immune to. **2** *his manner was unaffected* UNASSUMING, unpretentious, down-to-earth, natural, easy, uninhibited, open, artless, guileless, ingenuous, unsophisticated. **3** *she was welcomed with unaffected warmth* GENUINE, real, sincere, honest, earnest, wholehearted, heartfelt, true, bona fide, frank, open; *informal* upfront.
– OPPOSITES influenced, pretentious, feigned.
unafraid ● adjective UNDAUNTED, unabashed, fearless, brave, cour-

u

– DERIVATIVES **unanimity** /yo͞onənimmiti/ noun **unanimously** adverb.
– ORIGIN Latin *unanimus*, from *unus* 'one' + *animus* 'mind'.
unannounced ● adjective **1** not publicized. **2** without warning; unexpected.
unanswerable ● adjective **1** unable to be answered. **2** unable to be disclaimed or proved wrong.
unanswered ● adjective not answered or responded to.
unapologetic ● adjective not acknowledging or expressing regret.
– DERIVATIVES **unapologetically** adverb.
unappealing ● adjective not inviting or attractive.
– DERIVATIVES **unappealingly** adverb.
unappetizing (also **unappetising**) ● adjective not inviting or attractive.
– DERIVATIVES **unappetizingly** adverb.
unappreciated ● adjective not fully understood, recognized, or valued.
unappreciative ● adjective not fully understanding or recognizing something.
unapproachable ● adjective not welcoming or friendly.
unapproved ● adjective not officially accepted or sanctioned.
unarguable ● adjective **1** not open to disagreement; certain. **2** not able to be argued.
– DERIVATIVES **unarguably** adverb.
unarmed ● adjective not equipped with or carrying weapons.
unashamed ● adjective feeling or showing no guilt or embarrassment.
– DERIVATIVES **unashamedly** adverb.
unasked ● adjective **1** (of a question) not asked. **2** (often **unasked for**) not requested or sought.
unassailable ● adjective unable to be attacked, questioned, or defeated.
– DERIVATIVES **unassailability** noun **unassailably** adverb.
unassertive ● adjective not having or showing a confident and forceful personality.
unassisted ● adjective not helped by anyone or anything.
unassociated ● adjective not connected or associated.
unassuming ● adjective not pretentious or arrogant.
– DERIVATIVES **unassumingly** adverb.
unattached ● adjective **1** not working for or belonging to a particular organization. **2** without a husband or wife or established lover.
unattainable ● adjective not able to be reached or achieved.
– DERIVATIVES **unattainably** adverb.
unattended ● adjective **1** not dealt with. **2** not looked after.
unattractive ● adjective not pleasing, appealing, or inviting.
– DERIVATIVES **unattractively** adverb **unattractiveness** noun.
unattributed ● adjective (of a quotation, story, or work of art) of unknown or unpublished origin.
– DERIVATIVES **unattributable** adjective.
unauthorized (also **unauthorised**) ● adjective not having official permission or approval.
unavailable ● adjective **1** not at someone's disposal. **2** not free to do something.
– DERIVATIVES **unavailability** noun.
unavailing ● adjective achieving little or nothing.
– DERIVATIVES **unavailingly** adverb.
unavoidable ● adjective not able to be avoided or prevented; inevitable.
– DERIVATIVES **unavoidability** noun **unavoidably** adverb.
unaware ● adjective having no knowledge of a situation or fact.
– DERIVATIVES **unawareness** noun.
unawares (also **unaware**) ● adverb so as to surprise; unexpectedly.
unbalance ● verb **1** upset the balance of. **2** (**unbalanced**) de-

Thesaurus

ageous, plucky, intrepid, stout-hearted, bold, daring, confident, audacious, mettlesome, unshrinking; *informal* gutsy, spunky.
– OPPOSITES timid.
unanimous ● adjective **1** *doctors were unanimous about the effects* UNITED, in agreement, in accord, of one mind, in harmony, concordant, undivided. **2** *a unanimous vote* UNIFORM, consistent, united, concerted, congruent.
– OPPOSITES divided.
unanswerable ● adjective **1** *an unanswerable case* IRREFUTABLE, indisputable, undeniable, incontestable, incontrovertible; conclusive, absolute, positive. **2** *unanswerable questions* INSOLUBLE, unsolvable, insolvable, inexplicable, unexplainable.
– OPPOSITES weak, obvious.
unanswered ● adjective UNRESOLVED, undecided, unsettled, undetermined; pending, open to question, up in the air, doubtful, disputed.
unappetizing ● adjective UNPALATABLE, uninviting, unappealing, unpleasant, off-putting, disagreeable, distasteful, unsavoury, insipid, tasteless, flavourless, dull; inedible, uneatable, revolting; *informal* yucky, gross.
– OPPOSITES tempting.
unapproachable ● adjective **1** *unapproachable islands* INACCESSIBLE, unreachable, remote, out of the way, isolated, far-flung; *informal* off the beaten track, in the middle of nowhere, in the sticks, unget-at-able. **2** *her boss appeared unapproachable* ALOOF, distant, remote, detached, reserved, withdrawn, uncommunicative, guarded, undemonstrative, unresponsive, unforthcoming, unfriendly, unsympathetic, unsociable; cool, cold, frosty, stiff, formal; *informal* stand-offish.
– OPPOSITES accessible, friendly.
unarmed ● adjective DEFENCELESS, weaponless; unprotected, undefended, unguarded, unshielded, vulnerable, exposed, assailable, pregnable.
unassailable ● adjective **1** *an unassailable fortress* IMPREGNABLE, invulnerable, impenetrable, inviolable, invincible, unconquerable; secure, safe, strong, indestructible. **2** *his logic was unassailable* INDISPUTABLE, undeniable, unquestionable, incontestable, incontrovertible, irrefutable, indubitable, watertight, sound, good, sure, manifest, patent, obvious.
– OPPOSITES defenceless.
unassertive ● adjective PASSIVE, retiring, unforthcoming, submissive, unassuming, self-effacing, shy, timid, modest, humble, meek, unconfident, diffident, insecure; *informal* mousy.
– OPPOSITES bold.

u

unassuming ● adjective MODEST, self-effacing, humble, meek, reserved, diffident; unobtrusive, unostentatious, unpretentious, unaffected, natural, artless, ingenuous.
unattached ● adjective **1** *they were both unattached* SINGLE, unmarried, unwed, partnerless, uncommitted, available, footloose and fancy free, on one's own; on the shelf, unloved. **2** *we are unattached to any organization* UNAFFILIATED, unallied; autonomous, independent, non-aligned, self-governing, neutral, separate, unconnected, detached.
– OPPOSITES married.
unattended ● adjective **1** *his cries went unattended* IGNORED, disregarded, neglected, passed over. **2** *an unattended vehicle* UNGUARDED, unwatched, alone, solitary; abandoned. **3** *she had to walk there unattended* UNACCOMPANIED, unescorted, partnerless, unchaperoned, alone, on one's own, by oneself, solo; *informal* by one's lonesome; *Brit. informal* on one's tod, on one's Jack Jones; *Austral./NZ informal* on one's Pat Malone.
unattractive ● adjective PLAIN, ugly, ill-favoured, unappealing, unsightly, unlovely, unprepossessing, displeasing; hideous, monstrous, grotesque; *N. Amer.* homely; *informal* not much to look at, as ugly as sin; *Brit. informal* no oil painting.
– OPPOSITES beautiful.
unauthorized ● adjective UNOFFICIAL, unsanctioned, unaccredited, unlicensed, unwarranted, unapproved; disallowed, prohibited, banned, barred, forbidden, outlawed, illegal, illegitimate, illicit, proscribed.
– OPPOSITES official.
unavailing ● adjective INEFFECTIVE, ineffectual, inefficacious, vain, futile, useless, unsuccessful, fruitless, profitless, unprofitable, to no avail, abortive; *archaic* bootless.
– OPPOSITES effective.
unavoidable ● adjective INESCAPABLE, inevitable, inexorable, assured, certain, predestined, predetermined, ineluctable; necessary, compulsory, required, obligatory, mandatory.
unaware ● adjective IGNORANT, unknowing, unconscious, heedless, unmindful, oblivious, unsuspecting, uninformed, unenlightened, in the dark, unwitting, innocent; inattentive, unobservant, unperceptive, blind, deaf; *poetic/literary* nescient.
– OPPOSITES conscious.
unawares ● adverb **1** *brigands caught them unawares* BY SURPRISE, unexpectedly, without warning, suddenly, abruptly, unprepared, off-guard; *informal* with one's trousers down, napping; *Brit. informal* on the hop. **2** *the roach approached the pike unawares* UNKNOWINGLY, unwittingly, unconsciously; unintentionally, inadvertently, acci-

ranged. **3** (**unbalanced**) treating aspects of something unequally; partial.

unbearable ● adjective not able to be endured or tolerated.
– DERIVATIVES **unbearably** adverb.

unbeatable ● adjective **1** not able to be surpassed or defeated. **2** extremely good.

unbeaten ● adjective not defeated or surpassed.

unbecoming ● adjective **1** (especially of clothing) not flattering. **2** not fitting; unseemly.
– DERIVATIVES **unbecomingly** adverb.

unbeknown (also **unbeknownst**) ● adjective (**unbeknown to**) without the knowledge of.

unbelief ● noun lack of religious belief.
– DERIVATIVES **unbeliever** noun **unbelieving** adjective.

unbelievable ● adjective **1** unlikely to be true. **2** extraordinary.
– DERIVATIVES **unbelievably** adverb.

unbend ● verb (past and past part. **unbent**) **1** straighten. **2** become less reserved, formal, or strict.

unbending ● adjective austere and inflexible.

unbiased (also **unbiassed**) ● adjective showing no prejudice; impartial.

unbidden ● adjective **1** without having been invited. **2** arising without conscious effort.

unbleached ● adjective (especially of paper, cloth, or flour) not bleached.

unblock ● verb remove an obstruction from.

unblushing ● adjective not feeling or showing embarrassment or shame.
– DERIVATIVES **unblushingly** adverb.

unbolt ● verb open by drawing back a bolt.

unborn ● adjective (of a baby) not yet born.

unbosom ● verb archaic (**unbosom oneself**) disclose one's thoughts or secrets.

unbound ● adjective **1** not bound or restricted. **2** (of printed sheets) not bound together. **3** (of a bound book) not provided with a permanent cover.

unbounded ● adjective having no limits.

unbowed ● adjective not having submitted to pressure, demands, or accusations.

unbreakable ● adjective not liable to break or able to be broken.

unbreathable ● adjective (of air) not fit or pleasant to breathe.

unbridgeable ● adjective (of a gap or difference) not able to be bridged or made less significant.

unbridled ● adjective uncontrolled; unconstrained.

unbroken ● adjective **1** not broken; intact. **2** not interrupted. **3** not surpassed. **4** (of a horse) not broken in.

unbuckle ● verb unfasten the buckle of.

unbundle ● verb **1** market or charge for (items or services) separately rather than as part of a package. **2** split (a company or conglomerate) into its constituent businesses, especially prior to selling them off.

unburden ● verb **1** relieve of a burden. **2** (**unburden oneself**) be relieved of a cause of anxiety or distress through confiding in someone.

unburnt (also **unburned**) ● adjective not damaged or destroyed by fire.

unbutton ● verb **1** unfasten the buttons of. **2** informal relax and become less inhibited.

uncalled ● adjective **1** not summoned or invited. **2** (**uncalled for**) undesirable and unnecessary.

uncanny ● adjective (**uncannier**, **uncanniest**) strange or mysterious.
– DERIVATIVES **uncannily** adverb.

Thesaurus

dentally, by mistake.
– OPPOSITES prepared, knowingly.

unbalanced ● adjective **1** *he is unbalanced and dangerous* UNSTABLE, mentally ill, deranged, demented, disturbed, unhinged, insane, mad, out of one's mind, non compos mentis; *informal* crazy, loopy, loony, nuts, nutty, cracked, screwy, batty, dotty, cuckoo, bonkers, mental, off one's head, round the bend/twist; *Brit. informal* barmy, potty, crackers, barking, off one's rocker; *N. Amer. informal* nutso, squirrelly; *dated* touched. **2** *a most unbalanced article* BIASED, prejudiced, one-sided, partisan, inequitable, unjust, unfair, parti pris.
– OPPOSITES sane, unbiased.

unbearable ● adjective INTOLERABLE, insufferable, insupportable, unendurable, unacceptable, unmanageable, more than flesh and blood can stand, overpowering; *informal* too much.
– OPPOSITES tolerable.

unbeatable ● adjective INVINCIBLE, unstoppable, unassailable, indomitable, unconquerable, unsurpassable, matchless, peerless; supreme.

unbeaten ● adjective UNDEFEATED, unconquered, unsurpassed, unequalled, unrivalled; triumphant, victorious, supreme, matchless, second to none.

unbecoming ● adjective **1** *an unbecoming sundress* UNFLATTERING, unattractive, unsightly, plain, ugly, hideous; unsuitable. **2** *conduct unbecoming to the Senate* INAPPROPRIATE, unfitting, unbefitting, unsuitable, unsuited, inapt, out of keeping, untoward, incorrect, unacceptable; unworthy, improper, unseemly, undignified.
– OPPOSITES flattering, appropriate.

unbelief ● noun ATHEISM, non-belief, agnosticism, apostasy, irreligion, godlessness, nihilism; scepticism, cynicism, disbelief, doubt.
– OPPOSITES faith.

unbelievable ● adjective INCREDIBLE, beyond belief, inconceivable, unthinkable, unimaginable; unconvincing, far-fetched, implausible, improbable; *informal* hard to swallow.
– OPPOSITES credible.

unbend ● verb **1** *I couldn't unbend my knees* STRAIGHTEN (OUT), extend, flex, uncurl. **2** *if you'd only unbend a little* RELAX, unwind, de-stress, loosen up, let oneself go; *informal* let one's hair down, let it all hang out, hang loose.

unbending ● adjective **1** *an unbending man* ALOOF, formal, stiff, reserved, remote, forbidding, cool, unfeeling, unemotional, unfriendly, austere; *informal* uptight, stand-offish. **2** *unbending attitudes* UNCOMPROMISING, inflexible, unyielding, hard-line, tough, strict, firm, resolute, determined, unrelenting, relentless, inexorable, intransigent, immovable.

unbiased ● adjective IMPARTIAL, unprejudiced, neutral, non-partisan, disinterested, detached, dispassionate, objective, open-minded, equitable, even-handed, fair.
– OPPOSITES prejudiced.

unbidden ● adjective **1** *an unbidden guest* UNINVITED, unasked, unsolicited; unwanted, unwelcome. **2** *unbidden excitement* SPONTANEOUS, unprompted, voluntary, unforced, unplanned, unpremeditated; *informal* off-the-cuff.

unbind ● verb UNTIE, unchain, unfetter, unshackle, unfasten, untether, undo, loosen; release, free, liberate.

unblemished ● adjective IMPECCABLE, flawless, faultless, perfect, pure, whiter than white, clean, spotless, unsullied, unspoilt, undefiled, untouched, untarnished, unpolluted; incorrupt, guiltless, sinless, innocent, blameless; *informal* squeaky clean.
– OPPOSITES flawed.

unborn ● adjective **1** *your unborn child* EMBRYONIC, fetal, in utero; expected. **2** *the unborn generations* FUTURE, coming, forthcoming, subsequent.

unbounded ● adjective UNLIMITED, boundless, limitless, illimitable; unrestrained, unrestricted, unconstrained, uncontrolled, unchecked, unbridled; untold, immeasurable, endless, unending, interminable, everlasting, infinite, inexhaustible.
– OPPOSITES limited.

unbreakable ● adjective SHATTERPROOF, indestructible, imperishable, durable, long-lasting; toughened, sturdy, stout, resistant, hard-wearing, heavy-duty.
– OPPOSITES fragile.

unbridled ● adjective UNRESTRAINED, unconstrained, uncontrolled, uninhibited, unrestricted, unchecked, uncurbed, rampant, runaway, irrepressible, unstoppable, intemperate, immoderate.
– OPPOSITES restrained.

unbroken ● adjective **1** *the last unbroken window* UNDAMAGED, unimpaired, unharmed, unscathed, untouched, sound, intact, whole, perfect. **2** *an unbroken horse* UNTAMED, undomesticated, wild, feral. **3** *an unbroken chain of victories* UNINTERRUPTED, continuous, endless, constant, unremitting, ongoing. **4** *his record is still unbroken* UNBEATEN, undefeated, unsurpassed, unrivalled, unmatched, supreme.

unburden ● verb *she had a sudden wish to unburden herself* OPEN ONE'S HEART, confess, tell all; *informal* come clean; *archaic* unbosom oneself.

uncalled for ● adjective GRATUITOUS, unnecessary, needless, inessential; undeserved, unmerited, unwarranted, unjustified, unreasonable, unfair, inappropriate, pointless; unasked, unsolicited, unrequested, unprompted, unprovoked, unwelcome.

uncapped • adjective chiefly Brit. (of a player) never having been chosen as a member of a national sports team.
uncared • adjective (**uncared for**) not looked after properly.
uncaring • adjective **1** not displaying sympathy or concern for others. **2** not interested; unconcerned.
– DERIVATIVES **uncaringly** adverb.
unceasing • adjective not ceasing; continuous.
– DERIVATIVES **unceasingly** adverb.
unceremonious • adjective discourteous or abrupt.
– DERIVATIVES **unceremoniously** adverb.
uncertain • adjective **1** not known, reliable, or definite. **2** not completely confident or sure.
– PHRASES **in no uncertain terms** clearly and forcefully.
– DERIVATIVES **uncertainly** adverb.
uncertainty • noun (pl. **uncertainties**) **1** the state of being uncertain. **2** something that is uncertain or causes one to feel uncertain.
uncertainty principle • noun Physics the principle that the momentum and position of a particle cannot both be precisely determined at the same time.
unchallengeable • adjective not able to be disputed, opposed, or defeated.
unchallenged • adjective **1** not disputed, opposed, or defeated. **2** not called on to prove one's identity.
unchallenging • adjective not presenting a challenge.
unchangeable • adjective not liable to variation or able to be altered.
unchanged • adjective not changed; unaltered.
unchanging • adjective remaining the same.
– DERIVATIVES **unchangingly** adverb.
uncharacteristic • adjective not typical of a particular person or thing.
– DERIVATIVES **uncharacteristically** adverb.
uncharismatic • adjective lacking charisma.
uncharitable • adjective unkind or unsympathetic to others.
– DERIVATIVES **uncharitably** adverb.
uncharted • adjective (of an area of land or sea) not mapped or surveyed.
unchaste • adjective not chaste.
unchastened • adjective not restrained or demoralized by a reproof or misfortune.
unchecked • adjective (of something undesirable) not controlled or restrained.
unchivalrous • adjective (of a man) discourteous, especially towards women.
– DERIVATIVES **unchivalrously** adverb.
unchristian • adjective **1** not in accordance with the teachings of Christianity. **2** ungenerous or unfair.
uncial /unsiəl, unsh'l/ • adjective written in a majuscule script with rounded separated letters, which is found in manuscripts of the 4th–8th centuries and from which modern capital letters are derived. • noun an uncial letter, script, or manuscript.
– ORIGIN from Latin *unciales litterae* 'uncial letters', from *uncia* 'inch'; the connection is unclear.
uncircumcised • adjective (of a boy or man) not circumcised.
uncivil • adjective discourteous; impolite.
uncivilized (also **uncivilised**) • adjective **1** not socially or culturally advanced. **2** impolite; bad-mannered.
unclaimed • adjective not having been claimed.
unclasp • verb **1** unfasten (a clasp or similar device). **2** release the grip of.
unclassifiable • adjective not able to be classified.
unclassified • adjective not classified.
uncle • noun the brother of one's father or mother or the husband of one's aunt.
– ORIGIN Old French *oncle*, from Latin *avunculus* 'maternal uncle'.
unclean • adjective **1** dirty. **2** immoral. **3** (of food) regarded in a particular religion as impure and unfit for use or consumption. **4** (in biblical use, of a spirit) evil.
uncleanliness • noun the state of being dirty.
unclear • adjective **1** not easy to see, hear, or understand. **2** not obvious, definite, or certain.
uncleared • adjective **1** (of a cheque) not having passed through a clearing house and been paid into the payee's account. **2** (of land) not cleared of vegetation.
unclench • verb release (a clenched part of the body).
Uncle Sam • noun a personification of the federal government or citizens of the US.
– ORIGIN said to have arisen as a flippant expansion of the letters US.
Uncle Tom • noun derogatory, chiefly N. Amer. a black man considered to be excessively obedient or servile.
– ORIGIN the hero of H. B. Stowe's *Uncle Tom's Cabin* (1852).
unclimbed • adjective (of a mountain or rock face) not previously climbed.
– DERIVATIVES **unclimbable** adjective.
unclog • verb (**unclogged**, **unclogging**) remove accumulated matter from.
unclothed • adjective wearing no clothes; naked.

Thesaurus

uncanny • adjective **1** *the silence was uncanny* EERIE, unnatural, unearthly, other-worldly, ghostly, strange, abnormal, weird, bizarre, freakish; *Scottish* eldritch; *informal* creepy, spooky, freaky. **2** *an uncanny resemblance* STRIKING, remarkable, extraordinary, exceptional, incredible, noteworthy, notable, arresting.
unceasing • adjective INCESSANT, ceaseless, constant, continual, unabating, interminable, endless, unending, never-ending, everlasting, eternal, perpetual, continuous, non-stop, uninterrupted, unbroken, unremitting, persistent, relentless, unrelenting, unrelieved, sustained.
– OPPOSITES intermittent.
unceremonious • adjective **1** *an unceremonious dismissal* ABRUPT, sudden, hasty, hurried, summary, perfunctory, undignified; rude, impolite, discourteous, offhand. **2** *an unceremonious man* INFORMAL, casual, relaxed, easy-going, familiar, natural, open; *informal* laid-back.
– OPPOSITES formal.
uncertain • adjective **1** *the effects are uncertain* UNKNOWN, debatable, open to question, in doubt, undetermined, unsure, in the balance, up in the air; unpredictable, unforeseeable, incalculable; risky, chancy; *informal* iffy. **2** *uncertain weather* CHANGEABLE, variable, changeful, irregular, unpredictable, unreliable, unsettled, erratic, fluctuating. **3** *Ed was uncertain about the decision* UNSURE, doubtful, dubious, undecided, irresolute, hesitant, blowing hot and cold, vacillating, vague, unclear, ambivalent, in two minds. **4** *an uncertain smile* HESITANT, tentative, faltering, unsure, unconfident.
– OPPOSITES predictable, sure, confident.
unchangeable • adjective UNALTERABLE, immutable, invariable, changeless, fixed, hard and fast, cast-iron, set in stone, established, permanent, enduring, abiding, lasting, indestructible, ineradicable, irreversible.
– OPPOSITES variable.
unchanging • adjective CONSISTENT, constant, regular, unvarying, predictable, stable, steady, fixed, permanent, perpetual, eternal; sustained, lasting, persistent.
uncharitable • adjective MEAN, mean-spirited, unkind, selfish, self-centred, inconsiderate, thoughtless, insensitive, unfriendly, unsympathetic, uncaring, ungenerous, ungracious, unfair.
uncharted • adjective UNEXPLORED, unmapped, untravelled, undiscovered, unplumbed, unfamiliar, unknown.
uncivil • adjective IMPOLITE, rude, discourteous, disrespectful, unmannerly, bad-mannered, impertinent, impudent, ungracious; brusque, sharp, curt, offhand, gruff, churlish; *informal* off, fresh.
– OPPOSITES polite.
uncivilized • adjective UNCOUTH, coarse, rough, boorish, vulgar, philistine, uneducated, uncultured, uncultivated, benighted, unsophisticated, unpolished; ill-bred, ill-mannered, thuggish, loutish; barbarian, primitive, savage, brutish; *archaic* rude.
unclean • adjective **1** *unclean premises* DIRTY, filthy, grubby, grimy, mucky, foul, impure, tainted, soiled, unwashed; polluted, contaminated, infected, insanitary, unhygienic, unhealthy, germy, disease-ridden; *informal* yucky, cruddy; *Brit. informal* grotty, gungy. **2** *sex was considered unclean* SINFUL, immoral, bad, wicked, evil, corrupt, impure, unwholesome, sordid, disgusting, debased, degenerate, depraved. **3** *an unclean meat* IMPURE; forbidden, taboo.
– OPPOSITES pure, halal, kosher.
unclear • adjective UNCERTAIN, unsure, unsettled, up in the air, debatable, open to question, in doubt, doubtful; ambiguous, equivocal, indefinite, vague, mysterious, obscure, hazy, foggy, nebulous; *informal* iffy.
– OPPOSITES evident.
unclothed • adjective NAKED, bare, nude, stripped, undressed, in a state of nature; *informal* in one's birthday suit, in the buff, in the

u

unclouded ● adjective **1** (of the sky) not dark or overcast. **2** not troubled or spoiled by anything.
uncluttered ● adjective not cluttered by too many objects or elements.
uncoil ● verb straighten from a coiled or curled position.
uncoloured (US **uncolored**) ● adjective **1** having no colour. **2** not influenced.
uncombed ● adjective (of a person's hair) not combed.
uncomfortable ● adjective **1** not physically comfortable. **2** uneasy or awkward.
– DERIVATIVES **uncomfortably** adverb.
uncommercial ● adjective not making, intended to make, or allowing a profit.
uncommon ● adjective **1** out of the ordinary; unusual. **2** remarkably great.
– DERIVATIVES **uncommonly** adverb.
uncommunicative ● adjective unwilling to talk or give out information.
uncompetitive ● adjective not competitive or marked by fair competition.
uncomplaining ● adjective not complaining; stoical.
– DERIVATIVES **uncomplainingly** adverb.
uncomplicated ● adjective simple or straightforward.
uncomplimentary ● adjective not complimentary; negative or insulting.
uncomprehending ● adjective unable to comprehend something.
– DERIVATIVES **uncomprehendingly** adverb.
uncompromising ● adjective **1** unwilling to make concessions; resolute. **2** harsh or relentless.
– DERIVATIVES **uncompromisingly** adverb.
unconcealed ● adjective (especially of an emotion) not concealed; obvious.
unconcern ● noun a lack of worry or interest.
– DERIVATIVES **unconcerned** adjective **unconcernedly** adverb.
unconditional ● adjective not subject to any conditions.
– DERIVATIVES **unconditionally** adverb.
unconditioned ● adjective **1** unconditional. **2** relating to instinctive behaviour not formed or influenced by conditioning or learning. **3** not subjected to a conditioning process.
unconfident ● adjective not confident; hesitant.
unconfined ● adjective **1** not confined to a limited space. **2** (of joy or excitement) very great.
unconfirmed ● adjective not confirmed as to truth or validity.
uncongenial ● adjective **1** not friendly or pleasant to be with. **2** unsuitable and therefore unlikely to promote success or well-being.
unconnected ● adjective **1** not joined together or to something else. **2** not associated or linked in a sequence.
unconquerable ● adjective not conquerable.
– DERIVATIVES **unconquered** adjective.
unconscionable /unkonshənəb'l/ ● adjective not right or reasonable.
– DERIVATIVES **unconscionably** adverb.
– ORIGIN from obsolete *conscionable* 'conscientious'.
unconscious ● adjective **1** not awake and aware of and responding to one's environment. **2** done or existing without one realizing. **3** (**unconscious of**) unaware of. ● noun (**the unconscious**) the part of the mind which is inaccessible to the conscious mind but which affects behaviour and emotions.
– DERIVATIVES **unconsciously** adverb **unconsciousness** noun.
unconsecrated ● adjective not consecrated.
unconsidered ● adjective **1** disregarded and unappreciated. **2** not thought about in advance; rash.
unconsolable ● adjective inconsolable.
– DERIVATIVES **unconsolably** adverb.
unconstitutional ● adjective not in accordance with the political constitution or with procedural rules.
– DERIVATIVES **unconstitutionally** adverb.
unconstrained ● adjective not restricted or limited.
unconsummated ● adjective (of a marriage) not having been consummated.

Thesaurus

raw, in the altogether, in the nuddy; *Brit. informal* starkers; *Scottish informal* in the scud; *N. Amer. informal* buck naked.
– OPPOSITES dressed.
uncomfortable ● adjective **1** *an uncomfortable chair* PAINFUL, disagreeable, intolerable, unbearable, confining, cramped. **2** *I felt uncomfortable in her presence* UNEASY, awkward, nervous, tense, strained, edgy, restless, embarrassed, troubled, worried, anxious, unquiet, fraught; *informal* rattled, twitchy; *N. Amer. informal* discombobulated, antsy.
– OPPOSITES relaxed.
uncommitted ● adjective **1** *uncommitted voters* FLOATING, undecided, non-partisan, unaffiliated, neutral, impartial, independent, undeclared, uncertain; *informal* sitting on the fence. **2** *the uncommitted male* UNMARRIED, unattached, unwed, partnerless; footloose and fancy free, available, single, lone.
– OPPOSITES aligned, attached.
uncommon ● adjective **1** *an uncommon plant* UNUSUAL, abnormal, rare, atypical, unconventional, unfamiliar, strange, odd, curious, extraordinary, outlandish, novel, singular, peculiar, queer, bizarre; alien; *informal* weird, oddball, offbeat. **2** *abductions are uncommon* RARE, scarce, few and far between, exceptional, abnormal, isolated, infrequent, irregular; *Brit.* out of the common. **3** *an uncommon capacity for hard work* REMARKABLE, extraordinary, exceptional, singular, particular, marked, outstanding, noteworthy, significant, especial, special, signal, superior, unique, unparalleled, prodigious; *informal* mind-boggling.
uncommonly ● adverb UNUSUALLY, remarkably, extraordinarily, exceptionally, singularly, particularly, especially, decidedly, notably, eminently, extremely, very; *N. English* right; *informal* awfully, terribly, seriously; *Brit. informal* jolly, dead.
uncommunicative ● adjective TACITURN, quiet, unforthcoming, reserved, reticent, laconic, tongue-tied, mute, silent, tight-lipped; guarded, secretive, close, private; distant, remote, aloof, withdrawn, unsociable; *informal* mum, stand-offish.
– OPPOSITES talkative.
uncomplicated ● adjective SIMPLE, straightforward, clear, accessible, undemanding, unchallenging, unsophisticated, trouble-free, painless, effortless, easy, elementary, idiot-proof, plain sailing; *informal* a piece of cake, child's play, a cinch, a doddle, a breeze; *Brit. informal* easy-peasy.
– OPPOSITES complex.
uncompromising ● adjective INFLEXIBLE, unbending, unyielding, unshakeable, resolute, rigid, hard-line, immovable, intractable, firm, determined, iron-willed, obstinate, stubborn, adamant, obdurate, intransigent, headstrong, pig-headed; *Brit. informal* bloody-minded.
– OPPOSITES flexible.
unconcerned ● adjective **1** *he is unconcerned about their responses* INDIFFERENT, unmoved, apathetic, uninterested, incurious, dispassionate, heedless, unmindful; cool, lukewarm, unenthusiastic. **2** *she tried to look unconcerned* UNTROUBLED, unworried, unruffled, insouciant, nonchalant, blasé, carefree, casual, relaxed, at ease, {cool, calm, and collected}; *informal* laid-back.
– OPPOSITES interested, anxious.
unconditional ● adjective UNQUESTIONING, unqualified, unreserved, unlimited, unrestricted, wholehearted; complete, total, entire, full, absolute, out-and-out, unequivocal.
unconnected ● adjective **1** *the earth wire was unconnected* DETACHED, disconnected, loose. **2** *unconnected tasks* UNRELATED, dissociated, separate, independent, distinct, different, disparate, discrete. **3** *unconnected chains of thought* DISJOINTED, incoherent, disconnected, rambling, wandering, diffuse, disorderly, haphazard, disorganized, garbled, mixed, muddled, aimless.
– OPPOSITES attached, related, coherent.
unconscionable ● adjective **1** *the unconscionable use of test animals* UNETHICAL, amoral, immoral, unprincipled, indefensible, wrong; unscrupulous, unfair, underhand, dishonourable. **2** *we had to wait an unconscionable time* EXCESSIVE, unreasonable, unwarranted, uncalled for, unfair, inordinate, immoderate, undue, inexcusable, unnecessary, needless; *informal* over the top, OTT.
– OPPOSITES ethical, acceptable.
unconscious ● adjective **1** *she made sure he was unconscious* INSENSIBLE, senseless, insentient, insensate, comatose, inert, knocked out, stunned; motionless, immobile, prostrate; *informal* out cold, out for the count, dead to the world; *Brit. informal* spark out. **2** *she was unconscious of the pain* HEEDLESS, unmindful, disregarding, oblivious to, insensible to, impervious to, unaffected by, unconcerned by, indifferent to; unaware, unknowing. **3** *an unconscious desire* SUBCONSCIOUS, latent, suppressed, subliminal, sleeping, inherent, instinctive, involuntary, uncontrolled, spontaneous; unintentional, unthinking, unwitting, inadvertent; *informal* gut.

uncontainable ● adjective (especially of an emotion) very strong.
uncontaminated ● adjective not contaminated.
uncontentious ● adjective not contentious.
uncontested ● adjective not contested.
uncontrived ● adjective not artificially created.
uncontrollable ● adjective not controllable.
– DERIVATIVES **uncontrollably** adverb.
uncontrolled ● adjective not controlled.
uncontroversial ● adjective not controversial; avoiding controversy.
– DERIVATIVES **uncontroversially** adverb.
unconventional ● adjective not based on or conforming to what is generally done or believed.
– DERIVATIVES **unconventionality** noun **unconventionally** adverb.
unconvinced ● adjective not certain that something is true or can be relied on.
unconvincing ● adjective failing to convince or impress.
– DERIVATIVES **unconvincingly** adverb.
uncooked ● adjective not cooked; raw.
uncool ● adjective informal not fashionable or impressive.
uncooperative ● adjective unwilling to help others or do what they ask.
uncoordinated ● adjective **1** badly organized. **2** clumsy.
uncork ● verb pull the cork out of.
uncorroborated ● adjective not supported or confirmed by evidence.
uncountable ● adjective too many to be counted.
uncounted ● adjective **1** not counted. **2** very numerous.
uncouple ● verb disconnect or become disconnected.
uncouth ● adjective lacking good manners, refinement, or grace.
– ORIGIN Old English, 'unknown'.
uncover ● verb **1** remove a cover or covering from. **2** discover (something previously secret or unknown).
uncritical ● adjective not expressing criticism or using one's critical faculties.
– DERIVATIVES **uncritically** adverb.
uncross ● verb **1** move (something) back from a crossed position. **2** (**uncrossed**) Brit. (of a cheque) not crossed.
uncrowded ● adjective not crowded.
uncrowned ● adjective not formally crowned as a monarch.
unction /ungksh'n/ ● noun **1** formal the anointing of someone with oil or ointment as a religious rite or as a symbol of investiture as a monarch. **2** excessive or ingratiating politeness or effusiveness.
– ORIGIN Latin, from *unguere* 'anoint'.
unctuous /ungktyooəss/ ● adjective excessively flattering or ingratiating.
– DERIVATIVES **unctuously** adverb **unctuousness** noun.
uncultivated ● adjective **1** (of land) not used for growing crops. **2** not highly educated.
uncultured ● adjective not characterized by good taste, manners, or education.
uncured ● adjective not preserved by salting, drying, or smoking.
uncurl ● verb straighten from a curled position.
uncut ● adjective not cut.
undamaged ● adjective not harmed or damaged.
undated ● adjective not provided or marked with a date.
undaunted ● adjective not intimidated or discouraged by difficulty, danger, or disappointment.
undead ● adjective (of a fictional being) technically dead but still animate.
undecagon /undekkəgən/ ● noun another term for HENDECAGON.
– ORIGIN from Latin *undecim* 'eleven'.
undeceive ● verb tell (someone) that an idea or belief is mistaken.
undecided ● adjective **1** not having made a decision; uncertain. **2** not settled or resolved.
– DERIVATIVES **undecidedly** adverb.
undecipherable ● adjective (of speech or writing) not able to be read or understood.
undefeated ● adjective not defeated.
undefended ● adjective not defended.
undefined ● adjective not clear or defined.
– DERIVATIVES **undefinable** adjective.
undemanding ● adjective (especially of a task) not demanding.
undemocratic ● adjective not relating or according to democratic principles.
– DERIVATIVES **undemocratically** adverb.
undemonstrative ● adjective not tending to express feelings openly.

Thesaurus

– OPPOSITES aware, voluntary.
● noun *fantasies raging in the unconscious* SUBCONSCIOUS, psyche, ego, id, inner self.
uncontrollable ● adjective **1** *the crowds were uncontrollable* UNMANAGEABLE, out of control, ungovernable, wild, unruly, disorderly, recalcitrant, turbulent, disobedient, delinquent, defiant, undisciplined; formal refractory. **2** *an uncontrollable rage* UNGOVERNABLE, irrepressible, unstoppable, unquenchable; wild, violent, frenzied, furious, mad, hysterical, passionate.
– OPPOSITES compliant.
unconventional ● adjective UNUSUAL, irregular, unorthodox, unfamiliar, uncommon, unwonted, out of the ordinary, atypical, singular, alternative, different; new, novel, innovative, groundbreaking, pioneering, original, unprecedented; eccentric, idiosyncratic, quirky, odd, strange, bizarre, weird, outlandish, curious; abnormal, anomalous, aberrant, extraordinary; nonconformist, bohemian, avant-garde; informal way out, far out, offbeat, wacky, madcap, zany, hippy; Brit. informal rum; N. Amer. informal kooky, wacko.
– OPPOSITES orthodox.
unconvincing ● adjective IMPROBABLE, unlikely, implausible, incredible, unbelievable, questionable, dubious, doubtful; strained, laboured, far-fetched, unrealistic, fanciful, fantastic; feeble, weak, transparent, poor, lame, ineffectual, half-baked; informal hard to swallow.
– OPPOSITES persuasive.
uncooperative ● adjective UNHELPFUL, awkward, disobliging, recalcitrant, perverse, contrary, stubborn, wilful, stiff-necked, unyielding, unbending, inflexible, immovable, obstructive, difficult, obstreperous, disobedient; Brit. informal bloody-minded.
– OPPOSITES obliging.
uncoordinated ● adjective CLUMSY, awkward, blundering, bumbling, lumbering, flat-footed, heavy-handed, graceless, gawky, ungainly, ungraceful; inept, unhandy, unskilful, inexpert, maladroit, bungling; informal butterfingered, cack-handed, ham-fisted; Brit. informal all (fingers and) thumbs; N. Amer. informal klutzy.

u

– OPPOSITES dexterous.
uncouth ● adjective UNCIVILIZED, uncultured, uncultivated, unrefined, unpolished, unsophisticated, common, low, rough, coarse, crude, loutish, boorish, oafish; churlish, uncivil, rude, impolite, discourteous, disrespectful, unmannerly, bad-mannered, ill-bred, indecorous, vulgar, crass, indelicate; Brit. informal yobbish.
– OPPOSITES refined.
uncover ● verb **1** *she uncovered the sandwiches* EXPOSE, reveal, lay bare; unwrap, unveil; strip, denude. **2** *they uncovered a money-laundering plot* DETECT, discover, come across, stumble on, chance on, find, turn up, unearth, dig up; expose, bring to light, unmask, unveil, reveal, lay bare, make known, make public, betray, give away; informal blow the whistle on, pull the plug on.
unctuous ● adjective SYCOPHANTIC, ingratiating, obsequious, fawning, servile, grovelling, subservient, cringing, humble, hypocritical, insincere, gushing, effusive; glib, smooth, slick, slippery, oily, greasy; informal smarmy, slimy, sucky, soapy.
undaunted ● adjective UNAFRAID, undismayed, unflinching, unshrinking, unabashed, fearless, dauntless, intrepid, bold, valiant, brave, courageous, plucky, mettlesome, gritty, indomitable, confident, audacious, daring; informal gutsy, spunky.
– OPPOSITES fearful.
undecided ● adjective UNRESOLVED, uncertain, unsure, unclear, unsettled, indefinite, undetermined, unknown, in the balance, up in the air, debatable, arguable, moot, open to question, doubtful, dubious, borderline, ambiguous, vague; indecisive, irresolute, hesitant, tentative, wavering, vacillating, uncommitted, ambivalent, in two minds; informal iffy.
– OPPOSITES certain.
undefined ● adjective **1** *some matters are still undefined* UNSPECIFIED, unexplained, unspecific, indeterminate, unsettled; unclear, woolly, imprecise, inexact, indefinite, vague. **2** *undefined shapes* INDISTINCT, indefinite, formless, indistinguishable, vague, hazy, misty, shadowy, nebulous, blurred, blurry.
– OPPOSITES definite, distinct.
undemonstrative ● adjective UNEMOTIONAL, unaffectionate, impas-

undeniable ● adjective unable to be denied or disputed.
– DERIVATIVES **undeniably** adverb.

under ● preposition **1** extending or directly below. **2** below or behind (something covering or protecting). **3** at a lower level, layer, or grade than. **4** lower than (a specified amount, rate, or norm). **5** expressing submission or subordination. **6** as provided for by the rules of; in accordance with. **7** used to express grouping or classification. **8** undergoing (a process). ● adverb **1** extending or directly below something. **2** affected by an anaesthetic; unconscious.
– PHRASES **under way 1** (of a boat) moving through the water. **2** having started and making progress.
– ORIGIN Old English.

under- ● prefix **1** below; beneath: *undercover*. **2** lower in status; subordinate: *undersecretary*. **3** insufficiently; incompletely: *undernourished*.

underachieve ● verb do less well than is expected.
– DERIVATIVES **underachievement** noun **underachiever** noun.

under age ● adjective too young to engage legally in a particular activity.

underarm ● adjective & adverb (of a throw or stroke in sport) made with the arm or hand below shoulder level. ● noun a person's armpit.

underbelly ● noun (pl. **underbellies**) **1** the soft underside or abdomen of an animal, especially vulnerable to attack. **2** a hidden unpleasant or criminal part of society.

underbid ● verb (**underbidding**; past and past part. **underbid**) (in an auction) make a bid lower than another.

underbite ● noun the projection of the lower teeth beyond the upper.

underbrush ● noun N. Amer. undergrowth in a forest.

undercarriage ● noun **1** a wheeled structure beneath an aircraft which supports the aircraft on the ground. **2** the supporting frame under the body of a vehicle.

undercharge ● verb charge (someone) a price or amount that is too low.

underclass ● noun the lowest social class in a country or community, consisting of the poor and unemployed.

undercliff ● noun a terrace or lower cliff formed by a landslip.

underclothes ● plural noun clothes worn under others next to the skin.
– DERIVATIVES **underclothing** noun.

undercoat ● noun **1** a layer of paint applied after the primer and before the topcoat. **2** an animal's under layer of fur or down.

undercook ● verb cook insufficiently.

undercover ● adjective & adverb involving secret work for investigation or espionage.

undercroft ● noun the crypt of a church.
– ORIGIN from the rare term *croft* 'crypt', from Latin *crypta* in the same sense.

undercurrent ● noun **1** a current of water below the surface and moving in a different direction from any surface current. **2** an underlying feeling or influence.

undercut ● verb (**undercutting**; past and past part. **undercut**) **1** offer goods or services at a lower price than (a competitor). **2** cut or wear away the part under. **3** weaken; undermine. ● noun **1** a space formed by the removal or absence of material from the lower part of something. **2** Brit. the underside of a sirloin of beef.

underdeveloped ● adjective **1** not fully developed. **2** (of a country or region) not advanced economically.
– DERIVATIVES **underdevelopment** noun.

underdog ● noun a competitor thought to have little chance of winning a fight or contest.

underdone ● adjective (of food) insufficiently cooked.

underdress ● verb (also **be underdressed**) dress too plainly or too informally for a particular occasion.

underemphasize (also **underemphasise**) ● verb place insufficient emphasis on.

underemployed ● adjective not having sufficient or sufficiently demanding paid work.
– DERIVATIVES **underemployment** noun.

underestimate ● verb **1** estimate (something) to be smaller or less important than it really is. **2** regard (someone) as less capable than they really are. ● noun an estimate that is too low.
– DERIVATIVES **underestimation** noun.

underexpose ● verb Photography expose (film) for too short a time.
– DERIVATIVES **underexposure** noun.

underfed ● adjective insufficiently fed or nourished.

underfelt ● noun Brit. felt laid under a carpet for protection or support.

underflow ● noun an undercurrent.

underfoot ● adverb **1** under one's feet; on the ground. **2** constantly present and in one's way.

underfund ● verb provide with insufficient funding.
– DERIVATIVES **underfunding** noun.

undergarment ● noun an article of underclothing.

underglaze ● noun colour or decoration applied to pottery before the glaze is applied.

undergo ● verb (**undergoes**; past **underwent**; past part. **undergone**) experience or be subjected to (something unpleasant or arduous).
– ORIGIN Old English, 'undermine'.

undergrad ● noun informal an undergraduate.

undergraduate ● noun a student at a university who has not yet taken a first degree.

underground ● adjective & adverb **1** beneath the surface of the ground. **2** in secrecy or hiding. **3** favouring alternative forms of lifestyle or artistic expression; radical and experimental. ● noun **1** Brit. an underground railway. **2** a group or movement organized secretly to work against an existing regime.

undergrowth ● noun a dense growth of shrubs and other

Thesaurus

sive, dispassionate, restrained, reserved, unresponsive, uncommunicative, unforthcoming, stiff, guarded, aloof, distant, detached, remote, withdrawn; cool, cold, frosty, frigid; *informal* standoffish.

undeniable ● adjective INDISPUTABLE, indubitable, unquestionable, beyond doubt, beyond question, undebatable, incontrovertible, incontestable, irrefutable, unassailable; certain, sure, definite, positive, conclusive, plain, obvious, unmistakable, self-evident, patent, emphatic, categorical, unequivocal.
– OPPOSITES questionable.

under ● preposition **1** *they hid under a bush* BENEATH, below, underneath. **2** *the rent is under £250* LESS THAN, lower than, below. **3** *branch managers are under the retail director* SUBORDINATE TO, junior to, inferior to, subservient to, answerable to, responsible to, subject to, controlled by. **4** *forty homes are under construction* UNDERGOING, in the process of. **5** *the town was under water* FLOODED BY, immersed in, submerged by, sunk in, engulfed by, inundated by. **6** *our finances are under pressure* SUBJECT TO, liable to, at the mercy of.
– OPPOSITES above, over.
● adverb *coughing and spluttering she went under* DOWN, lower, below, underneath, beneath; underwater.

underclothes ● plural noun UNDERWEAR, undergarments, underclothing, lingerie, underthings; *informal* undies, frillies; *Brit. informal* smalls; *archaic* underlinen.

undercover ● adjective COVERT, secret, clandestine, underground, surreptitious, furtive, cloak-and-dagger, hole-and-corner, hugger-mugger, stealthy, hidden, concealed; *informal* hush-hush, sneaky.
– OPPOSITES overt.

undercurrent ● noun **1** *dangerous undercurrents in the cove* UNDERTOW, underflow, underswell, underset. **2** *the undercurrent of despair in his words* UNDERTONE, overtone, suggestion, connotation, intimation, hint, nuance, trace, suspicion, whisper, tinge; feeling, atmosphere, aura, echo; *informal* vibes.

undercut ● verb **1** *the firm undercut their rivals* CHARGE LESS THAN, undersell, underbid. **2** *his authority was being undercut* UNDERMINE, weaken, impair, sap, threaten, subvert, sabotage, ruin, destabilize, wreck.

underdog ● noun WEAKER PARTY, victim, loser, scapegoat; *informal* little guy, fall guy, stooge.

underestimate ● verb UNDERRATE, undervalue, do an injustice to, be wrong about, sell short, play down, understate; minimize, de-emphasize, underemphasize, diminish, downgrade, gloss over, trivialize; miscalculate, misjudge, misconstrue, misread.
– OPPOSITES exaggerate.

undergo ● verb GO THROUGH, experience, undertake, face, submit to, be subjected to, come in for, receive, sustain, endure, brave, bear, tolerate, stand, withstand, weather; *Brit. informal* wear.

underground ● adjective **1** *an underground car park* SUBTERRANEAN, buried, sunken, basement. **2** *underground organizations*

plants.

underhand (also **underhanded**) • adjective **1** acting or done in a secret or dishonest way. **2** underarm.

underlay[1] • verb (past and past part. **underlaid**) place something under (something else), especially to support or raise it. • noun material laid under a carpet for protection or support.

underlay[2] past tense of UNDERLIE.

underlie • verb (**underlying**; past **underlay**; past part. **underlain**) lie or be situated under.
– DERIVATIVES **underlying** adjective.

underline • verb **1** draw a line under (a word or phrase) to give emphasis or indicate special type. **2** emphasize. • noun a line drawn under a word or phrase.

underling • noun chiefly derogatory a subordinate.

underlip • noun the lower lip of a person or animal.

underlying present participle of UNDERLIE.

underman • verb (**undermanned**, **undermanning**) fail to provide with enough workers or crew.

undermine • verb **1** erode the base or foundation of (a rock formation). **2** dig or excavate beneath (a building or fortification) so as to make it collapse. **3** weaken gradually or insidiously.

underneath • preposition & adverb **1** situated directly below. **2** so as to be partly or wholly concealed by. • noun the part or side facing towards the ground; the underside.
– ORIGIN Old English.

undernourished • adjective having insufficient food for good health and condition.
– DERIVATIVES **undernourishment** noun.

underpaid past and past participle of UNDERPAY.

underpants • plural noun an undergarment covering the lower part of the body and having two holes for the legs.

underpart • noun a lower part or portion.

underpass • noun a road or pedestrian tunnel passing under another road or a railway.

underpay • verb (past and past part. **underpaid**) pay too little to (someone) or for (something).

underperform • verb perform less well than expected.
– DERIVATIVES **underperformance** noun.

underpin • verb (**underpinned**, **underpinning**) **1** support (a structure) from below by laying a solid foundation or substituting stronger for weaker materials. **2** support, justify, or form the basis for.

underplay • verb **1** perform (a role or part) in a restrained way. **2** represent (something) as being less important than it really is.

underpopulated • adjective having an insufficient or very small population.

underpowered • adjective lacking sufficient mechanical, electrical, or other power.

underprice • verb sell or offer at too low a price.

underprivileged • adjective not enjoying the same rights or standard of living as the majority of the population.

underrate • verb underestimate the extent, value, or importance of.
– DERIVATIVES **underrated** adjective.

under-represent • verb provide with insufficient or inadequate representation.

under-resourced • adjective provided with insufficient resources.

underscore • verb & noun another term for UNDERLINE.

undersea • adjective relating to or situated below the sea or the surface of the sea.

undersecretary • noun (pl. **undersecretaries**) **1** (in the UK) a junior minister or senior civil servant. **2** (in the US) the principal assistant to a member of the cabinet.

undersell • verb (past and past part. **undersold**) **1** sell something at a lower price than (a competitor). **2** promote or rate insufficiently.

undershirt • noun chiefly N. Amer. an undergarment worn under a shirt; a vest.

undershoot • verb (past and past part. **undershot**) **1** (of an aircraft) land short of (the runway). **2** fall short of (a point or target).

underside • noun the bottom or lower side or surface of something.

undersigned • noun (**the undersigned**) formal the person or people who have signed the document in question.

undersized (also **undersize**) • adjective of less than the usual size.

underskirt • noun a petticoat.

undersold past and past participle of UNDERSELL.

underspend • verb (past and past part. **underspent**) spend too little or less than has been planned. • noun an act of underspending.

understaff • verb provide (an organization) with too few members of staff to operate effectively.
– DERIVATIVES **understaffing** noun.

understand • verb (past and past part. **understood**) **1** perceive the intended meaning of (words, a language, or a speaker). **2** perceive the significance, explanation, or cause of. **3** interpret or view in a particular way. **4** infer from information received. **5** assume that (something) is present or is the case.

Thesaurus

CLANDESTINE, secret, surreptitious, covert, undercover, closet, hole-and-corner, cloak-and-dagger, hugger-mugger, back-alley, hidden, sneaky, furtive; resistance, subversive; *informal* hush-hush. **3** *the underground art scene* ALTERNATIVE, radical, revolutionary, unconventional, unorthodox, avant-garde, experimental, innovative.

• adverb **1** *the insects live underground* BELOW GROUND, in the earth. **2** *the rebels went underground* INTO HIDING, into seclusion, undercover.

• noun **1** *he took the underground* UNDERGROUND RAILWAY, metro; *N. Amer.* subway; *Brit. informal* tube. **2** *information from the French underground* RESISTANCE (MOVEMENT); partisans, guerrillas, freedom fighters; *historical* Maquis.

U

undergrowth • noun SHRUBBERY, vegetation, greenery, ground cover, underwood, brushwood, brush, scrub, covert, thicket, copse; bushes, plants, brambles, herbage; *N. Amer.* underbrush.

underhand • adjective DECEITFUL, dishonest, dishonourable, disreputable, unethical, unprincipled, immoral, unscrupulous, fraudulent, dubious, unfair; treacherous, duplicitous, double-dealing; devious, artful, crafty, conniving, scheming, sly, wily; clandestine, sneaky, furtive, covert, cloak-and-dagger; *N. Amer.* snide; *informal* crooked, shady, bent, low-down; *Brit. informal* dodgy; *Austral./NZ informal* shonky.
– OPPOSITES honest.

underline • verb **1** *she underlined a phrase* UNDERSCORE, mark, pick out, emphasize, highlight. **2** *the programme underlines the benefits of exercise* EMPHASIZE, stress, highlight, accentuate, accent, focus on, spotlight, point up, play up; *informal* rub in.

underling • noun SUBORDINATE, inferior, junior, minion, lackey, flunkey, menial, retainer, vassal, subject, hireling, servant, henchman, factotum; *informal* dogsbody, gofer; *Brit. informal* skivvy.
– OPPOSITES boss.

underlying • adjective **1** *the underlying aims of the research* FUNDAMENTAL, basic, primary, prime, central, principal, chief, key, elementary, intrinsic, essential. **2** *an underlying feeling of irritation* LATENT, repressed, suppressed, unrevealed, undisclosed, unexpressed, concealed, hidden, masked.

undermine • verb **1** *their integrity is being undermined* SUBVERT, sabotage, threaten, weaken, compromise, diminish, reduce, impair, mar, spoil, ruin, damage, hurt, injure, cripple, sap, shake; *informal* drag through the mud. **2** *we undermined the building* TUNNEL UNDER, dig under, burrow under, sap. **3** *the damp had so undermined the wall that it collapsed* ERODE, wear away, eat away at.
– OPPOSITES strengthen, support.

underprivileged • adjective NEEDY, deprived, disadvantaged, poor, destitute, in straitened circumstances, impoverished, poverty-stricken, indigent; *Brit.* on the breadline; *informal* on one's uppers, on one's beam-ends; *formal* penurious.
– OPPOSITES wealthy.

underrate • verb UNDERVALUE, underestimate, do an injustice to, sell short, play down, understate, minimize, diminish, downgrade, trivialize.
– OPPOSITES exaggerate.

undersized • adjective UNDERDEVELOPED, stunted, small, short, little, tiny, petite, slight, compact, miniature, mini, diminutive, dwarfish, pygmy; *Scottish* wee; *informal* pint-sized, pocket-sized, knee-high to a grasshopper, baby, teeny-weeny, itsy-bitsy.
– OPPOSITES overgrown.

understand • verb **1** *he couldn't understand anything we said* COMPREHEND, grasp, take in, see, apprehend, follow, make sense of, fathom; unravel, decipher, interpret; *informal* work out, figure out, make head or tail of, get one's head around, take on board, get

understandable • adjective **1** able to be understood. **2** to be expected; natural, reasonable, or forgivable.
– DERIVATIVES **understandably** adverb.
understanding • noun **1** the ability to understand something. **2** the power of abstract thought; intellect. **3** an individual's perception or judgement of a situation. **4** sympathetic awareness or tolerance. **5** an informal or unspoken agreement or arrangement. • adjective sympathetically aware of other people's feelings.
– DERIVATIVES **understandingly** adverb.
understate • verb describe or represent (something) as being smaller or less significant than it really is.
– DERIVATIVES **understatement** noun.
understated • adjective presented or expressed in a subtle and effective way.
– DERIVATIVES **understatedly** adverb.
understeer • verb (of a motor vehicle) have a tendency to turn less sharply than is intended.
understood past and past participle of UNDERSTAND.
understorey • noun (pl. **understoreys**) Ecology a layer of vegetation beneath the main canopy of a forest.
understudy • noun (pl. **understudies**) an actor who learns another's role in order to be able to act in their absence. • verb (**understudies**, **understudied**) study (a role or actor) as an understudy.
undersubscribed • adjective (of a course or event) having more places available than applications.
undertake • verb (past **undertook**; past part. **undertaken**) **1** commit oneself to and begin (an enterprise or responsibility); take on. **2** formally guarantee or promise.
undertaker • noun a person whose business is preparing dead bodies for burial or cremation and making arrangements for funerals.
undertaking • noun **1** a formal pledge or promise to do something. **2** a task that is taken on; an enterprise. **3** the management of funerals as a profession.
undertone • noun **1** a subdued or muted tone of sound or colour. **2** an underlying quality or feeling.
undertow • noun another term for UNDERCURRENT.
underuse • verb /undəryo͞oz/ use (something) below the optimum level. • noun /undəryo͞oss/ insufficient use.
– DERIVATIVES **underused** adjective.
underutilize (also **underutilise**) • verb underuse.
undervalue • verb (**undervalues**, **undervalued**, **undervaluing**) **1** rate insufficiently highly; fail to appreciate. **2** underestimate the financial value of.
underwater • adjective & adverb situated or occurring beneath the surface of the water.
underwear • noun clothing worn under other clothes next to the skin.
underweight • adjective below a weight considered normal or desirable.
underwent past of UNDERGO.
underwhelm • verb humorous fail to impress or make a positive impact on.
– ORIGIN suggested by OVERWHELM.
underwired • adjective (of a bra) having a semicircular wire support stitched under each cup.
underwood • noun small trees and shrubs growing beneath taller timber trees.
underwork • verb impose too little work on.
underworld • noun **1** the world of criminals or of organized crime. **2** the mythical abode of the dead, imagined as being under the earth.
underwrite • verb (past **underwrote**; past part. **underwritten**) **1** sign and accept liability under (an insurance policy). **2** undertake to finance or otherwise support or guarantee.
– DERIVATIVES **underwriter** noun.
undescended • adjective Medicine (of a testicle) remaining in the abdomen instead of descending normally into the scrotum.
undeserved • adjective not warranted, merited, or earned.
– DERIVATIVES **undeservedly** adverb.
undeserving • adjective not deserving or worthy of something positive.
undesirable • adjective not wanted or desirable because harmful, objectionable, or unpleasant. • noun an objectionable person.
– DERIVATIVES **undesirability** noun **undesirably** adverb.

Thesaurus

the drift of, catch on to, get; Brit. informal twig, suss (out). **2** *she understood how hard he'd worked* APPRECIATE, recognize, realize, acknowledge, know, be aware of, be conscious of; informal be wise to; formal be cognizant of. **3** *I understand that you wish to go* BELIEVE, gather, take it, hear (tell), notice, see, learn; conclude, infer, assume, surmise, fancy.
understandable • adjective **1** *make it understandable to the layman* COMPREHENSIBLE, intelligible, coherent, clear, explicit, unambiguous, transparent, plain, straightforward, digestible, user-friendly. **2** *an understandable desire to be happy* UNSURPRISING, expected, predictable, inevitable; reasonable, acceptable, logical, rational, normal, natural; justifiable, justified, defensible, excusable, pardonable, forgivable.
understanding • noun **1** *test your understanding of the language* COMPREHENSION, apprehension, grasp, mastery, appreciation, assimilation, absorption; knowledge, awareness, insight, skill, expertise, proficiency; informal know-how; formal cognizance. **2** *a young man of brilliant understanding* INTELLECT, intelligence, brainpower, brains, judgement, reasoning, mentality; insight, intuition, shrewdness, acumen, sagacity, wisdom, wit; informal nous, savvy, know-how. **3** *it was my understanding that this was free* BELIEF, perception, view, conviction, feeling, opinion, intuition, impression, assumption, supposition. **4** *he treated me with understanding* COMPASSION, sympathy, pity, feeling, concern, consideration, kindness, sensitivity, decency, humanity, charity, goodwill, mercy, tolerance. **5** *we had a tacit understanding* AGREEMENT, arrangement, deal, bargain, settlement, pledge, pact, compact, contract, covenant, bond.
– OPPOSITES ignorance, indifference.
• adjective *an understanding friend* COMPASSIONATE, sympathetic, sensitive, considerate, tender, kind, thoughtful, tolerant, patient, forbearing, lenient, merciful, forgiving, humane; approachable, supportive, perceptive.
understate • verb PLAY DOWN, downplay, underrate, underplay, de-emphasize, trivialize, minimize, diminish, downgrade, brush aside, gloss over; informal soft-pedal, sell short.
– OPPOSITES exaggerate.
understudy • noun STAND-IN, substitute, replacement, reserve, fill-in, locum, proxy, back-up, relief, standby, stopgap, second, ancillary; informal sub; N. Amer. informal pinch-hitter.
undertake • verb TACKLE, take on, assume, shoulder, handle, manage, deal with, be responsible for; engage in, take part in, go about, set about, get down to, get to grips with, embark on; attempt, try, endeavour; informal have a go at; formal essay.
undertaker • noun FUNERAL DIRECTOR; N. Amer. mortician.
undertaking • noun **1** *a risky undertaking* ENTERPRISE, venture, project, campaign, scheme, plan, operation, endeavour, effort, task, activity, pursuit, exploit, business, affair, procedure; mission, quest. **2** *sign this undertaking to comply with the rules* PLEDGE, agreement, promise, oath, covenant, vow, commitment, guarantee, assurance, contract.
undertone • noun **1** *he said something in an undertone* LOW VOICE, murmur, whisper, mutter. **2** *the story's dark undertones* UNDERCURRENT, overtone, suggestion, nuance, vein, atmosphere, aura, tenor, flavour; vibrations.
undervalue • verb UNDERRATE, underestimate, play down, understate, underemphasize, diminish, minimize, downgrade, reduce, brush aside, gloss over, trivialize, hold cheap; informal sell short.
underwater • adjective SUBMERGED, immersed, sunken, subaqueous; undersea, submarine.
underwear • noun UNDERCLOTHES, underclothing, undergarments, underthings, lingerie; informal undies, frillies; Brit. informal smalls; archaic underlinen.
underworld • noun **1** *Osiris, god of the underworld* THE NETHERWORLD, the nether regions, hell, the abyss; eternal damnation; Gehenna, Tophet, Sheol, Hades; Brit. the other place; poetic/literary the pit. **2** *the violent underworld of Southwark* CRIMINAL WORLD, gangland; criminals, gangsters; informal mobsters.
– OPPOSITES heaven.
underwrite • verb SPONSOR, support, back, insure, indemnify, subsidize, pay for, finance, fund; informal foot the bill for; N. Amer. informal bankroll.
undesirable • adjective **1** *undesirable side effects* UNPLEASANT, disagreeable, nasty, unwelcome, unwanted, unfortunate, infelicitous. **2** *some very undesirable people* UNPLEASANT, disagreeable, distasteful, obnoxious, nasty, awful, terrible, dreadful, frightful, repul-

undesired • adjective not wanted or desired.
undetectable • adjective not able to be detected.
– DERIVATIVES **undetectably** adverb.
undetected • adjective not detected or discovered.
undetermined • adjective not firmly decided or settled.
undeterred • adjective persevering despite setbacks.
undeveloped • adjective not having developed or been developed.
undeviating • adjective showing no deviation; constant and steady.
undiagnosed • adjective not diagnosed.
undid past of UNDO.
undies • plural noun informal articles of underwear.
undifferentiated • adjective not different or differentiated.
undigested • adjective **1** (of food) not digested. **2** (of information) not having been properly understood or absorbed.
undignified • adjective appearing foolish and unseemly; lacking in dignity.
undiluted • adjective **1** (of a liquid) not diluted. **2** not moderated or weakened.
undiminished • adjective not reduced or lessened.
undiplomatic • adjective insensitive and tactless.
– DERIVATIVES **undiplomatically** adverb.
undirected • adjective without a coherent plan or purpose.
undiscerning • adjective lacking judgement, insight, or taste.
undisciplined • adjective lacking in discipline; uncontrolled in behaviour or manner.
undisclosed • adjective not revealed or made known.
undiscovered • adjective not discovered.
undiscriminating • adjective lacking good judgement or taste.
undisguised • adjective (of a feeling) not disguised or concealed; open.
undismayed • adjective not dismayed or discouraged by a setback.
undisputed • adjective not disputed or called in question; accepted.
undistinguished • adjective lacking distinction; unexceptional.
undisturbed • adjective not disturbed.
undivided • adjective **1** not divided, separated, or broken into parts. **2** devoted completely to one object: *my undivided attention.*
undo • verb (**undoes**; past **undid**; past part. **undone**) **1** unfasten or loosen. **2** cancel or reverse the effects of (a previous action or measure). **3** formal cause the downfall or ruin of.
undocumented • adjective not recorded in or proved by documents.
undoing • noun a person's ruin or downfall.
undomesticated • adjective **1** (of an animal) not tamed. **2** not accustomed to domestic tasks.
undone • adjective **1** not tied or fastened. **2** not done or finished. **3** formal or humorous ruined by a disastrous setback.
undoubted • adjective not questioned or doubted by anyone.
– DERIVATIVES **undoubtedly** adverb.
undramatic • adjective **1** lacking the qualities expected in drama. **2** unexciting.
undraped • adjective **1** not covered with cloth or drapery. **2** (of a model or subject in art) naked.
undreamed /undreemd, undremt/ (Brit. also **undreamt** /undremt/) • adjective (**undreamed of**) not previously thought to be possible.
undress • verb **1** (also **get undressed**) take off one's clothes. **2** take the clothes off (someone else). • noun **1** the state of being naked or only partially clothed. **2** Military ordinary clothing or uniform, as opposed to full dress.
undressed • adjective **1** wearing no clothes; naked. **2** not treated, processed, or prepared for use. **3** (of food) not having a dressing.
undrinkable • adjective not fit to be drunk because of impurity or poor quality.
undue • adjective excessive or disproportionate.
– DERIVATIVES **unduly** adverb.
undulant /undyoolənt/ • adjective undulating.
undulant fever • noun brucellosis in humans.
– ORIGIN so named because of the intermittent fever associated with the disease.
undulate /undyoolayt/ • verb **1** move with a smooth wave-like

Thesaurus

sive, repellent, abhorrent, loathsome, hateful, detestable, deplorable, appalling, insufferable, intolerable, despicable, contemptible, odious, vile, unsavoury; *informal* ghastly, horrible, horrid; *Brit. informal* beastly.
– OPPOSITES pleasant, agreeable.
undignified • adjective UNSEEMLY, demeaning, unbecoming, unworthy, unbefitting, degrading, shameful, dishonourable, ignominious, discreditable, ignoble, untoward, unsuitable; scandalous, disgraceful, indecent, low, base; *informal* infra dig.
undisciplined • adjective UNRULY, disorderly, disobedient, badly behaved, recalcitrant, wilful, wayward, delinquent, naughty, rebellious, insubordinate, disruptive, errant, out of control, uncontrollable, wild; disorganized, unsystematic, unmethodical, lax, slapdash, slipshod, sloppy; *Brit. informal* stroppy, bolshie; *formal* refractory.
undisguised • adjective OBVIOUS, evident, patent, manifest, transparent, overt, unconcealed, unhidden, unmistakable, undeniable, plain, clear, clear-cut, explicit, naked, visible; blatant, flagrant, glaring, bold; *informal* standing/sticking out a mile.
undisputed • adjective UNDOUBTED, indubitable, uncontested, incontestable, unchallenged, incontrovertible, unequivocal, undeniable, irrefutable, unmistakable, sure, certain, definite, accepted, acknowledged, recognized.
– OPPOSITES doubtful.
undistinguished • adjective UNEXCEPTIONAL, indifferent, run-of-the-mill, middle-of-the-road, ordinary, average, commonplace, mediocre, humdrum, lacklustre, forgettable, uninspired, uneventful, unremarkable, inconsequential, featureless, nondescript, middling, moderate; *N. Amer.* garden-variety; *informal* nothing special, no great shakes, nothing to write home about, OK, so-so, bog standard; *Brit. informal* common or garden; *N. Amer. informal* bush-league.
– OPPOSITES extraordinary.
undivided • adjective COMPLETE, full, total, whole, entire, absolute, unqualified, unreserved, unmitigated, unbroken, consistent, thorough, exclusive, dedicated; focused, engrossed, absorbed, attentive, committed.
undo • verb **1** *he undid another button* UNFASTEN, unbutton, unhook, untie, unlace; unlock, unbolt; loosen, disentangle, extricate, release, detach, free, open; disconnect, disengage, separate. **2** *they will undo a decision by the law lords* REVOKE, overrule, overturn, repeal, rescind, reverse, countermand, cancel, annul, nullify, invalidate, void, negate; *Law* vacate; *formal* abrogate. **3** *she undid much of the good work done* RUIN, undermine, subvert, overturn, scotch, sabotage, spoil, impair, mar, destroy, wreck, eradicate, obliterate; cancel out, neutralize, thwart, foil, frustrate, hamper, hinder, obstruct; *informal* blow, put the kibosh on, foul up, muck up; *Brit. informal* scupper, throw a spanner in the works of; *N. Amer. informal* rain on someone's parade.
– OPPOSITES fasten, ratify, enhance.
undoing • noun **1** *she plotted the king's undoing* DOWNFALL, defeat, conquest, deposition, overthrow, ruin, ruination, elimination, end, collapse, failure, debasement; Waterloo. **2** *their complacency was their undoing* FATAL FLAW, Achilles' heel, weakness, weak point, failing, misfortune, affliction, curse.
undone • adjective **1** *some work was left undone* UNFINISHED, incomplete, half-done, unaccomplished, unfulfilled, unconcluded; omitted, neglected, disregarded, ignored; remaining, outstanding, deferred, pending, on ice; *informal* on the back burner. **2** *(formal) she had lost and was utterly undone* DONE FOR, finished, ruined, destroyed, doomed, lost, defeated, beaten; *informal* washed up.
– OPPOSITES finished, successful.
undoubted • adjective UNDISPUTED, unchallenged, unquestioned, indubitable, incontrovertible, irrefutable, incontestable, sure, certain, unmistakable; definite, accepted, acknowledged, recognized.
undoubtedly • adverb DOUBTLESS, indubitably, doubtlessly, no doubt, without (a) doubt; unquestionably, indisputably, undeniably, incontrovertibly, clearly, obviously, patently, certainly, definitely, surely, of course, indeed.
undress • verb *he undressed and got into bed* STRIP (OFF), disrobe, take off one's clothes; *Brit. informal* peel off.
– PHRASES **in a state of undress** NAKED, (in the) nude, bare, stripped, unclothed, undressed, in a state of nature; *informal* in one's birthday suit, in the raw, in the buff, in the nuddy; *Brit. informal* starkers.
undue • adjective EXCESSIVE, immoderate, intemperate, inordinate, disproportionate; uncalled for, unneeded, unnecessary, nonessential, needless, unwarranted, unjustified, unreasonable; in-

motion. **2** have a wavy form or outline.
– DERIVATIVES **undulation** noun **undulatory** adjective.
– ORIGIN from Latin *undulatus*, from *unda* 'a wave'.
undyed • adjective (of fabric) not dyed; of its natural colour.
undying • adjective lasting forever.
unearned • adjective not earned or deserved.
unearned income • noun income from investments rather than from work.
unearth • verb **1** find in the ground by digging. **2** discover by investigation or searching.
unearthly • adjective **1** unnatural or mysterious. **2** informal unreasonably early or inconvenient: *an unearthly hour.*
unease • noun anxiety or discontent.
uneasy • adjective (**uneasier**, **uneasiest**) causing or feeling anxiety; troubled or uncomfortable.
– DERIVATIVES **uneasily** adverb **uneasiness** noun.
uneatable • adjective not fit to be eaten.
uneaten • adjective not eaten.
uneconomic • adjective not profitable or making efficient use of resources.
uneconomical • adjective wasteful of money or other resources; not economical.
– DERIVATIVES **uneconomically** adverb.
unedifying • adjective distasteful or unpleasant.
unedited • adjective (of material for publication or broadcasting) not edited.
uneducated • adjective poorly educated.
unelectable • adjective very likely to be defeated at an election.
unelected • adjective (of an official) not elected.
unembarrassed • adjective not feeling or showing embarrassment.
unembellished • adjective not embellished or decorated.
unemotional • adjective not having or showing strong feelings.
– DERIVATIVES **unemotionally** adverb.
unemphatic • adjective not emphatic.
unemployable • adjective not able or likely to get paid employment because of a lack of skills or qualifications.
unemployed • adjective **1** without a paid job but available to work. **2** (of a thing) not in use.
unemployment • noun **1** the state of being unemployed. **2** the number or proportion of unemployed people.
unemployment benefit • noun payment made by the state or a trade union to an unemployed person.
unenclosed • adjective (especially of land) not enclosed.
unencumbered • adjective not having any burden or impediment.
unending • adjective **1** having or seeming to have no end. **2** countless or continual.
unendowed • adjective not endowed.
unendurable • adjective not able to be tolerated or endured.
unenforceable • adjective impossible to enforce.
un-English • adjective not characteristic of English people or the English language.
unenlightened • adjective not enlightened in outlook.
– DERIVATIVES **unenlightening** adjective.
unenterprising • adjective lacking initiative or entrepreneurial ability.
unenthusiastic • adjective not having or showing enthusiasm.
– DERIVATIVES **unenthusiastically** adverb.
unenviable • adjective difficult, undesirable, or unpleasant.
unequal • adjective **1** not equal in quantity, size, or value. **2** not fair, evenly balanced, or having equal advantage. **3** (usu. **unequal to**) not having the ability or resources to meet a challenge.
– DERIVATIVES **unequally** adverb.
unequalled (US **unequaled**) • adjective superior to all others in performance or extent.
unequipped • adjective not equipped with the necessary items or skills.
unequivocal • adjective leaving no doubt; unambiguous.
– DERIVATIVES **unequivocally** adverb.
unerring • adjective always right or accurate.
– DERIVATIVES **unerringly** adverb.
unescapable • adjective unable to be avoided or denied.
UNESCO /yo͞oneskō/ • abbreviation United Nations Educational, Scientific, and Cultural Organization.
unescorted • adjective not escorted.
unessential • adjective inessential.
unethical • adjective not morally correct.
– DERIVATIVES **unethically** adverb.

Thesaurus

appropriate, unmerited, unsuitable, improper.
– OPPOSITES appropriate.
undulate • verb RISE AND FALL, surge, swell, heave, ripple, flow; wind, wobble, oscillate.
undying • adjective ABIDING, lasting, enduring, permanent, constant, infinite; unceasing, perpetual, ceaseless, incessant, unending, never-ending; immortal, eternal, deathless.
unearth • verb **1** *workmen unearthed an artillery shell* DIG UP, excavate, exhume, disinter, root out, unbury. **2** *I unearthed an interesting fact* DISCOVER, uncover, find, come across, hit on, bring to light, expose, turn up, hunt out, nose out.
unearthly • adjective **1** *an unearthly chill in the air* OTHER-WORLDLY, supernatural, preternatural, alien; ghostly, spectral, phantom, mysterious, spine-chilling, hair-raising; uncanny, eerie, strange, weird, unnatural, bizarre; *Scottish* eldritch; *informal* spooky, creepy, scary. **2** *(informal) they rose at some unearthly hour* UNREASONABLE, preposterous, abnormal, extraordinary, absurd, ridiculous, unheard of; *informal* ungodly, unholy.
– OPPOSITES normal, reasonable.
uneasy • adjective **1** *the doctor made him feel uneasy* WORRIED, anxious, troubled, disturbed, agitated, nervous, tense, overwrought, edgy, apprehensive, restless, discomfited, perturbed, fearful, uncomfortable, unsettled; *informal* jittery, nervy. **2** *he had an uneasy feeling* WORRYING, disturbing, troubling, alarming, dismaying, disquieting, unsettling, disconcerting, upsetting. **3** *the victory ensured an uneasy peace* TENSE, awkward, strained, fraught; precarious, unstable, insecure.
– OPPOSITES calm, stable.
uneconomic, uneconomical • adjective UNPROFITABLE, uncommercial, non-viable, loss-making, worthless; wasteful, inefficient, improvident.
uneducated • adjective UNTAUGHT, unschooled, untutored, untrained, unread, unscholarly, illiterate, unlettered, ignorant, ill-informed, uninformed; uncouth, unsophisticated, uncultured, unaccomplished, unenlightened, philistine, benighted, backward.
– OPPOSITES learned.
unemotional • adjective RESERVED, undemonstrative, restrained, passionless, emotionless, sober, unsentimental, unexcitable, impassive, phlegmatic, stoical, equable; cold, cool, unfeeling.
unemployed • adjective JOBLESS, out of work, between jobs, unwaged, unoccupied, redundant, laid off; on benefit; *Brit.* signing on; *N. Amer.* on welfare; *Brit. informal* on the dole, 'resting'.
unending • adjective ENDLESS, never-ending, interminable, perpetual, eternal, ceaseless, incessant, unceasing, non-stop, uninterrupted, continuous, continual, constant, persistent, unbroken, unabating, unremitting, relentless.
unendurable • adjective INTOLERABLE, unbearable, insufferable, insupportable, more than flesh and blood can stand.
unenthusiastic • adjective INDIFFERENT, apathetic, half-hearted, lukewarm, casual, cool, lacklustre, offhand, unmoved; cursory, perfunctory.
– OPPOSITES keen.
unenviable • adjective DISAGREEABLE, unpleasant, undesirable, nasty, horrible, thankless; unwanted, unwished-for.
unequal • adjective **1** *they are unequal in length* DIFFERENT, dissimilar, unlike, unalike, disparate, unmatched, uneven, irregular, varying, variable. **2** *the unequal distribution of wealth* UNFAIR, unjust, disproportionate, inequitable, biased. **3** *an unequal contest* ONE-SIDED, uneven, unfair, ill-matched, unbalanced, lopsided. **4** *she felt unequal to the task* INADEQUATE FOR, incapable of, unqualified for, unsuited to, incompetent at, not up to; *informal* not cut out for.
– OPPOSITES identical, fair.
unequalled • adjective UNBEATEN, unmatched, matchless, unrivalled, unsurpassed, unparalleled, peerless, incomparable, inimitable, second to none, unique.
unequivocal • adjective UNAMBIGUOUS, unmistakable, indisputable, incontrovertible, indubitable, undeniable; clear, clear-cut, plain, explicit, specific, categorical, straightforward, blunt, candid, emphatic, manifest.
– OPPOSITES ambiguous.
unerring • adjective UNFAILING, infallible, perfect, flawless, faultless, impeccable, unimpeachable; sure, true, assured, deadly; *informal* sure-fire.
unethical • adjective IMMORAL, amoral, unprincipled, unscrupu-

uneven ● adjective **1** not level or smooth. **2** not regular, consistent, or equal.
– DERIVATIVES **unevenly** adverb **unevenness** noun.
uneventful ● adjective not marked by interesting or exciting events.
– DERIVATIVES **uneventfully** adverb **uneventfulness** noun.
unexamined ● adjective not investigated or examined.
unexceptionable ● adjective not open to objection, but not particularly new or exciting.
– DERIVATIVES **unexceptionably** adverb.
unexceptional ● adjective not out of the ordinary; usual.
– DERIVATIVES **unexceptionally** adverb.
unexcitable ● adjective not easily excited.
unexciting ● adjective not exciting; dull.
unexercised ● adjective **1** not made use of or put into practice. **2** not taking exercise; unfit.
unexpected ● adjective not expected or regarded as likely to happen.
– DERIVATIVES **unexpectedly** adverb **unexpectedness** noun.
unexpired ● adjective (of an agreement or period of time) not yet having come to an end.
unexplained ● adjective not made clear or accounted for.
– DERIVATIVES **unexplainable** adjective.
unexploded ● adjective (of an explosive device) not having exploded.
unexploited ● adjective (of resources) not used to maximum benefit.
unexplored ● adjective not explored, investigated, or evaluated.
unexposed ● adjective **1** not exposed. **2** (**unexposed to**) not introduced to or acquainted with.
unexpressed ● adjective (of a thought or feeling) not communicated or made known.
unexpurgated ● adjective (of a text) complete and containing all the original material; not censored.
unfailing ● adjective **1** without error. **2** reliable or constant.
– DERIVATIVES **unfailingly** adverb.
unfair ● adjective not based on or showing fairness; unjust.
– DERIVATIVES **unfairly** adverb **unfairness** noun.
unfaithful ● adjective **1** not faithful; disloyal. **2** engaging in sexual relations with a person other than one's lover or spouse.
– DERIVATIVES **unfaithfully** adverb **unfaithfulness** noun.
unfaltering ● adjective not faltering; steady or resolute.
– DERIVATIVES **unfalteringly** adverb.
unfamiliar ● adjective **1** not known or recognized; uncharacteristic. **2** (**unfamiliar with**) not having knowledge or experience of.
– DERIVATIVES **unfamiliarity** noun.
unfancied ● adjective not considered likely to win.
unfashionable ● adjective not fashionable or popular.
– DERIVATIVES **unfashionably** adverb.
unfasten ● verb open the fastening of; undo.
unfathomable ● adjective **1** incapable of being fully explored or understood. **2** impossible to measure the depth or extent of.
– DERIVATIVES **unfathomably** adverb **unfathomed** adjective.
unfavourable (US **unfavorable**) ● adjective **1** expressing lack of approval. **2** adverse; inauspicious.
– DERIVATIVES **unfavourably** adverb.
unfazed ● adjective informal not disconcerted or perturbed.
unfeasible ● adjective inconvenient or impractical.
– DERIVATIVES **unfeasibly** adverb.
unfeeling ● adjective **1** unsympathetic, harsh, or callous. **2** lacking physical sensation.
unfeigned ● adjective genuine; sincere.
unfeminine ● adjective lacking feminine qualities.
unfermented ● adjective not fermented.
unfertilized (also **unfertilised**) ● adjective not fertilized.
unfettered ● adjective unrestrained or uninhibited.
unfilled ● adjective not filled; vacant or empty.
unfiltered ● adjective not filtered.
unfinished ● adjective **1** not finished; incomplete. **2** not having been given an attractive surface appearance in manufacture.
unfit ● adjective **1** unsuitable or inadequate for something. **2** not in good physical condition.

Thesaurus

lous, dishonourable, wrong, dishonest, deceitful, unconscionable, fraudulent, underhand, wicked, evil, corrupt; unprofessional, improper.
uneven ● adjective **1** *uneven ground* BUMPY, rough, lumpy, stony, rocky, potholed, rutted, pitted, jagged. **2** *uneven teeth* IRREGULAR, unequal, unbalanced, lopsided, askew, crooked, asymmetrical, unsymmetrical. **3** *uneven quality* INCONSISTENT, variable, varying, fluctuating, irregular, erratic, patchy. **4** *an uneven contest* ONE-SIDED, unequal, unfair, unjust, inequitable, ill-matched, unbalanced.
– OPPOSITES flat, regular, equal.
uneventful ● adjective UNEXCITING, uninteresting, monotonous, boring, dull, tedious, humdrum, routine, unvaried, ordinary, run-of-the-mill, pedestrian, mundane, predictable.
– OPPOSITES exciting.
unexceptional ● adjective ORDINARY, average, typical, everyday, run-of-the-mill, middle-of-the-road, mediocre, indifferent; *informal* OK, so-so, nothing special, no great shakes, fair-to-middling.
unexpected ● adjective UNFORESEEN, unanticipated, unpredicted, unlooked for, without warning; sudden, abrupt, surprising, out of the blue.
unfailing ● adjective *his unfailing good humour* CONSTANT, reliable, dependable, steadfast, steady; endless, undying, unfading, inexhaustible, boundless, ceaseless.
unfair ● adjective **1** *the trial was unfair* UNJUST, inequitable, prejudiced, biased, discriminatory; one-sided, unequal, uneven, unbalanced, partisan. **2** *his comments were unfair* UNDESERVED, unmerited, uncalled for, unreasonable, unjustified; *Brit. informal* out of order. **3** *unfair play* UNSPORTING, unsportsmanlike, dirty, below the belt, underhand, dishonourable. **4** *you're being very unfair* INCONSIDERATE, thoughtless, insensitive, selfish, mean, unkind, unreasonable.
– OPPOSITES just, justified.
unfaithful ● adjective **1** *her husband had been unfaithful* ADULTEROUS, faithless, fickle, untrue, inconstant; *informal* cheating, two-timing. **2** *an unfaithful friend* DISLOYAL, treacherous, traitorous, untrustworthy, unreliable, undependable, false, two-faced, double-crossing, deceitful; *poetic/literary* perfidious.
– OPPOSITES loyal.
unfaltering ● adjective STEADY, resolute, resolved, firm, steadfast, fixed, decided, unswerving, unwavering, tireless, indefatigable, persistent, unyielding, relentless, unremitting, unrelenting.
– OPPOSITES unsteady.
unfamiliar ● adjective **1** *an unfamiliar part of the city* UNKNOWN, new, strange, foreign, alien. **2** *the unfamiliar sounds* UNUSUAL, uncommon, unconventional, novel, different, exotic, unorthodox, odd, peculiar, curious, uncharacteristic, anomalous, out of the ordinary. **3** *investors unfamiliar with the stock market* UNACQUAINTED, unused, unaccustomed, unconversant, inexperienced, uninformed, unenlightened, ignorant, new to, a stranger to.
unfashionable ● adjective OUT OF FASHION, outdated, old-fashioned, outmoded, out of style, dated, unstylish, passé, démodé; *informal* out, square, out of the ark.
unfasten ● verb UNDO, open, disconnect, remove, untie, unbutton, unzip, loose, loosen, free, unlock, unbolt.
unfathomable ● adjective **1** *dark unfathomable eyes* INSCRUTABLE, incomprehensible, enigmatic, indecipherable, obscure, esoteric, mysterious, mystifying, deep, profound. **2** *unfathomable water* DEEP, immeasurable, unfathomed, unplumbed, bottomless.
– OPPOSITES penetrable.
unfavourable ● adjective **1** *unfavourable comment* ADVERSE, critical, hostile, inimical, unfriendly, unsympathetic, negative; discouraging, disapproving, uncomplimentary, unflattering. **2** *the unfavourable economic climate* DISADVANTAGEOUS, adverse, inauspicious, unpropitious, gloomy; unsuitable, inappropriate, inopportune.
– OPPOSITES positive.
unfeeling ● adjective UNCARING, unsympathetic, unemotional, uncharitable; hard-hearted, heartless, hard, harsh, austere, cold, cold-hearted.
– OPPOSITES compassionate.
unfeigned ● adjective SINCERE, genuine, real, true, honest, unaffected, unforced, heartfelt, wholehearted.
– OPPOSITES insincere.
unfettered ● adjective UNRESTRAINED, unrestricted, unconstrained, free, unbridled, unchecked, uncontrolled.
– OPPOSITES restricted.
unfinished ● adjective **1** *an unfinished essay* INCOMPLETE, uncompleted; partial, undone, half-done; imperfect, unpolished, unrefined, sketchy, fragmentary, rough. **2** *the door can be supplied unfinished* UNPAINTED, unvarnished, untreated.
– OPPOSITES complete.

unfitted ● adjective **1** unfit for something. **2** (of furniture, linen, etc.) not fitted.
unfitting ● adjective unsuitable or unbecoming.
unfixed ● adjective **1** unfastened; loose. **2** uncertain or variable.
unflagging ● adjective tireless or persistent.
– DERIVATIVES **unflaggingly** adverb.
unflappable ● adjective informal calm in a crisis.
unflattering ● adjective not flattering.
– DERIVATIVES **unflatteringly** adverb.
unflinching ● adjective not afraid or hesitant.
– DERIVATIVES **unflinchingly** adverb.
unfocused (also **unfocussed**) ● adjective **1** not focused; out of focus. **2** without a specific aim or direction.
unfold ● verb **1** open or spread out from a folded position. **2** reveal or be revealed.
unforced ● adjective **1** produced naturally and without effort. **2** not compelled.
unforeseen ● adjective not anticipated or predicted.
– DERIVATIVES **unforeseeable** adjective.
unforgettable ● adjective highly memorable.
– DERIVATIVES **unforgettably** adverb.
unforgivable ● adjective so bad as to be unable to be forgiven or excused.
– DERIVATIVES **unforgivably** adverb.
unforgiven ● adjective not forgiven.
unforgiving ● adjective **1** not willing to forgive or excuse faults. **2** (of conditions) harsh; hostile.
unformed ● adjective **1** without a definite form. **2** not fully developed.
unforthcoming ● adjective **1** not willing to divulge information. **2** not available when needed.
unfortunate ● adjective **1** having bad fortune; unlucky. **2** regrettable or inappropriate. ● noun a person who suffers bad fortune.
– DERIVATIVES **unfortunately** adverb.
unfounded ● adjective having no foundation or basis in fact.
unfree ● adjective deprived or devoid of liberty.
unfreeze ● verb (past **unfroze**; past part. **unfrozen**) **1** thaw. **2** remove restrictions on the use of (an asset).
unfrequented ● adjective visited only rarely.
unfriendly ● adjective (**unfriendier**, **unfriendliest**) not friendly.
– DERIVATIVES **unfriendliness** noun.
unfrock ● verb another term for DEFROCK.
unfroze past of UNFREEZE.
unfrozen past participle of UNFREEZE.
unfulfilled ● adjective not fulfilled.
– DERIVATIVES **unfulfillable** adjective **unfulfilling** adjective.
unfunded ● adjective not receiving funds; not having a fund.
unfunny ● adjective (**unfunnier**, **unfunniest**) not amusing.
unfurl ● verb spread out from a rolled or folded state.
unfurnished ● adjective **1** without furniture. **2** archaic not supplied.
ungainly ● adjective clumsy; awkward.
– DERIVATIVES **ungainliness** noun.
– ORIGIN from obsolete *gainly* 'graceful', from an Old Norse word meaning 'straight'.
ungenerous ● adjective not generous; mean.
– DERIVATIVES **ungenerously** adverb.
ungentlemanly ● adjective not appropriate to or behaving like a gentleman.
unglazed ● adjective not glazed.
unglued ● adjective **1** not or no longer stuck. **2** informal confused and emotionally strained.
ungodly ● adjective **1** irreligious or immoral. **2** informal unreasonably early or inconvenient: *calls at ungodly hours.*
– DERIVATIVES **ungodliness** noun.
ungovernable ● adjective impossible to control or govern.
– DERIVATIVES **ungovernability** noun.
ungraceful ● adjective lacking in grace; clumsy.
– DERIVATIVES **ungracefully** adverb.
ungracious ● adjective not gracious.
– DERIVATIVES **ungraciously** adverb.
ungrammatical ● adjective not conforming to grammatical rules.
– DERIVATIVES **ungrammatically** adverb.
ungrateful ● adjective not feeling or showing gratitude.
– DERIVATIVES **ungratefully** adverb **ungratefulness** noun.
ungrounded ● adjective **1** groundless. **2** not electrically earthed. **3** (**ungrounded in**) not properly instructed or proficient in.
unguarded ● adjective **1** without protection or a guard. **2** not well considered; careless.

Thesaurus

unfit ● adjective **1** *the film is unfit for children | unfit for duty* UNSUITABLE, unsuited, inappropriate, unequipped, inadequate, not designed; incapable of, unable to do something, not up to, not equal to; *informal* not cut out for, not up to scratch. **2** *I am unfit* UNHEALTHY, out of condition/shape, in poor condition/shape.
– OPPOSITES suitable.
unflagging ● adjective TIRELESS, persistent, dogged, tenacious, determined, resolute, staunch, single-minded, unrelenting, unfaltering, unfailing.
– OPPOSITES inconstant.
unflappable ● adjective *(informal)* IMPERTURBABLE, unexcitable, cool, calm, {cool, calm, and collected}, self-controlled, cool-headed, level-headed; *informal* laid-back.
– OPPOSITES excitable.
unflattering ● adjective **1** *an unflattering review* UNFAVOURABLE, uncomplimentary, harsh, unsympathetic, critical, hostile, scathing. **2** *an unflattering dress* UNATTRACTIVE, unbecoming, unsightly, ugly, plain, ill-fitting.
– OPPOSITES complimentary, becoming.
unflinching ● adjective RESOLUTE, determined, single-minded, dogged, resolved, firm, committed, steady, unwavering, unflagging, unswerving, unfaltering, untiring, undaunted, fearless.
unfold ● verb **1** *May unfolded the map* OPEN OUT, spread out, flatten, straighten out, unroll. **2** *she unfolded her tale to Joanna* NARRATE, relate, recount, tell, reveal, disclose, divulge, communicate, report, recite, give an account of. **3** *I watched the events unfold* DEVELOP, evolve, happen, take place, occur, transpire, progress.
unforeseen ● adjective UNPREDICTED, unexpected, unanticipated, unplanned, unlooked for, not bargained for.
– OPPOSITES expected.
unforgettable ● adjective MEMORABLE, not/never to be forgotten, haunting, catchy; striking, impressive, outstanding, extraordinary, exceptional.
– OPPOSITES unexceptional.
unforgivable ● adjective INEXCUSABLE, unpardonable, unjustifiable, indefensible, inexpiable, irremissible.
– OPPOSITES venial.
unfortunate ● adjective **1** *unfortunate people* UNLUCKY, hapless, out of luck, luckless, wretched, miserable, forlorn, poor, pitiful; *informal* down on one's luck. **2** *an unfortunate start to our holiday* ADVERSE, disadvantageous, unfavourable, unlucky, unwelcome, unpromising, inauspicious, unpropitious; *formal* grievous. **3** *an unfortunate remark* REGRETTABLE, inappropriate, unsuitable, infelicitous, tactless, injudicious.
– OPPOSITES lucky, auspicious.
unfortunately ● adverb UNLUCKILY, sadly, regrettably, unhappily, alas, sad to say; *informal* worse luck.
unfounded ● adjective GROUNDLESS, baseless, unsubstantiated, unproven, unsupported, uncorroborated, unconfirmed, unverified, unattested, without basis, without foundation, speculative, conjectural.
– OPPOSITES proven.
unfriendly ● adjective **1** *an unfriendly look* HOSTILE, disagreeable, antagonistic, aggressive; ill-natured, unpleasant, surly, sour, unamicable, uncongenial; inhospitable, unneighbourly, unwelcoming, unkind, unsympathetic; unsociable, antisocial; aloof, cold, cool, frosty, distant, unapproachable; *informal* stand-offish, starchy. **2** *unfriendly terrain* UNFAVOURABLE, disadvantageous, unpropitious, inauspicious, hostile.
– OPPOSITES amiable, favourable.
ungainly ● adjective AWKWARD, clumsy, ungraceful, graceless, inelegant, gawky, maladroit, gauche, uncoordinated; *archaic* lubberly.
– OPPOSITES graceful.
ungodly ● adjective **1** *ungodly behaviour* UNHOLY, godless, irreligious, impious, blasphemous, sacrilegious; immoral, corrupt, depraved, sinful, wicked, evil, iniquitous. **2** *(informal) he called at an ungodly hour* UNREASONABLE, unsocial, antisocial; *informal* unearthly.
ungovernable ● adjective UNCONTROLLABLE, unmanageable, anarchic, intractable; unruly, disorderly, rebellious, riotous, wild, mutinous, undisciplined.
ungracious ● adjective RUDE, impolite, uncivil, discourteous, ill-mannered, bad-mannered, uncouth, disrespectful, insolent, impertinent, offhand.
– OPPOSITES polite.

unguent /unggwənt/ ● noun a soft greasy or viscous substance used as ointment or for lubrication.
– ORIGIN Latin *unguentum*, from *unguere* 'anoint'.
ungulate /unggyoolət, -layt/ ● noun Zoology a hoofed mammal.
– ORIGIN Latin *ungulatus*, from *ungula* 'hoof'.
unhand ● verb archaic or humorous release from one's grasp.
unhappy ● adjective (**unhappier**, **unhappiest**) **1** not happy. **2** unfortunate.
– DERIVATIVES **unhappily** adverb **unhappiness** noun.
unharmed ● adjective not harmed; uninjured.
unharness ● verb remove a harness from.
unhatched ● adjective not yet hatched.
UNHCR ● abbreviation United Nations High Commission for Refugees.
unhealthy ● adjective (**unhealthier**, **unhealthiest**) **1** in poor health. **2** not conducive to health.
– DERIVATIVES **unhealthily** adverb **unhealthiness** noun.
unheard ● adjective **1** not heard or listened to. **2** (**unheard of**) previously unknown.
unheated ● adjective not heated.
unheeded ● adjective heard or noticed but disregarded.
unheeding ● adjective not paying attention.
unhelpful ● adjective not helpful.
– DERIVATIVES **unhelpfully** adverb **unhelpfulness** noun.
unheralded ● adjective not previously announced, expected, or recognized.
unhesitating ● adjective without doubt or hesitation.
– DERIVATIVES **unhesitatingly** adverb.
unhinge ● verb **1** make mentally unbalanced. **2** take (a door) off its hinges.
unhistorical ● adjective not in accordance with history or historical analysis.
– DERIVATIVES **unhistorically** adverb.
unhitch ● verb unhook or unfasten.
unholy ● adjective (**unholier**, **unholiest**) **1** sinful; wicked. **2** (of an alliance) unnatural and potentially harmful. **3** informal dreadful: *an unholy row.*
unhook ● verb unfasten or detach (something held by a hook).
unhoped ● adjective (**unhoped for**) exceeding hope or expectation.
unhorse ● verb drag or cause to fall from a horse.
unhoused ● adjective having no accommodation or shelter.
unhurried ● adjective moving, acting, or taking place without haste or urgency.
– DERIVATIVES **unhurriedly** adverb.
unhurt ● adjective not hurt or harmed.
unhygienic ● adjective not hygienic.
– DERIVATIVES **unhygienically** adverb.
unhyphenated ● adjective not written with a hyphen.
uni ● noun (pl. **unis**) informal university.
uni- ● combining form one; having or consisting of one: *unicycle.*
– ORIGIN from Latin *unus.*
Uniate /yoōniayt/ (also **Uniat** /yoōniat/) ● adjective denoting any Christian community in eastern Europe or the Near East acknowledging papal supremacy but with its own liturgy.
– ORIGIN Russian *uniat*, from Latin *unio* 'unity'.
unicameral /yoōnikammərəl/ ● adjective (of a legislative body) having a single legislative chamber.
– ORIGIN from Latin *camera* 'chamber'.
UNICEF /yoōnisef/ ● abbreviation United Nations Children's (originally International Children's Emergency) Fund.
unicellular ● adjective Biology consisting of a single cell.
unicorn ● noun a mythical animal represented as a horse with a single straight horn projecting from its forehead.
– ORIGIN Latin *unicornis*, from *cornu* 'horn'.
unicycle ● noun a cycle with a single wheel, chiefly used by acrobats.
– DERIVATIVES **unicyclist** noun.
unidentifiable ● adjective unable to be identified.
unidentified ● adjective not recognized or identified.
unidiomatic ● adjective not using or containing expressions natural to a native speaker of a language.
unidirectional ● adjective moving or operating in a single direction.
unification ● noun the process of being unified.
Unification Church ● noun an evangelistic religious and political organization founded in 1954 in Korea by Sun Myung Moon.
uniform ● adjective not varying in form or character; the same in all cases and at all times. ● noun the distinctive clothing worn by members of the same organization or body or by children attending certain schools.
– DERIVATIVES **uniformed** adjective **uniformity** noun **uniformly** adverb.
– ORIGIN Latin *uniformis.*

Thesaurus

ungrateful ● adjective UNAPPRECIATIVE, unthankful, ungracious.
– OPPOSITES thankful.
unguarded ● adjective **1** *an unguarded frontier* UNDEFENDED, unprotected, unfortified; vulnerable, insecure, open to attack. **2** *an unguarded remark* CARELESS, ill-considered, incautious, thoughtless, rash, foolhardy, foolish, indiscreet, imprudent, injudicious, ill-judged, insensitive; poetic/literary temerarious. **3** *an unguarded moment* UNWARY, inattentive, off guard, distracted, absent-minded.
unhappiness ● noun SADNESS, sorrow, dejection, depression, misery, cheerlessness, downheartedness, despondency, despair, desolation, wretchedness, glumness, gloom, gloominess, dolefulness; melancholy, low spirits, mournfulness, woe, heartache, distress, chagrin, grief, pain; informal the blues.
unhappy ● adjective **1** *an unhappy childhood* SAD, miserable, sorrowful, dejected, despondent, disconsolate, morose, brokenhearted, heartbroken, down, downcast, dispirited, downhearted, depressed, melancholy, gloomy, glum, mournful, despairing, doleful, forlorn, woebegone, woeful, long-faced, joyless, cheerless; informal down in the mouth/dumps, fed up, blue. **2** *in the unhappy event of litigation* UNFORTUNATE, unlucky, luckless; ill-starred, ill-fated, doomed; informal jinxed; poetic/literary star-crossed. **3** *I was unhappy with the service I received* DISSATISFIED, displeased, discontented, disappointed, disgruntled. **4** *'disorganized capitalism' seems an unhappy term* INAPPROPRIATE, unsuitable, inapt, unfortunate; regrettable, ill-chosen.
– OPPOSITES cheerful.
unharmed ● adjective **1** *they released the hostage unharmed* UNINJURED, unhurt, unscathed, safe (and sound), alive and well, in one piece, without a scratch. **2** *the tomb was unharmed* UNDAMAGED, unbroken, unmarred, unspoiled, unsullied, unmarked; sound, intact, perfect, unblemished, pristine.
– OPPOSITES injured, damaged.
unhealthy ● adjective **1** *an unhealthy lifestyle* HARMFUL, detrimental, destructive, injurious, damaging, deleterious; malign, noxious, poisonous, insalubrious, baleful. **2** *an unhealthy pallor* ILL-LOOKING, ill, unwell, in poor health, ailing, sick, sickly, poorly, indisposed, weak, frail, delicate, infirm, washed out, run down, peaky. **3** *an unhealthy obsession with drugs* UNWHOLESOME, morbid, macabre, twisted, warped, depraved, abnormal, unnatural; informal sick.
unheard of ● adjective **1** *such behaviour was unheard of* UNPRECEDENTED, exceptional, extraordinary, out of the ordinary, unthought of, undreamed of, unbelievable, inconceivable, unimaginable, unthinkable; formal unexampled. **2** *a game unheard of in the UK* UNKNOWN, unfamiliar, new.
– OPPOSITES common, well known.
unheeded ● adjective DISREGARDED, ignored, neglected, overlooked, unnoted, unrecognized.
unhinged ● adjective DERANGED, demented, unbalanced, out of one's mind, crazed, mad, insane, disturbed; informal crazy, mental, bonkers, batty, loopy, bananas, touched.
– OPPOSITES sane.
unholy ● adjective **1** *a grin of unholy amusement* UNGODLY, godless, irreligious, impious, blasphemous, sacrilegious, profane, irreverent; wicked, evil, immoral, corrupt, depraved, sinful. **2** (informal) *an unholy row* SHOCKING, dreadful, outrageous, appalling, terrible, horrendous, frightful. **3** *an unholy alliance* UNNATURAL, unusual, improbable, made in Hell.
unhoped for ● adjective UNEXPECTED, unanticipated, unforeseen, unlooked-for, undreamed of, out of the blue.
– OPPOSITES expected.
unhurried ● adjective LEISURELY, easy, easy-going, relaxed, slow, deliberate, measured, calm.
– OPPOSITES hasty.
unhygienic ● adjective INSANITARY, unsanitary, dirty, filthy, contaminated, unhealthy, unwholesome, insalubrious, polluted, foul.
– OPPOSITES sanitary.
unidentified ● adjective UNKNOWN, unnamed, anonymous, incognito, nameless, unfamiliar, strange.
– OPPOSITES known.

unify /yoonifi/ ● verb (**unifies**, **unified**) make or become united or uniform.
– DERIVATIVES **unifier** noun.
– ORIGIN Latin *unificare*.
unilateral ● adjective **1** performed by or affecting only one person, group, etc. **2** relating to or affecting only one side of an organ, the body, etc.
– DERIVATIVES **unilateralism** noun **unilateralist** noun & adjective **unilaterally** adverb.
unimaginable ● adjective impossible to imagine or comprehend.
– DERIVATIVES **unimaginably** adverb.
unimaginative ● adjective not using or displaying imagination; stolid and dull.
– DERIVATIVES **unimaginatively** adverb.
unimpaired ● adjective not weakened or damaged.
unimpeachable ● adjective beyond reproach.
– DERIVATIVES **unimpeachably** adverb.
unimpeded ● adjective not obstructed or hindered.
unimportant ● adjective lacking in importance.
– DERIVATIVES **unimportance** noun.
unimpressed ● adjective not impressed.
unimpressive ● adjective not impressive.
unimproved ● adjective not improved.
unincorporated ● adjective **1** not formed into a legal corporation. **2** not included as part of a whole.
uninflected ● adjective not varied by inflection.
uninfluenced ● adjective not influenced.
uninformative ● adjective not providing useful or interesting information.
uninformed ● adjective lacking awareness or understanding of the facts.
uninhabitable ● adjective unsuitable for living in.
uninhabited ● adjective without inhabitants.
uninhibited ● adjective expressing oneself or acting without restraint.
– DERIVATIVES **uninhibitedly** adverb.
uninitiated ● adjective without special knowledge or experience.
uninjured ● adjective not harmed or damaged.
uninspired ● adjective **1** unimaginative; dull. **2** not filled with excitement.
uninspiring ● adjective not producing excitement or interest.
uninsurable ● adjective not eligible for insurance cover.
uninsured ● adjective not covered by insurance.
unintelligent ● adjective lacking intelligence.
– DERIVATIVES **unintelligence** noun **unintelligently** adverb.
unintelligible ● adjective impossible to understand.
– DERIVATIVES **unintelligibility** noun **unintelligibly** adverb.
unintended ● adjective not planned or meant.
unintentional ● adjective not done on purpose.
– DERIVATIVES **unintentionally** adverb.
uninterested ● adjective not interested or concerned.
– USAGE On the meaning and use of **uninterested** and **disinterested**, see DISINTERESTED.
uninteresting ● adjective not interesting.
uninterrupted ● adjective **1** continuous. **2** unobstructed.
– DERIVATIVES **uninterruptedly** adverb.
uninventive ● adjective not inventive.
uninvited ● adjective arriving or acting without invitation.
uninviting ● adjective not attractive; unpleasant.
– DERIVATIVES **uninvitingly** adverb.
uninvolved ● adjective not involved.
union ● noun **1** the action or fact of uniting or being united. **2** a state of harmony or agreement. **3** a marriage. **4** a club, society, or association formed by people with a common interest or purpose. **5** (also **Union**) a political unit consisting of a number of states or provinces with the same central government. **6** (**the Union**) the northern states of the US in the American Civil War. **7** a fabric made of different yarns, typically cotton and linen or silk.
– ORIGIN Latin, 'unity'.
unionist ● noun **1** a member of a trade union. **2** (**Unionist**) a

Thesaurus

unification ● noun UNION, merger, fusion, fusing, amalgamation, coalition, combination, confederation, federation, synthesis, joining.
uniform ● adjective **1** *a uniform temperature* CONSTANT, consistent, steady, invariable, unvarying, unfluctuating, unchanging, stable, static, regular, fixed, even, equal. **2** *pieces of uniform size* IDENTICAL, matching, similar, equal; same, like, homogeneous, consistent.
– OPPOSITES variable.
● noun *a soldier in uniform* COSTUME, livery, regalia, suit, ensemble, outfit; regimentals, colours; *informal* get-up, rig, gear; *archaic* habit.
uniformity ● noun **1** *uniformity in tax law* CONSTANCY, consistency, conformity, invariability, stability, regularity, evenness, homogeneity, homogeneousness, equality. **2** *a dull uniformity* MONOTONY, tedium, tediousness, dullness, dreariness, flatness, sameness.
– OPPOSITES variation, variety.
unify ● verb UNITE, bring together, join (together), merge, fuse, amalgamate, coalesce, combine, blend, mix, bind, consolidate.
– OPPOSITES separate.
unimaginable ● adjective UNTHINKABLE, inconceivable, incredible, unbelievable, unheard of, unthought of, untold, undreamed of, beyond one's wildest dreams.
unimaginative ● adjective UNINSPIRED, uninventive, unoriginal, uncreative, commonplace, pedestrian, mundane, ordinary, routine, humdrum, workaday, run-of-the-mill, hackneyed, trite.
unimpeachable ● adjective TRUSTWORTHY, reliable, dependable, above suspicion, irreproachable.
– OPPOSITES unreliable.
unimpeded ● adjective UNRESTRICTED, unhindered, unblocked, unhampered, free, clear.
unimportant ● adjective INSIGNIFICANT, inconsequential, trivial, minor, trifling, of little/no importance, of little/no consequence, of no account, irrelevant, peripheral, extraneous, petty, paltry; *informal* piddling; *formal* of no moment.
uninhabited ● adjective **1** *much of this land was uninhabited* UNPOPULATED, unpeopled, unsettled. **2** *an uninhabited hut* VACANT, empty, unoccupied, untenanted, to let.
uninhibited ● adjective **1** *uninhibited dancing* UNRESTRAINED, unrepressed, abandoned, wild, reckless; unrestricted, uncontrolled, unchecked, intemperate, wanton. **2** *I'm pretty uninhibited* UNRESERVED, unrepressed, liberated, unselfconscious, free and easy, relaxed, informal, open, outgoing, extrovert, outspoken, frank, forthright; *informal* upfront.
– OPPOSITES repressed.
uninspired ● adjective UNIMAGINATIVE, uninventive, pedestrian, mundane, unoriginal, commonplace, ordinary, routine, humdrum, run-of-the-mill, hackneyed, trite; spiritless, passionless.
uninspiring ● adjective BORING, dull, dreary, unexciting, unstimulating; dry, colourless, bland, lacklustre, tedious, humdrum, run-of-the-mill.
unintelligent ● adjective STUPID, ignorant, dense, brainless, mindless, foolish, dull-witted, slow, simple-minded, vacuous, vapid, idiotic, obtuse; *informal* thick, dim, dumb, dopey, half-witted, dozy.
unintelligible ● adjective **1** *unintelligible sounds* INCOMPREHENSIBLE, indiscernible, mumbled, indistinct, unclear, slurred, inarticulate, incoherent, garbled. **2** *unintelligible graffiti* ILLEGIBLE, indecipherable, unreadable.
unintentional ● adjective UNINTENDED, accidental, inadvertent, involuntary, unwitting, unthinking, unpremeditated, unconscious.
– OPPOSITES deliberate.
uninterested ● adjective INDIFFERENT, unconcerned, uninvolved, apathetic, lukewarm, unenthusiastic.
uninteresting ● adjective UNEXCITING, boring, dull, tiresome, wearisome, tedious, dreary, lifeless, humdrum, colourless, bland, insipid, banal, dry, pedestrian; *informal* samey.
– OPPOSITES exciting.
uninterrupted ● adjective UNBROKEN, continuous, continual, undisturbed, untroubled.
– OPPOSITES intermittent.
uninvited ● adjective **1** *an uninvited guest* UNASKED, unexpected; unwelcome, unwanted. **2** *uninvited suggestions* UNSOLICITED, unrequested, unsought.
uninviting ● adjective UNAPPEALING, unattractive, unappetizing, off-putting; bleak, cheerless, dreary, dismal, depressing, grim, inhospitable.
– OPPOSITES tempting.
union ● noun **1** *the union of art and nature* UNIFICATION, uniting, joining, merging, merger, fusion, fusing, amalgamating, amalgamation, coalition, combination, synthesis, blend, blending, mingling. **2** *the crowd moved in union* UNITY, accord, unison, harmony, agreement, concurrence; *formal* concord. **3** *his daughter's*

person in Northern Ireland in favour of union with Great Britain.
– DERIVATIVES **unionism** noun.
unionize (also **unionise**) ● verb become or cause to become members of a trade union.
– DERIVATIVES **unionization** noun.
Union Jack (also **Union flag**) ● noun the national flag of the United Kingdom.
unipolar ● adjective having or relating to a single pole or extremity.
unique ● adjective **1** being the only one of its kind; unlike anything else. **2** (**unique to**) belonging or connected to (one particular person, group, or place). **3** remarkable or unusual.
– DERIVATIVES **uniquely** adverb **uniqueness** noun.
– ORIGIN French, from Latin *unus* 'one'.
unisex ● adjective designed to be suitable for both sexes.
unisexual ● adjective **1** of one sex. **2** (of a flower) having either stamens or pistils but not both.
– DERIVATIVES **unisexuality** noun.
unison ● noun **1** simultaneous action or utterance. **2** Music a coincidence in pitch of sounds or notes. ● adjective performed in unison.
– ORIGIN Latin *unisonus*, from *sonus* 'sound'.
unit ● noun **1** an individual thing or person regarded as single and complete; each of the individual components making up a larger whole. **2** a device, part, or item of furniture with a specified function: *a sink unit.* **3** a self-contained or distinct section of a building or group of buildings. **4** a subdivision of a larger military grouping. **5** a standard quantity in terms of which other quantities may be expressed. **6** one as a number or quantity.
– DERIVATIVES **unitize** (also **unitise**) verb.
– ORIGIN from Latin *unus*, probably suggested by DIGIT.
unitard /yo͞onitaard/ ● noun a tight-fitting one-piece garment covering the whole body.
– ORIGIN from UNI- + LEOTARD.
Unitarian /yo͞onitairiən/ Christian Theology ● adjective referring to belief in the unity of God and rejection of the doctrine of the Trinity. ● noun a Christian holding this belief.
– DERIVATIVES **Unitarianism** noun.
– ORIGIN Latin *unitarius*, from *unitas* 'unity'.
unitary ● adjective **1** single; uniform. **2** relating to a unit or units.
unitary authority (also **unitary council**) ● noun (chiefly in the UK) a division of local government established in place of a two-tier system of local councils.
unit cell ● noun the smallest group of atoms from which an entire crystal can be built up by repetition.
unite ● verb **1** come or bring together for a common purpose or to form a whole. **2** archaic join in marriage.
– DERIVATIVES **united** adjective **unitive** adjective.
– ORIGIN Latin *unire* 'join together', from *unus* 'one'.
unit trust ● noun Brit. a trust managing a portfolio of stock exchange securities, in which small investors can buy units.
unity ● noun (pl. **unities**) **1** the state of being united or forming a whole. **2** a thing forming a complex whole. **3** Mathematics the number one.
universal ● adjective of, affecting, or done by all people or things in the world or in a particular group; applicable to all cases.
– DERIVATIVES **universality** noun **universally** adverb.
universalist ● noun **1** Christian Theology a person who believes that all humankind will eventually be saved. **2** a person advocating concern for everyone without regard to national or sectional allegiances.
– DERIVATIVES **universalism** noun **universalistic** adjective.
universalize (also **universalise**) ● verb make universal.
– DERIVATIVES **universalization** noun.
universal joint ● noun a joint which can transmit rotary power by a shaft at any selected angle.
universal suffrage ● noun the right of all adults (with minor exceptions) to vote in political elections.
universe ● noun **1** all existing matter and space considered as a whole; the cosmos. **2** a particular sphere of activity or experience.
– ORIGIN from Latin *universus* 'combined into one, whole'.
university ● noun (pl. **universities**) a high-level educational institution in which students study for degrees and academic research is done.
– ORIGIN Latin *universitas* 'the whole', later 'guild', from *universus* (see UNIVERSE).
unjoined ● adjective not joined together.
unjointed ● adjective lacking a joint or joints; consisting of a single piece.
unjust ● adjective not just; unfair.
– DERIVATIVES **unjustly** adverb.
unjustifiable ● adjective impossible to justify.
– DERIVATIVES **unjustifiably** adverb.
unjustified ● adjective not justified.

Thesaurus

union MARRIAGE, wedding, alliance; coupling, intercourse, copulation. **4** *representation by a union* ASSOCIATION, trade union, league, guild, confederation, federation.
– OPPOSITES separation, parting.
unique ● adjective **1** *each site is unique* DISTINCTIVE, individual, special, idiosyncratic; single, sole, lone, unrepeated, unrepeatable, solitary, exclusive, rare, uncommon, unusual; *informal* one-off. **2** *a unique insight into history* REMARKABLE, special, singular, noteworthy, notable, extraordinary; unequalled, unparalleled, unmatched, unsurpassed, incomparable; *formal* unexampled. **3** *species unique to the island* PECULIAR, specific.
unison ● noun
– PHRASES **in unison 1** *they lifted their arms in unison* SIMULTANEOUSLY, at (one and) the same time, (all) at once, (all) together. **2** *we are in complete unison* IN AGREEMENT, in accord, in harmony, as one; *formal* in concord.
unit ● noun **1** *the family is the fundamental unit of society* COMPONENT, element, constituent, subdivision. **2** *a unit of currency* QUANTITY, measure, denomination. **3** *a guerrilla unit* DETACHMENT, contingent, division, company, squadron, corps, regiment, brigade, platoon, battalion; cell, faction.
unite ● verb **1** *uniting the nation* UNIFY, join, link, connect, combine, amalgamate, fuse, weld, bond, bring together, knit together. **2** *environmentalists and activists united* JOIN TOGETHER, join forces, combine, band together, ally, cooperate, collaborate, work together, pull together, team up. **3** *he sought to unite comfort with elegance* MERGE, mix, blend, mingle, combine; *poetic/literary* commingle.
– OPPOSITES divide.
united ● adjective **1** *a united Germany* UNIFIED, integrated, amalgamated, joined, merged; federal, confederate. **2** *a united response* COMMON, shared, joint, combined, communal, cooperative, collective, collaborative, concerted. **3** *they were united in their views* IN AGREEMENT, agreed, in unison, of the same opinion, like-minded, as one, in accord, in harmony, in unity.
United States of America ● noun AMERICA; *informal* the States, the US of A, Uncle Sam; *poetic/literary* Columbia.
unity ● noun **1** *European unity* UNION, unification, integration, amalgamation; coalition, federation, confederation. **2** *unity between opposing factions* HARMONY, accord, cooperation, collaboration, agreement, consensus, solidarity; *formal* concord. **3** *the organic unity of the universe* ONENESS, singleness, wholeness, uniformity, homogeneity.
– OPPOSITES division, discord.
universal ● adjective GENERAL, ubiquitous, comprehensive, common, omnipresent, all-inclusive; global, worldwide, international, widespread.
– OPPOSITES restricted, local.
universally ● adverb INVARIABLY, always, without exception, in all cases; everywhere, worldwide, globally, internationally; widely, commonly, generally.
universe ● noun **1** *the physical universe* COSMOS, macrocosm, totality; infinity, all existence. **2** *the universe of computer hardware* PROVINCE, world, sphere, preserve, domain.
– RELATED TERMS cosmic.
university ● noun COLLEGE, academy, institute; *N. Amer.* school; *historical* polytechnic.
unjust ● adjective **1** *the attack was unjust* BIASED, prejudiced, unfair, inequitable, discriminatory, partisan, partial, one-sided. **2** *an unjust law* WRONGFUL, unfair, undeserved, unmerited, unwarranted, uncalled for, unreasonable, unjustifiable, indefensible.
– OPPOSITES fair.
unjustifiable ● adjective **1** *an unjustifiable extravagance* INDEFENSIBLE, inexcusable, unforgivable, unpardonable, uncalled for, without justification, unwarrantable; excessive, immoderate. **2** *an unjustifiable slur on his character* GROUNDLESS, unfounded, base-

unkempt ● adjective having an untidy or dishevelled appearance.
– ORIGIN from archaic *kempt* 'combed'.
unkept ● adjective **1** (of an undertaking) not honoured. **2** not tidy or cared for.
unkind ● adjective inconsiderate and harsh.
– DERIVATIVES **unkindly** adverb **unkindness** noun.
unkink ● verb make or become straight.
unknowable ● adjective not able to be known.
– DERIVATIVES **unknowability** noun.
unknowing ● adjective not knowing or aware. ● noun literary ignorance.
– DERIVATIVES **unknowingly** adverb.
unknown ● adjective not known or familiar. ● noun an unknown person or thing.
– PHRASES **unknown to** without the knowledge of.
unknown quantity ● noun a person or thing whose nature, value, or significance is not known.
Unknown Soldier ● noun an unidentified representative member of a country's armed forces killed in war, buried with special honours in a national memorial.
unlabelled (US **unlabeled**) ● adjective without a label.
unlace ● verb undo the laces of.
unladen ● adjective not carrying a load.
unladylike ● adjective not appropriate to or behaving like a lady.
unlaid ● adjective not laid.
unlamented ● adjective not mourned or regretted.
unlash ● verb unfasten (something securely tied down).
unlatch ● verb unfasten the latch of.
unlawful ● adjective not conforming to or permitted by law or rules.
– DERIVATIVES **unlawfully** adverb **unlawfulness** noun.
– USAGE The adjectives **unlawful** and **illegal** can both mean 'contrary to or forbidden by law', but **unlawful** has a broader meaning 'not permitted by rules': thus handball in soccer is **unlawful**, but not **illegal**.
unleaded ● adjective (especially of petrol) without added lead.
unlearn ● verb (past and past part. **unlearned** or **unlearnt**) aim to discard (something learned) from one's memory.
unlearned[1] /unlernid/ ● adjective not well educated.
unlearned[2] /unlernd/ (also **unlearnt** /unlernt/) ● adjective not having been learned.
unleash ● verb release from a leash or restraint.
unleavened ● adjective made without yeast or other raising agent.
unless ● conjunction except when; if not.
– ORIGIN from ON or IN + LESS.
unlettered ● adjective poorly educated or illiterate.
unlicensed ● adjective not having an official licence, especially for the sale of alcoholic liquor.
unlike ● preposition **1** different from; not like. **2** in contrast to. **3** uncharacteristic of. ● adjective dissimilar or different from each other.
– DERIVATIVES **unlikeness** noun.
unlikely ● adjective (**unlikelier**, **unlikeliest**) not likely; improbable.
– DERIVATIVES **unlikelihood** noun.
unlimited ● adjective not limited or restricted; infinite.
unlined[1] ● adjective not marked with lines or wrinkles.
unlined[2] ● adjective without a lining.
unlink ● verb make no longer connected.
unlisted ● adjective not included on a list, especially of stock exchange prices or telephone numbers.
unlit ● adjective **1** not provided with lighting. **2** not having been lit.
unlivable ● adjective uninhabitable.
unlived-in ● adjective not appearing to be inhabited.
unload ● verb **1** remove a load from. **2** remove (goods) from a vehicle, ship, etc. **3** informal get rid of. **4** remove (ammunition) from a gun or (film) from a camera.
– DERIVATIVES **unloader** noun.
unlock ● verb **1** undo the lock of (something) using a key. **2** make (something previously inaccessible or unexploited) available.
unlooked ● adjective (**unlooked for**) unexpected; unforeseen.
unloose ● verb undo; let free.
unloosen ● verb another term for UNLOOSE.
unloved ● adjective loved by no one.
unlovely ● adjective not attractive; ugly.
unlucky ● adjective (**unluckier**, **unluckiest**) having, bringing, or resulting from bad luck.
– DERIVATIVES **unluckily** adverb.
unmade ● adjective **1** (of a bed) not arranged tidily. **2** Brit. (of a

Thesaurus

less, unsubstantiated, unconfirmed, uncorroborated.
– OPPOSITES reasonable.
unkempt ● adjective UNTIDY, messy, scruffy, disordered, dishevelled, disarranged, rumpled, wind-blown, ungroomed, bedraggled, in a mess, messed up; tousled, uncombed; *N. Amer. informal* mussed up.
– OPPOSITES tidy.
unkind ● adjective **1** *everyone was being unkind to him* UNCHARITABLE, unpleasant, disagreeable, nasty, mean, mean-spirited, cruel, vicious, spiteful, malicious, callous, unsympathetic, unfeeling, uncaring, hurtful, ill-natured, hard-hearted, cold-hearted; unfriendly, uncivil, inconsiderate, insensitive, hostile; *informal* bitchy, catty; *Brit. informal* beastly. **2** *unkind weather* INCLEMENT, intemperate, rough, severe, filthy.
unkindness ● noun NASTINESS, unpleasantness, disagreeableness, cruelty, malice, meanness, mean-spiritedness, viciousness, callousness, hard-heartedness, cold-heartedness; unfriendliness, inconsiderateness, hostility; *informal* bitchiness, cattiness.
unknown ● adjective **1** *the outcome was unknown* UNDISCLOSED, unrevealed, secret; undetermined, undecided, unresolved, unsettled, unsure, unascertained. **2** *unknown country* UNEXPLORED, uncharted, unmapped, untravelled, undiscovered. **3** *persons unknown* UNIDENTIFIED, unnamed, nameless, anonymous. **4** *firearms were unknown to the Indians* UNFAMILIAR, unheard of, new, novel, strange. **5** *unknown artists* OBSCURE, unheard of, unsung, minor, insignificant, unimportant, undistinguished.
– OPPOSITES familiar.
unlawful ● adjective ILLEGAL, illicit, illegitimate, against the law; criminal, felonious; prohibited, banned, outlawed, proscribed, forbidden.
– OPPOSITES legal.
unleash ● verb LET LOOSE, release, (set) free, unloose, untie, untether, unchain.
unlettered ● adjective ILLITERATE, uneducated, poorly educated, unschooled, unlearned, ignorant.
– OPPOSITES educated.
unlike ● preposition **1** *England is totally unlike Jamaica* DIFFERENT FROM, unalike, dissimilar to. **2** *unlike Linda, Chrissy was a bit of a radical* IN CONTRAST TO, as opposed to.
– OPPOSITES similar too.
● adjective *a meeting of unlike minds* DISSIMILAR, unalike, disparate, contrasting, antithetical, different, diverse, heterogeneous, divergent, at variance, varying, at odds; *informal* like chalk and cheese.
unlikely ● adjective **1** *it is unlikely they will ever recover* IMPROBABLE, doubtful, dubious. **2** *an unlikely story* IMPLAUSIBLE, improbable, questionable, unconvincing, far-fetched, unrealistic, incredible, unbelievable, inconceivable, unimaginable; *informal* tall, cock and bull.
– OPPOSITES probable, believable.
unlimited ● adjective **1** *unlimited supplies of water* INEXHAUSTIBLE, limitless, illimitable, boundless, immeasurable, incalculable, untold, infinite, endless, never-ending. **2** *unlimited travel* UNRESTRICTED, unconstrained, unrestrained, unchecked, unbridled, uncurbed. **3** *unlimited power* TOTAL, unqualified, unconditional, unrestricted, absolute, supreme.
– OPPOSITES finite, restricted.
unload ● verb **1** *we unloaded the van* UNPACK, empty; *archaic* unlade. **2** *they unloaded the cases from the lorry* REMOVE, offload, discharge. **3** *the state unloaded its 25 per cent stake* SELL, discard, jettison, offload, get rid of, dispose of; palm something off on someone, foist something on someone, fob something off on someone; *informal* dump, junk, get shot/shut of.
unlock ● verb UNBOLT, unlatch, unbar, unfasten, open.
unlooked-for ● adjective UNEXPECTED, unforeseen, unanticipated, unsought, undreamed of, unpredicted, fortuitous, chance, serendipitous.
unloved ● adjective UNCARED-FOR, unwanted, friendless, unvalued; rejected, unwelcome, shunned, spurned, neglected, abandoned.
unlucky ● adjective **1** *he was unlucky not to score* UNFORTUNATE, luckless, out of luck, hapless, ill-fated, ill-starred, unhappy; *informal*

road) without a hard, smooth surface.
unmake • verb (past and past part. **unmade**) reverse or undo the making of; annul or destroy.
unman • verb (**unmanned**, **unmanning**) literary deprive of manly qualities such as self-control or courage.
unmanageable • adjective difficult or impossible to manage or control.
– DERIVATIVES **unmanageably** adverb.
unmanned • adjective not having or needing a crew or staff.
unmannerly • adjective not well mannered.
unmarked • adjective **1** not marked. **2** not noticed.
unmarried • adjective not married; single.
unmask • verb expose the true character of.
unmatched • adjective not matched or equalled.
unmeasurable • adjective not able to be measured objectively.
unmeasured • adjective not having been measured.
unmelodious • adjective not melodious; discordant.
unmentionable • adjective too embarrassing or offensive to be spoken about. • noun humorous an unmentionable thing.
unmerciful • adjective showing no mercy.
– DERIVATIVES **unmercifully** adverb.
unmerited • adjective not deserved or merited.
unmetalled • adjective Brit. (of a road) not having a hard surface.
unmetrical • adjective not composed in or using metre.
unmindful • adjective (**unmindful of**) not conscious or aware of.
unmissable • adjective that should not or cannot be missed.
unmistakable (also **unmistakeable**) • adjective not able to be mistaken for anything else.
– DERIVATIVES **unmistakably** adverb.
unmitigated • adjective absolute; unqualified.
– DERIVATIVES **unmitigatedly** adverb.
unmixed • adjective not mixed.
unmodulated • adjective not modulated.
unmoor • verb release the moorings of.
unmotivated • adjective **1** not motivated. **2** without apparent motive.
unmoved • adjective **1** not affected by emotion or excitement. **2** not changed in purpose or position.
– DERIVATIVES **unmovable** (also **unmoveable**) adjective.
unmoving • adjective **1** not moving; still. **2** not stirring any emotion.
unmusical • adjective **1** not pleasing to the ear. **2** unskilled in or indifferent to music.
unmuzzle • verb **1** remove a muzzle from. **2** allow freedom of expression to.
unnameable (also **unnamable**) • adjective unmentionable.
unnatural • adjective **1** contrary to nature; abnormal or artificial. **2** affected; not spontaneous.
– DERIVATIVES **unnaturally** adverb **unnaturalness** noun.
unnavigable • adjective not able to be sailed on by ships or boats.
unnecessary • adjective not necessary; more than is necessary.
– DERIVATIVES **unnecessarily** adverb.
unnerve • verb deprive of courage or confidence.
– DERIVATIVES **unnerving** adjective.
unnoticeable • adjective not easily observed or noticed.
– DERIVATIVES **unnoticeably** adverb.
unnoticed • adjective not noticed.
unnumbered • adjective **1** not assigned a number. **2** not counted; countless.
unobliging • adjective not helpful or cooperative.
unobserved • adjective not observed; unseen.
unobstructed • adjective not obstructed.
unobtainable • adjective not able to be obtained.
unobtrusive • adjective not conspicuous or attracting attention.
– DERIVATIVES **unobtrusively** adverb **unobtrusiveness** noun.
unoccupied • adjective not occupied.
unofficial • adjective not officially authorized or confirmed.
– DERIVATIVES **unofficially** adverb.
unopened • adjective not opened.
unopposed • adjective not opposed; unchallenged.

Thesaurus

down on one's luck; *poetic/literary* star-crossed. **2** *an unlucky number* UNFAVOURABLE, inauspicious, unpropitious, ominous, cursed, ill-fated, ill-omened, disadvantageous, unfortunate.
– OPPOSITES fortunate, favourable.
unmanageable • adjective **1** *the huge house was unmanageable* TROUBLESOME, awkward, inconvenient; cumbersome, bulky, unwieldy. **2** *his behaviour was becoming unmanageable* UNCONTROLLABLE, ungovernable, unruly, disorderly, out of hand, difficult, disruptive, undisciplined, wayward; *informal* stroppy; *archaic* contumacious.
unmanly • adjective EFFEMINATE, effete, unmasculine; weak, soft, timid, timorous, limp-wristed; *informal* sissy, wimpish, wimpy.
– OPPOSITES virile.
unmannerly • adjective RUDE, impolite, uncivil, discourteous, bad-mannered, ill-mannered, disrespectful, impertinent, impudent, insolent; uncouth, boorish, oafish, loutish, ill-bred, coarse.
– OPPOSITES polite.
unmarried • adjective UNWED(DED), single; spinster, bachelor; unattached, available, eligible, free.
unmatched • adjective **1** *a talent for publicity unmatched by any other politician* UNEQUALLED, unrivalled, unparalleled, unsurpassed. **2** *unmatched clarity and balance* PEERLESS, matchless, without equal, without parallel, incomparable, inimitable, superlative, second to none, in a class of its own.
unmentionable • adjective TABOO, censored, forbidden, banned, proscribed, prohibited, not to be spoken of, ineffable, unspeakable, unutterable, unprintable, off limits; *informal* no go.
unmerciful • adjective RUTHLESS, cruel, harsh, merciless, pitiless, cold-blooded, hard-hearted, callous, brutal, severe, unforgiving, inhumane, inhuman, heartless, unsympathetic, unfeeling.
unmistakable • adjective DISTINCTIVE, distinct, telltale, indisputable, indubitable, undoubted; plain, clear, definite, obvious, evident, self-evident, manifest, patent, unambiguous, unequivocal, pronounced, as plain as the nose on your face.
unmitigated • adjective ABSOLUTE, unqualified, categorical, complete, total, downright, outright, utter, out-and-out, undiluted, unequivocal, veritable, perfect, consummate, pure, sheer.
unmoved • adjective **1** *he was totally unmoved by her outburst* UNAFFECTED, untouched, unimpressed, undismayed, unworried; aloof, cool, cold, dry-eyed; unconcerned, uncaring, indifferent, impassive, unemotional, stoical, phlegmatic, equable; impervious (to), oblivious (to), heedless (of), deaf to. **2** *he remained unmoved on the crucial issues* STEADFAST, firm, unwavering, unswerving, resolute, decided, resolved, inflexible, unbending, implacable, adamant.
unnatural • adjective **1** *the life of a battery hen is completely unnatural* ABNORMAL, unusual, uncommon, extraordinary, strange, freak, odd, peculiar, unorthodox, exceptional, irregular, untypical. **2** *a flash of unnatural colour* ARTIFICIAL, man-made, synthetic, manufactured. **3** *unnatural vice* PERVERTED, warped, twisted, deviant, depraved, degenerate; *informal* kinky, pervy, sick. **4** *her voice sounded unnatural* AFFECTED, artificial, stilted, forced, laboured, strained, false, fake, insincere; *informal* put on, phoney. **5** *they condemned her as an unnatural woman* UNCARING, unfeeling, heartless, cold-blooded, hard-hearted, callous, cruel, inhumane.
– OPPOSITES normal, genuine.
unnecessary • adjective UNNEEDED, inessential, not required, uncalled for, useless, unwarranted, unwanted, undesired, dispensable, unimportant, optional, extraneous, expendable, disposable, redundant, pointless, purposeless.
– OPPOSITES essential.
unnerve • verb DEMORALIZE, discourage, dishearten, dispirit, daunt, alarm, frighten, dismay, disconcert, discompose, perturb, upset, discomfit, take aback, unsettle, disquiet, fluster, agitate, shake, ruffle, throw off balance; *informal* rattle, faze, shake up; *Brit. informal* put the wind up; *N. Amer. informal* discombobulate.
– OPPOSITES hearten.
unobtrusive • adjective **1** *she was unobtrusive and shy* SELF-EFFACING, retiring, unassuming, quiet; shy, bashful, timid, timorous, reserved, withdrawn, introvert(ed), unforthcoming, unassertive. **2** *unobtrusive service* INCONSPICUOUS, unnoticeable, low-key, discreet, circumspect, understated, unostentatious.
– OPPOSITES extrovert, conspicuous.
unoccupied • adjective **1** *an unoccupied house* VACANT, empty, uninhabited; free, available, to let. **2** *an unoccupied territory* UNINHABITED, unpopulated, unpeopled, unsettled. **3** *many young people were unoccupied* AT LEISURE, idle, free, with time on one's hands, at a loose end.
– OPPOSITES inhabited, populated, busy.
unofficial • adjective **1** *unofficial figures* UNAUTHENTICATED, unconfirmed, uncorroborated, unsubstantiated, off the record. **2** *an unofficial committee* INFORMAL, casual; unauthorized, unsanc-

u

unorganized (also **unorganised**) ● adjective **1** not organized. **2** not unionized.
unoriginal ● adjective lacking originality; derivative.
– DERIVATIVES **unoriginality** noun **unoriginally** adverb.
unorthodox ● adjective contrary to what is usual, traditional, or accepted.
– DERIVATIVES **unorthodoxy** noun.
unostentatious ● adjective not ostentatious.
– DERIVATIVES **unostentatiously** adverb.
unpack ● verb **1** open and remove the contents of (a suitcase or container). **2** remove from a packed container. **3** analyse into component elements.
unpaid ● adjective **1** (of a debt) not yet paid. **2** (of work or leave) undertaken without payment. **3** not receiving payment for work done.
unpaired ● adjective **1** not arranged in pairs. **2** not forming one of a pair.
unpalatable ● adjective **1** not pleasant to taste. **2** difficult to put up with or accept.
unparalleled ● adjective having no parallel or equal; exceptional.
unpardonable ● adjective (of a fault or offence) unforgivable.
– DERIVATIVES **unpardonably** adverb.
unparliamentary ● adjective (especially of language) contrary to the rules or procedures of parliament.
unpasteurized (also **unpasteurised**) ● adjective not pasteurized.
unpatriotic ● adjective not patriotic.
– DERIVATIVES **unpatriotically** adverb.
unpaved ● adjective lacking a metalled or paved surface.
unpeopled ● adjective emptied of people; depopulated.
unperson ● noun (pl. **unpersons**) a person whose name or existence is officially denied or ignored.
unperturbed ● adjective not perturbed or concerned.
unpick ● verb **1** undo the sewing of (stitches or a garment). **2** carefully analyse the different elements of.
unpin ● verb (**unpinned**, **unpinning**) unfasten or detach by removing a pin or pins.
unpitying ● adjective not feeling or showing pity.
unplaced ● adjective **1** not having or assigned to a specific place. **2** chiefly Horse Racing not one of the first three (sometimes four) to finish in a race.
unplanned ● adjective not planned.
unplayable ● adjective **1** not able to be played or played on. **2** (of music) too difficult or bad to perform.
unpleasant ● adjective not pleasant; disagreeable.
– DERIVATIVES **unpleasantly** adverb.
unpleasantness ● noun **1** the state or quality of being unpleasant. **2** bad feeling or quarrelling between people.
unploughed (US **unplowed**) ● adjective (of land) not having been ploughed.
unplug ● verb (**unplugged**, **unplugging**) **1** disconnect (an electrical device) by removing its plug from a socket. **2** remove an obstacle or blockage from.
unplugged ● adjective trademark (of pop or rock music) performed or recorded with acoustic rather than electrically amplified instruments.
unplumbed ● adjective **1** not provided with plumbing. **2** not fully explored or understood.
– DERIVATIVES **unplumbable** adjective.
unpolished ● adjective **1** not having a polished surface. **2** (of a work) not polished.
unpolled ● adjective **1** (of a voter) not having voted, or registered to vote, at an election. **2** (of a vote) not cast at or registered for an election. **3** (of a person) not included in an opinion poll.
unpopular ● adjective not liked or popular.
– DERIVATIVES **unpopularity** noun.
unpopulated ● adjective without inhabitants.
unpowered ● adjective having no fuel-burning source of power for propulsion.
unpractised (US **unpracticed**) ● adjective not trained or experienced.
unprecedented ● adjective never done or known before.
– DERIVATIVES **unprecedentedly** adverb.
unpredictable ● adjective not able to be predicted; changeable.
– DERIVATIVES **unpredictability** noun **unpredictably** adverb.
unprejudiced ● adjective without prejudice; unbiased.
unpremeditated ● adjective not thought out or planned beforehand.
unprepared ● adjective **1** not ready or able to deal with something. **2** not made ready for use.
unprepossessing ● adjective not attractive or appealing to the eye.
unpressurized (also **unpressurised**) ● adjective **1** (of a gas or its container) not having raised pressure that is produced or

Thesaurus

tioned, unaccredited.
– OPPOSITES confirmed, formal.
unorthodox ● adjective **1** *unorthodox views on management* UNCONVENTIONAL, unusual, radical, nonconformist, avant-garde, eccentric; *informal* off the wall, way out, offbeat. **2** *unorthodox religious views* HETERODOX, heretical, nonconformist, dissenting.
– OPPOSITES conventional.
unpaid ● adjective **1** *unpaid bills* UNSETTLED, outstanding, due, overdue, owing, owed, payable, undischarged; *N. Amer.* delinquent, past due. **2** *unpaid charity work* VOLUNTARY, volunteer, honorary, unremunerative, unsalaried, pro bono (publico).
unpalatable ● adjective **1** *unpalatable food* UNAPPETIZING, unappealing, unsavoury, inedible, uneatable; disgusting, revolting, nauseating, tasteless, flavourless. **2** *the unpalatable truth* DISAGREEABLE, unpleasant, regrettable, unwelcome, lamentable, dreadful, hateful.
– OPPOSITES tasty.
unparalleled ● adjective EXCEPTIONAL, unique, singular, rare, unprecedented, without parallel, without equal, unequalled; matchless, peerless, unrivalled, unsurpassed, unexcelled, incomparable, second to none; *formal* unexampled.
unperturbed ● adjective UNTROUBLED, undisturbed, unworried, unconcerned, unmoved, unflustered, unruffled, undismayed; calm, composed, cool, collected, unemotional, self-possessed, self-assured, level-headed, unfazed, laid-back.
unpleasant ● adjective **1** *a very unpleasant situation* DISAGREEABLE, irksome, troublesome, annoying, irritating, vexatious, displeasing, distressing, nasty, horrible, terrible, awful, dreadful, hateful, miserable, invidious, objectionable, offensive, obnoxious, repugnant, repulsive, repellent, revolting, disgusting, distasteful, nauseating, unsavoury. **2** *an unpleasant man* UNLIKABLE, unlovable, disagreeable; unfriendly, rude, impolite, obnoxious, nasty, spiteful, mean, mean-spirited; insufferable, unbearable, annoying, irritating. **3** *an unpleasant taste* UNAPPETIZING, unpalatable, unsavoury, unappealing, bitter, sour, rancid; disgusting, revolting, nauseating, sickening.
– OPPOSITES agreeable, likable.
unpolished ● adjective **1** *unpolished wood* UNVARNISHED, unfinished, untreated, natural. **2** *his unpolished ways* UNSOPHISTICATED, unrefined, uncultured, uncultivated, coarse, crude, rough (and ready), awkward, clumsy, gauche, vulgar. **3** *an unpolished performance* SLIPSHOD, rough, crude, uneven.
– OPPOSITES varnished, sophisticated.
unpopular ● adjective DISLIKED, friendless, unliked, unloved; unwelcome, avoided, ignored, rejected, shunned, spurned, cold-shouldered.
unprecedented ● adjective UNPARALLELED, unequalled, unmatched, unrivalled, without parallel, without equal, out of the ordinary, unusual, exceptional, singular, remarkable, unique; unheard of, unknown, new, ground-breaking, revolutionary, pioneering; *formal* unexampled.
unpredictable ● adjective **1** *unpredictable results* UNFORESEEABLE, uncertain, unsure, doubtful, dubious, in the balance, up in the air, arbitrary. **2** *unpredictable behaviour* ERRATIC, moody, volatile, unstable, capricious, temperamental, mercurial, changeable, variable.
unprejudiced ● adjective **1** *unprejudiced observation* OBJECTIVE, impartial, unbiased, neutral, non-partisan, detached, disinterested. **2** *unprejudiced attitudes* UNBIASED, non-discriminatory, tolerant, liberal, broad-minded, unbigoted.
– OPPOSITES partisan, intolerant.
unpremeditated ● adjective UNPLANNED, spontaneous, unprepared, impromptu, spur-of-the-moment, unrehearsed; *informal* off-the-cuff.
– OPPOSITES planned.
unprepared ● adjective **1** *we were unprepared for the new VAT regime* UNREADY, off (one's) guard, surprised, taken aback; *informal* caught napping, caught on the hop. **2** *they are unprepared to sup-*

u

maintained artificially. **2** (of an aircraft cabin) not having normal atmospheric pressure maintained at a high altitude.

unpretending • adjective archaic not pretentious or false.

unpretentious • adjective not pretentious; modest.

– DERIVATIVES **unpretentiously** adverb **unpretentiousness** noun.

unprincipled • adjective not acting in accordance with moral principles.

unprintable • adjective (of words, comments, or thoughts) too offensive or shocking to be published.

unproblematic • adjective not presenting a problem or difficulty.

– DERIVATIVES **unproblematically** adverb.

unprocessed • adjective not processed.

unproductive • adjective **1** not producing or able to produce large amounts of goods, crops, etc. **2** not achieving much; not very useful.

unprofessional • adjective below or contrary to the standards expected in a particular profession.

– DERIVATIVES **unprofessionally** adverb.

unprofitable • adjective **1** not yielding a profit. **2** not beneficial or useful.

unpromising • adjective not giving hope of future success or good results.

– DERIVATIVES **unpromisingly** adverb.

unprompted • adjective without being prompted.

unpronounceable • adjective too difficult to pronounce.

unprotected • adjective **1** not protected or kept safe from harm. **2** (of sexual intercourse) performed without a condom.

unproven /unproōv'n, -prō-/ (also **unproved**) • adjective **1** not demonstrated by evidence or argument as true or existing. **2** not tried and tested.

unprovoked • adjective (of an attack, crime, etc.) not directly provoked.

unpublished • adjective **1** (of a work) not published. **2** (of an author) having no writings published.

– DERIVATIVES **unpublishable** adjective.

unpunished • adjective (of an offence or offender) not receiving any punishment or penalty.

unputdownable • adjective informal (of a book) so engrossing that one cannot stop reading it.

unqualified • adjective **1** not having the necessary qualifications or requirements. **2** without reservation or limitation; total: *an unqualified success.*

unquantifiable • adjective impossible to express or measure.

unquenchable • adjective not able to be quenched.

unquestionable • adjective not able to be disputed or doubted.

– DERIVATIVES **unquestionably** adverb.

unquestioned • adjective **1** not disputed or doubted; certain. **2** accepted without question. **3** not subjected to questioning.

– DERIVATIVES **unquestioning** adjective.

unquiet • adjective **1** unable to be still; restless. **2** uneasy; anxious.

– DERIVATIVES **unquietly** adverb.

unquoted • adjective not quoted or listed on a stock exchange.

unravel • verb (**unravelled**, **unravelling**; US **unraveled**, **unraveling**) **1** undo (twisted, knitted, or woven threads); unwind. **2** become undone. **3** investigate and solve (a mystery or puzzle). **4** begin to fail or collapse.

unreachable • adjective unable to be reached or contacted.

unreactive • adjective having little tendency to react chemically.

unread • adjective not having been read.

unreadable • adjective **1** not clear enough to read; illegible. **2** too dull or difficult to be worth reading.

– DERIVATIVES **unreadability** noun **unreadably** adverb.

unready • adjective not ready or prepared.

unreal • adjective **1** imaginary; not seeming real. **2** unrealistic. **3** informal, chiefly N. Amer. incredible; amazing.

– DERIVATIVES **unreality** noun **unreally** adverb.

unrealistic • adjective not realistic.

– DERIVATIVES **unrealistically** adverb.

unrealized (also **unrealised**) • adjective **1** not achieved or created. **2** not converted into money: *unrealized property assets.*

unreason • noun irrationality; lack of reasonable thought.

– DERIVATIVES **unreasoned** adjective.

unreasonable • adjective **1** not guided by or based on good sense. **2** beyond the limits of acceptability.

– DERIVATIVES **unreasonableness** noun **unreasonably** adverb.

unreasoning • adjective not guided by or based on reason; illogical.

unreceptive • adjective not receptive.

unreciprocated • adjective not reciprocated; unrequited.

unrecognizable (also **unrecognisable**) • adjective not able to be recognized.

– DERIVATIVES **unrecognizably** adverb.

unrecognized (also **unrecognised**) • adjective **1** not identified

Thesaurus

port the reforms UNWILLING, disinclined, loath, reluctant, resistant, opposed.

– OPPOSITES ready, willing.

unpretentious • adjective **1** *he was thoroughly unpretentious* UNAFFECTED, modest, unassuming, without airs, natural, straightforward, open, honest, sincere, frank. **2** *an unpretentious hotel* SIMPLE, plain, modest, humble, unostentatious, homely, unsophisticated.

unprincipled • adjective IMMORAL, unethical, unscrupulous, dishonourable, dishonest, deceitful, devious, corrupt, crooked, wicked, evil, villainous, shameless, base, low.

– OPPOSITES ethical.

unproductive • adjective **1** *unproductive soil* STERILE, barren, infertile, unfruitful, poor. **2** *unproductive meetings* FRUITLESS, futile, vain, idle, useless, worthless, valueless, pointless, ineffective, ineffectual, unprofitable, unrewarding.

– OPPOSITES fruitful.

unprofessional • adjective **1** *unprofessional conduct* IMPROPER, unethical, unprincipled, unscrupulous, dishonourable, disreputable, unseemly, unbecoming, indecorous; *informal* shady, crooked. **2** *he accused the detectives of being unprofessional* AMATEURISH, amateur, unskilled, unskilful, inexpert, unqualified, inexperienced, incompetent, second-rate, inefficient.

unpromising • adjective INAUSPICIOUS, unfavourable, unpropitious, discouraging, disheartening, gloomy, bleak, black, portentous, ominous, ill-omened.

– OPPOSITES auspicious.

unqualified • adjective **1** *an unqualified accountant* UNCERTIFICATED, unlicensed, untrained, inexperienced. **2** *those unqualified to look after children* UNSUITABLE, unfit, ineligible, incompetent, unable, incapable. **3** *unqualified support* UNCONDITIONAL, unreserved, unlimited, without reservations, categorical, unequivocal, unambiguous, wholehearted; complete, absolute, downright, undivided, total, utter.

unquestionable • adjective INDUBITABLE, undoubted, beyond question, beyond doubt, indisputable, undeniable, irrefutable, incontestable, incontrovertible, unequivocal; certain, sure, definite, self-evident, evident, manifest, obvious, apparent, patent.

unravel • verb **1** *he unravelled the strands* UNTANGLE, disentangle, separate out, unwind, untwist. **2** *detectives are trying to unravel the mystery* SOLVE, resolve, clear up, puzzle out, get to the bottom of, explain, clarify, make head or tail of; *informal* figure out, suss (out). **3** *society is starting to unravel* FALL APART, fail, collapse, go wrong.

– OPPOSITES entangle.

unreadable • adjective **1** *unreadable writing* ILLEGIBLE, hard to read, indecipherable, unintelligible, scrawled, crabbed. **2** *heavy, unreadable novels* DULL, tedious, boring, uninteresting, dry, wearisome, difficult, heavy. **3** *Nathan's expression was unreadable* INSCRUTABLE, enigmatic, impenetrable, cryptic, mysterious, deadpan; *informal* poker-faced.

– OPPOSITES legible, accessible.

unreal • adjective IMAGINARY, fictitious, pretend, make-believe, made-up, dreamed-up, mock, false, illusory, mythical, fanciful; hypothetical, theoretical; *informal* phoney.

unrealistic • adjective **1** *it is unrealistic to expect changes overnight* IMPRACTICAL, impracticable, unfeasible, non-viable; unreasonable, irrational, illogical, senseless, silly, foolish, fanciful, idealistic, romantic, starry-eyed. **2** *unrealistic images* UNLIFELIKE, non-realistic, unnatural, non-representational, abstract.

– OPPOSITES pragmatic, lifelike.

unreasonable • adjective **1** *an unreasonable woman* UNCOOPERATIVE, unhelpful, disobliging, unaccommodating, awkward, contrary, difficult; obstinate, obdurate, wilful, headstrong, pigheaded, intractable, intransigent, inflexible; irrational, illogical, prejudiced, intolerant. **2** *unreasonable demands* UNACCEPTABLE, preposterous, outrageous; excessive, immoderate, disproportionate, undue, inordinate, intolerable, unjustified, unwarranted, uncalled

from previous encounters or knowledge. **2** not acknowledged as valid.
unreconciled • adjective not reconciled.
unreconstructed • adjective not reconciled or converted to the current political theory or movement.
unrecorded • adjective not recorded.
unredeemed • adjective not redeemed.
unreel • verb **1** unwind. **2** (of a film) wind from one reel to another during projection.
unrefined • adjective **1** not processed to remove impurities. **2** not elegant or cultured.
unregenerate /unrijennərət/ • adjective not reforming or showing repentance; obstinately wrong or bad.
unregistered • adjective not officially recognized and recorded.
unregulated • adjective not controlled or supervised by regulations or laws.
unrehearsed • adjective not rehearsed.
unrelated • adjective not related.
unreleased • adjective (especially of a film or recording) not released.
unrelenting • adjective not yielding in strength, severity, or determination.
– DERIVATIVES **unrelentingly** adverb.
unreliable • adjective not able to be relied upon.
– DERIVATIVES **unreliability** noun **unreliably** adverb.
unrelieved • adjective **1** lacking variation or change; monotonous. **2** not provided with aid or assistance.
– DERIVATIVES **unrelievedly** adverb.
unremarkable • adjective not particularly interesting or surprising.
unremarked • adjective not remarked upon; unnoticed.
unremitting • adjective never relaxing or slackening.
– DERIVATIVES **unremittingly** adverb.
unremunerative • adjective bringing little or no profit or income.
unrepeatable • adjective **1** not able to be repeated. **2** too offensive or shocking to be said again.
unrepentant • adjective showing no regret for one's wrongdoings.
– DERIVATIVES **unrepentantly** adverb.
unreported • adjective not reported.
unrepresentative • adjective not typical of a class, group, or body of opinion.
unrequited • adjective (of a feeling, especially love) not returned or rewarded.
unreserved • adjective **1** without reservations; complete. **2** frank and open. **3** not set apart or booked in advance.
– DERIVATIVES **unreservedly** adverb.
unresolved • adjective (of a problem, dispute, etc.) not resolved.
unresponsive • adjective not responsive.
– DERIVATIVES **unresponsively** adverb **unresponsiveness** noun.
unrest • noun **1** a state of rebellious dissatisfaction in a group of people. **2** a state of uneasiness or disturbance.
unrestrained • adjective not restrained or restricted.
– DERIVATIVES **unrestrainedly** adverb.
unrestricted • adjective not limited or restricted.
unrewarding • adjective not rewarding or satisfying.
unripe • adjective not ripe.
unrivalled (US **unrivaled**) • adjective surpassing all others.
unroll • verb open or cause to open out from a rolled-up state.
unromantic • adjective not romantic.
unruffled • adjective **1** not disordered or disturbed. **2** (of a person) not agitated; calm.
unruly • adjective (**unrulier**, **unruliest**) disorderly and disruptive; difficult to control.
– DERIVATIVES **unruliness** noun.
– ORIGIN from archaic *ruly* 'disciplined, orderly', from RULE.
unsaddle • verb remove the saddle from.
unsafe • adjective **1** not safe; dangerous. **2** Law (of a verdict or conviction) not based on reliable evidence and likely to constitute a miscarriage of justice. **3** referring to sexual activity in which precautions are not taken to reduce the risk of spreading sexually transmitted diseases.
unsaid past and past participle of UNSAY. • adjective not said or uttered.
unsaleable (also **unsalable**) • adjective not able to be sold.
unsalted • adjective not salted.
unsanitary • adjective not sanitary.

Thesaurus

for.
unrecognizable • adjective UNIDENTIFIABLE, unknowable; disguised.
unrefined • adjective **1** *unrefined clay* UNPROCESSED, untreated, crude, raw, natural, unprepared, unfinished. **2** *unrefined men* UNCULTURED, uncultivated, uncivilized, uneducated, unsophisticated; boorish, oafish, loutish, coarse, vulgar, rude, uncouth.
– OPPOSITES processed.
unrelated • adjective **1** *unrelated incidents* SEPARATE, unconnected, independent, unassociated, distinct, discrete, disparate. **2** *a reason unrelated to my work* IRRELEVANT, immaterial, inapplicable, unconcerned, off the subject, beside the point, not pertinent, not germane.
unrelenting • adjective **1** *the unrelenting heat* CONTINUAL, constant, continuous, relentless, unremitting, unabating, unrelieved, incessant, unceasing, endless, unending, persistent. **2** *an unrelenting opponent* IMPLACABLE, inflexible, uncompromising, unyielding, unbending, relentless, determined, dogged, tireless, unflagging, unshakeable, unswerving, unwavering.
– OPPOSITES intermittent.
unreliable • adjective **1** *unreliable volunteers* UNDEPENDABLE, untrustworthy, irresponsible, fickle, capricious, erratic, unpredictable, inconstant, faithless. **2** *an unreliable indicator* QUESTIONABLE, open to doubt, doubtful, dubious, suspect, unsound, tenuous, fallible; risky, chancy, inaccurate; *informal* iffy, dicey.
unremitting • adjective RELENTLESS, unrelenting, continual, constant, continuous, unabating, unrelieved, sustained, unceasing, ceaseless, endless, unending, persistent, perpetual, interminable.
unrepentant • adjective IMPENITENT, unrepenting, remorseless, unashamed, unapologetic, unabashed.
unreserved • adjective **1** *unreserved support* UNCONDITIONAL, unqualified, without reservations, unlimited, categorical, unequivocal, unambiguous; absolute, complete, thorough, wholehearted, total, utter, undivided. **2** *an unreserved young man* UNINHIBITED, extrovert, outgoing, unrestrained, open, unconstrained, unselfconscious, outspoken, frank, candid. **3** *unreserved seats* UNBOOKED, unallocated, unoccupied, free, empty, vacant.
– OPPOSITES qualified, reticent, booked.
unresolved • adjective UNDECIDED, unsettled, undetermined, uncertain, open, pending, open to debate/question, doubtful, in doubt, up in the air.
– OPPOSITES decided.
unrest • noun DISRUPTION, disturbance, trouble, turmoil, disorder, chaos, anarchy; discord, dissension, dissent, strife, protest, rebellion, uprising, rioting.
– OPPOSITES peace.
unrestrained • adjective UNCONTROLLED, unconstrained, unrestricted, unchecked, unbridled, unlimited, unfettered, uninhibited, unbounded, undisciplined.
unrestricted • adjective UNLIMITED, open, free, clear, unhindered, unimpeded, unhampered, unchecked, unrestrained, unconstrained, unblocked, unbounded, unconfined, unqualified.
– OPPOSITES limited.
unripe • adjective IMMATURE, unready, green, sour.
unrivalled • adjective UNEQUALLED, without equal, unparalleled, without parallel, unmatched, unsurpassed, unexcelled, incomparable, beyond compare, inimitable, second to none.
unruffled • adjective **1** *an unruffled voice* CALM, composed, self-controlled, self-possessed, untroubled, unperturbed, at ease, relaxed, serene, cool, {cool, calm, and collected}, cool-headed, unemotional, equanimous, equable, stoical; *informal* unfazed. **2** *an unruffled sea* TRANQUIL, calm, smooth, still, flat, motionless, placid, waveless, pacific, like a millpond.
unruly • adjective DISORDERLY, rowdy, wild, unmanageable, uncontrollable, disobedient, disruptive, undisciplined, wayward, wilful, headstrong, irrepressible, obstreperous, difficult, intractable, out of hand, recalcitrant; boisterous, lively; *formal* refractory; *archaic* contumacious.
– OPPOSITES disciplined.
unsafe • adjective **1** *the building was unsafe* DANGEROUS, risky, perilous, hazardous, life-threatening, high-risk, treacherous, insecure, unsound; harmful, injurious, toxic. **2** *the verdict was unsafe* UNRELIABLE, insecure, unsound, questionable, doubtful, dubious, open to question/doubt, suspect, fallible; *informal* iffy.
– OPPOSITES harmless, secure.
unsaid • adjective UNSPOKEN, unuttered, unstated, unexpressed, un-

u

unsatisfactory • adjective **1** unacceptable because poor or not good enough. **2** Law another term for UNSAFE.
– DERIVATIVES **unsatisfactorily** adverb.
unsatisfied • adjective not satisfied.
unsatisfying • adjective not satisfying.
– DERIVATIVES **unsatisfyingly** adverb.
unsaturated • adjective Chemistry (of organic molecules) having carbon–carbon double or triple bonds and therefore not containing the greatest possible number of hydrogen atoms.
– DERIVATIVES **unsaturation** noun.
unsaved • adjective not saved, in particular (in Christian use) not having had one's soul saved from damnation.
unsavoury (US **unsavory**) • adjective **1** disagreeable to taste, smell, or look at. **2** objectionable; disreputable.
unsay • verb (past and past part. **unsaid**) withdraw or retract (a statement).
unsayable • adjective not able to be said, especially because considered too controversial or offensive.
unscarred • adjective not scarred or damaged.
unscathed • adjective without suffering any injury, damage, or harm.
unscented • adjective not scented.
unscheduled • adjective not scheduled.
unschooled • adjective **1** lacking schooling or training. **2** not affected; natural and spontaneous.
unscientific • adjective **1** not in accordance with scientific principles or methodology. **2** lacking knowledge of or interest in science.
– DERIVATIVES **unscientifically** adverb.
unscramble • verb restore or convert to an intelligible or readable state.
unscreened • adjective **1** not subjected to screening. **2** not shown or broadcast. **3** not provided with a screen.
unscrew • verb unfasten by twisting.
unscripted • adjective said or delivered without a prepared script; impromptu.
unscrupulous • adjective without moral scruples.
– DERIVATIVES **unscrupulously** adverb **unscrupulousness** noun.
unseal • verb remove or break the seal of.
unsealed • adjective not sealed.
unseasonable • adjective (of weather) unusual for the time of year.
– DERIVATIVES **unseasonably** adverb.
unseasonal • adjective (especially of weather) unusual or inappropriate for the time of year.
unseasoned • adjective **1** (of food) not flavoured with salt, pepper, or other spices. **2** (of timber) not treated or matured. **3** inexperienced.
unseat • verb **1** cause to fall from a saddle or seat. **2** remove from a position of power.
unsecured • adjective **1** (of a loan) made without an asset given as security. **2** not made secure or safe.
unseeded • adjective **1** (of a competitor in a sports tournament) not seeded. **2** without seeds.
unseeing • adjective with one's eyes open but without noticing or seeing anything.
– DERIVATIVES **unseeingly** adverb.
unseemly • adjective (of behaviour or actions) not proper or appropriate.
– DERIVATIVES **unseemliness** noun.
unseen • adjective **1** not seen or noticed. **2** chiefly Brit. (of a passage for translation in an examination) not previously read or prepared.
unselfconscious • adjective not shy or embarrassed.
– DERIVATIVES **unselfconsciously** adverb **unselfconsciousness** noun.
unselfish • adjective not selfish.
– DERIVATIVES **unselfishly** adverb **unselfishness** noun.
unsentimental • adjective not displaying or influenced by sentimental feelings.
– DERIVATIVES **unsentimentally** adverb.
unserious • adjective not serious; light-hearted.
unserviceable • adjective not in working order; unfit for use.
unsettle • verb cause to be anxious or uneasy; disturb.
– DERIVATIVES **unsettling** adjective.
unsettled • adjective **1** lacking stability; changeable or liable to change. **2** agitated; uneasy. **3** not yet resolved. **4** (of an area) having no settlers or inhabitants.
unsex • verb deprive of gender, sexuality, or the characteristic attributes of one or other sex.
unshackle • verb release from shackles or other restraints.
unshakeable (also **unshakable**) • adjective (of a belief, feeling, etc.) firm and unable to be changed or disputed.
unshaken • adjective steadfast and unwavering.
unshaven • adjective not having shaved or been shaved.
unsheathe • verb draw or pull out (a knife or similar weapon) from a sheath.
unshed • adjective (of tears) welling in a person's eyes but not falling.
unshelled • adjective not extracted from its shell.
unship • verb (**unshipped**, **unshipping**) chiefly Nautical **1** remove (an oar, mast, or other object) from a fixed or regular position.

Thesaurus

voiced, untalked-of, suppressed; tacit, implicit, understood, not spelt out, taken as read, inferred, implied.
unsanitary • adjective UNHYGIENIC, insanitary, dirty, filthy, unclean, contaminated, unhealthy, germ-ridden, disease-ridden, infested, insalubrious, polluted.
– OPPOSITES hygienic.
unsatisfactory • adjective DISAPPOINTING, dissatisfying, undesirable, disagreeable, displeasing; inadequate, unacceptable, poor, bad, substandard, weak, mediocre, not good enough, not up to par, defective, deficient, imperfect, inferior; *informal* leaving a lot to be desired, no great shakes, not much cop.
unsavoury • adjective **1** *unsavoury portions of food* UNPALATABLE, unappetizing, distasteful, disagreeable, unappealing, unattractive; inedible, uneatable, disgusting, revolting, nauseating, sickening, foul, nasty, vile; tasteless, bland, flavourless; *informal* yucky. **2** *an unsavoury character* DISREPUTABLE, unpleasant, disagreeable, nasty, mean, rough; immoral, degenerate, dishonourable, dishonest, unprincipled, unscrupulous, villainous; *informal* shady, crooked.
– OPPOSITES tasty, appetizing.
unscathed • adjective UNHARMED, unhurt, uninjured, undamaged, in one piece, intact, safe (and sound), unmarked, untouched, unscratched.
– OPPOSITES harmed, injured.
unscrupulous • adjective UNPRINCIPLED, unethical, immoral, conscienceless, shameless, reprobate, exploitative, corrupt, dishonest, dishonourable, deceitful, devious, underhand, unsavoury, disreputable, evil, wicked, villainous; *informal* crooked, shady; *dated* dastardly.
unseat • verb **1** *the horse unseated his rider* DISLODGE, throw, dismount, upset, unhorse. **2** *an attempt to unseat the party leader* DEPOSE, oust, remove from office, topple, overthrow, bring down, dislodge, supplant, usurp, overturn, eject.
unseemly • adjective INDECOROUS, improper, unbecoming, unfitting, unbefitting, unworthy, undignified, indiscreet, indelicate, ungentlemanly, unladylike.
– OPPOSITES decorous.
unseen • adjective HIDDEN, concealed, obscured, camouflaged, out of sight, imperceptible, undetectable, unnoticeable, unnoticed, unobserved.
unselfish • adjective ALTRUISTIC, disinterested, selfless, self-denying, self-sacrificing; generous, philanthropic, public-spirited, charitable, benevolent, caring, kind, considerate, noble.
unsettle • verb DISCOMPOSE, unnerve, upset, disturb, disquiet, perturb, discomfit, disconcert, alarm, dismay, trouble, bother, agitate, fluster, ruffle, shake (up), throw, unbalance, destabilize; *informal* rattle, faze.
unsettled • adjective **1** *an unsettled life* AIMLESS, directionless, purposeless, without purpose; rootless, nomadic. **2** *an unsettled child* RESTLESS, restive, fidgety, anxious, worried, troubled, fretful; agitated, ruffled, uneasy, disconcerted, discomposed, unnerved, ill at ease, edgy, on edge, tense, nervous, apprehensive, disturbed, perturbed; *informal* rattled, fazed. **3** *unsettled weather* CHANGEABLE, changing, variable, varying, inconstant, inconsistent, ever-changing, erratic, unstable, undependable, unreliable, uncertain, unpredictable, protean. **4** *the question remains unsettled* UNDECIDED, to be decided, unresolved, undetermined, uncertain, open to debate, doubtful, in doubt, up in the air, in a state of uncertainty. **5** *the debt remains unsettled* UNPAID, payable, outstanding, owing, owed, to be paid, due, undischarged; *N. Amer.* delinquent, past due. **6** *unsettled areas* UNINHABITED, unpopulated, unpeopled, desolate, lonely.
unshakeable • adjective STEADFAST, resolute, staunch, firm, de-

u

2 unload (a cargo) from a ship or boat.
unshockable • adjective impossible to shock.
unshorn • adjective (of hair or wool) not cut or shorn.
unsighted • adjective **1** lacking the power of sight. **2** (especially in sport) prevented from having a clear view.
unsightly • adjective unpleasant to look at; ugly.
– DERIVATIVES **unsightliness** noun.
unsigned • adjective **1** not bearing a person's signature. **2** (of a musician or sports player) not having signed a contract of employment.
unsinkable • adjective unable to be sunk.
unskilful (also chiefly US **unskillful**) • adjective not having or showing skill.
– DERIVATIVES **unskilfully** adverb.
unskilled • adjective not having or requiring special skill or training.
unsling • verb (past and past part. **unslung**) remove from a position of being slung or suspended.
unsmiling • adjective not smiling; serious or unfriendly.
– DERIVATIVES **unsmilingly** adverb.
unsmoked • adjective **1** (of meat or fish) not cured by exposure to smoke. **2** (of tobacco or a cigarette) not having been smoked.
unsnap • verb (**unsnapped**, **unsnapping**) unfasten or open with a brisk movement and a sharp sound.
unsociable • adjective **1** not enjoying the company of others. **2** not conducive to friendly social relations.
unsocial • adjective **1** (of the hours of work of a job) falling outside the normal working day and thus socially inconvenient. **2** antisocial.
– DERIVATIVES **unsocially** adverb.
unsold • adjective (of an item) not sold.
unsolicited • adjective not asked for; given or done voluntarily.
unsolved • adjective not solved.
unsophisticated • adjective **1** lacking refined worldly knowledge or tastes. **2** not complicated or highly developed; basic.
unsorted • adjective not sorted or arranged.
unsound • adjective **1** not safe or robust; in poor condition. **2** not based on sound evidence or reasoning; unreliable or unacceptable.
– DERIVATIVES **unsoundness** noun.
unsparing • adjective merciless; severe.
– DERIVATIVES **unsparingly** adverb.
unspeakable • adjective **1** not able to be expressed in words. **2** too bad or horrific to express in words.
– DERIVATIVES **unspeakably** adverb.
unspecialized (also **unspecialised**) • adjective not specialized.
unspecific • adjective not specific; vague.
unspecified • adjective not stated clearly or exactly.
unspectacular • adjective not spectacular; unremarkable.
unspoilt (also **unspoiled**) • adjective not spoilt, in particular (of a place) not marred by development.
unspoken • adjective not expressed in speech; tacit.
unspool • verb **1** unwind from or as if from a spool. **2** (of a film) be screened.
unsporting • adjective not fair or sportsmanlike.
– DERIVATIVES **unsportingly** adverb.
unsportsmanlike • adjective unsporting.
unsprung • adjective not provided with springs.
unstable • adjective (**unstabler**, **unstablest**) **1** prone to change or collapse; not stable. **2** prone to psychiatric problems or sudden changes of mood.
unstained • adjective not stained.
unstated • adjective not stated or declared.
unsteady • adjective (**unsteadier**, **unsteadiest**) **1** liable to fall or shake; not firm. **2** not uniform or regular.
– DERIVATIVES **unsteadily** adverb **unsteadiness** noun.
unstick • verb (past and past part. **unstuck**) cause to become no longer stuck together.
– PHRASES **come unstuck** informal fail.
unstinting • adjective given or giving without restraint; unsparing.
– DERIVATIVES **unstinted** adjective **unstintingly** adverb.
unstoppable • adjective impossible to stop or prevent.
– DERIVATIVES **unstoppably** adverb.
unstopper • verb remove the stopper from (a container).
unstressed • adjective **1** Phonetics (of a syllable) not pronounced with stress. **2** not subjected to stress.
unstring • verb (past and past part. **unstrung**) **1** (**unstrung**) unnerved: *a mind unstrung by loneliness.* **2** remove or relax the string or strings of (a bow or musical instrument).

Thesaurus

cided, determined, unswerving, unwavering; unyielding, inflexible, dogged, obstinate, persistent, indefatigable, tireless, unflagging, unremitting, unrelenting, relentless.
unsightly • adjective UGLY, unattractive, unprepossessing, unlovely, disagreeable, displeasing, hideous, horrible, repulsive, revolting, offensive, grotesque, monstrous, ghastly.
– OPPOSITES attractive.
unskilful • adjective INEXPERT, incompetent, inept, unskilled, amateurish, unprofessional, inexperienced, untrained, unpractised; *informal* ham-fisted, ham-handed, cack-handed.
unskilled • adjective UNTRAINED, unqualified; manual, blue-collar, labouring, menial; inexpert, inexperienced, unpractised, amateurish, unprofessional.
unsociable • adjective UNFRIENDLY, uncongenial, unneighbourly, unapproachable, introverted, reticent, reserved, withdrawn, aloof, distant, remote, detached, unsocial, antisocial, taciturn, silent, quiet; *informal* stand-offish.
– OPPOSITES friendly.
unsolicited • adjective UNINVITED, unsought, unasked for, unrequested.
unsophisticated • adjective **1** *she seemed terribly unsophisticated* UNWORLDLY, naive, simple, innocent, ignorant, green, immature, callow, inexperienced, childlike, artless, guileless, ingenuous, natural, unaffected, unassuming, unpretentious. **2** *unsophisticated software* SIMPLE, crude, basic, rudimentary, primitive, rough and ready; straightforward, uncomplicated, uninvolved.
unsound • adjective **1** *structurally unsound* RICKETY, flimsy, wobbly, unstable, crumbling, damaged, rotten, ramshackle, insubstantial, unsafe, dangerous. **2** *this submission appears unsound* UNTENABLE, flawed, defective, faulty, ill-founded, flimsy, unreliable, questionable, dubious, tenuous, suspect, fallacious, fallible; *informal* iffy. **3** *of unsound mind* DISORDERED, deranged, disturbed, demented, unstable, unbalanced, unhinged, insane; *informal* touched.
– OPPOSITES strong.
unsparing • adjective **1** *he is unsparing in his criticism* MERCILESS, pitiless, ruthless, relentless, remorseless, unmerciful, unforgiving, implacable, uncompromising; stern, strict, severe, harsh, tough, rigorous. **2** *unsparing approval* UNGRUDGING, unstinting, willingly given, free, free-handed, ready; lavish, liberal, generous, magnanimous, open-handed.
unspeakable • adjective **1** *unspeakable delights* INDESCRIBABLE, beyond description, inexpressible, unutterable, indefinable, unimaginable, inconceivable, marvellous, wonderful. **2** *an unspeakable crime* DREADFUL, awful, appalling, horrific, horrifying, horrendous, abominable, frightful, fearful, shocking, ghastly, gruesome, monstrous, heinous, egregious, deplorable, despicable, execrable, vile.
unspecified • adjective UNNAMED, unstated, unidentified, undesignated, undefined, unfixed, undecided, undetermined, uncertain; nameless, unknown, indefinite, indeterminate, vague.
unspectacular • adjective UNREMARKABLE, unexceptional, undistinguished, unmemorable; ordinary, average, commonplace, mediocre, run-of-the-mill, indifferent.
– OPPOSITES remarkable.
unspoilt • adjective UNIMPAIRED, as good as new/before, perfect, pristine, immaculate, unblemished, unharmed, unflawed, undamaged, untouched, unmarked, untainted.
unspoken • adjective UNSTATED, unexpressed, unuttered, unsaid, unvoiced, unarticulated, undeclared, not spelt out; tacit, implicit, implied, understood, taken as read.
– OPPOSITES explicit.
unstable • adjective **1** *icebergs are notoriously unstable* UNSTEADY, rocky, wobbly, rickety, shaky, unsafe, insecure, precarious. **2** *unstable coffee prices* CHANGEABLE, volatile, variable, fluctuating, irregular, unpredictable, erratic. **3** *he was mentally unstable* UNBALANCED, of unsound mind, mentally ill, deranged, demented, disturbed, unhinged.
– OPPOSITES steady, firm.
unsteady • adjective **1** *she was unsteady on her feet* UNSTABLE, rocky, wobbly, rickety, shaky, tottery, doddery, insecure. **2** *an unsteady flow* IRREGULAR, uneven, varying, variable, erratic, spasmodic, changeable, changing, fluctuating, inconstant, intermittent, fitful.
– OPPOSITES stable, regular.

unstructured • adjective without formal organization or structure.
unstuck past and past participle of UNSTICK.
unstudied • adjective not laboured or artificial; natural.
unstuffy • adjective friendly, informal, and approachable.
unsubstantial • adjective having little or no solidity, reality, or factual basis.
unsubstantiated • adjective not supported or proven by evidence.
unsubtle • adjective obvious; clumsy.
– DERIVATIVES **unsubtly** adverb.
unsuccessful • adjective not successful.
– DERIVATIVES **unsuccessfully** adverb.
unsuitable • adjective not fitting or appropriate.
– DERIVATIVES **unsuitability** noun **unsuitably** adverb.
unsuited • adjective not right or appropriate.
unsullied • adjective not spoiled or made impure.
unsung • adjective not celebrated or praised: *unsung heroes.*
unsupervised • adjective not done or acting under supervision.
unsupportable • adjective insupportable.
unsupported • adjective **1** not supported. **2** not borne out by evidence or facts.
unsure • adjective **1** lacking confidence. **2** not fixed or certain.
– DERIVATIVES **unsurely** adverb **unsureness** noun.
unsurfaced • adjective (of a road or path) not provided with a durable upper layer.
unsurpassable • adjective not able to be surpassed.
unsurpassed • adjective better or greater than any other.
unsurprising • adjective not unexpected and so not causing surprise.
– DERIVATIVES **unsurprisingly** adverb.
unsuspected • adjective **1** not known or thought to exist; not imagined as possible. **2** not regarded with suspicion.
unsuspecting • adjective not aware of the presence of danger; feeling no suspicion.
– DERIVATIVES **unsuspectingly** adverb.
unsustainable • adjective **1** not able to be maintained at the current rate or level. **2** not able to be upheld or defended. **3** upsetting the ecological balance by depleting natural resources.
– DERIVATIVES **unsustainably** adverb.
unswayed • adjective not influenced or affected.
unsweetened • adjective (of food or drink) without added sugar or sweetener.
unswerving • adjective not changing or becoming weaker.
– DERIVATIVES **unswervingly** adverb.
unsymmetrical • adjective not symmetrical; asymmetrical.
unsympathetic • adjective **1** not sympathetic. **2** not showing approval of an idea or action. **3** not likeable.
– DERIVATIVES **unsympathetically** adverb.
unsystematic • adjective not done or acting according to a fixed plan or system.
– DERIVATIVES **unsystematically** adverb.
untainted • adjective not contaminated or tainted.
untameable (also **untamable**) • adjective not capable of being tamed or controlled.
untamed • adjective not tamed or controlled.
untangle • verb **1** free from tangles. **2** free from complications or confusion.
untapped • adjective (of a resource) not yet exploited or used.
untarnished • adjective **1** (of metal) not tarnished. **2** not spoiled or ruined.
untasted • adjective (of food or drink) not sampled.
untaught • adjective **1** not having been taught or educated. **2** not acquired by teaching; natural or spontaneous.
unteachable • adjective (of a pupil or skill) unable to be taught.
untempered • adjective not moderated or lessened.
untenable • adjective not able to be maintained or defended against attack or objection.
untended • adjective not cared for or looked after; neglected.
untenured • adjective (of a college teacher or post) without tenure.
Untermensch /ŏŏntərmensh/ • noun (pl. **Untermenschen** /ŏŏntərmenshən/) a person considered racially or socially inferior.
– ORIGIN German, 'underperson'.
untested • adjective not subjected to testing; unproven.
– DERIVATIVES **untestable** adjective.
unthinkable • adjective too unlikely or undesirable to be considered a possibility.
– DERIVATIVES **unthinkably** adverb.
unthinking • adjective without proper consideration.
– DERIVATIVES **unthinkingly** adverb.

Thesaurus

unstinted, unstinting • adjective *unstinted praise* LAVISH, liberal, generous, open-handed, ungrudging, unsparing, willingly given, ready, profuse, abundant, ample.
unstudied • adjective NATURAL, easy, unaffected, unforced, uncontrived, unstilted, unpretentious, without airs, artless.
unsubstantiated • adjective UNCONFIRMED, unsupported, uncorroborated, unverified, unattested, unproven; unfounded, groundless, baseless, without foundation.
unsuccessful • adjective **1** *an unsuccessful attempt* FAILED, without success, abortive, ineffective, fruitless, profitless, unproductive; vain, futile, useless, pointless, worthless. **2** *an unsuccessful business* UNPROFITABLE, loss-making. **3** *an unsuccessful candidate* FAILED, losing, beaten; unlucky, out of luck.
unsuitable • adjective **1** *programmes unsuitable for children* INAPPROPRIATE, unsuited, ill-suited, inapt, inapposite, unacceptable, unfitting, unbefitting, incompatible, out of place/keeping. **2** *an unsuitable moment* INOPPORTUNE, infelicitous; *formal* malapropos.
– OPPOSITES appropriate, opportune.
unsullied • adjective SPOTLESS, untarnished, unblemished, untainted, impeccable, undamaged, unspoilt, unimpaired, stainless, immaculate, unflawed.
– OPPOSITES tarnished.
unsung • adjective UNACKNOWLEDGED, uncelebrated, unacclaimed, unapplauded, unhailed; neglected, unrecognized, overlooked, forgotten.
– OPPOSITES celebrated.
unsure • adjective **1** *she felt very unsure* UNCONFIDENT, unassertive, insecure, hesitant, diffident, anxious, apprehensive. **2** *Sally was unsure what to do* UNDECIDED, irresolute, dithering, equivocating, in two minds, in a quandary. **3** *some teachers are unsure about the proposed strike* DUBIOUS, doubtful, sceptical, uncertain, unconvinced. **4** *the date is unsure* NOT FIXED, undecided, uncertain.
– OPPOSITES confident.
unsurpassed • adjective UNMATCHED, unrivalled, unparalleled, unequalled, matchless, peerless, without equal, inimitable, incomparable, unsurpassable; *formal* unexampled.
unsurprising • adjective PREDICTABLE, foreseeable, (only) to be expected, foreseen, anticipated, par for the course; *informal* inevitable, on the cards.
unsuspecting • adjective UNSUSPICIOUS, unwary, unaware, unconscious, ignorant, unwitting; trusting, gullible, credulous, ingenuous, naive.
– OPPOSITES wary.
unswerving • adjective UNWAVERING, unfaltering, steadfast, unshakeable, staunch, firm, resolute, stalwart, dedicated, committed, constant, single-minded, dogged, indefatigable, unyielding, unbending, indomitable.
unsympathetic • adjective **1** *unsympathetic staff* UNCARING, unconcerned, unfeeling, insensitive, unkind, pitiless, heartless, hard-hearted. **2** *the government was unsympathetic to these views* OPPOSED, against, (dead) set against, antagonistic, ill-disposed; *informal* anti. **3** *an unsympathetic character* UNLIKEABLE, disagreeable, unpleasant, objectionable, unsavoury; uncongenial, unfriendly, unneighbourly, unapproachable.
– OPPOSITES caring.
unsystematic • adjective UNMETHODICAL, uncoordinated, disorganized, unplanned, indiscriminate; random, inconsistent, irregular, erratic, casual, haphazard, chaotic.
untamed • adjective WILD, feral, undomesticated, unbroken.
untangle • verb **1** *I untangled the fishing tackle* DISENTANGLE, unravel, unsnarl, straighten out, untwist, untwine, unknot. **2** *untangling a mystery* SOLVE, find the/an answer to, resolve, puzzle out, fathom, clear up, clarify, get to the bottom of; *informal* figure out; *Brit. informal* suss out.
untarnished • adjective UNSULLIED, unblemished, untainted, impeccable, undamaged, unspoilt, unimpaired, spotless, stainless.
untenable • adjective INDEFENSIBLE, undefendable, insupportable, unsustainable, unjustified, unjustifiable, flimsy, weak, shaky.
unthinkable • adjective UNIMAGINABLE, inconceivable, unbelievable, incredible, beyond belief, implausible.
unthinking • adjective **1** *an unthinking woman* THOUGHTLESS, inconsiderate, insensitive; tactless, undiplomatic, indiscreet. **2** *an*

unthought ● adjective (**unthought of**) not imagined or dreamed of.
unthreatening ● adjective not threatening.
untidy ● adjective (**untidier**, **untidiest**) **1** not arranged tidily. **2** not inclined to be neat.
– DERIVATIVES **untidily** adverb **untidiness** noun.
untie ● verb (**untying**) undo or unfasten (something tied).
untied ● adjective not fastened or knotted.
until ● preposition & conjunction up to (the point in time or the event mentioned).
– ORIGIN from Old Norse *und* 'as far as' + TILL[1] (the sense thus duplicated).
untimely ● adjective **1** happening or done at an unsuitable time; inappropriate. **2** (of a death or end) happening too soon or sooner than normal.
– DERIVATIVES **untimeliness** noun.
untiring ● adjective continuing at the same rate without loss of vigour.
– DERIVATIVES **untiringly** adverb.
untitled ● adjective **1** (of a book or other work) having no title. **2** not having a title indicating high social or official rank.
unto ● preposition **1** archaic term for TO. **2** archaic term for UNTIL.
– ORIGIN from UNTIL, with TO replacing TILL[1] (in its northern dialect meaning 'to').
untold ● adjective **1** too much or too many to be counted; indescribable. **2** not narrated or recounted.
untouchable ● adjective **1** not able to be touched or affected. **2** unable to be matched or rivalled. **3** historical of or belonging to the lowest-caste Hindu group or the people outside the caste system. ● noun historical a member of the lowest-caste Hindu group.
– DERIVATIVES **untouchability** noun.
– USAGE In senses relating to the traditional Hindu caste system, the term **untouchable** and the social restrictions accompanying it were declared illegal in the constitution of India in 1949 and of Pakistan in 1953. The official term today is **scheduled caste.**
untouched ● adjective **1** not handled, used, or tasted. **2** (of a subject) not treated or discussed. **3** not affected, changed, or damaged in any way.
untoward ● adjective unexpected and inappropriate or adverse.
untraceable ● adjective unable to be found or traced.
untracked ● adjective (of land) not previously traversed; without tracks.
untrained ● adjective not having been trained in a particular skill.
untrammelled (US also **untrammeled**) ● adjective not restricted or hampered.
untranslatable ● adjective not able to be translated.
untreatable ● adjective for whom or which no medical care is available or possible.
untreated ● adjective **1** not given medical care. **2** not treated by the use of a chemical, physical, or biological agent.
untried ● adjective not yet tested; inexperienced.
untrodden ● adjective not having been walked on.
untroubled ● adjective not troubled.
untrue ● adjective **1** false or incorrect. **2** not faithful or loyal.
untrustworthy ● adjective unable to be trusted.
– DERIVATIVES **untrustworthiness** noun.
untruth ● noun (pl. **untruths**) **1** a lie. **2** the quality of being false.
untruthful ● adjective not truthful.
– DERIVATIVES **untruthfully** adverb **untruthfulness** noun.
untuck ● verb free from being tucked in or up.
untuned ● adjective not tuned or in tune.
unturned ● adjective not turned.
untutored ● adjective not formally taught.
untwist ● verb open from a twisted position.
untying present participle of UNTIE.
untypical ● adjective unusual or uncharacteristic.
– DERIVATIVES **untypically** adverb.
unusable ● adjective not fit to be used.

Thesaurus

unthinking remark ABSENT-MINDED, heedless, thoughtless, careless, injudicious, imprudent, unwise, foolish, reckless, rash, precipitate; involuntary, inadvertent, unintentional, spontaneous, impulsive, unpremeditated.
– OPPOSITES thoughtful, intentional.
untidy ● adjective **1** *untidy hair* SCRUFFY, tousled, dishevelled, unkempt, messy, disordered, disarranged, messed up, rumpled, bedraggled, uncombed, ungroomed, straggly, ruffled, tangled, matted, wind-blown; informal mussed up; N. Amer. informal raggedy. **2** *the room was untidy* DISORDERED, messy, in a mess, disorderly, disorganized, in disorder, cluttered, in a clutter, in a muddle, muddled, in chaos, chaotic, haywire, topsy-turvy, in disarray, at sixes and sevens; informal higgledy-piggledy.
– OPPOSITES neat, orderly.
untie ● verb UNDO, unknot, unbind, unfasten, unlace, untether, unhitch, unmoor; loose, (set) free, release, let go.
until ● preposition & conjunction **1** *I was working until midnight* (UP) TILL, up to, up until, as late as; N. Amer. through. **2** *this did not happen until 1998* BEFORE, prior to, previous to, up to, up until, (up) till, earlier than.
untimely ● adjective **1** *an untimely interruption* ILL-TIMED, badly timed, mistimed; inopportune, inappropriate; inconvenient, unwelcome, infelicitous; formal malapropos. **2** *his untimely death* PREMATURE, (too) early, too soon, before time.
– OPPOSITES opportune.
untiring ● adjective VIGOROUS, energetic, determined, resolute, enthusiastic, keen, zealous, spirited, dogged, tenacious, persistent, persevering, staunch; tireless, unflagging, unfailing, unfaltering, unwavering, indefatigable, unrelenting, unswerving; formal pertinacious.
untold ● adjective **1** *untold damage* BOUNDLESS, measureless, limitless, unlimited, infinite, immeasurable, incalculable. **2** *untold billions* COUNTLESS, innumerable, endless, limitless, numberless, an infinite number of, without number, uncountable; numerous, many, multiple; poetic/literary multitudinous, myriad. **3** *the untold story* UNREPORTED, unrecounted, unrevealed, undisclosed, undivulged, unpublished.
– OPPOSITES limited.
untouched ● adjective **1** *the food was untouched* UNEATEN, unconsumed, undrunk. **2** *one of the few untouched areas* UNSPOILT, unmarked, unblemished, unsullied, undefiled, undamaged, unharmed; pristine, natural, immaculate, in perfect condition, unaffected, unchanged, unaltered.
untoward ● adjective UNEXPECTED, unanticipated, unforeseen, unpredictable, unpredicted, surprising, unusual; unwelcome, unfavourable, adverse, unfortunate, infelicitous; formal malapropos.
untrained ● adjective UNSKILLED, untaught, unschooled, untutored, unpractised, inexperienced; unqualified, unlicensed, amateur, non-professional.
untried ● adjective UNTESTED, unestablished, new, experimental, unattempted, trial, test, pilot, unproven.
– OPPOSITES established.
untroubled ● adjective UNWORRIED, unperturbed, unconcerned, unruffled, undismayed, unbothered, unagitated, unflustered; insouciant, nonchalant, blasé, carefree, serene, relaxed, at ease, happy-go-lucky; informal laid-back.
untrue ● adjective **1** *these suggestions are totally untrue* FALSE, untruthful, fabricated, made up, invented, concocted, trumped up; erroneous, wrong, incorrect, inaccurate; fallacious, unsound, unfounded, misguided. **2** *he was untrue to his friends* UNFAITHFUL, disloyal, faithless, false, treacherous, traitorous, deceitful, deceiving, duplicitous, double-dealing, insincere, unreliable, undependable, inconstant; informal two-timing; poetic/literary perfidious.
– OPPOSITES correct, faithful.
untrustworthy ● adjective DISHONEST, deceitful, double-dealing, treacherous, traitorous, two-faced, duplicitous, dishonourable, unprincipled, unscrupulous, corrupt; unreliable, undependable.
– OPPOSITES reliable.
untruth ● noun **1** *a patent untruth* LIE, falsehood, fib, fabrication, invention, falsification, cock-and-bull story, half-truth, exaggeration; story, myth, piece of fiction; informal tall story, fairy tale, whopper; Brit. informal porky (pie). **2** *the total untruth of the story* FALSITY, falsehood, falseness, untruthfulness, fallaciousness, fictitiousness; fabrication, dishonesty, deceit, deceitfulness.
untruthful ● adjective **1** *the answers may be untruthful* FALSE, untrue, fabricated, made up, invented, trumped up; erroneous, wrong, incorrect, inaccurate, fallacious, fictitious. **2** *an untruthful person* LYING, mendacious, dishonest, deceitful, duplicitous, false, double-dealing, two-faced; informal crooked, bent; poetic/literary perfidious.
– OPPOSITES honest.
untutored ● adjective UNEDUCATED, untaught, unschooled, ignorant, unsophisticated, uncultured, unenlightened.
– OPPOSITES educated.

unused ● adjective **1** not used. **2** (**unused to**) not accustomed to.
unusual ● adjective **1** not habitually or commonly done or occurring. **2** remarkable; exceptional.
– DERIVATIVES **unusually** adverb **unusualness** noun.
unutterable ● adjective too great or awful to describe.
– DERIVATIVES **unutterably** adverb.
unuttered ● adjective not spoken or expressed.
unvalued ● adjective not valued.
unvaried ● adjective not varied.
unvarnished ● adjective **1** not varnished. **2** plain and straightforward.
unvarying ● adjective not varying.
– DERIVATIVES **unvaryingly** adverb.
unveil ● verb **1** remove a veil or covering from. **2** show or announce publicly for the first time.
unventilated ● adjective not ventilated.
unverifiable ● adjective unable to be verified.
unverified ● adjective not verified.
unversed ● adjective (**unversed in**) not experienced or skilled in.
unviable ● adjective not capable of working successfully.
unvisited ● adjective not visited.
unvoiced ● adjective **1** not expressed in words; unuttered. **2** Phonetics (of a speech sound) uttered without vibration of the vocal cords.
unwaged ● adjective chiefly Brit. **1** unemployed or doing unpaid work. **2** (of work) unpaid.
unwalled ● adjective without walls.
unwanted ● adjective not wanted.
unwarrantable ● adjective unjustifiable.
– DERIVATIVES **unwarrantably** adverb.
unwarranted ● adjective not warranted.
unwary ● adjective not cautious.
– DERIVATIVES **unwarily** adverb.
unwashed ● adjective not washed.
– PHRASES **the (great) unwashed** derogatory the multitude of ordinary people.
unwatchable ● adjective disturbing or uninteresting to watch.
unwatched ● adjective not watched.
unwavering ● adjective not wavering.
– DERIVATIVES **unwaveringly** adverb.
unweaned ● adjective not weaned.
unwearable ● adjective not fit to be worn.
unwearied ● adjective not wearied.
unwearying ● adjective never tiring or slackening.
unwed (also **unwedded**) ● adjective not married.
unweighted ● adjective not weighted.
unwelcome ● adjective not welcome.
unwelcoming ● adjective unfriendly or inhospitable.
unwell ● adjective ill.
unwholesome ● adjective not wholesome.
unwieldy ● adjective (**unwieldier**, **unwieldiest**) hard to move or manage because of its size, shape, or weight.
– DERIVATIVES **unwieldiness** noun.
– ORIGIN originally in the sense 'lacking strength': from WIELDY (in the obsolete sense 'active').
unwilling ● adjective not willing.
– DERIVATIVES **unwillingly** adverb **unwillingness** noun.
unwind ● verb (past and past part. **unwound**) **1** undo after winding. **2** relax after a period of work or tension.
unwinking ● adjective (of a stare or light) unwavering.
unwinnable ● adjective not winnable.

Thesaurus

untwine ● verb. See UNTWIST.
untwist ● verb UNTWINE, disentangle, unravel, unsnarl, unwind, unroll, uncoil, unfurl, open (out), straighten (out).
unused ● adjective **1** *the notebook is unused | unused food* UNUTILIZED, unemployed, unexploited, not in service; left over, remaining, uneaten, unconsumed, unneeded, not required, to spare, surplus. **2** *he was unused to such directness* UNACCUSTOMED, new, a stranger, unfamiliar, unconversant, unacquainted; *archaic* strange.
– OPPOSITES accustomed.
unusual ● adjective **1** *an unusual sight* UNCOMMON, abnormal, atypical, unexpected, surprising, unfamiliar, different; strange, odd, curious, out of the ordinary, extraordinary, unorthodox, unconventional, outlandish, singular, peculiar, bizarre; rare, scarce, few and far between, thin on the ground, exceptional, isolated, occasional, infrequent; *informal* weird, offbeat, way out, freaky. **2** *a man of unusual talent* REMARKABLE, extraordinary, exceptional, singular, particular, outstanding, notable, noteworthy, distinctive, striking, significant, special, unique, unparalleled, prodigious.
– OPPOSITES common.
unutterable ● adjective **1** *an existence of unutterable boredom* INDESCRIBABLE, beyond description, inexpressible, unspeakable, undefinable, inconceivable; extreme, great, overwhelming; dreadful, awful, appalling, terrible. **2** *unutterable joy* MARVELLOUS, wonderful, superb, splendid, unimaginable, profound, deep.
unvarnished ● adjective **1** *unvarnished wood* BARE, unpainted, unpolished, unfinished, untreated. **2** *the unvarnished truth* STRAIGHTFORWARD, plain, simple, stark; truthful, realistic, candid, honest, frank, forthright, direct, blunt, straight from the shoulder.
unveil ● verb REVEAL, present, disclose, divulge, make known, make public, communicate, publish, broadcast; display, show, exhibit, put on display; release, bring out.
unwanted ● adjective **1** *an unwanted development* UNWELCOME, undesirable, undesired, unpopular, unfortunate, unlucky, unfavourable, untoward; unpleasant, disagreeable, displeasing, distasteful, objectionable; regrettable, deplorable, lamentable; unacceptable, intolerable, awful, terrible, wretched, appalling. **2** *tins of unwanted pet food* UNUSED, left over, surplus, superfluous; uneaten, unconsumed, untouched. **3** *an unwanted guest* UNINVITED, unbidden, unasked, unrequested, unsolicited. **4** *many ageing people feel unwanted* FRIENDLESS, unloved, uncared-for, forsaken, rejected, shunned; superfluous, useless, unnecessary.
– OPPOSITES welcome.
unwarranted ● adjective **1** *the criticism is unwarranted* UNJUSTIFIED, unjustifiable, indefensible, inexcusable, unforgivable, unpardonable, uncalled for, unnecessary, unreasonable, unjust, groundless, excessive, immoderate, disproportionate. **2** *an unwarranted invasion of privacy* UNAUTHORIZED, unsanctioned, unapproved, uncertified, unlicensed; illegal, unlawful, illicit, illegitimate, criminal, actionable.
– OPPOSITES justified.
unwary ● adjective INCAUTIOUS, careless, thoughtless, heedless, inattentive, unwatchful, off one's guard.
unwavering ● adjective STEADY, fixed, resolute, resolved, firm, steadfast, unswerving, unfaltering, untiring, tireless, indefatigable, unyielding, relentless, unremitting, unrelenting, sustained.
– OPPOSITES unsteady.
unwelcome ● adjective **1** *I was made to feel unwelcome* UNWANTED, uninvited. **2** *even a small increase is unwelcome* UNDESIRABLE, undesired, unpopular, unfortunate, unlucky; disappointing, upsetting, distressing, disagreeable, displeasing; regrettable, deplorable, lamentable.
unwell ● adjective ILL, sick, poorly, indisposed, ailing, not (very) well, not oneself, under/below par, peaky, queasy, nauseous; *Brit.* off colour; *informal* under the weather, not up to snuff, funny, peculiar, lousy, rough; *Brit. informal* grotty; *Austral./NZ informal* crook; *dated* queer.
unwholesome ● adjective **1** *unwholesome air* UNHEALTHY, noxious, poisonous; insalubrious, unhygienic, insanitary; harmful, injurious, detrimental, destructive, damaging, deleterious, baleful. **2** *unwholesome Web pages* IMPROPER, immoral, indecent, corrupting, depraving, salacious.
– OPPOSITES healthy, seemly.
unwieldy ● adjective CUMBERSOME, unmanageable, unmanoeuvrable; awkward, clumsy, massive, heavy, hefty, bulky, weighty.
– OPPOSITES manageable.
unwilling ● adjective **1** *unwilling conscripts* RELUCTANT, unenthusiastic, hesitant, resistant, grudging, involuntary, forced. **2** *he was unwilling to take on that responsibility* DISINCLINED, reluctant, averse, loath; (**be unwilling to do something**) not have the heart to, baulk at, demur at, shy away from, flinch from, shrink from, have qualms about, have misgivings about, have reservations about.
– OPPOSITES keen.
unwillingness ● adjective DISINCLINATION, reluctance, hesitation, diffidence, wavering, vacillation, resistance, objection, opposition, doubts, second thoughts, scruples, qualms, misgivings; *archaic* disrelish.
unwind ● verb **1** *Ella unwound the scarf from her neck* UNROLL, uncoil, unravel, untwine, untwist, disentangle, open (out), straighten (out). **2** *unwinding after work* RELAX, loosen up, ease up/off, slow down, de-stress, unbend, rest, put one's feet up, take it easy;

unwisdom ● noun folly.
unwise ● adjective foolish.
– DERIVATIVES **unwisely** adverb.
unwitting ● adjective **1** not aware of the full facts. **2** not done on purpose; unintentional.
– DERIVATIVES **unwittingly** adverb.
– ORIGIN Old English, 'not knowing or realizing'.
unwomanly ● adjective not womanly.
unwonted /unwōntid/ ● adjective unaccustomed or unusual.
– DERIVATIVES **unwontedly** adverb.
unworkable ● adjective impractical.
unworked ● adjective not cultivated, mined, or carved.
unworldly ● adjective **1** having little awareness of the realities of life. **2** not seeming to belong to this world.
– DERIVATIVES **unworldliness** noun.
unworn ● adjective not worn.
unworried ● adjective not worried.
unworthy ● adjective (**unworthier**, **unworthiest**) not worthy.
– DERIVATIVES **unworthily** adverb **unworthiness** noun.
unwound[1] ● adjective (of a clock or watch) not wound or wound up.
unwound[2] past and past participle of UNWIND.
unwounded ● adjective not wounded.
unwrap ● verb (**unwrapped**, **unwrapping**) remove the wrapping from.
unwrinkled ● adjective not wrinkled.
unwritable ● adjective not able to be written.
unwritten ● adjective **1** not written. **2** (especially of a law) resting originally on custom or judicial decision rather than on statute.
unyielding ● adjective not yielding.
unyoke ● verb release (animals) from a yoke.
unzip ● verb (**unzipped**, **unzipping**) **1** unfasten the zip of. **2** Computing decompress (a compressed file).
up ● adverb **1** towards a higher place or position. **2** to or at a place perceived as higher. **3** to the place where someone is. **4** at or to a higher level or value. **5** into the desired or a proper condition. **6** out of bed. **7** in a publicly visible place. **8** (of the sun) visible in the sky. **9** towards the north. **10** Brit. towards or in the capital or a major city. **11** into a happy mood. **12** winning by a specified margin. **13** Brit. at or to a university, especially Oxford or Cambridge. ● preposition **1** from a lower to a higher point of. **2** from one end to another of (a street or other area). ● adjective **1** directed or moving towards a higher place or position. **2** at an end. **3** (of the road) being repaired. **4** cheerful. **5** (of a computer system) working properly. ● noun informal a period of good fortune. ● verb (**upped**, **upping**) increase (a level or amount).
– PHRASES **it is all up with** informal it is the end or there is no hope for. **on the up and up** Brit. informal steadily improving. **something is up** informal something unusual or undesirable is happening. **up against 1** close to or touching. **2** informal confronted with. **up and —** informal do (something) abruptly or boldly. **up and down** in various places throughout. **up before** appearing for a hearing in the presence of (a judge, magistrate, etc.). **up for 1** available for. **2** due or being considered for. **3** informal ready to take part in. **up on** well informed about. **up to 1** as far as. **2** (also **up until**) until. **3** indicating a maximum amount. **4** good enough for. **5** capable of. **6** the duty or choice of. **7** informal occupied with. **up top** Brit. informal in the way of intelligence. **up yours** vulgar slang expressing contemptuous defiance or rejection. **what's up?** informal **1** what is going on? **2** what is the matter?
– ORIGIN Old English.
up- ● prefix **1** (added to verbs and their derivatives) upwards: *upturned.* **2** (added to verbs and their derivatives) to a more recent time: *update.* **3** (added to nouns) denoting motion up: *uphill.* **4** (added to nouns) higher: *upland.*
up-and-coming ● adjective likely to become successful.
– DERIVATIVES **up-and-comer** noun.
up-and-over ● adjective (of a door) opened by being raised and pushed back into a horizontal position.
Upanishad /ōōpannishad/ ● noun each of a series of Hindu sacred books written in Sanskrit and explaining the philosophy introduced in the Veda.
– ORIGIN Sanskrit, 'sitting near (i.e. at the feet of a master)'.
upbeat ● noun (in music) an unaccented beat preceding an accented beat. ● adjective informal cheerful; optimistic.
upbraid ● verb scold or reproach.
– ORIGIN Old English, 'allege as a basis for censure', from BRAID in the obsolete sense 'brandish'.
upbringing ● noun the treatment and instruction received throughout one's childhood.
upchuck ● verb & noun N. Amer. informal vomit.
upcoming ● adjective forthcoming.
upcountry ● adverb & adjective inland.
update ● verb /updayt/ **1** make more modern. **2** give the latest information to. ● noun /**up**dayt/ an act of updating or an updated version.
– DERIVATIVES **updatable** adjective (Computing).
updraught (US **updraft**) ● noun an upward current of air.
upend ● verb set or turn on its end or upside down.
upfield ● adverb (in sport) in or to a position nearer to the opponents' end of a field.
upfront informal ● adverb (usu. **up front**) **1** at the front; in front. **2** (of a payment) in advance. ● adjective **1** bold and frank. **2** (of a payment) made in advance.
upgrade ● verb raise to a higher standard or rank. ● noun an act

Thesaurus

informal wind down, let it all hang out, unbutton; *N. Amer. informal* hang loose, chill out.
unwise ● adjective INJUDICIOUS, ill-advised, imprudent, foolish, silly, inadvisable, impolitic, misguided, foolhardy, irresponsible, rash, hasty, overhasty, reckless.
– OPPOSITES sensible.
unwitting ● adjective **1** *an unwitting accomplice* UNKNOWING, unconscious, unsuspecting, oblivious, unaware, innocent. **2** *an unwitting mistake* UNINTENTIONAL, unintended, inadvertent, involuntary, unconscious, accidental.
– OPPOSITES conscious.
unwonted ● adjective UNUSUAL, uncommon, unaccustomed, unfamiliar, unprecedented, exceptional, extraordinary, remarkable, singular, surprising.
– OPPOSITES usual.
unworldly ● adjective **1** *a gauche, unworldly girl* NAIVE, simple, inexperienced, innocent, green, raw, callow, immature, unsophisticated, gullible, ingenuous, artless, guileless, childlike, trusting, credulous. **2** *unworldly beauty* UNEARTHLY, other-worldly, ethereal, ghostly, preternatural, supernatural, paranormal, mystical; *rare* extramundane. **3** *an unworldly religious order* NON-MATERIALISTIC, spiritualistic, religious.
unworthy ● adjective **1** *he was unworthy of trust* UNDESERVING, ineligible, unqualified, unfit. **2** *unworthy behaviour* UNBECOMING, unsuitable, inappropriate, unbefitting, unfitting, unseemly, improper; discreditable, shameful, dishonourable, despicable, ignoble, contemptible, reprehensible.
– OPPOSITES deserving, becoming.
unwritten ● adjective TACIT, implicit, unvoiced, taken for granted, accepted, recognized, understood; traditional, customary, conventional; oral, verbal, spoken, vocal, word-of-mouth.
unyielding ● adjective **1** *unyielding spikes of cane* STIFF, inflexible, unbending, inelastic, firm, hard, solid, tough, tight, compact, compressed, dense. **2** *an unyielding policy* RESOLUTE, inflexible, uncompromising, unbending, unshakeable, unwavering, immovable, intractable, intransigent, rigid, stiff, firm, determined, dogged, obstinate, stubborn, adamant, obdurate, tenacious, relentless, implacable, single-minded; *formal* pertinacious.
up-and-coming ● adjective PROMISING, budding, rising, on the up and up, with potential; talented, gifted, able.
upbeat ● adjective *(informal)* OPTIMISTIC, cheerful, cheery, positive, confident, hopeful, sanguine, bullish, buoyant.
– OPPOSITES pessimistic, negative.
upbraid ● verb REPRIMAND, rebuke, admonish, chastise, chide, reprove, reproach, scold, berate, take to task, lambaste, give someone a piece of one's mind, haul over the coals, lecture; *informal* tell off, give someone a talking-to, dress down, give someone an earful, rap over the knuckles, bawl out, lay into; *Brit. informal* tick off, carpet, tear off a strip, give someone what for, give someone a rocket/rollicking; *N. Amer. informal* chew out, ream out; *Austral. informal* monster; *formal* castigate; *rare* reprehend.
upbringing ● noun CHILDHOOD, early life, formative years, teaching, instruction, care, bringing-up, rearing.
update ● verb **1** *security measures are continually updated* MODERNIZE, upgrade, bring up to date, improve, overhaul; *N. Amer.* bring up to code. **2** *I'll update him on today's developments* BRIEF, bring

of upgrading or an upgraded version.
– DERIVATIVES **upgradeable** (also **upgradable**) adjective.
upheaval ● noun a violent or sudden change or disruption.
upheave ● verb literary heave or lift up.
uphill ● adverb towards the top of a slope. ● adjective **1** sloping upwards. **2** difficult: *an uphill struggle*. ● noun an upward slope.
uphold ● verb (past and past part. **upheld**) **1** confirm or support. **2** maintain (a custom or practice).
– DERIVATIVES **upholder** noun.
upholster /uphōlstər/ ● verb **1** provide (furniture) with a soft, padded covering. **2** cover the walls or furniture in (a room) with textiles.
upholsterer ● noun a person who upholsters furniture.
– ORIGIN from the obsolete noun *upholster*, from UPHOLD in the obsolete sense 'keep in repair'.
upholstery ● noun **1** soft, padded textile covering used to upholster furniture. **2** the art or practice of upholstering.
upkeep ● noun **1** the process of keeping something in good condition. **2** the cost of this or of supporting a person.
upland ● noun (also **uplands**) an area of high or hilly land.
uplift ● verb **1** raise. **2** (**be uplifted**) (of an island, mountain, etc.) be created by an upward movement of the earth's surface. **3** elevate morally or spiritually. ● noun **1** an act of uplifting. **2** support from a garment for a woman's bust. **3** a morally or spiritually uplifting influence.
– DERIVATIVES **uplifter** noun.
uplighter ● noun a lamp designed to throw light upwards.
– DERIVATIVES **uplighting** noun.
uplink ● noun a communications link to a satellite. ● verb provide with or send by such a link.
upload Computing ● verb transfer (data) to a larger computer system. ● noun the action or process of uploading.
upmarket ● adjective & adverb chiefly Brit. towards or relating to the more expensive or affluent sector of the market.
upon ● preposition more formal term for ON.
upper ● adjective **1** situated above another part. **2** higher in position or status. **3** situated on higher ground. **4** (in place names) situated to the north. ● noun **1** the part of a boot or shoe above the sole. **2** informal a stimulating drug, especially amphetamine.
– PHRASES **have the upper hand** have an advantage or control. **on one's uppers** informal extremely short of money. **the upper crust** informal the upper classes.
upper case ● noun capital letters.
upper chamber ● noun another term for UPPER HOUSE.
upper class ● noun (treated as sing. or pl.) the social group with the highest status, especially the aristocracy. ● adjective relating to the upper class.
uppercut ● noun a punch delivered with an upwards motion and the arm bent.
upper house ● noun **1** the higher house in a bicameral parliament or similar legislature. **2** (**the Upper House**) (in the UK) the House of Lords.
uppermost ● adjective highest in place, rank, or importance. ● adverb at or to the uppermost position.
upper school ● noun **1** a secondary school for children aged from about fourteen upwards. **2** the section of a school comprising or catering for the older pupils.
uppish ● adjective informal arrogantly self-assertive.
uppity ● adjective informal self-important.
– ORIGIN from UP.
upraise ● verb raise to a higher level.
uprate ● verb **1** increase the value of. **2** improve the performance of.
upright ● adjective **1** vertical; erect. **2** greater in height than breadth. **3** strictly honourable or honest. **4** (of a piano) having vertical strings. ● adverb in or into an upright position. ● noun **1** a vertical post, structure, or line. **2** an upright piano.
– DERIVATIVES **uprightly** adverb **uprightness** noun.
uprise ● verb (past **uprose**; past part. **uprisen**) archaic or literary rise up.
uprising ● noun an act of resistance or rebellion.
upriver ● adverb & adjective towards or situated at a point nearer the source of a river.
uproar ● noun **1** a loud and impassioned noise or disturbance. **2** a public expression of outrage.
– ORIGIN Dutch *uproer*, from *op* 'up' + *roer* 'confusion', associated with ROAR.
uproarious ● adjective **1** characterized by or provoking uproar. **2** very funny.
– DERIVATIVES **uproariously** adverb **uproariousness** noun.

Thesaurus

up to date, inform, fill in, tell, notify, apprise, keep posted; *informal* clue in, put in the picture, bring/keep up to speed.
upgrade ● verb **1** *there are plans to upgrade the rail system* IMPROVE, modernize, update, bring up to date, make better, ameliorate, reform; rehabilitate, recondition, refurbish, renovate; *N. Amer.* bring up to code. **2** *he was upgraded to a seat in the cabinet* PROMOTE, give promotion to, elevate, move up, raise; *archaic* prefer.
– OPPOSITES downgrade, demote.
upheaval ● noun DISRUPTION, disturbance, trouble, turbulence, disorder, confusion, turmoil, pandemonium, chaos, mayhem, cataclysm; revolution, change.
uphill ● adjective **1** *an uphill path* UPWARD, rising, ascending, climbing. **2** *an uphill job* ARDUOUS, difficult, hard, tough, taxing, demanding, exacting, stiff, formidable, exhausting, tiring, wearisome, laborious, gruelling, back-breaking, punishing, burdensome, onerous, Herculean; *informal* no picnic, killing; *archaic* toilsome.
– OPPOSITES downhill.
uphold ● verb **1** *the court upheld his claim for damages* CONFIRM, endorse, sustain, approve, support, back (up), stand by, champion, defend. **2** *they've a tradition to uphold* MAINTAIN, sustain, continue, preserve, protect, keep, hold to, keep alive, keep going.
– OPPOSITES overturn, oppose.
upkeep ● noun **1** *the upkeep of the road* MAINTENANCE, repair(s), service, servicing, care, preservation, conservation; running. **2** *the child's upkeep* (FINANCIAL) SUPPORT, maintenance, keep, subsistence, care.
uplift ● verb *she needs something to uplift her spirits* BOOST, raise, buoy up, lift, cheer up, perk up, enliven, brighten up, lighten, stimulate, inspire, ginger up, revive, restore; *informal* buck up.
uplifted ● adjective *his uplifted face* RAISED, upraised, elevated, upthrust; held high, erect, proud.
uplifting ● adjective INSPIRING, stirring, inspirational, rousing, moving, touching, affecting, cheering, heartening, encouraging.
upper ● adjective **1** *the upper floor* HIGHER, superior; top. **2** *the upper echelons of the party* SENIOR, superior, higher-level, higher-ranking, top.
– OPPOSITES lower.
– PHRASES **the upper hand** AN ADVANTAGE, the edge, the whip hand, a lead, a head start, ascendancy, superiority, supremacy, sway, control, power, mastery, dominance, command.
upper-class ● adjective ARISTOCRATIC, noble, of noble birth, patrician, titled, blue-blooded, high-born, well born, elite, landowning, landed, born with a silver spoon in one's mouth; *Brit.* county, upmarket; *informal* upper-crust, top-drawer, {huntin', shootin', and fishin'}, classy; *Brit. informal* posh; *archaic* gentle, of gentle birth.
uppermost ● adjective **1** *the uppermost branches* HIGHEST, top, topmost. **2** *their own problems remained uppermost in their minds* PREDOMINANT, of greatest importance, to the fore, foremost, dominant, principal, chief, main, paramount, major.
uppish ● adjective *(informal)* ARROGANT, bumptious, full of oneself, puffed up, conceited, swollen-headed, pompous, self-assertive, overbearing, throwing one's weight about, cocky, self-important, superior, presumptuous, overweening; *informal* snooty, uppity, high and mighty, too big for one's boots.
upright ● adjective **1** *an upright position* VERTICAL, perpendicular, plumb, straight (up), straight up and down, bolt upright, erect, on end; on one's feet; *Heraldry* rampant. **2** *an upright member of the community* HONEST, honourable, upstanding, respectable, high-minded, law-abiding, right-minded, worthy, moral, ethical, righteous, decent, good, virtuous, principled, high-principled, of principle, noble, incorruptible.
– OPPOSITES horizontal, dishonourable.
uprising ● noun REBELLION, revolt, insurrection, mutiny, revolution, insurgence, rioting, riot; civil disobedience, unrest, anarchy, fighting in the streets; coup, coup d'état, putsch.
uproar ● noun **1** *the uproar in the kitchen continued for some time* TURMOIL, disorder, confusion, chaos, commotion, disturbance, rumpus, tumult, turbulence, mayhem, pandemonium, bedlam, noise, din, clamour, hubbub, racket; shouting, yelling, babel; *informal* hullabaloo; *Brit. informal* row. **2** *there was an uproar when he was dismissed* OUTCRY, furore, howl of protest; fuss, commotion, hue and cry, rumpus, ruckus, brouhaha; *informal* hullabaloo, stink,

uproot ● verb **1** pull (a plant, tree, etc.) out of the ground. **2** move (someone) from their home or a familiar location.
uprose past of UPRISE.
uprush ● noun a sudden upward surge or flow.
UPS ● abbreviation Computing uninterruptible power supply.
upsadaisy ● exclamation variant spelling of UPSY-DAISY.
upscale ● adjective & adverb N. Amer. upmarket.
upset ● verb /upset/ (**upsetting**; past and past part. **upset**) **1** make unhappy, disappointed, or worried. **2** knock over. **3** disrupt or disturb. ● noun /upset/ **1** a state of being upset. **2** an unexpected result or situation. ● adjective **1** /upset/ unhappy, disappointed, or worried. **2** /upset/ (of a person's stomach) having disturbed digestion.
– DERIVATIVES **upsetting** adjective.
upshift ● verb **1** change to a higher gear. **2** increase. ● noun an act or instance of upshifting.
upshot ● noun the eventual outcome or conclusion.
upside ● noun the positive aspect of something.
upside down ● adverb & adjective **1** with the upper part where the lower part should be. **2** in or into total disorder.
– ORIGIN from *up so down*, perhaps in the sense 'up as if down'.
upsides ● adverb (especially in horse racing) alongside.
upsilon /upsīlən/ ● noun the twentieth letter of the Greek alphabet (Υ, υ), transliterated as 'u' or (chiefly in English words derived through Latin) as 'y'.
– ORIGIN Greek, 'slender U'.
upsize ● verb chiefly N. Amer. increase or cause to increase in size or complexity.
upslope ● noun an upward slope. ● adverb & adjective at or towards a higher point on a slope.
upstage ● adverb & adjective at or towards the back of a stage. ● verb **1** divert attention from (someone) towards oneself. **2** (of an actor) move towards the back of a stage to make (another actor) face away from the audience.
upstairs ● adverb on or to an upper floor. ● adjective (also **upstair**) situated on an upper floor. ● noun an upper floor.
upstand ● noun an upright structure or object.
upstanding ● adjective **1** respectable. **2** erect.
upstart ● noun derogatory a person who has risen suddenly to prominence and behaves arrogantly.
upstate US ● adjective & adverb of, in, or to a part of a state remote from its large cities, especially the northern part. ● noun an upstate area.
upstream ● adverb & adjective situated or moving in the direction opposite to that in which a stream or river flows.
upstroke ● noun an upwards stroke.
upsurge ● noun an increase.
upswept ● adjective **1** curved, sloping, or directed upwards. **2** (of the hair) brushed upwards and off the face.
upswing ● noun an upward trend.
upsy-daisy (also **upsadaisy**) ● exclamation expressing encouragement to a child who has fallen or is being lifted.
uptake ● noun the action of taking up or making use of something.
– PHRASES **be quick** (or **slow**) **on the uptake** informal be quick (or slow) to understand something.
uptempo ● adjective & adverb Music played with a fast or increased tempo.
upthrust ● noun **1** Physics the upward force that a fluid exerts on a body floating in it. **2** Geology the upward movement of part of the earth's surface. ● verb (as adj. **upthrust**) thrust upwards.
uptick ● noun N. Amer. a small increase.
uptight ● adjective informal **1** nervously tense or angry. **2** conventional or repressed.
uptime ● noun time during which a machine, especially a computer, is in operation.
up to date ● adjective incorporating or aware of the latest developments and trends.
uptown chiefly N. Amer. ● adjective & adverb **1** of, in, or into the residential area of a town or city. **2** (as adjective) of or characteristic of an affluent area or people. ● noun an uptown area.
upturn ● noun an improvement or upward trend. ● verb (**upturned**) turned upwards or upside down.
uPVC ● abbreviation unplasticized polyvinyl chloride, a rigid form of PVC used for pipework and window frames.
upward ● adverb (also **upwards**) towards a higher point or level. ● adjective moving or leading towards a higher point or level.
– PHRASES **upwards of** more than.
– DERIVATIVES **upwardly** adverb.
upwelling ● noun a rising up of seawater, magma, or other liquid. ● adjective (especially of emotion) building up.
upwind ● adverb & adjective into the wind.
ur- /oor/ ● combining form primitive; original; earliest: *urtext*.
– ORIGIN German.
Uranian /yooraynīən/ ● adjective relating to the planet Uranus.

Thesaurus

ructions; Brit. informal row.
– OPPOSITES calm.
uproarious ● adjective **1** *an uproarious party* RIOTOUS, rowdy, noisy, loud, wild, unrestrained, unruly, rip-roaring, rollicking, boisterous; Brit. informal rumbustious; N. Amer. informal rambunctious. **2** *an uproarious joke* HILARIOUS, hysterically funny, too funny for words, rib-tickling; informal priceless, side-splitting, a scream, a hoot; informal, dated killing.
– OPPOSITES quiet.
uproot ● verb **1** *don't pick or uproot wild flowers* PULL UP, root out, deracinate, grub out/up. **2** *a revolution is necessary to uproot the social order* ERADICATE, get rid of, eliminate, root out, destroy, put an end to, do away with, wipe out, stamp out.
– OPPOSITES plant.
upset ● verb **1** *the accusation upset her* DISTRESS, trouble, perturb, dismay, disturb, discompose, unsettle, disconcert, disquiet, worry, bother, agitate, fluster, throw, ruffle, unnerve, shake; hurt, sadden, grieve. **2** *he upset a tureen of soup* KNOCK OVER, overturn, upend, tip over, topple (over); spill; archaic overset. **3** *the dam will upset the ecological balance* DISRUPT, interfere with, disturb, throw out, turn topsy-turvy, throw into confusion, mess up.
● noun **1** *a legal dispute will cause worry and upset* DISTRESS, trouble, perturbation, dismay, disquiet, worry, bother, agitation; hurt, grief. **2** *a stomach upset* DISORDER, complaint, ailment, illness, sickness, malady; informal bug; Brit. informal lurgy.
● adjective **1** *I was upset by the news* DISTRESSED, troubled, perturbed, dismayed, disturbed, unsettled, disconcerted, worried, bothered, anxious, agitated, flustered, ruffled, unnerved, shaken; hurt, saddened, grieved; informal cut up, choked; Brit. informal gutted. **2** *an upset stomach* DISTURBED, unsettled, queasy, bad, poorly; informal gippy.
– OPPOSITES unperturbed, calm.
upshot ● noun RESULT, end result, consequence, outcome, conclusion; effect, repercussion, reverberations, ramification; dated issue.
– OPPOSITES cause.
upside down ● adjective **1** *an upside-down canoe* UPTURNED, upended, wrong side up, overturned, inverted; capsized. **2** *they left the flat upside down* IN DISARRAY, in disorder, jumbled up, in a muddle, untidy, disorganized, chaotic, all over the place, in chaos, in confusion, topsy-turvy, at sixes and sevens; informal higgledy-piggledy.
upstanding ● adjective **1** *an upstanding member of the community* HONEST, honourable, upright, respectable, high-minded, law-abiding, right-minded, worthy, moral, ethical, righteous, decent, good, virtuous, principled, high-principled, of principle, noble, incorruptible. **2** *the upstanding feathered plumes* UPRIGHT, erect, vertical; standing, in a standing position, on one's feet; Heraldry rampant.
– OPPOSITES dishonourable.
upstart ● noun PARVENU(E), arriviste, nouveau riche, vulgarian; status seeker, social climber.
up to date ● adjective **1** *up-to-date equipment* MODERN, contemporary, the latest, state-of-the-art, new, present-day, up to the minute; advanced; informal bang up to date, mod. **2** *the newsletter will keep you up to date* INFORMED, up to speed, in the picture, in touch, au fait, au courant, conversant, familiar, knowledgeable, acquainted, aware.
– OPPOSITES out of date, old-fashioned.
upturn ● noun IMPROVEMENT, upswing, turn for the better; recovery, revival, rally, resurgence, increase, rise, jump, leap, upsurge, boost, escalation.
– OPPOSITES fall, slump.
upward ● adjective *an upward trend* RISING, on the rise, ascending, climbing, mounting; uphill.
– OPPOSITES downward.
● adverb *the smoke drifts upward.* See UPWARDS.
upwards ● adverb *he inched his way upwards* UP, upward, uphill; to the top.

uranium /yooraynɪəm/ ● noun a grey dense radioactive metallic chemical element used as a fuel in nuclear reactors.
– ORIGIN from the planet *Uranus*.
urban ● adjective relating to or characteristic of a town or city.
– DERIVATIVES **urbanism** noun **urbanist** noun **urbanize** (also **urbanise**) verb.
– ORIGIN Latin *urbanus*, from *urbs* 'city'.
urban district ● noun Brit. historical a group of urban communities governed by an elected council.
urbane /urbayn/ ● adjective (especially of a man) suave, courteous, and refined.
– DERIVATIVES **urbanely** adverb.
– ORIGIN originally in the sense 'urban': from Latin *urbanus*.
urbanite ● noun informal a town or city dweller.
urbanity ● noun **1** an urbane quality or manner. **2** urban life.
urban myth (also chiefly N. Amer. **urban legend**) ● noun an entertaining story or piece of information of uncertain origin that is circulated as though true.
urban renewal ● noun the redevelopment of slum areas in a large city.
urchin ● noun **1** a mischievous child, especially a raggedly dressed one. **2** archaic a goblin. **3** a sea urchin.
– ORIGIN Old French *herichon* 'hedgehog', from Latin *hericius*.
Urdu /oordōō, ur-/ ● noun an Indic language closely related to Hindi.
– ORIGIN from Persian, 'language of the camp' (because it developed as a lingua franca after the Muslim invasions between the occupying armies and the people of Delhi in the 12th century), from Turkish *ordu* (see HORDE).
-ure ● suffix forming nouns: **1** denoting an action, process, or result: *closure*. **2** denoting an office or function: *judicature*. **3** denoting a collective: *legislature*.
– ORIGIN Latin *-ura*.
urea /yooreeə/ ● noun Biochemistry a colourless crystalline compound which is the main nitrogenous breakdown product of proteins in the body and is excreted in urine.
– ORIGIN Latin, from Greek *ouron* 'urine'.
ureter /yooreetə/ ● noun the duct by which urine passes from the kidney to the bladder or cloaca.
– DERIVATIVES **ureteral** adjective **ureteric** /yooriterrik/ adjective.
– ORIGIN Greek *ourētēr*, from *ourein* 'urinate'.
urethane /yoorithayn/ ● noun **1** Chemistry a synthetic crystalline compound used to make pesticides and fungicides. **2** short for POLYURETHANE.
urethra /yooreethrə/ ● noun Anatomy & Zoology the duct by which urine is conveyed out of the body, and which in male vertebrates also conveys semen.
– DERIVATIVES **urethral** adjective.
– ORIGIN Greek *ourēthra*, from *ourein* 'urinate'.
urethritis /yooreethrītiss/ ● noun Medicine inflammation of the urethra.
urge ● verb **1** encourage or entreat earnestly to do something. **2** strongly recommend. ● noun a strong desire or impulse.
– ORIGIN Latin *urgere* 'press, drive'.
urgent ● adjective **1** requiring immediate action or attention. **2** earnest and insistent.
– DERIVATIVES **urgency** noun **urgently** adverb.
uric acid ● noun Biochemistry an insoluble nitrogenous compound which is the main excretory product of birds, reptiles, and insects.
– ORIGIN French *urique*, from URINE.
urinal /yoorīn'l/ ● noun a receptacle into which men may urinate, typically attached to the wall in a public toilet.
urinary ● adjective **1** relating to urine. **2** referring to the organs, structures, and ducts in which urine is produced and discharged.
urinate ● verb discharge urine.
– DERIVATIVES **urination** noun.
– ORIGIN Latin *urinare*.
urine /yoorin/ ● noun a pale yellowish fluid stored in the bladder and discharged through the urethra, consisting of excess water and waste substances removed from the blood by the kidneys.
– ORIGIN Latin *urina*.
URL ● abbreviation uniform (or universal) resource locator, the address of a World Wide Web page.
urn ● noun **1** a tall, rounded vase with a stem and base, especially one for storing a cremated person's ashes. **2** a large metal container with a tap, in which tea or coffee is made and kept hot.
– ORIGIN Latin *urna*.
urogenital ● adjective referring to both the urinary and genital organs.
urology /yoorolləji/ ● noun the branch of medicine concerned with the urinary system.
– DERIVATIVES **urological** adjective **urologist** noun.
ursine /ursīn/ ● adjective relating to or resembling bears.
– ORIGIN Latin *ursinus*, from *ursus* 'bear'.
Ursuline /ursyoolīn/ ● noun a nun of an order founded in northern Italy in 1535 for nursing the sick and teaching girls. ● adjective relating to this order.
– ORIGIN from St *Ursula*, the founder's patron saint.
urticaria /urtikairiə/ ● noun Medicine a rash of round, red weals on the skin which itch intensely, caused by an allergic reaction.
– ORIGIN Latin, from *urtica* 'nettle'.
Uruguayan /yoorəgwīən/ ● noun a person from Uruguay. ● adjective relating to Uruguay.
US ● abbreviation United States.
us ● pronoun (first person pl.) **1** used by a speaker to refer to himself or herself and one or more others as the object of a verb or preposition. **2** used after the verb 'to be' and after 'than' or 'as'. **3** informal me.
– USAGE On whether to use **us** or **we** following **than**, see the note at THAN.
– ORIGIN Old English.
USA ● abbreviation United States of America.
usable (also **useable**) ● adjective able to be used.
– DERIVATIVES **usability** noun.
USAF ● abbreviation United States Air Force.
usage ● noun **1** the action of using something or the fact of being used. **2** habitual or customary practice.
USB ● abbreviation Computing universal serial bus, a connector which enables any of a variety of peripheral devices to be plugged in to a computer.
use ● verb /yōōz/ **1** take, hold, or deploy as a means of achieving

Thesaurus

– OPPOSITES downward.
– PHRASES **upward(s) of** MORE THAN, above, over, in excess of, exceeding, beyond.
urban ● adjective TOWN, city, municipal, metropolitan, built-up, inner-city, suburban.
– OPPOSITES rural.
urbane ● adjective SUAVE, sophisticated, debonair, worldly, cultivated, cultured, civilized; smooth, polished, refined, self-possessed; courteous, polite, civil, well mannered, mannerly, charming, gentlemanly, gallant.
– OPPOSITES uncouth, unsophisticated.
urchin ● noun RAGAMUFFIN, waif, stray; imp, rascal; *derogatory* guttersnipe; *dated* gamin; *archaic* mudlark, scapegrace, street Arab.
urge ● verb **1** *she urged him to try again* ENCOURAGE, exhort, enjoin, press, entreat, implore, call on, appeal to, beg, plead with; egg on, spur, push, pressure, pressurize; *formal* adjure; *poetic/literary* beseech. **2** *she urged her horse down the lane* SPUR (ON), force, drive, impel. **3** *I urge caution in interpreting these results* ADVISE, counsel, advocate, recommend.
● noun *his urge to travel* DESIRE, wish, need, compulsion, longing, yearning, hankering, craving, appetite, hunger, thirst; fancy, impulse; *informal* yen, itch.
urgent ● adjective **1** *the urgent need for more funding* ACUTE, pressing, dire, desperate, critical, serious, grave, intense, crying, burning, compelling, extreme, high-priority, top-priority; life-and-death. **2** *an urgent whisper* INSISTENT, persistent, importunate, earnest, pleading, begging.
urinate ● verb PASS WATER, relieve oneself; *informal* spend a penny, have/take a leak, pee, piddle, widdle, have a tinkle; *Brit. informal* wee, have a Jimmy (Riddle), have a slash; *N. Amer. informal* take a whizz; *formal* micturate.
usable ● adjective READY/FIT FOR USE, able to be used, at someone's disposal, disposable; working, in working order, functioning, functional, serviceable, operational, up and running.
usage ● noun **1** *energy usage* USE, consumption, utilization. **2** *the usage of equipment* USE, utilization, operation, manipulation, running, handling. **3** *the intricacies of English usage* PHRASEOLOGY, parlance, idiom, way of speaking/writing, mode of expression;

something. **2** (**use up**) consume or expend the whole of. **3** treat in a particular way. **4** exploit unfairly. **5** /yo͞ost/ (**used to**) did repeatedly or existed in the past. **6** /yo͞ost/ (**be/get used to**) be or become familiar with through experience. **7** informal take (an illegal drug). ● noun /yo͞oss/ **1** the action of using or the state of being used. **2** the ability or power to exercise or manipulate something: *he lost the use of his legs.* **3** a purpose for or way in which something can be used. **4** value; advantage.
– PHRASES **have no use for** informal dislike or be impatient with. **make use of** use.
– ORIGIN Old French *user*, from Latin *uti.*
useable ● adjective variant spelling of USABLE.
use-by date ● noun chiefly Brit. the recommended date by which a perishable product should be used or consumed.
used ● adjective **1** having already been used. **2** second-hand.
useful ● adjective **1** able to be used for a practical purpose or in several ways. **2** informal very able or competent.
– DERIVATIVES **usefully** adverb **usefulness** noun.
useless ● adjective **1** serving no purpose. **2** informal having little ability or skill.
– DERIVATIVES **uselessly** adverb **uselessness** noun.
Usenet ● noun Computing an Internet service consisting of thousands of newsgroups.
user ● noun **1** a person who uses or operates something. **2** a person who exploits others.
user-friendly ● adjective easy to use or understand.
– DERIVATIVES **user-friendliness** noun.
usher ● noun **1** a person who shows people to their seats in a theatre or cinema or in church. **2** an official in a law court who swears in jurors and witnesses and keeps order. **3** Brit. a person employed to walk before a person of high rank on special occasions. ● verb show or guide somewhere.
– ORIGIN Old French *usser* 'doorkeeper', from Latin *ostium* 'door'.
usherette ● noun a woman who shows people to their seats in a cinema or theatre.
USN ● abbreviation United States Navy.
USS ● abbreviation United States Ship.
USSR ● abbreviation historical Union of Soviet Socialist Republics.
usual ● adjective habitually or typically occurring or done. ● noun informal **1** the drink someone habitually prefers. **2** the thing which is typically done or present.
– DERIVATIVES **usually** adverb.
– ORIGIN Latin *usualis*, from *usus* 'a use'.
usufruct /yo͞ozyoofrukt/ ● noun Roman Law the right to enjoy the use of another's property short of the destruction or waste of its substance.
– ORIGIN from Latin *usus et fructus* 'use and enjoyment'.
usurer /yo͞ozhərər/ ● noun a person who lends money at unreasonably high rates of interest.
usurious /yo͞ozhooriəss/ ● adjective relating to usury.
usurp /yoozurp/ ● verb **1** take (a position of power) illegally or by force. **2** take the place of (someone in power) illegally.
– DERIVATIVES **usurpation** noun **usurper** noun.
– ORIGIN Latin *usurpare* 'seize for use'.
usury /yo͞ozhəri/ ● noun the practice of lending money at unreasonably high rates of interest.
– ORIGIN Latin *usura*, from *usus* 'a use'.
UT ● abbreviation **1** Universal Time. **2** Utah.
Ute /yo͞ot/ ● noun (pl. same or **Utes**) a member of an American Indian people of Colorado, Utah, and New Mexico.
– ORIGIN Spanish *Yuta.*
ute /yo͞ot/ ● noun N. Amer. & Austral./NZ informal a utility vehicle.
utensil ● noun a tool or container, especially for household use.
– ORIGIN from Latin *utensilis* 'usable', from *uti* 'to use'.
uteri plural of UTERUS.
uterine /yo͞otərin/ ● adjective **1** of or relating to the uterus. **2** having the same mother but not the same father.
uterus /yo͞otərəss/ ● noun (pl. **uteri** /yo͞otərī/) the womb.
– ORIGIN Latin.
utilitarian /yo͞otilitairiən/ ● adjective **1** useful or practical rather than attractive. **2** relating to or adhering to utilitarianism. ● noun an adherent of utilitarianism.
utilitarianism ● noun **1** the doctrine that actions are right if they are useful or for the benefit of a majority. **2** the doctrine that the greatest happiness of the greatest number should be the guiding principle of conduct.
utility ● noun (pl. **utilities**) **1** the state of being useful, profitable, or beneficial. **2** a public utility. **3** Computing a utility program. ● adjective useful, especially through having several functions.
– ORIGIN Latin *utilitas*, from *utilis* 'useful'.
utility knife ● noun a Stanley knife.
utility program ● noun Computing a program for carrying out a

Thesaurus

idiolect. **4** *the usages of polite society* CUSTOM, practice, habit, tradition, convention, rule, observance; way, procedure, form, wont; formal praxis; (**usages**) mores.
use ● verb **1** *she used her key to open the front door* UTILIZE, make use of, avail oneself of, employ, work, operate, wield, ply, apply, manoeuvre, manipulate, put to use, put into service. **2** *the court will use its discretion in making an order* EXERCISE, employ, bring into play, practise, apply. **3** *use your troops well and they will not let you down* MANAGE, handle, treat, deal with, behave/act towards, conduct oneself towards. **4** *I couldn't help feeling that she was using me* TAKE ADVANTAGE OF, exploit, manipulate, take liberties with, impose on, abuse; capitalize on, profit from, trade on, milk; informal cash in on, walk all over. **5** *we have used all the available funds* CONSUME, get/go through, exhaust, deplete, expend, spend; waste, fritter away, squander, dissipate.
● noun **1** *the use of such weapons* UTILIZATION, usage, application, employment, operation, manipulation. **2** *his use of other people for his own ends* EXPLOITATION, manipulation; abuse. **3** *what is the use of that?* ADVANTAGE, benefit, service, utility, usefulness, help, good, gain, avail, profit, value, worth, point, object, purpose, sense, reason. **4** *composers have not found much use for the device* NEED, necessity, call, demand, requirement.
used ● adjective *a used car* SECOND-HAND, pre-owned, nearly new, old; worn, hand-me-down, handed-down, cast-off; Brit. informal reach-me-down.
– OPPOSITES new.
– PHRASES **used to** ACCUSTOMED TO, no stranger to, familiar with, at home with, in the habit of, experienced in, versed in, conversant with, acquainted with.
useful ● adjective **1** *a useful multi-purpose tool* FUNCTIONAL, practical, handy, convenient, utilitarian, serviceable, of use, of service; informal nifty. **2** *a useful experience* BENEFICIAL, advantageous, helpful, worthwhile, profitable, rewarding, productive, constructive, valuable, fruitful. **3** (informal) *they had some very useful players* COMPETENT, capable, able, skilful, skilled, talented, proficient, accomplished, good, handy.
– OPPOSITES useless, disadvantageous, incompetent.
useless ● adjective **1** *it was useless to try* | *a piece of useless knowledge* FUTILE, to no avail, in vain, vain, pointless, to no purpose, unavailing, hopeless, ineffectual, ineffective, to no effect, fruitless, unprofitable, profitless, unproductive; broken, kaput; archaic bootless. **2** (informal) *he was useless at his job* INCOMPETENT, inept, ineffective, incapable, inadequate, hopeless, bad; informal pathetic, a dead loss.
– OPPOSITES useful, beneficial, competent.
usher ● verb *she ushered him to a window seat* ESCORT, accompany, take, show, see, lead, conduct, guide, steer, shepherd.
● noun *ushers showed them to their seats* GUIDE, attendant, escort.
– PHRASES **usher something in** HERALD, mark the start of, signal, ring in, show in, set the scene for, pave the way for; start, begin, introduce, open the door to, get going, set in motion, get under way, kick off, launch.
usual ● adjective HABITUAL, customary, accustomed, wonted, normal, routine, regular, standard, typical, established, set, settled, stock, conventional, traditional, expected, predictable, familiar; average, general, ordinary, everyday.
– OPPOSITES unusual, exceptional.
usually ● adverb NORMALLY, generally, habitually, customarily, routinely, typically, ordinarily, commonly, conventionally, traditionally; as a rule, in general, more often than not, in the main, mainly, mostly, for the most part.
usurp ● verb **1** *Richard usurped the throne* SEIZE, take over, take possession of, take, commandeer, assume. **2** *the Hanoverian dynasty had usurped the Stuarts* OUST, overthrow, remove, topple, unseat, depose, dethrone; supplant, replace.
utensil ● noun IMPLEMENT, tool, instrument, device, apparatus, gadget, appliance, contrivance, contraption, aid; informal gizmo.
utilitarian ● adjective PRACTICAL, functional, serviceable, useful, sensible, efficient, utility, workaday; plain, unadorned, undecorative.
– OPPOSITES decorative.
utility ● noun USEFULNESS, use, benefit, value, advantage, advan-

routine function.

utility room ● noun a room with appliances for washing and other domestic work.

utility vehicle (also **utility truck**) ● noun a truck having low sides and used for small loads.

utilize (also **utilise**) ● verb make practical and effective use of.
– DERIVATIVES **utilizable** adjective **utilization** noun.
– ORIGIN French *utiliser*, from Latin *uti* 'to use'.

utmost ● adjective most extreme; greatest. ● noun (**the utmost**) the greatest or most extreme extent or amount.
– ORIGIN Old English, 'outermost'.

Utopia /yootōpiə/ ● noun an imagined perfect place or state of things.
– ORIGIN the title of a book (1516) by Sir Thomas More, from Greek *ou* 'not' + *topos* 'place'.

utopian ● adjective idealistic. ● noun an idealistic reformer.
– DERIVATIVES **utopianism** noun.

utter[1] ● adjective complete; absolute.
– DERIVATIVES **utterly** adverb.
– ORIGIN Old English, 'outer'.

utter[2] ● verb **1** make (a sound) or say (something). **2** Law put (forged money) into circulation.
– DERIVATIVES **utterable** adjective **utterer** noun.
– ORIGIN Dutch *ūteren* 'speak, make known, give currency to (coins)'.

utterance ● noun **1** a word, statement, or sound uttered. **2** the action of uttering.

uttermost ● adjective & noun another term for UTMOST.

U-turn ● noun **1** the turning of a vehicle in a U-shaped course so as to face the opposite way. **2** a reversal of policy.

UV ● abbreviation ultraviolet.

UVA ● abbreviation ultraviolet radiation of relatively long wavelengths.

UVB ● abbreviation ultraviolet radiation of relatively short wavelengths.

UVC ● abbreviation ultraviolet radiation of very short wavelengths, which does not penetrate the earth's ozone layer.

uvula /yōōvyoolə/ ● noun (pl. **uvulae** /yōōvyoolee/) a fleshy extension at the back of the soft palate which hangs above the throat.
– ORIGIN Latin, 'little grape'.

uxorial /uksoriəl/ ● adjective of or relating to a wife.

uxoricide /uksorrisīd/ ● noun **1** the killing of one's wife. **2** a man who kills his wife.

uxorious /uksoriəss/ ● adjective showing great or excessive fondness for one's wife.
– DERIVATIVES **uxoriousness** noun.
– ORIGIN Latin *uxoriosus*, from *uxor* 'wife'.

Uzbek /ŏŏzbek/ ● noun **1** a member of a people living mainly in Uzbekistan. **2** a person from Uzbekistan. **3** the language of Uzbekistan.
– ORIGIN Uzbek.

Uzi /ŏŏzi/ ● noun a type of sub-machine gun.
– ORIGIN from *Uziel* Gal, the Israeli army officer who designed it.

Thesaurus

tageousness, help, helpfulness, profitability, practicality, effectiveness, avail, service; *formal* efficacy.

utilize ● verb USE, make use of, put to use, employ, avail oneself of, bring/press into service, bring into play, deploy, draw on, exploit.

utmost ● adjective **1** *a matter of the utmost importance* GREATEST, highest, maximum, most, uttermost; extreme, supreme, paramount. **2** *the utmost tip of Shetland* FURTHEST, farthest, furthermost, farthermost, extreme, very, uttermost, outermost, endmost. ● noun *a plot that stretches credulity to the utmost* UTTERMOST, maximum, limit.

Utopia ● noun PARADISE, heaven, heaven on earth, Eden, Garden of Eden, Shangri-La, Elysium; idyll, nirvana, ideal place; *poetic/literary* Arcadia.

Utopian ● adjective IDEALISTIC, visionary, romantic, starry-eyed, fanciful, unrealistic; ideal, perfect, paradisal, heavenly, idyllic, blissful, Elysian; *poetic/literary* Arcadian.

utter[1] ● adjective *that's utter nonsense* COMPLETE, total, absolute, thorough, perfect, downright, out-and-out, outright, thoroughgoing, all-out, sheer, arrant, positive, prize, rank, pure, real, veritable, consummate, categorical, unmitigated, unqualified, unadulterated, unalloyed.

utter[2] ● verb **1** *he uttered an exasperated snort* EMIT, let out, give, produce. **2** *he hardly uttered a word* SAY, speak, voice, express, articulate, pronounce, enunciate, verbalize, vocalize.

utterance ● noun REMARK, comment, word, statement, observation, declaration, pronouncement.

utterly ● adverb COMPLETELY, totally, absolutely, entirely, wholly, fully, thoroughly, quite, altogether, one hundred per cent, downright, outright, in all respects, unconditionally, perfectly, really, to the hilt, to the core; *informal* dead.

uttermost ● adjective & noun. See UTMOST.

U-turn ● noun *a complete U-turn in economic policy* VOLTE-FACE, turnaround, about-face, reversal, shift, change of heart, change of mind, backtracking, change of plan; *Brit.* about-turn.

u

Vv

V[1] (also **v**) ● noun (pl. **Vs** or **V's**) **1** the twenty-second letter of the alphabet. **2** the Roman numeral for five.
V[2] ● abbreviation volt(s). ● symbol **1** the chemical element vanadium. **2** voltage or potential difference. **3** (in mathematical formulae) volume.
v ● abbreviation **1** Grammar verb. **2** versus. **3** very. ● symbol velocity.
V-1 ● noun a small bomb powered by a simple jet engine, used by the Germans in the Second World War.
– ORIGIN abbreviation of German *Vergeltungswaffe* 'reprisal weapon'.
V-2 ● noun a rocket-powered flying bomb used by the Germans in the Second World War.
– ORIGIN see V-1.
VA ● abbreviation **1** (in the UK) Order of Victoria and Albert. **2** Virginia.
vac ● noun Brit. informal **1** a vacation. **2** a vacuum cleaner.
vacancy ● noun (pl. **vacancies**) **1** an unoccupied position or job. **2** an available room in a hotel, guest house, etc. **3** empty space. **4** lack of intelligence or understanding.
vacant ● adjective **1** not occupied; empty. **2** (of a position) not filled. **3** showing no intelligence or interest.
– DERIVATIVES **vacantly** adverb.
vacant possession ● noun Brit. ownership of a property on completion of a sale, any previous occupant having moved out.
vacate /vaykayt/ ● verb **1** leave (a place). **2** give up (a position or job).
– ORIGIN Latin *vacare* 'leave empty'.
vacation ● noun **1** a holiday period between terms in universities and law courts. **2** chiefly N. Amer. a holiday. **3** the action of vacating. ● verb chiefly N. Amer. take a holiday.
– DERIVATIVES **vacationer** noun **vacationist** noun.
vaccinate /vaksinayt/ ● verb treat with a vaccine to produce immunity against a disease.
– DERIVATIVES **vaccination** noun.
vaccine /vakseen/ ● noun Medicine a substance used to stimulate the production of antibodies and provide immunity against one or several diseases, prepared from the causative agent of a disease or a synthetic substitute.
– ORIGIN Latin *vaccinus*, from *vacca* 'cow' (because of the early use of the cowpox virus against smallpox).
vaccinia /vaksinniə/ ● noun Medicine cowpox, or the virus causing it.
vacillate /vassilayt/ ● verb waver between different opinions or actions.
– DERIVATIVES **vacillation** noun.
– ORIGIN Latin *vacillare* 'sway'.
vacuole /vakyoo-ōl/ ● noun Biology a space or vesicle inside a cell, enclosed by a membrane and typically containing fluid.
– ORIGIN from Latin *vacuus* 'empty'.
vacuous /vakyooəss/ ● adjective showing a lack of thought or intelligence.
– DERIVATIVES **vacuity** /vəkyōoiti/ noun **vacuously** adverb **vacuousness** noun.
– ORIGIN Latin *vacuus* 'empty'.
vacuum /vakyooəm/ ● noun (pl. **vacuums** or **vacua** /vakyooə/) **1** a space entirely devoid of matter. **2** a space from which the air has been completely or partly removed. **3** a gap left by the loss or departure of someone or something important. **4** (pl. **vacuums**) informal a vacuum cleaner. ● verb informal clean with a vacuum cleaner.
– PHRASES **in a vacuum** in isolation from the normal context.
– ORIGIN Latin, from *vacuus* 'empty'.
vacuum cleaner ● noun an electrical apparatus that collects dust from floors and other surfaces by means of suction.
vacuum flask ● noun chiefly Brit. a container that keeps a substance hot or cold by means of a double wall enclosing a vacuum.
vacuum-pack ● verb seal (a product) in a pack or wrapping with the air removed.
vacuum tube ● noun a sealed glass tube containing a near vacuum which allows the free passage of electric current.
vade mecum /vaadi maykəm/ ● noun a handbook or guide kept constantly at hand.
– ORIGIN Latin, 'go with me'.
vagabond ● noun **1** a vagrant. **2** informal, dated a rogue. ● adjective having no settled home.
– ORIGIN Latin *vagabundus*, from *vagari* 'wander'.
vagary /vaygəri/ ● noun (pl. **vagaries**) an unexpected and inexplicable change.
– ORIGIN from Latin *vagari* 'wander'.
vagina /vəjīnə/ ● noun (pl. **vaginas** or **vaginae** /vəjīnee/) the muscular tube leading from the vulva to the cervix in women and most female mammals.
– DERIVATIVES **vaginal** adjective.
– ORIGIN Latin, 'sheath, scabbard'.
vaginismus /vajinizməss/ ● noun painful contraction of the vagina in response to physical contact or pressure.
vaginitis /vajinītiss/ ● noun inflammation of the vagina.
vagrant /vaygrənt/ ● noun **1** a person without a home or job. **2** archaic a wanderer. ● adjective relating to or living like a vagrant; wandering.
– DERIVATIVES **vagrancy** noun.

Thesaurus

vacancy ● noun **1** *there are vacancies for computer technicians* OPENING, position, situation vacant, post, job, opportunity, place. **2** *Cathy stared into vacancy, seeing nothing* EMPTY SPACE, emptiness, nothingness, void. **3** *a vacancy of mind* EMPTY-HEADEDNESS, lack of intelligence, brainlessness, vacuousness, vacuity, stupidity.
vacant ● adjective **1** *a vacant house* EMPTY, unoccupied, available, not in use, free, unfilled; uninhabited, untenanted. **2** *a vacant look* BLANK, expressionless, unresponsive, emotionless, impassive, uninterested, vacuous, empty, glazed, glassy; unintelligent, dull-witted, dense, brainless, empty-headed.
– OPPOSITES full, occupied, expressive.
vacate ● verb **1** *he was forced to vacate the premises* LEAVE, move out of, evacuate, quit, depart from; abandon, desert. **2** *he will be vacating his post next year* RESIGN FROM, leave, stand down from, give up, bow out of, relinquish, retire from; *informal* quit.
– OPPOSITES occupy, take up.
vacation ● noun **1** *his summer vacations in France* HOLIDAY, trip, tour, break, mini-break; leave, time off, recess, furlough; *informal* hol, vac; *formal* sojourn. **2** *the squatters' vacation of the occupied land* DEPARTURE, evacuation, abandonment, desertion.
vacillate ● verb DITHER, be indecisive, be undecided, waver, hesitate, be in two minds, blow hot and cold, keep changing one's mind; *Brit.* haver, hum and haw; *informal* dilly-dally, shilly-shally.
vacillating ● adjective IRRESOLUTE, indecisive, dithering, undecided, hesitant, wavering, ambivalent, divided, uncertain, in two minds, blowing hot and cold; *informal* dilly-dallying, shilly-shallying.
– OPPOSITES resolute.
vacuous ● adjective SILLY, inane, unintelligent, foolish, stupid, fatuous, idiotic, brainless, witless, vapid, vacant, empty-headed; *informal* dumb, gormless, moronic, brain-dead.
– OPPOSITES intelligent.
vacuum ● noun **1** *people longing to fill the spiritual vacuum in their lives* EMPTINESS, void, nothingness, vacancy. **2** *the political vacuum left by the Emperor's death* GAP, space, lacuna, void. **3** (*informal*) *I use the vacuum for cleaning the rug* VACUUM CLEANER; *Brit. informal* vac; *trademark* Hoover.
vagabond ● noun. See VAGRANT noun.
vagary ● noun CHANGE, fluctuation, variation, quirk, peculiarity,

– ORIGIN from Old French *vagarant* 'wandering about', from *vagrer* 'wander'.

vague ● adjective **1** of uncertain or indefinite character or meaning. **2** imprecise in thought or expression.
– DERIVATIVES **vaguely** adverb **vagueness** noun.
– ORIGIN Latin *vagus* 'wandering, uncertain'.

vagus /vaygəss/ ● noun (pl. **vagi** /vaygī/) Anatomy each of the pair of cranial nerves supplying the heart, lungs, and other organs of the chest and abdomen.
– DERIVATIVES **vagal** adjective.
– ORIGIN Latin.

vain ● adjective **1** having or showing an excessively high opinion of one's appearance or abilities. **2** useless or meaningless: *a vain boast.*
– PHRASES **in vain** without success. **take someone's name in vain** use someone's name in a way that shows a lack of respect.
– DERIVATIVES **vainly** adverb.
– ORIGIN Latin *vanus* 'empty, without substance'.

vainglory ● noun literary excessive vanity.
– DERIVATIVES **vainglorious** adjective **vaingloriously** adverb.

Vaisya /vīsyə/ (also **Vaishya**) ● noun a member of the third of the four Hindu castes, comprising merchants and farmers.
– ORIGIN Sanskrit, 'peasant, labourer'.

valance /valənss/ (also **valence**) ● noun **1** a length of decorative drapery attached to the canopy or frame of a bed to screen the structure or space beneath it. **2** a length of decorative drapery screening the curtain fittings above a window.
– DERIVATIVES **valanced** adjective.
– ORIGIN perhaps from Old French *avaler* 'lower, descend'.

vale ● noun chiefly literary a valley.
– PHRASES **vale of tears** the world as a scene of trouble or sorrow.
– ORIGIN Latin *vallis.*

valediction /validiksh'n/ ● noun **1** the action of saying farewell. **2** a farewell address or statement.
– ORIGIN from Latin *vale* 'goodbye' + *dicere* 'to say'.

valedictorian /validiktoriən/ ● noun (in North America) a student who delivers the valedictory at a graduation ceremony.

valedictory /validiktəri/ ● adjective serving as a farewell. ● noun (pl. **valedictories**) a farewell address.

valence[1] /vayl ənss/ ● noun Chemistry another term for VALENCY.

valence[2] ● noun variant spelling of VALANCE.

valency /vaylənsi/ ● noun (pl. **valencies**) Chemistry the combining power of an element, especially as measured by the number of hydrogen atoms it can displace or combine with.
– ORIGIN Latin *valentia* 'power, competence'.

valentine ● noun **1** a card sent, often anonymously, on St Valentine's Day (14 February) to a person one loves or is attracted to. **2** a person to whom one sends such a card.

valerian /vəleeriən/ ● noun **1** a plant bearing clusters of small pink, red, or white flowers. **2** a sedative drug obtained from a valerian root.
– ORIGIN Latin *valeriana*, apparently from *Valerianus* 'of Valerius' (a personal name).

valet /valit, valay/ ● noun **1** a man's personal male attendant, responsible for his clothes and appearance. **2** a hotel employee performing such duties for guests. **3** a person employed to clean or park cars. ● verb (**valeted**, **valeting**) **1** act as a valet to. **2** clean (a car).
– ORIGIN originally denoting a footman acting as an attendant to a horseman: from French, related to VASSAL.

valetudinarian /valityōōdinairiən/ ● noun a person in poor health or who is unduly anxious about their health. ● adjective in poor health or showing undue concern about one's health.
– ORIGIN from Latin *valetudinarius* 'in ill health'.

Valhalla /valhalə/ ● noun Scandinavian Mythology a palace in which heroes killed in battle feasted for eternity.
– ORIGIN Old Norse, 'hall of the slain'.

valiant ● adjective showing courage or determination.
– DERIVATIVES **valiantly** adverb.
– ORIGIN Old French *vailant*, from Latin *valere* 'be strong'.

valid ● adjective **1** (of a reason, argument, etc.) well based or logical. **2** legally binding or acceptable.
– DERIVATIVES **validity** noun **validly** adverb.
– ORIGIN Latin *validus* 'strong'.

validate ● verb **1** check or prove the validity of. **2** make or declare legally valid.
– DERIVATIVES **validation** noun.

valine /vayleen/ ● noun Biochemistry an amino acid which is a constituent of most proteins and is an essential nutrient in the diet.
– ORIGIN from *valeric acid*, a related compound, from VALERIAN.

valise /vəleez/ ● noun a small travelling bag or suitcase.
– ORIGIN French, from Italian *valigia.*

Valium /valiəm/ ● noun trademark for DIAZEPAM.
– ORIGIN of unknown origin.

Valkyrie /valkeeri, valkiri/ ● noun Scandinavian Mythology each of Odin's twelve handmaids who conducted slain warriors of their choice to Valhalla.
– ORIGIN Old Norse, 'chooser of the slain'.

Thesaurus

oddity, eccentricity, unpredictability, caprice, foible, whim, whimsy, fancy.

vagrant ● noun *a temporary home for vagrants* TRAMP, drifter, down-and-out, derelict, beggar, itinerant, wanderer, nomad, traveller, vagabond, transient, homeless person, beachcomber; *informal* knight of the road; *N. Amer.* hobo; *Austral.* bagman; *informal* bag lady; *N. Amer. informal* bum; *poetic/literary* wayfarer.
● adjective *vagrant beggars* HOMELESS, drifting, transient, roving, roaming, itinerant, wandering, nomadic, travelling, vagabond, rootless, of no fixed address/abode.

vague ● adjective **1** *a vague shape* INDISTINCT, indefinite, indeterminate, unclear, ill-defined; hazy, fuzzy, misty, blurred, blurry, out of focus, faint, shadowy, dim, obscure, nebulous, amorphous. **2** *a vague description* IMPRECISE, rough, approximate, inexact, non-specific, generalized, ambiguous, equivocal, hazy, woolly. **3** *they had only vague plans* HAZY, uncertain, undecided, unsure, unclear, unsettled, indefinite, indeterminate, unconfirmed, up in the air, speculative. **4** *she was so vague in everyday life* ABSENT-MINDED, forgetful, dreamy, abstracted, with one's head in the clouds; *informal* scatty, not with it.
– OPPOSITES clear, precise, certain.

V

vaguely ● adverb **1** *she looks vaguely familiar* SLIGHTLY, a little, a bit, somewhat, rather, in a way; faintly, obscurely; *informal* sort of, kind of. **2** *he fired his rifle vaguely in our direction* ROUGHLY, more or less, approximately. **3** *he smiled vaguely* ABSENT-MINDEDLY, abstractedly, vacantly.
– OPPOSITES very, exactly.

vain ● adjective **1** *he was vain about his looks* CONCEITED, narcissistic, self-loving, in love with oneself, self-admiring, self-regarding, egotistic, egotistical; proud, arrogant, boastful, cocky, immodest, swaggering; *informal* big-headed; *poetic/literary* vainglorious. **2** *a vain attempt* FUTILE, useless, pointless, to no purpose, in vain; ineffective, ineffectual, inefficacious, impotent, unavailing, to no avail, fruitless, profitless, unproductive, unsuccessful, failed, abortive, for nothing; thwarted, frustrated, foiled; *archaic* bootless.
– OPPOSITES modest, successful.
– PHRASES **in vain 1** *they tried in vain to save him* UNSUCCESSFULLY, without success, to no avail, to no purpose, fruitlessly. **2** *his efforts were in vain.* See VAIN sense 2.

valediction ● noun FAREWELL, goodbye, adieu, leave-taking.

valedictory ● adjective FAREWELL, goodbye, leaving, parting; last, final.

valet ● noun MANSERVANT, man, personal attendant, gentleman's gentleman, Jeeves; *Military, dated* batman.

valetudinarian ● noun *an elderly valetudinarian* HYPOCHONDRIAC; invalid.
● adjective *he was earnest, fussy, and valetudinarian* HYPOCHONDRIAC, obsessed with one's health, neurotic; sickly, ailing, poorly, in poor health, weak, infirm, valetudinary.

valiant ● adjective BRAVE, courageous, plucky, valorous, intrepid, heroic, gallant, lionhearted, bold, fearless, daring, audacious; unflinching, unshrinking, unafraid, dauntless, undaunted, doughty, indomitable, mettlesome, stout-hearted, spirited; *informal* game, gutsy, spunky.
– OPPOSITES cowardly.

valid ● adjective **1** *a valid criticism* WELL FOUNDED, sound, reasonable, rational, logical, justifiable, defensible, viable, bona fide; cogent, effective, powerful, convincing, credible, forceful, strong, weighty. **2** *a valid contract* LEGALLY BINDING, lawful, legal, official, signed and sealed, contractual; in force, in effect, effective.

validate ● verb **1** *clinical trials now exist to validate this claim* PROVE, substantiate, corroborate, verify, support, back up, bear out, confirm, justify, vindicate, authenticate. **2** *250 course proposals were validated* RATIFY, endorse, approve, agree to, accept,

valley ● noun (pl. **valleys**) a low area between hills or mountains, typically with a river or stream flowing through it.
– ORIGIN Latin *vallis.*

valor ● noun US spelling of VALOUR.

valorize /valərīz/ (also **valorise**) ● verb give or ascribe value or validity to.
– DERIVATIVES **valorization** noun.
– ORIGIN from French *valorisation,* from *valeur* 'value'.

valour (US **valor**) ● noun courage in the face of danger.
– DERIVATIVES **valorous** adjective.
– ORIGIN Latin *valor,* from *valere* 'be strong'.

valuable ● adjective **1** worth a great deal of money. **2** extremely useful or important. ● noun (**valuables**) valuable items.
– DERIVATIVES **valuably** adverb.

valuation ● noun an estimation of something's worth.
– DERIVATIVES **valuate** verb (chiefly N. Amer.).

value ● noun **1** the regard that something is held to deserve; importance or worth. **2** material or monetary worth. **3** (**values**) principles or standards of behaviour. **4** the numerical amount denoted by an algebraic term; a magnitude, quantity, or number. **5** Music the relative duration of the sound signified by a note. ● verb (**values, valued, valuing**) **1** estimate the value of. **2** consider to be important or beneficial.
– DERIVATIVES **valueless** adjective **valuer** noun.
– ORIGIN Old French, from Latin *valere.*

value added tax ● noun a tax on the amount by which the value of an article has been increased at each stage of its production or distribution.

value judgement ● noun an assessment of something as good or bad in terms of one's standards or priorities.

valve ● noun **1** a device for controlling the passage of fluid through a pipe or duct. **2** a cylindrical mechanism to vary the effective length of the tube in a brass musical instrument. **3** Anatomy & Zoology a membranous fold which allows blood or other fluid to flow in one direction through a vessel or organ. **4** Zoology each of the halves of the hinged shell of a bivalve mollusc or brachiopod.
– DERIVATIVES **valved** adjective.
– ORIGIN Latin *valva* 'leaf of a folding or double door'.

valvular ● adjective relating to, having, or acting as a valve or valves.

vamoose /vəmo͞os/ ● verb informal depart hurriedly.
– ORIGIN from Spanish *vamos* 'let us go'.

vamp[1] ● noun **1** the upper front part of a boot or shoe. **2** (in jazz and popular music) a short, simple introductory passage, usually repeated several times until otherwise instructed. ● verb **1** (**vamp up**) informal repair or improve. **2** repeat a short, simple passage of music.
– ORIGIN originally denoting the foot of a stocking: from Old French *avant* 'before' + *pie* 'foot'.

vamp[2] informal ● noun a woman who uses sexual attraction to exploit men. ● verb blatantly set out to attract (a man).
– DERIVATIVES **vampish** adjective **vampy** adjective.
– ORIGIN abbreviation of VAMPIRE.

vampire /vampīr/ ● noun **1** (in folklore) a corpse supposed to leave its grave at night to drink the blood of the living. **2** (also **vampire bat**) a small bat that feeds on blood by piercing the skin with its incisor teeth, found mainly in tropical America.
– DERIVATIVES **vampiric** /vampirrik/ adjective **vampirism** noun.
– ORIGIN Hungarian *vampir,* perhaps from Turkish *uber* 'witch'.

van[1] ● noun **1** a covered motor vehicle used for transporting goods or people. **2** Brit. a railway carriage for conveying luggage, mail, etc. **3** Brit. a caravan.
– ORIGIN shortening of CARAVAN.

van[2] ● noun (**the van**) **1** the foremost part of an advancing group of people. **2** the forefront.
– ORIGIN abbreviation of VANGUARD.

vanadium /vənaydiəm/ ● noun a hard grey metallic chemical element, used to make alloy steels.
– ORIGIN Latin, from an Old Norse name of the Scandinavian goddess Freyja.

Van Allen belt ● noun each of two regions of intense radiation partly surrounding the earth at heights of several thousand kilometres.
– ORIGIN named after the American physicist James A. *Van Allen* (born 1914).

vandal ● noun **1** a person who deliberately destroys or damages property. **2** (**Vandal**) a member of a Germanic people that ravaged Gaul, Spain, Rome, and North Africa in the 4th–5th centuries.
– DERIVATIVES **vandalism** noun.
– ORIGIN Latin *Vandalus.*

vandalize (also **vandalise**) ● verb deliberately destroy or damage (property).

Vandyke /vandīk/ ● noun **1** a broad lace or linen collar with an edge deeply cut into large points, fashionable in the 18th century. **2** (also **Vandyke beard**) a neat pointed beard.
– ORIGIN named after the Flemish painter Sir Anthony *Van Dyck* (1599–1641), whose portraits frequently depict such styles.

vane ● noun **1** a broad blade attached to a rotating axis or wheel which pushes or is pushed by wind or water, forming part of a device such as a windmill, propeller, or turbine. **2** a weathervane. **3** a projecting surface designed to guide the motion of a projectile, e.g. a fin on a torpedo.
– ORIGIN from obsolete *fane* 'banner', from Germanic.

vanguard ● noun **1** the foremost part of an advancing army or naval force. **2** a group of people leading the way in new developments or ideas.
– ORIGIN Old French *avantgarde,* from *avant* 'before' + *garde* 'guard'.

vanilla ● noun a substance obtained from the pods of a tropical climbing orchid or produced artificially, used as a flavouring and in the manufacture of cosmetics.
– ORIGIN Spanish *vainilla* 'pod', from Latin *vagina* 'sheath'.

vanillin ● noun Chemistry a fragrant compound which is the essential constituent of vanilla.

vanish ● verb **1** disappear suddenly and completely. **2** gradually cease to exist. **3** Mathematics become zero.

Thesaurus

authorize, legalize, legitimize, warrant, license, certify, recognize.
– OPPOSITES invalidate, disprove.

valley ● noun DALE, vale; hollow, gully, gorge, ravine, canyon, rift; *Brit.* combe, dene; *N. English* clough; *Scottish* glen, strath; *poetic/literary* dell, dingle.

valour ● noun BRAVERY, courage, pluck, intrepidity, nerve, daring, fearlessness, audacity, boldness, dauntlessness, stout-heartedness, heroism, backbone, spirit; *informal* guts, spunk; *Brit. informal* bottle; *N. Amer. informal* moxie.
– OPPOSITES cowardice.

valuable ● adjective **1** *a valuable watch* PRECIOUS, costly, high-priced, high-cost, expensive, dear; worth its weight in gold, worth a king's ransom, priceless. **2** *a valuable contribution* USEFUL, helpful, beneficial, invaluable, productive, constructive, effective, advantageous, worthwhile, worthy, important.
– OPPOSITES cheap, worthless, useless.

valuables ● plural noun PRECIOUS ITEMS, costly items, prized possessions, personal effects, treasures.

value ● noun **1** *houses exceeding £250,000 in value* PRICE, cost, worth; market price, monetary value, face value. **2** *the value of adequate preparation cannot be understated* WORTH, usefulness, advantage, benefit, gain, profit, good, help, helpfulness, avail; importance, significance. **3** *society's values are passed on to us as children* PRINCIPLES, ethics, moral code, morals, standards, code of behaviour.
● verb **1** *his estate was valued at £45,000* EVALUATE, assess, estimate, appraise, price, put/set a price on. **2** *she valued his opinion* THINK HIGHLY OF, have a high opinion of, hold in high regard, rate highly, esteem, set (great) store by, appreciate, respect; prize, cherish, treasure.

valued ● adjective CHERISHED, treasured, dear, prized; esteemed, respected, highly regarded.

valueless ● adjective WORTHLESS, of no value, useless, to no purpose, (of) no use, profitless, futile, pointless, vain, in vain, to no avail, to no effect, fruitless, unproductive, idle, ineffective, unavailing; *archaic* bootless.

vamp[1] ● verb (*informal*) *the design had been vamped up* IMPROVE, revamp, redesign, remodel, restyle, rework, make over; renovate, refurbish, redecorate, recondition, rehabilitate, overhaul, repair; *informal* do up, give something a facelift; *N. Amer. informal* rehab.

vamp[2] ● noun (*informal*) *a raven-haired vamp* SEDUCTRESS, temptress, siren, femme fatale, Mata Hari; flirt, coquette, tease.

van ● noun *he was in the van of the movement.* See VANGUARD.

vanguard ● noun FOREFRONT, van, advance guard, spearhead, front, front line, fore, lead, cutting edge; leaders, founders, founding fathers, pioneers, trailblazers, trendsetters, innovators,

– DERIVATIVES **vanishing** adjective & noun **vanishingly** adverb.
– ORIGIN Old French *esvanir*, from Latin *evanescere* 'die away'.
vanishing point ● noun the point at which receding parallel lines viewed in perspective appear to converge.
vanity ● noun (pl. **vanities**) **1** excessive pride in or admiration of one's own appearance or achievements. **2** the quality of being worthless or futile.
– ORIGIN Latin *vanitas*, from *vanus* 'empty, without substance'.
vanity case ● noun a small case fitted with a mirror and compartments for make-up.
vanity plate ● noun N. Amer. a vehicle licence plate bearing a distinctive or personalized combination of letters or numbers.
vanity unit ● noun a unit consisting of a washbasin set into a flat top with cupboards beneath.
vanquish /vangkwish/ ● verb defeat thoroughly.
– DERIVATIVES **vanquisher** noun.
– ORIGIN Old French *vainquir*, from Latin *vincere* 'conquer'.
vantage /vaantij/ ● noun (usu. **vantage point**) a place or position affording a good view.
– ORIGIN Old French *avantage* 'advantage'.
Vanuatuan /vanōōaatōōən/ ● noun a person from Vanuatu, a country in the SW Pacific. ● adjective relating to Vanuatu.
vapid /vappid/ ● adjective offering nothing that is stimulating or challenging.
– DERIVATIVES **vapidity** noun **vapidly** adverb.
– ORIGIN Latin *vapidus*.
vapor ● noun US spelling of VAPOUR.
vaporetto /vappərettō/ ● noun (pl. **vaporetti** /vappəretti/ or **vaporettos**) (in Venice) a canal boat for public transport.
– ORIGIN Italian, from Latin *vapor* 'steam'.
vaporize (also **vaporise**) ● verb convert into vapour.
– DERIVATIVES **vaporization** noun.
vaporizer ● noun a device that generates a vapour, especially for medicinal inhalation.
vapour (US **vapor**) ● noun **1** moisture or another substance diffused or suspended in the air. **2** Physics a gaseous substance that can be liquefied by pressure alone. **3** (**the vapours**) dated a fit of faintness, nervousness or depression.
– DERIVATIVES **vaporous** adjective.
– ORIGIN Latin *vapor* 'steam, heat'.
vapour trail ● noun a trail of condensed water from an aircraft or rocket at high altitude, seen as a white streak against the sky.
vaquero /vəkairō/ ● noun (pl. **vaqueros**) (in Spanish-speaking parts of the USA) a cowboy; a cattle driver.
– ORIGIN Spanish, from *vaca* 'cow'.
variable ● adjective **1** not consistent or having a fixed pattern; liable to vary. **2** able to be changed or adapted. **3** Mathematics (of a quantity) able to assume different numerical values. ● noun **1** a variable element, feature, or quantity. **2** Astronomy a star whose brightness changes, either regularly or irregularly. **3** (**variables**) the region of light, variable winds to the north of the NE trade winds or (in the southern hemisphere) between the SE trade winds and the westerlies.
– DERIVATIVES **variability** noun **variably** adverb.
variance ● noun **1** (usu. in phrase **at variance with**) the fact or quality of being different or inconsistent. **2** the state of disagreeing or quarrelling. **3** chiefly Law a discrepancy between two statements or documents.
variant ● noun a form or version that varies from other forms of the same thing or from a standard.
variation ● noun **1** a change or slight difference in condition, amount, or level. **2** a different or distinct form or version. **3** Music a new but still recognizable version of a theme.
– DERIVATIVES **variational** adjective.
varicella /varrisellə/ ● noun Medicine technical term for CHICKENPOX.
– ORIGIN Latin, from VARIOLA.
varicoloured /vairikullərd/ (US **varicolored**) ● adjective consisting of several different colours.
varicose /varrikōss, -kəss/ ● adjective (of a vein, especially in the leg) swollen, twisted, and lengthened, as a result of poor circulation.
– ORIGIN Latin *varicosus*.
varied ● adjective incorporating a number of different types or elements.
– DERIVATIVES **variedly** adverb.
variegated /vairigaytid/ ● adjective exhibiting different colours, especially as irregular patches or streaks.
– DERIVATIVES **variegation** /vairigaysh'n/ noun.
– ORIGIN from Latin *variegare* 'make varied'.
varietal /vərīət'l/ ● adjective **1** (of a wine or grape) made from or belonging to a single specified variety of grape. **2** chiefly Botany & Zoology of, forming, or characteristic of a variety.
variety ● noun (pl. **varieties**) **1** the quality or state of being different or diverse. **2** (**a variety of**) a number of things of the same general class that are distinct in character or quality. **3** a thing which differs in some way from others of the same general class. **4** a form of entertainment consisting of a series of different types of act, such as singing, dancing, and comedy. **5** Biology a subspecies or cultivar.
– PHRASES **variety is the spice of life** proverb new and exciting ex-

Thesaurus

ground-breakers.
– OPPOSITES rear.
vanish ● verb **1** *he vanished into the darkness* DISAPPEAR, be lost to sight/view, become invisible, vanish into thin air, recede from view. **2** *all hope of freedom vanished* FADE (AWAY), evaporate, melt away, come to an end, end, cease to exist, pass away, die out, be no more.
– OPPOSITES appear, materialize.
vanity ● noun **1** *she had none of the vanity often associated with beautiful women* CONCEIT, narcissism, self-love, self-admiration, self-regard, egotism; pride, arrogance, boastfulness, cockiness, swagger; *informal* big-headedness; *poetic/literary* vainglory. **2** *the vanity of all desires of the will* FUTILITY, uselessness, pointlessness, worthlessness, fruitlessness.
– OPPOSITES modesty.
vanquish ● verb CONQUER, defeat, beat, trounce, rout, triumph over, be victorious over, get the better of, worst; overcome, overwhelm, overpower, overthrow, subdue, subjugate, quell, quash, crush, bring someone to their knees; *informal* lick, hammer, clobber, thrash, demolish, wipe the floor with, make mincemeat of, massacre, slaughter, annihilate; *Brit. informal* stuff; *N. Amer. informal* cream, shellac.
vapid ● adjective INSIPID, uninspired, colourless, uninteresting, feeble, flat, dull, boring, tedious, tired, unexciting, uninspiring, unimaginative, lifeless, tame, vacuous, bland, trite.
– OPPOSITES lively, colourful.
vapour ● noun HAZE, mist, steam, condensation; fumes, exhalation, fog, smog, smoke.
variable ● adjective CHANGEABLE, changing, varying, shifting, fluctuating, changeful, irregular, inconstant, inconsistent, fluid, unsteady, unstable, unsettled, fitful, mutable, protean, wavering, vacillating, capricious, fickle, volatile, unpredictable, unreliable; *informal* up and down.
– OPPOSITES constant.
variance ● noun DIFFERENCE, variation, discrepancy, dissimilarity, disagreement, conflict, divergence, deviation, contrast, contradiction, imbalance, incongruity.
– PHRASES **at variance 1** *his recollections were at variance with documentary evidence* INCONSISTENT, at odds, not in keeping, out of keeping, out of line, out of step, in conflict, in disagreement, different, differing, divergent, discrepant, dissimilar, contrary, incompatible, contradictory, irreconcilable, incongruous. **2** *they were at variance with their previous allies* IN DISAGREEMENT, at odds, at cross purposes, at loggerheads, in conflict, in dispute, at outs, quarrelling.
variant ● noun *there are a number of variants of the same idea* VARIATION, form, alternative, adaptation, alteration, modification, permutation.
● adjective *a variant spelling* ALTERNATIVE, other, different, divergent, derived, modified.
variation ● noun **1** *regional variations in farming practice* DIFFERENCE, dissimilarity; disparity, contrast, discrepancy, imbalance; *technical* differential; *formal* dissimilitude. **2** *opening times are subject to variation* CHANGE, alteration, modification; diversification. **3** *there was very little variation from an understood pattern* DEVIATION, variance, divergence, departure, fluctuation. **4** *hurling is an Irish variation of hockey* VARIANT, form, alternative form; development, adaptation, alteration, diversification, modification.
varied ● adjective DIVERSE, assorted, miscellaneous, mixed, sundry, heterogeneous, wide-ranging, multifarious; disparate, motley.
variegated ● adjective MULTICOLOURED, particoloured, multicolour, many-coloured, many-hued, polychromatic, colourful, prismatic,

V

periences make life more interesting.
– ORIGIN Latin *varietas*, from *varius* 'changing, diverse'.
varifocal /vairifōk'l/ ● **adjective** (of a lens) allowing an infinite number of focusing distances for near, intermediate, and far vision. ● **noun** (**varifocals**) varifocal glasses.
variform /vairiform/ ● **adjective** **1** (of a group of things) differing from one another in form. **2** (of a single thing or a mass) consisting of a variety of forms or things.
variola /vərīələ/ ● **noun** Medicine technical term for SMALLPOX.
– ORIGIN Latin, 'pustule, pock'.
variometer /vairiommitər/ ● **noun** **1** a device for indicating an aircraft's rate of climb or descent. **2** a device whose total inductance can be varied. **3** an instrument for measuring variations in the earth's magnetic field.
variorum /vairiorəm/ ● **adjective** (of an edition of an author's works) having notes by various editors or commentators.
– ORIGIN from Latin *editio cum notis variorum* 'edition with notes by various (commentators)'.
various ● **adjective** different from one another; of different kinds or sorts. ● **determiner & pronoun** more than one; individual and separate.
– DERIVATIVES **variously** adverb **variousness** noun.
– ORIGIN Latin *varius* 'changing, diverse'.
varlet /vaarlit/ ● **noun** **1** archaic an unprincipled rogue. **2** historical a male attendant or servant.
– ORIGIN Old French, variant of *valet* (see VALET).
varmint /vaarmint/ ● **noun** N. Amer. informal or dialect a troublesome or mischievous person or wild animal.
– ORIGIN alteration of VERMIN.
varna /vaarnə/ ● **noun** each of the four Hindu castes, Brahman, Kshatriya, Vaisya, and Sudra.
– ORIGIN Sanskrit, 'colour, class'.
varnish ● **noun** a substance consisting of resin dissolved in a liquid, applied to wood or another surface to give a hard, clear, shiny surface when dry. ● **verb** apply varnish to.
– ORIGIN Old French *vernis*, from Latin *veronix* 'fragrant resin'.
varsity ● **noun** (pl. **varsities**) **1** Brit. dated or S. African university. **2** chiefly N. Amer. a sports team representing a university or college.
– ORIGIN shortening of UNIVERSITY, reflecting an archaic pronunciation.
vary ● **verb** (**varies**, **varied**) **1** differ in size, degree, or nature from something else of the same general class. **2** change from one form or state to another. **3** modify or change (something) to make it less uniform.
– ORIGIN Latin *variare*, from *varius* 'diverse'.
vas /vass/ ● **noun** (pl. **vasa** /vaysə/) Anatomy a vessel or duct.
– ORIGIN Latin, 'vessel'.
vascular /vaskyoolər/ ● **adjective** relating to or denoting the system of vessels for carrying blood or (in plants) sap, water, and nutrients.
– DERIVATIVES **vascularity** /vaskyoolarriti/ noun **vascularize** (also **vascularise**) verb.
– ORIGIN Latin *vascularis*, from *vasculum* 'small vessel'.
vascular plants ● **plural noun** plants with vascular tissue, i.e. flowering plants, conifers, cycads, ferns, horsetails, and clubmosses.
vas deferens /vass deffərenz/ ● **noun** (pl. **vasa deferentia** /vaysə deffərenshə/) Anatomy the duct which conveys sperm from the testicle to the urethra.
– ORIGIN from VAS + Latin *deferens* 'carrying away'.
vase ● **noun** a decorative ceramic or glass container used as an ornament or for displaying cut flowers.
– ORIGIN French, from Latin *vas* 'vessel'.
vasectomy /vəsektəmi/ ● **noun** (pl. **vasectomies**) the surgical cutting and sealing of part of each vas deferens, especially as a means of sterilization.
vaseline /vassileen/ ● **noun** trademark a type of petroleum jelly used as an ointment and lubricant.
– ORIGIN from German *Wasser* 'water' + Greek *elaion* 'oil'.
vasoactive ● **adjective** another term for VASOMOTOR.
vasoconstriction ● **noun** the constriction of blood vessels, which increases blood pressure.
– DERIVATIVES **vasoconstrictive** adjective.
vasodilation /vayzōdīlaysh'n/ (also **vasodilatation** /vayzōdīlaytaysh'n/) ● **noun** the dilatation of blood vessels, which decreases blood pressure.
– DERIVATIVES **vasodilatory** adjective.
vasomotor ● **adjective** affecting the diameter of blood vessels (and hence blood pressure).
vasopressor /vayzōpressər/ ● **noun** Medicine a drug or other agent which causes narrowing of blood vessels.
vassal /vass'l/ ● **noun** **1** historical a holder of land by feudal tenure on conditions of homage and allegiance. **2** a person or country in a subordinate position to another.
– DERIVATIVES **vassalage** noun.
– ORIGIN Latin *vassallus* 'retainer'.
vast ● **adjective** of very great extent or quantity; immense.
– DERIVATIVES **vastly** adverb **vastness** noun.
– ORIGIN Latin *vastus* 'void, immense'.
VAT ● **abbreviation** value added tax.
vat ● **noun** a large tank or tub used to hold liquid.
– ORIGIN from obsolete *fat* 'container', from Germanic.
vatic /vattik/ ● **adjective** literary predicting what will happen in the future.
– ORIGIN from Latin *vates* 'prophet'.
Vatican ● **noun** the palace and official residence of the Pope in Rome.
vatu /vattoo/ ● **noun** (pl. same) the basic monetary unit of Vanuatu, equal to 100 centimes.
– ORIGIN from Bislama, the official language of Vanuatu.
vaudeville /vawdəvil, vō-/ ● **noun** a type of entertainment featuring a mixture of musical and comedy acts.
– DERIVATIVES **vaudevillian** adjective & noun.
– ORIGIN French; apparently denoting songs composed by Olivier Basselin, a fifteenth-century fuller born in *Vau de Vire* in Normandy.
vault[1] ● **noun** **1** a roof in the form of an arch or a series of arches. **2** a large room or chamber used for storage, especially an underground one. **3** a chamber beneath a church or in a graveyard used for burials. **4** Anatomy the arched roof of a cavity. ● **verb** (**vaulted**) having or formed into an arched roof.
– ORIGIN Old French *voute*, from Latin *volvere* 'to roll'.
vault[2] ● **verb** leap or spring while supporting or propelling oneself with the hands or a pole. ● **noun** an act of vaulting.
– DERIVATIVES **vaulter** noun.
– ORIGIN Old French *volter* 'to turn (a horse), gambol'.
vaulting ● **noun** ornamental work in a vaulted roof or ceiling.

Thesaurus

rainbow-like, kaleidoscopic; mottled, marbled, striated, streaked, speckled, flecked, dappled; *informal* splotchy, splodgy.
– OPPOSITES plain, monochrome.
variety ● **noun** **1** *the lack of variety in the curriculum* DIVERSITY, variation, diversification, multifariousness, heterogeneity, many-sidedness; change, difference. **2** *a wide variety of flowers and shrubs* ASSORTMENT, miscellany, range, array, collection, selection, mixture, medley, multiplicity; mixed bag, motley collection, potpourri. **3** *fifty varieties of pasta* SORT, kind, type, class, category, style, form; make, model, brand; strain, breed, genus.
– OPPOSITES uniformity.
various ● **adjective** DIVERSE, different, differing, varied, varying, a variety of, assorted, mixed, sundry, miscellaneous, heterogeneous, disparate, motley; *poetic/literary* divers.
varnish ● **noun & verb** LACQUER, shellac, japan, enamel, glaze; polish.
vary ● **verb** **1** *estimates of the development cost vary* DIFFER, be different, be dissimilar. **2** *rates of interest vary over time* FLUCTUATE, rise and fall, go up and down, change, alter, shift, swing. **3** *the diaphragm is used for varying the aperture of the lens* MODIFY, change, alter, adjust, regulate, control, set; diversify. **4** *the routine never varied* CHANGE, alter, deviate, differ, fluctuate.
vassal ● **noun** *(historical)* VILLEIN, liegeman, man, vavasour, serf, helot.
vast ● **adjective** HUGE, extensive, expansive, broad, wide, boundless, immeasurable, limitless, infinite; enormous, immense, great, massive, colossal, tremendous, mighty, prodigious, gigantic, gargantuan, mammoth, monumental; giant, towering, mountainous, titanic, Brobdingnagian; *informal* jumbo, mega, monster, whopping, humongous, astronomical; *Brit. informal* ginormous.
– OPPOSITES tiny.
vat ● **noun** TUB, tank, cistern, barrel, butt, cask, tun, drum, basin; vessel, receptacle, container, holder, reservoir.
vault[1] ● **noun** **1** *the highest Gothic vault in Europe* ARCHED ROOF, dome, arch. **2** *the vault under the church* CELLAR, basement, underground chamber; crypt, undercroft, catacomb, burial chamber.

vaulting horse • noun a padded wooden block used for vaulting over by gymnasts and athletes.
vaunt /vawnt/ • verb (usu. as adj. **vaunted**) boast about or praise.
– DERIVATIVES **vaunting** adjective.
– ORIGIN Latin *vantare*, from *vanus* 'vain, empty'.
VC • abbreviation Victoria Cross.
V-chip • noun a computer chip installed in a television receiver that can be programmed to block violent or sexually explicit material.
VCR • abbreviation video cassette recorder.
VD • abbreviation venereal disease.
VDU • abbreviation visual display unit.
've • abbreviation informal have.
veal • noun the flesh of a calf, used as food.
– ORIGIN Old French *veel*, from Latin *vitellus* 'small calf'.
vector /vektər/ • noun **1** Mathematics & Physics a quantity having direction as well as magnitude, especially as determining the position of one point in space relative to another. **2** an organism that transmits a particular disease or parasite from one animal or plant to another. **3** a course to be taken by an aircraft. • verb direct (an aircraft in flight) to a desired point.
– DERIVATIVES **vectorial** adjective.
– ORIGIN Latin, 'carrier'.
Veda /vaydə, veedə/ • noun (treated as sing. or pl.) the most ancient Hindu scriptures.
– ORIGIN Sanskrit, 'sacred knowledge'.
Vedanta /vidantə/ • noun a Hindu philosophy based on the teachings of the Upanishads.
– DERIVATIVES **Vedantic** adjective.
– ORIGIN Sanskrit, from words meaning 'sacred knowledge' and 'end'.
VE day • noun the day (8 May) marking the Allied victory in Europe in 1945.
– ORIGIN abbreviation of *Victory in Europe*.
Vedic /vaydik, vee-/ • noun the language of the Vedas, an early form of Sanskrit. • adjective relating to the Veda or Vedas.
veejay • noun informal, chiefly N. Amer. a video jockey.
– ORIGIN from *VJ*, short for *video jockey*.
veep • noun N. Amer. informal vice-president.
– ORIGIN from the initials *VP*.
veer • verb **1** change direction suddenly. **2** (of the wind) change direction clockwise around the points of the compass. **3** suddenly change in opinion, subject, etc. • noun a sudden change of direction.
– ORIGIN French *virer*.
veg[1] /vej/ • noun (pl. same) Brit. informal a vegetable or vegetables.
veg[2] /vej/ • verb (**vegges**, **vegging**, **vegged**) (often **veg out**) informal relax completely.
– ORIGIN from VEGETATE.
vegan • noun a person who does not eat or use animal products.
– ORIGIN from VEGETARIAN.
Vegeburger • noun trademark for VEGGIE BURGER.
Vegemite /vejimīt/ • noun Austral./NZ trademark a type of savoury spread made from concentrated yeast extract.
– ORIGIN from VEGETABLE, on the pattern of *marmite*.
vegetable /vejitəb'l, vejtəb'l/ • noun **1** a plant or part of a plant used as food. **2** informal, derogatory a person who is incapable of normal mental or physical activity, especially through brain damage.
– ORIGIN originally in the sense 'growing as a plant': from Latin *vegetabilis* 'animating', from *vegetare* 'enliven'.
vegetable oil • noun an oil derived from plants, e.g. olive oil or sunflower oil.
vegetable tallow • noun vegetable fat used as tallow.
vegetal /vejit'l/ • adjective formal relating to plants.
– ORIGIN Latin *vegetalis*, from *vegetare* 'animate'.
vegetarian • noun a person who does not eat meat for moral, religious, or health reasons. • adjective eating or including no meat.
– DERIVATIVES **vegetarianism** noun.
vegetate • verb **1** live or spend a period of time in a dull, inactive, unchallenging way. **2** dated (of a plant or seed) grow or sprout.
– ORIGIN Latin *vegetare* 'enliven'.
vegetated • adjective covered with vegetation or plant life.
vegetation • noun plants collectively.
– DERIVATIVES **vegetational** adjective.
vegetative /vejitətiv/ • adjective **1** relating to vegetation or the growth of plants. **2** Biology relating to or denoting reproduction or propagation achieved by asexual means. **3** Medicine alive but comatose and without apparent brain activity or responsiveness.
veggie (also **vegie**) • noun & adjective informal another term for VEGETARIAN or VEGETABLE.
veggie burger (also trademark **Vegeburger**) • noun a savoury cake resembling a hamburger but made with vegetable protein or soya instead of meat.
vehement /veeəmənt/ • adjective showing strong feeling; forceful, passionate, or intense.
– DERIVATIVES **vehemence** noun **vehemently** adverb.
– ORIGIN Latin, 'impetuous, violent'.
vehicle /veeik'l/ • noun **1** a thing used for transporting people or goods on land. **2** a means of expressing, embodying, or fulfilling something: *she used paint as a vehicle for her ideas.* **3** a film, programme, song, etc., intended to display the leading performer to the best advantage. **4** a substance that facilitates the use of a drug, pigment, or other material mixed with it.
– DERIVATIVES **vehicular** /vihikyoolər/ adjective.
– ORIGIN Latin *vehiculum*, from *vehere* 'carry'.
veil • noun **1** a piece of fine material worn to protect or conceal the face. **2** a piece of fabric forming part of a nun's headdress, resting on the head and shoulders. **3** a thing that conceals, disguises, or obscures. • verb **1** cover with or as if with a veil. **2** (**veiled**) partially concealed, disguised, or obscured.
– PHRASES **draw a veil over** avoid discussing or calling attention to (something embarrassing or unpleasant). **take the veil** become a nun.
– ORIGIN Latin *velum* 'sail, curtain, veil'.
vein • noun **1** any of the tubes forming part of the circulation system by which blood is conveyed from all parts of the body towards the heart. **2** (in general use) a blood vessel. **3** (in plants) a slender rib running through a leaf, containing vascular tissue. **4** (in insects) a hollow rib forming part of the supporting framework of a wing. **5** a streak or stripe of a different colour in wood, marble, cheese, etc. **6** a fracture in rock containing a deposit of minerals or ore. **7** a source of a specified quality: *a rich vein of satire.* **8** a distinctive quality, style, or tendency: *he concluded in a humorous vein.*
– DERIVATIVES **veined** adjective **veining** noun **veiny** adjective.
– ORIGIN Old French *veine*, from Latin *vena*.

Thesaurus

V

3 *valuables stored in the vault* STRONGROOM, safe deposit, safety deposit.
vault[2] • verb *he vaulted over the gate* JUMP OVER, leap over, spring over, bound over; hurdle, clear.
vaunt • verb BOAST ABOUT, brag about, make much of, crow about, parade, flaunt; acclaim, praise, extol, celebrate; *informal* show off about; *formal* laud.
veer • verb TURN, swerve, swing, sheer, career, weave, wheel; change direction/course, go off course, deviate.
vegetate • verb DO NOTHING, idle, languish, laze, lounge, loll; moulder, stagnate; *informal* veg out, slob out; *Brit. informal* slummock; *N. Amer. informal* bum around, lollygag.
vegetation • noun PLANTS, flora; greenery, foliage, herbage, verdure.
vehemence • noun PASSION, force, forcefulness, ardour, fervour, violence, urgency, strength, vigour, intensity, keenness, enthusiasm, zeal.
vehement • adjective PASSIONATE, forceful, ardent, impassioned, heated, spirited, urgent, fervent, violent, fierce, strong, forcible, powerful, emphatic, vigorous, intense, earnest, keen, enthusiastic, zealous.
– OPPOSITES mild, apathetic.
vehicle • noun **1** *a stolen vehicle* MEANS OF TRANSPORT, conveyance; car, automobile, motorcycle, motorbike, van, bus, coach, lorry, truck; *N. Amer. informal* auto. **2** *a vehicle for the communication of original ideas* CHANNEL, medium, means (of expression), agency, agent, instrument, mechanism, organ, apparatus.
veil • noun *a thin veil of high cloud made the sun hazy* COVERING, cover, screen, curtain, mantle, cloak, mask, blanket, shroud, canopy, cloud, pall.
• verb *the peak was veiled in mist* ENVELOP, surround, swathe, enfold, cover, conceal, hide, screen, shield, cloak, blanket, shroud; obscure; *poetic/literary* enshroud, mantle.
veiled • adjective *veiled threats* DISGUISED, camouflaged, masked, co-

veinous ● adjective having prominent or noticeable veins.
vela plural of VELUM.
velar /veelər/ ● adjective **1** relating to a veil or velum. **2** Phonetics (of a speech sound) pronounced with the back of the tongue near the soft palate, as in *k* and *g* in English.
Velcro ● noun trademark a fastener consisting of two strips of fabric which adhere when pressed together.
– DERIVATIVES **Velcroed** adjective.
– ORIGIN from French *velours croché* 'hooked velvet'.
veld /velt/ (also **veldt**) ● noun open, uncultivated country or grassland in southern Africa.
– ORIGIN Afrikaans, 'field'.
veleta /vəleetə/ (also **valeta**) ● noun a ballroom dance in triple time, faster than a waltz and with partners side by side.
– ORIGIN Spanish, 'weathervane'.
vellum /velləm/ ● noun fine parchment made originally from the skin of a calf.
– ORIGIN Old French *velin*, from *veel* 'veal', from Latin *vitellus* 'small calf'.
velocimeter /velləsimmitər/ ● noun an instrument for measuring velocity.
– DERIVATIVES **velocimetry** noun.
velocipede /vilossipeed/ ● noun **1** historical an early form of bicycle propelled by working pedals on cranks fitted to the front axle. **2** US a child's tricycle.
– ORIGIN French, from Latin *velox* 'swift' + *pes* 'foot'.
velociraptor /vilossiraptər/ ● noun a small, agile carnivorous dinosaur with a large slashing claw on each foot.
– ORIGIN Latin, from *velox* 'swift' + RAPTOR.
velocity /vilossiti/ ● noun (pl. **velocities**) **1** the speed of something in a given direction. **2** (in general use) speed.
– ORIGIN Latin *velocitas*, from *velox* 'swift'.
velodrome /vellədrōm/ ● noun a cycle-racing track with steeply banked curves.
– ORIGIN French, from *vélo* 'bicycle'.
velour /vəloor/ (also **velours**) ● noun a plush woven fabric resembling velvet.
– ORIGIN French *velours* 'velvet'.
velouté /vəlo͞otay/ ● noun a sauce made from a roux of butter and flour with chicken, veal, or pork stock.
– ORIGIN French, 'velvety'.
velum /veeləm/ ● noun (pl. **vela** /veelə/) **1** Zoology a membrane bordering a cavity, especially in certain molluscs and other invertebrates. **2** Anatomy the soft palate.
– ORIGIN Latin, 'sail, curtain, covering, veil'.
velvet ● noun **1** a closely woven fabric of silk, cotton, or nylon with a thick short pile on one side. **2** soft downy skin that covers a deer's antler while it is growing.
– DERIVATIVES **velvety** adjective.
– ORIGIN Old French *veluotte*, from Latin *villus* 'tuft, down'.
velveteen ● noun a cotton fabric with a pile resembling velvet.
vena cava /veenə kayvə/ ● noun (pl. **venae cavae** /veenee kayvee/) each of two large veins carrying deoxygenated blood into the heart.
– ORIGIN Latin, 'hollow vein'.
venal /veen'l/ ● adjective open to bribery.
– DERIVATIVES **venality** noun.
– ORIGIN originally in the sense 'available for purchase': from Latin *venalis*, from *venum* 'thing for sale'.
vend ● verb **1** offer (small items) for sale. **2** Law or formal sell.
– ORIGIN Latin *vendere* 'sell'.
vendetta /vendettə/ ● noun **1** a blood feud in which the family of a murdered person seeks vengeance on the murderer or the murderer's family. **2** a prolonged bitter quarrel with or campaign against someone.
– ORIGIN Italian, from Latin *vindicta* 'vengeance'.
vending machine ● noun a machine that dispenses small articles when a coin or token is inserted.
vendor (US also **vender**) ● noun **1** a person or company offering something for sale. **2** Law the seller in a sale, especially of property.
veneer /vəneer/ ● noun **1** a thin decorative covering of fine wood applied to a coarser wood or other material. **2** an attractive appearance that covers or disguises true nature or feelings. ● verb (**veneered**) covered with a veneer.
– DERIVATIVES **veneering** noun.
– ORIGIN from German *furnieren*, from Old French *fournir* 'furnish'.
venerable ● adjective **1** accorded great respect because of age, wisdom, or character. **2** (in the Anglican Church) a title given to an archdeacon. **3** (in the Roman Catholic Church) a title given to a deceased person who has attained a certain degree of sanctity but has not been fully beatified or canonized.
venerate /vennərayt/ ● verb regard with great respect.
– DERIVATIVES **veneration** noun **venerator** noun.
– ORIGIN Latin *venerari* 'adore, revere'.
venereal /vineeriəl/ ● adjective **1** relating to venereal disease. **2** formal relating to sexual desire or sexual intercourse.
– ORIGIN from Latin *venereus*, from *venus* 'sexual love'.
venereal disease ● noun a disease contracted by sexual intercourse with a person already infected.
venereology /vineeriolləji/ ● noun the branch of medicine concerned with venereal diseases.
– DERIVATIVES **venereologist** noun.
venery[1] /vennəri/ ● noun archaic sexual indulgence.
– ORIGIN Latin *veneria*, from *venus* 'sexual love'.
venery[2] /vennəri/ ● noun archaic hunting.
– ORIGIN from Latin *venari* 'to hunt'.
Venetian ● adjective relating to Venice. ● noun a person from Venice.
venetian blind ● noun a window blind consisting of horizontal slats which can be pivoted to control the amount of light that passes through.
Venezuelan /vennizwaylən/ ● noun a person from Venezuela. ● adjective relating to Venezuela.
vengeance /venjənss/ ● noun punishment inflicted or retribution exacted for an injury or wrong.
– PHRASES **with a vengeance** with great intensity.
– ORIGIN Old French, from *venger* 'avenge'.
vengeful ● adjective seeking to harm someone in return for a perceived injury.
– DERIVATIVES **vengefully** adverb **vengefulness** noun.
venial /veeniəl/ ● adjective **1** Christian Theology (of a sin) not regarded as depriving the soul of divine grace. Often contrasted with

Thesaurus

vert, hidden, concealed, suppressed, underlying, implicit, implied, indirect.
– OPPOSITES overt.
vein ● noun **1** *a vein in his neck pulsed* BLOOD VESSEL. **2** *the mineral veins in the rock* LAYER, lode, seam, stratum, stratification, deposit. **3** *white marble with grey veins* STREAK, marking, mark, line, stripe, strip, band, thread, strand; *technical* stria, striation. **4** *he closes the article in a humorous vein* MOOD, humour, frame of mind, temper, disposition, attitude, tenor, tone, key, spirit, character, feel, flavour, quality, atmosphere; manner, way, style.
– RELATED TERMS vascular.
velocity ● noun SPEED, pace, rate, tempo, momentum, impetus; swiftness, rapidity; *poetic/literary* fleetness, celerity.
venal ● adjective CORRUPT, corruptible, bribable, open to bribery; dishonest, dishonourable, untrustworthy, unscrupulous, unprincipled; mercenary, greedy; *informal* bent.
– OPPOSITES honourable, honest.
vendetta ● noun FEUD, blood feud, quarrel, argument, falling-out, dispute, fight, war; bad blood, enmity, rivalry, conflict, strife.
vendor ● noun SELLER, retailer, purveyor, dealer, trader, tradesman, shopkeeper, merchant, supplier, stockist; huckster, pedlar, hawker; *N. Amer.* storekeeper.
veneer ● noun **1** *American cherry wood with a maple veneer* SURFACE, lamination, layer, overlay, facing, covering, finish, exterior. **2** *a veneer of sophistication* FACADE, front, false front, show, outward display, appearance, impression, semblance, guise, disguise, mask, masquerade, pretence, camouflage, cover.
venerable ● adjective RESPECTED, venerated, revered, reverenced, honoured, esteemed, hallowed, august, distinguished, eminent, great.
venerate ● verb REVERE, reverence, worship, hallow, hold sacred, exalt, adore, honour, respect, esteem; *archaic* magnify.
veneration ● noun REVERENCE, worship, adoration, exaltation, devotion, honour, respect, esteem, high regard.
vengeance ● noun REVENGE, retribution, retaliation, requital, reprisal, satisfaction, an eye for an eye (and a tooth for a tooth).
– PHRASES **with a vengeance** VIGOROUSLY, strenuously, energetically, with a will, with might and main, with all the stops out, for all one is worth, all out, flat out, at full tilt; *informal* hammer and tongs, like crazy, like mad; *Brit. informal* like billy-o.

MORTAL. **2** (of a fault or offence) slight and pardonable.
– ORIGIN Latin *venialis*, from *venia* 'forgiveness'.
venison /vennis'n/ ● noun meat from a deer.
– ORIGIN Old French *venesoun*, from Latin *venatio* 'hunting'.
Venn diagram ● noun a diagram representing mathematical or logical sets as circles, common elements of the sets being represented by intersections of the circles.
– ORIGIN named after the English logician John *Venn* (1834–1923).
venom ● noun **1** poisonous fluid secreted by animals such as snakes and scorpions and typically injected by biting or stinging. **2** extreme malice, bitterness, or aggression.
– ORIGIN Old French *venim*, from Latin *venenum* 'poison'.
venomous ● adjective **1** secreting or capable of injecting venom. **2** very malicious, bitter, or aggressive.
– DERIVATIVES **venomously** adverb.
venous /veenəss/ ● adjective relating to a vein or the veins.
vent[1] ● noun **1** an opening that allows air, gas, or liquid to pass out of or into a confined space. **2** the anus or cloaca of a fish or other animal. ● verb **1** give free expression to (a strong emotion). **2** discharge (air, gas, or liquid) through an outlet.
– PHRASES **give vent to** release or express (a strong emotion).
– ORIGIN from French *vent* 'wind' or *éventer* 'expose to air', both from Latin *ventus* 'wind'.
vent[2] ● noun a slit in a garment.
– ORIGIN Old French *fente* 'slit', from Latin *findere* 'cleave'.
ventilate ● verb **1** cause air to enter and circulate freely in (a room or building). **2** discuss (an opinion or issue) in public. **3** Medicine subject to artificial respiration.
– DERIVATIVES **ventilation** noun.
– ORIGIN Latin *ventilare* 'blow, winnow', from *ventus* 'wind'.
ventilator ● noun **1** an appliance or opening for ventilating a room or other space. **2** Medicine an appliance for artificial respiration; a respirator.
– DERIVATIVES **ventilatory** adjective.
ventral ● adjective Anatomy, Zoology, & Botany on or relating to the underside; abdominal. Compare with DORSAL.
– DERIVATIVES **ventrally** adverb.
– ORIGIN from Latin *venter* 'belly'.
ventricle /ventrik'l/ ● noun Anatomy **1** each of the two larger and lower cavities of the heart. **2** each of four connected fluid-filled cavities in the centre of the brain.
– DERIVATIVES **ventricular** /ventrikyoolər/ adjective.
– ORIGIN Latin *ventriculus*, from *venter* 'belly'.
ventriloquist /ventrilləkwist/ ● noun an entertainer who makes their voice seem to come from a dummy of a person or animal.
– DERIVATIVES **ventriloquial** /ventrilōkwiəl/ adjective **ventriloquism** noun **ventriloquy** noun.
– ORIGIN from Latin *venter* 'belly' + *loqui* 'speak'.
venture ● noun **1** a risky or daring journey or undertaking. **2** a business enterprise involving considerable risk. ● verb **1** dare to do something dangerous or risky. **2** dare to say something that may be considered audacious.
– PHRASES **nothing ventured, nothing gained** proverb you can't expect to achieve anything if you never take any risks.
– DERIVATIVES **venturer** noun.
– ORIGIN shortening of ADVENTURE.
venture capital ● noun capital invested in a project in which there is a substantial element of risk.
Venture Scout ● noun a member of the Scout Association aged between 16 and 20.
venturesome ● adjective willing to take risks or embark on difficult or unusual courses of action.
venturi /ventyoori/ ● noun (pl. **venturis**) a short piece of narrow tube between wider sections for measuring flow rate or exerting suction.
– ORIGIN named after the Italian physicist Giovanni B. *Venturi* (1746–1822).
venue /venyoo/ ● noun the place where an event or meeting is held.
– ORIGIN Old French, 'a coming', from *venir* 'come'.
venule /venyool/ ● noun Anatomy a very small vein.
– ORIGIN Latin *venula*.
Venus flytrap ● noun a plant with hinged leaves that spring shut on and digest insects which land on them.
Venusian /vinyooziən/ ● adjective relating to the planet Venus. ● noun a supposed inhabitant of Venus.
veracious /vərayshəss/ ● adjective formal speaking or representing the truth.
– ORIGIN from Latin *verus* 'true'.
veracity /vərassiti/ ● noun **1** conformity to facts; accuracy. **2** habitual truthfulness.
veranda (also **verandah**) ● noun a roofed platform along the outside of a house, level with the ground floor.
– ORIGIN Portuguese *varanda* 'railing, balustrade'.
verb ● noun Grammar a word used to describe an action, state, or occurrence, such as *hear*, *become*, or *happen*.
– ORIGIN Latin *verbum* 'word, verb'.
verbal ● adjective **1** relating to or in the form of words. **2** spoken rather than written; oral. **3** Grammar relating to or derived from a verb. ● noun **1** Grammar a word or words functioning as a verb. **2** (also **verbals**) Brit. informal abuse; insults.
– DERIVATIVES **verbally** adverb.
verbalism ● noun **1** concentration on forms of expression rather than content. **2** a verbal expression.
verbalize (also **verbalise**) ● verb express in words, especially by speaking aloud.
– DERIVATIVES **verbalization** noun.
verbal noun ● noun Grammar a noun formed as an inflection of a verb and partly sharing its constructions, such as *smoking* in *smoking is forbidden*.
verbatim /verbaytim/ ● adverb & adjective in exactly the same words as were used originally.
– ORIGIN Latin, from *verbum* 'word'.
verbena /verbeenə/ ● noun an ornamental plant with heads of bright showy flowers.
– ORIGIN Latin, 'sacred bough'.
verbiage /verbi-ij/ ● noun excessively lengthy or technical speech or writing.
– ORIGIN French, from obsolete *verbeier* 'to chatter'.
verbose /verbōss/ ● adjective using or expressed in more words than are needed.

Thesaurus

vengeful ● adjective VINDICTIVE, revengeful, out for revenge, unforgiving, grudge-bearing.
– OPPOSITES forgiving.
venial ● adjective FORGIVABLE, pardonable, excusable, allowable, permissible; slight, minor, unimportant, insignificant, trivial, trifling.
– OPPOSITES unforgivable, mortal.
venom ● noun **1** *snake venom* POISON, toxin; archaic bane. **2** *his voice was full of venom* RANCOUR, malevolence, vitriol, spite, vindictiveness, malice, maliciousness, ill will, animosity, animus, bitterness, antagonism, hostility, bile, hate, hatred; informal bitchiness, cattiness.
venomous ● adjective **1** *a venomous snake | the spider's venomous bite* POISONOUS, toxic; dangerous, deadly, lethal, fatal, mortal. **2** *venomous remarks* VICIOUS, spiteful, rancorous, malevolent, vitriolic, vindictive, malicious, poisonous, virulent, bitter, acrimonious, antagonistic, hostile, cruel; informal bitchy, catty; poetic/literary malefic, maleficent.
– OPPOSITES harmless, benevolent.
vent ● noun *an air vent* OUTLET, INLET, opening, aperture, hole, gap, orifice, space; duct, flue, shaft, well, passage, airway.
● verb *the crowd vented their fury on the pitch* LET OUT, give vent to, give free rein to, release, pour out, express, give expression to, air, voice, give voice to, ventilate.
ventilate ● verb **1** *the greenhouse must be properly ventilated* AIR, aerate, oxygenate, air-condition; freshen, cool. **2** *the workers ventilated their discontent* EXPRESS, give expression to, air, bring into the open, communicate, voice, give voice to, verbalize, discuss, debate, talk over.
venture ● noun *a business venture* ENTERPRISE, undertaking, project, scheme, operation, endeavour, speculation, plunge, gamble, experiment.
● verb **1** *we ventured across the moor* SET OUT, go, travel, journey. **2** *may I venture an opinion?* PUT FORWARD, advance, proffer, offer, air, suggest, submit, propose, moot, ventilate. **3** *I ventured to ask her to come and dine with me* DARE, make so bold as, presume; take the liberty of; informal stick one's neck out, go out on a limb.
veracious ● adjective (formal). See TRUTHFUL senses 1, 2.
verbal ● adjective ORAL, spoken, stated, said, verbalized; unwritten.
verbatim ● adverb WORD FOR WORD, letter for letter, line for line, to the letter, literally, exactly, precisely, closely, faithfully; formal literatim.

– DERIVATIVES **verbosely** adverb **verbosity** noun.
– ORIGIN Latin *verbosus*, from *verbum* 'word'.
verboten /verbōt'n/ ● adjective forbidden by an authority.
– ORIGIN German.
verdant /verd'nt/ ● adjective green with grass or other lush vegetation.
– DERIVATIVES **verdancy** noun **verdantly** adverb.
– ORIGIN perhaps from Old French *verdeant*, from Latin *viridis* 'green'.
verderer /verdərər/ ● noun Brit. a judicial officer of a royal forest.
– ORIGIN Old French, from Latin *viridis* 'green'.
verdict ● noun **1** a decision on an issue of fact in a civil or criminal case or an inquest. **2** an opinion or judgement.
– ORIGIN Old French *verdit*, from *veir* 'true' + *dit* 'saying'.
verdigris /verdigree/ ● noun a bright bluish-green encrustation or patina formed on copper or brass by atmospheric oxidation.
– ORIGIN from Old French *vert de Grece* 'green of Greece'.
verdure /verdyər/ ● noun lush green vegetation.
– ORIGIN from Old French *verd* 'green'.
verge ● noun **1** an edge or border. **2** Brit. a grass edging by the side of a road or path. **3** an extreme limit beyond which something specified will happen: *on the verge of tears*. ● verb (**verge on**) be very close or similar to.
– ORIGIN Old French, from Latin *virga* 'rod'.
verger ● noun **1** an official in a church who acts as a caretaker and attendant. **2** an officer who carries a rod before a bishop or dean as a symbol of office.
– ORIGIN Old French, from Latin *virga* 'rod'.
Vergilian ● adjective variant spelling of VIRGILIAN.
verify /verrifī/ ● verb (**verifies**, **verified**) **1** make sure or demonstrate that (something) is true, accurate, or justified. **2** Law swear to or support (a statement) by affidavit.
– DERIVATIVES **verifiable** adjective **verification** noun **verifier** noun.
– ORIGIN Latin *verificare*, from *verus* 'true'.
verily ● adverb archaic truly; certainly.
– ORIGIN from VERY.
verisimilitude /verrisimillityoōd/ ● noun the appearance of being true or real.
– ORIGIN Latin *verisimilitudo*, from *verisimilis* 'probable'.
verismo /verizmō/ ● noun realism or authenticity, especially in the arts.
– ORIGIN Italian.
veritable ● adjective genuine; properly so called (used to qualify a metaphor): *a veritable price explosion.*
– DERIVATIVES **veritably** adverb.
vérité /verritay/ ● noun a genre of film and television emphasizing realism and naturalism.
– ORIGIN French, 'truth'.
verity ● noun (pl. **verities**) **1** a true principle or belief. **2** truth.
– ORIGIN Latin *veritas*, from *verus* 'true'.
vermicelli /vermichelli, -selli/ ● plural noun **1** pasta made in long slender threads. **2** Brit. shreds of chocolate used to decorate cakes.
– ORIGIN Italian, 'little worms'.
vermicide /vermisīd/ ● noun a substance that is poisonous to worms.
vermicular /vərmikyoolər/ ● adjective **1** like a worm in form or movement; vermiform. **2** relating to or caused by intestinal worms.
– ORIGIN from Latin *vermiculus* 'little worm'.
vermiculated ● adjective **1** marked with sinuous or wavy lines. **2** archaic worm-eaten.
vermiculite /vərmikyoolīt/ ● noun a yellow or brown mineral found as an alteration product of mica and other minerals, used for insulation or as a moisture-retentive medium for growing plants.
– ORIGIN from Latin *vermiculari* 'be full of worms' (because on expansion due to heat, it shoots out forms resembling small worms).
vermiform ● adjective chiefly Zoology or Anatomy resembling or having the form of a worm.
vermifuge /vermifyoōj/ ● noun Medicine a medicine used to destroy parasitic worms.
vermilion /vərmilyən/ (also **vermillion**) ● noun **1** a brilliant red pigment made from mercury sulphide (cinnabar). **2** a brilliant red colour.
– ORIGIN Old French *vermeillon*, from Latin *vermiculus* 'little worm'.
vermin ● noun (treated as pl.) **1** wild mammals and birds which are harmful to crops, farm animals, or game, or which carry disease. **2** parasitic worms or insects. **3** very unpleasant and destructive people.
– DERIVATIVES **verminous** adjective.
– ORIGIN Old French, from Latin *vermis* 'worm'.
vermouth /vermәth, vərmoōth/ ● noun a red or white wine flavoured with aromatic herbs.
– ORIGIN French *vermout*, from German *Wermut* 'wormwood'.
vernacular /vərnakyoolər/ ● noun **1** the language or dialect spoken by the ordinary people of a country or region. **2** informal the specialized terminology of a group or activity. ● adjective **1** spoken as or using one's mother tongue rather than a second language. **2** (of architecture) concerned with domestic and functional rather than monumental buildings.
– ORIGIN from Latin *vernaculus* 'domestic, native'.
vernal /vern'l/ ● adjective of, in, or appropriate to spring.
– ORIGIN Latin *vernalis*, from *ver* 'spring'.
vernal equinox ● noun the spring equinox.
vernalization (also **vernalisation**) ● noun the cooling of seed during germination in order to accelerate flowering when it is planted.
vernier /verniər/ ● noun a small movable graduated scale for obtaining fractional parts of subdivisions on a fixed main scale of a measuring instrument.
– ORIGIN named after the French mathematician Pierre *Vernier* (1580–1637).
vernix /verniks/ ● noun a greasy deposit covering the skin of a baby at birth.
– ORIGIN Latin, from *veronix* 'fragrant resin'.
veronica ● noun **1** a herbaceous plant with upright stems bearing narrow pointed leaves and spikes of blue or purple flowers. **2** a cloth supposedly impressed with an image of Christ's face.
– ORIGIN from the given name *Veronica*; sense 2 refers to St *Veronica*, who offered her headcloth to Christ on the way to Calvary, to wipe his face.
verruca /vəroōkə/ ● noun (pl. **verrucae** /vəroōsee/ or **verrucas**) **1** a contagious wart on the sole of the foot. **2** (in medical use) a wart of any kind.
– ORIGIN Latin.
versatile ● adjective able to adapt or be adapted to many different functions or activities.
– DERIVATIVES **versatility** noun.

Thesaurus

verbiage ● noun VERBOSITY, padding, wordiness, prolixity, long-windedness; *Brit. informal* waffle.
verbose ● adjective WORDY, loquacious, garrulous, talkative, voluble; long-winded, lengthy, prolix, tautological, pleonastic, periphrastic, circumlocutory, circuitous, discursive, digressive, rambling; *informal* mouthy, gabby; *Brit. informal* waffly.
– OPPOSITES succinct, laconic.
verbosity ● noun WORDINESS, loquacity, garrulity, talkativeness, volubility; long-windedness, lengthiness, verbiage, prolixity, tautology, circumlocution, discursiveness; *Brit. informal* waffle.
verdant ● adjective GREEN, leafy, grassy; lush, rich; *poetic/literary* verdured, verdurous.
verdict ● noun JUDGEMENT, adjudication, decision, finding, ruling, resolution, pronouncement, conclusion, opinion; *Law* determination.
verge ● noun **1** *the verge of the lake* EDGE, border, margin, side, brink, rim, lip; fringe, boundary, perimeter; *poetic/literary* bourn, marge, skirt. **2** *Spain was on the verge of an economic crisis* BRINK, threshold, edge, point.
● verb *a degree of caution that verged on the obsessive* APPROACH, border on, be close/near to, be tantamount to; tend towards, approximate to, resemble.
verification ● noun CONFIRMATION, substantiation, proof, corroboration, support, attestation, validation, authentication, endorsement.
verify ● verb SUBSTANTIATE, confirm, prove, corroborate, back up, bear out, justify, support, uphold, attest to, testify to, validate, authenticate, endorse, certify.
– OPPOSITES refute.
vernacular ● noun **1** *he wrote in the vernacular to reach a wider audience* EVERYDAY LANGUAGE, colloquial language, conversational language, common parlance; dialect, regional language, regional-

– ORIGIN Latin *versatilis*, from *versare* 'turn about, revolve'.
verse ● noun **1** writing arranged with a metrical rhythm. **2** a group of lines that form a unit in a poem or song. **3** each of the short numbered divisions of a chapter in the Bible or other scripture.
– ORIGIN Latin *versus* 'a turn of the plough, a furrow, a line of writing', from *vertere* 'to turn'.
versed ● adjective (**versed in**) experienced or skilled in; knowledgeable about.
– ORIGIN Latin *versatus*, from *versari* 'be engaged in'.
versicle /versik'l/ ● noun a short sentence said or sung by the minister in a church service, to which the congregation gives a response.
versify ● verb (**versifies**, **versified**) turn into or express in verse.
– DERIVATIVES **versification** noun **versifier** noun.
version ● noun **1** a particular form of something differing in certain respects from other forms of the same type of thing. **2** an account of a matter from a particular person's point of view.
– ORIGIN originally in the sense 'translation': from Latin, from *vertere* 'to turn'.
verso /versō/ ● noun (pl. **versos**) a left-hand page of an open book, or the back of a loose document. Contrasted with RECTO.
– ORIGIN from Latin *verso folio* 'on the turned leaf'.
versus ● preposition **1** against. **2** as opposed to; in contrast to.
– ORIGIN Latin, 'towards'.
vert /vert/ ● noun green, as a conventional heraldic colour.
– ORIGIN Old French, from Latin *viridis* 'green'.
vertebra /vertibrə/ ● noun (pl. **vertebrae** /vertibray, -bree/) each of the series of small bones forming the backbone.
– DERIVATIVES **vertebral** adjective.
– ORIGIN Latin, from *vertere* 'to turn'.
vertebrate /vertibrət/ ● noun an animal having a backbone, including mammals, birds, reptiles, amphibians, and fishes. ● adjective relating to such animals.
vertex /verteks/ ● noun (pl. **vertices** /vertiseez/ or **vertexes**) **1** the highest point; the top or apex. **2** Geometry each angular point of a polygon, polyhedron, or other figure. **3** a meeting point of two lines that form an angle. **4** Anatomy the crown of the head.
– ORIGIN Latin, 'whirlpool, crown of a head, vertex'.
vertical ● adjective at right angles to a horizontal plane; having the top directly above the bottom. ● noun **1** (**the vertical**) a vertical line or plane. **2** an upright structure.
– DERIVATIVES **verticality** noun **vertically** adverb.
– ORIGIN Latin *verticalis*, from VERTEX.
vertiginous /vərtijinəss/ ● adjective **1** causing vertigo, especially by being extremely high or steep. **2** relating to or affected by vertigo.
– DERIVATIVES **vertiginously** adverb.
vertigo /vertigō/ ● noun a sensation of giddiness and loss of balance, caused by looking down from a great height or by disease affecting the inner ear.
– ORIGIN Latin, 'whirling'.
vervain /vervayn/ ● noun a herbaceous plant with small blue, white, or purple flowers, used in herbal medicine.
– ORIGIN Old French *verveine*, from Latin *verbena* 'sacred bough'.
verve ● noun vigour, spirit, and style.
– ORIGIN originally denoting talent in writing: from French, 'vigour', from Latin *verba* 'words'.
vervet monkey /vervit/ ● noun a common African monkey with greenish-brown upper parts and a black face.
– ORIGIN French.
very ● adverb **1** in a high degree. **2** (with superlative or **own**) without qualification: *the very best quality*. ● adjective **1** actual; precise. **2** emphasizing an extreme point in time or space. **3** with no addition; mere. **4** archaic real; genuine.
– ORIGIN from Latin *verus* 'true'.
Very light /verri, veeri/ ● noun a flare fired into the air from a pistol for signalling or for temporary illumination.
– ORIGIN named after the American naval officer Edward W. *Very* (1847–1910).
Very Reverend ● adjective a title given to a dean in the Anglican Church.
vesical /vessik'l/ ● adjective Anatomy & Medicine relating to or affecting the urinary bladder.
– ORIGIN from Latin *vesica* 'bladder'.
vesicle /vessik'l/ ● noun **1** Anatomy & Zoology a small fluid-filled sac or cyst. **2** Medicine a blister full of clear fluid. **3** Botany an air-filled swelling in a seaweed or other plant. **4** Geology a small cavity in volcanic rock, produced by gas bubbles.
– DERIVATIVES **vesicular** adjective **vesiculation** noun.
– ORIGIN Latin *vesicula* 'small bladder'.
vesper ● noun evening prayer.
– ORIGIN Latin, 'evening'.
vespers ● noun a service of evening prayer, especially in the Western Christian Church.
– ORIGIN Latin *vesperas* 'evensong'.
vessel ● noun **1** a ship or large boat. **2** a hollow container used to hold liquid. **3** a tube or duct conveying a fluid within an animal body or plant structure. **4** (in or alluding to biblical use) a person regarded as embodying a particular quality: *giving honour unto the wife, as unto the weaker vessel*.
– ORIGIN Old French *vessele*, from Latin *vas* 'vessel'.
vest ● noun **1** Brit. an undergarment worn on the upper part of the body, typically having no sleeves. **2** a similar garment worn for a particular purpose: *a bulletproof vest*. **3** N. Amer. & Austral. a waistcoat or sleeveless jacket. ● verb **1** (**vest in**) confer or bestow (power, property, etc.) on. **2** give (someone) the legal right to power, property, etc.
– ORIGIN Latin *vestis* 'garment'.
vesta ● noun chiefly historical a short wooden or wax match.
– ORIGIN from *Vesta*, the Roman goddess of the hearth.
vestal ● adjective **1** relating to the Roman goddess Vesta. **2** literary chaste; pure. ● noun a vestal virgin.
vestal virgin ● noun (in ancient Rome) a virgin consecrated to the goddess Vesta and vowed to chastity.

Thesaurus

isms, patois; *informal* lingo, local lingo. **2** *(informal) the vernacular of today's youth* LANGUAGE, parlance; idiom, slang, jargon; *informal* lingo, -speak, -ese.
versatile ● adjective ADAPTABLE, flexible, all-round, multifaceted, multitalented, resourceful; adjustable, multi-purpose, all-purpose, handy.
verse ● noun **1** *Elizabethan verse* POETRY, versification; poems, balladry, lyrics; blank verse, heroic verse, free verse; *poetic/literary* poesy. **2** *a verse he'd composed to mark my anniversary* POEM, lyric, ballad, sonnet, ode, limerick, rhyme, ditty, lay. **3** *a poem with sixty verses* STANZA, canto, couplet; strophe.
– OPPOSITES prose.
version ● noun **1** *his version of events* ACCOUNT, report, statement, description, record, story, rendering, interpretation, explanation, understanding, reading, impression, side. **2** *the English version will be published next year* EDITION, translation, impression. **3** *they have replaced coal-burning fires with gas versions* FORM, sort, kind, type, variety, variant.
vertex ● noun APEX, peak, tip, top.
vertical ● adjective UPRIGHT, erect, perpendicular, plumb, straight up and down, on end, standing, upstanding, bolt upright, upended.
– OPPOSITES horizontal.
vertigo ● noun DIZZINESS, giddiness, light-headedness, loss of balance; *Veterinary Medicine* sturdy.
verve ● noun ENTHUSIASM, vigour, energy, pep, dynamism, go, elan, vitality, vivacity, buoyancy, liveliness, animation, zest, sparkle, spirit, ebullience, life, brio, gusto, eagerness, keenness, passion, zeal, relish, feeling, ardour, fire; *informal* zing, zip, vim, pizzazz, oomph.
very ● adverb *that's very kind of you* EXTREMELY, exceedingly, exceptionally, extraordinarily, tremendously, immensely, hugely, intensely, acutely, abundantly, singularly, uncommonly, unusually, decidedly, particularly, supremely, highly, remarkably, really, truly, mightily; *informal* terrifically, awfully, fearfully, terribly, devilishly, majorly, seriously, mega, ultra, damn, damned; *Brit. informal* ever so, well, hellish, dead, jolly; *N. Amer. informal* real, mighty, awful, darned; *informal, dated* devilish, frightfully; *archaic* exceeding.
– OPPOSITES slightly.
● adjective **1** *those were his very words* EXACT, actual, precise. **2** *the very thought of food made her feel ill* MERE, simple, pure; sheer.
vessel ● noun **1** *a fishing vessel* BOAT, ship, craft, watercraft; *poetic/literary* barque. **2** *pour the mixture into a heatproof vessel* CONTAINER, receptacle; basin, bowl, pan, pot; urn, cask, barrel, drum, butt, vat.

vested interest ● noun **1** Law an interest (usually in land or money held in trust) recognized as belonging to a particular person. **2** a personal stake in an undertaking or state of affairs.

vestibule /vestibyōol/ ● noun **1** an antechamber or hall just inside the outer door of a building. **2** Anatomy a chamber or channel opening into another.
– DERIVATIVES **vestibular** adjective (Anatomy).
– ORIGIN Latin *vestibulum* 'entrance court'.

vestige /vestij/ ● noun **1** a remaining trace of something that once existed: *the last vestiges of colonialism.* **2** the smallest amount.
– ORIGIN Latin *vestigium* 'footprint'.

vestigial /vestijiəl/ ● adjective **1** forming a very small remnant of something. **2** Biology (of an organ or part of the body) degenerate, rudimentary, or atrophied, having lost its function in the course of evolution.
– DERIVATIVES **vestigially** adverb.

vestment ● noun **1** a robe worn by the clergy or choristers during services. **2** archaic a garment, especially a ceremonial or official robe.
– ORIGIN Latin *vestimentum*, from *vestire* 'to clothe'.

vest-pocket ● adjective N. Amer. small enough to fit into a pocket.

vestry ● noun (pl. **vestries**) a room in or attached to a church, used as an office and for changing into ceremonial vestments.
– ORIGIN Latin *vestiarium.*

vet[1] ● noun a veterinary surgeon. ● verb (**vetted**, **vetting**) make a careful and critical examination of (someone or something, especially of a person prior to employment).

vet[2] ● noun N. Amer. informal a veteran.

vetch ● noun a leguminous plant with purple, pink, or yellow flowers, cultivated for silage or fodder.
– ORIGIN Old French *veche*, from Latin *vicia*.

veteran ● noun **1** a person who has had long experience in a particular field. **2** an ex-member of the armed forces.
– ORIGIN Latin *veteranus*, from *vetus* 'old'.

veteran car ● noun Brit. an old style or model of car, specifically one made before 1919 or (strictly) before 1905.

veterinarian ● noun North American term for VETERINARY SURGEON.

veterinary /vettərinəri/ ● adjective relating to the diseases, injuries, and treatment of farm and domestic animals.
– ORIGIN Latin *veterinarius*, from *veterinae* 'cattle'.

veterinary surgeon ● noun Brit. a person qualified to treat diseased or injured animals.

vetiver /vettivər/ (also **vetivert**) ● noun a fragrant extract or essential oil obtained from the root of an Indian grass, used in perfumery and aromatherapy.
– ORIGIN Tamil, 'root'.

veto /veetō/ ● noun (pl. **vetoes**) **1** a constitutional right to reject a decision or proposal made by a law-making body. **2** any prohibition. ● verb (**vetoes**, **vetoed**) exercise a veto against.
– ORIGIN from Latin, 'I forbid', used by Roman tribunes of the people when opposing measures of the Senate.

vex ● verb make annoyed or worried.
– DERIVATIVES **vexation** noun.
– ORIGIN Latin *vexare* 'shake, disturb'.

vexatious ● adjective **1** causing annoyance or worry. **2** Law denoting an action or the bringer of an action that is brought without sufficient grounds for winning, purely to cause annoyance to the defendant.

vexed ● adjective **1** difficult and much debated; problematic. **2** annoyed or worried.

VGA ● abbreviation videographics array, a standard for defining colour display screens for computers.

vgc ● abbreviation very good condition.

VHF ● abbreviation very high frequency.

VHS ● abbreviation trademark video home system (as used by domestic video recorders).

VI ● abbreviation Virgin Islands.

via ● preposition **1** travelling through (a place) en route to a destination. **2** by way of; through. **3** by means of.
– ORIGIN from Latin, 'way, road'.

viable /vīəb'l/ ● adjective **1** capable of working successfully; feasible. **2** Biology (of a plant, animal, or cell) capable of surviving or living successfully.
– DERIVATIVES **viability** noun **viably** adverb.
– ORIGIN French, from *vie* 'life'.

viaduct ● noun a long bridge-like structure carrying a road or railway across a valley or other low ground.
– ORIGIN from Latin *via* 'way', on the pattern of *aqueduct*.

Viagra /vīagrə/ ● noun trademark a synthetic compound used to enhance male potency.
– ORIGIN apparently a blend of *virility* and the name *Niagara*.

vial /vīəl/ ● noun a small container used especially for holding liquid medicines.
– ORIGIN alteration of PHIAL.

via media /veeə meddiə/ ● noun formal a middle way or compromise between extremes.
– ORIGIN Latin.

viand /vīənd/ ● noun archaic an item of food.
– ORIGIN Old French *viande* 'food', from Latin *vivenda* 'things to be lived on'.

viaticum /vīattikəm/ ● noun (pl. **viatica** /vīattikə/) the Eucharist as given to a person near or in danger of death.
– ORIGIN Latin, from *via* 'road'.

Thesaurus

vest ● verb *executive power is vested in the President* CONFER ON, entrust to, invest in, bestow on, grant to, give to; endow, lodge, lay, place.

vestibule ● noun ENTRANCE HALL, hall, hallway, entrance, porch, portico, foyer, lobby, ante-room, antechamber, waiting room.

vestige ● noun **1** *the last vestiges of colonialism* REMNANT, fragment, relic, echo, indication, sign, trace, mark, legacy, reminder; remains. **2** *she showed no vestige of emotion* BIT, touch, hint, suggestion, suspicion, shadow, scrap, tinge, speck, shred, jot, iota, whit, scintilla, glimmer; *informal* smidgen, tad.

vestigial ● adjective **1** *vestigial limbs* RUDIMENTARY, undeveloped; non-functional; *Biology* primitive. **2** *he felt a vestigial flicker of anger from last night* REMAINING, surviving, residual, leftover, lingering.

vet ● verb *press releases are vetted by an executive council* CHECK, examine, scrutinize, investigate, inspect, look over, screen, assess, evaluate, appraise; *informal* check out.
● noun *I took the cat to the vet* VETERINARY SURGEON, animal doctor, horse doctor; *N. Amer.* veterinarian; *dated* veterinary.

veteran ● noun *a veteran of 16 political campaigns* OLD HAND, past master, doyen; *informal* old-timer, old stager, old warhorse.
– OPPOSITES novice.
● adjective *a veteran diplomat* LONG-SERVING, seasoned, old, hardened; adept, expert, well trained, practised, experienced; *informal* battle-scarred.

veto ● noun *parliament's right of veto* REJECTION, dismissal; prohibition, proscription, embargo, ban, interdict; *informal* thumbs down, red light.
– OPPOSITES approval.
● verb *the president vetoed the bill* REJECT, turn down, throw out, dismiss; prohibit, forbid, interdict, proscribe, disallow, embargo, ban; *informal* kill, put the kibosh on, give the thumbs down to, give the red light to.
– OPPOSITES approve.

vex ● verb ANNOY, irritate, anger, infuriate, exasperate, irk, gall, pique, put out, antagonize, get on someone's nerves, ruffle someone's feathers, make someone's hackles rise; *Brit.* rub up the wrong way; *informal* aggravate, peeve, miff, rile, nettle, needle, get (to), bug, hack off, get up someone's nose, get someone's goat, get someone's back up, give someone the hump, get someone's dander up; *Brit. informal* wind up, nark, get on someone's wick; *N. Amer. informal* tee off, tick off, burn up, rankle; *informal, dated* give someone the pip.

vexation ● noun ANNOYANCE, irritation, exasperation, indignation, anger, crossness, displeasure, pique, disgruntlement; *informal* aggravation.

vexatious ● adjective ANNOYING, irritating, infuriating, exasperating, maddening, trying, tiresome, troublesome, bothersome, irksome, vexing, galling; *informal* aggravating, pesky.

vexed ● adjective **1** *a vexed expression* ANNOYED, irritated, cross, angry, infuriated, exasperated, irked, piqued, displeased, put out, disgruntled; *informal* aggravated, peeved, nettled, miffed, miffy, riled, hacked off, hot under the collar; *Brit. informal* narked, shirty; *N. Amer. informal* teed off, ticked off, sore, bent out of shape; *archaic* wroth. **2** *the vexed issue of immigration* DISPUTED, in dispute, contested, in contention, contentious, debated, at issue, controversial, moot; problematic, difficult, knotty, thorny.

viable ● adjective FEASIBLE, workable, practicable, practical, usable,

vibe • noun informal **1** the atmosphere or aura of a person or place as communicated to and felt by others. **2** (**vibes**) short for VIBRAPHONE.

vibrant • adjective **1** full of energy and enthusiasm. **2** (of sound) strong or resonant. **3** (of colour) bright or bold.
– DERIVATIVES **vibrancy** noun **vibrantly** adverb.
– ORIGIN from Latin *vibrare* 'shake to and fro'.

vibraphone /vībrəfōn/ • noun a musical percussion instrument with a double row of tuned metal bars, each above a tubular resonator containing a motor-driven rotating vane, giving a vibrato effect.
– DERIVATIVES **vibraphonist** noun.

vibrate • verb **1** move with small movements rapidly to and fro. **2** (of a sound) resonate.
– DERIVATIVES **vibrating** adjective.
– ORIGIN Latin *vibrare* 'move to and fro'.

vibration • noun **1** an instance or the state of vibrating. **2** (**vibrations**) informal an emotional state or atmosphere, as communicated to and felt by others.
– DERIVATIVES **vibrational** adjective.

vibrato /vibraatō/ • noun Music a rapid, slight variation in pitch in singing or playing some musical instruments, producing a stronger or richer tone.
– ORIGIN Italian, from *vibrare* 'vibrate'.

vibrator • noun **1** a device that vibrates or causes vibration. **2** a vibrating device used for massage or sexual stimulation.
– DERIVATIVES **vibratory** adjective.

vibrio /vibriō, vī-/ • noun (pl. **vibrios**) Medicine a curved, rod-like bacterium of a group including that causing cholera.
– ORIGIN from Latin *vibrare* 'vibrate'.

vibrissae /vībrissee/ • plural noun long stiff hairs growing around the mouth or elsewhere on the face of many mammals; whiskers.
– ORIGIN Latin, 'nostril hairs'.

viburnum /vīburnəm, vi-/ • noun a shrub or small tree, typically bearing clusters of small white flowers.
– ORIGIN Latin, 'wayfaring tree'.

vicar • noun **1** (in the Church of England) a priest in charge of a parish where tithes formerly passed to a person or group other than the incumbent. **2** (in other Anglican Churches) a member of the clergy deputizing for another. **3** (in the Roman Catholic Church) a representative or deputy of a bishop.
– ORIGIN Old French *vicaire*, from Latin *vicarius* 'substitute'.

vicarage • noun the residence of a vicar.

vicar general • noun (pl. **vicars general**) an official serving as a deputy or representative of a bishop or archbishop.

vicarious /vikairiəss/ • adjective **1** experienced in the imagination through the feelings or actions of another person. **2** acting or done for another.
– DERIVATIVES **vicariously** adverb.
– ORIGIN from Latin *vicarius* 'substitute'.

vice[1] • noun **1** immoral or wicked behaviour. **2** criminal activities involving prostitution, pornography, or drugs. **3** an immoral or wicked personal characteristic. **4** a weakness of character; a bad habit.
– ORIGIN Old French, from Latin *vitium*.

vice[2] (US **vise**) • noun a metal tool with movable jaws which are used to hold an object firmly in place while work is done on it.
– DERIVATIVES **vice-like** adjective.
– ORIGIN Old French *vis*, from Latin *vitis* 'vine'.

vice- • combining form next in rank to and typically able to deputize for: *vice-president.*
– ORIGIN from Latin *vice* 'in place of'.

vice admiral • noun a high rank of naval officer, above rear admiral and below admiral.

vice chancellor • noun a deputy chancellor, especially one of a British university who oversees its administration.

vice-president • noun an official or executive ranking below and deputizing for a president.

viceregal • adjective relating to a viceroy.

viceroy • noun a ruler exercising authority in a colony on behalf of a sovereign.
– DERIVATIVES **viceroyalty** noun (pl. **viceroyalties**).
– ORIGIN archaic French, from *vice-* 'in place of' + *roi* 'king'.

vice versa /vīss versə, vīsi/ • adverb with the main items in the preceding statement the other way round.
– ORIGIN Latin, 'in-turned position'.

vichyssoise /veesheeswaaz/ • noun a soup made with potatoes, leeks, and cream and typically served chilled.
– ORIGIN French, 'of *Vichy*' (a town in central France).

vicinal /vissin'l, visīn'l/ • adjective **1** neighbouring; adjacent. **2** Chemistry referring or relating to atoms or groups that are attached to adjacent atoms in a ring or chain.

vicinity • noun (pl. **vicinities**) the area near or surrounding a place.
– ORIGIN Latin *vicinitas*, from *vicinus* 'neighbour'.

vicious • adjective **1** cruel or violent. **2** (of an animal) wild and dangerous. **3** literary immoral.
– DERIVATIVES **viciously** adverb **viciousness** noun.
– ORIGIN Latin *vitiosus*, from *vitium* 'vice'.

vicious circle • noun a sequence of reciprocal cause and effect in which two or more elements intensify and aggravate each other.

vicissitudes /visissityoōdz/ • plural noun changes of circumstances or fortune.
– ORIGIN Latin *vicissitudo*, from *vicissim* 'by turns'.

vicomte /veekont/ • noun (pl. pronounced same) a French nobleman corresponding in rank to a British or Irish viscount.

Thesaurus

possible, realistic, achievable, attainable, realizable; *informal* doable.
– OPPOSITES impracticable.

vibrant • adjective **1** *a vibrant and passionate woman* SPIRITED, lively, full of life, energetic, vigorous, vital, full of vim and vigour, animated, sparkling, effervescent, vivacious, dynamic, stimulating, exciting, passionate, fiery; *informal* peppy, feisty. **2** *she was vibrant with excitement* QUIVERING, trembling, shaking, shivering, shuddering, quavering, quaking. **3** *vibrant colours* VIVID, bright, striking, brilliant, strong, rich. **4** *his vibrant voice* RESONANT, sonorous, reverberant, resounding, ringing, echoing; strong, rich, full.
– OPPOSITES lifeless, pale.

V

vibrate • verb **1** *the floor beneath them vibrated* QUIVER, shake, tremble, shiver, shudder, judder, throb, pulsate; rock, oscillate, swing, sway, move to and fro. **2** *a low rumbling sound began to vibrate through the car* REVERBERATE, resonate, resound, ring, echo.

vibration • noun TREMOR, shaking, quivering, quaking, judder, juddering, shuddering, throb, throbbing, pulsation.

vicar • noun MINISTER, rector, priest, parson, clergyman, clergywoman, cleric, churchman, churchwoman, ecclesiastic, pastor, father, man/woman of the cloth, man/woman of god, curate, chaplain, preacher; *Scottish* kirkman; *N. Amer.* dominie; *informal* reverend, padre, Holy Joe, sky pilot; *Austral. informal* josser; *dated* divine.

vicarious • adjective INDIRECT, second-hand, secondary, derivative, derived, surrogate, substitute; empathetic, empathic.

vice • noun **1** *youngsters may be driven to vice* IMMORALITY, wrongdoing, wickedness, badness, evil, iniquity, villainy, corruption, misconduct; sin, sinfulness, ungodliness; depravity, degeneracy, dissolution, dissipation, debauchery, decadence, lechery; crime, transgression; *formal* turpitude; *archaic* trespass. **2** *smoking is my only vice* SHORTCOMING, failing, flaw, fault, defect, weakness, deficiency, limitation, imperfection, blemish, foible, frailty.
– OPPOSITES virtue.

vice versa • adverb CONVERSELY, inversely, contrariwise; reciprocally.

vicinity • noun **1** *she lives in the vicinity* NEIGHBOURHOOD, surrounding area, locality, locale, (local) area, district, region, quarter, zone; environs, surroundings, precincts; *N. Amer.* vicinage; *informal* neck of the woods. **2** *(archaic) the forest's vicinity to the dockyards.* See PROXIMITY.
– PHRASES **in the vicinity of** AROUND, about, nearly, circa, approaching, roughly, something like, more or less; in the region of, in the neighbourhood of, near to, close to; *Brit.* getting on for.

vicious • adjective **1** *a vicious killer* BRUTAL, ferocious, savage, violent, dangerous, ruthless, remorseless, merciless, heartless, callous, cruel, harsh, cold-blooded, inhuman, fierce, barbarous, barbaric, brutish, bloodthirsty, fiendish, sadistic, monstrous, murderous, homicidal. **2** *a vicious hate campaign* MALICIOUS, malevolent, malignant, malign, spiteful, vindictive, venomous, poisonous, rancorous, mean, cruel, bitter, acrimonious, hostile, nasty; defamatory, slanderous; *informal* catty.
– OPPOSITES gentle, kindly.

vicissitude • noun CHANGE, alteration, transition, shift, reversal,

– ORIGIN French.
victim ● noun **1** a person harmed, injured, or killed as a result of a crime or accident. **2** a person who is tricked or duped. **3** an animal or person killed as a religious sacrifice.
– PHRASES **fall victim to** be hurt, killed, or destroyed by.
– ORIGIN Latin *victima.*
victimize (also **victimise**) ● verb single out for cruel or unjust treatment.
– DERIVATIVES **victimization** noun **victimizer** noun.
victimless ● adjective (of a crime) in which there is no injured party.
victimology ● noun (pl. **victimologies**) the study of the victims of crime and the psychological effects on them.
victor ● noun a person who defeats an opponent in a battle, game, or competition.
– ORIGIN Latin, from *vincere* 'conquer'.
Victorian ● adjective **1** relating to the reign of Queen Victoria (1837–1901). **2** relating to the attitudes and values associated with the Victorian period, especially those of prudishness and high moral tone. ● noun a person who lived during the Victorian period.
– DERIVATIVES **Victorianism** noun.
Victoriana ● plural noun articles, especially collectors' items, from the Victorian period.
Victoria plum ● noun Brit. a large red dessert plum.
Victoria sandwich (also **Victoria sponge**) ● noun Brit. a cake consisting of two layers of sponge with a jam filling.
victorious ● adjective having won a victory; triumphant.
– DERIVATIVES **victoriously** adverb.
victor ludorum /viktər loodorəm/ ● noun Brit. a boy or man who is the overall champion in a sports competition.
– ORIGIN Latin, 'victor of the games'.
victory ● noun (pl. **victories**) an act of defeating an opponent in a battle or competition.
– ORIGIN Latin *victoria.*
victual /vitt'l/ dated ● noun (**victuals**) food or provisions. ● verb (**victualled**, **victualling**; US **victualed**, **victualing**) provide with food or other stores.
– ORIGIN Latin *victualis,* from *victus* 'food'; the pronunciation represents the early spelling *vittel.*
victualler /vitt'lər/ (US **victualer**) ● noun **1** Brit. a person who is licensed to sell alcoholic liquor. **2** dated a person providing or selling food or other provisions.
vicuña /vikoonyə/ ● noun **1** a wild relative of the llama, valued for its fine silky wool. **2** cloth made from this wool.
– ORIGIN Quechua.
vid ● noun informal short for VIDEO.
vide /vidday, veeday, vīdi/ ● verb see; consult (used as an instruction in a text to refer the reader elsewhere).
– ORIGIN Latin.
video ● noun (pl. **videos**) **1** the system of recording, reproducing, or broadcasting moving visual images on or from magnetic tape. **2** a film or other recording on magnetic tape. **3** a video cassette. **4** Brit. a video recorder. ● verb (**videoes**, **videoed**) film or make a video recording of.
– ORIGIN from Latin *videre* 'to see', on the pattern of *audio.*
videoconference ● noun an arrangement in which television sets linked to telephone lines are used to enable a group of people to communicate with and see each other.
– DERIVATIVES **videoconferencing** noun.
videodisc ● noun a CD-ROM or other disc used to store visual images.
video game ● noun a game played by electronically manipulating images produced by a computer program.
videography ● noun the process or art of making video films.
– DERIVATIVES **videographer** noun.
video jockey ● noun a person who introduces and plays music videos on television.
video-on-demand ● noun a system in which viewers choose their own filmed entertainment, by means of a PC or interactive TV system.
videophile ● noun an enthusiast for or devotee of video recordings or video technology.
videophone ● noun a telephone device transmitting and receiving a visual image as well as sound.
VideoPlus ● noun trademark a system for identifying broadcast television programmes by a numerical code which can be input into a video recorder in order to preset recording.
video recorder ● noun a device which, when linked to a television set, can be used for recording on and playing videotapes.
videotape ● noun **1** magnetic tape for recording and reproducing visual images and sound. **2** a video cassette. ● verb record on video.
vie ● verb (**vying**) compete eagerly with others in order to do or achieve something.
– ORIGIN probably from obsolete *envy,* from Latin *invitare* 'challenge'.
Viennese /veeəneez/ ● noun a person from Vienna. ● adjective relating to Vienna.
Vietcong /viətkong/ ● noun the Communist guerrilla force in Vietnam which fought the South Vietnamese government forces 1954–75 and opposed the South Vietnam and US forces in the Vietnam War.
– ORIGIN Vietnamese, 'Vietnamese Communist'.
Vietnamese ● noun (pl. same) **1** a person from Vietnam. **2** the language of Vietnam. ● adjective relating to Vietnam.
view ● noun **1** the ability to see something or to be seen from a particular position: *the mountains came into view.* **2** a sight or prospect from a particular position, typically an appealing one. **3** a way of regarding something; an attitude or opinion. **4** an inspection of things for sale by prospective purchasers. ● verb **1** look at or inspect. **2** regard in a particular light or with a particular attitude. **3** inspect (a house or other property) with the prospect of buying or renting. **4** watch on television.
– PHRASES **in full view** clearly visible. **in view 1** visible. **2** in one's mind or as one's aim. **in view of** because or as a result of. **with a view to** with the hope or intention of.
– DERIVATIVES **viewable** adjective.
– ORIGIN Old French *vieue,* from Latin *videre* 'to see'.
viewer ● noun **1** a person who views something. **2** a device for looking at film transparencies or similar photographic images.
viewership ● noun (treated as sing. or pl.) the audience for a par-

Thesaurus

downturn; inconstancy, instability, uncertainty, unpredictability, chanciness, fickleness, variability, changeability, fluctuation, vacillation; ups and downs.
victim ● noun **1** *a victim of crime* SUFFERER, injured party, casualty; fatality, loss; loser. **2** *the victim of a confidence trick* DUPE, stooge, gull, fool; target, prey, quarry, object, subject, focus, recipient; *informal* sucker, fall guy, chump, muggins, charlie; *N. Amer. informal* patsy, pigeon, sap. **3** *a sacrificial victim* SACRIFICE, (burnt) offering, scapegoat.
– PHRASES **fall victim to** FALL ILL WITH, be stricken with, catch, develop, contract, pick up; succumb to; *informal* go down with.
victimize ● verb PERSECUTE, pick on, push around, bully, abuse, discriminate against, ill-treat, mistreat, maltreat, terrorize; exploit, prey on, take advantage of, dupe, cheat, double-cross; *informal* get at, have it in for, give someone a hard time, hassle, lean on.
victor ● verb WINNER, champion, conqueror, vanquisher, hero; prizewinner, medallist; *informal* champ, top dog.
– OPPOSITES loser.
victorious ● adjective TRIUMPHANT, conquering, vanquishing, winning, champion, successful, top, first.
victory ● noun SUCCESS, triumph, conquest, win, favourable result, landslide, coup, vanquishment; mastery, superiority, supremacy; *informal* walkover, thrashing, trouncing.
– OPPOSITES defeat.
victuals ● plural noun *(dated).* See FOOD sense 1.
vie ● verb COMPETE, contend, contest, struggle, fight, battle, cross swords, lock horns, jockey; war, feud.
view ● noun **1** *the view from her flat* OUTLOOK, prospect, panorama, vista, scene, aspect, perspective, spectacle, sight; scenery, landscape. **2** *we agree with this view* OPINION, point of view, viewpoint, belief, judgement, thinking, notion, idea, conviction, persuasion, attitude, feeling, sentiment, concept, hypothesis, theory; stance, standpoint, approach. **3** *the church came into view* SIGHT, perspective, vision, visibility.
● verb **1** *they viewed the landscape* LOOK AT, eye, observe, gaze at, stare at, ogle, contemplate, regard, scan, survey, inspect, scrutinize; *informal* check out, get a load of, gawp at; *Brit. informal* clock; *N. Amer. informal* eyeball; *poetic/literary* espy, behold. **2** *the law was viewed as a last resort* CONSIDER, regard, look on, see, perceive, judge, deem, reckon.
– PHRASES **in view of** CONSIDERING, bearing in mind, taking into account, on account of, in the light of, owing to, because of, as a re-

ticular television programme or channel.

viewfinder ● noun a device on a camera showing the field of view of the lens, used in framing and focusing the picture.

viewpoint ● noun **1** a position affording a good view. **2** a point of view; an opinion.

viga /veegə/ ● noun US a rough-hewn roof timber, especially in an adobe building.
– ORIGIN Spanish.

vigil /vijil/ ● noun a period of staying awake during the time usually spent asleep, especially to keep watch or pray.
– ORIGIN from Latin, 'awake'.

vigilant ● adjective keeping careful watch for possible danger or difficulties.
– DERIVATIVES **vigilance** noun **vigilantly** adverb.
– ORIGIN from Latin *vigilare* 'keep awake'.

vigilante /vijilanti/ ● noun a member of a self-appointed group of people who undertake law enforcement in their community without legal authority.
– DERIVATIVES **vigilantism** noun.
– ORIGIN from Spanish, 'vigilant'.

vigneron /veenyəron/ ● noun a person who cultivates grapes for winemaking.
– ORIGIN French, from *vigne* 'vine'.

vignette /veenyet/ ● noun **1** a brief evocative description, account, or episode. **2** a small illustration or portrait photograph which fades into its background without a definite border. ● verb portray in the style of a vignette.
– ORIGIN originally also denoting a carved representation of a vine: from French, from *vigne* 'vine'.

vigor ● noun US spelling of VIGOUR.

vigorous ● adjective **1** strong, healthy, and full of energy. **2** characterized by or involving physical strength, effort, or energy. **3** (of language) forceful.
– DERIVATIVES **vigorously** adverb **vigorousness** noun.

vigour (US **vigor**) ● noun **1** physical strength and good health. **2** effort, energy, and enthusiasm.
– ORIGIN Latin *vigor*, from *vigere* 'be lively'.

Viking ● noun any of the Scandinavian seafaring pirates and traders who raided and settled in many parts of NW Europe in the 8th–11th centuries.
– ORIGIN Old Norse.

vile ● adjective **1** extremely unpleasant. **2** morally bad; wicked.
– DERIVATIVES **vilely** adverb **vileness** noun.
– ORIGIN Latin *vilis* 'cheap, base'.

vilify /villifi/ ● verb (**vilifies**, **vilified**) speak or write about in an abusively disparaging manner.
– DERIVATIVES **vilification** noun.
– ORIGIN Latin *vilificare*, from *vilis* 'cheap, base'.

villa ● noun **1** (especially in continental Europe) a large country residence in its own grounds. **2** Brit. a detached or semi-detached house in a residential district. **3** a rented holiday home abroad. **4** (in Roman times) a large country house, having an estate and consisting of buildings arranged around a courtyard.
– ORIGIN Latin.

village ● noun **1** a settlement in a rural area, larger than a hamlet and smaller than a town. **2** a self-contained district or community within a town or city.
– DERIVATIVES **villager** noun **villagey** adjective.
– ORIGIN Old French, from Latin *villa* 'country house'.

villain ● noun **1** a person who is guilty or capable of a crime or wickedness; a wrongdoer. **2** a character in a novel or play whose evil actions or motives are important to the plot.
– DERIVATIVES **villainous** adjective **villainy** noun.
– ORIGIN originally in the sense 'a rustic': from Old French *vilein*, from Latin *villa* 'country house'.

villanelle /villənel/ ● noun a pastoral or lyrical poem of nineteen lines, with only two rhymes throughout, and some lines repeated.
– ORIGIN Italian *villanella*, from *villanello* 'rural'.

villein /villin/ ● noun (in medieval England) a feudal tenant entirely subject to a lord or manor to whom he paid dues and services in return for land.
– ORIGIN variant of VILLAIN.

villi plural of VILLUS.

villus /villəss/ ● noun (pl. **villi** /villī/) Anatomy any of numerous minute elongated projections set closely together on a surface, especially in the absorbent lining of the small intestine.
– DERIVATIVES **villous** adjective.
– ORIGIN Latin, 'shaggy hair'.

vim ● noun informal energy; enthusiasm.
– ORIGIN perhaps from Latin, from *vis* 'energy'.

vinaigrette /vinnigret/ ● noun salad dressing of oil, wine vinegar, and seasoning.
– ORIGIN French, from *vinaigre* 'vinegar'.

vinca /vingkə/ ● noun another term for PERIWINKLE[1].
– ORIGIN Latin, from *pervinca* 'periwinkle'.

vindaloo /vindəloo/ ● noun a very hot Indian curry made with meat or fish.
– ORIGIN probably from Portuguese *vin d'alho* 'wine and garlic (sauce)'.

vindicate /vindikayt/ ● verb **1** clear of blame or suspicion. **2** show to be right or justified.
– DERIVATIVES **vindication** noun.
– ORIGIN Latin *vindicare* 'claim, avenge'.

vindictive ● adjective having or showing a strong or unreason-

Thesaurus

sult of. **on view** ON DISPLAY, on exhibition, on show.

viewer ● noun WATCHER, spectator, onlooker, observer; (**viewers**) audience, crowd; *poetic/literary* beholder.

viewpoint ● noun. See VIEW noun sense 2.

vigilant ● adjective WATCHFUL, observant, attentive, alert, eagle-eyed, hawk-eyed, on the lookout, on one's toes, on the qui vive; wide awake, on one's guard, cautious, wary, circumspect, heedful, mindful; *informal* beady-eyed.
– OPPOSITES inattentive.

vigorous ● adjective **1** *the child was vigorous* ROBUST, healthy, hale and hearty, strong, sturdy, fit; hardy, tough, athletic; bouncing, thriving, flourishing, blooming; energetic, lively, active, perky, spirited, vibrant, vital, zestful; *informal* peppy, bouncy, in the pink. **2** *a vigorous defence of policy* STRENUOUS, powerful, forceful, spirited, mettlesome, determined, aggressive, eager, zealous, ardent, fervent, vehement, passionate; tough, blunt, hard-hitting; *informal* punchy.
– OPPOSITES weak, feeble.

vigorously ● adverb STRENUOUSLY, strongly, powerfully, forcefully, energetically, heartily, with might and main, for dear life, for all one is worth, all out, fiercely, hard; *informal* like mad, like crazy; *Brit. informal* like billy-o.

vigour ● noun ROBUSTNESS, health, hardiness, strength, sturdiness, toughness; bloom, radiance, energy, life, vitality, verve, spirit; zeal, passion, determination, dynamism, zest, pep, drive; *informal* oomph, get-up-and-go; *Brit. informal* welly.
– OPPOSITES lethargy.

vile ● adjective FOUL, nasty, unpleasant, bad, disagreeable, horrid, horrible, dreadful, abominable, atrocious, offensive, obnoxious, odious, unsavoury, repulsive, disgusting, distasteful, loathsome, hateful, nauseating, sickening; disgraceful, appalling, shocking, sorry, shabby, shameful, dishonourable, execrable, heinous, abhorrent, deplorable, monstrous, wicked, evil, iniquitous, depraved, debased; contemptible, despicable, reprehensible; *informal* gross, God-awful, low-down, lousy; *Brit. informal* beastly; *archaic* scurvy.
– OPPOSITES pleasant.

vilify ● verb DISPARAGE, denigrate, defame, run down, revile, abuse, speak ill of, criticize, condemn; malign, slander, libel; *N. Amer.* slur; *informal* pull apart, lay into, slam, bad-mouth; *Brit. informal* rubbish, slate; *Austral./NZ informal* bag, monster; *formal* derogate, calumniate.
– OPPOSITES commend.

villain ● noun CRIMINAL, lawbreaker, offender, felon, convict, malefactor, miscreant, wrongdoer; gangster, gunman, thief, robber; rogue, scoundrel, reprobate, ruffian, hoodlum; *Law* malfeasant; *informal* crook, con, crim, baddy; *dated* cad, knave, blackguard.

villainous ● adjective WICKED, evil, iniquitous, sinful, nefarious, vile, foul, monstrous, outrageous, atrocious, abominable, reprehensible, hateful, odious, contemptible, horrible, heinous, egregious, diabolical, fiendish, vicious, murderous; criminal, illicit, unlawful, illegal, lawless; immoral, corrupt, degenerate, sordid, depraved, dishonourable, dishonest, unscrupulous, unprincipled; *informal* crooked, bent, low-down, dirty, shady; *dated* dastardly.
– OPPOSITES virtuous.

villainy ● noun WICKEDNESS, badness, evil, iniquity, wrongdoing, dishonesty, unscrupulousness, roguery, delinquency; crime, vice, criminality, lawlessness, lawbreaking, corruption; *Law* malfea-

ing desire for revenge.
– DERIVATIVES **vindictively** adverb **vindictiveness** noun.
– ORIGIN from Latin *vindicta* 'vengeance'.

vine ● noun **1** a climbing or trailing woody-stemmed plant. **2** the slender stem of a trailing or climbing plant.
– ORIGIN Latin *vinea* 'vineyard, vine', from *vinum* ('wine'.

vinegar ● noun **1** a sour-tasting liquid containing acetic acid, obtained by fermenting dilute alcoholic liquids and used as a condiment or for pickling. **2** sourness or peevishness of behaviour.
– DERIVATIVES **vinegary** adjective.
– ORIGIN from Old French *vyn egre*, from Latin *vinum* 'wine' + *acer* 'sour'.

vineyard ● noun a plantation of grapevines, typically producing grapes used in winemaking.

vingt-et-un /vaNtayŌN/ ● noun the card game pontoon or blackjack.
– ORIGIN French, 'twenty-one'.

vinho verde /veenō vairdi/ ● noun a young Portuguese wine, not allowed to mature.
– ORIGIN Portuguese, 'green wine'.

viniculture /vinnikulchər/ ● noun the cultivation of grapevines for winemaking.

vinification /vinnifikaysh'n/ ● noun the conversion of grape juice or other vegetable extract into wine by fermentation.
– DERIVATIVES **vinify** verb (**vinifies, vinified**).

vining /vīning/ ● noun the separation of leguminous crops from their vines and pods. ● adjective (of a plant) having climbing or trailing woody stems like a vine.

vino ● noun (pl. **vinos**) informal, chiefly Brit. wine, especially that which is cheap or of inferior quality.
– ORIGIN Spanish and Italian, 'wine'.

vin ordinaire /vaN ordinair/ ● noun (pl. **vins ordinaires**) cheap table wine for everyday use.
– ORIGIN French, 'ordinary wine'.

vinous /vīnəss/ ● adjective of, resembling, or associated with wine.

vintage ● noun **1** the year or place in which wine was produced. **2** a wine of high quality made from the crop of a single identified district in a good year. **3** the harvesting of grapes for winemaking. **4** the grapes or wine of a particular season. **5** the time that something was produced. ● adjective **1** referring to vintage wine. **2** referring to something from the past of high quality.
– ORIGIN Old French *vendange*, from Latin *vindemia*, from *vinum* 'wine' + *demere* 'remove'.

vintage car ● noun Brit. an old style or model of car, specifically one made between 1919 and 1930.

vintner /vintnər/ ● noun a wine merchant.
– ORIGIN Old French *vinetier*, from Latin *vinetum* 'vineyard'.

vinyl /vīn'l/ ● noun **1** synthetic resin or plastic based on polyvinyl chloride, used e.g. for wallpaper and emulsion paint and formerly for gramophone records. **2** /also -nīl/ Chemistry the unsaturated hydrocarbon radical $-CH=CH_2$, derived from ethylene.
– ORIGIN from Latin *vinum* 'wine' (suggested by the relationship of ethylene to ethyl alcohol).

viol /vīəl/ ● noun a musical instrument of the Renaissance and baroque periods, typically six-stringed, held vertically and played with a bow.
– ORIGIN Provençal *viola*.

viola[1] /viōlə/ ● noun an instrument of the violin family, larger than the violin and tuned a fifth lower.
– ORIGIN Italian and Spanish; compare with VIOL.

viola[2] /vīələ/ ● noun a plant of a genus that includes the pansies and violets.
– ORIGIN Latin, 'violet'.

violaceous /vīəlayshəss/ ● adjective of a violet colour.
– ORIGIN Latin *violaceus*, from *viola* 'violet'.

viola da gamba /viōlə da gambə/ ● noun a viol, specifically a bass viol (corresponding to the modern cello).
– ORIGIN Italian, 'viol for the leg'.

violate ● verb **1** break or fail to comply with (a rule or formal agreement). **2** treat with disrespect. **3** rape or sexually assault.
– DERIVATIVES **violation** noun **violator** noun.
– ORIGIN Latin *violare* 'treat violently'.

violence ● noun **1** behaviour involving physical force intended to hurt, damage, or kill. **2** strength of emotion or an unpleasant or destructive natural force.

violent ● adjective **1** using or involving violence. **2** very intense, forceful, or powerful.
– DERIVATIVES **violently** adverb.
– ORIGIN Latin, 'vehement, violent'.

violet ● noun **1** a small plant typically with purple, blue, or white five-petalled flowers. **2** a bluish-purple colour seen at the end of the spectrum opposite red.
– ORIGIN Old French *violette*, from Latin *viola* 'violet'.

violin ● noun a stringed musical instrument of treble pitch, having four strings and a body narrowed at the middle, played with a bow.
– DERIVATIVES **violinist** noun.
– ORIGIN Italian *violino* 'small viola'.

violist ● noun **1** /viōlist/ a viola player. **2** /vīəlist/ a viol player.

violoncello /vīələnchellō, veeə-/ ● noun formal term for CELLO.
– ORIGIN Italian.

VIP ● abbreviation very important person.

viper ● noun **1** a poisonous snake with large hinged fangs and a body typically with dark patterns on a lighter background. **2** a spiteful or treacherous person.
– DERIVATIVES **viperish** adjective **viperous** adjective.
– ORIGIN Latin *vipera*, from *vivus* 'alive' + *parere* 'bring forth' (because of a former belief that vipers bore live young).

viraemia /vīreemiə/ (also **viremia**) ● noun Medicine the presence of viruses in the blood.

Thesaurus

sance; *informal* crookedness; *formal* turpitude; *archaic* knavery.

vindicate ● verb **1** *he was vindicated by the jury* ACQUIT, clear, absolve, exonerate; discharge, liberate, free, redeem; *informal* let off (the hook); *formal* exculpate. **2** *I had fully vindicated my request* JUSTIFY, warrant, substantiate, ratify, authenticate, verify, confirm, corroborate, prove, defend, support, back, evidence, endorse.

vindictive ● adjective VENGEFUL, revengeful, unforgiving, resentful, acrimonious, bitter; spiteful, mean, rancorous, venomous, malicious, malevolent, nasty, cruel, unkind; *informal* catty.
– OPPOSITES forgiving.

vintage ● noun **1** *1986 was a classic vintage* YEAR. **2** *he lost a vintage through frost* (GRAPE) HARVEST, crop, yield. **3** *furniture of Louis XV vintage* PERIOD, era, epoch, time, origin; genre, style, kind, sort, type.
● adjective **1** *vintage French wine* HIGH-QUALITY, quality, choice, select, superior, best. **2** *vintage motor vehicles* CLASSIC, ageless, timeless; old, antique, heritage, historic. **3** *his reaction was vintage Francis* CHARACTERISTIC, typical, pure.

violate ● verb **1** *this violates fundamental human rights* CONTRAVENE, breach, infringe, break, transgress, overstep, disobey, defy, flout; disregard, ignore. **2** *the tomb was violated* DESECRATE, profane, defile, degrade, debase; damage, vandalize, deface, destroy. **3** *he drugged and then violated her* RAPE, assault, force oneself on, abuse, molest, interfere with; *dated* deflower, defile, dishonour, ruin; *poetic/literary* ravish.
– OPPOSITES respect.

violation ● noun **1** *a violation of human rights* CONTRAVENTION, breach, infringement, infraction, transgression, defiance; neglect. **2** *a violation of their private lives* INVASION, breach, infraction; trespass, intrusion, encroachment. **3** *she was threatened with violation* RAPE, (sexual) assault, (sexual) abuse, molestation, interference; *dated* defloration, defilement, dishonour; *archaic* ravishment.

violence ● noun **1** *police violence* BRUTALITY, brute force, ferocity, savagery, cruelty, sadism, barbarity, brutishness. **2** *the violence of the blow* FORCEFULNESS, force, power, strength, might, savagery, ferocity, brutality. **3** *the violence of his passion* INTENSITY, severity, strength, force, vehemence, power, potency, fervency, ardency, ferocity, fury.

violent ● adjective **1** *a violent alcoholic* BRUTAL, vicious, savage, rough, aggressive, threatening, fierce, wild, ferocious; barbarous, barbaric, thuggish, cut-throat, homicidal, murderous, cruel. **2** *a violent blow* POWERFUL, forceful, hard, sharp, smart, strong, vigorous, mighty, hefty; savage, ferocious, brutal, vicious. **3** *violent jealousy* INTENSE, extreme, strong, powerful, vehement, intemperate, unbridled, uncontrollable, ungovernable, inordinate, consuming, passionate.
– OPPOSITES gentle, weak, mild.

VIP ● noun CELEBRITY, famous person, very important person, personality, big name, star, superstar; dignitary, luminary, worthy,

– ORIGIN from VIRUS.
virago /viraagō/ ● noun (pl. **viragos** or **viragoes**) a domineering, violent, or bad-tempered woman.
– ORIGIN first used as the name given by Adam to Eve in the Vulgate version of the Bible: from Latin, 'heroic woman, female warrior', from *vir* 'man'.
viral ● adjective of the nature of, caused by, or relating to a virus or viruses.
– DERIVATIVES **virally** adverb.
viremia ● noun variant spelling of VIRAEMIA.
vireo /virriō/ ● noun (pl. **vireos**) a small American warbler-like songbird, typically green or grey.
– ORIGIN Latin, referring to a greenfinch or similar bird.
Virgilian /vurjilliən/ (also **Vergilian**) ● adjective relating to or in the style of the Roman poet Virgil (70–19 BC).
virgin ● noun **1** a person who has never had sexual intercourse. **2** (**the Virgin**) the Virgin Mary. **3** a person who is naive or inexperienced in a particular context: *a political virgin.* ● adjective **1** being, relating to, or appropriate for a virgin. **2** not yet used or exploited: *virgin forest.* **3** (of olive oil) obtained from the first pressing of olives.
– ORIGIN Latin *virgo*.
virginal ● adjective relating to or appropriate for a virgin. ● noun an early spinet with the strings parallel to the keyboard. [ORIGIN perhaps because usually played by young women.]
Virgin Birth ● noun the doctrine of Christ's birth from a mother, Mary, who was a virgin.
Virginia creeper ● noun a North American vine which is chiefly cultivated for its red autumn foliage.
virginity ● noun the state of being a virgin.
Virgo ● noun **1** Astronomy a large constellation (the Virgin), said to represent a maiden or goddess associated with the harvest. **2** Astrology the sixth sign of the zodiac, which the sun enters about 23 August.
– DERIVATIVES **Virgoan** noun & adjective.
– ORIGIN Latin.
viridescent /virridess'nt/ ● adjective greenish or becoming green.
– DERIVATIVES **viridescence** noun.
– ORIGIN from Latin *viridescere* 'become green'.
viridian /viriddiən/ ● noun **1** a bluish-green pigment containing chromium hydroxide. **2** a bluish-green colour.
– ORIGIN from Latin *viridis* 'green'.
virile ● adjective **1** (of a man) having strength, energy, and a strong sex drive. **2** vigorous, strong, and manly.
– DERIVATIVES **virility** noun.
– ORIGIN Latin *virilis*, from *vir* 'man'.
virology /vīrolləji/ ● noun the branch of science concerned with the study of viruses.
– DERIVATIVES **virological** adjective **virologist** noun.
virtual ● adjective **1** almost as described, but not completely or according to strict definition. **2** Computing not physically existing as such but made by software to appear to do so. **3** Optics relating to the points at which rays would meet if produced backwards.
– DERIVATIVES **virtuality** noun.
– ORIGIN Latin *virtualis*, from *virtus* 'virtue'.
virtually ● adverb **1** nearly; almost. **2** Computing by means of virtual reality techniques.
virtual memory (also **virtual storage**) ● noun Computing memory that appears to exist as main storage although most of it is supported by data held in secondary storage.
virtual reality ● noun Computing the computer-generated simulation of a three-dimensional image or environment that can be interacted with by using special electronic equipment.
virtue /vurtyōō/ ● noun **1** behaviour showing high moral standards. **2** a morally good or desirable quality. **3** a good or useful quality of a thing. **4** archaic virginity or chastity.
– PHRASES **by virtue of** because or as a result of.
– ORIGIN Latin *virtus* 'valour, merit, moral perfection', from *vir* 'man'.
virtuoso /vurtyoōōsō/ ● noun (pl. **virtuosi** /vurtyoōōsi/ or **virtuosos**) a person highly skilled in music or another artistic pursuit.
– DERIVATIVES **virtuosic** adjective **virtuosity** noun.
– ORIGIN from Italian, 'learned, skilful'.
virtuous ● adjective **1** having or showing high moral standards. **2** archaic chaste.
– DERIVATIVES **virtuously** adverb **virtuousness** noun.
virtuous circle ● noun a recurring cycle of events, the result of each one being to increase the beneficial effect of the next.
virulent /virrōōlənt, virryōō-/ ● adjective **1** (of a disease or poison) extremely severe or harmful in its effects. **2** (of a pathogen, especially a virus) highly infective. **3** bitterly hostile.
– DERIVATIVES **virulence** noun **virulently** adverb.
– ORIGIN originally describing a poisoned wound: from Latin *virulentus*, from *virus* (see VIRUS).
virus /vīrəss/ ● noun **1** a submicroscopic infective particle which

Thesaurus

grandee, lion, notable, notability, personage; *informal* heavyweight, celeb, bigwig, big shot, big cheese, nob, honcho, top dog, megastar; *N. Amer. informal* big wheel, (big) kahuna, high muckamuck.
virago ● noun HARRIDAN, shrew, dragon, termagant, vixen; fishwife, witch, hellcat, she-devil, tartar, martinet, spitfire, ogress; *informal* battleaxe; *archaic* scold.
virgin ● noun *she remained a virgin* chaste woman, celibate; *formal* virgo intacta; *poetic/literary* maiden, maid, vestal.
● adjective **1** *virgin forest* UNTOUCHED, unspoilt, untainted, immaculate, pristine, flawless; spotless, unsullied, unpolluted, undefiled, perfect; unchanged, intact; unexplored, uncharted, unmapped. **2** *virgin girls* CHASTE, virginal, celibate, abstinent; unmarried, unwed, maiden, maidenly; pure, uncorrupted, incorrupt, undefiled, unsullied, innocent; *poetic/literary* vestal.
virginal ● adjective. See VIRGIN adjective sense 2.
virginity ● noun CHASTITY, maidenhood, honour, purity, innocence; celibacy, abstinence; *informal* cherry; *archaic* virtue.
virile ● adjective MANLY, masculine, male; strong, tough, vigorous, robust, muscular, muscly, brawny, rugged, sturdy, husky; red-blooded, fertile; *informal* macho, laddish, butch, beefy, hunky.
– OPPOSITES effeminate.
virtual ● adjective EFFECTIVE, in effect, near (enough), essential, practical, to all intents and purposes; indirect, implied, implicit, unacknowledged, tacit.
virtually ● adverb EFFECTIVELY, in effect, all but, more or less, practically, almost, nearly, close to, verging on, just about, as good as, essentially, to all intents and purposes, as near as dammit; roughly, approximately; *informal* pretty much, pretty well; *poetic/literary* well nigh, nigh on.
virtue ● noun **1** *the simple virtue of peasant life* GOODNESS, virtuousness, righteousness, morality, integrity, dignity, rectitude, honour, decency, respectability, nobility, worthiness, purity; principles, ethics. **2** *promptness was not one of his virtues* GOOD POINT, good quality, strong point, asset, forte, attribute, strength, talent. **3** *(archaic) she lost her virtue in the city.* See VIRGINITY. **4** *I can see no virtue in this* MERIT, advantage, benefit, usefulness, strength, efficacy.
– OPPOSITES vice, failing, disadvantage.
– PHRASES **by virtue of** BECAUSE OF, on account of, by dint of, by means of, by way of, via, through, as a result of, as a consequence of, on the strength of, owing to, thanks to, due to, by reason of.
virtuosity ● noun SKILL, skilfulness, mastery, expertise, prowess, proficiency, ability, aptitude; excellence, brilliance, talent, genius, artistry, flair, panache, finesse, wizardry; *informal* know-how.
virtuoso ● noun *the pianist is clearly a virtuoso* GENIUS, expert, (past) master, maestro, artist, prodigy, marvel, adept, professional, doyen, veteran; star, champion; *informal* hotshot, wizard, pro, ace; *Brit. informal* dab hand.
– OPPOSITES duffer.
● adjective *a virtuoso violinist* SKILFUL, expert, accomplished, masterly, master, consummate, proficient, talented, gifted, adept, able, good, competent, capable; impressive, outstanding, exceptional, magnificent, supreme, first-rate, brilliant, excellent; *informal* superb, mean, ace.
– OPPOSITES incompetent.
virtuous ● adjective RIGHTEOUS, good, moral, ethical, upright, upstanding, high-minded, principled, exemplary; law-abiding, irreproachable, blameless, guiltless, unimpeachable, honest, honourable, reputable, decent, respectable, noble, worthy, meritorious; pure, whiter than white, saintly, angelic; *informal* squeaky clean.
virulent ● adjective **1** *virulent herbicides* POISONOUS, toxic, venomous, noxious, deadly, lethal, fatal, mortal, dangerous, harmful, injurious, pernicious, damaging, destructive; *poetic/literary* deathly, nocuous. **2** *a virulent epidemic* INFECTIOUS, infective, contagious, communicable, transmittable, transmissible, spreading, pestilen-

is able to multiply within the cells of a host organism and typically consists of nucleic acid coated in protein. **2** informal an infection or disease caused by such an agent. **3** (also **computer virus**) a piece of code surreptitiously introduced into a system in order to corrupt it or destroy data.
– ORIGIN originally denoting the venom of a snake: from Latin, 'slimy liquid, poison'.
visa /veezə/ ● **noun** an endorsement on a passport indicating that the holder is allowed to enter, leave, or stay for a specified period of time in a country.
– ORIGIN Latin, from *videre* 'to see'.
visage /vizzij/ ● **noun** literary a person's facial features or expression.
– DERIVATIVES **visaged** adjective.
– ORIGIN Old French, from Latin *visus* 'sight'.
vis-à-vis /veezaavee/ ● **preposition** in relation to.
– ORIGIN French, 'face to face'.
viscera /vissərə/ ● **plural noun** (sing. **viscus**) the internal organs in the main cavities of the body, especially those in the abdomen.
– ORIGIN Latin, plural of *viscus*.
visceral ● **adjective 1** relating to the viscera. **2** (of a feeling) deep and instinctive rather than rational.
– DERIVATIVES **viscerally** adverb.
viscid /vissid/ ● **adjective** glutinous; sticky.
– ORIGIN Latin *viscidus*, from *viscum* 'birdlime'.
viscoelastic /viskōilastik/ ● **adjective** Physics exhibiting both elastic and viscous behaviour.
– DERIVATIVES **viscoelasticity** noun.
viscose /viskōs/ ● **noun 1** a viscous orange-brown solution obtained by treating cellulose with sodium hydroxide and carbon disulphide, used as the basis of manufacturing rayon and transparent cellulose film. **2** rayon fabric or fibre made from this.
– ORIGIN from Latin *viscus* 'birdlime'.
viscosity /viskossiti/ ● **noun** (pl. **viscosties**) **1** the state of being viscous. **2** a quantity expressing the magnitude of internal friction in a fluid, as measured by the force per unit area resisting uniform flow.
viscount /vīkownt/ ● **noun** a British nobleman ranking above a baron and below an earl.
– ORIGIN Latin *vicecomes* (see VICE-, COUNT²).
viscountess /vīkowntiss/ ● **noun** the wife or widow of a viscount, or a woman holding the rank of viscount in her own right.
viscous /viskəss/ ● **adjective** having a thick, sticky consistency between solid and liquid; having a high viscosity.
– ORIGIN Latin *viscosus*, from *viscum* 'birdlime'.
viscus /viskəss/ singular form of VISCERA.
– ORIGIN Latin.

vise ● **noun** US spelling of VICE².
visibility ● **noun 1** the state of being able to see or be seen. **2** the distance one can see as determined by light and weather conditions.
visible ● **adjective 1** able to be seen or noticed. **2** Physics (of light) within the range of wavelengths to which the eye is sensitive. **3** of or relating to imports or exports of tangible commodities.
– DERIVATIVES **visibly** adverb.
– ORIGIN Latin *visibilis*, from *videre* 'to see'.
Visigoth /vizzigoth/ ● **noun** a member of the branch of the Goths who invaded the Roman Empire between the 3rd and 5th centuries AD.
– ORIGIN Latin *Visigothus*, possibly meaning 'West Goth'. Compare with OSTROGOTH.
vision ● **noun 1** the faculty or state of being able to see. **2** the ability to think about the future with imagination or wisdom. **3** a mental image of what the future will or could be like. **4** an experience of seeing something in a dream or trance, or as a supernatural apparition. **5** the images seen on a television screen. **6** a person or sight of unusual beauty.
– ORIGIN Latin, from *videre* 'to see'.
visionary ● **adjective 1** thinking about the future with imagination or wisdom. **2** relating to supernatural or dreamlike visions. ● **noun** (pl. **visionaries**) a visionary person.
visit ● **verb** (**visited**, **visiting**) **1** go to see and spend time with (someone) socially or as a guest. **2** go to see and spend time in (a place) as a tourist or guest. **3** go to see for a purpose. **4** (with reference to something harmful or unpleasant) inflict or be inflicted on someone. **5** N. Amer. informal chat. ● **noun 1** an act of visiting. **2** a temporary stay at a place. **3** N. Amer. an informal conversation.
– ORIGIN Latin *visitare* 'go to see'.
visitant ● **noun 1** chiefly literary a supernatural being; an apparition. **2** archaic a visitor or guest.
visitation ● **noun 1** an official or formal visit. **2** the appearance of a divine or supernatural being. **3** US Law a divorced person's right to spend time with their children in the custody of a former spouse. **4** a disaster or difficulty regarded as a divine punishment. **5** (**the Visitation**) the visit of the Virgin Mary to Elizabeth related in the Gospel of Luke, chapter 1.
visiting ● **adjective** (of an academic) working for a fixed period of time at another institution.
visiting card ● **noun** Brit. a card bearing a person's name and address, sent or left instead of a formal visit.
visitor ● **noun 1** a person visiting a person or place. **2** a migratory bird present in a locality for only part of the year.
visor /vīzər/ (also **vizor**) ● **noun 1** a movable part of a helmet that can be pulled down to cover the face. **2** a screen for protecting the eyes from unwanted light. **3** N. Amer. a stiff peak at the front of a cap.

Thesaurus

tial; *informal* catching. **3** *a virulent attack on morals* VITRIOLIC, malicious, malevolent, hostile, spiteful, venomous, vicious, vindictive, bitter, rancorous, acrimonious, scathing, caustic, withering, nasty, savage, harsh.
– OPPOSITES harmless, amicable.
viscous ● **adjective** STICKY, gummy, gluey, adhesive, tacky, adherent, treacly, syrupy; glutinous, gelatinous, thick, viscid, mucous, mucoid, mucilaginous; *informal* gooey, gloopy; *N. Amer. informal* gloppy.
visible ● **adjective** PERCEPTIBLE, perceivable, seeable, observable, noticeable, detectable, discernible; in sight, in/on view, on display; evident, apparent, manifest, transparent, plain, clear, conspicuous, obvious, patent, unmistakable, unconcealed, undisguised, prominent, salient, striking, glaring.
vision ● **noun 1** *her vision was blurred by tears* EYESIGHT, sight, observation, (visual) perception; eyes; view, perspective. **2** *visions of the ancestral pilgrims* APPARITION, spectre, phantom, ghost, wraith, manifestation; hallucination, illusion, mirage; *informal* spook; *poetic/literary* phantasm, shade. **3** *visions of a better future* DREAM, daydream, reverie; plan, hope; fantasy, pipe dream, delusion. **4** *his speech lacked vision* IMAGINATION, creativity, inventiveness, innovation, inspiration, intuition, perception, insight, foresight, prescience. **5** *Melissa was a vision in lilac* BEAUTIFUL SIGHT, feast for the eyes, pleasure to behold, delight, dream, beauty, picture, joy, marvel, sensation; *informal* sight for sore eyes, stunner, knockout, looker, peach; *Brit. informal* smasher.
visionary ● **adjective** *a visionary leader* INSPIRED, imaginative, creative, inventive, ingenious, enterprising, innovative; insightful, perceptive, intuitive, prescient, discerning, shrewd, wise, clever, resourceful; idealistic, romantic, quixotic, dreamy; *informal* starry-eyed.
● **noun 1** *a visionary pictured him in hell* SEER, mystic, oracle, prophet(ess), soothsayer, augur, diviner, clairvoyant, crystal-gazer; *Scottish* spaewife; *poetic/literary* sibyl. **2** *a visionary can't run a business effectively* DREAMER, daydreamer, idealist, romantic, fantasist, utopian.
visit ● **verb 1** *I visited my dear uncle* CALL ON, pay a visit to, go to see, look in on; stay with, holiday with; stop by, drop by; *N. Amer.* visit with, go see; *informal* pop in on, drop in on, look up. **2** *Alex was visiting America* STAY IN, stop over in, spend time in, holiday in, vacation in; tour, explore, see; *informal* do. **3** *they were visited with many epidemics* AFFLICT, attack, trouble, torment; *archaic* smite.
● **noun 1** *she paid a visit to her mum* (SOCIAL) CALL. **2** *a visit to the museum* TRIP TO, tour of, look round; stopover, stay; holiday, break, vacation; *formal* sojourn.
visitation ● **noun 1** *the bishop's pastoral visitations* (OFFICIAL) VISIT, tour of inspection, survey, examination. **2** *a visitation from God* APPARITION, vision, appearance, manifestation, materialization. **3** *Jehovah punished them by visitations* AFFLICTION, scourge, bane, curse, plague, blight, disaster, tragedy, catastrophe; punishment, retribution, vengeance.
visitor ● **noun 1** *I am expecting a visitor* GUEST, caller; company; *archaic* visitant. **2** *the monument attracts foreign visitors* TOURIST,

– DERIVATIVES **visored** adjective.
– ORIGIN Old French *viser*, from Latin *visus* 'sight'.
vista ● noun **1** a pleasing view, especially one seen through a long, narrow opening. **2** a mental view of an imagined future event or situation.
– ORIGIN Italian, 'view'.
visual ● adjective relating to seeing or sight. ● noun a picture, piece of film, or display used to illustrate or accompany something.
– DERIVATIVES **visually** adverb.
– ORIGIN Latin *visualis*, from *videre* 'to see'.
visual display unit ● noun Computing, chiefly Brit. a device for displaying input signals as characters on a screen.
visualize (also **visualise**) ● verb form a mental image of; imagine.
– DERIVATIVES **visualization** noun.
visuospatial /vizhyoo-ōspaysh'l/ ● adjective Psychology referring to the visual perception of the spatial relationships of objects.
vital ● adjective **1** absolutely necessary; essential. **2** essential for life: *the vital organs.* **3** full of energy; lively. ● noun (**vitals**) the body's important internal organs.
– DERIVATIVES **vitally** adverb.
– ORIGIN Latin *vitalis*, from *vita* 'life'.
vital capacity ● noun the greatest volume of air that can be expelled from the lungs after taking the deepest possible breath.
vital force ● noun the energy or spirit which animates living creatures.
vitalism ● noun the theory that the origin and phenomena of life are dependent on a force or principle distinct from purely chemical or physical forces.
– DERIVATIVES **vitalist** noun & adjective **vitalistic** adjective.
vitality ● noun **1** the state of being strong and active. **2** the power giving continuance of life, present in all living things.
vitalize (also **vitalise**) ● verb give strength and energy to.
vital signs ● plural noun clinical measurements, specifically pulse rate, temperature, respiration rate, and blood pressure, that indicate the state of a patient's essential body functions.
vital statistics ● plural noun **1** quantitative data concerning the population, such as the number of births, marriages, and deaths. **2** informal the measurements of a woman's bust, waist, and hips.
vitamin /vittəmin, vī-/ ● noun any of a group of organic compounds which are essential for normal nutrition and have to be supplied in the diet because they cannot be synthesized by the body.
– ORIGIN from Latin *vita* 'life' + AMINE, because vitamins were originally thought to contain an amino acid.
vitamin A ● noun another term for RETINOL.
vitamin B ● noun any of a group of substances essential for the working of certain enzymes in the body, including thiamine (**vitamin B_1**), riboflavin (**vitamin B_2**), pyridoxine (**vitamin B_6**), and cyanocobalamin (**vitamin B_{12}**).
vitamin C ● noun another term for ASCORBIC ACID.
vitamin D ● noun any of a group of compounds found in liver and fish oils, essential for the absorption of calcium and including calciferol (**vitamin D_2**) and cholecalciferol (**vitamin D_3**).
vitamin E ● noun another term for TOCOPHEROL.
vitamin K ● noun any of a group of compounds found mainly in green leaves and essential for the blood-clotting process, including phylloquinone (**vitamin K_1**) and menaquinone (**vitamin K_2**).
vitelline /vitellīn, vī-/ ● adjective Zoology & Embryology referring to the yolk (or yolk sac) of an egg or embryo, or to yolk-producing organs.
– ORIGIN Latin *vitellinus*, from *vitellus* 'yolk'.
vitiate /vishiayt/ ● verb formal **1** spoil or impair the quality or efficiency of. **2** destroy or impair the legal validity of.
– ORIGIN Latin *vitiare* 'impair'.
viticulture ● noun **1** the cultivation of grapevines. **2** the study of grape cultivation.
– DERIVATIVES **viticultural** adjective **viticulturist** noun.
– ORIGIN from Latin *vitis* 'vine'.
vitiligo /vitilīgō/ ● noun Medicine a condition in which the pigment is lost from areas of the skin, causing whitish patches.
– ORIGIN Latin.
vitreous /vitriəss/ ● adjective **1** like glass in appearance or physical properties. **2** (of a substance) derived from or containing glass.
– ORIGIN Latin *vitreus*, from *vitrum* 'glass'.
vitreous humour ● noun the transparent jelly-like tissue filling the eyeball behind the lens.
vitrify /vitrifī/ ● verb (**vitrifies, vitrified**) convert into glass or a glass-like substance, typically by exposure to heat.
– DERIVATIVES **vitrification** noun.
– ORIGIN from Latin *vitrum* 'glass'.
vitrine /vitreen/ ● noun a glass display case.
– ORIGIN French, from *vitre* 'glass pane'.
vitriol /vitriəl/ ● noun **1** archaic or literary sulphuric acid. **2** extreme bitterness or malice.
– DERIVATIVES **vitriolic** adjective **vitriolically** adverb.
– ORIGIN originally denoting the sulphate of various metals: from Latin *vitriolum*, from *vitrum* 'glass'.
vittle ● noun archaic variant spelling of VICTUAL.
vituperation ● noun bitter and abusive language.
– ORIGIN Latin, from *vituperare* 'censure, disparage'.
vituperative /vityōōpərətiv/ ● adjective bitter and abusive.
viva[1] /vīvə/ ● noun Brit. an oral examination, typically for an academic qualification.
– ORIGIN abbreviation of VIVA VOCE.
viva[2] /veevə/ ● exclamation long live! (used to express acclaim or support).
– ORIGIN Italian.
vivace /vivaachay/ ● adverb & adjective Music in a lively and brisk manner.
– ORIGIN Italian.
vivacious /vivayshəss/ ● adjective attractively lively and animated.
– DERIVATIVES **vivaciously** adverb **vivacity** noun.
– ORIGIN from Latin *vivax* 'lively, vigorous'.
vivarium /vīvairiəm, vi-/ ● noun (pl. **vivaria** /vīvairiə, vi-/) an enclosure or structure used for keeping animals under semi-natural conditions for observation or study or as pets.
– ORIGIN Latin, 'warren, fish pond'.

Thesaurus

traveller, holidaymaker, day tripper, tripper, vacationer, vacationist, sightseer; pilgrim; foreigner, outsider, stranger, alien; *Brit. informal* emmet, grockle.
vista ● noun VIEW, prospect, panorama, aspect, perspective, spectacle, sight; scenery, landscape.
visual ● adjective **1** *visual defects* OPTICAL, optic, ocular, eye; vision, sight. **2** *a visual indication that the alarm works* VISIBLE, perceptible, perceivable, discernible.
visualize ● verb ENVISAGE, envision, conjure up, picture, call to mind, see, imagine, evoke, dream up, fantasize about, conceptualize, contemplate.
vital ● adjective **1** *it is vital that action is taken* ESSENTIAL, of the essence, critical, crucial, indispensable, all-important, imperative, mandatory, urgent, pressing, burning, compelling, high-priority; *informal* earth-shattering, world-shaking. **2** *the vital organs* MAJOR, main, chief; essential, necessary. **3** *he is young and vital* LIVELY, energetic, active, sprightly, spry, spirited, vivacious, exuberant, bouncy, enthusiastic, vibrant, zestful, sparkling, dynamic, vigorous, lusty, hale and hearty; *informal* peppy, spunky, full of beans, bright-eyed and bushy-tailed.
– OPPOSITES unimportant, minor, listless.
vitality ● noun LIVELINESS, life, energy, spirit, vivacity, exuberance, buoyancy, bounce, verve, vim, pep, brio, zest, sparkle, dynamism, passion, fire, vigour, drive; *informal* get-up-and-go.
vitriolic ● adjective ACRIMONIOUS, rancorous, bitter, caustic, mordant, acerbic, trenchant, virulent, spiteful, savage, venomous, poisonous, malicious, splenetic; nasty, mean, cruel, unkind, harsh, vindictive, scathing, barbed, wounding, sharp, cutting, withering, sarcastic; *informal* bitchy, catty.
vituperate ● verb *(archaic)*. See REVILE.
vituperation ● noun INVECTIVE, revilement, condemnation, opprobrium, scolding, criticism, flak, disapprobation, fault-finding; blame, abuse, insults, vilification, denunciation, obloquy, denigration, disparagement, slander, libel, defamation, slurs, aspersions; vitriol, venom; *Brit. informal* stick; *formal* castigation.
– OPPOSITES praise.
vivacious ● adjective LIVELY, spirited, bubbly, ebullient, buoyant, sparkling, light-hearted, jaunty, merry, happy, jolly, full of fun, cheery, cheerful, perky, sunny, breezy, enthusiastic, irrepressible, vibrant, vital, zestful, energetic, dynamic; *informal* peppy,

viva voce /vīvə vōchi/ ● adjective (especially of an examination) oral rather than written. ● noun Brit. full form of VIVA[1].
– ORIGIN Latin, 'with the living voice'.
vivid ● adjective **1** producing powerful feelings or strong, clear images in the mind. **2** (of a colour) intensely deep or bright.
– DERIVATIVES **vividly** adverb **vividness** noun.
– ORIGIN originally in the sense 'lively, vigorous': from Latin *vividus*, from *vivere* 'to live'.
vivify /vivvifī/ ● verb (**vivifies, vivified**) enliven or animate.
– DERIVATIVES **vivification** noun.
– ORIGIN Latin *vivificare*, from *vivere* 'to live'.
viviparous /vivippərəss, vī-/ ● adjective **1** (of an animal) bringing forth live young which have developed inside the body of the parent. Compare with OVIPAROUS and OVOVIVIPAROUS. **2** (of a plant) reproducing from buds which form plantlets while still attached to the parent plant, or from seeds which germinate within the fruit.
– DERIVATIVES **viviparity** noun.
– ORIGIN Latin *viviparus*, from *vivus* 'alive' + *-parus* 'bearing'.
vivisection ● noun the practice of performing operations on live animals for scientific research (used by those opposed to such work).
– DERIVATIVES **vivisectionist** noun & adjective **vivisector** noun.
– ORIGIN from Latin *vivus* 'living', on the pattern of *dissection*.
vixen ● noun **1** a female fox. **2** a spiteful or quarrelsome woman.
– DERIVATIVES **vixenish** adjective.
– ORIGIN perhaps from an Old English word meaning 'of a fox'.
Viyella /vīellə/ ● noun trademark a fabric made from a twilled mixture of cotton and wool.
– ORIGIN from *Via Gellia*, a valley in Derbyshire.
viz. ● adverb namely; in other words.
– ORIGIN abbreviation of Latin *videlicet* in the same sense, *z* being a Latin symbol for *-et*.
vizier /vizeer/ ● noun historical a high official in some Muslim countries.
– ORIGIN Arabic, 'caliph's chief counsellor'.
vizor ● noun variant spelling of VISOR.
vizsla /vizlə/ ● noun a dog of a breed of golden-brown pointer with large drooping ears.
– ORIGIN named after the town of *Vizsla* in Hungary.
VJ day ● noun the day (15 August) in 1945 on which Japan ceased fighting in the Second World War, or the day (2 September) when Japan formally surrendered.
– ORIGIN *VJ*, abbreviation of *Victory over Japan*.
VLF ● abbreviation very low frequency (denoting radio waves of frequency 3–30 kilohertz and wavelength 10–100 kilometres).
VLSI ● abbreviation Electronics very large-scale integration.
V-neck ● noun a neckline having straight sides meeting at a point to form a V-shape.
– DERIVATIVES **V-necked** adjective.
VO ● abbreviation (in the UK) Royal Victorian Order.
vocabulary ● noun (pl. **vocabularies**) **1** the body of words used in a particular language or in a particular sphere. **2** the body of words known to an individual person. **3** a list of words with an explanation of their meanings. **4** a range of artistic or stylistic forms or techniques.
– ORIGIN Latin *vocabularius*, from *vocare* 'to call'.
vocal ● adjective **1** relating to the human voice. **2** expressing opinions or feelings freely or loudly. **3** (of music) consisting of or incorporating singing. ● noun **1** (also **vocals**) a musical performance involving singing. **2** a part of a piece of music that is sung.
– DERIVATIVES **vocally** adverb.
– ORIGIN Latin *vocalis*, from *vox* 'voice'.
vocal cords (also **vocal folds**) ● plural noun folds of the lining of the larynx whose edges vibrate in the airstream to produce the voice.
vocalese /vōkəleez/ ● noun a style of singing in which singers put words to jazz tunes or solos.
vocalic /vəkalik/ ● adjective Phonetics relating to or consisting of a vowel or vowels.
vocalise /vōkəleez/ ● noun Music **1** a singing exercise using individual syllables or vowel sounds. **2** a vocal passage consisting of a melody without words.
vocalist ● noun a singer, especially in jazz or popular music.
vocalize /vōkəlīz/ (also **vocalise**) ● verb **1** utter (a sound or word). **2** express (something) with words. **3** Music sing with several notes to one vowel.
– DERIVATIVES **vocalization** noun.
vocation ● noun **1** a strong feeling of suitability for a particular career or occupation. **2** a person's employment or main occupation, especially one requiring dedication. **3** a trade or profession.
– ORIGIN Latin, from *vocare* 'to call'.
vocational ● adjective **1** relating to an occupation or employment. **2** (of education or training) directed at a particular occupation and its skills.
– DERIVATIVES **vocationally** adverb.
vocative /vokkətiv/ ● adjective Grammar (of a case) used in addressing or invoking a person or thing.
– ORIGIN Latin *vocativus*, from *vocare* 'to call'.
vociferation ● noun noisy and vehement speech or argument.
– ORIGIN from Latin *vociferari* 'exclaim'.
vociferous /vəsiffərəss/ ● adjective vehement or clamorous.
– DERIVATIVES **vociferously** adverb **vociferousness** noun.
– ORIGIN from Latin *vociferari* 'exclaim'.
vocoder /vōkōdər/ ● noun a synthesizer that produces sounds from an analysis of speech input.
– ORIGIN from VOICE + CODE.
VOD ● abbreviation video-on-demand.
vodka ● noun an alcoholic spirit of Russian origin made by distillation of rye, wheat, or potatoes.
– ORIGIN Russian, 'little water'.
vodun /vōdo͞on/ ● noun another term for VOODOO.
– ORIGIN Fon (a language of Benin), 'fetish'.
voe /vō/ ● noun a small bay or creek in Orkney or Shetland.
– ORIGIN Old Norse.
vogue ● noun the prevailing fashion or style at a particular time.
– DERIVATIVES **voguish** adjective.
– ORIGIN French, from Italian *voga* 'rowing, fashion'.
voice ● noun **1** the sound produced in a person's larynx and uttered through the mouth, as speech or song. **2** the ability to speak or sing. **3** Music the range of pitch or type of tone with which a person sings. **4** Music a vocal part in a composition. **5** an opinion or attitude, or a means or agency by which it is expressed. **6** Grammar a form of a verb showing the relation of the subject to the action. ● verb **1** express in words. **2** (**voiced**) Phonetics (of a speech sound) uttered with resonance of the vocal cords.
– ORIGIN Old French *vois*, from Latin *vox*.
voice box ● noun the larynx.

Thesaurus

bouncy, upbeat, chirpy; *dated* gay.
– OPPOSITES dull.
vivid ● adjective **1** *a vivid blue sea* BRIGHT, colourful, brilliant, radiant, vibrant, strong, bold, deep, intense, rich, warm. **2** *a vivid account of urban poverty* GRAPHIC, evocative, realistic, lifelike, faithful, authentic, clear, detailed, lucid, striking, arresting, impressive, colourful, rich, dramatic, lively, stimulating, interesting, fascinating, scintillating; memorable, powerful, stirring, moving, haunting.
– OPPOSITES dull, vague.
viz. ● adverb NAMELY, that is to say, in other words, to wit, specifically; such as, as, like, for instance, for example; *formal* videlicet.
vocabulary ● noun **1** *she has an extensive vocabulary* LEXICON, lexis. **2** *we listed the terms in a vocabulary* WORDBOOK, dictionary, wordfinder, glossary, lexicon, thesaurus.
vocal ● adjective **1** *vocal sounds* VOCALIZED, voiced, uttered, articulated, oral; spoken, said. **2** *a vocal critic of the government* VOCIFEROUS, outspoken, forthright, plain-spoken, blunt, frank, candid, open; vehement, vigorous, emphatic, insistent, forceful, zealous, clamorous.
vocation ● noun CALLING, life's work, mission, purpose, function; profession, occupation, career, job, employment, trade, craft, business, line (of work), métier.
vociferous ● adjective. See VOCAL sense 2.
vogue ● noun *the skirt is enjoying a new vogue* FASHION, trend, fad, fancy, craze, rage, enthusiasm, passion, obsession, mania; fashionableness, popularity, currency, favour; *informal* trendiness.
– PHRASES **in vogue** FASHIONABLE, voguish, stylish, modish, up to date, up to the minute, modern, current; prevalent, popular, in favour, in demand, sought-after, all the rage; chic, smart, le dernier cri; *informal* trendy, hip, cool, big, happening, now, in, with it; *N.*

voiceless ● adjective **1** lacking a voice; speechless. **2** Phonetics (of a speech sound) uttered without resonance of the vocal cords.
voicemail ● noun a centralized electronic system which can store messages from telephone callers.
voice-over ● noun a piece of narration in a film or broadcast not accompanied by an image of the speaker.
voiceprint ● noun a visual record of speech, analysed with respect to frequency, duration, and amplitude.
void ● adjective **1** not valid or legally binding. **2** completely empty. **3** (**void of**) free from; lacking. ● noun a completely empty space. ● verb **1** chiefly N. Amer. declare to be not valid or legally binding. **2** discharge or drain away (water, gases, etc.). **3** chiefly Medicine excrete (waste matter).
– DERIVATIVES **voidable** adjective.
– ORIGIN Old French *vuide*; related to Latin *vacare* 'vacate'.
voila /vwaalaa/ ● exclamation there it is; there you are.
– ORIGIN French.
voile /voyl, vwaal/ ● noun a thin, semi-transparent fabric of cotton, wool, or silk.
– ORIGIN French, 'veil'.
volatile /vollətīl/ ● adjective **1** (of a substance) easily evaporated at normal temperatures. **2** liable to change rapidly and unpredictably, especially for the worse. ● noun a volatile substance.
– DERIVATIVES **volatility** noun **volatilize** (also **volatilise**) verb.
– ORIGIN originally in the sense 'creature that flies': from Latin *volatilis*, from *volare* 'to fly'.
volatile oil ● noun another term for ESSENTIAL OIL.
vol-au-vent /volləvon/ ● noun a small round case of puff pastry filled with a savoury mixture.
– ORIGIN French, 'flight in the wind'.
volcanic ● adjective **1** relating to or produced by a volcano or volcanoes. **2** (of a feeling or emotion) bursting out or liable to burst out violently.
– DERIVATIVES **volcanically** adverb.
volcanic glass ● noun obsidian.
volcanism (also **vulcanism**) ● noun Geology volcanic activity or phenomena.
volcano ● noun (pl. **volcanoes** or **volcanos**) a mountain or hill having a crater or vent through which lava, rock fragments, hot vapour, and gas are or have been erupted from the earth's crust.
– ORIGIN from Latin *Volcanus* 'Vulcan', the Roman god of fire.
volcanology /volkənolləji/ ● noun the scientific study of volcanoes.
– DERIVATIVES **volcanologist** noun.
vole ● noun a small mouse-like rodent with a rounded muzzle.
– ORIGIN from Norwegian *vollmus* 'field mouse'.
volition /vəlish'n/ ● noun (often in phrase **of one's own volition**) the faculty or power of using one's will.
– DERIVATIVES **volitional** adjective.
– ORIGIN Latin, from *volo* 'I wish'.
volley ● noun (pl. **volleys**) **1** a number of bullets, arrows, or other projectiles discharged at one time. **2** a series of utterances directed at someone in quick succession. **3** (in sport) a strike or kick of the ball made before it touches the ground. ● verb (**volleys**, **volleyed**) **1** strike or kick (the ball) before it touches the ground. **2** utter or discharge in quick succession.
– DERIVATIVES **volleyer** noun.
– ORIGIN French *volée*, from Latin *volare* 'to fly'.
volleyball ● noun a game for two teams in which a ball is hit by hand over a net and points are scored if the ball touches the ground on the opponent's side of the court.
volt ● noun the unit of electromotive force in the SI system, the difference of potential that would carry one ampere of current against a resistance of one ohm.
– ORIGIN named after the Italian physicist Alessandro *Volta* (1745–1827).
voltage ● noun an electromotive force or potential difference expressed in volts.
voltaic /voltayik/ ● adjective referring to electricity produced by chemical action in a primary battery; galvanic.
volte-face /voltfass/ ● noun **1** an act of turning round so as to face in the opposite direction. **2** an abrupt and complete reversal of attitude, opinion, or position.
– ORIGIN French, from Latin *volvere* 'to roll' + *facies* 'appearance, face'.
voltmeter ● noun an instrument for measuring electric potential in volts.
voluble /volyoob'l/ ● adjective speaking or spoken incessantly and fluently.
– DERIVATIVES **volubility** noun **volubly** adverb.
– ORIGIN originally in senses 'rotating about an axis' and 'tending to change': from Latin *volvere* 'to roll'.
volume ● noun **1** a book forming part of a work or series. **2** a single book or a bound collection of printed sheets. **3** a consecutive sequence of issues of a periodical. **4** the amount of space occupied by a substance or object or enclosed within a container. **5** the amount or quantity of something. **6** quantity or power of sound; degree of loudness. **7** fullness or expansive thickness of the hair.
– ORIGIN originally denoting a roll of parchment containing written matter: from Latin *volumen* 'a roll'.
volumetric /volyoometrik/ ● adjective relating to the measurement of volume.
– DERIVATIVES **volumetrically** adverb.
voluminous /vəlyoominəss/ ● adjective **1** (of clothing or drapery) loose and ample. **2** (of writing) very lengthy and full.
– DERIVATIVES **voluminously** adverb.
– ORIGIN partly from Latin *voluminosus* 'having many coils', partly from Latin *volumen* 'a roll'.

Thesaurus

Amer. informal tony, kicky.
voice ● noun **1** *she lost her voice* POWER OF SPEECH. **2** *he gave voice to his anger* EXPRESSION, utterance, verbalization, vocalization. **3** *the voice of the people* OPINION, view, feeling, wish, desire, vote, input. **4** *a powerful voice for conservation* MOUTHPIECE, representative, spokesperson, intermediary; forum, vehicle, instrument, channel, organ, agent.
● verb *they voiced their opposition* EXPRESS, vocalize, communicate, declare, state, assert, reveal, proclaim, announce, table, air, ventilate, vent; utter, say, speak, articulate; informal come out with.
void ● noun *the void of space* VACUUM, emptiness, nothingness, blankness, vacuity; (empty) space, gap, cavity, chasm, abyss, gulf, pit.
V
● verb **1** *the contract was voided* INVALIDATE, annul, nullify; negate, quash, cancel, countermand, repeal, revoke, rescind, retract, withdraw, reverse, undo, abolish; Law vacate; formal abrogate. **2** *they voided their bladders* EVACUATE, empty, drain, clear, purge. **3** *bacteria are voided in the urine* EJECT, expel, emit, discharge, pass, excrete, exude, eliminate.
– OPPOSITES validate, fill.
● adjective **1** *vast void spaces* EMPTY, vacant, blank, bare, clear, free, unfilled, unoccupied, uninhabited. **2** *a country void of man or beast* DEVOID OF, empty of, vacant of, bereft of, free from; lacking, wanting, without. **3** *the election was void* INVALID, null, ineffective, non-viable, useless, worthless, nugatory.
– OPPOSITES full, occupied, valid.
volatile ● adjective **1** *a volatile personality* UNPREDICTABLE, changeable, variable, inconstant, inconsistent, erratic, irregular, unstable, turbulent, blowing hot and cold, varying, shifting, fluctuating, fluid, mutable; mercurial, capricious, whimsical, fickle, flighty, impulsive, temperamental, highly strung, excitable, emotional, fiery, moody, tempestuous. **2** *the atmosphere is too volatile for an election* TENSE, strained, fraught, uneasy, uncomfortable, charged, explosive, inflammatory, turbulent; informal nail-biting; Brit. informal dodgy. **3** *a volatile organic compound* EVAPORATIVE, vaporous; explosive, inflammable; unstable, labile.
– OPPOSITES stable, calm.
volition ● noun
– PHRASES **of one's own volition** OF ONE'S OWN FREE WILL, of one's own accord, by choice, by preference; voluntarily, willingly, readily, freely, intentionally, consciously, deliberately, on purpose, purposely; gladly, with pleasure.
volley ● noun BARRAGE, cannonade, battery, bombardment, salvo, fusillade; storm, hail, shower, deluge, torrent; historical broadside.
voluble ● adjective TALKATIVE, loquacious, garrulous, verbose, wordy, chatty, gossipy, effusive, gushing, forthcoming, conversational, communicative, expansive; articulate, fluent; informal mouthy, gabby, gassy, windy.
– OPPOSITES taciturn.
volume ● noun **1** *a volume from the library* BOOK, publication, tome, hardback, paperback, title; manual, almanac, compendium. **2** *a glass syringe of known volume* CAPACITY, cubic measure, size, magnitude, mass, bulk, extent; dimensions, proportions, measurements. **3** *a huge volume of water* QUANTITY, amount, proportion,

volumize (also **volumise**) ● verb give volume or body to (hair).
voluntarism ● noun the principle of relying on voluntary action.
– DERIVATIVES **voluntarist** noun & adjective.
voluntary ● adjective **1** done, given, or acting of one's own free will. **2** working or done without payment. **3** Physiology under the conscious control of the brain. ● noun (pl. **voluntaries**) an organ solo played before, during, or after a church service.
– DERIVATIVES **voluntarily** adverb.
– ORIGIN Latin *voluntarius*, from *voluntas* 'will'.
voluntary-aided ● adjective (in the UK) referring to a voluntary school funded mainly by the local authority.
voluntary-controlled ● adjective (in the UK) denoting a voluntary school fully funded by the local authority.
voluntary school ● noun (in the UK) a school which, though not established by the local education authority, is funded mainly or entirely by it, and which typically encourages a particular set of religious beliefs.
voluntary simplicity ● noun a philosophy or way of life that rejects materialism, characterized by minimal consumption and environmental responsibility.
volunteer ● noun **1** a person who freely offers to do something. **2** a person who works for an organization without being paid. **3** a person who freely enrols for military service rather than being conscripted. ● verb **1** freely offer to do something. **2** say or suggest something without being asked. **3** freely enrol for military service rather than being conscripted. **4** commit (someone) to an undertaking.
– ORIGIN from French *volontaire* 'voluntary'.
volunteerism ● noun chiefly N. Amer. the use or involvement of volunteer labour, especially in community services.
voluptuary /vəluptyoori/ ● noun (pl. **voluptuaries**) a person devoted to luxury and sensual pleasure. ● adjective concerned with luxury and sensual pleasure.
– ORIGIN Latin *voluptuarius*, from *voluptas* 'pleasure'.
voluptuous /vəluptyooəss/ ● adjective **1** relating to or characterized by luxury or sensual pleasure. **2** (of a woman) curvaceous and sexually attractive.
– DERIVATIVES **voluptuously** adverb **voluptuousness** noun.
– ORIGIN Latin *voluptuosus*, from *voluptas* 'pleasure'.
volute /vəlyo͞ot/ ● noun Architecture a spiral scroll characteristic of Ionic capitals and also used in Corinthian and composite capitals.
– DERIVATIVES **voluted** adjective.
– ORIGIN Latin *voluta*, from *volvere* 'to roll'.
vomer /vōmər/ ● noun Anatomy the small thin bone separating the left and right nasal cavities in humans and most vertebrates.
– ORIGIN Latin, 'ploughshare' (because of the shape).
vomit ● verb (**vomited**, **vomiting**) **1** eject matter from the stomach through the mouth. **2** emit in an uncontrolled stream or flow. ● noun matter vomited from the stomach.
– ORIGIN Latin *vomere* 'to vomit'.
vomitous ● adjective chiefly N. Amer. nauseating.
voodoo ● noun a black religious cult practised in the Caribbean and the southern US, combining elements of Roman Catholic ritual with traditional African rites, and characterized by sorcery and spirit possession.
– DERIVATIVES **voodooism** noun **voodooist** noun.
– ORIGIN from Kwa (a Niger-Congo language).
voracious /vərayshəss/ ● adjective **1** wanting or devouring great quantities of food. **2** eagerly consuming something: *his voracious reading of literature.*
– DERIVATIVES **voraciously** adverb **voracity** noun.
– ORIGIN from Latin *vorax*, from *vorare* 'devour'.
-vorous /vərəss/ ● combining form feeding on a specified food: *carnivorous.*
– DERIVATIVES **-vore** combining form.
– ORIGIN Latin *-vorus*, from *vorare* 'devour'.
vortex /vorteks/ ● noun (pl. **vortexes** or **vortices** /vortiseez/) a whirling mass, especially a whirlpool or whirlwind.
– DERIVATIVES **vortical** adjective **vorticity** noun.
– ORIGIN Latin, 'eddy'.
Vorticism /vortisiz'm/ ● noun a British artistic movement of 1914–15 influenced by cubism and Futurism.
– DERIVATIVES **Vorticist** noun & adjective.
votary /vōtəri/ ● noun (pl. **votaries**) **1** a person who has made vows of dedication to religious service. **2** a devoted follower, adherent, or advocate.
– ORIGIN from Latin *vovere* 'vow'.
vote ● noun **1** a formal indication of a choice between two or more candidates or courses of action. **2** (**the vote**) the right to participate in an election. **3** (**the vote**) a particular body of electors or the votes cast by them: *the green vote.* ● verb **1** give or register a vote. **2** grant or confer by vote. **3** informal express a wish or suggestion.
– PHRASES **vote of (no) confidence** a vote showing that a majority continues to support (or no longer supports) the policy of a leader or governing body. **vote with one's feet** informal indicate an opinion by being present or absent or by some other course of action.
– DERIVATIVES **voter** noun.
– ORIGIN Latin *votum* 'a vow, wish', from *vovere* 'to vow'.
votive ● adjective offered or consecrated in fulfilment of a vow.
– ORIGIN Latin *votivus*, from *votum* 'a vow, wish'.
vouch ● verb (**vouch for**) **1** assert or confirm the truth or accuracy of. **2** confirm the identity or good character of.
– ORIGIN Old French *voucher* 'summon', from Latin *vocare* 'to call'.
voucher ● noun **1** a piece of paper that entitles the holder to a discount, or that may be exchanged for goods or services. **2** a receipt.

Thesaurus

measure, mass, bulk. **4** *she turned the volume down* LOUDNESS, sound, amplification.
voluminous ● adjective CAPACIOUS, roomy, spacious, ample, full, big, large, generous; billowing, baggy, loose-fitting; *formal* commodious.
voluntarily ● adverb OF ONE'S OWN FREE WILL, of one's own accord, of one's own volition, by choice, by preference; willingly, readily, freely, intentionally, deliberately, on purpose, purposely, spontaneously; gladly, with pleasure.
voluntary ● adjective **1** *attendance is voluntary* OPTIONAL, discretionary, elective, non-compulsory, volitional; *Law* permissive. **2** *voluntary work* UNPAID, unsalaried, for free, without charge, for nothing; honorary, volunteer; *Law* pro bono (publico).
– OPPOSITES compulsory, paid.
volunteer ● verb **1** *I volunteered my services* OFFER, tender, proffer, put forward, put up, venture. **2** *he volunteered as a driver* OFFER ONE'S SERVICES, present oneself, make oneself available.
● noun *each volunteer was tested three times* SUBJECT, participant, case, client, patient; *informal* guinea pig.
voluptuous ● adjective **1** *a voluptuous model* CURVACEOUS, shapely, ample, buxom, full-figured, Junoesque, Rubenesque; seductive, alluring, sultry, sensuous, sexy; *informal* curvy, busty, slinky. **2** *she was voluptuous by nature* HEDONISTIC, sybaritic, epicurean, pleasure-loving, self-indulgent; decadent, intemperate, immoderate, dissolute, sensual, licentious.
– OPPOSITES scrawny, ascetic.
vomit ● verb **1** *he needed to vomit* BE SICK, throw up, spew, fetch up; heave, retch, reach, gag; *N. Amer.* get sick; *informal* puke, chunder, chuck up, hurl; *Brit. informal* honk; *Scottish informal* boke; *N. Amer. informal* barf, upchuck. **2** *I vomited my breakfast* REGURGITATE, bring up, spew up, cough up; *informal* chuck up, throw up, puke; *Brit. informal* sick up; *N. Amer. informal* spit up. **3** *the printer is vomiting paper* EJECT, issue, emit, expel, discharge, disgorge, throw out, spew out, belch.
● noun *a coat stained with vomit* SICK; *informal* chunder, puke, spew; *N. Amer. informal* barf; *Medicine* vomitus.
voracious ● adjective INSATIABLE, unquenchable, unappeasable, prodigious, uncontrollable, compulsive, gluttonous, greedy, rapacious; enthusiastic, eager, keen, avid, desirous, hungry, ravenous; *informal* piggish.
vortex ● noun WHIRLWIND, whirlpool, gyre, maelstrom, eddy, swirl.
vote ● noun **1** *a rigged vote* BALLOT, poll, election, referendum, plebiscite; show of hands. **2** *in 1918 women got the vote* SUFFRAGE, voting rights, franchise, enfranchisement; voice, say.
● verb **1** *only half of them voted* GO TO THE POLLS, cast one's vote. **2** *I vote we have one more game* SUGGEST, propose, recommend, advocate, move, table, submit.
– PHRASES **vote someone in** ELECT, return, select, choose, pick, adopt, appoint, designate, opt for, plump for, decide on.
vouch ● verb
– PHRASES **vouch for** ATTEST TO, confirm, affirm, verify, swear to, testify to, bear out, back up, support, stick up for, corroborate,

vouchsafe ● verb give, grant, or disclose in a gracious or condescending manner.
– ORIGIN originally as the phrase *vouch* something *safe* on someone, i.e. 'warrant the secure conferment of'.
vow ● noun a solemn promise. ● verb solemnly promise to do something.
– ORIGIN Old French *vou*, from Latin *votum* 'a wish, vow'.
vowel ● noun **1** a speech sound in which the mouth is open and the tongue is not touching the top of the mouth, the teeth, or the lips. **2** a letter representing such a sound, such as *a, e, i, o, u*.
– ORIGIN Old French *vouel*, from Latin *vocalis littera* 'vocal letter'.
vox pop ● noun Brit. informal popular opinion as represented by informal comments from members of the public.
– ORIGIN abbreviation of VOX POPULI.
vox populi /voks **pop**yoolee/ ● noun the opinions or beliefs of the majority.
– ORIGIN Latin, 'the people's voice'.
voyage ● noun a long journey involving travel by sea or in space. ● verb go on a voyage.
– DERIVATIVES **voyager** noun.
– ORIGIN Old French *voiage*, from Latin *viaticum* 'provisions for a journey', later 'journey'.
voyeur /vwaayör, voy-/ ● noun **1** a person who gains sexual pleasure from watching others when they are naked or engaged in sexual activity. **2** a person who enjoys seeing the pain or distress of others.
– DERIVATIVES **voyeurism** noun **voyeuristic** adjective **voyeuristically** adverb.
– ORIGIN French, from *voir* 'see'.
VP ● abbreviation Vice-President.
VR ● abbreviation virtual reality.
VRML ● abbreviation Computing virtual reality modelling language.
vs ● abbreviation versus.
V-sign ● noun **1** Brit. a sign resembling the letter V made with the first two fingers pointing up and the back of the hand facing outwards, used as a gesture of abuse or contempt. **2** a similar sign made with the palm of the hand facing outwards, used as a symbol or gesture of victory.
VSO ● abbreviation Voluntary Service Overseas.
VSOP ● abbreviation Very Special Old Pale, a kind of brandy.
VT ● abbreviation Vermont.
VTOL ● abbreviation vertical take-off and landing.
vulcanism ● noun variant spelling of VOLCANISM.
vulcanite /vulkənīt/ ● noun hard black vulcanized rubber.
– ORIGIN from *Vulcan*, the Roman god of fire.
vulcanize /vulkənīz/ (also **vulcanise**) ● verb harden (rubber or rubber-like material) by treating it with sulphur at a high temperature.
– DERIVATIVES **vulcanization** noun.
vulcanology ● noun variant spelling of VOLCANOLOGY.
vulgar ● adjective **1** lacking sophistication or good taste. **2** making explicit and inappropriate reference to sex or bodily functions. **3** dated characteristic of or belonging to ordinary people.
– DERIVATIVES **vulgarity** noun (pl. **vulgarities**) **vulgarly** adverb.
– ORIGIN Latin *vulgaris*, from *vulgus* 'common people'.
vulgar fraction ● noun Brit. a fraction expressed by numerator and denominator, not decimally.
vulgarian /vulgairiən/ ● noun an unrefined person, especially one with newly acquired power or wealth.
vulgarism ● noun **1** a vulgar word or expression. **2** archaic an instance of rude or offensive behaviour.
vulgarize (also **vulgarise**) ● verb **1** make less refined. **2** make commonplace or less subtle or complex.
– DERIVATIVES **vulgarization** noun.
vulgar Latin ● noun informal Latin of classical times.
vulgar tongue ● noun the national or vernacular language of a people (especially as contrasted with Latin).
Vulgate /vulgayt/ ● noun the principal Latin version of the Bible, prepared in the 4th century and later revised and adopted as the official text for the Roman Catholic Church.
– ORIGIN from Latin *vulgata editio* 'edition prepared for the public'.
vulnerable ● adjective exposed to being attacked or harmed.
– DERIVATIVES **vulnerability** noun (pl. **vulnerabilities**) **vulnerably** adverb.
– ORIGIN Latin *vulnerabilis*, from *vulnerare* 'to wound'.
vulpine /vulpīn/ ● adjective relating to or reminiscent of a fox or foxes.
– ORIGIN Latin *vulpinus*, from *vulpes* 'fox'.
vulture /vulchər/ ● noun **1** a large bird of prey feeding chiefly on carrion, with the head and neck more or less bare of feathers. **2** a contemptible person who preys on or exploits others.
– ORIGIN Latin *vulturius*.
vulva /vulvə/ ● noun the female external genitals.
– DERIVATIVES **vulval** adjective.
– ORIGIN Latin, 'womb'.
vying present participle of VIE.

Thesaurus

substantiate, prove, uphold, give credence to, endorse, certify, warrant, validate.
voucher ● noun COUPON, token, ticket, licence, permit, carnet, pass; chit, slip, stub, docket; *Brit. informal* chitty; *N. Amer. informal* ducat, comp.
vouchsafe ● verb **1** *the grace which God had vouchsafed him* GRANT, give, accord; confer on, bestow on, favour with. **2** *you never vouchsafed that information before* DISCLOSE, reveal, divulge, impart, give away, make known, broadcast, air; *informal* blab, spill; *Brit. informal* cough. **3** *if he would only vouchsafe to talk with them* DEIGN, condescend, stoop, lower oneself, humble oneself, demean oneself.
– OPPOSITES withhold, conceal.
vow ● noun *a vow of silence* OATH, pledge, promise, bond, covenant, commitment, avowal, profession, affirmation, attestation, assurance, guarantee; word (of honour); *formal* troth.
– RELATED TERMS votive.
● verb *I vowed to do better* SWEAR, pledge, promise, avow, undertake, engage, make a commitment, give one's word, guarantee; *archaic* plight.
voyage ● noun *the voyage lasted 120 days* JOURNEY, trip, expedition, excursion, tour; hike, trek; pilgrimage, quest, crusade, odyssey; cruise, passage, flight, drive.
● verb *he voyaged through Peru* TRAVEL, journey, tour, globetrot; sail, steam, cruise, fly, drive; *informal* gallivant; *archaic* peregrinate.
vulgar ● adjective **1** *a vulgar joke* RUDE, indecent, indelicate, offensive, distasteful, coarse, crude, ribald, risqué, naughty, suggestive, racy, earthy, off colour, bawdy, obscene, lewd, salacious, smutty, dirty, filthy, pornographic, X-rated; *informal* sleazy, raunchy, blue, locker-room; *Brit. informal* saucy, close to the bone; *N. Amer. informal* gamy; *euphemistic* adult. **2** *the decor was lavish but vulgar* TASTELESS, crass, tawdry, ostentatious, flamboyant, overdone, showy, gaudy, garish, brassy, kitsch, tinselly, loud; *informal* flash, flashy, tacky, over the top. **3** *it was vulgar for a woman to whistle* IMPOLITE, ill-mannered, unmannerly, indecorous, unseemly, ill-bred, boorish, uncouth, crude, rough; unsophisticated, unrefined, common.
– OPPOSITES tasteful, decorous.
vulnerable ● adjective **1** *a vulnerable city* IN DANGER, in peril, in jeopardy, at risk, endangered, unsafe, unprotected, unguarded; open to attack, assailable, exposed, wide open; undefended, unfortified, unarmed, defenceless, helpless, pregnable. **2** *he is vulnerable to criticism* EXPOSED TO, open to, liable to, prone to, prey to, susceptible to, subject to, an easy target for; *archaic* susceptive of.
– OPPOSITES resilient.

Ww

W[1] (also **w**) ● noun (pl. **Ws** or **W's**) the twenty-third letter of the alphabet.
W[2] ● abbreviation **1** (in tables of sports results) games won. **2** watt(s). **3** West or Western. **4** Cricket (on scorecards) wicket(s). ● symbol the chemical element tungsten. [ORIGIN from Latin *wolframium*.]
w ● abbreviation **1** Cricket (on scorecards) wide(s). **2** with.
WA ● abbreviation **1** Washington (State). **2** Western Australia.
Waaf /waf/ ● noun historical (in the UK) a member of the Women's Auxiliary Air Force (1939–48).
wacko (also **whacko**) informal, chiefly N. Amer. ● adjective mad; insane. ● noun (pl. **wackos** or **wackoes**) a crazy person.
wacky (also **whacky**) ● adjective (**wackier**, **wackiest**) informal funny or amusing in a slightly odd way.
– DERIVATIVES **wackily** adverb **wackiness** noun.
– ORIGIN from WHACK.
wad /wod/ ● noun **1** a lump or bundle of a soft material, as used for padding, stuffing, or wiping. **2** a bundle of paper, banknotes, or documents. **3** informal a large amount of something, especially money. **4** chiefly historical a disc of felt or another material used to keep powder or shot in place in a gun barrel. ● verb (**wadded**, **wadding**) **1** compress (a soft material) into a wad. **2** line, stuff, or stop with soft material.
– DERIVATIVES **wadding** noun.
– ORIGIN perhaps related to Dutch *watten*, French *ouate* 'padding, cotton wool'.
waddle ● verb walk with short steps and a clumsy swaying motion. ● noun a waddling gait.
– ORIGIN perhaps related to WADE.
waddy /woddi/ ● noun (pl. **waddies**) **1** an Australian Aboriginal's war club. **2** Austral./NZ a club or stick, especially a walking stick.
– ORIGIN Dharuk (an Aboriginal language).
wade ● verb **1** walk through water or mud. **2** (**wade through**) read laboriously through (a long piece of writing). **3** (**wade in/into**) informal attack or intervene in a vigorous or forceful way. ● noun an act of wading.
– ORIGIN Old English, 'move onward', also 'penetrate'.
Wade–Giles /wayd jīlz/ ● noun a system of romanized spelling for transliterating Chinese, largely superseded by Pinyin.
– ORIGIN named after Sir T. F. *Wade* (1818–95) and H. A. *Giles* (1845–1935), professors of Chinese at Cambridge, who devised it.
wader ● noun **1** a sandpiper, plover, or other wading bird. **2** (**waders**) high waterproof boots, used by anglers.
wadi /waadi, woddi/ ● noun (pl. **wadis**) (in Arabic-speaking countries) a valley, ravine, or channel that is dry except in the rainy season.
– ORIGIN Arabic.
wafer ● noun **1** a very thin light, crisp sweet biscuit. **2** a thin disc of unleavened bread used in the Eucharist. **3** a disc of red paper stuck on a legal document as a seal. **4** Electronics a very thin slice of a semiconductor crystal used in solid-state circuitry.
– ORIGIN Old French *gaufre* 'honeycomb'; related to WAFFLE[2].
wafer-thin ● adjective very thin or thinly.
Waffen SS /vaff'n/ ● noun the combat units of the SS in Nazi Germany.
– ORIGIN German *Waffen* 'armed'.
waffle[1] informal ● verb speak or write at length in a vague or trivial manner. ● noun lengthy but vague or trivial talk or writing.
– DERIVATIVES **waffler** noun **waffly** adjective.
– ORIGIN from dialect *waff* 'yelp', of imitative origin.
waffle[2] ● noun a small crisp batter cake, baked in a waffle iron and eaten hot with butter or syrup.
– ORIGIN Dutch *wafel*; related to WAFER and GOFFER.
waffle iron ● noun a utensil for baking waffles, consisting of two shallow metal pans hinged together.
waft /woft, waaft/ ● verb pass easily or gently through the air. ● noun **1** a gentle movement of air. **2** a scent carried in the air.
– ORIGIN originally in the sense 'escort (a ship)', later 'convey by water': from Low German, Dutch *wachten* 'to guard'.
wag[1] ● verb (**wagged**, **wagging**) move rapidly to and fro. ● noun a wagging movement.
– ORIGIN Old English, 'to sway'.
wag[2] ● noun informal **1** a person fond of making jokes. **2** Austral./NZ informal a truant.
– ORIGIN originally denoting a young man or mischievous boy: probably from obsolete *waghalter* 'person likely to be hanged'.
wage ● noun (also **wages**) **1** a fixed regular payment for work, typically paid on a daily or weekly basis. **2** the result or effect of doing something wrong or unwise: *the wages of sin.* ● verb carry on (a war or campaign).
– DERIVATIVES **waged** adjective.
– ORIGIN Old French, related to GAGE[1] and WED.
wager ● noun & verb more formal term for BET.
– ORIGIN originally also in the sense 'solemn pledge': from Old French, 'to wage'.
waggish ● adjective informal humorous, playful, or facetious.
– DERIVATIVES **waggishly** adverb.
waggle ● verb move with short quick movements from side to side or up and down. ● noun an act of waggling.
– DERIVATIVES **waggler** noun **waggly** adjective.

Thesaurus

wacky ● adjective *(informal)*. See ECCENTRIC adjective.
wad ● noun **1** *a wad of cotton wool* LUMP, clump, mass, plug, pad, hunk, wedge, ball, cake, nugget; bit, piece; *Brit. informal* wodge. **2** *a wad of dollar bills* BUNDLE, roll, pile, stack, sheaf; *N. Amer.* bankroll. **3** *a wad of tobacco* QUID, twist, plug, chew.
● verb *the teddy bear was wadded with cotton* STUFF, pad, fill, pack; wrap, cover, cushion.
wadding ● noun STUFFING, filling, filler, packing, padding, cushioning, quilting.
waddle ● verb TODDLE, dodder, totter, wobble, shuffle; duckwalk.
wade ● verb **1** *they waded in the icy water* PADDLE, wallow, dabble, squelch; *informal* splosh. **2** *I had to wade through some hefty documents* PLOUGH, plod, trawl, labour, toil; study, browse; *informal* slog.
– PHRASES **wade in** *(informal)* SET TO WORK, buckle down, go to it, put one's shoulder to the wheel; *informal* plunge in, dive in, get stuck in, get cracking.
waffle *(Brit. informal)* ● verb *they waffled on about the baby* PRATTLE, chatter, babble, ramble, jabber, gibber, gabble, prate, drivel; *informal* blather; *Brit. informal* rabbit, witter, natter.
● noun *my panic reduced the interview to waffle* PRATTLE, drivel, nonsense, twaddle, gibberish, mumbo-jumbo; *informal* hot air, poppycock, bunk, hogwash, gobbledegook.
waft ● verb **1** *smoke wafted through the air* DRIFT, float, glide, whirl, travel. **2** *a breeze wafted the smell towards us* CONVEY, carry, transport, bear; blow, puff.
wag[1] ● verb **1** *the dog's tail wagged frantically* SWING, swish, waggle, switch, sway, shake, quiver, twitch, whip. **2** *he wagged his stick at them* SHAKE, wave, wiggle, flourish, brandish.
● noun **1** *a feeble wag of her tail* SWING, shake, swish, waggle, switch, quiver, twitch, whip. **2** *a wag of the finger* SHAKE, flourish, wiggle, waggle, wobble, wave.
wag[2] ● noun *(informal) he's a bit of a wag.* See JOKER.
wage ● noun **1** *the farm workers' wages* PAY, payment, remuneration, salary, stipend, fee, honorarium; income, revenue; profit, gain, reward; earnings; *formal* emolument. **2** *the wages of sin is death* REWARD, recompense, retribution; returns, deserts.
● verb *they waged war on the guerrillas* ENGAGE IN, carry on, conduct, execute, pursue, prosecute, proceed with.
wager ● noun *a wager of £100* BET, gamble, speculation; stake, pledge, ante; *Brit. informal* flutter.

– ORIGIN from WAG[1].
Wagnerian /vaagneeriən/ ● **adjective** relating to the German composer Richard Wagner (1813–83).
wagon (Brit. also **waggon**) ● **noun** **1** a vehicle, especially a horse-drawn one, for transporting goods. **2** Brit. a railway freight vehicle; a truck. **3** chiefly N. Amer. a wheeled cart or hut used as a food stall.
– PHRASES **on the wagon** informal teetotal.
– DERIVATIVES **wagonload** noun.
– ORIGIN Dutch *wagen*; related to WAIN.
wagoner (Brit. also **waggoner**) ● **noun** the driver of a horse-drawn wagon.
wagon-lit /vaggonlee/ ● **noun** (pl. **wagons-lits** pronunc. same) a sleeping car on a train in continental Europe.
– ORIGIN French, from *wagon* 'railway coach' + *lit* 'bed'.
wagon train ● **noun** historical a convoy of covered horse-drawn wagons, as used by pioneers or settlers in North America.
wagtail ● **noun** a slender songbird with a long tail that is frequently wagged up and down.
Wahhabi /wəhaabi/ (also **Wahabi**) ● **noun** (pl. **Wahabis**) a member of a strictly orthodox Sunni Muslim sect, the predominant religious force in Saudi Arabia.
– DERIVATIVES **Wahhabism** noun.
– ORIGIN named after the founder, Muhammad ibn Abd al-*Wahhab* (1703–92).
wah-wah ● **noun** a musical effect achieved on brass instruments by alternately applying and removing a mute and on an electric guitar by use of a pedal.
– ORIGIN imitative.
waif ● **noun** a homeless and helpless person, especially a neglected or abandoned child.
– DERIVATIVES **waifish** adjective.
– ORIGIN originally in *waif and stray*, denoting a piece of property found and, if unclaimed, falling to the lord of the manor: from Old French *gaif*.
wail ● **noun** **1** a prolonged high-pitched cry of pain, grief, or anger. **2** a sound resembling this. ● **verb** give or utter a wail.
– DERIVATIVES **wailer** noun.
– ORIGIN Old Norse, related to WOE.
wain ● **noun** archaic a wagon or cart.
– ORIGIN Old English, related to WAY and WEIGH.
wainscot /waynzkət/ ● **noun** an area of wooden panelling on the lower part of the walls of a room. ● **verb** (**wainscoted**, **wainscoting** or **wainscotted**, **wainscotting**) line (a room or wall) with wooden panelling.
– DERIVATIVES **wainscoting** (also **wainscotting**) noun.
– ORIGIN Low German *wagenschot*, apparently from *wagen* 'wagon' + *schot*, probably meaning 'partition'.
wainwright ● **noun** historical a wagon-builder.
waist ● **noun** **1** the part of the human body below the ribs and above the hips. **2** a narrow part in the middle of something such as a violin or hourglass.
– DERIVATIVES **waisted** adjective.
– ORIGIN probably from an Old English word related to WAX[2].
waistband ● **noun** a strip of cloth encircling the waist, attached to a skirt or a pair of trousers.
waistcoat /waystkōt, weskit/ ● **noun** Brit. a close-fitting waist-length garment with no sleeves or collar and buttoning down the front.
waistline ● **noun** **1** the measurement around a person's body at the waist. **2** the part of a garment that is shaped or constructed to fit at or near the waist.
wait ● **verb** **1** stay where one is or delay action until a particular time or event. **2** be delayed or deferred. **3** (**wait on/upon**) act as an attendant to. **4** act as a waiter or waitress. ● **noun** **1** a period of waiting. **2** (**waits**) Brit. archaic street singers of Christmas carols.
– PHRASES **in wait** watching for someone and preparing to attack them.
– ORIGIN Old French *waitier*; related to WAKE[1].
waiter ● **noun** a man whose job is to serve customers at their tables in a restaurant.
waiting list (N. Amer. **wait list**) ● **noun** a list of people waiting for something not immediately available.
waiting room ● **noun** a room for people waiting to see a medical practitioner or to catch a bus or train.
waitress ● **noun** a woman whose job is to serve customers at their tables in a restaurant.
– DERIVATIVES **waitressing** noun.
waive ● **verb** refrain from insisting on or applying (a right or claim).
– ORIGIN Old French *gaiver* 'allow to become a waif, abandon'.
waiver ● **noun** **1** an act or instance of waiving a right or claim. **2** a document recording this.
wake[1] ● **verb** (past **woke** or US, dialect, or archaic **waked**; past part. **woken** or US, dialect, or archaic **waked**) **1** (often **wake up**) emerge or cause to emerge from sleep. **2** cause to stir or come to life. **3** (**wake up to**) become alert to or aware of. ● **noun** **1** a watch or vigil held beside the body of someone who has died. **2** (especially in Ireland) a party held after a funeral. **3** (**wakes**) (treated as sing.) an annual festival and holiday in some parts of northern England.
– ORIGIN Old English, related to WATCH; sense 3 of the noun is probably from Old Norse.
wake[2] ● **noun** a trail of disturbed water or air left by the passage of a ship or aircraft.
– PHRASES **in the wake of** following as a consequence or result.
– ORIGIN probably from an Old Norse word meaning 'hole or opening in ice' (as made by a ship).
wakeful ● **adjective** **1** unable or not needing to sleep. **2** alert and vigilant.
– DERIVATIVES **wakefulness** noun.

Thesaurus

● **verb** *I'll wager a pound on the home team* BET, gamble, lay odds, put money on; stake, pledge, risk, venture, hazard, chance; *informal* punt.
waggle ● **verb.** See WAG[1] verb senses 1, 2.
waif ● **noun** RAGAMUFFIN, urchin; foundling, orphan, stray; *derogatory* guttersnipe; *dated* gamin.
wail ● **noun** *a wail of anguish* HOWL, bawl, yowl, cry, moan, groan; shriek, scream, yelp.
● **verb** *the children began to wail* HOWL, weep, cry, sob, moan, groan, keen, lament, yowl, snivel, whimper, whine, bawl, shriek, scream, yelp, caterwaul; *Scottish* greet; *informal* blubber, blub.
wait ● **verb** **1** *we'll wait in the airport* STAY (PUT), remain, rest, stop, halt, pause; linger, loiter, dally; *informal* stick around; *archaic* tarry. **2** *she had to wait until her bags arrived* STAND BY, hold back, bide one's time, hang fire, mark time, kill time, waste time, kick one's heels, twiddle one's thumbs; *informal* hold on, hang around, sit tight, hold one's horses. **3** *they were waiting for the kettle to boil* AWAIT; anticipate, expect, be ready. **4** *that job will have to wait* BE POSTPONED, be delayed, be put off, be deferred; *informal* be put on the back burner, be put on ice.
● **noun** *a long wait* DELAY, hold-up, interval, interlude, intermission, pause, break, stay, cessation, suspension, stoppage, halt, interruption, lull, respite, recess, moratorium, hiatus, gap, rest.
– PHRASES **wait on someone** SERVE, attend to, tend, cater for/to; minister to, take care of, look after, see to. **wait up** STAY AWAKE, stay up.
waiter, waitress ● **noun** SERVER, stewardess, steward, attendant, garçon; hostess, host; butler, servant, page; *N. Amer.* waitperson.
waive ● **verb** **1** *he waived his right to a hearing* RELINQUISH, renounce, give up, abandon, surrender, yield, reject, dispense with, abdicate, sacrifice, refuse, turn down, spurn. **2** *the manager waived the rules* DISREGARD, ignore, overlook, set aside, forgo, drop.
wake[1] ● **verb** **1** *at 4.30 am Mark woke up* AWAKE, waken (up), awaken, rouse oneself, stir, come to, come round, bestir oneself; get up, get out of bed; *formal* arise. **2** *she woke her husband* ROUSE, arouse, waken; *Brit. informal* knock up. **3** *a shock might wake him up a bit* ACTIVATE, stimulate, galvanize, enliven, stir up, spur on, ginger up, buoy up, invigorate, revitalize; *informal* perk up, pep up. **4** *they woke up to what we were saying* REALIZE, become aware of, become conscious of, become mindful of. **5** *the name woke an old memory* EVOKE, conjure up, rouse, stir, revive, awaken, rekindle, rejuvenate, stimulate.
– OPPOSITES sleep.
● **noun** *a mourner at a wake* VIGIL, watch; funeral.
wake[2] ● **noun** *the cruiser's wake* BACKWASH, wash, slipstream, turbulence; trail, path.
– PHRASES **in the wake of** IN THE AFTERMATH OF, after, subsequent to, following, as a result of, as a consequence of, on account of, because of, owing to.
wakeful ● **adjective** **1** *he had been wakeful all night* AWAKE, restless, restive, tossing and turning; *archaic* watchful. **2** *I was sudden-*

W

waken ● verb wake from sleep.
– ORIGIN Old English, 'be aroused'; related to WAKE[1].
Waldenses /woldenseez/ ● plural noun a puritan religious sect originating in southern France.
– DERIVATIVES **Waldensian** adjective & noun.
– ORIGIN named after the founder, Peter *Valdes* (died 1205).
Waldorf salad /wawldorf/ ● noun a salad made from apples, walnuts, celery, and mayonnaise.
– ORIGIN named after the *Waldorf*-Astoria Hotel in New York, where it was first served.
wale ● noun **1** a ridge on a textured woven fabric such as corduroy. **2** Nautical a horizontal wooden strip fitted as strengthening to a boat's side.
– ORIGIN Old English, 'stripe, weal'.
walk ● verb **1** move at a regular and fairly slow pace by lifting and setting down each foot in turn. **2** travel over (a route or area) on foot. **3** guide, accompany, or escort (someone) on foot. **4** take (a dog) out for exercise. **5** N. Amer. informal be released from suspicion or from a charge. ● noun **1** a journey on foot, especially for pleasure or exercise. **2** an unhurried rate of movement on foot. **3** a person's manner of walking. **4** a route or path for walking.
– PHRASES **walk (all) over** informal **1** treat in a thoughtless and exploitative manner. **2** defeat easily. **walk it** informal achieve a victory easily. **walk off with** (or **away with**) informal **1** steal. **2** win. **walk of life** the position within society that someone holds. **walk out 1** depart suddenly or angrily. **2** Brit. informal, dated go for walks in courtship.
– DERIVATIVES **walkable** adjective.
– ORIGIN Old English, 'roll, toss', also 'wander'.
walkabout ● noun **1** chiefly Brit. an informal stroll among a crowd conducted by an important visitor. **2** Austral. a journey on foot undertaken by an Australian Aboriginal in order to live in the traditional manner.
walkathon ● noun informal a long-distance walk organized as a fund-raising event.
walker ● noun **1** a person who walks. **2** a device for helping a baby learn to walk, consisting of a harness set into a frame on wheels.
walkie-talkie ● noun a portable two-way radio.
walk-in ● adjective (of a storage area) large enough to walk into.
walking frame ● noun Brit. a frame used by disabled or infirm people for support while walking.
walking stick ● noun a stick with a curved handle used for support when walking.
walking wounded ● plural noun people who have been injured in a battle or major accident but who are still able to walk.
Walkman ● noun (pl. **Walkmans** or **Walkmen**) trademark a type of personal stereo.
walk-on ● adjective (of a part in a play or film) small and not involving any speaking.
walkout ● noun a sudden angry departure, especially as a protest or strike.
walkover ● noun an easy victory.
walkway ● noun a raised passageway in a building, or a wide path in a park or garden.
wall ● noun **1** a continuous vertical brick or stone structure that encloses or divides an area of land. **2** a side of a building or room. **3** a protective or restrictive barrier: *a wall of silence.* **4** Soccer a line of defenders forming a barrier against a free kick taken near the penalty area. **5** the outer layer or lining of a bodily organ or cavity. ● verb **1** enclose within walls. **2** (**wall in/off/up**) block or seal by building a wall.
– PHRASES **drive up the wall** informal make very irritated. **go to the wall** informal (of a business) fail. **off the wall** informal **1** eccentric or unconventional. **2** angry. **3** (of an accusation) without basis or foundation. **walls have ears** proverb be careful what you say as people may be eavesdropping. **wall-to-wall 1** (of a carpet) fitted to cover an entire floor. **2** informal very numerous or plentiful.
– DERIVATIVES **walling** noun.
– ORIGIN Latin *vallum* 'rampart'.
wallaby ● noun (pl. **wallabies**) an Australasian marsupial similar to but smaller than a kangaroo.
– ORIGIN Dharuk (an Aboriginal language).
wallah /wollə/ ● noun Indian or informal a person of a specified kind or having a specified role.
– ORIGIN from a Hindi suffix meaning 'doer' (commonly taken to mean 'fellow').
wall bars ● plural noun Brit. parallel horizontal bars attached to the wall of a gymnasium, on which exercises are performed.
wallet ● noun **1** a pocket-sized, flat, folding holder for money and plastic cards. **2** archaic a bag for holding provisions when travelling.
– ORIGIN probably from a Germanic word related to WELL[2].
wall eye ● noun **1** an eye squinting outwards. **2** an eye with a streaked or opaque white iris. **3** (**walleye**) a large, predatory North American perch with opaque silvery eyes.
– DERIVATIVES **wall-eyed** adjective.
– ORIGIN Old Norse.
wallflower ● noun **1** a plant with fragrant flowers that bloom in early spring. **2** informal a girl who has no one to dance with at a dance or party.
Walloon /woloon/ ● noun **1** a member of a people who speak a French dialect and live in southern and eastern Belgium and neighbouring parts of France. Compare with FLEMING. **2** the French dialect spoken by this people.
– ORIGIN French *Wallon*; related to WELSH.
wallop informal ● verb (**walloped, walloping**) **1** strike or hit very hard. **2** heavily defeat (an opponent). **3** (**walloping**) strikingly large. ● noun **1** a heavy blow or punch. **2** Brit. alcoholic drink, especially beer.
– ORIGIN originally denoting a horse's gallop: from Old French *waloper*; related to WELL[1], LEAP, and GALLOP.

Thesaurus

ly wakeful ALERT, watchful, vigilant, on the lookout, on one's guard, attentive, heedful, wary.
– OPPOSITES asleep, inattentive.
waken ● verb. See WAKE[1] verb senses 1, 2.
Wales ● noun Cambria; *Brit.* the Principality.
walk ● verb **1** *they walked along the road* STROLL, saunter, amble, trudge, plod, hike, tramp, trek, march, stride, troop, patrol, step out, wander, ramble, tread, prowl, footslog, promenade, roam, traipse; stretch one's legs; *informal* mosey, pootle, hoof it; *Brit. informal* yomp; *formal* perambulate. **2** *he walked her home* ACCOMPANY, escort, guide, show, see, usher, take, chaperone, steer, shepherd.
● noun **1** *country walks* STROLL, saunter, amble, promenade; ramble, hike, tramp, march; turn, airing; *dated* constitutional. **2** *her elegant walk* GAIT, step, stride, tread. **3** *the riverside walk* PATHWAY, path, footpath, track, walkway, promenade, footway, pavement, trail, towpath.
– PHRASES **walk all over someone** *(informal)* **1** *be firm or they'll walk all over you* TAKE ADVANTAGE OF, impose on, exploit, use, abuse, misuse, manipulate, take liberties with; *informal* take for a ride, run rings around. **2** *we walked all over the home team.* See TROUNCE. **walk off/away with** *(informal)* **1** *she walked off with my car keys.* See STEAL verb sense 1. **2** *he walked off with four awards* WIN EASILY, win hands down, attain, earn, gain, receive, acquire, secure, collect, pick up, net; *informal* bag. **walk of life** CLASS, status, rank, caste, sphere, arena; profession, career, vocation, job, occupation, employment, business, trade, craft; province, field; *dated* station. **walk out 1** *he walked out in a temper* LEAVE, depart, get up and go, storm off/out, flounce out, absent oneself; *informal* take off. **2** *teachers walked out in protest* (GO ON) STRIKE, stop work; protest, mutiny, revolt; *Brit. informal* down tools. **walk out on someone** DESERT, abandon, leave, betray, throw over, jilt, run out on, rat on; *informal* chuck, dump, ditch.
walker ● noun HIKER, rambler, traveller, roamer, rover, stroller; pedestrian; *poetic/literary* wayfarer.
walkout ● noun STRIKE, stoppage, industrial action; revolt, rebellion.
walkover ● noun EASY VICTORY, rout, landslide; *informal* piece of cake, doddle, pushover, cinch, breeze, picnic, whitewash; *N. Amer. informal* duck soup; *dated* snip.
wall ● noun **1** *brick walls* BARRIER, partition, enclosure, screen, panel, separator. **2** *an ancient city wall* FORTIFICATION, rampart, barricade, bulwark, stockade. **3** *break down the walls that stop world trade* OBSTACLE, barrier, fence; impediment, hindrance, block, check.
– RELATED TERMS mural.
● verb **1** *tenements walled in the courtyard* ENCLOSE, bound, encircle, confine, hem, close in, shut in, fence in. **2** *the doorway had been walled up* BLOCK, seal, close, brick up.
– PHRASES **go to the wall** *(informal).* See FAIL sense 1. **off the wall** *(informal).* See UNCONVENTIONAL.

W

wallow ● verb **1** roll about or lie in mud or water. **2** (of a boat or aircraft) roll from side to side. **3** (**wallow in**) indulge without restraint in (something pleasurable). ● noun **1** an act of wallowing. **2** an area of mud or shallow water where mammals go to wallow.
– ORIGIN Old English.
wallpaper ● noun **1** paper pasted in strips over the walls of a room to provide a decorative or textured surface. **2** something, especially music, providing a bland or unvaried background. **3** Computing an optional background pattern or picture on a screen. ● verb apply wallpaper to (a wall or room).
wall pass ● noun Soccer a short pass to a teammate who immediately returns it; a one-two.
wally ● noun (pl. **wallies**) Brit. informal a silly or inept person.
– ORIGIN perhaps a shortened form of the given name *Walter*: the use possibly arose from an incident at a 1960s pop festival when a *Wally* became separated from his companions, his name being taken up as a chant by the crowd following numerous loudspeaker announcements.
walnut ● noun **1** an edible wrinkled nut enclosed by a hard round shell. **2** the tree which produces this nut, a source of valuable ornamental wood.
– ORIGIN Old English, from a compound meaning 'foreign nut'.
Walpurgis night /valpoorgiss/ ● noun (in German folklore) the night of April 30 (May Day's eve), when witches meet on the Brocken mountain and hold pagan rituals.
– ORIGIN named after St *Walburga*, whose feast day coincided with an ancient pagan festival.
walrus ● noun a large marine mammal having two large downward-pointing tusks, found in the Arctic Ocean.
– ORIGIN probably Dutch, perhaps from an Old Norse word meaning 'horse-whale'.
walrus moustache ● noun a long, thick, drooping moustache.
waltz /wawlts/ ● noun a dance in triple time performed by a couple, who turn rhythmically round and round as they progress around the dance floor. ● verb **1** dance a waltz. **2** move or act lightly, casually, or inconsiderately.
– ORIGIN German *Walzer*, from *walzen* 'revolve'.
waltzer ● noun **1** a person who dances the waltz. **2** a fairground ride in which cars spin round as they are carried round an undulating track.
wampum /wompəm/ ● noun historical a quantity of small cylindrical beads made by North American Indians from shells, strung together and worn as a decorative belt or used as money.
– ORIGIN Algonquian.
WAN ● abbreviation Computing wide area network.
wan /won/ ● adjective **1** (of a person) pale and giving the impression of illness or exhaustion. **2** (of light) pale; weak. **3** (of a smile) weak; strained.
– DERIVATIVES **wanly** adverb.
– ORIGIN Old English, 'dark, black', later 'of an unhealthy greyish colour, as if bruised'.
wand ● noun **1** a stick or rod thought to have magic properties, used in casting spells or performing tricks. **2** a slender staff or rod, especially one held as a symbol of office. **3** a hand-held electronic device passed over a bar code to read the encoded data.
– ORIGIN Old Norse, related to WEND and WIND².
wander ● verb **1** walk or move in a leisurely, casual, or aimless way. **2** move slowly away from a fixed point or place. ● noun an act or spell of wandering.
– DERIVATIVES **wanderer** noun.
– ORIGIN Old English, related to WEND and WIND².
wandering Jew ● noun **1** a legendary person said to have been condemned by Christ to wander the earth until the second coming. **2** a trailing plant with striped leaves suffused with purple.
wanderlust ● noun a strong desire to travel.
– ORIGIN German.
wane ● verb **1** (of the moon) have a progressively smaller part of its visible surface illuminated, so that it appears to decrease in size. **2** decrease in vigour or extent; become weaker.
– PHRASES **on the wane** becoming weaker or less vigorous.
– ORIGIN Old English, 'lessen'; related to VAIN.
wangle informal ● verb obtain (something desired) by persuading others to comply or by manipulating events. ● noun an instance of obtaining something in such a way.
– DERIVATIVES **wangler** noun.
– ORIGIN of unknown origin.
wank Brit. vulgar slang ● verb (also **wank off**) masturbate. ● noun an act of masturbating.
– ORIGIN of unknown origin.
wanker ● noun Brit. vulgar slang a stupid or contemptible person.
wanna ● contraction informal want to; want a.
wannabe /wonnəbee/ ● noun informal, derogatory a person who tries to be like someone else or to fit in with a particular group of people.
want ● verb **1** have a desire to possess or do; wish for. **2** desire sexually. **3** (**be wanted**) (of a suspected criminal) be sought by the police. **4** (often **want for**) lack or be short of something desirable or essential. **5** informal, chiefly Brit. ought to, should, or need to do something. **6** informal, chiefly Brit. (of a thing) require to be attended to. ● noun **1** a desire for something. **2** lack or deficiency. **3** lack of essentials; poverty.
– ORIGIN Old Norse, 'be lacking'.
wanting ● adjective **1** lacking in something required, necessary, or usual. **2** absent; not provided.

Thesaurus

wallet ● noun PURSE; *N. Amer.* billfold, pocketbook; *Brit. dated* notecase.
wallop ● verb *(informal)*. See THUMP verb sense 1.
wallow ● verb **1** *buffalo wallowed in the lake* LOLL ABOUT/AROUND, lie about/around, splash about/around; slosh, wade, paddle; *informal* splosh. **2** *a ship wallowing in stormy seas* ROLL, lurch, toss, plunge, reel, rock, flounder, keel, list; labour. **3** *she seems to wallow in self-pity* LUXURIATE, bask, take pleasure, take satisfaction, indulge (oneself), delight, revel, glory; enjoy, like, love, relish, savour; *informal* get a kick out of, get a buzz from.
wan ● adjective **1** *she looked so wan and frail* PALE, pallid, ashen, white, grey; anaemic, colourless, bloodless, waxen, chalky, pasty, peaky, sickly, washed out, drained, drawn, ghostly. **2** *the wan light of the moon* DIM, faint, weak, feeble, pale, watery.
– OPPOSITES flushed, bright.
wand ● noun BATON, stick, staff, bar, dowel, rod; twig, cane, birch, switch; *historical* caduceus.
wander ● verb **1** *I wandered around the estate* STROLL, amble, saunter, walk, dawdle, potter, ramble, meander; roam, rove, range, drift, prowl; *Scottish & Irish* stravaig; *informal* traipse, mosey, tootle; *Brit. informal* mooch. **2** *we are wandering from the point* STRAY, depart, diverge, veer, swerve, deviate, digress, drift, get sidetracked. **3** *the child wandered off* GET LOST, lose one's way, go astray. **4** *the road wanders along the shore* MEANDER, wind, twist, curve, zigzag, bend, snake.
● noun *let's go for a wander* STROLL, amble, saunter, walk, potter, ramble, prowl, promenade; turn, breather, airing; *informal* traipse, mosey, tootle; *Brit. informal* mooch; *dated* constitutional.
wanderer ● noun TRAVELLER, rambler, hiker, migrant, globetrotter, roamer, rover; itinerant, rolling stone, bird of passage, nomad; tramp, drifter, vagabond, vagrant; *Brit. informal* dosser; *N. Amer. informal* hobo, bum; *poetic/literary* wayfarer.
wane ● verb **1** *the moon is waning* DECREASE, diminish, dwindle. **2** *their support was waning* DECLINE, diminish, decrease, dwindle, shrink, tail off, ebb, fade (away), lessen, peter out, fall off, recede, slump, flag, weaken, give way, wither, evaporate, die out; *poetic/literary* evanesce.
– OPPOSITES wax, grow.
– PHRASES **on the wane** DECLINING, decreasing, diminishing, dwindling, shrinking, contracting, tapering off, subsiding, ebbing, fading away, dissolving, petering out, winding down, falling off, on the way out, receding, flagging, melting away, crumbling, withering, disintegrating, evaporating, dying out.
wangle ● verb *(informal)*. See CONTRIVE.
want ● verb **1** *do you want more coffee?* DESIRE, wish for, hope for, fancy, care for, like; long for, yearn for, crave, hanker after, hunger for, thirst for, cry out for, covet; need; *informal* have a yen for, be dying for. **2** *(informal) his toaster wants repairing* NEED, require, demand, cry out for. **3** *(informal) you want to be more careful* SHOULD, ought, need, must. **4** *(archaic) his poem wants a name* LACK, be without, have need of, be devoid of, be bereft of.
● noun **1** *his want of vigilance* LACK, absence, non-existence, unavailability; dearth, deficiency, inadequacy, insufficiency, paucity, shortage, scarcity, deficit. **2** *a time of want* NEED, neediness, austerity, privation, deprivation, poverty, impoverishment, penury, destitution; famine, drought. **3** *all her wants would be taken*

W

wanton ● adjective 1 (of a cruel or violent action) deliberate and unprovoked. 2 sexually immodest or promiscuous. 3 literary growing profusely; luxuriant. ● noun archaic a sexually immodest or promiscuous woman.
– DERIVATIVES **wantonly** adverb **wantonness** noun.
– ORIGIN originally in the sense 'rebellious, lacking discipline': from obsolete *wan-* 'badly' + Old English *togen* 'trained'.
WAP ● abbreviation Wireless Application Protocol, a means of enabling a mobile phone to browse the Internet and display data.
wapentake /woppəntayk/ ● noun historical a subdivision of certain northern and midland English counties, corresponding to a hundred in other counties.
– ORIGIN from Old Norse words meaning 'weapon' + 'take', perhaps with reference to voting in an assembly by a show of weapons.
wapiti /woppiti/ ● noun (pl. **wapitis**) a red deer of a large North American subspecies.
– ORIGIN Shawnee, 'white rump'.
War. ● abbreviation Warwickshire.
war ● noun 1 a state of armed conflict between different nations, states, or armed groups. 2 a sustained contest between rivals or campaign against something undesirable: *a war on drugs.* ● verb (**warred**, **warring**) engage in a war.
– PHRASES **be on the warpath** be very angry with someone. [ORIGIN with reference to American Indians heading towards a battle with an enemy.]
– ORIGIN from a variant of Old French *guerre* 'war'; related to WORSE.
waratah /worrətaa/ ● noun an Australian shrub with slender leathery leaves and clusters of crimson flowers.
– ORIGIN Dharuk (an Aboriginal language).
war baby ● noun a child born in wartime, especially one fathered illegitimately by a serviceman.
warble[1] ● verb 1 (of a bird) sing softly and with a succession of constantly changing notes. 2 (of a person) sing in a trilling or quavering voice. ● noun a warbling sound or utterance.
– ORIGIN Old French *werbler*; related to WHIRL.
warble[2] ● noun a swelling or abscess beneath the skin of cattle, horses, and other mammals, caused by the presence of the larva of the parasitic **warble fly**.
– ORIGIN origin uncertain.
warbler ● noun a small songbird typically living in trees and bushes and having a warbling song.
war chest ● noun a reserve of funds used for fighting a war.
war clouds ● plural noun a threatening situation of instability in international relations.
war crime ● noun an action carried out during the conduct of a war that violates accepted international rules of war.
ward ● noun 1 a room or division in a hospital for one or more patients. 2 an administrative division of a city or borough, represented by a councillor or councillors. 3 a child or young person under the care and control of a guardian appointed by their parents or a court. 4 any of the internal ridges or bars in a lock which prevent the turning of any key without corresponding grooves. 5 historical an area of ground enclosed by the encircling walls of a fortress or castle. ● verb (**ward off**) prevent from harming or affecting one.
– DERIVATIVES **wardship** noun.
– ORIGIN Old English, 'keep safe, guard'.
-ward (also **-wards**) ● suffix 1 (usu. **-wards**) (forming adverbs) towards the specified place or direction: *homewards.* 2 (usu. **-ward**) (forming adjectives) turned or tending towards: *upward.*
– ORIGIN Old English.
war dance ● noun a ceremonial dance performed before a battle or to celebrate victory.
warden ● noun 1 a person responsible for the supervision of a particular place or procedure. 2 Brit. the head of certain schools, colleges, or other institutions. 3 chiefly N. Amer. a prison governor.
– DERIVATIVES **wardenship** noun.
– ORIGIN Old French *wardein*, *guarden* 'guardian'.
warder ● noun (fem. **wardress**) chiefly Brit. a prison guard.
– ORIGIN from Old French *warder* 'to guard'.
ward of court ● noun a child or young person for whom a guardian has been appointed by the Court of Chancery or who has become directly subject to the authority of that court.
wardrobe ● noun 1 a large, tall cupboard in which clothes may be hung or stored. 2 a person's entire collection of clothes. 3 the costume department or costumes of a theatre or film company. 4 a department of a royal or noble household in charge of clothing.
– ORIGIN originally in the sense 'private chamber': from Old French *warderobe*, *garderobe* (see GARDEROBE).
wardroom ● noun a commissioned officers' mess on board a warship.
-wards ● suffix variant spelling of -WARD.
ware[1] ● noun 1 pottery, typically that of a specified type. 2 manufactured articles of a specified type. 3 (**wares**) articles offered for sale.
– ORIGIN Old English, 'commodities'.
ware[2] (also **'ware**) ● verb beware (used as a warning cry).
– ORIGIN Old English, 'be on one's guard'.
warehouse /wairhowss/ ● noun 1 a large building where raw materials or manufactured goods may be stored. 2 a large wholesale or retail store. ● verb /wairhowz/ store (goods) in a warehouse.
warfare ● noun engagement in or the state of war.
warfarin /wawrfərin/ ● noun a water-soluble compound with

Thesaurus

care of WISH, desire, demand, longing, yearning, fancy, craving, hankering; need, requirement; informal yen.
wanting ● adjective 1 *the defences were found wanting* DEFICIENT, inadequate, lacking, insufficient, imperfect, unacceptable, flawed, faulty, defective, unsound, substandard, inferior, second-rate, poor, shoddy; Brit. informal not much cop. 2 *the kneecap is wanting in amphibians* ABSENT, missing, lacking, non-existent. 3 *millions were left wanting for food* WITHOUT, lacking, deprived of, devoid of, bereft of, in need of; deficient in, short on; informal minus.
– OPPOSITES sufficient, present.
wanton ● adjective 1 *wanton destruction* DELIBERATE, wilful, malicious, spiteful, wicked, cruel; gratuitous, unprovoked, motiveless, arbitrary, groundless, unjustifiable, needless, unnecessary, uncalled for, senseless, pointless, purposeless, meaningless, empty. 2 *a wanton seductress* PROMISCUOUS, immoral, immodest, indecent, shameless, unchaste, fast, impure, abandoned, lustful, lecherous, lascivious, libidinous, licentious, dissolute, debauched, degenerate, corrupt, whorish, disreputable; dated loose.
– OPPOSITES justifiable, chaste.
war ● noun 1 *the Napoleonic wars* CONFLICT, warfare, combat, fighting, (military) action, bloodshed, struggle; battle, skirmish, fight, clash, engagement, encounter; offensive, attack, campaign; hostilities; jihad, crusade. 2 *the war against drugs* CAMPAIGN, crusade, battle, fight, struggle, movement, drive.
– RELATED TERMS belligerent, martial.
– OPPOSITES peace.
● verb *rival Emperors warred against each other* FIGHT, battle, combat, wage war, take up arms; feud, quarrel, struggle, contend, wrangle, cross swords; attack, engage, take on, skirmish with.
warble ● verb *larks warbled in the sky* TRILL, sing, chirp, chirrup, cheep, twitter, tweet, chatter, peep.
● noun *a warble pierced the air* TRILL, song, chirp, chirrup, chirr, cheep, twitter, tweet, chatter, peep, call.
ward ● noun 1 *the surgical ward* ROOM, department, unit, area. 2 *the most marginal ward in Westminster* DISTRICT, constituency, division, quarter, zone, parish. 3 *the boy is my ward* DEPENDANT, charge, protégé.
– PHRASES **ward someone off** FEND OFF, repel, repulse, beat back, chase away; informal send packing. **ward something off** 1 *she warded off the blow* PARRY, avert, deflect, block; evade, avoid, dodge. 2 *garlic is worn to ward off evil spirits* REBUFF, avert, keep at bay, fend off, stave off, resist, prevent, obstruct, foil, frustrate, thwart, check, stop.
warden ● noun 1 *the flats have a resident warden* SUPERINTENDENT, caretaker, janitor, porter, custodian, watchman, concierge, doorman. 2 *a game warden* RANGER, custodian, keeper, guardian, protector. 3 *he was handcuffed to a warden* PRISON OFFICER, guard, jailer, warder, wardress, keeper, sentry; informal screw. 4 *(Brit.) the college warden* PRINCIPAL, head, governor, master, mistress, rector, provost, president, director, chancellor; N. Amer. informal prexy.
warder, wardress ● noun. See WARDEN sense 3.
wardrobe ● noun 1 *she opened the wardrobe* CUPBOARD, cabinet, locker; N. Amer. closet. 2 *her wardrobe has an outfit for every mood* COLLECTION OF CLOTHES; garments, attire, outfits; trousseau.
warehouse ● noun STOREROOM, storehouse, store, depot, depository, stockroom; magazine; granary; informal lock-up.

anticoagulant properties, used as a rat poison and in the treatment of thrombosis.
– ORIGIN from the initial letters of *Wisconsin Alumni Research Foundation* + *-arin*.
war game ● noun **1** a military exercise carried out to test or improve tactical expertise. **2** a simulated military conflict carried out as a game or sport.
warhead ● noun the explosive head of a missile, torpedo, or similar weapon.
warhorse ● noun informal a veteran soldier, politician, sports player, etc. who has fought many campaigns or contests.
warlike ● adjective **1** disposed towards or threatening war; hostile. **2** directed towards or prepared for war.
war loan ● noun stock issued by the British government to raise funds at a time of war.
warlock ● noun a man who practises witchcraft.
– ORIGIN Old English, 'traitor, scoundrel, monster', also 'the Devil'.
warlord ● noun a military commander, especially one who autonomously commands a region.
warm ● adjective **1** of or at a fairly or comfortably high temperature. **2** (of clothes or coverings) made of a material that helps the body to retain heat. **3** enthusiastic, affectionate, or kind. **4** (of a colour) containing red, yellow, or orange tones. **5** (of a scent or trail) fresh; strong. **6** informal close to finding or guessing what is sought. ● verb **1** make or become warm. **2** (**warm to/towards**) become more interested in or enthusiastic about. ● noun **1** (**the warm**) a warm place or area. **2** an act of warming.
– PHRASES **warm up 1** prepare for physical exertion by doing gentle stretches and exercises. **2** (of an engine or electrical appliance) reach a temperature high enough to allow it to operate efficiently. **3** amuse or entertain (an audience or crowd) to make them more receptive to the main act.
– DERIVATIVES **warmer** noun **warmly** adverb **warmness** noun.
– ORIGIN Old English.
warm-blooded ● adjective **1** (of animals, chiefly mammals and birds) maintaining a constant body temperature by their metabolism. **2** ardent; passionate.
warm-hearted ● adjective sympathetic and kind.
warming pan ● noun historical a wide, flat brass pan on a long handle, filled with hot coals and used for warming a bed.
warmonger /wawrmunggər/ ● noun a person who seeks to bring about or promote war.
warmth ● noun **1** the quality, state, or sensation of being warm. **2** enthusiasm, affection, or kindness. **3** intensity of emotion.
warn ● verb **1** inform of a possible danger, problem, etc. **2** give (someone) cautionary advice about actions or conduct. **3** (**warn off**) order (someone) to keep away or to refrain from doing something.
– ORIGIN Old English, related to WARE².
warning ● noun **1** a statement or event that indicates a possible or impending danger or problem. **2** cautionary advice. **3** advance notice.
– DERIVATIVES **warningly** adverb.
warp ● verb **1** make or become bent or twisted, typically from the action of heat or damp. **2** make abnormal; distort. **3** move (a ship) along by hauling on a rope attached to a stationary object ashore. ● noun **1** a distortion or twist in shape. **2** the lengthwise threads on a loom over and under which the weft threads are passed to make cloth. **3** a rope attached at one end to a fixed point and used for moving or mooring a ship.
– ORIGIN Old English.
warpaint ● noun **1** paint traditionally used to decorate the face and body before battle, especially by North American Indians. **2** informal elaborate or excessive make-up.
warplane ● noun an aircraft designed and equipped to engage in air combat or to drop bombs.
warrant ● noun **1** an official authorization enabling the police or some other body to make an arrest, search premises, etc. **2** a document entitling the holder to receive goods, money, or services. **3** justification or authority. **4** an official certificate of appointment issued to an officer of lower rank than a commissioned officer. ● verb **1** justify or necessitate. **2** officially affirm or guarantee.
– PHRASES **I** (or **I'll**) **warrant** dated no doubt.
– DERIVATIVES **warrantable** adjective.
– ORIGIN originally in the senses 'protector', 'safeguard', and 'protect from danger': from Old French *guarant*; related to GUARANTEE.

Thesaurus

wares ● plural noun MERCHANDISE, goods, products, produce, stock, commodities; lines, range.
warfare ● noun FIGHTING, war, combat, conflict, (military) action, hostilities; bloodshed, battles, skirmishes.
warlike ● adjective AGGRESSIVE, belligerent, warring, bellicose, pugnacious, combative, bloodthirsty, jingoistic, sabre-rattling; hostile, threatening, quarrelsome; militaristic, militant; *informal* gung-ho.
warlock ● noun SORCERER, wizard, magus, (black) magician, enchanter; *archaic* mage.
warm ● adjective **1** *a warm kitchen* HOT, cosy, snug; *informal* toasty. **2** *a warm day in spring* BALMY, summery, sultry, hot, mild, temperate; sunny, fine. **3** *warm water* HEATED, tepid, lukewarm. **4** *a warm sweater* THICK, chunky, thermal, winter, woolly. **5** *a warm welcome* FRIENDLY, cordial, amiable, genial, kind, pleasant, fond; welcoming, hospitable, benevolent, benign, charitable; sincere, genuine, wholehearted, heartfelt, enthusiastic, eager, hearty. **6** (*informal*) *they haven't found it, but they're warm* CLOSE, near; *informal* hot.
– OPPOSITES cold, chilly, light, hostile.
● verb *warm the soup in that pan* HEAT (UP), reheat, cook; thaw (out), melt; *N. Amer.* warm over; *informal* zap; *Brit. informal* hot up.
– OPPOSITES chill.
– PHRASES **warm to/towards 1** *everyone warmed to him* LIKE, take to, get on (well) with, hit it off with, be on good terms with. **2** *he couldn't warm to the notion* BE ENTHUSIASTIC ABOUT, be supportive of, be excited about. **warm up** LIMBER UP, loosen up, stretch, work out, exercise; prepare, rehearse. **warm someone up** *the compère warmed up the crowd* ENLIVEN, liven, stimulate, animate, rouse, stir, excite; *informal* get going.
warm-blooded ● adjective **1** *mammals are warm-blooded Zoology* HOMEOTHERMIC, homeothermal. **2** *a warm-blooded woman* PASSIONATE, ardent, red-blooded, emotional, intense, impetuous, lively, spirited, fiery, tempestuous.
– OPPOSITES poikilothermic, reserved.
warmed-up ● adjective **1** *a warmed-up pasty* REHEATED; *N. Amer.* warmed-over. **2** *warmed-up ideas* UNORIGINAL, derivative, imitative, uninspired; copied, plagiarized, rehashed; hackneyed, stale, tired, banal; *informal* old hat.
– OPPOSITES original.
warm-hearted ● adjective KIND, warm, big-hearted, tender-hearted, tender, loving, caring, feeling, unselfish, selfless, benevolent, humane, good-natured; friendly, sympathetic, understanding, compassionate, charitable, generous.
warmonger ● noun MILITARIST, hawk, jingoist, sabre-rattler, aggressor, belligerent.
warmth ● noun **1** *the warmth of the fire* HEAT, warmness, hotness; cosiness. **2** *the warmth of their welcome* FRIENDLINESS, amiability, geniality, cordiality, kindness, tenderness, fondness; benevolence, charity; enthusiasm, eagerness, ardour, fervour, effusiveness.
warn ● verb **1** *David warned her that it was too late* NOTIFY, alert, apprise, inform, tell, make someone aware, forewarn, remind; *informal* tip off, put wise. **2** *police are warning galleries to be alert* ADVISE, exhort, urge, counsel, caution.
warning ● noun **1** *the earthquake came without warning* (ADVANCE) NOTICE, forewarning, alert; hint, signal, sign, alarm bells; *informal* a tip-off. **2** *a health warning* CAUTION, notification, information; exhortation, injunction; advice. **3** *a warning of things to come* OMEN, premonition, foreboding, prophecy, prediction, forecast, token, portent, signal, sign; *poetic/literary* foretoken. **4** *his sentence is a warning to other drunk drivers* EXAMPLE, deterrent, lesson, caution, exemplar, message, moral. **5** *a written warning* ADMONITION, caution, remonstrance, reprimand, censure; *informal* dressing-down, talking-to, telling-off.
warp ● verb **1** *timber which is too dry will warp* BUCKLE, twist, bend, distort, deform, misshape, malform, curve, bow, contort. **2** *he warped the mind of her child* CORRUPT, twist, pervert, deprave.
– OPPOSITES straighten.
warrant ● noun **1** *a warrant for his arrest* AUTHORIZATION, order, licence, permit, document; writ, summons, subpoena; mandate, decree, fiat, edict. **2** *a travel warrant* VOUCHER, chit, slip, ticket, coupon, pass. **3** *there's no warrant for this assumption* JUSTIFICATION, grounds, cause, rationale, basis, authority, licence, sanction, vin-

warrant officer ● noun a rank of officer in the army, RAF, or US navy, below the commissioned officers and above the NCOs.

warranty ● noun (pl. **warranties**) **1** a written guarantee promising to repair or replace an article if necessary within a specified period. **2** an engagement by an insured party that certain statements are true or that certain conditions shall be fulfilled.

warren ● noun **1** a network of interconnecting rabbit burrows. **2** a densely populated or labyrinthine building or district.
– ORIGIN Old French *garenne* 'game park'.

warrior ● noun (especially in former times) a brave or experienced soldier or fighter.
– ORIGIN Old French *werreior*, *guerreior*, from *guerre* 'war'.

warship ● noun a ship equipped with weapons and designed to take part in warfare at sea.

wart ● noun **1** a small, hard, benign growth on the skin. **2** any rounded protuberance on the skin of an animal or the surface of a plant.
– PHRASES **warts and all** informal including faults or unattractive qualities.
– DERIVATIVES **warty** adjective.
– ORIGIN Old English.

warthog ● noun an African wild pig with a large head, warty lumps on the face, and curved tusks.

wartime ● noun a period during which a war is taking place.

wary ● adjective (**warier**, **wariest**) (often **wary of**) cautious about possible dangers or problems.
– DERIVATIVES **warily** adverb **wariness** noun.
– ORIGIN from WARE[2].

was first and third person singular past of BE.

wasabi /wəsaabi/ ● noun a Japanese plant with a thick green root which tastes like strong horseradish and is used in cookery.
– ORIGIN Japanese.

wash ● verb **1** clean with water and, typically, soap or detergent. **2** (of flowing water) carry or move in a particular direction. **3** be carried by flowing water. **4** (**wash over**) occur all around without greatly affecting. **5** literary wet or moisten. **6** brush with a thin coat of dilute paint or ink. **7** informal seem convincing or genuine: *excuses just don't wash with us.* ● noun **1** an act of washing or an instance of being washed. **2** a quantity of clothes needing to be or just having been washed. **3** the water or air disturbed by a moving boat or aircraft. **4** a medicinal or cleansing solution. **5** a thin coating of paint or metal. **6** silt or gravel carried by water and deposited as sediment.
– PHRASES **be washed out** be postponed or cancelled because of rain. **come out in the wash** informal be resolved eventually. **wash one's dirty linen** (or **laundry**) **in public** informal discuss one's personal affairs in public. **wash one's hands of** disclaim responsibility for. [ORIGIN originally with biblical allusion to Pontius Pilate washing his hands after the condemnation of Christ (Gospel of Matthew, chapter 27).] **wash up 1** chiefly Brit. clean crockery and cutlery after use. **2** N. Amer. clean one's hands and face.
– DERIVATIVES **washable** adjective.
– ORIGIN Old English, related to WATER.

washbag ● noun Brit. a toilet bag.

washbasin ● noun a basin used for washing one's hands and face.

washboard ● noun **1** a board made of ridged wood or a sheet of corrugated zinc, against which clothes are scrubbed during washing. **2** a similar board played as a percussion instrument by scraping. **3** (before another noun) (of a man's stomach) lean and with well-defined muscles.

washed out ● adjective **1** faded by or as if by repeated washing. **2** pale and tired.

washed-up ● adjective informal no longer effective or successful.

washer ● noun **1** a person or device that washes. **2** a small flat ring fixed between a nut and bolt to spread the pressure or between two joining surfaces to act as a spacer or seal.

washer-dryer ● noun a washing machine with an inbuilt tumble-dryer.

washerwoman ● noun a woman whose occupation is washing clothes.

washing ● noun a quantity of clothes, bedlinen, etc. that is to be washed or has just been washed.

washing machine ● noun a machine for washing clothes, bedlinen, etc.

washing powder ● noun chiefly Brit. powdered detergent for washing laundry.

washing soda ● noun sodium carbonate, used dissolved in water for washing and cleaning.

washing-up ● noun Brit. crockery, cutlery, and other kitchen utensils that are to be washed.

washout ● noun **1** informal a disappointing failure. **2** a breach in a road or railway track caused by flooding.

washroom ● noun N. Amer. a room with washing and toilet facilities.

washstand ● noun chiefly historical a piece of furniture designed to hold a jug, bowl, or basin for washing one's hands and face.

washy ● adjective (**washier**, **washiest**) **1** (of food or drink) too watery. **2** insipid or pale.

wasn't ● contraction was not.

Wasp ● noun N. Amer. an upper- or middle-class American white Protestant, regarded as a member of the most powerful social group.
– ORIGIN from *white Anglo-Saxon Protestant*.

wasp ● noun a stinging winged insect which typically nests in complex colonies and has a black and yellow-striped body.
– ORIGIN Old English, perhaps related to WEAVE[1] (from the web-

Thesaurus

dication.
● verb **1** *the charges warranted a severe sentence* JUSTIFY, vindicate, call for, sanction, validate; permit, authorize; deserve, excuse, account for, legitimize; support, license, approve of; merit, qualify for, rate, be worthy of, be deserving of. **2** *we warrant that the texts do not infringe copyright* GUARANTEE, affirm, swear, promise, vow, pledge, undertake, state, assert, declare, profess, attest; vouch, testify, bear witness; *formal* aver.

warranty ● noun GUARANTEE, assurance, promise, commitment, undertaking, agreement.

warring ● adjective OPPOSING, conflicting, at war, fighting, battling, quarrelling; competing, hostile, rival.

warrior ● noun FIGHTER, soldier, serviceman, combatant.

wary ● adjective **1** *he was trained to be wary* CAUTIOUS, careful, circumspect, on one's guard, chary, alert, on the lookout, on one's toes, on the qui vive; attentive, heedful, watchful, vigilant, observant; *informal* wide awake. **2** *we are wary of strangers* SUSPICIOUS, chary, leery, careful, distrustful, mistrustful, sceptical, doubtful, dubious.
– OPPOSITES inattentive, trustful.

wash ● verb **1** *he washed in the bath* CLEAN ONESELF, have a wash; bathe, bath, shower, soak, freshen up; *formal* perform one's ablutions; *dated* make one's toilet. **2** *she washed her hands* CLEAN, cleanse, sponge, scrub, wipe, scour; shampoo, lather; sluice, swill, douse, swab, disinfect. **3** *she washed off the blood* REMOVE, expunge, eradicate; sponge off, scrub off, wipe off, rinse off. **4** *the women were washing clothes* LAUNDER, clean, rinse; *poetic/literary* lave. **5** *waves washed against the hull* SPLASH, lap, splosh, dash, break, beat, surge, ripple, roll. **6** *the wreckage was washed up downriver* SWEEP, carry, convey, transport; deposit. **7** *guilt washed over her* AFFECT, rush through, surge through, course through, flood over, flow over. **8** *the stonework was washed with pastel paint* PAINT, colour, tint, shade, dye, stain; coat, cover. **9** *(informal) this story just won't wash* BE ACCEPTED, be acceptable, be plausible, be convincing, hold up, hold water, stand up, bear scrutiny.
– OPPOSITES dirty, soil.
● noun **1** *she needs a wash* CLEAN, shower, dip, bath, soak; *formal* ablutions. **2** *that shirt should go in the wash* LAUNDRY, washing. **3** *antiseptic skin wash* LOTION, salve, preparation, rinse, liquid; liniment, embrocation. **4** *the wash of a motor boat* BACKWASH, wake, trail, path. **5** *the wash of the waves on the beach* SURGE, flow, swell, sweep, rise and fall, roll, splash. **6** *water thinned out the crayon into a wash* PAINT, stain, film.
– PHRASES **wash something away** ERODE, abrade, wear away, eat away, undermine. **wash one's hands of** DISOWN, renounce, reject, forswear, disavow, give up on, turn one's back on, cast aside, abandon; *formal* abjure. **wash up** WASH THE DISHES, do the dishes, do the washing-up.

washed out ● adjective **1** *a washed-out denim jacket* FADED, bleached, decolorized, stonewashed; pale, light, drab, muted. **2** *he looked washed out after his exams* EXHAUSTED, tired, worn out, weary, fatigued, spent, drained, enervated, run down; *informal* all in, done in, dog-tired, bushed, beat, zonked; *Brit. informal* knackered; *N. Amer. informal* pooped, tuckered out.

like form of its nest).

waspie ● noun (pl. **waspies**) a woman's corset or belt designed to accentuate a slender waist.

waspish ● adjective sharply irritable.
– DERIVATIVES **waspishly** adverb **waspishness** noun.

wasp-waisted ● adjective having a very narrow waist.

wassail /wossayl, woss'l/ archaic ● noun **1** spiced ale or mulled wine drunk during celebrations for Twelfth Night and Christmas Eve. **2** lively festivities involving the drinking of much alcohol. ● verb **1** make merry with much alcohol. **2** go from house to house at Christmas singing carols.
– DERIVATIVES **wassailer** noun.
– ORIGIN Old Norse, 'be in good health!'; compare with HAIL².

wast /wost, wəst/ archaic or dialect second person singular past of BE.

wastage ● noun **1** the action or process of wasting. **2** an amount wasted. **3** (also **natural wastage**) the reduction in the size of a workforce as a result of voluntary resignation or retirement rather than enforced redundancy.

waste ● verb **1** use carelessly, extravagantly, or to no purpose. **2** fail to make full or good use of. **3** (**be wasted on**) be unappreciated by. **4** (often **waste away**) become progressively weaker and more emaciated. **5** literary lay waste to. **6** N. Amer. informal kill or severely injure. **7** (**wasted**) informal under the influence of alcohol or illegal drugs. ● adjective **1** eliminated or discarded as no longer useful or required. **2** (of an area of land) not used, cultivated, or built on. ● noun **1** an act or instance of wasting. **2** unusable or unwanted material. **3** a large area of barren, uninhabited land.
– PHRASES **go to waste** be wasted. **lay waste** (**to**) completely destroy. **waste not, want not** proverb if you use a commodity or resource carefully and without extravagance you will never be in need.
– ORIGIN Old French, from Latin *vastus* 'unoccupied, uncultivated'.

waste-disposal unit ● noun an electrically operated device fitted to the waste pipe of a kitchen sink for grinding up food waste.

wasteful ● adjective using or expending something carelessly, extravagantly, or to no purpose.
– DERIVATIVES **wastefully** adverb **wastefulness** noun.

wasteland ● noun a barren or empty area of land.

waster ● noun **1** a wasteful person or thing. **2** informal a person who does little or nothing of value.

wastrel /waystrəl/ ● noun literary a wasteful or worthless person.
– ORIGIN originally denoting a strip of waste land.

watch ● verb **1** look at attentively. **2** keep under careful or protective observation. **3** exercise care, caution, or restraint about. **4** (**watch for**) look out for. **5** (**watch out**) be careful. **6** maintain an interest in. ● noun **1** a small timepiece worn typically on a strap on one's wrist. **2** an act or instance of watching. **3** a period of vigil, typically during the night. **4** a fixed period of duty on a ship, usually lasting four hours. **5** a shift worked by firefighters or police officers. **6** (also **night watch**) historical a watchman or group of watchmen who patrolled and guarded the streets of a town at night.
– PHRASES **keep watch** stay on the lookout for danger or trouble. **watch one's back** protect oneself against danger from an unexpected quarter. **the watches of the night** literary waking hours during the night.
– DERIVATIVES **watcher** noun.
– ORIGIN Old English, related to WAKE¹.

watchable ● adjective moderately enjoyable to watch.

watchdog ● noun **1** a dog kept to guard private property. **2** a person or group that monitors the practices of companies providing a particular service or utility.

watchful ● adjective **1** alert and vigilant. **2** archaic wakeful.
– DERIVATIVES **watchfully** adverb **watchfulness** noun.

watching brief ● noun **1** Brit. Law a brief held by a barrister to follow a case on behalf of a client who is not directly involved. **2** an interest in a proceeding in which one is not directly concerned.

watchman ● noun **1** a man employed to look after an empty building, especially at night. **2** historical a member of a night watch.

watchtower ● noun a tower built to create an elevated observation point.

watchword ● noun **1** a word or phrase expressing a core aim or belief. **2** archaic a military password.

water ● noun **1** the liquid which forms the seas, lakes, rivers,

Thesaurus

– OPPOSITES bold, energetic.

washout ● noun *(informal)*. See FAILURE senses 2, 3.

waspish ● adjective IRRITABLE, touchy, testy, cross, snappish, cantankerous, splenetic, short-tempered, bad-tempered, moody, crabby, crotchety, ratty; *informal* grouchy.

waste ● verb **1** *he doesn't like to waste money* SQUANDER, misspend, misuse, fritter away, throw away, lavish, dissipate, throw around; *informal* blow, splurge. **2** *kids are wasting away in the streets* GROW WEAK, grow thin, shrink, decline, wilt, fade, flag, deteriorate, degenerate, languish. **3** *the disease wasted his legs* EMACIATE, atrophy, wither, debilitate, shrivel, shrink, weaken, enfeeble. **4** *(poetic/literary) our country was wasted by the enemy.* See DEVASTATE sense 1. **5** *(N. Amer. informal) I saw them waste the guy.* See MURDER verb sense 1.
– OPPOSITES conserve, thrive.
● adjective **1** *waste material* UNWANTED, excess, superfluous, left over, scrap, useless, worthless; unusable, unprofitable. **2** *waste ground* UNCULTIVATED, barren, desert, arid, bare; desolate, void, uninhabited, unpopulated; wild.
● noun **1** *a waste of money* MISUSE, misapplication, misemployment, abuse; extravagance, wastefulness, lavishness. **2** *household waste* RUBBISH, refuse, litter, debris, dross, junk, detritus, scrap; dregs, scraps; sewage, effluent; *N. Amer.* garbage, trash. **3** *the frozen wastes of the South Pole* DESERT, wasteland, wilderness, emptiness, wilds.
– PHRASES **lay waste.** See LAY¹.

W

wasted ● adjective **1** *a wasted effort* SQUANDERED, misspent, misdirected, misused, dissipated; pointless, useless, needless, unnecessary. **2** *a wasted opportunity* MISSED, lost, forfeited, neglected, squandered, bungled; *informal* down the drain. **3** *I'm wasted in this job* UNDEREMPLOYED, underused, too good for; neglected, forgotten, disregarded. **4** *his wasted legs* EMACIATED, atrophied, withered, shrivelled, weak, frail, shrunken, skeletal, rickety, scrawny, wizened. **5** *(informal) everybody at the party was wasted.* See DRUNK adjective.

wasteful ● adjective PRODIGAL, profligate, uneconomical, extravagant, lavish, excessive, imprudent, improvident; thriftless, spendthrift; needless, useless.
– OPPOSITES frugal.

wasteland ● noun WILDERNESS, desert; wilds, wastes, badlands.

waster ● noun *(informal)* IDLER, loafer, good-for-nothing, ne'er-do-well, slob, lounger, shirker, sluggard, laggard; *informal* loser, skiver, slacker, lazybones; *N. Amer. informal* bum; *poetic/literary* wastrel.

wastrel ● noun *(poetic/literary)*. See WASTER.

watch ● verb **1** *she watched him as he spoke* OBSERVE, view, look at, eye, gaze at, stare at, gape at, peer at; contemplate, survey, keep an eye on; inspect, scrutinize, scan, examine, study, ogle, regard, mark; *informal* check out, get a load of, recce, eyeball; *Brit. informal* have a butcher's at; *poetic/literary* behold. **2** *he was being watched by the police* SPY ON, keep in sight, track, monitor, survey, follow, keep under surveillance; *informal* keep tabs on, stake out. **3** *will you watch the kids?* LOOK AFTER, mind, keep an eye on, take care of, supervise, tend, attend to; guard, safeguard, protect. **4** *we stayed to watch the boat* GUARD, protect, shield, defend, safeguard; cover, patrol, police. **5** *watch what you say* BE CAREFUL, mind, be aware of, pay attention to, consider, pay heed to.
– OPPOSITES ignore, neglect.
● noun **1** *Bill looked at his watch* TIMEPIECE, chronometer; wristwatch, pocket watch, stopwatch. **2** *we kept watch on the yacht* GUARD, vigil, lookout, an eye; observation, surveillance, vigilance.
– PHRASES **watch out/it/yourself** BE CAREFUL, be watchful, be on your guard, beware, be wary, be cautious, mind out, look out, pay attention, take heed, take care, keep an eye open/out, keep one's eyes peeled, be vigilant.

watchdog ● noun **1** *they use watchdogs to ward off trespassers* GUARD DOG. **2** *a consumer watchdog* OMBUDSMAN, monitor, scrutineer, inspector, supervisor; custodian, guardian, protector.

watcher ● noun ONLOOKER, spectator, observer, viewer, fly on the wall; witness, bystander; spy; *informal* rubberneck; *poetic/literary* beholder.

watchful ● adjective OBSERVANT, alert, vigilant, attentive, awake, aware, heedful, sharp-eyed, eagle-eyed; on the lookout, on the qui vive, wary, cautious, careful, chary.

and rain and is the basis of the fluids of living organisms. **2** (**waters**) an area of sea regarded as under the jurisdiction of a particular country. **3** (**the waters**) the water of a mineral spring as used medicinally. **4** (**waters**) amniotic fluid, especially as discharged shortly before birth. **5** urine. **6** one of the four elements (air, earth, fire, and water) in ancient and medieval philosophy and in astrology. **7** the quality of transparency and brilliance shown by a diamond or other gem. ● **verb 1** pour water over (a plant or an area of ground). **2** give a drink of water to (an animal). **3** (of the eyes or mouth) produce tears or saliva. **4** dilute (a drink) with water. **5** (**water down**) make less forceful or controversial by changing or leaving out certain details. **6** (of a river) flow through (an area).

– PHRASES **hold water** (of a theory) appear sound. **make water** (of a ship or boat) take in water through a leak. **of the first water 1** (of a diamond or pearl) of the greatest brilliance and transparency. **2** unsurpassed of their kind: *she was a bore of the first water*. **under water** submerged; flooded. **water on the brain** informal hydrocephalus. **water under the bridge** (or N. Amer. **water over the dam**) past events that are over and done with.

– DERIVATIVES **waterless** adjective.

– ORIGIN Old English.

water bailiff ● **noun** Brit. **1** an official who enforces fishing laws. **2** historical a customs officer at a port.

water-based ● **adjective** (of a substance or solution) using or having water as a medium or main ingredient.

waterbed ● **noun** a bed with a water-filled rubber or plastic mattress.

water birth ● **noun** a birth in which the mother spends the final stages of labour in a birthing pool.

water biscuit ● **noun** a thin, crisp unsweetened biscuit made from flour and water.

water boatman ● **noun** a predatory aquatic bug that swims on its back using its long back legs as oars.

water buffalo ● **noun** a large black buffalo with heavy swept-back horns, used as a beast of burden throughout the tropics.

water cannon ● **noun** a device that ejects a powerful jet of water, used to disperse a crowd.

water chestnut ● **noun** the crisp, white-fleshed tuber of a tropical aquatic sedge, used in oriental cookery.

water clock ● **noun** historical a clock that used the flow of water to measure time.

water closet ● **noun** dated a flush toilet.

watercolour (US **watercolor**) ● **noun 1** artists' paint made with a water-soluble binder, and thinned with water rather than oil. **2** a picture painted with watercolours. **3** the art of painting with watercolours.

– DERIVATIVES **watercolourist** noun.

watercourse ● **noun** a brook, stream, or artificially constructed water channel.

watercress ● **noun** a cress which grows in running water and whose pungent leaves are used in salad.

water cure ● **noun** chiefly historical a session of treatment by hydropathy.

water diviner ● **noun** Brit. a person who searches for underground water by using a dowsing rod.

watered silk ● **noun** silk that been treated in such a way as to give it a wavy lustrous finish.

waterfall ● **noun** a cascade of water falling from a height, formed when a river or stream flows over a precipice or steep incline.

waterfowl ● **plural noun** ducks, geese, or other large aquatic birds.

waterfront ● **noun** a part of a town or city alongside a body of water.

waterhole ● **noun** a depression in which water collects, typically one at which animals drink.

water ice ● **noun** a frozen dessert consisting of fruit juice or purée in a sugar syrup.

watering can ● **noun** a portable water container with a long spout and a detachable perforated cap, used for watering plants.

watering hole ● **noun 1** a waterhole from which animals regularly drink. **2** informal a pub or bar.

watering place ● **noun 1** a watering hole. **2** a spa or seaside resort.

water level ● **noun 1** the height reached by a body of water. **2** a water table.

water lily ● **noun** an ornamental aquatic plant with large round floating leaves and large cup-shaped flowers.

waterline ● **noun 1** the level normally reached by the water on the side of a ship. **2** a line on a shore, riverbank, etc. marking the level reached by the sea or a river.

waterlogged ● **adjective** saturated with or full of water.

– ORIGIN from archaic *waterlog* 'make a ship unmanageable by flooding', from WATER + LOG[1].

Waterloo /wawtərloo/ ● **noun** (usu. in phrase **meet one's Waterloo**) a decisive defeat or failure.

– ORIGIN from *Waterloo*, a village in what is now Belgium, site of a battle in 1815 in which Napoleon was finally defeated.

water main ● **noun** the main pipe in a water supply system.

waterman ● **noun 1** a boatman. **2** an oarsman of a specified level of knowledge or skill.

watermark ● **noun** a faint design made in some paper during manufacture that is visible when held against the light, identifying the maker. ● **verb** mark with such a design.

water meadow ● **noun** a meadow that is periodically flooded by a stream or river.

watermelon ● **noun** a large melon-like fruit with smooth green skin, red pulp, and watery juice.

watermill ● **noun** a mill worked by a waterwheel.

water nymph ● **noun** (in folklore and classical mythology) a nymph inhabiting or presiding over water, especially a naiad or nereid.

water pistol ● **noun** a toy pistol that shoots a jet of water.

water polo ● **noun** a seven-a-side game played by swimmers in a pool, with a ball like a football that is thrown into the opponents' net.

waterproof ● **adjective** impervious to water. ● **noun** Brit. a waterproof garment. ● **verb** make waterproof.

water rail ● **noun** a secretive rail (bird) inhabiting reedbeds, with a squealing call.

water rat ● **noun 1** a large semiaquatic rat-like rodent. **2** Brit. a water vole.

water-resistant ● **adjective** able to resist the penetration of water to some degree but not entirely.

watershed ● **noun 1** an area or ridge of land that separates waters flowing to different rivers, basins, or seas. **2** a turning point in a state of affairs. **3** Brit. the time after which programmes that are unsuitable for children are broadcast on television.

– ORIGIN from WATER + *shed* in the sense 'ridge of high ground' (related to SHED[2]).

waterside ● **noun** the area adjoining a sea, lake, or river.

waterski ● **noun** (pl. **waterskis**) each of a pair of skis enabling the wearer to skim the surface of the water when towed by a motor boat. ● **verb** travel on waterskis.

– DERIVATIVES **waterskier** noun.

water splash ● **noun** Brit. a water-filled dip in a road.

waterspout ● **noun** a rotating column of water and spray formed by a whirlwind occurring over the sea or other body of water.

water table ● **noun** the level below which the ground is satur-

Thesaurus

watchman ● **noun** SECURITY GUARD, custodian, warden; sentry, guard, patrolman, lookout, sentinel, scout, watch.

watchword ● **noun** GUIDING PRINCIPLE, motto, slogan, maxim, mantra, catchword, catchphrase, byword; *informal* buzzword.

water ● **noun 1** *a glass of water technical* H_2O; *dated* Adam's ale. **2** *a house down by the water* SEA, ocean; lake, river.

– RELATED TERMS aqueous, aqua-.

● **verb 1** *water the plants* SPRINKLE, moisten, dampen, wet, spray, splash; soak, douse, souse, drench, saturate; hose (down). **2** *my mouth watered* MOISTEN, become wet, leak; salivate. **3** *he watered the claret*. See WATER SOMETHING DOWN sense 1.

– PHRASES **hold water** BE TENABLE, ring true, bear scrutiny, make sense, stand up, hold up, be convincing, be plausible, be sound. **water something down 1** *staff had watered down the drinks* DILUTE, water, thin (out), weaken; adulterate, doctor, mix; *informal* cut. **2** *the proposals were watered down* MODERATE, temper, mitigate, tone down, soften, tame; understate, play down, soft-pedal.

waterfall ● **noun** CASCADE, cataract, falls, rapids; *N. English* force.

waterproof ● **adjective** *a waterproof jacket* WATERTIGHT, water-repellent, water-resistant, damp-proof; impermeable, impervious;

ated with water.

watertight ● adjective **1** closely sealed, fastened, or fitted so as to prevent the passage of water. **2** (of an argument or account) unable to be disputed or questioned.

water torture ● noun a form of torture in which the victim is exposed to the incessant dripping of water on the head or to the sound of dripping.

water tower ● noun a tower supporting an elevated water tank, whose height creates the pressure required to distribute the water through a piped system.

water vole ● noun a large semiaquatic vole which excavates burrows in the banks of rivers.

waterway ● noun a river, canal, or other route for travel by water.

waterweed ● noun vegetation growing in water.

waterwheel ● noun a large wheel driven by flowing water, used to work machinery or to raise water to a higher level.

water wings ● plural noun inflated floats fixed to the arms of someone learning to swim to give increased buoyancy.

waterworks ● plural noun **1** (treated as sing.) an establishment for managing a water supply. **2** informal the shedding of tears. **3** Brit. euphemistic, humorous the urinary system.

watery ● adjective **1** consisting of, containing, or resembling water. **2** (of food or drink) thin or tasteless as a result of containing too much water. **3** weak or pale.

watt ● noun the unit of power in the SI system, equivalent to one joule per second and corresponding to the rate of energy in an electric circuit where the potential difference is one volt and the current one ampere.

– ORIGIN named after the Scottish engineer James *Watt* (1736–1819).

wattage ● noun an amount of electrical power expressed in watts.

watt-hour ● noun a measure of electrical energy equivalent to a power consumption of one watt for one hour.

wattle[1] /wott'l/ ● noun **1** a material for making fences, walls, etc., consisting of rods or stakes interlaced with twigs or branches. **2** an Australian acacia with long pliant branches and cream, yellow, or golden flowers.

– ORIGIN Old English.

wattle[2] /wott'l/ ● noun a fleshy lobe hanging from the head or neck of the turkey and some other birds.

– ORIGIN of unknown origin.

wattle and daub ● noun a material formerly used in building walls, consisting of wattle covered with mud or clay.

wattlebird ● noun **1** an Australian songbird with a wattle hanging from each cheek. **2** a New Zealand songbird with wattles hanging from the base of the bill.

Watusi /wətōōsi/ (also **Watutsi** /wətōōtsi/) ● noun **1** (treated as pl.) the Tutsi people collectively (now dated in English use). **2** an energetic dance popular in the 1960s.

– ORIGIN a local name.

wave ● verb **1** move one's hand to and fro in greeting or as a signal. **2** move (one's hand or arm, or something held in one's hand) to and fro. **3** move to and fro with a swaying motion while remaining fixed to one point. **4** style (hair) so that it curls slightly. ● noun **1** a ridge of water curling into an arched form and breaking on the shore or between two depressions in open water. **2** a sudden occurrence of or increase in a phenomenon or emotion. **3** a gesture or signal made by waving one's hand. **4** a slightly curling lock of hair. **5** Physics a periodic disturbance of the particles of a substance which is propagated without net movement of the particles, as in the passage of undulating motion or sound. **6** Physics a similar variation of an electromagnetic field in the propagation of light or other radiation.

– PHRASES **make waves** informal **1** create a significant impression. **2** cause trouble.

– ORIGIN Old English, related to WAVER.

waveband ● noun a range of wavelengths between two given limits, used in radio transmission.

wave equation ● noun Mathematics a differential equation expressing the properties of motion in waves.

waveform ● noun Physics a curve showing the shape of a wave at a given time.

wavelength ● noun **1** Physics the distance between successive crests of a wave, especially as a distinctive feature of sound, light, radio waves, etc. **2** a person's way of thinking when communicated to another: *we weren't on the same wavelength.*

wavelet ● noun a small wave.

wave mechanics ● plural noun (treated as sing.) a method of analysis of the behaviour of atomic phenomena with particles represented by wave equations.

waver ● verb **1** move quiveringly; flicker. **2** begin to weaken; falter. **3** be indecisive.

– DERIVATIVES **waverer** noun **wavery** adjective.

– ORIGIN Old Norse, 'flicker'.

wavy ● adjective (**wavier**, **waviest**) having or consisting of a series of wave-like curves.

– DERIVATIVES **waviness** noun.

wax[1] ● noun **1** beeswax. **2** a soft solid oily substance that melts easily, used for making candles or polishes. ● verb **1** polish or treat with wax. **2** remove hair from (a part of the body) by applying wax and then peeling it off with the hairs. **3** informal make a recording of.

– DERIVATIVES **waxer** noun.

– ORIGIN Old English.

wax[2] ● verb **1** (of the moon) have a progressively larger part of its visible surface illuminated, so that it appears to increase in size. **2** literary become larger or stronger. **3** speak or write in the specified manner: *they waxed lyrical about the old days.*

– ORIGIN Old English.

wax[3] ● noun Brit. informal, dated a fit of anger.

– ORIGIN perhaps from phrases such as *wax angry* (see WAX[2]).

waxbill ● noun a small finch-like songbird with a red bill that resembles sealing wax in colour.

Thesaurus

rubberized, waxed.

● noun (*Brit.*) *she put on a waterproof* RAINCOAT, anorak, oilskin, cagoule; *Brit.* mackintosh; *Brit. informal* mac.

watertight ● adjective **1** *a watertight container* IMPERMEABLE, impervious, (hermetically) sealed; waterproof, water-repellent, water-resistant, damp-proof. **2** *a watertight alibi* INDISPUTABLE, unquestionable, incontrovertible, irrefutable, unassailable, impregnable; foolproof, sound, flawless, airtight, conclusive.

– OPPOSITES leaky, flawed.

watery ● adjective **1** *a watery discharge* LIQUID, fluid, aqueous; *technical* hydrous. **2** *a watery meadow* WET, damp, moist, sodden, soggy, squelchy, soft; saturated, waterlogged; marshy, boggy, swampy, miry, muddy. **3** *watery porridge* THIN, runny, weak, sloppy, dilute, diluted; tasteless, flavourless, insipid, bland. **4** *the light was watery and grey* PALE, wan, faint, weak, feeble; *informal* wishy-washy. **5** *watery eyes* TEARFUL, teary, moist, rheumy; *informal* weepy; *formal* lachrymose.

– OPPOSITES dry, thick, bright.

wave ● verb **1** *he waved his flag furiously* MOVE UP AND DOWN, move to and fro, wag, shake, swish, sweep, swing, brandish, flourish, wield; flick, flutter, waggle. **2** *the grass waved in the breeze* RIPPLE, flutter, undulate, stir, flap, sway, shake, quiver, move. **3** *the waiter waved them closer* GESTURE, gesticulate, signal, beckon, motion.

● noun **1** *she gave him a friendly wave* GESTURE, gesticulation; signal, sign, motion. **2** *he surfs the big waves* BREAKER, roller, comber, boomer, ripple, white horse; (**waves**) swell, surf, froth; *Austral.* bombora; *archaic* billow. **3** *a wave of emigration* FLOW, rush, surge, flood, stream, tide, deluge, spate. **4** *a wave of self-pity* SURGE, rush, stab, dart, upsurge; thrill, frisson; feeling. **5** *his hair grew in thick waves* CURL, kink, corkscrew, twist, ringlet, coil. **6** *electromagnetic waves* ripple, vibration, oscillation.

– PHRASES **make waves** (*informal*) CAUSE TROUBLE, be disruptive, be troublesome; make an impression, get noticed. **wave something aside** DISMISS, reject, brush aside, shrug off, disregard, ignore, discount, play down; *informal* pooh-pooh. **wave someone/something down** FLAG DOWN, hail, stop, summon, call, accost.

waver ● verb **1** *the candlelight wavered in the draught* FLICKER, quiver, twinkle, glimmer, wink, blink. **2** *his voice wavered* FALTER, wobble, tremble, quaver. **3** *he wavered between the choices* BE UNDECIDED, be irresolute, hesitate, dither, equivocate, vacillate, fluctuate; think twice, change one's mind, blow hot and cold; *Brit.* haver, hum and haw; *informal* shilly-shally, sit on the fence.

wavy ● adjective CURLY, curvy, curved, undulating, squiggly, rippled, crinkly, kinked, zigzag.

wax ● verb **1** *the moon is waxing* GET BIGGER, increase, enlarge. **2** (*poetic/literary*) *price sensitivity is waxing* INCREASE, grow, develop, rise, expand, escalate, intensify, spread, mushroom, snowball.

waxcloth (also **waxed cloth**) • noun cloth treated with wax to make it waterproof.

waxed jacket • noun an outdoor jacket made of a waxed waterproof fabric.

waxed paper • noun paper treated with wax to make it waterproof or greaseproof.

waxen • adjective **1** having a smooth, pale, translucent surface like that of wax. **2** archaic or literary made of wax.

waxwing • noun a crested songbird, mainly pinkish-brown and with bright red tips to some wing feathers.

waxwork • noun **1** a lifelike dummy modelled in wax. **2** (**waxworks**) (treated as sing.) an exhibition of waxworks.

waxy • adjective (**waxier**, **waxiest**) resembling wax in consistency or appearance.

– DERIVATIVES **waxiness** noun.

way • noun **1** a method, style, or manner of doing something. **2** the typical manner in which someone behaves or in which something happens. **3** a road, track, path, or street. **4** a route or means taken in order to reach, enter, or leave a place. **5** the route along which someone or something is travelling or would travel if unobstructed. **6** a specified direction. **7** the distance in space or time between two points. **8** informal a particular area or locality. **9** a particular aspect or respect. **10** a specified condition or state: *the family was in a poor way*. **11** (**ways**) parts into which something divides or is divided. **12** forward motion or momentum of a ship or boat through water. • adverb informal at or to a considerable distance or extent.

– PHRASES **by the way** incidentally. **by way of 1** via. **2** as a form of. **3** by means of. **come one's way** happen or become available to one. **get** (or **have**) **one's** (**own**) **way** get or do what one wants in spite of opposition. **give way 1** yield. **2** be unable to carry a load or withstand a force and collapse or break. **3** allow another to be or go first. **4** (**give way to**) be replaced or superseded by. **go one's own way** act as one wishes, especially against contrary advice. **go one's way 1** (of events, circumstances, etc.) be favourable to one. **2** leave. **have a way with** have a particular talent for dealing with or ability in. **have one's way with** humorous have sexual intercourse with. **in a way** (or **in some ways** or **in one way**) to a certain extent. **lead the way 1** go first along a route to show someone the way. **2** be a pioneer. **one way and another** (or **one way or the other**) **1** taking most aspects or considerations into account. **2** by some means. **3** whichever of two given alternatives is the case. **on the** (or **its**) **way** about to arrive or happen. **on the** (or **one's**) **way out** informal **1** going out of fashion or favour. **2** dying. **the other way round** (or **around**; Brit. also **about**) **1** in the opposite position or direction. **2** the opposite of what is expected or supposed. **out of the way 1** (of a place) remote. **2** dealt with or finished. **3** no longer an obstacle to someone's plans. **4** unusual or exceptional. **ways and means** the methods and resources for achieving something.

– ORIGIN Old English.

waybill • noun a list of passengers or goods being carried on a vehicle.

wayfarer • noun literary a person who travels on foot.

– DERIVATIVES **wayfaring** noun.

wayfaring tree • noun a white-flowered shrub which has berries turning from green through red to black.

waylay • verb (past and past part. **waylaid**) **1** intercept in order to attack. **2** intercept and detain with questions, conversation, etc.

waymark • noun (also **waymarker**) a sign forming one of a series used to mark out a footpath or similar route.

way-out • adjective informal unconventional or avant-garde.

-ways • suffix forming adjectives and adverbs of direction or manner: *lengthways*.

wayside • noun the edge of a road.

– PHRASES **fall by the wayside** fail to persist in an undertaking. [ORIGIN with biblical allusion to the Gospel of Luke, chapter 8.]

way station • noun N. Amer. a stopping place on a journey.

wayward • adjective self-willed and unpredictable; perverse.

– DERIVATIVES **waywardly** adverb **waywardness** noun.

– ORIGIN shortening of obsolete *awayward* 'turned away'.

wazzock /wazzək/ • noun Brit. informal a stupid or annoying person.

– ORIGIN of unknown origin.

Wb • abbreviation weber(s).

WBA • abbreviation World Boxing Association.

WBC • abbreviation World Boxing Council.

WC • abbreviation Brit. water closet.

we • pronoun (first person pl.) **1** used by a speaker to refer to himself or herself and one or more other people considered together. **2** people in general. **3** used in formal contexts for or by a royal person, or by a writer, to refer to himself or herself. **4** you (used condescendingly).

– USAGE On whether to use **we** or **us** following **than**, see the note at THAN.

– ORIGIN Old English.

weak • adjective **1** lacking physical strength and energy. **2** liable to break or give way under pressure. **3** not secure, stable, or firmly established. **4** lacking power, influence, or ability. **5** lacking intensity. **6** (of a liquid or solution) heavily diluted. **7** not convincing or forceful. **8** Grammar (of verbs) forming the past tense and past participle by addition of a suffix (in English, typically *-ed*).

– PHRASES **the weaker sex** (treated as sing. or pl.) dated women regarded collectively. **weak at the knees** helpless with emotion.

– ORIGIN Old English.

weaken • verb make or become weak.

Thesaurus

– OPPOSITES wane.

– PHRASES **wax lyrical** BE ENTHUSIASTIC, enthuse, rave, gush, get carried away.

waxen • adjective PALLID, pale, pasty, wan, ashen, colourless, anaemic, bloodless, washed out, white, grey, whitish, waxy, drained, sickly.

– OPPOSITES ruddy.

waxy • adjective. See WAXEN.

way • noun **1** *a way of reducing the damage* METHOD, process, procedure, technique, system; plan, strategy, scheme; means, mechanism, approach. **2** *she kissed him in her brisk way* MANNER, style, fashion, mode; modus operandi, MO. **3** *I've changed my ways* PRACTICE, wont, habit, custom, policy, procedure, convention, routine, modus vivendi; trait, attribute, peculiarity, idiosyncrasy; conduct, behaviour, manner, style, nature, personality, temperament, disposition, character. **4** *which way leads home?* ROUTE, course, direction; road, street, track, path. **5** *I'll go out the back way* DOOR, gate, exit, entrance, entry; route. **6** *a short way downstream* DISTANCE, length, stretch, journey; space, interval, span. **7** *April is a long way away* TIME, stretch, term, span, duration. **8** *a car coming the other way* DIRECTION, bearing, course, orientation, line, tack. **9** (*informal*) *what do they call it down your way?* AREA, region, district, neighbourhood, locality, locale; *informal* neck of the woods, parts; *Brit. informal* manor; *N. Amer. informal* hood, nabe. **10** *in some ways, he may be better off* RESPECT, regard, aspect, facet, sense; detail, point, particular. **11** *the country is in a bad way* STATE, condition, situation, circumstances, position; predicament, plight; *informal* shape.

– PHRASES **by the way** INCIDENTALLY, by the by, in passing, en passant. **give way 1** *the government gave way and passed the bill* YIELD, back down, surrender, concede defeat, give in, submit, succumb; acquiesce, agree, assent; *informal* throw in the towel/sponge, cave in. **2** *the door gave way* COLLAPSE, give, cave in, fall in, come apart, crumple. **3** *grief gave way to guilt* BE REPLACED BY, be succeeded by, be followed by, be supplanted by. **on the way** COMING, imminent, forthcoming, approaching, impending, close, near, on us; proceeding, en route, in transit.

wayfarer • noun (*poetic/literary*). See WANDERER.

waylay • verb **1** *we were waylaid and robbed* AMBUSH, hold up, attack, assail, rob; *informal* mug, stick up. **2** *several people waylaid her to chat* ACCOST, detain, intercept, take aside, pounce on, importune; *informal* buttonhole.

way-out • adjective (*informal*) UNCONVENTIONAL, avant-garde, outlandish, eccentric, quirky, unusual, bizarre, strange, peculiar, odd, uncommon; *informal* far out, offbeat, oddball, off the wall; *Brit. informal* rum.

– OPPOSITES ordinary.

wayward • adjective WILFUL, headstrong, stubborn, obstinate, obdurate, perverse, contrary, disobedient, insubordinate, undisciplined; rebellious, defiant, uncooperative, recalcitrant, unruly, wild, unmanageable, erratic; difficult, impossible; *formal* refractory.

– OPPOSITES docile.

weak • adjective **1** *they are too weak to move* FRAIL, feeble, delicate, fragile; infirm, sick, sickly, debilitated, incapacitated, ailing, indisposed, decrepit; tired, fatigued, exhausted; *informal* weedy.

W

weak-kneed ● adjective **1** weak and shaky from fear or excitement. **2** lacking in resolve or courage.
weakling ● noun a weak person or animal.
weakly ● adverb in a weak manner. ● adjective (**weaklier**, **weakliest**) weak or sickly.
weakness ● noun **1** the state or condition of being weak. **2** a disadvantage or fault. **3** a person or thing that one is unable to resist. **4** (**weakness for**) a self-indulgent liking for.
weal[1] /weel/ (also chiefly Medicine **wheal**) ● noun a red, swollen mark left on flesh by a blow or pressure.
– ORIGIN variant of WALE, influenced by obsolete *wheal* 'suppurate'.
weal[2] /weel/ ● noun formal that which is best for someone or something: *guardians of the public weal.*
– ORIGIN Old English, 'wealth, well-being'; related to WELL[1].
Wealden /weeldən/ ● adjective Brit. relating to the Weald, a formerly wooded district including parts of Kent, Surrey, and East Sussex.
wealth ● noun **1** an abundance of valuable possessions or money. **2** the state of being rich. **3** an abundance or profusion of something desirable.
– ORIGIN from WELL[1] or WEAL[2], on the pattern of *health.*
wealthy ● adjective (**wealthier**, **wealthiest**) having a great deal of money, resources, or assets; rich.
wean[1] ● verb **1** accustom (a young mammal) to food other than its mother's milk. **2** (often **wean off**) make (someone) give up a habit or addiction. **3** (**be weaned on**) be strongly influenced by (something) from an early age.
– ORIGIN Old English.
wean[2] ● noun Scottish & N. English a young child.
– ORIGIN contraction of *wee ane* 'little one'.
weanling ● noun a newly weaned animal.
weapon ● noun **1** a thing designed or used for inflicting bodily harm or physical damage. **2** a means of gaining an advantage or defending oneself.
– DERIVATIVES **weaponry** noun.
– ORIGIN Old English.
wear ● verb (past **wore**; past part. **worn**) **1** have on one's body as clothing, decoration, or protection. **2** exhibit or present (a particular facial expression or appearance). **3** damage or destroy or suffer damage or destruction by friction or use. **4** withstand continued use to a specified degree: *the fabric wears well wash after wash.* **5** (**wear off**) lose effectiveness or intensity. **6** (**wear down**) overcome by persistence. **7** (**wear out**) exhaust. **8** (**wearing**) mentally or physically tiring. **9** (**wear on**) (of time) pass slowly or tediously. ● noun **1** the action of wearing or the state of being worn. **2** clothing suitable for a particular purpose or of a particular type. **3** damage sustained from continuous use. **4** the capacity for withstanding such damage.
– PHRASES **wear thin** gradually dwindle or be used up.
– DERIVATIVES **wearable** adjective **wearer** noun.
– ORIGIN Old English.
weary ● adjective (**wearier**, **weariest**) **1** tired. **2** causing tiredness. **3** (often **weary of**) reluctant to experience any more of. ● verb (**wearies**, **wearied**) **1** make weary. **2** (**weary of**) grow tired of.
– DERIVATIVES **wearily** adverb **weariness** noun **wearisome** adjective.
– ORIGIN Old English.

Thesaurus

2 *bats have weak eyes* INADEQUATE, poor, feeble; defective, faulty, deficient, imperfect, substandard. **3** *a weak excuse* UNCONVINCING, untenable, tenuous, implausible, unsatisfactory, poor, inadequate, feeble, flimsy, lame, hollow; *informal* pathetic. **4** *I was too weak to be a rebel* SPINELESS, craven, cowardly, pusillanimous, timid; irresolute, indecisive, ineffectual, inept, effete, meek, tame, ineffective, impotent, soft, faint-hearted; *informal* yellow, weak-kneed, gutless, chicken. **5** *a weak light* DIM, pale, wan, faint, feeble, muted. **6** *a weak voice* INDISTINCT, muffled, muted, hushed, faint, low. **7** *weak coffee* WATERY, diluted, dilute, watered down, thin, tasteless, flavourless, bland, insipid, wishy-washy. **8** *a weak smile* UNENTHUSIASTIC, feeble, half-hearted, lame.
– OPPOSITES strong, powerful, convincing, resolute, bright, loud.
weaken ● verb **1** *the virus weakened him terribly* ENFEEBLE, debilitate, incapacitate, sap, enervate, tire, exhaust, wear out; wither, cripple, disable. **2** *she tried to weaken the shock for him* REDUCE, decrease, diminish, lessen, moderate, temper, dilute, blunt, mitigate, soften. **3** *our morale weakened* DECREASE, dwindle, diminish, wane, ebb, subside, peter out, fizzle out, tail off, decline, falter. **4** *the move weakened her authority* IMPAIR, undermine, compromise; invalidate, negate, discredit.
weakling ● noun MILKSOP, namby-pamby, coward, pushover; *informal* wimp, weed, sissy, drip, softie, doormat, chicken, yellow-belly, scaredy-cat; *N. Amer. informal* wuss, pussy.
weakness ● noun **1** *with old age came weakness* FRAILTY, feebleness, enfeeblement, fragility, delicacy; infirmity, sickness, sickliness, debility, incapacity, indisposition, decrepitude; *informal* weediness. **2** *he has worked on his weaknesses* FAULT, flaw, defect, deficiency, weak point, failing, shortcoming, imperfection, Achilles' heel. **3** *a weakness for champagne* FONDNESS, liking, partiality, preference, love, penchant, soft spot, predilection, inclination, taste, eye; enthusiasm, appetite. **4** *the President was accused of weakness* TIMIDITY, cravenness, cowardliness, pusillanimity; indecision, irresolution, ineffectuality, ineptitude, meekness, powerlessness, ineffectiveness, impotence. **5** *the weakness of this argument* UNTENABILITY, implausibility, poverty, inadequacy, transparency; flimsiness, hollowness. **6** *the weakness of the sound* INDISTINCTNESS, mutedness, faintness, feebleness, lowness; dimness, paleness.
weak-willed ● adjective SPINELESS, weak, irresolute, indecisive; impressionable, persuadable, persuasible, submissive, unassertive, compliant, pusillanimous; *informal* wimpish, chicken.
weal ● noun WELT, wound, lesion, swelling; scar, cicatrix, mark, blemish.
wealth ● noun **1** *a gentleman of wealth* AFFLUENCE, prosperity, riches, means, substance, fortune; money, cash, lucre, capital, treasure, finance; assets, possessions, resources, funds; property, stock, reserves, securities, holdings; *informal* wherewithal, dough, bread. **2** *a wealth of information* ABUNDANCE, profusion, plethora, mine, store, treasury, bounty, cornucopia; *informal* lot, load, heap, mass, mountain, stack, ton; *Brit. informal* shedload; *formal* plenitude.
– OPPOSITES poverty, dearth.
wealthy ● adjective RICH, affluent, moneyed, well off, well-to-do, prosperous, comfortable, propertied; of substance; *informal* well heeled, rolling in it, in the money, made of money, filthy rich, stinking rich, loaded, flush, quids in; *Austral./NZ informal* financial; *informal, dated* oofy.
– OPPOSITES poor.
wear ● verb **1** *he wore a suit* DRESS IN, be clothed in, have on, sport; put on, don. **2** *Barbara wore a smile* BEAR, have (on one's face), show, display, exhibit; give, put on, assume. **3** *the bricks have been worn down* ERODE, abrade, rub away, grind away, wash away, crumble (away), wear down; corrode, eat away (at), dissolve. **4** *the tyres are wearing well* LAST, endure, hold up, bear up, prove durable. **5** (*Brit. informal*) *I've asked him twice, but he won't wear it* ALLOW, permit, authorize, sanction, condone, indulge, agree to, approve of; put up with, take, stand, support; accept, swallow, tolerate, countenance; *informal* hack, abide, stomach; *Brit. informal* stick; *formal* brook; *archaic* suffer.
● noun **1** *you won't get much wear out of that* USE, wearing, service, utility, value; *informal* mileage. **2** *evening wear* CLOTHES, clothing, garments, dress, attire, garb, wardrobe; *informal* get-up, gear, togs; *Brit. informal* kit, clobber; *formal* apparel; *poetic/literary* array. **3** *the varnish which will withstand wear* DAMAGE, friction, erosion, attrition, abrasion.
– PHRASES **wear something down** *he wore down her resistance* GRADUALLY OVERCOME, slowly reduce, erode, wear away, exhaust, undermine. **wear off** *the novelty soon wore off* FADE, diminish, lessen, dwindle, decrease, wane, ebb, peter out, fizzle out, pall, disappear, vanish, run out. **wear on** *the afternoon wore on* PASS, elapse, proceed, advance, progress, go by, roll by, march on, slip by/away, fly by/past. **wear out** DETERIORATE, become worn, wear thin, fray, become threadbare, go into holes, wear through. **wear something out** USE UP, consume, go through. **wear someone out** FATIGUE, tire out, weary, exhaust, drain, sap, overtax, enervate, debilitate, jade, prostrate; *informal* whack, poop, shatter, frazzle, do in; *Brit. informal* knacker.
wearing ● adjective TIRING, exhausting, wearying, fatiguing, enervating, draining, sapping; demanding, exacting, taxing, arduous, gruelling, punishing, difficult, hard, tough, laborious, strenuous, rigorous.
wearisome ● adjective. See WEARING.
weary ● adjective **1** *he was weary after cycling* TIRED, worn out, exhausted, fatigued, sapped, dog-tired, spent, drained, prostrate, enervated; *informal* all in, done in, dead beat, ready to drop, bushed, worn to a frazzle, shattered; *Brit. informal* knackered, whacked; *N. Amer. informal* pooped, tuckered out. **2** *she was weary of*

weasel • noun **1** a small slender carnivorous mammal related to the stoat, with reddish-brown fur. **2** informal a deceitful or treacherous person. • verb (**weaselled**, **weaselling**; US **weaseled**, **weaseling**) achieve through cunning or deceit.
– DERIVATIVES **weaselly** adjective.
– ORIGIN Old English.
weasel words • plural noun statements that are intentionally ambiguous or misleading.
weather • noun **1** the state of the atmosphere at a place and time as regards temperature, wind, rain, etc. **2** (before another noun) denoting the side from which the wind is blowing; windward. Contrasted with LEE. • verb **1** wear away or change in form or appearance by long exposure to the weather. **2** come safely through.
– PHRASES **keep a weather eye on** be watchful for developments. **make heavy weather of** informal have unnecessary difficulty in dealing with (a task or problem). [ORIGIN from the nautical phrase *make good* or *bad weather of it*, referring to a ship in a storm.] **under the weather** informal slightly unwell or depressed.
– ORIGIN Old English.
weather balloon • noun a balloon equipped with meteorological apparatus which is sent into the atmosphere to provide information about the weather.
weather-beaten • adjective damaged, worn, or tanned by exposure to the weather.
weatherboard chiefly Brit. • noun **1** a sloping board attached to the bottom of an outside door to keep out the rain. **2** each of a series of horizontal boards nailed to outside walls with edges overlapping to keep out the rain.
– DERIVATIVES **weatherboarding** noun.
weathercock • noun a weathervane in the form of a cockerel.
weather house • noun a toy hygroscope in the form of a small house with figures of a man and woman standing in two porches, the man coming out in wet weather and the woman in dry.
weatherman (or **weatherwoman**) • noun a person who broadcasts a description and forecast of weather conditions.
weather station • noun an observation post where weather conditions and meteorological data are observed and recorded.
weatherstrip • noun a strip of material used to seal the edges of a door or window against rain and wind.
weathervane • noun a revolving pointer to show the direction of the wind.
weave[1] • verb (past **wove**; past part. **woven** or **wove**) **1** form (fabric) by interlacing long threads passing in one direction with others at a right angle to them. **2** (usu. as noun **weaving**) make fabric in this way. **3** make (basketwork or a wreath) by interlacing rods or flowers. **4** (**weave into**) make (interconnected elements) into (a story). • noun a particular style or manner in which fabric is woven: *cloth of a very fine weave.*
– ORIGIN Old English.
weave[2] • verb move from side to side to progress around obstructions.
– PHRASES **get weaving** Brit. informal set briskly to work.
– ORIGIN probably from an Old Norse word meaning 'to wave, brandish'.
weaver • noun **1** a person who weaves fabric. **2** (also **weaver bird**) a finch-like songbird of tropical Africa and Asia, which builds elaborately woven nests.
web • noun **1** a network of fine threads constructed by a spider, used to catch its prey. **2** a complex system of interconnected elements. **3** (**the Web**) short for WORLD WIDE WEB. **4** a membrane between the toes of a swimming bird or other aquatic animal. **5** a roll of paper used in a continuous printing process. **6** a piece of woven fabric.
– ORIGIN Old English, related to WEAVE[1].
webbed • adjective **1** (of an animal's feet) having the toes connected by a web. **2** Medicine (of fingers or toes) abnormally united by a fold of skin.
webbing • noun strong, closely woven fabric used chiefly for making straps and belts and for supporting the seats of upholstered chairs.
webcam (also **Webcam**) • noun (trademark in the US) a video camera connected to a computer connected to the Internet, so that its images can be seen by Internet users.
webcast • noun a live video broadcast of an event transmitted across the Internet.
weber /vaybər/ • noun the unit of magnetic flux in the SI system, sufficient to cause an electromotive force of one volt in a circuit of one turn when generated or removed in one second.
– ORIGIN named after the German physicist Wilhelm Eduard *Weber* (1804–91).
webmaster • noun Computing a person who is responsible for a particular server on the Internet.
web page • noun Computing a hypertext document accessible via the Internet.
website • noun Computing a location connected to the Internet that maintains one or more web pages.
wed • verb (**wedding**; past and past part. **wedded** or **wed**) **1** formal or literary marry. **2** formal or literary give or join in marriage. **3** (**wedded**) of or concerning marriage. **4** combine (two desirable factors or qualities). **5** (**be wedded to**) be entirely devoted to (an activity, belief, etc.).
– ORIGIN Old English, related to GAGE[1].
we'd • contraction **1** we had. **2** we should or we would.
wedding • noun a marriage ceremony.
wedding band • noun chiefly N. Amer. a wedding ring.
wedding breakfast • noun Brit. a celebratory meal eaten just after a wedding (at any time of day) by the couple and their guests.
wedding cake • noun a rich iced cake served at a wedding reception.
wedding march • noun a piece of march music played at the entrance of the bride or the exit of the couple at a wedding.
wedding ring • noun a ring worn by a married person, given to them by their spouse at their wedding.
wedge • noun **1** a piece of wood, metal, etc. with a thick end that tapers to a thin edge, that is driven between two objects or parts of an object to secure or separate them. **2** a wedge-shaped thing or piece. **3** a golf club with a low, angled face for max-

Thesaurus

the arguments TIRED OF, fed up with, bored by, sick of; *informal* have had it up to here with. **3** *a weary journey* TIRING, exhausting, wearying, fatiguing, enervating, draining, sapping, wearing, trying, demanding, taxing, arduous, gruelling, difficult, hard, tough.
– OPPOSITES fresh, keen, refreshing.
• verb **1** *she was wearied by her illness* TIRE, fatigue, wear out, overtire, exhaust, drain, sap, enervate, debilitate, enfeeble, prostrate; *informal* whack, bush, shatter, frazzle, poop, do in; *Brit. informal* knacker. **2** *don't risk wearying the reader* BORE, tire; irk, irritate, exasperate. **3** *he wearied of the struggle* TIRE OF, become fed up with, become bored by, sicken of; have had enough of.
– OPPOSITES refresh, interest.
wearying • adjective. See WEARING.
weather • noun *what's the weather like?* FORECAST, outlook; meteorological conditions, climate, atmospheric pressure, temperature; elements.
• verb *we weathered the recession* SURVIVE, come through, ride out, pull through; withstand, endure, rise above, surmount, overcome, resist; *informal* stick out.
– PHRASES **under the weather** *(informal)*. See ILL adjective sense 1.
weathered • adjective WEATHER-BEATEN, worn; tanned, bronzed; lined, creased, wrinkled, gnarled.
weave[1] • verb **1** *flowers were woven into their hair* ENTWINE, lace, twist, knit, intertwine, braid, plait. **2** *he weaves colourful plots* INVENT, make up, fabricate, construct, create, contrive, spin; tell, recount, relate.
weave[2] • verb *he had to weave his way through the crowds* THREAD, wind, wend; dodge, zigzag.
web • noun **1** *a spider's web* MESH, net, lattice, latticework, lacework, webbing; gauze, gossamer. **2** *a web of friendships* NETWORK, nexus, complex, set, chain.
wed • verb **1** *(formal) they are old enough to wed* MARRY, get married, become husband and wife; *informal* tie the knot, walk down the aisle, get spliced, get hitched. **2** *(formal) he will wed his girlfriend* MARRY, take as one's wife/husband, lead to the altar; *informal* make an honest woman of; *archaic* espouse. **3** *she wedded the two forms of spirituality* UNITE, unify, join, combine, amalgamate, fuse, integrate, bond, merge.
– OPPOSITES divorce, separate.
wedded • adjective **1** *wedded bliss* MARRIED, matrimonial, marital, conjugal, nuptial; *Law* spousal; *poetic/literary* connubial. **2** *he is wedded to his work* DEDICATED TO, devoted to, attached to, fixated on, single-minded about.
wedding • noun MARRIAGE (SERVICE/RITES), nuptials, union; *archaic*

imum loft. **4** a shoe with a fairly high heel forming a solid block with the sole. ● **verb 1** fix in position using a wedge. **2** force into a narrow space.
– PHRASES **drive a wedge between** cause a breach between. **the thin end of the wedge** informal an action of little importance in itself but likely to lead to more serious developments.
– ORIGIN Old English.
Wedgwood /wejwŏŏd/ ● **noun 1** trademark ceramic ware made by the English potter Josiah Wedgwood (1730–95) and his successors, especially a kind of stoneware with white embossed cameos. **2** a powder-blue colour characteristic of this stoneware.
wedlock ● **noun** the state of being married.
– PHRASES **born in** (or **out of**) **wedlock** born of married (or unmarried) parents.
– ORIGIN Old English, 'marriage vow'.
Wednesday ● **noun** the day of the week before Thursday and following Tuesday.
– ORIGIN Old English, named after the Germanic god *Odin*; translation of Latin *Mercurii dies* 'day of Mercury'.
wee[1] ● **adjective** (**weer**, **weest**) chiefly Scottish little.
– ORIGIN Old English.
wee[2] informal, chiefly Brit. ● **noun 1** an act of urinating. **2** urine. ● **verb** (**wees**, **weed**) urinate.
– ORIGIN imitative.
weed ● **noun 1** a wild plant growing where it is not wanted and in competition with cultivated plants. **2** informal cannabis. **3** (**the weed**) informal tobacco. **4** informal a weak or skinny person. ● **verb 1** remove weeds from. **2** (**weed out**) remove (inferior or unwanted items or members) from something.
– ORIGIN Old English.
weedkiller ● **noun** a substance used to destroy weeds.
weedy ● **adjective** (**weedier**, **weediest**) **1** containing or covered with many weeds. **2** informal thin and puny.
Wee Free ● **noun** a member of the minority group nicknamed the **Wee Free Kirk** which stood apart from the Free Church of Scotland when the majority amalgamated with the United Presbyterian Church to form the United Free Church in 1900.
week ● **noun 1** a period of seven days. **2** the period of seven days generally reckoned from and to midnight on Saturday night. **3** chiefly Brit. (preceded by a specified day) a week after (that day). **4** the five days from Monday to Friday, or the time spent working during this period.
– ORIGIN Old English.
weekday ● **noun** a day of the week other than Sunday or Saturday.
weekend ● **noun** Saturday and Sunday. ● **verb** informal spend a weekend somewhere.
weekender ● **noun** a person who spends weekends away from their main home.
weekly ● **adjective 1** done, produced, or occurring once a week. **2** calculated in terms of a week. ● **adverb** once a week. ● **noun** (pl. **weekies**) a newspaper or periodical issued every week.
weeny ● **adjective** (**weenier**, **weeniest**) informal tiny.
weep ● **verb** (past and past part. **wept**) **1** shed tears. **2** exude liquid. **3** (**weeping**) used in names of trees and shrubs with drooping branches, e.g. **weeping willow**. ● **noun** a fit or spell of shedding tears.
– ORIGIN Old English.
weepie (also **weepy**) ● **noun** (pl. **weepies**) informal a sentimental or emotional film, novel, or song.
weepy ● **adjective** (**weepier**, **weepiest**) informal **1** tearful; inclined to weep. **2** sentimental.
– DERIVATIVES **weepily** adverb **weepiness** noun.
weevil /weevil/ ● **noun** a small beetle with an elongated snout, several kinds of which are pests of crops or stored foodstuffs.
– ORIGIN Old English.
wee-wee informal, chiefly Brit. ● **noun** a child's word for urine. ● **verb** urinate.
– ORIGIN imitative.
w.e.f. ● **abbreviation** Brit. with effect from.
weft ● **noun** (in weaving) the crosswise threads that are passed over and under the warp threads on a loom to make cloth.
– ORIGIN Old English, related to WEAVE[1].
Wehrmacht /vairmaa<u>kh</u>t/ ● **noun** the German armed forces from 1921 to 1945.
– ORIGIN German, 'defensive force'.
weigh ● **verb 1** find out how heavy (someone or something) is. **2** have a specified weight. **3** (**weigh out**) measure and take out (a portion of a particular weight). **4** (**weigh down**) be heavy and cumbersome or oppressive to. **5** (**weigh on**) be depressing or worrying to. **6** (**weigh in**) (of a boxer or jockey) be officially weighed before or after a contest. **7** (often **weigh up**) assess the nature or importance of. **8** (often **weigh against**) influence a decision or action. **9** (**weigh in**) informal make a forceful contribution to a competition or argument. **10** (**weigh into**) join in or attack forcefully or enthusiastically.
– PHRASES **weigh anchor** Nautical take up the anchor when ready to sail.
– ORIGIN Old English.
weighbridge ● **noun** a machine for weighing vehicles, set into the ground to be driven on to.
weigh-in ● **noun** an official weighing, e.g. of boxers before a fight.
weight ● **noun 1** a body's relative mass or the quantity of matter contained by it, giving rise to a downward force; heaviness. **2** Physics the force exerted on the mass of a body by a gravitational field. **3** the quality of being heavy. **4** a unit or system of units used for expressing how much something weighs. **5** a piece of metal known to weigh a definite amount and used on scales to determine how heavy something is. **6** a heavy object. **7** (**weights**) heavy blocks or discs used in weightlifting or weight training. **8** ability to influence decisions or actions: *their recommendation will carry great weight.* **9** the importance attached to something. **10** a feeling of oppression or pressure. **11** the surface density of cloth, used as a measure of its quality. ● **verb 1** make heavier or keep in place with a weight. **2** attach importance or value to. **3** (**be weighted**) be planned or arranged so as to give someone or something an advantage.

Thesaurus

espousal.
– RELATED TERMS nuptial.
wedge ● **noun 1** *the door was secured by a wedge* TAPERED BLOCK, chock, stop. **2** *a wedge of cheese* TRIANGLE, segment, slice, section; chunk, lump, slab, hunk, block, piece.
● **verb** *she wedged her case between two bags* SQUEEZE, cram, jam, ram, force, push, shove; *informal* stuff, bung.
wedlock ● **noun** MARRIAGE, (holy) matrimony, married state, union.
wee ● **adjective** *(Scottish)* LITTLE, small, tiny, minute, miniature, mini, compact, undersized, diminutive, dwarf, midget, infinitesimal, microscopic, minuscule; *informal* teeny, teeny-weeny, itsy-bitsy, half-pint, dinky; *Brit. informal* titchy, diddy; *N. Amer. informal* little-bitty.
– OPPOSITES big.
weed ● **verb**
– PHRASES **weed something/someone out** ISOLATE, separate out, sort out, sift out, winnow out, filter out, set apart, segregate; eliminate, get rid of, remove; *informal* lose.
weedy ● **adjective** *(informal)* PUNY, feeble, weak, frail, undersized, slight, skinny; *informal* pint-sized.
weekly ● **adjective** *weekly instalments* ONCE A WEEK; lasting a week; *formal* hebdomadal.
● **adverb** *the directors meet weekly* ONCE A WEEK, every week, each week, on a weekly basis; by the week, per week, a week.
weep ● **verb** *even the toughest soldiers wept* CRY, shed tears, sob, snivel, whimper, whine, wail, bawl, keen; *Scottish* greet; *informal* boohoo, blub, blubber; *Brit. informal* grizzle.
● **noun** *you sit and have a weep* CRY, sob, snivel, whimper, bawl; *informal* blub, blubber; *Brit. informal* grizzle.
weepy ● **adjective** *(informal)* TEARFUL, close to tears, upset, distressed, sad, unhappy; in tears, crying, weeping, snivelling; *informal* teary; *formal* lachrymose.
weigh ● **verb 1** *she weighs the vegetables* MEASURE THE WEIGHT OF, put on the scales. **2** *he weighed 118 kg* HAVE A WEIGHT OF, tip the scales at. **3** *the situation weighed heavily on him.* See WEIGH SOMEONE DOWN sense 2. **4** *he has to weigh up the possibilities* CONSIDER, contemplate, think about, mull over, chew over, reflect on, ruminate about, muse on; assess, appraise, analyse, investigate, inquire into, look into, examine, review, explore, take stock of. **5** *they need to weigh benefit against risk* BALANCE, evaluate, compare, juxtapose, contrast.
– PHRASES **weigh someone down 1** *my fishing gear weighed me down* BURDEN, saddle, overload, overburden, encumber, hamper, handicap. **2** *the silence weighed me down* OPPRESS, depress, lie heavy on, burden, cast down, hang over, gnaw at, prey on (one's

– PHRASES **be worth one's weight in gold** be exceedingly useful or helpful. **throw one's weight about** (or **around**) informal be unpleasantly self-assertive.
– ORIGIN Old English.
weighting ● noun **1** allowance or adjustment made to take account of special circumstances or compensate for a distorting factor. **2** Brit. additional wages or salary paid to allow for a higher cost of living in a particular area.
weightless ● adjective (of a body) not apparently acted on by gravity.
– DERIVATIVES **weightlessly** adverb **weightlessness** noun.
weightlifting ● noun the sport or activity of lifting barbells or other heavy weights.
– DERIVATIVES **weightlifter** noun.
weight training ● noun physical training that involves lifting weights.
weight-watcher ● noun a person who is on a diet in order to lose weight.
weighty ● adjective (**weightier**, **weightiest**) **1** weighing a great deal; heavy. **2** very serious and important. **3** very influential.
– DERIVATIVES **weightily** adverb **weightiness** noun.
Weil's disease /vīlz/ ● noun an infectious bacterial disease transmitted by rats via contaminated water.
– ORIGIN named after the German physician H. Adolf *Weil* (1848–1916).
weir ● noun **1** a low dam built across a river to raise the level of water upstream or regulate its flow. **2** an enclosure of stakes set in a stream as a trap for fish.
– ORIGIN Old English.
weird ● adjective **1** suggesting something supernatural; uncanny. **2** informal very strange; bizarre.
– DERIVATIVES **weirdly** adverb **weirdness** noun.
– ORIGIN originally in the sense 'having the power to control destiny': from an Old English word meaning 'destiny, fate'.
weirdo ● noun (pl. **weirdos**) informal a strange or eccentric person.
weka /wekkə/ ● noun a large flightless New Zealand rail (bird).
– ORIGIN Maori, imitative of its cry.
welch /welch/ ● verb variant spelling of WELSH.
welcome ● noun **1** an instance or manner of greeting someone. **2** a pleased or approving reaction. ● exclamation used to greet someone in a glad or friendly way. ● verb **1** greet (someone arriving) in a glad, polite, or friendly way. **2** be glad to receive or hear of. ● adjective **1** (of a guest or new arrival) gladly received. **2** very pleasing because much needed or desired. **3** allowed or invited to do a specified thing. **4** (**welcome to**) used to indicate relief at relinquishing something to another: *you're welcome to it!*
– DERIVATIVES **welcomer** noun.
– ORIGIN Old English, 'a person whose coming is pleasing'.
weld ● verb **1** join together (metal parts) by heating the surfaces to the point of melting and pressing or hammering them together. **2** forge (an article) by such means. **3** cause to combine and form a whole. ● noun a welded joint.
– DERIVATIVES **welder** noun.
– ORIGIN alteration of WELL² in the obsolete sense 'melt or weld (heated metal)'.
welfare ● noun **1** the health, happiness, and fortunes of a person or group. **2** action or procedure designed to promote the basic physical and material well-being of people in need. **3** chiefly N. Amer. financial support given for this purpose.
– ORIGIN from WELL¹ + FARE.
welfare state ● noun a system whereby the state undertakes to protect the health and well-being of its citizens by means of grants, pensions, and other benefits.
welkin ● noun literary the sky or heaven.
– ORIGIN Old English, 'cloud, sky'.
well¹ ● adverb (**better**, **best**) **1** in a good or satisfactory way. **2** in a condition of prosperity or comfort. **3** in a favourable or approving manner. **4** in a thorough manner. **5** to a great extent or degree; very much. **6** Brit. informal very; extremely: *he was well out of order*. **7** very probably; in all likelihood. **8** without difficulty. **9** with good reason. **10** archaic luckily; opportunely: *hail fellow, well met*. ● adjective (**better**, **best**) **1** in good health; free or recovered from illness. **2** in a satisfactory state or position. **3** sensible; advisable. ● exclamation used to express surprise, anger, resignation, etc., or when pausing in speech.
– PHRASES **as well** in addition; too. **as well** (or **just as well**) **1** with equal reason or an equally good result. **2** sensible, appropriate, or desirable. **be well out of** Brit. informal be fortunate to be no longer involved in. **be well up on** know a great deal about. **leave** (or **let**) **well alone** refrain from interfering with or trying to improve something. **well and truly** completely.
– USAGE When **well** is used with a past participle, such as 'built', and the resulting compound precedes the noun, it is advisable to use a hyphen, as in *a tall, well-built man*; usually a hyphen is not used when the compound stands alone, as in *her remarks were well intentioned*.
– ORIGIN Old English, probably related to WILL¹.
well² ● noun **1** a shaft sunk into the ground to obtain water, oil, or gas. **2** a depression made to hold liquid. **3** a plentiful source or supply. **4** an enclosed space in the middle of a building, giving room for stairs or a lift or allowing light or ventilation. ● verb (often **well up**) **1** (of a liquid) rise up to the surface and spill or be about to spill. **2** (of an emotion) arise and become more intense.
– ORIGIN Old English.
we'll ● contraction we shall; we will.

Thesaurus

mind); trouble, worry, bother, disturb, upset, haunt, nag, torment, afflict, plague.
weight ● noun **1** *the weight of the book* HEAVINESS, mass, load, burden, pressure, force; poundage, tonnage. **2** *his recommendation will carry great weight* INFLUENCE, force, leverage, sway, pull, importance, significance, consequence, value, substance, power, authority; *informal* clout. **3** *a weight off her mind* BURDEN, load, millstone, albatross, encumbrance; trouble, worry, strain. **4** *the weight of the evidence is against him* PREPONDERANCE, majority, bulk, body, lion's share, predominance; most, almost all.
weighty ● adjective **1** *a weighty tome* HEAVY, thick, bulky, hefty, cumbersome, ponderous. **2** *a very weighty subject* IMPORTANT, significant, momentous, consequential, far-reaching, key, major, vital, critical, crucial; serious, grave, solemn. **3** *a weighty responsibility* BURDENSOME, onerous, heavy, oppressive, taxing, troublesome. **4** *weighty arguments* COMPELLING, cogent, strong, forceful, powerful, potent, effective, sound, valid, telling; impressive, persuasive, convincing, influential, authoritative.
– OPPOSITES light, trivial, weak.
weird ● adjective **1** *weird apparitions* UNCANNY, eerie, unnatural, supernatural, unearthly, other-worldly, ghostly, mysterious, strange, abnormal, unusual; *Scottish* eldritch; *informal* creepy, spooky, freaky. **2** *(informal) a weird sense of humour* BIZARRE, quirky, outlandish, eccentric, unconventional, unorthodox, idiosyncratic, surreal, crazy, peculiar, odd, strange, queer, freakish, zany, madcap, outré; *informal* wacky, freaky, way-out, offbeat, off the wall; *Brit. informal* rum; *N. Amer. informal* wacko.
– OPPOSITES normal, conventional.
weirdo ● noun *(informal)*. See ECCENTRIC noun.
welcome ● noun *a welcome from the vicar* GREETING, salutation; reception, hospitality; the red carpet.
● verb **1** *welcome your guests in their own language* GREET, salute, receive, meet, usher in. **2** *we welcomed their decision* BE PLEASED BY, be glad about, approve of, appreciate, embrace; *informal* give the thumbs up to.
● adjective *welcome news* PLEASING, agreeable, encouraging, gratifying, heartening, promising, favourable, pleasant; gladly received, wanted, appreciated, popular, desirable.
weld ● verb FUSE, bond, stick, join, attach, seal, splice, melt, solder.
welfare ● noun **1** *the welfare of children* WELL-BEING, health, comfort, security, safety, protection, prosperity, success, fortune; interest, good. **2** *we cannot claim welfare* SOCIAL SECURITY, (state) benefit, public assistance; pension, credit, support; sick pay, unemployment benefit; *Brit. informal* the dole.
well¹ ● adverb **1** *please behave well* SATISFACTORILY, nicely, correctly, properly, fittingly, suitably, appropriately. **2** *they get on well together* HARMONIOUSLY, agreeably, pleasantly, nicely, happily, amicably, amiably, peaceably; *informal* famously. **3** *he plays the piano well* SKILFULLY, ably, competently, proficiently, adeptly, deftly, expertly, admirably, excellently. **4** *treat your employees well* DECENTLY, fairly, kindly, generously, honestly. **5** *mix the ingredients well* THOROUGHLY, completely; effectively, rigorously, carefully. **6** *I know her quite well* INTIMATELY, thoroughly, deeply, profoundly, personally. **7** *they studied the car market well* CAREFULLY, closely, attentively, rigorously, in depth, exhaustively, in detail, meticulously, scrupulously, conscientiously, methodically, completely,

well advised ● adjective sensible; wise.
well appointed ● adjective (of a building or room) having a high standard of equipment or furnishing.
well-being ● noun the state of being comfortable, healthy, or happy.
well disposed ● adjective having a positive, sympathetic, or friendly attitude.
well done ● adjective **1** carried out successfully or satisfactorily. **2** (of food) thoroughly cooked. ● exclamation used to express congratulation or approval.
well earned ● adjective fully merited or deserved.
well endowed ● adjective **1** having plentiful supplies of a resource. **2** informal, humorous (of a man) having large genitals. **3** informal, humorous (of a woman) large-breasted.
well head ● noun **1** the place where a spring comes out of the ground. **2** the structure over a well.
well-heeled ● adjective informal wealthy.
well hung ● adjective informal, humorous (of a man) having large genitals.
wellie ● noun variant spelling of WELLY.
wellington (also **wellington boot**) ● noun chiefly Brit. a knee-length waterproof rubber or plastic boot.
– ORIGIN named after the British soldier and Prime Minister the 1st Duke of *Wellington* (1769–1852).
well knit ● adjective (of a person) strongly and compactly built.
well known ● adjective known widely or thoroughly.
well meaning (also **well meant**) ● adjective having good intentions but not necessarily the desired effect.
well-nigh ● adverb chiefly literary almost.
well off ● adjective **1** wealthy. **2** in a favourable situation or circumstances.
well oiled ● adjective **1** operating smoothly. **2** informal drunk.
well preserved ● adjective (of an old person) showing little sign of ageing.
well rounded ● adjective **1** having a pleasing curved shape. **2** (of a person) plump. **3** having a mature personality and varied interests.
well spoken ● adjective speaking in an educated and refined manner.
wellspring ● noun literary **1** a well head of a spring. **2** an abundant source of something.
well thumbed ● adjective (of a book) having been read often and bearing marks of frequent handling.
well-to-do ● adjective wealthy; prosperous.
well travelled ● adjective **1** (of a person) having travelled widely. **2** (of a route) much frequented by travellers.
well tried ● adjective having been used often and therefore known to be reliable.
well trodden ● adjective much frequented by travellers.
well turned ● adjective **1** (of a phrase or compliment) elegantly expressed. **2** (of a woman's ankle or leg) attractively shaped.
well-wisher ● noun a person who desires happiness or success for another, or who expresses such a desire.
well worn ● adjective **1** showing the signs of extensive use or wear. **2** (of a phrase or idea) used or repeated so often that it no longer has interest or significance.
welly (also **wellie**) ● noun (pl. **wellies**) Brit. informal **1** short for WELLINGTON. **2** power or vigour.
Welsh ● noun the language of Wales. ● adjective relating to Wales.
– DERIVATIVES **Welshness** noun.
– ORIGIN Old English, from Latin *Volcae*, the name of a Celtic people.
welsh (also **welch**) ● verb (**welsh on**) fail to honour (a debt or obligation).
– ORIGIN of unknown origin.
Welsh dresser ● noun a piece of wooden furniture with cupboards and drawers in the lower part and open shelves in the upper part.
Welsh rarebit (also **Welsh rabbit**) ● noun another term for RAREBIT.
welt ● noun **1** a leather rim round the edge of the upper of a shoe, to which the sole is attached. **2** a ribbed, reinforced, or decorative border of a garment or pocket. **3** a weal.
– ORIGIN of unknown origin.
Weltanschauung /veltaanshowŏŏng/ ● noun (pl. **Weltanschauungen** /veltaanshowŏŏngən/) a particular philosophy or

Thesaurus

comprehensively, fully, extensively. **8** *they speak well of him* ADMIRINGLY, highly, approvingly, favourably, appreciatively, warmly, enthusiastically, glowingly. **9** *she makes enough money to live well* COMFORTABLY, in (the lap of) luxury, prosperously. **10** *you may well be right* QUITE POSSIBLY, conceivably, probably; undoubtedly, certainly, unquestionably. **11** *he is well over forty* CONSIDERABLY, very much, a great deal, substantially, easily, comfortably, significantly. **12** *she could well afford it* EASILY, comfortably, readily, effortlessly.
– OPPOSITES badly, negligently, disparagingly, barely.
● adjective **1** *she was completely well again* HEALTHY, fine, fit, robust, strong, vigorous, blooming, thriving, hale and hearty, in good shape, in good condition, in good trim, in fine fettle; *informal* in the pink. **2** *all is not well* SATISFACTORY, all right, fine, in order, as it should be, acceptable; *informal* OK, hunky-dory; *N. Amer. & Austral./NZ informal* jake; *Brit. informal, dated* tickety-boo. **3** *it would be well to tell us in advance* ADVISABLE, sensible, prudent, politic, commonsensical, wise, judicious, expedient, recommended, advantageous, beneficial, profitable, desirable; a good idea.
– OPPOSITES poorly, unsatisfactory, inadvisable.
– PHRASES **as well** TOO, also, in addition, additionally, into the bargain, besides, furthermore, moreover, to boot. **as well as** TOGETHER WITH, along with, besides, plus, and, with, on top of, not to mention, to say nothing of, let alone.
well² ● noun **1** *she drew water from the well* BOREHOLE, bore, spring, waterhole. **2** *he's a bottomless well of forgiveness* SOURCE, supply, fount, reservoir, mine, fund, treasury.
● verb *tears welled from her eyes* FLOW, spill, stream, run, rush, gush, roll, cascade, flood, spout; seep, trickle; burst, issue.
well advised ● adjective WISE, prudent, sensible.
well balanced ● adjective. See BALANCED senses 1, 2, 3.
well behaved ● adjective ORDERLY, obedient, disciplined, peaceable, docile, controlled, restrained, cooperative, compliant; mannerly, polite, civil, courteous, respectful, proper, decorous, refined, polished.
– OPPOSITES naughty.
well-being ● noun. See WELFARE sense 1.
well bred ● adjective WELL BROUGHT UP, polite, civil, mannerly, courteous, respectful; ladylike, gentlemanly, genteel, cultivated, urbane, proper, refined, polished, well behaved.
well built ● adjective STURDY, strapping, brawny, burly, hefty, muscular, muscly, strong, rugged, lusty, Herculean; *informal* hunky, beefy, husky, hulking.
– OPPOSITES puny.
well dressed ● adjective SMART, fashionable, stylish, chic, modish, elegant, neat, spruce, trim, dapper; *N. Amer.* trig; *informal* snazzy, natty, snappy, sharp; *N. Amer. informal* spiffy, fly.
– OPPOSITES scruffy.
well founded ● adjective JUSTIFIABLE, justified, warranted, legitimate, defensible, valid, admissible, allowable, understandable, excusable, acceptable, reasonable, sensible, sound.
– OPPOSITES groundless.
well heeled ● adjective *(informal)*. See WEALTHY.
well known ● adjective **1** *well-known principles* FAMILIAR, widely known, popular, common, everyday, established. **2** *a well-known family of architects* FAMOUS, famed, prominent, notable, renowned, distinguished, eminent, illustrious, celebrated, acclaimed, important.
– OPPOSITES obscure.
well mannered ● adjective POLITE, courteous, civil, mannerly, genteel, decorous, respectful, refined, polished, civilized, urbane, well bred.
well-nigh ● adverb *(poetic/literary)* ALMOST, nearly, just about, more or less, practically, virtually, all but, as good as, nearing, approaching; roughly, approximately; *informal* pretty much, nigh on.
well off ● adjective **1** *her family's very well off.* See WELL-TO-DO. **2** *the prisoners were relatively well off* FORTUNATE, lucky, comfortable; *informal* sitting pretty. **3** *the island is not well off for harbours* WELL SUPPLIED WITH, well stocked with, well furnished with, well equipped with.
well read ● adjective KNOWLEDGEABLE, well informed, well versed, erudite, scholarly, literate, educated, cultured, bookish, studious; *dated* lettered.
– OPPOSITES ignorant.
well spoken ● adjective ARTICULATE, nicely spoken; refined, polite; *Brit. informal* posh.
well-to-do ● adjective WEALTHY, rich, affluent, moneyed, well off, prosperous, comfortable, propertied; *informal* rolling in it, in the

view of life; a world view.
– ORIGIN German, from *Welt* 'world' + *Anschauung* 'perception'.
welter • noun a large number of items in no order; a confused mass. • verb literary **1** move in a turbulent fashion. **2** lie steeped in blood.
– ORIGIN originally in the sense 'writhe, wallow': from Dutch, Low German *welteren*.
welterweight • noun a weight in boxing and other sports intermediate between lightweight and middleweight.
– ORIGIN of unknown origin.
wen[1] • noun a boil or other swelling or growth on the skin.
– ORIGIN Old English.
wen[2] (also **wyn**) • noun a runic letter, used in Old and Middle English, later replaced by *w*.
– ORIGIN Old English, 'joy'; so named because it is the first letter of this word.
wench /wench/ • noun archaic or humorous a girl or young woman.
– ORIGIN abbreviation of obsolete *wenchel* 'child, servant, prostitute'.
wend • verb (**wend one's way**) go slowly or by an indirect route.
– ORIGIN Old English, 'to turn, depart'; related to WIND[2].
Wendy house • noun Brit. a toy house large enough for children to play in.
– ORIGIN named after the house built around *Wendy* in J. M. Barrie's play *Peter Pan*.
Wensleydale /wenzlidayl/ • noun a type of white cheese with a crumbly texture.
– ORIGIN named after *Wensleydale* in Yorkshire.
went past of GO[1].
wept past and past participle of WEEP.
were second person singular past, plural past, and past subjunctive of BE.
we're • contraction we are.
weren't • contraction were not.
werewolf /weerwŏolf, wair-/ • noun (pl. **werewolves**) (in folklore) a person who periodically changes into a wolf, typically when there is a full moon.
– ORIGIN Old English; the first element has usually been identified with Old English *wer* 'man'.
wert /wert/ archaic second person singular past of BE.
Wesleyan • adjective relating to or denoting the teachings of the English preacher John Wesley (1703–91) or the main branch of the Methodist Church which he founded. • noun a follower of Wesley or adherent of the main Methodist tradition.
– DERIVATIVES **Wesleyanism** noun.
west • noun (usu. **the west**) **1** the direction towards the point of the horizon where the sun sets at the equinoxes, on the left-hand side of a person facing north. **2** the western part of a country, region, or town. **3** (**the West**) Europe and North America seen in contrast to other civilizations. **4** (**the West**) historical the non-Communist states of Europe and North America. • adjective **1** lying towards, near, or facing the west. **2** (of a wind) blowing from the west. • adverb to or towards the west.
– PHRASES **go west** Brit. informal be killed or lost.
– DERIVATIVES **westbound** adjective & adverb.
– ORIGIN Old English.
westerly • adjective & adverb **1** in a westward position or direction. **2** (of a wind) blowing from the west. • noun **1** a wind blowing from the west. **2** (**westerlies**) the belt of prevailing westerly winds in medium latitudes in the southern hemisphere.
western • adjective **1** situated in, directed towards, or facing the west. **2** (usu. **Western**) living in, coming from, or characteristic of the west, in particular Europe and North America. • noun a film or novel about cowboys in western North America.
– DERIVATIVES **westernmost** adjective.
Western Church • noun the part of the Christian Church originating in the Western Roman Empire, including the Roman Catholic, Anglican, Lutheran, and Reformed Churches.
westerner • noun a person from the west of a particular region or country.
westernize (also **westernise**) • verb bring or come under the influence of the cultural, economic, or political systems of Europe and North America.
– DERIVATIVES **westernization** noun **westernizer** noun.
West Indian • noun a person from the West Indies, or a person of West Indian descent. • adjective relating to the West Indies.
westing • noun **1** distance travelled or measured westward. **2** a figure or line representing westward distance on a map.
west-north-west • noun the direction or compass point midway between west and north-west.
west-south-west • noun the direction or compass point midway between west and south-west.
westward • adjective towards the west. • adverb (also **westwards**) in a westerly direction.
wet • adjective (**wetter**, **wettest**) **1** covered or saturated with liquid. **2** (of the weather) rainy. **3** involving the use of water or liquid. **4** (of paint, ink, etc.) not yet having dried or hardened. **5** Brit. informal lacking forcefulness or strength of character; feeble. **6** informal (of an area) allowing the free sale of alcoholic drink. • verb (**wetting**; past and past part. **wet** or **wetted**) **1** cover or touch with liquid. **2** (especially of a young child) urinate in or on. **3** (**wet oneself**) urinate involuntarily. • noun **1** liquid that makes something damp. **2** (**the wet**) rainy weather. **3** Brit. informal a feeble person. **4** Brit. a Conservative politician (especially in the 1980s) with liberal tendencies.
– PHRASES **wet the baby's head** Brit. informal celebrate a baby's birth with a drink. **wet behind the ears** informal lacking experience; immature. **wet one's whistle** informal have a drink.
– DERIVATIVES **wetly** adverb **wetness** noun.
– ORIGIN Old English, related to WATER.
weta /wettə/ • noun a large brown wingless insect with wood-boring larvae, found in New Zealand.
– ORIGIN Maori.
wet blanket • noun informal a person who spoils other people's enjoyment with their disapproving or unenthusiastic manner.
wet dream • noun an erotic dream that causes involuntary ejaculation of semen.
wet fish • noun fresh fish, as opposed to fish which has been frozen, cooked, or dried.
wet fly • noun an artificial fishing fly designed to sink below the surface of the water.
wether /wet͟hər/ • noun a castrated ram.
– ORIGIN Old English.
wetland • noun (also **wetlands**) swampy or marshy land.
wet look • noun a shiny appearance possessed by a clothing fabric or achieved by applying gel to the hair.
wet nurse • noun chiefly historical a woman employed to suckle another woman's child.
wet rot • noun a brown fungus causing decay in moist timber.
wetsuit • noun a close-fitting rubber garment covering the entire body, worn for warmth in water sports or diving.
we've • contraction we have.
whack informal • verb **1** strike forcefully with a sharp blow. **2** defeat heavily. **3** place or insert roughly or carelessly. **4** N. Amer. murder. • noun **1** a sharp or resounding blow. **2** a try or attempt. **3** Brit. a specified share of or contribution to something.
– PHRASES **out of whack** chiefly N. Amer. & Austral./NZ not working. **top** (or **full**) **whack** chiefly Brit. the maximum price or rate.
– ORIGIN imitative.

Thesaurus

money, loaded, well heeled, flush, made of money, quids in, worth a packet, on easy street.
welter • noun CONFUSION, jumble, tangle, mess, hotchpotch, mishmash, mass.
wend • verb MEANDER, wind one's way, wander, amble, stroll, saunter, drift, roam, swan, traipse, walk; journey, travel; *informal* mosey, tootle.
west • adjective WESTERN, westerly, occidental.
wet • adjective **1** *wet clothes* DAMP, moist, soaked, drenched, saturated, sopping, dripping, soggy; waterlogged, squelchy. **2** *it was cold and wet* RAINY, raining, pouring, teeming, showery, drizzly, drizzling; damp. **3** *the paint is still wet* STICKY, tacky; fresh. **4** *a wet mortar mix* AQUEOUS, watery, sloppy. **5** *(Brit. informal) the cadets were a bit wet* FEEBLE, silly, weak, foolish, inept, ineffectual, effete, soft, namby-pamby, timid, spiritless, cowardly, spineless; *informal* sissy, pathetic, drippy, wimpish, weedy, chicken; *Brit. informal* soppy.
– OPPOSITES dry, fine, brave.
• verb *wet the clothes before ironing them* DAMPEN, damp, moisten; sprinkle, spray, splash; soak, saturate, flood, douse, souse, drench.
– OPPOSITES dry.
• noun **1** *the wet of his tears* WETNESS, damp, moisture, moistness, sogginess; wateriness. **2** *the race was held in the wet* RAIN, drizzle, precipitation; spray, dew, damp. **3** *(Brit. informal) come on, don't be*

whacked (also **whacked out**) ● **adjective** informal **1** chiefly Brit. completely exhausted. **2** chiefly N. Amer. under the influence of drugs.
whacking ● **adjective** Brit. informal very large.
whacko ● **adjective & noun** (pl. **whackos**) variant spelling of WACKO.
whacky ● **adjective** variant spelling of WACKY.
whale ● **noun** (pl. same or **whales**) a very large marine mammal with a horizontal tail fin and a blowhole on top of the head for breathing.
– PHRASES **a whale of a ——** informal an exceedingly good example of something. **have a whale of a time** informal enjoy oneself very much.
– ORIGIN Old English.
whalebone ● **noun 1** an elastic horny substance which grows in a series of thin parallel plates in the upper jaw of some whales and is used by them to strain plankton from the seawater. **2** strips of this substance, formerly used as stays in corsets and dresses.
whaler ● **noun 1** a whaling ship. **2** a seaman engaged in whaling.
whaling ● **noun** the practice or industry of hunting and killing whales for their oil, meat, or whalebone.
wham informal ● **exclamation** used to express the sound of a forcible impact or the idea of a sudden and dramatic occurrence. ● **verb** (**whammed**, **whamming**) strike something forcefully.
whammy ● **noun** (pl. **whammies**) informal an event with a powerful and unpleasant effect; a blow.
whanau /waanow/ ● **noun** (pl. same) NZ an extended family or group of families living together in the same area.
– ORIGIN Maori.
whap ● **verb** (**whapped**, **whapping**) **& noun** chiefly N. Amer. variant spelling of WHOP.
whare /worri/ ● **noun** a Maori hut or house.
– ORIGIN Maori.
wharf /wawrf/ ● **noun** (pl. **wharves** or **wharfs**) a level quayside area to which a ship may be moored to load and unload.
– ORIGIN Old English.
wharfie ● **noun** Austral./NZ informal a dock labourer.
what ● **pronoun & determiner 1** asking for information specifying something. **2** (as pronoun) asking for repetition of something not heard or confirmation of something not understood. **3** (as pronoun) the thing or things that. **4** whatever. **5** used to emphasize something surprising or remarkable. ● **adverb 1** to what extent? **2** informal, dated used for emphasis or to invite agreement.
– PHRASES **give someone what for** informal, chiefly Brit. punish or scold someone severely. **what for?** informal for what reason? **what's what** informal what is useful or important. **what with** because of.
– ORIGIN Old English.
whatever ● **pronoun & determiner** used to emphasize a lack of restriction in referring to any thing; no matter what. ● **pronoun** used for emphasis instead of 'what' in questions. ● **adverb 1** at all; of any kind. **2** informal no matter what happens.
whatnot ● **noun** informal used to refer to an unidentified item or items having something in common with items already named.
whatsit ● **noun** informal a person or thing whose name one cannot recall, does not know, or does not wish to specify.
whatsoever ● **adverb** at all. ● **determiner & pronoun** archaic whatever.
wheal ● **noun** variant spelling of WEAL[1].
wheat ● **noun** a cereal widely grown in temperate countries, the grain of which is ground to make flour.
– ORIGIN Old English, related to WHITE.
wheatear ● **noun** a songbird with black and grey, buff, or white plumage and a white rump.
– ORIGIN apparently from WHITE + ARSE.
wheaten ● **adjective** made of wheat.
wheatgerm ● **noun** a nutritious foodstuff consisting of the extracted embryos of grains of wheat.
wheatgrass ● **noun** another term for COUCH[2].
wheatmeal ● **noun** flour made from wheat from which some of the bran and germ has been removed.
wheedle ● **verb** use endearments or flattery to persuade someone to do something.
– ORIGIN perhaps from German *wedeln* 'cringe, fawn'.
wheel ● **noun 1** a circular object that revolves on an axle, fixed below a vehicle to enable it to move along or forming part of a machine. **2** something resembling a wheel or having a wheel as its essential part. **3** (**wheels**) informal a car. **4** an instance of wheeling; a turn or rotation. **5** a recurring cycle of events: *he attempted to stop the wheel of history.* ● **verb 1** push or pull (a vehicle with wheels). **2** carry in or on a vehicle with wheels. **3** fly or turn in a wide circle or curve. **4** turn round quickly to face another way. **5** (**wheel in/on/out**) informal produce (something that is unimpressive because it has been frequently seen or heard before).
– PHRASES **wheel and deal** engage in commercial or political scheming. **the wheel of Fortune** the wheel which the deity Fortune is fabled to turn as a symbol of random luck or change. **wheels within wheels** secret or indirect influences affecting a complex situation.
– ORIGIN Old English.
wheelbarrow ● **noun** a small cart with a single wheel at the front and two supporting legs and two handles at the rear, used for carrying loads in building or gardening.
wheelbase ● **noun** the distance between the front and rear axles of a vehicle.
wheelchair ● **noun** a mobile wheeled chair for an invalid or disabled person.
wheel clamp ● **noun** a device for immobilizing an unlawfully parked car.
wheeler ● **noun** (in combination) a vehicle having a specified number of wheels: *a three-wheeler.*
wheeler-dealer (also **wheeler and dealer**) ● **noun** a person who engages in commercial or political scheming.
– DERIVATIVES **wheeler-dealing** noun.
wheelhouse ● **noun** a shelter for the person at the wheel of a boat or ship.
wheelie ● **noun** informal a manoeuvre whereby a bicycle or motorcycle is ridden for a short distance with the front wheel raised off the ground.
wheelie bin (also **wheely bin**) ● **noun** Brit. informal a large refuse bin set on wheels.
wheelspin ● **noun** rotation of a vehicle's wheels without traction.
wheelwright ● **noun** chiefly historical a person who makes or repairs wooden wheels.
wheeze ● **verb 1** breathe with a whistling or rattling sound in the chest, as a result of obstruction in the air passages. **2** (of a device) make an irregular rattling or spluttering sound. ● **noun 1** a sound of a person wheezing. **2** Brit. informal a clever or amusing scheme or trick.
– DERIVATIVES **wheezily** adverb **wheeziness** noun **wheezy** adjective.
– ORIGIN probably from an Old Norse word meaning 'to hiss'.
whelk ● **noun** a predatory marine mollusc with a heavy pointed spiral shell, some kinds of which are edible.
– ORIGIN Old English.
whelp ● **noun** chiefly archaic **1** a puppy. **2** derogatory a boy or young man. ● **verb** give birth to (a puppy).
– ORIGIN Old English.

Thesaurus

W

such a wet NAMBY-PAMBY, weakling, milksop, Milquetoast, baby, coward; *informal* wimp, weed, drip, sissy, softie, chicken, scaredy-cat; *Brit. informal* big girl's blouse; *N. Amer. informal* pantywaist, pussy.
whack *(informal)* ● **verb** *she whacked him on the head.* See STRIKE verb sense 1.
● **noun 1** *he got a whack with a stick.* See BLOW[2] sense 1. **2** *(Brit.) everyone will get their whack.* See SHARE noun.
wharf ● **noun** QUAY, pier, dock, berth, landing, jetty; harbour, dockyard, marina.
whatsit ● **noun** *(informal)* THING, so-and-so, whatever it's called; *informal* whatnot, doodah, what-d'you-call-it, what's-its-name, thingy, thingummy, thingamabob, thingamajig, oojamaflip; *Brit. informal* doings; *N. Amer. informal* doodad, doohickey.
wheedle ● **verb** COAX, cajole, inveigle, induce, entice, charm, tempt, beguile, flatter, persuade, influence, win someone over, bring someone round, convince, prevail on, get round; *informal* sweet-talk, soft-soap.
wheel ● **noun** *a wagon wheel* disc, hoop, ring, circle.
● **verb 1** *she wheeled the trolley away* PUSH, trundle, roll. **2** *the flock of doves wheeled round* TURN, go round, circle, orbit.
– PHRASES **at/behind the wheel** DRIVING, steering, in the driving seat.
wheeze ● **verb** *the illness left her wheezing* BREATHE NOISILY, gasp, whistle, hiss, rasp, croak, pant, cough.

when ● adverb **1** at what time? **2** how soon? **3** in what circumstances? **4** at which time or in which situation. ● conjunction **1** at or during the time that. **2** at any time that; whenever. **3** after which; and just then. **4** in view of the fact that. **5** although; whereas.
– ORIGIN Old English.

whence (also **from whence**) ● adverb formal or archaic **1** from what place or source? **2** from which; from where. **3** to the place from which. **4** as a consequence of which.
– USAGE **Whence** means 'from what place', as in *who are you and whence come you?* Strictly speaking, the preposition **from**, as in *the music store from whence the label was launched*, is redundant, but nevertheless **from whence** is usually accepted as good English.

whenever ● conjunction **1** at whatever time; on whatever occasion. **2** every time that. ● adverb used for emphasis instead of 'when' in questions.

whensoever ● conjunction & adverb formal word for WHENEVER.

where ● adverb **1** in or to what place or position? **2** in what direction or respect? **3** at, in, or to which. **4** the place or situation in which. **5** in or to a place or situation in which.
– ORIGIN Old English.

whereabouts ● adverb where or approximately where? ● noun (treated as sing. or pl.) the place where someone or something is.

whereafter ● adverb formal after which.

whereas ● conjunction **1** in contrast or comparison with the fact that. **2** taking into consideration the fact that.

whereat ● adverb & conjunction archaic or formal at which.

whereby ● adverb by which.

wherefore archaic ● adverb for what reason? ● adverb & conjunction as a result of which.

wherefrom ● adverb archaic from which or from where.

wherein ● adverb formal **1** in which. **2** in what place or respect?

whereof ● adverb formal of what or which.

whereon ● adverb archaic on which.

wheresoever ● adverb & conjunction formal word for WHEREVER.

whereto ● adverb archaic or formal to which.

whereupon ● conjunction immediately after which.

wherever ● adverb **1** in or to whatever place. **2** used for emphasis instead of 'where' in questions. ● conjunction in every case when.

wherewith ● adverb formal or archaic with or by which.

wherewithal ● noun the money or other resources needed for a particular purpose.

wherry /werri/ ● noun (pl. **wherries**) **1** a light rowing boat used chiefly for carrying passengers. **2** Brit. a large light barge.
– ORIGIN of unknown origin.

whet /wet/ ● verb (**whetted**, **whetting**) **1** sharpen the blade of (a tool or weapon). **2** excite or stimulate (someone's desire, interest, or appetite).
– ORIGIN Old English.

whether ● conjunction **1** expressing a doubt or choice between alternatives. **2** expressing an enquiry or investigation. **3** indicating that a statement applies whichever of the alternatives mentioned is the case.
– USAGE **Whether** and **if** are more or less interchangeable in sentences such as *I'll see whether he left an address* and *I'll see if he left an address*, although **whether** is more formal and more suitable for written use.
– ORIGIN Old English.

whetstone ● noun a fine-grained stone used for sharpening cutting tools.

whey /way/ ● noun the watery part of milk that remains after the formation of curds.
– ORIGIN Old English.

whey-faced ● adjective (of a person) pale.

which ● pronoun & determiner **1** asking for information specifying one or more people or things from a definite set. **2** used to refer to something previously mentioned when introducing a clause giving further information.
– ORIGIN Old English.

whichever ● determiner & pronoun **1** used to emphasize a lack of restriction in selecting one of a definite set of alternatives. **2** regardless of which.

whicker ● verb (of a horse) give a soft breathy whinny. ● noun a sound of this type.
– ORIGIN originally in the sense 'to snigger, titter': imitative.

whiff ● noun **1** a smell that is smelt only briefly or faintly. **2** Brit. informal an unpleasant smell. **3** a trace or hint of something bad or exciting. **4** a puff or breath of air or smoke. ● verb **1** get a brief or faint smell of. **2** Brit. informal give off an unpleasant smell.
– ORIGIN imitative.

whiffle ● verb **1** (of the wind) blow lightly in a specified direction. **2** blow or move with a puff of air. ● noun a slight movement of air.

whiffy ● adjective (**whiffier**, **whiffiest**) Brit. informal having an unpleasant smell.

Whig ● noun historical **1** a member of the British reforming party that sought the supremacy of Parliament, succeeded in the 19th century by the Liberal Party. **2** a supporter of the American Revolution. **3** a 17th-century Scottish Presbyterian.
– DERIVATIVES **Whiggery** noun **Whiggish** adjective **Whiggism** noun.
– ORIGIN probably a shortening of Scots *whiggamore*, the nickname of 17th-century Scottish rebels, from *whig* 'to drive' + MARE[1].

while ● noun **1** (**a while**) a period of time. **2** (**a while**) for some time. **3** (**the while**) at the same time; meanwhile. **4** (**the while**) literary during the time that. ● conjunction **1** at the same time as. **2** whereas (indicating a contrast). **3** although. ● adverb during which. ● verb (**while away**) pass (time) in a leisurely manner.
– PHRASES **worth while** (or **worth one's while**) worth the time or effort spent.
– ORIGIN Old English.

whilst ● conjunction & adverb chiefly Brit. while.

whim ● noun a sudden desire or change of mind.
– ORIGIN of unknown origin.

whimbrel /wimbrəl/ ● noun a small curlew with a striped crown and a trilling call.
– ORIGIN from WHIMPER or synonymous dialect *whimp* (imitative of the bird's call).

whimper ● verb make a series of low, feeble sounds expressive of fear, pain, or discontent. ● noun a whimpering sound.
– ORIGIN imitative.

whimsical ● adjective **1** playfully quaint or fanciful. **2** acting or behaving in a capricious manner.
– DERIVATIVES **whimsicality** noun **whimsically** adverb.

Thesaurus

● noun **1** *she still had a slight wheeze* RASP, croak, whistle, hiss, pant, cough. **2** (Brit. informal) *I've thought of a brilliant wheeze.* See RUSE.

whereabouts ● noun LOCATION, position, site, place, situation, spot, point, vicinity; home, address, locale, neighbourhood; bearings, orientation.

wherewithal ● noun MONEY, cash, capital, finance(s), funds; resources, means, ability, capability; informal dough, bread, loot, readies, the necessary, boodle, dibs, ducats; Brit. informal dosh, brass, lolly; N. Amer. informal bucks; US informal greenbacks.

whet ● verb **1** *he whetted his knife on a stone* SHARPEN, hone, strop, grind, file. **2** *something to whet your appetite* STIMULATE, excite, arouse, rouse, kindle, trigger, spark, quicken, stir, inspire, animate, fuel, fire, activate, tempt, galvanize.
– OPPOSITES blunt.

whiff ● noun **1** *I caught a whiff of perfume* FAINT SMELL, trace, sniff, scent, odour, aroma. **2** (Brit. informal) *there's a terrible whiff in here* STENCH, stink, smell, reek; Brit. informal pong, niff, hum; Scottish informal guff; N. Amer. informal funk. **3** *the faintest whiff of irony* TRACE, hint, suggestion, impression, suspicion, soupçon, nuance, intimation, tinge, vein, shred, whisper, air, element, overtone. **4** *whiffs of smoke from the boiler* PUFF, gust, flurry, breath, draught, waft.

while ● noun *we chatted for a while* TIME, spell, stretch, stint, span, interval, period; duration, phase; Brit. informal patch.
● verb *tennis helped to while away the time* PASS, spend, occupy, use up, kill.

whim ● noun **1** *she bought it on a whim* IMPULSE, urge, notion, fancy, foible, caprice, conceit, vagary, crotchet, inclination. **2** *our human whims* CAPRICIOUSNESS, whimsy, caprice, volatility, fickleness, idiosyncrasy.

whimper ● verb *he was whimpering in pain* WHINE, cry, sob, moan, snivel, wail, groan; Brit. informal grizzle.
● noun *she gave a whimper of protest* WHINE, cry, sob, moan, bleat, wail, groan.

whimsical ● adjective **1** *a whimsical sense of humour* FANCIFUL, playful, mischievous, waggish, quaint, curious, droll; eccentric, quirky, idiosyncratic, unconventional, outlandish, queer; informal offbeat, freaky. **2** *the whimsical arbitrariness of autocracy* VOLA-

W

whimsy (also **whimsey**) ● noun (pl. **whimsies** or **whimseys**) **1** playfully quaint or fanciful behaviour or humour. **2** a fanciful or odd thing. **3** a whim.
– ORIGIN probably from archaic *whim-wham* 'trinket, whim'.

whin ● noun chiefly N. English gorse.
– ORIGIN probably Scandinavian.

whinchat /winchat/ ● noun a small songbird related to the stonechat, with a brown back and orange-buff underparts.

whine ● noun **1** a long, high-pitched complaining cry. **2** a long, high-pitched unpleasant sound. **3** a feeble or petulant complaint. ● verb **1** give or make a whine. **2** complain in a feeble or petulant way.
– DERIVATIVES **whiner** noun **whiny** adjective.
– ORIGIN Old English, 'whistle through the air'; related to WHINGE.

whinge Brit. informal ● verb (**whingeing**) complain persistently and peevishly. ● noun an act of whingeing.
– DERIVATIVES **whinger** noun.
– ORIGIN Old English.

whinny ● noun (pl. **whinnies**) a gentle, high-pitched neigh. ● verb (**whinnies**, **whinnied**) (of a horse) make such a sound.
– ORIGIN imitative.

whip ● noun **1** a strip of leather or length of cord fastened to a handle, used for beating a person or urging on an animal. **2** an official of a political party appointed to maintain parliamentary discipline among its members. **3** Brit. a written notice from such an official requesting attendance for voting. **4** a dessert made from cream or eggs beaten into a light fluffy mass. **5** a violent striking or beating movement. ● verb (**whipped**, **whipping**) **1** strike with a whip. **2** (of a flexible object or rain or wind) strike or beat violently. **3** informal move or take out fast or suddenly. **4** beat (cream, eggs, etc.) into a froth. **5** Brit. informal steal. **6** bind with spirally wound twine.
– PHRASES **the whip hand** a position of power or control. **whip up 1** make or prepare very quickly. **2** deliberately excite or provoke. **3** stimulate (a particular feeling) in someone.
– DERIVATIVES **whipper** noun **whipping** noun.
– ORIGIN probably from Low German and Dutch *wippen* 'swing, leap, dance'.

whipcord ● noun **1** thin, tough, tightly twisted cord used for making the flexible end part of whips. **2** a closely woven ribbed worsted fabric.

whiplash ● noun **1** the lashing action of a whip. **2** the flexible part of a whip. **3** injury caused by a severe jerk to the head. ● verb jerk suddenly.

whipper-in ● noun (pl. **whippers-in**) a huntsman's assistant who brings straying hounds back into the pack.

whippersnapper ● noun informal a young and inexperienced person who is presumptuous or overconfident.
– ORIGIN perhaps representing *whipsnapper*, expressing noise and unimportance.

whippet ● noun a dog of a small slender breed, bred for racing.
– ORIGIN partly from obsolete *whippet* 'move briskly'.

whipping boy ● noun a person who is blamed or punished for the faults or incompetence of others.
– ORIGIN originally denoting a boy educated with a young prince and punished instead of him.

whippoorwill /wippərwill/ ● noun a North and Central American nightjar with a distinctive call.
– ORIGIN imitative of its call.

whippy ● adjective flexible; springy.

whip-round ● noun Brit. informal a collection of contributions of money for a particular purpose.

whipsaw ● noun a saw with a narrow blade and a handle at both ends. ● verb (past part. **whipsawn** or **whipsawed**) N. Amer. **1** cut with a whipsaw. **2** informal subject to two difficult situations or opposing pressures at the same time.

whirl ● verb **1** move rapidly round and round. **2** (of the head or mind) seem to spin round. ● noun **1** a rapid movement round and round. **2** frantic activity: *the mad social whirl*. **3** a sweet or biscuit with a spiral shape.
– PHRASES **give something a whirl** informal give something a try. **in a whirl** in a state of confusion.
– ORIGIN probably from an Old Norse word meaning 'turn about'.

whirligig ● noun **1** a toy that spins round, e.g. a top or windmill. **2** another term for ROUNDABOUT (in sense 2). **3** (also **whirligig beetle**) a small black water beetle which typically swims rapidly in circles on the surface.
– ORIGIN from WHIRL + obsolete *gig* 'toy for whipping'.

whirlpool ● noun **1** a quickly rotating mass of water in a river or sea into which objects may be drawn. **2** (also **whirlpool bath**) a heated pool in which hot aerated water is continuously circulated.

whirlwind ● noun **1** a column of air moving rapidly round and round in a cylindrical or funnel shape. **2** a very energetic or tumultuous person or process. **3** (before another noun) very rapid and unexpected: *a whirlwind romance*.
– PHRASES (**sow the wind and**) **reap the whirlwind** suffer serious consequences as a result of one's actions. [ORIGIN with biblical allusion to the Book of Hosea, chapter 8.]

whirr (also **whir**) ● verb (**whirred**, **whirring**) (of something rapidly rotating or moving to and fro) make a low, continuous, regular sound. ● noun a whirring sound.
– ORIGIN probably Scandinavian.

whisk ● verb **1** move or take suddenly, quickly, and lightly. **2** beat (a substance) with a light, rapid movement. ● noun **1** a utensil for whisking eggs or cream. **2** a bunch of grass, twigs, or bristles for flicking away dust or flies. **3** a brief, rapid action or movement.
– ORIGIN Scandinavian.

whisker ● noun **1** a long projecting hair or bristle growing from

Thesaurus

TILE, capricious, fickle, changeable, unpredictable, variable, erratic, mercurial, mutable, inconstant, inconsistent, unstable, protean.

whine ● noun **1** *the dog gave a whine* WHIMPER, cry, mewl, howl, yowl. **2** *the whine of the motor* HUM, drone. **3** *a whine about the quality of service* COMPLAINT, grouse, grumble, murmur; informal gripe, moan, grouch, whinge, bellyache, beef.
● verb **1** *a child was whining* WAIL, whimper, cry, mewl, moan, howl, yowl. **2** *the lift began to whine* HUM, drone. **3** *he's always whining about something* COMPLAIN, grouse, grouch, grumble, moan, carp, mutter, murmur; informal gripe, bellyache, whinge.

whinge (Brit. informal) ● verb *I whinged about the weather*. See WHINE verb sense 3.
● noun *his tale is one long whinge*. See WHINE noun sense 3.

whip ● noun *he would use a whip on his dogs* LASH, scourge, strap, belt; historical cat-o'-nine-tails.
● verb **1** *he whipped the boy* FLOG, scourge, flagellate, lash, strap, belt, thrash, beat, tan someone's hide. **2** *whip the cream* WHISK, beat. **3** *he whipped his listeners into a frenzy* ROUSE, stir up, excite, galvanize, electrify, stimulate, inspire, fire up, get someone going, inflame, agitate, goad, provoke. **4** (informal) *he whipped round the corner*. See DASH verb sense 1. **5** (informal) *he whipped out a revolver* PULL, whisk, snatch, pluck, jerk; informal yank; Scottish informal wheech. **6** (Brit. informal) *he whipped the necklace*. See STEAL verb sense 1.

whippersnapper ● noun (informal) UPSTART; informal pipsqueak, squirt; Brit. informal squit; N. Amer. informal snip.

whirl ● verb **1** *leaves whirled in eddies of wind* ROTATE, circle, wheel, turn, revolve, orbit, spin, twirl; Scottish birl. **2** *they whirled past* HURRY, race, dash, rush, run, sprint, bolt, dart, gallop, career, charge, shoot, hurtle, hare, fly, speed, scurry; informal tear, belt, pelt, scoot; Brit. informal bomb; N. Amer. informal hightail it. **3** *his mind was whirling* SPIN, reel, swim.
● noun **1** *a whirl of dust* SWIRL, flurry, eddy. **2** *the mad social whirl* HURLY-BURLY, activity, bustle, rush, flurry, fuss, turmoil, merry-go-round; informal to-do. **3** *Laura's mind was in a whirl* SPIN, daze, stupor, muddle, jumble; confusion; informal dither. **4** (informal) *go on, give it a whirl* TRY, test; informal go, shot, bash, stab.

whirlpool ● noun **1** *a river full of whirlpools* EDDY, vortex, maelstrom; N. Amer. informal suckhole. **2** *the health club has a whirlpool* JACUZZI, spa bath, hot tub.

whirlwind ● noun **1** *the building was hit by a whirlwind* TORNADO, hurricane, typhoon, cyclone, vortex; Austral. willy-willy; N. Amer. informal twister. **2** *a whirlwind of activity* MAELSTROM, welter, bedlam, mayhem, babel, swirl, tumult, hurly-burly, commotion, confusion; informal madhouse; N. Amer. three-ring circus.
● adjective *a whirlwind romance* RAPID, lightning, headlong, impulsive, breakneck, meteoric, sudden, swift, fast, quick, speedy; informal quickie.

whisk ● verb **1** *the cable car will whisk you to the top* SPEED, hurry, rush, sweep, hurtle, shoot; Scottish informal wheech. **2** *she whisked the cloth away* PULL, snatch, pluck, tug, jerk; informal whip, yank; Scottish informal wheech. **3** *he whisked out of sight* DASH, rush, race, bolt, dart, gallop, career, charge, shoot, hurtle, hare, fly, speed,

the face or snout of an animal. **2** (**whiskers**) the hair growing on a man's face. **3** (**a whisker**) informal a very small amount.
– DERIVATIVES **whiskered** adjective **whiskery** adjective.
– ORIGIN originally denoting a bundle of feathers, twigs, etc., used for whisking: from WHISK.
whisky (also Irish & US **whiskey**) • noun (pl. **whiskies**) a spirit distilled from malted grain, especially barley or rye.
– ORIGIN from Irish and Scottish Gaelic *uisge beatha* 'water of life'.
whisper • verb **1** speak very softly using one's breath rather than one's throat. **2** literary rustle or murmur softly. • noun **1** a whispered word or phrase, or a whispering tone of voice. **2** literary a soft rustling or murmuring sound. **3** a rumour or piece of gossip. **4** a slight trace.
– DERIVATIVES **whisperer** noun **whispery** adjective.
– ORIGIN Old English, related to WHISTLE.
whispering campaign • noun a systematic circulation of a rumour, especially in order to damage someone's reputation.
whist /wist/ • noun a card game in which points are scored according to the number of tricks won.
– ORIGIN earlier as *whisk*: perhaps from WHISK (with reference to whisking away the tricks).
whistle • noun **1** a clear, high-pitched sound made by forcing breath through pursed lips, or between one's teeth. **2** any similar sound. **3** an instrument used to produce such a sound. • verb **1** emit or produce a whistle. **2** produce (a tune) in such a way. **3** move rapidly through the air or a narrow opening with a whistling sound. **4** blow a whistle. **5** (**whistle for**) wish for or expect (something) in vain.
– PHRASES **blow the whistle on** informal bring (an illicit activity) to an end by informing on the person responsible. **(as) clean as a whistle** extremely clean or clear. **whistle down the wind** let go or abandon (something). **whistle in the dark** pretend to be unafraid.
– DERIVATIVES **whistler** noun.
– ORIGIN Old English.
whistle-blower • noun informal a person who informs on someone engaged in an illicit activity.
whistle-stop • adjective very fast and with only brief pauses.
whit /wit/ • noun a very small part or amount.
– PHRASES **not a whit** not at all.
– ORIGIN apparently from WIGHT in the obsolete sense 'small amount'.
white • adjective **1** of the colour of milk or fresh snow, due to the reflection of all visible rays of light. **2** very pale. **3** relating to a human group having light-coloured skin, especially of European ancestry. **4** morally or spiritually pure. **5** Brit. (of coffee or tea) served with milk or cream. **6** (of food such as bread or rice) light in colour through having been refined. **7** (of wine) made from white grapes, or dark grapes with the skins removed, and having a yellowish colour. • noun **1** white colour or pigment. **2** (also **whites**) white clothes or material. **3** the visible pale part of the eyeball around the iris. **4** the outer part which surrounds the yolk of an egg; the albumen. **5** a member of a light-skinned people. **6** a white or cream butterfly. • verb (**white out**) **1** turn white. **2** cover (a mistake) with white correction fluid. **3** lose colour vision as a prelude to losing consciousness.
– PHRASES **bleed white** drain of wealth or resources. **whited sepulchre** literary a hypocrite. [ORIGIN with biblical allusion to the Gospel of Matthew, chapter 23.]
– DERIVATIVES **whitely** adverb **whiteness** noun **whitish** adjective.
– ORIGIN Old English, related to WHEAT.
white admiral • noun a butterfly with dark brown wings bearing a broad white band.
white ant • noun another term for TERMITE.
whitebait • noun the small silvery-white young of herrings, sprats, and similar marine fish as food.
whitebeam • noun a tree related to the rowan, with red berries and hairy oval leaves that are white underneath.
white belt • noun a white belt worn by a beginner in judo or karate.
whiteboard • noun a wipeable board with a white surface used for teaching or presentations.
white-bread • adjective N. Amer. informal bland and unchallenging in a way thought characteristic of the white middle classes.
white cell • noun less technical term for LEUCOCYTE.
white Christmas • noun a Christmas during which there is snow on the ground.
white-collar • adjective relating to the work done or people who work in an office or other professional environment.
white dwarf • noun Astronomy a small, very dense star that is typically the size of a planet.
white elephant • noun a possession that is useless or troublesome.
– ORIGIN from the story that the kings of Siam gave such animals to courtiers they disliked, in order to ruin the recipient by the great expense incurred in maintaining the animal.
white feather • noun a white feather given to someone as a sign that they are considered a coward.
– ORIGIN with reference to a white feather in the tail of a game bird, being a mark of bad breeding.
whitefish • noun a mainly freshwater fish of the salmon family, widely used as food.
white flag • noun a white flag or cloth used as a symbol of surrender, truce, or a desire to negotiate.
whitefly • noun a minute winged bug covered with powdery white wax, damaging plants by feeding on sap and coating them with honeydew.
white gold • noun a silver-coloured alloy of gold with another metal.
white goods • plural noun large domestic electrical goods such as refrigerators and washing machines. Compare with BROWN GOODS.
whitehead • noun informal a pale or white-topped pustule on the skin.
white heat • noun the temperature or state of something that is so hot that it emits white light.
white hope (also **great white hope**) • noun a person expected to bring much success to a team or organization.
white horses • plural noun white-crested waves at sea.
white-hot • adjective so hot as to glow white.
white knight • noun a person or thing that comes to someone's aid.
white-knuckle • adjective causing fear or nervous excitement.
– ORIGIN with reference to the effect caused by gripping tightly to steady oneself on a fairground ride.
white lie • noun a harmless lie told to avoid hurting someone's feelings.
white light • noun apparently colourless light containing all the wavelengths of the visible spectrum at equal intensity (such as ordinary daylight).
white magic • noun magic used only for good purposes.
white meat • noun pale meat such as poultry, veal, and rabbit.

Thesaurus

zoom, scurry, scuttle, scamper; *informal* tear, belt, pelt, scoot, zip, whip. **4** *horses whisk their tails* FLICK, twitch, wave. **5** *whisk the egg yolks* WHIP, beat, mix.
• noun **1** *the horse gave a whisk of its tail* FLICK, twitch, wave, sweep. **2** *blend the eggs with a whisk* BEATER, mixer, blender.
whisper • verb **1** *Alison whispered in his ear* MURMUR, mutter, mumble, speak softly, breathe. **2** (*poetic/literary*) *the wind whispered in the grass* RUSTLE, murmur, sigh, moan, whoosh, whirr, swish, blow, breathe.
– OPPOSITES roar.
• noun **1** *she spoke in a whisper* MURMUR, mutter, mumble, low voice, undertone. **2** (*poetic/literary*) *the wind died to a whisper* RUSTLE, murmur, sigh, whoosh, swish. **3** *I heard a whisper that he's left town* RUMOUR, story, report, speculation, insinuation, suggestion, hint; *informal* buzz. **4** *not a whisper of interest.* See WHIT.
whit • noun SCRAP, bit, speck, iota, jot, atom, crumb, shred, grain, mite, touch, trace, shadow, suggestion, whisper, suspicion, scintilla; *informal* smidgen, smidge.
white • adjective **1** *apply a clean white bandage* COLOURLESS, unpigmented, bleached, natural; snowy, milky, chalky, ivory. **2** *her face was white with fear* PALE, pallid, wan, ashen, bloodless, waxen, chalky, pasty, peaky, washed out, drained, drawn, ghostly, deathly. **3** *white hair* SNOWY, grey, silver, silvery, hoary, grizzled. **4** *the early white settlers* CAUCASIAN, European. **5** *a whiter than white government* VIRTUOUS, moral, ethical, good, righteous, honourable, reputable, wholesome, honest, upright, upstanding, irreproachable; decent, worthy, noble; blameless, spotless, impeccable, unsullied, unblemished, uncorrupted, untainted; *informal* squeaky clean.
– OPPOSITES black, florid, immoral.

white metal • noun a white or silvery alloy.

whiten • verb make or become white.
– DERIVATIVES **whitener** noun.

white noise • noun Physics noise containing many frequencies with equal intensities.

white-out • noun **1** a dense blizzard. **2** a weather condition in which the features and horizon of snow-covered country are indistinguishable due to uniform light diffusion.

White Paper • noun (in the UK) a government report giving information or proposals on an issue.

white rose • noun the emblem of Yorkshire or the House of York in the Wars of the Roses.

White Russian • noun **1** a Belorussian. **2** an opponent of the Bolsheviks during the Russian Civil War. • adjective relating to White Russians.

white sauce • noun a sauce consisting of flour blended and cooked with butter and milk or stock.

white slave • noun a woman tricked or forced into prostitution in a foreign country.

white spirit • noun Brit. a volatile colourless liquid distilled from petroleum, used as a paint thinner and solvent.

white tie • noun **1** a white bow tie worn by men as part of full evening dress. **2** full evening dress.

white trash • noun N. Amer. derogatory poor white people.

white-van man • noun Brit. informal an aggressive male driver of a delivery or workman's van (typically white in colour).

whitewash • noun **1** a solution of lime and water or of whiting, size, and water, used for painting walls white. **2** a deliberate concealment of someone's mistakes or faults. **3** a victory by the same side in every game of a series. • verb **1** paint with whitewash. **2** conceal (mistakes or faults). **3** defeat with a whitewash.

white water • noun a fast shallow stretch of water in a river.

white wedding • noun Brit. a traditional wedding at which the bride wears a formal white dress.

white witch • noun a practitioner of witchcraft for altruistic purposes.

whitey • noun (pl. **whiteys**) informal, derogatory a white person.

whither archaic or literary • adverb **1** to what place or state? **2** what is the likely future of? **3** to which (with reference to a place). **4** to whatever place.
– ORIGIN Old English.

whiting[1] • noun (pl. same) a slender-bodied marine fish with edible white flesh.
– ORIGIN Dutch *wijting*, from *wijt* 'white'.

whiting[2] • noun ground chalk used for purposes such as whitewashing and cleaning metal plate.

whitlow /witlō/ • noun an abscess in the soft tissue near a fingernail or toenail.
– ORIGIN apparently from WHITE + FLAW.

Whitsun /witsən/ • noun Whitsuntide.

Whit Sunday • noun the seventh Sunday after Easter, a Christian festival commemorating the descent of the Holy Spirit at Pentecost (Acts, chapter 2).
– ORIGIN Old English, 'white Sunday', probably with reference to the white robes worn by the newly baptized at Pentecost.

Whitsuntide /witsəntīd/ • noun the weekend or week including Whit Sunday.

whittle • verb **1** carve (wood) by repeatedly cutting small slices from it. **2** make by whittling. **3** (**whittle away/down**) reduce by degrees.
– ORIGIN from dialect *whittle* 'knife', from an Old English word meaning 'cut, cut off'.

whiz-bang (also **whizz-bang**) • adjective informal, chiefly N. Amer. impressively lively and fast-paced.

whizz (also **whiz**) • verb (**whizzed**, **whizzing**) **1** move quickly through the air with a whistling or whooshing sound. **2** move or go fast. **3** (**whizz through**) do or deal with quickly. • noun **1** a whizzing sound. **2** informal a fast movement or brief journey. **3** (also **wiz**) informal a person who is extremely clever at something. [ORIGIN influenced by WIZARD.] **4** informal an act of urinating. **5** Brit. informal amphetamines.
– DERIVATIVES **whizzy** adjective.
– ORIGIN imitative.

whizz-kid (also **whiz-kid**) • noun informal a young person who is very successful or highly skilled.

WHO • abbreviation World Health Organization.

who • pronoun **1** what or which person or people? **2** introducing a clause giving further information about a person or people previously mentioned.
– USAGE According to formal grammar, **who** is used as the subject of a verb (*who decided this?*) and **whom** is used as the object of a verb or preposition (*to whom do you wish to speak?*). However, in modern English **who** is often used instead of **whom**, as in *who should we support?* and most people consider this to be acceptable.
– ORIGIN Old English.

whoa /wō/ (also **wo**) • exclamation used as a command to a horse to stop or slow down.

who'd • contraction **1** who had. **2** who would.

whodunnit (US **whodunit**) • noun informal a story or play about a murder in which the identity of the murderer is not revealed until the end.

whoever • pronoun **1** the person or people who; any person who. **2** regardless of who. **3** used for emphasis instead of 'who' in questions.

whole • adjective **1** complete; entire. **2** emphasizing a large extent or number: *a whole range of issues.* **3** in an unbroken or undamaged state. • noun **1** a thing that is complete in itself. **2** (**the whole**) all of something. • adverb informal entirely; wholly: *a whole new meaning.*
– PHRASES **as a whole** in general. **on the whole** taking everything into account; in general. **the whole nine yards** informal, chiefly N. Amer. everything possible or available.
– DERIVATIVES **wholeness** noun.
– ORIGIN Old English, related to HAIL[2].

wholefood • noun (also **wholefoods**) Brit. food that has been minimally processed and is free from additives.

wholehearted • adjective completely sincere and committed.
– DERIVATIVES **wholeheartedly** adverb.

wholemeal • adjective Brit. denoting flour or bread made from wholewheat, including the husk.

whole number • noun a number without fractions; an integer.

wholesale • noun the selling of goods in large quantities to be retailed by others. • adverb **1** being sold in such a way. **2** on a large scale. • adjective done on a large scale; extensive. • verb sell (goods) wholesale.
– DERIVATIVES **wholesaler** noun.

Thesaurus

white-collar • adjective CLERICAL, professional, executive, salaried, office.

whiten • verb MAKE WHITE, make pale, bleach, blanch, lighten, fade; *Brit. Military* blanco; *archaic* white.

whitewash • noun **1** *the report was a whitewash* COVER-UP, camouflage, deception, facade, veneer, pretext. **2** *a four-match whitewash* WALKOVER, rout, landslide; *informal* pushover, cinch, breeze.
– OPPOSITES exposé.
• verb *don't whitewash what happened* COVER UP, sweep under the carpet, hush up, suppress, draw a veil over, conceal, veil, obscure, keep secret; gloss over, downplay, soft-pedal.
– OPPOSITES expose.

whittle • verb **1** *he sat whittling a piece of wood* PARE, shave, trim, carve, shape, model. **2** *his powers were whittled away* ERODE, wear away, eat away, reduce, diminish, undermine, weaken, subvert, compromise, impair, impede, hinder, cripple, disable, enfeeble, sap. **3** *the ten teams have been whittled down to six* REDUCE, cut down, cut back, prune, trim, slim down, pare down, shrink, decrease, diminish.

whole • adjective **1** *the whole report* ENTIRE, complete, full, unabridged, uncut. **2** *a whole marble mantelpiece* INTACT, in one piece, unbroken; undamaged, flawless, faultless, unmarked, perfect.
– OPPOSITES incomplete.
• noun **1** *a single whole* ENTITY, unit, body, discrete item, ensemble. **2** *the whole of the year* ALL, every part, the lot, the sum (total).
– PHRASES **on the whole** OVERALL, all in all, all things considered, for the most part, in the main, in general, generally (speaking), as a (general) rule, by and large; normally, usually, more often than not, almost always, most of the time, typically, ordinarily.

wholehearted • adjective COMMITTED, positive, emphatic, devoted, dedicated, enthusiastic, unshakeable, unswerving; unqualified, unreserved, without reservations, unconditional, unequivocal, unmitigated; complete, full, total, absolute.
– OPPOSITES half-hearted.

wholesome ● adjective conducive to or promoting good health and physical or moral well-being.
– DERIVATIVES **wholesomely** adverb **wholesomeness** noun.

wholewheat ● noun whole grains of wheat including the husk.

wholly /hōlli/ ● adverb entirely; fully.

whom ● pronoun used instead of 'who' as the object of a verb or preposition.
– USAGE On the use of **who** and **whom**, see WHO.

whomever ● pronoun chiefly formal used instead of 'whoever' as the object of a verb or preposition.

whomp /womp/ informal ● verb strike heavily; thump. ● noun a thump.
– ORIGIN imitative.

whomsoever ● relative pronoun formal used instead of 'whosoever' as the object of a verb or preposition.

whoomph /wŏŏmf/ (also **whoomp** /wŏŏmp/) ● noun a loud muffled sound.
– ORIGIN imitative.

whoop /hŏŏp, wŏŏp/ ● noun **1** a loud cry of joy or excitement. **2** a long rasping indrawn breath. ● verb give or make a whoop.
– PHRASES **whoop it up** informal **1** enjoy oneself or celebrate unrestrainedly. **2** N. Amer. create a stir.
– ORIGIN probably imitative.

whoopee informal ● exclamation /wŏŏpee/ expressing wild excitement or joy. ● noun /wŏŏpee/ wild revelry.
– PHRASES **make whoopee 1** celebrate wildly. **2** have sexual intercourse.

whoopee cushion ● noun a rubber cushion that makes a sound like the breaking of wind when someone sits on it.

whooper swan /hŏŏpər/ ● noun a large swan with a black and yellow bill and a loud trumpeting call, breeding in northern Eurasia and Greenland.

whooping cough /hŏŏping/ ● noun a contagious bacterial disease chiefly affecting children, characterized by convulsive coughs followed by a whoop.

whoops (also **whoops-a-daisy**) ● exclamation informal expressing mild dismay.
– ORIGIN probably from UPSY-DAISY.

whoosh /woosh/ (also **woosh**) ● verb move quickly or suddenly and with a rushing sound. ● noun a whooshing movement.
– ORIGIN imitative.

whop /wop/ (chiefly N. Amer. also **whap**) informal ● verb (**whopped**, **whopping**) hit hard. ● noun a heavy blow or its sound.
– ORIGIN from dialect *wap* 'strike'.

whopper ● noun informal **1** a thing that is extremely large. **2** a gross or blatant lie.

whopping ● adjective informal extremely large.

whore ● noun derogatory a prostitute or promiscuous woman. ● verb **1** work as a prostitute. **2** use the services of prostitutes.
– DERIVATIVES **whorish** adjective.
– ORIGIN Old English.

whorehouse ● noun informal a brothel.

whorl /worl, wurl/ ● noun **1** Zoology each of the turns in the spiral shell of a mollusc. **2** Botany a set of leaves, flowers, or branches springing from a stem at the same level and encircling it. **3** a complete circle in a fingerprint.
– DERIVATIVES **whorled** adjective.
– ORIGIN originally denoting a small flywheel: apparently from WHIRL, influenced by an Old English word meaning 'small wheel or pulley fixed on a spindle'.

whortleberry /wurt'lbəri, -beri/ ● noun a bilberry.
– ORIGIN a dialect variant of obsolete *hurtleberry*, of unknown origin.

who's ● contraction **1** who is. **2** who has.
– USAGE A common mistake is to confuse **who's** with **whose**: **who's** is a contraction of **who is** or **who has**, while **whose** means 'belonging to associated with which person' or 'of whom or which' and is used in questions such as *whose is this?*

whose ● possessive determiner & pronoun **1** belonging to or associated with which person. **2** (as possessive determiner) of whom or which.
– ORIGIN Old English.

whosesoever ● relative pronoun & determiner formal whoever's.

whosever ● relative pronoun & determiner belonging to or associated with whichever person; whoever's.

whosoever ● pronoun formal term for WHOEVER.

whump /wump, wŏŏmp/ ● noun a dull thud. ● verb make a whump.
– ORIGIN imitative.

whup /wup/ ● verb (**whupped**, **whupping**) informal, chiefly N. Amer. beat; thrash.
– ORIGIN variant of WHIP.

why ● adverb **1** for what reason or purpose? **2** (with reference to a reason) on account of which; for which. **3** the reason for which. ● exclamation **1** expressing surprise or indignation. **2** used to add emphasis to a response. ● noun (pl. **whys**) a reason or explanation.
– ORIGIN Old English.

WI ● abbreviation **1** West Indies. **2** Wisconsin. **3** Brit. Women's Institute.

wibble ● verb informal **1** another term for WOBBLE. **2** Brit. speak or write at length and to no purpose.
– DERIVATIVES **wibbly** adjective.
– ORIGIN from *wibble-wobble*; sense 2 is perhaps a different word and influenced by DRIVEL.

Wicca /wikkə/ ● noun the religious cult of modern witchcraft.
– DERIVATIVES **Wiccan** adjective & noun.
– ORIGIN Old English, 'witch'.

wick[1] ● noun **1** a strip of porous material up which liquid fuel is drawn by capillary action to the flame in a candle, lamp, or lighter. **2** Medicine a gauze strip inserted in a wound to drain it. ● verb absorb or draw off (liquid) by capillary action.
– PHRASES **get on someone's wick** Brit. informal annoy someone.
– ORIGIN Old English.

wick[2] ● noun (in place names) a town, hamlet, or district.
– ORIGIN Old English, 'dwelling place', probably from Latin *vicus* 'street, village'.

wicked ● adjective **1** evil or morally wrong. **2** playfully mischievous. **3** informal excellent; wonderful.
– DERIVATIVES **wickedly** adverb **wickedness** noun.
– ORIGIN probably from WICCA.

wicker ● noun pliable twigs, typically of willow, plaited or

Thesaurus

wholesale ● adverb *images were removed wholesale* EXTENSIVELY, on a large scale, comprehensively; indiscriminately, without exception.
– OPPOSITES selectively.
● adjective *wholesale destruction* EXTENSIVE, widespread, large-scale, wide-ranging, comprehensive, total, mass; indiscriminate.
– OPPOSITES partial.

wholesome ● adjective **1** *wholesome food* HEALTHY, health-giving, healthful, good (for one), nutritious, nourishing; natural, uncontaminated, organic. **2** *wholesome fun* MORAL, ethical, good, clean, virtuous, pure, innocent, chaste; uplifting, edifying, proper, correct, decent; *informal* squeaky clean.

wholly ● adverb **1** *the measures were wholly inadequate* COMPLETELY, totally, absolutely, entirely, fully, thoroughly, utterly, quite, perfectly, downright, in every respect, in all respects; *informal* one hundred per cent. **2** *they rely wholly on you* EXCLUSIVELY, only, solely, purely, alone.

whoop ● noun *whoops of delight* SHOUT, cry, call, yell, roar, scream, shriek, screech, cheer; *informal* holler.
● verb *he whooped for joy* SHOUT, cry, call, yell, roar, scream, shriek, screech, cheer; *informal* holler.

whopper ● noun *(informal)* **1** *what a whopper!* MONSTER, brute, giant, colossus, mammoth, monstrosity; *informal* jumbo. **2** *Joseph's story is a whopper.* See LIE[1] noun.

whopping ● adjective *(informal).* See HUGE.

whore ● noun *the whores on the street.* See PROSTITUTE noun.
● verb **1** *she spent her life whoring* WORK AS A PROSTITUTE, sell one's body, sell oneself, be on the streets; *informal* be on the game. **2** *the men whored and drank* USE PROSTITUTES; *archaic* wench.

whorehouse ● noun. See BROTHEL.

whorl ● noun LOOP, coil, hoop, ring, curl, twirl, twist, spiral, helix.

wicked ● adjective **1** *wicked deeds* EVIL, sinful, immoral, wrong, morally wrong, wrongful, bad, iniquitous, corrupt, black-hearted, base, mean, vile; villainous, nefarious, erring, foul, monstrous, shocking, outrageous, atrocious, abominable, reprehensible, hateful, detestable, despicable, odious, contemptible, horrible, heinous, egregious, execrable, fiendish, vicious, murderous, barbarous; criminal, illicit, unlawful, illegal, lawless, felonious, dishonest, unscrupulous; *Law* malfeasant; *informal* crooked; *Brit. informal* beastly; *dated* dastardly; *rare* peccable. **2** *the wind was wicked* DISAGREEABLE, unpleasant, foul, bad, nasty, irksome, troublesome, annoying, irritating, displeasing, uncomfortable, hateful, detestable.

woven to make items such as furniture and baskets.
– DERIVATIVES **wickerwork** noun.
– ORIGIN Scandinavian.

wicket • noun **1** Cricket each of the sets of three stumps with two bails across the top at either end of the pitch, defended by a batsman. **2** a small door or gate, especially one beside or in a larger one.
– PHRASES **at the wicket** Cricket **1** batting. **2** by the wicketkeeper. **a sticky wicket 1** Cricket a pitch that has been drying after rain and is difficult to bat on. **2** informal a tricky or awkward situation.
– ORIGIN Old French *wiket*; probably related to an Old Norse word meaning 'to turn, move'.

wicketkeeper • noun Cricket a fielder stationed close behind a batsman's wicket.

widdershins /widdərshinz/ (also **withershins**) • adverb chiefly Scottish in a direction contrary to the sun's course (or anticlockwise), considered as unlucky.
– ORIGIN High German *widersinnes*, from *wider* 'against' + *sin* 'direction'.

widdle informal • verb urinate. • noun an act of urinating.
– ORIGIN from PIDDLE.

wide • adjective (**wider**, **widest**) **1** of great or more than average width. **2** (after a measurement and in questions) from side to side. **3** open to the full extent. **4** including a great variety of people or things. **5** spread among a large number or over a large area. **6** (in combination) extending over the whole of: *industry-wide*. **7** at a considerable or specified distance from a point or mark. **8** (especially in football) at or near the side of the field. • adverb **1** to the full extent. **2** far from a particular point or mark. **3** (especially in football) at or near the side of the field. • noun (also **wide ball**) Cricket a ball that is judged to be too wide of the stumps for the batsman to play.
– PHRASES **wide awake** fully awake. **wide of the mark 1** a long way from an intended target. **2** inaccurate. **wide open 1** (of a contest) of which the outcome is not predictable. **2** vulnerable to attack.
– DERIVATIVES **widely** adverb **wideness** noun.
– ORIGIN Old English.

wide-angle • adjective (of a lens) having a short focal length and hence a field covering a wide angle.

wide area network • noun a computer network in which the computers connected may be far apart, generally having a radius of more than 1 km.

wide boy • noun Brit. informal a man involved in petty criminal activities.

wide-eyed • adjective **1** having one's eyes wide open in amazement. **2** inexperienced; innocent.

widen • verb make or become wider.
– DERIVATIVES **widener** noun.

widescreen • adjective denoting a cinema or television screen presenting a wide field of vision in relation to height.

widespread • adjective spread among a large number or over a large area.

widgeon • noun variant spelling of WIGEON.

widget /wijit/ • noun informal a small gadget or mechanical device.
– ORIGIN perhaps an alteration of GADGET.

widow • noun **1** a woman who has lost her husband by death and has not married again. **2** humorous a woman whose husband is often away participating in a specified sport or activity: *a golf widow*. • verb (**be widowed**) become a widow or widower.
– ORIGIN Old English.

widower • noun a man who has lost his wife by death and has not married again.

widowhood • noun the state or period of being a widow or widower.

widow's mite • noun a small monetary contribution from someone who is poor.
– ORIGIN with biblical allusion to the Gospel of Mark, chapter 12.

widow's peak • noun a V-shaped growth of hair towards the centre of the forehead.

widow's weeds • plural noun black clothes worn by a widow in mourning.
– ORIGIN *weeds* is used in the obsolete sense 'garments' and is from Old English.

width /with, width/ • noun **1** the measurement or extent of something from side to side; the lesser or least of two or more dimensions of a body. **2** a piece of something at its full extent from side to side. **3** wide range or extent.

widthways (also **widthwise**) • adverb in a direction parallel with a thing's width.

wield • verb **1** hold and use (a weapon or tool). **2** have and be able to use (power or influence).
– DERIVATIVES **wielder** noun.
– ORIGIN Old English, 'govern, subdue, direct'.

wieldy • adjective (**wieldier**, **wieldiest**) easily controlled or handled.

Wiener schnitzel /veenər shnits'l/ • noun a thin slice of veal that is breaded and fried.
– ORIGIN German, 'Vienna cutlet'.

wife • noun (pl. **wives**) **1** a married woman considered in relation to her husband. **2** archaic or dialect a woman, especially an old or uneducated one.
– DERIVATIVES **wifely** adjective.
– ORIGIN Old English, 'woman'.

wig[1] • noun a covering for the head made of real or artificial hair.
– ORIGIN shortening of PERIWIG.

wig[2] • verb (**wigged**, **wigging**) informal **1** Brit. dated rebuke severely. **2** (**wig out**) chiefly N. Amer. become deliriously excited.
– ORIGIN apparently from WIG[1], perhaps from BIGWIG and associated

Thesaurus

3 *a wicked sense of humour* MISCHIEVOUS, playful, naughty, impish, roguish, arch, puckish, cheeky. **4** *(informal) Sophie makes wicked cakes.* See EXCELLENT.
– OPPOSITES virtuous.

wickedness • noun EVIL-DOING, evil, sin, sinfulness, iniquity, vileness, baseness, badness, wrongdoing, dishonesty, unscrupulousness, roguery, villainy, viciousness, degeneracy, depravity, immorality, vice, corruption, corruptness, devilry, fiendishness; *Law* malfeasance; *informal* crookedness; *formal* turpitude.

wide • adjective **1** *a wide river* BROAD, extensive, spacious, vast, spread out. **2** *their mouths were wide with shock* FULLY OPEN, agape, wide open. **3** *a wide range of opinion* COMPREHENSIVE, ample, broad, extensive, large, large-scale, wide-ranging, exhaustive, general, all-inclusive. **4** *his shot was wide* OFF TARGET, off the mark, wide of the mark/target, inaccurate.
– OPPOSITES narrow.
• adverb **1** *he opened his eyes wide* FULLY, to the fullest/furthest extent, as far/much as possible. **2** *he shot wide* OFF TARGET, wide of the mark/target, inaccurately.

wide awake • adjective FULLY AWAKE, conscious, sleepless, insomniac; *archaic* watchful.
– OPPOSITES asleep.

wide-eyed • adjective **1** *the whole class was wide-eyed* STARING IN AMAZEMENT, goggle-eyed, open-mouthed, dumbstruck, surprised, amazed, astonished, astounded, stunned, staggered; *informal* flabbergasted; *Brit. informal* gobsmacked. **2** *wide-eyed visitors* INNOCENT, naive, impressionable, ingenuous, childlike, credulous, trusting, unquestioning, unsophisticated, gullible.

widen • verb **1** *a proposal to widen the motorway* BROADEN, make/become wider, open up/out, expand, extend, enlarge. **2** *the Party must widen its support* INCREASE, augment, boost, swell, enlarge.

wide open • adjective **1** *his eyes were wide open* FULLY OPEN, open wide, agape. **2** *the championship is wide open* UNPREDICTABLE, uncertain, unsure, in the balance, up in the air; *informal* anyone's guess. **3** *they were wide open to attacks* VULNERABLE, exposed, unprotected, defenceless, undefended, at risk, in danger.

widespread • adjective GENERAL, extensive, universal, common, global, worldwide, international, omnipresent, ubiquitous, across the board, predominant, prevalent, rife, broad, rampant, pervasive.
– OPPOSITES limited.

width • noun **1** *the width of the river* WIDENESS, breadth, broadness, thickness, span, diameter, girth. **2** *the width of experience required* RANGE, breadth, compass, scope, span, scale, extent, extensiveness, comprehensiveness.
– OPPOSITES length, narrowness.

wield • verb **1** *he was wielding a sword* BRANDISH, flourish, wave, swing; use, employ, handle. **2** *he has wielded power since 1972* EXERCISE, exert, hold, maintain, command, control.

wife • noun SPOUSE, partner, mate, consort, woman, helpmate, helpmeet, bride; *informal* old lady, wifey, better half, missus; *Brit. in-*

with a rebuke given by a person in authority.

wigeon /wijən/ (also **widgeon**) ● noun a dabbling duck with mainly reddish-brown and grey plumage, the male having a whistling call.
– ORIGIN perhaps of imitative origin and suggested by PIGEON.

wiggle ● verb move with short movements up and down or from side to side. ● noun a wiggling movement.
– DERIVATIVES **wiggler** noun **wiggly** adjective (**wigglier**, **wiggliest**).
– ORIGIN Low German and Dutch *wiggelen*.

wight ● noun **1** archaic or dialect a person of a specified kind. **2** literary a spirit or ghost.
– ORIGIN Old English, 'thing, creature'.

wigwam ● noun a dome-shaped or conical dwelling made by fastening mats, skins, or bark over a framework of poles (as used formerly by some North American Indian peoples).
– ORIGIN Algonquian, 'their house'.

wild ● adjective **1** (of animals or plants) living or growing in the natural environment; not domesticated or cultivated. **2** (of people) not civilized. **3** (of scenery or a region) desolate-looking. **4** uncontrolled; unrestrained. **5** not based on reason or evidence: *a wild guess.* **6** informal very enthusiastic or excited. **7** informal very angry. **8** (of looks, appearance, etc.) indicating distraction. ● noun **1** (**the wild**) a natural state. **2** (also **the wilds**) a remote uninhabited area.
– PHRASES **run wild** grow or behave without restraint or discipline.
– DERIVATIVES **wildly** adverb **wildness** noun.
– ORIGIN Old English.

wild card ● noun **1** a playing card that can have any value, suit, colour, or other property in a game at the discretion of the player holding it. **2** a person or thing whose qualities are uncertain. **3** Computing a character that will match any character or sequence of characters in a search. **4** an opportunity to enter a sports competition without taking part in qualifying matches or being ranked at a particular level.

wildcat ● noun **1** a small Eurasian and African cat, typically grey with black markings and a bushy tail, believed to be the ancestor of the domestic cat. **2** a hot-tempered or ferocious person. **3** an exploratory oil well. ● adjective **1** (of a strike) sudden and unofficial. **2** commercially unsound or risky. ● verb US prospect for oil.
– DERIVATIVES **wildcatter** noun.

wild cherry ● noun another term for GEAN.

wild duck ● noun a mallard.

wildebeest /wildəbeest, vil-/ ● noun (pl. same or **wildebeests**) another term for GNU.
– ORIGIN Afrikaans, 'wild beast'.

wilderness ● noun **1** an uncultivated, uninhabited, and inhospitable region. **2** a position of disfavour.
– PHRASES **a voice in the wilderness** an unheeded advocate of reform (with allusion to the Gospel of Matthew, chapter 3).
– ORIGIN Old English, 'land inhabited only by wild animals'; related to DEER.

wildfire ● noun historical a highly flammable liquid used in warfare.
– PHRASES **spread like wildfire** spread with great speed.

wildfowl ● plural noun game birds, especially aquatic ones; waterfowl.

wild goose chase ● noun a foolish and hopeless search for or pursuit of something unattainable.

wildlife ● noun the native fauna (and sometimes flora) of a region.

wild oat ● noun a grass which is related to the cultivated oat and is found as a weed of other cereals.

wild rice ● noun a tall aquatic American grass with edible grains, related to rice.

wild silk ● noun coarse silk produced by wild silkworms, especially tussore.

wiles ● plural noun devious or cunning stratagems.
– ORIGIN perhaps related to an Old Norse word meaning 'craft'.

wilful (US also **willful**) ● adjective **1** intentional; deliberate. **2** stubborn and determined.
– DERIVATIVES **wilfully** adverb **wilfulness** noun.

will[1] ● modal verb (3rd sing. present **will**; past **would**) **1** expressing the future tense. **2** expressing a strong intention or assertion about the future. **3** expressing inevitable events. **4** expressing a request. **5** expressing desire, consent, or willingness. **6** expressing facts about ability or capacity. **7** expressing habitual behaviour. **8** expressing probability or expectation about something in the present.
– USAGE On the difference between **will** and **shall**, see the note at SHALL.
– ORIGIN Old English.

will[2] ● noun **1** the faculty by which a person decides on and initiates action. **2** (also **will power**) control or restraint deliberately exerted. **3** a desire or intention. **4** a legal document containing instructions for the disposition of one's money and property after one's death. ● verb **1** intend or desire to happen. **2** bring about by the exercise of mental powers. **3** bequeath in one's will.
– PHRASES **at will** at whatever time or in whatever way one pleases. **where there's a will there's a way** proverb determination will overcome any obstacle. **with a will** energetically and resolutely.
– ORIGIN Old English; related to WILL[1] and WELL[1].

willful ● adjective US variant spelling of WILFUL.

Thesaurus

formal other half, her indoors, trouble and strife.
– RELATED TERMS uxorial.

wiggle ● verb JIGGLE, wriggle, twitch, shimmy, joggle, wag, waggle, wobble, shake, twist, squirm, writhe.

wild ● adjective **1** *wild animals* UNTAMED, undomesticated, feral; fierce, ferocious, savage. **2** *wild flowers* UNCULTIVATED, native, indigenous. **3** *wild tribes* PRIMITIVE, uncivilized, uncultured; savage, barbarous, barbaric. **4** *wild hill country* UNINHABITED, unpopulated, uncultivated; rugged, rough, inhospitable, desolate, barren. **5** *a wild night* STORMY, squally, tempestuous, turbulent, boisterous. **6** *her wild black hair* DISHEVELLED, tousled, tangled, windswept, untidy, unkempt; *N. Amer.* mussed up. **7** *wild behaviour* UNCONTROLLED, unrestrained, out of control, undisciplined, unruly, rowdy, disorderly, riotous. **8** *wild with excitement* VERY EXCITED, delirious, in a frenzy; tumultuous, passionate, vehement, unrestrained. **9** *(informal) I was wild with jealousy* DISTRAUGHT, frantic, beside oneself, in a frenzy, hysterical, deranged, berserk; *informal* mad, crazy. **10** *(informal) Hank went wild when he found out.* See FURIOUS sense 1. **11** *(informal) his family weren't wild about me* VERY KEEN, very enthusiastic, enamoured, infatuated, smitten; *informal* crazy, mad, nutty/nuts. **12** *Bill's wild schemes* MADCAP, ridiculous, ludicrous, foolish, stupid, foolhardy, idiotic, absurd, silly, ill-considered, senseless, nonsensical; impractical, impracticable, unworkable; *informal* crazy, crackpot, cock-eyed. **13** *a wild guess* RANDOM, arbitrary, haphazard, uninformed.
– OPPOSITES tame, cultivated, calm, disciplined.
– PHRASES **run wild 1** *the garden had run wild* GROW UNCHECKED, grow profusely, run riot. **2** *the children are running wild* RUN AMOK, run riot, get out of control, be undisciplined.

wilderness ● noun **1** *the Siberian wilderness* WILDS, wastes, inhospitable region; desert. **2** *a litter-strewn wilderness* WASTELAND.

wildlife ● noun (WILD) ANIMALS, fauna.

wilds ● plural noun REMOTE AREAS, wilderness; backwoods; *N. Amer.* backcountry, backland; *Austral./NZ* outback, bush, backblocks, booay; *N. Amer. informal* boondocks, tall timbers.

wiles ● plural noun TRICKS, ruses, ploys, schemes, dodges, manoeuvres, subterfuges, artifices; guile, artfulness, cunning, craftiness.

wilful ● adjective **1** *wilful destruction* DELIBERATE, intentional, done on purpose, premeditated, planned, conscious. **2** *a wilful child* HEADSTRONG, strong-willed, obstinate, stubborn, pig-headed, recalcitrant, uncooperative, obstreperous, ungovernable, unmanageable; *Brit. informal* bloody-minded, bolshie; *N. Amer. informal* balky; *formal* refractory; *archaic* froward, contumacious.
– OPPOSITES accidental, amenable.

will[1] ● verb *accidents will happen* HAVE A TENDENCY TO, are bound to, do.

will[2] ● noun **1** *the will to succeed* DETERMINATION, will power, strength of character, resolution, resolve, resoluteness, single-mindedness, drive, commitment, dedication, doggedness, tenacity, tenaciousness, staying power. **2** *they stayed against their will* DESIRE, wish, preference, inclination, intention, intent. **3** *God's will* WISH, desire, decision, choice; decree, command. **4** *his father's will* (LAST WILL AND) TESTAMENT.
● verb **1** *do what you will* WANT, wish, please, see/think fit, think best, like, choose, prefer. **2** *God willed it* DECREE, order, ordain, command. **3** *she willed the money to her husband* BEQUEATH, leave, hand down, pass on, settle on; *Law* devise.

willie ● noun variant spelling of WILLY.

willies ● plural noun (**the willies**) informal a strong feeling of nervous discomfort.

– ORIGIN of unknown origin.

willing ● adjective **1** ready, eager, or prepared to do something. **2** given or done readily.

– DERIVATIVES **willingly** adverb **willingness** noun.

williwaw /williwaw/ ● noun a sudden violent squall blowing offshore from a mountainous coast.

– ORIGIN of unknown origin.

will-o'-the-wisp ● noun **1** a phosphorescent light seen hovering or floating at night on marshy ground, thought to result from the combustion of natural gases. **2** a person or thing that is difficult or impossible to reach or catch.

– ORIGIN originally as *Will with the wisp*, the sense of *wisp* being 'handful of lighted hay'.

willow ● noun a tree or shrub which typically grows near water, has narrow leaves and pliant branches, and bears catkins.

– ORIGIN Old English.

willowherb ● noun a plant with long narrow leaves and pink or pale purple flowers.

willow pattern ● noun a conventional design in pottery featuring a Chinese scene depicted in blue on white, typically including figures on a bridge, a willow tree, and birds.

willowy ● adjective **1** bordered, shaded, or covered by willows. **2** (of a person) tall, slim, and lithe.

willy (also **willie**) ● noun (pl. **willies**) Brit. informal a penis.

– ORIGIN familiar form of the given name *William*.

willy-nilly ● adverb **1** whether one likes it or not. **2** without direction or planning; haphazardly.

– ORIGIN later spelling of *will I, nill I* 'I am willing, I am unwilling'.

willy-willy ● noun (pl. **willy-willies**) Austral. a whirlwind or dust storm.

– ORIGIN Yindjibarndi (an Aboriginal language).

wilt[1] ● verb **1** (of a plant) become limp through loss of water, heat, or disease; droop. **2** (of a person) lose one's energy or vigour. ● noun any of a number of fungal or bacterial diseases of plants characterized by wilting of the foliage.

– ORIGIN perhaps from dialect *welk* 'lose freshness', of Low German origin.

wilt[2] archaic second person singular of WILL[1].

Wilts. ● abbreviation Wiltshire.

wily /wīli/ ● adjective (**wilier, wiliest**) skilled at gaining an advantage, especially deceitfully.

– DERIVATIVES **wiliness** noun.

wimp informal ● noun a weak and cowardly person. ● verb (**wimp out**) withdraw from something in a cowardly way.

– DERIVATIVES **wimpish** adjective **wimpy** adjective.

– ORIGIN origin uncertain, perhaps from WHIMPER.

wimple ● noun a cloth headdress covering the head, neck, and sides of the face, formerly worn by women and still by some nuns.

– ORIGIN Old English.

win ● verb (**winning**; past and past part. **won**) **1** be successful or victorious in (a contest or conflict). **2** gain as a result of success in a contest, conflict, etc. **3** gain (someone's attention, support, or love). **4** (**win over**) gain the support or favour of. **5** (**win out/through**) manage to succeed or achieve something by effort. ● noun a victory in a game or contest.

– PHRASES **win the day** be victorious. **win** (or **earn**) **one's spurs** **1** historical gain a knighthood by an act of bravery. **2** informal gain one's first distinction or honours.

– DERIVATIVES **winless** adjective **winnable** adjective.

– ORIGIN Old English, 'strive, contend', also 'subdue and take possession of, acquire'.

wince ● verb give a slight involuntary grimace or flinch due to pain or distress. ● noun an instance of wincing.

– ORIGIN Old French *guenchir* 'turn aside'.

winceyette /winsiet/ ● noun Brit. a lightweight brushed cotton fabric, used especially for nightclothes.

– ORIGIN from *wincey*, a lightweight wool and cotton fabric, from *woolsey* in LINSEY-WOOLSEY.

winch ● noun **1** a hauling or lifting device consisting of a rope or chain winding around a horizontal rotating drum, turned by a crank or by motor. **2** the crank of a wheel or axle. ● verb hoist or haul with a winch.

– ORIGIN Old English, 'reel, pulley'; related to WINK.

Winchester ● noun **1** (also **Winchester rifle**) trademark a breech-loading side-action repeating rifle. **2** (also **Winchester disk** or **drive**) Computing a disk drive in a sealed unit containing a high-capacity hard disk and the read-write heads.

– ORIGIN sense 1 named after the American rifle manufacturer Oliver F. *Winchester* (1810–80); sense 2 so named because its original numerical designation corresponded to the calibre of the rifle.

wind[1] /wind/ ● noun **1** the perceptible natural movement of the air, especially in the form of a current blowing from a particular direction. **2** breath as needed in physical exertion, speech, playing an instrument, etc. **3** Brit. air swallowed while eating or gas generated in the stomach and intestines by digestion. **4** meaningless talk. **5** (also **winds**) (treated as sing. or pl.) wind or woodwind instruments forming a band or section of an orchestra. ● verb **1** cause to have difficulty breathing because of exertion or a blow to the stomach. **2** Brit. make (a baby) bring up wind after feeding by patting its back.

– PHRASES **get wind of** informal hear a rumour of. **it's an ill wind that blows nobody any good** proverb few things are so bad that no one profits from them. **put the wind up** Brit. informal alarm or frighten. **sail close to** (or **near**) **the wind** **1** sail as nearly against the wind as is consistent with using its force. **2** informal verge on indecency, dishonesty, or disaster. **take the wind out of someone's sails** frustrate someone by anticipating an action or remark. **to the wind(s)** (or **the four winds**) in all directions. [ORIGIN from 'And fear of death deliver to the winds' (Milton's *Paradise Lost*).]

– DERIVATIVES **windless** adjective.

– ORIGIN Old English.

wind[2] /wīnd/ ● verb (past and past part. **wound** /wownd/) **1** move in or take a twisting or spiral course. **2** pass (something) around a

Thesaurus

– PHRASES **at will** AS ONE PLEASES, as one thinks fit, to suit oneself, at whim.

willing ● adjective **1** *I'm willing to give it a try* READY, prepared, disposed, inclined, of a mind, minded; happy, glad, pleased, agreeable, amenable; *informal* game. **2** *willing help* READILY GIVEN, willingly given, ungrudging.

– OPPOSITES reluctant.

willingly ● adverb VOLUNTARILY, of one's own free will, of one's own accord; readily, without reluctance, ungrudgingly, cheerfully, happily, gladly, with pleasure.

willingness ● noun READINESS, inclination, will, wish, desire.

willowy ● adjective TALL, SLIM, slender, svelte, lissom, sylphlike, long-limbed, graceful, lithe; *informal* slinky.

will power ● noun. See WILL[2] noun sense 1.

willy-nilly ● adverb **1** *cars were parked willy-nilly* HAPHAZARDLY, at random, randomly. **2** *we are, willy-nilly, in a different situation* WHETHER ONE LIKES IT OR NOT, of necessity; *informal* like it or lump it; *formal* perforce, nolens volens.

wilt ● verb **1** *the roses had begun to wilt* DROOP, sag, become limp, flop; wither, shrivel (up). **2** *wilting in the heat* LANGUISH, flag, droop, become listless. **3** *Shelley's happy mood wilted* FADE, ebb, wane, evaporate, melt away.

– OPPOSITES flourish.

wily ● adjective SHREWD, clever, sharp, sharp-witted, astute, canny, smart; crafty, cunning, artful, sly, scheming, calculating, devious; *informal* tricky, foxy; *archaic* subtle.

– OPPOSITES naive.

wimp ● noun (*informal*) COWARD, namby-pamby, milksop, weakling; *informal* drip, sissy, weed, wuss, pansy, scaredy-cat, chicken; *Brit. informal* wet, mummy's boy, big girl's blouse; *N. Amer. informal* cupcake, pantywaist, pussy; *Austral./NZ informal* sook; *archaic* poltroon.

win ● verb **1** *Steve won the race* BE THE VICTOR IN, be the winner of, come first in, take first prize in, triumph in, be successful in. **2** *she was determined to win* COME FIRST, be the winner, be victorious, carry/win the day, come out on top, succeed, triumph, prevail. **3** *he won a cash prize* SECURE, gain, collect, pick up, walk away/off with, carry off; *informal* land, net, bag, scoop. **4** *Ilona won his heart* CAPTIVATE, steal.

– OPPOSITES lose.

● noun *a 3–0 win* VICTORY, triumph, conquest.

– OPPOSITES defeat.

– PHRASES **win someone round/over** PERSUADE, talk round, convince, sway, prevail on.

wince ● verb *he winced at the pain* GRIMACE, pull a face, flinch,

W

thing or person so as to encircle or enfold them. **3** (with reference to a length of something) twist or be twisted around itself or a core. **4** make (a clockwork device) operate by turning a key or handle. **5** turn (a key or handle) repeatedly. **6** move (an audio or video tape or a film) back or forwards to a desired point. **7** hoist or draw with a windlass, winch, etc. ● **noun 1** a twist or turn in a course. **2** a single turn made when winding.
– PHRASES **wind down 1** (of a clockwork mechanism) gradually lose power. **2** draw or bring gradually to a close. **3** informal relax. **wind up 1** gradually bring to a conclusion. **2** informal end up in a specified state, situation, or place. **3** Brit. informal tease or irritate. **4** informal increase the tension or power of.
– ORIGIN Old English, 'go rapidly', 'twine'; related to WANDER and WEND.
windbag ● noun informal a person who talks a lot but says little of any value.
windbreak ● noun a row of trees, wall, or screen providing shelter from the wind.
windburn ● noun reddening and soreness of the skin caused by prolonged exposure to the wind.
– DERIVATIVES **windburned** (also **windburnt**) adjective.
windcheater ● noun chiefly Brit. a wind-resistant jacket with a close-fitting neck, waistband, and cuffs.
wind chill ● noun the cooling effect of wind on a surface.
wind chimes ● plural noun pieces of glass, metal rods, or similar items, suspended from a frame and typically hung near a door or window so as to chime in the draught.
winder /wīndər/ ● noun a device or mechanism for winding something, especially a watch, clock, or camera film.
windfall ● noun **1** an apple or other fruit blown from a tree by the wind. **2** a piece of unexpected good fortune, especially a legacy.
windfall tax (also **windfall profits tax**) ● noun a tax levied on an unexpectedly large profit, especially one regarded to be excessive or unfairly obtained.
wind farm ● noun an area containing a group of energy-producing windmills or wind turbines.
windflower ● noun an anemone.
winding /winding/ ● noun **1** a twisting movement or course. **2** a thing that winds or is wound round something. ● adjective having a twisting or spiral course.
winding sheet ● noun a shroud.
wind instrument ● noun **1** a musical instrument in which sound is produced by the vibration of air, typically by the player blowing into the instrument. **2** a woodwind instrument as distinct from a brass instrument.
windjammer ● noun historical a merchant sailing ship.
windlass ● noun a winch, especially one on a ship or in a harbour. ● verb haul or lift with a windlass.
– ORIGIN probably from an Old Norse word meaning 'winding pole'.
wind machine ● noun **1** a machine used in the theatre or in film-making for producing a blast of air or imitating the sound of wind. **2** a wind-driven turbine.
windmill ● noun a building with sails or vanes that turn in the wind and generate power to grind corn, generate electricity, or draw water. ● verb move (one's arms) in a manner suggestive of the sails of a windmill.
window ● noun **1** an opening in a wall or roof, fitted with glass in a frame to let in light or air and allow people to see out. **2** an opening through which customers are served in a bank, ticket office, etc. **3** a transparent panel in an envelope to show an address. **4** Computing a framed area on a display screen for viewing information. **5** (**window on/into/to**) a means of observing and learning about. **6** an interval or opportunity for action.
– PHRASES **go out of the window** informal (of a plan or behaviour) be abandoned or cease to exist. **windows of the soul** the eyes.
– DERIVATIVES **windowless** adjective.
– ORIGIN Old Norse, from words meaning 'wind' + 'eye'.
window box ● noun a long narrow box in which flowers and other plants are grown on an outside window sill.
window dressing ● noun **1** the arrangement of a display in a shop window. **2** the presentation of something in a superficially attractive way to give a favourable impression.
window frame ● noun a frame holding the glass of a window.
window ledge ● noun a window sill.
windowpane ● noun a pane of glass in a window.
window seat ● noun **1** a seat below a window, especially one in a bay or alcove. **2** a seat next to a window in an aircraft or train.
window-shop ● verb look at the goods displayed in shop windows, especially without intending to buy.
– DERIVATIVES **window-shopper** noun.
window sill ● noun a ledge or sill forming the bottom part of a window.
windpipe ● noun the trachea.
windscreen ● noun Brit. a glass screen at the front of a motor vehicle.
windscreen wiper ● noun Brit. a device for keeping a windscreen clear of rain, having a rubber blade on an arm that moves in an arc.
wind shear ● noun variation in wind velocity along a direction at right angles to the wind's direction, tending to exert a turning force.
windshield ● noun N. Amer. a windscreen.
windsock ● noun a light, flexible cylinder or cone mounted on a mast to show the direction and strength of the wind, especially at an airfield.
windstorm ● noun chiefly N. Amer. a gale.
windsurfing ● noun the sport of riding on water on a sailboard.
– DERIVATIVES **windsurf** verb **windsurfer** noun.
windswept ● adjective **1** exposed to strong winds. **2** (of a person's hair or appearance) untidy after being exposed to the wind.
wind tunnel ● noun a tunnel-like apparatus for producing an airstream past models of aircraft, buildings, etc., in order to investigate flow or the effect of wind on the full-size object.

Thesaurus

blench, start.
● noun *a wince of pain* GRIMACE, flinch, start.
wind[1] ● noun **1** *the trees were swaying in the wind* BREEZE, current of air; gale, hurricane; *informal* blow; *poetic/literary* zephyr. **2** *Jez got his wind back* BREATH; *informal* puff. **3** *you do talk a lot of wind.* See HOT AIR.
– RELATED TERMS aeolian.
– PHRASES **get wind of** *(informal)* HEAR ABOUT/OF, learn of, find out about, be told about, be informed of; *informal* hear something on the grapevine. **in the wind** ON THE WAY, coming, about to happen, in the offing, in the air, on the horizon, approaching, looming, brewing, afoot; *informal* on the cards. **put the wind up someone** *(Brit. informal)* SCARE, frighten, make afraid, make nervous, throw into a panic, alarm.
wind[2] ● verb **1** *the road winds up the mountain* TWIST (AND TURN), bend, curve, loop, zigzag, weave, snake. **2** *he wound a towel around his waist* WRAP, furl, entwine, lace. **3** *Anne wound the wool into a ball* COIL, roll, twist, twine.
– PHRASES **wind down 1** *(informal) he needed to wind down* RELAX, unwind, calm down, cool down/off, ease up/off, take it easy, rest, put one's feet up; *N. Amer. informal* hang loose, chill (out). **2** *the campaign was winding down* DRAW TO A CLOSE, come to an end, tail off, slack(en) off, slow down. **wind something down** BRING TO A CLOSE/END, wind up, close down. **wind up** *(informal)* END UP, finish up, find oneself, land up; *informal* fetch up. **wind someone up** *(Brit. informal)* **1** *Katie was just winding me up* TEASE, make fun of, chaff; *informal* take the mickey out of, send up, rib, josh, kid, have on, pull someone's leg; *N. Amer. informal* pull someone's chain; *Austral./NZ informal* poke mullock at. **2** *David was winding him up on purpose* ANNOY, anger, irritate, exasperate, get on someone's nerves, provoke, goad; *Brit.* rub up the wrong way; *informal* aggravate, rile, niggle, bug, put someone's back up, get up someone's nose, hack off; *Brit. informal* nark; *N. Amer. informal* ride. **wind something up 1** *Richard wound up the meeting* CONCLUDE, bring to an end/close, end, terminate; *informal* wrap up. **2** *the company has been wound up* CLOSE (DOWN), dissolve, put into liquidation.
winded ● adjective OUT OF BREATH, breathless, gasping for breath, panting, puffing, puffed out; *informal* out of puff.
windfall ● noun BONANZA, jackpot, pennies from heaven.
winding ● noun *the windings of the stream* TWIST, turn, turning, bend, loop, curve, zigzag, meander.
● adjective *the winding country roads* TWISTING AND TURNING, meandering, windy, twisty, bending, curving, zigzag, zigzagging, serpentine, sinuous, snaking.
– OPPOSITES straight.
windpipe ● noun TRACHEA, pharynx; throat.

wind-up ● noun **1** Brit. informal an attempt to tease or irritate someone. **2** an act of concluding something.

windward ● adjective & adverb facing the wind or on the side facing the wind. Contrasted with LEEWARD. ● noun the side from which the wind is blowing.

windy[1] /windi/ ● adjective (**windier**, **windiest**) **1** marked by or exposed to strong winds. **2** Brit. suffering from, marked by, or causing wind in the alimentary canal. **3** informal using or expressed in numerous words of little substance. **4** Brit. informal nervous or anxious.

– DERIVATIVES **windily** adverb **windiness** noun.

windy[2] /wīndi/ ● adjective following a winding course.

wine ● noun **1** an alcoholic drink made from fermented grape juice. **2** a fermented alcoholic drink made from other fruits or plants.

– PHRASES **good wine needs no bush** proverb there's no need to advertise or boast about something of good quality as people will always discover its merits. **wine and dine** entertain with drinks and a meal.

– DERIVATIVES **winey** (also **winy**) adjective.

– ORIGIN Old English, related to Latin *vinum*.

wine bar ● noun a bar or small restaurant that specializes in serving wine.

wine bottle ● noun a glass bottle for wine, the standard size holding 75 cl or 26⅔ fl. oz.

wine cellar ● noun **1** a cellar for storing wine. **2** a stock of wine.

wine glass ● noun a glass with a stem and foot, used for drinking wine.

winegrower ● noun a grower of grapes for wine.

wine gum ● noun a small coloured fruit-flavoured sweet made with gelatin.

wine list ● noun a list of the wines available in a restaurant.

winemaker ● noun a producer of wine.

– DERIVATIVES **winemaking** noun.

winery ● noun (pl. **wineries**) an establishment where wine is made.

wineskin ● noun an animal skin sewn up and used to hold wine.

wine tasting ● noun **1** the tasting of wine to assess its quality. **2** an occasion for this.

wine vinegar ● noun vinegar made from wine rather than malt.

wing ● noun **1** a modified forelimb or other appendage enabling a bird, bat, insect, or other creature to fly. **2** a rigid horizontal structure projecting from both sides of an aircraft and supporting it in the air. **3** a part of a large building, especially one that projects from the main part. **4** a group within an organization having particular views or a particular function. **5** (**the wings**) the sides of a theatre stage out of view of the audience. **6** the part of a soccer, rugby, or hockey field close to the sidelines. **7** (also **wing forward**) an attacking player positioned near the sidelines. **8** Brit. a raised part of the body of a vehicle above the wheel. **9** an air force unit of several squadrons or groups. **10** Botany a thin appendage of a fruit or seed dispersed by the wind. ● verb **1** fly, or move quickly as if flying. **2** shoot so as to wound in the wing or arm. **3** (**wing it**) informal speak or act without preparation.

– PHRASES **in the wings** ready for use or action at the appropriate time. **on the wing** (of a bird) in flight. **on a wing and a prayer** with only a small chance of success. [ORIGIN with reference to an emergency landing by an aircraft.] **spread** (or **stretch**) **one's wings** extend one's activities and interests. **take wing** fly away. **under one's wing** in or into one's protective care.

– DERIVATIVES **winged** adjective **wingless** adjective.

– ORIGIN Old Norse; sense 3 of the verb was originally theatrical slang referring to the playing of a role without proper knowledge of the text (by relying on a prompter in the wings or by studying in the wings between scenes).

wingbeat (also **wingstroke**) ● noun one complete set of motions of a wing in flying.

wing case ● noun each of a pair of modified toughened forewings covering the functional wings of a beetle or other insect.

wing chair ● noun an armchair with side pieces projecting forwards from a high back.

wing collar ● noun a high stiff shirt collar with turned-down corners.

wing commander ● noun a rank of RAF officer, above squadron leader and below group captain.

winger ● noun **1** an attacking player on the wing in soccer, hockey, etc. **2** (in combination) a member of a specified political wing: *a Tory right-winger.*

wing mirror ● noun a rear-view mirror projecting from the side of a vehicle.

wing nut ● noun a nut with a pair of projections for the fingers to turn it on a screw.

wingspan (also **wingspread**) ● noun the maximum extent across the wings of an aircraft, bird, etc., measured from tip to tip.

wink ● verb **1** close and open one eye quickly as a signal of affection or greeting or to convey a message. **2** shine or flash intermittently. ● noun an act of winking.

– PHRASES **as easy as winking** informal very easy or easily. **in the wink of an eye** (or **in a wink**) very quickly. **not sleep** (or **get**) **a wink** (or **not get a wink of sleep**) not sleep at all.

– ORIGIN Old English, related to WINCE.

winkle ● noun a small edible shore-dwelling mollusc with a spiral shell. ● verb (**winkle out**) chiefly Brit. extract or obtain with difficulty.

– ORIGIN shortening of PERIWINKLE[2].

winkle-picker ● noun Brit. informal a shoe with a long pointed toe, popular in the 1950s.

winner ● noun **1** a person or thing that wins. **2** informal a successful or highly promising thing.

winning ● adjective **1** gaining, resulting in, or relating to victory. **2** attractive; endearing. ● noun (**winnings**) money won, especially by gambling.

– DERIVATIVES **winningly** adverb.

winning post ● noun a post marking the end of a race.

winnow ● verb **1** blow air through (grain) in order to remove the chaff. **2** remove (chaff) from grain. **3** reduce the number in

Thesaurus

windswept ● adjective **1** *the windswept moors* EXPOSED, bleak, bare, desolate. **2** *his windswept hair* DISHEVELLED, tousled, unkempt, wind-blown, untidy; *N. Amer.* mussed up.

windy ● adjective **1** *a windy day* BREEZY, blowy, fresh, blustery, gusty; wild, stormy, squally, tempestuous, boisterous. **2** *a windy hillside* WINDSWEPT, exposed, open to the elements, bare, bleak. **3** *(informal) windy speeches.* See LONG-WINDED. **4** *(Brit. informal) she felt a bit windy.* See ANXIOUS sense 1.

– OPPOSITES still, sheltered.

W

wine ● noun *informal* plonk, vino, the grape; *poetic/literary* vintage.

– RELATED TERMS vinous, oeno-.

wing ● noun **1** *a bird's wings poetic/literary* pinion. **2** *the east wing of the house* PART, section, side; annexe, extension; *N. Amer.* ell. **3** *the radical wing of the party* FACTION, camp, caucus, arm, branch, group, section, set, coterie, cabal.

● verb **1** *a seagull winged its way over the sea* FLY, glide, soar. **2** *the bomb winged past* HURTLE, speed, shoot, whizz, zoom, streak, fly. **3** *she was shot at and winged* WOUND, graze, hit.

– PHRASES **wing it** *(informal)* IMPROVISE, play it by ear, extemporize, ad lib; *informal* busk it.

wink ● verb **1** *he winked an eye at her* BLINK, flutter, bat. **2** *the diamond winked in the moonlight* SPARKLE, twinkle, flash, glitter, gleam, shine, scintillate.

● noun *a wink of light* GLIMMER, gleam, glint, flash, flicker, twinkle, sparkle.

– PHRASES **in the wink of an eye** VERY QUICKLY, very soon, in a second, in a moment, in a trice, in a flash, in an instant, in no time at all; *N. Amer.* momentarily; *informal* in a jiffy, in two shakes (of a lamb's tail), in a sec, in the blink of an eye; *Brit. informal* in a tick, in a mo; *N. Amer. informal* in a snap. **wink at** TURN A BLIND EYE TO, close one's eyes to, ignore, overlook, disregard; connive at, condone, tolerate.

winkle ● verb

– PHRASES **winkle something out** *(Brit.)* WORM OUT, prise out, dig out, extract, draw out, obtain, get.

winner ● noun VICTOR, champion, conqueror, vanquisher, hero; medallist; *Brit.* victor ludorum; *informal* champ, top dog.

– OPPOSITES loser.

winning ● adjective **1** *the winning team* VICTORIOUS, successful, triumphant, vanquishing, conquering; first, top. **2** *a winning smile* ENGAGING, charming, appealing, endearing, sweet, cute, winsome, attractive, pretty, prepossessing, fetching, lovely, adorable, de-

a set of (people or things) gradually until only the best ones are left.
– ORIGIN Old English, related to WIND[1].
wino ● noun (pl. **winos**) informal a person who drinks excessive amounts of cheap wine or other alcohol.
winsome ● adjective attractive or appealing.
– DERIVATIVES **winsomely** adverb **winsomeness** noun.
– ORIGIN from an Old English word meaning 'joy'.
winter ● noun the coldest season of the year, after autumn and before spring. ● adjective **1** (of fruit) ripening late in the year. **2** (of crops) sown in autumn for harvesting the following year. ● verb spend the winter in a particular place.
– ORIGIN Old English.
wintergreen ● noun **1** a low-growing plant with spikes of white bell-shaped flowers. **2** an American shrub whose leaves produce oil. **3** (also **oil of wintergreen**) a pungent oil obtained from these plants or from birch bark, used medicinally and as a flavouring.
winterize (also **winterise**) ● verb (usu. **be winterized**) chiefly N. Amer. adapt or prepare for use in cold weather.
Winter Olympics ● plural noun an international contest of winter sports held every four years at a two-year interval from the Olympic games.
winter sports ● plural noun sports performed on snow or ice.
wintertime (also literary **winter-tide**) ● noun the season or period of winter.
wintry (also **wintery**) ● adjective (**wintrier**, **wintriest**) characteristic of winter, especially in being very cold or bleak.
wipe ● verb **1** clean or dry by rubbing with a cloth or one's hand. **2** remove (dirt or moisture) in this way. **3** erase (data) from a magnetic medium. **4** pass over an electronic reader, bar code, etc. ● noun **1** an act of wiping. **2** an absorbent disposable cleaning cloth.
– PHRASES **wipe the floor with** informal inflict a humiliating defeat on. **wipe off** subtract (an amount) from a value or debt. **wipe out 1** remove or eliminate. **2** kill (a large number of people). **3** ruin financially. **4** informal exhaust or intoxicate. **wipe the slate clean** make a fresh start.
– DERIVATIVES **wipeable** adjective **wiper** noun.
– ORIGIN Old English, related to WHIP.
wire ● noun **1** metal drawn out into a thin flexible thread or rod. **2** a length or quantity of wire used for fencing, to carry an electric current, etc. **3** a concealed electronic listening device. **4** informal a telegram. ● verb **1** install electric circuits or wires in. **2** provide, fasten, or reinforce with wire. **3** informal, chiefly N. Amer. send a telegram to.
– PHRASES **by wire** by telegraph. **down to the wire** informal until the very last minute.
– ORIGIN Old English, probably related to Latin *viere* 'plait, weave'.
wire brush ● noun a brush with tough wire bristles for cleaning hard surfaces.
wired ● adjective informal **1** making use of computers and information technology to transfer or receive information. **2** nervous, tense, or edgy. **3** intoxicated by drugs or alcohol.
wire grass ● noun chiefly N. Amer. & Austral. grass with tough wiry stems.
wire-haired ● adjective (especially of a dog breed) having wiry hair.
wireless ● noun dated, chiefly Brit. **1** a radio receiving set. **2** broadcasting or telegraphy using radio signals. ● adjective lacking or not requiring wires.
wire service ● noun N. Amer. a news agency that supplies syndicated news by teleprinter or other electronic means to newspapers, radio, and television stations.
wiretapping ● noun the practice of tapping a telephone line to monitor conversations secretly.
wire wool ● noun Brit. another term for STEEL WOOL.
wireworm ● noun the worm-like larva of a kind of beetle, which feeds on roots and can cause damage to crops.
wiring ● noun a system of wires providing electric circuits for a device or building.
wiry ● adjective (**wirier**, **wiriest**) **1** resembling wire in form and texture. **2** lean, tough, and sinewy.
wisdom ● noun **1** the quality of being wise. **2** the body of knowledge and experience that develops within a specified society or period.
wisdom tooth ● noun each of the four hindmost molars in humans, which usually appear at about the age of twenty.
wise[1] ● adjective **1** having or showing experience, knowledge, and good judgement. **2** (**wise to**) informal aware of. ● verb (**wise up**) informal become alert or aware.
– PHRASES **be wise after the event** understand and assess something only after its implications have become obvious.
– DERIVATIVES **wisely** adverb.
– ORIGIN Old English, related to WIT[2].
wise[2] ● noun archaic manner, way, or extent.
– PHRASES **in no wise** not at all.
– ORIGIN Old English, related to WIT[2].
-wise ● suffix **1** forming adjectives and adverbs of manner or respect: *clockwise*. **2** informal with respect to: *weather-wise*.
wiseacre /wīzaykər/ ● noun a person with an affectation of wisdom or knowledge.
– ORIGIN Dutch *wijsseggher* 'soothsayer'.
wisecrack informal ● noun a witty remark or joke. ● verb make a wisecrack.
– DERIVATIVES **wisecracker** noun.
wise guy ● noun informal a person who makes sarcastic or insolent remarks so as to demonstrate their cleverness.
wish ● verb **1** desire something that cannot or probably will not happen. **2** want to do something. **3** ask (someone) to do something or that (something) be done. **4** express a hope that (someone) has (happiness, success, etc.). **5** (**wish on**) hope that (something unpleasant) will happen to. ● noun **1** a desire or hope. **2** (**wishes**) an expression of a hope for someone's happiness, success, or welfare. **3** a thing wished for.
– PHRASES **if wishes were horses, beggars would ride** proverb if you could achieve your aims simply by wishing for them, life would be very easy. **the wish is father to the thought** proverb we believe a thing because we wish it to be true.

Thesaurus

lightful, disarming, captivating; *dated* taking.
winnings ● plural noun PRIZE MONEY, gains, prize, booty, spoils; proceeds, profits, takings, purse.
winnow ● verb SEPARATE (OUT), divide, sort out, sift out, filter out; isolate, find, identify; remove, get rid of.
winsome ● adjective. See WINNING sense 2.
wintry ● adjective **1** *wintry weather* BLEAK, cold, chilly, chill, frosty, freezing, icy, snowy, arctic, glacial, bitter, raw; *informal* nippy; *Brit. informal* parky. **2** *a wintry smile* UNFRIENDLY, unwelcoming, cool, cold, frosty, frigid.
– OPPOSITES summery, warm.
wipe ● verb **1** *Beth wiped the table* RUB, mop, sponge, swab; clean, dry, polish. **2** *he wiped the marks off the window* RUB OFF, clean off, clear up, remove, get rid of, take off, erase, efface. **3** *she wiped the memory from her mind* OBLITERATE, expunge, erase, blot out, blank out.
● noun *he gave the table a quick wipe* RUB, mop, sponge, swab; clean, polish.
– PHRASES **wipe someone/something out** DESTROY, annihilate, eradicate, eliminate; slaughter, massacre, kill, exterminate; demolish, raze to the ground; *informal* take out, zap; *N. Amer. informal* waste; *poetic/literary* slay.
wire ● noun CABLE, lead, flex.
wiry ● adjective **1** *a wiry man* SINEWY, tough, athletic, strong; lean, spare, thin, stringy, skinny. **2** *wiry hair* COARSE, rough, strong; curly, wavy.
– OPPOSITES flabby, smooth.
wisdom ● noun **1** *we questioned the wisdom of the decision* SAGACITY, intelligence, sense, common sense, shrewdness, astuteness, smartness, judiciousness, judgement, prudence, circumspection; logic, rationale, rationality, soundness, advisability. **2** *the wisdom of the East* KNOWLEDGE, learning, erudition, scholarship, philosophy; lore.
– OPPOSITES folly.
wise ● adjective *a wise old man* SAGE, sagacious, intelligent, clever, learned, knowledgeable, enlightened; astute, smart, shrewd, sharp-witted, canny, knowing; sensible, prudent, discerning, judicious, perceptive, insightful, perspicacious; rational, logical, sound, sane; *Brit. informal* fly; *formal* sapient.
– OPPOSITES foolish.
– PHRASES **put someone wise** *(informal)* TELL, inform, notify, apprise, make aware, put in the picture, fill in; warn, alert; *informal* clue in/up, tip off. **wise to** *(informal)* AWARE OF, familiar with, acquainted with; *formal* cognizant of.

– ORIGIN Old English, related to WONT.

wishbone • noun a forked bone between the neck and breast of a bird, especially one from a cooked bird which, when broken by two people, entitles the holder of the longer portion to make a wish.

wishful • adjective **1** having or expressing a wish for something to happen. **2** based on impractical wishes rather than facts.
– DERIVATIVES **wishfully** adverb.

wish-fulfilment • noun the satisfying of wishes or desires in dreams or fantasies.

wishing well • noun a well into which one drops a coin and makes a wish.

wishy-washy • adjective **1** (of a drink or soup) weak or thin. **2** feeble or insipid.

wisp • noun **1** a small thin bunch, strand, or amount of something. **2** a small thin person.
– DERIVATIVES **wispy** adjective (**wispier**, **wispiest**).
– ORIGIN origin uncertain.

wist past and past participle of WIT².

wisteria /wisteeriə/ (also **wistaria** /wistairiə/) • noun a climbing shrub with hanging clusters of pale bluish-lilac flowers.
– ORIGIN named after the American anatomist Caspar *Wistar* (or *Wister*) (1761–1818).

wistful • adjective having or showing a feeling of vague or regretful longing.
– DERIVATIVES **wistfully** adverb **wistfulness** noun.
– ORIGIN apparently from obsolete *wistly* 'intently', influenced by WISHFUL.

wit¹ • noun **1** (also **wits**) the capacity for inventive thought and quick understanding; keen intelligence. **2** a natural aptitude for using words and ideas in a quick and inventive way to create humour. **3** a person with this aptitude.
– PHRASES **be at one's wits' end** be completely at a loss as to what to do. **be frightened out of one's wits** be extremely frightened. **gather one's wits** allow oneself to think calmly and clearly in a demanding situation. **have** (or **keep**) **one's wits about one** be constantly alert. **live by one's wits** earn money by clever and sometimes dishonest means.
– DERIVATIVES **witted** adjective.
– ORIGIN Old English, related to WIT².

wit² • verb (**wot**, **witting**; past and past part. **wist**) **1** archaic know. **2** (**to wit**) that is to say.
– ORIGIN Old English.

witch • noun **1** a woman thought to have evil magic powers. **2** a follower or practitioner of modern witchcraft. **3** informal an ugly or unpleasant old woman. • verb archaic **1** practise witchcraft. **2** cast an evil spell on.
– DERIVATIVES **witchy** adjective.
– ORIGIN Old English.

witchcraft • noun the practice of magic, especially the use of spells and the invocation of evil spirits. See also WICCA.

witch doctor • noun a tribal magician credited with powers of healing, divination, and protection against the magic of others.

witch elm • noun variant spelling of WYCH ELM.

witchery • noun **1** the practice of magic. **2** bewitching quality or power.

witches' broom • noun dense twiggy growth in a tree caused by infection with fungus, mites, or viruses.

witches' sabbath • noun see SABBATH (sense 2).

witchetty /wichəti/ (also **witchetty grub**) • noun (pl. **witchetties**) a large whitish wood-eating larva of a beetle or moth, eaten as food by some Aboriginals.
– ORIGIN from words in an Aboriginal language meaning 'hooked stick for extracting grubs' + 'grub'.

witch hazel (also **wych hazel**) • noun **1** a shrub with fragrant yellow or orange flowers. **2** an astringent lotion made from the bark and leaves of this plant.
– ORIGIN for *wych*, see WYCH ELM.

witch-hunt • noun a campaign directed against a person or group holding views considered unorthodox or a threat to society.

witching hour • noun midnight, regarded as the time when witches are supposedly active.
– ORIGIN with allusion to *the witching time of night* from Shakespeare's *Hamlet* (III. ii. 377).

with • preposition **1** accompanied by. **2** in the same direction as. **3** possessing; having. **4** indicating the instrument used to perform an action or the material used for a purpose. **5** in opposition to or competition with. **6** indicating the manner or attitude in which a person does something. **7** indicating responsibility. **8** in relation to. **9** employed by. **10** using the services of. **11** affected by (a particular fact or condition). **12** indicating separation or removal from something.
– PHRASES **be with someone** informal follow someone's meaning. **with it** informal **1** up to date or fashionable. **2** alert and comprehending.
– ORIGIN Old English.

withal /withawl/ archaic • adverb **1** in addition. **2** nevertheless. • preposition with.

withdraw • verb (past **withdrew**; past part. **withdrawn**) **1** remove or take away. **2** take (money) out of an account. **3** discontinue or retract. **4** leave or cause to leave a place. **5** cease to participate in an activity or be a member of a team or organization. **6** depart to another place in search of quiet or privacy. **7** cease to take an addictive drug.

withdrawal • noun **1** the action or an act of withdrawing. **2** the process of ceasing to take an addictive drug.

withdrawn past participle of WITHDRAW. • adjective unusually shy

Thesaurus

wisecrack • noun (informal) JOKE, witticism, quip, jest, sally; pun, bon mot; *informal* crack, gag, funny, one-liner.

wish • verb **1** *I wished for power* DESIRE, want, hope for, covet, dream of, long for, yearn for, crave, hunger for, lust after; aspire to, set one's heart on, seek, fancy, hanker after; *informal* have a yen for, itch for; *archaic* be desirous of. **2** *they can do as they wish* WANT, desire, feel inclined, feel like, care; choose, please, think fit. **3** *I wish you to send them a message* WANT, desire, require. **4** *I wished him farewell* BID.
• noun **1** *his wish to own a Mercedes* DESIRE, longing, yearning, inclination, urge, whim, craving, hunger; hope, aspiration, aim, ambition, dream; *informal* hankering, yen, itch. **2** *her parents' wishes* REQUEST, requirement, bidding, instruction, direction, demand, order, command; want, desire; will; *poetic/literary* behest.

wishy-washy • adjective **1** *he's so wishy-washy* FEEBLE, ineffectual, weak, vapid, effete, spineless, limp, namby-pamby, spiritless, indecisive; *informal* wet, pathetic. **2** *wishy-washy soup* WATERY, weak, thin; tasteless, flavourless, insipid. **3** *a wishy-washy colour* PALE, insipid, pallid, muted.
– OPPOSITES strong, tasty, vibrant.

wisp • noun STRAND, tendril, lock; scrap, shred, thread.

wispy • adjective THIN, fine, feathery, flyaway.

wistful • adjective NOSTALGIC, yearning, longing; plaintive, regretful, rueful, melancholy, mournful; pensive, reflective, contemplative.

wit • noun **1** *he needed all his wits to escape* INTELLIGENCE, shrewdness, astuteness, cleverness, canniness, (common) sense, wisdom, sagacity, judgement, acumen, insight; brains, mind; *informal* nous, gumption, savvy, horse sense; *Brit. informal* common; *N. Amer. informal* smarts. **2** *my sparkling wit* WITTINESS, humour, funniness, drollery; repartee, badinage, banter, wordplay; jokes, witticisms, quips, puns. **3** *she's such a wit* COMEDIAN, humorist, comic, joker, jokester; *informal* wag; *informal, dated* card, caution.

witch • noun **1** *the witch cast a spell* SORCERESS, enchantress, hex; Wiccan; *archaic* pythoness. **2** *(informal) she's a right old witch* HAG, crone, harpy, harridan, she-devil; *informal* battleaxe.

witchcraft • noun SORCERY, (black) magic, witching, witchery, wizardry, thaumaturgy, spells, incantations; Wicca; *Irish* pishogue.

witch doctor • noun MEDICINE MAN, shaman, healer.

with • preposition ACCOMPANIED BY, escorted by; alongside, in addition to, as well as.

withdraw • verb **1** *she withdrew her hand from his* REMOVE, extract, pull out, take out; take back, take away. **2** *the ban on advertising was withdrawn* ABOLISH, cancel, lift, set aside, end, stop, remove, reverse, revoke, rescind, repeal, annul, void. **3** *she withdrew the allegation* RETRACT, take back, go back on, recant, disavow, disclaim, repudiate, renounce; back down, climb down, backtrack, back-pedal, do a U-turn, eat one's words. **4** *the troops withdrew from the city* LEAVE, pull out of, evacuate, quit, retreat from. **5** *his partner withdrew from the project* PULL OUT OF, back out of, bow out of; get cold feet. **6** *they withdrew to their rooms* RETIRE, retreat, adjourn, decamp; leave, depart, absent oneself; *formal* repair; *poetic/literary* betake oneself; *dated* remove.
– OPPOSITES insert, introduce, deposit, enter.

withdrawal • noun **1** *the withdrawal of subsidies* REMOVAL, abolition, cancellation, discontinuation, termination, elimination.

W

or reserved.

withe /with, wi**th**/ ● noun variant spelling of WITHY.

wither ● verb **1** (of a plant) become dry and shrivelled. **2** become shrunken or wrinkled from age or disease. **3** fall into decay or decline. **4** (**withering**) scornful.
– DERIVATIVES **witheringly** adverb.
– ORIGIN apparently a variant of WEATHER.

withers ● plural noun the highest part of a horse's back, lying at the base of the neck above the shoulders.
– ORIGIN apparently from obsolete *widersome*, from *wither-* 'against' (as the part that resists the strain of the collar).

withershins /wi**th**ərshinz/ ● adverb variant spelling of WIDDERSHINS.

withhold ● verb (past and past part. **withheld**) **1** refuse to give (something due to or desired by another). **2** suppress or restrain (an emotion or reaction).
– DERIVATIVES **withholder** noun.

within ● preposition **1** inside. **2** inside the range or bounds of. **3** occurring inside (a particular period of time). **4** not further off than (used with distances). ● adverb **1** inside; indoors. **2** internally or inwardly.

without ● preposition **1** not accompanied by or having the use of. **2** in which the action mentioned does not happen. **3** archaic or literary outside. ● adverb archaic or literary outside. ● conjunction archaic or dialect **1** without it being the case that. **2** unless.

withstand ● verb (past and past part. **withstood**) **1** remain undamaged or unaffected by. **2** offer strong resistance or opposition to.

withy /wi**th**i/ (also **withe**) ● noun (pl. **withies** or **withes**) **1** a tough flexible branch of an osier or other willow, used for tying, binding, or basketry. **2** an osier.
– ORIGIN Old English.

witless ● adjective foolish; stupid.
– DERIVATIVES **witlessly** adverb **witlessness** noun.

witness ● noun **1** a person who sees an event take place. **2** a person giving sworn testimony to a court of law or the police. **3** a person who is present at the signing of a document and signs it themselves to confirm this. **4** (**witness to**) evidence or proof of. **5** open profession of one's religious faith through words or actions. ● verb **1** be a witness to. **2** be the place, period, etc. in which (an event) takes place.
– ORIGIN Old English, from WIT[1].

witness box (N. Amer. **witness stand**) ● noun Law the place in a court where a witness stands to give evidence.

witter ● verb (usu. **witter on**) Brit. informal speak at length about trivial matters.
– ORIGIN probably imitative.

witticism ● noun a witty remark.

witting ● adjective **1** deliberate. **2** aware of the full facts.
– DERIVATIVES **wittingly** adverb.
– ORIGIN from WIT[2].

witty ● adjective (**wittier**, **wittiest**) showing or characterized by quick and inventive verbal humour.
– DERIVATIVES **wittily** adverb **wittiness** noun.

wives plural of WIFE.

wiz ● noun variant spelling of WHIZZ (in sense 3).

wizard ● noun **1** a man who has magical powers, especially in legends and fairy tales. **2** a person who is very skilled in a particular field or activity. ● adjective Brit. informal, dated excellent.
– DERIVATIVES **wizardly** adjective.
– ORIGIN originally in the sense 'philosopher, wise man': from WISE[1].

wizardry ● noun **1** the art or practice of magic. **2** great skill in a particular field or activity.

wizened /wizz'nd/ ● adjective shrivelled or wrinkled with age.
– ORIGIN from archaic *wizen* 'shrivel', from Old English.

WLTM ● abbreviation would like to meet.

WNW ● abbreviation west-north-west.

WO ● abbreviation Warrant Officer.

wo ● exclamation variant spelling of WHOA.

woad /wōd/ ● noun a yellow-flowered plant whose leaves were formerly used to make blue dye.
– ORIGIN Old English.

wobble ● verb **1** move unsteadily from side to side. **2** (of the voice) tremble. **3** waver between different courses of action. ● noun a wobbling movement or sound.
– ORIGIN Germanic, related to WAVE.

wobbleboard ● noun Austral. a piece of fibreboard used as a musical instrument, producing a low booming sound when flexed.

wobbler ● noun **1** a person or thing that wobbles. **2** another term for WOBBLY.

wobbly ● adjective (**wobblier**, **wobbliest**) **1** tending to wobble. **2** weak and unsteady from illness, tiredness, or anxiety. **3** uncertain or insecure. ● noun Brit. informal a fit of temper or panic.
– DERIVATIVES **wobbliness** noun.

wodge ● noun Brit. informal a large piece or amount.

Thesaurus

2 *the withdrawal of the troops* DEPARTURE, pull-out, exit, exodus, evacuation, retreat.

withdrawn ● adjective INTROVERTED, unsociable, inhibited, uncommunicative, unforthcoming, quiet, reticent, reserved, retiring, private, reclusive; shy, timid; aloof; *informal* stand-offish.
– OPPOSITES outgoing.

wither ● verb **1** *the flowers withered in the sun* SHRIVEL (UP), dry up; wilt, droop, go limp, fade, perish. **2** *the muscles in his leg withered* WASTE (AWAY), shrivel (up), shrink, atrophy. **3** *her confidence withered* DIMINISH, dwindle, shrink, lessen, fade, ebb, wane; evaporate, disappear.
– OPPOSITES thrive, grow.

withering ● adjective SCORNFUL, contemptuous, scathing, stinging, devastating; humiliating, mortifying.
– OPPOSITES admiring.

withhold ● verb **1** *he withheld the information* HOLD BACK, keep back, refuse to give; retain, hold on to; hide, conceal, keep secret; *informal* sit on. **2** *she could not withhold her tears* SUPPRESS, repress, hold back, fight back, choke back, control, check, restrain, contain.

within ● preposition **1** *within the prison walls* INSIDE, in, enclosed by, surrounded by; within the bounds of, within the confines of. **2** *within a few hours* IN LESS THAN, in under, in no more than, after only.
– OPPOSITES outside.

without ● preposition **1** *thousands were without food* LACKING, short of, deprived of, in need of, wanting, needing, requiring. **2** *I don't want to go without you* UNACCOMPANIED BY, unescorted by; in the absence of.

withstand ● verb RESIST, weather, survive, endure, cope with, stand, tolerate, bear, defy, brave, hold out against, bear up against; stand up to, face, confront.

witless ● adjective FOOLISH, stupid, unintelligent, idiotic, brainless, mindless; fatuous, inane, half-baked, empty-headed, slow-witted; *informal* thick, birdbrained, pea-brained, dopey, dim, dim-witted, half-witted, dippy, lamebrained, wooden-headed; *Brit. informal* daft; *Scottish & N. English informal* glaikit; *N. Amer. informal* dumb-ass.

witness ● noun **1** *witnesses claimed that he started the fight* OBSERVER, onlooker, eyewitness, spectator, viewer, watcher; bystander, passer-by. **2** *a whisky bottle was the only witness of his mood* EVIDENCE, indication, proof, testimony.
● verb **1** *who witnessed the incident?* SEE, observe, watch, view, notice, spot; be present at, attend; *poetic/literary* behold. **2** *the will is correctly witnessed* COUNTERSIGN, sign, endorse, validate; *N. Amer.* notarize. **3** *his writings witness an inner toughness* ATTEST TO, testify to, bear witness to, confirm, evidence, prove, verify, corroborate, substantiate; show, demonstrate, indicate, reveal, bespeak.

witter ● verb *(Brit. informal).* See GABBLE verb.

witticism ● noun JOKE, quip, jest, pun, play on words, bon mot; *informal* one-liner, gag, funny, crack, wisecrack.

witty ● adjective HUMOROUS, amusing, droll, funny, comic, comical; jocular, facetious, waggish; sparkling, scintillating, entertaining; clever, quick-witted.

wizard ● noun **1** *the wizard cast a spell over them* SORCERER, warlock, magus, (black) magician, enchanter; *archaic* mage. **2** *a financial wizard* GENIUS, expert, master, virtuoso, maestro, marvel, Wunderkind; *informal* hotshot, demon, whizz-kid, buff, pro, ace; *Brit. informal* dab hand; *N. Amer. informal* maven.

wizardry ● noun SORCERY, witchcraft, witchery, witching, (black) magic, enchantment; spells, charms; *Irish* pishogue.

wizened ● adjective WRINKLED, lined, creased, shrivelled (up), withered, weather-beaten, shrunken, gnarled.

wobble ● verb **1** *the table wobbled* ROCK, teeter, jiggle, sway, seesaw, shake. **2** *he wobbled across to the door* TEETER, totter, stagger, lurch. **3** *her voice wobbled* TREMBLE, shake, quiver, quaver, waver. **4** *for a few days the minister wobbled* HESITATE, vacillate, waver, dither, shilly-shally, blow hot and cold; *Scottish* swither.
● noun **1** *she stood up with a wobble* TOTTER, teeter, sway. **2** *the op-*

– ORIGIN alteration of WEDGE.

woe • noun literary **1** great sorrow or distress. **2** (**woes**) troubles.
– PHRASES **woe betide someone** humorous a person will be in trouble if they do a specified thing. **woe is me!** humorous an exclamation of sorrow or distress.
– ORIGIN Old English.

woebegone /wōbigon/ • adjective sad or miserable in appearance.
– ORIGIN from WOE + obsolete *begone* 'surrounded'.

woeful • adjective **1** full of sorrow; miserable. **2** very bad; deplorable.
– DERIVATIVES **woefully** adverb.

wog[1] • noun Brit. informal, offensive a person who is not white.
– ORIGIN of unknown origin.

wog[2] • noun Austral. informal a minor illness or infection.
– ORIGIN of unknown origin.

woggle • noun a loop or ring of leather or cord through which the ends of a Scout's neckerchief are threaded.
– ORIGIN of unknown origin.

wok • noun a bowl-shaped frying pan used in Chinese cookery.
– ORIGIN Chinese.

woke past of WAKE[1].

woken past participle of WAKE[1].

wold /wōld/ • noun (especially in British place names) a piece of high, open, uncultivated land or moor.
– ORIGIN Old English.

wolf • noun (pl. **wolves**) **1** a carnivorous mammal that lives and hunts in packs and is the largest member of the dog family. **2** informal a man who habitually seduces women. • verb (usu. **wolf down**) devour (food) greedily.
– PHRASES **cry wolf** raise repeated false alarms, so that a real cry for help is ignored. [ORIGIN with allusion to the fable of the shepherd boy who deluded people with false cries of 'Wolf!'] **keep the wolf from the door** have enough money to be able to buy food. **throw someone to the wolves** sacrifice someone in order to avoid trouble for oneself. **a wolf in sheep's clothing** a person who appears friendly but is really hostile. [ORIGIN with biblical allusion to the Book of Matthew, chapter 7.]
– DERIVATIVES **wolfish** adjective.
– ORIGIN Old English.

Wolf Cub • noun chiefly Brit. former term for **Cub Scout** (see CUB sense 2).

wolfhound • noun a dog of a large breed originally used to hunt wolves.

wolfram /wŏŏlfrəm/ • noun tungsten or its ore, especially as a commercial commodity.
– ORIGIN German, perhaps from *Wolf* 'wolf' + *rām* 'soot', probably originally a pejorative term used by miners in reference to the ore's inferiority to tin, with which it occurred.

wolf whistle • noun a whistle with a rising and falling pitch, used to express sexual attraction or admiration. • verb (**wolf-whistle**) whistle in such a way at.

wolverine /wŏŏlvəreen/ • noun a heavily built short-legged carnivorous mammal with a long brown coat and a bushy tail, native to northern tundra and forests.
– ORIGIN formed obscurely from *wolv-*, plural stem of WOLF.

wolves plural of WOLF.

woman • noun (pl. **women**) **1** an adult human female. **2** a female worker or employee. **3** a wife or lover.
– PHRASES **the little woman** a condescending way of referring to one's wife. **woman of the streets** euphemistic, dated a prostitute.
– DERIVATIVES **womanliness** noun **womanly** adjective.
– ORIGIN from the Old English words for WIFE and MAN.

womanhood • noun **1** the state or condition of being a woman. **2** women considered collectively. **3** the qualities traditionally associated with women.

womanish • adjective derogatory **1** suitable for or characteristic of a woman. **2** (of a man) effeminate.

womanize (also **womanise**) • verb (of a man) enter into numerous casual sexual relationships with women.
– DERIVATIVES **womanizer** noun.

womankind • noun women considered collectively.

womb • noun the organ in the lower body of a woman or female mammal where offspring are conceived and in which they develop before birth; the uterus.
– ORIGIN Old English.

wombat /wombat/ • noun a burrowing plant-eating Australian marsupial which resembles a small bear with short legs.
– ORIGIN from an extinct Aboriginal language.

women plural of WOMAN.

womenfolk • plural noun the women of a family or community considered collectively.

women's lib • noun informal short for WOMEN'S LIBERATION.
– DERIVATIVES **women's libber** noun.

women's liberation • noun the liberation of women from inequalities and subservient status in relation to men, and from attitudes causing these (now generally replaced by the term *feminism*).

won[1] past and past participle of WIN.

won[2] /won/ • noun (pl. same) the basic monetary unit of North and South Korea, equal to 100 jun in North Korea and 100 jeon in South Korea.

Thesaurus

eratic wobble in her voice TREMOR, quiver, quaver, trembling, vibrato.

wobbly • adjective **1** *a wobbly table* UNSTEADY, unstable, shaky, rocky, rickety; unsafe, precarious; uneven, unbalanced; *informal* wonky. **2** *her legs were a bit wobbly* SHAKY, quivery, weak, unsteady; *informal* trembly, like jelly. **3** *I feel so wobbly* FAINT, dizzy, light-headed, giddy, weak (at the knees), groggy, muzzy; *Brit. informal* woozy.
– OPPOSITES stable.

woe • noun **1** *a tale of woe* MISERY, sorrow, distress, wretchedness, sadness, unhappiness, heartache, heartbreak, despondency, despair, depression, gloom, melancholy; adversity, misfortune, disaster, suffering, hardship; *poetic/literary* dolour. **2** *financial woes* TROUBLE, difficulty, problem, trial, tribulation, misfortune, setback, reverse.
– OPPOSITES joy.

woebegone • adjective SAD, unhappy, miserable, dejected, disconsolate, forlorn, crestfallen, downcast, glum, gloomy, doleful, downhearted, despondent, melancholy, sorrowful, mournful, woeful, depressed, desolate, wretched; *informal* down in the mouth, down in the dumps, blue.
– OPPOSITES cheerful.

woeful • adjective **1** *her face was woeful.* See WOEBEGONE. **2** *a woeful tale* TRAGIC, sad, miserable, cheerless, sorry, pitiful, pathetic, gloomy, traumatic, depressing, heartbreaking, heart-rending, tear-jerking. **3** *the team's woeful performance* DREADFUL, awful, terrible, atrocious, disgraceful, deplorable, shameful, hopeless, lamentable; substandard, poor, inadequate, inferior, unsatisfactory; *informal* rotten, appalling, crummy, pathetic, pitiful, lousy, abysmal, dire; *Brit. informal* duff, chronic, rubbish.
– OPPOSITES cheerful, excellent.

wolf • verb DEVOUR, gobble (up), guzzle, gulp down, bolt; *informal* put away, demolish, shovel down, scoff (down), get outside of; *Brit. informal* gollop; *N. Amer. informal* scarf (down/up), snarf (down/up).
– OPPOSITES pick at.

wolfish • adjective *(informal)* LASCIVIOUS, lecherous, lustful; predatory, rapacious.

woman • noun **1** *a woman got out of the car* LADY, girl, female; matron; *Scottish & N. English* lass, lassie; *Irish* colleen; *informal* chick, girlie, filly, biddy; *Brit. informal* bird; *Scottish & N. English informal* wifie; *N. Amer. informal* sister, dame, broad, gal, jane; *Austral./NZ informal* sheila; *poetic/literary* maid, maiden, damsel; *archaic* wench, gentlewoman. **2** *he found himself a new woman* GIRLFRIEND, sweetheart, partner, significant other, inamorata, lover, mistress; fiancée; wife, spouse; *informal* bird, fancy woman, missus, better half; *Brit. informal* other half, Dutch, trouble and strife; *Irish informal* mot; *N. Amer. informal* squeeze; *dated* lady friend, lady love; *archaic* leman.
– RELATED TERMS female, gynaeco-.

womanhood • noun **1** *she was on the brink of womanhood* ADULTHOOD, maturity; *poetic/literary* muliebrity. **2** *she's an ideal of womanhood* WOMANLINESS, femininity. **3** *the stereotype of Soviet womanhood* WOMEN, womenfolk; womankind, womenkind, woman; the female sex.

womanish • adjective EFFEMINATE, girlish, girly, unmanly, unmasculine.
– OPPOSITES manly.

womanizer • noun PHILANDERER, Casanova, Don Juan, Romeo, Lothario, ladies' man, playboy, seducer, rake, roué, libertine, lecher; *informal* skirt-chaser, ladykiller, lech.

womankind • noun WOMEN, the female sex, womenkind, womanhood, womenfolk; woman.

womanly • adjective **1** *womanly virtues* FEMININE, female; *archaic*

W

– ORIGIN Korean.

wonder ● noun **1** a feeling of surprise and admiration, caused by something beautiful, unexpected, or unfamiliar. **2** a person or thing that causes such a feeling. **3** (before another noun) having remarkable properties or abilities: *a wonder drug.* ● verb **1** feel curious; desire to know. **2** feel doubt. **3** feel amazement and admiration.

– PHRASES **no** (or **little** or **small**) **wonder** it is not surprising. **nine days'** (or **seven-day** or **one-day**) **wonder** something that attracts great interest for a short while but is then forgotten. **wonders will never cease** often ironic an exclamation of surprise and pleasure. **work** (or **do**) **wonders** have a very beneficial effect.

– DERIVATIVES **wonderer** noun.

– ORIGIN Old English.

wonderful ● adjective extremely good, pleasant, or remarkable.

– DERIVATIVES **wonderfully** adverb **wonderfulness** noun.

wonderland ● noun a place full of wonderful things.

wonderment ● noun a state of awed admiration or respect.

wondrous ● adjective literary inspiring wonder. ● adverb archaic wonderfully.

– DERIVATIVES **wondrously** adverb.

wonk ● noun N. Amer. informal, derogatory a studious or hard-working person.

– ORIGIN of unknown origin.

wonky ● adjective (**wonkier**, **wonkiest**) Brit. informal **1** crooked; askew. **2** unsteady or faulty.

– DERIVATIVES **wonkily** adverb **wonkiness** noun.

– ORIGIN fanciful formation.

wont /wōnt/ ● adjective archaic or literary accustomed. ● noun (**one's wont**) formal or humorous one's customary behaviour. ● verb (3rd sing. present **wonts** or **wont**; past and past part. **wont** or **wonted**) archaic make or become accustomed.

– ORIGIN Old English.

won't ● contraction will not.

wonted /wōntid/ ● adjective archaic or literary usual.

wonton /wonton/ ● noun (in Chinese cookery) a small round dumpling with a savoury filling, typically served in soup.

– ORIGIN Chinese.

woo ● verb (**woos**, **wooed**) **1** try to gain the love of (a woman). **2** seek the support or custom of.

– DERIVATIVES **wooer** noun.

– ORIGIN Old English.

wood ● noun **1** the hard fibrous material forming the main substance of the trunk or branches of a tree or shrub, used for fuel or timber. **2** (also **woods**) a small forest. **3** (**the wood**) wooden barrels used for storing alcoholic drinks. **4** a golf club with a wooden or other head that is relatively broad from face to back. **5** another term for BOWL² (in sense 1).

– PHRASES **be unable to see the wood** (or N. Amer. **the forest**) **for the trees** fail to grasp the main issue because of over-attention to details. **out of the woods** out of danger or difficulty. **touch** (or chiefly N. Amer. **knock on**) **wood** touch something wooden to ward off bad luck.

– ORIGIN Old English.

wood alcohol ● noun crude methanol made by distillation from wood.

wood anemone ● noun a spring-flowering anemone with pink-tinged white flowers, growing in woodland and shady places.

woodbine ● noun **1** Brit. the common honeysuckle. **2** N. Amer. Virginia creeper.

woodblock ● noun **1** a block of wood from which woodcut prints are made. **2** a hollow wooden block used as a percussion instrument.

woodchip (also **woodchip paper**) ● noun chiefly Brit. wallpaper with small chips of wood embedded in it to give a grainy surface texture.

woodchuck ● noun a North American marmot with a heavy body and short legs.

– ORIGIN an alteration (by association with WOOD) of an American Indian name.

woodcock ● noun (pl. same) a long-billed woodland bird of the sandpiper family, with brown plumage.

woodcut ● noun a print of a type made from a design cut in relief in a block of wood.

woodcutter ● noun a person who cuts down wood.

wooded ● adjective (of land) covered with woods.

wooden ● adjective **1** made of wood. **2** resembling or characteristic of wood. **3** stiff and awkward.

– DERIVATIVES **woodenly** adverb **woodenness** noun.

wood engraving ● noun **1** a print made from a finely detailed design cut into the end grain of a block of wood. **2** the technique of making such prints.

– DERIVATIVES **wood engraver** noun.

wooden spoon ● noun chiefly Brit. a real or notional prize awarded to the person who is last in a race or competition.

– ORIGIN from the former practice of giving a spoon to the candidate coming last in the Cambridge mathematical tripos.

wood fibre ● noun fibre obtained from wood and used especially in the manufacture of paper.

woodgrain ● adjective denoting a surface or finish imitating the grain pattern of wood.

woodland ● noun (also **woodlands**) land covered with trees.

woodlouse ● noun (pl. **woodlice**) a small land crustacean with a greyish segmented body which it is able to roll into a ball.

woodpecker ● noun a bird with a strong bill and a stiff tail, typically pecking at tree trunks to find insects and drumming on dead wood to mark territory.

wood pigeon ● noun a common large pigeon, mainly grey with white patches forming a ring round its neck.

wood pulp ● noun wood fibre reduced chemically or mechanically to pulp and used in the manufacture of paper.

woodruff (also **sweet woodruff**) ● noun a white-flowered plant with sweet-scented leaves used to flavour drinks and in perfumery.

– ORIGIN Old English, from WOOD + an element of unknown meaning.

woodshed ● noun a shed where firewood is stored.

– PHRASES **something nasty in the woodshed** Brit. informal a

Thesaurus

feminal. **2** *her womanly figure* VOLUPTUOUS, curvaceous, shapely, ample, Junoesque, Rubenesque, buxom; *informal* curvy, busty.

– OPPOSITES masculine, boyish.

wonder ● noun **1** *she was speechless with wonder* AWE, admiration, wonderment, fascination; surprise, astonishment, amazement. **2** *the wonders of nature* MARVEL, miracle, phenomenon, sensation, spectacle, beauty; curiosity.

● verb **1** *I wondered what was on her mind* PONDER, think about, meditate on, reflect on, muse on, speculate about, conjecture; be curious about. **2** *I wonder you were so patient* BE SURPRISED, find it surprising. **3** *people wondered at such bravery* MARVEL, be amazed, be astonished, stand in awe, be dumbfounded, gape, goggle; *informal* be flabbergasted.

wonderful ● adjective MARVELLOUS, magnificent, superb, glorious, sublime, lovely, delightful; *informal* super, great, fantastic, terrific, tremendous, sensational, incredible, fabulous, fab, awesome, magic, ace, wicked, far out; *Brit. informal* smashing, brilliant, brill; *N. Amer. informal* peachy, dandy, neat; *Austral./NZ informal* beaut, bonzer; *Brit. informal, dated* champion, wizard, spiffing, topping; *N. Amer. informal, dated* swell.

– OPPOSITES awful.

wonky ● adjective *(Brit. informal)* **1** *a wonky picture.* See CROOKED sense 3. **2** *wonky stools.* See WOBBLY sense 1.

wont ● adjective *(poetic/literary) he was wont to arise at 5.30* ACCUSTOMED, used, given, inclined.

● noun *(formal) Paul drove fast, as was his wont* CUSTOM, habit, way, practice, convention, rule.

wonted ● adjective *(poetic/literary)* CUSTOMARY, habitual, usual, accustomed, familiar, normal, conventional, routine, common.

woo ● verb **1** *Richard wooed Joan* PAY COURT TO, pursue, chase (after); *dated* court, romance, seek the hand of, set one's cap at, make love to. **2** *the party wooed voters with promises* SEEK, pursue, curry favour with, try to win, try to attract, try to cultivate. **3** *an attempt to woo him out of retirement* ENTICE, tempt, coax, persuade, wheedle; *informal* sweet-talk.

wood ● noun **1** *polished wood* TIMBER, planks, planking; logs; *N. Amer.* lumber. **2** *a walk through the woods* FOREST, woodland, trees; copse, coppice, grove; *Brit.* spinney; *archaic* greenwood.

– RELATED TERMS ligneous.

wooded ● adjective FORESTED, afforested, tree-covered, woody; *poetic/literary* sylvan, bosky.

wooden ● adjective **1** *a wooden door* WOOD, timber, woody; ligneous. **2** *wooden acting* STILTED, stiff, unnatural, awkward, leaden; dry, flat, stodgy, lifeless, passionless, spiritless, soulless. **3** *her*

shocking or distasteful thing that has been kept secret. [ORIGIN from the novel *Cold Comfort Farm* by Stella Gibbons (1933).]

woodsman • noun a forester, hunter, or woodcutter.

wood sorrel • noun a woodland plant with clover-like leaves and pink or white flowers.

wood spirit • noun another term for WOOD ALCOHOL.

wood stain • noun a commercially produced substance for colouring wood.

woodsy • adjective N. Amer. of, relating to, or characteristic of wood or woodland.

woodturning • noun the activity of shaping wood with a lathe.
– DERIVATIVES **woodturner** noun.

woodwind • noun (treated as sing. or pl.) wind instruments other than brass instruments forming a section of an orchestra, including flutes, oboes, clarinets, and bassoons.

woodwork • noun **1** the wooden parts of a room, building, or other structure. **2** Brit. the activity or skill of making things from wood.
– PHRASES **come out of the woodwork** (of an unpleasant person or thing) emerge from obscurity.
– DERIVATIVES **woodworker** noun **woodworking** noun.

woodworm • noun **1** the wood-boring larva of a kind of small brown beetle. **2** the damaged condition of wood resulting from infestation with this larva.

woody • adjective (**woodier**, **woodiest**) **1** covered with trees. **2** made of, resembling, or suggestive of wood.
– DERIVATIVES **woodiness** noun.

woodyard • noun a yard where wood is chopped or stored.

woody nightshade • noun a climbing plant with purple flowers and poisonous red berry-like fruit.

woof[1] /wo͝of/ • noun the barking sound made by a dog. • verb bark.
– ORIGIN imitative.

woof[2] /wo͞of/ • noun another term for WEFT[1].
– ORIGIN Old English, from the base of WEAVE[1].

woofer /wo͝ofər/ • noun a loudspeaker designed to reproduce low frequencies.

wool • noun **1** the fine soft curly or wavy hair forming the coat of a sheep, goat, or similar animal, especially when shorn and made into cloth or yarn. **2** a metal or mineral made into a mass of fine fibres.
– PHRASES **pull the wool over someone's eyes** informal deceive someone.
– ORIGIN Old English.

wool-gathering • noun indulgence in aimless thought.

wool grower • noun a breeder of sheep for wool.

woollen (US **woolen**) • adjective **1** made wholly or partly of wool. **2** relating to the production of wool. • noun (**woollens**) woollen garments.

woolly • adjective (**woollier**, **woolliest**) **1** made of wool. **2** (of an animal or plant) covered with wool or hair resembling wool. **3** resembling wool in texture or appearance. **4** confused or unclear. • noun (pl. **woollies**) informal **1** chiefly Brit. a woollen garment, especially a pullover. **2** Austral./NZ a sheep.
– DERIVATIVES **woolliness** noun.

woolly bear • noun a large hairy caterpillar, especially that of a tiger moth.

Woolsack • noun (in the UK) the Lord Chancellor's wool-stuffed seat in the House of Lords.

woolshed • noun Austral./NZ a large shed for shearing and baling wool.

woomera /wo͞omərə/ • noun Austral. an Aboriginal stick used to throw a dart or spear more forcibly.
– ORIGIN Dharuk (an Aboriginal language).

Woop Woop /wo͝op wo͝op/ • noun Austral./NZ informal, humorous a remote outback town or district.
– ORIGIN mock Aboriginal.

woosh • verb & noun variant spelling of WHOOSH.

woozy • adjective (**woozier**, **wooziest**) informal unsteady, dizzy, or dazed.
– DERIVATIVES **woozily** adverb **wooziness** noun.
– ORIGIN of unknown origin.

wop • noun informal, offensive an Italian or other southern European.
– ORIGIN perhaps from Italian *guappo* 'bold, showy'.

Worcester sauce (also **Worcestershire sauce**) • noun a pungent sauce containing soy sauce and vinegar, first made in Worcester in England.

Worcs. • abbreviation Worcestershire.

word • noun **1** a single distinct meaningful element of speech or writing, used to form sentences with others. **2** a remark or statement. **3** (**a word**) even the smallest amount of something spoken or written: *don't believe a word.* **4** (**words**) angry talk. **5** (**the word**) a command, slogan, or signal. **6** (**one's word**) a person's account of the truth, especially when it differs from that of another person. **7** (**one's word**) a promise or assurance. **8** news. • verb express in particular words.
– PHRASES **be as good as one's word** do what one has promised. **have a word** speak briefly to someone. **have a word in someone's ear** speak to someone privately and discreetly. **in other words** that is to say. **in so many words** precisely in the way mentioned. **in a word** briefly. **a man** (or **woman**) **of his** (or **her**) **word** a person who keeps their promises. **on** (or **upon**) **my word** an exclamation of surprise or emphasis. **put words into someone's mouth 1** inaccurately report what someone has said. **2** prompt someone to say something inadvertently. **take someone at their word** assume that a person is speaking honestly or sincerely. **take the words out of someone's mouth** say what someone else was about to say. **take someone's word** (**for it**) believe what someone says or writes without checking for oneself. **too —— for words** informal extremely ——. **waste words** talk in vain. **word for word** in exactly the same or, when translated, exactly equivalent words. **word of honour** a solemn promise. **word of mouth** spoken communication as a means of transmitting information.
– DERIVATIVES **wordless** adjective.
– ORIGIN Old English.

word association • noun the spontaneous production of other words in response to a given word, used as a technique in psychiatric evaluation.

word class • noun a category of words of similar form or func-

Thesaurus

face was wooden EXPRESSIONLESS, impassive, poker-faced, emotionless, blank, vacant, unresponsive.

woodland • noun WOODS, wood, forest, trees; *archaic* greenwood.

woodwork • noun CARPENTRY, joinery.

wool • noun **1** *sheep's wool* FLEECE, hair, coat; floccus. **2** *a sweater made of cream wool* YARN.
– PHRASES **pull the wool over someone's eyes** *(informal)* DECEIVE, fool, trick, hoodwink, dupe, delude; *informal* lead up the garden path, put one over on, bamboozle, con.

wool-gathering • noun DAYDREAMING, dreaming, reverie, musing, abstraction, preoccupation; absent-mindedness, forgetfulness.

W

woolly • adjective **1** *a woolly hat* WOOLLEN, wool, fleecy. **2** *a sheep's woolly coat* FLEECY, shaggy, hairy, fluffy, flocculent. **3** *woolly generalizations* VAGUE, ill-defined, hazy, unclear, fuzzy, blurry, foggy, nebulous, imprecise, inexact, indefinite; confused, muddled.
• noun *(informal)* SWEATER, pullover, jersey, cardigan; *Brit.* jumper; *Brit. informal* cardy.

woozy • adjective *(informal)*. See GROGGY.

word • noun **1** *the Italian word for 'ham'* TERM, name, expression, designation, locution, vocable; *formal* appellation. **2** *his words were meant kindly* REMARK, comment, observation, statement, utterance, pronouncement. **3** *I've got three weeks to learn the words* SCRIPT, lyrics, libretto. **4** *I give you my word* PROMISE, word of honour, assurance, guarantee, undertaking; pledge, vow, oath, bond; *formal* troth. **5** *I want a word with you* TALK, conversation, chat, tête-à-tête, heart-to-heart, one-to-one; discussion, consultation; *informal* confab, powwow; *formal* confabulation. **6** *there's no word from the hospital* NEWS, information, communication, intelligence; message, report, communiqué, dispatch, bulletin; *informal* info, gen, dope; *poetic/literary* tidings. **7** *word has it he's turned over a new leaf* RUMOUR, hearsay, talk, gossip; *informal* the grapevine, the word on the street. **8** *I'm waiting for the word from HQ* INSTRUCTION, order, command; signal, prompt, cue, tip-off; *informal* go-ahead, thumbs up, green light. **9** *his word was law* COMMAND, order, decree, edict; bidding, will. **10** *our word now must be success* MOTTO, watchword, slogan, catchword, buzz word.
– RELATED TERMS verbal, lexical.
• verb *the question was carefully worded* PHRASE, express, put, couch, frame, formulate, style; say, utter.
– PHRASES **have words** QUARREL, argue, disagree, squabble, bicker, fight, wrangle, dispute, fall out, clash; *Brit. informal* row. **in a word** BRIEFLY, to be brief, in short, in a nutshell, to come to the point, to cut a long story short, not to put too fine a point on it; to sum up, to summarize, in summary. **word for word 1** *they took down the*

tion; a part of speech.

wording • noun the way in which something is worded.

word-perfect • adjective (of an actor or speaker) knowing one's part or speech by heart.

wordplay • noun the witty exploitation of the meanings and ambiguities of words.

word processor • noun a computer or program for storing, manipulating, and formatting text entered from a keyboard and providing a printout.

wordsmith • noun a skilled user of words.

wordy • adjective (**wordier**, **wordiest**) using or expressed in too many words.
– DERIVATIVES **wordily** adverb **wordiness** noun.

wore past of WEAR.

work • noun **1** activity involving mental or physical effort done in order to achieve a result. **2** such activity as a means of earning income. **3** a task or tasks to be undertaken. **4** a thing or things done or made; the result of an action. **5** (**works**) (treated as sing.) chiefly Brit. a place where industrial or manufacturing processes are carried out. **6** (**works**) chiefly Brit. operations of building or repair. **7** Military a defensive structure. **8** (**works**) the mechanism of a clock or other machine. **9** Physics the exertion of force overcoming resistance or producing molecular change. **10** (**the works**) informal everything needed, desired, or expected. • verb (past and past part. **worked** or archaic **wrought**) **1** do work, especially as one's job. **2** set to or keep at work. **3** (of a machine or system) function, especially properly or effectively. **4** (of a machine) be in operation. **5** have or bring about the desired result: *her plan worked admirably.* **6** bring (a material or mixture) to a desired shape or consistency. **7** produce (an article or design) using a specified material or sewing stitch. **8** cultivate (land) or extract materials from (a mine or quarry). **9** move gradually or with difficulty into another position. **10** (of a person's features) move violently or convulsively. **11** bring into a specified emotional state.
– PHRASES **get worked up** gradually come into a state of intense excitement, anger, or anxiety. **have one's work cut out** be faced with a hard or lengthy task. **in the works** being planned, worked on, or produced. **work in** try to include (something). **work off** reduce or eliminate by activity. **work on/upon** exert influence on. **work out 1** solve or be capable of being solved. **2** develop in a good or specified way. **3** plan in detail. **4** understand the character of. **5** engage in vigorous physical exercise. **work out at** be calculated at. **work over** informal beat up. **work one's passage** pay for one's journey on a ship with work instead of money. **work to rule** chiefly Brit. follow official working rules and hours exactly in order to reduce output and efficiency, as a form of industrial action. **work up to** proceed gradually towards (something more advanced). **work up** develop or improve (something) gradually.
– DERIVATIVES **workless** adjective.
– ORIGIN Old English.

workable • adjective **1** able to be worked. **2** capable of producing the desired result.
– DERIVATIVES **workability** noun **workably** adverb.

workaday • adjective not unusual or interesting; ordinary.

workaholic • noun informal a person who compulsively works excessively hard.
– DERIVATIVES **workaholism** noun.

workbench • noun a bench at which carpentry or other mechanical or practical work is done.

worker • noun **1** a person who works. **2** a person who achieves a specified thing: *a miracle-worker.* **3** a neuter or undeveloped female bee, wasp, ant, etc., large numbers of which perform the basic work of a colony.

work ethic • noun another term for PROTESTANT ETHIC.

work experience • noun short-term experience of employment, arranged for older pupils by schools.

workfare • noun a welfare system which requires some work or attendance for training from those receiving benefits.

workforce • noun (treated as sing. or pl.) the people engaged in or available for work in a particular area, firm, or industry.

Thesaurus

speeches word for word VERBATIM, letter for letter, to the letter; exactly, faithfully. **2** *a word-for-word translation* VERBATIM, literal, exact, direct, accurate, faithful; unadulterated, unabridged.

wording • noun PHRASING, phraseology, words, language, expression, terminology.

wordplay • noun PUNNING, puns, play on words; wit, witticisms, repartee.

wordy • adjective LONG-WINDED, verbose, prolix, lengthy, protracted, long-drawn-out, rambling, circumlocutory, periphrastic, pleonastic; loquacious, garrulous, voluble; *informal* windy; *Brit. informal* waffly.
– OPPOSITES succinct.

work • noun **1** *a day's work in the fields* LABOUR, toil, slog, drudgery, exertion, effort, industry, service; *informal* grind, sweat, elbow grease; *Brit. informal* graft, fag; *Austral./NZ informal* yakka; *poetic/literary* travail. **2** *I'm looking for work* EMPLOYMENT, a job, a post, a position, a situation; occupation, profession, career, vocation, calling. **3** *haven't you got any work?* TASKS, jobs, duties, assignments, projects; chores. **4** *works of literature* COMPOSITION, piece, creation; opus, oeuvre. **5** *this is the work of a radical faction* HANDIWORK, doing, act, deed. **6** *a lifetime spent doing good works* DEEDS, acts, actions. **7** *the complete works of Shakespeare* WRITINGS, oeuvre, canon, output. **8** *a car works* FACTORY, plant, mill, foundry, yard, workshop, shop. **9** *the works of a clock* MECHANISM, machinery, workings, parts, movement, action; *informal* insides. **10** *(informal) for only $60 you can get the works* EVERYTHING, the full treatment; *informal* the lot, the whole shebang, the full nine yards; *Brit. informal* the full monty.
– OPPOSITES leisure.
• verb **1** *staff worked late into the night* TOIL, labour, exert oneself, slave (away); keep at it, keep one's nose to the grindstone; *informal* slog (away), beaver away, plug away, put one's back into it, knock oneself out, sweat blood; *Brit. informal* graft, fag; *poetic/literary* travail. **2** *he worked in education for years* BE EMPLOYED, have a job, earn one's living, do business. **3** *farmers worked the land* CULTIVATE, farm, till, plough. **4** *his car was working perfectly* FUNCTION, go, run, operate; *informal* behave. **5** *how do I work this machine?* OPERATE, use, handle, control, manipulate, run. **6** *their ploy worked* SUCCEED, work out, turn out well, go as planned, get results, be effective; *informal* come off, pay off, do the trick; *N. Amer. informal* turn the trick. **7** *blusher can work miracles* BRING ABOUT, accomplish, achieve, produce, perform, create, engender, contrive, effect. **8** *(informal) the chairman was prepared to work it for Phil* ARRANGE, manipulate, contrive; pull strings; *N. Amer.* pull wires; *informal* fix, swing, wangle. **9** *he worked the crowd into a frenzy* STIR (UP), excite, drive, move, rouse, fire, galvanize; whip up, agitate. **10** *work the mixture into a paste* KNEAD, squeeze, form; mix, stir, blend. **11** *he worked the blade into the padlock* MANOEUVRE, manipulate, guide, edge. **12** *her mouth worked furiously* TWITCH, quiver, convulse. **13** *he worked his way through the crowd* MANOEUVRE, make, thread, wind, weave, wend.
– OPPOSITES rest, fail.
– PHRASES **work on someone** PERSUADE, manipulate, influence; coax, cajole, wheedle, soften up; *informal* twist someone's arm, lean on. **work out 1** *the bill works out at £50* AMOUNT TO, add up to, come to, total; *Brit.* tot up to. **2** *my idea worked out.* See WORK verb sense 6. **3** *things didn't work out the way she planned* END UP, turn out, go, come out, develop; happen, occur; *informal* pan out. **4** *he works out at the local gym* EXERCISE, train. **work something out 1** *work out what you can afford* CALCULATE, compute, reckon up, determine. **2** *I'm trying to work out what she meant* UNDERSTAND, comprehend, puzzle out, sort out, make sense of, get to the bottom of, make head or tail of, unravel, decipher, decode; *informal* figure out; *Brit. informal* suss out. **3** *they worked out a plan* DEVISE, formulate, draw up, put together, develop, construct, arrange, organize, contrive, concoct; hammer out, negotiate. **work something up** STIMULATE, rouse, raise, arouse, awaken, excite.

workable • adjective PRACTICABLE, feasible, viable, possible, achievable; realistic, reasonable, sensible, practical; *informal* doable.
– OPPOSITES impracticable.

workaday • adjective ORDINARY, average, run-of-the-mill, middle-of-the-road, conventional, unremarkable, unexceptional, undistinguished, commonplace, humdrum, mundane, pedestrian; routine, everyday, day-to-day; *N. Amer.* garden-variety; *informal* bog-standard, nothing to write home about, ten a penny, a dime a dozen; *Brit. informal* common or garden.
– OPPOSITES exceptional.

worker • noun **1** *a strike by 500 workers* EMPLOYEE, member of staff; workman, labourer, hand, operative, operator; proletarian; artisan, craftsman, craftswoman; wage-earner, breadwinner. **2** *(informal) I got a reputation for being a worker* HARD WORKER, toiler, workhorse; *informal* busy bee, eager beaver, workaholic; *N. Amer. in-*

workhorse ● noun a person or machine that works hard and reliably over a long period.
workhouse ● noun **1** historical (in the UK) a public institution in which poor people received board and lodging in return for work. **2** US a prison in which petty offenders are expected to work.
working ● adjective **1** having paid employment. **2** engaged in manual labour. **3** functioning or able to function. **4** good enough as the basis for work or argument and likely to be changed later: *a working title.* ● noun **1** a mine or a part of a mine from which minerals are being extracted. **2** (**workings**) the way in which a machine, organization, or system operates. **3** (**workings**) a record of the successive calculations made in solving a mathematical problem. **4** a scheduled duty or trip performed by a locomotive, bus, etc.
working capital ● noun the capital of a business which is used in its day-to-day trading operations.
working class ● noun the social group consisting of people who are employed for wages, especially in manual or industrial work.
working girl ● noun informal, euphemistic a prostitute.
working party (also **working group**) ● noun Brit. a group appointed to study and report on a particular question and make recommendations.
workload ● noun the amount of work to be done by someone or something.
workman ● noun **1** a man employed to do manual labour. **2** a person who works in a specified way.
– PHRASES **a bad workman always blames his tools** proverb a person who has done something badly will blame their equipment rather than admit their own lack of skill.
workmanlike ● adjective showing efficient competence.
workmanship ● noun the degree of skill with which a product is made or a job done.
workmate ● noun chiefly Brit. a person with whom one works; a colleague.
work of art ● noun a creative product with strong imaginative or aesthetic appeal.
workout ● noun a session of vigorous physical exercise.
work permit ● noun an official document giving a foreigner permission to take a job in a country.
workpiece ● noun an object being worked on with a tool or machine.
works council ● noun chiefly Brit. a group of employees representing a workforce in discussions with their employers.
worksheet ● noun **1** a paper listing questions or tasks for students. **2** a paper or table recording work done or in progress.
workshop ● noun **1** a room or building in which goods are manufactured or repaired. **2** a meeting at which a group engages in intensive discussion and activity on a particular subject or project.
work-shy ● adjective disinclined to work.
workspace ● noun **1** an area rented or sold for commercial purposes. **2** Computing a memory storage facility for temporary use.
workstation ● noun a desktop computer terminal, typically networked and more powerful than a personal computer.
worktop ● noun Brit. a flat surface for working on, especially in a kitchen.
world ● noun **1** (**the world**) the earth with all its countries and peoples. **2** a region or group of countries: *the English-speaking world.* **3** all that belongs to a particular period or sphere of activity: *the theatre world.* **4** (**one's world**) a person's life and activities. **5** (**the world**) secular or material matters as opposed to spiritual ones. **6** a planet. **7** (**a/the world**) a very large amount of: *that makes a world of difference.*
– PHRASES **the best of both** (or **all possible**) **worlds** the benefits of widely differing situations, enjoyed at the same time. **bring into the world** give birth to or assist at the birth of. **man** (or **woman**) **of the world** a person who is experienced in the ways of sophisticated society. **out of this world** informal extremely enjoyable or impressive. **the world and his wife** Brit. informal everybody. **the world, the flesh, and the devil** all forms of temptation to sin.
– ORIGIN Old English.
world-beater ● noun a person or thing that is better than all others in its field.
world-class ● adjective of or among the best in the world.
World Cup ● noun a competition between teams from several countries in a sport, in particular an international soccer tournament held every four years.
world English ● noun the English language including all of its regional varieties, such as North American, Australian, and South African English.
worldly ● adjective (**wordlier, wordliest**) **1** of or concerned with material affairs rather than spiritual ones. **2** experienced and sophisticated.
– PHRASES **worldly goods** (or **possessions** or **wealth**) everything that someone owns.
– DERIVATIVES **worldliness** noun.
worldly-wise ● adjective having sufficient experience not to be easily shocked or deceived.
world music ● noun music from the developing world incorporating traditional and/or popular elements.
world order ● noun a set of arrangements established internationally for preserving global political stability.
world power ● noun a country that has significant influence in international affairs.
world-ranking ● adjective among the best in the world.
world-shaking ● adjective very important; momentous.
world view ● noun a particular philosophy of life or conception of the world.
world war ● noun a war involving many large nations in all different parts of the world, especially the wars of 1914–18 and 1939–45.
world-weary ● adjective bored with or cynical about life.
worldwide ● adjective extending or applicable throughout the world. ● adverb throughout the world.

Thesaurus

formal wheel horse.
workforce ● noun EMPLOYEES, staff, personnel, workers, labour force, manpower; human resources; *informal* liveware.
working ● adjective **1** *working mothers* EMPLOYED, in (gainful) employment, in work, waged. **2** *a working waterwheel* FUNCTIONING, operating, running, active, operational, functional, serviceable; *informal* up and running. **3** *a working knowledge of contract law* SUFFICIENT, adequate, viable; useful, effective.
– OPPOSITES unemployed, faulty.
● noun **1** *the working of a carburettor* FUNCTIONING, operation, running, action, performance. **2** *the workings of a watch* MECHANISM, machinery, parts, movement, action, works; *informal* insides.
workman ● noun (MANUAL) WORKER, labourer, hand, operative, operator; employee; journeyman, artisan.
workmanlike ● adjective EFFICIENT, competent, professional, proficient, skilful, adept, masterly.
workmanship ● noun CRAFTSMANSHIP, artistry, craft, art, artisanship, handiwork; skill, expertise, technique.
workout ● noun EXERCISE SESSION, keep-fit session, training session, drill; warm-up; exercises, aerobics; *informal, dated* daily dozen.
workshop ● noun **1** *a car repair workshop* FACTORY, works, plant; garage. **2** *the craftsmen had a chilly workshop* WORKROOM, studio, atelier. **3** *a workshop on combating stress* STUDY GROUP, discussion group, seminar, class.
world ● noun **1** *he travelled the world* EARTH, globe, planet, sphere. **2** *life on other worlds* PLANET, satellite, moon, star, heavenly body, orb. **3** *the academic world* SPHERE, society, circle, arena, milieu, province, domain, orbit, preserve, realm, field, discipline, area. **4** *she would show the world that she was strong* EVERYONE, everybody, people, mankind, humankind, humanity, the (general) public, the population, the populace, all and sundry, every mother's son, {every Tom, Dick, and Harry}, every man jack. **5** *a world of difference* HUGE AMOUNT, good deal, great deal, abundance, wealth, profusion, mountain; plenty; *informal* heap, lot, load, ton, masses; *Brit. informal* shedload. **6** *she renounced the world* SOCIETY, secular interests, temporal concerns, earthly concerns.
– PHRASES **on top of the world** (*informal*). See OVERJOYED. **out of this world** (*informal*). See WONDERFUL.
worldly ● adjective **1** *his youth was wasted on worldly pursuits* EARTHLY, terrestrial, temporal, mundane; mortal, human, material, materialistic, physical, carnal, fleshly, bodily, corporeal, sensual. **2** *a worldly man* SOPHISTICATED, experienced, worldly-wise, knowledgeable, knowing, enlightened, shrewd, mature, seasoned, cosmopolitan, urbane, cultivated, cultured.
– OPPOSITES spiritual, naive.
worldly-wise ● adjective. See WORLDLY sense 2.

W

World Wide Web • noun Computing an extensive information system on the Internet providing facilities for documents to be connected to other documents by hypertext links.

worm • noun **1** an earthworm or other creeping or burrowing invertebrate animal having a long slender soft body and no limbs. **2** (**worms**) intestinal or other internal parasites. **3** a maggot regarded as eating dead bodies buried in the ground. **4** informal a weak or despicable person. • verb **1** move by crawling or wriggling. **2** (**worm one's way into**) insinuate one's way into. **3** (**worm out of**) obtain (information) from (someone) by cunning persistence. **4** treat (an animal) with a preparation designed to expel parasitic worms.
– PHRASES (**even**) **a worm will turn** proverb (even) a meek person will resist or retaliate if pushed too far.
– ORIGIN Old English.

worm cast • noun a convoluted mass of soil, mud, or sand thrown up at the surface by a burrowing worm.

worm-eaten • adjective (of wood) full of holes made by woodworm.

wormery • noun (pl. **wormeries**) a container in which worms are bred or kept for study.

worm gear • noun a mechanical arrangement consisting of a toothed wheel worked by a short revolving cylinder (worm) bearing a screw thread.

wormhole • noun **1** a hole made by a burrowing insect larva or worm in wood, fruit, etc. **2** Physics a hypothetical connection between widely separated regions of space–time.

worm's-eye view • noun a view as seen from below or from a humble position.

wormwheel • noun the wheel of a worm gear.

wormwood • noun **1** a woody shrub with a bitter aromatic taste, used as an ingredient of vermouth and absinthe and in medicine. **2** bitterness or grief, or a source of this.
– ORIGIN Old English.

wormy • adjective (**wormier, wormiest**) worm-eaten or full of worms.

worn past participle of WEAR. • adjective **1** suffering from wear. **2** very tired.

worn out • adjective **1** exhausted. **2** worn to the point of being no longer usable.

worried • adjective feeling, showing, or expressing anxiety.
– DERIVATIVES **worriedly** adverb.

worrisome • adjective causing anxiety or concern.

worry • verb (**worries, worried**) **1** feel or cause to feel troubled over actual or potential difficulties. **2** annoy or disturb. **3** (of a dog or other carnivorous animal) tear at or pull about with the teeth. **4** (of a dog) chase and attack (livestock, especially sheep). **5** (**worry at**) pull at or fiddle with repeatedly. **6** (**worry out**) discover or devise (a solution) by persistent thought. • noun (pl. **worries**) **1** the state of being worried. **2** a source of anxiety.
– PHRASES **no worries** informal, chiefly Austral. all right; fine.
– DERIVATIVES **worrier** noun **worrying** adjective.
– ORIGIN Old English, 'strangle'.

worry beads • plural noun a string of beads that one fingers so as to calm oneself.

worse • adjective **1** less good, satisfactory, or pleasing. **2** more serious or severe. **3** more ill or unhappy. • adverb **1** less well. **2** more seriously or severely. • noun a worse event or circumstance.
– PHRASES **none the worse for** not adversely affected by. **the worse for drink** rather drunk. **the worse for wear** informal **1** worn. **2** feeling rather unwell, especially as a result of drinking too much alcohol. **worse off** less fortunate or prosperous.
– ORIGIN Old English, related to WAR.

worsen • verb make or become worse.

worship • noun **1** the feeling or expression of reverence and adoration for a deity. **2** religious rites and ceremonies. **3** great admiration or devotion. **4** (**His/Your Worship**) chiefly Brit. a title of respect for a magistrate or mayor. • verb (**worshipped, worshipping**; US also **worshiped, worshiping**) **1** show reverence and adoration for (a deity). **2** feel great admiration or devotion for.
– DERIVATIVES **worshipper** noun.
– ORIGIN Old English, 'worthiness, acknowledgement of worth'.

worshipful • adjective **1** feeling or showing reverence and admiration. **2** (**Worshipful**) Brit. a title given to justices of the peace and to certain old companies or their officers.

worst • adjective most bad, severe, or serious. • adverb **1** most severely or seriously. **2** least well. • noun the worst part, event, or circumstance. • verb get the better of.
– PHRASES **at worst** in the worst possible case. **do one's worst** do as much damage as one can. **get** (or **have**) **the worst of it** suffer the most. **if the worst comes to the worst** if the most serious or difficult circumstances arise.
– ORIGIN Old English, related to WORSE.

worsted /wŏostid/ • noun **1** a fine smooth yarn spun from long

Thesaurus

worldwide • adjective GLOBAL, international, intercontinental, universal; ubiquitous, extensive, widespread, far-reaching, wide-ranging, all-embracing.
– OPPOSITES local.

worn • adjective **1** *his hat was worn* SHABBY, worn out, threadbare, tattered, in tatters, holey, falling to pieces, ragged, frayed, moth-eaten, scruffy, having seen better days; *informal* tatty, ratty, the worse for wear; *N. Amer. informal* raggedy. **2** *her face looked worn.* See WORN OUT sense 2.
– OPPOSITES smart, fresh.

worn out • adjective **1** *a worn-out shirt.* See WORN sense 1. **2** *by evening they looked worn out* EXHAUSTED, fatigued, tired (out), weary, drained, worn, drawn, wan, sapped, spent; careworn, haggard, hollow-eyed, pinched, pale, peaky; *informal* all in, done in, dog-tired, dead beat, fit to drop, shattered; *Brit. informal* knackered; *N. Amer. informal* pooped, tuckered out. **3** *worn-out ideas* OBSOLETE, antiquated, old, stale, hackneyed, trite, overused, overworked, clichéd, unoriginal, commonplace, pedestrian, prosaic, stock, conventional; *informal* played out, old hat.
– OPPOSITES smart, fresh.

worried • adjective ANXIOUS, perturbed, troubled, bothered, concerned, upset, distressed, distraught, disquieted, uneasy, fretful, agitated, nervous, edgy, on edge, tense, overwrought, worked up, keyed up, jumpy, stressed; apprehensive, fearful, afraid, frightened, scared; *informal* uptight, a bundle of nerves, on tenterhooks, jittery, twitchy, in a stew, all of a dither, in a flap, in a sweat, het up, rattled; *Brit. informal* windy, having kittens; *N. Amer. informal* antsy, squirrelly.
– OPPOSITES carefree.

worrisome • adjective. See WORRYING.

worry • verb **1** *she worries about his health* FRET, be concerned, be anxious, agonize, brood, panic, lose sleep, get worked up; *informal* get stressed, get in a flap, get in a state, stew, torment oneself. **2** *is something worrying you?* TROUBLE, bother, make anxious, disturb, distress, upset, concern, disquiet, fret, agitate, unsettle, perturb, scare, fluster, stress, tax, torment, plague, bedevil; prey on one's mind, weigh down, gnaw at; *informal* rattle, bug, get to. **3** *a dog worried his sheep* ATTACK, savage, maul, mutilate, mangle, go for; molest, torment, persecute.
• noun **1** *I'm beside myself with worry* ANXIETY, perturbation, distress, concern, uneasiness, unease, disquiet, fretfulness, restlessness, nervousness, nerves, agitation, edginess, tension, stress; apprehension, fear, dread, trepidation, misgiving, angst; *informal* butterflies (in the stomach), the willies, the heebie-jeebies. **2** *the rats are a worry* PROBLEM, cause for concern; nuisance, pest, plague, trial, trouble, vexation, bane, bugbear; *informal* pain (in the neck), headache, hassle, stress.

worrying • adjective ALARMING, worrisome, daunting, perturbing, niggling, bothersome, troublesome, unsettling, nerve-racking; distressing, disquieting, upsetting, traumatic, problematic; *informal* scary, hairy.

worsen • verb **1** *insomnia can worsen a patient's distress* AGGRAVATE, exacerbate, compound, add to, intensify, increase, magnify, heighten, inflame, augment; *informal* add fuel to the fire. **2** *the recession worsened* DETERIORATE, degenerate, decline; *informal* go downhill, go to pot, go to the dogs, hit the skids, nosedive.
– OPPOSITES improve.

worship • noun **1** *the worship of saints* REVERENCE, veneration, adoration, glorification, glory, exaltation; devotion, praise, thanksgiving, homage, honour; dulia, latria; *formal* laudation; *archaic* magnification. **2** *morning worship* SERVICE, religious rite, prayer, praise, devotion, religious observance; matins, vespers, evensong. **3** *he contemplated her with worship* ADMIRATION, adulation, idolization, lionization, hero-worship.
• verb *they worship pagan gods* REVERE, reverence, venerate, pay homage to, honour, adore, praise, pray to, glorify, exalt, extol; hold dear, cherish, treasure, esteem, adulate, idolize, deify, hero-worship, lionize; *informal* put on a pedestal; *formal* laud; *archaic* mag-

strands of combed wool. **2** fabric made from such yarn.
– ORIGIN from *Worstead*, a parish in Norfolk, England.
wort /wurt/ • noun the sweet infusion of ground malt or other grain before fermentation, used to produce beer and distilled malt liquors.
– ORIGIN Old English, related to ROOT[1].
worth • adjective **1** equivalent in value to the sum or item specified. **2** deserving to be treated or regarded in the way specified. **3** having income or property amounting to a specified sum. • noun **1** the value or merit of someone or something. **2** an amount of a commodity equivalent to a specified sum of money: *hundreds of pounds worth of clothes.*
– PHRASES **for all one is worth** informal as energetically or enthusiastically as one can.
– ORIGIN Old English.
worthless • adjective **1** having no real value or use. **2** having no good qualities.
– DERIVATIVES **worthlessly** adverb **worthlessness** noun.
worthwhile • adjective worth the time, money, or effort spent.
worthy • adjective (**worthier**, **worthiest**) **1** (often **worthy of**) deserving or good enough. **2** deserving effort, attention, or respect. **3** showing good intent but lacking in humour or imagination. • noun (pl. **worthies**) often humorous a person important in a particular sphere: *local worthies.*
– DERIVATIVES **worthily** adverb **worthiness** noun.
-worthy • combining form **1** deserving of a specified thing: *newsworthy.* **2** suitable for a specified thing: *roadworthy.*
wot singular present of WIT[2].
would • modal verb (3rd sing. present **would**) **1** past of WILL[1], in various senses. **2** (expressing the conditional mood) indicating the consequence of an imagined event. **3** expressing a desire or inclination. **4** expressing a polite request. **5** expressing a conjecture or opinion. **6** literary expressing a wish or regret.
– USAGE On the difference between **would** and **should**, see the note at SHOULD.
would-be • adjective often derogatory desiring or aspiring to be a specified type of person.
wouldn't • contraction would not.
wouldst archaic second person singular of WOULD.
wound[1] /wōōnd/ • noun **1** a bodily injury caused by a cut, blow, or other impact. **2** an injury to a person's feelings or reputation. • verb **1** inflict a wound on. **2** injure (a person's feelings).
– ORIGIN Old English.
wound[2] past and past participle of WIND[2].
wove past of WEAVE[1].
woven past participle of WEAVE[1].
wow[1] informal • exclamation (also **wowee**) expressing astonishment or admiration. • noun a sensational success. • verb impress and excite greatly.
wow[2] • noun Electronics slow pitch fluctuation in sound reproduction, perceptible in long notes. Compare with FLUTTER (in sense 4).
– ORIGIN imitative.
wowser /wowzər/ • noun Austral./NZ informal a puritanical person; a killjoy.
– ORIGIN of obscure origin.
WP • abbreviation word processing or word processor.
WPC • abbreviation (in the UK) woman police constable.
wpm • abbreviation words per minute (used after a number to indicate typing speed).
WRAC • abbreviation (in the UK, until 1993) Women's Royal Army Corps.
wrack[1] • verb variant spelling of RACK[1], RACK[3].
wrack[2] • noun a coarse brown seaweed which grows on the shoreline, often with air bladders providing buoyancy.
– ORIGIN apparently from archaic and dialect *wrack* 'shipwreck', from Dutch *wrak*.
wrack[3] (also **rack**) • noun a mass of high, thick, fast-moving cloud.
– ORIGIN originally denoting a rush or collision: probably Scandinavian.
WRAF • abbreviation (in the UK, until 1994) Women's Royal Air Force.
wraith /rayth/ • noun **1** a ghost or ghostly image of someone, especially one seen shortly before or after their death. **2** literary a wisp or faint trace.
– DERIVATIVES **wraithlike** adjective.
– ORIGIN of unknown origin.
wrangle • noun a long and complicated dispute or argument. • verb **1** engage in a wrangle. **2** N. Amer. round up or take charge of (livestock).
– DERIVATIVES **wrangler** noun.
– ORIGIN perhaps related to Low German *wrangen* 'to struggle'.
wrap • verb (**wrapped**, **wrapping**) **1** cover or enclose in paper or soft material. **2** arrange (paper or soft material) round something. **3** encircle or wind round: *he wrapped an arm around her waist.* **4** Computing cause (a word or unit of text) to be carried over to a new line automatically. **5** informal finish filming or recording. • noun **1** a loose outer garment or piece of material. **2** paper or material used for wrapping. **3** informal the end of a

Thesaurus

nify.
worst • verb DEFEAT, beat, prevail over, triumph over, trounce, rout, vanquish, conquer, master, overcome, overwhelm, overpower, crush; outdo, outclass, outstrip, surpass; *informal* thrash, lick, best, clobber, drub, slaughter, murder, wipe out, crucify, demolish, wipe the floor with, take to the cleaners, walk all over, make mincemeat of; *Brit. informal* stuff; *N. Amer. informal* shellac, cream.
worth • noun **1** *evidence of the rug's worth* VALUE, price, cost; valuation, quotation, estimate. **2** *the intrinsic worth of education* BENEFIT, advantage, use, value, virtue, utility, service, profit, help, aid; desirability, appeal; significance, sense; *informal* mileage, percentage; *archaic* behoof. **3** *a sense of personal worth* WORTHINESS, merit, value, excellence, calibre, quality, stature, eminence, consequence, importance, significance, distinction.
worthless • adjective **1** *the item was worthless* VALUELESS; poor quality, inferior, second-rate, low-grade, cheap, shoddy, tawdry; *informal* crummy, rubbishy, ten a penny; *Brit. informal* twopenny-halfpenny; *N. Amer. informal* nickel-and-dime. **2** *your conclusions are worthless* USELESS, no use, ineffective, ineffectual, fruitless, unproductive, unavailing, pointless, nugatory, valueless, inadequate, deficient, meaningless, senseless, insubstantial, empty, hollow, trifling, petty, inconsequential, lame, paltry, pathetic; *informal* a dead loss. **3** *his worthless son* GOOD-FOR-NOTHING, ne'er-do-well, useless, despicable, contemptible, low, ignominious, corrupt, villainous, degenerate, shiftless, feckless; *informal* no-good, lousy.
– OPPOSITES valuable, useful.
worthwhile • adjective VALUABLE, useful, of use, of service, beneficial, rewarding, advantageous, positive, helpful, profitable, gainful, fruitful, productive, constructive, effective, effectual, meaningful, worthy.
worthy • adjective *a worthy citizen* VIRTUOUS, righteous, good, moral, ethical, upright, upstanding, high-minded, principled, exemplary; law-abiding, irreproachable, blameless, guiltless, unimpeachable, honest, honourable, reputable, decent, respectable, noble, meritorious; pure, whiter than white, saintly, angelic; *informal* squeaky clean.
– OPPOSITES disreputable.
• noun *local worthies* DIGNITARY, personage, grandee, VIP, notable, notability, pillar of society, luminary, leading light, big name; *informal* heavyweight, bigwig, top dog, big shot, big cheese; *N. Amer. informal* big wheel, big kahuna.
– OPPOSITES nobody.
– PHRASES **be worthy of** DESERVE, merit, warrant, rate, justify, earn, be entitled to, qualify for.
would-be • adjective ASPIRING, budding, promising, prospective, potential, hopeful, keen, eager, ambitious; *informal* wannabe.
wound • noun **1** *a chest wound* INJURY, lesion, cut, gash, laceration, tear, slash; graze, scratch, abrasion; bruise, contusion; *Medicine* trauma. **2** *the wounds inflicted by the media* INSULT, blow, slight, offence, affront; hurt, damage, injury, pain, distress, grief, anguish, torment.
• verb **1** *he was critically wounded* INJURE, hurt, harm; maim, mutilate, disable, incapacitate, cripple; lacerate, cut, graze, gash, stab, slash. **2** *her words had wounded him* HURT, scar, damage, injure; insult, slight, offend, affront, distress, disturb, upset, trouble; grieve, sadden, pain, sting, shock, traumatize, torment.
wraith • noun GHOST, spectre, spirit, phantom, apparition, manifestation; *informal* spook; *poetic/literary* shade, phantasm.
wrangle • noun *a wrangle over money* ARGUMENT, dispute, disagreement, quarrel, falling-out, fight, squabble, altercation, war of words, shouting match, tiff; *informal* set-to, run-in, slanging match; *Brit. informal* barney, row, bust-up.
• verb *we wrangled over the details* ARGUE, quarrel, bicker, squab-

session of filming or recording. **4** Brit. informal a small packet of a powdered illegal drug. **5** a tortilla wrapped around a cold filling, eaten as a sandwich.
– PHRASES **under wraps** kept secret. **wrap up 1** put on or dress in warm clothes. **2** complete or conclude (a meeting or other process). **3** Brit. informal be quiet; stop talking. **4** (**wrapped up**) engrossed or absorbed to the exclusion of other things.
– DERIVATIVES **wrapping** noun.
– ORIGIN of unknown origin.
wrapped ● adjective Austral. informal overjoyed; delighted.
– ORIGIN blend of *wrapped up* 'engrossed' and RAPT.
wrapper ● noun **1** a piece of paper or other material used for wrapping something. **2** chiefly N. Amer. a loose robe or gown.
wrasse /rass/ ● noun (pl. same or **wrasses**) a brightly coloured marine fish with thick lips and strong teeth.
– ORIGIN Cornish *wrah*; related to Welsh *gwrach* 'old woman'.
wrath /roth, rawth/ ● noun extreme anger.
– ORIGIN Old English, related to WROTH.
wrathful ● adjective literary full of or characterized by intense anger.
– DERIVATIVES **wrathfully** adverb.
wreak ● verb **1** cause (a large amount of damage or harm). **2** inflict (vengeance).
– USAGE The past tense of **wreak** is **wreaked**, as in *rainstorms wreaked havoc yesterday*, not **wrought**. When **wrought** is used in the phrase **wrought havoc**, it is in fact an archaic past tense of **work**.
– ORIGIN Old English, 'drive (out), avenge'; related to WRECK and WRETCH.
wreath /reeth/ ● noun (pl. **wreaths** /reeths, reethz/) **1** an arrangement of flowers, leaves, or stems fastened in a ring and used for decoration or for laying on a grave. **2** a curl or ring of smoke or cloud.
– ORIGIN Old English, related to WRITHE.
wreathe /reeth/ ● verb **1** (usu. **be wreathed**) envelop, surround, or encircle. **2** (of smoke) move with a curling motion.
– ORIGIN from WRITHE, reinforced by WREATH.
wreck ● noun **1** the destruction of a ship at sea; a shipwreck. **2** a ship destroyed at sea. **3** a building, vehicle, etc. that has been destroyed or badly damaged. **4** N. Amer. a road or rail crash. **5** a person in a very bad physical or mental state. ● verb **1** cause the destruction of (a ship) by sinking or breaking up. **2** destroy or severely damage. **3** spoil completely. **4** (**wrecking**) historical the practice of causing a shipwreck in order to steal the cargo.
– ORIGIN Old French *wrec*, from Old Norse; related to WREAK.
wreckage ● noun the remains of something that has been badly damaged or destroyed.
wrecked ● adjective informal **1** exhausted. **2** drunk.
wrecker ● noun **1** a person or thing that wrecks something. **2** chiefly N. Amer. a person who breaks up damaged vehicles or demolishes old buildings to obtain usable spares or scrap.
Wren ● noun (in the UK) a member of the former Women's Royal Naval Service.
– ORIGIN from WRNS.
wren ● noun a very small short-winged songbird with a cocked tail.
– ORIGIN Old English.
wrench ● verb **1** pull or twist suddenly and violently. **2** injure (a part of the body) as a result of a sudden twisting movement. ● noun **1** a sudden violent twist or pull. **2** a feeling of abrupt pain and distress caused by one's own or another's departure. **3** an adjustable tool like a spanner, used for gripping and turning nuts or bolts.
– ORIGIN Old English.
wrest /rest/ ● verb **1** forcibly pull from a person's grasp. **2** take (power or control) after effort or resistance.
– ORIGIN Old English, 'twist, tighten'; related to WRIST.
wrestle ● verb **1** take part in a fight or contest that involves close grappling with one's opponent. **2** struggle with a difficulty or problem. **3** extract or manipulate (an object) with difficulty and some physical effort. ● noun **1** a wrestling bout or contest. **2** a hard struggle.
– DERIVATIVES **wrestler** noun **wrestling** noun.
wretch ● noun **1** an unfortunate person. **2** informal a contemptible person.
– ORIGIN Old English.
wretched ● adjective (**wretcheder**, **wretchedest**) **1** in a very unhappy or unfortunate state; miserable. **2** of poor quality; very bad. **3** used to express anger or annoyance: *she disliked the wretched man intensely.*
– DERIVATIVES **wretchedly** adverb **wretchedness** noun.

Thesaurus

ble, fall out, have words, disagree, be at odds, fight, battle, feud, clash; *informal* scrap; *Brit. informal* row.
wrap ● verb **1** *she wrapped herself in a towel* SWATHE, bundle, swaddle, muffle, cloak, enfold, envelop, encase, cover, fold, wind. **2** *I wrapped the vase carefully* PARCEL (UP), package, pack (up), bundle (up); gift-wrap.
● noun *he put a wrap round her* SHAWL, stole, cloak, cape, mantle, scarf, poncho, serape; *historical* pelisse.
– PHRASES **wrap up 1** *wrap up well — it's cold* DRESS WARMLY, muffle up. **2** *(Brit. informal) tell that child to wrap up.* See SHUT UP at SHUT.
wrap something up *(informal)* CONCLUDE, finish, end, wind up, round off, terminate, stop, cease, finalize, complete, tie up; *informal* sew up.
wrapper ● noun **1** *a sweet wrapper* WRAPPING, packaging, paper, cover, covering; jacket, sheath. **2** *(N. Amer.) she wore a cotton wrapper* HOUSECOAT, bathrobe, dressing gown, robe, kimono, peignoir.
wrath ● noun ANGER, rage, fury, outrage, spleen, vexation, (high) dudgeon, crossness, displeasure, annoyance, irritation; *poetic/literary* ire, choler.
– OPPOSITES happiness.
wreak ● verb INFLICT, bestow, mete out, administer, deliver, impose, exact, create, cause, result in, effect, engender, bring about, perpetrate, unleash, vent; *formal* effectuate.
wreath ● noun GARLAND, circlet, chaplet, crown, festoon, lei; ring, loop, circle.
wreathe ● verb **1** *a pulpit wreathed in holly* FESTOON, garland, drape, cover, bedeck, deck, decorate, ornament, adorn. **2** *blue smoke wreathed upwards* SPIRAL, coil, loop, wind, curl, twist, snake, curve.
wreck ● noun **1** *salvage teams landed on the wreck* SHIPWRECK, sunken ship, derelict; shell, hull. **2** *the wreck of a stolen car* WRECKAGE, debris, remainder, ruins, remains.
● verb **1** *he had wrecked her car* DEMOLISH, crash, smash up, damage, destroy; vandalize, deface, desecrate, write off; *N. Amer. informal* trash, total. **2** *his ship was wrecked* SHIPWRECK, sink, capsize, run aground. **3** *the crisis wrecked his plans* RUIN, spoil, disrupt, undo, put a stop to, frustrate, blight, crush, quash, dash, destroy, scotch, shatter, devastate, sabotage; *informal* mess up, screw up, foul up, put paid to, stymie, put the kibosh on, nix; *Brit. informal* scupper, dish.
wreckage ● noun. See WRECK noun senses 1, 2.
wrench ● noun **1** *she felt a wrench on her shoulders* TUG, pull, jerk, jolt, heave; *informal* yank. **2** *hold the piston with a wrench* SPANNER, monkey wrench. **3** *a wrench in his arm* SPRAIN, twist, strain, rick, crick. **4** *leaving was an immense wrench* PAINFUL PARTING, traumatic event; pang, trauma.
● verb **1** *he wrenched the gun from her hand* TUG, pull, jerk, wrest, heave, twist, pluck, grab, seize, snatch, force, prise; *N. Amer.* pry; *informal* yank. **2** *she wrenched her ankle* SPRAIN, twist, turn, strain, rick, crick, pull; injure, hurt.
wrest ● verb WRENCH, snatch, seize, grab, prise, pluck, tug, pull, jerk, dislodge; *N. Amer.* pry; *informal* yank.
wrestle ● verb GRAPPLE, fight, struggle, contend, vie, battle, wrangle; scuffle, tussle, brawl; *informal* scrap.
wretch ● noun **1** *the wretches killed themselves* POOR CREATURE, poor soul, poor thing, poor unfortunate; *informal* poor devil, poor beggar. **2** *I wouldn't trust the old wretch* SCOUNDREL, villain, ruffian, rogue, rascal, reprobate, criminal, miscreant, good-for-nothing; *informal* heel, creep, louse, rat, swine, dog, lowlife, scumbag; *informal, dated* rotter, bounder, blighter, blackguard.
wretched ● adjective **1** *I felt so wretched without you* MISERABLE, unhappy, sad, heartbroken, grief-stricken, sorrowful, distressed, desolate, devastated, despairing, disconsolate, downcast, dejected, crestfallen, cheerless, depressed, melancholy, morose, gloomy, mournful, doleful, dismal, forlorn, woebegone; *informal* blue; *poetic/literary* dolorous. **2** *I feel wretched* ILL, unwell, poorly, sick, below par; *Brit.* off colour; *informal* under the weather, out of sorts. **3** *their living conditions are wretched* HARSH, hard, grim, stark, difficult; poor, impoverished; pitiful, pathetic, miserable, cheerless, sordid, shabby, seedy, dilapidated; *informal* scummy; *Brit. informal* grotty. **4** *the wretched dweller in the shanty town* UNFORTUNATE, unlucky, luckless, ill-starred, blighted, hapless, poor, pitiable,

wriggle ● verb **1** twist and turn with quick writhing movements. **2** (**wriggle out of**) avoid by devious means. ● noun a wriggling movement.
– DERIVATIVES **wriggler** noun **wriggly** adjective.
– ORIGIN Low German *wriggelen*.

wright ● noun a maker or builder: *playwright*.
– ORIGIN Old English, related to WORK.

wring ● verb (past and past part. **wrung**) **1** squeeze and twist to force liquid from. **2** break (an animal's neck) by twisting forcibly. **3** squeeze (someone's hand) tightly. **4** (**wring from/out of**) obtain with difficulty or effort. **5** cause great pain or distress to. ● noun an act of wringing.
– PHRASES **wring one's hands** clasp and twist one's hands together as a gesture of distress or despair.
– ORIGIN Old English, related to WRONG.

wringer ● noun a device for wringing water from wet clothes or other objects.

wringing ● adjective extremely wet; soaked.

wrinkle ● noun **1** a slight line or fold, especially in fabric or the skin of the face. **2** informal a minor difficulty. **3** informal a clever innovation, or useful piece of information or advice. ● verb make or become wrinkled.
– DERIVATIVES **wrinkled** adjective.
– ORIGIN possibly from an Old English word meaning 'sinuous'.

wrinkly ● adjective (**wrinklier**, **wrinkliest**) having many wrinkles. ● noun (pl. **wrinklies**) Brit. informal, derogatory an old person.

wrist ● noun the joint connecting the hand with the forearm.
– ORIGIN Old English, probably related to WRITHE.

wristband ● noun a band word round the wrist, especially for identity purposes or as a sweatband.

wristwatch ● noun a watch worn on a strap round the wrist.

writ[1] ● noun **1** a form of written command in the name of a court or other legal authority, directing a person to act or refrain from acting in a specified way. **2** (**one's writ**) one's power to enforce compliance or submission.
– ORIGIN Old English, related to WRITE.

writ[2] ● verb archaic past participle of WRITE.
– PHRASES **writ large** in an obvious or exaggerated form.

write ● verb (past **wrote**; past part. **written**) **1** mark (letters, words, or other symbols) on a surface, with a pen, pencil, or similar implement. **2** write and send (a letter) to someone. **3** compose (a text or work) in writing. **4** compose (a musical work). **5** fill out or complete (a cheque or similar document). **6** Computing enter (data) into a specified storage medium or location in store. **7** underwrite (an insurance policy).
– PHRASES **be written all over one's face** informal be obvious from one's expression. **write off 1** dismiss as insignificant. **2** cancel the record of (a bad debt); acknowledge the failure to recover (an asset). **3** Brit. damage (a vehicle) so badly that it cannot be repaired or is not worth repairing.
– DERIVATIVES **writable** adjective (chiefly Computing).
– ORIGIN Old English.

write-off ● noun **1** a vehicle that is too badly damaged to be repaired. **2** a worthless or ineffectual person or thing.

writer ● noun **1** a person who has written a particular text, or who writes books or articles as an occupation. **2** Computing a device that writes data to a storage medium.

writerly ● adjective **1** of or characteristic of a professional author. **2** consciously literary.

writer's block ● noun the condition of being unable to think of what to write or how to proceed with writing.

writer's cramp ● noun pain or stiffness in the hand caused by excessive writing.

write-up ● noun a newspaper article giving an opinion of a recent event, performance, etc.; a review.

writhe /rīth/ ● verb twist or squirm in pain or as if in pain.
– ORIGIN Old English, 'make into coils, plait'.

writing ● noun **1** the activity or skill of writing. **2** written work. **3** (**writings**) books or other written works. **4** a sequence of letters or symbols forming coherent words.
– PHRASES **the writing is on the wall** there are clear signs that something unpleasant or unwelcome is going to happen. [ORIGIN with biblical allusion to Belshazzar's feast (Book of Daniel, chapter 5), at which mysterious writing appeared on the wall foretelling Belshazzar's overthrow.]

writ of execution ● noun Law a judicial order that a judgement be enforced.

written past participle of WRITE.

WRNS ● abbreviation historical (in the UK) Women's Royal Naval Service.

wrong ● adjective **1** not correct or true; mistaken or in error. **2** unjust, dishonest, or immoral. **3** in a bad or abnormal condition; amiss. ● adverb **1** in a mistaken or undesirable manner or direction. **2** with an incorrect result. ● noun an unjust, dishonest, or immoral action. ● verb **1** act unjustly or dishonestly towards. **2** mistakenly attribute bad motives to; misrepresent.
– PHRASES **get hold of the wrong end of the stick** misunderstand something. **get wrong** misunderstand (someone). **in the wrong** responsible for a mistake or offence. **on the wrong side of 1** out of favour with. **2** somewhat more than (a specified age). **two wrongs don't make a right** proverb the fact that someone has done something unjust or dishonest is no justification for acting in a similar way.
– DERIVATIVES **wrongly** adverb **wrongness** noun.
– ORIGIN Old Norse, 'awry, unjust'.

wrongdoing ● noun illegal or dishonest behaviour.

Thesaurus

downtrodden, oppressed; *poetic/literary* star-crossed. **5** *he's a wretched coward* DESPICABLE, contemptible, reprehensible, base, vile, loathsome, hateful, detestable, odious, ignoble, shameful, shabby, worthless; *informal* dirty, rotten, low-down, lousy. **6** *wretched weather* TERRIBLE, awful, dire, dreadful, atrocious, bad, poor, lamentable, deplorable; *informal* God-awful; *Brit. informal* beastly. **7** *I don't want the wretched money informal* damn, damned, blasted, blessed, flaming, confounded, rotten; *Brit. informal* flipping, blinking, blooming, bloody.
– OPPOSITES cheerful, well, comfortable, fortunate, excellent.

wriggle ● verb **1** *she tried to hug him but he wriggled* SQUIRM, writhe, wiggle, jiggle, jerk, thresh, flounder, flail, twitch, twist and turn; snake, worm, slither. **2** *he wriggled out of his responsibilities* AVOID, shirk, dodge, evade, elude, sidestep; escape from; *informal* duck.
● noun *the baby gave a wriggle* SQUIRM, jiggle, wiggle, twitch, twist.

wring ● verb **1** *wring out the clothes* TWIST, squeeze, screw, scrunch, knead, press, mangle. **2** *concessions were wrung from the government* EXTRACT, elicit, force, exact, wrest, wrench, squeeze, milk; *informal* bleed. **3** *his expression wrung her heart* REND, tear at, harrow, pierce, stab, wound, rack; distress, pain, hurt.

wrinkle ● noun **1** *fine wrinkles around her mouth* CREASE, fold, pucker, line, crinkle, furrow, ridge, groove; *informal* crow's feet. **2** (*informal*) *learn the wrinkles from someone more experienced* GUIDELINE, hint, tip, pointer, clue, suggestion; (**wrinkles**) guidance, advice.
● verb *his coat tails wrinkled up* CREASE, pucker, gather, line, crinkle, crimp, crumple, rumple, ruck up, scrunch up.

writ ● noun SUMMONS, subpoena, warrant, arraignment, indictment, citation, court order.

write ● verb **1** *he wrote her name in the book* PUT IN WRITING, write down, put down, jot down, note (down), take down, record, register, log, list; inscribe, sign, scribble, scrawl, pencil. **2** *I wrote a poem* COMPOSE, draft, think up, formulate, compile, pen, dash off, produce. **3** *he had her address and promised to write* CORRESPOND, write a letter, communicate, get in touch, keep in contact; *informal* drop someone a line.
– PHRASES **write someone/something off 1** *they have had to write off loans* FORGET ABOUT, disregard, give up on, cancel, annul, wipe out. **2** *he wrote off his new car* WRECK, smash up, crash, destroy, demolish, ruin; *N. Amer. informal* total. **3** *who would write off a player of his stature?* DISREGARD, dismiss, ignore.

writer ● noun AUTHOR, wordsmith, man/woman of letters, penman; novelist, essayist, biographer; journalist, columnist, correspondent; scriptwriter, playwright, dramatist, dramaturge, tragedian; poet; *informal* scribbler, scribe, pen-pusher, hack.

writhe ● verb SQUIRM, wriggle, thrash, flail, toss, toss and turn, twist, twist and turn, struggle.

writing ● noun **1** *I can't read his writing* HANDWRITING, hand, script, print; penmanship, calligraphy, chirography; *informal* scribble, scrawl. **2** *the writings of Gertrude Stein* WORKS, compositions, books, publications, oeuvre; papers, articles, essays.

wrong ● adjective **1** *the wrong answer* INCORRECT, mistaken, in error, erroneous, inaccurate, inexact, imprecise, fallacious, wide of the mark, off target, unsound, faulty; *informal* off beam, out. **2** *he knew he had said the wrong thing* INAPPROPRIATE, unsuitable, inapt, inapposite, undesirable; ill-advised, ill-considered, ill-judged, impolitic, injudicious, infelicitous, unfitting, out of keeping, im-

W

– DERIVATIVES **wrongdoer** noun.

wrong-foot • verb Brit. **1** (in a game) play so as to catch (an opponent) off balance. **2** place in a difficult or embarrassing situation by saying or doing something unexpected.

wrongful • adjective not fair, just, or legal.

– DERIVATIVES **wrongfully** adverb.

wrong-headed • adjective having or showing bad judgement; misguided.

wrote past tense of WRITE.

wroth /rōth, roth/ • adjective archaic angry.

– ORIGIN Old English, related to WRITHE.

wrought /rawt/ • adjective **1** (of metals) beaten out or shaped by hammering. **2** (in combination) made or fashioned in the specified way: *well-wrought*. **3** (**wrought up**) upset and anxious.

– ORIGIN archaic past and past participle of WORK.

wrought iron • noun a tough malleable form of iron suitable for forging or rolling rather than casting.

wrung past and past participle of WRING.

WRVS • abbreviation (in the UK) Women's Royal Voluntary Service.

wry /rī/ • adjective (**wryer**, **wryest** or **wrier**, **wriest**) **1** using or expressing dry, especially mocking, humour. **2** (of a person's face) twisted into an expression of disgust, disappointment, or annoyance. **3** bending or twisted to one side.

– DERIVATIVES **wryly** adverb **wryness** noun.

– ORIGIN from an Old English word meaning 'tend, incline', later 'swerve, contort'.

wrybill • noun a small New Zealand plover with a bill that bends to the right.

wryneck • noun a bird of the woodpecker family, with brown plumage and a habit of twisting its head backwards.

WSW • abbreviation west-south-west.

WTO • abbreviation World Trade Organization.

wunderkind /vŏŏndərkind/ • noun (pl. **wunderkinds** or **wunderkinder** /vŏŏndərkindər/) a person who achieves great success when relatively young.

– ORIGIN German, from *Wunder* 'wonder' + *Kind* 'child'.

Wurlitzer /wurlitsər/ • noun trademark a large pipe organ or electric organ.

– ORIGIN named after the American instrument-maker Rudolf *Wurlitzer* (1831–1914).

wurst /voorst, wurst/ • noun German or Austrian sausage.

– ORIGIN German.

wuss /wŏŏss/ • noun N. Amer. informal a weak or ineffectual person.

– ORIGIN of unknown origin.

WV • abbreviation West Virginia.

WWF • abbreviation **1** World Wide Fund for Nature. **2** World Wrestling Federation.

WWI • abbreviation World War I.

WWII • abbreviation World War II.

WWW • abbreviation World Wide Web.

WY • abbreviation Wyoming.

wych elm /wich/ (also **witch elm**) • noun a European elm with large rough leaves.

– ORIGIN *wych*, used in names of trees with pliant branches, is from Old English, apparently from a root meaning 'bend'.

wych hazel • noun variant spelling of WITCH HAZEL.

wyn /win/ • noun variant spelling of WEN².

WYSIWYG /wizziwig/ • adjective Computing denoting the representation of text on-screen in a form exactly corresponding to its appearance on a printout.

– ORIGIN acronym from *what you see is what you get*.

wyvern /wīvərn/ • noun Heraldry a winged two-legged dragon with a barbed tail.

– ORIGIN originally denoting a viper: from Old French *wivre*, from Latin *vipera*.

Thesaurus

proper; *informal* out of order. **3** *I've done nothing wrong* ILLEGAL, unlawful, illicit, criminal, dishonest, dishonourable, corrupt; unethical, immoral, bad, wicked, sinful, iniquitous, nefarious, blameworthy, reprehensible; *informal* crooked. **4** *there's something wrong with the engine* AMISS, awry, out of order, not right, faulty, defective.

– OPPOSITES right, correct, appropriate, legal.

• adverb *she guessed wrong* INCORRECTLY, wrongly, inaccurately, erroneously, mistakenly.

• noun **1** *the difference between right and wrong* IMMORALITY, sin, sinfulness, wickedness, evil; unlawfulness, crime, corruption, villainy, dishonesty, injustice, wrongdoing, misconduct, transgression. **2** *an attempt to make up for past wrongs* MISDEED, offence, injury, crime, transgression, peccadillo, sin; injustice, outrage, atrocity; *Law* tort; *archaic* trespass.

– OPPOSITES right.

• verb **1** *she was determined to forget the man who had wronged her* ILL-USE, mistreat, do an injustice to, do wrong to, ill-treat, abuse, harm, hurt, injure; *informal* do the dirty on. **2** *perhaps I am wronging him* MALIGN, misrepresent, do a disservice to, impugn, defame, slander, libel.

– PHRASES **get someone/something wrong** MISUNDERSTAND, misinterpret, misconstrue, mistake, misread, take amiss; get the wrong idea/impression; *informal* get the wrong end of the stick, be barking up the wrong tree. **go wrong 1** *I've gone wrong somewhere* MAKE A MISTAKE, make an error, make a blunder, blunder, miscalculate, trip up; *informal* slip up, screw up, make a boo-boo; *Brit. informal* boob. **2** *their plans went wrong* GO AWRY, go amiss, go off course, fail, be unsuccessful, fall through, come to nothing; backfire, misfire, rebound; *informal* come to grief, come a cropper, go up in smoke, bite the dust; *Brit. informal* go adrift. **3** *the radio's gone wrong* BREAK DOWN, malfunction, fail, stop working, crash, give out; *informal* be on the blink, conk out, go kaput; *Brit. informal* play up, pack up. **in the wrong** TO BLAME, blameworthy, at fault, reprehensible, responsible, culpable, answerable, guilty; *archaic* peccant.

wrongdoer • noun OFFENDER, lawbreaker, criminal, felon, delinquent, villain, culprit, evil-doer, sinner, transgressor, malefactor, miscreant, rogue, scoundrel; *informal* crook, wrong 'un; *Law* malfeasant; *archaic* trespasser.

wrongdoing • noun CRIME, lawbreaking, lawlessness, criminality, misconduct, misbehaviour, malpractice, corruption, immorality, sin, sinfulness, wickedness, evil, vice, iniquity, villainy; offence, felony, wrong, misdeed, misdemeanour, fault, peccadillo, transgression; *Law* malfeasance, tort; *formal* malversation; *archaic* trespass.

wrongful • adjective UNJUSTIFIED, unwarranted, unjust, unfair, undue, undeserved, unreasonable, groundless, indefensible, inappropriate, improper, unlawful, illegal, illegitimate.

– OPPOSITES rightful.

wrought up • adjective AGITATED, tense, stressed, overwrought, nervous, on edge, edgy, keyed up, worked up, jumpy, anxious, nervy, flustered, fretful, upset; *informal* in a state, in a stew, het up, wound up, uptight, in a tizz/tizzy; *Brit. informal* strung up; *N. Amer. informal* spooky, squirrelly.

– OPPOSITES calm.

wry • adjective **1** *his wry humour* IRONIC, sardonic, satirical, mocking, sarcastic; dry, droll, witty, humorous. **2** *a wry expression* UNIMPRESSED, displeased, annoyed, irritated, irked, vexed, piqued, disgruntled, dissatisfied; *informal* peeved. **3** *a wry neck* TWISTED, crooked, contorted, distorted, deformed, misshapen; *Scottish* thrawn.

Xx

X[1] (also **x**) ● **noun** (pl. **Xs** or **X's**) **1** the twenty-fourth letter of the alphabet. **2** denoting an unknown or unspecified person or thing. **3** the first unknown quantity in an algebraic expression. **4** referring to the principal or horizontal axis in a system of coordinates. **5** a cross-shaped written symbol, used to indicate an incorrect answer or to symbolize a kiss. **6** the Roman numeral for ten.

X[2] ● **symbol** films classified as suitable for adults only (replaced in the UK in 1983 by *18*, and in the US in 1990 by *NC-17*).

xanthine /zantheen/ ● **noun** Biochemistry any of a class of organic compounds including caffeine and other alkaloids.
– ORIGIN from Greek *xanthos* 'yellow'.

X chromosome ● **noun** Genetics (in humans and other mammals) a sex chromosome, two of which are normally present in female cells (designated XX) and only one in male cells (designated XY). Compare with Y CHROMOSOME.

Xe ● **symbol** the chemical element xenon.

xebec /zeebek/ ● **noun** historical a small three-masted Mediterranean sailing ship with lateen and square sails.
– ORIGIN Arabic.

xeno- ● **combining form 1** relating to a foreigner or foreigners: *xenophobia*. **2** other; different in origin: *xenograft*.
– ORIGIN from Greek *xenos* 'stranger', 'strange'.

xenobiotic /zennōbīottik/ ● **adjective** (of a substance) foreign to the body or to an ecological system.

xenograft ● **noun** a tissue graft or organ transplant from a donor of a different species from the recipient.

xenolith /zennəlith/ ● **noun** Geology a piece of rock within an igneous mass which is not derived from the original magma but has been introduced from elsewhere.

xenology /zenolləji/ ● **noun** (chiefly in science fiction) the scientific study of alien biology, cultures, etc.
– DERIVATIVES **xenologist** noun.

xenon /zennon/ ● **noun** an inert gaseous chemical element, present in trace amounts in the air and used in some kinds of electric light.

xenophobia ● **noun** intense or irrational dislike or fear of people from other countries.
– DERIVATIVES **xenophobe** noun **xenophobic** adjective.

xenotransplantation ● **noun** the process of grafting or transplanting organs or tissues between members of different species.
– DERIVATIVES **xenotransplant** noun.

xeriscape /zeeriskayp, zerr-/ ● **noun** chiefly N. Amer. a style of landscape design requiring little or no irrigation or other maintenance, used in arid regions.
– DERIVATIVES **xeriscaping** noun.
– ORIGIN from Greek *xēros* 'dry'.

xerography ● **noun** a dry copying process in which powder adheres to parts of a surface remaining electrically charged after being exposed to light from an image of the document to be copied.
– DERIVATIVES **xerographic** adjective.
– ORIGIN from Greek *xēros* 'dry'.

xerophyte /zeerəfīt, zerr-/ ● **noun** Botany a plant which needs very little water.
– DERIVATIVES **xerophytic** adjective.

Xerox /zeeroks/ ● **noun** trademark **1** a xerographic copying process. **2** a copy made using such a process. ● **verb** (**xerox**) copy (a document) by such a process.
– ORIGIN an invented name, based on XEROGRAPHY.

Xhosa /kōsə, kawsə/ ● **noun** (pl. same or **Xhosas**) **1** a member of a South African people traditionally living in the Eastern Cape Province. **2** the Bantu language of this people.
– ORIGIN Xhosa.

xi /ksī/ ● **noun** the fourteenth letter of the Greek alphabet (Ξ, ξ), transliterated as 'x'.
– ORIGIN Greek.

XL ● **abbreviation** extra large (as a clothes size).

Xmas /krisməss, eksməss/ ● **noun** informal term for CHRISTMAS.
– ORIGIN *X* representing the initial chi of Greek *Khristos* 'Christ'.

XML ● **abbreviation** Extensible Mark-up Language.

XOR ● **noun** Electronics exclusive OR (a Boolean operator).

X-rated ● **adjective 1** pornographic or indecent. **2** (formerly) denoting a film given an X classification.

X-ray ● **noun 1** an electromagnetic wave of very short wavelength, able to pass through many materials opaque to light. **2** a photograph or other image of the internal structure of an object produced by passing X-rays through the object. ● **verb** photograph or examine with X-rays.
– ORIGIN from *X-* (because, when discovered in 1895, the nature of the rays was unknown).

X-ray astronomy ● **noun** the branch of astronomy concerned with the detection and measurement of high-energy electromagnetic radiation emitted by celestial objects.

xu /soo/ ● **noun** (pl. same) a monetary unit of Vietnam, equal to one hundredth of a dong.
– ORIGIN Vietnamese, from French *sou*.

xylem /zīləm/ ● **noun** Botany the vascular tissue in plants which conducts water and dissolved nutrients upwards from the root and also helps to form the woody element in the stem.
– ORIGIN from Greek *xulon* 'wood'.

xylene /zīleen/ ● **noun** Chemistry a volatile liquid hydrocarbon resembling benzene, obtained by distilling wood, coal tar, or petroleum.
– ORIGIN from Greek *xulon* 'wood'.

xylophone /zīləfōn/ ● **noun** a musical instrument played by striking a row of wooden bars of graduated length with small beaters.
– ORIGIN from Greek *xulon* 'wood'.

Thesaurus

xenophobic ● **adjective** JINGOISTIC, chauvinistic, flag-waving, excessively nationalistic, isolationist; prejudiced, bigoted, intolerant.

Xerox ● **noun** *(trademark)* PHOTOCOPY, copy, duplicate, reproduction; *trademark* photostat.

Xmas ● **noun** *(informal)*. See CHRISTMAS.

X-ray ● **noun** RADIOGRAPH, X-ray image/picture/photograph, roentgenogram, radiogram.

Yy

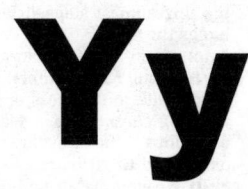

Y[1] (also **y**) ● noun (pl. **Ys** or **Y's**) **1** the twenty-fifth letter of the alphabet. **2** referring to an unknown or unspecified person or thing (coming second after 'x'). **3** (usu. *y*) the second unknown quantity in an algebraic expression. **4** referring to the secondary or vertical axis in a system of coordinates.
Y[2] ● abbreviation yen. ● symbol the chemical element yttrium.
y ● abbreviation year(s).
-y[1] ● suffix forming adjectives: **1** full of; having the quality of: *messy*. **2** inclined to; apt to: *sticky*.
– ORIGIN Old English.
-y[2] (also **-ey** or **-ie**) ● suffix **1** forming diminutive nouns, pet names, etc.: *granny*. **2** forming verbs: *shinny*.
– ORIGIN Scots.
-y[3] ● suffix forming nouns: **1** referring to a state or quality: *jealousy*. **2** referring to an action or its result: *victory*.
– ORIGIN from Latin *-ia*, *-ium* or Greek *-eia*, *-ia*.
yabby (also **yabbie**) ● noun (pl. **yabbies**) Austral. **1** a small freshwater crayfish. **2** a burrowing marine prawn, used as bait.
– ORIGIN Wemba-wemba (an Aboriginal language).
yacht /yot/ ● noun **1** a medium-sized sailing boat equipped for cruising or racing. **2** a powered boat equipped for cruising. ● verb race or cruise in a yacht.
– DERIVATIVES **yachting** noun.
– ORIGIN Dutch *jaghte*, from *jaghtschip* 'fast pirate ship'.
yack ● noun & verb variant spelling of YAK[2].
yacker ● noun variant spelling of YAKKA.
yah[1] ● exclamation yes (used in representations of upper-class speech).
yah[2] ● exclamation expressing derision.
yahoo /yaahoo, yəhoo/ ● noun informal a rude, coarse, or brutish person.
– ORIGIN named after an imaginary race in Jonathan Swift's *Gulliver's Travels* (1726).
Yahweh /yaaway/ ● noun a form of the Hebrew name of God used in the Bible.
– ORIGIN Hebrew.
yak[1] ● noun a large ox with shaggy hair and large horns, used in Tibet as a pack animal and for its milk, meat, and hide.
– ORIGIN Tibetan.
yak[2] (also **yack**) informal ● verb (**yakked**, **yakking**) talk at length about trivial or boring subjects. ● noun a trivial or lengthy conversation.
– ORIGIN imitative.
yakka /yakkər/ (also **yacker**) ● noun Austral./NZ informal work.
– ORIGIN Jagara (an Aboriginal language).
yakuza /yəkoozə/ ● noun (pl. same) (**the Yakuza**) a powerful Japanese criminal organization.
– ORIGIN Japanese, from the words for 'eight' + 'nine' + 'three', referring to the worst hand in a gambling game.
Yale ● noun trademark a type of lock with a latch bolt and a flat key with a serrated edge.
– ORIGIN named after the American locksmith Linus *Yale* Jr (1821–68).
yam ● noun **1** the edible starchy tuber of a tropical and subtropical climbing plant. **2** N. Amer. a sweet potato.
– ORIGIN from Portuguese *inhame* or obsolete Spanish *iñame*.
yammer informal ● verb **1** talk loudly and incessantly. **2** make a loud, incessant noise. ● noun loud and sustained noise.
– ORIGIN Old English, 'to lament'.
yang ● noun (in Chinese philosophy) the active male principle of the universe. Contrasted with YIN.
– ORIGIN Chinese, 'male genitals', 'sun', 'positive'.
Yank ● noun informal, often derogatory an American.
yank informal ● verb pull with a jerk. ● noun a sudden hard pull.
– ORIGIN of unknown origin.
Yankee ● noun informal **1** often derogatory an American. **2** US an inhabitant of New England or one of the northern states. **3** historical a Federal soldier in the Civil War. **4** a bet on four or more horses to win (or be placed) in different races.
– ORIGIN perhaps from Dutch *Janke*, from *Jan* 'John'.
Yanqui /yangki/ ● noun variant spelling of YANKEE, as used in Latin American contexts.
yap ● verb (**yapped**, **yapping**) **1** give a sharp, shrill bark. **2** informal talk at length in an irritating manner. ● noun a sharp, shrill bark.
– DERIVATIVES **yapper** noun **yappy** adjective (informal).
– ORIGIN imitative.
yard[1] ● noun **1** a unit of linear measure equal to 3 feet (0.9144 metre). **2** a square or cubic yard, especially of sand or other building materials. **3** a cylindrical spar slung across a ship's mast for a sail to hang from.
– PHRASES **by the yard** in large numbers or quantities.
– ORIGIN Old English.
yard[2] ● noun **1** chiefly Brit. a piece of uncultivated enclosed ground adjoining a building. **2** an area of land used for a particular purpose or business: *a builder's yard*. **3** N. Amer. the garden of a house.
– ORIGIN Old English, 'building, home, region'; related to GARDEN and ORCHARD.
yardage ● noun a distance or length measured in yards.
yardarm ● noun the outer extremity of a ship's yard.
Yardie informal ● noun **1** (among Jamaicans) a fellow Jamaican. **2** (in the UK) a member of a Jamaican or West Indian gang of criminals.
– ORIGIN from Jamaican English *yard* 'house, home'.
yardman ● noun **1** a person working in a railway or timber yard. **2** US a person who does various outdoor jobs.
yard of ale ● noun Brit. the amount of beer (typically two to three pints) held by a narrow glass about a yard high.
yard sale ● noun N. Amer. a sale of miscellaneous second-hand items held in the grounds of a private house.
yardstick ● noun **1** a measuring rod a yard long. **2** a standard used for comparison.
yarmulke /yaarmoolkə/ (also **yarmulka**) ● noun a skullcap worn in public by Orthodox Jewish men or during prayer by other Jewish men.
– ORIGIN Yiddish.
yarn ● noun **1** spun thread used for knitting, weaving, or sewing. **2** informal a long or rambling story. ● verb informal tell a yarn.
– ORIGIN Old English.
yarrow ● noun a plant with feathery leaves and heads of small white or pale pink flowers, used in herbal medicine.
– ORIGIN Old English.
yashmak /yashmak/ ● noun a veil concealing all of the face except the eyes, worn by some Muslim women in public.
– ORIGIN Turkish.
yatter informal ● verb talk incessantly; chatter. ● noun incessant talk.
– ORIGIN imitative.
yaw ● verb (of a moving ship or aircraft) twist or oscillate about a vertical axis. ● noun yawing movement of a ship or aircraft.
– ORIGIN of unknown origin.

Thesaurus

yahoo ● *(informal)* noun BOOR, lout, oaf, thug, barbarian, Neanderthal, brute, bully boy; *informal* clod, roughneck, bruiser; *Brit. informal* yobbo, yob, oik.
yank ● verb *(informal)* JERK, pull, tug, wrench; snatch, seize.
yap ● verb **1** *the dogs yapped about his heels* BARK, woof, yelp. **2** *(informal) what are they yapping on about?* See BABBLE verb sense 1.
yardstick ● noun STANDARD, measure, gauge, scale, guide, guideline, indicator, test, touchstone, barometer, criterion, benchmark, point of reference, model, pattern.
yarn ● noun **1** *you need to use a fine yarn* THREAD, cotton, wool,

yawl • noun a two-masted fore-and-aft-rigged sailing boat with the mizzenmast stepped far aft so that the mizzen boom overhangs the stern.
– ORIGIN from Low German *jolle* or Dutch *jol*.
yawn • verb **1** involuntarily open one's mouth wide and inhale deeply due to tiredness or boredom. **2** (**yawning**) wide open: *a yawning chasm.* • noun **1** an act of yawning. **2** informal a boring or tedious thing or event.
– ORIGIN Old English.
yawp • noun a harsh or hoarse cry or yelp. • verb shout or exclaim hoarsely.
– ORIGIN imitative.
yaws • plural noun (treated as sing.) a contagious tropical disease caused by a bacterium that enters skin abrasions and causes small lesions which may develop into deep ulcers.
– ORIGIN probably from Carib.
yay /yay/ (also **yea**) • adverb informal, chiefly N. Amer. (with measurements) so; to this extent.
– ORIGIN probably from YEA.
Yb • symb. the chemical element ytterbium.
Y chromosome • noun Genetics (in humans and other mammals) a sex chromosome which is normally present only in male cells, which are designated XY. Compare with X CHROMOSOME.
yd • abbreviation yard (measure).
ye[1] • pronoun (second person pl.) archaic or dialect plural of THOU[1].
– ORIGIN Old English.
ye[2] • determiner pseudo-archaic term for THE.
– ORIGIN from a misunderstanding of þ (see THORN), which could be written as y, so that *the* could be written *ye*; it was never, however, pronounced as 'ye'.
yea archaic or formal • adverb yes. • noun an affirmative answer.
– ORIGIN Old English.
yeah (also **yeh**) • exclamation & noun informal non-standard spelling of YES.
year • noun **1** the time taken by the earth to make one revolution around the sun. **2** (also **calendar year**) the period of 365 days (or 366 days in leap years) starting from the first of January, used for reckoning time in ordinary affairs. **3** a period of the same length as this starting at a different point. **4** a similar period used for reckoning time according to other calendars. **5** (**one's years**) one's age or time of life. **6** (**years**) informal a very long time. **7** a set of students grouped together as being of roughly similar ages.
– PHRASES **in the year of grace** (or **Our Lord**) —— in the year —— AD. **year in, year out** continuously or repeatedly over a period of years.
– ORIGIN Old English.
yearbook • noun **1** an annual publication giving current information about and listing events of the previous year. **2** N. Amer. an annual publication of the graduating class in a school or university, giving photographs of students and details of school activities in the previous year.
yearling • noun **1** an animal of a year old, or in its second year. **2** a racehorse in the calendar year after its year of foaling. • adjective having lived or existed for a year.
yearly • adjective & adverb happening or produced once a year or every year.
yearn /yern/ • verb have an intense feeling of loss and longing for something.
– DERIVATIVES **yearner** noun **yearning** noun.
– ORIGIN Old English, from a Germanic base meaning 'eager'.
year-on-year • adjective (of figures, prices, etc.) as compared with the corresponding ones from a year earlier.
year-round • adjective happening or continuing throughout the year.
yeast • noun **1** a microscopic single-celled fungus capable of converting sugar into alcohol and carbon dioxide. **2** a greyish-yellow preparation of this obtained chiefly from fermented beer, used as a fermenting agent, to raise bread dough, and as a food supplement. **3** Biology any single-celled fungus that reproduces vegetatively by budding or fission.
– ORIGIN Old English.
yeasty • adjective (**yeastier, yeastiest**) **1** of, resembling, or containing yeast. **2** turbulent or restless.
yell • noun **1** a loud, sharp cry, especially of pain, surprise, or delight. **2** N. Amer. an organized rhythmic cheer, especially one used to support a sports team. • verb shout in a loud or piercing way.
– ORIGIN Old English.
yellow • adjective **1** of the colour between green and orange in the spectrum, as of egg yolks or ripe lemons. **2** offensive having a yellowish or olive skin (as used to describe Chinese or Japanese people). **3** referring to a warning of danger which is thought to be near but not actually imminent. **4** informal cowardly. **5** (of a book or newspaper) unscrupulously sensational. • noun yellow colour or pigment. • verb become a yellow colour, especially with age.
– PHRASES **the yellow peril** offensive the political or military threat regarded as being posed by the Chinese or by the peoples of SE Asia.
– DERIVATIVES **yellowish** adjective **yellowness** noun **yellowy** adjective.
– ORIGIN Old English, related to GOLD.
yellow-belly • noun informal a coward.
– DERIVATIVES **yellow-bellied** adjective.
yellow card • noun (especially in soccer) a yellow card shown by the referee to a player being cautioned. • verb (**yellow-card**) (of the referee) show a yellow card to.
yellow dog • noun N. Amer. informal a contemptible person or thing.
yellow fever • noun a tropical disease caused by a virus transmitted by mosquitoes, causing fever and jaundice and often fatal.
yellowfin • noun a widely distributed, commercially important tuna that has yellow anal and dorsal fins.
yellow flag • noun a ship's yellow or quarantine flag, used to indicate the presence or absence of disease aboard.
yellowhammer • noun a common bunting, the male of which has a yellow head, neck, and breast.
– ORIGIN *-hammer* is perhaps from Old English *amore* (a kind of bird).
yellow jack • noun archaic term for YELLOW FEVER.
yellow jersey • noun (in a cycling race involving stages) a yellow jersey worn each day by the rider who is ahead on time over the whole race, and presented to the rider with the shortest overall time at the finish of the race.
Yellow Pages • plural noun (trademark in the UK) a telephone directory printed on yellow paper and listing businesses and other organizations according to the goods or services they offer.
yellow rattle • noun a partly parasitic yellow-flowered plant whose ripe seeds are shed into a pouch which rattles when shaken.
yelp • noun a short sharp cry. • verb utter a yelp or yelps.
– ORIGIN from Old English, 'to boast'.

Thesaurus

fibre, filament; ply. **2** *(informal) a far-fetched yarn* STORY, tale, anecdote, saga, narrative; *informal* tall tale/story, cock and bull story, shaggy-dog story, spiel.
yawning • adjective GAPING, wide open, wide, cavernous, deep; huge, great, big.
year • noun TWELVE-MONTH PERIOD, calendar year; *poetic/literary* sun, summer, winter; *archaic* twelvemonth.
– RELATED TERMS annual.
– PHRASES **year in, year out** REPEATEDLY, again and again, time and (time) again, time after time, over and over (again), {week in, week out}, {day in, day out}, recurrently, continuously, continually, constantly, habitually, regularly, without a break, unfailingly, always.
yearly • adjective *a yearly payment* ANNUAL, once a year, every year, each year.
• adverb *the guide is published yearly* ANNUALLY, once a year, per annum, by the year, every year, each year.
yearn • verb LONG, pine, crave, desire, want, wish, hanker, covet, lust, pant, hunger, thirst, ache, eat one's heart out, have one's heart set on; *informal* have a yen, itch.
yearning • noun LONGING, craving, desire, want, wish, hankering, urge, hunger, thirst, appetite, lust, ache; *informal* yen, itch.
yell • verb *he yelled in agony* CRY OUT, call out, call at the top of one's voice, shout, howl, yowl, wail, scream, shriek, screech, yelp, squeal; roar, bawl; *informal* holler.
• noun *a yell of rage* CRY, shout, howl, yowl, scream, shriek, screech, yelp, squeal; roar; *informal* holler.
yellow • adjective **1** *yellow hair | a yellow shirt* FLAXEN, golden, gold, blonde, fair; lemon, daffodil-yellow, mustard. **2** *(informal) he'll have to prove he's not yellow.* See COWARDLY.

Yemeni /yemməni/ • **adjective** a person from Yemen. • **adjective** relating to Yemen.
Yemenite • **noun & adjective** another term for YEMENI.
yen[1] • **noun** (pl. same) the basic monetary unit of Japan.
– ORIGIN from Japanese, 'round'.
yen[2] • **noun** informal a longing or yearning.
– ORIGIN originally in the sense 'craving for a drug': from Chinese.
yenta /yentə/ • **noun** N. Amer. informal a female gossip and busybody.
– ORIGIN Yiddish, originally a given name.
yeoman /yōmən/ • **noun** historical **1** a man holding a small landed estate; a freeholder. **2** a servant in a royal or noble household. **3** Brit. a member of the yeomanry force.
– PHRASES **yeoman service** efficient help.
– DERIVATIVES **yeomanly** adjective.
– ORIGIN probably from YOUNG + MAN.
Yeoman of the Guard • **noun** a member of the British sovereign's bodyguard (now having only ceremonial duties).
yeomanry • **noun** (treated as sing. or pl.) historical a body of yeomen, or yeomen collectively.
Yeoman Warder • **noun** a warder at the Tower of London.
yerba /yerbə/ • **noun** another term for MATÉ.
– ORIGIN Spanish, 'herb'.
yerba buena /yerbə bwaynə/ • **noun** a trailing aromatic herb related to savory and native to the western US, with whitish or lilac flowers.
– ORIGIN Spanish, 'good herb'.
yes • **exclamation** **1** used to give an affirmative response. **2** responding to someone addressing one or attracting one's attention. **3** questioning a remark. **4** expressing delight. • **noun** (pl. **yeses** or **yesses**) an affirmative answer, decision, or vote.
– ORIGIN Old English.
yeshiva /yəsheevə/ • **noun** an Orthodox Jewish college or seminary.
– ORIGIN Hebrew.
yes-man • **noun** informal a person who always agrees with their superiors.
yesterday • **adverb** on the day before today. • **noun** **1** the day before today. **2** the recent past.
– ORIGIN Old English.
yesteryear • **noun** literary last year or the recent past.
yet • **adverb** **1** up until now or then. **2** as soon as the present or a specified or implied time: *wait, don't go yet*. **3** from now into the future for a specified length of time. **4** referring to something that will or may happen in the future. **5** still; even (emphasizing increase or repetition). **6** in spite of that. • **conjunction** but at the same time.
– PHRASES **nor yet** and also not.
– ORIGIN Old English.
yeti /yetti/ • **noun** a large hairy manlike creature said to live in the highest part of the Himalayas.
– ORIGIN Tibetan, 'little manlike animal'.
yew • **noun** a coniferous tree with poisonous red berry-like fruit and dense, springy wood.
– ORIGIN Old English.
Y-fronts • **plural noun** Brit. trademark men's or boys' underpants with a seam at the front in the shape of an upside-down Y.
YHA • **abbreviation** (in the UK) Youth Hostels Association.
Yid • **noun** informal, offensive a Jew.
Yiddish /yiddish/ • **noun** a language used by Jews in or from central and eastern Europe, originally a German dialect with words from Hebrew and several modern languages. • **adjective** relating to this language.
– DERIVATIVES **Yiddisher** noun.
– ORIGIN from Yiddish *yidish daytsh* 'Jewish German'.
Yiddishism • **noun** a Yiddish word or idiom.
yield • **verb** **1** produce or provide (a natural, agricultural, or industrial product). **2** produce or generate (a result, gain, or financial return). **3** give way to demands or pressure. **4** relinquish possession of. **5** (of a mass or structure) give way under force or pressure. • **noun** an amount or result yielded.
– DERIVATIVES **yielder** noun.
– ORIGIN Old English, 'pay, repay'.
yikes • **exclamation** informal, humorous expressing shock and alarm.
– ORIGIN of unknown origin.
yin • **noun** (in Chinese philosophy) the passive female principle of the universe. Contrasted with YANG.
– ORIGIN Chinese, 'feminine', 'moon', 'shade'.
yip • **noun** a short, sharp cry or yelp, especially of excitement or delight. • **verb** (**yipped**, **yipping**) give a yip.
– ORIGIN imitative.
yippee • **exclamation** expressing wild excitement or delight.
yippie • **noun** (pl. **yippies**) a member of a group of young politically active hippies, originally in the US.
– ORIGIN acronym from *Youth International Party*, suggested by HIPPY[1].
Y2K • **abbreviation** year 2000 (with reference to the millennium bug).
ylang-ylang /eelangeelang/ • **noun** a sweet-scented essential oil obtained from the flowers of a tropical tree, used in perfumery and aromatherapy.
– ORIGIN Tagalog.
YMCA • **abbreviation** Young Men's Christian Association.
-yne • **suffix** Chemistry forming names of unsaturated hydrocarbons containing a triple bond.
– ORIGIN alteration of -INE[4].
yo • **exclamation** informal used to greet someone, attract their attention, or express excitement.
yob • **noun** Brit. informal a rude and loutish young man.
– DERIVATIVES **yobbery** noun **yobbish** adjective.
– ORIGIN from BOY (spelt backwards).
yobbo • **noun** (pl. **yobbos** or **yobboes**) Brit. informal a yob.
yocto- /yoktō/ • **combining form** used in units of measurement to indicate a factor of one million million million millionth (10^{-24}).
– ORIGIN adapted from OCTO-, on the pattern of combining forms such as *peta-*.
yodel /yōd'l/ • **verb** (**yodelled**, **yodelling**; US **yodeled**, **yodeling**) practise a form of singing or calling marked by rapid alternation between the normal voice and falsetto. • **noun** a song or call delivered in such a way.
– DERIVATIVES **yodeller** noun.
– ORIGIN German *jodeln*.
yoga • **noun** a Hindu spiritual and ascetic discipline, a part of which, including breath control, simple meditation, and the adoption of specific bodily postures, is widely practised for health and relaxation.
– DERIVATIVES **yogic** adjective.

Thesaurus

yelp • **noun & verb** SQUEAL, shriek, howl, yowl, yell, cry, shout, yawp; *informal* holler.
yen • **noun** *(informal)* HANKERING, yearning, longing, craving, urge, desire, want, wish, hunger, thirst, lust, appetite, ache; fancy, inclination; *informal* itch.
yes • **adverb** ALL RIGHT, very well, of course, by all means, sure, certainly, absolutely, indeed, affirmative, in the affirmative, agreed, roger; *Scottish, N. English, & archaic* aye; *Nautical* aye aye; *informal* yeah, yep, yup, uh-huh, okay, OK, okey-dokey, okey-doke; *Brit. informal* righto, righty-ho; *N. Amer. informal* surely; *archaic or formal* yea.
– OPPOSITES no.
yes-man • **noun** *(informal)* SYCOPHANT, toady, creep, fawner, flatterer, lickspittle, doormat; *informal* bootlicker; *Brit. informal* poodle; *N. Amer. informal* suck-up.
yet • **adverb** **1** *he hasn't made up his mind yet* SO FAR, thus far, as yet, up till/to now, until now. **2** *don't celebrate just yet* NOW, right now, at this time; already, so soon. **3** *he was doing nothing, yet he appeared purposeful* NEVERTHELESS, nonetheless, even so, but, however, still, notwithstanding, despite that, in spite of that, for all that, all the same, just the same, at the same time, be that as it may; *archaic* natheless. **4** *he supplied yet more unsolicited advice* EVEN, still, further, in addition, additionally, besides, into the bargain, to boot.
yield • **verb** **1** *too many projects yield poor returns* PRODUCE, bear, give, supply, provide, afford, return, bring in, earn, realize, generate, deliver, pay out. **2** *the nobility had yielded power to the new capitalist class* RELINQUISH, surrender, cede, remit, part with, hand over; make over, bequeath, leave. **3** *the Duke was forced to yield* SURRENDER, capitulate, submit, relent, admit defeat, back down, climb down, give in, give up the struggle, lay down one's arms, raise/show the white flag, throw in the towel/sponge. **4** *he yielded to her demands* GIVE IN TO, give way to, submit to, bow down to, comply with, agree to, consent to, go along with; grant, permit, allow; *informal* cave in to; *formal* accede to. **5** *the floorboards yielded underfoot* BEND, give, give way.
– OPPOSITES withhold, resist, defy.

– ORIGIN Sanskrit, 'union'.
yogi ● noun (pl. **yogis**) a person who is proficient in yoga.
– ORIGIN Sanskrit.
yogic flying ● noun a technique of Transcendental Meditation involving thrusting oneself off the ground while in the lotus position.
yogurt /yoggərt, yō-/ (also **yoghurt** or **yoghourt**) ● noun a semi-solid slightly sour food prepared from milk fermented by added bacteria.
– ORIGIN Turkish.
yoicks /yoyks/ ● exclamation used by fox-hunters to urge on the hounds.
– ORIGIN of unknown origin.
yoke ● noun **1** a wooden crosspiece that is fastened over the necks of two animals and attached to a plough or cart that they pull in unison. **2** (pl. same or **yokes**) a pair of yoked animals. **3** a frame fitting over the neck and shoulders of a person, used for carrying pails or baskets. **4** something that represents a bond between two parties: *the yoke of marriage.* **5** something oppressive or burdensome: *the yoke of imperialism.* **6** a part of a garment that fits over the shoulders and to which the main part of the garment is attached. ● verb couple or attach with or to a yoke.
– ORIGIN Old English.
yokel ● noun an unsophisticated country person.
– ORIGIN perhaps from dialect *yokel* 'green woodpecker'.
yolk /yōk/ ● noun the yellow internal part of a bird's egg, which is rich in protein and fat and nourishes the developing embryo.
– DERIVATIVES **yolked** adjective **yolky** adjective.
– ORIGIN Old English, related to YELLOW.
yolk sac ● noun Zoology a membranous sac containing yolk attached to the embryos of reptiles and birds and the larvae of some fishes.
Yom Kippur /yom kippər, kipoor/ ● noun the most solemn religious fast of the Jewish year, the last of the ten days of penitence that begin with Rosh Hashana (the Jewish New Year).
– ORIGIN Hebrew, 'day of atonement'.
yomp ● verb Brit. informal (of a soldier) march with heavy equipment over difficult terrain.
– ORIGIN of unknown origin.
yon literary or dialect ● determiner & adverb yonder; that. ● pronoun yonder person or thing.
– ORIGIN Old English.
yonder archaic or dialect ● adverb at some distance in the direction indicated; over there. ● determiner that or those (referring to something situated at a distance). ● noun (**the yonder**) the far distance.
yoni /yōni/ ● noun (pl. **yonis**) Hinduism the vulva, regarded as a symbol of divine procreative energy and conventionally represented by a circular stone.
– ORIGIN Sanskrit, 'source, womb, female genitals'.
yonks ● plural noun Brit. informal a very long time.
– ORIGIN perhaps related to **donkey's years** (see DONKEY).
yore ● noun (in phrase **of yore**) literary of former times or long ago.
– ORIGIN Old English.
yorker ● noun Cricket a ball bowled so that it pitches immediately under the bat.
– ORIGIN probably from *York*, suggesting its introduction by Yorkshire players.
Yorkist ● noun a follower of the House of York in the Wars of the Roses. ● adjective relating to the House of York.
Yorks. ● abbreviation Yorkshire.
Yorkshire pudding ● noun a baked batter pudding typically eaten with roast beef.
Yorkshire terrier ● noun a small long-haired blue-grey and tan breed of terrier.
Yoruba /yorroobə/ ● noun (pl. same or **Yorubas**) **1** a member of an African people of SW Nigeria and Benin. **2** the language of this people.
– ORIGIN the name in Yoruba.
yotta- /yottə/ ● combining form used in units of measurement to indicate a factor of one million million million million (10^{24}).
– ORIGIN from Italian *otto* 'eight'.
you ● pronoun (second person sing. or pl.) **1** used to refer to the person or people that the speaker is addressing. **2** used to refer to the person being addressed together with other people regarded in the same class. **3** used to refer to any person in general.
– ORIGIN Old English.
you'd ● contraction **1** you had. **2** you would.
you'll ● contraction you will; you shall.
young ● adjective (**younger**, **youngest**) **1** having lived or existed for only a short time. **2** relating to or characteristic of young people. ● noun (treated as pl.) young children or animals; offspring.
– DERIVATIVES **youngish** adjective.
– ORIGIN Old English.
young gun ● noun informal an energetic and assertive young man.
young offender ● noun Law (in the UK) a criminal between 14 and 17 years of age.
youngster ● noun a child, young person, or young animal.
Young Turk ● noun a young person eager for radical change to the established order.
– ORIGIN with reference to a revolutionary party active in the Ottoman Empire in the late 19th and early 20th centuries.
your ● possessive determiner **1** belonging to or associated with the person or people that the speaker is addressing. **2** belonging to or associated with any person in general. **3** (**Your**) used when addressing the holder of certain titles.
– ORIGIN Old English.
you're ● contraction you are.
yours ● possessive pronoun used to refer to something belonging to or associated with the person or people that the speaker is addressing.
yourself ● pronoun (second person sing.) (pl. **yourselves**) **1** used as the object of a verb or preposition when this is the same as the subject of the clause and the subject is the person or people being addressed. **2** (emphatic) you personally.
youse /yooz/ (also **yous**) ● pronoun dialect you (usually more than one person).
youth ● noun (pl. **youths**) **1** the period between childhood and adult age. **2** the qualities of vigour, freshness, immaturity, etc. associated with being young. **3** (treated as sing. or pl.) young people. **4** a young man.
– ORIGIN Old English, related to YOUNG.
youth club (also **youth centre**) ● noun a place or organization providing leisure activities for young people.
youthful ● adjective **1** young or seeming young. **2** characteristic of young people.
– DERIVATIVES **youthfully** adverb **youthfulness** noun.

Thesaurus

● noun *risky investments usually have higher yields* PROFIT, gain, return, dividend, earnings.
yob, yobbo ● noun *(Brit. informal).* See HOOLIGAN.
yoke ● noun **1** *the horses were loosened from the yoke* HARNESS, collar, coupling. **2** *countries struggling under the yoke of imperialism* TYRANNY, oppression, domination, hegemony, enslavement, servitude, subjugation, subjection, bondage, thrall; bonds, chains, fetters, shackles. **3** *the yoke of marriage* BOND, tie, connection, link.
● verb **1** *a pair of oxen were yoked together* HARNESS, hitch, couple, tether, fasten, attach, join. **2** *their aim of yoking biology and mechanics* UNITE, join, link, connect; tie, bind, bond.
yokel ● noun BUMPKIN, peasant, provincial, rustic, country cousin, countryman/woman; *Irish informal* culchie; *N. Amer. informal* hayseed, hillbilly, hick; *Austral. informal* bushy.
young ● adjective **1** *young people* YOUTHFUL, juvenile; junior, adolescent, teenage; in the springtime of life, in one's salad days. **2** *she's very young for her age* IMMATURE, childish, inexperienced, unsophisticated, naive, unworldly; *informal* wet behind the ears. **3** *the young microbrewery industry* FLEDGLING, developing, budding, in its infancy, emerging.
– OPPOSITES old, elderly, mature.
● noun **1** *a robin feeding its young* OFFSPRING, progeny, family, babies. **2** *the young don't care nowadays* YOUNG PEOPLE, children, boys and girls, youngsters, youth, the younger generation, juveniles, minors; *informal* kids, young 'uns.
youngster ● noun CHILD, teenager, adolescent, youth, juvenile, minor, junior; boy, girl; *Scottish & N. English* lass, lassie; *informal* lad, kid, whippersnapper, young 'un, teen.
youth ● noun **1** *he had been a keen sportsman in his youth* EARLY YEARS, young days, teens, teenage years, adolescence, boyhood, girlhood, childhood; minority; *formal* juvenescence. **2** *she had kept her youth and beauty* YOUTHFULNESS, freshness, bloom, vigour, energy. **3** *local youths* YOUNG MAN, boy, juvenile, teenager, adolescent, junior, minor; *informal* lad, kid. **4** *the youth of the nation* YOUNG

youth hostel ● noun a place providing cheap accommodation, aimed mainly at young people on holiday. ● verb (**youth-hostel**) take a holiday in which one stays overnight in youth hostels.
you've ● contraction you have.
yowl /yowl/ ● noun a loud wailing cry of pain or distress. ● verb make such a cry.
– ORIGIN imitative.
yo-yo ● noun (pl. **yo-yos**) **1** (trademark in the UK) a toy consisting of a pair of joined discs with a deep groove between them in which string is attached and wound, which can be spun alternately downward and upward by its weight and momentum as the string unwinds and rewinds. **2** a thing that repeatedly falls and rises again. ● verb (**yo-yoes**, **yo-yoed**) move up and down repeatedly; fluctuate.
– ORIGIN probably ultimately from a language of the Philippines.
YT ● abbreviation Yukon Territory.
YTS ● abbreviation Youth Training Scheme.
ytterbium /iterbiəm/ ● noun a silvery-white metallic chemical element of the lanthanide series.
– ORIGIN from *Ytterby* in Sweden, where minerals containing several rare-earth elements were found.
yttrium /itriəm/ ● noun a greyish-white metallic chemical element resembling the rare-earth elements.
– ORIGIN from *Ytterby* (see YTTERBIUM).
yuan /yooaan/ ● noun (pl. same) the basic monetary unit of China, equal to 10 jiao or 100 fen.
– ORIGIN from Chinese, 'round'.
yuca /yo͞okə/ ● noun chiefly US another term for CASSAVA.
– ORIGIN Carib.
yucca /yukkə/ ● noun a plant of the agave family with sword-like leaves and spikes of white bell-shaped flowers, native to warm regions of the US and Mexico.
– ORIGIN variant of YUCA.
yuck (also **yuk**) informal ● exclamation used to express strong distaste or disgust. ● noun something messy or disgusting.
– DERIVATIVES **yucky** (also **yukky**) adjective.
– ORIGIN imitative.
Yugoslav /yo͞ogəslaav/ ● noun a person from Yugoslavia.
– DERIVATIVES **Yugoslavian** noun & adjective.
– ORIGIN Austrian German *Jugoslav*, from Serbo-Croat *jug* 'south' + SLAV.
Yule (also **Yuletide**) ● noun archaic Christmas.
– ORIGIN Old English or Old Norse, originally applied to a pagan festival lasting twelve days; related to JOLLY.
yule log ● noun **1** a large log traditionally burnt in the hearth on Christmas Eve. **2** a log-shaped chocolate cake eaten at Christmas.
yummy ● adjective (**yummier**, **yummiest**) informal delicious.
Yupik /yo͞opik/ ● noun (pl. same or **Yupiks**) **1** a member of an Eskimo people of Siberia, the Aleutian Islands, and Alaska. **2** any of the languages of this people.
– ORIGIN Alaskan Yupik, 'real person'.
yuppie (also **yuppy**) ● noun (pl. **yuppies**) informal, derogatory a well-paid young middle-class professional working in a city.
– DERIVATIVES **yuppiedom** noun **yuppify** verb.
– ORIGIN from the acronym *young urban professional*.
yuppie flu ● noun informal derogatory term for CHRONIC FATIGUE SYNDROME.
yurt /yoort, yert/ ● noun a circular tent of felt or skins used by nomads in Mongolia, Siberia, and Turkey.
– ORIGIN Russian *yurta*.
YWCA ● abbreviation Young Women's Christian Association.

Thesaurus

PEOPLE, young, younger generation, next generation; *informal* kids.
– OPPOSITES adulthood, old age.
youthful ● adjective YOUNG-LOOKING, spry, sprightly, vigorous, active; young, boyish, girlish; fresh-faced, in the springtime of life, in one's salad days.
– OPPOSITES old, elderly.

Zz

Z /zed, US zee/ (also **z**) ● noun (pl. **Zs** or **Z's**) **1** the twenty-sixth letter of the alphabet. **2** (usu. *z*) the third unknown quantity in an algebraic expression. **3** used in repeated form to represent buzzing or snoring.

zabaglione /zabbalyōni/ ● noun an Italian dessert made of whipped egg yolks, sugar, and Marsala wine.
– ORIGIN Italian.

zag ● noun a sharp change of direction in a zigzag course. ● verb (**zagged**, **zagging**) make a zag.

zaire /zīeer/ ● noun (pl. same) the basic monetary unit of Zaire (Democratic Republic of Congo).

Zairean /zīeeriən/ (also **Zairian**) ● noun a person from Zaire (Democratic Republic of Congo). ● adjective relating to Zaire.

zakat /zəkaat/ ● noun obligatory payment made annually under Islamic law and used for charitable and religious purposes.
– ORIGIN Arabic, 'almsgiving'.

Zambian /zambiən/ ● noun a person from Zambia. ● adjective relating to Zambia.

zander /zandər/ ● noun (pl. same) a large freshwater perch native to northern and central Europe.
– ORIGIN German.

zany ● adjective (**zanier**, **zaniest**) amusingly unconventional and idiosyncratic. ● noun (pl. **zanies**) **1** a zany person. **2** historical a comic performer partnering a clown, whom he imitated in an amusing way.
– DERIVATIVES **zanily** adverb **zaniness** noun.
– ORIGIN Italian *zani* or *zanni*, Venetian form of *Gianni*, *Giovanni* 'John', stock name of the servants acting as clowns in the commedia dell'arte.

zap informal ● verb (**zapped**, **zapping**) **1** destroy or obliterate. **2** move or propel suddenly and rapidly. **3** use a remote control to change television channels, operate a video recorder, etc. ● noun a sudden burst of energy or sound.
– DERIVATIVES **zapper** noun **zappy** adjective.
– ORIGIN imitative.

zarzuela /thaarthwaylə, saarswaylə/ ● noun **1** a traditional Spanish form of musical comedy. **2** a Spanish dish of seafood cooked in a rich sauce.
– ORIGIN Spanish.

zazen /zaazen/ ● noun Zen meditation.
– ORIGIN Japanese.

zeal /zeel/ ● noun great energy or enthusiasm for a cause or objective.
– ORIGIN Greek *zēlos*.

zealot /zellət/ ● noun **1** a fanatical and uncompromising follower of a religion or policy. **2** (**Zealot**) a member of an ancient Jewish sect aiming at a world Jewish theocracy and resisting the Romans until AD 70.
– DERIVATIVES **zealotry** noun.

zealous /zelləss/ ● adjective having or showing zeal.
– DERIVATIVES **zealously** adverb **zealousness** noun.

zebra /zebrə, zee-/ ● noun an African wild horse with black-and-white stripes and an erect mane.
– ORIGIN from Italian, Spanish, or Portuguese, originally in the sense 'wild ass'.

zebra crossing ● noun Brit. a pedestrian street crossing marked with broad white stripes.

zebu /zeebōō/ ● noun a breed of domesticated ox with a humped back.
– ORIGIN French.

zeitgeist /zītgist/ ● noun the defining spirit or mood of a particular period of history.
– ORIGIN German, from *Zeit* 'time' + *Geist* 'spirit'.

Zen ● noun a Japanese school of Mahayana Buddhism emphasizing the value of meditation and intuition.
– ORIGIN Japanese, 'meditation'.

zenana /zinaanə/ ● noun (in India and Iran) the part of a house for the seclusion of women.
– ORIGIN from a Persian and Urdu word meaning 'woman'.

zenith /zennith/ ● noun **1** the point in the sky directly overhead. **2** the highest point in the sky reached by a given celestial object. **3** the time at which something is most powerful or successful.
– DERIVATIVES **zenithal** adjective.
– ORIGIN from an Arabic phrase meaning 'path over the head'.

zeolite /zeeəlīt/ ● noun any of a large group of silicate minerals used as cation exchangers and molecular sieves.
– ORIGIN from Greek *zein* 'to boil' (from their characteristic swelling when heated).

zephyr /zeffər/ ● noun literary a soft gentle breeze.
– ORIGIN Greek *zephuros* 'god of the west wind, west wind'.

Zeppelin /zeppəlin/ ● noun historical a large German dirigible airship of the early 20th century.
– ORIGIN named after Ferdinand, Count von *Zeppelin* (1838–1917), German airship pioneer.

zepto- /zeptō/ ● combining form used in units of measurement to indicate a factor of one thousand million million millionth (10^{-21}).
– ORIGIN adapted from SEPTI-, on the pattern of combining forms such as *peta-*.

zero /zeerō/ ● cardinal number (pl. **zeros**) **1** the figure 0; nought. **2** a temperature of 0°C (32°F), marking the freezing point of water. ● verb (**zeroes**, **zeroed**) **1** adjust (an instrument) to zero. **2** set the sights of (a gun) for firing. **3** (**zero in on**) take aim at or focus attention on.
– ORIGIN Arabic, 'cipher'.

zero hour ● noun the time at which a military or other operation is set to begin.

zero tolerance ● noun strict enforcement of the law regarding any form of anti-social behaviour.

Thesaurus

zany ● adjective ECCENTRIC, peculiar, odd, unconventional, strange, bizarre, weird; mad, crazy, comic, madcap, funny, quirky, idiosyncratic; *informal* wacky, screwy, nutty, oddball, off the wall; *Brit. informal* daft; *N. Amer. informal* kooky, wacko.
– OPPOSITES conventional, sensible.

zap ● verb (*informal*) **1** *they were zapped by anti-radar missiles.* See DESTROY sense 5. **2** *racing cars zapped past.* See SPEED verb sense 1.

zeal ● noun PASSION, ardour, love, fervour, fire, avidity, devotion, enthusiasm, eagerness, keenness, appetite, relish, gusto, vigour, energy, intensity; fanaticism.
– OPPOSITES apathy.

zealot ● noun FANATIC, enthusiast, extremist, radical, young Turk, diehard, activist, militant; bigot, dogmatist, sectarian, partisan; *informal* fiend, maniac, ultra, nut.

zealous ● adjective FERVENT, ardent, fervid, fanatical, passionate, impassioned, devout, devoted, committed, dedicated, enthusiastic, eager, keen, avid, vigorous, energetic, intense, fierce; *poetic/literary* perfervid.
– OPPOSITES apathetic.

zenith ● noun HIGHEST POINT, high point, crowning point, height, top, acme, peak, pinnacle, apex, apogee, crown, crest, summit, climax, culmination, prime, meridian.
– OPPOSITES nadir.

zero ● noun **1** *the sum's wrong—you've left off a zero* NOUGHT, nothing, nil, 0; *Computing* null character; *dated* cipher; *archaic* naught. **2** *I rated my chances as zero* NOTHING (AT ALL), nil, none; *N. English* nowt; *informal* zilch, nix, sweet Fanny Adams, sweet FA, not a dicky bird; *Brit. informal* damn all, not a sausage; *N. Amer. informal* zip, nada, diddly-squat; *archaic* naught, nought.
– PHRASES **zero in on** FOCUS ON, focus attention on, centre on, concentrate on, home in on, fix on, pinpoint, highlight, spotlight; *informal* zoom in on.

zest ● noun **1** great enthusiasm and energy. **2** excitement or piquancy. **3** the outer coloured part of the peel of citrus fruit, used as flavouring.
– DERIVATIVES **zestful** adjective **zesty** adjective.
– ORIGIN French *zeste*.

zester ● noun a kitchen utensil for scraping or peeling zest from citrus fruit.

zeta /zeetə/ ● noun the sixth letter of the Greek alphabet (Ζ, ζ), transliterated as 'z'.
– ORIGIN Greek.

zetta- /zettə/ ● combining form used in units of measurement to indicate a factor of one thousand million million million (10^{21}).
– ORIGIN from Italian *sette* 'seven'.

zeugma /zyoogmə/ ● noun a figure of speech in which a word applies to two others in different senses (e.g. *John and his driving licence expired last week*).
– ORIGIN Greek, from *zeugnunai* 'to yoke'.

zidovudine /zidovyoodeen/ ● noun Medicine an antiviral drug used to slow the growth of HIV infection in the body.

zig ● noun a sharp change of direction in a zigzag course. ● verb (**zigged**, **zigging**) make a zig.

ziggurat /ziggərat/ ● noun (in ancient Mesopotamia) a rectangular stepped tower, often with a temple on top.
– ORIGIN from an ancient Semitic language.

zigzag ● noun a line or course having abrupt alternate right and left turns. ● adjective & adverb veering to right and left alternately. ● verb (**zigzagged**, **zigzagging**) take a zigzag course.
– ORIGIN German *Zickzack*.

zilch /zilch/ informal, chiefly N. Amer. ● pronoun nothing. ● determiner not any; no.
– ORIGIN perhaps from a Mr *Zilch*, a character in the 1930s magazine *Ballyhoo*.

zillion ● cardinal number informal an extremely large number of people or things.
– DERIVATIVES **zillionaire** noun **zillionth** ordinal number.
– ORIGIN from *Z* (perhaps as a symbol of an unknown quantity) + MILLION.

Zimbabwean /zimbaabwiən/ ● noun a person from Zimbabwe. ● adjective relating to Zimbabwe.

Zimmer /zimmər/ (also **Zimmer frame**) ● noun trademark a kind of walking frame.
– ORIGIN from *Zimmer* Orthopaedic Limited, the name of the manufacturer.

zinc ● noun **1** a silvery-white metallic chemical element which is a constituent of brass and is used for galvanizing iron and steel. **2** galvanized iron or steel. ● verb (**zinced** /zingkt/) coated with zinc.
– ORIGIN German *Zink*.

Zinfandel /zinfandel/ ● noun a variety of black wine grape grown in California, from which a red or blush wine is made.
– ORIGIN of unknown origin.

zing informal ● noun energy, enthusiasm, or liveliness. ● verb **1** move swiftly. **2** N. Amer. criticize sharply.
– DERIVATIVES **zingy** adjective.
– ORIGIN imitative.

zinger ● noun informal, chiefly N. Amer. an outstanding person or thing.

zinnia /zinniə/ ● noun a plant of the daisy family, cultivated for its bright showy flowers.
– ORIGIN named after the German physician and botanist Johann G. *Zinn* (1727–59).

Zion /zīən/ (also **Sion**) ● noun **1** the hill of Jerusalem on which the city of David was built. **2** the Jewish people or religion. **3** (in Christian thought) the heavenly city or kingdom of heaven.
– ORIGIN Hebrew.

Zionism /zīəniz'm/ ● noun a movement for the development and protection of a Jewish nation in Israel.
– DERIVATIVES **Zionist** noun & adjective.

zip ● noun **1** chiefly Brit. a fastener consisting of two flexible strips of metal or plastic with interlocking projections closed or opened by pulling a slide along them. **2** informal energy; vigour. ● pronoun N. Amer. informal nothing at all. ● verb (**zipped**, **zipping**) **1** fasten with a zip. **2** informal move or propel at high speed. **3** Computing compress (a file) so that it takes up less space.
– ORIGIN imitative.

zip code (also **ZIP code**) ● noun US a postal code consisting of five or nine digits.
– ORIGIN acronym from *zone improvement plan*.

zipper chiefly N. Amer. ● noun a zip fastener. ● verb fasten with a zipper.

zippo ● pronoun N. Amer. informal zip; nothing.

zippy ● adjective (**zippier**, **zippiest**) informal **1** bright, fresh, or lively. **2** speedy.

zip-up ● adjective chiefly Brit. fastened with a zip.

zircon /zurkən/ ● noun a mineral consisting of zirconium silicate, typically brown but sometimes in translucent forms of gem quality.
– ORIGIN German *Zirkon*.

zirconium /zərkōniəm/ ● noun a hard silver-grey metallic chemical element.

zit ● noun informal, chiefly N. Amer. a spot on the skin.
– ORIGIN of unknown origin.

zither /zi<u>th</u>ər/ ● noun a musical instrument consisting of a flat wooden soundbox with numerous strings stretched across it, placed horizontally and played with the fingers and a plectrum.
– ORIGIN German, from Greek *kithara*, denoting a kind of harp; related to CITTERN.

zizz informal, chiefly Brit. ● noun **1** a whizzing or buzzing sound. **2** a short sleep. ● verb **1** make a whizzing or buzzing sound. **2** doze; sleep.
– ORIGIN imitative.

zloty /zlotti/ ● noun (pl. same, **zlotys**, or **zloties**) the basic monetary unit of Poland.
– ORIGIN from Polish, 'golden'.

Zn ● symbol the chemical element zinc.

zodiac /zōdiak/ ● noun a belt of the heavens within about 8° of the ecliptic, including all apparent positions of the sun, moon, and planets and divided by astrologers into twelve equal divisions or signs.
– DERIVATIVES **zodiacal** /zədīək'l/ adjective.
– ORIGIN Greek *zōidiakos*, from *zōidion* 'sculptured animal figure', from *zōion* 'animal'.

zoetrope /zōitrōp/ ● noun a cylinder with a series of pictures on the inner surface that, when viewed through slits with the cylinder rotating, give an impression of continuous motion.
– ORIGIN from Greek *zōē* 'life' + *-tropos* 'turning'.

zombie ● noun **1** a corpse supposedly revived by witchcraft, especially in certain African and Caribbean religions. **2** informal a lifeless, apathetic, or completely unresponsive person.
– DERIVATIVES **zombify** verb.
– ORIGIN West African.

zonation /zōnaysh'n/ ● noun distribution in or division into distinct zones.

zone ● noun **1** an area distinguished on the basis of a particular characteristic, use, restriction, etc. **2** (also **time zone**) a range of longitudes where a common standard time is used. **3** chiefly Botany & Zoology an encircling band or stripe of distinctive colour, texture, etc. ● verb divide into or assign to zones.
– DERIVATIVES **zonal** adjective.
– ORIGIN Greek, 'girdle'.

zonk ● verb informal **1** hit heavily. **2** (**zonk out**) fall suddenly and heavily asleep. **3** (**zonked**) under the influence of drugs or alcohol.
– ORIGIN imitative.

zoo ● noun **1** an establishment which keeps wild animals for

Thesaurus

zero hour ● noun THE APPOINTED TIME, the critical moment, the moment of truth, the point/moment of decision, the Rubicon, the crux; *informal* the crunch.

zest ● noun **1** *she had a great zest for life* ENTHUSIASM, gusto, relish, appetite, eagerness, keenness, avidity, zeal, fervour, ardour, passion; verve, vigour, liveliness, sparkle, fire, animation, vitality, dynamism, energy, brio, pep, spirit, exuberance, high spirits; *informal* zing, zip, oomph, vim, pizzazz, get-up-and-go. **2** *he wanted to add some zest to his life* PIQUANCY, tang, flavour, savour, taste, spice, spiciness, relish, bite; excitement, interest, an edge; *informal* kick, punch, zing, oomph. **3** *the zest of an orange* RIND, peel, skin.
– OPPOSITES apathy, indifference, blandness.

zigzag ● adjective TWISTING, twisty, full of twists and turns, serpentine, meandering, snaking, snaky, winding, crooked.
– OPPOSITES straight.

zing ● noun *(informal)*. See ZEST sense 1.

zone ● noun AREA, sector, section, belt, stretch, region, territory, district, quarter, precinct, locality, neighbourhood, province.

study, conservation, or display to the public. **2** informal a confused or chaotic situation.
– ORIGIN abbreviation of *zoological garden*, originally applied to the zoo at Regent's Park, London.
zoogeography /zōəjiogrəfi, zo͞oə-/ • noun the branch of zoology concerned with the geographical distribution of animals.
– DERIVATIVES **zoogeographer** noun **zoogeographic** adjective **zoogeographical** adjective.
zooid /zō-oyd, zo͞o-/ • noun Zoology an animal arising from another by budding or division, especially each of the individuals which make up a colonial organism.
zookeeper • noun an animal attendant employed in a zoo.
zoology /zo͞oolləji, zōolləji/ • noun **1** the scientific study of the behaviour, structure, physiology, classification, and distribution of animals. **2** the animal life of a particular region or geological period.
– DERIVATIVES **zoological** adjective **zoologically** adverb **zoologist** noun.
– ORIGIN from Greek *zōion* 'animal'.
zoom • verb **1** move or travel very quickly. **2** (of a camera) change smoothly from a long shot to a close-up or vice versa. • noun an act of a camera zooming.
– ORIGIN imitative.
zoom lens • noun a lens allowing a camera to zoom by varying the focal length.
zoomorphic /zōəmorfik, zo͞o-/ • adjective having or representing animal forms or gods of animal form.
– DERIVATIVES **zoomorphism** noun.
– ORIGIN from Greek *zōion* 'animal' + *morphē* 'form'.
zoonosis /zōənōsiss, zo͞oə-/ • noun (pl. **zoonoses** /zōənōseez, zo͞oə-/) Medicine any disease which can be transmitted to humans from animals.
– DERIVATIVES **zoonotic** adjective.
– ORIGIN from Greek *zōion* 'animal' + *nosos* 'disease'.
zoot suit • noun a man's suit characterized by a long loose jacket with padded shoulders and high-waisted tapering trousers, popular in the 1940s.
– ORIGIN rhyming formation on SUIT.
Zoroastrianism /zorrōastriəniz'm/ • noun a religion of ancient Persia based on the worship of a single god, founded by the prophet Zoroaster (also called Zarathustra) in the 6th century BC.
– DERIVATIVES **Zoroastrian** adjective & noun.
Zouave /zo͞oaav, zwaav/ • noun **1** a member of a French light-infantry corps, originally formed of Algerians and long retaining an oriental uniform. **2** (**zouaves**) women's trousers with wide tops, tapering to a narrow ankle.
– ORIGIN French, from *Zouaoua*, a Berber tribe living in Algeria.
zouk /zo͞ok/ • noun an exuberant style of popular music combining Caribbean and Western elements.
– ORIGIN from Guadeloupian Creole, 'to party'.
zounds /zowndz/ • exclamation archaic or humorous expressing surprise or indignation.
– ORIGIN a contraction from *God's wounds*.
Zr • symbol the chemical element zirconium.
zucchetto /tso͝okettō/ • noun (pl. **zucchettos**) a Roman Catholic cleric's skullcap, differing in colour according to rank.
– ORIGIN Italian *zucchetta* 'little gourd or head'.
zucchini /zo͞okeeni/ • noun (pl. same or **zucchinis**) chiefly N. Amer. a courgette.
– ORIGIN Italian, plural of *zucchino* 'little gourd'.
Zulu /zo͞olo͞o/ • noun **1** a member of a South African people living mainly in KwaZulu/Natal province. **2** the Bantu language of this people.
Zyban /zīban/ • noun trademark an antidepressant drug used to relieve nicotine withdrawal symptoms in those giving up smoking.
– ORIGIN an invented word.
zydeco /zīdikō/ • noun a kind of black American dance music originally from southern Louisiana, typically featuring accordion and guitar.
– ORIGIN Louisiana Creole, possibly from a pronunciation of French *les haricots* ('the beans') in a dance-tune title.
zygoma /zīgōmə, zi-/ • noun (pl. **zygomata** /zīgōmətə, zi-/) Anatomy the bony arch of the cheek, formed by connection of the zygomatic and temporal bones.
– DERIVATIVES **zygomatic** adjective.
– ORIGIN Greek *zugōma*, from *zugon* 'yoke'.
zygomatic bone • noun Anatomy the bone forming the prominent part of the cheek and the outer side of the eye socket.
zygote /zīgōt/ • noun Biology a cell resulting from the fusion of two gametes.
– DERIVATIVES **zygotic** /zīgottik/ adjective.
– ORIGIN from Greek *zugōtos* 'yoked'.

Wordpower Guide

Thematic Vocabulary Builder

This section gives a selection of words and phrases which are related to or associated with various keywords and which a conventional dictionary or thesaurus does not usually provide. It is intended both as a vocabulary builder and as a means of guiding you to a word or expression that may be on the tip of your tongue but that remains elusive.

acid ▶ alkali, base (*substances reacting with acid*), litmus test (*test for acid or alkali*), neutral (*neither acid nor alkaline*), pH (*scale of acidity or alkalinity*).

actor ▶ histrionic, thespian (*having to do with actors or drama*); cast (*list of actors in a play or film*), ham (*a bad actor*).

aircraft ▶ aileron, flaps, fuselage, rudder, spoiler, stabilizer, tailplane, undercarriage (*parts of aircraft*); jet, piston engine, ramjet, turbofan, turbojet (*kinds of aircraft engine*); aerodynamics, aeronautics (*science of aircraft flight*), aviation (*business of operating aircraft*), avionics (*aircraft electronics*).

alcohol ▶ teetotalism, temperance (*refusal to drink alcohol*), alcoholism, dipsomania (*addiction to alcohol*), Dutch courage (*confidence gained from drinking alcohol*).

alloy ▶ *some common alloys:* amalgam (*mercury with other metals*), brass (*copper and zinc*), bronze (*copper and tin*), pewter (*tin with copper and antimony*), solder (*usually lead and tin*), steel (*iron with carbon and other metals*).

angle ▶ acute (*less than 90°*), obtuse (*more than 90° and less than 180°*), reflex (*more than 180°*), right angle (*exactly 90°*); trigonometry (*branch of mathematics concerned with angles*).

animal ▶ fauna (*animals of a particular region*), invertebrates (*animals without backbones*), vertebrates (*animals with backbones*), zoology (*scientific study of animals*).

Arab ▶ Bedouin (*an Arab nomad living in the desert*), sheikh (*the leader of an Arab tribe, family, or village*), souk (*an Arab market*).

architecture ▶ *some architectural styles:* baroque, classical, Gothic, neoclassical, Palladian, rococo, Romanesque.

art ▶ *some art schools and styles:* art deco, art nouveau, baroque, classicism, cubism, Dada, expressionism, Fauvism, Impressionism, Mannerism, Pre-Raphaelitism, surrealism.

astrology ▶ cusp (*initial point of an astrological sign*), horoscope (*forecast of a person's future based on the position of the stars and planets*), sign (*each of the twelve divisions of the zodiac*), zodiac (*belt of the heavens including all the apparent positions of the sun, moon, and planets*).

atmosphere ▶ *layers of the earth's atmosphere (from lowest to highest):* troposphere, stratosphere, mesosphere, thermosphere, ionosphere.

back ▶ dorsal (*on the back or upper side*), lumbar (*relating to the lower back*), posterior (*further back in position*), supine (*lying on one's back*); lumbago (*back pain*).

bacteria ▶ bacillus (*rod-shaped bacterium*), coccus (*rounded bacterium*), sepsis, septicaemia (*presence of bacteria in tissues or blood*); *kinds of bacteria:* E. coli, legionella, listeria, meningococcus, pneumococcus, salmonella, staphylococcus, streptococcus.

bagpipes ▶ chanter (*pipe on which the melody is played*), drone (*pipe sounding a continuous low note*), pibroch (*elaborate Scottish music for bagpipes*), skirl (*shrill sound of bagpipes*), uillean pipes (*Irish bagpipes played using bellows worked by the elbow*).

ballet ▶ arabesque, entrechat, jeté, pirouette, plié (*ballet steps and movements*); barre (*bar used during exercises*), choreography (*design of dance movements*), pas de deux (*dance for two*), pointe (*tips of the toes*), tutu (*ballet dancer's dress*).

bankrupt ▶ insolvent (*relating to bankruptcy*), receiver (*official managing bankrupt business*), sequestrate (*take possession of property of bankrupt person*).

barrel ▶ cooper (*maker of barrels*), hogshead, keg, tun (*kinds of barrel*), hoop (*metal band around a barrel*), spigot (*plug for a barrel vent*), stave (*plank from which barrels are made*).

bear ▶ ursine (*of or like a bear*); grizzly bear, polar bear (*kinds of bear*); Ursa Major (*constellation, the Great Bear*), Ursa Minor (*constellation, the Little Bear*).

bee ▶ ambrosia (*bee bread*), apiary (*place where bees are kept*), apiculture (*keeping of bees*), drone (*male bee*), royal jelly (*food for queen bee larvae*).

beetle ▶ *some common beetles:* Colorado beetle, death-watch beetle, ladybird, scarab, weevil.

bell ▶ belfry (*place in a bell tower where bells are kept*), campanile (*a bell tower*), campanology (*art of bell-ringing*), knell (*sound of a bell, especially at a funeral*), peal (*ringing of bells, or set of bells*); tocsin (*alarm bell*).

biology ▶ cytology (*biology of cells*), ecology (*study of interrelations of organisms*), morphology (*study of forms of organisms*), physiology (*study of normal functions of organisms*), taxonomy (*classification of living organisms*).

bird ▶ avian (*having to do with birds*), aviary (*place where birds are kept*), oology (*study of birds' eggs*), ornithology (*study of birds*).

birth ▶ antenatal (*before birth*), Caesarean section (*operation to deliver child*), congenital (*present from birth*), natal (*having to do with the place and time of birth*), neonate (*newborn child*), obstetrics (*branch of medicine concerned with childbirth*), perinatal (*near to the time of birth*), postpartum (*following birth*).

blood ▶ *components of blood:* corpuscle, haemoglobin, plasma, platelet, rhesus factor, serum.

blue ▶ *shades of blue:* azure, cerulean, cobalt, cyan, indigo, lavender, navy, sapphire, saxe, teal, turquoise, ultramarine.

body ▶ corporal, corporeal, somatic (*having to do with the body*); metabolism (*the body's chemical processes*), posture (*a body position*).

bone ▶ marrow (*soft substance in the hollow of bones*), orthopaedics (*branch of medicine concerned with bone deformities*), osteoporosis (*brittleness of the bones*), osteoarthritis (*degeneration of joint cartilage*).

book ▶ appendix (*information at the end of a book*), bibliography (*list of books*), bibliophile (*collector or lover of books*), incunabulum (*early printed book*); recto (*right-hand page of an open book*), verso (*left-hand page of an open book*).

brass ▶ *brass musical instruments:* bugle, cornet, euphonium, flugelhorn, French horn, horn, sousaphone, trombone, trumpet, tuba.

bridge ▶ aqueduct (*bridge carrying water*), drawbridge (*bridge that can be raised*), humpback bridge (*small road bridge with a steep curve*), span (*part of a bridge between supports*), suspension bridge (*bridge suspended from cables*).

brother ▶ confraternity (*a brotherhood*), fraternal (*of or like a brother*), fratricide (*murder of one's own brother or sister*), sibling (*brother or sister*).

brown ▶ *shades of brown:* auburn, bronze, chestnut, chocolate, copper, dun, fawn, hazel, mahogany, sepia, tan, tawny, umber.

butterfly ▶ caterpillar (*butterfly larva*), chrysalis (*butterfly pupa*), lepidopteran (*having to do with butterflies and moths*), metamorphosis (*transformation of butterfly larva to adult*).

camp ▶ billy (*cooking pot used when camping*), bivouac (*temporary camp without tents*), canteen (*small water bottle used when camping*), latrine (*communal toilet in a camp*).

cancer ▶ *types of cancer:* carcinoma, lymphoma, melanoma; *treatments for cancer:* chemotherapy, radiotherapy; carcinogen (*substance causing cancer*); oncology (*branch of medicine concerned with cancer*).

candle ▶ candelabrum (*branched candlestick*), chandelier (*hanging light with branches for several candles*), menorah (*Jewish branched candlestick*), sconce (*ornamental candle holder on wall*).

castle ▶ *parts of a castle:* bailey, barbican, battlement, curtain wall, drawbridge, dungeon, keep, machicolation, moat, portcullis, rampart, turret.

cat ▶ feline (*of or like a cat or cats*); ailurophobia (*fear of cats*); *wild cats:* bobcat, cheetah, cougar, jaguar, leopard, lion, lynx, ocelot, panther, puma, tiger, wildcat.

cave ▶ grotto (*small picturesque cave*), potholer (*explorer of caves*), stalactite, stalagmite (*rock formations within cave*), speleology (*study or exploration of caves*), troglodyte (*cave-dweller*).

cell ▶ *kinds of cell:* erythrocyte (*red blood cell*), gamete (*sex cell*), leucocyte (*white blood cell*), neuron (*nerve cell*), zygote (*cell formed by fusion of gametes*); meiosis, mitosis (*division of cells*).

chemistry ▶ *branches of chemistry:* organic (*of carbon compounds*), inorganic (*of other substances*), physical (*application of physics to chemistry*); biochemistry (*of life*); alchemy (*medieval chemistry*).

child ▶ crèche (*a nursery*), infanticide (*murder of a child*), orphan (*child whose parents are dead*), paediatrics (*branch of medicine concerned with childhood diseases*).

Chinese ▶ *Chinese life and culture:* feng shui (*ancient Chinese system of designing and arranging buildings and objects*), kung fu, t'ai chi chuan (*Chinese martial arts*), mandarin (*official form of the Chinese language*), sinology (*study of Chinese language and culture*).

Christianity ▶ *dates in the Christian calendar:* Advent, Ascension, Christmas, Easter, Epiphany, Lent, Pentecost, Whit Sunday.

church ▶ *parts of a church:* aisle, apse, chancel, clerestory, crypt, nave, spire, steeple, transept, vestry.

circle ▶ *parts of a circle:* arc, chord, circumference, diameter, radius, segment.

city ▶ civic, urban (*having to do with a city*); citadel (*fortress protecting a city*), mayor (*elected head of a city*), metropolis (*main city of a region*), suburb (*district of private housing on outskirts of a city*).

coal ▶ anthracite, lignite (*kinds of coal*); Carboniferous (*geological period when many coal deposits were laid down*), coke (*fuel made by heating coal in the absence of air*), colliery (*coal mine*).

coast ▶ littoral (*relating to the coast or shore*); corniche (*road running along a coast*), harbour (*place on coast where ships may moor*), riviera (*coastal region with subtropical climate*).

code ▶ cipher (*simple kind of code*), cryptogram (*a text written in code*), cryptography (*art of writing or solving codes*), decipher, decrypt (*convert code into normal language*), encipher, encrypt (*convert normal language into code*).

coffin ▶ bier (*movable platform supporting a coffin*), catafalque (*wooden framework supporting a coffin*), hearse (*vehicle carrying a coffin*), pall (*cloth spread over a coffin*), sarcophagus (*stone coffin*).

coin ▶ numismatics (*study or collection of coins*), obverse (*side of coin bearing head or main design*), reverse (*secondary side of coin*), mint (*place where money is coined*).

collector ▶ *collectors and the objects they collect:* antiquarian (*ancient objects*), bibliophile (*books*), deltiologist (*postcards*), lepidopterist (*butterflies and moths*), numismatist (*coins*), philatelist (*stamps*).

comedy ▶ *kinds of comedy:* burlesque, farce, satire, slapstick, stand-up, vaudeville.

computer ▶ *kinds of computer:* desktop, laptop, mainframe, notebook, palmtop, word processor, workstation; *parts of a computer:* disk drive, hard disk, hardware, keyboard, monitor, mouse, software, VDU.

country ▶ *having to do with the country or the countryside:* bucolic, pastoral, rural, rustic.

craftsman ▶ *craftsmen and their products:* carpenter (*wooden objects*), cooper (*barrels*), cutler (*cutlery*), milliner (*hats*), potter (*ceramic ware*).

cross ▶ *types of cross:* crucifix, St George's cross, saltire, swastika; cruciform (*cross-shaped*).

cup ▶ chalice (*cup used for the Eucharist*), Grail (*cup used by Christ at the Last Supper*).

curve ▶ concave (*curving inwards*), convex (*curving outwards*); arc (*curve forming part of circumference of a circle*).

dance ▶ *some dances:* cancan, cha-cha, charleston, foxtrot, mambo, polka, rumba, salsa, tango, waltz; terpsichorean (*having to do with dancing*).

death ▶ autopsy, post-mortem (*examinations of a corpse to discover cause of death*), in extremis (*at the point of death*), inquest (*inquiry into the cause of a death*), memento mori (*object kept as a reminder of death*), rigor mortis (*stiffening of joints and muscles after death*), thanatology (*scientific study of death*).

devil ▶ diabolical (*of or like the Devil*); *names for the Devil:* Beelzebub, Lucifer, Old Nick, Satan.

dictionary ▶ gazetteer (*geographical dictionary*), lexicographer (*person who compiles dictionaries*), thesaurus (*book of synonyms*).

disease ▶ aetiology (*study of the causes of disease*), communicable, infectious (*referring to a disease which can be passed to others*), contagious (*referring to a disease spread by contact*), epidemic (*widespread occurrence of a disease*), epidemiology (*study of the spread of disease*), pathogen (*micro-organism that can cause disease*), pathology (*branch of medicine concerned with diseases*).

doctor ▶ *doctors and their specialties:* cardiologist (*disorders of the heart*), dermatologist (*disorders of the skin*), gynaecologist (*female reproductive system*), obstetrician (*childbirth*), oncology (*tumours*), ophthalmologist (*disorders of the eye*), paediatrician (*childhood disorders*), pathologist (*causes and effects of diseases*).

document ▶ archive (*collection of historical documents*), manuscript (*handwritten document*), pro forma (*standard document*), recto (*front of a loose document*), rubric (*heading on a document*), verso (*back of a loose document*).

dog ▶ canine (*of or like a dog or dogs*); *members of the dog family:* coyote, dingo, fox, jackal, wolf.

ear ▶ auditory (*having to do with hearing*), aural, otic (*having to do with the ear*), otology (*study of the ear*), tinnitus (*ringing in the ears*); *some parts of the ear:* auricle or pinna, cochlea, eardrum or tympanum.

earth ▶ circumnavigate (*travel around the earth*), geography (*study of physical features of the earth*), geology (*science of physical structure and substance of the earth*), terrestrial (*having to do with the earth*).

earthquake ▶ aftershock (*smaller earthquake following*

larger one), epicentre (*point on surface directly above focus*), focus (*point of origin of earthquake*), Richter scale (*measuring earthquake intensity*), seismic (*having to do with earthquakes*), seismograph, seismometer (*instruments for detecting or measuring earthquakes*), tsunami (*sea wave caused by earthquake*).

egg ▶ albumen (*egg white*), clutch (*set of eggs laid together*), incubate (*keep eggs warm for hatching*), ovate, oviform, ovoid (*egg-shaped*), oviparous (*egg-laying*), roe (*fish eggs*), spawn (*fish or amphibian eggs*).

eight ▶ octagon (*plane figure with eight straight sides and eight angles*), octahedron (*three-dimensional shape with eight faces*), octave (*series of eight musical notes between [and including] two notes*), octet (*group of eight musicians*).

election ▶ candidate (*person put forward for election*), canvass (*visit someone to seek their vote in an election*), hustings (*public political meetings before an election*), psephology (*statistical study of elections and voting*), suffrage (*the right to vote in political elections*).

element ▶ allotrope (*different form of a chemical element*), atom (*smallest particle of an element*), compound (*substance formed from two or more elements*), isotope (*form of the same element having different atomic mass*), periodic table (*table of the chemical elements*), valency (*combining power of an element*).

environment ▶ conservationist (*person dedicated to protecting the environment*), eco-friendly (*not harmful to the environment*), ecology (*study of organisms' relationships with each other and with the environment*), habitat (*natural environment of an organism*).

eye ▶ ocular (*having to do with the eye*); ophthalmologist (*specialist in eye diseases*), ophthalmoscope (*instrument for inspecting eyes*); *parts of the eye:* conjunctiva, cornea, iris, pupil, retina; *eye defects or diseases:* astigmatism, cataract, conjunctivitis, glaucoma, myopia (*short-sightedness*), ophthalmia.

feather ▶ down (*soft, fine feathers*), pinnate (*shaped like a feather*), plumage (*bird's feathers*), plume (*long, soft feather or arrangement of feathers*), preen (*of a bird: clean its feathers with its beak*); quill (*bird's main wing or tail feather*).

fetus ▶ amniocentesis (*procedure to check for abnormalities in the fetus*), amniotic fluid (*fluid surrounding a fetus*), caul (*membrane enclosing a fetus*), fetal (*relating to a fetus*), placenta (*organ that nourishes the fetus*), umbilical cord (*cord attaching the fetus to the placenta*).

figure ▶ *plane figures:* triangle (*three sides*), quadrilateral (*four sides*), pentagon (*five sides*), hexagon (*six sides*), heptagon (*seven sides*), octagon (*eight sides*), nonagon (*nine sides*), decagon (*ten sides*).

fire ▶ arson (*act of deliberately setting fire to property*); combustible, flammable, inflammable (*able to catch fire easily*); ember (*piece of burning wood or coal in a dying fire*), ignite (*catch fire or set on fire*).

five ▶ pentagon (*plane figure with five straight sides and five angles*), pentathlon (*athletic event made up of five different events*), quintet (*group of five musicians*), quintuplet (*each of five children born at one birth*).

flower ▶ *parts of a flower:* anther, bract, calyx, carpel, corolla, pistil, sepal, stamen, stigma, style.

foot ▶ chiropody, podiatry (*medical treatment of the feet*); athlete's foot (*ringworm infection of the feet*), corn (*painful area of thickened skin on the toes or foot*), metatarsus (*bones of the foot*), pedicure (*cosmetic treatment of the feet*), verruca (*wart on the sole of the foot*).

four ▶ quadrilateral (*four-sided figure*), quadruped (*animal with four feet*), quadruplet (*each of four children born at one birth*), quartet (*group or set of four; group of four musicians*).

fraction ▶ decimal fraction (*fraction with numbers either side of a decimal point*), denominator (*number below the line in a vulgar fraction*), numerator (*number above the line in a vulgar fraction*), vulgar fraction (*fraction expressed by numerator and denominator, not decimally*).

funeral ▶ cortège (*funeral procession*), hearse (*vehicle for conveying the coffin*), inter (*place a corpse in a grave or tomb*), obsequies (*funeral rites*), pall (*cloth spread over a coffin, hearse, or tomb*), wake (*party held after a funeral*).

gene ▶ allele (*one of two or more different forms of the same gene*), chromosome (*thread-like structure in a cell carrying genetic information*), clone (*genetically identical individual*), dominant (*gene expressed in offspring when inherited from only one parent*), Mendelism (*theory of heredity based on genes*), recessive (*gene expressed in offspring only when inherited from both parents*).

God ▶ atheism (*belief that God does not exist*), agnosticism (*belief that one cannot know whether or not God exists*), blasphemy (*irreverent talk about God*), divine (*having to do with God or a god*), pantheon (*all the gods of a people or religion*), polytheism (*belief in more than one god*).

gold ▶ bullion (*gold or silver in bulk before coining*), carat (*measure of purity for gold*), gild (*cover with gold*), Midas touch (*power of turning everything into gold*), nugget (*small lump of gold found in the earth*).

green ▶ *shades of green:* aquamarine, emerald, jade, lime, olive; chlorophyll (*green pigment in leaves*), patina, verdigris (*green sheen or film*), verdure (*lush green vegetation*).

hair ▶ alopecia (*abnormal hair loss*), depilate (*remove hair*), follicle (*sheath surrounding the root of a hair*), hirsute (*hairy*), toupee (*small wig worn to cover a bald spot*), trichology (*branch of medicine concerned with the hair and scalp*).

hand ▶ ambidextrous (*able to use right or left hands equally well*), dexterity (*skill with the hands*), manicure (*cosmetic treatment of the hands*), manual (*involving the hands*), metacarpus (*bones of the hand*).

health ▶ convalesce (*gradually recover one's health after illness*), hypochondriac (*person abnormally anxious about their health*), salubrious (*health-giving or healthy*), sanitary (*having to do with conditions affecting health*), valetudinarian (*person in poor health or overly concerned about their health*).

heart ▶ cardiac (*having to do with the heart*), cardiology (*branch of medicine concerned with the heart*), coronary (*having to do with the arteries that supply the heart*), pacemaker (*artificial device for regulating the heart muscle*); *parts of the heart:* aorta, atrium, mitral valve, vena cava, ventricle.

heartbeat ▶ arrhythmia (*irregular heartbeat*), bradycardia, (*abnormally slow heartbeat*), diastole (*phase when the heart muscle relaxes*), palpitation (*rapid, strong, or irregular heartbeat*), systole (*phase when the heart muscle contracts*), tachycardia (*abnormally rapid heart rate*).

heat ▶ *methods of transmitting heat:* conduction, convection, radiation; diathermy (*medical and surgical use of heat*), therm (*unit of heat*), thermal (*relating to heat*), thermodynamics (*science of heat and other forms of energy*).

Hinduism ▶ ashram (*Hindu religious retreat*), caste (*each of the hereditary classes of Hindu society*), guru (*Hindu spiritual teacher*), mahatma (*wise or holy Hindu teacher*).

horse ▶ equine (*of or like a horse or horses*); colt (*young uncastrated male horse*), foal (*young horse*), filly (*young female horse*), gelding (*castrated male horse*), mare (*female horse*), stallion (*uncastrated adult male horse*).

idea ▶ abstract (*having to do with ideas rather than objects*), ideology (*system of ideas*), plagiarism (*stealing someone else's idea*), sacred cow (*idea held to be above criticism*), stereotype (*widely held fixed idea of something*).

illusion ▶ hallucination (*illusion experienced as real*), mirage (*optical illusion caused by atmospheric conditions*), special effects (*illusions created for film and television*), trompe l'œil (*method of painting which creates an illusion*).

image ▶ definition (*degree of sharpness of an image*), graphic (*image on a computer screen*), hologram (*three-dimensional image*), iconography (*use or study of images*).

imitation ▶ burlesque (*comically exaggerated imitation*), ersatz (*referring to an inferior imitation of something*), parody (*mocking imitation*), pastiche (*imitation of artistic style*).

inherit ▶ disinherit (*prevent from inheriting*), heirloom (*valuable inherited article*), hereditary (*gained by inheritance*), legacy (*inherited amount of money or property*), primogeniture (*eldest son's right of inheritance*).

Indian ▶ *Indian life and culture:* monsoon (*seasonal wind and accompanying rainy season*), Raj (*period of British rule in India*), sitar (*large Indian lute*), tandoor (*clay oven*); *Indian languages:* Sanskrit (*ancient language of India*), Bengali, Gujarati, Hindi, Hindustani, Marathi, Tamil, Urdu.

injection ▶ ampoule (*glass capsule of liquid for injecting*), hypodermic (*referring to injection beneath the skin*), intravenous (*referring to injection into a vein*), syringe (*instrument for making injections*).

Internet ▶ bulletin board, chat room, newsgroup (*Internet forums for exchange of views or information*), dot-com (*company that conducts its business on the Internet*), e-commerce (*commerce conducted over the Internet*), home page (*web page introducing an Internet site*), portal (*Internet site providing directory of links to other sites*), surf (*browse the Internet*), webcam (*video camera connected to the Internet*), webcast (*a broadcast over the Internet*).

Irish ▶ *Irish life and culture:* Dail (*lower House of Parliament in the Irish Republic*), Hibernian (*relating to Ireland*), hurling (*game resembling hockey*), shamrock (*national emblem of Ireland*), Taoiseach (*Prime Minister of the Irish Republic*).

Islam ▶ ayatollah (*Shiite religious leader*), hajj (*pilgrimage to Mecca*), imam (*leader of prayers in a mosque*), jihad (*holy war undertaken by Muslims*), mosque (*Muslim place of worship*), minaret (*slender tower of a mosque*), muezzin (*man who calls Muslims to prayer*), Ramadan (*month of fasting*), Shia, Sunni (*main branches of Islam*).

island ▶ archipelago (*large group of islands*), atoll (*ring-shaped chain of islands*), insular (*relating to an island*), key (*low-lying island*).

Japanese ▶ *Japanese life and culture:* bonsai (*art of growing miniature trees*), futon (*padded mattress*), geisha (*hostess*), haiku (*poem of 17 syllables*), kabuki (*drama performed by men*), kimono (*loose robe*), manga (*fantasy cartoons and animation*), Noh (*traditional masked drama*), Shinto (*religion of spirit worship*), sumo (*wrestling*).

joint ▶ arthritis (*inflammation and stiffness of a joint of the body*), articulation (*the state of being jointed*), chiropractic (*manipulative treatment of joints*), dislocation (*injury in which a joint is disturbed*).

Judaism ▶ cantor (*person who leads prayers in a synagogue*), kosher (*referring to food prepared in accordance with Jewish law*), rabbi (*Jewish scholar, teacher, or religious leader*), synagogue (*building used for Jewish worship*).

kill ▶ euthanasia (*mercy killing*), genocide (*killing of a whole people*), homicide (*killing of another person*), manslaughter (*unintentional killing*), suicide (*killing of oneself*).

knight ▶ charger (*horse ridden by a knight*), chivalry (*medieval knights' code*), dub (*make someone a knight by touching their shoulder with a sword*), joust (*knights' mock combat*), quest (*a knight's expedition*).

know ▶ erudite (*knowing a great deal*), gnostic (*having to do with knowledge, especially mystical knowledge*), omniscient (*knowing everything*), philosophy (*study of nature of knowledge*), prescient (*knowing something in advance*).

language ▶ linguist (*person who studies language or languages*), monolingual (*speaking or expressed in only one language*), multilingual (*in or using several languages*), polyglot (*person who knows several languages*), vernacular (*language spoken by ordinary people*).

leaf ▶ deciduous (*referring to trees that shed leaves annually*), evergreen (*referring to trees that retain green leaves throughout the year*), frond (*leaf of a palm or fern*), vein (*slender rib running through a leaf*).

learning ▶ erudite (*having or showing learning*), polymath (*person of wide-ranging learning*), rote (*learning by mechanical repetition*).

light ▶ chiaroscuro (*treatment of light and shade in drawing and painting*); opaque (*not allowing light through*), translucent (*allowing light to pass through partially*), transparent (*allowing light to pass through so that objects behind can be clearly seen*).

lung ▶ pulmonary (*having to do with the lungs*); alveoli (*tiny air sacs in the lungs*), bronchi (*air passages of the lungs*), pleura (*membranes enclosing the lungs*), pneumonia (*lung infection in which pus collects in the lungs*).

magic ▶ amulet, talisman (*objects thought to have magical powers*); elixir (*magic potion*), incantation (*words said as a magic spell*), necromancy (*black magic*), numerology (*magical power of numbers*).

-mania ▶ dipsomania (*alcoholism*), egomania (*obsessive self-centredness*), kleptomania (*uncontrollable need to steal*), megalomania (*obsession with power*), monomania (*obsession with one thing*), nymphomania (*uncontrollable sexual desire in a woman*), pyromania (*obsession with setting things on fire*).

map ▶ cartography (*science of map-making*), Ordnance Survey (*official UK map-making organization*), projection (*way of representing the earth's surface on a map*), relief map (*map showing contours by shading*).

marriage ▶ banns (*announcement in church of intended marriage*), dowry (*money or property brought by bride on her marriage*), maiden name (*surname of woman before her marriage*), spouse (*husband or wife*); monogamy (*practice of having only one spouse at at a time*), bigamy (*crime of having more than one spouse at one time*), polygamy (*custom of having several spouses at one time*).

mathematics ▶ *branches of mathematics:* algebra, arithmetic, calculus, geometry, group theory, mechanics, number theory, statistics, trigonometry.

meaning ▶ antonym (*word which is opposite in meaning*), nuance (*slight difference in meaning*), synonym (*word which is the same in meaning*), semantics (*study of meaning*).

memory ▶ amnesia (*loss of memory*), flashback (*sudden vivid memory of past event*), keepsake (*small item kept in memory of person who gave or owned it*), memento (*item kept as a reminder*), mnemonic (*aid to memory*).

military ▶ court martial (*military court*), martial law (*government by the military forces of a country*), reconnaissance (*military observation of a region*), strategy (*long-term military plans*), tactics (*short-term military plans*).

missile ▶ ballistic missile (*guided missile falling on to its target by gravity*), cruise missile (*flying bomb guided by an on-board computer*), heat-seeking missile (*able to home in on heat emitted by target*), silo (*underground launcher for missile*), torpedo (*underwater missile*).

moisture ▶ dehydrated, desiccated (*lacking moisture*), hygroscopic (*tending to absorb moisture*), humidity (*amount of moisture in the air*), saturated (*full of moisture*).

monastery ▶ abbot (*head of a monastery*), chapter (*monastery's governing body*), cloister (*covered walk*), refectory (*dining hall*).

monk ▶ cowl (*monk's hood*), habit (*monk's robe*), novice, postulant (*beginner monk*), scapular (*monk's short cloak*), tonsure (*shaven part of monk's head*).

motion ▶ inertia (*tendency to remain in motion or motionless*), kinetic (*having to do with motion*); impetus, momentum (*energy associated with motion*).

mountain ▶ alpine (*having to do with high mountains*); arête (*sharp mountain ridge*), col (*high mountain pass*), peak (*pointed top of a mountain*), sierra (*long mountain chain*), summit (*highest point of a mountain*), tarn (*mountain lake*).

mouth ▶ oral, buccal (*having to do with the mouth*); epiglottis (*flap at the back of the mouth*), palate (*roof of the mouth*), saliva (*watery liquid produced in the mouth*), tonsil (*mass of tissue at the back of the mouth*), uvula (*fleshy part at the back of the mouth*).

music ▶ *some musical forms:* concerto, fantasia, fugue, march, opera, operetta, oratorio, prelude, rhapsody, requiem, sonata, song, symphony.

musician ▶ ensemble (*group of musicians performing together*), minstrel (*medieval musician*); maestro, virtuoso (*distinguished musician*).

name ▶ alias (*false name or identity*), anonymous (*not identified by name*), nom de plume (*pen name*), nomenclature (*body or system of names*), onomastics (*study of proper names*), pen name (*literary pseudonym*), pseudonym (*fictitious name*), toponym (*place name*).

newspaper ▶ article (*piece of writing in a newspaper*), broadsheet (*newspaper with a large format*), editorial (*newspaper article written by its editorial team, giving an opinion on an issue*), tabloid (*newspaper with pages half the size of a broadsheet, popular in style*).

number ▶ cardinal number (*number denoting quantity, e.g. five*), ordinal number (*number defining position in a series, e.g. fifth*), prime number (*number divisible only by itself and 1*), root (*number that when multiplied by itself gives a specified number*), square (*product of a number multiplied by itself*).

nun ▶ coif (*close-fitting cap worn under nun's veil*), convent (*community of nuns*), nunnery (*religious house of nuns*), wimple (*nun's headdress*).

oath ▶ affidavit (*statement confirmed by oath*), depose (*give evidence on oath*), perjury (*offence of lying in court under oath*).

office ▶ depose (*remove from office forcefully*), impeach (*charge holder of public office with misconduct*), inaugurate (*admit formally to office*), incumbency (*period during which someone holds an office*), tenure (*holding of an office*).

old ▶ antiquarian (*person who collects or studies old things*), dotage (*period of life when one is old and weak*), geriatric (*relating to old people*), senile (*mentally weakened through age*).

opera ▶ aria (*song for a soloist in an opera*), diva (*celebrated female opera singer*), libretto (*words of an opera*), prima donna (*chief female singer in an opera company*).

operation ▶ *some operations:* amputation (*cutting off of a limb*), angioplasty (*to repair or unblock a blood vessel*), Caesarean section (*delivery of a child by cutting through the mother's abdomen*), hysterectomy (*removal of all or part of the womb*), mastectomy (*removal of a breast*), tonsillectomy (*removal of the tonsils*).

page ▶ centrefold (*the two middle pages of a magazine*), flyleaf (*blank page at the start or end of a book*), footer (*line of text appearing at the bottom of each page of a document*), footnote (*piece of extra information printed at the bottom of a page*), header (*text printed at the top of each page of a document*), paginate (*number the pages of a book*).

pain ▶ anaesthetic (*drug making one unable to feel pain*), analgesic (*medicine relieving pain*), masochist (*person who enjoys experiencing pain*), neuralgia (*intense pain along a nerve*), sadist (*person who enjoys inflicting pain*).

parliament ▶ act (*law passed by parliament*), backbencher (*member of parliament who does not hold a government or opposition post*), bicameral (*referring to a parliament with two chambers*), bill (*draft of a proposed law presented to parliament*), Hansard (*record of UK parliamentary debates*), hung parliament (*with no party having a majority*), prorogue (*discontinue a session of parliament*).

people ▶ demotic, plebeian (*having to do with ordinary people*), hoi polloi, (*a derogatory term for common people*), proletariat (*working-class people*), vernacular (*language spoken by ordinary people*).

percussion ▶ *percussion instruments:* bells, castanets, cymbals, drum, glockenspiel, gong, Jew's harp, maracas, piano, tambourine, vibraphone, xylophone.

philosophy ▶ determinism (*belief that events are determined by external forces acting on the will*), dialectic (*philosophical debate*), empiricism (*theory that all knowledge is derived from experience*), epistemology (*philosophy of knowledge*), ethics (*philosophy of morals*), metaphysics (*philosophical study of abstract concepts*), ontology (*philosophy concerned with the nature of being*).

phobia ▶ *examples of phobias:* acrophobia (*heights*), agoraphobia (*open or public places*), arachnophobia (*spiders*), claustrophobia (*confined places*), homophobia (*homosexuals*), hydrophobia (*water*), necrophobia (*the dead*), neophobia (*the new*), nyctophobia (*night or darkness*), technophobia (*new technology*), xenophobia (*foreigners or strangers*).

photograph ▶ daguerreotype (*early kind of photograph*), darkroom (*room for developing photographs*), paparazzi (*photographers who try to photograph celebrities*), slide (*small piece of film set in a frame, viewed with a projector*), transparency (*photograph printed on plastic or glass, viewed with a projector*).

plant ▶ botany (*study of plants*), chlorophyll (*green pigment of plants*), flora (*plants of a region*), herbivorous (*feeding on plants*), transpiration (*loss of water vapour from the leaves of a plant*); annual (*plant living one year*), biennial (*two years*), perennial (*three or more years*).

play ▶ denouement (*final part of a play in which all is resolved*), dialogue (*conversation between people in a play*), dramatize (*turn something into a play*), epilogue (*address to the audience at the end of a play*), prologue (*address to the audience at the start of a play*), soliloquy (*speech in which a character speaks their thoughts aloud*); comedy, farce, melodrama, pantomime, tragedy (*types of play*).

poem ▶ blank verse (*unrhymed poetry*), metre (*rhythmic pattern of a poem*), prosody (*study of forms and rhythms of poetry*), stanza (*group of lines forming basic unit of a poem*); *forms of poem:* ballad, elegy, epic, haiku, limerick, lyric, ode, sonnet; anthology (*collection of poems*).

poison ▶ antidote (*medicine which works against a poison*), toxicology (*science of poisons*), toxin (*poison produced by a micro-organism*), venom (*snake poison*).

poll ▶ plebiscite, referendum (*public polls on a particular issue*); straw poll (*unofficial ballot to test opinion*).

pope ▶ papal, pontifical (*having to do with popes*); bull (*papal edict*), encyclical (*letter from the pope to all Catholic bishops*), papacy (*the position or role of the pope*), Vatican (*official residence of the pope*).

population ▶ census (*official survey of a population*), demography (*study of human populations*), overspill (*part of the population moving from an overcrowded place to live elsewhere*).

power ▶ carte blanche (*power to do whatever one wishes*), megalomaniac (*person obsessed with exercising power*), omnipotence (*unlimited power*), usurp (*seize power unlawfully*).

praise ▶ encomium, eulogy, panegyric (*speeches or texts praising someone*); laudatory (*expressing praise*).

prayer ▶ amen (*said at the end of a prayer*), Ave Maria (or Hail Mary) (*Roman Catholic prayer to the Virgin Mary*), collect (*short prayer*), intercession (*prayer said for others*), paternoster (*the Lord's Prayer, said in Latin*), rosary (*Roman Catholic prayer of repeated Hail Marys, or beads used in this*).

preach ▶ evangelism (*preaching of the Christian gospel*), lay reader (*lay person allowed to preach and conduct some services in the Anglican Church*), pulpit (*platform for preaching*).

pregnancy ▶ abortion (*deliberate bringing to an end of a pregnancy*), conceive (*become pregnant*), ectopic (*involving growth of the fetus outside the womb*), in vitro (*referring to conception achieved outside the body*); miscarriage (*birth of a fetus before it can survive independently*); progesterone (*hormone stimulating the uterus to prepare for pregnancy*).

pressure ▶ barometer (*device to measure pressure*), isobar (*line of equal pressure on a weather map*), pneumatic (*operated by air or gas under pressure*).

priest ▶ clerical (*having to do with priests*), neophyte (*newly ordained priest*), ordain (*make someone a priest*), presbytery (*house of a Roman Catholic parish priest*), seminary (*college for priests*).

printing ▶ compositor, typesetter (*person who arranges type for printing*); font (*set of type of a particular design*), impression (*copies of a book printed at one time*), justification (*spacing of words to fill width of page or column*), typography (*art of printing from types*).

prison ▶ custodial (*having to do with prisons and imprisonment*), incarcerate (*lock someone up in prison*), parole (*release of a prisoner on promise of good behaviour*), penology (*the study of prison management*), remission (*reduction of a prison sentence*).

protein ▶ albumin (*blood protein*), amino acids (*compounds which are building blocks of proteins*), casein (*milk protein*), gluten (*cereal protein*).

punishment ▶ penal (*having to do with punishment*), punitive (*intended as punishment*); impunity (*freedom from being punished*), nemesis (*unavoidable punishment*).

rabbit ▶ buck (*male rabbit*), doe (*female rabbit*), hutch (*box for housing rabbits*), kitten (*young rabbit*), myxomatosis (*disease of rabbits*), scut (*a rabbit's short tail*), warren (*network of rabbit burrows*).

read ▶ dyslexia (*reading disorder*), illegible (*not clear enough to be read*), illiterate (*unable to read or write*), literacy (*ability to read and write*).

reason ▶ a priori (*reasoning based on theory rather than observation*), deduction (*reasoning in which a general rule is used to draw a particular conclusion*), fallacy (*mistake in reasoning*), induction (*reasoning in which a general conclusion is drawn from particular examples*), logic (*science of reasoning*).

red ▶ *shades of red:* burgundy, carmine, cerise, cherry, claret, coral, crimson, maroon, puce, ruby, scarlet, vermilion.

religion ▶ *major religions:* Baha'i, Buddhism, Christianity, Hinduism, Islam, Jainism, Judaism, Shinto, Sikhism, Zoroastrianism; denomination (*recognized branch of a church or religion*), divinity, theology (*study of religion*), fundamentalism (*strict following of the doctrines of a religion*), scripture (*sacred writings of a religion*); proselytize (*convert from one religion to another*).

rifle ▶ bayonet (*blade fixed to the muzzle of a rifle*), breech (*back part of a rifle barrel*), carbine (*light automatic rifle*).

river ▶ backwater (*stretch of stagnant water on a river*), basin (*area drained by a river*), delta (*triangular area where a river branches at its mouth*), embankment (*wall or bank built to prevent a river flooding*), estuary (*mouth of a large river*), fluvial (*having to do with a river*), tributary (*river or stream flowing into a larger river*).

rock ▶ crevice (*narrow crack in rock*), lava (*hot molten rock*), pinnacle (*high pointed piece of rock*), precipice (*tall, steep rock face*); *types of rock:* igneous, metamorphic, sedimentary.

Russian ▶ *Russian life and culture:* dacha (*holiday home in the country*), Duma (*lower chamber of parliament*), glasnost (*policy of more open government*), kremlin (*citadel*), perestroika (*reforms introduced in the former Soviet Union in the 1980s*), samovar (*decorated tea urn*), steppe (*large area of flat grassland*).

sacred ▶ blaspheme (*speak irreverently of sacred things*), consecrate (*make or declare something sacred*), desecrate (*treat something holy with violent disrespect*), sacrilege (*the treating of something sacred with great disrespect*), sanctum (*sacred place*).

saddle ▶ *parts of a saddle:* cantle, crupper, girth, pommel, stirrup.

saint ▶ beatification (*the first step towards making someone a saint*), canonize (*officially declare someone a saint*), hagiography (*the writing of the lives of saints*).

salt ▶ brackish (*referring to water that is slightly salty*), brine (*very salty water*), desalinate (*remove salt from seawater*), saline (*containing salt*).

same ▶ coeval (*having the same age or date of origin*), concurrent (*existing or happening at the same time*), contemporary (*living or occurring at the same time*), synchronous (*existing or occurring at the same time*), synonym (*word that means that same as another word*).

school ▶ alma mater (*the school that one attended*), alumnus (*former student of a school*), catchment (*area from which a school's pupils are drawn*), scholastic (*having to do with schools and education*).

Scottish ▶ *Scottish life and culture:* Caledonian (*having to do with Scotland*), clan (*group of related families*), claymore (*large sword*), haggis (*dish consisting of offal and suet or oatmeal*), Highland fling (*vigorous dance*), Hogmanay (*New Year's Eve*).

sea ▶ marine (*having to do with the sea*), maritime (*having to do with shipping or the sea*); oceanography (*scientific study of the sea*), submarine (*existing or happening under the surface of the sea*).

sediment ▶ delta (*triangular area of sediment at the mouth of a river*), lees (*sediment of wine*), moraine (*mass of rock and sediment carried down and deposited by a glacier*), silt (*fine material carried by running water and deposited as sediment*).

seed ▶ seminal (*having to do with a seed*); dicotyledon (*plant whose seeds have two seed leaves*), germinate (*of a seed: begin to grow and put out seeds*), monocotyledon (*plant whose seeds have a single seed leaf*).

sense ▶ aural (*relating to the sense of hearing*), olfactory (*relating to the sense of smell*), sensory (*relating to the senses*), tactile (*relating to the sense of touch*), visual (*relating to the sense of sight*).

sentence ▶ clause (*group of words with a subject and verb, forming a sentence or part of one*), parse (*analyse structure of a sentence*), syntax (*arrangement of words to make well-formed sentences*).

seven ▶ heptagon (*plane figure with seven straight sides and seven angles*), heptathlon (*athletic contest made up of seven separate events*), septet (*group of seven musicians*), septuple (*made up of seven parts or elements*).

sew ▶ embroidery (*art of decorative sewing*), haberdasher (*seller of sewing materials*), needlewoman, seamstress (*woman skilled at sewing*); baste, tack (*sew loosely with long stitches*).

sex ▶ aphrodisiac (*arousing sexual desire*), celibate, chaste (*abstaining from sexual relations*), libido (*sexual desire*), Platonic (*referring to non-sexual love*), post-coital (*after sexual intercourse*).

sheep ▶ fleece (*wool coat of a sheep*), ovine (*of or like a sheep*); ewe (*female sheep*), mutton (*flesh of a mature sheep used as food*), ram (*male sheep*).

shell ▶ bivalve (*mollusc with two hinged shells*), carapace (*the hard upper shell of a tortoise or related animal*), crustacean (*animal with a hard shell, such as a crab*).

ship ▶ *kinds of ship:* bulk carrier, coaster, collier, container ship, ferry, freighter, liner, reefer, tanker, warship; bow (*front end of a ship*), port (*side of a ship on the left when one is facing* *forward*), starboard (*side of a ship on the right when one is facing forward*), stern (*rearmost part of a ship*); load line, Plimsoll line (*line on ship's side showing legal limit of submersion*).

side ▶ lateral (*of or at the side*); equilateral (*having equal sides*), juxtapose (*place side by side*), polygon (*figure with many sides*).

sin ▶ absolve (*declare someone free from sin*), mortal (*referring to serious sin believed to deprive the soul of divine grace*), redeem (*save someone from sin*), venial (*referring to sin that does not deprive the soul of divine grace*).

sister ▶ sororal (*of or like a sister*), sorority (*sisterhood*), sibling (*brother or sister*).

six ▶ hexagon (*plane figure with six straight sides and six angles*), hexagram (*six-pointed star*), sextet (*group of six musicians*), sextuple (*made up of six parts or elements*), sextuplet (*each of six children born at one birth*).

ski ▶ après-ski (*social activities following a day's skiing*), nursery slopes (*gentle ski slopes for beginners*), piste (*ski slope with compacted snow*), slalom (*ski race down a winding course*).

skin ▶ cutaneous (*having to do with the skin*), dermatology (*branch of medicine concerned with the skin*), dermis, epidermis (*layers of the skin*), dermatitis, eczema (*inflammation of the skin*).

skull ▶ cranial (*relating to the skull*); cranium (*part of skull containing the brain*), fontanelle (*soft area of a baby's skull*), phrenology (*study of skull shape as supposed indicator of character*), trepan (*saw used by surgeons to make holes in the skull*).

slave ▶ servile (*like a slave*); bondage, servitude (*state of being a slave*); emancipate, enfranchise (*release someone from slavery*).

sleep ▶ dormant (*in or as if in a deep sleep*), hibernate (*of an animal: spend the winter in a state like deep sleep*), hypnotic, sedative (*causing sleep*), insomnia (*inability to sleep*), somnambulism (*sleepwalking*), somnolent, soporific (*tending to cause sleep*).

soil ▶ agronomy (*science of soil management and crop production*), humus (*organic component of soil*), loam (*soil of clay and sand containing humus*), marl (*soil consisting of clay and lime*).

song ▶ *kinds of song:* anthem, aria, ballad, calypso, carol, ditty, fado, glee, hymn, lied, lullaby, madrigal, psalm, shanty, spiritual.

speech ▶ oral (*spoken rather than written*), oratory (*public speaking*), phonetic, phonic (*having to do with speech sounds*), phonetics (*study and classification of speech sounds*).

speed ▶ Mach number (*indicating ratio of speed to the speed of sound*), supersonic (*faster than the speed of sound*), tachometer (*instrument measuring the working speed of an engine*), tempo (*speed at which a piece of music is played*).

star ▶ astral, stellar (*having to do with a star or stars*); constellation (*group of stars forming a pattern*), interstellar (*occurring or situated between stars*), magnitude (*degree of brightness of a star*), nova (*star undergoing an increase in brightness*), supernova (*exploding star*).

story ▶ allegory (*story with symbolic meaning*), fable, parable (*story illustrating moral lesson*), folklore, legend, mythology (*traditional stories in a culture*), narrator (*storyteller*), raconteur (*skilled storyteller*).

string ▶ *stringed instruments:* banjo, cello, double bass, guitar, harp, lute, lyre, mandolin, sitar, viola, violin.

sugar ▶ diabetes (*disease characterized by excess sugar in the blood and urine*), hyperglycaemia (*excess of sugar in the blood*); molasses (*thick brown liquid containing sugar*), saccharin (*artificial sugar substitute*).

sun ▶ solar (*having to do with the sun*), heliocentric (*having the sun at the centre*), heliotropism (*growth or movement towards sunlight*), zenith (*sun's highest point in the sky*).

surgery ▶ amputation (*surgical removal of a body part*), ligature (*cord used in surgery to tie an artery*), prosthetics (*surgical fitting of artificial body parts*), scalpel (*sharp knife used by a surgeon*).

swim ▶ aqualung, scuba (*swimmer's underwater breathing apparatus*), flume (*water slide at a swimming pool*), lido (*public open-air swimming pool*), natation (*technical word for swimming*).

sword ▶ fencing (*sport of fighting with blunted swords*), hilt (*sword handle*), pommel (*knob on sword's handle*), scabbard (*sheath for sword*).

tax ▶ black economy (*part of country's economy not taxed by government*), excise (*tax payable on alcohol etc.*), fiscal (*having to do with taxes*), tariff (*tax to be paid on particular class of imports and exports*), tithe (*one tenth of income formerly paid as tax to support the Church*).

temperature ▶ absolute zero (*lowest temperature theoretically possible, equivalent to -273.15°C*), Celsius, centigrade (*referring to temperature scale on which water freezes at 0°*), Fahrenheit (*referring to temperature scale on which water freezes at 32°*).

ten ▶ decade (*period of ten years*), decagon (*plane figure with ten straight sides and ten angles*), decahedron (*solid figure with ten plane faces*), Decalogue (*the Ten Commandments*), decathlon (*athletic event in which each competitor takes part in the same ten events*), decimal (*referring to a number system based on the number ten*).

theatre ▶ thespian (*having to do with the theatre*); impresario (*person who finances theatrical productions*), repertory (*performance of a theatre company's repertoire at regular intervals*); *seats in a theatre, lowest to highest:* stalls, dress circle, circle, gallery (or balcony).

theology ▶ divinity (*study of religion*), eschatology (*part of theology concerned with death, judgement, and destiny*), scholasticism (*medieval system of theology and philosophy*).

three ▶ hat-trick (*three successes of the same kind*), triathlon (*athletic contest consisting of three different events*), triennial (*lasting for or recurring every three years*), trio (*group or set of three*), triumvirate (*group of three powerful people*).

tide ▶ ebb (*movement of the tide out to sea*), flood (*rising of the tide*), neap tide (*tide when there is least difference between high and low water*), spring tide (*tide when there is the greatest difference between high and low water*).

time ▶ anachronism (*something which seems to belong to another time period*), chronological (*relating to dates and time sequences*), horology (*study and measurement of time*), synchronous (*existing or occurring at the same time*), temporal (*having to do with time*).

toe ▶ bunion (*painful swelling on the big toe*), corn (*painful area of thickened skin on the toes or foot*), hammer toe (*toe that is bent downwards*), pedicure (*cosmetic treatment of the feet and toenails*).

tomb ▶ catacomb (*underground cemetery*), cromlech, dolmen (*megalithic tombs*), epitaph (*inscription on a tomb*), inter (*place someone in a tomb*), mausoleum (*building housing a tomb or tombs*), sepulchral (*relating to tombs or burial*), sepulchre (*stone tomb or monument*).

tooth ▶ dental (*relating to teeth*), dentist (*person qualified to treat the teeth*), dentition (*arrangement or condition of the teeth*), enamel (*hard substance covering the crown of a tooth*), orthodontics (*treatment of irregularities of the teeth*), plaque, tartar (*deposits which form on the teeth*); *human teeth:* bicuspids, canines, incisors, molars, premolars, tricuspids, wisdom teeth.

touch ▶ palpable (*able to be touched or felt*), tactile (*relating to the sense of touch*), tangible (*perceptible by touch*).

tower ▶ *types of tower:* belfry, campanile, donjon, keep, minaret, steeple, turret, watchtower, ziggurat.

tree ▶ arboreal (*having to do with trees*), deciduous (*referring to trees that shed their leaves annually*), dendrochronology (*technique of dating material by means of annual growth rings in tree trunks*), evergreen (*referring to trees that retain green leaves throughout the year*), silviculture (*growing and cultivation of trees*), topiary (*art of clipping shrubs or trees into attractive shapes*).

triangle ▶ *types of triangle:* equilateral (*having sides of equal length*), isosceles (*having two sides equal*), scalene (*having all sides unequal*).

twelve ▶ dodecagon (*plane figure with twelve straight sides and twelve angles*), dodecahedron (*three-dimensional shape with twelve faces*), duodecimal (*relating to a counting system based on twelve*), gross (*twelve dozen, 144*).

twin ▶ fraternal, dizygotic (*referring to twins derived from two separate ova*); identical, monozygotic (*referring to twins derived from one ovum*); conjoined, Siamese (*referring to twins whose bodies are joined at birth*).

two ▶ biennial (*taking place every two years*), binary (*composed of or involving two things*), bisect (*divide into two parts*), dichotomy (*separation or contrast between two things*), dual (*consisting of two parts, elements, or aspects*).

unconscious ▶ coma (*state of deep unconsciousness*), comatose (*deeply unconscious*), narcosis (*drug-induced unconsciousness*), resuscitate (*revive someone from unconsciousness*).

universe ▶ astronomy (*science of stars, planets, and the universe*), cosmic (*relating to the universe*), cosmology, cosmogony (*science of the origin and development of the universe*).

university ▶ alumnus (*former student of a particular university*), campus (*university site and buildings*), don (*university teacher*), fresher (*newly arrived first-year student*), graduation (*the receiving of a degree*), matriculation (*enrolment in a university*).

valley ▶ *kinds of valley:* basin, combe, dale, dene, dingle, glen, gorge, strath, wadi.

verse ▶ blank verse (*verse without rhyme*), couplet (*pair of successive lines of verse*), doggerel (*badly written verse*), scansion (*rhythm of a line of verse*).

vitamin ▶ *the main vitamins:* retinol (*vitamin A*), thiamine (*vitamin B_1*), riboflavin (*vitamin B_2*), pyridoxine (*vitamin B_6*), cyanocobalamin (*vitamin B_{12}*), ascorbic acid (*vitamin C*), calciferol (*vitamin D_2*), cholecalciferol (*vitamin D_3*), tocopherol (*vitamin E*), phylloquinone (*vitamin K_1*), menaquinone (*vitamin K_2*); *diseases caused by lack of a vitamin:* beriberi (*vitamin B_1*), pernicious anaemia (*vitamin B_{12}*), rickets (*vitamin D*), scurvy (*vitamin C*).

voice ▶ cadence (*rise and fall in pitch of the voice*), intonation (*rise and fall of the voice in speaking*), register (*particular part of the range of a person's voice*), timbre (*character of voice as distinct from its pitch and strength*), vocal (*relating to the human voice*).

volcano ▶ *states of a volcano:* active (*erupting or having erupted in the past*), dormant (*not currently erupting*), extinct (*not having erupted in recorded history*).

vote ▶ abstain (*formally choose not to vote*), disenfranchise (*deprive someone of the right to vote*), electoral roll (*official list of people in a district entitled to vote*), electorate (*people in a district entitled to vote*), enfranchise (*give someone the right to vote*), floating voter (*person who does not vote for the same party all the time*), franchise, suffrage (*the right to vote*), referendum (*general vote by the electorate on a single political question*).

walk ▶ ambulatory (*having to do with walking*), circumambulate (*walk all the way round*), pedestrian (*person walking on a road*), perambulate (*walk from place to place*), promenade (*place for public walking*).

war ▶ casus belli (*something provoking a war*), ceasefire (*temporary period in a war when fighting stops*), martial (*having to do with war*), neutral (*not supporting either side in a war*), pacifism (*belief that disputes should be settled through peaceful means rather than war*).

watch ▶ analogue (*referring to a watch with hands*), digital (*referring to a watch with a numerical display*), fob (*chain for a watch*), horology (*art of making clocks and watches*), synchronize (*set a watch to the same time as another*).

water ▶ aquatic (*living in water*), aqueduct (*bridge carrying water*), aqueous, hydrous (*containing water*), dehydrate (*remove water from something*), hydraulic (*operated by water*), hydrolysis (*chemical breakdown of substances in water*).

wave ▶ crest (*the top of the ridge of a wave*), spindrift (*spray blown from waves*), spume (*froth on waves*), tsunami (*tidal wave produced by an earthquake*), undulate (*move with a wave-like motion*).

wealth ▶ magnate, tycoon (*very wealthy businessman*); arriviste, nouveau riche, parvenu (*person who has recently become wealthy*); avarice (*excessive greed for wealth*), Mammon (*wealth seen as an evil influence*), plutocracy (*rule by rich people*).

wear ▶ attrition (*gradual wearing down*), corrosion (*wearing away by chemical action*), durable (*resistant to wear*), erosion (*wearing away by natural forces*).

Welsh ▶ *Welsh life and culture:* coracle (*small round wickerwork boat*), cromlech (*ancient stone tomb*), Cymru (*Welsh word for Wales*), eisteddfod (*competitive festival of music and poetry*), hwyl (*stirring emotional feeling associated with the Welsh*).

whale ▶ ambergris (*substance produced by sperm whales, used in making perfume*), blubber (*the fat of whales and other sea mammals*), baleen whales (*whales having plates of whalebone in the mouth for feeding on plankton*), cetacean (*a whale or related mammal, e.g. a dolphin or porpoise*), krill (*shrimp-like crustaceans eaten by whales*), pod (*group of whales*).

wheel ▶ hub, nave (*centre of a wheel*), linchpin (*pin through the end of an axle keeping a wheel in position*), sprocket (*projecting tooth on a wheel*).

will ▶ codicil (*supplement to a will*), executor (*person appointed to carry out the terms of a will*), intestate (*having left no will*), legacy (*something left to someone in a will*), probate (*official validation of a will*), testate (*having made a valid will*), testator (*a person making a will*).

wind ▶ anemometer (*instrument for measuring wind speed*), Beaufort Scale (*scale of wind speeds*), leeward (*on or towards the side sheltered from the wind*), windward (*on or towards the side facing the wind*).

window ▶ *types of window:* bay, casement, clerestory, dormer, fanlight, oriel, sash window, skylight.

wine ▶ bouquet, nose (*scent of a wine*), carafe (*flask for serving wine*), lees (*sediment in wine*), oenology (*study of wines*), vinous (*of or like wine*), vintage (*year or place in which wine was produced*), vintner (*wine merchant*); brut (*referring to very dry sparkling wine*), demi-sec (*medium dry*), pétillant (*slightly sparkling*), sec (*dry*).

witch ▶ coven (*group of witches*), familiar (*spirit accompanying and obeying a witch*), warlock (*man who practises witchcraft*), Wicca (*pagan religion of modern witchcraft*).

wood ▶ ligneous (*made or consisting of wood*), marquetry (*furniture decoration of inlaid wood*), parquet (*flooring of wooden blocks*), veneer (*thin decorative covering of wood*), wainscot (*area of wooden panelling in a room*).

woodwind ▶ *woodwind instruments:* bassoon, clarinet, cor anglais, flute, oboe, piccolo, recorder.

word ▶ verbal (*of or in words*), lexical (*relating to the vocabulary of a language*); acronym (*word formed from initial* *letters*), anagram (*word formed from the letters of another*), malapropism (*the use of a similar-sounding but wrong word*), neologism (*newly invented word*), nonce word (*word invented for a particular occasion*), onomatopoeic (*referring to a word imitating the sound of what it refers to*), palindrome (*word or phrase spelled the same backwards as forwards*), verbatim (*in exactly the same words*).

writing ▶ calligraphy (*decorative handwriting*), cursive (*referring to joined-up writing*), epistolary (*relating to the writing of letters*), graphology (*study of handwriting*), palaeography (*study of ancient writing systems*).

X-ray ▶ barium meal (*mixture swallowed to allow X-rays to be made of the stomach or intestines*), mammography (*the use of X-rays to diagnose tumours of the breasts*), radiography (*the production of images by X-rays*), radiology (*the science of X-rays*), radiotherapy (*the treatment of disease using X-rays*), tomography (*a technique for displaying a cross-section of a human body using X-rays or ultrasound*).

year ▶ annals (*history of events year by year*), annual (*occurring once a year; covering a year*), annuity (*sum of money paid to someone each year*), biannual (*occurring twice a year*), biennial (*occurring every other year*), per annum (*for each year*), perennial (*lasting through a year or several years*).

yellow ▶ *shades of yellow:* amber, canary, flaxen, gold, lemon, mustard, primrose, straw, topaz.

young ▶ juvenilia (*works produced by a writer or artist when young*), rejuvenate (*make someone younger or more energetic*), salad days (*period when one is young and inexperienced*), wunderkind (*very successful young person*).

zodiac ▶ *signs of the zodiac:* Aries (*Ram*), Taurus (*Bull*), Gemini (*Twins*), Cancer (*Crab*), Leo (*Lion*), Virgo (*Virgin*), Libra (*Scales*), Scorpio (*Scorpion*), Sagittarius (*Archer*), Capricorn (*Goat*), Aquarius (*Water Bearer*), Pisces (*Fish/Fishes*).

Collective Names for Animals and Birds

Many of these names are humorous terms which were probably rarely if ever used: they were taken up by Joseph Sturt in 'Sports & Pastimes of England' (1801) and by other antiquarian writers. The first list is arranged in the alphabetical order of the birds and animals and the second in the order of the collective names themselves.

1

a shrewdness of **apes**
a herd or pace of **asses**
a troop of **baboons**
a cete of **badgers**
a sloth of **bears**
a swarm, drift, hive, or erst of **bees**
a flock, flight, or pod of **birds**
a herd, gang, or obstinacy of **buffalo**
a bellowing of **bullfinches**
a drove of **bullocks**
a clowder or glaring of **cats**
an army of **caterpillars**
a herd or drove of **cattle**
a brood, clutch, or peep of **chickens**
a chattering of **choughs**
a rag or rake of **colts**
a covert of **coots**
a herd of **cranes**
a bask of **crocodiles**
a murder of **crows**
a litter of **cubs**
a herd of **curlew**
a herd or mob of **deer**
a pack or kennel of **dogs**
a school of **dolphins**
a trip of **dotterel**
a flight, dole, or piteousness of **doves**
a paddling of **ducks** (*on water*)
a safe of **ducks** (*on land*)
a fling of **dunlin**
a herd or parade of **elephants**
a herd or gang of **elk**
a busyness of **ferrets**
a charm of **finches**
a shoal or run of **fish**
a swarm or cloud of **flies**
a skulk of **foxes**
a gaggle of **geese** (*on land*)
a skein, team, or wedge of **geese** (*in flight*)
a herd of **giraffe**
a cloud of **gnats**
a flock, herd, or trip of **goats**
a band of **gorillas**
a pack or covey of **grouse**
a down, mute, or husk of **hares**
a cast of **hawks**
a siege of **herons**
a bloat of **hippopotami**
a drove, string, stud, or team of **horses**
a pack, cry, or kennel of **hounds**
a flight or swarm of **insects**
a fluther or smack of **jellyfish**
a mob or troop of **kangaroos**
a litter or kindle of **kittens**
a desert of **lapwings**
a bevy or exaltation of **larks**
a leap of **leopards**
a pride or sawt of **lions**
a tiding of **magpies**
a sord or suit of **mallard**
a stud of **mares**
a richesse of **martens**
a labour of **moles**
a troop of **monkeys**
a span or barren of **mules**
a watch of **nightingales**
a parliament or stare of **owls**
a yoke of **oxen**
a pandemonium of **parrots**
a covey of **partridges**
a muster of **peacocks**
a muster, parcel, or rookery of **penguins**
a bevy or head of **pheasants**
a litter or herd of **pigs**
a kit of **pigeons** (*in flight*)
a congregation, stand, or wing of **plovers**
a rush or flight of **pochards**
a pod, school, herd, or turmoil of **porpoises**
a covey of **ptarmigan**
a litter of **pups**
a bevy or drift of **quail**
a bury of **rabbits**
a string of **racehorses**
an unkindness of **ravens**
a crash of **rhinoceros**
a bevy of **roe deer**
a parliament, building, or rookery of **rooks**
a hill of **ruffs**
a pod, herd, or rookery of **seals**
a flock, herd, trip, or mob of **sheep**
a dopping of **sheldrake**
a wisp or walk of **snipe**
a host of **sparrows**
a murmuration of **starlings**
a flight of **swallows**
a game or herd of **swans** (*on land*)
a wedge of **swans** (*in flight*)
a drift, herd, or sounder of **swine**
a spring of **teal**
a knot of **toads**
a hover of **trout**
a rafter of **turkeys**
a bale or turn of **turtles**
a bunch or knob of **waterfowl**
a school, herd, pod, or gam of **whales**
a company or trip of **wigeon**
a sounder of **wild boar**
a dout or destruction of **wild cats**
a team of **wild ducks** (*in flight*)
a bunch, trip, plump, or knob of **wildfowl**
a pack or rout of **wolves**
a fall of **woodcock**
a descent of **woodpeckers**
a herd of **wrens**
a zeal of **zebras**

2

an **army** of caterpillars
a **bale** of turtles
a **band** of gorillas
a **barren** of mules
a **bask** of crocodiles
a **bellowing** of bullfinches
a **bevy** of larks, pheasants, quail, or roe deer
a **bloat** of hippopotami
a **brood** of chickens
a **building** of rooks
a **bunch** of waterfowl or wildfowl
a **bury** of rabbits
a **busyness** of ferrets
a **cast** of hawks
a **cete** of badgers
a **charm** of finches
a **chattering** of choughs
a **cloud** of flies or gnats
a **clowder** of cats
a **clutch** of chickens
a **company** of wigeon
a **congregation** of plovers
a **covert** of coots

a **covey** of grouse, partridges, or ptarmigan
a **crash** of rhinoceros
a **cry** of hounds
a **descent** of woodpeckers
a **desert** of lapwings
a **destruction** of wild cats
a **dole** of doves
a **dopping** of sheldrake
a **dout** of wild cats
a **down** of hares
a **drift** of bees, quail, or swine
a **drove** of bullocks, cattle, or horses
an **erst** of bees
an **exaltation** of larks
a **fall** of woodcock
a **flight** of birds, doves, insects, or swallows
a **fling** of dunlin
a **flock** of birds, goats, pochards, or sheep
a **fluther** of jellyfish
a **gaggle** of geese (*on land*)
a **gam** of whales
a **game** of swans (*on land*)
a **gang** of buffalo or elk
a **glaring** of cats
a **head** of pheasants
a **herd** of asses, buffalo, cattle, cranes, curlew, deer, elephants, elk, giraffe, goats, pigs, porpoises, seals, sheep, swans (*on land*), swine, whales, or wrens
a **hill** of ruffs
a **hive** of bees
a **host** of sparrows
a **hover** of trout
a **husk** of hares
a **kennel** of dogs or hounds
a **kindle** of kittens
a **kit** of pigeons (*in flight*)
a **knob** of waterfowl or wildfowl
a **knot** of toads
a **labour** of moles
a **leap** of leopards
a **litter** of cubs, kittens, pigs, or pups
a **mob** of deer, sheep, or kangaroos
a **murder** of crows
a **murmuration** of starlings
a **muster** of peacocks or penguins
a **mute** of hares
an **obstinacy** of buffalo
a **pace** of asses
a **pack** of dogs, grouse, hounds, or wolves
a **paddling** of ducks (*on water*)
a **pandemonium** of parrots
a **parade** of elephants
a **parcel** of penguins
a **parliament** of owls or rooks
a **peep** of chickens
a **piteousness** of doves
a **plump** of wildfowl
a **pod** of birds, porpoises, seals, or whales
a **pride** of lions
a **rag** of colts
a **rafter** of turkeys
a **rake** of colts
a **richesse** of martens
a **rookery** of penguins, rooks, or seals
a **rout** of wolves
a **run** of fish
a **rush** of pochards
a **safe** of ducks (*on land*)
a **sawt** of lions
a **school** of dolphins, porpoises, or whales
a **shoal** of fish
a **shrewdness** of apes
a **siege** of herons
a **skein** of geese (*in flight*)
a **skulk** of foxes
a **sloth** of bears
a **smack** of jellyfish
a **sord** of mallard
a **sounder** of swine or wild boar
a **span** of mules
a **spring** of teal
a **stand** of plovers
a **stare** of owls
a **string** of horses or racehorses
a **stud** of mares or horses
a **suit** of mallard
a **swarm** of bees, flies, or insects
a **team** of geese or wild ducks (*in flight*) or of horses
a **tiding** of magpies
a **trip** of dotterel, goats, sheep, wigeon, or wildfowl
a **troop** of baboons, kangaroos, or monkeys
a **turmoil** of porpoises
a **turn** of turtles
an **unkindness** of ravens
a **walk** of snipe
a **watch** of nightingales
a **wedge** of geese or swans (*in flight*)
a **wing** of plovers
a **wisp** of snipe
a **yoke** of oxen
a **zeal** of zebras

Foreign Words and Phrases

Over the centuries the English language has assimilated words and phrases from a variety of other languages and this process continues unabated. All the words and phrases listed here are likely to be encountered in British English, where they are often printed in italics. The illustrative examples provided are taken from a variety of sources including newspapers, magazines, journals, and books.

ab initio (Latin): from the beginning.

a cappella (Italian): sung without instrumental accompaniment: *an a cappella performance of a medieval mass.* [literally 'in chapel style']

à deux (French): for or involving two people: *dinner à deux.*

ad hoc (Latin): made or done for a particular purpose: *an ad hoc meeting of ministers and civil servants.* [literally 'to this']

ad infinitum (Latin): endlessly; forever. [literally 'to infinity']

ad interim (Latin): for the meantime.

ad nauseam (Latin): to a tiresomely excessive degree: *a phrase repeated ad nauseam in the media.* [literally 'to sickness']

a fortiori (Latin): with better reason; more conclusively. [literally 'from stronger']

agent provocateur (French): a person who tempts a suspected criminal to commit a crime and so be caught and convicted. [literally 'provocative agent']

à huis clos (French): in private. [literally 'with closed doors']

al dente (Italian): (of food) cooked so as to be still firm when bitten. [literally 'to the tooth']

alfresco (Italian): in the open air: *lunch was served alfresco.*

amour propre (French): self-respect. [literally 'love of oneself']

annus mirabilis (Latin): a remarkable or auspicious year.

a posteriori (Latin): based on reasoning from known facts or past events rather than on assumptions or predictions. [literally 'from what comes after']

a priori (Latin): based on deduction rather than experience: *a priori assumptions about human nature.* [literally 'from what is before']

au courant (French): well informed; up to date: *they're not au courant with the Japanese literary scene.* [literally 'in the (regular) course']

au fait (French): having a good or detailed knowledge: *he's evidently au fait with the technology.* [literally 'to the point']

au fond (French): basically; in essence: *au fond, she's quite a reasonable woman.* [literally 'at the bottom']

au naturel (French): in the most simple or natural way.

beau geste (French): a noble and generous act. [literally 'splendid gesture']

beau idéal (French): the highest standard of excellence. [literally 'ideal beauty']

beau monde (French): fashionable society. [literally 'fine world']

beaux arts (French): the fine arts.

bête noire (French): a person or thing one particularly dislikes. [literally 'black beast']

belles-lettres (French): literary works written and read for their elegant style. [literally 'fine letters']

billet-doux (French): a love letter. [literally 'sweet note']

blitzkrieg (German): an intense, violent military campaign intended to bring about a swift victory. [literally 'lightning war']

bona fide (Latin): genuine; real: *a bona fide money-back guarantee.* [literally 'with good faith']

bon mot (French): a clever or witty remark. [literally 'good word']

bon vivant (French): a person with a sociable and luxurious lifestyle. [literally 'person living well']

brasserie (French): an informal or inexpensive restaurant. [literally 'brewery']

carpe diem (Latin): make the most of the present time. [literally 'seize the day!']

carte blanche (French): complete freedom to act as one wishes: *he was given carte blanche to make whatever changes he saw fit.* [literally 'blank paper']

cause célèbre (French): a controversial issue attracting much public attention. [literally 'famous case']

caveat emptor (Latin): the buyer is responsible for checking the quality of goods before purchasing them. [literally 'let the buyer beware']

c'est la guerre (French): used as an expression of resigned acceptance. [literally 'that's war']

chacun à son gout (French): everyone to their own taste.

chef-d'œuvre (French): a masterpiece. [literally 'chief work']

cherchez la femme (French): there is certain to be a woman at the bottom of a problem or mystery. [literally 'look for the woman']

comme il faut (French): correct in behaviour or etiquette. [literally 'as is necessary']

compos mentis (Latin): sane; in full control of one's mind.

cognoscenti (Italian): people who are well informed about something: *a man regarded by the cognoscenti as the greatest pianist in Europe.* [literally 'people who know']

cordon sanitaire (French): a guarded line placed around an area infected by disease to prevent anyone from leaving. [literally 'sanitary line']

Cosa Nostra (Italian): a US criminal organization related to the Mafia. [literally 'our thing']

coup de foudre (French): love at first sight. [literally 'stroke of lightning']

coup de grâce (French): a blow by which a mortally wounded person or thing is mercifully killed. [literally 'stroke of grace']

coup de main (French): a sudden surprise attack. [literally 'stroke of hand']

coup d'état (French): a sudden violent seizure of power. [literally 'blow of state']

cri de cœur (French): a passionate appeal or protest. [literally 'cry from the heart']

cui bono? (Latin): who stands to gain (implying that this person may have been responsible for a crime)? [literally 'to whom (is it) a benefit?']

de facto (Latin): in fact, whether by right or not: *the de facto president of the republic.*

Dei gratia (Latin): by the grace of God.

déjà vu (French): the sense of having experienced the present situation before. [literally 'already seen']

de jure (Latin): rightful; by right: *a de jure claim to the territory.* [literally 'of law']

de nos jours (French): contemporary: *a kind of Oscar Wilde de nos jours.* [literally 'of our days']
Deo gratias (Latin): thanks be to God.
Deo volente (Latin): God willing.
de profundis (Latin): expressing one's deepest feelings. [literally 'from the depths']
de rigueur (French): obligatory; required by etiquette or current fashion: *black tie was de rigueur on such occasions.* [literally 'in strictness']
dernier cri (French): the very latest fashion: *a dark suit in the cut that was the dernier cri of that time.* [literally 'the last cry']
de trop (French): not wanted; superfluous: *she hovered uncertainly in the doorway, feeling rather de trop.* [literally 'excessive']
deus ex machina (Latin): an unexpected event that saves an apparently hopeless situation. [literally 'god from the machinery']
dolce far niente (Italian): pleasant idleness. [literally 'sweet doing nothing']
dolce vita (Italian): a life of pleasure and luxury. [literally 'sweet life']
doppelgänger (German): an apparition or double of a living person. [literally 'double-goer']
double entendre (French): a word or phrase with two possible interpretations. [from obsolete French, 'double understanding']
dramatis personae (Latin): the characters in a play. [literally 'persons of the drama']
embarras de richesse (French): more options or resources than one knows what to do with. [literally 'embarrassment of riches']
éminence grise (French): a person who has power or influence without holding an official position. [literally 'grey eminence']
en famille (French): with one's family; in an informal way: *we ate en famille at the kitchen table.* [literally 'in family']
enfant terrible (French): a person whose behaviour is unconventional or controversial. [literally 'terrible child']
en masse (French): all together: *the cabinet resigned en masse.* [literally 'in a mass']
en passant (French): by the way: *what is interesting, en passant, is that it is a pre-war model.* [literally 'in passing']
entente cordiale (French): a friendly understanding between states.
entre nous (French): between ourselves: *entre nous, I'll be glad when he retires.*
esprit de corps (French): a feeling of pride and loyalty uniting the members of a group. [literally 'spirit of the body']
ex gratia (Latin): (of payment) given as a favour rather than because of any legal obligation. [literally 'from favour']
ex officio (Latin): by virtue of one's position or status: *an ex officio member of the committee.* [literally 'out of duty']
fait accompli (French): a thing that has been done or decided and cannot now be altered. [literally 'accomplished fact']
faute de mieux (French): for want of a better alternative.
faux pas (French): an embarrassing blunder or indiscretion. [literally 'false step']
femme fatale (French): a seductive woman. [literally 'disastrous woman']
fête champêtre (French): an outdoor entertainment; a garden party. [literally 'rural festival']
fin de siècle (French): relating to the end of a century.
force majeure (French): superior strength.
folie de grandeur (French): delusions of grandeur.
gîte (French): a small furnished holiday house in France.
grande dame (French): a woman who is influential within a particular sphere: *the grande dame of British sculpture.* [literally 'grand lady']
haute couture (French): the designing and making of clothes by leading fashion houses. [literally 'high dressmaking']
haute cuisine (French): high-quality cooking. [literally 'high cookery']
haut monde (French): fashionable society. [literally 'high world']
hors de combat (French): out of action due to injury or damage: *the juke box is currently hors de combat.* [literally 'out of the fight']
ideé fixe (French): an obsession. [literally 'fixed idea']
in absentia (Latin): while not present: *he was sentenced to death in absentia.* [literally 'in absence']
in camera (Latin): in private: *the meeting will be held in camera.* [literally 'in the chamber']
in extremis (Latin): in an extremely difficult situation; at the point of death. [literally 'in the most extreme or furthest']
in loco parentis (Latin): in the place of a parent: *the head teacher was acting in loco parentis.*
in medias res (Latin): in or into the middle of a sequence of events: *he began his story in medias res.* [literally 'in the middle of things']
in propria persona (Latin): in his or her own person.
in situ (Latin): in the original or appropriate position. [literally 'in place']
inter alia (Latin): among other things: *charges of, inter alia, insider dealing* and *stock manipulation.* [literally 'among others']
in toto (Latin): as a whole: *he rejected the proposals in toto.*
ipso facto (Latin): by that very fact or act: *the enemy of one's enemy may be ipso facto a friend.* [literally 'by the fact itself']
je ne sais quoi (French): a quality that is hard to describe: *an actor possessed of that certain je ne sais quoi that makes someone a star.* [literally 'I do not know what']
jeu d'esprit (French): a light-hearted display of wit. [literally 'game of the mind']
jeunesse dorée (French): wealthy, fashionable young people. [literally 'gilded youth']
joie de vivre (French): exuberant enjoyment of life. [literally 'joy of living']
laissez-faire (French): a non-interventionist policy. [literally 'allow to do']
locum tenens (Latin): a temporary deputy or stand-in. [literally 'one holding a place']
locus classicus (Latin): the best known or most authoritative passage on a subject. [literally 'classical place']
magnum opus (Latin): the most important work of an artist, writer, etc. [literally 'great work']
manqué (French): having failed to become what one might have been: *an artist manqué.* [from *manquer*, 'to lack']
mea culpa (Latin): an acknowledgement that something is one's fault. [literally 'by my fault']
memento mori (Latin): something kept as a reminder that death is inevitable. [literally 'remember (that you have) to die']
ménage à trois (French): an arrangement in which a married couple and the lover of one of them live together. [literally 'household of three']
modus operandi (Latin): a way of doing something. [literally 'way of operating']
modus vivendi (Latin): an arrangement that allows conflicting parties to coexist peacefully. [literally 'way of living']

mot juste (French): the most exact or appropriate word or expression.

ne plus ultra (Latin): the best example of something: *the ne plus ultra of decorative splendour.* [literally 'not further beyond']

nil desperandum (Latin): do not despair. [literally 'no need to despair']

noblesse oblige (French): privilege entails responsibility. [literally 'nobility obligates']

nolens volens (Latin): whether one wants or likes something or not. [from *nolens* 'not willing' + *volens* 'willing']

non sequitur (Latin): a conclusion or statement that does not logically follow from the previous statement. [literally 'it does not follow']

nouveau riche (French): people who have recently become rich and who display their wealth ostentatiously. [literally 'new rich']

objet d'art (French): a small decorative or artistic object.

on dit (French): a piece of gossip. [literally 'they say']

par excellence (French): better or more than all others of the same kind: *a singer-songwriter par excellence.* [literally 'by excellence']

parti pris (French): a preconceived view; a bias. [literally 'side taken']

per annum (Latin): for each year.

per capita (Latin): for each person. [literally 'by heads']

per se (Latin): by or in itself or themselves: *Jack had nothing against women per se, but she had alarmed him.*

persona non grata (Latin): a person who is not welcome somewhere.

pièce de résistance (French): the most important or impressive item: *the pièce de résistance was chocolate cake laced with kirsch.* [literally 'piece (i.e. means) of resistance']

pied-à-terre (French): a small flat or house kept for occasional use. [literally 'foot to earth']

pis aller (French): a last resort. [from *pis* 'worse' + *aller* 'to go']

plat du jour (French): a special dish prepared by a restaurant on a particular day. [literally 'dish of the day']

plus ça change (French): used to express resigned acknowledgement of the fact that certain things never change. [from *plus ça change, plus c'est la même chose* 'the more it changes, the more it stays the same']

prima facie (Latin): accepted as so until proved otherwise: *a prima facie case of professional misconduct.* [from *primus* 'first' + *facies* 'face']

primus inter pares (Latin): the senior or representative member of a group. [literally 'first among equals']

pro rata (Latin): proportional; proportionally. [literally 'according to the rate']

proxime accessit (Latin): the person who comes second in an examination or is runner-up for an award. [literally 'came very near']

quid pro quo (Latin): a favour or advantage given in return for something. [literally 'something for something']

raison d'être (French): the most important reason for someone or something's existence: *football appeared to be his sole raison d'être.* [literally 'reason for being']

reductio ad absurdam (Latin): a method of disproving a premise by showing that its logical conclusion is absurd. [literally 'reduction to the absurd']

roman-à-clef (French): a novel in which real people or events appear with invented names. [literally 'novel with a key']

sangfroid (French): the ability to stay calm in difficult circumstances. [literally 'cold blood']

savoir faire (French): the ability to act appropriately in social situations. [literally 'know how to do']

sine die (Latin): (of proceedings) adjourned indefinitely. [literally 'without a day']

sine qua non (Latin): a thing that is absolutely essential: *tennis courts are a sine qua non for any summer camp.* [literally 'without which not']

soi-disant (French): self-styled; so-called: *a soi-disant novelist.* [from *soi* 'oneself' + *disant* 'saying']

sotto voce (Italian): in a quiet voice. [from *sotto* 'under' + *voce* 'voice']

sub judice (Latin): being considered by a court of law and therefore not to be publicly discussed elsewhere. [literally 'under a judge']

sub rosa (Latin): happening or done in secret: *the inspection must be sub rosa.* [literally 'under the rose']

sui generis (Latin): unique: *each of his novels is sui generis.* [literally 'of its own kind']

table d'hôte (French): a restaurant meal offered at a fixed price, with few if any choices. [literally 'host's table']

tant mieux (French): so much the better.

tant pis (French): so much the worse; too bad.

terra firma (Latin): dry land; the ground. [literally 'firm land']

terra incognita (Latin): unknown territory.

tête-à-tête (French): a private conversation. [literally 'head-to-head']

tour de force (French): a thing accomplished with great skill: *the aria is a musical tour de force.* [literally 'feat of strength']

tout de suite (French): at once. [literally 'quite in sequence']

verboten (German): forbidden: *smoking is absolutely verboten.*

via media (Latin): a compromise. [literally 'middle way']

victor ludorum (Latin): the overall champion in a sports competition. [literally 'victor of the games']

vis-à-vis (French): in relation to; as compared with: *the value of the dollar vis-à-vis other currencies.* [literally 'face-to-face']

vox populi (Latin): public opinion. [literally 'the people's voice']

zeitgeist (German): the characteristic spirit or mood of a particular historical period. [from *Zeit* 'time' + *Geist* 'spirit']

Selecting the Right Word

Words which share a similar basic meaning may have subtly different nuances and connotations. This section explains the distinctions of meaning between words which are close synonyms of each other in order to help you select the most appropriate word for the meaning you want to convey. The distinctions drawn are based on a careful analysis of how the words are actually used by native English speakers and the illustrative examples are taken from real evidence.

accurate: precise, exact

All these words apply to information or statements that are correct, usually helpfully and informatively so.

- An **accurate** statement or representation has been put together with great care and corresponds to the facts. It is likely to give people a good idea of the truth or be a reliable guide for action: *a frighteningly accurate description of her life.*
- **Precise** refers to minute attention to detail. It draws a contrast with something that may be correct but is more vague or approximate: *we have no precise figures for possible job losses.*
- **Exact** emphasizes that something has been definitely identified, with no margin for vagueness or error: *we may never know the exact number of deaths.* An *exact statement* is one that is both precise and truthful.

agree: consent, assent, acquiesce

More than one party is needed for an agreement, but the contributions made by each may be different.

- **Agreeing** is typically done between equals who cooperate in working out their final position: *we'll have to decide what compromise we can agree on. Agree* may also, however, be used of permission being given by someone in a position of superior power: *we can appoint him if we can get the Area Health Authority to agree.*
- Someone who **consents** to a proposal is presented with a suggestion in which they have some interest, because agreeing to it will require them to take action or affect them in some way: *she has the same capacity as an adult to consent to surgical treatment.* Normally, they have some degree of authority or control: their agreement is essential if a plan is to be put into action, and they are free to refuse it.
- Someone who **assents** to a proposal is generally a person whose approval is required, although they probably feel quite indifferent to it. They are free to accept or reject the proposal, but have played no part in working it out: they merely accept what is presented to them: *the inspector assented to the remark with a nod.*
- To **acquiesce** is to accept something by default through failing to resist. Often what is accepted is not something that the person really wants, and their acquiescence is due to exhaustion, attrition, or lack of real bargaining power: *the authorities believed that most refugees would eventually acquiesce.* Acquiescence can easily slip into passive connivance at something bad: *the company was accused of acquiescing in the pollution of the land.*

anticipate: expect, foresee

These words all relate to someone's knowledge of or attitude to future events.

- **Anticipate** is used when someone thinks that something is likely to occur, and takes action or makes plans to prepare for it: *the police anticipated trouble and drafted in reinforcements.* It can also mean 'look forward to eagerly': *the eve of the much-anticipated Pissarro exhibition.*
- To **expect** something is to be fairly confident that it will happen: *over 20,000 visitors are expected.* This is the most general word. *Expect* may also be used of something that is required or demanded, whether or not one thinks it is likely: *we expect total loyalty from all our employees.*
- **Foresee** is used of the ability to recognize the future course of events in advance: *no one can foresee whether tax will go up or down.*

artificial: synthetic, man-made

All these words refer to things that have been made or produced by human beings: they may also convey an implicit judgement about this fact.

- Something **artificial** has not occurred naturally but has been deliberately made by humans; the word is particularly applied to copies or replacements of natural objects, made from some synthetic material such as plastic: *an artificial heart.* The word comes from Latin *artificium* meaning 'workmanship' or 'making a work of art'. By extension, *artificial* is also used of hypocritical displays of emotion: *I thought his smile was artificial.* An *artificial distinction* is one that is discredited because it has no basis in reality.
- **Synthetic** materials are produced by humans through chemical processes, rather than grown naturally: *synthetic fabrics can imitate everything from silk to rubber.* The word is from Greek *synthesis* 'putting together'. There is often a hint that the imitation is inferior to its original: *set against native trees, Leyland green looks very synthetic.*
- **Man-made** is a more neutral term. Whereas both *artificial* and *synthetic* can carry a note of criticism or disapproval, *man-made fibres* or a *man-made lake* are presented as created by humans, without any implied comment on the desirability or otherwise of the procedure. Unlike the other two synonyms, it is applied solely to physical objects and materials.

autocratic: despotic, tyrannical

These words are all more or less critical descriptions of someone's exercise of power.

- **Autocratic** refers to a regime where all power is concentrated in the hands of a single ruler: *autocratic tsarist Russia*. It has come to be used of anyone in a position of power who refuses to share that power with others: *an autocratic management style*. Generally, *autocratic* implies no comment on the benevolence or otherwise of the exercise of power; if there is criticism, it is only of the exclusiveness.
- **Despotic** is a less common word. Taken from the Greek term for a master or absolute ruler, it now usually describes someone who not only holds great power but exercises it oppressively: *the cruel, corrupt, and despotic Shah*.
- **Tyrannical** also comes from a Greek term that originally simply meant an absolute ruler; but it now invariably refers to cruel exercise of power by someone who cannot be called to account: *a tyrannical landowner*.

bold: audacious, daring

These words all acknowledge someone's fearlessness.

- A **bold** person feels no fear of possible dangers, or at least is not deterred by them: *this difficult climb will appeal only to the bold*. Other people's opinions or possible anger do not trouble them either: *only one journalist was bold enough to tackle the Prime Minister*.
- **Audacious** carries a greater note of surprise at extreme readiness to take risks: *a series of audacious takeovers*. It is often used to describe actions rather than a character trait. *Audacious* acts typically show inventiveness in going beyond the boundaries of what has previously been considered possible.
- **Daring** typically refers to adventurousness undeterred by physical danger: *a daring mission to rescue wounded soldiers*. It can also refer to a readiness to shock (*smoking in the street was considered very daring in those days*), and is also used to mean 'provocative': *a pretty girl in daring clothes*.

border: boundary, frontier

There are all sorts of dividing lines, political, geographical, and metaphorical: some can be crossed with less trouble than others.

- **Border** generally means a national boundary, hence a significant division which may take time and effort to cross: *the building of a huge dam on the Thai–Laotian border*.
- A **boundary** marks the division between two areas or two concepts, usually clearly but generally not creating any difficulty in passing from one side to the other: *it is only a matter of time before the disease crosses the county boundary* | *technologies which cut across traditional boundaries between industrial sectors*.
- A **frontier** is generally difficult to cross: the word is used of national borders, especially borders between hostile powers, and may hint at armed surveillance and unsympathetic officials: *troops had been dispatched to Syria's frontier with Iraq*. *Frontier* can also denote the point beyond which no one as yet has gone or can go: *the frontiers of knowledge*.

busy: occupied, engaged, active

- Saying that someone is **busy** means that they have a great deal to do (*if I'm busy my husband does the cooking*) or are occupied with a specified activity (*he was busy with the preparations*). Either way, they are likely to have no time for further calls on their attention: *I'm too busy to write letters*.
- Someone who is **occupied** has something to do which takes up a good deal of their time or attention. There is a suggestion that this activity is a welcome means of filling empty time, but not unduly onerous: *a box of toys kept the children occupied all afternoon*.
- **Engaged** emphasizes the fact that someone has no time or attention left for any new activities or demands: *you'll have to wait to see her, she's engaged at present*.
- Someone who is **active** is doing a great deal, often in a particular context or area: *she has been active in local politics since 1985*.

calm: serene, tranquil, placid, peaceful

All these words indicate a freedom from disturbance or agitation.

- Someone who is **calm** remains, or at least appears, unruffled in worrying or frightening situations: *Hugh kept calm despite the extreme provocation*. *Calm* is often applied to a place where there has been fighting or unrest but which is now relatively peaceful.
- Describing someone as **serene** suggests that their calm appearance or behaviour springs from a deep inner peace. The word comes from Latin *serenus*, used of bright, clear skies, and the serene person has a radiance about them: *her eyes were happy and serene*.
- **Tranquil** is most commonly used of places. A *tranquil village* or *tranquil countryside* is relaxingly free from noise or disturbance.
- Someone with a **placid** nature is not easily worried or upset: *a placid, contented family man*. *Placid* can have critical overtones, suggesting that someone is too slow to react and rather dull: *a placid and unreflective temperament*. *Placid* is also used of quiet, docile animals, especially cows and horses.
- A **peaceful** place or atmosphere is relaxing and soothing. People are typically described as *peaceful* either when they have been in pain or distress and are now more at ease, or to convey their preference for avoiding violence or aggression: *Dad was a peaceful, law-abiding citizen*.

candid: frank, outspoken, forthright, blunt

These words show a combination of admiration for openness and honesty with a feeling that life would be more comfortable if some things were concealed.

- A **candid** person keeps no secrets and glosses over no distressing or discreditable facts: *he was candid about the difficulties*. There may be a suggestion that such total openness is found refreshing and appealing. The word is from Latin *candidus*, meaning 'white, pure'.

- **Frank**, while very close in meaning, can suggest a greater bluntness; it is also used for a down-to-earth openness on matters seen as sensitive or embarrassing: *frank discussion of sexual problems*. Behaviour or emotions that are not concealed even though one might expect them to be can also be described as *frank*: *she spoke with frank envy*.
- Someone who is **outspoken** is probably unusually ready to risk unpopularity or even danger by expressing controversial opinions: *an outspoken critic of the military*.
- Someone who is **forthright** says what they have to say, without fear or favour and in an uncompromising manner (*Mandela was forthright in his criticism of US policy*), while someone who is **blunt** may even take a perverse delight in mentioning sensitive issues or giving unwelcome news in a forthright way: *requests for an interview met with a blunt refusal*.

careless: heedless, thoughtless

- Someone who is **careless** is not giving their full attention to what they are doing, typically in a situation where this could result in harm to themselves or to others: *he was charged with causing death by careless driving*. *Careless* may also be used to indicate that someone is relaxed and casual (*she moved with careless grace*) or trying to appear so (*she managed to turn the wince into a careless shrug*).
- **Heedless** indicates that someone is taking no notice of factors which might be expected to influence their behaviour, either in their own interests (*she knelt on the floor, heedless of the cold stone*) or in those of others (*she talked on, heedless of her sister's strained silence*).
- A **thoughtless** person gives no consideration to the feelings or convenience of others. Thoughtlessness may be contrasted with actual intent to harm or regarded as blameworthy in itself: *to think that a few minutes of thoughtless pleasure could end in this | she was angry—he had been thoughtless and insensitive*.

characteristic: typical, distinctive

- A **characteristic** feature of someone or something is one that is immediately recognizable as an essential part of their nature: *he has behaved with characteristic generosity*.
- Something that is a **typical** member of a class of things has all the central defining features of the members of that class: *the facade is typical fourteenth-century work | the typical party member was male and middle class*. *Typical* is often used to express annoyance at some regular feature or habit: *he didn't turn up, which was absolutely typical*.
- A **distinctive** feature is not necessarily central or typical, but serves to distinguish one individual or class of items from all others: *he spotted the police station with its distinctive blue lamp*.

compel: force, coerce, oblige

All these words refer to making someone do something that they would not otherwise choose to do. (They are often used in the passive, underlining the sense that someone feels deprived of power or choice.)

- Someone who is **compelled** to do something is subjected to pressure that they feel unable to resist. Often, this pressure is applied by someone in authority and takes the form of the threat of penalties if the person should fail to comply: *companies are compelled to comply with the regulations*. Adverse circumstances may also *compel* someone to do something: *he was compelled to retire on grounds of ill health*.
- **Force** is a more general term for using superior power to make someone do what one wants them to. (It comes from Latin *fortis* 'strong'.) The superior power may be that of uncontrollable circumstances (*the firm has been forced to make nineteen workers redundant*) or that of someone physically stronger or better equipped (*the raider forced him to open the safe*). People may also *force* themselves to do something, steeling themselves for something necessary but unpleasant: *Lucy forced herself to sound calm*.
- **Coerce** lays the greatest emphasis on the fact that someone is reluctant to do what they are being made to. The pressure applied to them is severe and oppressive, and may involve violence or the threat of it: *he was coerced into giving evidence*.
- If someone is **obliged** to do something they find it necessary to do it. *Oblige* is particularly used of requirements imposed on someone by law or a legally binding agreement: *the Minister is obliged to report regularly to a parliamentary board*.

complicated: complex, intricate, involved

- Something **complicated** consists of or involves a number of different elements. The relation between these is not straightforward, so that the whole is difficult to understand (*a complicated system of voting*) or to manage or construct: *a complicated political and personal dilemma*.
- **Complex** emphasizes the number of interrelated parts, elements, or facets: *highly complex organisms | the organization became more complex*. Complexity may be more deeply seated in something's nature than complicatedness. *Complex* may also suggest that something is regarded as interesting or intriguing, rather than irritating, on account of its difficulty: *she knew his character to be deep and complex*.
- **Intricate** describes a complex interrelation of small details, calling for very close attention if it is to be appreciated or understood: *intricate political manoeuvres | intricate iron trellis-work*. The word suggests that there is a pattern or rationale to be discerned, though careful scrutiny is required to discover it.
- **Involved** suggests a confusing number of details, interrelated in such a way as to make understanding very difficult: *a long, involved conversation*. It often carries a note of criticism, suggesting that the confusion is unnecessary.

concise: succinct, terse

These words all denote brevity in statements or pieces of writing.

- **Concise** expresses approval of a statement that conveys a large amount of information briefly. It suggests that by keeping the words used to the necessary minimum, the speaker or writer has achieved greater clarity as well as brevity: *the instructions were clear and concise*.
- A **succinct** remark or expression is pithy, made more

forceful by its brevity: *each page is introduced by a succinct heading*. This forceful brevity may be achieved by including only the most important points in what is said.

- **Terse** comes from Latin *tergere* 'wipe, polish'. A *terse* statement or expression has had any dispensable words removed. The word may be used approvingly, suggesting elegance or forcefulness: *a terse and gritty thriller*. Frequently, however, it suggests a brevity verging on the harsh or unfriendly: *Luke's terse reply forbade further talk*.

confident: optimistic, sanguine, hopeful

All these words indicate that someone expects good things to come their way; but they vary in the degree of assurance or justification assigned to this expectation.

- When we say we are **confident**, the usual implication is that our expectation is doubt-free, probably because we have incontrovertible evidence: *he's confident of a successful outcome*.
- Someone who is **optimistic** has an assurance that is not quite so strong: they have good evidence, but it is not cast-iron: *Gilroy is optimistic about long-term growth*.
- A person who is **sanguine** about something is cheerfully optimistic about it, but this attitude may not be shared by others: *William's analysis is far too sanguine*.
- A **hopeful** person admits to themself a possibility of failure: *he was hopeful that the plan would be accepted*.

continual: continuous, constant, ceaseless

These words describe processes or situations which do not stop, but with different emphases.

- **Continual** applies mainly to an action or event that occurs repeatedly and at very short intervals over a period of time: *the continual criticisms of the committee*. It can also be used of a process or situation that never stops at all: *he was in continual pain*.
- **Continuous** describes something that extends without a break, either in space or in time: *a continuous stone wall | fighting was continuous, both night and day*.
- **Constant** can mean 'not changing' as well as 'not stopping'. When it is used to describe a continuing action or process, it often also carries the idea of remaining the same in nature or intensity: *she needs constant attention*. *Constant* can convey a sense that the continuation or repetition of something is felt to be exasperating or wearing: *coal supplies were reduced by constant cancellations of goods trains*.
- **Ceaseless** is most often used of something unpleasant, dangerous, or challenging, and suggests an unrelenting quality: *ceaseless rain made further progress impossible*.

danger: peril, hazard, risk

- **Danger** is the most general word for a real possibility of suffering harm or injury: *the danger faced by today's police officers*.
- **Peril** is a more formal or literary word, and marks out the danger as intense or the possible harm as very serious: *the immediate peril confronting the world in the early 1940s*.
- **Hazard** probably comes from an Arabic word meaning 'chance'. It suggests the possibility of unforeseen and unpredictable harm arising from an activity, situation, or object: *the hazards of travelling*.
- **Risk** indicates a more predictable possibility of harm arising from an action or a situation, or an action or object that predictably increases the likelihood of harm: *going on holiday without insurance is always a risk*. A risk may often be a danger that someone chooses to incur because it is outweighed by some other consideration: *the woman had the right to refuse a blood transfusion even at risk to her life*.

disgrace: dishonour, shame, ignominy

These words all apply to a situation in which someone has lost other people's respect.

- A person in **disgrace** has incurred general disapproval through behaviour considered unacceptable: *Nixon had resigned in disgrace*. There is a strong suggestion of outrage and scandal.
- **Dishonour** is less often used, perhaps because the notion of honour that it involves has itself become unfashionable. It indicates a situation in which someone's behaviour has caused people to regard them as having an ignoble character, in particular to condemn them for cowardice or dishonesty: *feelings which induce a man to prefer death to dishonour*.
- **Shame** carries a much stronger implication of an inner feeling than the other words. While someone in *disgrace* is disapproved of, someone who incurs *shame* feels deeply distressed at this disapproval: *deceit only brings shame*. There is a suggestion that such a person is avoided by other people or feels unable to mix with them.
- **Ignominy** is a formal word coming from a Latin expression for the loss of one's 'good name'. It indicates a condition of deep humiliation in the eyes of other people, resulting from failure or from particularly disgraceful behaviour: *the ignominy of an innings defeat*.

distant: remote, faraway, far-off

These words all describe something that is a long way away in space or time.

- **Distant** is the most general and neutral word for something that is a long way away: *fine views stretch to the distant mountains | the distant past*.
- **Remote** suggests that distance makes something isolated or inaccessible: *Indian tribes still living in remote areas of the Amazonian rainforests*.
- Describing something or somewhere as **faraway** may emphasize the difficulty of getting to it, but often it also suggests an exotic and romantic quality: *the perfect escape to faraway places*.
- Something that is **far-off** is a very long way away indeed, and is likely to be very different indeed from our ordinary, everyday world: *an adventure story set in a far-off mystical land*.

earn: deserve, merit

These words all express the idea that something is due to someone, whether or not they actually receive it.

- To **earn** something is to receive it after having behaved in such a way that it is just or appropriate that one should do so: *his achievements should earn him a place among the world's top ten players.*
- You may or may not receive what you **deserve**: *surely we deserved some reward for our efforts.* Someone or something may *deserve* something because of their general character, rather than a particular action: *she deserves some happiness.*
- **Merit** is a more formal term for deserving something: *she laughed with more enthusiasm than the joke merited.*

eccentric: unconventional, idiosyncratic, quirky

These words all describe people or things that are out of the ordinary. They express varying degrees of disapproval, interest, or curiosity.

- Someone described as **eccentric** behaves in a way that does not conform to what is usual or expected. The description always carries a reference to the person's supposed mental state, which is regarded as strange, maybe even to the point of insanity: *an eccentric millionaire who built his own UFO landing park.*
- **Unconventional** is less strong. It describes behaviour that is not bound by generally accepted rules or ways of doing things. *Unconventional* expresses interest rather than suspicion or disapproval: *he was one of the most unconventional men she had ever met.* An *unconventional* person deliberately cultivates an independent-minded approach to life.
- **Idiosyncratic** comes from Greek words meaning 'individual mix'. It emphasizes the fact that someone's ideas or behaviour are unique to them: *the band's approach is idiosyncratic.* This uniqueness may be appealing or unsettling.
- **Quirky** suggests an unusual, distinctive, and surprising or unpredictable character. There is a sense that this character makes someone or something amusing or intriguing: *a quirky sense of humour.*

fair: just, equitable

These words express judgements springing from a belief that everyone should get what they are entitled to.

- **Fair** is the most general term. It is an emotive word, expressing a very deep-seated sense of what is basically right, coupled with indignation if this is not achieved. Central to this is the idea that everyone should be treated alike, without favouritism or prejudice, so that what they receive is what they really deserve: *fair play should be seen to have taken place.* Being *fair* may involve going to particular trouble to take account of points in favour of people who are in danger of being judged harshly: *it would hardly be fair to blame them for giving in to such temptation. Fair* is used not only to judge people and their behaviour but also to complain about impersonal bad luck: *life's just not fair.*
- **Just** comes from Latin *ius* 'law'. It gives a more intellectual slant to the general idea of fairness by suggesting that there is an objective standard—originally a legal standard—of what is right and fair, against which someone's behaviour can be measured. Sometimes the standard is still that of the law: *he would continue to battle for a just settlement.* However, the standard may also be a moral rather than a legal one: *a just and more democratic society.*
- **Equitable** is a more uncommon and formal term. Coming ultimately from Latin *aequus* 'equal', it has a root sense of 'even-handed', 'fair to all'. It suggests fair and unbiased conclusions reached through reasoning, and is used particularly of financial and political policies: *the equitable distribution of costs among consumers.*

faithful: loyal, constant, true

All these words are used to describe an unwavering commitment to someone or something.

- Someone who is **faithful** shows unchanging affection or support for a person or cause, often in the face of difficulty or some temptation to desert: *a faithful lover | the party faithful.* The word is used humorously of inanimate objects regarded as absolutely reliable: *he drove his faithful Toyota overland from Saudi Arabia. Faithful* is also used specifically to refer to sexual fidelity: *her husband had always been faithful to her.*
- **Loyal** is used mainly to refer to commitment to a superior or employer: *a loyal subject of the king | years of loyal service.* A *loyal friend* will show unwavering support, particularly in the face of criticism or hostility from others.
- The main use of **constant** is to refer to an activity that is regularly repeated at short intervals over a long period of time. When used of a person's character, it is a rather literary term for unchanging and utterly reliable fidelity: *a constant friend.*
- **True** has a rather archaic ring when used to describe fidelity. This can be exploited to give a poetic or romantic note to a statement: *she is as true to me as the day is long.*

famous: celebrated, well known, renowned

All four of these adjectives assume that fame is desirable, and contrast with *notorious,* which refers to being well known for some crime or bad quality.

- Someone or something **famous** is known about and admired by very large numbers of people: *he became the most famous footballer in the side.* This is the most general word of the four.
- **Celebrated** suggests that someone or something is much talked about and praised: *one of Rodin's most celebrated works.* Something may be *celebrated* within a fairly small group—*the celebrated book 'Pedagogy of the Oppressed'* may be well known and highly regarded among its readers, but cannot be said to be famous.
- **Well known** conveys the idea of being recognized by a large number of people, but generally lacks the glamorous connotations of *famous*: *a well-known engineering company.* Someone may be *well known* without being admired, although the adjective itself (unlike *notorious*) does not carry any bad connotations.
- **Renowned** is a less common word than *famous.* It serves to emphasize general agreement about the good reputation of the person or thing in question: *standards of cuisine and service for which the hotel is renowned.*

forgive: pardon, excuse, condone

- **Forgive** is the standard word used when someone to whom a wrong has been done makes a deliberate decision to put aside the feelings of anger and blame occasioned by that wrong: *she could never forgive her friend's betrayal.*
- **Pardon** is used mainly to refer to the official remission of a punishment to which an offender has been sentenced: *the President pardoned nine prisoners.* When used as a synonym for *forgive*, it has a rather old-fashioned or mannered tone: *you have pardoned all their wrongs.*
- A circumstance that **excuses** an action provides reasons for seeing it as less blameworthy than it would otherwise be: *his friend's betrayal could be excused as a simple error of judgement.* (Forgiveness and pardon, in contrast, presuppose the guilt of the person being forgiven or pardoned.) Like *forgive*, *excuse* also describes a decision to put aside feelings of anger or blame, but generally it implies that the offence was a fairly minor one: *excuse my delay in writing.*
- **Condone** is a more critical term than the other three. It suggests that someone who does not condemn behaviour that is morally wrong is in turn wrong to be so forgiving: *union leaders cannot condone the use of violence.*

futile: fruitless, vain, pointless

All these words refer to unsuccessful actions, some more scornfully than others.

- An undertaking described as **futile** has no chance of success. There is an implication that this should have been obvious all along to the people concerned had they not been too stupid to realize it: *futile attempts to escape.*
- A **fruitless** undertaking ultimately proves unsuccessful, but this outcome could not have been predicted: *talks collapsed after months of fruitless negotiation.*
- **Vain** (from Latin *vanus* 'empty, without substance') is a more formal word, emphasizing the disappointment caused by an unsuccessful outcome: *a vain attempt to save a drowning man.*
- Something described as **pointless** is doomed from the outset to be unsuccessful or to serve no worthwhile purpose, so should not have been attempted in the first place: *I knew it would be pointless expecting him to change his mind.*

glib: slick, smooth, urbane

These words, with varying degrees of suspicion, describe extreme ease and confidence in speech or manner.

- To be **glib** is always bad. The word describes extreme ease and fluency in producing answers which are inadequate to deal with the complexity of an issue or are too readily produced to be sincere: *the glib phrases rolled off his tongue.* If the glib person is aiming to impress, the attempt is a failure, as their superficiality is obvious.
- **Slick** applies to actions as well as speech; it denotes technical mastery and the assurance that it produces. This technical perfection is generally viewed with suspicion; there is a suggestion that it is achieved at the expense of a proper concern with content or with honesty: *a slick public relations campaign.*
- Someone described as **smooth** is regarded as too charming to be trusted. Their charm, it is suggested, is probably being exercised in the dishonest pursuit of self-interest: *he was too smooth to be a real gentleman.*
- **Urbane** is the most neutral term, referring to a polished and relaxed ease and charm: *Neil was urbane, witty, and sophisticated.* An *urbane* person is generally pleasant to be with, and if their ease of manner is regarded with suspicion, this must be separately indicated.

grateful: thankful, appreciative

- Someone who is **grateful** realizes that someone else has helped them or treated them kindly, and therefore has warm feelings towards that person: *her whole family is grateful to the surgeons who saved her. Grateful*, in fact, suggests more of an impulse to thank someone than *thankful*.
- **Thankful** is more concerned with a person's attitude to their good fortune than with their feelings towards anyone responsible for it. It suggests that someone is relieved or pleased about a situation or turn of events, often one for which no particular person can be identified as responsible: *she was thankful that she felt so much better.*
- The main use of **appreciative** is to indicate that someone recognizes the merits or appeal of something and makes that recognition clear: *they were the most appreciative audience we'd played to.*

hinder: hamper, impede, obstruct

All these words apply to making progress slower or more difficult.

- **Hinder** comes from an Old English word meaning 'back'. It refers generally to the creation of difficulties or delays that hold people back from doing something: *ministers were suspected of deliberately hindering the progress of the bill.*
- **Hamper** comes from a Middle English term meaning 'shackle or entangle'. It is used of physical burdens that weigh someone down or make their movement awkward: *he was laden with parcels and further hampered by an enormous umbrella.* By extension, it is applied to problems and handicaps that interfere with effective action: *they were hampered by shortage of funds.*
- **Impede** comes from Latin *impedire* 'shackle the feet'. It refers to slowing something down or getting in the way: *rivers impeded north–south communications.*
- **Obstruct** is used primarily of a physical object that literally blocks the way: *a car was obstructing the entrance.* Its use is extended to the creation of non-physical obstacles, making something difficult though usually not impossible: *he was charged with obstructing the police investigation.*

hint: suggestion, innuendo, insinuation

- A **hint** is a message that one person conveys to another without stating it explicitly, often because it is a request or involves something that they are embarrassed to say directly. It may be conveyed verbally or through someone's behaviour:

she picked up her book, but Sandra did not take the hint. Hint can also refer to a piece of practical advice or information given explicitly: *handy hints for home buyers*.

- **Suggestion** refers to an idea or piece of advice about a possible course of action, put forward for consideration without any implication of indirectness or concealment: *he shrugged off suggestions that he was planning to quit politics*. What *suggestion* shares with the other words is a certain tentativeness.
- **Innuendo** is an indirect way of conveying an idea through the undertones and implications of what is said. The message conveyed typically has a sexual content or is to someone's discredit: *innuendos about his sources of finance*. Exploiting shared knowledge and double meanings, *innuendo* creates a complicity between speaker and listener, typically an unwelcome one.
- **Insinuation** is the most consistently pejorative of these words. Whereas *innuendo* may sometimes refer to an exploitation of implicit meanings that is intended simply to amuse, an *insinuation* is always meant to injure or distress someone by implying something to their discredit: *insinuations about her private life*.

illegal: unlawful, illicit

These words all apply to behaviour that transgresses in different ways against codes governing community life.

- An **illegal** action or activity is one that is specifically forbidden by law, especially criminal law: *illegal drug use*.
- Anything that is *illegal* is in virtue of that also **unlawful**. However, *unlawful* has a wider application than *illegal*, referring to actions that are not recognized by or in conformity with the law as well as to those that are specifically forbidden: *the use of unlawful violence*.
- **Illicit** can be used synonymously with *illegal*: *heroin or other illicit drugs*. It may also, however, refer to the breach of moral codes or other sets of rules that do not have the status of statute law: *the temptations of an illicit romance. Illicit* suggests the allure of what is secret and forbidden.

implicit: tacit, unspoken

These words all describe ideas that can be understood despite not being directly expressed.

- A meaning or message that is **implicit** is not stated openly but can be worked out by reasoning from what has been said. Similarly, an *implicit* attitude or belief can be inferred from the behaviour that it prompts: *the speech contained an implicit condemnation of nuclear weapons | we must examine assumptions implicit in the way the questions are asked*.
- **Tacit**, from the Latin for 'silent', suggests that the idea or attitude that is not made explicit is nonetheless understood and accepted by two or more people, and typically that it is important to their coexistence or ability to work successfully: *the government depended on a tacit agreement with other parties*. It is suggested that the mutual understanding is so clear that there is no need to make such ideas explicit, and frequently that they are so sensitive or controversial that it is more expedient not to do so.
- **Unspoken** basically means that something is not said aloud, and depending on context it can have opposite implications. Something may be *unspoken* because it is to be kept secret: *unspoken resentment. Unspoken* may also, however, describe a message that is made very clear and is possibly all the more effective for not being explicit: *every glance was an unspoken reproach*.

inconstant: changeable, capricious, fickle

These words all indicate that someone or something is liable to change and cannot be relied on.

- **Inconstant** is a rather literary word suggesting that changes are not only sudden and frequent but also inexplicable. It is applied particularly to someone who is not faithful in love: *a man who was inconstant in his affections*.
- **Changeable** is a more common word for people and things liable to frequent variation. It tends to suggest changes that are quite dramatic: *she experienced changeable moods and panic attacks. Changeable* is regularly used of weather: *outlook for tomorrow: changeable with rain at times*.
- **Capricious** emphasizes the fact that someone's changes of mind and of behaviour spring from irrational and unpredictable whims, making them totally unreliable: *he was capricious and manipulative*. A *capricious* person is both irresponsible and inconsiderate.
- Coming from an Old English word meaning 'deceitful', **fickle** is a strongly disapproving description of someone who changes their views and allegiances very rapidly: *voters are fickle*. A *fickle lover* is shallow and transfers their affections repeatedly from one person to another: *men are so fickle, always on the lookout for someone new*.

keen: acute, penetrating

- **Keen** is used of sensitive and powerful perception, both physical and mental (*his keen hearing | a keen intellect*); when applied to someone's eyes, it often suggests an appearance of alertness and perceptiveness as well as actual power: *his keen eyes went from Thomas to Ralf*. The impressions or attitudes resulting from *keen* mental perception are intense: *young people show a keen awareness of animal welfare*.
- Someone whose physical or mental perception is **acute** can detect small details that are not readily apparent to others: *young children have a particularly acute sense of smell*. An *acute thinker* will produce *acute comments* and *acute criticism*, identifying central issues and making perceptive points about them. Intense and insistent emotion may be described as *acute*: *acute grief at the loss of her parents*.
- **Penetrating** eyes may or may not have good sight, but they look as though they can see through you: *she was unable to meet his penetrating eyes*. A *penetrating mind* enables one to see deeply into a problem and think up *penetrating questions*, calculated to reveal important truths.

kind: kindly, benevolent

These words all apply to people who care about and try to promote the well-being and happiness of others.

- A **kind** person shows consideration for others, either by behaving helpfully, thoughtfully, and generously (*it was very kind of you to make her a cake*) or by being gentle and caring, especially to someone in trouble or distress (*the doctor was so* *kind when Daddy was ill*). *Kind* is also used in polite requests, where the speaker is not in fact concerned with the generous or kindly feelings of the person addressed: *please be so kind as to excuse me*.

- **Kindly** is often used of older people or of people with authority. It suggests a warm and tolerant kindness: *she was kindly, almost motherly*.
- The sense of authority or superiority is still stronger when someone is described as **benevolent**. A *benevolent ruler* or *benevolent dictatorship* has the good of the subjects at heart and acts to promote it. *Benevolent* can also be used of a parent or other older person who is detached from but pleased by the happiness of younger or less experienced people: *he was like a benevolent uncle*.

languid: lethargic, listless

These words all describe people (or their actions) that are or appear to be lacking in enthusiasm or energy.

- A **languid** person may very well be alert and focused, but if so, they do not show it: *his seemingly effortless, languid run-up to the wicket*. *Languid* implies disinclination rather than inability: it can also be used to describe a pleasantly lazy stretch of time: *a languid weekend at his Tuscan villa* (the implication being that the weekenders could have been more energetic if they had wanted to).
- A **lethargic** person has no control over their lack of energy (*I felt sluggish and lethargic*), a condition that may be due to exhaustion, illness, or climatic heat and humidity. *Lethargy* was originally a technical term meaning 'sleeping sickness' (a tropical disease in which sufferers cannot wake up). It was later extended to refer to torpor due to other causes.
- **Listless** originally meant 'lacking appetite or desire', from the archaic word *list* 'desire'. Someone who is listless has lost interest in pretty well everything: *after he lost his job he became listless and depressed*.

lazy: idle, indolent

- A **lazy** person is reluctant to expend any energy or go to any trouble, the implication generally being that there is a particular task that they could or should be doing and are not doing: *he's too lazy to mow the lawn*. This attitude tends to result in *lazy work* or *lazy thinking*, avoiding anything difficult or original.
- **Idle** is more strongly critical, as in *you're an idle scrounger*. But when applied to machines or factories, the word loses its critical overtones: *the mill had stood idle since 1914*. *Idle* can also be used of something that is unproductive because it is aimless (*idle curiosity*) or has no basis in reality (*idle threats* | *idle fears*).
- **Indolent** emphasizes disinclination to exert oneself: *all the girls were indolent and frivolous*. The word was originally a medical term meaning 'causing no pain' (*an indolent ulcer*), hence 'having no effect' and so 'doing nothing'.

linger: loiter, dawdle

The idea common to these words is that of prolonging an activity or staying longer than necessary.

- **Linger** is the most general word. A person may linger somewhere because they are enjoying being there, not merely because they are wasting time: *she lingered in the yard, enjoying the warm sunshine*. A person's eyes may linger on a pleasant sight, or one person's fingers may linger on another's, in a gesture of affection. More broadly, *linger* is used to refer to anything that lasts longer than is normal or expected, e.g. *a lingering death* | *suspicion still lingers*.
- There is an implication that someone who is **loitering** is up to no good: *teenagers loitering in front of a newsagent's, drinking shandy and smoking*.
- Someone who is **dawdling** should probably be somewhere else: *he dawdled aimlessly around the streets*. It is used of slow and idle movement and of wasting time generally.

malign: defame, slander, libel, traduce

All these verbs involve X making unfair or damaging critical remarks to Y about Z.

- **Malign** is a general term for making false or unjustifiable criticisms. One can malign someone unintentionally: *I could be maligning the lad—I haven't seen much of him lately*.
- To **defame** someone is to make an unfair critical or accusatory remark about them which, once known by others, will damage their reputation to such an extent that legal action may be called for: *he convinced the jurors that he had been defamed by the article*. Malicious intent is not necessarily implied; the test of defamation is the resultant damage.
- In legal usage **slandering** someone is saying something untrue about them so as to damage their reputation, whereas **libelling** them is making such a remark in written or other 'permanent' form (which is held to include broadcasting and the Internet).
- **Traduce** is a more formal term for the deliberate telling of damaging untruths: *he is traducing his colleagues with unsubstantiated accusations*.

meagre: sparse, scanty

All these words are applicable when there is not enough of something, or less than might have been expected.

- **Meagre** is generally used of necessities such as food and money. It suggests that there is not enough (*the meagre resources of the state pension*) or that what there is is of poor quality (*a bowl of meagre gruel*).
- **Sparse** means 'thinly dispersed'—that is, small or few in relation to the area covered or the space to be filled: *a sparse and scattered population*.
- **Scanty** means 'small' or 'inadequate'; it is now often used of skimpy or revealing clothing: *the women looked cold in their scanty bodices*.

moving: touching, affecting

All three words relate to the arousing of emotions, generally ones in which pleasure and pain are mixed.

- To find something **moving** is to have deep emotions aroused by it, often through sympathy with someone else's suffering:

a moving display of drawings by children in a concentration camp. The feelings may be experienced as both painful and uplifting: *a moving tribute to the power and determination of the human spirit*.

- Something **touching** inspires feelings of tenderness, sometimes verging on the sentimental: *there was a touching air of innocence about the boy*. *Touching* is less intense than *moving*. It can also convey someone's gratitude for an unexpected service or tribute: *your concern is most touching*.
- **Affecting** is a less common term for something arousing a sympathy or sadness that is experienced as pleasurable: *an affecting tale of romantic tragedy*.

naked: nude, bare

- The standard word for someone who isn't wearing any clothes is **naked**. This word also has several well-established metaphorical uses: *the naked eye* is unaided by a telescopic or similar instrument, while a *naked light bulb* is not shielded or dimmed by a shade. One might have expected *naked self-interest* to be hidden or disguised as something more respectable.
- **Nude**, from Latin *nudus*, is slightly more formal or euphemistic than the good old Anglo-Saxon word *naked*. It is used especially with reference to paintings and photographs of naked people.
- **Bare** is another Anglo-Saxon word, used typically to refer to a part of the body rather than the whole thing: *running about in bare feet*. Doing something *with your bare hands* implies that you are not using any tools, rather than that you have taken off your gloves. In its metaphorical uses, *bare* suggests the removal of everything that is not absolutely indispensable: *the bare bones of a news story | a small bare room containing only a single bed and a wooden chair*.

native: indigenous, aboriginal

It would be odd to describe a **native** New Yorker as **indigenous**, although both words refer to someone or something that is associated with a particular place by birth or origin.

- **Native**, related to *nativity* (meaning 'birth'), refers to the place where an individual was born (*he left his native Germany in his teens*). It often refers to qualities that someone has possessed since birth: *she possessed a certain amount of native wit*. In a sense that overlaps with *indigenous*, *native* denotes people or other living things which originated in the region or country being discussed (*native fauna*). *Native peoples*, with their *native cultures*, were looked down on in the days of the British Empire, so that native became a derogatory word when applied to a human being, but in expressions such as *native Australian* it is now recovering its dignity.
- **Indigenous** is a more technical word, used to refer to populations which have been in a particular place since time immemorial, and to their social, cultural, and economic systems: *the indigenous languages of Nigeria*.
- There are no longer any **aboriginal** New Yorkers. The word comes from the Latin phrase *ab origine*, 'from the beginning', and refers to the earliest known inhabitants of a place or to primitive peoples who have no known ancestors and have inhabited a region since long before the earliest historical time.

new: novel, fresh, original, newfangled

The more specific synonyms emphasize different aspects of being **new**.

- What is **novel** is interestingly new or unusual; the word may hint at surprise and approval: *an interesting and novel solution*.
- **Fresh** can mean 'new and different': *the trial was reopened to consider fresh evidence*. It can also mean 'good or active because new': *the memory was still fresh in their minds | use fresh vegetables, not tinned*.
- **Original** is used to refer to something that is not derived from anything else: *an interesting and original line of argument*.
- What is **newfangled** is new, but disapproved of or unwanted: *expecting them to sing newfangled and jolly hymns*. Someone who describes something as newfangled risks being perceived, often with some amusement, as merely giving voice to the querulous discontent of the elderly or reactionary.

obstinate: stubborn, headstrong, wilful

These words express an exasperated reaction to someone's determination to have their own way in the face of persuasion or pressure to the contrary.

- Someone who is **obstinate** resolutely refuses to listen to reason: *he sensed obstinate refusal rather than a willingness to bargain*.
- Someone who is **stubborn** is even more obstinate than someone who is *obstinate*. *Stubborn* can imply deliberate or irrational obstructiveness, rather than mere refusal to comply with persuasion: *you're not in a fit state to drive, but I assumed you'd be stubborn about it*. *Stubborn* is the word most immediately associated by speakers with animals, especially and proverbially mules.
- Whereas *obstinate* and *stubborn* imply refusal to act in accordance with the wishes of others, **headstrong** implies a determination to act in accordance with one's own wishes, regardless of the opinions of others: *a headstrong woman who had always flouted convention*.
- Someone described as **wilful** is being condemned for their determination to do what they want regardless of its effects or of others' feelings: *she was wilful, determined, and manipulative*. The wilful person is often seen as immature.

offensive: derogatory, insulting, rude

These words illustrate the delicacy required in dealing with others: offence and distress can be caused in various ways, unconsciously as well as intentionally.

- An **offensive** remark or expression makes someone deeply hurt, upset, or angry, whether or not the speaker realizes or intends this: *the allegations are very offensive | offensive language*. The person who is distressed is not necessarily the subject of the remarks.
- A **derogatory** comment, on the other hand, is deliberately intended to express a low opinion of someone: *she tells me I'm fat and is always making derogatory remarks*.

- **Insulting** language or behaviour shows a lack of respect: *the Minister's reply is arrogant and insulting | the cartoon is insulting to men.* It is generally intended to upset or annoy. Even if this is not the intended result, the speaker is not usually worried if this occurs.
- Someone who is **rude** ignores the rules of good manners. They show a lack of consideration for other people's feelings, either in what they say or in their manner: *Mandy's so rude and ungrateful | 'None of your business,' was his rude reply.*

opportune: timely, auspicious

- **Opportune** is used mainly to refer to a favourable occasion for doing something: *I waited for an opportune moment to discuss the idea.* When applied to actions or events occurring at favourable moments, it can suggest the role of chance in producing a happy outcome: *an opportune visit from the manager allowed him to air his views.*
- A **timely** action or event occurs at a moment when it can make the greatest difference to a situation: *the assassins were stopped only by the timely intervention of a patrol.* A *timely reminder* is given when it is much needed, if not overdue.
- Coming from Latin *auspex*, a word referring to someone who watched the flight of birds for favourable omens, **auspicious** can mean 'lucky': *an auspicious day was chosen for the wedding.* More generally, it is used of situations where all the circumstances are conducive to the success of a new undertaking: *he is waiting for the most auspicious moment to call an election.*

perceptible: palpable, appreciable, noticeable

- What is **perceptible** can be noticed, but only just: *barely perceptible hesitation.*
- Something that is **palpable** impinges far more forcefully on our consciousness. A more formal word, literally meaning 'able to be touched or felt', *palpable* is applied to something that is intellectually self-evident (*a palpable untruth*), or to an intense feeling or atmosphere: *the silence, like the sunlight, was palpable, sensuous.*
- Something **appreciable** is large or important enough to be easily perceived and to be taken into account in plans or calculations: *pupils may have to travel appreciable distances.*
- Something described as **noticeable** is not merely prominent enough to be perceived but conspicuous: *noticeable results guaranteed in 28 days.*

polite: civil, courteous

These three adjectives all describe people or actions that are considerate and well mannered: **polite** is the most common form.

- **Polite** can also mean 'civilized and cultured', and politeness can involve glossing over subjects felt to be coarse or embarrassing: *this is not what passes for humour in polite society.*
- Behaviour that is **civil** is formal and rather reserved, and may indeed be only the absolute minimum required to avoid actually being rude: *his replies were civil, but scarcely welcoming.*
- **Courteous** comes from a Middle English term meaning 'having manners fit for a royal court'; it suggests a particularly graceful and charming politeness: *friendly and courteous staff.*

quarrel: argue, wrangle, dispute, bicker

- **Quarrel** is used of people having an angry argument: *he married her for her money, so now they're always quarrelling.* One may also dispassionately *quarrel* with something in the sense of disagreeing with or objecting to it: *there was nothing in this document with which he could quarrel.*
- **Arguing** involves two people staunchly and sometimes even acrimoniously defending two different, incompatible points of view: *he and Martin used to argue for hours about the paranormal.*
- **Wrangle** suggests a long, complex, and sometimes intense debate or argument: *after considerable wrangling a compromise was reached.*
- People who **dispute** are expected to show more reasoned argument than if they are merely quarrelling. *Dispute* is mainly used of denying or arguing against a specified view: *people who dispute the official interpretation of their rights.*
- **Bickering** represents an argument as childish. The criticism may be of the logic employed, or of the triviality of the issue disputed: *the constant bickering between Mary and his mother.*

refuse: decline, reject, spurn

Choose the right word, and you can indicate not just *that* 'No' was said, but also *how* it was said.

- Simply saying 'No' to a request, suggestion, or offer is best indicated by **refuse**: *she refused to speak to the media.*
- A polite, rather formal refusal is indicated by **decline**: *he declined to speculate about a cancer cure.*
- **Reject** suggests that what is on offer is felt to be not good enough or not justified: *an article which her editor had rejected. Reject* is also used of the body's immune system when it kills a transplanted organ.
- **Spurn** suggests an even higher degree of distaste or contempt (*the younger brother he spurns as a liar*), although nowadays headline writers often use it in a looser sense: *pensions managers may spurn equities.*
- Both **spurn** and **reject** are also used of refusing affection to someone who used to be or might be expected to be the object of it: *a spurned lover | she didn't want him to feel rejected after his sister was born.*

religious: devout, pious

- **Religious** has the broadest sense: it is mostly used in factual statements conveying neither approval nor disapproval (*both men were deeply religious*). Sometimes *religious* is used in an extended sense to suggest that someone attaches particular importance to a secular object or pursuit; there may be a critical suggestion that this is not a fit object for such devotion: *he always had a religious obsession with fame.*

- **Devout** is used to indicate a deep and genuine religious commitment: *he was a devout Quaker and would not allow a pub in the village. Devout* is also used to convey total or uncritical enthusiasm for or commitment to a secular object or pursuit: *a devout soccer fan.*
- **Pious**, too, conveys religious commitment: *donations to the Church from pious laymen.* It may also be used to denote hypocritical religiosity: *I know what's under that pious face of yours.*

sarcastic: sardonic, ironic, caustic

All these words imply a mocking attitude, but some are nastier than others.

- A **sarcastic** comment conveys scorn and mockery which is meant to leave the person on the receiving end hurt and angry, while possibly entertaining others who may hear it. Sarcasm typically involves using an utterance to express the opposite of what it literally means: *'That's nice,' Broomhead said in his most sarcastic manner | the youngsters gave a sarcastic cheer.*
- **Sardonic** suggests a more cynical amusement. Sardonic people probably feel secure that their insight and freedom from illusion are superior to other people's—hence the frequency with which someone is said to give a *sardonic smile.*
- **Ironic** remarks or humour also spring from a sense of acute insight or perceptiveness, but without any element of scorn or cynicism. Like sarcasm, irony uses utterances to convey the opposite of their literal meaning, but more subtly and with an effect of wry amusement rather than blatant mockery.
- **Caustic** is even more scathing than *sarcastic.* It suggests the use of wit to make criticism or rejection all the more devastating: *she managed to bite back the caustic retort on the tip of her tongue.*

strange: odd, curious, peculiar

These words are all applied to things that are unusual or unfamiliar; they generally also suggest that something is in some way surprising.

- **Strange** is the most neutral term for something that is not expected or is hard to understand or explain: *this is strange behaviour for a left-wing party.*
- **Odd** gives a stronger sense of puzzlement: *what an odd thing to say.*
- Describing something as **curious** may suggest that one finds it not only strange or puzzling but also interesting: *the church has a curious history.*
- Something described as **peculiar** is felt to be very strange, even disturbingly so: *whoever thought up that joke has a peculiar sense of humour.*

stroll: saunter, amble

These words have in common the idea of relaxed and unhurried movement.

- People who are **strolling** are typically walking for pleasure, at a relaxed pace which allows them to enjoy their surroundings or company, or both: *a day for lovers to stroll through leafy woods.* They are definitely under no pressure to exert themselves.
- **Saunter** can be used in the same way, but it may also suggest a more self-conscious or conspicuous freedom from hurry or anxiety. Someone may saunter to emphasize their lack of concern when they might be expected to be nervous (*Jasper was sauntering past the police station*), or their feeling that they have no need for permission to be where they are (*Dana sauntered into Claudia's office*).
- Someone who is **ambling** is walking in a very slow or casual way, giving the impression that they have no particular destination or objective: *he ambled down the corridor, whistling.*

strut: swagger, parade

These words all refer to types of ostentatious movement.

- **Strut** is frequently used of birds as well of people—especially of birds engaged in courtship displays. It refers to a stiff, erect movement suggesting aggressive self-importance: *he strutted around his vast office like a peacock.* There is often a suggestion that this self-importance is combined with other qualities that the writer or speaker finds obnoxious or that it is used to conceal feelings of inadequacy.
- A **swagger** is an easier, more expansive and swinging movement, reflecting arrogant self-confidence: *he swaggered around the room in his new uniform.*
- Someone who is **parading** is walking in a way that is calculated to draw attention: *I've seen her parading round the village in her fur coat and jewellery.*

subject: topic, theme

- **Subject** is the most general term for something that is or could be written, talked, or thought about: *his mind was no longer on the subject of politics | please send questions on any subjects you would like discussed.*
- When distinguished from *subject*, **topic** can refer to a smaller and more specific area for discussion—a book on the *subject* of Victorian England might have chapters on *topics* such as wealth and poverty, women, and so forth. Idiomatically, something discussed in conversation is more likely to be a *topic* than a *subject.*
- A **theme** is typically associated with a relatively long work or discussion, recurring throughout it and unifying it: *she deals delicately with the themes of love and jealousy.* A *theme* is generally developed or elaborated rather than discussed or debated, in contrast with *subjects* or *topics.*

supersede: replace, supplant

- Something that has been **superseded** has had its place taken by something more up to date and consequently regarded as more efficient or otherwise preferable: *the older models have now been superseded.*
- **Replace** is a more neutral term. One person or thing may replace another as part of a normal process (*the interim*

government was replaced by an elected one) or in an emergency (*Heslop replaces Underwood, who has a broken jaw*); the person or thing replaced is not necessarily seen as outdated or inefficient.

- Someone or something that **supplants** another is often seen as having no rightful claim on the place they have taken, or as being in some respect a poor substitute: *he entertained dark suspicions about Jenkins' ambition to supplant him.*

sure: certain, positive, convinced, definite

The element that these words have in common is the implication that the person in question is confident that their belief is well founded, even indisputable. (Of course, they may be in for a nasty shock.)

- **Sure** and **certain** are very close in meaning, but someone who claims to be *certain* about something is making an even stronger, more emphatic claim than someone who is *sure* about it: *I'm certain he heard me* expresses a greater degree of confidence than *I'm sure he heard me.*
- **Positive** is typically used in speech or reported speech; it expresses absolute confidence: *'Are you sure she won't want to pursue the issue?' 'Positive'.*
- Someone who is **convinced** about something feels a certainty that has probably been growing over time: *I'm convinced the killer was someone local.*
- Someone with clear and confidently held views or beliefs may be **definite** in expressing them clearly and uncompromisingly: *'Not a chance.' Jean was definite.*

task: job, chore, duty

These words all apply to activities that people are obliged to do, whether they want to or not.

- **Task** is the broadest term, meaning 'a piece of work to be done': *he was given the task of drawing up a programme of action*. The *tasks* that someone has to do may be assigned to them by a person who has authority over them, or undertaken voluntarily.
- A **job** is primarily the occupation by which someone earns their living, in the course of which they may regularly have to perform a number of *tasks*: *he landed a job as a technical engineer*. A single piece of work for which someone is paid may also be referred to as a *job*: *the mechanic quoted him £50 for the job.*
- **Chores** are tedious routine tasks (*everyday chores like shopping or housework*) or tasks that are felt to be unpleasant but unavoidable (*financial planning is seen as a nasty chore*).
- **Duty** is used of tasks which, in some way or degree, one is required to perform: *her official duties. Duty* also highlights moral or legal obligation (*a sense of filial duty*).

threaten: menace, intimidate

- When one person **threatens** another they indicate or say that they will do something harmful or unpleasant if that person does not comply with their wishes: *robbers threatened the shop assistant with a gun. Threaten* can also be used of something that constitutes a danger (*the Amazonian forest is being threatened by a major oil extraction project*) and of undesirable events that are thought to be likely (*the slick threatens to become the world's largest*).
- **Menace** emphasizes the fear or unease produced by a serious threat (*the menacing gun was held low*) or by something perceived as sinister though in fact not necessarily dangerous (*the palace was a weird, menacing building*).
- To **intimidate** someone is to behave in such a way as to frighten them into submission or inaction: *one witness had disappeared and two more had been intimidated.* Someone or something may also intimidate another unintentionally, appearing so formidable that the person perceiving them loses confidence: *I was intimidated by the whole idea of Cambridge.*

unfortunate: unlucky, ill-starred, hapless

These words all express a recognition that something undesirable and probably undeserved has happened to someone, with some degree of sympathy for them.

- **Unfortunate** is the most general term for referring to the undesirability of a person's situation: *the unfortunate Cunningham was sacked.*
- Describing someone as **unlucky** lays greater emphasis on the element of chance involved in their misfortune: the undesirable outcome was a matter of chance, generally with no rational explanation: *one of the unlucky couples had their wedding cancelled. Unlucky* is often used of people who are unsuccessful despite their best efforts: *Cooper was unlucky, coming 11th.*
- **Ill-starred** is seldom found outside self-consciously literary writing. The stars are often associated with inexorable fate, so it is not surprising that *ill-starred* means 'doomed from the outset': *Scott's ill-starred Polar expedition.*
- Coming from *hap*, an old word meaning 'luck', **hapless** too is generally used self-consciously, aiming at a particular effect. The pity expressed for the *hapless* person is sometimes tinged with amusement or exasperation. It is strongly hinted that they have contributed to their own misfortune through incompetence or weakness: *the hapless Finnegan missed his putt*. The similarity in sound of 'hopeless' and 'helpless' may have played a part in the development of this implication.

vague: hazy, indistinct

These words all describe something that is hard to define or understand precisely.

- A **vague** idea or statement is too imprecise to have a single definite interpretation: *he had been very vague about his activities*. Physical objects may be described as *vague* if their outline is not sharp: *a vague, just perceptible shape.*
- **Hazy** is applied more often than *vague* to physical objects that are blurred and hard to perceive distinctly: *the coastline stretched away, hazy in the hot sunshine. Hazy* memories or ideas can be recalled or described only in a general way—the details are unclear or not fully understood: *I have only hazy memories of that event.*
- Something that is **indistinct** cannot be clearly focused on as a separate entity (and so cannot be identified) by the eye or the ear: *a banging and shouting, muffled and indistinct*. This sense is extended to ideas that cannot be identified and understood: *the line which the law draws is at the very least indistinct.*

valid: sound, cogent

- Something **valid** has force or power: the word comes from the Latin *validus*, meaning 'strong'. When applied to reasoning, the word indicates a power to convince: a *valid argument* contains no errors of logic, and a *valid conclusion* follows logically from the argument in its favour.
- **Sound** comes from Germanic words meaning 'healthy', and can also have the sense 'solid' or 'dependable'. An argument or position that is *sound* is secure against objections because it is based on good evidence and accurate reasoning: *scientifically sound papers*.
- **Cogent** (from Latin *cogere*, meaning 'compel') refers to arguments that compel the assent of anyone who has understood them: *an impassioned and cogent plea for judicial reform*.

woman: girl, lady

The neutral word for an adult female person is **woman**; other terms may cause offence. When used by a man, **girl** is held by some women to be patronizing and to suggest that a woman is not being seen as deserving serious attention. **Lady** is a rather old-fashioned term, which used to be the standard polite word, but now tends to be seen as having connotations of pretentiousness.

work: labour, toil

- **Work** is the general term for things that have to be done, either in order to earn a living or because they are necessary if someone is to achieve a particular aim: *clerical work* | *I've some work to do in the garden*. When applied to the actual doing of these things, *work* implies that effort is involved: *thank you for your hard work on the project*.
- **Labour** typically indicates physical work, especially when this is hard and exhausting: *long hours of manual labour*.
- **Toil** refers to exhausting, tedious, and seemingly unending hard work: *most of his life was spent in toil on the farm*.

yearn: long, pine, hanker

- To **yearn** is to experience an intense desire, usually for something impossible to obtain; recognition of this difficulty or impossibility means that the desire tends to be mixed with grief or sorrow: *she yearned for her missing father*.
- If you **long** for something, you also feel a deep desire for it: *she longed for a totally committed relationship*. You can also long for something quite trivial that you are likely to get fairly soon: *I'm longing for a cup of tea*.
- To **pine** is to long for someone or something that one has lost: *even though he had a new girlfriend she still pined for him*. The feeling may be so intense and obsessive that it results in physical illness and 'wasting away'.
- If someone **hankers** for something, they have a persistent, nagging feeling of desire for it: *he was still hankering for his home*. It may be used to refer to a form of daydreaming, wishing that some feature of one's life were different but recognizing that it will not change: *she had always hankered to be tall and fair*.

Weird and Wonderful Words

This section gives a wide selection of some of the more unusual and obscure words in the English language, together with information about their meanings, origins, pronunciations, and links to other words or word groups. Intended as interesting, colourful, and fun additions to your vocabulary, the words should also prove useful in word games and quizzes.

absquatulate ▶ to leave somewhere abruptly. The word was made up in the US in the mid 19th century with the intention of sounding like a Latin word: it is pronounced 'ab**skwot**yōōlayt'.

abomasum ▶ the fourth stomach of a ruminant (an animal that chews the cud, such as a cow or sheep). The three other stomachs are called the rumen, reticulum, and omasum: the abomasum secretes acid and digestive enzymes and is the one that corresponds to the stomach of other mammals. It is pronounced 'abō**may**sum'.

afreet ▶ a powerful jinn or demon in Arabian and Muslim mythology. The word comes from the Arabic *'ifrīt* and is pronounced 'afreet'.

amphibology ▶ a phrase or sentence that is grammatically ambiguous, such as *She sees more of her children than her husband*, which can mean either 'she sees more of her children than her husband does' or 'she sees more of her children than she does of her husband'. The term comes from the Greek word *amphibolos*, meaning 'ambiguous'.

amphisbaena ▶ a mythical serpent which has a head at each end and is able to move in either direction. The word comes from the Greek words *amphis*, meaning 'both ways' and *bainein*, meaning 'to go' and is pronounced 'amfis**bee**nə'.

anfractuous ▶ an adjective meaning 'winding or circuitous', as in *life's anfractuous journey*. It comes from the Latin word *anfractus*, meaning 'a bending'.

anguilliform ▶ an adjective meaning 'shaped like or resembling an eel', from the Latin word for eel, *anguilla*. It is pronounced 'ang**gwill**iform'.

aspergillum ▶ an implement such as a brush or perforated container, used for sprinkling holy water in religious ceremonies: it is pronounced 'aspə**jill**um'. The rite of sprinkling holy water at the beginning of the Mass is still practised occasionally in Catholic churches and is called *asperges*. This word comes from the first words of the Latin text of Psalm 50(51):9, *Asperges me*, translated by the King James Bible as 'Purge me'. The psalm is recited before Mass during the sprinkling of the holy water.

autotomy ▶ the casting off of a limb or other part of the body by an animal under threat. Certain lizards, for example, if seized by the tail by a predator, can shed their tails. The discarded tail continues to thrash about, thus distracting the attention of the predator and allowing the lizard to escape. The term comes from the Greek words *autos*, meaning 'self' and *-tomia*, meaning 'cutting'.

Barmecide ▶ an adjective meaning 'illusory or imaginary and therefore disappointing'. The word comes from *Barmkī*, the name of an Arabic prince in the *Arabian Nights' Entertainments*, who gave a beggar a feast consisting of a succession of ornate but empty dishes. Most English words ending in '-cide', such as **homicide** or **insecticide**, are nouns rather than adjectives and refer to a person or substance that kills, or an act of killing. In this class of words the ending or suffix '-cide' comes from the Latin verb *caedere*, meaning 'to kill'.

bibliopole ▶ a person who buys and sells books, especially rare ones. The word is based on the Greek word *biblion*, which means 'book'. Other related words are **bibliomania**, a passionate enthusiasm for collecting and possessing books, **bibliophile**, a person who has a great love of books, and **bibliotherapy**, the use of books as therapy in the treatment of mental or psychological disorders.

bilboes ▶ an iron bar with sliding shackles, used in the past to put round a prisoner's ankles. It has been suggested that the word may come from *Bilbao*: many of the instruments were supposedly manufactured there before being shipped on board the Spanish Armada to be used for shackling prisoners taken by the invading fleet. In fact the word occurs in English many years before 1588, the year of the Armada, so this suggestion is doubtful.

blatherskite ▶ a person who talks at great length without making much sense. The word originated in the 17th century; it was adopted into American colloquial speech during the War of Independence (1775–83) from a Scottish song *Maggie Lauder*, by F. Semphill, which was popular with the American troops. It is pronounced '**bla<u>th</u>**əskīt'.

borborygmus ▶ a rumbling or gurgling noise made by the movement of fluid and gas in the intestines. It comes from a Greek word with the same meaning, *borborugmos*, and is pronounced 'borbə**rig**məs'.

branks ▶ an instrument used in the past to punish a nagging woman, consisting of an iron framework for the head and a sharp metal gag for restraining the tongue. The word was in use from the 16th century but it is not clear how it originated: it has been compared with the German word *Pranger*, meaning 'a pillory', the Dutch *prang* 'a fetter', and with the late Middle English *barnacle(s)*, a word for a powerful bit used to restrain a horse. Another term for **branks** is **scold's bridle**.

bruxism ▶ involuntary and habitual grinding of the teeth, typically during sleep: the term is pronounced '**bruk**siz'm'. Another word that means 'tooth-grinding' is **thegosis**: this is used to refer to tooth-grinding by animals as a means of sharpening their teeth.

cachinnate ▶ to laugh loudly or raucously. The word comes from the Latin verb *cachinnare*, which probably originated as an imitation of the sound of raucous laughter, and it is pronounced '**kakk**inayt'.

cacoethes ▶ an urge to do something inadvisable. The term comes from the Greek words *kakos* 'bad' and *ēthos* 'disposition' and is pronounced 'kakō**ee**<u>th</u>eez'. Several English words are based on the Greek word *kakos*, including **cacodemon**, a malevolent spirit or person, **cacography**, bad handwriting or spelling, and **cacophony**, a harsh, discordant mixture of sounds.

caducity ▶ the physical and mental infirmity and frailty that may be experienced in old age: the word comes from the Latin adjective *caducus*, which means 'liable to fall'.

callithumpian ▶ an adjective meaning 'having to do with or resembling a band of discordant instruments or a noisy parade'. An American term whose first recorded use is in 1836, it may have developed from the old Southern English dialect word *gallithumpian*. This was a name for a heckler or troublemaker at parliamentary elections.

cantillate ▶ to chant or intone a passage of religious text. The word comes from the Latin verb *cantare* 'to sing'; other words based on this or on *canere*, another Latin verb with the same meaning, include **cantata**, **canticle**, **chant**, and **enchant**.

carphology ▶ convulsive or involuntary movements made by delirious patients, such as plucking at the bedclothes or grasping at imaginary objects. This word originated in the mid 19th century: it comes from the Greek words *karphos* 'straw' and *legein* 'to collect'. Another term for the same phenomenon is **floccillation**.

cereology ▶ the study or investigation of crop circles. The word comes from *Ceres*, the name of the goddess of corn, and its first recorded use was in 1990.

chiliad ▶ a group of a thousand things or a period of a thousand years, from the Greek word *khilioi*, meaning 'one thousand': it is pronounced '**kil**eead'. Most English words meaning 'a thousand of something' begin with the prefix *kilo-*, for example **kilogram**, **kilometre**, or **kilowatt**. This prefix, also taken from *khilioi*, was introduced in the French language at the institution of the metric system in 1795, as a way of describing weights and measures containing 1000 times the basic unit.

cicisbeo ▶ an archaic word for a married woman's male companion or lover, pronounced 'sisiz**bay**ō'. The word comes from Italian, and the *Vocabulario degli Accademici della Crusca*, a 17th-century Italian dictionary, speculates that it may have developed from an inversion of *bel cece* 'beautiful chick (pea)', but its origin remains obscure.

clepsydra ▶ an instrument used in the past to measure time by marking the flow of water into or out of a container. Its name comes from the Greek words *kleptein* 'to steal' and *hudōr* 'water', and it is pronounced '**klep**sidrə'.

coffle ▶ a line of animals or slaves fastened or driven along together. An 18th-century word, it comes from the Arabic word *ḳāfila*, which means 'caravan', in the sense of 'a group of people travelling together'.

colporteur ▶ a person who peddles books, newspapers, or other writings, especially someone employed by a society to travel about and sell or distribute bibles and religious tracts. The word's direct origin is French, but it probably comes ultimately from the Latin verb *comportare*, meaning 'to carry something with one'.

concinnity ▶ elegance or neatness of literary or artistic style, from Latin *concinnus*, meaning 'skilfully put together'. It is pronounced 'kən**sin**iti'.

coprolalia ▶ a technical term for the involuntary and repetitive use of obscene language that may occur as a symptom of certain mental illnesses or neurological disorders, e.g. Tourette's syndrome. It comes from the Greek words *kopros*, meaning 'dung' and *lalia* meaning 'speech or chatter' and is pronounced 'koprə**lay**liə'.

coriaceous ▶ an adjective meaning 'resembling or having the texture of leather', from the Latin noun *corium*, which means 'leather, skin, or hide'. Other English words which come from this include **cuirass**, a piece of armour originally made of leather, **currier**, a person who treats tanned leather, and **excoriate**, one meaning of which is 'to damage or remove the surface of skin'.

crinkum-crankum ▶ an archaic word for elaborate decoration or detail, coined in the mid 17th century. It is an example of a class of words formed by a process called 'reduplication', the repetition of a syllable or group of letters exactly or with a slight change, e.g. **dilly-dally**, **easy-peasy**, **pitter-patter**, **knick-knack**, or **hurly-burly**.

crottle ▶ a type of common lichen found on rocks, used in Scotland to make a golden-brown or reddish-brown dye for wool used in the manufacture of tweed.

cryptozoology ▶ the search for and study of animals whose existence or survival is disputed or unproven, such as the Loch Ness monster and the yeti. 'Crypto-' comes from the Greek word *kruptos*, meaning 'concealed, hidden': other English words based on this include **cryptic**, mysterious or obscure in meaning, **cryptogram**, a text written in code, and **cryptonym**, a code name.

cudbear ▶ a purple or violet powder used for dyeing, prepared from various types of lichen. The name was devised by Cuthbert Gordon, the 18th-century Scottish chemist who patented the powder, as a variation of his own first name.

dandiprat ▶ an archaic word for a young or insignificant person. The word arose in the early 16th century as a term for an English coin worth three halfpence, but its origin is unknown.

dariole ▶ a small round metal mould used in French cooking for baking and serving an individual sweet or savoury dish. The term comes from an Old French word for a small filled pasty.

decubitus ▶ a medical term (pronounced 'di**kyoo**bitəss') for the posture of someone who is lying down or lying in bed; **decubitus ulcer** is the technical term for a bedsore. The word comes from the Latin verb *decumbere*, which means 'to lie down': another English word which comes from this is the adjective **decumbent**, a botanical term describing a plant or part of a plant that is lying along the ground or other surface.

defervescence ▶ a medical term for the lessening of a fever, from the Latin verb *defervescere* meaning 'to stop boiling'. The English words **fervent**, **fervid**, and **fervour** all come from the Latin *fervere*, which means 'to boil'.

deglutition ▶ the action of process of swallowing. A technical term, it comes from the Latin verb *deglutire*, meaning 'to swallow something down'. The verb **swallow** comes from the Old English word *swelgan*.

degust ▶ to taste food or drink carefully, so as to fully appreciate it, from Latin *gustare* 'to taste'. A related word is **gustatory**, meaning 'having to do with tasting or the sense of taste', as in *asparagus is a gustatory treat*.

deipnosophist ▶ a person skilled in the art of dining and dinner-table conversation. The word comes from the Greek words *deipnon*, meaning 'dinner' and *sophist*, which means 'a wise man' and it is pronounced 'dīp**noss**əfist'. It is the title of a book written in about AD 228 by Atheneus, in which a group of learned men dine together, discussing subjects ranging from food and cookery to literary criticism.

deterge ▶ to cleanse something thoroughly. The word comes from the Latin verb *detergere*, meaning 'to wipe something away', as does the familiar noun, **detergent**.

discobolus ▶ a discus thrower in ancient Greece, from the Greek words *diskos* 'discus' and *-bolos* '-throwing'. The word is pronounced 'dis**kob**ələss'.

doryphore ▶ a person who is critical of others in a pedantic and annoyingly persistent way. The word was introduced into English in the 1950s by Sir Harold Nicholson: it comes from French, in which its literal meaning is 'Colorado beetle', but its ultimate origin is the Greek word *doruphoros*, which means 'spear-carrier'.

ecdysiast ▶ a striptease performer. The term was coined in the 1940s and it comes from the Greek word *ekdusis*, meaning 'shedding'. It is pronounced 'ek**diz**iast'.

edacious ▶ an adjective which means 'having to do with eating or fond of eating'. The term comes from the Greek verb *edere*, meaning 'to eat': other English words to do with food and eating which come from this verb are **comestibles** and **edible**.

eld ▶ old age, as in *the aches and pains of eld*. A word used mainly in poetry of the past, it comes from Old English, as do **elder** and **old**.

emacity ▶ fondness for buying things, from the Latin verb *emere*, meaning 'to buy'.

emmetropia ▶ the normal condition of the eye: perfect vision. The word was invented in the 19th century by F. C.

Donders, a Dutch physician, from the Greek adjective *emmetros* 'well-proportioned' and the ending or suffix '-opia'. This suffix is usually found in words for visual disorders, such as **myopia**, short-sightedness, **presbyopia**, long-sightedness, **protanopia**, a form of colour blindess, or **hemeralopia**, difficulty seeing in daylight.

energumen ▶ a person believed to be possessed by the devil or a spirit. Originating in the 18th century, the word also means an enthusiast or fanatic: it comes from the Greek verb *energein*, meaning 'to work in or upon', and is pronounced 'enəgyo͞omən'.

ensorcell ▶ to enchant or fascinate someone. It comes from the French word *sorcier*, meaning 'sorcerer'.

entomophagy ▶ the eating of insects, especially by people rather than animals or other insects: it is pronounced 'entə**moff**əji'. *Entomon* is the Greek word for 'insect' and the ending or suffix '-phagy' comes from the Greek verb *phagein*, meaning 'to eat': other English words with the same ending include **ichthyophagy**, the eating of fish, or **coprophagy**, the eating of faeces or dung.

etui ▶ a small ornamental case for holding needles, cosmetics, and other articles. Prounced 'e**twee**', the term comes from the Old French word *estui*, meaning 'prison'. Interestingly, the English word **tweezers** is related to **etui**. It developed from *etweese*, which is the plural form of **etui**.

eucatastrophe ▶ a happy ending in a story. The word originated in the mid 20th century and is said to have been coined by J. R. R. Tolkien. One of the meanings of *catastrophe* is 'the denouement of a drama', while the prefix 'eu-' (from Greek *eu* 'well') indicates something good or pleasant, as in **eupeptic**, which means 'having a good digestion', or **euphonious**, meaning 'pleasing to the ear'.

famulus ▶ an assistant or attendant, especially one working for a magician or scholar. In Latin, *famulus* means 'servant'.

fipple ▶ the mouthpiece of a recorder or similar wind instrument. The term was first used in the 17th century and may be related to the Icelandic word *flipi*, meaning 'horse's lip'.

flews ▶ the thick pendulous lips of a bloodhound or similar dog. The word's origin is unknown, but it has been in use since the late 16th century.

floccinaucinihilipilification ▶ the action or habit of estimating something as worthless. The term comes from the Latin words *flocci, nauci, nihili*, and *pili*, all of which mean 'at little value'. It is rarely, if ever, used seriously, and is generally only encountered in word games or as an example of an extremely long word.

frondeur ▶ a political rebel. A French word, it was used as a name for the members of the group of rebellious French noblemen who instigated the Fronde, a series of civil wars (1648–53) in which the aristocracy rose up against Mazarin and the court during the minority of Louis XIV. A *fronde* was the name for a type of sling used in a children's game played in the streets of Paris at the time of the rebellion, and the original, literal meaning of *frondeur* was 'slinger'.

frore ▶ an adjective meaning 'frozen or frosty'. A now obsolete past participle of **freeze**, it is found mainly in poetry of the past.

fugacious ▶ an adjective which means 'transient or fleeting', as in *she was acutely conscious of her fugacious youth*. Pronounced 'fyo͞o**gay**shəs', the word comes from the Latin verb *fugere*, meaning 'to flee': another English word based on the same Latin verb is **fugitive**.

funambulist a tightrope walker. The term comes from the Latin words *funis* 'rope' and *ambulare* 'to walk', and is pronounced 'fyo͞o**namb**yo͞olist'.

furuncle ▶ a boil. A technical term, it comes from the Latin word *furunculus*, whose literal meaning is 'petty thief'. An extended meaning in Latin is 'a knob on a vine', the knob being regarded as stealing the vine's sap, and the word's meaning in English developed from this sense. It is pronounced '**fyo͞or**ungk'l'.

fuscous ▶ an adjective meaning 'dark and sombre in colour', from Latin *fuscus* 'dark or dusky'. Other English words which are based on this Latin adjective are **obfuscate**, to make something obscure or unclear, and **subfusc**, the name for the dark formal clothing worn for examinations and ceremonial or formal occasions at some universities.

futhark ▶ the Scandinavian runic alphabet. Pronounced '**fo͞o**thark', the word is made up of the first six letters of this alphabet: *f, u, th, a, r*, and *k*.

galligaskins ▶ a type of loosely fitting breeches worn in the 16th and 17th centuries. The origin of the word is complicated and uncertain, but it may come from the Italian word *grechesco*, which means 'Greek'. The breeches in question were apparently originally described as *alla grechesca*, meaning 'in the Greek fashion'.

gasconade ▶ extravagant boasting. The word arose in the 17th century from the French verb *gasconner*, meaning 'to talk like a Gascon, to brag': the inhabitants of Gascony were apparently notorious at that time for their bragging. It is pronounced 'gaskə**nayd**'.

glabrous ▶ a technical term which refers to skin that is hairless or a leaf that has no down. It comes from the Latin word *glaber*, which means 'hairless, smooth' and is pronounced '**glay**brəss'.

gnathic ▶ an adjective which means 'having to do with the jaws'. The word comes from *gnathos*, the Greek word for jaw, and is pronounced '**nath**ik' or '**nayth**ik'. A related word is **prognathous**, an adjective which refers to a person with a projecting jaw or chin.

gobemouche ▶ a gullible or credulous listener. Pronounced '**gob**moosh', the word comes from the French *gobe-mouches*, which translates as 'fly-catcher', possibly alluding to a gullible listener's open-mouthed expression.

guddle ▶ to fish with one's hands by groping under the stones or banks of a stream. A Scottish term, its origin is unknown.

habile ▶ an adjective meaning 'deft or skilful', as in *his habile fingers*. The word was first used in the 15th century as a different spelling of 'able' and it is pronounced '**hab**il'.

hallux ▶ an anatomical term for the big toe. It comes from the Latin word *allex*.

haruspex ▶ a religious official in ancient Rome who inspected the entrails of sacrificial animals in order to foretell the future. The first part of the word is related to a Sanskrit word *hirā*, which means 'artery', while '-spex' comes from the Latin verb *specere*, meaning 'to look at'. The word is pronounced 'hə**russ**peks', and its plural, **haruspices**, is pronounced 'hə**russ**piseez'.

hodiernal ▶ an adjective meaning 'having to do with the present day', from the Latin word *hodie*, 'today'. It is pronounced 'hodi**urn**'l' or 'hōdi**urn**'l'.

hoggin ▶ a mixture of sand and gravel, used especially in road-building. The word's origin is unknown.

horripilation ▶ the standing up of hairs on the skin as a result of cold, fear, or excitement. The word comes from the Latin verb *horrere*, meaning 'to stand on end; to tremble or shudder'. Other English words based on this include **horrent**, a term used mainly in poetry to refer to hair that is standing on end, and also the familiar adjectives **horrible**, **horrid**, and **horrific**.

imbrue ▶ to stain one's hand or sword with blood. A poetic term, it comes from the Old French verb *embruer*, which means 'to bedaub something'.

incrassate ▶ an adjective meaning 'thickened in form or consistency'. Pronounced 'in**krass**ayt', it comes from the Latin word *incrassatus*, which means 'made thick'.

ingurgitate ▶ to swallow something greedily. The word comes from the Latin verb *ingurgitare*, meaning 'to pour in', and this verb is itself formed from *in-* 'into' and *gurges* 'whirpool, gulf'. Other English words which come from the word *gurges* include **regurgitate** and **gorge**.

inspissate ▶ to thicken or congeal, from the Latin word *inspissare*, meaning 'to thicken'.

izzard ▶ an old name for the letter Z, which apparently developed from the Greek word for Z, *zēta*.

kenspeckle ▶ an adjective meaning 'conspicuous or easily recognizable'. A Scottish word, it was first used in the 16th century and comes from Scandinavian: it is probably based on the Old Norse words *kenna*, meaning 'to know or perceive' and *spak-*, *spek-*, meaning 'wise or wisdom'.

lablab ▶ a tropical Asian plant of the pea family. The word comes from Arabic.

labarum ▶ a banner or flag bearing symbolic motifs. Pronounced '**lab**ərum', it was originally used of Constantine the Great's imperial standard which bore Christian symbolic imagery fused with the military symbols of the Roman Empire. The word's origin is unknown.

lactarium ▶ a dairy: it comes from the Latin word *lac*, which means 'milk'. Several other English words come from this, for example **lactate**, **lactic**, and **lactose**. A more surprising derivation is **lettuce**: called *lactuca* in Latin, this name alluded to the plant's milky juice.

loblolly ▶ a North American pine tree with very long slender needles. The word is first found in the 16th century as a name for a type of thick gruel, but its origin and the reason why it later became a name for the tree are unknown.

logomachy ▶ an argument about words, from the Greek words *logos*, meaning 'word' and *-makhia*, meaning 'fighting'. Several other unusual English words end in '-machy': for example **tauromachy**, bullfighting, **theomachy**, a fight against God or between gods, and **sciamachy**, a form of mock fighting engaged in for exercise or practice.

luculent ▶ an adjective (pronounced '**lo͝o**kyoolənt') referring to speech or writing that is clearly expressed, as in *his luculent prose.* The word comes from the Latin noun *lux*, 'light', as does **lucid**, a more familiar word with the same meaning as **luculent**.

lurdan ▶ an idle or incompetent person. An archaic word, it comes from the French adjective *lourd*, meaning 'heavy'.

merkin ▶ an artificial covering of hair for the pubic area. The word arose in the 17th century, apparently as a different spelling of the old word *malkin*, which was a pet form of the name *Matilda* or *Maud*.

merrythought ▶ a bird's wishbone. The word 'wishbone' alludes to the traditional custom in which this bone is taken from a cooked chicken, turkey, or similar bird and pulled by two people until it snaps: the person left holding the longer piece is then entitled to make a wish. The term 'merrythought' is also thought to refer to this practice.

misogamy ▶ the hatred of marriage. The word comes from the Greek words *misos*, meaning 'hatred' and *gamos*, which means 'marriage', and it is pronounced 'mi**sog**əmi'. **Monogamy**, **bigamy**, and **polygamy** are other examples of English words based on the Greek word for marriage.

mistigris ▶ a joker or other extra card played as a wild card in some versions of poker. Pronounced '**mis**tigris', the word comes from the French noun *mistigri*, meaning 'jack of clubs'.

monorchid ▶ an adjective meaning 'having only one testicle': the Greek word for testicle is *orkhis*.

moonraker ▶ a native of the county of Wiltshire. The name refers to an old Wiltshire tale about some men who were caught by tax collectors in the act of raking a pond for kegs of smuggled brandy. They feigned madness by claiming they were raking out the moon and so threw the tax collectors off the scent.

muktuk ▶ the skin and blubber of a whale, typically the narwhal or beluga whale, used as food by the Inuit people. The word comes from the Inuit language.

mumpsimus ▶ a traditional custom or notion that is adhered to although it has been shown to be unreasonable. The term comes from the story of a 16th-century illiterate English priest who, when reciting the Eucharist, mistakenly said *quod in ore mumpsimus* instead of *quod in ore sumpsimus* (which means 'which we have taken into the mouth'). When corrected, he is said to have replied 'I will not change my mumpsimus for your new sumpsimus'.

mundungus ▶ offal or refuse. Originating in the 17th century, the term came from the Spanish word *mondongo*, which means 'black pudding or tripe', and it was later used to refer to foul-smelling, cheap tobacco.

nacarat ▶ a bright orange-red colour. The word, pronounced '**nak**uhrat', may come from Spanish and Portuguese *nacarado*, an adjective meaning 'orange-red'.

naker ▶ an old word for a kettledrum. First appearing in Middle English, it comes from the Old French *nacaire*, a word for a musical instrument resembling a kettledrum that was apparently used by the Saracens.

nainsook ▶ a fine, soft cotton fabric, originally made in the Indian subcontinent. The word comes from the Hindi words *nain*, meaning 'eye' and *sukh*, meaning 'pleasure'.

noyade ▶ an execution carried out by drowning. The term originated in the 19th century, referring to a mass execution by drowning carried out in the French town of Nantes in 1794. A French word, its literal meaning is 'drowning', from the verb *noyer* 'to drown'. It is pronounced 'nwaa**yaard**'.

nugacity ▶ triviality or frivolity. The term comes from the Latin word *nugax*, which means 'trifling or frivolous'.

numbles ▶ an archaic word for the entrails of an animal, especially a deer, as used for food. The word comes from the Latin word *lumbus*, meaning 'loin'. Another archaic word with the same meaning is **umbles**.

obnubilate ▶ to darken, dim, or obscure something. The word comes from the Latin verb *obnubilare*, meaning 'to cover something with clouds or fog' and it is pronounced 'ob**nyo͞o**bilayt'.

ogdoad ▶ a group or set of eight, from the Greek word for eight, *oktō*. Another unusual word with the same meaning is **octad**.

onychophagist ▶ a person who bites their nails. The term comes from the Greek words *onux*, meaning 'fingernail' and *phagein*, which means 'to eat'. Another English word which comes from *onux* is *onyx*, because some varieties of this semi-precious stone resemble the colours of a fingernail.

orectic ▶ an adjective meaning 'having to do with desire or appetite'. The word originated in the 17th century as a noun meaning 'a stimulant for the appetite' from the Greek verb *oregein* 'to stretch out or reach for'. Its current sense dates from the late 18th century.

ortanique ▶ a citrus fruit which is a cross between an orange and a tangerine, developed in Jamaica in the 1920s. The name is a blend of parts of three separate words: 'orange', 'tangerine', and 'unique'.

otalgia ▶ earache. The ending '-algia' comes from the Greek word *algos*, meaning 'pain'. It is found in several English words which refer to pain in a particular part of the body, for example **neuralgia**, pain along the course of a nerve, or **myalgia**, pain in a muscle or group of muscles.

paludal ▶ an adjective meaning 'living or occurring in a marshy habitat'. A technical term, it comes from the Latin word for marsh, *palus*.

Pantagruelian ▶ pronounced 'pantəgro͞o**el**leeən', this adjective means 'enormous'. 'Pantagruel' is the name of a huge giant in *Gargantua and Pantagruel*, a work by the sixteenth-century French author François Rabelais:

gargantuan is another and rather more familiar adjective with the same meaning.

panurgic ▶ an adjective meaning 'able or ready to do anything'. It comes from the Greek words *pan* 'all' and *ergon* 'work'. **Energy**, **ergonomics**, and **surgeon** are examples of other English words based on *ergon*.

papabile ▶ an adjective meaning 'worthy of being or eligible to be pope'. Pronounced 'pə**paa**bilay', it comes from the Latin word for pope, *papa*.

paraph ▶ a flourish after a signature, originally used as a precaution against forgery. The word is first recorded in the 15th century and its first meaning was 'a paragraph'.

pavonine ▶ an adjective which means 'having to do with or resembling a peacock'. Pronounced '**pav**ənīn', the word comes from *pavo*, the Latin for peacock.

pedicular ▶ an adjective meaning 'having to do with or infested with lice'. The word looks as if it might have something to do with the feet, as it sounds a bit like **pedicure**, but the latter word comes from *pes*, the Latin for foot, while **pedicular** comes from *pediculus*, the Latin for louse.

periapt ▶ an item worn as a charm or amulet. It comes from the Greek words *peri*, meaning 'around' and *haptein*, which means 'to fasten'.

petcock ▶ a small valve in the pipe of a steam boiler or the cylinder of a steam engine, used for drainage or for reducing pressure. The origin of the word is uncertain.

peterman ▶ a person who breaks open and robs safes. The word originated in the early 20th century: 'peter' is a slang term among criminals for a safe, cash register, or till.

pettitoes ▶ pig's trotters, especially as food. First recorded in 1555, the word is still used occasionally: it may have developed from the Old French *petite oye*, meaning 'the giblets of a goose'.

pilgarlic ▶ a bald-headed man, or a person regarded with mild contempt. The word originated in the 16th century as a compound of *pil* 'peel' and 'garlic': the intention was to liken a man with a bald head to a peeled head of garlic.

pismire ▶ an ant. A Middle English word, it comes from *piss* (alluding to the smell of an anthill) and *mire*, an obsolete word for an ant.

pneumonoultramicroscopicsilicovolcano-coniosis ▶ an invented term said to mean 'a lung disease caused by inhaling very fine ash and sand dust', but rarely used except for its curiosity value as an example of an extremely long word.

pococurante ▶ an adjective meaning 'careless or nonchalant'. The word comes from Italian *poco*, meaning 'little' and *curante*, meaning 'caring': it can also be used as a noun to refer to a careless or nonchalant person.

pollex ▶ a technical word for the thumb. It comes from Latin.

posology ▶ the part of medicine concerned with the size or frequency of a dose of a medicine or a drug. *Posos* is a Greek word meaning 'how much': the word **dose** comes from another Greek word *dosis*, which means 'gift'.

probang ▶ a strip of flexible material with a sponge or tuft at the end, used to remove a foreign body from the throat or to apply medication to it. It was invented by Walter Rumsey (1584–1660), who called it a *provang*: the spelling change probably came about as a result of an analogy with the word **probe**.

prosopagnosia ▶ a term used in psychiatry for an inability to recognize the faces of familiar people, typically as a result of brain damage. It comes from the Greek words *prosōpon*, meaning 'face' and *agnōsia*, meaning 'ignorance' and it is pronounced 'prosōpag**nō**siə'.

pyknic ▶ a technical term used to refer to a stocky physique with a rounded body and head, thickset trunk, and a tendency to fat. It comes from the Greek word *puknos*, meaning 'thick' and was first used by the German psychiatrist Ernst Kretschmer (1888–1964) in his classification of human body types. The other two types were **asthenic**, referring to a lean, long-limbed, and narrow-shouldered physique, and **athletic**, referring to a physique characterized by large bones and well-developed muscles.

ratite ▶ a term used in ornithology to refer to birds that are unable to fly, such as the ostrich or emu. This class of birds have a flat breastbone without a **carina**, a ridge to which the flight muscles are attached. Birds which do have this ridge (and are able to fly) are known as **carinate**.

retiform ▶ an adjective which means 'resembling a net', from the Latin word for net, *rete*. Another English word based on this is **retina**.

rubiginous ▶ an adjective meaning 'rust-coloured', from the Latin word for rust, *rubigo*.

rubricate ▶ to add elaborate capital letters (typically red ones) or other decorations to a manuscript. The verb comes from the Latin word *rubrica*, which means 'red chalk or ochre'.

rutilant ▶ an adjective meaning 'glowing or glittering with red or golden light', as in *hands adorned with rutilant gems*. Used mainly in poetry or in self-consciously literary writing, it comes from the Latin word *rutilus*, meaning 'reddish'.

scaramouch ▶ an archaic word for a boastful but cowardly person, pronounced '**skarr**əmowtch' or '**skarr**əmootch'. It comes from *Scaramuccia*, the name of a stock character depicted as such a person in *commedia dell'arte*, a kind of comic drama popular in Italy in the 16th–18th centuries. This name itself came from *scaramuccia*, meaning 'skirmish'.

sciolist ▶ an archaic word for a person who pretends to be knowledgeable and well informed about something. Pronounced '**sī**əlist', it comes from the Latin verb *scire*, meaning 'to know'. Other English words based on this verb include **nescient**, lacking knowledge of something, **omniscient**, knowing everything, and **prescient**, knowing about something before it happens.

selkie ▶ a mythical sea creature that resembles a seal when it is in the water but is able to take on human form when on land. A Scottish term, it comes from *selch*, a word for a seal, and it can also be spelled **silkie** or **selky**.

serac ▶ a pinnacle or ridge of ice on the surface of a glacier. Originating in the mid 19th century, the term comes from the Swiss French word *sérac*, which was originally the name of a kind of white cheese.

sesquipedalian ▶ an adjective referring to a word with many syllables or to a piece of writing which uses many long words. It comes from the Latin words *sesqui-*, meaning 'one and a half', and *ped*, which means 'foot' and owes its origin to to the Roman writer Horace (65–8 BC). In his *Ars Poetica* he mentions *sesquipedalia verba* 'words which are a foot and a half long'.

shofar ▶ a ram's-horn trumpet used in Jewish religious ceremonies and in ancient times to sound a battle signal. Pronounced '**shō**fə', the word comes from Hebrew, and its plural form can be either **shofars** or **shofroth**.

skimmington ▶ a kind of procession, once common in villages and country districts, intended to make an example of a nagging wife or an unfaithful husband. The word was originally also used to refer to the man or woman playing the part of the offending husband or wife in such a procession: it may come from *skimming-ladle*, an implement used in mock beatings during the spectacle.

snollygoster ▶ a shrewd or unprincipled person, especially a politician. The word originated in America in the 19th century: some people have speculated that it may be connected with *snallygaster*, a word for a mythical monster supposedly found in Maryland, apparently invented to terrify ex-slaves and stop them voting.

sockdolager ▶ a heavy blow, especially one that knocks a person to the ground. The word is an American coinage, first recorded in 1838: its origin is uncertain, although the first syllable presumably comes from the verb *sock*, meaning 'to give someone a heavy blow'. It can also be used to refer to something exceptional, especially in terms of its size.

soucouyant ▶ in eastern Caribbean folklore, a kind of witch who is believed to shed her skin by night and suck the blood of her victims. The word comes from West Indian creole and is pronounced 'sōokōo**yon**'.

spaghettification ▶ the process by which (in some theories) an object would be stretched and ripped apart by gravitational forces on falling into a black hole.

spitchcock ▶ an eel that has been cut into sections, dressed with breadcrumbs and herbs, and grilled or fried. A similar word is **spatchcock**, which refers to a chicken or game bird split open and grilled: the origin of both words is uncertain.

splanchnic ▶ an adjective meaning 'having to do with the the viscera or internal organs, especially those of the abdomen'. Pronounced '**splank**nik', it comes from the Greek word *splankhna*, which means 'entrails'.

spurrier ▶ a very rare term for a person who makes spurs.

sternutator ▶ a technical word for something that causes sneezing. A more specialized sense of the word refers to a substance used in chemical warfare that causes irritation to the nose and eyes, pain in the chest, and nausea. The word comes from the Latin verb *sternuere*, meaning 'to sneeze'.

stercoraceous ▶ an adjective which means 'consisting of or resembling dung or faeces'. A technical term, it comes from the Latin word for dung, *stercus*.

strappado ▶ a form of punishment or torture used in the past. The victim was tied to a pulley, hoisted in the air, and then allowed to fall almost to the ground before being stopped with an abrupt jerk. The word also referred to the instrument used in this and it comes from the Italian verb *strappare*, meaning 'to snatch'.

strigil ▶ an instrument with a curved blade used by ancient Greeks and Romans to scrape sweat and dirt from the skin in a hot-air bath or after exercise. The word comes from the Latin verb *stringere*, which means 'to touch lightly', and it is pronounced '**strijil**'.

struthious ▶ an adjective meaning 'having to do with or resembling an ostrich'. It comes from the Latin word for ostrich, *struthio*.

succuss ▶ to shake something vigorously. The verb is now used chiefly in the context of preparing homeopathic remedies: it comes the Latin word *succutere*, meaning 'to shake' and is pronounced 'sə**kuss**'.

sudd ▶ **the sudd** is an area of floating vegetation in a stretch of the White Nile which is thick enough to impede navigation. **Sudd** comes from an Arabic word whose literal meaning is 'obstruction'.

temerarious ▶ an adjective meaning 'rash or reckless', as in *his temerarious deeds*. A literary word, it comes from Latin *temere* 'rashly', as does **temerity**, excessive confidence or boldness.

testudo ▶ a device used in siege warfare in ancient Rome. Consisting of a wheeled screen with an arched roof, it could be pushed up to the walls of a besieged city while the attacking troops sheltered underneath it. The word comes from Latin, in which its literal meaning is 'tortoise'.

thaumatrope ▶ a scientific toy devised in the 19th century. It consisted of a disc with a different picture on each of its two sides: when the disc was rotated rapidly these pictures appeared to combine into one image. The term comes from the Greek words *thauma*, meaning 'marvel' and *tropos*, which means 'turning'. Another English word based on *thauma* is **thaumaturge**, which means 'a magician'.

thurifer ▶ a person carrying a censer, or **thurible**, of burning incense during religious ceremonies. Both **thurifer** and **thurible** come from the Latin word for incense, *thus*.

tomalley ▶ a North American term for the digestive gland of a lobster. It turns green when cooked and is considered to be a gastronomic delicacy. Pronounced '**tom**əlee', the word comes from Carib (a South American language).

Torschlusspanik ▶ a sense of alarm or anxiety, said to be experienced particularly in middle age, caused by the suspicion that life's opportunities are passing one by or have in fact already passed. The word comes from German, in which its literal translation is 'shut door (or gate) panic'.

triskaidekaphobia ▶ extreme superstition about the number thirteen: the Greek for thirteen is *treiskaideka*. The word is pronounced 'triskīdekə**fō**biə.

triskelion ▶ a Celtic symbol consisting of three curved lines or three stylized human legs radiating from a centre: the emblem of the Isle of Man is an example of this kind of symbol. The term comes from the prefix 'tri-', meaning 'three', and the Greek word *skelos*, which means 'leg'.

turbary ▶ the legal right to cut turf or peat for fuel on common ground or on another person's ground. The term comes from the Old French word *tourbe*, meaning 'turf'.

umbriferous ▶ an adjective mean 'shady', as in *the garden's umbriferous trees*. It comes from the Latin word *umbra*, 'shade', as does **umbrage**, an English word familiar in the phrase *take umbrage*, meaning 'take offence'. In previous centuries, **umbrage** also meant 'shade or shadow cast by trees'.

uncinate ▶ an anatomical term meaning 'having a hooked shape', from the Latin word for hook, *uncinus*.

uniped ▶ a person or animal with only one foot or leg. The word is based on the Latin for foot, *pes*, as are **biped**, an animal with two feet, and **quadruped**, an animal with four feet.

uroboros ▶ a circular symbol depicting a snake (or a dragon) swallowing its tail, intended as an emblem of wholeness or infinity. The term comes from Greek *(drakōn) ouroboros* '(snake) devouring its tail' and it is pronounced 'yoo**rō**borəs'.

velleity ▶ a wish or inclination which is not strong enough to lead one to take action. The word comes from the Latin verb *velle*, meaning 'to wish' and is pronounced 'veleeiti'.

verjuice ▶ a sour juice obtained from crab apples or unripe grapes and used, in former times, in cooking and for medicinal purposes. The term comes from the French words *vert*, meaning 'green' and *jus*, meaning 'juice'.

vespertine ▶ an adjective which means 'having to do with or occurring in the evening', from the Latin word for evening, *vesper*. Another English word based on this is **vespers**, the name of a prayer service held in the evening or late afternoon in many Western Christian churches.

vexillology ▶ the study of flags. The term comes from the Latin for flag, *vexillum*, which itself comes from the verb *vehere*, meaning 'to carry'. **Vexillum** is used in modern English as a technical term for the large uppermost petal of the flowers of leguminous plants.

virescent ▶ an adjective meaning 'greenish in colour', as in *the virescent light*. A term used mainly in poetry, it comes from the Latin verb *virere*, which means 'to be green'.

wayzgoose ▶ an annual summer party held, in previous times, by a printing house for all its employees, usually taking the form of a dinner and an excursion into the country. Originally, the word referred to an annual entertainment given by a master printer for his workmen on or about St Bartholomew's Day (24 August) to mark the traditional end of summer and the beginning of the season of working by candlelight. The word's origin has not been established: all that is definitely known is that it was first spelled 'waygoose'.

wittol ▶ a man who knows of and tolerates his wife's infidelity. It apparently comes from the archaic verb *wit*, meaning 'to have knowledge' and an altered spelling of the last syllable of *cuckold*, a word which means 'the husband of an adulteress'.

wobbegong ▶ an Australian shark which is brown with pale markings and lives in shallow waters around reefs. It belongs to the family of sharks called Orectolobidae, also known as 'carpet sharks'. The name **wobbegong** probably comes from a New South Wales Aboriginal language.

ylem ▶ (in the big bang theory) the primordial matter of the universe. The term comes from the Latin word *hylem*, meaning 'matter': it is pronounced 'eelem'.

zoolatry ▶ the worship of animals. The ending or suffix '-latry' comes from the Greek word for worship, 'latria', and it is found in several English words indicating the worship of or excessive devotion to a particular thing, for example **idolatry**, the worship of idols, **hagiolatry**, the worship of saints, or **bardolatry**, a humorous term for an excessive admiration for Shakespeare.

Common Confusables

There are many words in the English language which look alike or sound alike but have quite different meanings. Such words are very easy to confuse and the following list explains the differences between the pairs (or trios) of words that commonly cause problems.

adopted, **adoptive**
children are **adopted**, but parents are **adoptive**.

accept, **except**
accept means 'agree', whereas **except** means 'not including'.

access, **excess**
access to somewhere is the means or opportunity to enter it or use it; an **excess** of something is more of it than is necessary or desirable.

adverse, **averse**
adverse means 'unfavourable, bad' whereas **averse** means 'strongly disliking or opposed to something' as in *I am not averse to helping out.*

affect, **effect**
affect means 'make a difference to someone or something', whereas **effect** means 'a result' or 'bring about a result'.

allusion, **illusion**
an **allusion** is an indirect reference to something; an **illusion** is a false idea or belief.

amoral, **immoral**
amoral means 'lacking any sense of morality', whereas **immoral** means 'not following accepted standards of morality'.

ante, **anti**
ante means 'before'; **anti** means 'against'.

appraise, **apprise**
to **appraise** something is to assess it, whereas to **apprise** someone of something is to inform them of it.

assent, **ascent**
assent means 'approval or agreement'; an **ascent** is an instance of going up something, as in *the first ascent of the Matterhorn.*

augur, **auger**
augur means 'be a sign of something in the future'; an **auger** is a tool used for boring holes in wood.

aural, **oral**
aural means 'relating to the ear or sense of hearing', whereas **oral** means 'relating to the mouth' or 'spoken rather than written'.

baited, **bated**
baited is an inflection of the verb 'to bait'; waiting for something with **bated** breath is to wait for it in a state of great suspense or excitement.

balmy, **barmy**
balmy means 'pleasantly warm', whereas **barmy** means 'mad, crazy'.

bass, **base**
bass denotes the lowest adult male singing voice; the **base** of something is its supporting part, foundation, or starting point.

biannual, **biennial**
biannual means 'occurring twice a year', whereas **biennial** means 'taking place every two years'.

breach, **breech**
a **breach** is a hole or gap, or an action that breaks a rule or agreement; the **breech** of a gun barrel is the back part of it.

cannon, **canon**
a **cannon** is a gun, whereas a **canon** is a clergyman, a rule or law, or a list of books or other works.

canvas, **canvass**
canvas is a kind of material; to **canvass** is to seek political support before an election or to seek people's opinions on something.

censure, **censor**, **censer**
to **censure** someone or something is to express strong disapproval of them, to **censor** a book or film is to suppress unacceptable parts of it, and a **censer** is a container in which incense is burnt.

chord, **cord**
a **chord** is group of musical notes sounded together; a **cord** is a length of string or an anatomical structure resembling this, as in *spinal cord* or *vocal cords.*

climactic, **climatic**
climactic means 'forming a climax', whereas **climatic** means 'relating to climate'.

complacent, **complaisant**
complacent means 'smug and self-satisfied'; **complaisant** means 'willing to please'.

complement, **compliment**
to **complement** something is to enhance it by adding extra features, whereas to **compliment** someone or something is to express praise or approval of them.

confidant, **confident**
a **confidant** (or **confidante** if the person is female) is a person in whom one confides; **confident** means 'self-assured' or 'certain'.

council, **counsel**
a **council** is an administrative or advisory body of people; **counsel** is advice or guidance.

councillor, **counsellor**
a **councillor** is a member of a council; a **counsellor** gives guidance on personal or psychological problems.

credible, creditable
credible means 'believable, convincing', whereas **creditable** means 'deserving praise'.

curb, kerb
a **curb** is a check or restraint, as in *curbs on public expenditure*; a **kerb** is the edge of a pavement.

currant, current
currants are dried fruits; a **current** is a flow of water, air, or electrically charged particles.

defuse, diffuse
defuse means 'remove the fuse from an explosive device' or 'reduce danger or tension in a difficult situation'; **diffuse** means 'spread over a wide area'.

desert, dessert
deserts are large waterless areas; **desserts** are puddings.

discreet, discrete
discreet means 'careful and judicious', whereas **discrete** means 'separate, distinct'.

draft, draught
in British English a **draft** means 'a preliminary version' or 'an order to pay a sum of money', while a **draught** means 'a current of air' or 'an act of drinking'; in American English the spelling **draft** is used for all senses.

elicit, illicit
elicit is a verb, meaning 'draw out a response or reaction'; **illicit** is an adjective meaning 'forbidden or unlawful'.

emigrate, immigrate
a person **emigrates** from their country and **immigrates** into another, leaving the first to settle permanently in the second.

envelop, envelope
to **envelop** something is to cover or surround it completely; an **envelope** encloses a letter or document.

equable, equitable
an **equable** person is calm and even-tempered; an **equitable** system is a fair one.

exceptionable, exceptional
exceptionable means 'causing disapproval or offence', whereas **exceptional** means 'not typical' or 'unusually good'.

fawn, faun
a **fawn** is a young deer and also a light brown colour; a **faun** is a Roman god portrayed as part man, part goat.

flaunt, flout
to **flaunt** something is to display it ostentatiously; to **flout** a rule or law is to openly disregard it.

flounder, founder
flounder generally means 'have trouble doing or understanding something', whereas **founder** means 'fail or come to nothing'.

forbear, forebear
to **forbear** from something is to stop oneself doing it; a **forebear** is an ancestor.

foreword, forward
a **foreword** is a short introduction to a book; **forward** means 'onward' or 'ahead'.

fractious, factious
fractious means 'bad-tempered'; **factious** means 'having opposing or dissenting views'.

freeze, frieze
freeze denotes the process by which liquids turn into solids as a result of extreme cold; a **frieze** is a band of sculpted or painted decoration on a wall.

Gallic, Gaelic
Gallic means 'French'; **Gaelic** means 'Celtic'.

grisly, grizzly
grisly means 'horrific or revolting'; a **grizzly** is a bear.

hangar, hanger
a **hangar** is a large building for housing aircraft; a **hanger** is something to hang clothes on.

hoard, horde
a **hoard** is a store of something valuable, whereas **horde** is a disparaging term for a large group of people.

hummus, humus
hummus (or **houmous**) is a dip made from ground chickpeas; **humus** is an organic component of soil.

incredible, incredulous
incredible means 'impossible or hard to believe', whereas **incredulous** means 'unwilling or unable to believe something'.

interment, internment
interment means 'burial'; **internment** means 'imprisonment'.

lama, llama
a **lama** is a Buddhist monk; a **llama** is a South American animal.

loath, loathe
if you are **loath** to do something, you are reluctant or unwilling to do it; to **loathe** someone or something is to dislike them greatly.

loose, lose
as a verb **loose** means 'unfasten or set free'; **lose** means 'no longer have' or 'become unable to find'.

luxuriant, luxurious
luxuriant means 'rich and profuse in growth', whereas **luxurious** means 'very comfortable, elegant, and expensive'.

marital, martial
marital means 'to do with marriage', whereas **martial** means 'to do with war'.

meter, metre
a **meter** is a measuring device, whereas a **metre** is a metric unit; **metre** is also the rhythm of a piece of poetry.

militate, mitigate
to **militate** against something is to be a strong factor in preventing it; to **mitigate** something unpleasant or unwelcome is to make it less severe.

naturist, naturalist
a **naturist** is a nudist; a **naturalist** is an expert in natural history.

omit, emit
to **omit** something is to leave it out; to **emit** something is to discharge it, as in *factories which emit pollutants into rivers.*

ordinance, ordnance
an **ordinance** is an official order or a religious rite; **ordnance** is a term for guns or munitions.

palate, palette, pallet
a person's **palate** is the roof of their mouth, a **palette** is a small board on which an artist mixes colours, and a **pallet** is a portable platform on which goods can be stacked or transported; a **pallet** is also a straw mattress.

pedal, peddle
a **pedal** is a foot-operated lever, to **pedal** is to move by means of pedals; to **peddle** goods is to sell them.

pole, poll
a **pole** is a long thin piece of wood and also each of the two opposite points of a magnet; **poll** denotes the process of voting in an election.

pour, pore
liquids **pour** or are poured; to **pore** over a book is to read it attentively.

practice, practise
in British spelling **practice** is the noun and **practise** the verb.

principal, principle
principal means 'most important, main'; a **principle** is a general law or rule used as a basis for a system of belief or behaviour.

proscribe, prescribe
to **proscribe** something is to forbid or condemn it; to **prescribe** something is either to recommend the use of a medicine or treatment or to state officially that something should be done.

sceptic, septic
a **sceptic** is someone who questions accepted beliefs or statements; a **septic** wound is one that has become infected with bacteria.

shear, sheer
to **shear** a sheep is to cut off its wool; to **sheer** means 'swerve or change course quickly' or 'avoid an unpleasant topic', as in *her mind sheered away from these unwelcome images.*

sight, site
sight is the ability to see or something seen; a **site** is a place where something is located or happens.

stationary, stationery
the adjective **stationary** means 'not moving or changing'; **stationery** is a noun meaning 'paper and other writing materials'.

story, storey
a **story** is a tale or account; a **storey** is a floor of a building.

swat, swot
to **swat** a fly is to hit or crush it with a sharp blow; to **swot** for an exam is to study hard for it.

team, teem
a **team** is a group of sports players; **teem** means 'to be full of something' or 'to pour with rain'.

titillate, titivate
to **titillate** someone is to excite them; to **titivate** someone or something is to make them smarter or more attractive.

tortuous, torturous
tortuous means 'full of twists and turns' or 'excessively lengthy and complex'; **torturous** means 'characterized by pain and suffering', as in *a torturous and lingering death.*

turbid, turgid
turbid liquids are cloudy or muddy, whereas a **turgid** river is swollen or overflowing; **turgid** can also be used to describe language that is pompous and boring.

unsociable, unsocial, antisocial
unsociable means 'not enjoying or engaging in activities with others'; **unsocial** usually means 'socially inconvenient' and typically refers to a job's hours of work; **antisocial** means 'contrary to accepted social behaviour and therefore annoying'.

venal, venial
venal means 'susceptible to bribery'; in Christian theology a **venial** sin (in contrast to a mortal sin) is one that will not deprive the soul of divine grace.

wreath, wreathe
a **wreath** is an arrangement of flowers; to **wreathe** is to surround or encircle.

Games and Puzzles Wordbuilder

Players of word games may be at an advantage if they have access to a supply of short words or words with unusual spellings. Two-letter words, words containing a *q* not followed by a *u*, and words beginning with *x* can be particularly useful and a wide selection is included in the following lists. Proper names and abbreviations which are not pronounced as they are spelt (such as *Dr* or *Mr*) are excluded from the lists as they are not allowed in most word games.

Two-letter words

aa: rough cindery lava
ab: an abdominal muscle
ad: an advertisement
ag (S. African): expressing various emotions, e.g. irritation, grief, or pleasure
ah: expressing surprise, sympathy, pleasure, etc.
ai: the three-toed sloth
am: the present tense of 'be'
an: a form of the indefinite article
as: used to convey relative extent or degree
at: expressing location or time
aw: expressing mild protest, entreaty, etc.
ba: (in Egyptian mythology) the soul
be: exist
bi: bisexual
bo: a kind of fig tree
by: beside
da: one's father
DJ: a disc jockey
do: perform (an action)
dy: a type of sediment
eh: seeking explanation or agreement
El: an elevated railway or section of railway
em: a measuring unit in printing
en: a measuring unit in printing
er: expressing doubt or hesitation
ex: a former spouse or partner
fa: a musical note
Ga: a member of a people living in Ghana
GI: a soldier in the US army
go: move or travel
ha: expressing surprise, triumph, etc.
he: a male person or animal previously mentioned
hi: used as a greeting
ho: expressing surprise, triumph, etc.
id: a part of the mind
if: introducing a conditional clause
in: within
io: a North American moth
is: the present tense of 'be'
it: a thing previously mentioned
ja (S. African): yes
jo (Scottish, old use): a sweetheart
Ju: used to designate a kind of Chinese pottery
ka: (in Egyptian mythology) the spirit
ki: a plant of the lily family
KO: a knockout in boxing match
la: a musical note
li: a Chinese unit of distance
lo (old use): used to draw attention to something
ma: one's mother
MD (Brit.): a managing director
me: the objective case of 'I'
mi: a musical note
mo: a moment
MP: a Member of Parliament
mu: the 12th letter of the Greek alphabet
my: belonging to me
no: not any
nu: the 13th letter of the Greek alphabet
ob: a type of gene
od: a power once thought to pervade the natural world
of: belonging to
og (Australian, old use): a shilling
oh: expressing surprise, anger, disappointment, etc.
oi: used to attract attention
OK: used to express assent, agreement, etc.
om: a mystic syllable which constitutes a sacred mantra
on: supported by or covering
op: an operation
or: used to link alternatives
os: a bone
ou: a Hawaiian bird
ow: expressing pain
ox: a cow or bull
oy: = oi
Oz: Australia
pa: one's father
pi: the 16th letter of the Greek alphabet
po: a chamber pot
qi: (in Chinese philosophy) the life force
ra: (in Norway and Sweden) a moraine
re: a musical note
ri: a Japanese unit of length
se: a Chinese musical instrument
si: = te
so: therefore
ta: thank you
te: a musical note
ti: = te
TV: (a) television
uh: expressing hesitation
um: expressing hesitation
up: towards a higher position
us: the objective case of 'we'
Wa: a member of a people living on the borders of China and Burma
we: oneself and others
Wu: a dialect of Chinese
xi: the 14th letter of the Greek alphabet
xu: a monetary unit of Vietnam
ye (old use): the plural form of 'thou'
Yi: a people living in parts of China
yo: used as a greeting
yu: an ancient Chinese wine container

Words with a q not followed by a u

qadi: a Muslim judge
qanat: an irrigation tunnel
qasida: an Arabic or Persian poem
qawwal: a qawwali singer
qawwali: Muslim devotional music
qi: (in Chinese philosophy) the life force
qibla: the direction towards Mecca
qigong: a Chinese system of physical exercises
qin: a Chinese musical instrument
qintar: a monetary unit of Albania
qiviut: wool from the musk ox
qwerty: the standard layout of typewriters and keyboards
tariqa: the Sufi method of spiritual learning

Words beginning with x

xanthan: a polysaccharide
xanthate: a chemical compound
xanthene: a chemical compound
xanthic: yellowish
xanthin: a yellow colouring matter
xanthine: a biochemical compound
xanthoma: a yellow patch on the skin
xebec: a sailing ship
xeme: a fork-tailed gull
xenia: gifts to a guest or guests
xenial: relating to hospitality
xenon: a noble gas
xeric: very dry
xeroma: abnormal dryness of a body part
xerox: to photocopy
Xhosa: a South African people or their language
xi: the 14th letter of the Greek alphabet
xiphoid: sword-shaped
Xmas: Christmas
xoanon: a wooden image of a god
xography: a photographic process
xu: a monetary unit of Vietnam
xylan: a compound found in wood
xylary: of or relating to xylem
xylem: plant tissue
xylene: a liquid hydrocarbon
xylite: a volatile liquid
xylol: = xylene
xylose: a plant sugar
xyrid: a sedge-like herb
xyster: a surgical instrument
xyston: an ancient Greek spear
xystus: an ancient Greek portico